Wine Spectator's

Ultimate Guide To Buying Wine

6TH EDITION

WINE SPECTATOR PRESS
New York

Contents

Michael Del Sol

Wine Spectator's Ultimate Guide to Buying Wine, Sixth Edition

Printed in the United States of America

ISBN: 1-881659-50-X
ISSN: 1058-5729

Published By
M. Shanken Communications, Inc.
387 Park Avenue South
New York, NY 10016

San Francisco office:
601 Van Ness Ave., Suite 2032
San Francisco, CA 94102

For subscriptions to *Wine Spectator*,
call (800) 752-7799 in the U.S. and Canada,
or write
PO Box 50462
Boulder, CO 80322-0462

Visit our website at:
www.winespectator.com

Distributed by Running Press Book Publishers
125 South Twenty-Second Street
Philadelphia, PA 19103-4399

Introduction

Get acquainted with *Wine Spectator*'s tasting system, and learn several ways to get the most for your wine-buying dollar.

Foreword **5**
Wine-Buying Strategies **6**
How We Taste Wine; The Tasters **10**
Vintage Charts **13**
The Top 100: 1997, 1996, 1995 . . . . **27**

Great Wine Values

Here's a quick-access list of terrific buys from four continents for $12 dollars or less—the best wines we've tasted in this price category since July 1997.

Argentina · Australia · Austria · Chile · France · Germany · Italy · New Zealand · Portugal · South Africa · Spain · USA · World Rosés · World Sparkling Wines · World Dessert Wines . . . **35**

Great Vintages, Great Wines

Geared especially to the collector, this section rates wines from the recent outstanding vintages of six of the world's most prestigious wine types.

Red Bordeaux **60**
Red Burgundy **72**
White Burgundy **102**
Vintage Port **126**
California Cabernet **130**
California Chardonnay **154**

Top-Rated Current Releases

Discover the best currently available wines in your favorite categories, and use this "shopping list" when you visit your local wine store.

Red Bordeaux **178**
Red Burgundy **179**
White Burgundy **181**
Champagne **186**
German Riesling **187**
Barolo & Barbaresco **190**
Chianti Classico **190**
Super Tuscans **191**
Vintage Port **191**
Rioja Red **192**

California Cabernet & Blends **192**
California Chardonnay **196**
California Merlot **201**
California Zinfandel **201**
California Pinot Noir **203**
California Sauvignon Blanc & Blends **205**
California Sparkling Wine **205**

The Main Listings: Wines by Country and Producer

Following a general introduction to the wines of each country—complete with maps of the major wine regions—you'll find *Wine Spectator*'s ratings and current retail prices for over 40,000 wines, and the many tasting notes that describe a wine's special character.

How to Use These Listings **208**
Australia **210**
Austria **248**
Chile **261**
France **277**
Germany **613**
Italy **639**
Portugal **745**
South Africa **764**
Spain **774**
Other International **799**
Argentina 799
Bulgaria 802
Canada 803
Greece 804
Hungary 805
Israel 807
Lebanon 807
New Zealand 807
Romania 812
Slovenia 812
Switzerland 812
USA **815**

Winery Index

Find the exact page number in the main listings on which each winery's ratings begin.

. . . . **1114**

Fred Seidman

Wine Spectator's Ultimate Guide to Buying Wine
Sixth Edition

Editor and Publisher Marvin R. Shanken

Executive Editor Michael Moaba
Managing Editor, *Wine Spectator* Jim Gordon

Editorial Director, Book Division Ann Berkhausen
Associate Editor Amy Lyons
Assistant Editor Steffanie Diamond Brown
Chief Proofreader Alan Richtmyer
Writer Ben Giliberti

Tasting Director Bruce Sanderson
Tasting Coordinators
James Molesworth, New York;
Thomas Garrett, San Francisco
Assistant Tasting Coordinators
Molly Ferrell, New York;
MaryAnn Worobiec, San Francisco
Copy Editor Cordelia Macintire
Chief Proofreader James Rothschild

Vice President, Creative Services Martin Leeds
Designer Jeffrey Felmus
Cover Art Director Ken Newbaker
Cover Designer Maria Taffera Lewis
Cover Photography Jeff Harris
Production Manager Connie McGilvray

President Robert Beleson
Senior Vice President, Marketing Jay Morris
Vice President, Director of Advertising Miriam Morgenstern
Vice President, Western Advertising Manager Cynthia A. McGregor
Vice President, Advertising Services Elizabeth Ferrero
Vice President, Circulation Laura Zandi

©1998 Beringer Vineyards, St. Helena, CA.

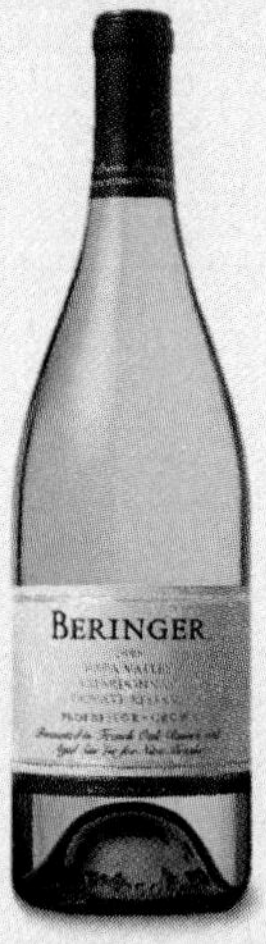

1996 Private Reserve Chardonnay

"This top-of-the-line Chardonnay lives up to its pedigree, showing ripe pear, smoky oak, fig and vanilla flavors, turning rich and elegant and revealing a fine

balance

and integration that let the flavors linger on and on."

Wine Spectator
Highly Recommended
3-31-98 - Rated 95

"Ripe, rich and flavorful, with layers of pear, apple, melon, fig and spice. Shows

depth, concentration

and complexity on a long, lively finish."

Wine Spectator
1-31-98 - Rated 90

1996 Napa Valley Chardonnay

BERINGER.

"Winery that makes the Best Chardonnay in California."

Second Year in a Row, *Readers' Choice Awards, Wine Spectator 6-30-98*

Foreword

Wine Spectator's Ultimate Guide to Buying Wine is back—bigger and more informative than ever. As always, we strive to publish the most authoritative and up-to-date wine buying guide available. This year we've added over 150 pages, completely revised all of the sections, and—as a bonus—included a handy pull-out vintage chart to keep in your wallet. An entirely new section entitled Great Wine Values lists over 850 top-scoring wines priced at $12 or less. And we've added overviews and greatly expanded the wine listings for two countries: South Africa and Austria.

Wine lovers around the world find the Ultimate Guide to Buying Wine an indispensable resource. We want you to be able to use this book at home to plan your wine purchases and take it with you to wine shops when you buy. It's like having at your fingertips the nearly 300 issues of *Wine Spectator* magazine that have been published since 1985, when we began our wine-tasting program in its current form.

The scope of the wines reviewed here is as broad as the charter of *Wine Spectator*, the world's most widely read consumer wine publication, founded in 1976. In exclusive tastings by our senior editors, we rate the best—and the best-selling—wines from California, Bordeaux, Burgundy, Italy, Washington, Germany, and Spain, to mention just a few regions. From Chardonnay and Cabernet Sauvignon, to Champagne and vintage Port, our editors give you their independent views on which are the best wines in each category.

Our guide enables you to quickly look up our editors' ratings of over 40,000 of the wines we've reviewed—including tasting notes with descriptions of aromas and flavors for nearly 20,000 wines from recent vintages, and advice on whether to drink it now or cellar for a while.

The Ultimate Guide to Buying Wine, Sixth Edition, is an incomparable reference for wine consumers and wine-trade members alike. We are always looking for ways to improve it, and we welcome your help. Please contact us with any criticisms or suggestions.

Finally, I invite you to visit us on the World Wide Web—at **www.winespectator.com** —where you'll find additional information about the world of wine, plus feature stories and databases on award-winning restaurants, recipes, hotels, travel, events, and much more.

Marvin R. Shanken
Editor and Publisher

Wine-Buying Strategies

By James Laube

If you're new to wine, you're in for an adventure. Devising a buying strategy can be as simple as choosing a few brands you like and sticking with them, or it can be as complex as collecting verticals of the world's greatest wines or buying wine futures.

For many wine drinkers, maintaining brand loyalty is a tried-and-true way to keep your cellar stocked with reliable wines that suit your taste and budget. More daring collectors expand their hobby of wine collecting into a more sophisticated enterprise. They keep tabs on new wines and vintages from old-guard producers in Bordeaux, Burgundy, Italy, Spain, or Germany, and a watchful eye on up-and-coming producers from the New World, such as California, Oregon, Washington, Australia, New Zealand, Chile, and South Africa.

Rick Mariani

Regardless of your level of interest in wine, you're in for some fun and challenges. Wine is a living thing and is constantly changing. Every year you'll be presented with a seemingly endless stream of new wines, producers, appellations and vintages. Even when you find a winery or style of wine that appeals to you, your taste will likely change over time, and you'll discover new things that appeal to you. The combination of possibilities is endless.

Rule No. 1 of buying wine is to trust your own taste. No one knows your taste preferences better than you, so it's important to be comfortable deciding which wines appeal to you and which don't. The best advice is to taste a wine by buying a single bottle before you commit to several bottles or a case. The importance of this rule is further magnified for expensive wines. It makes no sense to pay $20, $30 or $40 for a wine you've never tried and might not like. You'll be far happier with your buying decisions if you taste a wine and decide you like it before committing to more bottles. There's a big wine world to choose from, with literally thousands of different wines. Even if your friends or wine critics rave about a wine, there's no guarantee that you'll like it.

Gaining experience with the world's fine wines takes time, but it is a fascinating journey. You're likely to learn as much from your buying mistakes as you will from your triumphs. Part of the fun of wine is learning where and how it's grown and vinified, which food types match well with different wines, and which wine types and vintages improve with cellaring and bottle age.

Before you start buying wine, it's a good idea to assess your needs. How much wine do you drink and on what occasions? Do you want to cellar young wines for drinking in a few years? You may also decide to budget money for your wine hobby so you can determine how much you can realistically afford to spend on wine. For some people it's easy to identify their wine needs. For others it's wiser to plan a strategy before heading to the wine shop. Remember, it's easier to buy a case of wine than it is to drink it.

It's also easy to buy more wine than you realistically need. Buying wine on a whim can be fun, particularly when you spot a special bottle you've been looking for. But fanciful buying also increases the odds that you'll end up with a wine you may not need for which you may have paid too much. Planning ahead allows you to set aside a specific amount of money for buying wine by the case. Many retailers and wineries offer a 10 percent discount for case purchases. Discount stores, however, usually pass along the 10 percent discount on all purchases.

Once you've outlined your needs, you'll need a place to shop. Years ago, about the only source to buy fine wine was the traditional fine-wine merchant. Today, your options abound. You see fine wine in scores of discount chain stores and upscale supermarkets, some of which present a dazzling selection. Retailers have also become more aggressive with sales promotions, selling wine through ads in newspapers and magazines, and via telephone and toll-free "800" numbers. A growing list of retailers publish catalogs, especially during the holiday season, offering hundreds of wines and special gift packages. There are even wine-of-the-month clubs. Once you join, the club selects wines for you and ships them to your home for you to sample.

10 Tips to Better Wine Buying

1. Always taste before you buy. Don't get trapped buying what your friends or critics call the best. Trust your own palate. Taste a bottle before you buy six bottles or a case.

2. Diversify your collection. You may have passions for one kind of wine or another, but variety is the spice of life with wine, so shop around for different styles of wine.

3. Shop for values. Go out of your way to look for best buys to get the most mileage out of your wine dollar.

4. Drink your wines before they get too old. Even the most age-worthy reds from Bordeaux or California reach drinkability in 10 years. You've paid good money for your wines; don't let them slide over the hill.

5. Keep costs in perspective. A few fine wines are expensive, but far too many well-made, reasonably priced wines are ignored because they lack the image and prestige of higher-priced wines.

6. Buy wine by the case. Most retailers give you a 10 percent discount or one bottle free.

7. Beware of last year's superstar. Last year's hero could be this year's goat.

8. Stockpile wine you like so that you don't run out or hesitate to open the last bottle.

9. Investing in futures can be risky business.

10. Assemble your wines with rhyme and reason. Think about your needs before parting with your cash.

Most of the time, though, you'll be purchasing wine at a retail store, so it helps to get to know your local wine stores and merchants, including what kinds of wines they stock and their pricing strategies.

A well-informed retailer is an excellent source of sound buying advice and tips about what's new and interesting in his store. Retailers can also help find special wines that may be hard to find. Some retail stores even do the shopping for their customers. When a special wine comes in, they set aside a few bottles or a case and bill the customer, holding the wine until it's picked up.

James Suckling

While you're visiting wine shops, take special notice of how the wines are stored and if the temperature is cool. Light and heat are enemies of wine. Wine shops that are warm or hot in summer months may not be the best place to buy your wines. It's also wise to examine wine bottles to make sure the fill level is good—up to the neck of the bottle—and that wine hasn't leaked through the cork. If wine leaks out, that means air is getting into the bottle and oxidizing the wine. Avoid bottles with low fills or leaks.

Kim Marcus

As wine gets costlier, it makes greater sense to develop a buying strategy. One fun way to defray costs and taste a broad selection of wines is to join a club or group that tastes wines regularly. This way you can spread out some of the costs and taste expensive wines such as Château Lafite-Rothschild, Romanée-Conti, Gaja or Château d'Yquem. Each member brings a bottle of wine to the tasting and shares it among six, eight or 12 people. Some wine syndicates even order cases of wines together, which is another way to cut costs (with a 10 percent discount) and broaden your exposure to the world of fine wines.

For those who like to take risks, buying wine futures, where you pay a discounted price in advance of a wine's delivery, is one way to obtain hard-to-get wines, presumably at reduced prices. Buying futures works like this: Young, unbottled wines are sold at discounted prices through retailers or wineries. Once the wine is bottled and ready for sale, it is delivered to the consumer. Most of the time, consumers pay less for futures, and futures can be a good way to obtain hard-to-get wines.

Others buy wine futures for speculation purposes. They hope that the price they pay for futures is sufficiently lower than the price will be when the wine is released. If that's true, they can resell the wine at a profit. But there are risks in buying futures. The major danger is that you're buying a wine you haven't tried. Unless you're intimately familiar with the producer, vintage or style of wine, you're gambling. You could also pay more for a wine than is necessary. If the economy sours, the price on release may be far less than anticipated, reducing the savings you hoped to achieve. Finally, in buying futures you may tie up your money with one or two producers and miss out on some of the other bargains once that vintage is released. There's also the possibility that your retailer may go out of business before the wine is released, making your wine and your money difficult to recover.

When you're on the road touring wine country, you'll also discover that many wineries have specialty wines or older vintages no longer on the market that they sell only at the winery. Be on the lookout for some of those rarities, but don't necessarily expect to find great bargains. Most wineries give a 10 percent discount on sales, but they mark their wines up to full retail price. You can often find them less expensive at your local retail outlet.

How We Taste Wine

The wine ratings and tasting notes contained in this book are the result of thousands of tastings by the senior editors of *Wine Spectator*. Two types of tastings are used to review wines for the magazine and for this book. First are the weekly blind tastings of newly released wines by our editors in San Francisco and New York. Second are special blind tastings of a particular type or vintage of wine, frequently conducted on location around the world. (A small percentage of the scores in this book, notably those of very old vintages, were not conducted under blind conditions.)

The weekly blind tastings are arranged by our tasting coordinators, who bag and code the wine bottles. They do not participate in the tastings. All capsules and corks are removed from the bottles prior to tasting, and when necessary other efforts are made to conceal the wines' identity from the tasters. Tasters are told only the general type of wine (varietal or region) and the vintage. Price is not taken into account in scoring, although the notes are often edited after the scores are determined to include comments about price and value.

Wines are chosen for tasting from those sent to our offices for review and from wines we purchase at retail. Wines scoring below 70 are automatically retasted under blind conditions from a different bottle. We also retaste many other wines to confirm our impressions.

Wines are scored using *Wine Spectator's* 100-point scale. (See How to Use These Listings on page 208 for a fuller explanation.) Ratings reflect how highly our tasters regard each wine relative to other wines. Ratings are based on immediate quality, as well as on how good a wine will be when it's at its peak, regardless of how soon that will be.

A range of scores (for example, 85-89) indicates a preliminary evaluation, and is used in conjunction with barrel tastings, which are conducted before wines are released.

THE TASTERS

MARVIN R. SHANKEN
EDITOR AND PUBLISHER

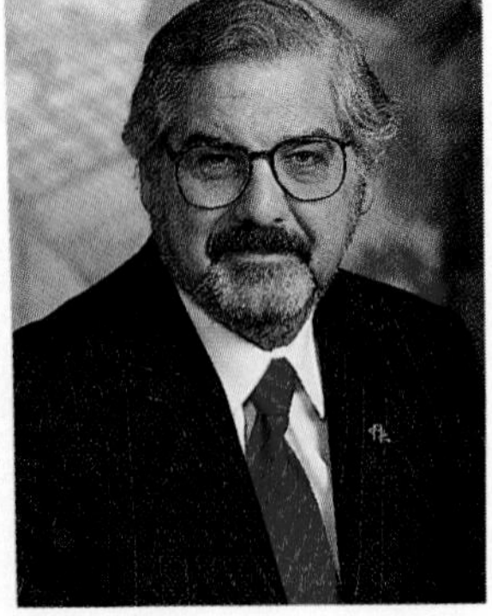

Marvin Shanken, 54, was a partner in a Wall Street investment firm—and a wine lover—in the early 1970s when he bought *Impact*, then a little-known beverage-industry newsletter. In 1979 he purchased *Wine Spectator*—today, the largest and most influential wine publication in the world. Shanken is chairman of M. Shanken Communications, Inc., publisher of *Cigar Aficionado, Hamptons Country, Aspen Country, Impact, Impact International, Market Watch,* and *Food Arts,* and event chairman of the New York and California Wine Experiences.

JIM GORDON
MANAGING EDITOR

Jim Gordon, 46, supervises the editorial staff and wine tasting operations in New York, San Francisco and Europe. His experience covering the wine industry goes back to 1979 when he began working as a journalist in Napa Valley. He joined *Wine Spectator* in San Francisco in 1984, and was promoted to managing editor in 1987. He moved to the magazine's New York headquarters in 1993. Gordon participates in weekly blind tastings and has traveled and reported extensively on U.S. and European wine regions.

HARVEY STEIMAN
EDITOR AT LARGE

Harvey Steiman, 51, tastes and reports on a wide variety of wine regions, including Australia, California and the Pacific Northwest. Steiman joined *Wine Spectator* in 1984, after serving as food and wine editor of the San Francisco Examiner. Among his accomplishments as a critic, Steiman sounded the alarm on the poor quality of the 1983 vintage in Burgundy and introduced readers to the era of modern winegrowing in Italy's Piedmont. Steiman is also a master at explaining the wonderful affinity between wine and good cooking. He creates the monthly *Wine Spectator* menus and has authored three cookbooks. His next book, for Wine Spectator Press, will be a general guide to enjoying wine.

JAMES SUCKLING
SENIOR EDITOR/EUROPEAN BUREAU CHIEF

James Suckling, 39, joined *Wine Spectator* in 1981, and in 1985 he was assigned to Europe. His specialties as a critic are Bordeaux, vintage Port and Tuscany. Suckling cut his teeth on the heralded 1982 vintage in Bordeaux and now blind tastes every vintage three times before the wines are released. Suckling was the first major critic to tip off Americans to the great quality of the 1989 and 1990 vintages in Bordeaux. His 1990 book, *Vintage Port*, is the Port aficionados' bible, and his writing was instrumental in bringing international acclaim to the modern wines of Tuscany.

JAMES LAUBE
SENIOR EDITOR

James Laube, 47, is *Wine Spectator*'s senior expert on the major wine types of California, most notably Cabernet Sauvignon and Chardonnay. He has been writing for the magazine since 1980, and joined the staff full-time in 1983. The second edition of Laube's third book, the award-winning *California Wine,* will be published in 1999. As the leading authority on California wine, Laube cautioned consumers about the troubled 1989 Chardonnay vintage while most other critics were defending the wineries, and he was the first major writer to recognize the excellence of the 1990 through 1992 Cabernet vintages. His reviewing and reporting have helped bring numerous wineries to the forefront of recognition.

PER-HENRIK MANSSON
SENIOR EDITOR

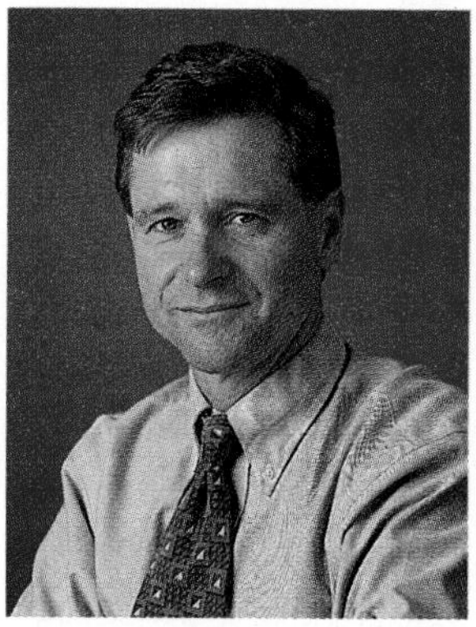

Per-Henrik Mansson, 47, is *Wine Spectator*'s leading expert on Burgundy, and also does regular tasting and reporting on Piedmont, Bordeaux, Tuscany and the Rhône. Mansson joined *Wine Spectator* in 1987 and has been based in Europe since 1989. His reviews of red Burgundy helped bring the excellent 1989 and classic 1990 vintage to the forefront of attention. But he also warned consumers off the much weaker 1991 and 1992 vintages and endured severe criticism from other critics and the wine trade for his tough stance. Mansson's reporting skills were developed in earlier jobs with daily newspapers.

THOMAS MATTHEWS
SENIOR EDITOR/NEW YORK BUREAU CHIEF

Thomas Matthews, 45, began writing for *Wine Spectator* in 1987, while living in Bordeaux. In 1988, he joined the magazine's staff as a reporter in the London bureau, moving back to the United States in 1989 to become *Wine Spectator*'s New York bureau chief. His first book, *A Village in the Vineyards,* was published in 1993.

Matthews got his start in the wine business in 1979, picking grapes in Bordeaux and Cognac. From 1982 to 1986, he worked in New York City as the wine buyer for Odeon Restaurant and Café Luxembourg. He has a bachelor's degree in literature and philosophy from Bennington College in Vermont and a master's degree in political science from Yale University in Connecticut.

KIM MARCUS
ASSISTANT MANAGING EDITOR

Kim Marcus, 39, joined the *Wine Spectator* staff in 1988 and has been a regular taster since 1990. Marcus is in charge of the magazine's Upfront section, and edits the annual vintage reports, which give readers a sneak preview of each vintage's potential quality in all the world's major wine regions. Marcus filed *Wine Spectator*'s first staff-written report from Chile in 1992. He also has been a key behind-the-scenes reporter on the California wine industry. His 1992 cover story, "California's Billion Dollar Nightmare," related the denial and damage that accompanied the phylloxera epidemic in the vineyards, and he writes *Wine Spectator*'s eagerly awaited twice-annual reports on great wine values.

BRUCE SANDERSON
TASTING DIRECTOR

Bruce Sanderson, 42, joined *Wine Spectator* in 1993 after working for the previous five years as a wine steward and in retail wine sales. He manages the tasting operations in New York, San Francisco and Europe, and is a regular taster in the New York office, where a wide variety of wines from Europe, South America, the eastern United States and other regions are reviewed. He writes the "Spectator Picks" column in the magazine's Buying Guide section. Sanderson has been studying toward a Master of Wine degree, and has taught wine appreciation classes.

JEFF MORGAN
WEST COAST EDITOR

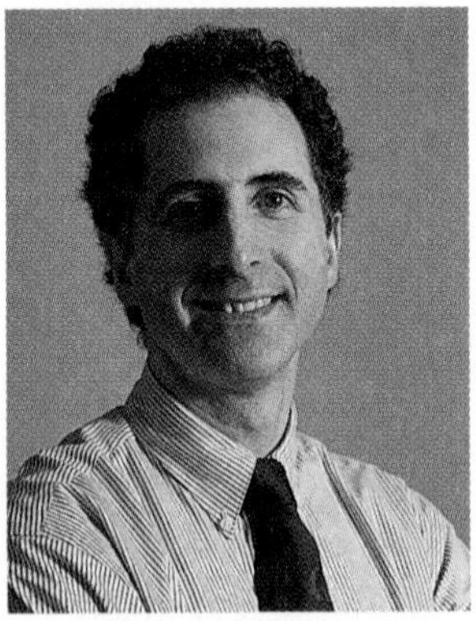

Jeff Morgan, 44, joined *Wine Spectator* full time in 1995 after writing for the magazine on a freelance basis since 1992. Morgan is now the magazine's principal West Coast news reporter, a feature writer and a wine taster. His in-depth story on the wines of California's South Central Coast brought overdue recognition to the Chardonnays, Pinot Noirs and other wines of this up-and-coming area. Morgan once worked as a winery manager and has written on wine for other national magazines and *The New York Times*.

Vintage Charts

The best guarantee of satisfaction in evaluating a wine for purchase is the quality behind the producer's name. Once you've picked a producer with a track record for quality, often the next question is, "Which vintage should I buy?" Knowing the relative merits of each vintage can help you make more informed buying decisions.

This section presents our qualitative ratings—using *Wine Spectator*'s 100-point scale—of vintages in the world's major wine regions for the past 10 or more years. The ratings have been updated according to ongoing wine evaluations by our senior editors. For each year listed you will find the score, a comment on the characteristics of that vintage or its wines, and our recommendation for when to drink.

Wine Spectator's 100-Point Scale

95-100—Classic, a great wine

90-94—Outstanding, a wine of superior character and style

80-89—Good to Very Good, a wine with special qualities

70-79—Average, a drinkable wine that may have minor flaws

60-69—Below Average, drinkable but not recommended

50-59—Poor, undrinkable, not recommended

Vintage charts are, by necessity, general in nature. Vintage ratings listed here are averages for region and year. A score range indicates that wines were tasted as barrel samples. Many good wines are produced in "bad" years, just as bad wines are produced in "good" years. Use our vintage charts as a general guide to overall quality.

■ ■ ■ ■

FRANCE | ALSACE

Vintage	Score	Rating	Comment	Drinkability
1997	87-91	Very Good-Outstanding	Ripe, rich, precocious wines; high yields, little botrytis	Not Released/ Drink or Hold
1996	92	Outstanding	Aromatic, racy, complex and long-lived; little botrytis, with pure fruit	Drink or Hold
1995	90	Outstanding	Small crop due to rot, but rich, vibrant Rieslings; uneven for other varietals and late-harvest wines	Drink or Hold
1994	91	Outstanding	Rainy September, but top producers made excellent dry wines and great late-harvest wines	Drink or Hold
1993	87	Very Good	Rainy year, but ripe grapes; intense, steely wines	Drink
1992	84	Good	A huge crop; producers who limited yields made solid wines	Drink
1991	77	Average	Harvest rains hurt quality; some late-harvest success	Drink
1990	93	Outstanding	Exceptionally ripe year; stunning Rieslings, some fine late-harvest wines	Drink or Hold
1989	96	Classic	A ripe year; rich, round wines and superb late-harvest gems	Drink or Hold
1988	95	Classic	Excellent balance; firm and opulent	Drink
1987	85	Very Good	Steely, lean and fresh	Drink
1986	84	Good	Light, elegant and delicious	Drink
1985	90	Outstanding	Concentrated and intensely fruity, with good backbone	Drink or Hold
1983	93	Outstanding	Very rich and superbly structured; many dessert wines	Drink

FRANCE | RED BORDEAUX

Vintage	Score	Rating	Comment	Drinkability
1997	81-85	Good–Very Good	Uneven quality; top names fruity, delicious; for early drinking; Right Bank best	Not Released
1996	85-89	Very Good	Typical clarets, silky and aromatic with medium body; with few exceptions, stick to Médoc	Not Released
1995	95	Classic	Warm, wonderful reds with opulent fruit and velvety tannins; harmonious and beautiful	Hold
1994	85	Very Good	Medium-bodied, with good fruit, firm tannins	Drink or Hold
1993	82	Good	Good color; perfumy, fruity and balanced	Drink
1992	72	Average	Light, simple, often diluted; early-maturing	Drink
1991	72	Average	Lean, tough and light; top names only	Drink
1990	97	Classic	Opulent, well structured and harmonious	Hold
1989	98	Classic	Bold, dramatic fruit character; tannic and long- aging	Hold
1988	93	Outstanding	Typical structure; racy, fruity wines; firm tannins; best in Pessac-Léognan, Pomerol, Pauillac	Drink or Hold
1987	76	Average	Delicate; ripe, yet diluted	Drink
1986	95	Classic	Powerful, intense and tannic; best in Médoc	Hold
1985	93	Outstanding	Balanced, supple and fruity; defines finesse	Drink or Hold
1984	70	Average	Unripe, astringent and dry; most fading	Drink

1983	86	Very Good	Rich and ripe in fruit and tannins; some overly tannic	Drink
1982	95	Classic	Intensely ripe fruit, plenty of round tannins; many still fresh, delicious; fabulous in Médoc	Drink or Hold
1981	82	Good	Elegant, balanced and charming; some starting to fade	Drink
1980	78	Average	Light, pleasant wines for early drinking	Drink
1979	83	Good	Supple, fruity and delicate; perfect now	Drink
1978	86	Very Good	Structured, fleshy and complex; best are improving	Drink or Hold
1977	60	Below Average	Poor, unripe and acidic; well past their prime	Drink
1976	80	Good	Early promise unfulfilled; fully matured now	Drink
1975	85	Very Good	Hard, tannic, slowly evolving; time will tell	Drink or Hold
1971	80	Good	Uneven quality; Pomerol and St.-Emilion still good	Drink
1970	91	Outstanding	Excellent all-around vintage; structured, with lots of fruit	Drink or Hold
1966	89	Very Good	Typical but hard wines; most at their peak	Drink
1964	80	Good	Uneven quality; outstanding in Pomerol and St.-Emilion	Drink
1961	99	Classic	Best since 1945; great concentration and structure	Drink or Hold

FRANCE | RED BURGUNDY

Vintage	Score	Rating	Comment	Drinkability
1996	93	Outstanding	Ripe, vibrant, charming and seductive; sweet, silky tannins. Large crop produced some diluted wines	Drink or Hold
1995	88	Very Good	Stick to Côte de Nuits; best are elegant but firm, with refined tannins. Many Côte de Beaune wines diluted	Hold
1994	81	Good	Uneven quality; good fruit and fine tannins in best wines; stick to top estates	Drink or Hold
1993	91	Outstanding	Top domaines made exuberant, racy, balanced wines	Hold
1992	79	Average	Pleasant at best, diluted and light at worst	Drink
1991	86	Very Good	Uneven quality, but some wines improving as they flesh out and tannins soften	Drink or hold
1990	98	Classic	Classic balance, formidable fruit and refined tannins	Drink or Hold
1989	93	Outstanding	Seductive and harmonious; delicious now	Drink
1988	90	Outstanding	Muscular and firm; some losing fruit, others improving	Drink or Hold
1987	85	Very Good	Lovely and supple; at their peak now	Drink
1986	79	Average	Lean and drying; some past their peak	Drink
1985	95	Classic	Ripe, supple and soft; very appealing; many peaking now	Drink
1984	74	Average	Many thin, watery wines	Drink
1983	79	Average	Most are drying and over-the-hill, but a few gems escaped widespread rot	Drink
1982	78	Average	Huge crop; some good, but many disappointing	Drink
1981	74	Average	Light and thin	Drink
1980	79	Average	Drinkable, but past their peak	Drink
1979	80	Good	The best are still good; others past their peak	Drink
1978	92	Outstanding	Best wines have extraordinary richness and finesse	Drink or Hold

1977	65	Below Average	Past their peak	Drink
1976	87	Very Good	Tough wines; some coming around	Drink or Hold
1972	81	Good	Lean wines with style	Drink
1971	89	Very Good	Fully mature vintage	Drink
1970	81	Good	Forgotten vintage; holding up	Drink
1969	93	Outstanding	Authentic structure; flavorful	Drink

FRANCE | WHITE BURGUNDY

Vintage	Score	Rating	Comment	Drinkability
1996	93	Outstanding	Elegant, racy, with well-defined, pure, clean flavors	Drink or Hold
1995	93	Outstanding	Rich, thick and generous, with good acidity and aging potential	Drink or Hold
1994	87	Very Good	Charming, soft, honeyed, fruity; many delicious upon release	Drink
1993	82	Good	Austere, lean; best are elegant	Drink
1992	89	Very Good	Balanced; great finesse and lovely fruit	Drink or Hold
1991	85	Very Good	Fruity, charming, delicious already	Drink
1990	92	Outstanding	Racy, graceful, round; will improve with age	Drink
1989	92	Outstanding	Rich, opulent; the best will age well	Drink or Hold
1988	88	Very Good	Firm; good concentration and balance	Drink or Hold
1987	84	Good	Fresh, simple; enjoy while fruit flavor lasts	Drink
1986	92	Outstanding	Seductive, opulent, honeyed; peaking now	Drink
1985	94	Outstanding	Bold, powerful; some remain tough	Drink or Hold
1984	78	Average	Light, tart, very simple	Drink
1983	85	Very Good	Uneven; some are rich and heavy	Drink
1982	83	Good	Some surprises, but generally light	Drink
1981	82	Good	Difficult, uneven vintage; high acidity	Drink

FRANCE | CHAMPAGNE

Vintage	Score	Rating	Comment	Drinkability
1990	94	Outstanding	Fine balance and full flavor	Drink or Hold
1989	90	Outstanding	Extremely ripe and generous	Drink or Hold
1988	93	Outstanding	Outstanding quality; beautifully balanced	Drink or Hold
1987	81	Good	Acceptable, but few vintage bottlings	Drink
1986	86	Very Good	Very good quality; lean in style	Drink
1985	96	Classic	Superb balance; great structure and flavor	Drink or Hold
1984	79	Average	Unexceptional quality; large harvest	Drink
1983	83	Good	Good, pleasant Champagnes	Drink
1982	94	Outstanding	Rich, complex, with abundant flavor	Drink
1981	84	Good	Angular and hard, with clean fruit; some surprises	Drink
1980	82	Good	Generous and very fruity with average structure	Drink
1979	91	Outstanding	Classy, elegant, aging well	Drink
1976	88	Very Good	Ripe, opulent year	Drink
1975	92	Outstanding	Bold but balanced Champagnes	Drink

NO POSTAGE
NECESSARY
IF MAILED
IN THE
UNITED STATES

BUSINESS REPLY MAIL

FIRST-CLASS MAIL PERMIT NO. 101 BOONE, IA

POSTAGE WILL BE PAID BY ADDRESSEE

Wine Spectator

P.O. BOX 37364
BOONE, IA 50037-2364

NO POSTAGE
NECESSARY
IF MAILED
IN THE
UNITED STATES

BUSINESS REPLY MAIL

FIRST-CLASS MAIL PERMIT NO. 101 BOONE, IA

POSTAGE WILL BE PAID BY ADDRESSEE

Wine Spectator

P.O. BOX 37368
BOONE, IA 50037-2368

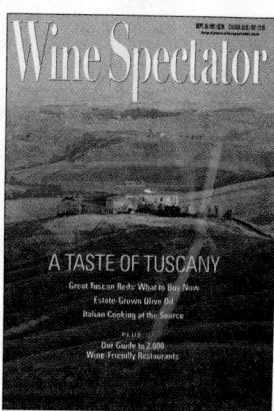

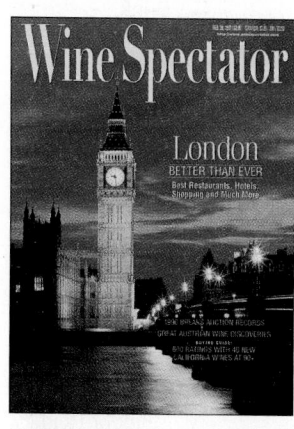

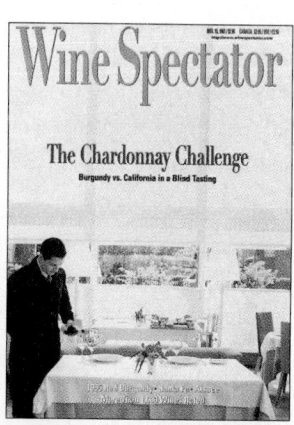

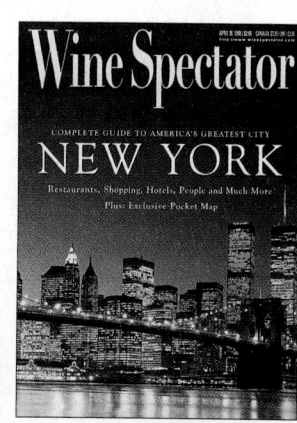

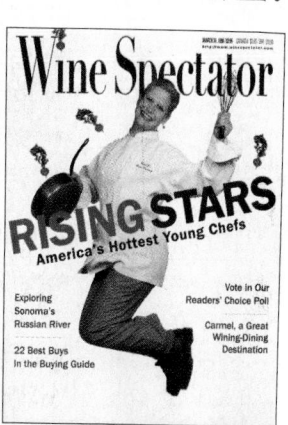

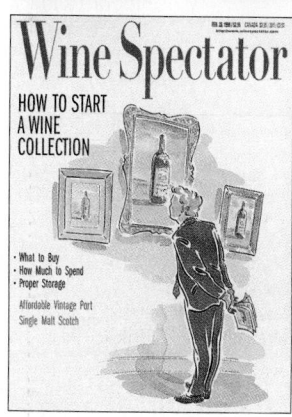

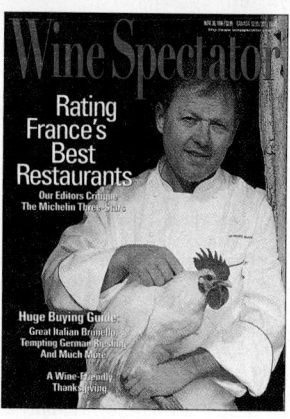

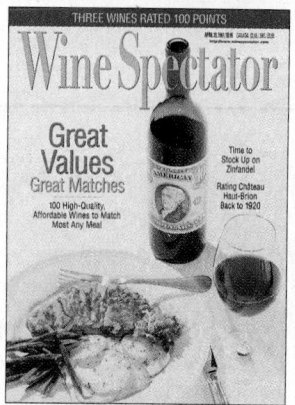

FRANCE | NORTHERN RHÔNE RED

Vintage	Score	Rating	Comment	Drinkability
1996	85-89	Very Good	Big but inconsistent; top producers made outstanding wines	Drink or Hold
1995	91	Outstanding	Red wines offer concentration and typicity	Drink or Hold
1994	88	Very Good	Concentrated, chewy reds; best will be long-agers	Drink or Hold
1993	75	Average	Wet harvest left many wines diluted	Drink
1992	78	Average	Light year; for early drinking	Drink
1991	89	Very Good	Elegant, with fine tannins and silky fruit; early-maturing	Drink or Hold
1990	97	Classic	Massive and rich, with loads of tannin and fruit	Hold
1989	92	Outstanding	Round and opulent, with great texture and backbone	Hold
1988	90	Outstanding	Solid and tough; excellent aging potential	Hold
1987	85	Very Good	Soft and short, but drinking well	Drink
1986	87	Very Good	Tannic and medium-bodied, very firm; starting to come around	Drink
1985	90	Outstanding	Rich, round, loads of fruit	Drink
1983	90	Outstanding	Big and tannic, very solid; best appellations need more time	Drink or Hold
1982	86	Very Good	Ripe and fruity; lacking in backbone but drinking well	Drink

FRANCE | SOUTHERN RHÔNE RED

Vintage	Score	Rating	Comment	Drinkability
1996	80-85	Good–Very Good	Light, fruity, pleasant, early-drinking reds	Drink or Hold
1995	88	Very Good	Intense, tannic, ripe reds to cellar	Drink or Hold
1994	86	Very Good	Less consistent than northern appellations; only top wines need aging	Drink or Hold
1993	78	Average	Inconsistent; best are balanced	Drink
1992	74	Average	Diluted, lean; few successful wines	Drink
1991	73	Average	Most wines hard and green	Drink
1990	95	Classic	Massive wines with great concentration	Hold
1989	96	Classic	Hot year; powerful, concentrated reds built for aging	Hold
1988	90	Outstanding	Dry and temperate year; balanced wines with focused fruit and firm backbone	Hold
1987	75	Average	Wet weather with rot prevalent; light, fruity wines, some lacking character	Drink
1986	88	Very Good	Racy wines with plenty of steely tannins and clean fruit; underrated	Hold
1985	86	Very Good	Ripe and exuberant, with loads of fruit that's evolving quickly	Drink or Hold
1983	89	Very Good	Small crop of Grenache; tannic, powerful wines coming into their own	Drink or Hold
1982	84	Good	Variable year, but many wines still fresh; balanced, with an abundance of fruit	Drink

There are hundreds
of time-saving, economical
ways to make wine.
©1998 Chateau Ste. Michelle Vineyards & Winery, Woodinville, WA 98072
And we ignore all of them.
All our Chardonnays are 100% barrel fermented and aged sur lie.
A practice as rare as the quality it creates.
Chateau Ste Michelle
VINEYARDS & WINERY

FRANCE | SAUTERNES

Vintage	Score	Rating	Comment	Drinkability
1992	72	Average	Light, straightforward, diluted and medium-sweet	Drink
1991	77	Average	Moderately sweet, attractive apéritif wines	Drink
1990	99	Classic	Fabulous balance; rich and racy, with power and elegance	Hold
1989	98	Classic	Incredibly rich, with lots of botrytis; built for aging	Hold
1988	93	Outstanding	Extremely fine and firm, well balanced and concentrated	Hold
1987	79	Average	Clean, appealing, with little botrytis	Drink
1986	90	Outstanding	Harmonious, charming, focused and honeyed; lively acidity	Hold
1985	85	Very Good	Little botrytis character; clean and sweet	Drink
1984	68	Below Average	A few good wines; a wet, difficult harvest	Drink
1983	95	Classic	Intense, complex and stylish; abundant botrytis character	Drink or Hold
1981	83	Good	Medium richness; finely balanced wines	Drink
1980	82	Good	Good year; balanced, lightly botrytized wines	Drink

GERMANY | RIESLING

Vintage	Score	Rating	Comment	Drinkability
1996	89	Very Good	Extremely late harvest; stunning in Rheingau; stick to top estates. Perfumed, ripe and high in acidity; age-worthy	Drink or Hold
1995	88	Very Good	Best estates made best wines; aromatic, fruity, with harmonious acidity	Drink
1994	86	Very Good	Solid quality, high acidity, medium extract; focus on top estates	Drink or Hold
1993	89	Very Good	Great surprise: plenty of fruit, acidity and character; stick to top estates	Drink or Hold
1992	88	Very Good	Uneven quality; some late-harvest, botrytized classics, but many soft, diluted wines	Drink or Hold
1991	85	Very Good	Crisp, racy acidity, but uneven quality	Drink or Hold
1990	97	Classic	Powerful; great acidity and extract, harmonious	Hold
1989	92	Outstanding	Exceptional for botrytized, late-harvest wines, but others tough and unexceptional	Drink or Hold
1988	93	Outstanding	Balanced, firm; best from middle Mosel	Drink
1987	83	Good	Fresh, light; high acidity; surprisingly good	Drink
1986	86	Very Good	Aromatic, elegant; best from Pfalz	Drink
1985	87	Very Good	Racy, well structured; some problems in Rheingau, Pfalz	Drink
1984	74	Average	Unripe, aggresive acidity; only top producers drinkable	Drink
1983	93	Outstanding	Very fruity, ripe, round; little botrytis	Drink or Hold
1981	81	Good	Clean, lean, light	Drink
1979	88	Very Good	Small crop; fresh, well structured	Drink
1976	96	Classic	Huge, ripe, powerful; plenty of botrytis	Drink
1975	93	Outstanding	Superb, great balance, firm structure	Drink
1973	84	Good	Better than expected; ripe acidity, good fruit	Drink
1971	97	Classic	Powerful, elegant, superb structure; long-lived	Drink

ITALY | PIEDMONT/BAROLO & BARBARESCO

Vintage	Score	Rating	Comment	Drinkability
1996	93-98	Outstanding-Classic	Could rival or exceed '90 and '89; lush, ripe, opulent Barolos and Barbarescos, some great vini da tavola	Not Released
1995	87-91	Very Good–Outstanding	Late-picked Barolos are concentrated, but poor weather produced uneven quality in some vineyards	Drink or Hold
1994	77	Average	Barbarescos show spice and modest fruit, lack concentration	Drink or Hold
1993	87	Very Good	Some are delicious and fruity; supple tannins	Drink or Hold
1992	76	Average	Diluted; many estates didn't bottle	Drink
1991	77	Average	Most wines light, some pleasant; a few very good	Drink
1990	97	Classic	Firm, ripe and long-aging	Hold
1989	97	Classic	Ripe, opulent and supple	Hold
1988	90	Outstanding	Firm, focused and generous	Drink or Hold
1987	83	Good	Light, but with pretty fruit	Drink
1986	86	Very Good	Soft and generous	Drink or Hold
1985	94	Outstanding	Rich, ripe, concentrated and elegant	Drink or Hold
1984	80	Good	Light style; spicy and fruity	Drink
1983	75	Average	Very light, sometimes thin	Drink
1982	90	Outstanding	Powerful, tannic and long-lived	Drink or Hold
1979	86	Very Good	Supple and flavorful	Drink or Hold
1978	90	Outstanding	Firm and classically built	Drink or Hold

ITALY | TUSCANY/BRUNELLO DI MONTALCINO

Vintage	Score	Rating	Comment	Drinkability
1992	76	Average	Aromatic, light and diluted; slightly unripe	Drink
1991	84	Good	Perfumed and fruity, with fresh tannins and good structure; some diluted	Drink or Hold
1990	98	Classic	Super structure; powerful and ripe, yet balanced	Drink or Hold
1989	80	Good	Light, aromatic and fresh	Drink
1988	94	Outstanding	Rich and harmonious, with outstanding structure	Drink or Hold
1987	81	Good	Lean and aromatic, with delicate fruit	Drink
1986	85	Very Good	Medium-weight; better than expected, with firm tannins	Drink or Hold
1985	94	Outstanding	Superripe, concentrated and powerful; some wines overdone	Drink or Hold
1984	72	Average	Light, diluted and weak	Drink
1983	88	Very Good	Well rounded, with luscious fruit and good tannins	Drink
1982	87	Very Good	Hot year; ripe, firm and delicious	Drink
1981	82	Good	Fine and fruity, with good structure; fading	Drink

ITALY | TUSCANY/CHIANTI AND SUPER TUSCAN REDS

Vintage	Score	Rating	Comment	Drinkability
1995	88	Very Good	Fruity, well-structured, with lively acidity, long finish	Drink or Hold
1994	86	Very Good	Aromatic, soft-textured and easy to drink	Drink or Hold
1993	84	Good	Fresh, clean and perfumed; firm tannins, crisp acidity	Drink or Hold
1992	77	Average	Very light, very diluted; buy only the best names	Drink
1991	81	Good	Delicate, aromatic, fresh wines for early drinking	Drink
1990	98	Classic	Concentrated, highly extracted, with firm tannins, fresh acidity	Drink or Hold
1989	79	Average	Some light, pleasant wines; others very diluted	Drink
1988	96	Classic	Balanced, with excellent concentration, firm acidity and fine tannins	Drink or Hold
1987	82	Good	Variable quality, but some good surprises	Drink
1986	86	Very Good	Slightly lean but solid wines, with good fruit	Drink
1985	95	Classic	Hot, superripe year; big and rich wines with tons of fruit	Drink
1984	75	Average	Light, difficult vintage; most wines insipid	Drink
1983	88	Very Good	Pretty wines, with good intensity and backbone	Drink
1982	90	Outstanding	Very ripe fruit, with plenty of tannins; rich, round wines	Drink
1981	85	Very Good	Focused fruit, firm tannins; some exceptional wines	Drink

PORTUGAL | VINTAGE PORT

Vintage	Score	Rating	Comment	Drinkability
1995	92	Outstanding	Fruity; well structured; good length	Hold
1994	99	Classic	Classic vintage, superlative structure, fabulous harmony	Hold
1992	94	Outstanding	Concentrated, tannic and fruity; best are classics	Hold
1991	93	Outstanding	Racy, harmonious, rich	Hold
1987	88	Very Good	Balanced and elegant, with good finesse	Hold
1986	80	Good	Firm, gutsy and a little simple	Hold
1985	93	Outstanding	Opulent and intense, but some variability	Drink or Hold
1984	81	Good	Lean, linear, one-dimensional	Drink or Hold
1983	92	Outstanding	Powerful, tannic and age-worthy	Hold
1982	84	Good	Sweet and raisiny; unbalanced	Drink or Hold
1980	87	Very Good	Solid and well structured, with focused fruit	Drink or Hold
1979	74	Average	Light, sweet and insipid	Drink
1978	84	Good	Fruity, soft and ready	Drink
1977	97	Classic	Tough, tannic and complex; ageless	Hold
1976	76	Average	Simple, variable and short	Drink
1975	80	Good	Light and one-dimensional, but fruity	Drink
1974	74	Average	Aromatic and angular; small production	Drink
1972	79	Average	Light, fragrant and easy to drink	Drink
1970	95	Classic	Harmonious and well structured, with intense fruit	Drink or Hold
1969	72	Average	Light and simple; tiny production	Drink
1968	77	Average	One-dimensional and fruity; small crop	Drink

1967	88	Very Good	Focused fruit; angular and elegant	Drink
1966	93	Outstanding	Iron backbone; fresh; good concentration	Drink or Hold
1965	80	Good	Rich and focused fruit; tiny production	Drink
1964	81	Good	Appealing fruit; stylish, soft and round	Drink
1963	98	Classic	Copious fruit; forceful and extremely age-worthy	Drink or Hold
1960	87	Very Good	Balanced, sweet and elegant; at their peak	Drink
1957	85	Very Good	Angular, tannic and lively; tiny production	Drink
1955	94	Outstanding	Harmonious, refined, fruity and solid	Drink
1954	85	Very Good	Fragrant, balanced, fresh and fruity	Drink
1950	86	Very Good	Subtle, sweet and soft	Drink
1948	99	Classic	Massive, superripe and powerful	Drink or Hold
1947	93	Outstanding	Balanced, integrated and attractive	Drink
1945	98	Classic	Youthful and concentrated; superlative quality	Drink or Hold
1942	86	Very Good	Pleasant, elegant and fruity	Drink
1935	95	Classic	Aromatic, refined and firmly structured	Drink
1934	93	Outstanding	Ripe, powerful and concentrated	Drink
1931	95	Classic	Luscious, rich and complete	Drink
1927	100	Classic	Superb concentration with balance and breeding; large production	Drink
1912	98	Classic	Concentrated, powerful and superbly structured	Drink
1908	94	Outstanding	Fine, balanced and flavorful	Drink
1904	90	Outstanding	Delicate, balanced and fruity	Drink
1900	90	Outstanding	Classy, balanced and delicate	Drink

UNITED STATES | CALIFORNIA/CABERNET SAUVIGNON

Vintage	Score	Rating	Comment	Drinkability
1996	90-94	Outstanding	Early signs point to ripe, flavorful wines	Not Released
1995	90-94	Outstanding	Rich, complex and flavorful	Hold
1994	96	Classic	Ripe, dark and concentrated; best since 1987	Hold
1993	90	Outstanding	Predominantly excellent vintage	Drink or Hold
1992	93	Outstanding	Supple, rich, fruity, with soft tannins	Hold
1991	94	Outstanding	Intense, tannic, age-worthy; best in Napa	Hold
1990	95	Classic	Ripe, supple, complex; best in Napa	Drink or Hold
1989	84	Good	Austere, tannic; uneven quality	Drink
1988	82	Good	Lean, crisp and simple	Drink
1987	96	Classic	Deep, rich, complex, tannic; best in Napa	Drink
1986	95	Classic	Classic structure, tight; best are still age-worthy	Drink
1985	97	Classic	California's finest; elegant, rich, stylish	Drink
1984	94	Outstanding	Rich, fruity, opulent	Drink
1983	81	Good	Lean, tannic; uneven quality	Drink
1982	78	Average	Austere, lean; uneven quality	Drink
1981	85	Very Good	Supple, charming, balanced	Drink

1980	84	Good	Ripe, firm; fading now	Drink
1979	88	Very Good	Austere but age-worthy; best are long-lived	Drink
1978	93	Outstanding	Ripe, flavorful, complex; past their prime	Drink
1977	82	Good	Elegant and charming	Drink
1976	75	Average	Ripe but awkward	Drink
1975	86	Very Good	Charming, supple, elegant, balanced	Drink
1974	91	Outstanding	Bold, rich, opulent, dramatic	Drink
1973	87	Very Good	Elegant, charming, subtle, balanced	Drink
1972	67	Below Average	Rainy harvest; simple, watery, uninspired	Drink
1971	68	Below Average	Rainy harvest; poor quality, mediocre	Drink
1970	95	Classic	Deep, complex, elegant, age-worthy	Drink
1969	92	Outstanding	Elegant, supple, balanced, charming	Drink
1968	96	Classic	Rich, concentrated, powerful, tannic	Drink
1967	82	Good	Elegant, supple and balanced, with early charm	Drink
1966	91	Outstanding	Rich, complex, balanced, delightful	Drink
1965	83	Good	Ripe, balanced and charming; serviceable	Drink
1964	91	Outstanding	Ripe, complex and balanced; enduring	Drink
1963	69	Below Average	Frost damage, short crop with uneven quality, not memorable	Drink
1962	69	Below Average	Frost damage, mediocre vintage, uninspiring	Drink
1961	71	Average	Severe frosts; decent quality but past their prime	Drink
1960	84	Good	Fruity, elegant and balanced; commendable	Drink
1959	87	Very Good	Elegant, balanced and complex; enduring	Drink
1958	95	Classic	Amazingly youthful; complex, elegant, age-worthy	Drink
1957	78	Average	Elegant, balanced and fruity; uneven quality	Drink
1956	86	Very Good	Supple, balanced, complex, age-worthy	Drink
1955	89	Very Good	Great depth, balance, finesse and ageability	Drink
1954	85	Very Good	Elegant, balanced, charming	Drink
1953	67	Below Average	Decent and drinkable, but not notable	Drink
1952	85	Very Good	Severe frosts; low expectations but sound wines	Drink
1951	94	Outstanding	Great depth, character and balance; age-worthy	Drink
1950	90	Outstanding	Fine depth, character and ageability	Drink
1949	86	Very Good	Heavy frosts; firm-structured and age-worthy	Drink
1948	69	Below Average	Wet spring, cool harvest with low sugars; uneven quality	Drink
1947	85	Very Good	Warm year; elegant, balanced, age-worthy	Drink
1946	91	Outstanding	Heavy frosts, early harvest; deeply flavored and early-maturing	Drink
1942	88	Very Good	Ripe and balanced, aging well	Drink
1941	89	Very Good	Rich, deep, concentrated, age-worthy	Drink
1939	87	Very Good	Ripe, balanced, age-worthy	Drink

UNITED STATES | CALIFORNIA/CHARDONNAY

Vintage	Score	Rating	Comment	Drinkability
1996	97	Classic	Tremendous flavors, finesse and concentration	Drink or Hold
1995	97	Classic	Great depth, richness, complexity and finesse	Drink or Hold
1994	95	Classic	Lots of superb wines; uniformly ripe, rich, complex	Drink or Hold
1993	88	Very Good	Forward, fruity and balanced, but many lean and simple; variable quality	Drink
1992	93	Outstanding	Elegant and flavorful, with fine depth	Drink
1991	92	Outstanding	Intense, ripe, complex and balanced	Drink
1990	92	Outstanding	Ripe, rich and concentrated, with fine depth	Drink
1989	85	Very Good	Uneven quality, but some are fine	Drink
1988	89	Very Good	Ripe, balanced, delicate, forward	Drink
1987	85	Very Good	Hard, austere, uneven quality, but some are fine	Drink
1986	91	Outstanding	Deep, rich, concentrated, complex	Drink
1985	92	Outstanding	Ripe, elegant, concentrated, harmonious	Drink
1984	87	Very Good	Very ripe, fleshy, early-maturing	Drink
1983	81	Good	Austere, uneven quality; most have faded	Drink
1982	79	Average	Huge crop; very ripe but unbalanced	Drink
1981	87	Very Good	Ripe, forward, charming	Drink
1980	86	Very Good	Very rich, ripe, full-bodied	Drink

UNITED STATES | CALIFORNIA/MERLOT

Vintage	Score	Rating	Comment	Drinkability
1995	90-94	Outstanding	Shows great promise	Hold
1994	92	Outstanding	Best since '90; complex, age-worthy	Drink or Hold
1993	83	Good	Variable quality, with a few stars	Drink or Hold
1992	89	Very Good	Complex wines; best are well-balanced	Drink or Hold
1991	88	Very Good	Ripe, large crop; well-balanced	Drink or Hold
1990	90	Outstanding	Ripe and complex	Drink or Hold
1989	84	Good	Large crop, but uneven quality	Drink
1988	86	Very Good	Small crop; fruity and balanced	Drink
1987	91	Outstanding	Rich and complex; best of decade	Drink
1986	87	Very Good	Huge crop; ripe and powerful	Drink
1985	88	Very Good	Ripe and balanced, but variable	Drink
1984	86	Very Good	Fleshy, ripe and forward	Drink
1983	86	Very Good	Intense and tannic; better than Cabernet	Drink

UNITED STATES | CALIFORNIA/PINOT NOIR

Vintage	Score	Rating	Comment	Drinkability
1995	88	Very Good	Elegant, fruity, balanced, but a small crop in many areas	Drink or Hold
1994	95	Classic	Excellent; rich and dark	Drink or Hold
1993	86	Very Good	Light in color and body, but appealing	Drink

1992	92	Outstanding	Ripe and fruity; best in Russian River	Drink or Hold
1991	91	Outstanding	Complex and concentrated; best in Russian River	Drink or Hold
1990	92	Outstanding	Rich, complex and concentrated	Drink or Hold
1989	84	Good	Huge crop, uneven quality, light style	Drink
1988	87	Very Good	Forward, balanced, pleasant wines	Drink
1987	85	Very Good	Light, simple, pleasant	Drink
1986	89	Very Good	Firm, deep and intense; has aged well	Drink
1985	88	Very Good	Elegant, balanced, complex	Drink
1984	86	Very Good	Ripe, opulent and complex	Drink

UNITED STATES | CALIFORNIA/ZINFANDEL

Vintage	Score	Rating	Comment	Drinkability
1996	87	Very Good	Variable quality; best are well-balanced	Drink or Hold
1995	96	Classic	Brilliant fruit; ripe, complex, intense, balanced	Drink or Hold
1994	95	Classic	Dark, rich, intense, complex; classy	Drink or Hold
1993	88	Very Good	Fruity, complex; fine balance	Drink or Hold
1992	93	Outstanding	Very ripe, opulent and complex	Drink or Hold
1991	92	Outstanding	Ripe, elegant, complex	Drink or Hold
1990	93	Outstanding	Rich, complex and concentrated	Drink or Hold
1989	82	Good	Huge crop; uneven quality, tannic	Drink
1988	84	Good	Uneven crop; forward-balanced wines	Drink
1987	92	Outstanding	Bright, rich and complex	Drink
1986	91	Outstanding	Firm, intense, tannic yet; age-worthy	Drink
1985	93	Outstanding	Wonderful balance and harmony	Drink
1984	88	Very Good	Ripe, opulent and complex	Drink

UNITED STATES | OREGON/PINOT NOIR

Vintage	Score	Rating	Comment	Drinkability
1996	87	Very Good	Light but generally ripe; most wines on the tannic side	Hold
1995	81	Good	Some successes, but many wines hollow, short	Drink or Hold
1994	92	Outstanding	Very ripe, exotic wines dominate the vintage	Drink or Hold
1993	85	Very Good	Uneven, but the best wines are elegant	Drink
1992	90	Outstanding	Underrated by many; numerous opulent wines	Drink
1991	86	Very Good	Generally ripe flavors; starting to fade	Drink
1990	85	Very Good	Many drinkable wines; starting to fade	Drink
1989	85	Very Good	Drinkable; some starting to fade	Drink
1988	85	Very Good	Ripe flavors; starting to fade	Drink
1987	75	Average	Thin, light and simple	Drink
1986	82	Good	Lean, hard and tannic	Drink
1985	88	Very Good	Very ripe early, but most have faded	Drink

The Top 100

Each year the editors of *Wine Spectator* choose 100 of the most exciting wines from the thousands reviewed to present our Top 100 Wines of the Year in the December 31 issue. All of the wines considered for our Top 100 were evaluated in blind tastings in our offices or on location in Europe. The result each year is 100 wine choices that would make for splendid drinking for even the toughest wine critic.

We could have simply given you a list of the highest-scoring wines, but that would only be part of the story. A wine's score simply reflects how good it is, regardless of price or where it comes from. Many of the most exciting wines we review are worth special attention because they represent a unique style or make a real contribution to the great diversity that makes wine so much fun. Absolute quality is only one component of this "excitement factor." Listed below are some additional criteria that we consider.

Overall Value
We expect more of higher-priced wines. A $100 Bordeaux has to carry an extremely high rating to make the Top 100. Conversely, a $10 Cabernet Sauvignon could make the Top 100 with a lower score.

Relative Value within Type
The Top 100 favors highly rated wines that are priced below average for their type. For example, a $25 Chassagne-Montrachet is a good relative value. A $25 Chilean Chardonnay is not.

Availability
Overall, the Top 100 favors wines that are not in extemely short supply. However, some wines made in tiny quantities, such as *cru* Burgundies, were so highly rated and reasonably priced in their categories that we decided they are well worth searching for. We made exceptions to the rule for wines such as these.

Rarity of Excellence within Type
We like to find outstanding wines in categories that don't usually produce outstanding quality. For example, the best Sauvignon Blanc may make the list while a Chardonnay with the same score and price may not, because we find fewer outstanding Sauvignon Blancs.

In the following pages are the Top 100 rankings for 1997, 1996 and 1995.

The Top 100: 1997

RANK	SCORE	PRICE*	WINE
1	100	$55	**FONSECA** Vintage Port 1994
1	100	$55	**TAYLOR FLADGATE** Vintage Port 1994
3	96	$70	**JOSEPH PHELPS** Insignia Napa Valley 1994
4	96	$60	**ARAUJO** Cabernet Sauvignon Napa Valley Eisele Vineyard 1994
5	95	$30	**ROBERT MONDAVI** Chardonnay Napa Valley Reserve 1994
6	97	$160	**CHATEAU D'YQUEM** Sauternes 1990
7	94	$17	**CLOUDY BAY** Sauvignon Blanc Marlborough 1996
8	95	$25	**BODEGAS REYES** Ribera del Duero Teófilo Reyes 1994
9	95	$36	**CAYMUS** Cabernet Sauvignon Napa Valley 1994
10	93	$30	**SAINTSBURY** Chardonnay Carneros Reserve 1995
11	94	$29	**BERINGER** Chardonnay Napa Valley Private Reserve 1995
12	94	$75	**DOMINUS ESTATE** Napa Valley Napanook Vineyard 1994
13	94	$90	**OPUS ONE** Napa Valley 1994
14	98	$35	**DOMAINE DES BAUMARD** Quarts de Chaume 1995
15	95	$45	**WARRE** Vintage Port 1994
16	95	$35	**DIDIER DAGUENEAU** Pouilly-Fumé Pur Sang 1995
17	93	$18	**MERRYVALE** Chardonnay Napa Valley Starmont 1995
18	97	$60	**JACQUES PRIEUR** Puligny-Montrachet Les Combettes 1995
19	95	$47	**DENIS MORTET** Gevrey-Chambertin En Motrot 1995
20	93	$75	**PAUL JABOULET AÎNÉ** Hermitage La Chapelle 1995
21	94	$31	**ALLEGRINI** Amarone della Valpolicella Classico Superiore 1990
22	95	$30	**MARTINEZ** Vintage Port 1994
23	94	$45	**LEONETTI** Cabernet Sauvignon Columbia Valley 1994
24	94	$60	**SHAFER** Cabernet Sauvignon Stags Leap District Hillside Select 1993
25	96	$100	**CASTELLO DI AMA** Vigna l'Apparita 1993
26	95	$60	**BODEGAS ALEJANDRO FERNANDEZ** Ribera del Duero Pesquera Janus Reserva 1994
27	94	$60	**J.L. CHAVE** Hermitage 1994
28	94	$60	**TRIMBACH** Riesling Alsace Clos Ste.-Hune 1991
29	94	$18	**JEAN-PAUL DROIN** Chablis Montée de Tonnerre 1996
30	94	$35	**VERGET** Puligny-Montrachet Les Enseignères 1995
31	93	$24	**CHALK HILL** Chardonnay Chalk Hill 1995
32	94	$30	**MATANZAS CREEK** Chardonnay Sonoma Valley 1995
33	94	$35	**PETER MICHAEL** Les Pavots Knights Valley 1994
34	93	$30	**VIADER** Napa Valley 1994
35	93	$70	**BONNEAU DU MARTRAY** Corton-Charlemagne 1995
36	94	$125	**ALDO CONTERNO** Barolo Cicala 1993
37	93	$115	**CHÂTEAU LAFITE ROTHSCHILD** Pauillac 1994
38	92	$16	**ESTANCIA** Meritage Red Alexander Valley 1994
39	93	$29	**GÉRARD CHAVY** Puligny-Montrachet 1995
40	92	$18	**VILLA MT. EDEN** Chardonnay California Grand Reserve 1995
41	93	$85	**CHÂTEAU CLINET** Pomerol 1994
42	92	$43	**MATANZAS CREEK** Merlot Sonoma Valley 1994
43	92	$21	**FERRARI-CARANO** Chardonnay Alexander Valley 1995
44	92	$15	**ALAIN GRAILLOT** Crozes-Hermitage 1995
45	91	$12	**ROSEMOUNT** Shiraz South Eastern Australia 1996
46	92	$12	**LOLONIS** Zinfandel Mendocino County 1994
47	93	$40	**ROSEMOUNT** Syrah McLaren Vale Balmoral 1994
48	92	$23	**RIDGE** Lytton Springs Dry Creek Valley 1995
49	93	$115	**CHÂTEAU HAUT-BRION** Pessac-Léognan 1994
50	92	$25	**CAKEBREAD** Cabernet Sauvignon Napa Valley 1994

*PRICE ON RELEASE

The Top 100: 1997

RANK	SCORE	PRICE*	WINE
51	92	$24	**ROCHIOLI** Pinot Noir Russian River Valley 1995
52	92	$13	**RABBIT RIDGE** Sangiovese Sonoma County Coniglio Selezione 1994
53	92	$15	**FLORA SPRINGS** Sangiovese Napa Valley 1995
54	92	$35	**FATTORIA DI FELSINA** Chianti Classico Rancia Riserva 1994
55	93	$45	**COSTERS DEL SIURANA** Priorat Clos de L'Obac 1995
56	91	$14	**COLUMBIA CREST** Chardonnay Columbia Valley Estate Series 1995
57	92	$28	**GRGICH HILLS** Chardonnay Napa Valley 1995
58	92	$15	**CHARLES KRUG** Merlot Napa Valley Peter Mondavi Family 1995
59	92	$85	**CHATEAU L'ANGÉLUS** St.-Emilion 1994
60	92	$21	**ROEDERER ESTATE** Brut Rosé Anderson Valley NV
61	91	$16	**THE HESS COLLECTION** Chardonnay Napa Valley 1995
62	91	$20	**BERINGER** Cabernet Sauvignon Knights Valley 1994
63	92	$45	**PENFOLDS** Cabernet Sauvignon South Australia Bin 707 1993
64	91	$15	**LOCKWOOD** Chardonnay Monterey 1995
65	91	$18	**SANFORD** Chardonnay Santa Barbara County 1995
66	92	$25	**SONOMA-CUTRER** Chardonnay Sonoma Coast The Cutrer Vineyard 1994
67	93	$15 (375ml)	**BONNY DOON** Muscat California Vin de Glacière 1996
68	93	$18	**PETER LEHMANN** Clancy's Gold Preference Barossa Valley 1994
69	91	$20	**KANONKOP** Pinotage Stellenbosch 1995
70	91	$33	**E. GUIGAL** Côte-Rôtie Côtes Brune et Blonde 1993
71	91	$40	**HENRIOT** Brut Champagne Millésimé 1989
72	92	$61	**DOMAINE WEINBACH** Riesling Alsace Grand Cru Schlossberg Cuvée Ste.-Cathérine 1996
73	90	$11	**KURT DARTING** Riesling Kabinett Pfalz Ungsteiner Bettelhaus 1996
74	90	$11	**COLUMBIA CREST** Cabernet Sauvignon Columbia Valley 1994
75	90	$15	**BEAULIEU VINEYARD** Cabernet Sauvignon Rutherford 1994
76	91	$13	**BEAULIEU VINEYARD** Zinfandel Napa Valley 1995
77	91	$13	**LEASINGHAM** Shiraz Clare Valley Domain 1995
78	92	$40	**LOUIS CARILLON** Puligny-Montrachet 1995
79	92	$35	**VINCENT GIRARDIN** Volnay Clos des Chênes 1995
80	90	$18	**STEELE** Pinot Noir Carneros 1995
81	91	$19	**BODEGAS ISMAEL ARROYO** Ribera del Duero Val Sotillo Crianza 1994
82	90	$15	**DRY CREEK** Chardonnay Sonoma County 1995
83	91	$15	**GHISLAINE & JEAN-HUGUES GOISOT** Chardonnay Bourgogne Côtes d'Auxerre Corps de Garde 1995
84	90	$14	**RAYMOND** Chardonnay Napa Valley Reserve 1995
85	90	$17	**CONDADO DE HAZA** Ribera del Duero 1995
86	90	$15	**CASA LAPOSTOLLE** Merlot Rapel Valley Cuvée Alexandre 1995
87	90	$18	**CHATEAU ST. JEAN** Merlot Sonoma County 1994
88	91	$45	**CHATEAU COS-D'ESTOURNEL** St.-Estèphe 1994
89	90	$17	**PASCAL JOLIVET** Sancerre 1995
90	90	$9	**GIESEN** Sauvignon Blanc Marlborough 1996
91	90	$12	**MARKHAM** Sauvignon Blanc Napa Valley 1996
92	92	$15	**MARKHAM** Cabernet Sauvignon Napa Valley 1994
93	91	$25	**CHÂTEAU BOUSCASSÉ** Madiran Vieilles Vignes 1995
94	90	$13	**RABBIT RIDGE** Zinfandel Sonoma County 1995
95	91	$30	**MONTAUDON** Brut Champagne NV
96	91	$30	**CATTIER** Brut Champagne Antique NV
97	90	$17	**BYRON** Pinot Noir Santa Barbara County 1995
98	90	$19	**ROBERT WEIL** Riesling Kabinett Rheingau 1996
99	90	$7	**HOGUE** White Riesling Late Harvest Columbia Valley 1996
100	91	$23	**TRUCHARD** Pinot Noir Carneros 1995

*PRICE ON RELEASE

The Top 100: 1996

RANK	SCORE	PRICE*	WINE
1	95	$20	**BERINGER** Chardonnay Napa Valley Private Reserve 1994
2	98	$70	**GROTH** Cabernet Sauvignon Napa Valley Reserve 1992
3	93	$20	**CHALK HILL** Chardonnay Chalk Hill 1994
4	93	$22	**HENSCHKE** Shiraz-Cabernet-Malbec Eden Valley Barossa Valley Keyneton Estate 1993
5	93	$23	**SHAFER** Chardonnay Napa Valley Carneros Red Shoulder Ranch 1994
6	93	$29	**KUMEU RIVER** Chardonnay Kumeu 1994
7	92	$13	**LINDEMANS** Chardonnay Padthaway 1994
8	92	$16	**GALLO-SONOMA** Chardonnay Russian River Valley Laguna Ranch Vineyard 1994
9	92	$15	**ALAIN GRAILLOT** Crozes-Hermitage 1994
10	92	$27	**ARROWOOD** Cabernet Sauvignon Sonoma County 1993
11	92	$30	**CHÂTEAU CANON-LA GAFFELIÈRE** St.-Emilion 1993
12	91	$16	**CONCHA Y TORO** Cabernet Sauvignon Maipo Puente Alto Vineyard Don Melchor Private Reserve 1993
13	92	$18	**CHATEAU ST. JEAN** Chardonnay Alexander Valley Belle Terre Vineyards 1994
14	92	$18	**STEELE** Chardonnay California 1994
15	95	$34	**NIEPOORT** Tawny Port Colheita 1983
16	91	$12	**CHATEAU SOUVERAIN** Chardonnay Sonoma County 1994
17	91	$17	**FERRARI-CARANO** Fumé Blanc Sonoma County Reserve 1995
18	92	$12	**CHATEAU REYNELLA** Shiraz McLaren Vale Basket Pressed 1994
19	95	$25	**SAINTSBURY** Chardonnay Carneros Reserve 1994
20	94	$20	**HARDYS** Shiraz Padthaway-McLaren Vale-Clare Valley Eileen Hardy 1993
21	94	$40	**LEONETTI** Merlot Washington 1994
22	93	$45	**SILVER OAK** Cabernet Sauvignon Napa Valley 1992
23	94	$19	**TRUCHARD** Chardonnay Napa Valley Carneros 1994
24	94	$25	**BROADLEY** Pinot Noir Oregon Claudia's Choice 1994
25	93	$28	**BYRON** Chardonnay Santa Maria Valley Estate 1993
26	93	$40	**SIMI** Cabernet Sauvignon Alexander Valley Reserve 1992
27	93	$50	**SILVER OAK** Cabernet Sauvignon Napa Valley Bonny's Vineyard 1991
28	93	$28 (375ml)	**DE BORTOLI** Sémillon Australia Noble One 1993
29	97	$84	**CAMPOGIOVANNI** Brunello di Montalcino Vigna del Quercione Riserva 1990
30	96	$27	**TURLEY** Zinfandel Napa Valley Hayne Vineyard 1994
31	96	$34	**HENSCHKE** Shiraz Keyneton Mount Edelstone 1993
32	96	$48	**ROCHIOLI** Pinot Noir Russian River Valley West Block Reserve 1994
33	96	$60	**CHÂTEAU PAPE CLÉMENT** Pessac-Léognan White 1994
34	95	$38	**CHATEAU ST. JEAN** Cabernet Sauvignon Sonoma County Reserve 1990
35	92	$22	**LINDEMANS** Cabernet Sauvignon Coonawarra St. George Vineyard 1991
36	92	$24	**ST. FRANCIS** Merlot Sonoma Valley Reserve Estate 1992
37	91	$14	**PAUL JABOULET** Aîné Crozes-Hermitage Les Jalets 1994
38	91	$18	**PENFOLDS** Shiraz South Australia Kalimna Bin 28 1993
39	91	$18	**BOLLA** Amarone della Valpolicella Classico 1988
40	95	$52	**ARGIANO** Brunello di Montalcino Riserva 1990
41	95	$100	**CASTELLO BANFI** Brunello di Montalcino Poggio all'Oro Riserva 1990
42	95	$110	**PENFOLDS** Shiraz South Australia Grange 1991
43	94	$32	**JEAN GRIVOT** Vosne-Romanée Les Beaux Monts 1993
44	94	$50	**CHÂTEAU LA FLEUR DE GAY** Pomerol 1993
45	92	$16	**VILLA MT. EDEN** Chardonnay Napa Valley Grand Reserve 1994
46	92	$16	**TYRRELL'S** Pinot Chardonnay Hunter Valley Vat 47 1994
47	93	$14	**NAVARRO** White Riesling Late Harvest Anderson Valley Sweet 1994
48	93	$19	**ROBERT BIALE** Zinfandel Napa Valley Aldo's Vineyard Proprietor's Series 1994
49	93	$27	**ST. HALLETT** Shiraz Barossa Old Block 1993

*PRICE ON RELEASE

The Top 100: 1996

RANK	SCORE	PRICE*	WINE
50	93	$40	**MICHEL COLIN-DELÉGER** Chassagne-Montrachet En Remilly 1994
51	93	$40	**BEAUX FRÈRES** Pinot Noir Yamhill County Beaux Frères Vineyard 1994
52	93	$75	**POGGIO ANTICO** Brunello di Montalcino Riserva 1990
53	92	$19	**SADDLEBACK** Cabernet Sauvignon Napa Valley 1993
54	92	$20	**ROSENBLUM** Zinfandel Mount Veeder Brandlin Ranch 1994
55	92	$29	**TRIMBACH** Riesling Alsace Cuvée Frédéric Emile 1992
56	92	$30	**MARQUIS D'ANGERVILLE** Volnay Premier Cru 1993
57	92	$31	**QUILCEDA CREEK** Cabernet Sauvignon Washington 1992
58	92	$46	**LOUIS ROEDERER** Brut Champagne 1990
59	91	$16	**LANDMARK** Chardonnay Sonoma County Overlook 1994
60	91	$16	**CARMENET** Chardonnay Sonoma Valley Carneros Sangiacomo Vineyard 1993
61	91	$15	**MCGUIGAN BROTHERS** Cabernet Sauvignon Australia Personal Reserve 1993
62	91	$16	**MITCHELTON** Chardonnay Victoria Reserve 1994
63	91	$16	**ROBERT MONDAVI** Zinfandel Napa Valley 1994
64	91	$17	**CASTELLO BANFI** Chardonnay Tuscany Fontanelle 1993
65	91	$18	**STEELE** Zinfandel Mendocino Du Pratt Vineyard 1993
66	91	$20	**RIDGE** Geyserville Sonoma County 1994
67	91	$15	**VALETTE** Mâcon-Chaintré Vieilles Vignes 1994
68	91	$22	**CHATEAU ST. JEAN** Cabernet Sauvignon Sonoma County Cinq Cépages 1993
69	91	$22	**JEAN-PIERRE GROSSOT** Chablis Les Fourneaux 1994
70	90	$10	**MARTINELLI** Gewürztraminer Russian River Valley 1995
71	90	$10	**TALTARNI** Sauvignon Blanc Victoria 1995
72	90	$10	**VOSS** Sauvignon Blanc Napa Valley 1995
73	90	$11	**BERINGER** Chardonnay Napa Valley 1994
74	90	$11	**CHATEAU ST. JEAN** Chardonnay Sonoma County 1994

*PRICE ON RELEASE

RANK	SCORE	PRICE	WINE
75	90	$12	**DECOY** Migration Red Napa Valley 1993
76	90	$12	**J. LOHR** Chardonnay Monterey Riverstone 1994
77	90	$12	**WYNNS** Chardonnay Coonawarra 1994
78	90	$12	**SILVAN RIDGE** Early Muscat Oregon Semi-Sparkling 1994
79	90	$13	**FRANCISCAN** Chardonnay Napa Valley Oakville Estate Barrel Fermented 1994
80	90	$14	**PETER LEHMANN** Cabernet Sauvignon Barossa 1993
81	90	$14	**CHATEAU ST. JEAN** Merlot Sonoma County 1993
82	90	$14	**CHALK HILL** Sauvignon Blanc Chalk Hill 1994
83	90	$15	**BERNARDUS** Chardonnay Monterey County 1994
84	90	$15	**CASA LAPOSTOLLE** Merlot Rapel Valley Cuvée Alexandre 1994
85	90	$15	**GREENWOOD RIDGE** Zinfandel Sonoma County Scherrer Vineyards 1994
86	90	$16	**CHÂTEAU D'OLIVIER** Pessac-Léognan White 1994
87	91	$25	**CHÂTEAU LA LOUVIÈRE** Pessac-Léognan White 1994
88	91	$25	**CAYMUS** Cabernet Sauvignon Napa Valley 1993
89	90	$16	**SAXENBURG** Shiraz Stellenbosch Private Collection 1993
90	90	$17	**RAYMOND** Cabernet Sauvignon Napa Valley Reserve 1993
91	90	$18	**DOMAINES SCHLUMBERGER** Gewürztraminer Alsace Fleur de Guebwiller 1993
92	90	$18	**WATERBROOK** Merlot Columbia Valley 1993
93	90	$18	**HEDGES** Cabernet Sauvignon Columbia Valley Three Vineyards at Red Mountain 1994
94	90	$18	**KUNDE** Viognier Sonoma Valley 1995
95	90	$19	**GARY FARRELL** Pinot Noir Russian River Valley 1994
96	90	$20	**STEELE** Pinot Noir Santa Barbara County Bien Nacido Vineyard 1994
97	90	$21	**PANTHER CREEK** Pinot Noir Willamette Valley Reserve 1993
98	90	$21	**KEN WRIGHT** Pinot Noir Willamette Valley 1994
99	90	$22	**ALION** Ribera del Duero 1992
100	90	$30	**DRAPPIER** Brut Champagne Carte Blanche NV

■ ■ ■ ■

The Top 100: 1995

RANK	SCORE	PRICE*	WINE
1	97	$100	**PENFOLDS** Shiraz South Australia Grange **1990**
2	99	$100	**CAYMUS** Cabernet Sauvignon Napa Valley Special Selection **1991**
3	94	$18	**THE HESS COLLECTION** Cabernet Sauvignon Napa Valley **1992**
4	96	$45	**FONSECA** Vintage Port **1992**
5	96	$140	**COMTE GEORGES DE VOGÜÉ** Musigny Cuvée Vieilles Vignes **1993**
6	94	$13	**ZACA MESA** Syrah Santa Barbara County Zaca Vineyards **1993**
7	95	$43	**CAMPOGIOVANNI** Brunello di Montalcino **1990**
8	94	$40	**KISTLER** Chardonnay Sonoma Valley Kistler Vineyard **1992**
9	95	$45	**BERINGER** Cabernet Sauvignon Napa Valley Private Reserve **1992**
10	96	$27	**TRIMBACH** Riesling Alsace Cuvée Frédéric Emile **1990**
11	95	$22	**TURLEY** Zinfandel Napa Valley Hayne Vineyard **1993**
12	98	$60	**ALTESINO** Brunello di Montalcino Montosoli **1990**
13	97	$150	**E. GUIGAL** Côte-Rôtie La Landonne **1991**
14	96	$40	**ARAUJO** California Cabernet Sauvignon Eisele Vineyard **1992**
15	97	$90	**DANIEL RION** Clos Vougeot **1993**
16	96	$28 (375ml)	**ARROWOOD** California White Riesling Late Harvest Russian River Valley Oak Meadow Vineyard Special Select **1993**
17	96	$40	**FLORA SPRINGS** Cabernet Sauvignon Napa Valley Rutherford Reserve **1992**
18	95	$37	**TAYLOR FLADGATE** Vintage Port **1992**
19	94	$30	**LEWIS** Cabernet Sauvignon Napa Valley Oakville Ranch **1992**
20	93	$30	**ANDERSON'S** Conn Valley Cabernet Sauvignon Napa Valley Estate Reserve **1992**
21	93	$45	**FAR NIENTE** Cabernet Sauvignon Napa Valley **1992**
22	95	$72	**CAPARZO** Brunello di Montalcino Vigna la Casa **1990**
23	96	$185	**LEROY** Volnay-Santenots **1993**
24	93	$9 (375ml)	**CHATEAU STE. MICHELLE** Washington White Riesling Late Harvest Columbia Valley Chateau Reserve **1991**
25	93	$30	**JEAN-MARC BOILLOT** Volnay **1993**
26	94	$15	**BONNY DOON** California Muscat Canelli Vin de Glacière **1994** (375ml)
27	94	$26	**MONTICELLO** Chardonnay Napa Valley Corley Estate Reserve **1992**
28	93	$44	**MONTHELIE-DOUHAIRET** Volnay En Champans **1993**
29	92	$16	**PENFOLDS** South Australia Cabernet-Shiraz Bin 389 **1992**
30	93	$18	**RABBIT RIDGE** Zinfandel Sonoma Country San Lorenzo Reserve **1993**
31	92	$17	**A. RAFANELLI** Cabernet Sauvignon Dry Creek Valley **1992**
32	92	$18	**ROMBAUER** Chardonnay Carneros **1993**
33	92	$20	**BERINGER** Chardonnay Napa Valley Private Reserve **1993**
34	94	$27	**MASTROJANNI** Brunello di Montalcino **1990**
35	94	$49	**QUINTA DO VESÚVIO** Vintage Port **1992**
36	93	$28	**WHITEHALL LANE** Cabernet Sauvignon Napa Valley Morisoli Vineyard **1992**
37	91	$20	**GROTH** Cabernet Sauvignon Napa Valley **1992**
38	93	$60	**MÉO-CAMUZET** Nuits-St.-Georges Aux Murgers **1993**
39	93	$30	**FORMAN** Cabernet Sauvignon Napa Valley **1992**
40	93	$45	**SHAFER** Cabernet Sauvignon Stags Leap District Hillside Select **1991**
41	93	$55	**DOMINUS** Napa Valley Napanook Vineyard **1991**
42	93	$30	**ETUDE** Cabernet Sauvignon Napa Valley **1992**
43	92	$29	**BERINGER** Merlot Howell Mountain Bancroft Ranch **1992**
44	92	$30	**CHATEAU MONTELENA** Cabernet Sauvignon Napa Valley The Montelena Estate **1991**
45	92	$40	**PENFOLDS** Cabernet Sauvignon South Australia Bin 707 **1992**
46	93	$59	**ORNELLAIA** Masseto **1992**
47	92	$20	**ALION** Ribera del Duero Reserva **1991**
48	91	$17	**MARKHAM** Chardonnay Napa Valley Barrel Fermented **1993**
49	93	$30	**CASTELLO BANFI** Brunello di Montalcino **1990**

*PRICE ON RELEASE

The Top 100: 1995

RANK	SCORE	PRICE*	WINE
50	93	$42	**OLIVIER LEFLAIVE FRÈRES** Volnay Frémiets **1993**
51	91	$23	**MATANZAS CREEK** Chardonnay Sonoma Valley **1993**
52	92	$25	**ARROWOOD** Cabernet Sauvignon Sonoma County **1992**
53	93	$54	**CONTI COSTANTI** Brunello di Montalcino **1990**
54	91	$16	**BODEGAS ESMERALDA** Cabernet Sauvignon Mendoza Agrelo Vineyard Catena **1992**
55	92	$180	**BODEGAS VEGA SICILIA** Ribera del Duero Unico Reserva **1970**
56	92	$65	**DOMAINE LEFLAIVE** Puligny-Montrachet Clavaillon **1992**
57	92	$35	**DOMAINE ZIND-HUMBRECHT** Gewürztraminer Grand Cru Goldert **1993**
58	92	$35	**HENSCHKE** Cabernet Sauvignon Eden Valley Cyril Henschke **1991**
59	92	$20	**RIDGE** California Chardonnay Santa Cruz Mountains **1992**
60	91	$15	**GLORIA FERRER** Chardonnay Carneros **1993**
61	92	$27	**KUMEU RIVER** Chardonnay Kumeu **1993**
62	91	$17	**CAYMUS** California Conundrum **1994**
63	91	$12	**MARIENBERG** Shiraz McLaren Vale **1992**
64	92	$35	**SIMI** Cabernet Sauvignon Alexander Valley Reserve **1991**
65	91	$19	**CHALK HILL** Chardonnay Chalk Hill **1993**
66	91	$20	**FERRARI-CARANO** Chardonnay Alexander Valley **1993**
67	91	$30	**EL MOLINO** Pinot Noir Napa Valley **1992**
68	92	$68	**MONGEARD-MUGNERET** Echezeaux Vieilles Vignes **1993**
69	92	$21	**STONESTREET** Chardonnay Sonoma County **1993**
70	92	$45	**NOZZOLE** Il Pareto **1993**
71	92	$28	**ROSEMOUNT** Chardonnay Hunter Valley Roxburgh **1991**
72	91	$12	**KIONA** Merlot Columbia Valley **1992**
73	90	$11	**MARQUÉS DE RISCAL** Rioja Riserva **1989**
74	90	$10	**ROSEMOUNT** Shiraz South Australia **1994**
75	91	$29	**LEONETTI WASHINGTON** Merlot **1992**
76	91	$32	**SILVER OAK** Cabernet Sauvignon Alexander Valley **1991**
77	91	$30	**MATANZAS CREEK** Merlot Alexander Valley **1993**
78	91	$55	**ROBERT MONDAVI** Cabernet Sauvignon, Napa Valley Reserve **1992**
79	91	$20	**RIDGE** Zinfandel Blend Sonoma County Geyserville **1993**
80	90	$12	**FRANCISCAN** Chardonnay Napa Valley Oakville Estate Barrel Fermented **1993**
81	91	$37	**RUINART** Champagne R de Ruinart **NV**
82	91	$25	**TALBOTT** Chardonnay Monterey **1992**
83	91	$30	**HENSCHKE** Shiraz Keyneton Mount Edelstone **1992**
84	91	$18	**ST. FRANCIS** Zinfandel Sonoma Valley Old Vines **1993**
85	91	$20	**MARIMAR TORRES** Chardonnay Sonoma County Green Valley Don Miguel **1992**
86	90	$25	**CHATEAU STE. MICHELLE** Chardonnay Columbia Valley Cold Creek Vineyard **1993**
87	90	$15	**FERRARI-CARANO** Fumé Blanc Sonoma County Reserve **1994**
88	90	$18	**FONTODI** Chianti Classico Riserva **1991**
89	90	$14	**E. & J. GALLO** Zinfandel Dry Creek Valley Frei Ranch Vineyard Gallo **1990**
90	90	$20	**GLEN CARLOU** Chardonnay Paarl **1994**
91	90	$15	**GREEN & RED** Zinfandel Napa Valley Chiles Mill Vineyard **1993**
92	90	$18	**HEITZ** Cabernet Sauvignon Napa Valley **1990**
93	90	$32	**LAURENT PERRIER** Champagne Brut L.P. **NV**
94	90	$18	**SIRO PANCENTI** Rosso di Montalcino **1993**
95	90	$18	**SANFORD** Chardonnay Santa Barbara County **1993**
96	90	$18	**STEELE** Pinot Noir Carneros **1993**
97	90	$20	**THELEMA** Cabernet Sauvignon-Merlot Stellenbosch **1992**
98	90	$16	**ROEDERER ESTATE** Anderson Valley Brut **NV**
99	90	$65	**ANTINORI** Solaia **1991**
100	91	$89	**MOËT & CHANDON** Cuvée Dom Pérignon **1988**

*PRICE ON RELEASE

Great Wine Values

To help you find many of the outstanding values in wine that this book covers, we have included the following handy list of over 850 wines. Each wine costs $12 or less, and each one scored 85 points or more on *Wine Spectator's* 100-point scale.

The wines are organized by country of origin, then by whether they're red or white, and then by type or category. At the end are three special categories—rosés, sparkling wines, and dessert wines—that bring together wines from all over the world. A star at the end of a listing (✪) indicates a wine that should be relatively easy to obtain from your local shop, since at least 15,000 cases were produced.

For complete tasting notes on these wines, look in the main listings under the country of origin and the winery's name.

• Argentina •

RED

Cabernet Sauvignon

87 **TRAPICHE** Cabernet Sauvignon Mendoza Oak Cask 1993 • $9
85 **BODEGA NORTON** Cabernet Sauvignon Mendoza 1994 • $9
85 **BODEGAS ESMERALDA** Cabernet Sauvignon Maipu Trumpeter 1995 • $9
85 **J. & F. LURTON** Cabernet Sauvignon Mendoza 1996 • $6
85 **J. & F. LURTON** Cabernet Sauvignon Mendoza Gran Lurton Reserva 1996 • $12

Malbec and Malbec Blends

88 **J. & F. LURTON** Malbec Mendoza 1996 • $6
86 **BODEGA NORTON** Malbec Mendoza 1996 • $9
86 **MARIPOSA** Malbec Mendoza 1996 • $10
86 **SANTA JULIA** Malbec-Cabernet Sauvignon Mendoza 1995 • $7
85 **BODEGAS DOMECQ** Malbec-Syrah Mendoza Balbi Vineyard 1997 • $7
85 **LA AGRICOLA** Malbec-Cabernet Sauvignon Mendoza Uvas del Sol 1995 • $8
85 **TRAPICHE** Malbec Mendoza 1995 • $6 ✪

Other Red

87 **SANTA JULIA** Syrah Mendoza Don Alberto 1996 • $7
86 **BODEGA NORTON** Merlot Mendoza 1994 • $9
85 **COMPASS** Merlot Mendoza 1996 • $9

WHITE

86 **J. & F. LURTON** Chardonnay Mendoza 1996 • $6

• Australia •

RED

Cabernet Sauvignon and Cabernet Blends

87 **BULLETIN PLACE** Cabernet Sauvignon Australia 1994 • $10
87 **NORMANS** Cabernet Sauvignon South Australia Bin C106 1995 • $12
87 **ROSEMOUNT** Cabernet Sauvignon South Eastern Australia 1996 • $11 ✪
86 **BLACK OPAL** Cabernet Sauvignon South Eastern Australia 1996 • $11 ✪
86 **HARDYS** Cabernet-Shiraz South Eastern Australia Signature 1995 • $11
86 **JAMIESONS RUN** Cabernet Sauvignon-Shiraz-Cabernet Franc Coonawarra 1995 • $11
86 **MCGUIGAN** Cabernet Sauvignon South Eastern Australia Bin 4000 1997 • $9
86 **SEAVIEW** Cabernet Sauvignon South Australia 1994 • $9
85 **HASELGROVE** Cabernet Sauvignon South Eastern Australia Sovereign 1996 • $10
85 **ORLANDO** Cabernet Sauvignon South Eastern Australia Jacob's Creek 1995 • $9 ✪
85 **SEAVIEW** Cabernet Sauvignon South Australia 1995 • $9
85 **YARRA RIDGE** Cabernet Sauvignon Yarra Valley 1996 • $12

Grenache and Grenache Blends

88 **ST. HALLETT** Gamekeeper's Reserve Red Barossa 1997 • $10
87 **BASEDOW** Grenache Barossa Bush Vine 1995 • $10
87 **D'ARENBERG** Red Ochre McLaren Vale 1996 • $9
86 **CHAIN OF PONDS** Grenache-Sangiovese Adelaide Hills Novello Rosso 1997 • $12
86 **COCKATOO RIDGE** Grenache-Shiraz South Eastern Australia 1996 • $9 ✪
85 **ST. HALLETT** Gamekeeper's Reserve Red Barossa 1996 • $10

Shiraz and Shiraz Blends

91 **ROSEMOUNT** Shiraz South Eastern Australia 1996 • $12 ✪
89 **ALLANDALE** Shiraz Hunter River Valley Matthew 1995 • $12
88 **BANROCK STATION** Shiraz-Cabernet Sauvignon South Eastern Australia 1997 • $6
88 **SEAVIEW** Shiraz McLaren Vale 1994 • $9
87 **BANROCK STATION** Shiraz South Eastern Australia 1997 • $7
87 **BLACK OPAL** Shiraz South Eastern Australia 1996 • $11 ✪
87 **BULLETIN PLACE** Shiraz Australia 1995 • $10
87 **FOX RIVER** Classic Red Australia 1996 • $12
87 **HASELGROVE** Shiraz South Australia Sovereign 1997 • $10
87 **HERMITAGE ROAD** Shiraz South Eastern Australia 1997 • $10
87 **PENFOLDS** Shiraz-Mourvèdre South Eastern Australia Bin 2 1996 • $9
87 **WOLF BLASS** Shiraz South Australia 1996 • $12
86 **BANROCK STATION** Shiraz-Cabernet Sauvignon South Eastern Australia 1996 • $6 ✪
86 **ORLANDO** Shiraz-Cabernet South Eastern Australia Jacob's Creek 1996 • $9 ✪
86 **MCGUIGAN** Shiraz South Eastern Australia Millenium Bin 2000 1997 • $10
86 **MITCHELTON** Shiraz South Eastern Australia Thomas Mitchell 1995 • $10
86 **QUEEN ADELAIDE** Shiraz-Cabernet South Eastern Australia 1995 • $6
86 **ROSEMOUNT** Shiraz-Cabernet South Eastern Australia 1997 • $9 ✪
86 **SEAVIEW** Shiraz McLaren Vale 1996 • $9
86 **TYRRELL'S** Shiraz South Australia Moore's Creek 1996 • $8 ✪

Other Red

87 **CHARLES STURT** University Red South Eastern Australia 1995 • $10
85 **YARRA RIDGE** Pinot Noir Yarra Valley 1997 • $12
85 **YARRA RIDGE** Pinot Noir Victoria 1996 • $12

WHITE

Chardonnay and Chardonnay Blends

90 **CHATEAU REYNELLA** Chardonnay McLaren Vale 1996 • $12
89 **SEPPELT** Chardonnay Australia Corella Ridge 1996 • $12
89 **WATER WHEEL** Chardonnay Bendigo 1996 • $12
88 **HERMITAGE ROAD** Chardonnay South Eastern Australia 1996 • $11
88 **LEASINGHAM** Chardonnay Clare Valley Domain 1996 • $10
88 **WYNNS COONAWARRA ESTATE** Chardonnay Coonawarra 1997 • $12
87 **ALICE WHITE** Chardonnay South Eastern Australia 1996 • $7 ✪
87 **BEST'S** Chardonnay-Sauvignon Blanc Swan Hill 1996 • $9
87 **BULLETIN PLACE** Chardonnay Australia 1996 • $10
87 **DEAKIN ESTATE** Chardonnay Victoria 1996 • $12
87 **HARDYS** Chardonnay South Eastern Australia Signature 1997 • $9
87 **TYRRELL'S** Chardonnay South Eastern Australia Old Winery 1997 • $11 ✪
86 **BRIEN** Chardonnay-Gordo Victoria Family Selection 1996 • $11

86 **BROKE FORDWICH** Chardonnay Hunter Valley 1997 • $12
86 **GALLANT** Chardonnay Mornington Peninsula 1996 • $11
86 **HARDYS** Chardonnay Padthaway 1996 • $11
86 **NORMANS** Chardonnay South Australia Bin C207 1996 • $12
86 **OXFORD LANDING** Chardonnay South Eastern Australia 1997 • $8 ✪
86 **SALISBURY** Chardonnay Victoria 1997 • $8 ✪
85 **BLACK OPAL** Chardonnay South Eastern Australia 1997 • $11 ✪
85 **COCKATOO RIDGE** Chardonnay South Eastern Australia 1996 • $9
85 **FOX CREEK** Chardonnay McLaren Vale Unwooded 1996 • $10
85 **JAMIESONS RUN** Chardonnay South Eastern Australia 1996 • $11
85 **LINDEMANS** Chardonnay South Eastern Australia Bin 65 1997 • $8 ✪
85 **MILBURN PARK** Chardonnay South Eastern Australia Reserve 1997 • $9 ✪
85 **ORLANDO** Chardonnay South Eastern Australia Jacob's Creek 1997 • $9 ✪
85 **QUEEN ADELAIDE** Chardonnay South Eastern Australia 1997 • $7
85 **ROSEMOUNT** Chardonnay South Eastern Australia 1997 • $10 ✪
85 **TYRRELL'S** Chardonnay-Sémillon South Eastern Australia Long Flat 1997 • $8 ✪

Sauvignon Blanc

87 **WIRILDA CREEK** Sauvignon Blanc McLaren Vale 1996 • $11
86 **SALISBURY** Sauvignon Blanc Victoria 1997 • $8
85 **JAMIESONS RUN** Sauvignon Blanc South Eastern Australia 1997 • $11
85 **WATER WHEEL** Sauvignon Blanc Bendigo 1996 • $9

Sémillon and Sémillon Blends

88 **PETER LEHMANN** Sémillon Barossa 1996 • $12
87 **PETER LEHMANN** Sémillon Barossa 1997 • $12
86 **EVANS WINE COMPANY** Sémillon Hunter Valley 1997 • $12
86 **TYRRELL'S** Sémillon-Sauvignon Blanc South Eastern Australia Old Winery 1997 • $11
85 **BASEDOW** Sémillon Barossa 1996 • $10
85 **PENFOLDS** Sémillon-Chardonnay South Australia Koonunga Hill 1997 • $8
85 **SEAVIEW** Sémillon-Sauvignon Blanc McLaren Vale 1996 • $8
85 **TYRRELL'S** Sémillon Hunter Valley Old Winery 1997 • $11

Other White

89 **LEASINGHAM** Riesling Clare Valley 1996 • $8
86 **D'ARENBERG** White Ochre McLaren Vale 1996 • $9
86 **ST. HALLETT** Poacher's Blend White Barossa 1997 • $10 ✪
85 **MITCHELTON** Marsanne South Eastern Australia Thomas Mitchell 1996 • $10

• Austria •

RED

85 **JOHANNESHOF REINISCH** Zweigelt Qualitätswein Thermenregion 1996 • $12

WHITE

87 **HÖPLER** Pinot Blanc Kabinett Neusiedlersee 1995 • $10
87 **PFAFFL** Grüner Veltliner Qualitätswein Weinviertel Hundsleiten-Sandtal 1995 • $12
86 **DINSTLGUT LOIBEN** Grüner Veltliner Qualitätswein Wachau Loibner Loibenberg 1996 • $11

85 **E. & M. BERGER** Grüner Veltliner Kabinett Kremstal Gedersdorfer Lössterrassen 1996 • $11
85 **HÖPLER** Grüner Veltliner Qualitätswein Burgenland 1996 • $9
85 **MARKOWITSCH** Grüner Veltliner Qualitätswein Carnuntum Ried Schanzäcker 1996 • $9
85 **W. GLATZER** Weissburgunder Kabinett Carnuntum 1996 • $10

• Chile •

RED

CABERNET SAUVIGNON

87 **CALITERRA** Cabernet Sauvignon Central Valley Reserva 1995 • $12
87 **DE MARTINO** Cabernet Sauvignon Maipo Valley Prima Reserve 1995 • $12 ✪
87 **LAS CASAS DEL TOQUI** Cabernet Sauvignon Totihue-Cachapoal Valley Réserve Prestige 1995 • $12
86 **ERRAZURIZ** Cabernet Sauvignon Aconcagua Valley El Ceibo Estate 1996 • $9 ✪
86 **MONTGRAS** Cabernet Sauvignon Colchagua Valley 1996 • $8
85 **LAS CASAS DEL TOQUI** Cabernet Sauvignon Totihue-Cachapoal Valley Réserve 1995 • $9
85 **VIÑA TARAPACÁ** Cabernet Sauvignon Central Valley 1996 • $7

MERLOT AND OTHER RED

86 **DE MARTINO** Malbec Maipo Valley Prima Reserve 1996 • $12
85 **CALITERRA** Merlot Central Valley 1996 • $8
85 **CONCHA Y TORO** Merlot Peumo Valley Trio 1996 • $9 ✪
85 **DE MARTINO** Carmenère Maipo Valley Prima Reserve 1996 • $12
85 **VIÑA GRACIA** Merlot Maipo Valley Curioso 1996 • $8 ✪

WHITE

86 **ECHEVERRIA** Chardonnay Molina Reserva 1996 • $9
86 **J. & F. LURTON** Chardonnay Lontue Valley Araucano 1996 • $7
85 **CALITERRA** Chardonnay Aconcagua Valley Reserva 1996 • $11
85 **UNDURRAGA** Sauvignon Blanc Lontue Valley 1997 • $8
85 **VERAMONTE** Chardonnay Casablanca Valley 1996 • $10 ✪

• France •

RED

BEAUJOLAIS

89 **OLIVIER RAVIER** Morgon Côte du Puy 1996 • $10
88 **MOMMESSIN** Morgon 1996 • $11
86 **CHÂTEAU DE PIZAY** Régnié 1995 • $11
86 **GEORGES DUBOEUF** Brouilly Château de Nervers 1996 • $11
86 **GEORGES DUBOEUF** Brouilly Grand Cuvée Flower Label 1996 • $11
86 **GEORGES DUBOEUF** Chénas Domaine des Darroux 1996 • $10
86 **GEORGES DUBOEUF** Chénas Flower Label 1996 • $10
86 **MOMMESSIN** Brouilly 1996 • $11 ✪

86 **MOMMESSIN** Brouilly Château de Briante 1996 • $12
86 **MOMMESSIN** Juliénas 1996 • $11
86 **MOMMESSIN** Juliénas Domaine de la Conseillère 1996 • $12
86 **OLIVIER RAVIER** Juliénas Château de la Bottière 1996 • $10
85 **CHÂTEAU DE PIZAY** Morgon 1995 • $11
85 **GEORGES DUBOEUF** Brouilly Domaine de Combillaty 1996 • $11
85 **GEORGES DUBOEUF** Chiroubles Domaine Desmures 1996 • $10
85 **GEORGES DUBOEUF** Chiroubles Flower Label 1996 • $10
85 **GEORGES DUBOEUF** Morgon Jean Descombes 1996 • $11
85 **GEORGES DUBOEUF** Régnié Flower Label 1996 • $10
85 **HENRY FESSY** Beaujolais-Villages Domaine de la Roche 1996 • $7
85 **JEAN-MARC AUJOUX** Brouilly 1996 • $11 ✪
85 **JEAN-MARC AUJOUX** Juliénas 1996 • $11 ✪
85 **OLIVIER RAVIER** Régnié 1996 • $8

BORDEAUX

90 **CHÂTEAU FERRANDE** Graves 1995 • $12 ✪
88 **CHÂTEAU BARREYRES** Haut-Médoc 1995 • $12 ✪
88 **CHÂTEAU D'ARCINS** Haut-Médoc 1995 • $12 ✪
87 **LE CHARME LABORY** St.-Estèphe 1995 • $12
86 **CHÂTEAU LA FREYNELLE** Bordeaux 1995 • $8
86 **CHÂTEAU TOUR-PRIGNAC** Médoc 1995 • $10 ✪
86 **PIERRE DOURTHE** Bordeaux Numéro 1 1995 • $9
86 **SIRIUS** Bordeaux 1995 • $12
85 **BLASON D'ISSAN** Margaux 1995 • $12
85 **CHÂTEAU CARDUS** Médoc 1995 • $12
85 **CHÂTEAU DU BOUSQUET** Côtes de Bourg 1995 • $9 ✪
85 **CHÂTEAU JONQUEYRES** Bordeaux Supérieur 1995 • $12
85 **CHÂTEAU MIREFLEURS** Bordeaux Supérieur 1995 • $8 ✪
85 **CHÂTEAU TOUR DU MAYNE** Haut-Médoc 1995 • $9

LANGUEDOC-ROUSSILLON

91 **CHÂTEAU ST.-GERMAIN** Coteaux du Languedoc 1995 • $12
90 **BORIE LA VITARÈLE** St.-Chinian 1995 • $10
89 **DOMAINE CLAVEL** Coteaux du Languedoc Terroir de la Méjanelle Les Garrigues 1995 • $10
89 **DOMAINE DU MAS CREMAT** Côtes du Roussillon 1995 • $12
88 **CANET VALETTE** St.-Chinian 1995 • $10
88 **DOMAINE CLAVEL** Coteaux du Languedoc Terroir de la Méjanelle Mas de Clavel Vieilles Vignes 1995 • $7
88 **DOMAINE MARIS** Minervois Carte Noire 1995 • $9
87 **CHATEAU DE LA NEGLY** Syrah-Grenache Coteaux du Languedoc 1995 • $10
87 **CHÂTEAU LES PINS** Côtes du Roussillon-Villages 1995 • $11
87 **DOMAINE DES MURETTES** Minervois Clos de l'Olivier 1995 • $11
87 **DOMAINE GUY DE SAUVANES** Faugères Cuvée Sarah 1995 • $8
87 **DOMAINE PICCININI** Minervois 1996 • $10
87 **DOMAINE PIQUEMAL** Côtes du Roussillon 1995 • $10
87 **DOMAINE ST.-ANTONIN** Faugères 1996 • $10
87 **ETANG DU MOULIN** Minervois Réserve 1996 • $8
87 **MAS CHAMPART** Coteaux du Languedoc 1995 • $12
86 **CATHERINE DE ST.-JUERY** Syrah Coteaux du Languedoc 1995 • $9
86 **CHÂTEAU CAPENDU** Corbières L'Excellence 1995 • $9

86 **CHÂTEAU PUECH-HAUT** Coteaux du Languedoc St.-Drézéry 1995 • $10
86 **DOMAINE LEON BARRAL** Faugères 1994 • $10
85 **CHÂTEAU DE CABRIAC** Corbières Cuvée Marquise de Puivert 1995 • $10
85 **CHÂTEAU DE JAU** Côtes du Roussillon-Villages 1995 • $10
85 **CHÂTEAU DE PENA** Côtes du Roussillon-Villages 1995 • $9
85 **CHÂTEAU SAINTE EULALIE** Minervois Cuvée Tradition 1995 • $9
85 **CLOS DE VILLEMAJOU** Corbières 1994 • $8
85 **DOMAINE BORIE DE MAUREL** Syrah Minervois 1996 • $9
85 **DOMAINE CROS** Minervois 1995 • $7

Loire

86 **CAVE DES VIGNERONS DE SAUMUR** Saumur Red Cuvée Tradition 1996 • $7
86 **PHILIPPE DELESVAUX** Anjou Red 1996 • $11
85 **CAVE DES VIGNERONS DE SAUMUR** Saumur-Champigny Cuvée Tradition 1996 • $9
85 **DOMAINE DE LA CHANTELEUSERIE** Bourgueil Cuvée Alouettes 1996 • $11
85 **SAUVION & FILS** Saumur-Champigny 1996 • $9

Rhône

88 **DOMAINE DU COLOMBIER** Crozes-Hermitage 1995 • $12
88 **J. VIDAL-FLEURY** Côtes du Rhône 1995 • $9
88 **PERRIN RÉSERVE** Côtes du Rhône 1995 • $10 ✪
88 **VIGNERONS DE ST.-GERVAIS** Syrah Côtes du Rhône-Villages 1996 • $10
87 **PAUL JABOULET AÎNÉ** Côtes du Rhône Parallèle 45 1996 • $10 ✪
86 **DOMAINE DE LA ROQUETTE** Vin de Pays de la Principauté d'Orange Le Pigeoulet 1996 • $10
85 **DELAS** Côtes du Rhône St.-Esprit 1996 • $8
85 **DELAS** Côtes du Rhône St.-Esprit 1995 • $8
85 **DOMAINE DE LA RÉMÉJEANNE** Côtes du Rhône Les Arbousiers 1996 • $12
85 **DOMAINE DE LA RÉMÉJEANNE** Côtes du Rhône Les Chevrefeuilles 1995 • $9
85 **DOMAINE DE PÉRILLIÈRE** Côtes du Rhône-Villages 1995 • $10
85 **DOMAINE DE PIAUGIER** Gigondas 1995 • $10
85 **DOMAINE DU TRAPADIS** Côtes du Rhône 1995 • $11
85 **J. VIDAL-FLEURY** Côtes du Rhône-Villages 1994 • $10
85 **LA VIEILLE FERME** Côtes du Ventoux 1995 • $8
85 **PERRIN RÉSERVE** Côtes du Rhône 1996 • $10 ✪

Vin de Pays d'Oc Merlot

86 **J. & F. LURTON** Merlot Vin de Pays d'Oc Domaine des Salices 1996 • $7
85 **BARTON & GUESTIER** Merlot Vin de Pays d'Oc 1996 • $7 ✪
85 **DULONG** Merlot Vin de Pays d'Oc 1996 • $7 ✪
85 **MÉDITÉO** Merlot Vin de Pays d'Oc 1996 • $7

Vin de Pays d'Oc Syrah

87 **DOMAINE MIQUEL** Syrah Vin de Pays d'Oc 1995 • $12
87 **J. & F. LURTON** Syrah Vin de Pays d'Oc Domaine des Salices 1996 • $7
87 **RICHEMONT** Syrah Vin de Pays d'Oc Reserve 1995 • $7
86 **MÉDITÉO** Syrah Vin de Pays d'Oc 1996 • $7
86 **MICHEL PICARD** Syrah Vin de Pays d'Oc 1996 • $10 ✪
85 **DOMAINE LA CHEVALIÈRE** Syrah Vin de Pays d'Oc Réserve 1996 • $10
85 **SUNFLOWER VALLEY** Syrah Vin de Pays d'Oc 1996 • $7

OTHER RED

89 **CHÂTEAU DE PERRON** Madiran 1995 • $12
88 **DOMAINE BÉNAZETH** Vin de Pays de l'Aude 1995 • $10
87 **DOMAINE BIBIAN** Madiran 1995 • $11
87 **DOMAINE CAZES** Vin de Pays des Côtes Catalanes Le Credo 1994 • $12
87 **J. & F. LURTON** Vin de Pays d'Oc Domaine de Bachellery 1994 • $6
87 **LES VIGNERONS DE BUZET** Buzet Baron d'Ardeuil 1991 • $11
87 **MAS DE GOURGONNIER** Les Baux de Provence Réserve du Mas 1994 • $12
87 **MAS DE LE DAME** Les Baux de Provence Cuvée Gourmande 1995 • $11
86 **J. & F. LURTON** Grenache Vin de Pays d'Oc Domaine de Bachellery 1995 • $6
85 **CHÂTEAU CALISSANNE** Coteaux d'Aix-en-Provence Cuvée du Château 1995 • $10
85 **CHÂTEAU CALISSANNE** Coteaux d'Aix-en-Provence Cuvée du Château 1994 • $10
85 **CHÂTEAU DE PADERE** Buzet 1994 • $11
85 **CHÂTEAU LAGREZETTE** Cahors Moulin Lagrezette 1995 • $11
85 **CHÂTEAU RICHARD** Côtes de Bergerac 1994 • $12
85 **RICHEMONT** Cabernet Sauvignon Vin de Pays d'Oc Reserve 1995 • $7
85 **YVON MAU** Merlot Vin de Pays des Côtes de Gascogne 1996 • $6 ✪

WHITE

ALSACE

91 **PIERRE SPARR** Tokay Pinot Gris Alsace Réserve 1996 • $12
89 **PIERRE SPARR** Gewürztraminer Alsace Réserve 1996 • $12
88 **CHARLES WANTZ** Riesling Alsace Réserve Particulière 1996 • $12
87 **CHARLES WANTZ** Pinot Blanc Alsace Réserve Particulière 1996 • $12
87 **LUCIEN ALBRECHT** Riesling Alsace 1995 • $12
87 **MEYER-FONNÉ** Pinot Blanc Alsace Vieilles Vignes 1996 • $10
87 **PIERRE SPARR** Pinot Blanc Alsace Diamant d'Alsace Réserve 1996 • $8 ✪
87 **PIERRE SPARR** Riesling Alsace Carte d'Or 1996 • $9
86 **DOMAINE BRUNO HUNOLD** Pinot Blanc Alsace 1995 • $9
86 **PIERRE SPARR** Tokay Pinot Gris Alsace Carte d'Or 1996 • $10
85 **DOMAINE BOTT-GEYL** Sylvaner Alsace Béblenheim 1995 • $10
85 **HUGEL** Alsace Gentil 1996 • $10
85 **PIERRE SPARR** Gewürztraminer Alsace Carte d'Or 1996 • $10

BORDEAUX

89 **MICHEL LYNCH** Sauvignon Blanc Bordeaux 1996 • $9 ✪
87 **CHÂTEAU COUCHEROY** Pessac-Léognan White 1995 • $11
86 **CHÂTEAU DE CRUZEAU** Pessac-Léognan White 1995 • $12
86 **SIRIUS** Bordeaux White 1995 • $10
85 **CHÂTEAU BONNET** Entre-Deux-Mers 1995 • $10
85 **J.M. ARCAUTE** Sauvignon Blanc Bordeaux 1995 • $7

BURGUNDY

89 **LE MANOIR MURISALTIEN** Mâcon-Fuissé 1996 • $12
88 **JEAN MANCIAT** Mâcon 1996 • $12
88 **JEAN-MARC BROCARD** Bourgogne sur Portlandien White 1996 • $8
88 **L'HÉRITIER-GUYOT** Mâcon-Villages 1996 • $9
87 **DIDIER TRIPOZ** Charnay-lès-Mâcon Clos des Tournons 1996 • $9
87 **HENRI CLERC & FILS** Bourgogne Les Riaux White 1995 • $12
86 **PAUL BOURGEON** Mâcon-Villages 1996 • $11

86 **ROGER LUQUET** Mâcon Clos de Condemine 1996 • $11
85 **GROUPEMENT DE PRODUCTEURS DE PRISSÉ** Mâcon-Villages 1996 • $11 ✪
85 **LE MANOIR MURISALTIEN** Mâcon-Cruzilles 1996 • $10
85 **MICHEL BARAT** Chablis 1996 • $12
85 **MOMMESSIN** Bourgogne White 1995 • $12
85 **ROUX PÈRE & FILS** Bourgogne White 1995 • $9

Languedoc-Roussillon

86 **CHÂTEAU LA ROQUE** Coteaux du Languedoc White Pic St.-Loup 1996 • $9
85 **LES TERRASSES DE GUILHEM** Vin de Pays de l'Herault White 1996 • $9

Loire

86 **J.-C. PICHOT** Vouvray Domaine Le Peu de la Moriette 1996 • $8
86 **LUC & ANDRÉE-MARIE CHOBLET** Muscadet-Côtes de Grandlieu Sur Lie Clos de la Sénaigerie 1996 • $10
85 **CHÉREAU-CARRÉ** Muscadet de Sèvre et Maine Sur Lie Château de la Gravelle 1996 • $11
85 **DOMAINE DE MAISON BLANCHE** Quincy 1995 • $10 ✪
85 **JEAN-CLAUDE BOUGRIER** Vouvray 1996 • $9
85 **LES FRÈRES COUILLAUD** Muscadet de Sèvre et Maine Sur Lie Château La Morinière 1996 • $8

Rhône

89 **DOMAINE PÉLAQUIÉ** Côtes du Rhône-Villages White Laudun 1996 • $12
87 **CAVE DE TAIN L'HERMITAGE** St.-Péray Les Nobles Rives 1995 • $11
87 **DOMAINE DU COLOMBIER** Crozes-Hermitage White 1996 • $12
85 **CAVES DES PAPES** Côtes du Rhône White 1996 • $7
85 **DOMAINE DE LA RÉMÉJEANNE** Côtes du Rhône White Les Arbousiers 1996 • $11
85 **E. GUIGAL** Côtes du Rhône White 1996 • $10

Other White

86 **DOMAINE DU TARIQUET** Vin de Pays des Côtes de Gascogne White Cuvée Bois 1995 • $11
86 **LA LIAISON** Chardonnay Vin de Pays d'Oc 1996 • $10
85 **CHÂTEAU RICHARD** Bergerac White 1995 • $9
85 **DOMAINE DU MAGE** Ugni Blanc-Colombard Vin de Pays des Côtes de Gascogne 1996 • $7
85 **J. & F. LURTON** Sauvignon Blanc Vin de Pays d'Oc Les Fumées Blanches 1996 • $6 ✪
85 **LA PEROUSE** Vin de Pays d'Oc Cuvée Blanc 1995 • $8
85 **MÉDITÉO** Chardonnay Vin de Pays d'Oc 1996 • $7
85 **PLAIMONT** Vin de Pays des Côtes de Gascogne White Colombelle 1996 • $6 ✪

• Germany •

WHITE

Riesling

90 **KURT DARTING** Riesling Kabinett Pfalz Ungsteiner Bettelhaus 1996 • $11
89 **KURT DARTING** Riesling Spätlese Pfalz Dürkheimer Spielberg 1996 • $12
87 **BALTHASAR RESS** Riesling Kabinett Rheingau Hattenheimer Schützenhaus 1996 • $10
87 **FITZ-RITTER** Riesling Spätlese Pfalz Ungsteiner Herrenberg 1995 • $12
87 **HEYL ZU HERRNSHEIM** Riesling Kabinett Rheinhessen Schloss Mathildenhof 1996 • $12
87 **HEYL ZU HERRNSHEIM** Riesling Kabinett Trocken Rheinhessen Niersteiner Pettental 1996 • $12
87 **JOH. JOS. CHRISTOFFEL ERBEN** Riesling Kabinett Mosel-Saar-Ruwer Erdener Treppchen 1996 • $11
87 **JOH. JOS. PRÜM** Riesling Qba Mosel-Saar-Ruwer Dr. M. Prüm 1996 • $11

87 **LANGWERTH VON SIMMERN** Riesling Kabinett Rheingau Hattenheimer Mannberg 1996 • $
87 **LINGENFELDER** Riesling Kabinett Halbtrocken Pfalz Freinsheimer Musikantenbuckel 1996 • $12
87 **REICHSRAT VON BUHL** Riesling QbA Halbtrocken Pfalz Deidesheimer 1996 • $12
87 **STAATSWEINGÜTER KLOSTER EBERBACH** Riesling QbA Rheingau Steinberger 1996 • $12
86 **BALTHASAR RESS** Riesling QbA Trocken Rheingau 1996 • $9
86 **C. VON SCHUBERT** Riesling QbA Mosel-Saar-Ruwer Maximin Grünhäuser Bruderberg 1996 • $12
86 **FREIHERR ZU KNYPHAUSEN** Riesling Kabinett Rheingau 1996 • $12
86 **FREIHERR ZU KNYPHAUSEN** Riesling Kabinett Trocken Rheingau Erbacher Steinmorgen 1996 • $12
86 **JOH. JOS. CHRISTOFFEL ERBEN** Riesling Kabinett Mosel-Saar-Ruwer Ürziger Würzgarten 1996 • $11
86 **LANGWERTH VON SIMMERN** Riesling Kabinett Rheingau 1996 • $11
86 **LANGWERTH VON SIMMERN** Riesling Qualitätswein Rheingau Riesling 1996 • $10
86 **SCHMITGES** Riesling Qualitätswein Mosel-Saar-Ruwer 1996 • $10
86 **ZILLIKEN** Riesling QbA Halbtrocken Mosel-Saar-Ruwer Zilliken Gutsriesling 1996 • $11
85 **DR. BÜRKLIN-WOLF** Riesling QbA Pfalz Forster 1996 • $10
85 **FREIHERR ZU KNYPHAUSEN** Riesling Kabinett Rheingau Baron zu Knyphausen Erbacher Steinmorgen 1996 • $12
85 **FREIHERR ZU KNYPHAUSEN** Riesling QbA Rheingau Baron zu Knyphausen Charta 1996 • $12
85 **H. DÖNNHOFF** Riesling QbA Nahe 1996 • $12
85 **J. WEGELER ERBEN** Riesling QbA Trocken Rheingau 1996 • $9
85 **STEPHAN EHLEN** Riesling Kabinett Mosel-Saar-Ruwer Erdener Treppchen 1996 • $12

Scheurebe

87 **KURT DARTING** Scheurebe Spätlese Pfalz Dürkheimer Spielberg 1996 • $11

• Italy •

RED

Chianti

88 **FATTORIA DI BASCIANO** Chianti Rufina Riserva 1994 • $11
87 **CASTELLO DI LILLIANO** Chianti Classico 1995 • $11
86 **CASTELLO DI QUERCETO** Chianti Classico 1994 • $12
86 **CONTE FERDINANDO GUICCIARDINI** Chianti Colli Fiorentini Il Cortile del Castello di Poppiano 1994 • $9
86 **DIEVOLE** Chianti Classico 1995 • $12
86 **FATTORIA DI BASCIANO** Chianti Rufina 1995 • $7
86 **LA TORRACCIA** Chianti Classico Il Tarocco 1993 • $11
86 **TENUTA BORGO SCOPETO** Chianti Classico 1994 • $12
86 **SELVAPIANA** Chianti Rufina 1994 • $11
85 **BARONE RICASOLI** Chianti Classico San Ripolo 1995 • $10 ✪
85 **RICCARDO FALCHINI** Chianti Colli Senesi Titolato Colombaia 1996 • $9
85 **SAN FELICE** Chianti Classico 1995 • $12
85 **SAN LUIGI** Chianti Colli Senesi 1994 • $11
85 **TENUTA DI GHIZZANO** Chianti 1996 • $10

Other Tuscan Red

88 **SIRO PACENTI** Rosso di Montalcino 1995 • $12
87 **FATTORIA DEI BARBI** Brusco dei Barbi 1996 • $10
87 **TENUTA DI GRACCIANO DELLA SETA** Rosso di Montepulciano 1995 • $10

86 **ENZO TIEZZI** Rosso di Montalcino 1995 • $12
86 **FATTORIA DEL CERRO** Rosso di Montepulciano 1996 • $11
85 **BARONE RICASOLI** Toscana Formulae 1995 • $12
85 **CARPINETO** Dogajolo 1996 • $11 ✪
85 **CECCHI** Sangiovese di Toscana 1995 • $8 ✪
85 **ROCCA DELLE MACIE** Rubizzo 1995 • $10

Dolcetto d'Alba

88 **GIUSEPPE CORTESE** Dolcetto d'Alba Trifolera 1996 • $11
87 **SCRIMAGLIO** Dolcetto d'Alba 1996 • $10
86 **STEFANO FARINA** Dolcetto d'Alba 1996 • $10
85 **BEL COLLE** Dolcetto d'Alba Borgo Castagni in Verduno 1996 • $12
85 **BENI DI BATASIOLO** Dolcetto d'Alba 1996 • $11
85 **PUNSET** Dolcetto d'Alba Organically Grown 1995 • $12

Other Piedmont Red

90 **CA' DEL RE** Barbera d'Alba 1996 • $10
89 **ALFREDO PRUNOTTO** Barbera d'Asti Fiulot 1996 • $11
85 **CANTINE GIACOMO ASCHERI** Barbera d'Alba Vigna Fontanelle 1995 • $12
85 **STEFANO FARINA** Barbera d'Alba 1995 • $9

Merlot

86 **FANTINEL** Merlot Grave del Friuli Barone Rosso 1997 • $9
86 **PRAVINI** Merlot Trentino 1995 • $9
85 **PETER ZEMMER** Merlot Alto Adige 1995 • $12

Other Red

86 **BERTANI** Valpolicella Valpantena Secco-Bertani 1995 • $10 ✪
86 **LEONE DE CASTRIS** Salice Salentino Riserva 1994 • $12
86 **UMANI RONCHI** Montepulciano d'Abruzzo Jorio 1995 • $11
85 **ACINUM** Valpolicella Classico Superiore 1995 • $12
85 **BORGO AL CASTELLO** Primitivo Tarantino Mother Zin 1996 • $10
85 **FALESCO** Vitiano 1996 • $10
85 **FANTINEL** Cabernet Franc Grave del Friuli F Sigillo Oro 1997 • $12
85 **FARNESE** Sangiovese Abruzzi 1995 • $6 ✪
85 **LEONE DE CASTRIS** Salice Salentino Maiana 1995 • $8
85 **MEZZACORONA** Cabernet Sauvignon Trentino 1995 • $8 ✪
85 **TERRE DI GINESTRA** Sicily Red 1995 • $9
85 **VILLA CERVIA** Montepulciano d'Abruzzo 1995 • $6 ✪

WHITE

Chardonnay

85 **ANTINORI** Chardonnay Umbria Castello della Sala 1996 • $12
85 **FURLAN CASTELCOSA** Chardonnay delle Venezie 1996 • $12
85 **VIALA** Chardonnay delle Venezie 1996 • $6

Pinot Grigio and Pinot Bianco

86 **CA'VIT** Pinot Grigio delle Venezie 1997 • $8 ✪
86 **ENO-FRIULIA** Pinot Bianco Collio 1997 • $12
86 **FRATELLI PIGHIN** Pinot Grigio Grave del Friuli 1996 • $12
85 **BOLLINI** Pinot Grigio Trentino 1997 • $11 ✪

85 **CAMPANILE** Pinot Grigio Grave del Friuli 1997 • $11
85 **ECCO DOMANI** Pinot Bianco delle Venezie 1996 • $10 ✪
85 **ENO-FRIULIA** Pinot Grigio Collio 1997 • $12
85 **FONTANA CANDIDA** Pinot Grigio delle Venezie 1996 • $8
85 **SANTI** Pinot Grigio Trentino Vigneto Sortesele 1996 • $12
85 **TIEFENBRUNNER** Pinot Grigio Alto Adige 1996 • $11
85 **VILLA ABA** Pinot Grigio Grave del Friuli 1996 • $12

Tuscan White

87 **RUFFINO** Libaio 1996 • $10
85 **BADIA A COLTIBUONO** Trappoline 1995 • $10
85 **CASTELLARE DI CASTELLINA** Spartito 1994 • $10
85 **MONTENIDOLI** Vernaccia di San Gimignano Fiore 1995 • $9
85 **SAN FELICE** Belcaro 1996 • $11

Other White

86 **CAVALCHINA** Bianco di Custoza 1997 • $10
85 **BANEAR** Sauvignon Grave del Friuli 1995 • $12
85 **CA' RUGATE** Soave Classico 1996 • $12
85 **CONTADI CASTALDI** Terre de Franciacorta White 1996 • $10
85 **FAZI-BATTAGLIA** Verdicchio dei Castelli di Jesi Classico Le Moie 1994 • $12
85 **FURLAN CASTELCOSA** Castelcosa Grigio 1996 • $12
85 **SALVIANO** Orvieto Classico 1996 • $12
85 **ZENATO** Lugana S. Benedetto 1996 • $12

• New Zealand •

Sauvignon Blanc

90 **GIESEN** Sauvignon Blanc Marlborough 1996 • $9
88 **GIESEN** Sauvignon Blanc Marlborough 1997 • $12
88 **VILLA MARIA** Sauvignon Blanc Marlborough-Te Kauwhata-Hawke's Bay Private Bin 1996 • $10
87 **MISSION** Sauvignon Blanc Hawkes Bay 1997 • $12
86 **SELWYN RIVER** Sauvignon Blanc Marlborough 1996 • $9

Other White

90 **ST. CLAIR** Riesling Marlborough 1997 • $12
87 **MISSION** Pinot Gris Hawkes Bay 1996 • $11
87 **SELWYN RIVER** Chardonnay Marlborough 1996 • $10
85 **GIESEN** Riesling Canterbury 1996 • $11

• Portugal •

RED

Douro

88 **RAMOS-PINTO** Douro 1994 • $11
86 **QUINTA DO CRASTO** Douro 1995 • $11
85 **CAVES VELHAS** Douro Lagar Velho Reserva 1990 • $10

Other Red

87 **CASA CADAVAL** Trincadeira Preta Ribatejo 1994 • $12
87 **LUIS PATO** Bairrada Quinta do Ribeirinho Primeira Escolha 1995 • $12
86 **CAVES DOM TEODÓSIO** Dão Cardeal Reserva 1990 • $9
85 **CAVES DOM TEODÓSIO** Dão Cardeal 1995 • $7
85 **CAVES DOM TEODÓSIO** Tomar Quinta de S. João Batista 1994 • $7
85 **HERDADE DO ESPORÃO** Reguengos 1993 • $12

WHITE

85 **QUINTA DO CÔTTO** Douro White 1996 • $12
85 **SOGRAPE** Dão White Duque de Viseu 1996 • $8

• South Africa •

RED

Cabernet Sauvignon and Cabernet Blends

88 **BACKSBERG** Cabernet Sauvignon Paarl 1995 • $12
87 **KANONKOP** Kadette Stellenbosch 1995 • $10
86 **CATHEDRAL CELLAR** Cabernet Sauvignon Coastal Region 1994 • $12
85 **SPRINGBOK** Cabernet Sauvignon Western Cape 1995 • $8 ✪

Merlot

87 **SPRINGBOK** Merlot Western Cape 1995 • $8
85 **BACKSBERG** Merlot Paarl 1995 • $12
85 **NEETHLINGSHOF** Merlot Stellenbosch 1994 • $10
85 **SWARTLAND WINERY** Merlot Swartland Region 1997 • $10 ✪

Other Red

89 **BACKSBERG** Shiraz Paarl 1995 • $12
87 **CLOS MALVERNE** Pinotage Stellenbosch 1996 • $12
87 **LIEVLAND** Lievlander Red Stellenbosch 1995 • $8
86 **SPRINGBOK** Pinotage Western Cape 1995 • $9 ✪

WHITE

88 **BACKSBERG** Chardonnay Paarl 1996 • $12
88 **SAVANHA** Chardonnay Western Cape Agulhas Bank 1996 • $9
87 **NEIL ELLIS** Sauvignon Blanc Groenkloof 1997 • $12
86 **CHEETAH VALLEY** Chardonnay Western Cape 1997 • $10
85 **NEETHLINGSHOF** Chardonnay Stellenbosch 1995 • $10
85 **NEETHLINGSHOF** Weisser Riesling Stellenbosch 1996 • $10

• Spain •

RED

Navarra

87 **BODEGAS PIEDEMONTE** Cabernet Sauvignon Navarra Oligitum 1995 • $6
87 **BODEGAS PIEDEMONTE** Navarra Coupage Crianza 1994 • $8
86 **BODEGAS GUELBENZU** Navarra 1995 • $10
86 **BODEGAS PIEDEMONTE** Cabernet Sauvignon Navarra Crianza 1994 • $8
85 **BODEGAS PIEDEMONTE** Navarra Oligitum 1995 • $6
85 **PALACIO DE LA VEGA** Navarra Crianza 1994 • $12 ✪
85 **PALACIO DE LA VEGA** Tempranillo Navarra 1996 • $9

Ribera del Duero

89 **BODEGA SAN JORGE** Ribera del Duero Arroyo Crianza 1994 • $12
87 **HIJOS DE ANTONIO BARCELO** Ribera del Duero Viña Mayor 1996 • $6 ✪
85 **BODEGA SAN JORGE** Ribera del Duero Arroyo 1996 • $7 ✪
85 **BODEGAS FELIX CALLEJO** Ribera del Duero Cuatro Meses en Barrica 1996 • $12
85 **HIJOS DE ANTONIO BARCELO** Ribera del Duero Viña Mayor Crianza 1994 • $8 ✪

Rioja

88 **BODEGAS MUERZA** Rioja Vega Crianza 1994 • $10
87 **BODEGAS AGE** Rioja Siglo Reserva 1988 • $12
87 **BODEGAS CAMPO VIEJO** Rioja Reserva 1990 • $11
87 **BODEGAS LAN** Rioja Reserva 1988 • $12 ✪
87 **MARQUÉS DE GRIÑON** Rioja 1995 • $10 ✪
86 **ARTADI** Rioja Crianza 1994 • $12
86 **BODEGAS MONTECILLO** Rioja Reserva 1989 • $12
86 **BODEGAS MONTECILLO** Rioja Viña Cumbrero Crianza 1994 • $8
86 **BODEGAS PRIMICIA** Rioja Viña Diezmo Crianza 1994 • $10 ✪
86 **MARQUÉS DE CÁCERES** Rioja Crianza 1994 • $12
86 **R. DE AYALA LETE E HIJOS** Rioja Viña Santurnia Crianza 1994 • $7
85 **BODEGAS PALACIOS REMONDO** Rioja Herencia Remondo Crianza 1994 • $10 ✪
85 **MARQUÉS DEL PUERTO** Rioja Crianza 1994 • $9

Other Red

87 **ABADIA RETUERTA** Viño de Mesa de Castilla y Leon Rivola 1996 • $10 ✪
87 **ONIX** Priorat 1995 • $8
85 **SCALA DEI** Priorat El Cipres 1995 • $8

WHITE

Rias Baixas

88 **ADEGAS DAS EIRAS** Rias Baixas Terras Gauda 1996 • $12
88 **BODEGAS DE VILARIÑO-CAMBADOS** Albariño Rias Baixas Burgáns 1996 • $10
87 **VALDUMIA** Albariño Rias Baixas 1996 • $12 ✪
86 **ADEGAS DAS EIRAS** Albariño Rias Baixas Abadia de San Campio 1996 • $12

Rioja

90 **R. LÓPEZ DE HEREDIA VIÑA TONDONIA** Rioja White Viña Gravonia Crianza 1988 • $12
87 **CUNE** Rioja White Monopole 1994 • $12

86 **BODEGAS MARQUÉS DE MURRIETA** Rioja White Misela 1993 • $8 ✪
86 **MARQUÉS DE CÁCERES** Rioja White Antea 1994 • $9
85 **BODEGAS BERONIA** Viura Rioja White Barrel Fermented 1996 • $11
85 **BODEGAS BRETÓN** Rioja White Loriñon Barrel Fermented 1996 • $10

OTHER WHITE

86 **COMPANIA DE VINOS DE LA GRANJA** Rueda Basa 1996 • $7 ✪
85 **BODEGA NEKEAS** Viura-Chardonnay Navarra Vega Sindoa 1996 • $6
85 **MARQUÉS DE RISCAL** Rueda 1996 • $7

• United States •

RED

CABERNET SAUVIGNON AND CABERNET BLENDS

California

87 **BEAULIEU VINEYARD** Cabernet Sauvignon Napa Valley Beautour 1994 • $11 ✪
87 **DREYER SONOMA** Cabernet Sauvignon Sonoma County 1995 • $11
87 **NAPA RIDGE** Cabernet Sauvignon Central Coast Oak Barrel 1995 • $9 ✪
87 **TERRA ROSA** Cabernet Sauvignon North Coast 1995 • $11
86 **HESS SELECT** Cabernet Sauvignon California 1995 • $10 ✪
86 **MERIDIAN** Cabernet Sauvignon California 1994 • $11
86 **RUTHERFORD VINTNERS** Cabernet Sauvignon Sonoma County Barrel Select 1995 • $9
86 **VILLA MT. EDEN** Cabernet Sauvignon California 1994 • $12 ✪
85 **ARCIERO** Cabernet Sauvignon Paso Robles 1994 • $11
85 **BOEGER** Cabernet Sauvignon El Dorado 1994 • $12
85 **CHARLES B. MITCHELL** Cabernet Sauvignon El Dorado Vintner's Cuvee 1995 • $11
85 **FIRESTONE** Cabernet Sauvignon Santa Ynez Valley 1994 • $12
85 **GOSSAMER BAY** Cabernet Sauvignon California 1995 • $9
85 **HAWK CREST** Cabernet Sauvignon California 1995 • $12 ✪
85 **ROBERT MONDAVI** Cabernet Sauvignon North Coast Coastal 1995 • $11
85 **ROUND HILL** Cabernet Sauvignon California 1995 • $8 ✪
85 **TURNING LEAF** Cabernet Sauvignon California 1995 • $8
85 **WENTE** Cabernet Sauvignon Livermore Valley 1995 • $11

Oregon

86 **VALLEY VIEW** Cabernet Sauvignon Rogue Valley 1995 • $12
85 **EDGEFIELD** Oregon Black Rabbit Red 1996 • $11

Washington

90 **COLUMBIA CREST** Cabernet Sauvignon Columbia Valley 1994 • $11 ✪
89 **SILVER LAKE** Cabernet Sauvignon Columbia Valley Reserve 1994 • $12
88 **KNIPPRATH** Cabernet Sauvignon Columbia Valley 1994 • $12
87 **COLUMBIA CREST** Cabernet Sauvignon Columbia Valley 1995 • $11 ✪
86 **BADGER MOUNTAIN** Cabernet-Merlot Columbia Valley 1996 • $12
86 **DUCK POND** Cabernet Sauvignon Columbia Valley Fries Vineyard-Wahluke Slope 1995 • $10
86 **HYATT** Cabernet Sauvignon Yakima Valley 1993 • $12
86 **POWERS** Cabernet-Merlot Columbia Valley 1995 • $12
85 **ARBOR CREST** Cabernet Sauvignon-Merlot Washington 1995 • $12

85 **HEDGES** Cabernet Sauvignon-Merlot Washington 1996 • $11 ✪
85 **HOGUE** Cabernet-Merlot Columbia Valley 1995 • $10 ✪
85 **SILVER LAKE** Cabernet-Merlot Columbia Valley 1995 • $9

GAMAY

California

87 **PRESTON** Gamay Beaujolais Dry Creek Valley 1996 • $11
86 **PRESTON** Gamay Dry Creek Valley 1997 • $12
85 **BERINGER** Gamay California Beaujolais Nouveau 1997 • $7

LEMBERGER

Washington

86 **HOODSPORT** Lemberger-Cabernet Yakima Valley 1995 • $11
86 **LATAH CREEK** Lemberger Washington 1995 • $9
85 **HOGUE** Lemberger Columbia Valley Genesis Blue Franc 1995 • $12
85 **OAKWOOD** Lemberger Yakima Valley 1993 • $10

MERLOT

California

86 **BEAULIEU VINEYARD** Merlot California Coastal 1995 • $10 ✪
86 **SEA RIDGE COASTAL** Merlot California 1996 • $10
86 **STEVENOT** Merlot California Reserve 1995 • $12
86 **TURNING LEAF** Merlot Sonoma County Sonoma Reserve 1994 • $10 ✪
85 **PEPPERWOOD GROVE** Merlot California 1996 • $7

Oregon/Washington

86 **ASHLAND VINEYARDS** Merlot Rogue Valley (Oregon) 1995 • $12
86 **VALLEY VIEW** Merlot Rogue Valley (Oregon) 1995 • $12
85 **DUCK POND** Merlot Columbia Valley Fries' Desert Wind Vineyad Wahluke Slope (Washington) 1996 • $12

PETITE SIRAH

California

86 **FOPPIANO** Petite Sirah Russian River Valley 1994 • $11
86 **PARDUCCI** Petite Sirah California Old Vines 1995 • $10 ✪
85 **BOGLE** Petite Sirah California 1995 • $9

PINOT NOIR

California

87 **ANAPAMU** Pinot Noir Monterey County 1995 • $12 ✪
87 **CEDAR BROOK** Pinot Noir California 1995 • $9
87 **ESTANCIA** Pinot Noir Monterey Pinnacles 1996 • $12
85 **MIRASSOU** Pinot Noir Central Coast Family Selection 1995 • $11
85 **SONOMA CREEK** Pinot Noir Sonoma County 1995 • $12
85 **TALUS** Pinot Noir California 1995 • $10 ✪
85 **VILLA MT. EDEN** Pinot Noir California 1996 • $12

Oregon/Washington

88 **HIGH PASS** Pinot Noir Willamette Valley 1995 • $11
85 **BETHEL HEIGHTS** Pinot Noir Willamette Valley Eola Hills Cuvée 1996 • $12
85 **KNIPPRATH** Pinot Noir Columbia Valley 1994 • $10
85 **LAUREL RIDGE** Pinot Noir Willamette Valley 1995 • $12

Rhone Blend

California

86 **DOMAINE DE LA TERRE ROUGE** Tête-à-Tête Sierra Red Foothills 1996 • $11
85 **CLINE** Vin Rouge California Côtes d'Oakley 1996 • $9 ✪
85 **PRESTON** Faux Dry Creek Valley 1995 • $10
85 **RABBIT RIDGE** Allure Red California 1995 • $7 ✪

Syrah

California

88 **FOREST GLEN** Shiraz California Barrel Select 1995 • $10
88 **SHOOTING STAR** Syrah Lake County 1996 • $12
87 **IRONSTONE** Shiraz California 1995 • $11
87 **MCDOWELL** Syrah Mendocino 1996 • $10
87 **MONTHAVEN** Syrah California 1995 • $10
86 **PARDUCCI** Syrah Mendocino Old Vines 1995 • $10
86 **SIERRA VISTA** Syrah El Dorado 1995 • $10

Zinfandel

California

90 **VIANO** Zinfandel Contra Costa County Sand Rock Hill Reserve Selection 1994 • $10
89 **CHATEAU SOUVERAIN** Zinfandel Dry Creek Valley 1995 • $12 ✪
88 **BERINGER** Zinfandel North Coast Appellation Collection 1995 • $12
87 **ARCIERO** Zinfandel Paso Robles 1995 • $11
87 **BERINGER** Zinfandel North Coast 1994 • $12
87 **GALLO OF SONOMA** Zinfandel Sonoma County 1995 • $10
87 **TURNING LEAF** Zinfandel California 1996 • $8
86 **FETZER** Zinfandel California 1995 • $9 ✪
86 **FOPPIANO** Zinfandel Dry Creek Valley 1994 • $11
86 **NAPA RIDGE** Zinfandel Central Coast 1995 • $9 ✪
86 **ROSENBLUM** Zinfandel California Vintners Cuvée XVI NV • $10
86 **SHOOTING STAR** Zinfandel Lake County 1996 • $11
85 **BEAULIEU VINEYARD** Zinfandel California Beautour 1996 • $10 ✪
85 **BLACK SHEEP** Zinfandel Sierra Foothills 1995 • $12
85 **CLINE** Zinfandel California 1996 • $10 ✪
85 **MADROÑA** Zinfandel El Dorado 1995 • $10
85 **ROBERT MONDAVI** Zinfandel North Coast Coastal 1995 • $10
85 **RUTHERFORD VINTNERS** Zinfandel Lodi Barrel Select 1995 • $9
85 **SHENANDOAH** Zinfandel Amador County Special Reserve 1996 • $9
85 **VILLA MT. EDEN** Zinfandel California 1995 • $12
85 **WOODBRIDGE** Zinfandel California 1995 • $6

Other Red

California

87 **FOUNTAIN GROVE** Petit Noir Russian River Valley 1995 • $8
87 **MONTEVIÑA** Refosco Amador County 1995 • $8
87 **PARDUCCI** Charbono Mendocino Old Vines 1994 • $10
87 **SHOOTING STAR** Cabernet Franc Clear Lake 1995 • $10
86 **IL PODERE DELL'OLIVOS** Barbera Santa Barbara County Ragazzo Legnoso Riserva 1995 • $12
86 **J. LOHR** Valdiguié Monterey Wildflower 1996 • $8
86 **MONTEVIÑA** Barbera Amador County 1995 • $12
85 **AMADOR FOOTHILL** Sangiovese Shenandoah Valley 1994 • $12

85 **NOCETO** Sangiovese Shenandoah Valley 1995 • $12
85 **RABBIT RIDGE** Montepiano Red California 1995 • $10
85 **RABBIT RIDGE** Dolcetto Paso Robles 1995 • $12

Washington

88 **ARBOR CREST** Cabernet Franc Washington 1994 • $12
88 **SHOOTING STAR** Grenache Washington Côte de Columbia 1996 • $9
85 **PAUL THOMAS** Rattlesnake Red Washington 1995 • $10

WHITE

CHARDONNAY AND CHARDONNAY BLENDS

California

89 **R.H. PHILLIPS** Chardonnay Dunnigan Hills Toasted Head 1996 • $12
88 **BRUTOCAO** Chardonnay Mendocino Bliss Vineyard 1995 • $12
88 **ESTANCIA** Chardonnay Monterey County Pinnacles 1996 • $11 ✪
88 **MIRASSOU** Chardonnay Monterey County Family Selection 1996 • $12 ✪
88 **SEBASTIANI** Chardonnay California 1996 • $12 ✪
88 **STEVENOT** Chardonnay Sierra Foothills 1996 • $10
87 **BEAULIEU VINEYARD** Chardonnay California Beautour 1996 • $10 ✪
87 **BONTERRA** Chardonnay Mendocino County 1996 • $12
87 **EXPRESSIONS** Chardonnay Sonoma County 1995 • $10
87 **GALLO OF SONOMA** Chardonnay Sonoma County 1995 • $10 ✪
87 **HESS SELECT** Chardonnay California 1996 • $10
87 **MERIDIAN** Chardonnay Santa Barbara County 1996 • $11
87 **RABBIT RIDGE** Chardonnay Sonoma County 1996 • $12
87 **SEVEN PEAKS** Chardonnay California 1996 • $12 ✪
87 **TURNING LEAF** Chardonnay Sonoma County Sonoma Reserve 1995 • $10
87 **WILLIAM HILL** Chardonnay Napa Valley 1995 • $12
86 **ANAPAMU** Chardonnay Central Coast 1996 • $12 ✪
86 **BANDIERA** Chardonnay California Coastal 1996 • $9 ✪
86 **BUENA VISTA** Chardonnay Carneros 1995 • $12 ✪
86 **CEDAR BROOK** Chardonnay California 1995 • $9
86 **CONCANNON** Chardonnay Central Coast Selected Vineyard 1996 • $10 ✪
86 **EBERLE** Chardonnay Paso Robles 1995 • $12
86 **FETZER** Chardonnay Mendocino Barrel Select 1996 • $12
86 **HAWK CREST** Chardonnay California 1996 • $10 ✪
86 **INDIGO HILLS** Chardonnay Mendocino County 1995 • $9
86 **MADROÑA** Chardonnay El Dorado 1996 • $12
86 **NAPA RIDGE** Chardonnay North Coast Coastal Vines 1996 • $9 ✪
86 **R.H. PHILLIPS** Chardonnay Dunnigan Hills Barrel Cuvée 1996 • $8 ✪
86 **ROUND HILL** Chardonnay Napa Valley 1995 • $12
86 **TAFT STREET** Chardonnay Sonoma County 1996 • $10 ✪
86 **VENTANA** Chardonnay Monterey Gold Stripe 1996 • $12
85 **BELVEDERE** Chardonnay Sonoma County 1996 • $11 ✪
85 **CANYON ROAD** Chardonnay California 1997 • $8 ✪
85 **ESTANCIA** Chardonnay Monterey County Pinnacles 1995 • $10 ✪
85 **FETZER** Chardonnay California Sundial 1997 • $8 ✪
85 **FOUNTAIN GROVE** Chardonnay California 1995 • $10
85 **INDIGO HILLS** Chardonnay Mendocino County 1996 • $10 ✪

85 **JOLIESSE** Chardonnay California Reserve 1995 • $7 ✪
85 **LAWRENCE J. BARGETTO** Chardonnay Central Coast Cypress 1996 • $10
85 **LAZY CREEK** Chardonnay Anderson Valley 1995 • $10
85 **LEEWARD** Chardonnay Central Coast 1996 • $11
85 **NAPA RIDGE** Chardonnay Central Coast Coastal Vines 1996 • $9
85 **PEIRANO ESTATE** Chardonnay Lodi 1995 • $9
85 **RUTHERFORD VINTNERS** Chardonnay Lodi Barrel Select 1996 • $9
85 **SILVER RIDGE** Chardonnay California 1995 • $10
85 **ST. FRANCIS** Chardonnay Sonoma County 1996 • $12 ✪
85 **STRATFORD** Chardonnay California 1996 • $12
85 **TALUS** Chardonnay California 1995 • $8 ✪

New York

87 **FOX RUN** Chardonnay Finger Lakes Reserve 1996 • $12
85 **PELLEGRINI VINEYARDS** Chardonnay North Fork of Long Island Eastend Select 1996 • $9

Oregon

89 **COOPER MOUNTAIN** Chardonnay Willamette Valley 1995 • $12
87 **ASHLAND VINEYARDS** Chardonnay Rogue Valley 1995 • $10
87 **BRIDGEVIEW** Chardonnay Oregon Blue Moon 1996 • $10
87 **VAN DUZER** Chardonnay Oregon Eola Selection 1995 • $12
87 **WILLAMETTE VALLEY** Chardonnay Oregon 1996 • $10
86 **BRIDGEVIEW** Chardonnay Oregon Barrel Select 1995 • $10
86 **EOLA HILLS** Chardonnay Oregon 1996 • $10
86 **WEISINGER'S** Chardonnay-Sémillon Rogue Valley NV • $11
85 **BRIDGEVIEW** Chardonnay Oregon 1996 • $6
85 **BRIDGEVIEW** Chardonnay Oregon Barrel Select 1994 • $10
85 **DUCK POND** Chardonnay Willamette Valley 1996 • $8
85 **MONTINORE** Chardonnay Willamette Valley Vintner's Cuvée 1996 • $5

Washington

89 **E.B. FOOTE** Chardonnay Columbia Valley 1995 • $12
89 **LATAH CREEK** Chardonnay Washington 1996 • $11
88 **ARBOR CREST** Chardonnay Washington Cameo Reserve 1995 • $12
88 **COLUMBIA CREST** Chardonnay Columbia Valley 1996 • $9 ✪
88 **HOGUE** Chardonnay Washington 1996 • $9 ✪
88 **PRESTON PREMIUM WINES** Chardonnay Columbia Valley 1995 • $11
87 **COLUMBIA CREST** Chardonnay Columbia Valley 1995 • $9 ✪
87 **DUCK POND** Chardonnay Columbia Valley 1996 • $8
87 **HYATT** Chardonnay Yakima Valley 1995 • $10
87 **WATERBROOK** Chardonnay Columbia Valley 1996 • $11
86 **CANOE RIDGE** Chardonnay Columbia Valley 1996 • $12
86 **HOGUE** Chardonnay Columbia Valley 1995 • $10
86 **HOODSPORT** Chardonnay Yakima Valley Skagit Valley Tulip Festival 1995 • $11
85 **ARBOR CREST** Chardonnay Washington 1995 • $9
85 **SILVER LAKE** Chardonnay Columbia Valley 1995 • $10

CHENIN BLANC

California

87 **GAN EDEN** Chenin Blanc Lake County 1995 • $9
86 **DANIEL GEHRS** Chenin Blanc Monterey County Carmel Vineyard Le Cheniere 1996 • $9
86 **DRY CREEK** Chenin Blanc Clarksburg Dry 1996 • $8

85 **ALEXANDER VALLEY VINEYARDS** Chenin Blanc Alexander Valley Dry Wetzel Family Estate 1995 • $9
85 **PINE RIDGE** Chenin Blanc California 1996 • $8 ✪

Washington
85 **HOGUE** Chenin Blanc Columbia Valley 1996 • $7
85 **WASHINGTON HILLS** Chenin Blanc Columbia Valley Varietal Select Dry 1996 • $6

Gewürztraminer

California
89 **HANDLEY** Gewürztraminer Anderson Valley 1996 • $11
88 **BONNY DOON** Gewürztraminer Monterey County Pacific Rim 1996 • $12
88 **LOUIS M. MARTINI** Gewürztraminer Russian River Valley 1996 • $12
86 **ADLER FELS** Gewürztraminer Sonoma County 1996 • $11
86 **ROSENBLUM** Gewürztraminer California 1996 • $10
85 **ALDERBROOK** Gewürztraminer Russian River Valley Saralee's Vineyard 1996 • $11
85 **BOUCHAINE** Gewürztraminer Russian River Valley Dry 1996 • $12
85 **DE LOACH** Gewürztraminer Russian River Valley Early Harvest 1996 • $12
85 **FETZER** Gewürztraminer California 1997 • $7 ✪
85 **GUNDLACH BUNDSCHU** Gewürztraminer Sonoma Valley Rhinefarm Vineyards 1996 • $10

New York
87 **STANDING STONE** Gewürztraminer Finger Lakes 1996 • $11

Oregon
87 **AMITY** Gewürztraminer Oregon Dry 1996 • $10
87 **MONTINORE** Gewürztraminer Willamette Valley 1996 • $5
87 **WILLAMETTE VALLEY** Gewürztraminer Oregon 1996 • $8
86 **BRIDGEVIEW** Gewürztraminer Oregon 1996 • $6

Washington
87 **COLUMBIA** Gewürztraminer Yakima Valley 1996 • $7
86 **WORDEN** Gewürztraminer Washington 1995 • $7

Pinot Gris

Oregon
87 **DUCK POND** Pinot Gris Willamette Valley 1996 • $12
86 **BRIDGEVIEW** Pinot Gris Oregon Cuvée Spéciale 1996 • $11
86 **COOPER MOUNTAIN** Pinot Gris Willamette Valley 1996 • $12
86 **EDGEFIELD** Pinot Gris Willamette Valley 1996 • $11
85 **CHAMPOEG** Pinot Gris Willamette Valley Estate 1996 • $12

Washington
89 **COLUMBIA** Pinot Gris Yakima Valley 1996 • $10
85 **TEFFT** Pinot Grigio Columbia Valley Crystal Pheasant Vineyard 1997 • $8

Riesling

California
87 **ARROWOOD** White Riesling Sonoma County Domaine du Grand Archer 1996 • $11
87 **PARAISO SPRINGS** Johannisberg Riesling Santa Lucia Highlands 1996 • $9
87 **VENTANA** Riesling Monterey Dry 1996 • $8
85 **CLAIBORNE & CHURCHILL** Riesling Central Coast Dry Alsatian Style 1997 • $12
85 **DA VINCI** Riesling Sierra Foothills NV • $7
85 **KENDALL-JACKSON** Johannisberg Riesling California Vintner's Reserve 1996 • $11

New York

86 **STANDING STONE** Riesling Finger Lakes Dry 1996 • $11

Oregon

89 **WILLAMETTE VALLEY** Riesling Oregon Dry 1996 • $8
87 **ARGYLE** Riesling Willamette Valley Dry Reserve 1996 • $11
87 **EDGEFIELD** White Riesling Yamhill County Hyland Vineyards Vineyard Select 1996 • $12

Washington

88 **COVEY RUN** Riesling Dry Columbia Valley 1996 • $6
87 **KIONA** White Riesling Columbia Valley 1996 • $6
87 **WASHINGTON HILLS** Johannisberg Riesling Columbia Valley Varietal Select 1996 • $6
86 **BOOKWALTER** Riesling Washington Vintner's Select 1996 • $8
86 **COLUMBIA** Riesling Columbia Valley Cellarmaster's Reserve 1996 • $7 ✪
86 **COVEY RUN** Johannisberg Riesling Columbia Valley 1996 • $6
86 **HOGUE** Johannisberg Riesling Washington 1997 • $7 ✪
85 **COLUMBIA CREST** Johannisberg Riesling Columbia Valley 1996 • $7 ✪
85 **HYATT** Johannisberg Riesling Yakima Valley 1995 • $6
85 **LATAH CREEK** Johannisberg Riesling Washington 1996 • $7
85 **PAUL THOMAS** Johannisberg Riesling Columbia Valley 1995 • $6

Sauvignon Blanc and Blends

California

91 **MASON** Sauvignon Blanc Napa Valley 1996 • $12
90 **BERINGER** Sauvignon Blanc Napa Valley 1996 • $9
90 **MARKHAM** Sauvignon Blanc Napa Valley 1996 • $12 ✪
89 **J. FRITZ** Sauvignon Blanc Russian River Valley Poplar Vineyard 1996 • $12
89 **SANTINO** Fumé Blanc Amador County 1995 • $9
88 **BECKMEN** Sauvignon Blanc Santa Barbara County Beckmen Vineyards 1995 • $12
88 **BOEGER** Sauvignon Blanc El Dorado 1997 • $10
88 **CALLAWAY** Sauvignon Blanc Temecula 1997 • $8 ✪
88 **DRY CREEK** Fumé Blanc Sonoma County 1996 • $12 ✪
88 **FOUNTAIN GROVE** Sauvignon Blanc California 1996 • $9
88 **GEYSER PEAK** Sauvignon Blanc Sonoma County 1997 • $7 ✪
88 **KENWOOD** Sauvignon Blanc Sonoma County 1996 • $11 ✪
88 **RANCHO SISQUOC** Sauvignon Blanc Santa Maria Valley 1996 • $12
88 **RENAISSANCE** Sauvignon Blanc North Yuba Barrel Select 1996 • $12
88 **RODNEY STRONG** Sauvignon Blanc Northern Sonoma Charlotte's Home 1997 • $10 ✪
88 **STEVENOT** Sauvignon Blanc Calaveras County 1996 • $10
88 **VENTANA** Sauvignon Blanc Monterey 1996 • $10
88 **WENTE** Sauvignon Blanc Livermore Valley 1996 • $8
87 **BEAULIEU VINEYARD** Sauvignon Blanc Napa Valley 1996 • $11
87 **BENZIGER** Fumé Blanc Sonoma County 1996 • $10 ✪
87 **BERINGER** Sauvignon Blanc-Sémillon Knights Valley Meritage 1994 • $9
87 **BRANDER** Sauvignon Blanc Santa Ynez Valley 1996 • $11
87 **CANYON ROAD** Sauvignon Blanc California 1997 • $7 ✪
87 **CHARLES B. MITCHELL** Sauvignon Blanc Sierra Foothills 1996 • $8
87 **CHARLES B. MITCHELL** Sauvignon Blanc-Sémillon El Dorado 1995 • $11
87 **CHATEAU POTELLE** Sauvignon Blanc Napa Valley 1996 • $11
87 **CLOS DU LAC** Sauvignon Blanc Sierra Foothills 1996 • $10
87 **J. FRITZ** Sauvignon Blanc Dry Creek Valley Jenner Vineyard 1996 • $12
87 **MARTINELLI** Sauvignon Blanc Russian River Valley Martinelli Vineyard 1996 • $12

87 **NORMAN** Sauvignon Blanc Paso Robles Morrow Vineyard 1996 • $12
87 **PRESTON** Sauvignon Blanc Dry Creek Valley Cuvée de Fumé 1996 • $12
87 **QUIVIRA** Sauvignon Blanc Dry Creek Valley 1995 • $10
87 **ROBERT MONDAVI** Fumé Blanc Napa Valley 1996 • $12
87 **RUTHERFORD RANCH** Sauvignon Blanc Napa Valley 1994 • $7
87 **SCHUG** Sauvignon Blanc North Coast 1996 • $12
86 **BUTTONWOOD** Sauvignon Blanc Santa Ynez Valley 1996 • $10
86 **CONCANNON** Sauvignon Blanc Livermore Valley Selected Vineyard 1997 • $8 ✪
86 **FIELD STONE** Sauvignon Blanc Sonoma County 1995 • $10
86 **FIELDBROOK** Sauvignon Blanc Redwood Valley Elizabeth Vineyard 1996 • $11
86 **FIRESTONE** Sauvignon Blanc Santa Barbara County 1996 • $9
86 **FREESTONE** Sauvignon Blanc Napa Valley 1996 • $11
86 **HANNA** Sauvignon Blanc Russian River Valley 1996 • $11
86 **MONTHAVEN** Sauvignon Blanc Napa Valley 1996 • $9
86 **MORGAN** Sauvignon Blanc Sonoma & Monterey 1996 • $11
86 **NAPA RIDGE** Sauvignon Blanc North Coast 1996 • $6 ✪
86 **ONE VINEYARD** Sauvignon Blanc Napa Valley 1995 • $11
86 **RABBIT RIDGE** Sauvignon Blanc Russian River Valley 1997 • $10
86 **RAYMOND** Sauvignon Blanc Napa Valley Reserve 1996 • $11
86 **ROBERT MONDAVI** Sauvignon Blanc North Coast Coastal 1996 • $9
86 **ROBERT PECOTA** Sauvignon Blanc California 1997 • $11
86 **SHENANDOAH** Sauvignon Blanc Amador County 1997 • $8
86 **STONEHEDGE** Sauvignon Blanc California 1996 • $8 ✪
85 **BECKMEN** Sauvignon Blanc Santa Barbara County 1996 • $12
85 **BRANDER** Sauvignon Blanc Santa Ynez Valley 1997 • $11
85 **CHATEAU ST. JEAN** Fumé Blanc Sonoma County 1996 • $9
85 **FARELLA-PARK** Sauvignon Blanc Napa Valley 1995 • $10
85 **FOX MOUNTAIN** Sauvignon Blanc Sonoma County Limited Release 1996 • $10
85 **HIDDEN CELLARS** Sauvignon Blanc Mendocino 1996 • $11
85 **INDIGO HILLS** Sauvignon Blanc Mendocino County 1996 • $10 ✪
85 **KUNDE** Sauvignon Blanc Sonoma Valley Magnolia Lane 1996 • $11
85 **LOCKWOOD** Sauvignon Blanc Monterey 1996 • $10
85 **MERIDIAN** Sauvignon Blanc California 1996 • $9
85 **QUAIL RIDGE** Sauvignon Blanc Napa Valley 1996 • $10
85 **STERLING** Sauvignon Blanc North Coast 1996 • $8 ✪
85 **SUTTER HOME** Sauvignon Blanc California 1996 • $5 ✪

Oregon

88 **LAUREL RIDGE** Sauvignon Blanc Willamette Valley Vintner's Reserve 1995 • $10
85 **DI STEFANO** Fumé Blanc Willamette Valley 1996 • $9

Washington

88 **COLUMBIA CREST** Sauvignon Blanc Columbia Valley Estate Series 1996 • $12
87 **CATERINA** Sauvignon Blanc Columbia Valley 1996 • $9
87 **HOGUE** Fumé Blanc Columbia Valley 1996 • $9 ✪
87 **TAGARIS** Fumé Blanc Columbia Valley 1996 • $8
86 **COVEY RUN** Sauvignon Blanc Yakima Valley Reserve 1995 • $10
86 **PRESTON PREMIUM WINES** Fumé Blanc Columbia Valley 1995 • $8
86 **WATERBROOK** Sauvignon Blanc Columbia Valley 1996 • $11
85 **ARBOR CREST** Grand Cépage Washington 1995 • $9
85 **ARBOR CREST** Sauvignon Blanc Washington 1996 • $8
85 **HOODSPORT** Sauvignon Blanc Yakima Valley 1996 • $9

Sémillon and Blends

Washington

- **88** **WASHINGTON HILLS** Sémillon-Chardonnay Columbia Valley Varietal Select 1995 • $8
- **86** **HOGUE** Sémillon Columbia Valley 1996 • $8 ✪
- **86** **HOGUE** Sémillon-Chardonnay Columbia Valley 1995 • $9
- **85** **HOGUE** Sémillon Yakima Valley Genesis 1996 • $12
- **85** **SILVER LAKE** Sémillon Chardonnay Columbia Valley 1995 • $7

Other White

California

- **87** **CHAPPELLET** Old Vine Cuvée White Napa Valley Special Select 1995 • $12
- **87** **MARTINI & PRATI** Pinot Bianco Monterey 1996 • $10
- **86** **BUTTONWOOD** Marsanne Santa Ynez Valley 1996 • $12
- **86** **DECOY** Migration White Napa Valley 1996 • $10
- **86** **EXPRESSIONS** Viognier San Benito 1995 • $10/375ml
- **86** **LOCKWOOD** Pinot Blanc Monterey 1996 • $12
- **86** **MORGAN** Malvasia Bianca Monterey 1996 • $12
- **85** **MADDALENA** Muscat Canelli Central Coast 1996 • $8
- **85** **MARTINI & PRATI** Vino Grigio California 1996 • $10
- **85** **PINE RIDGE** La Petite Vigne TSIFG White Napa Valley 1996 • $12

Oregon

- **88** **BRIDGEVIEW** Early Muscat Oregon 1996 • $8
- **85** **AMITY** Pinot Blanc Willamette Valley Helmick Vineyards 1996 • $12
- **85** **TUALATIN** Müller-Thurgau Willamette Valley 1996 • $7

Washington

- **85** **LATAH CREEK** Muscat Canelli Washington 1996 • $8
- **85** **POWERS** Muscat Canelli Columbia Valley 1996 • $7

• World Rosés •

United States

- **87** **COOPER MOUNTAIN** White Pinot Noir Willamette Valley (Oregon)1996 • $7
- **87** **SANFORD** Pinot Noir Carneros Vin Gris (California) 1996 • $12
- **86** **BEAULIEU VINEYARD** Grenache San Benito South Hart Vineyard Signet Collection (California) 1995 • $10
- **85** **BRIDGEVIEW** Rosé de Pinot Oregon 1996 • $12
- **85** **ZACA MESA** Z Gris Santa Barbara County Rosé (California) 1996 • $8

Other

- **86** **CHAIN OF PONDS** Grenache-Sangiovese Adelaide Hills (Australia) Novello Rosso 1997 • $12
- **86** **REMY PANNIER** Cabernet Franc Rosé Vin de Pays du Jardin de la France 1996 • $6 ✪
- **85** **DOMAINE DE LA RÉMÉJEANNE** Côtes du Rhône Rosé Les Arbousiers 1995 (France) • $10
- **85** **BODEGAS MARTINEZ BUJANDA** Rioja Rosado Conde de Valdemar (Spain) 1996 • $8 ✪

• World Sparkling Wines •

United States

89 **BENZIGER** Brut Blanc de Blancs Carneros Late Disgorged 1990 • $10
89 **KORBEL** Natural California NV • $12 ✪
88 **DOMAINE CHANDON** Blanc de Noirs Carneros Cuvée 393 NV • $11 ✪
88 **DOMAINE CHANDON** Brut Napa-Sonoma Counties Cuvée 194 NV • $11 ✪
88 **INDIGO HILLS** Brut Chardonnay North Coast NV • $9
87 **MOUNTAIN DOME** Brut Washington NV • $10
87 **TOTT'S** Brut California Reserve Cuvée NV • $7
86 **EDEN ROC** Brut California NV • $5
86 **MIRABELLE** Brut North Coast NV • $12

Other

86 **PAUL CHENEAU** Brut Blanc de Blancs Cava (Spain) NV • $9
86 **MONT-MARÇAL** Brut Cava Reserva (Spain) NV • $12 ✪
85 **MARWOOD** Brut (Italy) NV • $9
85 **CADEAUX** Brut Blanc de Blancs Royal Crown Cuvée Privée (France) NV • $10
85 **SEAVIEW** Brut South Eastern Australia 1996 • $8

• World Dessert Wines •

Muscat

88 **LA VICOMTÉ DE LA PEYRADE** Muscat de Frontignan (France) NV • $10
87 **MARKHAM** Muscat Napa Valley Blanc (California) 1996 • $9/375ml
87 **ROBERT PECOTA** Muscat Canelli Napa Valley Moscato d'Andrea (California) 1996 • $9/375ml
86 **MICHELE CHIARLO** Moscato d'Asti Nivole (Italy) 1996 • $9
86 **NEIRANO** Moscato d'Asti (Italy) 1995 • $10
85 **CHÂTEAU DE PENA** Muscat de Rivesaltes (France) 1996 • $9
85 **CLOS DU LAC** Muscat Amador County Vin Doux Naturel (California) 1996 • $12/375ml

Port

88 **LINDEMANS** Tawny Port Barossa Valley Macquarie Very Special (Australia) NV • $10
88 **SEPPELT** Tawny Port Barossa Valley Trafford D.P. 30 (Australia) NV • $12
87 **QUADY** Port Amador County (California) LBV 1993 • $12
85 **BARROS** White Port Lagrima (Portugal) NV • $9
85 **FORIS** Ruby Oregon 1995 • $10/375ml

Riesling

90 **HOGUE** White Riesling Late Harvest Columbia Valley (Washington) 1996 • $7 ✪
88 **LAUREL RIDGE** Riesling Willamette Valley Select Harvest (Oregon) 1995 • $8/375ml
86 **AMITY** Riesling Late Harvest Oregon Juliard Vineyard 1996 • $10
86 **COVEY RUN** White Riesling Columbia Valley Late Harvest (Washington) 1996 • $9
85 **WASHINGTON HILLS** White Riesling Late Harvest Columbia Valley Varietal Select (Washington) 1996 • $8

Other

88 **ERRAZURIZ** Sauvignon Blanc Late Harvest Casablanca Valley (Chile) 1996 • $7
87 **DOMAINE DE LA MOTTE** Coteaux du Layon Rochefort (France) 1996 • $12
85 **COLLAVINI** Pinot Grigio Collio Villa di Canlungo Vendemmia Tardiva (Italy) 1996 • $12
85 **CHÂTEAU LA RAME** Ste.-Croix-du-Mont (France) 1993 • $11

Great Vintages, Great Wines

In the following pages you will find *Wine Spectator*'s ratings for the recent outstanding vintages of six of the world's most prestigious—and therefore collectible—wine types: red Bordeaux, red Burgundy, white Burgundy, vintage Port, California Cabernet and blends, and California Chardonnay. Also listed are current retail or auction prices.

The wines are organized in descending order of score, to make it easy to identify the best wines of each vintage. If you know the name of a wine already and you want to look up its score and tasting note, turn to the main listings section and look under the country name and then under the producer's name.

Château Mouton-Rothschild in Pauillac, Gironde.

Red Bordeaux

Here are *Wine Spectator*'s ratings and prices for the major château wines from the four best recent vintages—1995, 1990, 1989 and 1988. The wines are organized by vintage and then in descending order of score, to make it easy to identify the best wines of each vintage. For ratings from years omitted from this section, turn to the main listings section, where you will find complete ratings under the château names.

The 1995 vintage created a lot of excitement among Bordeaux drinkers and collectors because it was the first truly outstanding-quality vintage in five years. From 1991 through 1994 a number of good wines were produced, and they can be good purchases for drinking now and in the next few years. "Futures" purchases of the 1996 and 1997 vintages are available, too, but neither of these vintages will be as good as 1995. *Wine Spectator* bureau chief James Suckling rates 1996 at 85-89 points out of 100 and 1997 at 81-85, based on blind tastings of barrel samples. 1995 is still the vintage to buy and hold for further consumption at maturity. That period might be from 2005 to 2025.

1995 RED BORDEAUX | VINTAGE RATING: 95

100 **CHÂTEAU MARGAUX** Margaux 1995 • $145 Ⓐ • (01/31/98) • CS

98 **CHÂTEAU PÉTRUS** Pomerol 1995 • $900 • (01/31/98) • CS

97 **CHÂTEAU DUCRU-BEAUCAILLOU** St.-Julien 1995 • $48 Ⓐ • (01/31/98) • CS

97 **CHÂTEAU LAFITE ROTHSCHILD** Pauillac 1995 • $275 • (01/31/98) • CS

97 **CHÂTEAU TROTANOY** Pomerol 1995 • $160 • (01/31/98) • HR

96 **CHÂTEAU CALON-SÉGUR** St.-Estèphe 1995 • $75 • (01/31/98) • SS

96 **CHÂTEAU L'EGLISE CLINET** Pomerol 1995 • $275 • (01/31/98)

96 **CHÂTEAU MOUTON-ROTHSCHILD** Pauillac 1995 • $180 Ⓐ • (01/31/98) • CS

96 **CHÂTEAU PICHON-LONGUEVILLE-LALANDE** Pauillac 1995 • $160 • (01/31/98) • CS

95 **CHÂTEAU AUSONE** St.-Emilion 1995 • $250 • (01/31/98) • HR

95 **CHÂTEAU CANON-LA GAFFELIÈRE** St.-Emilion 1995 • $60 • (01/31/98)

95 **CHÂTEAU CLERC MILON** Pauillac 1995 • $60 • (01/31/98) • SS

Key: SS—Spectator Selection CS—Cellar Selection HR—Highly Recommended BB—Best Buy $NA—Price not available Ⓐ—Auction Price
Dates in parentheses indicate the issues in which the ratings were published.

95 **CHÂTEAU CLINET** Pomerol 1995 • $140 Ⓐ • (01/31/98)

95 **CHÂTEAU FIGEAC** St.-Emilion 1995 • $60 • (01/31/98)

95 **CHÂTEAU LAFLEUR** Pomerol 1995 • $250 • (01/31/98)

95 **VIEUX-CHÂTEAU-CERTAN** Pomerol 1995 • $80 • (01/31/98)

94 **CHÂTEAU ANGÉLUS** St.-Emilion 1995 • $160 • (01/31/98)

94 **CHÂTEAU CHEVAL-BLANC** St.-Emilion 1995 • $220 • (01/31/98)

94 **CHÂTEAU FERRIÈRE** Margaux 1995 • $30 • (01/31/98)

94 **CHÂTEAU HAUT-BRION** Pessac-Léognan 1995 • $146 Ⓐ • (01/31/98)

94 **CHÂTEAU LA CONSEILLANTE** Pomerol 1995 • $68 Ⓐ • (01/31/98)

94 **CHÂTEAU LATOUR** Pauillac 1995 • $150 Ⓐ • (01/31/98) • CS

94 **CHÂTEAU LYNCH-BAGES** Pauillac 1995 • $48 Ⓐ • (01/31/98)

94 **CHÂTEAU PALMER** Margaux 1995 • $67 • (01/31/98)

94 **CHÂTEAU PONTET-CANET** Pauillac 1995 • $22 Ⓐ • (01/31/98) • SS

94 **CHÂTEAU RAUZAN-SÉGLA** Margaux 1995 • $48 • (01/31/98)

93 **CHÂTEAU COS-D'ESTOURNEL** St.-Estèphe 1995 • $80 • (01/31/98)

93 **CHÂTEAU KIRWAN** Margaux 1995 • $30 • (01/31/98)

93 **CHÂTEAU LA MISSION-HAUT-BRION** Pessac-Léognan 1995 • $130 • (01/31/98)

93 **CHÂTEAU LA POINTE** Pomerol 1995 • $25 • (01/31/98)

Red Bordeaux

93 **CHÂTEAU LAFON-ROCHET** St.-Estèphe 1995 • $33 • (01/31/98)
93 **CHÂTEAU LANGOA BARTON** St.-Julien 1995 • $30 • (01/31/98)
93 **CHÂTEAU LARMANDE** St.-Emilion 1995 • $20 Ⓐ • (01/31/98)
93 **CHÂTEAU LE PIN** Pomerol 1995 • $955 Ⓐ • (01/31/98)
93 **CHÂTEAU LÉOVILLE BARTON** St.-Julien 1995 • $50 • (01/31/98)
93 **CHÂTEAU LÉOVILLE POYFERRÉ** St.-Julien 1995 • $36 • (01/31/98)
93 **CHÂTEAU PAVIE-MACQUIN** St.-Emilion 1995 • $35 • (01/31/98)
93 **CHÂTEAU SIRAN** Margaux 1995 • $30 • (01/31/98)
93 **CHÂTEAU DE VALANDRAUD** St.-Emilion 1995 • $300 • (01/31/98)
93 **PENSÉES DE LAFLEUR** Pomerol 1995 • $75 • (01/31/98)
92 **CHÂTEAU BOURGNEUF** Pomerol 1995 • $30 • (01/31/98)
92 **CHÂTEAU DAUZAC** Margaux 1995 • $25 • (01/31/98)
92 **CHÂTEAU GISCOURS** Margaux 1995 • $24 Ⓐ • (01/31/98)
92 **CHÂTEAU GRAND-PUY-LACOSTE** Pauillac 1995 • $29 Ⓐ • (01/31/98)
92 **CHÂTEAU HAUT-BAILLY** Pessac-Léognan 1995 • $40 • (01/31/98)
92 **CHÂTEAU LASCOMBES** Margaux 1995 • $30 • (01/31/98)
92 **CHÂTEAU MONBOUSQUET** St.-Emilion 1995 • $30 • (01/31/98)
92 **CHÂTEAU MOULIN-ST.-GEORGES** St.-Emilion 1995 • $24 • (01/31/98)
92 **CHÂTEAU PAPE CLÉMENT** Pessac-Léognan 1995 • $40 • (01/31/98)
92 **CHÂTEAU POUJEAUX** Moulis 1995 • $24 • (01/31/98)
92 **CHÂTEAU TROPLONG-MONDOT** St.-Emilion 1995 • $36 Ⓐ • (01/31/98)
92 **CHÂTEAU D'ARMAILHAC** Pauillac 1995 • $25 • (01/31/98)
91 **CHÂTEAU BEAUREGARD** Pomerol 1995 • $21 Ⓐ • (01/31/98)
91 **CHÂTEAU HAUT-MARBUZET** St.-Estèphe 1995 • $22 Ⓐ • (01/31/98)
91 **CHÂTEAU LA SERRE** St.-Emilion 1995 • $28 • (01/31/98)
91 **CHÂTEAU LAGRANGE** St.-Julien 1995 • $21 Ⓐ • (01/31/98)
91 **CHÂTEAU MAGDELAINE** St.-Emilion 1995 • $40 • (01/31/98)
91 **CHÂTEAU MALESCOT-ST.-EXUPÉRY** Margaux 1995 • $35 • (01/31/98)
91 **CHÂTEAU PAVIE-DECESSE** St.-Emilion 1995 • $28 • (01/31/98)
91 **CHÂTEAU RAUZAN-GASSIES** Margaux 1995 • $30 • (01/31/98)
91 **CHÂTEAU SOCIANDO-MALLET** Haut-Médoc 1995 • $27 Ⓐ • (01/31/98)
91 **CHÂTEAU DE FIEUZAL** Pessac-Léognan 1995 • $30 • (01/31/98)
91 **CLOS L'EGLISE** Pomerol 1995 • $30 • (01/31/98)
91 **LES FORTS DE LATOUR** Pauillac 1995 • $43 Ⓐ • (01/31/98)

Key: SS—Spectator Selection CS—Cellar Selection HR—Highly Recommended BB—Best Buy $NA—Price not available Ⓐ—Auction Price
Dates in parentheses indicate the issues in which the ratings were published.

91 **PAVILLON ROUGE DU CHÂTEAU MARGAUX** Margaux 1995 • $22 Ⓐ • (01/31/98)
90 **CARRUADES DE LAFITE ROTHSCHILD** Pauillac 1995 • $30 • (01/31/98)
90 **CHÂTEAU CANUET** Margaux 1995 • $20 • (01/31/98)
90 **CHÂTEAU CHASSE-SPLEEN** Moulis 1995 • $26 • (01/31/98)
90 **CHÂTEAU CLOS DES JACOBINS** St.-Emilion 1995 • $30 • (01/31/98)
90 **CHÂTEAU DUHART-MILON ROTHSCHILD** Pauillac 1995 • $25 • (01/31/98)
90 **CHÂTEAU FAIZEAU** Montagne-St.-Emilion Sélection Vieilles Vignes 1995 • $18 • (01/31/98)
90 **CHÂTEAU FERRANDE** Graves 1995 • $12 • (01/31/98)
90 **CHÂTEAU FONTENIL** Fronsac 1995 • $15 • (01/31/98)
90 **CHÂTEAU GAZIN** Pomerol 1995 • $45 • (01/31/98)
90 **CHÂTEAU GLORIA** St.-Julien 1995 • $22 Ⓐ • (01/31/98)
90 **CHÂTEAU GRAND MOULINET** Pomerol 1995 • $20 • (01/31/98)
90 **CHÂTEAU HAUT-BAGES-LIBÉRAL** Pauillac 1995 • $20 • (01/31/98)
90 **CHÂTEAU HAUT-BATAILLEY** Pauillac 1995 • $19 Ⓐ • (01/31/98)
90 **CHÂTEAU HAUT-LAGRANGE** Pessac-Léognan 1995 • $20 • (01/31/98)
90 **CHÂTEAU LA CARDONNE** Médoc 1995 • $18 • (01/31/98)
90 **CHÂTEAU LA FLEUR DE GAY** Pomerol 1995 • $80 • (01/31/98)
90 **CHÂTEAU LA GARDE** Pessac-Léognan 1995 • $15 • (01/31/98)
90 **CHÂTEAU LA GURGUE** Margaux 1995 • $25 • (01/31/98)
90 **CHÂTEAU LAFLEUR-GAZIN** Pomerol 1995 • $30 • (01/31/98)
90 **CHÂTEAU LE BON-PASTEUR** Pomerol 1995 • $38 • (01/31/98)
90 **CHÂTEAU MOULIN PEY-LABRIE** Canon-Fronsac 1995 • $18 • (01/31/98)
90 **CHÂTEAU PRIEURÉ-LICHINE** Margaux 1995 • $18 Ⓐ • (01/31/98)
90 **CHÂTEAU SMITH-HAUT-LAFITTE** Pessac-Léognan 1995 • $35 • (01/31/98)
90 **CHÂTEAU ST.-PIERRE** St.-Julien 1995 • $30 • (01/31/98)
90 **CHÂTEAU TERTRE DAUGAY** St.-Emilion 1995 • $44 • (01/31/98)
90 **CHÂTEAU DE CRUZEAU** Pessac-Léognan 1995 • $15 • (01/31/98)
90 **CLOS FOURTET** St.-Emilion 1995 • $25 • (01/31/98)
90 **CLOS DE L'ORATOIRE** St.-Emilion 1995 • $30 • (01/31/98)
90 **DOMAINE DE COURTEILLAC** Bordeaux Supérieur 1995 • $18 • (01/31/98)
89 **CHÂTEAU BATAILLEY** Pauillac 1995 • $22 • (01/31/98)
89 **CHÂTEAU BEAUSÉJOUR** St.-Emilion 1995 • $35 • (01/31/98)
89 **CHÂTEAU BEYCHEVELLE** St.-Julien 1995 • $22 Ⓐ • (01/31/98)
89 **CHÂTEAU CARBONNIEUX** Pessac-Léognan 1995 • $25 • (01/31/98)
89 **CHÂTEAU CARONNE-STE.-GEMME** Haut-Médoc 1995 • $20 • (01/31/98)
89 **CHÂTEAU HAUT LARIVEAU** Canon-Fronsac 1995 • $20 • (01/31/98)
89 **CHÂTEAU HAUT-BAGES-AVÉROUS** Pauillac 1995 • $25 • (01/31/98)
89 **CHÂTEAU HAUT-GARDÈRE** Pessac-Léognan 1995 • $15 • (01/31/98)

89 **CHÂTEAU LA CROIX-DE-GAY** Pomerol 1995 • $25 • (01/31/98)

89 **CHÂTEAU LA CROIX DU CASSE** Pomerol 1995 • $23 • (01/31/98)

89 **CHÂTEAU LA DOMINIQUE** St.-Emilion 1995 • $30 Ⓐ • (01/31/98)

89 **CHÂTEAU LA FLEUR-PÉTRUS** Pomerol 1995 • $65 • (01/31/98)

89 **CHÂTEAU LA GAFFELIÈRE** St.-Emilion 1995 • $37 • (01/31/98)

89 **CHÂTEAU LA TOURETTE** Pauillac 1995 • $22 • (01/31/98)

89 **CHÂTEAU LA VIEILLE CURE** Fronsac 1995 • $20 • (01/31/98)

89 **CHÂTEAU D'ISSAN** Margaux 1995 • $20 Ⓐ • (01/31/98)

89 **CHÂTEAU DE LA DAUPHINE** Fronsac 1995 • $20 • (01/31/98)

89 **CHÂTEAU LABÉGORCE-ZÉDÉ** Margaux 1995 • $22 • (01/31/98)

89 **CHÂTEAU LATOUR À POMEROL** Pomerol 1995 • $55 • (01/31/98)

89 **CHÂTEAU OLIVIER** Pessac-Léognan 1995 • $25 • (01/31/98)

89 **CHÂTEAU ROBIN** Côtes de Castillon 1995 • $15 • (01/31/98)

89 **CHÂTEAU ST.-ROBERT** Graves Cuvée Poncet-Deville 1995 • $25 • (01/31/98)

89 **CHÂTEAU TRONQUOY-LALANDE** St.-Estèphe 1995 • $20 • (01/31/98)

89 **DOMAINE DE LARRIVET** Pessac-Léognan 1995 • $20 • (01/31/98)

89 **SÉGLA** Margaux 1995 • $25 • (01/31/98)

88 **CHÂTEAU BARREYRES** Haut-Médoc 1995 • $12 • (01/31/98)

88 **CHÂTEAU BEAUMONT** Haut-Médoc 1995 • $15 • (01/31/98)

88 **CHÂTEAU BROWN** Pessac-Léognan 1995 • $18 • (01/31/98)

88 **CHÂTEAU CANTELYS** Pessac-Léognan 1995 • $30 • (01/31/98)

88 **CHÂTEAU CANTENAC-BROWN** Margaux 1995 • $25 • (01/31/98)

88 **CHÂTEAU CAP DE HAUT** Haut-Médoc 1995 • $NA • (01/01/97)

88 **CHÂTEAU COS-LABORY** St.-Estèphe 1995 • $22 • (01/31/98)

88 **CHÂTEAU FONPLÉGADE** St.-Emilion 1995 • $24 • (01/31/98)

88 **CHÂTEAU GRAND VILLAGE** Bordeaux Supérieur 1995 • $15 • (01/31/98)

88 **CHÂTEAU GRIVIÈRE** Médoc 1995 • $18 • (01/31/98)

88 **CHÂTEAU GRUAUD-LAROSE** St.-Julien 1995 • $45 • (01/31/98)

88 **CHÂTEAU LA TOUR-HAUT-BRION** Pessac-Léognan 1995 • $35 • (01/31/98)

88 **CHÂTEAU LARCIS-DUCASSE** St.-Emilion 1995 • $20 • (01/31/98)

88 **CHÂTEAU LE BOSCQ** St.-Estèphe 1995 • $20 • (01/31/98)

88 **CHÂTEAU LES CHARMES-GODARD** Côtes de Francs 1995 • $18 • (01/31/98)

88 **CHÂTEAU MALARTIC-LAGRAVIÈRE** Pessac-Léognan 1995 • $25 • (01/31/98)

88 **CHÂTEAU MARSAU** Côtes de Francs 1995 • $15 • (01/31/98)

88 **CHÂTEAU MONTROSE** St.-Estèphe 1995 • $33 Ⓐ • (01/31/98)

88 **CHÂTEAU PAVIE** St.-Emilion 1995 • $30 Ⓐ • (01/31/98)

88 **CHÂTEAU PETIT-VILLAGE** Pomerol 1995 • $40 • (01/31/98)

88 **CHÂTEAU PHÉLAN-SÉGUR** St.-Estèphe 1995 • $25 • (01/31/98)

88 **CHÂTEAU PIBRAN** Pauillac 1995 • $20 • (01/31/98)

88 **CHÂTEAU PICHON-LONGUEVILLE-BARON** Pauillac 1995 • $39 Ⓐ • (01/31/98)

88 **CHÂTEAU TOUMALIN** Canon-Fronsac 1995 • $18 • (01/31/98)

88 **CHÂTEAU D'ANGLUDET** Margaux 1995 • $30 • (01/31/98)

88 **CHÂTEAU D'ARCINS** Haut-Médoc 1995 • $12 • (01/31/98)

88 **CHÂTEAU DE LA TOUR** Bordeaux Supérieur Réserve du Château 1995 • $16 • (01/31/98)

88 **CLOS MARSALETTE** Pessac-Léognan 1995 • $20 • (01/31/98)

88 **DOMAINE DE L'EGLISE** Pomerol 1995 • $21 • (01/31/98)

88 **LA PARDE DE HAUT-BAILLY** Pessac-Léognan 1995 • $15 • (01/31/98)

88 **LES CHARMES DE KIRWAN** Margaux 1995 • $18 • (01/31/98)

88 **LES FIEFS DE LAGRANGE** St.-Julien 1995 • $19 • (01/31/98)

88 **RÉSERVE DE LA COMTESSE** Pauillac 1995 • $25 • (01/31/98)

87 **CHÂTEAU ANDRON-BLANQUET** St.-Estèphe 1995 • $20 • (01/31/98)

87 **CHÂTEAU BERGAT** St.-Emilion 1995 • $25 • (01/31/98)

87 **CHÂTEAU BONNET** Bordeaux 1995 • $15 • (01/31/98)

87 **CHÂTEAU CADET-BON** St.-Emilion 1995 • $28 • (01/31/98)

87 **CHÂTEAU CANON-MOUEIX** Canon-Fronsac 1995 • $21 • (01/31/98)

87 **CHÂTEAU CHANTE-ALOUETTE** St.-Emilion 1995 • $28 • (01/31/98)

87 **CHÂTEAU CITRAN** Haut-Médoc 1995 • $20 • (01/31/98)

87 **CHÂTEAU CLOS CHAUMONT** Premières Côtes de Bordeaux 1995 • $18 • (01/31/98)

87 **CHÂTEAU COUFRAN** Haut-Médoc 1995 • $25 • (01/31/98)

87 **CHÂTEAU FLEUR-CARDINALE** St.-Emilion 1995 • $22 • (01/31/98)

87 **CHÂTEAU HAUT-SURGET** Lalande-de-Pomerol 1995 • $15 • (01/31/98)

87 **CHÂTEAU LA CROIX ST.-GEORGES** Pomerol 1995 • $44 • (01/31/98)

87 **CHÂTEAU LA LOUVIÈRE** Pessac-Léognan 1995 • $25 • (01/31/98)

87 **CHÂTEAU LA TOUR CARNET** Haut-Médoc 1995 • $15 • (01/31/98)

87 **CHÂTEAU LABAT** Haut-Médoc 1995 • $22 • (01/31/98)

87 **CHÂTEAU LE CROCK** St.-Estèphe 1995 • $16 • (01/31/98)

87 **CHÂTEAU LYNCH-MOUSSAS** Pauillac 1995 • $22 • (01/31/98)

87 **CHÂTEAU MONBRISON** Margaux 1995 • $22 • (01/31/98)

87 **CHÂTEAU PUYGUERAUD** Côtes de Francs 1995 • $16 • (01/31/98)

87 **CHÂTEAU RAMAFORT** Médoc 1995 • $18 • (01/31/98)

87 **CHÂTEAU ST.-ANDRÉ-CORBIN** St.-Georges-St.-Emilion 1995 • $14 • (01/31/98)

87 **CHÂTEAU TALBOT** St.-Julien 1995 • $21 Ⓐ • (01/31/98)

87 **CHÂTEAU TOUR DE MIRAMBEAU** Bordeaux Cuvée Passion 1995 • $NA • (01/01/97)

87 **CHÂTEAU DU GLANA** St.-Julien Vieilles Vignes 1995 • $15 • (01/31/98)
87 **CHÂTEAU LE VIVIER** Médoc 1995 • $15 • (01/31/98)
87 **DOMAINE DE CHEVALIER** Pessac-Léognan 1995 • $25 Ⓐ • (01/31/98)
87 **JEAN-PIERRE MOUEIX** St.-Emilion 1995 • $16 • (01/31/98)
87 **LA BASTIDE DE SIRAN** Margaux 1995 • $15 • (01/31/98)
87 **LA RÉSERVE DE LÉOVILLE BARTON** St.-Julien 1995 • $22 • (01/31/98)
87 **LE CHARME LABORY** St.-Estèphe 1995 • $12 • (01/31/98)
87 **LES PAGODES DE COS** St.-Estèphe 1995 • $27 • (01/31/98)
87 **TOURELLES DE LONGUEVILLE** Pauillac 1995 • $25 • (01/31/98)
86 **ABEILLE DE FIEUZAL** Pessac-Léognan 1995 • $15 • (01/31/98)
86 **CHÂTEAU BARET** Pessac-Léognan 1995 • $18 • (01/31/98)
86 **CHÂTEAU BEAU-SITE** St.-Estèphe 1995 • $24 • (01/31/98)
86 **CHÂTEAU BEL-ORME-TRONQUOY-DE-LALANDE** Haut-Médoc 1995 • $20 • (01/31/98)
86 **CHÂTEAU BOUSCAUT** Pessac-Léognan 1995 • $22 • (01/31/98)
86 **CHÂTEAU CANON** St.-Emilion 1995 • $27 Ⓐ • (01/31/98)
86 **CHÂTEAU CANON-DE-BREM** Canon-Fronsac 1995 • $18 • (01/31/98)
86 **CHÂTEAU CLARKE** Listrac 1995 • $26 • (10/15/97)
86 **CHÂTEAU CLÉMENT PICHON** Haut-Médoc 1995 • $15 • (01/31/98)
86 **CHÂTEAU CROIZET-BAGES** Pauillac 1995 • $20 • (01/31/98)
86 **CHÂTEAU CURÉ-BON** St.-Emilion 1995 • $26 • (01/31/98)
86 **CHÂTEAU LA FREYNELLE** Bordeaux 1995 • $8 • (01/31/98)
86 **CHÂTEAU LA TOUR LÉOGNAN** Pessac-Léognan 1995 • $NA • (01/31/98)
86 **CHÂTEAU LARRIVET-HAUT-BRION** Pessac-Léognan 1995 • $20 • (01/31/98)
86 **CHÂTEAU LE DOYENNÉ** Premières Côtes de Bordeaux 1995 • $14 • (01/31/98)
86 **CHÂTEAU LE SARTRE** Pessac-Léognan 1995 • $22 • (01/31/98)
86 **CHÂTEAU LUSSEAU** St.-Emilion 1995 • $24 • (01/31/98)
86 **CHÂTEAU ROYLLAND** St.-Emilion 1995 • $NA • (01/01/97)
86 **CHÂTEAU TEYSSIER** Montagne-St.-Emilion 1995 • $NA • (01/31/98)
86 **CHÂTEAU TOUR-PRIGNAC** Médoc 1995 • $10 • (01/31/98)
86 **CHÂTEAU D'ARCHE** Haut-Médoc 1995 • $15 • (01/31/98)
86 **MONDOT** St.-Emilion 1995 • $25 • (01/31/98)
86 **PIERRE DOURTHE** Bordeaux Numéro 1 1995 • $9 • (01/31/98)
86 **SIRIUS** Bordeaux 1995 • $12 • (01/31/98)
85 **BLASON D'ISSAN** Margaux 1995 • $12 • (01/31/98)

Key: SS—Spectator Selection CS—Cellar Selection HR—Highly Recommended BB—Best Buy $NA—Price not available Ⓐ—Auction Price
Dates in parentheses indicate the issues in which the ratings were published.

85 **CHÂTEAU ARNAULD** Haut-Médoc 1995 • $20 • (01/31/98)
85 **CHÂTEAU BELGRAVE** Haut-Médoc 1995 • $25 • (01/31/98)
85 **CHÂTEAU CARDUS** Médoc 1995 • $12 • (01/31/98)
85 **CHÂTEAU COUCHEROY** Pessac-Léognan 1995 • $18 • (01/31/98)
85 **CHÂTEAU JONQUEYRES** Bordeaux Supérieur 1995 • $12 • (01/31/98)
85 **CHÂTEAU LA FLEUR** St.-Emilion 1995 • $18 • (01/31/98)
85 **CHÂTEAU LA FLEUR-ST.-GEORGES** Lalande-de-Pomerol 1995 • $20 • (01/31/98)
85 **CHÂTEAU LA GRANGE DE GRENET** Bordeaux 1995 • $8 • (06/30/97)
85 **CHÂTEAU LILIAN LADOUYS** St.-Estèphe 1995 • $18 • (01/31/98)
85 **CHÂTEAU LIVERSAN** Haut-Médoc 1995 • $15 • (01/31/98)
85 **CHÂTEAU MARBUZET** St.-Estèphe 1995 • $26 • (01/31/98)
85 **CHÂTEAU MEYNEY** St.-Estèphe 1995 • $21 Ⓐ • (01/31/98)
85 **CHÂTEAU MIREFLEURS** Bordeaux Supérieur 1995 • $8 • (01/31/98)
85 **CHÂTEAU MOULIN RICHE** St.-Julien 1995 • $25 • (01/31/98)
85 **CHÂTEAU SAINT-YZANS** Médoc 1995 • $NA • (01/01/97)
85 **CHÂTEAU TOUR DU MAYNE** Haut-Médoc 1995 • $9 • (01/31/98)
85 **CHÂTEAU DE REIGNAC** Bordeaux Supérieur Cuvée Prestige 1995 • $13 • (01/31/98)
85 **CHÂTEAU DU BOUSQUET** Côtes de Bourg 1995 • $9 • (01/31/98)
85 **CHÂTEAU DU TERTRE** Margaux 1995 • $15 Ⓐ • (01/31/98)
85 **DOMAINE DE LA ROQUETTE** Pessac-Léognan 1995 • $NA • (01/31/98)
85 **FRANK PHÉLAN** St.-Estèphe 1995 • $14 • (01/31/98)
85 **HAUTS DE SMITH** Pessac-Léognan 1995 • $18 • (01/31/98)
85 **LA DAME DE MONTROSE** St.-Estèphe 1995 • $30 • (01/31/98)
85 **LA SIRÈNE DE GISCOURS** Margaux 1995 • $14 • (01/31/98)
85 **SARGET DE GRUAUD-LAROSE** St.-Julien 1995 • $24 • (01/31/98)

1990 Red Bordeaux
Vintage Rating: 97

100 **CHÂTEAU LATOUR** Pauillac 1990 • $425 Ⓐ • (03/31/93)
98 **CHÂTEAU PÉTRUS** Pomerol 1990 • $228 Ⓐ • (03/31/93)
97 **CHÂTEAU LE PIN** Pomerol 1990 • $479 Ⓐ • (03/31/93)
97 **CHÂTEAU LAFITE ROTHSCHILD** Pauillac 1990 • $550 • (03/31/93)
96 **CHÂTEAU HAUT-BRION** Pessac-Léognan 1990 • $190 Ⓐ • (04/30/93) • CS
96 **CHÂTEAU LE GAY** Pomerol 1990 • $49 • (03/31/93)
96 **CHÂTEAU MARGAUX** Margaux 1990 • $253 Ⓐ • (03/31/93)
95 **CHÂTEAU BEAUSÉJOUR** St.-Emilion 1990 • $85 • (03/31/93)
95 **CHÂTEAU CANON-LA GAFFELIÈRE** St.-Emilion 1990 • $39 • (03/15/93) • HR
95 **CHÂTEAU CORDEILLAN-BAGES** Pauillac 1990 • $33 • (03/31/93)

95 **CHÂTEAU GRAND-PUY-LACOSTE** Pauillac 1990 • $26 • (03/31/93)
95 **CHÂTEAU LA FLEUR DE GAY** Pomerol 1990 • $100 • (03/31/93)
95 **CHÂTEAU LA LAGUNE** Haut-Médoc 1990 • $52 Ⓐ • (10/15/94)
95 **CHÂTEAU LA MISSION-HAUT-BRION** Pessac-Léognan 1990 • $63 Ⓐ • (03/31/93)
95 **CHÂTEAU LAFLEUR** Pomerol 1990 • $424 Ⓐ • (05/15/94)
95 **CHÂTEAU LAGRANGE** Pomerol 1990 • $30 • (03/31/93)
95 **CHÂTEAU LAGRANGE** St.-Julien 1990 • $30 • (03/31/93) • SS
95 **CHÂTEAU MOUTON-ROTHSCHILD** Pauillac 1990 • $96 Ⓐ • (05/15/93) • CS
94 **CHÂTEAU AUSONE** St.-Emilion 1990 • $95 Ⓐ • (03/31/93)
94 **CHÂTEAU BOURGNEUF** Pomerol 1990 • $23 • (03/31/93)
94 **CHÂTEAU CLERC MILON** Pauillac 1990 • $30 • (03/31/93)
94 **CHÂTEAU COS-LABORY** St.-Estèphe 1990 • $25 • (03/31/93)
94 **CHÂTEAU FONROQUE** St.-Emilion 1990 • $28 • (03/31/93)
94 **CHÂTEAU LA CONSEILLANTE** Pomerol 1990 • $110 Ⓐ • (03/31/93)
94 **CHÂTEAU LA CROIX-DE-GAY** Pomerol 1990 • $28 • (03/31/93)
94 **CHÂTEAU LA LOUVIÈRE** Pessac-Léognan 1990 • $21 • (03/31/93)
94 **CHÂTEAU LARMANDE** St.-Emilion 1990 • $24 • (03/31/93)
94 **CHÂTEAU LYNCH-BAGES** Pauillac 1990 • $58 Ⓐ • (03/31/93)
94 **CHÂTEAU MONTROSE** St.-Estèphe 1990 • $96 Ⓐ • (03/31/93)
94 **CHÂTEAU PAVIE** St.-Emilion 1990 • $38 • (03/31/93)
94 **CHÂTEAU PICHON-LONGUEVILLE-LALANDE** Pauillac 1990 • $86 Ⓐ • (11/15/97)
94 **CLOS DE L'ORATOIRE** St.-Emilion 1990 • $28 • (03/31/93)
94 **LES FORTS DE LATOUR** Pauillac 1990 • $75 • (03/31/93)
93 **CHÂTEAU L'ANGÉLUS** St.-Emilion 1990 • $71 Ⓐ • (03/31/93)
93 **CHÂTEAU LA TOUR-HAUT-BRION** Pessac-Léognan 1990 • $35 • (03/31/93)
93 **CHÂTEAU LE BON-PASTEUR** Pomerol 1990 • $43 • (03/31/93)
93 **CHÂTEAU LÉOVILLE BARTON** St.-Julien 1990 • $48 • (03/31/93)
93 **CHÂTEAU LES ORMES-DE-PEZ** St.-Estèphe 1990 • $22 • (03/31/93)
93 **CHÂTEAU PAVIE-DECESSE** St.-Emilion 1990 • $22 • (03/31/93)
93 **CHÂTEAU PIBRAN** Pauillac 1990 • $25 • (03/31/93)
93 **CHÂTEAU SMITH-HAUT-LAFITTE** Pessac-Léognan 1990 • $22 • (03/31/93)
93 **CHÂTEAU TALBOT** St.-Julien 1990 • $24 Ⓐ • (03/31/93)
93 **CHÂTEAU DE PEZ** St.-Estèphe 1990 • $20 • (03/31/93)
92 **CHÂTEAU CANTENAC-BROWN** Margaux 1990 • $24 • (03/31/93)
92 **CHÂTEAU DUHART-MILON ROTHSCHILD** Pauillac 1990 • $25 • (10/15/94)
92 **CHÂTEAU FIGEAC** St.-Emilion 1990 • $105 • (03/31/93)
92 **CHÂTEAU GISCOURS** Margaux 1990 • $12 Ⓐ • (03/31/93)
92 **CHÂTEAU HAUT-MARBUZET** St.-Estèphe 1990 • $33 Ⓐ • (03/31/93)
92 **CHÂTEAU L'EVANGILE** Pomerol 1990 • $110 Ⓐ • (03/31/93)
92 **CHÂTEAU LA GRAVE À POMEROL** Pomerol 1990 • $28 • (03/31/93)
92 **CHÂTEAU LÉOVILLE POYFERRÉ** St.-Julien 1990 • $64 • (03/31/93)
92 **CHÂTEAU PAPE CLÉMENT** Pessac-Léognan 1990 • $47 • (03/31/93)
92 **CHÂTEAU PETIT-VILLAGE** Pomerol 1990 • $47 • (03/31/93)
92 **CHÂTEAU ST.-PIERRE** St.-Julien 1990 • $26 • (03/31/93)
92 **CHÂTEAU TROTANOY** Pomerol 1990 • $80 Ⓐ • (05/15/94)
92 **CHÂTEAU VILLEMAURINE** St.-Emilion 1990 • $28 • (03/31/93)
92 **CHÂTEAU DE FIEUZAL** Pessac-Léognan 1990 • $29 • (03/31/93)
92 **DOMAINE DE CHEVALIER** Pessac-Léognan 1990 • $42 • (03/31/93)
91 **CHÂTEAU BRANE-CANTENAC** Margaux 1990 • $28 • (03/31/93)
91 **CHÂTEAU CANON** St.-Emilion 1990 • $54 Ⓐ • (04/30/95)
91 **CHÂTEAU CERTAN DE MAY** Pomerol 1990 • $60 Ⓐ • (10/15/94)
91 **CHÂTEAU CHEVAL-BLANC** St.-Emilion 1990 • $182 Ⓐ • (03/31/93)
91 **CHÂTEAU DESMIRAIL** Margaux 1990 • $27 • (03/31/93)
91 **CHÂTEAU FONTENIL** Fronsac 1990 • $17 • (03/31/93)
91 **CHÂTEAU FRANC-MAYNE** St.-Emilion 1990 • $23 • (03/31/93)
91 **CHÂTEAU HAUT-BAGES-AVÉROUS** Pauillac 1990 • $22 • (03/31/93)
91 **CHÂTEAU HAUT-CORBIN** St.-Emilion 1990 • $18 • (03/31/93)
91 **CHÂTEAU LA TOUR MARTILLAC** Pessac-Léognan 1990 • $25 • (03/31/93)
91 **CHÂTEAU LANGOA BARTON** St.-Julien 1990 • $27 • (03/31/93)
91 **CHÂTEAU LÉOVILLE LAS CASES** St.-Julien 1990 • $73 • (09/15/96)
91 **CHÂTEAU MONBRISON** Margaux 1990 • $22 Ⓐ • (03/31/93)
91 **CHÂTEAU MOULIN DU CADET** St.-Emilion 1990 • $NA • (03/31/93)
91 **CHÂTEAU PALMER** Margaux 1990 • $42 Ⓐ • (03/31/93)
91 **CHÂTEAU PHÉLAN-SÉGUR** St.-Estèphe 1990 • $27 • (03/31/93)
91 **CHÂTEAU PICHON-LONGUEVILLE-BARON** Pauillac 1990 • $96 Ⓐ • (09/15/96)
91 **CHÂTEAU POUGET** Margaux 1990 • $22 • (03/31/93)
91 **CHÂTEAU SOCIANDO-MALLET** Haut-Médoc 1990 • $29 Ⓐ • (03/31/93)
91 **CHÂTEAU TROPLONG-MONDOT** St.-Emilion 1990 • $110 • (03/31/93)
91 **CHÂTEAU TROTTEVIEILLE** St.-Emilion 1990 • $29 • (03/31/93)
91 **CHÂTEAU DE CRUZEAU** Pessac-Léognan 1990 • $16 • (03/31/93)
90 **CHÂTEAU BEAU-SITE** St.-Estèphe 1990 • $23 • (03/31/93)
90 **CHÂTEAU BRANAIRE-DUCRU** St.-Julien 1990 • $38 • (03/31/93)
90 **CHÂTEAU BÉLAIR** St.-Emilion 1990 • $35 • (03/31/93)
90 **CHÂTEAU CHASSE-SPLEEN** Moulis 1990 • $27 • (03/31/93)

90 **CHÂTEAU COS-D'ESTOURNEL** St.-Estèphe 1990 • $72 Ⓐ • (03/31/93)
90 **CHÂTEAU FONPLÉGADE** St.-Emilion 1990 • $25 • (03/31/93)
90 **CHÂTEAU GRUAUD-LAROSE** St.-Julien 1990 • $35 • (03/31/93)
90 **CHÂTEAU KIRWAN** Margaux 1990 • $28 • (03/31/93)
90 **CHÂTEAU LA FLEUR-PÉTRUS** Pomerol 1990 • $70 • (03/31/93)
90 **CHÂTEAU LAFLEUR-GAZIN** Pomerol 1990 • $30 • (03/31/93)
90 **CHÂTEAU LALANDE-BORIE** St.-Julien 1990 • $19 • (03/31/93)
90 **CHÂTEAU LARCIS-DUCASSE** St.-Emilion 1990 • $25 • (03/31/93)
90 **CHÂTEAU LATOUR À POMEROL** Pomerol 1990 • $60 • (10/15/94)
90 **CHÂTEAU MAGDELAINE** St.-Emilion 1990 • $36 Ⓐ • (03/31/93)
90 **CHÂTEAU MEYNEY** St.-Estèphe 1990 • $25 • (03/31/93)
90 **CHÂTEAU PETIT-FIGEAC** St.-Emilion 1990 • $24 • (03/31/93)
90 **CHÂTEAU SIRAN** Margaux 1990 • $22 • (03/31/93)
90 **CHÂTEAU D'OLIVIER** Pessac-Léognan 1990 • $20 • (12/31/92) • HR
90 **CLOS FOURTET** St.-Emilion 1990 • $30 • (03/31/93)
90 **TOURELLES DE LONGUEVILLE** Pauillac 1990 • $24 • (03/31/93)
89 **CHÂTEAU CANON-DE-BREM** Canon-Fronsac 1990 • $17 • (03/31/93)
89 **CHÂTEAU CANUET** Margaux 1990 • $18 • (03/31/93)
89 **CHÂTEAU FAIZEAU** Montagne-St.-Emilion Sélection Vieilles Vignes 1990 • $15 • (03/31/93)
89 **CHÂTEAU GLORIA** St.-Julien 1990 • $27 • (03/31/93)
89 **CHÂTEAU LA FLEUR** St.-Emilion 1990 • $22 • (03/31/93)
89 **CHÂTEAU LA TOUR DE MONS** Margaux 1990 • $20 • (03/31/93)
89 **CHÂTEAU LABÉGORCE-ZÉDÉ** Margaux 1990 • $22 • (03/31/93)
89 **CHÂTEAU LAFON-ROCHET** St.-Estèphe 1990 • $21 • (03/31/93)
89 **CHÂTEAU LIVERSAN** Haut-Médoc 1990 • $19 • (03/31/93)
89 **CHÂTEAU MALMAISON** Moulis 1990 • $14 • (03/31/93)
89 **CHÂTEAU MOULIN HAUT-LAROQUE** Fronsac 1990 • $14 • (03/31/93)
89 **CHÂTEAU TOUR HAUT-CAUSSAN** Médoc 1990 • $17 • (03/31/93)
89 **CHÂTEAU D'ARMAILHAC** Pauillac 1990 • $22 • (03/31/93)
89 **CHÂTEAU DE ROCHEMORIN** Pessac-Léognan 1990 • $12 • (03/31/93)
89 **PAUILLAC DE CHÂTEAU LATOUR** Pauillac 1990 • $29 Ⓐ • (03/31/93)
89 **VIEUX-CHÂTEAU-CERTAN** Pomerol 1990 • $61 Ⓐ • (03/31/93)
88 **CHÂTEAU ANDRON-BLANQUET** St.-Estèphe 1990 • $18 • (03/31/93)
88 **CHÂTEAU BOUSCAUT** Pessac-Léognan 1990 • $18 • (03/31/93)
88 **CHÂTEAU CISSAC** Haut-Médoc 1990 • $18 • (03/31/93)

Key: SS—Spectator Selection CS—Cellar Selection HR—Highly Recommended BB—Best Buy $NA—Price not available Ⓐ—Auction Price
Dates in parentheses indicate the issues in which the ratings were published.

88 **CHÂTEAU COUFRAN** Haut-Médoc 1990 • $17 • (03/31/93)
88 **CHÂTEAU DUCRU-BEAUCAILLOU** St.-Julien 1990 • $51 Ⓐ • (03/31/93)
88 **CHÂTEAU DURFORT-VIVENS** Margaux 1990 • $22 • (03/31/93)
88 **CHÂTEAU GAZIN** Pomerol 1990 • $60 • (03/31/93)
88 **CHÂTEAU HAUT-BAILLY** Pessac-Léognan 1990 • $28 • (03/31/93)
88 **CHÂTEAU HAUT-MAILLET** Pomerol 1990 • $25 • (03/31/93)
88 **CHÂTEAU LA DOMINIQUE** St.-Emilion 1990 • $60 • (03/31/93)
88 **CHÂTEAU LA FLEUR-ST.-GEORGES** Lalande-de-Pomerol 1990 • $NA • (03/31/93)
88 **CHÂTEAU LA SERRE** St.-Emilion 1990 • $22 • (03/31/93)
88 **CHÂTEAU LA VIEILLE CURE** Fronsac 1990 • $19 • (03/31/93)
88 **CHÂTEAU LACHESNAYE** Haut-Médoc 1990 • $17 • (03/31/93)
88 **CHÂTEAU LESTAGE** Listrac 1990 • $18 • (03/31/93)
88 **CHÂTEAU MAZERIS-BELLEVUE** Canon-Fronsac 1990 • $15 • (03/31/93)
88 **CHÂTEAU MOULIN PEY-LABRIE** Canon-Fronsac 1990 • $16 • (03/31/93)
88 **CHÂTEAU NENIN** Pomerol 1990 • $25 Ⓐ • (03/31/93)
88 **CHÂTEAU POUJEAUX** Moulis 1990 • $20 • (03/31/93)
88 **CHÂTEAU ST.-ANDRÉ-CORBIN** St.-Georges-St.-Emilion 1990 • $15 • (03/31/93)
88 **CHÂTEAU DE CHANTEGRIVE** Graves Cuvée Edouard 1990 • $16 • (03/31/93)
88 **CHÂTEAU DU GLANA** St.-Julien 1990 • $20 • (03/31/93)
88 **LES FIEFS DE LAGRANGE** St.-Julien 1990 • $18 • (03/31/93)
87 **CHÂTEAU BEYCHEVELLE** St.-Julien 1990 • $48 • (03/31/93)
87 **CHÂTEAU BRILLETTE** Moulis 1990 • $18 • (03/31/93)
87 **CHÂTEAU CARBONNIEUX** Pessac-Léognan 1990 • $19 • (03/31/93)
87 **CHÂTEAU LA CABANNE** Pomerol 1990 • $27 • (03/31/93)
87 **CHÂTEAU LA GURGUE** Margaux 1990 • $27 • (03/31/93)
87 **CHÂTEAU LA TOUR LÉOGNAN** Pessac-Léognan 1990 • $21 • (03/31/93)
87 **CHÂTEAU LE SARTRE** Pessac-Léognan 1990 • $19 • (03/31/93)
87 **CHÂTEAU LOUDENNE** Médoc 1990 • $17 • (03/31/93)
87 **CHÂTEAU LYNCH-MOUSSAS** Pauillac 1990 • $18 • (03/31/93)
87 **CHÂTEAU MALESCOT-ST.-EXUPÉRY** Margaux 1990 • $24 • (02/28/94)
87 **CHÂTEAU PUY-BLANQUET** St.-Emilion 1990 • $13 • (03/31/93)
87 **CHÂTEAU RAUSAN-SÉGLA** Margaux 1990 • $38 • (03/31/93)
87 **CHÂTEAU DE CHANTEGRIVE** Graves 1990 • $14 • (03/31/93)
87 **DOMAINE DE L'EGLISE** Pomerol 1990 • $37 • (03/31/93)
87 **LACOSTE-BORIE** Pauillac 1990 • $18 • (03/31/93)
86 **CHÂTEAU ARNAULD** Haut-Médoc 1990 • $19 • (03/31/93)
86 **CHÂTEAU BERGAT** St.-Emilion 1990 • $19 • (03/31/93)
86 **CHÂTEAU CHAMBERT-MARBUZET** St.-Estèphe 1990 • $25 • (03/31/93)
86 **CHÂTEAU CITRAN** Haut-Médoc 1990 • $20 • (03/31/93)
86 **CHÂTEAU DALEM** Fronsac 1990 • $20 • (03/31/93)

86 **CHÂTEAU L'EGLISE CLINET** Pomerol 1990 • $45 Ⓐ • (06/15/93)
86 **CHÂTEAU LA FLEUR-POURRET** St.-Emilion 1990 • $23 • (03/31/93)
86 **CHÂTEAU LA POINTE** Pomerol 1990 • $27 • (03/31/93)
86 **CHÂTEAU LANESSAN** Haut-Médoc 1990 • $16 • (03/31/93)
86 **CHÂTEAU LASCOMBES** Margaux 1990 • $22 • (03/31/93)
86 **CHÂTEAU PRIEURÉ-LICHINE** Margaux 1990 • $20 • (03/31/93)
86 **CHÂTEAU ST.-GEORGES** St.-Georges-St.-Emilion 1990 • $23 • (08/31/95)
86 **CHÂTEAU TRIMOULET** St.-Emilion 1990 • $20 • (09/15/93)
86 **CHÂTEAU YON-FIGEAC** St.-Emilion 1990 • $24 • (03/31/93)
86 **CHÂTEAU D'ANGLUDET** Margaux 1990 • $22 • (03/31/93)
86 **CHÂTEAU D'ISSAN** Margaux 1990 • $25 • (03/31/93)
86 **CHÂTEAU DE LAMARQUE** Haut-Médoc 1990 • $18 • (03/31/93)
86 **CHÂTEAU DE MARBUZET** St.-Estèphe 1990 • $19 • (09/15/93)
85 **CHÂTEAU BALAC** Haut-Médoc 1990 • $12 • (09/15/93)
85 **CHÂTEAU CANON** Canon-Fronsac 1990 • $18 • (03/31/93)
85 **CHÂTEAU DAUZAC** Margaux 1990 • $23 • (03/31/93)
85 **CHÂTEAU FOURCAS-HOSTEN** Listrac 1990 • $20 • (03/31/93)
85 **CHÂTEAU VERDIGNAN** Haut-Médoc 1990 • $17 • (03/31/93)
85 **CHÂTEAU DE FRANCE** Pessac-Léognan 1990 • $20 • (03/31/93)
85 **CLOS LARCIS** St.-Emilion 1990 • $25 • (03/31/93)

1989 Red Bordeaux
Vintage Rating: 98

99 **CHÂTEAU MARGAUX** Margaux 1989 • $173 Ⓐ • (03/15/92) • CS
99 **CHÂTEAU MOUTON-ROTHSCHILD** Pauillac 1989 • $150 Ⓐ • (03/15/92)
98 **CHÂTEAU LA FLEUR DE GAY** Pomerol 1989 • $139 Ⓐ • (03/15/92)
98 **CHÂTEAU LYNCH-BAGES** Pauillac 1989 • $99 Ⓐ • (03/15/92)
98 **CHÂTEAU PICHON-LONGUEVILLE-BARON** Pauillac 1989 • $87 Ⓐ • (03/15/92)
97 **CHÂTEAU HAUT-BRION** Pessac-Léognan 1989 • $352 Ⓐ • (03/15/92)
97 **CHÂTEAU LATOUR** Pauillac 1989 • $147 Ⓐ • (03/15/92)
96 **CHÂTEAU CLERC MILON** Pauillac 1989 • $44 • (03/15/92) • HR
96 **CHÂTEAU CORDEILLAN-BAGES** Pauillac 1989 • $24 • (03/15/92)
96 **CHÂTEAU L'EGLISE CLINET** Pomerol 1989 • $69 • (08/31/92) • HR
96 **CHÂTEAU LA MISSION-HAUT-BRION** Pessac-Léognan 1989 • $237 Ⓐ • (03/15/92)
96 **CHÂTEAU LAFLEUR** Pomerol 1989 • $303 Ⓐ • (03/15/92)
96 **DOMAINE DE CHEVALIER** Pessac-Léognan 1989 • $42 Ⓐ • (03/15/92)
95 **CHÂTEAU BEYCHEVELLE** St.-Julien 1989 • $50 Ⓐ • (03/15/92)
95 **CHÂTEAU CALON-SÉGUR** St.-Estèphe 1989 • $27 Ⓐ • (03/15/92)
95 **CHÂTEAU CHASSE-SPLEEN** Moulis 1989 • $58 Ⓐ • (03/15/92)
95 **CHÂTEAU COS-D'ESTOURNEL** St.-Estèphe 1989 • $46 Ⓐ • (03/15/92)
95 **CHÂTEAU LA POINTE** Pomerol 1989 • $23 Ⓐ • (03/15/92)
95 **CHÂTEAU LA TOUR-HAUT-BRION** Pessac-Léognan 1989 • $46 Ⓐ • (03/15/92)
95 **CHÂTEAU LAFITE ROTHSCHILD** Pauillac 1989 • $113 Ⓐ • (03/15/92)
95 **CHÂTEAU LAGRANGE** St.-Julien 1989 • $39 Ⓐ • (03/15/92)
95 **CHÂTEAU LARMANDE** St.-Emilion 1989 • $18 Ⓐ • (03/15/92)
95 **CHÂTEAU MONTROSE** St.-Estèphe 1989 • $67 Ⓐ • (03/15/92)
95 **CHÂTEAU PALMER** Margaux 1989 • $105 Ⓐ • (03/15/92)
95 **CHÂTEAU PIBRAN** Pauillac 1989 • $25 • (03/15/92)
95 **CHÂTEAU PICHON-LONGUEVILLE-LALANDE** Pauillac 1989 • $96 Ⓐ • (11/15/97)
95 **CHÂTEAU OLIVIER** Pessac-Léognan 1989 • $23 • (03/15/92) • SS
95 **CHÂTEAU DE FIEUZAL** Pessac-Léognan 1989 • $38 Ⓐ • (03/15/92) • HR
94 **CHÂTEAU BRANE-CANTENAC** Margaux 1989 • $40 Ⓐ • (03/15/92)
94 **CHÂTEAU FRANC-MAYNE** St.-Emilion 1989 • $28 • (03/15/92)
94 **CHÂTEAU L'ANGÉLUS** St.-Emilion 1989 • $142 Ⓐ • (03/15/92)
94 **CHÂTEAU LANGOA BARTON** St.-Julien 1989 • $39 Ⓐ • (03/15/92)
94 **CHÂTEAU LE PIN** Pomerol 1989 • $680 Ⓐ • (05/15/94)
94 **CHÂTEAU LÉOVILLE BARTON** St.-Julien 1989 • $33 Ⓐ • (03/15/92)
94 **CHÂTEAU D'ARMAILHAC** Pauillac 1989 • $30 Ⓐ • (03/15/92)
94 **TOURELLES DE LONGUEVILLE** Pauillac 1989 • $27 • (03/15/92)
93 **CHÂTEAU AUSONE** St.-Emilion 1989 • $101 Ⓐ • (03/15/92)
93 **CHÂTEAU BARET** Pessac-Léognan 1989 • $18 • (03/15/92)
93 **CHÂTEAU BOUSCAUT** Pessac-Léognan 1989 • $22 • (03/15/92)
93 **CHÂTEAU CITRAN** Haut-Médoc 1989 • $20 • (03/15/92)
93 **CHÂTEAU COS-LABORY** St.-Estèphe 1989 • $18 • (03/15/92)
93 **CHÂTEAU FIGEAC** St.-Emilion 1989 • $49 Ⓐ • (03/15/92)
93 **CHÂTEAU GRAND-MAYNE** St.-Emilion 1989 • $22 • (03/15/92)
93 **CHÂTEAU GRUAUD-LAROSE** St.-Julien 1989 • $36 Ⓐ • (03/15/92)
93 **CHÂTEAU L'ARROSÉE** St.-Emilion 1989 • $49 Ⓐ • (04/30/92) • HR
93 **CHÂTEAU LATOUR À POMEROL** Pomerol 1989 • $55 • (05/15/94)
93 **CHÂTEAU LE TERTRE ROTEBOEUF** St.-Emilion 1989 • $79 Ⓐ • (03/15/92)
93 **CHÂTEAU MEYNEY** St.-Estèphe 1989 • $40 Ⓐ • (03/15/92) • HR
93 **CHÂTEAU MONBRISON** Margaux 1989 • $27 Ⓐ • (03/15/92)

93 **CHÂTEAU VILLEMAURINE** St.-Emilion 1989 • $30 • (03/15/92)
93 **DOMAINE DE L'EGLISE** Pomerol 1989 • $49 Ⓐ • (03/15/92)
92 **CHÂTEAU DURFORT-VIVENS** Margaux 1989 • $28 • (03/15/92)
92 **CHÂTEAU GISCOURS** Margaux 1989 • $40 Ⓐ • (03/15/92)
92 **CHÂTEAU HAUT-BAILLY** Pessac-Léognan 1989 • $40 Ⓐ • (03/15/92)
92 **CHÂTEAU L'EVANGILE** Pomerol 1989 • $70 Ⓐ • (03/15/92)
92 **CHÂTEAU LA CABANNE** Pomerol 1989 • $20 Ⓐ • (03/15/92)
92 **CHÂTEAU LA COMMANDERIE** St.-Emilion 1989 • $19 • (03/15/92)
92 **CHÂTEAU LA CONSEILLANTE** Pomerol 1989 • $173 Ⓐ • (03/15/92)
92 **CHÂTEAU LA GURGUE** Margaux 1989 • $30 • (03/15/92)
92 **CHÂTEAU LA TOUR CARNET** Haut-Médoc 1989 • $24 • (03/15/92)
92 **CHÂTEAU LAFON-ROCHET** St.-Estèphe 1989 • $34 Ⓐ • (03/15/92)
92 **CLOS LARCIS** St.-Emilion 1989 • $28 • (03/15/92)
91 **CHÂTEAU BEAUSÉJOUR** St.-Emilion 1989 • $44 • (03/15/92)
91 **CHÂTEAU CANTEMERLE** Haut-Médoc 1989 • $48 Ⓐ • (03/15/92)
91 **CHÂTEAU DUCRU-BEAUCAILLOU** St.-Julien 1989 • $26 Ⓐ • (10/15/92)
91 **CHÂTEAU GAZIN** Pomerol 1989 • $37 Ⓐ • (03/15/92)
91 **CHÂTEAU GRAND-PUY-LACOSTE** Pauillac 1989 • $45 Ⓐ • (03/15/92)
91 **CHÂTEAU LA DOMINIQUE** St.-Emilion 1989 • $65 Ⓐ • (03/15/92)
91 **CHÂTEAU LA LOUVIÈRE** Pessac-Léognan 1989 • $22 • (03/15/92) • HR
91 **CHÂTEAU LARCIS-DUCASSE** St.-Emilion 1989 • $28 • (03/15/92)
91 **CHÂTEAU LE GAY** Pomerol 1989 • $63 Ⓐ • (03/15/92)
91 **CHÂTEAU SMITH-HAUT-LAFITTE** Pessac-Léognan 1989 • $26 Ⓐ • (03/15/92)
91 **CHÂTEAU ST.-ANDRÉ-CORBIN** St.-Georges-St.-Emilion 1989 • $15 • (04/30/92)
91 **CHÂTEAU ST.-PIERRE** St.-Julien 1989 • $21 Ⓐ • (10/15/92)
91 **LES FORTS DE LATOUR** Pauillac 1989 • $42 Ⓐ • (03/15/92)
91 **VIEUX-CHÂTEAU-CERTAN** Pomerol 1989 • $46 Ⓐ • (03/15/92)
90 **CHÂTEAU BAHANS HAUT-BRION** Pessac-Léognan 1989 • $36 Ⓐ • (03/15/92)
90 **CHÂTEAU BEAU-SITE** St.-Estèphe 1989 • $20 • (03/15/92)
90 **CHÂTEAU BOURGNEUF** Pomerol 1989 • $32 • (03/15/92)
90 **CHÂTEAU BRANAIRE-DUCRU** St.-Julien 1989 • $42 Ⓐ • (03/15/92)
90 **CHÂTEAU CANON** St.-Emilion 1989 • $49 Ⓐ • (04/30/95)
90 **CHÂTEAU CHEVAL-BLANC** St.-Emilion 1989 • $114 Ⓐ • (03/15/92)
90 **CHÂTEAU DAUZAC** Margaux 1989 • $22 Ⓐ • (03/15/92)

Key: SS—Spectator Selection CS—Cellar Selection HR—Highly Recommended BB—Best Buy $NA—Price not available Ⓐ—Auction Price
Dates in parentheses indicate the issues in which the ratings were published.

90 **CHÂTEAU DUHART-MILON ROTHSCHILD** Pauillac 1989 • $25 Ⓐ • (03/15/92)
90 **CHÂTEAU HAUT-BAGES-AVÉROUS** Pauillac 1989 • $26 • (03/15/92)
90 **CHÂTEAU HAUT-MARBUZET** St.-Estèphe 1989 • $35 Ⓐ • (03/15/92)
90 **CHÂTEAU LYNCH-MOUSSAS** Pauillac 1989 • $18 • (03/15/92)
90 **CHÂTEAU LÉOVILLE POYFERRÉ** St.-Julien 1989 • $42 • (03/15/92)
90 **CHÂTEAU PAVIE** St.-Emilion 1989 • $36 Ⓐ • (03/15/92)
90 **CHÂTEAU PAVIE-DECESSE** St.-Emilion 1989 • $29 • (03/15/92)
90 **CHÂTEAU PETIT-FIGEAC** St.-Emilion 1989 • $21 • (03/15/92)
90 **CHÂTEAU POUJEAUX** Moulis 1989 • $21 • (03/15/92)
90 **CHÂTEAU PUY-BLANQUET** St.-Emilion 1989 • $14 • (03/15/92)
90 **CHÂTEAU SOCIANDO-MALLET** Haut-Médoc 1989 • $41 Ⓐ • (03/15/92)
90 **CHÂTEAU TALBOT** St.-Julien 1989 • $62 Ⓐ • (03/15/92)
90 **CHÂTEAU TROTANOY** Pomerol 1989 • $124 Ⓐ • (05/15/94)
90 **CHÂTEAU TROTTEVIEILLE** St.-Emilion 1989 • $44 • (03/15/92)
90 **CHÂTEAU VERDIGNAN** Haut-Médoc 1989 • $17 • (03/15/92)
90 **CHÂTEAU DE MALLERET** Haut-Médoc 1989 • $NA • (03/15/92)
90 **CHÂTEAU DU TERTRE** Margaux 1989 • $25 Ⓐ • (03/15/92)
89 **BARON PHILIPPE DE ROTHSCHILD** Médoc 1989 • $11 • (11/15/94) • HR
89 **CARRUADES DE LAFITE ROTHSCHILD** Pauillac 1989 • $34 Ⓐ • (03/15/92)
89 **CHÂTEAU BARON DE BRANE** Margaux 1989 • $NA • (03/15/92)
89 **CHÂTEAU BÉLAIR** St.-Emilion 1989 • $37 • (03/15/92)
89 **CHÂTEAU CANTENAC-BROWN** Margaux 1989 • $30 Ⓐ • (03/15/92)
89 **CHÂTEAU CERTAN DE MAY** Pomerol 1989 • $55 Ⓐ • (10/15/94)
89 **CHÂTEAU COUFRAN** Haut-Médoc 1989 • $14 • (03/15/92)
89 **CHÂTEAU GLORIA** St.-Julien 1989 • $22 Ⓐ • (10/15/92)
89 **CHÂTEAU HAUT-BAGES-LIBÉRAL** Pauillac 1989 • $24 Ⓐ • (03/15/92)
89 **CHÂTEAU HAUT-CORBIN** St.-Emilion 1989 • $26 • (03/15/92)
89 **CHÂTEAU LARRIVET-HAUT-BRION** Pessac-Léognan 1989 • $22 Ⓐ • (03/15/92)
89 **CHÂTEAU PONTET-CANET** Pauillac 1989 • $30 Ⓐ • (03/15/92)
89 **CHÂTEAU TROPLONG-MONDOT** St.-Emilion 1989 • $103 Ⓐ • (03/15/92)
89 **CHÂTEAU DE FRANCE** Pessac-Léognan 1989 • $22 • (03/15/92)
89 **CHÂTEAU DE LAMARQUE** Haut-Médoc 1989 • $26 • (03/15/92)
89 **CHÂTEAU DE MARBUZET** St.-Estèphe 1989 • $21 • (03/15/92)
89 **CHÂTEAU DE PEZ** St.-Estèphe 1989 • $27 Ⓐ • (03/15/92)
89 **CLOS FOURTET** St.-Emilion 1989 • $28 • (03/15/92)
89 **COUVENT DES JACOBINS** St.-Emilion 1989 • $28 • (04/30/92)
89 **LACOSTE-BORIE** Pauillac 1989 • $15 • (03/15/92)

88 **CHÂTEAU ARNAULD** Haut-Médoc 1989 • $14 • (03/15/92)

88 **CHÂTEAU CANON-LA GAFFELIÈRE** St.-Emilion 1989 • $36 Ⓐ • (03/15/92)

88 **CHÂTEAU DUPLESSIS-FABRE** Moulis 1989 • $9 • (03/15/92)

88 **CHÂTEAU FONROQUE** St.-Emilion 1989 • $24 • (03/15/92)

88 **CHÂTEAU GRANDES-MURAILLES** St.-Emilion 1989 • $NA • (03/15/92)

88 **CHÂTEAU LA CLAVERIE** Côtes de Francs 1989 • $21 • (03/15/92)

88 **CHÂTEAU LA CROIX-DE-GAY** Pomerol 1989 • $27 • (03/15/92)

88 **CHÂTEAU LA FLEUR-PÉTRUS** Pomerol 1989 • $78 Ⓐ • (03/15/92)

88 **CHÂTEAU LA GRAVE À POMEROL** Pomerol 1989 • $35 • (03/15/92)

88 **CHÂTEAU LA TOUR DE MONS** Margaux 1989 • $25 • (03/15/92)

88 **CHÂTEAU LA VIEILLE CURE** Fronsac 1989 • $16 • (03/15/92)

88 **CHÂTEAU LALANDE-BORIE** St.-Julien 1989 • $17 • (03/15/92)

88 **CHÂTEAU LE BON-PASTEUR** Pomerol 1989 • $37 Ⓐ • (04/30/92)

88 **CHÂTEAU MAGDELAINE** St.-Emilion 1989 • $49 Ⓐ • (03/15/92)

88 **CHÂTEAU PAPE CLÉMENT** Pessac-Léognan 1989 • $43 • (03/15/92)

88 **CHÂTEAU PETIT-VILLAGE** Pomerol 1989 • $41 Ⓐ • (03/15/92)

88 **CHÂTEAU PLAGNAC** Médoc 1989 • $12 • (03/15/92)

88 **CHÂTEAU RAMAGE LA BÂTISSE** Haut-Médoc 1989 • $15 • (03/15/92)

88 **CHÂTEAU RAUSAN-SÉGLA** Margaux 1989 • $48 Ⓐ • (03/15/92)

88 **CHÂTEAU SIRAN** Margaux 1989 • $25 • (03/15/92)

88 **CHÂTEAU D'AGASSAC** Haut-Médoc 1989 • $20 • (03/15/92)

88 **CHÂTEAU DE CHANTEGRIVE** Graves 1989 • $20 • (03/15/92)

88 **CHÂTEAU DE ROCHEMORIN** Pessac-Léognan 1989 • $16 • (03/15/92)

87 **CHÂTEAU CAP DE MOURLIN** St.-Emilion 1989 • $23 • (03/15/92)

87 **CHÂTEAU FOURCAS-HOSTEN** Listrac 1989 • $19 • (03/15/92)

87 **CHÂTEAU HAUT-BATAILLEY** Pauillac 1989 • $29 Ⓐ • (03/15/92)

87 **CHÂTEAU KIRWAN** Margaux 1989 • $20 Ⓐ • (03/15/92)

87 **CHÂTEAU LA LAGUNE** Haut-Médoc 1989 • $41 Ⓐ • (10/15/94)

87 **CHÂTEAU LA TOUR-DE-BESSAN** Margaux 1989 • $NA • (03/15/92)

87 **CHÂTEAU LAFLEUR-GAZIN** Pomerol 1989 • $NA • (03/15/92)

87 **CHÂTEAU LAGRANGE** Pomerol 1989 • $39 Ⓐ • (03/15/92)

87 **CHÂTEAU LAROSE-TRINTAUDON** Haut-Médoc 1989 • $12 • (03/15/92)

87 **CHÂTEAU LIVERSAN** Haut-Médoc 1989 • $18 • (03/15/92)

87 **CHÂTEAU MALESCOT-ST.-EXUPÉRY** Margaux 1989 • $27 • (03/15/92)

87 **CHÂTEAU SOUTARD** St.-Emilion 1989 • $27 • (09/15/93)

87 **CHÂTEAU TOUR HAUT-CAUSSAN** Médoc 1989 • $20 • (03/15/92)

87 **CHÂTEAU D'ANGLUDET** Margaux 1989 • $67 Ⓐ • (03/15/92)

87 **CHÂTEAU DU GLANA** St.-Julien 1989 • $NA • (03/15/92)

87 **PAVILLON ROUGE DU CHÂTEAU MARGAUX** Margaux 1989 • $28 Ⓐ • (04/30/92)

86 **CHÂTEAU BRILLETTE** Moulis 1989 • $17 • (03/15/92)

86 **CHÂTEAU CANON-MOUEIX** Canon-Fronsac 1989 • $22 • (03/15/92)

86 **CHÂTEAU DESMIRAIL** Margaux 1989 • $27 • (03/15/92)

86 **CHÂTEAU FOURCAS-DUPRÉ** Listrac 1989 • $25 • (03/15/92)

86 **CHÂTEAU GRAND-PUY-DUCASSE** Pauillac 1989 • $29 Ⓐ • (04/30/92)

86 **CHÂTEAU LABÉGORCE-ZÉDÉ** Margaux 1989 • $20 • (03/15/92)

86 **CHÂTEAU LES CHARMES-GODARD** Côtes de Francs 1989 • $NA • (03/15/92)

86 **CHÂTEAU LES ORMES-DE-PEZ** St.-Estèphe 1989 • $24 • (03/15/92)

86 **CHÂTEAU MOULIN DU CADET** St.-Emilion 1989 • $NA • (03/15/92)

86 **CHÂTEAU PLAISANCE** Premières Côtes de Bordeaux Cuvée Spéciale 1989 • $13 • (01/31/92)

86 **CHÂTEAU PRIEURÉ-LICHINE** Margaux 1989 • $36 Ⓐ • (03/15/92)

86 **CHÂTEAU DE CAMENSAC** Haut-Médoc 1989 • $16 • (03/15/92)

86 **CHÂTEAU DE CRUZEAU** Pessac-Léognan 1989 • $14 • (03/15/92)

85 **CHÂTEAU BALESTARD-LA-TONNELLE** St.-Emilion 1989 • $28 • (03/15/92)

85 **CHÂTEAU BELLEGRAVE-VAN DER VOORT** Pauillac 1989 • $20 • (09/15/93)

85 **CHÂTEAU CARBONNIEUX** Pessac-Léognan 1989 • $26 • (03/15/92)

85 **CHÂTEAU CISSAC** Haut-Médoc 1989 • $23 Ⓐ • (03/15/92)

85 **CHÂTEAU CLARKE** Listrac 1989 • $16 • (03/15/92)

85 **CHÂTEAU CLOS DES JACOBINS** St.-Emilion 1989 • $45 • (03/15/92)

85 **CHÂTEAU LA SALLE DE POUJEAUX** Moulis 1989 • $15 • (03/15/92)

85 **CHÂTEAU LA TOUR-DE-BY** Médoc 1989 • $19 • (03/15/92)

85 **CHÂTEAU LANESSAN** Haut-Médoc 1989 • $20 • (03/15/92)

85 **CHÂTEAU MALARTIC-LAGRAVIÈRE** Pessac-Léognan 1989 • $24 • (03/15/92)

85 **CHÂTEAU MALMAISON** Moulis 1989 • $16 • (03/15/92)

85 **CHÂTEAU PHÉLAN-SÉGUR** St.-Estèphe 1989 • $29 Ⓐ • (03/15/92)

85 **CHÂTEAU SOUDARS** Haut-Médoc 1989 • $15 • (03/15/92)

85 **CHÂTEAU DE CHANTEGRIVE** Graves Cuvée Edouard 1989 • $22 • (03/15/92)

1988 RED BORDEAUX
VINTAGE RATING: 93

97 **CHÂTEAU LYNCH-BAGES** Pauillac 1988 • $64 Ⓐ • (10/15/94)

97 **CHÂTEAU MARGAUX** Margaux 1988 • $133 Ⓐ • (03/31/91) • CS

96 **CHÂTEAU PALMER** Margaux 1988 • $68 Ⓐ • (02/28/91) • CS

95 **CHÂTEAU COS-D'ESTOURNEL** St.-Estèphe 1988 • $36 Ⓐ • (07/15/91) • CS
95 **CHÂTEAU LE PIN** Pomerol 1988 • $497 Ⓐ • (05/15/94)
95 **CHÂTEAU LÉOVILLE LAS CASES** St.-Julien 1988 • $46 Ⓐ • (02/15/92)
95 **CHÂTEAU PICHON-LONGUEVILLE-BARON** Pauillac 1988 • $55 Ⓐ • (03/31/91) • SS
94 **CHÂTEAU CLERC MILON** Pauillac 1988 • $26 • (04/30/91) • SS
94 **CHÂTEAU HAUT-BAILLY** Pessac-Léognan 1988 • $34 Ⓐ • (04/30/91)
94 **CHÂTEAU L'ARROSÉE** St.-Emilion 1988 • $33 Ⓐ • (03/15/91) • HR
94 **CHÂTEAU LA FLEUR DE GAY** Pomerol 1988 • $86 Ⓐ • (06/30/91) • HR
94 **CHÂTEAU LAFITE ROTHSCHILD** Pauillac 1988 • $104 Ⓐ • (11/30/91)
94 **CHÂTEAU LARRIVET-HAUT-BRION** Pessac-Léognan 1988 • $25 • (04/30/91)
94 **CHÂTEAU PAVIE-DECESSE** St.-Emilion 1988 • $16 Ⓐ • (03/31/91) • HR
94 **CHÂTEAU PÉTRUS** Pomerol 1988 • $355 Ⓐ • (08/31/91)
93 **CHÂTEAU BEYCHEVELLE** St.-Julien 1988 • $46 Ⓐ • (04/30/91)
93 **CHÂTEAU CHEVAL-BLANC** St.-Emilion 1988 • $63 Ⓐ • (12/31/90) • CS
93 **CHÂTEAU FIGEAC** St.-Emilion 1988 • $46 Ⓐ • (06/30/91) • HR
93 **CHÂTEAU HAUT-BAGES-AVÉROUS** Pauillac 1988 • $20 • (04/30/91)
93 **CHÂTEAU L'ANGÉLUS** St.-Emilion 1988 • $53 Ⓐ • (03/31/91)
93 **CHÂTEAU LATOUR** Pauillac 1988 • $118 Ⓐ • (04/30/91)
93 **CHÂTEAU PAPE CLÉMENT** Pessac-Léognan 1988 • $40 • (12/31/90) • HR
92 **CHÂTEAU CLINET** Pomerol 1988 • $80 Ⓐ • (02/28/91) • HR
92 **CHÂTEAU DUCRU-BEAUCAILLOU** St.-Julien 1988 • $30 Ⓐ • (10/15/92)
92 **CHÂTEAU HAUT-BRION** Pessac-Léognan 1988 • $105 Ⓐ • (04/30/97)
92 **CHÂTEAU HAUT-BRION** Pessac-Léognan 1988 • $105 Ⓐ • (04/30/97)
92 **CHÂTEAU LA LOUVIÈRE** Pessac-Léognan 1988 • $24 • (08/31/91) • SS
92 **CHÂTEAU MARQUIS DE TERME** Margaux 1988 • $23 • (04/30/91)
92 **CHÂTEAU MONBRISON** Margaux 1988 • $24 Ⓐ • (02/28/91) • HR
92 **CHÂTEAU RAUSAN-SÉGLA** Margaux 1988 • $51 Ⓐ • (03/15/91) • HR
92 **CHÂTEAU DE FRANCE** Pessac-Léognan 1988 • $18 • (02/28/91) • SS
92 **CHÂTEAU DE MARBUZET** St.-Estèphe 1988 • $17 • (07/15/91) • SS
92 **LES FIEFS DE LAGRANGE** St.-Julien 1988 • $17 • (04/30/91)
91 **CHÂTEAU BALESTARD-LA-TONNELLE** St.-Emilion 1988 • $25 • (04/30/91)
91 **CHÂTEAU CITRAN** Haut-Médoc 1988 • $20 • (04/30/91)
91 **CHÂTEAU FRANC-BIGAROUX** St.-Emilion 1988 • $24 • (07/31/91) • HR

Key: SS—Spectator Selection CS—Cellar Selection HR—Highly Recommended BB—Best Buy $NA—Price not available Ⓐ—Auction Price
Dates in parentheses indicate the issues in which the ratings were published.

91 **CHÂTEAU HAUT-MARBUZET** St.-Estèphe 1988 • $29 Ⓐ • (12/31/90) • SS
91 **CHÂTEAU L'EGLISE CLINET** Pomerol 1988 • $47 • (12/31/90)
91 **CHÂTEAU LA LAGUNE** Haut-Médoc 1988 • $34 Ⓐ • (04/30/91)
91 **CHÂTEAU LA TOUR-HAUT-BRION** Pessac-Léognan 1988 • $29 Ⓐ • (06/15/91) • CS
91 **CHÂTEAU LAFLEUR** Pomerol 1988 • $194 Ⓐ • (05/15/94)
91 **CHÂTEAU LÉOVILLE BARTON** St.-Julien 1988 • $29 Ⓐ • (03/31/91) • HR
91 **CHÂTEAU TAILHAS** Pomerol 1988 • $20 • (04/30/91)
91 **CHÂTEAU TRIMOULET** St.-Emilion 1988 • $16 • (06/15/91) • HR
91 **CHÂTEAU OLIVIER** Pessac-Léognan 1988 • $25 • (02/15/91) • HR
91 **CHÂTEAU DE FIEUZAL** Pessac-Léognan 1988 • $33 Ⓐ • (04/30/91)
91 **DOMAINE DE CHEVALIER** Pessac-Léognan 1988 • $42 Ⓐ • (07/15/91) • HR
91 **VIEUX-CHÂTEAU-CERTAN** Pomerol 1988 • $39 Ⓐ • (03/31/91)
90 **CHÂTEAU BATAILLEY** Pauillac 1988 • $29 Ⓐ • (04/30/91)
90 **CHÂTEAU BEAUREGARD** Pomerol 1988 • $21 Ⓐ • (07/31/91) • HR
90 **CHÂTEAU BOURGNEUF** Pomerol 1988 • $19 • (06/30/91)
90 **CHÂTEAU CERTAN DE MAY** Pomerol 1988 • $67 Ⓐ • (06/30/91)
90 **CHÂTEAU CLOS DES JACOBINS** St.-Emilion 1988 • $26 • (04/15/91) • HR
90 **CHÂTEAU DAUZAC** Margaux 1988 • $20 • (06/30/91) • HR
90 **CHÂTEAU GRAND-PUY-LACOSTE** Pauillac 1988 • $72 Ⓐ • (04/30/91)
90 **CHÂTEAU LA CONSEILLANTE** Pomerol 1988 • $45 Ⓐ • (03/31/91)
90 **CHÂTEAU LA GURGUE** Margaux 1988 • $34 • (04/30/91)
90 **CHÂTEAU LA MISSION-HAUT-BRION** Pessac-Léognan 1988 • $68 Ⓐ • (11/15/91)
90 **CHÂTEAU LATOUR À POMEROL** Pomerol 1988 • $29 Ⓐ • (10/15/94)
90 **CHÂTEAU LE TERTRE ROTEBOEUF** St.-Emilion 1988 • $56 Ⓐ • (06/15/91)
90 **CHÂTEAU MOUTON-BARONNE-PHILIPPE** Pauillac 1988 • $32 Ⓐ • (04/30/91)
90 **CHÂTEAU PRIEURÉ-LICHINE** Margaux 1988 • $24 Ⓐ • (04/30/91)
90 **CHÂTEAU TALBOT** St.-Julien 1988 • $43 Ⓐ • (03/15/91)
89 **CHÂTEAU CADET-PIOLA** St.-Emilion 1988 • $20 • (07/15/91)
89 **CHÂTEAU CANTENAC-BROWN** Margaux 1988 • $27 Ⓐ • (04/30/91)
89 **CHÂTEAU CERTAN-GIRAUD** Pomerol 1988 • $23 • (02/28/91)
89 **CHÂTEAU CHASSE-SPLEEN** Moulis 1988 • $33 Ⓐ • (03/31/91)
89 **CHÂTEAU FONBADET** Pauillac 1988 • $16 • (08/31/91)
89 **CHÂTEAU GISCOURS** Margaux 1988 • $30 Ⓐ • (04/30/91)
89 **CHÂTEAU GRAND-MAYNE** St.-Emilion 1988 • $20 • (04/30/91)
89 **CHÂTEAU GRAND-PUY-DUCASSE** Pauillac 1988 • $24 Ⓐ • (04/30/91)

89 **CHÂTEAU LA CROIX-DE-GAY** Pomerol 1988 • $30 • (06/30/91)
89 **CHÂTEAU MALESCOT-ST.-EXUPÉRY** Margaux 1988 • $20 • (04/30/91)
89 **CHÂTEAU PAVIE** St.-Emilion 1988 • $45 Ⓐ • (03/31/91)
89 **CHÂTEAU TROTANOY** Pomerol 1988 • $52 Ⓐ • (08/31/91)
89 **LACOSTE-BORIE** Pauillac 1988 • $19 • (04/30/91)
89 **LE PETIT CHEVAL** St.-Emilion 1988 • $35 • (03/31/91)
88 **CHÂTEAU CANON** St.-Emilion 1988 • $52 Ⓐ • (04/30/95)
88 **CHÂTEAU CLOS RENÉ** Pomerol 1988 • $24 • (04/30/91)
88 **CHÂTEAU DUHART-MILON ROTHSCHILD** Pauillac 1988 • $24 • (08/31/91)
88 **CHÂTEAU GLORIA** St.-Julien 1988 • $18 • (10/15/92)
88 **CHÂTEAU HAUT-BAGES-LIBÉRAL** Pauillac 1988 • $22 Ⓐ • (03/15/91)
88 **CHÂTEAU LA TOUR MARTILLAC** Pessac-Léognan 1988 • $24 • (02/28/91)
88 **CHÂTEAU LES ORMES-DE-PEZ** St.-Estèphe 1988 • $21 • (04/30/91)
88 **CHÂTEAU MOULINET** Pomerol 1988 • $17 • (07/31/91)
88 **CHÂTEAU POUJEAUX** Moulis 1988 • $15 • (02/28/91)
88 **CHÂTEAU SIRAN** Margaux 1988 • $19 • (06/30/91)
88 **CHÂTEAU SOUDARS** Haut-Médoc 1988 • $15 • (04/30/91)
88 **CHÂTEAU ST.-PIERRE** St.-Julien 1988 • $27 • (10/15/92)
88 **CHÂTEAU TOUR-DU-HAUT-MOULIN** Haut-Médoc 1988 • $20 • (04/30/91)
88 **CHÂTEAU D'ISSAN** Margaux 1988 • $29 Ⓐ • (04/30/91)
88 **PAVILLON ROUGE DU CHÂTEAU MARGAUX** Margaux 1988 • $37 Ⓐ • (04/30/91)
88 **RÉSERVE DE LA COMTESSE** Pauillac 1988 • $26 • (03/15/91)
87 **CHÂTEAU BEAU-SÉJOUR BÉCOT** St.-Emilion 1988 • $21 • (06/30/91)
87 **CHÂTEAU BEAUSÉJOUR** St.-Emilion 1988 • $28 Ⓐ • (04/30/91)
87 **CHÂTEAU BOUSCAUT** Pessac-Léognan 1988 • $20 • (04/30/91)
87 **CHÂTEAU GAZIN** Pomerol 1988 • $40 Ⓐ • (06/30/91)
87 **CHÂTEAU GREYSAC** Médoc 1988 • $15 • (04/30/91)
87 **CHÂTEAU HAUT-BATAILLEY** Pauillac 1988 • $27 Ⓐ • (08/31/91)
87 **CHÂTEAU KIRWAN** Margaux 1988 • $21 Ⓐ • (04/30/91)
87 **CHÂTEAU L'EVANGILE** Pomerol 1988 • $50 Ⓐ • (06/30/91)
87 **CHÂTEAU LALANDE-BORIE** St.-Julien 1988 • $17 • (04/30/91)
87 **CHÂTEAU LE BONNAT** Graves 1988 • $18 • (12/31/90)
87 **CHÂTEAU LIVERSAN** Haut-Médoc 1988 • $15 Ⓐ • (07/31/91)
87 **CHÂTEAU MONTROSE** St.-Estèphe 1988 • $42 Ⓐ • (03/31/91)
87 **CHÂTEAU PHÉLAN-SÉGUR** St.-Estèphe 1988 • $29 Ⓐ • (07/15/91)
87 **CHÂTEAU PICHON-LONGUEVILLE-LALANDE** Pauillac 1988 • $77 Ⓐ • (11/15/97)
87 **CHÂTEAU ROCHER BELLEVUE FIGEAC** St.-Emilion 1988 • $18 • (04/30/91)
87 **CHÂTEAU SOCIANDO-MALLET** Haut-Médoc 1988 • $34 Ⓐ • (03/31/91)
87 **CHÂTEAU TAILLEFER** Pomerol 1988 • $22 • (06/30/91)
87 **CHÂTEAU DE CRUZEAU** Pessac-Léognan 1988 • $14 • (02/28/91)
86 **CHÂTEAU AUSONE** St.-Emilion 1988 • $87 Ⓐ • (10/15/94)
86 **CHÂTEAU CANON-LA GAFFELIÈRE** St.-Emilion 1988 • $30 • (06/30/91)
86 **CHÂTEAU CARBONNIEUX** Pessac-Léognan 1988 • $19 Ⓐ • (02/28/91)
86 **CHÂTEAU GRAND-PONTET** St.-Emilion 1988 • $21 • (07/15/91)
86 **CHÂTEAU LA DOMINIQUE** St.-Emilion 1988 • $25 • (06/30/91)
86 **CHÂTEAU LA TOUR-DE-BY** Médoc 1988 • $13 • (06/15/91)
86 **CHÂTEAU LANGOA BARTON** St.-Julien 1988 • $35 Ⓐ • (07/15/91)
86 **CHÂTEAU LARMANDE** St.-Emilion 1988 • $46 Ⓐ • (04/30/91)
86 **CHÂTEAU VERDIGNAN** Haut-Médoc 1988 • $15 • (04/30/91)
86 **CHÂTEAU DE LAMARQUE** Haut-Médoc 1988 • $20 • (04/30/91)
86 **CHÂTEAU DE LA DAME** Margaux 1988 • $15 • (02/15/91)
86 **CHÂTEAU DU TERTRE** Margaux 1988 • $35 Ⓐ • (06/30/91)
86 **CLOS FOURTET** St.-Emilion 1988 • $25 Ⓐ • (10/31/91)
85 **CHÂTEAU BEL AIR** Haut-Médoc 1988 • $15 • (04/30/91)
85 **CHÂTEAU BERTINERIE** Premières Côtes de Blaye 1988 • $10 • (07/15/90)
85 **CHÂTEAU CALON-SÉGUR** St.-Estèphe 1988 • $25 Ⓐ • (07/15/91)
85 **CHÂTEAU CANTEMERLE** Haut-Médoc 1988 • $29 Ⓐ • (03/15/91)
85 **CHÂTEAU CORMEIL-FIGEAC** St.-Emilion 1988 • $20 • (04/30/91)
85 **CHÂTEAU COS-LABORY** St.-Estèphe 1988 • $20 • (04/30/91)
85 **CHÂTEAU FOMBRAUGE** St.-Emilion 1988 • $14 Ⓐ • (11/30/92)
85 **CHÂTEAU FONPLÉGADE** St.-Emilion 1988 • $18 • (06/30/91)
85 **CHÂTEAU L'ENCLOS** Pomerol 1988 • $20 • (03/15/91)
85 **CHÂTEAU LE BON-PASTEUR** Pomerol 1988 • $43 Ⓐ • (02/28/91)
85 **CHÂTEAU LYNCH-MOUSSAS** Pauillac 1988 • $25 • (08/31/91)
85 **CHÂTEAU RAUZAN-GASSIES** Margaux 1988 • $35 • (08/31/91)
85 **CHÂTEAU TERTRE DAUGAY** St.-Emilion 1988 • $20 • (04/30/91)
85 **CHÂTEAU TROPLONG-MONDOT** St.-Emilion 1988 • $46 Ⓐ • (07/15/91)
85 **CHÂTEAU TROTTEVIEILLE** St.-Emilion 1988 • $51 • (04/30/91)
85 **CHÂTEAU D'ANGLUDET** Margaux 1988 • $20 Ⓐ • (02/28/91)
85 **PIERRE JEAN** St.-Emilion 1988 • $10 • (06/30/91) • BB

Domaine Méo-Camuzet.

Red Burgundy

The six highest-scoring recent vintages of red Burgundy on the market—1996, 1995, 1993, 1990, 1989 and 1988—are listed in this section, with ratings and prices. The wines are organized by vintage and then in descending order of score, to make it easy to identify the best wines of each year. For ratings of wines from other vintages, see the main listings.

Burgundy lovers should jump on the 1996 vintage, which will arrive in stores during the fall of 1998, because *Wine Spectator's* Burgundy expert, Per-Henrik Mansson, rates it slightly higher than either 1995 or 1993. Those two vintages have many great wines, but they are years in which careful shopping is recommended because not everything was of high quality. This contrasts with 1990, a vintage in which you can hardly go wrong when buying. We skipped over 1991, 1992 and 1994 in this section; none of these years was a washout, and 1991 in particular produced some very good wines, but these three years are significantly weaker overall than the years covered here.

Red Burgundy is generally made in small quantities, and many of the best wines are bought up quickly upon release. But diligent shoppers can find them on sale at retail, at auction and on restaurant wine lists.

Note: Our 1996 Red Burgundy tastings were completed too close to publication of this book to include full tasting notes for this vintage in the main listings section.

1996 RED BURGUNDY | VINTAGE RATING: 93

99 **DENIS MORTET** Clos de Vougeot 1996 • $87 • (09/30/98)

99 **ROBERT JAYER-GILLES** Echézeaux du Dessus 1996 • $140 • (09/30/98)

98 **DOMAINE LEROY** Romanée St.-Vivant 1996 • $610 • (09/30/98)

97 **SÉRAFIN PÈRE & FILS** Charmes-Chambertin 1996 • $120 • (09/30/98)

96 **BOUCHARD PÈRE & FILS** Clos Vougeot 1996 • $88 • (09/30/98)

96 **JACQUES PRIEUR** Musigny 1996 • $162 • (09/30/98) • CS

96 **LOUIS JADOT** Chambertin-Clos de Bèze 1996 • $115 • (09/30/98)

96 **MÉO-CAMUZET** Vosne-Romanée Les Chaumes 1996 • $78 • (09/30/98)

95 **DENIS MORTET** Chambertin 1996 • $125 • (09/30/98)

95 **DOMAINE D'AUVENAY** Bonnes Mares 1996 • $660 • (09/30/98)

95 **DOMAINE LEROY** Musigny 1996 • $660 • (09/30/98)

95 **DOMAINE LEROY** Richebourg 1996 • $610 • (09/30/98)

95 **MÉO-CAMUZET** Clos de Vougeot 1996 • $98 • (09/30/98)

Key: SS—Spectator Selection CS—Cellar Selection HR—Highly Recommended BB—Best Buy $NA—Price not available Ⓐ—Auction Price
Dates in parentheses indicate the issues in which the ratings were published.

95 **MÉO-CAMUZET** Richebourg 1996 • $260 • (09/30/98)

95 **SÉRAFIN PÈRE & FILS** Gevrey-Chambertin Vieilles Vignes 1996 • $60 • (09/30/98)

94 **CLAUDE DUGAT** Gevrey-Chambertin Lavaux St.-Jacques 1996 • $80 • (09/30/98)

94 **CLAUDE DUGAT** Gevrey-Chambertin Premier Cru 1996 • $80 • (09/30/98)

94 **DOMAINE LEROY** Chambolle-Musigny Les Fremières 1996 • $165 • (09/30/98)

94 **DOMAINE LEROY** Latricières-Chambertin 1996 • $610 • (09/30/98)

94 **DOMAINE LEROY** Savigny-lès-Beaune Les Narbantons 1996 • $85 • (09/30/98)

94 **DOMAINE D'AUVENAY** Mazis-Chambertin 1996 • $660 • (09/30/98)

94 **FOUGERAY DE BEAUCLAIR** Bonnes Mares 1996 • $82 • (09/30/98)

94 **HENRI GOUGES** Nuits-St.-Georges Les Pruliers 1996 • $45 • (09/30/98)

94 **SÉRAFIN PÈRE & FILS** Gevrey-Chambertin Le Fonteny 1996 • $75 • (09/30/98)

94 **SÉRAFIN PÈRE & FILS** Gevrey-Chambertin Les Cazetiers 1996 • $80 • (09/30/98)

94 **SÉRAFIN PÈRE & FILS** Gevrey-Chambertin Les Corbeaux 1996 • $75 • (09/30/98)

93 **BERTRAND AMBROISE** Nuits-St.-Georges Les Vaucrains 1996 • $60 • (09/30/98)

Fred Seidman

93 **CHÂTEAU DE LA TOUR** Clos Vougeot 1996 • $65 • (09/30/98)

93 **DOMAINE LEROY** Chambertin 1996 • $660 • (09/30/98)

93 **DOMAINE LEROY** Nuits-St.-Georges Aux Boudots 1996 • $255 • (09/30/98)

93 **DOMAINE LEROY** Volnay Santenots 1996 • $180 • (09/30/98)

93 **DROUHIN-LAROZE** Chambertin-Clos de Bèze 1996 • $93 • (09/30/98)

93 **JACQUES PRIEUR** Echézeaux 1996 • $120 • (09/30/98)

93 **JEAN GRIVOT** Richebourg 1996 • $165 • (09/30/98)

93 **JEAN-MARC BOILLOT** Pommard Rugiens 1996 • $93 • (09/30/98)

93 **MAISON AMBROISE** Vougeot Les Cras 1996 • $60 • (09/30/98)

93 **VINCENT GIRARDIN** Pommard Clos des Lambots Vieilles Vignes 1996 • $46 • (09/30/98) • HR

93 **VINCENT GIRARDIN** Pommard Les Chanlins Vieilles Vignes 1996 • $59 • (09/30/98)

92 **ANNE GROS** Richebourg 1996 • $200 • (09/30/98)

92 **BERTRAND AMBROISE** Nuits-St.-Georges Cuvée Vieilles Vignes 1996 • $40 • (09/30/98)

92 **BOUCHARD PÈRE & FILS** Chambertin-Clos de Bèze 1996 • $142 • (09/30/98)

92 **BOUCHARD-AÎNÉ & FILS** Echézeaux 1996 • $NA • (09/30/98)

92 **DANIEL RION** Nuits-St.-Georges Les Grandes Vignes 1996 • $32 • (09/30/98)

92 **DANIEL RION** Vosne-Romanée Les Beaux-Monts 1996 • $48 • (09/30/98)

92 **DANIEL RION** Vosne-Romanée Les Chaumes 1996 • $51 • (09/30/98)

92 **DENIS MORTET** Gevrey-Chambertin Les Champeaux 1996 • $63 • (09/30/98)

92 **DOMAINE LEROY** Clos de Vougeot 1996 • $435 • (09/30/98)

92 **DROUHIN-LAROZE** Musigny 1996 • $260 • (09/30/98)

92 **HENRI GOUGES** Nuits-St.-Georges Les St.-Georges 1996 • $60 • (09/30/98)

92 **JACQUES PRIEUR** Volnay Clos des Santenots 1996 • $64 • (09/30/98)

92 **LEROY** Vosne-Romanée Aux Beaumonts 1996 • $255 • (09/30/98)

92 **MAISON AMBROISE** Pommard Les Saussilles 1996 • $45 • (09/30/98)

92 **MÉO-CAMUZET** Nuits-St.-Georges Aux Boudots 1996 • $89 • (09/30/98)

92 **MÉO-CAMUZET** Vosne-Romanée Aux Brûlées 1996 • $130 • (09/30/98)

92 **ROBERT ARNOUX** Romanée St.-Vivant 1996 • $220 • (09/30/98)

92 **ROBERT JAYER-GILLES** Côte de Nuits-Villages 1996 • $45 • (09/30/98)

92 **ROBERT JAYER-GILLES** Nuits-St.-Georges Les Haut Poirets 1996 • $75 • (09/30/98)

91 **DANIEL RION** Chambolle-Musigny Les Charmes 1996 • $59 • (09/30/98)

91 **DANIEL RION** Nuits-St.-Georges Les Lavières 1996 • $32 • (09/30/98)

91 **DANIEL RION** Vosne-Romanée 1996 • $32 • (09/30/98)

Key: SS—Spectator Selection CS—Cellar Selection HR—Highly Recommended BB—Best Buy $NA—Price not available Ⓐ—Auction Price
Dates in parentheses indicate the issues in which the ratings were published.

91 **DENIS MORTET** Chambolle-Musigny Aux Beaux Bruns 1996 • $63 • (09/30/98)

91 **DENIS MORTET** Gevrey-Chambertin Lavaux St.-Jacques 1996 • $63 • (09/30/98)

91 **DOMAINE LEROY** Corton Renardes 1996 • $305 • (09/30/98)

91 **JACQUES PRIEUR** Volnay Champans 1996 • $60 • (09/30/98)

91 **JEAN BOILLOT** Volnay Les Caillerets 1996 • $66 • (09/30/98)

91 **JEAN GRIVOT** Clos de Vougeot 1996 • $58 • (09/30/98)

91 **LÉCHENEAUT** Chambolle-Musigny Premier Cru 1996 • $65 • (09/30/98)

91 **LÉCHENEAUT** Clos de la Roche 1996 • $110 • (09/30/98)

91 **MÉO-CAMUZET** Nuits-St.-Georges Aux Murgers 1996 • $89 • (09/30/98)

91 **ROBERT ARNOUX** Echézeaux 1996 • $90 • (09/30/98)

91 **ROBERT JAYER-GILLES** Nuits-St.-Georges Les Damodes 1996 • $85 • (09/30/98)

90 **BERTRAND AMBROISE** Clos de Vougeot 1996 • $85 • (09/30/98)

90 **BERTRAND AMBROISE** Volnay Santenots Hospices de Beaune Cuvée Jehan de Massol 1996 • $90 • (09/30/98)

90 **BONNEAU DU MARTRAY** Corton 1996 • $55 • (09/30/98)

90 **BOUCHARD PÈRE & FILS** Bonnes Mares 1996 • $99 • (09/30/98)

90 **BRUNO CLAIR** Savigny-lès-Beaune La Dominode 1996 • $56 • (09/30/98)

90 **CLAUDE DUGAT** Charmes-Chambertin 1996 • $125 • (09/30/98)

90 **DANIEL RION** Chambolle-Musigny Les Beaux-Bruns 1996 • $48 • (09/30/98)

90 **DANIEL RION** Nuits-St.-Georges Clos des Argillières 1996 • $49 • (09/30/98)

90 **DENIS MORTET** Gevrey-Chambertin 1996 • $42 • (09/30/98)

90 **DENIS MORTET** Gevrey-Chambertin En Champs Vieille Vigne 1996 • $53 • (09/30/98)

90 **DENIS MORTET** Gevrey-Chambertin En Motrot 1996 • $48 • (09/30/98)

90 **DOMAINE LEROY** Chambolle-Musigny Les Charmes 1996 • $255 • (09/30/98)

90 **DOMAINE LEROY** Nuits-St.-Georges Aux Vignes Rondes 1996 • $255 • (09/30/98)

90 **DOMAINE DU CHÂTEAU DE VOSNE-ROMANÉE** La Romanée 1996 • $300 • (09/30/98)

90 **DROUHIN-LAROZE** Clos de Vougeot 1996 • $85 • (09/30/98)

90 **JACQUES PRIEUR** Chambertin 1996 • $130 • (09/30/98)

90 **JACQUES PRIEUR** Clos Vougeot 1996 • $90 • (09/30/98)

90 **JACQUES PRIEUR** Volnay Santenots 1996 • $58 • (09/30/98)

90 **JEAN & JEAN-LOUIS TRAPET** Chambertin 1996 • $100 • (09/30/98)

90 **JEAN BOILLOT** Beaune Clos du Roi 1996 • $48 • (09/30/98)

90 **JEAN GRIVOT** Nuits-St.-Georges Les Boudots 1996 • $47 • (09/30/98)

90 **JEAN GRIVOT** Vosne-Romanée Les Beaux Monts 1996 • $47 • (09/30/98)

90 **JEAN-MARC BOILLOT** Beaune Montrevenots 1996 • $36 • (09/30/98)

90 **JOSEPH DROUHIN** Bonnes Mares 1996 • $118 • (09/30/98)
90 **JOSEPH DROUHIN** Clos de Vougeot 1996 • $85 • (09/30/98)
90 **LAURENT ROUMIER** Chambolle-Musigny 1996 • $NA • (09/30/98)
90 **LÉCHENEAUT** Nuits-St.-Georges Les Cailles 1996 • $65 • (09/30/98)
90 **LEROY** Vosne-Romanée Aux Genevrères 1996 • $115 • (09/30/98)
90 **MAILLARD PÈRE & FILS** Corton Renardes 1996 • $55 • (09/30/98)
90 **MÉO-CAMUZET** Nuits-St.-Georges 1996 • $49 • (09/30/98)
90 **PHILIPPE CHARLOPIN-PARIZOT** Gevrey-Chambertin Cuvée Vieilles Vignes 1996 • $38 • (09/30/98)
90 **ROBERT ARNOUX** Clos de Vougeot 1996 • $90 • (09/30/98)
90 **ROBERT ARNOUX** Vosne-Romanée Les Suchots 1996 • $100 • (09/30/98)
90 **VINCENT GIRARDIN** Pommard Les Grands Epenots Vieilles Vignes 1996 • $70 • (09/30/98)
90 **VINCENT GIRARDIN** Pommard Les Rugiens 1996 • $74 • (09/30/98)
89 **ANNE GROS** Chambolle-Musigny La Combe d'Orveau 1996 • $50 • (09/30/98)
89 **ARMAND ROUSSEAU** Chambertin-Clos de Bèze 1996 • $NA • (09/30/98)
89 **BRUNO CLAIR** Gevrey-Chambertin Cazetiers 1996 • $96 • (09/30/98)
89 **CORON PÈRE & FILS** Clos Vougeot 1996 • $56 • (09/30/98)
89 **DANIEL RION** Nuits-St.-Georges Les Vignes Rondes 1996 • $48 • (09/30/98)
89 **DOMAINE LEROY** Gevrey-Chambertin Les Combottes 1996 • $255 • (09/30/98)
89 **DOMAINE LEROY** Nuits-St.-Georges Au Bas de Combe 1996 • $115 • (09/30/98)
89 **DOMAINE LEROY** Nuits-St.-Georges Aux Lavières 1996 • $115 • (09/30/98)
89 **DOMAINE THOMAS-MOILLARD** Corton Clos du Roi 1996 • $49 • (09/30/98)
89 **DOMAINE DES ORBIERS** Volnay Clos des Chênes 1996 • $NA • (09/30/98)
89 **DOMAINE DU CHÂTEAU DE VOSNE-ROMANÉE** Vosne-Romanée Aux Reignots 1996 • $73 • (09/30/98)
89 **DROUHIN-LAROZE** Gevrey-Chambertin Premier Cru 1996 • $50 • (09/30/98)
89 **DROUHIN-LAROZE** Latricières-Chambertin 1996 • $80 • (09/30/98)
89 **EDMOND CORNU** Corton Bressandes 1996 • $60 • (09/30/98)
89 **HENRI CLERC & FILS** Clos de Vougeot 1996 • $60 • (09/30/98)
89 **JEAN BOILLOT** Nuits-St.-Georges Les Cailles 1996 • $66 • (09/30/98)
89 **JEAN BOILLOT** Volnay Les Fremiets 1996 • $66 • (09/30/98)
89 **JEAN GRIVOT** Echézeaux 1996 • $47 • (09/30/98)
89 **JEAN-MARC BOILLOT** Volnay Carelle sous la Chapelle 1996 • $53 • (09/30/98)
89 **LALEURE-PIOT** Corton Bressandes 1996 • $68 • (09/30/98)
89 **LÉCHENEAUT** Nuits-St.-Georges Les Damodes 1996 • $65 • (09/30/98)
89 **LEROY** Vosne-Romanée Aux Brûlées 1996 • $255 • (09/30/98)
89 **LUCIEN MUZARD & FILS** Pommard Les Cras 1996 • $NA • (09/30/98)
89 **MOMMESSIN** Clos de Tart 1996 • $110 • (09/30/98)
89 **MONGEARD-MUGNERET** Echézeaux Vieille Vigne 1996 • $60 • (09/30/98)
89 **PASCAL PRUNIER** Monthélie Les Vignes Rondes 1996 • $20 • (09/30/98)
89 **PHILIPPE CHARLOPIN-PARIZOT** Mazis-Chambertin 1996 • $92 • (09/30/98)
89 **PIERRE ANDRÉ** Corton Pougets 1996 • $NA • (09/30/98)
89 **PRINCE FLORENT DE MÉRODE** Pommard Clos de la Platière 1996 • $37 • (09/30/98)
89 **ROBERT ARNOUX** Vosne-Romanée Aux Reignots 1996 • $55 • (09/30/98)
89 **ROBERT JAYER-GILLES** Hautes Côtes de Nuits 1996 • $33 • (09/30/98)
89 **THIERRY MORTET** Chambolle-Musigny 1996 • $NA • (09/30/98)
89 **TOLLOT-BEAUT & FILS** Aloxe-Corton Les Vercots 1996 • $42 • (09/30/98)
89 **TOLLOT-BEAUT & FILS** Beaune Clos du Roi 1996 • $42 • (09/30/98)
88 **ANNE GROS** Clos Vougeot Le Grand Maupertuis 1996 • $90 • (09/30/98)
88 **ANNE GROS** Vosne-Romanée Les Barreaux 1996 • $NA • (09/30/98)
88 **ANTONIN GUYON** Corton Bressandes 1996 • $48 • (09/30/98)
88 **ANTONIN RODET** Gevrey-Chambertin Les Cazetiers 1996 • $52 • (09/30/98)
88 **BOUCHARD PÈRE & FILS** Pommard Premier Cru 1996 • $48 • (09/30/98)
88 **BOUCHARD-AÎNÉ & FILS** Gevrey-Chambertin 1996 • $NA • (09/30/98)
88 **CHAUVENET-CHOPIN** Nuits-St.-Georges Aux Argillas 1996 • $55 • (09/30/98)
88 **CORON PÈRE & FILS** Nuits-St.-Georges Les Cailles 1996 • $43 • (09/30/98)
88 **DENIS MORTET** Bourgogne Les Charmes au Châtelain 1996 • $NA • (09/30/98)
88 **DENIS MORTET** Gevrey-Chambertin Au Vellé 1996 • $48 • (09/30/98)
88 **DOMAINE LEROY** Pommard Les Vignots 1996 • $115 • (09/30/98)
88 **DOMAINE DU CHÂTEAU DE PREMEAUX** Nuits-St.-Georges 1996 • $28 • (09/30/98)
88 **DOMAINE DU CLOS FRANTIN** Clos de Vougeot 1996 • $65 • (09/30/98)
88 **DOMAINE DU CLOS FRANTIN** Echézeaux 1996 • $63 • (09/30/98)
88 **DOUDET-NAUDIN** Savigny-lès-Beaune 1996 • $16 • (09/30/98)
88 **JACQUES PRIEUR** Beaune Clos de la Feguine 1996 • $50 • (09/30/98)
88 **JEAN BOILLOT** Beaune Les Epenottes 1996 • $48 • (09/30/98)
88 **JEAN BOILLOT** Volnay Les Chevrets 1996 • $66 • (09/30/98)
88 **JEAN-MARC BOILLOT** Pommard Jarollières 1996 • $60 • (09/30/98)
88 **JEAN-MARC BOILLOT** Volnay 1996 • $36 • (09/30/98)
88 **JOSEPH DROUHIN** Musigny 1996 • $160 • (09/30/98)

88 **LALEURE-PIOT** Pernand-Vergelesses Ile des Vergelesses 1996 • $45 • (09/30/98)

88 **MAILLARD PÈRE & FILS** Aloxe-Corton Les Grandes Lollières 1996 • $34 • (09/30/98)

88 **MONGEARD-MUGNERET** Vosne-Romanée Les Orveaux 1996 • $40 • (09/30/98)

88 **MONTHÉLIE-DOUHAIRET** Monthélie Clos Le Meix Garnier 1996 • $27 • (09/30/98)

88 **MONTHÉLIE-DOUHAIRET** Monthélie Le Meix Bataille 1996 • $30 • (09/30/98)

88 **MUSSY** Pommard Saussilles 1996 • $39 • (09/30/98)

88 **P. DUBREUIL-FONTAINE PÈRE & FILS** Corton Bressandes 1996 • $60 • (09/30/98)

88 **P. DUBREUIL-FONTAINE PÈRE & FILS** Corton Clos du Roi 1996 • $62 • (09/30/98)

88 **PIERRE LABET** Beaune Clos des Monsnières 1996 • $28 • (09/30/98)

88 **ROBERT ARNOUX** Nuits-St.-Georges Les Procès 1996 • $56 • (09/30/98)

88 **ROBERT GROFFIER** Chambolle-Musigny Les Sentiers 1996 • $69 • (09/30/98)

88 **SIMON BIZE & FILS** Savigny-lès-Beaune Aux Grands Liards 1996 • $34 • (09/30/98)

88 **TOLLOT-BEAUT & FILS** Corton 1996 • $62 • (09/30/98)

88 **VINCENT GIRARDIN** Santenay Les Gravières Vieilles Vignes 1996 • $34 • (09/30/98)

87 **ANTONIN RODET** Gevrey-Chambertin 1996 • $44 • (09/30/98)

87 **ARMAND ROUSSEAU** Ruchottes-Chambertin Clos des Ruchottes 1996 • $85 • (09/30/98)

87 **BRUNO CLAIR** Vosne-Romanée Les Champs Perdrix 1996 • $55 • (09/30/98)

87 **CHANTAL LESCURE** Chambolle-Musigny Les Mombies 1996 • $34 • (09/30/98)

87 **CHÂTEAU DE POMMARD** Pommard 1996 • $45 • (09/30/98)

87 **CORON PÈRE & FILS** Vosne-Romanée Les Suchots 1996 • $42 • (09/30/98)

87 **DANIEL RION** Nuits-St.-Georges Les Hauts-Pruliers 1996 • $48 • (09/30/98)

87 **DOMAINE BORGEOT** Chassagne-Montrachet Red Clos St.-Jean 1996 • $40 • (09/30/98)

87 **DOMAINE LEROY** Clos de la Roche 1996 • $610 • (09/30/98)

87 **DOMAINE LEROY** Nuits-St.-Georges Aux Allots 1996 • $115 • (09/30/98)

87 **DOMAINE DU CHÂTEAU DE PREMEAUX** Nuits-St.-Georges Clos des Argillières 1996 • $36 • (09/30/98)

87 **DOMAINE DU CLOS DU PAVILLON** Pommard 1996 • $36 • (09/30/98)

87 **DROUHIN-LAROZE** Bonnes Mares 1996 • $90 • (09/30/98)

87 **FOUGERAY DE BEAUCLAIR** Côte de Nuits-Villages 1996 • $20 • (09/30/98)

87 **FOUGERAY DE BEAUCLAIR** Fixin Clos Marion 1996 • $26 • (09/30/98)

87 **FRÉDÉRIC ESMONIN** Gevrey-Chambertin Lavaux St.-Jacques 1996 • $30 • (09/30/98)

87 **JEAN & JEAN-LOUIS TRAPET** Latricières-Chambertin 1996 • $75 • (09/30/98)

Key: SS—Spectator Selection CS—Cellar Selection HR—Highly Recommended BB—Best Buy $NA—Price not available Ⓐ—Auction Price

Dates in parentheses indicate the issues in which the ratings were published.

87 **JEAN GRIVOT** Vosne-Romanée 1996 • $32 • (09/30/98)

87 **JEAN-NOËL GAGNARD** Santenay Clos des Tavannes 1996 • $NA • (09/30/98)

87 **JOSEPH DROUHIN** Beaune Clos des Mouches 1996 • $53 • (09/30/98)

87 **JOSEPH DROUHIN** Grands Echézeaux 1996 • $135 • (09/30/98)

87 **LALEURE-PIOT** Corton Le Rognet 1996 • $64 • (09/30/98)

87 **MAILLARD PÈRE & FILS** Beaune 1996 • $23 • (09/30/98)

87 **MAILLARD PÈRE & FILS** Chorey-lès-Beaune 1996 • $20 • (09/30/98)

87 **MICHELE & PATRICE RION** Bourgogne Les Bons Bâtons 1996 • $18 • (09/30/98)

87 **MICHELE & PATRICE RION** Chambolle-Musigny Les Cras 1996 • $48 • (09/30/98)

87 **MONTHÉLIE-DOUHAIRET** Monthélie Les Duresses 1996 • $30 • (09/30/98)

87 **MONTHÉLIE-DOUHAIRET** Pommard Les Fremiers 1996 • $54 • (09/30/98)

87 **MONTHÉLIE-DOUHAIRET** Volnay En Champans 1996 • $43 • (09/30/98)

87 **PHILIPPE CHARLOPIN-PARIZOT** Charmes-Chambertin 1996 • $92 • (09/30/98)

87 **PIERRE GUILLEMOT** Savigny-lès-Beaune Serpentières 1996 • $26 • (09/30/98)

87 **ROBERT ARNOUX** Vosne-Romanée Les Hautes Maizières 1996 • $50 • (09/30/98)

87 **ROBERT JAYER-GILLES** Hautes Côtes de Beaune 1996 • $33 • (09/30/98)

87 **SIMON BIZE & FILS** Savigny-lès-Beaune Les Fournaux 1996 • $40 • (09/30/98)

87 **THIERRY MORTET** Gevrey-Chambertin Clos Prieur 1996 • $NA • (09/30/98)

87 **VINCENT GIRARDIN** Chassagne-Montrachet Red Clos de la Boudriotte 1996 • $44 • (09/30/98)

87 **VINCENT GIRARDIN** Corton Perrières 1996 • $69 • (09/30/98)

87 **VINCENT GIRARDIN** Volnay Les Santenots 1996 • $49 • (09/30/98)

86 **ALAIN GRAS** St.-Romain Red 1996 • $19 • (09/30/98)

86 **ANTONIN RODET** Savigny-lès-Beaune Les Gravains 1996 • $29 • (09/30/98)

86 **ARNOUX PÈRE & FILS** Bourgogne 1996 • $12 • (09/30/98)

86 **BRUNO CLAIR** Gevrey-Chambertin 1996 • $56 • (09/30/98)

86 **BRUNO CLAIR** Marsannay Les Vaudenelles 1996 • $26 • (09/30/98)

86 **CORON PÈRE & FILS** Echézeaux Domaine du Château de Bligny 1996 • $56 • (09/30/98)

86 **CORON PÈRE & FILS** Gevrey-Chambertin 1996 • $30 • (09/30/98)

86 **CORON PÈRE & FILS** Gevrey-Chambertin Les Champeaux 1996 • $44 • (09/30/98)

86 **CORON PÈRE & FILS** Nuits-St.-Georges 1996 • $30 • (09/30/98)

86 **DOMAINE DU CLOS ST.-MARC** Nuits-St.-Georges Clos St.-Marc 1996 • $55 • (09/30/98)

86 **FOUGERAY DE BEAUCLAIR** Marsannay St.-Jacques 1996 • $25 • (09/30/98)

86 **HENRI CLERC & FILS** Echézeaux 1996 • $50 • (09/30/98)

86 **HENRI NAUDIN-FERRAND** Côte de Nuits-Villages Le Clos de Magny 1996 • $17 • (09/30/98)

86 **JEAN & JEAN-LOUIS TRAPET** Gevrey-Chambertin Petite Chapelle 1996 • $35 • (09/30/98)

86 **JEAN-NOËL GAGNARD** Chassagne-Montrachet Red Clos St.-Jean 1996 • $25 • (09/30/98)

86 **JOSEPH DROUHIN** Griotte-Chambertin 1996 • $105 • (09/30/98)

86 **JOSEPH DROUHIN** Romanée St.-Vivant 1996 • $160 • (09/30/98)

86 **LUCIEN MUZARD & FILS** Chassagne-Montrachet Red Vieilles Vignes 1996 • $NA • (09/30/98)

86 **LUCIEN MUZARD & FILS** Santenay Maladière 1996 • $22 • (09/30/98)

86 **MAILLARD PÈRE & FILS** Aloxe-Corton 1996 • $30 • (09/30/98)

86 **PASCAL PRUNIER** Monthélie 1996 • $17 • (09/30/98)

86 **PRINCE FLORENT DE MÉRODE** Ladoix Les Chaillots 1996 • $22 • (09/30/98)

86 **RENÉ MONNIER** Beaune Cent Vignes 1996 • $NA • (09/30/98)

86 **TOLLOT-BEAUT & FILS** Beaune Grèves 1996 • $42 • (09/30/98)

86 **VINCENT GIRARDIN** Beaune Clos des Vignes Franches 1996 • $39 • (09/30/98)

86 **VINCENT GIRARDIN** Chassagne-Montrachet Red Morgeot 1996 • $41 • (09/30/98)

85 **ALAIN GRAS** Auxey-Duresses 1996 • $23 • (09/30/98)

85 **ALBERT BICHOT** Pommard Clos Micault 1996 • $39 • (09/30/98)

85 **ANTONIN RODET** Clos de Vougeot 1996 • $69 • (09/30/98)

85 **ANTONIN RODET** Nuits-St.-Georges Les St.-Georges 1996 • $57 • (09/30/98)

85 **ARMAND ROUSSEAU** Gevrey-Chambertin Clos St.-Jacques 1996 • $100 • (09/30/98)

85 **BOUCHARD PÈRE & FILS** Corton 1996 • $63 • (09/30/98)

85 **BRUNO CLAIR** Chambolle-Musigny Les Veroilles 1996 • $46 • (09/30/98)

85 **BRUNO CLAIR** Gevrey-Chambertin Clos du Fonteny 1996 • $73 • (09/30/98)

85 **BRUNO CLAIR** Gevrey-Chambertin Petite Chapelle 1996 • $70 • (09/30/98)

85 **BRUNO CLAIR** Morey-St.-Denis En la Rue de Vergy 1996 • $47 • (09/30/98)

85 **CHANTAL LESCURE** Pommard Les Vaumuriens 1996 • $NA • (09/30/98)

85 **CHANTAL LESCURE** Vosne-Romanée Les Suchots 1996 • $52 • (09/30/98)

85 **DOMAINE DU CLOS FRANTIN** Vosne-Romanée 1996 • $38 • (09/30/98)

85 **DOUDET-NAUDIN** Corton Maréchaudes Vieille Vigne 1996 • $45 • (09/30/98)

85 **DOUDET-NAUDIN** Vosne-Romanée Les Suchots 1996 • $45 • (09/30/98)

85 **EDMOND CORNU** Bourgogne 1996 • $17 • (09/30/98)

85 **FOUGERAY DE BEAUCLAIR** Marsannay Les Favières 1996 • $19 • (09/30/98)

85 **HENRI CLERC & FILS** Santenay Les Potets 1996 • $22 • (09/30/98)

85 **JACQUES PRIEUR** Beaune Grèves 1996 • $44 • (09/30/98)

85 **JEAN-NOËL GAGNARD** Chassagne-Montrachet Red Morgeot 1996 • $27 • (09/30/98)

85 **MAILLARD PÈRE & FILS** Savigny-lès-Beaune 1996 • $23 • (09/30/98)

85 **MOILLARD** Monthélie 1996 • $17 • (09/30/98)

85 **MONTHÉLIE-DOUHAIRET** Pommard Les Chanlins 1996 • $54 • (09/30/98)

85 **OLIVIER LEFLAIVE FRÈRES** Pommard 1996 • $45 • (09/30/98)

85 **P. DUBREUIL-FONTAINE PÈRE & FILS** Aloxe-Corton Les Vercots 1996 • $39 • (09/30/98)

85 **PASCAL PRUNIER** Auxey-Duresses Les Duresses 1996 • $21 • (09/30/98)

85 **PHILIPPE CHARLOPIN-PARIZOT** Chambertin 1996 • $105 • (09/30/98)

85 **PHILIPPE CHARLOPIN-PARIZOT** Gevrey-Chambertin La Justice 1996 • $34 • (09/30/98)

85 **PIERRE ANDRÉ** Vosne-Romanée Les Suchots 1996 • $NA • (09/30/98)

85 **ROBERT GROFFIER** Bourgogne 1996 • $26 • (09/30/98)

85 **SIMON BIZE & FILS** Savigny-lès-Beaune Les Bourgeots 1996 • $29 • (09/30/98)

85 **THIERRY MORTET** Chambolle-Musigny Les Beaux Bruns 1996 • $NA • (09/30/98)

85 **TOLLOT-BEAUT & FILS** Chorey-lès-Beaune 1996 • $22 • (09/30/98)

85 **TOLLOT-BEAUT & FILS** Savigny-lès-Beaune Lavières 1996 • $32 • (09/30/98)

85 **VINCENT GIRARDIN** Maranges Clos des Loyères Vieilles Vignes 1996 • $26 • (09/30/98)

85 **VINCENT GIRARDIN** Santenay La Maladière 1996 • $33 • (09/30/98)

85 **VINCENT GIRARDIN** Volnay Clos des Chênes 1996 • $53 • (09/30/98)

1995 Red Burgundy
Vintage Rating: 88

98 **DOMAINE LEROY** Romanée St.-Vivant 1995 • $600 • (11/15/97) • CS

97 **DENIS MORTET** Chambolle-Musigny Aux Beaux Bruns 1995 • $59 • (11/15/97) • HR

96 **ARMAND ROUSSEAU** Chambertin 1995 • $195 Ⓐ • (11/15/97)

96 **LÉCHENEAUT** Chambolle-Musigny Premier Cru 1995 • $60 • (11/15/97)

96 **PHILIPPE CHARLOPIN-PARIZOT** Charmes-Chambertin 1995 • $87 • (11/15/97)

96 **ROBERT GROFFIER** Bonnes Mares 1995 • $90 • (01/31/98)

96 **SÉRAFIN PÈRE & FILS** Charmes-Chambertin 1995 • $95 • (11/15/97)

95 **BERNARD DUGAT-PY** Gevrey-Chambertin Coeur de Roy Vieilles Vignes 1995 • $40 • (01/31/98) • HR

95 **BOUCHARD PÈRE & FILS** La Romanée Château de Vosne-Romanée 1995 • $210 • (11/15/97)

95 **DENIS MORTET** Clos Vougeot 1995 • $81 • (11/15/97)

95 **DENIS MORTET** Gevrey-Chambertin En Motrot 1995 • $47 • (11/15/97)

95 **DOMAINE LEROY** Richebourg 1995 • $600 • (11/15/97)

95 **FRÉDÉRIC ESMONIN** Mazis-Chambertin Hospices de Beaune Cuvée Madeleine Collignon 1995 • $85 • (11/15/97)

95 **PHILIPPE CHARLOPIN-PARIZOT** Chambertin 1995 • $95 • (11/15/97)

95 **ROBERT GROFFIER** Chambolle-Musigny Les Sentiers 1995 • $55 • (01/31/98) • HR

95 **ROBERT JAYER-GILLES** Echézeaux du Dessus 1995 • $150 • (11/15/97)

Red Burgundy

94 **COMTE GEORGES DE VOGÜÉ** Chambolle-Musigny Les Amoureuses 1995 • $175 • (11/15/97)

94 **J. FAIVELEY** Mazis-Chambertin 1995 • $97 • (11/15/97)

94 **JEAN GRIVOT** Echézeaux 1995 • $60 • (11/15/97)

93 **ANNE GROS** Vosne-Romanée Les Barreaux 1995 • $55 • (11/15/97)

93 **CLAUDE DUGAT** Charmes-Chambertin 1995 • $110 • (11/15/97)

93 **DENIS MORTET** Chambertin 1995 • $115 • (11/15/97)

93 **DENIS MORTET** Gevrey-Chambertin En Champs Vieille Vigne 1995 • $55 • (11/15/97)

93 **DENIS MORTET** Gevrey-Chambertin Lavaux St.-Jacques 1995 • $59 • (11/15/97)

93 **DOMAINE LEROY** Nuits-St.-Georges Aux Boudots 1995 • $250 • (11/15/97)

93 **DOMAINE D'AUVENAY** Bonnes Mares 1995 • $503 Ⓐ • (11/15/97)

93 **PHILIPPE CHARLOPIN-PARIZOT** Clos St.-Denis 1995 • $80 • (11/15/97)

92 **ANNE GROS** Clos Vougeot Le Grand Maupertuis 1995 • $80 • (11/15/97)

92 **BOUCHARD PÈRE & FILS** Bonnes Mares 1995 • $89 • (11/15/97)

92 **CHOPIN-GROFFIER** Clos Vougeot 1995 • $92 • (11/15/97)

92 **DANIEL RION** Vosne-Romanée Les Beaux Monts 1995 • $66 • (11/15/97)

92 **DENIS MORTET** Gevrey-Chambertin Au Vellé 1995 • $47 • (11/15/97)

92 **DOMAINE LEROY** Pommard Les Vignots 1995 • $110 • (11/15/97)

92 **DOMAINE LEROY** Vosne-Romanée Les Beaux Monts 1995 • $250 • (11/15/97)

92 **LOUIS JADOT** Chambertin-Clos de Bèze 1995 • $90 • (11/15/97)

92 **MÉO-CAMUZET** Clos de Vougeot 1995 • $70 • (11/15/97)

92 **MICHELE & PATRICE RION** Chambolle-Musigny Les Cras 1995 • $48 • (11/15/97)

92 **ROBERT JAYER-GILLES** Nuits-St.-Georges Les Hauts Poirets 1995 • $85 • (11/15/97)

92 **VINCENT GIRARDIN** Volnay Clos des Chênes 1995 • $35 • (11/15/97)

91 **ARMAND ROUSSEAU** Ruchottes-Chambertin 1995 • $85 • (11/15/97)

91 **BERTRAND AMBROISE** Clos de Vougeot 1995 • $90 • (11/15/97)

91 **BRUNO CLAIR** Savigny-lès-Beaune La Dominode 1995 • $40 • (11/15/97)

91 **COMTE GEORGES DE VOGÜÉ** Bonnes Mares 1995 • $175 • (11/15/97)

91 **DANIEL RION** Clos Vougeot 1995 • $99 • (11/15/97)

91 **DENIS BACHELET** Gevrey-Chambertin Vieilles Vignes 1995 • $45 • (01/31/98)

91 **DENIS MORTET** Gevrey-Chambertin 1995 • $42 • (11/15/97)

91 **DOMAINE LEROY** Latricières-Chambertin 1995 • $600 • (11/15/97)

91 **DOMAINE THOMAS-MOILLARD** Corton Le Clos du Roi 1995 • $43 • (11/15/97)

Key: SS—Spectator Selection CS—Cellar Selection HR—Highly Recommended BB—Best Buy $NA—Price not available Ⓐ—Auction Price

Dates in parentheses indicate the issues in which the ratings were published.

91 **PHILIPPE CHARLOPIN-PARIZOT** Morey-St.-Denis 1995 • $32 • (11/15/97)

90 **ANNE GROS** Richebourg 1995 • $170 • (11/15/97)

90 **BERTRAND AMBROISE** Corton Le Rognet 1995 • $80 • (11/15/97)

90 **BERTRAND AMBROISE** Nuits-St.-Georges Les Vaucrains 1995 • $58 • (11/15/97)

90 **CORON PÈRE & FILS** Clos de Vougeot 1995 • $63 • (11/15/97)

90 **DANIEL RION** Nuits-St.-Georges Clos des Argillières 1995 • $66 • (11/15/97)

90 **DANIEL RION** Nuits-St.-Georges Les Grandes Vignes 1995 • $44 • (11/15/97)

90 **DANIEL RION** Vosne-Romanée 1995 • $44 • (11/15/97)

90 **DOMAINE LEROY** Corton Les Renardes 1995 • $250 • (11/15/97)

90 **DOMAINE LEROY** Gevrey-Chambertin Aux Combottes 1995 • $NA • (11/15/97)

90 **FRANÇOIS LAMARCHE** La Grand Rue 1995 • $98 • (11/15/97)

90 **J. FAIVELEY** Clos de la Roche 1995 • $93 • (11/15/97)

90 **JEAN GRIVOT** Richebourg 1995 • $150 • (11/15/97)

90 **JEAN-JACQUES CONFURON** Vosne-Romanée Les Beaux Monts 1995 • $70 • (11/15/97)

90 **JOSEPH DROUHIN** Charmes-Chambertin 1995 • $85 • (11/15/97)

90 **JOSEPH DROUHIN** Griotte-Chambertin 1995 • $95 • (11/15/97)

90 **JOSEPH DROUHIN** Musigny 1995 • $110 • (01/31/98)

90 **PHILIPPE CHARLOPIN-PARIZOT** Gevrey-Chambertin Cuvée Vieilles Vignes 1995 • $37 • (11/15/97)

90 **PHILIPPE CHARLOPIN-PARIZOT** Vosne-Romanée 1995 • $37 • (11/15/97)

90 **ROBERT GROFFIER** Chambolle-Musigny Les Amoureuses 1995 • $75 • (01/31/98)

90 **ROSSIGNOL-TRAPET** Chambertin 1995 • $68 • (11/15/97)

90 **SÉRAFIN PÈRE & FILS** Gevrey-Chambertin 1995 • $46 • (11/15/97)

90 **SÉRAFIN PÈRE & FILS** Gevrey-Chambertin Les Cazetiers 1995 • $72 • (11/15/97)

90 **TOLLOT-BEAUT & FILS** Beaune Clos du Roi 1995 • $40 • (11/15/97)

90 **VINCENT GIRARDIN** Chassagne-Montrachet Clos de la Boudriotte Red 1995 • $30 • (11/15/97)

90 **VINCENT GIRARDIN** Pommard Les Chanlins Vieilles Vignes 1995 • $40 • (11/15/97)

89 **BRUNO CLAIR** Marsannay Les Vaudenelles 1995 • $20 • (11/15/97)

89 **CHAUVENET-CHOPIN** Nuits-St.-Georges Aux Murgers 1995 • $54 • (11/15/97)

89 **DOMAINE DE LA POUSSE D'OR** Volnay Les Caillerets 1995 • $52 • (11/15/97)

89 **DOMAINE DE LA POUSSE D'OR** Volnay Les Caillerets-Clos des 60 Ouvrées 1995 • $55 • (11/15/97)

89 **FRANÇOIS BUFFET** Volnay Champans 1995 • $30 • (11/15/97)

89 **FRANÇOIS LAMARCHE** Echézeaux 1995 • $61 • (11/15/97)

89 **J. CONFURON-COTETIDOT** Nuits-St.-Georges 1995 • $50 • (11/15/97)

89 **J. FAIVELEY** Chambolle-Musigny La Combe d'Orveau 1995 • $61 • (11/15/97)

89 **JACQUES PRIEUR** Volnay En Champans 1995 • $50 • (11/15/97)

89 **JEAN & JEAN-LOUIS TRAPET** Latricières-Chambertin 1995 • $62 • (11/15/97)
89 **JEAN GRIVOT** Vosne-Romanée Les Beaux Monts 1995 • $45 • (11/15/97)
89 **JOSEPH DROUHIN** Chambolle-Musigny 1995 • $34 • (11/15/97)
89 **LECHENEAUT** Clos de la Roche 1995 • $100 • (11/15/97)
89 **MOMMESSIN** Aloxe-Corton 1995 • $26 • (11/15/97)
89 **MOMMESSIN** Clos de Tart 1995 • $103 • (11/15/97)
89 **MONGEARD-MUGNERET** Grands Echézeaux 1995 • $83 • (11/15/97)
89 **SÉRAFIN PÈRE & FILS** Gevrey-Chambertin Fonteny 1995 • $60 • (11/15/97)
88 **ALETH GIRARDIN** Pommard Rugiens 1995 • $44 • (11/15/97)
88 **BOUCHARD PÈRE & FILS** Clos de Vougeot 1995 • $80 • (11/15/97)
88 **BRUNO CLAIR** Chambertin-Clos de Bèze 1995 • $100 • (11/15/97)
88 **CHOPIN-GROFFIER** Nuits-St.-Georges Aux Chaignots 1995 • $56 • (11/15/97)
88 **CLAUDE DUGAT** Gevrey-Chambertin 1995 • $48 • (11/15/97)
88 **COMTE GEORGES DE VOGÜÉ** Chambolle-Musigny Premier Cru 1995 • $100 • (11/15/97)
88 **CORON PÈRE & FILS** Vosne-Romanée Les Suchots 1995 • $54 • (11/15/97)
88 **DOMAINE DE LA POUSSE D'OR** Pommard Les Jarollières 1995 • $60 • (11/15/97)
88 **DROUHIN-LAROZE** Chambertin-Clos de Bèze 1995 • $58 • (11/15/97)
88 **DROUHIN-LAROZE** Clos de Vougeot 1995 • $56 • (11/15/97)
88 **EMILE JUILLOT** Mercurey Les Combins 1995 • $NA • (11/15/97)
88 **EMMANUEL ROUGET** Nuits-St.-Georges 1995 • $35 • (01/31/98)
88 **FRANÇOIS LAMARCHE** Clos de Vougeot 1995 • $64 • (11/15/97)
88 **JEAN GRIVOT** Clos de Vougeot 1995 • $60 • (11/15/97)
88 **JEAN GRIVOT** Nuits-St.-Georges Aux Boudots 1995 • $45 • (11/15/97)
88 **JOSEPH DROUHIN** Beaune Clos des Mouches 1995 • $45 • (01/31/98)
88 **LOUIS JADOT** Beaune Clos des Ursules 1995 • $35 • (11/15/97)
88 **LÉCHENEAUT** Chambolle-Musigny 1995 • $40 • (11/15/97)
88 **MOILLARD** Gevrey-Chambertin 1995 • $26 • (01/31/98)
88 **MOMMESSIN** Vosne-Romanée Les Suchots 1995 • $45 • (11/15/97)
88 **PHILIPPE CHARLOPIN-PARIZOT** Fixin 1995 • $NA • (11/15/97)
88 **ROBERT JAYER-GILLES** Côte de Nuits-Villages 1995 • $40 • (11/15/97)
88 **VINCENT GIRARDIN** Pommard Les Rugiens Vieilles Vignes 1995 • $44 • (11/15/97)
87 **ALETH GIRARDIN** Pommard Les Epenots 1995 • $44 • (11/15/97)
87 **BERTRAND AMBROISE** Nuits-St.-Georges En Rue de Chaux 1995 • $48 • (11/15/97)
87 **BONNEAU DU MARTRAY** Corton 1995 • $60 • (11/15/97)
87 **BRUNO CLAIR** Chambolle-Musigny Les Véroilles 1995 • $33 • (11/15/97)
87 **CLAUDE DUGAT** Gevrey-Chambertin Premier Cru 1995 • $60 • (11/15/97)
87 **CORON PÈRE & FILS** Pommard Les Epenots 1995 • $54 • (11/15/97)
87 **DANIEL RION** Chambolle-Musigny Les Charmes 1995 • $82 • (11/15/97)
87 **DANIEL RION** Vosne-Romanée Les Chaumes 1995 • $66 • (11/15/97)
87 **DANIEL SENARD** Corton En Charlemagne 1995 • $72 • (11/15/97)
87 **EDMOND CORNU** Aloxe-Corton Les Valozières 1995 • $40 • (11/15/97)
87 **FONTAINE-GAGNARD** Chassagne-Montrachet Morgeot Red 1995 • $36 • (11/15/97)
87 **FONTAINE-GAGNARD** Pommard Les Rugiens 1995 • $60 • (11/15/97)
87 **G. BARTET** Gevrey-Chambertin Clos St.-Jacques 1995 • $71 • (11/15/97)
87 **J. CONFURON-COTETIDOT** Vosne-Romanée 1995 • $48 • (11/15/97)
87 **JACQUES PRIEUR** Musigny 1995 • $140 • (11/15/97)
87 **JEAN & JEAN-LOUIS TRAPET** Chambertin 1995 • $76 • (11/15/97)
87 **JEAN & JEAN-LOUIS TRAPET** Chapelle-Chambertin 1995 • $62 • (11/15/97)
87 **JOSEPH DROUHIN** Bonnes Mares 1995 • $100 • (11/15/97)
87 **JOSEPH DROUHIN** Clos St.-Denis 1995 • $75 • (01/31/98)
87 **LALEURE-PIOT** Corton Le Rognet 1995 • $59 • (11/15/97)
87 **LALEURE-PIOT** Corton Les Bressandes 1995 • $62 • (11/15/97)
87 **MÉO-CAMUZET** Vosne-Romanée Aux Brûlées 1995 • $70 • (11/15/97)
87 **MOMMESSIN** Morey-St.-Denis La Forge 1995 • $52 • (11/15/97)
87 **MONGEARD-MUGNERET** Vosne-Romanée 1995 • $29 • (11/15/97)
87 **PHILIPPE CHARLOPIN-PARIZOT** Marsannay En Montchenevoy Red 1995 • $20 • (11/15/97)
87 **ROBERT JAYER-GILLES** Hautes Côtes de Beaune 1995 • $30 • (11/15/97)
87 **TOLLOT-BEAUT & FILS** Corton Les Bressandes 1995 • $70 • (11/15/97)
86 **A.-F. GROS** Echézeaux 1995 • $85 • (11/15/97)
86 **ANTONIN RODET** Savigny-lès-Beaune 1995 • $25 • (11/15/97)
86 **BERTRAND AMBROISE** Nuits-St.-Georges 1995 • $33 • (11/15/97)
86 **BOUCHARD PÈRE & FILS** Beaune Les Grèves Vigne de l'Enfant Jésus 1995 • $63 • (11/15/97)
86 **BRUNO CLAIR** Gevrey-Chambertin Clos du Fonteny 1995 • $54 • (11/15/97)
86 **BRUNO CLAIR** Marsannay Les Longeroies 1995 • $21 • (11/15/97)
86 **BRUNO CLAIR** Morey-St.-Denis En la Rue de Vergy 1995 • $34 • (11/15/97)
86 **CHOFFLET-VALDENAIRE** Givry Clos Jus 1995 • $18 • (11/15/97)
86 **CORON PÈRE & FILS** Nuits-St.-Georges Les Cailles 1995 • $52 • (11/15/97)
86 **DANIEL RION** Nuits-St.-Georges Aux Vignerondes 1995 • $66 • (11/15/97)
86 **DANIEL RION** Nuits-St.-Georges Les Hauts Pruliers 1995 • $66 • (11/15/97)

Red Burgundy

86 **HENRI CLERC & FILS** Clos de Vougeot 1995 • $NA • (11/15/97)

86 **JEAN BOILLOT** Beaune Clos du Roi 1995 • $44 • (11/15/97)

86 **JEAN BOILLOT** Volnay Les Caillerets 1995 • $59 • (11/15/97)

86 **JOSEPH DROUHIN** Chambertin 1995 • $100 • (11/15/97)

86 **JOSEPH DROUHIN** Nuits-St.-Georges 1995 • $35 • (11/15/97)

86 **LALEURE-PIOT** Côte de Nuits-Villages Les Bellevues 1995 • $22 • (01/31/98)

86 **LALEURE-PIOT** Pernand-Vergelesses Les Vergelesses 1995 • $31 • (11/15/97)

86 **LECHENEAUT** Nuits-St.-Georges Les Cailles 1995 • $60 • (11/15/97)

86 **LOUIS JADOT** Gevrey-Chambertin Le Clos St.-Jacques 1995 • $60 • (11/15/97)

86 **MICHEL & MARC ROSSIGNOL** Volnay Les Pitures 1995 • $33 • (01/31/98)

86 **MOILLARD** Morey-St.-Denis Monts Luisants 1995 • $26 • (11/15/97)

86 **MOMMESSIN** Beaune Les Cents Vignes 1995 • $26 • (11/15/97)

86 **MOMMESSIN** Vosne-Romanée 1995 • $30 • (11/15/97)

86 **PHILIPPE CHARLOPIN-PARIZOT** Gevrey-Chambertin La Justice 1995 • $NA • (11/15/97)

86 **ROGER CAILLOT** Volnay Clos des Chênes 1995 • $27 • (11/15/97)

86 **ROSSIGNOL-TRAPET** Latricières-Chambertin 1995 • $55 • (11/15/97)

86 **VINCENT GIRARDIN** Beaune Clos des Vignes Franches 1995 • $27 • (11/15/97)

86 **VINCENT GIRARDIN** Pommard Les Vignots 1995 • $31 • (11/15/97)

85 **ALAIN GRAS** Auxey-Duresses Red 1995 • $23 • (11/15/97)

85 **ALETH GIRARDIN** Pommard 1995 • $27 • (11/15/97)

85 **ANTONIN RODET** Gevrey-Chambertin Estournelles St.-Jacques 1995 • $50 • (11/15/97)

85 **ARMAND ROUSSEAU** Gevrey-Chambertin Le Clos St.-Jacques 1995 • $100 • (11/15/97)

85 **BERTRAND AMBROISE** Côte de Nuits-Villages 1995 • $20 • (11/15/97)

85 **BERTRAND AMBROISE** Vosne-Romanée Aux Damaudes 1995 • $38 • (11/15/97)

85 **BILLARD-GONNET** Pommard Les Chaponnières 1995 • $45 • (11/15/97)

85 **BILLARD-GONNET** Pommard Les Pezerolles 1995 • $45 • (11/15/97)

85 **BOUCHARD PÈRE & FILS** Le Corton 1995 • $63 • (11/15/97)

85 **BOUCHARD PÈRE & FILS** Volnay Caillerets Ancienne Cuvée Carnot Domaines du Château de Beaune 1995 • $44 • (11/15/97)

85 **CHANTAL LESCURE** Beaune Les Chouacheux 1995 • $32 • (01/31/98)

85 **CHANTAL LESCURE** Côte de Beaune La Grande Chatelaine 1995 • $23 • (01/31/98)

Key: SS—Spectator Selection CS—Cellar Selection HR—Highly Recommended BB—Best Buy $NA—Price not available Ⓐ—Auction Price
Dates in parentheses indicate the issues in which the ratings were published.

85 **CHANTAL LESCURE** Pommard Les Bertins 1995 • $46 • (01/31/98)

85 **CHANTAL LESCURE** Pommard Les Vaumuriens 1995 • $36 • (01/31/98)

85 **CHOFFLET-VALDENAIRE** Givry Clos de Choue 1995 • $18 • (11/15/97)

85 **CLAUDE DUGAT** Gevrey-Chambertin Lavaux St.-Jacques 1995 • $70 • (11/15/97)

85 **COMTE GEORGES DE VOGÜÉ** Chambolle-Musigny 1995 • $75 • (11/15/97)

85 **CORON PÈRE & FILS** Beaune 1995 • $25 • (11/15/97)

85 **CORON PÈRE & FILS** Beaune Le Clos des Mouches 1995 • $43 • (11/15/97)

85 **DOMAINE LEROY** Savigny-lès-Beaune Les Narbantons 1995 • $80 • (11/15/97)

85 **DOMAINE THOMAS-MOILLARD** Beaune Grèves 1995 • $28 • (11/15/97)

85 **DOMAINE THOMAS-MOILLARD** Nuits-St.-Georges Clos de Thorey 1995 • $39 • (01/31/98)

85 **DOMAINE THOMAS-MOILLARD** Vosne-Romanée Aux Malconsorts 1995 • $43 • (03/31/98)

85 **EMILE JUILLOT** Mercurey Les Croichots 1995 • $NA • (11/15/97)

85 **FONTAINE-GAGNARD** Chassagne-Montrachet Clos St.-Jean Red 1995 • $36 • (11/15/97)

85 **HERVÉ SIGAUT** Chambolle-Musigny Les Sentiers 1995 • $39 • (11/15/97)

85 **HERVÉ SIGAUT** Morey-St.-Denis Les Charrières 1995 • $39 • (11/15/97)

85 **J. CONFURON-COTETIDOT** Gevrey-Chambertin Lavaut St.-Jacques 1995 • $70 • (11/15/97)

85 **J. CONFURON-COTETIDOT** Vosne-Romanée Les Suchots 1995 • $60 • (11/15/97)

85 **J. FAIVELEY** Bourgogne 1995 • $13 • (11/15/97)

85 **JACQUES PRIEUR** Corton Les Bressandes 1995 • $92 • (11/15/97)

85 **JEAN & JEAN-LOUIS TRAPET** Gevrey-Chambertin Cuvée Vieilles Vignes 1995 • $25 • (11/15/97)

85 **JEAN-JACQUES CONFURON** Nuits-St.-Georges Aux Boudots 1995 • $62 • (11/15/97)

85 **LECHENEAUT** Nuits-St.-Georges Les Damodes 1995 • $53 • (11/15/97)

85 **LOUIS JADOT** Corton Les Pougets 1995 • $54 • (11/15/97)

85 **LOUIS JADOT** Echézeaux 1995 • $90 • (11/15/97)

85 **LOUIS JADOT** Gevrey-Chambertin 1995 • $30 • (11/15/97)

85 **MOMMESSIN** Nuits-St.-Georges 1995 • $30 • (11/15/97)

85 **MONGEARD-MUGNERET** Savigny-lès-Beaune Les Narbantons 1995 • $23 • (11/15/97)

85 **P. DUBREUIL-FONTAINE PÈRE & FILS** Pommard Les Epenots 1995 • $55 • (11/15/97)

85 **PAUL DU COUËDIC** Mercurey Les Veleys 1995 • $20 • (11/15/97)

85 **PHILIPPE CHARLOPIN-PARIZOT** Bourgogne 1995 • $14 • (11/15/97)

85 **THIERRY MORTET** Chambolle-Musigny Aux Beaux Bruns 1995 • $62 • (11/15/97)

85 **TOLLOT-BEAUT & FILS** Savigny-lès-Beaune Les Lavières 1995 • $32 • (11/15/97)

85 **VINCENT GIRARDIN** Corton Perrières 1995 • $46 • (11/15/97)

85 **VINCENT GIRARDIN** Volnay Les Champans 1995 • $35 • (11/15/97)

85 **VINCENT GIRARDIN** Volnay-Santenots 1995 • $35 • (11/15/97)

1993 Red Burgundy
Vintage Rating: 91

99 **DOMAINE LEROY** Romanée St.-Vivant 1993 • $500 • (12/15/96)
98 **DOMAINE LEROY** Chambertin 1993 • $500 • (12/15/96)
98 **DOMAINE LEROY** Musigny 1993 • $500 • (12/15/96)
98 **DOMINIQUE LAURENT** Mazis-Chambertin 1993 • $117 • (05/15/96)
97 **BERTRAND AMBROISE** Corton Le Rognet 1993 • $75 • (11/15/95) • CS
97 **DANIEL RION** Clos Vougeot 1993 • $90 • (11/15/95) • HR
97 **LEROY** Musigny 1993 • $1082 Ⓐ • (11/15/95) • CS
96 **BERTRAND AMBROISE** Clos de Vougeot 1993 • $90 • (11/15/95)
96 **COMTE GEORGES DE VOGÜÉ** Musigny Cuvée Vieilles Vignes 1993 • $140 • (11/15/95) • CS
96 **DOMINIQUE LAURENT** Ruchottes-Chambertin 1993 • $117 • (05/15/96)
96 **JEAN GRIVOT** Richebourg 1993 • $128 • (05/15/96)
96 **LEROY** Clos de Vougeot 1993 • $403 Ⓐ • (11/15/95)
96 **LEROY** Richebourg 1993 • $989 Ⓐ • (11/15/95) • CS
96 **LEROY** Volnay-Santenots 1993 • $138 Ⓐ • (11/15/95)
96 **SÉRAFIN PÈRE & FILS** Charmes-Chambertin 1993 • $90 • (11/15/95)
95 **ANNE & FRANÇOIS GROS** Clos Vougeot Le Grand Maupertuis 1993 • $55 • (11/15/95)
95 **ARMAND ROUSSEAU** Chambertin 1993 • $111 Ⓐ • (09/15/96)
95 **DOMAINE LEROY** Latricières-Chambertin 1993 • $325 • (12/15/96)
95 **DOMAINE LEROY** Richebourg 1993 • $500 • (12/15/96)
95 **DOMINIQUE LAURENT** Gevrey-Chambertin Vieilles Vignes 1993 • $NA • (05/15/96)
95 **EMMANUEL ROUGET** Echézeaux 1993 • $80 • (05/15/96)
95 **EMMANUEL ROUGET** Vosne-Romanée Cros Parantoux 1993 • $72 • (05/15/96)
95 **LEROY** Chambertin 1993 • $690 Ⓐ • (11/15/95)
95 **LEROY** Nuits-St.-Georges Aux Vignerondes 1993 • $185 • (11/15/95)
95 **LEROY** Romanée St.-Vivant 1993 • $500 • (11/15/95)
95 **ROBERT JAYER-GILLES** Echézeaux du Dessus 1993 • $135 • (11/15/95)
94 **COMTE GEORGES DE VOGÜÉ** Bonnes Mares 1993 • $115 • (11/15/95)
94 **COMTE GEORGES DE VOGÜÉ** Chambolle-Musigny Les Amoureuses 1993 • $125 • (11/15/95)
94 **DANIEL RION** Nuits-St.-Georges Aux Vignerondes 1993 • $50 • (11/15/95)
94 **DENIS MORTET** Chambertin 1993 • $115 • (11/15/95)
94 **DENIS MORTET** Clos Vougeot 1993 • $80 • (11/15/95)
94 **DOMAINE LEROY** Clos de la Roche 1993 • $325 • (12/15/96)
94 **DOMAINE DE LA ROMANÉE-CONTI** La Tâche 1993 • $241 Ⓐ • (05/15/96) • CS
94 **DOMAINE DE LA ROMANÉE-CONTI** Romanée-Conti 1993 • $1725 Ⓐ • (05/15/96) • CS
94 **DOMINIQUE LAURENT** Clos Vougeot 1993 • $NA • (05/15/96)
94 **GROS FRÈRE & SOEUR** Richebourg 1993 • $110 • (11/15/95)
94 **J. CONFURON-COTETIDOT** Gevrey-Chambertin 1993 • $NA • (05/15/96)
94 **JACQUES PRIEUR** Musigny 1993 • $63 • (11/15/95)
94 **JEAN GRIVOT** Vosne-Romanée Les Beaux Monts 1993 • $32 • (05/15/96) • HR
94 **JEAN GROS** Richebourg 1993 • $160 • (11/15/95)
94 **JEAN-JACQUES CONFURON** Chambolle-Musigny Premier Cru 1993 • $60 • (11/15/95) • HR
94 **JEAN-JACQUES CONFURON** Vosne-Romanée Les Beaux Monts 1993 • $63 • (11/15/95)
94 **LEROY** Clos de la Roche 1993 • $1082 Ⓐ • (11/15/95)
94 **LEROY** Vosne-Romanée Les Beaux Monts 1993 • $392 Ⓐ • (11/15/95)
94 **MÉO-CAMUZET** Richebourg 1993 • $175 • (11/15/95)
94 **PHILIPPE CHARLOPIN-PARIZOT** Charmes-Chambertin 1993 • $94 • (05/15/96)
93 **ARMAND ROUSSEAU** Chambertin-Clos de Bèze 1993 • $100 Ⓐ • (09/15/96)
93 **ARMAND ROUSSEAU** Ruchottes-Chambertin Clos des Ruchottes 1993 • $92 Ⓐ • (09/15/96)
93 **DANIEL RION** Nuits-St.-Georges Les Grandes Vignes 1993 • $32 • (11/15/95)
93 **DANIEL RION** Vosne-Romanée Les Chaumes 1993 • $50 • (11/15/95)
93 **DOMAINE DES COMTES LAFON** Volnay-Santenots Les Santenots du Milieu 1993 • $53 Ⓐ • (05/15/96)
93 **DOMINIQUE LAURENT** Pommard Les Epenots 1993 • $85 • (05/15/96)
93 **DOMINIQUE LAURENT** Pommard Vieilles Vignes 1993 • $48 • (05/15/96)
93 **GROS FRÈRE & SOEUR** Grands Echézeaux 1993 • $69 • (11/15/95)
93 **JEAN-MARC BOILLOT** Volnay 1993 • $30 • (11/15/95)
93 **JOSEPH DROUHIN** Corton Les Bressandes 1993 • $70 • (11/15/95)
93 **LECHENEAUT** Chambolle-Musigny Premier Cru 1993 • $68 • (11/15/95)
93 **LECHENEAUT** Nuits-St.-Georges Les Damodes 1993 • $68 • (11/15/95)
93 **LEROY** Vosne-Romanée Les Brûlées 1993 • $185 • (11/15/95)
93 **MAURICE ECARD** Savigny-lès-Beaune Aux Serpentières 1993 • $25 • (05/15/96)
93 **MÉO-CAMUZET** Nuits-St.-Georges Aux Murgers 1993 • $60 • (11/15/95)
93 **MÉO-CAMUZET** Vosne-Romanée Aux Brûlées 1993 • $75 • (11/15/95)
93 **MÉO-CAMUZET** Vosne-Romanée Les Chaumes 1993 • $70 • (11/15/95)
93 **MICHEL LAFARGE** Volnay Clos du Château des Ducs 1993 • $65 • (11/15/95)
93 **MONGEARD-MUGNERET** Clos de Vougeot 1993 • $60 Ⓐ • (11/15/95)
93 **MONTHÉLIE-DOUHAIRET** Volnay Champans 1993 • $44 • (11/15/95)
93 **OLIVIER LEFLAIVE FRÈRES** Volnay Frémiets 1993 • $42 • (11/15/95)
93 **ROBERT ARNOUX** Romanée St.-Vivant 1993 • $NA • (11/15/95)
93 **ROBERT JAYER-GILLES** Nuits-St.-Georges Les Poirets 1993 • $70 • (11/15/95)
92 **ARMAND ROUSSEAU** Gevrey-Chambertin Le Clos St.-Jacques 1993 • $67 Ⓐ • (09/15/96)

■ ■ ■ ■

Red Burgundy

92 **CLAUDE DUGAT** Gevrey-Chambertin Lavaux St.-Jacques 1993 • $65 • (11/15/95)

92 **DANIEL RION** Chambolle-Musigny Les Charmes 1993 • $63 • (11/15/95)

92 **DANIEL RION** Vosne-Romanée Les Beaux Monts 1993 • $50 • (11/15/95)

92 **DOMAINE DE L'ARLOT** Nuits-St.-Georges Clos des Forêts St.-Georges 1993 • $40 • (05/15/96)

92 **DOMAINE DE LA ROMANÉE-CONTI** Romanée St.-Vivant 1993 • $135 • (05/15/96)

92 **FOREY PÈRE & FILS** Vosne-Romanée Les Gaudichots 1993 • $45 • (11/15/95)

92 **JACQUES PRIEUR** Clos Vougeot 1993 • $54 • (11/15/95)

92 **JACQUES-FRÉDÉRIC MUGNIER** Bonnes Mares 1993 • $90 • (05/15/96)

92 **JEAN & JEAN-LOUIS TRAPET** Chambertin 1993 • $NA • (05/15/96)

92 **JEAN GRIVOT** Clos de Vougeot 1993 • $45 • (05/15/96) • CS

92 **JEAN GRIVOT** Echézeaux 1993 • $45 • (05/15/96)

92 **JEAN-MARC BOILLOT** Volnay Pitures 1993 • $42 • (11/15/95)

92 **LEROY** Corton Les Renardes 1993 • $185 • (11/15/95)

92 **LEROY** Pommard Les Vignots 1993 • $128 Ⓐ • (11/15/95)

92 **LOUIS JADOT** Clos Vougeot 1993 • $NA • (11/15/95)

92 **LOUIS JADOT** Corton Les Pougets 1993 • $46 • (11/15/95)

92 **MARQUIS D'ANGERVILLE** Volnay Premier Cru 1993 • $30 • (05/15/96)

92 **MONGEARD-MUGNERET** Echézeaux Vieille Vigne 1993 • $50 Ⓐ • (11/15/95)

92 **ROBERT JAYER-GILLES** Nuits-St.-Georges Les Damodes 1993 • $85 • (11/15/95)

92 **ROSSIGNOL-TRAPET** Latricières-Chambertin 1993 • $64 • (11/15/95)

92 **THIERRY MORTET** Gevrey-Chambertin 1993 • $42 • (09/15/96)

91 **ANNE & FRANÇOIS GROS** Richebourg 1993 • $100 • (11/15/95)

91 **ARMAND GIRARDIN** Pommard Les Charmots 1993 • $60 • (11/15/95)

91 **CLAUDE DUGAT** Gevrey-Chambertin Premier Cru 1993 • $50 • (11/15/95)

91 **DENIS MORTET** Chambolle-Musigny Aux Beaux Bruns 1993 • $43 • (11/15/95)

91 **DUJAC** Clos St.-Denis 1993 • $79 • (05/15/96)

91 **EMMANUEL ROUGET** Vosne-Romanée Les Beaux Monts 1993 • $55 • (05/15/96)

91 **FOREY PÈRE & FILS** Echézeaux 1993 • $45 • (11/15/95)

91 **GROS FRÈRE & SOEUR** Vosne-Romanée 1993 • $35 • (11/15/95)

91 **J. FAIVELEY** Chambertin-Clos de Bèze 1993 • $113 • (05/15/96)

91 **J. FAIVELEY** Echézeaux 1993 • $56 • (05/15/96)

91 **JACQUES PRIEUR** Volnay-Santenots 1993 • $34 • (11/15/95)

91 **JEAN GROS** Vosne-Romanée Clos des Réas 1993 • $60 • (11/15/95)

Key: SS—Spectator Selection CS—Cellar Selection HR—Highly Recommended BB—Best Buy $NA—Price not available Ⓐ—Auction Price

Dates in parentheses indicate the issues in which the ratings were published.

91 **JOSEPH DROUHIN** Chambertin 1993 • $119 • (11/15/95)

91 **LALEURE-PIOT** Corton Les Bressandes 1993 • $51 • (11/15/95)

91 **LECHENEAUT** Clos de la Roche 1993 • $90 • (11/15/95)

91 **LEROY** Latricières-Chambertin 1993 • $325 • (11/15/95)

91 **LEROY** Nuits-St.-Georges Aux Boudots 1993 • $185 • (11/15/95)

91 **LUCIEN BOILLOT** Pommard Les Fremiers 1993 • $38 • (11/15/95)

91 **LUCIEN BOILLOT** Volnay Les Caillerets 1993 • $38 • (11/15/95)

91 **MICHEL GROS** Chambolle-Musigny 1993 • $35 • (11/15/95)

91 **MONGEARD-MUGNERET** Echézeaux 1993 • $50 • (11/15/95)

91 **PIERRE DAMOY** Chambertin 1993 • $69 • (11/15/95)

91 **PIERRE DAMOY** Chambertin-Clos de Bèze 1993 • $55 • (11/15/95)

91 **PIERRE DAMOY** Chapelle-Chambertin 1993 • $57 • (11/15/95)

91 **ROBERT ARNOUX** Clos de Vougeot 1993 • $80 • (11/15/95)

91 **SÉRAFIN PÈRE & FILS** Gevrey-Chambertin Fonteny 1993 • $65 • (11/15/95)

91 **SÉRAFIN PÈRE & FILS** Gevrey-Chambertin Les Cazetiers 1993 • $70 • (11/15/95)

91 **TOLLOT-BEAUT & FILS** Corton 1993 • $57 • (11/15/95)

90 **ALETH GIRARDIN** Beaune Le Clos des Mouches 1993 • $48 • (11/15/95)

90 **ARMAND GIRARDIN** Pommard Les Epenots 1993 • $60 • (11/15/95)

90 **BERTAGNA** Clos St.-Denis 1993 • $71 • (05/15/96)

90 **BERTRAND AMBROISE** Nuits-St.-Georges Les Vaucrains 1993 • $65 • (11/15/95)

90 **BOUCHARD PÈRE & FILS** La Romanée Château de Vosne-Romanée 1993 • $116 Ⓐ • (11/15/95)

90 **CLAUDE DUGAT** Charmes-Chambertin 1993 • $90 • (11/15/95)

90 **CLAUDE DUGAT** Gevrey-Chambertin 1993 • $40 • (11/15/95)

90 **COSTE-CAUMARTIN** Pommard Les Boucherottes 1993 • $42 • (11/15/95)

90 **DANIEL RION** Vosne-Romanée 1993 • $32 • (11/15/95)

90 **DENIS MORTET** Gevrey-Chambertin 1993 • $42 • (09/15/96)

90 **DENIS MORTET** Gevrey-Chambertin Champeaux 1993 • $58 • (11/15/95)

90 **DENIS MORTET** Gevrey-Chambertin En Champs Vieille Vigne 1993 • $50 • (11/15/95)

90 **DENIS MORTET** Gevrey-Chambertin En Motrot 1993 • $46 • (11/15/95)

90 **DENIS MORTET** Gevrey-Chambertin Lavaut St.-Jacques 1993 • $58 • (11/15/95)

90 **DOMAINE DE COURCEL** Pommard Les Rugiens 1993 • $42 • (11/15/95)

90 **DOMAINE DE LA ROMANÉE-CONTI** Echézeaux 1993 • $101 Ⓐ • (05/15/96)

90 **DOMAINE DE LA ROMANÉE-CONTI** Richebourg 1993 • $207 Ⓐ • (05/15/96)

90 **EMMANUEL ROUGET** Nuits-St.-Georges 1993 • $NA • (05/15/96)

90 **FONTAINE-GAGNARD** Volnay Clos des Chênes 1993 • $43 • (11/15/95)

90 **FRÉDÉRIC ESMONIN** Ruchottes-Chambertin 1993 • $65 • (11/15/95)

90 **GEANTET-PANSIOT** Charmes-Chambertin 1993 • $60 • (05/15/96)

90 **GEANTET-PANSIOT** Gevrey-Chambertin Poissenot 1993 • $45 • (05/15/96)

90 **J. FAIVELEY** Nuits-St.-Georges Porrets St.-Georges 1993 • $43 • (05/15/96)

90 **JACQUES PRIEUR** Volnay-Santenots Clos des Santenots 1993 • $37 • (11/15/95)

90 **JEAN GRIVOT** Nuits-St.-Georges Aux Boudots 1993 • $32 • (05/15/96)

90 **JEAN-JACQUES CONFURON** Clos Vougeot 1993 • $85 • (11/15/95)

90 **JEAN-JACQUES CONFURON** Nuits-St.-Georges Les Fleurières 1993 • $45 • (11/15/95)

90 **JEAN-MARC BOILLOT** Pommard Les Jarolières 1993 • $50 • (11/15/95)

90 **JEAN-MARC PAVELOT** Savigny-lès-Beaune Aux Guettes 1993 • $28 • (11/15/95)

90 **JEAN-MARC PAVELOT** Savigny-lès-Beaune La Dominode 1993 • $28 • (11/15/95)

90 **LECHENEAUT** Nuits-St.-Georges Premier Cru 1993 • $60 • (11/15/95)

90 **LEROY** Chambolle-Musigny Les Charmes 1993 • $200 • (11/15/95)

90 **LOUIS JADOT** Chambertin-Clos de Bèze 1993 • $87 • (11/15/95)

90 **MARQUIS D'ANGERVILLE** Volnay Champans 1993 • $29 • (05/15/96)

90 **MAUME** Gevrey-Chambertin 1993 • $NA • (05/15/96)

90 **MÉO-CAMUZET** Nuits-St.-Georges Aux Boudots 1993 • $60 • (11/15/95)

90 **MICHELE & PATRICE RION** Chambolle-Musigny Les Cras 1993 • $38 • (11/15/95)

90 **PARENT** Corton Les Renardes 1993 • $62 • (11/15/95)

90 **PHILIPPE CHARLOPIN-PARIZOT** Clos St.-Denis 1993 • $94 • (05/15/96)

90 **PHILIPPE ROSSIGNOL** Gevrey-Chambertin Les Corbeaux Cuvée Vieilles Vignes 1993 • $NA • (05/15/96)

90 **PRINCE FLORENT DE MÉRODE** Ladoix Les Chaillots 1993 • $17 • (11/15/95)

90 **ROBERT JAYER-GILLES** Côte de Nuits-Villages 1993 • $36 • (11/15/95)

90 **ROBERT JAYER-GILLES** Hautes Côtes de Beaune 1993 • $22 • (11/15/95)

90 **ROSSIGNOL-TRAPET** Beaune Teurons 1993 • $33 • (11/15/95)

90 **ROSSIGNOL-TRAPET** Chambertin 1993 • $77 • (11/15/95)

90 **TOLLOT-BEAUT & FILS** Corton Les Bressandes 1993 • $57 • (11/15/95)

90 **TOLLOT-BEAUT & FILS** Savigny-lès-Beaune Les Lavières 1993 • $25 • (11/15/95)

89 **DENIS MORTET** Marsannay Les Longeroies Red 1993 • $30 • (11/15/95)

89 **DOMAINE DE L'ARLOT** Nuits-St.-Georges Clos de L'Arlot 1993 • $34 • (05/15/96)

89 **DOMAINE DE LA POUSSE D'OR** Volnay Les Caillerets-Clos des 60 Ouvrées 1993 • $60 • (11/15/95)

89 **DOMAINE DES LAMBRAYS** Clos des Lambrays 1993 • $50 • (05/15/96)

89 **DOMINIQUE LAURENT** Nuits-St.-Georges Les Vaucrains 1993 • $NA • (05/15/96)

89 **DROUHIN-LAROZE** Clos de Vougeot 1993 • $62 • (11/15/95)

89 **EDMOND CORNU** Ladoix Les Carrières 1993 • $27 • (11/15/95)

89 **EMMANUEL ROUGET** Savigny-lès-Beaune 1993 • $NA • (05/15/96)

89 **FONTAINE-GAGNARD** Chassagne-Montrachet Morgeot Red 1993 • $27 • (11/15/95)

89 **HAEGELEN-JAYER** Clos de Vougeot 1993 • $NA • (05/15/96)

89 **J. CONFURON-COTETIDOT** Clos de Vougeot 1993 • $NA • (05/15/96)

89 **J. CONFURON-COTETIDOT** Nuits-St.-Georges 1993 • $NA • (05/15/96)

89 **J. CONFURON-COTETIDOT** Nuits-St.-Georges Premier Cru 1993 • $NA • (05/15/96)

89 **JACQUES PRIEUR** Chambertin 1993 • $90 • (05/15/96)

89 **JACQUES-FRÉDÉRIC MUGNIER** Chambolle-Musigny Les Fuées 1993 • $69 • (05/15/96)

89 **JEAN GROS** Vosne-Romanée 1993 • $35 • (11/15/95)

89 **JEAN-JACQUES CONFURON** Nuits-St.-Georges Les Chaboeufs 1993 • $60 • (11/15/95)

89 **JEAN-JACQUES CONFURON** Romanée St.-Vivant 1993 • $150 • (11/15/95)

89 **JEAN-MARC BOILLOT** Volnay Carelle Sous La Chapelle 1993 • $42 • (11/15/95)

89 **JEAN-MARC PAVELOT** Savigny-lès-Beaune Aux Gravains 1993 • $30 • (11/15/95)

89 **LABOURÉ-ROI** Echézeaux 1993 • $54 • (11/15/95)

89 **LALEURE-PIOT** Corton Le Rognet 1993 • $47 • (11/15/95)

89 **LÉONARD DE ST.-AUBIN** Volnay 1993 • $26 • (05/15/96)

89 **LEROY** Gevrey-Chambertin Aux Combottes 1993 • $220 • (11/15/95)

89 **LEROY** Nuits-St.-Georges 1993 • $110 • (11/15/95)

89 **LEROY** Savigny-lès-Beaune Les Narbantons 1993 • $70 • (11/15/95)

89 **LOUIS JADOT** Gevrey-Chambertin Estournelles St.-Jacques 1993 • $48 • (11/15/95)

89 **LOUIS LATOUR** Romanée St.-Vivant Les Quatre Journaux 1993 • $NA • (05/15/96)

89 **MACHARD DE GRAMONT** Nuits-St.-Georges Les Hauts Poirets 1993 • $34 • (09/15/96)

89 **MICHEL ESMONIN** Gevrey-Chambertin Le Clos St.-Jacques 1993 • $64 • (11/15/95)

89 **MOMMESSIN** Beaune Les Cents Vignes 1993 • $30 • (11/15/95)

89 **MOMMESSIN** Bonnes Mares 1993 • $80 • (11/15/95)

89 **PHILIPPE ROSSIGNOL** Gevrey-Chambertin Les Corbeaux 1993 • $NA • (05/15/96)

89 **PIERRE DAMOY** Gevrey-Chambertin Clos Tamisot 1993 • $30 • (11/15/95)

89 **ROBERT ARNOUX** Echézeaux 1993 • $80 • (11/15/95)

89 **TOLLOT-BEAUT & FILS** Aloxe-Corton Les Vercots 1993 • $37 • (11/15/95)

88 **ANNE & FRANÇOIS GROS** Chambolle-Musigny La Combe d'Orveau 1993 • $29 • (11/15/95)

88 **ANNE & FRANÇOIS GROS** Vosne-Romanée 1993 • $40 • (11/15/95)

88 **ANTONIN RODET** Nuits-St.-Georges Roncière 1993 • $45 • (11/15/95)

88 **BERTAGNA** Clos de Vougeot 1993 • $90 • (05/15/96)

88 **BERTRAND AMBROISE** Vosne-Romanée Les Damaudes 1993 • $45 • (11/15/95)

88 **BONNEAU DU MARTRAY** Corton 1993 • $45 • (11/15/95)

■ ■ ■ ■

Red Burgundy

88 **BOUCHARD PÈRE & FILS** Chambolle-Musigny 1993 • $36 • (11/15/95)

88 **BOUCHARD PÈRE & FILS** Vosne-Romanée Aux Raignots Château de Vosne-Romanée 1993 • $51 • (11/15/95)

88 **CHOPIN-GROFFIER** Clos Vougeot 1993 • $85 • (11/15/95)

88 **CHÂTEAU DE POMMARD** Pommard 1993 • $36 • (11/15/95)

88 **COMTE GEORGES DE VOGÜÉ** Chambolle-Musigny 1993 • $60 • (11/15/95)

88 **COSTE-CAUMARTIN** Pommard Les Fremiers 1993 • $NA • (05/15/96)

88 **DANIEL RION** Nuits-St.-Georges Clos des Argillières 1993 • $50 • (11/15/95)

88 **DANIEL RION** Nuits-St.-Georges Les Pruliers 1993 • $50 • (11/15/95)

88 **DENIS MORTET** Bourgogne Les Charmes au Châtelain 1993 • $15 • (11/15/95)

88 **DENIS MORTET** Gevrey-Chambertin Au Vellé 1993 • $46 • (11/15/95)

88 **DOMAINE DE COURCEL** Pommard Les Grands Epenots 1993 • $33 • (11/15/95)

88 **DOMAINE DE L'ARLOT** Nuits-St.-Georges 1993 • $22 • (05/15/96)

88 **DOMAINE DE LA POUSSE D'OR** Volnay Clos de la Bousse d'Or 1993 • $70 • (11/15/95)

88 **DOMAINE DE LA ROMANÉE-CONTI** Grands Echézeaux 1993 • $135 • (05/15/96)

88 **DOMAINE DES COMTES LAFON** Volnay Clos des Chênes 1993 • $NA • (05/15/96)

88 **DOMAINE DU CLOS FRANTIN** Grands Echézeaux 1993 • $60 • (11/15/95)

88 **DUJAC** Gevrey-Chambertin Aux Combottes 1993 • $65 • (05/15/96)

88 **DUJAC** Morey-St.-Denis 1993 • $37 • (05/15/96)

88 **FONTAINE-GAGNARD** Bourgogne 1993 • $14 • (11/15/95)

88 **FOREY PÈRE & FILS** Vosne-Romanée 1993 • $26 • (11/15/95)

88 **GEORGES MUGNERET** Nuits-St.-Georges Aux Chaignots 1993 • $NA • (05/15/96)

88 **J. CONFURON-COTETIDOT** Chambolle-Musigny 1993 • $NA • (05/15/96)

88 **JACQUES PRIEUR** Beaune Clos de la Féguine 1993 • $30 • (11/15/95)

88 **JACQUES PRIEUR** Corton Les Bressandes 1993 • $70 • (11/15/95)

88 **JACQUES PRIEUR** Volnay En Champans 1993 • $36 • (11/15/95)

88 **JACQUES-FRÉDÉRIC MUGNIER** Chambolle-Musigny 1993 • $39 • (05/15/96)

88 **JEAN GRIVOT** Vosne-Romanée 1993 • $22 • (05/15/96)

88 **JOSEPH DROUHIN** Bonnes Mares 1993 • $100 • (11/15/95)

88 **JOSEPH DROUHIN** Musigny 1993 • $77 Ⓐ • (11/15/95)

88 **JOSEPH DROUHIN** Volnay En Chevret 1993 • $38 • (11/15/95)

88 **LECHENEAUT** Chambolle-Musigny 1993 • $48 • (11/15/95)

Key: SS—Spectator Selection CS—Cellar Selection HR—Highly Recommended BB—Best Buy $NA—Price not available Ⓐ—Auction Price
Dates in parentheses indicate the issues in which the ratings were published.

88 **LEJEUNE** Pommard Les Argillières 1993 • $36 • (11/15/95)

88 **LEROY** Chambolle-Musigny Les Fremières 1993 • $125 • (11/15/95)

88 **LOUIS JADOT** Beaune Clos des Ursules 1993 • $35 • (11/15/95)

88 **LOUIS JADOT** Romanée St.-Vivant 1993 • $135 • (11/15/95)

88 **LOUIS JADOT** Vosne-Romanée Les Suchots 1993 • $46 • (11/15/95)

88 **LOUIS LATOUR** Corton Château Corton Grancey 1993 • $43 • (11/15/95)

88 **LUCIEN BOILLOT** Gevrey-Chambertin Cherbaudes 1993 • $40 • (11/15/95)

88 **MÉO-CAMUZET** Clos de Vougeot 1993 • $55 • (11/15/95)

88 **MICHEL LAFARGE** Volnay Clos des Chênes 1993 • $94 • (05/15/96)

88 **MICHELE & PATRICE RION** Bourgogne Les Bons Bâtons 1993 • $15 • (11/15/95)

88 **MOMMESSIN** Chambolle-Musigny Premier Cru 1993 • $45 • (11/15/95)

88 **MONGEARD-MUGNERET** Richebourg 1993 • $110 • (11/15/95)

88 **P. DUBREUIL-FONTAINE PÈRE & FILS** Corton Les Bressandes 1993 • $NA • (05/15/96)

88 **P. DUBREUIL-FONTAINE PÈRE & FILS** Corton Les Perrières 1993 • $NA • (05/15/96)

88 **PHILIPPE CHARLOPIN-PARIZOT** Gevrey-Chambertin Cuvée Vieilles Vignes 1993 • $NA • (05/15/96)

88 **PRINCE FLORENT DE MÉRODE** Corton Le Clos du Roi 1993 • $44 • (11/15/95)

88 **PRINCE FLORENT DE MÉRODE** Pommard La Platière 1993 • $31 • (11/15/95)

88 **ROBERT ARNOUX** Vosne-Romanée Les Chaumes 1993 • $55 • (11/15/95)

88 **ROBERT JAYER-GILLES** Bourgogne Hautes-Côtes de Nuits 1993 • $22 • (05/15/96)

88 **ROSSIGNOL-TRAPET** Gevrey-Chambertin Petite Chapelle 1993 • $43 • (11/15/95)

88 **THIERRY MORTET** Gevrey-Chambertin Clos Prieur 1993 • $50 • (05/15/96)

88 **TOLLOT-BEAUT & FILS** Beaune Clos du Roi 1993 • $35 • (11/15/95)

87 **A.-F. GROS** Vosne-Romanée Aux Réas 1993 • $44 • (11/15/95)

87 **A.-F. GROS** Vosne-Romanée Maizières 1993 • $50 • (11/15/95)

87 **BOUCHARD PÈRE & FILS** Chassagne-Montrachet Red 1993 • $25 • (11/15/95)

87 **DANIEL RION** Côte de Nuits-Villages 1993 • $17 • (11/15/95)

87 **DOMAINE DE LA POUSSE D'OR** Santenay Clos de Tavannes 1993 • $40 • (11/15/95)

87 **DOMAINE DU CLOS FRANTIN** Vosne-Romanée Aux Malconsorts 1993 • $NA • (11/15/95)

87 **EDMOND CORNU** Corton Les Bressandes 1993 • $57 • (11/15/95)

87 **FONTAINE-GAGNARD** Chassagne-Montrachet Red 1993 • $23 • (11/15/95)

87 **JEAN & JEAN-LOUIS TRAPET** Chapelle-Chambertin 1993 • $NA • (05/15/96)

87 **JEAN-MARC PAVELOT** Savigny-lès-Beaune Les Narbantons 1993 • $29 • (11/15/95)

87 **JOSEPH DROUHIN** Chambolle-Musigny Premier Cru 1993 • $45 • (11/15/95)

87 **JOSEPH DROUHIN** Morey-St.-Denis Clos Sorbè 1993 • $43 • (11/15/95)

87 **LABOURÉ-ROI** Gevrey-Chambertin 1993 • $22 • (11/15/95)

87 **LALEURE-PIOT** Chorey-lès-Beaune Les Champs Longs 1993 • $17 • (11/15/95)

87 **LOUIS JADOT** Beaune Clos des Couchereaux 1993 • $25 • (11/15/95)

87 **LOUIS JADOT** Fixin 1993 • $18 • (11/15/95)

87 **LUCIEN BOILLOT** Gevrey-Chambertin Les Corbeaux 1993 • $40 • (11/15/95)

87 **LUCIEN BOILLOT** Volnay Les Brouillards 1993 • $37 • (11/15/95)

87 **MACHARD DE GRAMONT** Nuits-St.-Georges Les Hauts Pruliers 1993 • $34 • (09/15/96)

87 **MICHEL GROS** Vosne-Romanée Clos de la Fontaine 1993 • $NA • (05/15/96)

87 **MOMMESSIN** Nuits-St.-Georges Aux Chaignots 1993 • $57 • (11/15/95)

87 **MOMMESSIN** Savigny-lès-Beaune 1993 • $21 • (11/15/95)

87 **MOMMESSIN** Vosne-Romanée Premier Cru 1993 • $46 • (11/15/95)

87 **MONGEARD-MUGNERET** Grands Echézeaux 1993 • $83 Ⓐ • (11/15/95)

87 **MONGEARD-MUGNERET** Savigny-lès-Beaune 1993 • $22 • (11/15/95)

87 **P. DUBREUIL-FONTAINE PÈRE & FILS** Corton Le Clos du Roi 1993 • $NA • (05/15/96)

87 **PARENT** Pommard Les Epenots 1993 • $57 • (11/15/95)

87 **PIERRE LABET** Beaune Les Monsnières 1993 • $20 • (11/15/95)

87 **PRINCE FLORENT DE MÉRODE** Corton Les Maréchaudes 1993 • $32 • (11/15/95)

87 **ROBERT ARNOUX** Vosne-Romanée Les Suchots 1993 • $80 • (11/15/95)

87 **ROSSIGNOL-TRAPET** Chapelle-Chambertin 1993 • $77 • (11/15/95)

87 **ROSSIGNOL-TRAPET** Gevrey-Chambertin 1993 • $28 • (11/15/95)

87 **THIERRY MORTET** Chambolle-Musigny Aux Beaux Bruns 1993 • $58 • (05/15/96)

87 **TOLLOT-BEAUT & FILS** Beaune Les Grèves 1993 • $35 • (11/15/95)

87 **TOLLOT-BEAUT & FILS** Chorey-Côte de Beaune 1993 • $18 • (11/15/95)

86 **ALAIN GRAS** Auxey-Duresses Red 1993 • $20 • (11/15/95)

86 **ANTONIN RODET** Vosne-Romanée 1993 • $30 • (11/15/95)

86 **BERTAGNA** Vougeot Clos de la Perrière 1993 • $58 • (05/15/96)

86 **BERTRAND AMBROISE** Nuits-St.-Georges 1993 • $40 • (11/15/95)

86 **BOUCHARD PÈRE & FILS** Beaune Les Teurons Domaines du Château de Beaune 1993 • $28 • (11/15/95)

86 **BOUCHARD PÈRE & FILS** Gevrey-Chambertin 1993 • $29 • (11/15/95)

86 **BRUNO CLAIR** Gevrey-Chambertin 1993 • $47 • (05/15/96)

86 **BRUNO CLAIR** Marsannay Les Grasses Têtes 1993 • $25 • (05/15/96)

86 **CHOFFLET-VALDENAIRE** Givry 1993 • $20 • (05/15/96)

86 **DOMINIQUE LAURENT** Beaune Premier Cru Vieilles Vignes 1993 • $NA • (05/15/96)

86 **DOMINIQUE LAURENT** Volnay 1993 • $NA • (05/15/96)

86 **DOMINIQUE LAURENT** Vosne-Romanée 1993 • $NA • (05/15/96)

86 **DUJAC** Chambolle-Musigny 1993 • $37 • (05/15/96)

86 **F. CHAUVENET** Charmes-Chambertin 1993 • $78 • (11/15/95)

86 **FRÉDERIC ESMONIN** Gevrey-Chambertin Clos Prieur 1993 • $30 • (11/15/95)

86 **JAFFELIN** Volnay 1993 • $24 • (11/15/95)

86 **JEAN & JEAN-LOUIS TRAPET** Latricières-Chambertin 1993 • $NA • (05/15/96)

86 **JEAN-MARC BOILLOT** Bourgogne 1993 • $17 • (11/15/95)

86 **JEAN-MARC MILLOT** Echézeaux 1993 • $NA • (05/15/96)

86 **JOSEPH DROUHIN** Beaune Clos des Mouches 1993 • $50 • (11/15/95)

86 **L'HÉRITIER-GUYOT** Corton Les Renardes 1993 • $60 • (11/15/95)

86 **LABOURÉ-ROI** Charmes-Chambertin 1993 • $59 • (11/15/95)

86 **LABOURÉ-ROI** Pommard Les Bertins 1993 • $29 • (11/15/95)

86 **LALEURE-PIOT** Savigny-lès-Beaune Aux Vergelesses 1993 • $25 • (11/15/95)

86 **MAUME** Gevrey-Chambertin Lavaut St.-Jacques 1993 • $NA • (05/15/96)

86 **MICHEL VOARICK** Corton Les Renardes 1993 • $60 • (11/15/95)

86 **OLIVIER LEFLAIVE FRÈRES** Pommard Les Rugiens 1993 • $48 • (11/15/95)

86 **PARENT** Pommard Les Chaponnières 1993 • $50 • (11/15/95)

86 **PRINCE FLORENT DE MÉRODE** Corton Les Bressandes 1993 • $37 • (11/15/95)

86 **SIMON BIZE & FILS** Savigny-lès-Beaune Les Marconnets 1993 • $25 • (05/15/96)

86 **TOLLOT-BEAUT & FILS** Aloxe-Corton 1993 • $29 • (11/15/95)

85 **BOUCHARD PÈRE & FILS** Beaune Le Clos de la Mousse 1993 • $28 • (11/15/95)

85 **BRUNO CLAIR** Marsannay Les Vaudenelles 1993 • $22 • (05/15/96)

85 **COMTE ARMAND** Pommard Clos des Epeneaux 1993 • $60 Ⓐ • (05/15/96)

85 **DOMAINE DE LA POUSSE D'OR** Pommard Les Jarolières 1993 • $65 • (11/15/95)

85 **DOMAINE DE LA POUSSE D'OR** Volnay Les Caillerets 1993 • $53 • (11/15/95)

85 **DOMAINE DES COMTES LAFON** Volnay En Champans 1993 • $NA • (05/15/96)

85 **DOMAINE DU CLOS FRANTIN** Echézeaux 1993 • $NA • (11/15/95)

85 **EDMOND CORNU** Savigny-lès-Beaune 1993 • $22 • (11/15/95)

85 **FOREY PÈRE & FILS** Nuits-St.-Georges Les Perrières 1993 • $33 • (11/15/95)

85 **JACQUES-FRÉDÉRIC MUGNIER** Chambolle-Musigny Les Amoureuses 1993 • $100 • (05/15/96)

85 **JEAN & JEAN-LOUIS TRAPET** Gevrey-Chambertin 1993 • $NA • (05/15/96)

85 **JEAN GRIVOT** Vosne-Romanée Les Suchots 1993 • $NA • (05/15/96)

85 **JEAN-MARC BOILLOT** Beaune Les Montrevenots 1993 • $30 • (11/15/95)

85 **JEAN-MARC PAVELOT** Savigny-lès-Beaune 1993 • $22 • (11/15/95)

85 **JOSEPH DROUHIN** Charmes-Chambertin 1993 • $84 • (11/15/95)

85 **JOSEPH DROUHIN** Pommard Les Epenots 1993 • $35 • (11/15/95)

85 **LALEURE-PIOT** Pernand-Vergelesses Ile des Vergelesses 1993 • $33 • (11/15/95)

85 **LEJEUNE** Pommard Les Poutures 1993 • $31 • (11/15/95)

85 **LÉONARD DE ST.-AUBIN** Pommard 1993 • $27 • (05/15/96)

85 **LOUIS JADOT** Santenay Clos de Malte 1993 • $16 • (11/15/95)

85 **LUCIEN BOILLOT** Nuits-St.-Georges Les Pruliers 1993 • $40 • (11/15/95)

85 **MACHARD DE GRAMONT** Beaune Les Chouacheux 1993 • $28 • (09/15/96)

85 **MACHARD DE GRAMONT** Pommard Clos Blanc 1993 • $40 • (09/15/96)

85 **MICHEL VOARICK** Corton Le Clos du Roi 1993 • $60 • (11/15/95)

85 **MICHEL VOARICK** Pernand-Vergelesses 1993 • $20 • (11/15/95)

85 **MOMMESSIN** Beaune 1993 • $23 • (11/15/95)

85 **MOMMESSIN** Charmes-Chambertin 1993 • $68 • (11/15/95)

85 **MONGEARD-MUGNERET** Hautes Côtes de Nuits 1993 • $17 • (11/15/95)

85 **P. DUBREUIL-FONTAINE PÈRE & FILS** Pernand-Vergelesses 1993 • $NA • (05/15/96)

85 **PARENT** Beaune Les Epenottes 1993 • $57 • (11/15/95)

85 **PRINCE FLORENT DE MÉRODE** Corton Les Renardes 1993 • $37 • (11/15/95)

85 **ROBERT ARNOUX** Pinot Noir Bourgogne 1993 • $18 • (05/15/96)

85 **ROPITEAU FRÈRES** Santenay 1993 • $16 • (11/15/95)

85 **SÉRAFIN PÈRE & FILS** Gevrey-Chambertin Vieilles Vignes 1993 • $55 • (11/15/95)

1990 Red Burgundy
Vintage Rating: 98

99 **COMTE GEORGES DE VOGÜÉ** Bonnes Mares 1990 • $110 Ⓐ • (12/15/92)

99 **COMTE GEORGES DE VOGÜÉ** Musigny Cuvée Vieilles Vignes 1990 • $135 • (02/28/95)

99 **MÉO-CAMUZET** Vosne-Romanée Cros Parantoux 1990 • $81 • (06/15/93)

98 **DOMAINE LEROY** Musigny 1990 • $1073 • (12/15/96)

98 **LEROY** Richebourg 1990 • $299 • (12/15/92)

97 **ANNE & FRANÇOIS GROS** Richebourg 1990 • $130 • (12/15/92)

97 **CHRISTOPHE ROUMIER** Ruchottes-Chambertin 1990 • $80 • (12/15/92)

97 **DANIEL RION** Clos Vougeot 1990 • $100 • (12/15/92)

97 **LEROY** Clos de la Roche 1990 • $289 Ⓐ • (12/15/92)

97 **LEROY** Clos de Vougeot 1990 • $155 Ⓐ • (12/15/92)

Key: SS—Spectator Selection CS—Cellar Selection HR—Highly Recommended BB—Best Buy $NA—Price not available Ⓐ—Auction Price
Dates in parentheses indicate the issues in which the ratings were published.

97 **LEROY** Pommard Les Vignots 1990 • $74 • (12/15/92)

97 **LEROY** Romanée St.-Vivant 1990 • $299 • (12/15/92)

97 **LEROY** Vosne-Romanée Aux Réas 1990 • $58 • (12/15/92)

97 **MÉO-CAMUZET** Richebourg 1990 • $242 • (06/15/93)

97 **ROBERT JAYER-GILLES** Echézeaux du Dessus 1990 • $100 • (12/15/92)

97 **ROBERT JAYER-GILLES** Nuits-St.-Georges Les Poirets 1990 • $48 • (12/15/92)

97 **ROSSIGNOL-TRAPET** Latricières-Chambertin 1990 • $83 • (12/15/92)

96 **ARMAND ROUSSEAU** Ruchottes-Chambertin Clos des Ruchottes 1990 • $80 • (12/15/92)

96 **DOMAINE LEROY** Chambertin 1990 • $481 • (12/15/96)

96 **DOMAINE LEROY** Richebourg 1990 • $575 • (12/15/96)

96 **G. ROUMIER** Bonnes Mares 1990 • $100 • (12/15/92)

96 **GROS FRÈRE & SOEUR** Richebourg 1990 • $51 • (12/15/92)

96 **JOSEPH DROUHIN** Charmes-Chambertin 1990 • $81 • (12/15/92)

96 **LEROY** Chambertin 1990 • $456 Ⓐ • (12/15/92)

96 **LEROY** Latricières-Chambertin 1990 • $204 • (12/15/92)

96 **MOMMESSIN** Charmes-Chambertin 1990 • $45 • (12/15/92)

96 **TOLLOT-BEAUT & FILS** Corton Les Bressandes 1990 • $40 • (02/28/95)

95 **ANNE & FRANÇOIS GROS** Clos Vougeot Le Grand Maupertuis 1990 • $75 • (12/15/92)

95 **ARMAND ROUSSEAU** Chambertin-Clos de Bèze 1990 • $135 • (12/15/92)

95 **COSTE-CAUMARTIN** Pommard Les Boucherottes 1990 • $37 • (12/15/92)

95 **F. CHAUVENET** Clos St.-Denis 1990 • $65 • (12/15/92)

95 **JOSEPH DROUHIN** Musigny 1990 • $129 • (12/15/92)

95 **LEROY** Nuits-St.-Georges Aux Allots 1990 • $67 • (12/15/92)

95 **LEROY** Nuits-St.-Georges Aux Vignerondes 1990 • $100 • (12/15/92)

95 **LEROY** Pommard Trois Follots 1990 • $69 • (12/15/92)

95 **LEROY** Vosne-Romanée Aux Genaivrières 1990 • $61 • (12/15/92)

95 **LEROY** Vosne-Romanée Les Beaux Monts 1990 • $200 Ⓐ • (12/15/92) • HR

95 **MICHEL LAFARGE** Volnay Clos du Château des Ducs 1990 • $75 • (12/15/92)

95 **MOMMESSIN** Clos de Tart 1990 • $96 • (12/15/92)

95 **ROSSIGNOL-TRAPET** Chambertin 1990 • $106 • (12/15/92)

95 **ROSSIGNOL-TRAPET** Chapelle-Chambertin 1990 • $83 • (12/15/92)

94 **A.-F. GROS** Richebourg 1990 • $180 • (12/15/92)

94 **BERTRAND AMBROISE** Corton Le Rognet 1990 • $60 • (12/15/92)

94 **BOUCHARD PÈRE & FILS** Pommard Premier Cru Domaines du Château de Beaune 1990 • $39 • (12/15/92)

94 **CHÂTEAU DE LA TOUR** Clos Vougeot 1990 • $22 Ⓐ • (12/15/92)

94 **CHOPIN-GROFFIER** Clos Vougeot 1990 • $70 • (12/15/92)

94 **COMTE GEORGES DE VOGÜÉ** Chambolle-Musigny Les Amoureuses 1990 • $66 • (12/15/92)

94 **COSTE-CAUMARTIN** Pommard 1990 • $28 • (12/15/92)

94 **COSTE-CAUMARTIN** Pommard Les Fremiers 1990 • $32 • (12/15/92)

94 **DENIS BACHELET** Charmes-Chambertin 1990 • $53 • (12/15/92)

94 **DOMAINE LEROY** Clos de la Roche 1990 • $413 • (12/15/96)

94 **DOMAINE DE LA ROMANÉE-CONTI** Echézeaux 1990 • $182 Ⓐ • (12/31/93) • CS

94 **DOMAINE DE LA ROMANÉE-CONTI** Grands Echézeaux 1990 • $160 • (12/31/93) • CS

94 **F. CHAUVENET** Corton 1990 • $60 • (12/15/92)

94 **GUY CASTAGNIER** Bonnes Mares 1990 • $NA • (12/15/92)

94 **GUY CASTAGNIER** Mazis-Chambertin Mazy-Chambertin 1990 • $NA • (12/15/92)

94 **JEAN GROS** Richebourg 1990 • $150 • (12/15/92)

94 **JEAN-MARC BOILLOT** Pommard Les Jarolières 1990 • $67 • (12/15/92)

94 **JEAN-MARC BOILLOT** Volnay Pitures 1990 • $55 • (12/15/92)

94 **JOSEPH DROUHIN** Griotte-Chambertin 1990 • $84 • (12/15/92)

94 **LEROY** Chambolle-Musigny Les Fremières 1990 • $79 • (12/15/92)

94 **LEROY** Nuits-St.-Georges Aux Lavières 1990 • $59 • (12/15/92)

94 **LEROY** Nuits-St.-Georges Aux Boudots 1990 • $108 • (12/15/92)

94 **MÉO-CAMUZET** Vosne-Romanée Les Chaumes 1990 • $55 • (02/15/93)

94 **MICHEL LAFARGE** Volnay Clos des Chênes 1990 • $75 • (02/28/95)

94 **MORTET & FILS** Clos de Vougeot 1990 • $NA • (12/15/92)

94 **PHILIPPE CHARLOPIN-PARIZOT** Chambertin 1990 • $90 • (08/31/92)

94 **PRINCE FLORENT DE MÉRODE** Corton Les Renardes 1990 • $54 • (12/15/92)

94 **TOLLOT-BEAUT & FILS** Corton 1990 • $56 • (12/15/92)

93 **ARMAND ROUSSEAU** Mazis-Chambertin Mazy-Chambertin 1990 • $75 • (12/15/92)

93 **BOUCHARD PÈRE & FILS** Beaune Les Marconnets Domaines du Château de Beaune 1990 • $28 • (12/15/92)

93 **BRUNO CLAIR** Chambertin-Clos de Bèze 1990 • $70 • (12/15/92)

93 **CHOPIN-GROFFIER** Vougeot 1990 • $44 • (12/15/92)

93 **CHRISTOPHE ROUMIER** Charmes-Chambertin 1990 • $105 • (12/15/92)

93 **COMTE ARMAND** Pommard Clos des Epeneaux 1990 • $57 • (12/15/92)

93 **DANIEL RION** Nuits-St.-Georges Les Argillières 1990 • $52 Ⓐ • (12/15/92)

93 **DANIEL RION** Vosne-Romanée Les Chaumes 1990 • $70 • (02/28/95)

93 **DANIEL SENARD** Corton En Charlemagne 1990 • $NA • (12/15/92)

93 **DANIEL SENARD** Corton Le Clos du Roi 1990 • $55 • (12/15/92)

93 **DANIEL SENARD** Corton Les Meix 1990 • $NA • (12/15/92)

93 **DOMAINE LEROY** Latricières-Chambertin 1990 • $250 • (12/15/96)

93 **DOMAINE DE LA POUSSE D'OR** Volnay Clos de la Bousse d'Or 1990 • $75 • (11/30/92) • CS

93 **DOMAINE DE LA ROMANÉE-CONTI** Romanée-Conti 1990 • $750 • (12/31/93) • CS

93 **GEORGES MUGNERET** Ruchottes-Chambertin 1990 • $78 • (12/15/92)

93 **GHISLAINE BARTHOD** Chambolle-Musigny Aux Beaux Bruns 1990 • $50 • (12/15/92)

93 **GROS FRÈRE & SOEUR** Clos Vougeot Musigny 1990 • $68 Ⓐ • (12/15/92)

93 **GUY CASTAGNIER** Clos St.-Denis 1990 • $NA • (12/15/92)

93 **J. FAIVELEY** Chambertin-Clos de Bèze 1990 • $130 • (12/15/92)

93 **JAFFELIN** Romanée St.-Vivant 1990 • $75 • (12/15/92)

93 **JEAN GROS** Vosne-Romanée Clos des Réas 1990 • $48 • (12/15/92)

93 **JOSEPH DROUHIN** Beaune Clos des Mouches 1990 • $52 • (12/15/92)

93 **JOSEPH DROUHIN** Bonnes Mares 1990 • $91 • (12/15/92)

93 **JOSEPH DROUHIN** Chambolle-Musigny Les Amoureuses 1990 • $80 • (12/15/92)

93 **JOSEPH DROUHIN** Volnay Clos des Chênes 1990 • $42 • (12/15/92)

93 **MÉO-CAMUZET** Vosne-Romanée 1990 • $36 • (02/15/93)

93 **MÉO-CAMUZET** Vosne-Romanée Aux Brûlées 1990 • $81 • (06/15/93)

93 **MORTET & FILS** Gevrey-Chambertin Clos Prieur 1990 • $38 • (12/15/92)

93 **MUGNERET-GIBOURG** Echézeaux 1990 • $66 • (12/15/92)

93 **P. DUBREUIL-FONTAINE PÈRE & FILS** Corton Le Clos du Roi 1990 • $61 • (12/15/92)

93 **PHILIPPE BATACCHI** Clos de la Roche 1990 • $59 • (12/15/92)

93 **PHILIPPE BATACCHI** Morey-St.-Denis Premier Cru 1990 • $44 • (12/15/92)

93 **TOLLOT-BEAUT & FILS** Aloxe-Corton 1990 • $38 • (12/15/92)

92 **ARMAND ROUSSEAU** Chambertin 1990 • $150 • (12/15/92)

92 **ARMAND ROUSSEAU** Clos de la Roche 1990 • $78 • (12/15/92)

92 **BOUCHARD PÈRE & FILS** Volnay Taille Pieds Domaines du Château de Beaune 1990 • $34 Ⓐ • (12/15/92)

92 **BRUNO CLAIR** Gevrey-Chambertin Fonteny 1990 • $45 • (12/15/92)

92 **BRUNO CLAIR** Savigny-lès-Beaune La Dominode 1990 • $32 • (12/15/92)

92 **DANIEL RION** Nuits-St.-Georges Aux Vignerondes 1990 • $70 • (12/15/92)

92 **DANIEL RION** Nuits-St.-Georges Les Grandes Vignes 1990 • $42 • (12/15/92)

92 **DANIEL RION** Vosne-Romanée Les Beaux Monts 1990 • $70 • (12/15/92)

92 **DOMAINE LEROY** Romanée St.-Vivant 1990 • $405 • (12/15/96)

92 **DUJAC** Charmes-Chambertin 1990 • $75 • (12/15/92)

92 **DUJAC** Clos de la Roche 1990 • $83 • (12/15/92)

92 **DUJAC** Gevrey-Chambertin Aux Combottes 1990 • $67 • (12/15/92)

92 **F. CHAUVENET** Clos de Vougeot 1990 • $69 • (12/15/92)

92 **FOREY PÈRE & FILS** Echézeaux 1990 • $65 • (12/15/92)

Red Burgundy

92 **G. ROUMIER** Chambolle-Musigny Les Amoureuses 1990 • $55 • (12/15/92)

92 **G. ROUMIER** Clos Vougeot 1990 • $65 • (12/15/92)

92 **HENRI GOUGES** Nuits-St.-Georges Clos des Porrets St.-Georges 1990 • $58 • (12/15/92)

92 **HENRI GOUGES** Nuits-St.-Georges Les St.-Georges 1990 • $60 • (12/15/92)

92 **HUBERT LIGNIER** Clos de la Roche 1990 • $90 • (12/15/92)

92 **J. FAIVELEY** Clos de Vougeot 1990 • $50 Ⓐ • (12/15/92)

92 **J. FAIVELEY** Gevrey-Chambertin Les Marchais 1990 • $45 • (12/15/92)

92 **J. FAIVELEY** Morey-St.-Denis Clos des Ormes 1990 • $12 Ⓐ • (12/15/92)

92 **JAFFELIN** Charmes-Chambertin 1990 • $55 • (12/15/92)

92 **JEAN-MARC BOILLOT** Beaune Les Montrevenots 1990 • $39 • (12/15/92)

92 **JEAN-MARC BOILLOT** Pommard Les Saussilles 1990 • $48 • (12/15/92)

92 **JEAN-MARC BOILLOT** Volnay 1990 • $40 • (12/15/92)

92 **JEAN-MARC PAVELOT** Savigny-lès-Beaune Aux Guettes 1990 • $33 • (12/15/92)

92 **LEJEUNE** Pommard Les Rugiens 1990 • $49 • (12/15/92)

92 **LEROY** Corton Les Renardes 1990 • $111 • (12/15/92)

92 **LEROY** Gevrey-Chambertin Aux Combottes 1990 • $111 • (12/15/92)

92 **LEROY** Savigny-lès-Beaune Les Narbantons 1990 • $138 Ⓐ • (12/15/92)

92 **LOUIS JADOT** Chambertin-Clos de Bèze 1990 • $105 • (02/28/95)

92 **LOUIS JADOT** Vosne-Romanée 1990 • $30 • (12/15/92)

92 **MOMMESSIN** Volnay Taille Pieds 1990 • $23 • (12/15/92)

92 **OLIVIER LEFLAIVE FRÈRES** Pommard 1990 • $30 • (12/15/92)

92 **OLIVIER LEFLAIVE FRÈRES** Volnay Clos de la Barre 1990 • $36 • (12/15/92)

92 **OLIVIER LEFLAIVE FRÈRES** Volnay Frémiets Premier Cru 1990 • $35 • (12/15/92)

92 **PHILIPPE CHARLOPIN-PARIZOT** Charmes-Chambertin 1990 • $70 • (08/31/92)

92 **PHILIPPE LECLERC** Gevrey-Chambertin Combe au Moine 1990 • $70 • (12/15/92)

92 **PONSOT** Clos de la Roche Cuvée Vieilles Vignes 1990 • $150 • (03/15/93)

92 **ROBERT CHEVILLON** Nuits-St.-Georges Les St.-Georges 1990 • $62 Ⓐ • (02/28/95)

92 **TOLLOT-BEAUT & FILS** Beaune Les Grèves 1990 • $40 • (12/15/92)

91 **BERNARD SERVEAU** Chambolle-Musigny Les Amoureuses 1990 • $68 • (12/15/92)

91 **BERNARD SERVEAU** Nuits-St.-Georges Chaines Carteaux 1990 • $46 • (12/15/92)

91 **BOUCHARD PÈRE & FILS** Corton Le Corton Domaines du Château de Beaune 1990 • $50 • (12/15/92)

91 **CHOPIN-GROFFIER** Nuits-St.-Georges Aux Chaignots 1990 • $40 • (12/15/92)

Key: SS—Spectator Selection CS—Cellar Selection HR—Highly Recommended BB—Best Buy $NA—Price not available Ⓐ—Auction Price
Dates in parentheses indicate the issues in which the ratings were published.

91 **DANIEL RION** Vosne-Romanée 1990 • $42 • (12/15/92)

91 **DENIS BACHELET** Gevrey-Chambertin Vieilles Vignes 1990 • $43 • (12/15/92)

91 **DOMAINE DE LA POUSSE D'OR** Volnay Les Caillerets-Clos des 60 Ouvrées 1990 • $62 • (12/15/92) • HR

91 **DOMAINE DE LA ROMANÉE-CONTI** La Tâche 1990 • $428 Ⓐ • (12/31/93)

91 **DOMAINE DE LA ROMANÉE-CONTI** Richebourg 1990 • $310 Ⓐ • (12/31/93)

91 **DOMAINE TAUPENOT-MERME** Charmes-Chambertin 1990 • $58 • (11/30/94)

91 **DUJAC** Echézeaux 1990 • $88 • (12/15/92)

91 **F. CHAUVENET** Echézeaux 1990 • $62 • (12/15/92)

91 **GEORGES MUGNERET** Clos Vougeot 1990 • $89 • (12/15/92)

91 **GROS FRÈRE & SOEUR** Grands Echézeaux 1990 • $85 • (12/15/92)

91 **HENRI GOUGES** Nuits-St.-Georges Les Vaucrains 1990 • $60 • (12/15/92)

91 **J. CONFURON-COTETIDOT** Echézeaux 1990 • $65 • (12/15/92)

91 **J. CONFURON-COTETIDOT** Nuits-St.-Georges Premier Cru 1990 • $28 • (12/15/92)

91 **J. FAIVELEY** Echézeaux 1990 • $71 Ⓐ • (12/15/92)

91 **J. FAIVELEY** Mazis-Chambertin 1990 • $52 Ⓐ • (12/15/92)

91 **J. FAIVELEY** Nuits-St.-Georges Les Damodes 1990 • $45 • (12/15/92)

91 **JACQUES GERMAIN** Beaune Les Teurons 1990 • $48 • (12/15/92)

91 **JACQUES GERMAIN** Beaune Les Cents Vignes 1990 • $46 • (12/15/92)

91 **JACQUES GERMAIN** Beaune Les Vignes Franches 1990 • $46 • (12/15/92)

91 **JAFFELIN** Gevrey-Chambertin Lavaut St.-Jacques 1990 • $42 • (12/15/92)

91 **JEAN GARAUDET** Pommard Les Charmots 1990 • $48 • (08/31/92)

91 **JOSEPH DROUHIN** Chambertin 1990 • $113 • (12/15/92)

91 **JOSEPH DROUHIN** Clos de Vougeot 1990 • $71 • (12/15/92)

91 **JOSEPH DROUHIN** Echézeaux 1990 • $69 • (12/15/92)

91 **JOSEPH DROUHIN** Gevrey-Chambertin Champeaux 1990 • $70 • (12/15/92)

91 **JOSEPH DROUHIN** Grands Echézeaux 1990 • $100 • (02/28/95)

91 **JOSEPH DROUHIN** Pommard Les Epenots 1990 • $48 • (12/15/92)

91 **LOUIS JADOT** Beaune Clos des Ursules 1990 • $44 • (12/15/92)

91 **LOUIS JADOT** Bonnes Mares 1990 • $75 • (12/15/92)

91 **LOUIS JADOT** Chambolle-Musigny 1990 • $30 • (12/15/92)

91 **LOUIS JADOT** Clos Vougeot 1990 • $55 • (12/15/92)

91 **LOUIS JADOT** Griotte-Chambertin 1990 • $70 • (12/15/92)

91 **MÉO-CAMUZET** Nuits-St.-Georges Aux Boudots 1990 • $68 • (02/15/93)

91 **MOILLARD** Beaune Les Grèves Domaine Thomas-Moillard 1990 • $40 • (12/15/92)

91 **MOMMESSIN** Aloxe-Corton 1990 • $20 • (12/15/92)

91 **MOMMESSIN** Vosne-Romanée Les Suchots 1990 • $35 • (12/15/92)

91 **MORTET & FILS** Gevrey-Chambertin Champeaux 1990 • $45 • (12/15/92)

91 **OLIVIER LEFLAIVE FRÈRES** Pommard Les Rugiens 1990 • $35 • (12/15/92)

91 **P. DUBREUIL-FONTAINE PÈRE & FILS** Pommard Les Epenots 1990 • $59 • (12/15/92)

91 **PHILIPPE BATACCHI** Gevrey-Chambertin Les Evosselles 1990 • $32 Ⓐ • (12/15/92)

91 **PHILIPPE LECLERC** Gevrey-Chambertin Champeaux 1990 • $50 • (12/15/92)

91 **PONSOT** Morey-St.-Denis 1990 • $68 • (03/15/93)

91 **ROSSIGNOL-TRAPET** Beaune Teurons 1990 • $46 • (12/15/92)

91 **SÉRAFIN PÈRE & FILS** Gevrey-Chambertin Les Cazetiers 1990 • $56 • (12/15/92)

90 **A.-F. GROS** Echézeaux 1990 • $90 • (12/15/92)

90 **ALAIN BURGUET** Gevrey-Chambertin Vieilles Vignes 1990 • $43 • (12/15/92)

90 **ARMAND ROUSSEAU** Gevrey-Chambertin Le Clos St.-Jacques 1990 • $85 • (12/15/92)

90 **BERTRAND AMBROISE** Nuits-St.-Georges Les Vaucrains 1990 • $44 Ⓐ • (12/15/92)

90 **BERTRAND AMBROISE** Nuits-St.-Georges Rue de Chaux 1990 • $48 • (12/15/92)

90 **BOUCHARD PÈRE & FILS** Volnay Caillerets Ancienne Cuvée Carnot Domaines du Château de Beaune 1990 • $37 • (12/15/92)

90 **BOURÉE PÈRE & FILS** Clos de la Roche 1990 • $70 • (12/15/92)

90 **BOURÉE PÈRE & FILS** Gevrey-Chambertin Le Clos St.-Jacques 1990 • $60 • (12/15/92)

90 **BRUNO CLAIR** Morey-St.-Denis En la Rue de Vergy 1990 • $37 • (12/15/92)

90 **COMTE GEORGES DE VOGÜÉ** Chambolle-Musigny 1990 • $45 • (12/15/92)

90 **DANIEL RION** Nuits-St.-Georges Les Pruliers 1990 • $70 • (12/15/92)

90 **DOMAINE TAUPENOT-MERME** Chambolle-Musigny 1990 • $22 • (11/30/94) • HR

90 **DOMAINE DE LA ROMANÉE-CONTI** Romanée St.-Vivant 1990 • $175 • (12/31/93)

90 **DUJAC** Clos St.-Denis 1990 • $83 • (12/15/92)

90 **F. CHAUVENET** Gevrey-Chambertin Lavaut St.-Jacques 1990 • $56 • (12/15/92)

90 **F. CHAUVENET** Nuits-St.-Georges Les Pruliers 1990 • $52 • (12/15/92)

90 **GHISLAINE BARTHOD** Chambolle-Musigny Les Charmes 1990 • $50 • (12/15/92)

90 **GHISLAINE BARTHOD** Chambolle-Musigny Les Véroilles 1990 • $50 • (12/15/92)

90 **GUY CASTAGNIER** Clos de la Roche 1990 • $NA • (12/15/92)

90 **HENRI GOUGES** Nuits-St.-Georges Les Pruliers 1990 • $58 • (12/15/92)

90 **J. FAIVELEY** Corton Clos des Cortons 1990 • $86 • (12/15/92)

90 **J. FAIVELEY** Pommard Les Chaponnières 1990 • $65 • (12/15/92)

90 **J. FAIVELEY** Nuits-St.-Georges Aux Chaignots 1990 • $48 • (12/15/92)

90 **J. FAIVELEY** Nuits-St.-Georges Clos de la Maréchale 1990 • $36 Ⓐ • (11/30/92) • HR

90 **J. FAIVELEY** Nuits-St.-Georges Porrets St.-Georges 1990 • $45 • (12/15/92)

90 **JAFFELIN** Beaune Champs Pimont 1990 • $25 • (12/15/92)

90 **JEAN-MICHEL GAUNOUX** Volnay Clos des Chênes 1990 • $NA • (12/15/92)

90 **JOSEPH DROUHIN** Volnay 1990 • $33 • (12/15/92)

90 **JOSEPH DROUHIN** Vosne-Romanée Les Petits Monts 1990 • $NA • (12/15/92)

90 **LALEURE-PIOT** Corton Les Bressandes 1990 • $NA • (12/15/92)

90 **LALEURE-PIOT** Pernand-Vergelesses Ile des Vergelesses 1990 • $NA • (12/15/92)

90 **LOUIS JADOT** Corton Les Pougets 1990 • $50 • (12/15/92)

90 **LOUIS JADOT** Gevrey-Chambertin Le Clos St.-Jacques 1990 • $48 • (12/15/92)

90 **LOUIS JADOT** Mazis-Chambertin 1990 • $70 • (12/15/92)

90 **LOUIS JADOT** Pommard Les Arvelets 1990 • $42 • (12/15/92)

90 **LUCIEN BOILLOT** Volnay Les Brouillards 1990 • $32 • (12/15/92)

90 **MÉO-CAMUZET** Nuits-St.-Georges Aux Murgers 1990 • $68 • (02/15/93)

90 **MICHEL LAFARGE** Volnay 1990 • $43 • (12/15/92)

90 **MOILLARD** Morey-St.-Denis Monts Luisants 1990 • $33 • (12/15/92)

90 **MOMMESSIN** Beaune Les Cents Vignes 1990 • $20 • (12/15/92)

90 **MOMMESSIN** Gevrey-Chambertin Lavaut St.-Jacques 1990 • $45 • (12/15/92)

90 **MOMMESSIN** Nuits-St.-Georges Aux Chaignots 1990 • $29 • (12/15/92)

90 **MOMMESSIN** Savigny-lès-Beaune 1990 • $14 • (12/15/92)

90 **MORTET & FILS** Chambolle-Musigny Aux Beaux Bruns 1990 • $45 • (12/15/92)

90 **MORTET & FILS** Gevrey-Chambertin 1990 • $NA • (12/15/92)

90 **OLIVIER LEFLAIVE FRÈRES** Pommard Les Epenots 1990 • $35 • (12/15/92)

90 **PAUL PERNOT** Beaune Les Teurons 1990 • $33 • (04/30/92)

90 **PHILIPPE BATACCHI** Gevrey-Chambertin Les Jeunes Rois 1990 • $38 • (12/15/92)

90 **PHILIPPE CHARLOPIN-PARIZOT** Gevrey-Chambertin Cuvée Vieilles Vignes 1990 • $40 • (04/30/92)

90 **PHILIPPE LECLERC** Gevrey-Chambertin La Platière 1990 • $35 • (12/15/92)

90 **PRINCE FLORENT DE MÉRODE** Corton Le Clos du Roi 1990 • $38 • (12/15/92)

90 **PRINCE FLORENT DE MÉRODE** Pommard La Platière 1990 • $48 • (12/15/92)

90 **ROBERT JAYER-GILLES** Côte de Nuits-Villages 1990 • $34 • (12/15/92)

90 **ROSSIGNOL-TRAPET** Gevrey-Chambertin Petite Chapelle 1990 • $21 Ⓐ • (12/15/92)

90 **SIMON BIZE & FILS** Savigny-lès-Beaune Aux Vergelesses 1990 • $29 • (12/15/92)

90 **SIMON BIZE & FILS** Savigny-lès-Beaune Les Marconnets 1990 • $33 • (12/15/92)

90 **TOLLOT-BEAUT & FILS** Beaune Clos du Roi 1990 • $48 • (12/15/92)

90 **TOLLOT-BEAUT & FILS** Savigny-lès-Beaune Les Lavières 1990 • $35 • (12/15/92)

89 **ALAIN BURGUET** Gevrey-Chambertin 1990 • $NA • (12/15/92)

89 **BERTAGNA** Nuits-St.-Georges Aux Murgers 1990 • $NA • (12/15/92)

89 **BERTRAND AMBROISE** Nuits-St.-Georges 1990 • $38 • (12/15/92)

89 **BOUCHARD PÈRE & FILS** Echézeaux 1990 • $42 • (10/31/92)

89 **BRUNO CLAIR** Gevrey-Chambertin Les Cazetiers 1990 • $55 • (12/15/92)

89 **CHÂTEAU DES HERBEAUX** Chambertin 1990 • $75 • (02/15/93)

89 **CHOPIN-GROFFIER** Nuits-St.-Georges 1990 • $43 • (12/15/92)

89 **EDMOND CORNU** Corton Les Bressandes 1990 • $60 • (12/15/92)

89 **F. CHAUVENET** Beaune Les Grèves 1990 • $35 • (12/15/92)

89 **F. CHAUVENET** Gevrey-Chambertin Estournelles St.-Jacques 1990 • $56 • (12/15/92)

89 **G. ROUMIER** Morey-St.-Denis Clos de la Bussière 1990 • $53 • (12/15/92)

89 **GUY CASTAGNIER** Charmes-Chambertin 1990 • $NA • (12/15/92)

89 **GUY CASTAGNIER** Latricières-Chambertin 1990 • $NA • (12/15/92)

89 **J. FAIVELEY** Chambolle-Musigny Les Fuées 1990 • $36 Ⓐ • (12/15/92)

89 **J. FAIVELEY** Gevrey-Chambertin Les Cazetiers 1990 • $49 • (12/15/92)

89 **JACQUES GERMAIN** Beaune Aux Cras 1990 • $46 • (12/15/92)

89 **JACQUES GERMAIN** Beaune Les Boucherottes 1990 • $42 • (12/15/92)

89 **JAFFELIN** Pommard 1990 • $30 • (12/15/92)

89 **JEAN-MARC PAVELOT** Savigny-lès-Beaune 1990 • $22 • (12/15/92)

89 **JOSEPH DROUHIN** Clos de la Roche 1990 • $69 • (12/15/92)

89 **LALEURE-PIOT** Pernand-Vergelesses Les Vergelesses 1990 • $NA • (12/15/92)

89 **LOUIS LATOUR** Corton Château Corton Grancey 1990 • $43 • (12/15/92)

89 **LOUIS LATOUR** Romanée St.-Vivant Les Quatre Journaux 1990 • $139 • (12/15/92)

89 **MACHARD DE GRAMONT** Nuits-St.-Georges Les Damodes 1990 • $48 • (05/31/95)

89 **MÉO-CAMUZET** Corton Le Rognet 1990 • $68 • (06/15/93)

89 **MOILLARD** Corton Clos des Vergennes 1990 • $53 • (12/15/92)

89 **P. DUBREUIL-FONTAINE PÈRE & FILS** Corton Les Bressandes 1990 • $59 • (12/15/92)

89 **PARENT** Pommard Les Epenots 1990 • $NA • (12/15/92)

89 **PHILIPPE CHARLOPIN-PARIZOT** Clos St.-Denis 1990 • $76 • (08/31/92)

89 **PIERRE GUILLEMOT** Savigny-lès-Beaune Aux Serpentières 1990 • $24 • (12/15/92)

89 **PIERRE LABET** Beaune Les Monsnières 1990 • $30 • (12/15/92)

89 **SÉRAFIN PÈRE & FILS** Gevrey-Chambertin 1990 • $45 • (12/15/92)

Key: SS—Spectator Selection CS—Cellar Selection HR—Highly Recommended BB—Best Buy $NA—Price not available Ⓐ—Auction Price

Dates in parentheses indicate the issues in which the ratings were published.

89 **SIMON BIZE & FILS** Savigny-lès-Beaune Aux Fournaux 1990 • $28 • (12/15/92)

88 **BERNARD SERVEAU** Chambolle-Musigny Les Sentiers 1990 • $35 • (12/15/92)

88 **BOUCHARD PÈRE & FILS** Aloxe-Corton Domaines du Château de Beaune 1990 • $30 • (12/15/92)

88 **BOUCHARD PÈRE & FILS** Beaune Les Grèves Vigne de l'Enfant Jésus Domaines du Château de Beaune 1990 • $55 • (02/28/95)

88 **BOUCHARD PÈRE & FILS** Chambertin Domaines du Château de Beaune 1990 • $NA • (12/15/92)

88 **CHÂTEAU DE POMMARD** Pommard 1990 • $60 • (12/15/92)

88 **COSTE-CAUMARTIN** Bourgogne 1990 • $16 • (12/15/92)

88 **DANIEL SENARD** Corton Les Bressandes 1990 • $NA • (12/15/92)

88 **DOMAINE DU CLOS FRANTIN** Echézeaux 1990 • $42 • (11/30/92)

88 **DOMAINE TAUPENOT-MERME** Morey-St.-Denis 1990 • $22 • (11/30/94)

88 **FRANÇOIS LEGROS** Chambolle-Musigny Les Noirots 1990 • $40 • (03/15/93)

88 **FRANÇOIS LEGROS** Nuits-St.-Georges Les Perrières 1990 • $39 • (03/15/93)

88 **G. ROUMIER** Chambolle-Musigny 1990 • $28 • (12/15/92)

88 **GEORGES MUGNERET** Nuits-St.-Georges Aux Chaignots 1990 • $45 • (12/15/92)

88 **HENRI GOUGES** Nuits-St.-Georges 1990 • $40 • (12/15/92)

88 **HENRI GOUGES** Nuits-St.-Georges Les Vaucrains Premier Cru 1990 • $60 • (12/31/94)

88 **HUBERT LIGNIER** Morey-St.-Denis Premier Cru 1990 • $36 • (12/15/92)

88 **JAFFELIN** Monthélie 1990 • $17 • (12/15/92)

88 **JEAN GARAUDET** Pommard Les Noizons 1990 • $40 • (08/31/92)

88 **JEAN-MARC BOILLOT** Bourgogne 1990 • $19 • (12/15/92)

88 **JOSEPH DROUHIN** Aloxe-Corton 1990 • $33 • (12/15/92)

88 **JOSEPH DROUHIN** Beaune Hospices de Beaune Cuvée Maurice Drouhin 1990 • $NA • (12/15/92)

88 **JOSEPH DROUHIN** Chambolle-Musigny Les Hauts Doix 1990 • $53 • (12/15/92)

88 **JOSEPH DROUHIN** Corton 1990 • $58 • (12/15/92)

88 **JOSEPH DROUHIN** Gevrey-Chambertin 1990 • $36 • (12/15/92)

88 **JOSEPH DROUHIN** Morey-St.-Denis 1990 • $33 • (12/15/92)

88 **JOSEPH DROUHIN** Nuits-St.-Georges Aux Boudots 1990 • $57 • (12/15/92)

88 **LEJEUNE** Pommard Les Argillières 1990 • $40 • (12/15/92)

88 **LEROY** Nuits-St.-Georges Au Bas de Combe 1990 • $58 • (12/15/92)

88 **LOUIS JADOT** Pernand-Vergelesses Clos de la Croix de Pierre 1990 • $18 • (12/15/92)

88 **LOUIS JADOT** Savigny-lès-Beaune La Dominode 1990 • $23 • (12/15/92)

88 **LOUIS JADOT** Vosne-Romanée Les Suchots 1990 • $49 • (12/15/92)

88 **LOUIS LATOUR** Pommard Les Epenots 1990 • $37 • (02/28/95)

88 **LUCIEN BOILLOT** Gevrey-Chambertin Les Corbeaux 1990 • $33 • (12/15/92)

88 **MÉO-CAMUZET** Nuits-St.-Georges 1990 • $38 • (02/15/93)

88 **MOILLARD** Savigny-lès-Beaune Domaine Thomas-Moillard 1990 • $20 • (12/15/92)

88 **P. DUBREUIL-FONTAINE PÈRE & FILS** Pernand-Vergelesses Ile des Vergelesses 1990 • $37 • (12/15/92)

88 **PHILIPPE BATACCHI** Côte de Nuits-Villages 1990 • $20 • (12/15/92)

88 **PIERRE BITOUZET** Aloxe-Corton Les Valozières 1990 • $NA • (12/15/92)

88 **PIERRE BITOUZET** Savigny-lès-Beaune Les Lavières 1990 • $NA • (12/15/92)

88 **PIERRE LABET** Beaune Aux Coucherias 1990 • $35 • (12/15/92)

88 **PRINCE FLORENT DE MÉRODE** Ladoix Les Chaillots 1990 • $23 • (12/15/92)

87 **A. & P. DE VILLAINE** Bouzeron La Digoine Red 1990 • $16 • (11/30/92)

87 **DOMAINE DE L'ARLOT** Nuits-St.-Georges Clos des Forêts St.-Georges 1990 • $49 • (12/15/92)

87 **DUJAC** Morey-St.-Denis 1990 • $41 • (12/15/92)

87 **F. CHAUVENET** Clos de la Roche 1990 • $76 • (12/15/92)

87 **F. CHAUVENET** Monthélie Les Champs Fulliot 1990 • $NA • (12/15/92)

87 **F. CHAUVENET** Pommard Les Chanlins 1990 • $59 • (12/15/92)

87 **FRANÇOIS LEGROS** Nuits-St.-Georges Aux Bousselots 1990 • $39 • (03/15/93)

87 **FRANÇOIS LEGROS** Vougeot Les Crâs 1990 • $45 • (03/15/93)

87 **GHISLAINE BARTHOD** Chambolle-Musigny 1990 • $25 • (12/15/92)

87 **GHISLAINE BARTHOD** Chambolle-Musigny Les Cras 1990 • $50 • (12/15/92)

87 **GUY CASTAGNIER** Chambolle-Musigny 1990 • $NA • (12/15/92)

87 **GUY CASTAGNIER** Clos de Vougeot 1990 • $NA • (12/15/92)

87 **GUY CASTAGNIER** Gevrey-Chambertin 1990 • $NA • (12/15/92)

87 **HENRI PERROT-MINOT** Morey-St.-Denis En la Rue de Vergy 1990 • $25 • (03/15/94)

87 **JAFFELIN** Beaune Les Bressandes 1990 • $27 • (12/15/92)

87 **JEAN GARAUDET** Beaune Le Clos des Mouches 1990 • $35 • (08/31/92)

87 **JEAN-LUC DUBOIS** Chorey-lès-Beaune 1990 • $30 • (06/15/93)

87 **JOSEPH DROUHIN** Chambolle-Musigny 1990 • $36 • (12/15/92)

87 **JOSEPH DROUHIN** Pernand-Vergelesses 1990 • $21 • (12/15/92)

87 **LOUIS JADOT** Beaune Les Avaux 1990 • $28 • (12/15/92)

87 **LOUIS JADOT** Côte de Beaune-Villages 1990 • $15 • (12/15/92)

87 **LOUIS JADOT** Santenay Clos de Malte 1990 • $18 • (12/15/92)

87 **LOUIS JADOT** Volnay 1990 • $28 • (12/15/92)

87 **LOUIS LATOUR** Beaune Domaine Latour 1990 • $21 • (12/15/92)

87 **LUCIEN BOILLOT** Volnay Les Angles 1990 • $32 • (12/15/92)

87 **MARIUS DELARCHE PÈRE & FILS** Corton Les Renardes 1990 • $49 • (06/15/93)

87 **MARIUS DELARCHE PÈRE & FILS** Pernand-Vergelesses Ile des Vergelesses 1990 • $28 • (06/15/93)

87 **MOILLARD** Beaune 1990 • $26 • (12/15/92)

87 **MORTET & FILS** Bourgogne Les Charmes au Châtelain 1990 • $NA • (12/15/92)

87 **MUSSY** Beaune Les Montrevenots 1990 • $45 • (12/15/92)

87 **PHILIPPE BATACCHI** Fixin 1990 • $23 • (12/15/92)

87 **SÉRAFIN PÈRE & FILS** Gevrey-Chambertin Fonteny 1990 • $63 • (12/15/92)

87 **SÉRAFIN PÈRE & FILS** Gevrey-Chambertin Vieilles Vignes 1990 • $50 • (12/15/92)

87 **SIMON BIZE & FILS** Savigny-lès-Beaune Aux Grands Liards 1990 • $22 • (12/15/92)

87 **SIMON BIZE & FILS** Bourgogne Les Perrières 1990 • $17 • (12/15/92)

87 **YVON CLERGET** Volnay Premier Cru 1990 • $37 • (12/15/92)

86 **ALAIN GRAS** St.-Romain Red 1990 • $24 • (12/15/92)

86 **ALBERT MOROT** Beaune Les Bressandes 1990 • $38 • (12/15/92)

86 **BOUCHARD PÈRE & FILS** Chambolle-Musigny 1990 • $NA • (12/15/92)

86 **BOUCHARD PÈRE & FILS** Volnay Frémiets-Clos de la Rougeotte Domaines du Château de Beaune 1990 • $NA • (12/15/92)

86 **BOUCHARD PÈRE & FILS** Nuits-St.-Georges Les Argillières 1990 • $31 • (12/15/92)

86 **DOMAINE DU CLOS FRANTIN** Vosne-Romanée Aux Malconsorts 1990 • $37 • (11/30/92)

86 **F. CHAUVENET** Pommard 1990 • $45 • (12/15/92)

86 **F. CHAUVENET** Volnay Clos de Chênes 1990 • $58 • (12/15/92)

86 **FRÉDÉRIC ESMONIN** Ruchottes-Chambertin 1990 • $71 • (10/31/92)

86 **GEISWELLER & FILS** Bourgogne 1990 • $NA • (12/15/92)

86 **GROS FRÈRE & SOEUR** Côte de Nuits-Villages 1990 • $18 • (12/15/92)

86 **HENRI PERROT-MINOT** Morey-St.-Denis La Riotte 1990 • $40 • (12/31/93)

86 **HUBERT LIGNIER** Morey-St.-Denis 1990 • $36 • (12/15/92)

86 **JAFFELIN** Clos de Vougeot 1990 • $55 • (12/15/92)

86 **JEAN-NOËL GAGNARD** Chassagne-Montrachet Morgeot Red 1990 • $25 • (02/15/93)

86 **JOSEPH DROUHIN** Vosne-Romanée Les Suchots 1990 • $58 • (12/15/92)

86 **LABOURÉ-ROI** Nuits-St.-Georges 1990 • $20 • (06/15/93)

86 **LEROY** Bourgogne Leroy 1990 • $18 • (12/15/92)

86 **LOUIS JADOT** Monthélie 1990 • $18 • (12/15/92)

86 **LOUIS LATOUR** Bourgogne Cuvée Latour 1990 • $11 • (12/15/92)

86 **LUCIEN BOILLOT** Bourgogne 1990 • $14 • (12/15/92)

86 **MÉO-CAMUZET** Bourgogne Passe-tout-grains 1990 • $17 • (03/31/92)

86 **MOILLARD** Pommard Les Rugiens 1990 • $50 • (12/15/92)

86 **MOMMESSIN** Chambolle-Musigny 1990 • $22 • (12/15/92)

86 **MOMMESSIN** Santenay Clos Rousseau 1990 • $14 • (12/15/92)

86 **MORTET & FILS** Chambertin 1990 • $92 • (12/15/92)

86 **MUGNERET-GIBOURG** Bourgogne 1990 • $18 • (12/15/92)

86 **MUSSY** Pommard Les Epenots 1990 • $50 • (12/15/92)

86 **PIERRE PONNELLE** Bonnes Mares 1990 • $56 • (01/01/94)

86 **PIERRE PONNELLE** Clos de Vougeot 1990 • $48 • (01/01/94)

86 **PRIEUR-BRUNET** Beaune Clos du Roi 1990 • $32 • (02/15/93)

86 **PRINCE FLORENT DE MÉRODE** Aloxe-Corton Premier Cru 1990 • $37 • (12/15/92)

86 **PRINCE FLORENT DE MÉRODE** Corton Les Maréchaudes 1990 • $49 • (12/15/92)

86 **SIMON BIZE & FILS** Savigny-lès-Beaune Aux Guettes 1990 • $33 • (12/15/92)

86 **TOLLOT-BEAUT & FILS** Chorey-Côte de Beaune 1990 • $26 • (12/15/92)

86 **YVON CLERGET** Volnay Les Caillerets 1990 • $45 • (12/15/92)

85 **ALAIN GRAS** Auxey-Duresses Red 1990 • $29 • (12/15/92)

85 **ALBERT MOROT** Beaune Les Teurons 1990 • $39 • (12/15/92)

85 **BERNARD MOREY** Chassagne-Montrachet Red 1990 • $28 • (06/15/93)

85 **BERNARD SERVEAU** Chambolle-Musigny Les Chabiots 1990 • $35 • (12/15/92)

85 **BERTAGNA** Vougeot Clos de la Perrière 1990 • $NA • (12/15/92)

85 **BOUCHARD PÈRE & FILS** Vosne-Romanée Aux Raignots Château de Vosne-Romanée 1990 • $53 • (12/15/92)

85 **DANIEL RION** Côte de Nuits-Villages 1990 • $25 • (12/15/92)

85 **EDMOND CORNU** Bourgogne 1990 • $15 • (12/15/92)

85 **F. CHAUVENET** Chambolle-Musigny 1990 • $45 • (12/15/92)

85 **FOREY PÈRE & FILS** Vosne-Romanée 1990 • $30 • (12/15/92)

85 **GUY CASTAGNIER** Morey-St.-Denis 1990 • $NA • (12/15/92)

85 **J. FAIVELEY** Bourgogne 1990 • $11 • (12/15/92)

85 **J. FAIVELEY** Nuits-St.-Georges 1990 • $36 • (12/15/92)

85 **JACQUES GERMAIN** Chorey-Côte de Beaune Château de Chorey-lès-Beaune 1990 • $24 • (12/15/92)

85 **JAFFELIN** Chassagne-Montrachet Red 1990 • $16 • (12/15/92)

85 **JAFFELIN** Pernand-Vergelesses 1990 • $16 • (12/15/92)

85 **JAFFELIN** Santenay 1990 • $16 • (12/15/92)

85 **JAFFELIN** Volnay 1990 • $24 • (12/15/92)

85 **JEAN CHARTRON** Bourgogne Clos de la Combe 1990 • $11 • (03/31/92)

85 **JEAN GARAUDET** Monthélie 1990 • $25 • (08/31/92)

85 **JEAN GROS** Nuits-St.-Georges 1990 • $30 • (12/15/92)

85 **LABOURÉ-ROI** Charmes-Chambertin 1990 • $45 • (06/15/93)

85 **LABOURÉ-ROI** Pommard 1990 • $20 • (06/15/93)

85 **LEJEUNE** Bourgogne 1990 • $18 • (12/15/92)

Key: SS—Spectator Selection CS—Cellar Selection HR—Highly Recommended BB—Best Buy $NA—Price not available Ⓐ—Auction Price

Dates in parentheses indicate the issues in which the ratings were published.

85 **LOUIS JADOT** Fixin 1990 • $15 • (12/15/92)

85 **LOUIS JADOT** Nuits-St.-Georges Clos des Corvées 1990 • $36 • (12/15/92)

85 **LUCIEN BOILLOT** Gevrey-Chambertin Cherbaudes 1990 • $35 • (12/15/92)

85 **MÉO-CAMUZET** Bourgogne 1990 • $20 • (06/15/93)

85 **MICHEL GROS** Côte de Nuits-Villages 1990 • $NA • (12/15/92)

85 **MOILLARD** Fixin Clos de la Perrière 1990 • $30 • (12/15/92)

85 **MOILLARD** Gevrey-Chambertin 1990 • $33 • (12/15/92)

85 **OLIVIER LEFLAIVE FRÈRES** Chassagne-Montrachet Red 1990 • $17 • (12/15/92)

85 **OLIVIER LEFLAIVE FRÈRES** Santenay Les Gravières 1990 • $17 • (12/15/92)

85 **PARENT** Beaune Les Epenottes 1990 • $NA • (12/15/92)

85 **PHILIPPE LECLERC** Gevrey-Chambertin Les Cazetiers 1990 • $65 • (12/15/92)

85 **PRIEUR-BRUNET** Pommard La Platière 1990 • $40 • (02/15/93)

85 **PRIEUR-BRUNET** Volnay-Santenots 1990 • $35 • (02/15/93)

85 **PRIEURÉ-ROCH** Vosne-Romanée Les Clous 1990 • $30 • (06/15/93)

85 **PRINCE FLORENT DE MÉRODE** Corton Les Bressandes 1990 • $54 • (12/15/92)

85 **SIMON BIZE & FILS** Savigny-lès-Beaune 1990 • $20 • (12/15/92)

1989 Red Burgundy
Vintage Rating: 93

98 **JEAN GROS** Richebourg 1989 • $173 Ⓐ • (01/31/92)

97 **A.-F. GROS** Richebourg 1989 • $130 • (01/31/92)

97 **DOMAINE DE LA ROMANÉE-CONTI** Romanée-Conti 1989 • $850 • (10/31/92)

97 **MÉO-CAMUZET** Richebourg 1989 • $270 • (11/15/91)

96 **G. ROUMIER** Musigny 1989 • $95 • (01/31/92)

96 **LEROY** Pommard Les Vignots 1989 • $60 Ⓐ • (01/31/92)

96 **LEROY** Richebourg 1989 • $287 Ⓐ • (01/31/92)

95 **DOMAINE DU CLOS FRANTIN** Richebourg 1989 • $117 • (01/31/92)

95 **GROS FRÈRE & SOEUR** Richebourg 1989 • $81 • (01/31/92)

95 **J. FAIVELEY** Mazis-Chambertin 1989 • $46 Ⓐ • (01/31/92)

95 **LEROY** Clos de Vougeot 1989 • $173 Ⓐ • (01/31/92)

95 **LEROY** Corton Les Renardes 1989 • $117 • (01/31/92)

95 **LEROY** Nuits-St.-Georges Aux Boudots 1989 • $117 • (01/31/92)

95 **LEROY** Romanée St.-Vivant 1989 • $197 Ⓐ • (01/31/92)

95 **MÉO-CAMUZET** Vosne-Romanée Cros Parantoux 1989 • $91 • (11/15/91)

94 **BERTRAND AMBROISE** Nuits-St.-Georges Les Vaucrains 1989 • $38 • (01/31/92)

94 **BOUCHARD PÈRE & FILS** Volnay Caillerets Ancienne Cuvée Carnot Domaines du Château de Beaune 1989 • $52 • (02/29/92) • CS

94 **BOURÉE PÈRE & FILS** Clos de la Roche 1989 • $65 • (01/31/92)

94 **CHARLES MORTET** Chambertin 1989 • $68 • (01/31/92)

94 **CHOPIN-GROFFIER** Clos Vougeot 1989 • $72 • (01/31/92)

94 **CHRISTOPHE ROUMIER** Ruchottes-Chambertin 1989 • $70 • (01/31/92)

94 **COMTE GEORGES DE VOGÜÉ** Bonnes Mares 1989 • $93 • (01/31/92)

94 **EMMANUEL ROUGET** Vosne-Romanée Cros Parantoux 1989 • $83 • (11/15/91)

94 **F. CHAUVENET** Pommard Les Epenots 1989 • $45 • (01/31/92)

94 **JAFFELIN** Clos St.-Denis 1989 • $53 • (01/31/92)

94 **LEROY** Chambolle-Musigny Les Fremières 1989 • $80 • (01/31/92)

94 **LEROY** Clos de la Roche 1989 • $148 Ⓐ • (01/31/92)

94 **LEROY** Vosne-Romanée Les Brûlées 1989 • $111 Ⓐ • (01/31/92)

94 **MÉO-CAMUZET** Clos de Vougeot 1989 • $91 • (11/15/91) • CS

94 **MÉO-CAMUZET** Nuits-St.-Georges Aux Murgers 1989 • $81 • (11/15/91)

94 **MÉO-CAMUZET** Vosne-Romanée Aux Brûlées 1989 • $91 • (11/15/91)

94 **MICHEL LAFARGE** Volnay Clos du Château des Ducs 1989 • $67 • (01/31/92)

94 **MONGEARD-MUGNERET** Vosne-Romanée Les Orveaux 1989 • $43 • (01/31/92)

94 **ROBERT JAYER-GILLES** Echézeaux 1989 • $101 • (01/31/92)

94 **TOLLOT-BEAUT & FILS** Corton Les Bressandes 1989 • $58 • (02/28/95)

93 **ARMAND ROUSSEAU** Chambertin-Clos de Bèze 1989 • $104 Ⓐ • (01/31/92)

93 **BERNARD SERVEAU** Chambolle-Musigny Les Sentiers 1989 • $30 • (01/31/92)

93 **BERTRAND AMBROISE** Corton Le Rognet 1989 • $45 • (01/31/92)

93 **BOUCHARD PÈRE & FILS** Vosne-Romanée Aux Raignots Château de Vosne-Romanée 1989 • $55 • (01/31/92)

93 **CHOPIN-GROFFIER** Nuits-St.-Georges Aux Chaignots 1989 • $40 • (01/31/92)

93 **COMTE GEORGES DE VOGÜÉ** Chambolle-Musigny Les Amoureuses 1989 • $93 • (01/31/92)

93 **COMTE GEORGES DE VOGÜÉ** Musigny Cuvée Vieilles Vignes 1989 • $134 • (02/28/95)

93 **DANIEL RION** Nuits-St.-Georges Aux Vignerondes 1989 • $63 • (01/31/92)

93 **DOMAINE DE LA ROMANÉE-CONTI** Grands Echézeaux 1989 • $111 Ⓐ • (10/31/92) • HR

93 **DOMAINE DU CLOS FRANTIN** Echézeaux 1989 • $45 • (01/31/92)

93 **F. CHAUVENET** Corton 1989 • $50 • (01/31/92)

93 **G. ROUMIER** Bonnes Mares 1989 • $46 Ⓐ • (01/31/92)

93 **GUY CASTAGNIER** Latricières-Chambertin 1989 • $62 • (01/31/92)

93 **GUY CASTAGNIER** Mazis-Chambertin Mazy-Chambertin 1989 • $62 • (01/31/92)

93 **JEAN GRIVOT** Richebourg 1989 • $178 Ⓐ • (01/31/92)

93 **JOSEPH DROUHIN** Bonnes Mares 1989 • $99 • (01/31/92)

93 **LEROY** Chambertin 1989 • $264 Ⓐ • (01/31/92)

93 **LEROY** Gevrey-Chambertin Aux Combottes 1989 • $68 Ⓐ • (01/31/92)

93 **LEROY** Latricières-Chambertin 1989 • $151 Ⓐ • (01/31/92)

93 **LOUIS JADOT** Corton Les Pougets 1989 • $64 • (01/31/92)

93 **LOUIS LATOUR** Bonnes Mares 1989 • $60 • (01/31/92)

93 **LOUIS LATOUR** Romanée St.-Vivant Les Quatre Journaux 1989 • $140 • (01/31/92)

93 **MÉO-CAMUZET** Corton 1989 • $76 • (11/15/91)

93 **MICHEL LAFARGE** Volnay Clos des Chênes 1989 • $67 • (02/28/95)

93 **MOILLARD** Vosne-Romanée Aux Malconsorts Domaine Thomas-Moillard 1989 • $60 • (01/31/92)

93 **MONGEARD-MUGNERET** Echézeaux Vieille Vigne 1989 • $43 Ⓐ • (01/31/92)

93 **MONGEARD-MUGNERET** Grands Echézeaux 1989 • $82 Ⓐ • (01/31/92)

93 **MONGEARD-MUGNERET** Vougeot Les Crâs 1989 • $NA • (01/31/92)

93 **OLIVIER LEFLAIVE FRÈRES** Clos St.-Denis 1989 • $56 • (01/31/92)

92 **BOUCHARD PÈRE & FILS** Chambertin Clos de Bèze 1989 • $92 • (01/31/92)

92 **BOUCHARD PÈRE & FILS** Corton Le Corton Domaines du Château de Beaune 1989 • $79 • (01/31/92)

92 **BOUCHARD PÈRE & FILS** Pommard Clos du Pavillon 1989 • $NA • (01/31/92)

92 **COSTE-CAUMARTIN** Pommard Les Boucherottes 1989 • $38 • (01/31/92)

92 **COSTE-CAUMARTIN** Pommard Les Fremiers 1989 • $35 • (01/31/92)

92 **DANIEL RION** Clos Vougeot 1989 • $94 • (01/31/92)

92 **DANIEL RION** Nuits-St.-Georges Les Pruliers 1989 • $63 • (01/31/92)

92 **DOMAINE DE LA POUSSE D'OR** Volnay Clos de l'Audignac 1989 • $45 • (01/31/92)

92 **F. CHAUVENET** Echézeaux 1989 • $56 • (01/31/92)

92 **FRANÇOIS LEGROS** Chambolle-Musigny Les Noirots 1989 • $30 • (11/15/91)

92 **FRÉDÉRIC ESMONIN** Griotte-Chambertin 1989 • $80 • (03/31/92)

92 **GROS FRÈRE & SOEUR** Grands Echézeaux 1989 • $80 • (01/31/92)

92 **J. FAIVELEY** Nuits-St.-Georges Les St.-Georges 1989 • $28 Ⓐ • (01/31/92)

92 **JACQUES GERMAIN** Beaune Les Teurons 1989 • $50 • (01/31/92)

92 **JEAN GROS** Vosne-Romanée Clos des Réas 1989 • $70 • (01/31/92)

92 **JOSEPH DROUHIN** Beaune Clos des Mouches 1989 • $42 Ⓐ • (02/29/92)

92 **JOSEPH DROUHIN** Chambolle-Musigny Les Feusselottes 1989 • $55 • (01/31/92)

92 **JOSEPH DROUHIN** Chambolle-Musigny Les Sentiers 1989 • $55 • (01/31/92)

92 **JOSEPH DROUHIN** Charmes-Chambertin 1989 • $80 • (01/31/92)

92 **JOSEPH DROUHIN** Mazis-Chambertin 1989 • $86 • (01/31/92)

92 **JOSEPH DROUHIN** Romanée St.-Vivant 1989 • $94 • (01/31/92)

92 **LABOURÉ-ROI** Bonnes Mares 1989 • $55 • (08/31/92)

92 **LEROY** Nuits-St.-Georges Aux Allots 1989 • $45 Ⓐ • (01/31/92)

92 **LEROY** Nuits-St.-Georges Les Vignerondes 1989 • $53 Ⓐ • (01/31/92)

92 **LEROY** Vosne-Romanée Les Beaux Monts 1989 • $142 Ⓐ • (01/31/92)

92 **MÉO-CAMUZET** Nuits-St.-Georges 1989 • $52 • (11/15/91)

92 **MOMMESSIN** Clos de Tart 1989 • $52 • (01/31/92)

92 **MONGEARD-MUGNERET** Richebourg 1989 • $63 Ⓐ • (01/31/92)

92 **OLIVIER LEFLAIVE FRÈRES** Volnay Clos de la Barre 1989 • $38 • (01/31/92)

92 **P. DUBREUIL-FONTAINE PÈRE & FILS** Corton Le Clos du Roi 1989 • $63 • (01/31/92)

92 **SÉRAFIN PÈRE & FILS** Charmes-Chambertin 1989 • $43 Ⓐ • (01/31/92)

92 **SÉRAFIN PÈRE & FILS** Gevrey-Chambertin Vieilles Vignes 1989 • $45 • (01/31/92)

91 **BERTRAND AMBROISE** Nuits-St.-Georges Rue de Chaux 1989 • $38 • (01/31/92)

91 **BOUCHARD PÈRE & FILS** Beaune Les Grèves Vigne de l'Enfant Jésus Domaines du Château de Beaune 1989 • $59 • (02/28/95)

91 **BOURÉE PÈRE & FILS** Beaune Les Epenotes 1989 • $30 • (01/31/92)

91 **BRUNO CLAIR** Vosne-Romanée Aux Champs Perdrix 1989 • $30 • (01/31/92)

91 **CHOPIN-GROFFIER** Nuits-St.-Georges 1989 • $32 • (01/31/92)

91 **DANIEL RION** Nuits-St.-Georges Les Argillières 1989 • $63 • (01/31/92)

91 **DOMAINE LEROY** Chambertin 1989 • $310 • (12/15/96)

91 **DOMAINE LEROY** Musigny 1989 • $225 • (12/15/96)

91 **DOMAINE DE LA POUSSE D'OR** Santenay Clos de Tavannes 1989 • $29 • (01/31/92)

91 **DOMAINE DE LA ROMANÉE-CONTI** La Tâche 1989 • $368 Ⓐ • (10/31/92)

91 **DOMAINE DE LA ROMANÉE-CONTI** Romanée St.-Vivant 1989 • $118 Ⓐ • (10/31/92)

91 **DOMAINE DU CLOS FRANTIN** Clos de Vougeot 1989 • $56 • (01/31/92)

91 **DOMAINE DU CLOS FRANTIN** Nuits-St.-Georges 1989 • $29 • (02/29/92)

91 **DUJAC** Clos St.-Denis 1989 • $80 • (01/31/92)

91 **EMMANUEL ROUGET** Vosne-Romanée 1989 • $48 • (11/15/91)

91 **F. CHAUVENET** Beaune Les Grèves 1989 • $30 • (01/31/92)

91 **F. CHAUVENET** Gevrey-Chambertin Estournelles St.-Jacques 1989 • $40 • (01/31/92)

91 **F. CHAUVENET** Nuits-St.-Georges Aux Chaignots 1989 • $45 • (01/31/92)

91 **FRÉDÉRIC ESMONIN** Ruchottes-Chambertin 1989 • $80 • (03/31/92)

91 **GEORGES MUGNERET** Ruchottes-Chambertin 1989 • $66 • (04/30/92)

91 **GROS FRÈRE & SOEUR** Clos Vougeot Musigny 1989 • $80 Ⓐ • (01/31/92)

91 **GROS FRÈRE & SOEUR** Vosne-Romanée 1989 • $39 • (01/31/92)

91 **GUY CASTAGNIER** Bonnes Mares 1989 • $67 • (01/31/92)

91 **GUY CASTAGNIER** Clos St.-Denis 1989 • $62 • (01/31/92)

Key: SS—Spectator Selection CS—Cellar Selection HR—Highly Recommended BB—Best Buy $NA—Price not available Ⓐ—Auction Price
Dates in parentheses indicate the issues in which the ratings were published.

91 **J. CONFURON-COTETIDOT** Clos de Vougeot 1989 • $60 • (09/15/92) • HR

91 **J. FAIVELEY** Corton Clos des Cortons 1989 • $68 • (01/31/92)

91 **JACQUES GERMAIN** Beaune Les Vignes Franches 1989 • $45 • (01/31/92)

91 **JACQUES-FRÉDÉRIC MUGNIER** Chambolle-Musigny 1989 • $41 • (01/31/92)

91 **JAFFELIN** Corton 1989 • $54 • (01/31/92)

91 **JAFFELIN** Echézeaux 1989 • $60 • (01/31/92)

91 **JAFFELIN** Romanée St.-Vivant 1989 • $80 • (01/31/92)

91 **JEAN GARAUDET** Beaune Le Clos des Mouches 1989 • $32 • (11/15/91)

91 **JEAN GARAUDET** Pommard Les Noizons 1989 • $34 • (11/15/91)

91 **JOSEPH DROUHIN** Chambolle-Musigny 1989 • $41 • (01/31/92)

91 **JOSEPH DROUHIN** Clos St.-Denis 1989 • $76 • (01/31/92)

91 **JOSEPH DROUHIN** Gevrey-Chambertin Les Cazetiers 1989 • $70 • (01/31/92)

91 **JOSEPH DROUHIN** Griotte-Chambertin 1989 • $90 • (01/31/92)

91 **JOSEPH DROUHIN** Volnay Clos des Chênes 1989 • $50 • (01/31/92)

91 **JOSEPH DROUHIN** Vosne-Romanée Les Beaux Monts 1989 • $70 • (01/31/92)

91 **LEROY** Savigny-lès-Beaune Les Narbantons 1989 • $65 • (01/31/92)

91 **LEROY** Vosne-Romanée Aux Genaivrières 1989 • $75 • (01/31/92)

91 **LOUIS JADOT** Beaune Clos des Ursules 1989 • $73 Ⓐ • (02/29/92)

91 **LOUIS LATOUR** Beaune Domaine Latour 1989 • $22 • (01/31/92)

91 **MÉO-CAMUZET** Vosne-Romanée 1989 • $47 • (11/15/91)

91 **MÉO-CAMUZET** Vosne-Romanée Les Chaumes 1989 • $62 • (01/31/92)

91 **MOMMESSIN** Corton Les Grèves 1989 • $45 • (01/31/92)

91 **PHILIPPE CHARLOPIN-PARIZOT** Chambertin 1989 • $35 • (11/15/91)

91 **TOLLOT-BEAUT & FILS** Beaune Clos du Roi 1989 • $52 • (01/31/92)

90 **A.-F. GROS** Clos Vougeot Le Grand Maupertuis 1989 • $NA • (01/31/92)

90 **ARMAND ROUSSEAU** Gevrey-Chambertin Le Clos St.-Jacques 1989 • $72 Ⓐ • (01/31/92)

90 **ARMAND ROUSSEAU** Mazis-Chambertin Mazy-Chambertin 1989 • $80 • (01/31/92)

90 **ARMAND ROUSSEAU** Ruchottes-Chambertin Clos des Ruchottes 1989 • $85 • (01/31/92)

90 **BERTRAND AMBROISE** Nuits-St.-Georges 1989 • $30 • (01/31/92)

90 **BOUCHARD PÈRE & FILS** Beaune Les Marconnets Domaines du Château de Beaune 1989 • $39 • (01/31/92)

90 **BRUNO CLAIR** Morey-St.-Denis En la Rue de Vergy 1989 • $36 • (01/31/92)

90 **CHARLES MORTET** Gevrey-Chambertin Champeaux 1989 • $34 • (01/31/92)

90 **CHOPIN-GROFFIER** Chambolle-Musigny 1989 • $32 • (01/31/92)

90 **DANIEL RION** Vosne-Romanée Les Beaux Monts 1989 • $63 • (01/31/92)

90 **DOMAINE DE L'ARLOT** Nuits-St.-Georges Clos des Forêts St.-Georges 1989 • $55 • (01/31/92)

90 **DOMAINE DE LA POUSSE D'OR** Volnay Clos de la Bousse d'Or 1989 • $60 • (01/31/92)

90 **DOMAINE DE LA ROMANÉE-CONTI** Echézeaux 1989 • $114 • (10/31/92)

90 **DOMAINE DE LA ROMANÉE-CONTI** Richebourg 1989 • $214 Ⓐ • (10/31/92)

90 **DOMAINE DU CLOS FRANTIN** Grands Echézeaux 1989 • $56 • (01/31/92)

90 **DUJAC** Charmes-Chambertin 1989 • $72 • (01/31/92)

90 **F. CHAUVENET** Clos de Vougeot 1989 • $60 • (01/31/92)

90 **F. CHAUVENET** Volnay Clos de Chênes 1989 • $40 • (01/31/92)

90 **FOREY PÈRE & FILS** Echézeaux 1989 • $NA • (01/31/92)

90 **G. ROUMIER** Chambolle-Musigny 1989 • $38 • (01/31/92)

90 **GUY CASTAGNIER** Charmes-Chambertin 1989 • $62 • (01/31/92)

90 **GUY CASTAGNIER** Clos de la Roche 1989 • $62 • (01/31/92)

90 **HENRI GOUGES** Nuits-St.-Georges Les Vaucrains 1989 • $49 • (01/31/92)

90 **J. FAIVELEY** Beaune Champs Pimont 1989 • $34 • (01/31/92)

90 **J. FAIVELEY** Chambertin-Clos de Bèze 1989 • $63 Ⓐ • (01/31/92)

90 **J. FAIVELEY** Nuits-St.-Georges Les Damodes 1989 • $45 • (01/31/92)

90 **J. FAIVELEY** Pommard Les Chaponnières 1989 • $50 • (01/31/92)

90 **JACQUES GERMAIN** Beaune Aux Cras 1989 • $48 • (01/31/92)

90 **JACQUES-FRÉDÉRIC MUGNIER** Chambolle-Musigny Les Amoureuses 1989 • $62 • (01/31/92)

90 **JAFFELIN** Nuits-St.-Georges Les Damodes 1989 • $36 • (01/31/92)

90 **JEAN GROS** Vosne-Romanée 1989 • $39 • (01/31/92)

90 **JEAN-JACQUES CONFURON** Romanée St.-Vivant 1989 • $113 • (10/31/92)

90 **JOBLOT** Givry Clos du Cellier-aux-Moines 1989 • $25 • (01/31/92)

90 **JOSEPH DROUHIN** Chambertin 1989 • $114 • (01/31/92)

90 **JOSEPH DROUHIN** Grands Echézeaux 1989 • $114 • (02/28/95)

90 **JOSEPH DROUHIN** Volnay En Chevret 1989 • $50 • (01/31/92)

90 **LOUIS JADOT** Beaune Les Boucherottes 1989 • $38 • (01/31/92)

90 **LOUIS JADOT** Gevrey-Chambertin Le Clos St.-Jacques 1989 • $22 Ⓐ • (01/31/92)

90 **MÉO-CAMUZET** Nuits-St.-Georges Aux Boudots 1989 • $81 • (11/15/91)

90 **MOMMESSIN** Beaune 1989 • $18 • (01/31/92)

90 **MOMMESSIN** Nuits-St.-Georges Les Vaucrains 1989 • $45 • (01/31/92)

90 **RENÉ ENGEL** Grands Echézeaux 1989 • $75 • (11/15/91)

90 **TOLLOT-BEAUT & FILS** Aloxe-Corton 1989 • $60 Ⓐ • (01/31/92)

90 **TOLLOT-BEAUT & FILS** Beaune Les Grèves 1989 • $44 • (01/31/92)

90 **TOLLOT-BEAUT & FILS** Corton 1989 • $67 • (01/31/92)

90 **TOLLOT-BEAUT & FILS** Savigny-lès-Beaune Les Lavières 1989 • $38 • (01/31/92)

89 **BOUCHARD PÈRE & FILS** Clos de la Roche 1989 • $NA • (01/31/92)

89 **BOUCHARD PÈRE & FILS** Nuits-St.-Georges Clos St.-Marc 1989 • $59 • (01/31/92)

89 **BOUCHARD PÈRE & FILS** Nuits-St.-Georges La Richemone 1989 • $NA • (01/31/92)

89 **BRUNO CLAIR** Gevrey-Chambertin Les Cazetiers 1989 • $61 • (01/31/92)

89 **BRUNO CLAIR** Savigny-lès-Beaune La Dominode 1989 • $24 Ⓐ • (01/31/92)

89 **CHANTAL LESCURE** Vosne-Romanée Les Suchots 1989 • $25 • (08/31/92)

89 **CHARLES MORTET** Chambolle-Musigny Aux Beaux Bruns 1989 • $34 • (01/31/92)

89 **COMTE GEORGES DE VOGÜÉ** Chambolle-Musigny 1989 • $44 • (01/31/92)

89 **DANIEL RION** Chambolle-Musigny Aux Beaux Bruns 1989 • $45 • (01/31/92)

89 **DANIEL RION** Vosne-Romanée 1989 • $37 • (01/31/92)

89 **DOMAINE DU CLOS FRANTIN** Vosne-Romanée 1989 • $30 • (01/31/92)

89 **DOMAINE LEROY** Romanée St.-Vivant 1989 • $197 • (12/15/96)

89 **DUJAC** Clos de la Roche 1989 • $80 • (01/31/92)

89 **F. CHAUVENET** Gevrey-Chambertin Le Clos St.-Jacques 1989 • $45 • (01/31/92)

89 **FOREY PÈRE & FILS** Nuits-St.-Georges Les Perrières 1989 • $NA • (01/31/92)

89 **FRÉDÉRIC ESMONIN** Mazis-Chambertin Mazy-Chambertin 1989 • $80 • (03/31/92)

89 **HENRI GOUGES** Nuits-St.-Georges Les St.-Georges 1989 • $49 • (01/31/92)

89 **HENRI GOUGES** Nuits-St.-Georges Les Vaucrains Premier Cru 1989 • $49 • (12/31/94)

89 **J. CONFURON-COTETIDOT** Chambolle-Musigny 1989 • $32 • (11/30/92)

89 **J. CONFURON-COTETIDOT** Vosne-Romanée 1989 • $27 • (10/31/92)

89 **J. FAIVELEY** Echézeaux 1989 • $53 Ⓐ • (01/31/92)

89 **J. FAIVELEY** Gevrey-Chambertin Les Cazetiers 1989 • $47 • (01/31/92)

89 **J. FAIVELEY** Latricières-Chambertin 1989 • $53 Ⓐ • (01/31/92)

89 **JAFFELIN** Aloxe-Corton 1989 • $27 • (01/31/92)

89 **JAFFELIN** Beaune Champs Pimonts 1989 • $27 • (01/31/92)

89 **JAFFELIN** Chambolle-Musigny 1989 • $28 • (01/31/92)

89 **JAFFELIN** Clos de Vougeot 1989 • $60 • (01/31/92)

89 **JAFFELIN** Volnay 1989 • $29 • (01/31/92)

89 **JOSEPH DROUHIN** Aloxe-Corton 1989 • $27 • (01/31/92)

89 **JOSEPH DROUHIN** Chambolle-Musigny Les Baudes 1989 • $52 • (01/31/92)

89 **JOSEPH DROUHIN** Chambolle-Musigny Premier Cru 1989 • $50 • (01/31/92)

89 **JOSEPH DROUHIN** Pommard Les Epenots 1989 • $56 • (01/31/92)

89 **JOSEPH DROUHIN** Vosne-Romanée Les Suchots 1989 • $70 • (01/31/92)

89 **LEROY** Nuits-St.-Georges Aux Lavières 1989 • $75 • (01/31/92)

89 **LOUIS JADOT** Vosne-Romanée 1989 • $40 • (01/31/92)

Red Burgundy

89 **LOUIS LATOUR** Corton Château Corton Grancey 1989 • $48 • (01/31/92)

89 **MOILLARD** Beaune Les Grèves Domaine Thomas-Moillard 1989 • $28 • (01/31/92)

89 **MOILLARD** Corton Clos des Vergennes 1989 • $40 • (01/31/92)

89 **MOILLARD** Morey-St.-Denis Monts Luisants 1989 • $28 • (01/31/92)

89 **MOILLARD** Nuits-St.-Georges Clos de Thorey Domaine Thomas-Moillard 1989 • $35 • (01/31/92)

89 **MOMMESSIN** Vosne-Romanée Aux Brûlées 1989 • $38 • (01/31/92)

89 **RENÉ ENGEL** Echézeaux 1989 • $47 • (11/15/91)

89 **ROBERT CHEVILLON** Nuits-St.-Georges 1989 • $36 • (01/31/92)

89 **ROBERT CHEVILLON** Nuits-St.-Georges Les Vaucrains 1989 • $65 • (01/31/92)

89 **ROBERT DROUHIN** Clos de Vougeot 1989 • $88 • (01/31/92)

89 **SÉRAFIN PÈRE & FILS** Gevrey-Chambertin Les Cazetiers 1989 • $54 • (01/31/92)

88 **ALBERT BICHOT** Corton Hospices de Beaune Cuvée Docteur-Peste 1989 • $100 • (01/31/92)

88 **ARMAND ROUSSEAU** Gevrey-Chambertin 1989 • $30 Ⓐ • (01/31/92)

88 **BOUCHARD PÈRE & FILS** Echézeaux 1989 • $62 • (01/31/92)

88 **BOUCHARD PÈRE & FILS** Volnay Taille Pieds Domaines du Château de Beaune 1989 • $48 • (01/31/92)

88 **BOUCHARD-AÎNÉ & FILS** Chambertin Clos de Bèze Domaine Marion 1989 • $NA • (01/31/92)

88 **CHANTAL LESCURE** Beaune Les Chouacheux 1989 • $19 • (08/31/92)

88 **CHARLES MORTET** Gevrey-Chambertin Clos Prieur 1989 • $30 • (01/31/92)

88 **CHARLES MORTET** Gevrey-Chambertin 1989 • $25 • (01/31/92)

88 **DANIEL RION** Nuits-St.-Georges Les Grandes Vignes 1989 • $38 • (01/31/92)

88 **DOMAINE D'AUVENAY** Auxey-Duresses Red 1989 • $42 • (01/31/92)

88 **DOMAINE DU CLOS FRANTIN** Chambertin 1989 • $73 • (01/31/92)

88 **F. CHAUVENET** Gevrey-Chambertin Lavaut St.-Jacques 1989 • $45 • (01/31/92)

88 **F. CHAUVENET** Nuits-St.-Georges Les Pruliers 1989 • $45 • (01/31/92)

88 **F. CHAUVENET** Volnay Premier Cru 1989 • $36 • (01/31/92)

88 **FRÉDÉRIC ESMONIN** Gevrey-Chambertin Lavaut St.-Jacques 1989 • $42 • (03/31/92)

88 **FRÉDÉRIC ESMONIN** Gevrey-Chambertin Les Corbeaux 1989 • $42 • (03/31/92)

88 **G. ROUMIER** Chambolle-Musigny Les Amoureuses 1989 • $62 • (01/31/92)

88 **GUY CASTAGNIER** Chambolle-Musigny 1989 • $39 • (01/31/92)

88 **J. FAIVELEY** Morey-St.-Denis Clos des Ormes 1989 • $44 • (01/31/92)

88 **J. FAIVELEY** Vosne-Romanée 1989 • $35 • (01/31/92)

Key: SS—Spectator Selection CS—Cellar Selection HR—Highly Recommended BB—Best Buy $NA—Price not available Ⓐ—Auction Price

Dates in parentheses indicate the issues in which the ratings were published.

88 **JACQUES-FRÉDÉRIC MUGNIER** Musigny 1989 • $125 • (01/31/92)

88 **JAFFELIN** Gevrey-Chambertin 1989 • $30 • (01/31/92)

88 **JOBLOT** Givry Clos de la Servoisine 1989 • $25 • (01/31/92)

88 **JOSEPH DROUHIN** Beaune Grèves 1989 • $47 • (01/31/92)

88 **JOSEPH DROUHIN** Clos de la Roche 1989 • $77 • (01/31/92)

88 **LABOURÉ-ROI** Chambertin 1989 • $55 • (08/31/92)

88 **LOUIS JADOT** Chambertin-Clos de Bèze 1989 • $100 • (02/28/95)

88 **LOUIS JADOT** Fixin 1989 • $21 • (01/31/92)

88 **LOUIS JADOT** Pommard Les Grands Epenots 1989 • $50 • (01/31/92)

88 **MARIE-PIERRE GERMAIN** Aloxe-Corton Les Vercots 1989 • $NA • (01/31/92)

88 **MAURICE ECARD** Savigny-lès-Beaune Aux Serpentières 1989 • $25 • (11/15/91)

88 **MICHEL LAFARGE** Volnay 1989 • $41 • (01/31/92)

88 **MOILLARD** Fixin 1989 • $NA • (01/31/92)

88 **MOMMESSIN** Aloxe-Corton Les Valozières 1989 • $28 • (01/31/92)

88 **MOMMESSIN** Pommard 1989 • $28 • (01/31/92)

88 **MUGNERET-GIBOURG** Echézeaux 1989 • $62 • (04/30/92)

88 **OLIVIER LEFLAIVE FRÈRES** Charmes-Chambertin 1989 • $60 • (01/31/92)

88 **OLIVIER LEFLAIVE FRÈRES** Pommard Les Epenots 1989 • $40 • (01/31/92)

88 **PHILIPPE CHARLOPIN-PARIZOT** Gevrey-Chambertin Cuvée Vieilles Vignes 1989 • $75 • (11/15/91)

88 **POTHIER-RIEUSSET** Beaune Les Boucherottes 1989 • $28 • (11/30/92)

87 **BOUCHARD PÈRE & FILS** Aloxe-Corton Domaines du Château de Beaune 1989 • $36 • (01/31/92)

87 **BRUNO CLAIR** Marsannay Les Longeroies 1989 • $18 • (01/31/92)

87 **CHANTAL LESCURE** Pommard Les Bertins 1989 • $25 • (08/31/92)

87 **CHARLES MORTET** Bourgogne 1989 • $14 • (01/31/92)

87 **COSTE-CAUMARTIN** Bourgogne 1989 • $15 • (01/31/92)

87 **F. CHAUVENET** Clos St.-Denis 1989 • $60 • (01/31/92)

87 **FRANÇOIS LEGROS** Nuits-St.-Georges Les Perrières 1989 • $29 • (11/15/91)

87 **G. ROUMIER** Clos Vougeot 1989 • $62 • (01/31/92)

87 **GEORGES MUGNERET** Chambolle-Musigny Les Feusselottes 1989 • $47 • (04/30/92)

87 **HENRI GOUGES** Nuits-St.-Georges Clos des Porrets St.-Georges 1989 • $45 • (01/31/92)

87 **J. FAIVELEY** Gevrey-Chambertin 1989 • $34 • (01/31/92)

87 **J. FAIVELEY** Gevrey-Chambertin Combe au Moine 1989 • $47 • (01/31/92)

87 **JAFFELIN** Charmes-Chambertin 1989 • $66 • (01/31/92)

87 **JAFFELIN** Monthélie 1989 • $19 • (01/31/92)

87 **JEAN GROS** Nuits-St.-Georges 1989 • $39 • (01/31/92)

87 **JEAN-NOËL GAGNARD** Chassagne-Montrachet Morgeot Red 1989 • $25 • (11/15/91)

87 **JOSEPH DROUHIN** Chassagne-Montrachet Red 1989 • $23 • (01/31/92)

87 **JOSEPH DROUHIN** Pommard Les Rugiens 1989 • $56 • (01/31/92)

87 **JOSEPH DROUHIN** Santenay 1989 • $44 • (01/31/92)

87 **JOSEPH DROUHIN** Savigny-lès-Beaune 1989 • $23 • (01/31/92)

87 **LOUIS JADOT** Clos Vougeot 1989 • $74 • (01/31/92)

87 **LOUIS JADOT** Monthélie 1989 • $21 • (01/31/92)

87 **LOUIS LATOUR** Gevrey-Chambertin 1989 • $35 • (01/31/92)

87 **MAURICE ECARD** Savigny-lès-Beaune Les Peuillets 1989 • $25 • (11/15/91)

87 **MOMMESSIN** Fixin 1989 • $15 • (01/31/92)

87 **MOMMESSIN** Maranges 1989 • $13 • (01/31/92)

87 **MONGEARD-MUGNERET** Clos de Vougeot 1989 • $41 Ⓐ • (01/31/92)

87 **OLIVIER LEFLAIVE FRÈRES** Morey-St.-Denis 1989 • $30 • (01/31/92)

87 **RENÉ ENGEL** Vosne-Romanée Les Brûlées 1989 • $35 • (11/15/91)

87 **SIMON BIZE & FILS** Savigny-lès-Beaune Aux Vergelesses 1989 • $27 • (01/31/92)

87 **TOLLOT-BEAUT & FILS** Chorey-Côte de Beaune 1989 • $28 • (01/31/92)

86 **ALBERT BICHOT** Pommard Hospices de Beaune Cuvée Cyrot-Chaudron 1989 • $70 • (01/31/92)

86 **BERNARD SERVEAU** Morey-St.-Denis Les Sorbès 1989 • $30 • (01/31/92)

86 **CHARLES MORTET** Clos de Vougeot 1989 • $47 • (01/31/92)

86 **CHÂTEAU DE POMMARD** Pommard 1989 • $65 • (01/31/92)

86 **DOMAINE DU CLOS FRANTIN** Corton 1989 • $58 • (01/31/92)

86 **DUJAC** Gevrey-Chambertin Aux Combottes 1989 • $65 • (01/31/92)

86 **EMMANUEL ROUGET** Nuits-St.-Georges 1989 • $48 • (11/15/91)

86 **F. CHAUVENET** Pommard Les Chanlins 1989 • $45 • (01/31/92)

86 **FRÉDÉRIC ESMONIN** Gevrey-Chambertin Estournelles St.-Jacques 1989 • $42 • (03/31/92)

86 **GEORGES MUGNERET** Nuits-St.-Georges Aux Chaignots 1989 • $43 • (04/30/92)

86 **GUY CASTAGNIER** Morey-St.-Denis 1989 • $NA • (01/31/92)

86 **HENRI GOUGES** Nuits-St.-Georges Les Pruliers 1989 • $45 • (01/31/92)

86 **JAFFELIN** Chassagne-Montrachet Red 1989 • $18 • (01/31/92)

86 **JAFFELIN** Morey-St.-Denis Les Ruchots 1989 • $30 • (01/31/92)

86 **JAFFELIN** Pernand-Vergelesses 1989 • $19 • (01/31/92)

86 **JAFFELIN** Vosne-Romanée 1989 • $29 • (01/31/92)

86 **JEAN GARAUDET** Monthélie 1989 • $22 • (11/15/91)

86 **JOSEPH DROUHIN** Gevrey-Chambertin Lavaut St.-Jacques 1989 • $70 • (01/31/92)

86 **JOSEPH DROUHIN** Morey-St.-Denis Clos Sorbè 1989 • $45 • (01/31/92)

86 **LOUIS JADOT** Pernand-Vergelesses Clos de la Croix de Pierre 1989 • $21 • (01/31/92)

86 **LUPÉ-CHOLET** Bourgogne Comte de Lupé 1989 • $8 • (01/31/92)

86 **MOILLARD** Fixin Clos d'Entre Deux Velles 1989 • $28 • (01/31/92)

86 **MOMMESSIN** Beaune Les Cents Vignes 1989 • $23 • (01/31/92)

86 **PRINCE FLORENT DE MÉRODE** Pommard La Platière 1989 • $48 • (11/30/92)

86 **ROBERT CHEVILLON** Nuits-St.-Georges Les St.-Georges 1989 • $53 • (02/28/95)

86 **ROBERT JAYER-GILLES** Hautes Côtes de Nuits 1989 • $24 • (01/31/92)

86 **SÉRAFIN PÈRE & FILS** Gevrey-Chambertin Fonteny 1989 • $50 • (01/31/92)

85 **ALBERT BICHOT** Bourgogne Château de Montpatey 1989 • $10 • (06/15/92) • BB

85 **BERNARD SERVEAU** Chambolle-Musigny Les Amoureuses 1989 • $50 • (01/31/92)

85 **BOURÉE PÈRE & FILS** Gevrey-Chambertin 1989 • $35 • (01/31/92)

85 **DANIEL RION** Vosne-Romanée Les Chaumes 1989 • $63 • (02/28/95)

85 **DOMAINE LEROY** Clos de la Roche 1989 • $147 • (12/15/96)

85 **DOMAINE LEROY** Richebourg 1989 • $206 • (12/15/96)

85 **F. ROBLET-MONNOT** Volnay Les Caillerets 1989 • $37 • (11/15/93)

85 **FOREY PÈRE & FILS** Vosne-Romanée 1989 • $NA • (01/31/92)

85 **G. ROUMIER** Morey-St.-Denis Clos de la Bussière 1989 • $38 • (01/31/92)

85 **GUY CASTAGNIER** Clos de Vougeot 1989 • $64 • (01/31/92)

85 **J. FAIVELEY** Chambolle-Musigny 1989 • $34 • (01/31/92)

85 **J. FAIVELEY** Clos de Vougeot 1989 • $41 Ⓐ • (01/31/92)

85 **J. FAIVELEY** Fixin 1989 • $21 • (01/31/92)

85 **J. FAIVELEY** Nuits-St.-Georges Clos de la Maréchale 1989 • $25 Ⓐ • (01/31/92)

85 **JAFFELIN** Auxey-Duresses Red 1989 • $16 • (01/31/92)

85 **JAFFELIN** Beaune Les Bressandes 1989 • $28 • (01/31/92)

85 **JAFFELIN** Fixin 1989 • $18 • (01/31/92)

85 **JAFFELIN** Ladoix Côte de Beaune 1989 • $13 • (01/31/92)

85 **JAFFELIN** Pommard 1989 • $33 • (01/31/92)

85 **JAFFELIN** Santenay 1989 • $17 • (01/31/92)

85 **JAFFELIN** Savigny-lès-Beaune 1989 • $18 • (01/31/92)

85 **JEAN-NOËL GAGNARD** Santenay Clos de Tavannes 1989 • $25 • (11/15/91)

85 **JOSEPH DROUHIN** Bourgogne Laforêt 1989 • $9 • (04/30/91) • BB

85 **JOSEPH DROUHIN** Maranges Premier Cru 1989 • $20 • (01/31/92)

85 **JOSEPH DROUHIN** Pommard 1989 • $43 • (01/31/92)

85 **LEROY** Bourgogne Leroy 1989 • $18 • (01/31/92)

85 **LEROY** Nuits-St.-Georges La Richemone 1989 • $NA • (12/15/96)

85 **LOUIS JADOT** Nuits-St.-Georges Clos des Corvées 1989 • $56 • (01/31/92)

85 **LOUIS LATOUR** Pommard Les Epenots 1989 • $38 • (02/28/95)

85 **MICHEL JUILLOT** Mercurey Clos Tonnerre 1989 • $24 • (08/31/92)

85 **MICHEL LAFARGE** Pinot Noir Bourgogne 1989 • $19 • (01/31/92)

85 **MOILLARD** Corton Le Clos du Roi Domaine Thomas-Moillard 1989 • $41 • (01/31/92)

85 **MOILLARD** Ladoix Côte de Beaune 1989 • $NA • (01/31/92)

85 **MOMMESSIN** Gevrey-Chambertin Lavaut St.-Jacques 1989 • $45 • (01/31/92)

85 **MONGEARD-MUGNERET** Bourgogne 1989 • $10 • (01/31/92)

85 **MONGEARD-MUGNERET** Vosne-Romanée 1989 • $34 • (01/31/92)

85 **RENÉ ENGEL** Clos Vougeot 1989 • $66 • (11/15/91)

85 **RENÉ ENGEL** Vosne-Romanée 1989 • $34 • (11/15/91)

85 **SAIER** Clos des Lambrays 1989 • $68 • (11/15/91)

85 **SIMON BIZE & FILS** Savigny-lès-Beaune Les Bourgeots 1989 • $19 • (01/31/92)

1988 Red Burgundy
Vintage Rating: 90

98 **JEAN GROS** Richebourg 1988 • $125 Ⓐ • (02/28/91)

97 **A.-F. GROS** Richebourg 1988 • $190 • (02/15/91)

96 **EMMANUEL ROUGET** Echézeaux 1988 • $81 • (11/15/90)

96 **MÉO-CAMUZET** Richebourg 1988 • $253 • (11/30/90)

95 **ARMAND ROUSSEAU** Chambertin-Clos de Bèze 1988 • $188 • (05/15/91)

95 **LEROY** Romanée St.-Vivant 1988 • $431 Ⓐ • (04/30/91)

94 **DOMAINE DE LA ROMANÉE-CONTI** Richebourg 1988 • $238 Ⓐ • (04/30/91)

94 **HENRI JAYER** Echézeaux 1988 • $59 Ⓐ • (05/15/91)

94 **JEAN GROS** Vosne-Romanée Clos des Réas 1988 • $81 Ⓐ • (02/28/91) • HR

94 **JOSEPH DROUHIN** Chambertin 1988 • $83 • (02/15/91)

94 **LOUIS JADOT** Griotte-Chambertin 1988 • $75 • (03/15/91)

94 **MÉO-CAMUZET** Vosne-Romanée Cros Parantoux 1988 • $84 • (11/30/90)

93 **ARMAND ROUSSEAU** Chambertin 1988 • $96 Ⓐ • (05/15/91)

93 **BERTRAND AMBROISE** Nuits-St.-Georges Rue de Chaux 1988 • $40 • (05/15/91)

93 **DANIEL RION** Nuits-St.-Georges Aux Lavières 1988 • $33 • (02/15/91) • HR

93 **DOMAINE CECI** Clos de Vougeot 1988 • $48 • (07/15/91)

93 **DROUHIN-LAROZE** Bonnes Mares 1988 • $81 • (12/31/90)

93 **GUY CASTAGNIER** Latricières-Chambertin 1988 • $63 • (07/15/91)

93 **HENRI JAYER** Vosne-Romanée Cros Parantoux 1988 • $180 • (05/15/91)

93 **JOSEPH DROUHIN** Echézeaux 1988 • $60 • (11/15/90) • HR

93 **JOSEPH DROUHIN** Charmes-Chambertin 1988 • $58 Ⓐ • (11/15/90)

93 **JOSEPH DROUHIN** Clos de la Roche 1988 • $73 • (02/15/91)

93 **LEROY** Nuits-St.-Georges Aux Boudots 1988 • $230 • (04/30/91)

93 **LEROY** Vosne-Romanée Les Beaux Monts 1988 • $81 Ⓐ • (04/30/91)

Key: SS—Spectator Selection CS—Cellar Selection HR—Highly Recommended BB—Best Buy $NA—Price not available Ⓐ—Auction Price
Dates in parentheses indicate the issues in which the ratings were published.

93 **LOUIS JADOT** Chapelle-Chambertin 1988 • $75 • (03/15/91)

93 **LOUIS JADOT** Corton Les Pougets 1988 • $61 • (03/31/91)

93 **ROBERT GROFFIER** Chambolle-Musigny Les Amoureuses 1988 • $66 • (11/15/90)

92 **BERTRAND AMBROISE** Corton Le Rognet 1988 • $43 • (11/30/90)

92 **CHOPIN-GROFFIER** Vougeot 1988 • $32 • (05/15/91)

92 **DANIEL RION** Clos Vougeot 1988 • $53 Ⓐ • (01/31/91)

92 **DANIEL RION** Nuits-St.-Georges Aux Vignerondes 1988 • $54 • (01/31/91)

92 **DANIEL RION** Vosne-Romanée Les Beaux Monts 1988 • $48 • (02/15/91)

92 **DOMAINE DE LA ROMANÉE-CONTI** Echézeaux 1988 • $124 Ⓐ • (04/30/91)

92 **DOMAINE DE LA ROMANÉE-CONTI** Grands Echézeaux 1988 • $153 Ⓐ • (04/30/91)

92 **DROUHIN-LAROZE** Chambertin-Clos de Bèze 1988 • $88 • (12/31/90)

92 **GEORGES MUGNERET** Ruchottes-Chambertin 1988 • $69 • (11/15/90)

92 **GROS FRÈRE & SOEUR** Clos Vougeot Musigny 1988 • $95 • (03/31/91)

92 **JOSEPH DROUHIN** Corton Les Bressandes 1988 • $60 • (11/15/90)

92 **JOSEPH DROUHIN** Morey-St.-Denis Monts Luisants 1988 • $38 • (02/28/91)

92 **LOUIS JADOT** Beaune Les Boucherottes 1988 • $33 • (03/31/91)

92 **LOUIS TRAPET** Chambertin 1988 • $41 Ⓐ • (07/15/91)

92 **MÉO-CAMUZET** Clos de Vougeot 1988 • $95 • (11/30/90)

92 **MÉO-CAMUZET** Nuits-St.-Georges Aux Boudots 1988 • $80 • (11/30/90)

92 **PONSOT** Chambolle-Musigny Les Charmes 1988 • $58 • (04/30/91)

92 **RENÉ ENGEL** Echézeaux 1988 • $37 Ⓐ • (03/31/91)

92 **ROSSIGNOL-FEVRIER** Volnay 1988 • $32 • (03/31/91)

92 **SÉRAFIN PÈRE & FILS** Gevrey-Chambertin 1988 • $35 • (03/31/91)

92 **SÉRAFIN PÈRE & FILS** Gevrey-Chambertin Fonteny 1988 • $50 • (05/15/91)

92 **TOLLOT-BEAUT & FILS** Corton Les Bressandes 1988 • $59 • (02/28/95)

91 **A. CHOPIN** Nuits-St.-Georges Aux Murgers 1988 • $28 • (07/15/90)

91 **A.-F. GROS** Echézeaux 1988 • $84 • (02/15/91)

91 **ALAIN MICHELOT** Nuits-St.-Georges 1988 • $39 • (07/15/91)

91 **ALBERT MOROT** Beaune Les Cents Vignes 1988 • $30 • (04/30/91)

91 **ARMAND ROUSSEAU** Clos de la Roche 1988 • $62 Ⓐ • (05/15/91)

91 **BOUCHARD PÈRE & FILS** Corton Le Corton Domaines du Château de Beaune 1988 • $77 • (03/31/91)

91 **BOURÉE PÈRE & FILS** Clos de la Roche 1988 • $85 • (03/31/91)

91 **CHARLES MORTET** Gevrey-Chambertin Clos Prieur 1988 • $41 • (02/15/91)

91 **DANIEL RION** Nuits-St.-Georges Les Argillières 1988 • $48 • (01/31/91) • HR

91 **DANIEL RION** Nuits-St.-Georges Les Pruliers 1988 • $54 • (01/31/91)

91 **DANIEL RION** Vosne-Romanée Les Chaumes 1988 • $54 • (02/28/95)

91 **DOMAINE CECI** Chambolle-Musigny Aux Echanges 1988 • $33 • (07/15/91)

91 **DROUHIN-LAROZE** Latricières-Chambertin 1988 • $68 • (12/31/90)

91 **GROS FRÈRE & SOEUR** Richebourg 1988 • $192 • (02/28/91)

91 **GUY CASTAGNIER** Clos de la Roche 1988 • $63 • (07/15/91)

91 **GUY CASTAGNIER** Mazis-Chambertin Mazy-Chambertin 1988 • $63 • (07/15/91)

91 **J. JAYER** Echézeaux 1988 • $65 Ⓐ • (03/15/91)

91 **J. LABET & N. DECHELETTE** Clos Vougeot Château de la Tour 1988 • $50 • (11/30/90)

91 **JOSEPH DROUHIN** Griotte-Chambertin 1988 • $81 • (11/15/90)

91 **LOUIS JADOT** Beaune Clos des Ursules 1988 • $43 Ⓐ • (03/31/91)

91 **LOUIS JADOT** Gevrey-Chambertin Estournelles St.-Jacques 1988 • $50 • (03/15/91)

91 **LOUIS JADOT** Ruchottes-Chambertin 1988 • $48 Ⓐ • (03/15/91)

91 **MÉO-CAMUZET** Nuits-St.-Georges 1988 • $50 • (11/30/90)

91 **MÉO-CAMUZET** Nuits-St.-Georges Aux Murgers 1988 • $80 • (11/30/90)

91 **MOILLARD** Morey-St.-Denis Monts Luisants 1988 • $30 • (12/15/90) • HR

91 **PONSOT** Latricières-Chambertin 1988 • $150 • (05/15/91)

91 **RENÉ ENGEL** Clos Vougeot 1988 • $37 Ⓐ • (03/15/91)

91 **ROBERT ARNOUX** Romanée St.-Vivant 1988 • $250 • (11/15/90)

91 **SAIER** Clos des Lambrays 1988 • $75 • (03/31/91)

91 **SÉRAFIN PÈRE & FILS** Gevrey-Chambertin Les Cazetiers 1988 • $53 • (05/15/91)

90 **ALAIN MICHELOT** Nuits-St.-Georges Aux Chaignots 1988 • $56 • (05/15/91)

90 **BERNARD HERESZTYN** Gevrey-Chambertin Les Goulots 1988 • $44 • (07/15/91)

90 **BOUCHARD PÈRE & FILS** Pommard 1988 • $37 • (04/30/91) • HR

90 **COMTE ARMAND** Pommard Clos des Epeneaux 1988 • $58 Ⓐ • (02/28/91)

90 **COMTE GEORGES DE VOGÜÉ** Musigny Cuvée Vieilles Vignes 1988 • $108 • (02/28/95)

90 **DOMAINE DES CHEZEAUX** Griotte-Chambertin 1988 • $110 • (05/15/91)

90 **DUJAC** Clos de la Roche 1988 • $75 • (03/31/91)

90 **DUJAC** Echézeaux 1988 • $70 • (03/31/91)

90 **J. FAIVELEY** Corton Clos des Cortons 1988 • $120 • (03/31/91)

90 **JACQUES GERMAIN** Beaune Les Teurons 1988 • $42 • (02/15/91)

90 **JEAN GARAUDET** Pommard Les Charmots 1988 • $46 • (11/15/90)

90 **JEAN GROS** Vosne-Romanée 1988 • $29 Ⓐ • (02/28/91)

90 **JEANNE-MARIE DE CHAMPS** Nuits-St.-Georges Les Terres Blanches 1988 • $39 • (07/15/91)

90 **JOSEPH DROUHIN** Clos de Vougeot 1988 • $85 • (02/15/91)

90 **JOSEPH DROUHIN** Vosne-Romanée Les Suchots 1988 • $57 • (02/28/91)

90 **LOUIS JADOT** Beaune Clos des Couchereaux 1988 • $35 • (03/31/91)

90 **MICHEL LAFARGE** Volnay Clos du Château des Ducs 1988 • $65 • (07/15/91)

90 **REMOISSENET PÈRE & FILS** Beaune Les Grèves 1988 • $38 • (11/30/90) • HR

90 **ROBERT CHEVILLON** Nuits-St.-Georges Les St.-Georges 1988 • $59 • (02/28/95)

90 **ROBERT GROFFIER** Bonnes Mares 1988 • $80 • (11/15/90)

89 **ALAIN MICHELOT** Nuits-St.-Georges La Richemone 1988 • $54 • (05/15/91)

89 **BOUCHARD PÈRE & FILS** Chambertin Clos de Bèze 1988 • $82 • (04/30/91)

89 **BOUCHARD PÈRE & FILS** Pommard Premier Cru Domaines du Château de Beaune 1988 • $53 • (03/31/91)

89 **BOURÉE PÈRE & FILS** Charmes-Chambertin 1988 • $75 • (03/31/91)

89 **CHANDON DE BRIAILLES** Corton Les Bressandes 1988 • $75 • (02/28/91)

89 **CHARLES MORTET** Gevrey-Chambertin 1988 • $35 • (02/15/91)

89 **COMTE GEORGES DE VOGÜÉ** Bonnes Mares 1988 • $65 Ⓐ • (03/31/91)

89 **COMTE GEORGES DE VOGÜÉ** Chambolle-Musigny Les Amoureuses 1988 • $93 • (02/28/91)

89 **DROUHIN-LAROZE** Clos de Vougeot 1988 • $81 • (12/31/90)

89 **G. ROUMIER** Chambolle-Musigny 1988 • $30 • (07/15/91)

89 **GROS FRÈRE & SOEUR** Vosne-Romanée 1988 • $46 • (03/31/91)

89 **GUY CASTAGNIER** Clos St.-Denis 1988 • $63 • (07/15/91)

89 **HAEGELEN-JAYER** Nuits-St.-Georges Les Damodes 1988 • $39 • (05/15/91)

89 **HENRI JAYER** Vosne-Romanée Les Beaux Monts 1988 • $160 • (05/15/91)

89 **J. FAIVELEY** Gevrey-Chambertin Les Cazetiers 1988 • $57 • (03/31/91)

89 **JACQUES THEVENOT-MACHAL** Volnay-Santenots 1988 • $36 • (11/15/90)

89 **JACQUES-FRÉDÉRIC MUGNIER** Chambolle-Musigny Les Fuées 1988 • $60 • (05/15/91)

89 **JEAN GRIVOT** Nuits-St.-Georges Les Pruliers 1988 • $53 • (04/30/91)

89 **JEANNE-MARIE DE CHAMPS** Nuits-St.-Georges Les Didiers Hospices de Nuits Cuvée Jacques Duret 1988 • $49 • (09/30/90)

89 **LEROY** Clos de Vougeot 1988 • $177 Ⓐ • (04/30/91)

89 **LEROY** Nuits-St.-Georges Aux Allots 1988 • $49 Ⓐ • (04/30/91)

89 **LOUIS JADOT** Nuits-St.-Georges Clos des Corvées 1988 • $49 • (02/28/91)

89 **LOUIS TRAPET** Chambertin Cuvée Vieilles Vignes 1988 • $119 • (07/15/91)

89 **LOUIS TRAPET** Chapelle-Chambertin 1988 • $84 • (07/15/91)

89 **MACHARD DE GRAMONT** Vosne-Romanée Les Réas 1988 • $32 • (07/15/91)

89 **MÉO-CAMUZET** Vosne-Romanée Aux Brûlées 1988 • $84 • (11/30/90)

89 **MICHEL LAFARGE** Volnay Clos des Chênes 1988 • $72 • (02/28/95)

89 **MOILLARD** Nuits-St.-Georges Clos de Thorey Domaine Thomas-Moillard 1988 • $50 • (12/31/90)

Red Burgundy

89 **MOILLARD** Nuits-St.-Georges Hospices de Nuits Cuvée Jacques Duret 1988 • $68 • (08/31/91)

89 **MUGNERET-GIBOURG** Echézeaux 1988 • $70 • (11/15/90)

89 **PIERRE AMIOT** Gevrey-Chambertin Aux Combottes 1988 • $64 • (03/15/91)

89 **PONSOT** Clos de la Roche Cuvée William 1988 • $150 • (05/15/91)

89 **PONSOT** Griotte-Chambertin 1988 • $150 • (05/15/91)

89 **RENÉ ENGEL** Vosne-Romanée Les Brûlées 1988 • $45 • (02/28/91)

89 **ROBERT GROFFIER** Chambolle-Musigny Les Sentiers 1988 • $45 • (11/15/90)

88 **ALAIN BURGUET** Gevrey-Chambertin Vieilles Vignes 1988 • $45 • (12/31/90)

88 **BERNARD SERVEAU** Morey-St.-Denis Les Sorbès 1988 • $35 • (02/28/91)

88 **BOUCHARD PÈRE & FILS** Volnay Taille Pieds Domaines du Château de Beaune 1988 • $50 • (03/31/91)

88 **CHANTAL LESCURE** Pommard Les Bertins 1988 • $22 Ⓐ • (11/30/90)

88 **CHÂTEAU DES HERBEAUX** Volnay-Santenots 1988 • $36 • (11/30/90)

88 **DOMAINE LEROY** Chambertin 1988 • $480 • (12/15/96)

88 **DOMAINE LEROY** Musigny 1988 • $480 • (12/15/96)

88 **DOMAINE LEROY** Romanée St.-Vivant 1988 • $431 • (12/15/96)

88 **DOMAINE DE LA POUSSE D'OR** Pommard Les Jarolières 1988 • $27 Ⓐ • (08/31/91)

88 **DROUHIN-LAROZE** Chapelle-Chambertin 1988 • $68 • (12/31/90)

88 **DROUHIN-LAROZE** Gevrey-Chambertin Clos Prieur 1988 • $44 • (12/31/90)

88 **GHISLAINE BARTHOD** Chambolle-Musigny 1988 • $50 • (03/15/91)

88 **JAFFELIN** Chambolle-Musigny 1988 • $32 • (12/31/90)

88 **JAFFELIN** Gevrey-Chambertin 1988 • $25 • (08/31/91)

88 **JAFFELIN** Volnay 1988 • $30 • (08/31/91)

88 **JEAN CHARTRON** Beaune Hospices de Beaune Cuvée Cyrot-Chaudron 1988 • $40 • (02/15/91)

88 **JEAN GARAUDET** Monthélie 1988 • $23 • (11/15/90)

88 **JEAN GARAUDET** Pommard 1988 • $37 • (11/15/90)

88 **JEAN-MARC BOILLOT** Beaune Les Montrevenots 1988 • $37 • (05/15/91)

88 **JOSEPH DROUHIN** Beaune Clos des Mouches 1988 • $38 Ⓐ • (02/15/91)

88 **JOSEPH DROUHIN** Grands Echézeaux 1988 • $85 • (02/28/95)

88 **LEROY** Pommard Les Vignots 1988 • $125 Ⓐ • (04/30/91)

88 **LOUIS JADOT** Bonnes Mares 1988 • $46 Ⓐ • (03/15/91)

88 **LOUIS JADOT** Chambertin-Clos de Bèze 1988 • $90 • (02/28/95)

88 **LOUIS JADOT** Gevrey-Chambertin Le Clos St.-Jacques 1988 • $52 • (03/15/91)

88 **LOUIS JADOT** Nuits-St.-Georges Aux Boudots 1988 • $49 • (02/28/91)

88 **MACHARD DE GRAMONT** Nuits-St.-Georges Les Pruliers 1988 • $37 • (07/15/91)

Key: SS—Spectator Selection CS—Cellar Selection HR—Highly Recommended BB—Best Buy $NA—Price not available Ⓐ—Auction Price
Dates in parentheses indicate the issues in which the ratings were published.

88 **MARQUIS D'ANGERVILLE** Volnay Clos des Ducs 1988 • $47 • (10/31/93)

88 **MOILLARD** Beaune Hospices de Beaune Cuvée Clos des Avaux 1988 • $80 • (08/31/91)

88 **MOILLARD** Vosne-Romanée Aux Malconsorts Domaine Thomas-Moillard 1988 • $50 • (03/31/91)

88 **MONGEARD-MUGNERET** Echézeaux Vieille Vigne 1988 • $67 Ⓐ • (02/15/91)

88 **PONSOT** Clos de la Roche Cuvée Vieilles Vignes 1988 • $185 • (05/15/91)

88 **POTHIER-RIEUSSET** Beaune Les Boucherottes 1988 • $35 • (11/30/90)

88 **ROBERT JAYER-GILLES** Hautes Côtes de Beaune 1988 • $26 • (05/15/91)

88 **TOLLOT-BEAUT & FILS** Chorey-lès-Beaune 1988 • $25 • (12/31/90)

87 **ALAIN MICHELOT** Nuits-St.-Georges Les Vaucrains 1988 • $56 • (05/15/91)

87 **ALBERT BICHOT** Pommard 1988 • $25 • (08/31/90)

87 **ALBERT BICHOT** Volnay Cuvée Blondeau Hospices de Beaune 1988 • $60 • (06/15/92)

87 **ALBERT BICHOT** Vosne-Romanée Les Beaux Monts 1988 • $34 • (07/15/90)

87 **ALBERT MOROT** Beaune Les Bressandes 1988 • $30 • (03/31/91)

87 **ALETH GIRARDIN** Pommard Les Charmots 1988 • $44 • (07/15/91)

87 **CHANSON PÈRE & FILS** Vosne-Romanée Les Suchots 1988 • $55 • (09/30/90)

87 **CHARLES MORTET** Gevrey-Chambertin Champeaux 1988 • $46 • (03/15/91)

87 **CHARTRON & TRÉBUCHET** Pommard Les Epenots 1988 • $45 • (02/28/91)

87 **CHÂTEAU DE MEURSAULT** Volnay Clos des Chênes 1988 • $47 • (07/15/91)

87 **CHÂTEAU DE POMMARD** Pommard 1988 • $53 • (09/15/92)

87 **CHÂTEAU DES HERBEAUX** Chambertin 1988 • $75 • (12/31/90)

87 **CHOPIN-GROFFIER** Clos Vougeot 1988 • $70 • (05/15/91)

87 **DANIEL RION** Chambolle-Musigny Aux Beaux Bruns 1988 • $37 • (01/31/91)

87 **DOMAINE LEROY** Richebourg 1988 • $345 • (12/15/96)

87 **DOMAINE DE L'ARLOT** Nuits-St.-Georges Clos de L'Arlot 1988 • $43 • (03/31/91)

87 **DOMAINE DU CLOS FRANTIN** Gevrey-Chambertin 1988 • $37 • (07/15/90)

87 **GHISLAINE BARTHOD** Chambolle-Musigny Les Cras 1988 • $45 • (02/28/91)

87 **GUY CASTAGNIER** Bonnes Mares 1988 • $67 • (07/15/91)

87 **JEAN GRIVOT** Nuits-St.-Georges Aux Boudots 1988 • $54 • (04/30/91)

87 **JOSEPH DROUHIN** Chambolle-Musigny Les Amoureuses 1988 • $76 • (12/31/90)

87 **JOSEPH DROUHIN** Latricières-Chambertin 1988 • $72 • (02/15/91)

87 **LAROCHE** Nuits-St.-Georges 1988 • $28 • (11/15/90)

87 **LEROY** Bourgogne d'Auvenay 1988 • $15 • (04/30/91)

87 **MÉO-CAMUZET** Vosne-Romanée 1988 • $50 • (12/31/90)

87 **MICHEL LAFARGE** Volnay Premier Cru 1988 • $44 • (07/15/91)

86 **ALBERT MOROT** Beaune Les Grèves 1988 • $32 • (07/15/91)

86 **ALBERT MOROT** Savigny-lès-Beaune Aux Vergelesses La Bataillère 1988 • $26 • (03/31/91)

86 **BERNARD SERVEAU** Chambolle-Musigny Les Chabiots 1988 • $39 • (02/28/91)

86 **CHANDON DE BRIAILLES** Savigny-lès-Beaune Les Lavières 1988 • $31 • (02/28/91)

86 **CHÂTEAU DES HERBEAUX** Clos Vougeot 1988 • $65 • (11/30/90)

86 **DUJAC** Gevrey-Chambertin Aux Combottes 1988 • $54 • (03/31/91)

86 **GEORGES MUGNERET** Chambolle-Musigny Les Feusselottes 1988 • $54 • (11/15/90)

86 **GÉRARD MUGNERET** Vosne-Romanée 1988 • $37 • (02/28/91)

86 **GUY CASTAGNIER** Clos de Vougeot 1988 • $65 • (08/31/91)

86 **JACQUES-FRÉDÉRIC MUGNIER** Chambolle-Musigny 1988 • $96 Ⓐ • (05/15/91)

86 **JACQUES-FRÉDÉRIC MUGNIER** Chambolle-Musigny Les Amoureuses 1988 • $80 • (05/15/91)

86 **JEAN GARAUDET** Beaune Le Clos des Mouches 1988 • $40 • (11/15/90)

86 **JEAN-NOËL GAGNARD** Chassagne-Montrachet Morgeot Red 1988 • $20 • (12/31/90)

86 **JESSIAUME PÈRE & FILS** Santenay Les Gravières 1988 • $21 • (03/31/91)

86 **LABOURÉ-ROI** Chambolle-Musigny 1988 • $35 • (02/28/91)

86 **LOUIS JADOT** Pernand-Vergelesses Clos de la Croix de Pierre 1988 • $17 • (03/31/91)

86 **LOUIS JADOT** Pommard Les Grands Epenots 1988 • $38 • (03/31/91)

86 **MAUME** Charmes-Chambertin 1988 • $60 • (07/15/91)

86 **PAUL PERNOT** Beaune Les Teurons 1988 • $33 • (03/31/91)

86 **PIERRE AMIOT** Clos de la Roche 1988 • $75 • (03/15/91)

86 **ROBERT ARNOUX** Vosne-Romanée Les Suchots 1988 • $60 • (02/28/91)

86 **ROUX PÈRE & FILS** Volnay En Champans 1988 • $35 • (03/31/90)

86 **TOLLOT-BEAUT & FILS** Beaune Clos du Roi 1988 • $53 • (02/28/91)

85 **BOUCHARD PÈRE & FILS** Beaune Les Grèves Vigne de l'Enfant Jésus Domaines du Château de Beaune 1988 • $59 • (02/28/95)

85 **BOUCHARD PÈRE & FILS** Chassagne-Montrachet Red 1988 • $22 • (04/30/91)

85 **CHANSON PÈRE & FILS** Pernand-Vergelesses Les Vergelesses 1988 • $24 • (08/31/90)

85 **DOMAINE DE L'ARLOT** Nuits-St.-Georges Clos des Forêts St.-Georges 1988 • $53 • (03/31/91)

85 **DOMAINE DE LA POUSSE D'OR** Volnay Les Caillerets 1988 • $49 • (08/31/91)

85 **DUJAC** Charmes-Chambertin 1988 • $60 • (03/31/91)

85 **FRANÇOISE & DENIS CLAIR** Santenay La Comme 1988 • $25 • (06/15/92)

85 **G. VACHET-ROUSSEAU** Gevrey-Chambertin 1988 • $30 • (12/31/90)

85 **J. FAIVELEY** Nuits-St.-Georges Les Damodes 1988 • $52 • (03/31/91)

85 **JEAN GRIVOT** Clos de Vougeot 1988 • $70 • (04/30/91)

85 **JOSEPH DROUHIN** Volnay Clos des Chênes 1988 • $45 • (02/15/91)

85 **LEROY** Auxey-Duresses Les Clous Red 1988 • $52 • (05/15/91)

85 **LOUIS JADOT** Chassagne-Montrachet Morgeot Clos de la Chapelle Duc de Magenta Red 1988 • $20 • (03/31/91)

85 **MARC MOREY** Beaune Les Paules 1988 • $24 • (08/31/90)

85 **PIERRE BOILLOT** Volnay-Santenots 1988 • $37 • (08/31/90)

85 **PONSOT** Clos St.-Denis Cuvée Vieilles Vignes 1988 • $165 • (07/15/91)

85 **PONSOT** Morey-St.-Denis Monts Luisants 1988 • $40 • (04/30/91)

85 **PRIEUR-BRUNET** Volnay-Santenots 1988 • $35 • (11/30/90)

Domaine du Château de Puligny-Montrachet in Côte de Beaune.

White Burgundy

Here are *Wine Spectator*'s ratings and prices for the five best recent vintages of white Burgundy—1996, 1995, 1994, 1992 and 1990. These Burgundian Chardonnays are organized by vintage and then in descending order of score, to make it easy to identify the best wines of each vintage.

The two most recent vintages on sale, 1995 and 1996, are both rated outstanding. Note that 1996 is a year for longer-aging white wines, while 1995 is more friendly to drink now. If you can find the increasingly rare 1990s—and 1989s—for sale at reliable wine shops where you believe they have been properly stored, they are worth buying. Both vintages are rated Outstanding (92) by *Wine Spectator*. The 1992 and 1994 vintages are very good, but perhaps not quite as remarkable. 1991 and 1993 weren't as good overall, and make for riskier shopping.

1996 WHITE BURGUNDY | VINTAGE RATING: 93

99 **LAROCHE** Chablis Les Clos 1996 • $82 • (05/31/98) • CS

99 **MARC COLIN** Montrachet 1996 • $250 • (05/31/98)

98 **J. MOREAU & FILS** Chablis Les Clos 1996 • $47 • (05/31/98)

98 **JOSEPH DROUHIN** Chablis Les Clos 1996 • $50 • (05/31/98)

98 **LAROCHE** Chablis Réserve de l'Obédience 1996 • $110 • (05/31/98)

98 **VERGET** Chablis Vaillons 1996 • $29 • (05/31/98)

97 **BLAIN-GAGNARD** Bâtard-Montrachet 1996 • $110 • (05/31/98) • CS

97 **JEAN CHARTRON** Chevalier-Montrachet Clos des Chevaliers 1996 • $170 • (05/31/98)

97 **MARC COLIN** Bâtard-Montrachet 1996 • $130 • (05/31/98)

96 **BOUCHARD PÈRE & FILS** Chevalier-Montrachet 1996 • $150 • (05/31/98)

96 **JEAN-MARC BOILLOT** Puligny-Montrachet La Truffière 1996 • $72 • (05/31/98)

96 **JEAN-PAUL DROIN** Chablis Les Clos 1996 • $40 • (05/31/98)

Key: SS—Spectator Selection CS—Cellar Selection HR—Highly Recommended BB—Best Buy $NA—Price not available Ⓐ—Auction Price
Dates in parentheses indicate the issues in which the ratings were published.

96 **VERGET** Chablis Montée de Tonnerre 1996 • $30 • (05/31/98)

95 **A. LONG-DEPAQUIT** Chablis Les Preuses 1996 • $35 • (05/31/98)

95 **BLAIN-GAGNARD** Criots-Bâtard-Montrachet 1996 • $110 • (05/31/98)

95 **BOUCHARD PÈRE & FILS** Corton-Charlemagne 1996 • $110 • (05/31/98)

95 **JEAN-MARC BOILLOT** Puligny-Montrachet Les Referts 1996 • $62 • (05/31/98)

95 **JEAN-MARC BROCARD** Chablis Beauregard 1996 • $25 • (05/31/98)

95 **JEAN-PAUL DROIN** Chablis Valmur 1996 • $40 • (05/31/98)

95 **JEAN-PAUL DROIN** Chablis Vaudésir 1996 • $40 • (05/31/98)

95 **ROGER BELLAND** Criots-Bâtard-Montrachet 1996 • $90 • (05/31/98)

95 **VINCENT GIRARDIN** Meursault Les Perrières 1996 • $65 • (05/31/98)

94 **ALBERT GRIVAULT** Meursault Les Perrières 1996 • $50 • (05/31/98)

94 **BILLAUD-SIMON** Chablis Les Clos 1996 • $NA • (05/31/98)

94 **CORDIER PÈRE & FILS** Pouilly-Fuissé Vieilles Vignes 1996 • $29 • (05/31/98)

94 **DOMAINE DES MALANDES** Chablis Côte de Léchet 1996 • $17 • (05/31/98)

■ ■ ■ ■

White Burgundy

94 **JEAN DAUVISSAT** Chablis Vaillons 1996 • $25 • (05/31/98)

94 **JEAN PILLOT** Chevalier-Montrachet 1996 • $150 • (05/31/98)

94 **JEAN-MARC BOILLOT** Puligny-Montrachet Les Combettes 1996 • $72 • (05/31/98)

94 **JEAN-MARC BOILLOT** Puligny-Montrachet Les Pucelles 1996 • $62 • (05/31/98)

94 **JEAN-PAUL DROIN** Chablis Montée de Tonnerre 1996 • $18 • (08/31/97)

94 **JEAN-PAUL DROIN** Chablis Montmains 1996 • $23 • (05/31/98)

94 **JEAN-PAUL DROIN** Chablis Vaillons 1996 • $23 • (05/31/98)

94 **JEAN-PAUL DROIN** Chablis Vosgros 1996 • $23 • (05/31/98)

94 **LA CHABLISIENNE** Chablis Bougros 1996 • $42 • (05/31/98)

94 **LA CHABLISIENNE** Chablis Les Fourchaumes 1996 • $27 • (05/31/98)

94 **LA CHABLISIENNE** Chablis Montée de Tonnerre 1996 • $27 • (05/31/98)

94 **LA CHABLISIENNE** Chablis Valmur 1996 • $42 • (05/31/98)

94 **LAROCHE** Chablis Les Fourchaumes 1996 • $40 • (05/31/98)

94 **LOUIS MICHEL** Chablis Les Clos 1996 • $46 • (05/31/98)

94 **MICHEL BARAT** Chablis Côte de Léchet 1996 • $15 • (05/31/98)

94 **MICHEL BARAT** Chablis Monts de Milieu 1996 • $15 • (05/31/98)

94 **MICHEL JUILLOT** Corton-Charlemagne 1996 • $95 • (05/31/98)

94 **VINCENT GIRARDIN** Corton-Charlemagne 1996 • $83 • (05/31/98)

93 **BILLAUD-SIMON** Chablis Montée de Tonnerre 1996 • $24 • (05/31/98)

93 **CHÂTEAU DE MALIGNY** Chablis Fourchaume 1996 • $25 • (08/31/97)

93 **CHÂTEAU DE VIVIERS** Chablis Blanchots 1996 • $44 • (05/31/98)

93 **CHÂTEAU DE VIVIERS** Chablis Vaillons 1996 • $26 • (05/31/98)

93 **DOMAINE BORGEOT** Santenay Les Gravières White 1996 • $26 • (05/31/98)

93 **DOMAINE DE VAUDON** Chablis 1996 • $20 • (05/31/98)

93 **FONTAINE-GAGNARD** Criots-Bâtard-Montrachet 1996 • $148 • (05/31/98)

93 **FONTAINE-GAGNARD** Montrachet 1996 • $336 • (05/31/98)

93 **J. MOREAU & FILS** Chablis Valmur 1996 • $46 • (05/31/98)

93 **JEAN PILLOT** Chassagne-Montrachet Morgeot 1996 • $40 • (05/31/98)

93 **JEAN-MARC BOILLOT** Meursault 1996 • $39 • (05/31/98)

93 **JEAN-MARC BOILLOT** Puligny-Montrachet Les Folatières 1996 • $56 • (05/31/98)

Key: SS—Spectator Selection CS—Cellar Selection HR—Highly Recommended BB—Best Buy $NA—Price not available Ⓐ—Auction Price
Dates in parentheses indicate the issues in which the ratings were published.

93 **JEAN-MARC BROCARD** Chablis Bougros 1996 • $45 • (05/31/98)

93 **JEAN-MARC BROCARD** Chablis Fourchaume 1996 • $25 • (05/31/98)

93 **JEAN-MARC BROCARD** Chablis Les Clos 1996 • $45 • (05/31/98)

93 **LA CHABLISIENNE** Chablis Montmain 1996 • $25 • (05/31/98)

93 **LA CHABLISIENNE** Chablis Premier Cru Vieilles Vignes 1996 • $25 • (05/31/98)

93 **LA CHABLISIENNE** Chablis Vaillon 1996 • $25 • (05/31/98)

93 **LALEURE-PIOT** Corton-Charlemagne 1996 • $96 • (05/31/98)

93 **LOUIS MICHEL** Chablis Montée de Tonnerre 1996 • $30 • (05/31/98)

93 **LOUIS PINSON** Chablis Mont de Milieu 1996 • $22 • (05/31/98)

93 **MARC COLIN** St.-Aubin Le Charmois White 1996 • $35 • (05/31/98)

93 **MARC COLIN** St.-Aubin Les Combes White 1996 • $35 • (05/31/98)

93 **MARC MOREY** Chassagne-Montrachet Les Vergers 1996 • $48 • (05/31/98)

93 **MAROSLAVAC-LEGER** Puligny-Montrachet Les Folatières 1996 • $50 • (05/31/98)

93 **MICHEL BARAT** Chablis Vaillons 1996 • $15 • (05/31/98)

93 **MICHEL BOUZEREAU & FILS** Meursault Les Genevrières 1996 • $NA • (05/31/98)

93 **MONTHÉLIE-DOUHAIRET** Meursault Les Santenots 1996 • $53 • (05/31/98)

93 **PASCAL BOUCHARD** Chablis Vaudésir 1996 • $44 • (05/31/98)

93 **RÉMI JOBARD** Meursault Les Genevrières 1996 • $55 • (05/31/98)

93 **VERGET** Pouilly-Fuissé Tête de Cuvée 1996 • $15 • (05/31/98) • HR

93 **VINCENT GIRARDIN** Chassagne-Montrachet Morgeot Vieilles Vignes 1996 • $NA • (05/31/98)

93 **VINCENT GIRARDIN** Meursault Les Narvaux 1996 • $42 • (05/31/98)

92 **A. LONG-DEPAQUIT** Chablis Les Vaillons 1996 • $25 • (05/31/98)

92 **ALBERT GRIVAULT** Meursault Clos des Perrières 1996 • $60 • (05/31/98)

92 **BILLAUD-SIMON** Chablis Les Blanchots Vieilles Vignes 1996 • $60 • (05/31/98)

92 **BOUCHARD PÈRE & FILS** Beaune Premier Cru White 1996 • $38 • (05/31/98)

92 **BOUCHARD PÈRE & FILS** Puligny-Montrachet Les Pucelles 1996 • $68 • (05/31/98)

92 **CHÂTEAU DE PULIGNY-MONTRACHET** Meursault 1996 • $26 • (05/31/98)

92 **CHÂTEAU DE VIVIERS** Chablis 1996 • $18 • (05/31/98)

92 **CHÂTEAU DE VIVIERS** Chablis Vaucopins 1996 • $25 • (05/31/98)

92 **CHÂTEAU DE LA MALTROYE** Chassagne-Montrachet Grandes Ruchottes 1996 • $50 • (05/31/98)

92 **CLAUDE ET HUBERT CHAVY-CHOUET** Puligny-Montrachet Les Enseignères 1996 • $45 • (05/31/98)

92 **CORSIN** Pouilly-Fuissé 1996 • $23 • (05/31/98)

92 **ETIENNE BOILEAU** Chablis Montée de Tonnerre 1996 • $25 • (05/31/98)

92 **FRANÇOIS D'ALLAINES** Mâcon La Roche Vineuse 1996 • $NA • (05/31/98)

92 **GÉRARD CHAVY** Puligny-Montrachet Les Perrières 1996 • $40 • (05/31/98)

92 **GHISLAINE & JEAN-HUGUES GOISOT** Sauvignon de St.-Bris 1996 • $14 • (05/31/98)

92 **HENRI CLERC & FILS** Chevalier-Montrachet 1996 • $120 • (05/31/98)

92 **HUBERT LAMY** St.-Aubin Clos de la Chatenière White 1996 • $22 • (05/31/98)

92 **HUBERT LAMY** St.-Aubin Les Murgers des Dents de Chien White 1996 • $28 • (05/31/98)

92 **HUBERT LAMY** Chassagne-Montrachet Les Macherelles 1996 • $38 • (05/31/98)

92 **HUBERT LAMY** St.-Aubin En Remilly White 1996 • $22 • (05/31/98)

92 **JACQUES BURRIER** Pouilly-Fuissé Château de Beauregard Cuvée Prestige 1996 • $21 • (05/31/98)

92 **JEAN DAUVISSAT** Chablis 1996 • $18 • (05/31/98)

92 **JEAN DAUVISSAT** Chablis Séchet 1996 • $23 • (05/31/98)

92 **JEAN-CLAUDE COURTAULT** Chablis 1996 • $NA • (08/31/97)

92 **JOSEPH DROUHIN** Corton-Charlemagne 1996 • $92 • (05/31/98)

92 **JOSEPH DROUHIN** Puligny-Montrachet Clos de la Garenne 1996 • $65 • (05/31/98)

92 **LAMBLIN & FILS** Chablis Fourchaume 1996 • $NA • (08/31/97)

92 **SIMONNET-FEBVRE** Chablis Fourchaume 1996 • $23 • (05/31/98)

92 **VINCENT GIRARDIN** Savigny-lès-Beaune Dessus les Vermots White 1996 • $28 • (05/31/98)

92 **WILLIAM FÈVRE** Chablis Montée de Tonnerre 1996 • $22 • (05/31/98)

91 **BERNARD LÉGLAND** Chablis Montmains 1996 • $24 • (05/31/98)

91 **BILLAUD-SIMON** Chablis Mont de Milieu 1996 • $24 • (05/31/98)

91 **BILLAUD-SIMON** Chablis Mont de Milieu Vieilles Vignes 1996 • $27 • (05/31/98)

91 **BLAIN-GAGNARD** Chassagne-Montrachet Morgeot 1996 • $45 • (05/31/98)

91 **BOUCHARD PÈRE & FILS** Puligny-Montrachet Les Chalumeaux 1996 • $50 • (05/31/98)

91 **CHÂTEAU FUISSÉ** Pouilly-Fuissé Vieilles Vignes 1996 • $49 • (05/31/98)

91 **CORSIN** Mâcon-Villages 1996 • $13 • (08/31/97)

91 **FONTAINE-GAGNARD** Bâtard-Montrachet 1996 • $148 • (05/31/98)

91 **GHISLAINE & JEAN-HUGUES GOISOT** Bourgogne Aligoté 1996 • $14 • (05/31/98)

91 **HUBERT LAMY** St.-Aubin Les Frionnes White 1996 • $20 • (05/31/98)

91 **J.-A. FERRET** Pouilly-Fuissé Les Scélés 1996 • $26 • (05/31/98)

91 **JACQUES BURRIER** Pouilly-Fuissé Château de Beauregard 1996 • $21 • (05/31/98)

91 **JEAN-MARC BOILLOT** Montagny Premier Cru 1996 • $20 • (05/31/98)

91 **JEAN-MARC BROCARD** Bourgogne sur Kimmeridjien White 1996 • $15 • (08/31/97)

91 **JEAN-MARC BROCARD** Chablis Vieilles Vignes 1996 • $21 • (08/31/97)

91 **MARC COLIN** Chassagne-Montrachet Caillerets 1996 • $50 • (05/31/98)

91 **MARC MOREY** Chassagne-Montrachet Les Chenevottes 1996 • $44 • (05/31/98)

91 **MARC MOREY** Chassagne-Montrachet Morgeot 1996 • $50 • (05/31/98)

91 **MAROSLAVAC-LEGER** Meursault Au Murger de Monthélie 1996 • $36 • (05/31/98)

91 **MICHEL BOUZEREAU & FILS** Meursault Les Grands Charrons 1996 • $36 • (05/31/98)

91 **MICHEL BOUZEREAU & FILS** Puligny-Montrachet Champ Gain 1996 • $55 • (05/31/98)

91 **MICHEL MOREY-COFFINET** Chassagne-Montrachet La Romanée 1996 • $47 • (05/31/98)

91 **PASCAL BOUCHARD** Chablis Blanchots 1996 • $44 • (05/31/98)

91 **RÉMI JOBARD** Meursault Sous La Velle 1996 • $35 • (05/31/98)

91 **SIMONNET-FEBVRE** Chablis 1996 • $15 • (08/31/97)

91 **VERGET** Chablis 1996 • $20 • (05/31/98)

91 **VERGET** St.-Aubin Premier Cru White 1996 • $28 • (05/31/98)

90 **A. LONG-DEPAQUIT** Chablis Les Beugnons 1996 • $25 • (05/31/98)

90 **BILLAUD-SIMON** Chablis Fourchaume 1996 • $26 • (05/31/98)

90 **BOUCHARD PÈRE & FILS** Beaune Clos St.-Landry White 1996 • $50 • (05/31/98)

90 **BOUCHARD PÈRE & FILS** Chassagne-Montrachet 1996 • $39 • (05/31/98)

90 **BOUCHARD PÈRE & FILS** Meursault 1996 • $35 • (05/31/98)

90 **BOUCHARD PÈRE & FILS** Puligny-Montrachet Les Folatières 1996 • $55 • (05/31/98)

90 **CHARTRON & TRÉBUCHET** St.-Aubin La Chatenière White 1996 • $25 • (05/31/98)

90 **CLAUDE ET HUBERT CHAVY-CHOUET** Puligny-Montrachet Hameau de Blagny Vieille Vigne 1996 • $60 • (05/31/98)

90 **CORDIER PÈRE & FILS** Pouilly-Fuissé Au Metertiere 1996 • $32 • (05/31/98)

90 **DANIEL BARRAUD** Pouilly-Fuissé La Verchère 1996 • $25 • (05/31/98)

90 **DEMESSEY** Pernand-Vergelesses Sous le Bois de Noël et Belles Filles White 1996 • $19 • (05/31/98)

90 **DOMAINE DE LA BONGRAN** Mâcon-Clessé Quintaine Cuvée Tradition 1996 • $25 • (05/31/98)

90 **FONTAINE-GAGNARD** Chassagne-Montrachet Clos St.-Jean Clos Les Murées 1996 • $60 • (05/31/98)

90 **FONTAINE-GAGNARD** Chassagne-Montrachet Caillerets 1996 • $60 • (05/31/98)

90 **FRANCINE ET OLIVIER SAVARY** Chablis 1996 • $NA • (08/31/97)

90 **GILBERT PICQ** Chablis Vosgros 1996 • $22 • (05/31/98)

90 **H. & P. JACQUESON** Rully La Pucelle White 1996 • $20 • (05/31/98)

90 **JEAN CHARTRON** Puligny-Montrachet Clos du Cailleret 1996 • $60 • (05/31/98)

90 **JEAN PILLOT** Chassagne-Montrachet Les Champs Gain 1996 • $38 • (05/31/98)

90 **JEAN PILLOT** Chassagne-Montrachet Les Chenevottes 1996 • $35 • (05/31/98)

90 **JEAN-CLAUDE THÉVENET** Mâcon-Pierreclos 1996 • $13 • (08/31/97)

■ ■ ■ ■

White Burgundy

90 **JEAN-MARC BOILLOT** Rully Grésigny White 1996 • $21 • (05/31/98)

90 **JEAN-MARC BROCARD** Petit Chablis 1996 • $18 • (08/31/97)

90 **JEAN-PIERRE GROSSOT** Chablis Les Fourneaux 1996 • $22 • (05/31/98)

90 **JEAN-PIERRE GROSSOT** Chablis Vaucoupin 1996 • $25 • (05/31/98)

90 **JOSEPH DROUHIN** Beaune Clos des Mouches White 1996 • $78 • (05/31/98)

90 **JOSEPH DROUHIN** Chablis Premier Cru 1996 • $25 • (08/31/97) • SS

90 **LAMBLIN & FILS** Chablis 1996 • $NA • (08/31/97)

90 **LOUIS PINSON** Chablis Les Clos 1996 • $33 • (05/31/98)

90 **MARC COLIN** Puligny-Montrachet La Garenne 1996 • $50 • (05/31/98)

90 **MARC COLIN** St.-Aubin En Remilly White 1996 • $35 • (05/31/98)

90 **MARC COLIN** St.-Aubin La Chatenière White 1996 • $35 • (05/31/98)

90 **MARC COLIN** St.-Aubin Les Cortons White 1996 • $35 • (05/31/98)

90 **MARC MOREY** Chassagne-Montrachet 1996 • $32 • (05/31/98)

90 **MARC MOREY** Chassagne-Montrachet En Virondot 1996 • $44 • (05/31/98)

90 **MAROSLAVAC-LEGER** Puligny-Montrachet Les Combettes 1996 • $50 • (05/31/98)

90 **MICHEL BOUZEREAU & FILS** Meursault Le Limozin 1996 • $NA • (05/31/98)

90 **MICHEL BOUZEREAU & FILS** Meursault Les Charmes-Dessus 1996 • $NA • (05/31/98)

90 **PASCAL BOUCHARD** Chablis Les Clos 1996 • $44 • (05/31/98)

90 **PAUL GARAUDET** Meursault Vieilles Vignes 1996 • $32 • (05/31/98)

90 **PIERRE LABET** Beaune Clos des Monsnières White 1996 • $33 • (05/31/98)

90 **RAPET PÈRE & FILS** Corton-Charlemagne 1996 • $79 • (05/31/98)

90 **RÉMI JOBARD** Bourgogne White 1996 • $20 • (05/31/98)

90 **RÉMI JOBARD** Meursault Le Poruzot-Dessus 1996 • $52 • (05/31/98)

90 **SERVIN** Chablis Bougros 1996 • $42 • (05/31/98)

90 **SERVIN** Chablis Les Clos 1996 • $45 • (05/31/98)

90 **SERVIN** Chablis Montée de Tonnerre 1996 • $26 • (05/31/98)

90 **THIERRY HAMELIN** Chablis 1996 • $17 • (08/31/97)

90 **THIERRY HAMELIN** Petit Chablis 1996 • $14 • (08/31/97)

90 **VERGET** St.-Véran 1996 • $13 • (05/31/98)

90 **VESSIGAUD PÈRE & FILS** Pouilly-Fuissé Vieilles Vignes 1996 • $27 • (05/31/98)

89 **A. LONG-DEPAQUIT** Chablis Les Lys 1996 • $25 • (05/31/98)

89 **ANDRÉ AUVIGUE** Pouilly-Fuissé Solutré 1996 • $18 • (05/31/98)

Key: SS—Spectator Selection CS—Cellar Selection HR—Highly Recommended BB—Best Buy $NA—Price not available Ⓐ—Auction Price

Dates in parentheses indicate the issues in which the ratings were published.

89 **BERNARD DEFAIX** Chablis Côte de Léchet 1996 • $26 • (05/31/98)

89 **BILLAUD-SIMON** Chablis Vaudésir 1996 • $40 • (05/31/98)

89 **BOUCHARD PÈRE & FILS** Puligny-Montrachet 1996 • $39 • (05/31/98)

89 **CATHERINE & PASCAL ROLLET** Pouilly-Fuissé Au Coeur du Cru 1996 • $NA • (05/31/98)

89 **CHÂTEAU DE MALIGNY** Chablis Vau de Vey 1996 • $25 • (05/31/98)

89 **CHÂTEAU DE PULIGNY-MONTRACHET** Monthélie White 1996 • $22 • (05/31/98)

89 **DOMAINE DE LA SOUFRANDISE** Pouilly-Fuissé Vieilles Vignes 1996 • $21 • (05/31/98)

89 **DOMAINE DES DEUX ROCHES** Mâcon-Davayé 1996 • $14 • (08/31/97)

89 **FONTAINE-GAGNARD** Chassagne-Montrachet Morgeot 1996 • $60 • (05/31/98)

89 **FONTAINE-GAGNARD** Chassagne-Montrachet La Maltroie 1996 • $60 • (05/31/98)

89 **GHISLAINE & JEAN-HUGUES GOISOT** Bourgogne Côtes d'Auxerre White 1996 • $15 • (05/31/98)

89 **GILBERT PICQ** Chablis 1996 • $19 • (08/31/97)

89 **JACQUES SAUMAIZE** Pouilly-Fuissé Vigne Blanche 1996 • $NA • (05/31/98)

89 **JEAN-MARC BOILLOT** Puligny-Montrachet 1996 • $42 • (05/31/98)

89 **JEANNE PAULE FILIPPI** Chablis Vaillons 1996 • $25 • (05/31/98)

89 **JEANNE PAULE FILIPPI** Chablis Montée de Tonnerre 1996 • $25 • (05/31/98)

89 **JOSEPH DROUHIN** Chablis Vaudésir 1996 • $48 • (05/31/98)

89 **LALEURE-PIOT** Pernand-Vergelesses White 1996 • $27 • (05/31/98)

89 **LE MANOIR MURISALTIEN** Mâcon-Fuissé 1996 • $12 • (05/31/98)

89 **LOUIS LATOUR** Chablis Beauroy 1996 • $27 • (05/31/98)

89 **MAROSLAVAC-LEGER** Puligny-Montrachet Champs Gain 1996 • $50 • (05/31/98)

89 **MICHEL JUILLOT** Mercurey Les Champs Martins White 1996 • $30 • (05/31/98)

89 **MICHEL MOREY-COFFINET** Chassagne-Montrachet 1996 • $35 • (05/31/98)

89 **MICHEL PRUNIER** Meursault Les Clous 1996 • $NA • (05/31/98)

89 **PAUL GARAUDET** Puligny-Montrachet 1996 • $32 • (05/31/98)

89 **RÉMI JOBARD** Meursault En Luraule 1996 • $37 • (05/31/98)

89 **SAUMAIZE-MICHELIN** Pouilly-Fuissé Clos de la Roche 1996 • $23 • (05/31/98)

89 **SIMONNET-FEBVRE** Chablis Montée de Tonnerre 1996 • $20 • (05/31/98)

89 **SIMONNET-FEBVRE** Chablis Vaillons 1996 • $19 • (05/31/98)

89 **VERGET** Bourgogne White 1996 • $16 • (05/31/98)

89 **VINCENT GIRARDIN** Puligny-Montrachet Les Referts 1996 • $NA • (05/31/98)

88 **A. LONG-DEPAQUIT** Chablis Les Vaucopins 1996 • $25 • (05/31/98)

88 **ALBERT BICHOT** Chablis 1996 • $22 • (05/31/98)

88 **BERNARD MOREAU** Chassagne-Montrachet Les Chenevottes 1996 • $38 • (05/31/98)

88 **BERNARD MOREAU** Chassagne-Montrachet Morgeot 1996 • $38 • (05/31/98)

88 **BERNARD MOREY** Chassagne-Montrachet La Maltroie 1996 • $45 • (05/31/98)

88 **BLAIN-GAGNARD** Chassagne-Montrachet Clos St.-Jean 1996 • $45 • (05/31/98)

88 **BRUNO CLAIR** Marsannay White 1996 • $29 • (05/31/98)

88 **CHÂTEAU FUISSÉ** Pouilly-Fuissé 1996 • $32 • (05/31/98)

88 **CHÂTEAU FUISSÉ** Pouilly-Fuissé Les Combettes 1996 • $37 • (05/31/98)

88 **CORDIER PÈRE & FILS** Pouilly-Fuissé Vieilles Vignes Grapillage 1996 • $63 • (05/31/98)

88 **CORDIER PÈRE & FILS** Pouilly-Fuissé Vignes Blanches 1996 • $32 • (05/31/98)

88 **CORDIER PÈRE & FILS** St.-Véran Clos à la Côte 1996 • $21 • (05/31/98)

88 **CORSIN** St.-Véran 1996 • $16 • (05/31/98)

88 **GEORGES DUBOEUF** Pouilly-Fuissé Domaine Béranger 1996 • $20 • (05/31/98)

88 **GHISLAINE & JEAN-HUGUES GOISOT** Bourgogne Côtes d'Auxerre Corps de Garde White 1996 • $17 • (05/31/98)

88 **GÉRARD CHAVY** Puligny-Montrachet Les Folatières 1996 • $40 • (05/31/98)

88 **JEAN CHARTRON** Puligny-Montrachet Les Folatières 1996 • $55 • (05/31/98)

88 **JEAN MANCIAT** Mâcon 1996 • $12 • (05/31/98)

88 **JEAN PILLOT** Chassagne-Montrachet Les Vergers 1996 • $38 • (05/31/98)

88 **JEAN-MARC BOILLOT** Puligny-Montrachet Champ Canet 1996 • $62 • (05/31/98)

88 **JEAN-MARC BROCARD** Bourgogne sur Portlandien White 1996 • $8 • (05/31/98)

88 **JEANNE PAULE FILIPPI** Chablis Champs Royaux 1996 • $17 • (05/31/98)

88 **L'HÉRITIER-GUYOT** Mâcon-Villages 1996 • $9 • (08/31/97)

88 **LA CHABLISIENNE** Chablis Les Clos 1996 • $58 • (05/31/98)

88 **LA CHABLISIENNE** Chablis Mont de Milieu 1996 • $27 • (05/31/98)

88 **LA GOUZOTTE D'OR** St.-Romain White 1996 • $14 • (05/31/98)

88 **LAROCHE** Chablis St.-Martin 1996 • $23 • (05/31/98)

88 **LAURENT TRIBUT** Chablis 1996 • $22 • (05/31/98)

88 **LE MANOIR MURISALTIEN** Pouilly-Fuissé 1996 • $18 • (05/31/98)

88 **LOUIS MICHEL** Chablis Grenouilles 1996 • $48 • (05/31/98)

88 **MICHEL BOUZEREAU & FILS** Bourgogne White 1996 • $NA • (05/31/98)

88 **OLIVIER LEFLAIVE FRÈRES** St.-Aubin En Remilly White 1996 • $29 • (05/31/98)

88 **PASCAL BOUCHARD** Chablis Montmains 1996 • $29 • (05/31/98)

88 **SERVIN** Chablis Vaillons 1996 • $24 • (05/31/98)

88 **THIERRY GUÉRIN** Pouilly-Fuissé La Roche 1996 • $24 • (05/31/98)

88 **VERGET** Mâcon-Villages Tête de Cuvée 1996 • $15 • (05/31/98)

88 **VINCENT GIRARDIN** Chassagne-Montrachet Le Cailleret 1996 • $51 • (05/31/98)

88 **VINCENT GIRARDIN** Santenay Le Beaurepaire White 1996 • $33 • (05/31/98)

88 **VINCENT GIRARDIN** Santenay Les Gravières White 1996 • $33 • (05/31/98)

87 **ALAIN GEOFFROY** Chablis 1996 • $NA • (08/31/97)

87 **ANTONIN RODET** Mâcon-Villages 1996 • $14 • (08/31/97)

87 **BERNARD MOREAU** Chassagne-Montrachet 1996 • $30 • (05/31/98)

87 **BILLAUD-SIMON** Chablis 1996 • $NA • (08/31/97)

87 **BOUCHARD PÈRE & FILS** Auxey-Duresses White 1996 • $22 • (05/31/98)

87 **CATHERINE & PASCAL ROLLET** Pouilly-Fuissé Domaine de la Chapelle Vieilles Vignes 1996 • $20 • (05/31/98)

87 **CHARTRON & TRÉBUCHET** Meursault 1996 • $35 • (05/31/98)

87 **CHARTRON & TRÉBUCHET** Puligny-Montrachet 1996 • $45 • (05/31/98)

87 **DEMESSEY** Mâcon-Cruzilles Cuvée Spéciale 1996 • $14 • (08/31/97)

87 **DENIS POMMIER** Chablis Beauroy 1996 • $NA • (05/31/98)

87 **DIDIER TRIPOZ** Charnay-lès-Mâcon Clos des Tournons 1996 • $9 • (08/31/97)

87 **DOMAINE DE LALANDE** Pouilly-Fuissé Clos Reyssié 1996 • $NA • (05/31/98)

87 **FONTAINE-GAGNARD** Chassagne-Montrachet Les Chenevottes 1996 • $60 • (05/31/98)

87 **GEORGES DUBOEUF** Pouilly-Fuissé 1996 • $19 • (05/31/98)

87 **GEORGES DUBOEUF** Pouilly-Fuissé Elevé en Fût de Chêne 1996 • $20 • (05/31/98)

87 **HENRI NAUDIN-FERRAND** Hautes-Côtes de Beaune White 1996 • $14 • (05/31/98)

87 **HENRI NAUDIN-FERRAND** Hautes Côtes de Nuits White 1996 • $14 • (05/31/98)

87 **HUBERT LAMY** St.-Aubin Les Cortons White 1996 • $22 • (05/31/98)

87 **JEAN DAUVISSAT** Chablis Les Preuses 1996 • $45 • (05/31/98)

87 **JEAN DAUVISSAT** Chablis Vaillons Vieilles Vignes 1996 • $30 • (05/31/98)

87 **JEAN-CLAUDE COURTAULT** Chablis Montmain Domaine de la Tour 1996 • $NA • (05/31/98)

87 **JEAN-MARC BROCARD** Chablis Montmains 1996 • $23 • (05/31/98)

87 **JOSEPH DROUHIN** Chablis 1996 • $19 • (08/31/97)

87 **JOSEPH DROUHIN** Puligny-Montrachet Les Folatières 1996 • $65 • (05/31/98)

87 **LA CHABLISIENNE** Chablis Côte de Léchet 1996 • $25 • (05/31/98)

87 **LA GOUZOTTE D'OR** Chablis 1996 • $18 • (05/31/98)

87 **LOUIS MOREAU** Chablis Les Fourneaux 1996 • $25 • (05/31/98)

87 **LOUIS MOREAU** Chablis Vaulignot 1996 • $22 • (05/31/98)

87 **LYNE & JEAN-BERNARD MARCHIVE** Petit Chablis 1996 • $NA • (08/31/97)

87 **MARC COLIN** Puligny-Montrachet Le Trézin 1996 • $40 • (05/31/98)

87 **MICHEL PICARD** Pouilly-Fuissé 1996 • $24 • (01/31/98)

87 **SYLVAIN MOSNIER** Chablis Côte de Lechet 1996 • $24 • (05/31/98)

87 **THOMAS** St.-Véran Vieilles Vignes 1996 • $18 • (05/31/98)

87 **VERGET** Chassagne-Montrachet 1996 • $35 • (05/31/98)

87 **VERGET** Santenay White 1996 • $24 • (05/31/98)

87 **VESSIGAUD PÈRE & FILS** Mâcon-Fuissé 1996 • $16 • (05/31/98)

87 **VINCENT GIRARDIN** Santenay Clos du Beauregard White 1996 • $NA • (05/31/98)

87 **VINCENT GIRARDIN** Savigny-lès-Beaune Les Vergelesses White 1996 • $32 • (05/31/98)

86 **ALAIN GEOFFROY** Chablis Beauroy 1996 • $20 • (05/31/98)

86 **ALAIN GEOFFROY** Petit Chablis 1996 • $NA • (08/31/97)

86 **AUVIGUE & REVEL** Mâcon-Fuissé Vendanges Manuelles 1996 • $15 • (08/31/97)

86 **BILLAUD-SIMON** Chablis Les Vaillons 1996 • $22 • (05/31/98)

86 **CHARTRON & TRÉBUCHET** Chassagne-Montrachet 1996 • $40 • (05/31/98)

86 **CORDIER PÈRE & FILS** Pouilly-Fuissé Vieilles Vignes 2ème Tri Sélection 1996 • $63 • (05/31/98)

86 **CORSIN** St.-Véran Tirage Précoce 1996 • $15 • (05/31/98)

86 **DOMAINE DE LA SOUFRANDISE** Pouilly-Fuissé Clos la Soufrandise 1996 • $17 • (05/31/98)

86 **DOMAINE DES VELANGES** Mâcon-Davayé 1996 • $NA • (08/31/97)

86 **FONTAINE-GAGNARD** Chassagne-Montrachet Les Vergers 1996 • $60 • (05/31/98)

86 **JEAN-CLAUDE COURTAULT** Petit Chablis 1996 • $NA • (08/31/97)

86 **JEAN-MARC BOILLOT** Givry White 1996 • $21 • (05/31/98)

86 **JEAN-MARC PILLOT** Puligny-Montrachet Le Caillerets 1996 • $NA • (05/31/98)

86 **JEAN-PIERRE GROSSOT** Chablis 1996 • $18 • (08/31/97)

86 **JOSEPH DROUHIN** Pouilly-Fuissé 1996 • $15 • (05/31/98)

86 **JOSEPH DROUHIN** Rully White 1996 • $21 • (05/31/98)

86 **JOSEPH DROUHIN** St.-Aubin White 1996 • $32 • (05/31/98)

86 **JOSEPH DROUHIN** St.-Véran 1996 • $13 • (05/31/98)

86 **LYNE & JEAN-BERNARD MARCHIVE** Chablis 1996 • $NA • (08/31/97)

86 **OLIVIER LEFLAIVE FRÈRES** Mercurey White 1996 • $23 • (05/31/98)

86 **PASCAL BOUCHARD** Chablis 1996 • $21 • (08/31/97)

86 **PASCAL BOUCHARD** Chablis Mont de Milieu 1996 • $29 • (05/31/98)

86 **PAUL BOURGEON** Mâcon-Villages 1996 • $11 • (05/31/98)

86 **ROGER LUQUET** Mâcon Clos de Condemine 1996 • $11 • (05/31/98)

86 **SIMONNET-FEBVRE** Chablis Mont de Milieu 1996 • $20 • (08/31/97)

86 **THOMAS** Pouilly-Fuissé Vieilles Vignes 1996 • $25 • (05/31/98)

85 **A. LONG-DEPAQUIT** Chablis 1996 • $NA • (08/31/97)

Key: SS—Spectator Selection CS—Cellar Selection HR—Highly Recommended BB—Best Buy $NA—Price not available Ⓐ—Auction Price

Dates in parentheses indicate the issues in which the ratings were published.

85 **ALAIN GEOFFROY** Chablis Domaine le Verger Cuvée Vieilles Vignes 1996 • $NA • (08/31/97)

85 **BLAIN-GAGNARD** Chassagne-Montrachet Caillerets 1996 • $45 • (05/31/98)

85 **BRUNO CLAIR** Morey-St.-Denis En la Rue de Vergy White 1996 • $55 • (05/31/98)

85 **CHARTRON & TRÉBUCHET** Montagny Les Grandes Vignes 1996 • $17 • (05/31/98)

85 **CHARTRON & TRÉBUCHET** Montrachet 1996 • $240 • (05/31/98)

85 **CHARTRON & TRÉBUCHET** Rully La Chaume White 1996 • $19 • (05/31/98)

85 **CHARTRON & TRÉBUCHET** St.-Véran Château de Chasselas 1996 • $14 • (05/31/98)

85 **CHÂTEAU VITALLIS** Pouilly-Fuissé 1996 • $15 • (05/31/98)

85 **CHÂTEAU DE MALIGNY** Chablis 1996 • $18 • (08/31/97)

85 **DOMAINE DE LA SOUFRANDISE** Mâcon-Fuissé Le Ronté 1996 • $14 • (05/31/98)

85 **ETIENNE BOILEAU** Chablis Vaillons Domaine du Chardonnay 1996 • $NA • (05/31/98)

85 **GHISLAINE & JEAN-HUGUES GOISOT** Sauvignon de St.-Bris Corps de Garde Gourmand Fié Gris 1996 • $NA • (05/31/98)

85 **GROUPEMENT DE PRODUCTEURS DE PRISSÉ** Mâcon-Villages 1996 • $11 • (08/31/97)

85 **J.-A. FERRET** Pouilly-Fuissé Les Moulins 1996 • $25 • (05/31/98)

85 **JEAN PILLOT** Puligny-Montrachet 1996 • $30 • (05/31/98)

85 **JEAN-CLAUDE THÉVENET** St.-Véran Vieilles Vignes 1996 • $18 • (05/31/98)

85 **JEAN-JACQUES MARTIN** Pouilly-Fuissé Les Chevrières 1996 • $19 • (05/31/98)

85 **JEAN-MARC BOILLOT** Bâtard-Montrachet 1996 • $126 • (05/31/98)

85 **JEAN-PAUL DROIN** Chablis Grenouille 1996 • $45 • (05/31/98)

85 **LA CHABLISIENNE** Chablis 1996 • $20 • (08/31/97)

85 **LE MANOIR MURISALTIEN** Mâcon-Cruzilles 1996 • $10 • (05/31/98)

85 **LOUIS LATOUR** Chablis Montmains 1996 • $28 • (05/31/98)

85 **LOUIS PINSON** Chablis 1996 • $19 • (05/31/98)

85 **MAROSLAVAC-LEGER** Puligny-Montrachet Les Corvées des Vignes 1996 • $40 • (05/31/98)

85 **MICHEL BARAT** Chablis 1996 • $12 • (08/31/97)

85 **MICHEL PICARD** Chablis 1996 • $22 • (01/31/98)

85 **MICHEL PRUNIER** Auxey-Duresses Vieilles Vignes White 1996 • $NA • (05/31/98)

85 **MONTHÉLIE-DOUHAIRET** Monthélie Les Duresses White 1996 • $35 • (05/31/98)

85 **P. DUBREUIL-FONTAINE PÈRE & FILS** Pernand-Vergelesses Clos Berthet White 1996 • $33 • (05/31/98)

85 **PAUL BEAUDET** St.-Véran Domaine du Poète 1996 • $14 • (05/31/98)

85 **PAUL GARAUDET** Monthélie Les Champs Fulliot White 1996 • $24 • (05/31/98)

85 **R. BALLOT-MILLOT & FILS** Meursault Genevrières 1996 • $54 • (05/31/98)

85 **RAPET PÈRE & FILS** Pernand-Vergelesses Premier Cru White 1996 • $28 • (05/31/98)

85 **ROBERT JAYER-GILLES** Hautes Côtes de Nuits White 1996 • $24 • (05/31/98)

85 **ROGER BELLAND** Chassagne-Montrachet Morgeot-Clos Pitois 1996 • $50 • (05/31/98)

85 **THIBERT PÈRE & FILS** Mâcon-Fuissé 1996 • $19 • (08/31/97)

85 **THOMAS** St.-Véran Cuvée No. 2 1996 • $15 • (05/31/98)

85 **TRENEL & FILS** Mâcon-Villages 1996 • $NA • (08/31/97)

1995 White Burgundy
Vintage Rating: 93

99 **DOMAINE D'AUVENAY** Chevalier-Montrachet 1995 • $479 Ⓐ • (08/31/97) • HR

99 **JACQUES PRIEUR** Montrachet 1995 • $290 • (08/31/97) • HR

99 **VERGET** Bâtard-Montrachet 1995 • $180 • (05/31/97)

98 **DOMAINE D'AUVENAY** Criots-Bâtard-Montrachet 1995 • $498 • (08/31/97)

98 **DOMAINE D'AUVENAY** Puligny-Montrachet Les Folatières 1995 • $133 • (08/31/97)

98 **DOMAINE DES COMTES LAFON** Montrachet 1995 • $400 • (05/31/98)

98 **ETIENNE SAUZET** Chevalier-Montrachet 1995 • $219 • (08/31/97)

98 **J.-F. COCHE-DURY** Corton-Charlemagne 1995 • $175 • (05/31/98)

98 **MARC COLIN** Montrachet 1995 • $250 • (05/31/97)

98 **P. DUBREUIL-FONTAINE PÈRE & FILS** Corton-Charlemagne 1995 • $74 • (05/31/97)

98 **RAPET PÈRE & FILS** Corton-Charlemagne 1995 • $NA • (05/31/97)

97 **DOMAINE D'AUVENAY** Meursault Les Narvaux 1995 • $155 • (08/31/97)

97 **DOMAINE DES COMTES LAFON** Meursault Charmes 1995 • $80 • (05/31/98)

97 **J.-F. COCHE-DURY** Meursault Perrières 1995 • $130 • (05/31/98)

97 **JACQUES PRIEUR** Puligny-Montrachet Les Combettes 1995 • $60 • (08/31/97)

97 **LATOUR-GIRAUD** Meursault Les Genevrières 1995 • $NA • (08/31/97)

97 **RAMONET** Chassagne-Montrachet Les Grandes Ruchottes 1995 • $70 • (08/31/97)

96 **ANTONIN GUYON** Corton-Charlemagne 1995 • $65 • (05/31/97)

96 **ETIENNE SAUZET** Bienvenues-Bâtard-Montrachet 1995 • $185 • (08/31/97)

96 **JACQUES PRIEUR** Meursault Les Perrières 1995 • $80 • (08/31/97)

96 **JACQUES THEVENOT-MACHAL** Meursault Les Charmes 1995 • $30 • (08/31/97)

96 **JEAN-NOËL GAGNARD** Chassagne-Montrachet Clos de la Maltroye 1995 • $55 • (08/31/97)

96 **MARIUS DELARCHE PÈRE & FILS** Corton-Charlemagne 1995 • $NA • (05/31/97)

95 **MAROSLAVAC-LEGER** Puligny-Montrachet Les Combettes 1995 • $40 • (08/31/97)

95 **DOMAINE DES COMTES LAFON** Meursault Les Perrières 1995 • $90 • (05/31/98)

95 **ETIENNE SAUZET** Bâtard-Montrachet 1995 • $187 • (08/31/97)

95 **GUY ROULOT** Meursault Les Charmes 1995 • $80 • (08/31/97)

95 **GUY ROULOT** Meursault Les Perrières 1995 • $80 • (08/31/97)

95 **JACQUES PRIEUR** Chevalier-Montrachet 1995 • $175 • (08/31/97)

95 **JEAN-MARC BOILLOT** Puligny-Montrachet Champ Canet 1995 • $58 • (08/31/97)

95 **JEAN-MARC BOILLOT** Puligny-Montrachet La Truffière 1995 • $74 • (05/31/97)

95 **LOUIS LATOUR** Bâtard-Montrachet 1995 • $134 Ⓐ • (08/31/97)

95 **MARC MOREY** Puligny-Montrachet Les Pucelles 1995 • $45 • (05/31/97)

95 **MICHEL BOUZEREAU & FILS** Puligny-Montrachet Champ Gain 1995 • $50 • (05/31/97)

95 **MICHEL NIELLON** Chassagne-Montrachet Les Champs Gain 1995 • $50 • (08/31/97)

95 **MICHEL NIELLON** Chevalier-Montrachet 1995 • $130 • (08/31/97)

95 **RAMONET** Chassagne-Montrachet Caillerets 1995 • $45 • (05/31/97)

95 **ROGER CAILLOT** Bâtard-Montrachet 1995 • $92 • (08/31/97)

94 **CHARLES & RÉMI JOBARD** Meursault Le Porusot-Dessus 1995 • $45 • (05/31/97)

94 **DOMAINE DE LA BONGRAN** Mâcon-Clessé Quintaine Cuvée Tradition 1995 • $25 • (05/31/98)

94 **DOMAINE DES COMTES LAFON** Meursault Clos de la Barre 1995 • $55 • (05/31/98)

94 **ETIENNE SAUZET** Puligny-Montrachet Les Combettes 1995 • $112 • (08/31/97)

94 **ETIENNE SAUZET** Puligny-Montrachet Les Perrières 1995 • $83 • (08/31/97)

94 **GUY ROULOT** Meursault Les Tessons Clos de Mon Plaisir 1995 • $50 • (05/31/98)

94 **HENRI CLERC & FILS** Puligny-Montrachet Les Folatières 1995 • $45 • (05/31/97) • HR

94 **JACQUES SAUMAIZE** St.-Véran Poncetys 1995 • $NA • (05/31/98)

94 **JEAN PILLOT** Chassagne-Montrachet Les Champs Gain 1995 • $35 • (05/31/97)

94 **JEAN-MARC BOILLOT** Puligny-Montrachet Les Combettes 1995 • $75 • (08/31/97)

94 **JOSEPH DROUHIN** Meursault Les Perrières 1995 • $60 • (05/31/97)

94 **LOUIS JADOT** Corton-Charlemagne 1995 • $54 Ⓐ • (08/31/97)

94 **LOUIS JADOT** Puligny-Montrachet Clos de la Garenne Duc de Magenta 1995 • $58 • (08/31/97)

94 **MICHEL COLIN-DELÉGER** Chassagne-Montrachet En Remilly 1995 • $50 • (05/31/97)

94 **ROGER CAILLOT** Meursault Le Limozin 1995 • $32 • (08/31/97)

94 **TOLLOT-BEAUT & FILS** Corton-Charlemagne 1995 • $90 • (08/31/97)

94 **VERGET** Chassagne-Montrachet La Maltroie Cuvée Vieilles Vignes 1995 • $44 • (08/31/97)

94 **VERGET** Puligny-Montrachet Les Enseignères 1995 • $35 • (05/31/97)

93 **ANTONIN RODET** Corton-Charlemagne 1995 • $75 • (05/31/97)

93 **BLAIN-GAGNARD** Chassagne-Montrachet La Boudriotte 1995 • $45 • (08/31/97)

93 **BONNEAU DU MARTRAY** Corton-Charlemagne 1995 • $70 • (08/31/97)

White Burgundy

93 **CHARLES & RÉMI JOBARD** Meursault Les Genevrières 1995 • $47 • (05/31/97)

93 **CHÂTEAU DE PULIGNY-MONTRACHET** Meursault Les Perrières 1995 • $36 • (01/31/98)

93 **CHÂTEAU DE PULIGNY-MONTRACHET** Meursault Les Poruzots 1995 • $42 • (01/31/98)

93 **DOMAINE DE ROALLY** Mâcon-Viré 1995 • $23 • (05/31/97)

93 **DOMAINE DES COMTES LAFON** Meursault 1995 • $50 • (05/31/98)

93 **DOMAINE DES COMTES LAFON** Meursault Désirée 1995 • $NA • (05/31/98)

93 **DOMAINE DES COMTES LAFON** Puligny-Montrachet Champ-Gain 1995 • $NA • (05/31/98)

93 **ETIENNE SAUZET** Puligny-Montrachet Champ Canet 1995 • $97 • (08/31/97)

93 **ETIENNE SAUZET** Puligny-Montrachet La Garenne 1995 • $87 • (08/31/97)

93 **ETIENNE SAUZET** Puligny-Montrachet Les Referts 1995 • $83 • (08/31/97)

93 **GUY ROULOT** Meursault Le Tesson Clos de Mon Plaisir 1995 • $50 • (08/31/97)

93 **GUY ROULOT** Meursault Les Luchets 1995 • $45 • (05/31/97)

93 **GÉRARD CHAVY** Puligny-Montrachet 1995 • $29 • (05/31/97)

93 **GÉRARD CHAVY** Puligny-Montrachet Clavaillon 1995 • $35 • (05/31/97)

93 **HENRI CLERC & FILS** Chevalier-Montrachet 1995 • $110 • (05/31/97)

93 **J.-F. COCHE-DURY** Meursault Les Rougeots 1995 • $80 • (05/31/98)

93 **JEAN-MARC BOILLOT** Bâtard-Montrachet 1995 • $131 • (05/31/97)

93 **JEAN-NOËL GAGNARD** Chassagne-Montrachet Caillerets 1995 • $65 • (08/31/97)

93 **JEAN-NOËL GAGNARD** Chassagne-Montrachet Les Chenevottes 1995 • $65 • (08/31/97)

93 **JOSEPH DROUHIN** Montrachet Marquis de Laguiche 1995 • $300 • (08/31/97)

93 **JOSEPH MATROT** Meursault-Blagny 1995 • $46 • (08/31/97)

93 **LATOUR-GIRAUD** Meursault Les Perrières 1995 • $NA • (05/31/97)

93 **LOUIS CARILLON** Puligny-Montrachet Champ Canet 1995 • $57 • (08/31/97)

93 **LOUIS JADOT** Criots-Bâtard-Montrachet 1995 • $135 • (08/31/97)

93 **LOUIS LATOUR** Corton-Charlemagne 1995 • $71 Ⓐ • (08/31/97) • CS

93 **MARC COLIN** Chassagne-Montrachet Les Champs Gain 1995 • $NA • (05/31/97)

93 **MAROSLAVAC-LEGER** Puligny-Montrachet Les Folatières 1995 • $40 • (08/31/97)

93 **MICHEL COLIN-DELÉGER** Chassagne-Montrachet Les Chaumées 1995 • $47 • (05/31/97)

93 **RAMONET** Chassagne-Montrachet 1995 • $40 • (08/31/97)

93 **RAMONET** Chassagne-Montrachet La Boudriotte 1995 • $50 • (08/31/97)

Key: SS—Spectator Selection CS—Cellar Selection HR—Highly Recommended BB—Best Buy $NA—Price not available Ⓐ—Auction Price
Dates in parentheses indicate the issues in which the ratings were published.

93 **ROGER CAILLOT** Puligny-Montrachet Les Folatières 1995 • $45 • (08/31/97)

93 **ROUX PÈRE & FILS** Chassagne-Montrachet Les Macherelles 1995 • $35 • (05/31/97)

93 **VERGET** Chassagne-Montrachet Morgeot Cuvée Vieilles Vignes 1995 • $46 • (08/31/97)

93 **VERGET** Meursault Le Porusots 1995 • $50 • (05/31/97)

92 **ANTONIN RODET** Mercurey Château de Chamirey White 1995 • $18 • (08/31/97)

92 **BERNARD MOREAU** Chassagne-Montrachet Morgeot 1995 • $35 • (05/31/97)

92 **BOUCHARD PÈRE & FILS** Beaune Premier Cru White 1995 • $38 • (08/31/97)

92 **BOUCHARD PÈRE & FILS** Montrachet 1995 • $320 • (08/31/97)

92 **CORDIER PÈRE & FILS** Pouilly-Fuissé Lot No. 2 1995 • $25 • (05/31/97)

92 **ETIENNE SAUZET** Chassagne-Montrachet 1995 • $53 • (08/31/97)

92 **ETIENNE SAUZET** Puligny-Montrachet 1995 • $55 • (08/31/97)

92 **GUY AMIOT** Chassagne-Montrachet Clos St.-Jean 1995 • $40 • (08/31/97)

92 **GUY BOCARD** Meursault Les Charmes 1995 • $NA • (08/31/97)

92 **JACQUES THEVENOT-MACHAL** Puligny-Montrachet Les Folatières 1995 • $30 • (08/31/97)

92 **JEAN PILLOT** Chassagne-Montrachet Les Chenevottes 1995 • $33 • (05/31/97)

92 **JEAN-MARC BOILLOT** Puligny-Montrachet 1995 • $41 • (08/31/97)

92 **JEAN-MARC BOILLOT** Puligny-Montrachet Les Referts 1995 • $58 • (05/31/97)

92 **JOSEPH MATROT** Puligny-Montrachet Les Chalumaux 1995 • $44 • (05/31/97)

92 **LOUIS CARILLON** Puligny-Montrachet 1995 • $40 • (05/31/97)

92 **LOUIS CARILLON** Puligny-Montrachet Les Perrières 1995 • $53 • (08/31/97)

92 **LOUIS JADOT** Puligny-Montrachet Les Folatières 1995 • $51 • (08/31/97)

92 **LOUIS JADOT** Chevalier-Montrachet Les Demoiselles 1995 • $170 • (08/31/97)

92 **LOUIS LATOUR** Puligny-Montrachet Les Folatières 1995 • $56 • (08/31/97)

92 **MICHEL BOUZEREAU & FILS** Meursault Les Charmes-Dessus 1995 • $50 • (05/31/97)

92 **MICHEL COLIN-DELÉGER** Puligny-Montrachet La Truffière 1995 • $70 • (05/31/97)

92 **MICHEL MOREY-COFFINET** Chassagne-Montrachet La Romanée 1995 • $45 • (08/31/97)

92 **OLIVIER LEFLAIVE FRÈRES** Criots-Bâtard-Montrachet 1995 • $125 • (08/31/97)

92 **OLIVIER LEFLAIVE FRÈRES** Montrachet 1995 • $270 • (08/31/97)

92 **PRIEUR-BRUNET** Meursault Les Chevalières 1995 • $36 • (08/31/97)

92 **RAMONET** Chassagne-Montrachet Les Vergers 1995 • $50 • (05/31/97)

92 **RAMONET** Puligny-Montrachet Champ Canet 1995 • $70 • (08/31/97)

92 **ROGER CAILLOT** Meursault en la Barre Clos Marguerite 1995 • $32 • (08/31/97)

92 **VALETTE** Pouilly-Fuissé Clos Reyssié Réserve Particulière 1995 • $40 • (05/31/97)

92 **VERGET** Chablis Montée de Tonnerre 1995 • $29 • (06/15/97)

91 **BLAIN-GAGNARD** Chassagne-Montrachet Caillerets 1995 • $45 • (05/31/97)

91 **BOUCHARD PÈRE & FILS** Meursault Les Genevrières 1995 • $66 • (05/31/97)

91 **BRUNO CLAIR** Morey-St.-Denis En la Rue de Vergy White 1995 • $49 • (05/31/97)

91 **CHÂTEAU FUISSÉ** Pouilly-Fuissé Vieilles Vignes 1995 • $48 • (05/31/97)

91 **DOMAINE D'AUVENAY** Auxey-Duresses White 1995 • $56 • (08/31/97)

91 **GÉRARD CHAVY** Puligny-Montrachet Les Folatières 1995 • $35 • (05/31/97)

91 **GHISLAINE & JEAN-HUGUES GOISOT** Bourgogne Côtes d'Auxerre Corps de Garde White 1995 • $15 • (06/15/97)

91 **GUFFENS-HEYNEN** Mâcon-Pierreclos En Chavigne 1995 • $20 • (05/31/97)

91 **J.-A. FERRET** Pouilly-Fuissé Les Ménétrières 1995 • $41 • (05/31/98)

91 **JACQUES PRIEUR** Beaune Clos de la Féguine White 1995 • $45 • (08/31/97)

91 **JEAN-MARC BROCARD** Chablis Bougros 1995 • $43 • (06/15/97)

91 **LOUIS MICHEL** Chablis Grenouilles 1995 • $46 • (06/15/97)

91 **MARC COLIN** Puligny-Montrachet La Garenne 1995 • $NA • (05/31/97)

91 **MAROSLAVAC-LEGER** Meursault Au Murger de Monthélie 1995 • $28 • (08/31/97)

91 **MICHEL BOUZEREAU & FILS** Meursault Les Grands Charrons 1995 • $40 • (05/31/97)

91 **MICHEL COLIN-DELÉGER** Chassagne-Montrachet Les Chenevottes 1995 • $50 • (05/31/97)

91 **MICHEL COLIN-DELÉGER** Chassagne-Montrachet Les Vergers 1995 • $50 • (08/31/97)

91 **OLIVIER LEFLAIVE FRÈRES** Meursault Les Charmes 1995 • $62 • (08/31/97)

91 **OLIVIER LEFLAIVE FRÈRES** Puligny-Montrachet Champ Gain 1995 • $52 • (08/31/97)

91 **PATRICK JAVILLIER** Meursault Clos du Cromin Cuvée Spéciale Mise Tardive 1995 • $40 • (08/31/97)

91 **PAUL GARAUDET** Monthélie Les Champs Fulliot White 1995 • $23 • (05/31/97)

91 **R. BALLOT-MILLOT & FILS** Meursault Les Genevrières 1995 • $50 • (05/31/97)

91 **ROUX PÈRE & FILS** Puligny-Montrachet Les Enseignères 1995 • $38 • (05/31/97)

91 **VERGET** Chablis Valmur 1995 • $142 Ⓐ • (06/15/97)

91 **VERGET** Meursault Les Casse-Têtes 1995 • $35 • (05/31/97)

91 **VERGET** Meursault Les Charmes Cuvée Vieilles Vignes 1995 • $65 • (05/31/97)

90 **ALBERT GRIVAULT** Meursault Clos des Perrières 1995 • $62 • (05/31/97)

90 **ALBERT GRIVAULT** Meursault Les Perrières 1995 • $46 • (05/31/97)

90 **ANTONIN RODET** Chassagne-Montrachet La Grande Montagne 1995 • $54 • (05/31/97)

90 **BERNARD MOREAU** Chassagne-Montrachet Les Chenevottes 1995 • $35 • (05/31/97)

90 **BILLAUD-SIMON** Chablis Vaudésir 1995 • $36 • (06/15/97)

90 **BOUCHARD PÈRE & FILS** Corton-Charlemagne 1995 • $110 • (08/31/97)

90 **CHARLES & RÉMI JOBARD** Meursault Les Chevalières 1995 • $35 • (05/31/97)

90 **CHARLES & RÉMI JOBARD** Meursault Sous la Velle 1995 • $33 • (05/31/97)

90 **CHÂTEAU GRENOUILLES** Chablis Grenouilles 1995 • $NA • (06/15/97)

90 **CHÂTEAU DE PULIGNY-MONTRACHET** Monthélie White 1995 • $20 • (01/31/98)

90 **CHÂTEAU DE PULIGNY-MONTRACHET** Puligny-Montrachet 1995 • $32 • (08/31/97)

90 **CHÂTEAU DE PULIGNY-MONTRACHET** Puligny-Montrachet Les Folatières 1995 • $48 • (01/31/98)

90 **DEMESSEY** Chassagne-Montrachet Morgeot 1995 • $39 • (05/31/97)

90 **GHISLAINE & JEAN-HUGUES GOISOT** Sauvignon de St.-Bris 1995 • $14 • (06/15/97)

90 **GUFFENS-HEYNEN** Pouilly-Fuissé 1995 • $34 • (05/31/98)

90 **GUY BOCARD** Meursault Le Limozin 1995 • $NA • (05/31/97)

90 **GUY ROULOT** Bourgogne White 1995 • $20 • (08/31/97)

90 **GUY ROULOT** Meursault Les Meix Chavaux 1995 • $45 • (05/31/97)

90 **GUY ROULOT** Meursault Les Vireuils 1995 • $45 • (05/31/97)

90 **HENRI CLERC & FILS** Meursault-Blagny Sous le Dos d'Ane 1995 • $50 • (08/31/97)

90 **HENRY LAMY** St.-Aubin En Remilly White 1995 • $22 • (05/31/97)

90 **JACQUES PRIEUR** Corton-Charlemagne 1995 • $90 • (08/31/97)

90 **JACQUES PRIEUR** Meursault Clos de Mazeray 1995 • $42 • (08/31/97)

90 **JACQUES THEVENOT-MACHAL** Puligny-Montrachet 1995 • $25 • (08/31/97)

90 **JEAN PILLOT** Chassagne-Montrachet Morgeot 1995 • $38 • (05/31/97)

90 **JEAN PILLOT** Puligny-Montrachet 1995 • $30 • (05/31/97)

90 **JEAN-PIERRE DICONNE** Meursault Clos des Luchets 1995 • $NA • (05/31/97)

90 **JEAN-PIERRE GROSSOT** Chablis Vaucoupin 1995 • $24 • (06/15/97)

90 **JOSEPH DROUHIN** Beaune Clos des Mouches White 1995 • $70 • (08/31/97)

90 **JOSEPH DROUHIN** Chassagne-Montrachet Marquis de Laguiche 1995 • $58 Ⓐ • (08/31/97)

90 **JOSEPH MATROT** Meursault Les Charmes 1995 • $NA • (05/31/97)

90 **LA CHABLISIENNE** Chablis Mont de Milieu 1995 • $30 • (06/15/97)

90 **LOUIS JADOT** St.-Aubin White 1995 • $21 • (08/31/97)

90 **LOUIS LATOUR** Chassagne-Montrachet Morgeot 1995 • $43 • (08/31/97)

90 **LOUIS LATOUR** Meursault 1995 • $30 • (05/31/97)

90 **LOUIS LATOUR** Meursault-Blagny 1995 • $42 • (05/31/97)

90 **LOUIS LATOUR** Meursault Les Charmes 1995 • $52 • (08/31/97)

■ ■ ■ ■

White Burgundy

90 **LOUIS LATOUR** Meursault Les Gouttes d'Or 1995 • $49 • (08/31/97)

90 **LOUIS LATOUR** Puligny-Montrachet La Garenne 1995 • $49 • (08/31/97)

90 **LOUIS PINSON** Chablis Mont de Milieu 1995 • $23 • (06/15/97)

90 **LOUIS SERVIN** Chablis Montée de Tonnerre 1995 • $17 • (06/15/97)

90 **MARC MOREY** Chassagne-Montrachet En Virondot 1995 • $45 • (05/31/97)

90 **MICHEL COLIN-DELÉGER** Chassagne-Montrachet Morgeot 1995 • $50 • (08/31/97)

90 **MICHEL MOREY-COFFINET** Chassagne-Montrachet 1995 • $32 • (08/31/97)

90 **MICHEL NIELLON** Chassagne-Montrachet Clos de la Maltroie 1995 • $50 • (08/31/97)

90 **OLIVIER LEFLAIVE FRÈRES** Chassagne-Montrachet Morgeot 1995 • $52 • (08/31/97)

90 **OLIVIER LEFLAIVE FRÈRES** Mercurey White 1995 • $16 • (08/31/97) • SS

90 **OLIVIER LEFLAIVE FRÈRES** Meursault 1995 • $41 • (08/31/97)

90 **OLIVIER LEFLAIVE FRÈRES** Puligny-Montrachet Les Folatières 1995 • $62 • (08/31/97)

90 **PATRICK JAVILLIER** Meursault Les Charmes 1995 • $50 • (08/31/97)

90 **PATRICK JAVILLIER** Meursault Les Narvaux 1995 • $NA • (05/31/97)

90 **PIERRE MATROT** Puligny-Montrachet Les Combettes 1995 • $50 • (05/31/97)

90 **R. BALLOT-MILLOT & FILS** Meursault 1995 • $35 • (05/31/97)

90 **RENÉ & VINCENT DAUVISSAT** Chablis Séchet 1995 • $32 • (06/15/97)

90 **RENÉ MONNIER** Meursault Les Chevalières 1995 • $NA • (08/31/97)

90 **ROGER CAILLOT** Meursault Le Tesson 1995 • $31 • (08/31/97)

90 **ROGER CAILLOT** Puligny-Montrachet Les Pucelles 1995 • $68 • (08/31/97)

90 **ROUX PÈRE & FILS** Meursault Clos des Porusots 1995 • $32 • (05/31/97)

90 **TOLLOT-BEAUT & FILS** Bourgogne White 1995 • $20 • (08/31/97)

90 **VOCORET & FILS** Chablis Blanchot 1995 • $40 • (06/15/97)

89 **A. LONG-DEPAQUIT** Chablis Moutonne 1995 • $36 • (06/15/97)

89 **ANTONIN GUYON** Meursault Les Charmes 1995 • $40 • (05/31/97)

89 **ANTONIN RODET** Meursault Les Perrières Cave Privée 1995 • $58 • (05/31/97)

89 **BERNARD MOREAU** Chassagne-Montrachet Les Grandes Ruchottes 1995 • $39 • (08/31/97)

89 **BILLAUD-SIMON** Chablis Les Blanchots Vieilles Vignes 1995 • $56 • (06/15/97)

89 **BILLAUD-SIMON** Chablis Mont de Milieu 1995 • $21 • (06/15/97)

89 **BILLAUD-SIMON** Chablis Mont de Milieu Vieilles Vignes 1995 • $25 • (06/15/97)

Key: SS—Spectator Selection CS—Cellar Selection HR—Highly Recommended BB—Best Buy $NA—Price not available Ⓐ—Auction Price

Dates in parentheses indicate the issues in which the ratings were published.

89 **BOUCHARD PÈRE & FILS** Beaune Clos St.-Landry White 1995 • $50 • (08/31/97)

89 **CORDIER PÈRE & FILS** Pouilly-Fuissé Lot No. 3 1995 • $25 • (05/31/97)

89 **DOMAINE DES COMTES LAFON** Meursault Goutte d'Or 1995 • $65 • (05/31/98)

89 **ETIENNE BOILEAU** Chablis Montmains 1995 • $25 • (06/15/97)

89 **J.-A. FERRET** Pouilly-Fuissé Les Clos 1995 • $33 • (05/31/98)

89 **JEAN DAUVISSAT** Chablis Séchet 1995 • $23 • (06/15/97)

89 **JEAN DAUVISSAT** Chablis Vaillons Vieilles Vignes 1995 • $30 • (06/15/97)

89 **JEAN-MARC BROCARD** Bourgogne sur Jurassique White 1995 • $13 • (06/15/97)

89 **JEAN-MARC BROCARD** Chablis Beauregard 1995 • $23 • (06/15/97)

89 **JEAN-MARC BROCARD** Chablis Montmains 1995 • $23 • (06/15/97)

89 **LA CHABLISIENNE** Chablis Blanchot 1995 • $25 • (06/15/97)

89 **LA CHABLISIENNE** Chablis Fourchaume 1995 • $25 • (06/15/97)

89 **LA CHABLISIENNE** Chablis Fourchaumes Les Vaulorents 1995 • $25 • (06/15/97)

89 **LA CHABLISIENNE** Chablis Premier Cru Vieilles Vignes 1995 • $23 • (06/15/97)

89 **LA CHABLISIENNE** Chablis Valmur 1995 • $30 • (06/15/97)

89 **LAROCHE** Chablis Les Blanchots 1995 • $32 • (06/15/97)

89 **LAROCHE** Chablis Vaillons 1995 • $30 • (06/15/97)

89 **LOUIS MICHEL** Chablis Montée de Tonnerre 1995 • $27 • (06/15/97)

89 **LOUIS MICHEL** Chablis Montmain 1995 • $26 • (06/15/97)

89 **LOUIS MICHEL** Chablis Vaudésir 1995 • $44 • (06/15/97)

89 **LOUIS MOREAU** Chablis Vaulignot 1995 • $NA • (06/15/97)

89 **MARC COLIN** St.-Aubin La Chatenière White 1995 • $33 • (05/31/97)

89 **MARC COLIN** St.-Aubin Les Combes White 1995 • $33 • (05/31/97)

89 **MARC MOREY** Chassagne-Montrachet Caillerets 1995 • $50 • (08/31/97)

89 **MARC MOREY** Chassagne-Montrachet Les Chenevottes 1995 • $42 • (08/31/97)

89 **MARC MOREY** Chassagne-Montrachet Morgeot 1995 • $50 • (08/31/97)

89 **MICHEL BARAT** Chablis Côte de Léchet 1995 • $15 • (06/15/97)

89 **MONTHÉLIE-DOUHAIRET** Meursault Les Santenots 1995 • $50 • (05/31/97)

89 **OLIVIER LEFLAIVE FRÈRES** Bâtard-Montrachet 1995 • $130 • (08/31/97)

89 **PATRICK JAVILLIER** Meursault Les Tillets 1995 • $39 • (08/31/97)

89 **PIERRE FERRAUD & FILS** Pouilly-Fuissé La Chardonneraie 1995 • $16 • (05/31/97)

89 **PRIEUR-BRUNET** Meursault 1995 • $30 • (08/31/97)

89 **PRIEUR-BRUNET** Meursault Les Charmes 1995 • $40 • (08/31/97)

89 **RAMONET** Bourgogne Aligoté 1995 • $20 • (08/31/97)

89 **ROGER CAILLOT** Bourgogne Les Herbeux White 1995 • $16 • (08/31/97)

89 **ROGER CAILLOT** Meursault Clos du Cromin 1995 • $32 • (08/31/97)

88 **ALAIN GEOFFROY** Chablis Beauroy 1995 • $20 • (06/15/97)

88 **ALAIN ROY-THEVENIN** Montagny Les Burnins 1995 • $19 • (05/31/97)

88 **ALBERT GRIVAULT** Meursault 1995 • $28 • (05/31/97)

88 **BERNARD LÉGLAND** Chablis Montmains 1995 • $22 • (06/15/97)

88 **BERNARD MOREAU** Chassagne-Montrachet 1995 • $30 • (08/31/97)

88 **BILLAUD-SIMON** Chablis Les Preuses 1995 • $36 • (06/15/97)

88 **CORSIN** Mâcon-Villages 1995 • $NA • (08/31/96)

88 **CORSIN** St.-Véran Tirage Précoce 1995 • $NA • (08/31/96)

88 **DOMAINE DES DEUX ROCHES** St.-Véran Les Terres Noires 1995 • $NA • (08/31/96)

88 **DOMAINE DES VELANGES** St.-Véran Cuvée Hors Classé 1995 • $12 • (05/31/97)

88 **DOMAINE MICHELOT** Meursault Les Perrières 1995 • $75 • (05/31/97)

88 **ETIENNE SAUZET** Bourgogne White 1995 • $28 • (08/31/97)

88 **FRANÇOIS LUMPP** Givry Petit Marole White 1995 • $20 • (05/31/97)

88 **GHISLAINE & JEAN-HUGUES GOISOT** Bourgogne Côtes d'Auxerre White 1995 • $13 • (06/15/97)

88 **HUBERT LAMY** Chassagne-Montrachet 1995 • $NA • (05/31/97)

88 **HUBERT LAMY** St.-Aubin Les Murgers des Dents de Chien White 1995 • $NA • (05/31/97)

88 **J. MOREAU & FILS** Chablis Vaillons Cuvée Préstige Guy Moreau 1995 • $27 • (06/15/97)

88 **JACQUES PRIEUR** Bourgogne White 1995 • $15 • (08/31/97)

88 **JEAN PILLOT** Chassagne-Montrachet 1995 • $28 • (05/31/97)

88 **JEAN-MARC BROCARD** Bourgogne sur Kimmeridjien White 1995 • $14 • (06/15/97)

88 **JEAN-PIERRE GROSSOT** Chablis Les Fourneaux 1995 • $24 • (06/15/97)

88 **JOSEPH DROUHIN** Montagny 1995 • $22 • (05/31/97)

88 **JOSEPH MATROT** Meursault Les Chevalières 1995 • $30 • (08/31/97)

88 **L'HÉRITIER-GUYOT** Vougeot Clos Blanc de Vougeot White 1995 • $43 • (08/31/97)

88 **LA CHABLISIENNE** Chablis Montmain 1995 • $25 • (06/15/97)

88 **LATOUR-GIRAUD** Meursault Le Porusots 1995 • $NA • (05/31/97)

88 **LOUIS JADOT** Meursault Les Perrières 1995 • $51 • (08/31/97)

88 **LOUIS LATOUR** Auxey-Duresses White 1995 • $19 • (08/31/97)

88 **LOUIS LATOUR** Chassagne-Montrachet 1995 • $38 • (05/31/97)

88 **MAROSLAVAC-LEGER** Puligny-Montrachet Corvées des Vignes 1995 • $30 • (08/31/97)

88 **MICHEL BOUZEREAU & FILS** Meursault Le Tesson 1995 • $NA • (05/31/97)

88 **MICHEL JUILLOT** Corton-Charlemagne 1995 • $95 • (05/31/97)

88 **MONTHÉLIE-DOUHAIRET** Monthélie Les Duresses White 1995 • $37 • (05/31/97)

88 **OLIVIER LEFLAIVE FRÈRES** Meursault Les Perrières 1995 • $58 • (08/31/97)

88 **PIERRE BITOUZET** Savigny-lès-Beaune Les Talmettes White 1995 • $NA • (08/31/97)

88 **RENÉ BOURGEON** Givry Clos de la Brûlée White 1995 • $NA • (05/31/97)

88 **ROBERT MARTIN** St.-Véran Domaine de la Denante 1995 • $NA • (08/31/96)

88 **ROGER CAILLOT** Santenay White 1995 • $18 • (08/31/97)

88 **THIERRY HAMELIN** Chablis Vau Ligneau 1995 • $21 • (06/15/97)

88 **THOMAS** St.-Véran Vieille Vigne 1995 • $NA • (08/31/96)

88 **VERGET** Puligny-Montrachet Sous le Puits 1995 • $43 • (08/31/97)

87 **ALAIN ROY-THEVENIN** Montagny Premier Cru 1995 • $17 • (05/31/97)

87 **ANTONIN RODET** Meursault Goutte d'Or Cave Privée 1995 • $54 • (05/31/97)

87 **AUVIGUE & REVEL** St.-Véran 1995 • $13 • (05/31/97)

87 **BILLAUD-SIMON** Chablis Montée de Tonnerre 1995 • $24 • (06/15/97)

87 **BOUCHARD PÈRE & FILS** Chevalier-Montrachet 1995 • $150 • (08/31/97)

87 **BRUNO CLAIR** Corton-Charlemagne 1995 • $89 • (08/31/97)

87 **CHÂTEAU FUISSÉ** Pouilly-Fuissé Les Brûlées 1995 • $37 • (05/31/97)

87 **CHÂTEAU FUISSÉ** St.-Véran 1995 • $15 • (05/31/97)

87 **CORSIN** Pouilly-Fuissé 1995 • $20 • (05/31/97)

87 **DOMAINE MICHELOT** Meursault Le Limozin 1995 • $40 • (05/31/97)

87 **DOMAINE MICHELOT** Meursault Les Narvaux 1995 • $45 • (05/31/97)

87 **DOMAINE DE LA SOUFRANDISE** Pouilly-Fuissé Vieilles Vignes 1995 • $25 • (05/31/97)

87 **DOMAINE DES DEUX ROCHES** Mâcon-Villages 1995 • $NA • (08/31/96)

87 **FRANÇOISE & DENIS CLAIR** St.-Aubin Les Murgers des Dents de Chien White 1995 • $28 • (05/31/97)

87 **GILBERT PICQ** Chablis Vaucoupin 1995 • $17 • (06/15/97)

87 **GUY AMIOT** Chassagne-Montrachet Les Macherelles 1995 • $37 • (05/31/97)

87 **HENRI CLERC & FILS** Bourgogne Les Riaux White 1995 • $12 • (08/31/97)

87 **HUBERT LAMY** St.-Aubin Les Cortons White 1995 • $22 • (05/31/97)

87 **J. MOREAU & FILS** Chablis Vaudésir 1995 • $43 • (06/15/97)

87 **JEAN COLLET** Chablis Montée de Tonnerre 1995 • $35 • (06/15/97)

87 **JEAN DAUVISSAT** Chablis Montmain 1995 • $NA • (06/15/97)

87 **JEAN-PIERRE GROSSOT** Chablis 1995 • $16 • (10/15/97)

87 **JOSEPH DROUHIN** Meursault 1995 • $42 • (05/31/97)

87 **JOSEPH DROUHIN** Puligny-Montrachet 1995 • $47 • (08/31/97)

87 **JOSEPH DROUHIN** Rully White 1995 • $22 • (08/31/97)

87 **LA CHABLISIENNE** Chablis Bougros 1995 • $25 • (06/15/97)

White Burgundy

87 **LAURENT TRIBUT** Chablis Beauroy 1995 • $30 • (06/15/97)

87 **LOUIS JADOT** Santenay Clos de Malte White 1995 • $22 • (08/31/97)

87 **LOUIS MICHEL** Chablis Vaillons 1995 • $26 • (06/15/97)

87 **MAILLARD PÈRE & FILS** Corton-Charlemagne 1995 • $50 • (05/31/97)

87 **MARC COLIN** St.-Aubin En Remilly White 1995 • $34 • (05/31/97)

87 **MICHEL BARAT** Chablis Vaillons 1995 • $15 • (06/15/97)

87 **MICHEL BOUZEREAU & FILS** Meursault Le Limozin 1995 • $NA • (05/31/97)

87 **OLIVIER LEFLAIVE FRÈRES** Chassagne-Montrachet 1995 • $41 • (08/31/97)

87 **OLIVIER LEFLAIVE FRÈRES** Puligny-Montrachet Champ Canet 1995 • $52 • (08/31/97)

87 **OLIVIER LEFLAIVE FRÈRES** St.-Aubin En Remilly White 1995 • $26 • (05/31/97)

87 **PATRICK JAVILLIER** Bourgogne Cuvée des Forgets White 1995 • $20 • (08/31/97)

87 **PATRICK JAVILLIER** Savigny-lès-Beaune Dessus de Montchenevoy White 1995 • $25 • (08/31/97)

87 **R. BALLOT-MILLOT & FILS** Meursault Les Narvaux 1995 • $40 • (05/31/97)

87 **RAMONET** St.-Aubin Les Charmois White 1995 • $35 • (05/31/97)

87 **RENÉ & VINCENT DAUVISSAT** Chablis La Forêt 1995 • $32 • (06/15/97)

87 **RENÉ & VINCENT DAUVISSAT** Chablis Vaillons 1995 • $32 • (06/15/97)

87 **ROUX PÈRE & FILS** St.-Aubin La Chatenière White 1995 • $29 • (05/31/97)

87 **SAUMAIZE-MICHELIN** Pouilly-Fuissé Les Ronchevats 1995 • $29 • (05/31/97)

87 **SYLVAIN MOSNIER** Chablis Côte de Léchet 1995 • $NA • (06/15/97)

87 **THIERRY GUÉRIN** Pouilly-Fuissé La Roche 1995 • $20 • (05/31/97)

87 **VOCORET & FILS** Chablis Montée de Tonnerre 1995 • $22 • (06/15/97)

86 **BOUCHARD PÈRE & FILS** Pouilly-Fuissé 1995 • $22 • (05/31/97)

86 **CATHERINE & PASCAL ROLLET** Mâcon-Solutré-Pouilly 1995 • $11 • (05/31/97)

86 **CHÂTEAU DE MALIGNY** Chablis L'Homme Mort 1995 • $22 • (06/15/97)

86 **CORDIER PÈRE & FILS** Mâcon 1995 • $12 • (05/31/98)

86 **DIDIER TRIPOZ** Charnay-lès-Mâcon Clos des Tournons 1995 • $NA • (08/31/96)

86 **DOMAINE DE LA CHAPELLE** Pouilly-Fuissé Vieilles Vignes 1995 • $20 • (05/31/97)

86 **DOMAINE DE LALANDE** Pouilly-Fuissé Clos Reyssié 1995 • $NA • (05/31/97)

86 **DOMAINE DE LA SOUFRANDISE** Mâcon-Fuissé 1995 • $16 • (05/31/97)

86 **DOMAINE DE LA SOUFRANDISE** Pouilly-Fuissé Levrouté 1995 • $29 • (05/31/97)

Key: SS—Spectator Selection CS—Cellar Selection HR—Highly Recommended BB—Best Buy $NA—Price not available Ⓐ—Auction Price
Dates in parentheses indicate the issues in which the ratings were published.

86 **DOMAINE MICHELOT** Puligny-Montrachet La Garenne 1995 • $50 • (05/31/97)

86 **DOMAINE DES DEUX ROCHES** St.-Véran 1995 • $NA • (08/31/96)

86 **E.A.R.L. HAMELIN** Chablis Beauroy 1995 • $21 • (06/15/97)

86 **GEORGES PICO** Chablis Montmains Domaine de Bois d'Yver 1995 • $NA • (06/15/97)

86 **HENRI NAUDIN-FERRAND** Hautes Côtes de Nuits White 1995 • $18 • (08/31/97)

86 **JEAN DAUVISSAT** Chablis Les Preuses 1995 • $45 • (06/15/97)

86 **JEAN-JACQUES MARTIN** St.-Véran 1995 • $NA • (08/31/96)

86 **JEAN-MARC BROCARD** Chablis Montée de Tonnerre 1995 • $23 • (06/15/97)

86 **JEAN-MARC BROCARD** Sauvignon de St.-Bris 1995 • $12 • (06/15/97)

86 **JEAN-NOËL GAGNARD** Chassagne-Montrachet Les Champs Gain 1995 • $65 • (08/31/97)

86 **JEAN-PIERRE DICONNE** Auxey-Duresses White 1995 • $NA • (08/31/97)

86 **LA CHABLISIENNE** Chablis Beauroy 1995 • $25 • (06/15/97)

86 **LA CHABLISIENNE** Chablis Côte de Léchet 1995 • $25 • (06/15/97)

86 **LA CHABLISIENNE** Chablis Vaillon 1995 • $25 • (06/15/97)

86 **LA CHABLISIENNE** Chablis Vaudésir 1995 • $30 • (06/15/97)

86 **LOUIS MOREAU** Chablis Les Fourneaux 1995 • $NA • (06/15/97)

86 **MICHEL BARAT** Chablis Monts de Milieu 1995 • $15 • (06/15/97)

86 **MICHEL COLIN-DELÉGER** Chassagne-Montrachet La Maltroie 1995 • $47 • (05/31/97)

86 **MONTHÉLIE-DOUHAIRET** Meursault 1995 • $41 • (05/31/97)

86 **MONTHÉLIE-DOUHAIRET** Monthélie White 1995 • $30 • (05/31/97)

86 **PATRICK JAVILLIER** Meursault Au Murger de Monthélie 1995 • $45 • (08/31/97)

86 **PATRICK JAVILLIER** Meursault 1995 • $35 • (08/31/97)

86 **PIERRE BITOUZET** Savigny-lès-Beaune Les Goudelettes White 1995 • $NA • (08/31/97)

86 **PIERRE COLIN** Bâtard-Montrachet 1995 • $NA • (05/31/97)

86 **PRIEUR-BRUNET** Santenay Clos Rousseau White 1995 • $33 • (08/31/97)

86 **SAUMAIZE-MICHELIN** Pouilly-Fuissé Clos de la Roche 1995 • $28 • (05/31/97)

86 **SIMONNET-FEBVRE** Chablis Mont de Milieu 1995 • $22 • (06/15/97)

86 **SYLVAIN MOSNIER** Chablis Beauroy 1995 • $NA • (06/15/97)

86 **THIERRY GUÉRIN** St.-Véran Clos des Pierres Brûlées 1995 • $16 • (05/31/97)

86 **VERGET** Mâcon-Villages Tête de Cuvée 1995 • $13 • (05/31/97)

86 **VERGET** Pouilly-Fuissé 1995 • $15 • (05/31/97)

86 **WILLIAM FÈVRE** Chablis Vaudésir 1995 • $32 • (06/15/97)

85 **A. LONG-DEPAQUIT** Chablis Les Vaucopins 1995 • $21 • (06/15/97)

85 **A. LONG-DEPAQUIT** Chablis Les Vaudésirs 1995 • $29 • (06/15/97)

85 **BILLAUD-SIMON** Chablis Vaillons 1995 • $21 • (06/15/97)

85 **BRUNO CLAIR** Marsannay White 1995 • $21 • (05/31/97)

85 **CATHERINE & PASCAL ROLLET** Pouilly-Fuissé Domaine de la Chapelle 1995 • $18 • (05/31/98)

85 **CHÂTEAU FUISSÉ** Pouilly-Fuissé 1995 • $16 • (05/31/97)

85 **CHÂTEAU FUISSÉ** Pouilly-Fuissé Le Clos 1995 • $37 • (05/31/97)

85 **CHÂTEAU DE MALIGNY** Chablis Fourchaume 1995 • $22 • (06/15/97)

85 **CHÂTEAU DE MALIGNY** Chablis Montée de Tonnerre 1995 • $22 • (06/15/97)

85 **CHÂTEAU DE RULLY** Rully White 1995 • $18 • (08/31/97)

85 **DOMAINE MICHELOT** Meursault Sous la Velle 1995 • $33 • (05/31/97)

85 **DOMAINE DES DEUX ROCHES** St.-Véran Vieilles Vignes 1995 • $24 • (05/31/97)

85 **DOMAINE DES MALANDES** Chablis Côte de Léchet 1995 • $20 • (06/15/97)

85 **GÉRARD TREMBLAY** Chablis Fourchaume 1995 • $NA • (06/15/97)

85 **GUY AMIOT** Bourgogne Aligoté 1995 • $15 • (08/31/97)

85 **GUY AMIOT** Montrachet 1995 • $250 • (05/31/97)

85 **HENRI PLUMET HÉRITIERS** Pouilly-Fuissé Clos du Chalet Pouilly 1995 • $24 • (05/31/97)

85 **JEAN COLLET** Chablis Mont de Milieu 1995 • $35 • (06/15/97)

85 **JEAN COLLET** Chablis Vaillons 1995 • $25 • (06/15/97)

85 **JOSEPH DROUHIN** Mâcon-Villages 1995 • $NA • (08/31/96)

85 **JOSEPH MATROT** Meursault 1995 • $32 • (08/31/97)

85 **L'HÉRITIER-GUYOT** Corton-Charlemagne 1995 • $50 • (08/31/97)

85 **LA CHABLISIENNE** Chablis Montée de Tonnerre 1995 • $25 • (06/15/97)

85 **LAROCHE** Chablis Les Fourchaumes 1995 • $32 • (06/15/97)

85 **LAURENT TRIBUT** Chablis Côte de Léchet 1995 • $30 • (06/15/97)

85 **LE MOULIN DU PONT** St.-Véran Vendanges Manuelles 1995 • $NA • (08/31/96)

85 **LOUIS JADOT** Pernand-Vergelesses White 1995 • $21 • (08/31/97)

85 **LOUIS LATOUR** Montagny La Grande Roche 1995 • $14 • (05/31/97)

85 **LOUIS LATOUR** Pernand-Vergelesses White 1995 • $21 • (08/31/97)

85 **LOUIS LATOUR** Pouilly-Fuissé 1995 • $15 • (05/31/98)

85 **LOUIS MOREAU** Chablis 1er Cru 1995 • $NA • (06/15/97)

85 **MAURICE BERTRAND** Montagny Premier Cru 1995 • $NA • (05/31/97)

85 **MOMMESSIN** Bourgogne White 1995 • $12 • (08/31/97)

85 **OLIVIER LEFLAIVE FRÈRES** Puligny-Montrachet 1995 • $41 • (08/31/97)

85 **PAUL BEAUDET** Mâcon-Viré 1995 • $NA • (05/31/97)

85 **PAUL GARAUDET** Meursault Vieille Vigne 1995 • $NA • (05/31/97)

85 **ROBERT JAYER-GILLES** Hautes Côtes de Nuits White 1995 • $27 • (08/31/97)

85 **ROBERT MARTIN** Mâcon-Villages Domaine de la Denante 1995 • $NA • (08/31/96)

85 **ROUX PÈRE & FILS** Bourgogne White 1995 • $9 • (08/31/97)

85 **ROUX PÈRE & FILS** Chassagne-Montrachet 1995 • $31 • (08/31/97)

85 **THIERRY HAMELIN** Chablis 1995 • $15 • (08/31/96)

1994 White Burgundy
Vintage Rating: 87

96 **ETIENNE SAUZET** Montrachet 1994 • $278 • (08/31/96)

96 **MARC COLIN** Montrachet 1994 • $200 • (05/31/96)

96 **RAMONET** Montrachet 1994 • $250 • (05/31/97)

96 **VERGET** Montrachet 1994 • $160 • (05/31/96)

95 **BERTRAND AMBROISE** Corton-Charlemagne 1994 • $75 • (08/31/96) • CS

95 **J.-F. COCHE-DURY** Corton-Charlemagne 1994 • $312 Ⓐ • (05/31/97)

95 **J.-F. COCHE-DURY** Meursault Les Perrières 1994 • $80 • (08/31/96)

95 **MICHEL BOUZEREAU & FILS** Meursault Les Genevrières 1994 • $45 • (05/31/96)

95 **RAMONET** Chassagne-Montrachet Les Grandes Ruchottes 1994 • $65 • (05/31/97)

94 **BOUCHARD PÈRE & FILS** Montrachet 1994 • $185 • (05/31/96)

94 **DOMAINE LEFLAIVE** Bâtard-Montrachet 1994 • $NA • (08/31/96)

94 **DOMAINE DES COMTES LAFON** Montrachet 1994 • $403 Ⓐ • (05/31/97)

94 **MICHEL BOUZEREAU & FILS** Puligny-Montrachet Champ Gain 1994 • $45 • (05/31/96)

94 **PIERRE COLIN** Bâtard-Montrachet 1994 • $NA • (05/31/96)

93 **CHARLES & RÉMI JOBARD** Meursault Les Genevrières 1994 • $45 • (05/31/96)

93 **GUFFENS-HEYNEN** Pouilly-Fuissé La Roche 1994 • $40 • (05/31/96)

93 **J.-A. FERRET** Pouilly-Fuissé Tournant de Pouilly 1994 • $45 • (05/31/96)

93 **JACQUES PRIEUR** Chevalier-Montrachet 1994 • $150 • (05/31/96)

93 **JEAN PILLOT** Chassagne-Montrachet Les Vergers 1994 • $32 • (05/31/96)

93 **JEAN THÉVENET** Mâcon-Clessé Domaine de la Bongran Quintaine Cuvée Tradition 1994 • $25 • (05/31/97)

93 **JEAN-MARC BOILLOT** Puligny-Montrachet Les Combettes 1994 • $62 • (05/31/96)

93 **JEAN-NOËL GAGNARD** Chassagne-Montrachet Caillerets 1994 • $NA • (08/31/96)

93 **JOSEPH DROUHIN** Montrachet Marquis de Laguiche 1994 • $125 Ⓐ • (05/31/97)

93 **LOUIS CARILLON** Puligny-Montrachet Les Perrières 1994 • $50 • (08/31/96) • HR

93 **MICHEL COLIN-DELÉGER** Chassagne-Montrachet En Remilly 1994 • $40 • (05/31/96)

93 **MICHEL COLIN-DELÉGER** Puligny-Montrachet La Truffière 1994 • $NA • (08/31/96)

93 **RAMONET** Bâtard-Montrachet 1994 • $80 • (05/31/97)

93 **ROBERT & RAYMOND JACOB** Corton-Charlemagne 1994 • $NA • (05/31/96)

■ ■ ■ ■

White Burgundy

92 **ANTONIN GUYON** Meursault Les Charmes-Dessus 1994 • $32 • (05/31/96)

92 **BOUCHARD PÈRE & FILS** Chevalier-Montrachet 1994 • $125 • (05/31/97)

92 **DOMAINE LEFLAIVE** Bienvenues-Bâtard-Montrachet 1994 • $NA • (08/31/96)

92 **EMILIAN GILLET** Mâcon-Viré Quintaine 1994 • $18 • (05/31/98)

92 **ETIENNE SAUZET** Bâtard-Montrachet 1994 • $177 • (08/31/96)

92 **GUFFENS-HEYNEN** Pouilly-Fuissé Clos des Petits-Croux 1994 • $34 • (05/31/96)

92 **GUY ROULOT** Meursault Les Charmes 1994 • $63 • (05/31/96)

92 **JACQUES PRIEUR** Montrachet 1994 • $200 • (08/31/96)

92 **MICHEL NIELLON** Chevalier-Montrachet 1994 • $135 • (05/31/96)

92 **OLIVIER LEFLAIVE FRÈRES** Puligny-Montrachet Champ Gain 1994 • $41 • (08/31/96) • HR

92 **PATRICK JAVILLIER** Meursault Les Casse-Têtes 1994 • $NA • (08/31/96)

92 **VERGET** Chassagne-Montrachet La Romanée 1994 • $50 • (05/31/96)

92 **VERGET** Corton-Charlemagne Cuvée Vieilles Vignes 1994 • $57 • (05/31/96)

92 **VERGET** Meursault Le Porusot 1994 • $44 • (05/31/96)

91 **BONNEAU DU MARTRAY** Corton-Charlemagne 1994 • $55 • (08/31/96) • CS

91 **BOUCHARD PÈRE & FILS** Corton-Charlemagne 1994 • $60 • (05/31/96)

91 **ETIENNE SAUZET** Puligny-Montrachet Champ Canet 1994 • $NA • (08/31/96)

91 **GUY ROULOT** Meursault Le Tesson Clos de Mon Plaisir 1994 • $43 • (05/31/96)

91 **HENRI CLERC & FILS** Bienvenues-Bâtard-Montrachet 1994 • $90 • (08/31/96)

91 **HENRI CLERC & FILS** Puligny-Montrachet Champ Gain 1994 • $NA • (08/31/96)

91 **HENRI CLERC & FILS** Puligny-Montrachet Les Folatières 1994 • $NA • (08/31/96)

91 **J.-F. COCHE-DURY** Meursault Les Chevalières 1994 • $NA • (08/31/96)

91 **JEAN-NOËL GAGNARD** Chassagne-Montrachet Les Chenevottes 1994 • $NA • (08/31/96)

91 **JOSEPH DROUHIN** Puligny-Montrachet Les Folatières 1994 • $54 • (05/31/96)

91 **LOUIS JADOT** Chevalier-Montrachet Les Demoiselles 1994 • $NA • (08/31/96)

91 **LOUIS JADOT** Puligny-Montrachet Les Perrières 1994 • $38 • (05/31/96)

91 **MICHEL NIELLON** Bâtard-Montrachet 1994 • $135 • (08/31/96)

91 **OLIVIER LEFLAIVE FRÈRES** Meursault Les Perrières 1994 • $NA • (08/31/96)

91 **OLIVIER LEFLAIVE FRÈRES** Rully Premier Cru White 1994 • $19 • (05/31/96)

91 **VERGET** Meursault Les Charmes Cuvée Vieilles Vignes 1994 • $52 • (05/31/96)

90 **ALBERT GRIVAULT** Meursault Les Perrières 1994 • $39 • (05/31/96)

Key: SS—Spectator Selection CS—Cellar Selection HR—Highly Recommended BB—Best Buy $NA—Price not available Ⓐ—Auction Price

Dates in parentheses indicate the issues in which the ratings were published.

90 **BLAIN-GAGNARD** Chassagne-Montrachet Morgeot 1994 • $45 • (05/31/96)

90 **CHARTRON & TRÉBUCHET** Puligny-Montrachet 1994 • $26 • (05/31/96)

90 **CHÂTEAU FUISSÉ** Pouilly-Fuissé Vieilles Vignes 1994 • $44 • (05/31/96)

90 **DOMAINE LEFLAIVE** Puligny-Montrachet Clavoillon 1994 • $48 Ⓐ • (08/31/96)

90 **DOMAINE LEFLAIVE** Puligny-Montrachet Les Combettes 1994 • $NA • (08/31/96)

90 **DOMAINE LEFLAIVE** Puligny-Montrachet Les Folatières 1994 • $NA • (08/31/96)

90 **DOMAINE DES COMTES LAFON** Meursault Les Charmes 1994 • $90 • (05/31/97)

90 **DOMAINE DES COMTES LAFON** Meursault Les Genevrières 1994 • $NA • (05/31/97)

90 **ETIENNE SAUZET** Chevalier-Montrachet 1994 • $NA • (08/31/96)

90 **ETIENNE SAUZET** Puligny-Montrachet Les Combettes 1994 • $NA • (08/31/96)

90 **ETIENNE SAUZET** Puligny-Montrachet Les Referts 1994 • $NA • (08/31/96)

90 **FERNAND PILLOT** Chassagne-Montrachet Les Vergers 1994 • $NA • (05/31/96)

90 **FERNAND PILLOT** Chassagne-Montrachet Vide Bourse 1994 • $NA • (05/31/96)

90 **FRANÇOISE & DENIS CLAIR** St.-Aubin Les Murgers des Dents de Chien White 1994 • $27 • (05/31/96)

90 **G. MICHELOT** Meursault 1994 • $NA • (05/31/96)

90 **GUY ROULOT** Meursault Les Meix Chavaux 1994 • $NA • (08/31/96)

90 **J.-F. COCHE-DURY** Meursault 1994 • $NA • (08/31/96)

90 **J.-F. COCHE-DURY** Meursault Les Rougeots 1994 • $NA • (08/31/96)

90 **JACQUES PRIEUR** Meursault Clos de Mazeray 1994 • $35 • (05/31/96)

90 **JACQUES PRIEUR** Puligny-Montrachet Les Combettes 1994 • $50 • (05/31/96)

90 **JEAN BOILLOT** Puligny-Montrachet Les Pucelles 1994 • $45 • (05/31/96)

90 **JEAN-MARC BOILLOT** Puligny-Montrachet Les Folatières 1994 • $51 • (05/31/96)

90 **JEAN-MARC BOILLOT** Puligny-Montrachet Les Pucelles 1994 • $58 • (05/31/96)

90 **JEAN-NOËL GAGNARD** Bâtard-Montrachet 1994 • $NA • (08/31/96)

90 **JOSEPH DROUHIN** Bâtard-Montrachet 1994 • $NA • (08/31/96)

90 **JOSEPH DROUHIN** St.-Aubin White 1994 • $22 • (05/31/96)

90 **LOUIS CARILLON** Puligny-Montrachet Champ Canet 1994 • $NA • (08/31/96)

90 **LOUIS LATOUR** Corton-Charlemagne 1994 • $96 Ⓐ • (05/31/96)

90 **MARC COLIN** Chassagne-Montrachet Vide Bourse 1994 • $38 • (05/31/96)

90 **MARC MOREY** Chassagne-Montrachet Les Vergers 1994 • $40 • (05/31/96)

90 **MICHEL BOUZEREAU & FILS** Meursault Les Charmes 1994 • $45 • (05/31/96)

90 **MICHEL NIELLON** Chassagne-Montrachet Clos de la Maltroie 1994 • $NA • (05/31/96)

90 **MOILLARD** Bâtard-Montrachet 1994 • $85 • (05/31/96)

90 **OLIVIER LEFLAIVE FRÈRES** Chevalier-Montrachet 1994 • $181 • (05/31/97)

90 **OLIVIER LEFLAIVE FRÈRES** Montrachet 1994 • $NA • (08/31/96)

90 **OLIVIER LEFLAIVE FRÈRES** Puligny-Montrachet Champ Canet 1994 • $NA • (08/31/96)

90 **PATRICK JAVILLIER** Meursault Les Clous 1994 • $NA • (08/31/96)

90 **PATRICK JAVILLIER** Puligny-Montrachet Les Levrons 1994 • $NA • (05/31/96)

90 **PATRICK JAVILLIER** Savigny-lès-Beaune Dessus de Montchenevoy White 1994 • $NA • (08/31/96)

90 **ROBERT JAYER-GILLES** Hautes Côtes de Nuits White 1994 • $25 • (08/31/96)

90 **TOLLOT-BEAUT & FILS** Corton-Charlemagne 1994 • $NA • (08/31/96)

90 **VALETTE** Pouilly-Fuissé Tradition 1994 • $33 • (05/31/97)

90 **VERGET** Meursault Les Genevrières Hospices de Beaune 1994 • $35 • (05/31/96)

89 **CHARTRON & TRÉBUCHET** Chassagne-Montrachet Morgeot 1994 • $25 • (05/31/96)

89 **CHARTRON & TRÉBUCHET** Santenay White 1994 • $15 • (05/31/96)

89 **CHÂTEAU FUISSÉ** Pouilly-Fuissé Le Clos 1994 • $34 • (05/31/96)

89 **CHÂTEAU FUISSÉ** Pouilly-Fuissé Les Combettes 1994 • $34 • (05/31/96)

89 **DOMAINE DES COMTES LAFON** Meursault Clos de la Barre 1994 • $60 • (05/31/97)

89 **FRANÇOISE & DENIS CLAIR** Puligny-Montrachet La Garenne 1994 • $44 • (05/31/96)

89 **GUY AMIOT** Chassagne-Montrachet Les Champs Gain 1994 • $44 • (05/31/96)

89 **JEAN PILLOT** Chassagne-Montrachet Morgeot 1994 • $NA • (05/31/96)

89 **JEAN-JACQUES MARTIN** Pouilly-Fuissé Les Chevrières 1994 • $NA • (05/31/96)

89 **L'HÉRITIER-GUYOT** Vougeot Clos Blanc de Vougeot White 1994 • $40 • (05/31/96)

89 **LOUIS JADOT** Meursault Les Perrières 1994 • $38 • (05/31/96)

89 **MICHEL COLIN-DELÉGER** Chassagne-Montrachet Les Chenevottes 1994 • $45 • (05/31/96)

89 **MICHEL GROS** Hautes Côtes de Nuits White 1994 • $NA • (08/31/97)

89 **MICHEL NIELLON** Chassagne-Montrachet Clos St.-Jean 1994 • $NA • (05/31/96)

89 **MOILLARD** Meursault Les Charmes 1994 • $37 • (05/31/96)

89 **OLIVIER LEFLAIVE FRÈRES** Bâtard-Montrachet 1994 • $NA • (08/31/96)

89 **PAUL GARAUDET** Meursault Vieille Vigne 1994 • $26 • (05/31/96)

89 **PRIEUR-BRUNET** Meursault Les Forges Dessus 1994 • $NA • (08/31/96)

89 **RAMONET** Puligny-Montrachet Champ Canet 1994 • $50 • (05/31/97)

89 **RENÉ MONNIER** Puligny-Montrachet Les Folatières 1994 • $NA • (08/31/96)

89 **VERGET** Pouilly-Fuissé Tête de Cuvée 1994 • $25 • (05/31/96)

89 **VERGET** Puligny-Montrachet Les Enseignères 1994 • $33 • (05/31/96)

88 **ALBERT GRIVAULT** Meursault 1994 • $25 • (05/31/96)

88 **CORDIER PÈRE & FILS** Pouilly-Fuissé Lot No.1 1994 • $21 • (05/31/96)

88 **DOMAINE LEFLAIVE** Puligny-Montrachet Les Pucelles 1994 • $NA • (08/31/96)

88 **ETIENNE SAUZET** Bienvenues-Bâtard-Montrachet 1994 • $177 • (08/31/96)

88 **FERNAND PILLOT** Chassagne-Montrachet Les Grandes Ruchottes 1994 • $NA • (05/31/96)

88 **FERNAND PILLOT** Puligny-Montrachet 1994 • $NA • (05/31/96)

88 **FONTAINE-GAGNARD** Criots-Bâtard-Montrachet 1994 • $90 • (05/31/96)

88 **GHISLAINE & JEAN-HUGUES GOISOT** Bourgogne Aligoté 1994 • $NA • (05/31/96)

88 **GUY ROULOT** Meursault Les Luchets 1994 • $36 • (05/31/96)

88 **HENRI NAUDIN-FERRAND** Bourgogne Hautes-Côtes de Beaune White 1994 • $NA • (05/31/96)

88 **JEAN CHARTRON** Puligny-Montrachet Les Pucelles 1994 • $NA • (05/31/96)

88 **JEAN PILLOT** Chassagne-Montrachet Les Macherelles 1994 • $NA • (05/31/96)

88 **JEAN-MARC BOILLOT** Chassagne-Montrachet 1994 • $NA • (08/31/96)

88 **LALEURE-PIOT** Pernand-Vergelesses Premier Cru White 1994 • $34 • (05/31/96)

88 **LOUIS LATOUR** Bâtard-Montrachet 1994 • $120 • (08/31/96)

88 **MICHEL COLIN-DELÉGER** Chassagne-Montrachet Morgeot 1994 • $40 • (05/31/96)

88 **MICHEL MOREY-COFFINET** Chassagne-Montrachet Caillerets 1994 • $34 • (05/31/96)

88 **MICHEL MOREY-COFFINET** Chassagne-Montrachet La Romanée 1994 • $37 • (05/31/96)

88 **MICHEL NIELLON** Chassagne-Montrachet 1994 • $45 • (05/31/96)

88 **MOMMESSIN** Pouilly-Fuissé 1994 • $25 • (05/31/96)

88 **OLIVIER LEFLAIVE FRÈRES** Puligny-Montrachet Les Folatières 1994 • $NA • (08/31/96)

88 **PATRICK JAVILLIER** Meursault Au Murger de Monthélie 1994 • $NA • (08/31/96)

88 **ROUX PÈRE & FILS** Corton-Charlemagne 1994 • $NA • (08/31/96)

88 **THIBERT PÈRE & FILS** Pouilly-Fuissé 1994 • $15 • (05/31/96)

88 **THOMAS** Pouilly-Fuissé Vieilles Vignes 1994 • $25 • (05/31/96)

88 **THOMAS** St.-Véran Vieille Vigne Cuvée Préstige 1994 • $16 • (08/31/95)

87 **ANTONIN GUYON** Corton-Charlemagne 1994 • $65 • (08/31/96)

87 **BACHELET-RAMONET** Chassagne-Montrachet Caillerets 1994 • $NA • (05/31/96)

87 **BLAIN-GAGNARD** Chassagne-Montrachet Caillerets 1994 • $45 • (05/31/96)

87 **BOUCHARD PÈRE & FILS** Bâtard-Montrachet 1994 • $96 • (05/31/96)

87 **BOUCHARD PÈRE & FILS** Beaune Clos St.-Landry Domaines du Château de Beaune White 1994 • $32 • (05/31/96)

87 **BOUCHARD PÈRE & FILS** Beaune Premier Cru White 1994 • $28 • (05/31/96)

87 **BOUCHARD PÈRE & FILS** Puligny-Montrachet Les Pucelles 1994 • $46 • (05/31/96)

87 **BRUNO CLAIR** Morey-St.-Denis En la Rue de Vergy White 1994 • $NA • (08/31/96)

White Burgundy

87 **CHARTRON & TRÉBUCHET** Bourgogne White 1994 • $10 • (05/31/96)

87 **CORDIER PÈRE & FILS** Pouilly-Fuissé Les Vignes Blanches 1994 • $34 • (05/31/96)

87 **CORSIN** St.-Véran 1994 • $15 • (08/31/95)

87 **DANIEL BARRAUD** Pouilly-Fuissé La Verchère 1994 • $21 • (05/31/96)

87 **DOMAINE MICHELOT** Meursault Les Narvaux 1994 • $40 • (05/31/96)

87 **DOMAINE DE ROALLY** Mâcon-Viré 1994 • $18 • (05/31/97)

87 **DOMAINE DES COMTES LAFON** Meursault Désirée 1994 • $75 • (05/31/97)

87 **ETIENNE SAUZET** Puligny-Montrachet 1994 • $NA • (08/31/96)

87 **GEORGES DUBOEUF** Pouilly-Fuissé Oak-Aged 1994 • $17 • (05/31/96)

87 **GUFFENS-HEYNEN** Mâcon-Pierreclos En Chavigne 1994 • $20 • (08/31/96)

87 **GUY AMIOT** Chassagne-Montrachet Clos St.-Jean 1994 • $44 • (05/31/96)

87 **GUY AMIOT** Chassagne-Montrachet Les Vergers 1994 • $44 • (05/31/96)

87 **J.-A. FERRET** Pouilly-Fuissé Les Vernays 1994 • $NA • (08/31/96)

87 **JACQUES SAUMAIZE** Pouilly-Fuissé Clos de La Roche 1994 • $17 • (05/31/96)

87 **JEAN PILLOT** Chassagne-Montrachet Les Chenevottes 1994 • $30 • (05/31/96)

87 **JEAN-CLAUDE THÉVENET** St.-Véran Clos de l'Ermitage Cuvée Vieilles Vignes 1994 • $16 • (08/31/95)

87 **JEAN-MARC BOILLOT** Puligny-Montrachet Les Referts 1994 • $47 • (05/31/96)

87 **JEAN-NOËL GAGNARD** Chassagne-Montrachet Les Masures 1994 • $NA • (08/31/96)

87 **JEAN-NOËL GAGNARD** Chassagne-Montrachet Morgeot 1994 • $NA • (08/31/96)

87 **JOSEPH DROUHIN** Puligny-Montrachet 1994 • $39 • (05/31/96)

87 **LOUIS CARILLON** Puligny-Montrachet 1994 • $35 • (05/31/96)

87 **MARC MOREY** Chassagne-Montrachet Morgeot 1994 • $48 • (05/31/96)

87 **MOILLARD** Corton-Charlemagne 1994 • $60 • (05/31/96)

87 **MOILLARD** Puligny-Montrachet Les Perrières 1994 • $39 • (05/31/96)

87 **OLIVIER LEFLAIVE FRÈRES** St.-Aubin En Remilly White 1994 • $22 • (05/31/96)

87 **PHILIPPE CHAVY** Puligny-Montrachet Corvée des Vignes 1994 • $30 • (05/31/96)

87 **RAMONET** Bienvenues-Bâtard-Montrachet 1994 • $80 • (05/31/97)

87 **ROUX PÈRE & FILS** Chardonnay Bourgogne 1994 • $NA • (05/31/96)

87 **TOLLOT-BEAUT & FILS** Bourgogne White 1994 • $NA • (08/31/96)

87 **VERGET** Chassagne-Montrachet Premier Cru 1994 • $27 • (05/31/96)

Key: SS—Spectator Selection CS—Cellar Selection HR—Highly Recommended BB—Best Buy $NA—Price not available Ⓐ—Auction Price
Dates in parentheses indicate the issues in which the ratings were published.

87 **VINCENT PRUNIER** Puligny-Montrachet La Garenne 1994 • $NA • (05/31/96)

86 **ANTONIN RODET** Meursault Les Perrières 1994 • $53 • (05/31/96)

86 **BLAIN-GAGNARD** Criots-Bâtard-Montrachet 1994 • $95 • (05/31/96)

86 **CHÂTEAU DE LA MALTROYE** Chassagne-Montrachet Clos du Château de la Maltroye 1994 • $NA • (08/31/96)

86 **CHÂTEAU DE PULIGNY-MONTRACHET** Puligny-Montrachet 1994 • $16 • (05/31/96)

86 **CORSIN** Mâcon-Villages 1994 • $12 • (08/31/95)

86 **FONTAINE-GAGNARD** Bâtard-Montrachet 1994 • $90 • (05/31/96)

86 **FONTAINE-GAGNARD** Chassagne-Montrachet La Boudriotte 1994 • $46 • (05/31/96)

86 **GEORGES BURRIER** Pouilly-Fuissé 1994 • $18 • (05/31/96)

86 **GEORGES DUBOEUF** Mâcon-Lugny Fête des Fleurs 1994 • $8 • (06/30/95) • BB

86 **GEORGES DUBOEUF** Pouilly-Fuissé Flower Label 1994 • $16 • (06/30/95)

86 **GEORGES DUBOEUF** St.-Véran 1994 • $9 • (06/30/95)

86 **GUY AMIOT** Chassagne-Montrachet Les Macherelles 1994 • $39 • (05/31/96)

86 **GUY ROULOT** Meursault Les Vireuils 1994 • $NA • (08/31/96)

86 **JACQUES PRIEUR** Corton-Charlemagne 1994 • $NA • (08/31/96)

86 **JEAN-MARC BOILLOT** Puligny-Montrachet 1994 • $37 • (05/31/96)

86 **JEAN-MARC BROCARD** Bourgogne Domaine Ste.-Claire White 1994 • $11 • (05/31/96)

86 **LÉONARD DE ST.-AUBIN** Puligny-Montrachet 1994 • $27 • (05/31/96)

86 **L'HÉRITIER-GUYOT** St.-Romain White 1994 • $16 • (05/31/96)

86 **LOUIS JADOT** Beaune Les Grèves White 1994 • $38 • (05/31/96)

86 **LOUIS JADOT** Corton-Charlemagne 1994 • $NA • (08/31/96)

86 **LOUIS LATOUR** Chevalier-Montrachet Les Demoiselles 1994 • $160 • (08/31/96)

86 **LOUIS LATOUR** Montrachet 1994 • $230 • (05/31/96)

86 **MARC MOREY** Chassagne-Montrachet Les Chenevottes 1994 • $40 • (05/31/96)

86 **MARC MOREY** Puligny-Montrachet Les Pucelles 1994 • $60 • (05/31/96)

86 **MICHEL JUILLOT** Mercurey White 1994 • $23 • (05/31/96)

86 **MOILLARD** Puligny-Montrachet 1994 • $30 • (05/31/96)

86 **MOMMESSIN** Meursault 1994 • $NA • (08/31/96)

86 **OLIVIER LEFLAIVE FRÈRES** Meursault 1994 • $NA • (08/31/96)

86 **OLIVIER LEFLAIVE FRÈRES** Puligny-Montrachet 1994 • $NA • (08/31/96)

86 **PIERRE BITOUZET** Corton-Charlemagne 1994 • $50 • (05/31/96)

86 **PRIEUR-BRUNET** Meursault 1994 • $NA • (08/31/96)

86 **PRIEUR-BRUNET** Santenay Clos Rousseau White 1994 • $NA • (08/31/96)

86 **RAPET PÈRE & FILS** Corton-Charlemagne 1994 • $70 • (05/31/96)

86 **RENÉ GUÉRIN** Pouilly-Fuissé La Roche Sélection Vieilles Vignes Cuvée No. 1 1994 • $NA • (05/31/96)

86 **RENÉ GUÉRIN** Pouilly-Fuissé La Roche Sélection Vieilles Vignes No. 2 1994 • $21 • (05/31/96)

86 **ROGER BELLAND** Chassagne-Montrachet Morgeot 1994 • $NA • (05/31/96)

86 **THIBERT PÈRE & FILS** Pouilly-Fuissé Vieilles Vignes 1994 • $16 • (05/31/96)

86 **VERGET** Meursault Les Rougeots 1994 • $31 • (05/31/96)

86 **VERGET** Puligny-Montrachet Sous le Puits 1994 • $38 • (05/31/96)

85 **ANDRÉ AUVIGUE** Pouilly-Fuissé Solutré 1994 • $18 • (05/31/96)

85 **BERTRAND AMBROISE** St.-Romain White 1994 • $17 • (08/31/96)

85 **BLAIN-GAGNARD** Chassagne-Montrachet Clos St.-Jean 1994 • $45 • (05/31/96)

85 **BLAIN-GAGNARD** Chassagne-Montrachet La Boudriotte 1994 • $45 • (05/31/96)

85 **BOUCHARD PÈRE & FILS** Meursault Les Genevrières 1994 • $46 • (05/31/96)

85 **CATHERINE & PASCAL ROLLET** Pouilly-Fuissé Domaine de la Chapelle 1994 • $16 • (05/31/96)

85 **CATHERINE & PASCAL ROLLET** Pouilly-Fuissé Domaine de la Chapelle Vieilles Vignes 1994 • $19 • (05/31/96)

85 **CAVE DE VIRÉ** Mâcon-Viré Cuvée Spéciale 1994 • $NA • (08/31/95)

85 **CHARLES & RÉMI JOBARD** Chardonnay Bourgogne 1994 • $20 • (05/31/96)

85 **CHARTRON & TRÉBUCHET** Auxey-Duresses White 1994 • $14 • (05/31/96)

85 **CHARTRON & TRÉBUCHET** Meursault 1994 • $22 • (05/31/96)

85 **CHARTRON & TRÉBUCHET** Pernand-Vergelesses White 1994 • $15 • (05/31/96)

85 **CHARTRON & TRÉBUCHET** St.-Aubin La Chatenière White 1994 • $17 • (05/31/96)

85 **CHÂTEAU DE PULIGNY-MONTRACHET** St.-Aubin En Remilly White 1994 • $11 • (05/31/96)

85 **CHÂTEAU POUILLY** Pouilly-Fuissé 1994 • $27 • (05/31/96)

85 **DOMAINE MICHELOT** Meursault Clos du Cromin 1994 • $38 • (05/31/96)

85 **DOMAINE MICHELOT** Meursault Les Charmes 1994 • $50 • (05/31/96)

85 **DOMAINE MICHELOT** Meursault Les Perrières 1994 • $60 • (05/31/96)

85 **DOMAINE MICHELOT** Meursault Sous la Velle 1994 • $30 • (05/31/96)

85 **DOMAINE DES DEUX ROCHES** Mâcon-Villages 1994 • $13 • (08/31/95)

85 **DOMAINE DES DEUX ROCHES** St.-Véran 1994 • $15 • (08/31/95)

85 **FERNAND PILLOT** Chassagne-Montrachet 1994 • $NA • (05/31/96)

85 **FERNAND PILLOT** Chassagne-Montrachet Morgeot 1994 • $NA • (05/31/96)

85 **FONTAINE-GAGNARD** Chassagne-Montrachet La Maltroie 1994 • $46 • (05/31/96)

85 **GUY AMIOT** Chassagne-Montrachet Caillerets 1994 • $50 • (05/31/96)

85 **HENRI PLUMET HÉRITIERS** Pouilly-Fuissé Clos du Chalet Pouilly 1994 • $NA • (05/31/96)

85 **J.-A. FERRET** Pouilly-Fuissé Tête de Cru 1994 • $40 • (05/31/96)

85 **JACQUES PRIEUR** Meursault Les Perrières 1994 • $70 • (05/31/96)

85 **JACQUES SAUMAIZE** Pouilly-Fuissé Vigne Blanche 1994 • $NA • (05/31/96)

85 **JEAN BOILLOT** Puligny-Montrachet Clos de la Mouchère 1994 • $44 • (05/31/96)

85 **JEAN CHARTRON** Chevalier-Montrachet 1994 • $NA • (08/31/96)

85 **JEAN CHARTRON** Puligny-Montrachet Le Cailleret 1994 • $42 • (05/31/96)

85 **JEAN PILLOT** Chassagne-Montrachet Caillerets 1994 • $42 • (05/31/96)

85 **JEAN PILLOT** Chassagne-Montrachet Les Champs Gain 1994 • $32 • (05/31/96)

85 **JEAN PILLOT** Puligny-Montrachet 1994 • $NA • (05/31/96)

85 **JEAN-NOËL GAGNARD** Chassagne-Montrachet Les Champs Gain 1994 • $NA • (08/31/96)

85 **LATOUR-GIRAUD** Puligny-Montrachet Champ Canet 1994 • $NA • (05/31/96)

85 **LOUIS LATOUR** Chassagne-Montrachet Les Chenevottes 1994 • $37 • (05/31/96)

85 **LOUIS LATOUR** Puligny-Montrachet La Garenne 1994 • $NA • (08/31/96)

85 **LUPÉ-CHOLET** Chassagne-Montrachet 1994 • $NA • (05/31/96)

85 **MARC COLIN** Chassagne-Montrachet Caillerets 1994 • $45 • (05/31/96)

85 **MARC COLIN** Chassagne-Montrachet Les Champs Gain 1994 • $40 • (05/31/96)

85 **MARC COLIN** Puligny-Montrachet Le Trézin 1994 • $40 • (05/31/96)

85 **MARC COLIN** St.-Aubin Le Charmois White 1994 • $24 • (05/31/96)

85 **MARC COLIN** St.-Aubin Les Cortons White 1994 • $24 • (05/31/96)

85 **MARC MOREY** Chassagne-Montrachet 1994 • $33 • (05/31/96)

85 **MARC MOREY** Chassagne-Montrachet En Virondot 1994 • $40 • (05/31/96)

85 **MICHEL BOUZEREAU & FILS** Meursault Le Tesson 1994 • $35 • (05/31/96)

85 **MICHEL BOUZEREAU & FILS** Meursault Les Grands Charrons 1994 • $30 • (05/31/96)

85 **MICHEL NIELLON** Chassagne-Montrachet Les Champs Gain 1994 • $55 • (05/31/96)

85 **MOILLARD** Meursault 1994 • $29 • (05/31/96)

85 **PIERRE ANDRÉ** Meursault 1994 • $NA • (08/31/96)

85 **PRIEUR-BRUNET** Chassagne-Montrachet Les Embazées 1994 • $NA • (08/31/96)

85 **PRIEUR-BRUNET** Meursault Les Charmes 1994 • $NA • (08/31/96)

85 **RAPET PÈRE & FILS** Pernand-Vergelesses White 1994 • $21 • (05/31/96)

85 **RENÉ GUÉRIN** Pouilly-Fuissé La Roche 1994 • $22 • (05/31/97)

85 **RENÉ MONNIER** Meursault Les Chevalières 1994 • $NA • (08/31/96)

85 **ROGER BELLAND** Puligny-Montrachet Champ Gain 1994 • $NA • (05/31/96)

85 **ROGER LUQUET** Pouilly-Fuissé Clos du Bourg 1994 • $19 • (05/31/96)

85 **ROUX PÈRE & FILS** Chassagne-Montrachet 1994 • $NA • (05/31/96)

85 **SAUMAIZE-MICHELIN** Pouilly-Fuissé Les Ronchevats 1994 • $NA • (05/31/96)

85 **THIERRY GUÉRIN** Pouilly-Fuissé La Roche Vieilles Vignes 1994 • $22 • (05/31/96)

85 **THOMAS** St.-Véran 1994 • $12 • (08/31/95)

1992 White Burgundy
Vintage Rating: 89

97 **JACQUES PRIEUR** Montrachet 1992 • $200 • (08/31/94) • HR

96 **JEAN CHARTRON** Chevalier-Montrachet Clos des Chevaliers 1992 • $95 • (08/31/94) • HR

95 **LOUIS LATOUR** Montrachet 1992 • $206 Ⓐ • (08/31/94) • CS

95 **PIERRE COLIN** Bâtard-Montrachet 1992 • $50 • (08/31/94)

95 **RAMONET** Montrachet 1992 • $268 • (05/15/95)

94 **BOUCHARD PÈRE & FILS** Chevalier-Montrachet Domaines du Château de Beaune 1992 • $81 • (08/31/94) • HR

94 **DOMAINE DES COMTES LAFON** Meursault Les Genevrières 1992 • $75 • (01/01/96)

94 **ETIENNE SAUZET** Bienvenues-Bâtard-Montrachet 1992 • $127 • (08/31/94)

94 **JEAN-NOËL GAGNARD** Bâtard-Montrachet 1992 • $100 • (08/31/94)

94 **JOSEPH DROUHIN** Montrachet Marquis de Laguiche 1992 • $184 Ⓐ • (08/31/94)

94 **RAMONET** Bâtard-Montrachet 1992 • $NA • (05/15/95)

93 **DOMAINE LEFLAIVE** Chevalier-Montrachet 1992 • $241 Ⓐ • (05/15/95)

93 **DOMAINE DES COMTES LAFON** Meursault Les Charmes 1992 • $109 Ⓐ • (01/01/96)

93 **ETIENNE SAUZET** Puligny-Montrachet Champ Canet 1992 • $68 • (08/31/94)

93 **GUFFENS-HEYNEN** Pouilly-Fuissé Clos des Petits-Croux 1992 • $NA • (05/15/95)

93 **J.-F. COCHE-DURY** Corton-Charlemagne 1992 • $748 Ⓐ • (08/31/94)

93 **J.-F. COCHE-DURY** Meursault Les Perrières 1992 • $83 • (05/15/95)

93 **J.-F. COCHE-DURY** Meursault Les Rougeots 1992 • $NA • (05/15/95)

93 **LOUIS JADOT** Corton-Charlemagne 1992 • $74 Ⓐ • (08/31/94) • HR

93 **MARC MOREY** Bâtard-Montrachet 1992 • $92 • (08/31/94)

93 **VERGET** Bâtard-Montrachet 1992 • $125 • (08/31/94)

93 **VERGET** Puligny-Montrachet Sous le Puits 1992 • $38 • (08/31/94) • HR

92 **CHARTRON & TRÉBUCHET** Bâtard-Montrachet 1992 • $82 • (07/31/94)

92 **CHÂTEAU DE PULIGNY-MONTRACHET** Meursault Le Porusot 1992 • $30 • (08/31/94)

92 **DOMAINE LEFLAIVE** Puligny-Montrachet Clavoillon 1992 • $73 Ⓐ • (05/15/95) • CS

92 **ETIENNE SAUZET** Chevalier-Montrachet 1992 • $114 Ⓐ • (08/31/94)

Key: SS—Spectator Selection CS—Cellar Selection HR—Highly Recommended BB—Best Buy $NA—Price not available Ⓐ—Auction Price
Dates in parentheses indicate the issues in which the ratings were published.

92 **JACQUES PRIEUR** Meursault Les Perriéres 1992 • $45 • (08/31/94)

92 **JACQUES PRIEUR** Puligny-Montrachet Les Combettes 1992 • $44 • (08/31/94)

92 **JOSEPH DROUHIN** Bâtard-Montrachet 1992 • $120 • (08/31/94)

92 **JOSEPH DROUHIN** Puligny-Montrachet La Garenne 1992 • $43 • (08/31/94)

92 **LOUIS JADOT** Puligny-Montrachet Clos de la Garenne Duc de Magenta 1992 • $33 • (08/31/94)

92 **OLIVIER LEFLAIVE FRÈRES** Bâtard-Montrachet 1992 • $100 • (05/15/95)

92 **OLIVIER LEFLAIVE FRÈRES** Bienvenues-Bâtard-Montrachet 1992 • $85 • (05/15/95)

92 **PATRICK JAVILLIER** Meursault Les Narvaux 1992 • $35 • (08/31/94)

92 **TOLLOT-BEAUT & FILS** Corton-Charlemagne 1992 • $70 • (08/31/94)

91 **AMIOT-BONFILS** Puligny-Montrachet Les Demoiselles 1992 • $65 • (08/31/94)

91 **DOMAINE LEFLAIVE** Puligny-Montrachet Les Combettes 1992 • $115 Ⓐ • (05/15/95)

91 **DOMAINE RENÉ MANUEL** Meursault Les Bouchères 1992 • $NA • (08/31/94)

91 **ETIENNE SAUZET** Bâtard-Montrachet 1992 • $127 • (08/31/94)

91 **ETIENNE SAUZET** Puligny-Montrachet Les Folatières 1992 • $68 • (08/31/94)

91 **G. MICHELOT** Meursault Le Cromin 1992 • $38 • (08/31/94)

91 **GUY ROULOT** Meursault Les Perrières 1992 • $58 • (08/31/94)

91 **J. FAIVELEY** Corton-Charlemagne 1992 • $62 • (08/31/94)

91 **JEAN-MARC BOILLOT** Puligny-Montrachet Les Referts 1992 • $NA • (08/31/94)

91 **LOUIS JADOT** Chevalier-Montrachet Les Demoiselles 1992 • $108 Ⓐ • (08/31/94)

91 **MICHELOT-BUISSON** Meursault Les Charmes 1992 • $57 • (08/31/94)

91 **RAMONET** Chassagne-Montrachet Caillerets 1992 • $52 • (05/15/95)

91 **RAMONET** Chassagne-Montrachet Les Vergers 1992 • $NA • (05/15/95)

91 **VAUCHER** Corton-Charlemagne 1992 • $NA • (08/31/94)

90 **BERNARD LÉGER-PLUMET** Pouilly-Fuissé Domaine des Gerbaux Fût de Chêne 1992 • $NA • (05/15/95)

90 **BONNEAU DU MARTRAY** Corton-Charlemagne 1992 • $44 Ⓐ • (08/31/94)

90 **C. MICHELOT** Meursault Les Grands Charrons 1992 • $NA • (08/31/94)

90 **CHARTRON & TRÉBUCHET** Puligny-Montrachet 1992 • $25 • (07/31/94) • HR

90 **CHARTRON & TRÉBUCHET** Puligny-Montrachet Les Referts 1992 • $28 • (08/31/94)

90 **DOMAINE D'AUVENAY** Meursault Les Narvaux 1992 • $64 • (08/31/94)

90 **DOMAINE D'AUVENAY** Puligny-Montrachet Les Folatières 1992 • $96 • (08/31/94)

90 **DOMAINE DES COMTES LAFON** Meursault Clos de la Barre 1992 • $55 • (01/01/96)

90 **DOMAINE DES COMTES LAFON** Meursault Les Perrières 1992 • $80 • (01/01/96)

90 **GUY ROULOT** Meursault Les Luchets 1992 • $32 • (08/31/94)

90 **HENRI GERMAIN** Meursault Le Limozin 1992 • $33 • (08/31/94)

90 **J.-F. COCHE-DURY** Meursault 1992 • $NA • (08/31/94)

90 **JEAN CHARTRON** Puligny-Montrachet Le Cailleret 1992 • $34 • (08/31/94)

90 **JEAN PILLOT** Chassagne-Montrachet Les Champs Gain 1992 • $32 • (08/31/94)

90 **JOSEPH DROUHIN** Beaune Clos des Mouches White 1992 • $55 • (08/31/94)

90 **LOUIS CARILLON** Puligny-Montrachet 1992 • $33 • (08/31/94)

90 **LOUIS CARILLON** Puligny-Montrachet Champ Canet 1992 • $43 • (08/31/94)

90 **LOUIS CARILLON** Puligny-Montrachet Les Perrières 1992 • $41 • (08/31/94)

90 **LOUIS LATOUR** Corton-Charlemagne 1992 • $77 Ⓐ • (08/31/94)

90 **MARC MOREY** Chassagne-Montrachet En Virondot 1992 • $35 • (08/31/94)

90 **MARC MOREY** Puligny-Montrachet Les Pucelles 1992 • $53 • (08/31/94)

90 **OLIVIER LEFLAIVE FRÈRES** Puligny-Montrachet Les Folatières 1992 • $52 • (08/31/94)

90 **VERGET** Pouilly-Fuissé 1992 • $17 • (05/15/95)

89 **BERNARD MOREY** Chassagne-Montrachet Morgeot 1992 • $33 • (02/28/94)

89 **BLAIN-GAGNARD** Bâtard-Montrachet 1992 • $86 Ⓐ • (08/31/94)

89 **BOUCHARD PÈRE & FILS** Corton-Charlemagne Domaines du Château de Beaune 1992 • $50 • (08/31/94)

89 **CHÂTEAU DE PULIGNY-MONTRACHET** Puligny-Montrachet Les Folatières 1992 • $34 • (08/31/94)

89 **DOMAINE LEFLAIVE** Puligny-Montrachet Les Pucelles 1992 • $115 Ⓐ • (05/15/95)

89 **FRANÇOIS JOBARD** Meursault Le Porusot 1992 • $50 • (05/15/95)

89 **JEAN CHARTRON** Puligny-Montrachet Les Pucelles 1992 • $36 • (08/31/94)

89 **JEAN PILLOT** Chassagne-Montrachet Les Chenevottes 1992 • $30 • (08/31/94)

89 **JOSEPH MATROT** Meursault Les Charmes 1992 • $33 • (08/31/94)

89 **LOUIS JADOT** Meursault Les Charmes 1992 • $35 • (08/31/94)

89 **LOUIS LATOUR** Meursault Les Gouttes d'Or 1992 • $31 • (08/31/94)

89 **LOUIS LATOUR** Puligny-Montrachet Les Folatières 1992 • $34 • (08/31/94)

89 **MESTRE-MICHELOT** Meursault Le Limozin 1992 • $38 • (08/31/94)

89 **MESTRE-MICHELOT** Meursault Le Porusot 1992 • $NA • (08/31/94)

89 **MICHEL BOUZEREAU & FILS** Meursault Les Grands Charrons 1992 • $NA • (08/31/94)

89 **MOMMESSIN** Corton-Charlemagne 1992 • $70 • (08/31/94)

89 **PATRICK JAVILLIER** Meursault Les Tillets 1992 • $33 • (08/31/94)

89 **PIERRE BITOUZET** Corton-Charlemagne 1992 • $52 • (08/31/94)

89 **RENÉ MONNIER** Meursault Les Charmes 1992 • $40 • (08/31/94)

88 **ALBERT GRIVAULT** Meursault 1992 • $28 • (08/31/94)

88 **ANTONIN RODET** Corton-Charlemagne 1992 • $NA • (08/31/94)

88 **BOUCHARD PÈRE & FILS** Puligny-Montrachet Les Pucelles 1992 • $30 • (08/31/94)

88 **CHARTRON & TRÉBUCHET** Corton-Charlemagne 1992 • $56 • (07/31/94)

88 **DOMAINE DES COMTES LAFON** Meursault 1992 • $48 • (05/15/95)

88 **ETIENNE SAUZET** Puligny-Montrachet La Garenne 1992 • $62 • (08/31/94)

88 **ETIENNE SAUZET** Puligny-Montrachet Les Combettes 1992 • $79 • (08/31/94)

88 **JAFFELIN** Meursault Les Cras 1992 • $34 • (08/31/94)

88 **JOSEPH DROUHIN** Meursault Les Perrières 1992 • $40 • (08/31/94)

88 **MICHEL BOUZEREAU & FILS** Meursault Les Genevrières 1992 • $NA • (08/31/94)

88 **MICHEL COLIN-DELÉGER** Chassagne-Montrachet Les Chenevottes 1992 • $36 • (08/31/94)

88 **MICHEL NIELLON** Chassagne-Montrachet Clos St.-Jean 1992 • $NA • (08/31/94)

88 **MOMMESSIN** Meursault 1992 • $25 • (08/31/94)

88 **PIERRE MATROT** Meursault 1992 • $20 • (08/31/94)

88 **VAUCHER** Puligny-Montrachet 1992 • $NA • (08/31/94)

87 **ALBERT GRIVAULT** Meursault Les Perrières 1992 • $80 • (08/31/94)

87 **BERNARD MOREY** Chassagne-Montrachet Les Baudines 1992 • $33 • (02/28/94)

87 **CHARTRON & TRÉBUCHET** Chassagne-Montrachet Morgeot 1992 • $22 • (08/31/94)

87 **CHÂTEAU DE PULIGNY-MONTRACHET** Puligny-Montrachet 1992 • $26 • (08/31/94)

87 **DOMAINE LEFLAIVE** Puligny-Montrachet 1992 • $53 Ⓐ • (05/15/95)

87 **FRANÇOIS JOBARD** Meursault Les Genevrières 1992 • $50 • (05/15/95)

87 **GUY ROULOT** Meursault Le Tesson Clos de Mon Plaisir 1992 • $40 • (08/31/94)

87 **JEAN PILLOT** Puligny-Montrachet 1992 • $26 • (08/31/94)

87 **JEAN-CLAUDE BOISSET** Meursault 1992 • $15 • (05/31/94)

87 **JEAN-MARC BOILLOT** Puligny-Montrachet 1992 • $NA • (08/31/94)

87 **JEAN-NOËL GAGNARD** Chassagne-Montrachet Caillerets 1992 • $47 • (08/31/94)

87 **JOSEPH MATROT** Meursault Les Chevalières 1992 • $25 • (05/15/95)

87 **LABOURÉ-ROI** Meursault 1992 • $NA • (08/31/94)

87 **LÉONARD DE ST.-AUBIN** Puligny-Montrachet 1992 • $24 • (11/15/94)

87 **LOUIS LATOUR** Puligny-Montrachet 1992 • $27 • (08/31/94)

87 **MICHEL COLIN-DELÉGER** Chassagne-Montrachet Les Chaumées 1992 • $45 • (08/31/94)

87 **MICHEL MOREY-COFFINET** Chassagne-Montrachet La Romanée 1992 • $39 • (07/31/94)

87 **MICHEL NIELLON** Chassagne-Montrachet Clos de la Maltroie 1992 • $NA • (08/31/94)

87 **MOMMESSIN** Meursault Les Charmes 1992 • $34 • (08/31/94)

87 **OLIVIER LEFLAIVE FRÈRES** Meursault Les Perrières 1992 • $45 • (08/31/94)

87 **OLIVIER LEFLAIVE FRÈRES** Montrachet 1992 • $175 • (05/15/95)

87 **RAMONET** Chassagne-Montrachet Les Ruchottes 1992 • $68 • (05/15/95)

87 **VALETTE** Pouilly-Fuissé Clos Reyssié 1992 • $NA • (05/15/95)

87 **VERGET** Chassagne-Montrachet Morgeot 1992 • $44 • (08/31/94)

87 **VERGET** Meursault Genevrières 1992 • $50 • (08/31/94)

86 **GUY BOCARD** Meursault Charmes Premier Cru 1992 • $36 • (06/15/95)

86 **J.J. VINCENT & FILS** Pouilly-Fuissé Château Fuissé 1992 • $37 • (11/15/94)

86 **J.J. VINCENT & FILS** Pouilly-Fuissé Château Fuissé Vieilles Vignes 1992 • $50 • (11/15/94)

86 **JEAN CHARTRON** Puligny-Montrachet Les Folatières 1992 • $35 • (07/31/94)

86 **JEAN-CLAUDE BOISSET** Rully White 1992 • $10 • (02/28/95) • BB

86 **LOUIS JADOT** Chassagne-Montrachet 1992 • $23 • (08/31/94)

86 **MARC COLIN** Chassagne-Montrachet Caillerets 1992 • $32 • (08/31/94)

86 **MICHEL BOUZEREAU & FILS** Meursault Le Tesson 1992 • $29 Ⓐ • (08/31/94)

86 **MICHEL COLIN-DELÉGER** Chassagne-Montrachet Les Vergers 1992 • $47 Ⓐ • (08/31/94)

86 **MICHEL NIELLON** Chassagne-Montrachet 1992 • $32 • (08/31/94)

86 **OLIVIER LEFLAIVE FRÈRES** Puligny-Montrachet Champ Canet 1992 • $50 • (08/31/94)

86 **RAMONET** Chassagne-Montrachet Morgeot 1992 • $50 • (05/15/95)

86 **RENÉ MONNIER** Meursault Les Chevalières 1992 • $25 • (08/31/94)

86 **VERGET** Chassagne-Montrachet La Romanée 1992 • $50 • (08/31/94)

85 **ALBERT MOREY** Bâtard-Montrachet 1992 • $114 • (02/28/94)

85 **ANTONIN RODET** Meursault Rodet 1992 • $NA • (08/31/94)

85 **CHARTRON & TRÉBUCHET** Auxey-Duresses White 1992 • $18 • (07/31/94)

85 **CHARTRON & TRÉBUCHET** Chassagne-Montrachet Les Vergers Clos St.-Marc 1992 • $30 • (07/31/94)

85 **DOMAINE DANIEL COLBOIS** Chablis Premier Cru Cuvée Alexis 1992 • $25 • (06/15/97)

85 **ETIENNE SAUZET** Puligny-Montrachet Les Referts 1992 • $62 • (08/31/94)

85 **GUY AMIOT** Chassagne-Montrachet 1992 • $NA • (08/31/94)

85 **HENRI GERMAIN** Chassagne-Montrachet Morgeot 1992 • $39 • (08/31/94)

85 **J. FAIVELEY** Bourgogne White 1992 • $16 • (08/31/94)

85 **J.J. VINCENT & FILS** St.-Véran 1992 • $9 • (01/01/94)

85 **JEAN-NOËL GAGNARD** Chassagne-Montrachet Les Chenevottes 1992 • $36 • (08/31/94)

85 **JOSEPH DROUHIN** Chassagne-Montrachet Marquis de Laguiche 1992 • $42 • (08/31/94)

Key: SS—Spectator Selection CS—Cellar Selection HR—Highly Recommended BB—Best Buy $NA—Price not available Ⓐ—Auction Price
Dates in parentheses indicate the issues in which the ratings were published.

85 **LA REINE PÉDAUQUE** Meursault Les Charmes 1992 • $29 • (08/31/94)

85 **MARC MOREY** Chassagne-Montrachet Morgeot 1992 • $36 • (08/31/94)

85 **MOMMESSIN** Puligny-Montrachet 1992 • $27 • (08/31/94)

85 **OLIVIER LEFLAIVE FRÈRES** Chassagne-Montrachet Morgeot 1992 • $45 • (08/31/94)

85 **OLIVIER LEFLAIVE FRÈRES** Corton-Charlemagne 1992 • $65 • (05/15/95)

85 **PATRICK JAVILLIER** Meursault Les Casse-Têtes 1992 • $30 • (08/31/94)

85 **PIERRE ANDRÉ** Puligny-Montrachet Les Folatières 1992 • $28 • (08/31/94)

85 **PIERRE MATROT** Puligny-Montrachet Les Chalumaux 1992 • $30 • (08/31/94)

85 **SYLVAIN LANGOUREAU** Meursault La Pièce sous le Bois 1992 • $32 • (08/31/94)

85 **TOLLOT-BEAUT & FILS** Bourgogne White 1992 • $15 • (08/31/94)

1990 White Burgundy
Vintage Rating: 92

100 **DOMAINE DES COMTES LAFON** Montrachet 1990 • $413 • (10/15/93) • CS

97 **DOMAINE DE LA ROMANÉE-CONTI** Montrachet 1990 • $500 • (10/15/93)

97 **PAUL PERNOT** Bâtard-Montrachet 1990 • $175 • (02/28/93)

97 **PIERRE MOREY** Montrachet 1990 • $375 • (01/31/93)

96 **DOMAINE DE LA ROMANÉE-CONTI** Montrachet 1990 • $978 Ⓐ • (11/15/95)

96 **LOUIS LATOUR** Montrachet 1990 • $195 • (10/15/93)

96 **RAMONET** Montrachet 1990 • $500 • (11/15/95)

95 **DOMAINE LEFLAIVE** Bâtard-Montrachet 1990 • $150 • (10/15/93)

95 **DOMAINE LEFLAIVE** Chevalier-Montrachet 1990 • $165 • (01/31/93) • HR

95 **ETIENNE SAUZET** Bâtard-Montrachet 1990 • $188 • (11/30/92)

95 **LOUIS LATOUR** Corton-Charlemagne 1990 • $62 Ⓐ • (09/30/93) • CS

95 **RAMONET** Montrachet 1990 • $350 • (11/30/92)

94 **DOMAINE DES COMTES LAFON** Meursault Désirée 1990 • $71 • (10/15/93)

94 **DOMAINE DES COMTES LAFON** Meursault Les Charmes 1990 • $85 Ⓐ • (10/15/93)

94 **DOMAINE DES COMTES LAFON** Meursault Les Genevrières 1990 • $109 • (10/15/93)

94 **G. MICHELOT** Meursault Les Tillets 1990 • $NA • (10/15/93)

94 **J.-F. COCHE-DURY** Corton-Charlemagne 1990 • $150 • (10/15/93)

94 **LOUIS LATOUR** Chevalier-Montrachet Les Demoiselles 1990 • $133 • (10/15/93)

94 **MESTRE-MICHELOT** Meursault Le Limozin 1990 • $NA • (10/15/93)

94 **RAMONET** Bâtard-Montrachet 1990 • $200 • (02/28/93)

94 **RAMONET** Bienvenues-Bâtard-Montrachet 1990 • $180 • (01/31/93)

94 **RAMONET** Chassagne-Montrachet Les Ruchottes 1990 • $49 • (11/30/92)

93 **BOUCHARD PÈRE & FILS** Chevalier-Montrachet 1990 • $124 • (10/15/93)
93 **BOUCHARD PÈRE & FILS** Montrachet 1990 • $210 • (10/15/93)
93 **DOMAINE D'AUVENAY** Puligny-Montrachet Les Folatières 1990 • $100 • (10/15/93)
93 **DOMAINE DES COMTES LAFON** Meursault Clos de la Barre 1990 • $69 • (10/15/93) • HR
93 **GUY ROULOT** Meursault Les Perrières 1990 • $48 • (10/15/93)
93 **J.-F. COCHE-DURY** Meursault 1990 • $36 • (10/15/93)
93 **JEAN THÉVENET** Mâcon-Clessé Domaine de la Bongran Quintaine Cuvée Spéciale Levroutée 1990 • $59 • (05/31/97)
93 **LABOURÉ-ROI** Montrachet 1990 • $160 • (07/15/92)
93 **LOUIS JADOT** Chevalier-Montrachet Les Demoiselles 1990 • $34 Ⓐ • (07/31/93)
93 **LOUIS JADOT** Puligny-Montrachet Les Pucelles 1990 • $NA • (10/15/93)
93 **LOUIS LATOUR** Meursault Les Gouttes d'Or 1990 • $35 • (10/15/93)
92 **BONNEAU DU MARTRAY** Corton-Charlemagne 1990 • $60 • (10/15/93) • HR
92 **DOMAINE LEFLAIVE** Puligny-Montrachet Les Pucelles 1990 • $88 • (10/15/93)
92 **DOMAINE DES COMTES LAFON** Meursault 1990 • $68 • (10/15/93)
92 **DOMAINE DES COMTES LAFON** Meursault Les Perrières 1990 • $120 • (10/15/93)
92 **ETIENNE SAUZET** Puligny-Montrachet Les Referts 1990 • $83 • (01/31/93)
92 **GUFFENS-HEYNEN** Pouilly-Fuissé Clos des Petits-Croux 1990 • $50 • (07/31/92)
92 **GUY ROULOT** Meursault Le Tesson Clos de Mon Plaisir 1990 • $34 • (10/15/93)
92 **J. FAIVELEY** Corton-Charlemagne 1990 • $125 • (10/15/93)
92 **JOSEPH DROUHIN** Beaune Clos des Mouches White 1990 • $64 • (05/15/92) • CS
92 **JOSEPH DROUHIN** Corton-Charlemagne 1990 • $75 • (05/15/92)
92 **LOUIS JADOT** Corton-Charlemagne 1990 • $67 • (10/15/93)
92 **LOUIS LATOUR** Puligny-Montrachet Les Folatières 1990 • $37 • (10/15/93)
92 **OLIVIER LEFLAIVE FRÈRES** Meursault Le Porusot 1990 • $40 • (10/15/93)
92 **OLIVIER LEFLAIVE FRÈRES** Puligny-Montrachet Champ Canet 1990 • $40 • (10/15/93)
92 **OLIVIER LEFLAIVE FRÈRES** Puligny-Montrachet Champ Gain 1990 • $40 • (10/15/93) • HR
92 **PIERRE BITOUZET** Corton-Charlemagne 1990 • $84 • (08/31/92)
91 **BOUCHARD PÈRE & FILS** Beaune Domaines du Château de Beaune White 1990 • $78 • (08/31/92)
91 **CHARTRON & TRÉBUCHET** Bâtard-Montrachet 1990 • $108 • (03/31/92)
91 **GUY ROULOT** Meursault Les Charmes 1990 • $48 • (10/15/93)
91 **JEAN CHARTRON** Puligny-Montrachet Les Pucelles 1990 • $53 • (03/31/92) • HR
91 **JEAN-NOËL GAGNARD** Chassagne-Montrachet Morgeot 1990 • $60 • (08/31/92)
91 **JOSEPH DROUHIN** Meursault 1990 • $32 • (05/15/92) • HR
91 **LOUIS JADOT** Meursault 1990 • $25 • (10/15/93)
91 **LOUIS LATOUR** Bienvenues-Bâtard-Montrachet 1990 • $107 • (10/15/93)
91 **LOUIS LATOUR** Chassagne-Montrachet Morgeot 1990 • $NA • (10/15/93)
91 **LOUIS LATOUR** Puligny-Montrachet 1990 • $31 • (09/30/93) • HR
91 **MICHEL COLIN-DELÉGER** Chassagne-Montrachet Les Chaumées 1990 • $45 • (02/28/93)
91 **MICHEL COLIN-DELÉGER** Chassagne-Montrachet Les Vergers 1990 • $38 • (10/15/93)
91 **MICHEL COLIN-DELÉGER** Chassagne-Montrachet Morgeot 1990 • $38 • (10/15/93)
91 **MICHELOT-BUISSON** Meursault Genevrières 1990 • $NA • (10/15/93)
91 **OLIVIER LEFLAIVE FRÈRES** Puligny-Montrachet Les Folatières 1990 • $42 • (10/15/93)
91 **PAUL PERNOT** Puligny-Montrachet Les Folatières 1990 • $60 • (04/15/92) • HR
91 **TOLLOT-BEAUT & FILS** Corton-Charlemagne 1990 • $95 • (10/15/93)
90 **BOUCHARD PÈRE & FILS** Meursault Les Genevrières 1990 • $51 • (10/15/93)
90 **CHÂTEAU DES HERBEAUX** Puligny-Montrachet Les Combettes 1990 • $45 • (12/15/92)
90 **DOMAINE LEFLAIVE** Bienvenues-Bâtard-Montrachet 1990 • $109 • (10/15/93)
90 **DOMAINE LEFLAIVE** Puligny-Montrachet 1990 • $53 • (10/15/93)
90 **DOMAINE LEFLAIVE** Puligny-Montrachet Les Combettes 1990 • $86 • (10/15/93)
90 **ETIENNE SAUZET** Chassagne-Montrachet 1990 • $50 • (02/28/93)
90 **ETIENNE SAUZET** Puligny-Montrachet Champ Canet 1990 • $83 • (01/31/93)
90 **GUFFENS-HEYNEN** Pouilly-Fuissé La Roche 1990 • $45 • (07/31/92) • HR
90 **GUY ROULOT** Meursault Les Luchets 1990 • $34 • (10/15/93)
90 **J. FAIVELEY** Meursault 1990 • $39 • (10/15/93)
90 **JEAN-MARC BOILLOT** Meursault 1990 • $50 • (10/15/93)
90 **JOSEPH DROUHIN** Bâtard-Montrachet 1990 • $128 • (05/15/92)
90 **JOSEPH DROUHIN** Meursault Les Charmes 1990 • $48 • (05/15/92)
90 **JOSEPH MATROT** Meursault 1990 • $37 • (08/31/92)
90 **LABOURÉ-ROI** Corton-Charlemagne 1990 • $48 • (07/15/92) • HR
90 **LEQUIN-ROUSSOT** Chassagne-Montrachet Morgeot 1990 • $34 • (08/31/92)
90 **LOUIS JADOT** Meursault Genevrières 1990 • $NA • (10/15/93)
90 **LOUIS JADOT** Meursault Les Perrières 1990 • $39 • (10/15/93)
90 **MARC COLIN** Chassagne-Montrachet Caillerets 1990 • $40 • (10/15/93)
90 **MICHELOT-BUISSON** Meursault Les Perrières 1990 • $NA • (10/15/93)
90 **VALETTE** Pouilly-Fuissé Clos Reyssié Réserve Particulière 1990 • $NA • (01/01/95)
89 **ALBERT MOREY** Chassagne-Montrachet Morgeot 1990 • $40 • (08/31/92)

89 **BOUCHARD PÈRE & FILS** Meursault Les Genevrières Domaines du Château de Beaune 1990 • $35 • (08/31/92)

89 **ETIENNE SAUZET** Puligny-Montrachet Les Combettes 1990 • $99 • (01/31/93)

89 **ETIENNE SAUZET** Puligny-Montrachet Les Perrières 1990 • $83 • (01/31/93)

89 **FERNAND COFFINET** Bâtard-Montrachet 1990 • $112 • (06/15/93)

89 **JEAN CHARTRON** Puligny-Montrachet Les Folatières 1990 • $48 • (03/31/92)

89 **JEAN-MARC BOILLOT** Bâtard-Montrachet 1990 • $105 Ⓐ • (10/15/93)

89 **JEAN-MARC BOILLOT** Chassagne-Montrachet Morgeot 1990 • $75 • (10/15/93)

89 **JEAN-NOËL GAGNARD** Chassagne-Montrachet Premier Cru 1990 • $55 • (08/31/92)

89 **JEAN-MARC BOILLOT** Puligny-Montrachet 1990 • $55 • (10/15/93)

89 **JEAN-MARC BOILLOT** Puligny-Montrachet La Truffière 1990 • $45 • (11/30/92)

89 **LOUIS JADOT** Pernand-Vergelesses White 1990 • $18 • (10/15/93)

89 **LOUIS LATOUR** Meursault 1990 • $27 • (10/15/93)

89 **MADAME FRANÇOIS COLIN** Puligny-Montrachet Les Demoiselles 1990 • $75 • (01/31/93)

89 **MARC COLIN** Chassagne-Montrachet 1990 • $30 • (10/15/93)

89 **PAUL PERNOT** Puligny-Montrachet Les Pucelles 1990 • $75 • (07/15/92)

89 **R. BALLOT-MILLOT & FILS** Meursault Charmes 1990 • $38 • (10/15/93)

89 **RAMONET** Chassagne-Montrachet Caillerets 1990 • $49 • (11/30/92)

88 **BOUCHARD PÈRE & FILS** Meursault Clos des Corvées de Coteaux 1990 • $50 • (10/15/93)

88 **CHÂTEAU DE PULIGNY-MONTRACHET** Puligny-Montrachet 1990 • $62 • (08/31/92)

88 **DOMAINE DU CLOS FRANTIN** Corton-Charlemagne 1990 • $50 • (05/15/93)

88 **JACQUES SAUMAIZE** Pouilly-Fuissé Les Ronchevats 1990 • $29 • (11/30/92)

88 **JEAN CHARTRON** Puligny-Montrachet Le Cailleret 1990 • $57 • (03/31/92)

88 **JEAN-MARC MOREY** Chassagne-Montrachet Caillerets 1990 • $47 • (02/28/93)

88 **JOSEPH MATROT** Puligny-Montrachet Les Chalumaux 1990 • $55 • (08/31/92)

88 **LABOURÉ-ROI** Chassagne-Montrachet Morgeot 1990 • $25 • (07/15/92)

88 **LEQUIN-ROUSSOT** Bâtard-Montrachet 1990 • $86 • (08/31/92)

88 **LEQUIN-ROUSSOT** Chassagne-Montrachet Caillerets 1990 • $34 • (08/31/92)

88 **LOUIS LATOUR** Chassagne-Montrachet 1990 • $30 • (10/15/93)

88 **LOUIS LATOUR** Meursault-Blagny Château de Blagny 1990 • $32 • (10/15/93)

88 **MICHEL COLIN-DELÉGER** Chassagne-Montrachet En Remilly 1990 • $36 • (10/15/93)

Key: SS—Spectator Selection CS—Cellar Selection HR—Highly Recommended BB—Best Buy $NA—Price not available Ⓐ—Auction Price
Dates in parentheses indicate the issues in which the ratings were published.

88 **MOILLARD** Meursault Les Charmes 1990 • $45 • (08/31/92)

88 **OLIVIER LEFLAIVE FRÈRES** Bâtard-Montrachet 1990 • $100 • (10/15/93)

88 **OLIVIER LEFLAIVE FRÈRES** Meursault 1990 • $28 • (10/15/93)

88 **PIERRE MOREY** Bâtard-Montrachet 1990 • $122 Ⓐ • (06/15/93)

88 **RAMONET** Chassagne-Montrachet Les Vergers 1990 • $41 • (11/30/92)

87 **BERNARD MOREY** Chassagne-Montrachet Les Embazées 1990 • $34 • (08/31/92)

87 **BERNARD MOREY** Chassagne-Montrachet Morgeot 1990 • $34 • (08/31/92)

87 **BERNARD MOREY** Puligny-Montrachet Sous le Puits 1990 • $40 • (08/31/92)

87 **CHARTRON & TRÉBUCHET** Meursault Les Charmes 1990 • $44 • (03/31/92)

87 **CHÂTEAU DE PULIGNY-MONTRACHET** Côte de Nuits-Villages White 1990 • $24 • (08/31/92)

87 **ETIENNE SAUZET** Puligny-Montrachet 1990 • $50 • (12/15/92)

87 **J. FAIVELEY** Chassagne-Montrachet 1990 • $42 • (10/15/93)

87 **J. FAIVELEY** Puligny-Montrachet Champ Gain 1990 • $47 • (10/15/93)

87 **JAFFELIN** Puligny-Montrachet 1990 • $28 • (05/15/92)

87 **JEAN-NOËL GAGNARD** Chassagne-Montrachet Caillerets 1990 • $62 • (08/31/92)

87 **JOSEPH DROUHIN** Meursault Les Perrières 1990 • $48 • (05/15/92)

87 **LOUIS JADOT** Beaune Les Grèves White 1990 • $38 • (10/15/93)

87 **LOUIS JADOT** Savigny-lès-Beaune White 1990 • $18 • (07/31/93)

87 **LOUIS LATOUR** Puligny-Montrachet La Truffière 1990 • $38 • (10/15/93)

87 **MICHEL COLIN-DELÉGER** Chassagne-Montrachet Les Chenevottes 1990 • $36 • (10/15/93)

87 **OLIVIER LEFLAIVE FRÈRES** Puligny-Montrachet 1990 • $35 • (10/15/93)

87 **PIERRE MOREY** Meursault Le Tesson 1990 • $50 • (01/31/93)

86 **BOUCHARD PÈRE & FILS** Beaune Premier Cru White 1990 • $NA • (10/15/93)

86 **BOUCHARD PÈRE & FILS** Puligny-Montrachet 1990 • $34 • (10/15/93)

86 **CHARTRON & TRÉBUCHET** Chassagne-Montrachet Morgeot 1990 • $40 • (03/31/92)

86 **CHARTRON & TRÉBUCHET** St.-Romain White 1990 • $20 • (03/31/92)

86 **DOMAINE D'AUVENAY** Auxey-Duresses White 1990 • $40 • (10/15/93)

86 **JACQUES SAUMAIZE** Pouilly-Fuissé Vigne Blanche 1990 • $25 • (03/31/93)

86 **JEAN CHARTRON** Chevalier-Montrachet 1990 • $120 • (03/31/92)

86 **JEAN-MARC MOREY** Chassagne-Montrachet Les Chaumées 1990 • $47 • (02/28/93)

86 **JOSEPH DROUHIN** Chassagne-Montrachet Marquis de Laguiche 1990 • $37 Ⓐ • (07/15/92)

86 **JOSEPH DROUHIN** Puligny-Montrachet Les Pucelles 1990 • $64 • (05/15/92)

86 **LEQUIN-ROUSSOT** Chassagne-Montrachet Les Vergers 1990 • $34 • (08/31/92)

86 **LEROY** Corton-Charlemagne 1990 • $153 Ⓐ • (05/15/93)

86 **LEROY** Meursault Les Narvaux 1990 • $75 • (01/31/93)

86 **LOUIS JADOT** Chassagne-Montrachet 1990 • $28 • (10/15/93)

86 **LOUIS JADOT** Chassagne-Montrachet Morgeot Clos de la Chapelle Duc de Magenta 1990 • $32 • (10/15/93)

86 **LOUIS JADOT** Puligny-Montrachet Champ Gain 1990 • $35 • (07/31/94)

86 **MARC COLIN** Chassagne-Montrachet Les Champs Gain 1990 • $40 • (10/15/93)

86 **MARC COLIN** St.-Aubin Les Combes White 1990 • $30 • (10/15/93)

86 **MARIUS DELARCHE PÈRE & FILS** Pernand-Vergelesses White 1990 • $16 • (12/15/92)

86 **MICHELOT-BUISSON** Meursault Les Charmes 1990 • $NA • (10/15/93)

86 **MOILLARD** Meursault Clos du Cromin 1990 • $27 • (10/15/93)

86 **OLIVIER LEFLAIVE FRÈRES** Meursault Les Perrières 1990 • $40 • (10/15/93)

86 **OLIVIER LEFLAIVE FRÈRES** Puligny-Montrachet Les Referts 1990 • $40 • (10/15/93)

86 **PIERRE MOREY** Meursault Les Perrières 1990 • $67 • (12/15/92)

86 **PRIEUR-BRUNET** Meursault Chevalières 1990 • $27 • (12/15/92)

85 **ALBERT MOREY** Chassagne-Montrachet 1990 • $47 • (08/31/92)

85 **BERNARD MOREY** Chassagne-Montrachet Les Baudines 1990 • $34 • (11/30/92)

85 **CHÂTEAU DE MEURSAULT** Meursault 1990 • $40 • (06/15/95)

85 **DOMAINE RENÉ MANUEL** Meursault Clos de la Baronne 1990 • $22 Ⓐ • (08/31/92)

85 **GUFFENS-HEYNEN** Pouilly-Fuissé Les Croux 1990 • $34 • (07/31/92)

85 **J. FAIVELEY** Puligny-Montrachet 1990 • $42 • (10/15/93)

85 **JAFFELIN** Bâtard-Montrachet 1990 • $75 • (04/15/92)

85 **JAFFELIN** Chassagne-Montrachet Les Vergers 1990 • $32 • (04/15/92)

85 **JAFFELIN** Puligny-Montrachet La Garenne 1990 • $34 • (04/15/92)

85 **JEAN-MARC MOREY** Chassagne-Montrachet Les Chenevottes 1990 • $47 • (02/28/93)

85 **JOSEPH DROUHIN** Chassagne-Montrachet 1990 • $36 • (05/15/92)

85 **JOSEPH DROUHIN** Puligny-Montrachet Les Folatières 1990 • $60 • (05/15/92)

85 **LABOURÉ-ROI** Bâtard-Montrachet 1990 • $80 • (07/15/92)

85 **LEQUIN-ROUSSOT** Santenay Clos Rousseau White 1990 • $24 • (08/31/92)

85 **LOUIS JADOT** Pouilly-Fuissé Cuvée Réserve Spéciale 1990 • $22 • (11/30/92)

85 **MARC COLIN** St.-Aubin La Chatenière White 1990 • $30 • (10/15/93)

85 **MICHEL COLIN-DELÉGER** Chassagne-Montrachet 1990 • $39 • (02/28/93)

85 **PIERRE PONNELLE** Côte de Beaune Les Pierres Blanches White 1990 • $12 • (07/31/94)

A view from Quinta do Napoli.

Vintage Port

Here are *Wine Spectator*'s ratings and prices for the eight most recent "declared" vintages of vintage Port. The Ports are organized by vintage and in descending order of score, to make it easy to identify the best labels in each vintage.

Listed here are scores from the 1995, 1994, 1992, 1991, 1987, 1985, 1983 and 1977 vintages. The 1994 vintage created big headlines for its super-high quality, and Port lovers rushed to buy these wines, pushing up prices as they increased the demand. *Wine Spectator* named the 1994 Taylor and 1994 Fonseca as twin Wines of the Year in the December 31, 1997–January 15, 1998 issue. Because of all this attention on 1994, the 1995 vintage is a relative bargain—very high quality Ports were made, and yet the demand has been lower.

1995 VINTAGE PORT | VINTAGE RATING: 92

95 **QUINTA DO VESUVIO** Vintage Port 1995 • $60 • (04/30/98) • CS
95 **TAYLOR FLADGATE** Vintage Port Quinta de Vargellas Vinha Velha 1995 • $NA • (04/30/98)
92 **DELAFORCE** Vintage Port Quinta da Corte 1995 • $40 • (04/30/98)
92 **FONSECA** Vintage Port Guimaraens 1995 • $39 • (04/30/98) • CS
92 **SMITH WOODHOUSE** Vintage Port Madalena 1995 • $32 • (04/30/98) • CS
92 **TAYLOR FLADGATE** Vintage Port Quinta de Vargellas 1995 • $39 • (04/30/98) • CS
92 **WARRE** Vintage Port Quinta da Cavadinha 1995 • $33 • (04/30/98) • CS
91 **CHURCHILL** Vintage Port Agua Alta 1995 • $40 • (04/30/98)
91 **CROFT** Vintage Port Quinta da Roeda 1995 • $45 • (04/30/98)
90 **COCKBURN** Vintage Port Quinta dos Canais 1995 • $39 • (04/30/98)
90 **DOW** Vintage Port Quinta do Bomfim 1995 • $38 • (04/30/98)
90 **FEIST** Vintage Port 1995 • $25 • (04/30/98)
90 **FERREIRA** Vintage Port 1995 • $37 • (04/30/98)
90 **MARTINEZ** Vintage Port Quinta da Eira Velha 1995 • $45 • (04/30/98)
90 **QUINTA DO CRASTO** Vintage Port 1995 • $33 • (04/30/98)
90 **QUINTA DO NOVAL** Vintage Port Quinta do Roriz 1995 • $45 • (04/30/98)
90 **QUINTA DO NOVAL** Vintage Port 1995 • $55 • (04/30/98)
90 **TAYLOR FLADGATE** Vintage Port Quinta de Terra Feita 1995 • $NA • (04/30/98)

Key: SS—Spectator Selection CS—Cellar Selection HR—Highly Recommended BB—Best Buy $NA—Price not available Ⓐ—Auction Price
Dates in parentheses indicate the issues in which the ratings were published.

89 **GRAHAM** Vintage Port Malvedos 1995 • $43 • (04/30/98)
88 **BURMESTER** Vintage Port 1995 • $22 • (04/30/98)
88 **QUINTA DO NOVAL** Vintage Port Quinta da Silval 1995 • $45 • (04/30/98)
88 **ROZES** Vintage Port 1995 • $45 • (04/30/98)
87 **BARROS** Vintage Port 1995 • $22 • (04/30/98)
87 **DUFF GORDON** Vintage Port 1995 • $40 • (04/30/98)
87 **FEUERHEERD** Vintage Port 1995 • $28 • (04/30/98)
87 **OSBORNE** Vintage Port 1995 • $30 • (04/30/98)
86 **CALEM** Vintage Port Quinta da Foz 1995 • $19 • (04/30/98)
86 **KOPKE** Vintage Port 1995 • $NA • (04/30/98)
86 **OFFLEY** Vintage Port Boa Vista 1995 • $35 • (04/30/98)
86 **PORTO POCAS** Vintage Port 1995 • $30 • (04/30/98)
86 **QUINTA DO PASSADOURO** Vintage Port 1995 • $54 • (04/30/98)
85 **GILBERT'S** Vintage Port 1995 • $45 • (04/30/98)
85 **QUINTA DE LA ROSA** Vintage Port 1995 • $39 • (04/30/98)

1994 VINTAGE PORT
VINTAGE RATING: 99

100 **FONSECA** Vintage Port 1994 • $120 • (04/30/97) • CS
100 **QUINTA DO NOVAL** Vintage Port Nacional 1994 • $400 • (04/30/97) • CS
100 **TAYLOR FLADGATE** Vintage Port 1994 • $120 • (04/30/97) • CS
97 **DOW** Vintage Port 1994 • $80 • (04/30/97)
97 **MARTINEZ** Vintage Port Quinta da Eira Velha 1994 • $30 • (04/30/97)
96 **CROFT** Vintage Port 1994 • $50 • (04/30/97)
96 **QUINTA DO VESUVIO** Vintage Port 1994 • $70 • (04/30/97)
95 **GRAHAM** Vintage Port 1994 • $100 • (04/30/97)
95 **MARTINEZ** Vintage Port 1994 • $30 • (04/30/97)

95 **QUINTA DO NOVAL** Vintage Port 1994 • $50 • (04/30/97)
95 **WARRE** Vintage Port 1994 • $60 • (04/30/97)
93 **CHURCHILL** Vintage Port 1994 • $35 • (04/30/97)
93 **QUINTA DO CRASTO** Vintage Port 1994 • $35 • (04/30/97)
92 **COCKBURN** Vintage Port 1994 • $45 • (04/30/97)
92 **DELAFORCE** Vintage Port 1994 • $40 • (04/30/97)
92 **GOULD CAMPBELL** Vintage Port 1994 • $55 • (04/30/97)
91 **NIEPOORT** Vintage Port 1994 • $45 • (04/30/97)
91 **OSBORNE** Vintage Port 1994 • $30 • (04/30/97)
89 **CALEM** Vintage Port Quinta do Sagrado 1994 • $38 • (04/30/97)
89 **FERREIRA** Vintage Port 1994 • $42 • (04/30/97)
88 **QUINTA DO PASSADOURO** Vintage Port 1994 • $45 • (04/30/97)
88 **RAMOS-PINTO** Vintage Port Quinta da Ervamoira 1994 • $50 • (04/30/97)
88 **TUKE HOLDSWORTH** Vintage Port 1994 • $33 • (04/30/97)
87 **QUARLES HARRIS** Vintage Port 1994 • $55 • (04/30/97)
87 **RAMOS-PINTO** Vintage Port 1994 • $45 • (04/30/97)
86 **BARROS** Vintage Port 1994 • $20 • (04/30/97)
86 **GILBERT** Vintage Port 1994 • $NA • (04/30/97)
86 **KOPKE** Vintage Port 1994 • $NA • (04/30/97)
86 **PORTO POCAS** Vintage Port 1994 • $51 • (04/30/97)
86 **QUINTA DE LA ROSA** Vintage Port 1994 • $40 • (04/30/97)
86 **ROZES** Vintage Port 1994 • $NA • (01/01/97)
86 **SMITH WOODHOUSE** Vintage Port 1994 • $45 • (04/30/97)
85 **SANDEMAN** Vintage Port 1994 • $40 • (04/30/97)

1992 Vintage Port
Vintage Rating: 94

96 **FONSECA** Vintage Port 1992 • $30 • (06/15/95) • CS
95 **TAYLOR FLADGATE** Vintage Port 1992 • $37 • (06/15/95)
94 **QUINTA DO VESÚVIO** Vintage Port 1992 • $49 • (06/15/95)
92 **DOW** Vintage Port Quinta do Bomfim 1992 • $30 • (06/30/95)
91 **GRAHAM** Vintage Port Malvedos 1992 • $39 • (06/30/95)
91 **WARRE** Vintage Port Quinta da Cavadinha 1992 • $26 • (06/30/95)
90 **DELAFORCE** Vintage Port 1992 • $35 • (06/15/95)
90 **NIEPOORT** Vintage Port 1992 • $33 • (06/15/95)
90 **QUINTA DO INFANTADO** Vintage Port 1992 • $35 • (06/15/95)
89 **CHURCHILL** Vintage Port Agua Alta 1992 • $35 • (06/15/95)
89 **COCKBURN** Vintage Port Quinta da Canias 1992 • $35 • (06/15/95)
89 **MARTINEZ** Vintage Port Quinta da Eira Velha 1992 • $NA • (06/15/95)
88 **OSBORNE** Vintage Port 1992 • $28 • (06/15/95)
89 **QUINTA DA ROMANEIRA** Vintage Port Quinta das Liceiras 1992 • $NA • (06/15/95)
88 **QUINTA DE LA ROSA** Vintage Port 1992 • $NA • (06/15/95)
88 **QUINTA DO PASSADOURO** Vintage Port 1992 • $NA • (06/15/95)
88 **SMITH WOODHOUSE** Vintage Port 1992 • $33 • (06/15/95)
87 **BURMESTER** Vintage Port Quinta do Nova 1992 • $NA • (06/15/95)
86 **CALEM** Vintage Port Quinta do Foz 1992 • $NA • (06/15/95)
85 **BURMESTER** Vintage Port 1992 • $NA • (06/15/95)
85 **GILBERT** Vintage Port 1992 • $NA • (06/15/95)

1991 Vintage Port
Vintage Rating: 93

94 **CROFT** Vintage Port 1991 • $32 • (07/31/94)
94 **TAYLOR FLADGATE** Vintage Port Quinta de Vargellas 1991 • $NA • (07/31/94)
93 **FONSECA** Vintage Port 1991 • $NA • (07/31/94)
93 **FONSECA** Vintage Port Guimaraens 1991 • $35 • (07/31/94)
93 **GRAHAM** Vintage Port 1991 • $45 • (07/31/94)
93 **QUINTA DO NOVAL** Vintage Port Nacional 1991 • $180 • (06/15/98) • CS
92 **GOULD CAMPBELL** Vintage Port 1991 • $35 • (07/31/94)
91 **CHURCHILL** Vintage Port 1991 • $35 • (07/31/94)
91 **DOW** Vintage Port 1991 • $42 • (07/31/94)
91 **FERREIRA** Vintage Port 1991 • $19 • (07/31/94)
91 **QUINTA DO VESÚVIO** Vintage Port 1991 • $48 • (07/31/94)
91 **WARRE** Vintage Port 1991 • $35 • (07/31/94)
88 **COCKBURN** Vintage Port 1991 • $36 • (07/31/94)
87 **DELAFORCE** Vintage Port Quinta da Corte 1991 • $29 • (07/31/94)
87 **QUINTA DO NOVAL** Vintage Port 1991 • $25 • (07/31/94)
87 **ROZES** Vintage Port 1991 • $23 • (07/31/94)
87 **SMITH WOODHOUSE** Vintage Port 1991 • $36 • (07/31/94)
86 **BURMESTER** Vintage Port 1991 • $NA • (07/31/94)
86 **QUINTA DE LA ROSA** Vintage Port 1991 • $NA • (07/31/94)
86 **RAMOS-PINTO** Vintage Port 1991 • $26 • (07/31/94)
85 **GILBERT** Vintage Port 1991 • $NA • (07/31/94)
85 **MARTINEZ** Vintage Port 1991 • $NA • (07/31/94)
85 **NIEPOORT** Vintage Port 1991 • $NA • (07/31/94)
85 **QUINTA DO INFANTADO** Vintage Port 1991 • $25 • (07/31/94)

1987 Vintage Port
Vintage Rating: 88

94 **QUINTA DO NOVAL** Vintage Port Nacional 1987 • $145 • (01/01/90)
93 **TAYLOR FLADGATE** Vintage Port Quinta de Vargellas 1987 • $NA • (02/01/90)
91 **GRAHAM** Vintage Port Malvedos 1987 • $NA • (02/01/90)
91 **NIEPOORT** Vintage Port 1987 • $17 Ⓐ • (11/01/89)
90 **FONSECA** Vintage Port Guimaraens 1987 • $NA • (02/01/90)
89 **COCKBURN** Vintage Port Quinta do Tua 1987 • $28 • (06/15/93)
89 **QUINTA DO NOVAL** Vintage Port 1987 • $30 • (01/01/90)

Key: SS—Spectator Selection CS—Cellar Selection HR—Highly Recommended BB—Best Buy $NA—Price not available Ⓐ—Auction Price
Dates in parentheses indicate the issues in which the ratings were published.

88 **FERREIRA** Vintage Port 1987 • $NA • (11/01/89)
88 **OFFLEY** Vintage Port Boa Vista 1987 • $NA • (01/01/90)
87 **DELAFORCE** Vintage Port Quinta da Corte 1987 • $NA • (02/01/90)
86 **DOW** Vintage Port Quinta do Bomfim 1987 • $NA • (02/01/90)
86 **KOPKE** Vintage Port 1987 • $24 • (01/01/90)
86 **QUINTA DA EIRA VELHA** Vintage Port 1987 • $NA • (05/01/90)
86 **ROZES** Vintage Port 1987 • $NA • (06/01/90)
86 **WARRE** Vintage Port Quinta da Cavadinha 1987 • $NA • (02/01/90)

1985 Vintage Port
Vintage Rating: 93

96 **GRAHAM** Vintage Port 1985 • $42 • (06/01/90)
95 **FONSECA** Vintage Port 1985 • $32 • (06/01/90)
95 **QUINTA DO NOVAL** Vintage Port Nacional 1985 • $225 • (11/01/89)
93 **BURMESTER** Vintage Port 1985 • $25 • (01/01/90)
92 **NIEPOORT** Vintage Port 1985 • $44 • (06/01/90)
91 **QUINTA DO NOVAL** Vintage Port 1985 • $NA • (10/31/88)
91 **WARRE** Vintage Port 1985 • $18 Ⓐ • (06/01/90)
90 **COCKBURN** Vintage Port 1985 • $16 Ⓐ • (06/01/90)
90 **KOPKE** Vintage Port 1985 • $14 Ⓐ • (01/01/90)
90 **TAYLOR FLADGATE** Vintage Port 1985 • $40 • (06/01/90)
89 **DOW** Vintage Port 1985 • $23 Ⓐ • (06/01/90)
89 **MARTINEZ** Vintage Port 1985 • $16 Ⓐ • (06/01/90)
89 **OFFLEY** Vintage Port Boa Vista 1985 • $31 • (06/01/90)
89 **SMITH WOODHOUSE** Vintage Port 1985 • $33 • (06/01/90)
88 **CALEM** Vintage Port 1985 • $42 • (06/01/90)
88 **ROCHA** Vintage Port 1985 • $32 • (04/15/91)
87 **FERREIRA** Vintage Port 1985 • $20 • (11/01/89)
87 **VAN ZELLER** Vintage Port Quinta do Roriz 1985 • $NA • (07/01/90)
85 **GOULD CAMPBELL** Vintage Port 1985 • $23 • (06/01/90)
85 **MORGAN** Vintage Port 1985 • $NA • (02/01/90)
85 **POCAS JUNIOR** Vintage Port 1985 • $19 • (02/01/90)
85 **QUARLES HARRIS** Vintage Port 1985 • $27 • (06/01/90)
85 **RAMOS-PINTO** Vintage Port 1985 • $21 • (11/01/89)

1983 Vintage Port
Vintage Rating: 92

97 **COCKBURN** Vintage Port 1983 • $30 Ⓐ • (06/01/90)
94 **DOW** Vintage Port 1983 • $20 Ⓐ • (06/01/90)
93 **GRAHAM** Vintage Port 1983 • $40 • (06/01/90)
92 **SMITH WOODHOUSE** Vintage Port 1983 • $12 Ⓐ • (06/01/90)
91 **FERREIRA** Vintage Port 1983 • $14 • (11/01/89)
91 **OFFLEY** Vintage Port Boa Vista 1983 • $35 • (01/01/90)
90 **FONSECA** Vintage Port 1983 • $34 • (06/01/90)
90 **GOULD CAMPBELL** Vintage Port 1983 • $31 • (06/01/90)
89 **QUARLES HARRIS** Vintage Port 1983 • $31 • (02/01/90)
89 **RAMOS-PINTO** Vintage Port 1983 • $35 • (11/01/89)
89 **TAYLOR FLADGATE** Vintage Port 1983 • $35 • (06/01/90)
88 **WARRE** Vintage Port 1983 • $16 Ⓐ • (06/01/90)
85 **CROFT** Vintage Port Quinta da Roeda 1983 • $22 • (02/01/90)
85 **KOPKE** Vintage Port 1983 • $23 • (01/01/90)

1977 Vintage Port
Vintage Rating: 97

100 **FONSECA** Vintage Port 1977 • $16 • (04/01/90)
98 **TAYLOR FLADGATE** Vintage Port 1977 • $70 • (04/01/90)
94 **DOW** Vintage Port 1977 • $43 Ⓐ • (04/01/90)
93 **GOULD CAMPBELL** Vintage Port 1977 • $29 Ⓐ • (02/01/90)
92 **WARRE** Vintage Port 1977 • $32 Ⓐ • (04/01/90)
90 **GRAHAM** Vintage Port 1977 • $46 Ⓐ • (04/01/90)
89 **NIEPOORT** Vintage Port 1977 • $50 • (04/01/90)
89 **QUARLES HARRIS** Vintage Port 1977 • $43 • (02/01/90)
89 **REBELLO-VALENTE** Vintage Port 1977 • $40 • (02/01/90)
89 **SMITH WOODHOUSE** Vintage Port 1977 • $25 Ⓐ • (02/01/90)
88 **OFFLEY** Vintage Port Boa Vista 1977 • $18 Ⓐ • (01/01/90)
86 **FERREIRA** Vintage Port 1977 • $49 • (11/01/89)
85 **CROFT** Vintage Port 1977 • $25 Ⓐ • (04/01/90)
85 **SANDEMAN** Vintage Port 1977 • $28 Ⓐ • (06/01/90)

Beringer Vineyards in St. Helena, Napa Valley.

California Cabernet

Here are *Wine Spectator*'s ratings and prices for the five most recent outstanding vintages of California Cabernet Sauvignon and Bordeaux-style blends, including red Meritage wines. The wines are organized in descending order of score, to make it easy to identify the best wines of each vintage.

The vintages included here are 1994, 1992, 1991, 1990 and 1987. 1994 is the highest rated year since 1987, in the judgment of *Wine Spectator* critic James Laube. Cabernets from 1995, 1996 and 1997 are all potentially outstanding in quality, but too few had been released and reviewed in time to include here. We omitted 1993 because it is not rated quite as highly as the listed years, but it nonetheless ranks as outstanding. Wines from this and other years are to be found in the main listings.

1994 CALIFORNIA CABERNET | VINTAGE RATING: 96

97 **BERINGER** Cabernet Sauvignon Napa Valley Bancroft Vineyard 1994 • $85 • (10/31/97)

96 **ARAUJO** Cabernet Sauvignon Napa Valley Eisele Vineyard 1994 • $204 Ⓐ • (10/15/97) • HR

96 **FLORA SPRINGS** Cabernet Sauvignon Napa Valley Rutherford Hillside Reserve 1994 • $65 • (10/15/97) • HR

96 **GROTH** Cabernet Sauvignon Napa Valley Reserve 1994 • $100 • (05/15/98) • CS

96 **JOSEPH PHELPS** Insignia Napa Valley 1994 • $70 • (09/30/97) • CS

95 **CAYMUS** Cabernet Sauvignon Napa Valley 1994 • $77 Ⓐ • (05/31/97) • CS

95 **CAYMUS** Cabernet Sauvignon Napa Valley Special Selection 1994 • $153 Ⓐ • (12/31/97) • CS

95 **COLGIN** Cabernet Sauvignon Napa Valley Herb Lamb Vineyard 1994 • $368 Ⓐ • (07/31/97) • HR

95 **DALLA VALLE** Maya Napa Valley 1994 • $333 Ⓐ • (10/31/97) • HR

95 **HARLAN ESTATE** Napa Valley 1994 • $100 • (05/15/98) • CS

95 **SCREAMING EAGLE** Cabernet Sauvignon Napa Valley 1994 • $604 Ⓐ • (10/31/97)

95 **SHAFER** Cabernet Sauvignon Stags Leap District Hillside Select 1994 • $75 • (10/15/97)

94 **ARROWOOD** Cabernet Sauvignon Sonoma County Réserve Spéciale 1994 • $50 • (07/31/98)

94 **BRYANT FAMILY** Cabernet Sauvignon Napa Valley 1994 • $370 Ⓐ • (11/30/97)

Key: SS—Spectator Selection CS—Cellar Selection HR—Highly Recommended BB—Best Buy $NA—Price not available Ⓐ—Auction Price
Dates in parentheses indicate the issues in which the ratings were published.

94 **DIAMOND CREEK** Cabernet Sauvignon Napa Valley Lake 1994 • $125 Ⓐ • (03/31/97) • HR

94 **DIAMOND CREEK** Cabernet Sauvignon Napa Valley Volcanic Hill 1994 • $60 • (03/31/97) • CS

94 **DOMINUS ESTATE** Napa Valley Napanook Vineyard 1994 • $75 • (07/31/97) • CS

94 **GRACE FAMILY** Cabernet Sauvignon Napa Valley 1994 • $307 Ⓐ • (05/31/97) • CS

94 **HARTWELL** Cabernet Sauvignon Stags Leap District Grace Vineyard 1994 • $63 • (11/30/97)

94 **LEWIS CELLARS** Cabernet Sauvignon Napa Valley Reserve 1994 • $36 • (06/15/97) • HR

94 **LIVINGSTON** Cabernet Sauvignon Napa Valley Moffett Vineyard 1994 • $36 • (10/31/97) • HR

94 **OPUS ONE** Napa Valley 1994 • $90 • (10/15/97) • CS

94 **PETER MICHAEL** Les Pavots Knights Valley 1994 • $35 • (08/31/97) • CS

94 **ROBERT CRAIG** Affinity Napa Valley 1994 • $28 • (08/31/97) • HR

94 **ROBERT CRAIG** Cabernet Sauvignon Mount Veeder 1994 • $28 • (11/15/97)

94 **ROBERT MONDAVI** Cabernet Sauvignon Napa Valley Reserve 1994 • $64 Ⓐ • (07/31/97) • CS

93 **BEAULIEU VINEYARD** Cabernet Sauvignon Napa Valley Georges de Latour Private Reserve 1994 • $50 • (10/15/97) • CS

93 **BEAULIEU VINEYARD** Cabernet Sauvignon Rutherford Clone 6 Signet Collection 1994 • $100 • (11/15/97)

93 **CHATEAU SOUVERAIN** Cabernet Sauvignon Alexander Valley Winemaker's Reserve 1994 • $30 • (10/15/97)

93 **CORNERSTONE** Cabernet Sauvignon Howell Mountain Beatty Ranch 1994 • $35 • (10/31/97)

93 **DALLA VALLE** Cabernet Sauvignon Napa Valley 1994 • $40 • (10/31/97) • CS

93 **DIAMOND CREEK** Cabernet Sauvignon Napa Valley Gravelly Meadow 1994 • $100 • (06/15/98)

93 **DIAMOND CREEK** Cabernet Sauvignon Napa Valley Lake 1994 • $125 Ⓐ • (06/15/98)

93 **DIAMOND CREEK** Cabernet Sauvignon Napa Valley Red Rock Terrace 1994 • $60 • (03/31/97) • CS

93 **DIAMOND CREEK** Cabernet Sauvignon Napa Valley Red Rock Terrace Microclimate 2 1994 • $150 • (06/15/98)

93 **ETUDE** Cabernet Sauvignon Napa Valley 1994 • $38 • (09/30/97)

93 **GIRARD** Cabernet Sauvignon Napa Valley Reserve 1994 • $40 • (11/15/97)

93 **GUENOC** Cabernet Sauvignon Napa Valley Beckstoffer IV Vineyard Reserve 1994 • $40 • (10/31/97)

93 **HARRISON** Cabernet Sauvignon Napa Valley 1994 • $33 • (07/31/97) • HR

93 **LA JOTA** Cabernet Sauvignon Howell Mountain 13th Anniversary Release 1994 • $46 • (04/30/97)

93 **LIPARITA** Cabernet Sauvignon Howell Mountain 1994 • $32 • (05/15/98) • HR

93 **PINE RIDGE** Andrus Reserve Napa Valley 1994 • $85 • (07/31/97)

93 **RAYMOND** Cabernet Sauvignon Napa Valley Generations 1994 • $35 • (10/31/97) • SS

93 **RIDGE** Monte Bello Santa Cruz Mountains 1994 • $100 • (09/30/97)

93 **ROCKLAND** Cabernet Sauvignon Napa Valley 1994 • $30 • (11/15/96)

93 **ST. FRANCIS** Cabernet Sauvignon Sonoma Valley Reserve 1994 • $30 • (10/15/97) • SS

93 **SILVERADO VINEYARDS** Cabernet Sauvignon Napa Valley Limited Reserve 1994 • $72 Ⓐ • (11/30/97) • HR

93 **STAG'S LEAP WINE CELLARS** Cask 23 Napa Valley 1994 • $100 • (03/31/98) • CS

93 **STONESTREET** Legacy Alexander Valley 1994 • $50 • (10/15/97) • HR

93 **VIADER** Napa Valley 1994 • $30 • (05/31/97)

93 **WHITE COTTAGE** Cabernet Sauvignon Howell Mountain 1994 • $35 • (10/15/97)

92 **BEHRENS & HITCHCOCK** Cabernet Sauvignon Napa Valley Staglin Vineyard 1994 • $28 • (11/30/97)

92 **BERINGER** Cabernet Sauvignon Napa Valley Chabot Vineyard 1994 • $85 • (10/31/97)

92 **BERINGER** Cabernet Sauvignon Napa Valley Marston Vineyard 1994 • $85 • (10/31/97)

92 **CAKEBREAD** Cabernet Sauvignon Napa Valley 1994 • $25 • (07/31/97) • SS

92 **CLARK-CLAUDON** Cabernet Sauvignon Napa Valley 1994 • $45 • (05/31/97)

92 **CUVAISON** Cabernet Sauvignon Napa Valley ATS 1994 • $50 • (04/30/98)

92 **DEL DOTTO** Cabernet Sauvignon Napa Valley 1994 • $42 • (10/31/97)

92 **ESTANCIA** Meritage Alexander Valley 1994 • $16 • (05/15/97) • SS

92 **FISHER** Cabernet Sauvignon Napa Valley Lamb Vineyard 1994 • $50 • (10/31/97)

92 **FORMAN** Cabernet Sauvignon Napa Valley 1994 • $35 • (05/31/97)

92 **JUSTIN** Isosceles Paso Robles 1994 • $33 • (10/31/97)

Key: SS—Spectator Selection CS—Cellar Selection HR—Highly Recommended BB—Best Buy $NA—Price not available Ⓐ—Auction Price

Dates in parentheses indicate the issues in which the ratings were published.

92 **MARKHAM** Cabernet Sauvignon Napa Valley 1994 • $15 • (10/31/97) • SS

92 **NIEBAUM-COPPOLA** Rubicon Rutherford 1994 • $65 • (06/15/98) • CS

92 **PAHLMEYER** Napa Valley 1994 • $40 • (11/30/96) • HR

92 **PARADIGM** Cabernet Sauvignon Napa Valley Oakville 1994 • $30 • (09/30/97)

92 **PEJU** Cabernet Sauvignon Napa Valley HB Vineyard 1994 • $55 • (10/31/97)

92 **PINE RIDGE** Cabernet Sauvignon Stags Leap District 1994 • $35 • (10/31/97)

92 **ST. CLEMENT** Cabernet Sauvignon Howell Mountain White Cottage Ranch 1994 • $45 • (09/30/97)

92 **SPOTTSWOODE** Cabernet Sauvignon Napa Valley 1994 • $45 • (10/15/97) • CS

92 **STAG'S LEAP WINE CELLARS** Cabernet Sauvignon Napa Valley Fay 1994 • $50 • (03/31/98) • CS

92 **VILLA MT. EDEN** Cabernet Sauvignon Mendocino Signature Series 1994 • $50 • (10/31/97)

92 **VON STRASSER** Cabernet Sauvignon Napa Valley Diamond Mountain 1994 • $32 • (10/31/97)

92 **WHITEHALL LANE** Cabernet Sauvignon Rutherford Morisoli Vineyard Reserve 1994 • $36 • (09/30/97)

91 **ALTAMURA** Cabernet Sauvignon Napa Valley 1994 • $33 • (12/15/97)

91 **ANDERSON'S CONN VALLEY** Cabernet Sauvignon Napa Valley Estate Reserve 1994 • $40 • (10/15/97)

91 **ARROWOOD** Cabernet Sauvignon Sonoma County 1994 • $34 • (10/15/97)

91 **BEAULIEU VINEYARD** Tapestry Reserve Napa Valley 1994 • $20 • (10/31/97) • SS

91 **BERINGER** Cabernet Sauvignon Knights Valley 1994 • $20 • (07/31/97) • SS

91 **CHATEAU ST. JEAN** Cabernet Sauvignon Sonoma County Cinq Cépages 1994 • $24 • (09/30/97) • SS

91 **CHIMNEY ROCK** Cabernet Sauvignon Stags Leap District Reserve 1994 • $50 • (10/15/97)

91 **COSENTINO** M. Coz Napa Valley Meritage 1994 • $60 • (11/15/97)

91 **DEHLINGER** Cabernet Sauvignon Russian River Valley Estate 1994 • $25 • (09/30/97)

91 **DIAMOND CREEK** Cabernet Sauvignon Napa Valley Red Rock Terrace 1994 • $100 • (06/15/98)

91 **DIAMOND CREEK** Cabernet Sauvignon Napa Valley Volcanic Hill 1994 • $100 • (06/15/98)

91 **DUNN** Cabernet Sauvignon Howell Mountain 1994 • $45 • (05/15/98) • CS

91 **FAR NIENTE** Cabernet Sauvignon Napa Valley 1994 • $55 • (02/28/97)

91 **GALLERON** Cabernet Sauvignon Napa Valley 1994 • $50 • (09/30/97)

91 **GEYSER PEAK** Réserve Alexandre Alexander Valley 1994 • $28 • (10/31/97)

91 **LAMBERT BRIDGE** Crane Creek Cuvée Dry Creek Valley 1994 • $28 • (11/15/97)

91 **PAUL HOBBS** Cabernet Sauvignon Howell Mountain Liparita Vineyard 1994 • $45 • (10/31/97)

91 **PRIDE** Cabernet Sauvignon Napa Valley Reserve 1994 • $65 • (03/31/98)

91 **QUINTESSA** Rutherford Napa Valley 1994 • $70 • (11/30/97)

91 **S. ANDERSON** Cabernet Sauvignon Stags Leap District Richard Chambers Vineyard 1994 • $50 • (10/31/97)

91 **SADDLEBACK** Cabernet Sauvignon Napa Valley 1994 • $23 • (09/30/97)

91 **ST. CLEMENT** Cabernet Sauvignon Napa Valley 1994 • $27 • (07/31/97)

91 **ST. CLEMENT** Oroppas Napa Valley 1994 • $30 • (11/15/96)

91 **STAG'S LEAP WINE CELLARS** Cabernet Sauvignon Napa Valley S.L.V. 1994 • $50 • (11/30/97) • CS

91 **STEELE** Cabernet Sauvignon Anderson Valley 1994 • $24 • (12/15/97)

91 **STONESTREET** Cabernet Sauvignon Alexander Valley 1994 • $35 • (10/31/97)

91 **SWANSON** Alexis Napa Valley 1994 • $33 • (03/31/97)

91 **SWANSON** Cabernet Sauvignon Napa Valley 1994 • $24 • (07/31/97)

91 **TRUCHARD** Cabernet Sauvignon Napa Valley Carneros 1994 • $24 • (09/30/97)

91 **VENEZIA** Cabernet Sauvignon Alexander Valley Meola Vineyards 1994 • $25 • (05/15/97)

90 **BEAULIEU VINEYARD** Cabernet Sauvignon Rutherford 1994 • $15 • (07/31/97) • SS

90 **BENZIGER** Cabernet Sauvignon Sonoma County Five Bordeaux Varietals 1994 • $14 • (04/30/97) • SS

90 **BERINGER** Alluvium Knights Valley 1994 • $25 • (03/31/98)

90 **BERNARDUS** Marinus Carmel Valley 1994 • $30 • (04/30/97)

90 **BUEHLER** Cabernet Sauvignon Napa Valley Estate 1994 • $35 • (11/15/97)

90 **CARMENET** Meritage Red Sonoma Valley Moon Mountain Estate Reserve 1994 • $40 • (11/15/97)

90 **CHIMNEY ROCK** Cabernet Sauvignon Napa Valley 1994 • $24 • (07/31/97)

90 **CLOS DU BOIS** Marlstone Vineyard Alexander Valley 1994 • $25 • (05/15/98)

90 **CLOS PEGASE** Cabernet Sauvignon Napa Valley Hommage Artist Series Reserve 1994 • $40 • (09/30/97)

90 **CRONIN** Concerto Stags Leap District Robinson Vineyard 1994 • $23 • (04/30/98)

90 **DE LOACH** Cabernet Sauvignon Russian River Valley O.F.S. 1994 • $28 • (09/30/97)

90 **DUCKHORN** Cabernet Sauvignon Napa Valley 1994 • $28 • (05/31/97)

90 **FLORA SPRINGS** Trilogy Napa Valley 1994 • $33 • (10/15/97)

90 **GUENOC** Cabernet Sauvignon Napa Valley Bella Vista Vineyard Reserve 1994 • $26 • (09/30/97)

90 **GUENOC** Langtry Napa Valley Meritage Red 1994 • $41 • (09/30/97)

90 **LA JOTA** Cabernet Sauvignon Howell Mountain Howell Mountain Selection 1994 • $28 • (05/15/97)

90 **LONG** Cabernet Sauvignon Napa Valley 1994 • $35 • (01/31/97)

90 **MORAGA** Red Bel Air 1994 • $55 • (05/15/98)

90 **PHILIP TOGNI** Cabernet Sauvignon Napa Valley 1994 • $39 • (11/15/96)

90 **PINE RIDGE** Cabernet Sauvignon Howell Mountain 1994 • $35 • (10/31/97)

90 **PRIDE** Cabernet Sauvignon Napa Valley 1994 • $24 • (10/31/97)

90 **RAVENSWOOD** Pickberry Sonoma Mountain 1994 • $30 • (03/31/97)

90 **ROBERT CRAIG** Cabernet Sauvignon Howell Mountain 1994 • $28 • (11/30/97)

90 **ROBERT MONDAVI** Cabernet Sauvignon Napa Valley 1994 • $22 • (11/15/97)

90 **ROCKING HORSE** Cabernet Sauvignon Napa Valley Garvey Family Vineyard 1994 • $24 • (11/30/97)

90 **ROMBAUER** Cabernet Sauvignon Napa Valley Diamond Mountain Selection 1994 • $50 • (11/15/97)

90 **ROSENTHAL-THE MALIBU ESTATE** Cabernet Sauvignon Malibu & Newton Canyon 1994 • $25 • (05/15/98)

90 **SIGNORELLO** Cabernet Sauvignon Napa Valley Founder's Reserve 1994 • $55 • (09/30/97)

90 **SONOMA CREEK** Cabernet Sauvignon Sonoma Valley Rancho Salina Vineyard 1994 • $28 • (10/31/97)

90 **SPRING MOUNTAIN** Red Napa Valley 1994 • $36 • (04/30/98)

90 **STAGLIN FAMILY** Cabernet Sauvignon Rutherford 1994 • $40 • (06/15/97)

90 **TOM EDDY** Cabernet Sauvignon Napa Valley 1994 • $50 • (05/15/98)

90 **VINE CLIFF** Cabernet Sauvignon Napa Valley Oakville Estate 1994 • $36 • (10/15/97)

90 **VINEYARD 29** Cabernet Sauvignon Napa Valley 1994 • $55 • (09/30/97)

90 **ZD WINES** Cabernet Sauvignon Napa Valley Reserve 1994 • $55 • (05/15/98)

89 **ARNS** Cabernet Sauvignon Napa Valley 1994 • $35 • (10/31/97)

89 **B.R. COHN** Cabernet Sauvignon Sonoma Valley Olive Hill Vineyard 1994 • $35 • (02/28/97)

89 **CAFARO** Cabernet Sauvignon Napa Valley 1994 • $30 • (10/31/97)

89 **CHALK HILL** Cabernet Sauvignon Chalk Hill 1994 • $26 • (10/31/97)

89 **CHARLES KRUG** Cabernet Sauvignon Napa Valley Peter Mondavi Family 1994 • $14 • (08/31/97)

89 **CHATEAU SOUVERAIN** Cabernet Sauvignon Alexander Valley 1994 • $15 • (06/30/97) • SS

89 **CLOS DU BOIS** Cabernet Sauvignon Alexander Valley Briarcrest Vineyard 1994 • $23 • (06/15/98)

89 **COSENTINO** Cabernet Sauvignon Napa Valley Reserve 1994 • $40 • (10/15/97)

89 **COSENTINO** The Poet Napa Valley Meritage 1994 • $30 • (11/15/97)

89 **CUVAISON** Cabernet Sauvignon Napa Valley 1994 • $25 • (11/15/97)

89 **DRY CREEK** Cabernet Sauvignon Dry Creek Valley 25th Anniversary 1994 • $30 • (03/31/98)

89 **ELLIOTT** Cabernet Sauvignon Napa Valley 1994 • $24 • (11/15/97)

89 **FETZER** Cabernet Sauvignon Napa Valley Usibelli Vineyard Reserve 1994 • $24 • (11/15/97)

89 **FRANCISCAN** Magnificat Napa Valley Meritage 1994 • $25 • (11/30/97)

89 **FREEMARK ABBEY** Cabernet Sauvignon Napa Valley 1994 • $18 • (10/31/97)

89 **FRICK** Cabernet Sauvignon Dry Creek Valley 1994 • $20 • (09/15/97)

89 **GEYSER PEAK** Cabernet Sauvignon Alexander Valley Reserve 1994 • $28 • (05/31/97)

89 **GREENWOOD RIDGE** Cabernet Sauvignon Anderson Valley 1994 • $36 • (11/15/97)

89 **HARTWELL** Cabernet Sauvignon Stags Leap District Sunshine Vineyard 1994 • $40 • (11/30/97)

89 **JOSEPH PHELPS** Cabernet Sauvignon Napa Valley 1994 • $24 • (02/28/97)

89 **JOSEPH PHELPS** Cabernet Sauvignon Napa Valley Backus Vineyard 1994 • $70 • (10/15/97)

89 **JUSTIN** Cabernet Sauvignon San Luis Obispo County Reserve 1994 • $20 • (03/31/97)

89 **LAMBERT BRIDGE** Cabernet Sauvignon Dry Creek Valley 1994 • $20 • (11/15/97)

89 **MURPHY-GOODE** Cabernet Sauvignon Alexander Valley Brenda Block Reserve 1994 • $30 • (07/31/97)

89 **NEWTON** Cabernet Sauvignon Napa Valley 1994 • $30 • (01/31/98)

89 **OPTIMA** Cabernet Sauvignon Alexander Valley 1994 • $28 • (08/31/97)

89 **PAUL HOBBS** Cabernet Sauvignon Napa Valley Carneros Hyde Vineyard 1994 • $40 • (10/31/97)

89 **PEZZI KING** Cabernet Sauvignon Dry Creek Valley 1994 • $18 • (04/30/97)

89 **PINE RIDGE** Cabernet Sauvignon Rutherford 1994 • $22 • (10/31/97)

89 **RAYMOND** Cabernet Sauvignon Napa Valley Reserve 1994 • $20 • (05/31/97)

89 **S. ANDERSON** Cabernet Sauvignon Stags Leap District 1994 • $24 • (10/31/97)

89 **SCHUG** Cabernet Sauvignon Sonoma Valley Heritage Reserve 1994 • $30 • (12/15/97)

89 **SEAVEY** Cabernet Sauvignon Napa Valley 1994 • $30 • (12/31/97)

89 **VIANSA** Cabernet Sauvignon Napa Valley Reserve 1994 • $30 • (11/30/97)

89 **WHITEHALL LANE** Cabernet Sauvignon Napa Valley 1994 • $18 • (11/15/96)

88 **A. RAFANELLI** Cabernet Sauvignon Dry Creek Valley 1994 • $20 • (09/30/97)

88 **ADELAIDA** Cabernet Sauvignon San Luis Obispo County 1994 • $21 • (05/31/98)

88 **BARTHOLOMEW PARK** Cabernet Sauvignon Sonoma Valley Desnudos Vineyard 1994 • $20 • (10/31/97)

88 **BENZIGER** Cabernet Sauvignon Sonoma Mountain Reserve 1994 • $32 • (06/30/98)

88 **BUENA VISTA** Cabernet Sauvignon Carneros 1994 • $16 • (08/31/97)

88 **CAIN** Five Napa Valley 1994 • $45 • (10/31/97)

88 **CHAPPELLET** Cabernet Sauvignon Napa Valley Signature 1994 • $22 • (12/31/97)

88 **CHARLES KRUG** Cabernet Sauvignon Napa Valley Vintage Selection 1994 • $35 • (10/31/97)

88 **CHATEAU MONTELENA** Cabernet Sauvignon Napa Valley Calistoga Cuvée 1994 • $18 • (11/15/96)

88 **CHIMNEY ROCK** Elevage Stags Leap District 1994 • $40 • (10/15/97)

88 **CINNABAR** Cabernet Sauvignon Santa Cruz Mountains Saratoga Vineyard 1994 • $25 • (11/15/97)

88 **CRONIN** Cabernet Sauvignon Santa Cruz Mountains 1994 • $23 • (04/30/98)

88 **DAVID COFFARO** Cabernet Sauvignon Dry Creek Valley Coffaro Estate Vineyard Old Vines 1994 • $16 • (09/15/96)

88 **DAYDREAM** Cabernet Sauvignon Napa Valley 1994 • $24 • (11/30/97)

88 **DELECTUS** Cabernet Sauvignon Napa Valley 1994 • $42 • (07/31/97)

88 **DOUGLASS HILL** Cabernet Sauvignon Napa Valley 1994 • $13 • (10/15/97)

88 **DRY CREEK** Meritage Dry Creek Valley 1994 • $25 • (08/31/97)

88 **DUNCAN PEAK** Cabernet Sauvignon Mendocino 1994 • $20 • (11/15/97)

88 **DUNN** Cabernet Sauvignon Napa Valley 1994 • $39 • (05/15/98)

88 **EDGEWOOD** Cabernet Sauvignon Napa Valley 1994 • $20 • (04/30/98)

88 **ESTANCIA** Cabernet Sauvignon Sonoma-Napa Counties 1994 • $11 • (03/31/97) • BB

Key: SS—Spectator Selection CS—Cellar Selection HR—Highly Recommended BB—Best Buy $NA—Price not available Ⓐ—Auction Price
Dates in parentheses indicate the issues in which the ratings were published.

88 **FETZER** Cabernet Sauvignon North Coast Barrel Select 1994 • $14 • (09/30/97)

88 **FIELD STONE** Cabernet Sauvignon Alexander Valley Staten Family Reserve 1994 • $28 • (07/31/98)

88 **FISHER** Cabernet Sauvignon Sonoma County Wedding Vineyard 1994 • $50 • (10/31/97)

88 **FOXEN** Cabernet Sauvignon Santa Barbara County 1994 • $24 • (11/15/96)

88 **FRANCISCAN** Cabernet Sauvignon Napa Valley 1994 • $16 • (05/15/97)

88 **FROG'S LEAP** Cabernet Sauvignon Napa Valley 1994 • $20 • (11/15/96)

88 **GIRARD** Cabernet Sauvignon Napa Valley 1994 • $25 • (10/31/97)

88 **GRGICH HILLS** Cabernet Sauvignon Napa Valley 1994 • $30 • (10/31/97)

88 **GROTH** Cabernet Sauvignon Napa Valley 1994 • $27 • (08/31/97)

88 **HUSCH** Cabernet Sauvignon Mendocino La Ribera Vineyards 1994 • $15 • (10/15/97)

88 **IRON HORSE** Cabernet Sauvignon Alexander Valley Barrel Fermented 1994 • $19 • (11/30/97)

88 **JORDAN** Cabernet Sauvignon Alexander Valley 1994 • $34 • (06/30/98)

88 **KARL LAWRENCE** Cabernet Sauvignon Napa Valley 1994 • $28 • (09/30/97)

88 **KENDALL-JACKSON** Cabernet Sauvignon Alexander Valley Buckeye Vineyard Single Vineyard Series 1994 • $24 • (08/31/97)

88 **KENWOOD** Cabernet Sauvignon Sonoma Valley 1994 • $18 • (10/31/97)

88 **KENWOOD** Cabernet Sauvignon Sonoma Valley Jack London Vineyard 1994 • $25 • (10/31/97)

88 **LOCKWOOD** Cabernet Sauvignon Monterey 1994 • $15 • (05/31/97)

88 **LOCKWOOD** Cabernet Sauvignon Monterey Partners' Reserve 1994 • $21 • (11/15/97)

88 **MARTIN RAY** Cabernet Sauvignon California Saratoga Cuvée 1994 • $30 • (12/15/97)

88 **MEEKER** Cabernet Sauvignon Dry Creek Valley Gold Leaf Cuvée 1994 • $18 • (11/15/97)

88 **MOUNT EDEN** Cabernet Sauvignon Santa Cruz Mountains 1994 • $20 • (05/15/97)

88 **MOUNT VEEDER** Cabernet Sauvignon Napa Valley 1994 • $25 • (08/31/97)

88 **MURPHY-GOODE** Cabernet Sauvignon Alexander Valley Murphy Ranch 1994 • $18 • (11/15/96)

88 **OAKVILLE RANCH** Cabernet Sauvignon Napa Valley 1994 • $30 • (07/31/97)

88 **RAVENSWOOD** Cabernet Sauvignon Sonoma Valley Gregory Vineyard 1994 • $20 • (02/28/97)

88 **ROBERT MONDAVI** Cabernet Sauvignon Napa Valley Oakville District 1994 • $28 • (06/30/97)

88 **ROBERT PECOTA** Cabernet Sauvignon Napa Valley Kara's Vineyard 1994 • $23 • (11/15/96)

88 **ROSENBLUM** Holbrook Mitchell Trio Napa Valley 1994 • $24 • (11/30/96)

88 **SCHUG** Cabernet Sauvignon Napa Valley 1994 • $18 • (12/15/97)

88 **SHAFER** Cabernet Sauvignon Stags Leap District 1994 • $28 • (06/30/97)

88 **SIGNORELLO** Cabernet Sauvignon Napa Valley 1994 • $30 • (11/15/97)

88 **SIMI** Cabernet Sauvignon Alexander Valley 1994 • $18 • (10/31/97)

88 **STAG'S LEAP WINE CELLARS** Cabernet Sauvignon Napa Valley 1994 • $19 Ⓐ • (05/15/97)

88 **STERLING** Reserve Napa Valley 1994 • $40 • (12/15/97)

88 **THE HESS COLLECTION** Cabernet Sauvignon Napa Valley 1994 • $20 • (05/15/98)

88 **V. SATTUI** Cabernet Sauvignon Napa Valley Morisoli Vineyard 1994 • $27 • (05/15/97)

88 **WILLIAM HILL** Cabernet Sauvignon Napa Valley Reserve 1994 • $27 • (12/15/97)

88 **ZD WINES** Cabernet Sauvignon Napa Valley 1994 • $30 • (07/31/97)

87 **ALEXANDER VALLEY VINEYARDS** Cabernet Sauvignon Alexander Valley Wetzel Family Estate 1994 • $15 • (11/15/97)

87 **BEAULIEU VINEYARD** Cabernet Sauvignon Napa Valley Beautour 1994 • $11 • (10/15/97)

87 **BENZIGER** A Tribute Sonoma Mountain 1994 • $25 • (10/31/97)

87 **BUEHLER** Cabernet Sauvignon Napa Valley 1994 • $20 • (07/31/97)

87 **BURGESS** Cabernet Sauvignon Napa Valley Vintage Selection 1994 • $22 • (11/30/97)

87 **CHARLES KRUG** Generations Napa Valley Peter Mondavi Family 1994 • $30 • (10/31/97)

87 **CHATEAU CHRISTINA** Cabernet Sauvignon Carmel Valley 1994 • $25 • (11/15/97)

87 **COOPER-GARROD** Cabernet Sauvignon Santa Cruz Mountains 1994 • $25 • (11/30/97)

87 **CORISON** Cabernet Sauvignon Napa Valley 1994 • $35 • (09/30/97)

87 **DAVIS BYNUM** Cabernet Sauvignon Russian River Valley Hedin Vineyard Limited Edition 1994 • $20 • (12/15/97)

87 **DAVIS BYNUM** Eclipse Sonoma County 1994 • $28 • (04/30/98)

87 **DRY CREEK** Cabernet Sauvignon Dry Creek Valley Reserve 1994 • $25 • (11/30/96)

87 **FISHER** Cabernet Sauvignon Napa Valley Coach Insignia 1994 • $24 • (10/31/97)

87 **HARMONY CELLARS** Cabernet Sauvignon Paso Robles 1994 • $14 • (10/15/97)

87 **IRON HORSE** Cabernet Sauvignon Alexander Valley Cuveé Joy 1994 • $25 • (11/15/97)

87 **J. LOHR** Cabernet Sauvignon Paso Robles Seven Oaks 1994 • $14 • (07/31/97)

87 **JOHNSON TURNBULL** Cabernet Sauvignon Napa Valley Oakville 1994 • $22 • (04/30/97)

87 **JUDD'S HILL** Cabernet Sauvignon Napa Valley 1994 • $30 • (05/15/98)

87 **KENDALL-JACKSON** Cabernet Sauvignon California Grand Reserve 1994 • $39 • (07/31/97)

87 **LOUIS M. MARTINI** Cabernet Sauvignon Sonoma Valley Monte Rosso Vineyard Selection Heritage Collection 1994 • $30 • (11/30/97)

87 **MEEKER** Four Kings Scharf Family Vineyard Sonoma County 1994 • $20 • (11/15/97)

87 **MERRYVALE** Cabernet Sauvignon Napa Valley 1994 • $27 • (10/31/97)

87 **NAPA RIDGE** Cabernet Sauvignon Central Coast Oak Barrel 1994 • $8 • (02/28/97) • BB

87 **NAPA RIDGE** Cabernet Sauvignon Napa Valley Reserve 1994 • $15 • (10/15/97)

87 **NAPA RIDGE** Cabernet Sauvignon North Coast Oak Barrel 1994 • $8 • (11/15/96) • BB

87 **NEWLAN** Cabernet Sauvignon Napa Valley 1994 • $19 • (10/15/97)

87 **PAOLETTI** Cabernet Sauvignon Napa Valley 1994 • $30 • (12/15/97)

87 **PER SEMPRE** Cabernet Sauvignon Napa Valley 1994 • $35 • (01/31/98)

87 **RABBIT RIDGE** Cabernet Sauvignon Russian River Valley Rabbit Ridge Ranch Winemaker's Grand Reserve 1994 • $40 • (03/31/98)

87 **RAVENSWOOD** Rancho Salina Vineyards Sonoma Valley 1994 • $25 • (02/28/97)

87 **RAYMOND** Cabernet Sauvignon Napa Valley Estates 1994 • $14 • (05/31/97)

87 **ROMBAUER** Cabernet Sauvignon Napa Valley 1994 • $27 • (11/15/97)

87 **SEBASTIANI** Cabernet Sauvignon Sonoma County 1994 • $10 • (04/30/97) • BB

87 **SOQUEL** Cabernet Sauvignon Santa Cruz Mountains 1994 • $22 • (10/31/97)

87 **TITUS** Cabernet Sauvignon Napa Valley 1994 • $22 • (04/30/98)

87 **TREFETHEN** Cabernet Sauvignon Napa Valley 1994 • $24 • (11/15/97)

87 **TULOCAY** Cabernet Sauvignon Napa Valley Cliff Vineyard 1994 • $22 • (11/30/97)

87 **TURNBULL** Cabernet Sauvignon Napa Valley Oakville 1994 • $22 • (04/30/97)

87 **VOLKER EISELE** Cabernet Sauvignon Napa Valley 1994 • $30 • (10/31/97)

87 **WELLINGTON** Cabernet Sauvignon Sonoma County Mohrhardt Ridge Vineyard 1994 • $15 • (11/15/97)

86 **ALDERBROOK** Cabernet Sauvignon Dry Creek Valley 1994 • $17 • (05/15/97)

86 **AMICI** Cabernet Sauvignon Napa Valley 1994 • $22 • (05/31/98)

86 **BARTHOLOMEW PARK** Cabernet Sauvignon Sonoma Valley Alta Vista Vineyard 1994 • $18 • (10/31/97)

86 **CLOS DU BOIS** Cabernet Sauvignon Sonoma County 1994 • $13 • (11/15/96)

86 **CLOS DU VAL** Cabernet Sauvignon Napa Valley 1994 • $24 • (03/31/98)

86 **CLOS PEGASE** Cabernet Sauvignon Napa Valley 1994 • $23 • (10/31/97)

86 **DELORIMIER** Mosaic Alexander Valley Meritage 1994 • $20 • (11/15/97)

86 **DRY CREEK** Cabernet Sauvignon Dry Creek Valley 1994 • $17 • (11/30/96)

86 **DUNNING** Cabernet Sauvignon Paso Robles Westside 1994 • $14 • (11/30/96)

86 **EBERLE** Cabernet Sauvignon Paso Robles 1994 • $18 • (11/15/97)

86 **GALANTE** Cabernet Sauvignon Carmel Valley Blackjack Pasture 1994 • $30 • (10/15/96)

86 **GEYSER PEAK** Cabernet Sauvignon Sonoma County 1994 • $10 • (11/15/96) • BB

86 **GUENOC** Meritage Red Lake County 1994 • $15 • (11/15/97)

86 **IRON HORSE** Cabernet Sauvignon Alexander Valley 1994 • $19 • (11/30/97)

86 **LAUREL GLEN** Cabernet Sauvignon Sonoma Mountain 1994 • $35 • (08/31/97)

86 **MERIDIAN** Cabernet Sauvignon California 1994 • $11 • (09/30/97)

86 **NORMAN** Cabernet Sauvignon Paso Robles 1994 • $16 • (11/15/97)

86 **NORMAN** No Nonsense Red Claret Paso Robles 1994 • $12 • (11/15/96)

86 **PEACHY CANYON** Para Siempre Central Coast 1994 • $28 • (08/31/97) • BB

86 **PER SEMPRE** Cabernet Sauvignon Napa Valley Select Reserve 1994 • $43 • (01/31/98)

86 **RENAISSANCE** Cabernet Sauvignon North Yuba 1994 • $13 • (10/31/97)

86 **RENAISSANCE** Cabernet Sauvignon North Yuba Reserve 1994 • $20 • (07/31/98)

86 **RICHARDSON** Synergy Sonoma Valley 1994 • $15 • (12/15/95)

86 **RODNEY STRONG** Cabernet Sauvignon Northern Sonoma Alexander's Crown Vineyard 1994 • $23 • (03/31/98)

86 **RUTZ** Cabernet Sauvignon Napa Valley 1994 • $26 • (11/30/97)

86 **ST. FRANCIS** Cabernet Sauvignon Sonoma County 1994 • $10 • (10/15/96) • BB

86 **SHENANDOAH** Cabernet Sauvignon Amador County 1994 • $10 • (11/30/96)

86 **SMITH & HOOK** Cabernet Sauvignon Santa Lucia Highlands Masterpiece Edition 1994 • $35 • (11/30/97)

86 **VILLA MT. EDEN** Cabernet Sauvignon California 1994 • $12 • (10/15/97)

86 **VOILÀ!** Melange Napa Valley 1994 • $18 • (07/31/98)

86 **WILD HORSE** Cabernet Sauvignon San Luis Obispo County 1994 • $16 • (12/15/96)

86 **WILLIAM HILL** Cabernet Sauvignon Napa Valley 1994 • $14 • (09/30/97)

85 **ARCIERO** Cabernet Sauvignon Paso Robles 1994 • $11 • (09/30/97)

85 **BEAULIEU VINEYARD** Cabernet Sauvignon Napa Valley 1994 • $15 • (07/31/97)

85 **BOEGER** Cabernet Sauvignon El Dorado 1994 • $12 • (10/15/97)

85 **CAIN** Cuvée Napa Valley 1994 • $19 • (07/31/97)

85 **CLOS DU BOIS** Cabernet Sauvignon Alexander Valley 1994 • $17 • (05/15/97)

85 **FIELD STONE** Cabernet Sauvignon Alexander Valley 1994 • $18 • (07/31/98)

85 **FIRESTONE** Cabernet Sauvignon Santa Ynez Valley 1994 • $12 • (10/31/97)

85 **FREESTONE** Cabernet Sauvignon Napa Valley 1994 • $15 • (10/15/97)

85 **GALANTE** Cabernet Sauvignon Carmel Valley Red Rose Hill 1994 • $25 • (10/15/96)

85 **LE DUCQ** Red Napa Valley 1994 • $99 • (03/31/98)

85 **MARIO PERELLI-MINETTI** Cabernet Sauvignon Napa Valley 1994 • $NA • (03/31/98)

85 **MIDNIGHT CELLARS** Cabernet Sauvignon Paso Robles 1994 • $16 • (09/15/97)

85 **MIRASSOU** Cabernet Sauvignon Napa Valley Harvest Reserve Limited Bottling 1994 • $18 • (05/15/97)

85 **NEWTON** Claret Napa Valley 1994 • $16 • (02/28/97)

85 **QUATRO** Cabernet Sauvignon Sonoma County 1994 • $18 • (08/31/97)

85 **ROBERT MONDAVI** Cabernet Sauvignon North Coast Coastal 1994 • $11 • (12/31/96)

85 **ROSENBLUM** Cabernet Sauvignon Napa Valley Yountville Vineyards 1994 • $20 • (11/30/96)

85 **SMITH & HOOK** Cabernet Sauvignon Santa Lucia Highlands 1994 • $18 • (09/30/97)

85 **STERLING** Cabernet Sauvignon Napa Valley Diamond Mountain Ranch Vineyard 1994 • $18 • (10/31/97)

85 **TREFETHEN** Cabernet Sauvignon California Eshcol 1994 • $10 • (11/30/96) • BB

Key: SS—Spectator Selection CS—Cellar Selection HR—Highly Recommended BB—Best Buy $NA—Price not available Ⓐ—Auction Price
Dates in parentheses indicate the issues in which the ratings were published.

84 **BOEGER** Meritage Reserve El Dorado 1994 • $15 • (07/31/98)

84 **SUNSTONE** Equinox Santa Barbara County 1994 • $21 • (12/15/96)

83 **JESSANDRA VITTORIA** Santa Vittoria Sonoma Valley 1994 • $25 • (08/31/96)

82 **SONOMA CREEK** Meritage Sonoma County 1994 • $18 • (10/31/97)

1992 California Cabernet
Vintage Rating: 93

98 **GROTH** Cabernet Sauvignon Napa Valley Reserve 1992 • $125 Ⓐ • (04/30/96) • CS

96 **ARAUJO** Cabernet Sauvignon Napa Valley Eisele Vineyard 1992 • $40 • (11/15/95) • CS

96 **FLORA SPRINGS** Cabernet Sauvignon Napa Valley Rutherford Reserve 1992 • $40 • (11/15/95) • HR

95 **BERINGER** Cabernet Sauvignon Napa Valley Private Reserve 1992 • $45 • (11/15/95) • CS

95 **ST. CLEMENT** Oroppas Napa Valley 1992 • $25 • (09/30/94) • CS

94 **DALLA VALLE** Maya Napa Valley 1992 • $377 Ⓐ • (12/15/95)

94 **DIAMOND CREEK** Cabernet Sauvignon Napa Valley Lake 1992 • $121 Ⓐ • (06/15/98)

94 **LEWIS CELLARS** Cabernet Sauvignon Napa Valley Oakville Ranch 1992 • $30 • (11/30/95) • HR

94 **SCREAMING EAGLE** Cabernet Sauvignon Napa Valley 1992 • $678 Ⓐ • (02/29/96)

94 **STAG'S LEAP WINE CELLARS** Cask 23 Napa Valley 1992 • $80 • (12/15/95) • CS

94 **THE HESS COLLECTION** Cabernet Sauvignon Napa Valley 1992 • $18 • (11/15/95) • SS

93 **ANDERSON'S CONN VALLEY** Cabernet Sauvignon Napa Valley Estate Reserve 1992 • $30 • (11/15/95) • HR

93 **BERINGER** Cabernet Sauvignon Napa Valley Chabot Vineyard 1992 • $100 • (12/15/96)

93 **CRONIN** Concerto Stags Leap District Robinson Vineyard 1992 • $17 • (04/30/96)

93 **ETUDE** Cabernet Sauvignon Napa Valley 1992 • $30 • (11/30/95) • HR

93 **FAR NIENTE** Cabernet Sauvignon Napa Valley 1992 • $45 • (11/15/95) • HR

93 **FORMAN** Cabernet Sauvignon Napa Valley 1992 • $36 Ⓐ • (06/15/95) • CS

93 **FREEMARK ABBEY** Cabernet Sauvignon Napa Valley Bosché 1992 • $32 • (09/30/97) • CS

93 **HEITZ** Cabernet Sauvignon Napa Valley Martha's Vineyard 1992 • $67 Ⓐ • (05/31/97) • CS

93 **PAUL HOBBS** Cabernet Sauvignon Napa Valley Carneros Hyde Vineyard 1992 • $30 • (12/15/95) • HR

93 **SHAFER** Cabernet Sauvignon Stags Leap District Hillside Select 1992 • $50 • (11/15/96) • HR

93 **SILVER OAK** Cabernet Sauvignon Napa Valley 1992 • $75 Ⓐ • (11/15/96) • CS

93 **SIMI** Cabernet Sauvignon Alexander Valley Reserve 1992 • $31 Ⓐ • (11/15/96) • CS

93 **WHITEHALL LANE** Cabernet Sauvignon Napa Valley Morisoli Vineyard 1992 • $28 • (10/15/95) • HR

92 **A. RAFANELLI** Cabernet Sauvignon Dry Creek Valley 1992 • $17 • (09/30/95) • SS

92 **ALTAMURA** Cabernet Sauvignon Napa Valley 1992 • $28 • (08/31/96) • HR

92 **ARROWOOD** Cabernet Sauvignon Sonoma County 1992 • $25 • (11/15/95) • HR

92 **ARROWOOD** Cabernet Sauvignon Sonoma County Réserve Spéciale 1992 • $35 • (12/15/95) • HR

92 **CAYMUS** Cabernet Sauvignon Napa Valley Special Selection 1992 • $120 Ⓐ • (05/15/96) • CS

92 **CHATEAU ST. JEAN** Cabernet Sauvignon Sonoma County Reserve 1992 • $45 • (09/30/97)

92 **CHIMNEY ROCK** Reserve Stags Leap District 1992 • $30 • (12/15/95)

92 **COLGIN** Cabernet Sauvignon Napa Valley Herb Lamb Vineyard 1992 • $29 • (10/15/95) • HR

92 **CORISON** Cabernet Sauvignon Napa Valley 1992 • $28 • (11/30/95) • CS

92 **COSENTINO** M. Coz Napa Valley Meritage 1992 • $45 • (12/15/95)

92 **DALLA VALLE** Cabernet Sauvignon Napa Valley 1992 • $83 Ⓐ • (12/15/95) • CS

92 **DIAMOND CREEK** Cabernet Sauvignon Napa Valley Gravelly Meadow 1992 • $50 • (06/15/98)

92 **DIAMOND CREEK** Cabernet Sauvignon Napa Valley Volcanic Hill 1992 • $50 Ⓐ • (06/15/98)

92 **E. & J. GALLO** Cabernet Sauvignon Northern Sonoma Estate Bottled 1992 • $45 • (11/15/96)

92 **FLORA SPRINGS** Trilogy Napa Valley 1992 • $27 • (11/30/95) • CS

92 **JUSTIN** Isosceles San Luis Obispo County Reserve 1992 • $25 • (12/15/95) • HR

92 **NIEBAUM-COPPOLA** Rubicon Rutherford 1992 • $50 • (05/31/97)

92 **ST. FRANCIS** Cabernet Sauvignon Sonoma County Reserve 1992 • $24 • (11/30/95) • HR

92 **STONESTREET** Legacy Alexander Valley 1992 • $35 • (09/30/95) • CS

92 **VILLA MT. EDEN** Cabernet Sauvignon Mendocino Signature Series 1992 • $45 • (03/31/95) • HR

92 **WHITEHALL LANE** Cabernet Sauvignon Napa Valley Reserve 1992 • $23 • (10/15/95) • HR

91 **CHATEAU MONTELENA** Cabernet Sauvignon Napa Valley The Montelena Estate 1972-1992 Anniversary 1992 • $36 • (11/15/96) • CS

91 **DIAMOND CREEK** Cabernet Sauvignon Napa Valley Red Rock Terrace 1992 • $58 • (06/15/98)

91 **DIAMOND CREEK** Cabernet Sauvignon Napa Valley Volcanic Hill 1992 • $50 Ⓐ • (11/15/94)

91 **ELAN** Cabernet Sauvignon Atlas Peak 1992 • $30 • (11/30/97)

91 **FERRARI-CARANO** Reserve Red Sonoma County 1992 • $47 • (09/30/97)

91 **GROTH** Cabernet Sauvignon Napa Valley 1992 • $20 • (09/30/95) • CS

91 **HARLAN ESTATE** Napa Valley 1992 • $75 • (11/15/96)

91 **JUDD'S HILL** Cabernet Sauvignon Napa Valley 1992 • $26 • (12/15/95)

91 **KENDALL-JACKSON** Cabernet Sauvignon California Grand Reserve 1992 • $35 • (11/30/95)

91 **KENWOOD** Cabernet Sauvignon Sonoma Valley Artist Series 1992 • $50 • (12/15/96)

91 **OPUS ONE** Napa Valley 1992 • $75 • (12/15/95) • CS

91 **PEJU** Cabernet Sauvignon Napa Valley HB Vineyard 1992 • $35 • (12/15/95)

91 **PHILIP TOGNI** Cabernet Sauvignon Napa Valley 1992 • $32 • (11/15/94) • CS

91 **PINE RIDGE** Cabernet Sauvignon Napa Valley Rutherford Cuvée 1992 • $16 • (11/15/95) • SS

91 **RIDGE** Monte Bello Santa Cruz Mountains 1992 • $80 • (11/15/96) • CS

91 **ROBERT MONDAVI** Cabernet Sauvignon Napa Valley Oakville District 1992 • $28 • (12/15/95)

91 **ROBERT MONDAVI** Cabernet Sauvignon Napa Valley Reserve 1992 • $55 • (07/31/95) • CS

91 **SHAFER** Cabernet Sauvignon Stags Leap District 1992 • $22 • (09/30/95) • CS

91 **STAG'S LEAP WINE CELLARS** Cabernet Sauvignon Napa Valley Fay 1992 • $35 • (12/15/95) • CS

91 **STAGLIN FAMILY** Cabernet Sauvignon Napa Valley 1992 • $28 • (12/15/95)

91 **STONESTREET** Cabernet Sauvignon Alexander Valley 1992 • $25 • (10/31/95) • HR

90 **BURGESS** Cabernet Sauvignon Napa Valley Vintage Selection 1992 • $22 • (11/15/96) • SS

90 **CHATEAU MONTELENA** Cabernet Sauvignon Napa Valley Calistoga Cuvée 1992 • $15 • (11/15/94) • SS

90 **CONN CREEK** Anthology Napa Valley 1992 • $30 • (12/15/95)

90 **CORNERSTONE** Cabernet Sauvignon Howell Mountain Beatty Ranch 1992 • $33 • (12/15/95)

90 **DIAMOND CREEK** Cabernet Sauvignon Napa Valley Gravelly Meadow-Lake 1992 • $NA • (06/15/98)

90 **DIAMOND CREEK** Cabernet Sauvignon Napa Valley Red Rock Terrace 1992 • $50 • (11/15/94)

90 **DUCKHORN** Cabernet Sauvignon Napa Valley 1992 • $24 • (10/31/95) • SS

90 **GUENOC** Cabernet Sauvignon Napa Valley Beckstoffer IV Vineyard Reserve 1992 • $40 • (12/15/95)

90 **GUENOC** Cabernet Sauvignon Napa Valley Bella Vista Vineyard Reserve 1992 • $25 • (12/15/95)

90 **GUNDLACH BUNDSCHU** Cabernet Sauvignon Sonoma Valley Rhinefarm Vineyards Vintage Reserve 1992 • $30 • (11/15/96)

90 **HARRISON** Cabernet Sauvignon Napa Valley 1992 • $33 • (11/15/95)

90 **HARTWELL** Cabernet Sauvignon Stags Leap District 1992 • $50 • (11/15/95)

90 **HEITZ** Cabernet Sauvignon Napa Valley Trailside Vineyard 1992 • $48 • (09/30/97)

90 **JARVIS** Cabernet Sauvignon Napa Valley 1992 • $48 • (08/31/95)

90 **JOSEPH PHELPS** Insignia Napa Valley 1992 • $100 Ⓐ • (09/30/95) • CS

90 **MOUNT EDEN** Cabernet Sauvignon Santa Cruz Mountains Old Vine Reserve 1992 • $35 • (06/15/96)

90 **OAKVILLE RANCH** Cabernet Sauvignon Napa Valley 1992 • $24 • (12/15/95)

90 **PETER MICHAEL** Cabernet Sauvignon Knights Valley Les Pavots 1992 • $29 • (12/15/95)

90 **PINE RIDGE** Cabernet Sauvignon Stags Leap District 1992 • $31 • (12/15/95)

90 **RAYMOND** Cabernet Sauvignon Napa Valley Private Reserve 1992 • $26 • (11/15/96)

90 **ST. CLEMENT** Cabernet Sauvignon Napa Valley 1992 • $24 • (10/31/95)

90 **SEQUOIA GROVE** Cabernet Sauvignon Napa Valley 1992 • $18 • (07/31/95) • SS

90 **SIGNORELLO** Cabernet Sauvignon Napa Valley Founder's Reserve 1992 • $32 • (09/15/95) • CS

90 **SILVER OAK** Cabernet Sauvignon Alexander Valley 1992 • $58 Ⓐ • (11/15/96)

90 **SILVERADO VINEYARDS** Cabernet Sauvignon Napa Valley 1992 • $19 • (03/31/95) • SS

90 **SPOTTSWOODE** Cabernet Sauvignon Napa Valley 1992 • $39 • (11/30/95) • CS

90 **SWANSON** Cabernet Sauvignon Napa Valley 1992 • $22 • (12/15/95)

90 **THE HESS COLLECTION** Cabernet Sauvignon Napa Valley Reserve 1992 • $39 • (11/15/96)

■ ■ ■ ■

California Cabernet

90 **THOMAS FOGARTY** Cabernet Sauvignon Napa Valley Vallerga Vineyards 1992 • $25 • (04/30/96)

90 **ZIA** Cabernet Sauvignon Napa Valley 1992 • $24 • (04/30/96)

89 **ATLAS PEAK** Cabernet Sauvignon Atlas Peak 1992 • $18 • (12/15/95)

89 **BEAULIEU VINEYARD** Cabernet Sauvignon Napa Valley Georges de Latour Private Reserve 1992 • $40 • (12/15/95)

89 **BELL** Cabernet Sauvignon Rutherford Baritelle Vineyard 1992 • $50 • (07/31/97)

89 **BRYANT FAMILY** Cabernet Sauvignon Napa Valley 1992 • $246 Ⓐ • (05/31/96)

89 **CARDINALE** Meritage California 1992 • $60 • (11/15/96)

89 **CARMENET** Meritage Red Sonoma Valley Moon Mountain Estate Vineyard 1992 • $25 • (11/30/96)

89 **CAYMUS** Cabernet Sauvignon Napa Valley 1992 • $58 Ⓐ • (09/30/95)

89 **CHATEAU ST. JEAN** Cabernet Sauvignon Sonoma County Cinq Cépages 1992 • $18 • (02/29/96)

89 **CHATEAU SOUVERAIN** Cabernet Sauvignon Alexander Valley Winemaker's Reserve 1992 • $16 • (12/15/95)

89 **CLOS DU BOIS** Cabernet Sauvignon Alexander Valley Briarcrest Vineyard 1992 • $20 • (11/30/95)

89 **CLOS DU BOIS** Marlstone Vineyard Alexander Valley 1992 • $21 • (11/30/95)

89 **CLOS DU VAL** Cabernet Sauvignon Napa Valley Reserve 1992 • $45 • (12/31/96)

89 **DE LOACH** Cabernet Sauvignon Russian River Valley O.F.S. 1992 • $25 • (09/30/96)

89 **DRY CREEK** Cabernet Sauvignon Dry Creek Valley 1992 • $16 • (10/15/95)

89 **ELYSE** Cabernet Sauvignon Napa Valley Morisoli Vineyard 1992 • $30 • (04/30/96)

89 **ESTANCIA** Meritage Alexander Valley 1992 • $15 • (09/30/95)

89 **FERRARI-CARANO** Cabernet Sauvignon Sonoma County 1992 • $22 • (11/15/96)

89 **FREEMARK ABBEY** Cabernet Sauvignon Napa Valley Sycamore Vineyards 1992 • $30 • (09/30/97)

89 **GALLO OF SONOMA** Cabernet Sauvignon Dry Creek Valley Frei Ranch Vineyard 1992 • $16 • (11/15/95)

89 **GARY FARRELL** Cabernet Sauvignon Sonoma County Ladi's Vineyard 1992 • $20 • (07/31/95)

89 **GREENWOOD RIDGE** Cabernet Sauvignon Anderson Valley 1992 • $18 • (09/15/95)

89 **GUENOC** Langtry California Meritage Red 1992 • $35 • (12/15/95)

89 **HEITZ** Cabernet Sauvignon Napa Valley 1992 • $20 • (05/31/97)

89 **JOSEPH PHELPS** Cabernet Sauvignon Napa Valley Backus Vineyard 1992 • $51 Ⓐ • (12/15/95)

89 **LA JOTA** Cabernet Sauvignon Howell Mountain 11th Anniversary Release 1992 • $42 • (01/01/97)

89 **LIVINGSTON** Cabernet Sauvignon Napa Valley Moffett Vineyard 1992 • $30 • (12/15/95)

89 **MARTIN RAY** Cabernet Sauvignon California Saratoga Cuvée 1992 • $28 • (10/31/95)

89 **MONTICELLO** Cabernet Sauvignon Napa Valley Jefferson Cuvée 1992 • $18 • (12/15/95)

Key: SS—Spectator Selection CS—Cellar Selection HR—Highly Recommended BB—Best Buy $NA—Price not available Ⓐ—Auction Price
Dates in parentheses indicate the issues in which the ratings were published.

89 **NAVARRO** Cabernet Sauvignon Mendocino 1992 • $19 • (11/15/97)

89 **OAKFORD** Cabernet Sauvignon Napa Valley 1992 • $30 • (11/15/96)

89 **OPTIMA** Cabernet Sauvignon Alexander Valley 1992 • $25 • (12/15/95)

89 **PAHLMEYER** Napa Valley 1992 • $34 • (12/15/95)

89 **RIDGE** Cabernet Sauvignon Santa Cruz Mountains 1992 • $16 • (11/15/94)

89 **RODNEY STRONG** Cabernet Sauvignon Northern Sonoma Reserve 1992 • $30 • (11/15/96)

89 **ROSENTHAL-THE MALIBU ESTATE** Cabernet Sauvignon California 1992 • $22 • (12/15/95)

89 **S. ANDERSON** Cabernet Sauvignon Stags Leap District Richard Chambers Vineyard 1992 • $46 • (12/15/95)

89 **SEBASTIANI** Cabernet Sauvignon Sonoma Valley Cherryblock Old Vines 1992 • $35 • (04/30/97)

89 **SEQUOIA GROVE** Cabernet Sauvignon Rutherford Estate Reserve 1992 • $30 • (07/31/95)

89 **SIMI** Cabernet Sauvignon Alexander Valley 1992 • $15 • (10/15/95)

89 **STONEHEDGE** Cabernet Sauvignon Napa Valley Winemaker's Reserve 1992 • $10 • (11/30/95) • BB

88 **ADELAIDA** Cabernet Sauvignon San Luis Obispo County 1992 • $19 • (11/15/96)

88 **BEAULIEU VINEYARD** Tapestry Napa Valley Reserve 1992 • $20 • (04/30/96)

88 **CAFARO** Cabernet Sauvignon Napa Valley 1992 • $26 • (12/15/95)

88 **CHATEAU POTELLE** Cabernet Sauvignon Mount Veeder V.G.S. 1992 • $39 • (11/30/96)

88 **CHIMNEY ROCK** Elevage Stags Leap District 1992 • $30 • (12/15/95)

88 **CINNABAR** Cabernet Sauvignon Santa Cruz Mountains Saratoga Vineyard 1992 • $20 • (12/15/95)

88 **CLOS LACHANCE** Cabernet Sauvignon Santa Cruz Mountains 1992 • $20 • (07/31/95)

88 **CLOS PEGASE** Cabernet Sauvignon Napa Valley 1992 • $19 • (10/15/95)

88 **CONN CREEK** Cabernet Sauvignon Napa Valley Limited Release 1992 • $18 • (12/15/95)

88 **COSENTINO** Cabernet Sauvignon Napa Valley Punched Cap Fermented Unfined 1992 • $16 • (09/15/95)

88 **CRONIN** Cabernet Sauvignon Santa Cruz Mountains 1992 • $20 • (01/01/97)

88 **CUVAISON** Cabernet Sauvignon Napa Valley 1992 • $26 • (12/15/95)

88 **DUNN** Cabernet Sauvignon Napa Valley 1992 • $39 Ⓐ • (12/15/95)

88 **EHLERS GROVE** Cabernet Sauvignon Napa Valley 1992 • $15 • (12/15/95)

88 **GIRARD** Cabernet Sauvignon Napa Valley Reserve 1992 • $40 • (12/15/95)

88 **GUENOC** Meritage Red Lake County 1992 • $15 • (12/15/95)

88 **JUSTIN** Cabernet Sauvignon San Luis Obispo County 1992 • $18 • (12/15/95)

88 **LA JOTA** Cabernet Sauvignon Howell Mountain Selection 1992 • $18 • (06/15/95)

88 **LAUREL GLEN** Cabernet Sauvignon Sonoma Mountain Counterpoint 1992 • $16 • (12/15/95)

88 **MARKHAM** Cabernet Sauvignon Napa Valley 1992 • $17 • (11/30/95)

88 **MAZZOCCO** Cabernet Sauvignon Sonoma County 1992 • $18 • (04/30/96)

88 **MERRYVALE** Cabernet Sauvignon Napa Valley 1992 • $24 • (12/15/95)

88 **MERRYVALE** Profile Napa Valley 1992 • $36 • (11/15/96)

88 **MIRASSOU** Cabernet Sauvignon Monterey County Harvest Reserve 1992 • $15 • (11/15/96)

88 **MOUNT VEEDER** Reserve Napa Valley 1992 • $40 • (08/31/96)

88 **NEWTON** Claret Napa Valley 1992 • $13 • (11/15/94)

88 **PAHLMEYER** Jayson Napa Valley 1992 • $20 • (12/31/94)

88 **PARDUCCI** Cabernet Sauvignon Mendocino County 1992 • $8 • (11/15/95) • BB

88 **PLAM** Cabernet Sauvignon Napa Valley 1992 • $30 • (11/15/94)

88 **RAYMOND** Cabernet Sauvignon Napa Valley 1992 • $17 • (11/30/95)

88 **REMICK RIDGE** Cabernet Sauvignon Sonoma Valley 1992 • $19 • (05/31/96)

88 **RUBISSOW-SARGENT** Cabernet Sauvignon Mount Veeder 1992 • $19 • (11/15/97)

88 **RUBISSOW-SARGENT** Les Trompettes Mount Veeder 1992 • $22 • (11/15/97)

88 **SAUSAL** Cabernet Sauvignon Alexander Valley 1992 • $14 • (10/31/95)

88 **SEAVEY** Cabernet Sauvignon Napa Valley 1992 • $28 • (07/31/96)

88 **SHENANDOAH** Cabernet Sauvignon Amador County 1992 • $10 • (11/15/94) • BB

88 **SMITH & HOOK** Cabernet Sauvignon Santa Lucia Highlands Masterpiece Edition 1992 • $30 • (12/15/95)

88 **STAG'S LEAP WINE CELLARS** Cabernet Sauvignon Napa Valley S.L.V. 1992 • $35 • (12/15/95)

88 **STERLING** Cabernet Sauvignon Napa Valley Diamond Mountain Ranch Vineyard 1992 • $17 • (10/31/95)

88 **TERRA ROSA** Cabernet Sauvignon North Coast 1992 • $10 • (04/30/95) • SS

88 **TERRACES** Cabernet Sauvignon Napa Valley 1992 • $40 • (02/28/97)

88 **TOM EDDY** Cabernet Sauvignon Napa Valley 1992 • $36 • (05/15/96)

88 **TRUCHARD** Cabernet Sauvignon Napa Valley Carneros 1992 • $20 • (03/31/96)

88 **VENGE** Cabernet Sauvignon Napa Valley Family Reserve 1992 • $35 • (08/31/96)

88 **VIADER** Napa Valley 1992 • $28 • (07/31/95)

88 **VILLA MT. EDEN** Cabernet Sauvignon Napa Valley Grand Reserve 1992 • $16 • (04/30/96)

88 **VOLKER EISELE** Cabernet Sauvignon Napa Valley 1992 • $26 • (05/15/97)

88 **VON STRASSER** Cabernet Sauvignon Napa Valley Diamond Mountain 1992 • $28 • (02/28/95)

88 **ZD WINES** Cabernet Sauvignon Napa Valley Reserve 1992 • $34 • (04/30/96)

87 **ARROWOOD** Cabernet Sauvignon Sonoma County Domaine du Grand Archer 1992 • $10 • (11/15/94)

87 **BARNETT** Cabernet Sauvignon Spring Mountain 1992 • $32 • (05/31/95)

87 **BAYVIEW CELLARS** Cabernet Sauvignon Napa Valley 1992 • $16 • (09/15/96)

87 **BENZIGER** Cabernet Sauvignon Sonoma County 1992 • $13 • (09/15/95)

87 **BENZIGER** Estate Tribute Red Sonoma Mountain 1992 • $20 • (10/15/96)

87 **BERINGER** Cabernet Sauvignon Knights Valley 1992 • $15 • (08/31/95)

87 **BERINGER** Meritage Knights Valley 1992 • $13 • (11/15/95)

87 **BYINGTON** Cabernet Sauvignon Alexander Valley Smith Reichel Vineyard 1992 • $15 • (12/15/95)

87 **CAKEBREAD** Cabernet Sauvignon Napa Valley Rutherford Reserve 1992 • $44 • (07/31/97)

87 **CARMENET** Cabernet Sauvignon Sonoma County Moon Mountain Dynamite Cabernet 1992 • $15 • (09/15/95)

87 **COSENTINO** The Poet Napa Valley Meritage 1992 • $24 • (12/15/95)

87 **FOXEN** Cabernet Sauvignon Santa Barbara County 1992 • $20 • (10/31/94)

87 **FRANCISCAN** Cabernet Sauvignon Napa Valley Oakville Estate 1992 • $15 • (12/15/95)

87 **GALLO OF SONOMA** Cabernet Sauvignon Sonoma County 1992 • $12 • (11/15/95)

87 **GUNDLACH BUNDSCHU** Cabernet Sauvignon Sonoma Valley Rhinefarm Vineyards 1992 • $15 • (10/31/95)

87 **HELENA VIEW** Cabernet Sauvignon Napa Valley 1992 • $12 • (11/30/96)

87 **HESS SELECT** Cabernet Sauvignon California 1992 • $10 • (11/15/94) • BB

87 **HILL & THOMA WINEGROWERS** Cabernet Sauvignon Napa Valley Clos Fontaine du Mont Reserve 1992 • $32 • (12/15/95)

87 **JEKEL** Cabernet Sauvignon Arroyo Seco Sanctuary Estate 1992 • $13 • (12/15/95)

87 **JOSEPH PHELPS** Cabernet Sauvignon Napa Valley 1992 • $46 Ⓐ • (09/30/95)

87 **JUSTIN** Justification San Luis Obispo County 1992 • $20 • (05/15/95)

87 **KATHRYN KENNEDY** Cabernet Sauvignon Santa Cruz Mountains 1992 • $35 Ⓐ • (07/31/96)

87 **KENWOOD** Cabernet Sauvignon Sonoma Valley Jack London Vineyard 1992 • $20 • (10/31/95)

87 **LAMBERT BRIDGE** Cabernet Sauvignon Sonoma County 1992 • $15 • (12/15/95)

87 **LIVINGSTON** Cabernet Sauvignon Napa Valley Stanley's Selection 1992 • $18 • (08/31/95)

87 **LYETH** A Red Blend Alexander Valley 1992 • $18 • (08/31/95)

87 **MAZZOCCO** Matrix Dry Creek Valley 1992 • $28 • (08/31/96)

87 **MOUNT VEEDER** Cabernet Sauvignon Napa Valley 1992 • $25 • (12/15/95)

87 **MURPHY-GOODE** Cabernet Sauvignon Alexander Valley Murphy Ranch 1992 • $15 • (05/15/95)

87 **NAPA RIDGE** Cabernet Sauvignon Central Coast 1992 • $8 • (10/15/95) • BB

87 **NORMAN** Cabernet Sauvignon Paso Robles 1992 • $13 • (11/15/94)

87 **PARADIGM** Cabernet Sauvignon Napa Valley 1992 • $28 • (12/15/95)

87 **PEACHY CANYON** Cabernet Sauvignon Central Coast 1992 • $18 • (11/15/94)

87 **PEJU** Meritage Napa Valley 1992 • $24 • (11/15/94)

87 **POPE VALLEY** Cabernet Sauvignon Napa Valley La Dolce DeVita Vineyard 1992 • $15 • (12/15/95)

87 **PRIDE** Cabernet Sauvignon Napa Valley 1992 • $18 • (12/15/95)

87 **ROBERT CRAIG** Cabernet Sauvignon Napa Valley 1992 • $20 • (10/15/95)

87 **RODNEY STRONG** Cabernet Sauvignon Northern Sonoma Alexander's Crown Vineyard 1992 • $20 • (09/15/96)

87 **RUTHERFORD RANCH** Cabernet Sauvignon Napa Valley 1992 • $11 • (11/15/96)

87 **RUTHERFORD VINEYARDS** Cabernet Sauvignon Napa Valley Rutherford Bench 1992 • $8 • (12/15/95)

87 **SADDLEBACK** Cabernet Sauvignon Napa Valley 1992 • $17 • (12/15/95)

87 **SEBASTIANI** Cabernet Sauvignon Sonoma County 1992 • $10 • (11/15/95) • BB

87 **SILVERADO HILL CELLARS** Cabernet Sauvignon Napa Valley 1992 • $15 • (11/15/96)

87 **STERLING** Reserve Napa Valley 1992 • $40 • (12/15/95)

87 **SUMMIT LAKE** Cabernet Sauvignon Howell Mountain Emily Kestrel 1992 • $25 • (11/30/96)

87 **SUTTER HOME** Cabernet Sauvignon Napa Valley Reserve 1992 • $12 • (11/15/96)

87 **TREFETHEN** Cabernet Sauvignon Napa Valley 1992 • $21 • (02/29/96)

87 **V. SATTUI** Cabernet Sauvignon Napa Valley Julian Schwinger Reserve Stock 1992 • $50 • (04/30/96)

87 **VICHON** Cabernet Sauvignon California Coastal Selection 1992 • $9 • (01/31/95) • BB

87 **VICHON** Cabernet Sauvignon Napa Valley 1992 • $16 • (12/15/95)

87 **WHITE ROCK** Claret Napa Valley 1992 • $24 • (05/15/97)

87 **WHITEHALL LANE** Cabernet Sauvignon Napa Valley 1992 • $15 • (10/15/95)

86 **ALEXANDER VALLEY VINEYARDS** Cabernet Sauvignon Alexander Valley Wetzel Family Estate 1992 • $14 • (05/31/95)

86 **BARON HERZOG** Cabernet Sauvignon California 1992 • $9 • (12/31/94) • BB

86 **BEAULIEU VINEYARD** Cabernet Sauvignon Napa Valley Rutherford 1992 • $12 • (11/30/95)

86 **CAIN** Five Napa Valley 1992 • $40 • (12/15/96)

86 **CHAPPELLET** Cabernet Sauvignon Napa Valley Pritchard Hill Estates 1992 • $15 • (09/15/95)

86 **CHÂTEAU JULIEN** Cabernet Sauvignon Monterey County Private Reserve 1992 • $18 • (11/30/96)

86 **CIRRI** Cabernet Sauvignon Alexander Valley 1992 • $10 • (12/15/95)

86 **CONCANNON** Assemblage Red Central Coast Reserve 1992 • $15 • (12/15/95)

86 **DE LOACH** Cabernet Sauvignon Russian River Valley 1992 • $15 • (12/15/95)

86 **DEHLINGER** Cabernet Sauvignon Russian River Valley 1992 • $18 • (08/31/96)

86 **DURNEY** Cabernet Sauvignon Carmel Valley Dances On Your Palate 1992 • $21 • (11/30/96)

86 **DURNEY** Cabernet Sauvignon Carmel Valley Dances On Your Palate Private Reserve 1992 • $31 • (03/31/96)

86 **ELAN** Cabernet Sauvignon Napa Valley 1992 • $29 • (05/15/97)

86 **ELLIOTT VINEYARD** Cabernet Sauvignon Napa Valley 1992 • $14 • (11/15/96)

86 **FATHOM** Cabernet Sauvignon Santa Ynez Valley 1992 • $24 • (11/15/94)

86 **FETZER** Cabernet Sauvignon Sonoma County Reserve 1992 • $24 • (04/30/97)

86 **HICKOK** Claret Napa Valley 1992 • $25 • (11/15/97)

86 **IVÁN TAMÁS** Cabernet Sauvignon Livermore Valley Reserve 1992 • $14 • (09/15/97)

86 **J. LOHR** Cabernet Sauvignon California Cypress 1992 • $9 • (11/30/95) • BB

86 **KENWOOD** Cabernet Sauvignon Sonoma Valley 25th Anniversary Vintage 1992 • $16 • (10/31/95)

Key: SS—Spectator Selection CS—Cellar Selection HR—Highly Recommended BB—Best Buy $NA—Price not available Ⓐ—Auction Price
Dates in parentheses indicate the issues in which the ratings were published.

86 **LOCKWOOD** Cabernet Sauvignon Monterey 1992 • $14 • (09/30/95)

86 **LOUIS M. MARTINI** Cabernet Sauvignon Napa Valley Reserve 1992 • $15 • (07/31/97)

86 **MARTIN RAY** Cabernet Sauvignon Napa Valley 1992 • $28 • (10/31/95)

86 **MENDOCINO HILL** Cabernet Sauvignon Mendocino County Private Reserve 1992 • $14 • (09/15/97)

86 **RAVENSWOOD** Cabernet Sauvignon Sonoma County 1992 • $15 • (11/15/94)

86 **ROCKING HORSE** Cabernet Sauvignon Stags Leap District Robinson Vineyard 1992 • $24 • (04/15/95)

86 **SANTA BARBARA WINERY** Cabernet Sauvignon Santa Ynez Valley Reserve 1992 • $16 • (12/15/95)

86 **SCHUG** Cabernet Sauvignon Sonoma Valley Heritage Reserve 1992 • $25 • (11/15/94)

86 **VINEYARD 29** Cabernet Sauvignon Napa Valley 1992 • $50 • (09/15/96)

85 **CHÂTEAU MARGARITE** Cabernet Sauvignon Napa Valley 1992 • $15 • (12/15/95)

85 **CHATEAU SOUVERAIN** Cabernet Sauvignon Alexander Valley 1992 • $12 • (03/31/95)

85 **DELORIMIER** Mosaic Alexander Valley Meritage 1992 • $18 • (03/31/96)

85 **DOMAINE SAINT GEORGE** Cabernet Sauvignon California Vintage Reserve 1992 • $6 • (11/15/94) • BB

85 **DUNCAN PEAK** Cabernet Sauvignon Mendocino County 1992 • $16 • (11/15/94)

85 **FETZER** Cabernet Sauvignon North Coast Barrel Select 1992 • $12 • (12/15/95)

85 **FIELD STONE** Cabernet Sauvignon Alexander Valley 1992 • $16 • (11/30/96)

85 **GUENOC** Cabernet Sauvignon Lake County 1992 • $15 • (12/15/95)

85 **HOPE FARMS** Cabernet Sauvignon Paso Robles 1992 • $13 • (11/30/96)

85 **KONRAD** Mélange à Trois Mendocino 1992 • $13 • (12/15/95)

85 **LAUREL GLEN** Cabernet Sauvignon Sonoma Mountain 1992 • $33 • (12/15/95)

85 **LOS ENCANTOS** Cabernet Sauvignon Napa Valley Covenant Reserve 1992 • $14 • (02/29/96)

85 **M.G. VALLEJO** Cabernet Sauvignon California 1992 • $6 • (11/30/95) • BB

85 **MCDOWELL** Cabernet Sauvignon Mendocino 1992 • $10 • (12/15/95)

85 **MILL CREEK** Cabernet Sauvignon Dry Creek Valley 1992 • $12 • (12/15/95)

85 **MIRASSOU** Cabernet Sauvignon Monterey County 1992 • $11 • (12/15/96)

85 **PHOENIX** Cabernet Sauvignon Napa Valley 1992 • $16 • (11/30/96)

85 **ROSENBLUM** Holbrook Mitchell Trio Napa Valley 1992 • $23 • (11/15/94)

85 **ROUND HILL** Cabernet Sauvignon Napa Valley 1992 • $12 • (12/15/95)

85 **ST. FRANCIS** Cabernet Sauvignon Sonoma County 1992 • $10 • (11/15/94)

85 **STERLING** Cabernet Sauvignon Napa Valley 1992 • $14 • (11/30/95)

85 **TAFT STREET** Cabernet Sauvignon California 1992 • $10 • (12/15/95)

85 **TITUS** Cabernet Sauvignon Napa Valley 1992 • $19 • (12/15/95)

85 **WEINSTOCK** Cabernet Sauvignon Sonoma County 1992 • $9 • (05/31/95)

85 **WHITE OAK** Cabernet Sauvignon Alexander Valley 1992 • $14 • (12/15/95)

85 **WILLIAM HILL** Cabernet Sauvignon Napa Valley Reserve 1992 • $24 • (12/15/95)

84 **CHARLES KRUG** Generations Napa Valley Peter Mondavi Family 1992 • $30 • (02/28/97)

1991 California Cabernet
Vintage Rating: 94

99 **CAYMUS** Cabernet Sauvignon Napa Valley Special Selection 1991 • $155 Ⓐ • (04/15/95) • CS

97 **FLORA SPRINGS** Cabernet Sauvignon Napa Valley Reserve 1991 • $33 • (09/30/94) • CS

95 **GROTH** Cabernet Sauvignon Napa Valley Reserve 1991 • $58 Ⓐ • (04/15/95) • CS

94 **BERINGER** Cabernet Sauvignon Napa Valley Private Reserve 1991 • $40 • (03/31/95) • CS

94 **DIAMOND CREEK** Cabernet Sauvignon Napa Valley Red Rock Terrace 1991 • $25 Ⓐ • (06/15/98)

94 **DIAMOND CREEK** Cabernet Sauvignon Napa Valley Red Rock Terrace Micro-Climate 3 1991 • $50 • (11/15/93) • CS

94 **GUENOC** Cabernet Sauvignon Napa Valley Beckstoffer Vineyard Reserve 1991 • $35 • (09/30/94) • CS

94 **MARTIN RAY** Cabernet Sauvignon Napa Valley 1991 • $28 • (11/15/94) • HR

94 **ST. CLEMENT** Oroppas Napa Valley 1991 • $22 • (10/31/93) • HR

93 **CAYMUS** Cabernet Sauvignon Napa Valley 1991 • $36 Ⓐ • (11/15/94) • SS

93 **CONN CREEK** Anthology Napa Valley 1991 • $30 • (09/30/94) • CS

93 **CORNERSTONE** Cabernet Sauvignon Howell Mountain Beatty Ranch 1991 • $33 • (11/15/94) • HR

93 **DIAMOND CREEK** Cabernet Sauvignon Napa Valley Volcanic Hill 1991 • $37 Ⓐ • (06/15/98)

93 **DIAMOND CREEK** Cabernet Sauvignon Napa Valley Volcanic Hill Micro-Climate 4 1991 • $50 • (11/15/93) • CS

93 **DOMINUS ESTATE** Napa Valley Napanook Vineyard 1991 • $55 • (11/15/95) • CS

93 **JUDD'S HILL** Cabernet Sauvignon Napa Valley 1991 • $24 • (09/30/94) • SS

93 **NEWTON** Cabernet Sauvignon Napa County 1991 • $NA • (01/01/97)

93 **OPUS ONE** Napa Valley 1991 • $65 • (11/15/94) • CS

93 **SHAFER** Cabernet Sauvignon Stags Leap District Hillside Select 1991 • $45 • (11/15/95) • CS

93 **SILVER OAK** Cabernet Sauvignon Napa Valley Bonny's Vineyard 1991 • $125 Ⓐ • (09/15/96) • CS

93 **SILVERADO VINEYARDS** Cabernet Sauvignon Stags Leap District 1991 • $17 • (04/30/94) • SS

93 **SILVERADO VINEYARDS** Cabernet Sauvignon Stags Leap District Limited Reserve 1991 • $40 • (11/15/94) • CS

93 **SPOTTSWOODE** Cabernet Sauvignon Napa Valley 1991 • $40 • (11/15/94) • CS

92 **CHATEAU MONTELENA** Cabernet Sauvignon Napa Valley The Montelena Estate 1991 • $40 • (05/31/95) • SS

92 **CHATEAU ST. JEAN** Cabernet Sauvignon Sonoma County Reserve 1991 • $39 • (11/15/96)

92 **CLOS DU BOIS** Cabernet Sauvignon Alexander Valley Winemaker's Reserve 1991 • $30 • (10/15/94) • CS

92 **DALLA VALLE** Cabernet Sauvignon Napa Valley 1991 • $110 Ⓐ • (11/15/94) • SS

92 **DIAMOND CREEK** Cabernet Sauvignon Napa Valley Gravelly Meadow 1991 • $48 Ⓐ • (06/15/98)

92 **DIAMOND CREEK** Cabernet Sauvignon Napa Valley Volcanic Hill Microclimate 1991 • $150 • (06/15/98)

92 **HARTWELL** Cabernet Sauvignon Stags Leap District 1991 • $55 • (11/15/94)

92 **OAKVILLE RANCH** Cabernet Sauvignon Napa Valley Reserve 1991 • $32 • (05/15/95) • HR

92 **PRIDE** Cabernet Sauvignon Napa Valley 1991 • $18 • (05/15/94) • HR

92 **SIMI** Cabernet Sauvignon Alexander Valley Reserve 1991 • $35 • (10/15/95) • HR

92 **STAG'S LEAP WINE CELLARS** Cask 23 Napa Valley 1991 • $70 • (12/31/94) • CS

92 **THE HESS COLLECTION** Cabernet Sauvignon Napa Valley 1991 • $34 Ⓐ • (11/15/94) • SS

91 **ARROWOOD** Cabernet Sauvignon Sonoma County 1991 • $25 • (09/30/94) • SS

91 **B.R. COHN** Cabernet Sauvignon Sonoma Valley Olive Hill Vineyard 1991 • $31 Ⓐ • (04/15/95) • HR

91 **BUEHLER** Cabernet Sauvignon Napa Valley Reserve 1991 • $25 • (09/30/95)

91 **CHATEAU ST. JEAN** Cabernet Sauvignon Sonoma County Cinq Cépages 1991 • $18 • (11/15/95) • HR

91 **CHATEAU SOUVERAIN** Cabernet Sauvignon Alexander Valley Winemaker's Reserve 1991 • $14 • (10/31/94) • HR

91 **DIAMOND CREEK** Cabernet Sauvignon Napa Valley Volcanic Hill 1991 • $50 • (11/15/93) • CS

91 **DUNN** Cabernet Sauvignon Howell Mountain 1991 • $79 Ⓐ • (12/15/95) • CS

91 **E. & J. GALLO** Cabernet Sauvignon Northern Sonoma Estate Bottled 1991 • $50 • (11/15/94) • HR

91 **EBERLE** Cabernet Sauvignon Paso Robles Reserve 1991 • $35 • (11/15/97)

91 **GEYSER PEAK** Réserve Alexandre Alexander Valley 1991 • $30 • (07/31/94) • CS

91 **GUENOC** Langtry California Meritage Red 1991 • $35 • (09/30/94) • HR

91 **HEITZ** Cabernet Sauvignon Napa Valley Martha's Vineyard 1991 • $62 Ⓐ • (04/30/96) • CS

91 **KENDALL-JACKSON** Cardinale California Meritage 1991 • $60 • (12/15/95)

91 **NIEBAUM-COPPOLA** Rubicon Rutherford 1991 • $40 • (09/15/96) • CS

91 **OAKVILLE RANCH** Cabernet Sauvignon Napa Valley Lewis Select 1991 • $28 • (09/30/94)

91 **PAUL HOBBS** Cabernet Sauvignon Napa Valley Carneros Hyde Vineyard 1991 • $30 • (10/31/94) • HR

91 **RIDGE** Monte Bello Santa Cruz Mountains 1991 • $75 • (11/15/95) • CS

91 **ROBERT PECOTA** Cabernet Sauvignon Napa Valley Kara's Vineyard 1991 • $20 • (09/15/94) • HR

91 **ROSENTHAL-THE MALIBU ESTATE** Cabernet Sauvignon California 1991 • $20 • (11/15/94)

91 **S. ANDERSON** Cabernet Sauvignon Stags Leap District Richard Chambers Vineyard 1991 • $46 • (12/31/94) • HR

91 **SEQUOIA GROVE** Cabernet Sauvignon Napa Valley Estate Reserve 1991 • $26 • (07/31/94)

91 **SILVER OAK** Cabernet Sauvignon Alexander Valley 1991 • $32 • (11/15/95) • HR

91 **STONESTREET** Legacy Alexander Valley 1991 • $35 • (11/15/94)

91 **THE HESS COLLECTION** Cabernet Sauvignon Napa Valley Reserve 1991 • $39 • (04/30/96)

91 **VIADER** Napa Valley 1991 • $28 • (11/15/94) • HR

90 **A. RAFANELLI** Cabernet Sauvignon Dry Creek Valley 1991 • $15 • (09/15/94) • SS

90 **ARAUJO** Cabernet Sauvignon Napa Valley Eisele Vineyard 1991 • $169 Ⓐ • (10/15/94) • CS

90 **BEAULIEU VINEYARD** Cabernet Sauvignon Napa Valley Georges de Latour Private Reserve 1991 • $40 • (12/15/95)

90 **CHIMNEY ROCK** Elevage Stags Leap District 1991 • $30 • (11/15/94)

90 **COSENTINO** Cabernet Sauvignon Napa Valley Reserve 1991 • $30 • (12/15/95)

90 **DALLA VALLE** Maya Napa Valley 1991 • $354 Ⓐ • (11/15/94)

90 **DIAMOND CREEK** Cabernet Sauvignon Napa Valley Gravelly Meadow Lake Blend 1991 • $50 • (11/15/93)

90 **DIAMOND CREEK** Cabernet Sauvignon Napa Valley Gravelly Meadow Microclimate 1991 • $150 • (06/15/98)

90 **DIAMOND CREEK** Cabernet Sauvignon Napa Valley Red Rock Terrace 1991 • $50 • (11/15/93)

90 **FERRARI-CARANO** Reserve Red Sonoma County 1991 • $47 • (11/15/96)

90 **FOXEN** Cabernet Sauvignon Santa Barbara County 1991 • $20 • (02/28/94) • HR

90 **FREEMARK ABBEY** Cabernet Sauvignon Napa Valley Bosché 1991 • $24 • (11/30/96)

90 **GALLO OF SONOMA** Cabernet Sauvignon Sonoma County 1991 • $12 • (03/31/95) • SS

90 **GEYSER PEAK** Cabernet Sauvignon Alexander Valley Reserve 1991 • $20 • (03/15/94) • SS

90 **GROTH** Cabernet Sauvignon Napa Valley 1991 • $55 Ⓐ • (10/15/94) • SS

90 **HARLAN ESTATE** Napa Valley 1991 • $65 • (11/30/95)

90 **JOSEPH PHELPS** Cabernet Sauvignon Napa Valley Backus Vineyard 1991 • $33 Ⓐ • (10/15/94) • CS

90 **JOSEPH PHELPS** Insignia Napa Valley 1991 • $62 Ⓐ • (05/31/95) • CS

90 **KISTLER** Cabernet Sauvignon Sonoma Valley Kistler Estate Vineyard 1991 • $30 • (06/15/95) • HR

90 **LA JOTA** Cabernet Sauvignon Howell Mountain 10th Anniversary Release 1991 • $38 • (06/15/94) • CS

90 **LAUREL GLEN** Cabernet Sauvignon Sonoma Mountain Counterpoint 1991 • $15 • (11/30/93) • SS

90 **MERRYVALE** Profile Napa Valley 1991 • $36 • (12/15/95)

90 **PARADIGM** Cabernet Sauvignon Napa Valley 1991 • $26 • (11/15/94)

90 **PEACHY CANYON** Cabernet Sauvignon Paso Robles 1991 • $18 • (11/15/93)

90 **PHILIP TOGNI** Cabernet Sauvignon Napa Valley 1991 • $30 • (11/15/93)

90 **ROBERT MONDAVI** Cabernet Sauvignon Napa Valley Reserve 1991 • $68 Ⓐ • (11/15/94)

90 **ROBERT MONDAVI** Cabernet Sauvignon Napa Valley Unfiltered 1991 • $18 • (11/15/94) • SS

90 **ROCKING HORSE** Cabernet Sauvignon Stags Leap District Robinson Vineyard 1991 • $24 • (03/31/94) • HR

90 **ROSENBLUM** Cabernet Sauvignon Napa Valley Holbrook Mitchell Vineyard 1991 • $14 • (10/31/94) • HR

90 **SADDLEBACK** Cabernet Sauvignon Napa Valley 1991 • $17 • (10/31/94) • HR

90 **ST. CLEMENT** Cabernet Sauvignon Napa Valley 1991 • $23 • (09/30/94) • SS

90 **SHAFER** Cabernet Sauvignon Stags Leap District 1991 • $21 • (08/31/94) • HR

Key: SS—Spectator Selection CS—Cellar Selection HR—Highly Recommended BB—Best Buy $NA—Price not available Ⓐ—Auction Price

Dates in parentheses indicate the issues in which the ratings were published.

90 **SIGNORELLO** Cabernet Sauvignon Napa Valley Founder's Reserve 1991 • $30 • (09/30/94)

90 **SILVER OAK** Cabernet Sauvignon Napa Valley 1991 • $36 • (11/15/95)

90 **TOM EDDY** Cabernet Sauvignon Napa Valley 1991 • $32 • (04/30/95)

90 **V. SATTUI** Cabernet Sauvignon Napa Valley Mario's Reserve Stock 1991 • $35 • (11/15/94)

89 **ADELAIDA** Cabernet Sauvignon San Luis Obispo County 1991 • $19 • (11/30/96)

89 **ARROWOOD** Domaine du Grand Archer Sonoma County 1991 • $8 • (04/30/94) • SS

89 **CAIN** Five Napa Valley 1991 • $40 • (12/15/95)

89 **CAKEBREAD** Cabernet Sauvignon Napa Valley Rutherford Reserve 1991 • $42 • (11/15/96)

89 **CHAPPELLET** Cabernet Sauvignon Napa Valley 1991 • $20 • (11/15/94)

89 **CHARLES KRUG** Cabernet Sauvignon Napa Valley Vintage Selection 1991 • $28 • (12/15/95)

89 **CORISON** Cabernet Sauvignon Napa Valley 1991 • $26 • (10/15/94)

89 **COSENTINO** M. Coz Napa Valley Meritage 1991 • $45 • (11/15/94)

89 **CRONIN** Cabernet Sauvignon Santa Cruz Mountains 1991 • $17 • (04/30/96)

89 **DE LOACH** Cabernet Sauvignon Russian River Valley O.F.S. 1991 • $25 • (09/30/95)

89 **DRY CREEK** Cabernet Sauvignon Dry Creek Valley Reserve 1991 • $20 • (10/31/94)

89 **FAR NIENTE** Cabernet Sauvignon Napa Valley 1991 • $40 • (09/15/94)

89 **FIRESTONE** Vintage Reserve Santa Ynez Valley 1991 • $22 • (12/15/95)

89 **FORMAN** Cabernet Sauvignon Napa Valley 1991 • $30 • (03/15/94) • CS

89 **FRANCISCAN** Meritage Magnificat Oakville Estate Napa Valley 1991 • $20 • (12/15/95)

89 **GRGICH HILLS** Cabernet Sauvignon Napa Valley Yountville Selection 1991 • $35 • (12/15/95)

89 **GUENOC** Meritage Red Lake County 1991 • $15 • (10/31/94) • SS

89 **JOHNSON TURNBULL** Cabernet Sauvignon Napa Valley 1991 • $18 • (10/31/94)

89 **JOSEPH PHELPS** Cabernet Sauvignon Napa Valley 1991 • $23 Ⓐ • (10/15/94)

89 **JOSEPH PHELPS** Cabernet Sauvignon Napa Valley Eisele Vineyard 1991 • $48 Ⓐ • (10/15/94)

89 **KENDALL-JACKSON** Cabernet Sauvignon California Grand Reserve 1991 • $30 • (11/15/94)

89 **KENWOOD** Cabernet Sauvignon Sonoma Valley Artist Series 1991 • $34 Ⓐ • (11/15/94)

89 **LAUREL GLEN** Cabernet Sauvignon Sonoma Mountain 1991 • $42 Ⓐ • (11/15/94)

89 **LIVINGSTON** Cabernet Sauvignon Napa Valley Moffett Vineyard 1991 • $30 • (11/15/94)

89 **LYETH** A Red Blend Alexander Valley 1991 • $14 • (10/15/94) • SS

89 **MARTIN BROTHERS** Etrusco Paso Robles 1991 • $18 • (06/30/93)

89 **NEWLAN** Cabernet Sauvignon Napa Valley 1991 • $16 • (11/30/95)

89 **OAKVILLE RANCH** Cabernet Sauvignon Napa Valley 1991 • $24 • (09/30/94)

89 **RICHARDSON** Cabernet Sauvignon Sonoma Valley Horne 1991 • $14 • (11/15/93)

89 **RIDGE** Cabernet Sauvignon Santa Cruz Mountains 1991 • $16 • (10/15/93)

89 **SEAVEY** Cabernet Sauvignon Napa Valley 1991 • $26 • (07/31/95)
89 **STAGLIN FAMILY** Cabernet Sauvignon Napa Valley 1991 • $26 • (11/15/94)
89 **SWANSON** Cabernet Sauvignon Napa Valley 1991 • $20 • (11/15/94)
89 **WHITEHALL LANE** Cabernet Sauvignon Napa Valley Morisoli Vineyard 1991 • $36 • (05/31/95)
89 **WHITEHALL LANE** Cabernet Sauvignon Napa Valley Reserve 1991 • $26 • (05/31/95)
88 **ALTAMURA** Cabernet Sauvignon Napa Valley 1991 • $25 • (05/31/96)
88 **ANDERSON'S CONN VALLEY** Cabernet Sauvignon Napa Valley Estate Reserve 1991 • $30 • (11/15/94)
88 **BENZIGER** Cabernet Sauvignon Sonoma County 1991 • $13 • (03/15/94)
88 **BERINGER** Meritage Knights Valley 1991 • $13 • (09/15/94)
88 **CAFARO** Cabernet Sauvignon Napa Valley 1991 • $28 • (09/15/95)
88 **CAKEBREAD** Cabernet Sauvignon Napa Valley 1991 • $22 • (11/15/94)
88 **CARMENET** Meritage Red Sonoma Valley Moon Mountain Estate Vineyard 1991 • $25 • (11/15/96)
88 **CLOS DU BOIS** Marlstone Vineyard Alexander Valley 1991 • $18 • (01/31/95)
88 **CLOS PEGASE** Cabernet Sauvignon Napa Valley 1991 • $17 • (06/30/94)
88 **CONN CREEK** Cabernet Sauvignon Napa Valley Limited Release 1991 • $18 • (11/15/94)
88 **CUVAISON** Cabernet Sauvignon Napa Valley 1991 • $22 • (11/15/94)
88 **DEHLINGER** Cabernet Sauvignon Russian River Valley 1991 • $15 • (05/15/95)
88 **DUNCAN PEAK** Cabernet Sauvignon Mendocino County 1991 • $12 • (10/31/93)
88 **DUNN** Cabernet Sauvignon Napa Valley 1991 • $38 Ⓐ • (11/15/94)
88 **EBERLE** Cabernet Sauvignon Paso Robles 1991 • $16 • (04/15/95)
88 **FISHER** Cabernet Sauvignon Sonoma County Wedding Vineyard 1991 • $28 • (11/15/94)
88 **FREEMARK ABBEY** Cabernet Sauvignon Napa Valley Sycamore Vineyards 1991 • $22 • (11/30/96)
88 **GRACE FAMILY** Cabernet Sauvignon Napa Valley 1991 • $238 Ⓐ • (11/15/94)
88 **GUILLIAMS** Cabernet Sauvignon Spring Mountain 1991 • $17 • (12/15/95)
88 **GUNDLACH BUNDSCHU** Cabernet Sauvignon Sonoma Valley Rhinefarm Vineyards 1991 • $15 • (10/31/94)
88 **HEITZ** Cabernet Sauvignon Napa Valley Trailside Vineyard 1991 • $45 • (11/15/96)
88 **JUSTIN** Cabernet Sauvignon San Luis Obispo County Society Reserve 1991 • $19 • (11/15/94)
88 **LOCKWOOD** Cabernet Sauvignon Monterey 1991 • $12 • (10/31/93)
88 **MARKHAM** Cabernet Sauvignon Napa Valley 1991 • $17 • (11/15/94)
88 **MAZZOCCO** Cabernet Sauvignon Sonoma County 1991 • $18 • (11/15/94)
88 **MORGAN** Cabernet Sauvignon Carmel Valley 1991 • $15 • (11/15/94)
88 **MOUNT EDEN** Cabernet Sauvignon Santa Cruz Mountains Old Vine Reserve 1991 • $35 • (04/15/95)
88 **NAVARRO** Cabernet Sauvignon Mendocino 1991 • $18 • (11/15/96)
88 **OAKFORD** Cabernet Sauvignon Napa Valley 1991 • $30 • (12/15/95)
88 **OPTIMA** Cabernet Sauvignon Alexander Valley 1991 • $25 • (02/28/95)
88 **PINE RIDGE** Cabernet Sauvignon Stags Leap District 1991 • $30 • (11/15/94)
88 **RAYMOND** Cabernet Sauvignon Napa Valley 1991 • $17 • (11/15/94)
88 **ROBERT SINSKEY** Claret Stags Leap District 1991 • $28 • (11/15/94)
88 **ROSENBLUM** Cabernet Sauvignon Napa Valley George Hendry Vineyard Reserve 1991 • $30 • (11/15/94)
88 **ST. FRANCIS** Cabernet Sauvignon Sonoma County Reserve 1991 • $24 • (11/15/94)
88 **ST. SUPÉRY** Cabernet Sauvignon Napa Valley Dollarhide Ranch 1991 • $15 • (11/15/96)
88 **ST. SUPERY** Cabernet Sauvignon Napa Valley Dollarhide Ranch Limited Edition 1991 • $25 • (11/15/96)
88 **SEBASTIANI** Cabernet Sauvignon Sonoma Valley Cherryblock Old Vines 1991 • $24 • (11/15/94)
88 **SEQUOIA GROVE** Cabernet Sauvignon Napa Valley 1991 • $18 • (11/15/94)
88 **STAG'S LEAP WINE CELLARS** Cabernet Sauvignon Napa Valley Fay 1991 • $30 • (12/31/94)
88 **STERLING** Reserve Napa Valley 1991 • $30 • (11/15/94)
88 **STONESTREET** Cabernet Sauvignon Alexander Valley 1991 • $22 • (05/15/95)
88 **TERRACES** Cabernet Sauvignon Napa Valley 1991 • $40 • (10/31/95)
88 **VICHON** Cabernet Sauvignon Stags Leap District 1991 • $28 • (12/15/95)
88 **VINE CLIFF** Cabernet Sauvignon Napa Valley 1991 • $25 • (04/30/95)
88 **WHITEHALL LANE** Cabernet Sauvignon Napa Valley 1991 • $14 • (11/15/94)
88 **VON STRASSER** Cabernet Sauvignon Napa Valley Diamond Mountain 1991 • $25 • (03/31/94)
87 **BEAULIEU VINEYARD** Cabernet Sauvignon Napa Valley Rutherford 1991 • $13 • (10/15/94)
87 **BEAULIEU VINEYARD** Tapestry Napa Valley Signet Collection 1991 • $20 • (12/15/95)
87 **BERINGER** Cabernet Sauvignon Knights Valley 1991 • $13 • (05/31/94)
87 **BERNARD PRADEL** Cabernet Sauvignon Howell Mountain Ranch 1991 • $21 • (09/15/95)
87 **BUENA VISTA** Cabernet Sauvignon Carneros 1991 • $12 • (10/15/94)
87 **CHÂTEAU MARGARITE** Cabernet Sauvignon Napa Valley 1991 • $15 • (11/15/93)
87 **CLOS DU BOIS** Cabernet Sauvignon Alexander Valley Briarcrest Vineyard 1991 • $18 • (11/15/94)
87 **CLOS DU VAL** Cabernet Sauvignon Stags Leap District 1991 • $20 • (09/30/95)
87 **CRONIN** Concerto Stags Leap District Robinson Vineyard 1991 • $17 • (02/28/95)
87 **DRY CREEK** Cabernet Sauvignon Sonoma County 1991 • $15 • (11/15/93)
87 **GARY FARRELL** Cabernet Sauvignon Sonoma County Ladi's Vineyard 1991 • $18 • (08/31/94)
87 **GIRARD** Cabernet Sauvignon Napa Valley Reserve 1991 • $35 • (11/15/94)
87 **IRON HORSE** Cabernets Alexander Valley T-T Vineyards 1991 • $19 • (12/15/95)
87 **J. LOHR** Cabernet Sauvignon Paso Robles VS 1991 • $22 • (11/30/95)
87 **KATHRYN KENNEDY** Cabernet Sauvignon Santa Cruz Mountains 1991 • $54 • (11/15/94)
87 **MAZZOCCO** Matrix Dry Creek Valley 1991 • $28 • (12/15/95)

87 **MERRYVALE** Cabernet Sauvignon Napa Valley 1991 • $23 • (11/15/94)

87 **MIRASSOU** Cabernet Sauvignon Monterey County Fifth Generation Harvest Reserve 1991 • $12 • (12/15/95)

87 **NAPA RIDGE** Cabernet Sauvignon North Coast Reserve 1991 • $13 • (10/15/95)

87 **NEWTON** Claret Napa Valley 1991 • $12 • (06/15/93)

87 **PETER MICHAEL** Cabernet Sauvignon Knights Valley Les Pavots 1991 • $46 Ⓐ • (05/15/95)

87 **RAYMOND** Meritage Napa Valley Private Reserve 1991 • $40 • (12/15/95)

87 **ROCHIOLI** Cabernet Sauvignon Russian River Valley Neoma's Vineyard Reserve 1991 • $26 • (12/15/95)

87 **RUSTRIDGE** Cabernet Sauvignon Napa Valley 1991 • $20 • (12/15/95)

87 **STAG'S LEAP WINE CELLARS** Cabernet Sauvignon Napa Valley 1991 • $18 • (03/31/94)

87 **TRUCHARD** Cabernet Sauvignon Napa Valley Carneros 1991 • $18 • (11/15/94)

87 **TULOCAY** Cabernet Sauvignon Napa Valley De Celles Vineyard 1991 • $12 • (11/15/94)

87 **V. SATTUI** Cabernet Sauvignon Napa Valley Preston Vineyard 1991 • $22 • (11/15/94)

86 **ATLAS PEAK** Cabernet Sauvignon Atlas Peak 1991 • $18 • (09/15/95)

86 **BOEGER** Meritage El Dorado 1991 • $15 • (12/15/95)

86 **BUEHLER** Cabernet Sauvignon Napa Valley 1991 • $13 • (09/15/94)

86 **CHATEAU POTELLE** Cabernet Sauvignon Napa Valley 1991 • $18 • (10/15/96)

86 **CLOS DU BOIS** Cabernet Sauvignon Alexander Valley 1991 • $12 • (02/28/94)

86 **CLOS PEGASE** Hommage Napa Valley 1991 • $25 • (11/15/94)

86 **COSENTINO** Cabernet Sauvignon Napa Valley 1991 • $16 • (10/31/94)

86 **CUVAISON** Meritage Napa Valley Reserve 1991 • $50 • (12/15/95)

86 **DORCICH CELLARS** Cabernet Sauvignon Santa Clara County 1991 • $18 • (07/31/95)

86 **ESTANCIA** Cabernet Sauvignon Alexander Valley 1991 • $9 • (10/31/93) • BB

86 **FERRARI-CARANO** Cabernet Sauvignon Sonoma County 1991 • $16 • (09/15/95)

86 **FIELD STONE** Cabernet Sauvignon Alexander Valley Staten Family Reserve 1991 • $23 • (11/30/96)

86 **FLORA SPRINGS** Trilogy Napa Valley 1991 • $25 • (11/15/94)

86 **GIRARD** Cabernet Sauvignon Napa Valley 1991 • $18 • (05/31/94)

86 **KATHRYN KENNEDY** Lateral California 1991 • $18 • (11/15/93)

86 **KONRAD** Mélange à Trois Mendocino 1991 • $12 • (03/15/94)

86 **LIPARITA** Cabernet Sauvignon Howell Mountain 1991 • $28 • (11/15/94)

86 **MARIO PERELLI-MINETTI** Cabernet Sauvignon Napa Valley 1991 • $13 • (05/31/96)

86 **PEJU** Cabernet Sauvignon Napa Valley HB Vineyard 1991 • $35 • (09/15/95)

86 **ROBERT PEPI** Cabernet Sauvignon Napa Valley Vine Hill Ranch 1991 • $18 • (12/15/95)

Key: SS—Spectator Selection CS—Cellar Selection HR—Highly Recommended BB—Best Buy $NA—Price not available Ⓐ—Auction Price
Dates in parentheses indicate the issues in which the ratings were published.

86 **RODNEY STRONG** Cabernet Sauvignon Northern Sonoma Alexander's Crown Vineyard 1991 • $20 • (12/15/95)

86 **RODNEY STRONG** Cabernet Sauvignon Northern Sonoma Reserve 1991 • $30 • (12/15/95)

86 **ROSENBLUM** Holbrook Mitchell Trio Napa Valley 1991 • $22 • (11/15/93)

86 **RUTHERFORD RANCH** Cabernet Sauvignon Napa Valley 1991 • $10 • (11/15/94)

86 **RUTHERFORD RANCH** Quintessence Napa Valley Meritage 1991 • $20 • (12/15/95)

86 **SANTA CRUZ MOUNTAIN** Cabernet Sauvignon Santa Cruz Mountains Bates Ranch 1991 • $18 • (11/15/96)

86 **SIERRA VISTA** Cabernet Sauvignon El Dorado Five Star Reserve 1991 • $22 • (11/15/94)

86 **SMITH & HOOK** Cabernet Sauvignon Santa Lucia Highlands 1991 • $18 • (11/15/94)

86 **SOQUEL** Cabernet Sauvignon Santa Cruz Mountains 1991 • $20 • (04/15/94)

86 **STERLING** Cabernet Sauvignon Napa Valley Diamond Mountain Ranch Vineyard 1991 • $18 • (11/15/94)

86 **TOBIN JAMES** Cabernet Sauvignon San Luis Obispo County Twilight 1991 • $12 • (11/15/93)

86 **TREFETHEN** Cabernet Sauvignon Napa Valley Reserve 1991 • $40 • (11/15/96)

86 **TULOCAY** Cabernet Sauvignon Napa Valley Cliff Vineyard 1991 • $12 • (11/15/94)

86 **V. SATTUI** Cabernet Sauvignon Napa Valley Suzanne's Vineyard 1991 • $16 • (11/15/94)

86 **WELLINGTON** Victory Reserve Sonoma County 1991 • $20 • (09/15/96)

85 **BANDIERA** Cabernet Sauvignon Napa Valley 1991 • $7 • (09/30/94) • BB

85 **CARMENET** Cabernet Sauvignon Sonoma Valley Dynamite Cabernet 1991 • $15 • (11/15/93)

85 **CHALK HILL** Cabernet Sauvignon Chalk Hill 1991 • $21 • (11/15/94)

85 **CHARLES KRUG** Generations Napa Valley Peter Mondavi Family 1991 • $30 • (09/15/96)

85 **CHATEAU SOUVERAIN** Cabernet Sauvignon Alexander Valley 1991 • $11 • (06/30/94)

85 **CONN CREEK** Cabernet Sauvignon Napa Valley Barrel Select 1991 • $18 • (11/15/94)

85 **CRESTON** Cabernet Sauvignon Paso Robles Winemaker's Selection 1991 • $19 • (11/30/96)

85 **DELORIMIER** Mosaic Alexander Valley Meritage 1991 • $18 • (08/31/95)

85 **ESTANCIA** Meritage Alexander Valley 1991 • $14 • (09/15/94)

85 **FARELLA-PARK** Cabernet Sauvignon Napa Valley 1991 • $25 • (02/28/95)

85 **FOREST GLEN** Cabernet Sauvignon Sonoma County 1991 • $10 • (04/30/94)

85 **FREEMARK ABBEY** Cabernet Sauvignon Napa Valley 1991 • $17 • (11/15/94)

85 **GUENOC** Cabernet Sauvignon Lake County 1991 • $15 • (11/15/94)

85 **HANNA** Cabernet Sauvignon Alexander Valley 1991 • $14 • (02/28/95)

85 **HEITZ** Cabernet Sauvignon Napa Valley 1991 • $29 Ⓐ • (04/30/96)

85 **HILL & THOMA WINEGROWERS** Cabernet Sauvignon Napa Valley Clos Fontaine du Mont Reserve 1991 • $32 • (12/31/94)

85 **KEENAN** Cabernet Sauvignon Napa Valley 1991 • $21 • (12/15/95)

85 **KUNDE** Cabernet Sauvignon Sonoma Valley Reserve 1991 • $23 • (05/31/96)

85 **MONTICELLO** Cabernet Sauvignon Napa Valley Corley Select Reserve 1991 • $25 • (12/15/95)

85 **MOUNT VEEDER** Cabernet Sauvignon Napa Valley 1991 • $18 • (01/31/95)

85 **PEJU** Cabernet Sauvignon Napa Valley 1991 • $18 • (09/15/95)

85 **PINE RIDGE** Cabernet Sauvignon Napa Valley Andrus Reserve 1991 • $60 • (11/15/93)

85 **RIDGE** Cabernet Sauvignon Napa County York Creek 1991 • $16 • (11/15/94)

85 **RITCHIE CREEK** Cabernet Sauvignon Napa Valley 1991 • $18 • (04/15/95)

85 **SEBASTIANI** Cabernet Sauvignon Sonoma County 1991 • $10 • (11/15/94)

85 **STAGS' LEAP WINERY** Cabernet Sauvignon Napa Valley 1991 • $20 • (11/15/94)

85 **STELTZNER** Cabernet Sauvignon Stags Leap District 1991 • $18 • (03/31/95)

85 **STELTZNER** Cabernet Sauvignon Stags Leap District Commemorative 1991 • $45 • (03/31/95)

85 **SULLIVAN** Cabernet Sauvignon Napa Valley 1991 • $23 • (11/15/94)

85 **V. SATTUI** Cabernet Sauvignon Napa Valley 1991 • $14 • (11/15/94)

85 **WELLINGTON** Cabernet Sauvignon Sonoma County Mohrhardt Ridge Vineyard 1991 • $14 • (11/15/94)

85 **WHITE ROCK** Claret Napa Valley 1991 • $22 • (12/15/95)

85 **WHITEHALL LANE** Meritage Napa Valley 1991 • $15 • (11/15/94)

1990 California Cabernet
Vintage Rating: 95

98 **CAYMUS** Cabernet Sauvignon Napa Valley Special Selection 1990 • $192 Ⓐ • (03/31/94) • CS

97 **SILVERADO VINEYARDS** Cabernet Sauvignon Napa Valley Limited Reserve 1990 • $40 • (10/31/93) • CS

95 **CHATEAU ST. JEAN** Cabernet Sauvignon Sonoma County Reserve 1990 • $38 • (04/30/96) • CS

95 **STAG'S LEAP WINE CELLARS** Cask 23 Napa Valley 1990 • $80 • (09/15/96)

94 **GROTH** Cabernet Sauvignon Napa Valley Reserve 1990 • $73 Ⓐ • (11/15/94) • CS

94 **MOUNT VEEDER** Cabernet Sauvignon Napa Valley 1990 • $15 • (10/31/93) • SS

93 **CAIN** Five Napa Valley 1990 • $34 • (09/15/94) • CS

93 **DALLA VALLE** Cabernet Sauvignon Napa Valley 1990 • $25 • (09/30/93) • HR

93 **DIAMOND CREEK** Cabernet Sauvignon Napa Valley Volcanic Hill 1990 • $38 Ⓐ • (06/15/98)

93 **DUCKHORN** Cabernet Sauvignon Napa Valley 1990 • $20 • (07/31/93) • CS

93 **E. & J. GALLO** Cabernet Sauvignon Northern Sonoma Estate Bottled 1990 • $60 • (10/31/93) • CS

93 **OAKVILLE RANCH** Cabernet Sauvignon Napa Valley 1990 • $23 • (10/15/93) • HR

93 **SPOTTSWOODE** Cabernet Sauvignon Napa Valley 1990 • $69 • (09/15/96)

93 **STAG'S LEAP WINE CELLARS** Cask 23 Napa Valley 1990 • $80 • (09/15/96)

92 **BERINGER** Cabernet Sauvignon Napa Valley Private Reserve 1990 • $40 • (11/15/94) • CS

92 **COSENTINO** M. Coz Napa Valley Meritage 1990 • $45 • (11/15/93)

92 **DIAMOND CREEK** Cabernet Sauvignon Napa Valley Lake 1990 • $191 Ⓐ • (06/15/98)

92 **DIAMOND CREEK** Cabernet Sauvignon Napa Valley Volcanic Hill 1990 • $50 • (11/15/92) • CS

92 **DUNN** Cabernet Sauvignon Napa Valley 1990 • $41 Ⓐ • (11/15/93) • CS

92 **GUENOC** Cabernet Sauvignon Napa Valley Beckstoffer Vineyard Reserve 1990 • $35 • (11/15/93) • HR

92 **MOUNT VEEDER** Reserve Napa Valley 1990 • $25 • (09/15/94) • CS

92 **OPUS ONE** Napa Valley 1990 • $65 • (11/30/93) • CS

92 **PHILIP TOGNI** Cabernet Sauvignon Napa Valley 1990 • $30 • (11/15/92)

92 **SIGNORELLO** Cabernet Sauvignon Napa Valley Founder's Reserve 1990 • $30 • (10/15/93)

92 **STAG'S LEAP WINE CELLARS** Cask 23 Napa Valley 1990 • $80 • (10/31/93) • CS

91 **ARROWOOD** Cabernet Sauvignon Sonoma County 1990 • $24 • (10/31/93) • SS

91 **CLOS PEGASE** Cabernet Sauvignon Napa Valley 1990 • $17 • (11/15/93) • SS

91 **CORISON** Cabernet Sauvignon Napa Valley 1990 • $24 • (10/15/93) • HR

91 **DIAMOND CREEK** Cabernet Sauvignon Napa Valley Red Rock Terrace 1990 • $50 • (11/15/92)

91 **DOMINUS ESTATE** Napa Valley 1990 • $64 Ⓐ • (06/30/94) • SS

91 **FERRARI-CARANO** Reserve Red Sonoma County 1990 • $47 • (11/30/95)

91 **GUENOC** Langtry Lake County Meritage Red 1990 • $35 • (11/15/93) • HR

91 **GUENOC** Meritage Red Lake County 1990 • $18 Ⓐ • (11/15/93) • SS

91 **HARRISON** Cabernet Sauvignon Napa Valley Reserve 1990 • $40 • (10/15/94)

91 **HEITZ** Cabernet Sauvignon Napa Valley Trailside Vineyard 1990 • $45 • (10/15/95) • CS

91 **KENDALL-JACKSON** Cardinale California Meritage 1990 • $50 • (10/15/94) • HR

91 **LIVINGSTON** Cabernet Sauvignon Napa Valley Moffett Vineyard 1990 • $30 • (11/15/93) • HR

91 **RIDGE** Monte Bello Santa Cruz Mountains 1990 • $53 • (09/15/96)

91 **ROBERT MONDAVI** Cabernet Sauvignon Napa Valley Reserve 1990 • $55 • (10/31/93) • HR

91 **ROCKING HORSE** Cabernet Sauvignon Stags Leap District Robinson Vineyard 1990 • $22 • (02/15/93)

91 **ST. FRANCIS** Cabernet Sauvignon Sonoma County Reserve 1990 • $24 • (09/30/93) • HR

91 **SILVER OAK** Cabernet Sauvignon Napa Valley 1990 • $78 Ⓐ • (11/15/94) • CS

91 **SPOTTSWOODE** Cabernet Sauvignon Napa Valley 1990 • $56 Ⓐ • (10/31/93) • CS

91 **STAG'S LEAP WINE CELLARS** Cabernet Sauvignon Napa Valley 1990 • $18 • (05/15/93) • SS

91 **VIADER** Napa Valley 1990 • $25 • (07/15/93) • HR

91 **VICHON** Cabernet Sauvignon Stags Leap District 1990 • $24 • (11/15/93) • HR

90 **A. RAFANELLI** Cabernet Sauvignon Dry Creek Valley 1990 • $15 • (09/15/93) • HR

90 **ANDERSON'S CONN VALLEY** Cabernet Sauvignon Napa Valley Estate Reserve 1990 • $25 • (11/15/93)

90 **B.R. COHN** Cabernet Sauvignon Sonoma Valley Olive Hill Vineyard 1990 • $25 • (11/15/93)

90 **BERINGER** Cabernet Sauvignon Knights Valley 1990 • $13 • (11/15/93) • SS

90 **CAYMUS** Cabernet Sauvignon Napa Valley 1990 • $115 Ⓐ • (12/15/93) • SS

90 **CHATEAU MONTELENA** Cabernet Sauvignon Napa Valley The Montelena Estate 1990 • $46 Ⓐ • (11/15/94) • CS

90 **CHATEAU SOUVERAIN** Cabernet Sauvignon Alexander Valley 1990 • $11 • (11/15/93) • SS

90 **DIAMOND CREEK** Cabernet Sauvignon Napa Valley Lake 1990 • $176 Ⓐ • (02/15/93)

90 **ESTANCIA** Meritage Alexander Valley 1990 • $14 • (10/15/93) • SS

90 **GARY FARRELL** Cabernet Sauvignon Sonoma County Ladi's Vineyard 1990 • $18 • (11/15/92)

90 **GEYSER PEAK** Cabernet Sauvignon Alexander Valley Reserve 1990 • $15 • (06/15/93) • HR

90 **GEYSER PEAK** Réserve Alexandre Alexander Valley 1990 • $30 • (11/15/93)

90 **GRACE FAMILY** Cabernet Sauvignon Napa Valley 1990 • $225 Ⓐ • (08/31/93)

90 **GROTH** Cabernet Sauvignon Napa Valley 1990 • $17 • (09/30/93) • SS

90 **HEITZ** Cabernet Sauvignon Napa Valley 1990 • $18 • (04/30/95) • HR

90 **HEITZ** Cabernet Sauvignon Napa Valley Martha's Vineyard 1990 • $63 Ⓐ • (04/30/95) • CS

90 **KENDALL-JACKSON** Cabernet Sauvignon California Grand Reserve 1990 • $30 • (11/15/93)

90 **MARKHAM** Cabernet Sauvignon Napa Valley 1990 • $17 • (11/15/93) • SS

90 **NIEBAUM-COPPOLA** Rubicon Napa Valley 1990 • $35 • (12/15/95)

90 **PAHLMEYER** Caldwell Vineyard Napa Valley 1990 • $32 • (10/15/93)

90 **RAYMOND** Meritage Napa Valley Private Reserve 1990 • $40 • (10/31/94) • HR

90 **RIDGE** Monte Bello Santa Cruz Mountains 1990 • $53 • (09/15/96)

90 **ROBERT MONDAVI** Cabernet Sauvignon Napa Valley 1990 • $15 • (10/31/93) • SS

90 **ROMBAUER** Le Meilleur du Chai Napa Valley 1990 • $40 • (08/31/97)

90 **S. ANDERSON** Cabernet Sauvignon Stags Leap District Richard Chambers Vineyard 1990 • $42 • (11/15/93)

90 **ST. CLEMENT** Cabernet Sauvignon Napa Valley 1990 • $22 • (10/31/93)

90 **SEQUOIA GROVE** Cabernet Sauvignon Napa Valley 1990 • $16 • (03/31/94) • SS

90 **SEQUOIA GROVE** Cabernet Sauvignon Napa Valley Estate Reserve 1990 • $25 • (12/15/93)

90 **SHAFER** Cabernet Sauvignon Stags Leap District 1990 • $20 • (11/15/93)

90 **SHAFER** Cabernet Sauvignon Stags Leap District Hillside Select 1990 • $38 • (12/15/95)

90 **SILVERADO VINEYARDS** Cabernet Sauvignon Stags Leap District 1990 • $17 • (06/30/93) • HR

90 **THE HESS COLLECTION** Cabernet Sauvignon Napa Valley 1990 • $18 • (04/15/94) • CS

90 **THE HESS COLLECTION** Cabernet Sauvignon Napa Valley Reserve 1990 • $38 • (11/15/94)

89 **BEAULIEU VINEYARD** Cabernet Sauvignon Napa Valley Georges de Latour Private Reserve 1990 • $40 • (11/15/94)

89 **BRAREN PAULI** Cabernet Sauvignon Dry Creek Valley 1990 • $13 • (10/31/93)

Key: SS—Spectator Selection CS—Cellar Selection HR—Highly Recommended BB—Best Buy $NA—Price not available Ⓐ—Auction Price

Dates in parentheses indicate the issues in which the ratings were published.

89 **CHATEAU SOUVERAIN** Cabernet Sauvignon Alexander Valley Winemaker's Reserve 1990 • $14 • (05/31/94)

89 **CLOS DU BOIS** Cabernet Sauvignon Alexander Valley Briarcrest Vineyard 1990 • $19 • (04/15/94)

89 **CLOS DU VAL** Cabernet Sauvignon Napa Valley Reserve 1990 • $45 • (04/30/95)

89 **DALLA VALLE** Maya Napa Valley 1990 • $50 • (09/30/93)

89 **DIAMOND CREEK** Cabernet Sauvignon Napa Valley Gravelly Meadow 1990 • $50 • (11/15/92)

89 **DIAMOND CREEK** Cabernet Sauvignon Napa Valley Red Rock Terrace 1990 • $34 Ⓐ • (06/15/98)

89 **DRY CREEK** Meritage Dry Creek Valley 1990 • $18 • (11/15/94)

89 **DUNN** Cabernet Sauvignon Howell Mountain 1990 • $39 • (05/15/94)

89 **DURNEY** Cabernet Sauvignon Carmel Valley 1990 • $17 • (11/15/94)

89 **FERRARI-CARANO** Cabernet Sauvignon Sonoma County 1990 • $15 • (09/30/94)

89 **FORMAN** Cabernet Sauvignon Napa Valley 1990 • $30 • (07/15/93)

89 **KATHRYN KENNEDY** Cabernet Sauvignon Santa Cruz Mountains 1990 • $54 • (06/15/94)

89 **LAUREL GLEN** Cabernet Sauvignon Sonoma Mountain 1990 • $22 Ⓐ • (11/15/93)

89 **LIPARITA** Cabernet Sauvignon Howell Mountain 1990 • $28 • (11/15/93)

89 **LONG** Cabernet Sauvignon Napa Valley 1990 • $30 • (08/31/93)

89 **MURRIETA'S WELL** Vendimia Livermore Valley 1990 • $28 • (11/15/94)

89 **RIDGE** Monte Bello Santa Cruz Mountains 1990 • $60 • (11/15/93)

89 **ST. FRANCIS** Cabernet Sauvignon Sonoma County 1990 • $10 • (09/30/93)

89 **SEAVEY** Cabernet Sauvignon Napa Valley 1990 • $24 • (08/31/94)

89 **SILVER OAK** Cabernet Sauvignon Alexander Valley 1990 • $64 Ⓐ • (11/15/94)

89 **SILVER OAK** Cabernet Sauvignon Napa Valley 1990 • $78 Ⓐ • (09/15/96)

89 **STAG'S LEAP WINE CELLARS** Cabernet Sauvignon Napa Valley S.L.V. 1990 • $30 • (03/31/94) • HR

89 **SWANSON** Cabernet Sauvignon Napa Valley 1990 • $23 • (11/15/93)

89 **TERRA ROSA** Cabernet Sauvignon Napa Valley 1990 • $9 • (09/30/93) • BB

89 **VICHON** Cabernet Sauvignon Napa Valley 1990 • $16 • (08/31/93) • HR

88 **ALEXANDER VALLEY VINEYARDS** Cabernet Sauvignon Alexander Valley Wetzel Family Estate 1990 • $14 • (06/15/93)

88 **ALTAMURA** Cabernet Sauvignon Napa Valley 1990 • $25 • (09/15/95)

88 **BURGESS** Cabernet Sauvignon Napa Valley Vintage Selection 1990 • $18 • (10/15/94)

88 **CHARLES KRUG** Cabernet Sauvignon Napa Valley 1990 • $12 • (10/31/93)

88 **CHIMNEY ROCK** Elevage Stags Leap District 1990 • $30 • (11/15/93)

88 **CLOS DU BOIS** Marlstone Vineyard Alexander Valley 1990 • $20 • (11/15/93)

88 **CUTLER CELLAR** Cabernet Sauvignon Sonoma Valley 1990 • $19 • (11/15/94)

88 **DEER PARK** Cabernet Sauvignon Howell Mountain Beatty Ranch Reserve 1990 • $24 • (10/31/94)

88 **DIAMOND CREEK** Cabernet Sauvignon Napa Valley Gravelly Meadow 1990 • $41 Ⓐ • (06/15/98)

88 **DIAMOND CREEK** Cabernet Sauvignon Napa Valley Three Vineyard Blend 1990 • $150 • (06/15/98)

88 **DUNN** Cabernet Sauvignon Howell Mountain 1990 • $92 Ⓐ • (09/15/96)

88 **FAR NIENTE** Cabernet Sauvignon Napa Valley 1990 • $36 • (09/15/93)

88 **FRANCISCAN** Cabernet Sauvignon Napa Valley Oakville Estate 1990 • $13 • (10/31/93)

88 **FREEMARK ABBEY** Cabernet Sauvignon Napa Valley Sycamore Vineyards 1990 • $23 • (12/15/95)

88 **FROG'S LEAP** Cabernet Sauvignon Napa Valley 1990 • $17 • (09/30/93)

88 **HOMEWOOD** Cabernet Sauvignon Alexander Valley 1990 • $14 • (11/30/96)

88 **HUSCH** Cabernet Sauvignon Mendocino La Ribera Vineyards 1990 • $14 • (08/31/93)

88 **INNISFREE** Cabernet Sauvignon Napa Valley 1990 • $11 • (04/30/93)

88 **IRON HORSE** Cabernets Alexander Valley 1990 • $19 • (11/15/93)

88 **J. LOHR** Cabernet Sauvignon Paso Robles Seven Oaks 1990 • $11 • (11/15/93)

88 **J. LOHR** Cabernet Sauvignon Paso Robles VS.1 1990 • $22 • (03/31/95)

88 **JOSEPH PHELPS** Cabernet Sauvignon Napa Valley Backus Vineyard 1990 • $30 • (11/15/93)

88 **JUSTIN** Isosceles San Luis Obispo County Reserve 1990 • $23 • (11/15/93)

88 **KATHRYN KENNEDY** Lateral California 1990 • $17 • (10/15/92)

88 **KUNDE** Cabernet Sauvignon Sonoma Valley 1990 • $15 • (03/15/93)

88 **KUNDE** Claret Sonoma Valley Louis Kunde Founder's Reserve 1990 • $17 • (11/15/93)

88 **LAUREL GLEN** Cabernet Sauvignon Sonoma Mountain Reserve 1990 • $75 • (11/15/93)

88 **LIVINGSTON** Cabernet Sauvignon Napa Valley Stanley's Selection 1990 • $20 • (03/15/93)

88 **LOCKWOOD** Cabernet Sauvignon Monterey Partners' Reserve 1990 • $18 • (10/31/93)

88 **MARIO PERELLI-MINETTI** Cabernet Sauvignon Napa Valley 1990 • $15 • (11/15/94)

88 **MERRYVALE** Cabernet Sauvignon Napa Valley 1990 • $20 • (06/30/93)

88 **MONTICELLO** Cabernet Sauvignon Napa Valley Corley Reserve 1990 • $25 • (11/15/93)

88 **MOUNT EDEN** Cabernet Sauvignon Santa Cruz Mountains Lathweisen Ridge 1990 • $15 • (06/15/93)

88 **NAVARRO** Cabernet Sauvignon Mendocino 1990 • $17 • (10/15/95)

88 **OAKFORD** Cabernet Sauvignon Napa Valley 1990 • $25 • (11/15/94)

88 **PEJU** Cabernet Sauvignon Napa Valley HB Vineyard 1990 • $35 • (11/15/94)

88 **PRESTON** Cabernet Sauvignon Dry Creek Valley 1990 • $12 • (11/15/94)

88 **RANCHO SISQUOC** Cellar Select Red Santa Maria Valley 1990 • $25 • (11/15/93)

88 **RAYMOND** Cabernet Sauvignon Napa Valley 1990 • $17 • (11/15/93)

88 **RAYMOND** Cabernet Sauvignon Napa Valley Private Reserve 1990 • $25 • (10/31/94)

88 **RIDGE** Cabernet Sauvignon Napa County York Creek 1990 • $16 • (11/15/93)

88 **RODNEY STRONG** Cabernet Sauvignon Northern Sonoma Reserve 1990 • $30 • (06/15/94)

88 **SAN SABA** Cabernet Sauvignon Monterey 1990 • $15 • (11/15/94)

88 **SOQUEL** Cabernet Sauvignon Santa Cruz Mountains 1990 • $16 • (03/31/93)

88 **STAG'S LEAP WINE CELLARS** Cabernet Sauvignon Napa Valley Fay 1990 • $30 • (03/31/94)

88 **STELTZNER** Claret Stags Leap District 1990 • $11 • (11/15/92)

88 **TUDAL** Cabernet Sauvignon Napa Valley 1990 • $17 • (02/28/94)

88 **VINCENT ARROYO** Cabernet Sauvignon Napa Valley 1990 • $15 • (11/15/92)

88 **WHITE ROCK** Claret Napa Valley 1990 • $19 • (04/15/94)

88 **WHITEHALL LANE** Cabernet Sauvignon Napa Valley Reserve 1990 • $23 • (02/28/95)

88 **WHITEHALL LANE** Cabernet Sauvignon Napa Valley 1990 • $13 • (12/15/93)

88 **WILLIAM HILL** Cabernet Sauvignon Napa Valley Reserve 1990 • $24 • (11/15/93)

88 **WINDEMERE** Cabernet Sauvignon Napa Valley Diamond Mountain 1990 • $14 • (08/31/93)

87 **ARIES** Cabernet Sauvignon Napa Valley 1990 • $11 • (10/31/93)

87 **ATLAS PEAK** Consenso Atlas Peak 1990 • $22 • (12/15/95)

87 **BANDIERA** Cabernet Sauvignon Napa Valley 1990 • $7 • (04/15/94) • BB

87 **CAKEBREAD** Cabernet Sauvignon Napa Valley Rutherford Reserve 1990 • $42 • (12/15/95)

87 **CHATEAU ST. JEAN** Cabernet Sauvignon Sonoma County Cinq Cépages 1990 • $18 • (09/30/94)

87 **CLOS DU BOIS** Cabernet Sauvignon Alexander Valley 1990 • $13 • (03/31/93)

87 **CLOS PEGASE** Hommage Napa Valley 1990 • $20 • (04/15/94)

87 **COSENTINO** Cabernet Sauvignon Napa Valley Reserve 1990 • $25 • (11/15/94)

87 **FETZER** Cabernet Sauvignon California Barrel Select 1990 • $12 • (11/15/93)

87 **GIRARD** Cabernet Sauvignon Napa Valley 1990 • $16 • (11/15/93)

87 **GRGICH HILLS** Cabernet Sauvignon Napa Valley 1990 • $22 • (04/30/95)

87 **HANNA** Cabernet Sauvignon Alexander Valley 1990 • $18 • (11/15/93)

87 **HARRISON** Cabernet Sauvignon Napa Valley 1990 • $30 • (07/15/93)

87 **HUSCH** Cabernet Sauvignon Mendocino North Field Select 1990 • $18 • (11/15/93)

87 **JOHNSON TURNBULL** Cabernet Sauvignon Napa Valley Vineyard Selection 67 1990 • $34 • (04/30/94)

87 **JORDAN** Cabernet Sauvignon Alexander Valley 1990 • $25 • (06/30/94)

87 **LAKESPRING** Cabernet Sauvignon Napa Valley 1990 • $10 • (05/15/94)

87 **LAUREL GLEN** Cabernet Sauvignon Sonoma Mountain Counterpoint 1990 • $15 • (03/15/93)

87 **LYETH** A Red Blend Alexander Valley 1990 • $13 • (06/30/93)

87 **MERIDIAN** Cabernet Sauvignon Paso Robles 1990 • $14 • (09/30/93)

87 **MURPHY-GOODE** Cabernet Sauvignon Alexander Valley Murphy Ranch 1990 • $15 • (10/15/93)

87 **ROBERT SINSKEY** Claret Carneros 1990 • $28 • (05/15/94)

87 **ROSENBLUM** Holbrook Mitchell Trio Napa Valley 1990 • $22 • (11/15/92)

87 **SMITH & HOOK** Cabernet Sauvignon Santa Lucia Highlands 1990 • $18 • (03/31/94)

87 **SMOTHERS BROTHERS** Cabernet Sauvignon Sonoma Valley Remick Ridge Ranch 1990 • $18 • (11/15/94)

87 **STERLING** Reserve Napa Valley 1990 • $30 • (11/15/94)

87 **STONESTREET** Cabernet Sauvignon Alexander Valley 1990 • $20 • (11/15/94)

87 **SUTTER HOME** Cabernet Sauvignon Napa Valley Centennial Selection Reserve 1990 • $12 • (10/31/93)

87 **TREFETHEN** Cabernet Sauvignon Napa Valley 1990 • $19 • (11/15/95)

87 **TRUCHARD** Cabernet Sauvignon Napa Valley Carneros 1990 • $18 • (11/15/93)

87 **WHITE OAK** Cabernet Sauvignon Alexander Valley 1990 • $14 • (11/15/93)

87 **VON STRASSER** Cabernet Sauvignon Napa Valley Diamond Mountain 1990 • $25 • (11/15/93)

86 **BEAUCANON** Cabernet Sauvignon Napa Valley 1990 • $11 • (02/28/95)

86 **BENZIGER** Cabernet Sauvignon Sonoma County 1990 • $13 • (09/30/93)

86 **CHALK HILL** Cabernet Sauvignon Chalk Hill 1990 • $17 • (12/15/93)

86 **CHÂTEAU MARGARITE** Cabernet Sauvignon Napa Valley 1990 • $12 • (11/15/93)

86 **CHATEAU POTELLE** Cabernet Sauvignon Napa Valley Cuvée 95 1990 • $16 • (10/15/94)

86 **COSENTINO** Cabernet Sauvignon Napa Valley 1990 • $15 • (11/15/93)

86 **COSENTINO** The Poet California Meritage 1990 • $23 • (05/15/95)

86 **CRONIN** Joe's Cuvée California 1990 • $27 • (03/15/94)

86 **ESTANCIA** Cabernet Sauvignon Alexander Valley 1990 • $9 • (06/15/93) • BB

86 **FISHER** Cabernet Sauvignon Napa & Sonoma Counties Coach Insignia 1990 • $20 • (06/15/93)

86 **GALLO OF SONOMA** Cabernet Sauvignon Sonoma County 1990 • $10 • (11/15/94) • BB

86 **GIRARD** Cabernet Sauvignon Napa Valley Reserve 1990 • $25 • (04/15/94)

86 **GUILLIAMS** Cabernet Sauvignon Napa Valley Spring Mountain District 1990 • $15 • (11/15/94)

86 **HALLCREST** Cabernet Sauvignon El Dorado County Covington Vineyard 1990 • $19 • (11/15/94)

86 **HAMBRECHT** Cabernet Sauvignon Dry Creek Valley Bradford Mountain Vineyard 1990 • $13 • (11/15/93)

86 **IRON HORSE** Cabernets Alexander Valley T-T Vineyards 1990 • $15 • (10/31/94)

86 **J. LOHR** Cabernet Sauvignon California Cypress 1990 • $8 • (11/15/93) • BB

86 **JOSEPH PHELPS** Insignia Napa Valley 1990 • $53 Ⓐ • (11/15/94)

86 **KENWOOD** Cabernet Sauvignon Sonoma Valley Artist Series 1990 • $30 • (12/15/93)

86 **KISTLER** Cabernet Sauvignon Sonoma Valley Kistler Estate Vineyard 1990 • $30 • (02/28/94)

86 **NEWLAN** Cabernet Sauvignon Napa Valley 1990 • $26 • (02/28/95)

Key: SS—Spectator Selection CS—Cellar Selection HR—Highly Recommended BB—Best Buy $NA—Price not available Ⓐ—Auction Price

Dates in parentheses indicate the issues in which the ratings were published.

86 **RABBIT RIDGE** Cabernet Sauvignon Sonoma County Rabbit Ridge Ranch Estate Reserve 1990 • $20 • (11/15/94)

86 **RAVENSWOOD** Pickberry Sonoma Mountain 1990 • $26 • (11/15/93)

86 **ROBERT PECOTA** Cabernet Sauvignon Napa Valley Kara's Vineyard 1990 • $17 • (09/15/93)

86 **ROCHIOLI** Cabernet Sauvignon Russian River Valley Neoma's Vineyard Reserve 1990 • $24 • (06/15/93)

86 **RODNEY STRONG** Cabernet Sauvignon Northern Sonoma Alexander's Crown Vineyard 1990 • $20 • (11/15/93)

86 **ROMBAUER** Cabernet Sauvignon Napa Valley 1990 • $18 • (11/15/94)

86 **ST. SUPÉRY** Cabernet Sauvignon Napa Valley Dollarhide Ranch 1990 • $14 • (05/15/94)

86 **STEVENOT** Cabernet Sauvignon Calaveras County Reserve 1990 • $10 • (07/31/93)

86 **TERRACES** Cabernet Sauvignon Napa Valley 1990 • $40 • (11/15/94)

86 **VILLA MT. EDEN** Cabernet Sauvignon Napa Valley Grand Reserve 1990 • $16 • (11/15/93)

86 **WELLINGTON** Cabernet Sauvignon Mount Veeder Random Ridge 1990 • $16 • (10/15/93)

86 **WENTE** Cabernet Sauvignon Livermore Valley Charles Wetmore Vineyard Reserve 1990 • $16 • (08/31/94)

86 **ZD WINES** Cabernet Sauvignon Napa Valley 1990 • $20 • (11/15/92)

85 **BEAULIEU VINEYARD** Cabernet Sauvignon Napa Valley Rutherford 1990 • $11 • (10/31/93)

85 **BEAULIEU VINEYARD** Meritage Napa Valley 1990 • $20 • (11/15/94)

85 **BERNARD PRADEL** Cabernet Sauvignon Napa Valley Limited Barrel Selection 1990 • $14 • (09/15/95)

85 **BYRON** Cabernet Sauvignon Santa Barbara County 1990 • $16 • (08/31/92)

85 **CARMENET** Meritage Red Sonoma Valley Moon Mountain Estate Vineyard 1990 • $25 • (11/15/93)

85 **CHIMNEY ROCK** Cabernet Sauvignon Stags Leap District 1990 • $20 • (04/30/94)

85 **CRONIN** Cabernet Sauvignon Santa Cruz Mountains 1990 • $17 • (02/28/95)

85 **CUVAISON** Cabernet Sauvignon Napa Valley 1990 • $18 • (03/31/94)

85 **DE LOACH** Cabernet Sauvignon Russian River Valley 1990 • $16 • (03/31/93)

85 **DORCICH CELLARS** Cabernet Sauvignon Santa Clara County 1990 • $20 • (07/31/95)

85 **FIRESTONE** Cabernet Sauvignon Santa Ynez Valley Reserve 1990 • $20 • (11/15/94)

85 **FLORA SPRINGS** Cabernet Sauvignon Napa Valley Reserve 1990 • $33 • (02/28/94)

85 **FLORA SPRINGS** Trilogy Napa Valley 1990 • $33 • (02/28/94)

85 **FRANCISCAN** Meritage Magnificat Napa Valley 1990 • $20 • (11/15/94)

85 **HALLCREST** Cabernet Sauvignon El Dorado County De Cascabel Vineyard Proprietors Reserve 1990 • $13 • (11/15/94)

85 **HEITZ** Cabernet Sauvignon Napa Valley Bella Oaks Vineyard 1990 • $44 Ⓐ • (04/30/95)

85 **JOSEPH PHELPS** Cabernet Sauvignon Napa Valley 1990 • $24 Ⓐ • (06/15/93)

85 **LA JOTA** Cabernet Sauvignon Howell Mountain 1990 • $28 • (11/15/93)

85 **LAWRENCE J. BARGETTO** Cabernet Sauvignon Santa Cruz Mountains Bates Ranch 1990 • $16 • (12/15/95)

85 **LOUIS M. MARTINI** Cabernet Sauvignon Sonoma Valley Monte Rosso 1990 • $23 • (09/30/94)

85 **MARKHAM** Laurent Napa Valley Reserve 1990 • $25 • (12/31/94)

85 **MARTIN BROTHERS** Etrusco Paso Robles 1990 • $18 • (11/15/92)

85 **MAYACAMAS** Cabernet Sauvignon Napa Valley 1990 • $26 Ⓐ • (12/15/95)

85 **MOUNT EDEN** Cabernet Sauvignon Santa Cruz Mountains Old Vine Reserve 1990 • $30 • (11/15/93)

85 **NALLE** Cabernet Sauvignon Dry Creek Valley 1990 • $18 • (11/15/93)

85 **PEACHY CANYON** Cabernet Sauvignon Paso Robles 1990 • $15 • (03/31/93)

85 **QUAIL RIDGE** Cabernet Sauvignon Napa Valley 1990 • $13 • (11/15/94)

85 **QUIVIRA** Cabernet Cuvée Dry Creek Valley 1990 • $15 • (11/15/94)

85 **RIDGE** Cabernet Sauvignon Santa Cruz Mountains 1990 • $14 • (02/15/93)

85 **ROUND HILL** Cabernet Sauvignon Napa Valley Signature Reserve 1990 • $20 • (09/15/96)

85 **RUBISSOW-SARGENT** Les Trompettes Mount Veeder 1990 • $18 • (11/15/94)

85 **SANTA CRUZ MOUNTAIN** Cabernet Sauvignon Santa Cruz Mountains Bates Ranch 1990 • $15 • (12/15/95)

85 **STONESTREET** Legacy Alexander Valley 1990 • $35 • (11/15/93)

85 **THE NEGOCIANTS** Cabernet Sauvignon Napa Valley 1990 • $10 • (03/31/94)

85 **VINE CLIFF** Cabernet Sauvignon Napa Valley 1990 • $35 • (11/15/93)

85 **WINTERBROOK** Cabernet Sauvignon Napa Valley Grand Reserve 1990 • $19 • (09/15/93)

85 **YORK MOUNTAIN** Cabernet Sauvignon San Luis Obispo County 1990 • $14 • (12/15/95)

1987 California Cabernet
Vintage Rating: 96

98 **CAYMUS** Cabernet Sauvignon Napa Valley Special Selection 1987 • $175 Ⓐ • (10/31/91) • CS

97 **BERINGER** Cabernet Sauvignon Napa Valley Private Reserve 1987 • $86 Ⓐ • (12/15/97)

97 **DUNN** Cabernet Sauvignon Howell Mountain 1987 • $82 Ⓐ • (12/15/97)

97 **GRACE FAMILY** Cabernet Sauvignon Napa Valley 1987 • $242 Ⓐ • (06/30/90)

97 **OPUS ONE** Napa Valley 1987 • $96 Ⓐ • (11/15/90) • CS

96 **JOSEPH PHELPS** Insignia Napa Valley 1987 • $71 Ⓐ • (12/15/97)

96 **SHAFER** Cabernet Sauvignon Stags Leap District Hillside Select 1987 • $56 • (12/15/97)

96 **SILVERADO VINEYARDS** Cabernet Sauvignon Napa Valley Limited Reserve 1987 • $69 Ⓐ • (12/15/97)

96 **SPOTTSWOODE** Cabernet Sauvignon Napa Valley 1987 • $62 Ⓐ • (09/15/90) • SS

95 **CHATEAU MONTELENA** Cabernet Sauvignon Napa Valley 1987 • $109 Ⓐ • (10/31/91) • SS

95 **DIAMOND CREEK** Cabernet Sauvignon Napa Valley Volcanic Hill 1987 • $67 Ⓐ • (12/15/89)

95 **DUCKHORN** Cabernet Sauvignon Napa Valley 1987 • $55 Ⓐ • (06/30/90) • CS

95 **HEITZ** Cabernet Sauvignon Napa Valley Martha's Vineyard 1987 • $96 Ⓐ • (03/31/92) • CS

95 **KENDALL-JACKSON** Cardinale California Meritage 1987 • $44 Ⓐ • (03/31/92) • HR

95 **LA JOTA** Cabernet Sauvignon Howell Mountain 1987 • $31 Ⓐ • (07/31/90) • SS

95 **SILVER OAK** Cabernet Sauvignon Napa Valley Bonny's Vineyard 1987 • $85 • (12/15/97)

95 **SPOTTSWOODE** Cabernet Sauvignon Napa Valley 1987 • $77 • (12/15/97)

95 **WILLIAM HILL** Cabernet Sauvignon Napa Valley Reserve 1987 • $39 • (11/15/90) • SS

94 **BERINGER** Cabernet Sauvignon Napa Valley Private Reserve 1987 • $86 Ⓐ • (10/31/91) • HR

94 **DIAMOND CREEK** Cabernet Sauvignon Napa Valley Red Rock Terrace 1987 • $40 Ⓐ • (12/15/89)

94 **DUNN** Cabernet Sauvignon Howell Mountain 1987 • $82 Ⓐ • (04/15/91) • HR

94 **FROG'S LEAP** Cabernet Sauvignon Napa Valley 1987 • $39 • (12/31/89) • SS

94 **GRACE FAMILY** Cabernet Sauvignon Napa Valley 1987 • $242 Ⓐ • (12/15/97)

94 **LAUREL GLEN** Cabernet Sauvignon Sonoma Mountain Counterpoint 1987 • $13 • (10/31/89)

94 **LIVINGSTON** Cabernet Sauvignon Napa Valley Moffett Vineyard 1987 • $63 • (12/15/97)

94 **OPUS ONE** Napa Valley 1987 • $164 • (12/15/97)

94 **PHILIP TOGNI** Cabernet Sauvignon Napa Valley 1987 • $24 • (08/31/90)

94 **THE HESS COLLECTION** Cabernet Sauvignon Napa Valley 1987 • $30 Ⓐ • (12/15/97)

94 **THE HESS COLLECTION** Cabernet Sauvignon Napa Valley Reserve 1987 • $41 Ⓐ • (12/15/97)

93 **ARROWOOD** Cabernet Sauvignon Sonoma County 1987 • $26 • (12/15/97)

93 **BERINGER** Cabernet Sauvignon Napa Valley Chabot Vineyard 1987 • $80 • (12/15/97)

93 **BENZIGER** Cabernet Sauvignon Sonoma County 1987 • $22 • (09/30/90) • SS

93 **CAYMUS** Cabernet Sauvignon Napa Valley 1987 • $58 Ⓐ • (09/15/90)

93 **CHATEAU MONTELENA** Cabernet Sauvignon Napa Valley 1987 • $109 Ⓐ • (12/15/97)

93 **CLOS DU VAL** Cabernet Sauvignon Napa Valley Reserve 1987 • $100 • (12/15/97)

93 **DIAMOND CREEK** Cabernet Sauvignon Napa Valley Lake 1987 • $242 Ⓐ • (06/15/98)

93 **DUNN** Cabernet Sauvignon Napa Valley 1987 • $65 Ⓐ • (11/15/90)

93 **FORMAN** Cabernet Sauvignon Napa Valley 1987 • $41 Ⓐ • (09/30/90) • CS

93 **LAUREL GLEN** Cabernet Sauvignon Sonoma Mountain 1987 • $38 Ⓐ • (12/15/97)

93 **LOUIS M. MARTINI** Cabernet Sauvignon Sonoma Valley Monte Rosso 1987 • $20 • (11/15/90) • HR

93 **MAZZOCCO** Cabernet Sauvignon Alexander Valley Claret Style 1987 • $20 • (08/31/90)

93 **PHILIP TOGNI** Cabernet Sauvignon Napa Valley 1987 • $72 • (12/15/97)

93 **QUAIL RIDGE** Cabernet Sauvignon Napa Valley 1987 • $16 • (09/30/91) • HR

93 **ROBERT MONDAVI** Cabernet Sauvignon Napa Valley Reserve 1987 • $81 Ⓐ • (12/15/97)

93 **SILVER OAK** Cabernet Sauvignon Alexander Valley 1987 • $72 Ⓐ • (12/15/97)

93 **SILVERADO VINEYARDS** Cabernet Sauvignon Stags Leap District Limited Reserve 1987 • $45 • (10/31/91) • HR

93 **STERLING** Reserve Napa Valley 1987 • $43 • (11/15/90)

92 **B.R. COHN** Cabernet Sauvignon Sonoma Valley Olive Hill Vineyard 1987 • $36 Ⓐ • (06/30/90)

92 **BEAULIEU VINEYARD** Cabernet Sauvignon Napa Valley Georges de Latour Private Reserve 1987 • $38 Ⓐ • (11/15/91)

92 **CAIN** Cabernet Sauvignon Napa Valley Estate 1987 • $25 • (10/15/90)

92 **CHAPPELLET** Cabernet Sauvignon Napa Valley Reserve 1987 • $27 • (02/15/93)

92 **CHATEAU ST. JEAN** Cabernet Sauvignon Alexander Valley 1987 • $16 • (06/30/91) • SS

92 **CHATEAU ST. JEAN** Cabernet Sauvignon Alexander Valley Reserve 1987 • $38 • (07/31/92) • CS

92 **CLOS DU VAL** Cabernet Sauvignon Stags Leap District 1987 • $17 • (06/30/91) • HR

92 **CLOS DU VAL** Reserve Stags Leap District 1987 • $45 • (07/15/92) • CS

92 **CORISON** Cabernet Sauvignon Napa Valley 1987 • $41 • (11/15/90)

92 **CUVAISON** Cabernet Sauvignon Napa Valley 1987 • $36 • (10/31/90) • HR

92 **DOMINUS ESTATE** Napa Valley 1987 • $72 • (12/15/97)

92 **DUCKHORN** Cabernet Sauvignon Napa Valley 1987 • $55 Ⓐ • (12/15/97)

92 **ETUDE** Cabernet Sauvignon Napa Valley 1987 • $36 • (12/15/97)

92 **FOLIE À DEUX** Cabernet Sauvignon Napa Valley 1987 • $18 • (11/15/90)

92 **GEYSER PEAK** Réserve Alexandre Alexander Valley 1987 • $18 • (12/15/97)

92 **GUENOC** Cabernet Sauvignon Napa Valley Beckstoffer Vineyard Reserve 1987 • $24 • (06/30/91)

92 **HEITZ** Cabernet Sauvignon Napa Valley Martha's Vineyard 1987 • $96 Ⓐ • (12/15/97)

92 **KATHRYN KENNEDY** Cabernet Sauvignon Santa Cruz Mountains 1987 • $100 • (12/15/97)

92 **KENWOOD** Cabernet Sauvignon Sonoma Valley Jack London Vineyard 1987 • $19 • (01/31/91) • HR

92 **MORGAN** Cabernet Sauvignon Carmel Valley 1987 • $16 • (09/30/90)

92 **OPTIMA** Cabernet Sauvignon Sonoma County 1987 • $22 • (12/15/90) • HR

92 **RODNEY STRONG** Cabernet Sauvignon Alexander Valley Reserve 1987 • $28 • (09/30/91) • HR

92 **SHAFER** Cabernet Sauvignon Stags Leap District 1987 • $19 • (07/31/90)

92 **SILVERADO VINEYARDS** Cabernet Sauvignon Napa Valley 1987 • $41 Ⓐ • (12/15/97)

92 **SILVERADO VINEYARDS** Cabernet Sauvignon Stags Leap District 1987 • $25 • (04/15/90) • SS

92 **SIMI** Cabernet Sauvignon Alexander Valley Reserve 1987 • $29 Ⓐ • (12/15/97)

92 **SWANSON** Cabernet Sauvignon Napa Valley 1987 • $25 • (10/15/91)

92 **TERRACES** Cabernet Sauvignon Napa Valley 1987 • $38 • (02/29/92)

91 **A. RAFANELLI** Cabernet Sauvignon Dry Creek Valley 1987 • $NA • (12/15/97)

91 **BEAULIEU VINEYARD** Cabernet Sauvignon Napa Valley Georges de Latour Private Reserve 1987 • $44 • (12/15/97)

91 **CAIN** Five Napa Valley 1987 • $30 • (04/30/91) • HR

91 **CAKEBREAD** Cabernet Sauvignon Napa Valley Rutherford Reserve 1987 • $23 • (09/15/93) • HR

91 **CLOS DU BOIS** Cabernet Sauvignon Alexander Valley Briarcrest Vineyard 1987 • $48 • (12/15/97)

Key: SS—Spectator Selection CS—Cellar Selection HR—Highly Recommended BB—Best Buy $NA—Price not available Ⓐ—Auction Price
Dates in parentheses indicate the issues in which the ratings were published.

91 **DIAMOND CREEK** Cabernet Sauvignon Napa Valley Lake 1987 • $242 Ⓐ • (11/15/90)

91 **EDMUNDS ST. JOHN** Les Fleurs du Chaparral Napa Valley 1987 • $15 • (08/31/90)

91 **FAR NIENTE** Cabernet Sauvignon Napa Valley 1987 • $46 • (12/15/97)

91 **FLORA SPRINGS** Cabernet Sauvignon Napa Valley Cellar Select 1987 • $25 • (11/15/90)

91 **GUENOC** Cabernet Sauvignon Napa Valley Beckstoffer Vineyard Reserve 1987 • $65 • (12/15/97)

91 **HACIENDA** Antares Sonoma County 1987 • $28 • (11/15/90)

91 **KENWOOD** Cabernet Sauvignon Sonoma Valley Artist Series 1987 • $32 Ⓐ • (12/15/97)

91 **MAZZOCCO** Matrix Sonoma County 1987 • $28 • (01/31/92)

91 **OAKFORD** Cabernet Sauvignon Napa Valley 1987 • $25 • (11/15/90)

91 **PAHLMEYER** Caldwell Vineyard Napa Valley 1987 • $41 Ⓐ • (11/15/90)

91 **SANTA CRUZ MOUNTAIN** Cabernet Sauvignon Santa Cruz Mountains Bates Ranch 1987 • $16 • (11/15/92)

91 **STERLING** Cabernet Sauvignon Napa Valley 1987 • $14 • (05/15/90)

91 **STERLING** Cabernet Sauvignon Napa Valley Diamond Mountain Ranch 1987 • $16 • (11/15/90)

91 **VINCENT ARROYO** Cabernet Sauvignon Napa Valley 1987 • $12 • (11/15/90)

90 **BERINGER** Cabernet Sauvignon Knights Valley 1987 • $20 • (11/15/90) • HR

90 **CAKEBREAD** Cabernet Sauvignon Napa Valley 1987 • $25 • (10/15/90)

90 **CHAPPELLET** Cabernet Sauvignon Napa Valley Reserve 1987 • $19 Ⓐ • (12/15/97)

90 **CHATEAU ST. JEAN** Cabernet Sauvignon Alexander Valley Reserve 1987 • $50 • (12/15/97)

90 **CHIMNEY ROCK** Cabernet Sauvignon Stags Leap District 1987 • $29 • (07/31/91) • SS

90 **CLOS DU BOIS** Marlstone Vineyard Alexander Valley 1987 • $27 • (07/31/91) • HR

90 **CLOS PEGASE** Hommage California 1987 • $20 • (08/31/91) • HR

90 **CUTLER CELLAR** Cabernet Sauvignon Sonoma Valley Batto Ranch 1987 • $17 • (03/31/92) • HR

90 **CUVAISON** Cabernet Sauvignon Napa Valley 1987 • $36 • (12/15/97)

90 **DIAMOND CREEK** Cabernet Sauvignon Napa Valley Gravelly Meadow 1987 • $67 Ⓐ • (12/15/89)

90 **FLORA SPRINGS** Trilogy Napa Valley 1987 • $33 • (05/15/91)

90 **FORMAN** Cabernet Sauvignon Napa Valley 1987 • $41 Ⓐ • (12/15/97)

90 **FREEMARK ABBEY** Cabernet Sauvignon Napa Valley Sycamore Vineyards 1987 • $25 • (11/15/93)

90 **GAN EDEN** Cabernet Sauvignon Alexander Valley 1987 • $18 • (03/31/91)

90 **GROTH** Cabernet Sauvignon Napa Valley Reserve 1987 • $77 Ⓐ • (12/15/97)

90 **HEITZ** Cabernet Sauvignon Napa Valley 1987 • $60 Ⓐ • (04/15/92) • SS

90 **HUSCH** Cabernet Sauvignon Mendocino La Ribera Vineyards 1987 • $12 • (11/15/90)

90 **JORDAN** Cabernet Sauvignon Alexander Valley 1987 • $26 Ⓐ • (11/15/91) • HR

90 **JUSTIN** Reserve Paso Robles 1987 • $NA • (12/15/97)

90 **KENWOOD** Cabernet Sauvignon Sonoma Valley 1987 • $15 • (07/15/91)

90 **LAUREL GLEN** Cabernet Sauvignon Sonoma Mountain 1987 • $38 Ⓐ • (09/15/90)

90 **MONTICELLO** Cabernet Sauvignon Napa Valley Corley Reserve 1987 • $26 Ⓐ • (11/15/90)

90 **MONTICELLO** Cabernet Sauvignon Napa Valley Jefferson Cuvée 1987 • $14 • (09/30/90)

90 **RAYMOND** Cabernet Sauvignon Napa Valley Private Reserve 1987 • $20 • (12/15/97)

90 **ROBERT MONDAVI** Cabernet Sauvignon Napa Valley 1987 • $72 Ⓐ • (12/15/97)

90 **ROBERT MONDAVI** Cabernet Sauvignon Napa Valley Reserve 1987 • $81 Ⓐ • (08/31/90)

90 **ROBERT PECOTA** Cabernet Sauvignon Napa Valley Kara's Vineyard 1987 • $16 • (10/15/90)

90 **ROBERT PEPI** Cabernet Sauvignon Napa Valley Vine Hill Ranch 1987 • $24 • (04/30/91) • HR

90 **ST. CLEMENT** Cabernet Sauvignon Napa Valley 1987 • $18 • (12/15/97)

90 **STERLING** Reserve Napa Valley 1987 • $43 • (12/15/97)

90 **STRATFORD** Cabernet Sauvignon Napa Valley Partners' Reserve 1987 • $16 • (04/30/91)

90 **TERRACES** Cabernet Sauvignon Napa Valley 1987 • $38 • (12/15/97)

90 **WHITEHALL LANE** Cabernet Sauvignon Napa Valley Reserve 1987 • $28 • (11/15/91)

90 **ZD WINES** Cabernet Sauvignon Napa Valley Estate Bottled 1987 • $40 • (01/31/91)

89 **ABREU** Cabernet Sauvignon Napa Valley Madrona Ranch 1987 • $25 • (07/31/91)

89 **ADELAIDA** Cabernet Sauvignon Paso Robles 1987 • $14 • (02/28/91)

89 **ALEXANDER VALLEY VINEYARDS** Cabernet Sauvignon Alexander Valley Wetzel Family Estate 1987 • $28 • (12/15/97)

89 **BANDIERA** Cabernet Sauvignon Napa Valley 1987 • $7 • (11/15/91) • BB

89 **CAIN** Five Napa Valley 1987 • $70 • (12/15/97)

89 **CARMENET** Red Sonoma Valley 1987 • $20 • (11/15/90)

89 **CONN CREEK** Triomphe Napa Valley 1987 • $26 • (07/15/92)

89 **CORISON** Cabernet Sauvignon Napa Valley 1987 • $41 • (12/15/97)

89 **CRONIN** Cabernet Sauvignon-Merlot Stags Leap District Robinson Vineyard 1987 • $17 • (02/28/91)

89 **CUTLER CELLAR** Satyre Sonoma Valley 1987 • $20 • (07/15/92)

89 **DIAMOND CREEK** Cabernet Sauvignon Napa Valley Gravelly Meadow 1987 • $67 Ⓐ • (06/15/98)

89 **DIAMOND CREEK** Cabernet Sauvignon Napa Valley Volcanic Hill 1987 • $67 Ⓐ • (12/15/97)

89 **DOMINUS ESTATE** Napa Valley 1987 • $43 Ⓐ • (11/15/91)

89 **DRY CREEK** Meritage Dry Creek Valley 1987 • $45 • (12/15/97)

89 **FRANCISCAN** Cabernet Sauvignon Napa Valley Oakville Estate 1987 • $12 • (02/15/91)

89 **GEYSER PEAK** Cabernet Sauvignon Alexander Valley Estate Reserve 1987 • $28 • (12/15/97)

89 **GEYSER PEAK** Cabernet Sauvignon Alexander Valley Reserve 1987 • $14 • (06/15/91)

89 **GUENOC** Cabernet Sauvignon Lake County 1987 • $12 • (07/15/91)

89 **GUNDLACH BUNDSCHU** Cabernet Sauvignon Sonoma Valley Rhinefarm Vineyards Vintage Reserve 1987 • $22 • (07/31/92)

89 **GUSTAVE NIEBAUM** Cabernet Sauvignon Napa Valley Mast Vineyard 1987 • $14 • (08/31/92)

89 **HUSCH** Cabernet Sauvignon Mendocino La Ribera Vineyards 1987 • $25 • (12/15/97)

89 **INGLENOOK-NAPA VALLEY** Cabernet Sauvignon Napa Valley Reserve Cask 1987 • $21 • (11/15/92)

89 **JOHNSON TURNBULL** Cabernet Sauvignon Napa Valley Vineyard Selection 67 1987 • $22 • (06/30/91)

89 **KATHRYN KENNEDY** Cabernet Sauvignon Santa Cruz Mountains 1987 • $46 • (01/31/91)

89 **KENWOOD** Cabernet Sauvignon Sonoma Valley Jack London Vineyard 1987 • $45 • (12/15/97)

89 **MURPHY-GOODE** Cabernet Sauvignon Alexander Valley Premier Vineyard 1987 • $17 • (05/31/90)

89 **NALLE** Cabernet Sauvignon Dry Creek Valley 1987 • $18 • (01/31/91)

89 **ROBERT KEEBLE** Cabernet Sauvignon Napa Valley 1987 • $14 • (10/15/91)

89 **RODNEY STRONG** Cabernet Sauvignon Alexander Valley Alexander's Crown Vineyard 1987 • $17 • (07/15/91)

89 **SANTA CRUZ MOUNTAIN** Cabernet Sauvignon Santa Cruz Mountains Bates Ranch 1987 • $NA • (12/15/97)

89 **SILVER OAK** Cabernet Sauvignon Alexander Valley 1987 • $72 Ⓐ • (10/15/91)

89 **SILVER OAK** Cabernet Sauvignon Napa Valley 1987 • $89 Ⓐ • (10/15/91)

89 **SILVER OAK** Cabernet Sauvignon Napa Valley Bonny's Vineyard 1987 • $87 • (10/31/92)

89 **SIMI** Cabernet Sauvignon Sonoma County 1987 • $17 • (05/15/91)

89 **STAGS' LEAP WINERY** Cabernet Sauvignon Napa Valley 1987 • $18 • (06/30/91)

88 **CAYMUS** Cabernet Sauvignon Napa Valley Special Selection 1987 • $175 Ⓐ • (12/15/97)

88 **CLOS DU BOIS** Cabernet Sauvignon Alexander Valley Briarcrest Vineyard 1987 • $18 • (11/15/91)

88 **DEHLINGER** Cabernet Sauvignon Russian River Valley 1987 • $13 • (02/28/91)

88 **DIAMOND CREEK** Cabernet Sauvignon Napa Valley Red Rock Terrace 1987 • $40 Ⓐ • (12/15/97)

88 **ESTANCIA** Meritage Alexander Valley 1987 • $12 • (01/31/91)

88 **FAR NIENTE** Cabernet Sauvignon Napa Valley 1987 • $46 • (11/15/90)

88 **FETZER** Cabernet Sauvignon Sonoma County Reserve 1987 • $22 • (09/30/93)

88 **FREEMARK ABBEY** Cabernet Sauvignon Napa Valley 1987 • $29 • (12/15/97)

88 **FREEMARK ABBEY** Cabernet Sauvignon Napa Valley Bosché 1987 • $22 Ⓐ • (12/15/97)

88 **GEYSER PEAK** Cabernet Sauvignon Sonoma County 1987 • $9 • (11/30/90) • BB

88 **GIRARD** Cabernet Sauvignon Napa Valley Reserve 1987 • $25 • (11/15/91)

88 **GRGICH HILLS** Cabernet Sauvignon Napa Valley 1987 • $NA • (12/15/97)

88 **GROTH** Cabernet Sauvignon Napa Valley Reserve 1987 • $77 Ⓐ • (03/31/92)

88 **GUENOC** Langtry Lake-Napa Counties Meritage Red 1987 • $35 • (04/15/91)

88 **HAGAFEN** Cabernet Sauvignon Napa Valley 1987 • $20 • (04/30/90)

88 **JOSEPH PHELPS** Cabernet Sauvignon Napa Valley Backus Vineyard 1987 • $48 Ⓐ • (07/15/91)

88 **KENWOOD** Cabernet Sauvignon Sonoma Valley 1987 • $25 • (12/15/97)

88 **KENWOOD** Cabernet Sauvignon Sonoma Valley Artist Series 1987 • $32 Ⓐ • (11/15/90)

88 **LYTTON SPRINGS** Cabernet Sauvignon Mendocino County Private Reserve 1987 • $18 • (09/15/90)

88 **MAZZOCCO** Cabernet Sauvignon Alexander Valley Claret Style 1987 • $20 • (12/15/97)

88 **NAVARRO** Cabernet Sauvignon Mendocino 1987 • $16 • (11/15/92)

88 **NEWLAN** Cabernet Sauvignon Napa Valley 1987 • $15 • (11/15/92)

88 **NIEBAUM-COPPOLA** Rubicon Napa Valley 1987 • $30 • (11/15/93)

88 **PRESTON** Cabernet Sauvignon Dry Creek Valley 1987 • $14 • (10/31/90)

88 **RAYMOND** Cabernet Sauvignon Napa Valley 1987 • $26 • (12/15/97)

88 **RENAISSANCE** Cabernet Sauvignon North Yuba Reserve 1987 • $35 • (12/15/95)

88 **RIDGE** Cabernet Sauvignon Santa Cruz Mountains Monte Bello 1987 • $44 Ⓐ • (11/15/90)

88 **SHAFER** Cabernet Sauvignon Stags Leap District Hillside Select 1987 • $56 • (07/31/92)

88 **SIMI** Cabernet Sauvignon Alexander Valley Reserve 1987 • $29 • (07/15/92)

88 **STAR HILL** Cabernet Sauvignon Napa Valley Doc's Reserve 1987 • $24 • (11/15/91)

88 **SWANSON** Cabernet Sauvignon Napa Valley 1987 • $25 • (12/15/97)

88 **TREFETHEN** Cabernet Sauvignon Napa Valley 1987 • $50 • (12/15/97)

88 **V. SATTUI** Cabernet Sauvignon Napa Valley Preston Vineyard Reserve Stock 1987 • $35 • (11/15/92)

88 **VILLA MT. EDEN** Cabernet Sauvignon Napa Valley 1987 • $13 • (02/15/91)

88 **WILD HORSE** Cabernet Sauvignon Paso Robles 1987 • $13 • (04/30/91)

87 **ALEXANDER VALLEY VINEYARDS** Cabernet Sauvignon Alexander Valley 1987 • $12 • (05/31/90)

87 **ARROWOOD** Cabernet Sauvignon Sonoma County 1987 • $26 • (11/15/90)

87 **B.R. COHN** Cabernet Sauvignon Sonoma Valley Olive Hill Vineyard 1987 • $36 Ⓐ • (12/15/97)

87 **CHATEAU SOUVERAIN** Cabernet Sauvignon Alexander Valley 1987 • $10 • (11/15/90)

87 **CHATEAU SOUVERAIN** Cabernet Sauvignon Alexander Valley Private Reserve 1987 • $26 • (12/15/97)

87 **CONN CREEK** Cabernet Sauvignon Napa Valley Barrel Select 1987 • $17 • (07/15/91)

87 **CONN CREEK** Cabernet Sauvignon Napa Valley Reserve 1987 • $23 • (08/31/92)

87 **DE LOACH** Cabernet Sauvignon Russian River Valley O.F.S. 1987 • $50 • (12/15/97)

87 **DIAMOND CREEK** Cabernet Sauvignon Napa Valley Red Rock Terrace 1987 • $40 Ⓐ • (06/15/98)

87 **DIAMOND CREEK** Cabernet Sauvignon Napa Valley Volcanic Hill 1987 • $67 Ⓐ • (06/15/98)

87 **DRY CREEK** Meritage Dry Creek Valley 1987 • $24 • (01/31/92)

87 **FETZER** Cabernet Sauvignon Sonoma County Reserve 1987 • $75 • (12/15/97)

87 **FRANCISCAN** Meritage Napa Valley 1987 • $17 • (04/30/91)

87 **FREEMARK ABBEY** Cabernet Sauvignon Napa Valley Bosché 1987 • $22 Ⓐ • (11/15/91)

Key: SS—Spectator Selection CS—Cellar Selection HR—Highly Recommended BB—Best Buy $NA—Price not available Ⓐ—Auction Price
Dates in parentheses indicate the issues in which the ratings were published.

87 **GARY FARRELL** Cabernet Sauvignon Sonoma County 1987 • $16 • (10/31/90)

87 **GEYSER PEAK** Réserve Alexandre Alexander Valley 1987 • $18 • (05/15/93)

87 **GRGICH HILLS** Cabernet Sauvignon Napa Valley 1987 • $22 • (11/15/92)

87 **HUSCH** Cabernet Sauvignon Mendocino North Field Select 1987 • $16 • (11/15/90)

87 **KENDALL-JACKSON** Cabernet Sauvignon California Proprietor's Grand Reserve 1987 • $16 • (03/31/92)

87 **KLEIN** Cabernet Sauvignon Santa Cruz Mountains 1987 • $19 • (10/15/90)

87 **LOUIS M. MARTINI** Cabernet Sauvignon Napa Valley Reserve 1987 • $14 • (10/15/90)

87 **MARIETTA** Cabernet Sauvignon Sonoma County 1987 • $10 • (02/28/91)

87 **MARKHAM** Cabernet Sauvignon Napa Valley 1987 • $17 • (08/31/91)

87 **MAYACAMAS** Cabernet Sauvignon Napa Valley 1987 • $45 • (12/15/97)

87 **MAZZOCCO** Matrix Sonoma County 1987 • $28 • (12/15/97)

87 **MEEKER** Cabernet Sauvignon Dry Creek Valley 1987 • $14 • (10/15/91)

87 **MOUNT VEEDER** Cabernet Sauvignon Napa Valley Mount Veeder Vineyards 1987 • $50 • (12/15/97)

87 **NEWTON** Cabernet Sauvignon Napa Valley 1987 • $17 • (11/15/91)

87 **PEJU** Cabernet Sauvignon Napa Valley HB Vineyard 1987 • $20 • (11/15/90)

87 **QUAIL RIDGE** Cabernet Sauvignon Napa Valley Reserve 1987 • $25 • (11/15/92)

87 **QUIVIRA** Cabernet Sauvignon Dry Creek Valley 1987 • $15 • (11/15/90)

87 **RAVENSWOOD** Pickberry Sonoma Mountain 1987 • $48 • (12/15/97)

87 **ROBERT MONDAVI** Cabernet Sauvignon Napa Valley 1987 • $72 Ⓐ • (05/31/90)

87 **ROMBAUER** Cabernet Sauvignon Napa Valley 1987 • $17 • (11/15/91)

87 **SEQUOIA GROVE** Cabernet Sauvignon Napa Valley Estate 1987 • $31 • (11/15/91)

87 **SILVER OAK** Cabernet Sauvignon Napa Valley 1987 • $89 Ⓐ • (12/15/97)

87 **STAG'S LEAP WINE CELLARS** Cask 23 Napa Valley 1987 • $78 • (12/15/97)

87 **STERLING** Three Palms Vineyard Napa Valley 1987 • $23 • (11/15/90)

87 **VICHON** Cabernet Sauvignon Stags Leap District 1987 • $17 • (07/31/90)

87 **WINDSOR** Cabernet Sauvignon Russian River Valley River West Vineyard 1987 • $20 • (11/15/92)

86 **BERNARD PRADEL** Cabernet Sauvignon Napa Valley 1987 • $20 • (10/15/90)

86 **BYINGTON** Cabernet Sauvignon Napa Valley 1987 • $16 • (11/15/91)

86 **CLOS DU BOIS** Cabernet Sauvignon Alexander Valley 1987 • $11 • (02/15/90)

86 **COSENTINO** Cabernet Sauvignon North Coast Reserve 1987 • $28 • (02/28/91)

86 **EBERLE** Cabernet Sauvignon Paso Robles Reserve 1987 • $26 • (11/15/93)

86 **FRANCISCAN** Cabernet Sauvignon Napa Valley Library Selection 1987 • $20 • (12/15/97)

86 **FREEMARK ABBEY** Cabernet Sauvignon Napa Valley 1987 • $22 Ⓐ • (07/31/91)

86 **GIRARD** Cabernet Sauvignon Napa Valley 1987 • $16 • (11/15/90)

86 **INGLENOOK-NAPA VALLEY** Cabernet Sauvignon Napa Valley 1987 • $10 • (11/15/91)

86 **IRON HORSE** Cabernets Alexander Valley 1987 • $20 • (03/15/91)

86 **J. LOHR** Cabernet Sauvignon Paso Robles Seven Oaks 1987 • $12 • (04/30/91)

86 **KEENAN** Cabernet Sauvignon Napa Valley 1987 • $19 • (05/31/90)

86 **MARKHAM** Cabernet Sauvignon Napa Valley 1987 • $15 • (12/15/97)

86 **MIRASSOU** Cabernet Sauvignon Monterey County Harvest Reserve 1987 • $13 • (11/15/91)

86 **PAHLMEYER** Caldwell Vineyard Napa Valley 1987 • $41 Ⓐ • (12/15/97)

86 **ROLLING HILLS** Cabernet Sauvignon California 1987 • $7 • (12/15/89) • BB

86 **RUTHERFORD HILL** Cabernet Sauvignon Napa Valley XVS 1987 • $26 • (11/15/92)

86 **SEBASTIANI** Wildwood Sonoma Valley 1987 • $15 • (08/31/91)

86 **STELTZNER** Cabernet Sauvignon Napa Valley Stags Leap District 1987 • $25 • (11/15/91)

86 **STONEGATE** Meritage Reserve Napa Valley 1987 • $17 • (11/15/93)

86 **TERRA ROSA** Red Napa Valley 1987 • $14 • (07/31/90)

86 **TREFETHEN** Cabernet Sauvignon Napa Valley 1987 • $16 • (11/15/90)

86 **WENTE** Cabernet Sauvignon Livermore Valley Charles Wetmore Vineyard Reserve 1987 • $18 • (04/30/91)

85 **BEAULIEU VINEYARD** Cabernet Sauvignon Napa Valley Rutherford 1987 • $11 Ⓐ • (12/15/90)

85 **BENZIGER** A Tribute Red Sonoma Mountain 1987 • $20 • (12/31/90)

85 **BENZIGER** Cabernet Sauvignon Sonoma Valley Estate Bottled 1987 • $12 • (11/15/90)

85 **BOEGER** Cabernet Sauvignon El Dorado 1987 • $11 • (03/15/91)

85 **BUEHLER** Cabernet Sauvignon Napa Valley 1987 • $21 • (07/31/90)

85 **BURGESS** Cabernet Sauvignon Napa Valley Vintage Selection 1987 • $20 • (10/15/91)

85 **CHAUFFE-EAU** Cabernet Sauvignon Alexander Valley 1987 • $16 • (08/31/92)

85 **COSENTINO** The Poet California Meritage 1987 • $25 • (09/15/90)

85 **DE LOACH** Cabernet Sauvignon Russian River Valley O.F.S. 1987 • $22 • (10/15/90)

85 **ETUDE** Cabernet Sauvignon Napa Valley 1987 • $36 • (11/10/90)

85 **FIELD STONE** Cabernet Sauvignon Alexander Valley 1987 • $14 • (02/28/91)

85 **GRAND CRU** Cabernet Sauvignon Sonoma County Premium Selection 1987 • $12 • (11/15/91)

85 **GUNDLACH BUNDSCHU** Cabernet Sauvignon Sonoma Valley Rhinefarm Vineyards 1987 • $15 • (05/15/91)

85 **HEITZ** Cabernet Sauvignon Napa Valley Bella Oaks Vineyard 1987 • $33 • (06/30/92)

85 **MOUNT EDEN** Cabernet Sauvignon Santa Cruz Mountains Young Vine Cuvée 1987 • $12 • (04/15/90)

85 **MOUNT VEEDER** Cabernet Sauvignon Napa Valley 1987 • $22 • (04/30/91)

85 **PEDRONCELLI** Cabernet Sauvignon Dry Creek Valley 1987 • $9 • (11/15/90) • BB

85 **PINE RIDGE** Cabernet Sauvignon Stags Leap District 1987 • $28 • (01/31/92)

85 **RIDGE** Cabernet Sauvignon Napa County York Creek 1987 • $21 • (11/15/92)

85 **RODNEY STRONG** Cabernet Sauvignon Sonoma County 1987 • $10 • (06/30/91)

85 **ROMBAUER** Cabernet Sauvignon Napa Valley 1987 • $50 • (12/15/97)

85 **RUTHERFORD HILL** Cabernet Sauvignon Napa Valley 1987 • $16 • (11/15/92)

85 **ST. SUPÉRY** Cabernet Sauvignon Napa Valley Dollarhide Ranch 1987 • $13 • (07/15/90)

85 **SEGHESIO** Cabernet Sauvignon Sonoma County 1987 • $9 • (04/30/91)

85 **STRATFORD** Cabernet Sauvignon Napa Valley 1987 • $12 • (04/30/90)

85 **VIANSA** Obsidian Napa & Sonoma Counties 1987 • $65 • (07/15/91)

85 **WHITE OAK** Cabernet Sauvignon Sonoma County 1987 • $14 • (02/29/92)

85 **WILLIAM HILL** Cabernet Sauvignon Napa Valley Silver Label 1987 • $14 • (11/15/90)

Sequoia Grove Vineyards in St. Helena, Napa Valley.

California Chardonnay

Here are *Wine Spectator*'s ratings and prices for the four most recent vintages of California Chardonnay. All are of exceptional quality, and the choice of excellent Chardonnay has never been better. The most recently released year, 1996, is perhaps the easiest vintage in which to find a great bottle of Chardonnay, followed closely by 1995, 1994 and 1993.

The wines are organized in descending order of score, to make it easy to identify the best wines of each vintage. If you know the name of a wine already and you want to look up its score and tasting note, turn to the main listings section of this book and look under United States and then under the winery name.

1996 California Chardonnay | Vintage Rating: 97

95 **BERINGER** Chardonnay Napa Valley Private Reserve 1996 • $32 • (03/31/98) • HR

95 **VILLA MT. EDEN** Chardonnay Santa Maria Valley Bien Nacido Vineyards Signature Series 1996 • $35 • (05/31/98) • HR

94 **BERINGER** Chardonnay Napa Valley Sbragia Limited Release 1996 • $35 • (07/31/98) • HR

94 **PATZ & HALL** Chardonnay Napa Valley 1996 • $29 • (01/31/98) • HR

94 **ROCHIOLI** Chardonnay Russian River Valley Allen Vineyard 1996 • $38 • (07/31/98)

93 **CHALK HILL** Chardonnay Chalk Hill 1996 • $28 • (06/15/98) • SS

93 **GARY FARRELL** Chardonnay Russian River Valley Allen Vineyard 1996 • $28 • (06/30/98)

93 **LANDMARK** Chardonnay Russian River Valley Lorenzo 1996 • $35 • (06/30/98)

93 **LEWIS CELLARS** Chardonnay Napa Valley Reserve 1996 • $32 • (05/15/98)

93 **NEYERS** Chardonnay Sonoma Coast Thieriot Vineyard 1996 • $35 • (11/15/97)

93 **PATZ & HALL** Chardonnay Carneros Hyde Vineyard 1996 • $35 • (01/31/98)

93 **PATZ & HALL** Chardonnay Mount Veeder Carr Vineyard 1996 • $42 • (06/30/98) • HR

93 **PATZ & HALL** Chardonnay Russian River Valley 1996 • $29 • (01/31/98)

93 **PETER MICHAEL** Chardonnay Knights Valley Belle Côte 1996 • $42 • (07/31/98)

Key: SS—Spectator Selection CS—Cellar Selection HR—Highly Recommended BB—Best Buy $NA—Price not available Ⓐ—Auction Price
Dates in parentheses indicate the issues in which the ratings were published.

93 **PETER MICHAEL** Chardonnay Napa County Clos du Ciel 1996 • $38 • (07/31/98) • HR

93 **ROCHIOLI** Chardonnay Russian River Valley River Block 1996 • $32 • (07/31/98)

93 **SIGNORELLO** Chardonnay Napa Valley Founder's Reserve 1996 • $48 • (07/31/98) • HR

93 **STEELE** Chardonnay Carneros Durell Vineyard 1996 • $24 • (06/30/98)

93 **STEELE** Chardonnay Mendocino Lolonis Vineyard 1996 • $26 • (06/30/98)

93 **TALLEY** Chardonnay Arroyo Grande Valley Rincon Vineyard 1996 • $30 • (07/31/98)

93 **TALLEY** Chardonnay Arroyo Grande Valley Rosemary's Vineyard 1996 • $30 • (07/31/98)

93 **VINE CLIFF** Chardonnay Napa Valley 1996 • $25 • (04/30/98) • HR

92 **AU BON CLIMAT** Chardonnay Arroyo Grande Valley Reserve Talley 1996 • $25 • (07/31/98)

92 **AUGUST BRIGGS** Chardonnay Carneros Leveroni Vineyards 1996 • $25 • (01/31/98)

92 **AUGUST BRIGGS** Chardonnay Russian River Valley 1996 • $25 • (01/31/98)

92 **BABCOCK** Chardonnay Santa Ynez Valley Grand Cuvee 1996 • $30 • (06/30/98)

92 **BABCOCK** Chardonnay Santa Ynez Valley Mt. Carmel Vineyard 1996 • $30 • (06/30/98)

92 **CHATEAU SOUVERAIN** Chardonnay Russian River Valley Winemaker's Reserve 1996 • $20 • (07/31/98) • HR

92 **DE LOACH** Chardonnay Russian River Valley O.F.S. 1996 • $28 • (06/30/98) • SS

92 **GUENOC** Chardonnay Guenoc Valley Genevieve Magoon Vineyard Unfiltered Reserve 1996 • $30 • (06/30/98)

92 **HARRISON** Chardonnay Napa Valley 1996 • $32 • (07/31/98)

92 **LANDMARK** Chardonnay Sonoma County Damaris Reserve 1996 • $32 • (06/30/98)

92 **LANDMARK** Chardonnay Sonoma County Overlook 1996 • $21 • (03/31/98) • SS

92 **LIVINGSTON** Chardonnay Napa Valley 1996 • $40 • (05/31/98)

92 **MERIDIAN** Chardonnay Edna Valley Coastal Reserve 1996 • $14 • (03/31/98) • SS

92 **MERRYVALE** Chardonnay Napa Valley Reserve 1996 • $30 • (07/31/98)

92 **NEYERS** Chardonnay Carneros 1996 • $25 • (11/15/97)

92 **OAKVILLE RANCH** Chardonnay Napa Valley ORV 1996 • $32 • (05/15/98)

92 **RIDGE** Chardonnay Santa Cruz Mountains 1996 • $25 • (06/30/98)

92 **SANFORD** Chardonnay Santa Barbara County Barrel Select 1996 • $30 • (06/30/98)

92 **SHAFER** Chardonnay Napa Valley Carneros Red Shoulder Ranch 1996 • $30 • (05/31/98) • HR

92 **SIGNORELLO** Chardonnay Napa Valley 1996 • $30 • (07/31/98)

92 **STEELE** Chardonnay Mendocino DuPratt Vineyard 1996 • $26 • (06/30/98)

92 **STEELE** Chardonnay Santa Barbara County Bien Nacido Vineyard 1996 • $26 • (05/31/98)

92 **STEELE** Chardonnay Santa Barbara County Goodchild Vineyard 1996 • $26 • (05/31/98)

92 **TALLEY** Chardonnay Edna Valley Oliver's Vineyard 1996 • $18 • (12/31/97) • SS

92 **THUNDER MOUNTAIN** Chardonnay Santa Cruz Mountains Matteson Vineyard 1996 • $29 • (06/30/98)

92 **TRUCHARD** Chardonnay Napa Valley Carneros 1996 • $24 • (04/30/98)

91 **BABCOCK** Chardonnay Santa Maria Valley Bien Nacido Vineyard Block W Gravelly Vein 1996 • $30 • (05/31/98)

91 **BENZIGER** Chardonnay Carneros Reserve 1996 • $25 • (06/30/98)

91 **BENZIGER** Chardonnay Carneros Yamakawa Vineyards Reserve 1996 • $25 • (05/31/98)

91 **BERNARDUS** Chardonnay Monterey County 1996 • $18 • (06/30/98) • SS

91 **BYINGTON** Chardonnay Santa Cruz Mountains Dirk Vineyard Special Reserve Vineyards 1996 • $24 • (06/30/98)

91 **CARNEROS BIGHORN RANCH** Chardonnay Napa Valley Reserve 1996 • $20 • (05/31/98) • SS

91 **CHALONE** Chardonnay Chalone 1996 • $27 • (05/31/98)

91 **CHATEAU ST. JEAN** Chardonnay Alexander Valley Belle Terre Vineyard 1996 • $22 • (05/15/98)

91 **FLORA SPRINGS** Chardonnay Napa Valley 1996 • $20 • (06/30/98)

91 **FLORA SPRINGS** Chardonnay Napa Valley Lavender Hill Vineyard 1996 • $23 • (06/30/98)

91 **GAINEY** Chardonnay Santa Barbara County Limited Selection 1996 • $25 • (07/31/98)

91 **GALLO OF SONOMA** Chardonnay Russian River Valley Laguna Ranch Vineyard 1996 • $18 • (05/31/98) • SS

91 **J. FRITZ** Chardonnay Russian River Valley Dutton Vineyard Shop Block 1996 • $30 • (06/30/98)

Key: SS—Spectator Selection CS—Cellar Selection HR—Highly Recommended BB—Best Buy $NA—Price not available Ⓐ—Auction Price

Dates in parentheses indicate the issues in which the ratings were published.

91 **J. FRITZ** Chardonnay Russian River Valley Dutton Ranch 1996 • $20 • (06/30/98)

91 **LAETITIA** Chardonnay San Luis Obispo County Laetitia Vineyard 1996 • $25 • (06/30/98)

91 **LONG** Chardonnay Napa Valley 1996 • $31 • (05/31/98)

91 **LONGORIA** Chardonnay Santa Ynez Valley Santa Rita Cuvée 1996 • $25 • (06/30/98)

91 **MERRYVALE** Chardonnay Napa Valley Starmont 1996 • $18 • (07/31/98) • SS

91 **MIRASSOU** Chardonnay Monterey County Showcase Selection Harvest Reserve 1996 • $28 • (06/30/98)

91 **MOUNT EDEN** Chardonnay Edna Valley MacGregor Vineyard 1996 • $16 • (03/31/98) • SS

91 **NEWTON** Chardonnay Napa-Sonoma Counties 1996 • $22 • (11/15/97) • SS

91 **NEYERS** Chardonnay Napa Valley 1996 • $25 • (11/15/97)

91 **NICHOLS** Chardonnay Santa Barbara County Cottonwood Canyon Vineyard 1996 • $30 • (11/30/97)

91 **PAUL HOBBS** Chardonnay Sonoma Valley Kunde Vineyard 1996 • $35 • (06/30/98)

91 **PAUL HOBBS** Chardonnay Sonoma Mountain Richard Dinner Vineyard 1996 • $39 • (06/30/98)

91 **PINE RIDGE** Chardonnay Stags Leap District Dijon Clones 1996 • $34 • (05/15/98)

91 **PRIDE** Chardonnay Napa Valley 1996 • $20 • (05/15/98)

91 **RAYMOND** Chardonnay Napa Valley Generations 1996 • $27 • (05/15/98)

91 **ROCHIOLI** Chardonnay Russian River Valley 1996 • $24 • (05/31/98)

91 **SANFORD** Chardonnay Santa Ynez Valley Estate Bottled 1996 • $26 • (06/30/98)

91 **SEBASTIANI** Chardonnay Russian River Valley Dutton Ranch 1996 • $30 • (07/31/98)

91 **SIMI** Chardonnay Carneros 1996 • $21 • (07/31/98)

91 **STAG'S LEAP WINE CELLARS** Chardonnay Napa Valley Beckstoffer Ranch 1996 • $28 • (05/15/98)

91 **STAG'S LEAP WINE CELLARS** Chardonnay Napa Valley Reserve 1996 • $37 • (05/15/98)

91 **THUNDER MOUNTAIN** Chardonnay Santa Cruz Mountains Bald Mountain Vineyard 1996 • $29 • (06/30/98)

90 **AU BON CLIMAT** Chardonnay Edna Valley Alban Vineyard 1996 • $20 • (11/15/97)

90 **BERINGER** Chardonnay Napa Valley 1996 • $15 • (01/31/98)

90 **BUEHLER** Chardonnay Russian River Valley Reserve 1996 • $30 • (04/30/98)

90 **BYINGTON** Chardonnay Santa Cruz Mountains 1996 • $20 • (06/30/98)

90 **BYINGTON** Chardonnay Santa Cruz Mountains Bald Mountain Vineyard Special Reserve Vineyards 1996 • $24 • (07/31/98)

90 **CALERA** Chardonnay Central Coast 1996 • $16 • (03/31/98)

90 **CALLE CIELO** Chardonnay Santa Cruz Mountains 1996 • $25 • (06/30/98)

90 **CAMBRIA** Chardonnay Santa Maria Valley Katherine's Vineyard 1996 • $18 • (04/30/98)

90 **CHAPPELLET** Chardonnay Napa Valley Signature Series 1996 • $24 • (03/31/98)

90 **CHATEAU SOUVERAIN** Chardonnay Sonoma County 1996 • $13 • (01/31/98) • SS

90 **CLOS LACHANCE** Chardonnay Santa Cruz Mountains Vintner's Reserve 1996 • $29 • (06/30/98)

90 **COSENTINO** Chardonnay Napa Valley The Sculptor Reserve 1996 • $30 • (05/15/98)

90 **DEHLINGER** Chardonnay Russian River Valley 1996 • $20 • (06/30/98)

90 **EL MOLINO** Chardonnay Napa Valley 1996 • $38 • (06/30/98)

90 **ESTANCIA** Chardonnay Monterey Reserve 1996 • $19 • (06/30/98)

90 **FAR NIENTE** Chardonnay Napa Valley 1996 • $40 • (06/30/98)

90 **FERRARI-CARANO** Chardonnay Alexander Valley 1996 • $21 • (07/31/98) • SS

90 **FESS PARKER** Chardonnay Santa Barbara County Marcella's Vineyard American Tradition Reserve 1996 • $24 • (06/30/98)

90 **FORMAN** Chardonnay Napa Valley 1996 • $27 • (11/30/97)

90 **FRANCISCAN OAKVILLE ESTATE** Chardonnay Napa Valley 1996 • $15 • (06/30/98) • SS

90 **GLORIA FERRER** Chardonnay Carneros 1996 • $19 • (05/15/98) • SS

90 **GUENOC** Chardonnay Guenoc Valley Genevieve Magoon Vineyard Reserve 1996 • $25 • (06/30/98)

90 **MCILROY** Chardonnay Russian River Valley Aquarius Ranch 1996 • $18 • (06/30/98)

90 **MORGAN** Chardonnay Monterey 1996 • $18 • (04/30/98) • SS

90 **MUELLER** Chardonnay Russian River Valley LB 1996 • $18 • (06/30/98)

90 **MUELLER** Chardonnay Russian River Valley Oak Meadow Vineyard 1996 • $18 • (07/31/98)

90 **MURPHY-GOODE** Chardonnay Alexander Valley Island Block Reserve 1996 • $24 • (05/15/98)

90 **OAKVILLE RANCH** Chardonnay Napa Valley Vista Vineyard 1996 • $26 • (05/31/98)

90 **PAHLMEYER** Chardonnay Napa Valley 1996 • $50 • (05/31/98)

90 **PINE RIDGE** Chardonnay Napa Valley Carneros Dijon Clones 1996 • $20 • (01/31/98)

90 **ROBERT MONDAVI** Chardonnay Napa Valley 1996 • $19 • (07/31/98)

90 **ST. FRANCIS** Chardonnay Sonoma Valley Reserve 1996 • $22 • (03/31/98)

90 **SCHUG** Chardonnay Carneros 1996 • $18 • (05/15/98)

90 **SELBY** Chardonnay Sonoma County 1996 • $23 • (04/30/98)

90 **SIMI** Chardonnay Sonoma County 1996 • $17 • (07/31/98)

90 **STEELE** Chardonnay California Steele Cuvée 1996 • $19 • (05/31/98) • SS

90 **STEELE** Chardonnay Carneros Sangiacomo Vineyard 1996 • $24 • (05/15/98)

90 **STEELE** Chardonnay Sonoma Valley Parmelee-Hill Vineyard 1996 • $26 • (06/30/98)

90 **STUHLMULLER** Chardonnay Alexander Valley 1996 • $21 • (07/31/98)

90 **TALLEY** Chardonnay Arroyo Grande Valley 1996 • $20 • (07/31/98) • SS

90 **THE HESS COLLECTION** Chardonnay Napa Valley 1996 • $18 • (06/30/98)

90 **VON STRASSER** Chardonnay Napa Valley 1996 • $30 • (05/31/98)

89 **ALDERBROOK** Chardonnay Dry Creek Valley 1996 • $13 • (02/28/98) • SS

89 **ARROWOOD** Chardonnay Sonoma County Domaine du Grand Archer 1996 • $14 • (03/31/98)

89 **BEAUCANON** Chardonnay Napa Valley Jacques de Coninck 1996 • $28 • (05/15/98)

89 **CARMENET** Chardonnay Sonoma Valley Carneros Sangiacomo Vineyard 1996 • $17 • (05/31/98)

89 **CHATEAU ST. JEAN** Chardonnay Sonoma County 1996 • $13 • (12/31/97) • SS

89 **CLOS DU BOIS** Chardonnay Alexander Valley Alexander Valley Selection 1996 • $15 • (03/31/98)

89 **DE LOACH** Chardonnay Russian River Valley Estate Bottled 1996 • $20 • (04/30/98)

89 **EDNA VALLEY** Chardonnay Edna Valley Paragon 1996 • $17 • (05/15/98)

89 **GEYSER PEAK** Chardonnay Alexander Valley Reserve 1996 • $20 • (07/31/98)

89 **GRGICH HILLS** Chardonnay Napa Valley 1996 • $30 • (07/31/98)

89 **KENDALL-JACKSON** Chardonnay California Grand Reserve 1996 • $26 • (05/31/98)

89 **KENT RASMUSSEN** Chardonnay Napa Valley 1996 • $23 • (05/31/98)

89 **MARTIN RAY** Chardonnay California Mariage 1996 • $25 • (07/31/98)

89 **MIRASSOU** Chardonnay Monterey County Harvest Reserve 1996 • $16 • (05/15/98)

89 **MURPHY-GOODE** Chardonnay Russian River Valley J & K Murphy Vineyard Reserve 1996 • $24 • (05/15/98)

89 **NICHOLS** Chardonnay Central Coast Blend 1996 • $30 • (11/30/97)

89 **NICHOLS** Chardonnay Central Coast Blend 1996 • $NA • (03/31/98)

89 **PEZZI KING** Chardonnay Sonoma County 1996 • $17 • (04/30/98)

89 **QUPÉ** Chardonnay Santa Barbara County Bien Nacido Vineyard 1996 • $18 • (11/15/97)

89 **R.H. PHILLIPS** Chardonnay Dunnigan Hills Toasted Head 1996 • $12 • (06/30/98) • HR

89 **RABBIT RIDGE** Chardonnay Russian River Valley Rabbit Ridge Ranch Estate Reserve 1996 • $18 • (04/30/98)

89 **RUTZ** Chardonnay Russian River Valley Dutton Ranch 1996 • $30 • (05/15/98)

89 **ST. CLEMENT** Chardonnay Napa Valley Carneros Abbott's Vineyard 1996 • $20 • (05/31/98)

89 **SONOMA-CUTRER** Chardonnay Sonoma Coast Russian River Ranches 1996 • $17 • (03/31/98)

89 **SONOMA-LOEB** Chardonnay Sonoma County 1996 • $20 • (11/30/97)

89 **SOQUEL** Chardonnay Santa Cruz Mountains 1996 • $20 • (06/30/98)

89 **STAG'S LEAP WINE CELLARS** Chardonnay Napa Valley 1996 • $24 • (04/30/98)

89 **STEPHEN ROSS** Chardonnay Edna Valley Edna Ranch 1996 • $18 • (07/31/98)

89 **WHITCRAFT** Chardonnay Santa Maria Valley Bien Nacido Vineyard 1996 • $22 • (11/30/97)

89 **ZACA MESA** Chardonnay Santa Barbara County Zaca Vineyards 1996 • $14 • (05/15/98)

88 **ADASTRA** Chardonnay Napa Valley Carneros 1996 • $22 • (12/31/97)

88 **AU BON CLIMAT** Chardonnay Santa Barbara County 1996 • $18 • (11/15/97)

88 **AU BON CLIMAT** Chardonnay Santa Barbara County Le Bouge D'à Côté 1996 • $25 • (07/31/98)

88 **BECKMEN** Chardonnay Santa Barbara County Barrel Select 1996 • $20 • (06/15/98)

88 **BYINGTON** Chardonnay Napa Valley Twin Mountains 1996 • $15 • (07/31/98)

88 **BYRON** Chardonnay Santa Maria Valley 1996 • $17 • (07/31/98)

88 **CAKEBREAD** Chardonnay Napa Valley 1996 • $25 • (05/31/98)

88 **CALE** Chardonnay Carneros Sangiacomo Vineyards 1996 • $20 • (05/15/98)

88 **CANEPA** Chardonnay Alexander Valley Gauer Vineyard Adobe III 1996 • $26 • (05/15/98)

88 **CHAUFFE-EAU** Chardonnay Carneros Sangiacomo Vineyard 1996 • $20 • (06/15/98)

88 **CLOS LACHANCE** Chardonnay Santa Cruz Mountains 1996 • $22 • (06/30/98)

88 **CUVAISON** Chardonnay Napa Valley Carneros 1996 • $21 • (06/15/98)

88 **DRY CREEK** Chardonnay Sonoma County 1996 • $15 • (06/30/98)

88 **EHLERS GROVE** Chardonnay Sonoma & Napa Counties Winery Reserve 1996 • $25 • (06/30/98)

88 **ESTANCIA** Chardonnay Monterey County Pinnacles 1996 • $11 • (06/30/98)

88 **FOXEN** Chardonnay Santa Maria Valley 1996 • $20 • (07/31/98)

88 **FREEMARK ABBEY** Chardonnay Napa Valley 1996 • $17 • (04/30/98)

88 **FREEMARK ABBEY** Chardonnay Napa Valley Carpy Ranch 1996 • $24 • (05/15/98)

88 **GALLO OF SONOMA** Chardonnay Dry Creek Valley Stefani Vineyard 1996 • $16 • (05/31/98)

88 **GREENWOOD RIDGE** Chardonnay Anderson Valley Du Pratt Vineyard 1996 • $22 • (03/31/98)

88 **GROTH** Chardonnay Napa Valley 1996 • $18 • (03/31/98)

88 **HANDLEY** Chardonnay Dry Creek Valley Handley Vineyard 1996 • $17 • (05/31/98)

88 **HANNA** Chardonnay Russian River Valley 1996 • $16 • (12/15/97)

88 **HENDRY RANCH** Chardonnay Napa Valley Block 9 1996 • $22 • (05/31/98)

88 **IRON HORSE** Chardonnay Sonoma County Green Valley 1996 • $22 • (07/31/98)

88 **J. LOHR** Chardonnay Monterey Riverstone 1996 • $14 • (06/15/98)

88 **JOSEPH PHELPS** Chardonnay Los Carneros 1996 • $20 • (05/31/98)

88 **JOSEPH SWAN** Chardonnay Russian River Valley Estate 1996 • $25 • (07/31/98)

88 **KENDALL-JACKSON** Chardonnay Arroyo Seco Paradise Vineyard Single Vineyard Series 1996 • $20 • (06/15/98)

88 **KENWOOD** Chardonnay Sonoma County-Santa Maria Valley Reserve 1996 • $22 • (07/31/98)

88 **KORBEL** Chardonnay Russian River Valley Heck Family Cellar Selection 1996 • $15 • (03/31/98)

88 **LAETITIA** Chardonnay San Luis Obispo County Reserve 1996 • $17 • (06/30/98)

88 **LAMBERT BRIDGE** Chardonnay Sonoma County 1996 • $17 • (07/31/98)

88 **LIPARITA** Chardonnay Howell Mountain 1996 • $24 • (05/15/98)

88 **LAURIER** Chardonnay Sonoma County 1996 • $15 • (07/31/98)

88 **M. TRINCHERO** Chardonnay Napa Valley 1996 • $35 • (07/31/98)

88 **MIDNIGHT CELLARS** Chardonnay Central Coast 1996 • $16 • (07/31/98)

88 **MIRASSOU** Chardonnay Monterey County Family Selection 1996 • $12 • (12/31/97)

Key: SS—Spectator Selection CS—Cellar Selection HR—Highly Recommended BB—Best Buy $NA—Price not available Ⓐ—Auction Price
Dates in parentheses indicate the issues in which the ratings were published.

88 **MOROVINO** Chardonnay Santa Barbara County 1996 • $16 • (06/15/98)

88 **NICHOLS** Chardonnay Arroyo Grande Valley Talley Vineyard 1996 • $28 • (07/31/98)

88 **NICHOLS** Chardonnay Central Coast Reserve 1996 • $33 • (02/28/98)

88 **RUTZ** Chardonnay Russian River Valley 1996 • $22 • (06/30/98)

88 **SAINTSBURY** Chardonnay Carneros 1996 • $17 • (05/15/98)

88 **SANFORD** Chardonnay Santa Barbara County 1996 • $18 • (01/31/98)

88 **SEBASTIANI** Chardonnay California 1996 • $12 • (06/15/98)

88 **SEVEN PEAKS** Chardonnay Edna Valley Reserve 1996 • $18 • (06/30/98)

88 **STEVENOT** Chardonnay Sierra Foothills 1996 • $10 • (11/30/97) • BB

88 **SWANSON** Chardonnay Napa Valley Carneros 1996 • $26 • (05/31/98)

88 **WILD HORSE** Chardonnay Central Coast 1996 • $16 • (07/31/98)

88 **ZD WINES** Chardonnay California 1996 • $25 • (07/31/98)

87 **B.R. COHN** Chardonnay Carneros Joseph Herman Vineyard Reserve 1996 • $24 • (05/15/98)

87 **B.R. COHN** Chardonnay Sonoma Valley 1996 • $14 • (07/31/98)

87 **BEAULIEU VINEYARD** Chardonnay California Beautour 1996 • $10 • (02/28/98) • BB

87 **BEAULIEU VINEYARD** Chardonnay Carneros 1996 • $14 • (05/15/98)

87 **BECKMEN** Chardonnay Santa Barbara County 1996 • $16 • (05/15/98)

87 **BELVEDERE** Chardonnay Alexander Valley 1996 • $14 • (05/15/98)

87 **BELVEDERE** Chardonnay Russian River Valley 1996 • $17 • (06/30/98)

87 **BONTERRA** Chardonnay Mendocino County 1996 • $12 • (06/30/98)

87 **CARNEROS CREEK** Chardonnay Carneros 1996 • $16 • (05/15/98)

87 **CASTLE CREEK** Chardonnay California 1996 • $15 • (05/31/98)

87 **CLAIBORNE & CHURCHILL** Chardonnay Edna Valley MacGregor Vineyard 1996 • $18 • (07/31/98)

87 **CLOS DU VAL** Chardonnay Napa Valley Carneros 1996 • $17 • (04/30/98)

87 **CLOS PEGASE** Chardonnay Napa Valley Carneros Mitsuko's Vineyard 1996 • $19 • (07/31/98)

87 **CLOS DU BOIS** Chardonnay Alexander Valley Calcaire Vineyard 1996 • $18 • (04/30/98)

87 **CLOS DU BOIS** Chardonnay Dry Creek Valley Flintwood Vineyards 1996 • $17 • (05/15/98)

87 **COBBLESTONE** Chardonnay Arroyo Seco 1996 • $23 • (01/31/98)

87 **COLBY** Chardonnay Napa Valley 1996 • $14 • (07/31/98)

87 **CONCANNON** Chardonnay Livermore Valley Reserve 1996 • $16 • (07/31/98)

87 **COSENTINO** Chardonnay Napa County 1996 • $18 • (05/15/98)

87 **DE LOACH** Chardonnay Sonoma County Sonoma Cuvée 1996 • $13 • (07/31/98)

87 **DRY CREEK** Chardonnay Sonoma County Reserve 1996 • $20 • (04/30/98)

87 **FIELD STONE** Chardonnay Sonoma County 1996 • $15 • (06/30/98)

87 **FIRESTONE** Chardonnay Santa Ynez Valley 1996 • $13 • (07/31/98)

87 **GEYSER PEAK** Chardonnay Sonoma County 1996 • $14 • (06/15/98)

87 **GUENOC** Chardonnay North Coast 1996 • $16 • (05/15/98)

87 **GUNDLACH BUNDSCHU** Chardonnay Sonoma Valley Carneros Sangiacomo Ranch 1996 • $16 • (07/31/98)

87 **HESS SELECT** Chardonnay California 1996 • $10 • (01/31/98) • BB

87 **J. FRITZ** Chardonnay Russian River Valley Dutton Vineyard Ruxton Ranch 1996 • $26 • (06/30/98)

87 **J. FRITZ** Chardonnay Russian River Valley Poplar Vineyard 1996 • $22 • (06/30/98)

87 **KENWOOD** Chardonnay Sonoma County 1996 • $15 • (06/15/98)

87 **KUNDE** Chardonnay Sonoma Valley 1996 • $15 • (04/30/98)

87 **LAWRENCE J. BARGETTO** Chardonnay Santa Cruz Mountains Regan Vineyard 1996 • $18 • (12/15/97)

87 **MACROSTIE** Chardonnay Carneros 1996 • $18 • (07/31/98)

87 **MARKHAM** Chardonnay Napa Valley 1996 • $16 • (05/15/98)

87 **MAZZOCCO** Chardonnay Sonoma County River Lane 1996 • $15 • (12/15/97)

87 **MERIDIAN** Chardonnay Santa Barbara County 1996 • $11 • (11/15/97)

87 **MONT ST. JOHN** Chardonnay Carneros 1996 • $15 • (07/31/98)

87 **MURPHY-GOODE** Chardonnay Sonoma County 1996 • $15 • (02/28/98)

87 **NICHOLS** Chardonnay Edna Valley Paragon Vineyard 1996 • $28 • (03/31/98)

87 **NICHOLS** Chardonnay Santa Barbara County Bien Nacido Vineyards 1996 • $26 • (03/31/98)

87 **OJAI** Chardonnay Santa Barbara County Bien Nacido Vineyard 1996 • $20 • (12/15/97)

87 **PINE RIDGE** Chardonnay Napa Valley Knollside Cuvée 1996 • $18 • (02/28/98)

87 **RABBIT RIDGE** Chardonnay Sonoma County 1996 • $12 • (05/15/98)

87 **RAVENSWOOD** Chardonnay Sonoma Valley Sangiacomo 1996 • $20 • (07/31/98)

87 **RODNEY STRONG** Chardonnay Chalk Hill Chalk Hill Vineyard 1996 • $16 • (02/28/98)

87 **ROSENBLUM** Chardonnay Edna Valley 1996 • $24 • (12/15/97)

87 **S. ANDERSON** Chardonnay Napa Valley Carneros District 1996 • $22 • (01/31/98)

87 **SADDLEBACK** Chardonnay Napa Valley 1996 • $18 • (12/31/97)

87 **SAN SABA** Chardonnay Monterey 1996 • $20 • (05/31/98)

87 **SANTA CRUZ MOUNTAIN** Chardonnay Santa Cruz Mountains S. Miller Vineyard 1996 • $19 • (07/31/98)

87 **SCHUG** Chardonnay Carneros Heritage Reserve 1996 • $25 • (05/15/98)

87 **SCHUG** Chardonnay North Coast 1996 • $14 • (06/30/98)

87 **SEBASTOPOL** Chardonnay Russian River Valley Dutton Ranch 1996 • $24 • (05/15/98)

87 **SEQUOIA GROVE** Chardonnay Napa Valley Carneros 1996 • $18 • (05/15/98)

87 **SEVEN PEAKS** Chardonnay California 1996 • $12 • (09/30/97)

87 **SOQUEL** Chardonnay Monterey County 1996 • $16 • (06/30/98)

87 **STEPHEN ROSS** Chardonnay Edna Valley Linda's Vineyard 1996 • $18 • (07/31/98)

87 **STERLING** Chardonnay Napa Valley 1996 • $14 • (01/31/98)

87 **STERLING** Chardonnay Napa Valley Diamond Mountain Ranch Vineyard 1996 • $18 • (05/31/98)

87 **SUNSTONE** Chardonnay Santa Barbara County 1996 • $18 • (07/31/98)

87 **UNALII** Chardonnay Sonoma County Hillside Estates 1996 • $14 • (01/31/98)

87 **WHITE OAK** Chardonnay Sonoma County Myers Limited Reserve 1996 • $20 • (05/15/98)

87 **WHITE ROCK** Chardonnay Napa Valley 1996 • $20 • (05/15/98)

87 **WILLIAM HILL** Chardonnay Napa Valley 1996 • $15 • (04/30/98)

87 **WILLIAM HILL** Chardonnay Napa Valley Reserve 1996 • $20 • (06/30/98)

87 **WINDSOR** Chardonnay Russian River Valley Signature Series 1996 • $16 • (06/30/98)

87 **DELORIMIER** Chardonnay Alexander Valley 1996 • $16 • (03/31/98)

86 **ADLER FELS** Chardonnay Sonoma County Coleman Reserve 1996 • $16 • (03/31/98)

86 **ALEXANDER VALLEY VINEYARDS** Chardonnay Alexander Valley Wetzel Family Reserve 1996 • $24 • (05/31/98)

86 **ANAPAMU** Chardonnay Central Coast 1996 • $12 • (06/30/98)

86 **ATLAS PEAK** Chardonnay Atlas Peak 1996 • $16 • (04/30/98)

86 **BANDIERA** Chardonnay California Coastal 1996 • $9 • (07/31/97)

86 **BRAREN PAULI** Chardonnay Mendocino Busch Creek Vineyard 1996 • $13 • (12/15/97)

86 **CHARLES KRUG** Chardonnay Carneros Peter Mondavi Family Reserve 1996 • $20 • (05/15/98)

86 **CHIMNEY ROCK** Chardonnay Carneros 1996 • $17 • (05/31/98)

86 **CONCANNON** Chardonnay Central Coast Selected Vineyard 1996 • $10 • (07/31/98) • BB

86 **DAVID ARTHUR** Chardonnay Napa Valley Reserve 1996 • $28 • (03/31/98)

86 **DE LOACH** Chardonnay Russian River Valley 1996 • $18 • (04/30/98)

86 **DEERFIELD RANCH** Chardonnay North Coast 1996 • $24 • (07/31/98)

86 **DOMAINE SANTA BARBARA** Chardonnay Santa Barbara County Los Olivos Vineyard 1996 • $19 • (07/31/98)

86 **FETZER** Chardonnay Mendocino Barrel Select 1996 • $12 • (03/31/98)

86 **GARY FARRELL** Chardonnay Santa Barbara County Bien Nacido Vineyard 1996 • $22 • (04/30/98)

86 **HARMONY CELLARS** Chardonnay San Luis Obispo 1996 • $14 • (07/31/98)

86 **HAWK CREST** Chardonnay California 1996 • $10 • (01/31/98) • BB

86 **JEKEL** Chardonnay Monterey County Gravelstone 1996 • $15 • (05/31/98)

86 **KEENAN** Chardonnay Napa Valley 1996 • $20 • (07/31/98)

86 **LAKE SONOMA** Chardonnay Russian River Valley 1996 • $15 • (07/31/98)

86 **LAWRENCE J. BARGETTO** Chardonnay Santa Clara & Santa Cruz Counties Coastal Reserve 1996 • $15 • (03/31/98)

86 **LOGAN** Chardonnay Monterey 1996 • $17 • (07/31/98)

86 **MADROÑA** Chardonnay El Dorado 1996 • $12 • (07/31/98)

86 **MARK WEST** Chardonnay Russian River Valley 1996 • $15 • (05/15/98)

86 **MONTEREY PENINSULA** Chardonnay Central Coast 1996 • $13 • (01/31/98)

86 **NAPA RIDGE** Chardonnay North Coast Coastal Vines 1996 • $9 • (05/31/98) • BB

86 **PYRAMIDS** Chardonnay Sonoma County 1996 • $16 • (06/15/98)

86 **R.H. PHILLIPS** Chardonnay Dunnigan Hills Barrel Cuvée 1996 • $8 • (09/15/97) • BB

86 **RAYMOND** Chardonnay Napa Valley Reserve 1996 • $15 • (05/15/98)

86 **RUTZ** Chardonnay Russian River Valley Maison Grand Cru 1996 • $25 • (05/15/98)

86 **SANTA BARBARA WINERY** Chardonnay Santa Barbara County 1996 • $15 • (07/31/98)

86 **STERLING** Chardonnay Napa Valley Carneros Winery Lake Vineyard 1996 • $18 • (05/31/98)

86 **TAFT STREET** Chardonnay Sonoma County 1996 • $10 • (07/31/98) • BB

86 **VENTANA** Chardonnay Monterey Gold Stripe 1996 • $12 • (12/15/97)

86 **WELLINGTON** Chardonnay Sonoma County 1996 • $13 • (06/30/98)

85 **ACACIA** Chardonnay Carneros 1996 • $20 • (05/31/98)

85 **BELVEDERE** Chardonnay Sonoma County 1996 • $11 • (03/31/98)

85 **BUEHLER** Chardonnay Russian River Valley 1996 • $15 • (04/30/98)

85 **COOPER-GARROD** Chardonnay Santa Cruz Mountains 1996 • $20 • (07/31/98)

85 **DOMAINE SANTA BARBARA** Chardonnay Santa Barbara County Bien Nacido Vineyard 1996 • $20 • (07/31/98)

85 **EOS** Chardonnay Paso Robles Astraeus Vineyard 1996 • $15 • (07/31/98)

85 **FROG'S LEAP** Chardonnay Carneros 1996 • $19 • (05/15/98)

85 **INDIGO HILLS** Chardonnay Mendocino County 1996 • $10 • (03/31/98) • BB

85 **LAWRENCE J. BARGETTO** Chardonnay Central Coast Cypress 1996 • $10 • (12/15/97) • BB

85 **LEEWARD** Chardonnay Central Coast 1996 • $11 • (12/15/97)

85 **LOCKWOOD** Chardonnay Monterey 1996 • $16 • (03/31/98)

85 **LOS ENCANTOS** Chardonnay Edna Valley Covenant Reserve 1996 • $16 • (11/30/97)

85 **MAYO** Chardonnay Sonoma Valley 1996 • $17 • (05/15/98)

85 **MILL CREEK** Chardonnay Dry Creek Valley 1996 • $13 • (11/30/97)

85 **NAPA RIDGE** Chardonnay Central Coast Coastal Vines 1996 • $9 • (12/15/97)

85 **RUTHERFORD VINTNERS** Chardonnay Lodi Barrel Select 1996 • $9 • (11/30/97)

85 **ST. FRANCIS** Chardonnay Sonoma County 1996 • $12 • (03/31/98)

85 **STEVENOT** Chardonnay Calaveras County Shaw Ranch 1996 • $20 • (05/31/98)

85 **STRATFORD** Chardonnay California 1996 • $12 • (05/15/98)

85 **VENTANA** Chardonnay Monterey J. Douglas Meador Winegrower's Grand Reserve 1996 • $25 • (05/15/98)

Key: SS—Spectator Selection CS—Cellar Selection HR—Highly Recommended BB—Best Buy $NA—Price not available Ⓐ—Auction Price

Dates in parentheses indicate the issues in which the ratings were published.

1995 CALIFORNIA CHARDONNAY
VINTAGE RATING: 97

95 **KISTLER** Chardonnay Sonoma Coast Camp Meeting Ridge 1995 • $42 • (04/30/98) • HR

95 **MARCASSIN** Chardonnay Carneros Hudson Vineyards E Block 1995 • $45 • (06/30/97) • HR

95 **WILLIAMS SELYEM** Chardonnay Russian River Valley Allen Vineyard 1995 • $42 • (03/31/98)

94 **BERINGER** Chardonnay Napa Valley Private Reserve 1995 • $29 • (04/30/97) • HR

94 **E. & J. GALLO** Chardonnay Northern Sonoma Estate Bottled 1995 • $35 • (02/28/98) • HR

94 **KISTLER** Chardonnay Russian River Valley Vine Hill Vineyard 1995 • $42 • (06/30/98) • HR

94 **MARCASSIN** Chardonnay Alexander Valley Gauer Vineyard Upper Barn 1995 • $45 • (06/15/97)

94 **MATANZAS CREEK** Chardonnay Sonoma Valley 1995 • $30 • (10/15/97) • CS

94 **PATZ & HALL** Chardonnay Mount Veeder Carr Vineyard 1995 • $40 • (05/15/97) • HR

94 **PAUL HOBBS** Chardonnay Sonoma Mountain Richard Dinner Vineyard 1995 • $30 • (05/31/97) • HR

94 **PETER MICHAEL** Chardonnay Napa County Clos du Ciel 1995 • $35 • (05/31/97)

94 **ROCHIOLI** Chardonnay Russian River Valley Allen Vineyard Reserve 1995 • $35 • (05/31/97)

94 **ROCHIOLI** Chardonnay Russian River Valley South River Vineyard Reserve 1995 • $40 • (11/15/97)

93 **ARROWOOD** Chardonnay Sonoma County Cuvée Michel Berthoud Réserve Spéciale 1995 • $33 • (09/30/97) • HR

93 **BEAULIEU VINEYARD** Chardonnay Carneros Reserve 1995 • $20 • (05/31/97) • SS

93 **BERINGER** Chardonnay Napa Valley Sbragia Limited Release 1995 • $35 • (06/15/98)

93 **BYINGTON** Chardonnay Santa Cruz Mountains 1995 • $20 • (06/15/97)

93 **CHALK HILL** Chardonnay Chalk Hill 1995 • $24 • (05/31/97) • SS

93 **CUVAISON** Chardonnay Napa Valley Carneros ATS Selection 1995 • $43 • (04/30/98)

93 **DEHLINGER** Chardonnay Russian River Valley 1995 • $18 • (05/31/97)

93 **FERRARI-CARANO** Chardonnay Napa & Sonoma Counties Reserve 1995 • $34 • (05/15/98) • HR

93 **FLORA SPRINGS** Chardonnay Napa Valley Reserve 1995 • $20 • (04/30/97)

93 **GAINEY** Chardonnay Santa Ynez Valley Limited Selection 1995 • $25 • (06/15/97)

93 **GUENOC** Chardonnay Guenoc Valley Genevieve Magoon Vineyard Unfiltered Reserve 1995 • $30 • (05/31/97)

93 **KISTLER** Chardonnay Sonoma Mountain McCrea Vineyard 1995 • $42 • (03/31/98) • CS

93 **KISTLER** Chardonnay Sonoma Valley Durell Vineyard 1995 • $40 • (03/31/98) • CS

93 **LEWIS CELLARS** Chardonnay Napa Valley Reserve 1995 • $30 • (06/15/97)

93 **MARTINELLI** Chardonnay Russian River Valley Gold Ridge 1995 • $20 • (05/31/97)

93 **MERRYVALE** Chardonnay Napa Valley Reserve 1995 • $25 • (06/15/97)

93 **MERRYVALE** Chardonnay Napa Valley Starmont 1995 • $18 • (06/15/97) • SS

93 **NEWTON** Chardonnay Napa-Sonoma Counties 1995 • $20 • (05/15/97) • SS

93 **OAKVILLE RANCH** Chardonnay Napa Valley Vista Vineyard 1995 • $22 • (05/31/97)

93 **PATZ & HALL** Chardonnay Napa Valley 1995 • $27 • (12/31/96) • HR
93 **PAUL HOBBS** Chardonnay Sonoma Mountain Kunde Vineyard 1995 • $28 • (05/31/97)
93 **RIDGE** Chardonnay Santa Cruz Mountains Monte Bello Ridge Vineyards 1995 • $23 • (05/31/97)
93 **ROCHIOLI** Chardonnay Russian River Valley Estate Cuvée Reserve 1995 • $30 • (05/31/97)
93 **SAINTSBURY** Chardonnay Carneros Reserve 1995 • $30 • (05/31/97)
93 **SIGNORELLO** Chardonnay Napa Valley Hope's Cuvée 1995 • $60 • (06/15/97)
93 **SIMI** Chardonnay Sonoma County Reserve 1995 • $29 • (07/31/98)
93 **STAG'S LEAP WINE CELLARS** Chardonnay Napa Valley Reserve 1995 • $35 • (05/31/97)
93 **STEELE** Chardonnay Carneros Sangiacomo Vineyard 1995 • $22 • (05/15/97)
93 **TALBOTT** Chardonnay Monterey Sleepy Hollow Vineyard 1995 • $30 • (06/30/98) • SS
93 **TALLEY** Chardonnay Arroyo Grande Valley Rosemary's Vineyard 1995 • $30 • (05/31/97)
93 **VINE CLIFF** Chardonnay Napa Valley 1995 • $23 • (04/30/97)
92 **ARROWOOD** Chardonnay Sonoma County 1995 • $22 • (05/31/97)
92 **AU BON CLIMAT** Chardonnay Santa Barbara County Le Bouge Bien Nacido Vineyard 1995 • $25 • (07/31/97)
92 **BYRON** Chardonnay Santa Maria Valley Estate 1995 • $32 • (07/31/98)
92 **CARMENET** Chardonnay Sonoma Valley Carneros Sangiacomo Vineyard 1995 • $17 • (05/31/97)
92 **CHATEAU POTELLE** Chardonnay Mount Veeder V.G.S. 1995 • $35 • (06/30/98)
92 **CHATEAU ST. JEAN** Chardonnay Alexander Valley Belle Terre Vineyard 1995 • $22 • (05/31/97)
92 **CLOS LACHANCE** Chardonnay Santa Cruz Mountains 1995 • $19 • (06/15/97)
92 **DE LOACH** Chardonnay Russian River Valley O.F.S. 1995 • $25 • (02/28/97)
92 **FAR NIENTE** Chardonnay Napa Valley 1995 • $36 • (02/28/97)
92 **FERRARI-CARANO** Chardonnay Alexander Valley 1995 • $21 • (05/31/97) • SS
92 **FERRARI-CARANO** Chardonnay Alexander Valley Tre Terre 1995 • $26 • (09/30/97)
92 **FLORA SPRINGS** Chardonnay Carneros 1995 • $24 • (04/30/97)
92 **GARY FARRELL** Chardonnay Russian River Valley Allen Vineyard 1995 • $22 • (05/31/97)
92 **GRGICH HILLS** Chardonnay Napa Valley 1995 • $28 • (05/31/97) • HR
92 **GUENOC** Chardonnay Guenoc Valley Genevieve Magoon Vineyard Reserve 1995 • $23 • (05/31/97)
92 **HANZELL** Chardonnay Sonoma Valley 1995 • $30 • (01/31/98) • CS
92 **IRON HORSE** Chardonnay Sonoma County Green Valley Cuvée Joy 1995 • $50 • (05/31/97)
92 **KENT RASMUSSEN** Chardonnay Napa Valley 1995 • $21 • (06/15/97)
92 **KENWOOD** Chardonnay Santa Maria-Sonoma Reserve 1995 • $20 • (05/31/97)
92 **KISTLER** Chardonnay Sonoma Coast 1995 • $31 • (05/15/97)
92 **KISTLER** Chardonnay Carneros Hudson Vineyard 1995 • $48 • (06/30/98)
92 **LANDMARK** Chardonnay Sonoma Valley Damaris Reserve 1995 • $28 • (03/31/97) • HR
92 **MARCASSIN** Chardonnay Sonoma Coast Lorenzo Vineyard 1995 • $45 • (06/15/97)
92 **MARKHAM** Chardonnay Napa Valley Reserve 1995 • $28 • (08/31/97)
92 **MUELLER** Chardonnay Russian River Valley 1995 • $15 • (06/30/97) • HR
92 **NICHOLS** Chardonnay Arroyo Grande Valley Talley Vineyards 1995 • $28 • (05/15/97)
92 **PAHLMEYER** Chardonnay Napa Valley 1995 • $40 • (05/31/97)
92 **PINE RIDGE** Chardonnay Stags Leap District 1995 • $30 • (03/31/98)
92 **ROBERT MONDAVI** Chardonnay Carneros 1995 • $23 • (05/31/97)
92 **S. ANDERSON** Chardonnay Napa Valley Proprietor's Reserve 1995 • $30 • (05/31/97)
92 **SAINTSBURY** Chardonnay Carneros 1995 • $17 • (05/31/97) • SS
92 **SIGNORELLO** Chardonnay Napa Valley 1995 • $28 • (06/15/97)
92 **SIGNORELLO** Chardonnay Napa Valley Founder's Reserve 1995 • $44 • (06/15/97)
92 **SONOMA-LOEB** Chardonnay Sonoma County Private Reserve 1995 • $30 • (05/31/97)
92 **STAG'S LEAP WINE CELLARS** Chardonnay Napa Valley Beckstoffer Ranch 1995 • $28 • (10/15/97)
92 **STEELE** Chardonnay Mendocino DuPratt Vineyard 1995 • $25 • (05/15/97)
92 **STEELE** Chardonnay Santa Barbara County Bien Nacido Vineyard 1995 • $25 • (05/31/97)
92 **STEELE** Chardonnay Santa Barbara County Goodchild Vineyard 1995 • $24 • (09/30/97)
92 **STEELE** Chardonnay Sonoma Valley Durell Vineyard 1995 • $24 • (08/31/97)
92 **TALBOTT** Chardonnay Monterey Cuvée Cynthia 1995 • $45 • (06/30/98)
92 **TESTAROSSA** Chardonnay California George Troquato Signature Reserve 1995 • $38 • (03/31/98)
92 **TESTAROSSA** Chardonnay Santa Barbara County Bien Nacido Vineyard 1995 • $27 • (03/31/98)
92 **VILLA MT. EDEN** Chardonnay California Grand Reserve 1995 • $18 • (08/31/97)
92 **VILLA MT. EDEN** Chardonnay Santa Maria Valley Signature Series Bien Nacido Vineyards 1995 • $35 • (01/01/98)
92 **VINE CLIFF** Chardonnay Napa Valley Proprietress Reserve 1995 • $34 • (11/15/97)
91 **ANDERSON'S CONN VALLEY** Chardonnay Napa Valley Feurnier Vineyard 1995 • $40 • (04/30/98)
91 **AU BON CLIMAT** Chardonnay Santa Ynez Valley Sanford & Benedict Reserve 1995 • $35 • (11/15/97)
91 **B.R. COHN** Chardonnay Carneros Joseph Herman Vineyard Reserve 1995 • $24 • (03/31/97)
91 **BANNISTER** Chardonnay Russian River Valley Porter-Bass Vineyard 1995 • $20 • (06/15/97)
91 **BELVEDERE** Chardonnay Russian River Valley 1995 • $15 • (06/15/97)
91 **BENZIGER** Chardonnay Carneros Reserve 1995 • $22 • (05/15/97)
91 **BUEHLER** Chardonnay Russian River Valley Reserve 1995 • $25 • (06/15/97)
91 **BYINGTON** Chardonnay Santa Cruz Mountains Dirk Vineyard Special Reserve Vineyards 1995 • $24 • (06/15/97)
91 **CALERA** Chardonnay Central Coast 1995 • $16 • (12/15/96) • SS
91 **CAMBRIA** Chardonnay Santa Maria Valley Katherine's Vineyard 1995 • $20 • (05/31/97)

91 **CANEPA** Chardonnay Alexander Valley Gauer Vineyard Adobe III 1995 • $24 • (06/15/97)

91 **CHALONE** Chardonnay Chalone 1995 • $27 • (05/31/97)

91 **CHATEAU ST. JEAN** Chardonnay Alexander Valley Robert Young Vineyard 1995 • $24 • (11/30/97)

91 **CHATEAU SOUVERAIN** Chardonnay Russian River Valley Winemaker's Reserve 1995 • $20 • (05/31/97)

91 **CLOS DU VAL** Chardonnay Napa Valley Carneros Reserve 1995 • $24 • (06/15/97)

91 **COSENTINO** Chardonnay Napa Valley The Sculptor Reserve 1995 • $26 • (05/15/97)

91 **CRONIN** Chardonnay Alexander Valley Stuhlmuller Vineyard 1995 • $18 • (05/15/98)

91 **DRY CREEK** Chardonnay Sonoma County Reserve 1995 • $20 • (06/15/97)

91 **EL MOLINO** Chardonnay Napa Valley 1995 • $38 • (05/31/97)

91 **ESTANCIA** Chardonnay Monterey Reserve 1995 • $20 • (05/15/97)

91 **FLOWERS** Chardonnay Sonoma Coast Camp Meeting Ridge Vineyard 1995 • $36 • (04/30/98)

91 **FORMAN** Chardonnay Napa Valley 1995 • $28 • (02/28/97)

91 **FRANCISCAN OAKVILLE ESTATE** Chardonnay Napa Valley Cuvée Sauvage 1995 • $30 • (01/31/98)

91 **GALLO OF SONOMA** Chardonnay Dry Creek Valley Stefani Vineyard 1995 • $14 • (05/15/97) • SS

91 **GARY FARRELL** Chardonnay Santa Barbara County Bien Nacido Vineyard 1995 • $22 • (05/15/97)

91 **GIRARD** Chardonnay Napa Valley 1995 • $25 • (05/31/97)

91 **GIRARD** Chardonnay Napa Valley Reserve 1995 • $40 • (05/31/97)

91 **KENDALL-JACKSON** Chardonnay California Grand Reserve 1995 • $26 • (05/15/97)

91 **KENDALL-JACKSON** Chardonnay Santa Maria Valley Camelot Vineyard 1995 • $18 • (02/28/97)

91 **KENDALL-JACKSON** Chardonnay Santa Maria Valley Camelot Vineyard Single Vineyard Series 1995 • $18 • (02/28/97)

91 **KISTLER** Chardonnay Russian River Valley Dutton Ranch 1995 • $42 • (07/31/98)

91 **LANDMARK** Chardonnay Sonoma County Overlook 1995 • $18 • (03/31/97) • SS

91 **LOCKWOOD** Chardonnay Monterey 1995 • $15 • (02/28/97) • SS

91 **LONG** Chardonnay Napa Valley 1995 • $31 • (05/31/97)

91 **MACROSTIE** Chardonnay Carneros 1995 • $18 • (06/15/97) • SS

91 **MARTINELLI** Chardonnay Sonoma Coast Charles Ranch 1995 • $25 • (02/28/98)

91 **MER SOLEIL** Chardonnay Central Coast 1995 • $36 • (01/31/98)

91 **MERIDIAN** Chardonnay Santa Barbara County Limited Release 1995 • $25 • (05/31/97)

91 **MIRASSOU** Chardonnay Monterey Showcase 1995 • $25 • (06/30/97)

91 **MOUNT EDEN** Chardonnay Santa Cruz Mountains 1995 • $38 • (09/30/97)

Key: SS—Spectator Selection CS—Cellar Selection HR—Highly Recommended BB—Best Buy $NA—Price not available Ⓐ—Auction Price

Dates in parentheses indicate the issues in which the ratings were published.

91 **MURPHY-GOODE** Chardonnay Russian River Valley J & K Murphy Vineyard Reserve 1995 • $24 • (06/15/97)

91 **NAPA RIDGE** Chardonnay Napa Valley Reserve 1995 • $15 • (01/31/98)

91 **NEWTON** Chardonnay Napa Valley Unfiltered 1995 • $NA • (01/31/98)

91 **OAKVILLE RANCH** Chardonnay Napa Valley ORV 1995 • $30 • (05/31/97)

91 **PATZ & HALL** Chardonnay Russian River Valley 1995 • $27 • (12/31/96)

91 **RABBIT RIDGE** Chardonnay Sonoma County Winemaker's Grand Reserve 1995 • $30 • (03/31/98)

91 **RAYMOND** Chardonnay Napa Valley Generations 1995 • $25 • (05/31/97)

91 **ROMBAUER** Chardonnay Carneros 1995 • $24 • (02/28/97) • SS

91 **S. ANDERSON** Chardonnay Napa Valley Carneros 1995 • $20 • (05/31/97)

91 **SANFORD** Chardonnay Santa Barbara County 1995 • $18 • (05/31/97)

91 **SANFORD** Chardonnay Santa Barbara County Barrel Select 1995 • $30 • (01/31/98)

91 **SEAVEY** Chardonnay Napa Valley 1995 • $18 • (06/15/97)

91 **SHAFER** Chardonnay Napa Valley Carneros Red Shoulder Ranch 1995 • $30 • (05/31/97)

91 **STEELE** Chardonnay California Steele Cuvée 1995 • $18 • (05/15/97)

91 **STEELE** Chardonnay Mendocino Lolonis Vineyard 1995 • $26 • (08/31/97)

91 **STONESTREET** Chardonnay Sonoma County 1995 • $25 • (05/31/97)

91 **TALBOTT** Chardonnay Monterey Diamond T Estate 1995 • $45 • (07/31/98)

91 **TALLEY** Chardonnay Arroyo Grande Valley 1995 • $20 • (05/31/97)

91 **TESTAROSSA** Chardonnay Chalone 1995 • $28 • (03/31/98)

91 **THE HESS COLLECTION** Chardonnay Napa Valley 1995 • $16 • (06/30/97)

91 **TRUCHARD** Chardonnay Napa Valley Carneros 1995 • $22 • (05/15/97)

91 **VENEZIA** Chardonnay Alexander Valley Beaterra Vineyard 1995 • $20 • (09/30/97)

91 **VENEZIA** Chardonnay Napa Valley Regusci Vineyard 1995 • $20 • (04/30/97)

91 **WHITCRAFT** Chardonnay Santa Maria Valley 1995 • $22 • (05/31/97)

91 **WHITCRAFT** Chardonnay Santa Ynez Valley Sanford & Benedict Vineyard 1995 • $35 • (05/31/97)

90 **ACACIA** Chardonnay Carneros 1995 • $19 • (05/31/97)

90 **ACACIA** Chardonnay Carneros Reserve 1995 • $30 • (07/31/98)

90 **AU BON CLIMAT** Chardonnay Santa Barbara County 1995 • $18 • (11/30/96)

90 **BABCOCK** Chardonnay Santa Ynez Valley Grand Cuvee 1995 • $35 • (05/31/97)

90 **BANNISTER** Chardonnay Russian River Valley Allen Vineyard 1995 • $22 • (06/15/97)

90 **BELVEDERE** Chardonnay Sonoma County Preferred Stock 1995 • $21 • (05/15/98)

90 **BERNARDUS** Chardonnay Monterey County 1995 • $17 • (05/31/97)

90 **BYRON** Chardonnay Santa Barbara County 1995 • $17 • (05/31/97)

90 **CAKEBREAD** Chardonnay Napa Valley 1995 • $23 • (06/15/97)

90 **CALE** Chardonnay Carneros Sangiacomo Vineyard 1995 • $20 • (02/28/97)

90 **CALERA** Chardonnay Mount Harlan Twentieth Anniversary Vintage 1995 • $30 • (03/31/98)

90 **CHATEAU MONTELENA** Chardonnay Napa Valley 1995 • $25 • (06/30/98)

90 **CHIMNEY ROCK** Chardonnay Carneros 1995 • $17 • (05/31/97)

90 **CLOS DU VAL** Chardonnay Napa Valley Carneros 1995 • $16 • (04/30/97) • HR

90 **CLOS PEGASE** Chardonnay Napa Valley Carneros Mitsuko's Vineyard 1995 • $19 • (05/31/97)

90 **CRONIN** Chardonnay Santa Cruz Mountains 1995 • $20 • (05/15/98)

90 **CUVAISON** Chardonnay Napa Valley Carneros Reserve 1995 • $28 • (05/15/98)

90 **DE LOACH** Chardonnay Russian River Valley 1995 • $16 • (06/15/97) • SS

90 **DRY CREEK** Chardonnay Sonoma County 1995 • $15 • (05/15/97) • SS

90 **FIRESTONE** Chardonnay Santa Ynez Valley 1995 • $13 • (06/15/97)

90 **FISHER** Chardonnay Sonoma County Coach Insignia 1995 • $18 • (05/31/97)

90 **GALLO OF SONOMA** Chardonnay Russian River Valley Laguna Ranch Vineyard 1995 • $16 • (09/30/97) • SS

90 **GEYSER PEAK** Chardonnay Alexander Valley Reserve 1995 • $23 • (05/31/97)

90 **GLORIA FERRER** Chardonnay Carneros 1995 • $17 • (06/15/97)

90 **HARRISON** Chardonnay Napa Valley 1995 • $30 • (05/15/97)

90 **J. LOHR** Chardonnay Monterey Riverstone 1995 • $14 • (04/30/97) • SS

90 **JOSEPH PHELPS** Chardonnay Los Carneros 1995 • $19 • (05/15/97)

90 **LA CREMA** Chardonnay Sonoma Coast 1995 • $20 • (06/15/97)

90 **LAETITIA** Chardonnay San Luis Obispo County Laetitia Vineyard 1995 • $25 • (10/15/97)

90 **LAMBERT BRIDGE** Chardonnay Sonoma County 1995 • $16 • (06/15/97)

90 **LITTORAI** Chardonnay Sonoma Coast Occidental 1995 • $30 • (12/31/97)

90 **LOCKWOOD** Chardonnay Monterey Partners' Reserve 1995 • $21 • (05/31/97)

90 **MACROSTIE** Chardonnay Carneros Reserve 1995 • $25 • (07/31/98)

90 **MARIMAR TORRES** Chardonnay Sonoma County Green Valley Don Miguel Vineyard 1995 • $22 • (10/15/97) • SS

90 **MARK WEST** Chardonnay Russian River Valley Reserve 1995 • $20 • (06/15/97)

90 **MERIDIAN** Chardonnay Edna Valley Reserve 1995 • $15 • (05/15/97)

90 **MIRASSOU** Chardonnay Monterey County 1995 • $12 • (05/15/97)

90 **MIRASSOU** Chardonnay Monterey County Harvest Reserve Limited Bottling 1995 • $16 • (05/15/97)

90 **MORGAN** Chardonnay Monterey 1995 • $18 • (05/31/97)

90 **MUELLER** Chardonnay Alexander Valley Gauer Ranch 1995 • $18 • (08/31/97)

90 **NEYERS** Chardonnay Carneros 1995 • $22 • (11/30/96)

90 **NEYERS** Chardonnay Sonoma Coast Thieriot Vineyard 1995 • $30 • (12/15/96)

90 **PEJU** Chardonnay Napa Valley 1995 • $16 • (05/15/97)

90 **PEZZI KING** Chardonnay Sonoma County 1995 • $20 • (12/31/97)

90 **RAYMOND** Chardonnay Napa Valley Reserve 1995 • $14 • (06/15/97)

90 **ROBERT MONDAVI** Chardonnay Napa Valley Reserve 1995 • $31 • (11/30/97)

90 **ROSENBLUM** Chardonnay Edna Valley 1995 • $16 • (06/30/97)

90 **ST. CLEMENT** Chardonnay Napa Valley Carneros Abbott's Vineyard 1995 • $20 • (06/15/97)

90 **SCHUG** Chardonnay Carneros Heritage Reserve 1995 • $25 • (04/30/98)

90 **SEBASTIANI** Chardonnay Russian River Valley Dutton Ranch 1995 • $25 • (05/31/97)

90 **SEBASTOPOL** Chardonnay Russian River Valley Dutton Ranch 1995 • $18 • (01/31/98)

90 **SELBY** Chardonnay Sonoma County 1995 • $20 • (06/15/97)

90 **SIMI** Chardonnay Sonoma County 1995 • $18 • (05/31/97)

90 **SOLITUDE** Chardonnay Carneros Sangiacomo Vineyard 1995 • $20 • (12/15/96) • SS

90 **SONOMA-CUTRER** Chardonnay Russian River Valley Russian River Ranches 1995 • $16 • (04/30/97)

90 **SONOMA-CUTRER** Chardonnay Sonoma Coast Cutrer Vineyard 1995 • $28 • (03/31/98)

90 **SONOMA-CUTRER** Chardonnay Sonoma Coast Russian River Ranches 1995 • $16 • (04/30/97)

90 **STAG'S LEAP WINE CELLARS** Chardonnay Napa Valley 1995 • $24 • (05/15/97)

90 **STEELE** Chardonnay Mendocino Dennison Vineyard 1995 • $22 • (08/31/97)

89 **ALDERBROOK** Chardonnay Dry Creek Valley 1995 • $12 • (05/15/97)

89 **ALDERBROOK** Chardonnay Dry Creek Valley Dorothy's Vineyard 1995 • $20 • (03/31/98)

89 **AU BON CLIMAT** Chardonnay Arroyo Grande Valley Talley Reserve 1995 • $30 • (07/31/97)

89 **BABCOCK** Chardonnay Santa Barbara County One Ton Per Acre 1995 • $20 • (06/15/97)

89 **BEARBOAT** Chardonnay Russian River Valley 1995 • $18 • (05/15/97)

89 **BERINGER** Chardonnay Napa Valley 1995 • $15 • (01/31/97)

89 **B.R. COHN** Chardonnay Sonoma Valley 1995 • $14 • (04/30/97)

89 **BUENA VISTA** Chardonnay Carneros Grand Reserve 1995 • $24 • (12/15/97)

89 **CHAPPELLET** Chardonnay Napa Valley 1995 • $14 • (06/15/97)

89 **CHATEAU SOUVERAIN** Chardonnay Sonoma County 1995 • $13 • (04/30/97)

89 **CINNABAR** Chardonnay Santa Cruz Mountains Saratoga Vineyard 1995 • $23 • (02/28/97)

89 **CLOS DU BOIS** Chardonnay Alexander Valley Calcaire Vineyard 1995 • $18 • (07/31/97)

89 **CONCANNON** Chardonnay Livermore Valley Reserve 1995 • $15 • (07/31/97)

89 **CUVAISON** Chardonnay Napa Valley Carneros 1995 • $16 • (12/31/96) • SS

89 **DE LOACH** Chardonnay Russian River Valley Sonoma Cuvée 1995 • $12 • (06/15/97)

89 **EDNA VALLEY** Chardonnay Edna Valley Paragon 1995 • $17 • (06/30/97) • SS

89 **FISHER** Chardonnay Sonoma County Whitney's Vineyard 1995 • $26 • (06/15/97)

89 **FRANCISCAN** Chardonnay Napa Valley 1995 • $16 • (07/31/97)

89 **GUENOC** Chardonnay Guenoc Valley 1995 • $15 • (06/15/97)

89 **HART'S DESIRE** Chardonnay Edna Valley MacGregor Vineyard 1995 • $15 • (09/30/97)

89 **LAWRENCE J. BARGETTO** Chardonnay Santa Cruz Mountains 1995 • $18 • (04/30/97)

89 **LIPARITA** Chardonnay Howell Mountain 1995 • $22 • (05/15/97)

89 **MAZZOCCO** Chardonnay Sonoma County River Lane 1995 • $15 • (05/15/97)

89 **MORGAN** Chardonnay Monterey Reserve 1995 • $26 • (03/31/98)

89 **MOUNT EDEN** Chardonnay Edna Valley MacGregor Vineyard 1995 • $16 • (06/30/97)

89 **NAVARRO** Chardonnay Mendocino 1995 • $12 • (06/15/97)

89 **OJAI** Chardonnay Arroyo Grande Valley 1995 • $16 • (06/30/97)

89 **OPTIMA** Chardonnay Carneros 1995 • $28 • (06/15/97)

89 **PINE RIDGE** Chardonnay Napa Valley Knollside Cuvée 1995 • $17 • (06/15/97)

89 **PRIDE** Chardonnay Napa Valley 1995 • $18 • (07/31/97)

89 **RABBIT RIDGE** Chardonnay Carneros Sangiacomo Vineyard Reserve 1995 • $18 • (12/15/96)

89 **RAYMOND** Chardonnay Monterey Estates 1995 • $12 • (06/15/97)

89 **RUTZ** Chardonnay Russian River Valley Dutton Ranch 1995 • $30 • (01/01/98)

89 **SANTA BARBARA WINERY** Chardonnay Santa Barbara County 1995 • $14 • (06/30/97)

89 **SILVERADO VINEYARDS** Chardonnay Napa Valley 1995 • $18 • (04/30/97)

89 **SONOMA-CUTRER** Chardonnay Sonoma Coast Les Pierres 1995 • $28 • (03/31/98)

89 **SONOMA-LOEB** Chardonnay Sonoma County 1995 • $20 • (12/15/96)

89 **SWANSON** Chardonnay Napa Valley Carneros 1995 • $24 • (04/30/97)

89 **THOMAS FOGARTY** Chardonnay Santa Cruz Mountains Estate Reserve 1995 • $28 • (12/31/97)

89 **WENTE** Chardonnay Livermore Valley Herman Wente Reserve 1995 • $23 • (04/30/98)

89 **WHITE ROCK** Chardonnay Napa Valley 1995 • $19 • (05/15/97)

89 **WILLIAM HILL** Chardonnay Napa Valley Reserve 1995 • $18 • (06/15/97)

88 **ADELAIDA** Chardonnay San Luis Obispo County 1995 • $20 • (07/31/98)

88 **BELVEDERE** Chardonnay Sonoma County 1995 • $10 • (04/30/97) • BB

88 **BENZIGER** Chardonnay Carneros 1995 • $14 • (04/30/97)

88 **BRUTOCAO** Chardonnay Mendocino Bliss Vineyard 1995 • $12 • (12/15/97)

88 **BYINGTON** Chardonnay Napa Valley Twin Mountains 1995 • $15 • (06/15/97)

88 **CAMBRIA** Chardonnay Santa Maria Valley Reserve 1995 • $36 • (04/30/98)

88 **CARNEROS BIGHORN RANCH** Chardonnay Napa Valley Carneros Reserve 1995 • $18 • (05/15/97)

Key: SS—Spectator Selection CS—Cellar Selection HR—Highly Recommended BB—Best Buy $NA—Price not available Ⓐ—Auction Price
Dates in parentheses indicate the issues in which the ratings were published.

88 **CHASSEUR** Chardonnay Russian River Valley Dutton 1995 • $28 • (04/30/98)

88 **CHATEAU JULIEN** Chardonnay Monterey County Private Reserve 1995 • $20 • (07/31/97)

88 **CHATEAU POTELLE** Chardonnay Central Coast 1995 • $16 • (07/31/98)

88 **CHATEAU WOLTNER** Chardonnay Howell Mountain Frederique Vineyard 1995 • $40 • (12/31/97)

88 **CHATEAU WOLTNER** Chardonnay Howell Mountain Titus Vineyard 1995 • $40 • (12/31/97)

88 **CLOS DU BOIS** Chardonnay Dry Creek Valley Flintwood Vineyard 1995 • $17 • (07/31/97)

88 **CLOS DU BOIS** Chardonnay Sonoma County 1995 • $13 • (07/31/97)

88 **COBBLESTONE** Chardonnay Monterey County 1995 • $17 • (06/15/97)

88 **CRONIN** Chardonnay Monterey County 1995 • $16 • (05/15/98)

88 **CURTIS** Chardonnay Santa Barbara County 1995 • $17 • (07/31/97)

88 **EDMEADES** Chardonnay Anderson Valley 1995 • $18 • (06/15/98)

88 **FESS PARKER** Chardonnay Santa Barbara County American Tradition Reserve 1995 • $22 • (07/31/97)

88 **FETZER** Chardonnay Mendocino County Barrel Select 1995 • $11 • (04/30/97)

88 **FETZER** Chardonnay Sonoma County Carneros Sangiacomo Vineyard 1995 • $17 • (04/30/97)

88 **FLORA SPRINGS** Chardonnay Napa Valley 1995 • $13 • (04/30/97)

88 **FOREST HILL** Chardonnay Napa Valley Private Reserve 1995 • $30 • (04/30/98)

88 **FROG'S LEAP** Chardonnay Carneros 1995 • $19 • (06/15/97)

88 **GREENWOOD RIDGE** Chardonnay Anderson Valley Du Pratt Vineyard 1995 • $20 • (02/28/97)

88 **GROTH** Chardonnay Napa Valley 1995 • $15 • (05/15/97)

88 **HARMONY CELLARS** Chardonnay San Luis Obispo County 1995 • $13 • (01/31/98)

88 **IVÁN TAMÁS** Chardonnay Central Coast Reserve 1995 • $14 • (07/31/98)

88 **JORDAN** Chardonnay Sonoma County 1995 • $24 • (05/15/98)

88 **KUNDE** Chardonnay Sonoma Valley Kinneybrook 1995 • $20 • (03/31/98)

88 **KYNSI** Chardonnay Santa Ynez Valley Sanford & Benedict Vineyard 1995 • $25 • (03/31/98)

88 **LA CREMA** Chardonnay Sonoma Coast Reserve 1995 • $26 • (12/15/97)

88 **LAURIER** Chardonnay Sonoma County 1995 • $15 • (03/31/98)

88 **LOUIS M. MARTINI** Chardonnay Russian River Valley Reserve 1995 • $18 • (06/15/97)

88 **MARCELINA** Chardonnay Napa Valley 1995 • $18 • (12/15/97)

88 **MARKHAM** Chardonnay Napa Valley 1995 • $15 • (12/31/96)

88 **MARTIN RAY** Chardonnay California Mariage 1995 • $28 • (07/31/97)

88 **MAYO** Chardonnay Sonoma Valley 1995 • $15 • (06/15/97)

88 **MAYO** Chardonnay Sonoma Valley Barrel Select 1995 • $20 • (06/15/97)

88 **MERIDIAN** Chardonnay Santa Barbara County 1995 • $11 • (01/31/97) • HR

88 **MONTICELLO** Chardonnay Napa Valley Corley Estate Reserve 1995 • $26 • (07/31/98)

88 **MURPHY-GOODE** Chardonnay Alexander Valley Island Block Reserve 1995 • $24 • (06/15/97)
88 **NAVARRO** Chardonnay Anderson Valley Première Reserve 1995 • $16 • (06/15/97)
88 **OLIVET LANE** Chardonnay Russian River Valley 1995 • $14 • (03/31/97)
88 **PARAISO SPRINGS** Chardonnay Santa Lucia Highlands 1995 • $13 • (07/31/97)
88 **PEJU** Chardonnay Napa Valley HB Vineyard 1995 • $24 • (05/15/97)
88 **R.H. PHILLIPS** Chardonnay Dunnigan Hills Toasted Head 1995 • $12 • (06/15/97)
88 **RANCHO SISQUOC** Chardonnay Santa Maria Valley 1995 • $15 • (09/30/97)
88 **ROBERT MONDAVI** Chardonnay Napa Valley 1995 • $17 • (04/30/97)
88 **ROCHIOLI** Chardonnay Russian River Valley 1995 • $18 • (12/31/96)
88 **RODNEY STRONG** Chardonnay Chalk Hill Chalk Hill Vineyard 1995 • $15 • (04/30/97)
88 **ST. FRANCIS** Chardonnay Sonoma Valley Reserve 1995 • $20 • (01/31/97)
88 **SANTA BARBARA WINERY** Chardonnay Santa Barbara County Reserve 1995 • $23 • (07/31/97)
88 **SANTA CRUZ MOUNTAIN** Chardonnay Santa Cruz Mountains S. Miller Vineyard 1995 • $18 • (07/31/97)
88 **SCHUG** Chardonnay Carneros 1995 • $18 • (04/30/98)
88 **SEBASTIANI** Chardonnay Sonoma County 1995 • $10 • (04/30/97) • BB
88 **SEQUOIA GROVE** Chardonnay Napa Valley Carneros 1995 • $14 • (05/15/97)
88 **SEQUOIA GROVE** Chardonnay Rutherford Estate Reserve 1995 • $18 • (06/15/97)
88 **SILVERADO VINEYARDS** Chardonnay Napa Valley Limited Reserve 1995 • $36 • (03/31/98)
88 **STERLING** Chardonnay Napa Valley Carneros Winery Lake Vineyard 1995 • $18 • (01/31/97)
88 **STONEHEDGE** Chardonnay Napa Valley 1995 • $13 • (12/31/96)
88 **STONESTREET** Chardonnay Alexander Valley Upper Barn Block Alexander Mountain Estate 1995 • $30 • (12/15/97)
88 **STORRS** Chardonnay Santa Cruz Mountains Meyley Vineyard 1995 • $20 • (03/31/98)
88 **TESTAROSSA** Chardonnay Chalone Michaud Vineyard Reserve 1995 • $38 • (03/31/98)
88 **VILLA MT. EDEN** Chardonnay California 1995 • $9 • (02/28/97) • BB
88 **WHITEHALL LANE** Chardonnay Napa Valley 1995 • $15 • (08/31/97)
88 **DELORIMIER** Chardonnay Alexander Valley 1995 • $16 • (05/15/97)
87 **ANAPAMU** Chardonnay Central Coast 1995 • $10 • (06/15/97) • BB
87 **ATLAS PEAK** Chardonnay Atlas Peak 1995 • $16 • (03/31/97)
87 **AU BON CLIMAT** Chardonnay Edna Valley Alban Vineyard 1995 • $20 • (11/30/96)
87 **BELVEDERE** Chardonnay Alexander Valley 1995 • $12 • (06/15/97)
87 **BONTERRA** Chardonnay Mendocino County 1995 • $12 • (02/28/97)
87 **CHARLES KRUG** Chardonnay Carneros Peter Mondavi Family Reserve 1995 • $20 • (06/15/97)
87 **CHATEAU JULIEN** Chardonnay Monterey County Grand Reserve 1995 • $8 • (06/15/97)
87 **CHATEAU WOLTNER** Chardonnay Howell Mountain St. Thomas Vineyard 1995 • $23 • (12/31/97)
87 **CLOS DU BOIS** Chardonnay Alexander Valley Alexander Valley Selection 1995 • $15 • (04/30/97)
87 **COOPER-GARROD** Chardonnay Santa Cruz Mountains 1995 • $20 • (07/31/97)
87 **DAVIS BYNUM** Chardonnay Russian River Valley Limited Edition 1995 • $17 • (11/30/97)
87 **EXPRESSIONS** Chardonnay Sonoma County 1995 • $10 • (11/15/97) • BB
87 **FESS PARKER** Chardonnay Santa Barbara County 1995 • $16 • (07/31/97)
87 **FLEUR DE CARNEROS CELLARS** Chardonnay California 1995 • $12 • (12/31/96)
87 **GALLO OF SONOMA** Chardonnay Sonoma County 1995 • $10 • (11/30/97) • BB
87 **GREEN & RED** Chardonnay Napa Valley Catacula Vineyard 1995 • $18 • (06/15/97)
87 **HAGAFEN** Chardonnay Napa Valley 1995 • $14 • (06/15/97)
87 **HAGAFEN** Chardonnay Napa Valley Reserve 1995 • $18 • (01/31/98)
87 **JEPSON** Chardonnay Mendocino County Estate Select 1995 • $14 • (09/15/97)
87 **KEEGAN** Chardonnay Knights Valley 1995 • $20 • (11/30/97)
87 **KENDALL-JACKSON** Chardonnay Arroyo Seco Paradise Vineyard 1995 • $19 • (07/31/97)
87 **KENDALL-JACKSON** Chardonnay California Vintner's Reserve 1995 • $15 • (01/31/97)
87 **KUNDE** Chardonnay Sonoma Valley Reserve 1995 • $22 • (12/15/97)
87 **KUNDE** Chardonnay Sonoma Valley Wildwood Vineyard 1995 • $20 • (03/31/98)
87 **LAKESPRING** Chardonnay California 1995 • $11 • (12/31/96)
87 **LAWRENCE J. BARGETTO** Chardonnay Central Coast Cypress 1995 • $10 • (04/30/97)
87 **LONGORIA** Chardonnay Santa Ynez Valley Santa Rita Cuvée 1995 • $23 • (06/15/97)
87 **MARK WEST** Chardonnay Russian River Valley 1995 • $14 • (06/15/97)
87 **MCILROY** Chardonnay Russian River Valley Aquarius Ranch 1995 • $18 • (06/15/97)
87 **MEEKER** Chardonnay Sonoma County Incognito 1995 • $18 • (07/31/97)
87 **MURPHY-GOODE** Chardonnay Alexander Valley 1995 • $14 • (01/31/97)
87 **NAPA RIDGE** Chardonnay North Coast Coastal Vines 1995 • $8 • (02/28/97)
87 **NIEBAUM-COPPOLA** Chardonnay Napa Valley Francis Coppola Family Wines 1995 • $18 • (11/15/96)
87 **PYRAMIDS** Chardonnay Sonoma County Ranch Vineyards 1995 • $16 • (05/15/98)
87 **RENAISSANCE** Chardonnay North Yuba 1995 • $18 • (07/31/97)
87 **ROBERT MONDAVI** Chardonnay Central Coast Coastal 1995 • $11 • (01/31/97)
87 **RODNEY STRONG** Chardonnay Sonoma County 1995 • $12 • (04/30/97)
87 **S. ANDERSON** Chardonnay Stags Leap District 1995 • $20 • (06/15/97)
87 **SADDLEBACK** Chardonnay Napa Valley 1995 • $16 • (06/15/97)
87 **STEPHEN ROSS** Chardonnay Edna Valley Edna Ranch 1995 • $18 • (06/15/97)
87 **STERLING** Chardonnay Napa Valley 1995 • $14 • (05/15/97)
87 **STEVENOT** Chardonnay Calaveras County Shaw Ranch 1995 • $18 • (06/15/97)

87 **STONEHEDGE** Chardonnay California Barrel Fermented 1995 • $10 • (12/31/96) • BB

87 **TURNING LEAF** Chardonnay Sonoma County Sonoma Reserve 1995 • $10 • (07/31/98)

87 **VON STRASSER** Chardonnay Napa Valley 1995 • $30 • (11/30/97)

87 **WHITE OAK** Chardonnay Sonoma County 1995 • $13 • (06/15/97)

87 **WILD HORSE** Chardonnay Central Coast 1995 • $14 • (12/15/96)

87 **WILLIAM HILL** Chardonnay Napa Valley 1995 • $12 • (07/31/97)

87 **ZACA MESA** Chardonnay Santa Barbara County Zaca Vineyards 1995 • $15 • (07/31/97)

87 **ZD WINES** Chardonnay California 1995 • $24 • (07/31/97)

86 **ADLER FELS** Chardonnay Sonoma County 1995 • $14 • (07/31/97)

86 **BANDIERA** Chardonnay California Coastal 1995 • $8 • (12/31/96)

86 **BEAULIEU VINEYARD** Chardonnay Carneros 1995 • $13 • (12/31/96)

86 **BECKMEN** Chardonnay Santa Barbara County 1995 • $15 • (03/31/98)

86 **BUEHLER** Chardonnay Russian River Valley 1995 • $15 • (07/31/97)

86 **BUENA VISTA** Chardonnay Carneros 1995 • $12 • (07/31/97)

86 **CASTORO** Chardonnay Paso Robles Reserve 1995 • $16 • (07/31/98)

86 **CEDAR BROOK** Chardonnay California 1995 • $9 • (07/31/97)

86 **DREYER SONOMA** Chardonnay Sonoma County 1995 • $10 • (04/30/97)

86 **EBERLE** Chardonnay Paso Robles 1995 • $12 • (07/31/97)

86 **FESS PARKER** Chardonnay Santa Barbara County Marcella's Vineyard American Tradition Reserve 1995 • $28 • (07/31/97)

86 **GODWIN** Chardonnay Alexander Valley 1995 • $20 • (07/31/97)

86 **GUNDLACH BUNDSCHU** Chardonnay Sonoma Valley Sangiacomo Ranch 1995 • $17 • (02/28/97)

86 **HESS SELECT** Chardonnay California 1995 • $10 • (01/31/97) • BB

86 **INDIGO HILLS** Chardonnay Mendocino County 1995 • $9 • (12/15/97)

86 **JASON** Chardonnay California 1995 • $6 • (06/15/97)

86 **LAETITIA** Chardonnay San Luis Obispo County Reserve 1995 • $17 • (12/15/97)

86 **MIDNIGHT CELLARS** Chardonnay Central Coast 1995 • $15 • (01/31/98)

86 **PARDUCCI** Chardonnay North Coast 1995 • $10 • (11/30/96)

86 **ROUND HILL** Chardonnay California 1995 • $8 • (02/28/97) • BB

86 **ROUND HILL** Chardonnay Napa Valley 1995 • $12 • (11/30/97)

86 **STEPHEN ROSS** Chardonnay Santa Maria Valley Bien Nacido Vineyard 1995 • $18 • (07/31/97)

86 **WELLINGTON** Chardonnay Sonoma Valley Reserve 1995 • $16 • (07/31/97)

Key: SS—Spectator Selection CS—Cellar Selection HR—Highly Recommended BB—Best Buy $NA—Price not available Ⓐ—Auction Price

Dates in parentheses indicate the issues in which the ratings were published.

86 **WHITE OAK** Chardonnay Sonoma County Myers Limited Reserve 1995 • $17 • (07/31/97)

85 **BOEGER** Chardonnay El Dorado 1995 • $12 • (12/31/96)

85 **CAMELOT** Chardonnay Santa Barbara County 1995 • $16 • (11/30/97)

85 **CANYON ROAD** Chardonnay Russian River Valley Reserve 1995 • $18 • (11/15/97)

85 **CARNEROS CREEK** Chardonnay Carneros 1995 • $17 • (01/31/97)

85 **CHARLES KRUG** Chardonnay Napa Valley Peter Mondavi Family 1995 • $13 • (07/31/97)

85 **ESTANCIA** Chardonnay Monterey County Pinnacles 1995 • $10 • (07/31/97)

85 **FOUNTAIN GROVE** Chardonnay California 1995 • $10 • (07/31/97)

85 **FREEMARK ABBEY** Chardonnay Napa Valley 1995 • $18 • (03/31/98)

85 **GEYSER PEAK** Chardonnay Sonoma County 1995 • $12 • (01/31/97)

85 **HANDLEY** Chardonnay Dry Creek Valley 1995 • $18 • (07/31/97)

85 **HIDDEN CELLARS** Chardonnay Mendocino Mendocino Heritage 1995 • $25 • (12/31/97)

85 **IRON HORSE** Chardonnay Sonoma County Green Valley 1995 • $18 • (07/31/97)

85 **JOLIESSE** Chardonnay California Reserve 1995 • $7 • (07/31/97)

85 **KEENAN** Chardonnay Napa Valley 1995 • $17 • (07/31/97)

85 **KENWOOD** Chardonnay Sonoma County 25th Anniversary Vintage 1995 • $15 • (11/15/96)

85 **KUNDE** Chardonnay Sonoma Valley 1995 • $14 • (11/30/96)

85 **LAZY CREEK** Chardonnay Anderson Valley 1995 • $10 • (07/31/97)

85 **LEEWARD** Chardonnay Central Coast 1995 • $11 • (12/15/96)

85 **MICHEL-SCHLUMBERGER** Chardonnay Dry Creek Valley 1995 • $20 • (12/15/97)

85 **NAPA RIDGE** Chardonnay Central Coast Coastal Vines 1995 • $8 • (11/30/96)

85 **OJAI** Chardonnay Arroyo Grande Valley Reserve 1995 • $28 • (12/15/97)

85 **PEIRANO ESTATE** Chardonnay Lodi 1995 • $9 • (09/30/97)

85 **SCHEID** Chardonnay Monterey 1995 • $16 • (01/31/98)

85 **SILVER RIDGE** Chardonnay California 1995 • $10 • (07/31/97)

85 **STONEGATE** Chardonnay Sonoma County Bella Vista Vineyard 1995 • $14 • (07/31/97)

85 **SUMMERFIELD** Chardonnay California Vintner's Reserve 1995 • $8 • (12/31/96)

85 **TALUS** Chardonnay California 1995 • $8 • (07/31/97)

1994 CALIFORNIA CHARDONNAY
VINTAGE RATING: 95

95 **BERINGER** Chardonnay Napa Valley Private Reserve 1994 • $55 Ⓐ • (04/30/96) • SS

95 **KISTLER** Chardonnay Russian River Valley Vine Hill Vineyard 1994 • $38 • (06/30/97) • HR

95 **KISTLER** Chardonnay Sonoma Mountain McCrea Vineyard 1994 • $38 • (02/28/97) • HR

95 **PETER MICHAEL** Chardonnay Sonoma County Cuvée Indigène 1994 • $60 • (12/31/96)

95 **ROBERT MONDAVI** Chardonnay Napa Valley Reserve 1994 • $30 • (04/30/97) • HR
95 **ROCHIOLI** Chardonnay Russian River Valley Reserve 1994 • $28 • (04/30/96)
95 **SAINTSBURY** Chardonnay Carneros Reserve 1994 • $25 • (05/31/96) • HR
94 **BERINGER** Chardonnay Napa Valley Sbragia Limited Release 1994 • $25 • (05/15/96) • HR
94 **KISTLER** Chardonnay Russian River Valley Dutton Ranch 1994 • $36 • (02/28/97)
94 **MARCASSIN** Chardonnay Alexander Valley Gauer Vineyard Upper Barn 1994 • $39 • (05/15/96) • CS
94 **PATZ & HALL** Chardonnay Mount Veeder Carr Vineyard 1994 • $38 • (02/29/96)
94 **PETER MICHAEL** Chardonnay Sonoma County Mon Plaisir 1994 • $40 • (12/31/96) • HR
94 **SANFORD** Chardonnay Santa Ynez Valley 1994 • $24 • (05/31/97)
94 **TRUCHARD** Chardonnay Napa Valley Carneros 1994 • $19 • (03/31/96) • HR
94 **VILLA MT. EDEN** Chardonnay Santa Maria Valley Bien Nacido Vineyard Signature Series 1994 • $30 • (05/31/96)
93 **CHALK HILL** Chardonnay Chalk Hill 1994 • $20 • (06/15/96) • SS
93 **CUVAISON** Chardonnay Napa Valley Carneros ATS Selection 1994 • $40 • (05/31/97)
93 **FERRARI-CARANO** Chardonnay Napa & Sonoma Counties Reserve 1994 • $32 • (05/31/97)
93 **GIRARD** Chardonnay Napa Valley Reserve 1994 • $32 • (05/31/96)
93 **KISTLER** Chardonnay Sonoma County Cuvée Cathleen 1994 • $50 • (06/30/97)
93 **MARCASSIN** Chardonnay Carneros Hudson Vineyard 1994 • $39 • (05/15/96)
93 **MARTIN RAY** Chardonnay California Mariage 1994 • $25 • (05/31/96)
93 **MER SOLEIL** Chardonnay Central Coast 1994 • $32 • (05/31/96) • HR
93 **PINE RIDGE** Chardonnay Stags Leap District 1994 • $25 • (05/31/96) • HR
93 **ROMBAUER** Chardonnay Carneros 1994 • $21 • (12/31/95) • SS
93 **SHAFER** Chardonnay Napa Valley Carneros Red Shoulder Ranch 1994 • $23 • (06/15/96) • HR
93 **SILVERADO VINEYARDS** Chardonnay Napa Valley Limited Reserve 1994 • $36 • (05/31/97)
93 **STEELE** Chardonnay Carneros Sangiacomo Vineyard 1994 • $22 • (05/31/96)
92 **ARROWOOD** Chardonnay Sonoma County Cuvée Michel Berthoud Réserve Spéciale 1994 • $27 • (05/31/96) • HR
92 **BYRON** Chardonnay Santa Maria Valley Estate 1994 • $30 • (06/30/97)
92 **CHALK HILL** Chardonnay Chalk Hill Estate Vineyard Selection 1994 • $36 • (10/15/97)
92 **CHATEAU POTELLE** Chardonnay Mount Veeder V.G.S. 1994 • $35 • (05/31/97)
92 **CHATEAU ST. JEAN** Chardonnay Alexander Valley Belle Terre Vineyards 1994 • $18 • (04/30/96) • HR
92 **CHATEAU ST. JEAN** Chardonnay Alexander Valley Robert Young Vineyard 1994 • $24 • (05/31/97)
92 **CRONIN** Chardonnay Santa Cruz Mountains Nancy's Cuvée 1994 • $27 • (06/15/97)
92 **CUVAISON** Chardonnay Napa Valley Carneros Reserve 1994 • $30 • (08/31/96) • HR
92 **E. & J. GALLO** Chardonnay Northern Sonoma Estate Bottled 1994 • $30 • (09/30/96)
92 **GALLO OF SONOMA** Chardonnay Russian River Valley Laguna Ranch Vineyard 1994 • $16 • (04/30/96) • HR
92 **GARY FARRELL** Chardonnay Russian River Valley Allen Vineyard 1994 • $20 • (04/30/96)
92 **GARY FARRELL** Chardonnay Russian River Valley 1994 • $17 • (05/15/96)
92 **JOSEPH PHELPS** Chardonnay Napa Valley Ovation 1994 • $30 • (09/15/96)
92 **KISTLER** Chardonnay Sonoma Valley Kistler Vineyard 1994 • $45 • (06/30/97)
92 **LIPARITA** Chardonnay Howell Mountain 1994 • $18 • (04/30/96)
92 **LITTORAI** Chardonnay Sonoma Coast Occidental 1994 • $28 • (11/30/96)
92 **MARTINELLI** Chardonnay Russian River Valley Gold Ridge 1994 • $18 • (11/15/96)
92 **MOUNT EDEN** Chardonnay Santa Cruz Mountains 1994 • $36 • (02/28/97)
92 **NEWTON** Chardonnay Napa Valley Unfiltered 1994 • $30 • (02/28/97)
92 **NICHOLS** Chardonnay Arroyo Grande Valley Talley Vineyards 1994 • $23 • (04/30/96)
92 **PAHLMEYER** Chardonnay Napa Valley 1994 • $41 Ⓐ • (05/31/96)
92 **PINE RIDGE** Chardonnay Stags Leap District 1994 • $25 • (11/30/97)
92 **SANFORD** Chardonnay Santa Barbara County Barrel Select 1994 • $30 • (05/31/97)
92 **SARAH'S VINEYARD** Chardonnay Santa Clara County Gold Label 1994 • $45 • (03/31/98)
92 **SIGNORELLO** Chardonnay Napa Valley Founder's Reserve 1994 • $30 • (05/15/96)
92 **SONOMA-CUTRER** Chardonnay Sonoma Coast Cutrer Vineyard 1994 • $25 • (05/31/97)
92 **STEELE** Chardonnay California 1994 • $18 • (05/15/96) • SS
92 **STEELE** Chardonnay Mendocino DuPratt Vineyard 1994 • $24 • (05/31/96)
92 **STEELE** Chardonnay Santa Barbara County Goodchild Vineyard 1994 • $24 • (05/31/96)
92 **VILLA MT. EDEN** Chardonnay Napa Valley Grand Reserve 1994 • $16 • (04/30/96)
91 **ACACIA** Chardonnay Carneros Reserve 1994 • $28 • (05/31/97)
91 **BEAULIEU VINEYARD** Chardonnay Carneros Reserve 1994 • $18 • (04/30/96)
91 **CALERA** Chardonnay Mount Harlan 1994 • $30 • (12/15/96)
91 **CHALONE** Chardonnay Chalone 1994 • $26 Ⓐ • (06/15/96) • CS
91 **CHATEAU MONTELENA** Chardonnay Napa Valley 1994 • $25 • (06/15/97) • SS
91 **CHATEAU ST. JEAN** Chardonnay Sonoma County Private Chateau Select 1994 • $18 • (06/15/97)
91 **CHATEAU SOUVERAIN** Chardonnay Carneros Winemaker's Reserve 1994 • $16 • (06/15/96)
91 **CHATEAU SOUVERAIN** Chardonnay Sonoma County 1994 • $12 • (04/30/96) • SS
91 **CLOS DU BOIS** Chardonnay Alexander Valley Calcaire Vineyard 1994 • $18 • (04/30/96) • SS
91 **EL MOLINO** Chardonnay Napa Valley 1994 • $35 • (05/31/96)
91 **FERRARI-CARANO** Chardonnay Alexander Valley Tre Terre 1994 • $24 • (05/15/96)
91 **FORMAN** Chardonnay Napa Valley 1994 • $23 • (07/31/96) • HR
91 **GIRARD** Chardonnay Napa Valley 1994 • $18 • (06/15/96) • SS

California Chardonnay

91 **LANDMARK** Chardonnay Sonoma County Overlook 1994 • $16 • (03/31/96) • SS

91 **LONG** Chardonnay Napa Valley 1994 • $30 • (02/28/97)

91 **MACROSTIE** Chardonnay Carneros 1994 • $17 • (04/30/96)

91 **PATZ & HALL** Chardonnay Napa Valley 1994 • $28 • (02/29/96) • HR

91 **SIMI** Chardonnay Sonoma County Reserve 1994 • $28 • (05/31/97)

91 **SOLITUDE** Chardonnay Carneros Sangiacomo Vineyard 1994 • $19 • (01/31/96)

91 **STAG'S LEAP WINE CELLARS** Chardonnay Napa Valley Beckstoffer Ranch 1994 • $24 • (05/31/96)

91 **STAG'S LEAP WINE CELLARS** Chardonnay Napa Valley Reserve 1994 • $32 • (05/15/97)

91 **STEELE** Chardonnay Santa Barbara County Bien Nacido Vineyard 1994 • $24 • (05/31/96)

91 **STONESTREET** Chardonnay Sonoma County 1994 • $25 • (05/31/96) • SS

91 **TALBOTT** Chardonnay Monterey Cuvée Cynthia 1994 • $45 • (02/28/97)

91 **TESTAROSSA** Chardonnay Chalone 1994 • $22 • (12/15/96)

91 **THOMAS FOGARTY** Chardonnay Santa Cruz Mountains Estate Reserve 1994 • $23 • (06/30/96)

91 **VINE CLIFF** Chardonnay Napa Valley Proprietress Reserve 1994 • $30 • (11/15/96)

90 **ACACIA** Chardonnay Carneros 1994 • $18 • (04/30/96) • SS

90 **BELVEDERE** Chardonnay Sonoma County Preferred Stock 1994 • $22 • (04/30/97)

90 **BERINGER** Chardonnay Napa Valley 1994 • $11 • (03/31/96) • SS

90 **BERNARDUS** Chardonnay Monterey County 1994 • $15 • (05/15/96) • SS

90 **BYINGTON** Chardonnay Santa Cruz Mountains Special Reserve Vineyards Spring Ridge Vineyard 1994 • $23 • (06/30/96)

90 **BYRON** Chardonnay Santa Barbara County Reserve 1994 • $23 • (05/31/96)

90 **CALERA** Chardonnay Central Coast 1994 • $15 • (12/31/95) • SS

90 **CHALONE** Chardonnay Chalone Reserve 1994 • $45 • (05/31/96)

90 **CHATEAU JULIEN** Chardonnay Monterey County Private Reserve 1994 • $13 • (07/31/96)

90 **CHATEAU ST. JEAN** Chardonnay Alexander Valley Robert Young Vineyards Reserve 1994 • $57 • (04/30/98)

90 **CHATEAU ST. JEAN** Chardonnay Sonoma County 1994 • $11 • (04/30/96) • SS

90 **DAVIS BYNUM** Chardonnay Russian River Valley Allen & McIlroy Vineyards Limited Edition 1994 • $18 • (05/15/97)

90 **DRY CREEK** Chardonnay Dry Creek Valley Reserve 1994 • $17 • (05/15/96)

90 **ESTANCIA** Chardonnay Monterey Reserve 1994 • $20 • (05/31/96)

90 **FERRARI-CARANO** Chardonnay Alexander Valley 1994 • $22 • (05/15/96) • SS

90 **FRANCISCAN** Chardonnay Napa Valley Oakville Estate Barrel Fermented 1994 • $13 • (04/30/96)

Key: SS—Spectator Selection CS—Cellar Selection HR—Highly Recommended BB—Best Buy $NA—Price not available Ⓐ—Auction Price

Dates in parentheses indicate the issues in which the ratings were published.

90 **FREEMARK ABBEY** Chardonnay Napa Valley Carpy Ranch 1994 • $24 • (05/31/97)

90 **GREENWOOD RIDGE** Chardonnay Anderson Valley Du Pratt Vineyard 1994 • $19 • (04/30/96)

90 **GRGICH HILLS** Chardonnay Napa Valley 1994 • $26 • (05/31/96)

90 **HANZELL** Chardonnay Sonoma Valley 1994 • $28 • (11/30/96)

90 **HARRISON** Chardonnay Napa Valley 1994 • $26 • (04/30/96)

90 **J. LOHR** Chardonnay Monterey Riverstone 1994 • $12 • (02/29/96) • SS

90 **JOSEPH PHELPS** Chardonnay Los Carneros 1994 • $17 • (07/31/96) • SS

90 **KENDALL-JACKSON** Chardonnay California Grand Reserve 1994 • $26 • (03/31/96)

90 **KENDALL-JACKSON** Chardonnay Santa Maria Valley Camelot Vineyard 1994 • $18 • (03/31/96) • SS

90 **LAURIER** Chardonnay Sonoma County 1994 • $15 • (05/31/97)

90 **LEWIS CELLARS** Chardonnay Napa Valley Oakville Ranch Reserve 1994 • $28 • (05/15/96)

90 **LOCKWOOD** Chardonnay Monterey Partners' Reserve 1994 • $21 • (05/31/97)

90 **MARIMAR TORRES** Chardonnay Sonoma County Green Valley Don Miguel Vineyard 1994 • $20 • (11/15/96)

90 **MARKHAM** Chardonnay Napa Valley 1994 • $15 • (06/15/96) • SS

90 **MATANZAS CREEK** Chardonnay Sonoma Valley 1994 • $18 Ⓐ • (05/31/96)

90 **MONTICELLO** Chardonnay Napa Valley Corley Family Vineyards 1994 • $18 • (07/31/97)

90 **MUELLER** Chardonnay Russian River Valley 1994 • $13 • (05/15/96)

90 **NEWTON** Chardonnay Napa Valley 1994 • $19 • (03/31/96)

90 **RIDGE** Chardonnay Santa Cruz Mountains Monte Bello Ridge Vineyards 1994 • $20 • (05/15/96)

90 **S. ANDERSON** Chardonnay Stags Leap District 1994 • $20 • (04/30/96)

90 **ST. FRANCIS** Chardonnay Sonoma Valley Reserve 1994 • $20 • (05/15/96)

90 **SANFORD** Chardonnay Santa Barbara County 1994 • $17 • (05/31/96) • SS

90 **SELBY** Chardonnay Sonoma County 1994 • $18 • (04/30/96)

90 **STEELE** Chardonnay Mendocino Dennison Vineyard 1994 • $22 • (05/31/96)

90 **TALBOTT** Chardonnay Monterey Diamond T Estate 1994 • $40 • (07/31/97)

90 **TALBOTT** Chardonnay Monterey Sleepy Hollow Vineyard 1994 • $28 • (02/28/97)

90 **TALLEY** Chardonnay Arroyo Grande Valley Rincon Vineyard 1994 • $28 • (11/30/96)

90 **THOMAS FOGARTY** Chardonnay Santa Cruz Mountains 1994 • $17 • (02/29/96) • HR

90 **VINE CLIFF** Chardonnay Napa Valley 1994 • $23 • (05/31/96)

89 **ALDERBROOK** Chardonnay Dry Creek Valley Dorothy's Vineyard 1994 • $19 • (05/15/97)

89 **AU BON CLIMAT** Chardonnay Santa Ynez Valley Sanford & Benedict Reserve 1994 • $35 • (11/30/96)

89 **BENZIGER** Chardonnay Carneros Reserve 1994 • $13 • (03/31/96) • HR

89 **CAKEBREAD** Chardonnay Napa Valley Reserve 1994 • $33 • (06/15/97)

89 **CAMELOT** Chardonnay Central Coast 1994 • $11 • (06/15/96)

89 **CHATEAU WOLTNER** Chardonnay Howell Mountain St. Thomas Vineyard 1994 • $23 • (05/15/97)

89 **CHATEAU WOLTNER** Chardonnay Howell Mountain Titus Vineyard 1994 • $40 • (05/15/97)

89 **CLOS LACHANCE** Chardonnay Santa Cruz Mountains 1994 • $18 • (05/31/96)

89 **CLOS PEGASE** Chardonnay Napa Valley Carneros Pegase Circle Reserve 1994 • $23 • (05/15/96)

89 **CLOS DU BOIS** Chardonnay Dry Creek Valley Flintwood Vineyard 1994 • $17 • (04/30/96)

89 **COOPER-GARROD** Chardonnay Santa Cruz Mountains 1994 • $18 • (02/29/96)

89 **DE LOACH** Chardonnay Russian River Valley O.F.S. 1994 • $25 • (05/15/96)

89 **DRY CREEK** Chardonnay Sonoma County Barrel Fermented 1994 • $14 • (03/31/96)

89 **ESTANCIA** Chardonnay Monterey County 1994 • $10 • (10/15/96) • SS

89 **FLORA SPRINGS** Chardonnay Carneros 1994 • $20 • (06/30/96)

89 **GEYSER PEAK** Chardonnay Alexander Valley Reserve 1994 • $20 • (05/15/96)

89 **GLORIA FERRER** Chardonnay Carneros 1994 • $16 • (07/31/96)

89 **J. FRITZ** Chardonnay Russian River Valley Dutton Ranch Cuvée de Terre 1994 • $20 • (11/30/96)

89 **J. LOHR** Chardonnay Arroyo Seco VS 1994 • $23 • (06/15/96)

89 **JORDAN** Chardonnay Sonoma County 1994 • $20 • (06/15/97)

89 **JUSTIN** Chardonnay San Luis Obispo County 1994 • $17 • (04/30/97)

89 **KUNDE** Chardonnay Sonoma Valley Kinneybrook 1994 • $20 • (05/31/96)

89 **KUNDE** Chardonnay Sonoma Valley Wildwood 1994 • $20 • (05/31/96)

89 **LANDMARK** Chardonnay Sonoma County Damaris Reserve 1994 • $23 • (03/31/96)

89 **MERIDIAN** Chardonnay Santa Barbara County 1994 • $10 • (02/29/96) • BB

89 **MONTICELLO** Chardonnay Napa Valley Corley Estate Reserve 1994 • $26 • (06/15/97)

89 **MORGAN** Chardonnay Monterey Reserve 1994 • $24 • (04/30/97)

89 **MUELLER** Chardonnay Alexander Valley Gauer Ranch 1994 • $15 • (05/15/96)

89 **MURPHY-GOODE** Chardonnay Alexander Valley Island Block Reserve 1994 • $24 • (01/31/96)

89 **MURPHY-GOODE** Chardonnay Russian River Valley J & K Murphy Vineyard Reserve 1994 • $24 • (05/31/96)

89 **NAVARRO** Chardonnay Anderson Valley Première Reserve 1994 • $15 • (06/15/96)

89 **OAKVILLE RANCH** Chardonnay Napa Valley ORV 1994 • $28 • (05/15/96)

89 **PAUL HOBBS** Chardonnay Sonoma Mountain Richard Dinner Vineyard 1994 • $28 • (06/30/96)

89 **RAYMOND** Chardonnay Napa Valley Private Reserve 1994 • $18 • (05/31/96)

89 **RAYMOND** Chardonnay Napa Valley Reserve 1994 • $14 • (05/31/96)

89 **ROBERT MONDAVI** Chardonnay Carneros 1994 • $23 • (12/31/96) • HR

89 **ROBERT MONDAVI** Chardonnay Napa Valley 1994 • $17 • (05/31/96)

89 **ROCHIOLI** Chardonnay Russian River Valley 1994 • $17 • (06/15/96)

89 **SIGNORELLO** Chardonnay Napa Valley 1994 • $20 • (03/31/96)

89 **SONOMA-CUTRER** Chardonnay Sonoma Coast Russian River Ranches 1994 • $15 • (07/31/96)

89 **STAG'S LEAP WINE CELLARS** Chardonnay Napa Valley 1994 • $22 • (06/15/96)

89 **TALLEY** Chardonnay Arroyo Grande Valley 1994 • $18 • (11/30/96)

89 **VICHON** Chardonnay Napa Valley 1994 • $NA • (02/29/96)

89 **WILD HORSE** Chardonnay Central Coast 1994 • $14 • (06/30/96) • SS

88 **ARROWOOD** Chardonnay Sonoma County 1994 • $21 • (05/31/96)

88 **AU BON CLIMAT** Chardonnay Santa Barbara County 1994 • $15 • (01/31/96)

88 **BABCOCK** Chardonnay Santa Ynez Valley Mt. Carmel Vineyard 1994 • $27 • (01/31/96)

88 **BANNISTER** Chardonnay Russian River Valley Allen Vineyard 1994 • $20 • (05/31/96)

88 **BEAULIEU VINEYARD** Chardonnay Napa Valley Carneros 1994 • $13 • (02/29/96)

88 **BECKMEN** Chardonnay Santa Ynez Valley 1994 • $14 • (06/15/97)

88 **BELVEDERE** Chardonnay Russian River Valley 1994 • $13 • (02/29/96)

88 **BELVEDERE** Chardonnay Sonoma County 1994 • $9 • (02/29/96) • BB

88 **BUENA VISTA** Chardonnay Carneros Grand Reserve 1994 • $22 • (06/15/96)

88 **BYRON** Chardonnay Santa Barbara County 1994 • $16 • (05/31/96)

88 **CAMBRIA** Chardonnay Santa Barbara County 1994 • $15 • (02/29/96)

88 **CAMBRIA** Chardonnay Santa Maria Valley Reserve 1994 • $30 • (06/15/96)

88 **CHALONE** Chardonnay Chalone Gavilan 1994 • $16 • (06/15/96)

88 **CHATEAU WOLTNER** Chardonnay Howell Mountain Frederique Vineyard 1994 • $40 • (05/15/97)

88 **CINNABAR** Chardonnay Santa Cruz Mountains Saratoga Vineyard 1994 • $23 • (06/15/96)

88 **CLAIBORNE & CHURCHILL** Chardonnay Edna Valley MacGregor Vineyard 1994 • $18 • (05/31/96)

88 **CLOS PEGASE** Chardonnay Napa Valley Carneros Mitsuko's Vineyard 1994 • $17 • (05/15/96)

88 **DEHLINGER** Chardonnay Russian River Valley 1994 • $16 • (05/31/96)

88 **DRY CREEK** Chardonnay Dry Creek Valley Wolcott Vineyard Barrel Fermented Reserve 1994 • $22 • (02/29/96)

88 **EDMEADES** Chardonnay Anderson Valley 1994 • $18 • (05/15/96)

88 **EXPRESSIONS** Chardonnay Sonoma County 1994 • $10 • (04/30/96) • BB

88 **FESS PARKER** Chardonnay Santa Barbara County American Tradition Reserve 1994 • $22 • (11/30/96)

88 **GAINEY** Chardonnay Santa Ynez Valley Limited Selection 1994 • $25 • (06/30/96)

88 **GUENOC** Chardonnay Guenoc Valley Genevieve Magoon Vineyard Reserve 1994 • $23 • (04/30/96)

88 **GUENOC** Chardonnay Guenoc Valley Genevieve Magoon Vineyard Unfiltered Reserve 1994 • $30 • (05/15/96)

88 **HANDLEY** Chardonnay Dry Creek Valley 1994 • $17 • (07/31/96)

88 **LA CREMA** Chardonnay Sonoma County 1994 • $15 • (03/31/96)

88 **LAKESPRING** Chardonnay Napa Valley 1994 • $12 • (02/29/96)

88 **LONGORIA** Chardonnay Santa Ynez Valley Huber Vineyard 1994 • $21 • (06/30/96)

88 **LOS ENCANTOS** Chardonnay Santa Maria Covenant Reserve 1994 • $14 • (02/29/96)

88 **LYNMAR** Chardonnay Russian River Valley Quail Hill Vineyard 1994 • $20 • (06/15/97)

88 **MACROSTIE** Chardonnay Carneros Reserve 1994 • $25 • (11/15/96)

88 **MAZZOCCO** Chardonnay Sonoma County Winemaker's Select 1994 • $18 • (05/15/97)

88 **MERRYVALE** Chardonnay Napa Valley Starmont 1994 • $16 • (05/31/96)

88 **MIRASSOU** Chardonnay Monterey County Fifth Generation Family Selection 1994 • $11 • (06/15/96)

88 **NAVARRO** Chardonnay Mendocino Special 1994 • $16 • (11/30/96)

88 **NORMAN** Chardonnay San Luis Obispo County 1994 • $12 • (05/15/96)

88 **OAKVILLE RANCH** Chardonnay Napa Valley Vista Vineyard 1994 • $20 • (05/15/96)

88 **PINE RIDGE** Chardonnay Napa Valley Knollside Cuvée 1994 • $16 • (05/31/96)

88 **QUPÉ** Chardonnay Santa Barbara County Sierra Madre Reserve 1994 • $25 • (05/31/96)

88 **REMICK RIDGE** Chardonnay Sonoma Valley 1994 • $16 • (06/15/96)

88 **RUTZ** Chardonnay Russian River Valley Dutton Ranch 1994 • $25 • (10/15/96)

88 **SAINTSBURY** Chardonnay Carneros 1994 • $15 • (07/31/96)

88 **SALAMANDRE** Chardonnay Santa Cruz Mountains Matteson Vineyard 1994 • $24 • (07/31/96)

88 **SCHUG** Chardonnay Carneros Heritage Reserve 1994 • $25 • (06/30/96)

88 **SEAVEY** Chardonnay Napa Valley 1994 • $16 • (05/15/96)

88 **SEQUOIA GROVE** Chardonnay Rutherford Estate Reserve 1994 • $21 • (07/31/96)

88 **SONOMA-CUTRER** Chardonnay Sonoma Coast Les Pierres 1994 • $28 • (07/31/97)

88 **SONOMA-LOEB** Chardonnay Sonoma County 1994 • $18 • (03/31/96)

88 **SONOMA-LOEB** Chardonnay Sonoma County Private Reserve 1994 • $25 • (02/29/96)

88 **STEELE** Chardonnay Mendocino Lolonis Vineyard 1994 • $26 • (05/31/96)

88 **STEELE** Chardonnay Sonoma Valley Durell Vineyard 1994 • $24 • (05/31/96)

88 **WENTE** Chardonnay Arroyo Seco Riva Ranch Reserve 1994 • $15 • (04/30/98)

88 **WENTE** Chardonnay Livermore Valley Herman Wente Reserve 1994 • $22 • (06/30/96)

88 **WHITCRAFT** Chardonnay Santa Maria Valley Bien Nacido Vineyard 1994 • $17 • (06/15/96)

88 **WHITCRAFT** Chardonnay Santa Ynez Valley Sanford & Benedict Vineyard 1994 • $35 • (05/15/96)

88 **DELORIMIER** Chardonnay Alexander Valley Clonal Select 1994 • $20 • (06/30/96)

87 **ADELAIDA** Chardonnay San Luis Obispo County 1994 • $19 • (06/15/97)

87 **AU BON CLIMAT** Chardonnay Santa Barbara County Le Bouge D'à Côté 1994 • $25 • (07/31/96)

Key: SS—Spectator Selection CS—Cellar Selection HR—Highly Recommended BB—Best Buy $NA—Price not available Ⓐ—Auction Price
Dates in parentheses indicate the issues in which the ratings were published.

87 **BYINGTON** Chardonnay Santa Cruz Mountains Special Reserve Vineyards 1994 • $18 • (06/30/96)

87 **CAKEBREAD** Chardonnay Napa Valley 1994 • $23 • (01/31/96)

87 **CALE** Chardonnay Carneros Sangiacomo Vineyard 1994 • $20 • (05/15/96)

87 **CAMELOT** Chardonnay Santa Barbara County 1994 • $18 • (06/15/96)

87 **CARPE DIEM** Chardonnay San Luis Obispo County 1994 • $19 • (02/29/96)

87 **CHAPPELLET** Chardonnay Napa Valley Signature 1994 • $24 • (06/15/96)

87 **COBBLESTONE VINEYARDS** Chardonnay Monterey County 1994 • $15 • (07/31/96)

87 **CRONIN** Chardonnay Alexander Valley Stuhlmuller Vineyard 1994 • $18 • (09/15/96)

87 **DREYER SONOMA** Chardonnay Sonoma County 1994 • $9 • (04/30/96)

87 **EDMEADES** Chardonnay Anderson Valley Anderson Crest Vineyard 1994 • $20 • (06/15/96)

87 **ESTATE WILLIAM BACCALA** Chardonnay Sonoma County 1994 • $11 • (07/31/96)

87 **FESS PARKER** Chardonnay Santa Barbara County 1994 • $16 • (06/30/96)

87 **FIELD STONE** Chardonnay Sonoma County 1994 • $14 • (12/15/96)

87 **FIELDBROOK** Chardonnay Trinity County Meredith Vineyard 1994 • $14 • (07/31/96)

87 **FIRESTONE** Chardonnay Santa Ynez Valley 1994 • $13 • (07/31/96) • HR

87 **FISHER** Chardonnay Sonoma County Whitney's Vineyard 1994 • $26 • (06/15/96)

87 **FLORA SPRINGS** Chardonnay Napa Valley Reserve 1994 • $18 • (07/31/96)

87 **GALLO OF SONOMA** Chardonnay Dry Creek Valley Stefani Vineyard 1994 • $16 • (05/15/96)

87 **GUENOC** Chardonnay Guenoc Valley 1994 • $15 • (04/30/96)

87 **HANDLEY** Chardonnay Anderson Valley 1994 • $13 • (07/31/96)

87 **HESS SELECT** Chardonnay California 1994 • $10 • (06/30/96) • BB

87 **IRON HORSE** Chardonnay Sonoma County Green Valley 1994 • $18 • (05/15/96)

87 **JARVIS** Chardonnay Napa Valley 1994 • $36 • (05/15/97)

87 **JOULLIAN** Chardonnay Monterey 1994 • $12 • (06/15/96)

87 **KENWOOD** Chardonnay Sonoma County 25th Anniversary Vintage 1994 • $14 • (12/15/95)

87 **KUNDE** Chardonnay Sonoma Valley Reserve 1994 • $22 • (06/15/96)

87 **LA CREMA** Chardonnay Sonoma County Sonoma Reserve 1994 • $23 • (09/15/96)

87 **LAMBERT BRIDGE** Chardonnay Sonoma County 1994 • $15 • (07/31/96)

87 **LOCKWOOD** Chardonnay Monterey 1994 • $15 • (04/30/96)

87 **LOGAN** Chardonnay Monterey 1994 • $14 • (05/15/96)

87 **LOUIS M. MARTINI** Chardonnay Napa Valley 1994 • $11 • (06/15/96)

87 **LYETH** Chardonnay Sonoma County 1994 • $11 • (02/29/96)

87 **MAZZOCCO** Chardonnay Sonoma County River Lane 1994 • $14 • (06/30/96)

87 **MIRASSOU** Chardonnay Monterey County Fifth Generation Harvest Reserve Limited Bottling 1994 • $15 • (07/31/96)

87 **OLIVET LANE** Chardonnay Russian River Valley Pellegrini Family Vineyards 1994 • $12 • (02/29/96)
87 **OPTIMA** Chardonnay Carneros 1994 • $28 • (02/29/96)
87 **PARDUCCI** Chardonnay Mendocino County 1994 • $8 • (09/30/95) • BB
87 **PETER MICHAEL** Chardonnay Napa County Clos du Ciel 1994 • $32 • (06/15/96)
87 **PRIDE** Chardonnay Napa Valley 1994 • $18 • (05/15/96)
87 **R.H. PHILLIPS** Chardonnay Dunnigan Hills Barrel Cuvée 1994 • $8 • (05/31/96) • BB
87 **RABBIT RIDGE** Chardonnay Russian River Valley Rabbit Ridge Ranch Estate Reserve 1994 • $16 • (05/15/96)
87 **RAYMOND** Chardonnay Monterey Estates 1994 • $12 • (03/31/96)
87 **RODNEY STRONG** Chardonnay Sonoma County 1994 • $11 • (06/15/96)
87 **SANTA BARBARA WINERY** Chardonnay Santa Ynez Valley Lafond Vineyard 1994 • $30 • (06/15/97)
87 **SANTA BARBARA WINERY** Chardonnay Santa Ynez Valley Reserve 1994 • $22 • (06/30/96)
87 **SEQUOIA GROVE** Chardonnay Napa Valley Carneros 1994 • $16 • (10/15/96)
87 **SILVER HORSE** Chardonnay Paso Robles 1994 • $11 • (02/29/96)
87 **SILVERADO VINEYARDS** Chardonnay Napa Valley 1994 • $11 • (07/31/96)
87 **SWANSON** Chardonnay Napa Valley Carneros 1994 • $22 • (05/15/96)
87 **TALLEY** Chardonnay Edna Valley Oliver's Vineyard 1994 • $15 • (06/15/96)
87 **THE HESS COLLECTION** Chardonnay Napa Valley 1994 • $12 • (07/31/96)
87 **V. SATTUI** Chardonnay Napa Valley Carsi Vineyard 1994 • $19 • (07/31/96)
87 **ZACA MESA** Chardonnay Santa Barbara County Zaca Vineyards 1994 • $13 • (05/15/96)
86 **ARCIERO** Chardonnay Paso Robles 1994 • $9 • (06/15/96) • BB
86 **BANDIERA** Chardonnay Napa Valley 1994 • $8 • (09/30/95) • BB
86 **BELVEDERE** Chardonnay Alexander Valley 1994 • $12 • (04/30/96)
86 **BOUCHAINE** Chardonnay Carneros 1994 • $17 • (11/30/96)
86 **BOUCHAINE** Chardonnay Napa Valley Carneros Estate Reserve 1994 • $24 • (07/31/97)
86 **CAMBRIA** Chardonnay Santa Maria Valley Katherine's Vineyard 1994 • $18 • (02/29/96)
86 **CATHY MACGREGOR** Chardonnay Edna Valley MacGregor Vineyard 1994 • $22 • (07/31/97)
86 **CLOS DU BOIS** Chardonnay Alexander Valley Winemaker's Reserve 1994 • $24 • (09/15/96)
86 **CÔTES DE SONOMA** Chardonnay Sonoma County 1994 • $8 • (10/15/95) • BB
86 **FAR NIENTE** Chardonnay Napa Valley 1994 • $32 • (02/29/96)
86 **FERMENTATIONS & MORE** Chardonnay Edna Valley MacGregor Vineyard 1994 • $13 • (04/30/96)
86 **FETZER** Chardonnay North Coast Barrel Select 1994 • $10 • (06/15/96)
86 **FISHER** Chardonnay Sonoma County Coach Insignia 1994 • $18 • (06/15/96)
86 **FRANCISCAN** Chardonnay Napa Valley Oakville Estate Cuvée Sauvage 1994 • $30 • (10/15/96)
86 **H.W. HELMS** Chardonnay Carneros 1994 • $11 • (07/31/96)
86 **HILL & THOMA WINEGROWERS** Chardonnay Napa Valley Carneros Bighorn Ranch Reserve 1994 • $19 • (09/15/96)
86 **JOLIESSE** Chardonnay California Reserve 1994 • $7 • (05/31/96) • BB
86 **KENDALL-JACKSON** Chardonnay California Vintner's Reserve 1994 • $14 • (12/15/95)
86 **KENT RASMUSSEN** Chardonnay Napa Valley 1994 • $21 • (02/29/96)
86 **KUNDE** Chardonnay Sonoma Valley 1994 • $14 • (01/31/96)
86 **LEEWARD** Chardonnay Monterey County Reserve 1994 • $15 • (12/15/96)
86 **MERIDIAN** Chardonnay Santa Barbara County Limited Release 1994 • $17 • (06/30/96)
86 **MICHAEL SULLBERG** Chardonnay Knights Valley Lot 54 Barrel Fermented 1994 • $8 • (02/29/96)
86 **MILL CREEK** Chardonnay Dry Creek Valley 1994 • $12 • (06/30/96)
86 **MURPHY-GOODE** Chardonnay Alexander Valley 1994 • $14 • (12/31/95)
86 **NAPA RIDGE** Chardonnay Napa Valley Reserve 1994 • $12 • (06/30/96)
86 **P. & M. STAIGER** Chardonnay Santa Cruz Mountains 1994 • $12 • (06/15/96)
86 **PEJU** Chardonnay Napa Valley 1994 • $15 • (06/30/96)
86 **RUTHERFORD RANCH** Chardonnay Napa Valley 1994 • $10 • (12/15/96)
86 **RUTZ** Chardonnay Russian River Valley 1994 • $20 • (10/15/96)
86 **S. ANDERSON** Chardonnay Napa Valley Carneros 1994 • $18 • (05/15/96)
86 **SEBASTIANI** Chardonnay Russian River Valley Dutton Ranch 1994 • $18 • (06/30/96)
86 **SILVER RIDGE** Chardonnay California Barrel Fermented 1994 • $10 • (06/30/96)
86 **SUNSTONE** Chardonnay Santa Barbara County 1994 • $18 • (07/31/96)
86 **TAFT STREET** Chardonnay Sonoma County 1994 • $10 • (06/15/96) • BB
86 **ZACA MESA** Chardonnay Santa Barbara County Chapel Vineyard 1994 • $18 • (07/31/96)
86 **VON STRASSER** Chardonnay Napa Valley 1994 • $30 • (06/15/96)
85 **BARNETT** Chardonnay Napa Valley 1994 • $18 • (07/31/97)
85 **BEL ARBORS** Chardonnay California Vintner's Selection 1994 • $5 • (05/31/96) • BB
85 **BUEHLER** Chardonnay Russian River Valley 1994 • $13 • (05/15/96)
85 **BUENA VISTA** Chardonnay Carneros 1994 • $12 • (12/15/96)
85 **CAMELOT** Chardonnay Monterey Reserve 1994 • $22 • (06/15/96)
85 **CANEPA** Chardonnay Alexander Valley Gauer Vineyard Adobe III 1994 • $24 • (04/30/96)
85 **CASTLE VINEYARDS** Chardonnay Sonoma Valley 1994 • $15 • (07/31/96)
85 **CHATEAU POTELLE** Chardonnay Napa Valley-Central Coast 1994 • $10 • (10/15/95)
85 **COSENTINO** Chardonnay Napa Valley 1994 • $14 • (06/30/96)
85 **COSENTINO** Chardonnay Napa Valley The Sculptor Reserve 1994 • $25 • (06/30/96)
85 **CUVAISON** Chardonnay Napa Valley Carneros Twenty-Fifth Anniversary Harvest 1994 • $16 • (06/30/96)
85 **DE LOACH** Chardonnay Russian River Valley 1994 • $15 • (06/30/96)

85 **FOREST GLEN** Chardonnay California Barrel Fermented 1994 • $10 • (05/15/96)

85 **GUNDLACH BUNDSCHU** Chardonnay Sonoma Valley Sangiacomo Ranch 1994 • $15 • (07/31/96)

85 **HAYWOOD** Chardonnay California Vintner's Select 1994 • $8 • (11/15/95) • BB

85 **HIDDEN CELLARS** Chardonnay Mendocino County 1994 • $13 • (07/31/96)

85 **MARK WEST** Chardonnay Russian River Valley 1994 • $13 • (01/01/97)

85 **MERIDIAN** Chardonnay Edna Valley Reserve 1994 • $14 • (06/30/96)

85 **MISSION VIEW** Chardonnay Paso Robles 1994 • $10 • (10/31/95)

85 **MONTICELLO** Chardonnay Napa Valley Corley Wild Yeast Estate Reserve 1994 • $33 • (06/15/96)

85 **MORGAN** Chardonnay Monterey 1994 • $18 • (07/31/96)

85 **NAPA RIDGE** Chardonnay Central Coast Coastal Vines 1994 • $8 • (10/15/95)

85 **NAPA RIDGE** Chardonnay Napa Valley Frisinger Vineyard 1994 • $11 • (06/30/96)

85 **NAVARRO** Chardonnay Mendocino 1994 • $8 • (02/29/96)

85 **RANCHO SISQUOC** Chardonnay Santa Maria Valley 1994 • $15 • (07/31/96)

85 **RENAISSANCE** Chardonnay North Yuba Reserve 1994 • $35 • (07/31/97)

85 **RODNEY STRONG** Chardonnay Chalk Hill Chalk Hill Vineyard 1994 • $14 • (04/30/96)

85 **RUTZ** Chardonnay Russian River Valley Quail Hill Vineyard 1994 • $25 • (10/15/96)

85 **SCHUG** Chardonnay Carneros 1994 • $18 • (06/30/96)

85 **SCHUG** Chardonnay Sonoma Valley 1994 • $14 • (06/30/96)

85 **SILVERADO HILL CELLARS** Chardonnay Napa Valley 1994 • $10 • (06/15/96)

85 **SONOMA CREEK** Chardonnay Carneros Reserve 1994 • $15 • (07/31/96)

85 **TURNING LEAF** Chardonnay Sonoma County Sonoma Reserve 1994 • $10 • (12/31/96)

85 **VITA NOVA** Chardonnay Santa Barbara County Rancho Vinedo Vineyards 1994 • $15 • (07/31/96)

85 **WILLIAM HILL** Chardonnay Napa Valley Reserve 1994 • $18 • (12/31/96)

85 **YORK MOUNTAIN** Chardonnay San Luis Obispo County 1994 • $12 • (06/30/96)

1993 California Chardonnay
Vintage Rating: 88

95 **MATANZAS CREEK** Chardonnay Sonoma Valley Journey 1993 • $75 • (02/28/97) • HR

94 **KISTLER** Chardonnay Sonoma Valley Kistler Vineyard 1993 • $40 • (06/30/96) • CS

93 **AU BON CLIMAT** Chardonnay Santa Ynez Valley Sanford & Benedict Reserve 1993 • $34 • (01/31/96)

93 **BYRON** Chardonnay Santa Maria Valley Estate 1993 • $28 • (04/30/96) • HR

93 **FERRARI-CARANO** Chardonnay Alexander Valley Tre Terre 1993 • $22 • (02/29/96)

Key: SS—Spectator Selection CS—Cellar Selection HR—Highly Recommended BB—Best Buy $NA—Price not available Ⓐ—Auction Price
Dates in parentheses indicate the issues in which the ratings were published.

93 **PETER MICHAEL** Chardonnay Sonoma County Cuvée Indigène 1993 • $40 • (01/31/96)

93 **PETER MICHAEL** Chardonnay Sonoma County Mon Plaisir 1993 • $35 • (01/31/96) • HR

93 **VILLA MT. EDEN** Chardonnay Santa Barbara County Signature Series 1993 • $30 • (07/31/95) • HR

92 **BERINGER** Chardonnay Napa Valley Private Reserve 1993 • $20 • (03/31/95) • SS

92 **CHATEAU DE BAUN** Chardonnay Russian River Valley Creekside Vineyard Reserve 1993 • $18 • (02/29/96)

92 **GARY FARRELL** Chardonnay Russian River Valley Allen Vineyard 1993 • $18 • (04/15/95) • HR

92 **KISTLER** Chardonnay Russian River Valley Vine Hill Vineyard 1993 • $35 • (06/30/96)

92 **MACROSTIE** Chardonnay Carneros Reserve 1993 • $23 • (01/31/96)

92 **MARCASSIN** Chardonnay Alexander Valley Gauer Vineyard Upper Barn 1993 • $36 • (06/30/95) • HR

92 **ROMBAUER** Chardonnay Carneros 1993 • $18 • (03/31/95) • SS

92 **SIMI** Chardonnay Sonoma County Reserve 1993 • $28 • (06/15/96) • HR

92 **STONESTREET** Chardonnay Sonoma County 1993 • $21 • (04/30/95) • SS

91 **ADLER FELS** Chardonnay Sonoma County 1993 • $12 • (03/31/96) • HR

91 **ARROWOOD** Chardonnay Sonoma County Cuvée Michel Berthoud Réserve Spéciale 1993 • $24 • (06/15/95) • HR

91 **BYRON** Chardonnay Santa Barbara County Reserve 1993 • $23 • (07/31/95) • HR

91 **CAMBRIA** Chardonnay Santa Maria Valley Reserve 1993 • $25 • (05/31/95) • SS

91 **CARMENET** Chardonnay Sonoma Valley Carneros Sangiacomo Vineyard 1993 • $16 • (06/30/96) • SS

91 **CHALK HILL** Chardonnay Chalk Hill 1993 • $19 • (05/15/95) • SS

91 **CHATEAU ST. JEAN** Chardonnay Alexander Valley Robert Young Vineyard Reserve 1993 • $58 • (05/31/97)

91 **FERRARI-CARANO** Chardonnay Alexander Valley 1993 • $20 • (04/30/95) • SS

91 **FERRARI-CARANO** Chardonnay Napa-Sonoma Counties Reserve 1993 • $30 • (05/15/96)

91 **GAINEY** Chardonnay Santa Ynez Valley Limited Selection 1993 • $25 • (07/31/95)

91 **GLORIA FERRER** Chardonnay Carneros 1993 • $15 • (03/31/95) • SS

91 **KISTLER** Chardonnay Sonoma Mountain McCrea Vineyard 1993 • $35 • (06/30/96) • HR

91 **KISTLER** Chardonnay Sonoma Valley Durell Vineyard 1993 • $34 • (06/15/95) • HR

91 **LITTORAI** Chardonnay Russian River Valley Mays Canyon 1993 • $25 • (12/31/95)

91 **MARCASSIN** Chardonnay Sonoma Coast Lorenzo Vineyard 1993 • $36 • (06/30/95)

91 **MARKHAM** Chardonnay Napa Valley Barrel Fermented 1993 • $17 • (06/15/95) • SS

91 **MATANZAS CREEK** Chardonnay Sonoma Valley 1993 • $23 • (09/30/95) • SS

91 **PATZ & HALL** Chardonnay Napa Valley 1993 • $25 • (06/15/95) • HR

91 **ROBERT MONDAVI** Chardonnay Napa Valley Reserve 1993 • $29 • (07/31/95) • HR

91 **STEELE** Chardonnay Mendocino DuPratt Vineyard 1993 • $24 • (07/31/95)

91 **TALBOTT** Chardonnay Monterey Sleepy Hollow Vineyard 1993 • $26 • (12/31/95) • CS

91 **VILLA MT. EDEN** Chardonnay Carneros Grand Reserve 1993 • $14 • (04/30/95) • HR

91 **WILLIAMS SELYEM** Chardonnay Russian River Valley Allen Vineyard 1993 • $35 • (06/30/95)

90 **ACACIA** Chardonnay Carneros Reserve 1993 • $25 • (04/30/96)

90 **AU BON CLIMAT** Chardonnay Arroyo Grande Valley Talley Vineyard Talley Reserve 1993 • $25 • (07/31/95)

90 **BYRON** Chardonnay Santa Barbara County 1993 • $15 • (07/31/95) • SS

90 **CAMELOT** Chardonnay Santa Barbara County 1993 • $12 • (01/31/95) • HR

90 **DE LOACH** Chardonnay Russian River Valley O.F.S. 1993 • $25 • (09/30/95) • HR

90 **FOXEN** Chardonnay Santa Maria Valley 1993 • $20 • (04/15/95) • HR

90 **FRANCISCAN** Chardonnay Napa Valley Oakville Estate Barrel Fermented 1993 • $12 • (04/15/95) • SS

90 **GEYSER PEAK** Chardonnay Alexander Valley Reserve 1993 • $20 • (04/15/95) • HR

90 **GUENOC** Chardonnay Guenoc Valley Genevieve Magoon Vineyard Reserve 1993 • $25 • (05/31/95) • HR

90 **HANZELL** Chardonnay Sonoma Valley 1993 • $26 • (10/15/96) • CS

90 **IRON HORSE** Chardonnay Sonoma County Cuvée Joy 1993 • $19 • (05/15/95)

90 **KENDALL-JACKSON** Chardonnay California Grand Reserve 1993 • $24 • (06/30/95) • HR

90 **KISTLER** Chardonnay Sonoma County Cuvée Cathleen 1993 • $50 • (06/30/96)

90 **KUNDE** Chardonnay Sonoma Valley Kinneybrook 1993 • $17 • (01/31/96)

90 **LANDMARK** Chardonnay Alexander Valley Damaris Reserve 1993 • $19 • (12/31/94) • HR

90 **LEWIS CELLARS** Chardonnay Napa Valley Oakville Ranch Reserve 1993 • $26 • (07/31/95)

90 **LIPARITA** Chardonnay Howell Mountain 1993 • $16 • (10/31/95) • HR

90 **LONG** Chardonnay Napa Valley 1993 • $30 • (01/31/96)

90 **LOS OLIVOS** Chardonnay Santa Barbara County 1993 • $18 • (09/30/95)

90 **MARCASSIN** Chardonnay Carneros Hudson Vineyard 1993 • $36 • (06/30/95)

90 **MOUNT EDEN** Chardonnay Edna Valley MacGregor Vineyard 1993 • $15 • (03/31/95) • SS

90 **MURPHY-GOODE** Chardonnay Russian River Valley J & K Murphy Vineyard Reserve 1993 • $24 • (07/31/95)

90 **OAKVILLE RANCH** Chardonnay Napa Valley Vista Vineyards 1993 • $18 • (06/15/95) • HR

90 **QUPÉ** Chardonnay Santa Barbara County Sierra Madre Vineyards 1993 • $11 • (04/30/95) • SS

90 **ROCHIOLI** Chardonnay Russian River Valley Reserve 1993 • $28 • (06/15/95)

90 **ST. FRANCIS** Chardonnay Sonoma Valley Reserve 1993 • $19 • (04/15/95) • HR

90 **SANFORD** Chardonnay Santa Barbara County 1993 • $18 • (06/30/95) • SS

90 **SANFORD** Chardonnay Santa Barbara County Barrel Select 1993 • $30 • (07/31/96)

90 **SANTA BARBARA WINERY** Chardonnay Santa Ynez Valley Lafond Vineyard 1993 • $30 • (05/15/96)

90 **SIGNORELLO** Chardonnay Napa Valley Founder's Reserve 1993 • $30 • (07/31/95)

90 **SOLITUDE** Chardonnay Carneros Sangiacomo Vineyard 1993 • $18 • (05/31/95) • HR

90 **STEELE** Chardonnay Mendocino Lolonis Vineyard 1993 • $20 • (07/31/95)

90 **TALBOTT** Chardonnay Monterey Diamond T Estate 1993 • $34 • (05/31/96)

89 **AU BON CLIMAT** Chardonnay Santa Maria Valley Gold Coast Vineyard 1993 • $20 • (07/31/95)

89 **BANNISTER** Chardonnay Russian River Valley Allen Vineyard 1993 • $18 • (06/15/95)

89 **CHATEAU SOUVERAIN** Chardonnay Russian River Valley Rochioli Vineyard Reserve 1993 • $16 • (04/30/95)

89 **CLOS LACHANCE** Chardonnay Santa Cruz Mountains 1993 • $18 • (07/31/95)

89 **CLOS DU BOIS** Chardonnay Alexander Valley Calcaire Vineyard 1993 • $18 • (05/15/95)

89 **FRANCISCAN** Chardonnay Napa Valley Oakville Estate Cuvée Sauvage 1993 • $30 • (05/31/95)

89 **GARY FARRELL** Chardonnay Russian River Valley Westside Farms 1993 • $18 • (07/31/95)

89 **GUNDLACH BUNDSCHU** Chardonnay Sonoma Valley Sangiacomo Ranch Special Selection 1993 • $15 • (11/15/95)

89 **HANDLEY** Chardonnay Dry Creek Valley Cellar Select 1993 • $20 • (06/15/97)

89 **HOP KILN** Chardonnay Russian River Valley M. Griffin Vineyards 1993 • $15 • (02/28/95)

89 **JOSEPH PHELPS** Chardonnay Los Carneros 1993 • $17 • (08/31/95) • HR

89 **KISTLER** Chardonnay Russian River Valley Dutton Ranch 1993 • $35 • (06/30/96)

89 **KISTLER** Chardonnay Sonoma Coast 1993 • $26 • (06/15/95)

89 **KUNDE** Chardonnay Sonoma Valley Reserve 1993 • $20 • (07/31/96)

89 **KUNDE** Chardonnay Sonoma Valley Wildwood 1993 • $17 • (01/31/96)

89 **MARK WEST** Chardonnay Russian River Valley 1993 • $13 • (05/31/96) • SS

89 **MARTIN RAY** Chardonnay California Mariage 1993 • $24 • (08/31/95)

89 **MERRYVALE** Chardonnay Napa Valley Silhouette 1993 • $36 • (05/31/96)

89 **MILLBROOK** Chardonnay Central Coast Mistral Vineyard 1993 • $8 • (02/28/95)

89 **OPTIMA** Chardonnay Carneros 1993 • $25 • (10/15/95)

89 **PAHLMEYER** Chardonnay Napa Valley 1993 • $26 Ⓐ • (04/30/95)

89 **PINE RIDGE** Chardonnay Stags Leap District 1993 • $25 • (06/30/95)

89 **SAINTSBURY** Chardonnay Carneros Reserve 1993 • $25 • (05/31/95)

89 **SANTA BARBARA WINERY** Chardonnay Santa Ynez Valley Reserve 1993 • $20 • (07/31/95)

89 **SARAH'S VINEYARD** Chardonnay Santa Clara County 1993 • $42 • (07/31/95)

89 **SEBASTIANI** Chardonnay Russian River Valley Dutton Ranch 1993 • $18 • (05/31/95)

89 **SONOMA-LOEB** Chardonnay Sonoma County Private Reserve 1993 • $26 • (07/31/95)

89 **STAG'S LEAP WINE CELLARS** Chardonnay Napa Valley Reserve 1993 • $28 • (05/31/95)

89 **V. SATTUI** Chardonnay Napa Valley Carsi Vineyard 1993 • $18 • (02/28/95)

89 **VINE CLIFF** Chardonnay Napa Valley Proprietress Reserve 1993 • $35 • (05/31/95)

89 **VOSS** Chardonnay Napa Valley 1993 • $NA • (02/29/96)

89 **WHITCRAFT** Chardonnay Santa Maria Valley Bien Nacido Vineyard 1993 • $22 • (05/31/95)

88 **BAILEYANA** Chardonnay Edna Valley Paragon Vineyard 1993 • $15 • (07/31/95)

88 **BEAULIEU VINEYARD** Chardonnay Carneros Reserve 1993 • $18 • (12/31/95)

88 **CALE** Chardonnay Carneros Sangiacomo Vineyard 1993 • $18 • (06/15/95)

88 **CALERA** Chardonnay Central Coast 1993 • $15 • (02/28/95)

88 **CAMELOT** Chardonnay Central Coast 1993 • $12 • (07/31/95)

88 **CANEPA** Chardonnay Alexander Valley Canepa Vineyard 1993 • $20 • (12/15/95)

88 **COBBLESTONE VINEYARDS** Chardonnay Monterey County 1993 • $15 • (07/31/96)

88 **CUVAISON** Chardonnay Napa Valley Carneros Reserve 1993 • $28 • (07/31/95)

88 **DEHLINGER** Chardonnay Russian River Valley 1993 • $15 • (05/31/95)

88 **E. & J. GALLO** Chardonnay Northern Sonoma Estate Bottled 1993 • $30 • (07/31/95)

88 **EDNA VALLEY** Chardonnay Edna Valley 1993 • $15 • (06/30/95)

88 **EL MOLINO** Chardonnay Napa Valley 1993 • $30 • (07/31/95)

88 **FESS PARKER** Chardonnay Santa Barbara County American Tradition Reserve 1993 • $18 • (06/15/95)

88 **FETZER** Chardonnay Mendocino Reserve 1993 • $24 • (07/31/95)

88 **GAN EDEN** Chardonnay Sonoma County 1993 • $12 • (07/31/95)

88 **GIRARD** Chardonnay Napa Valley Old Vines 1993 • $19 • (12/15/95)

88 **HILL & THOMA WINEGROWERS** Chardonnay Napa Valley Clos Fontaine du Mont Reserve 1993 • $20 • (05/31/96)

88 **JARVIS** Chardonnay Napa Valley 1993 • $34 • (07/31/96)

88 **KEENAN** Chardonnay Napa Valley 1993 • $15 • (10/15/95)

88 **KENDALL-JACKSON** Chardonnay Santa Maria Valley Camelot Vineyard 1993 • $16 • (07/31/95)

88 **LANDMARK** Chardonnay Sonoma County Overlook 1993 • $14 • (02/28/95)

88 **LAURIER** Chardonnay Sonoma County 1993 • $15 • (03/31/96)

88 **MARIMAR TORRES** Chardonnay Sonoma County Green Valley Don Miguel Vineyard 1993 • $20 • (05/15/96)

88 **MAYACAMAS** Chardonnay Napa Valley 1993 • $18 • (05/15/96)

88 **MERRYVALE** Chardonnay Napa Valley Reserve 1993 • $25 • (07/31/95)

88 **MORGAN** Chardonnay Monterey Reserve 1993 • $23 • (06/15/96)

88 **MUELLER** Chardonnay Sonoma County Gauer Ranch 1993 • $15 • (03/31/96)

88 **NAPA RIDGE** Chardonnay Napa Valley Frisinger Vineyard 1993 • $11 • (04/15/95)

88 **NAVARRO** Chardonnay Anderson Valley Première Reserve 1993 • $NA • (02/29/96)

88 **PEJU** Chardonnay Napa Valley HB Vineyard 1993 • $22 • (12/31/94)

Key: SS—Spectator Selection CS—Cellar Selection HR—Highly Recommended BB—Best Buy $NA—Price not available Ⓐ—Auction Price
Dates in parentheses indicate the issues in which the ratings were published.

88 **QUPÉ** Chardonnay Santa Barbara County Sierra Madre Reserve 1993 • $25 • (07/31/95)

88 **RABBIT RIDGE** Chardonnay Russian River Valley Rabbit Ridge Ranch Estate Reserve 1993 • $16 • (07/31/95)

88 **ROBERT MONDAVI** Chardonnay Carneros 1993 • $23 • (05/15/96)

88 **SCHUG** Chardonnay Carneros Heritage Reserve 1993 • $25 • (07/31/95)

88 **SIGNORELLO** Chardonnay Napa Valley 1993 • $20 • (04/15/95)

88 **STAG'S LEAP WINE CELLARS** Chardonnay Napa Valley 1993 • $19 • (07/31/95)

88 **STEELE** Chardonnay Santa Barbara County Bien Nacido Vineyard 1993 • $22 • (07/31/95)

88 **SWANSON** Chardonnay Napa Valley Carneros 1993 • $20 • (07/31/95)

88 **TALLEY** Chardonnay Arroyo Grande Valley 1993 • $18 • (07/31/95)

88 **TERRA** Chardonnay Carneros Sangiacomo Vineyard 1993 • $19 • (06/30/96)

88 **WENTE** Chardonnay Livermore Valley Herman Wente Reserve 1993 • $14 • (09/30/95)

88 **WILD HORSE** Chardonnay Central Coast 1993 • $13 • (01/31/95)

88 **ZACA MESA** Chardonnay Santa Barbara County Alumni Winemaker Series James A. Clendenen 1993 • $18 • (02/29/96)

87 **ARROWOOD** Chardonnay Sonoma County 1993 • $20 • (06/15/95)

87 **AU BON CLIMAT** Chardonnay Santa Barbara County 1993 • $16 • (07/31/95)

87 **BEAUCANON** Chardonnay Napa Valley 1993 • $12 • (07/31/95)

87 **BELVEDERE** Chardonnay Russian River Valley 1993 • $12 • (10/15/95)

87 **BERNARDUS** Chardonnay Monterey County 1993 • $15 • (06/30/95)

87 **CAMBRIA** Chardonnay Santa Maria Valley Katherine's Vineyard 1993 • $16 • (02/28/95)

87 **CARNEROS CREEK** Chardonnay California Fleur de Carneros 1993 • $9 • (09/30/95) • BB

87 **CHALONE** Chardonnay Chalone 1993 • $27 • (07/31/95)

87 **CHATEAU DE BAUN** Chardonnay Russian River Valley 1993 • $10 • (04/30/95)

87 **CHAUFFE-EAU** Chardonnay Carneros Sans Filtrage Sangiacomo 1993 • $17 • (07/31/95)

87 **CLAIBORNE & CHURCHILL** Chardonnay Edna Valley MacGregor Vineyard 1993 • $17 • (07/31/95)

87 **CLOS DANIELLE** Chardonnay Carneros Private Reserve 1993 • $9 • (01/31/95) • BB

87 **CLOS PEGASE** Chardonnay Napa Valley Carneros Pegase Circle Reserve 1993 • $20 • (07/31/95)

87 **CONCANNON** Chardonnay Livermore Valley Reserve 1993 • $15 • (07/31/95)

87 **DURNEY** Chardonnay Carmel Valley Dances On Your Palate 1993 • $18 • (07/31/96)

87 **ESTANCIA** Chardonnay Monterey County 1993 • $9 • (04/15/95) • BB

87 **ESTANCIA** Chardonnay Monterey County Reserve 1993 • $20 • (07/31/95)

87 **FESS PARKER** Chardonnay Santa Barbara County 1993 • $13 • (01/31/95)

87 **FETZER** Chardonnay North Coast Barrel Select 1993 • $11 • (06/30/95)

87 **FIRESTONE** Chardonnay Santa Ynez Valley Barrel Fermented 1993 • $12 • (11/30/94)

87 **GALLO OF SONOMA** Chardonnay Sonoma County 1993 • $12 • (06/30/95)

87 **GIRARD** Chardonnay Napa Valley Viridian Vineyard 1993 • $38 • (12/15/95)

87 **HANDLEY** Chardonnay Dry Creek Valley 1993 • $15 • (06/30/96)

87 **IRON HORSE** Chardonnay Sonoma County Green Valley 1993 • $18 • (05/15/95)

87 **J. LOHR** Chardonnay Monterey Riverstone 1993 • $12 • (12/15/95)

87 **MILL CREEK** Chardonnay Dry Creek Valley 1993 • $12 • (05/15/95)

87 **MIRASSOU** Chardonnay Monterey County Fifth Generation Harvest Reserve 1993 • $12 • (07/31/95)

87 **NAPA RIDGE** Chardonnay Central Coast 1993 • $7 • (06/15/94) • BB

87 **NICHOLS** Chardonnay Arroyo Grande Valley Talley Vineyards 1993 • $20 • (12/31/95)

87 **OJAI** Chardonnay Santa Barbara County Reserve 1993 • $21 • (07/31/95)

87 **PRIDE** Chardonnay Napa Valley 1993 • $18 • (07/31/95)

87 **RAYMOND** Chardonnay Napa Valley 1993 • $14 • (12/15/95)

87 **ROBERT SINSKEY** Chardonnay Napa Valley Los Carneros 1993 • $20 • (07/31/95)

87 **SEBASTIANI** Chardonnay Sonoma County 1993 • $10 • (06/15/95) • BB

87 **SHAFER** Chardonnay Napa Valley Barrel Select 1993 • $16 • (04/30/95)

87 **SILVERADO VINEYARDS** Chardonnay Napa Valley 1993 • $15 • (05/31/95)

87 **TRUCHARD** Chardonnay Napa Valley Carneros 1993 • $17 • (07/31/95)

87 **WHITE OAK** Chardonnay Sonoma County Myers Limited Reserve 1993 • $16 • (10/15/95)

87 **WILLIAM HILL** Chardonnay Napa Valley Reserve 1993 • $18 • (12/15/96)

87 **WILSON DANIELS** Chardonnay Napa Valley 1993 • $10 • (05/15/96)

87 **ZACA MESA** Chardonnay Santa Barbara County Zaca Vineyards 1993 • $12 • (01/31/95)

86 **BEAULIEU VINEYARD** Chardonnay Napa Valley Beautour 1993 • $10 • (04/30/95) • BB

86 **BURGESS** Chardonnay Napa Valley Barrel Fermented Debourbage 1993 • $15 • (07/31/95)

86 **CHAPPELLET** Chardonnay Napa Valley 1993 • $15 • (10/31/95)

86 **CHATEAU ST. JEAN** Chardonnay Alexander Valley Belle Terre Vineyards 1993 • $18 • (07/31/95)

86 **CHATEAU WOLTNER** Chardonnay Howell Mountain 1993 • $10 • (09/30/94)

86 **CHAUFFE-EAU** Chardonnay Russian River Valley Sans Filtrage Dutton 1993 • $18 • (07/31/95)

86 **CLOS DU VAL** Chardonnay Carneros Special Select 1993 • $20 • (04/30/95)

86 **CLOS PEGASE** Chardonnay Napa Valley Carneros 1993 • $15 • (09/30/95)

86 **CLOS DU BOIS** Chardonnay Dry Creek Valley Flintwood Vineyard 1993 • $17 • (07/31/95)

86 **COSENTINO** Chardonnay Napa Valley The Sculptor Reserve 1993 • $24 • (02/28/95)

86 **CUVAISON** Chardonnay Napa Valley Carneros 1993 • $15 • (07/31/95)

86 **GAINEY** Chardonnay Santa Barbara County 1993 • $14 • (07/31/95)

86 **GRGICH HILLS** Chardonnay Napa Valley 1993 • $24 • (12/15/95)

86 **GUENOC** Chardonnay Guenoc Valley 1993 • $15 • (02/28/95)

86 **HARRISON** Chardonnay Napa Valley 1993 • $26 • (07/31/95)

86 **HESS SELECT** Chardonnay California 1993 • $10 • (12/15/94) • BB

86 **HIDDEN CELLARS** Chardonnay Mendocino County Organically Grown Grapes 1993 • $10 • (09/30/95)

86 **JOULLIAN** Chardonnay Monterey Family Reserve 1993 • $20 • (06/15/96)

86 **LAMBERT BRIDGE** Chardonnay Sonoma County Barrel Fermented 1993 • $13 • (04/15/95)

86 **LEEWARD** Chardonnay Edna Valley Reserve 1993 • $15 • (05/31/95)

86 **LOCKWOOD** Chardonnay Monterey 1993 • $15 • (12/15/95)

86 **LOCKWOOD** Chardonnay Monterey Partners' Reserve 1993 • $17 • (06/30/96)

86 **LONGORIA** Chardonnay Santa Ynez Valley Huber Vineyard 1993 • $16 • (07/31/95)

86 **MURPHY-GOODE** Chardonnay Alexander Valley 1993 • $13 • (07/31/95)

86 **NAPA RIDGE** Chardonnay Napa Valley Reserve 1993 • $13 • (07/31/95)

86 **NEVADA CITY** Chardonnay Nevada County Barrel Fermented 1993 • $11 • (07/31/95)

86 **NEYERS** Chardonnay Carneros 1993 • $16 • (02/28/95)

86 **OJAI** Chardonnay Arroyo Grande Valley 1993 • $18 • (07/31/95)

86 **PARAISO SPRINGS** Chardonnay Santa Lucia Highlands 1993 • $12 • (07/31/95)

86 **PAUL HOBBS** Chardonnay Sonoma Mountain Richard Dinner Vineyard 1993 • $28 • (07/31/95)

86 **PEJU** Chardonnay Napa Valley 1993 • $16 • (07/31/95)

86 **ROUND HILL** Chardonnay California 1993 • $7 • (04/30/95) • BB

86 **RUTHERFORD VINEYARDS** Chardonnay Napa Valley 1993 • $8 • (06/15/95) • BB

86 **S. ANDERSON** Chardonnay Napa Valley Carneros 1993 • $18 • (04/30/95)

86 **SALAMANDRE** Chardonnay Santa Cruz Mountains Matteson Vineyard 1993 • $16 • (07/31/95)

86 **SANFORD** Chardonnay Santa Ynez Valley 1993 • $24 • (07/31/95)

86 **SONOMA-LOEB** Chardonnay Sonoma County 1993 • $16 • (07/31/95)

86 **SOQUEL** Chardonnay California Coastal Cellars 1993 • $6 • (07/31/96)

86 **STEELE** Chardonnay California 1993 • $18 • (07/31/95)

86 **STONY HILL** Chardonnay Napa Valley SHV 1993 • $23 • (07/31/95)

86 **STORRS** Chardonnay Santa Cruz Mountains Vanumanutagi Vineyards 1993 • $19 • (05/31/95)

86 **TAFT STREET** Chardonnay Sonoma County 1993 • $10 • (01/31/95) • BB

85 **ATLAS PEAK** Chardonnay Atlas Peak 1993 • $16 • (07/31/95)

85 **BABCOCK** Chardonnay San Luis Obispo Talley Vineyard 1993 • $25 • (01/31/95)

85 **BABCOCK** Chardonnay Santa Barbara County 1993 • $16 • (01/31/95)

85 **BEAULIEU VINEYARD** Chardonnay Napa Valley Carneros 1993 • $13 • (09/30/95)

85 **BENZIGER** Chardonnay Carneros 1993 • $13 • (06/30/95)

85 **BOUCHAINE** Chardonnay Carneros 1993 • $15 • (02/29/96)

85 **BOUCHAINE** Chardonnay Napa Valley Carneros Estate Reserve 1993 • $22 • (06/30/96)

85 **BUEHLER** Chardonnay Russian River Valley 1993 • $13 • (01/31/95)

85 **BURGESS** Chardonnay Napa Valley Triere Vineyard Reserve 1993 • $22 • (11/30/96)

85 **CHATEAU ST. JEAN** Chardonnay Sonoma County 1993 • $11 • (05/15/96)

85 **CHATEAU SOUVERAIN** Chardonnay Sonoma County Barrel Fermented 1993 • $12 • (06/15/95)

85 **CLOS DU VAL** Chardonnay Napa Valley Carneros 1993 • $15 • (12/15/95)

85 **CRONIN** Chardonnay Alexander Valley Stuhlmuller Vineyard 1993 • $18 • (07/31/95)

85 **CRONIN** Chardonnay Napa Valley 1993 • $18 • (07/31/95)

85 **DE LOACH** Chardonnay Russian River Valley 1993 • $15 • (02/29/96)

85 **EDMEADES** Chardonnay Anderson Valley Dennison Vineyard 1993 • $20 • (07/31/95)

85 **ELKHORN PEAK** Chardonnay Napa Valley Fagan Creek Vineyards 1993 • $15 • (07/31/95)

85 **ESTATE WILLIAM BACCALA** Chardonnay Sonoma County 1993 • $13 • (02/29/96)

85 **FAR NIENTE** Chardonnay Napa Valley 1993 • $32 • (07/31/95)

85 **FISHER** Chardonnay Sonoma County Whitney's Vineyard 1993 • $26 • (07/31/95)

85 **FOREST HILL** Chardonnay Napa Valley Private Reserve 1993 • $28 • (07/31/95)

85 **FOXEN** Chardonnay Santa Maria Valley Tinaquaic Vineyard 1993 • $28 • (07/31/95)

85 **GEYSER PEAK** Chardonnay Sonoma County 1993 • $10 • (12/15/94) • BB

85 **GLEN ELLEN** Chardonnay California Proprietor's Reserve 1993 • $5 • (07/31/95) • BB

85 **GODSPEED** Chardonnay Mount Veeder 1993 • $15 • (07/31/95)

85 **HAHN** Chardonnay Monterey 1993 • $10 • (03/31/95)

85 **HANNA** Chardonnay Russian River Valley Reserve 1993 • $18 • (06/30/96)

85 **HUSCH** Chardonnay Mendocino 1993 • $12 • (11/30/94)

85 **J. LOHR** Chardonnay California Cypress 1993 • $9 • (12/15/95)

85 **KENDALL-JACKSON** Chardonnay California Vintner's Reserve 1993 • $14 • (09/15/94)

85 **KORBEL** Chardonnay Russian River Valley 1993 • $15 • (06/30/95)

85 **LA CREMA** Chardonnay California Grand Cuvée 1993 • $20 • (05/31/95)

85 **LA CREMA** Chardonnay California Reserve 1993 • $12 • (05/31/95)

85 **MACROSTIE** Chardonnay Carneros 1993 • $16 • (02/28/95)

85 **MADROÑA** Chardonnay El Dorado 1993 • $12 • (07/31/95)

85 **MERIDIAN** Chardonnay Edna Valley 1993 • $14 • (04/30/95)

85 **MERIDIAN** Chardonnay Santa Barbara County 1993 • $10 • (06/15/95)

Key: SS—Spectator Selection CS—Cellar Selection HR—Highly Recommended BB—Best Buy $NA—Price not available Ⓐ—Auction Price
Dates in parentheses indicate the issues in which the ratings were published.

85 **MONT ST. JOHN** Chardonnay Carneros Organically Grown Grapes 1993 • $13 • (07/31/95)

85 **MONTEREY VINEYARD** Chardonnay Monterey County Limited Release 1993 • $13 • (07/31/95)

85 **NAPA RIDGE** Chardonnay Central Coast Coastal Vines 1993 • $8 • (11/30/94) • BB

85 **PETER MCCOY** Chardonnay Knights Valley Clos des Pierres 1993 • $20 • (06/15/96)

85 **R.H. PHILLIPS** Chardonnay California Barrel Cuvée 1993 • $7 • (06/30/95) • BB

85 **ROBERT MONDAVI** Chardonnay Napa Valley Unfiltered 1993 • $15 • (07/31/95)

85 **ROCHIOLI** Chardonnay Russian River Valley 1993 • $16 • (07/31/95)

85 **RODNEY STRONG** Chardonnay Chalk Hill Chalk Hill Vineyard 1993 • $14 • (07/31/95)

85 **SAINT GREGORY** Chardonnay Mendocino 1993 • $16 • (07/31/96)

85 **SAINTSBURY** Chardonnay Carneros 1993 • $15 • (07/31/95)

85 **SALMON CREEK** Chardonnay Carneros 1993 • $12 • (07/31/95)

85 **SCHUG** Chardonnay Sonoma Valley 1993 • $12 • (11/30/94)

85 **STERLING** Chardonnay Napa Valley Z Lot 1993 • $20 • (07/31/95)

85 **STONY HILL** Chardonnay Napa Valley 1993 • $21 Ⓐ • (06/15/96)

85 **STORRS** Chardonnay Santa Cruz Mountains Christie Vineyard Mountain Vineyard Collection 1993 • $17 • (07/31/95)

85 **TREFETHEN** Chardonnay Napa Valley 1993 • $19 • (07/31/95)

85 **VILLA MT. EDEN** Chardonnay California Cellar Select 1993 • $8 • (04/30/95)

85 **WENTE** Chardonnay Arroyo Seco Riva Ranch 1993 • $8 • (05/15/96)

85 **WENTE** Chardonnay Central Coast 1993 • $9 • (04/30/95)

85 **WILDHURST** Chardonnay California 1993 • $10 • (07/31/95)

85 **ZD WINES** Chardonnay California 1993 • $23 • (02/28/95)

85 **DELORIMIER** Chardonnay Alexander Valley 1993 • $14 • (02/29/96)

Top-Rated Current Releases

By Wine Type

This section of the book is where you look if you are interested in a particular wine type and want a "shopping list" of the best currently available wines of that type. (The main listings section, which follows, is where you look if you have a specific wine in mind and want to know *Wine Spectator*'s rating and price.)

Seventeen popular wine types are covered here, with the top-rated wines of each type listed in descending order by score. These cover the most recent vintages reviewed, those that you will find in most wine shops.

RED BORDEAUX

100 **CHÂTEAU LATOUR** Pauillac 1990 • $NA • (12/15/97)
100 **CHÂTEAU MARGAUX** Margaux 1995 • $120 • (01/31/98) • CS
98 **CHÂTEAU LATOUR** Pauillac 1989 • $95 • (12/15/97)
98 **CHÂTEAU PÉTRUS** Pomerol 1995 • $650 • (01/31/98) • CS
97 **CHÂTEAU DUCRU-BEAUCAILLOU** St.-Julien 1995 • $50 • (01/31/98) • CS
97 **CHÂTEAU LAFITE ROTHSCHILD** Pauillac 1995 • $120 • (01/31/98) • CS
97 **CHÂTEAU TROTANOY** Pomerol 1995 • $75 • (01/31/98) • HR
96 **CHÂTEAU CALON-SÉGUR** St.-Estèphe 1995 • $30 • (01/31/98) • SS
96 **CHÂTEAU L'EGLISE CLINET** Pomerol 1995 • $200 • (01/31/98)
96 **CHÂTEAU MOUTON-ROTHSCHILD** Pauillac 1995 • $120 • (01/31/98) • CS
96 **CHÂTEAU PICHON-LONGUEVILLE-LALANDE** Pauillac 1995 • $75 • (01/31/98) • CS
95 **CHÂTEAU AUSONE** St.-Emilion 1995 • $120 • (01/31/98) • HR
95 **CHÂTEAU CANON-LA GAFFELIÈRE** St.-Emilion 1995 • $45 • (01/31/98)
95 **CHÂTEAU CLERC MILON** Pauillac 1995 • $25 • (01/31/98) • SS
95 **CHÂTEAU CLINET** Pomerol 1995 • $120 • (01/31/98)
95 **CHÂTEAU FIGEAC** St.-Emilion 1995 • $45 • (01/31/98)
95 **CHÂTEAU LAFLEUR** Pomerol 1995 • $75 • (01/31/98)
95 **CHÂTEAU PICHON-LONGUEVILLE-LALANDE** Pauillac 1989 • $NA • (11/15/97)
95 **VIEUX-CHÂTEAU-CERTAN** Pomerol 1995 • $55 • (01/31/98)
94 **CHÂTEAU ANGÉLUS** St.-Emilion 1995 • $70 • (01/31/98)
94 **CHÂTEAU CHEVAL-BLANC** St.-Emilion 1995 • $120 • (01/31/98)
94 **CHÂTEAU FERRIÈRE** Margaux 1995 • $25 • (01/31/98)
94 **CHÂTEAU HAUT-BRION** Pessac-Léognan 1995 • $120 • (01/31/98)
94 **CHÂTEAU LA CONSEILLANTE** Pomerol 1995 • $80 • (01/31/98)
94 **CHÂTEAU LATOUR** Pauillac 1995 • $120 • (01/31/98) • CS
94 **CHÂTEAU LYNCH-BAGES** Pauillac 1995 • $40 • (01/31/98)
94 **CHÂTEAU PALMER** Margaux 1995 • $60 • (01/31/98)
94 **CHÂTEAU PICHON-LONGUEVILLE-LALANDE** Pauillac 1990 • $NA • (11/15/97)
94 **CHÂTEAU PONTET-CANET** Pauillac 1995 • $35 • (01/31/98) • SS
94 **CHÂTEAU RAUZAN-SÉGLA** Margaux 1995 • $35 • (01/31/98)
93 **CHÂTEAU COS-D'ESTOURNEL** St.-Estèphe 1995 • $45 • (01/31/98)
93 **CHÂTEAU KIRWAN** Margaux 1995 • $25 • (01/31/98)
93 **CHÂTEAU LAFON-ROCHET** St.-Estèphe 1995 • $33 • (01/31/98)
93 **CHÂTEAU LANGOA BARTON** St.-Julien 1995 • $30 • (01/31/98)
93 **CHÂTEAU LARMANDE** St.-Emilion 1995 • $30 • (01/31/98)
93 **CHÂTEAU LA MISSION-HAUT-BRION** Pessac-Léognan 1995 • $65 • (01/31/98)
93 **CHÂTEAU LÉOVILLE BARTON** St.-Julien 1995 • $45 • (01/31/98)
93 **CHÂTEAU LÉOVILLE POYFERRÉ** St.-Julien 1995 • $30 • (01/31/98)
93 **CHÂTEAU PAVIE-MACQUIN** St.-Emilion 1995 • $35 • (01/31/98)
93 **PENSÉES DE LAFLEUR** Pomerol 1995 • $75 • (01/31/98)
93 **CHÂTEAU LE PIN** Pomerol 1995 • $500 • (01/31/98)
93 **CHÂTEAU LA POINTE** Pomerol 1995 • $25 • (01/31/98)
93 **CHÂTEAU SIRAN** Margaux 1995 • $25 • (01/31/98)
93 **CHÂTEAU DE VALANDRAUD** St.-Emilion 1995 • $150 • (01/31/98)
92 **CHÂTEAU D'ARMAILHAC** Pauillac 1995 • $20 • (01/31/98)
92 **CHÂTEAU BOURGNEUF** Pomerol 1995 • $30 • (01/31/98)
92 **CHÂTEAU DAUZAC** Margaux 1995 • $20 • (01/31/98)
92 **CHÂTEAU GISCOURS** Margaux 1995 • $25 • (01/31/98)
92 **CHÂTEAU GRAND-PUY-LACOSTE** Pauillac 1995 • $35 • (01/31/98)
92 **CHÂTEAU HAUT-BAILLY** Pessac-Léognan 1995 • $40 • (01/31/98)
92 **CHÂTEAU LASCOMBES** Margaux 1995 • $30 • (01/31/98)
92 **CHÂTEAU MONBOUSQUET** St.-Emilion 1995 • $25 • (01/31/98)
92 **CHÂTEAU MOULIN-ST.-GEORGES** St.-Emilion 1995 • $24 • (01/31/98)
92 **CHÂTEAU PAPE CLÉMENT** Pessac-Léognan 1995 • $40 • (01/31/98)
92 **CHÂTEAU POUJEAUX** Moulis 1995 • $24 • (01/31/98)
92 **CHÂTEAU TROPLONG-MONDOT** St.-Emilion 1995 • $50 • (01/31/98)
91 **CHÂTEAU BEAUREGARD** Pomerol 1995 • $50 • (01/31/98)
91 **CLOS DE L'EGLISE** Pomerol 1995 • $30 • (01/31/98)
91 **CHÂTEAU DE FIEUZAL** Pessac-Léognan 1995 • $30 • (01/31/98)
91 **CHÂTEAU HAUT-MARBUZET** St.-Estèphe 1995 • $35 • (01/31/98)
91 **CHÂTEAU LAGRANGE** St.-Julien 1995 • $30 • (01/31/98)
91 **CHÂTEAU MAGDELAINE** St.-Emilion 1995 • $40 • (01/31/98)
91 **CHÂTEAU MALESCOT-ST.-EXUPÉRY** Margaux 1995 • $35 • (01/31/98)
91 **CHÂTEAU PAVIE-DECESSE** St.-Emilion 1995 • $28 • (01/31/98)
91 **CHÂTEAU RAUZAN-GASSIES** Margaux 1995 • $30 • (01/31/98)
91 **CHÂTEAU LA SERRE** St.-Emilion 1995 • $28 • (01/31/98)
91 **CHÂTEAU SOCIANDO-MALLET** Haut-Médoc 1995 • $25 • (01/31/98)
91 **LES FORTS DE LATOUR** Pauillac 1995 • $39 • (01/31/98)
91 **PAVILLON ROUGE DU CHÂTEAU MARGAUX** Margaux 1995 • $38 • (01/31/98)
90 **CARRUADES DE LAFITE ROTHSCHILD** Pauillac 1995 • $30 • (01/31/98)
90 **CHÂTEAU LE BON-PASTEUR** Pomerol 1995 • $38 • (01/31/98)
90 **CHÂTEAU CANUET** Margaux 1995 • $20 • (01/31/98)
90 **CHÂTEAU LA CARDONNE** Médoc 1995 • $18 • (01/31/98)
90 **CHÂTEAU CHASSE-SPLEEN** Moulis 1995 • $26 • (01/31/98)
90 **CHÂTEAU CLOS DES JACOBINS** St.-Emilion 1995 • $30 • (01/31/98)
90 **CLOS DE L'ORATOIRE** St.-Emilion 1995 • $30 • (01/31/98)
90 **CLOS FOURTET** St.-Emilion 1995 • $25 • (01/31/98)
90 **DOMAINE DE COURTEILLAC** Bordeaux Supérieur 1995 • $18 • (01/31/98)
90 **CHÂTEAU DE CRUZEAU** Pessac-Léognan 1995 • $15 • (01/31/98)
90 **CHÂTEAU DUHART-MILON ROTHSCHILD** Pauillac 1995 • $25 • (01/31/98)
90 **CHÂTEAU FAIZEAU** Montagne-St.-Emilion Sélection Vieilles Vignes 1995 • $18 • (01/31/98)
90 **CHÂTEAU FERRANDE** Graves 1995 • $12 • (01/31/98)

Key: SS—Spectator Selection CS—Cellar Selection HR—Highly Recommended BB—Best Buy $NA—Price not available Ⓐ—Auction Price
Dates in parentheses indicate the issues in which the ratings were published.

90 **CHÂTEAU LA FLEUR DE GAY** Pomerol 1995 • $80 • (01/31/98)
90 **CHÂTEAU FONTENIL** Fronsac 1995 • $15 • (01/31/98)
90 **CHÂTEAU LA GARDE** Pessac-Léognan 1995 • $15 • (01/31/98)
90 **CHÂTEAU GAZIN** Pomerol 1995 • $45 • (01/31/98)
90 **CHÂTEAU GLORIA** St.-Julien 1995 • $25 • (01/31/98)
90 **CHÂTEAU GRAND MOULINET** Pomerol 1995 • $20 • (01/31/98)
90 **CHÂTEAU LA GURGUE** Margaux 1995 • $25 • (01/31/98)
90 **CHÂTEAU HAUT-BAGES-LIBÉRAL** Pauillac 1995 • $20 • (01/31/98)
90 **CHÂTEAU HAUT-BATAILLEY** Pauillac 1995 • $30 • (01/31/98)
90 **CHÂTEAU HAUT-LAGRANGE** Pessac-Léognan 1995 • $20 • (01/31/98)
90 **CHÂTEAU LAFLEUR-GAZIN** Pomerol 1995 • $30 • (01/31/98)
90 **CHÂTEAU LATOUR** Pauillac 1994 • $92 • (12/15/97)
90 **CHÂTEAU MOULIN PEY-LABRIE** Canon-Fronsac 1995 • $18 • (01/31/98)
90 **CHÂTEAU PRIEURÉ-LICHINE** Margaux 1995 • $27 • (01/31/98)
90 **CHÂTEAU ST.-PIERRE** St.-Julien 1995 • $25 • (01/31/98)
90 **CHÂTEAU SMITH-HAUT-LAFITTE** Pessac-Léognan 1995 • $30 • (01/31/98)
90 **CHÂTEAU TERTRE DAUGAY** St.-Emilion 1995 • $44 • (01/31/98)
89 **CHÂTEAU BATAILLEY** Pauillac 1995 • $22 • (01/31/98)
89 **CHÂTEAU BEAUSÉJOUR** St.-Emilion 1995 • $35 • (01/31/98)
89 **CHÂTEAU BEYCHEVELLE** St.-Julien 1995 • $30 • (01/31/98)
89 **CHÂTEAU CARBONNIEUX** Pessac-Léognan 1995 • $20 • (01/31/98)
89 **CHÂTEAU LA CARDONNE** Médoc 1994 • $16 • (11/30/97)
89 **CHÂTEAU CARONNE-STE.-GEMME** Haut-Médoc 1995 • $20 • (01/31/98)
89 **CHÂTEAU LA CROIX-DE-GAY** Pomerol 1995 • $25 • (01/31/98)
89 **CHÂTEAU LA CROIX DU CASSE** Pomerol 1995 • $23 • (01/31/98)
89 **CHÂTEAU DE LA DAUPHINE** Fronsac 1995 • $20 • (01/31/98)
89 **CHÂTEAU LA DOMINIQUE** St.-Emilion 1995 • $40 • (01/31/98)
89 **CHÂTEAU LA FLEUR-PÉTRUS** Pomerol 1995 • $65 • (01/31/98)
89 **CHÂTEAU LA GAFFELIÈRE** St.-Emilion 1995 • $37 • (01/31/98)
89 **CHÂTEAU HAUT-BAGES-AVÉROUS** Pauillac 1995 • $25 • (01/31/98)
89 **CHÂTEAU HAUT-GARDÈRE** Pessac-Léognan 1995 • $15 • (01/31/98)
89 **CHÂTEAU HAUT LARIVEAU** Canon-Fronsac 1995 • $20 • (01/31/98)
89 **CHÂTEAU D'ISSAN** Margaux 1995 • $25 • (01/31/98)
89 **CHÂTEAU LABÉGORCE-ZÉDÉ** Margaux 1995 • $22 • (01/31/98)
89 **DOMAINE DE LARRIVET** Pessac-Léognan 1995 • $20 • (01/31/98)
89 **CHÂTEAU LATOUR** Pauillac 1993 • $60 • (12/15/97)
89 **CHÂTEAU LATOUR À POMEROL** Pomerol 1995 • $50 • (01/31/98)
89 **CHÂTEAU D'OLIVIER** Pessac-Léognan 1995 • $25 • (01/31/98)
89 **CHÂTEAU ROBIN** Côtes de Castillon 1995 • $15 • (01/31/98)
89 **CHÂTEAU ST.-ROBERT** Graves Cuvée Poncet-Deville 1995 • $25 • (01/31/98)
89 **SÉGLA** Margaux 1995 • $25 • (01/31/98)
89 **CHÂTEAU LA TOURETTE** Pauillac 1995 • $22 • (01/31/98)
89 **CHÂTEAU TRONQUOY-LALANDE** St.-Estèphe 1995 • $20 • (01/31/98)
89 **CHÂTEAU LA VIEILLE CURE** Fronsac 1995 • $20 • (01/31/98)
88 **CHÂTEAU D'ANGLUDET** Margaux 1995 • $30 • (01/31/98)
88 **CHÂTEAU D'ARCINS** Haut-Médoc 1995 • $12 • (01/31/98)
88 **CHÂTEAU BARREYRES** Haut-Médoc 1995 • $12 • (01/31/98)
88 **CHÂTEAU BEAUMONT** Haut-Médoc 1995 • $15 • (01/31/98)
88 **CHÂTEAU LE BOSCQ** St.-Estèphe 1995 • $20 • (01/31/98)
88 **CHÂTEAU BROWN** Pessac-Léognan 1995 • $18 • (01/31/98)
88 **CHÂTEAU CANTELYS** Pessac-Léognan 1995 • $30 • (01/31/98)
88 **CHÂTEAU CANTENAC-BROWN** Margaux 1995 • $25 • (01/31/98)
88 **LES CHARMES DE KIRWAN** Margaux 1995 • $18 • (01/31/98)
88 **CHÂTEAU LES CHARMES-GODARD** Côtes de Francs 1995 • $18 • (01/31/98)
88 **CLOS MARSALETTE** Pessac-Léognan 1995 • $20 • (01/31/98)
88 **CHÂTEAU COS-LABORY** St.-Estèphe 1995 • $20 • (01/31/98)
88 **DOMAINE DE L'EGLISE** Pomerol 1995 • $21 • (01/31/98)
88 **LES FIEFS DE LAGRANGE** St.-Julien 1995 • $19 • (01/31/98)
88 **CHÂTEAU FONPLÉGADE** St.-Emilion 1995 • $24 • (01/31/98)
88 **CHÂTEAU GRAND VILLAGE** Bordeaux Supérieur 1995 • $15 • (01/31/98)
88 **CHÂTEAU GRIVIÈRE** Médoc 1995 • $18 • (01/31/98)
88 **CHÂTEAU GRUAUD-LAROSE** St.-Julien 1995 • $45 • (01/31/98)
88 **CHÂTEAU LARCIS-DUCASSE** St.-Emilion 1995 • $20 • (01/31/98)
88 **CHÂTEAU LATOUR** Pauillac 1991 • $65 • (12/15/97)
88 **CHÂTEAU MALARTIC-LAGRAVIÈRE** Pessac-Léognan 1995 • $25 • (01/31/98)
88 **CHÂTEAU MARSAU** Côtes de Francs 1995 • $15 • (01/31/98)
88 **CHÂTEAU MONTROSE** St.-Estèphe 1995 • $40 • (01/31/98)
88 **LA PARDE DE HAUT-BAILLY** Pessac-Léognan 1995 • $15 • (01/31/98)
88 **CHÂTEAU PAVIE** St.-Emilion 1995 • $30 • (01/31/98)
88 **CHÂTEAU PETIT-VILLAGE** Pomerol 1995 • $40 • (01/31/98)
88 **CHÂTEAU PHÉLAN-SÉGUR** St.-Estèphe 1995 • $25 • (01/31/98)
88 **CHÂTEAU PIBRAN** Pauillac 1995 • $20 • (01/31/98)
88 **CHÂTEAU PICHON-LONGUEVILLE-BARON** Pauillac 1995 • $35 • (01/31/98)
88 **CHÂTEAU PICHON-LONGUEVILLE-LALANDE** Pauillac 1994 • $NA • (11/15/97)
88 **RÉSERVE DE LA COMTESSE** Pauillac 1995 • $25 • (01/31/98)
88 **CHÂTEAU TOUMALIN** Canon-Fronsac 1995 • $18 • (01/31/98)
88 **CHÂTEAU LA TOUR-HAUT-BRION** Pessac-Léognan 1995 • $35 • (01/31/98)
88 **CHÂTEAU DE LA TOUR** Bordeaux Supérieur Réserve du Château 1995 • $16 • (01/31/98)

RED BURGUNDY

98 **DOMAINE LEROY** Romanée St.-Vivant 1995 • $600 • (11/15/97) • CS
97 **DOMINIQUE LAURENT** Echézeaux 1994 • $75 • (09/30/97)
97 **DENIS MORTET** Chambolle-Musigny Aux Beaux Bruns 1995 • $59 • (11/15/97) • HR
96 **PHILIPPE CHARLOPIN-PARIZOT** Charmes-Chambertin 1995 • $87 • (11/15/97)
96 **ROBERT GROFFIER** Bonnes Mares 1995 • $90 • (01/31/98)
96 **DOMINIQUE LAURENT** Bonnes Mares 1994 • $160 • (09/30/97)
96 **LÉCHENEAUT** Chambolle-Musigny Premier Cru 1995 • $60 • (11/15/97)
96 **ARMAND ROUSSEAU** Chambertin 1995 • $130 • (11/15/97)
96 **SÉRAFIN PÈRE & FILS** Charmes-Chambertin 1995 • $95 • (11/15/97)

95 **BOUCHARD PÈRE & FILS** La Romanée Château de Vosne-Romanée 1995 • $210 • (11/15/97)

95 **PHILIPPE CHARLOPIN-PARIZOT** Chambertin 1995 • $95 • (11/15/97)

95 **BERNARD DUGAT-PY** Gevrey-Chambertin Coeur de Roy Vieilles Vignes 1995 • $40 • (01/31/98) • HR

95 **FRÉDÉRIC ESMONIN** Mazis-Chambertin Hospices de Beaune Cuvée Madeleine Collignon 1995 • $85 • (11/15/97)

95 **ROBERT GROFFIER** Chambolle-Musigny Les Sentiers 1995 • $55 • (01/31/98) • HR

95 **ROBERT JAYER-GILLES** Echézeaux du Dessus 1995 • $150 • (11/15/97)

95 **DOMAINE LEROY** Richebourg 1995 • $600 • (11/15/97)

95 **DENIS MORTET** Clos Vougeot 1995 • $81 • (11/15/97)

95 **DENIS MORTET** Gevrey-Chambertin En Motrot 1995 • $47 • (11/15/97)

94 **J. FAIVELEY** Mazis-Chambertin 1995 • $97 • (11/15/97)

94 **JEAN GRIVOT** Echézeaux 1995 • $60 • (11/15/97)

94 **DOMINIQUE LAURENT** Chambolle-Musigny Les Sentiers 1994 • $95 • (09/30/97)

94 **DOMINIQUE LAURENT** Pommard Les Epenots 1994 • $95 • (09/30/97)

94 **COMTE GEORGES DE VOGÜÉ** Chambolle-Musigny Les Amoureuses 1995 • $175 • (11/15/97)

93 **DOMAINE D'AUVENAY** Bonnes Mares 1995 • $550 • (11/15/97)

93 **DOMAINE D'AUVENAY** Bonnes Mares 1994 • $459 • (09/30/97)

93 **DOMAINE D'AUVENAY** Mazis-Chambertin 1994 • $459 • (09/30/97)

93 **PHILIPPE CHARLOPIN-PARIZOT** Clos St.-Denis 1995 • $80 • (11/15/97)

93 **CLAUDE DUGAT** Charmes-Chambertin 1995 • $110 • (11/15/97)

93 **ANNE GROS** Vosne-Romanée Les Barreaux 1995 • $55 • (11/15/97)

93 **DOMINIQUE LAURENT** Chambertin-Clos de Bèze 1994 • $150 • (09/30/97)

93 **DOMINIQUE LAURENT** Gevrey-Chambertin Lavaux St.-Jacques 1994 • $80 • (09/30/97)

93 **DOMAINE LEROY** Nuits-St.-Georges Aux Boudots 1995 • $250 • (11/15/97)

93 **DOMAINE LEROY** Romanée St.-Vivant 1994 • $475 • (09/30/97)

93 **DENIS MORTET** Chambertin 1995 • $115 • (11/15/97)

93 **DENIS MORTET** Gevrey-Chambertin En Champs Vieille Vigne 1995 • $55 • (11/15/97)

93 **DENIS MORTET** Gevrey-Chambertin Lavaux St.-Jacques 1995 • $59 • (11/15/97)

92 **BOUCHARD PÈRE & FILS** Bonnes Mares 1995 • $89 • (11/15/97)

92 **CHOPIN-GROFFIER** Clos Vougeot 1995 • $92 • (11/15/97)

92 **BERNARD DUGAT-PY** Gevrey-Chambertin Petite-Chapelle 1994 • $43 • (09/30/97)

92 **VINCENT GIRARDIN** Volnay Clos des Chênes 1995 • $35 • (11/15/97)

92 **ANNE GROS** Clos Vougeot Le Grand Maupertuis 1995 • $80 • (11/15/97)

92 **LOUIS JADOT** Chambertin-Clos de Bèze 1995 • $90 • (11/15/97)

92 **LOUIS JADOT** Chapelle-Chambertin 1994 • $56 • (09/30/97)

Key: SS—Spectator Selection CS—Cellar Selection HR—Highly Recommended BB—Best Buy $NA—Price not available Ⓐ—Auction Price

Dates in parentheses indicate the issues in which the ratings were published.

92 **ROBERT JAYER-GILLES** Nuits-St.-Georges Les Hauts Poirets 1995 • $85 • (11/15/97)

92 **MICHEL LAFARGE** Volnay Clos des Chênes 1994 • $70 • (09/30/97)

92 **DOMAINE DES COMTES LAFON** Volnay-Santenots Les Santenots du Milieu 1994 • $55 • (09/30/97)

92 **DOMINIQUE LAURENT** Nuits-St.-Georges La Richemone 1994 • $75 • (09/30/97)

92 **DOMAINE LEROY** Pommard Les Vignots 1995 • $110 • (11/15/97)

92 **DOMAINE LEROY** Vosne-Romanée Les Beaux Monts 1995 • $250 • (11/15/97)

92 **MÉO-CAMUZET** Clos de Vougeot 1995 • $70 • (11/15/97)

92 **DENIS MORTET** Gevrey-Chambertin Au Vellé 1995 • $47 • (11/15/97)

92 **DANIEL RION** Vosne-Romanée Les Beaux Monts 1995 • $66 • (11/15/97)

92 **MICHELE & PATRICE RION** Chambolle-Musigny Les Cras 1995 • $48 • (11/15/97)

91 **BERTRAND AMBROISE** Clos de Vougeot 1995 • $90 • (11/15/97)

91 **DENIS BACHELET** Gevrey-Chambertin Vieilles Vignes 1995 • $45 • (01/31/98)

91 **PHILIPPE CHARLOPIN-PARIZOT** Morey-St.-Denis 1995 • $32 • (11/15/97)

91 **BRUNO CLAIR** Savigny-lès-Beaune La Dominode 1995 • $40 • (11/15/97)

91 **JEAN GRIVOT** Richebourg 1994 • $160 • (09/30/97)

91 **DOMAINE LEROY** Latricières-Chambertin 1995 • $600 • (11/15/97)

91 **DENIS MORTET** Gevrey-Chambertin 1995 • $42 • (11/15/97)

91 **DANIEL RION** Clos Vougeot 1995 • $99 • (11/15/97)

91 **ARMAND ROUSSEAU** Ruchottes-Chambertin 1995 • $85 • (11/15/97)

91 **DOMAINE THOMAS-MOILLARD** Corton Le Clos du Roi 1995 • $43 • (11/15/97)

91 **COMTE GEORGES DE VOGÜÉ** Bonnes Mares 1995 • $175 • (11/15/97)

90 **BERTRAND AMBROISE** Corton Le Rognet 1995 • $80 • (11/15/97)

90 **BERTRAND AMBROISE** Nuits-St.-Georges Les Vaucrains 1995 • $58 • (11/15/97)

90 **PHILIPPE CHARLOPIN-PARIZOT** Gevrey-Chambertin Cuvée Vieilles Vignes 1995 • $37 • (11/15/97)

90 **PHILIPPE CHARLOPIN-PARIZOT** Vosne-Romanée 1995 • $37 • (11/15/97)

90 **JEAN-JACQUES CONFURON** Vosne-Romanée Les Beaux Monts 1995 • $70 • (11/15/97)

90 **CORON PÈRE & FILS** Clos de Vougeot 1995 • $63 • (11/15/97)

90 **JOSEPH DROUHIN** Charmes-Chambertin 1995 • $85 • (11/15/97)

90 **JOSEPH DROUHIN** Griotte-Chambertin 1995 • $95 • (11/15/97)

90 **JOSEPH DROUHIN** Musigny 1995 • $110 • (01/31/98)

90 **J. FAIVELEY** Clos de la Roche 1995 • $93 • (11/15/97)

90 **VINCENT GIRARDIN** Chassagne-Montrachet Clos de la Boudriotte Red 1995 • $30 • (11/15/97)

90 **VINCENT GIRARDIN** Pommard Les Chanlins Vieilles Vignes 1995 • $40 • (11/15/97)

90 **JEAN GRIVOT** Echézeaux 1994 • $50 • (09/30/97)

90 **JEAN GRIVOT** Richebourg 1995 • $150 • (11/15/97)

90 **ROBERT GROFFIER** Chambolle-Musigny Les Amoureuses 1995 • $75 • (01/31/98)

90 **ANNE GROS** Richebourg 1995 • $170 • (11/15/97)

90 **DOMAINE DES COMTES LAFON** Volnay Clos des Chênes 1994 • $55 • (09/30/97)

90 **DOMAINE FRANÇOIS LAMARCHE** La Grand Rue 1995 • $98 • (11/15/97)
90 **DOMINIQUE LAURENT** Grands Echézeaux 1994 • $125 • (09/30/97)
90 **DOMAINE LEROY** Corton Les Renardes 1995 • $250 • (11/15/97)
90 **DOMAINE LEROY** Gevrey-Chambertin Aux Combottes 1995 • $NA • (11/15/97)
90 **DANIEL RION** Nuits-St.-Georges Clos des Argillières 1995 • $66 • (11/15/97)
90 **DANIEL RION** Nuits-St.-Georges Les Grandes Vignes 1995 • $44 • (11/15/97)
90 **DANIEL RION** Vosne-Romanée 1995 • $44 • (11/15/97)
90 **DOMAINE DE LA ROMANÉE-CONTI** Richebourg 1994 • $190 • (09/30/97)
90 **ROSSIGNOL-TRAPET** Chambertin 1995 • $68 • (11/15/97)
90 **SÉRAFIN PÈRE & FILS** Gevrey-Chambertin 1995 • $46 • (11/15/97)
90 **SÉRAFIN PÈRE & FILS** Gevrey-Chambertin Les Cazetiers 1995 • $72 • (11/15/97)
90 **TOLLOT-BEAUT & FILS** Beaune Clos du Roi 1995 • $40 • (11/15/97)
89 **FRANÇOIS BUFFET** Volnay Champans 1995 • $30 • (11/15/97)
89 **CHAUVENET-CHOPIN** Nuits-St.-Georges Les Murgers 1995 • $54 • (11/15/97)
89 **BRUNO CLAIR** Marsannay Les Vaudenelles 1995 • $20 • (11/15/97)
89 **J. CONFURON-COTETIDOT** Nuits-St.-Georges 1995 • $50 • (11/15/97)
89 **JOSEPH DROUHIN** Chambolle-Musigny 1995 • $34 • (11/15/97)
89 **J. FAIVELEY** Chambolle-Musigny La Combe d'Orveau 1995 • $61 • (11/15/97)
89 **JEAN GRIVOT** Vosne-Romanée Les Beaux Monts 1995 • $45 • (11/15/97)
89 **FRANÇOIS LAMARCHE** Echézeaux 1995 • $61 • (11/15/97)
89 **DOMINIQUE LAURENT** Bourgogne Cuvée No. 1 1994 • $18 • (09/30/97)
89 **LECHENEAUT** Clos de la Roche 1995 • $100 • (11/15/97)
89 **MOMMESSIN** Aloxe-Corton 1995 • $26 • (11/15/97)
89 **MOMMESSIN** Clos de Tart 1995 • $103 • (11/15/97)
89 **MONGEARD-MUGNERET** Grands Echézeaux 1995 • $83 • (11/15/97)
89 **DOMAINE DE LA POUSSE D'OR** Volnay Les Caillerets 1995 • $52 • (11/15/97)
89 **DOMAINE DE LA POUSSE D'OR** Volnay Les Caillerets-Clos des 60 Ouvrées 1995 • $55 • (11/15/97)
89 **JACQUES PRIEUR** Volnay Champans 1995 • $50 • (11/15/97)
89 **DOMAINE DE LA ROMANÉE-CONTI** Grands Echézeaux 1994 • $115 • (09/30/97)
89 **SÉRAFIN PÈRE & FILS** Gevrey-Chambertin Fonteny 1995 • $60 • (11/15/97)
89 **JEAN & JEAN-LOUIS TRAPET** Latricières-Chambertin 1995 • $62 • (11/15/97)
88 **BOUCHARD PÈRE & FILS** Clos Vougeot 1995 • $80 • (11/15/97)
88 **PHILIPPE CHARLOPIN-PARIZOT** Fixin 1995 • $NA • (11/15/97)
88 **CHOPIN-GROFFIER** Nuits-St.-Georges Aux Chaignots 1995 • $56 • (11/15/97)
88 **BRUNO CLAIR** Chambertin-Clos de Bèze 1995 • $100 • (11/15/97)
88 **CORON PÈRE & FILS** Vosne-Romanée Les Suchots 1995 • $54 • (11/15/97)
88 **DROUHIN-LAROZE** Chambertin-Clos de Bèze 1995 • $58 • (11/15/97)
88 **DROUHIN-LAROZE** Clos de Vougeot 1995 • $56 • (11/15/97)
88 **JOSEPH DROUHIN** Beaune Clos des Mouches 1995 • $45 • (01/31/98)
88 **CLAUDE DUGAT** Gevrey-Chambertin 1995 • $48 • (11/15/97)
88 **ALETH GIRARDIN** Pommard Rugiens 1995 • $44 • (11/15/97)
88 **VINCENT GIRARDIN** Pommard Les Rugiens Vieilles Vignes 1995 • $44 • (11/15/97)
88 **JEAN GRIVOT** Clos de Vougeot 1995 • $60 • (11/15/97)
88 **JEAN GRIVOT** Nuits-St.-Georges Aux Boudots 1995 • $45 • (11/15/97)
88 **LOUIS JADOT** Beaune Clos des Ursules 1995 • $35 • (11/15/97)
88 **ROBERT JAYER-GILLES** Côte de Nuits-Villages 1995 • $40 • (11/15/97)
88 **EMILE JUILLOT** Mercurey Les Combins 1995 • $NA • (11/15/97)
88 **DOMAINE FRANÇOIS LAMARCHE** Clos de Vougeot 1995 • $64 • (11/15/97)
88 **LÉCHENEAUT** Chambolle-Musigny 1995 • $40 • (11/15/97)
88 **MOILLARD** Gevrey-Chambertin 1995 • $26 • (01/31/98)
88 **MOMMESSIN** Vosne-Romanée Les Suchots 1995 • $45 • (11/15/97)
88 **DOMAINE DE LA POUSSE D'OR** Pommard Les Jarollières 1995 • $60 • (11/15/97)
88 **DOMAINE DE LA ROMANÉE-CONTI** Echézeaux 1994 • $90 • (09/30/97)
88 **EMMANUEL ROUGET** Nuits-St.-Georges 1995 • $35 • (01/31/98)
88 **COMTE GEORGES DE VOGÜÉ** Chambolle-Musigny Premier Cru 1995 • $100 • (11/15/97)

WHITE BURGUNDY

99 **DOMAINE D'AUVENAY** Chevalier-Montrachet 1995 • $492 • (08/31/97) • HR
99 **MARC COLIN** Montrachet 1996 • $250 • (05/31/98)
99 **JACQUES PRIEUR** Montrachet 1995 • $290 • (08/31/97) • HR
98 **DOMAINE D'AUVENAY** Criots-Bâtard-Montrachet 1995 • $498 • (08/31/97)
98 **DOMAINE D'AUVENAY** Puligny-Montrachet Les Folatières 1995 • $133 • (08/31/97)
98 **J.-F. COCHE-DURY** Corton-Charlemagne 1995 • $175 • (05/31/98)
98 **DOMAINE DES COMTES LAFON** Montrachet 1995 • $400 • (05/31/98)
98 **LOUIS LATOUR** Chevalier-Montrachet Les Demoiselles 1995 • $186 • (08/31/97)
98 **ETIENNE SAUZET** Chevalier-Montrachet 1995 • $219 • (08/31/97)
97 **DOMAINE D'AUVENAY** Meursault Les Narvaux 1995 • $155 • (08/31/97)
97 **BLAIN-GAGNARD** Bâtard-Montrachet 1996 • $110 • (05/31/98) • CS
97 **JEAN CHARTRON** Chevalier-Montrachet Clos des Chevaliers 1996 • $170 • (05/31/98)
97 **J.-F. COCHE-DURY** Meursault Perrières 1995 • $130 • (05/31/98)
97 **MARC COLIN** Bâtard-Montrachet 1996 • $130 • (05/31/98)
97 **DOMAINE DES COMTES LAFON** Meursault Charmes 1995 • $80 • (05/31/98)
97 **LATOUR-GIRAUD** Meursault Les Genevrières 1995 • $NA • (08/31/97)
97 **JACQUES PRIEUR** Puligny-Montrachet Les Combettes 1995 • $60 • (08/31/97)
97 **RAMONET** Chassagne-Montrachet Les Grandes Ruchottes 1995 • $70 • (08/31/97)

96 **JEAN-MARC BOILLOT** Puligny-Montrachet La Truffière 1996 • $72 • (05/31/98)

96 **BOUCHARD PÈRE & FILS** Chevalier-Montrachet 1996 • $150 • (05/31/98)

96 **JEAN-NOËL GAGNARD** Chassagne-Montrachet Clos de la Maltroye 1995 • $55 • (08/31/97)

96 **JACQUES PRIEUR** Meursault Les Perrières 1995 • $80 • (08/31/97)

96 **ETIENNE SAUZET** Bienvenues-Bâtard-Montrachet 1995 • $185 • (08/31/97)

96 **JACQUES THEVENOT-MACHAL** Meursault Les Charmes 1995 • $30 • (08/31/97)

95 **ROGER BELLAND** Criots-Bâtard-Montrachet 1996 • $90 • (05/31/98)

95 **BLAIN-GAGNARD** Criots-Bâtard-Montrachet 1996 • $110 • (05/31/98)

95 **JEAN-MARC BOILLOT** Puligny-Montrachet Champ Canet 1995 • $58 • (08/31/97)

95 **JEAN-MARC BOILLOT** Puligny-Montrachet Les Referts 1996 • $62 • (05/31/98)

95 **BOUCHARD PÈRE & FILS** Corton-Charlemagne 1996 • $110 • (05/31/98)

95 **ROGER CAILLOT** Bâtard-Montrachet 1995 • $92 • (08/31/97)

95 **VINCENT GIRARDIN** Meursault Les Perrières 1996 • $65 • (05/31/98)

95 **DOMAINE DES COMTES LAFON** Meursault Les Perrières 1995 • $90 • (05/31/98)

95 **LOUIS LATOUR** Bâtard-Montrachet 1995 • $157 • (08/31/97)

95 **ROLAND MAROSLAVAC-LEGER** Puligny-Montrachet Les Combettes 1995 • $40 • (08/31/97)

95 **MICHEL NIELLON** Chassagne-Montrachet Les Champs Gain 1995 • $50 • (08/31/97)

95 **MICHEL NIELLON** Chevalier-Montrachet 1995 • $130 • (08/31/97)

95 **JACQUES PRIEUR** Chevalier-Montrachet 1995 • $175 • (08/31/97)

95 **GUY ROULOT** Meursault Les Charmes 1995 • $80 • (08/31/97)

95 **GUY ROULOT** Meursault Les Perrières 1995 • $80 • (08/31/97)

95 **ETIENNE SAUZET** Bâtard-Montrachet 1995 • $187 • (08/31/97)

94 **JEAN-MARC BOILLOT** Puligny-Montrachet Les Combettes 1996 • $72 • (05/31/98)

94 **JEAN-MARC BOILLOT** Puligny-Montrachet Les Combettes 1995 • $75 • (08/31/97)

94 **JEAN-MARC BOILLOT** Puligny-Montrachet Les Pucelles 1996 • $62 • (05/31/98)

94 **DOMAINE DE LA BONGRAN** Mâcon-Clessé Quintaine Cuvée Tradition 1995 • $25 • (05/31/98)

94 **ROGER CAILLOT** Meursault Le Limozin 1995 • $32 • (08/31/97)

94 **CORDIER PÈRE & FILS** Pouilly-Fuissé Vieilles Vignes 1996 • $29 • (05/31/98)

94 **VINCENT GIRARDIN** Corton-Charlemagne 1996 • $83 • (05/31/98)

94 **ALBERT GRIVAULT** Meursault Les Perrières 1996 • $50 • (05/31/98)

94 **LOUIS JADOT** Corton-Charlemagne 1995 • $82 • (08/31/97)

94 **LOUIS JADOT** Puligny-Montrachet Clos de la Garenne Duc de Magenta 1995 • $NA • (08/31/97)

Key: SS—Spectator Selection CS—Cellar Selection HR—Highly Recommended BB—Best Buy $NA—Price not available Ⓐ—Auction Price
Dates in parentheses indicate the issues in which the ratings were published.

94 **MICHEL JUILLOT** Corton-Charlemagne 1996 • $95 • (05/31/98)

94 **DOMAINE DES COMTES LAFON** Meursault Clos de la Barre 1995 • $55 • (05/31/98)

94 **JEAN PILLOT** Chevalier-Montrachet 1996 • $150 • (05/31/98)

94 **GUY ROULOT** Meursault Les Tessons Clos de Mon Plaisir 1995 • $50 • (05/31/98)

94 **JACQUES SAUMAIZE** St.-Véran Poncetys 1995 • $NA • (05/31/98)

94 **ETIENNE SAUZET** Puligny-Montrachet Les Combettes 1995 • $112 • (08/31/97)

94 **ETIENNE SAUZET** Puligny-Montrachet Les Perrières 1995 • $83 • (08/31/97)

94 **TOLLOT-BEAUT & FILS** Corton-Charlemagne 1995 • $90 • (08/31/97)

94 **VERGET** Chassagne-Montrachet La Maltroie Cuvée Vieilles Vignes 1995 • $44 • (08/31/97)

93 **BLAIN-GAGNARD** Chassagne-Montrachet La Boudriotte 1995 • $45 • (08/31/97)

93 **JEAN-MARC BOILLOT** Meursault 1996 • $39 • (05/31/98)

93 **JEAN-MARC BOILLOT** Puligny-Montrachet Les Folatières 1996 • $56 • (05/31/98)

93 **BONNEAU DU MARTRAY** Corton-Charlemagne 1995 • $70 • (08/31/97)

93 **DOMAINE BORGEOT** Santenay Les Gravières White 1996 • $26 • (05/31/98)

93 **MICHEL BOUZEREAU & FILS** Meursault Les Genevrières 1996 • $NA • (05/31/98)

93 **ROGER CAILLOT** Puligny-Montrachet Les Folatières 1995 • $45 • (08/31/97)

93 **LOUIS CARILLON** Puligny-Montrachet Champ Canet 1995 • $57 • (08/31/97)

93 **J.-F. COCHE-DURY** Meursault Les Rougeots 1995 • $80 • (05/31/98)

93 **MARC COLIN** St.-Aubin Le Charmois White 1996 • $35 • (05/31/98)

93 **MARC COLIN** St.-Aubin Les Combes White 1996 • $35 • (05/31/98)

93 **JOSEPH DROUHIN** Montrachet Marquis de Laguiche 1995 • $300 • (08/31/97)

93 **FONTAINE-GAGNARD** Criots-Bâtard-Montrachet 1996 • $148 • (05/31/98)

93 **FONTAINE-GAGNARD** Montrachet 1996 • $336 • (05/31/98)

93 **JEAN-NOËL GAGNARD** Chassagne-Montrachet Caillerets 1995 • $65 • (08/31/97)

93 **JEAN-NOËL GAGNARD** Chassagne-Montrachet Les Chenevottes 1995 • $65 • (08/31/97)

93 **VINCENT GIRARDIN** Chassagne-Montrachet Morgeot Vieilles Vignes 1996 • $NA • (05/31/98)

93 **VINCENT GIRARDIN** Meursault Les Narvaux 1996 • $42 • (05/31/98)

93 **LOUIS JADOT** Criots-Bâtard-Montrachet 1995 • $135 • (08/31/97)

93 **RÉMI JOBARD** Meursault Les Genevrières 1996 • $55 • (05/31/98)

93 **DOMAINE DES COMTES LAFON** Meursault 1995 • $50 • (05/31/98)

93 **DOMAINE DES COMTES LAFON** Meursault Désirée 1995 • $NA • (05/31/98)

93 **DOMAINE DES COMTES LAFON** Puligny-Montrachet Champ-Gain 1995 • $NA • (05/31/98)

93 **LALEURE-PIOT** Corton-Charlemagne 1996 • $96 • (05/31/98)

93 **LOUIS LATOUR** Corton-Charlemagne 1995 • $80 • (08/31/97) • CS

93 **MAROSLAVAC-LEGER** Puligny-Montrachet Les Folatières 1996 • $50 • (05/31/98)

93 **ROLAND MAROSLAVAC-LEGER** Puligny-Montrachet Les Folatières 1995 • $40 • (08/31/97)
93 **JOSEPH MATROT** Meursault-Blagny 1995 • $46 • (08/31/97)
93 **MONTHÉLIE-DOUHAIRET** Meursault Les Santenots 1996 • $53 • (05/31/98)
93 **MARC MOREY** Chassagne-Montrachet Les Vergers 1996 • $48 • (05/31/98)
93 **JEAN PILLOT** Chassagne-Montrachet Morgeot 1996 • $40 • (05/31/98)
93 **CHÂTEAU DE PULIGNY-MONTRACHET** Meursault Les Perrières 1995 • $36 • (01/31/98)
93 **CHÂTEAU DE PULIGNY-MONTRACHET** Meursault Les Poruzots 1995 • $42 • (01/31/98)
93 **RAMONET** Chassagne-Montrachet 1995 • $40 • (08/31/97)
93 **RAMONET** Chassagne-Montrachet La Boudriotte 1995 • $50 • (08/31/97)
93 **GUY ROULOT** Meursault Le Tesson Clos de Mon Plaisir 1995 • $50 • (08/31/97)
93 **ETIENNE SAUZET** Puligny-Montrachet Champ Canet 1995 • $97 • (08/31/97)
93 **ETIENNE SAUZET** Puligny-Montrachet La Garenne 1995 • $87 • (08/31/97)
93 **ETIENNE SAUZET** Puligny-Montrachet Les Referts 1995 • $83 • (08/31/97)
93 **VERGET** Chassagne-Montrachet Morgeot Cuvée Vieilles Vignes 1995 • $46 • (08/31/97)
93 **VERGET** Pouilly-Fuissé Tête de Cuvée 1996 • $15 • (05/31/98) • HR
92 **FRANÇOIS D'ALLAINES** Mâcon La Roche Vineuse 1996 • $NA • (05/31/98)
92 **GUY AMIOT** Chassagne-Montrachet Clos St.-Jean 1995 • $40 • (08/31/97)
92 **GUY BOCARD** Meursault Les Charmes 1995 • $NA • (08/31/97)
92 **JEAN-MARC BOILLOT** Puligny-Montrachet 1995 • $41 • (08/31/97)
92 **BOUCHARD PÈRE & FILS** Beaune Premier Cru White 1996 • $38 • (05/31/98)
92 **BOUCHARD PÈRE & FILS** Beaune Premier Cru White 1995 • $38 • (08/31/97)
92 **BOUCHARD PÈRE & FILS** Montrachet 1995 • $320 • (08/31/97)
92 **BOUCHARD PÈRE & FILS** Puligny-Montrachet Les Pucelles 1996 • $68 • (05/31/98)
92 **JACQUES BURRIER** Pouilly-Fuissé Château de Beauregard Cuvée Prestige 1996 • $21 • (05/31/98)
92 **ROGER CAILLOT** Meursault en la Barre Clos Marguerite 1995 • $32 • (08/31/97)
92 **LOUIS CARILLON** Puligny-Montrachet Les Perrières 1995 • $53 • (08/31/97)
92 **CLAUDE ET HUBERT CHAVY-CHOUET** Puligny-Montrachet Les Enseignères 1996 • $45 • (05/31/98)
92 **GÉRARD CHAVY** Puligny-Montrachet Les Perrières 1996 • $40 • (05/31/98)
92 **HENRI CLERC & FILS** Chevalier-Montrachet 1996 • $120 • (05/31/98)
92 **CORSIN** Pouilly-Fuissé 1996 • $23 • (05/31/98)
92 **JOSEPH DROUHIN** Corton-Charlemagne 1996 • $92 • (05/31/98)
92 **JOSEPH DROUHIN** Puligny-Montrachet Clos de la Garenne 1996 • $65 • (05/31/98)
92 **EMILIAN GILLET** Mâcon-Viré Quintaine 1994 • $18 • (05/31/98)
92 **VINCENT GIRARDIN** Savigny-lès-Beaune Dessus les Vermots White 1996 • $28 • (05/31/98)
92 **GHISLAINE & JEAN-HUGUES GOISOT** Sauvignon de St.-Bris 1996 • $14 • (05/31/98)
92 **ALBERT GRIVAULT** Meursault Clos des Perrières 1996 • $60 • (05/31/98)
92 **LOUIS JADOT** Chevalier-Montrachet Les Demoiselles 1995 • $170 • (08/31/97)
92 **LOUIS JADOT** Puligny-Montrachet Les Folatières 1995 • $51 • (08/31/97)
92 **HUBERT LAMY** Chassagne-Montrachet Les Macherelles 1996 • $38 • (05/31/98)
92 **HUBERT LAMY** St.-Aubin Clos de la Chatenière White 1996 • $22 • (05/31/98)
92 **HUBERT LAMY** St.-Aubin En Remilly White 1996 • $22 • (05/31/98)
92 **HUBERT LAMY** St.-Aubin Les Murgers des Dents de Chien White 1996 • $28 • (05/31/98)
92 **LOUIS LATOUR** Puligny-Montrachet Les Folatières 1995 • $56 • (08/31/97)
92 **OLIVIER LEFLAIVE FRÈRES** Criots-Bâtard-Montrachet 1995 • $125 • (08/31/97)
92 **OLIVIER LEFLAIVE FRÈRES** Montrachet 1995 • $270 • (08/31/97)
92 **CHÂTEAU DE LA MALTROYE** Chassagne-Montrachet Grandes Ruchottes 1996 • $50 • (05/31/98)
92 **MICHEL MOREY-COFFINET** Chassagne-Montrachet La Romanée 1995 • $45 • (08/31/97)
92 **PRIEUR-BRUNET** Meursault Les Chevalières 1995 • $36 • (08/31/97)
92 **CHÂTEAU DE PULIGNY-MONTRACHET** Meursault 1996 • $26 • (05/31/98)
92 **RAMONET** Puligny-Montrachet Champ Canet 1995 • $70 • (08/31/97)
92 **ANTONIN RODET** Mercurey Château de Chamirey White 1995 • $18 • (08/31/97)
92 **ETIENNE SAUZET** Chassagne-Montrachet 1995 • $53 • (08/31/97)
92 **ETIENNE SAUZET** Puligny-Montrachet 1995 • $55 • (08/31/97)
92 **JACQUES THEVENOT-MACHAL** Puligny-Montrachet Les Folatières 1995 • $30 • (08/31/97)
91 **DOMAINE D'AUVENAY** Auxey-Duresses White 1995 • $56 • (08/31/97)
91 **BLAIN-GAGNARD** Chassagne-Montrachet Morgeot 1996 • $45 • (05/31/98)
91 **JEAN-MARC BOILLOT** Montagny Premier Cru 1996 • $20 • (05/31/98)
91 **BOUCHARD PÈRE & FILS** Puligny-Montrachet Les Chalumeaux 1996 • $50 • (05/31/98)
91 **MICHEL BOUZEREAU & FILS** Meursault Les Grands Charrons 1996 • $36 • (05/31/98)
91 **MICHEL BOUZEREAU & FILS** Puligny-Montrachet Champ Gain 1996 • $55 • (05/31/98)
91 **JEAN-MARC BROCARD** Bourgogne sur Kimmeridjien White 1996 • $15 • (08/31/97)
91 **JACQUES BURRIER** Pouilly-Fuissé Château de Beauregard 1996 • $21 • (05/31/98)
91 **MICHEL COLIN-DELÉGER** Chassagne-Montrachet Les Vergers 1995 • $50 • (08/31/97)
91 **MARC COLIN** Chassagne-Montrachet Caillerets 1996 • $50 • (05/31/98)
91 **CORSIN** Mâcon-Villages 1996 • $13 • (08/31/97)
91 **J.-A. FERRET** Pouilly-Fuissé Les Ménétrières 1995 • $41 • (05/31/98)
91 **J.-A. FERRET** Pouilly-Fuissé Les Scélés 1996 • $26 • (05/31/98)
91 **FONTAINE-GAGNARD** Bâtard-Montrachet 1996 • $148 • (05/31/98)
91 **CHÂTEAU FUISSÉ** Pouilly-Fuissé Vieilles Vignes 1996 • $49 • (05/31/98)

91 **GHISLAINE & JEAN-HUGUES GOISOT** Bourgogne Aligoté 1996 • $14 • (05/31/98)

91 **PATRICK JAVILLIER** Meursault Clos du Cromin Cuvée Spéciale Mise Tardive 1995 • $40 • (08/31/97)

91 **RÉMI JOBARD** Meursault Sous La Velle 1996 • $35 • (05/31/98)

91 **HUBERT LAMY** St.-Aubin Les Frionnes White 1996 • $20 • (05/31/98)

91 **OLIVIER LEFLAIVE FRÈRES** Meursault Les Charmes 1995 • $62 • (08/31/97)

91 **OLIVIER LEFLAIVE FRÈRES** Puligny-Montrachet Champ Gain 1995 • $52 • (08/31/97)

91 **MAROSLAVAC-LEGER** Meursault Au Murger de Monthélie 1996 • $36 • (05/31/98)

91 **MAROSLAVAC-LEGER** Meursault Au Murger de Monthélie 1995 • $28 • (08/31/97)

91 **MICHEL MOREY-COFFINET** Chassagne-Montrachet La Romanée 1996 • $47 • (05/31/98)

91 **MARC MOREY** Chassagne-Montrachet Les Chenevottes 1996 • $44 • (05/31/98)

91 **MARC MOREY** Chassagne-Montrachet Morgeot 1996 • $50 • (05/31/98)

91 **JACQUES PRIEUR** Beaune Clos de la Féguine White 1995 • $45 • (08/31/97)

91 **VERGET** St.-Aubin Premier Cru White 1996 • $28 • (05/31/98)

90 **DANIEL BARRAUD** Pouilly-Fuissé La Verchère 1996 • $25 • (05/31/98)

90 **JEAN-MARC BOILLOT** Rully Grésigny White 1996 • $21 • (05/31/98)

90 **DOMAINE DE LA BONGRAN** Mâcon-Clessé Quintaine Cuvée Tradition 1996 • $25 • (05/31/98)

90 **BOUCHARD PÈRE & FILS** Beaune Clos St.-Landry White 1996 • $50 • (05/31/98)

90 **BOUCHARD PÈRE & FILS** Chassagne-Montrachet 1996 • $39 • (05/31/98)

90 **BOUCHARD PÈRE & FILS** Corton-Charlemagne 1995 • $110 • (08/31/97)

90 **BOUCHARD PÈRE & FILS** Meursault 1996 • $35 • (05/31/98)

90 **BOUCHARD PÈRE & FILS** Puligny-Montrachet Les Folatières 1996 • $55 • (05/31/98)

90 **MICHEL BOUZEREAU & FILS** Meursault Les Charmes-Dessus 1996 • $NA • (05/31/98)

90 **MICHEL BOUZEREAU & FILS** Meursault Le Limozin 1996 • $NA • (05/31/98)

90 **ROGER CAILLOT** Meursault Le Tesson 1995 • $31 • (08/31/97)

90 **ROGER CAILLOT** Puligny-Montrachet Les Pucelles 1995 • $68 • (08/31/97)

90 **CHARTRON & TRÉBUCHET** St.-Aubin La Chatenière White 1996 • $25 • (05/31/98)

90 **JEAN CHARTRON** Puligny-Montrachet Clos du Cailleret 1996 • $60 • (05/31/98)

90 **CLAUDE ET HUBERT CHAVY-CHOUET** Puligny-Montrachet Hameau de Blagny Vieille Vigne 1996 • $60 • (05/31/98)

90 **HENRI CLERC & FILS** Meursault-Blagny Sous le Dos d'Ane 1995 • $50 • (08/31/97)

90 **MICHEL COLIN-DELÉGER** Chassagne-Montrachet Morgeot 1995 • $50 • (08/31/97)

90 **MARC COLIN** Puligny-Montrachet Les Garennes 1996 • $50 • (05/31/98)

Key: SS—Spectator Selection CS—Cellar Selection HR—Highly Recommended BB—Best Buy $NA—Price not available Ⓐ—Auction Price
Dates in parentheses indicate the issues in which the ratings were published.

90 **MARC COLIN** St.-Aubin La Chatenière White 1996 • $35 • (05/31/98)

90 **MARC COLIN** St.-Aubin Les Cortons White 1996 • $35 • (05/31/98)

90 **MARC COLIN** St.-Aubin En Remilly White 1996 • $35 • (05/31/98)

90 **CORDIER PÈRE & FILS** Pouilly-Fuissé Au Metertiere 1996 • $32 • (05/31/98)

90 **DEMESSEY** Pernand-Vergelesses Sous le Bois de Noël et Belles Filles White 1996 • $19 • (05/31/98)

90 **JOSEPH DROUHIN** Beaune Clos des Mouches White 1996 • $78 • (05/31/98)

90 **JOSEPH DROUHIN** Beaune Clos des Mouches White 1995 • $70 • (08/31/97)

90 **JOSEPH DROUHIN** Chassagne-Montrachet Marquis de Laguiche 1995 • $65 • (08/31/97)

90 **FONTAINE-GAGNARD** Chassagne-Montrachet Caillerets 1996 • $60 • (05/31/98)

90 **FONTAINE-GAGNARD** Chassagne-Montrachet Clos St.-Jean Clos Les Murées 1996 • $60 • (05/31/98)

90 **PAUL GARAUDET** Meursault Vieilles Vignes 1996 • $32 • (05/31/98)

90 **GUFFENS-HEYNEN** Pouilly-Fuissé 1995 • $34 • (05/31/98)

90 **H. & P. JACQUESON** Rully La Pucelle White 1996 • $20 • (05/31/98)

90 **LOUIS JADOT** St.-Aubin White 1995 • $21 • (08/31/97)

90 **PATRICK JAVILLIER** Meursault Les Charmes 1995 • $50 • (08/31/97)

90 **RÉMI JOBARD** Bourgogne White 1996 • $20 • (05/31/98)

90 **RÉMI JOBARD** Meursault Le Poruzot-Dessus 1996 • $52 • (05/31/98)

90 **PIERRE LABET** Beaune Clos des Monsnières White 1996 • $33 • (05/31/98)

90 **LOUIS LATOUR** Chassagne-Montrachet Morgeot 1995 • $43 • (08/31/97)

90 **LOUIS LATOUR** Meursault Les Charmes 1995 • $52 • (08/31/97)

90 **LOUIS LATOUR** Meursault Les Gouttes d'Or 1995 • $49 • (08/31/97)

90 **LOUIS LATOUR** Puligny-Montrachet La Garenne 1995 • $49 • (08/31/97)

90 **OLIVIER LEFLAIVE FRÈRES** Chassagne-Montrachet Morgeot 1995 • $52 • (08/31/97)

90 **OLIVIER LEFLAIVE FRÈRES** Mercurey White 1995 • $16 • (08/31/97) • SS

90 **OLIVIER LEFLAIVE FRÈRES** Meursault 1995 • $41 • (08/31/97)

90 **OLIVIER LEFLAIVE FRÈRES** Puligny-Montrachet Les Folatières 1995 • $62 • (08/31/97)

90 **MAROSLAVAC-LEGER** Puligny-Montrachet Les Combettes 1996 • $50 • (05/31/98)

90 **RENÉ MONNIER** Meursault Les Chevalières 1995 • $NA • (08/31/97)

90 **MICHEL MOREY-COFFINET** Chassagne-Montrachet 1995 • $32 • (08/31/97)

90 **MARC MOREY** Chassagne-Montrachet 1996 • $32 • (05/31/98)

90 **MARC MOREY** Chassagne-Montrachet En Virondot 1996 • $44 • (05/31/98)

90 **MICHEL NIELLON** Chassagne-Montrachet Clos de la Maltroie 1995 • $50 • (08/31/97)

90 **JEAN PILLOT** Chassagne-Montrachet Les Champs Gain 1996 • $38 • (05/31/98)

90 **JEAN PILLOT** Chassagne-Montrachet Les Chenevottes 1996 • $35 • (05/31/98)

90 **JACQUES PRIEUR** Corton-Charlemagne 1995 • $90 • (08/31/97)

90 **JACQUES PRIEUR** Meursault Clos de Mazeray 1995 • $42 • (08/31/97)

90 **CHÂTEAU DE PULIGNY-MONTRACHET** Puligny-Montrachet Les Folatières 1995 • $48 • (01/31/98)

90 **CHÂTEAU DE PULIGNY-MONTRACHET** Monthélie White 1995 • $20 • (01/31/98)

90 **CHÂTEAU DE PULIGNY-MONTRACHET** Puligny-Montrachet 1995 • $32 • (08/31/97)

90 **RAPET PÈRE & FILS** Corton-Charlemagne 1996 • $79 • (05/31/98)

90 **GUY ROULOT** Bourgogne White 1995 • $20 • (08/31/97)

90 **JEAN-CLAUDE THÉVENET** Mâcon-Pierreclos 1996 • $13 • (08/31/97)

90 **JACQUES THEVENOT-MACHAL** Puligny-Montrachet 1995 • $25 • (08/31/97)

90 **TOLLOT-BEAUT & FILS** Bourgogne White 1995 • $20 • (08/31/97)

90 **VERGET** St.-Véran 1996 • $13 • (05/31/98)

90 **VESSIGAUD PÈRE & FILS** Pouilly-Fuissé Vieilles Vignes 1996 • $27 • (05/31/98)

89 **ANDRÉ AUVIGUE** Pouilly-Fuissé Solutré 1996 • $18 • (05/31/98)

89 **JEAN-MARC BOILLOT** Puligny-Montrachet 1996 • $42 • (05/31/98)

89 **BOUCHARD PÈRE & FILS** Beaune Clos St.-Landry White 1995 • $50 • (08/31/97)

89 **BOUCHARD PÈRE & FILS** Puligny-Montrachet 1996 • $39 • (05/31/98)

89 **ROGER CAILLOT** Bourgogne Les Herbeux White 1995 • $16 • (08/31/97)

89 **ROGER CAILLOT** Meursault Clos du Cromin 1995 • $32 • (08/31/97)

89 **DOMAINE DES DEUX ROCHES** Mâcon-Davayé 1996 • $14 • (08/31/97)

89 **J.-A. FERRET** Pouilly-Fuissé Les Clos 1995 • $33 • (05/31/98)

89 **FONTAINE-GAGNARD** Chassagne-Montrachet La Maltroie 1996 • $60 • (05/31/98)

89 **FONTAINE-GAGNARD** Chassagne-Montrachet Morgeot 1996 • $60 • (05/31/98)

89 **PAUL GARAUDET** Puligny-Montrachet 1996 • $32 • (05/31/98)

89 **VINCENT GIRARDIN** Puligny-Montrachet Les Referts 1996 • $NA • (05/31/98)

89 **GHISLAINE & JEAN-HUGUES GOISOT** Bourgogne Côtes d'Auxerre White 1996 • $15 • (05/31/98)

89 **MICHEL GROS** Hautes Côtes de Nuits White 1994 • $NA • (08/31/97)

89 **PATRICK JAVILLIER** Meursault Les Tillets 1995 • $39 • (08/31/97)

89 **RÉMI JOBARD** Meursault En Luraule 1996 • $37 • (05/31/98)

89 **MICHEL JUILLOT** Mercurey Les Champs Martins White 1996 • $30 • (05/31/98)

89 **DOMAINE DES COMTES LAFON** Meursault Goutte d'Or 1995 • $65 • (05/31/98)

89 **LALEURE-PIOT** Pernand-Vergelesses White 1996 • $27 • (05/31/98)

89 **OLIVIER LEFLAIVE FRÈRES** Bâtard-Montrachet 1995 • $130 • (08/31/97)

89 **MAROSLAVAC-LEGER** Puligny-Montrachet Champs Gain 1996 • $50 • (05/31/98)

89 **BERNARD MOREAU** Chassagne-Montrachet Les Grandes Ruchottes 1995 • $39 • (08/31/97)

89 **MICHEL MOREY-COFFINET** Chassagne-Montrachet 1996 • $35 • (05/31/98)

89 **MARC MOREY** Chassagne-Montrachet Caillerets 1995 • $50 • (08/31/97)

89 **MARC MOREY** Chassagne-Montrachet Les Chenevottes 1995 • $42 • (08/31/97)

89 **MARC MOREY** Chassagne-Montrachet Morgeot 1995 • $50 • (08/31/97)

89 **LE MANOIR MURISALTIEN** Mâcon-Fuissé 1996 • $12 • (05/31/98)

89 **PRIEUR-BRUNET** Meursault 1995 • $30 • (08/31/97)

89 **PRIEUR-BRUNET** Meursault Les Charmes 1995 • $40 • (08/31/97)

89 **MICHEL PRUNIER** Meursault Les Clous 1996 • $NA • (05/31/98)

89 **CHÂTEAU DE PULIGNY-MONTRACHET** Monthélie White 1996 • $22 • (05/31/98)

89 **RAMONET** Bourgogne Aligoté 1995 • $20 • (08/31/97)

89 **CATHERINE & PASCAL ROLLET** Pouilly-Fuissé Au Coeur du Cru 1996 • $NA • (05/31/98)

89 **SAUMAIZE-MICHELIN** Pouilly-Fuissé Clos de la Roche 1996 • $23 • (05/31/98)

89 **JACQUES SAUMAIZE** Pouilly-Fuissé Vigne Blanche 1996 • $NA • (05/31/98)

89 **DOMAINE DE LA SOUFRANDISE** Pouilly-Fuissé Vieilles Vignes 1996 • $21 • (05/31/98)

89 **VERGET** Bourgogne White 1996 • $16 • (05/31/98)

88 **PIERRE BITOUZET** Savigny-lès-Beaune Les Talmettes White 1995 • $NA • (08/31/97)

88 **BLAIN-GAGNARD** Chassagne-Montrachet Clos St.-Jean 1996 • $45 • (05/31/98)

88 **JEAN-MARC BOILLOT** Puligny-Montrachet Champ Canet 1996 • $62 • (05/31/98)

88 **MICHEL BOUZEREAU & FILS** Bourgogne White 1996 • $NA • (05/31/98)

88 **JEAN-MARC BROCARD** Bourgogne sur Portlandien White 1996 • $8 • (05/31/98)

88 **ROGER CAILLOT** Santenay White 1995 • $18 • (08/31/97)

88 **JEAN CHARTRON** Puligny-Montrachet Les Folatières 1996 • $55 • (05/31/98)

88 **GÉRARD CHAVY** Puligny-Montrachet Les Folatières 1996 • $40 • (05/31/98)

88 **BRUNO CLAIR** Marsannay White 1996 • $29 • (05/31/98)

88 **CORDIER PÈRE & FILS** Pouilly-Fuissé Vieilles Vignes Grapillage 1996 • $63 • (05/31/98)

88 **CORDIER PÈRE & FILS** Pouilly-Fuissé Vignes Blanches 1996 • $32 • (05/31/98)

88 **CORDIER PÈRE & FILS** St.-Véran Clos à la Côte 1996 • $21 • (05/31/98)

88 **CORSIN** St.-Véran 1996 • $16 • (05/31/98)

88 **GEORGES DUBOEUF** Pouilly-Fuissé Domaine Béranger 1996 • $20 • (05/31/98)

88 **CHÂTEAU FUISSÉ** Pouilly-Fuissé 1996 • $32 • (05/31/98)

88 **CHÂTEAU FUISSÉ** Pouilly-Fuissé Les Combettes 1996 • $37 • (05/31/98)

88 **VINCENT GIRARDIN** Chassagne-Montrachet Le Cailleret 1996 • $51 • (05/31/98)

88 **VINCENT GIRARDIN** Santenay Le Beaurepaire White 1996 • $33 • (05/31/98)

88 **VINCENT GIRARDIN** Santenay Les Gravières White 1996 • $33 • (05/31/98)

88 **GHISLAINE & JEAN-HUGUES GOISOT** Bourgogne Côtes d'Auxerre Corps de Garde White 1996 • $17 • (05/31/98)

88 **LA GOUZOTTE D'OR** St.-Romain White 1996 • $14 • (05/31/98)

88 **THIERRY GUÉRIN** Pouilly-Fuissé La Roche 1996 • $24 • (05/31/98)

88 **L'HÉRITIER-GUYOT** Mâcon-Villages 1996 • $9 • (08/31/97)

88 **L'HÉRITIER-GUYOT** Vougeot Clos Blanc de Vougeot White 1995 • $43 • (08/31/97)

88 **LOUIS JADOT** Meursault Les Perrières 1995 • $51 • (08/31/97)

88 **LOUIS LATOUR** Auxey-Duresses White 1995 • $19 • (08/31/97)

88 **OLIVIER LEFLAIVE FRÈRES** Meursault Les Perrières 1995 • $58 • (08/31/97)

88 **OLIVIER LEFLAIVE FRÈRES** St.-Aubin En Remilly White 1996 • $29 • (05/31/98)

88 **JEAN MANCIAT** Mâcon 1996 • $12 • (05/31/98)

88 **MAROSLAVAC-LEGER** Puligny-Montrachet Corvée des Vignes 1995 • $30 • (08/31/97)

88 **JOSEPH MATROT** Meursault Les Chevalières 1995 • $30 • (08/31/97)

88 **BERNARD MOREAU** Chassagne-Montrachet 1995 • $30 • (08/31/97)

88 **BERNARD MOREAU** Chassagne-Montrachet Les Chenevottes 1996 • $38 • (05/31/98)

88 **BERNARD MOREAU** Chassagne-Montrachet Morgeot 1996 • $38 • (05/31/98)

88 **BERNARD MOREY** Chassagne-Montrachet La Maltroie 1996 • $45 • (05/31/98)

88 **LE MANOIR MURISALTIEN** Pouilly-Fuissé 1996 • $18 • (05/31/98)

88 **JEAN PILLOT** Chassagne-Montrachet Les Vergers 1996 • $38 • (05/31/98)

88 **JACQUES PRIEUR** Bourgogne White 1995 • $15 • (08/31/97)

88 **ETIENNE SAUZET** Bourgogne White 1995 • $28 • (08/31/97)

88 **VERGET** Mâcon-Villages Tête de Cuvée 1996 • $15 • (05/31/98)

88 **VERGET** Puligny-Montrachet Sous le Puits 1995 • $43 • (08/31/97)

CHAMPAGNE

96 **KRUG** Brut Blanc de Blancs Champagne Clos du Mesnil 1985 • $210 • (12/31/97)

95 **CHARLES HEIDSIECK** Brut Rosé Champagne 1985 • $55 • (12/31/97)

95 **KRUG** Brut Rosé Champagne NV • $150 • (12/31/97)

95 **UNION CHAMPAGNE** Brut Blanc de Blancs Champagne Cuvée Orpale 1985 • $49 • (12/31/97)

94 **CHARLES HEIDSIECK** Brut Blanc de Blancs Champagne Blanc des Millénaires 1985 • $70 • (11/30/97)

94 **KRUG** Brut Champagne 1989 • $125 • (11/30/97) • CS

94 **DE VENOGE** Brut Champagne des Princes 1990 • $79 • (12/31/97)

94 **VEUVE CLICQUOT** Brut Champagne La Grande Dame 1989 • $100 • (11/30/97) • HR

94 **VEUVE CLICQUOT** Brut Rosé Champagne La Grande Dame 1988 • $195 • (09/30/97) • HR

93 **BOLLINGER** Brut Champagne Grande Année 1989 • $70 • (12/31/97)

93 **NICOLAS FEUILLATTE** Brut Champagne Premier Cru Cuvée Spéciale 1988 • $50 • (11/30/97)

93 **KRUG** Brut Champagne Collection 1976 • $280 • (12/31/97)

93 **PALMER & CO.** Brut Blanc de Blancs Champagne 1988 • $40 • (12/31/97)

93 **PHILIPPONNAT** Brut Champagne Grand Blanc 1989 • $50 • (11/30/97)

93 **POMMERY** Brut Champagne Louise 1988 • $95 • (09/30/97)

92 **BOLLINGER** Brut Rosé Champagne 1988 • $60 • (12/31/97)

Key: SS—Spectator Selection CS—Cellar Selection HR—Highly Recommended BB—Best Buy $NA—Price not available Ⓐ—Auction Price

Dates in parentheses indicate the issues in which the ratings were published.

92 **BOLLINGER** Extra Brut Champagne R.D. 1985 • $135 • (12/31/97)

92 **CHARLES DE CAZANOVE** Brut Champagne 1990 • $30 • (11/30/97)

92 **GASTON CHIQUET** Brut Champagne Special Club 1990 • $39 • (11/30/97)

92 **DEUTZ** Brut Blanc de Blancs Champagne 1989 • $45 • (12/31/97)

92 **KRUG** Brut Champagne Private Cuvée 1947 • $NA • (07/31/97)

92 **LECLERC-BRIANT** Brut Champagne Divine 1989 • $55 • (11/30/97)

92 **ALAIN ROBERT** Brut Blanc de Blancs Champagne Le Mesnil 1985 • $50 • (11/15/97)

91 **BRICOUT** Brut Champagne Cuvée Prestige 1991 • $26 • (04/30/98) • SS

91 **CATTIER** Brut Champagne Antique NV • $30 • (10/31/97) • HR

91 **DRAPPIER** Brut Champagne Carte d'Or 1990 • $45 • (12/31/97)

91 **DRAPPIER** Brut Champagne Grande Sendrée 1989 • $76 • (12/31/97)

91 **CHARLES HEIDSIECK** Brut Champagne Réserve NV • $34 • (05/31/98)

91 **HENRIOT** Brut Champagne Millésimé 1989 • $40 • (08/31/97) • HR

91 **J. LASSALLE** Brut Rosé Champagne Réserve des Grandes Années NV • $40 • (11/30/97)

91 **LECHERE** Brut Champagne Orient Express Cuvée Speciale NV • $50 • (11/30/97)

91 **MOËT & CHANDON** Brut Rosé Champagne Cuvée Dom Pérignon 1986 • $190 • (11/30/97)

91 **MONTAUDON** Brut Champagne NV • $30 • (11/30/97) • SS

91 **PANNIER** Brut Champagne Egérie 1990 • $49 • (11/15/97)

91 **PHILIPPONNAT** Brut Champagne Clos des Goisses 1988 • $99 • (11/30/97)

91 **LOUIS ROEDERER** Brut Blanc de Blancs Champagne 1990 • $54 • (12/31/97)

91 **RUINART** Brut Blanc de Blancs Champagne Dom Ruinart 1988 • $97 • (12/31/97)

91 **UNION CHAMPAGNE** Brut Blanc de Blancs Champagne de St.-Gall 1990 • $34 • (12/31/97)

90 **HENRI ABELÉ** Brut Champagne 1986 • $85 • (11/30/97)

90 **PAUL BARA** Brut Champagne 1989 • $40 • (12/31/97)

90 **BEAUMONT DES CRAYÈRES** Brut Champagne Nostalgie 1990 • $32 • (11/30/97)

90 **HENRI BILLIOT** Brut Champagne 1990 • $39 • (11/30/97)

90 **BONNAIRE** Brut Blanc de Blancs Champagne Cramant 1990 • $40 • (12/31/97)

90 **BONNAIRE** Brut Blanc de Blancs Champagne Special Club 1989 • $48 • (12/31/97)

90 **CHARTOGNE-TAILLET** Brut Champagne Cuvée Ste.-Anne NV • $30 • (11/30/97)

90 **DELBECK** Brut Champagne 1990 • $34 • (04/30/98)

90 **NICOLAS FEUILLATTE** Brut Champagne Cuvée Palmes d'Or 1990 • $95 • (08/31/97)

90 **ALFRED GRATIEN** Brut Rosé Champagne Cuvée Paradis NV • $95 • (11/30/97)

90 **MARC HÉBRART** Brut Champagne Special Club 1990 • $47 • (04/30/98)

90 **JACQUESSON** Brut Champagne Signature 1989 • $55 • (12/31/97)

90 **JEAN LAURENT** Brut Rosé Champagne NV • $29 • (04/30/98)

90 **A.R. LENOBLE** Brut Blanc de Blancs Champagne NV • $30 • (11/30/97)

90 **A. MARGAINE** Brut Blanc de Blancs Champagne Special Club 1989 • $43 • (11/30/97)
90 **SERGE MATHIEU** Brut Rosé Champagne NV • $37 • (11/30/97)
90 **G.H. MUMM** Brut Champagne Cordon Rouge NV • $25 • (11/15/97) • SS
90 **PALMER & CO.** Brut Rosé Champagne NV • $34 • (11/30/97)
90 **JOSEPH PERRIER** Brut Champagne Cuvée Joséphine 1985 • $96 • (12/31/97)
90 **POMMERY** Brut Champagne Brut Royal Apanage NV • $27 • (07/31/97) • HR
90 **POMMERY** Brut Rosé Champagne Louise 1990 • $119 • (11/30/97)
90 **SALON** Brut Blanc de Blancs Champagne Le Mesnil 1988 • $130 • (11/30/97)
90 **UNION CHAMPAGNE** Brut Blanc de Blancs Champagne de St.-Gall NV • $28 • (12/31/97)
90 **DE VENOGE** Brut Blanc de Blancs Champagne 1990 • $35 • (12/31/97)
89 **BEAUMONT DES CRAYÈRES** Brut Champagne Cuvée de Prestige NV • $28 • (11/15/97)
89 **BEAUMONT DES CRAYÈRES** Brut Champagne Cuvée de Réserve NV • $22 • (10/31/97)
89 **BOLLINGER** Brut Champagne Special Cuvée NV • $30 • (11/15/97)
89 **A. CHARBAUT & FILS** Brut Blanc de Blancs Champagne 1990 • $45 • (12/31/97)
89 **COMTE AUDOIN DE DAMPIERRE** Brut Champagne Grande Année 1990 • $49 • (04/30/98)
89 **DEUTZ** Brut Champagne 1990 • $35 • (12/31/97)
89 **DEUTZ** Brut Champagne Cuvée William Deutz 1988 • $85 • (12/31/97)
89 **EGLY-OURIET** Brut Champagne Cuvée Spéciale NV • $40 • (04/30/98)
89 **EGLY-OURIET** Brut Champagne Tradition NV • $30 • (04/30/98)
89 **EGLY-OURIET** Brut Rosé Champagne NV • $35 • (04/30/98)
89 **PIERRE GIMONNET & FILS** Brut Blanc de Blancs Champagne Fleuron 1990 • $40 • (11/30/97)
89 **HENRIOT** Brut Champagne Cuvée des Enchanteleurs 1985 • $70 • (08/31/97)
89 **HENRIOT** Brut Champagne Souverain NV • $29 • (07/31/97)
89 **LANSON** Brut Champagne 1990 • $30 • (11/30/97)
89 **LANSON** Extra Dry Champagne Ivory Label NV • $22 • (11/15/97)
89 **LECHERE** Brut Blanc de Blancs Champagne 1990 • $40 • (11/30/97)
89 **MOËT & CHANDON** Brut Champagne Cuvée Dom Pérignon 1990 • $110 • (11/30/97)
89 **MOËT & CHANDON** Brut Rosé Champagne Impérial NV • $40 • (11/30/97)
89 **BRUNO PAILLARD** Brut Champagne 1989 • $50 • (04/30/98)
89 **BRUNO PAILLARD** Brut Champagne Première Cuvée NV • $27 • (04/30/98)
89 **PALMER & CO.** Brut Champagne 1989 • $40 • (12/31/97)
89 **PHILIPPONNAT** Brut Champagne Le Reflet NV • $40 • (11/15/97)
89 **PIPER-HEIDSIECK** Brut Rosé Champagne NV • $48 • (11/30/97)
89 **PIPER-HEIDSIECK** Extra Dry Champagne NV • $28 • (10/31/97)
89 **RUINART** Brut Rosé Champagne Dom Ruinart 1986 • $112 • (12/31/97)
89 **TAITTINGER** Brut Blanc de Blancs Champagne Comtes de Champagne 1989 • $113 • (11/30/97)
89 **TAITTINGER** Brut Champagne La Française NV • $38 • (11/30/97)
89 **TAITTINGER** Brut Rosé Champagne Comtes de Champagne 1993 • $152 • (11/30/97)
89 **DE VENOGE** Brut Champagne Cordon Bleu NV • $27 • (10/31/97)
89 **VEUVE CLICQUOT** Brut Rosé Champagne Réserve 1988 • $60 • (12/31/97)
89 **VILMART** Brut Champagne Cuvée du Nouveau Monde NV • $63 • (11/30/97)
89 **VRANKEN** Brut Champagne Demoiselle Grande Cuvée NV • $28 • (11/15/97)
89 **VRANKEN** Brut Champagne Demoiselle Tête de Cuvée 1990 • $60 • (09/30/97)
88 **ALLOUCHERY-PERSEVAL** Brut Champagne Réserve NV • $27 • (11/15/97)
88 **HENRI BILLIOT** Brut Champagne Cuvée Laetitia NV • $54 • (11/30/97)
88 **DELBECK** Brut Champagne Heritage NV • $29 • (04/30/98)
88 **DRAPPIER** Brut Rosé Champagne Grande Sendrée 1989 • $72 • (11/30/97)
88 **ALFRED GRATIEN** Brut Champagne Classique NV • $35 • (10/31/97)
88 **ALFRED GRATIEN** Brut Champagne Cuvée Paradis NV • $90 • (11/15/97)
88 **CHARLES HEIDSIECK** Brut Champagne 1990 • $48 • (08/31/97)
88 **LARMANDIER-BERNIER** Brut Blanc de Blancs Champagne NV • $30 • (11/30/97)
88 **LAURENT-PERRIER** Brut Rosé Champagne Grand Siècle Alexandra 1988 • $110 • (04/30/98)
88 **JEAN LAURENT** Brut Blanc de Blancs Champagne NV • $27 • (04/30/98)
88 **JEAN LAURENT** Brut Blanc de Noirs Champagne NV • $25 • (04/30/98)
88 **JEAN LAURENT** Brut Champagne Millésime 1989 • $35 • (04/30/98)
88 **A.R. LENOBLE** Brut Champagne 1988 • $35 • (11/15/97)
88 **MOËT & CHANDON** Brut Rosé Champagne Impérial 1992 • $55 • (11/30/97)
88 **BRUNO PAILLARD** Brut Rosé Champagne Première Cuvée NV • $38 • (04/30/98)
88 **PERRIER-JOUËT** Brut Rosé Champagne Fleur de Champagne Belle Epoque 1988 • $110 • (12/31/97)
88 **PHILIPPONNAT** Brut Champagne Royale Réserve NV • $25 • (10/31/97)
88 **POL ROGER** Brut Champagne Cuvée Sir Winston Churchill 1986 • $100 • (12/31/97)
88 **RUINART** Brut Champagne R de Ruinart NV • $38 • (11/15/97)
88 **RUINART** Brut Rosé Champagne R de Ruinart NV • $71 • (11/30/97)
88 **J. DE TELMONT** Brut Champagne Grand Vintage 1988 • $30 • (12/31/97)
88 **DE VENOGE** Brut Rosé Champagne Princesse NV • $35 • (11/30/97)
88 **DE VENOGE** Demi-Sec Champagne NV • $27 • (11/30/97)
88 **VEUVE CLICQUOT** Brut Champagne NV • $45 • (05/31/98)

GERMAN RIESLING

100 **GUNDERLOCH** Riesling Trockenbeerenauslese Rheinhessen Nackenheim Rothenberg 1996 • $251 • (11/30/97) • HR
97 **ROBERT WEIL** Riesling Trockenbeerenauslese Rheingau Kiedrich Gräfenberg 1996 • $310 • (11/30/97) • CS
96 **ROBERT WEIL** Riesling Eiswein Rheingau Kiedrich Gräfenberg 1996 • $200 • (11/30/97)

95 **CRUSIUS** Riesling Eiswein Nahe Traiser 1996 • $150 • (11/30/97)

95 **STAATSWEINGÜTER KLOSTER EBERBACH** Riesling Eiswein Gold Cap Rheingau Erbacher Marcobrunn 1996 • $320 • (07/31/98)

95 **EGON MÜLLER** Riesling Eiswein Mosel-Saar-Ruwer Scharzhofberger Nr. 103 1996 • $NA • (11/30/97)

95 **WILLI SCHAEFER** Riesling Auslese Mosel-Saar-Ruwer Graacher Domprobst 1996 • $55 • (04/30/98) • HR

94 **FRANZ KÜNSTLER** Riesling Eiswein Rheingau Hochheimer Reichestal 1996 • $195 • (11/30/97)

94 **EGON MÜLLER** Riesling Auslese Mosel-Saar-Ruwer Scharzhofberger Cask Nr. B 1996 • $NA • (11/30/97)

94 **DR. PAULY-BERGWEILER** Riesling Eiswein Mosel-Saar-Ruwer Bernkasteler Lay 1996 • $139 • (11/30/97)

94 **SCHLOSS SCHONBORN** Riesling Beerenauslese Rheingau Rüdesheimer Berg Schlossberg 1996 • $NA • (07/31/98)

93 **JOSEF BIFFAR** Riesling Eiswein Pfalz Deidesheimer Mäushöhle 1996 • $NA • (11/30/97)

93 **GEORG BREUER** Riesling Eiswein Gold Cap Rheingau Rüdesheimer Bischofsberg 1996 • $300 • (11/30/97)

93 **REICHSRAT VON BUHL** Riesling Trockenbeerenauslese Pfalz Forster Ungeheuer 1996 • $183 • (11/30/97)

93 **GUNDERLOCH** Riesling Beerenauslese Rheinhessen Nackenheimer Rothenberg 1996 • $99 • (11/30/97)

93 **REINHOLD HAART** Riesling Beerenauslese Mosel-Saar-Ruwer Piesporter Goldtröpfchen 1996 • $162 • (11/30/97)

93 **SCHLOSS JOHANNISBERG** Riesling Eiswein Rheingau 1996 • $222 • (11/30/97)

93 **PETER NICOLAY** Riesling Trockenbeerenauslese Mosel-Saar-Ruwer Ürziger Würzgarten 1996 • $500 • (11/30/97)

92 **REICHSRAT VON BUHL** Riesling Eiswein Pfalz Forster Jesuitengarten 1996 • $89 • (11/30/97)

92 **STAATSWEINGÜTER KLOSTER EBERBACH** Riesling Auslese Rheingau Rauenthaler Baiken 1996 • $18 • (07/31/98)

92 **LE GALLAIS** Riesling Auslese Gold Cap Mosel-Saar-Ruwer Wiltinger Braune Kupp 1996 • $NA • (11/30/97)

92 **SCHLOSS JOHANNISBERG** Riesling Beerenauslese Rheingau 1996 • $NA • (11/30/97)

92 **FRANZ KÜNSTLER** Riesling Spätlese Rheingau Hochheimer Kirchenstück 1996 • $30 • (11/30/97)

92 **MÜLLER-CATOIR** Riesling Spätlese Pfalz Haardter Herzog 1996 • $31 • (11/30/97)

92 **DR. H. THANISCH** Riesling Auslese Long Gold Cap Mosel-Saar-Ruwer Bernkasteler Doctor AP Nr. 5 1996 • $163 • (11/30/97)

92 **SCHLOSS VOLLRADS** Riesling Eiswein Gold Cap Rheingau 1996 • $NA • (11/30/97)

92 **ROBERT WEIL** Riesling Auslese Gold Cap Rheingau Kiedricher Gräfenberg 1996 • $299 • (11/30/97)

92 **ROBERT WEIL** Riesling Spätlese Rheingau Kiedricher Gräfenberg 1996 • $41 • (11/30/97)

91 **DR. BÜRKLIN-WOLF** Riesling Beerenauslese Pfalz Wachenheimer Gerümpel 1996 • $72 • (11/30/97)

91 **SCHLOSSGUT DIEL** Riesling Auslese Nahe 1996 • $41 • (11/30/97)

91 **STAATSWEINGÜTER KLOSTER EBERBACH** Riesling Spätlese Rheingau Erbacher Marcobrunn 1996 • $24 • (07/31/98)

91 **REINHOLD HAART** Riesling Spätlese Mosel-Saar-Ruwer Piesporter Goldtröpfchen 1996 • $28 • (11/30/97)

91 **SCHLOSS JOHANNISBERG** Riesling Auslese Rheingau 1996 • $74 • (11/30/97)

Key: SS—Spectator Selection CS—Cellar Selection HR—Highly Recommended BB—Best Buy $NA—Price not available Ⓐ—Auction Price
Dates in parentheses indicate the issues in which the ratings were published.

91 **FRANZ KÜNSTLER** Riesling Beerenauslese Rheingau Hochheimer Hölle 1996 • $113 • (11/30/97)

91 **DR. LOOSEN** Riesling Auslese Mosel-Saar-Ruwer Erdener Prälat 1996 • $49 • (11/30/97)

91 **MÜLLER-CATOIR** Riesling Eiswein Pfalz Haardter Bürgergarten 1996 • $94 • (11/30/97)

91 **WILLI SCHAEFER** Riesling Spätlese Mosel-Saar-Ruwer Graacher Himmelreich 1996 • $17 • (04/30/98) • HR

91 **LANGWERTH VON SIMMERN** Riesling Auslese Rheingau Hattenheimer Nussbrunnen 1996 • $45 • (11/30/97)

90 **BASSERMANN-JORDAN** Riesling Eiswein Pfalz Forster Ungeheuer 1996 • $119 • (11/30/97)

90 **JOSEF BIFFAR** Riesling Auslese Pfalz Deidesheimer Kieselberg 1996 • $34 • (11/30/97)

90 **GEORG BREUER** Riesling QbA Rheingau Montosa Charta 1996 • $20 • (11/30/97)

90 **REICHSRAT VON BUHL** Riesling Auslese Gold Cap Pfalz Forster Ungeheuer 1996 • $27 • (11/30/97)

90 **KURT DARTING** Riesling Kabinett Pfalz Ungsteiner Bettelhaus 1996 • $11 • (11/30/97)

90 **H. DÖNNHOFF** Riesling Eiswein Nahe Oberhäuser Brücke 1996 • $93 • (11/30/97)

90 **STAATSWEINGÜTER KLOSTER EBERBACH** Riesling Spätlese Rheingau Rüdesheimer Berg Rottland 1996 • $18 • (07/31/98)

90 **REINHOLD HAART** Riesling Kabinett Mosel-Saar-Ruwer Piesporter Goldtröpfchen 1996 • $19 • (11/30/97)

90 **SCHLOSS JOHANNISBERG** Riesling Spätlese Rheingau 1996 • $28 • (11/30/97)

90 **SCHLOSS JOHANNISBERG** Riesling Spätlese Trocken Rheingau 1996 • $27 • (11/30/97)

90 **TONI JOST** Riesling Auslese Mittelrhein Bacharacher Hahn 1996 • $37 • (04/30/98)

90 **KARTHÄUSERHOF** Riesling Kabinett Mosel-Saar-Ruwer Eitelsbacher Karthäuserhofberg 1996 • $17 • (01/01/98)

90 **REICHSGRAF VON KESSELSTATT** Riesling Beerenauslese Mosel-Saar-Ruwer Scharzhofberger 1996 • $65 • (11/30/97)

90 **REICHSGRAF VON KESSELSTATT** Riesling Spätlese Mosel-Saar-Ruwer Scharzhofberger 1996 • $19 • (11/30/97)

90 **LINGENFELDER** Riesling Spätlese Halbtrocken Pfalz Grosskarlbacher Osterberg 1996 • $14 • (11/30/97)

90 **DR. LOOSEN** Riesling Auslese Mosel-Saar-Ruwer Ürziger Würzgarten 1996 • $36 • (11/30/97)

90 **DR. LOOSEN** Riesling Beerenauslese Mosel-Saar-Ruwer Erdener Treppchen 1996 • $153 • (11/30/97)

90 **DR. LOOSEN** Riesling Spätlese Mosel-Saar-Ruwer Ürziger Würzgarten 1996 • $27 • (11/30/97)

90 **ALFRED MERKELBACH** Riesling Auslese Mosel-Saar-Ruwer Ürziger Würzgarten No. 12 1996 • $18 • (04/30/98)

90 **MAX FERD. RICHTER** Riesling Trockenbeerenauslese Mosel-Saar-Ruwer Brauneberger Juffer-Sonnenuhr 1996 • $142 • (11/30/97)

90 **SCHLOSS SCHONBORN** Riesling Spätlese Rheingau Geisenheimer Rothenberg-Lothar Franz 1996 • $NA • (07/31/98)

90 **C. VON SCHUBERT** Riesling Eiswein Mosel-Saar-Ruwer Maximin Grünhäuser Herrenberg 1996 • $85 • (11/30/97)

90 **C. VON SCHUBERT** Riesling Kabinett Mosel-Saar-Ruwer Maximin Grünhäuser Herrenberg 1996 • $18 • (11/30/97)

90 **SELBACH-OSTER** Riesling Eiswein Mosel-Saar-Ruwer Bernkasteler Badstube 1996 • $NA • (11/30/97)

90 **SELBACH-OSTER** Riesling Trockenbeerenauslese Mosel-Saar-Ruwer Zeltinger Sonnenuhr 1996 • $NA • (11/30/97)

90 **J. WEGELER ERBEN** Riesling Eiswein Rheingau Oestricher Lenchen Geheimrat Wegeler 1996 • $NA • (11/30/97)

90 **ROBERT WEIL** Riesling Kabinett Rheingau 1996 • $19 • (11/30/97)

90 **ZILLIKEN** Riesling Spätlese Mosel-Saar-Ruwer Saarburger Rausch 1996 • $21 • (11/30/97)

89 **BALBACH** Riesling Eiswein Rheinhessen Nierstein Oelberg 1996 • $NA • (11/30/97)

89 **DR. BÜRKLIN-WOLF** Riesling Spätlese Trocken Pfalz Forster Kirchenstück 1996 • $25 • (11/30/97)

89 **JOH. JOS. CHRISTOFFEL ERBEN** Riesling Auslese Mosel-Saar-Ruwer Ürziger Würzgarten Two Stars 1996 • $23 • (11/30/97)

89 **KURT DARTING** Riesling Spätlese Pfalz Dürkheimer Spielberg 1996 • $12 • (11/30/97)

89 **H. DÖNNHOFF** Riesling Auslese Nahe Niederhäuser Hermannshöhle 1996 • $27 • (11/30/97)

89 **REINHOLD HAART** Riesling Auslese Mosel-Saar-Ruwer Piesporter Goldtröpfchen AP Nr. 8 1996 • $36 • (11/30/97)

89 **AUGUST KESSELER** Riesling Spätlese Rheingau Rüdesheimer Berg Rottland 1996 • $36 • (11/30/97)

89 **REICHSGRAF VON KESSELSTATT** Riesling Spätlese Mosel-Saar-Ruwer Josephshöfer 1996 • $21 • (11/30/97)

89 **KOEHLER-RUPRECHT** Riesling Kabinett Halbtrocken Pfalz Kallstadter Steinacker 1996 • $NA • (11/30/97)

89 **KRUGER-RUMPF** Riesling Auslese Nahe Münsterer Dautenpflänzer 1996 • $20 • (04/30/98)

89 **KRUGER-RUMPF** Riesling Spätlese Nahe Münsterer Dautenpflänzer 1996 • $16 • (04/30/98)

89 **LINGENFELDER** Riesling Auslese Trocken Pfalz Freinsheimer Goldberg 1996 • $NA • (11/30/97)

89 **DR. LOOSEN** Riesling Kabinett Mosel-Saar-Ruwer Wehlener Sonnenuhr 1996 • $17 • (11/30/97)

89 **DR. LOOSEN** Riesling Spätlese Mosel-Saar-Ruwer Wehlener Sonnenuhr 1996 • $23 • (11/30/97)

89 **ALFRED MERKELBACH** Riesling Spätlese Mosel-Saar-Ruwer Erdener Treppchen No. 9 1996 • $15 • (04/30/98)

89 **MÜLLER-CATOIR** Riesling Spätlese Trocken Pfalz Haardter Herrenletten 1996 • $29 • (11/30/97)

89 **VON OTHEGRAVEN** Riesling Spätlese Mosel-Saar-Ruwer Kanzemer Altenberg 1996 • $19 • (03/31/98)

89 **SCHLOSS REINHARTSHAUSEN** Riesling Trockenbeerenauslese Rheingau Erbacher Siegelsberg 1996 • $NA • (11/30/97)

89 **MAX FERD. RICHTER** Riesling Spätlese Mosel-Saar-Ruwer Wehlener Sonnenuhr 1996 • $18 • (11/30/97)

89 **SCHLOSS SCHONBORN** Riesling Kabinett Rheingau Hattenheimer Pfaffenberg 1996 • $NA • (07/31/98)

89 **C. VON SCHUBERT** Riesling Spätlese Mosel-Saar-Ruwer Maximin Grünhäuser Abtsberg 1996 • $24 • (11/30/97)

89 **HEINRICH SEEBRICH** Riesling Eiswein Rheinhessen Niersteiner Rosenberg 1996 • $38 • (04/30/98)

89 **SELBACH-OSTER** Riesling Spätlese Mosel-Saar-Ruwer Wehlener Sonnenuhr 1996 • $20 • (11/30/97)

89 **LANGWERTH VON SIMMERN** Riesling Spätlese Rheingau Rauenthaler Baiken 1996 • $23 • (11/30/97)

89 **DR. H. THANISCH** Riesling Spätlese Mosel-Saar-Ruwer Bernkasteler Doctor 1996 • $51 • (11/30/97)

89 **SCHLOSS VOLLRADS** Riesling Spätlese Rheingau 1996 • $24 • (07/31/98)

89 **J. WEGELER ERBEN** Riesling Spätlese Rheingau Charta Geheimrat Wegeler Erben 1996 • $NA • (11/30/97)

89 **J. WEGELER ERBEN** Riesling Trockenbeerenauslese Rheingau Geisenheimer Rothenberg Geheimrat Wegeler 1996 • $NA • (11/30/97)

89 **ROBERT WEIL** Riesling Auslese Rheingau Kiedricher Gräfenberg 1996 • $41 • (11/30/97)

88 **JOSEF BIFFAR** Riesling Spätlese Halbtrocken Pfalz Deidesheimer Mäushöhle 1996 • $21 • (11/30/97)

88 **GEORG BREUER** Riesling Auslese Gold Cap Rheingau Rüdesheimer Berg Schlossberg 1996 • $100 • (11/30/97)

88 **REICHSRAT VON BUHL** Riesling Kabinett Pfalz Armand 1996 • $15 • (11/30/97)

88 **DR. BÜRKLIN-WOLF** Riesling Eiswein Pfalz Wachenheimer Gerümpel 1996 • $185 • (11/30/97)

88 **DR. BÜRKLIN-WOLF** Riesling Spätlese Pfalz Wachenheimer Gerümpel 1996 • $16 • (11/30/97)

88 **JOH. JOS. CHRISTOFFEL ERBEN** Riesling Auslese Mosel-Saar-Ruwer Ürziger Würzgarten One Star 1996 • $20 • (11/30/97)

88 **SCHLOSSGUT DIEL** Riesling Kabinett Nahe Dorsheimer Pittermännchen 1996 • $20 • (11/30/97)

88 **SCHLOSSGUT DIEL** Riesling Spätlese Nahe Dorsheimer Burgberg 1996 • $25 • (11/30/97)

88 **STAATSWEINGÜTER KLOSTER EBERBACH** Riesling Eiswein Rheingau Rauenthaler Baiken 1996 • $130 • (07/31/98)

88 **GUNDERLOCH** Riesling Spätlese Rheinhessen Nackenheimer Rothenberg 1996 • $24 • (11/30/97)

88 **FRITZ HAAG** Riesling Kabinett Mosel-Saar-Ruwer Brauneberger Juffer 1996 • $15 • (04/30/98)

88 **JOHANN HAART** Riesling Auslese Mosel-Saar-Ruwer Piesporter Goldtröpfchen 1996 • $24 • (04/30/98)

88 **HEYL ZU HERRNSHEIM** Riesling Auslese Rheinhessen Niersteiner Pettenthal 1996 • $22 • (11/30/97)

88 **HEYL ZU HERRNSHEIM** Riesling Spätlese Rheinhessen Niersteiner Brudersberg 1996 • $18 • (11/30/97)

88 **SCHLOSS JOHANNISBERG** Riesling Kabinett Rheingau 1996 • $23 • (11/30/97)

88 **TONI JOST** Riesling Kabinett Mittelrhein Bacharacher Hahn 1996 • $17 • (04/30/98)

88 **KARTHÄUSERHOF** Riesling QbA Mosel-Saar-Ruwer Eitelsbacher Karthäuserhofberg 1996 • $14 • (11/30/97)

88 **AUGUST KESSELER** Riesling Kabinett Rheingau 1996 • $18 • (11/30/97)

88 **REICHSGRAF VON KESSELSTATT** Riesling Auslese Gold Cap Mosel-Saar-Ruwer Josephshöfer 1996 • $26 • (11/30/97)

88 **REICHSGRAF VON KESSELSTATT** Riesling Eiswein Mosel-Saar-Ruwer Scharzhofberger 1996 • $107 • (11/30/97)

88 **REICHSGRAF VON KESSELSTATT** Riesling Kabinett Mosel-Saar-Ruwer Piesporter Goldtröpfchen 1996 • $15 • (11/30/97)

88 **REICHSGRAF VON KESSELSTATT** Riesling Kabinett Mosel-Saar-Ruwer Scharzhofberger 1996 • $15 • (11/30/97)

88 **REICHSGRAF VON KESSELSTATT** Riesling Spätlese Mosel-Saar-Ruwer Graacher Domprobst 1996 • $18 • (11/30/97)

88 **REICHSGRAF VON KESSELSTATT** Riesling Spätlese Mosel-Saar-Ruwer Kaseler Nies'chen 1996 • $18 • (11/30/97)

88 **KOEHLER-RUPRECHT** Riesling Spätlese Halbtrocken Pfalz Kallstadter Saumagen 1996 • $19 • (11/30/97)

88 **FRANZ KÜNSTLER** Riesling Spätlese Trocken Rheingau Hochheimer Hölle 1996 • $34 • (11/30/97)

88 **LINGENFELDER** Riesling Spätlese Pfalz Grosskarlbacher Osterberg 1996 • $15 • (11/30/97)

88 **ALFRED MERKELBACH** Riesling Auslese Mosel-Saar-Ruwer Ürziger Würzgarten No. 11 1996 • $18 • (04/30/98)

88 **EGON MÜLLER** Riesling QbA Mosel-Saar-Ruwer Scharzhofberger 1996 • $16 • (11/30/97)

88 **VON OTHEGRAVEN** Riesling Auslese Mosel-Saar-Ruwer Kanzemer Altenberg Cask No. 12 1996 • $30 • (03/31/98)

88 **DR. PAULY-BERGWEILER** Riesling Spätlese Mosel-Saar-Ruwer Wehlener Sonnenuhr 1996 • $23 • (11/30/97)

88 **PFEFFINGEN** Riesling Kabinett Halbtrocken Pfalz Pfeffo 1996 • $15 • (04/30/98)

88 **MAX FERD. RICHTER** Riesling Beerenauslese Mosel-Saar-Ruwer Graacher Dompropst 1996 • $72 • (11/30/97)

88 **MAX FERD. RICHTER** Riesling Kabinett Mosel-Saar-Ruwer Brauneberger Juffer 1996 • $15 • (11/30/97)

88 **MAX FERD. RICHTER** Riesling Kabinett Mosel-Saar-Ruwer Wehlener Sonnenuhr 1996 • $15 • (11/30/97)

88 **SCHLOSS SCHONBORN** Riesling Spätlese Rheingau Hattenheimer Pfaffenberg 1996 • $NA • (07/31/98)

88 **C. VON SCHUBERT** Riesling Auslese Mosel-Saar-Ruwer Maximin Grünhäuser Abtsberg Cask No. 55 1996 • $28 • (11/30/97)
88 **LANGWERTH VON SIMMERN** Riesling Kabinett Rheingau Erbacher Marcobrunn 1996 • $14 • (11/30/97)
88 **DR. H. THANISCH (MÜLLER-BURGGRAEF)** Riesling Auslese Mosel-Saar-Ruwer Bernkasteler Doctor 1996 • $NA • (11/30/97)
88 **DR. H. THANISCH** Riesling Auslese Gold Cap Mosel-Saar-Ruwer Bernkasteler Doctor AP Nr. 6 1996 • $110 • (11/30/97)
88 **J. WEGELER ERBEN** Riesling Spätlese Rheingau Geisenheimer Rothenberg Geheimrat J. Wegeler Erben 1996 • $20 • (11/30/97)
88 **J. WEGELER ERBEN** Riesling Spätlese Trocken Rheingau Geheimrat J. 1996 • $NA • (11/30/97)
88 **ZILLIKEN** Riesling Kabinett Mosel-Saar-Ruwer Ockfener Bockstein 1996 • $14 • (11/30/97)

BAROLO & BARBARESCO

94 **ALDO CONTERNO** Barolo Cicala 1993 • $125 • (10/31/97)
93 **AZELIA** Barolo Bricco Fiasco 1993 • $41 • (10/31/97)
93 **DOMENICO CLERICO** Barolo Pajana 1993 • $44 • (10/31/97)
92 **CIABOT BERTON** Barolo Roggeri 1993 • $28 • (10/31/97)
92 **PAOLO SCAVINO** Barolo Bric dël Fiasc 1993 • $53 • (10/31/97)
92 **PAOLO SCAVINO** Barolo Cannubi 1993 • $53 • (10/31/97)
91 **CASCINA BONGIOVANNI** Barolo 1993 • $40 • (10/31/97)
91 **DOMENICO CLERICO** Barolo Ciabot Mentin Ginestra 1993 • $44 • (10/31/97)
91 **GAJA** Barbaresco 1994 • $70 • (10/31/97)
90 **MICHELE CHIARLO** Barolo Vigna Rionda 1993 • $64 • (10/31/97)
90 **CORINO** Barolo Vigneto Rocche 1993 • $35 • (10/31/97)
90 **SILVIO GRASSO** Barolo Ciabot Manzoni 1993 • $35 • (10/31/97)
90 **FRATELLI ODDERO** Barolo Mondoca di Bussia Soprana 1993 • $29 • (10/31/97)
90 **ALFREDO PRUNOTTO** Barolo Bussia 1993 • $50 • (10/31/97)
90 **RENATO RATTI** Barolo Marcenasco 1993 • $40 • (10/31/97)
90 **GIOVANNI VIBERTI** Barolo Riserva La Volta 1993 • $NA • (10/31/97)
89 **BENI DI BATASIOLO** Barolo 1993 • $20 • (10/31/97)
89 **FRATELLI BROVIA** Barolo Villero 1993 • $40 • (10/31/97)
89 **BRUNO GIACOSA** Barolo Collina Rionda 1993 • $110 • (10/31/97)
89 **SILVIO GRASSO** Barolo 1993 • $30 • (10/31/97)
89 **MASSOLINO** Barolo Vigna Parafada 1993 • $45 • (10/31/97)
89 **GIOVANNI VIBERTI** Barolo 1993 • $NA • (10/31/97)
88 **CANTINE GIACOMO ASCHERI** Barolo Vigna Farina 1993 • $35 • (10/31/97)
88 **FRATELLI CERETTO** Barolo Brunate 1993 • $49 • (10/31/97)
88 **MICHELE CHIARLO** Barolo Cannubi 1993 • $77 • (10/31/97)
88 **GAJA** Barolo Sperss 1993 • $100 • (10/31/97)
88 **GIOVANNI MANZONE** Barolo Le Gramolere 1993 • $33 • (10/31/97)
88 **ARMANDO PARUSSO** Barolo Bussia Vigna Munie 1993 • $37 • (10/31/97)

Key: SS—Spectator Selection CS—Cellar Selection HR—Highly Recommended BB—Best Buy $NA—Price not available Ⓐ—Auction Price
Dates in parentheses indicate the issues in which the ratings were published.

88 **PODERI ROCCHE DEI MANZONI** Barolo Vigna Rocche 1993 • $22 • (10/31/97)
88 **GIOVANNI VIBERTI** Barolo San Pietro 1993 • $NA • (10/31/97)
88 **VIETTI** Barolo Brunate 1993 • $59 • (10/31/97)
88 **VIETTI** Barolo Castiglione 1993 • $40 • (10/31/97)

CHIANTI CLASSICO

95 **CASTELLO DI AMA** Chianti Classico Bellavista Riserva 1990 • $NA • (09/30/97)
92 **FATTORIA DI FELSINA** Chianti Classico Rancia Riserva 1994 • $35 • (09/30/97)
92 **FATTORIA DI FELSINA** Chianti Classico Rancia Riserva 1993 • $33 • (09/30/97)
92 **POGGERINO** Chianti Classico Bugialla Riserva 1990 • $NA • (09/30/97)
92 **SAN FELICE** Chianti Classico Poggio Rosso Riserva 1990 • $NA • (09/30/97)
91 **CASTELLO DI AMA** Chianti Classico Bellavista Riserva 1994 • $40 • (09/30/97)
90 **CENNATOIO** Chianti Classico Riserva 1994 • $NA • (09/30/97)
90 **FATTORIA DI FELSINA** Chianti Classico Berardenga Riserva 1994 • $23 • (09/30/97)
90 **FONTODI** Chianti Classico Vigna del Sorbo Riserva 1994 • $30 • (09/30/97)
90 **FONTODI** Chianti Classico Vigna del Sorbo Riserva 1993 • $28 • (09/30/97)
90 **POGGERINO** Chianti Classico Bugialla Riserva 1994 • $42 • (09/30/97)
90 **SAN FELICE** Chianti Classico Poggio Rosso Riserva 1994 • $27 • (09/30/97)
90 **SAN FELICE** Chianti Classico Poggio Rosso Riserva 1993 • $30 • (09/30/97)
89 **CASA EMMA** Chianti Classico Riserva 1994 • $35 • (09/30/97)
89 **CASTEL RUGGERO** Chianti Classico Riserva 1993 • $NA • (10/31/96)
89 **FATTORIA DI FELSINA** Chianti Classico Riserva 1993 • $19 • (10/31/96)
89 **CASTELLO DI FONTERUTOLI** Chianti Classico Riserva 1995 • $NA • (01/01/97)
89 **CASTELLO DI FONTERUTOLI** Chianti Classico Ser Lapo Riserva 1994 • $32 • (09/30/97)
89 **FONTODI** Chianti Classico Riserva 1993 • $19 • (10/31/96)
89 **FONTODI** Chianti Classico Vigna del Sorbo Riserva 1990 • $NA • (09/30/97)
88 **ANTINORI** Chianti Classico Badia a Passignano Riserva 1994 • $30 • (09/30/97)
88 **BROLIO** Chianti Classico Riserva 1994 • $17 • (09/30/97)
88 **CASTEL RUGGERO** Chianti Classico 1994 • $NA • (10/31/96)
88 **LE CORTI** Chianti Classico Cortevecchia Riserva 1994 • $25 • (09/30/97)
88 **FATTORIA DI FELSINA** Chianti Classico 1995 • $18 • (09/30/97)
88 **FATTORIA DI FELSINA** Chianti Classico Berardenga 1994 • $14 • (10/31/96)
88 **FATTORIA DI FELSINA** Chianti Classico Rancia Riserva 1990 • $NA • (09/30/97)
88 **LE FILIGARE** Chianti Classico Riserva 1994 • $28 • (04/30/98)
88 **FONTODI** Chianti Classico 1995 • $18 • (09/30/97)
88 **FONTODI** Chianti Classico 1994 • $15 • (10/31/96)
88 **FONTODI** Chianti Classico Riserva 1994 • $23 • (09/30/97)

88 **CASTELLO DI LILLIANO** Chianti Classico Riserva 1994 • $25 • (09/30/97)
88 **CASTELLO DI LILLIANO** Chianti Classico Riserva 1993 • $24 • (10/31/96)
88 **POGGERINO** Chianti Classico Bugialla Riserva 1993 • $28 • (10/31/96)
88 **FATTORIA QUERCIABELLA** Chianti Classico Riserva 1994 • $25 • (09/30/97)
88 **RIECINE** Chianti Classico Riserva 1994 • $33 • (09/30/97)
88 **RUFFINO** Chianti Classico Ducale Gold Label Riserva 1993 • $NA • (09/30/97)
88 **SOLATIONE** Chianti Classico Riserva 1993 • $20 • (04/30/98)
88 **VECCHIE TERRE DI MONTEFILI** Chianti Classico 1994 • $20 • (10/31/96)

SUPER TUSCANS

96 **CASTELLO DI AMA** Vigna l'Apparita 1993 • $100 • (09/30/97) • HR
94 **ARGIANO** Solengo 1995 • $50 • (12/31/97) • HR
93 **ANTINORI** Solaia 1994 • $97 • (09/30/97) • CS
93 **PODERE POGGIO SCALETTE** Il Carbonaione 1993 • $55 • (09/30/97)
92 **CASTELLO DEI RAMPOLLA** Sammarco 1994 • $65 • (09/30/97)
91 **COL D'ORCIA** Olmaia 1993 • $39 • (09/30/97)
91 **ISOLE E OLENA** Cepparello 1995 • $34 • (09/30/97)
90 **CASTELLO BANFI** Excelsus 1993 • $45 • (09/30/97)
90 **CASTELLO BANFI** Summus 1994 • $40 • (09/30/97)
90 **JACOPO BIONDI-SANTI** Schidione 1993 • $107 • (09/30/97)
90 **CARPINETO** Farnito 1994 • $20 • (09/30/97)
90 **CASTELLARE DI CASTELLINA** Coniale di Castellare 1993 • $35 • (09/30/97)
90 **FATTORIA DI FELSINA** Fontalloro 1993 • $40 • (09/30/97)
90 **ISOLE E OLENA** Cabernet Sauvignon Tuscany Collezione de Marchi 1994 • $32 • (09/30/97)
90 **LUCE** Luce della Vite 1993 • $55 • (09/30/97)
90 **FATTORIA MONSANTO** Sangiovese Tuscany Fabrizio Bianchi 1993 • $26 • (07/31/97)
90 **MONTECALVI** Rosso dell'Alta Valle della Greve 1995 • $36 • (10/31/97)
90 **MONTEVERTINE** Le Pergole Torte 1994 • $59 • (09/30/97)
90 **PODERE POGGIO SCALETTE** Il Carbonaione 1994 • $55 • (09/30/97)
90 **RIECINE** La Gioia 1994 • $40 • (09/30/97)
90 **RUFFINO** Cabreo Il Borgo 1995 • $28 • (09/30/97)
90 **TERRABIANCA** Campaccio Barriques Speciale 1993 • $58 • (09/30/97)
89 **ANTINORI** Tignanello 1994 • $55 • (09/30/97)
89 **CASTELLO BANFI** Tavernelle 1994 • $25 • (09/30/97)
89 **GUICCIARDINI STROZZI** Millanni 1994 • $42 • (09/30/97)
89 **ISOLE E OLENA** Syrah Tuscany Collezione de Marchi 1994 • $34 • (09/30/97)
89 **LUCE** Luce della Vite 1994 • $55 • (09/30/97)
89 **POLIZIANO** Elegia 1995 • $35 • (09/30/97)
89 **CASTELLO DI QUERCETO** La Corte 1993 • $30 • (09/30/97)
89 **SAN FELICE** Vigorello 1994 • $24 • (09/30/97)
89 **FATTORIA UCCELLIERA** Castellaccio 1993 • $26 • (09/30/97)
89 **VECCHIE TERRE DI MONTEFILI** Anfiteatro 1994 • $50 • (09/30/97)
89 **VILLA LA SELVA** Selvamaggio 1993 • $25 • (09/30/97)
89 **VISTARENNI** Codirosso 1993 • $24 • (09/30/97)
88 **AVIGNONESI** Grifi 1994 • $43 • (09/30/97)
88 **BADIA A COLTIBUONO** Sangioveto di Coltibuono 1994 • $35 • (09/30/97)
88 **JACOPO BIONDI-SANTI** Sassoalloro 1994 • $28 • (09/30/97)
88 **LA CALONICA** Girifalco 1995 • $29 • (09/30/97)
88 **DEI** Santa Catharina 1995 • $35 • (09/30/97)
88 **FATTORIA LE FILIGARE** Podere Le Rocce 1994 • $38 • (04/30/98)
88 **CASTELLO DI FONTERUTOLI** Siepi 1995 • $50 • (09/30/97)
88 **FONTODI** Case Via 1994 • $38 • (09/30/97)
88 **FONTODI** Flaccianello 1994 • $40 • (09/30/97)
88 **CASTELLO DI GABBIANO** per Ania 1990 • $30 • (09/30/97)
88 **GUICCIARDINI STROZZI** Sòdole 1994 • $26 • (09/30/97)
88 **FATTORIA MONSANTO** Nemo 1994 • $33 • (10/31/97)
88 **FATTORIA PETROLO** Torrione 1994 • $32 • (09/30/97)
88 **ROCCA DELLE MACIE** Roccato 1994 • $26 • (09/30/97)
88 **TERRABIANCA** Piano del Cipresso 1993 • $31 • (09/30/97)
88 **TENUTA VALDIPIATTA** Trefonti 1994 • $30 • (09/30/97)
88 **VECCHIE TERRE DI MONTEFILI** Bruno di Rocca 1994 • $50 • (09/30/97)
88 **FATTORIA DI VIGNAMAGGIO** Gherardino 1993 • $36 • (09/30/97)
88 **VILLA CAFAGGIO** Cortaccio 1994 • $46 • (09/30/97)
88 **VILLA CAFAGGIO** San Martino 1994 • $41 • (09/30/97)
88 **VITICCIO** Monile 1994 • $40 • (09/30/97)

VINTAGE PORT

95 **TAYLOR FLADGATE** Vintage Port Quinta de Vargellas Vinha Velha 1995 • $NA • (04/30/98)
95 **QUINTA DO VESUVIO** Vintage Port 1995 • $60 • (04/30/98) • CS
93 **QUINTA DO NOVAL** Vintage Port Nacional 1991 • $180 • (06/15/98) • CS
92 **DELAFORCE** Vintage Port Quinta da Corte 1995 • $40 • (04/30/98)
92 **FONSECA** Vintage Port Guimaraens 1995 • $39 • (04/30/98) • CS
92 **SMITH WOODHOUSE** Vintage Port Madalena 1995 • $32 • (04/30/98) • CS
92 **TAYLOR FLADGATE** Vintage Port Quinta de Vargellas 1995 • $39 • (04/30/98) • CS
92 **WARRE** Vintage Port Quinta da Cavadinha 1995 • $33 • (04/30/98) • CS
91 **CHURCHILL** Vintage Port Agua Alta 1995 • $40 • (04/30/98)
91 **CROFT** Vintage Port Quinta da Roeda 1995 • $45 • (04/30/98)
90 **COCKBURN** Vintage Port Quinta dos Canais 1995 • $39 • (04/30/98)
90 **QUINTA DO CRASTO** Vintage Port 1995 • $33 • (04/30/98)
90 **DOW** Vintage Port Quinta do Bomfim 1995 • $38 • (04/30/98)
90 **FEIST** Vintage Port 1995 • $25 • (04/30/98)
90 **FERREIRA** Vintage Port 1995 • $37 • (04/30/98)
90 **MARTINEZ** Vintage Port Quinta da Eira Velha 1995 • $45 • (04/30/98)
90 **QUINTA DO NOVAL** Vintage Port 1995 • $55 • (04/30/98)
90 **QUINTA DO NOVAL** Vintage Port Quinta do Roriz 1995 • $45 • (04/30/98)
90 **TAYLOR FLADGATE** Vintage Port Quinta de Terra Feita 1995 • $NA • (04/30/98)
89 **GRAHAM** Vintage Port Malvedos 1995 • $43 • (04/30/98)
88 **BURMESTER** Vintage Port 1995 • $22 • (04/30/98)
88 **QUINTA DO NOVAL** Vintage Port Quinta da Silval 1995 • $45 • (04/30/98)
88 **ROZES** Vintage Port 1995 • $45 • (04/30/98)

RIOJA RED

92 **SEÑORIO DE SAN VICENTE** Tempranillo Rioja 1994 • $25 • (02/28/98)

91 **BODEGAS MUGA** Rioja Torre Muga Reserva 1991 • $50 • (02/28/98) • CS

89 **MARQUÉS DE GRIÑON** Rioja Colección Personal Reserva 1990 • $18 • (10/15/97)

89 **BODEGAS MARQUÉS DE MURRIETA** Rioja Ygay Reserva Especial 1989 • $20 • (11/15/97) • SS

88 **BODEGAS BRETÓN** Rioja Loriñon Reserva 1991 • $17 • (10/15/97)

88 **BODEGAS MUERZA** Rioja Vega Crianza 1994 • $10 • (11/30/97) • BB

88 **LA GRANJA NUESTRA SEÑORA DE REMELLURI** Rioja 1994 • $16 • (02/28/98)

88 **LA GRANJA NUESTRA SEÑORA DE REMELLURI** Rioja Gran Reserva 1990 • $40 • (02/28/98)

87 **BODEGAS CAMPO VIEJO** Rioja Reserva 1990 • $11 • (11/15/97)

87 **CUNE** Rioja Imperial Gran Reserva 1989 • $33 • (11/30/97)

87 **MARQUÉS DE GRIÑON** Rioja 1995 • $10 • (10/15/97)

87 **BODEGAS MARTINEZ BUJANDA** Rioja Conde de Valdemar Gran Reserva 1990 • $21 • (11/15/97)

87 **SEÑORIO DE SAN VICENTE** Tempranillo Rioja Reserva 1991 • $25 • (02/28/98)

86 **ARTADI** Rioja Crianza 1994 • $12 • (02/28/98)

86 **R. DE AYALA LETE E HIJOS** Rioja Viña Santurnia Crianza 1994 • $7 • (05/31/98)

86 **MARQUÉS DE CÁCERES** Rioja Crianza 1994 • $12 • (10/15/97)

86 **MARQUÉS DE CÁCERES** Rioja Reserva 1990 • $17 • (10/15/97)

86 **R. LÓPEZ DE HEREDIA VIÑA TONDONIA** Rioja Viña Tondonia Reserva 1989 • $17 • (10/15/97)

86 **BODEGAS MONTECILLO** Rioja Reserva 1989 • $12 • (10/15/97)

86 **BODEGAS MONTECILLO** Rioja Viña Cumbrero Crianza 1994 • $8 • (10/15/97)

86 **BODEGAS PRIMICIA** Rioja Viña Diezmo Crianza 1994 • $10 • (11/15/97) • BB

86 **BODEGAS VIÑEGRAS** Rioja Don Teófilo I Crianza 1994 • $17 • (05/31/98)

85 **CONTINO** Rioja Reserva 1990 • $22 • (10/15/97)

85 **LA RIOJA ALTA** Rioja Viña Arana Reserva 1991 • $18 • (05/31/98)

85 **MARQUÉS DEL PUERTO** Rioja Crianza 1994 • $9 • (11/15/97)

85 **BODEGAS LAN** Rioja Viña Lanciano Reserva 1991 • $17 • (05/31/98)

85 **R. LÓPEZ DE HEREDIA VIÑA TONDONIA** Rioja Viña Tondonia Reserva 1990 • $17 • (11/15/97)

85 **BODEGAS MARQUÉS DE MURRIETA** Rioja Ygay Reserva 1992 • $15 • (10/15/97)

85 **BODEGAS PALACIOS REMONDO** Rioja Herencia Remondo Crianza 1994 • $10 • (02/28/98) • BB

85 **BODEGAS PRIMICIA** Rioja Viña Diezmo Reserva 1989 • $14 • (11/15/97)

Key: SS—Spectator Selection CS—Cellar Selection HR—Highly Recommended BB—Best Buy $NA—Price not available Ⓐ—Auction Price

Dates in parentheses indicate the issues in which the ratings were published.

CALIFORNIA CABERNET SAUVIGNON & CABERNET BLENDS

97 **BERINGER** Cabernet Sauvignon Napa Valley Bancroft Vineyard 1994 • $85 • (10/31/97)

96 **ARAUJO** Cabernet Sauvignon Napa Valley Eisele Vineyard 1994 • $60 • (10/15/97) • HR

96 **DIAMOND CREEK** Cabernet Sauvignon Napa Valley Gravelly Meadow 1995 • $NA • (06/15/98)

96 **DIAMOND CREEK** Cabernet Sauvignon Napa Valley Red Rock Terrace 1995 • $NA • (06/15/98)

96 **FLORA SPRINGS** Cabernet Sauvignon Napa Valley Rutherford Hillside Reserve 1994 • $65 • (10/15/97) • HR

96 **GROTH** Cabernet Sauvignon Napa Valley Reserve 1994 • $100 • (05/15/98) • CS

96 **JOSEPH PHELPS** Insignia Napa Valley 1994 • $70 • (09/30/97) • CS

95 **CAYMUS** Cabernet Sauvignon Napa Valley Special Selection 1994 • $100 • (12/31/97) • CS

95 **COLGIN** Cabernet Sauvignon Napa Valley Herb Lamb Vineyard 1994 • $50 • (07/31/97) • HR

95 **DALLA VALLE** Maya Napa Valley 1994 • $80 • (10/31/97) • HR

95 **HARLAN ESTATE** Napa Valley 1994 • $100 • (05/15/98) • CS

95 **MARTIN RAY** Cabernet Sauvignon Napa Valley Diamond Mountain 1995 • $45 • (07/31/98)

95 **SCREAMING EAGLE** Cabernet Sauvignon Napa Valley 1994 • $75 • (10/31/97)

95 **SHAFER** Cabernet Sauvignon Stags Leap District Hillside Select 1994 • $75 • (10/15/97)

94 **ARROWOOD** Cabernet Sauvignon Sonoma County Réserve Spéciale 1994 • $50 • (07/31/98)

94 **BRYANT FAMILY** Cabernet Sauvignon Napa Valley 1994 • $50 • (11/30/97)

94 **ROBERT CRAIG** Affinity Napa Valley 1994 • $28 • (08/31/97) • HR

94 **ROBERT CRAIG** Cabernet Sauvignon Mount Veeder 1994 • $28 • (11/15/97)

94 **DIAMOND CREEK** Cabernet Sauvignon Napa Valley Volcanic Hill 1995 • $NA • (06/15/98)

94 **DOMINUS ESTATE** Napa Valley Napanook Vineyard 1994 • $75 • (07/31/97) • CS

94 **HARTWELL** Cabernet Sauvignon Stags Leap District Grace Vineyard 1994 • $63 • (11/30/97)

94 **LIVINGSTON** Cabernet Sauvignon Napa Valley Moffett Vineyard 1994 • $36 • (10/31/97) • HR

94 **PETER MICHAEL** Les Pavots Knights Valley 1994 • $35 • (08/31/97) • CS

94 **ROBERT MONDAVI** Cabernet Sauvignon Napa Valley Reserve 1995 • $80 • (07/31/98)

94 **ROBERT MONDAVI** Cabernet Sauvignon Napa Valley Reserve 1994 • $74 • (07/31/97) • CS

94 **OPUS ONE** Napa Valley 1994 • $90 • (10/15/97) • CS

94 **SHAFER** Cabernet Sauvignon Stags Leap District Hillside Select 1993 • $60 • (10/31/97) • CS

93 **BEAULIEU VINEYARD** Cabernet Sauvignon Napa Valley Georges de Latour Private Reserve 1994 • $50 • (10/15/97) • CS

93 **BEAULIEU VINEYARD** Cabernet Sauvignon Rutherford Clone 6 Signet Collection 1994 • $100 • (11/15/97)

93 **CHATEAU SOUVERAIN** Cabernet Sauvignon Alexander Valley Winemaker's Reserve 1994 • $30 • (10/15/97)

93 **CORNERSTONE** Cabernet Sauvignon Howell Mountain Beatty Ranch 1994 • $35 • (10/31/97)

93 **DALLA VALLE** Cabernet Sauvignon Napa Valley 1994 • $40 • (10/31/97) • CS

93 **DIAMOND CREEK** Cabernet Sauvignon Napa Valley Gravelly Meadow 1994 • $NA • (06/15/98)
93 **DIAMOND CREEK** Cabernet Sauvignon Napa Valley Lake 1994 • $NA • (06/15/98)
93 **DIAMOND CREEK** Cabernet Sauvignon Napa Valley Red Rock Terrace Microclimate 2 1994 • $NA • (06/15/98)
93 **ETUDE** Cabernet Sauvignon Napa Valley 1994 • $38 • (09/30/97)
93 **FREEMARK ABBEY** Cabernet Sauvignon Napa Valley Bosché 1992 • $32 • (09/30/97) • CS
93 **GIRARD** Cabernet Sauvignon Napa Valley Reserve 1994 • $40 • (11/15/97)
93 **GUENOC** Cabernet Sauvignon Napa Valley Beckstoffer IV Vineyard Reserve 1994 • $40 • (10/31/97)
93 **HARLAN ESTATE** Napa Valley 1993 • $85 • (10/15/97)
93 **HARRISON** Cabernet Sauvignon Napa Valley 1994 • $33 • (07/31/97) • HR
93 **LEWIS CELLARS** Cabernet Sauvignon Napa Valley Reserve 1995 • $40 • (05/15/98) • HR
93 **LIPARITA** Cabernet Sauvignon Howell Mountain 1994 • $32 • (05/15/98) • HR
93 **PETER MICHAEL** Les Pavots Knights Valley 1995 • $50 • (07/31/98)
93 **PINE RIDGE** Andrus Reserve Napa Valley 1994 • $85 • (07/31/97)
93 **RAYMOND** Cabernet Sauvignon Napa Valley Generations 1994 • $35 • (10/31/97) • SS
93 **RIDGE** Monte Bello Santa Cruz Mountains 1994 • $100 • (09/30/97)
93 **ST. CLEMENT** Oroppas Napa Valley 1995 • $35 • (08/31/97)
93 **ST. FRANCIS** Cabernet Sauvignon Sonoma Valley Reserve 1994 • $30 • (10/15/97) • SS
93 **SIGNORELLO** Cabernet Sauvignon Napa Valley 1995 • $30 • (07/31/98)
93 **SIGNORELLO** Cabernet Sauvignon Napa Valley Founder's Reserve 1995 • $55 • (07/31/98)
93 **SILVERADO VINEYARDS** Cabernet Sauvignon Napa Valley Limited Reserve 1994 • $50 • (11/30/97) • HR
93 **STAG'S LEAP WINE CELLARS** Cask 23 Napa Valley 1994 • $100 • (03/31/98) • CS
93 **STONESTREET** Legacy Alexander Valley 1994 • $50 • (10/15/97) • HR
93 **VON STRASSER** Cabernet Sauvignon Napa Valley Diamond Mountain 1995 • $36 • (07/31/98)
93 **WHITE COTTAGE** Cabernet Sauvignon Howell Mountain 1994 • $35 • (10/15/97)
92 **BEHRENS & HITCHCOCK** Cabernet Sauvignon Napa Valley Staglin Vineyard 1994 • $28 • (11/30/97)
92 **BERINGER** Cabernet Sauvignon Napa Valley Chabot Vineyard 1994 • $85 • (10/31/97)
92 **BERINGER** Cabernet Sauvignon Napa Valley Marston Vineyard 1994 • $85 • (10/31/97)
92 **CAKEBREAD** Cabernet Sauvignon Napa Valley 1994 • $25 • (07/31/97) • SS
92 **CARDINALE** Napa-Alexander Valleys 1995 • $70 • (07/31/98)
92 **CHATEAU ST. JEAN** Cabernet Sauvignon Sonoma County Reserve 1992 • $45 • (09/30/97)
92 **CUVAISON** Cabernet Sauvignon Napa Valley ATS 1994 • $50 • (04/30/98)
92 **DEL DOTTO** Cabernet Sauvignon Napa Valley 1994 • $42 • (10/31/97)
92 **FAR NIENTE** Cabernet Sauvignon Napa Valley 1995 • $70 • (06/30/98) • HR
92 **FISHER** Cabernet Sauvignon Napa Valley Lamb Vineyard 1994 • $50 • (10/31/97)
92 **FREEMARK ABBEY** Cabernet Bosché Napa Valley Bosché Estate 1993 • $35 • (06/30/98) • CS
92 **GRACE FAMILY** Cabernet Sauvignon Napa Valley 1995 • $475 • (06/15/98)
92 **HARTWELL** Cabernet Sauvignon Stags Leap District Sunshine Vineyard 1995 • $50 • (05/15/98)
92 **JUSTIN** Isosceles Paso Robles 1994 • $33 • (10/31/97)
92 **MARKHAM** Cabernet Sauvignon Napa Valley 1994 • $15 • (10/31/97) • SS
92 **NIEBAUM-COPPOLA** Rubicon Rutherford 1994 • $65 • (06/15/98) • CS
92 **PARADIGM** Cabernet Sauvignon Napa Valley Oakville 1994 • $30 • (09/30/97)
92 **PEJU** Cabernet Sauvignon Napa Valley HB Vineyard 1994 • $55 • (10/31/97)
92 **PINE RIDGE** Andrus Reserve Napa Valley 1995 • $85 • (06/30/98)
92 **PINE RIDGE** Cabernet Sauvignon Stags Leap District 1994 • $35 • (10/31/97)
92 **PLUMPJACK** Cabernet Sauvignon Napa Valley McWilliam's Mt. Eden Vineyard 1995 • $30 • (11/15/97)
92 **PLUMPJACK** Cabernet Sauvignon Napa Valley McWilliam's Mt. Eden Vineyard Reserve 1995 • $65 • (11/15/97)
92 **ST. CLEMENT** Cabernet Sauvignon Howell Mountain White Cottage Ranch 1994 • $45 • (09/30/97)
92 **SNOWDEN** Cabernet Sauvignon Napa Valley 1993 • $35 • (07/31/97)
92 **SPOTTSWOODE** Cabernet Sauvignon Napa Valley 1994 • $45 • (10/15/97) • CS
92 **STAG'S LEAP WINE CELLARS** Cabernet Sauvignon Napa Valley Fay 1994 • $50 • (03/31/98) • CS
92 **SWANSON** Alexis Napa Valley 1995 • $40 • (12/15/97) • HR
92 **VIADER** Napa Valley 1995 • $33 • (01/31/98) • HR
92 **VILLA MT. EDEN** Cabernet Sauvignon Mendocino Signature Series 1994 • $50 • (10/31/97)
92 **VON STRASSER** Cabernet Sauvignon Napa Valley Diamond Mountain 1994 • $32 • (10/31/97)
92 **WHITEHALL LANE** Cabernet Sauvignon Rutherford Morisoli Vineyard Reserve 1994 • $36 • (09/30/97)
91 **ALTAMURA** Cabernet Sauvignon Napa Valley 1994 • $33 • (12/15/97)
91 **ANDERSON'S CONN VALLEY** Cabernet Sauvignon Napa Valley Estate Reserve 1994 • $40 • (10/15/97)
91 **S. ANDERSON** Cabernet Sauvignon Stags Leap District Richard Chambers Vineyard 1994 • $50 • (10/31/97)
91 **ARROWOOD** Cabernet Sauvignon Sonoma County 1994 • $34 • (10/15/97)
91 **BEAULIEU VINEYARD** Tapestry Reserve Napa Valley 1994 • $20 • (10/31/97) • SS
91 **BERINGER** Cabernet Sauvignon Knights Valley 1994 • $20 • (07/31/97) • SS
91 **BERINGER** Cabernet Sauvignon Knights Valley Appellation Collection 1995 • $NA • (06/15/98)
91 **CHATEAU ST. JEAN** Cabernet Sauvignon Sonoma County Cinq Cépages 1994 • $24 • (09/30/97) • SS
91 **CHIMNEY ROCK** Cabernet Sauvignon Stags Leap District Reserve 1994 • $50 • (10/15/97)
91 **CLOS DU VAL** Cabernet Sauvignon Napa Valley Reserve 1993 • $50 • (10/31/97)
91 **B.R. COHN** Cabernet Sauvignon Sonoma Valley Olive Hill Estate Vineyards 1995 • $35 • (07/31/98)
91 **COSENTINO** M. Coz Napa Valley Meritage 1994 • $60 • (11/15/97)
91 **ROBERT CRAIG** Affinity Napa Valley 1995 • $34 • (06/15/98) • CS
91 **DEHLINGER** Cabernet Sauvignon Russian River Valley Estate 1994 • $25 • (09/30/97)
91 **DELECTUS** Cabernet Sauvignon Napa Valley 1995 • $42 • (07/31/98)

91 **DIAMOND CREEK** Cabernet Sauvignon Napa Valley Red Rock Terrace 1994 • $NA • (06/15/98)

91 **DIAMOND CREEK** Cabernet Sauvignon Napa Valley Volcanic Hill 1994 • $NA • (06/15/98)

91 **DUNN** Cabernet Sauvignon Howell Mountain 1994 • $45 • (05/15/98) • CS

91 **EBERLE** Cabernet Sauvignon Paso Robles Reserve 1991 • $35 • (11/15/97)

91 **ELAN** Cabernet Sauvignon Atlas Peak 1992 • $30 • (11/30/97)

91 **FERRARI-CARANO** Reserve Red Sonoma County 1992 • $47 • (09/30/97)

91 **FORMAN** Cabernet Sauvignon Napa Valley 1995 • $38 • (06/30/98)

91 **GALLERON** Cabernet Sauvignon Napa Valley 1994 • $50 • (09/30/97)

91 **GEYSER PEAK** Réserve Alexandre Alexander Valley 1994 • $28 • (10/31/97)

91 **HEITZ** Cabernet Sauvignon Napa Valley Bella Oaks Vineyard 1993 • $28 • (05/15/98) • CS

91 **PAUL HOBBS** Cabernet Sauvignon Howell Mountain Liparita Vineyard 1994 • $45 • (10/31/97)

91 **KATHRYN KENNEDY** Cabernet Sauvignon Santa Cruz Mountains 1993 • $70 • (10/31/97)

91 **LAMBERT BRIDGE** Crane Creek Cuvée Dry Creek Valley 1994 • $28 • (11/15/97)

91 **MORAGA** Bel Air 1993 • $50 • (07/31/97)

91 **JOSEPH PHELPS** Cabernet Sauvignon Napa Valley 1995 • $27 • (06/30/98) • SS

91 **PRIDE** Cabernet Sauvignon Napa Valley Reserve 1994 • $65 • (03/31/98)

91 **PRIDE** Cabernet Sauvignon Napa Valley 1995 • $24 • (11/30/97) • HR

91 **QUINTESSA** Rutherford Napa Valley 1994 • $70 • (11/30/97)

91 **SADDLEBACK** Cabernet Sauvignon Napa Valley 1994 • $23 • (09/30/97)

91 **ST. CLEMENT** Cabernet Sauvignon Napa Valley 1994 • $27 • (07/31/97)

91 **STAG'S LEAP WINE CELLARS** Cabernet Sauvignon Napa Valley S.L.V. 1994 • $50 • (11/30/97) • CS

91 **STEELE** Cabernet Sauvignon Anderson Valley 1994 • $24 • (12/15/97)

91 **STONESTREET** Cabernet Sauvignon Alexander Valley 1994 • $35 • (10/31/97)

91 **SWANSON** Cabernet Sauvignon Napa Valley 1995 • $26 • (07/31/98)

91 **SWANSON** Cabernet Sauvignon Napa Valley 1994 • $24 • (07/31/97)

91 **TERRACES** Cabernet Sauvignon Napa Valley 1993 • $40 • (11/30/97)

91 **TRUCHARD** Cabernet Sauvignon Napa Valley Carneros 1994 • $24 • (09/30/97)

91 **ZD WINES** Cabernet Sauvignon Napa Valley 1995 • $32 • (05/15/98)

90 **ADELAIDA** Cabernet Sauvignon San Luis Obispo County 1993 • $19 • (08/31/97)

90 **BEAULIEU VINEYARD** Cabernet Sauvignon Rutherford 1994 • $15 • (07/31/97) • SS

90 **BERINGER** Alluvium Knights Valley 1994 • $25 • (03/31/98)

90 **BERINGER** Cabernet Sauvignon Napa Valley Chabot Vineyard 1993 • $100 • (06/15/98)

Key: SS—Spectator Selection CS—Cellar Selection HR—Highly Recommended BB—Best Buy $NA—Price not available Ⓐ—Auction Price

Dates in parentheses indicate the issues in which the ratings were published.

90 **BUEHLER** Cabernet Sauvignon Napa Valley Estate 1994 • $35 • (11/15/97)

90 **BUENA VISTA** Cabernet Sauvignon Carneros Grand Reserve 1993 • $26 • (08/31/97)

90 **CARMENET** Meritage Red Sonoma Valley Moon Mountain Estate Reserve 1994 • $40 • (11/15/97)

90 **CHIMNEY ROCK** Cabernet Sauvignon Napa Valley 1995 • $28 • (05/15/98) • SS

90 **CHIMNEY ROCK** Cabernet Sauvignon Napa Valley 1994 • $24 • (07/31/97)

90 **CLOS DU BOIS** Marlstone Vineyard Alexander Valley 1994 • $25 • (05/15/98)

90 **CLOS PEGASE** Cabernet Sauvignon Napa Valley Hommage Artist Series Reserve 1994 • $40 • (09/30/97)

90 **B.R. COHN** Cabernet Sauvignon Sonoma Valley Olive Hill Estate Vineyards Special Selection 1995 • $80 • (06/15/98)

90 **ROBERT CRAIG** Cabernet Sauvignon Howell Mountain 1994 • $28 • (11/30/97)

90 **CRONIN** Concerto Stags Leap District Robinson Vineyard 1994 • $23 • (04/30/98)

90 **DE LOACH** Cabernet Sauvignon Russian River Valley O.F.S. 1994 • $28 • (09/30/97)

90 **TOM EDDY** Cabernet Sauvignon Napa Valley 1994 • $50 • (05/15/98)

90 **TOM EDDY** Cabernet Sauvignon Napa Valley 1993 • $40 • (10/31/97)

90 **E. & J. GALLO** Cabernet Sauvignon Northern Sonoma Estate Bottled 1993 • $45 • (10/31/97)

90 **FIFE** Cabernet Sauvignon Napa Valley Estate Vineyard 1995 • $24 • (05/15/98)

90 **FLORA SPRINGS** Trilogy Napa Valley 1994 • $33 • (10/15/97)

90 **GUENOC** Cabernet Sauvignon Napa Valley Bella Vista Vineyard Reserve 1994 • $26 • (09/30/97)

90 **GUENOC** Langtry Napa Valley Meritage Red 1994 • $41 • (09/30/97)

90 **HEITZ** Cabernet Sauvignon Napa Valley Trailside Vineyard 1992 • $48 • (09/30/97)

90 **HENDRY RANCH** Cabernet Sauvignon Napa Valley Block 8 1995 • $24 • (05/15/98)

90 **THE HESS COLLECTION** Cabernet Sauvignon Napa Valley Reserve 1993 • $40 • (05/15/98)

90 **KENWOOD** Cabernet Sauvignon Sonoma Valley Artist Series 1993 • $50 • (10/31/97) • CS

90 **LONG** Cabernet Sauvignon Napa Valley 1995 • $40 • (03/31/98)

90 **ROBERT MONDAVI** Cabernet Sauvignon Napa Valley 1994 • $22 • (11/15/97)

90 **MORAGA** Red Bel Air 1994 • $55 • (05/15/98)

90 **MOUNT VEEDER** Reserve Napa Valley 1993 • $40 • (08/31/97)

90 **NIEBAUM-COPPOLA** Rubicon Rutherford 1993 • $55 • (05/15/98)

90 **ROBERT PECOTA** Cabernet Sauvignon Napa Valley Kara's Vineyard 1995 • $25 • (05/31/98)

90 **PINE RIDGE** Cabernet Sauvignon Howell Mountain 1994 • $35 • (10/31/97)

90 **PINE RIDGE** Cabernet Sauvignon Stags Leap District 1995 • $38 • (06/15/98)

90 **PRIDE** Cabernet Sauvignon Napa Valley 1994 • $24 • (10/31/97)

90 **ROCKING HORSE** Cabernet Sauvignon Napa Valley Garvey Family Vineyard 1994 • $24 • (11/30/97)

90 **ROMBAUER** Cabernet Sauvignon Napa Valley Diamond Mountain Selection 1994 • $50 • (11/15/97)

90 **ROMBAUER** Le Meilleur du Chai Napa Valley 1990 • $40 • (08/31/97)

90 **ROSENTHAL-THE MALIBU ESTATE** Cabernet Sauvignon Malibu & Newton Canyon 1994 • $25 • (05/15/98)

90 **SIGNORELLO** Cabernet Sauvignon Napa Valley Founder's Reserve 1994 • $55 • (09/30/97)

90 **SILVER OAK** Cabernet Sauvignon Alexander Valley 1993 • $40 • (09/30/97) • CS

90 **SONOMA CREEK** Cabernet Sauvignon Sonoma Valley Rancho Salina Vineyard 1994 • $28 • (10/31/97)

90 **SPRING MOUNTAIN** Red Napa Valley 1994 • $36 • (04/30/98)

90 **VINE CLIFF** Cabernet Sauvignon Napa Valley Oakville Estate 1994 • $36 • (10/15/97)

90 **VINEYARD 29** Cabernet Sauvignon Napa Valley 1994 • $55 • (09/30/97)

90 **ZD WINES** Cabernet Sauvignon Napa Valley Reserve 1994 • $55 • (05/15/98)

89 **ALDERBROOK** Cabernet Sauvignon Sonoma County 1995 • $16 • (08/31/97)

89 **S. ANDERSON** Cabernet Sauvignon Stags Leap District 1994 • $24 • (10/31/97)

89 **ARNS** Cabernet Sauvignon Napa Valley 1994 • $35 • (10/31/97)

89 **BELL** Cabernet Sauvignon Rutherford Baritelle Vineyard 1992 • $50 • (07/31/97)

89 **CAFARO** Cabernet Sauvignon Napa Valley 1994 • $30 • (10/31/97)

89 **CHALK HILL** Cabernet Sauvignon Chalk Hill 1994 • $26 • (10/31/97)

89 **CHATEAU SOUVERAIN** Cabernet Sauvignon Alexander Valley 1995 • $17 • (06/30/98) • HR

89 **CLOS DU BOIS** Cabernet Sauvignon Alexander Valley Briarcrest Vineyard 1994 • $23 • (06/15/98)

89 **COSENTINO** Cabernet Sauvignon Napa Valley Reserve 1994 • $40 • (10/15/97)

89 **COSENTINO** The Poet Napa Valley Meritage 1994 • $30 • (11/15/97)

89 **CUVAISON** Cabernet Sauvignon Napa Valley 1994 • $25 • (11/15/97)

89 **DIAMOND CREEK** Cabernet Sauvignon Napa Valley Red Rock Terrace 1995 • $75 • (11/30/97)

89 **DRY CREEK** Cabernet Sauvignon Dry Creek Valley 25th Anniversary 1994 • $30 • (03/31/98)

89 **DRY CREEK** Meritage Dry Creek Valley 1995 • $25 • (04/30/98)

89 **ELLIOTT** Cabernet Sauvignon Napa Valley 1994 • $24 • (11/15/97)

89 **FETZER** Cabernet Sauvignon Napa Valley Usibelli Vineyard Reserve 1994 • $24 • (11/15/97)

89 **FRANCISCAN** Magnificat Napa Valley Meritage 1994 • $25 • (11/30/97)

89 **FREEMARK ABBEY** Cabernet Sauvignon Napa Valley 1994 • $18 • (10/31/97)

89 **FREEMARK ABBEY** Cabernet Sauvignon Napa Valley Sycamore Vineyards 1992 • $30 • (09/30/97)

89 **FRICK** Cabernet Sauvignon Dry Creek Valley 1994 • $20 • (09/15/97)

89 **GREENWOOD RIDGE** Cabernet Sauvignon Anderson Valley 1994 • $36 • (11/15/97)

89 **HARTWELL** Cabernet Sauvignon Stags Leap District Sunshine Vineyard 1994 • $40 • (11/30/97)

89 **PAUL HOBBS** Cabernet Sauvignon Napa Valley Carneros Hyde Vineyard 1994 • $40 • (10/31/97)

89 **HONIG** Cabernet Sauvignon Napa Valley 1995 • $22 • (05/15/98)

89 **CHARLES KRUG** Cabernet Sauvignon Napa Valley Peter Mondavi Family 1994 • $14 • (08/31/97)

89 **LA JOTA** Cabernet Sauvignon Howell Mountain 14th Anniversary Release 1995 • $48 • (06/30/98)

89 **LAMBERT BRIDGE** Cabernet Sauvignon Dry Creek Valley 1994 • $20 • (11/15/97)

89 **LANG & REED** Cabernet Franc Napa Valley 1996 • $18 • (03/31/98)

89 **MURPHY-GOODE** Cabernet Sauvignon Alexander Valley Brenda Block Reserve 1994 • $30 • (07/31/97)

89 **NAVARRO** Cabernet Sauvignon Mendocino 1992 • $19 • (11/15/97)

89 **NEWTON** Cabernet Sauvignon Napa Valley 1994 • $30 • (01/31/98)

89 **OPTIMA** Cabernet Sauvignon Alexander Valley 1994 • $28 • (08/31/97)

89 **JOSEPH PHELPS** Cabernet Sauvignon Napa Valley Backus Vineyard 1994 • $70 • (10/15/97)

89 **PINE RIDGE** Cabernet Sauvignon Rutherford 1995 • $24 • (03/31/98)

89 **PINE RIDGE** Cabernet Sauvignon Rutherford 1994 • $22 • (10/31/97)

89 **RIDGE** Monte Bello Santa Cruz Mountains 1993 • $80 • (10/15/97)

89 **ROSENBLUM** Cabernet Sauvignon Napa Valley Holbrook Mitchell Vineyard 1995 • $30 • (04/30/98)

89 **SCHUG** Cabernet Sauvignon Sonoma Valley Heritage Reserve 1994 • $30 • (12/15/97)

89 **SEAVEY** Cabernet Sauvignon Napa Valley 1994 • $30 • (12/31/97)

89 **ROBERT SINSKEY** Claret Stags Leap District 1993 • $30 • (05/15/98)

89 **VIANSA** Cabernet Sauvignon Napa Valley Reserve 1994 • $30 • (11/30/97)

89 **VIGIL** Cabernet Franc Napa Valley 1995 • $20 • (11/30/97)

88 **ADELAIDA** Cabernet Sauvignon San Luis Obispo County 1994 • $21 • (05/31/98)

88 **ARBIOS** Cabernet Sauvignon Alexander Valley 1995 • $30 • (06/15/98)

88 **ARROWOOD** Cabernet Sauvignon Sonoma County Domaine du Grand Archer 1995 • $16 • (03/31/98)

88 **DAVID ARTHUR** Meritagío Red Napa Valley 1995 • $32 • (04/30/98)

88 **BARTHOLOMEW PARK** Cabernet Sauvignon Sonoma Valley Desnudos Vineyard 1994 • $20 • (10/31/97)

88 **BENZIGER** Cabernet Sauvignon Sonoma Mountain Reserve 1994 • $32 • (06/30/98)

88 **BUENA VISTA** Cabernet Sauvignon Carneros 1994 • $16 • (08/31/97)

88 **CAIN** Five Napa Valley 1994 • $45 • (10/31/97)

88 **CHAPPELLET** Cabernet Sauvignon Napa Valley Signature 1994 • $22 • (12/31/97)

88 **CHATEAU POTELLE** Cabernet Sauvignon Mount Veeder V.G.S. 1993 • $39 • (07/31/98)

88 **CHAUFFE-EAU** Cabernet Sauvignon Alexander Valley Smith-Reichel Vineyard 1995 • $19 • (06/30/98)

88 **CHIMNEY ROCK** Elevage Stags Leap District 1994 • $40 • (10/15/97)

88 **CINNABAR** Cabernet Sauvignon Santa Cruz Mountains Saratoga Vineyard 1994 • $25 • (11/15/97)

88 **CLOS DU BOIS** Cabernet Sauvignon Alexander Valley Alexander Valley Selection 1995 • $18 • (04/30/98)

88 **CLOS DU BOIS** Cabernet Sauvignon Alexander Valley Briarcrest Vineyard 1993 • $21 • (07/31/97)

88 **CRONIN** Cabernet Sauvignon Santa Cruz Mountains 1994 • $23 • (04/30/98)

88 **CURTIS** Cabernet Franc Santa Ynez Valley Kingsley Vineyard 1994 • $18 • (07/31/97)

88 **DAYDREAM** Cabernet Sauvignon Napa Valley 1994 • $24 • (11/30/97)

88 **DELECTUS** Cabernet Sauvignon Napa Valley 1994 • $42 • (07/31/97)

88 **DIAMOND CREEK** Cabernet Sauvignon Napa Valley Volcanic Hill 1995 • $75 • (11/30/97)

88 **DIAMOND CREEK** Cabernet Sauvignon Napa Valley Volcanic Hill 1993 • $NA • (06/15/98)

88 **DOUGLASS HILL** Cabernet Sauvignon Napa Valley 1994 • $13 • (10/15/97)

88 **DRY CREEK** Meritage Dry Creek Valley 1994 • $25 • (08/31/97)

88 **DUNCAN PEAK** Cabernet Sauvignon Mendocino 1994 • $20 • (11/15/97)

88 **DUNN** Cabernet Sauvignon Napa Valley 1994 • $39 • (05/15/98)

88 **EDGEWOOD** Cabernet Sauvignon Napa Valley 1994 • $20 • (04/30/98)

88 **ESTANCIA** Duo Alexander Valley 1995 • $18 • (11/30/97)

88 **FETZER** Cabernet Sauvignon North Coast Barrel Select 1994 • $14 • (09/30/97)

88 **FIELD STONE** Cabernet Sauvignon Alexander Valley Staten Family Reserve 1994 • $28 • (07/31/98)

88 **FISHER** Cabernet Sauvignon Sonoma County Wedding Vineyard 1994 • $50 • (10/31/97)

88 **FOLIE À DEUX** Cabernet Sauvignon Napa Valley Reserve 1995 • $22 • (11/30/97)

88 **GEYSER PEAK** Cabernet Sauvignon Sonoma County 1995 • $15 • (10/31/97)

88 **GIRARD** Cabernet Sauvignon Napa Valley 1994 • $25 • (10/31/97)

88 **GRGICH HILLS** Cabernet Sauvignon Napa Valley 1994 • $30 • (10/31/97)

88 **GROTH** Cabernet Sauvignon Napa Valley 1994 • $27 • (08/31/97)

88 **HEITZ** Cabernet Sauvignon Napa Valley 1993 • $21 • (05/15/98)

88 **THE HESS COLLECTION** Cabernet Sauvignon Napa Valley 1994 • $20 • (05/15/98)

88 **WILLIAM HILL** Cabernet Sauvignon Napa Valley Reserve 1994 • $27 • (12/15/97)

88 **HUSCH** Cabernet Sauvignon Mendocino La Ribera Vineyards 1994 • $15 • (10/15/97)

88 **IRON HORSE** Cabernet Sauvignon Alexander Valley Barrel Fermented 1994 • $19 • (11/30/97)

88 **JORDAN** Cabernet Sauvignon Alexander Valley 1994 • $34 • (06/30/98)

88 **KARL LAWRENCE** Cabernet Sauvignon Napa Valley 1994 • $28 • (09/30/97)

88 **KENDALL-JACKSON** Cabernet Sauvignon Alexander Valley Buckeye Vineyard Single Vineyard Series 1994 • $24 • (08/31/97)

88 **KENWOOD** Cabernet Sauvignon Sonoma Valley 1994 • $18 • (10/31/97)

88 **KENWOOD** Cabernet Sauvignon Sonoma Valley Jack London Vineyard 1994 • $25 • (10/31/97)

88 **CHARLES KRUG** Cabernet Sauvignon Napa Valley Vintage Selection 1994 • $35 • (10/31/97)

88 **LANG & REED** Cabernet Franc Napa Valley 1993 • $20 • (03/31/98)

88 **LEWELLING** Cabernet Sauvignon Napa Valley 1993 • $30 • (05/31/98)

88 **LIVINGSTON** Cabernet Sauvignon Napa Valley Stanley's Selection 1995 • $22 • (03/31/98)

88 **LOCKWOOD** Cabernet Sauvignon Monterey Partners' Reserve 1994 • $21 • (11/15/97)

88 **MEEKER** Cabernet Sauvignon Dry Creek Valley Gold Leaf Cuvée 1994 • $18 • (11/15/97)

Key: SS—Spectator Selection CS—Cellar Selection HR—Highly Recommended BB—Best Buy $NA—Price not available Ⓐ—Auction Price
Dates in parentheses indicate the issues in which the ratings were published.

88 **MIDNIGHT CELLARS** Cabernet Franc Paso Robles Crescent 1995 • $15 • (05/31/98)

88 **MOUNT VEEDER** Cabernet Sauvignon Napa Valley 1994 • $25 • (08/31/97)

88 **NEYERS** Cabernet Sauvignon Napa Valley 1995 • $40 • (05/31/98)

88 **NIEBAUM-COPPOLA** Cabernet Franc Napa Valley Francis Coppola Family Wines 1995 • $20 • (12/15/97)

88 **OAKVILLE RANCH** Cabernet Sauvignon Napa Valley 1994 • $30 • (07/31/97)

88 **PEZZI KING** Cabernet Sauvignon Dry Creek Valley 1995 • $20 • (04/30/98)

88 **PINE RIDGE** Cabernet Sauvignon Howell Mountain 1995 • $38 • (04/30/98)

88 **A. RAFANELLI** Cabernet Sauvignon Dry Creek Valley 1994 • $20 • (09/30/97)

88 **MARTIN RAY** Cabernet Sauvignon California Saratoga Cuvée 1994 • $30 • (12/15/97)

88 **ROSENBLUM** Cabernet Sauvignon Napa Valley Hendry Vineyard Reserve 1995 • $40 • (05/31/98)

88 **ROSENBLUM** Holbrook Mitchell Trio Napa Valley 1995 • $35 • (04/30/98)

88 **RUBISSOW-SARGENT** Cabernet Sauvignon Mount Veeder 1992 • $19 • (11/15/97)

88 **RUBISSOW-SARGENT** Les Trompettes Mount Veeder 1992 • $22 • (11/15/97)

88 **SCHUG** Cabernet Sauvignon Napa Valley 1994 • $18 • (12/15/97)

88 **SEQUOIA GROVE** Cabernet Sauvignon Napa Valley 1995 • $22 • (06/15/98)

88 **SIGNORELLO** Cabernet Sauvignon Napa Valley 1994 • $30 • (11/15/97)

88 **SILVER OAK** Cabernet Sauvignon Napa Valley 1993 • $50 • (10/15/97)

88 **SIMI** Cabernet Sauvignon Alexander Valley 1994 • $18 • (10/31/97)

88 **STERLING** Cabernet Sauvignon Napa Valley 1995 • $14 • (04/30/98) • HR

88 **STERLING** Reserve Napa Valley 1994 • $40 • (12/15/97)

88 **RODNEY STRONG** Cabernet Sauvignon Northern Sonoma Alexander's Crown Vineyard 1993 • $22 • (08/31/97)

88 **SULLIVAN** Coeur de Vigne Napa Valley Private Reserve 1993 • $40 • (11/30/97)

88 **VOLKER EISELE** Cabernet Sauvignon Napa Valley 1995 • $35 • (07/31/98)

88 **WHITEHALL LANE** Cabernet Sauvignon Napa Valley 1995 • $20 • (04/30/98)

88 **ZD WINES** Cabernet Sauvignon Napa Valley 1994 • $30 • (07/31/97)

CALIFORNIA CHARDONNAY

95 **BERINGER** Chardonnay Napa Valley Private Reserve 1996 • $32 • (03/31/98) • HR

95 **KISTLER** Chardonnay Sonoma Coast Camp Meeting Ridge 1995 • $42 • (04/30/98) • HR

95 **VILLA MT. EDEN** Chardonnay Santa Maria Valley Bien Nacido Vineyards Signature Series 1996 • $35 • (05/31/98) • HR

95 **WILLIAMS SELYEM** Chardonnay Russian River Valley Allen Vineyard 1995 • $42 • (03/31/98)

94 **E. & J. GALLO** Chardonnay Northern Sonoma Estate Bottled 1995 • $35 • (02/28/98) • HR

94 **KISTLER** Chardonnay Russian River Valley Vine Hill Vineyard 1995 • $42 • (06/30/98) • HR

94 **MATANZAS CREEK** Chardonnay Sonoma Valley 1995 • $30 • (10/15/97) • CS

94 **PATZ & HALL** Chardonnay Napa Valley 1996 • $29 • (01/31/98) • HR

94 **ROCHIOLI** Chardonnay Russian River Valley South River Vineyard Reserve 1995 • $40 • (11/15/97)

93 **ARROWOOD** Chardonnay Sonoma County Cuvée Michel Berthoud Réserve Spéciale 1995 • $33 • (09/30/97) • HR

93 **BERINGER** Chardonnay Napa Valley Sbragia Limited Release 1995 • $35 • (06/15/98)

93 **CHALK HILL** Chardonnay Chalk Hill 1996 • $28 • (06/15/98) • SS

93 **CUVAISON** Chardonnay Napa Valley Carneros ATS Selection 1995 • $43 • (04/30/98)

93 **GARY FARRELL** Chardonnay Russian River Valley Allen Vineyard 1996 • $28 • (06/30/98)

93 **FERRARI-CARANO** Chardonnay Napa & Sonoma Counties Reserve 1995 • $34 • (05/15/98) • HR

93 **KISTLER** Chardonnay Sonoma Mountain McCrea Vineyard 1995 • $42 • (03/31/98) • CS

93 **KISTLER** Chardonnay Sonoma Valley Durell Vineyard 1995 • $40 • (03/31/98) • CS

93 **LANDMARK** Chardonnay Russian River Valley Lorenzo 1996 • $35 • (06/30/98)

93 **LEWIS CELLARS** Chardonnay Napa Valley Reserve 1996 • $32 • (05/15/98)

93 **NEYERS** Chardonnay Sonoma Coast Thieriot Vineyard 1996 • $35 • (11/15/97)

93 **PATZ & HALL** Chardonnay Carneros Hyde Vineyard 1996 • $35 • (01/31/98)

93 **PATZ & HALL** Chardonnay Mount Veeder Carr Vineyard 1996 • $42 • (06/30/98) • HR

93 **PATZ & HALL** Chardonnay Russian River Valley 1996 • $29 • (01/31/98)

93 **STEELE** Chardonnay Carneros Durell Vineyard 1996 • $24 • (06/30/98)

93 **STEELE** Chardonnay Mendocino Lolonis Vineyard 1996 • $26 • (06/30/98)

93 **TALBOTT** Chardonnay Monterey Sleepy Hollow Vineyard 1995 • $30 • (06/30/98) • SS

93 **VINE CLIFF** Chardonnay Napa Valley 1996 • $25 • (04/30/98) • HR

92 **AU BON CLIMAT** Chardonnay Santa Barbara County Le Bouge Bien Nacido Vineyard 1995 • $25 • (07/31/97)

92 **BABCOCK** Chardonnay Santa Ynez Valley Grand Cuvee 1996 • $30 • (06/30/98)

92 **BABCOCK** Chardonnay Santa Ynez Valley Mt. Carmel Vineyard 1996 • $30 • (06/30/98)

92 **AUGUST BRIGGS** Chardonnay Carneros Leveroni Vineyards 1996 • $25 • (01/31/98)

92 **AUGUST BRIGGS** Chardonnay Russian River Valley 1996 • $25 • (01/31/98)

92 **CHALK HILL** Chardonnay Chalk Hill Estate Vineyard Selection 1994 • $36 • (10/15/97)

92 **CHATEAU POTELLE** Chardonnay Mount Veeder V.G.S. 1995 • $35 • (06/30/98)

92 **DE LOACH** Chardonnay Russian River Valley O.F.S. 1996 • $28 • (06/30/98) • SS

92 **FERRARI-CARANO** Chardonnay Alexander Valley Tre Terre 1995 • $26 • (09/30/97)

92 **GUENOC** Chardonnay Guenoc Valley Genevieve Magoon Vineyard Unfiltered Reserve 1996 • $30 • (06/30/98)

92 **HANZELL** Chardonnay Sonoma Valley 1995 • $30 • (01/31/98) • CS

92 **KISTLER** Chardonnay Carneros Hudson Vineyard 1995 • $48 • (06/30/98)

92 **LANDMARK** Chardonnay Sonoma County Damaris Reserve 1996 • $32 • (06/30/98)

92 **LANDMARK** Chardonnay Sonoma County Overlook 1996 • $21 • (03/31/98) • SS

92 **LIVINGSTON** Chardonnay Napa Valley 1996 • $40 • (05/31/98)

92 **MARKHAM** Chardonnay Napa Valley Reserve 1995 • $28 • (08/31/97)

92 **MERIDIAN** Chardonnay Edna Valley Coastal Reserve 1996 • $14 • (03/31/98) • SS

92 **NEYERS** Chardonnay Carneros 1996 • $25 • (11/15/97)

92 **OAKVILLE RANCH** Chardonnay Napa Valley ORV 1996 • $32 • (05/15/98)

92 **PINE RIDGE** Chardonnay Stags Leap District 1995 • $30 • (03/31/98)

92 **PINE RIDGE** Chardonnay Stags Leap District 1994 • $25 • (11/30/97)

92 **RIDGE** Chardonnay Santa Cruz Mountains 1996 • $25 • (06/30/98)

92 **SANFORD** Chardonnay Santa Barbara County Barrel Select 1996 • $30 • (06/30/98)

92 **SARAH'S VINEYARD** Chardonnay Santa Clara County Gold Label 1994 • $45 • (03/31/98)

92 **SHAFER** Chardonnay Napa Valley Carneros Red Shoulder Ranch 1996 • $30 • (05/31/98) • HR

92 **STAG'S LEAP WINE CELLARS** Chardonnay Napa Valley Beckstoffer Ranch 1995 • $28 • (10/15/97)

92 **STEELE** Chardonnay Santa Barbara County Bien Nacido Vineyard 1996 • $26 • (05/31/98)

92 **STEELE** Chardonnay Santa Barbara County Goodchild Vineyard 1996 • $26 • (05/31/98)

92 **STEELE** Chardonnay Santa Barbara County Goodchild Vineyard 1995 • $24 • (09/30/97)

92 **STEELE** Chardonnay Mendocino DuPratt Vineyard 1996 • $26 • (06/30/98)

92 **STEELE** Chardonnay Sonoma Valley Durell Vineyard 1995 • $24 • (08/31/97)

92 **TALBOTT** Chardonnay Monterey Cuvée Cynthia 1995 • $45 • (06/30/98)

92 **TALLEY** Chardonnay Edna Valley Oliver's Vineyard 1996 • $18 • (12/31/97) • SS

92 **TESTAROSSA** Chardonnay California George Troquato Signature Reserve 1995 • $38 • (03/31/98)

92 **TESTAROSSA** Chardonnay Santa Barbara County Bien Nacido Vineyard 1995 • $27 • (03/31/98)

92 **THUNDER MOUNTAIN** Chardonnay Santa Cruz Mountains Matteson Vineyard 1996 • $29 • (06/30/98)

92 **TRUCHARD** Chardonnay Napa Valley Carneros 1996 • $24 • (04/30/98)

92 **VILLA MT. EDEN** Chardonnay California Grand Reserve 1995 • $18 • (08/31/97)

92 **VILLA MT. EDEN** Chardonnay Santa Maria Valley Bien Nacido Vineyard Signature Series 1995 • $35 • (01/01/98)

92 **VINE CLIFF** Chardonnay Napa Valley Proprietress Reserve 1995 • $34 • (11/15/97)

91 **ANDERSON'S CONN VALLEY** Chardonnay Napa Valley Feurnier Vineyard 1995 • $40 • (04/30/98)

91 **AU BON CLIMAT** Chardonnay Santa Ynez Valley Sanford & Benedict Reserve 1995 • $35 • (11/15/97)

91 **BABCOCK** Chardonnay Santa Maria Valley Bien Nacido Vineyard Block W Gravelly Vein 1996 • $30 • (05/31/98)

91 **BENZIGER** Chardonnay Carneros Reserve 1996 • $25 • (06/30/98)

91 **BENZIGER** Chardonnay Carneros Yamakawa Vineyards Reserve 1996 • $25 • (05/31/98)

91 **BERNARDUS** Chardonnay Monterey County 1996 • $18 • (06/30/98) • SS

91 **BYINGTON** Chardonnay Santa Cruz Mountains Dirk Vineyard Special Reserve Vineyards 1996 • $24 • (06/30/98)

91 **CARNEROS BIGHORN RANCH** Chardonnay Napa Valley Reserve 1996 • $20 • (05/31/98) • SS

91 **CHALONE** Chardonnay Chalone 1996 • $27 • (05/31/98)

91 **CHATEAU ST. JEAN** Chardonnay Alexander Valley Belle Terre Vineyard 1996 • $22 • (05/15/98)

91 **CHATEAU ST. JEAN** Chardonnay Alexander Valley Robert Young Vineyard 1995 • $24 • (11/30/97)

91 **CRONIN** Chardonnay Alexander Valley Stuhlmuller Vineyard 1995 • $18 • (05/15/98)

91 **FLORA SPRINGS** Chardonnay Napa Valley 1996 • $20 • (06/30/98)

91 **FLORA SPRINGS** Chardonnay Napa Valley Lavender Hill Vineyard 1996 • $23 • (06/30/98)

91 **FLOWERS** Chardonnay Sonoma Coast Camp Meeting Ridge Vineyard 1995 • $36 • (04/30/98)

91 **FRANCISCAN OAKVILLE ESTATE** Chardonnay Napa Valley Cuvée Sauvage 1995 • $30 • (01/31/98)

91 **J. FRITZ** Chardonnay Russian River Valley Dutton Ranch 1996 • $20 • (06/30/98)

91 **J. FRITZ** Chardonnay Russian River Valley Dutton Vineyard Shop Block 1996 • $30 • (06/30/98)

91 **GALLO OF SONOMA** Chardonnay Russian River Valley Laguna Ranch Vineyard 1996 • $18 • (05/31/98) • SS

91 **PAUL HOBBS** Chardonnay Sonoma Mountain Richard Dinner Vineyard 1996 • $39 • (06/30/98)

91 **PAUL HOBBS** Chardonnay Sonoma Valley Kunde Vineyard 1996 • $35 • (06/30/98)

91 **LAETITIA** Chardonnay San Luis Obispo County Laetitia Vineyard 1996 • $25 • (06/30/98)

91 **LONG** Chardonnay Napa Valley 1996 • $31 • (05/31/98)

91 **LONGORIA** Chardonnay Santa Ynez Valley Santa Rita Cuvée 1996 • $25 • (06/30/98)

91 **MARTINELLI** Chardonnay Sonoma Coast Charles Ranch 1995 • $25 • (02/28/98)

91 **MER SOLEIL** Chardonnay Central Coast 1995 • $36 • (01/31/98)

91 **MIRASSOU** Chardonnay Monterey County Showcase Selection Harvest Reserve 1996 • $28 • (06/30/98)

91 **MOUNT EDEN** Chardonnay Edna Valley MacGregor Vineyard 1996 • $16 • (03/31/98) • SS

91 **MOUNT EDEN** Chardonnay Santa Cruz Mountains 1995 • $38 • (09/30/97)

91 **NAPA RIDGE** Chardonnay Napa Valley Reserve 1995 • $15 • (01/31/98)

91 **NEWTON** Chardonnay Napa-Sonoma Counties 1996 • $22 • (11/15/97) • SS

91 **NEWTON** Chardonnay Napa Valley Unfiltered 1995 • $NA • (01/31/98)

91 **NEYERS** Chardonnay Napa Valley 1996 • $25 • (11/15/97)

91 **NICHOLS** Chardonnay Santa Barbara County Cottonwood Canyon Vineyard 1996 • $30 • (11/30/97)

91 **PINE RIDGE** Chardonnay Stags Leap District Dijon Clones 1996 • $34 • (05/15/98)

91 **PRIDE** Chardonnay Napa Valley 1996 • $20 • (05/15/98)

91 **RABBIT RIDGE** Chardonnay Sonoma County Winemaker's Grand Reserve 1995 • $30 • (03/31/98)

91 **RAYMOND** Chardonnay Napa Valley Generations 1996 • $27 • (05/15/98)

91 **ROCHIOLI** Chardonnay Russian River Valley 1996 • $24 • (05/31/98)

91 **SANFORD** Chardonnay Santa Barbara County Barrel Select 1995 • $30 • (01/31/98)

91 **SANFORD** Chardonnay Santa Ynez Valley Estate Bottled 1996 • $26 • (06/30/98)

Key: SS—Spectator Selection CS—Cellar Selection HR—Highly Recommended BB—Best Buy $NA—Price not available Ⓐ—Auction Price

Dates in parentheses indicate the issues in which the ratings were published.

91 **STAG'S LEAP WINE CELLARS** Chardonnay Napa Valley Beckstoffer Ranch 1996 • $28 • (05/15/98)

91 **STAG'S LEAP WINE CELLARS** Chardonnay Napa Valley Reserve 1996 • $37 • (05/15/98)

91 **STEELE** Chardonnay Mendocino Lolonis Vineyard 1995 • $26 • (08/31/97)

91 **TESTAROSSA** Chardonnay Chalone 1995 • $28 • (03/31/98)

91 **THUNDER MOUNTAIN** Chardonnay Santa Cruz Mountains Bald Mountain Vineyard 1996 • $29 • (06/30/98)

91 **VENEZIA** Chardonnay Alexander Valley Beaterra Vineyard 1995 • $20 • (09/30/97)

90 **AU BON CLIMAT** Chardonnay Edna Valley Alban Vineyard 1996 • $20 • (11/15/97)

90 **BELVEDERE** Chardonnay Sonoma County Preferred Stock 1995 • $21 • (05/15/98)

90 **BERINGER** Chardonnay Napa Valley 1996 • $15 • (01/31/98)

90 **BUEHLER** Chardonnay Russian River Valley Reserve 1996 • $30 • (04/30/98)

90 **BYINGTON** Chardonnay Santa Cruz Mountains 1996 • $20 • (06/30/98)

90 **CALERA** Chardonnay Central Coast 1996 • $16 • (03/31/98)

90 **CALERA** Chardonnay Mount Harlan Twentieth Anniversary Vintage 1995 • $30 • (03/31/98)

90 **CALLE CIELO** Chardonnay Santa Cruz Mountains 1996 • $25 • (06/30/98)

90 **CAMBRIA** Chardonnay Santa Maria Valley Katherine's Vineyard 1996 • $18 • (04/30/98)

90 **CHAPPELLET** Chardonnay Napa Valley Signature Series 1996 • $24 • (03/31/98)

90 **CHATEAU MONTELENA** Chardonnay Napa Valley 1995 • $25 • (06/30/98)

90 **CHATEAU ST. JEAN** Chardonnay Alexander Valley Robert Young Vineyards Reserve 1994 • $57 • (04/30/98)

90 **CHATEAU SOUVERAIN** Chardonnay Sonoma County 1996 • $13 • (01/31/98) • SS

90 **CLOS LACHANCE** Chardonnay Santa Cruz Mountains Vintner's Reserve 1996 • $29 • (06/30/98)

90 **COSENTINO** Chardonnay Napa Valley The Sculptor Reserve 1996 • $30 • (05/15/98)

90 **CRONIN** Chardonnay Santa Cruz Mountains 1995 • $20 • (05/15/98)

90 **CUVAISON** Chardonnay Napa Valley Carneros Reserve 1995 • $28 • (05/15/98)

90 **DEHLINGER** Chardonnay Russian River Valley 1996 • $20 • (06/30/98)

90 **EL MOLINO** Chardonnay Napa Valley 1996 • $38 • (06/30/98)

90 **ESTANCIA** Chardonnay Monterey Reserve 1996 • $19 • (06/30/98)

90 **FAR NIENTE** Chardonnay Napa Valley 1996 • $40 • (06/30/98)

90 **FORMAN** Chardonnay Napa Valley 1996 • $27 • (11/30/97)

90 **FRANCISCAN OAKVILLE ESTATE** Chardonnay Napa Valley 1996 • $15 • (06/30/98) • SS

90 **GALLO OF SONOMA** Chardonnay Russian River Valley Laguna Ranch Vineyard 1995 • $16 • (09/30/97) • SS

90 **GLORIA FERRER** Chardonnay Carneros 1996 • $19 • (05/15/98) • SS

90 **GUENOC** Chardonnay Guenoc Valley Genevieve Magoon Vineyard Reserve 1996 • $25 • (06/30/98)

90 **THE HESS COLLECTION** Chardonnay Napa Valley 1996 • $18 • (06/30/98)

90 **LAETITIA** Chardonnay San Luis Obispo County Laetitia Vineyard 1995 • $25 • (10/15/97)

90 **LITTORAI** Chardonnay Sonoma Coast Occidental 1995 • $30 • (12/31/97)

90 **MCILROY** Chardonnay Russian River Valley Aquarius Ranch 1996 • $18 • (06/30/98)

90 **ROBERT MONDAVI** Chardonnay Napa Valley Reserve 1995 • $31 • (11/30/97)

90 **MONTICELLO** Chardonnay Napa Valley Corley Family Vineyards 1994 • $18 • (07/31/97)

90 **MORGAN** Chardonnay Monterey 1996 • $18 • (04/30/98) • SS

90 **MUELLER** Chardonnay Alexander Valley Gauer Ranch 1995 • $18 • (08/31/97)

90 **MUELLER** Chardonnay Russian River Valley LB 1996 • $18 • (06/30/98)

90 **MURPHY-GOODE** Chardonnay Alexander Valley Island Block Reserve 1996 • $24 • (05/15/98)

90 **OAKVILLE RANCH** Chardonnay Napa Valley Vista Vineyard 1996 • $26 • (05/31/98)

90 **PAHLMEYER** Chardonnay Napa Valley 1996 • $50 • (05/31/98)

90 **FESS PARKER** Chardonnay Santa Barbara County Marcella's Vineyard American Tradition Reserve 1996 • $24 • (06/30/98)

90 **PEZZI KING** Chardonnay Sonoma County 1995 • $20 • (12/31/97)

90 **PINE RIDGE** Chardonnay Napa Valley Carneros Dijon Clones 1996 • $20 • (01/31/98)

90 **ST. FRANCIS** Chardonnay Sonoma Valley Reserve 1996 • $22 • (03/31/98)

90 **SCHUG** Chardonnay Carneros 1996 • $18 • (05/15/98)

90 **SCHUG** Chardonnay Carneros Heritage Reserve 1995 • $25 • (04/30/98)

90 **SEBASTOPOL** Chardonnay Russian River Valley Dutton Ranch 1995 • $18 • (01/31/98)

90 **SELBY** Chardonnay Sonoma County 1996 • $23 • (04/30/98)

90 **SONOMA-CUTRER** Chardonnay Sonoma Coast Cutrer Vineyard 1995 • $28 • (03/31/98)

90 **STEELE** Chardonnay California Steele Cuvée 1996 • $19 • (05/31/98) • SS

90 **STEELE** Chardonnay Carneros Sangiacomo Vineyard 1996 • $24 • (05/15/98)

90 **STEELE** Chardonnay Mendocino Dennison Vineyard 1995 • $22 • (08/31/97)

90 **STEELE** Chardonnay Sonoma Valley Parmelee-Hill Vineyard 1996 • $26 • (06/30/98)

90 **TALBOTT** Chardonnay Monterey Diamond T Estate 1994 • $40 • (07/31/97)

90 **MARIMAR TORRES** Chardonnay Sonoma County Green Valley Don Miguel Vineyard 1995 • $22 • (10/15/97) • SS

90 **VON STRASSER** Chardonnay Napa Valley 1996 • $30 • (05/31/98)

89 **ALDERBROOK** Chardonnay Dry Creek Valley 1996 • $13 • (02/28/98) • SS

89 **ALDERBROOK** Chardonnay Dry Creek Valley Dorothy's Vineyard 1995 • $20 • (03/31/98)

89 **ARROWOOD** Chardonnay Sonoma County Domaine du Grand Archer 1996 • $14 • (03/31/98)

89 **AU BON CLIMAT** Chardonnay Arroyo Grande Valley Talley Reserve 1995 • $30 • (07/31/97)

89 **BEAUCANON** Chardonnay Napa Valley Jacques de Coninck 1996 • $28 • (05/15/98)

89 **BUENA VISTA** Chardonnay Carneros Grand Reserve 1995 • $24 • (12/15/97)

89 **CARMENET** Chardonnay Sonoma Valley Carneros Sangiacomo Vineyard 1996 • $17 • (05/31/98)

89 **CHATEAU ST. JEAN** Chardonnay Sonoma County 1996 • $13 • (12/31/97) • SS

89 **CLOS DU BOIS** Chardonnay Alexander Valley Alexander Valley Selection 1996 • $15 • (03/31/98)

89 **CLOS DU BOIS** Chardonnay Alexander Valley Calcaire Vineyard 1995 • $18 • (07/31/97)

89 **CONCANNON** Chardonnay Livermore Valley Reserve 1995 • $15 • (07/31/97)

89 **DE LOACH** Chardonnay Russian River Valley Estate Bottled 1996 • $20 • (04/30/98)

89 **EDNA VALLEY** Chardonnay Edna Valley Paragon 1996 • $17 • (05/15/98)

89 **THOMAS FOGARTY** Chardonnay Santa Cruz Mountains Estate Reserve 1995 • $28 • (12/31/97)

89 **FRANCISCAN** Chardonnay Napa Valley 1995 • $16 • (07/31/97)

89 **HART'S DESIRE** Chardonnay Edna Valley MacGregor Vineyard 1995 • $15 • (09/30/97)

89 **KENDALL-JACKSON** Chardonnay California Grand Reserve 1996 • $26 • (05/31/98)

89 **MIRASSOU** Chardonnay Monterey County Harvest Reserve 1996 • $16 • (05/15/98)

89 **MORGAN** Chardonnay Monterey Reserve 1995 • $26 • (03/31/98)

89 **MURPHY-GOODE** Chardonnay Russian River Valley J & K Murphy Vineyard Reserve 1996 • $24 • (05/15/98)

89 **NICHOLS** Chardonnay Central Coast Blend 1996 • $NA • (03/31/98)

89 **PEZZI KING** Chardonnay Sonoma County 1996 • $17 • (04/30/98)

89 **R.H. PHILLIPS** Chardonnay Dunnigan Hills Toasted Head 1996 • $12 • (06/30/98) • HR

89 **PRIDE** Chardonnay Napa Valley 1995 • $18 • (07/31/97)

89 **QUPÉ** Chardonnay Santa Barbara County Bien Nacido Vineyard 1996 • $18 • (11/15/97)

89 **RABBIT RIDGE** Chardonnay Russian River Valley Rabbit Ridge Ranch Estate Reserve 1996 • $18 • (04/30/98)

89 **KENT RASMUSSEN** Chardonnay Napa Valley 1996 • $23 • (05/31/98)

89 **RUTZ** Chardonnay Russian River Valley Dutton Ranch 1996 • $30 • (05/15/98)

89 **RUTZ** Chardonnay Russian River Valley Dutton Ranch 1995 • $30 • (01/01/98)

89 **ST. CLEMENT** Chardonnay Napa Valley Carneros Abbott's Vineyard 1996 • $20 • (05/31/98)

89 **SONOMA-CUTRER** Chardonnay Sonoma Coast Les Pierres 1995 • $28 • (03/31/98)

89 **SONOMA-CUTRER** Chardonnay Sonoma Coast Russian River Ranches 1996 • $17 • (03/31/98)

89 **SONOMA-LOEB** Chardonnay Sonoma County 1996 • $20 • (11/30/97)

89 **SOQUEL** Chardonnay Santa Cruz Mountains 1996 • $20 • (06/30/98)

89 **STAG'S LEAP WINE CELLARS** Chardonnay Napa Valley 1996 • $24 • (04/30/98)

89 **WENTE** Chardonnay Livermore Valley Herman Wente Reserve 1995 • $23 • (04/30/98)

89 **WHITCRAFT** Chardonnay Santa Maria Valley Bien Nacido Vineyard 1996 • $22 • (11/30/97)

89 **ZACA MESA** Chardonnay Santa Barbara County Zaca Vineyards 1996 • $14 • (05/15/98)

88 **ADASTRA** Chardonnay Napa Valley Carneros 1996 • $22 • (12/31/97)

88 **AU BON CLIMAT** Chardonnay Santa Barbara County 1996 • $18 • (11/15/97)

88 **BECKMEN** Chardonnay Santa Barbara County Barrel Select 1996 • $20 • (06/15/98)

88 **BRUTOCAO** Chardonnay Mendocino Bliss Vineyard 1995 • $12 • (12/15/97)

88 **CAKEBREAD** Chardonnay Napa Valley 1996 • $25 • (05/31/98)

88 **CALE** Chardonnay Carneros Sangiacomo Vineyards 1996 • $20 • (05/15/98)

88 **CAMBRIA** Chardonnay Santa Maria Valley Reserve 1995 • $36 • (04/30/98)

88 **CANEPA** Chardonnay Alexander Valley Gauer Vineyard Adobe III 1996 • $26 • (05/15/98)

88 **CHASSEUR** Chardonnay Russian River Valley Dutton 1995 • $28 • (04/30/98)

88 **CHATEAU JULIEN** Chardonnay Monterey County Private Reserve 1995 • $20 • (07/31/97)

88 **CHATEAU WOLTNER** Chardonnay Howell Mountain Frederique Vineyard 1995 • $40 • (12/31/97)

88 **CHATEAU WOLTNER** Chardonnay Howell Mountain Titus Vineyard 1995 • $40 • (12/31/97)

88 **CHAUFFE-EAU** Chardonnay Carneros Sangiacomo Vineyard 1996 • $20 • (06/15/98)

88 **CLOS DU BOIS** Chardonnay Dry Creek Valley Flintwood Vineyard 1995 • $17 • (07/31/97)

88 **CLOS DU BOIS** Chardonnay Sonoma County 1995 • $13 • (07/31/97)

88 **CLOS LACHANCE** Chardonnay Santa Cruz Mountains 1996 • $22 • (06/30/98)

88 **CRONIN** Chardonnay Monterey County 1995 • $16 • (05/15/98)

88 **CURTIS** Chardonnay Santa Barbara County 1995 • $17 • (07/31/97)

88 **CUVAISON** Chardonnay Napa Valley Carneros 1996 • $21 • (06/15/98)

88 **DRY CREEK** Chardonnay Sonoma County 1996 • $15 • (06/30/98)

88 **EDMEADES** Chardonnay Anderson Valley 1995 • $18 • (06/15/98)

88 **EHLERS GROVE** Chardonnay Sonoma & Napa Counties Winery Reserve 1996 • $25 • (06/30/98)

88 **ESTANCIA** Chardonnay Monterey County Pinnacles 1996 • $11 • (06/30/98)

88 **FOREST HILL** Chardonnay Napa Valley Private Reserve 1995 • $30 • (04/30/98)

88 **FREEMARK ABBEY** Chardonnay Napa Valley 1996 • $17 • (04/30/98)

88 **FREEMARK ABBEY** Chardonnay Napa Valley Carpy Ranch 1996 • $24 • (05/15/98)

88 **GALLO OF SONOMA** Chardonnay Dry Creek Valley Stefani Vineyard 1996 • $16 • (05/31/98)

88 **GREENWOOD RIDGE** Chardonnay Anderson Valley Du Pratt Vineyard 1996 • $22 • (03/31/98)

88 **GROTH** Chardonnay Napa Valley 1996 • $18 • (03/31/98)

88 **HANDLEY** Chardonnay Dry Creek Valley Handley Vineyard 1996 • $17 • (05/31/98)

88 **HANNA** Chardonnay Russian River Valley 1996 • $16 • (12/15/97)

88 **HARMONY CELLARS** Chardonnay San Luis Obispo County 1995 • $13 • (01/31/98)

88 **HENDRY RANCH** Chardonnay Napa Valley Block 9 1996 • $22 • (05/31/98)

88 **JORDAN** Chardonnay Sonoma County 1995 • $24 • (05/15/98)

88 **KENDALL-JACKSON** Chardonnay Arroyo Seco Paradise Vineyard Single Vineyard Series 1996 • $20 • (06/15/98)

88 **KORBEL** Chardonnay Russian River Valley Heck Family Cellar Selection 1996 • $15 • (03/31/98)

88 **KUNDE** Chardonnay Sonoma Valley Kinneybrook 1995 • $20 • (03/31/98)

Key: SS—Spectator Selection CS—Cellar Selection HR—Highly Recommended BB—Best Buy $NA—Price not available Ⓐ—Auction Price
Dates in parentheses indicate the issues in which the ratings were published.

88 **KYNSI** Chardonnay Santa Ynez Valley Sanford & Benedict Vineyard 1995 • $25 • (03/31/98)

88 **LA CREMA** Chardonnay Sonoma Coast Reserve 1995 • $26 • (12/15/97)

88 **LAETITIA** Chardonnay San Luis Obispo County Reserve 1996 • $17 • (06/30/98)

88 **LAURIER** Chardonnay Sonoma County 1995 • $15 • (03/31/98)

88 **LIPARITA** Chardonnay Howell Mountain 1996 • $24 • (05/15/98)

88 **J. LOHR** Chardonnay Monterey Riverstone 1996 • $14 • (06/15/98)

88 **MARCELINA** Chardonnay Napa Valley 1995 • $18 • (12/15/97)

88 **MIRASSOU** Chardonnay Monterey County Family Selection 1996 • $12 • (12/31/97)

88 **MOROVINO** Chardonnay Santa Barbara County 1996 • $16 • (06/15/98)

88 **NICHOLS** Chardonnay Central Coast Reserve 1996 • $33 • (02/28/98)

88 **PARAISO SPRINGS** Chardonnay Santa Lucia Highlands 1995 • $13 • (07/31/97)

88 **FESS PARKER** Chardonnay Santa Barbara County American Tradition Reserve 1995 • $22 • (07/31/97)

88 **JOSEPH PHELPS** Chardonnay Los Carneros 1996 • $20 • (05/31/98)

88 **RANCHO SISQUOC** Chardonnay Santa Maria Valley 1995 • $15 • (09/30/97)

88 **MARTIN RAY** Chardonnay California Mariage 1995 • $28 • (07/31/97)

88 **RUTZ** Chardonnay Russian River Valley 1996 • $22 • (06/30/98)

88 **SAINTSBURY** Chardonnay Carneros 1996 • $17 • (05/15/98)

88 **SANFORD** Chardonnay Santa Barbara County 1996 • $18 • (01/31/98)

88 **SANTA BARBARA WINERY** Chardonnay Santa Barbara County Reserve 1995 • $23 • (07/31/97)

88 **SANTA CRUZ MOUNTAIN** Chardonnay Santa Cruz Mountains S. Miller Vineyard 1995 • $18 • (07/31/97)

88 **SCHUG** Chardonnay Carneros 1995 • $18 • (04/30/98)

88 **SEBASTIANI** Chardonnay California 1996 • $12 • (06/15/98)

88 **SEVEN PEAKS** Chardonnay Edna Valley Reserve 1996 • $18 • (06/30/98)

88 **SILVERADO VINEYARDS** Chardonnay Napa Valley Limited Reserve 1995 • $36 • (03/31/98)

88 **SONOMA-CUTRER** Chardonnay Sonoma Coast Les Pierres 1994 • $28 • (07/31/97)

88 **STEVENOT** Chardonnay Sierra Foothills 1996 • $10 • (11/30/97) • BB

88 **STONESTREET** Chardonnay Alexander Valley Upper Barn Block Alexander Mountain Estate 1995 • $30 • (12/15/97)

88 **STORRS** Chardonnay Santa Cruz Mountains Meyley Vineyard 1995 • $20 • (03/31/98)

88 **SWANSON** Chardonnay Napa Valley Carneros 1996 • $26 • (05/31/98)

88 **TESTAROSSA** Chardonnay Chalone Michaud Vineyard Reserve 1995 • $38 • (03/31/98)

88 **WENTE** Chardonnay Arroyo Seco Riva Ranch Reserve 1994 • $15 • (04/30/98)

88 **WHITEHALL LANE** Chardonnay Napa Valley 1995 • $15 • (08/31/97)

CALIFORNIA MERLOT

92 **ARROWOOD** Merlot Sonoma County 1994 • $35 • (07/31/97)
92 **COSENTINO** Merlot Napa Valley Oakville 1995 • $50 • (07/31/97)
92 **CHARLES KRUG** Merlot Napa Valley Peter Mondavi Family 1995 • $15 • (07/31/97) • SS
92 **OAKVILLE RANCH** Merlot Napa Valley 1994 • $28 • (07/31/97)
92 **WHITEHALL LANE** Merlot Napa Valley 1995 • $20 • (11/15/97) • SS
91 **LEWIS CELLARS** Merlot Napa Valley Reserve 1995 • $45 • (05/31/98)
91 **MARKHAM** Merlot Napa Valley Reserve 1994 • $35 • (08/31/97)
91 **NEYERS** Merlot Napa Valley 1995 • $25 • (11/15/97)
91 **NEYERS** Merlot Napa Valley Neyers Ranch-Conn Valley 1995 • $35 • (11/15/97)
91 **SEAVEY** Merlot Napa Valley 1994 • $24 • (11/30/97)
91 **TRUCHARD** Merlot Napa Valley Carneros 1995 • $24 • (05/15/98)
90 **CHATEAU ST. JEAN** Merlot Sonoma County Reserve 1993 • $35 • (05/15/98)
90 **COTTONWOOD CANYON** Merlot Central Coast 1994 • $25 • (07/31/97)
90 **PAHLMEYER** Merlot Napa Valley 1995 • $50 • (05/31/98)
90 **PALOMA** Merlot Napa Valley 1995 • $26 • (12/15/97)
90 **PINE RIDGE** Merlot Napa Valley Carneros 1995 • $33 • (03/31/98)
90 **WHITEHALL LANE** Merlot Napa Valley Leonardini Vineyard Reserve 1995 • $36 • (09/30/97)
89 **BALLENTINE** Merlot Napa Valley 1994 • $18 • (07/31/97)
89 **BELVEDERE** Merlot Dry Creek Valley Preferred Stock 1994 • $22 • (07/31/97)
89 **BERINGER** Merlot Howell Mountain Bancroft Ranch 1994 • $45 • (04/30/98)
89 **CAKEBREAD** Merlot Napa Valley 1994 • $27 • (07/31/97)
89 **FLORA SPRINGS** Merlot Napa Valley Windfall Vineyard 1995 • $40 • (03/31/98)
89 **FORMAN** Merlot Napa Valley 1994 • $40 • (09/15/97)
89 **GREENWOOD RIDGE** Merlot Anderson Valley 1995 • $22 • (11/30/97)
89 **LOCKWOOD** Merlot Monterey Partners' Reserve 1995 • $25 • (03/31/98)
89 **PRIDE** Merlot Napa Valley 1995 • $24 • (09/30/97)
89 **RABBIT RIDGE** Merlot Carneros Sangiacomo Vineyard Reserve 1995 • $23 • (04/30/98)
89 **RUTHERFORD HILL** Merlot Napa Valley Reserve 1995 • $40 • (05/15/98)
89 **SWANSON** Merlot Napa Valley 1995 • $24 • (09/30/97)
88 **ANTARES** Merlot California 1995 • $22 • (12/15/97)
88 **ARMIDA** Merlot Russian River Valley 1994 • $16 • (07/31/97)
88 **ARROWOOD** Merlot Sonoma County Domaine du Grand Archer 1995 • $19 • (03/31/98)
88 **AZALEA SPRINGS** Merlot Napa Valley 1995 • $30 • (03/31/98)
88 **BEHRENS & HITCHCOCK** Merlot Napa Valley Oakville 1995 • $25 • (11/30/97)
88 **BUENA VISTA** Merlot Carneros Grand Reserve 1994 • $26 • (07/31/97)
88 **CAFARO** Merlot Napa Valley 1994 • $30 • (11/15/97)
88 **CLOVERDALE RANCH** Merlot Alexander Valley Estate Cuvée 1995 • $14 • (09/15/97)
88 **DUCKHORN** Merlot Howell Mountain 1993 • $35 • (07/31/97)
88 **DUCKHORN** Merlot Napa Valley 1995 • $28 • (03/31/98)
88 **ERIC ROSS** Merlot Sonoma County 1995 • $22 • (03/31/98)
88 **ESTATE WILLIAM BACCALA** Merlot Napa Valley 1994 • $14 • (11/30/97)
88 **GARY FARRELL** Merlot Russian River Valley 1995 • $23 • (04/30/98)
88 **FOLIE À DEUX** Merlot Napa Valley Reserve 1995 • $22 • (11/30/97)
88 **FOXEN** Merlot Santa Barbara County 1995 • $24 • (04/30/98)
88 **FREEMARK ABBEY** Merlot Napa Valley 1995 • $21 • (04/30/98)
88 **THE HESS COLLECTION** Merlot Napa Valley 1994 • $20 • (05/15/98)
88 **LOCKWOOD** Merlot Monterey 1995 • $17 • (11/30/97)
88 **LONGORIA** Merlot Santa Ynez Valley 1994 • $21 • (07/31/97)
88 **MIDNIGHT CELLARS** Merlot Paso Robles Eclipse 1995 • $19 • (04/30/98)
88 **NIEBAUM-COPPOLA** Merlot Napa Valley Francis Coppola Family Wines 1995 • $32 • (05/15/98)
88 **RANCHO SISQUOC** Merlot Santa Maria Valley 1994 • $16 • (07/31/97)
88 **RICHARDSON** Merlot Carneros Sangiacomo Vineyard 1995 • $17 • (07/31/97)
88 **ROSENBLUM** Merlot Russian River Valley Lone Oak Vineyard 1995 • $20 • (03/31/98)
88 **ST. CLEMENT** Merlot Napa Valley 1995 • $24 • (04/30/98)
88 **SONOMA CREEK** Merlot Sonoma Valley Sangiacomo Vineyard 1994 • $28 • (07/31/97)
88 **SUMMERS RANCH** Merlot Knights Valley 1995 • $24 • (04/30/98)
88 **VENGE** Merlot Napa Valley 1995 • $28 • (03/31/98)
88 **VINE CLIFF** Merlot Napa Valley 1995 • $27 • (04/30/98)
88 **VOSS** Merlot Napa Valley 1995 • $18 • (04/30/98)
88 **VOSS** Merlot Napa Valley 1994 • $18 • (07/31/97)

CALIFORNIA ZINFANDEL

95 **TURLEY** Zinfandel Howell Mountain Black-Sears Vineyard 1995 • $26 • (07/31/97) • HR
95 **TURLEY** Zinfandel Oakley Duarte Vineyard 1995 • $22 • (07/31/97) • HR
94 **KUNDE** Zinfandel Sonoma Valley Robusto 1995 • $24 • (07/31/97)
93 **TURLEY** Zinfandel Dry Creek Valley Grist Vineyard 1995 • $30 • (07/31/97)
94 **TURLEY** Zinfandel Napa Valley Hayne Vineyard 1995 • $35 • (07/31/97)
93 **TURLEY** Zinfandel Napa Valley Moore "Earthquake" Vineyard 1995 • $30 • (07/31/97)
92 **LOLONIS** Zinfandel Mendocino County Private Reserve 1994 • $19 • (12/31/97) • SS
92 **RABBIT RIDGE** Zinfandel Sonoma County 0VZ Reserve 1995 • $26 • (09/30/97)
92 **RAVENSWOOD** Zinfandel Sonoma Valley Old Hill Vineyard Limited Edition 1995 • $24 • (09/30/97)
92 **RIDGE** Zinfandel Sonoma Valley Pagani Ranch 1995 • $25 • (10/31/97) • SS
92 **ROSENBLUM** Zinfandel Alexander Valley Harris Kratka Vineyard 1995 • $20 • (08/31/97)
92 **ROSENBLUM** Zinfandel Sonoma Valley Samsel Vineyard Maggie's Reserve 1995 • $25 • (09/30/97)
92 **ST. FRANCIS** Zinfandel Sonoma Valley Pagani Vineyard Reserve 1995 • $28 • (08/31/97)
92 **TERRACES** Zinfandel Napa Valley 1995 • $20 • (12/15/97)
91 **AUGUST BRIGGS** Zinfandel Napa Valley 1995 • $18 • (08/31/97)

91 **CHATEAU POTELLE** Zinfandel Mount Veeder V.G.S 1995 • $35 • (04/30/98)

91 **JC CELLARS** Zinfandel Redwood Valley Rhodes 1996 • $27 • (06/15/98)

91 **NIEBAUM-COPPOLA** Zinfandel Napa Valley Edizione Pennino 1995 • $24 • (03/31/98) • SS

91 **RABBIT RIDGE** Zinfandel Sonoma County Winemaker's Grand Reserve 1995 • $30 • (03/31/98)

91 **RAVENSWOOD** Zinfandel Sonoma Valley Cooke 1995 • $22 • (09/30/97)

91 **ROSENBLUM** Zinfandel Mount Veeder Brandlin Ranch 1996 • $23 • (06/15/98)

91 **STEELE** Zinfandel Clear Lake Catfish Vineyard 1994 • $18 • (10/31/97)

91 **JOSEPH SWAN** Zinfandel Russian River Valley Frati Ranch 1995 • $24 • (06/15/98)

91 **TRUCHARD** Zinfandel Napa Valley Carneros 1996 • $18 • (05/31/98)

90 **DAVID COFFARO** Zinfandel Dry Creek Valley Coffaro Estate Vineyard 1996 • $19 • (05/31/98)

90 **DE LOACH** Zinfandel Russian River Valley O.F.S. 1996 • $28 • (03/31/98)

90 **GARY FARRELL** Zinfandel Russian River Valley 1995 • $20 • (08/31/97)

90 **GALLO OF SONOMA** Zinfandel Alexander Valley Barrelli Creek Vineyard 1995 • $14 • (06/15/98) • SS

90 **HARTFORD COURT** Zinfandel Russian River Valley Hartford Vineyard 1995 • $32 • (10/31/97)

90 **HAYWOOD** Zinfandel Sonoma Valley Los Chamizal Vineyard Rocky Terrace 1995 • $25 • (06/15/98)

90 **HIDDEN CELLARS** Zinfandel Mendocino Ford & Hitzman Vineyards Mendocino Heritage 1995 • $30 • (03/31/98)

90 **LAMBORN FAMILY** Zinfandel Howell Mountain The French Connection 1995 • $19 • (09/15/97)

90 **MICHAEL-SCOTT** Zinfandel Napa Valley 1996 • $22 • (04/30/98)

90 **RABBIT RIDGE** Zinfandel Sonoma County Winemaker's Grand Reserve 1996 • $32 • (06/15/98)

90 **A. RAFANELLI** Zinfandel Dry Creek Valley 1995 • $18 • (12/15/97) • SS

90 **ROMBAUER** Zinfandel Napa Valley 1995 • $20 • (06/15/98)

90 **ROSENBLUM** Zinfandel Napa Valley Hendry Vineyard Reserve 1995 • $25 • (04/30/98)

90 **ST. FRANCIS** Zinfandel Sonoma Valley Pagani Vineyard Reserve 1996 • $28 • (06/15/98)

90 **SEGHESIO** Zinfandel Sonoma County Old Vine 1996 • $21 • (06/15/98)

90 **SEGHESIO** Zinfandel Sonoma County Old Vine 1995 • $20 • (04/30/98)

90 **SPENKER** Zinfandel Lodi 1995 • $14 • (07/31/97)

90 **STEELE** Zinfandel Mendocino Pacini Vineyard 1996 • $20 • (05/31/98)

90 **JOSEPH SWAN** Zinfandel Russian River Valley Zeigler Vineyard 1995 • $20 • (06/15/98)

90 **JOSEPH SWAN** Zinfandel Sonoma Valley Stellwagen Vineyard 1995 • $20 • (06/15/98)

90 **TURLEY** Zinfandel Napa Valley Aïda Vineyard 1995 • $25 • (07/31/97)

90 **TURLEY** Zinfandel Napa Valley Whitney Tennessee Vineyard 1995 • $25 • (07/31/97)

90 **VIANO** Zinfandel Contra Costa County Sand Rock Hill Reserve Selection 1994 • $10 • (12/15/97)

Key: SS—Spectator Selection CS—Cellar Selection HR—Highly Recommended BB—Best Buy $NA—Price not available Ⓐ—Auction Price
Dates in parentheses indicate the issues in which the ratings were published.

89 **ALDERBROOK** Zinfandel Russian River Valley Gamba Vineyard 1996 • $20 • (03/31/98)

89 **BUEHLER** Zinfandel Napa Valley Estate 1995 • $20 • (04/30/98)

89 **CHATEAU SOUVERAIN** Zinfandel Dry Creek Valley 1995 • $12 • (12/15/97) • SS

89 **CLINE** Zinfandel Contra Costa County Live Oak 1995 • $24 • (11/15/97)

89 **FANUCCHI** Zinfandel Russian River Valley Old Vine 1996 • $33 • (03/31/98)

89 **FIFE** Zinfandel Napa Valley Old Vines 1995 • $19 • (09/30/97)

89 **FRANUS** Zinfandel Contra Costa County Planchon Vineyard 1996 • $17 • (06/15/98)

89 **HAYWOOD** Zinfandel Sonoma Valley Rocky Terrace Los Chamizal Vineyard 1994 • $25 • (01/01/98)

89 **HOWELL MOUNTAIN VINEYARD** Zinfandel Howell Mountain 1995 • $16 • (08/31/97)

89 **KARLY** Zinfandel Amador County Warrior Fires 1995 • $20 • (06/15/98)

89 **LOLONIS** Zinfandel Mendocino County 1995 • $16 • (06/15/98)

89 **MARKHAM** Zinfandel Napa Valley 1994 • $17 • (08/31/97)

89 **MARTINELLI** Zinfandel Russian River Valley Jackass Vineyard 1996 • $25 • (06/15/98)

89 **PARADIGM** Zinfandel Oakville 1995 • $22 • (06/15/98)

89 **RAVENSWOOD** Zinfandel Napa Valley Dickerson 1995 • $22 • (09/30/97)

89 **RAVENSWOOD** Zinfandel Sonoma Valley Monte Rosso 1995 • $22 • (09/30/97)

89 **RENWOOD** Zinfandel Amador County Jack Rabbit Flat Fox Creek Vineyard 1995 • $25 • (11/15/97)

89 **RENWOOD** Zinfandel Fiddletown Eschen Vineyard 1995 • $23 • (11/15/97)

89 **RIDGE** Zinfandel Paso Robles Dusi Ranch 1996 • $20 • (05/31/98)

89 **ROCHIOLI** Zinfandel Russian River Valley 1996 • $20 • (06/15/98)

89 **ROSENBLUM** Zinfandel Mount Veeder Brandlin Ranch 1995 • $23 • (09/30/97)

89 **ROSENBLUM** Zinfandel Napa Valley 1995 • $18 • (04/30/98)

89 **ROSENBLUM** Zinfandel Redwood Valley Rhodes Vineyard Annette's Reserve 1996 • $22 • (06/15/98)

89 **ROSENBLUM** Zinfandel Sonoma County St. Peters Church Vineyard 1996 • $20 • (06/15/98)

89 **STEELE** Zinfandel Mendocino DuPratt Vineyard 1995 • $20 • (10/31/97)

89 **STONEHEDGE** Zinfandel Napa Valley 1994 • $13 • (11/15/97)

89 **WHITEHALL LANE** Zinfandel Napa Valley 1995 • $20 • (09/30/97)

88 **BALLENTINE** Zinfandel Napa Valley 1995 • $16 • (11/30/97)

88 **BERINGER** Zinfandel North Coast Appellation Collection 1995 • $12 • (06/15/98)

88 **BOEGER** Zinfandel El Dorado Walker Vineyard 1995 • $15 • (05/15/98)

88 **DAVID BRUCE** Zinfandel Paso Robles Ranchita Canyon Vineyard 1995 • $15 • (03/31/98)

88 **DE LOACH** Zinfandel Russian River Valley Saitone Ranch 1996 • $20 • (03/31/98)

88 **DRY CREEK** Zinfandel Sonoma County Reserve 1995 • $25 • (06/15/98)

88 **EDMEADES** Zinfandel Mendocino Ciapusci Vineyard 1995 • $28 • (06/15/98)

88 **GARY FARRELL** Zinfandel Dry Creek Valley Grist Ranch 1995 • $20 • (06/15/98)

88 **FIFE** Zinfandel Redwood Valley Redhead Vineyard 1995 • $19 • (09/30/97)

88 **FOLIE À DEUX** Zinfandel Amador County Old Vine 1995 • $16 • (09/15/97)
88 **J. FRITZ** Zinfandel Dry Creek Valley Old Vine 1996 • $20 • (06/15/98)
88 **GRGICH HILLS** Zinfandel Sonoma County 1995 • $18 • (03/31/98)
88 **GUNDLACH BUNDSCHU** Zinfandel Sonoma Valley Rhinefarm Vineyards 1996 • $16 • (06/15/98)
88 **HAYWOOD** Zinfandel Sonoma Valley Los Chamizal Vineyard 1994 • $16 • (01/01/98)
88 **HIDDEN CELLARS** Zinfandel Mendocino Hildreth Ranch Mendocino Heritage 1995 • $25 • (03/31/98)
88 **JACUZZI** Zinfandel Contra Costa County Reserve 1994 • $40 • (11/15/97)
88 **LONETREE** Zinfandel Mendocino 1996 • $14 • (06/15/98)
88 **LORENZA-LAKE** Zinfandel Napa Valley Blockheadia Ringnosii 1996 • $20 • (05/15/98)
88 **MCILROY** Zinfandel Russian River Valley Porter-Bass Vineyard 1995 • $18 • (01/01/98)
88 **MURPHY-GOODE** Zinfandel Dry Creek-Alexander Valleys 1995 • $16 • (12/15/97)
88 **MURPHY-GOODE** Zinfandel Sonoma County 1996 • $16 • (05/31/98)
88 **PRESTON** Zinfandel Dry Creek Valley Old Vines-Old Clones 1996 • $18 • (05/15/98)
88 **RABBIT RIDGE** Zinfandel Dry Creek Valley Olson Vineyard Reserve 1996 • $23 • (05/31/98)
88 **RAVENSWOOD** Zinfandel Russian River Valley Wood Road Belloni 1995 • $22 • (09/30/97)
88 **RENWOOD** Zinfandel Amador County Grandpère 1995 • $23 • (11/15/97)
88 **RIDGE** Zinfandel Sonoma County Sonoma Station 1996 • $16 • (05/31/98)
88 **RIDGE** Zinfandel Spring Mountain York Creek 1995 • $23 • (11/15/97)
88 **ROSENBLUM** Zinfandel Alexander Valley Harris Kratka Vineyard 1996 • $22 • (06/15/98)
88 **ROSENBLUM** Zinfandel Napa Valley Hendry Vineyard Reserve 1996 • $26 • (06/15/98)
88 **ROSENBLUM** Zinfandel Paso Robles Richard Sauret Vineyard 1996 • $17 • (05/15/98)
88 **ROSENBLUM** Zinfandel Sonoma Valley Samsel Vineyard Maggie's Reserve 1996 • $28 • (06/15/98)
88 **ERIC ROSS** Zinfandel Sonoma County Old Vine 1995 • $22 • (03/31/98)
88 **ST. FRANCIS** Zinfandel Sonoma County Old Vines 1996 • $20 • (05/31/98)
88 **ST. FRANCIS** Zinfandel Sonoma County Old Vines 1995 • $22 • (08/31/97)
88 **SAUSAL** Zinfandel Alexander Valley Century Vines 1995 • $18 • (06/15/98)
88 **SAUSAL** Zinfandel Alexander Valley Private Reserve 1995 • $16 • (06/15/98)
88 **SEGHESIO** Zinfandel Alexander Valley San Lorenzo 1995 • $20 • (05/15/98)
88 **SOBON ESTATE** Zinfandel Fiddletown 1995 • $15 • (08/31/97)
88 **SOBON ESTATE** Zinfandel Shenandoah Valley Rocky Top 1996 • $15 • (05/31/98)
88 **SOBON ESTATE** Zinfandel Shenandoah Valley Rocky Top 1995 • $15 • (08/31/97)
88 **STEELE** Zinfandel Mendocino Pacini Vineyard 1995 • $16 • (10/31/97)
88 **STORYBOOK MOUNTAIN** Zinfandel Napa Valley Mayacamas Range 1996 • $17 • (05/31/98)
88 **TRIA** Zinfandel Dry Creek Valley 1996 • $18 • (05/31/98)
88 **ZOOM** Zinfandel Contra Costa County 102-Year-Old Vines 1996 • $20 • (05/31/98)
92 **RIDGE** Lytton Springs Dry Creek Valley 1995 • $23 • (07/31/97) • SS
90 **RIDGE** Geyserville Sonoma County 1996 • $NA • (05/31/98)
89 **RIDGE** Geyserville Sonoma County 1995 • $25 • (11/15/97)
88 **RIDGE** Lytton Springs Dry Creek Valley 1996 • $25 • (05/31/98)

CALIFORNIA PINOT NOIR

94 **DEHLINGER** Pinot Noir Russian River Valley 1995 • $28 • (12/31/97) • HR
94 **WILLIAMS SELYEM** Pinot Noir Russian River Valley Rochioli Vineyard 1995 • $65 • (12/31/97)
94 **WILLIAMS SELYEM** Pinot Noir Sonoma Coast Hirsch Vineyard 1995 • $40 • (10/31/97)
93 **SAINTSBURY** Pinot Noir Carneros Reserve 1995 • $35 • (01/31/98) • HR
93 **W.H. SMITH WINES** Pinot Noir Sonoma Coast Hellenthal Vineyard 1995 • $32 • (07/31/97)
93 **STEELE** Pinot Noir Santa Barbara County Bien Nacido Vineyard 1995 • $38 • (10/31/97)
93 **TALLEY** Pinot Noir Arroyo Grande Valley Rosemary's Vineyard 1995 • $32 • (12/15/97)
93 **WILLIAMS SELYEM** Pinot Noir Russian River Valley Allen Vineyard 1995 • $36 • (10/31/97)
93 **WILLIAMS SELYEM** Pinot Noir Russian River Valley Olivet Lane 1995 • $36 • (10/31/97)
93 **WILLIAMS SELYEM** Pinot Noir Russian River Valley Rochioli Vineyard 1994 • $60 • (10/31/97)
92 **AU BON CLIMAT** Pinot Noir Santa Barbara County Bien Nacido Vineyard La Bauge 1995 • $30 • (08/31/97)
92 **DAVID BRUCE** Pinot Noir Chalone 1995 • $30 • (12/15/97) • HR
92 **GARY FARRELL** Pinot Noir Russian River Valley Rochioli Vineyard 1995 • $50 • (12/31/97)
92 **ROCHIOLI** Pinot Noir Russian River Valley 1995 • $24 • (07/31/97)
92 **STEELE** Pinot Noir Mendocino DuPratt Vineyard 1995 • $28 • (10/15/97)
92 **TALLEY** Pinot Noir Arroyo Grande Valley Rincon Vineyard 1995 • $30 • (12/15/97)
92 **WILLIAMS SELYEM** Pinot Noir Russian River Valley Allen Vineyard 1994 • $42 • (10/31/97)
92 **WILLIAMS SELYEM** Pinot Noir Sonoma Coast Coastlands Vineyard 1995 • $40 • (12/31/97)
92 **WILLIAMS SELYEM** Pinot Noir Sonoma Coast Coastlands Vineyard 1994 • $38 • (10/31/97)
92 **WILLIAMS SELYEM** Pinot Noir Sonoma Coast Hirsch Vineyard 1994 • $36 • (10/31/97)
91 **BEAULIEU VINEYARD** Pinot Noir Carneros Reserve 1995 • $30 • (01/31/98) • SS
91 **BERNARDUS** Pinot Noir Santa Barbara County Bien Nacido Vineyard 1995 • $35 • (01/31/98)
91 **CUVAISON** Pinot Noir Napa Valley Carneros 1995 • $30 • (01/31/98)
91 **DEHLINGER** Pinot Noir Russian River Valley Goldridge Vineyard 1995 • $23 • (08/31/97)
91 **MERIDIAN** Pinot Noir Santa Barbara & San Luis Obispo Counties Reserve 1995 • $20 • (03/31/98)
91 **ROBERT MONDAVI** Pinot Noir Napa Valley Reserve 1995 • $31 • (08/31/97)
91 **MUELLER** Pinot Noir Russian River Valley Emily's Cuvée 1995 • $22 • (07/31/97)
91 **OJAI** Pinot Noir Santa Barbara County Bien Nacido Vineyard Benjamin Lorenzo 1995 • $36 • (01/31/98)
91 **SANFORD** Pinot Noir Santa Barbara County Sanford & Benedict Vineyard Barrel Select 1995 • $34 • (01/31/98)

91 **MARIMAR TORRES** Pinot Noir Sonoma County Green Valley Don Miguel Vineyard 1995 • $25 • (02/28/98) • SS

91 **TRUCHARD** Pinot Noir Napa Valley Carneros 1995 • $23 • (08/31/97)

91 **WILLIAMS SELYEM** Pinot Noir Anderson Valley Ferrington Vineyard 1994 • $38 • (10/31/97)

91 **WILLIAMS SELYEM** Pinot Noir Russian River Valley Riverblock Vineyard 1994 • $35 • (10/31/97)

90 **ACACIA** Pinot Noir Carneros Reserve 1995 • $30 • (02/28/98)

90 **AU BON CLIMAT** Pinot Noir Central Coast Mistral Vineyard 1995 • $25 • (07/31/97)

90 **BABCOCK** Pinot Noir Santa Ynez Valley Estate Grown 1996 • $30 • (02/28/98)

90 **BERINGER** Pinot Noir Napa Valley Stanly Ranch 1994 • $20 • (12/31/97)

90 **BYRON** Pinot Noir Santa Barbara County 1995 • $17 • (11/30/97) • SS

90 **GARY FARRELL** Pinot Noir Russian River Valley Allen Vineyard 1995 • $40 • (12/31/97) • HR

90 **HITCHING POST** Pinot Noir Santa Ynez Valley Sanford & Benedict Vineyard 1995 • $30 • (01/31/98)

90 **KISTLER** Pinot Noir Sonoma Coast Hirsch Vineyard 1995 • $50 • (06/30/98)

90 **LANDMARK** Pinot Noir Sonoma County Grand Detour 1995 • $30 • (09/15/97)

90 **MORGAN** Pinot Noir Monterey Reserve 1995 • $28 • (01/31/98)

90 **SANFORD** Pinot Noir Santa Barbara County 1995 • $20 • (10/31/97) • SS

90 **STEELE** Pinot Noir Carneros 1995 • $18 • (10/15/97) • SS

90 **STEELE** Pinot Noir Carneros Sangiacomo Vineyard 1995 • $24 • (10/15/97)

90 **WILLIAMS SELYEM** Pinot Noir Anderson Valley Ferrington Vineyard 1995 • $40 • (10/31/97)

90 **WILLIAMS SELYEM** Pinot Noir Russian River Valley 1995 • $35 • (10/31/97)

90 **WILLIAMS SELYEM** Pinot Noir Russian River Valley Riverblock Vineyard 1995 • $36 • (12/31/97)

89 **DAVID BRUCE** Pinot Noir Russian River Valley Reserve 1995 • $25 • (12/31/97)

89 **COSENTINO** Pinot Noir Russian River Valley 1996 • $50 • (02/28/98)

89 **CUVAISON** Pinot Noir Napa Valley Carneros Eris 1995 • $19 • (12/15/97)

89 **DE LOACH** Pinot Noir Russian River Valley O.F.S. 1996 • $28 • (12/31/97)

89 **GARY FARRELL** Pinot Noir Russian River Valley 1996 • $23 • (06/30/98)

89 **NICHOLS** Pinot Noir Central Coast Reserve 1996 • $45 • (02/28/98)

89 **NICHOLS** Pinot Noir Edna Valley Paragon Vineyard 1996 • $28 • (02/28/98)

89 **NICHOLS** Pinot Noir Monterey County Pisoni Vineyards 1996 • $42 • (02/28/98)

89 **ROCHIOLI** Pinot Noir Russian River Valley Little Hill Block Reserve 1995 • $38 • (11/15/97)

89 **ROCHIOLI** Pinot Noir Russian River Valley Three Corner Vineyard Reserve 1995 • $40 • (11/15/97)

89 **ROCHIOLI** Pinot Noir Russian River Valley West Block Reserve 1995 • $50 • (11/15/97)

Key: SS—Spectator Selection CS—Cellar Selection HR—Highly Recommended BB—Best Buy $NA—Price not available Ⓐ—Auction Price
Dates in parentheses indicate the issues in which the ratings were published.

89 **SANTA CRUZ MOUNTAIN** Pinot Noir Santa Cruz Mountains Matteson Vineyard 1995 • $18 • (01/31/98)

89 **STONESTREET** Pinot Noir Russian River Valley 1995 • $30 • (12/15/97)

89 **VILLA MT. EDEN** Pinot Noir Santa Maria Valley Bien Nacido Vineyard 1995 • $20 • (10/31/97)

89 **WILLIAMS SELYEM** Pinot Noir Russian River Valley 1994 • $28 • (10/31/97)

89 **WILLIAMS SELYEM** Pinot Noir Sonoma Coast 1994 • $30 • (10/31/97)

88 **ACACIA** Pinot Noir Carneros 1995 • $19 • (07/31/97)

88 **ACACIA** Pinot Noir Carneros St. Clair Vineyard Reserve 1994 • $38 • (03/31/98)

88 **ANCIEN WINES** Pinot Noir Carneros 1995 • $23 • (07/31/97)

88 **AU BON CLIMAT** Pinot Noir California Isabelle 1995 • $50 • (10/31/97)

88 **AU BON CLIMAT** Pinot Noir Central Coast 1995 • $18 • (08/31/97)

88 **BANNISTER** Pinot Noir Russian River Valley 1995 • $20 • (08/31/97)

88 **AUGUST BRIGGS** Pinot Noir Carneros 1995 • $25 • (07/31/97)

88 **DAVID BRUCE** Pinot Noir Sonoma County 1995 • $18 • (01/31/98)

88 **CALERA** Pinot Noir Central Coast 1995 • $16 • (11/30/97)

88 **CALERA** Pinot Noir Mount Harlan Jensen 1994 • $38 • (07/31/97)

88 **CALERA** Pinot Noir Mount Harlan Mills 1994 • $35 • (02/28/98)

88 **CALERA** Pinot Noir Mount Harlan Reed 1994 • $35 • (03/31/98)

88 **CHALONE** Pinot Noir Chalone 1994 • $27 • (01/31/98)

88 **DOMAINE CARNEROS** Pinot Noir Carneros 1995 • $20 • (08/31/97)

88 **DOMAINE CARNEROS** Pinot Noir Carneros The Famous Gate 1995 • $32 • (09/30/97)

88 **EL MOLINO** Pinot Noir Napa Valley 1995 • $38 • (01/31/98)

88 **ESTANCIA** Pinot Noir Monterey Reserve 1995 • $18 • (08/31/97)

88 **ETUDE** Pinot Noir Carneros 1995 • $30 • (10/31/97)

88 **FLORA SPRINGS** Pinot Noir Carneros Lavender Hill Vineyard 1996 • $30 • (04/30/98)

88 **FOWLER** Pinot Noir Central Coast 1995 • $32 • (08/31/97)

88 **FOXEN** Pinot Noir Santa Maria Valley Bien Nacido Vineyard 1995 • $30 • (07/31/97)

88 **FOXEN** Pinot Noir Santa Ynez Valley Sanford & Benedict Vineyard 1995 • $30 • (09/30/97)

88 **GABRIELLI** Pinot Noir Mendocino Reserve 1995 • $25 • (09/30/97)

88 **GREENWOOD RIDGE** Pinot Noir Anderson Valley 1996 • $22 • (02/28/98)

88 **HARMONY CELLARS** Pinot Noir Paso Robles 1994 • $13 • (09/30/97)

88 **IRON HORSE** Pinot Noir Sonoma County Green Valley 1996 • $23 • (01/31/98)

88 **KYNSI** Pinot Noir Edna Valley 1995 • $18 • (03/31/98)

88 **LA CREMA** Pinot Noir Sonoma Coast Reserve 1995 • $26 • (12/15/97)

88 **LAETITIA** Pinot Noir San Luis Obispo County Laetitia Vineyard 1995 • $25 • (10/15/97)

88 **LONGORIA** Pinot Noir Santa Maria Valley Bien Nacido Vineyard 1995 • $32 • (01/31/98)

88 **MACROSTIE** Pinot Noir Carneros 1995 • $18 • (12/15/97)

88 **MACROSTIE** Pinot Noir Carneros Reserve 1995 • $26 • (12/15/97)

88 **MONTICELLO** Pinot Noir Napa Valley Corley Estate Reserve 1995 • $32 • (01/31/98)

88 **MOSHIN** Pinot Noir Russian River Valley Proprietor's Select 1995 • $24 • (01/31/98)
88 **NAVARRO** Pinot Noir Anderson Valley Méthode à l'Ancienne 1994 • $18 • (02/28/98)
88 **NAVARRO** Pinot Noir Mendocino 1995 • $13 • (10/15/97)
88 **NICHOLS** Pinot Noir Central Coast Blend 1996 • $36 • (02/28/98)
88 **PATZ & HALL** Pinot Noir Carneros Hyde Vineyard 1996 • $35 • (06/30/98)
88 **SAINTSBURY** Pinot Noir Carneros 1996 • $20 • (01/31/98)
88 **SANTA BARBARA WINERY** Pinot Noir Santa Barbara County 1995 • $20 • (11/15/97)
88 **SIGNORELLO** Pinot Noir Carneros Las Amigas Vineyard 1995 • $48 • (03/31/98)
88 **STEELE** Pinot Noir Anderson Valley 1995 • $22 • (10/15/97)
88 **STEELE** Pinot Noir Carneros Durell Vineyard 1995 • $24 • (10/31/97)
88 **STEPHEN ROSS** Pinot Noir Santa Maria Valley Bien Nacido Vineyard 1996 • $24 • (01/31/98)
88 **VILLA MT. EDEN** Pinot Noir Santa Maria Valley Bien Nacido Vineyard Grand Reserve 1996 • $20 • (01/31/98)
88 **WHITCRAFT** Pinot Noir Santa Maria Valley Bien Nacido Vineyard 1996 • $35 • (01/31/98)
88 **WHITCRAFT** Pinot Noir Santa Maria Valley Bien Nacido Vineyard Q Block 1996 • $40 • (01/31/98)
88 **WILD HORSE** Pinot Noir Central Coast Cheval Sauvage 1994 • $35 • (09/30/97)
88 **WILLIAMS SELYEM** Pinot Noir Russian River Valley Olivet Lane 1994 • $34 • (10/31/97)
88 **WILLIAMS SELYEM** Pinot Noir Sonoma Coast 1995 • $30 • (10/31/97)

CALIFORNIA SAUVIGNON BLANC & BLENDS

91 **CAYMUS** Sauvignon Blanc Napa Valley 1996 • $14 • (01/31/98) • SS
91 **MASON** Sauvignon Blanc Napa Valley 1996 • $12 • (07/31/97)
91 **ROCHIOLI** Sauvignon Blanc Russian River Valley 1997 • $14 • (06/30/98) • SS
90 **BERINGER** Sauvignon Blanc Napa Valley 1996 • $9 • (01/31/98) • BB
90 **CAIN** Sauvignon Blanc Monterey Ventana Vineyard Musqué 1996 • $17 • (01/31/98)
90 **CHALK HILL** Sauvignon Blanc Chalk Hill 1995 • $16 • (07/31/97)
90 **DUCKHORN** Sauvignon Blanc Napa Valley 1996 • $15 • (01/31/98) • HR
90 **GRGICH HILLS** Fumé Blanc Napa Valley 1996 • $15 • (03/31/98) • SS
90 **MARKHAM** Sauvignon Blanc Napa Valley 1996 • $12 • (09/15/97) • SS
90 **MASON** Sauvignon Blanc Napa Valley 1997 • $14 • (05/31/98)
90 **MURPHY-GOODE** Sauvignon Blanc Alexander Valley Fumé II The Deuce 1996 • $24 • (03/31/98)
90 **NAVARRO** Sauvignon Blanc Mendocino Cuvée 128 1996 • $13 • (03/31/98)
90 **ROCHIOLI** Sauvignon Blanc Russian River Valley Old Vines Reserve 1996 • $20 • (11/30/97)
89 **BABCOCK** Sauvignon Blanc Santa Ynez Valley Eleven Oaks 1996 • $20 • (03/31/98)
89 **BLAKE** Sauvignon Blanc Napa Valley 1995 • $16 • (10/15/97)
89 **FLORA SPRINGS** Sauvignon Blanc Napa Valley 1996 • $15 • (03/31/98)
89 **J. FRITZ** Sauvignon Blanc Russian River Valley Poplar Vineyard 1996 • $12 • (03/31/98)
89 **ROBERT MONDAVI** Fumé Blanc Napa Valley To-Kalon Vineyard I Block 1995 • $50 • (04/30/98)
89 **SANTINO** Fumé Blanc Amador County 1995 • $9 • (10/15/97)
89 **WATTLE CREEK** Sauvignon Blanc Alexander Valley 1996 • $16 • (09/15/97)
88 **BECKMEN** Sauvignon Blanc Santa Barbara County Beckmen Vineyards 1995 • $12 • (09/15/97)
88 **BOEGER** Sauvignon Blanc El Dorado 1997 • $10 • (04/30/98)
88 **CALLAWAY** Sauvignon Blanc Temecula 1997 • $8 • (05/15/98) • BB
88 **DRAXTON** Sauvignon Blanc Alexander Valley 1995 • $NA • (01/31/98)
88 **DRY CREEK** Fumé Blanc Sonoma County 1996 • $12 • (11/15/97)
88 **FOUNTAIN GROVE** Sauvignon Blanc California 1996 • $9 • (03/31/98)
88 **GEYSER PEAK** Sauvignon Blanc Sonoma County 1997 • $7 • (05/15/98) • BB
88 **HANNA** Sauvignon Blanc Russian River Valley Reserve 1996 • $21 • (01/31/98)
88 **KENWOOD** Sauvignon Blanc Sonoma County 1996 • $11 • (07/31/97) • BB
88 **KENWOOD** Sauvignon Blanc Sonoma Valley Reserve 1996 • $15 • (03/31/98)
88 **ROBERT MONDAVI** Fumé Blanc Napa Valley To-Kalon Vineyard Reserve 1995 • $22 • (11/30/97)
88 **MURPHY-GOODE** Fumé Blanc Alexander Valley Reserve 1996 • $17 • (03/31/98)
88 **RANCHO SISQUOC** Sauvignon Blanc Santa Maria Valley 1996 • $12 • (04/30/98)
88 **RENAISSANCE** Sauvignon Blanc North Yuba Barrel Select 1996 • $12 • (04/30/98)
88 **STAG'S LEAP WINE CELLARS** Sauvignon Blanc Napa Valley 1996 • $15 • (04/30/98)
88 **STEVENOT** Sauvignon Blanc Calaveras County 1996 • $10 • (03/31/98)
88 **RODNEY STRONG** Sauvignon Blanc Northern Sonoma Charlotte's Home 1997 • $10 • (06/30/98) • BB
88 **SUTTER HOME** Sauvignon Blanc Monterey County Signature Series 1997 • $14 • (05/31/98)
88 **VENTANA** Sauvignon Blanc Monterey 1996 • $10 • (07/31/97)
88 **WENTE** Sauvignon Blanc Livermore Valley 1996 • $8 • (03/31/98) • BB

CALIFORNIA SPARKLING WINE

92 **S. ANDERSON** Brut Napa Valley 1993 • $24 • (04/30/98) • SS
92 **SCHRAMSBERG** J. Schram Napa Valley 1990 • $50 • (11/30/97)
91 **S. ANDERSON** Brut Napa Valley 1992 • $24 • (11/30/97)
91 **GLORIA FERRER** Brut Carneros Carneros Cuvée Late Disgorged 1989 • $28 • (06/30/98)
91 **KORBEL** Le Premier Reserve California 1991 • $20 • (12/15/97) • HR
91 **MUMM CUVÉE NAPA** DVX Napa Valley 1993 • $40 • (11/30/97)
90 **S. ANDERSON** Blanc de Noirs Napa Valley 1993 • $23 • (11/30/97)
90 **CODORNIU NAPA** Reserve Napa Valley 1991 • $23 • (11/30/97)
90 **KRISTONE** Blanc de Blancs California 1992 • $40 • (11/30/97)

90 **PACIFIC ECHO** Brut Mendocino County Private Reserve 1992 • $30 • (06/30/98)
90 **ROEDERER ESTATE** Brut Anderson Valley L'Ermitage 1992 • $33 • (11/30/97)
89 **BENZIGER** Brut Blanc de Blancs Carneros Late Disgorged 1990 • $10 • (11/30/97)
89 **HANDLEY** Brut Anderson Valley 1992 • $20 • (11/30/97)
89 **IRON HORSE** Vrais Amis Sonoma County Green Valley 1992 • $24 • (11/30/97)
89 **J** Sonoma County 1993 • $25 • (11/30/97)
88 **BUENA VISTA** Brut Blanc de Blanc Carneros 1991 • $17 • (04/30/98)
88 **GLORIA FERRER** Brut Carneros Royal Cuveé 1989 • $19 • (11/30/97)
88 **ROBERT HUNTER** Brut de Noirs Sonoma Valley Extended Tirage 1992 • $25 • (06/15/98)
88 **IRON HORSE** Brut Rosé Sonoma County Green Valley 1992 • $25 • (11/30/97)
88 **SCHRAMSBERG** Blanc de Noirs Napa Valley 1990 • $26 • (11/30/97)
88 **SCHRAMSBERG** Brut Rosé Napa Valley Cuvée de Pinot 1994 • $25 • (11/30/97)

Key: SS—Spectator Selection CS—Cellar Selection HR—Highly Recommended BB—Best Buy $NA—Price not available Ⓐ—Auction Price
Dates in parentheses indicate the issues in which the ratings were published.

The Main Listings

Wines by Country and Producer

This is the *Ultimate Guide*'s main listings section. Here you will find "nuts-and-bolts" information—producer, appellation, vintage, price, date of rating, and score—on over 40,000 wines reviewed by *Wine Spectator* since 1984. Listings of the 20,000 most recently tasted wines also contain descriptive notes that will help you get a sense of what the wine actually tastes like.

Turn the page for detailed information that will help you to understand and make use of our listings.

How to Use These Listings

The wine ratings contained in this guide are taken from the tasting results that have been published in *Wine Spectator* since 1984. While the majority of the ratings in this book are quite recent, some ratings are not as current.

While we feel that these older ratings can be very useful in presenting a nearly complete vertical representation of a particular wine, we also feel the need to caution you to pay particular attention to the date on each of the ratings. This will tell you how current the rating is.

Ratings and tasting notes included here are by *Wine Spectator*'s senior editors, and include tastings conducted by an editor as part of the research for one of our Wine Spectator Press books.

Wine Spectator's 100-Point Scale

95-100—Classic; a great wine
90-94—Outstanding; superior character and style
80-89—Good to very good; wine with special qualities
70-79—Average; drinkable wine that may have minor flaws
60-69—Below average; drinkable but not recommended
50-59—Poor; undrinkable, not recommended

There is one other type of rating you will see in this book, primarily in the listings for red Bordeaux and California Cabernet. These are ratings based on barrel tastings, which are tastings conducted on wines before they have been bottled and released for sale. These are, by definition, very preliminary ratings and should be treated as such. Many things can happen to a wine between the time it is tasted in barrel and the time that you purchase it at your local store; wines can improve or decline during that time, and can show signs of poor shipping or storage conditions. Barrel-tasting ratings are indicated by the code (BT) and by a range of scores (e.g. 85-89).

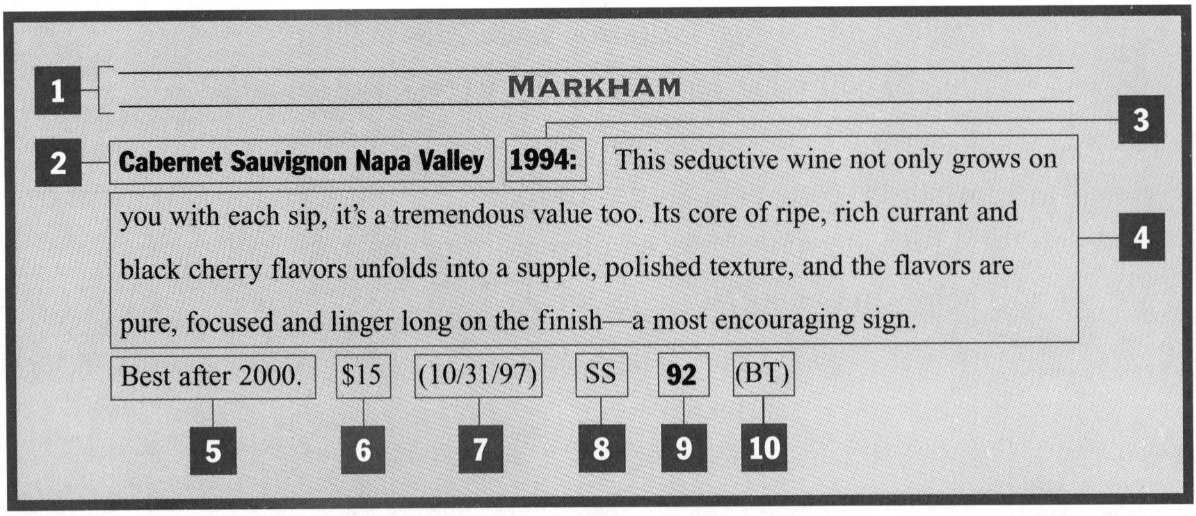

1
MARKHAM
2
Cabernet Sauvignon Napa Valley
1994:
3
This seductive wine not only grows on you with each sip, it's a tremendous value too. Its core of ripe, rich currant and black cherry flavors unfolds into a supple, polished texture, and the flavors are pure, focused and linger long on the finish—a most encouraging sign.
4
Best after 2000.
$15
(10/31/97)
SS
92
(BT)
5
6
7
8
9
10

The Ratings: Piece by Piece

Because of the very large number of ratings presented here, each wine listing must be as brief as possible. Therefore, we have used abbreviations and shortcuts throughout this book. A key to these symbols can be found in the lower left-hand corner of every left-hand page in the main listings. At left is a typical wine listing and an explanation for each of the elements.

1. Producer's Name—The name of the winery or producer.

Producers whose names are preceded by "Château," "Domaine," "Bodegas" and the like are listed by the name following these designations. For example, Château Margaux will be listed under "M" as "Margaux, Château." The United States and other English-speaking countries are an exception to this rule, however. (Thus, Chateau St. Jean in California is found under "C.")

Producers' names that include given names are listed alphabetically under the surname. For example, Robert Mondavi will be found under "M" as "Mondavi, Robert."

Producers' names that begin with English and foreign articles such as a, the, de, di, le, la, los, etc., are listed under the main word following the article. Thus, La Vieille Ferme is listed as "Vieille Ferme, La."

Producers' names that begin with "St." or "Ste." are alphabetized as though this word were spelled out. For example, "Saint Laurent, Château" follows "St.-Jovian."

2. Wine Type/Description—Contains the wine type and any varietal name, appellation, or other vineyard or special designation, such as Sonoma Valley or Cask 23.

3. Vintage—The year the wine was harvested and vinified.

4. Tasting Note—The tasting note for the wine, as published in *Wine Spectator* (or, in rare cases, a Wine Spectator Press book). These notes give the tasters' impressions of the wine, and thus present a more complete picture than the score alone.

5. Drinkability—Tasting notes may also include our estimate as to when a wine will be at its best.

6. Price Data—The wine's price information can come in three distinct forms:

—A single price, such as $37, signifies the suggested retail price *on release*. Bottle age, scarcity, and exceptional quality can all cause a wine's price to escalate, so please note—**prices will vary**.

—$NA means that no price data was available; it occurs typically with older wines, very new ones, and wines which are not imported into the U.S.

—A price followed by the symbol Ⓐ is an average of recent auction prices, for older or collectible wines.

7. Issue Date—The date of the issue of *Wine Spectator* in which the rating was first published. In general, the wines were tasted within two months prior to this date.

An issue date of January 1 indicates a tasting note which, for various reasons, was never published in the magazine. In general, wines with an issue date of 01/01/97 were tasted between November 1996 and May 1997; 01/01/98 denotes wines tasted between October 1997 and April 1998.

8. Special Ratings—The special designations used here are:

SS (Spectator Selection) — *Wine Spectator*'s highest recommendations in a given issue. Not necessarily the highest-scoring wines, they are the wines we think represent the most outstanding values when quality is balanced against price.

CS (Cellar Selection) — The wines we believe are the best candidates for addition to your cellar. They should improve with bottle age, and they show the greatest potential as collectibles.

BB (Best Buy) — Outstanding quality at modest prices. Note: because of their attractive prices, these wines tend to disappear from retail shelves quickly.

HR (Highly Recommended) — Other noteworthy wines selected from among the highest-scoring wines in a given issue. Price is not a consideration.

9. Score—This is the number, from the *Wine Spectator*'s 100-point scale, that represents the taster's evaluation of the wine's quality relative to other wines.

Ratings are based on immediate quality, as well as on how good a wine will be when it's at its peak, regardless of how soon that will be.

A range of scores (90-94, for example) indicates a preliminary rating, and is used in conjunction with a barrel tasting.

10. Barrel Tasting—The code (BT) appearing after a range of scores indicates a barrel tasting, as described on the previous page.

Australia

With more than 1000 wineries in production, Australia has become a formidable source of quality wine. Almost every major grape variety is cultivated here, and Australia's best wines compete with the elite of Bordeaux, Burgundy and California in price as well as quality.

Australian wines are stylistically similar to California's. Their flavors tend to be full and hearty, and new oak (often the vanilla-tasting American oak) is frequently employed in their production. Also, as in California, there is an increasing concentration here on a few major red and white varietals. Cabernet Sauvignon and Chardonnay are extremely successful and are widely planted. The more traditional Shiraz (known as Syrah elsewhere) also thrives here, producing a rich wine that takes oak aging quite well. Sémillon, often blended with Chardonnay, shows unusual viscosity and freshness.

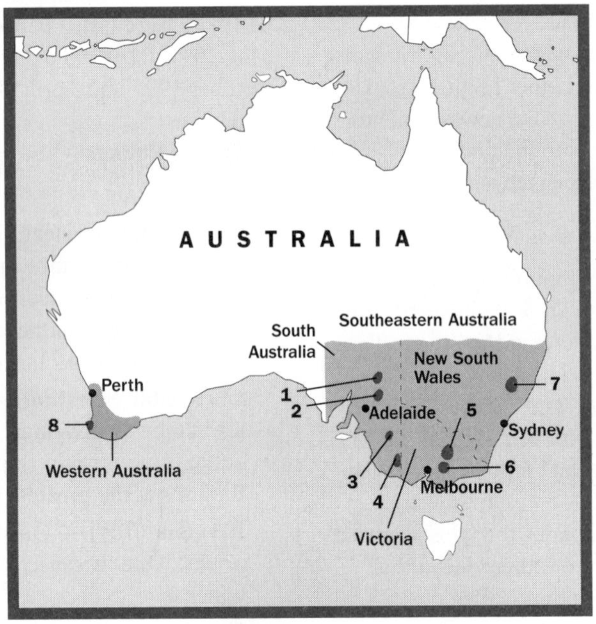

1. Clare
2. Barossa Valley
3. Padthaway
4. Coonawarra
5. Goulburn Valley
6. Yarra Valley
7. Hunter Valley
8. Margaret River

HISTORY OF AUSTRALIAN WINE PRODUCTION

The first vines arrived in Australia with the British Expeditionary Fleet in 1778. However, serious commercial wine production did not begin until the 1890s, in Southeastern Australia, where the vast majority of wine production still takes place. Most wineries were established as family enterprises. Many of these family names—for example, Tyrell's, Yalumba and McWilliams—remain important in the present-day Australian wine industry.

Before 1950, Australian wine production focused on fortified wines. A red wine boom in the 1960s was followed by a white wine boom in the 1980s. There was a sudden upswing in prices of hot wines in the 1980s, and again in the mid-1900s, but there are still plenty of good low- and mid-priced wines available.

AUSTRALIAN WINE REGIONS

Australia's chief wine regions are South Australia, New South Wales and Victoria. Often wines from all three regions are blended and sold under the catch-all Southeastern Australia denomination. The only other significant wine region is Western Australia, located near Perth on the West Coast.

South Australia

More than 60 percent of the country's wine production come from the South Australia region, which includes the well-known Barossa Valley, located about 60 kilometers from Adelaide. Barossa is also the headquarters of many of the country's most famous wineries, including Penfolds, Seppelt, Peter Lehmann, and Wolf Blass. South Australia is also the source of Penfolds Grange (formerly Grange Hermitage), generally regarded as Australia's greatest red wine. Made from almost 100 percent Shiraz and always aged in new American oak, it was created by the late Max Schubert, the legendary former head of Penfolds winemaking operations.

The chief grape varieties in South Australia are Shiraz and Grenache for reds, and Sémillon and Riesling for whites. However, Cabernet Sauvignon and Chardonnay are becoming increasingly important, particularly for export markets.

South Australia's finest Cabernet-based reds come from the Coonawarra district, which, like the Médoc of France and Napa Valley, excels in producing an ageworthy, well-structured Cabernet Sauvignon. Although Coonawarra's climate is cooler than Barossa's, the key feature of its *terroir* is its unique soil, called *terra rossa*, which consists of a rich layer of rust-colored earth laid over a thick layer of limestone and clay. The cigar-shaped Coonawarra district, only a mile wide and seven miles long, is virtually the only place in Australia that contains significant acreage of this prized soil. Wynns and Parker Estate are perhaps the most famous wineries located in Coonawarra, but many other wineries, such as Lindemans, Penfolds, Petaluma, Seppelt, and Rosemount, obtain considerable production from the region.

South Australia also boasts what many consider Australia's finest white wine district: Padthaway, which is located about 65 miles north of Coonawarra. Padthaway's Chardonnays are particularly distinguished, seeming to combine a California-like generosity with a European-style minerally austerity. The Clare region, north of Adelaide, has developed an excellent reputation for its Riesling and its crisp style of Shiraz.

John Duval

The vineyards at Petaluma—a top wine producer—located in South Australia.

New South Wales

Although South Australia now outranks it in production, New South Wales was Australia's first important wine region; some of its vineyards date back to the 1820s. While Cabernet Sauvignon and Chardonnay have been extensively planted in New South Wales in recent decades, the traditional Shiraz and Sémillon remain the most distinctive wines of the region.

The Hunter Valley, about 100 miles north of Sydney, is the most important wine region of New South Wales. Major Hunter Valley wineries include Tyrell's, McWilliams, Wyndham Estate, and Rothbury Estate, all of which have achieved international reputations.

Though not widely planted until the 1970s, a subregion called the Upper Hunter Valley—home of the Rosemount winery—seems to have a special facility for producing Chardonnays and Shiraz with vigorous fruit and alcoholic richness.

Victoria

Victoria is not as well-known as the other major Australian wine regions, but its wines have great potential. Foremost among these regions is the cool Yarra Valley, which excels at Burgundian-style Pinot Noirs and Chardonnays. Yarra Valley wines often sell at top prices, reflecting the low yields and painstaking production methods typically maintained by the wineries there.

Victoria also excels in the production of sparkling wines, owing to a cool climate that allows the grapes to obtain excellent acidity along with concentrated fruit. Although some of the traditional Champagne grapes, such as Pinot Noir and Chardonnay, are cultivated here, the Sémillon is the dominant sparkling wine grape in Victoria. This variety lends Victoria's sparkling wines a unique herbal dimension that is quite appealing. Well-known sparkling wine producers in Victoria include Yellowglen and Seppelt.

Western Australia

Lying on the western coast near Perth, the Western Australia region is far removed geographically from the rest of Australian winemaking and it accounts for a relatively small percentage of total production. Located at its southwestern extreme is the Margaret River area, Western Australia's most prestigious wine producing area. With high natural acidity and firm tannins, Margaret River products are considered by many the most European-style wines of Australia. Leading Margaret River producers, which tend to be "boutique" wineries (meaning that their wines can be hard to find and expensive), include Leeuwin and Goundrey.

AUSTRALIAN DESSERT WINES

Sweet dessert wines are an Australian specialty. Among the best known is the hazelnut-scented Yalumba Galway Pipe Port, which is similar to a Portuguese tawny, with a bit more almondy sweetness. Also well regarded is the pineapple- and butterscotch-scented Peter Lehmann Sémillon Sauternes, which has proven itself a genuine value through the years. Best of all are the liqueur Muscats and Tokays, primarily from Rutherglen, which are among the most complex and distinctive dessert wines in the world.

ABBEY VALE

Cabernet Merlot Margaret River 1995: A distinct herbal layer runs through the smooth-textured berry and red plum flavors. Light in style, this red shows more depth than it initially seems to possess. Drink now. 400 cases made. • $20 • (11/30/97) • **87**

Sauvignon Blanc Margaret River 1997: Smooth and gentle, with lively peach and floral flavors. Drink now. 500 cases made. • $17 • (11/30/97) • **86**

ADAMS, TIM

Grenache Clare Valley The Fergus 1996: Soft, fruity style of Grenache, emphasizing pretty plum and pepper flavors and suppleness on the finish. Drink now. • $20 • (04/30/98) • **85**

Riesling Clare Valley 1994 • $15 • (06/30/95) • **86**

Sémillon Clare Valley 1996: This appellation isn't known for Sémillon, but this wine has plenty of flavor and a lively, promising finish. Fig, citrus and lanolin flavors balance on a fulcrum of crisp acidity. Should age well through 2000 to 2005. • $20 • (04/30/98) • **88**

Sémillon Clare Valley 1994 • $17 • (06/30/95) • **87**

Sémillon Clare Valley 1993 • $15 • (06/30/95) • **84**

Shiraz Clare Valley 1992 • $16 • (11/15/95) • **83**

ALL SAINTS

Merlot Rutherglen-Victoria Classic Release 1994: Crisp in texture, but showing some nice, ripe currant and blackberry flavors that linger on the straightforward finish. Soft tannins make it best from 1999. 30,000 cases made. • $14 • (05/31/97) • **85**

ALLANDALE

Chardonnay Hunter River Valley 1995: Has more intensity that most Aussie Chardonnays, with resinous pear and mineral flavors on a firm frame. Finishes with lots of spice. Drinkable now. 15,000 cases made. • $12 • (05/31/97) • **88**

Shiraz Hunter River Valley Matthew 1996: Gamy flavors add an interesting bass note to the chorus of black cherry and spice character, balancing this medium-weight red nicely. 1,000 cases made. • $17 • (05/15/98) • **86**

Shiraz Hunter River Valley Matthew 1995: Ripe and round, a beefy wine with terrific, earthy berry and spice flavors, slightly dipping in intensity before the finish. Should be at its best after 2000. 1,000 cases made. • $12 • (09/30/97) • **89**

ALLANMERE

Chardonnay Australia Durham 1996: Simple and fresh, appealing for its melon and vanilla flavors. Has a slightly resinous finish. Try now. 800 cases made. • $13 • (10/31/97) • **84**

ALLINDA

Chardonnay Yarra Valley 1996: Earthy, smoky flavors dominate this silky-textured, complex wine. Offers some apple and spice flavors on the finish and a nice layer of rich honey. 300 cases made. • $25 • (05/15/98) • **89**

Riesling Yarra Valley 1996: Bright and jazzy, with citrusy green apple and resin flavors. Best from 1999 through 2004. 300 cases made. • $19 • (05/31/98) • **88**

Sauvignon Blanc Yarra Valley 1997: Crisp in texture, with light citrus and melon flavors, hinting at fig on the finish. Very youthful and fresh. 300 cases made. • $22 • (05/15/98) • **85**

ALTA

Sauvignon Blanc Victoria 1994 • $14 • (06/30/95) • **85**

Key: SS—Spectator Selection. CS—Cellar Selection. BB—Best Buy. HR—Highly Recommended. $NA—Price not available. (BT)—Barrel tasting. (A)—Auction Price.
Dates in parentheses represent the issues in which the ratings were published.

ANTIPODEAN

Sauvignon Blanc-Sémillon-Viognier Yarra Valley 1997: Bright and fruity, with a mouthful of pear and pineapple flavor and just a hint of sage on the finish. 5,000 cases made. • $15 • (06/15/98) • **84**

Shiraz-Mourvèdre-Grenache-Viognier Barossa 1996: Firm and focused, nicely shaped to show off the ripe plum and anise flavors beaming through the mildly chewy finish. 5,000 cases made. • $15 • (06/15/98) • **87**

ARROWFIELD

Cabernet Merlot Australia 1990 • $10 • (03/31/93) • **84**
Cabernet Merlot South Eastern Australia 1993 • $11 • (06/30/95) • **81**
Cabernet Merlot South Eastern Australia 1991 • $10 • (08/31/94) • **83**
Cabernet Sauvignon Australia Show Reserve 1990 • $15 • (11/30/92) • **84**
Cabernet Sauvignon Hunter Valley Show Reserve 1991 • $18 • (07/31/94) • **86**
Cabernet Sauvignon McLaren Vale Show Reserve 1992 • $22 • (04/30/96) • **87**
Chardonnay South Eastern Australia 1994 • $11 • (06/30/95) • **81**
Chardonnay South Eastern Australia Show Reserve 1994 • $22 • (04/30/96) • **88**
Chardonnay South Eastern Australia Show Reserve 1993 • $20 • (05/15/95) HR • **90**
Gewürztraminer South Eastern Australia Late Harvest 1993 • $11 • (05/15/95) • **88**
Rhine Riesling Late Harvest Cowra Show Reserve 1993 • $22/375ml • (05/15/96) • **90**
Sémillon Chardonnay Hunter Valley 1993 • $8 • (09/30/94) • **81**
Sémillon South Eastern Australia Show Reserve 1993 • $20 • (06/30/95) • **86**
Shiraz Australia Show Reserve 1990 • $15 • (11/30/92) • **85**
Shiraz Cabernet Australia 1990 • $10 • (11/30/92) • **87**
Shiraz Hunter Valley Show Reserve 1991 • $18 • (09/30/94) • **89**
Shiraz South Eastern Australia 1993 • $11 • (05/15/95) • **84**
Shiraz South Eastern Australia 1991 • $10 • (09/30/94) • **82**
Shiraz South Eastern Australia Show Reserve 1992 • $20 • (05/15/95) • **88**

ARUNDA

Chardonnay South Eastern Australia 1996: Fresh and ever-so-slightly spicy, with a core of straightforward apple and pear flavors. Drink now. 2,000 cases made. • $9 • (04/30/97) • **82**

Shiraz Cabernet South Eastern Australia 1996: On the lighter side, but nicely balanced to show off plum and currant flavors shaded by hints of anise and other spices. Drink now. 2,000 cases made. • $9 • (04/30/97) • **84**

Shiraz Cabernet South Eastern Australia 1990 • $6 • (05/31/93) • **81**

ASHWOOD GROVE

Cabernet Sauvignon Riverina 1991 • $10 • (07/15/93) • **84**
Cabernet Sauvignon Riverland 1992 • $9 • (06/30/95) • **83**
River Willow Red Riverland 1991 • $7 • (05/31/93) • **85**
River Willow White Riverland 1993 • $7 • (06/30/95) • **73**
Sémillon-Sauvignon Blanc Riverland 1994 • $8 • (06/30/95) • **80**
Shiraz Riverina 1991 • $9 • (05/31/93) • **84**
Shiraz Riverland 1993 • $9 • (03/31/96) • **83**
Shiraz Riverland 1992 • $9 • (06/30/95) • **83**

AUSVETIA

Shiraz South Australia 1994: Goes for elegance over power without sacrificing a bit of its anise-scented black cherry, plum and chocolate flavors that glide smoothly over the finish. Good now; best from 2000 through 2010. • $60 • (05/15/98) • **92**

BALDIVIS

Cabernet Sauvignon Merlot Western Australia 1991 • $9 • (12/15/93) • **84**
Cabernet Sauvignon Merlot Western Australia 1990 • $9 • (06/30/93) • **80**

BANNOCKBURN

Pinot Noir Geelong 1990 • $NA • (06/30/93) • **87**
Pinot Noir Geelong 1986 • $26 • (01/31/90) • **73**

Pinot Noir Geelong 1985 • $17 • (03/15/88) • **74**
Shiraz Geelong 1984 • $13 • (10/31/89) • **81**

BANROCK STATION

Chardonnay South Eastern Australia Unwooded 1997: Pretty, straightforward Chardonnay with citrus, pear and vanilla notes floating through. 20,000 cases made. • $7 • (11/30/97) • **84**

Sémillon Chardonnay South Eastern Australia 1997: Soft, silky, almost sweet-tasting, with pretty pineapple, fig and citrus flavors swirling through the juicy finish. 20,000 cases made. • $6 • (11/30/97) • **83**

Shiraz South Eastern Australia 1997: This Aussie Shiraz is a lot of wine for the price. It's smooth, ripe and lively on the palate, with spicy anise notes around a plush core of black cherry flavor, turning velvety on the finish. Enjoyable now, it's also easy to find and easy on the pocketbook. 10,000 cases made. • $7 • (02/28/98) BB • **87**

Shiraz Cabernet Sauvignon South Eastern Australia 1997: Youthful, firm-textured and appealing for its nicely articulated berry and herb flavors that linger on the finish. 15,000 cases made. • $6 • (05/31/98) BB • **88**

Shiraz Cabernet Sauvignon South Eastern Australia 1996: Ripe and generous, on a modest frame, this Shiraz blend takes off in a racy style before softening on the finish and highlighting toasty currant and berry flavors. It's ready to drink, and won't strain your budget when the occasion calls for a few bottles. 20,000 cases made. • $6 • (11/30/97) BB • **86**

BAROSSA VALLEY ESTATE

Cabernet Sauvignon South Australia 1987 • $11 • (01/31/90) • **83**

Chardonnay Barossa Valley Ebenezer 1996: Smooth and creamy, and though a bit green around the edges, it has good spicy flavors and finishes harmoniously and subtly with more spice and some toasty character. 2,100 cases made. • $18 • (05/31/97) • **89**

Shiraz Barossa Valley E & E Black Pepper 1994: Dense and chewy, solidly packed with dark berry, raspberry, anise and pepper flavors that turn just a bit rough on the finish. Has lots of personality, though could be more graceful. Best from 2000. 2,950 cases made. • $60 • (06/15/97) • **87**

Shiraz Barossa Valley Ebenezer 1994: Chewy in texture but not very dense, with a nice mouthful of spicy blackberry and licorice flavors that linger on the finish. Drinkable now. 5,200 cases made. • $25 • (05/31/97) • **88**

Shiraz Cabernet Sauvignon Barossa Valley 1985 • $8 • (09/30/89) BB • **86**

BARRATT

Chardonnay Adelaide Hills Piccadilly Valley 1996: Elegant, refined style of Chardonnay, offering plenty of pear and spice flavors that linger neatly and harmoniously on the nicely defined finish. Delicious now. 2,000 cases made. • $20 • (04/30/98) • **88**

Pinot Noir Adelaide Hills Piccadilly Valley 1996: Light and direct, appealing for its fresh berry flavors, accented by a touch of pickle barrel. Drinkable now. 1,000 cases made. • $21 • (04/30/98) • **82**

BARRIER REEF

Cabernet Sauvignon South Eastern Australia 1993: Supple and appealing for its well-rounded berry and cedar flavors that glide smoothly through the finish. 5,000 cases made. • $7 • (10/15/96) • **84**

Cabernet Sauvignon South Eastern Australia 1992 • $8 • (11/30/95) • **85**

Cabernet Shiraz South Eastern Australia 1991 • $7 • (06/30/93) • **76**

Chardonnay South Eastern Australia 1994: In a broad style, focusing on butterscotch and spice flavors more than fruit, and finishing softly. 5,000 cases made. • $7 • (10/15/96) • **82**

Chardonnay South Eastern Australia 1993 • $8 • (12/31/95) • **85**

Sauvignon Blanc South Eastern Australia 1994: A solid effort, but a slightly salty, bitter edge takes away from the charm. 4,000 cases made. • $6 • (10/15/96) • **81**

Sauvignon Blanc South Eastern Australia 1993 • $7 • (06/30/96) BB • **83**

BARRY, BRIAN

Cabernet Sauvignon Clare Valley Juds Hill Vineyard 1994: Racy acidity runs through this ripe-flavored red, focusing on black cherry and cedar notes. 500 cases made. • $16 • (05/31/98) • **85**

BARRY, JIM

Cabernet-Malbec Clare Valley McCrae Wood 1995: Crisp in texture, with an odd balance of tarry, ripe black cherry and mint flavors. Best from 2000. 60 percent Cabernet Sauvignon, 40 percent Malbec. 1,000 cases made. • $31 • (06/15/98) • **85**

Shiraz Clare Valley McCrae Wood 1995: Crisp in texture, generous in flavor, layered with berry, plum, chocolate and spice notes that linger on the finish. Smooth already; drink now through 2002. 1,000 cases made. • $31 • (06/15/98) • **88**

Shiraz Clare Valley McCrae Wood 1994: A chewy style of Shiraz, with a racy acidity that balances the ripe blackberry and pepper flavors. Has the purity of flavor and austerity of structure to become an elegant wine by 2000 to 2001. • $30 • (05/31/97) • **89**

Shiraz Clare Valley The Armagh 1995: Ripe and intense, with well-defined blackberry, anise and pepper flavors, hinting at chocolate and eucalyptus on the firm finish. Veers toward tartness, but it has impressive, if eccentric, character. Best from 1999 through 2005. • $76 • (06/15/98) • **92**

Shiraz Clare Valley The Armagh 1994: A distinctive wine with lots of personality, this has big ripe flavors that fill the lean, sinewy frame with mouth-filling, juicy character. Intense, it needs until 1999 to 2000 to show what it has. • $75 • (05/31/97) • **91**

BARWANG

Cabernet Sauvignon New South Wales 1994 • $16 • (04/30/96) • **88**
Cabernet Sauvignon New South Wales 1993 • $18 • (10/15/95) • **85**
Cabernet Sauvignon Australia 1992 • $18 • (09/30/94) • **89**
Chardonnay New South Wales 1995 • $16 • (04/30/96) • **81**
Chardonnay New South Wales 1994 • $18 • (09/30/95) • **86**
Chardonnay Australia 1993 • $18 • (09/30/94) • **83**
Shiraz New South Wales 1994 • $16 • (04/30/96) • **86**
Shiraz New South Wales 1992 • $18 • (11/15/95) • **85**
Shiraz Australia 1991 • $18 • (09/30/94) • **84**

BASEDOW

Chardonnay Barossa 1996: Soft and spicy, with lots of pineapple flowing through it, this ripe wine has modest pretensions and good flavor. Drinkable now. 1,000 cases made. • $17 • (11/30/97) • **85**

Grenache Barossa Bush Vine 1995: Ripe and spicy like many Barossa reds, finishing with refreshing lightness, polish and zip. Drink now. • $10 • (11/30/97) • **87**

Sémillon Barossa 1996: This soft, spice cookie of a wine is supple and generous with its pineapple and fig flavor, but tightens up a bit on the finish. Best from 1999 to 2000. 500 cases made. • $10 • (11/30/97) • **85**

Shiraz Barossa 1995: Bright and atypically tart for Barossa, its anise and black cherry flavors are shaded with hints of dill and smoke. Best from 1999 or 2000. 1,000 cases made. • $17 • (11/30/97) • **85**

BASS PHILLIP

Pinot Noir Victoria 1995: Fruity, fresh and lively, with strawberry and floral flavors that linger on the crisp finish. Drinkable now. 20 cases made. • $35 • (08/31/97) • **86**

Pinot Noir Victoria Premium 1995: Smooth, supple, generous with its tobacco-scented plum, berry and spice flavors, this is a harmonious, subtle wine with impressive depth and resonance. It vibrates with richness yet maintains an elegant feel. Drink now. 44 cases made. • $55 • (08/31/97) • **91**

Pinot Noir Victoria Reserve 1995: Smells pretty, with its sweet berry, floral and vanilla character, delivers silky texture and pretty flavors on the palate. Drink now. 6 cases made. • $75 • (08/31/97) • **89**

BENJAMIN

Tawny Port Australia NV: A multilayered dessert wine with waves of supple, complex flavors, rich but not overwhelming notes of cinnamon, nutmeg, walnut, spice and sweet berry, even touches of brown sugar and malt on the silky finish. Fine drinking, and a fine value. 20,000 cases made. • $10 • (06/15/97) BB • **91**

BERRI ESTATES

Cabernet Sauvignon Barossa Valley 1985 • $7 • (04/30/88) • **76**
Cabernet Shiraz Australia 1985 • $10 • (07/01/87) • **89**

BEST'S

Cabernet Shiraz South Australia Vintage Selection 1986 • $10 • (03/15/88) • **80**
Shiraz Barossa Valley 1985 • $9 • (02/15/88) • **85**

BEST'S

Chardonnay-Sauvignon Blanc Swan Hill 1996: A crisp, generous white with spicy, citrusy flavors that last through the snappy finish. Refreshing now. 600 cases made. • $9 • (10/31/97) • **87**

BETHANY CREEK

Chardonnay South Eastern Australia Premium Selection 1996: Big, bright and spicy, with zingy pear and spice flavors swirling through the smooth, polished finish. Drinkable now. 12,000 cases made. • $11 • (04/30/97) • **85**
Shiraz South Eastern Australia 1996: A medicinal, bitter, green character cuts a wide swath through the fruit flavors. 3,000 cases made. • $11 • (04/30/97) • **70**

BLACK OPAL

Cabernet Merlot Coonawarra Reserve 1995: Strives for elegance, but ends up shy on the nose and unfocused in flavor. Currant, berry and herb notes finally sneak in on the finish. May be better in 2000 to 2004. 8,000 cases made. • $16 • (05/15/97) • **83**
Cabernet Merlot South Australia Reserve 1994 • $14 • (04/30/96) • **80**
Cabernet Merlot South Eastern Australia 1996: On the light side, with an herbal edge to the modest black cherry and toasty flavors in this simple red. Drinkable now. 50,000 cases made. • $11 • (11/30/97) • **82**
Cabernet Merlot South Eastern Australia 1995: Soft and spicy, with a pickle-barrel, mineral character in front of the modest berry flavors. Drinkable now. 25,000 cases made. • $10 • (01/31/97) • **79**
Cabernet Merlot South Eastern Australia 1994 • $9 • (04/30/96) • **83**
Cabernet Merlot South Eastern Australia 1992 • $10 • (04/30/94) • **81**
Cabernet Merlot South Eastern Australia 1990 • $9 • (04/15/93) BB • **87**
Cabernet Merlot South Eastern Australia 1989 • $9 • (11/30/92) • **82**
Cabernet Sauvignon Hunter Valley 1985 • $8 • (07/15/88) BB • **81**
Cabernet Sauvignon South Eastern Australia 1996: Supple and elegantly balanced, with a core of pretty plum and berry flavors and light layers of spice and earth wafting across it. Very tasty now. 50,000 cases made. • $11 • (11/30/97) • **86**
Cabernet Sauvignon South Eastern Australia 1995: A simple, round wine, enjoyable for its sweet plummy flavors. Drinkable now. 25,000 cases made. • $10 • (01/31/97) • **80**
Cabernet Sauvignon South Eastern Australia 1994 • $9 • (04/30/96) • **85**
Cabernet Sauvignon South Eastern Australia 1992 • $10 • (04/30/94) • **83**
Cabernet Sauvignon South Eastern Australia 1989 • $9 • (11/30/92) • **78**
Cabernet Sauvignon South Eastern Australia 1987 • $8 • (02/28/90) BB • **85**
Chardonnay Padthaway Reserve 1996: A bright, open-textured Chardonnay with flavors reminiscent of canned pears, mineral and spice. Drink now. 8,000 cases made. • $16 • (05/15/97) • **84**
Chardonnay South Australia Reserve 1995 • $14 • (04/30/96) • **88**
Chardonnay South Eastern Australia 1997: Has a sweet-spicy component threading its way through the pear and melon flavors. Youthful and exuberant. Drink now. 80,000 cases made. • $11 • (03/31/98) • **85**
Chardonnay South Eastern Australia 1996: A solid wine, with spicy pear flavors that linger on the finish. Could use a bit more finesse. Try now. 25,000 cases made. • $10 • (01/31/97) • **81**
Chardonnay South Eastern Australia 1995 • $9 • (04/30/96) • **83**
Chardonnay South Eastern Australia 1993 • $10 • (09/30/94) • **75**
Shiraz South Eastern Australia 1996: Ripe and distinctively spicy, with a jazzy anise note complementing the dark berry flavors. Drink now. 70,000 cases made. • $11 • (03/31/98) BB • **87**
Shiraz South Eastern Australia 1995: Ripe and supple. Generous, spicy, anise-scented black cherry flavors up front, fading a bit on the finish. Ready now. 25,000 cases made. • $10 • (02/28/97) • **84**
Shiraz South Eastern Australia 1994 • $9 • (04/30/96) • **82**
Shiraz South Eastern Australia 1991 • $10 • (03/31/94) • **83**
Shiraz South Eastern Australia 1990 • $8 • (11/30/92) • **80**

Key: SS—Spectator Selection. CS—Cellar Selection. BB—Best Buy. HR—Highly Recommended. $NA—Price not available. (BT)—Barrel tasting. Ⓐ—Auction Price.
Dates in parentheses represent the issues in which the ratings were published.

BLACK ROCK

Cabernet Sauvignon Coonawarra 1995: Showing restraint and elegance, this crisp-textured wine displays carefully articulated currant and pepper aromas and flavors, and finishes with polish. Best from 2000. 2,500 cases made. • $22 • (11/30/97) • **87**
Chardonnay McLaren Vale 1996: Supple and appealing for its pretty, vanilla-scented passion fruit and pear flavors, which linger nicely on the generous, nutmeg-scented finish. Drinkable now. 2,500 cases made. • $16 • (11/30/97) • **88**

BLACK SILK

White South Australia 1993 • $7 • (04/30/94) • **78**

BLASS, WOLF

Cabernet Blend South Australia Black Label 1986 • $26 • (04/30/94) • **87**
Cabernet Merlot South Australia Black Label 1983 • $25 • (04/30/89) • **77**
Cabernet Sauvignon Shiraz Merlot South Australia Black Label 1986 • $25 • (05/31/93) • **90**
Cabernet Sauvignon Shiraz South Australia Bilyara Black Label 1992: Rich, ripe, round and warm, with a generous bead of spicy black cherry, chocolate and coffee flavors that swirl beautifully through the supple finish. Try now. 2,000 cases made. • $40 • (07/31/96) • **89**
Cabernet Sauvignon Shiraz South Australia Black Label 1987 • $26 • (08/31/94) • **87**
Cabernet Sauvignon South Australia President's Selection 1994: Earthy, gamy, eucalyptus nuances course through the overripe blackberry and anise flavors. A solid wine, but its flavors won't charm everyone. Try in 1999. 5,000 cases made. • $16 • (04/30/97) • **86**
Cabernet Sauvignon South Australia President's Selection 1993 • $16 • (06/15/96) • **87**
Cabernet Sauvignon South Australia President's Selection 1989 • $15 • (08/31/94) • **83**
Cabernet Sauvignon South Australia President's Selection 1987 • $15 • (05/31/93) • **85**
Cabernet Sauvignon South Australia President's Selection 1986 • $18 • (03/15/92) • **78**
Cabernet Sauvignon South Australia President's Selection 1983 • $14 • (04/30/88) • **76**
Cabernet Sauvignon South Australia Yellow Label 1996: Distinctly herbal, with minty, peppery character around a light core of pretty blackberry flavor. Drink now. 30,000 cases made. • $12 • (03/31/98) • **84**
Cabernet Sauvignon South Australia Yellow Label 1995: Fresh and focused, it's a spicy Cabernet that shows modest, ripe black cherry flavors, anise and tar notes. Drink now. 90,000 cases made. • $12 • (05/15/97) • **83**
Cabernet Sauvignon South Australia Yellow Label 1994 • $11 • (06/15/96) • **86**
Cabernet Sauvignon South Australia Yellow Label 1992 • $10 • (08/31/94) • **85**
Cabernet Sauvignon South Australia Yellow Label 1990 • $10 • (05/31/93) • **86**
Cabernet Sauvignon South Australia Yellow Label 1989 • $10 • (06/30/93) • **81**
Cabernet Sauvignon South Australia Yellow Label 1988 • $10 • (03/15/92) • **88**
Cabernet Sauvignon South Australia Yellow Label 1984 • $10 • (04/30/89) • **78**
Cabernet Sauvignon South Australia Yellow Label 1983 • $9 • (12/15/87) • **86**
Cabernet Shiraz Australia Black Label 1980 • $18 • (07/01/87) • **89**
Cabernet Shiraz Australia Yellow Label 1983 • $8 • (07/01/87) • **87**
Cabernet Shiraz Clare Barossa Valleys Black Label 1982 • $25 • (04/15/88) • **88**
Cabernet Shiraz Langhorne Creek 1981 • $18 • (07/01/87) • **90**
Chardonnay President's Selection McLaren Vale 1996: Smooth in texture, tangy in flavor, with zingy grapefruit, pear and floral flavors that linger on the crisp finish. Try now. 7,800 cases made. • $15 • (05/31/97) • **87**
Chardonnay President's Selection South Australia 1995 • $14 • (05/31/96) • **85**
Chardonnay President's Selection South Australia Bilyara Cellars 1994 • $13 • (03/31/95) HR • **91**
Chardonnay-Sémillon South Eastern Australia 1996: Ripe and generous, with pineapple and tropical fruit flavors and a smooth finish. 2,000 cases made. • $9 • (11/30/97) • **84**

Chardonnay South Australia 1997: Bright, youthful and simple, with a spicy edge to the green apple flavors. Best in 1999. 30,000 cases made. • $12 • (03/31/98) • **84**

Chardonnay South Australia 1996: Spicy, toasty flavors predominate in this crisp, medium-weight wine, with hints of green apple on the finish. Drink now. 15,000 cases made. • $11 • (04/30/97) • **84**

Chardonnay South Australia 1995 • $11 • (05/31/96) • **87**

Chardonnay South Australia Barrel Fermented 1993 • $10 • (09/30/94) • **82**

Grenache Clare Valley Old Vine Presidents Selection 1995: Bright, fresh and spicy, this is a jazzy mouthful of berry, mint and anise flavors that linger on the open-textured finish. Try now. 1,500 cases made. • $19 • (11/30/97) • **87**

Riesling South Australia Gold Label 1996: A dry and flavorful style, offering a marvelous array of citrus, apple, floral and apricot notes that spin smartly through the lively, just off-dry finish. This Aussie Riesling is delicious now, but try to wait until 2000 to 2001 to see what develops. 60,000 cases made. • $12 • (06/15/97) SS • **90**

Shiraz-Cabernet Sauvignon South Australia Red Label 1996: Smooth and spicy, with a nice, ripe currant note at the core, finishing with a wee bitterness on the otherwise supple finish. Drink now. • $NA • (03/31/98) • **85**

Shiraz-Cabernet Sauvignon South Australia Red Label 1995: Smooth, warm and rich with spicy plum flavors that are supple and inviting, though not deep. Ready now. 15,000 cases made. • $11 • (01/31/97) • **85**

Shiraz South Australia 1996: Has a lean, crisp style, offering a generous bead of blueberry and blackberry flavors that linger on the slightly peppery finish. Appealing now, best from 1999 through 2002. 10,000 cases made. • $12 • (05/15/98) • **87**

Shiraz South Australia President's Selection 1994: Generous with its spicy black cherry and toast flavors, it's smooth and nicely balanced in a non-aggressive style. Drink now. 3,000 cases made. • $16 • (04/30/97) • **86**

Shiraz South Australia President's Selection 1990 • $13 • (09/30/94) • **86**

Shiraz South Australia President's Selection 1988 • $15 • (05/31/93) • **85**

BLEASDALE

Cabernet Sauvignon Australia Langhorne Creek 1990 • $8 • (06/30/95) BB • **86**

Langhorne Creek White Burgundy Australia 1995 • $8 • (03/31/96) • **85**

Langhorne Creek White Burgundy Australia 1994 • $7 • (04/15/95) • **84**

Malbec Langhorne Creek 1992 • $8 • (03/31/96) • **80**

Shiraz Australia Langhorne Creek 1992 • $7 • (05/15/95) BB • **87**

Shiraz Cabernet Sauvignon Langhorne Creek 1992 • $8 • (03/31/96) • **87**

Shiraz Cabernet Sauvignon Langhorne Creek 1989 • $7 • (05/31/93) • **78**

Shiraz Langhorne Creek 1993 • $8 • (03/31/96) • **87**

Shiraz Langhorne Creek 1987 • $7 • (05/31/93) • **71**

Shiraz Langhorne Creek Bremerview 1994: Smooth and lively, with personality, showing bright red cherry and berry flavors on a velvety frame. Drinkable now. 65,000 cases made. • $11 • (06/15/97) • **85**

BLUE PYRENEES

Cabernet Sauvignon Australia 1982 • $20 • (05/31/87) • **89**

Chardonnay Victoria 1996: Elegant, supple, seductive and delicious, offering layers of pear, honey, spice and mineral flavors that keep swirling through the long finish. Drink now through at least 2000. 6,000 cases made. • $24 • (04/30/98) • **91**

Red Victoria Estate 1995: A distinctive mouthful of red wine, tart on balance, but with gobs of ripe black cherry and game flavors, and interesting hints of pepper on the finish. Best after 2000. A blend of 65 percent Cabernet Sauvignon, 16 percent Shiraz, 6 percent Cabernet Franc, 13 percent Merlot. 11,200 cases made. • $24 • (05/15/98) • **88**

Sparkling Australia Midnight Cuvée NV: Bright and refreshing, a lively sparkler, with pretty pear and vanilla flavors, hinting at citrus and cream on the finish. 376 cases made. • $26 • (05/31/98) • **87**

BOULDER OPAL

Chardonnay South Eastern Australia Malo-Oak 1996: Open-textured, and generous with its pear and spice flavors that linger pleasantly on the soft finish. Drinkable now. 5,000 cases made. • $13 • (09/15/97) • **86**

BOWEN ESTATE

Cabernet Sauvignon Coonawarra 1992 • $22 • (10/31/95) • **89**

Red Coonawarra 1992 • $22 • (10/31/95) • **89**

Shiraz Coonawarra 1995: Very crisp, even bordering on sour, with an earthy edge to the citrusy berry flavors. Could improve after 1999. 7,000 cases made. • $11 • (06/15/97) • **82**

BOYNTON'S OF BRIGHT

Sémillon Ovens Valley 1997: Fresh and fruity, generous with its spicy pear and melon flavors. Has a nice touch of honey on the finish. 1,000 cases made. • $16 • (05/15/98) • **85**

Shiraz Ovens Valley 1997: Polished and generous with its plum and berry flavors, this is an exuberant wine with lovely fruit that lingers on the gentle finish. 800 cases made. • $23 • (05/15/98) • **86**

BRANDS LAIRA

Cabernet Sauvignon Coonawarra 1991 • $13 • (09/30/94) • **84**

Cabernet Sauvignon Coonawarra Laira 1993 • $15 • (06/30/95) • **87**

Chardonnay Coonawarra 1994 • $15 • (04/30/96) • **91**

Chardonnay Coonawarra Laira 1993 • $15 • (04/15/95) • **83**

Shiraz Coonawarra 1994 • $15 • (04/30/96) • **90**

Shiraz Coonawarra 1992 • $15 • (06/30/95) • **84**

Shiraz Coonawarra 1990 • $13 • (10/31/93) • **86**

BRIAR RIDGE

Cabernet Sauvignon Hunter Valley 1996: Open-textured and straightforward, with cedary raspberry and spice flavors. 2,000 cases made. • $17 • (05/31/98) • **83**

Chardonnay Hunter Valley Hand Picked 1997: Bright and appealing for its straightforward, juicy nectarine and spice flavors. 3,000 cases made. • $17 • (05/31/98) • **85**

Shiraz Hunter Valley Old Vines 1996: Soft, smooth and generous with its plum, currant and rust flavors that linger with sharp focus on the finish. The texture could grow more plush with cellaring. 2,000 cases made. • $17 • (05/31/98) • **87**

BRIDGEWATER MILL

Shiraz McLaren Vale Millstone 1993 • $15 • (05/31/96) • **88**

BRIEN

Chardonnay-Gordo Victoria Family Selection 1996: Effusive with its brightly defined fruit character, oozing with nectarine, pear, apple and spice flavors that remain lively through the polished finish. Drinkable now. Gordo is an Aussie name for Muscat of Alexandria. • $11 • (04/30/98) • **86**

Shiraz-Cabernet Victoria Family Selection 1996: Flavors lean heavily toward earth and game in this light-textured, almost watery red. Fizzing, probably refermenting. Tasted twice, with consistent notes. • $14 • (04/30/98) • **71**

BROKE ESTATE

Cabernet Sauvignon-Franc Hunter Valley 1993 • $20 • (06/30/95) • **78**

Chardonnay Hunter Valley 1993 • $20 • (04/30/95) • **86**

BROKE FORDWICH

Chardonnay Hunter Valley 1997: Crisp in texture, with generous pear, vanilla and peach flavors that remain fresh through the solid finish. 10,000 cases made. • $12 • (06/15/98) • **86**

BROKENWOOD

Cabernet Sauvignon South Eastern Australia 1990 • $15 • (05/15/94) • **82**

Shiraz South Eastern Australia 1990 • $15 • (10/31/93) • **86**

BROWN BROTHERS

Cabernet Sauvignon King Valley Family Selection 1991 • $10 • (06/30/94) • **80**

Cabernet Sauvignon Victoria 1987 • $9 • (07/15/90) • **82**

Cabernet Sauvignon Victoria 1985 • $7 • (05/15/89) • **76**

Cabernet Sauvignon Victoria Family Selection Reserve 1988 • $17 • (04/30/95) • **88**

Cabernet Sauvignon Victoria Reserve 1987 • $12 • (09/15/90) • **83**

Cabernet Sauvignon Victoria St.-George Vineyard 1984 • $8 • (05/31/87) • **86**
Everton Family Selection Cabernet Blend King Valley 1992 • $9 • (06/30/95) • **85**
Everton Family Selection Cabernet Blend Victoria 1990 • $7 • (03/31/95) • **81**
Muscat Victoria Lexia Family Selection 1993 • $9 • (05/15/95) • **87**
Muscat of Alexandria Victoria Lexia 1987 • $8 • (07/31/90) • **73**
Muscat of Alexandria Victoria Lexia 1986 • $8 • (05/15/89) • **77**
Pinot Noir Victoria 1983 • $9 • (07/01/87) • **83**
Port Victoria 1987 • $13 • (07/31/90) • **84**
Port Victoria Family Selection Wood Matured Reserve NV • $8 • (03/31/95) BB • **86**
Sauvignon Blanc King Valley Family Selection 1993 • $10 • (01/31/95) • **83**
Shiraz Australia 1983 • $9 • (07/15/87) • **92**
Shiraz Cabernet Sauvignon Victoria 1988 • $9 • (05/31/93) • **83**
Shiraz King Valley Family Selection 1991 • $9 • (09/30/94) • **85**
Shiraz Mondeuse Cabernet Sauvignon Australia 1983 • $10 • (07/01/87) • **87**
Shiraz Victoria 1990 • $9 • (05/31/93) • **82**
Shiraz Victoria 1986 • $8 • (07/15/90) • **85**
Shiraz Victoria 1985 • $7 • (05/15/89) BB • **83**
Tarrango Victoria 1993 • $8 • (01/31/95) • **83**

BROWNS' OF PADTHAWAY

Cabernet Sauvignon Padthaway Family Reserve 1995: Soft and toasty, generous with its ripe berry, anise and smoke flavors. Finishes smooth and appealing at this stage. 1,000 cases made. • $19 • (05/31/98) • **87**
Shiraz Padthaway T-Trellis 1995: Light and spicy, with a modest level of plum and cherry notes that finish with a hint of pickle-barrel flavor. 1,000 cases made. • $19 • (05/15/98) • **85**

BULLER & SON, R.L.

Cabernet-Shiraz North West Victoria The Magee 1995: A vegetable-juice character intrudes on the ripe black cherry flavors of this richly textured wine. Not for everyone. 25,000 cases made. • $10 • (01/01/97) • **78**

BULLETIN PLACE

Cabernet Sauvignon Australia 1994: A serious wine with layers of ripe cherry, coffee, spice and raspberry flavors gliding smoothly through the finish on a supple frame. Delicious now, perhaps best after 2000. • $10 • (10/31/97) • **87**
Chardonnay Australia 1996: Has some intensity behind its spicy pear flavors, picking up floral and resinlike nuances on the jazzy finish. Drinkable now. • $10 • (10/31/97) • **87**
Shiraz Australia 1995: Ripe and generous, with appealing cherry and currant flavors that linger gently. Modestly built, has elegance and grace. Try now. • $10 • (10/31/97) • **87**

CAPE MENTELLE

Cabernet Sauvignon Margaret River 1993: Herbal, vegetal flavors shoulder past the rustic black cherry flavors in this rough-textured red. 200 cases made. • $24 • (05/31/98) • **85**
Cabernet Sauvignon Margaret River 1992 • $20 • (06/15/96) • **83**
Cabernet Sauvignon Margaret River 1991 • $19 • (10/31/95) • **77**
Cabernet Sauvignon Margaret River 1988 • $19 • (06/30/92) • **79**
Cabernet Sauvignon Western Australia 1987 • $19 • (03/31/91) • **84**
Chardonnay Margaret River 1996: Big, ripe and forward, with layers of pear and mineral flavors that are harmonious and distinctive. Not your typical Chardonnay, but one with personality. 250 cases made. • $23 • (05/31/98) • **88**
Chardonnay Margaret River 1994: Ripe and spicy, showing all the richness and flavor of barrel fermentation along with touches of lime and pear. A bit heavy-handed about it, but loaded with flavor. Drink now. • $20 • (05/15/97) • **86**
Chardonnay Margaret River 1993 • $19 • (06/30/95) • **87**

Key: SS—Spectator Selection. CS—Cellar Selection. BB—Best Buy. HR—Highly Recommended. $NA—Price not available. (BT)—Barrel tasting. Ⓐ—Auction Price.
Dates in parentheses represent the issues in which the ratings were published.

Shiraz Margaret River 1994: Tight, and more than a little green in flavor. A chewy wine with only a bit of plummy, anise-scented fruit flavors to brighten it up. Try in 2000. • $15 • (10/31/96) • **83**
Shiraz Margaret River 1992 • $15 • (10/31/95) • **85**
Shiraz Margaret River 1989 • $15 • (05/31/92) • **84**
Shiraz Margaret River 1988 • $15 • (02/28/91) • **88**

CAPEL VALE

Chardonnay Western Australia 1995 • $14 • (03/31/96) • **87**
Shiraz Western Australia 1994 • $14 • (03/31/96) • **84**
Shiraz Western Australia 1990 • $11 • (05/31/93) • **70**

CASSEGRAIN

Cabernet Sauvignon Hunter Valley Vintage Selection 1990 • $16 • (06/30/94) • **87**
Cabernet Sauvignon Merlot Hastings River 1996: Light and supple, with pretty currant and spice flavors that linger on the soft finish. 1,800 cases made. • $15 • (05/31/98) • **85**
Cabernet Sauvignon Merlot South Eastern Australia 1988 • $15 • (08/31/92) • **86**
Cabernet Sauvignon Pokolbin 1986 • $18 • (03/31/91) • **83**
Cabernet Sauvignon Shiraz Merlot Hastings River 1997: A solid red, offering black cherry and spice flavors on a rustic frame. 3,300 cases made. • $13 • (05/31/98) • **82**
Cabernet Sauvignon Shiraz Merlot South Eastern Australia 1991 • $8 • (11/30/93) • **77**
Cabernet Sauvignon Shiraz Merlot South Eastern Australia 1988 • $8 • (09/30/91) • **69**
Chambourcin Hastings Valley 1993 • $13 • (01/31/95) • **82**
Chambourcin New South Wales 1992 • $12 • (04/30/94) • **83**
Chambourcin South Eastern Australia 1990 • $12 • (02/15/92) • **77**
Chardonnay Hastings Valley 1994 • $16 • (04/15/95) • **86**
Chardonnay Hastings Valley 1993 • $16 • (01/31/95) SS • **91**
Pinot Noir Hastings River Cellar Selection 1997: Youthful, with berry-centered aromas and flavors and a firm texture. Vibrant, with welcome persistence on the finish. 1,300 cases made. • $15 • (05/31/98) • **87**
Pinot Noir Hastings River Reserve 1997: Firm in texture, with a spicy, tobacco-scented complexity surrounding the chewy black currant and berry flavors. Needs time. 500 cases made. • $20 • (05/31/98) • **88**
Pinot Noir New South Wales Morrillon Vineyard 1988 • $20 • (02/29/92) • **80**
Sémillon New South Wales Black Label 1993 • $16 • (06/30/95) • **85**
Shiraz Hastings River 1997: A youthful, bright wine with pretty raspberry and blackberry notes. Finishes with a light touch of spice. 900 cases made. • $15 • (05/31/98) • **83**
Shiraz Hastings Valley 1993 • $16 • (03/31/95) • **88**
Shiraz Hunter Valley Foundation 1989 • $11 • (05/31/93) • **75**
Shiraz Hunter Valley Vintage Selection 1983 • $18 • (05/31/93) • **72**
Shiraz New South Wales Black Label 1993 • $16 • (03/31/95) • **86**
Shiraz Pokolbin Leonard Select Vineyard 1987 • $20 • (03/15/91) • **87**
Shiraz South Eastern Australia 1988 • $13 • (02/15/92) • **77**
Shiraz South Eastern Australia Black Label 1989 • $16 • (03/31/94) • **82**

CEDAR CREEK

Cabernet Sauvignon South Eastern Australia Bin 99 1994 • $11/1.5 liter • (04/30/96) • **72**
Cabernet Sauvignon South Eastern Australia Bin 99 1992 • $6 • (09/30/94) • **78**
Cabernet Sauvignon South Eastern Australia Bin 99 1990 • $6 • (03/31/93) BB • **82**
Chardonnay South Eastern Australia Bin 33 1995 • $7 • (03/31/96) • **80**
Chardonnay South Eastern Australia Bin 33 1993 • $6 • (09/30/94) • **77**
Sémillon Blend South Eastern Australia Bin 11 1994 • $6 • (03/31/96) • **81**
Shiraz-Cabernet South Eastern Australia 1997: A firm-textured red with pretty flavors, offering cherry tones with a foxy accent. 70 percent Shiraz, 30 percent Cabernet Sauvignon. 20,000 cases made. • $10 • (05/31/98) • **83**
Shiraz-Cabernet South Eastern Australia Bin 21 1995 • $10/1.5 liter • (04/30/96) • **75**
Shiraz-Cabernet South Eastern Australia Bin 21 1991 • $5 • (09/30/94) • **79**
Shiraz-Merlot South Eastern Australia 1997: Light in texture, with modest tobacco-scented berry flavors. 85 percent Shiraz, 15 percent Merlot. 20,000 cases made. • $10 • (05/31/98) • **82**

Shiraz South Eastern Australia 1997: Light and smooth, with plum flavors, but an earthy streak keeps it from being as charming as it could be. 20,000 cases made. • $10 • (05/31/98) • **81**

CHAIN OF PONDS

Cabernet Sauvignon Adelaide Hills Amadeus 1994: Ripe in flavor and generous in style. A soft, almost plush red with marvelous black cherry, currant and smoke flavors that linger on the slightly chewy finish. Best from 2000. • $25 • (04/30/98) • **89**
Chardonnay Adelaide Hills 1994: Ripe, spicy and lightly honeyed; already mature-tasting, finishing smooth and with good balance. Drink now. • $23 • (04/30/98) • **85**
Grenache-Sangiovese Adelaide Hills Novello Rosso 1997: Soft and refreshing for its distinctive strawberry and spice flavors that linger on the gently fading finish. Blush style. Really tastes of Grenache and Sangiovese. • $12 • (05/15/98) • **86**

CHAMBERS

Muscat Rutherglen Rosewood Vineyards NV: Rich and spicy, it's a tower of nut, coffee and black cherry flavors that keep building upon one another, finishing explosively with more cherry, caramel and coffee notes on the long finish. 300 cases imported. • $13/375ml • (09/15/97) • **92**
Muscat Rutherglen Rosewood Vineyards Rare NV: Powerful, spicy and imposing, it's a dark, brooding, grand wine with a decadent edge to the sweet coffee, sassafras, bay leaf and dark cherry flavors that persist through the smoky, caramel-scented finish. Very long and powerful, but drink in small doses. 25 cases imported. • $130/375ml • (09/15/97) • **94**
Muscat Rutherglen Rosewood Vineyards Special NV: Incredibly intense, rich and smoky, with black cherry, clove, cola and anise flavors in profusion. Long and redolent of tar and smoke on the sweet finish. 100 cases imported. • $45/375ml • (09/15/97) • **95**
Tokay Rutherglen Rosewood Vineyards NV: Sweet and rich, its core of walnut flavors gaining complexity with exotic spice and orange peel overtones, finishing sweet and smoky, with a sense of elegance. 300 cases imported. • $13/375ml • (09/15/97) • **90**
Tokay Rutherglen Rosewood Vineyards Rare NV: Has the color of blackstrap molasses, kind of smells like it, too, but the texture and balance are so elegant and refined that the flavors play out like a peacock's tail opening. Smoky prune, molasses and raspberry swirl around the nucleus, with orbits of thyme, hazelnut, walnut and coffee skittering around. Sensational. 130 cases imported. • $130/375ml • (09/15/97) HR • **98**
Tokay Rutherglen Rosewood Vineyards Special NV: Satiny and silky, with sweet, rich textures and deep flavors of smoky, hazelnut-scented black plum with overtones of exotic spices. Hints at dark chocolate on the creamy finish. 100 cases imported. • $60/375ml • (09/15/97) • **95**

CHAPEL HILL

Shiraz McLaren Vale 1994: Rich and ripe, this is bursting with delicious Shiraz flavors, dripping with plum, blackberry and anise notes that keep throbbing through a mouthfilling finish. Approachable now, likely best from 2000. • $20 • (05/15/97) • **91**

CHATEAU REYNELLA

Cabernet Merlot McLaren Vale 1990 • $8 • (09/30/94) • **79**
Cabernet Merlot McLaren Vale Basket Pressed 1995: Bright, tight and remarkably well focused, brimming with currant, plum and berry flavors that remain sharp and jazzy through the finish. Nice now. 5,000 cases made. • $25 • (03/31/98) • **88**
Cabernet Merlot McLaren Vale Basket Pressed 1993 • $10 • (03/31/96) • **86**
Cabernet Merlot McLaren Vale Basket Pressed 1992 • $10 • (12/15/95) BB • **87**
Cabernet Sauvignon Coonawarra 1988 • $8 • (04/30/91) • **86**
Cabernet Sauvignon Coonawarra 1984 • $7 • (04/30/88) • **80**
Cabernet Sauvignon Coonawarra 1980 • $15 • (05/31/87) • **84**
Cabernet Sauvignon McLaren Vale Basket Pressed 1995: Ripe and generous, with flavors centering around currant and mint. Strongly herbal on the finish. 3,000 cases made. • $22 • (05/31/98) • **86**
Cabernet Sauvignon McLaren Vale 1994 • $12 • (06/30/96) • **88**
Cabernet Sauvignon McLaren Vale Basket Pressed 1993 • $12 • (03/31/96) • **85**
Cabernet Sauvignon McLaren Vale Basket Pressed 1992 • $10 • (06/30/95) • **86**
Cabernet Sauvignon McLaren Vale Basket Pressed 1991 • $8 • (07/31/94) BB • **84**
Cabernet Sauvignon McLaren Vale Basket Pressed 1990 • $9 • (05/15/94) • **82**
Chardonnay McLaren Vale 1996: A supple, delicious example of ripe, straightforward Chardonnay, offering a pretty range of pineapple, pear and spice flavors that linger gently on the finish, echoing spice and honey. 5,000 cases made. • $12 • (05/31/98) HR • **90**
Chardonnay McLaren Vale 1994 • $10 • (03/31/96) • **88**
Chardonnay McLaren Vale 1993 • $8 • (09/30/94) • **84**
Port McLaren Vale Museum Release 1981: Ripe and spicy, this sweet, supple Port plays out its vanilla-scented plum, blackberry and tar flavors with elegance. Could use a bit more grip, but it should be fine through 2010 to 2020. 1,500 cases made. • $15 • (05/31/97) • **93**
Port South Australia 1981 • $12 • (11/15/91) • **85**
Shiraz McLaren Vale Basket Pressed 1995: Smooth and nicely focused to show off the pretty plum and berry flavors. Chewy enough on the finish to want some time in the cellar. 3,000 cases made. • $22 • (05/31/98) • **88**
Shiraz McLaren Vale Basket Pressed 1994 • $12 • (06/30/96) HR • **92**
Shiraz McLaren Vale Basket Pressed 1993 • $10 • (03/31/96) • **86**
Shiraz McLaren Vale Basket Pressed 1991 • $8 • (09/30/94) • **81**
Tawny Port McLaren Vale Old Cave NV: Very sweet, almost syrupy, with lots of caramel and coffee flavors, finishing with elegance and a nice hint of berry flavor. 4,000 cases made. • $15 • (05/31/97) • **90**
Vintage Port McLaren Vale 1992 • $13 • (06/30/95) • **79**

CHATEAU TAHBILK

Cabernet Sauvignon Goulburn Valley 1993: In a soft, earthy style that centers around a nice core of berry flavor, with leather and spice notes around the edges. Best from 1999 to 2002. • $14 • (12/31/96) • **85**
Cabernet Sauvignon Goulburn Valley 1992: A solid red, though not much about it that says Cabernet. A bit chewy, but shows enough tarry berry flavors to make it worth cellaring until 2002 to 2005. • $14 • (08/31/96) • **85**
Cabernet Sauvignon Goulburn Valley 1990 • $11 • (06/15/94) • **83**
Cabernet Sauvignon Goulburn Valley 1989 • $12 • (11/30/92) • **83**
Cabernet Sauvignon Goulburn Valley 1988 • $12 • (03/31/91) • **87**
Cabernet Sauvignon Goulburn Valley 1987 • $11 • (07/31/90) • **89**
Cabernet Sauvignon Goulburn Valley 1986 • $10 • (03/31/89) • **88**
Cabernet Sauvignon Goulburn Valley 1984 • $7 • (11/15/87) • **81**
Cabernet Sauvignon Victoria 1990 • $11 • (06/30/93) • **78**
Chardonnay Goulburn Valley 1994: Spicy, toasty, nutty flavors dominate this medium-weight, slightly resiny white. Drink now. • $14 • (08/31/96) • **83**
Marsanne Goulburn Valley 1995: Fresh and tangy, with lively citrus and pear flavors. A hint of rose petal on the silky finish. • $11 • (08/31/96) • **84**
Marsanne Goulburn Valley 1993 • $10 • (04/15/95) BB • **87**
Shiraz 1988 • $10 • (02/15/92) • **82**
Shiraz Goulburn Valley 1993: A rustic style, earthy and spicy, with modest orange peel and leather flavors that barely fill it out. Try in 1999. • $14 • (12/31/96) • **82**
Shiraz Goulburn Valley 1992: Earthy and chewy. Packing enough berry, anise and spice flavor to warrant cellaring until the modest but hard tannins subside—see what develops around 2000 to 2005. • $14 • (08/31/96) • **86**
Shiraz Goulburn Valley 1991 • $10 • (06/15/94) • **84**
Shiraz Goulburn Valley 1989 • $11 • (11/30/92) • **73**
Shiraz Goulburn Valley 1987 • $11 • (03/15/91) • **87**
Shiraz Goulburn Valley 1984 • $6 • (11/15/87) • **77**
Shiraz Victoria 1990 • $10 • (05/31/93) • **84**
Shiraz Victoria 1986 • $10 • (03/31/89) • **88**

CHITTERING

Cabernet Sauvignon Merlot Western Australia 1988 • $18 • (09/30/91) • **79**

CIMICKY, CHARLES

Barossa Valley Red 1995: Deliciously smooth and spicy. A lovely mouthful of cherry, raspberry, cinnamon and coffee flavors that swirl delicately through the spicy finish. Appealing now, but feels like it might deepen by 2000 or 2001. A blend of Cabernet Sauvignon, Merlot and Cabernet Franc. 500 cases made. • $20 • (03/31/98) • **91**
Shiraz Barossa Valley Signature 1995: Ripe, round and spicy, with the plum-pudding flavors that characterize Barossa Shiraz, finishing with chewy tannins and a hint of oak to balance the medium-weight blackberry and cherry flavors. 1,500 cases made. • $NA • (05/15/98) • **88**

Shiraz Barossa Valley Signature 1994: Ripe and just a bit gamy in character, with distinctive black cherry and anise flavors that stay smooth and silky through the lingering finish. Drink now. 7,000 cases made. • $16 • (05/31/97) • **88**

CLANCY'S

Red Barossa Valley Gold Preference 1992 • $16 • (04/30/96) • **86**

CLARENDON HILLS

Chardonnay Clarendon Kangarilla Vineyard 1996: Spicy, earthy flavors dominate this hard-edged Chardonnay; the fruit character feels raw and rough now. Try in 2000. Tasted twice, with consistent notes. 300 cases made. • $37 • (04/30/98) • **79**

Grenache Australia Old Vines 1994: Reminiscent of Châteauneuf-du-Pape, this is spicy up front and redolent of blackberry, mint and smoke flavors that knock around exuberantly on the finish. Drink now. • $25 • (12/15/96) • **90**

Grenache Clarendon Blewitt Springs Vineyard 1995: Dense and spicy, with gobs of nutmeg- and clove-scented plum, blackberry and raspberry flavors that slink through the finish. Never loses its sense of balance despite a layer of chewy tannins and a spicy whack of oak on the finish. Approachable now, best from 2000. 375 cases made. • $28 • (05/31/97) • **92**

Grenache Clarendon Blewitt Springs Vineyard Old Vines 1996: Very dark and dense, with gobs of boysenberry, anise and smoke flavors that swirl through the biting tannins on the finish. Promises big things when it matures, after 2000 or 2002. 600 cases made. • $34 • (04/30/98) • **88**

Grenache Clarendon Clarendon Vineyard Old Vines 1995: A dramatic wine, lean in structure but packed with spice, black cherry and leather flavors that just don't quit on the long finish. Try now. 475 cases made. • $28 • (06/15/97) • **89**

Grenache Clarendon Kangarilla Vineyard Old Vines 1996: Bright, jazzy, a mouthfilling red packed with raspberry and spice flavors that linger on the solid finish. Nice now with hearty food, best from 2000. 600 cases made. • $34 • (04/30/98) • **88**

Merlot Clarendon 1995: Supple in texture, but chewy, with fine tannins supporting the pure blueberry, plum and mineral flavors that become increasingly exotic with each sip and echo long on the finish. Tempting now, but best from 2000. 400 cases made. • $35 • (05/31/97) • **91**

Shiraz Clarendon 1996: Dense and chewy. A solid mouthful of berry flavor with tough, chewy tannins earmarking it for the cellar. Give it until 2001 to 2003 to see what that anise note on the finish develops into. 600 cases made. • $38 • (04/30/98) • **87**

Shiraz Clarendon 1995: Dense and unusually Rhône-like for an Aussie Shiraz, with plenty of earth, leather and gamelike overtones to the supple core of black cherry and dark plum flavors. Distinctive, somewhat unique, a wine of great style and character. Best from 2000. 800 cases made. • $33 • (06/15/97) • **92**

Shiraz Clarendon Astralis 1996: A huge mouthful of plum, blackberry and blueberry flavors on a supple, elegant frame. Doesn't quite have the grandeur of the '95, but it's beautifully balanced to show off its pretty mint, cedar and spice nuances. Delicious now, it feels like it should develop through 2002. 450 cases made. • $125 • (04/30/98) • **92**

Shiraz Clarendon Astralis 1995: Deep, dark and juicy, this is a dense wine with crisp acidity to balance the solid blackberry, spice and hints of dill on the jazzy finish. Has a distinctive personality and impressive length—there's nothing else quite like it. Best from 1999. 450 cases made. • $120 • (06/15/97) • **95**

CLEVELAND

Pinot Noir Australia Macedon Ranges 1996: Light in flavor and texture, this finishes with nice hints of plum and mint. Drink now. • $18 • (04/30/98) • **81**

CLYDE PARK

Cabernet Sauvignon Geelong 1984 • $15 • (03/15/88) • **79**

Key: SS—Spectator Selection. CS—Cellar Selection. BB—Best Buy. HR—Highly Recommended. $NA—Price not available. (BT)—Barrel tasting. Ⓐ—Auction Price.
Dates in parentheses represent the issues in which the ratings were published.

COCKATOO RIDGE

Cabernet Blend South Eastern Australia 1994 • $9 • (03/31/96) • **82**

Cabernet Merlot South Eastern Australia 1995: A nice, light red wine with modest cedar notes to complement the basic berry flavors. Has a raw edge. Drink now. • $9 • (12/31/97) • **81**

Cabernet Merlot South Eastern Australia 1993 • $7 • (10/15/95) • **84**

Cabernet Merlot South Eastern Australia 1992 • $6 • (05/15/94) BB • **84**

Cabernet Merlot South Eastern Australia 1990 • $7 • (06/30/92) BB • **82**

Chardonnay South Eastern Australia 1996: Fresh and appealing for its straightforward pear and melon flavors, finishing with a hint of mineral. Drink now. • $9 • (06/30/97) • **85**

Chardonnay South Eastern Australia 1995: Soft and round, enlivened by a little spiciness. A pleasant, polished wine for early drinking. • $9 • (11/30/96) • **81**

Chardonnay South Eastern Australia 1994 • $9 • (03/31/96) • **82**

Chardonnay South Eastern Australia 1993 • $6 • (03/15/94) • **80**

Grenache-Shiraz South Eastern Australia 1996: This interesting red from Down Under is light in color and texture, but lively and seductive in flavor, layering its raspberry, strawberry, plum and spice flavors on a silky frame. It's a very good value, and it's ready to drink. 20,000 cases made. • $9 • (12/31/97) BB • **86**

COLDRIDGE

Sémillon Chardonnay South Eastern Australia 1993 • $6 • (09/30/94) • **78**

Shiraz Cabernet South Eastern Australia 1994 • $7 • (06/30/95) • **82**

Shiraz Cabernet South Eastern Australia 1993 • $6 • (06/15/94) • **80**

Shiraz Cabernet South Eastern Australia 1992 • $6 • (10/31/93) BB • **82**

Shiraz Cabernet Victoria 1989 • $6 • (08/31/92) BB • **81**

COLDSTREAM HILLS

Cabernet Sauvignon Lilydale 1987 • $20 • (01/31/90) • **84**

Pinot Noir Yarra Valley 1992 • $15 • (04/30/94) • **88**

CORIOLE

Cabernet-Merlot McLaren Vale Mary Kathleen 1995: Earthy, gamy notes add a little extra personality to the basic currant and plum flavors, finishing with a solid feel of firm tannins. 67 percent Cabernet Sauvignon, 22 percent Merlot, 11 percent Cabernet Franc. 500 cases made. • $44 • (05/31/98) • **86**

Cabernet Sauvignon McLaren Vale 1994: Lean, focused and spicy, centered around anise-scented blackberry flavors, with mint and a hint of raisin on the finish. The texture is silky, making it approachable now, but it should improve through 2001. 4,000 cases made. • $20 • (04/30/97) • **90**

Cabernet Sauvignon McLaren Vale 1993 • $20 • (04/30/96) • **89**

Chardonnay McLaren Vale 1996: A solid white, with pretty peach and floral flavors that linger on the generous finish. Ready to drink. 500 cases made. • $20 • (10/31/97) • **87**

Grenache McLaren Vale Lalla Rookh Old Vines 1996: Ripe, rich and chewy with blackberry and cola flavors that linger on the earthy finish. 200 cases made. • $24 • (05/15/98) • **86**

Redstone McLaren Vale Red 1995: Packs a lot of flavor onto a taut frame—lots of blackberry, anise, pepper and earth flavors. Has a layer of scratchy tannins that needs until 2000 to 2001 to soften. A blend of Syrah, Cabernet Sauvignon and Grenache. 1,500 cases made. • $17 • (09/30/97) • **88**

Redstone McLaren Vale Shiraz-Cabernet 1994: 5,000 cases made. • $17 • (02/28/97) • **89**

Redstone McLaren Vale Shiraz-Cabernet 1993 • $15 • (04/30/96) • **87**

Sangiovese McLaren Vale 1994 • $16 • (04/30/96) • **86**

Sémillon-Sauvignon Blanc McLaren Vale 1997: Has the distinctive fig and tobacco flavors of Sémillon on a crisp frame, harmonious and persistent on the lean finish. 70 percent Sémillon, 30 percent Sauvignon Blanc. 1,000 cases made. • $17 • (05/15/98) • **86**

Sémillon-Sauvignon Blanc McLaren Vale 1996: Firm in texture, a bit chewy, with modest peach, tobacco and spice flavors. Ready to drink. 800 cases made. • $17 • (10/31/97) • **83**

Sémillon-Sauvignon Blanc McLaren Vale 1994 • $14 • (04/30/96) • **87**

Shiraz McLaren Vale 1996: A pretty red, with focused blackberry, plum and black pepper flavors, finishing with a layer of fine tannins. 2,000 cases made. • $25 • (05/15/98) • **87**

Shiraz McLaren Vale 1995: Crisp and brightly focused around a core of blackberry and plum flavor, which keeps sailing smoothly through the well-rounded finish. Silky, and ready now, but could improve through 2000 to 2001. 2,500 cases made. • $20 • (09/30/97) • **91**

Shiraz McLaren Vale 1994: Has a wild, almost animal edge to its ripe cherry and dusky spice flavors, a bit tannic and rough at this stage. May be best from 1999 to 2001. 5,000 cases made. • $20 • (02/28/97) • **88**

Shiraz McLaren Vale 1993 • $20 • (04/30/96) • **87**

Shiraz McLaren Vale Lloyd Reserve 1993: Ripe and generous with its spicy plum, black cherry and anise aromas and flavors. A mouthfilling wine that never gets heavy or syrupy, just focused and bright with character. Appealing now for its youthful vigor, but best from 2000 to 2001. 500 cases made. • $36 • (02/28/97) • **92**

COWRA

Cabernet Sauvignon New South Wales 1988 • $10 • (03/31/93) • **62**

CRANSWICK

Cabernet Sauvignon Riverina 1991 • $8 • (06/15/94) • **82**

Sémillon-Chardonnay South Eastern Australia 1995: Pleasantly round in the mouth, and fruity, with a hazelnut accent to the pear flavors. • $8 • (10/31/96) • **83**

Shiraz-Cabernet South Eastern Australia 1995: Lean and tart, with beefy flavors and barnyard aromas that never quite get revved up. • $8 • (10/31/96) • **78**

Shiraz-Cabernet South Eastern Australia 1990 • $7 • (05/31/93) • **82**

Shiraz-Merlot South Eastern Australia 1995: Light, smooth and brightly fruity, with lots of berry and currant flavors singing through the finish. Drinkable now. 10,000 cases made. • $8 • (11/30/96) • **83**

Shiraz-Merlot South Eastern Australia 1990 • $7 • (04/15/93) • **80**

CRITTENDEN, GARRY

Barbera Victoria 1996: Packed with jazzy berry flavors, definitely on the tart side. Hints at mint on the crisp finish, which echoes the berry notes. Tasty now, perhaps best from 1999 or 2000. 500 cases made. • $19 • (04/30/98) • **87**

I Riserva Red King Valley 1995: Crisp and bright, with simple berry flavors and hints of citrus at the edges. A blend of 80 percent Nebbiolo and 20 percent Barbera. 480 cases made. • $18 • (05/31/97) • **82**

Sangiovese Victoria 1996: Earthy, gamy flavors are most prominent in this firm-textured red, folding in just enough berry flavor to make things pleasant on the finish. 200 cases made. • $19 • (05/15/98) • **82**

CULLEN

Cabernet-Merlot Margaret River 1995: Open-textured and generous, focusing on ripe raspberry and cherry flavors on a supple frame. Cedary, herbal flavors become prominent on the finish. Firm now. • $40 • (05/15/98) • **88**

Cabernet-Merlot Margaret River 1985 • $15 • (11/15/87) • **87**

Chardonnay Margaret River 1996: Crisp, bright and lively. A pretty wine with layers of spice and cream seeping in on the finish. Feels light but has plenty of apple and pear flavors, with a finish that lasts and lasts. Best from 1999. • $30 • (05/15/98) • **89**

Chardonnay Margaret River 1995: Beautifully proportioned, harmonious and smooth, with rich pear, honey and sage flavors that swirl nicely through the finish. 56 cases made. • $30 • (10/15/97) • **90**

Sauvignon Blanc-Sémillon Margaret River Reserve 1996: Bright and bracing, snappy with grapefruit and quince flavors, with a touch of herb on the crisp finish. Try now. 50 percent Sauvignon Blanc, 50 percent Sémillon. • $30 • (05/15/98) • **88**

DALFARRAS

Cabernet Sauvignon Australia 1989 • $8 • (09/30/93) • **77**

DALWHINNIE

Cabernet Sauvignon Victoria 1994: Lean and spicy, a toasty wine with a sense of elegance but not much richness or flavor. Try in 2000. • $40 • (02/28/97) • **84**

Chardonnay Victoria 1996: A jazzy mouthful of citrus, passion fruit and honey-hazelnut flavors that swirl and linger on the polished finish, this has style and harmony and promises to be just lovely by 1999. • $39 • (04/30/98) • **91**

Chardonnay Victoria 1994: Ripe, buttery and redolent of tropical fruit flavors, particularly a touch of banana, that may not appeal to everyone. Has a distinctive spicy-caramel note on the finish. A big, complex wine. Drink now. • $35 • (02/28/97) • **87**

Shiraz Victoria 1994: An elegant red with distinct floral, almost violet-tinged, plum and anise flavors that wrap around a velvety, supple structure. Has length and character, just needs time to develop it all. Best from 2001 to 2003. 700 cases made. • $42 • (02/28/97) • **90**

D'ARENBERG

Cabernet Sauvignon McLaren Vale Coppermine Road 1995: Nicely articulated blackberry and currant flavors take on a lovely tinge of spice, cedar and just a hint of mint on the long, solid finish. Drinkable now. 100 cases made. • $40 • (07/31/97) • **88**

Cabernet Sauvignon McLaren Vale The High Trellis 1995: Ripe and generous, with a bit of earthy character to make the raspberry and red plum flavors more interesting. Nicely shaped, harmonious and supple. • $15 • (05/15/98) • **87**

Cabernet Sauvignon McLaren Vale The High Trellis 1994: Crisp and bright, with pleasant black raspberry and currant flavors. Its fine-grained tannins might benefit from cellaring until 1999 to 2000. 200 cases made. • $15 • (07/31/97) • **87**

Cabernet Sauvignon McLaren Vale The High Trellis 1989 • $8 • (07/15/93) • **82**

Chambourcin McLaren Vale The Peppermint Paddock 1995: Ripe and jammy. Has raspberry flavors and a gamy streak that adds interest, if not charm. Drink now. 300 cases made. • $21 • (07/31/97) • **86**

Chardonnay McLaren Vale The Olive Grove 1996: Lean, bright and racy, with lots of pear and mineral flavors that linger on the finish. 1,200 cases made. • $15 • (07/31/97) • **88**

Chardonnay McLaren Vale The Otherside 1996: Distinctive. Crisp and spicy, with a modest character of nectarine and slate that finishes with a touch of tobacco. Drink now. 100 cases made. • $35 • (07/31/97) • **87**

Grenache McLaren Vale The Custodian 1996: A snazzy mouthful of red berry flavor, brimming with raspberry and red currant jamminess, finishing sturdy. Drink sooner rather than later. 500 cases made. • $21 • (07/31/97) • **86**

Grenache-Shiraz McLaren Vale Ironstone Pressings 1995: On the lighter side, but the nice mouthful of blackberry and black cherry flavors holds through the solid finish. Drink now. 200 cases made. • $25 • (07/31/97) • **87**

Grenache-Shiraz McLaren Vale Red Ochre 1996: Lithe, supple and generous in style, with appetizing notes of spicy, sage-scented black cherry and plum, this Australian red blend is packed with flavor, yet reined-in enough to qualify as charming. Well worth trying at this price and score. Enjoy now through 2001. A blend of 82 percent Grenache, 18 percent Shiraz. 3,000 cases imported. • $9 • (06/15/98) BB • **87**

Ironstone Pressings Australia Red 1991 • $15 • (01/31/95) • **87**

Ironstone Pressings McLaren Vale Red 1989 • $11 • (05/31/93) • **86**

Mourvèdre McLaren Vale The Twenty Eight Road 1996: Firm and flavorful, chewy in texture, with lovely black cherry and mineral flavors that linger on the generous finish. • $22 • (05/15/98) • **86**

Mourvèdre McLaren Vale The Twenty Eight Road 1995: A jazzy wine, with lots of wild berry and fragrant iris notes, finishing with some snappy spice tones. Drink now. 120 cases made. • $21 • (07/31/97) • **85**

Riesling Blend McLaren Vale White Ochre 1996: Bright and mouthfilling, a juicy wine with broad structure and plenty of green apple and floral flavors, plus a hint of mint on the finish. • $9 • (06/15/98) • **86**

Riesling McLaren Vale Noble 1996: Sweet but not syrupy, this is a rich mouthful of gorgeous pear, apricot, caramel, honey and floral flavors, echoing the floral and honey on the long finish. • $25/375ml • (05/31/98) • **91**

Shiraz Australia Old Vine 1990 • $11 • (03/31/95) • **75**

Shiraz-Grenache McLaren Vale d'Arry's Original 1995: Chock-full of smoky berry and black cherry flavors, this firm, focused wine delivers polished character. A bit resinous and oaky on the finish, try in 1999. 1,000 cases made. • $15 • (07/31/97) • **87**

Shiraz McLaren Vale Old Vine 1995: Brimming with beautifully focused black cherry and cola flavors that swirl and glide through the polished, satiny finish. Should gain elegance with cellaring until 1999 to 2000. 950 cases made. • $15 • (07/31/97) • **91**

Shiraz McLaren Vale Old Vine 1989 • $8 • (05/31/93) BB • **85**

Shiraz McLaren Vale The Dead Arm 1995: Firm, chewy, and packed with blackberry and anise flavors. However, the oak character and tannin clamp down a bit on the finish. Echoes tobacco and berry flavors. Give it until 2000. 200 cases made. • $50 • (07/31/97) • **92**

Tawny Port Australia Nostalgia Very Old NV • $16 • (03/31/95) • **83**

Vintage Port Australia 1987 • $16 • (03/31/95) • **85**

DE BORTOLI

Sémillon Australia Noble One 1993 • $28/375ml • (06/15/96) • **93**

DEAKIN

Chardonnay Victoria 1996: Ripe and generous on a lithe frame, offering smooth-textured pear and citrus flavors that linger nicely on the racy finish. Better in 1999. • $12 • (04/30/98) • **87**

Chardonnay Victoria Alfred 1996: Bright and refreshing. A lighter style of Chardonnay with pretty pear and spice flavors, grabbing a nip of acidity on the finish. Try now. • $15 • (04/30/98) • **86**

DEVIL'S LAIR

Margaret River Cabernet Blend 1995: Ripe and supple, almost plush in texture, with distinctly herbal, almost vegetal overtones to the rhubarb and black cherry flavors. Try now. A blend of Cabernet Sauvignon, Merlot and Cabernet Franc. 500 cases made. • $25 • (02/28/98) • **83**

Cabernet Sauvignon Margaret River 1992 • $20 • (10/15/95) • **82**

Chardonnay Margaret River 1996: Rich, ripe and gorgeously balanced, wrapped in a silky blanket of spice and vanilla, glowing from the core with pear, citrus and delicate pineapple notes that enrich and linger as they finish. Delicious now. 500 cases made. • $25 • (02/28/98) • **89**

Chardonnay Margaret River 1994 • $19 • (06/30/95) • **87**

Chardonnay Margaret River 1993 • $17 • (06/30/95) • **88**

DRAYTON'S

Cabernet Sauvignon Hunter Valley 1993 • $10 • (10/31/95) • **84**

Cabernet Sauvignon Hunter Valley 1991 • $10 • (09/30/94) • **79**

Chardonnay C-6 South Eastern Australia 1996: Simple and appealing for its nectarine flavors and spicy, toasty overtones that linger refreshingly. 12,000 cases made. • $8 • (04/30/97) • **85**

Chardonnay C-6 South Eastern Australia 1995 • $8 • (04/30/96) • **81**

Chardonnay C-6 Hunter Valley 1994 • $7 • (12/15/94) BB • **85**

Chardonnay C-6 Hunter Valley 1993 • $7 • (04/15/94) BB • **85**

Chardonnay Hunter Valley 1995 • $9 • (06/30/96) • **85**

Chardonnay Hunter Valley 1994 • $8 • (12/15/94) • **85**

Chardonnay Hunter Valley 1993 • $8 • (04/15/94) BB • **88**

Chardonnay South Eastern Australia 1996: Solid in texture and refreshing for its herbal pineapple and caramel flavors. 12,000 cases made. • $9 • (04/30/97) • **84**

Chardonnay South Eastern Australia 1995 • $9 • (04/30/96) • **85**

Port Australia Fine Old Pioneer NV • $10 • (03/31/95) • **82**

Sémillon Chardonnay Hunter Valley Oakey Creek 1994 • $7 • (10/15/95) • **85**

Sémillon Hunter Valley 1993 • $8 • (10/31/95) • **85**

Shiraz Cabernet Sauvignon Hunter Valley Oakey Creek 1993 • $7 • (06/15/94) • **82**

Shiraz Hunter Valley Bin 5555 1994 • $9 • (12/15/95) • **73**

Shiraz Hunter Valley Bin 5555 1990 • $10 • (04/15/94) • **82**

Shiraz Hunter Valley William 1991 • $23 • (10/31/95) • **83**

Shiraz Hunter Valley William 1989 • $30 • (09/30/94) • **85**

Shiraz S-5 South Eastern Australia 1996: Not a lot of fruit apparent for such a young wine, it's a bit rough and leathery. 8,000 cases made. • $7 • (04/30/97) • **79**

Shiraz S-5 South Eastern Australia 1995 • $7 • (04/30/96) • **84**

Shiraz S-5 Hunter Valley 1994 • $7 • (10/31/95) • **82**

Shiraz South Eastern Australia 1995: Light for a Shiraz, with simple berry and spice flavors. Drink now. 8,000 cases made. • $14 • (04/30/97) • **82**

Tawny Port Hunter Valley Old Log Press NV • $18 • (03/31/95) • **88**

Verdelho Hunter Valley 1995 • $10 • (03/31/96) • **86**

Verdelho Hunter Valley 1994 • $10 • (10/31/95) • **83**

Key: SS—Spectator Selection. CS—Cellar Selection. BB—Best Buy. HR—Highly Recommended. $NA—Price not available. (BT)—Barrel tasting. (A)—Auction Price.

Dates in parentheses represent the issues in which the ratings were published.

DROMANA

Chardonnay Mornington Peninsula Reserve 1995: Emphasizes spice and butter over fruit, then gets really zingy on the rich, complex finish. A distinctive wine with deep flavors and a bite of acidity on the finish. 160 cases made. • $36 • (04/30/98) • **87**

ELDERTON

Cabernet Sauvignon Merlot Barossa Valley 1984 • $11 • (04/30/88) • **86**

Cabernet Sauvignon Shiraz Merlot Barossa Valley 1995: Ripe, jammy and generous. A serious mouthful of black cherry, dried berry, chocolate, cedar and brown sugar flavors that linger on the finish, and at the same time show some restraint. 950 cases made. • $33 • (04/30/98) • **88**

Sémillon South Eastern Australia Golden 1996: Copper in color, but sweet and juicy, with bright apricot and melon flavors that start off with richness and finish with some length. Yummy. Drink now. • $18/375ml • (05/31/97) • **88**

Shiraz Barossa Valley 1995: Nicely proportioned, with a harmonious chorus of berry, black cherry, sweet anise and earth flavors. A bit raw with tannin on the finish, but just give this beauty until 1999 to 2000 to show all it has. • $20 • (06/15/97) • **91**

Shiraz Barossa Valley Command 1992: Rich, ripe and amazingly concentrated, this is almost explosive in the way it offers up its spicy blackberry, black cherry and dark plum flavors, shaded with fascinating nuances of licorice and herbs. • $34 • (12/15/96) • **94**

EVANS WINE COMPANY

Chardonnay Hunter Valley 1996: Ripe and juicy, almost racy with its zippy acidity, and beautifully balanced to show off pear, spice and melon flavors that linger enticingly on the polished finish. Try now. • $13 • (10/31/97) • **90**

Sémillon Hunter Valley 1997: Fresh and lively, with a light tobacco scent wafting through the pear and almond notes. Attractive now, hold until 2001 to 2003 to see what happens. • $12 • (03/31/98) • **86**

Shiraz South Eastern Australia 1996: Has a freshness and liveliness that lets its red cherry and blackberry flavor shine through the velvety, slightly chewy tannins—making this charming from start to finish. Drinkable now. • $15 • (11/15/97) • **88**

Verdelho Hunter Valley 1997: Fresh and appealing for its ripe melon and almond flavors. Drinkable now. • $12 • (03/31/98) • **84**

EVANS & TATE

Cabernet Merlot Barrique 61 Western Australia 1995: Has a distinctively herbal, greenish edge to the modest raspberry flavors, with a hint of cinnamon also. Drink now. 5,000 cases made. • $15 • (10/31/97) • **83**

Cabernet Merlot Barrique 61 Australia 1994 • $14 • (04/30/96) • **88**

Cabernet Sauvignon Margaret River 1991 • $14 • (11/15/93) • **82**

Chardonnay Margaret River 1996: Aims for restraint, packing plenty of green apple, spice and honey flavors into a focused, elegant package. Flavors linger enticingly on the finish. Has the stuff to improve with cellaring through 1999 to 2000. 500 cases made. • $28 • (11/30/97) • **90**

Chardonnay Two Vineyards Western Australia 1996: A solid Chardonnay, but it has a bite of earthy tobacco character that keeps the pretty pear and melon flavors from emerging as enticingly as they could. Drinkable now. 5,000 cases made. • $15 • (10/31/97) • **85**

Chardonnay Two Vineyards Australia 1995 • $14 • (04/30/96) • **86**

Chardonnay Two Vineyards Australia 1994 • $14 • (06/30/95) • **80**

Chardonnay Two Vineyards Western Australia 1993 • $14 • (03/15/94) • **81**

Merlot Australia Margaret River 1992 • $15 • (05/31/95) • **85**

Merlot Margaret River 1995: Showing lovely herb- and chocolate-scented berry flavors up front, this smooth-textured wine has extra tannins on the finish that nudge past the flavors. Best after 2000. 500 cases made. • $22 • (11/30/97) • **86**

Merlot Margaret River 1994: Minty, herbal, earthy flavors dominate the fruit in this simple, modest wine. • $16 • (08/31/96) • **79**

Merlot Margaret River 1992 • $15 • (09/30/94) • **82**

Merlot Margaret River 1991 • $16 • (04/30/94) • **70**

Merlot Margaret River 1990 • $15 • (12/15/93) • **82**

Sauvignon Blanc Western Australia 1995: Light, with a smooth frame. Citrusy herb flavors have a hint of mint. • $14 • (08/31/96) • **82**

Sémillon Sauvignon Blanc Margaret River Classic 1993 • $12 • (12/31/93) • **84**

Shiraz Cabernet Western Australia Gnangara 1992 • $12 • (03/31/94) • **82**
Shiraz Cabernet Western Australia Gnangara 1991 • $10 • (11/30/93) • **80**
Shiraz Gnangara Western Australia 1995: A lighter style of Shiraz, with pretty berry and beet flavors that linger gently on the soft finish. Nicely balanced. Drink now. 10,000 cases made. • $15 • (10/31/97) • **86**
Shiraz Gnangara Australia 1993 • $10 • (06/30/95) • **85**
Shiraz Margaret River Hermitage 1991 • $14 • (10/31/93) • **87**

FIFTH LEG

Margaret River Red 1996: Bright and supple. A smooth mouthful of blackberry and anise flavors that linger on the chewy finish. Best after 1999. A blend of Merlot, Cabernet Sauvignon and Shiraz. From Devil's Lair. 250 cases made. • $15 • (02/28/98) • **85**
Margaret River White 1997: Distinctly spicy and herbal, with a lovely core of generous pear and passion fruit flavor, finishing smooth and silky. Drink now. A blend of Chardonnay, Sémillon and Sauvignon Blanc. 640 cases made. • $15 • (03/31/98) • **87**

FIVE MILE HOLLOW

Chardonnay Sémillon Sauvignon Blanc Australia 1993 • $10 • (07/31/94) • **84**
Red Hastings River 1994 • $12 • (04/30/96) • **80**
Red Hastings Valley 1993 • $12 • (05/31/95) • **85**
Sémillon Chardonnay Hastings River 1997: Rich, focused and sinewy, focusing its distinctive citrus, pineapple and earthy honey flavors. 65 percent Sémillon, 35 percent Chardonnay. 6,000 cases made. • $13 • (05/31/98) • **87**
Shiraz Cabernet Merlot Australia 1992 • $10 • (09/30/94) • **85**
White Hastings River 1995 • $12 • (04/30/96) • **82**
White Hastings Valley 1994 • $12 • (05/31/95) • **85**

FLAME OPAL

Chardonnay South Eastern Australia 1996: Fresh and appealing for its tropical fruit and pear flavors. 5,000 cases made. • $13 • (09/15/97) • **83**

FOUR SISTERS

Sauvignon Blanc-Sémillon South Eastern Australia 1996: Light and open-textured, with modest fig and apple flavors that soften on the finish. Drink now. • $14 • (04/30/98) • **83**

FOX CREEK

Chardonnay McLaren Vale Unwooded 1996: Ripe and spicy, soft in texture but not expansive, it's a tight wine with modest pear and apricot flavors. Drink now. 1,000 cases made. • $10 • (10/31/97) • **85**

FOX RIVER

Chardonnay Australia 1997: Fresh and simple, with pretty tropical fruit-cocktail flavors that remain refreshing on the finish. 3,000 cases made. • $12 • (06/15/98) • **84**
Classic Red Australia 1996: Firm in texture, nicely balanced to show off its ripe blackberry and blueberry flavors, hinting at tar and herbs on the lithe finish. A blend of Shiraz and Cabernet Sauvignon. 6,000 cases made. • $12 • (06/15/98) • **87**
Classic Red Western Australia 1995: Light, and herbal in character, with some nice plum notes at the center but little heft. A blend of Cabernet and Shiraz. 5,000 cases made. • $12 • (05/15/97) • **79**
Classic White Western Australia 1996: Crisp and resiny, with bright, citrus-accented pear and peach flavors weaving through the snappy finish. Drink now. A blend of Chardonnay, Sémillon and Riesling. 15,000 cases made. • $12 • (05/15/97) • **86**
Pinot Noir Western Australia 1997: So light you can read through it, with more tea and herb character than fruit on the slightly chewy finish. 2,500 cases made. • $12 • (06/15/98) • **80**

FRANKLAND

Olmo's Reward Red Western Australia 1994: Aims for elegance. A lean, lithe bundle of currant and plum flavors surrounded by hints of cedar, mint and spice, all nicely wrapped with gentle tannins. Smooth, with not-too-crisp acidity, it's approachable now but should improve through 2001 to 2004. A blend of Cabernet Franc, Merlot, Cabernet Sauvignon, Malbec, and Petit Verdot. 1,900 cases made. • $24 • (04/30/98) • **88**
Olmo's Reward Red Western Australia 1993: Shows tarry black cherry flavors with an earthy, gamy streak, finishing on the lighter side. Drinkable now. 1,500 cases made. • $20 • (06/15/97) • **84**
Riesling Western Australia 1996: Dry, with a pretty layer of spicy green apple and floral flavor that wraps around the soft core. Finishes with a nice touch of mineral. Drinkable now. 1,600 cases made. • $16 • (04/30/98) • **88**
Shiraz Western Australia Isolation Ridge 1995: Has a strong herb and tobacco current through the ripe black cherry flavors, a chewy texture and a bit more acidity than most Aussie Shirazes. Drink from 1999. 1,800 cases made. • $19 • (06/30/98) • **83**
Shiraz Western Australia Isolation Ridge 1994: Lean and juicy, a different kind of Shiraz with jazzy lime and other citrusy overtones to the berry and anise flavors. Best from 1999. 1,500 cases made. • $16 • (06/15/97) • **86**

GALLANT

Chardonnay Mornington Peninsula 1996: Light and aromatic, a delicate style that offers some attractive lime and floral flavors that linger on the lively finish. Drink now. 1,000 cases made. • $11 • (10/31/97) • **86**

GARRETT, ANDREW

Cabernet Blend Australia McLarens Red 1991 • $7 • (11/30/92) • **81**
Cabernet Merlot Australia French Oak Matured 1990 • $10 • (11/30/92) • **83**
Cabernet Merlot South Eastern Australia 1991 • $11 • (04/30/94) • **85**
Shiraz Australia Bold Style 1991 • $9 • (11/30/92) • **87**
Shiraz South Australia Clarendon Estate 1982 • $8 • (11/15/87) • **80**
Shiraz South Eastern Australia Black Shiraz 1992 • $10 • (03/31/94) • **81**

GLEESON'S RIDGE

Riesling Clare Valley 1996: Dry and refreshing for its bright, floral apple and pear flavors, which persist on the polished finish. Ready to drink. 500 cases made. • $14 • (03/31/98) • **87**

GOUNDREY

Cabernet-Merlot Mount Barker 1996: Lean in texture, generous with its herb-scented cherry and leather flavors. Approachable now; best from 2000 through 2005. 18,000 cases made. • $14 • (06/15/98) • **87**
Cabernet-Merlot Mount Barker 1995: A crisp, straightforward red, with tarry notes to complement the basic black cherry and citrus flavors. Drinkable now. 11,500 cases made. • $10 • (05/15/97) • **81**
Cabernet Sauvignon Mount Barker Reserve Selection 1995: Supple, minty, generous and dripping with flavor, layering sweet plum, berry and vanilla flavors, hinting at smoke and sage on the long, multilayered finish. Impressive now; best from 2000 through 2005. 1,700 cases made. • $24 • (06/15/98) • **90**
Chardonnay Mount Barker Reserve Selection 1997: Silky, polished and spicy, with lovely nutmeg-scented pear, peach and hazelnut flavors swirling through the artfully balanced finish. Shows plenty of depth and richness. 2,500 cases made. • $24 • (06/15/98) • **91**
Chardonnay Mount Barker Reserve Selection 1995: Appealing for its harmony and many layers of flavors and textures, this is delicious—ripe, spicy, smooth and generous with its honey-scented fig, nutmeg and raisin character. Drink now. 900 cases made. • $18 • (05/15/97) • **93**
Chardonnay Mount Barker Unwooded 1997: Lively and generous with its pear, apple and spice flavors, hinting at vanilla and peach on the long, amiable finish. Delicious fruit flavors make this wonderful already, so why wait? 70,000 cases made. • $14 • (06/15/98) • **88**
Chardonnay Mount Barker Unwooded 1996: From Australia comes this ready-to-drink white, fresh and lively, highlighted by jazzy passion fruit, apple and spice flavors that step gracefully around a silky core. Very nicely done, and there's enough of this reasonably priced wine to go around. 28,000 cases made. • $10 • (05/15/97) BB • **88**
Chenin Blanc Mount Barker 1997: Fresh and appealing, on the dry side, with pretty melon and apple flavors that keep shining on the bright finish. 10,000 cases made. • $14 • (06/15/98) • **87**
Merlot Mount Barker Reserve 1995: Mint and eucalyptus flavors meld with smoothly textured berry and spicy oak notes to create a distinctive wine with polish and class. Drink now. 700 cases made. • $25 • (05/15/97) • **86**

Riesling Mount Barker Late Picked 1996: Soft and round, with vanilla-scented pear flavors that linger on the subtle, slightly sweet finish. 1,000 cases made. • $14 • (06/15/98) • **87**

Riesling Mount Barker Reserve Selection 1997: Lots of floral, citrus and melon flavors make for a jazzy wine, dry and sprightly on the finish, echoing all the extra hints of peach, apricot and quince. 1,500 cases made. • $20 • (06/15/98) • **88**

Sauvignon Blanc Mount Barker Reserve 1996: Light in texture but bright in flavor, with plenty of fig, apricot, mineral and tobacco notes weaving through to the finish. 1,000 cases made. • $15 • (05/15/97) • **87**

Shiraz Mount Barker Reserve Selection 1996: Lean, with a pickle-barrel edge to the modest berry flavors. Folds in more herb flavors than do most Aussie Shirazes. 1,600 cases made. • $23 • (06/15/98) • **86**

Shiraz Mount Barker Reserve Selection 1995: Has a distinctive herbal streak running through plum and tobacco flavors on a moderate frame. Finishes with a bit of acidic bite. Try in 2000. 3,000 cases made. • $15 • (05/15/97) • **85**

GRANT SMITH LTD.

Shiraz Cabernet Riverina Valley Bin 95 Vintner's Reserve 1990 • $6 • (12/15/93) BB • **83**

Shiraz Merlot Riverina Bin 101 Vintner's Reserve 1990 • $6 • (04/15/94) BB • **85**

GREEN POINT

Blanc de Blanc Australia Cuvée 1992: Crisp and spicy, this sparkling wine has more delicacy than most, offering ginger, pear and toast flavors that linger on the finish. 50 cases made. • $30 • (09/30/97) • **89**

Blanc de Noir Australia Cuvée 1991: Earthy, toasty flavors weave through this crisp sparkling wine, but it picks up enough richness and finesse to spread on the finish. • $30 • (09/30/97) • **89**

Brut Australia 1994: Fresh, floral and generous pear and bright spice flavors, it then finishes creamily and with a touch of lemon. 600 cases made. • $30 • (07/31/97) • **87**

Brut Rosé Australia 1993: Pale salmon color, delicate rose-scented raspberry flavors and a nice mouthful of crisp, lemony tartness make this a bracing, charming example of rosé fizz. • $30 • (09/30/97) • **88**

Brut Rosé South Eastern Australia 1994: Copper-colored, with fresh, delicate plum and spice flavors that turn floral on the light finish. 100 cases made. • $30 • (07/31/97) • **86**

Chardonnay Yarra Valley 1996: Slick, polished and lithe, balancing its apricot, pear and mineral flavors on a compact frame, finishing generously. Best from 1999. 200 cases made. • $25 • (07/31/97) • **89**

GROSSET

Riesling Clare Valley Polish Hill 1997: Dry, with zingy grapefruit and apple sailing along through the lively finish. Exuberant now, should be stylish when it settles down, by 1999 or 2000. 2,800 cases made. • $21 • (04/30/98) • **89**

Riesling Clare Valley Polish Hill 1996: A technicolor, dry Riesling, this is bright and zingy, with layers of peach, mineral, pine and apple flavors that remain lively through the long finish and are just crisp enough to create a charming balance. Lovely now, better after 2000. 1,800 cases made. • $19 • (05/31/97) • **91**

HAMILTON, RICHARD

Cabernet Sauvignon Coonawarra Reserve 1994: Supple, generous and harmonious, following up its ripe plum, currant and vanilla flavors with some firm tannins on the finish. Best after 1999. • $21 • (11/15/96) • **88**

Chardonnay McLaren Vale 1996: Bright in flavor, with refreshing citrus and apple tones that linger on the lively finish. Nice now, may be better in 1999. • $18 • (04/30/98) • **86**

Grenache-Shiraz McLaren Vale Burton's Vineyard 1995: Going for power over finesse, this is rich, concentrated and spicy, a mouthful of raw fruit with exotic spice and herbal overtones. Best now to 2000. 750 cases made. • $15 • (02/28/97) • **87**

Key: SS—Spectator Selection. CS—Cellar Selection. BB—Best Buy. HR—Highly Recommended. $NA—Price not available. (BT)—Barrel tasting. Ⓐ—Auction Price.
Dates in parentheses represent the issues in which the ratings were published.

Grenache-Shiraz McLaren Vale Burton's Vineyard 1994: Light and effusively fruity, offering plenty of blackberry, cherry and cola flavors that linger on the finish, where they pick up a smoky note. Try now. 700 cases made. • $12 • (10/31/96) • **87**

Merlot McLaren Vale Reserve 1996: Loaded with personality, lean and crisp, with juicy currant flavor gliding through tight tannins and sharp acidity. One for the cellar; could become more friendly by 2000. • $24 • (04/30/98) • **86**

Shiraz McLaren Vale Old Vine Reserve 1995: Feels youthful and tart, with a range of berry, anise and game flavors running through. Drinkable now. 1,500 cases made. • $23 • (02/28/97) • **86**

HANWOOD

Cabernet Sauvignon Australia 1993 • $8 • (06/30/95) • **81**
Cabernet Sauvignon South Eastern Australia 1994 • $7 • (04/30/96) • **83**
Chardonnay Australia 1993 • $8 • (06/30/95) • **84**
Chardonnay South Eastern Australia 1995 • $7 • (04/30/96) • **84**
Sémillon Chardonnay Australia 1993 • $6 • (10/15/95) BB • **86**
Shiraz South Eastern Australia 1994 • $7 • (04/30/96) • **81**

HAPPS

Shiraz Margaret River 1990 • $11 • (03/31/94) • **83**

HARDYS

Cabernet Malbec Reynella McLaren Vale Collection No. 9 1984 • $6 • (07/15/88) • **76**

Cabernet Sauvignon Coonawarra 1995: Has plenty of ripe blackberry and currant flavors up front, hinting at anise and smoke on the softening finish. 4,000 cases made. • $18 • (05/31/98) • **86**

Cabernet Sauvignon Coonawarra 1994: Packs in some delicious currant, tar and cedar flavors, is generous but not overwhelmingly so, and finishes with a green accent. Tasty now, but the tannins want until 1999 to 2000. 12,500 cases made. • $11 • (10/15/96) HR • **88**

Cabernet Sauvignon Coonawarra 1993 • $11 • (03/31/96) • **86**
Cabernet Sauvignon Coonawarra 1992 • $10 • (06/30/95) BB • **87**
Cabernet Sauvignon Coonawarra 1987 • $11 • (07/15/90) • **81**
Cabernet Sauvignon Coonawarra Collection 1990 • $10 • (06/30/94) BB • **88**
Cabernet Sauvignon Coonawarra Regional Collection 1992 • $10 • (08/31/94) BB • **89**
Cabernet Sauvignon Coonawarra Regional Collection 1991 • $10 • (06/30/94) • **84**

Cabernet Sauvignon Coonawarra Thomas Hardy 1993: Showing maturity, with some pleasant cherry and mint flavors at the core, this supple wine has velvety tannins and a touch of cedar on the narrowing finish. 1,000 cases made. • $50 • (05/31/98) • **87**

Cabernet Sauvignon Coonawarra Thomas Hardy 1992: Bright, with pinpoint-focus, this juicy mouthful of plum, blackberry and mint flavors remains jazzy and exquisitely balanced through the very long finish. Harmonious and polished, it should be best after 2000. 1,000 cases made. • $45 • (05/31/97) • **92**

Cabernet Sauvignon Coonawarra Thomas Hardy 1991 • $20 • (03/31/96) • **89**
Cabernet Sauvignon Coonawarra Thomas Hardy 1989 • $27 • (03/31/95) • **88**
Cabernet Sauvignon Keppoch 1986 • $7 • (07/15/90) • **79**
Cabernet Sauvignon Keppoch 1985 • $7 • (10/31/88) • **80**
Cabernet Sauvignon Keppoch Bird Series 1985 • $6 • (09/30/88) BB • **81**
Cabernet Sauvignon McLaren Vale Captain's Selection 1985 • $4 • (07/15/88) • **75**
Cabernet Sauvignon McLaren Vale Collection No. 8 1986 • $11 • (01/31/89) • **76**
Cabernet Sauvignon Shiraz South Eastern Australia Bird Series 1990 • $7 • (05/15/94) • **82**
Cabernet Sauvignon South Australia Bird Series 1988 • $8 • (03/15/92) BB • **83**
Cabernet Sauvignon South Australia Collection 1989 • $12 • (05/31/93) • **83**
Cabernet Sauvignon South Australia Collection 1988 • $10 • (02/15/91) • **83**
Cabernet Sauvignon South Australia Nottage Hill 1989 • $8 • (11/30/92) • **80**
Cabernet Sauvignon South Eastern Australia 1994 • $8 • (06/30/95) • **81**
Cabernet Sauvignon South Eastern Australia Nottage Hill 1992 • $7 • (07/31/94) • **82**
Cabernet Sauvignon South Eastern Australia Nottage Hill 1990 • $8 • (03/31/93) • **77**

Cabernet-Shiraz South Eastern Australia Nottage Hill 1996: Light in texture, with ripe raspberry and anise flavors that finish with some polish. 30,000 cases made. • $7 • (06/15/98) • **83**

Cabernet-Shiraz South Eastern Australia Nottage Hill 1995: Smooth, silky and simple, with appealing berry flavors that linger nicely on the finish. 25,000 cases made. • $7 • (05/15/97) • **84**

Cabernet-Shiraz South Eastern Australia Nottage Hill 1994 • $7 • (04/30/96) • **86**

Cabernet-Shiraz South Eastern Australia Nottage Hill 1993 • $7 • (04/30/95) • **85**

Cabernet-Shiraz South Eastern Australia Signature 1995: Has a sweet, licoricelike edge to the bright blackberry and blueberry flavors. A crisp wine with pretty flavors that last on the finish. Best from 1999. 5,000 cases made. • $11 • (02/28/98) • **86**

Chardonnay Padthaway 1996: Supple, rich and generous with tropical fruit, melon, pear and spice flavors up front. Finishes a bit narrow. 4,000 cases made. • $11 • (06/15/98) • **86**

Chardonnay Padthaway 1995: A delicious Australian Chardonnay that folds its peach, melon, pear and spice flavors together with fine style and impressive length. 14,000 cases made. • $11 • (09/30/96) HR • **89**

Chardonnay Padthaway 1994 • $11 • (03/31/96) BB • **88**

Chardonnay Padthaway Eileen Hardy Yarra Valley Adelaide Hills 1995: Ripe and generous. An attractive mouthful of smooth-textured pineapple, honey and citrus flavors that pick up a touch of spicy oak on the long finish. Drinkable now. 3,000 cases made. • $24 • (04/30/97) • **89**

Chardonnay Padthaway Eileen Hardy Yarra Glen 1994 • $18 • (06/30/96) • **85**

Chardonnay Padthaway Eileen Hardy 1993 • $19 • (05/15/95) • **89**

Chardonnay South Eastern Australia 1994 • $8 • (06/30/95) • **82**

Chardonnay South Eastern Australia Bird Series 1993 • $9 • (09/30/94) • **83**

Chardonnay South Eastern Australia Nottage Hill 1997: Refreshing for its pretty nectarine and pear flavors, this is a simple wine with some flair on the light finish. 60,000 cases made. • $7 • (06/15/98) • **84**

Chardonnay South Eastern Australia Nottage Hill 1996: Fresh, zippy and bright with green apple and pear flavors. A hint of citrus balances a touch of spice on the finish. 250,000 cases made. • $7 • (12/31/96) BB • **84**

Chardonnay South Eastern Australia Nottage Hill 1995 • $7 • (03/31/96) BB • **84**

Chardonnay South Eastern Australia Nottage Hill 1994 • $7 • (06/30/95) BB • **84**

Chardonnay South Eastern Australia Nottage Hill 1993 • $7 • (03/31/95) BB • **83**

Chardonnay South Eastern Australia Signature 1997: Light and tangy, fruit-centered, with a bracing green pineapple edge to the pear and apple flavors. Try now. 5,000 cases made. • $9 • (02/28/98) • **87**

Merlot South Eastern Australia Nottage Hill 1996: This modest red has some pretty currant and berry flavors weaving through a slightly chewy texture. 30,000 cases made. • $7 • (06/15/98) • **83**

Merlot South Eastern Australia Nottage Hill 1994 • $8 • (03/31/96) • **85**

Merlot South Eastern Australia Nottage Hill 1993 • $7 • (05/31/95) BB • **86**

Port McLaren Vale 1983: Mature Port, with low-profile black cherry and anise flavors, a very soft grip, and leather-spice overtones on the finish. 900 cases made. • $14 • (06/15/98) • **86**

Premium Classic Dry Red McLaren Vale 1986 • $6 • (05/15/89) • **75**

Premium Classic Dry Red South Australia 1988 • $5 • (07/31/90) BB • **78**

Sémillon Chardonnay South Eastern Australia Captain's Selection 1993 • $7 • (09/30/94) • **74**

Sémillon Chardonnay South Eastern Australia Stamps of Australia 1993 • $6 • (09/30/94) • **78**

Shiraz Cabernet Sauvignon South Eastern Australia Bird Series 1991 • $10 • (09/30/94) • **83**

Shiraz Cabernet Sauvignon South Eastern Australia Captain's Selection 1993 • $6 • (09/30/94) • **83**

Shiraz Cabernet Sauvignon South Eastern Australia Captain's Selection 1992 • $7 • (09/30/94) • **76**

Shiraz Cabernet Sauvignon South Eastern Australia Captain's Selection 1991 • $6 • (05/31/93) BB • **84**

Shiraz Cabernet Sauvignon South Eastern Australia Captain's Selection 1990 • $6 • (06/30/92) BB • **82**

Shiraz Cabernet Sauvignon South Eastern Australia Stamps of Australia 1993 • $7 • (09/30/94) • **81**

Shiraz Cabernet Sauvignon South Eastern Australia Stamps of Australia 1992 • $6 • (09/30/94) • **82**

Shiraz McLaren Vale 1987 • $7 • (07/15/90) BB • **87**

Shiraz McLaren Vale 1986 • $7 • (12/31/88) BB • **89**

Shiraz McLaren Vale Bird Series 1991 • $7 • (04/15/94) BB • **84**

Shiraz McLaren Vale Bird Series 1990 • $7 • (05/31/93) • **80**

Shiraz McLaren Vale Bird Series 1988 • $7 • (09/30/91) BB • **84**

Shiraz McLaren Vale Padthaway Bird Series 1984 • $5 • (07/15/88) • **79**

Shiraz McLaren Vale Padthaway Clare Valley Eileen Hardy 1994: Beautifully proportioned, dense and dark, showing layer upon layer of flavor, with black cherry, blackberry and spice, and hints of cedar on the finish. Should be best from 1999. 1,000 cases made. • $45 • (05/31/97) • **90**

Shiraz McLaren Vale Padthaway Clare Valley Eileen Hardy 1993 • $20 • (04/30/96) • **94**

Shiraz South Australia Eileen Hardy 1992 • $20 • (05/15/95) • **87**

Shiraz South Australia Eileen Hardy 1990 • $20 • (03/31/94) • **86**

Shiraz South Australia Eileen Hardy 1989 • $20 • (05/31/93) • **84**

Shiraz South Australia Eileen Hardy 1988 • $19 • (02/15/92) HR • **91**

Shiraz South Eastern Australia Nottage Hill 1995: Simple and refreshing for its mineral and tobacco-scented berry flavors, finishing smoothly. 20,000 cases made. • $7 • (05/15/97) • **82**

Shiraz South Eastern Australia Nottage Hill 1994: Delivers a rich, spicy nose and bright cherry flavors, then veers off into a tart finish and slightly drying tannins. 11,000 cases made. • $7 • (10/15/96) • **82**

Shiraz South Eastern Australia Nottage Hill 1993 • $7 • (11/15/95) • **82**

Sparkling Shiraz Australia NV: Sparkling Shiraz is an Aussie specialty that hasn't been exported much, but the spicy berry and anise flavors taste fine as fizz. Try with cheeses. 1,500 cases made. • $19 • (11/30/97) • **86**

Tawny Port Australia Tall Ships NV • $10 • (03/31/95) • **86**

Tawny Port South Australia Whiskers Blake NV: Succulent and smooth, this tremendously complex tawny is layered with caramel, walnut, coffee, almond and orange peel flavors, long, elegant and spicy in the mouth. 5,000 cases made. • $13 • (05/31/97) HR • **94**

Vintage Port Australia 1983 • $15 • (06/30/95) • **73**

Vintage Port Australia 1982 • $15 • (03/31/95) • **85**

HARVARD

Shiraz Cabernet South Eastern Australia 1990 • $6 • (05/31/93) • **78**

HASELGROVE

Cabernet-Merlot-Shiraz McLaren Vale 1996: Firm in texture, with nicely focused black cherry and tobacco flavors that linger on the finish. A bit chewy. A blend of 68 percent Cabernet Sauvignon, 22 percent Merlot, and 10 percent Shiraz. 3,100 cases made. • $16 • (05/31/98) • **86**

Cabernet Sauvignon South Eastern Australia Sovereign 1996: Soft and generous with its bright raspberry and currant flavors, finishing with a supple feel. 9,000 cases made. • $10 • (05/31/98) • **85**

Chardonnay McLaren Vale 1997: Fresh and appealing for its nectarine and melon flavors, lightly accented with spicy oak. 2,000 cases made. • $13 • (05/15/98) • **86**

Chardonnay McLaren Vale H Reserve 1996: A beguiling mouthful of pear, pineapple and spicy oak flavors that lingers through the long and generous finish. Best from 1999. 300 cases made. • $15 • (05/15/98) • **88**

Chardonnay South Eastern Australia Sovereign 1997: Fresh and fruity, with pineapple and spice flavors on a medium frame. 20,000 cases made. • $9 • (05/15/98) • **84**

Grenache South Eastern Australia Sovereign 1996: Light and smooth, here's a gentle wine with spicy raspberry and chocolate flavors that linger on the soft finish. 5,000 cases made. • $10 • (05/15/98) • **84**

Sauvignon Blanc McLaren Vale 1997: Bright in flavor, with open-textured pear, green melon and herb flavors that linger on the tobacco-scented finish. 2,150 cases made. • $13 • (05/15/98) • **86**

Shiraz McLaren Vale H Garnet SG-4 NV: Dark purple in color, with lots of spice and pepper flavors popping through the soft, slightly sweet berry flavors on the finish. A very interesting wine. 650 cases made. • $20 • (05/31/98) • **86**

Shiraz McLaren Vale H Reserve 1996: A huge mouthful of spice and fruit flavors. Marked by lots of oak aromas and flavors, it also has a solid core of ripe black cherry and black currant flavor for it all to wrap around. Drink now. 1,600 cases made. • $29 • (05/31/98) HR • **92**

Shiraz South Australia Sovereign 1997: Supple and generous, with spicy black cherry and berry flavors shaded with hints of smoke and vanilla. Best from 1999 through 2001. 4,000 cases made. • $10 • (05/15/98) • **87**

HAWTHORN HILL

Merlot South Eastern Australia Bin 8000 1990 • $7 • (11/30/92) • **78**

Shiraz South Eastern Australia Bin 5000 1990 • $7 • (11/30/92) BB • **85**

HEGGIES

Cabernet Blend Cabernets 1985 • $15 • (03/31/93) • **84**
Chardonnay Eden Valley 1996: Soft and ripe, with pretty fig and honey notes around the modest core of pear flavor. • $15 • (06/15/98) • **84**
Chardonnay Eden Valley 1994 • $15 • (05/15/96) • **90**
Merlot Eden Valley 1993: A solid red wine. Chewy with tannin but not exactly packed with flavor. Try now or hold. • $15 • (05/31/97) • **85**
Merlot Eden Valley 1992 • $16 • (06/30/96) • **80**
Rhine Riesling Late Harvest Barossa Valley Botrytis Affected 1986 • $8/375ml • (02/15/88) • **92**
Riesling Eden Valley Botrytis 1997: Very sweet, silky-smooth and satiny. A lush mouthful of pear, floral, vanilla and honey flavors that glide smoothly and effortlessly through the polished finish. 1,000 cases made. • $16/375ml • (06/15/98) • **94**
Riesling Eden Valley Botrytis 1996: Remarkable for its harmony, this weaves together floral, apricot and honey flavors, juicy sweetness and balancing acidity. Flavors linger gracefully on the finish, echoing sweet fruit. Just delicious. 1,000 cases made. • $14/375ml • (05/31/97) • **92**
Riesling Eden Valley Botrytis Affected 1995: Rich in flavor. Plenty of honey, apricot and spice flavors, the sweetness firmly supported by tangy acidity, all extending into a long, fat finish. Drinkable now. 1,000 cases made. • $15 • (10/31/96) • **90**
Viognier Eden Valley 1994 • $15 • (09/30/95) • **86**

HENSCHKE

Cabernet Blend Keyneton Estate 1988 • $14 • (06/30/92) • **82**
Cabernet Blend Keyneton Estate 1985 • $12 • (03/31/89) • **79**
Cabernet Blend Keyneton Estate 1984 • $12 • (02/15/88) • **85**
Cabernet Sauvignon Eden Valley Cyril Henschke 1994: Very ripe and concentrated, dense and sharply focused, its blackberry-scented currant, plum and tar flavors swirl through the deep finish. Delicious now. • $49 • (06/15/98) • **92**
Cabernet Sauvignon Eden Valley Cyril Henschke 1993: Smooth, ripe and complex with coffee, spice and cinnamon overtones to the minty black cherry and ripe currant flavors, rich and round on the smoky finish. Loaded with personality, it has enough finely grained tannins to want cellaring until 2000 to 2004. • $66 • (05/31/97) • **94**
Cabernet Sauvignon Eden Valley Cyril Henschke 1992 • $36 • (04/30/96) • **92**
Cabernet Sauvignon Eden Valley Cyril Henschke 1990 • $28 • (08/31/94) • **84**
Cabernet Sauvignon Eden Valley Cyril Henschke 1989 • $23 • (05/31/93) • **86**
Cabernet Sauvignon Keyneton Cyril Henschke 1991 • $35 • (06/15/95) CS • **92**
Cabernet Sauvignon Keyneton Cyril Henschke 1988 • $23 • (06/30/92) • **85**
Cabernet Sauvignon Keyneton Cyril Henschke 1986 • $23 • (09/15/89) • **91**
Cabernet Sauvignon Keyneton Cyril Henschke 1985 • $21 • (01/31/89) • **90**
Cabernet Sauvignon Keyneton Cyril Henschke 1984 • $19 • (12/15/87) • **94**
Chardonnay Eden Valley Barossa Ranges 1997: Bright and flavorsome. A lithe wine with pretty pineapple and apple flavors that linger on the gentle finish. • $25 • (06/15/98) • **86**
Johann's Garden Barossa Valley 1996: Chewy texture, friendly wine, with generous berry and plum flavors that echo nicely and pick up an overlay of earthy spice on the finish. A blend of 80 percent Bush Vine Grenache, 10 percent Mourvèdre and 10 percent Shiraz. • $30 • (06/15/98) • **87**
Riesling Eden Valley Julius 1996: Fresh and floral, with almond-accented, light melon flavors, stylish and graceful. Drinkable now. • $18 • (05/31/97) • **88**
Sémillon Eden Valley Louis 1997: Fresh and youthful, with some pretty pineapple and citrus flavors, finishing with a hint of bitterness. • $23 • (06/15/98) • **84**
Sémillon Eden Valley Louis 1996: Bright and spicy, with hints of honey and oatmeal sneaking in between the citrus and pineapple flavors. Balanced, it's drinkable now but could improve through 1999 to 2000. • $21 • (05/31/97) • **87**
Sémillon Eden Valley Louis 1995 • $17 • (03/31/96) • **87**
Sémillon Eden Valley Matured in French Oak 1994 • $11 • (10/31/95) • **77**

Key: SS—Spectator Selection. CS—Cellar Selection. BB—Best Buy. HR—Highly Recommended. $NA—Price not available. (BT)—Barrel tasting. (A)—Auction Price.
Dates in parentheses represent the issues in which the ratings were published.

Shiraz Cabernet Malbec Australia Keyneton Estate 1992 • $19 • (06/15/95) • **86**
Shiraz Cabernet Malbec Australia Keyneton Estate 1991 • $12 • (08/31/94) • **85**
Shiraz Cabernet Malbec Eden Valley/Barossa Valley Keyneton Estate 1994: Smooth and elegant, with a rich core of bright berry and plum flavors that pick up hints of spice and cedar on the long, supple finish. The fine tannins can use cellaring until 2000. A blend of 75 percent Shiraz, 15 percent Cabernet Sauvignon, and 10 percent Malbec. • $30 • (05/31/97) • **91**
Shiraz Cabernet Malbec Eden Valley/Barossa Valley Keyneton Estate 1993 • $22 • (03/31/96) HR • **93**
Shiraz Cabernet Merlot Eden Valley/Barossa Valley Keyneton Estate 1995: Ripe and generous, dripping with spice, blackberry, blueberry and plum flavors, echoing anise and pepper on the raw finish. • $36 • (06/15/98) • **87**
Shiraz Eden Valley Mount Edelstone Vineyard 1995: Feel the depth, feel the elegance, taste the lovely range of ripe plum, prune, anise, black cherry and spice flavors that linger with real style and grace in this Australian red. Delicious now, at its best from 2000 through 2010. 500 cases made. • $56 • (06/15/98) HR • **93**
Shiraz Keyneton Estate 1989 • $14 • (05/31/93) • **83**
Shiraz Keyneton Hill of Grace 1992: Earthy, almost decadent-tasting, but there are plenty of ripe plum, prune and black cherry flavors to accompany the gamy streak and hints of black pepper in this distinctive wine. Impressive now, better in 2000 or 2002. • $107 • (11/15/97) • **94**
Shiraz Keyneton Hill of Grace 1991 • $65 • (06/30/95) • **91**
Shiraz Keyneton Hill of Grace 1989 • $31 • (05/31/93) • **91**
Shiraz Keyneton Hill of Grace 1988 • $27 • (05/31/92) • **88**
Shiraz Keyneton Hill of Grace 1987 • $27 • (05/31/92) CS • **91**
Shiraz Keyneton Hill of Grace 1986 • $26 • (09/30/89) • **87**
Shiraz Keyneton Mount Edelstone 1994: Ripe and rich, offering plenty of blackberry, pepper and anise flavors that remain vibrant through the finish. The tannins have some bite to them, so best to cellar into 1999. • $48 • (11/15/97) • **89**
Shiraz Keyneton Mount Edelstone 1993 • $34 • (03/31/96) CS • **96**
Shiraz Keyneton Mount Edelstone 1992 • $30 • (06/15/95) SS • **91**
Shiraz Keyneton Mount Edelstone 1991 • $18 • (09/30/94) • **87**
Shiraz Keyneton Mount Edelstone 1990 • $17 • (05/31/93) • **84**
Shiraz Keyneton Mount Edelstone 1989 • $17 • (05/31/92) • **88**
Shiraz Keyneton Mount Edelstone 1988 • $17 • (05/31/92) HR • **90**
Shiraz Keyneton Mount Edelstone 1987 • $17 • (05/31/91) • **86**
Shiraz Keyneton Mount Edelstone 1986 • $17 • (10/31/89) HR • **90**
Shiraz Keyneton Mount Edelstone 1985 • $15 • (03/31/89) • **81**
Shiraz Keyneton Mount Edelstone 1984 • $14 • (02/15/88) • **90**

HERITAGE

Sémillon Barossa Valley Steve Hoff 1994: The crisp texture lets the pineapple and tobacco flavors emerge brightly on the finish. Perhaps best after 1999. 5,500 cases made. • $10 • (05/31/97) • **84**

HERMITAGE ROAD

Chardonnay Hunter Valley Reserve 1996: Ripe, spicy and rich in texture, with flavors that lean strongly to the woody side. Finishes with a nice touch of honey. Try now. 1,000 cases made. • $16 • (11/15/97) • **86**
Chardonnay South Eastern Australia 1996: Light, fruity, fresh and distinctive. Has a pleasant apricot quality to the green apple flavor, and it lasts on the finish. Drink now. 4,000 cases made. • $11 • (11/15/97) • **88**
Shiraz South Eastern Australia 1997: Bright, jazzy and tasty. A lush-textured mouthful of currant and raspberry flavor that lingers on the smooth finish. Yummy now, so why wait? • $10 • (05/15/98) • **87**

HIGHBANK

Red Coonawarra Basket Pressed 1996: Soft and ripe, with a strong spicy streak running through the berry flavors. Firms up as gentle tannins sweep through the finish. Give it until 2000 to 2002. A blend of Cabernet Sauvignon, Merlot and Cabernet Franc. 800 cases made. • $38 • (04/30/98) • **86**

HILL-SMITH ESTATE

Cabernet Sauvignon Barossa Valley 1984 • $9 • (08/31/87) • **75**
Cabernet Sauvignon Barossa Valley 1981 • $9 • (07/16/86) • **82**

Cabernet-Shiraz Adelaide Hills Terra Rossa Block 1988 • $11 • (11/30/92) • **81**

Cabernet-Shiraz Eden Valley Terra Rossa Block 1994: A bright mouthful of jazzy flavors, centering around black plum, chocolate, vanilla and spice, finishing with supple intensity and more spice notes. Drink now. • $12 • (05/15/97) • **86**

Cabernet-Shiraz Eden Valley Terra Rossa Block 1992 • $12 • (05/15/96) • **87**

Chardonnay Eden Valley Air-Strip Block 1994 • $12 • (05/15/96) • **89**

Sauvignon Blanc Eden Valley Air-Strip Block 1996: Crisp and refreshing, with a core of grapefruit flavor and bright, grassy, green apple overtones. Drink now. 1,000 cases made. • $12 • (11/30/96) • **87**

Sémillon Chenin Blanc Varietal White Barossa Valley 1984 • $4 • (11/15/86) BB • **78**

Sémillon Late Harvest Barossa Valley Autumn Harvest Botrytis 1986 • $10/375ml • (03/15/89) • **84**

Sémillon Late Harvest Barossa Valley Autumn Harvest Botrytis 1985 • $8/375ml • (02/15/88) • **88**

Sémillon Late Harvest Barossa Valley Autumn Harvest Botrytis 1983 • $8/375ml • (08/31/86) • **84**

Shiraz Barossa Valley 1986 • $9 • (02/28/91) BB • **86**

Shiraz Barossa Valley 1984 • $6 • (05/15/87) • **82**

Varietal Red Barossa Valley 1985 • $4 • (01/31/88) • **75**

HILLSTOWE

Chardonnay Adelaide Hills Udy's Mill 1995: Distinctively smooth, ripe and spicy, with pretty nutmeg, pepper and smoke notes to color the lively pear and citrus flavors. Beautifully balanced to drink now. 2,100 cases made. • $20 • (02/28/98) • **88**

Chardonnay Adelaide Hills Udy's Mill 1994: Crisp, focused and on the lean side. Delicately floral, with a resiny peach flavor that lingers. Drink now. • $22 • (08/31/96) • **87**

Chardonnay McLaren Vale Buxton 1995: Inauspiciously dark, this has more spice and toast than fruit flavor; fades on the finish. 3,800 cases made. • $12 • (03/31/98) • **79**

Merlot-Cabernet McLaren Vale Buxton 1994: Light, almost tart, with a layer of ripe currant and blackberry flavor wrapped around a tight core of spice and zingy acidity. Appealing now. 2,400 cases made. • $15 • (03/31/98) • **86**

Pinot Noir Adelaide Hills 1991 • $15 • (06/30/93) • **88**

Pinot Noir Adelaide Hills Udy's Mill 1994: Light, soft and pretty. A lovely mouthful of delicate berry, cherry and toast flavors that linger gently on the supple finish. Drinkable now. 900 cases made. • $19 • (03/31/98) • **86**

Pinot Noir Yarra Valley 1992 • $21 • (07/31/94) • **83**

Shiraz McLaren Vale Buxton 1994: Bursting with delicious berry, black cherry and spice flavors, this lushly aromatic Shiraz goes for liveliness over smoothness. Give it until 1999 to soften. 300 cases made. • $20 • (03/31/98) • **87**

HOUGHTON

Cabernet Sauvignon Frankland River Wildflower Ridge 1988 • $9 • (07/15/91) • **78**

Cabernet Sauvignon Western Australia Wildflower Ridge 1992 • $8 • (10/31/95) BB • **88**

Cabernet Sauvignon Western Australia Wildflower Ridge 1991 • $7 • (09/30/94) • **82**

Cabernet Sauvignon Western Australia Wildflower Ridge 1990 • $7 • (09/30/94) • **82**

Cabernet Shiraz McLaren Vale Wildflower Ridge 1985 • $9 • (12/31/88) • **88**

Chardonnay Western Australia Wildflower Ridge 1995: Simple, fruity and spicy, with an appealing freshness. 3,000 cases made. • $8 • (07/31/96) • **81**

Chardonnay Western Australia Wildflower Ridge 1993 • $7 • (09/30/94) • **74**

Shiraz McLaren Vale Wildflower Ridge 1985 • $9 • (12/31/88) • **88**

Shiraz Western Australia Wildflower Ridge 1994 • $8 • (06/30/96) • **85**

Shiraz Western Australia Wildflower Ridge 1993 • $8 • (10/31/95) • **84**

Shiraz Western Australia Wildflower Ridge 1991 • $7 • (06/15/94) BB • **84**

Shiraz Western Australia Wildflower Ridge 1990 • $9 • (05/31/93) • **84**

Shiraz Western Australia Wildflower Ridge 1989 • $9 • (11/30/92) • **83**

White Burgundy Western Australia 1993 • $6 • (09/30/94) • **77**

HOWARD PARK

Cabernet M Western Australia 1994: Dark and ripe, with herbal berry and black cherry flavors that wrap smoothly around the fine-grained tannins on the generous finish. Approachable now. • $48 • (06/15/97) • **87**

Chardonnay Western Australia 1995: A powerfully focused wine that fills the mouth with pear, peach, spice and mineral flavors that linger enticingly on the finish. Ripe and generous, it has remarkable depth and harmony already, but should be best from 1999 or 2000. 1,100 cases made. • $28 • (04/30/97) • **90**

Riesling Western Australia 1997: Light, lithe and subtle. A pretty wine with almond and mineral overtones to the delicate pear flavors. Finishes a bit raw now, but should be terrific by 1999. • $20 • (04/30/98) • **86**

Riesling Western Australia 1996: Dry, nicely balanced, not particularly effusive, but shows some pleasant peach and kerosene aromas that kick in on the finish. Drink now. 3,000 cases made. • $20 • (04/30/97) • **85**

HUGO

Chardonnay McLaren Flat 1995: Lean and crisp, with mineral-accented citruslike flavors and a clean, sharp finish. 5,000 cases made. • $10 • (05/31/97) • **85**

Shiraz McLaren Vale 1996: Ripe and supple, brimming with spicy blackberry flavors and finishing with a gentle spin of vanilla and plum. Best from 1999 through 2004. 3,000 cases made. • $15 • (06/15/98) • **89**

Shiraz McLaren Vale 1995: Dense and chewy, a solid mouthful of earthy, gamy and ripe blackberry flavors that never quite lift off. May be better in 1999. 3,500 cases made. • $16 • (09/15/97) • **84**

HUNGERFORD HILL

Cabernet Merlot Hunter Valley 1985 • $10 • (02/28/90) • **80**

Cabernet Sauvignon Coonawarra 1984 • $11 • (03/15/88) • **79**

Pinot Noir Hunter Valley 1986 • $12 • (02/28/90) • **74**

Pinot Noir Hunter Valley 1984 • $11 • (03/15/88) • **70**

Shiraz Hunter Valley 1988 • $10 • (02/28/90) • **80**

HUNTER PARK

Chardonnay Hunter Valley 1994 • $11 • (06/15/96) • **83**

Chardonnay Hunter Valley Kenmarie Vineyard 1994 • $15 • (06/15/96) • **88**

Chardonnay Hunter Valley Kenmarie Vineyard 1993 • $20 • (01/31/95) • **89**

HUNTER RIDGE

Chardonnay South Eastern Australia Grand Show Reserve 1995: A concentrated mouthful of spicy, earthy, mineral-scented pineapple and honey flavors, finishing with a slight kick of bitterness and some spicy oak notes. Try now. 500 cases made. • $17 • (04/30/97) • **86**

Chardonnay South Eastern Australia Vanessa's Vale 1996: Smooth, spicy and leaning strongly toward the mineral and resin overtones that shade the green apple, pineapple and melon flavors. Try now. 10,000 cases made. • $9 • (04/30/97) • **85**

Chardonnay South Eastern Australia Vanessa's Vale 1995 • $9 • (03/31/96) • **88**

Merlot South Eastern Australia Grand Show Reserve 1995: Light and crisp, with modest berry and smoke flavors that fade on the finish. 500 cases made. • $17 • (04/30/97) • **80**

Merlot South Eastern Australia Vanessa's Vale 1996: Firm, compact and tightly balanced to show its modest blackberry, earth and anise flavors. Finish is a bit short. Drinkable now. 9,000 cases made. • $9 • (04/30/97) • **81**

Merlot South Eastern Australia Vanessa's Vale 1995 • $9 • (03/31/96) • **87**

Shiraz South Eastern Australia Vanessa's Vale 1996: Light and minty, with more herb than fruit flavor, finishing simply. Drinkable now. 6,000 cases made. • $9 • (04/30/97) • **79**

Shiraz South Eastern Australia Vanessa's Vale 1995 • $9 • (03/31/96) • **85**

Tawny Port South Eastern Australia Grand Show NV: Dark, rich and complex, swirling with spice-, walnut- and nutmeg-scented coffee, chocolate and orange peel flavors, all elegantly balanced and finishing without any syrupy feel. Try now. 500 cases made. • $18/500ml • (04/30/97) • **91**

HUNTERS

Chardonnay Hunter River Valley 747 1994 • $7 • (03/31/96) • **79**

Merlot Hunter River Valley 565 1993 • $7 • (03/31/96) • **77**

JABIRU

Cabernet Sauvignon Australia 1993 • $8 • (03/31/95) BB • **85**
Chardonnay South Eastern Australia 1994 • $8 • (01/31/95) BB • **84**
Sauvignon Blanc South Eastern Australia 1993 • $8 • (01/31/95) • **79**

JAMIESONS RUN

Cabernet Sauvignon-Shiraz-Cabernet Franc Coonawarra 1995: A chunky wine, firm in texture, with pretty currant and floral flavors that persist on the open-textured finish. Best from 1999 or 2000. 10,000 cases made. • $11 • (03/31/98) • **86**
Cabernet Sauvignon-Shiraz Coonawarra 1994: Brilliant flavors have a hot edge to them, but the ripe currant, berry and cedar flavors swirl through to the finish. Drink with hearty food. 10,000 cases made. • $9 • (02/28/97) • **84**
Chardonnay Coonawarra 1993 • $10 • (09/30/94) • **83**
Chardonnay South Australia 1995: Fresh and lively, delivering a nice mouthful of pear and citrus flavors that linger on the slightly raw finish. Try now. 10,000 cases made. • $10 • (01/31/97) BB • **85**
Chardonnay South Eastern Australia 1996: Smooth and bright. Appealing for its snappy green-apple and vanilla flavors, finishing on a creamy note. Drinkable now. 10,000 cases made. • $11 • (03/31/98) • **85**
Pinot Noir South Eastern Australia 1997: Light and fruity, with red raspberry flavors dominating. Very young and fresh. Drink soon. 2,000 cases made. • $11 • (05/15/98) • **80**
Sauvignon Blanc South Eastern Australia 1997: Light and bright, with the zing of citrus and green apple plus a touch of herb on the finish. Drink now. 8,000 cases made. • $11 • (03/31/98) • **85**
Sauvignon Blanc South Eastern Australia 1996: Has a sweet-tart balance, showing hints of passion fruit and grapefruit to go along with peach and vanilla notes. Fresh and simple finish. 50,000 cases made. • $11 • (06/15/97) • **83**
Shiraz Cabernet Coonawarra 1991 • $10 • (09/30/94) • **81**
Shiraz Cabernet Coonawarra 1990 • $10 • (09/30/94) • **77**

JASPER HILL

Riesling Heathcote Georgia's Paddock 1996: Bright and refreshing, with straightforward green-apple and floral flavors that linger nicely. 16 cases made. • $25 • (09/30/97) • **85**
Shiraz Heathcote Georgia's Paddock 1995: Remarkable for its intensity, this red is packed to bursting with smoky, gamy, herb-scented licorice and dark plum flavors that persist on the complex, powerful finish. A tightly wound Australian beauty that needs until 2001 to 2003 to show what it has. 104 cases made. • $44 • (08/31/97) HR • **94**

KAESLER

Shiraz Barossa Valley Old Vine 1995: Lithe in texture, rich in flavor, with anise-scented blackberry and cherry flavors that linger with concentration on the finish. Best from 1999 to 2000. 500 cases made. • $30 • (03/31/98) • **88**
Shiraz Barossa Valley Old Vine 1994: Rich and mouthfilling, this is a full-bodied Shiraz with toasty berry and plum flavors that show hints of licorice on the velvety finish. Drink now. 3,000 cases made. • $13 • (06/15/97) • **87**

KATNOOK

Cabernet Sauvignon Coonawarra 1994: Dense in color and flavor without a lot of weight, melding a harmonious chorus of earthy blackberry and plum notes with a mossy edge. Best from 2000 or 2002. 1,200 cases made. • $27 • (05/31/97) • **87**
Cabernet Sauvignon Coonawarra 1992: A solid effort that packs plenty of black pepper-scented berry and currant flavors into a chewy frame. Has the length to warrant cellaring until 2000 or 2002. • $29 • (11/15/96) • **87**

Key: SS—Spectator Selection. CS—Cellar Selection. BB—Best Buy. HR—Highly Recommended. $NA—Price not available. (BT)—Barrel tasting. Ⓐ—Auction Price.
Dates in parentheses represent the issues in which the ratings were published.

Chardonnay Coonawarra 1994: Rich, ripe and powerful, dense with apple, spice and mineral flavors, echoing with buttery overtones on the solid finish. Try now. 4,000 cases made. • $26 • (02/28/97) • **88**
Merlot Coonawarra 1995: Smooth and generous with its mint-scented cherry and earth flavors, hanging appealingly on a crisp frame, finishing with polish and elegance. Nice now, best from 2000 or 2001. • $28 • (04/30/98) • **86**
Merlot Coonawarra 1994: Starts off aristocratically, with elegant structure and a nice range of herb, tobacco- and chocolate-scented cherry flavors, fading a bit on the velvety finish. Try now. 1,500 cases made. • $26 • (02/28/97) • **86**
Merlot Coonawarra 1993: Has the structure and the balance, but the modest Merlot flavors never quite burst through the surface of fine tannins. • $26 • (11/15/96) • **84**
Sauvignon Blanc Coonawarra 1996: A distinctively herbal Sauvignon Blanc, with rosemary and sage overtones to its green gooseberry flavors, which linger nicely. 1,000 cases made. • $23 • (05/31/97) • **86**
Sauvignon Blanc Coonawarra 1995: Distinctly varietal, with herb, anise and apple flavors jostling for attention. Drinkable now. • $19 • (11/15/96) • **84**

KINGSTON ESTATE

Cabernet Sauvignon Riverland 1992 • $10 • (03/31/96) • **82**
Cabernet Sauvignon South Australia Riverland 1991 • $10 • (07/31/94) • **85**
Chardonnay Riverland 1995: Fresh and appealing, with bright apple and pear flavors and, on the finish, some spicy oak notes. Drink now. 3,000 cases made. • $9 • (05/15/97) • **82**
Chardonnay Riverland Reserve 1993: An attractive wine, soft and generous with honey, spice and caramel flavors. Finishes with a silky texture, more honey notes. Drink soon. 500 cases made. • $15 • (05/15/97) • **86**
Merlot Riverland 1995: A light and simple red, with modest herb-accented berry flavors that turn mineral-like on the finish. 6,000 cases made. • $9 • (05/15/97) • **80**
Merlot Riverland 1993 • $10 • (03/31/96) • **84**
Merlot Riverland Reserve 1991: A jazzy wine with ripe flavors, crisp texture and some simple, spicy grape notes adding interest. Drinkable now. 500 cases made. • $15 • (05/15/97) • **82**
Merlot South Australia Riverland Reserve 1989 • $15 • (09/30/94) • **83**
Mourvèdre Riverland 1993 • $10 • (03/31/96) • **83**
Sémillon South Australia Riverland 1993 • $9 • (09/30/94) • **81**
Shiraz Riverland 1993 • $10 • (03/31/96) • **86**
Shiraz South Australia Riverland 1991 • $9 • (09/30/94) • **84**
Shiraz South Australia Riverland Reserve 1991 • $15 • (01/31/95) • **85**

KOALA RIDGE

Cabernet Sauvignon Barossa Valley 1990 • $9 • (03/31/93) BB • **84**
Cabernet Sauvignon Barossa Valley 1988 • $10 • (03/15/92) • **83**
Cabernet Sauvignon Barossa Valley 1985 • $9 • (01/31/89) • **84**
Chardonnay Eden Valley 1993 • $10 • (09/30/94) • **81**
Hermitage Barossa Valley 1985 • $9 • (01/31/90) • **80**
Hermitage Barossa Valley 1984 • $8 • (08/31/87) • **71**

KOOKABURRA

Cabernet Sauvignon South Eastern Australia 1992 • $8 • (06/30/95) • **74**
Chardonnay South Eastern Australia 1993 • $6 • (04/15/95) • **80**
Shiraz South Eastern Australia 1992 • $6 • (03/31/95) • **81**

LEASINGHAM

Cabernet Malbec Australia Bin 56 Winemakers Selection 1984 • $7 • (11/15/87) • **84**
Cabernet Malbec Clare Valley 1994: Balanced on the tart side, but the flavors are brilliant—centering around blackberry and currant, with hints of anise and cedar. Tightly wound now, may develop more generosity by 2000 to 2003. 5,000 cases made. • $12 • (10/15/96) • **87**
Cabernet Malbec Clare Valley Domaine 1993 • $12 • (03/31/96) • **80**
Cabernet Malbec Clare Valley Domaine 1992 • $8 • (06/30/94) • **89**
Cabernet Malbec Clare Valley Domaine 1989 • $8 • (08/31/92) • **82**
Cabernet Sauvignon Australia Bin 49 Winemakers Selection 1982 • $7 • (11/15/87) • **83**
Cabernet Sauvignon Clare Valley Classic 1995: Has the racy Clare Valley acidity but also plenty of ripe berry and currant flavors to balance, with a smoky-toasty cloud over the finish. Drink now. 1,500 cases made. • $29 • (05/31/98) • **88**

Cabernet Sauvignon Clare Valley Classic 1992 • $16 • (06/15/95) • **90**
Cabernet Shiraz Australia Bin 68 1983 • $5 • (11/15/87) • **79**
Chardonnay Clare Valley 1993 • $9 • (06/30/95) • **84**
Chardonnay Clare Valley Domain 1996: Crisp and vibrant with its citrus and tart pineapple flavors that linger jazzily on the finish. A mouthfilling Chardonnay that's appealing now. 6,000 cases made. • $10 • (10/15/97) • **88**
Chardonnay South Australia Hutt Creek 1993 • $6 • (09/30/94) • **81**
Domaine Red Clare Valley 1995: Crisp in texture, with considerable doses of lime and other citrusy notes to go with the berry and smoke flavors. Drinkable now. A blend of 85 percent Cabernet Sauvignon and 15 percent Malbec. 5,000 cases made. • $13 • (10/31/97) • **82**
Riesling Clare Valley 1996: Dry, delicate and crisp, floating its lovely pear, apple, citrus and floral flavors on a gentle contour of texture, finishing long and lovely. Delicious now, even more interesting by 2000 to 2002. 2,000 cases made. • $8 • (10/31/97) • **89**
Sauvignon Blanc South Australia Hutt Creek 1993 • $6 • (09/30/94) • **80**
Shiraz Cabernet Malbec Australia Hutt Creek Claret 1984 • $4 • (09/30/87) BB • **81**
Shiraz Cabernet Sauvignon South Australia Hutt Creek 1991 • $6 • (09/30/94) • **82**
Shiraz Cabernet Sauvignon South Australia Hutt Creek 1989 • $5 • (08/31/92) BB • **87**
Shiraz Clare Valley 1992 • $8 • (09/30/94) • **83**
Shiraz Clare Valley Classic Clare 1995: Crisp in texture, exuberant in flavor, hitting all sorts of raspberry, blackberry and pepper notes, lingering enticingly on the firm finish. Fun to drink. 1,500 cases made. • $29 • (05/31/98) • **90**
Shiraz Clare Valley Classic Clare 1994: Rich, smooth and powerful, its layers of blackberry, black cherry and licorice flavors swirling with coffee and toasty oak notes. Has intensity of color, flavor and length. Drink now. 1,500 cases made. • $24 • (11/30/96) • **93**
Shiraz Clare Valley Classic Clare 1992 • $16 • (06/30/95) • **86**
Shiraz Clare Valley Domain 1995: From Australia comes this elegantly built Shiraz, remarkable for its rich flavor profile, with cascades of lovely cherry, blackberry, raspberry and spice flavors that swirl together smoothly on the taut finish. Delicious, but will be at its best from 1999 or 2000. 5,000 cases made. • $13 • (10/31/97) HR • **91**
Shiraz Clare Valley Domaine 1994: Rich and flavorful, offering appealing cola-scented black cherry and licorice flavors that jangle enticingly through the finish. Drink now. Tasted twice, with consistent notes. 6,000 cases made. • $13 • (11/30/96) • **89**
Shiraz Clare Valley Domaine 1993 • $9 • (02/29/96) • **86**
Shiraz Clare Valley Domaine 1992 • $9 • (06/30/95) BB • **85**

LEEUWIN

Cabernet Sauvignon Margaret River 1993: Minty herbal aromas and flavors dominate up front, while polished, supple currant and plum flavors valiantly try to balance on the finish. Check it out in 2000 to 2002 to see which wins. 260 cases made. • $35 • (07/31/97) • **87**
Cabernet Sauvignon Margaret River 1988 • $18 • (07/31/94) • **84**
Cabernet Sauvignon Margaret River 1983 • $18 • (05/31/88) • **86**
Cabernet Sauvignon Margaret River 1979 • $20 • (09/15/89) • **79**
Cabernet Sauvignon Margaret River Art Series 1987 • $20 • (11/30/92) • **70**
Cabernet Sauvignon Margaret River Redgum Ridge 1990 • $15 • (11/15/93) • **83**
Chardonnay Margaret River 1994: Ripe, rich and marvelously balanced at once, its dense pear and pineapple flavors shaded by hints of oatmeal and brown sugar, its finish tangy, bright and extremely long. Gorgeous now, it should do nothing but deepen through at least 2001. 260 cases made. 260 cases made. • $40 • (07/31/97) HR • **94**
Pinot Noir Margaret River Art Series 1988 • $20 • (11/30/92) • **81**
Riesling Margaret River 1996: Lithe and lean, but mouthfilling with its jazzy nectarine, apple and spice flavors that linger appealingly on the concentrated finish. Elegant now, but has a track record for being at its best after age eight. 200 cases made. • $20 • (07/31/97) • **91**
Riesling Margaret River 1995: A subtle style, dry and inviting for its pretty citrus and peach flavors, touch of floral character on the finish. Should develop further with cellaring until 2000. 100 cases made. • $20 • (09/30/97) • **86**

LEHMANN, PETER

Cabernet Blend Barossa Valley 1986 • $8 • (02/28/91) • **78**
Cabernet Sauvignon Barossa Valley 1995: Silky, smooth and ripe. A lovely mouthful of black cherry, currant, plum and spice flavors that linger with intensity on the rich finish. Delicious now, should improve through 2001. 10,000 cases made. • $17 • (09/30/97) • **89**
Cabernet Sauvignon Barossa Valley 1994: Dense and chewy, but the berry, spice and chocolate flavors never quite open up. May be better after 1999. 10,000 cases made. • $15 • (01/31/97) • **85**
Cabernet Sauvignon Barossa Valley 1993 • $14 • (04/30/96) HR • **90**
Cabernet Sauvignon Barossa Valley 1992 • $13 • (06/30/95) • **80**
Cabernet Sauvignon Barossa Valley 1987 • $8 • (03/31/91) • **80**
Cabernet Sauvignon Barossa Valley 1986 • $9 • (01/31/90) • **85**
Cabernet Sauvignon Barossa Valley 1983 • $9 • (07/01/87) • **81**
Chardonnay Barossa Valley 1997: Lean in texture, with fresh apple and melon flavors to liven it up. Has nice touches of honey and spice on the finish. 5,000 cases made. • $16 • (05/15/98) • **85**
Chardonnay Barossa Valley 1996: Ripe, bright and appealing for its juicy pineapple and citrus flavors. Try now. 5,000 cases made. • $16 • (10/15/97) • **86**
Chardonnay Barossa Valley 1995: In a sturdy, straightforward style, this never develops much charm or depth, although the finish has some nice spicy notes. 6,000 cases made. • $15 • (10/15/96) • **82**
Clancy's Barossa Valley Red 1996: Shows lots of ripe fruit in a smooth package, offering lots of pretty plum, raspberry, spice and smoke flavors that linger enticingly. Delicious now. A blend of 43 percent Shiraz, 26 percent Cabernet Sauvignon, 17 percent Merlot, 14 percent Cabernet Franc. 2,000 cases made. • $19 • (05/31/98) • **89**
Clancy's Gold Preference Barossa Valley 1995: Strives for elegance and achieves a fine balance between spicy intensity and silky texture. Not a big wine, but the flavors vibrate along a live-wire of blackberry, earth and pepper that lingers long. Best from 2000. 41 percent Shiraz, 36 percent Cabernet Sauvignon, 12 percent Merlot, 11 percent Cabernet Franc. 2,000 cases made. • $18 • (09/30/97) • **92**
Clancy's Gold Preference Barossa Valley 1994: Rich, spicy and complex, disarmingly seductive with plum, black cherry and exotic spices mingling on the plush finish. Has style and power, but finishes with welcome harmony. Absolutely stunning now, but should keep developing through 2000 to 2005. A blend of Shiraz, Cabernet Sauvignon, Merlot, and Cabernet Franc. 5,000 cases made. • $18 • (02/28/97) • **93**
Clancy's Gold Preference Barossa Valley 1991 • $15 • (06/30/95) • **77**
Mentor Red Barossa Valley 1993: Firm in texture, with pretty black cherry and berry flavors emerging from the gauzy layer of fine tannins. A blend of 55 percent Cabernet Sauvignon, 20 percent Malbec, 18 percent Shiraz, 7 percent Merlot. 500 cases made. • $32 • (05/31/98) • **85**
Mentor Red Barossa Valley 1991: Broad and chewy, with a tart balance of ripe berry and chocolate flavors. Softens on the finish. Drink now. 500 cases made. • $35 • (09/30/96) • **88**
Port Barossa Valley Bin AD 2016 1995: Dusky spice nuances run through the dark cherry and anise flavors, with a hint of gaminess on the soft finish. Best from 2002. 1,000 cases made. • $20 • (06/15/98) • **85**
Port Barossa Valley Bin AD 2010 1989 • $15 • (04/15/95) • **85**
Sémillon Barossa Valley 1997: Light in texture, almost silky, with pretty fig, melon and pepper aromas and flavors that linger on the delicate finish. 5,000 cases made. • $12 • (05/15/98) • **87**
Sémillon Barossa Valley 1996: Bright, smooth and generous with its pineapple, tobacco and citrus flavors, it's fun to drink now, should develop extra nuances with cellaring until 1999 or beyond. 6,000 cases made. • $12 • (09/30/97) • **88**
Sémillon Barossa Valley 1995: Shows elegance and restraint, but the citrus, pear and floral flavors emerge gracefully on the round finish. Appealing now, best after 2000. 8,000 cases made. • $11 • (10/31/96) HR • **88**
Sémillon Barossa Valley 1994 • $10 • (01/31/95) • **85**
Sémillon Barossa Valley Botrytis Sauternes 1996: Golden-colored and sweet, with vanilla-scented fig and honey flavors wrapped in spicy oak notes. Distinctive spicecake character on the finish suggests it will be at its best from 2000 to 2004. 5,000 cases made. • $16/375ml • (11/30/97) • **88**
Sémillon Barossa Valley Botrytis Sauternes 1995: Generously sweet, with nice honey and butter flavors supported by bright acidity. 4,000 cases made. • $15/375ml • (10/15/96) • **85**
Sémillon Late Harvest Barossa Valley Botrytis Sauternes 1992 • $12 • (06/30/95) • **83**
Sémillon Late Harvest Barossa Valley Botrytis Sauternes 1988 • $6/375ml • (04/15/91) BB • **83**
Sémillon Late Harvest Barossa Valley Botrytis Sauternes 1987 • $8/375ml • (10/31/89) • **89**
Sémillon Late Harvest Barossa Valley Botrytis Sauternes 1984 • $15 • (07/01/87) • **89**

Shiraz Barossa Valley 1996: Smooth and generous, this supple Shiraz focuses on pretty black cherry and berry flavors. Good now, best from 1999 through 2003. 30,000 cases made. • $15 • (05/15/98) • **87**

Shiraz Barossa Valley 1995: Ripe, gooey and harmonious, with rich flavors of red cherry, tobacco, raspberry and anise, finishing long and in remarkable balance. Tempting now, but has all the pieces to age into a beauty by 2001 to 2003. 30,000 cases made. • $13 • (09/30/97) • **89**

Shiraz Barossa Valley 1994: Rich, ripe and spicy, its generous blackberry, cinnamon and buttery-caramel flavors persisting through a solid finish. Drinkable now. 12,000 cases made. • $11 • (09/30/96) • **87**

Shiraz Barossa Valley 1993 • $10 • (04/30/96) • **88**

Shiraz Barossa Valley 1992 • $10 • (01/31/95) • **81**

Shiraz Barossa Valley 1987 • $8 • (04/15/91) BB • **84**

Shiraz Barossa Valley 1983 • $7 • (07/01/87) • **81**

Shiraz Barossa Valley Dry Red 1985 • $7 • (07/31/89) BB • **84**

Shiraz Barossa Valley Dry Red 1983 • $5 • (04/30/87) • **79**

Shiraz Barossa Valley Stonewell 1991: A solid Barossa Shiraz, full of spice and gooey with chocolate and molasses notes. It's ripe with berry flavor that gets a little tarry on the velvety finish. Best from 2000 or 2002. 500 cases made. • $36 • (02/28/97) • **89**

Shiraz Cabernet Sauvignon Barossa Valley 1985 • $7 • (01/31/90) • **83**

LENSWOOD

Cabernet Lenswood 1994: A lighter style of red that emphasizes the spicy, herbal, minty side of the flavor spectrum. Drinkable now. 530 cases made. • $25 • (06/15/97) • **86**

Chardonnay Lenswood 1995: Fresh and immensely appealing for the spicy, citrusy intensity that swirls around the core of ripe pear and honey flavors. A serious Chardonnay, it's approachable now, but should improve through 2000. 2,000 cases made. • $21 • (05/31/97) • **91**

Pinot Noir Lenswood 1996: Crisp in texture, with a lively blast of ripe blackberry and currant flavor that remains pure and focused through the finish. Has a hard edge that needs until 1999 to soften. One of the better Aussie PNs to make it to these shores. 855 cases made. • $31 • (04/30/98) • **87**

Pinot Noir Lenswood 1995: A lighter style, with appealing currant and wild berry flavors and a soft and simple finish. Drinkable now. 1,050 cases made. • $28 • (05/31/97) • **83**

Sauvignon Blanc Lenswood 1997: A crisp, lemony wine with floral overtones and a bite of green berry on the finish. Drink while it's fresh. 2,400 cases made. • $21 • (04/30/98) • **85**

Sauvignon Blanc South Australia 1996: Brilliant tropical fruit—especially passion fruit—character leaps from the glass and hangs on through the very crisp, borderline-acidic finish. 2,000 cases made. • $21 • (06/15/97) • **87**

LEYDENS VALE

Chardonnay Victoria 1996: Spicy and ripe, with peach and pear flavors that course through the palate. Shows harmony and plenty of style. 1,000 cases made. • $20 • (05/31/98) • **89**

Merlot Victoria 1995: Crisp, lean and decidedly minty, with modest berry-candy flavors sneaking through on the finish. Drinkable now. 508 cases made. • $20 • (04/30/98) • **82**

Pinot Noir Victoria 1995: Light in color and texture, with firm tannins and modest portions of berry and toast flavors. A solid wine, best from 1999. 1,400 cases made. • $20 • (04/30/98) • **84**

Riesling Victoria 1995: Lush, almost creamy. A dry wine with rich texture and lovely apple, honey, peach and spice flavors that linger gently on the finish. Drinkable now. 800 cases made. • $20 • (04/30/98) • **88**

Shiraz Victoria 1996: Fresh, bright and packed with dazzling berry and spice flavors that persist on the jazzy finish, picking up a tinge of pickle barrel and bell pepper. Very distinctive. Drink from 1999 or 2000. 4,200 cases made. • $20 • (04/30/98) • **87**

LILLYDALE

Cabernet Merlot Yarra Valley 1990 • $14 • (06/30/95) • **82**

Chardonnay Yarra Valley 1993 • $14 • (06/30/95) • **81**

Pinot Noir Yarra Valley 1990 • $14 • (06/30/95) • **77**

Key: SS—Spectator Selection. CS—Cellar Selection. BB—Best Buy. HR—Highly Recommended. $NA—Price not available. (BT)—Barrel tasting. Ⓐ—Auction Price.

Dates in parentheses represent the issues in which the ratings were published.

LINDEMANS

Cabernet Blend Coonawarra Pyrus 1994: Firm and focused, a tightly wound red with cedary overtones to the core of currant and dark berry flavors. Approachable now, best from 2000 through 2005. A blend of 70 percent Cabernet Sauvignon, 10 percent Merlot, 10 percent Cabernet Franc, 10 percent Malbec. • $28 • (05/15/98) • **88**

Cabernet Blend Coonawarra Pyrus 1993: Lean and juicy, focusing its blackberry and herb flavors in a fine beam that cuts through the chewy tannins. Finishes with some length, making it best from 2000. 370 cases made. • $28 • (05/31/97) • **87**

Cabernet Blend Coonawarra Pyrus 1991 • $22 • (04/30/96) • **87**

Cabernet Blend Coonawarra Pyrus 1987 • $25 • (05/31/93) • **84**

Cabernet Blend Coonawarra Pyrus 1986 • $25 • (06/30/92) • **77**

Cabernet Blend Coonawarra Pyrus 1985 • $20 • (05/31/88) • **87**

Cabernet Merlot Padthaway 1995: A solid red, with spicy blackberry and a touch of herbs riding on a solid foundation. Fine tannins and soft structure. Drinkable now. 10,676 cases made. • $15 • (11/15/97) • **86**

Cabernet Merlot Padthaway 1994: Soft, open and fresh, this offers a lovely mouthful of Cabernet flavor with hints of cola and anise on the slightly chewy finish. Approachable now. 10,270 cases made. • $15 • (12/31/96) • **87**

Cabernet Merlot South Australia Padthaway 1990 • $13 • (04/15/93) • **83**

Cabernet Sauvignon Coonawarra 1986 • $14 • (10/31/90) • **83**

Cabernet Sauvignon Coonawarra 1985 • $14 • (04/30/89) • **86**

Cabernet Sauvignon Coonawarra 1984 • $12 • (02/15/88) • **84**

Cabernet Sauvignon Coonawarra 1982 • $8 • (09/30/86) • **79**

Cabernet Sauvignon Coonawarra 150 Years Sequicentenary 1990 • $13 • (03/31/95) • **80**

Cabernet Sauvignon Coonawarra St.-George Vineyard 1994: Dense in flavor and chewy in texture. Sharply focused to show off its cedary currant and blackberry flavors, shaded with hints of mineral and sage. Has style and length. • $28 • (05/15/98) • **89**

Cabernet Sauvignon Coonawarra St.-George Vineyard 1993: Smooth in texture, with minty, herbal flavors dominating the ripe cherry and plum notes, which fade into the background. Tries for elegance and comes up sort of soft. Try in 1999 to 2000. 375 cases made. • $28 • (05/31/97) • **87**

Cabernet Sauvignon Coonawarra St.-George Vineyard 1991 • $22 • (04/30/96) • **92**

Cabernet Sauvignon Coonawarra St.-George Vineyard 1986 • $25 • (06/30/92) • **82**

Cabernet Sauvignon Coonawarra St.-George Vineyard 1985 • $21 • (04/30/89) • **80**

Cabernet Sauvignon Coonawarra St.-George Vineyard 1984 • $15 • (01/31/88) • **88**

Cabernet Sauvignon Coonawarra Special Selection 1995: Firm and generous with fruity currant. Red pepper and herb overtones swirl through the soft finish. • $15 • (06/30/98) • **86**

Cabernet Sauvignon Coonawarra Special Selection 1994: Dense and chewy, an elegant wine with lots of stuffing, offering smoky currant and boysenberry flavors that linger nicely on the smooth finish. Best from 2000. 5,200 cases made. • $15 • (05/31/97) • **88**

Cabernet Sauvignon Coonawarra Special Selection 1993 • $15 • (04/30/96) • **85**

Cabernet Sauvignon Coonawarra Special Selection 1991 • $13 • (11/30/95) • **85**

Cabernet Sauvignon Coonawarra Vineyard 1990 • $22 • (03/31/95) • **85**

Cabernet Sauvignon South Eastern Australia Bin 45 1996: Fresh and simple. A straightforward red with a pleasant smoky edge to the basic blackberry flavors. Drinkable now. 83,000 cases made. • $8 • (03/31/98) • **83**

Cabernet Sauvignon South Eastern Australia Bin 45 1995: Packs a lot of ripe, juicy Cabernet flavor into a velvety, supple frame, aiming for purity of character and achieving more clarity and finesse than many Aussie Cabernets. Most appealing for its approachable texture. 24,290 cases made. • $8 • (05/31/97) • **87**

Cabernet Sauvignon South Eastern Australia Bin 45 1994 • $7 • (04/30/96) • **85**

Cabernet Sauvignon South Eastern Australia Bin 45 1993 • $7 • (11/30/95) • **83**

Cabernet Sauvignon South Eastern Australia Bin 45 1992 • $7 • (03/31/95) BB • **86**

Cabernet Sauvignon South Eastern Australia Bin 45 1991 • $7 • (04/30/94) BB • **82**

Cabernet Sauvignon South Eastern Australia Bin 45 1990 • $7 • (04/15/93) • **80**

Cabernet Sauvignon South Eastern Australia Bin 45 1989 • $6 • (08/31/92) BB • **81**

Cabernet Sauvignon South Eastern Australia Bin 45 1985 • $6 • (01/31/88) • **79**

Cabernet Shiraz Coonawarra Limestone Ridge 1984 • $15 • (07/01/87) • **87**

Chardonnay Coonawarra 1994 • $15 • (04/30/95) • **87**

Chardonnay Padthaway 1996: The newest Chardonnay vintage from this Australian winery is remarkably generous and open-textured, bubbling over with citrusy pineapple and pear flavors, shaded nicely with gentle spicy notes that linger enticingly on the elegant finish. Delicious. 6,891 cases made. • $13 • (11/30/97) SS • **90**

Chardonnay Padthaway 1995: Ripe, round and juicily bright. Delivers tropical fruit, pear and citrus flavors, and hints of toast and nutmeg on the long finish. Generous and stylish. Try now. 32,800 cases made. • $13 • (12/31/96) SS • **91**

Chardonnay Padthaway 1994 • $13 • (04/30/96) • **92**

Chardonnay Padthaway Vineyard 1993 • $13 • (03/31/95) • **87**

Chardonnay Padthaway Winemaker's Reserve 1995: Ripe, round and generous, this lovely mouthful balances honey, spice and baked apple flavors harmoniously on the long finish. Delicious now through 2000. • $25 • (05/15/98) • **91**

Chardonnay South Eastern Australia Bin 65 1997: Light, bright and citrusy in style, echoing grapefruit and spice notes on the generous finish. It's ready to drink, widely available, and the asking price is a bargain in todays Chardonnay market. 429,000 cases made. • $8 • (03/31/98) BB • **85**

Chardonnay South Eastern Australia Bin 65 1996: Fresh, and a little zingier than most because of the spicy, toasty edge to the green apple and leesy flavors. Drink now. • $7 • (05/15/97) • **85**

Chardonnay South Eastern Australia Bin 65 1995 • $7 • (03/31/96) • **83**

Chardonnay South Eastern Australia Bin 65 1994 • $7 • (03/31/95) BB • **85**

Chardonnay South Eastern Australia Bin 65 1993 • $7 • (04/15/94) BB • **83**

Merlot South Australia Reserve 1995: Light and silky, this is a pretty red with berry, herb and vanilla flavors that linger on the straightforward finish. Drinkable now. 6,168 cases made. • $15 • (11/15/97) • **85**

Merlot South Australia Reserve 1993 • $13 • (12/15/95) • **86**

Merlot Bin 40 South Eastern Australia 1996: Light and pretty for its raspberry and sandalwood flavors that echo lightly on the finish. Drink now. 94,500 cases made. • $9 • (03/31/98) • **82**

Merlot Bin 40 South Australia 1995: Soft, with herbal and tea-leaf aromas and flavors looking for some fruit to balance. Drinkable now. • $7 • (02/28/97) • **81**

Merlot Bin 40 South Australia 1994 • $7 • (03/31/96) • **82**

Merlot Bin 40 South Australia 1993 • $8 • (04/15/95) BB • **87**

Merlot Bin 40 South Eastern Australia 1992 • $7 • (09/30/94) • **80**

Pinot Noir Padthaway 1996: A sturdy red with appealing, ripe berry flavors, finishing with a solid feel. • $15 • (05/15/98) • **83**

Pinot Noir Padthaway 1995: Smooth and bright with strawberry and cream flavors that linger nicely on the supple finish. Drink now. 600 cases made. • $15 • (05/31/97) • **86**

Pinot Noir Padthaway 1986 • $12 • (09/15/89) • **73**

Pinot Noir Padthaway 1984 • $12 • (02/15/88) • **82**

Pinot Noir South Australia Bin 99 1996: Soft and spicy, generous with its minty berry flavors, finishing with a bite of tannin. Drink now. 26,300 cases made. • $9 • (10/31/97) • **82**

Sauvignon Blanc South Eastern Australia Bin 95 1995: Soft and simple, with pleasant grape flavors and a hint of melon on the finish. • $7 • (05/15/97) • **81**

Sémillon Chardonnay South Eastern Australia Bin 77 1996: Supple and friendly, this is generous with its pear and citrus flavors. Drink now. • $7 • (05/15/97) • **83**

Sémillon Chardonnay South Eastern Australia Bin 77 1995 • $7 • (04/30/96) • **83**

Sémillon Chardonnay South Eastern Australia Bin 77 1994 • $7 • (06/15/95) BB • **85**

Sémillon Hunter River Valley Hunter River Bin 8655 1995: Has a strange flavor, reminiscent of wint-o'-green Life Savers—it's distinctive but puzzling. Try in 2000. 1,000 cases made. • $10 • (10/31/97) • **82**

Sémillon Late Harvest Padthaway Botrytis Griffith 1988 • $12/375ml • (07/31/90) • **83**

Sémillon Late Harvest Padthaway Botrytis Griffith 1987 • $12/375ml • (10/31/89) • **91**

Shiraz Barossa Valley 1986 • $12 • (05/15/89) • **83**

Shiraz Cabernet Coonawarra Limestone Ridge Lindemans Classic 1982 • $38 • (07/31/90) • **70**

Shiraz Cabernet Coonawarra Limestone Ridge Vineyard 1994: Firm and flavorful, a succulent mouthful of anise-scented blackberry and mineral flavors. Has a density and intensity that promises much with cellaring. Nice now, best from 2000 through 2005. 54 percent Shiraz, 46 percent Cabernet Sauvignon. • $28 • (05/15/98) • **91**

Shiraz Cabernet Coonawarra Limestone Ridge Vineyard 1993: Jazzy stuff, dazzling with its juicy blackberry, spice and vanilla flavors, almost breathtaking for its purity of fruit and long, surprisingly harmonious finish. Appealing now, but just wait until 2002 to 2004. 84 percent Shiraz, 16 percent Cabernet Sauvignon. 587 cases made. • $28 • (05/31/97) • **94**

Shiraz Cabernet Coonawarra Limestone Ridge Vineyard 1991 • $22 • (04/30/96) • **91**

Shiraz Cabernet Coonawarra Limestone Ridge Vineyard 1990 • $22 • (01/31/95) • **87**

Shiraz Cabernet Coonawarra Limestone Ridge Vineyard 1986 • $25 • (06/30/92) • **86**

Shiraz Cabernet Coonawarra Limestone Ridge Vineyard 1985 • $21 • (07/31/89) • **68**

Shiraz Cabernet Sauvignon South Eastern Australia Henry Lindeman 1991 • $6 • (05/31/93) • **79**

Shiraz Hunter Valley 1987 • $10 • (02/15/91) • **81**

Shiraz Hunter Valley Bin 3110 Lindemans Classic 1965 • $95 • (09/15/89) • **96**

Shiraz Hunter Valley Bin 4110 Lindemans Classic 1970 • $60 • (09/15/89) • **89**

Shiraz Hunter Valley Bin 5910 Lindemans Classic 1980 • $30 • (07/31/90) • **73**

Shiraz Padthaway 1995: Firm, open-textured and nicely focused to show off the pretty plum and blackberry fruit. Finishes with grace. • $15 • (06/30/98) • **87**

Shiraz Padthaway 1994: A lighter, leaner Shiraz in structure, but it's not shy on flavor, offering ripe plum, currant and pepper galore. It all comes together nicely on the harmonious finish. • $15 • (05/15/98) • **89**

Shiraz South Australia Bin 50 1996: Smooth and pretty, with floral and spicy notes adding interest to the light berry flavors. Drink now. 28,500 cases made. • $8 • (03/31/98) • **84**

Shiraz South Australia Bin 50 1995: Ripe and chunky, with an earthy, gamy streak running through the anise-scented black cherry flavors. Try now. • $7 • (02/28/97) • **85**

Shiraz South Australia Bin 50 1994 • $8 • (06/30/96) • **86**

Shiraz South Australia Bin 50 1993 • $7 • (12/15/95) • **84**

Shiraz South Eastern Australia Bin 50 1992 • $7 • (01/31/95) • **82**

Shiraz South Eastern Australia Bin 50 1989 • $6 • (05/31/92) • **80**

Shiraz South Eastern Australia Bin 50 1987 • $5 • (07/15/90) BB • **84**

Shiraz South Australia Bin 50 1986 • $5 • (05/15/89) • **78**

Tawny Port Australia Macquarie Very Special Wood Matured NV • $11 • (07/31/90) • **84**

Tawny Port Barossa Valley Macquarie Very Special NV: A lighter style of Port, its modest sweetness emphasizing the cinnamon-spiced, dusky, mineral-scented caramel and berry flavors. Finishes with balance and harmony. 5,000 cases made. • $10 • (04/30/98) • **88**

LITTLE'S

Sémillon-Chardonnay Hunter Valley 1995: Refreshing for its smooth, bright, golden apple and pineapple flavors that linger, with a touch of cream, on the finish. Drink now. 6,000 cases made. • $11 • (05/31/97) • **87**

LURTON, J. & F.

Fleurieu Heritage McLaren Vale 1996: A nice mouthful of peppery pear and citrus flavors that finish smoothly and invitingly. A blend of Sauvignon Blanc and Sémillon. • $15 • (09/15/97) • **85**

MACKENZIE ESTATES

Sémillon Chardonnay Hunter Valley 1994 • $8 • (04/30/96) • **77**

Shiraz Hunter Valley 1994 • $8 • (04/30/96) • **77**

MADFISH BAY

Chardonnay Western Australia 1996: Bright and sassy. A lively wine with appealing passion fruit, pear and apple flavors that resonate through the finish. Drink now. Second label of Howard Park. 8,000 cases made. • $17 • (04/30/97) • **87**

MARIENBERG

Cabernet Sauvignon McLaren Vale 1992 • $12 • (10/15/95) • **84**
Cabernet Sauvignon South Eastern Australia Reserve 1994: Tart and jazzy, this is a spicy wine with red cherry and tobacco notes lending interest. Best from 1999. 2,500 cases made. • $13 • (10/31/97) • **85**
Chardonnay McLaren Vale 1994 • $12 • (06/30/95) • **86**
Chardonnay South Eastern Australia 1993 • $11 • (03/31/96) • **78**
Chardonnay South Eastern Australia Reserve 1996: Rich and spicy, layered with pear, smoke and orange-peel notes that finish with a definite thwack of oak. Try now. 2,500 cases made. • $13 • (10/31/97) • **85**
Cottage Classic Cabernet Blend South Australia 1995: On the lean side, but there's plenty of flavor behind the crisp acidity and fine tannins, with ripe berry and mint notes that echo on the lightish finish. Drink now. A blend of 65 percent Cabernet, 25 percent Mourvèdre and 10 percent Grenache. 4,000 cases made. • $10 • (10/31/97) • **84**
Lavinia Classic Dry White McLaren Vale 1994 • $10 • (06/30/95) • **81**
Riesling McLaren Vale Cottage Classic 1994 • $10 • (06/30/95) • **84**
Sémillon Chardonnay McLaren Vale 1994 • $11 • (06/15/95) • **86**
Shiraz McLaren Vale 1993 • $12 • (04/30/96) • **85**
Shiraz McLaren Vale 1992 • $12 • (10/31/95) HR • **91**
Shiraz South Eastern Australia Reserve 1994: Earthy, gamy flavors add a different dimension to this smooth-textured, firm red, with pretty berry and anise flavors echoing on the finish. Drink now. 2,500 cases made. • $13 • (10/31/97) • **85**

MCALISTER

Red South East Gippsland 1994: Light and simple, an easy-drinking wine with modest red fruit and spice flavors. Try now. 48 cases made. • $35 • (10/15/97) • **82**

MCGUIGAN

Black Shiraz South Eastern Australia 1994 • $7 • (11/15/95) BB • **85**
Black Shiraz South Eastern Australia 1992 • $7 • (10/31/93) BB • **83**
Black Shiraz South Eastern Australia 1991 • $7 • (05/31/93) BB • **82**
Cabernet Merlot Hunter Valley Shareholders Reserve 1991 • $11 • (02/28/93) • **86**
Cabernet Sauvignon South Eastern Australia Bin 4000 1997: Soft and generous, with pretty plum and currant flavors that linger nicely on the drink-me-now finish. 10,000 cases made. • $9 • (05/31/98) BB • **86**
Cabernet Sauvignon South Eastern Australia Bin 4000 1991 • $8 • (06/15/94) • **80**
Cabernet Sauvignon South Eastern Australia Personal Reserve 1996: Soft, ripe and generous, with prune and plum notes adding interest to the currant and anise flavors. Impressive for its transparency, but needs to fill in the missing pieces. May be better after 1999. 2,500 cases made. • $20 • (11/30/97) • **87**
Cabernet Sauvignon Australia Personal Reserve 1993 • $15 • (04/30/96) • **91**
Chardonnay South Eastern Australia Bin 7000 1997: Fresh and generous, with flavors that are more spicy than fruity, finishing with a smoky edge. 15,000 cases made. • $9 • (05/15/98) • **83**
Chardonnay South Eastern Australia Bin 7000 1996: A fresh and zingy style, providing an interesting mouthful of star fruit, apple and pineapple flavors that linger on the solid finish. 9,000 cases made. • $8 • (04/30/97) • **86**
Chardonnay South Eastern Australia Reserve 1996: A full-on barrel-fermented style, polished to a fare-thee-well and leaning more toward nutmeg and other spice flavors than fruit. Drink now. 2,000 cases made. • $20 • (11/30/97) • **85**
Chardonnay South Eastern Australia Personal Reserve 1995: Soft, bordering on blowsy. Oaky flavors dominate up front, while the finish shows rich honey and spice flavors that go on and on. A highly quirky wine (even to the tall, straight-shoulder-shaped bottle), but it has a sense of drama. 1,500 cases made. • $20 • (11/30/96) • **87**
Merlot South Eastern Australia Bin 3000 1997: Firm in texture, tightly packed with black cherry and anise flavors, all on a relatively small scale. 15,000 cases made. • $9 • (05/31/98) • **84**
Merlot South Eastern Australia Bin 3000 1996: Lean, light and modestly flavored, with nice hints of mint and prune on the soft finish. 12,000 cases made. • $9 • (04/30/97) • **83**
Merlot South Eastern Australia Bin 3000 1995 • $8 • (04/30/96) • **85**
Merlot South Eastern Australia Bin 3000 Soft Mellow Dry Red 1994 • $9 • (06/30/96) • **81**
Merlot South Eastern Australia Bin 3000 1993 • $8 • (04/15/95) • **85**
Sauvignon Blanc South Eastern Australia Bin 8000 1997: Simple and a bit earthy, with a steely edge to the herbal flavors. 6,000 cases made. • $8 • (03/31/98) • **80**
Sauvignon Blanc South Eastern Australia Bin 8000 1996: Bracing, refreshing style emphasizing zingy citrus, passion fruit and green apple flavors that remain vibrant through the lingering finish. Has plenty of personality but nothing bizarre. 2,500 cases made. • $8 • (04/30/97) • **88**
Sémillon Chardonnay South Eastern Australia 1994 • $7 • (10/31/95) BB • **85**
Sémillon South Eastern Australia Botrytis Personal Reserve 1995: Dark and caramel-scented, it's a lot lighter and more elegant in flavor than the dark, burnished-gold color would suggest. Delivers lots of flavor up front and finishes with a nice hint of citrus to balance the sweetness. 1,100 cases made. • $11/500ml • (04/30/97) • **88**
Shiraz South Eastern Australia Millenium Bin 2000 1997: Round and fresh, with lots of plum and blackberry flavors at the core, and finishing with a polished texture, this young red is not only tasty, it's a smart buy. 10,000 cases made. • $10 • (05/15/98) BB • **86**
Shiraz South Eastern Australia Personal Reserve 1996: Bold, youthful and vibrant, with berry and spice flavors, this is nicely packed with character and shaded with fine tannins. Best after 2000. 2,500 cases made. • $20 • (11/30/97) • **88**
Shiraz Hunter Valley Hermitage Personal Reserve 1993 • $15 • (04/30/96) • **91**
Tawny Port South Eastern Australia Brian McGuigan's Private Reserve NV: Darker than most tawny Ports, showing a bit more fruit as well, this is mature and smooth with nice spikes of black cherry, spice and caramel flavor. Drink now. 1,650 cases made. • $18 • (01/31/97) • **87**
The Black Label South Eastern Australia Red 1996: Light in texture, with youthful, ebullient berry and anise flavors that finish with modest intensity. Ready to drink. A blend of Shiraz, Mourvèdre and Malbec. 25,000 cases made. • $8 • (04/30/97) • **83**

MCLARENS

Chardonnay South Eastern Australia 1993 • $9 • (12/15/94) BB • **86**
Classic Dry White South Eastern Australia 1993 • $7 • (01/31/95) • **82**
Sémillon Chardonnay South Eastern Australia 1992 • $9 • (01/31/95) • **83**
Shiraz Cabernet Sauvignon South Eastern Australia 1992 • $9 • (01/31/95) • **82**
Shiraz South Eastern Australia 1992 • $8 • (04/15/94) BB • **85**
Shiraz South Eastern Australia 1991 • $8 • (11/30/93) BB • **87**

MCWILLIAM'S

Cabernet Sauvignon Australia Hanwood Estate 1991 • $7 • (12/15/93) • **82**
Cabernet Sauvignon South Eastern Australia Mount Pleasant 1992 • $10 • (09/30/94) • **85**
Cabernet Sauvignon South Eastern Australia Mount Pleasant 1991 • $10 • (12/15/93) • **80**
Shiraz Australia Hanwood 1993 • $7 • (09/30/94) • **77**

MEADOWBANK

Pinot Noir Tasmania 1995: Light in color, very spicy, with a red cherry note peeking through the cinnamon and leather flavors that persist on the finish. Drink now. 500 cases made. • $19 • (03/31/98) • **83**

MELTON, CHARLES

Grenache Barossa Valley Rosé of Virginia 1997: Soft and pretty, offering a lovely mouthful of red cherry and rose petal flavors that remain vivid through the generous, off-dry finish. Try now. • $16 • (04/30/98) • **86**
Nine Popes Red Barossa Valley 1996: Bright and crisp in texture, packed with deep cherry, berry and anise flavors that come together nicely on the finish, skewing toward fruit as they linger. Best from 1999 or 2000. A blend of Grenache, Shiraz and Mourvèdre. • $45 • (04/30/98) • **88**
Nine Popes Red Barossa Valley 1995: Ripe, rich, exuberantly fruity and flavorful, a gonzo wine with elegance. For all the raspberry, blueberry, plum

Key: SS—Spectator Selection. CS—Cellar Selection. BB—Best Buy. HR—Highly Recommended. $NA—Price not available. (BT)—Barrel tasting. (A)—Auction Price.
Dates in parentheses represent the issues in which the ratings were published.

and anise flavors, it ends up smooth and balanced through the finish. Tempting now, should keep growing through 1999 to 2000. A blend of 68 percent Grenache, 30 percent Shiraz and 2 percent Mourvèdre. 1,500 cases made. • $35 • (04/30/97) • **92**

MENZIES

Cabernet Sauvignon Coonawarra 1993: Lean and chewy, a dense, tart, zingy wine with unfocused berry flavors that soften on the finish. Try after 1999. • $17 • (05/31/97) • **84**

Cabernet Sauvignon Coonawarra 1992: Ripe, generous and distinctive for its mouthfilling black currant, black cherry and minty, spicy overtones that linger on the chewy but well-modulated finish. Has style and grace, and the stuffing to improve through 2002, at least. 2,000 cases made. • $18 • (11/30/96) • **90**

MERRILL, GEOFF

Cabernet Sauvignon South Australia 1992: Lithe and spicy, in a crisp style that compacts its berry and herb flavors into a racy frame. Drink now. • $24 • (11/30/96) • **83**

Cabernet Sauvignon-Merlot South Eastern Australia Owen's Estate 1994: The tart, earthy flavors obscure any charm in this medium-weight blend. • $14 • (10/15/96) • **78**

Chardonnay South Eastern Australia 1994: Smooth and appealing, offering straightforward apple, spice and vanilla flavors that fade a bit on the finish. • $22 • (11/30/96) • **85**

Chardonnay South Eastern Australia Owen's Estate 1995: Tasty, with resiny citrus and apple flavors that remain vibrant through the finish. Beautifully articulated fruit flavors carry it. Try now. • $14 • (12/31/96) • **88**

Chardonnay South Eastern Australia Owen's Estate 1994: Starts off bright and crisp, with an appealing layer of fresh melon and apple flavors, then narrows a bit on the finish as it strives for delicacy. Drinkable now. • $14 • (01/31/97) • **86**

Sauvignon Blanc McLaren Vale Owen's Estate 1996: Fresh and appealing for its spot-on pear and herb flavors. Refreshingly straightforward and open-textured. • $14 • (12/31/96) • **85**

Sauvignon Blanc South Eastern Australia Owen's Estate 1995: Dry, even a bit austere, with zingy citrus and celery flavors that linger. • $14 • (10/15/96) • **83**

MILBURN PARK

Cabernet Sauvignon South Eastern Australia 1996: Supple, generous and appealing for its ripe currant and berry flavors. 8,000 cases made. • $9 • (05/31/98) • **84**

Cabernet Sauvignon Victoria 1995: Light, with piney flavors dominating modest berry character. Finish is tight. Drinkable now. 15,000 cases made. • $9 • (02/28/97) • **80**

Cabernet Sauvignon Victoria 1994 • $9 • (03/31/96) • **85**

Chardonnay South Eastern Australia Reserve 1997: Open-textured, generous with its apple and spice flavors, straightforward and immediately likable. 18,000 cases made. • $9 • (05/31/98) • **85**

Chardonnay Victoria 1995: Soft in texture and generous with its citrusy pear and mineral flavors that grow creamy on the finish. Balanced by a delicate zing of acidity. Drinkable now. 20,000 cases made. • $9 • (02/28/97) BB • **87**

Chardonnay Victoria 1994 • $9 • (03/31/96) BB • **88**

Sauvignon Blanc Victoria 1995: Smooth and mild in flavor, with just a hint of herbality to the modest apple flavors. Ready to drink. 10,000 cases made. • $8 • (04/30/97) • **83**

Sauvignon Blanc Victoria 1994 • $8 • (03/31/96) BB • **85**

MILDARA

Cabernet Merlot Coonawarra 1985 • $5 • (01/31/88) BB • **80**

Cabernet Merlot Coonawarra 1984 • $5 • (06/15/87) BB • **82**

Cabernet Merlot Murray River Valley 1986 • $7 • (03/31/89) • **80**

Cabernet Sauvignon Coonawarra 1986 • $10 • (01/31/89) • **90**

Cabernet Sauvignon Coonawarra 1985 • $8 • (04/15/88) BB • **89**

Cabernet Sauvignon Coonawarra 1984 • $6 • (04/30/87) • **77**

Cabernet Sauvignon McLaren Vale Private Reserve 1985 • $13 • (01/31/89) • **85**

Cabernet Sauvignon Murray River Valley 1986 • $8 • (01/31/89) • **80**

Shiraz Coonawarra 1986 • $9 • (12/31/88) • **89**

MITCHELL

Sémillon Clare Valley 1995: Bright and refreshing for its pear and pineapple flavors. A lively wine with a stony edge to the solid finish. Drink now. 18,000 cases made. • $11 • (05/31/97) • **87**

Shiraz Clare Valley Peppertree Vineyard 1989 • $11 • (02/15/92) • **76**

MITCHELTON

Cabernet Blend South Eastern Australia 1993 • $10 • (06/30/95) • **82**

Cabernet Blend South Eastern Australia 1992 • $9 • (05/15/94) • **84**

Cabernet Merlot Australia Print Label 1985 • $17 • (01/31/90) • **78**

Cabernet Sauvignon Goulburn Valley 1988 • $13 • (04/15/91) • **86**

Cabernet Sauvignon Goulburn Valley 1986 • $13 • (01/31/90) • **73**

Cabernet Sauvignon Goulburn Valley Reserve 1990 • $18 • (03/31/93) • **82**

Cabernet Sauvignon South Eastern Australia Reserve 1992 • $16 • (01/31/95) • **80**

Cabernet Sauvignon South Eastern Australia Reserve 1991 • $14 • (11/15/93) • **81**

Cabernet Sauvignon Victoria Reserve 1994: Bright in flavor, supple in texture, with smoke-tinged berry and currant flavors that remain tight and spicy through the finish. Best after 1999. 7,000 cases made. • $20 • (11/30/96) • **87**

Cabernet Sauvignon Victoria Reserve 1993 • $16 • (11/30/95) • **90**

Cabernet Shiraz Cabernet Franc South Eastern Australia Thomas Mitchell 1994 • $10 • (04/30/96) • **80**

Cabernet Shiraz Merlot South Eastern Australia 1991 • $10 • (11/30/93) • **82**

Cabernet Shiraz Merlot Victoria 1990 • $10 • (08/31/92) • **87**

Cabernet Shiraz Merlot Victoria 1987 • $9 • (01/31/90) • **86**

Cabernet Shiraz South Eastern Australia Thomas Mitchell 1995: Lean and chewy, not very forward, but it has some pretty berry and toast flavors lurking in the background. It should open up by 1999. 14,000 cases made. • $10 • (07/31/97) • **84**

Chardonnay Victoria 1994 • $10 • (06/30/95) • **82**

Chardonnay Victoria 1993 • $9 • (07/31/94) BB • **85**

Chardonnay Victoria Reserve 1994: Supple, generous and beautifully proportioned, this is a sleek wine with lovely buttery, spicy pear and apple flavors that extend into a long and glorious finish. Has depth and harmony. Drinkable now. 5,000 cases made. • $16 • (11/30/96) • **91**

Chardonnay Victoria Reserve 1993 • $16 • (06/30/96) • **89**

Marsanne Goulburn Valley 1996: A solid white wine, with nice grace notes of almond and smoke to the pear flavors that linger on the generous, slightly raw finish. Drink by 1999. 5,000 cases made. • $17 • (11/30/97) • **86**

Marsanne South Eastern Australia 1995 • $10 • (04/30/96) • **83**

Marsanne South Eastern Australia 1993 • $9 • (07/31/94) • **81**

Marsanne South Eastern Australia Thomas Mitchell 1996: Has pretty fruit and floral flavors that linger on the soft, sweet-tasting finish. Drink soon. 7,000 cases made. • $10 • (11/30/97) • **85**

Marsanne Victoria Reserve 1993 • $16 • (04/30/96) • **81**

MCM Cab Mac Victoria Red 1992 • $9 • (03/31/93) • **85**

Shiraz Goulburn Valley 1995: Packed with flavor, here is a rousing mouthful of blackberry, anise, mint and plum flavors that persist on the solid finish. Impressive now, best after it picks up some polish by 1999 or 2000. 5,000 cases made. • $17 • (11/30/97) • **88**

Shiraz Goulburn Valley 1989 • $8 • (02/15/92) • **80**

Shiraz Goulburn Valley 1988 • $8 • (03/15/91) BB • **86**

Shiraz South Eastern Australia 1993 • $10 • (06/30/95) • **85**

Shiraz South Eastern Australia Thomas Mitchell 1995: Supple, jazzy and nicely balanced to show off its raspberry and blackberry flavors. A drink-me-now quaffer. 5,000 cases made. • $10 • (11/30/97) • **86**

Shiraz South Eastern Australia Thomas Mitchell 1994 • $10 • (04/30/96) • **83**

Shiraz Victoria 1991 • $9 • (05/31/93) • **84**

Shiraz Victoria 1990 • $8 • (11/30/92) BB • **84**

Shiraz Victoria Print Label 1991 • $18 • (09/30/94) • **87**

Shiraz Victoria Print Label 1990 • $17 • (05/31/93) • **88**

Shiraz Victoria Reserve 1993 • $16 • (06/30/96) • **91**

White Goulburn Valley 1994: Dry, crisp and appealing, but not especially intense, offering light nectarine and spice flavors. 3,000 cases made. • $16 • (01/31/97) • **83**

MONTROSE

Cabernet Sauvignon Mudgee 1987 • $10 • (02/28/91) • **81**

Cabernet Sauvignon Mudgee 1986 • $8 • (07/31/89) • **86**

Cabernet Sauvignon Mudgee 1984 • $10 • (04/30/88) • **88**
Cabernet Sauvignon Mudgee Special Reserve 1985 • $16 • (01/31/90) • **80**
Chardonnay South Eastern Australia Poet's Corner 1996: Soft and smooth, with bright melon and spice flavors that finish with a seeming touch of sweetness. 13,000 cases made. • $10 • (05/15/97) • **82**
Poet's Corner Red South Eastern Australia 1991 • $6 • (03/31/93) BB • **82**
Shiraz Mudgee 1988 • $9 • (03/15/91) • **78**
Shiraz Mudgee 1984 • $10 • (07/01/87) • **87**
Shiraz Mudgee 1983 • $7 • (03/15/88) • **86**
Shiraz South Eastern Australia Poet's Corner 1995: Light, supple and easy to drink. A smooth wine with appealing berry, cherry and spice flavors. 10,000 cases made. • $10 • (05/15/97) • **84**

MOUNT HORROCKS

Riesling Clare Valley Cordon Cut 1997: Very sweet, satiny smooth, with pretty pear, vanilla and cream flavors that linger on the finish. Might gain depth with cellaring. 1,300 cases made. • $18/375ml • (05/31/98) • **92**
Riesling Watervale Cordon Cut 1996: A rich, luscious dessert wine with melon, apricot, honey and pineapple flavors that cascade through the silky finish and plenty of mouthwatering acidity to balance to the sweetness. Try now. 800 cases made. • $17/375ml • (05/31/97) • **94**

MOUNT LANGI GHIRAN

Cabernet Merlot Victoria Langi 1994: Burnt, gamy flavors aren't for everyone, but this has plenty of pretty plum and berry notes that make it worth cellaring until 1999 to 2000. • $30 • (11/30/97) • **86**
Cabernet Merlot Victoria 1993: Chunky, chewy and packs a nice dose of berry and cherry flavors between the hard covers of toasty oak and firm tannins. Needs until 1998 to 2000 to soften the edges. 1,200 cases made. • $24 • (11/30/96) • **90**
Shiraz Victoria Langi 1995: A lot of character in a silky, elegant package, offering flavors of blueberry, plum, licorice, black pepper and other spices, all lingering forever on the finish. Delicious now, better evolved in 2000. 2,800 cases made. • $30 • (07/31/97) • **91**
Shiraz Victoria 1994 • $24 • (06/15/96) • **92**

MOUNT MARY

Quintet Lilydale 1994: Smooth in texture, with earthy, peppery, tarry notes accenting the modest berry flavors. Seems ready now, but has a reputation for improving with much cellaring. 64 cases made. • $65 • (09/30/97) • **85**

MOUNT PLEASANT

Chardonnay Hunter Valley 1995 • $13 • (04/30/96) • **87**
Chardonnay Hunter Valley 1993 • $12 • (06/30/95) • **88**
Shiraz Hunter Valley 1993 • $11 • (04/30/96) • **82**
Shiraz Hunter Valley 1992 • $12 • (11/30/95) • **83**

MOUNTADAM

Chardonnay Australia 1993 • $25 • (09/30/95) HR • **90**
Chardonnay Eden Valley 1995: Smooth and inviting, with spicy caramel and honey overtones to the silky core of sweet pear and apple flavors. Finishes with harmony and style. 4,000 cases made. • $25 • (06/15/97) • **88**
Chardonnay Eden Valley 1994 • $26 • (04/30/96) • **90**
Pinot Noir Eden Valley 1993 • $26 • (04/30/96) • **81**
Pinot Noir Eden Valley 1992 • $20 • (07/31/94) • **88**
Pinot Noir Eden Valley 1988 • $25 • (03/31/91) • **86**

MURRINDINDI

Chardonnay Victoria 1995: Bright and tart, here's a juicy wine with lovely nectarine and spice flavors that bounce along pleasantly through the finish. Nice now, better in 1999. 4,000 cases made. • $17 • (04/30/98) • **88**

Key: SS—Spectator Selection. CS—Cellar Selection. BB—Best Buy. HR—Highly Recommended. $NA—Price not available. (BT)—Barrel tasting. Ⓐ—Auction Price.
Dates in parentheses represent the issues in which the ratings were published.

NOON'S

Cabernet-Shiraz Langhorne Creek 1995: Light in structure but dripping with ripe cherry and anise flavors. A solid wine to drink now with hearty food. 55 percent Cabernet Sauvignon, 45 percent Shiraz. 600 cases made. • $17 • (05/31/98) • **85**

NORMANS

Cabernet Sauvignon McLaren Vale Chais Clarendon 1995: Has a pretty mint and cedar overlay to the basic black cherry and currant flavors, finishes with a gamy edge. Nicely crafted, but the flavors won't appeal to everyone. Best from 1999 or 2000. 500 cases made. • $18 • (03/31/98) • **84**
Cabernet Sauvignon South Australia Chais Clarendon 1991 • $20 • (06/30/95) • **78**
Cabernet Sauvignon South Australia Chais Clarendon 1989 • $19 • (09/30/94) • **78**
Cabernet Sauvignon South Australia Bin C106 1995: Nicely packed with generous currant and blackberry flavors, this is a solidly built wine with polished tannins and a long finish. Hold until 2000 to 2001 to see if it will develop more nuance. • $12 • (11/30/97) • **87**
Cabernet Sauvignon South Australia Family Reserve 1993: Ripe and plush at first, with a tangy twist to the blackberry and cola flavors, finishing with a touch of lime. Best from 2000. • $8 • (05/15/97) • **83**
Cabernet Sauvignon South Australia Family Reserve 1992 • $10 • (09/30/94) • **79**
Chardonnay Padthaway Chais Clarendon 1996: Broad and ripe, with spicy pear flavors that linger smoothly on the generous finish. Gets richer and spicier on the long finish. Drink now. 500 cases made. • $15 • (03/31/98) • **88**
Chardonnay South Australia Bin C207 1996: Ripe, robust style of Chardonnay, offering plenty of pear and floral flavors, hinting at resin on the soft finish. Drink now. 1,500 cases made. • $12 • (03/31/98) • **86**
Chardonnay South Australia Chandlers Hill 1994 • $8 • (01/31/95) • **81**
Chardonnay South Australia Chandlers Hill 1993 • $8 • (09/30/94) • **84**
Chardonnay South Australia Family Reserve 1994 • $10 • (04/15/95) • **87**
Chardonnay South Australia Family Reserve 1993 • $10 • (09/30/94) • **83**
Chardonnay South Eastern Australia Lone Gum 1996: Nice, straightforward Chardonnay, with citrusy pear and spice flavors on a modest scale. Drink now. • $9 • (11/30/97) • **83**
Sémillon-Chardonnay South Eastern Australia Lone Gum 1996: Soft, fruity style emphasizes bright apple and pear flavors over any complications. Drink now. 10,000 cases made. • $8 • (03/31/98) • **82**
Shiraz-Cabernet South Eastern Australia Lone Gum 1996: Crisp and simple, with appealing blackberry and currant flavors. Hints of smoke on the polished, gentle finish. Drink now. 30,000 cases made. • $8 • (03/31/98) • **83**
Shiraz McLaren Vale Chais Clarendon 1995: A lovely Shiraz of spice and fruit flavor, offering a solid core of boysenberry and plum with grace notes of coffee, anise and mineral. Approachable now, best from 1999 or 2000. 500 cases made. • $18 • (03/31/98) • **88**
Shiraz South Australia Chais Clarendon 1992 • $20 • (04/15/95) • **87**
Shiraz South Australia Chais Clarendon 1990 • $19 • (06/15/94) • **86**
Shiraz South Australia Chandlers Hill 1993 • $8 • (04/15/95) • **79**
Shiraz South Australia Chandlers Hill 1992 • $8 • (06/15/94) • **82**
Shiraz South Eastern Australia Lone Gum 1996: Light, bright and supple, offering pretty black cherry and cinnamon flavors that finish soft and polished. Drink now. 20,000 cases made. • $9 • (03/31/98) • **84**

ORLANDO

Brut Australia Carrington Extra Brut NV: Soft, almost creamy in texture, with spicy, toasty flavors and hints of honey and pineapple. Likeable for its grace, ultimately simple. 120,000 cases made. • $9 • (03/31/98) • **84**
Cabernet Sauvignon Coonawarra Jacaranda Ridge 1989 • $35 • (10/31/95) • **83**
Cabernet Sauvignon Coonawarra St.-Hugo 1993: Solidly built to show off its layers of spicy, herbal Cabernet flavors, wrapped in velvety tannins and lingering with spicy juiciness. Best from 2000 to 2002. 200 cases made. • $28 • (06/15/97) • **90**
Cabernet Sauvignon Coonawarra St.-Hugo 1989 • $15 • (12/15/93) • **86**
Cabernet Sauvignon Coonawarra St.-Hugo 1987 • $15 • (05/31/91) • **78**
Cabernet Sauvignon Coonawarra St.-Hugo 1986 • $8 • (02/28/91) • **81**
Cabernet Sauvignon Coonawarra St.-Hugo 1985 • $15 • (04/30/89) • **90**
Cabernet Sauvignon South Eastern Australia Jacob's Creek 1995: Solid in texture and flavorful, with pretty black cherry and currant. Finishes soft, with a hint of herbs. 24,200 cases made. • $9 • (05/31/98) • **85**

Cabernet Sauvignon South Eastern Australia Jacob's Creek 1994: A soft, slightly caramel-like red wine, light and tangy. Not very reminiscent of Cabernet. 40,000 cases made. • $8 • (05/15/97) • **79**
Cabernet Sauvignon South Eastern Australia Jacob's Creek 1990 • $8 • (12/15/93) • **78**
Cabernet Sauvignon South Eastern Australia Jacob's Creek 1989 • $7 • (06/30/92) • **77**
Cabernet Sauvignon South Eastern Australia Jacob's Creek 1988 • $7 • (07/15/91) BB • **83**
Cabernet Sauvignon South Eastern Australia Jacob's Creek 1987 • $7 • (07/31/90) BB • **85**
Cabernet Sauvignon South Eastern Australia Jacob's Creek 1986 • $7 • (05/15/89) BB • **87**
Chardonnay Padthaway St. Hilary 1996: Here's an aromatic, spicy and beautifully focused white, almost resinous in flavor as it spreads its oak-scented pineapple, pear and honey tones over the finish. Nicely done; good price, too. 10,000 cases made. • $16 • (05/15/98) SS • **90**
Chardonnay South Eastern Australia Jacob's Creek 1997: A fresh and fruity white, more like Riesling than Chardonnay, with peach and citrus flavors that linger enticingly on the light finish. Made in a quantity that suggests availability, it's also reasonably priced. 70,800 cases made. • $9 • (05/15/98) BB • **85**
Chardonnay South Eastern Australia Jacob's Creek 1996: Light and fruity, with some resinous notes adding character. Finish is simple and refreshing. 100,000 cases made. • $8 • (05/15/97) • **81**
Chardonnay South Eastern Australia Jacob's Creek 1995 • $7 • (03/31/96) • **81**
Chardonnay South Eastern Australia Jacob's Creek 1993 • $7 • (06/30/94) BB • **82**
Merlot South Eastern Australia Jacob's Creek 1996: Light and silky, a pretty wine with modest plum and cola flavors. 46,300 cases made. • $9 • (05/31/98) • **83**
Merlot South Eastern Australia Jacob's Creek 1995: Light and supple, with a modest portion of mint and red berry flavors. Try now. 30,000 cases made. • $9 • (05/15/97) • **80**
Merlot South Eastern Australia Jacob's Creek 1994 • $7 • (03/31/96) • **80**
Merlot South Eastern Australia Jacob's Creek 1992 • $8 • (09/30/94) • **77**
Merlot South Eastern Australia Jacob's Creek 1991 • $8 • (12/15/93) • **81**
Merlot South Eastern Australia Jacob's Creek 1990 • $7 • (06/30/92) • **79**
Merlot South Eastern Australia Jacob's Creek 1989 • $7 • (09/30/91) • **82**
Riesling South Eastern Australia Dry 1997: Light, soft and appealing in its simple apple and resin flavors. 266 cases made. • $9 • (05/31/98) • **84**
Riesling South Eastern Australia Jacob's Creek 1996: Dry, but soft enough to land gently on the palate with its peach, floral and slightly oily flavors. Drink now. • $7 • (06/30/97) • **84**
Sémillon Chardonnay South Eastern Australia Jacob's Creek 1997: Soft and spicy, generous with its melon flavor at the core, agreeable for current drinking. 80 percent Sémillon, 20 percent Chardonnay. 12,200 cases made. • $9 • (05/15/98) • **82**
Sémillon Chardonnay South Eastern Australia Jacob's Creek 1996: Smooth and spicy, a small-scale wine with pretty pear and butterscotch notes. • $7 • (06/30/97) • **82**
Sémillon Chardonnay South Eastern Australia Jacob's Creek 1995 • $7 • (03/31/96) • **80**
Shiraz Cabernet South Eastern Australia Jacob's Creek 1996: A jazzy mouthful of bright raspberry and black cherry flavors, with hints of coffee and tobacco sneaking in on the finish. Nicely balanced to show the pretty flavors. 25,100 cases made. • $9 • (05/31/98) BB • **86**
Shiraz Cabernet South Eastern Australia Jacob's Creek 1995: Has the sturdy backbone of a Cabernet with the ripe, chewy flavors of Shiraz, leaning toward dark plum and anise. Not big or rich, but the flavor profile is on the mark. Try now. 60,000 cases made. • $7 • (05/15/97) • **82**
Shiraz Cabernet South Eastern Australia Jacob's Creek 1994 • $7 • (03/31/96) • **82**
Shiraz Cabernet South Eastern Australia Jacob's Creek 1991 • $8 • (10/31/93) • **80**
Shiraz Padthaway Lawson's 1992: Crisp structure and bright flavors characterize this racy Shiraz, offering peppery currant notes that persist on the finish. 2,600 cases made. • $26 • (05/15/98) • **87**
Shiraz Padthaway Lawson's 1991 • $22 • (02/29/96) • **89**

O'SHEA, MAURICE

Chardonnay Australia 1994 • $25 • (04/30/96) • **82**
Shiraz Hunter Valley 1993 • $25 • (04/30/96) • **86**

OXFORD LANDING

Cabernet Shiraz South Eastern Australia 1997: Crisp and bright, with red cherry and currant flavors on a light, supple frame. 80,000 cases made. • $9 • (06/15/98) • **84**
Cabernet Shiraz South Eastern Australia 1995: On the light side, with a nice core of cherry flavor and a vegetal edge which detracts from its charm. Drinkable now. • $8 • (02/28/97) • **82**
Cabernet Shiraz South Eastern Australia 1993 • $7 • (11/30/95) BB • **85**
Cabernet Shiraz South Eastern Australia 1992 • $7 • (06/30/95) • **84**
Cabernet Shiraz South Eastern Australia 1991 • $7 • (04/30/94) • **81**
Chardonnay South Eastern Australia 1997: Here's a find in high-quality, value-oriented Australian Chardonnay. This one's supple and appealing for its pear and melon flavors, which remain pure and last nicely on the wide-open finish. Good for drinking now through 1999 to 2000. 130,000 cases made. • $8 • (12/31/97) BB • **86**
Chardonnay South Eastern Australia 1996: Fruity and fresh, with sharp acidity cutting through the fresh citrus and apple flavors. Needs food to balance the acidity. • $8 • (02/28/97) • **83**
Chardonnay South Eastern Australia 1995 • $8 • (03/31/96) • **84**
Chardonnay South Eastern Australia 1994 • $10 • (05/15/95) • **86**
Chardonnay South Eastern Australia 1993 • $7 • (03/15/94) • **83**
Merlot South Eastern Australia 1994 • $7 • (06/30/96) • **78**
Merlot South Eastern Australia 1993 • $7 • (06/30/96) BB • **85**
Sauvignon Blanc South Australia 1997: Light, smooth and spicy, with a hint of root beer sneaking in with the light citrus and apple flavors. Try now. • $9 • (01/31/98) BB • **84**
Sauvignon Blanc South Eastern Australia 1996: Light but fragrant, with distinctive herb and green berry flavors that finish a bit soft. • $8 • (05/15/97) • **83**
Sauvignon Blanc South Eastern Australia 1994 • $7 • (03/31/96) • **80**
Sauvignon Blanc South Eastern Australia 1993 • $7 • (04/30/94) • **80**

PARKER COONAWARRA ESTATE

Cabernet Blend Coonawarra Terra Rossa First Growth 1994: Chewy and focused to show off the tarry currant flavors which linger on the solid finish. Needs to settle down, perhaps by 2001 to 2004. 2,000 cases made. • $45 • (09/30/97) • **88**
Cabernet Blend Coonawarra Terra Rossa First Growth 1990 • $38 • (09/30/94) • **80**
Cabernet Blend Coonawarra Terra Rossa First Growth 1989 • $35 • (05/31/93) • **89**
Cabernet Sauvignon Coonawarra Terra Rossa 1995: Minty, earthy flavors dominate this rustic, solidly built red. May show more charm if cellared until 2000. 2,000 cases made. • $25 • (09/30/97) • **85**
Cabernet Sauvignon Coonawarra Terra Rossa 1994: Feels almost crisp, keeping a tight rein on its pickle barrel-scented berry and leather flavors. Finishes with enough style to warrant cellaring until 1999 to 2000 to see what develops. 1,200 cases made. • $22 • (09/30/96) • **88**
Cabernet Sauvignon Coonawarra Terra Rossa 1992 • $20 • (03/31/95) • **74**
Cabernet Sauvignon Coonawarra Terra Rossa 1991 • $22 • (09/30/94) • **82**
Cabernet Sauvignon Coonawarra Terra Rossa 1989 • $20 • (05/31/93) • **83**
Terra Rossa First Growth Coonawarra 1993: A light claret style with stewed fruit and herbal notes and chocolaty, spicy currant flavors. Firm tannins need until 1999 or 2000 to soften. 850 cases made. • $45 • (01/31/97) • **86**
Terra Rossa First Growth Coonawarra 1991 • $39 • (03/31/95) • **87**

PENFOLDS

Cabernet Sauvignon South Australia Bin 407 1994: Dark, dense and tarry, this is a serious mouthful of flavor and tannin that needs cellaring until 2002 to 2005. 4,600 cases made. • $17 • (09/15/97) • **87**
Cabernet Sauvignon South Australia Bin 407 1993 • $16 • (04/30/96) • **88**
Cabernet Sauvignon South Australia Bin 407 1992 • $16 • (03/31/96) • **85**
Cabernet Sauvignon South Australia Bin 407 1991 • $16 • (11/30/94) • **86**
Cabernet Sauvignon South Australia Bin 407 1990 • $16 • (03/31/93) • **78**
Cabernet Sauvignon South Australia Bin 707 1994: Bright and fruity, with a firm backbone to support the well-articulated currant and blackberry flavors. Finishes with a nice echo of fruit, but doesn't show the depth and extra dimensions we've come to expect of this wine. Approachable now, best from 2000. 2,700 cases made. • $45 • (03/31/98) • **88**
Cabernet Sauvignon South Australia Bin 707 1993: Lovely, graceful style, with a generous core of plum and blueberry flavors that swirl around nicely, with some coffee and herb overtones on the artfully integrated finish.

Progressively builds in character with each sip. Approachable now, but try to wait until 2003 to 2005. 7,638 cases made. • $45 • (04/30/97) • **92**

Cabernet Sauvignon South Australia Bin 707 1992 • $40 • (10/15/95) CS • **92**

Cabernet Sauvignon South Australia Bin 707 1990 • $51 Ⓐ • (03/31/95) CS • **92**

Cabernet Sauvignon South Australia Bin 707 1989 • $40 • (05/31/93) • **85**

Cabernet Sauvignon South Australia Bin 707 1987 • $57 Ⓐ • (05/31/91) • **83**

Cabernet Sauvignon South Australia Bin 707 1986 • $58 Ⓐ • (09/30/89) • **90**

Cabernet Sauvignon South Australia Bin 707 1981 • $18 • (07/01/87) • **90**

Cabernet Shiraz Coonawarra Bin 920 1990 • $110 • (05/15/96) • **86**

Cabernet Shiraz Clare Valley 1995: Lean in structure, minty in flavor, with modest berry notes to keep it in balance, but it seems pretty tame at this point. Try in 1999. 2,188 cases made. • $10 • (05/31/97) • **84**

Cabernet Shiraz South Australia Bin 389 1994: An effusive mouthful of Cabernet, with floral-scented blackberry and spice flavors that remain smooth through the finish. Try now. 9,300 cases made. • $19 • (09/15/97) • **86**

Cabernet Shiraz South Australia Bin 389 1993 • $18 • (04/30/96) • **87**

Cabernet Shiraz South Australia Bin 389 1992 • $16 • (11/30/95) SS • **92**

Cabernet Shiraz South Australia Bin 389 1991 • $16 • (11/30/95) • **90**

Cabernet Shiraz South Australia Bin 389 1990 • $16 • (01/31/95) • **86**

Cabernet Shiraz South Australia Bin 389 1989 • $16 • (04/15/94) • **87**

Cabernet Shiraz South Australia Bin 389 1989 • $16 • (06/30/93) • **83**

Cabernet Shiraz South Australia Bin 389 1988 • $16 • (03/31/93) • **81**

Cabernet Shiraz South Australia Bin 389 1987 • $14 • (02/28/91) • **88**

Cabernet Shiraz South Australia Bin 389 1986 • $15 • (01/31/90) • **83**

Cabernet Shiraz South Australia Bin 389 1985 • $14 • (12/31/88) • **86**

Cabernet Shiraz South Australia Bin 389 1983 • $15 • (07/01/87) • **91**

Cabernet Shiraz South Australia Koonunga Hill 1991 • $9 • (03/31/95) BB • **85**

Cabernet Shiraz South Australia Koonunga Hill 1987 • $7 • (02/28/91) BB • **86**

Cabernet Shiraz South Australia Koonunga Hill 1986 • $7 • (05/15/89) • **78**

Cabernet Shiraz South Australia Koonunga Hill 1984 • $7 • (07/01/87) • **89**

Chardonnay Koonunga Hill South Eastern Australia 1997: Distinctly floral and more than a little sweet, with nectarine flavors emerging on the finish. 20,800 cases made. • $9 • (05/15/98) • **84**

Chardonnay Koonunga Hill South Australia 1996: Crisp and spicy, here's a bright, open-textured Chardonnay that's easy to like for its pear and peach flavors. Try now. 30,236 cases made. • $9 • (05/31/97) • **85**

Chardonnay Koonunga Hill Australia 1995 • $9 • (04/30/96) • **88**

Chardonnay Sauvignon Blanc Clare Valley Organically Grown Grapes 1993 • $10 • (01/31/95) • **85**

Chardonnay South Australia 1994 • $9 • (05/15/96) • **84**

Chardonnay South Australia 1993 • $9 • (04/30/95) • **87**

Chardonnay South Australia Barrel Fermented Reserve 1994 • $12 • (03/31/96) • **88**

Chardonnay South Australia The Valleys 1995: Bright and almost chewy with flavor, this is packed with pineapple and pear notes that echo on the finish, with a touch of earth. Try now. 2,538 cases made. • $13 • (05/31/97) • **87**

Grange Shiraz South Australia 1992: Ripe, smoky and spicy, this is a wine of extraordinary subtlety and complexity, powerful without showing too much muscle. It layers its anise, black cherry and blackberry flavors to keep them zingy through the finish. Shows a lot of depth and surprising restraint. Best to cellar until 2002 to 2005. 2,049 cases made. • $110 • (10/15/97) CS • **94**

Grange Shiraz South Australia 1991: Rich, chewy, spicy and full of currant and blackberry character, this is distinctive for the harmony that's beneath the hedonistic fanfare of flavors. A stunning wine with all the Grange characteristics. Try from 2005 to 2015. • $110 • (01/31/97) • **95**

Grange Shiraz South Australia 1990: Magnificent, exotic, a veritable cascade of opulent flavors—earthy currant, black cherry and licorice—on a grand frame of incredible length, wrapped in finely-grained tannins. Feels like it can age through 2010 or 2020, at least. • $150 • (01/31/97) • **98**

Grange Hermitage South Australia Bin 95 1989: Amazingly ripe and lush, this bubbles with vibrant fruit like a mouthful of cassis syrup, concentrated, elegant and remarkably silky in texture. Blackberry, currant and vanilla flavors ooze over the palate, making for a thoroughly hedonistic drink. Wonderful now or wait until it calms down, perhaps by 2003 or 2005. • $207 • (01/31/97) • **96**

Key: SS—Spectator Selection. CS—Cellar Selection. BB—Best Buy. HR—Highly Recommended. $NA—Price not available. (BT)—Barrel tasting. Ⓐ—Auction Price.
Dates in parentheses represent the issues in which the ratings were published.

Grange Hermitage South Australia Bin 95 1988: A rich wine that never forgets to be elegant, this is plush, focused and generous with its berry, plum and anise flavors that remain sweet and supple through the long finish. • $162 • (01/31/97) • **91**

Grange Hermitage South Australia Bin 95 1987: Extemely spicy on the nose, with zingy berry and plum character coursing through the palate of typical Grange flavors. Chewy with tannins, but they're finely grained. Needs until 2005 or so. • $90 • (01/31/97) • **90**

Grange Hermitage South Australia Bin 95 1986: Approaching full maturity, this has developed into a huge mouthful of cherry, raspberry, plum, prune, anise and mineral flavors that keep expanding on the palate. Sensational now, but still has room to grow, at least until 2006 to 2010. • $307 • (01/31/97) • **98**

Grange Hermitage South Australia Bin 95 1985: Atypical of an 11-year-old wine, this is youthful but graceful. It began lean and elegant, but has developed sweet, deep and heady berry, plum, vanilla and spice flavors that swirl through. Delicious now, but should keep developing until 2010 or 2015, possibly beyond. • $84 • (01/31/97) • **94**

Grange Hermitage South Australia Bin 95 1984: A big wine, deep and chewy, firm and focused. Offers harmonious, youthful berry flavors that pick up cedar and anise accents on the finish. Best to hold until 2005. • $80 • (01/31/97) • **91**

Grange Hermitage South Australia Bin 95 1983: Deep, dense and chewy, this is packed with plum and mineral flavors that are dominated by the structure now, but will have fleshed out by 2003 to 2006. • $84 • (01/31/97) • **90**

Grange Hermitage South Australia Bin 95 1982: Packed with bright flavors, raspberry and red plum dominating, with great length and sweet tannins to suggest a long life. Harmonious and elegant beneath focused power. Best from 2007 to 2010. • $170 • (01/31/97) • **92**

Grange Hermitage South Australia Bin 95 1981: Seems lean and earthy at first, but develops in the glass into an impeccably balanced, intense mouthful of smoky plum, bacon, herb and licorice flavors. A stylish package. • $177 • (01/31/97) • **89**

Grange Hermitage South Australia Bin 95 1980: Rich, sweet and silky, delivering a lovely mouthful of lush fruit flavors, centering around currant and plum, with hints of licorice and leather at the edges. Expands and deepens on the finish. Approachable now, but should continue to improve for years. • $NA • (01/31/97) • **93**

Grange Hermitage South Australia Bin 95 1979: Big and broad, this wine is gloriously spicy and rich, pouring out its licorice-scented plum, prune, berry and smoke flavors like a fountain, yet remaining harmonious and marvelously balanced. Drink now, or let it grow. • $212 • (01/31/97) • **94**

Grange Hermitage South Australia Bin 95 1978: Earthy, pruny, very mature flavors in a smoothly grained texture. Seems to be losing its freshness, but it's still relatively complex. • $339 • (01/31/97) • **83**

Grange Hermitage South Australia Bin 95 1977: Big-boned, rich and packed with berry, beetroot and mineral flavors that shine through the fine layer of firm tannins. A great example of a maturing Grange. Still growing in the bottle; aim for 2000 to 2005. • $208 • (01/31/97) • **90**

Grange Hermitage South Australia Bin 95 1976: Solid, vibrant and rich with black cherry, red plum, spice and vanilla flavors shaded with hints of anise and currant. Reaching its peak, but still remarkably fresh and concentrated. • $706 • (01/31/97) • **93**

Grange Hermitage South Australia Bin 95 1975: Harmonious and supple, laced with licorice character, focused but not especially grand. Drinkable now, but can improve further. • $328 • (01/31/97) • **87**

Grange Hermitage South Australia Bin 95 1974: Generous with its fresh-tasting plum and raspberry flavors that bubble up beautifully through a layer of finely grained tannins. A harmonious wine, exhibiting both grace and a modicum of power. • $354 • (01/31/97) • **90**

Grange Hermitage South Australia Bin 95 1973: Firm in texture, with velvety prune and blackberry flavors weaving around a distinctive licorice note. A bit on the chunky side. • $310 • (01/31/97) • **87**

Grange Hermitage South Australia Bin 95 1972: Firm and ever-so-slightly chewy, still showing a nice core of black cherry and plum flavors. Has some room to grow, but it's appealing now. • $NA • (01/31/97) • **88**

Grange Hermitage South Australia Bin 95 1971: This is the wine that made Grange's reputation in Europe. It's become harmonious, velvety and rich with plum, raspberry, spice, leather and cedar flavors that extend into a long finish. • $638 • (01/31/97) • **92**

Grange Hermitage South Australia Bin 95 1970: More sharply pointed than usual for Grange, but the bright beam of raspberry and plum flavor cuts through the fine-grained tannins. Has some nice mineral nuances, too. • $443 • (01/31/97) • **89**

Grange Hermitage South Australia Bin 95 1969: Very mature, with an earthy, mushroomy character, but it still feels alive and velvety. • $443 • (01/31/97) • **86**

Grange Hermitage South Australia Bin 95 1968: A solid, medium-weight, fully mature red. Not especially Grange-like, but pleasantly spicy and it gently folds in some nice prune and smoke notes. • $549 • (01/31/97) • **85**

Grange Hermitage South Australia Bin 95 1967: Rich and harmonious, though not huge, it's a supple Grange with gorgeous anise-scented plum and cherry flavors that last on the pointedly long finish. • $NA • (01/31/97) • **91**

Grange Hermitage South Australia Bin 95 1966: Mature, earthy, leathery flavors dominate up front, followed by sweet plum and cedar flavors, but not showing the expected opulence. • $589 • (01/31/97) • **87**

Grange Hermitage South Australia Bin 95 1965: Has a nice core of hard-edged black cherry and prune flavors, with a bit of mushroom on the finish. Still feels youthful, but it's polished enough to drink easily now. • $NA • (01/31/97) • **88**

Grange Hermitage South Australia Bin 95 1964: Ripe, sweet and pruny. A lithe, mature wine with a decidedly spicy accent to its nicely focused, floral-scented fruit flavors. • $NA • (01/31/97) • **86**

Grange Hermitage South Australia Bin 95 1963: Mature and velvety, if a bit raucous, with tightly packed raspberry, chocolate, cedar and anise flavors. Firm and focused on the finish. • $NA • (01/31/97) • **89**

Grange Hermitage South Australia Bin 95 1962: A bit sharp with acidity, but has a welcome freshness of spicy, coffee-scented complexity that opens to a core of dark raspberry and cherry flavors. Hits some cedar notes on the finish. • $NA • (01/31/97) • **87**

Grange Hermitage South Australia Bin 95 1961: Rich, mature and gloriously alive, with concentrated cherry, plum, spice and vanilla flavors that rev up and ring through the long finish. Elegant and in perfect shape. • $NA • (01/31/97) • **92**

Grange Hermitage South Australia Bin 95 1960: Chocolate, prune and floral notes swirl nicely in a smooth texture, finishing gently and with some elegance. • $NA • (01/31/97) • **87**

Grange Hermitage South Australia Bin 95 1959: A good wine, but it has a metallic accent that detracts from the typical prune and cherry flavors. • $NA • (01/31/97) • **80**

Grange Hermitage South Australia Bin 95 1958: It's flavors are getting tired, veering toward coffee, caramel and smoke, the fruit fading. Has velvety texture, but is short on richness. • $NA • (01/31/97) • **84**

Grange Hermitage South Australia Bin 95 1957: Spice and coffee notes dominate, with fresh, youthful fruit flavors and a chewy texture on the palate. Has remarkable freshness and intensity, but lacks the polish of the 1956. • $NA • (01/31/97) • **89**

Grange Hermitage South Australia Bin 95 1956: Deep, spicy and warm, showing caramel and coffee flavors with volatile accents. Berry and black cherry notes come through on the rich finish. • $NA • (01/31/97) • **86**

Grange Hermitage South Australia Bin 95 1955: Complex and quite aromatic, offering a wide range of smoky, spicy dried-tomato aromas that narrow and get chewy on a tight, tart palate that reveals it's flavors on the long finish. First commercial Grange bottling. • $NA • (01/31/97) • **90**

Grenache Shiraz Mourvèdre Barossa Valley Old Vine 1994: Ripe and open-textured, with black cherry and anise flavors swirling through the wide-open finish. • $17 • (05/15/98) • **88**

Port Australia Club NV • $9 • (05/15/96) • **89**

Rhine Riesling Late Harvest South Australia 1987 • $5/375ml • (03/15/89) BB • **88**

Riesling South Australia Bin 202 1993 • $7 • (04/30/94) • **82**

Sémillon Chardonnay South Australia Koonunga Hill 1997: Bright in flavor, round in texture, with pretty apple and cream notes that linger on the fresh finish. 70 percent Sémillon, 30 percent Chardonnay. • $8 • (05/15/98) • **85**

Sémillon Chardonnay South Australia Koonunga Hill 1996: This easy-drinking white blend is smooth in texture, its appealing, creamy pear flavors enlivened by hints of citrus and green apple that linger on the finish. Seldom is a wine this good this affordable. Drink now. 20,000 cases made. • $7 • (05/31/97) BB • **86**

Sémillon Chardonnay South Australia Koonunga Hill 1995 • $8 • (04/30/96) • **87**

Sémillon Chardonnay South Australia Koonunga Hill 1994 • $9 • (03/31/96) • **85**

Sémillon Chardonnay South Australia Koonunga Hill 1993 • $9 • (05/31/95) • **83**

Sémillon Late Harvest South Australia 1987 • $6/375ml • (03/15/89) • **84**

Shiraz Coonawarra Bin 128 1994: A crisp, jazzy style of Shiraz that centers its charm around a generous layer of berry and plum flavors, with just a hint of licorice at the edge. Drink now. 5,500 cases made. • $14 • (09/15/97) • **87**

Shiraz Coonawarra Bin 128 1993 • $14 • (04/30/96) • **86**

Shiraz Coonawarra Bin 128 1992 • $13 • (11/30/95) • **88**

Shiraz Coonawarra Bin 128 1990 • $15 • (03/31/94) • **83**

Shiraz Kalimna Bin 28 South Australia 1994: Dark, chewy and spicy, with licorice notes threaded through the tough-edged blackberry and vanilla flavors. Best from 1999. 2,100 cases made. • $19 • (09/15/97) • **86**

Shiraz Kalimna Bin 28 South Australia 1993 • $18 • (04/30/96) • **91**

Shiraz Kalimna Bin 28 South Australia 1992 • $16 • (11/15/95) • **85**

Shiraz Magill Estate 1994: Rich and generous in flavor, this is a complete wine, with spicy blackberry and chocolate flavors swirling through a finish that eases off a bit, making it feel elegant. 3,200 cases made. • $44 • (05/15/98) • **90**

Shiraz Magill Estate 1993: A nicely shaped Shiraz, less opulent than most, but lovely for its spice, sandalwood and other exotic notes on an elegant frame. Finishes with a cedary note. Nice now, better after 2000. 580 cases made. • $44 • (11/30/97) • **89**

Shiraz Magill Estate Vineyard South Australia 1988 • $44 • (05/31/93) • **85**

Shiraz Magill Estate Vineyard South Australia 1985 • $45 • (07/31/89) • **87**

Shiraz South Australia St.-Henri 1992: Gamy flavors provide an earthy counterpoint to the chewy plum, spice and toast flavors in this firm-textured Shiraz. Give it until 1999 to soften. • $21 • (04/30/97) • **88**

Shiraz-Cabernet Koonunga Hill South Australia 1995: Soft, fruity and mildly spicy, offering a nice brown-sugar and prune character. An easy-drinking red for current consumption. 19,000 cases made. • $9 • (07/31/97) • **83**

Shiraz-Cabernet Koonunga Hill Australia 1994 • $9 • (04/30/96) • **85**

Shiraz-Cabernet Koonunga Hill South Australia 1993 • $9 • (03/31/96) • **78**

Shiraz-Cabernet Koonunga Hill South Australia 1992 • $NA • (06/30/95) • **84**

Shiraz-Cabernet Koonunga Hill South Australia 1990 • $9 • (02/28/93) BB • **86**

Shiraz-Cabernet South Australia Bin 80A 1980: A blend of Barossa Shiraz and Coonawarra Cabernet Sauvignon, this has more backbone than the straight Shiraz, with sweet currant and cedar notes swirling on the long, focused finish. • $212 • (01/31/97) • **92**

Shiraz-Cabernet South Australia Bin 820 1982: An all-Coonawarra blend of Cabernet Sauvignon and Shiraz. Lean and juicy, it's a marvelous mouthful of berry flavor, with hints of mineral and mint. Still feels youthful. Best from 2002 to 2005. • $NA • (01/31/97) • **88**

Shiraz-Cabernet South Australia Bin 920 1990: A blend of Coonawarra Cabernet Sauvignon and Shiraz. Juicy, lively and pointedly dazzling with distinctly mineral-scented currant and blackberry flavors. Less opulent than your typical Shiraz but elegant in structure. Delicious now, but give until 2002 to 2005. • $NA • (01/31/97) • **92**

Shiraz-Mourvèdre South Eastern Australia Bin 2 1996: A soft and velvety red blend, this generous mouthful of black cherry, plum and spice flavors hints at mineral on the supple finish. Well worth a try, especially at this low price. 80 percent Shiraz, 20 percent Mourvèdre. 6,700 cases made. • $9 • (05/15/98) BB • **87**

Shiraz-Mourvèdre South Eastern Australia Bin 2 1995: Elegant, vibrant, generous with its red berry, plum and fresh anise flavors, finishing with a crisp bite and impressive length. Not as exuberant as some Rhône-style wines, but it has class. Drinkable now. A blend of 79 percent Shiraz and 21percent Mourvèdre. • $9 • (04/30/97) • **85**

Shiraz-Mourvèdre South Eastern Australia Bin 2 1994: Firm in texture, with a solid dose of spicy plum and black cherry flavors that pick up a hint of anise on the supple finish, as it fades away. Drink now. • $10 • (11/15/96) BB • **86**

PENLEY

Cabernet Sauvignon Coonawarra 1994: A bright, peppery style of Cabernet that packs lots of snazzy plum and berry flavors into its streamlined frame, and echoes anise and herbs. Tannins can use until 1999 to 2000. 120 cases made. • $40 • (08/31/97) • **89**

Cabernet Sauvignon Coonawarra Phoenix 1995: Bursts on the palate with bright plum, currant and spice flavors, with hints of herbs and coffee on the zingy finish. Tempting now, best from 1999. 165 cases made. • $23 • (08/31/97) • **90**

Chardonnay South Australia 1995: Golden-colored, soft, rich and generous, dripping with spice, honey and pineapple flavors, it's a smooth, harmonious package. Flavors linger on the seductive finish. Drinkable now, better in 1999. 160 cases made. • $24 • (08/31/97) • **91**

Shiraz-Cabernet South Australia 1994: A solid wine, rife with boysenberry and currant flavors that expand through the jazzy finish. Has style, grace and plenty of spice overtones. 100 cases made. • $24 • (08/31/97) • **91**

PEPPER TREE

Chardonnay Hunter-Coonawarra 1995: Light, silky and tangy, with orange and apple flavors that finish with a burst of spiciness. Try now. 18,000 cases made. • $13 • (05/31/97) • **89**

Shiraz Hunter Valley & McLaren Vale Hunter Vineyards 1996: Open-textured and generous with its smoky, meaty beet and black cherry flavors that echo on the finish. 3,000 cases made. • $17 • (05/31/98) • **86**

PETALUMA

Cabernet Merlot Coonawarra 1988 • $21 • (12/15/93) • **85**

Cabernet Merlot Coonawarra 1986 • $25 • (05/31/91) • **87**

Cabernet Merlot Coonawarra 1984 • $18 • (05/31/87) • **92**

Cabernet Sauvignon Coonawarra 1991 • $20 • (04/30/95) • **88**

Cabernet Sauvignon Coonawarra 1984 • $18 • (05/31/87) • **91**

Cabernet Shiraz Coonawarra 1982 • $16 • (07/01/87) • **89**

Chardonnay Australia 1994 • $22 • (06/15/96) • **86**

Chardonnay South Australia Piccadilly Valley 1995: Has elegance and subtlety that set it apart from many Aussie whites. Nicely balanced to show off its spicy, tobacco-scented side, it develops some meaty notes to mix with the pear and peach flavors on the harmonious finish. 5,000 cases made. • $21 • (05/31/97) • **90**

Coonawarra Red 1994: A leaner style of Cabernet showing hints of chocolate and spice amid the basic black cherry and currant flavors and finishing with a swirl of spicy oak. Best from 2001 on. 60 percent Cabernet Sauvignon, 40 percent Merlot. 4,000 cases made. • $21 • (05/31/97) • **89**

Riesling Clare Valley 1996: Dripping with ripe Riesling flavors, this white offers melon and green apple notes tinged with honey and a vibrant, open-textured, dry finish. Terrific. Drink now. 4,000 cases made. • $16 • (05/15/97) • **88**

Riesling Clare Valley 1995 • $16 • (05/31/96) • **90**

PEWSEY VALE

Cabernet Sauvignon Australia Individual Vineyard Selection 1989 • $11 • (04/15/93) • **78**

Rhine Riesling Late Harvest Barossa Valley Botrytis 1986 • $8/375ml • (02/15/88) • **90**

Rhine Riesling Late Harvest Barossa Valley Botrytis Individual Vineyard Selection 1987 • $9/375ml • (10/31/89) • **71**

PIBBIN

Pinot Noir Adelaide Hills 1995: Not for everyone, but distinctive. Light, with slightly gamy flavors and modest cherry notes competing against a minty edge. A swirl of flavor lingers on the finish. Best from 1999. 500 cases made. • $14 • (10/31/97) • **85**

PIERRO

Chardonnay Australia 1994 • $32 • (03/31/96) • **92**

Chardonnay Margaret River 1995: A big, mouthfilling wine that scatters its mineral, orange, pear and toast flavors rather than pulling them together into a harmonious whole. Drinkable now. • $38 • (02/28/97) • **89**

PIKES

Cabernet Sauvignon Clare Valley 1995: Crisp and juicy, with ripe blackberry and anise flavors hovering over the stony, earthy notes gliding beneath. Good now, better after 2000. 500 cases made. • $16 • (05/31/97) • **87**

Riesling Clare Valley 1997: Bright, clear and open-textured, this is a crisp mouthful of pear, pineapple and floral flavors that linger nicely on the finish. Very good now, maybe better by 2000 to 2002. 8,000 cases made. • $14 • (04/30/98) • **88**

Riesling Clare Valley 1996: A subtle wine, dry and intense, with chalk, mineral and green apple flavors that glide smoothly through a long, elegant finish. Needs to develop more depth, but it could do that by 2000. 8,000 cases made. • $14 • (05/31/97) • **88**

Shiraz Clare Valley 1995: Earthy, gamy flavors course through the bright berry and plum flavors in this jazzy Shiraz. Has lots of personality and charm, but it's not for the faint of heart. Best from 1999. 1,500 cases made. • $17 • (05/31/97) • **88**

PIPERS BROOK

Pinot Noir Tasmania 1990 • $25 • (02/29/92) • **81**

PLUNKETT

Chardonnay Victoria Strathbogie Ranges Unwooded 1995: On the lighter side, with a sense of elegance and hints of spice and cream to offset the tangy, citrusy flavors, all shining through on the finish. 6,000 cases made. • $11 • (05/31/97) • **86**

PREECE

Cabernet Sauvignon Goulburn Valley 1990 • $14 • (11/30/92) • **85**

Cabernet Sauvignon Goulburn Valley 1989 • $13 • (03/15/92) • **84**

Cabernet Sauvignon South Eastern Australia 1994: A solid Cabernet, with low-intensity plum and berry flavors, and lots of tar and cedar notes wafting through the piney finish. Firm enough to want until 2000 to 2002. 4,000 cases made. • $15 • (10/15/96) • **85**

Cabernet Sauvignon South Eastern Australia 1993 • $12 • (06/30/95) • **82**

Cabernet Sauvignon South Eastern Australia 1992 • $12 • (04/30/94) • **86**

Cabernet Sauvignon Victoria 1995: Light in texture for a Cabernet, with some pretty fruit and mint flavors that turn a bit lean on the finish. 10,000 cases made. • $15 • (05/15/97) • **83**

Chardonnay South Eastern Australia 1994 • $12 • (06/30/95) • **83**

Chardonnay South Eastern Australia 1993 • $11 • (09/30/94) • **86**

Chardonnay Victoria 1996: A fruit-centered wine, fresh and brilliant with pear and nectarine flavors. Smooth and refreshing finish. 10,000 cases made. • $15 • (05/15/97) • **88**

Chardonnay Victoria 1995: Gentle and smooth, with appealing, but somewhat subdued, apple and spice flavors. 6,000 cases made. • $15 • (10/15/96) • **83**

Merlot Victoria 1995: Ripe, polished and distinctly fruity, with wild berry and raspberry flavors prominent. Finishes with style. 5,000 cases made. • $15 • (05/15/97) • **86**

Merlot Victoria 1994: Firm in texture, but the flavors are reticent touches of ripe plum and smoke running through the chewy structure and need until 2000 to 2001. 6,000 cases made. • $15 • (10/31/96) • **85**

QUEEN ADELAIDE

Chardonnay South Eastern Australia 1997: Fresh and fragrant, a nice package of pear, spice and slightly resinous flavors, balanced and appealing. 1,500 cases made. • $7 • (05/15/98) • **85**

Chardonnay South Eastern Australia 1995: Soft, almost sweet, with a fruity character that emphasizes peach and pear notes. 15,000 cases made. • $6 • (10/15/96) • **81**

Chardonnay South Eastern Australia 1994 • $6 • (12/15/95) • **81**

Chardonnay South Eastern Australia 1993 • $6 • (06/30/95) • **81**

Pinot Noir South Australia 1996: Very light in color and flavor, but the plum and spice flavors are nice. Finishes with a touch of bitterness. Try now. • $6 • (05/15/97) • **82**

Shiraz Cabernet South Eastern Australia 1995: A spicy style, folding some earthy notes into the mix of berry and anise flavors. Lean and smooth. Should benefit from cellaring until 1999. 2,400 cases made. • $6 • (10/31/97) • **86**

Shiraz Cabernet South Eastern Australia 1993 • $6 • (10/15/95) • **83**

Shiraz Cabernet South Eastern Australia 1992 • $6 • (06/30/95) BB • **82**

Shiraz Cabernet South Eastern Australia 1991 • $6 • (10/31/93) • **80**

RANDALL BRIDGE

Chardonnay South Eastern Australia 1996: Ripe and generous, a broadly structured wine with pear, spice and toast notes that soften on the finish. 13,000 cases made. • $5 • (07/31/97) • **82**

Key: SS—Spectator Selection. CS—Cellar Selection. BB—Best Buy. HR—Highly Recommended. $NA—Price not available. (BT)—Barrel tasting. Ⓐ—Auction Price.

Dates in parentheses represent the issues in which the ratings were published.

REDBANK

Cabernet Blend South Eastern Australia Sally's Paddock 1986 • $32 • (01/31/90) • **86**

Cabernet Sauvignon South Eastern Australia Long Paddock 1986 • $13 • (01/31/90) • **74**

Cabernet Sauvignon South Eastern Australia Long Paddock 1985 • $7 • (07/15/91) • **74**

Cabernet Sauvignon South Eastern Australia Redbank Cabernet 1986 • $54 • (01/31/90) • **89**

Cabernet Sauvignon Victoria Redbank Cabernet 1991 • $37 • (10/15/95) • **87**

Chardonnay South Eastern Australia Long Paddock 1996: Light and refreshing for its pear and resin flavors that linger on the open-textured finish, gaining richness with each sip. Try now. • $11 • (06/30/97) • **86**

Chardonnay South Eastern Australia Long Paddock 1994 • $10 • (03/31/96) • **84**

Chardonnay South Eastern Australia Long Paddock 1993 • $10 • (06/30/96) • **84**

Sally's Paddock Red Victoria 1993 • $57 • (04/30/96) • **85**

Sémillon South Eastern Australia Long Paddock 1994 • $10 • (03/31/96) • **84**

Shiraz South Eastern Australia Long Paddock 1996: Soft in texture, with a racy streak of anise and other spices running through the ripe plum and cherry flavors. Flavors never get above *mezzo forte*, but it's appealing for current drinking. • $12 • (06/30/97) • **83**

Shiraz South Eastern Australia Long Paddock 1991 • $9 • (11/30/93) • **82**

Shiraz Victoria Mountain Creek 1985 • $9 • (09/30/91) • **84**

REYNOLDS

Cabernet Merlot Orange-Hunter Districts 1996: On the light side, with firm tannins and minty flavors that weave in hints of cherry and tar on the finish. 50 percent Cabernet Sauvignon, 50 percent Merlot. 1,720 cases made. • $16 • (06/15/98) • **85**

Cabernet Merlot Orange District Hunter Valley Yarraman 1995: Bright, ripe and decidedly minty, this is a distinctive wine with a supple texture and a nice array of Cabernet flavors. Finishes with a hint of spicy oak. Try now. 1,000 cases made. • $16 • (05/15/97) • **86**

Cabernet Sauvignon Hunter Valley Orange District 1995: A sturdy red, offering minty herbal notes that ring through the modest black cherry and tar flavors. Best from 2000. 700 cases made. • $24 • (06/15/98) • **83**

Cabernet Sauvignon Hunter Valley Orange District 1994: Decidedly minty, with bright berry flavors beneath, this is a lightish, supple style of Cabernet that's best in 1998 to 2000. 900 cases made. • $23 • (05/15/97) • **83**

Chardonnay Hunter Valley Orange District 1996: Crisp in texture, with bright, lemony pear flavors that glide gently through the smooth finish. 1,250 cases made. • $22 • (06/15/98) • **86**

Chardonnay Hunter Valley Orange District 1995: Simple and moderately flavorful, with its generous apple and beeswax flavors sustained through the finish. 1,000 cases made. • $22 • (05/15/97) • **84**

Chardonnay Hunter Valley Yarraman 1995: An earthy, sappy character intrudes on the modest fruit and spice flavors—this won't appeal to everyone. Try now. Tasted twice, with consistent notes. • $16 • (06/15/97) • **78**

Sémillon Hunter Valley Yarraman 1996: Has a slightly bitter edge to its muted orange and tobacco flavors. Try now. 2,500 cases made. • $14 • (05/15/97) • **80**

Shiraz Hunter Valley Yarraman 1995: A distinctive wine, bright in flavor, its density balanced with elegance and harmony. Attractive chocolate and smoke-scented berry and vanilla flavors, polished and graceful finish. Drink now. 700 cases made. • $16 • (05/15/97) • **89**

RIDDOCH

Shiraz Coonawarra 1995: Lean, taut style of Shiraz featuring anise-scented blackberry and smoke flavors, hinting lightly at gaminess on the nicely drawn finish. Approachable now, best from 2000. • $18 • (04/30/98) • **86**

ROBERTSON'S WELL

Cabernet Sauvignon Coonawarra 1995: Generous in flavor, open-textured and supple, with pretty blackberry, tar and coffee flavors that linger on the well-modulated finish. Approachable now; best from 1999 through 2004. 3,000 cases made. • $16 • (06/15/98) • **87**

Cabernet Sauvignon Coonawarra 1994: The firm texture and chewy, tarry blackberry and anise flavors could develop a bit more flesh with cellaring until 1999 to 2001. 20,000 cases made. • $15 • (06/15/97) • **83**

Chardonnay Victoria 1996: A pretty Chardonnay, with flavors centered around nectarine and apple on a light, silky frame. Has style and harmony. Drink now. 8,000 cases made. • $15 • (05/15/97) • **87**

ROBSON, MURRAY

Chardonnay Hunter Valley 1997: Has a sense of elegance and grace, offering pretty melon, apple and spice flavors that linger on the smooth finish. 300 cases made. • $24 • (05/15/98) • **88**

Gewürztraminer Hunter Valley 1997: Brightly aromatic, rife with spicy pineapple flavors overlaid with rose petal. Only a slightly bitter bite on the finish strikes a cautious note. 210 cases made. • $22 • (05/31/98) • **85**

Sémillon Hunter Valley 1997: Youthful and vibrant, this smooth-textured wine has pretty pear and earthy spice flavors that linger on the finish. 250 cases made. • $22 • (05/31/98) • **86**

ROO'S LEAP

Cabernet Sauvignon McLaren Vale 1990 • $10 • (03/31/93) • **81**

Cabernet Sauvignon McLaren Vale 1985 • $10 • (11/30/88) • **89**

Cabernet Sauvignon McLaren Vale Limited Edition 1986 • $9 • (01/31/90) • **85**

Chardonnay Coonawarra Barrel Fermented 1993 • $12 • (06/30/94) • **85**

Pinot Noir McLaren Vale 1988 • $8 • (02/28/91) • **86**

ROSEMOUNT

Brut South Eastern Australia 1994 • $8 • (05/31/95) BB • **85**

Brut South Eastern Australia 1989 • $15 • (08/31/92) • **88**

Cabernet Sauvignon Coonawarra Kirri Billi Vineyard 1986 • $20 • (10/31/90) • **88**

Cabernet Sauvignon Coonawarra Reserve 1994: Jammed with flavors. Layers ripe berry, smoke and herbal notes that swirl through the finish with hints of pepper and anise, all wrapped with polished tannins. Tempting now, best after 2000. 5,000 cases made. • $19 • (10/31/97) • **88**

Cabernet Sauvignon Coonawarra Show Reserve 1993 • $17 • (03/31/96) • **88**

Cabernet Sauvignon Coonawarra Show Reserve 1992 • $17 • (11/30/95) HR • **93**

Cabernet Sauvignon Coonawarra Show Reserve 1991 • $17 • (04/30/94) • **80**

Cabernet Sauvignon Coonawarra Show Reserve 1989 • $17 • (11/30/92) • **85**

Cabernet Sauvignon Coonawarra Show Reserve 1988 • $16 • (05/31/91) • **89**

Cabernet Sauvignon Coonawarra Show Reserve 1987 • $15 • (02/28/91) • **88**

Cabernet Sauvignon Coonawarra Show Reserve 1985 • $14 • (01/31/89) • **82**

Cabernet Sauvignon Coonawarra Show Reserve 1984 • $14 • (02/28/87) • **86**

Cabernet Sauvignon Hunter Valley 1989 • $10 • (09/30/91) • **82**

Cabernet Sauvignon Hunter Valley 1988 • $10 • (01/31/90) • **76**

Cabernet Sauvignon Hunter Valley 1987 • $10 • (07/31/89) • **83**

Cabernet Sauvignon Hunter Valley 1986 • $11 • (01/31/89) SS • **93**

Cabernet Sauvignon Hunter Valley 1985 • $9 • (01/31/88) • **85**

Cabernet Sauvignon Hunter Valley 1984 • $9 • (04/30/87) • **78**

Cabernet Sauvignon South Eastern Australia 1996: This crisp Cabernet is appealing for its fresh berry and currant flavors, picking up some nice hints of brown sugar and spice on the finish. Rosemount does it again, at an affordable price. Best from 1999 or 2000. 98,000 cases made. • $11 • (04/30/98) BB • **87**

Cabernet Sauvignon South Australia 1995: Smooth and spicy, with a nice mouthful of bright blackberry flavors that linger on the solid finish. Drinkable now, better in 1999. 35,000 cases made. • $11 • (02/28/97) • **85**

Cabernet Sauvignon South Australia 1994 • $10 • (10/15/95) • **84**

Cabernet Sauvignon South Australia 1993 • $10 • (04/30/95) • **85**

Cabernet Sauvignon South Eastern Australia 1992 • $10 • (07/31/94) • **83**

Cabernet Sauvignon South Eastern Australia 1991 • $9 • (03/31/93) • **86**

Cabernet Shiraz South Eastern Australia 1989 • $6 • (07/31/90) BB • **81**

Chardonnay Hunter Valley 1995 • $10 • (04/30/96) SS • **89**

Chardonnay Hunter Valley 1994 • $10 • (06/30/95) • **82**

Chardonnay Hunter Valley 1993 • $10 • (06/30/94) • **87**

Chardonnay Hunter Valley Reserve 1996: Smooth and ripe, generous with its apricot, melon and spice flavors that linger on the solid finish. Drinkable now. • $19 • (10/31/97) • **89**

Chardonnay Hunter Valley Roxburgh 1993 • $30 • (03/31/96) CS • **92**

Chardonnay Hunter Valley Show Reserve 1995: Rich, spicy and prettily floral, with a nutmeg accent to the apple flavors. Beautifully balanced to show off the spicy overtones, keeping the solid core of bright fruit. Drink now. 6,000 cases made. • $19 • (02/28/97) • **89**

Chardonnay Hunter Valley Show Reserve 1994 • $17 • (12/15/95) • **89**

Chardonnay Hunter Valley Show Reserve 1993 • $16 • (04/30/95) SS • **89**

Chardonnay South Australia 1996: Smooth and polished, this is appealing for its spicy vanilla and pear flavors that are shaded by sage and mineral nuances on the finish. 250,000 cases made. • $10 • (11/30/96) BB • **86**

Chardonnay South Eastern Australia 1997: Lots of flavor for the price, fresh and round, generous with its melon and spice character, finishing with a slightly thick texture. Best from 1999. 50,000 cases made. • $10 • (05/15/98) • **85**

Dry Red Diamond Reserve Hunter Valley 1988 • $6 • (02/28/90) BB • **83**

Dry Red Diamond Reserve Hunter Valley 1986 • $6 • (09/15/87) BB • **86**

Fumé Blanc Hunter Valley 1994 • $10 • (06/30/96) • **84**

Fumé Blanc South Eastern Australia 1993 • $10 • (01/01/96) • **83**

Grenache-Shiraz South Eastern Australia 1997: Soft and generous, with a strong floral note ringing alongside the basic berry flavors. A drink-me-now red. 65 percent Grenache, 35 percent Shiraz. 35,000 cases made. • $8 • (05/15/98) • **84**

Grenache-Shiraz South Eastern Australia 1996: This Rhône-style red blend is marked by dazzling, almost neon-purple color and exuberant plum and grape flavors, but even while it's rich and dense it remains appealingly fresh. A ready-to-drink bargain from a reliable producer. 20,000 cases made. • $8 • (05/15/97) BB • **86**

GSM Grenache-Syrah-Mourvèdre McLaren Vale 1995: Jazzy, flavorful red, with layers of blackberry, plum and anise flavors on a lightish frame. Ripe flavors persist on the lively finish. 5,000 cases made. • $17 • (06/30/98) • **88**

GSM McLaren Vale 1994: Remarkably distinctive, with layers of spice, plum and berry flavors and earthy mushroom grace notes that take off like a rocket. Smooth and harmonious, but the flavors really soar. Delicious now. A blend of Grenache, Shiraz and Mourvèdre. 900 cases made. • $16 • (01/31/97) • **91**

Merlot South Eastern Australia 1992 • $11 • (12/15/93) • **82**

Pinot Noir Hunter Valley 1989 • $10 • (09/30/91) • **81**

Pinot Noir Hunter Valley 1985 • $9 • (04/30/87) • **84**

Pinot Noir Hunter Valley Giants Creek Vineyard 1987 • $20 • (02/28/90) • **84**

Riesling South Eastern Australia Traminer Riesling 1994 • $8 • (04/15/95) • **85**

Riesling South Eastern Australia Traminer Riesling 1993 • $8 • (09/30/94) • **84**

Sauvignon Blanc Hunter Valley 1996: Distinctly herbal, with anise-accented, modest apple flavors; a bit tired on the finish. Drink now. • $10 • (02/28/97) • **84**

Sauvignon Blanc South Eastern Australia 1997: Crisp and appealing for its lively pear, floral and sage flavors. 15,000 cases made. • $10 • (06/30/98) • **84**

Sémillon Hunter Valley 1996: Light and almost crisp, with a tight bud of pear and earthy mineral flavors that shows more charm than most Hunter Sémillons at this stage. 20,000 cases made. • $10 • (05/15/97) • **86**

Sémillon-Chardonnay South Eastern Australia 1997: Earthy, floral notes add a nice fillip to the basic pear flavors in this pleasant white wine. 175,000 cases made. • $8 • (04/30/98) • **84**

Sémillon-Chardonnay South Eastern Australia 1996: Its spicy pear and pineapple flavors are ripe, generous and fresh through the lively finish. Ready now. 41,000 cases made. • $7 • (01/31/97) BB • **86**

Sémillon-Chardonnay South Eastern Australia 1995 • $8 • (06/15/96) • **83**

Sémillon-Chardonnay South Eastern Australia 1993 • $8 • (09/30/94) • **84**

Shiraz Cabernet Australia 1995 • $10 • (06/15/96) BB • **86**

Shiraz Cabernet Mudgee Mountain Blue 1994: Shows some very pretty berry flavors on a frame that's lighter and less dense than that of most Aussie Shirazes, and finishes modestly. Try now. 90 percent Shiraz, 10 percent Cabernet Sauvignon. 2,500 cases made. • $25 • (06/15/97) • **87**

Shiraz Cabernet South Eastern Australia 1997: Light and fragrant, this red blend is a jazzy mouthful of straight-on blackberry flavor with a hint of spice around the edges. It's drinkable now and represents real value in the face of ever-rising prices for quality Aussie wines. 125,000 cases made. • $9 • (02/28/98) BB • **86**

Shiraz Cabernet South Eastern Australia 1996: Fresh, youthful and lively with berry and plum flavors. Not a rich wine, but likeable for its freshness. Drink now. 62,000 cases made. • $7 • (01/31/97) BB • **85**

Shiraz Cabernet South Eastern Australia 1993 • $8 • (06/30/94) • **85**

Shiraz Cabernet South Eastern Australia 1992 • $7 • (10/31/93) BB • **86**

Shiraz Cabernet South Eastern Australia 1991 • $7 • (11/30/92) • **67**

Shiraz Cabernet South Eastern Australia 1990 • $7 • (07/15/91) BB • **84**

Shiraz Hunter Valley 1989 • $8 • (02/15/91) SS • **91**

Shiraz Hunter Valley 1988 • $8 • (01/31/90) SS • **90**

Shiraz Hunter Valley 1987 • $9 • (07/31/89) • **87**

Shiraz Hunter Valley 1986 • $9 • (04/15/89) • **92**

Shiraz Hunter Valley 1985 • $8 • (02/15/88) • **80**

Shiraz Hunter Valley 1984 • $7 • (04/30/87) • **83**

Shiraz McLaren Vale Show Reserve 1989 • $15 • (02/29/92) • **89**

Shiraz South Eastern Australia 1996: Bursting with fruit, here's a lively, generous, amazingly supple Shiraz—a mouthful of blackberry, anise, chocolate and spice notes that remain rich and vibrant through the finish. Approachable now, at its best from 2000. From a trusted winery, and reasonably priced. 150,000 cases made. • $12 • (11/30/97) SS • **91**

Shiraz South Australia 1995: A zinger of a wine, this is packed with rich black cherry and dark plum flavors, on a crisp frame. It's certainly approachable now, but should flesh out if cellared until 1999 or 2000. 75,000 cases made. • $10 • (11/30/96) SS • **90**

Shiraz South Australia 1994 • $10 • (10/31/95) SS • **90**

Shiraz South Australia 1993 • $10 • (01/31/95) • **83**

Shiraz South Eastern Australia 1992 • $10 • (01/31/94) SS • **89**

Shiraz South Eastern Australia 1991 • $9 • (04/15/93) HR • **89**

Shiraz South Eastern Australia 1990 • $8 • (02/15/92) SS • **92**

Syrah McLaren Vale Balmoral 1994: Deep and aristocratic, this is an elegant wine with power. Layers and layers of blueberry, blackberry, pepper and cream flavors make it stunning to drink now, but best to give the fine mesh of tannins until 2000 to 2003 to resolve. 2,500 cases made. • $40 • (05/31/97) • **93**

Syrah McLaren Vale Balmoral 1993 • $28 • (03/31/96) • **90**

Syrah McLaren Vale Balmoral 1992 • $25 • (03/31/95) CS • **93**

Syrah McLaren Vale Show Reserve 1991 • $17 • (01/31/94) SS • **90**

Syrah McLaren Vale Show Reserve 1990 • $16 • (04/15/93) HR • **92**

Traminer-Riesling South Eastern Australia 1997: A pretty wine, soft and fragrant, with spicy pear flavors and a touch of honey. Drink now. 25,000 cases made. • $8 • (02/28/98) • **84**

Traminer-Riesling South Eastern Australia 1996: A generous, richly-textured wine; ripe and floral, with appealing peach, rose petal and pear flavors that linger on the full finish. Drink now. 13,000 cases made. • $7 • (01/31/97) • **86**

Traminer-Riesling South Eastern Australia 1995 • $8 • (05/15/96) • **87**

ROTHBURY

Cabernet Sauvignon South Eastern Australia 1994 • $9 • (06/15/96) • **84**

Chardonnay Hunter Valley 1996: A soft wine with modest fruit character and an earthy bite, this tries for elegance but loses some charm via a strong sappy, resiny streak. Try now. 20,000 cases made. • $8 • (05/15/97) • **85**

Chardonnay Hunter Valley 1995 • $8 • (05/31/96) • **85**

Chardonnay Hunter Valley 1993 • $9 • (12/15/94) BB • **86**

Chardonnay Hunter Valley Barrel Fermented 1993 • $11 • (03/31/95) • **85**

Chardonnay Hunter Valley Reserve Bottling 1994 • $14 • (06/15/96) • **89**

Chardonnay Hunter Valley Reserve Bottling 1993 • $13 • (03/31/95) • **86**

Hermitage Hunter Valley 1984 • $10 • (07/01/87) • **90**

Hermitage Hunter Valley 1983 • $15 • (07/01/87) • **90**

Pinot Noir Hunter Valley 1983 • $10 • (07/01/87) • **87**

Pinot Noir Hunter Valley Director's Reserve 1983 • $15 • (07/01/87) • **89**

Shiraz Hunter Valley Herlstone Vineyard 1987 • $9 • (05/31/91) • **85**

Shiraz Hunter Valley Herlstone Vineyard 1986 • $11 • (07/31/89) • **76**

Shiraz Hunter Valley Herlstone Vineyard 1985 • $11 • (03/31/89) • **78**

Shiraz Hunter Valley Herlstone Vineyard 1984 • $9 • (05/15/87) • **90**

Shiraz Hunter Valley Reserve Bottling 1993 • $20 • (06/30/96) • **88**

Shiraz South Eastern Australia 1994: A lighter style of Shiraz, but still packed with plenty of berry, chocolate and anise flavors. Finishes with appealing length and harmony. 10,000 cases made. • $8 • (05/15/97) • **87**

Shiraz South Eastern Australia 1993 • $8 • (05/31/96) BB • **85**

Shiraz South Eastern Australia 1992 • $9 • (11/30/94) BB • **85**

Syrah Hunter Valley 1989 • $11 • (05/31/93) • **78**

ROVALLEY RIDGE

Cabernet Shiraz Barossa Valley Limited Release 1991 • $NA • (06/30/96) • **85**

Cabernet Shiraz Eden Valley Show Reserve 1992 • $NA • (01/01/96) • **92**

Cabernet Barossa Valley 1992 • $NA • (06/30/96) • **85**

Key: SS—Spectator Selection. CS—Cellar Selection. BB—Best Buy. HR—Highly Recommended. $NA—Price not available. (BT)—Barrel tasting. (A)—Auction Price.
Dates in parentheses represent the issues in which the ratings were published.

Chardonnay Eden Valley Show Reserve 1993 • $NA • (01/01/96) • **89**
Chardonnay New South Wales 1993 • $8 • (09/30/94) • **78**
Red New South Wales 1992 • $6 • (09/30/94) • **81**
Shiraz Barossa Valley Old Vine Show Reserve 1992 • $NA • (06/30/96) • **85**
Shiraz Barossa Valley Old Vine Show Reserve 1991 • $18 • (05/15/95) HR • **92**
Show Reserve Eden Valley 1991 • $18 • (06/30/95) • **82**

RUMBALL, PETER

Sparkling Shiraz South Eastern Australia Special Cuvée SB9 NV: Jazzy aromas and flavors of black cherry, raspberry, tealeaf and lots and lots of mint course through this distinctive, daringly dry wine. Ready now for a special occasion. 500 cases made. • $23 • (03/31/98) • **89**

RYECROFT

Shiraz McLaren Vale Flame Tree 1992 • $8 • (04/30/93) BB • **88**

RYMILL

Cabernet Sauvignon Coonawarra 1995: Light in texture, sprightly in flavor, this is a lovely, elegant Cabernet with berry, currant and mint flavors swirling through the polished finish. 5,613 cases made. • $16 • (06/15/98) • **87**
Chardonnay Coonawarra 1996: Supple, ripe style of Chardonnay offers plenty of spicy pear and melon flavors, hinting at honey and caramel on the delicate finish. 6,195 cases made. • $14 • (06/15/98) • **87**
Chardonnay Coonawarra 1995: Tastes very mature for a '95, dominated by a distinctly floral, toasty component, offering some nice honey notes on the finish. Drink soon. • $13 • (02/28/98) • **83**
Merlot Cabernets Coonawarra 1995: Earthy, herbal notes mix with a core of black cherry and balsamic flavors that brighten a bit on the finish. Best from 2001. A blend of Merlot, Cabernet Franc and Cabernet Sauvignon. 3,778 cases made. • $15 • (06/15/98) • **80**
Merlot Cabernets Coonawarra 1994: Elegant, lithe and crisp, with sharply focused blackberry, tar and citrus flavors that remain beautifully defined through the long finish. Approachable now, but should keep growing through 2002. A blend of Merlot, Cabernet Franc and Cabernet Sauvignon. • $15 • (02/28/98) • **88**
Shiraz Coonawarra 1995: Dark and dense up front, but it lightens up as the jazzy black raspberry and cherry flavors expand on the finish. Echoes fruit and pepper. Tannins need time. 6,195 cases made. • $16 • (06/15/98) • **88**

SADDLER'S CREEK

Cabernet Sauvignon Australia Bluegrass 1995: Ripe, warm and generous, this is a big-shouldered wine with herb and eucalyptus nuances laced through the black cherry and smoke flavors. Supple enough to drink now. Best now through 1999. 1,500 cases made. • $19 • (11/15/96) • **88**
Chardonnay Australia Marrowbone 1995: Firm in texture and offering a nice range of spice, vanilla and golden pear flavors that linger lightly on the finish. 1,500 cases made. • $19 • (11/15/96) • **88**
Shiraz Australia Marrowbone 1994: A soft, supple expression of Shiraz, offering pretty plum, cola and cherry flavors that finish with a cascade of spice notes. Drink now. 1,500 cases made. • $19 • (11/15/96) • **87**

ST. HALLETT

Gamekeeper's Reserve Barossa Red 1997: A fascinating blend. Lighter than a typical Shiraz, its flavors center around pretty raspberry and tobacco notes, yet it's firm in texture and impressively focused. A blend of Grenache, Mourvèdre and Touriga. 8,000 cases made. • $10 • (06/15/98) • **88**
Gamekeeper's Reserve Barossa 1996: Tastes like a straight-on Grenache, light and crisp with cherry candy flavors. A blend of Grenache, Mourvèdre and Touriga. • $10 • (07/31/97) • **85**
Gamekeeper's Reserve Barossa 1994 • $10 • (03/31/96) • **86**
Poacher's Blend Barossa White 1997: Light in texture, with pretty melon and spice flavors that remain simple and refreshing through the finish, this blend of Chenin Blanc, Sémillon and Sauvignon Blanc arrives just in time for summer sipping at a price that won't pinch. 30,000 cases made. • $10 • (06/15/98) BB • **86**
Poacher's Blend Barossa White 1996: Light, crisp and refreshing, showing a slightly grassy accent to its apricot and pear flavors. Finishes gracefully, and with much charm. 3,000 cases made. • $10 • (11/30/96) • **88**
Poacher's Blend Barossa White 1995 • $10 • (04/30/96) • **84**
Shiraz Barossa Faith 1996: Supple, refreshing and brimming with plum, currant and blackberry, remaining round and polished through the juicy finish. Each sip calls for another as the anise, tar and vanilla notes chime in on the finish. 1,000 cases made. • $33 • (06/15/98) • **90**
Shiraz Barossa Faith 1995: Crisp and flavorful, with very ripe, almost decadent flavors on an austere frame, this offers plenty of tarry, berry character and a smooth, smoky finish. Best from 2000. • $17 • (05/31/97) • **88**
Shiraz Barossa Faith 1994: Spicy and ripe-tasting, it's generous with its cranberry-scented plum and anise flavors that linger on the round, mouth-filling finish. Tempting now, but wait until 1999 for the oak to meld. 2,000 cases made. • $18 • (04/30/97) • **88**
Shiraz Barossa Old Block 1994: Silky smooth and supple, brimming with plum, berry and anise flavors, yet balanced to show a real sense of elegance. Flavors persist on the finish. Tempting now; best from 2000 through 2010. 1,000 cases made. • $33 • (06/15/98) • **91**
Shiraz Barossa Old Block 1993: Rich, spicy and complex, its generous plum and red cherry flavors cradled in a nest of sweet cinnamon, nutmeg, vanilla and meaty, roasted notes. Full-bodied, but gentle enough in texture to be approachable now. Best from 2000. 1,500 cases made. • $27 • (11/30/96) HR • **93**
Shiraz Barossa Old Block 1992 • $23 • (03/31/96) CS • **92**

SALISBURY

Cabernet Sauvignon Victoria 1996: Light in texture, with soft currant and floral flavors that echo on the silky finish. 19,000 cases made. • $8 • (05/31/98) • **84**
Cabernet Sauvignon Victoria 1995: Light and fragrant with spicy oak and hints of raspberry, this smooth-textured wine is designed for early drinking. • $8 • (06/15/97) • **83**
Chardonnay Victoria 1997: Supple and lithe, open in texture, showing off its pretty pear and spice flavors that linger gently on the finish. 81,500 cases made. • $8 • (05/31/98) BB • **86**
Chardonnay Victoria 1996: Check the bargain price on this bright and sharply focused Chardonnay, its fresh apple and citrus flavors, finishing with a touch of spicy oak. Drink now. 20,000 cases made. • $8 • (05/31/97) BB • **85**
Sauvignon Blanc Victoria 1997: Silky, bright and lively, with spicy, honey-tinged pineapple and citrus flavors that linger on the generous finish. 9,500 cases made. • $8 • (05/31/98) • **86**
Sauvignon Blanc Victoria 1996: Light and gently spicy, with a fragile thread of citrus and pear flavors, finishing soft. 6,000 cases made. • $8 • (06/15/97) • **82**

SALITAGE

Chardonnay Pemberton 1996: Exotic, spicy and distinctive for its pineapple, honey and mineral flavors, finishing with a hint of nutmeg. Drinkable now, better in 1999. 500 cases made. • $35 • (07/31/97) • **87**
Pinot Noir Pemberton 1995: Tastes more of mint, eucalyptus and flower stalks than fruit, but it's a distinctive red that could develop into something special with cellaring until 1999. 300 cases made. • $35 • (07/31/97) • **80**
Red Pemberton 1995: Bright, focused and tightly woven, firm tannins wrapping around a solid core of plum and currant flavors. Needs cellaring to soften the rougher edges. Best from 2000. A blend of Cabernet Sauvignon, Cabernet Franc, Merlot, and Petit Verdot. 200 cases made. • $40 • (07/31/97) • **88**

SALTRAM

Cabernet Sauvignon Coonawarra Pinnacle Selection 1988 • $12 • (06/30/93) • **82**
Cabernet Sauvignon Coonawarra Pinnacle Selection 1984 • $13 • (11/30/92) • **76**
Cabernet Sauvignon Hazelwood 1985 • $8 • (07/31/89) • **79**
Cabernet Sauvignon Shiraz Barossa Valley 1984 • $12 • (01/31/90) • **89**
Cabernet Sauvignon South Australia Classic 1987 • $7 • (06/30/93) • **79**
Shiraz Cabernet South Eastern Australia 1988 • $6 • (05/31/93) • **76**
Shiraz Hazelwood 1984 • $8 • (07/31/89) • **81**

SANDALFORD

Cabernet Sauvignon Margaret River & Mount Barker 1994: A crisp red, with expansive, earth-scented blackberry and juicy currant flavors resonating nicely on the long finish. Pretty graceful now for a hard-edged wine that needs until 2000 to 2004 to fill out. • $18 • (05/31/97) • **88**

Chardonnay Margaret River & Mount Barker 1995: Has some distinctive, peppery orange flavors that enhance the basic Chardonnay flavors, then finishes softly. Try now. • $18 • (06/30/97) • **83**

Shiraz Australia 1995: Ripe and tangy at the same time, this is a nice mouthful of berry and red currant flavors that finish with surprising gentleness. Try now. • $18 • (12/31/97) • **85**

SCARBOROUGH

Chardonnay Hunter Valley 1996: Dripping with butter and spice flavors around a core of pear and pineapple, ripe and generous. Persistent finish bodes well. 1,500 cases made. • $16 • (05/15/98) • **87**

Chardonnay Hunter Valley 1995 • $15 • (04/30/96) • **85**

SCOTCHMANS HILL

Chardonnay Geelong 1996: Ripe, spicy and generous with its honey-scented pear and pineapple flavors, hinting at smoke on the round finish. Texture is wonderful and flavors follow smoothly. Good now, better from 1999. 5,000 cases made. • $25 • (04/30/98) • **90**

Chardonnay Geelong 1994 • $20 • (12/15/95) • **88**

Pinot Noir Geelong 1996: Big, chewy, gamy Pinot Noir offering mint and cherry flavors and a rough layer of tannin. Try in 2000. 6,000 cases made. • $24 • (04/30/98) • **83**

Pinot Noir Geelong 1995: Tea leaf, plum and earth flavors mingle gently in this smooth-textured, nicely polished wine. Has more character than most Aussie Pinots, finishing light. • $NA • (01/01/97) • **85**

Pinot Noir Geelong 1994 • $20 • (12/15/95) • **87**

SEAVIEW

Brut Pinot Noir Chardonnay South Eastern Australia 1993: Emphasizes mature, baked bread and smoke flavors, sneaking in a perfumy note that lingers on the finish. • $13 • (03/31/98) • **86**

Brut South Eastern Australia 1996: Fresh and spicy, a lively, youthful glass of fizz that nicely melds its apple and bread-dough character. 10,000 cases made. • $8 • (03/31/98) BB • **85**

Brut South Eastern Australia 1995: Light, creamy and bright with spicy, floral overtones to the peach and vanilla flavors. Refreshing, although it has a touch of bitterness. • $9 • (04/30/97) • **84**

Brut South Australia 1990 • $9 • (07/15/93) • **80**

Brut South Australia 1988 • $9 • (11/15/91) • **83**

Cabernet Sauvignon McLaren Vale 1993 • $8 • (03/31/96) • **85**

Cabernet Sauvignon McLaren Vale Edwards & Chaffey 1994: Rich in flavor and texture, this is loaded with spicy currant, plum and chocolate flavors that persist through the long, chewy finish. Drinkable now. 1,800 cases made. • $27 • (09/30/96) • **91**

Cabernet Sauvignon South Australia 1995: Smooth and ripe, this is a straightforward mouthful of berry and spice flavors, finishing with just enough chewy tannin to want cellaring. 2,200 cases made. • $9 • (05/15/98) • **85**

Cabernet Sauvignon South Australia 1994: Hard to beat the price for this dark, dense and chewy, but not tough, Cabernet, with its polished frame that showcases the mineral-scented currant and berry flavors stylishly. It's drinking well now, even better after 1999. 12,400 cases made. 12,400 cases made. • $9 • (09/30/97) BB • **86**

Cabernet Sauvignon South Australia 1992 • $7 • (10/31/95) • **83**

Cabernet Sauvignon South Australia 1989 • $6 • (05/15/94) BB • **82**

Cabernet Sauvignon South Australia 1986 • $10 • (07/31/90) • **88**

Cabernet Shiraz South Australia 1987 • $8 • (09/30/91) BB • **82**

Chardonnay McLaren Vale 1996: Fresh and lively, with lots of appealing pear, apple, spice and vanilla flavors that linger on the well-buffed finish. Has style and elegance, but mostly lots of vivid flavors. This is more than worth its asking price and ready to drink now. 76,000 cases made. • $9 • (02/28/97) BB • **88**

Chardonnay McLaren Vale 1995 • $8 • (03/31/96) • **83**

Chardonnay McLaren Vale 1994 • $7 • (04/30/95) SS • **90**

Key: SS—Spectator Selection. CS—Cellar Selection. BB—Best Buy. HR—Highly Recommended. $NA—Price not available. (BT)—Barrel tasting. Ⓐ—Auction Price.
Dates in parentheses represent the issues in which the ratings were published.

Chardonnay McLaren Vale Edwards & Chaffey 1995: Nicely packed with citrus and apple flavors, plus a veneer of spicy oak and a touch of mineral. Drink now. 1,000 cases made. • $25 • (09/15/97) • **88**

Chardonnay McLaren Vale Edwards & Chaffey 1994: Ripe, spicy and complex; a fascinating mouthful of nutmeg-scented pear, orange and honey flavors that linger nicely on the long finish. Drink now. 2,972 cases made. • $25 • (08/31/96) • **89**

Port Australia Flagship NV • $9 • (11/15/91) • **79**

Sauvignon Blanc McLaren Vale 1996: Light, smooth and simple, fragrant with apple and melon character, finishing with a touch of herb. • $8 • (05/15/98) • **84**

Sauvignon Blanc McLaren Vale 1994 • $9 • (05/31/96) • **84**

Sauvignon Blanc McLaren Vale 1993 • $8 • (06/30/95) • **82**

Sémillon Sauvignon Blanc McLaren Vale 1996: Soft and pleasant for its tobacco-scented pineapple and peach flavors, favoring roundness and silkiness right through the finish. 74 percent Sémillon, 26 percent Sauvignon Blanc. • $8 • (05/15/98) • **85**

Sémillon Sauvignon Blanc McLaren Vale 1994 • $9 • (05/31/96) • **85**

Shiraz Cabernet South Australia 1991 • $6 • (05/15/94) BB • **84**

Shiraz McLaren Vale 1996: Dense and chewy, with bright berry flavor peeking through the anise and mineral character. 6,355 cases made. • $9 • (05/15/98) • **86**

Shiraz McLaren Vale 1994: Solid, chewy and flavorful, offering a broad range of blackberry, anise and pepper flavors that linger, with a touch of smoke on the finish. Approachable now, best from 1999. 9,400 cases made. • $9 • (09/30/97) • **88**

Shiraz McLaren Vale 1993 • $8 • (03/31/96) • **85**

Shiraz McLaren Vale 1992 • $7 • (06/30/96) BB • **86**

Shiraz McLaren Vale Edwards & Chaffey 1995: Smooth in texture, appealing for its pretty berry and spice flavors, echoing hints of black cherry on the finish. • $27 • (05/31/98) • **88**

Shiraz McLaren Vale Edwards & Chaffey 1994: A real beauty. Has depth, richness, power and elegance in one package, layering its plum, berry, nutmeg and vanilla flavors in abundance. This Aussie red is delicious now, but should improve through 1999 or 2000. 2,663 cases made. • $27 • (09/30/96) HR • **92**

Shiraz South Australia 1987 • $10 • (09/30/91) • **86**

Shiraz South Eastern Australia 1989 • $6 • (09/30/94) • **71**

SEPPELT

Amontillado Australia Seppeltsfield Show D.P. 116 NV: Smooth and sensual, with spicy toasty walnut and buttery flavors that pick up some caramel notes on the off-dry finish. 500 cases made. • $20/375ml • (10/15/96) • **89**

Amontillado Barossa Show D.P. 116 NV: Has a lovely sense of richness; dry and nutty, with walnut, almond and hints of anise swirling through the flavor profile. • $16/375ml • (05/31/98) • **88**

Brut Australia Fleur de Lys 1985 • $18 • (12/31/88) • **85**

Cabernet Sauvignon Australia Dorrien 1989 • $26 • (06/30/95) • **83**

Cabernet Sauvignon Barossa Valley Dorrien 1992: Dense and chewy, this is an earthy wine with gamy overtones to the ripe, black cherry flavors. Finishing a bit chewily, it needs until 2000 to sort itself out. 2,000 cases made. • $28 • (05/31/97) • **86**

Cabernet Sauvignon Barossa Valley Dorrien 1990 • $26 • (03/31/96) • **89**

Cabernet Sauvignon Barossa Valley Dorrien 1987 • $22 • (03/31/93) • **85**

Cabernet Sauvignon Padthaway Black Label 1988 • $12 • (03/31/91) • **81**

Cabernet Sauvignon South Australia Black Label 1994: Ripe, tarry flavors dominate. Soft-textured and straightforward. Drinkable now. 2,600 cases made. • $11 • (08/31/96) • **85**

Cabernet Sauvignon South Australia Black Label 1993 • $10 • (04/30/96) • **80**

Cabernet Sauvignon South Australia Black Label 1992 • $10 • (10/31/95) HR • **90**

Cabernet Sauvignon South Australia Black Label 1991 • $10 • (07/31/94) • **86**

Cabernet Sauvignon South Australia Black Label 1990 • $10 • (11/15/93) • **82**

Cabernet Sauvignon South Eastern Australia Black Label 1982 • $13 • (04/01/86) • **78**

Cabernet Sauvignon South Eastern Australia Murray River 1987 • $5 • (04/15/88) • **77**

Cabernet Sauvignon South Australia Reserve Bin 1993 • $8 • (10/31/95) • **82**

Cabernet Sauvignon South Eastern Australia Reserve Bin 1991 • $8 • (06/15/94) • **82**

Cabernet Sauvignon South Eastern Australia Reserve Bin 1990 • $8 • (11/15/93) • **84**

Cabernet Sauvignon South Eastern Australia Reserve Bin 1988 • $9 • (07/15/91) • **82**

Cabernet Sauvignon Victoria Drumborg 1989 • $30 • (06/30/95) • **72**

Cabernet Sauvignon Victoria Harpers Range 1994: Lively, with a supple texture. Bursting with fruit; bright currant, berry and slightly tarry flavors. Approachable now, but worth cellaring until 1999 to 2000. 1,000 cases made. • $16 • (08/31/96) • **89**

Cabernet Shiraz South Australia Classic 1994 • $6 • (04/30/96) • **79**

Cabernet Shiraz South Australia Classic 1992 • $6 • (04/15/95) BB • **87**

Cabernet Shiraz South Eastern Australia Classic 1990 • $6 • (11/30/93) • **76**

Cabernet Shiraz South Eastern Australia 1986 • $8 • (01/31/90) • **82**

Cabernet Shiraz South Eastern Australia Moyston 1989 • $8 • (11/30/92) • **79**

Chardonnay Adelaide Hills Partalunga Vineyard 1996: This fresh, generous style of Chardonnay emphasizes peach and apple flavors, smooth texture and an uncomplicated structure. 320 cases made. • $30 • (05/15/98) • **88**

Chardonnay Australia Corella Ridge 1996: A straightforward, refreshing style of Chardonnay, its flavors centering on pretty apricot and melon notes that linger on the smooth finish. Delicious now, but it could grow through 1999. 2,000 cases made. • $12 • (10/31/97) • **89**

Chardonnay South Australia Black Label 1995: Lean and spicy, with a citrusy green apple flavor that lingers and gains focus on the finish. 3,800 cases made. • $11 • (08/31/96) • **85**

Chardonnay South Australia Black Label 1994 • $10 • (12/15/95) • **87**

Chardonnay South Eastern Australia Reserve Bin 1996: Chardonnay at this price and score is a rare find, and this one is both stylish and flavorful. It's shaped for elegance, lean and delicate up front, gaining richness as the ripe pear, peach and spice flavors pile up on the finish. Appealing now and should improve through 1999. 20,000 cases made. • $9 • (05/15/97) BB • **88**

Chardonnay South Eastern Australia Reserve Bin 1994 • $8 • (03/31/96) • **81**

Chardonnay South Eastern Australia Reserve Bin 1993 • $8 • (09/30/94) • **80**

Chardonnay Victoria Corella Ridge Victorian Portfolio 1995: A very pretty Chardonnay, delicate in aroma and rich in flavor and texture, layering spicy pineapple, toast, mineral and pear notes in profusion. Finishes with length and grace. Delicious now, could improve through 1999. 510 cases made. • $14 • (05/15/97) • **90**

Fino Australia Seppeltsfield Show D.P. 117 NV: Shows marvelous almond, dried citrus peel and honey notes on the nose, but tastes tart and almost waxy. 500 cases made. • $20/375ml • (10/15/96) • **85**

Fino Barossa Valley Show D.P. 117 NV: Very light in color, dry, with almond-scented floral flavors. Drink now, slightly chilled. 100 cases made. • $16/375ml • (05/31/98) • **83**

Muscat Rutherglen Show D.P. 63 NV: A dark, dense and exotic wine, sweet, rich and redolent of spices and hints of black cherry, walnut and hazelnut. Cascades its flavors with elegance. A serious hit of flavor to finish a dinner. (1997 bottling.) 700 cases made. • $19/375ml • (12/31/97) • **92**

Oloroso Australia Seppeltsfield Show D.P. 38 NV: Feels hot, but becomes sweet and silky as the walnut, dried apricot and toast flavors play across the palate. 500 cases made. • $20/375ml • (10/15/96) • **88**

Oloroso Barossa Show D.P. 38 NV: Dark, almost amber in color, with lovely scents of orange peel, almond, cinnamon and sandalwood spinning through the soft finish. • $16/375ml • (05/31/98) • **89**

Port Australia Para No. 113 NV • $25 • (11/15/91) • **83**

Port Barossa Valley Para Port Bin 109 NV • $25 • (02/15/88) • **92**

Port Barossa Valley Para Port No. 110 NV • $25 • (03/15/89) • **79**

Port McLaren Flat Barossa 1978 • $15 • (02/15/88) • **70**

Sémillon Chardonnay South Eastern Australia Classic 1997: A pleasant wine, round and soft, with modest melon and tobacco flavors. 76 percent Sémillon, 24 percent Chardonnay. 1,200 cases made. • $7 • (05/15/98) • **82**

Sémillon Chardonnay South Eastern Australia 1994 • $6 • (03/31/96) • **82**

Sémillon Chardonnay South Eastern Australia Classic 1993 • $6 • (09/30/94) • **81**

Shiraz Australia Great Western Vineyards Hermitage 1988 • $25 • (04/15/95) • **82**

Shiraz Black Label South Eastern Australia 1994: Soft, spicy and appealing. Modest berry and tobacco flavors pick up some tannins on the finish. Drinkable now. 2,000 cases made. • $11 • (08/31/96) • **84**

Shiraz Black Label South Australia 1993 • $10 • (04/30/96) • **87**

Shiraz Black Label Victoria 1992 • $10 • (10/31/95) • **87**

Shiraz Black Label South Australia 1990 • $10 • (10/31/93) • **82**

Shiraz Black Label South Australia 1989 • $10 • (05/31/93) • **85**

Shiraz Black Label Victoria 1988 • $12 • (08/31/92) • **86**

Shiraz Black Label South Eastern Australia 1984 • $12 • (12/31/88) • **87**

Shiraz Black Label South Eastern Australia 1983 • $10 • (02/15/88) • **74**

Shiraz South Australia Reserve Bin 1995: Light in weight but firmly chewy, with fine-grained tannins around the modest plum and eucalyptus flavors. Drink now. 5,000 cases made. • $9 • (05/15/97) • **81**

Shiraz South Australia Reserve Bin 1994: Starts off with brilliant fruit character, but suffers from a green astringency and a fading finish. 2,500 cases made. • $9 • (10/15/96) • **80**

Shiraz South Eastern Australia Reserve Bin 1993 • $8 • (10/31/95) • **83**

Shiraz South Australia Reserve Bin 1992 • $7 • (04/15/95) BB • **87**

Shiraz South Eastern Australia Reserve Bin 1991 • $8 • (09/30/94) • **78**

Shiraz South Eastern Australia Reserve Bin 1990 • $8 • (10/31/93) • **82**

Shiraz South Eastern Australia Reserve Bin 1989 • $9 • (08/31/92) • **84**

Shiraz Victoria Chalambar 1994: Ripe, and silky smooth. Generous flavors—berry, black cherry, plum, anise and vanilla—that linger enticingly on the long finish. Delicious now, but could keep gaining depth through 2002. 900 cases made. • $14 • (08/31/96) • **92**

Shiraz Victoria Great Western Vineyards Hermitage 1988 • $25 • (10/31/95) • **85**

Sparkling South Eastern Australia Salinger 1992: Creamy texture and honey-scented flavors make this softly-styled, easy-going sparkler appealing. 15,000 cases made. • $15 • (05/15/97) • **87**

Sparkling Australia Salinger 1991: A straightforward mouthful of crisp apple and mineral flavors that remain lively through the finish. Sparkling wine. • $15 • (11/30/96) • **82**

Sparkling Shiraz South Eastern Australia Harpers Range 1993: A fine example of a distinctive Aussie wine, this is dry, spicy, redolent of berries and anise with a cedary overtone, made lively via its effervescent texture. 1,500 cases made. • $13 • (10/31/97) • **87**

Tawny Port Barossa Valley Trafford D.P. 30 NV: Rich and spicy, sweet and heady, with cinnamon, nutmeg, rose petal and sandalwood aromas and flavors. Nicely made, and not as sticky as some. 5,500 cases made. • $12 • (12/31/97) • **88**

Tokay Rutherglen Show D.P. 57 NV: Amber, bordering on chestnut brown in color, this deep, exotic wine shows generous walnut, black cherry and seductive spice flavors. Sweet but not cloying, it's delicious wine for topping off a serious dinner. (1996 bottling.) 600 cases made. • $19/375ml • (06/30/98) • **91**

SEVENHILL

Port Clare Valley 1988: Gamy, earthy aromas are strong, but there's enough fruit for the wine to finish with some nice spice and black cherry notes. 500 cases made. • $31 • (06/15/98) • **85**

Port Clare Valley 1987: Ripe, almost overripe, with anise and earth notes drowning out anything more pleasant. 500 cases made. • $31 • (06/15/98) • **77**

Riesling Clare Valley 1994 • $14 • (06/30/95) • **86**

Tawny Port Clare Valley NV: Offers plenty of pretty berry and cherry flavors, with hints of prune and cola on the finish. 500 cases made. • $23 • (06/15/98) • **87**

Tokay Clare Valley Liqueur NV: Spice and citrus overtones give this lightly sweet, amber-colored dessert wine extra dimension. Has lovely dried-apricot character at the center, with butter and cinnamon notes on the finish. 400 cases made. • $31 • (06/15/98) • **92**

Verdelho Clare Valley NV: Light amber in color, sweet but not cloying, with walnut, floral and green almond flavors folding in on the finish. 500 cases made. • $31 • (06/15/98) • **87**

SHAW & SMITH

Chardonnay Reserve South Australia 1996: Smooth and spicy, a nicely turned wine showing pretty apricot and pear flavors that linger on the finish. Ready now. 1,400 cases made. • $19 • (05/15/98) • **88**

Chardonnay Reserve South Australia 1995: Shows reserve and an unusual range of flavors, more mineral and lemon, with a layer of vanilla on the long-lasting finish. Nice now, best from 1999. 1,600 cases made. • $19 • (05/15/98) • **87**

Chardonnay Reserve Australia 1994: Its attractive aromas are more herbal and mineral-like than usual for Chardonnay, but its richness, complexity and elegance make it worth paying attention to. Hints at tropical fruit and spice flavors on the finish. 1,600 cases made. • $21 • (10/15/96) • **89**

Chardonnay Unoaked South Australia 1996: A tart, vibrant white with jazzy citrus and apple flavors. Without oak, it feels like a Sauvignon Blanc, but not quite as vibrant. Drink now. 5,500 cases made. • $14 • (05/15/98) • **86**

Chardonnay Unoaked Australia 1995: Bright, zingy and generous, with its passion fruit, citrus and pear flavors tempered by attractive mineral qualities that fold together smoothly on the finish. 4,500 cases made. • $16 • (10/15/96) • **88**

Sauvignon Blanc South Australia 1997: Light and appealing for its pear and herb flavors, finishing smooth and refreshing. Drink now. 11,000 cases made. • $14 • (05/15/98) • **88**

Sauvignon Blanc South Australia 1996: Bright and fresh, appealing for its zingy passion fruit and nectarine flavors that linger beautifully on the disarmingly pure finish. Drink soon. 9,000 cases made. • $14 • (05/15/98) • **90**

Sauvignon Blanc Australia 1995: Crisp and lively, this is a vibrant wine with bay leaf and orange peel notes that give it more character than most. 5,500 cases made. • $16 • (10/15/96) • **87**

SHELDRAKE

Chardonnay Western Australia 1996: Dark, ripe and spicy, slightly tired-feeling, with floral, nutmeg, clove and brown sugar overtones to the basic pineapple and pear flavors. Drink soon. 10,000 cases made. • $12 • (04/30/98) • **84**

Chardonnay Western Australia 1995: A sturdy white wine, bright and solidly built to showcase its pretty apple and spice flavors. Drink now. 4,000 cases made. • $13 • (04/30/97) • **85**

Merlot Western Australia 1996: Soft and herbal, with minty, cedary flavors overlaying the modest berry ones. Not too tannic, but feels undefined. 2,000 cases made. • $16 • (04/30/98) • **81**

Merlot Western Australia 1995: Ripe and minty, this is a complex wine with supple texture and lightish flavors. Echoes of mint and chocolate on the finish. Drink now. 1,600 cases made. • $16 • (04/30/97) • **83**

Shiraz Western Australia 1995: Smells and tastes minty, but it pours some delicious plum, anise and raspberry flavors into the mix, finishing with some richness of texture and a sense of restraint. Drinkable now. • $13 • (02/28/97) • **88**

Tawny Port Australia NV: Has a lovely garnet color and a spicy, almost Muscat-like flavor that zings through the supple berry and almond character. Not terribly sweet, but smooth, spicy and immediately appealing. 750 cases made. • $13 • (02/28/98) • **88**

SIENNA RIDGE

Red South Eastern Australia 1994: Smooth and ripe. Generous, spicy black cherry and plum flavors play against a licorice accent in the finish. 15,000 cases made. • $6 • (07/31/96) • **84**

White South Eastern Australia 1995: Simple, bright and modestly fruity, with hints of almond mixed in. 15,000 cases made. • $6 • (07/31/96) • **79**

SINGING CREEK

Red South Eastern Australia 1995: Crisp and fruity, with ripe plum and spice flavors that echo through the finish. 15,000 cases made. • $6 • (07/31/96) • **82**

White South Eastern Australia 1995: Bright, expansive and fruity, with pineapple and almond flavors. 15,000 cases made. • $6 • (07/31/96) • **82**

STAFFORD RIDGE

Cabernet-Merlot South Australia Geoff Weaver 1992: A smooth, supple style of Cabernet showing simple plum and berry flavors, finishing softly and gently. Drinkable now, and through 2004. 4,000 cases made. • $15 • (05/31/97) • **84**

STANLEY BROTHERS

Cabernet Sauvignon Barossa Valley Thoroughbred 1995: Lean and crisp for a Barossa red, but it has the characteristic spicy, tarry blackberry flavors that remain zippy through the finish. 1,000 cases made. • $19 • (06/15/98) • **87**

Key: SS—Spectator Selection. CS—Cellar Selection. BB—Best Buy. HR—Highly Recommended. $NA—Price not available. (BT)—Barrel tasting. (A)—Auction Price.
Dates in parentheses represent the issues in which the ratings were published.

STANTON & KILLEEN

Muscat Rutherglen Collectors NV: Dark, dense, and sweet, with a bite of alcohol cutting through the coffee, smoke and anise flavors. Very nice, despite a hint of harshness on the finish. • $48/375ml • (04/30/98) • **87**

Muscat Rutherglen Premium NV: Impressively spicy, with layers of cinnamon and nutmeg weaving through the dark coffee and anise flavors, picking up dried cherry and pear on the finish. • $30/375ml • (04/30/98) • **91**

Tokay Rutherglen Premium NV: Sweet, lush and lively, with just enough alcohol and acidity to balance the rich, spicy litchi and berry flavors that linger on the firm finish. • $30/375ml • (04/30/98) • **90**

STONIER'S

Cabernet Sauvignon Mornington Peninsula 1992 • $20 • (10/15/95) • **84**
Chardonnay Mornington Peninsula Reserve 1994 • $24 • (04/30/96) • **87**

STURT, CHARLES

University Red South Eastern Australia 1995: Ripe and smooth, with a chewy texture beneath the generous plum and currant flavors. Lingers gently on the spicy finish. Drink now. A blend of 55 percent Cabernet Sauvignon, 30 percent Syrah, 15 percent Merlot. 500 cases made. • $10 • (10/31/97) • **87**

SUNNYCLIFF

Cabernet Sauvignon Coonawarra 1991 • $7 • (09/30/94) • **79**
Cabernet Sauvignon Coonawarra 1990 • $7 • (04/15/93) BB • **84**
Chardonnay Victoria 1993 • $7 • (09/30/94) • **79**

SWANN, MARK

Cabernet Sauvignon Coonawarra 1987 • $7 • (02/28/91) BB • **84**
Cabernet Sauvignon Coonawarra 1985 • $7 • (10/31/88) BB • **88**
Cabernet Sauvignon Coonawarra 1984 • $8 • (08/31/87) • **77**
Cabernet Sauvignon Coonawarra 1982 • $7 • (03/16/84) • **78**
Cabernet Sauvignon South Australia 1990 • $7 • (03/31/93) • **75**
Cabernet Sauvignon South Australia 1989 • $8 • (03/15/92) • **81**
Cabernet Sauvignon South Australia Proprietor's Reserve 1988 • $5 • (02/28/91) BB • **86**
Cabernet Sauvignon South Australia Proprietor's Reserve 1987 • $5 • (07/31/89) BB • **81**
Cabernet Sauvignon South Australia Proprietor's Reserve 1986 • $5 • (10/31/88) • **78**
Dessert Rutherglen Gold Vintner's Select NV • $10/375ml • (12/31/88) • **92**
Port Australia Vintage 1980 • $10 • (04/16/84) • **78**
Shiraz Eden Valley 1980 • $6 • (03/16/84) • **80**

TALTARNI

Cabernet Sauvignon Victoria 1993: A solid Cabernet, rich and inviting for its supple, generous red cherry, currant and herbal flavors. Finishes with plush texture. Best from 1999. • $15 • (08/31/97) • **89**

Cabernet Sauvignon Victoria 1992: Minty, herbal flavors dominate the fruit flavor in this lean but supple Cabernet. Drink now. Tasted twice, with consistent notes. • $15 • (11/30/96) • **80**

Cabernet Sauvignon Victoria 1990 • $15 • (04/30/96) • **89**
Cabernet Sauvignon Victoria 1989 • $15 • (06/30/95) • **87**
Cabernet Sauvignon Victoria 1988 • $12 • (06/30/94) • **86**
Cabernet Sauvignon Victoria 1987 • $12 • (08/31/92) • **80**
Cabernet Sauvignon Victoria 1986 • $10 • (09/30/91) • **81**
Cabernet Sauvignon Victoria 1984 • $9 • (11/15/87) • **85**
Cabernet Sauvignon Victoria 1982 • $9 • (04/30/87) • **84**
Cabernet Sauvignon Victoria 1981 • $7 • (05/16/85) • **80**
Cabernet Sauvignon Victoria 1980 • $6 • (03/01/84) • **81**
Merlot Cabernet Franc Victoria 1990 • $12 • (07/31/94) • **85**
Merlot Victoria 1992 • $15 • (04/30/96) • **89**
Merlot Victoria 1991 • $15 • (04/15/95) • **83**

Sauvignon Blanc Victoria 1997: A bright, lively and juicy wine with plenty of melon and spice up front, touches of passion fruit and herb on the finish. 5,100 cases made. • $13 • (05/15/98) • **88**

Sauvignon Blanc Victoria 1996: Bright and fresh, with a mouthful of appealing nectarine and apple flavors that linger, with a generous grassy note on the finish. 2,000 cases made. • $10 • (11/30/96) • **88**

Sauvignon Blanc Victoria 1995 • $10 • (04/30/96) • **90**
Sauvignon Blanc Victoria 1993 • $12 • (05/31/95) • **89**
Shiraz Victoria 1995: Lean and lithe, well balanced to show off the modest blueberry and plum flavors under a layer of mineral and earth notes. Approachable now, best from 2000. • $16 • (03/31/98) • **86**
Shiraz Victoria 1993 • $15 • (04/30/96) • **90**
Shiraz Victoria 1992 • $15 • (03/31/95) • **89**
Shiraz Victoria 1991 • $13 • (09/30/94) • **88**
Shiraz Victoria 1990 • $13 • (04/30/93) • **92**
Shiraz Victoria 1989 • $14 • (08/31/92) • **88**
Shiraz Victoria 1988 • $14 • (05/31/92) • **89**
Shiraz Victoria 1987 • $10 • (09/30/91) • **82**
Shiraz Victoria 1986 • $10 • (10/31/90) • **84**
Shiraz Victoria 1985 • $10 • (11/30/88) SS • **91**
Shiraz Victoria 1984 • $9 • (02/15/88) • **75**
Shiraz Victoria 1982 • $9 • (04/30/87) • **86**
Shiraz Victoria 1980 • $6 • (03/16/84) • **77**

TAMBURLAINE

The Chapel Reserve Hunter Valley NV: Decidedly herbal, almost weedy, with a strong minty streak running through the metallic berry flavors. May be best after 1999. A blend of Shiraz, Cabernet Sauvignon and Chambourcin. 1,200 cases made. • $14 • (09/30/97) • **80**

TARRAWARRA

Pinot Noir Yarra Glen 1989 • $28 • (04/15/92) • **80**
Pinot Noir Yarra Glen 1988 • $25 • (12/31/90) • **86**
Pinot Noir Yarra Valley 1991 • $26 • (07/31/94) • **85**
Pinot Noir Yarra Valley 1990 • $27 • (08/31/92) • **87**
Pinot Noir Yarra Valley Tunnel Hill 1991 • $15 • (06/30/93) • **81**

TEMPLE BRUER

Cabernet Sauvignon-Merlot-Cabernet Franc South Australia 1989 • $11 • (03/31/95) • **84**
Grenache South Australia Cornucopia 1994: Light and fruity, this is an easy-drinking wine with modest berry and black cherry flavors and a hint of almond on the finish. Drink soon. • $10 • (05/15/97) • **83**
Shiraz Malbec Langhorne Creek 1991: Soft and inviting, with plum, currant and a hint of black cherry predominating, and some flavors reminiscent of Malbec in the blend. Drinkable now. 1,000 cases made. • $15 • (06/15/97) • **87**
Shiraz Malbec South Australia 1994: Bright berry and earthy herbal flavors carry this crisp, tart wine through, echoing strawberry on the finish. Best from 1999. 500 cases made. • $14 • (04/30/98) • **85**
Shiraz Malbec South Australia 1990 • $11 • (01/31/95) • **80**

THISTLE HILL

Cabernet Sauvignon Mudgee 1988 • $18 • (04/30/94) • **79**

TRENTHAM

Cabernet Merlot Murray River Valley 1996: Bright and spicy, refreshingly centered around soft berry and cigar-box flavors that linger gently on the finish. A blend of 60 percent Cabernet Sauvignon and 40 percent Merlot. 1,000 cases made. • $15 • (05/31/98) • **86**
Chardonnay Riverland 1995: Smooth and creamy, with fresh nectarine, spice and vanilla flavors that linger sweetly on the soft finish. 30,000 cases made. • $11 • (05/31/97) • **86**

TUNNEL HILL

Pinot Noir Yarra Valley 1990 • $16 • (02/29/92) • **84**

TURKEY FLAT

Grenache Noir Barossa Valley 1996: Ripe, concentrated, bursting with spicy cherry and tobacco flavors, it's intense and rich enough to achieve a sort of grandeur. Impressive now, best from 1999. 1,000 cases made. • $20 • (10/15/97) • **90**
Shiraz Barossa Valley 1995: Ripe and jazzy. A full-throated roar of an Australian Shiraz that rides its raw power to a surprisingly soft landing. It's a thrill ride packed with fresh plum, spice and berry flavors that gain momentum from a touch of smoky oak that weaves through the finish. Best from 2000. 3,000 cases made. • $28 • (09/15/97) HR • **93**

TYRRELL'S

Brut Pinot Noir Hunter Valley 1983 • $19 • (09/30/88) • **82**
Cabernet Merlot South Australia Old Winery 1997: Light and appealing for its herbal berry flavors and supple texture. 85 percent Cabernet Sauvignon, 15 percent Merlot. 35,000 cases made. • $11 • (05/31/98) • **84**
Cabernet Merlot South Australia Old Winery 1996: Bright and refreshing, with simple herb-scented raspberry flavors that get a bit chewy on the finish. Try now. 3,500 cases made. • $10 • (05/15/97) • **82**
Cabernet Merlot South Eastern Australia Old Winery 1994 • $8 • (03/31/96) • **84**
Cabernet Merlot South Eastern Australia Old Winery 1992 • $8 • (06/30/95) • **84**
Cabernet Merlot South Eastern Australia Old Winery 1991 • $8 • (12/15/93) • **81**
Cabernet Merlot South Eastern Australia Old Winery 1990 • $9 • (03/31/93) • **78**
Cabernet Merlot Australia Old Winery 1988 • $7 • (03/31/91) BB • **84**
Cabernet Merlot Hunter Valley 1987 • $7 • (09/15/90) • **79**
Cabernet Merlot Hunter Valley 1986 • $8 • (01/31/90) BB • **88**
Cabernet Merlot Hunter Valley 1985 • $9 • (07/31/89) • **84**
Cabernet Merlot Hunter Valley 1984 • $9 • (07/15/88) • **82**
Cabernet Merlot New South Wales Victoria 1983 • $8 • (03/15/88) • **84**
Cabernet Sauvignon South Eastern Australia Old Winery 1992 • $8 • (06/30/95) BB • **83**
Cabernet Sauvignon South Eastern Australia Old Winery 1991 • $8 • (11/15/93) • **80**
Cabernet Sauvignon South Eastern Australia Old Winery 1986 • $9 • (03/15/92) • **84**
Cabernet Sauvignon Hunter Valley Classic 1984 • $7 • (09/15/90) BB • **88**
Cabernet Sauvignon Hunter Valley Premier Selection 1983 • $8 • (04/30/88) BB • **87**
Chardonnay Hunter Valley Moon Mountain Individual Vineyards 1996: Lean in structure, with a nice bead of grapefruit and pear flavor that extends into a sturdy finish. 8,000 cases made. • $25 • (05/31/98) • **88**
Chardonnay Hunter Valley Moon Mountain Individual Vineyards 1995: This has personality. Distinctively spicy and rich, with lanolin and nutmeg overtones to ripe pear and caramel flavors that linger on the finish, with a touch of zingy tangerine. 1,500 cases made. • $20 • (05/15/97) • **88**
Chardonnay Hunter Valley Shee-Oak Individual Vineyard 1997: Bright and vibrant, a lively wine with layers of green apple, citrus and honey flavors that extend nicely into a long finish. Very pretty now. 8,000 cases made. • $25 • (05/31/98) • **90**
Chardonnay Hunter Valley Shee-Oak 1996: Bright and spicy, with lively pear and honey flavors that gain layers of spice and vanilla on the elegant finish. Delicious. Drinkable now, best from 1999. 6,000 cases made. • $20 • (05/15/97) • **90**
Chardonnay Hunter Valley Shee-Oak Individual Vineyard Non-Wooded 1995 • $10 • (04/30/96) • **88**
Chardonnay Hunter Valley Shee-Oak Individual Vineyard Non-Wooded 1994 • $10 • (03/31/96) • **88**
Chardonnay South Eastern Australia Old Winery 1997: A lively mouthful of green apple, pear and spice flavors, finishing with a touch of citrus. Refreshing to drink now. 35,000 cases made. • $11 • (05/31/98) BB • **87**
Chardonnay South Eastern Australia Old Winery 1996: Ripe, charming and almost delicate after all, with spicy pear and mineral flavors that linger on the subtle finish. 35,000 cases made. • $10 • (05/15/97) • **86**
Chardonnay South Eastern Australia Old Winery Premier Selection 1995 • $7 • (04/30/96) • **87**
Chardonnay South Eastern Australia Old Winery Premier Selection 1994 • $8 • (03/31/96) BB • **85**
Chardonnay South Eastern Australia Old Winery 1993 • $8 • (06/30/95) BB • **85**
Chardonnay Sémillon South Eastern Australia Long Flat 1997: Smooth and appealing for its bright apple and pear flavors, hinting at fig on the finish. 90,000 cases made. • $8 • (05/31/98) • **85**
Dry Red Vat 9 Hunter Valley 1987 • $15 • (04/15/93) • **81**
Dry Red Vat 9 Hunter River Winemaker's Selection 1984 • $15 • (02/15/92) • **83**
Hermitage Australia 1982 • $8 • (07/01/87) • **84**
Long Flat Red South Eastern Australia 1997: On the light side, with a firm core of raspberry and spice flavors that linger gently on the finish. A blend

of Cabernet Sauvignon, Shiraz, and Malbec. 120,000 cases made. • $8 • (05/31/98) • **84**
Long Flat Red South Eastern Australia 1994 • $6 • (06/30/95) • **79**
Long Flat Red South Eastern Australia 1992 • $6 • (05/31/95) • **83**
Long Flat Red South Eastern Australia 1991 • $7 • (05/31/93) • **82**
Long Flat Red South Eastern Australia 1990 • $6 • (08/31/92) BB • **84**
Long Flat Red South Eastern Australia 1988 • $7 • (02/15/92) BB • **84**
Long Flat Red Hunter Valley 1986 • $6 • (01/31/90) • **79**
Long Flat Red Hunter Valley 1985 • $5 • (07/31/89) BB • **81**
Long Flat Red Hunter Valley 1984 • $6 • (09/30/88) BB • **83**
Long Flat Red Hunter Valley 1983 • $6 • (04/15/88) • **79**
Long Flat White South Eastern Australia 1997: Very fragrant, with floral, citrusy pear and litchi flavors that remain juicy and sprightly through the finish. A blend of Sémillon, Traminer and Trebbiano. 100 cases made. • $8 • (05/31/98) • **85**
Long Flat White South Eastern Australia 1995 • $6 • (03/31/96) BB • **84**
Long Flat White South Eastern Australia 1994 • $6 • (05/31/95) BB • **84**
Pinot Chardonnay Hunter Valley Vat 47 1997: Very smooth in texture, with spicy, toasty pear and melon flavors that lean toward the earthy side on the harmonious finish. Has some lovely citrusy overtones as well. 5,000 cases made. • $40 • (05/31/98) • **89**
Pinot Chardonnay Hunter Valley Vat 47 1996: A many-layered wine with smooth texture and spicy pear and honey flavors in profusion. Ripe, long and dramatic, it should continue to gain depth through 1999 to 2000. 8,000 cases made. • $30 • (05/15/97) • **89**
Pinot Chardonnay Hunter Valley Vat 47 1995 • $15 • (04/30/96) • **83**
Pinot Chardonnay Hunter Valley Vat 47 1994 • $16 • (04/30/96) HR • **92**
Pinot Chardonnay Hunter Valley Vat 47 1993 • $15 • (06/30/95) • **86**
Pinot Noir Hunter River 1985 • $10 • (07/01/87) • **87**
Pinot Noir Hunter Valley Eclipse Individual Vineyards 1996: Light in texture, modestly endowed with spicy plum and tea leaf aromas and flavors. Nicely balanced. 2,000 cases made. • $25 • (05/31/98) • **85**
Pinot Noir South Eastern Australia Old Winery 1997: Light and velvety, with pretty blackberry and pepper flavors that echo lightly on the finish. 12,000 cases made. • $11 • (05/31/98) • **83**
Pinot Noir South Eastern Australia Old Winery 1996: Light in texture with flavors that center around bright berry, but it also slides in some greenish notes. Best from 1999. 8,000 cases made. • $10 • (05/15/97) • **82**
Pinot Noir Hunter Valley Old Winery 1995 • $7 • (04/30/96) • **84**
Pinot Noir South Eastern Australia Old Winery 1993 • $8 • (06/15/95) BB • **88**
Sémillon Chardonnay South Eastern Australia Long Flat 1995 • $6 • (03/31/96) • **82**
Sémillon Hunter Valley Old Winery 1997: Light in texture, with resiny pineapple and green apple flavors that soften on the finish. 5,000 cases made. • $11 • (05/31/98) • **85**
Sémillon Hunter Valley Old Winery 1996 • $10 • (05/15/97) • **84**
Sémillon Hunter Valley Vat 1 1993: A subtle wine, with earthy tobacco and pineapple flavors gliding gently over the palate. Drinkable now, but known to age well. Try through 2000. 5,000 cases made. • $40 • (05/31/98) • **87**
Sémillon Sauvignon Blanc South Eastern Australia Old Winery 1997: Bright and refreshing for its pretty green apple and pineapple character. 50 percent Sémillon, 50 percent Sauvignon Blanc. 5,000 cases made. • $11 • (05/31/98) • **86**
Shiraz Hunter Valley Brokenback Individual Vineyards 1996: Its crisp structure favors herbal tartness over lush fruit, echoing mint and plum on the finish. 6,000 cases made. • $25 • (05/31/98) • **83**
Shiraz Hunter Valley Stevens 1994: Ripe, and well focused to show off its bright blackberry and plum flavors, this feels round and generous right through the finish, which echoes fruit and anise. Has all the ingredients to be enjoyed now, but it could develop through 2000 to 2003. 2,000 cases made. • $20 • (05/15/97) • **88**
Shiraz Hunter Valley Vat 9 1994: Has some pretty blackberry flavor at the core, but this medium-weight wine is dripping with game, anise and tar flavors. Best from 1999 through 2002. 3,000 cases made. • $40 • (05/31/98) • **86**
Shiraz Hunter Valley Vat 9 1993: Lots of earthy anise character runs through the chewy blackberry flavors of this quirky red. Should develop some depth by 2000 to 2002. 6,000 cases made. • $30 • (05/15/97) • **84**
Shiraz Hunter Valley Vat 9 1991 • $11 • (04/30/96) • **88**
Shiraz Hunter Valley Vat 9 Aged Release 1990 • $12 • (02/29/96) • **87**

Key: SS—Spectator Selection. CS—Cellar Selection. BB—Best Buy. HR—Highly Recommended. $NA—Price not available. (BT)—Barrel tasting. Ⓐ—Auction Price.
Dates in parentheses represent the issues in which the ratings were published.

Shiraz Hunter Valley Hunter River Vat 9 1989 • $12 • (06/30/95) • **77**
Shiraz Hunter Valley Dry Red Vat 9 1987 • $10 • (06/15/94) • **82**
Shiraz Hunter Valley Classic 1986 • $8 • (01/31/90) BB • **84**
Shiraz South Australia Moore's Creek 1996: Ripe and generous, this ready-to-drink red is packed with ripe currant and black cherry flavors that linger on the open-textured finish. A good, affordable choice if you need a couple of bottles for tonight; drink through 2001. 20,000 cases made. • $8 • (05/15/98) BB • **86**
Shiraz South Eastern Australia Old Winery 1996: This solid red has some pretty black cherry and plum flavors, with all sorts of herb, anise and earthy flavors swirling around it. Not for all tastes. 25,000 cases made. • $11 • (05/31/98) • **83**
Shiraz South Eastern Australia Old Winery 1995: Firm in texture, this is a chewy wine with modest berry and mineral flavors that finish crisply. Drink now. 15,000 cases made. • $10 • (05/15/97) • **83**
Shiraz Hunter Valley Old Winery Premier Selection 1993 • $8 • (02/29/96) • **86**
Shiraz Hunter Valley Old Winery 1990 • $8 • (06/30/95) • **83**
Shiraz Hunter Valley Old Winery 1988 • $10 • (05/31/93) • **77**
Tawny Port Australia 8 Barrels NV • $9 • (05/15/96) • **87**
Tawny Port Australia 8-Year-Old Fine Aged NV • $9 • (06/30/95) • **81**
Verdelho Hunter Valley Fordwich 1996: Fat and generous with its spicy pear flavors, finishing with a hard-edged mineral note. Tasty. Drink now. 2,000 cases made. • $20 • (05/15/97) • **83**

VASSE FELIX

Cabernet Merlot Margaret River Classic Dry Red 1991 • $12 • (04/30/94) • **82**
Cabernet Merlot Western Australia 1995: Strongly minty, it's an herbal, cedary red with layers of black cherry and anise flavors. Not for everyone, but a distinctive wine. 3,000 cases made. • $16 • (06/15/97) • **86**
Cabernet Sauvignon Margaret River 1995: Chewy in texture, with cedary boysenberry and red raspberry flavors, touches of earth and game on the taut finish. Best from 2000. 2,500 cases made. • $24 • (06/15/97) • **83**
Cabernet Sauvignon Margaret River 1990 • $14 • (04/30/94) • **85**
Chardonnay Western Australia 1996: Dripping with personality, this rolls out spicy pear and distinctive earthy, tarry overtones that linger on the smoky finish. Delicious now, likely better after 1999. 4,000 cases made. • $21 • (06/15/97) • **90**
Sauvignon Blanc-Sémillon-Chardonnay Western Australia 1996: Light, nicely polished, shining with spicy citrus and apple flavors and sliding in a touch of herb on the finish. Ready to drink. A blend of 38 percent Sauvignon Blanc, 36 percent Sémillon, 26 percent Chardonnay. 3,000 cases made. • $16 • (06/15/97) • **87**
Shiraz Margaret River 1995: Has a strong, minty edge to the rich, anise-scented berry and beetroot flavors—an unusual range of flavors for Shiraz. Best from 1999. 1,000 cases made. • $26 • (06/15/97) • **83**

VIRGIN HILLS

Red Keyneton 1994: Lean, lithe and elegant. A wiry wine with finely textured tannins, snappy acidity and a juicy mixture of plum, currant and berry flavors that echo on the finish, with more than a hint of pickle barrel. Best from 1999. A blend of Cabernet Sauvignon, Shiraz, Malbec, and Merlot. 200 cases made. • $33 • (07/31/97) • **89**

WAKEFIELD

Cabernet Sauvignon Clare Valley 1994: Rich, supple and intense, remarkable for its generosity and a smoothness that swirls over a frame of racy acidity. Flavors center around blueberry and currant. Delicious now. 1,500 cases made. • $13 • (10/31/97) • **89**
Riesling Clare Valley Clare 1994: Light and airy, with a creamy mineral note adding interest to the basic peach and apple flavors. Gently lingering finish. • $10 • (05/31/97) • **85**

WATER WHEEL

Cabernet Sauvignon Bendigo 1996: Firm in texture, this chewy wine places its berry and currant flavors under a deep layer of tannins that sort of clamps down on the finish. Best after 2002. 6,000 cases made. • $14 • (04/30/98) • **85**
Chardonnay Bendigo 1996: Soft, ripe and generous with its pear and peach flavors, lingering with a touch of smoky spice on the finish. Impressive for

its purity of flavor and harmony. Best from late this year. 6,000 cases made. • $12 • (04/30/98) • **89**

Sauvignon Blanc Bendigo 1996: Fresh and appealing for its pretty melon and citrus flavors, with just a hint of herb or grass around the edges. Drink now. 6,000 cases made. • $9 • (04/30/98) • **85**

Shiraz Bendigo 1996: Ripe and jazzy, with pretty blueberry and plum flavors shaded with a touch of spice. Chewy tannins need until 2001 to settle down. 2,000 cases made. • $14 • (04/30/98) • **86**

WHITE, ALICE

Chardonnay South Eastern Australia 1996: Here's a pretty Australian Chardonnay, brimming with pear and gentle spice flavors. It's appealing to drink sooner rather than later, and at this price and score it's a smart choice when the occasion demands more than one bottle. 100,000 cases made. • $7 • (10/31/97) BB • **87**

WHITE OPAL

Chardonnay South Eastern Australia 1996: Light and refreshing for its bright, peppery apple and guava flavors. Drink now. 25,000 cases made. • $10 • (01/31/97) • **83**

WILDERNESS

Chardonnay Hunter Valley Reserve 1996: Strongly floral, so much so as to interfere with the pretty citrus and apricot flavors. Finishes a tad sour. 7,000 cases made. • $15 • (10/31/97) • **81**

Merlot Hunter Valley 1995: Herbal, vegetal flavors overcome the modest fruit; not the range of flavors destined to please too many palates. 5,000 cases made. • $15 • (10/31/97) • **77**

Shiraz Hunter Valley 1995: Spicy, with a thin bead of plum and berry flavor losing out to a green, resiny edge. Drink now. Tasted twice, with consistent notes. 5,000 cases made. • $15 • (10/31/97) • **79**

WILKINSON, AUDREY

Cabernet Sauvignon Hunter Valley 1986 • $14 • (09/30/91) • **87**

Shiraz Hunter Valley Hermitage 1985 • $13 • (09/30/91) • **79**

WILLESPIE

Cabernet Sauvignon Margaret River 1993: Generous with its herbal, tobacco and blackberry flavors that linger on the supple finish. A sturdy, stylish wine that promises better things by 1999 to 2000. 500 cases made. • $14 • (10/31/97) • **87**

Cabernet Sauvignon Margaret River 1990 • $13 • (11/15/93) • **79**

Cabernet Sauvignon Margaret River 1989 • $13 • (06/30/93) • **82**

WILTON

Sémillon New South Wales Botrytis 1995: Very dark color, sweet but not unctuous, offering straightforward pineapple and apricot flavors that echo hints of spice and fig on the finish. Nice now, but give it until 2000 to see what develops. • $24/375ml • (06/30/98) • **88**

WIRILDA CREEK

Sauvignon Blanc McLaren Vale 1996: Bright, focused and spicy, with gentle hints of herb mingling with the pretty nectarine and pear flavors. Delicious now. 300 cases made. • $11 • (10/31/97) • **87**

WOODLEY

Shiraz-Cabernet South Eastern Australia Queen Adelaide 1992 • $6 • (06/30/95) • **82**

Shiraz-Cabernet South Eastern Australia Queen Adelaide 1989 • $7 • (05/31/93) • **74**

Shiraz-Cabernet South Eastern Australia Queen Adelaide 1988 • $7 • (02/29/92) BB • **82**

Tawny Port South Australia Queen Adelaide NV • $7 • (04/15/95) BB • **87**

WYNDHAM

Cabernet Merlot Hunter Valley Bin 888 1990 • $8 • (09/30/94) • **77**

Cabernet Sauvignon South Eastern Australia Bin 444 1995: Big, chewy and bursting with brilliant flavors. A cascade of currant, blackberry, sage and spice character extends into a long, elegant finish. Tannins are beautifully integrated. Has the goods to develop through 2005 and beyond. • $10 • (06/15/97) • **88**

Cabernet Sauvignon South Eastern Australia Bin 444 1993 • $7 • (05/15/96) • **79**

Cabernet Sauvignon South Eastern Australia Bin 444 1992 • $9 • (11/30/94) • **84**

Cabernet Sauvignon South Eastern Australia Bin 444 1991 • $7 • (01/31/95) • **83**

Cabernet Sauvignon Hunter Valley Bin 444 1988 • $7 • (06/30/92) • **80**

Cabernet Sauvignon Hunter Valley Bin 444 1983 • $6 • (07/15/88) BB • **82**

Cabernet Shiraz South Eastern Australia 1989 • $7 • (06/30/92) • **76**

Cabernet Shiraz Hunter Valley 1987 • $7 • (01/31/90) BB • **91**

Cabernet Shiraz Hunter Valley 1986 • $6 • (12/31/88) BB • **87**

Cabernet Shiraz Hunter Valley 1985 • $6 • (03/15/88) BB • **87**

Chardonnay Hunter Valley Oak Cask 1995: Broad and spicy. A soft wine with a bitter edge to the otherwise pretty floral and pear flavors. Drink now. 12,000 cases made. • $9 • (02/28/97) • **82**

Chardonnay South Eastern Australia Oak Cask 1993 • $9 • (04/30/95) BB • **88**

Chardonnay South Eastern Australia Bin 222 1997: Soft and appealing, with pretty apple and vanilla flavors. 60,000 cases made. • $8 • (06/30/98) • **82**

Chardonnay South Eastern Australia Bin 222 1993 • $7 • (06/30/95) • **83**

Merlot Hunter Valley 1986 • $8 • (01/31/90) BB • **85**

Pinot Noir South Eastern Australia Bin 333 1994 • $7 • (05/15/96) • **85**

Pinot Noir South Eastern Australia Bin 333 1987 • $7 • (08/31/92) • **78**

Sémillon-Chardonnay South Eastern Australia Bin 777 1995 • $6 • (05/15/96) BB • **85**

Shiraz South Eastern Australia Bin 555 1993 • $8 • (06/15/96) • **82**

Shiraz South Eastern Australia Bin 555 1991 • $9 • (09/30/94) • **81**

Shiraz South Eastern Australia Bin 555 1990 • $7 • (02/15/93) BB • **85**

Shiraz South Eastern Australia Bin 555 1988 • $7 • (06/30/92) • **83**

Shiraz Hunter Valley Bin 555 1986 • $7 • (01/31/90) BB • **85**

TR2 Vintage Reserve South Eastern Australia 1995: Smells like an old Traminer or Riesling, more kerosene than fruit marks the character and it finishes soft and flabby. • $9 • (04/30/97) • **74**

TR2 Reserve Bin Medium Dry White South Eastern Australia 1993 • $4 • (09/30/94) • **87**

WYNN, DAVID

Cabernet Sauvignon Eden Valley 1996: Polished and supple, this lean wine with soft edges and appealing anise and berry flavors is ready now. 4,000 cases made. • $14 • (11/30/97) • **85**

Cabernet Sauvignon Eden Valley 1995: Crisp and lively. A juicy little wine, not a grand style of Cabernet but one that with its pretty berry flavors can complement dinner. Drink now. 4,000 cases made. • $12 • (02/28/97) • **85**

Chardonnay South Eastern Australia 1994 • $10 • (12/15/95) • **84**

Chardonnay South Eastern Australia Unwooded 1996: A different style, bright and fruity, with a juicy freshness to the passion fruit, apple and citrus flavors that linger appealingly. Drink now. 8,000 cases made. • $12 • (02/28/97) • **87**

Sémillon Chardonnay South Eastern Australia 1993 • $9 • (10/15/95) • **83**

Shiraz Eden Valley Patriarch 1995: Firm, crisp, focused and generous with its anise- and herb-scented black cherry and blackberry flavors. Finishes with backbone and style. Best from 1999 or 2000. 2,000 cases made. • $25 • (11/30/97) • **89**

Shiraz Eden Valley Patriarch 1994: Round and supple, with focused blackberry, plum and spice flavors that finish with a cedary accent, this wine balances plushness with a touch of austerity. Drink now. 3,000 cases made. • $22 • (05/15/97) • **90**

Shiraz South Eastern Australia Patriarch 1993 • $15 • (10/31/95) • **86**

Shiraz Eden Valley Unwooded 1996: Fresh and jammy, a nose- and mouthful of raspberry flavor, straightforward and nicely rounded on the finish. Drink now. 6,000 cases made. • $12 • (02/28/97) • **83**

WYNNS COONAWARRA ESTATE

Cabernet Hermitage Coonawarra 1984 • $10 • (12/31/88) • **79**

Cabernet Sauvignon Coonawarra 1995: Firm and chewy, with earthy currant and plum flavors sneaking past the fine-grained tannins. • $14 • (06/15/98) • **86**

Cabernet Sauvignon Coonawarra 1993: A very crisp, hard-edged style with emphasis on mint character on the back palate. Chunky tannins will require until 2002 or 2004 to settle down, but the flavors feel like they can hold until then, too. • $12 • (12/15/96) • **86**

Cabernet Sauvignon Coonawarra 1991 • $12 • (04/30/95) • **85**

Cabernet Sauvignon Coonawarra 1989 • $12 • (04/30/94) • **82**

Cabernet Sauvignon Coonawarra 1982 • $15 • (11/30/88) • **90**

Cabernet Sauvignon Coonawarra Estate 1989 • $12 • (04/15/93) • **86**

Cabernet Sauvignon Coonawarra John Riddoch 1992 • $40 • (04/30/96) • **91**

Cabernet Sauvignon Coonawarra John Riddoch Limited Release 1990 • $22 • (11/30/94) SS • **92**

Cabernet Sauvignon Coonawarra John Riddoch Limited Release 1988 • $22 • (03/31/93) • **84**

Cabernet Shiraz Coonawarra 1990 • $11 • (04/30/94) • **83**

Cabernet Shiraz Merlot Coonawarra 1995: Tart and tarry, with lots of anise and black pepper running through the chewy black cherry flavors. Best from 1999. 50 percent Cabernet Sauvignon, 35 percent Shiraz, 15 percent Merlot. • $11 • (06/15/98) • **83**

Chardonnay Coonawarra 1997: Bright and vibrant, with spicy apple and pear flavors hinting at resin on the lively finish. • $12 • (06/15/98) • **88**

Chardonnay Coonawarra 1994 • $12 • (04/30/96) • **90**

Chardonnay Coonawarra 1993 • $12 • (06/30/95) • **88**

Shiraz Coonawarra 1996: Distinctively spicy, with an anise and poppy seed shading to the dark cherry and blackberry lurking in the crisp background. Nicely balanced so all sorts of nuances come through. • $13 • (06/15/98) • **88**

Shiraz Coonawarra 1993: Crisp and juicy, delivering a nice mouthful of ripe berry flavor, with a citrus accent. Needs to be cellared to develop some richness, so try in 2000 or 2002. • $12 • (12/15/96) • **87**

Shiraz Coonawarra 1992 • $11 • (03/31/95) • **84**

Shiraz Coonawarra 1991 • $11 • (03/31/94) • **84**

Shiraz Coonawarra Michael 1993: Crisp in texture, with spicy berry and prune flavors that expand and gain a touch of anise on the finish. Has impressive length; needs until 1999 to 2000 to soften. 4,693 cases made. • $40 • (08/31/96) • **90**

YALUMBA

Brut de Brut Australia 1984 • $8 • (03/15/88) • **84**

Cabernet-Merlot South Australia Barrel Select Family Reserve 1995: Silky and simple, with pleasant red berry and strawberry flavors that linger nicely on the smooth finish. Drink now. • $12 • (05/31/97) • **85**

Cabernet-Merlot South Australia Family Reserve 1994: Sweet prune and currant flavors show a spicy floral accent at the start, then mellow on the firm finish, picking up some chocolaty notes. Drink now. 2,000 cases made. • $12 • (09/30/96) • **88**

Cabernet Sauvignon Coonawarra Family Reserve 1989 • $9 • (02/28/93) BB • **84**

Cabernet Sauvignon Coonawarra Octavius 1988 • $30 • (05/15/94) • **90**

Cabernet Sauvignon Coonawarra The Menzies 1994: Big, ripe and generous. A chunky wine with solid blackberry and anise flavors that turn chewy on the finish. Best after 1999. • $21 • (02/28/98) • **86**

Cabernet Shiraz Coonawarra 1984 • $6 • (01/31/88) • **78**

Chardonnay Australia Show Reserve 1993 • $NA • (06/30/96) • **88**

Chardonnay Barossa 1997: A solidly built white, with pretty pear and vanilla flavors. Could be more polished. 3,000 cases made. • $13 • (06/15/98) • **85**

Chardonnay Barossa Reserve 1995: Bright and refreshing, with creamy pear and grapefruit flavors that ride smoothly through the finish. Drink now. • $13 • (05/31/97) • **88**

Chardonnay Barossa Barrel Select Family Reserve 1996: Ripe and effusive with its spicy, creamy, golden apple flavors, this mouthfilling white doesn't get heavy. Drink now. • $11 • (05/31/97) • **87**

Chardonnay South Australia Family Reserve 1995: Smooth, bright and appealing for its spicy apple flavors that linger on the well-proportioned finish. 5,000 cases made. • $11 • (11/30/96) • **86**

Chardonnay Barossa Valley Family Reserve 1994 • $12 • (03/31/96) • **84**

Chardonnay South Eastern Australia Oxford Landing 1994 • $7 • (05/15/95) • **86**

Chardonnay Yarra Valley Eden Valley Show Reserve 1993 • $12 • (03/31/96) • **90**

Grenache Barossa Bush Vine Reserve 1995: Bright in flavor, soft in texture, with warm, chocolaty raspberry and ripe strawberry flavors that remain generous through the supple finish. Has style and character, and it's ready to drink. • $12 • (06/30/97) • **88**

Grenache Barossa Bush Vine 1994 • $12 • (04/30/96) • **80**

Merlot South Eastern Australia Oxford Landing 1992 • $8 • (09/30/94) • **78**

Muscat Museum Victoria Museum Release NV: This Australian "sticky" rivals the quality of many more-prestigious versions, at a fraction of the price. It's a gorgeous mouthful of spice and walnut, sweet and opulent, and is deep with clove, coffee, dried litchi and berry flavors that linger with hints of tangerine-peel on the finish. Yummy. • $15/375ml • (02/28/98) HR • **94**

Muscat Rutherglen Museum Show Reserve NV • $12/375ml • (09/15/94) HR • **98**

Old Sweet Wine Barossa Museum Release NV: Leaner and less opulent than most liqueur wines, but very subtle and complex, sharp with acidity on the finish, and very pretty for its raspberry and spice flavors. • $15/375ml • (02/28/98) • **89**

Oxford Landing South Eastern Australia 1992 • $7 • (06/30/95) • **84**

Port Galway Pipe NV • $19 • (05/31/96) • **92**

Sémillon Botrytis South Australia Family Reserve 1995: Rich, sweet and spicy, this offers a mouthful of generous butter, fig, pineapple and allspice. Already fully developed, drink it soon. 2,000 cases made. • $13/375ml • (10/15/96) • **89**

Sémillon Late Harvest Barossa Valley Botrytis Family Reserve 1994 • $12/375ml • (12/31/95) HR • **94**

Sémillon Late Harvest Barossa Valley Botrytis Sémillon Family Reserve 1993 • $11 • (09/30/95) • **93**

Sémillon Late Harvest Eden Valley Botrytis Family Reserve 1991 • $10 • (09/15/94) • **86**

Sémillon Late Harvest Barossa Valley Botrytis Affected 1984 • $5/375ml • (03/15/89) • **83**

Sémillon-Sauvignon Blanc Griffith & Barossa Botrytis 1997: Sweet, spicy and silky, with generous layers of fig, honey, dried pear and guava swirling through the polished finish. Showing a nice balance of sweetness and acidity, this Aussie sweetie should age beautifully. 2,000 cases made. • $15/375ml • (06/15/98) HR • **91**

Sémillon-Sauvignon Blanc South Australia Botrytis Family Reserve 1996: Dark and sweet without being exceedingly rich, but its orange, apricot and honey flavors seem restrained. Not as rich or as sweet as in recent years. • $12/375ml • (05/31/97) • **86**

Shiraz Barossa Valley Family Reserve 1995: A richly textured wine, ripe and smoky, with lots of sweet spice, plum and anise flavors that linger on the tarry finish. Approachable now, best from 2000 to 2005. • $12 • (05/31/97) • **90**

Shiraz Barossa Valley Family Reserve 1994: Supple, with disarmingly fresh and delicious sweet berry and vanilla flavors, although there's not much on the nose yet. Drinkable now. • $12 • (10/15/96) • **87**

Shiraz Barossa Valley Family Reserve 1993 • $10 • (03/31/96) • **86**

Shiraz Barossa Valley Family Reserve 1991 • $10 • (09/30/94) • **88**

Shiraz Barossa Valley Family Reserve 1989 • $9 • (11/30/92) • **86**

Shiraz Barossa Octavius 1993: Smooth, polished and generous, with toasty black cherry and anise flavors, not terribly intense but balanced and harmonious. Drink now. • $40 • (05/31/97) • **88**

Shiraz Barossa Octavius Old Vine 1992: A rich, generous Shiraz with a minty accent to the ripe blackberry, spicecake and tar flavors and a hint of anise on the long, elegant, chewy finish. Yummy now, but should keep growing through 1999 or 2000. 500 cases made. • $40 • (11/30/96) • **92**

Tawny Antique Barossa Museum Release NV: Lightly sweet and elegant, not a huge, mouthfilling style but one that unfolds its walnut, nutmeg, cinnamon and coffee flavors on a lithe, silky sweet background. • $15/375ml • (02/28/98) • **92**

Tawny Port South Australia Clocktower NV • $10 • (05/15/96) BB • **89**

Viognier Barossa Reserve 1996: Has the forward spice and honeysuckle character of Viognier without the broad texture and power the grape usually produces. Nicely done. • $13 • (06/30/97) • **85**

Viognier Barossa Reserve 1995: Nicely crafted to show off the creamy melon and spice flavors. Ripe and round, without excessive weight to bog it down. 800 cases made. • $13 • (09/30/96) • **87**

YARRA RIDGE

Cabernet Sauvignon Yarra Valley 1996: On the lighter side for a Cabernet, with pretty raspberry and herbal flavors that linger gently on the lean finish. 2,000 cases made. • $12 • (05/15/98) • **85**

Cabernet Sauvignon Yarra Valley Reserve 1995: Tight and firm, with a layer of hard tannins over a nice core of currant and ripe blackberry. Needs until 2001 to see what will become of the tannins. • $NA • (03/31/98) • **86**

Key: SS—Spectator Selection. CS—Cellar Selection. BB—Best Buy. HR—Highly Recommended. $NA—Price not available. (BT)—Barrel tasting. (A)—Auction Price.
Dates in parentheses represent the issues in which the ratings were published.

Cabernet Sauvignon Victoria 1994: Rich and chewy, with a strong mint component to the supple plum and black cherry flavors, softening on the finish. Drink now. 10,000 cases made. • $11 • (01/31/97) • **83**

Chardonnay Yarra Valley 1995: Shows some nice green apple, toast and earth notes and strives for elegance, but the elements have not yet achieved harmony. May be best from 1999. 25,000 cases made. • $12 • (05/15/97) • **85**

Pinot Noir Yarra Valley 1997: Youthful and fragrant, with spicy berry flavors. Finishes a bit sharp, but it's promising. Try in 1999. 200 cases made. • $12 • (03/31/98) • **85**

Pinot Noir Victoria 1996: Lots of mint and earth nuances weave their way through the pretty berry flavors. Firm tannins keep it from being as charming as it could be. Try in 1999. 5,000 cases made. • $12 • (08/31/97) • **85**

Pinot Noir Victoria 1995: A light, supple red with modest Pinot Noir character, offering currant and toast notes that linger gently on the finish. Drink now. 8,500 cases made. • $12 • (05/15/97) • **85**

Pinot Noir Victoria 1993 • $12 • (06/30/95) • **74**

Sauvignon Blanc South Eastern Australia 1994 • $12 • (06/30/95) • **82**

Sauvignon Blanc Victoria 1996: Lively and zingy. Its bright passion fruit, citrus and apple flavors compete for attention, yet are harmonious. Try now. 10,000 cases made. • $11 • (01/31/97) • **88**

YARRA YERING

Dry Red No. 1 Yarra Valley 1994: Ripe, deep, and gamy around the edges, with a meaty feel to the solid black cherry, anise and smoke flavors. A distinguished wine with room to grow through 2005. 85 percent Cabernet Sauvignon. 75 cases made. • $40 • (08/31/97) • **89**

Dry Red No. 2 Yarra Valley 1994: Rich and leathery, with a core of ripe berry, plum and distinctly gamy flavors that stay round and generous on the finish, with a stroke of mint at the end. Has more of a Rhône-like feel than do most Aussie Shiraz. 95 percent Shiraz, 5 percent Viognier. 60 cases made. • $40 • (08/31/97) • **89**

Pinot Noir Yarra Valley 1994: Ripe and concentrated, showing lots of smoky blackberry, plum and pepper flavors, it's one of the more focused Australian Pinot Noirs. Best from 1999. 50 cases made. • $50 • (08/31/97) • **85**

Shiraz Yarra Valley Underhill 1994: Dark and chewy, a distinctive, raw mouthful of blackberry, licorice and vanilla flavors that smooth out a bit on the harmonious finish. Built for long-term cellaring, it should come together by 1999, and keep improving through 2005 and beyond. 200 cases made. • $40 • (08/31/97) • **92**

YARRAMAN

Cabernet-Shiraz Australia Wybong 1994: Ripe, rich and generous, layering its plum, berry, toast, vanilla and spice flavors on a smooth, velvety background. Has a minty accent that adds extra interest. Needs time to develop and expand. Best after 2000. 500 cases made. • $22 • (10/31/96) • **89**

Chardonnay Hunter Valley Barrington 1995: Woody aromas and flavors predominate in this serious-minded but dull wine. 1,500 cases made. • $22 • (10/15/96) • **80**

YARRAMAN ROAD

Cabernet-Shiraz South Eastern Australia 1995: Firm and chunky, offering a solid mouthful of anise-scented black cherry and berry flavors that linger on the softly chewy finish. Drinkable now. A blend of 60 percent Cabernet Sauvignon and 40 percent Shiraz. 5,000 cases made. • $20 • (10/15/97) • **87**

Chardonnay Hunter Valley Barrington 1995: Wonderful texture—smooth, soft, silky and spicy, and some pretty apple, earth and nutmeg flavors. Drink now. 1,500 cases made. • $22 • (01/31/97) • **87**

YERING STATION

Red Yarra Valley 1995: A solid red, nicely packed with berry, currant and plum flavors, this is a tight wine that promises richness by 2000 or so. Tannins are well-integrated and the cedary flavors add interest on the finish. A blend of 70 percent Cabernet Sauvignon, 15 percent Merlot and 15 percent Cabernet Franc. 600 cases made. • $14 • (10/31/97) • **86**

YERINGBERG

Yarra Valley Red 1995: A distinctive wine, with bright strawberry, currant and mint character that lingers enticingly on the finish, nicely packed with generous, supple flavor. Approachable now, best from 1999 or 2000. 56 cases made. • $40 • (09/30/97) • **90**

Yarra Valley White 1996: Spice, mineral and floral notes add a nice nuance to the apple and melon flavors in this solid, approachable white that's ready to drink. A blend of Marsanne and Roussanne. 28 cases made. • $30 • (10/31/97) • **84**

Austria

For most wine drinkers outside of Europe, Austrian wines remain an unknown quantity. They've been long overshadowed by wines from neighbor-to-the-northwest Germany, with which they share a number of features: a predominance of white grapes, a particular strength in sweet wines—and labels that the average American consumer finds impenetrable. In fact, because of Austria's more southerly location and more varied climate, its range of grapes and wines is notably wider than Germany's.

Austria's "national grape" and most widely planted variety is the versatile Grüner Veltliner, which can be made into light, dry (*Trocken*) table wines, or complex, ageable sweet wines. Some of the most exciting recent developments in Austrian whites, though, involve Riesling—a probable 19th-century immigrant from Germany—made in both dry and off-dry styles. Other Austrian whites include the unrelated native Welschriesling, Weissburgunder (Pinot Blanc), Grauburgunder (Pinot Gris), Scheurebe (a cross between Riesling and Sylvaner), and Bouvier, which was originally a table grape. The ubiquitous Chardonnay (also called Morillon here) has begun to appear as well, even—astonishingly—in the form of superb botrytized dessert wines.

Red grapes, while in the minority, are found in most of Austria's winegrowing regions. Varieties include the native Zweigelt or Blauer Zweigelt, now sometimes blended with Cabernet Sauvignon; Blaufränkisch, the same grape known in the American Northwest as Lemberger; and Spätburgunder (Pinot Noir) and its likely relative St.-Laurent.

1. Wachau
2. Kremstal
3. Kamptal
4. Neusiedlersee-Hügelland
5. Neusiedlersee

Most Austrian wine labels bear the same quality/ripeness designations as German wines, but to complicate matters a bit further, the region of Wachau (see below) uses its own equivalent system: Qualitätswein = Steinfeder (in Wachau), Kabinett = Federspiel, and Spätlese = Smaragd (a word referring to the emerald color of the tiny lizards that live in the vineyards!)

WINE REGIONS

The winegrowing areas of Austria lie entirely within the eastern third of the country. The northernmost, bordering on the Czech and Slovak Republics, is Niederösterreich, which includes the highly respected wine districts of Kamptal, Kremstal and Wachau; these are the source of many of the country's best dry Rieslings and Grüner Veltliners. The capital city of Vienna (Wien) is unique in being the center of its own small viticultural area, and there are even some vines within the city limits.

Neusiedlersee and Neusiedlersee-Hügelland occupy eastern Austria's central latitudes, bordering Hungary. Most of the extraordinary Beerenauslese and Trockenbeerenauslese dessert wines that have reached the market over the last few years originated here, as does Austria's most traditional sweet wine, Ausbruch Rust.

Further south lies Burgenland, heartland of Austria's red wine industry. The traditional varieties of Blaufränkisch and Blauer Zweigelt are grown in abundance here, but the region is also a hotbed of experimentation with western European "noble" grapes such as Cabernet Sauvignon. West of Burgenland is Steiermark, source of a wide variety of dry white wines.

ALZINGER

Riesling Auslese Wachau Dürnsteiner Hollerin 1995: Gorgeous Riesling. Racy. Very fine wine, with spicy lemon and lime, honey and cut apple aromas and flavors. Medium-bodied, medium sweet, with a long aftertaste. Lots going on in this glass. Drink now or hold. • $NA/375ml • (02/28/98) • **91**

Riesling Smaragd Wachau Loibner Steinertal 1995: Mature marzipan and petrol notes display the richness of the 1995 vintage. Vibrant, with lime and apple character and a rich texture. Best now through 2002. • $NA • (02/28/98) • **88**

ANGERHOF

Muscat Ottonel Trockenbeerenauslese Neusiedlersee 1995: Gorgeous sweety, with exotic yet classy character. Subtle aromas of honeycomb, tea and cedar with light tropical fruit and hints of vanilla. Full-bodied and very sweet, with wonderful intensity of flavors and crisp acidity. Long, long finish. Better after 1999. 125 cases made. • $NA/375ml • (02/28/98) • **94**

Sämling 88 Trockenbeerenauslese Neusiedlersee 1995: Subtle now, but explodes at the finish. Aromas of apricot are followed by plenty of citrus peel, grapefruit and honey flavors, and it's all lively and balanced between sweetness and acidity. Tangy finish. Drink from 2000 through 2005. 140 cases made. • $NA/375ml • (02/28/98) • **92**

Zweigelt Strohwein Neusiedlersee Vin de Paille Rosé 1995: Light colored and aromatic. Shows honey and raisin, with some spice accents. Rich and sweet, it's not unlike a white varietal but for the hint of tannin at the end. Drink now through 2002. • $NA/375ml • (02/28/98) • **87**

BERGER, E .& M.

Blauer Zweigelt Qualitätswein Trocken Kremstal Barrique 1994: Wild berry and spice are the predominant flavors, supported by enough tannin to deliver some astringency on the finish. 333 cases made. • $14 • (02/28/97) • **83**

Chardonnay Kabinett Kremstal Gedersdorfer Altmandl 1996: A *vin de terroir*. The flavors are more from the soil than the grapes, with mineral, earthy notes and a firm, stony texture. Not big in fruit but very expressive and concentrated, with a long, subtle finish. Drink now through 2002. 416 cases made. • $NA • (02/28/98) • **88**

Grüner Veltliner Kabinett Kremstal Gedersdorfer Lössterrassen 1996: Richness and decent intensity of herb, citrus and mineral flavors carry through on the finish. Drink now through 2002. 583 cases made. • $11 • (02/28/98) • **85**

Grüner Veltliner Kabinett Trocken Kremstal Lössterrassen 1995: Pretty spice and floral character on the nose but slightly dull on the palate. Medium-bodied, with a light, spicy finish. 833 cases made. • $12 • (12/15/96) • **84**

Grüner Veltliner Qualitätswein Trocken Kremstal 1995: Vibrant and spicy, this has an intensity of intriguing, floral-accented pear flavor that carries through the finish. 4,166 cases made. • $8/liter • (12/15/96) • **85**

Riesling Kabinett Kremstal Gedersdorf Steingraben + Lissen 1996: Dry, lean and spicy, revealing mineral, chamomile and hazelnut character in a forward, immediate style. Drink now, with light food. 250 cases made. • $14 • (02/28/98) • **87**

Riesling Qualitätswein Trocken Kremstal Gedersdorf Steingraben + Spiegel 1995: A deeply colored, mineral-accented Riesling exhibiting honey and apple flavors. It's lively but not that intense. 416 cases made. • $16 • (12/15/96) • **84**

BOCKFLIESS

Pinot Blanc Qualitätswein Weinviertel Riede Hochfeld 1996: If you like ginger-snap cookies, you'll love this wine. Racy and taut, with a distinct mineral character, though not typical of Pinot Blanc. Needs food. Drink now. • $15 • (02/28/98) • **84**

BRUNDLMAYER

Brut Kamptal 1993: A lively texture and rich fruit flavors accented by vanilla give this well-balanced bubbly depth and length. Drink now. 2,083 cases made. • $NA • (02/28/98) • **86**

Chardonnay Auslese Kamptal 1994: A medium-sweet Chardonnay, with ripe tropical fruit on nose and palate, good acidity and a sweet finish. A strange bird of a wine. • $36 • (02/28/97) • **83**

Grüner Veltliner Auslese Kamptal Loiser Berg 1995: A lovely sipping wine, with spice, honey and perfume aromas and flavors. Medium-bodied and moderately sweet, with a fresh, clean, though slightly one-dimensional, finish. 220 cases made. • $NA • (02/28/97) • **87**

Grüner Veltliner Auslese Kamptal Ried Loiser Berg 1995: Seems diluted, with only modest flavors of marzipan and herbs. Better than the first bottle. 290 cases made. • $29 • (02/28/98) • **78**

Grüner Veltliner Beerenauslese Kamptal Ried Loiser Berg 1995: Gorgeous dessert wine. Aromas of botrytis, spice, honey and minerals are followed by an intense apricot, orange-peel component on the palate. Thick and concentrated, with beautiful acidity for balance and great length. Delicious now, even better after 2000. • $NA • (02/28/98) • **93**

Grüner Veltliner Qualitätswein Kamptal Alte Reben 1996: An impressive Grüner. Quite ripe, with vanilla and apricot flavors. Rich texture. Plenty of acidity for backbone suggests this wine may need until 2000 to integrate. 292 cases made. • $20 • (02/28/98) • **87**

Grüner Veltliner Qualitätswein Kamptal Ried Lamm 1996: Loads of vanilla and a smoky note. Rich, showing good depth of flavor as well as balance and structure, it's one of the successes of the vintage. Drink from 1999 through 2003. 250 cases made. • $20 • (02/28/98) • **88**

Grüner Veltliner Qualitätswein Trocken Kamptal Alte Reben 1995: Intense, with peach, citrus and white pepper flavors that are buoyed along by lively acidity, then climax in a complex and lingering finish. A wine with amplitude, matched by precision balance. 220 cases made. • $21 • (12/15/96) • **90**

Grüner Veltliner Qualitätswein Trocken Kamptal Langenloiser Berg Vogelsang 1995: Silky and caressing on the palate, this wine serves up ample aromas and flavors of pear and spice, with crisp acidity. 2,000 cases made. • $16 • (12/15/96) • **84**

Pinot Noir Qualitätswein Kamptal Cécile 1994: Smooth texture, but the cherry notes are one-dimensional. The finish is somewhat astringent. • $NA • (02/28/98) • **79**

Riesling Auslese Kamptal Ried Zöbinger Heiligenstein 1995: Intense and powerful, bursting with floral, apple and lime character accented by almond. All the elements are well integrated, with lively acidity on an elegant framework. Drink now through 2002. 250 cases made. • $36 • (02/28/98) • **90**

Riesling Auslese Kamptal Zöbinger Heiligenstein 1995: Oozing honey and freshly cut fruit, especially melon, flavors. Medium-bodied, with fine acidity and a sweet fruit and spice finish. A lovely apéritif. Drink now. 220 cases made. • $37 • (12/15/96) • **88**

Riesling Beerenauslese Kamptal Zöbinger Heiligenstein 1995: Tropical scents of pineapple, banana and orange-peel combine with honey and tropical fruit flavors, all kept fresh and vivid by acidity. Moderately sweet and delicate, this is delicious. Drink now through 2002. • $NA • (02/28/98) • **90**

Riesling Kabinett Trocken Kamptal 1995: This is firm, dry and floral, with plenty of up-front apple character, but it drops off quickly. 2,000 cases made. • $17 • (12/15/96) • **84**

Riesling Kabinett Trocken Kamptal Zöbinger Heiligenstein 1995: Lovely, rich pear and peach flavors dominate this round, vibrant white. Has a soft, almost lush texture and a dry, refreshing finish. 1,800 cases made. • $22 • (12/15/96) • **88**

Riesling Qualitätswein Kamptal Zöbinger Heiligenstein Alte Reben 1996: Ripe and developed for a 1996, showing passion fruit and marzipan as well as lime and mineral elements, this has richness and acidity. Drink now through 2002. 375 cases made. • $32 • (02/28/98) • **89**

Riesling Qualitätswein Kamptal Zöbinger Heiligenstein Alte Reben 1995: A fruity and soft-textured Riesling that's verging on off-dry. Medium-bodied, with licorice and honey flavors and a long, succulent finish. 220 cases made. • $31 • (12/15/96) • **85**

St. Laurent Kamptal Ried Ladner 1993: A medium-bodied, serviceable red showing plum and herbal flavors. Drinkable now. • $NA • (02/28/97) • **80**

CHORHERREN KLOSTERNEUBERG

Chardonnay Auslese Wien Ried Altweingarten 1996: Ripe and full-bodied, its apricot and smoke flavors are backed by lots of acidity. Very good for the vintage. Drink now through 2000. 383 cases made. • $22 • (02/28/98) • **85**

Gewürztraminer Auslese Wien Ried Gebhardin 1996: Fairly dry, full of racy acidity and just a hint of honey adding an extra dimension to the apple and spice flavors. Full-bodied, powerful, this would be great with a cheese course. Drink now through 2005. 750 cases made. • $23/500ml • (02/28/98) • **90**

Pinot Blanc Auslese Wien Ried Kuchelviertel 1995: Distinctly smoky, there's also ripe peach and mineral notes, all on a firm backbone. Delicious. Drink now. 333 cases made. • $18 • (02/28/98) • **84**

AUSTRIA

FEILER-ARTINGER

Ruster Ausbruch Neusiedlersee-Hügelland 1995: Lovely aromas of honey, vanilla and apricot waft from the glass. Thick and sweet, showing appealing notes of orange and apricot with some botrytis accents, balancing acidity and a moderate finish. Drink now through 2003. 700 cases made. • $NA/375ml • (02/28/98) • **90**

Ruster Ausbruch Neusiedlersee-Hügelland Essenz 1995: Supersweet and thick with apricot and spice flavors that fan out and intensify, culminating in a long finish. No shortage of acidity here, which keeps everything lively. Not currently available in the U.S. Drink now through 2005. 500 cases made. • $NA/375ml • (02/28/98) • **92**

Ruster Ausbruch Neusiedlersee-Hügelland Pinot Cuvée 1995: Very pungent, with a watercress pepperiness in the aromas. On the palate, the flavors are all honey and peaches. Viscous texture. Sweet and just a touch cloying on the finish. Drink now through 2002. 530 cases made. • $NA/375ml • (02/28/98) • **88**

FREIE WEINGARTNER WACHAU

Grüner Veltliner Federspiel Trocken Wachau Weissenkirchner Vorderseiber 1995: Shows some decent fruit flavors, but it's rather light and watery on the finish. Not much to it, really. • $11 • (12/15/96) • **78**

Grüner Veltliner Qualitätswein Trocken Wachau Pfarre Weissenkirchen Wachauer Pfarr-Veltliner 1995: Aromas of pear, hay and a hint of almond are followed by a refreshing, rich mouthful of wine. A good value that's ready now. • $10/1 liter.(12/15/96) • **84**

Grüner Veltliner Smaragd Wachau Weissenkirchner Achleiten 1996: Pear and grass flavors are the hallmarks of this dry, austere white. Well balanced and concentrated, it needs time to integrate. Drink from 1999 through 2002. 1,050 cases made. • $20 • (02/28/98) • **86**

Grüner Veltliner Smaragd Wachau Weissenkirchner Achleiten 1995: Shows a distinctive earthiness alongside almond and herbal components. Medium-bodied, with moderate intensity and length. Earthy finish. 600 cases made. • $20 • (02/28/98) • **85**

Riesling Federspiel Trocken Wachau Terrassen Thal 1995: A wine with loads of grapefruit aromas and flavors, and a good pinch of spice as well. Medium-bodied, dry and spicy on the finish. • $16 • (12/15/96) • **87**

Riesling Smaragd Trocken Wachau Dürnsteiner Kellerberg 1995: Shows an abundance of grapefruit and spice aromas and flavors wrapped up in a medium-bodied package with fine acidity and a crisp finish. • $25 • (12/15/96) • **87**

Riesling Smaragd Trocken Wachau Spitzer Singerriedel 1995: Not as intense as some in this category, but there's plenty of rose petal, honey and almond aromas and flavors. Medium body, medium acidity and a light finish. • $25 • (12/15/96) • **86**

Riesling Smaragd Trocken Wachau Weissenkirchner Achleiten 1995: Extremely ripe and intense, offering loads of piecrust, pineapple and tropical fruit flavors and aromas. Full-bodied, yet it's lively and refined. Long, fruity finish. Drink now. • $25 • (12/15/96) • **90**

Riesling Smaragd Wachau Weissenkirchner Achleiten 1996: Offers apple and lemon notes, with a hint of mineral, in a light-bodied style. Lean structure and a moderate finish. 500 cases made. • $28 • (02/28/98) • **85**

FRITSCH, WEINBERGHOF

Blauer Burgunder Qualitätswein Donauland Ried Kreuzberg-Ruppersthal 1995: Smells and tastes like cherry candy. 125 cases made. • $NA • (02/28/98) • **74**

Blauer Spätburgunder Qualitätswein Trocken Donauland Perfektion Ried Kreuzberg-Ruppersthal 1994: The rich, velvety texture complements the aromas and flavors of black fruits and smoky oak. Well made and intriguing. • $NA • (02/28/97) • **85**

Foggathal Donauland Red 1995: Has some vanilla and wood character combined with a medium structure but not much fruit. 250 cases made. • $22 • (02/28/98) • **78**

Foggathal Qualitätswein Trocken Donauland 1994: A serious attempt at winemaking, but it's not quite there yet. Light and fresh, with pretty berry, Port-like flavors and a hint of new wood. Drink now. 166 cases made. • $24 • (02/28/97) • **84**

Key: SS—Spectator Selection CS—Cellar Selection HR—Highly Recommended BB—Best Buy $NA—Price not available Ⓐ—Auction Price (BT)—Barrel Tasting

Dates in parentheses indicate the issues in which the ratings were published.

Grüner Veltliner Kabinett Donauland Ried Zeiselgraben-Mitterstockstall 1996: Lovely almond, pear and floral aromas, but the flavors don't hold up. Soft, slightly flat. • $NA • (02/28/98) • **80**

Grüner Veltliner Qualitätswein Trocken Donauland Windspiel 1995: Crisp and zingy, with attractive floral and pear aromas and flavors and a clean finish. Light- to medium-bodied. 1,000 cases made. • $12 • (12/15/96) • **83**

Grüner Veltliner Spätlese Donauland 1996: Ripe and rich, full of honey, apple and herb flavors. Falls a bit short. Balanced on the soft side for early consumption. Drink now through 2000. 250 cases made. • $19 • (02/28/98) • **84**

Grüner Veltliner Spätlese Trocken Donauland Ried: Schlossberg Oberstockstall Wagramer Selektion 1995: Wonderfully ripe, with grapefruit and apricot aromas and flavors. Full-bodied and dry, with a lovely, fruity finish. Delicious. 291 cases made. • $18 • (12/15/96) • **88**

Merlot Qualitätswein Trocken Donauland Kreuzberg-Ruppersthal 1994: Good, in a lighter style. Offers berry, vanilla and raspberry character, light tannins and a light, fruity finish. 83 cases made. • $24 • (02/28/97) • **84**

Riesling Kabinett Trocken Donauland Ried Zeiselgraben Mitterstockstall 1995: Slighty heavier style of Riesling with a flinty, earthy character on the nose and palate. Medium-bodied, with medium acidity and a light finish. 250 cases made. • $15 • (12/15/96) • **85**

Riesling Qualitätswein Donauland 1996: Plenty of weight and density, with flavors of peach and almond, and an intriguing tropical note. Moderately high acidity keeps it lively, but the finish lacks length. 416 cases made. • $15 • (02/28/98) • **87**

Riesling Qualitätswein Trocken Donauland Perfektion Ried: Mordthal Ruppertsthal 1995: Subtle and elegant, its delicate peach and lime flavors accented by a lingering, minerally finish. Ready to drink. 166 cases made. • $18 • (12/15/96) • **86**

Weissburgunder-Chardonnay Donauland Schlossberg-Oberstockstall 1996: Tropical fruit and floral notes mark this round, exotic white, then the acidity and smoky flavors take over, leaving a refreshing, tangy aftertaste. Drink now. 250 cases made. • $NA • (02/28/98) • **85**

Zweigelt Qualitätswein Trocken Donauland 1994: Good, light red, with berry, spice aromas and flavors, and a hint of vanilla. Medium body, with medium tannins and a light finish. Slightly one-dimensional. Drink now. 416 cases made. • $13 • (02/28/97) • **85**

GEYMULLER, DOMAINE BARON

Riesling Qualitätswein Trocken Kremstal Hollenburger Goldberg 1995: There's a bounty of ripe fruit, honey and hazelnut character to this wine—especially on the nose. Medium-bodied, with moderate acidity and a round, caressing texture. • $NA • (02/28/97) • **88**

GLATZER, W.

Blauer Zweigelt Qualitätswein Carnuntum Dornen Vogel 1996: Delicious, packed with blackberry character, rich texture and firm structure. Concentrated, with a good finish. Best now through 2002. 333 cases made. • $16 • (02/28/98) • **86**

Blauer Zweigelt Qualitätswein Carnuntum Rieden Cuvée 1996: Solid, with plenty of grapey, fresh fruit flavors bolstered by moderate tannins and vibrant acidity. 1,667 cases made. • $10 • (02/28/98) • **82**

Blaufränkisch Qualitätswein Carnuntum Reserve 1995: Gorgeous character of smoky blackberry and vanilla is married to a medium-bodied, lean frame sporting good acidity. Well balanced, with moderate tannins. Best now through 2000. 333 cases made. • $14 • (02/28/98) • **87**

Blaufränkisch Qualitätswein Trocken Carnuntum 1995: Rich, Port-like aromas, followed by a fruity palate that turns lean and astringent. Perhaps food would soften it. 583 cases made. • $11 • (02/28/97) • **82**

Grüner Veltliner Kabinett Trocken Carnuntum Dornenvogel 1995: Good intensity of spicy, white pepper character, with fresh fruit flavors and crisp acidity. Slightly short finish. 500 cases made. • $12 • (12/15/96) • **85**

Grüner Veltliner Qualitätswein Carnuntum 1996: A good, solid Grüner displaying a vanilla aroma and the characteristic lentil flavor, this will stand up to food. Drink now through 2002. 250 cases made. • $8 • (02/28/98) • **84**

Weissburgunder Kabinett Carnuntum 1996: Broad-shouldered for Pinot Blanc, with appley, floral and nutty flavors, firm acidity and a long finish. Try with seafood or chicken. Drink now. 583 cases made. • $10 • (02/28/98) • **85**

Weissburgunder Kabinett Trocken Carnuntum 1995: Not very Sauvignon-like in character, but it's fresh and vibrant, with lemon and mineral flavors. 500 cases made. • $12 • (02/28/97) • **82**

Zweigelt Qualitätswein Trocken Carnuntum Dornenvogl 1995: Bright cherry flavors are interwoven with accents of vanilla and spice. Medium-bodied, with good concentration and a lively finish. 416 cases made. • $16 • (02/28/97) • **85**

Zweigelt Qualitätswein Trocken Carnuntum Riedencuvée 1995: Plum and spice notes introduce this crisp, light-bodied red. It's immediate and refreshing in its appeal. 1,666 cases made. • $11 • (02/28/97) • **83**

GOBELSBURG, SCHLOSS

Grüner Veltliner Kabinett Trocken Kamptal Allerheiligenstiftung 1995: Lovely aromas of roses and pears waft from this elegant, distinctive wine. Very dry, with a subtle, lingering finish. 833 cases made. • $15 • (12/15/96) • **86**

Grüner Veltliner Qualitätswein Kamptal Ried Lamm 1996: Nectarine and grapefruit flavors indicate ripeness, and the rich texture delivers those flavors through the long finish. Balanced and appealing. Drink now through 2000. 167 cases made. • $21 • (02/28/98) • **85**

Grüner Veltliner Trocken Kamptal Messwein 1995: Fresh and inviting, with a subtle interplay of green apple, almond and grasslike flavors. The finish is firm and lingering. 4,166 cases made. • $12 • (12/15/96) • **85**

Grüner Veltliner Trocken Kamptal Niederösterreichischer Landwein 1995: Pretty, perfumed spice and almond aromas, but it's slightly dull on the palate with plenty of green apple-skin character. 5,000 cases made. • $8/liter • (12/15/96) • **82**

Riesling Qualitätswein Trocken Kamptal Ried Gaisberg-Kammern 1995: A pretty, steely wine with lovely mineral and spice aromas and flavors and a racy, refreshing finish. 416 cases made. • $21 • (12/15/96) • **86**

GRAF HARDEGG

Riesling Eiswein Weinviertel Steinbügel-Seefeld 1996: Intense. Smells and tastes of peanuts and caramel. Quite thick, yet shows searing acidity and a smoky finish. Drink from 2000 to 2007. 167 cases made. • $29/375ml • (02/28/98) • **89**

Riesling Eiswein Weinviertel Steinbügel-Seefeld 1995: Terrific. Haunting aromas of Poire William and honey are followed by apple and apricot notes that take on a smoky quality on the finish. The viscous texture is smartly balanced by racy acidity. Hard to keep your hands off it now. Drink from 1999 through 2005. 167 cases made. • $25/375ml • (02/28/98) • **92**

GSELLMANN & GSELLMANN

Red Qualitätswein Neusiedlersee Alte Lagen 1995: Vivid and plush, with plum and vanilla character. Pleasant texture and flavors, if not particularly complex. Ready to drink. 500 cases made. • $16 • (02/28/98) • **85**

HEINRICH

Blauer Zweigelt Qualitätswein Neusiedlersee 1996: Deeply colored, with aromas of smoky black fruits and just a hint of gaminess. Rich and smooth, full of blackberry flavors, balanced and moderately concentrated, though not that complex. Drink now through 2001. 2,000 cases made. • $15 • (02/28/98) • **86**

Blauer Zweigelt Qualitätswein Trocken Neusiedlersee 1994: Pleasant quaffing red with spicy berry and raspberry character. Medium-bodied, with light tannins and a fresh finish. • $16 • (02/28/97) • **84**

Blaufränkisch Qualitätswein Trocken Neusiedlersee 1994: Tastes like a good-quality, standard Beaujolais, with berry and cherry aromas and flavors. Medium-bodied, with soft tannins and a fresh, fruity finish. Drink now. • $16 • (02/28/97) • **84**

Weissburgunder Qualitätswein Neusiedlersee 1996: Apples and peaches are the dominant themes. Vibrant and light-bodied, the flavors continue through a moderate finish. Drink now. 800 cases made. • $14 • (02/28/98) • **82**

Weissburgunder Qualitätswein Trocken Neusiedlersee 1995: The aromas and flavors are minerally and herbal in this dry, medium-bodied wine. Finish is a little austere. • $14 • (02/28/97) • **82**

HIEDLER

Chardonnay Qualitätswein Kamptal Langenloiser Kittmannsberg 1996: Crisp, minerally and appley, with good concentration and a very lively acidic structure, this Chardonnay would be an excellent partner for lighter dishes like salmon or chicken. Best now through 2002. • $22 • (02/28/98) • **85**

Grüner Veltliner Auslese Halbtrocken Kamptal Langenloiser Thal 1994: There's a wax, apple and mineral quality to this white, with a light structure, a touch of vanilla on the finish. Still, it's diluted. • $20 • (02/28/98) • **84**

Grüner Veltliner Qualitätswein Kamptal Langenloiser Thal 1996: Straightforward flavors of thyme and lemon, followed by mineral notes on the finish. Lacks the concentration and depth to really stand out. • $17 • (02/28/98) • **84**

Grüner Veltliner Qualitätswein Kamptal Vier Weinberge 1996: A zippy Grüner that starts off with mineral and stone character, and finishes on a lemon note. • $14 • (02/28/98) • **84**

Grüner Veltliner Qualitätswein Trocken Kamptal Langenloiser Thal 1995: Racy, showing steely, flinty and floral aromas and flavors, off-dry, with good spice notes. Fresh finish. 300 cases made. • $15 • (12/15/96) • **84**

Grüner Veltliner Qualitätswein Trocken Kamptal Langloiser Weingärtencuvée 1995: An extremely ripe style, featuring peach, mineral and bitter almond flavors, with a firm structure that supports the palate nicely. Good length. 308 cases made. • $13 • (12/15/96) • **86**

Riesling Qualitätswein Trocken Kamptal Zöbinger Heiligenstein 1995: Very aromatic, dominated by floral and citrus notes with a touch of petrol. The palate is crisp, vibrant and delivers moderate flavors of apple and peach that linger on the finish. 183 cases made. • $20 • (01/31/97) • **85**

Weissburgunder Beerenauslese Kamptal Langenloiser Spiegel Süss 1994: This is a crowd-pleaser. Rich and weighty, exhibiting nuances of coconut flavor from some new-oak treatment and plenty of acidity to keep the flavors and texture in balance. 66 cases made. • $33/500 ml • (12/15/96) • **90**

Weissburgunder Qualitätswein Halbtrocken Kamptal Langenloiser Schenkenbichl 1996: Focused and direct citrus and nut character. Vibrant, compact and short. Ready to drink. • $20 • (02/28/98) • **82**

Weissburgunder Qualitätswein Trocken Kamptal Langenloiser Schenkenbichl 1995: Shows some good, ripe fruit flavors and acidity, with a medium body, but it's slightly dull and volatile on the finish. 208 cases made. • $16 • (02/28/97) • **80**

Weissburgunder Qualitätswein Trocken Kamptal Langenloiser Schenkenbichl 1994: Steely and closed up—not giving much fruit on the palate, but the texture is vibrant and the acidity fresh. Try now. 325 cases made. • $16 • (02/28/97) • **84**

HIRTZBERGER, FRANZ

Grauburgunder Smaragd Trocken Wachau Pluris 1995: A smoky, nutty, minerally character is allied to power and restraint in this intense Pinot Gris. It seems to be holding back, and shows promise of more in the future. Try now. • $31 • (12/15/96) • **87**

Grüner Veltliner Federspiel Trocken Wachau Rotes Tor 1995: A beauty, from its aromas and flavors of ripe apricot and flowers to its long finish, reminiscent of grilled almonds and grapefruit. Complex, balanced and harmonious. • $15 • (12/15/96) • **86**

Grüner Veltliner Smaragd Trocken Wachau Honivogl 1995: Oily and rich, verging on being fat. A full-bodied wine, with very ripe apricot and pineapple flavors, moderate acidity and a short finish. • $35 • (12/15/96) • **85**

Grüner Veltliner Smaragd Trocken Wachau Rotes Tor 1995: Big and fruity, with impressive aromas and flavors of spices, flowers and almonds, good acidity and a fruity, slightly sweet finish. • $26 • (12/15/96) • **87**

Grüner Veltliner Smaragd Wachau Honivogl 1996: Ripe aromas of honey and vanilla custard lead into peach and chamomile notes, all in a medium-bodied and harmonious package that tails off a little on the finish. 404 cases made. • $35 • (02/28/98) • **87**

Grüner Veltliner Smaragd Wachau Rotes Tor 1996: Austere and spicy, there's a density and texture to the apple flavors, and all the elements hang together nicely. Loads of mineral, especially on the finish. Needs food. 212 cases made. • $26 • (02/28/98) • **86**

Riesling Federspiel Trocken Wachau Steinterrassen 1995: A medium-bodied wine of good intensity, showing applelike character and a lean stoniness that carries into the long finish. • $26 • (12/15/96) • **86**

Riesling Smaragd Trocken Wachau Hochrain 1995: Very ripe, with loads of tropical fruit character on the nose. Full-bodied, with medium acidity. Drink now. • $41 • (12/15/96) • **88**

Riesling Smaragd Trocken Wachau Singerriedel 1995: Inviting, this features lime, apple and passion-fruit flavors with medium body and intensity. The finish is bracing, and suggests pairing with food. • $50 • (12/15/96) • **89**

Riesling Smaragd Wachau Singerriedel 1996: So minerally, it's like drinking the soil, yet complex notes of talc, peach, apple and spice make it intriguing. Very structured, concentrated and lean, with an intensity that cannot be denied. Best beyond 2000. • $50 • (02/28/98) • **91**

HOPLER

Grüner Veltliner Qualitätswein Burgenland 1996: Shows some fine stony elements, along with white pepper and lemon accents. Lean and racy, with a bit of alcohol on the finish. 3,000 cases made. • $9 • (02/28/98) • **85**

Grüner Veltliner Qualitätswein Trocken Neusiedlersee 1995: A different style of Grüner, from the deep color and tropical accents to the lush, rich passion fruit and melon flavors. Pleasant, but lacks zip. 20,000 cases made. • $9 • (01/31/97) • **82**

Pinot Blanc Kabinett Neusiedlersee 1995: Shows the quality of the '95 harvest. Pungent aromas of tropical fruit and marzipan. Thickly textured and concentrated, with a firm backbone. Long finish. Drink now. 2,500 cases made. • $10 • (02/28/98) • **87**

Pinot Blanc Qualitätswein Trocken Neusiedlersee 1994: Rich flavors of apple and vanilla underscored by a refreshing lemon note, finishing crisply. Ready to drink. 5,000 cases made. • $10 • (01/31/97) • **83**

Pinot Blanc Spätlese Neusiedlersee 1995: Rich apricot notes and tropical nuances reflect the ripeness of the 1995 vintage. Very concentrated yet with high acidity. Delicious. Drink now through 2000. 1,000 cases made. • $13 • (02/28/98) • **86**

Pinot Blanc Trockenbeerenauslese Neusiedlersee 1995: A subtle yet complex dessert wine, this TBA builds on the palate with nutmeg, clove, honey, apricot and citrus accents that gracefully blossom. It's gentle and deftly balanced, with a long aftertaste. 2,000 cases made. • $25/375ml • (02/28/98) HR • **93**

Pinot Gris Qualitätswein Burgenland 1996: Good Pinot Gris character. Smells like violets and tastes like apricots, with a rich texture, balanced on the soft side. Drink now. 1,000 cases made. • $11 • (02/28/98) • **84**

Pinot Noir Qualitätswein Burgenland 1995: Lively acidity and a vanilla and currant edge keep pulsing until the finish, where it falls a bit short. Ready to drink. 3,500 cases made. • $13 • (02/28/98) • **83**

Pinot Noir Qualitätswein Trocken Neusiedlersee 1994: Dull and muddled, with jammy fruit flavors and a tobacco note. Not very exciting. 4,000 cases made. • $10 • (01/31/97) • **73**

Zweigelt Qualitätswein Trocken Neusiedlersee Alesio 1994: Soft berry flavors of moderate concentration give this wine a pleasant, straightforward appeal. Ready to drink. 1,000 cases made. • $11 • (01/31/97) • **82**

JAMEK, JOSEF

Grüner Veltliner Auslese Wachau Ried Achleiten 1994: An auslese with a hint of sweetness to match its ripe pear, tobacco and spice character. Concludes with a touch of bitterness on the dry finish. Ready to drink. 183 cases made. • $35 • (12/15/96) • **87**

Grüner Veltliner Federspiel Trocken Wachau Ried Achleiten 1995: Deep greenish-gold in color, and yields smoky, tropical fruit aromas. There's weight and concentration, but it comes off a bit heavy. 1,333 cases made. • $18 • (12/15/96) • **83**

Grüner Veltliner Federspiel Trocken Wachau Stein Am Rain 1994: A lively white, exhibiting flavors of pear, tobacco and a hint of pine. Refreshing and balanced, finishing short. • $14 • (01/31/97) • **83**

Riesling Federspiel Trocken Wachau Jochinger Pichl 1995: Subtle, with white peach and light spice aromas and flavors. Medium-bodied, with fine acidity and a fresh and light finish. 600 cases made. • $20 • (12/15/96) • **88**

Riesling Federspiel Trocken Wachau Jochinger Pichl 1994: A rich, full style for Riesling. Dry, with a mineral, apple and peach character allied to a firm structure. A plentiful mouthful with a long finish. Ready now. • $20 • (02/28/97) • **89**

Riesling Federspiel Trocken Wachau Ried Klaus 1995: A lot of ripeness, with citrus and almond aromas and flavors, and enough acidity to keep it all harmonious on the finish. 1,041 cases made. • $25 • (12/15/96) • **89**

Riesling Smaragd Trocken Wachau Zwerithaler 1995: Terrific. Sporting loads of tropical fruit flavors, especially tangerine, as well as bracing acidity for balance and a mineral nuance. Beautiful length. Approachable now, but should develop through 2001. 250 cases made. • $NA • (02/28/97) • **90**

Riesling Smaragd Trocken Wachau Zwerithaler 1994: A leaner, racier version, with lime and mineral flavors that unfold gracefully. Tangy and concentrated, it could use a bit more time to develop fully, though it's drinkable now. Would go well with food. • $33 • (02/28/97) • **91**

JURIS

Pinot Noir Qualitätswein Neusiedlersee 1995: Pretty, with red berry, cherry and hints of spice. Silky on the palate. Everything is in the right proportion. Good length. Drink now through 2000. • $21 • (02/28/98) • **85**

Key: SS—Spectator Selection CS—Cellar Selection HR—Highly Recommended BB—Best Buy $NA—Price not available Ⓐ—Auction Price (BT)—Barrel Tasting
Dates in parentheses indicate the issues in which the ratings were published.

St. Georg Red Qualitätswein Neusiedlersee 1995: New oak character accents the cherry notes. Light-bodied, balanced and supple. Drink now through 2000. • $18 • (02/28/98) • **84**

Saint Laurent Qualitätswein Neusiedlersee 1995: There's a whiff of smoke and blackberries in this modern-styled red of moderate concentration, integrated with acidity and light tannins. Best now through 2000. • $21 • (02/28/98) • **85**

KNOLL

Grüner Veltliner Auslese Wachau Loibner 1995: An amazing wine for food. Intense aromas of honey and white pepper, with a hint of spices. Full-bodied and off-dry, with wonderfully wild and spicy flavors. Long, long finish. 250 cases made. • $NA/500ml • (02/28/98) • **92**

Grüner Veltliner Federspiel Trocken Wachau Kreutles 1994: Very exotic. Lime, passion fruit and floral flavors are underscored by tobacco notes. Dry, but turns short on the finish. • $18 • (12/15/96) • **84**

Grüner Veltliner Smaragd Trocken Wachau Ried Loibenberg 1995: This is floral in character, and intense, with plenty of ripe apricot and spice flavors that turn dry and minerally. Long and enticing finish. Try with food. • $28 • (12/15/96) • **89**

Grüner Veltliner Smaragd Trocken Wachau Ried Loibenberg 1994: More like a kabinett due to its elegant weight and style, this is medium-bodied, with a clean, spicy floral character and a crisp, lively finish. • $27 • (12/15/96) • **86**

Grüner Veltliner Smaragd Wachau Ried Loibenberg 1996: Rich and textured, dry and spicy, it has weight and density of flavor. Tobacco and herb notes are broad and long, but finish short. Drink from 1999 through 2003. 333 cases made. • $28 • (02/28/98) • **87**

Riesling Beerenauslese Wachau Ried Pfaffenberg Steiner Süss 1995: Fabulous aromas of apricots, minerals and flowers are followed by peach and honey flavors, all wrapped in an elegant, lively package. Light and airy, with a lingering finish. Enjoy now. • $38/500 ml • (12/15/96) • **90**

Riesling Smaragd Trocken Wachau Ried Loibenberg 1994: Obviously ripe, but this delivers more on the nose than on the palate. Medium-bodied, with spicy flavors. Clean finish. • $34 • (12/15/96) • **87**

Riesling Smaragd Trocken Wachau Ried Schütt Dürnsteiner 1995: A combination of lime, peach and herb notes give complexity to this vibrant, exciting wine. A touch of botrytis adds interest, and the finish is long. • $65 • (12/15/96) • **88**

Riesling Smaragd Wachau Ried Schütt Dürnsteiner 1996: Elegant, displaying lime, apple and almond notes, all in a harmonious and rich package. The lime and mineral character reverberates on the finish. Best from 1999 through 2002. 450 cases made. • $56 • (02/28/98) • **89**

KRACHER

Auslese Neusiedlersee 1994: A medium-sweet wine full of apricot and honey flavors that are enticing at first, then turn dry and fall short. • $30 • (02/28/97) • **83**

Beerenauslese Neusiedlersee Nouvelle Vague 1993: Tasting this is like biting into a piece of pecan pie. Full-bodied and very sweet with wild coconut and honey flavors. Long, long finish. A unique wine. • $75/375ml • (12/15/96) • **92**

Beerenauslese Neusiedlersee Weinlaubenhof Grande Cuvée 1995: A fruit bomb. Packed with apricot, honey and orange-zest flavors that deliver immediate gratification, then turn subtle yet lingering. Very elegant, despite the rich texture. • $90/375ml • (02/28/98) • **91**

Beerenauslese Neusiedlersee Weinlaubenhof Grande Cuvée 1994: There's an abundance of dried fruit and honey flavors in this full-bodied wine. It's very sweet, with an oily texture and a long, sweet-and-spicy finish. • $53/375ml • (12/15/96) • **87**

Beerenauslese Neusiedlersee Weinlaubenhof Grande Cuvée 1991: Quite sweet and thick, with intense, burnt almond, toffee and syrup aromas and flavors. Only needing a bit more acidity to score outstanding. • $53/375ml • (02/28/97) • **89**

Beerenauslese Neusiedlersee 1995: A concentrated yet well-balanced wine. Honey and vanilla aromas, with a touch of honeydew, apple and apricot. Medium- to full-bodied, with spicy flavors and a long, sweet, oily texture. Crème brûlée in a glass. Drink now or hold. • $NA/375ml • (02/28/98) • **90**

Chardonnay Nouvelle Vague Neusiedlersee 1994: We've never tasted a Chardonnay like this. It's thick as honey and just as sweet, with exotic tropical fruit, spice and burnt almond aromas and flavors and a long, sweet finish. An amazing sticky. • $75/375ml • (12/15/96) • **93**

Chardonnay Trockenbeerenauslese Neusiedlersee Nouvelle Vague No. 13 1995: A white chocolate dream. Incredibly concentrated and viscous, lively and complex at the same time. The white chocolate is augmented by lemon peel, vanilla custard and apricot flavors that pulse through the finish. Try in 2000. • $100/375ml • (02/28/98) • **98**

Chardonnay-Welschriesling Trockenbeerenauslese Neusiedlersee Nouvelle Vague No. 7 1995: This dessert white from Austria is very aromatic, sporting floral elements alongside passion fruit and butterscotch flavors, especially on the finish. A beam of acidity running throughout makes it sing. Drink now through 2005. • $90/375ml • (02/28/98) HR • **97**

Muscat Ottonel Trockenbeerenauslese Neusiedlersee Zwischen den Seen No. 5 1995: Delicate in style, with rose petal, citrus and raisin flavors, this dessert wine glides across the palate gracefully, where the bright acidity delivers the honey and raisin on the lingering finish. Beautifully crafted. • $90/375ml • (02/28/98) • **93**

Muscat Ottonel Trockenbeerenauslese Neusiedlersee Zwischen den Seen No. 11 1995: Incredibly dense and rich, displaying nutmeg, citrus peel and apricot essence, all the while maintaining a lovely sense of harmony. Not searingly high acidity but enough to keep the finish clean and lively, with a white-chocolate aftertaste. • $95/375ml • (02/28/98) • **93**

Qualitätswein Neusiedlersee Days of Wine and Roses 1994: Very aromatic, sporting exotic floral and almond notes, then turning dry and astringent, as if it can't decide what it wants to be. • $15 • (02/28/97) • **81**

Scheurebe Beerenauslese Neusiedlersee 1994: Slightly dumb in style, but offers lots of superripe, raisinlike aromas and flavors. It's full-bodied, very sweet and has an oily texture. • $23/375ml • (12/15/96) • **84**

Scheurebe Beerenauslese Neusiedlersee Zwischen den Seen 1994: A leafy note runs through this dessert wine, adding complexity to the honey and peach flavors. Great intensity and concentration, with a flourish on the finish. • $43/375ml • (12/15/96) • **90**

Scheurebe Beerenauslese Neusiedlersee Zwischen den Seen 1993: Terrific interplay of sweetness and acidity gives this wine harmony and finesse. Apricot and butterscotch flavors are the headliners. • $53/375ml • (12/15/96) • **89**

Scheurebe Beerenauslese Neusiedlersee Zwischen den Seen 1991: An herbal note adds complexity to the honey and nectarine flavors, all supported by whopping acidity. It's fresh, bracing and delicious. • $43/375ml • (12/15/96) • **90**

Scheurebe Trockenbeerenauslese Neusiedlersee Zwischen den Seen No. 3 1995: Floral and peach aromas are accented by spicy botrytis notes in this racy TBA. Everything is in the right proportion, from the honey and lime flavors to the medium weight and texture, and it finishes long and complex. Drinkable now, better in 2000. • $72/375ml • (02/28/98) • **92**

Scheurebe Trockenbeerenauslese Neusiedlersee Zwischen den Seen No. 4 1995: Heavily botrytized and a little monolithic at this stage, but there's plenty of concentration and vibrant acidity to offset the sweetness and apricot, honey and citrus flavors. Should come together by 2000. • $90/375ml • (02/28/98) • **94**

Scheurebe Trockenbeerenauslese Neusiedlersee Zwischen den Seen No. 6 1995: Deliciously rich, the honey, truffle and grapefruit character is enticing, but it's on the soft side, lacking the zing to warrant long cellaring. Drink now. • $75/375ml • (02/28/98) • **88**

Scheurebe Trockenbeerenauslese Neusiedlersee Zwischen den Seen No. 14 1995: Assertive Scheurebe character shows through in this thickly textured, sweet wine that absolutely melts in the mouth. Smoke and grapefruit aromas augment the honey and apricot flavors, with good acidity beneath. Drink now through 2003. • $100/375ml • (02/28/98) • **91**

Traminer Trockenbeerenauslese Neusiedlersee Nouvelle Vague No. 8 1995: Thick and honeyed. Brilliant yellow, with gold hue. Honey, syrup and burnt almond aromas with a hint of tropical fruit. Full-bodied, very sweet, with a honey, apple and almond aftertaste. Sweet finish. Drink now or hold. • $90/375ml • (02/28/98) • **91**

Welschriesling Beerenauslese Neusiedlersee Zwischen den Seen 1994: Harmonious and sweet, with almond, spice and honey notes on nose and palate. Full-bodied, with moderate acidity and soft texture. Medium-sweet finish. Not a full-blown dessert wine. Try with fresh berries. • $75/375ml • (12/15/96) • **88**

Welschriesling Trockenbeerenauslese Neusiedlersee Zwischen den Seen No. 1 1995: Quite delicate and elegant. Floral, nectarine and honey notes stay fresh and luscious, and the botrytis component is played down. Long, raisiny aftertaste. Delicious on its own or with light desserts. • $65/375ml • (02/28/98) • **91**

Welschriesling Trockenbeerenauslese Neusiedlersee Zwischen den Seen No. 2 1995: Rich and silky-smooth, full of raisinlike flavors, baked apple and honey. Super acidity cleanses the palate, leaving an impression of a wine lighter than this actually is. Drink from now through 2005. • $75/375ml • (02/28/98) • **96**

Welschriesling Trockenbeerenauslese Neusiedlersee Zwischen den Seen No. 15 1995: Young, intense and grapey, with honey and apricot, but there isn't enough acidity to keep the flavors pumping, so the thick texture coats the palate without direction. Nice smoky finish, though. • $110/375ml • (02/28/98) • **88**

Zweigelt Rosé Neusiedlersee Trockenbeerenauslese Nouvelle Vague No. 10 "tu es adorable" 1995: Delicious dessert wine, with everything in the right proportions. Apricot, crème brûlée and raisin character in spades, without being too sweet. Just when you think it's too much, the acidity sweeps the palate clean. Well done. Drink now through 2005. • $90/375ml • (02/28/98) • **93**

KRAFT

Blauer Burgunder Beerenauslese Neusiedlersee-Hügelland 1995: Raisin and tealike character in a light-bodied frame, with moderate acidity but an astringent finish. 1,500 cases made. • $NA/500ml • (02/28/98) • **77**

Chardonnay Ruster Ausbruch Neusiedlersee-Hügelland 1995: Very exotic, showing a heavy botrytis element plus orange, cinnamon and marzipan flavors, all on a medium-bodied frame. Sweet, yet has enough acidity to keep it from cloying. Drink now through 2003. 133 cases made. • $NA/500ml • (02/28/98) • **90**

LANG

Chardonnay Ausbruch Neusiedlersee 1995: Very rich, with plenty of botrytis and apricot notes and a hint of nuts. Thickly textured, it's forward and slightly heavy, with an aftertaste of honey. 100 cases made. • $NA/375ml • (02/28/98) • **87**

Chardonnay Ausbruch Neusiedlersee Barrique 1994: Gold colored, with honey, petrol and spice aromas. Full-bodied and very sweet, with oily, beeswax flavors and a long, oily finish. Thick but simple. 42 cases made. • $NA/375ml • (02/28/98) • **86**

Chardonnay Trockenbeerenauslese Neusiedlersee 1995: Broad, sweet and full-bodied, though not showing the range of flavors found in some other varieties. Well balanced and lengthy, with some enticing spice and vanilla notes. Drink now through 2002. • $NA/375ml • (02/28/98) • **89**

Pinot Noir Trockenbeerenauslese Neusiedlersee 1995: Sweet and thick. Just sits on the palate; all structure with insufficient flavor. 116 cases made. • $NA/375ml • (02/28/98) • **80**

Sämling 88 Trockenbeerenauslese Neusiedlersee 1994: Wow! Unbelievable ripeness and intensity of flavors here. The passion fruit, apricot and truffle flavors in this super-botrytized dessert wine simply melt in your mouth; totally integrated with the acid and alcohol to create a sublime taste experience. The finish is clean, subtle and long. 833 cases made. • $NA/375ml • (02/28/98) • **95**

Welschriesling Trockenbeerenauslese Neusiedlersee 1995: Superlative dessert wine. Raisin, white chocolate and orange flavors coat the palate, and the unctuous texture is just kept in check by the acidity. Delicious. Drink now through 2005. 167 cases made. • $NA/375ml • (02/28/98) • **91**

LENZ MOSER

Beerenauslese White Neusiedlersee Prestige 1995: Not as sweet as some but rich and fruity. Try with food. A rich and oily white with botrytis spice, lemon and cedar aromas and flavors. Medium-to-full body. Lemon-lime aftertaste. Drink now. • $NA/350ml • (02/28/98) • **88**

Grüner Veltliner Qualitätswein Austria Prestige Mailberg 1996: Shows the lentil and herbal side of Grüner Veltliner, with moderate richness and cleansing acidity on the finish. • $9 • (02/28/98) • **82**

Trockenbeerenauslese White Neusiedlersee Prestige 1995: A big and rich TBA with a slightly one-dimensional flavor profile but good intensity of sweetness and character. Thick and oily, with honey, vanilla and a hint of spice. Full-bodied, very sweet, with a long aftertaste and a creamy texture. Better after 1999. • $NA/375ml • (02/28/98) • **89**

LOIBEN, DINSTLGUT

Grüner Veltliner Kabinett Trocken Wachau Loibner Mühlpoint 1995: Elegant, with a goodly amount of floral, spice and honey aromas and flavors. It's medium in body, has fine acidity and a clean, fresh finish. • $10 • (12/15/96) • **86**

Grüner Veltliner Qualitätswein Wachau Loibner Loibenberg 1996: An expressive Grüner, displaying apple, peach and mineral character, rich texture and refreshing acidity. Drink now through 2002. 1,667 cases made. • $11 • (02/28/98) • **86**

Grüner Veltliner Qualitätswein Wachau Loibner Schütt 1996: Firm, showing modest concentration and length, notes of grapefruit and herbs. Needs some food to perk it up. 1,000 cases made. • $10 • (02/28/98) • **83**

Riesling Qualitätswein Kremstal Kremser Pfaffenberg 1996: Enticing stone, fruit and mineral aromas give way to a steely palette of lemony citrus and mineral flavors. 1,041 cases made. • $13 • (02/28/98) • **84**

LOIMER

Chardonnay Auslese Kamptal 1995: A lovely combination of apple, nectarine, honey and white pepper aromas and flavors are carried on a dazzling structure with vibrant acidity in this lightly sweet white. Hints of vanilla carry through on the finish. Try with foie gras. 80 cases made. • $NA/375ml • (02/28/98) • **89**

Grüner Veltliner Beerenauslese Kamptal Spiegel 1995: A very good BA to sip on its own. Intense aromas of lemon, beeswax and spice. Full-bodied, medium sweet, with honey, orange-peel and apricot aftertaste. Drink now. 83 cases made. • $NA/350ml • (02/28/98) • **87**

Grüner Veltliner Qualitätswein Kamptal Langenloiser Spiegel 1996: Could there be new oak here? Vanilla and smoky notes dominate the rich texture, with an impression of acidity and tannins on the finish. A bit awkward overall. 333 cases made. • $16 • (02/28/98) • **83**

Grüner Veltliner Qualitätswein Trocken Kamptal Langenloiser Spiegel 1995: Rich aromas of apricot and passion fruit are underscored by a firm palate of citrus and spice flavors. Beautiful. Drink now. • $15 • (12/15/96) • **87**

Qualitätswein Trocken Kamptal Spiegel Langenlois Alte Reben Erste Lage 1995: This has the texture of a big Chardonnay and the spicy, mineral character of Riesling. Full-bodied, with ample acidity and a rich, fruity finish. Perfect with food. • $30 • (12/15/96) • **87**

Riesling Qualitätswein Kamptal Langenloiser Steinmassl 1996: Distinctly earthy, with white pepper and citrus accents. Solid, medium-bodied, sporting vibrant acidity. Lacks integration at this stage, but the components are there. Should complement food. Try in 2000. 416 cases made. • $24 • (02/28/98) • **87**

Riesling Qualitätswein Trocken Kamptal Langenloiser Steinmassl 1995: This shows plenty of ripeness on the nose, with spice and melon notes dominating. Medium-bodied, with firm acidity and a light finish. • $26 • (12/15/96) • **87**

MALAT

Chardonnay Trockenbeerenauslese Kremstal 1995: Completely mindblowing! Smells like a chocolate and apricot dessert with truffle sauce. In the mouth, the chocolate and truffle theme continues. The texture is mouthcoatingly unctuous, only to be cleansed by a laserlike acidity that prepares you for the endless finish. Extremely powerful and unevolved; wait until 2003, but should last well into the next century. • $NA/375ml • (02/28/98) • **97**

Sauvignon Blanc Qualitätswein Kremstal 1996: Broad and waxy, tasting more like Chenin Blanc than Sauvignon Blanc. Though rich and mouthfilling, it lacks vibrancy. • $NA • (02/28/98) • **81**

MALTESER RITTERORDEN

Cabernet Sauvignon-Merlot Kommende Mailberg Weinviertel 1994: A distinctive clove note adds complexity to the black currant and vanilla tones. Firmly structured. Still youthful; will the fruit survive the tannins? Drink now through 2000. • $20 • (02/28/98) • **84**

Grüner Veltliner Qualitätswein Weinviertel Hundschupfen 1996: Moderate richness, with an herbal, gooseberry quality, but it's neutral and short on the finish. • $10 • (02/28/98) • **78**

MANTLERHOF

Grüner Veltliner Kabinett Kremstal Speigel 1996: Lemony, herbal character is the main feature of this medium-bodied wine. Tart finish. 400 cases made. • $16 • (02/28/98) • **81**

Grüner Veltliner Qualitätswein Trocken Kremstal Erste Lage Spiegel 1995: A big and rich Grüner with loads of apricot and grapefruit character and hints of spice. Full-bodied and oily, yet fresh and crisp with very good acidity. Impressive. If you like big Gewürz from Alsace, try this. 333 cases made. • $18 • (12/15/96) • **89**

Riesling Auslese Kremstal Tiefenthal 1995: A medium-sweet version, this is rich and spicy, featuring floral and honey notes with a hint of grapefruit. Dry on the finish. 166 cases made. • $25 • (12/15/96) • **88**

Riesling Qualitätswein Kremstal 1996: Straightforward and fruity, with a hint of sweetness, displaying peach and mineral flavors. Finishes short. 250 cases made. • $18 • (02/28/98) • **84**

Key: SS—Spectator Selection CS—Cellar Selection HR—Highly Recommended BB—Best Buy $NA—Price not available Ⓐ—Auction Price (BT)—Barrel Tasting

Dates in parentheses indicate the issues in which the ratings were published.

Roter Veltliner Beerenauslese Kremstal 1995: An attractive dessert wine that brings you back for more. Deep gold colored, with an earth and honey perfume. Full-bodied, sweet and oily textured. Grapefruit and honey aftertaste. Drink now. 100 cases made. • $34/500 ml • (02/28/98) • **88**

Roter Veltliner Qualitätswein Trocken Kremstal Reisenthal 1995: The aromas are subtle, but there's plenty of honey and apple flavors and the texture is rich. Full-bodied and a bit alcoholic, though enjoyable. 333 cases made. • $18 • (02/28/97) • **84**

MARKOWITSCH

Chardonnay Qualitätswein Carnuntum Reserve 1995: Quite mature compared to others from '95, with a broad, rich profile and butter and vanilla flavors. Well balanced and lively, but the oaky character won't make this a long-term wine. Drink now. 600 cases made. • $17 • (02/28/98) • **84**

Grüner Veltliner Qualitätswein Carnuntum Ried Schanzäcker 1996: Rich and balanced. Delicate floral and talc aromas segue into lemon, apple and peach flavors. Tender, but there's good acidity for balance. 833 cases made. • $9 • (02/28/98) • **85**

Pinot Gris Qualitätswein Carnuntum Reserve 1995: A modern-style Pinot Gris, showing plenty of new oak aromas and flavors along with peach and tropical notes. Finishes with a touch of oak tannin. Not what you might expect, but tasty. Drink now through 2000. 667 cases made. • $17 • (02/28/98) • **85**

MAYER, FRANZ

Grüner Veltliner Grinzinger Kabinett Wien Schenkenberg 1996: Fresh and grapey, with cassis aromas followed by white pepper and tobacco notes. Tender, yet the acidity is prominent on the finish. 2,500 cases made. • $9 • (02/28/98) • **83**

Kabinett Wien Nussberger Symphony 1996: An exuberant white, bursting with melon and gooseberry character. Starts out soft, yet there's firm acidity. Drink now. A blend of six white grapes. 2,500 cases made. • $10 • (02/28/98) • **83**

Rheinriesling Kabinett Wien "Vienna Classic" 1996: Lean and on the tart side, showing the more herbal, grassy component of Riesling. • $11 • (02/28/98) • **83**

MICHLITS-STADLMANN

Grüner Veltliner Strohwein Neusiedlersee 1992: A pungent nose, with botrytis accents of dried apricots and raisins. Quite elegant for this degree of ripeness. Finish is clean and refreshing. 50 cases made. • $36/375ml • (12/15/96) • **86**

Traminer Ausbruch Neusiedlersee 1995: Very ripe and spicy. Dark gold in color, with an amber tint. Honey, almond flavors, with a floral hint. Full-bodied and thick, with oily, honeyed texture. Spicy, almond aftertaste. Drink now. • $25/375ml • (02/28/98) • **88**

Weissburgunder Trockenbeerenauslese Neusiedlersee 1995: Slightly volatile white, with wonderfully ripe fruit, but odd. Full-bodied and very sweet, with a milky, ripe fruit aftertaste. • $38/375ml • (02/28/98) • **79**

Zweigelt-Blau Falstaff Prämiert Extra Trocken Neusiedlersee 1993: Some decent berry aromas and flavors, with a rather stemmy character beneath. Medium-bodied, with medium, very soft tannins and a fruity finish. • $15 • (02/28/97) • **84**

MORANDELL

Grüner Veltliner Qualitätswein Trocken Kamptal 1994: Dull and out of sorts, with candy and marzipan flavors. Tasted twice, with consistent notes. • $7 • (01/31/97) • **70**

MUNZENRIEDER

Bouvier Trockenbeerenauslese Neusiedlersee 1995: Vivid and superbly defined, with amazing concentration of fruit and sweetness. Aromas of honey, lemon, mango and grapefruit. Full-bodied and very sweet, with a long, long aftertaste. Drink now or hold. • $NA/375ml • (02/28/98) • **95**

Bouvier Trockenbeerenauslese Neusiedlersee 1994: Displays distinctive floral and smoky character, with honey and vanilla custard notes. Loads of acidity. The finish is a little coarse, detracting slightly from the overall appeal. Drink now through 2001. • $NA/375ml • (02/28/98) • **90**

Sämling 88 Trockenbeerenauslese Neusiedlersee 1995: Gorgeous dessert wine displaying exotic, botrytized notes in addition to the honey, orange and crème brûlée flavors, all riding on a thick, luscious texture. Concentrated and dense, one can only imagine the acid level to balance this degree of sweetness. Stunning now; should improve through 2005. 580 cases made. • $NA/375ml • (02/28/98) • **92**

Sämling 88 Trockenbeerenauslese Neusiedlersee Pannonia Weingut 1991: Straightforward flavors of canned peaches and honey with a touch of botrytis to add interest, but this lacks the zippy acidity to prolong the flavors on the finish. Viscous, and balanced on the soft side, it's ready now through 2000. 250 cases made. • $NA/375ml • (02/28/98) • **89**

Welschriesling Trockenbeerenauslese Neusiedlersee 1995: Hold on tight. Ultrarich, smoky apricot aromas lead into a sweet, multidimensional dessert wine sporting honey, apricot, butterscotch and citrus flavors. The whole package seems weightless thanks to superb balance and refreshing acidity. Long, smoky finish. 250 cases made. • $20/375ml • (02/28/98) • **95**

NEKOWITSCH

Strohwein White Neusiedlersee Schilfwein Tradition 1995: Loads of perfume, with a heady mix of roses, violets and raisins wafting from the glass, followed by the taste of apricots and oranges. Thickly textured without being heavy, its appeal is upfront. 208 cases made. • $45/375ml • (02/28/98) • **87**

NIGL

Grüner Veltliner Beerenauslese Kremstal 1995: Plenty of botrytis notches up the exotic element in this dessert wine. Luscious, yet it maintains an elegance and harmony to the honey, mushroom and vanilla notes. Finishes well, but a bit hot. • $28/375ml • (02/28/98) • **87**

Grüner Veltliner Kremstal Alte Reben 1996: Delicious. Exhibits floral, litchi and vanilla flavors on a soft texture, yet the underlying acidity comes to the fore on the finish, where a lemony component lingers. Drink now through 2002. 208 cases made. • $18 • (02/28/98) • **87**

Grüner Veltliner Qualitätswein Trocken Kremstal Kremser Alte Reben 1995: A big Grüner, with ripe, tropical fruit flavors that start off almost sweet, then turn dry and minerally, with a touch of bitterness at the end. Enjoyable now. • $21 • (12/15/96) • **86**

Grüner Veltliner Qualitätswein Trocken Kremstal Senftenberger Piri 1995: Excellent intensity of ripe fruit and spice flavors, especially white pepper flavor. Medium-bodied, with fresh acidity, it's crisp and clean. 250 cases made. • $18 • (12/15/96) • **88**

Riesling Qualitätswein Trocken Kremstal Privat Senftenberger Piri 1995: Beautifully aromatic, with scents of pine needles, flowers and honey. Medium-bodied, with pine-accented fruit flavors, and fresh and fruity acidity. Delicious. • $35 • (12/15/96) • **88**

Riesling Qualitätswein Trocken Kremstal Urgesteins Kremser Kremsleiten 1995: A fresh, floral component lends appeal to this soft, straightforward Riesling. Medium-bodied. Ready now. • $25 • (12/15/96) • **84**

Riesling Qualitätswein Trocken Kremstal Urgesteins Senftenberger Ried Hochäcker 1995: Starts out soft and floral, then turns very dry. The lime and melon flavors are concentrated, with a moderate finish. • $29 • (12/15/96) • **84**

Urgesteins-Riesling Kremstal Kremser Kremsleiten 1996: Intense and spicy, this has density of flavor and an elegant structure. The lime, apple and honeysuckle character carries through to the dry, almost pungent finish. Drinkable now; better in 2000. 330 cases made. • $25 • (02/28/98) • **91**

Urgesteins-Riesling Kremstal Senftenberger Hochächer 1996: Beautiful. Beguiling spice and mineral character holds court, with lime and apple notes lurking in the background. Very tightly wound, vibrant, showing depth and a rich texture. Try in 2000. 208 cases made. • $29 • (02/28/98) • **90**

Veltliner-Privat Kremstal Senftenberger Piri 1996: Elegant and flavorful. Lovely interplay of talc, litchi and peach. Wonderfully balanced. The litchi note echoes on the finish, along with lemony acidity. Well done for the vintage. 167 cases made. • $25 • (02/28/98) • **89**

NIKOLAIHOF

Grüner Veltliner Federspiel Trocken Wachau Im Weingebirge 1995: Aromas of almonds and white pepper, in spades. Rich and round, exhibiting flavors of green apple, with spice accents, but lacks the vibrancy and intensity to score higher. 1,666 cases made. • $23 • (12/15/96) • **82**

Grüner Veltliner Federspiel Trocken Wachau Im Weingebirge 1994: Very racy, displaying apple, pear, mineral and some tropical fruit nuances. Intense and focused, it lingers on the finish. Delicious now. 900 cases made. • $20 • (01/31/97) • **87**

Grüner Veltliner Federspiel Wachau Im Weinebirge 1996: Delicate and floral-scented, displaying citrus flavors on a firm backbone and minerally undercurrent. Drink from 1999 through 2003. • $23 • (02/28/98) • **85**

Riesling Federspiel Trocken Wachau Vom Stein 1994: Big and rich, this shows masses of lemon and lime aromas and flavors, with hints of spice and piecrust. Full-bodied, with excellent acidity and a long, flavorful finish. Drink now or hold. 2,083 cases made. • $29 • (12/15/96) • **91**

Riesling Federspiel Wachau Vom Stein 1995: A delicate, vibrant style that exhibits density and richness, along with some good apple and lime notes. Drink now through 2000. • $25 • (02/28/98) • **87**

Riesling Kabinett Trocken Kremstal Steiner Hund 1994: Refined and sleek, with lovely spicy, steely and fruity character. Medium-bodied, with ultrafine acidity and a long, vibrantly fruity finish. 291 cases made. • $30 • (12/15/96) • **90**

Riesling Smaragd Wachau Vom Stein 1995: Tropical aromas and flavors of banana and mango accent the peach. Lean texture, with moderate concentration. • $32 • (02/28/98) • **84**

OPITZ, WILLI

Bouvier Trockenbeerenauslese Neusiedlersee 1995: Not as powerful and sweet as similar wines in this category but very good. Subtle, lively TBA with very spicy, white pepper character. Medium-bodied, sweet, with a pepper and honey aftertaste. Drink now. • $85/375ml • (02/28/98) • **87**

Gewürztraminer Trockenbeerenauslese Neusiedlersee 1995: A study in contrasts. Amazing balance of lush texture and racy acidity meshes in an ethereal package, making this TBA elegant and seductive. Delicious apricot, spice, honey and caramel flavors with accents of botrytis, followed by a long finish. 125 cases made. • $95/375ml • (02/28/98) • **95**

Neusiedlersee Weisser Schilfmandl 1995: Very distinctive, with Muscat and overwhelming pine-resin aromas. Thick and rich, with a touch of astringency on the finish. • $75/375ml • (02/28/98) • **79**

Neusiedlersee Weisser Schilfmandl 1994: Basil, mint and pine come to mind with this fat, ripe, sweet wine. Easy to like, though one wishes for a bit more structure. 166 cases made. • $75/375ml • (10/31/97) • **86**

Pinot Gris Trockenbeerenauslese Neusiedlersee 1995: Showing some smoke and clove notes in addition to honey and orange, here's a viscous, concentrated dessert wine with good acidity to balance the sweetness. Beautifully integrated, with a fresh, lingering finish. • $90/375ml • (02/28/98) • **91**

Trockenbeerenauslese Neusiedlersee Opitz One 1995: The aroma has a wood ash note, while the light berry and honey flavors are allied with a fresh, elegant structure. Delicate yet sweet, this may be best drunk on its own. Drink now through 2001. • $80/375ml • (02/28/98) • **88**

Trockenbeerenauslese Neusiedlersee Opitz One 1994: Incredibly sweet and rich, this is a red dessert wine with tempting figgy, nutty aromas, sweet, plummy flavors and a long finish. Drink now or cellar through 2010. 80 cases made. • $80/375ml • (10/31/97) • **90**

Welschriesling/Scheurebe Trockenbeerenauslese Neusiedlersee Goldackerl 1995: Shows a lot of raisin character along with some very ripe melon notes, but there's good underlying acidity. Lacks the concentration of the best of the vintage, however. • $85 • (02/28/98) • **89**

PFAFFL

Chardonnay Qualitätswein Weinviertel 1995: Lean and crisp, this is more like a Riesling than Chardonnay, with floral, apple and mineral flavors. Good intensity and a moderate finish. Drink now through 2000. 667 cases made. • $13 • (02/28/98) • **84**

Chardonnay Qualitätswein Weinviertel Exklusiv 1996: Lean and appley, with smoky, vanilla notes from new oak that don't mesh at this point. May come together with time. Best from 1999 through 2003. 667 cases made. • $13 • (02/28/98) • **79**

Grüner Veltliner Qualitätswein Weinviertel Hundsleiten-Sandtal 1995: Grapefruit and mineral are the dominant themes, with herbal notes for accent. Well integrated and compact now, it should unfold nicely by 2000. 416 cases made. • $12 • (02/28/98) • **87**

Sauvignon Blanc Qualitätswein Weinviertel 1996: Austere, concentrated and dry almost to the point of chalkiness, with flavors reminiscent of earth, stones and grapefruit peel. Needs food. Best now through 2000. 583 cases made. • $18 • (02/28/98) • **83**

Sauvignon Blanc Qualitätswein Weinviertel 1995: Very ripe and fleshy, displaying cassis and marzipan notes on a rich texture, and vibrant acidity. Concentrated, dense and long, this is absolutely delicious. Best now through 2000. 500 cases made. • $17 • (02/28/98) • **89**

Zweigelt-Cabernet Sauvignon Weinviertel Excellent 1995: Leafy and herbal, with some berry accents, this has medium body, modest concentration and tannin on the finish. Ready to drink. 667 cases made. • $17 • (02/28/98) • **82**

PICHLER, F.X.

Grüner Veltliner Federspiel Trocken Wachau Loibner Klostersatz 1995: Plenty of spicy, white pepper character to this medium-bodied wine. Fine acidity and a dry, crisp finish. A good match for food. • $22 • (12/15/96) • **86**

Grüner Veltliner Smaragd Trocken Wachau Dürnsteiner Kellerberg 1995: Rich floral and apricot notes give a weighty feeling without being fat, and the vibrant acidity and spicy, dry finish keep everything in check. Drink now. • $40 • (12/15/96) • **88**

Grüner Veltliner Smaragd Wachau Dürnsteiner Kellerberg 1996: Smells like banana candy, but in the mouth it's dry and spicy, with a firm, almost searing intensity from the citrusy acidity and alcohol. Try now. 375 cases made. • $40 • (02/28/98) • **88**

Riesling Smaragd Trocken Wachau Dürnsteiner Kellerberg 1996: Shows character of apple, mineral, and banana-marshmallow candy. Good structure and presence, but lacks concentration of fruit flavors. Try from 1999 through 2002. 458 cases made. • $50 • (02/28/98) • **86**

Riesling Smaragd Trocken Wachau Dürnsteiner Kellerberg 1995: Tropical flavors of passion fruit and litchi add dimension to the racy, citrusy acidity in this lively, focused Riesling. Elegance and finesse make this an electrifying presentation. • $50 • (12/15/96) • **90**

Riesling Smaragd Trocken Wachau Loibner Berg 1995: A superb Riesling, with a concentration of spicy lemon-lime and slate character. Full-bodied, with firm acidity and a long, intensely flavored finish. • $45 • (12/15/96) • **90**

PICHLER, RUDOLF

Grüner Veltliner Smaragd Wachau Wösendorfer Hochrain 1996: Round and rich, redolent of honey and apple, this is finely balanced and broad, with a tangy acidity at the end. Enough structure for future development. Drink now through 2002. 150 cases made. • $34 • (02/28/98) • **88**

Grüner Veltliner Smaragd Wachau Wösendorfer Hochrain 1995: Already showing mature marzipan and honey notes, the quality of the 1995 vintage is evident in the richness, harmony and length of this wine. Firm underlying acidity. Delicious. Drink now through 2002. 150 cases made. • $32 • (02/28/98) • **88**

Riesling Smaragd Trocken Wachau Wösendorfer Kirchweg 1995: Floral and herbal character marks this austere, lean wine. 150 cases made. • $29 • (02/28/98) • **81**

POCKL

Admiral Qualitätswein Trocken Neusiedlersee 1994: Fresh, spicy cherry flavor and a leafy note are accented by new oak in this internationally styled red. The finish packs a wallop of tannins, so try with food. • $32 • (02/28/97) • **84**

Pinot Noir Qualitätswein Neusiedlersee 1995: Seductive, earthy and herbal Pinot Noir character, along with a note of red berry and mouth-watering acidity. Good length. Ready to drink. 250 cases made. • $34 • (02/28/98) • **85**

Rosso e Nero Red Neusiedlersee 1994: Smoky black cherry notes enliven the rich yet firm texture in this red blend. Finishes less generously than it begins, but food should temper that. Ready to drink. 250 cases made. • $30 • (02/28/98) • **86**

Zweigelt Qualitätswein Trocken Neusiedlersee Classique 1995: Strange aromas of nail polish and grape skins detract from the quality of this light red. • $14 • (02/28/97) • **76**

POLZ, ERICH & WALTER

Grauburgunder Qualitätswein Südsteiermark Grassnitzberg 1996: Very floral and delicate. A straightforward, easy-drinking white without a lot of fruit character or concentration. Drink now. • $15 • (02/28/98) • **80**

Morillon Qualitätswein Trocken Südsteiermark Hochgrassnitzberg 1995: A broad-shouldered white, full of honeysuckle and apple flavors. Finish is a bit lean and short, though. • $22 • (02/28/97) • **84**

Morillon Qualitätswein Trocken Südsteiermark Steirsche Klassik 1995: A no-nonsense Chardonnay. Features apple and melon flavors, medium body and clean finish. • $18 • (02/28/97) • **84**

Riesling Qualitätswein Trocken Südsteiermark 1994: An austere, spicy style, showing hints of rose petal and tropical fruit flavors. The dry, almost chalky finish tails off quickly. • $14 • (12/15/96) • **82**

Sauvignon Blanc Qualitätswein Südsteiermark Hochgrassnitzberg 1996: Rich and flavorful, with characteristic Sauvignon Blanc grass, melon and grapefruit notes, all supported by lively acidity. Best now through 2000. • $31 • (02/28/98) • **86**

Sauvignon Blanc Qualitätswein Trocken Südsteiermark 1995: An initial sweaty note disappears to reveal a bracing, mineral- and grass-flavored wine that should pair well with white meat and fish dishes. Ready now. • $18 • (02/28/97) • **83**

Sauvignon Blanc Qualitätswein Trocken Südsteiermark Hochgrassnitzberg 1995: A clean and crisp Sauvignon with pretty mineral and melon aromas and flavors and moderate acidity. Light finish. • $26 • (12/15/96) • **85**

Weissburgunder Qualitätswein Trocken Südsteiermark Grassnitzberg 1995: An extra dose of ripeness rounds out this wine's melon and fig character. Lovely balance and a good finish make for easy drinking now. • $18 • (12/15/96) • **85**

PRAGER

Feinburgunder Smaragd Trocken Wachau 1995: Exotic. Smells and tastes like Pinot Gris with its abundant character of almond, spice, smoke, sweet pepper and tropical fruit. Full-bodied and rich, with a long, wild finish. • $31 • (12/15/96) • **90**

Grüner Veltliner Federspiel Wachau Weissenkirchen 1994: Good concentration of fruit for a kabinett. This is medium-bodied, with fine acidity and a salty, spicy character. • $19 • (12/15/96) • **87**

Grüner Veltliner Federspiel Wachau Weissenkirchner Hinter der Burg 1995: A flinty, leesy aroma is followed by a rich herb and white pepper character that's fresh and straightforward. • $21 • (01/31/97) • **85**

Grüner Veltliner Smaragd Trocken Wachau Weissenkirchner Achleiten 1995: Loads of passion fruit, apricot and toast flavors coast into a long, intense finish of bone-dry character, somewhat startling after the ripe, exotic beginning. • $29 • (12/15/96) • **90**

Grüner Veltliner Smaragd Wachau Weissenkirchner Achleiten 1996: Delicious from start to finish, this Grüner adds a touch of lime to the white pepper and chamomile character, all in a vibrant, deftly balanced presentation. Plenty of richness and a lingering aftertaste. Structured to drink well now through 2003. 300 cases made. • $29 • (02/28/98) • **90**

Riesling Federspiel Trocken Wachau Weissenkirchner Steinriegl 1995: Subtle spice and honey aromas and flavors in this medium-bodied wine. It's dry, with fresh acidity and a steely finish. • $24 • (12/15/96) • **88**

Riesling Federspiel Wachau Weissenkirchner Steinriegl 1996: A live wire, exhibiting lime-tinged apple and mineral flavors that virtually crackle in the mouth. Firmly structured and lean, with a taut, expressive character. Enjoy from 2000 through 2005. 2,000 cases made. • $24 • (02/28/98) • **89**

Riesling Federspiel Wachau Weissenkirchner Steinriegl 1994: Extremely rich, full of mineral and green plum flavors that close up on the almond- and petrol-accented finish of this tightly structured wine. Needs time to open. Try now. • $22 • (12/15/96) • **90**

Riesling Smaragd Trocken Wachau Weissenkirchner Achleiten 1995: The ripe fruit flavors are underlaid by firm structure. It's tightly wound at this stage, with a light finish. • $35 • (12/15/96) • **86**

Riesling Smaragd Trocken Wachau Weissenkirchner Klaus 1995: A blockbuster of a Riesling, with aromas and flavors of spice, grapefruit, passion fruit—you name it. Full-bodied, with great acidity and a long, flavorful finish. Drink now or hold. • $35 • (12/15/96) • **93**

Riesling Smaragd Trocken Wachau Weissenkirchner Steinriegl 1995: Rich and fat for a top-class Riesling, with slight, mature petrol, spice and honey aromas and flavors. Full-bodied, with medium acidity and a long, fruity finish. • $35 • (12/15/96) • **87**

Riesling Smaragd Wachau Weissenkirchner Achleiten 1996: Austere yet what extract! Floral, apple and mineral character, densely textured and concentrated. Keeps building in the mouth to a rich finish. Great balance and intensity. Best from now through 2005. 350 cases made. • $35 • (02/28/98) • **91**

Riesling Smaragd Wachau Weissenkirchner Achleiten 1994: A wine that sneaks up on your palate and then gives you a blast of flavor. Medium-bodied, with fine acidity and loads of lemon-lime, spice and honey on the finish. Drink now or cellar. • $32 • (12/15/96) • **90**

Riesling Smaragd Wachau Weissenkirchner Klaus 1996: Marked by fragrant, floral aromas and lime and apple flavors. Turns crisp and zingy on the finish. An appealing peach note lingers. Best now through 2002. 250 cases made. • $35 • (02/28/98) • **89**

Riesling Smaragd Wachau Weissenkirchner Klaus 1994: Reminiscent of Alsace with its spicy, petrol personality. Beginning to show some development, it needs food to smooth out the steely structure. An almond flavor rounds out the finish. • $32 • (12/15/96) • **88**

Riesling Smaragd Wachau Weissenkirchner Steinriegl 1996: Shows lime, apple, honey and mineral character. Rich, striking and well balanced, with racy acidity underneath. Try now. 500 cases made. • $35 • (02/28/98) • **89**

Key: SS—Spectator Selection CS—Cellar Selection HR—Highly Recommended BB—Best Buy $NA—Price not available Ⓐ—Auction Price (BT)—Barrel Tasting
Dates in parentheses indicate the issues in which the ratings were published.

Riesling Smaragd Wachau Weissenkirchner Steinriegl 1994: Fabulous lemon-lime and spice notes, underscored by a steely mineral character. It's lean and intense; try now with food. • $32 • (12/15/96) • **91**

Smaragd Wachau Feinburgunder 1996: A racy, delineated white full of mineral intensity. Citrus and nutlike notes complete the flavor range. Should be more expressive from 1999 through 2003. 250 cases made. • $31 • (02/28/98) • **85**

REBENHOF

Sauvignon Blanc Trocken Südsteiermark Nussberg 1995: Elegant and refined, with its melon and mineral aromas and flavors crisp and inviting. Ripe fruit notes on the finish. Ready to drink. • $NA • (02/28/97) • **86**

Weissburgunder Trocken Südsteiermark 1995: Impressively rich, with plenty of creamy melon aromas and flavors. Medium-bodied and round, with a lively, ripe, fruit-flavored finish. Delicious. • $NA • (02/28/97) • **87**

REINISCH, JOHANNESHOF

Cabernet Sauvignon Qualitätswein Thermenregion Reserve 1994: Plenty of herbal flavors and some plum notes as well. Has some richness, modest depth, ends on a tannic note. 490 cases made. • $29 • (06/15/97) • **84**

Chardonnay Qualitätswein Thermenregion 1995: Rich and nearly sweet in character, this Chardonnay is dripping with butterscotch and honey flavors backed by fresh fruit and a smooth texture. 580 cases made. • $16 • (06/15/97) • **85**

Chardonnay Qualitätswein Thermenregion Reserve 1996: Nuances of vanilla from new oak clash with the high acidity in this racy, lean Chardonnay. One wishes for more fruit concentration also. Best now through 2003. 125 cases made. • $22 • (02/28/98) • **82**

Chardonnay Trockenbeerenauslese Thermenregion 1995: An extravagantly rich but vividly defined dessert wine that has the intrigue of a great Sauternes and the verve of a classic Riesling. Honey, peach and grapefruit flavors, great balance and a long, long finish make this an extraordinary taste experience. Should age through at least 2010. 130 cases made. • $60/375ml • (06/15/97) • **94**

Eiswein Thermenregion 1995: Vibrantly fruity dessert wine, with vivid grapefruit and honey flavors and zingy acidity that give it complexity, length and a refreshing texture. Delicious now, but has the balance to improve through 2005, at least. 65 cases made. • $50/375ml • (06/15/97) • **90**

Pinot Blanc Qualitätswein Thermenregion 1996: Lively and fresh, with flavors of canned peaches and a smoky, earthy note on the finish. Drink now. 1,150 cases made. • $11 • (02/28/98) • **79**

Pinot Blanc Qualitätswein Thermenregion 1995: Very soft, reminiscent of flowers and talcum powder, yet it's deftly balanced with lemony acidity, ending on a nutty note. Good length. 840 cases made. • $11 • (06/15/97) • **85**

Pinot Noir Qualitätswein Thermenregion Reserve 1994: Lovely. Spicy blackberries combine with a silky texture and vibrant acidity in this medium-bodied red. Food should soften the somewhat tannic finish. 583 cases made. • $17 • (02/28/98) • **86**

Saint Laurent Qualitätswein Thermenregion Reserve 1995: Aromas of fresh beets give way to cherry, cedar, dill and vanilla flavors. Medium-bodied, lightly tannic. Ready to drink. 416 cases made. • $23 • (02/28/98) • **82**

Saint Laurent Qualitätswein Thermenregion Reserve 1994: Green tasting, with only modest plum and herb flavors. Has concentration, but turns a bit astringent. 1,250 cases made. • $19 • (06/15/97) • **81**

Zweigelt Qualitätswein Thermenregion 1996: Shows a lovely sense of harmony between the structure, the texture and the cherry and spice flavors. Try now through 2003. 1,650 cases made. • $12 • (02/28/98) • **85**

Zweigelt Qualitätswein Thermenregion 1995: Focused and a bit on the light side, with peppery and beefy flavors. Unique flavors for barbecue fare. 1,600 cases made. • $12 • (06/15/97) • **83**

ROSENHOF

Bouvier Trockenbeerenauslese Neusiedlersee 1995: A wine with wonderful definition and sweet flavors. Gold color, with a brilliant orange hue. Intense orange peel, raisin and spice aromas. Full-bodied and very sweet, with a maple, toffee and tobacco flavor. Long, long, sweet finish. Drink now or hold. • $NA/375ml • (02/28/98) • **90**

Chardonnay Trockenbeerenauslese Neusiedlersee Barrique 1995: Very exotic, showing pear and almond notes along with the honey and spice, elegant for a TBA. Tart acidity at this stage, which will integrate with the concentrated fruit flavors and sweetness in time. Try in 2002. • $NA/375ml • (02/28/98) • **93**

Muscat Ottonel Beerenauslese Neusiedlersee 1995: Pretty sticky. Thick and powerful, with lots of spicy orange peel and tea aromas and flavors. Medium- to full-bodied, with lots of sweet fruit flavors and a long, sweet finish. Good acidity. Drink now. • $NA/375ml • (02/28/98) • **90**

SALOMON-WEINGUT UNDHOF, ERICH

Gewürztraminer Auslese Kremstal Kremser Wachtberg 1995: A powerful, spicy wine that needs food. Slightly overdone. Wonderful aromas of mineral, spice and honey with a hint of almonds. Medium-bodied, off-dry, with big, intense flavors. Long aftertaste. Drink now. • $30/375ml • (02/28/98) • **89**

Riesling Auslese Kremstal Kremser Kögl 1995: A lovely, delicate white, just off-dry, redolent of peaches, lime blossoms and minerals. Well balanced and lively, yet the finish is slightly cloying. May improve in a year or two. • $25 • (02/28/98) • **88**

Riesling Auslese Kremstal Steiner Pfaffenberg 1995: Soft and easy on the palate, with fresh aromas and flavors of spice, honey and melon. Medium-bodied, with a sweet, fruity finish. 250 cases made. • $25 • (12/15/96) • **85**

Riesling Kabinett Kremstal Kremser Kögl 1995: There's an earthy component to the aroma, but the intense, minerally streak will appeal to fans of lean, austerely styled Rieslings. This is firm and needs food. 833 cases made. • $19 • (12/15/96) • **88**

Riesling Kabinett Trocken Kremstal Steiner Pfaffenberg 1994: Firmly structured and broad, with a mineral note running throughout. Impressive, with a hint of marzipan flavor at the end, but lacks a bit of zip. 250 cases made. • $19 • (12/15/96) • **86**

Riesling Qualitätswein Kremstal Steiner Pfaffenberg 1996: A perfect example of site expressing itself through the grape. Austere, minerally and mouth-watering, with subtle peach and lime flavors hinting at petrol, this is firm, with a rich texture and lively finish. Try now through 2003. 333 cases made. • $18 • (02/28/98) • **90**

Riesling Spätlese Kremstal Kremser Kögl 1995: Totally seductive. Combines ripe, tropical fruit flavors with a round yet vibrant structure. Dovetails into a long finish. A pleasure to drink now. 250 cases made. • $21 • (12/15/96) • **89**

SATTLERHOF

Chardonnay Qualitätswein Südsteiermark 1996: New oak notes add complexity but sit apart from the apple flavors and citrus acidity. Flavorful, but a little awkward and slightly tart on the finish. Drink now. • $13 • (02/28/98) • **82**

Sauvignon Blanc Qualitätswein Südsteiermark 1996: Tasty. Full of gooseberry, herb and lemon flavors, well-integrated acidity and a juicy texture. • $17 • (02/28/98) • **84**

SCHLUMBERGER

Brut 1987 • $17 • (02/28/95) • **87**

Brut Blanc de Blancs Wien NV: A light, simply flavored sparkling wine with assertive yeasty aromas. Drink now. 500 cases made. • $12 • (02/28/98) • **80**

Brut Wien Cuvée Klimt Der Kuss NV: A good, solid, basic bubbly with straightforward, crisp flavors and a touch of aged complexity. Drink now. 750 cases made. • $NA • (02/28/98) • **81**

Brut Wien Cuvée Klimt Judith I NV: An innocuous bottle of bubbly that's clean and well balanced, with bland flavors. Drink now. 750 cases made. • $NA • (02/28/98) • **77**

Cabernet-Merlot Thermenregion Privat-Keller 1993: Lovely, mature Cabernet aromas of coffee and cedar are followed by cassis and spice notes. Medium-bodied, slightly austere. Needs steaks, roasts or cheeses to show well. Ready to drink. 1,000 cases made. • $NA • (02/28/98) • **86**

Cabernet-Merlot Thermenregion Vöslauer Goldeck 1994: Age has mellowed the cherry character. Shows smoke and barnyard notes. Lean in profile and firmly structured, the tannins need hearty food. 2,083 cases made. • $NA • (02/28/98) • **83**

SCHROCK, HEIDI

Ausbruch Neusiedlersee-Hugelland Ruster 1993: Impressive for its honey, baked apple and butterscotch character, but lacks the intensity and dimension to score higher. Falls short on the finish. • $41/375ml • (12/15/96) • **86**

Muscat Qualitätswein Neusiedlersee-Hügelland Ruster 1996: Light, dry and spicy, with mineral character and a hint of soapiness. Lemony acidity gets the juices flowing. 125 cases made. • $20 • (02/28/98) • **79**

Ruster Ausbruch Neusiedlersee-Hügelland 1996: Lovely honey and vanilla custard aromas and flavors denote this white of medium body and sweetness. There's good zip to it, though the balance leans toward softness. Drink now through 2002. 83 cases made. • $45/500ml • (02/28/98) • **88**

Ruster Ausbruch Neusiedlersee-Hügelland 1995: Light on its feet, this shows moderate citrus, vanilla and apple character with fresh acidity, yet it dissipates quickly. Try with less-sweet desserts or cheeses. 250 cases made. • $40/500ml • (02/28/98) • **86**

Ruster Ausbruch Neusiedlersee-Hügelland Fumé 1995: This hints of apricots, with rather narrow flavors of raisins and honey that turn astringent on the finish. 167 cases made. • $45/500ml • (02/28/98) • **83**

Weissburgunder Qualitätswein Neusiedlersee-Hügelland Ruster 1996: An appealing Pinot Blanc whose apple and vanilla custard notes are married to a crisp, lean structure. Refreshing finish. Best with light foods. Drink now. 350 cases made. • $20 • (02/28/98) • **83**

Welschriesling Auslese Neusiedlersee-Hügelland Vogelsang 1996: A spice monster, displaying white pepper, nutmeg and vanilla, but lacks intensity and vibrancy, finishing a bit cloying. Drinkable now. 60 cases made. • $20 • (02/28/98) • **86**

SEIGENDORF, KLOSTERKELLER

Weissburgunder Kabinett Neusiedlersee 1996: Clean and fresh, with apple, citrus and almond flavors on a light-bodied frame. Good as an apéritif. Drink now. • $NA • (02/28/98) • **82**

SEPP MOSER

Blauer Burgunder Qualitätswein Kremstal Riede Gebling 1995: Browning already. Flavors of earth, smoke and autumn leaves. Lacks the silky texture of the best Pinot/Blauer Burgunders. • $17 • (02/28/98) • **80**

Blauer Zweigelt Qualitätswein Burgenland Riede Hedwighof 1995: Cedar notes add interest to the licorice flavor, but there's not enough fruit to balance the tannin. Medium-bodied. Drink now. • $17 • (02/28/98) • **81**

Zweigelt-Cabernet Burgenland Cuvée Hedwighof 1995: Rich, chewy and concentrated, showing black cherry, plum and smoke notes, all married to a firm structure. Vanilla accents linger on the finish. A good match for food. Best now through 2002. A Zweigelt-Cabernet blend. • $19 • (02/28/98) • **87**

SERVUS

Burgenland White 1994 • $NA • (11/30/95) • **82**

SETZER

Grüner Veltliner Qualitätswein Weinviertel Ried Eichholz 1996: Smells and tastes like white pepper and herbs. A nutty character and a fat texture, yet it's not flabby. Soft and fleshy. Drinkable now. 208 cases made. • $NA • (02/28/98) • **85**

Grüner Veltliner Qualitätswein Weinviertel Ried Eichholz 1995: Has an added dimension of ripeness and amplitude. Already beginning to show a mature marzipan note alongside white peach, tobacco and lentil, it's viscous and medium- to full-bodied, broad, yet with just enough acidity to keep from being flabby. Drink now through 2000. 208 cases made. • $NA • (02/28/98) • **89**

Sauvignon Blanc Qualitätswein Weinviertel Hohenwarther 1995: Lively, crisp and tangy, with moderately intense flavors of lemon alongside character of mineral and grass. 250 cases made. • $NA • (02/28/98) • **84**

SONNHOF

Grüner Veltliner Qualitätswein Kamptal Loiserberg 1996: A racy, delineated white, evoking floral and spicy aromas and flavors. Richly textured in the middle palate, then the crisp acidity takes over. Finishes long. Drink from 1999 to 2003. 650 cases made. • $16 • (02/28/98) • **88**

Pinot Blanc Qualitätswein Kamptal 1996: Full of verve, with floral and mineral notes augmenting the peach and apple character. Beautifully balanced and subtle, with a lingering finish. Drink now. 1,200 cases made. • $16 • (02/28/98) • **88**

Urgesteins-Riesling Kamptal Zöbinger Heiligenstein 1996: Apple flavors are accented by a floral, talcum-powder note that softens the wine despite high acidity. Seems a bit underripe. 500 cases made. • $19 • (02/28/98) • **83**

Key: SS—Spectator Selection CS—Cellar Selection HR—Highly Recommended BB—Best Buy $NA—Price not available Ⓐ—Auction Price (BT)—Barrel Tasting

Dates in parentheses indicate the issues in which the ratings were published.

TEMENT, E. & M.

Morillon Qualitätswein Südsteiermark Zieregg 1995: Vanilla and nutmeg character from new oak works well with the apple and citrus flavors, though it's a bit dominant at this stage. Vibrant and rich, with a long, butterscotch finish, it needs time to settle down. Best from 1999 through 2002. 208 cases made. • $NA • (02/28/98) • **87**

Morillon Qualitätswein Trocken Südsteiermark 1995: Crisp, with good melon and apple flavors, slightly simple. Medium-bodied, clean finish. • $19 • (02/28/97) • **81**

Sauvignon Blanc Qualitätswein Südsteiermark 1996: Richly textured, showing good balance, but the flavors lack vividness and concentration. Still, a pleasant drink. 833 cases made. • $20 • (02/28/98) • **80**

Sauvignon Blanc Qualitätswein Südsteiermark Zieregg 1996: Round and rich, plenty of zippy acidity carries the melon, vanilla and apple flavors to a lingering finish. Best now through 2000. 250 cases made. • $34 • (02/28/98) • **85**

Sauvignon Blanc Qualitätswein Trocken Südsteiermark 1995: Clean and simple, offering melon and citrus aromas and flavors. Light- to medium-bodied, with a light finish. • $20 • (02/28/97) • **84**

Sauvignon Blanc Qualitätswein Trocken Südsteiermark Zieregg 1995: Expressive melon and herb notes are the hallmarks of this direct, fruity Sauvignon. Refreshing, and drinkable now. • $36 • (12/15/96) • **85**

TERRA GALOS

Furmint Beerenauslese Neusiedlersee 1995: A balanced, interesting wine. Pretty honeycomb, spice and tea. Medium body, medium sweet, with smoke, honey and oak. Medium aftertaste. Drink now. • $NA/500ml • (02/28/98) • **87**

Müller-Thurgau Trockenbeerenauslese Neusiedlersee-Hügelland 1995: Big, fat and raisiny. A bit rustic but amazingly concentrated. Gold colored, with an amber hue. Full-bodied and incredibly sweet, with massive raisin, dried fruit flavors and a burnt toffee undertone. Long, long, sweet finish. Drink now. • $NA/375ml • (02/28/98) • **90**

Pinot Noir Trockenbeerenauslese Neusiedlersee-Hügelland 1995: The Pinot Noir flavors of berry and spice are present, along with honey notes, in this sweet and vibrant dessert red. Finishes a little short. • $NA/375ml • (02/28/98) • **87**

THIEL, RICHARD

Pinot Chardonnay Cuvée Qualitätswein Trocken Thermenregion 1995: Medium-bodied and fruity, this has fresh aromas and flavors of melon and vanilla, with fine acidity and an almost off-dry finish. Drink now. • $18 • (02/28/97) • **84**

Riesling Qualitätswein Thermenregion 1996: Ripe and lively, with a spice and nectarine quality backed by a firm, tight structure that needs until 2000 to unfold. Just lacks the extra depth and dimension of the very best. 550 cases made. • $16 • (02/28/98) • **88**

Riesling Qualitätswein Trocken Thermenregion Gumpoldskirchner 1995: Fabulously spicy and slatey on the nose, wonderfully perfumed. The palate, however, doesn't follow through—it's of medium body, moderate flavor-intensity and crisp on the finish. • $14 • (12/15/96) • **86**

Riesling Thermenregion Das Beste Vom 1996: Dry and powerful, with stone, citrus and green plum notes on a medium-bodied frame. Rich texture. Austere, flavorful and long on the finish. Try with roasted pork. 200 cases made. • $20 • (02/28/98) • **88**

Rotgipfler Qualitätswein Trocken Thermenregion 1995: Rich and extroverted, this displays pear and floral flavors, with smoky notes that dovetail into a crisp, dry, minerally finish. Balanced and delicious. Drink now. • $14 • (12/15/96) • **86**

Spätrot Rotgipfler Spätlese Thermenregion 1994: Rather cloying and fat, this has some ripe fruit flavors, but there's a disproportionate amount of sweetness on the finish. • $18 • (02/28/97) • **72**

Zierfandler Gumpoldskirchner Thermenregion Classic Cuvée 1996: Rich and fat, yet it retains enough acidity for balance. The flavors are floral and citrus, the structure will stand up to light foods. 750 cases made. • $20 • (02/28/98) • **83**

Zierfandler-Rotgipfler Trockenbeerenauslese Thermenregion Gumpoldskirchner 1995: Harmonious and well made. More like a dessert wine from white grapes, this displays loads of honey and butter notes, a touch of botrytis and fine, racy acidity. Drink now through 2004. 167 cases made. • $60/375ml • (02/28/98) • **90**

AUSTRIA

TRIEBAUMER, ERNST

Blaufränkisch Qualitätswein Neusiedlersee Ried Oberer Wald 1995: Looks purple and inky, and tastes the same. A spicy, succulent red bursting with ripe, red fruits that seem barely out of the fermenting vat. Not a lot of structure here. 410 cases made. • $22 • (02/28/98) • **85**

Sauvignon Blanc Ruster Ausbruch Neusiedlersee-Hügelland 1995: Intensely spicy, here's an assertive dessert wine showing racy acidity and power to match the apricot, honey and citrus-peel flavors. It finishes a bit hot, but the bold flavors are concentrated and cannot be denied. 200 cases made. • $39 • (02/28/98) • **90**

Traminer Ausbruch Neusiedlersee-Hügelland Ried Mitterkräften 1995: Big and powerful but slightly overdone. Yellow, gold with a green tinge. Spice, honey and almond-skin aromas. Full-bodied and sweet, with loads of botrytis, spice and a long, honey finish. A little hot on the finish. Drink now. 170 cases made. • $35/375ml • (02/28/98) • **88**

UMATHUM

Pinot Noir Qualitätswein Neusiedlersee Junger Berg 1995: Smooth texture, yet the flavors are firm and compact, remaining curranty throughout, with a hint of chocolate. 530 cases made. • $15 • (02/28/98) • **83**

Pinot Noir Qualitätswein Trocken Neusiedlersee Blauburgunder 1994: New oak adds butterscotch character, but there's not enough fruit flavor to match, and the finish is tough. • $20 • (02/28/97) • **78**

Red Qualitätswein Trocken Neusiedlersee Ried Hallebühl 1992: Pretty use of new, toasty oak which marries well with the fruit, but it's a bit too light and lacks the ripeness to merit more attention. Drink now. • $37 • (02/28/97) • **81**

St. Laurent Qualitätswein Trocken Neusiedlersee vom Stein 1993: In a full-blown, exaggerated style with some hints of barnyard flavor and a resinous, woody element. More vegetal than fruity in character. • $38 • (02/28/97) • **74**

Urgesteins-Riesling Halbtrocken Neusiedlersee Hackelsberg 1996: Delicate. Aromas of flowers and limes are followed by apple and mineral flavors. Balanced, appealing presentation. Tangy finish. 125 cases made. • $15 • (02/28/98) • **86**

Zweigelt Qualitätswein Neusiedlersee 1996: A curranty edge runs through this rich, supple red, augmenting the black cherry flavor. Quite full-bodied, with a lingering finish. 2,100 cases made. • $10 • (02/28/98) • **84**

Zweigelt Qualitätswein Trocken Neusiedlersee 1995: Light, thin and rather weedy, with some fruit character and a light structure. • $17 • (02/28/97) • **77**

VELICH

Beerenauslese Neusiedlersee Seewinkel 1995: Intense aromas of honey, apricots, passion fruit and botrytis. Medium weight and intensity, with the exotic flavors up front, but could use a touch more acidity to keep it lively and lingering. • $NA/375ml • (02/28/98) • **87**

Chardonnay Qualitätswein Neusiedlersee Tiglat 1995: An international-style that marries new oak with appley fruit, adding nutmeg and vanilla accents. Well structured and medium-bodied, it's a bit marked by the oak now, but should settle down in the next year. Best now through 2003. • $NA • (02/28/98) • **87**

Muscat Ottonel Beerenauslese Neusiedlersee 1995: Flavor-packed, harmonious wine. Intense aromas of shiitake mushroom and spices with an undertone of lemon, ripe fruit. Full-bodied, medium sweet, with fresh acidity, a long, lemon-and-honey aftertaste. Good length. Drink now or hold. • $NA/375ml • (02/28/98) • **90**

Neuburger Ausbruch Neusiedlersee 1991: Orange-colored, with an amber hue. Toffee, coffee and tobacco aromas. Full-bodied and very oily, medium sweet, with raisiny flavors and a long finish. A bit overdone. Drink now. • $NA/375ml • (02/28/98) • **85**

Welschriesling Trockenbeerenauslese Neusiedlersee 1995: Incredibly viscous and intense, the aromas and flavors range from coconut to apricot and chocolate with a bit of orange-peel. Seems monolithic now, but the vibrant acidity suggests trying in 1999. • $NA/375ml • (02/28/98) • **93**

Welschriesling Trockenbeerenauslese Neusiedlersee 1991: Caramel is the major theme in this rich, sweet wine, but the overall impression is straightforward and simple, lacking intensity and zip. Drinkable now. • $NA/375ml • (02/28/98) • **86**

WALZER, EWALD

Grüner Veltliner Qualitätswein Halbtrocken Kremstal Kremser Gebling 1996: Aroma of pear concentrate is accented by lemon on the palate. Broad, but lacks depth and length. 83 cases made. • $15 • (02/28/98) • **82**

Grüner Veltliner Qualitätswein Halbtrocken Kremstal Kremser Gebling 1995: A mixture of sweet and sour that doesn't quite mesh. 60 cases made. • $23 • (02/28/98) • **76**

Riesling Urgesteins-Riesling Kremstal Kremser Gebling 1995: Earthy aromas give way to almond and peach flavors. Thickly textured, with balance and personality. Drink now. 67 cases made. • $25 • (02/28/98) • **84**

WIENINGER

Chardonnay Kabinett Trocken Vienna 1995: Offering a little more character than is usual for an Austrian Chardonnay, with mineral, honey and straw notes highlighting the apple and melon flavors. Crisp finish. Ready to drink. • $19 • (12/15/96) • **86**

Chardonnay Kabinett Vienna 1996: Well made Chardonnay. Broad apple and nutty aromas and flavors, rich texture, with a lively structure that keeps the whole presentation fresh and interesting. Definitely a food wine. Drink now through 2000. 1,250 cases made. • $15 • (02/28/98) • **86**

Chardonnay Qualitätswein Vienna Grand Select 1995: Rich, oaky and stylish, displaying nutmeg, fig and smoke aromas in addition to appley fruit, this is a very good version of the international style. Firmly structured and dry, it should pair well with food. Drink now through 2001. 125 cases made. • $NA • (02/28/98) • **88**

Chardonnay Qualitätswein Vienna Select 1996: Offering loads of tropical fruit, citrus and vanilla flavors with searingly high acidity, this is appealing, though it doesn't really scream Chardonnay. Needs food. Best now through 2002. 500 cases made. • $22 • (02/28/98) • **84**

Grüner Veltliner Qualitätswein Trocken Vienna Herrenholz 1995: Reveals a ripe, exotic note that adds an extra dimension to the herb and pear flavors. Good weight, concentration and length add up to a tasty wine. Drink now. • $17 • (12/15/96) • **86**

Grüner Veltliner Qualitätswein Vienna Herrenholz 1996: Very perfumed, floral aromas, with flavors of green bean. Thin and awkward. 333 cases made. • $17 • (02/28/98) • **77**

Riesling Kabinett Trocken Vienna 1995: Sleek, spicy and exciting, with a lovely silky texture and zingy fruit character. Medium-bodied, with fine acidity and a long finish. A very good Riesling. • $19 • (12/15/96) • **90**

Riesling Qualitätswein Vienna Select 1996: Inviting talc and rose petal aromas, hints of peach and apple and a firm, minerally structure that turns more lean and austere on the finish. Try with food, now through 2000. 83 cases made. • $15 • (02/28/98) • **86**

WINKLER-HERMADEN

Blauer Zweigelt Qualitätswein Trocken Südoststeiermark 1994: A crisp, berry-flavored red for easy quaffing. Simple and direct. • $12 • (01/31/97) • **78**

Gewürztraminer Qualitätswein Trocken Südoststeiermark 1994: Smells like eggnog, then the butterscotch and vanilla flavors (from new oak) take over. Nowhere in the mix does it say Gewürz. Strange. • $13 • (01/31/97) • **76**

Pinot Gris Qualitätswein Trocken Südoststeiermark 1995: Broad and ripe, it gives an impression of sweetness that is enhanced by a dose of new oak, while maintaining balance and harmony. Ready now. • $13 • (01/31/97) • **88**

WINZER KREMS

Grüner Veltliner Kabinett Trocken Kremstal Kremser Goldberg Kellermeister Privat 1996: Dry and spicy. Nicely balanced, with moderate structure for early drinking. Flavors of herbs and minerals. 2,500 cases made. • $NA • (02/28/98) • **84**

Grüner Veltliner Kabinett Trocken Kremstal Kremser Sandgrube 1996: Succulent. Interesting character of red cherry, almond and lemon. Fresh, with a clean, lingering finish. Drink now. 10,000 cases made. • $NA • (02/28/98) • **84**

Riesling Kabinett Trocken Kremstal Kremser Kremsleiten Kellermeister 1996: A spicy, pungent federspiel/kabinett that shows good depth on an elegant framework. Forward and light, with immediate appeal. Drink now through 2000. 1,667 cases made. • $NA • (02/28/98) • **88**

WINZERHAUS

Blauer Zweigelt Qualitätswein Weinviertel 1996: Elegant, showing currant and strawberry flavors. Medium-bodied, with refreshing, vibrant acidity. Should match light meat and poultry dishes. Drink now through 2000. 5,833 cases made. • $8 • (02/28/98) • **82**

Grüner Veltliner Qualitätswein Weinviertel 1995: Herbal flavors are prominent, but the overall presentation is a bit blunt, with bitterness on the finish. 16,666 cases made. • $8 • (12/15/96) • **78**

Pinot Blanc Beerenauslese Neusiedlersee 1995: Delicate, with honey and apricot character and medium sweetness balanced by refreshing acidity, keeping everything lively and pulsing through the finish. Hints of orange add depth to the flavors. 450 cases made. • $NA/375ml • (02/28/98) • **88**

ZIMMERMANN

Grüner Veltliner Kabinett Kremstal Gedersdorfer Gernlüssen 1995: Very dry, with almond and apple flavors and a touch of citrus that lingers on the finish. Medium-bodied, with a hint of bitterness at the end. A good match for food. 416 cases made. • $NA • (02/28/98) • **84**

Grüner Veltliner Qualitätswein Kremstal Kremser Gebling 1995: A bit closed right now, but shows the density and structure of a great vintage, finishing with tangy acidity. The flavors are celery, lemon and mineral. Try in 2000. 133 cases made. • $NA • (02/28/98) • **88**

Riesling Qualitätswein Kremstal Rohrendorfer Rosshimmel 1995: Distinctive, showing marzipan, beeswax and nectarine flavors on a thick, rich texture that turns dry and tart on the finish. Needs until 2000 to open up. 83 cases made. • $13 • (02/28/98) • **88**

ZULL, FAMILIE

Grüner Veltliner Qualitätswein Trocken Weinviertel Ödfeld 1995: Offers nicely ripe fruit flavors, with almond, orange-peel and grapefruit character. Medium-bodied, with bright acidity and a long, clean finish. • $11 • (12/15/96) • **87**

Riesling Kabinett Trocken Weinviertel Innere Bergen Steinbreiten 1995: Deep, concentrated flavors of pear, citrus and spice resonate throughout. Quite big and powerful, with the fruit, acidity and weight all in harmony. Drinkable now through 2000. • $14 • (12/15/96) • **90**

Riesling Qualitätswein Trocken Weinviertel Innere Bergen 1995: Thick and oily for a Riesling, with honey and spice, especially clove, aromas and flavors. Medium in body, acidity and finish. • $17/500 ml • (12/15/96) • **85**

Key: SS—Spectator Selection CS—Cellar Selection HR—Highly Recommended BB—Best Buy $NA—Price not available Ⓐ—Auction Price (BT)—Barrel Tasting
Dates in parentheses indicate the issues in which the ratings were published.

Chile

Chile has been called a paradise for the production of fine wine. Stretching more than 2500 miles from its northern border in the Atacama Desert to Tierra del Fuego in the south, Chile is squeezed between the cool Pacific in the west and the high Andes Mountains in the east. Because Chile has never been touched by phylloxera, it is one of the few places where vinifera vines can be planted on their own roots, without the necessity of being grafted onto phylloxera-resistant American rootstock. Clean, abundant water from the Andes makes irrigation reliable, and grape vines thrive in Chile's naturally fertile, light soil. Prices for Chilean wines are often quite modest, with many good bottlings in the $6 to $12 range.

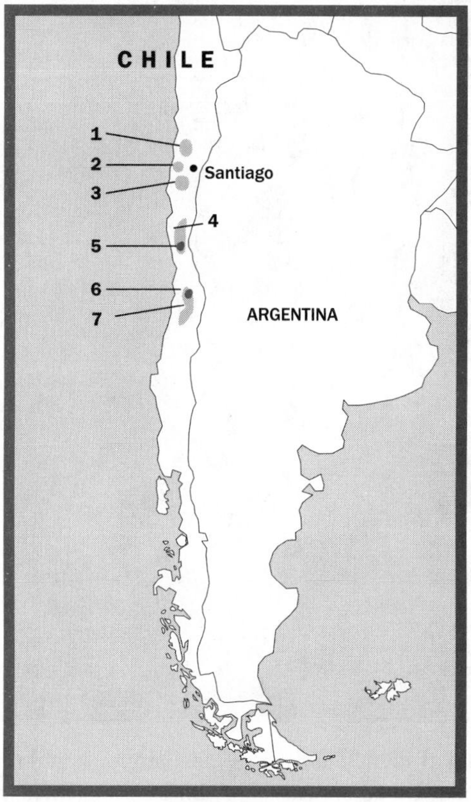

1. Aconcagua
2. Casablanca
3. Maipo
4. Rapel
5. Colchagua
6. Curicó
7. Maule

HISTORY OF CHILEAN WINEMAKING

Chilean viticulture dates back to the 1850s, when a wave of French immigrants settled in the Santiago region, bringing with them native French grape types such as Cabernet Sauvignon, Malbec, Merlot, Sémillon and Sauvignon Blanc. The French winemaking tradition remains strong here. Chilean wines still tend more toward the elegant, European style than they do toward the heavier, more concentrated style found in much of the rest of the New World (though this is partly attributable to the light Chilean soil).

For many years Chile was held back by a lack of capital and foreign investment. As recently as the early 1980s, for example, Chilean wines were still being fermented and aged in wood barrels made from the local rauli (beech) tree. Much of this wood was musty and old, leading to oxidized whites and tired reds that lacked fruit.

The situation changed dramatically in the mid-1980s, when Chile began to aggressively develop its wine industry as a source of export income. Chilean, American and European interests, including Domaine Rothschild (of Lafite), owners of the Los Vascos estate in Peralillo, the Torres family of Spain and Kendall-Jackson of California have invested in the Chilean wine industry, bringing with them the latest winemaking technology. In addition, leading enologists such as Bordeaux's Michel Rolland and California's Greg Upton have been retained as consultants at leading estates.

CHILEAN WINE REGIONS

Located in the northern part of Chile's central valley, a narrow, 300-mile long valley set between the Andes and a coastal range of mountains to the west, is the Maipo Valley. Starting just below Santiago and extending 25 miles south to the town of Buin, the Maipo is the heart of the Chilean wine industry. The wines from vineyards closer to Santiago, such as Cousiño-Macul and the Bruno Paul estate (a joint venture between Bruno Prats of Château Cos-d'Estournel and Paul Pontallier of Château Margaux), have a distinctly earthy taste that is reminiscent of a red Graves. Further south in the Rapel and Maule regions of the valley, a number of newer sub-regions are being quickly developed. These include Lontue, Colchagua, Curicó and Rancagua. Many producers blend wines from a number of these regions, with the object of producing well balanced reds and whites that combine the flavors of several regions.

MAJOR CHILEAN GRAPE VARIETIES

The grounds of Viña Santa Rita in the Maipo Valley south of Santiago.

Mark Vaughn

Much like California wines, Chilean wines are marketed primarily by varietal labeling (for instance, "Chardonnay") rather than by regional appellations such as "Maipo Valley." The most important grape types remain the traditional red and white Bordeaux varieties, with Chardonnay receiving more and more attention.

Cabernet Sauvignon is widely planted. Many Cabernets display the cedary nuances and gentle herbal notes of a red Bordeaux. In place of the old rauli barrels of the past, many winemakers are using combinations of French and American oak to season the wine, adding an appealing vanilla note to the Cabernet varietal character. Concha y Toro, the largest producer, makes wines ranging from light, everyday clarets to impressive oak-aged reservas such as the Don Melchor line, a regular strong performer in *Wine Spectator* tastings. Errazuriz and Santa Rita have also established themselves as fine Cabernet producers.

Because Chilean Cabernet is soft and round, it has rarely needed the softening effect of Merlot to achieve balance. As a result, until recently, Chile had not produced much Merlot, which was thought of primarily as a blending grape. However, with Merlot's rise as a popular varietal in its own right throughout the world, production has increased. Chilean Merlots are of a high quality, displaying soft, luscious fruit and a nice Graves-like *goût de terroir.* Particularly exciting is Casa Lapostolle, whose first two vintages of Merlot Cuvée Alexandre scored very well.

Most Chilean wineries also produce decent, sometimes delicious, white wines. Sauvignon Blanc remains the most consistent of the white varieties. Most is now cold-fermented in stainless steel vats, yielding wines that are fresh and ready to be drunk upon release. A more serious style, made in the manner of a white Graves (using barrel fermentation), is also beginning to appear at a somewhat higher price.

Chardonnay is also becoming important, largely because of the almost insatiable international demand for this popular varietal. Generally warm conditions in many regions have meant that Chilean Chardonnays often lack crispness and definition. Several producers, including Los Vascos, Concha y Toro, Santa Rita and Vina Calina are experimenting with barrel fermentation, lees stirring and more careful selection of grapes in an effort to produce Chardonnays with more character.

ALAMEDA

Cabernet Sauvignon Maipo Valley 1994: Light-bodied, but firm, with aromas of smoke and cedar, flavors of cherries and tomatoes. This is Chile's traditional style. 200,000 cases made. • $5 • (02/28/97) • **82**

Cabernet Sauvignon Maipo Valley 1988 • $6 • (06/15/92) BB • **84**

Cabernet Sauvignon Maipo Valley Santa Maria Vineyard 1993 • $7 • (02/29/96) • **81**

Cabernet Sauvignon Maipo Valley Vintner's Selection 1995: A round red offering well-balanced cherry flavors and firm tannins. Smoky aromas add a rustic note. Drinkable now. 250,000 cases made. • $5 • (02/28/97) • **83**

Cabernet Sauvignon Maipo Valley Vintner's Selection 1993 • $5 • (02/29/96) BB • **85**

Cabernet Sauvignon Maipo Valley Vintner's Selection 1992 • $5 • (04/30/95) BB • **85**

Chardonnay Maipo Valley 1995: Round and soft, with ripe apple, vanilla and light cinnamon flavors that turn slightly sweet on the finish. Makes a pleasant apéritif. 70,000 cases made. • $7 • (02/28/97) • **82**

Chardonnay Maipo Valley Los Arboles Special Reserve 1996: Expressive oak-induced flavors of vanilla and hazelnut provide immediate appeal. Crisp acidity keeps the balance, while apple and melon flavors keep it interesting. 12,500 cases made. • $8 • (05/31/97) • **85**

Chardonnay Maipo Valley Santa Maria Vineyard 1996: Straightforward and quite full on the palate, with clean, crisp acidity softened by vanilla notes and light apple flavors. Fresh, if rather neutral. 150,000 cases made. • $6 • (06/30/97) • **84**

Chardonnay Maipo Valley Santa Maria Vineyard 1994 • $6 • (04/30/95) • **84**

Merlot Maipo Valley Santa Maria Vineyard 1995: A silky wine with a strong backbone. Medium-bodied, with modest cherry, herb and smoke flavors, balanced, and with enough grip to match food. 250,000 cases made. • $6 • (02/28/97) • **83**

Merlot Maipo Valley Santa Maria Vineyard 1994: Plenty of oak, plus firm tannins, with the dark fruit and slightly meaty flavors typical of the varietal. Even if the parts exceed the whole, it's an interesting wine. 200,000 cases made. • $6 • (04/30/97) • **84**

Merlot Maipo Valley Santa Maria Vineyard 1993 • $6 • (02/29/96) BB • **86**

Merlot Maipo Valley Santa Maria Vineyard 1992 • $6 • (06/15/95) • **84**

Merlot Maipo Valley Santa Maria Vineyard 1987 • $6 • (06/15/92) BB • **82**

Sauvignon Blanc Maipo Valley 1995: Crisp, lemony acidity brightens up the palate before giving way to riper flavors of pear and melon on the lingering finish. A subtle style, underpinned by good nerve and intensity. 50,000 cases made. • $5 • (04/30/97) BB • **85**

Sauvignon Blanc Maipo Valley Vintner's Selection 1994 • $5 • (06/30/96) • **81**

ARRIGORRIAGA

Cabernet Sauvignon San Fernando 1996: Black cherry and blackberry flavors are generous in this round red, and the tannins are firm enough for food. Fresh and straightforward; drinkable now. From William Fèvre. • $12 • (06/30/97) • **84**

Chardonnay Maipo Valley 1995: Tasty butterscotch and vanilla flavors stand out in this well-oaked wine, with pineapple and melon flavors to balance, and enough acidity to keep it fresh. From William Fèvre. • $12 • (06/30/97) • **86**

BEL ARBOR

Cabernet Sauvignon Valle Central Vintner's Selection 1996: Cherry and berry flavors are fresh but light in this velvety red, with its soft tannins and accents of spice and toast. A sweet, pretty wine for drinking now. • $6 • (10/31/97) • **83**

Cabernet Sauvignon Valle Central Vintner's Selection 1995: Soft, round and fruity, showing black cherry and licorice flavors with hints of spice and toast. Bright acidity and soft tannins make it appealing now. • $6 • (02/28/97) • **85**

Chardonnay Valle Central Vintner's Selection 1996: Charming Chilean white offers creamy texture with ripe melon and subtle pineapple flavors. Nicely integrated sweet oak notes emerge on the finish. All this at a price that invites you to imbibe freely. 100,000 cases made. • $6 • (02/28/97) BB • **87**

BOLDOS, CHATEAU LOS

Cabernet Sauvignon Requinoa 1995: Ripe and a bit rustic, displaying black cherry, raisin and light earth notes with enough tannin to match food. • $6 • (04/30/97) • **83**

Cabernet Sauvignon Requinoa 1991 • $8 • (06/15/95) • **75**

Chardonnay Requinoa 1996: A full-bore white. Honey, toast and spice flavors and some tropical fruit notes provide the interest. A bit heavy-handed, but it makes an impression. • $8 • (04/30/97) • **86**

Sauvignon Blanc Requinoa 1996: Crisp and light, animated by tart citrus flavors. Refreshing except for a slight metallic note that sneaks into the herbal finish. • $6 • (04/30/97) • **81**

BOUCHON, VIÑEDOS J.

Sauvignon Blanc Maule Valley Las Mercedes 1997: Nutty and earthy aromas and flavors are more prominent than the modest apple ones. 5,000 cases made. • $8 • (05/31/98) • **79**

BRUNO, DOMAINE PAUL

Cabernet Sauvignon Maipo Valley 1994 • $15 • (06/30/96) • **74**

CABALLERO DE CHILE

Cabernet Sauvignon Valle Central Reserva 1995: Earthy and herbal notes predominate in this round, rather soft red. Ripe flavors of plum and raisin are juicy, and soft tannins make it easy to drink. 45,000 cases made. • $7 • (03/31/98) • **82**

Sauvignon Blanc Valle Central Reserva 1996: Despite intriguing herbal, waxy aromas, this soft white turns a bit brassy and dull on the palate. Past its prime. 30,000 cases made. • $6 • (05/31/98) • **79**

CALINA

Cabernet Sauvignon Valle Central 1995: This ripe, fleshy red offers plenty of blackberry and black cherry flavors backed up by sweet, toasty oak notes. It's round and soft, but has enough structure for food. Drink now. Second label of Viña Calina. 5,000 cases made. • $8 • (06/30/97) • **87**

Chardonnay Valle de Itata 1996: This exuberant white shows sweet, simple oak and melon flavors, fresh and juicy. A good beginner's Chardonnay. 5,000 cases made. • $8 • (06/30/97) • **82**

CALITERRA

Cabernet Sauvignon Central Valley 1995: Shows good concentration. Very firm tannins block the plum and black cherry flavors, while the finish is clean but neutral. Try now. • $8 • (10/31/97) • **84**

Cabernet Sauvignon Central Valley Reserva 1995: Cocoa and coffee aromas give way to dark flavors of chocolate, plum and black pepper in this rich, well-structured red. Shows good concentration and balance. Try now. • $12 • (10/31/97) • **87**

Cabernet Sauvignon Maipo Valley 1994: Black cherry, herb and smoke flavors mingle in this firm, lean red. Has some concentration but lacks generosity. Try now. 24,000 cases made. • $8 • (02/28/97) • **83**

Cabernet Sauvignon Maipo Valley 1992 • $NA • (04/30/95) • **78**

Cabernet Sauvignon Maipo Valley 1991 • $6 • (04/30/93) • **83**

Cabernet Sauvignon Maipo Valley 1990 • $5 • (03/15/93) BB • **84**

Cabernet Sauvignon Maipo Valley 1989 • $6 • (06/15/92) BB • **87**

Cabernet Sauvignon Maipo Valley 1988 • $6 • (10/15/91) • **79**

Cabernet Sauvignon Maipo Valley 1987 • $6 • (09/15/90) BB • **86**

Cabernet Sauvignon Maipo Valley 1986 • $6 • (07/31/89) BB • **85**

Cabernet Sauvignon Maipo Valley Reserva 1994: Supple, with a mingling of smoke, bright cherry and tart cranberry flavors. Good concentration. Try now. 5,000 cases made. • $11 • (02/28/97) • **85**

Cabernet Sauvignon Maipo Valley Reserva 1988 • $9 • (12/15/92) • **86**

Chardonnay Aconcagua Valley Reserva 1996: Floral and spicy aromas give way to toast, spice and ripe apple flavors in this silky, well-balanced white. It's fresh and has enough acidity for lighter foods. • $11 • (11/15/97) • **85**

Chardonnay Central Valley 1996: Refreshing, with a clean, lively texture, and good acidity, but the fruit flavors are subtle, almost neutral, with notes of apple, pear and hazelnut. A discreet complement to food. 51,500 cases made. • $8 • (06/30/97) • **84**

Chardonnay Maipo Valley Reserva 1995: Honey and butterscotch flavors give this full-bodied wine a sweet appeal, but there's enough acidity in the apple and melon flavors for balance. Richer than most Chilean Chards. 6,000 cases made. • $11 • (02/28/97) • **87**

Merlot Central Valley 1996: Plump and fruity, this generous red shows plum, chocolate and cola flavors with ripe tannins and a round, soft texture. Big enough for food. Drink now. • $8 • (10/31/97) • **85**

Merlot Curicó Valley 1995: Well balanced, with a pleasantly chewy texture, but the fruit flavors are muted. Try now. 29,000 cases made. • $8 • (02/28/97) • **84**

Sauvignon Blanc Central Valley 1996: Lean and crisp. A straightforward wine with light citrus, herb and apple flavors and plenty of firm acidity. A nice complement to food. 30,000 cases made. • $6 • (02/28/97) • **83**

CANEPA

Cabernet Sauvignon Curicó Magnificum 1990 • $19 • (05/31/95) • **86**

Cabernet Sauvignon Maipo Valley 1995: Vivid cassis aromas are alluring, but the flavors lean toward the herbal and the vegetal, and the tannins are severe. 12,000 cases made. • $7 • (06/30/97) • **76**

Cabernet Sauvignon Maipo Valley 1994 • $7 • (06/30/95) • **82**

Cabernet Sauvignon Maipo Valley 1993 • $6 • (04/30/95) • **79**

Cabernet Sauvignon Maipo Valley 1991 • $6 • (04/30/93) • **82**

Cabernet Sauvignon Maipo Valley 1990 • $6 • (06/15/92) BB • **81**

Cabernet Sauvignon Maipo Valley 1986 • $6 • (06/15/90) • **75**

Cabernet Sauvignon Maipo Valley 1985 • $4 • (11/15/87) • **75**

Cabernet Sauvignon Maipo Valley Finisimo 1983 • $9 • (06/30/90) • **76**

Cabernet Sauvignon Maipo Valley Finisimo Estate Reserve 1990 • $NA • (06/30/96) • **83**

Cabernet Sauvignon Maipo Valley Private Reserve 1994: Sweet oak and ripe plum flavors with unusually tart acidity. Refreshing, if a bit off-balance. Try now. 9,000 cases made. • $10 • (04/30/97) • **83**

Cabernet Sauvignon Maipo Valley Private Reserve 1993: Lush and ripe. With vivid berry and sweet vanilla flavors and a hint of game underneath, this is concentrated but a bit disjointed; sacrifices harmony for power. • $10 • (02/28/97) • **85**

Cabernet Sauvignon Maipo Valley Private Reserve 1992 • $8 • (04/30/95) BB • **88**

Cabernet Sauvignon Maipo Valley Reserva 1988 • $6 • (06/15/90) BB • **84**

Cabernet Sauvignon-Malbec Curicó 1996: Soft and simple, offering the grapey fruitiness of a Beaujolais nouveau. Try slightly chilled; drink now. 10,000 cases made. • $6 • (02/28/97) • **77**

Cabernet Sauvignon-Malbec Curicó 1994 • $5 • (10/31/95) • **85**

Cabernet Sauvignon-Malbec Maipo Valley 1984 • $4 • (03/15/88) • **74**

Cabernet Sauvignon-Malbec Sagrada Familia 1993 • $5 • (05/31/95) • **84**

Chardonnay Rancagua 1996: Lively fruit flavors of melon, pineapple and banana complement a buttery vanilla character. A firm core of acidity holds it all together. 15,000 cases made. • $7 • (02/28/97) • **85**

Chardonnay Rancagua 1994 • $6 • (04/30/95) • **84**

Chardonnay Rancagua Private Reserve 1995: Bold and muscular in style. Toasty oak aromas jump from the glass, as do the pineapple and melon flavors, and remain vivid through this full-bodied wine. Bigger than most Chilean Chards, but well balanced. Offers real value at this price and score. 10,000 cases made. • $9 • (05/31/97) BB • **87**

Merlot Curicó 1996: Light, fresh and fruity, almost like a Beaujolais nouveau. Shows pleasant cherry candy flavors and a soft texture. 20,000 cases made. • $7 • (04/30/97) • **83**

Merlot Curicó 1994 • $6 • (06/15/95) • **81**

Merlot Maipo Valley 1990 • $6 • (06/15/92) BB • **84**

Merlot Maipo Valley 1988 • $6 • (06/30/90) BB • **79**

Sauvignon Blanc Curicó 1996: Tart lemon and pineapple flavors are bright and crisp. Light and clean, it's refreshing but needs food to soften the pucker. 20,000 cases made. • $6 • (02/28/97) • **83**

Sauvignon Blanc Curicó 1994 • $5 • (05/15/95) • **85**

CARMEN

Cabernet Sauvignon Maipo Valley 1993 • $6 • (06/30/96) • **78**

Cabernet Sauvignon Maipo Valley 1990 • $6 • (05/31/94) • **70**

Cabernet Sauvignon Maipo Valley Alto Jahuel 1990 • $6 • (07/15/93) BB • **82**

Key: SS—Spectator Selection CS—Cellar Selection HR—Highly Recommended BB—Best Buy $NA—Price not available Ⓐ—Auction Price (BT)—Barrel Tasting
Dates in parentheses indicate the issues in which the ratings were published.

Cabernet Sauvignon Maipo Valley Alto Jahuel Reserve 1989 • $8 • (07/15/93) • **81**

Cabernet Sauvignon Maipo Valley Barrel Select Gold Reserve 1993 • $18 • (01/31/95) • **86**

Cabernet Sauvignon Maipo Valley Gold Reserve 1993: Spice and cedar accents add depth to the ripe plum and raisin flavors. Velvety, with good concentration and balance. Showing some maturity. Drink now. 2,000 cases made. • $25 • (02/28/97) • **86**

Cabernet Sauvignon Maipo Valley Grand Vidure Reserve 1995: A fruit-driven wine with bright blackberry and cherry flavors and a silky texture. Not complex, but it draws you back for another sip. Enjoyable now. 4,000 cases made. • $13 • (02/28/97) • **86**

Cabernet Sauvignon Maipo Valley Grand Vidure Reserve 1994: Bright flavors of blackberry and toast make a vivid impact in this round, chewy red. It's vibrant and fresh. Drink now. • $12 • (02/28/97) • **85**

Cabernet Sauvignon Maipo Valley Reserve 1995: Good depth here. Deeply colored, highly extracted, with concentrated dark fruit flavors and plenty of toast and spice notes. Tannins are firm yet well integrated. Drinkable now. 15,000 cases made. • $13 • (06/30/97) • **88**

Cabernet Sauvignon Maipo Valley Reserve 1994: Solid, with some complexity. Ripe plum and black cherry flavors nicely framed by toasty oak and supported by firm yet well-integrated tannins. Balanced and clean. Drink now. • $10 • (01/01/97) • **87**

Cabernet Sauvignon Maipo Valley Reserve 1992 • $10 • (06/30/96) • **78**

Cabernet Sauvignon Maipo Valley Reserve 1991 • $9 • (01/31/95) • **80**

Cabernet Sauvignon Maipo Valley Reserve 1990 • $8 • (05/31/94) • **72**

Cabernet Sauvignon Rapel Valley 1992 • $6 • (04/30/95) BB • **87**

Cabernet Sauvignon Valle Central 1994: Supple and straightforward, with light cherry and licorice flavors. What it lacks in concentration, it makes up in harmony. 60,000 cases made. • $8 • (01/01/97) • **83**

Chardonnay Maipo Valley Reserve 1995: Straightforward, clean and showing good varietal character. Its apple, light citrus and vanilla flavors are well balanced and fresh. 1,600 cases made. • $14 • (02/28/97) • **84**

Chardonnay Maipo Valley Reserve 1994 • $9 • (04/30/95) BB • **87**

Chardonnay Rapel Valley 1994 • $6 • (02/28/95) BB • **84**

Chardonnay Valle Central 1996: A mix of sweet cooked-apple and earth flavors leaves this a bit flat on the palate. It's round and soft, but not enticing. 50,000 cases made. • $8 • (02/28/97) • **79**

Chardonnay Valle Central 1995 • $6 • (06/30/96) • **83**

Merlot Maipo Valley Alto Jahuel 1990 • $6 • (01/31/94) • **80**

Merlot Maipo Valley Reserve 1993 • $9 • (01/31/95) • **85**

Merlot Maule Valley 1994 • $6 • (05/31/96) • **82**

Merlot Maule Valley 1993 • $6 • (06/15/95) • **83**

Merlot Maule Valley Reserve 1994 • $10 • (05/31/96) • **80**

Merlot Rapel Valley 1992 • $6 • (05/31/94) • **82**

Merlot Rapel Valley Reserve 1995: Lush and velvety, packed with ripe plum and blackberry flavors accented with plenty of vanilla, mint and spice notes and supported by round tannins. Lots of voluptuous, up-front pleasure in this red from Chile. 4,000 cases made. • $13 • (02/28/97) HR • **89**

Merlot Rapel Valley Reserve 1993 • $9 • (05/15/95) BB • **88**

Merlot Valle Central 1995: Ripe, rich and fleshy, with plum, chocolate and spice flavors wrapped in mouth-coating tannins and finishing hot with alcohol. Shows concentration. Try now. • $8 • (02/28/97) • **85**

Petite Sirah Maipo Valley Reserve 1995: Brawnier than most Chilean reds, from its dark purple color to its firm tannins and layer of smoky oak. The flavors range from plum to licorice to black pepper, and linger on the finish. 1,000 cases made. • $13 • (06/30/97) • **87**

Sauvignon Blanc Casablanca Valley Reserve 1997: Aromas of pineapple and lime follow through on the palate in this ripe, exuberant white. It's well balanced and refreshing, akin to the New Zealand style of Sauvignon Blanc. • $15 • (05/31/98) • **86**

Sauvignon Blanc Casablanca Valley Reserve 1996: Vibrant with bright citrus and pear aromas followed by pear, herb and smoke flavors. It's lively and flavorful, with good varietal character. 3,000 cases made. • $13 • (02/28/97) • **86**

Sauvignon Blanc Rapel Valley 1996: Straightforward, simple apple and light herb flavors. Clean but a bit diluted. An easy apéritif, but won't stand up to any but the lightest foods. 19,000 cases made. • $8 • (02/28/97) • **80**

Sauvignon Blanc Rapel Valley 1995 • $6 • (06/30/96) • **78**

Sauvignon Blanc Rapel Valley 1994 • $6 • (05/15/95) • **87**

Sauvignon Blanc Valle Central 1997: Light and crisp, this lean white offers smoke, mineral and citrus flavors with a firm backbone of acidity. Good with shellfish. • $8 • (05/31/98) • **83**

CARTA VIEJA

Cabernet Sauvignon Maule Valley 1995: Light and simple, with herb and berry flavors and light, firm tannins. A modest accompaniment to lighter dishes. • $5 • (06/30/97) • **80**
Cabernet Sauvignon Maule Valley 1994: Round and supple, with thick black cherry and toast flavors, soft tannins and a jammy, slightly sweet finish. A quaffing wine for early drinking. • $5 • (02/28/97) • **83**
Cabernet Sauvignon Maule Valley 1993 • $4 • (04/30/95) • **82**
Cabernet Sauvignon Maule Valley 1991 • $4 • (05/31/94) • **76**
Cabernet Sauvignon Maule Valley 1990 • $4 • (02/28/93) BB • **81**
Cabernet Sauvignon Maule Valley 1987 • $6 • (06/15/91) • **78**
Cabernet Sauvignon Maule Valley 1986 • $4 • (06/15/90) • **75**
Cabernet Sauvignon Maule Valley Antiqua Selection 1988 • $8 • (04/30/93) • **76**
Cabernet Sauvignon Maule Valley Antiqua Selection 1986 • $8 • (06/15/91) • **75**
Chardonnay Maule Valley 1996: Apple and citrus flavors are light and clean in this tart white, then fade quickly. A pleasant apéritif. • $5 • (06/30/97) • **80**
Chardonnay Maule Valley 1995: Fresh, clean and rather neutral in style. With its lively acidity and modest apple and citrus flavors, it makes a crisp backdrop for food. • $5 • (02/28/97) • **83**
Chardonnay Maule Valley 1994 • $4 • (04/30/95) • **78**
Merlot Maule Valley 1996: Light and fresh, offering alluring aromas of chocolate and black cherry, but it turns a bit bitter on the finish. Soft enough for drinking now. • $5 • (06/30/97) • **80**
Merlot Maule Valley 1993 • $4 • (06/15/95) • **80**
Merlot Maule Valley 1991 • $4 • (02/28/93) BB • **81**
Sauvignon Blanc Maule Valley 1996: Herbal and grasslike notes predominate in this light, tart white. Acidic on its own, but may soften with food. • $5 • (06/30/97) • **79**
Sauvignon Blanc Maule Valley 1995: Pretty pear aromas give way to searing acidity and a touch of earthiness in this hard, tart wine. Try with food. • $5 • (02/28/97) • **78**

CASAS DEL TOQUI, LAS

Cabernet Sauvignon Cachapoal 1995 • $10 • (06/30/96) • **84**
Cabernet Sauvignon Totihue-Cachapoal Valley Réserve 1995: Clean and polished, with toasty oak aromas and flavors framing the berry and light herb flavors. Tannins are firm; finish is spicy but a bit dry. A solid wine. 11,000 cases made. • $9 • (10/31/97) • **85**
Cabernet Sauvignon Totihue-Cachapoal Valley Réserve Prestige 1995: A healthy dollop of oak gives this ripe red attractive vanilla and toast nuances that marry well with the bright berry and black cherry flavors. Tannins are firm but well integrated. Drink now. 3,000 cases made. • $12 • (10/31/97) • **87**
Chardonnay Cachapoal Grande Réserve 1995 • $10 • (06/30/96) • **83**
Chardonnay Totihue-Cachapoal Valley 1996: Has some decent pear and apple flavors, but it ends up somewhat coarse. 14,500 cases made. • $7 • (10/31/97) • **78**
Chardonnay Totihue-Cachapoal Valley Grande Réserve 1996: A good, quaffable Chardonnay with pear and spice flavors. A bit awkward on the finish, but nothing out of bounds. 6,500 cases made. • $10 • (10/31/97) • **82**
Sémillon Cachapoal 1995 • $8 • (06/30/96) • **78**
Sémillon Totihue-Cachapoal Valley 1996: Smoky, herbal aromas and flavors give a distinctive personality, and it has the body and balance to stand up to food. Not much fruit, but a peachy note emerges on the finish. 13,000 cases made. • $6 • (10/31/97) • **83**

CASTILLO DEL RIO

Chardonnay Chile 1995: Straightforward, with crisp, clean, fresh apple flavors. Simple, but refreshing. 4,000 cases made. • $6 • (06/30/97) • **83**
Merlot-Cabernet Sauvignon Chile 1995: Sharp and firmly tannic, with earth and licorice notes predominating. Turns slightly bitter on the finish. 4,000 cases made. • $6 • (06/30/97) • **77**
Merlot Chile 1995: Black cherry and herb flavors mingle in this soft, fleshy red. Firm tannins emerge on the finish. It's sturdy, and will stand up to food. 4,000 cases made. • $6 • (06/30/97) • **84**
Sauvignon Blanc Chile 1995: Lively, fresh and well balanced, with apple, citrus and light herb flavors, and a pleasant hint of vanilla. Focused and food-friendly. 2,000 cases made. • $6 • (06/30/97) • **87**

CONCHA Y TORO

Cabernet Sauvignon Maipo 1989 • $5 • (04/30/93) • **81**
Cabernet Sauvignon Maipo 1984 • $5 • (04/30/88) BB • **89**
Cabernet Sauvignon Maipo Casillero del Diablo 1995: Rich yet vivid, this fleshy red balances toasty oak and ripe fruit flavors with notes of plum, vanilla and chocolate, all echoing on the long finish. From a Chilean producer known for good wine at good value. 8,000 cases made. • $10 • (05/31/97) BB • **86**
Cabernet Sauvignon Maipo Casillero del Diablo Reserva Special 1984 • $7 • (11/15/87) • **85**
Cabernet Sauvignon Maipo Pirque Vineyard Casillero del Diablo 1992 • $8 • (04/30/95) • **82**
Cabernet Sauvignon Maipo Pirque Vineyard Casillero del Diablo 1984 • $9 • (06/15/92) • **74**
Cabernet Sauvignon Maipo Pirque Vineyard Casillero del Diablo Special Reserve 1991 • $9 • (05/31/94) • **81**
Cabernet Sauvignon Maipo Pirque Vineyard Casillero del Diablo Special Reserve 1988 • $9 • (12/15/92) • **81**
Cabernet Sauvignon Maipo Puente Alto Vineyard Don Melchor Private Reserve 1994: This big, highly extracted reserve shows interesting ripe flavors of plum, black olive, toast and mint, with very firm tannins and a rather hot finish. Not many Chilean reds offer this much structure and concentration, but it's no surprise from this reputable estate. Try now. 4,000 cases made. • $23 • (05/31/97) HR • **90**
Cabernet Sauvignon Maipo Puente Alto Vineyard Don Melchor Private Reserve 1993 • $16 • (06/30/96) CS • **91**
Cabernet Sauvignon Maipo Don Melchor Private Reserve 1991 • $13 • (04/30/95) • **87**
Cabernet Sauvignon Maipo Don Melchor Private Reserve 1990 • $13 • (04/15/94) • **84**
Cabernet Sauvignon Maipo Puente Alto Vineyard Don Melchor Private Reserve 1989 • $14 • (07/15/93) • **78**
Cabernet Sauvignon Maipo Puente Alto Vineyard Don Melchor Private Reserve 1988 • $15 • (04/30/93) • **74**
Cabernet Sauvignon Maipo Puente Alto Vineyard Don Melchor Private Reserve 1987 • $13 • (06/30/90) • **85**
Cabernet Sauvignon Maipo Puente Alto Vineyard Marqués de Casa Concha 1994: Smoke and herb flavors keep this firm red austere, but it's well balanced, with very good concentration, and has the grip for food. Try now. 2,000 cases made. • $13 • (05/31/97) • **86**
Cabernet Sauvignon Maipo Puente Alto Vineyard Marqués de Casa Concha 1991 • $10 • (05/31/94) • **81**
Cabernet Sauvignon Maipo Puente Alto Vineyard Marqués de Casa Concha 1989 • $11 • (06/30/96) • **76**
Cabernet Sauvignon Maipo Puente Alto Vineyard Marqués de Casa Concha 1988 • $11 • (04/30/93) • **73**
Cabernet Sauvignon Maipo Puente Alto Vineyard Marqués de Casa Concha 1987 • $9 • (06/15/92) • **67**
Cabernet Sauvignon Maipo Puente Alto Vineyard Marqués de Casa Concha Special Reserve 1983 • $8 • (09/15/90) • **75**
Cabernet Sauvignon Maipo Special Reserve 1981 • $6 • (04/30/88) • **80**
Cabernet Sauvignon Maipo Valley Trio 1995: Smoke, earth and herbs are the predominant flavors in this medium-bodied but tough-textured red. It has real grip, but lacks finesse. Try now. 20,000 cases made. • $9 • (11/30/97) • **84**
Cabernet Sauvignon Maipo Valley Trio 1994 • $8 • (06/30/96) • **84**
Cabernet Sauvignon-Merlot Rapel 1990 • $5 • (04/30/93) • **78**
Cabernet Sauvignon-Merlot Rapel 1988 • $5 • (07/31/92) • **79**
Cabernet Sauvignon-Merlot Rapel 1986 • $4 • (09/15/90) BB • **80**
Cabernet Sauvignon-Merlot Valle Central 1997: Ripe-tasting, with some good dark plum, chocolate and leather flavors. Has an appetizing gamy note on the finish. Smooth, ready to drink. • $8/1.5 liter • (05/15/98) • **82**
Chardonnay Aconcagua Valley Casillero del Diablo 1996: Muscular, with toasty oak and ripe melon flavors, as well as firm acidity. Has more impact than most Chilean whites, with perhaps a shade too much oak for true balance. • $10 • (05/31/97) • **85**
Chardonnay Casablanca Valley Amelia Private Reserve 1995: Exuberant and jammed with tropical fruit, smoke and butter flavors. It's ripe, yet has enough acidity to complement food. 1,500 cases made. • $15 • (05/31/97) • **86**
Chardonnay Casablanca Valley Casillero del Diablo 1994 • $9 • (06/30/96) • **84**
Chardonnay Casablanca Valley Trio 1996: Tangy tropical fruit flavors and aromas give this white some punch, but a toasty, nearly charred note on the

finish drags it down. May settle down with food. 30,000 cases made. • $9 • (11/15/97) • **82**
Chardonnay Casablanca Valley Trio 1995 • $8 • (06/30/96) • **84**
Chardonnay Maipo Valley Santa Isabel Vineyard Marqués de Casa Concha 1994 • $10 • (04/30/95) • **85**
Chardonnay Maipo Valley Santa Isabel de Pirque Marqués de Casa Concha 1995: Light and crisp, this marries delicate apple and melon flavors with light vanilla notes. Balanced and clean on the finish. 2,000 cases made. • $13 • (05/31/97) • **85**
Chardonnay Valle Central 1997: A nice, fruity wine with pear and honey flavors and an appealing mineral note. A good, clean-tasting Chardonnay. • $8/1.5 liter • (05/15/98) • **84**
Merlot Peumo Valley Trio 1996: Here's yet another value-quality combination from this Chilean winery. This beguiling red offers a pleasing medley of toasty oak, chocolate and ripe blackberry flavors, with accents of game and herbs. Soft and juicy on the palate, it's made for drinking now. 50,000 cases made. • $9 • (11/15/97) BB • **85**
Merlot Peumo Valley Trio 1995 • $8 • (06/30/96) • **85**
Merlot Rapel 1990 • $5 • (04/30/93) BB • **83**
Merlot Rapel 1986 • $4 • (03/15/90) • **76**
Merlot Rapel Casillero del Diablo 1996: A soft and fleshy red from Chile, dark and delicious with its ripe plum, licorice and black coffee flavors. Light tannins and a fruity finish tie it up with a bow. It's balanced, easy drinking and fairly priced. 10,000 cases made. • $10 • (06/30/97) BB • **86**
Merlot Rapel Peumo Vineyard Casillero del Diablo 1994 • $8 • (05/15/95) • **85**
Merlot Rapel Peumo Vineyard Marqués de Casa Concha 1994: This big red offers ripe fruit and good concentration, with voluptuous plum and coffee flavors underpinned by ripe, firm tannins. It's a gutsy, well-balanced wine that should improve through 2000. 3,000 cases made. • $13 • (06/30/97) • **89**
Merlot Rapel Peumo Vineyard Marqués de Casa Concha 1993 • $10 • (05/15/95) BB • **89**
Merlot Rapel Peumo Vineyard Marqués de Casa Concha 1992 • $10 • (05/31/94) • **85**
Merlot Rapel Peumo Vineyard Marqués de Casa Concha 1990 • $11 • (04/30/93) • **76**
Merlot Rapel Peumo Vineyard Marqués de Casa Concha 1989 • $9 • (05/15/92) • **85**
Merlot Valle Central 1997: A plush Merlot, with a pleasant core of plum flavors and a good herbal edge. Finishes on a slightly sweet note. • $8/1.5 liter • (05/15/98) • **83**
Sauvignon Blanc Curicó Valley Sunrise 1996: The toast and vanilla flavors show an oak influence that overwhelms the apple and pear in this round white. Has just enough acidity for balance, and finishes clean. • $NA • (05/31/98) • **82**
Sauvignon Blanc Maipo Valley Casillero del Diablo 1996: Round, with flavors of fig, apple and melon, vanilla notes and a creamy texture; even so, it retains enough acidity for balance. 2,000 cases made. • $10 • (06/30/97) • **86**
Sauvignon Blanc Maipo Valley Casillero del Diablo 1994 • $8 • (05/15/95) • **86**

CONO SUR

Cabernet Sauvignon 1993 • $6 • (04/30/95) • **82**
Cabernet Sauvignon Selection Reserve 1992 • $10 • (04/30/95) • **85**
Pinot Noir 1994 • $6 • (04/15/95) • **80**
Pinot Noir Selection Reserve 1994 • $10 • (04/15/95) • **81**

COUSIÑO-MACUL

Cabernet Sauvignon Maipo Valley 1995: Raisin, leather and herb flavors are ripe in this unusually evolved red. Has plenty of stuffing but lacks fresh fruit. • $6 • (06/30/97) • **80**
Cabernet Sauvignon Maipo Valley 1991 • $7 • (05/31/94) • **79**
Cabernet Sauvignon Maipo Valley 1990 • $8 • (04/30/93) • **75**
Cabernet Sauvignon Maipo Valley 1988 • $8 • (05/15/92) • **81**
Cabernet Sauvignon Maipo Valley 1987 • $6 • (09/15/90) • **71**
Cabernet Sauvignon Maipo Valley 1986 • $8 • (09/15/90) • **72**
Cabernet Sauvignon Maipo Valley 1984 • $5 • (02/15/89) BB • **86**
Cabernet Sauvignon Maipo Valley 1983 • $6 • (05/15/88) BB • **85**
Cabernet Sauvignon Maipo Valley Antiguas Reservas 1993: Firmly structured, with plum, smoke and burnt toast flavors. Distinctive, but lacks sufficient fruit for balance. • $9 • (06/30/97) • **80**
Cabernet Sauvignon Maipo Valley Antiguas Reservas 1990 • $9 • (06/15/95) • **82**
Cabernet Sauvignon Maipo Valley Antiguas Reservas 1989 • $12 • (05/31/94) • **80**
Cabernet Sauvignon Maipo Valley Antiguas Reservas 1988 • $11 • (04/30/93) • **74**
Cabernet Sauvignon Maipo Valley Antiguas Reservas 1987 • $10 • (06/15/92) • **82**
Cabernet Sauvignon Maipo Valley Antiguas Reservas 1986 • $10 • (05/31/92) • **83**
Cabernet Sauvignon Maipo Valley Antiguas Reservas 1985 • $11 • (10/15/91) • **81**
Cabernet Sauvignon Maipo Valley Antiguas Reservas 1984 • $9 • (09/15/90) • **77**
Cabernet Sauvignon Maipo Valley Antiguas Reservas 1981 • $9 • (02/15/89) • **80**
Cabernet Sauvignon Maipo Valley Antiguas Reservas 1980 • $8 • (05/15/88) • **80**
Chardonnay Maipo Valley 1996: Ripe melon and banana flavors turn almost sweet with thick vanilla notes in this round, soft white. Needs a bit more acidity, but has an immediate appeal. • $8 • (06/30/97) • **83**
Chardonnay Maipo Valley 1995: Ripe and round, with melon and light honey flavors and a slight smoke note on the finish. Soft, easy to drink. • $7 • (06/30/97) • **83**
Finis Terrae Maipo Valley 1993: This big, powerful red is packed with ripe fruit, toasty oak and firm tannins. Shows good varietal character, and a smoky, herbal note typical of Maipo. Lacks clarity, but will stand up to the richest foods. • $30 • (06/30/97) • **87**
Finis Terrae Maipo Valley 1992 • $25 • (06/30/96) • **83**
Merlot Maipo Valley 1994: Black cherry and plum flavors are appealing, but a slightly burnt note detracts and firm tannins grip tightly on the finish. Try now. • $14 • (06/30/97) • **81**
Merlot Maipo Valley Limited Release 1991 • $11 • (06/15/95) • **78**
Merlot Maipo Valley Limited Release 1990 • $11 • (05/31/94) • **83**
Merlot Maipo Valley Limited Release 1989 • $11 • (05/31/92) • **85**
Merlot Maipo Valley Limited Release 1988 • $11 • (05/31/92) • **84**

CRANE LAKE

Cabernet Sauvignon Colchagua Valley 1992 • $5 • (04/30/95) BB • **86**
Merlot Colchagua Valley 1992 • $5 • (06/15/95) • **84**
Sauvignon Blanc Colchagua Valley 1994 • $5 • (06/15/95) • **79**

CREMASCHI FURLOTTI

Cabernet Sauvignon Maule Valley 1995: Smoky, toasty aromas give way to light berry and chocolate flavors that barely register under the mouthfilling tannins of this overoaked red. It has appealing elements, but lacks balance. • $8 • (10/31/97) • **81**
Chardonnay Maule Valley 1996: This very crisp white is quite lively, with vanilla, herb and light apple flavors. A bit disjointed, but it finishes clean and refreshing. • $8 • (10/31/97) • **83**

DE MARTINO

Cabernet Sauvignon Maipo Valley 1995: Fresh and straightforward, this red is quite tannic, with cherry, black olive and herb flavors. Not that expressive on its own, but a good match for hearty dishes. 50,000 cases made. • $9 • (11/30/97) • **84**
Cabernet Sauvignon Maipo Valley Prima Reserve 1995: This polished red offers a deft mix of toast, coffee, ripe plum, black olive and licorice flavors. The structure is firm, but the wine is lively and balanced. Drink now. 25,000 cases made. • $12 • (10/31/97) • **87**
Cabernet Sauvignon Maipo Valley Prima Reserve 1994 • $5 • (02/29/96) • **84**
Cabernet Sauvignon Maipo Valley Prima Reserve 1993 • $8 • (02/29/96) • **87**
Cabernet Sauvignon Maipo Valley Santa Ines Vineyard 1991 • $6 • (04/30/95) • **77**
Cabernet Sauvignon Maipo Valley Santa Ines Vineyard 1990 • $5 • (03/15/93) BB • **85**

Key: SS—Spectator Selection CS—Cellar Selection HR—Highly Recommended BB—Best Buy $NA—Price not available Ⓐ—Auction Price (BT)—Barrel Tasting
Dates in parentheses indicate the issues in which the ratings were published.

Carmenère Maipo Valley 1996: Vivid plum, licorice and smoke flavors give this lively red distinctive character. It has light tannins and lacks a bit of structure. Accessible now. 5,000 cases made. • $9 • (10/31/97) • **83**

Carmenère Maipo Valley Prima Reserve 1996: This chewy red offers plum, licorice and smoke flavors, with thick texture and firm tannins. Has enough structure to stand up to food. Drinkable now. 3,000 cases made. • $12 • (10/31/97) • **85**

Chardonnay Maipo Valley 1996: This big-boned white makes an impact on the palate with its muscular acidity and toasty oak flavors. Its fruit flavors are rather neutral, with light notes of apple and lime, but it should match well with food. 7,300 cases made. • $9 • (10/31/97) • **84**

Chardonnay Maipo Valley Prima Reserve 1996: Vanilla and toast flavors dominate this medium-bodied white. There's enough acidity to keep it lively, but it lacks fruit for balance. For fans of oak. 7,200 cases made. • $12 • (10/31/97) • **83**

Chardonnay Maipo Valley Prima Reserve 1995 • $6 • (02/29/96) • **81**

Malbec Maipo Valley 1996: This vivid red packs a real punch of flavor, with smoky, gamy notes giving way to ripe cherry and plum flavors. Balanced and fresh, it's drinkable now through 2000. 5,000 cases made. • $9 • (10/31/97) • **84**

Malbec Maipo Valley Prima Reserve 1996: This firm red shows polished, ripe black cherry and toast flavors and meaty, smoky notes. Try now. 3,000 cases made. • $12 • (10/31/97) • **86**

Merlot Maipo Valley 1996: Leans towards the meaty, herbal side of the varietal, with light plum notes. It has firm tannins and a clean finish with coffee accents. Drinkable now. 17,300 cases made. • $9 • (10/31/97) • **83**

Merlot Maipo Valley Prima Reserve 1994 • $6 • (02/29/96) • **82**

Merlot Maipo Valley Santa Ines Vineyard 1993 • $6 • (06/15/95) • **80**

Sauvignon Blanc Maipo Valley 1996: Quite rich, with melon, pineapple and vanilla flavors and firm acidity. It's powerful enough to match with food, though a light earthy note on the finish detracts a bit. 25,500 cases made. • $9 • (10/31/97) • **83**

Sauvignon Blanc Maipo Valley Prima Reserve 1996: A round, silky white, offering sunny flavors of melon, apple and cream, with just enough acidity to keep it fresh. Not much varietal flavor, but tasty. 3,900 cases made. • $10 • (10/31/97) • **84**

Sauvignon Blanc Maipo Valley Prima Reserve 1995 • $7 • (02/29/96) • **83**

Sauvignon Blanc Maipo Valley Santa Ines Vineyard 1994 • $6 • (06/15/95) • **78**

DOÑA SOL

Cabernet Sauvignon Colchagua Valley 1992 • $6 • (04/30/95) • **85**

Chardonnay Colchagua Valley 1994 • $6 • (04/30/95) • **81**

Merlot Colchagua Valley 1992 • $6 • (06/15/95) • **77**

Sauvignon Blanc Colchagua Valley 1994 • $6 • (06/15/95) • **80**

DONOSO, CASA

Cabernet Sauvignon Maule Valley 1993: The ripe blackberry and light herb flavors show varietal character, and it's well concentrated. A healthy dollop of oak adds sweet vanilla and smoke flavors. • $9 • (04/30/97) • **88**

Chardonnay Maule Valley 1996: This lively white shows a mix of apple, banana and cream flavors. Appealing, but a bit simple. An easy quaff. • $10 • (06/30/97) • **82**

Merlot Maule Valley 1996: This velvety red offers deep plum, blackberry and toast flavors, thick on the palate but only moderately tannic. It's balanced and well defined. • $9 • (04/30/97) • **86**

Sauvignon Blanc Maule Valley 1996: A medium-bodied white showing good structure, but the flavors are rather subdued, with light pear and almond notes. A modest complement to simple dishes. • $9 • (04/30/97) • **82**

ECHEVERRIA

Cabernet Sauvignon Molina 1996: Good grip in this firmly structured red, but the tannins nearly overwhelm the black cherry, cola and herb flavors. Try now. 30,000 cases made. • $7 • (06/30/97) • **84**

Cabernet Sauvignon Molina 1995: Smoke and earth aromas give way to plum and wood flavors in this firm red. It shows more structure than generosity. Try now. 30,000 cases made. • $7 • (06/30/97) • **85**

Cabernet Sauvignon Molina Reserva 1995: A gorgeous red in the international style, this has plenty of vanilla and chocolate oak notes, ripe, lush, black-fruit flavors and a firm, polished texture. It's more a showstopper than a food wine, but appealing nonetheless. 20,000 cases made. • $9 • (06/30/97) • **88**

Cabernet Sauvignon Molina Reserva 1994: Light body and supple texture, with bright black cherry and licorice flavors. Vivid and well defined. Not an ager, but pleasant to drink now. 30,000 cases made. • $9 • (02/28/97) • **84**

Chardonnay Molina Reserva 1996: Pretty aromas of vanilla and toast give way to a smooth texture and round flavors of vanilla, melon and lime in this luscious white from Chile. It's well balanced and firm enough for food. Represents solid value for all that it offers. 10,000 cases made. • $9 • (10/31/97) BB • **86**

Chardonnay Molina Unwooded 1996: Bright acidity enlivens the modest apple and pear flavors. Fresh, light-bodied, simple but refreshing. 8,000 cases made. • $7 • (02/28/97) • **81**

Sauvignon Blanc Molina 1996: Rich and round. With its melon, fig and light honey flavors, this tastes almost Californian in style, with a hint of fruity sweetness balancing the moderate acidity. 20,000 cases made. • $6 • (02/28/97) BB • **86**

EDWARDS, LUIS FELIPE

Cabernet Sauvignon Chile Pupilla 1995: Herb and black olive aromas say Cabernet, and black cherry and plum flavors back it up. This is a balanced, fruity wine for drinking now. • $7 • (04/30/97) • **86**

Cabernet Sauvignon Colchagua 1994: Smoke and bell pepper flavors dominate this medium-bodied yet firmly tannic red. Tasted twice, with consistent notes. • $8 • (06/30/97) • **79**

Cabernet Sauvignon Colchagua Reserva 1994: Simple and a bit cloying, with strong flavors of vanilla and toasty oak that override the light cherry and berry flavors. • $12 • (06/30/97) • **79**

Chardonnay Colchagua 1996: A nice balance of smoky oak and crisp, clean fruit gives this wine allure. The peach, vanilla and orange flavors draw you back for another sip. • $8 • (04/30/97) • **87**

ERRAZURIZ

Cabernet Sauvignon Aconcagua Valley 1987 • $9 • (09/15/90) • **82**

Cabernet Sauvignon Aconcagua Valley 1985 • $5 • (09/15/88) • **82**

Cabernet Sauvignon Aconcagua Valley Don Maximiano Antigua Reserva 1984 • $7 • (09/15/88) BB • **87**

Cabernet Sauvignon Aconcagua Valley Don Maximiano Estate Reserva 1995: This rugged red offers plum, coffee and herb flavors, wrapped around very firm tannins. Though a bit hot and coarse, it has concentration and distinctive character. 8,000 cases made. • $15 • (02/28/98) • **84**

Cabernet Sauvignon Aconcagua Valley Don Maximiano Estate Reserva 1994: Distinctive and exuberant, this vibrant red offers mint, cassis, coffee and cigar-box flavors, with good concentration, ripe, firm tannins and a long, spicy finish. Though not a textbook Cabernet, it shows more character than most Chilean reds. Try now. 7,000 cases made. • $15 • (10/31/97) • **89**

Cabernet Sauvignon Aconcagua Valley Don Maximiano Estate Reserva 1993 • $12 • (10/31/95) • **87**

Cabernet Sauvignon Aconcagua Valley Don Maximiano Estate Reserva 1991 • $9 • (04/15/94) • **82**

Cabernet Sauvignon Aconcagua Valley Don Maximiano Estate Reserva 1990 • $9 • (04/30/93) • **88**

Cabernet Sauvignon Aconcagua Valley Don Maximiano Estate Reserva 1989 • $10 • (06/15/92) • **87**

Cabernet Sauvignon Aconcagua Valley Don Maximiano Estate Reserva 1988 • $9 • (06/15/92) • **85**

Cabernet Sauvignon Aconcagua Valley Don Maximiano Estate Special Reserva 1993: Distinctive mint and herb notes give character to this rich wine. It's ripe and concentrated, with massive tannins and lots of plum, cassis and raisin flavors. Impressive, though not for everyone. 1,500 cases made. • $25 • (04/30/97) • **88**

Cabernet Sauvignon Aconcagua Valley Don Maximiano Estate Special Reserva 1989 • $9 • (04/30/93) • **83**

Cabernet Sauvignon Aconcagua Valley El Ceibo Estate 1996: From Chile comes this muscular red, showing firm tannins under chocolate, licorice, black olive and plum flavors. A good, affordable option in Cabernet, it's rich enough for food and balanced enough to improve through 2000. 60,000 cases made. • $9 • (10/31/97) BB • **86**

Cabernet Sauvignon Aconcagua Valley Reserva 1993: The cherry and herb flavors are undermined by a persistent earthy note. Medium-bodied, but dryly tannic. 7,000 cases made. • $15 • (06/30/97) • **78**

Cabernet Sauvignon Curicó Valley El Descanso Estate 1995: A soft and lush, ripe and round Cabernet, with plum, cinnamon and chocolate flavors, velvety texture and enough tannin to hold it in focus. A good match for beef or lamb dishes and inexpensive enough for everyday drinking. 45,000 cases made. • $9 • (04/30/97) BB • **87**

Chardonnay Casablanca Valley La Escultura Estate 1997: This soft, easy-drinking white offers floral aromas and flavors of apple, honey and smoke. The texture is creamy, the finish clean and short. 45,000 cases made. • $9 • (03/31/98) • **82**

Chardonnay Casablanca Valley La Escultura Estate 1996: Light and soft, with tropical fruit aromas that fade on the palate. A polished but simple wine with a short finish. 45,000 cases made. • $9 • (04/30/97) • **82**

Chardonnay Casablanca Valley La Escultura Estate Reserva 1996: A smooth white, displaying ripe apple and melon flavors with light herbal accents. It's clean but a bit soft; serve well chilled. 7,000 cases made. • $15 • (10/31/97) • **83**

Chardonnay Casablanca Valley Reserva 1995: Good intensity and adequate balance. The tropical fruit, honey and spice flavors are bold, but the wine is heavy, with just enough acidity to keep it on its feet. 7,000 cases made. • $15 • (04/30/97) • **84**

Chardonnay Casablanca Valley Wild Ferment 1996: A round, firm white, with apple, toast and lemon flavors that are clean, balanced and harmonious and linger on the finish, drawing you back for another sip. 1,000 cases made. • $19 • (10/31/97) • **87**

Chardonnay Maipo Valley Wild Ferment 1995: Full-bodied, almost oily, with very ripe, tropical fruit flavors that are almost sweet. Heavy with vanilla notes. An unusual style for Chile, but has a voluptuous appeal. 500 cases made. • $19 • (05/31/97) • **86**

Chardonnay Maule Valley 1995 • $NA • (10/31/95) • **78**

Chardonnay Maule Valley Reserva 1994 • $12 • (10/31/95) • **84**

Don Maximiano Founder's Reserve Aconcagua Valley 1994: This full-bodied red shows more concentration than character, as the ripe, plush flavors of plum, prune, chocolate and tobacco are dominated by the thick texture and full tannins. Try now. A blend of 87 percent Cabernet Sauvignon, 8 percent Merlot and 5 percent Cabernet Franc. 1,600 cases made. • $25 • (10/31/97) • **89**

Merlot Aconcagua Valley Reserva 1996: Power with finesse. Deep color, vibrant aromas of crushed blackberry and dark chocolate, a muscular but balanced texture and ripe fruit flavors combine in this powerful yet still refreshing red. Harmonious enough to give pleasure now and should improve through 2000. 600 cases made. • $19 • (10/31/97) • **89**

Merlot Aconcagua Valley Reserva 1995: Rich and smooth, with ripe flavors of blackberry and plum, sweet as jam. There's plenty of tannin for backbone, but it's well integrated, and the harmony continues through the lingering finish. 200 cases made. • $19 • (04/30/97) • **88**

Merlot Curicó Valley El Descanso Estate 1996: Bright cherry flavors, with a hint of herbaceousness, run through this silky, light-bodied Merlot. An easy quaff for drinking now. 50,000 cases made. • $9 • (04/30/97) • **82**

Merlot Maule Valley 1994 • $8 • (06/30/96) • **75**

Merlot Maule Valley 1992 • $8 • (03/31/93) BB • **85**

Merlot Maule Valley 1991 • $8 • (12/15/92) • **83**

Sauvignon Blanc Casablanca Valley La Escultura Estate 1997: Exuberant aromas of tropical fruit give way to more straightforward flavors of apple and lime in this round yet crisp wine. Well balanced, with a clean, fresh finish. 38,000 cases made. • $8 • (05/31/98) • **84**

Sauvignon Blanc Casablanca Valley La Escultura Estate 1996: Tropical flavors of mango and pineapple give personality, while firm acidity keeps it crisp. Fresh and light, it's a fine apéritif. 25,000 cases made. • $8 • (04/30/97) • **85**

Sauvignon Blanc Late Harvest Casablanca Valley 1996: A bold, striking dessert wine that's sweet, rich, lively and concentrated. Like taking Sauvignon into another dimension. 600 cases made. • $7/375ml • (10/31/97) • **88**

Sauvignon Blanc Late Harvest Casablanca Valley 1995: Like an herb-infused liqueur, this sweet wine is velvety, lush and flavored with apricot, candied lemon and herb notes. A well-made curiosity. 350 cases made. • $7/375ml • (04/30/97) • **87**

Sauvignon Blanc Maule 1995 • $8 • (02/29/96) • **80**

GARZAS, LAS

Cabernet Sauvignon Colchagua Valley 1990 • $7 • (04/30/93) • **80**

Cabernet Sauvignon Colchagua Valley Proprietor Reserve 1990 • $7 • (05/31/94) • **77**

Key: SS—Spectator Selection CS—Cellar Selection HR—Highly Recommended BB—Best Buy $NA—Price not available Ⓐ—Auction Price (BT)—Barrel Tasting

Dates in parentheses indicate the issues in which the ratings were published.

JOYA, CHATEAU LA

Sauvignon Blanc Colchagua Valley 1996: Herbal and smoky aromas give way to lean, very crisp flavors of citrus and mineral. Rather tart and austere on its own, but should complement grilled fish. • $8 • (05/31/98) • **82**

JULIA, CASA

Merlot San Fernando Valley 1995: Balanced but a bit diluted, showing cherry, herb and mildly vegetal flavors and slightly lean tannins. 4,500 cases made. • $8 • (02/28/97) • **79**

Sauvignon Blanc Lontue Valley 1996: Vivid, with round apple and fig flavors mingling with fresh herbal notes. Shows better definition than most Chilean whites, and finishes with an appetizing bitterness. 4,000 cases made. • $8 • (06/30/97) • **85**

L'HÉRITAGE

Brut Chile 1993: This smells spoiled and vegetal, and tastes bitter and coarse. Tasted twice, with consistent notes. 3,500 cases made. • $10 • (07/31/96) • **63**

LAPOSTOLLE, CASA

Cabernet Sauvignon Colchagua 1994 • $9 • (06/30/96) BB • **87**

Cabernet Sauvignon Rapel Valley 1995: Lean, with tart cranberry and light herb flavors. Fresh and firmly tannic. Has balance; try now. • $10 • (05/31/97) • **85**

Cabernet Sauvignon Rapel Valley Cuvée Alexandre 1995: This big red shows ripe plum, licorice and tar notes over powerful tannins, with a long fruity, smoky finish. Impressive. Try now. • $15 • (06/30/97) • **89**

Chardonnay Casablanca Valley Cuvée Alexandre 1995: Lush, ripe and full-bodied, with serious oak flavors of butter and vanilla, apple and melon notes underneath. Rich, but comes across a bit heavy-handed. • $15 • (05/31/97) • **85**

Chardonnay Colchagua Selection 1994 • $9 • (10/31/95) • **81**

Chardonnay Rapel Valley 1995: A little age has softened this wine and accentuated its herbal notes, while a rich overlay of wood adds sweet vanilla flavors. A bit dull. • $10 • (06/30/97) • **81**

Merlot Colchagua Selection 1994 • $9 • (05/15/95) • **87**

Merlot Rapel Valley 1995: The black cherry flavor is enticing, but the oak influence is a bit raw, with blunt, toasty flavors and aggressive tannins. May settle down with food. • $10 • (04/30/97) • **83**

Merlot Rapel Valley Cuvée Alexandre 1995: Richly textured, packed with ripe blackberry, plum, chocolate and tobacco flavors with muscular but well-integrated tannins, this shows more definition and depth than most Chilean Merlots. A beautiful example of the international style, it's delicious now. 10,000 cases made. • $15 • (04/30/97) • **90**

Merlot Rapel Valley Cuvée Alexandre 1994 • $15 • (06/30/96) HR • **90**

Sauvignon Blanc Colchagua 1995 • $8 • (06/30/96) • **76**

Sauvignon Blanc Colchagua 1994 • $7 • (05/15/95) • **85**

Sauvignon Blanc Rapel Valley 1996: Soft, round and full-bodied, with coconut and vanilla flavors and a strongly smoky finish. Has character, but not of typical Sauvignon Blanc. Tasted twice, with consistent notes. • $10 • (06/30/97) • **80**

LURTON, J. & F.

Chardonnay Lontue Valley Araucano 1996: Firm and nicely balanced, with ripe melon and apple flavors, a judicious touch of toasty oak and enough acidity to match well with food. It's clean, with pleasant smoky notes that linger on the finish. • $7 • (10/31/97) • **86**

Merlot Lontue Valley 1995: This solid red offers black cherry, coffee and herb flavors, with firm, slightly drying tannins that shut down the finish. Big enough for food; try now. • $7 • (10/31/97) • **84**

Sauvignon Blanc Lontue Valley Araucano 1996: Crisp and clean. Basically neutral in flavor with light notes of apple and herb, but it makes a refreshing apéritif. • $7 • (10/31/97) • **80**

MAISON DU LAC

Cabernet Sauvignon Maipo Valley 1994: Friendly fruit, a mix of fresh and candied cherries and a sweet vanilla note give this simple appeal. Firm tannins give it a chance with food. • $6 • (02/28/97) • **83**

Cabernet Sauvignon Maipo Valley 1989: Hanging in there. Though it hasn't developed much complexity, it still shows firm structure and some fresh cherry flavor. Try with food. 3,000 cases made. • $6 • (02/28/97) • **83**

Merlot Maipo Valley 1994: Attractive, vibrant berry and cherry flavors, with chocolate accents and enough tannin for balance. Not a big wine, but pleasant now. • $8 • (02/28/97) • **84**

Merlot Maipo Valley 1992: Coffee and smoke flavors overwhelm the modest fruit flavors of this medium-bodied, dry red. 3,000 cases made. • $7 • (02/28/97) • **74**

Merlot Maipo Valley 1990 • $7 • (01/31/94) • **81**

MONTES

Cabernet Sauvignon Curicó Valley 1994: Herb and bell pepper flavors predominate in this light red. Offers some sweet cherry fruit and light tannins. 15,000 cases made. • $10 • (02/28/98) • **79**

Cabernet Sauvignon Curicó Valley 1993: Oak plus ripe fruit equals this soft red with nearly sweet flavors of cherry jam and vanilla. It's appealing at first, a bit cloying after a few sips. 20,000 cases made. • $8 • (04/30/97) • **84**

Cabernet Sauvignon Curicó 1992 • $8 • (06/30/96) • **84**

Cabernet Sauvignon Curicó 1991 • $8 • (02/29/96) BB • **88**

Cabernet Sauvignon Curicó 1990 • $8 • (04/30/95) • **78**

Cabernet Sauvignon Curicó 1989 • $8 • (05/31/94) • **80**

Cabernet Sauvignon Curicó Valley La Finca Estate 1995: Notes of blackberry and bell pepper mingle in this lean, firm wine. It's well focused, but lacks generosity. May show more breadth with food. 6,000 cases made. • $9 • (04/30/97) • **84**

Cabernet Sauvignon Curicó Valley Montes Alpha 1994: Ripe and fruity, this pretty red offers bright cherry, blueberry and blackberry flavors with spicy oak accents and enough tannin to keep it firm. The ripe fruit lingers on the finish. 5,000 cases made. • $17 • (03/31/98) • **87**

Cabernet Sauvignon Curicó Valley Montes Alpha 1993: A rich wine with good varietal character, this Chilean Cabernet is concentrated, well balanced and seamlessly presented, integrating smoky oak notes, ripe, sweet blackberry flavors and ripe tannins. A fine match for hearty foods. 10,000 cases made. • $15 • (04/30/97) BB • **89**

Cabernet Sauvignon Curicó Montes Alpha 1992 • $14 • (06/30/96) • **78**

Cabernet Sauvignon Curicó Montes Alpha 1991 • $14 • (06/15/95) • **87**

Cabernet Sauvignon Curicó Montes Alpha 1990 • $14 • (04/30/95) • **84**

Cabernet Sauvignon Curicó Montes Alpha 1989 • $12 • (02/28/94) • **78**

Cabernet Sauvignon Curicó Montes Alpha Private Selection 1988 • $14 • (05/15/92) • **87**

Cabernet Sauvignon Curicó Villa Montes 1993 • $7 • (02/29/96) • **82**

Cabernet Sauvignon Curicó Villa Montes 1992 • $6 • (04/30/95) • **83**

Cabernet Sauvignon Curicó Villa Montes 1991 • $6 • (02/28/94) • **79**

Cabernet Sauvignon Curicó Villa Montes 1990 • $6 • (02/28/93) BB • **84**

Cabernet Sauvignon Curicó Villa Montes 1989 • $6 • (06/15/92) BB • **84**

Cabernet Sauvignon Curicó Villa Montes 1988 • $4 • (02/15/90) • **73**

Cabernet Sauvignon Curicó Villa Montes 1987 • $7 • (02/15/90) BB • **84**

Cabernet Sauvignon Curicó Villa Montes Special Selection 1987 • $12 • (09/15/90) • **84**

Chardonnay Curicó Montes Alpha Special Cuvée 1995 • $NA • (06/30/96) • **79**

Chardonnay Curicó Montes Alpha Special Cuvée 1994 • $10 • (06/15/95) • **85**

Chardonnay Curicó Valley Oak Barrel Fermented 1996: Sweet vanilla notes dominate this round, somewhat flat white. Light apple flavors are submerged; finish is a bit cloying. 25,000 cases made. • $8 • (04/30/97) • **78**

Chardonnay Curicó Oak Barrel Fermented 1995 • $8 • (02/29/96) • **79**

Chardonnay Curicó Oak Barrel Fermented 1994 • $8 • (04/30/95) • **84**

Chardonnay Curicó Valley Special Cuvée 1996: A wine to sink your teeth into. Buttery but balanced, with delicious pear, ripe apple and cream flavors. Spicy notes on the finish. 10,000 cases made. • $16 • (10/31/97) • **87**

Fumé Blanc Curicó Valley 1996: Fleshy and round, with smoke and hazelnut flavors more prominent than fruity ones. Distinctive, but lacks classic varietal character, instead echoing traditional Chilean domestic style. 1,500 cases made. • $9 • (02/28/97) • **84**

Malbec Colchagua 1996: Well made, marked by bright fruit flavor, good balance and the gamy, licorice note typical of the varietal. Medium-bodied, with moderate tannins, it's pleasant for drinking now. 10,000 cases made. • $8 • (06/30/97) • **87**

Malbec Colchagua 1995 • $8 • (06/30/96) • **86**

Merlot Curicó 1991 • $8 • (01/31/94) • **82**

Merlot Curicó 1990 • $8 • (04/30/93) BB • **83**

Merlot Curicó Montes Alpha Special Reserve Aged in French Oak 1994 • $14 • (06/30/95) • **86**

Merlot Curicó Special Cuvée 1994 • $8 • (05/31/96) • **85**

Merlot Curicó Special Cuvée 1993 • $8 • (12/31/95) • **86**

Merlot Curicó Valley Montes Alpha 1995: Round and ripe, with luscious, jammy flavors of plum and cassis mingling with sweet vanilla notes. Made in a lush, California style, it's irresistible, but perhaps not perfect for food. 5,000 cases made. • $15 • (05/31/97) • **89**

Merlot Curicó Valley Montes Alpha Special Reserve 1994: Appealing, oak-induced flavors of vanilla and light toast are dominant, but there's enough black cherry flavor to keep the balance, and enough tannin for food. • $10 • (04/30/97) • **85**

Merlot Curicó Valley Special Cuvée 1996: There's a Spanish accent to this spicy, cinnamon-scented red, with its smooth texture, predominant oak and sweet cherry flavors. Not an ager, it offers easy drinking now. 20,000 cases made. • $9 • (10/31/97) • **83**

Merlot Curicó Valley Special Cuvée 1995: Perked up by bright berry and cherry flavors, with a pleasant hint of chocolate on the finish. It's fresh, lively and harmonious. 20,000 cases made. • $8 • (04/30/97) • **85**

Merlot Curicó Valley Special Cuvée 1992 • $8 • (05/31/94) • **83**

Merlot Curicó Villa Montes 1995 • $7 • (05/31/96) BB • **85**

Merlot Curicó Villa Montes 1994 • $8 • (02/29/96) • **83**

Merlot Curicó Villa Montes 1993 • $7 • (06/15/95) • **83**

Merlot Curicó Villa Montes 1991 • $7 • (01/31/94) • **80**

Merlot Curicó Valley Villa Montes 1989 • $7 • (09/15/90) • **79**

Sauvignon Blanc Curicó Valley Fumé Blanc 1997: This lush, vanilla-scented white has distinctive personality, with a nice mix of oaky and citrusy flavors, and enough acidity to keep it fresh. Not a classic Sauvignon Blanc, but will please fans of oak. 12,000 cases made. • $9 • (05/31/98) • **84**

Sauvignon Blanc Curicó Villa Montes 1994 • $6 • (06/15/95) • **77**

MONTGRAS

Cabernet Sauvignon Colchagua Valley 1996: Spicy oak aromas draw you into this balanced, fruity red. Ripe plum flavors are supported by round, ripe tannins, and the finish is spicy and long. A well-crafted wine for drinking now. • $8 • (10/31/97) • **86**

Cabernet Sauvignon Colchagua Valley 1995: Light, fresh berry and herb flavors are dominated by heavy, drying tannins in this flavorful but unbalanced red. May soften with food. • $8 • (10/31/97) • **78**

Cabernet Sauvignon Colchagua Valley 1994: Aggressive flavors of tobacco and game give this tannic red a hard edge. There's cherry flavor, too. Tasted twice, with consistent notes. • $8 • (02/28/97) • **78**

Cabernet Sauvignon Colchagua Valley Reserva 1995: Sweet vanilla flavors dominate this fleshy red, with black cherry and toast notes under firm tannins. Has good concentration, and will please fans of oak. • $11 • (06/30/97) • **84**

Chardonnay Colchagua Valley 1996: Smoky, almost charred, oak aromas and flavors dominate this light-bodied white. It has good, crisp acidity, but lacks fruit to balance the oak. • $8 • (10/31/97) • **82**

Chardonnay Colchagua Valley 1995: Tempting hazelnut and apple flavors run through this balanced white. It aims for elegance rather than power and largely hits the mark. • $8 • (02/28/97) • **85**

Merlot Colchagua Valley 1996: Fresh and balanced, its flavors of chocolate and cherry backed by firm but unobtrusive tannins make a clean, lively wine that's accessible now. • $8 • (10/31/97) • **84**

Merlot Colchagua Valley 1995: Offers ripe red berry and light smoke flavors; bright acidity keeps it lively. Light and fresh, with good, straightforward varietal character. Drink now. • $8 • (02/28/97) • **84**

MOONSHINE VINEYARD

Merlot Rancagua Valley 1994: Packed with flavors of sweet blackberry and chocolate. Round and soft on the palate. Doesn't have serious structure, but it's delightful now. 12,000 cases made. • $12 • (06/30/97) • **85**

MORNING STAR

Cabernet Sauvignon Rapel Valley 1995: This lush red offers plenty of toast and cola notes from oak aging, and just enough plum flavor for balance. Soft on the palate. 17,000 cases made. • $8 • (06/30/97) • **84**

Merlot Rapel Valley 1995: This straightforward red offers cherry and grape flavors with hints of vanilla. It's supple and fresh. 13,600 cases made. • $8 • (06/30/97) • **81**

PARTAGER

Cabernet Sauvignon Maule Valley 1995: Light-bodied but dry-textured, with brown sugar and raisin flavors that taste added-on. This is jug wine with a varietal label. • $10/1.5 liter • (02/28/97) • **75**

Chardonnay Maule Valley 1995: Light and simple, with a musty undertone. A jug wine with little varietal character. • $10/1.5 liter • (02/28/97) • **73**

PIDUCO CREEK

Cabernet Sauvignon Maule Valley 1995: Fleshy, with jammy berry and prune flavors that are thick and a bit soft. Has good concentration but lacks focus. • $7 • (06/30/97) • **83**

Chardonnay Maule Valley 1996: In a straightforward style, with apple and light vanilla flavors in a round body. Quite delicate, it's best as an apéritif. • $7 • (04/30/97) • **83**

Merlot Maule Valley 1996: This grapey red tastes like a nouveau, with herbal and smoky accents that leave a slightly bitter finish, some black cherry flavors and light tannins. • $7 • (06/30/97) • **79**

Sauvignon Blanc Maule Valley 1996: Light and lively, offering green apple and herb flavors, with good acidity keeping them fresh. A slight earthy note competes with the fruit, but will fade with food. • $7 • (04/30/97) • **80**

CHILE

PLAYA, LA

Cabernet Sauvignon Maipo Valley 1992 • $6 • (06/30/96) • **61**

Cabernet Sauvignon Maipo Valley 1989 • $6 • (05/31/94) • **77**

Cabernet Sauvignon Maipo Valley 1988 • $5 • (04/30/93) BB • **81**

Cabernet Sauvignon Maipo Valley 1986 • $4 • (03/15/90) • **74**

Cabernet Sauvignon Maipo Valley Estate Reserve 1992: Evolving nicely, this is soft but still fresh, with sweet cherry and vanilla flavors and supple tannins. Won't stand up to rich foods, but it's pleasant on its own. 4,000 cases made. • $10 • (04/30/97) • **84**

Cabernet Sauvignon Maipo Valley Estate Reserve 1990 • $8 • (06/15/95) • **72**

Cabernet Sauvignon Maipo Valley Estate Reserve 1988 • $8 • (05/31/94) • **81**

Chardonnay Maipo Valley 1995 • $6 • (02/29/96) • **78**

Merlot Maipo Valley 1994: Nice, smooth, with good fruit flavors and enough complexity to hold interest. Enjoyable, easy to drink. 60,000 cases made. • $6 • (04/30/97) • **84**

Merlot Maipo Valley 1990 • $6 • (05/31/94) BB • **86**

Merlot Maipo Valley 1988 • $5 • (04/30/93) BB • **81**

Merlot Maipo Valley 1987 • $4 • (03/15/90) • **75**

Merlot Maipo Valley Reserve 1994: Smooth, polished and handsome. A tasty, seamlessly made Merlot with rather light tannins, subtle fruit and oak flavors that are well integrated and a lingering, spicy finish. 2,500 cases made. • $12 • (04/30/97) • **88**

PORTA, CASA

Cabernet Sauvignon Cachapoal Valley 1996: Soft and round, this simple red offers black cherry and herb flavors over light but slightly drying tannins. Drinkable, but anonymous. • $7 • (10/31/97) • **79**

Chardonnay Central Valley 1996: Though clean and fresh, this medium-bodied white is almost neutral in flavor, with hints of apple, toast and lime. Well balanced, but lacks personality. • $7 • (11/15/97) • **82**

Sauvignon Blanc Rapel Valley 1997: Juicy, with bright, citrusy acidity and round flavors of apple and melon. It's simple but clean, with enough body to stand up to food. 1,500 cases made. • $6 • (05/31/98) • **82**

PORTAL DEL ALTO

Cabernet Sauvignon Maipo Valley 1992 • $4 • (05/31/94) • **77**

Cabernet Sauvignon Maipo Valley 1990 • $4 • (03/15/93) BB • **84**

Cabernet Sauvignon Maipo Valley 1987 • $3 • (06/15/92) BB • **83**

Cabernet Sauvignon Maipo Valley 1984 • $3 • (03/15/90) • **77**

Cabernet Sauvignon Maipo Valley Gran Reserva 1989 • $4 • (04/30/93) • **72**

Key: SS—Spectator Selection CS—Cellar Selection HR—Highly Recommended BB—Best Buy $NA—Price not available Ⓐ—Auction Price (BT)—Barrel Tasting

Dates in parentheses indicate the issues in which the ratings were published.

Cabernet Sauvignon Maipo Valley Gran Reserva 1986 • $3 • (06/15/92) BB • **79**

Cabernet Sauvignon Maipo Valley Gran Reserva 1983 • $4 • (09/15/90) BB • **82**

Merlot Maipo Valley 1992 • $4 • (05/31/94) • **78**

Merlot Maipo Valley 1990 • $4 • (04/30/93) • **77**

Sauvignon Blanc Maipo Valley 1997: This round white has good body, with clean flavors of lemon and herb. There's not much fruit flavor to balance the acidity, but a light vanilla note adds interest. • $7 • (05/31/98) • **81**

PROSPERITY

Merlot Colchagua Valley 1995: Straightforward and soft, with ripe cherry flavor and sweet vanilla accents. Not much structure, but balanced. Made by Firestone Vineyard in California. Drink now. • $7 • (02/28/97) • **83**

RABAT, DOMAINE

Cabernet Sauvignon Colchagua Valley Apalta Vineyard Reserva 1990 • $7 • (04/30/95) • **85**

Cabernet Sauvignon Maipo Valley 1991 • $5 • (04/30/95) • **72**

Merlot Colchagua Valley Apalta Vineyard Reserva 1992 • $7 • (06/15/95) • **86**

RACO, CAVAS DEL

Cabernet Sauvignon Alto Maipo 1990 • $10 • (06/30/96) • **71**

Cabernet Sauvignon Maipo Valley 1994: Very ripe and somewhat top-heavy, marked by flavors of candied fruit, smoke and herb. Has personality. 3,300 cases made. • $8 • (06/30/97) • **80**

Chardonnay Maipo Valley 1995: Garish. Overdone herb and vanilla aromas give way to a flabby wine with little fruit or definition. A poor bet with food. 3,300 cases made. • $8 • (04/30/97) • **76**

RIVER FALLS

Cabernet Sauvignon Colchagua 1995: Straightforward, with cherry flavors that taste jammy, almost cooked. Supple on the palate, but firm on the finish; try with food. 20,000 cases made. • $7 • (02/28/97) • **82**

Chardonnay Colchagua 1995: Soft and light, with a touch of sweetness to its apple, vanilla and butter flavors. It's harmonious, if not very intense. 20,000 cases made. • $7 • (02/28/97) • **82**

Merlot Colchagua 1994 • $6 • (12/31/95) • **83**

Merlot Maule 1995: Plum, raisin and chocolate flavors give a sweet, soft appeal. Round tannins add some structure, but it's a bit short on acidity. Drinkable now. 20,000 cases made. • $7 • (02/28/97) • **84**

SAINT MORILLON

Cabernet Sauvignon Lontue 1995: This light red offers cherry and marked herb flavors. A bit soft and diluted but clean and fresh on the finish, with light cocoa flavors from oak. 25,000 cases made. • $7 • (03/31/98) • **82**

Cabernet Sauvignon Lontue 1993: Dried cherry and vanilla flavors give pleasant sweetness, and soft tannins make it drinkable now. A soft, rather simple red. • $7 • (06/30/97) • **83**

Cabernet Sauvignon Lontue 1992 • $5 • (04/30/95) • **76**

Cabernet Sauvignon Lontue 1986 • $5 • (10/15/91) BB • **83**

Cabernet Sauvignon Lontue 1985 • $4 • (09/15/90) • **75**

Cabernet Sauvignon Maipo 1990 • $6 • (05/31/94) BB • **85**

Cabernet Sauvignon Maipo 1987 • $6 • (03/15/93) BB • **81**

Cabernet Sauvignon Maipo 1986 • $5 • (07/31/92) • **76**

Chardonnay Lontue 1997: This soft white tastes like candy, with strong caramel and honey notes, dripping over cooked apple and banana flavors. 18,000 cases made. • $7 • (03/31/98) • **77**

Chardonnay Lontue 1996: Crisp and rather light, with straightforward flavors of apple and light smoke with good acidity. A modest wine that will complement food. • $7 • (06/30/97) • **83**

Merlot Lontue 1995: Nice toast, coffee and black cherry flavors. Quite spritzy on the palate. Tasted twice, with consistent notes. • $7 • (06/30/97) • **68**

Sauvignon Blanc Lontue 1997: Sharp acidity and modest fruit combine to make this lean white tart and neutral. Try now as a spritzer. 15,000 cases made. • $7 • (05/31/98) • **78**

Sauvignon Blanc Lontue 1995: This has snap and heft. It's rich for Sauvignon Blanc, but still lively with acidity. Flavors are pleasant—citrus and hay—with an herbal note at the finish. • $6 • (07/31/96) • **83**

Sauvignon Blanc Lontue 1994 • $5 • (06/15/95) • **79**

SAN CARLOS

Cabernet Sauvignon Colchagua Valley 1995: Ripe flavors are appealing, but strong vegetal and smoke notes and aggressive tannins throw it out of balance. • $7 • (06/30/97) • **77**
Cabernet Sauvignon Colchagua Valley 1994: Supple, with good varietal character and black cherry, herb and black olive flavors. Just enough grip for food. • $6 • (06/30/97) • **83**
Cabernet Sauvignon Colchagua Valley 1991 • $7 • (10/31/95) • **77**
Chardonnay Colchagua 1995 • $6 • (10/31/95) • **82**
Chardonnay Colchagua Valley 1996: Round, with ripe apple, light vanilla and smoke flavors running through, this wine is expressive, but soft and short on the finish. • $6 • (06/30/97) • **82**
Malbec Colchagua Valley 1996: This exuberant, polished red offers bright black cherry and attractive smoke flavors, with light but firm tannins and light oak notes. Shows good varietal character. • $7 • (06/30/97) • **86**
Malbec Colchagua Valley Oak Aged 1994 • $6 • (02/29/96) • **86**
Merlot Colchagua Valley 1996: Firm, with plenty of ripe black cherry flavors, but an earthy note detracts from the pleasure. The finish is clean and long. Try now. • $6 • (05/31/97) • **83**
Merlot Colchagua Valley 1994 • $6 • (12/31/95) • **85**
Sauvignon Blanc Colchagua Valley 1996: Ripe and round, this white offers apple, melon and light herb flavors, but lacks the acidity to go well with food. Try as an apéritif. • $6 • (06/30/97) • **81**
Sauvignon Blanc Colchagua Valley 1994 • $6 • (02/29/96) • **82**

SAN JOSE DE SANTIAGO

Cabernet Sauvignon Colchagua Valley 1990 • $5 • (05/15/92) BB • **85**
Cabernet Sauvignon Maule 1993 • $7 • (06/30/96) • **79**

SAN PEDRO

Cabernet Sauvignon Lontue Castillo de Molina 1982 • $7 • (02/15/89) • **78**
Cabernet Sauvignon Lontue Castillo de Molina 1981 • $7 • (11/15/87) BB • **83**
Cabernet Sauvignon Lontue Castillo de Molina 1979 • $7 • (03/15/87) • **81**
Cabernet Sauvignon Lontue Gato de Oro 1986 • $4 • (02/15/90) BB • **85**
Cabernet Sauvignon Lontue Gato Negro 1989 • $4 • (06/15/92) • **75**
Cabernet Sauvignon Lontue Gato Negro 1985 • $4 • (11/15/88) BB • **80**
Cabernet Sauvignon Lontue Gato Negro 1984 • $4 • (05/15/88) BB • **83**
Cabernet Sauvignon Lontue Gato Negro 1983 • $4 • (03/15/87) • **76**
Cabernet Sauvignon Lontue Las Encinas Vino Tinto Seco 1987 • $NA • (06/15/92) • **80**
Merlot Lontue 1989 • $7 • (05/31/92) BB • **89**
Merlot Lontue 1988 • $5 • (12/31/90) BB • **84**
Merlot Lontue Gato de Oro 1987 • $6 • (02/15/89) BB • **81**

SANTA ALICIA

Cabernet Sauvignon Maipo Valley 1990 • $6 • (10/31/95) • **82**
Cabernet Sauvignon Maipo Valley Reserve 1992: Herbal, gamy and barnyard-like flavors crowd out the light cherry. Drink up. 10,000 cases made. • $8 • (02/28/97) • **78**
Cabernet Sauvignon Maipo Valley Reserve 1990 • $8 • (10/31/95) • **83**
Chardonnay Maipo Valley Reserve 1995: Cooked apple and butter flavors mark this soft, flabby white, with a rubber note on the finish. 5,000 cases made. • $8 • (02/28/97) • **73**
Chardonnay-Sémillon Vintage Select Curicó Valley 1993 • $5 • (02/29/96) • **73**
Fumé Blanc Maipo Valley Reserve 1995: This crisp white shows varietal character in its herbaceous, grassy notes, but there's not much fruit to counter its tart acidity. May soften with food. 20,000 cases made. • $8 • (06/30/97) • **80**
Merlot Maipo Valley 1992 • $6 • (12/31/95) • **79**
Merlot Maipo Valley Limited Production 1993: A crisp, tart red with flavors of cranberry and cherry. It's lively and fresh, but the acidity is strong. 25,000 cases made. • $6 • (04/30/97) • **80**
Merlot Maipo Valley Reserve 1992 • $8 • (12/31/95) BB • **88**
Merlot-Cabernet Sauvignon Curicó Valley Vintage Select 1992 • $5 • (10/31/95) • **76**
Sauvignon Blanc Maipo Valley Limited Production 1996: Crisp citrus and herb aromas are appealing, but don't quite carry through on the soft, smoky palate. Clean but one-dimensional. 20,000 cases made. • $6 • (06/30/97) • **79**

SANTA AMELIA

Cabernet Sauvignon Colchagua 1995: Herb and cedar flavors compete with the light berry flavors in this light yet drying wine. 30,000 cases made. • $7 • (02/28/97) • **79**
Cabernet Sauvignon Colchagua 1994 • $6 • (10/31/95) BB • **88**
Chardonnay Colchagua 1995: Relatively simple but clean and engaging, with bright apple and citrus flavors and plenty of refreshing acidity to match with food. 30,000 cases made. • $7 • (02/28/97) • **84**
Chardonnay Colchagua 1994 • $6 • (10/31/95) • **82**
Merlot Colchagua 1995: A solid core of ripe fruit gains intensity from spice and tobacco accents. Though firm, it's lively and light on its feet. A good food wine that also enchants with its price. Drinkable now. 30,000 cases made. • $7 • (02/28/97) BB • **86**
Merlot Colchagua 1994 • $6 • (12/31/95) BB • **86**

SANTA ANA DE CURICO

Cabernet Sauvignon Colchagua Valley Santiago 1541 1995: Soft and round, with sweet fruit and toasty oak, moderate tannins and a short finish. Drinkable now. • $5 • (06/30/97) • **84**
Chardonnay Maipo Valley Santiago 1541 1995: Smoky, nutty and sweet vanilla flavors stand out in this broadly oaked white, with apple and hazelnut notes beneath. • $6 • (06/30/97) • **83**
Merlot Colchagua Valley Santiago 1541 1995: This fleshy red offers an appealing mix of black cherry, smoke and herb flavors. Soft and round on the palate. Drinkable now. • $6 • (06/30/97) • **84**
Sauvignon Blanc Lontue Valley Santiago 1541 1996: Grassy and herbal flavors dominate this thin wine. It has good acidity, but is otherwise fairly neutral. • $5 • (06/30/97) • **78**

SANTA EMA

Cabernet Sauvignon Maipo Valley 1994: Soft and simple, this has pleasant cherry and herb flavors, but lacks personality. Drink now. 25,000 cases made. • $7 • (02/28/97) • **79**
Cabernet Sauvignon Maipo Valley Super Premium 1992: Sweet and soft, with so much vanilla flavor it tastes like custard with a raspberry purée. 15,000 cases made. • $9 • (02/28/97) • **82**
Chardonnay Maipo Valley 1997: This simple white offers vanilla, lemon and light honey flavors, with a smoky, slightly bitter finish. An acceptable apéritif. 12,000 cases made. • $7 • (05/15/98) • **80**
Chardonnay Maipo Valley 1996: Light and crisp, this offers some pleasant apple flavors, but a strong note of smoke leaves it unbalanced. 25,000 cases made. • $7 • (06/30/97) • **78**
Chardonnay Maipo Valley Reserve 1996: Firm and clean, this well-structured white has clean, crisp acidity and good grip on the palate. The fruit flavors are muted, but should open with food. 10,000 cases made. • $11 • (05/15/98) • **84**
Chardonnay Maipo Valley Super Premium 1995: This expressive white isn't sophisticated, but offers ripe, vivid flavors of vanilla, coconut and melon that linger sweetly on the finish. Significantly better than an earlier sample. 15,000 cases made. • $9 • (06/30/97) • **84**
Merlot Maipo Valley 1994: Well-balanced cherry and berry flavors with just enough tannin for grip. Fresh and light; pleasant with food. 25,000 cases made. • $7 • (02/28/97) • **83**
Merlot Maipo Valley Super Premium 1994: Sweet oak and roasted fruit flavors give a jamlike character that's appealing, if not very varietal. Drinkable now. 15,000 cases made. • $9 • (04/30/97) • **83**

SANTA MARVISTA

Cabernet Sauvignon Rapel 1995: Herb and bell pepper flavors dominate this somewhat tannic red. A bit austere, but might open up with food. 25,000 cases made. • $7 • (06/30/97) • **82**
Chardonnay Rapel 1996: Racy and very crisp, with vivid apple and floral flavors. Lively and refreshing, it's not powerful, but can stand up to lighter foods. 35,000 cases made. • $7 • (06/30/97) • **84**
Merlot Rapel 1996: Big and well concentrated, but it's somewhat harsh, with bitter herb, smoke and plum flavors. Tannins are firm and balanced. Try now. 50,000 cases made. • $7 • (05/31/97) • **84**

SANTA MONICA

Cabernet Sauvignon Rancagua 1994: Shows herb, smoke and light cherry flavors, with light tannins and a short finish. Simple, easy to drink. 10,000 cases made. • $8 • (06/30/97) • **80**
Cabernet Sauvignon Rancagua 1993 • $6 • (06/30/96) • **77**
Cabernet Sauvignon Rancagua 1992 • $6 • (06/30/96) • **77**
Cabernet Sauvignon Rancagua 1991 • $6 • (04/30/95) • **77**
Cabernet Sauvignon Rancagua 1989 • $5 • (10/15/91) BB • **85**
Cabernet Sauvignon Rancagua 1988 • $6 • (03/15/90) BB • **86**
Cabernet Sauvignon Rancagua Tierra de Sol 1985 • $NA • (06/15/92) • **74**
Cabernet Sauvignon Rancagua Tierra de Sol Reserva 1990 • $12 • (04/30/95) • **81**
Chardonnay Rancagua 1996: Quite delicate, its floral and light herb flavors kept lively by crisp acidity, with apple notes lingering on the finish. 8,000 cases made. • $8 • (06/30/97) • **84**
Chardonnay Rancagua 1995 • $6 • (06/30/96) • **83**
Chardonnay Rancagua Tierra de Sol Reserva 1995: Fans of oak will enjoy the sweet, soft vanilla flavor, accentuated by ripe melon and pineapple. Not a food wine, but fine for a cocktail party. • $12 • (02/28/97) • **83**
Merlot Rancagua 1994 • $6 • (06/30/96) • **73**
Merlot Rancagua 1993 • $5 • (06/15/95) • **79**
Merlot Rancagua 1992 • $6 • (01/31/94) • **79**
Sauvignon Blanc Rancagua 1994 • $6 • (06/30/96) • **77**
Sémillon Rancagua 1994 • $5 • (06/30/96) • **83**

CHILE

SANTA RITA

Cabernet Sauvignon Maipo Valley 120 1990 • $6 • (05/31/94) • **83**
Cabernet Sauvignon Maipo Valley 120 1989 • $7 • (02/15/93) BB • **85**
Cabernet Sauvignon Maipo Valley 120 1988 • $6 • (05/31/92) BB • **86**
Cabernet Sauvignon Maipo Valley 120 1987 • $11 • (06/15/90) • **78**
Cabernet Sauvignon Maipo Valley 120 1986 • $5 • (05/15/89) BB • **83**
Cabernet Sauvignon Maipo Valley 120 1984 • $9 • (07/15/87) • **87**
Cabernet Sauvignon Maipo Valley Casa Real 1994: This well-balanced red offers black cherry, herb and light coffee flavors, with firm but unobtrusive tannins. Both flavorful and refreshing, it's a fine food wine. Tasted twice, with consistent notes. • $25 • (06/30/97) • **86**
Cabernet Sauvignon Maipo Valley Casa Real 1993 • $25 • (06/30/96) • **88**
Cabernet Sauvignon Maipo Valley Casa Real 1989 • $NA • (06/15/92) • **81**
Cabernet Sauvignon Maipo Valley Medalla Real 1994: Ripe flavors of plum, raisin and chocolate give immediate appeal. It's soft on the palate and finishes with a pleasant herbal note. • $13 • (06/30/97) • **84**
Cabernet Sauvignon Maipo Valley Medalla Real 1993 • $13 • (06/30/96) • **85**
Cabernet Sauvignon Maipo Valley Medalla Real 1992 • $12 • (04/30/95) • **87**
Cabernet Sauvignon Maipo Valley Medalla Real 1990 • $11 • (04/15/94) • **87**
Cabernet Sauvignon Maipo Valley Medalla Real 1989 • $12 • (02/15/93) HR • **89**
Cabernet Sauvignon Maipo Valley Medalla Real 1988 • $11 • (05/15/92) • **88**
Cabernet Sauvignon Maipo Valley Medalla Real 1987 • $12 • (06/15/91) • **82**
Cabernet Sauvignon Maipo Valley Medalla Real 1986 • $5 • (03/15/90) • **78**
Cabernet Sauvignon Maipo Valley Medalla Real 1985 • $8 • (03/31/88) • **75**
Cabernet Sauvignon Maipo Valley Reserva 1994: Smooth and well integrated, exhibiting ripe plum flavors with nice smoky accents and firm yet polished tannins. A hearty wine for hearty dishes. • $10 • (04/30/97) • **86**
Cabernet Sauvignon Maipo Valley Reserva 1993 • $10 • (06/30/96) • **85**
Cabernet Sauvignon Maipo Valley Reserva 1992 • $9 • (04/30/95) • **81**
Cabernet Sauvignon Maipo Valley Reserva 1990 • $9 • (04/15/94) • **85**
Cabernet Sauvignon Maipo Valley Reserva 1989 • $10 • (04/30/93) • **83**
Cabernet Sauvignon Maipo Valley Reserva 1988 • $9 • (06/15/92) • **86**
Cabernet Sauvignon Maipo Valley Reserva 1987 • $12 • (09/15/90) • **85**
Cabernet Sauvignon Maipo Valley Reserva 1986 • $6 • (05/15/89) BB • **87**
Cabernet Sauvignon Rapel Valley 120 1994: This light, supple red mingles berry, herb and light, earthlike flavors. It's balanced, but rather simple. • $8 • (06/30/97) • **80**
Cabernet Sauvignon Rapel Valley 120 1992 • $7 • (04/30/95) • **85**
Chardonnay Casablanca Valley Medalla Real 1996: Bright, citrusy acidity keeps this lean white lively, while fresh pineapple and light vanilla flavors give interest. A good match for lighter dishes. • $13 • (06/30/97) • **85**

Key: SS—Spectator Selection CS—Cellar Selection HR—Highly Recommended BB—Best Buy $NA—Price not available Ⓐ—Auction Price (BT)—Barrel Tasting
Dates in parentheses indicate the issues in which the ratings were published.

Chardonnay Casablanca Valley Medalla Real 1995: Harmonious, with balanced flavors of apple, citrus, toast and herb. Has good body, but remains crisp and clean. A good, food-friendly wine. • $13 • (05/31/97) • **86**
Chardonnay Lontue Valley 120 1996: A nice balance of ripe fruit flavors, vanilla notes and crisp acidity adds up to harmony and verve. Refreshing; draws you back for another sip. • $8 • (05/31/97) • **85**
Chardonnay Maipo Valley Medalla Real 1994 • $13 • (04/30/95) • **82**
Chardonnay Maipo Valley Reserva 1996: A nice blend of smoke, melon and light citrus flavors in this straightforward, balanced white. It would make a fine, modest complement to food. • $9 • (06/30/97) • **85**
Chardonnay Maipo Valley Reserva 1995 • $10 • (06/30/96) • **84**
Chardonnay Maipo Valley Reserva 1994 • $9 • (04/30/95) • **82**
Chardonnay Maule Valley 120 1995 • $6 • (06/30/96) • **82**
Chardonnay Maule Valley 120 1994 • $7 • (04/30/95) • **80**
Merlot Maule Valley 120 1994 • $6 • (06/30/96) • **79**
Merlot Maule Valley 120 1992 • $7 • (06/15/95) • **82**
Merlot Maipo Valley 120 1990 • $7 • (04/30/93) • **78**
Merlot Maipo Valley 120 1989 • $7 • (06/15/91) BB • **80**
Merlot Rapel Valley 120 1991 • $6 • (05/31/94) • **81**
Sauvignon Blanc Lontue Valley 120 1997: Crisp and clean, this straightforward white offers apple and pear flavors with some concentration and good balance. Will blossom with food. • $8 • (05/31/98) • **84**
Sauvignon Blanc Maule Valley 120 1995 • $6 • (06/30/96) • **83**
Sauvignon Blanc Maule Valley 120 1994 • $7 • (06/15/95) • **83**
Sauvignon Blanc Maule Valley Reserva 1995 • $10 • (06/30/96) • **80**
Sauvignon Blanc Maule Valley Reserva 1994 • $8 • (05/15/95) • **85**
Sauvignon Blanc Rapel Valley Medalla Real 1996: Fresh and balanced but fairly neutral in flavor, with light, citrusy acidity and hints of herbs. Makes a pleasant apéritif. • $11 • (06/30/97) • **82**

SOUTH VALLEY

Cabernet Sauvignon Chile 1989: Silky, with light flavors of dried cherry, spice and cinnamon and soft tannins that turn a bit dry on the finish. It has held up well, but hasn't gained much with age. Drink up. 2,000 cases made. • $9 • (10/31/97) • **81**
Cabernet Sauvignon Rancagua 1989 • $9 • (02/28/94) • **83**

STONELAKE

Cabernet Sauvignon Lontue 1995: Toasty oak and ripe blueberry and plum flavors make a winning combination in this luscious, round red. It's a pretty, international-style Cab. 4,500 cases made. • $13 • (02/28/98) • **86**
Cabernet Sauvignon Lontue 1994: A big, friendly wine with plenty of sweet vanilla and ripe blackberry flavors. Aims for drinkability and hits it. 2,150 cases imported. • $12 • (02/28/97) • **85**
Cabernet Sauvignon Lontue 1993 • $13 • (06/30/96) • **85**
Chardonnay Lontue 1995: Fans of oak: This is your wine. There's plenty of sweet vanilla, butter and piecrust flavors, along with enough fruit flavor to keep it honest. • $12 • (04/30/97) • **84**
Chardonnay Lontue La Primavera Vineyard 1996: Toasty oak aromas are appealing and carry through to the creamy palate, where melon, apple and vanilla flavors linger on the finish. Crisp acidity keeps it lively. 1,200 cases made. • $13 • (02/28/98) • **85**
Chardonnay Lontue La Primavera Vineyard 1994 • $13 • (06/30/96) • **84**
Merlot Lontue 1995: Juicy black cherry and blackberry flavors are sweet and inviting in this ripe fruit bomb. It's saved from jamminess by firm tannins and toasty oak flavors. Well made, with good concentration. 4,000 cases imported. • $12 • (02/28/97) • **87**
Merlot Lontue 1994 • $13 • (05/31/96) • **84**
Pinot Noir Lontue 1995: Attractive toasty, smoky notes add depth to the sweet plum and oak flavors. Tannins are firm, and there's sufficient concentration for compatibility with food. • $13 • (06/30/97) • **85**
Pinot Noir Lontue La Primavera Vineyard 1996: Has some nice richness to it, with pleasant berry, cherry and spice flavors, that linger on the finish. A good, solid Pinot Noir that will go well with food. 4,000 cases made. • $14 • (02/28/98) • **84**
Pinot Noir Lontue La Primavera Vineyard 1994 • $14 • (06/30/96) • **85**

STONY HOLLOW

Cabernet Sauvignon Rapel 1995: Supple, with light cherry, cedar and herb flavors, and light tannins that kick in on the finish. A bit thick and dull. 20,000 cases made. • $6 • (06/30/97) • **78**
Cabernet Sauvignon San Fernando 1988 • $6 • (06/15/92) BB • **84**

Chardonnay Rapel 1996: Crisp and herb-scented, this light, lively white is a good match for shellfish. It's a bit austere, but well balanced and fresh. 25,000 cases made. • $6 • (06/30/97) • **83**

Merlot Rapel 1996: Grape and herb flavors mingle uneasily in this light, and lightly tannic, wine. Tastes like a nouveau. 40,000 cases made. • $6 • (06/30/97) • **79**

TERRA NOVA

Cabernet Sauvignon Maipo Valley 1993: Dead leaves and dried fruit are the dominant flavors. Light-bodied. Drink up. Tasted twice, with consistent notes. 8,000 cases made. • $10 • (02/28/97) • **76**

Chardonnay Maipo Valley 1995: Light-bodied and soft, its dried apple and cinnamon flavors have just enough acidity for freshness. Simple, with some varietal character. 8,000 cases made. • $10 • (02/28/97) • **81**

Merlot Maipo Valley 1994: Light-bodied, pleasant and simple, with straightforward cherry flavors and just enough tannin and acidity for balance. 6,000 cases made. • $10 • (02/28/97) • **80**

Sauvignon Blanc Maipo Valley 1996: Light-bodied, this has ripe apple, melon and smoke flavors with crisp, underlying acidity. A bit dull, but some intriguing pear and herb notes sneak in on the finish. 2,000 cases made. • $10 • (02/28/97) • **83**

TERRA ROSA

Cabernet Sauvignon Central Valley 1995: Light, with slightly candied, vanilla-accented flavors of raspberry and strawberry over the slightly drying tannins. Drinkable now. Made by Laurel Glen, which also offers a Terra Rosa bottling from California grapes. • $10 • (10/31/97) • **80**

TERRANOBLE

Merlot Maule 1994 • $8 • (06/15/95) • **77**

Sauvignon Blanc Maule 1994 • $8 • (06/15/95) • **81**

TOLVA, DOMAINE

Cabernet Sauvignon Maule Valley 1991 • $5 • (05/31/94) BB • **82**

Cabernet Sauvignon Maule Valley 1989 • $5 • (12/15/92) • **74**

Merlot Maule Valley 1992 • $5 • (05/31/94) BB • **83**

TORREÓN DE PAREDES

Sauvignon Blanc Rengo 1997: Round, with ripe apple and melon flavors and light smoky and earthy accents. Has just enough acidity to keep it balanced. 5,000 cases made. • $10 • (05/31/98) • **81**

TORRES, MIGUEL

Cabernet Sauvignon Curicó 1992 • $7 • (06/15/95) • **78**

Cabernet Sauvignon Curicó 1991 • $7 • (05/31/94) • **78**

Cabernet Sauvignon Curicó 1990 • $7 • (06/15/92) BB • **85**

Cabernet Sauvignon Curicó 1989 • $7 • (06/15/91) BB • **82**

Cabernet Sauvignon Curicó 1988 • $4 • (09/15/90) BB • **87**

Cabernet Sauvignon Curicó 1985 • $5 • (03/31/88) • **73**

Cabernet Sauvignon Curicó 1984 • $4 • (01/31/87) • **79**

Cabernet Sauvignon Curicó District Manso de Velasco Reserva 1995: This muscular red shows good concentration, with dark, rich flavors of currant, cassis, game and tar. The tannins are a bit top-heavy now, but by 1999 or so this should be beautiful. • $14 • (10/31/97) • **88**

Cabernet Sauvignon Curicó District Manso de Velasco Reserva 1994: Shows good concentration, with ripe plum and cassis flavors, but the oak is heavy-handed, turning dry on the finish. Try now. 2,400 cases made. • $15 • (04/30/97) • **84**

Cabernet Sauvignon Curicó District Manso de Velasco Reserve 1993 • $16 • (10/31/95) • **84**

Cabernet Sauvignon Curicó District Manso de Velasco Reserve 1990 • $15 • (05/31/95) • **84**

Cabernet Sauvignon Curicó District Manso de Velasco Reserve 1989 • $15 • (06/15/95) • **83**

Chardonnay Curicó Chardonnay de la Cordillera 1994 • $8 • (02/29/96) • **77**

Santa Digna Red Chile 1985 • $NA • (02/16/86) • **76**

Santa Digna Red Chile 1983 • $NA • (02/16/86) • **78**

Sauvignon Blanc Chile Santa Digna 1996: This lively white has vivid acidity, with grapefruit, grass and mineral flavors. Racy and clean, it makes a crisp apéritif. • $8 • (06/30/97) • **85**

Sauvignon Blanc Curicó District 1997: This crisp white offers lively flavors of grapefruit and herb with strong grassy accents. It's a bit disjointed, but youthful exuberance makes it appealing. • $7 • (10/31/97) • **83**

Sauvignon Blanc Curicó District 1995 • $7 • (02/29/96) • **74**

Sauvignon Blanc Curicó District 1994 • $7 • (05/15/95) • **84**

TRAVERSO, SERGIO

Cabernet Sauvignon Colchagua 1992 • $7 • (06/15/95) • **76**

Cabernet Sauvignon Colchagua 1990 • $6 • (12/15/92) • **79**

Cabernet Sauvignon Rapel Reserva 1994: Soft, round and simple, offering some cherry and raisin flavors, light tannins and an herbal finish. Drink now. 5,000 cases made. • $7 • (02/28/97) • **81**

Chardonnay Rapel Reserva 1995: Full-blown style, bursting with tropical fruit and sweet oak flavors—imagine a pineapple sundae. Not refined, but makes a powerful impression. 5,000 cases made. • $8 • (02/28/97) • **86**

Merlot Colchagua 1992 • $7 • (06/30/96) • **77**

Merlot Colchagua 1990 • $6 • (12/15/92) BB • **83**

Merlot Rapel Reserva 1994: A friendly, unobtrusive wine, straightforward in style, with cherry and light earth flavors and just enough tannin to stand up to food. 10,000 cases made. • $8 • (04/30/97) • **83**

Sauvignon Blanc Rapel Reserva 1995: Straightforward, basically neutral in flavor, with good acidity and light apple and earthlike flavors. 5,000 cases made. • $7 • (04/30/97) • **79**

UNDURRAGA

Cabernet Sauvignon Colchagua Valley 1996: This soft red offers straightforward cherry and herb flavors, with light tannins and a short finish. • $7 • (03/31/98) • **78**

Cabernet Sauvignon Colchagua Valley 1995: Lively, with herb-accented berry and spice flavors and just enough tannin for grip. Nice minty notes linger on the finish. • $7 • (02/28/97) • **84**

Cabernet Sauvignon Maipo Valley 1992 • $6 • (04/30/95) • **84**

Cabernet Sauvignon Maipo Valley 1991 • $5 • (05/31/94) • **77**

Cabernet Sauvignon Maipo Valley 1990 • $6 • (07/15/93) • **79**

Cabernet Sauvignon Maipo Valley 1989 • $6 • (06/15/92) • **74**

Cabernet Sauvignon Maipo Valley 1988 • $5 • (09/15/90) BB • **83**

Cabernet Sauvignon Maipo Valley 1987 • $5 • (02/15/90) BB • **87**

Cabernet Sauvignon Maipo Valley Reserva 1994: Its bright fruit and good balance give it solid appeal; its herb and spice overtones and firm underlying tannins give it character. Well crafted. Drink now. 2,100 cases made. • $9 • (02/28/97) • **87**

Cabernet Sauvignon Maipo Valley Reserve Selection 1991 • $9 • (05/31/95) • **88**

Cabernet Sauvignon Maipo Valley Reserve Selection 1989 • $8 • (05/31/94) • **82**

Cabernet Sauvignon Maipo Valley Reserve Selection 1988 • $9 • (04/30/93) • **81**

Cabernet Sauvignon Maipo Valley Reserve Selection 1987 • $8 • (06/15/92) BB • **87**

Cabernet Sauvignon Maipo Valley Reserve Selection 1986 • $8 • (06/15/91) BB • **83**

Cabernet Sauvignon Maipo Valley Reserve Selection 1985 • $7 • (03/15/90) BB • **85**

Cabernet Sauvignon Maipo Valley Santa Ana 1985 • $5 • (11/15/87) • **78**

Chardonnay Colchagua Valley 1996: A full-bodied marriage of ripe melon and toasty oak flavors, held together by firm acidity. Not complex, but balanced and bold. • $7 • (02/28/97) • **85**

Chardonnay Maipo Valley 1995 • $6 • (06/30/96) • **77**

Chardonnay Maipo Valley 1994 • $6 • (04/30/95) • **83**

Chardonnay Maipo Valley Reserva 1996: Oaky flavors dominate this thick white, tasting of newly cut lumber and sugared vanilla. Apple and lemon notes are buried in the mix. • $10 • (03/31/98) • **78**

Chardonnay Maipo Valley Reserva 1995: Understated but quite attractive, this offers pear, vanilla and hazelnut flavors. Balanced and fresh, with a fine, subtle finish. Try with light foods. • $10 • (02/28/97) • **86**

Merlot Colchagua Valley 1995: Soft, velvety texture is enticing, while the flavors lean toward the herbal side of Merlot, with cherry accents. Drink now. • $6 • (02/28/97) • **82**

Merlot Maipo Valley 1993 • $6 • (01/01/95) • **82**

Merlot Maipo Valley 1992 • $6 • (04/30/93) • **76**

Pinot Noir Maipo Valley 1995: Varietal character is evident in this round, fruity wine, which offers bright berry flavors, light spice notes and a hint of herb. • $8 • (06/30/97) • **83**

Pinot Noir Maipo Valley 1992 • $7 • (04/15/95) • **78**

Sauvignon Blanc Lontue Valley 1997: Pretty floral and mineral aromas are followed by clean, crisp flavors of grapefruit and herb in this fresh, balanced wine. A well-focused match for lighter fish dishes. • $NA • (05/31/98) • **85**

Sauvignon Blanc Maipo 1996: Lean, very crisp and dominated by lemony acidity, with only light herb and apple flavors to flesh it out. A bit tart on its own, it should soften with food. • $7 • (02/28/97) • **81**

Sauvignon Blanc Maipo Valley 1995 • $6 • (06/30/96) • **80**

Sauvignon Blanc Maipo Valley 1994 • $6 • (06/15/95) • **81**

VALDIVIESO

Cabernet Sauvignon Maipo Valley 1986 • $7 • (04/30/93) • **83**

Cabernet Sauvignon Maipo Valley 1984 • $8 • (06/15/92) • **71**

Merlot Maipo Valley 1989 • $8 • (06/15/92) • **79**

VALLE DE SAN FERNANDO

Cabernet Sauvignon San Fernando 1988 • $5 • (06/15/92) BB • **83**

Cabernet Sauvignon San Fernando 1985 • $7 • (07/31/89) • **79**

Cabernet Sauvignon San Fernando 1983 • $4 • (11/15/88) • **77**

Cabernet Sauvignon San Fernando Gran Reserva 1986 • $6 • (04/30/93) • **79**

Cabernet Sauvignon San Fernando Gran Reserva 1984 • $6 • (09/15/90) BB • **81**

Cabernet Sauvignon San Fernando Gran Reserva 1982 • $6 • (11/15/88) BB • **81**

Merlot San Fernando 1990 • $5 • (06/15/92) • **75**

VASCOS, LOS

Cabernet Sauvignon Colchagua 1995: Soft and simple, with cherry, herb and light spice flavors that are appealing but lack depth. A quaffing wine that's ready now. • $7 • (06/30/97) • **80**

Cabernet Sauvignon Colchagua 1993 • $7 • (04/30/95) BB • **85**

Cabernet Sauvignon Colchagua 1992 • $7 • (05/31/94) BB • **83**

Cabernet Sauvignon Colchagua 1991 • $9 • (04/15/94) • **82**

Cabernet Sauvignon Colchagua 1990 • $7 • (05/31/92) BB • **88**

Cabernet Sauvignon Colchagua 1989 • $7 • (06/15/92) BB • **83**

Cabernet Sauvignon Colchagua 1988 • $7 • (06/15/91) BB • **82**

Cabernet Sauvignon Colchagua 1987 • $5 • (09/15/90) BB • **86**

Cabernet Sauvignon Colchagua 1985 • $5 • (11/15/87) • **84**

Cabernet Sauvignon Colchagua 1984 • $4 • (04/30/88) BB • **88**

Cabernet Sauvignon Colchagua Grande Reserve 1991 • $12 • (05/31/94) • **83**

Cabernet Sauvignon Colchagua Reserve 1994: Supple, with toasty oak aromas and sweet vanilla, cherry and light smoke flavors. Has a candylike appeal. 25,000 cases made. • $12 • (06/30/97) • **82**

Cabernet Sauvignon Colchagua Reserve 1993: Supple and balanced, this round red offers cherry and brown sugar flavors. Straightforward and slightly jammy, with just enough tannin to keep it fresh. • $10 • (02/28/97) • **83**

Cabernet Sauvignon Colchagua Reserve 1992 • $12 • (04/30/95) • **84**

Cabernet Sauvignon Colchagua Reserve 1990 • $12 • (05/31/94) • **81**

Cabernet Sauvignon Colchagua Reserve 1989 • $11 • (06/15/92) • **84**

Chardonnay Colchagua 1995: Round and simple, exhibiting good balance and straightforward apple and citrus flavors. A slight mustiness detracts. • $7 • (04/30/97) • **81**

Chardonnay Colchagua 1994 • $7 • (04/30/95) • **75**

Sauvignon Blanc Colchagua 1996: Lively fruit aromas of apple and melon, with flavors of herb, almond and coconut. Full-bodied, ripe and round, it's appealing if not typical for the varietal. • $7 • (06/30/97) • **84**

Sauvignon Blanc Colchagua 1994 • $5 • (05/31/95) • **71**

Key: SS—Spectator Selection CS—Cellar Selection HR—Highly Recommended BB—Best Buy $NA—Price not available Ⓐ—Auction Price (BT)—Barrel Tasting

Dates in parentheses indicate the issues in which the ratings were published.

VERAMONTE

Cabernet Sauvignon Curicó Valley 1995: Ripe fruit and a jolt of oak give this Cab more volume than most Chilean reds. It offers pleasant plum and blackberry flavors with toast and licorice undertones and firm, round tannins. Drinks well now, at a consumer-friendly price. A blend of 85 percent Cabernet Sauvignon and 15 percent Carmenère. 18,000 cases made. • $10 • (02/28/97) BB • **86**

Chardonnay Casablanca Valley 1996: This exuberant white offers tropical fruit notes of mango and melon, while a strong dose of oak adds sweet vanilla flavors, yet it's still crisp enough to draw you back for another sip. A solid value from Chile. 30,000 cases made. • $10 • (02/28/98) BB • **85**

Chardonnay Casablanca Valley 1995: Well made, delicate yet vivid, with pineapple, vanilla and nutmeg flavors that are fresh and well balanced and linger on the finish. 5,000 cases made. • $10 • (02/28/97) • **86**

Merlot Casablanca Valley Primus 1995: A chewy red with ripe plum, light herb and rich coffee flavors and firm tannins. It's concentrated, but oak dominates. Try now. 1,500 cases made. • $15 • (06/30/97) • **85**

VILLA RICA

Cabernet Sauvignon Colchagua Valley La Nobleza 1994: Thin and slightly sweet. Brown sugar and cedar dominate the strawberry flavors. It bears a resemblance to an old-style Rioja. 3,000 cases made. • $10 • (02/28/97) • **78**

VILLARD

Cabernet Sauvignon Rancagua 1992 • $8 • (04/30/95) • **81**

Cabernet Sauvignon Rancagua 1991 • $8 • (05/31/94) • **76**

Merlot Cachapoal 1992 • $8 • (06/15/95) • **87**

Sauvignon Blanc Aconcagua Casablanca Vineyard 1996: Coconut and honey aromas give way to round, oaky flavors in this full-bodied, deeply colored white. Its fruit flavors are modest, and there's not much Sauvignon Blanc character, but the wine has distinctive personality. 6,000 cases made. • $8 • (05/31/98) • **83**

Sauvignon Blanc Aconcagua Casablanca Vineyard 1994 • $7 • (05/15/95) • **85**

VIÑA CALINA

Cabernet Franc Chile 1994 • $20 • (02/29/96) • **84**

Cabernet Sauvignon Chile 1993 • $20 • (02/29/96) • **84**

Cabernet Sauvignon Chile Selección de Las Lomas 1994: Lovely cassis, chocolate and smoke flavors give this wine both pizzazz and depth. A flashy California style that makes delicious drinking. 2,000 cases made. • $20 • (06/30/97) • **88**

Chardonnay Chile Selección de Las Lomas 1996: Its rich butter and vanilla flavors will please fans of oak, but its melon and pineapple flavors are a bit overwhelmed. Nice acidity keeps it lively, though. 4,000 cases made. • $16 • (06/30/97) • **84**

Chardonnay Chile Selección de Las Lomas 1995 • $16 • (06/30/96) • **86**

Merlot Chile 1994 • $20 • (02/29/96) • **83**

Merlot Chile Selección de Las Lomas 1995: This ambitious red has an inky color, firm tannins and ripe flavors of plum, raisin and black coffee. It's concentrated, but a bit disjointed. Try now. 2,000 cases made. • $20 • (06/30/97) • **85**

VIÑA DEL MAR

Cabernet Sauvignon Curicó Selección Especial 35 1988 • $6 • (06/15/91) BB • **81**

Cabernet Sauvignon Curicó Selección Especial 35 1987 • $6 • (09/15/90) BB • **83**

Cabernet Sauvignon Lontue 1988 • $6 • (06/15/92) • **79**

Cabernet Sauvignon Lontue 1985 • $6 • (04/30/88) BB • **86**

Cabernet Sauvignon Lontue Selección Especial 17 1986 • $6 • (02/15/90) BB • **80**

Cabernet Sauvignon Maipo Valley 1992 • $6 • (04/30/95) • **78**

Cabernet Sauvignon Maipo Valley 1990 • $6 • (05/31/94) • **82**

Cabernet Sauvignon Maipo Valley Reserve 1988 • $9 • (06/15/95) • **77**

Cabernet Sauvignon Maipo Valley Reserve 1987 • $10 • (05/31/94) • **83**

Cabernet Sauvignon Maipo Valley Reserve 1986 • $9 • (06/15/92) • **78**

Chardonnay Maipo Valley 1994 • $7 • (06/15/95) • **73**

Fumé Blanc Maipo Valley 1994 • $6 • (06/15/95) • **76**

Merlot Curicó Selección Especial 12 1989 • $6 • (06/15/91) BB • **80**
Merlot Curicó Selección Especial 12 1988 • $6 • (09/15/90) BB • **82**
Merlot Lontue 1990 • $6 • (06/15/92) BB • **83**
Merlot Lontue 1988 • $6 • (07/31/89) BB • **80**
Merlot Maipo Reserve 1989 • $9 • (05/15/92) • **78**
Merlot Maipo Valley 1992 • $6 • (06/15/95) • **77**
Merlot Maipo Valley 1991 • $6 • (05/31/94) BB • **82**

VIÑA GRACIA

Cabernet Sauvignon Cachapoal Conversado Reserva 1993: Fleshy, with sweet vanilla and berry flavors, round, soft tannins and no sharp edges. Not complex, but brings you back for another sip. Would show well with chocolate desserts. 3,000 cases made. • $10 • (05/31/97) • **85**
Cabernet Sauvignon Maipo Celebrado 1995: Has concentration, but strong tobacco and herb flavors dominate, and firm tannins shut down the finish. Try now. 20,000 cases made. • $8 • (06/30/97) • **83**
Chardonnay Cachapoal Reposado 1996: Lively, with zesty citrus and pineapple flavors. Deft use of oak adds spice and smoke notes. A bit tart on its own; fine with food. 15,000 cases made. • $8 • (05/31/97) • **85**
Merlot Maipo Valley Curioso 1996: Displaying ripe flavors of plum and prune, plenty of chocolate-scented oak and a thick, jammy texture, this Chilean red is reasonably priced. Much better than samples reviewed earlier sent by an unauthorized importer. Try now. 20,000 cases made. • $8 • (10/31/97) BB • **85**

VIÑA MORANDÉ

Sauvignon Blanc Valle Central Pionero 1997: This very crisp white offers herbal and grassy character and light flavors of lime and grapefruit. Leans toward the Loire Valley style. 9,000 cases made. • $6 • (05/31/98) • **82**

VIÑA PORTA

Cabernet Sauvignon Cachapoal Valley 1996: Smoky, herbal aromas follow through on the palate, joined by light cherry and spice flavors in this soft, juicy red. Drinkable now. • $9 • (10/31/97) • **82**
Cabernet Sauvignon Valle del Cachapoal 1994 • $9 • (06/30/96) • **83**
Cabernet Sauvignon Valle del Cachapoal 1993 • $9 • (12/31/95) • **84**
Cabernet Sauvignon Valle del Cachapoal 1992 • $9 • (04/30/95) BB • **87**
Cabernet Sauvignon Valle del Cachapoal Reserva 1992 • $11 • (04/30/95) • **88**
Chardonnay Cachapoal Valley 1996: This easy-quaffing white is smooth and soft on the palate, with light melon, apple and vanilla flavors. It's fresh and well balanced; a nice apéritif. • $9 • (11/15/97) • **84**
Chardonnay Valle del Cachapoal 1995 • $9 • (06/30/96) • **82**
Chardonnay Valle del Cachapoal 1994 • $9 • (02/29/96) • **84**

VIÑA SANTA CAROLINA

Cabernet Sauvignon Maipo Valley Estrella de Oro 1982 • $8 • (03/15/90) • **76**
Cabernet Sauvignon Maipo Valley Los Toros Vineyard Reserva 1985 • $8 • (04/30/93) BB • **84**
Cabernet Sauvignon Maipo Valley Los Toros Vineyard Special Reserve 1988 • $8 • (04/30/93) • **83**
Cabernet Sauvignon Maipo Valley Reserva 1995: A nice balance of fruit and oak provides harmony, while round tannins make it accessible yet firm enough for food. The finish is long and fruity. • $7 • (05/31/97) • **85**
Cabernet Sauvignon Maipo Valley Santa Rosa Vineyard 1986 • $4 • (04/30/88) • **78**
Cabernet Sauvignon Maipo Valley Santa Rosa Vineyard Gran Reserva Cinco Estrellas 1987 • $14 • (02/28/94) • **84**
Cabernet Sauvignon Maipo Valley Santa Rosa Vineyard Reserva 1990 • $8 • (05/31/95) • **84**
Cabernet Sauvignon-Merlot Colchagua Valley 1995: Supple, with plum, smoke and light herb flavors. A bit light for food, but well balanced and accessible. • $8/1.5 liter • (06/30/97) • **82**
Chardonnay Lontue Valley 1994 • $6 • (06/15/95) • **80**
Chardonnay Maipo Valley Reserva 1996: A California style. Lush and tropical, with coconut and pineapple flavors and just enough acidity to balance the sweet fruit-and-oak character. • $7 • (05/31/97) • **86**
Chardonnay-Sauvignon Blanc Colchagua Valley 1996: Simple, clean and straightforward, with light apple and peach flavors. An easy quaff. • $8/1.5 liter • (06/30/97) • **80**
Merlot-Cabernet Sauvignon Colchagua Valley 1995: Fruity, with an almost jammy texture, flavors of black cherry and plum and light tannins. Easy to drink. • $8/1.5 liter • (05/31/97) • **83**
Merlot-Cabernet Sauvignon San Fernando Valley 1993 • $6 • (05/15/95) • **85**
Merlot Maipo Valley Santa Rosa Vineyard 1993 • $6 • (05/15/95) BB • **86**
Merlot Maipo Valley Santa Rosa Vineyard 1989 • $6 • (03/31/93) BB • **82**
Merlot Maipo Valley Santa Rosa Vineyard Reserva 1991 • $8 • (04/15/94) • **84**
Merlot Maipo Valley Santa Rosa Vineyard Reserva 1990 • $8 • (04/30/93) • **82**
Merlot Maipo Valley Santa Rosa Vineyard Reserva 1989 • $8 • (04/30/93) BB • **82**
Merlot Maipo Valley Santa Rosa Vineyard Reserva Especial 1989 • $8 • (06/15/92) BB • **83**
Merlot Maule Valley Reserva 1995: Soft, with sweet raspberry and vanilla flavors that produce a pleasant, candylike appeal. Simple, but fun. • $7 • (06/30/97) • **82**
Merlot San Fernando Valley Gran Reserva Cinco Estrellas 1993 • $10 • (05/15/95) • **86**
Merlot San Fernando Valley Reserva 1993 • $8 • (06/15/95) • **81**
Pinot Noir Maipo Valley Reserva Santa Rosa Vineyard 1994 • $8 • (06/15/95) • **77**

VIÑA SEGÚ OLLÉ

Cabernet Sauvignon Maule Valley Doña Consuelo 1995: Firm, its fruit flavors muted by herb and smoke flavors and slightly aggressive tannins. Try with food. 30,000 cases made. • $6 • (06/30/97) • **81**
Cabernet Sauvignon Maule Valley Doña Consuelo 1994 • $6 • (06/30/96) • **75**
Cabernet Sauvignon Maule Valley Doña Consuelo 1992 • $6 • (04/30/95) • **77**
Cabernet Sauvignon Maule Valley Doña Consuelo Reserve 1994: Delivers cherry and chocolate flavors that carry through to the finish, with alluring toast and chocolate notes from lavish use of new oak. Not balanced for aging, but seductive now. 5,000 cases made. • $8 • (04/30/97) • **86**
Cabernet Sauvignon Maule Valley Doña Consuelo Reserve 1993 • $8 • (06/15/96) • **83**
Cabernet Sauvignon Maule Valley Doña Consuelo Reserve 1992 • $8 • (06/30/96) • **84**
Cabernet Sauvignon Maule Valley Doña Consuelo Reserve 1991 • $14 • (06/30/96) • **76**
Chardonnay Maule Valley Doña Consuelo 1995 • $6 • (06/30/96) • **79**
Chardonnay Maule Valley Doña Consuelo 1994 • $6 • (04/30/95) • **78**
Chardonnay Maule Valley Doña Consuelo Reserve 1994: Still has a good backbone of acidity, but the flavors have matured into earthy and austere smoky tones that won't appeal to everyone. Best with food. 5,000 cases made. • $8 • (04/30/97) • **82**
Merlot Maule Valley Doña Consuelo 1995 • $6 • (05/31/96) • **81**
Merlot Maule Valley Doña Consuelo 1994 • $6 • (06/15/95) • **78**
Moscatel de Alejandria Maule Valley Doña Consuelo 1995: Dry, with light, exotic aromas and flavors of spice, orange peel and almond. Round on the palate, but kept crisp by good acidity. A nice apéritif. 15,000 cases made. • $6 • (06/30/97) • **84**
Moscatel de Alejandria Maule Valley Doña Consuelo 1994 • $6 • (06/30/96) • **81**
Red Maule Valley 1995: Light-bodied, with simple cherry flavors, herbaceous accents and lean tannins. It has varietal character, but remains simple. • $7/1.5 liter • (06/30/97) • **81**
Sauvignon Blanc Maule Valley Doña Consuelo 1996: Lean and underripe, this is quite herbal, with a marked earthy note and not much fruit. 15,000 cases made. • $6 • (06/30/97) • **76**
Sauvignon Blanc Maule Valley Doña Consuelo 1995: Straightforward and a bit dull, a round wine, with clean acidity and light apple flavors. 15,000 cases made. • $6 • (02/28/97) • **79**
Sauvignon Blanc Maule Valley Doña Consuelo 1994 • $6 • (06/30/96) • **83**
Sauvignon Blanc Sémillon Maule Valley 1995: Nutty, cooked apple flavors are round, but the underlying acidity is firm. Finishes cleanly, and may find more balance with food. 15,000 cases made. • $5 • (02/28/97) • **79**
White Maule Valley Chardonnay Sauvignon Blanc 1995: Very crisp but rather neutral in character, with hints of herb and tobacco on the palate. Clean but not very inviting. • $7/1.5 liter • (06/30/97) • **78**

VIÑA TARAPACÁ

Cabernet Sauvignon Central Valley 1996: Bright blackberry and light herb flavors are well defined and firm in this nicely structured red. It's harmonious and accessible now. • $7 • (11/30/97) • **85**

Cabernet Sauvignon Maipo Valley Reserva 1993: What a deal in quality Cabernet Sauvignon. This red from Chile is a model of deft winemaking, with harmonious and firm black cherry, toast and tobacco notes. An understated style that will blossom with food. 10,000 cases made. • $10 • (05/31/97) BB • **88**

Chardonnay Maipo Valley 1997: Toasty, smoky aromas and flavors are appealing in this solid white, but the appley fruit is simple and a bit overwhelmed by oak. Still, firm acidity keeps it crisp. • $7 • (03/31/98) • **82**

Chardonnay Maipo Valley 1996: Clean, crisp and lean, with delicate floral and apple flavors and toasty bottom notes. Quite lively, with a strongly oaked finish. • $7 • (06/30/97) • **84**

Chardonnay Maipo Valley Reserva 1996: This well-balanced white offers a nice mix of peach and melon flavors with toasty, smoky accents. It's subtle yet complex. • $10 • (06/30/97) • **87**

Merlot Maipo Valley 1995: Distinctly smoky aromas and flavors give a slightly bitter character with firm tannins and concentrated plum flavors. Try now. • $7 • (05/31/97) • **84**

Sauvignon Blanc Valle Central 1997: Lively, clean and fresh, with mineral and herb aromas and flavors and very firm acidity. Balanced and well defined, it's a nice match for lighter dishes. • $7 • (05/31/98) • **84**

VIÑA TERRA ANDINA

Cabernet Sauvignon Valle Central 1995: Ripe fruit flavors of black cherry and plum make for easy-drinking appeal. Balanced, with just enough tannin for food. • $7 • (06/30/97) • **84**

Chardonnay Valle Central 1996: Full-bodied, with a healthy dose of oak. There's enough acidity, but it lacks a bit in fruit. Has enough grip to match with food. • $7 • (06/30/97) • **83**

Sémillon Valle Central 1996: Pretty peach aromas give way to a round, fruity white with just a hint of sweetness. Though not complex, it's inviting and makes a delightful apéritif. • $7 • (06/30/97) • **85**

VINAPORTA

Cabernet Sauvignon Valle del Cachapoal 1991 • $9 • (05/31/94) • **79**

VIÑOS DE CHILE

Blush Lontue Gato Rosado 1994 • $5 • (08/31/95) • **84**
Cabernet Sauvignon Lontue Gato Negro 1993 • $5 • (04/30/95) • **75**
Sauvignon Blanc Lontue Gato Blanco 1994 • $5 • (05/31/95) BB • **86**

VIÑOS EXPOSICION

Cabernet Sauvignon Talca Conde del Maule 1988 • $6 • (06/15/92) • **79**
Cabernet Sauvignon Talca Escudo de Talca 1990 • $5 • (06/15/92) BB • **82**
Cabernet Sauvignon Talca Molino Viejo 1990 • $5 • (06/15/92) BB • **82**
Cabernet Sauvignon Talca Reserva de Talca 1989 • $6 • (06/15/92) • **77**

VINTERRA

Cabernet Sauvignon Maipo & Napa Valleys NV • $7 • (02/15/90) BB • **86**

VIU MANENT

Cabernet Sauvignon Colchagua Valley Proprietor's Reserve 1992: Distinctive, with alluring and harmonious aromas and flavors of cassis, toast and dark chocolate backed with firm, round tannins. Drinkable now. • $9 • (05/31/97) • **87**

Cabernet Sauvignon Colchagua Valley Proprietor's Reserve 1991 • $6 • (10/31/95) • **85**

Key: SS—Spectator Selection CS—Cellar Selection HR—Highly Recommended BB—Best Buy $NA—Price not available Ⓐ—Auction Price (BT)—Barrel Tasting
Dates in parentheses indicate the issues in which the ratings were published.

Cabernet Sauvignon Colchagua Valley Reserve 1993: Appealing, ripe and well balanced, with fresh plum, chocolate and vanilla flavors, and round tannins that will match well with food. Drink now. • $8 • (05/31/97) • **86**

Chardonnay Colchagua Proprietor's Reserve 1994 • $NA • (10/31/95) • **73**

Malbec Colchagua Valley 1995: This round red marries soft black cherry and earth flavors with light oak accents and firm tannins. Modest, but well balanced. Should complement food. • $8 • (06/30/97) • **85**

WALNUT CREST

Cabernet Sauvignon Maipo 1987 • $5 • (04/30/93) BB • **82**
Cabernet Sauvignon Maipo 1985 • $4 • (06/30/90) BB • **80**

Cabernet Sauvignon Rapel Valley 1995: Mouth-coating, this wine is thick with ripe fruit and round tannins, offering berry, tobacco and herb flavors. Rich, but a bit clumsy. 150,000 cases made. • $6 • (06/30/97) • **84**

Chardonnay Rapel Valley 1996: Crisp, clean and light-bodied, with floral, apple and light herb flavors. Lean and delicate; nice as an apéritif. 250,000 cases made. • $6 • (06/30/97) • **83**

Merlot Rapel Valley 1996: This Chilean red is generous, harmonious and lush, with plenty of plum and cassis flavors wrapped around ripe tannins and well-integrated notes of toast and smoke. A bargain at twice the price. 300,000 cases made. • $7 • (05/31/97) BB • **87**

Merlot Rapel Valley 1993 • $5 • (05/15/95) BB • **86**
Merlot Rapel Valley 1992 • $5 • (05/31/94) • **79**
Merlot Rapel Valley 1990 • $5 • (04/30/93) BB • **84**
Merlot Rapel Valley 1989 • $4 • (05/15/92) BB • **83**
Merlot Rapel Valley 1987 • $4 • (06/30/90) BB • **85**

France

Although France is not the largest producer of wine, it produces more great wine than any other country. The wines of Bordeaux, Burgundy, the Rhône and Champagne all testify to the centuries-old reputation of quality French wine. Yet, France is not just about tradition. In recent decades, less well-known regions of France such as the Languedoc, Provence, the Ardèche and the Jardin de la France have undergone a viticultural revolution. Where once these vineyards produced simple *vin ordinaire* for everyday domestic consumption, many now turn out quality wines of all types.

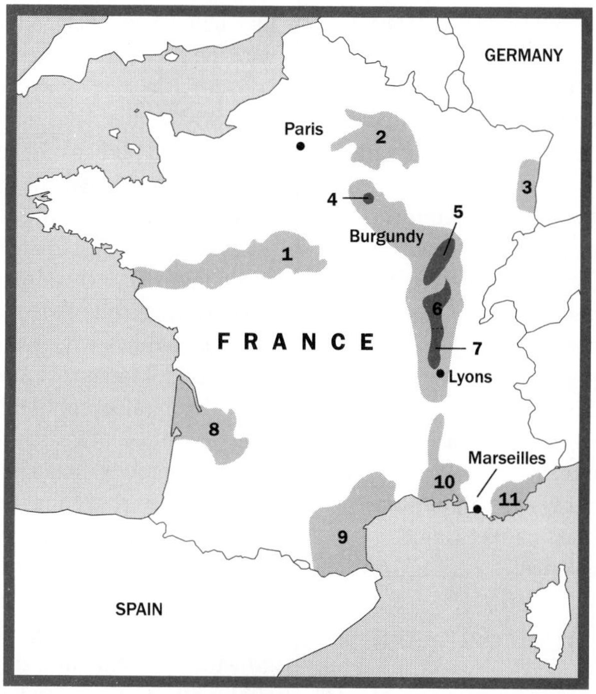

1. Loire
2. Champagne
3. Alsace
4. Chablis
5. Côte d'Or
6. Mâcon
7. Beaujolais
8. Bordeaux
9. Languedoc-Roussillion (d'Oc)
10. Rhône
11. Provence

THE FRENCH APPELLATION SYSTEM

Established in the 1930s, the *Appellation (d'Origine) Controllée* laws (AC) are key to understanding French wines. Though widely misperceived as a guarantee of quality, what the AC laws are, in fact, is a guarantee of authenticity—in other words, that the wine in the bottle actually comes from the place stated on its label. This system reflects the basic philosophical underpinning of French winemaking: that soils are unique and that the character and quality of wine flows from the precise interplay of soil, climate, grape variety and the human element contributed by the winemaker.

There are roughly 250 recognized AC wine types, ranging from large regional appellations, such as "AC Bordeaux," which covers tens of thousands of acres, to mini-appellations, such as "Château Grillet," which covers a single estate. As a general rule, the more tightly specified the AC, the better the quality of the soil and the wine that comes from it. Thus, to take Bordeaux as an example, at the top of the AC hierarchy are the specific communes, such as Pauillac, St.-Julien, Margaux and Pomerol. At the base of the pyramid are the basic Bordeaux wines, which can come from anywhere in the region. In between are intermediate levels such as Médoc and Haut-Médoc. As one moves up the pyramid, specifications as to yields per acre, alcoholic content, and other factors grow increasingly tighter. Most of the other important regions—including Burgundy, the Rhône, and the Loire—have similar gradations of specificity and quality within their respective appellations.

With the vast improvements in winemaking and viticulture that have taken place in recent decades, the traditional appellation control system has become somewhat inadequate; it does not embrace the dynamic growth and improvement in quality going on outside the original ACs. An intermediate experiment with a category called VDQS (*vins delimités de qualité supérieure*) was initiated in 1949, to recognize regions of special merit that had not quite achieved the quality and consistency expected of a wine in the AC category. This VDQS category has now largely disappeared as many of its original members have been elevated to full AC status.

Many of the most exciting recent developments have taken place in a category created in 1973 called *vin de pays* (VDP). There are now roughly a hundred defined areas that have the right to use this term on their labels. Some of the best known include Vin de Pays d'Oc, Vin de Pays de l'Hérault and Vin de Pays des Côtes du Gascogne. More than 75 percent of the *vins de pays* are from the vast Midi region on France's Mediterranean coast, which in the past had been devoted almost solely to bulk wine production.

The VDP category has become extremely important and now accounts for about one-fifth of total wine production. Development here has been aided by the simple fact that vineyard land in the better-known ACs has become prohibitively expensive. Large, established AC firms such as Louis Latour, Moreau, and Baron de Rothschild (Mouton) have invested heavily in VDP production, believing that with the right production techniques and better vineyard practices, there is significant potential for quality wines.

Many of the VDP wines are sold under their varietal names—as "Chardonnay," for instance—in a frank recognition of the realities of the modern consumer market; consumers appear to understand varietal labels much better than they do the more complex appellation system. This represents a major shift away from the traditional *appellation controllée* philosophy, which has always emphasized geography over grape varieties. It is a safe bet that both systems will continue to coexist and prosper, with the AC wines being marketed to a sophisticated audience of collectors and connoisseurs, while the varietal wines will be sold with increasing success to a mass market which demands good quality at a fair price.

FRENCH WINE REGIONS

Bordeaux

Of all the wines entitled to AC status, Bordeaux accounts for the largest percentage of production by far, about 20 to 25 percent in good years. At more than sixty million cases annually, it also accounts for about 10 percent of total French wine production. Almost 250,000 acres of vineyards are entitled to the Bordeaux appellation, and 80 percent of the total production is devoted to red wines.

The most important Bordeaux grape is Cabernet Sauvignon, which forms the backbone of many of its wines. However, Merlot is more widely planted, and accounts for nearly half of all acreage. Cabernet Franc, Petit Verdot and Malbec are also significant here. Most Bordeaux wines are blends of two or more of these varieties.

The most widely planted white grape variety in Bordeaux is the Sémillon, followed closely by the Sauvignon Blanc. Muscadelle, Colombard and Ugni Blanc account for most of the remaining white production. Like the reds, most white Bordeaux is a blend of two or more varieties.

The Médoc remains the most important Bordeaux appellation. Cabernet Sauvignon is dominant here, accounting for the sturdy structure and long aging potential of classic Médoc clarets. Four major subregions of the Médoc are held in high regard; each has its own distinctive style. Margaux is known for its delicate bouquet and aristocratic svelteness; St.-Julien may be the best balanced, combining Margaux finesse with the classic characteristics of its neighbor Pauillac, known for its black currant aromas and powerful structure. St.-Estèphe, with the heaviest soil, produces the sturdiest and perhaps the most reliable claret, seeming to obtain a reasonable degree of concentration and depth even in difficult years.

In 1855, the best châteaux of the Médoc were classified into five levels, from first to fifth growth. The first growths, called the *premiers crus*, are perhaps the most famous wine names in the world: Lafite-Rothschild, Margaux, Latour, Mouton-Rothschild and Haut-Brion (although the latter is actually in the Graves). In recent years the quality of several lower classified growths has improved to the point where they can now challenge the first growths in every way but price. These so-called super-seconds include Léoville Las Cases, Ducru-Beaucaillou, Cos d'Estournel, Palmer (actually a third growth) and Pichon-Longueville-Lalarde. Just below the classified growths are the many excellent *crus bourgeois*, several of which (Gloria and Chasse-Spleen, for instance) would almost certainly be ranked with the classified growths in the unlikely event of a reclassification.

Because it is close to the port of Bordeaux, the Médoc dominated the Bordeaux wine trade for centuries. In the last two decades, however, Saint-Emilion and Pomerol, on the so-called right bank of the Dordogne River, have achieved their rightful places alongside the great wines of the Médoc. Pomerol is dominated by Merlot. Its estates tend to be tiny, and demand for their best wines vastly outstrips supply. The most famous estate, Petrus, now sells its wines for more than any Médoc *premier cru*. Other top Pomerol properties include Trotanoy, L'Evangile, La Conseillante, Lafleur, Vieux Château Certan, Clinet, and the microscopic Le Pin.

St.-Emilion is a larger region than Pomerol, and the quality of its estates is more variable. Merlot is the most important grape, but here it is often blended with significant quantities of Cabernet Franc, Malbec and, less often, Cabernet Sauvignon. Unlike Pomerol, which has never had a classification, St.-Emilion was first classified in 1954, and had a subsequent reclassification in 1985. Its two top wines, Cheval Blanc and Ausone, are considered on a par with the Médoc first growths. Just below them are a dozen or so other fine estates that would rank with the better second and third growths of the Médoc. These include Figeac, Canon, Pavie, Magdelaine, and Clos Fourtet.

The Graves region, which surrounds the town of Pessac, a suburb of the city of Bordeaux, is unusual in that its reputation rests equally on the quality of its reds and whites. Many of the top estates, such as Haut-Brion, La Mission Haut-Brion, Domaine de Chevalier and Olivier produce exquisite whites from a blend of Sémillon and Sauvignon Blanc. Reds here rely more heavily on Merlot than do the wines of the Médoc, located just to the north. As a result, a red Graves tends to mature more quickly than a typical Médoc, though it shares the Médoc's robust structure.

Contained within the southern part of the Graves, the regions of Sauternes and Barsac produce one of the world's great sweet dessert wines, mostly from Sémillon, but with some Sauvignon Blanc used at certain estates. Like the great German late-harvest wines, the key to superlative Sauternes is the development of noble rot (*Botrytis cinerea*), which gradually draws water out of the grape, shriveling it and greatly concentrating the flavors of the grape. Among the wines of Sauternes, Château d'Yquem has no equal. However, great Sauternes are also made at Château Rieussec, Climens, Guiraud, Suduiraut and others.

Sara Matthews

Château Beychevelle, in the St.-Julien region of Bordeaux.

Burgundy

No region has suffered so much for its fame as has Burgundy. Its name was appropriated by bulk producers worldwide to represent any generic red, and many were heavy and sweet. It was also a victim of its own abuses, as many producers let grape yields soar in the late 1960s and 1970s. But with yields under control and a renewed commitment to conscientious cellar practices, there can be little doubt that today Burgundy is producing some of the best wines in its illustrious history.

The heart of Burgundy is the Côte d'Or, which at 20,000 acres, is less than a tenth the size of Bordeaux. The northern half of the Côte d'Or, the Côte de Nuits, specializes in red Burgundy, which is made exclusively from the Pinot Noir grape. The southern half of the Côte d'Or, the Côte de Beaune, produces both red and white Burgundy; the latter is made almost exclusively from Chardonnay. Red and white Burgundies are extraordinarily complex, and are among the most avidly sought-after by collectors of great wine.

The appellation system of Burgundy is complicated. At the top of the Burgundy hierarchy are the *grands crus* vineyards. The best known of these include Le Chambertin, Le Musigny, Romanée-Conti, Richebourg, La Tâche and Clos de Vougeot for red wines; Le Montrachet, Chevalier-Montrachet, Bâtard-Montrachet and Corton-Charlemagne for white wines. Classified below the *grands crus* are the *premiers crus*, some of which produce wines that are virtually on a par with *grands crus* and are usually less expensive. The best-known *premiers crus* in the Côte de Nuits include Gevrey-Chambertin le Cazetiers, Chambolle-Musigny Les Amoureuses, Chambolle-Musigny Les Charmes and Vosne-Romanée Les Suchots. In the Côte de Beaune, *premiers crus* include Beaune Clos des Mouches (white and red), Beaune Les Grèves (red), Pommard Les Epenots (red), Volnay

Clos des Ducs (red), Meursault Charmes (white), Puligny-Montrachet Les Combettes (white) and Puligny-Montrachet Les Pucelles (white).

Somewhat confusingly, many of the *grands crus* have had their names appended to the nearby villages. Thus, the villages of Gevrey-Chambertin, Chambolle-Musigny, Vosne-Romanée, Puligny-Montrachet and Aloxe-Corton all produce wines under their names. While often quite good, these never have the depth and dimension of top *grands crus* or *premiers crus*, which must come from a single vineyard.

It's important to note that most great Burgundy vineyards have more than one owner (Clos de Vougeot, for example, has nearly 80), and the range in quality between the best and the worst producers is enormous. The best way for consumers to assure themselves of a quality product is to consult a reliable wine publication (such as *Wine Spectator)* for ratings of individual producers' wines.

An important emerging region of Burgundy is the small Côte Chalonnaise, immediately south of the Côte de Beaune, which is developing a reputation for reasonably priced reds and whites. The four major appellations of the Chalonnaise are Mercurey, Givry, Rully and Montagny. The first two are noted for their red wines, most of which are made exclusively from Pinot Noir (rather than the less exalted Gamay of Beaujolais). Both are more similar to the soft, fruity style of the Côte de Beaune than to the denser, earthier reds of the Côte de Nuits. While Mercurey is larger than Givry, the latter boasts several exceptionally fine vineyards—Cellier-aux-Moines and Domaine Thenard among them—which give it the stronger following among connoisseurs. Rully also makes good reds, but both it and Montagny are better known for their whites, which are made from Chardonnay.

The Mâconnais is a considerably larger—and quite exciting—area of Burgundy. Mâcon wines are made largely from Chardonnay, and top producers here make Chardonnays rivalling those of the Côte de Beaune. Among the most interesting are Jean Thevenet, Verget, and Guffens-Heynen.

South of the Mâconnais lies the highly productive region of Beaujolais, an excellent source of affordable everyday red wines. Beaujolais is made from the vigorously fruity Gamay grape. Of particular distinction are the ten *crus* of Beaujolais, which offer greater complexity and concentration; the most prominent are Moulin-à-Vent, Fleurie, and Morgon. Many wine lovers find the debut of Beaujolais Nouveau, a grapey wine that is released the third Thursday of each November, a reason for special celebration.

The Rhône

Though they are often lumped together, the northern and southern regions of the Rhône are best viewed separately. Northern Rhône has a continental climate, with moderate summers; its wines are firmly structured and tannic. The southern Rhône is primarily Mediterranean, with much hotter summers. The warmth produces wines that are higher in alcohol, with a riper, softer edge. Vintages differ as well. For example, 1991 was mediocre at best in the south, while in the north it was very good, even outstanding in some areas.

The major appellations of the north are Côte Rôtie, Hermitage, Crozes-Hermitage, St.-Joseph and Cornas for reds and Condrieu for whites. Hermitage, Crozes-Hermitage and St.-Joseph also make whites, primarily from Marsanne; Condrieu uses Viognier. All northern reds rely on the Syrah grape.

Châteauneuf-du-Pape, located in the southern Rhône, is without doubt the most famous appellation of the entire Rhône. The south also produces 80 percent of the region's Côtes-du-Rhône. Though inexpensive, Côtes-du-Rhône can be good to very good, in styles ranging from grapey Beaujolais types to serious wines that could almost pass for Châteauneuf-du-Papes. In the south, the major grape varieties include Grenache, Mourvèdre, Cinsault, Syrah and Cournoise. In recent years, Grenache has been de-emphasized in favor of the more complex Mourvèdre and Syrah. White grapes are less important in the south than in the north. However, Roussanne and Marsanne produce small cuvées of superb whites in Châteauneuf-du-Pape.

Other French Regions

The Loire is known for its crisp white wines; the best known is probably Muscadet, which is made from the Muscadet grape, sometimes called the *melon de Bourgogne*. Muscadet is made to be drunk when it is young and vigorous, though a few examples, which are labeled *sur lie* (meaning aged on yeasty sediment), can improve with short-term aging. The Chenin Blanc grape also produces a number of distinctive Loire wines. The best known

Per-Henrick Mansson

The vineyards of Fortant de France, located in the Midi region in southern France.

is Vouvray, which can range from bone dry to quite sweet, depending on the style chosen by the producer. However, the best dry whites of the Loire are Sancerre and Pouilly Fumé. Both are made from the Sauvignon Blanc grape, which here produces an especially crisp, flinty style of wine quite unlike examples from Bordeaux and California.

Red Loire is a relative rarity, but a few interesting types are made. These include Chinon rouge, made from Cabernet Franc, and Sancerre rouge, made from Pinot Noir.

Alsace lies on the French-German border and utilizes the major German varietals, including Riesling, Gewürztraminer and Sylvaner. Unlike German wines, which tend to be off-dry or sweet, most Alsatian wines are dry. However, in especially ripe years, the region produces late harvest wines called *vendange tardive*, some of which can be sweet, and *sélections de grains nobles*, always sweet.

Champagne

Champagne is widely imitated around the world, but true Champagne can only come from the Champagne region of France. It must be made by the *méthode champenoise*, in which a secondary fermentation takes place in the bottle. Most Champagne is made from a blend of Pinot Noir, Pinot Meunier and Chardonnay; when only the latter is used, the Champagne is called *blanc de blancs*. Most Champagne is a blend of different vintages, which helps ensure a consistently reliable product. In exceptional years, however, many houses produce a vintage-dated Champagne. While not necessarily better than non-vintage, vintage Champagne is usually more distinctive and commands a higher price. Most houses also produce a luxurious—and expensive—prestige cuvée (formerly called the *tète de cuvée)*. Dom Perignon is the best known, but it is rare to find a prestige cuvée that does not deliver the very best the house has to offer.

ABARBANEL

Cabernet Sauvignon Vin de Pays d'Oc 1996: Smells reduced, with a minimal core of cherry flavor and clumsy tannins. Not recommended. Kosher. Tasted three times, with consistent notes. Past its prime. 2,500 cases made. • $9 • (12/15/97) • **65**

Cabernet Sauvignon Vin de Pays de Cassan 1994: Its herb and green olive character says Cabernet, but there's a candied quality to the fruit flavors, and the tannins are too prominent. Kosher. • $8 • (12/15/96) • **77**

Chardonnay Vin de Pays d'Oc 1996: Tired and flabby, with canned-fruit flavors. Kosher. 2,000 cases made. • $10 • (09/30/97) • **72**

Chardonnay Vin de Pays d'Oc 1995: Odd and off-tasting, with nutty, oxidized aromas and canned-fruit flavors. Tasted twice. Kosher. • $9 • (02/28/97) • **71**

Grenache Rosé Vin de Pays d'Oc French Blush 1996: Shows some dried cherry and herbal flavors, but it seems a bit dried out in the end. Kosher. 1,000 cases made. • $9 • (09/30/97) • **76**

Grenache Rosé Vin de Pays de Cassan French Blush 1995: Dry, with oxidized aromas and only faint fruit flavors of watermelon and cherry. Kosher. • $8 • (12/15/96) • **76**

Merlot Vin de Pays d'Oc 1996: Smells like cough syrup with a heavy menthol aroma. Tastes dried out and cloying. Kosher. 2,500 cases made. • $9 • (11/15/97) • **72**

Merlot Vin de Pays d'Oc 1995: A good, solid wine with ample fruit flavor and a firm texture. Somewhat tannic and turns lean on the finish. Kosher. • $8 • (12/15/96) • **81**

ABBAYE DE THOLOMIES

Minervois Réserve 1993: This inky red has a chewy texture and ripe flavors of sweet plums, raisins and chocolate. The tannins are firm but well-integrated. Try now. • $11 • (06/30/97) • **85**

ABBAYE DE VALMAGNE

Coteaux du Languedoc 1994: Don't be fooled by the lush texture and soft raspberry and dried herb flavors—there's plenty of structure lurking in the shadows of this satisfying red. Try with roasted chicken or grilled meats. • $11 • (05/15/97) • **85**

Coteaux du Languedoc 1991 • $10 • (03/15/94) • **87**

Coteaux du Languedoc 1989 • $10 • (10/31/92) • **72**

Coteaux du Languedoc 1988 • $12 • (08/31/91) • **80**

ABEILLE DE FIEUZAL

Pessac-Léognan 1995: Aromas of crushed berries and mushrooms. Full-bodied with velvety, full tannins. Rather astringent on the finish. Second label of Château de Fieuzal. Best after 1999. • $15 • (01/31/98) • **86**

Pessac-Léognan White 1995: Plenty of coconut and apple aromas and flavors. Medium-bodied, with fresh acidity, but slightly diluted on the finish. Second label of Château de Fieuzal. Drink now. • $16 • (04/30/98) • **84**

ABELÉ, HENRI

Brut Champagne 1986: A fully mature, dry, bracing and lean style that turns tight on the finish. Combines mineral, lemon and toast flavors in a subtle, enticing blend. Drink now. 2,275 cases made. • $85 • (11/30/97) • **90**

Brut Champagne NV: An atypical but very attractive bubbly that's lively in flavor, bracing in balance and quite citruslike in character. A toasty yeast note adds complexity on the finish. 10,800 cases made. • $25 • (10/31/97) • **87**

Brut Champagne Grande Marque Impériale 1982: Classically yeasty and toasty, with creamy texture and rich flavors of vanilla, fig and grapefruit, complex and spicy, lovely, nicely crafted Champagne in a restrained, elegant style. • $29 • (07/31/87) • **90**

Brut Champagne Le Sourire de Reims 1986: Vibrant flavors and elegant texture; enjoyably mature but still fresh. Balanced toward the lean side, as crisp citrus notes and firm acidity are accented by subtle butter and vanilla. 2,275 cases made. • $85 • (11/30/95) • **89**

Key: SS—Spectator Selection CS—Cellar Selection HR—Highly Recommended BB—Best Buy $NA—Price not available Ⓐ—Auction Price (BT)—Barrel Tasting
Dates in parentheses indicate the issues in which the ratings were published.

Brut Rosé Champagne Cuvée Reservée 1983: Crisp and fruity, with intensely focused apple and spice aromas and flavors that hint at nutmeg and almond on the finish. Drinkable now. • $50 • (03/31/92) • **88**

Brut Rosé Champagne Grande Marque Impériale 1982: Rich and creamy, with lots of almond and smoke notes to the basic pear and grapefruit flavors that linger through the finish, modifying themselves and becoming more complex on the aftertaste. Drink now. • $25 • (03/31/92) • **88**

ACACIAS, DOMAINE DES

Touraine Sauvignon 1995: Round, almost soft, with peach-tart flavors that mingle fruit, dough and cinnamon notes. A pretty wine, accessible and beguiling. Drink now. 2,000 cases made. • $10 • (05/15/97) • **85**

ADAM, J.-B.

Alsace Kaefferkopf 1994: Spicy, floral Gewürztraminer notes dominate this blend. Has personality, but is rather light on the palate. Finishes with a pleasing bitter note. Drink now. • $19 • (10/15/96) • **82**

Alsace Kaefferkopf Traditionnelle 1996: Big-boned and powerful for a Riesling, revealing plenty of floral, tropical fruit and spice nuances, with a dry, minerally finish. Drinkable now, yet balanced to develop through 2003. • $20 • (11/15/97) • **88**

Gewürztraminer Alsace 1994: Broad texture and blunt flavors of melon and chocolate combine to make a heavy, rather dull wine. • $14 • (10/15/96) • **79**

Gewürztraminer Alsace Kaefferkopf Cuvée Jean-Baptiste 1995: Floral and honey flavors are muted, yet there's an underlying power and a spicy, mineral character. Tangible ripeness and weight. More structure than fruit overall. • $21 • (09/30/97) • **84**

Gewürztraminer Alsace Kaefferkopf Cuvée Jean-Bapiste 1994: Straightforward, simple and rather subdued for Gewürz. Broad, and slightly flat, offering light flavors of melons and juniper. • $19 • (10/15/96) • **82**

Gewürztraminer Alsace Réserve 1996: Well-focused, showing pure flavors of litchi, pear and roses wrapped in a smooth texture. Finish has a touch of grapefruit. Delicious now. • $16 • (09/30/97) • **87**

Gewürztraminer Alsace Réserve 1993 • $12 • (09/15/95) • **83**

Gewürztraminer Alsace Sélection de Grains Noble 1989 • $52 • (09/30/94) • **93**

Gewürztraminer Alsace Vendange Tardive 1994: Shows powerful apricot, rose petal and spice aromas and a sleek, thick texture loaded with spicy fruit flavors and braced by firm acidity. Balanced and harmonious; not overly sweet. • $39 • 500ml (10/15/96) • **89**

Muscat Alsace 1995: Exuberant, appealing bright lime and grapefruit flavors with spicy accents. There's also a fruity softness unusual in Alsace Muscats. • $13 • (09/30/96) • **84**

Muscat Alsace Réserve 1993 • $10 • (09/15/95) • **84**

Pinot Blanc Alsace 1994: Round and soft, with some attractive spice and honey notes, but it turns a bit earthy on the palate and finishes without crispness or pep. Drink now. • $11 • (10/15/96) • **80**

Pinot Blanc Alsace Réserve 1996: Vibrant, with straightforward appeal from its earthy apple and almond flavors. A bit metallic at the end. • $11 • (09/30/97) • **79**

Pinot Blanc Alsace Réserve 1993 • $9 • (07/31/95) • **84**

Pinot Gris Alsace Cuvée Jean-Baptiste 1995: Seductive, ripe and creamy, like vanilla pudding, with dashes of spice and citrus. Full-bodied and slightly coarse on the finish. • $19 • (09/30/97) • **84**

Pinot Gris Alsace Réserve 1996: Soft and lush, with just enough acidity to keep everything lively, this young white has peach and honey flavors that say "drink me." • $15 • (09/30/97) • **85**

Pinot Noir Alsace Cuvée Jean-Baptiste 1995: Like a rosé in color and body, this Pinot Noir has vivid aromas and flavors of raspberry and spice, with just a hint of licorice. Attractive and enjoyable now. Best slightly chilled. • $18 • (11/15/97) • **84**

Riesling Alsace 1994: Assertive, but a bit disjointed. This mingles very tart grapefruit flavors with herbal and lightly earthy notes. Try now. • $12 • (10/15/96) • **83**

Riesling Alsace Kaefferkopf Cuvée Jean-Baptiste 1995: Soft and straightforward, with almond and apple flavors culminating in a dry, crisp finish. Ready now. • $20 • (09/30/97) • **84**

Riesling Alsace Kaefferkopf Cuvée Jean-Baptiste 1994: Clean and elegant. Classic mineral aromas give way to light floral and fruit flavors, especially lime and pineapple. Very fresh, if lacking in concentration. • $19 • (10/15/96) • **85**

Riesling Alsace Letzenberg Cuvée Jean-Baptiste 1994: Grapefruit and mineral notes are shy but clean, making this a supportive but unobtrusive complement to food. • $15 • (10/15/96) • **83**

Riesling Alsace Réserve 1995: An austere style of Riesling characterized by pine and diesel flavors, with accents of apple and marzipan. Try now. • $14 • (09/30/97) • **84**

Riesling Alsace Réserve 1993 • $9 • (09/15/95) BB • **88**

Sylvaner Alsace Réserve 1993 • $9 • (09/15/95) • **86**

Tokay Pinot Gris Alsace 1994: Thick, almost viscous, yet dry, with herbal and pear flavors. Try now. • $14 • (09/30/96) • **87**

Tokay Pinot Gris Alsace Cuvée Jean-Baptiste 1994: Melon and pear flavors carry though this round but somewhat restrained wine; it has enough body and firm acidity to marry well with food. • $18 • (10/15/96) • **86**

Tokay Pinot Gris Alsace Réserve 1993 • $12 • (09/15/95) • **81**

Tokay Pinot Gris Alsace Sélection de Grains Nobles 1994: Rich yet delicate, with flavors and aromas of honey, coconut, almond and pear that mingle nicely. Sweet but not cloying; spice and citrus notes keep it lively and harmonious. Very appealing for its balance and delicacy. • $60/500ml • (10/15/96) • **91**

Tokay Pinot Gris Alsace Sélection de Grains Noble 1990 • $52 • (09/30/94) • **89**

AGASSAC, CHÂTEAU D'

Haut-Médoc 1989 • $20 • (03/15/92) • **88**

AIGLON, MAISON L'

Chardonnay Vin de Pays d'Oc Grand Reserve 1995: A nice, easy-going, fruity tasting Chardonnay with a soft texture and pleasant flavors. 15,000 cases made. • $7 • (02/28/97) • **82**

St.-Chinian Grand Reserve 1994: Fresh and fruity, with loads of plum and and berry flavors. A nice, juicy quality adds to its appeal. Spicy flavors linger on the finish. 10,000 cases made. • $7 • (06/15/97) • **86**

St.-Chinian Grand Réserve 1993: The aromas are promising and it doesn't diasappoint. Packed with gamy, chewy black cherry, this brawny red makes up in flavor what it lacks in finesse. • $8 • (07/31/96) • **85**

St.-Chinian Grand Réserve 1990 • $6 • (07/15/92) BB • **83**

AIGUELIÈRE, DOMAINE L'

Coteaux du Languedoc Grenat 1995: Quite leathery-tasting, but still fresh with plum and cherry notes. Finishes on a distinctly gamy note. Interesting, but not for everyone. Drink now. • $15 • (03/31/98) • **83**

Coteaux du Languedoc Montpeyroux 1995: Meaty and gamy aromas and flavors predominate in this inky Mediterranean red. It's quite lush on the palate, but tannins are firm. Has distinctive personality despite muted fruit flavors. Drink now. • $17 • (12/15/97) • **84**

Coteaux du Languedoc Montpeyroux 1991 • $12 • (03/15/94) • **86**

Coteaux du Languedoc Montpeyroux 1989 • $11 • (04/15/93) • **77**

Coteaux du Languedoc Montpeyroux Côte Dorée 1993: Intense and powerful, quite distinctive and gutsy with layers of flavor. Dominated by beefy and leathery flavors, with dried cherry, bitter chocolate and cedary components too. Incredibly concentrated, still quite tannic and firm. Best from 1999 through 2005. • $38 • (03/31/98) • **89**

Coteaux du Languedoc Montpeyroux Côte Dorée 1991 • $NA • (03/15/94) • **89**

Coteaux du Languedoc Montpeyroux Côte Rousse 1991 • $NA • (03/15/94) • **87**

Coteaux du Languedoc Montpeyroux Tradition 1995: A tannic red offering meaty and earthy aromas and flavors that turn slightly bitter on the finish. A rustic wine that needs food to soften. Drink now. • $20 • (12/15/97) • **82**

AIGUILLOUX, CHÂTEAU

Corbières 1991 • $7 • (03/15/94) • **83**

ALADAME, STEPHANE

Montagny Premier Cru 1995: Woody and slightly heavy, showing persistent candle wax, floral and perfume notes. 417 cases made. • $NA • (05/31/97) • **70**

ALARY, DOMAINE

Côtes du Rhône-Villages Cairanne 1995: Very fruity. Light and quite crisp, with red berry, cherry, spice and white pepper flavors. Rather long on the finish. Drink now. 2,083 cases made. • $13 • (10/15/97) • **80**

Côtes du Rhône-Villages Cairanne Réserve du Vigneron 1995: Fruity and crisp, with fresh red berry aromas. Light- to medium-bodied, it has ripe tannins and well-integrated oak flavors that make it lush and supple. Lingering finish. Well made. Drink now. 583 cases made. • $18 • (10/15/97) • **85**

ALBRECHT, LUCIEN

Gewürztraminer Alsace 1996: Take a bouquet of flowers, add some honeysuckle, litchi and a touch of grapefruit-peel on the finish and you have this forward white. Attractive, but lacks concentration. Tasted twice, with consistent notes. • $15 • (11/15/97) • **82**

Gewürztraminer Alsace Sélection de Grains Nobles 1989 • $NA • (11/15/90) • **93**

Gewürztraminer Alsace Vendange Tardive 1994: This late-harvest Gewürz shows lovely balance and the rose and litchi flavors are subdued. It finishes a bit short and coarse for this vintage and level of ripeness. • $45 • (10/15/97) • **87**

Pinot Blanc Alsace 1996: Ripe and exotic, with a leesy character, it's fat and round in the mouth, where there are ripe apple flavors. Short finish. • $16 • (09/15/97) • **83**

Pinot Blanc Alsace 1993 • $10 • (11/15/94) • **78**

Riesling Alsace 1995: Ripe peach, apricot and a floral talcum-powder quality are the hallmarks of this rich, opulent Riesling. Has good acidity and should develop well over the next few years. • $12 • (09/15/97) • **87**

Riesling Alsace Pfingstberg Sélection de Grains Nobles 1989 • $NA • (11/15/90) • **87**

Riesling Alsace Vendange Tardive 1994: This late-harvest white exhibits some apple, honey and mineral flavors, yet it appears hollow and on the earthy side. • $45 • (11/15/97) • **84**

Tokay Pinot Gris Alsace Sélection de Grains Nobles 1994: A luscious dessert wine, its sweetness balanced deftly by honey, apricot and mushroom flavors and a touch of mandarin orange to keep the finish bright. • $75 • (10/15/97) • **90**

Tokay Pinot Gris Alsace Vendange Tardive 1994: An internal structure of steel is within this towering Pinot Gris. Intense flavors of ripe mango and apricot with smoky, nutty accents persist through the finish, which is a touch hot. It's moderately sweet and all the elements are there, so give it until 1999 to settle down. • $45 • (10/15/97) • **90**

ALLAINES, FRANÇOIS D'

Mâcon La Roche Vineuse 1996: Extraordinary Mâcon from a producer who is a discovery for us. Tender and gentle, this lush, full-bodied, honeyed and floral '96 makes for a soft-textured, delicious drink. Kicks in with subtle oak, spice, fruit and citrus flavors on the super-supple finish. Not imported into the U.S. Drink now through 2000. 250 cases made. • $NA • (05/31/98) • **92**

ALLEMAND, THIERRY

Cornas 1991 • $NA • (05/31/94) • **84**

Cornas Chaillot 1991 • $27 • (05/31/94) • **86**

ALLIET, PHILIPPE

Chinon Vieilles Vignes 1995: A plush, powerful red, with very deep color, explosive aromas of toast, vanilla and plum, and deep, rich flavors of plum, coffee, tobacco and game. Full tannins are well-integrated, and the long finish echoes with mineral, game and coffee notes. An international style applied to classic Loire character. Best from 1999 through 2005. • $16 • (06/15/98) HR • **91**

ALLOUCHERY-PERSEVAL

Brut Champagne Réserve NV: Generous in flavor and elegant in texture, this is a thoroughly pleasing Champagne with ripe fruit notes accented by vanilla and fig on the finish. Drink now. 2,000 cases made. • $27 • (11/15/97) • **88**

FRANCE

Brut Champagne Tradition NV: A good all-around Champagne with enough lively fruit flavors to fill out the smooth but crisp texture and linger a bit on the finish. 3,500 cases made. • $23 • (12/31/97) • **85**

ALQUIER, GILBERT

Faugères 1995: Beautiful raspberry and wild herb aromas and flavors are buoyed on a fresh, vibrant structure. An appealing red, with light tannins that suggest food. • $14 • (08/31/97) • **86**

Faugères 1991 • $9 • (03/15/94) • **87**

Faugères 1990 • $9 • (03/15/94) • **84**

Faugères 1985 • $7 • (09/30/87) • **78**

Faugères La Maison Jaune Réserve 1995: Exotic-tasting, with flavors of lavender and sagebrush. Ripe and focused with an appealing mineral edge to it, it's a hearty wine that's both rustic and refined. Drink now through 2000. • $13 • (03/31/98) • **86**

Faugères Les Bastides Réserve 1995: Here's a mouthful of plummy, spicy fruit flavor from France, with a mineral and tobacco edge. It's full, round and warm, like baked bricks, yet has a firmness to it that supports the rich flavors and texture. Unique and compelling, with great length. Made from a blend of Syrah, Grenache and Mourvèdre. • $17 • (12/15/97) HR • **91**

Faugères Les Bastides Réserve 1991 • $15 • (03/15/94) • **87**

AMADIEU, PIERRE

Côtes du Rhône Roulepierre 1995: Pretty ripe cherry and smoke notes are bright and accessible. Light and fruity, but it has just enough tannins to stand up to food. Drink now. 5,000 cases made. • $6 • (02/28/97) • **84**

Gigondas Romane-Machotte 1995: Light in color and in body, with some decent red berry flavors. More Côtes du Rhône than Gigondas. Still, fairly delicate. Drink now. 11,667 cases made. • $NA • (10/15/97) • **80**

AMBROISE, BERTRAND

Bourgogne White 1994: Pretty, and quite oaky, though honey and lemon aromas and flavors struggle to balance the wood. Decent length. Medium-bodied. Try now. • $14 • (08/31/96) • **84**

Chardonnay St.-Romain 1993: Rather ripe, beautiful pear and sweet melon tones. Harmonious, clean mineral flavors and a round, sound finish. Drink now. • $17 • (05/15/95) • **85**

Clos de Vougeot 1995: Very oaky, from the coffee, vanilla and spice notes to the chewy, woody finish and beautifully integrated tannins. Perhaps too much wood for balance over the long haul. 75 cases made. • $90 • (11/15/97) • **91**

Clos de Vougeot 1994: A seductive wine with impressive clarity of pure currant and plum flavors that acquire exotic licorice, spice and coffee overtones, narrow on the palate, then extend into a lively finish with crisp tannins. Best from 2000. • $75 • (11/15/96) • **93**

Clos de Vougeot 1993: An awesome blockbuster, boasting layers of ripe fruit, mineral and spice character. Full in body and mega-tannic, but if you are patient this will bring huge returns of pleasure. Try in 2004. • $90 • (11/15/95) • **96**

Corton-Charlemagne 1994: A masterpiece in this vintage. Beautifully concentrated, full-bodied, fresh, and sweet tasting. Packed with apricot, peach, toasty oak and honey flavors. Long and balanced finish. Delicious now and through 2000. • $75 • (08/31/96) CS • **95**

Corton-Charlemagne 1993: Rich and fat, showing pear, pineapple and toasty coconut flavors. Somewhat heavy-handed on the finish. Drinkable now. From a producer known for his great reds. • $60 • (05/15/95) • **87**

Corton Le Rognet 1995: Fabulous and exotic, this full-bodied '95 explodes with pure, fresh cassis, toasty oak, Oriental spices, violet and wet earth character. It's ripe and rich, but the wall of tannins will need until 2000 to soften. 250 cases made. • $80 • (11/15/97) • **90**

Corton Le Rognet 1994: Solid, youthful and packed with plum, vanilla and toasty aromas and flavors, showing some power and lots of lovely fruit character. Needs cellaring to polish the chewy tannins. Best after 1999 or 2000. • $60 • (11/15/96) • **90**

Corton Le Rognet 1993: Just as monumental now, in bottle, as we remember from a barrel sample earlier this year. An amazing red that boasts masses of plum, currant flavors with wood-scented dark chocolate and vanilla character. Full in body, with loads of fine tannins and a long, elegant finish. Try in 2006. 80 cases made. • $75 • (11/15/95) CS • **97**

Corton Le Rognet 1992: Brilliant deep color and concentrated berry notes pick up some nice cedar and spice overtones, finishing with gravelly tannins. Flavors come through nicely. Try now. 80 cases made. • $55 • (12/15/94) • **89**

Corton Le Rognet 1991: Firm, austere and light, but has bright raspberry and red currant flavors. Focused and lively on the finish, albeit a bit stemmy. Drinkable now. 225 cases made. • $49 Ⓐ • (01/31/94) • **85**

Corton Le Rognet 1990: Combining the beauty with the beast, this supercharged red is big yet delicate, with great, ripe berry characteristics and a lot of well-integrated wood notes. Try now. • $60 • (12/15/92) • **94**

Corton Le Rognet 1989 • $45 • (01/31/92) • **93**

Corton Le Rognet 1988 • $43 • (11/30/90) • **92**

Corton Le Rognet 1987 • $38 • (03/31/90) • **90**

Côte de Nuits-Villages 1995: Toasty, smoky, packed with black cherry flavor, this is a pumped up Côte de Nuits-Village that shows ambition for the appellation. Delicious now, better in 1999. 750 cases made. • $20 • (11/15/97) • **85**

Côte de Nuits-Villages 1994: Firm in texture, with a bright beam of berry flavor that reaches only half-intensity. Ready now. • $20 • (11/15/96) • **80**

Côte de Nuits-Villages 1992: Lean and smooth, with a gamy component to the black cherry flavor. Finishes solid; drinkable now. • $19 • (12/15/94) • **79**

Côte de Nuits-Villages 1987 • $15 • (02/28/90) • **82**

Nuits-St.-Georges 1995: Impressive oak treatment in this sweet, fat Nuits. Has a lively attack but fades a bit in the middle, turns slightly astringent on the finish. 750 cases made. • $33 • (11/15/97) • **86**

Nuits-St.-Georges 1994: Gets a lift from lots of new oak, but lacks the intensity of flavor to balance it. • $30 • (11/15/96) • **79**

Nuits-St.-Georges 1993: Very well-crafted, featuring a nice use of new wood, medium body, soft tannins and medium toasty oak and berry finish. Better in 1999. • $40 • (11/15/95) • **86**

Nuits-St.-Georges 1992: Chunky, chewy tannins make it hard to find the flavors in this sturdy wine. Drink now. • $NA • (12/15/94) • **77**

Nuits-St.-Georges 1991: Modest currant and tobacco aromas and flavors are light, simple and directly appealing. Polished and already drinkable. 375 cases made. • $28 Ⓐ • (01/31/94) • **83**

Nuits-St.-Georges 1990: Bright and lively, with an abundance of cherry, berry and earth aromas and flavors and chewy tannins. Drinkable now. • $38 • (12/15/92) • **89**

Nuits-St.-Georges 1989 • $30 • (01/31/92) • **90**

Nuits-St.-Georges En Rue de Chaux 1995: Balanced, sweet-tasting, ripe and supple, of medium body and intensity, with charming plum, cherry, mint and blackberry flavors. Firm tannins on the finish, but should be nice to drink from 1999. 175 cases made. • $48 • (11/15/97) • **87**

Nuits-St.-Georges En Rue de Chaux 1994: Showing an impressively dense texture for the vintage, this offers plenty of wood-scented spice, black cherry and plum flavors and a smoky, lingering finish. Medium body. Try now. • $40 • (11/15/96) • **87**

Nuits-St.-Georges Les Vaucrains 1995: Powerful and rugged, this monster Nuit shows impressive dark color, great concentration and a solid backbone of tannins and fruit. Offers oak-infused tar, petrol, cassis and wet earth complexity, but it's a bit rough. Try after 2000. 75 cases made. • $58 • (11/15/97) • **90**

Nuits-St.-Georges Les Vaucrains 1994: Has chewy tannins, but also a modicum of pretty currant and vanilla flavors that hold on and echo through the finish. Try now. • $45 • (11/15/96) • **83**

Nuits-St.-Georges Les Vaucrains 1993: Extremely smooth, offering lovely, velvety tannins and a solid core of fruit. Full body, firm tannins and a long, flavorful finish. Try after 2000. • $65 • (11/15/95) • **90**

Nuits-St.-Georges Les Vaucrains 1992: Deep and rich but extremely tannic. Oaky and concentrated with currant flavors. Too much green tannin for us. • $44 • (12/15/94) • **78**

Nuits-St.-Georges Les Vaucrains 1991: Attractive wild berry and wildflower aromas carry on in the flavors, showing a thin thread running through the firm tannins and echoing on the finish. Drinkable now. 50 cases made. • $39 Ⓐ • (01/31/94) • **85**

Nuits-St.-Georges Les Vaucrains 1990: Decadent, with rich earth, truffle and fruit aromas and flavors and lots of firm tannins, yet has a fine mouthfeel. Drink now. • $44 Ⓐ • (12/15/92) • **90**

Nuits-St.-Georges Les Vaucrains 1989 • $38 • (01/31/92) • **94**

Nuits-St.-Georges Rue de Chaux 1992: Perfumed and rather deep for a '92. Chewy and flavorful, delivering a ripe texture, with plum, currant and tobacco notes. Drinkable now. • $38 • (12/15/94) • **85**

Key: SS—Spectator Selection CS—Cellar Selection HR—Highly Recommended BB—Best Buy $NA—Price not available Ⓐ—Auction Price (BT)—Barrel Tasting

Dates in parentheses indicate the issues in which the ratings were published.

Nuits-St.-Georges Rue de Chaux 1991: Vibrant currant and wild berry aromas and flavors shade toward toast on the finish of this firm, juicy, charming wine. Drinkable now. 125 cases made. • $36 Ⓐ • (01/31/94) • **86**

Nuits-St.-Georges Rue de Chaux 1990: Very rich, but shows restraint. Offers loads of black cherry and earth characteristics along with masses of silky tannins. Drink now. • $48 • (12/15/92) • **90**

Nuits-St.-Georges Rue de Chaux 1989 • $38 • (01/31/92) • **91**

Nuits-St.-Georges Rue de Chaux 1988 • $40 • (05/15/91) • **93**

Nuits-St.-Georges Vieilles Vignes 1994: An oaky style, with tough cherry flavors and a drying layer of tannins on the finish. • $35 • (11/15/96) • **79**

St.-Romain White 1995: Showy, with loads of toasty nuts and honey, its chewy texture lacks a bit in finesse, but it's full-bodied. Lemony and slightly disjointed on the crisp finish. • $18 • (08/31/97) • **80**

St.-Romain White 1994: Good quality for a simple Saint-Romain. Medium-bodied, and lively with citrus, green apple, peach and honey flavors. Long finish. A pleasure to drink now. • $17 • (08/31/96) • **85**

Vosne-Romanée 1994: Tough in texture, thin and stale in flavor. • $32 • (11/15/96) • **77**

Vosne-Romanée Aux Damaudes 1995: Ripe and round, with a slight tomato note married to the fresh blackberry, earth and chocolate flavors. Turns dry and tannic on the finish. • $38 • (11/15/97) • **85**

Vosne-Romanée Les Damaudes 1993: Elegant red, showing wood, plum, fruit and tannins in just the right proportions. Medium-to-light body, fine tannins and a fresh finish. Drink in 1999. • $45 • (11/15/95) • **88**

AMBROISE, MAISON

Bourgogne White 1996: Straightforward, with oak, tart green apple, lime and cilantro notes. Light-bodied, with a crisp finish that's a bit bitter. 800 cases made. • $18 • (05/31/98) • **79**

Ladoix Les Gréchons White 1996: Quite oaky, but this medium-bodied '96 offers supple texture, crisp acidity, ripe fruit and toasty oak shadings. Succulent, it's tempting now through 2005. 250 cases made. • $25 • (05/31/98) • **84**

St.-Romain White 1996: Steely and vibrant, with freshly cut grass, green apple, grapefruit and some pear flavors, a tart finish. Medium-bodied, closed on the nose and tough now, it needs time; try in 1999. 350 cases made. • $25 • (05/31/98) • **83**

AMIOT, GUY

Bourgogne Aligoté 1995: Fairly rich and seductive, especially for an Aligoté. Has pear, peach, lime flavors and a slightly hot finish. Drink now through 2000. • $15 • (08/31/97) • **85**

Bourgogne White 1995: Shows the oily, full-bodied character of many '95s, with some lime, mineral and ripe fruit notes. Quite nice, but a bit rough on the finish. Try now. • $18 • (08/31/97) • **80**

Chassagne-Montrachet 1995: Odd-tasting, with notes of wax, perfume, Poire William and kirsch to the modest fruit flavors. Supple, medium-bodied, with a one-dimensional finish. Drink now. • $30 • (05/31/97) • **77**

Chassagne-Montrachet 1993: An early-drinking '93, featuring an apple, cream and chalk character, medium body and a delicious vanilla, apple finish. • $NA • (05/15/95) • **85**

Chassagne-Montrachet 1992: Toasty, smoky aromas combine with honey and pear on the palate to make a very flavorful white. Drinkable now. • $NA • (08/31/94) • **85**

Chassagne-Montrachet Caillerets 1995: Rich, showing good, medium intensity and ripe fruit and honey character, but it comes off as a bit rustic and coarse. • $40 • (05/31/97) • **80**

Chassagne-Montrachet Caillerets 1994: Lovely, medium-bodied '94, featuring enough spice, mineral and ripe fruit flavors to keep anybody happy. Modest intensity. • $50 • (05/31/96) • **85**

Chassagne-Montrachet Clos St.-Jean 1995: Beautiful, with stony, minerally, ripe tropical flavors, and a handsome, full-bodied, oily structure. Rather intense and crisp on the finish, but give it time to develop its full range. Try after 2000. • $40 • (08/31/97) • **92**

Chassagne-Montrachet Clos St.-Jean 1994: Crisp and refeshing, but showing some body and character, ripe pear and honey and a slight vegetal note. Good concentration on the lively finish. Drinkable now. • $44 • (05/31/96) • **87**

Chassagne-Montrachet Clos St.-Jean 1993: Chewy and chalky, quite smooth for a '93, showing lime, pear and green apple flavor. Try now. • $43 • (05/15/95) • **83**

Chassagne-Montrachet Les Champs Gain 1995: Full-bodied and rather closed, with a lactic, diluted honey and cardboard flavor. Not very clean or elegant, and a bit dry on the finish. Drink now. • $40 • (05/31/97) • **79**

Chassagne-Montrachet Les Champs Gain 1994: Very intense and vibrant, as distinctive dried herb notes mingle with fresh lemon and honey character. Medium body, long finish. Needs time; try in 1999. • $44 • (05/31/96) • **89**

Chassagne-Montrachet Les Champs Gain 1993: Toasty oak and green apple flavors; medium body, firm acidity and a light, toasty finish. • $43 • (05/15/95) • **84**

Chassagne-Montrachet Les Macherelles 1995: Lively, sweet-tasting and eminently pleasant, with a slightly wood-dominated character of citrus, ripe pear and honey. Full-bodied, of medium intensity, it's nicely balanced. Try now through 2000. • $37 • (05/31/97) • **87**

Chassagne-Montrachet Les Macherelles 1994: Some concentrated ripe pear and apple flavors, inserting a basil, oregano touch for added complexity. Medium- to full-bodied, this *premier cru* tastes crisp and fresh. Drinkable now. • $39 • (05/31/96) • **86**

Chassagne-Montrachet Les Vergers 1995: Tastes odd, with a less-than-clean, cardboardlike character. May have suffered from recent bottling because underneath are nice, ripe flavors. Drinkable now. • $42 • (05/31/97) • **78**

Chassagne-Montrachet Les Vergers 1994: Flavorful and seductive, offering pretty lemon, honey and herbal notes, medium body and a chewy, chalky texture. Lovely, pure and clean. Try now. • $44 • (05/31/96) • **87**

Chassagne-Montrachet Les Vergers 1992: A bit simple, with a nice balance of crisp lemon and apple flavors and an earthy touch. A smooth, round finish. 260 cases made. • $56 • (08/31/94) • **82**

Montrachet 1995: Medium- to-full body, with clean, fairly rich fruit and mineral flavors, some lightly toasty oak and spice notes; a bit of coarseness on the finish. A bit disappointing for a Montrachet. May be better after 2000. • $250 • (05/31/97) • **85**

Puligny-Montrachet Les Demoiselles 1995: Round and fairly rich with full body and distinctive herbality underpinning toasty, spicy notes. Finish is clumsy and overly woody. Drink now to 2000. • $45 • (05/31/97) • **83**

Puligny-Montrachet Les Demoiselles 1994: Lovely, creamy texture, with some butter and herbal notes marrying nicely in this harmonious, full-bodied '94. Fresh dried herbs and toasty oak add complexity. Try in 1999. • $60 • (05/31/96) • **84**

St.-Aubin En Remilly White 1995: Rich, but rustic and heavy, leaving a slighty bitter aftertaste. More spice, caramel and oak notes than fruit flavors. • $25 • (05/31/97) • **78**

AMIOT, PIERRE

Clos de la Roche 1988 • $75 • (03/15/91) • **86**

Clos de la Roche 1987 • $49 • (12/15/89) • **86**

Clos de la Roche 1982 • $28 • (06/16/85) SS • **93**

Gevrey-Chambertin Aux Combottes 1988 • $64 • (03/15/91) • **89**

Gevrey-Chambertin Aux Combottes 1987 • $42 • (12/15/89) • **88**

Morey-St.-Denis Aux Charmes 1982 • $18 • (07/01/85) • **88**

Morey-St.-Denis Les Ruchots 1988 • $57 • (02/28/91) • **80**

AMIOT-BONFILS

Puligny-Montrachet Les Demoiselles 1992: A tightly-wound white Burgundy with ample pear and peach flavors that are held in check by firm acidity. Drinkable now. 100 cases made. • $65 • (08/31/94) • **91**

AMIRAL DE BEYCHEVELLE

St.-Julien 1995: A slightly lean red, but with some pretty berry, mineral and cherry aromas and flavors. Silky finish. Second label of Château Beychevelle. Drink now. • $13 • (01/31/98) • **80**

AMOURIERS, DOMAINE DES

Corbières Vieilles Vignes 1991 • $8 • (03/15/94) • **82**

Côtes du Rhône 1994: Fairly ripe and thick, with some cherry, currant and plum flavors. Flavorful and attractive. Drink now. • $9 • (10/15/97) • **80**

Vacqueyras 1995: A smooth and easy ride; nicely balanced, medium-bodied, with moderate intensity of plum, cherry and toasty oak flavors. Enjoy now. • $9 • (10/15/97) • **84**

Vin de Pays de Vaucluse 1996: Light and crisp, with straightforward herbal, wild berry and stemmy flavors. Simple. Drink chilled. • $7 • (10/15/97) • **79**

FRANCE

ANDRÉ, PIERRE

Aloxe-Corton 1993: Very light and papery. Not much there really. Short finish. 416 cases made. • $35 • (11/15/95) • **72**

Beaune Clos des Avaux 1994: Light in color and in body, lean and delicate, with a little strawberry and earth flavor on a quaffable finish. • $23 • (11/15/96) • **79**

Chassagne-Montrachet Chanvennes 1994: A bit oaky, but otherwise seductive and opulent. A nice blend of fruit, spice, honey, hazelnut and caramel aromas and flavors. A good effort. Try now. • $NA • (08/31/96) • **84**

Chassagne-Montrachet Chanvennes 1993: Subtle mineral, flint and mushroom character, medium body, well-integrated acidity and fresh, elegant finish. Drinkable now. 1,000 cases made. • $30 • (08/31/95) • **83**

Chassagne-Montrachet Chanvennes Red 1993: Light, diluted and watery, with weedy, strawlike, musty character. 1,000 cases made. • $25 • (11/15/95) • **73**

Châteauneuf-du-Pape 1990: Earthy, barnyardlike overtones tend to obscure the fruit, but what's there is decent enough. Seems a little tired, but it's drinkable. • $21 • (04/15/93) • **77**

Châteauneuf-du-Pape 1988 • $23 • (03/31/91) • **84**

Clos Vougeot 1993: Unusually dry tannins, adding a dry cherry component. Firm yet not fruity enough to hold up to the tannins. Tough finish. • $70 • (11/15/95) • **77**

Corton 1994: Sweet, in a gooey way, this tastes syrupy and like sour-cherry candy. Not very fancy. Tasted twice with consistent notes. • $75 • (11/15/96) • **72**

Corton-Charlemagne 1994: Elegant and light-textured, with some mineral, pear, apple and toasty oak flavors. Pleasant, light-to-medium body. A bit short on the finish. Ready to drink. • $NA • (08/31/96) • **80**

Corton-Charlemagne 1993: A bit dumb with earthy, overripe apple and candied character. Rather dull and metallic on the finish. 750 cases made. • $65 • (08/31/95) • **81**

Corton-Charlemagne 1992: Simple and straightforward, showing stale fruit flavors that verge on cardboard notes. Modest apple and pear here. It's a shame to release such average Corton-Charlemagne. 830 cases made. • $52 • (08/31/94) • **79**

Corton Hautes Mourottes 1992: Very light, with a candied strawberry character dominating the modest flavors. Drinkable now. 233 cases made. • $36 • (12/15/94) • **74**

Corton Le Clos du Roi 1985 • $45 • (07/15/88) • **88**

Corton Les Pougets 1993: A delicate red offering some pretty dried plum and berry character, light body and silky finish. Better in 1999. 500 cases made. • $48 • (11/15/95) • **84**

Corton Les Pougets 1985 • $45 • (07/15/88) • **90**

Gevrey-Chambertin Champlain 1994: Nicely balanced and fairly ripe and rich, with a core of licorice, plum and black cherry flavors. Lacks a bit in intensity, but delivers some manageable tannins. Drink in 1999. • $29 • (11/15/96) • **82**

Gevrey-Chambertin Champlain 1993: Elegant, focused cherry and plum character, medium body, fine tannins and a delicate finish. Better in 1999. 750 cases made. • $21 • (11/15/95) • **82**

Gevrey-Chambertin Champlain 1992: Bright and flavorful, a little chewy in tannins, but shows nice berry and currant flavors and a touch of mineral. Drinkable now. 750 cases made. • $21 • (12/15/94) • **82**

Ladoix Clos des Chagnots 1993: Delicate style, rather light and nicely supple, offering a minty, plummy character but not much structure. Drinkable now. 1,000 cases made. • $20 • (11/15/95) • **79**

Ladoix Le Rognet White 1994: Fairly lush and ripe. Medium-to-full body and good fruit intensity, but slightly coarse finish. A reductive aroma detracts. Try now. • $NA • (08/31/96) • **79**

Ladoix Le Rognet White 1992: A wine with personality; chewy, with lively spice, herb and apple flavors that offer balance and a satisfying drinking experience. 333 cases made. • $17 • (08/31/94) • **83**

Mâcon-Villages Mâcon André 1994: Sour and odd: cardboardlike flavors taste flat and dull. Not recommended. Tasted twice, with consistent notes. 7,000 cases made. • $9 • (08/31/95) • **67**

Meursault 1994: A good effort—very ripe and rich, even by the standards of this vintage. Aromas and flavors of mango, fig, honey and toasty coconut. Full-bodied, but slightly heavy finish. Drink now. • $NA • (08/31/96) • **85**

Meursault 1993: Lean and austere revealing mineral, lime and grapefruit character. Light-bodied; hard acidity. 667 cases made. • $26 • (05/15/95) • **79**

Meursault Les Charmes 1993: A bit dull: apple, cider and vanilla aromas and flavors, with a short finish. 200 cases made. • $40 • (08/31/95) • **76**

Nuits-St.-Georges 1993: Straightforward and very light, tasting more like water than wine, adding a hint of strawberry and cherry notes. Dry, short finish. • $30 • (11/15/95) • **76**

Pommard Premier Cru 1993: Silky, pretty berry and chocolate character, medium body, light tannins and fresh fnish. Drinkable now. 750 cases made. • $38 • (11/15/95) • **80**

Pouilly-Fuissé Domaine des Vieilles Pierres 1993: Wet straw, herbal, tart flavors are a bit one-dimensional, but are clean and straightforward. Drink now. • $17 • (05/15/95) • **77**

Puligny-Montrachet 1993: Green, citrusy, herbal flavors dominate at first, finishing with slightly astringent honey and earth notes. Try now. 417 cases made. • $27 • (05/15/95) • **78**

Puligny-Montrachet Les Folatières 1994: Distinctive, with flavors ranging from mineral and chalk to floral, butterscotch and cardboard. Supple, medium-bodied, and turns a bit dry on the finish. • $NA • (08/31/96) • **78**

Puligny-Montrachet Les Folatières 1993: Very steely mineral, floral and fruit character. Medium to light-bodied; light finish. 500 cases made. • $37 • (05/15/95) • **79**

Puligny-Montrachet Les Folatières 1992: This tastes crisp, lively and fruity, with lime, grapefruit and apple flavors. Straightforward and solid. 1,000 cases made. • $28 • (08/31/94) • **85**

St.-Aubin Les Anges White 1994: A slightly odd *premier cru*. Has mint mixing with cardboard- and paperlike aromas and flavors. Modest fruit. Turns dry on the finish. • $NA • (08/31/96) • **77**

St.-Aubin Les Anges White 1993: Attractive lemon, lime, cream and mineral aromas, but very light-bodied with a crisp, almost neutral finish. 500 cases made. • $20 • (05/15/95) • **79**

St.-Véran 1994: Some decent pear and lemon flavors, but also showing odd cardboard notes. Drying, slightly burning, finish. 5,000 cases made. • $9 • (08/31/95) • **73**

Santenay Domaine du Prieuré Sainte Agathe 1993: A straightforward Burgundy, somewhat disappointing for its lack of fresh fruit. Offers only modest flavors. Drinkable now. 583 cases made. • $18 • (11/15/95) • **79**

Savigny-lès-Beaune Aux Guettes 1993: A round and soft red offering plummy, tobacco character, medium body and tannins and smooth, succulent texture. Drinkable now. 1,000 cases made. • $25 • (11/15/95) • **82**

Savigny-lès-Beaune Aux Guettes 1985 • $20 • (07/31/88) • **85**

Savigny-lès-Beaune Le Champier White 1994: Thick and full-bodied, with a chalky, chunky texture. Moderately fruity flavors. Slightly drying finish with a cardboardlike note. • $NA • (08/31/96) • **75**

Savigny-lès-Beaune Le Champier White 1993: Soft, round lemony, creamy, earthy flavors, with a somewhat odd, papery note. Slight dilution. Drinkable now. 750 cases made. • $21 • (05/15/95) • **74**

Volnay 1994: Earthy, eucalyptus aromas and flavors cut through the coarse tannins and some berry flavor. Not terribly charming. • $30 • (11/15/96) • **76**

ANDRON-BLANQUET, CHÂTEAU

St.-Estèphe 1995: Enchanting aromas of berries, minerals and flowers. Medium- to full-bodied with racy tannins and an enduring aftertaste of berries and earth. Slightly astringent. Best after 2000. 7,500 cases made. • $20 • (01/31/98) • **87**

St.-Estèphe 1994: A joy to smell, this shows plenty of vanilla, berry and plum character. Medium-bodied, with chewy tannins and a fruity finish. Slightly simple. Try now. • $18 • (01/31/97) • **83**

St.-Estèphe 1993: Light- to medium-bodied, delivering red berry flavors but also a slight herbaceous note. Some dilution on the finish. Drinkable now. 9,000 cases made. • $18 • (01/31/96) • **79**

St.-Estèphe 1990: A no-nonsense wine, with berry, cassis and light spice aromas and flavors and silky tannins. Drinkable now. 6,500 cases made. • $18 • (03/31/93) • **88**

ANGÉLIQUE DE MONBOUSQUET, CHÂTEAU

St.-Emilion 1995: Rather light, with some berry character but weedy and light on the finish. Not much here. 3,000 cases made. • $23 • (01/31/98) • **76**

Key: SS—Spectator Selection CS—Cellar Selection HR—Highly Recommended BB—Best Buy $NA—Price not available Ⓐ—Auction Price (BT)—Barrel Tasting
Dates in parentheses indicate the issues in which the ratings were published.

ANGÉLUS, CHÂTEAU

St.-Emilion 1997: Dark-colored, with mint, tobacco and cherry aromas. Medium-to-full body, with velvety tannins but a slightly hollow midpalate. Almost outstanding. • $NA • (06/15/98) (BT) • **85-89**

St.-Emilion 1996: Ink-colored, with intense blackberry and spice aromas. Full-bodied, with velvety tannins and a tar and tobacco aftertaste. Solid, new-wave Bordeaux. • $115 • (06/15/98) (BT) • **90-94**

St.-Emilion 1995: A stunning red. Dark and inky, with masses of coffee, blackberry, cherry and wild flower aromas. Full-bodied and tannic, with loads of fruit and tons of oak on the long, long finish. Perhaps a bit too much new wood on the finish? Best after 2003. • $160 • (01/31/98) • **94**

St.-Emilion 1994: Angélus continues its hot streak. Super color and concentration for the vintage. Exotic aromas of berries, red fruits, toasty oak and minerals. Full-bodied, with full, silky tannins and a long minty, fruity finish. Fine for drinking now, better in 2000 and beyond. 10,000 cases made. • $115 • (01/31/97) HR • **92**

St.-Emilion 1993: As outstanding as we remember from the barrel. Ripe and seductive, a full-bodied St.-Emilion that stands out for this vintage. Oozes with plum, red berry, chocolate, tobacco and smoke flavors. Beautiful texture, elegant tannins and an impressive finish. Try now. 9,583 cases made. • $53 Ⓐ • (01/31/96) • **90**

St.-Emilion 1992: Extraordinarily good; one of the stars of this weakling vintage. Black cherry and berry flavors, full-bodied, velvety and fresh. Long, long finish. Drinkable now. • $45 Ⓐ • (05/15/96) • **89**

St.-Emilion 1991: Well-crafted with smoky, berry, earthy aromas and flavors. Medium-bodied, tannic and lean finish. Drinkable now. • $32 • (03/31/94) • **80**

St.-Emilion 1990: Giant wine with loads of toasty oak, meat, plum, black coffee character, tons of velvety tannins and a long, tannic finish. Drink now. 12,000 cases made. • $71 Ⓐ • (03/31/93) • **93**

St.-Emilion 1989 • $142 Ⓐ • (03/15/92) • **94**

St.-Emilion 1988 • $53 Ⓐ • (03/31/91) • **93**

St.-Emilion 1987 • $27 • (05/15/90) • **85**

St.-Emilion 1986 • $55 Ⓐ • (06/30/89) • **94**

St.-Emilion 1985 • $60 Ⓐ • (10/15/94) • **89**

St.-Emilion 1983 • $46 Ⓐ • (10/15/94) • **83**

St.-Emilion 1982 • $21 Ⓐ • (03/16/85) • **85**

St.-Emilion 1981 • $17 Ⓐ • (10/15/94) • **84**

St.-Emilion 1979 • $24 Ⓐ • (10/15/89) • **82**

St.-Emilion 1947: Crisp, but not overly acidic, with raspberry sour-candy flavors that linger on the finish. • $NA • (05/31/97) • **85**

ANGERVILLE, MARQUIS D'

Volnay Champans 1993: Bright, fresh fruit flavors and assertive oak notes make this a big, showy Volnay. Has black cherry, clove and spice notes, all in balance, and the finish really lingers. • $29 • (05/15/96) • **90**

Volnay Champans 1992: Firm in texture; fresh fruit flavor is supported by enough tannin and acidity to make it well balanced and appealing. Drinkable now. • $25 • (05/15/95) • **84**

Volnay Champans 1953 • $NA • (12/31/94) • **92**

Volnay Clos des Ducs 1992: Well-balanced black cherry flavors are accented by smoky, leathery, spicy notes. Firm in tannins, brightened by acidity and long on the finish. Drink now. • $32 • (05/15/95) • **87**

Volnay Clos des Ducs 1988 • $47 • (10/31/93) • **88**

Volnay Clos des Ducs 1985 • $62 Ⓐ • (03/15/88) • **80**

Volnay Les Caillerets 1992: Firm-textured, young and lively; needs time to develop. Has a rather lean profile but good depth of fruit and lingering, plummy, spicy finish. Drink now. • $30 • (05/15/95) • **87**

Volnay Premier Cru 1993: Great fruit combines with intriguing, spicy accents for a full-flavored, complex, interesting Burgundy sporting a lingering aftertaste. Elegant but concentrated, firmly tannic but not harsh. Tempting now, but best in 1999. 400 cases made. • $30 • (05/15/96) • **92**

Volnay Taillepieds 1992: Quite concentrated for a light vintage, showing plenty of currant and black cherry flavors framed by firm tannins and lively acidity. Great balance and lingering finish. Drink now. • $27 • (05/15/95) • **86**

ANGLUDET, CHÂTEAU D'

Margaux 1997: Medium-bodied, with silky tannins and mineral and berry character. Medium finish. Very good. • $NA • (06/15/98) (BT) • **85-89**

Margaux 1996: Well presented, with medium, fine tannins and attractive mint and berry character. Medium-bodied, with a medium finish. Needs more concentration of ripe fruit to be outstanding. • $32 • (06/15/98) (BT) • **85-89**

Margaux 1995: Refined, pretty '95. Currants, blackberries and green tobacco aromas. Medium-bodied, with fine tannins and plenty of tobacco and fruit on the finish. Best after 2000. 10,500 cases made. • $30 • (01/31/98) • **88**

Margaux 1994: Showing attractive berry and vanilla aromas and flavors, this is medium-bodied, with medium tannins and a slightly short finish. Drink now or hold. 10,500 cases made. • $19 Ⓐ • (01/31/97) • **84**

Margaux 1993: Rather lean but some good black cherry and dried herb character. Medium-bodied with firm tannins and a light finish. • $30 • (01/31/96) • **80**

Margaux 1990: Vibrant and delicate, with refreshing fruit and lively tannins. Not a blockbuster, but it's fun to taste. Drinkable now. 12,500 cases made. • $22 • (03/31/93) • **86**

Margaux 1989 • $67 Ⓐ • (03/15/92) • **87**

Margaux 1988 • $20 Ⓐ • (02/28/91) • **85**

Margaux 1987 • $12 • (05/15/90) • **78**

Margaux 1986 • $38 Ⓐ • (11/30/89) • **90**

Margaux 1985 • $34 Ⓐ • (04/15/88) • **90**

Margaux 1983 • $39 Ⓐ • (10/15/86) • **93**

Margaux 1982 • $23 Ⓐ • (08/31/92) • **91**

Margaux 1961 • $28 • (04/30/96) • **84**

ANSELME, PERE

Châteauneuf-du-Pape 1989 • $16 • (03/31/94) • **83**

Châteauneuf-du-Pape 1986 • $14 • (10/15/91) • **84**

Châteauneuf-du-Pape 1985 • $14 • (10/15/91) • **86**

Châteauneuf-du-Pape 1983 • $13 • (10/15/91) • **89**

Châteauneuf-du-Pape 1981 • $NA • (10/15/91) • **88**

Châteauneuf-du-Pape Clos-Bimard 1989 • $NA • (10/15/91) • **84**

Châteauneuf-du-Pape Cuvée Prestige Clos Bimard 1988 • $20 • (10/15/91) • **88**

Châteauneuf-du-Pape La Fiole 1990: Ripe and spicy, with strawberry and raspberry jamlike flavors that give it a light, fruity profile. The tannins don't really show until the finish, but they remind you that this is a young wine that can stand cellaring. Drinkable now. • $17 • (04/15/93) • **85**

Châteauneuf-du-Pape La Fiole 1984 • $12 • (10/31/87) • **88**

Châteauneuf-du-Pape La Fiole Grand Cuvée 1984 • $13 • (10/31/87) • **74**

Châteauneuf-du-Pape La Fiole du Pape NV • $14 • (09/30/89) • **86**

Châteauneuf-du-Pape La Fiole du Pape Uno Bono Fiolo NV • $13 • (01/31/88) • **82**

Côtes du Rhône-Villages 1994: Pretty and quite elegant, with bright cherry, berry and plum character, and lively, fresh acidity on the finish. Has held up well, and the tannins are smooth. Not very concentrated. Drink now. 2,222 cases made. • $14 • (10/15/97) • **85**

Côtes du Rhône-Villages Marescal 1985 • $5 • (12/31/87) • **75**

Côtes du Rhône-Villages Seguret 1990 • $9 • (04/15/93) • **83**

Côtes du Rhône-Villages Seguret 1986 • $5 • (05/15/89) • **72**

Côtes du Ventoux 1991 • $7 • (06/15/93) BB • **84**

Crozes-Hermitage 1986 • $7 • (07/31/89) • **80**

Crozes-Hermitage 1983 • $7 • (10/15/87) BB • **84**

Gigondas 1989 • $14 • (04/15/93) • **78**

Merlot Vin de Pays des Côteaux d'Enserune NV • $5 • (07/15/89) • **78**

ANTONIN, AUGUSTE

Côte de Brouilly 1995: Firm and rather austere for Beaujolais, this shows cherry and game flavors with a tannic backbone suitable for food. Has typicity and muscle. 2,000 cases made. • $17 • (04/30/97) • **86**

APOLLINE, CHÂTEAU L'

St.-Emilion Cuvée Anais 1997: Straightforward and grapey, with a slight raisin character. Medium-bodied, with slightly hard tannins. Fluid finish. A bit overdone? • $NA • (06/15/98) (BT) • **75-79**

AQUÉRIA, CHÂTEAU D'

Tavel 1996: A rosé with character, showing a grip of chewy texture, with dried herbs, lemon, raspberry flavors. Medium-to-full body, it has good acidity and freshness on the finish. Drink now. 23,000 cases made. • $15 • (10/15/97) • **85**

Tavel 1995: This dry rosé offers fresh, assertive berry and herb flavors. It's full-bodied, yet very crisp. The rosy pink color is lovely, too. 24,000 cases made. • $15 • (12/15/96) • **84**

ARCAUTE, J.M.

Merlot Bordeaux 1995: Straightforward, with berry, light chocolate and a hint of earth. Medium- to light-bodied, with light tannins and a fruity finish. Drink now. 12,000 cases made. • $9 • (01/31/98) • **81**

Merlot Bordeaux 1994: Plum and light coffee flavors with firm tannins on the finish. The round structure is more evident than the fruit, but it will match well with grilled meats. • $8 • (07/31/96) • **81**

Sauvignon Blanc Bordeaux 1995: A very good but restrained white with lean citrus and mineral flavors, a crisp texture and a tangy finish. 2,000 cases made. • $7 • (02/28/98) • **85**

ARCHAMBAULT, PIERRE

Sancerre Cave du Clos La Perrière 1993 • $14 • (12/15/95) • **75**

Sancerre Domaine de la Perrière 1996: Clean and fresh, this straightforward white offers apple and citrus flavors with light herbal notes. Light but vibrant, it makes a good match with shellfish. Drink now through 1999. • $16 • (05/31/98) • **85**

Sancerre Domaine de la Perrière 1995: Marked by herb and light smoke flavors that give this white a distinctive, if rather austere, personality. Try now. 10,000 cases made. • $15 • (05/31/97) • **85**

ARCHAMBEAU, CHÂTEAU

Cérons 1994: Fresh, sweet and appealing, this is a citrus-accented dessert wine. 6,000 cases made. • $9 • (10/15/97) • **83**

ARCHE, CHÂTEAU D'

Haut-Médoc 1997: Pleasant plum and berry aromas and flavors. Medium-to-light body, with moderate tannins and a light finish. • $NA • (06/15/98) (BT) • **80-84**

Haut-Médoc 1996: Attractive red berry character, with violets and currants. Medium-bodied, with medium, fine tannins and a short, slightly fluid finish. • $15 • (06/15/98) (BT) • **80-84**

Haut-Médoc 1995: Loads of blackberry character in this wine. Full-bodied and very thick with masses of fruit. A bit disjointed, though. Try after 1999. • $15 • (01/31/98) • **86**

Sauternes 1990: Thick, lush and extremely impressive honey, lemon, vanilla and cream flavors. So sweet, it is a dessert in itself. Drinkable now or hold past 2000. • $31 • (04/15/95) • **93**

Sauternes 1989: Racy, sweet and tart, showing a lot of botrytis character and bitter orange marmalade, spice, dried apricot and honey flavors. Medium body; a long, elegant finish. Drinkable now. • $26 • (04/15/95) • **91**

Sauternes 1988: Exotic style; loads of new wood and spicy clove, vanilla and butter flavors. The medium body and sweetness end in a zingy finish. Drink now. • $25 • (04/15/95) • **88**

Sauternes 1987: • $32 • (06/15/90) • **85**

Sauternes 1986: A beauty that offers lovely harmony. Of botrytis character, with spice, toasty coconut, vanilla, lemon and smoke aromas and flavors. • $23 • (04/15/95) • **93**

Sauternes 1983: A pleasant surprise and a fine value, delicious now but with the structure and intensity to age gracefully. Deep gold, beautifully proportioned, with the fruit flavors of fig and apricot in balance with the wood and tobacco, • $23 • (01/31/88) • **93**

ARCHE-LAFAURIE, CHÂTEAU D'

Sauternes 1947: Crisp and zingy, with a dried apricot and caramel character against a tight, acidic background. • $NA • (05/31/97) • **84**

ARCINS, CHÂTEAU D'

Haut-Médoc 1995: A great value. This spicy, smooth and polished Bordeaux has stylish oak accents along with seemingly sweet cherry and plum flavors. Not very tannic; it melts in your mouth. Drink now through 2000. 40,000 cases made. • $12 • (01/31/98) • **88**

Key: SS—Spectator Selection CS—Cellar Selection HR—Highly Recommended BB—Best Buy $NA—Price not available Ⓐ—Auction Price (BT)—Barrel Tasting

Dates in parentheses indicate the issues in which the ratings were published.

ARDECHOIS, VIGNERONS

Vin de Pays des Côteaux de l'Ardeche 1988 • $4 • (04/30/90) BB • **79**

ARFEULIÈRE, DOMAINE DE L'

Mâcon-Uchizy Les Maranches 1996: Bottle shock? Slightly spritzy, it smells overly earthy and tastes tart. Too bad because there is decent concentration. 250 cases made. • $10 • (05/31/98) • **73**

Mâcon-Uchizy Les Maranches 1995: Good, solid Mâcon, made in the traditional style. Crisp, flavorful, light- to medium-bodied, with focused pear, apple and hay flavors. Balanced, ready to drink. 1,600 cases made. • $13 • (05/31/97) • **84**

ARJOLLE, DOMAINE DE L'

Cabernet Sauvignon Vin de Pays des Côtes de Thongue 1995: A mouthful of tannins, with pretty spice notes and strong leather and dark plum flavors. Good concentration, but needs to settle down. Best from 1999 through 2002. 4,500 cases made. • $16 • (06/15/98) • **84**

Sauvignon Blanc Vin de Pays des Côtes de Thongue 1996: Tastes somewhat oxidized. Modest fruit flavors. Some richness, but no finesse. 3,300 cases made. • $9 • (05/15/98) • **78**

Vin de Pays des Côtes de Thongue Cuvée de l'Arjolle 1995: Full-bodied, very tannic and rustic in texture and fruity in flavor, this deep-colored, smoky and gamy red needs equally robust food. A blend of 70 percent Cabernet Sauvignon and 30 percent Merlot. Drink now. 5,500 cases made. • $11 • (07/31/98) • **84**

ARLOT, DOMAINE DE L'

Côte de Nuits-Villages Clos du Châpeau 1989 • $24 • (01/31/92) • **83**

Côte de Nuits-Villages Clos du Châpeau 1988 • $21 • (03/31/91) • **80**

Nuits-St.-Georges 1993: Combines great, pure fruit flavors with spicy, oaky accents in a firm-textured, firmly tannic, nicely balanced package. Focused and enjoyable. Best in 1999. • $22 • (05/15/96) • **88**

Nuits-St.-Georges 1990: An interesting wine, with black truffle and berry flavors and silky tannins. Could use a little more concentration of fruit; seems somewhat alcoholic. Drinkable now. 250 cases made. • $33 • (12/15/92) • **79**

Nuits-St.-Georges Clos de L'Arlot 1993: Leathery, smoky aromas and oaky, spicy, stemmy flavors. Not much fruit showing now. It's concentrated and quite tannic but still smooth, and has a long finish. Try after 2000. • $34 • (05/15/96) • **89**

Nuits-St.-Georges Clos de L'Arlot 1990: Very raisiny in flavor, but rather light in body. Offers decent fruit flavors, but seems rather light on the finish. Drinkable now. 800 cases made. • $45 • (12/15/92) • **78**

Nuits-St.-Georges Clos de L'Arlot 1989 • $48 • (01/31/92) • **78**

Nuits-St.-Georges Clos de L'Arlot 1988 • $43 • (03/31/91) • **87**

Nuits-St.-Georges Clos des Forêts St.-Georges 1993: Balanced like a tightrope walker. Really fruity and focused. Bright and juicy in flavor, offering ripe cherry and strawberry notes accented by spice and smoke. Firmly tannic, but broad and chewy rather than tough in texture. Lively and long on the finish. Drink now. • $40 • (05/15/96) • **92**

Nuits-St.-Georges Clos des Forêts St.-Georges 1990: Traditional in style, with spicy, woody chocolate and fruit flavors, medium tannins and a long finish. Drinkable now. 1,400 cases made. • $49 • (12/15/92) • **87**

Nuits-St.-Georges Clos des Forêts St.-Georges 1989 • $55 • (01/31/92) • **90**

Nuits-St.-Georges Clos des Forêts St.-Georges 1988 • $53 • (03/31/91) • **85**

Nuits-St.-Georges Clos des Forêts St.-Georges 1987 • $43 • (03/31/90) • **83**

ARMAILHAC, CHÂTEAU D'

Pauillac 1997: Medium-bodied, with soft tannins and a grapefruit and green bell-pepper character on the nose and palate. • $NA • (06/15/98) (BT) • **80-84**

Pauillac 1996: As elegant as ever, with well-integrated tannins and pretty berry and cherry aromas and flavors. Medium-to-full in body. • $27 • (06/15/98) (BT) • **85-89**

Pauillac 1995: Loads of fruit in this wine, with concentrated tobacco, cherry and cedar. Full-bodied, with big, velvety tannins and a long, succulent aftertaste. Best after 2002. • $25 • (01/31/98) • **92**

Pauillac 1994: Clearly defined and well-made, with violet, berry character and fine tannins. Not quite as good as from the barrel. Tasted twice with consistent notes. Drink now or hold. • $27 • (01/31/97) • **86**

Pauillac 1993: Beautifully balanced, boasting lovely currant, mineral and black cherry flavors, medium-to-full body, good complexity and well-integrated tannins. Should improve with age; try in 1999. • $25 • (01/31/96) • **89**

Pauillac 1992: Slightly one-dimensional, showing raspberry character and firm tannins; has a racy texture but is somewhat aggressive. Drinkable now. • $20 • (04/15/95) • **80**

Pauillac 1991: An alluring smoky, nutty, fruity quality in this wine that has a soft, round mouthfeel. • $20 • (03/31/94) • **85**

Pauillac 1990: A pretty wine, with delicacy and a good concentration of ripe fruit. There's plenty of tobacco, blackberry and brown sugar character and firm tannins. Drink now. 18,000 cases made. • $22 • (03/31/93) • **89**

Pauillac 1989 • $30 Ⓐ • (03/15/92) • **94**

Pauillac 1985 • $24 • (10/15/94) • **91**

ARMAND, COMTE

Pommard Clos des Epeneaux 1993: Excellent concentration, but this dark-colored *premier cru* also tastes very woody at this stage, showing cedar, cigar box, chestnut and spice flavors and some fine cassis and cherry notes. A drying finish keeps it from scoring higher. Better in 2000? • $60 Ⓐ • (05/15/96) • **85**

Pommard Clos des Epeneaux 1990: Big and massive; packed to the brim with fruit and tannins. Shows elegance that bodes well for cellaring; drinkable now. 1,500 cases made. • $57 • (12/15/92) • **93**

Pommard Clos des Epeneaux 1989 • $50 • (11/30/92) • **82**

Pommard Clos des Epeneaux 1988 • $58 Ⓐ • (02/28/91) • **90**

Pommard Clos des Epeneaux 1987 • $41 • (08/31/90) • **81**

Pommard Clos des Epeneaux 1985 • $44 • (03/15/88) • **91**

ARNAULD, CHÂTEAU

Haut-Médoc 1997: Slightly raisiny and grassy, with medium body, moderate tannins and a medium finish. • $NA • (06/15/98) (BT) • **75-79**

Haut-Médoc 1996: Medium-bodied, with fine, silky tannins and a mint and berry aftertaste. Well-crafted and solid. 12,000 cases made. • $20 • (06/15/98) (BT) • **85-89**

Haut-Médoc 1995: A bit lean, but offers some pretty spice, coffee and vanilla aromas and flavors. Medium-bodied, with medium, velvety tannins and a fresh fruit aftertaste. Best after 2000. • $20 • (01/31/98) • **85**

Haut-Médoc 1993: A bit light and simple, but it offers some pretty currant and cherry flavors. Drinkable now. • $17 • (01/31/96) • **81**

Haut-Médoc 1992: Herb and cassis aromas and flavors accompany medium body, medium tannins and an herbal finish. • $11 • (04/15/95) • **78**

Haut-Médoc 1991: Pleasant plum, vanilla character with round texture and a light finish. • $11 • (03/31/94) • **77**

Haut-Médoc 1990: This offers an impressively chunky texture and well-focused herbal and tomato flavors. Drinkable now. 9,000 cases made. • $19 • (03/31/93) • **86**

Haut-Médoc 1989 • $14 • (03/15/92) • **88**

Haut-Médoc 1988 • $15 • (04/30/91) • **84**

Haut-Médoc 1987 • $13 • (11/30/89) • **79**

Haut-Médoc 1986 • $18 • (11/30/89) • **82**

Haut-Médoc 1985 • $15 • (02/15/88) • **82**

Haut-Médoc 1983 • $9 • (01/01/86) • **75**

Haut-Médoc 1982 • $17 • (11/30/89) • **71**

ARNOUX, ROBERT

Bourgogne 1994: Ready to drink, this is light and refreshing for its pretty strawberry and floral flavors. • $16 • (11/15/96) • **80**

Clos de Vougeot 1994: Lean, earthy and a bit gamy up front, picking up some pretty raspberry and anise flavors on the midpalate before it skids into a drying finish. Try now. • $75 • (11/15/96) • **81**

Clos de Vougeot 1993: Racy red sporting sleek tannins and loads of smoky, berry, raspberry character. Medium-bodied and finely tannic, with a super-fruity finish. Better in 2000. • $80 • (11/15/95) • **91**

Clos de Vougeot 1991: Ripe and chewy, leaning toward anise and spice in the otherwise sweet raspberry fruit, with a stemmy note on the finish. Drinkable now. • $60 • (08/31/94) • **86**

Clos de Vougeot 1988 • $70 • (03/15/91) • **78**

Echézeaux 1994: Built for the long haul, with its broad, coarse tannins, but underneath it's packed with ripe, rich flavors of currant, mineral and berry. It will always be tannic, but the flavors are lovely. • $73 • (11/15/96) • **89**

Echézeaux 1993: Beautiful plum and floral character, medium body, soft tannins and sweet fruit finish. Not a heavyweight but a joy to taste. • $80 • (11/15/95) • **89**

Echézeaux 1991: An appealing, lighter style displaying ample cherry and plum flavors, firm tannins, with a smooth texture and a lingering finish. Drinkable now. • $72 • (05/31/95) • **87**

Nuits-St.-Georges 1991: Generous, fruity and easy to like, sporting good balance and firm tannins. Drinkable now. • $30 • (05/31/95) • **86**

Nuits-St.-Georges Aux Corvées Pagets 1994: Crisp and lively, with a polished bead of spicy currant flavor that weaves through the fine tannins. Try in 1999. • $50 • (11/15/96) • **83**

Nuits-St.-Georges Aux Corvées Pagets 1993: Delicate mocha, vanilla and berry character, medium body, soft tannins and a fresh finish. Better in 1999. • $55 • (11/15/95) • **81**

Nuits-St.-Georges Aux Corvées Pagets 1991: Aromas of cinnamon and vanilla indicate lots of oak influence in this attractive, fruity but slightly tough red Burgundy. Drink now. • $55 • (05/31/95) • **88**

Nuits-St.-Georges Les Poisets 1994: Firm, a little drying in texture, but shines a lovely beam of blackberry and currant flavors that brighten up the palate and linger on the finish. Try now. • $44 • (11/15/96) • **84**

Nuits-St.-Georges Les Poisets 1993: Rather meager but attractive spicy, fruity flavors, light-to-medium body, light tannins and a fresh finish. Drink now. • $50 • (11/15/95) • **81**

Nuits-St.-Georges Les Poisets 1991: Generous in fruity, gamy flavors and balanced well by crisp acidity and firm tannins. A complete, enjoyable package that is developing an alluring, spicy aroma. Drinkable now. • $55 • (05/31/95) • **87**

Pinot Noir Bourgogne 1993: A solid little Burgundy showing fresh fruit flavors, velvety texture, firm tannins and good balance. Drinkable now. 900 cases made. • $18 • (05/15/96) • **85**

Romanée St.-Vivant 1994: Has amazing density and power, without losing grace. Deep-colored, with complex aromas and rich flavors. Delicous from start to finish, jumping with fresh, grapey aromas and plenty of currant, plum, violet and toasty oak notes. Has a clean, pure, lingering finish. • $160 • (11/15/96) • **92**

Romanée St.-Vivant 1993: Seductively velvety, this soft-styled, full-bodied red unfolds its charm in a cascade of rose petal, plum, mocha and spice flavors. It shows its pedigree in the seamless body and finish. Tempting now, but try to hold off until 1999. • $NA • (11/15/95) • **93**

Romanée St.-Vivant 1991: There is dazzling flavor intensity in this seductively rich and fruity Burgundy. It has ample cherry and berry aromas, ripe black cherry flavors accented by oak, firm, fine tannins, lively acidity and a long, long finish. Tempting to drink now, but will improve through about 1999. • $210 • (05/31/95) • **92**

Romanée St.-Vivant 1988 • $250 • (11/15/90) • **91**

Vosne-Romanée 1992: Rather tough and tight now, but solid, chewy fruit flavors give it life and hints of vanilla add complexity. Try now. • $38 • (05/15/95) • **84**

Vosne-Romanée Aux Raignots 1994: Firm in texture, with a layer of charming berry and rose petal flavors lurking under the blanket of grainy tannins. Best from 1999. • $60 • (11/15/96) • **84**

Vosne-Romanée Hautes Maizières 1994: Very light in color, offering pretty strawberry and rose petal flavors. The finish is simple and fragrant. Drink now. • $40 • (11/15/96) • **82**

Vosne-Romanée Hautes Maizières 1993: Nice and sweet, but quite light. Tastes of raspberries and strawberries, showing tannins that seem somewhat drying. Try now. • $50 • (11/15/95) • **78**

Vosne-Romanée Hautes Maizières 1991: Elegant, well-balanced and complete, exhibiting intrguing aromas of tea, spice and cherry, solid fruit flavors and a firm but smooth texture. Drinkable now. • $40 • (05/31/95) • **86**

Vosne-Romanée Les Chaumes 1994: A tannic, chewy texture overlays the nice core of bright currant flavor, which echoes on the finish. May be better in 1999. • $52 • (11/15/96) • **82**

Vosne-Romanée Les Chaumes 1993: Pretty plum, vanilla and cherry character, medium-to-light body, light tannins and a soft finish. Better in 1999. • $55 • (11/15/95) • **88**

Vosne-Romanée Les Chaumes 1991: Firm-textured, young and tannic; needs time to develop, yet has enough fruit stuffing to age nicely. Try now. • $50 • (05/31/95) • **89**

Vosne-Romanée Les Chaumes 1988 • $45 • (02/28/91) • **80**

Vosne-Romanée Les Suchots 1994: Gamy, leathery flavors hack through the ripe currant flavors. Finish shows drying tannins. • $75 • (11/15/96) • **79**

Vosne-Romanée Les Suchots 1993: Some good ripe fruit character, but slightly diluted on the center palate. Medium in body and tannins and a short finish. Drink now. • $80 • (11/15/95) • **87**

Vosne-Romanée Les Suchots 1991: Nicely mature and complex, demonstrating the subtle bottle bouquet we look for in aged Burgundy, but with enough bright fruit and acidity to keep it balanced. Drinkable now. • $70 • (05/31/95) • **88**
Vosne-Romanée Les Suchots 1988 • $60 • (02/28/91) • **86**
Vosne-Romanée Les Suchots 1985 • $52 • (07/31/88) • **90**

ARNOUX PÈRE & FILS

Chorey-lès-Beaune Confrelin 1994: Light, chewy, with a musty edge to the thin fruit flavors. • $NA • (11/15/96) • **75**
Savigny-lès-Beaune 1994: A simple wine, unremarkable in character. Not too tannic. • $NA • (11/15/96) • **78**

ARROMANS, CHÂTEAU LES

Entre-Deux-Mers 1993 • $8 • (05/31/95) • **79**

ARROSÉE, CHÂTEAU L'

St.-Emilion 1989 • $49 Ⓐ • (04/30/92) HR • **93**
St.-Emilion 1988 • $33 Ⓐ • (03/15/91) HR • **94**
St.-Emilion 1987 • $28 • (05/15/90) • **82**
St.-Emilion 1986 • $62 Ⓐ • (02/15/89) • **87**
St.-Emilion 1985 • $55 Ⓐ • (02/29/88) • **85**
St.-Emilion 1983 • $38 Ⓐ • (05/16/86) • **87**
St.-Emilion 1982 • $66 Ⓐ • (05/15/89) • **91**
St.-Emilion 1970 • $50 • (05/15/93) • **90**

FRANCE

ARSAC, CHÂTEAU D'

Haut-Médoc 1989 • $9 • (03/15/92) • **82**
Haut-Médoc 1985 • $5 • (02/15/89) • **75**

ARVIGNY, CHÂTEAU D'

Haut-Médoc 1997: Light and simple, with berry flavors and hints of oak. Light in body and finish. • $NA • (06/15/98) (BT) • **75-79**
Haut-Médoc 1996: Decent fruit character and medium tannins, but slightly diluted on the palate. Medium-bodied. Simple finish. • $18 • (06/15/98) (BT) • **80-84**

AUBERT, DOMAINE MAX

Châteauneuf-du-Pape La Nonciature 1995: Lacks the stuffing of the best '95s, but offers pretty cherry and spicy flavors, with a slightly herbal finish. It's light-bodied and drinkable now. 4,000 cases made. • $20 • (10/15/97) • **80**
Châteauneuf-du-Pape La Nonciature 1994: Straightforward and fruity, this was rushed to the market to be drunk young while it's still fresh. Soft tannins accompany the smooth texture. • $20 • (10/15/95) • **82**
Châteauneuf-du-Pape White La Nonciature 1996: Exotic, offering layers of peach and apricot character. Medium-bodied, with fairly good concentration. Stands out in its category; has almost late-harvest aromas. Succulent finish. Try now through 1999. 2,500 cases made. • $20 • (10/15/97) • **87**
Châteauneuf-du-Pape White La Nonciature 1995: The fruit has faded a bit, and it's somewhat oxidized, showing muted pear and cooked apple flavors. Medium-bodied, with a chewy, drying finish. 2,500 cases made. • $20 • (10/15/97) • **78**
Châteauneuf-du-Pape White La Nonciature 1994: A fresh, clean white sporting floral, nutty, fruity flavors and enough body to provide lingering aftertaste. Fine as a substitute for Chardonnay. • $22 • (10/15/95) • **85**
Châteauneuf-du-Pape White La Nonciature Grande Réserve 1996: Of medium weight, it shows decent concentration of fruit and mineral character. Rather harmonious and fairly long, and could improve through 1998. 500 cases made. • $36 • (10/15/97) • **85**
Côtes du Rhône Château de Galliffet 1995: Very pretty, with nicely focused red berry, smoke and toasty spice flavors. Give it until 1998 to '99 to smooth out; has thick texture and a supple, fruity finish. 900 cases made. • $18 • (10/15/97) • **85**

Key: SS—Spectator Selection CS—Cellar Selection HR—Highly Recommended BB—Best Buy $NA—Price not available Ⓐ—Auction Price (BT)—Barrel Tasting
Dates in parentheses indicate the issues in which the ratings were published.

Côtes du Rhône Domaine de la Présidente 1995: Focused and well balanced, this round red offers black cherry, licorice and light herbal flavors with moderate tannins. Appealing now, but should be more expressive in 1997. A bargain in a French red. 10,000 cases made. • $9 • (10/15/96) BB • **85**
Côtes du Rhône Domaine de la Présidente 1994 • $10 • (11/15/95) • **79**
Côtes du Rhône Domaine de la Présidente Blanc de Blancs 1995: Full-bodied yet still crisp and refreshing, offering modest herbal and apple flavors; it would make a pleasantly subtle accompaniment to grilled chicken. 2,500 cases made. • $9 • (12/15/96) • **82**
Côtes du Rhône Domaine de la Présidente Blanc de Blancs 1994 • $10 • (09/30/95) • **82**
Côtes du Rhône Domaine de la Présidente Blanc de Blancs Réserve 1996: This white offers ripe melon and pear flavors with appealing hints of herbs, yet firm acidity kicks in and keeps it fresh. A good match for food. 1,200 cases made. • $14 • (10/15/97) • **83**
Côtes du Rhône Domaine de la Présidente Blanc de Blancs Réserve 1994: Round, rustic and a bit flabby, with dull flavors of butter and earth. An old-style wine that needs drinking now. 1,200 cases made. • $14 • (10/15/97) • **74**
Côtes du Rhône Rosé Domaine de la Présidente 1995: Clean and dry, this offers light herb and berry flavors with a refreshing, slightly bitter finish. A good base for a fruit punch. 4,500 cases made. • $9 • (10/15/96) • **80**
Côtes du Rhône-Villages Cairanne Goutillonnage 1995: Light to medium in body, very flavorful, showing lovely black pepper, red berry character. Firm tannins lead to a rather intense, slightly crisp finish. Drink now through 1999. 800 cases made. • $16 • (10/15/97) • **84**
Côtes du Rhône-Villages Cairanne Goutillonnage 1994: A bit dry, with some cherry and spice flavors, and distinctive, gamy, leathery flavors that are interesting. Lacks a bit of opulence; medium-bodied, ready to drink. 800 cases made. • $16 • (10/15/97) • **80**
Côtes du Rhône-Villages Domaine de la Présidente Cairanne 1995: Light and diluted, with little fruit flavor. A bit tart. Short finish. 12,000 cases made. • $10 • (10/15/97) • **70**
Côtes du Rhône-Villages Domaine de la Présidente Cairanne 1994 • $12 • (11/15/95) • **83**
Côtes du Rhône-Villages Domaine de la Présidente Cairanne Goutillonnage 1994 • $14 • (09/30/95) • **86**

AUBUISIÈRES, DOMAINE DES

Vouvray Demi-Sec Le Bouchet 1993 • $14 • (12/15/95) • **87**
Vouvray Moelleux Le Marigny 1993 • $14 • (12/15/95) • **87**
Vouvray Moelleux Les Girardières 2ème Trie 1996: This moderately sweet, pleasant white offers lemon meringue and cooked apple flavors, with hints of spice and toast. Firm acidity keeps it balanced. Drink now. • $22 • (05/31/98) • **83**
Vouvray Sec Le Marigny 1993 • $14 • (12/15/95) • **79**

AUGEY

Bordeaux 1993: Sturdy and simple, with rustic tannins, but enough berry and cherry show through to make it drinkable, especially with food. • $7 • (12/15/95) • **80**
Bordeaux White 1994 • $7 • (02/29/96) • **84**

AUJOUX, JEAN-MARC

Beaujolais 1996: Light but slightly bitter, this grapey wine offers earthy, smoky flavors under tart cherry. 300,000 cases made. • $6 • (09/15/97) • **76**
Beaujolais-Villages 1996: Ripe, with earthy, spicy notes to the core of plum flavors. It's soft and round, yet has grip on the finish. Will complement food. 200,000 cases made. • $8 • (09/15/97) • **84**
Beaujolais-Villages RT Limited Edition 1993 • $7 • (06/30/94) • **79**
Brouilly 1996: Bright, balanced and supple, with well-defined flavors of cherries, raspberries and light spices. Versatile, it will work well as an apéritif or with food. 25,000 cases made. • $11 • (07/31/97) BB • **85**
Brouilly Domaine François Chevalier 1996: Ripe, round and almost chunky, showing plum, coffee and cinnamon flavors, full tannins and a spicy finish. 6,000 cases made. • $14 • (09/15/97) • **84**
Brouilly RT 1994 • $8 • (06/15/95) • **84**
Brouilly RT Limited Edition 1993 • $8 • (06/30/94) • **80**
Chiroubles RT 1994 • $9 • (07/31/95) • **79**
Chiroubles RT Limited Edition 1993 • $9 • (06/30/94) • **84**
Fleurie RT 1994 • $10 • (06/15/95) • **85**
Fleurie RT Limited Edition 1993 • $10 • (06/30/94) • **84**

Juliénas 1996: Rich and assertive, marrying crisp black cherry with light, earthy flavors in a traditional style. Drinkable now. 20,000 cases made. • $11 • (09/15/97) • **85**

Juliénas Château de la Prat 1996: Good concentration. This dark crimson-colored wine is redolent of spices, game and ripe dark fruits, and the rich tones carry onto the muscular palate. A traditional style that's meant for food and will improve through 2000. 5,000 cases made. • $14 • (08/31/97) • **88**

Juliénas RT 1994 • $9 • (07/31/95) • **82**

Juliénas RT Limited Edition 1993 • $9 • (06/30/94) • **83**

Mâcon-Villages 1994: Mineral and earth flavors give distinctive character, but it's lean and light, showing apple and lemon notes. 4,000 cases made. • $9 • (06/30/95) • **77**

Morgon 1996: Bright and crisp, this offers snappy black cherry and blackberry flavors on a firm, clean frame. Drinkable now. 30,000 cases made. • $11 • (09/15/97) • **84**

Morgon Côte de Py Domaine Charles Jenny 1996: With firm, gripping tannins and slightly earthy tones, it's fairly rustic in style, but is kept pleasurable by a core of cherry flavor. 3,000 cases made. • $14 • (09/15/97) • **80**

Morgon RT 1994 • $8 • (07/31/95) • **83**

Morgon RT Limited Edition 1993 • $8 • (06/30/94) • **86**

Moulin-à-Vent 1996: Round and supple, a ripe red with spicy plum and smoke flavors, round, soft tannins and a clean, fresh finish. Generous; accessible now. 20,000 cases made. • $12 • (09/15/97) • **84**

Moulin-à-Vent RT 1994 • $10 • (07/31/95) • **83**

Moulin-à-Vent RT Limited Edition 1993 • $10 • (06/30/94) • **86**

St.-Amour RT 1994 • $10 • (07/31/95) • **81**

St.-Amour RT Limited Edition 1993 • $10 • (06/30/94) • **82**

St.-Véran 1994: Crisp and pleasant, but seems a bit square and rough despite some nice pear, apple and wet earth flavors. Slightly diluted on the finish. 416 cases made. • $11 • (08/31/95) • **80**

AUPILHAC, DOMAINE D'

Coteaux du Languedoc Montpeyroux 1992 • $9 • (03/15/94) • **87**

Vin de Pays du Mont Baudille Le Carignan 1992 • $8 • (03/15/94) • **88**

AUSONE, CHÂTEAU

St.-Emilion 1997: Reserved yet beautiful. Medium-bodied and silky, with lovely mineral and spice character. Fresh finish. Almost outstanding. • $NA • (06/15/98) (BT) • **85-89**

St.-Emilion 1996: This has certainly improved since last year. Wonderful. Extremely well crafted, with fruit and tannins in all the right places. Medium- to full-bodied, with fine tannins and a fresh finish. Almost classic quality. • $350 • (06/15/98) (BT) • **90-94**

St.-Emilion 1995: Awesome Ausone. Modern yet classic. Made from one of the best vineyard sites in Bordeaux, this wine offers berry, strawberry jam and vanilla aromas with hints of minerals. Full-bodied, with full yet fine tannins. Long, long finish. Polished and smooth. Best after 2001. • $250 • (01/31/98) HR • **95**

St.-Emilion 1993: Features plenty of seductive toasty oak and sweet fruit character, medium body, delicate tannins and a long vanilla, tobacco and plum finish. Delicious now. • $90 • (01/31/96) • **88**

St.-Emilion 1990: An alluring wine with gorgeous plum, blackberry and toasty oak character, full silky tannins and a long rich finish. Drinkable now. 2,150 cases made. • $95 Ⓐ • (03/31/93) • **94**

St.-Emilion 1989 • $101 Ⓐ • (03/15/92) • **93**

St.-Emilion 1988 • $87 Ⓐ • (10/15/94) • **86**

St.-Emilion 1986 • $84 Ⓐ • (10/15/94) • **89**

St.-Emilion 1985 • $94 Ⓐ • (10/15/94) • **92**

St.-Emilion 1983 • $109 Ⓐ • (10/15/94) • **90**

St.-Emilion 1982 • $181 • (08/31/92) • **90**

St.-Emilion 1981 • $86 Ⓐ • (10/15/94) • **88**

St.-Emilion 1980 • $40 Ⓐ • (11/30/87) • **86**

St.-Emilion 1979 • $68 Ⓐ • (10/15/89) • **92**

St.-Emilion 1978 • $102 Ⓐ • (11/30/87) • **93**

St.-Emilion 1977 • $29 • (11/30/87) • **83**

St.-Emilion 1976 • $105 Ⓐ • (11/30/87) • **89**

St.-Emilion 1974 • $28 • (11/30/87) • **76**

St.-Emilion 1973 • $42 Ⓐ • (11/30/87) • **77**

St.-Emilion 1972 • $30 • (11/30/87) • **75**

St.-Emilion 1971 • $90 • (11/30/87) • **83**

St.-Emilion 1970 • $38 Ⓐ • (05/15/93) • **89**

St.-Emilion 1969 • $173 Ⓐ • (11/30/87) • **76**

St.-Emilion 1967 • $55 Ⓐ • (11/30/87) • **79**

St.-Emilion 1966 • $52 Ⓐ • (11/30/87) • **85**

St.-Emilion 1964 • $87 Ⓐ • (11/30/87) • **78**

St.-Emilion 1962 • $55 Ⓐ • (11/30/87) • **85**

St.-Emilion 1961 • $311 Ⓐ • (04/30/96) • **89**

St.-Emilion 1959 • $211 Ⓐ • (10/15/90) • **79**

St.-Emilion 1958 • $95 • (11/30/87) • **79**

St.-Emilion 1957 • $67 Ⓐ • (11/30/87) • **74**

St.-Emilion 1956 • $175 • (11/30/87) • **86**

St.-Emilion 1955 • $163 Ⓐ • (11/30/87) • **91**

St.-Emilion 1954 • $180 • (11/30/87) • **87**

St.-Emilion 1953 • $240 • (11/30/87) • **78**

St.-Emilion 1952 • $130 Ⓐ • (11/30/87) • **85**

St.-Emilion 1950 • $153 Ⓐ • (11/30/87) • **78**

St.-Emilion 1949 • $350 • (11/30/87) • **91**

St.-Emilion 1947: A bit watery, but nicely evocative of fresh earth and spices, finishing with a vague nuance of plum. • $439 Ⓐ • (05/31/97) • **84**

St.-Emilion 1945 • $748 Ⓐ • (03/16/86) • **75**

St.-Emilion 1943 • $99 Ⓐ • (11/30/87) • **84**

St.-Emilion 1942 • $250 • (11/30/87) • **81**

St.-Emilion 1937 • $93 Ⓐ • (11/30/87) • **83**

St.-Emilion 1936 • $300 • (11/30/87) • **82**

St.-Emilion 1929 • $350 Ⓐ • (11/30/87) • **83**

St.-Emilion 1928 • $313 Ⓐ • (11/30/87) • **83**

St.-Emilion 1926 • $680 • (11/30/87) • **82**

St.-Emilion 1925 • $175 • (11/30/87) • **75**

St.-Emilion 1924 • $483 Ⓐ • (11/30/87) • **95**

St.-Emilion 1923 • $200 • (11/30/87) • **76**

St.-Emilion 1921 • $1150 • (11/30/87) • **94**

St.-Emilion 1918 • $850 • (11/30/87) • **87**

St.-Emilion 1916 • $430 • (11/30/87) • **86**

St.-Emilion 1914 • $380 • (11/30/87) • **79**

St.-Emilion 1913 • $380 • (11/30/87) • **81**

St.-Emilion 1912 • $380 • (11/30/87) • **79**

St.-Emilion 1905 • $600 • (11/30/87) • **82**

St.-Emilion 1902 • $300 • (11/30/87) • **83**

St.-Emilion 1900 • $1545 Ⓐ • (11/30/87) • **78**

St.-Emilion 1899 • $1250 • (11/30/87) • **77**

St.-Emilion 1894 • $800 • (11/30/87) • **85**

St.-Emilion 1879 • $1137 Ⓐ • (11/30/87) • **93**

St.-Emilion 1877 • $933 Ⓐ • (11/30/87) • **92**

AUTARD, DOMAINE PAUL

Châteauneuf-du-Pape 1993: Fruity and focused, showing fresh, ripe raspberry and black cherry flavors that echo on the finish. Nicely balanced and elegant in texture, adding just a hint of tannin. 7,000 cases made. • $17 • (10/15/95) • **84**

Côtes du Rhône 1995: Ripe and round, with raisin and cinnamon flavors that are a bit candied. Has personality, but resembles a dessert wine more than a table red. 2,000 cases made. • $9 • (02/28/97) • **79**

Côtes du Rhône 1994 • $8 • (11/15/95) • **80**

AUVENAY, DOMAINE D'

Auxey-Duresses Red 1989 • $42 • (01/31/92) • **88**

Auxey-Duresses White 1995: Well made, this wine is tightly built around a core of clean, fresh fruit and spicy oak. You can taste the concentration in the silky texture. Medium- to full-bodied, ripe and sweet-tasting, it still shows an edge to its muscular framework that suggests cellaring until at least 2000 for more complexity. • $56 • (08/31/97) • **91**

Auxey-Duresses White 1993: Impressive for the vintage. Quite rich, displaying apple, truffle, mushroom and cream character, medium-to-full body and a smooth texture. Drinkable now. • $35 • (05/15/95) • **86**

Bonnes Mares 1995: Distinctive, with superb *goût de terroir* and racy fruit flavor. This full, fleshy, beautiful wine shows great depth. Rich, it fans out on the palate, with lovely oak. Fabulous balance, great length. An ager. Try after 2002. • $503 Ⓐ • (11/15/97) • **93**

Bonnes Mares 1994: Rather sweet and ripe, with supple tannins; very round and charming, showing great texture. Lovely plum, currant and mineral character. Well made, it's a wine of great depth. Needs time to show all it has. Try after 2002. • $459 • (09/30/97) • **93**

Chevalier-Montrachet 1995: Unique. Amazingly rich, ripe, bordering on raisiny, and almost thicker than extra-virgin olive oil. It offers apricot and cherry flavors and the *goût de terroir* of flint, wet soil and matchstick notes. For all that, though, it's clean and pure, and the balance is flawless.

FRANCE

A memorable drinking experience now, it will be best after 2000 and might benefit from decanting. • $479 Ⓐ • (08/31/97) HR • **99**

Criots-Bâtard-Montrachet 1995: Very lush and opulent. It's a generous and showy wine, offering plenty of crème brûlée, toasty bread, coconut, pear tart and grilled pineapple flavors. The texture like velvet, it's a pleasure to taste, though some may find the smoky, toasty notes excessive. Drink now through 2005. 144 bottles made. • $498 • (08/31/97) • **98**

Mazis-Chambertin 1994: Beautiful and concentrated, with excellent extract of cassis and cassis bush character. It has a sweet, ripe flavor, supple tannins, much personality. All in all, it's a great, full-bodied '94 that is not overly tannic or overoaked, but emphasizes its fruit and earth. Try after 2005. • $459 • (09/30/97) • **93**

Meursault Les Narvaux 1995: Stunning. Sexy, exotic and very distinctive, so thick it's more like food than wine, more like cream than white Burgundy. It's fat, rich, opulent and generous without tasting heavy. Still a bit closed on the nose, but offers plenty of rose petals, jasmine, peach, apricot and dried herb flavors, along with honey and toasty oak notes. Perfectly balanced, immensely flavorful and elegant. Drink now or hold for decades. 96 cases made. • $155 • (08/31/97) • **97**

Meursault Les Narvaux 1992: Beautiful, with elegant yet very flavorful character; delivers attractive fig, toasty bread, honey and spice flavors and a lingering finish. Drinkable now. 162 cases made. • $64 • (08/31/94) • **90**

Puligny-Montrachet Les Folatières 1995: Aficionados of white Burgundy, here is something truly distinctive and unusual: a *premier cru* that's just greater than 99 percent of all *grand crus*. Lovely from start to finish, it smells of rose petals and tastes of exotic spices and fruits. Full-bodied, it blends intensity with a super-concentrated, velvety texture in such a way as to make you swoon. Bravo for this mindboggling wine! (Just a hair below the quality of Madame Bize's Chevalier-Montrachet.) Try now through 2005. 96 cases made. • $133 • (08/31/97) • **98**

Puligny-Montrachet Les Folatières 1993: Ripe and delicious. Deep yellow color, medium body, vanilla, lemon and lime flavors and toasty oak finish. Wonderfully sweet fruit. • $NA • (08/31/95) • **86**

Puligny-Montrachet Les Folatières 1992: An exotic, rich, floral style of Puligny that smells like vanilla and ginger, tastes like honey, pear and nutmeg and has a long finish. Smooth and supple in texture. Very inviting. 170 cases made. • $96 • (08/31/94) • **90**

AUVIGUE, ANDRÉ

Pouilly-Fuissé Solutré 1996: A beauty, with seamless balance and harmonious interplay between lime, tropical, spice, mineral, pear and apple flavors. Full-bodied, it's a touch spicy and smoky on the succulent finish. Tempting now through 2000. 2,080 cases made. • $18 • (05/31/98) • **89**

Pouilly-Fuissé Solutré 1995: Fairly pleasant, with some pear, honey, and citrus flavors. Of medium body, it's rather subtle, but also a bit diluted. Drink now. 2,500 cases made. • $18 • (05/31/97) • **81**

Pouilly-Fuissé Solutré 1994: Very good intensity of fruit, offering green apple, pineapple and pear notes. Clean and crisp, a medium-bodied white that delivers plenty of flavors. Drinkable now. • $18 • (05/31/96) • **85**

Pouilly-Fuissé Solutré 1993: Tart and sharp. The lime, apple skin and grassy aromas and flavors round off on the finish, unfolding some decent, ripe pear, mineral and grapefruit flavors. Drinkable now. 2,083 cases made. • $14 • (05/15/95) • **80**

Pouilly-Fuissé Vieilles Vignes 1994: A middle-of-the road white, of light-to-medium body. Slightly awkward, offering stale aromas but some fresh, crisp fruit flavors. Could use more harmony. 916 cases made. • $24 • (05/31/96) • **77**

Pouilly-Fuissé Vieilles Vignes 1993: Good intensity, with earthy, buttery, yeasty aromas echoed on the palate. Lots of fresh lemon in the chewy, chalky finish. Try now. 813 cases made. • $22 • (05/15/95) • **83**

AUVIGUE & REVEL

Mâcon-Fuissé Vendanges Manuelles 1996: Ripe and full-bodied, yet with plenty of zesty, vibrant, lime-tasting character, this wine gives the palate a jolt. Has some lovely honey, pear and tropical flavors lurking beneath that acidic blanket. Drink now through 1999. • $15 • (08/31/97) • **86**

Mâcon-Villages Vendanges Manuelles 1996: Light and a bit diluted, tasting green and unripe. Tart finish. • $15 • (08/31/97) • **75**

Key: SS—Spectator Selection CS—Cellar Selection HR—Highly Recommended BB—Best Buy $NA—Price not available Ⓐ—Auction Price (BT)—Barrel Tasting

Dates in parentheses indicate the issues in which the ratings were published.

St.-Véran 1995: A very pretty St.-Véran; sweet and ripe, with nice fruit flavor and a smooth texture, but a crisp finish. Drink now. 1,333 cases made. • $13 • (05/31/97) • **87**

AVERY

Richebourg 1947: Seems lean and zingy, with lots of spice notes and elegance. It's not particularly deep, but it's sound stuff. • $NA • (05/31/97) • **88**

AVRIL, PASCAL & CATHERINE

Touraine Red 1995: Good structure for a Touraine, with firm tannins and ripe plum flavors. A bit green and lean on the palate, but a smoky note emerges on the finish. Drink now through 1999. 2,800 cases made. • $12 • (06/15/98) • **84**

AYALA

Brut Blanc de Blancs Champagne 1988: Assertive and complex in style, this full-bodied bubbly has toasty, nutty aromas, similarly bold, but still fresh, fruit flavors and an appealing, lingering finish. Great to drink now or hold through 2000. Has matured nicely since first reviewed in 1992. 1,200 cases made. • $44 • (11/30/96) • **90**

Brut Blanc de Blancs Champagne 1982: Dry, medium-bodied and pleasant in a fruity, slightly herbal style. Well-balanced with acid and clean and refreshing on the finish. • $29 • (04/15/88) • **85**

Brut Champagne 1983: Simple, straightforward and uncomplicated, with dough, spice and vanilla flavors that are somewhat ponderous on the palate. A touch of caramel on the finish makes it more interesting. • $30 • (12/31/89) • **80**

Brut Champagne 1982: Full and nicely mature in style. Shows mature appley, slightly butterscotchy flavors and a smooth, mouthfilling texture. Very well made. • $27 • (04/15/88) • **86**

Brut Champagne Grand Cuvée 1985: A slightly herbal style of Champagne, with earthy aromas and full, lemony flavors. Crisp but round in texture. • $57 • (12/31/89) • **84**

Brut Champagne Grand Cuvée 1982: Nicely tart style with crisp, subdued citrus flavors and just a hint of maturity. Drinkable now. • $52 • (04/15/88) • **87**

AYDIE, CHÂTEAU D'

Madiran 1993: Ripe and fairly rich with good flavors of black cherry, leather and plum. Somewhat rustic tasting in the end, but has plenty of character and tannins. • $17 • (06/15/97) • **85**

Madiran 1991 • $14 • (06/30/94) • **87**

AZO, HERVÉ

Chablis 1994 • $15 • (08/31/95) • **85**

Chablis Côte de Léchet 1994 • $20 • (05/31/96) • **82**

Chablis Côte de Léchet 1993 • $19 • (08/31/95) • **75**

Chablis Vaudevey 1994 • $20 • (05/31/96) • **83**

Chablis Vaudevey 1993 • $20 • (08/31/95) • **83**

BACHELET, DENIS

Charmes-Chambertin 1990: Dense and chunky, like a rich raspberry sauce. Has plenty of tannins and fresh acidity, making it a wine to lay away for decades. Try now. 175 cases made. • $53 • (12/15/92) • **94**

Charmes-Chambertin Vieilles Vignes 1986 • $43 • (07/15/89) • **87**

Côte de Nuits-Villages 1990: This charmer displays plenty of raspberry and sweet berry flavors and medium tannins. Drinkable now. • $18 • (12/15/92) • **84**

Gevrey-Chambertin Les Corbeaux Vieilles Vignes 1986 • $30 • (07/15/89) • **83**

Gevrey-Chambertin Vieilles Vignes 1995: An elegant and racy red, with true Pinot Noir character. It grows on you, from the elegant, spicy oak, wild raspberry and strawberry character to the fresh, vibrant, citrusy texture. Long finish. Drink after 2000. • $45 • (01/31/98) • **91**

Gevrey-Chambertin Vieilles Vignes 1990: So seductive you can almost drink it now, with fresh raspberry and cherry flavors and a hint of toastiness. Really turns up the volume in the end. Drink now. 400 cases made. • $43 • (12/15/92) • **91**

Gevrey-Chambertin Vieilles Vignes 1986 • $24 • (07/15/89) • **88**

BACHELET-RAMONET

Bâtard-Montrachet 1994: Has some elegance and a core of citrus, pear, herb and mineral flavors, but this medium-bodied white is very tart on aftertaste. Try now • $NA • (05/31/96) • **79**

Chassagne-Montrachet Caillerets 1994: A serious, medium-bodied white Burgundy, delivering plenty of punchy character, mineral, wet earth and citrus flavors and a long finish. • $NA • (05/31/96) • **87**

Chassagne-Montrachet La Grande Montagne 1994: Clean, crisp and straightforward, a *premier cru* delivering modest mineral, green apple and vegetal flavors. Quite a sharp, tart finish. • $NA • (05/31/96) • **80**

Chassagne-Montrachet Les Grandes Ruchottes 1994: Fairly crisp, but has slightly odd flavors—chalk, wood and cardboard. Medium-body and dry finish. Tasted twice, with consistent notes. • $45 • (08/31/96) • **70**

BAHANS HAUT-BRION, CHÂTEAU

Pessac-Léognan 1997: Round and ripe, with berry and tobacco on the nose and palate. Medium-bodied, with medium tannins. • $NA • (06/15/98) (BT) • **85-89**

Pessac-Léognan 1996: A lovely red, with berry, cherry, cedar and earth aromas and flavors. Medium- to full-bodied, with fine tannins and a sweet fruit finish. • $40 • (06/15/98) (BT) • **85-89**

Pessac-Léognan 1995: Remember the stunning '89 Bahans? Try this. It's full-bodied, with wonderfully ripe, well-knit tannins and a bounty of fruit, tobacco and chocolate notes. Finish is sooo long. Better than previous tasting. • $25 • (05/15/97) (BT) • **90-94**

Pessac-Léognan 1989 • $36 Ⓐ • (03/15/92) • **90**

Pessac-Léognan 1986 • $27 Ⓐ • (09/15/89) • **86**

BAILLAT, DOMAINE

Corbières 1995: Packed with savory flavors of pepper and anise, with some rich plummy notes. Nicely concentrated, with a dash of leather on the finish. Drink now through 1999. 2,000 cases made. • $8 • (04/30/98) • **84**

BAILLY, FRANCK & JEAN-FRANÇOIS

Sancerre Cuvée Chavignol 1996: Muscular, full-bodied and concentrated, with assertive melon, green apple and smoke flavors, firm acidity, even some tannin. Though not a classically-styled Sancerre, it has character and power, and should improve with time. Drink now through 2003. • $17 • (05/31/98) • **88**

Sancerre Cuvée Chavignol 1995: This muscular white offers rich texture, very firm acidity and light flavors of citrus, apple and herbs. Good structure; muted fruit. Try now. • $19 • (06/15/97) • **87**

BALAC, CHÂTEAU

Haut-Médoc 1990: Full-bodied and fruity, offering nice cherry and raspberry flavors. Firm and fairly tannic, with good aromas. A sturdy Bordeaux that's best to drink now. • $12 • (09/15/93) • **85**

BALESTARD, CHÂTEAU

Bordeaux 1997: Unbelievable. Seriously good jam juice. Medium- to full-bodied, with loads of fruit and soft tannins. Medium finish. Napa meets Bordeaux. • $NA • (06/15/98) (BT) • **85-89**

BALESTARD-LA-TONNELLE, CHÂTEAU

St.-Emilion 1989 • $28 • (03/15/92) • **85**

St.-Emilion 1988 • $25 • (04/30/91) • **91**

St.-Emilion 1982 • $24 Ⓐ • (08/31/92) • **82**

BALLAND, DOMAINE JEAN-PAUL

Sancerre 1995: This big white's apple and pear flavors are round and ripe, making it almost Californian in style, but it shows the classic cut hay notes of the region, with balanced acidity. • $15 • (06/15/97) • **88**

Sancerre 1994 • $15 • (12/15/95) • **80**

Sancerre 1993 • $13 • (10/31/94) • **86**

BALLENA

Cabernet Sauvignon Vin de Pays d'Oc 1995: Wild, jammy, grapey flavors mark this medium-bodied, ready-to-drink red. It's hearty in flavor, yet fairly smooth in texture. 30,000 cases made. • $7 • (07/31/97) • **83**

Chardonnay Vin de Pays d'Oc 1996: A soft, fruity wine with lots of pear and banana flavors. Simple and satisfying. 30,000 cases made. • $7 • (06/30/97) • **82**

Merlot Vin de Pays d'Oc 1995: A fresh, grapey, jammy-tasting red with lots of flavor and very little tannin. Smooth, soft and easy to drink. 30,000 cases made. • $7 • (07/31/97) • **84**

BALLOT-MILLOT & FILS, R.

Meursault 1995: Deft winemaking underlies this pure, clean, understated village wine that stresses fruit and *terroir* over showy oak flavors. It's full-bodied, with subtle quince, mineral, wet stone, vanilla bean, pear and hazelnut flavors that glide to a graceful, cream-textured finish. Drink now through 2005. 292 cases made. • $35 • (05/31/97) • **90**

Meursault 1993: Somewhat hard but very lively, offering green apple, mineral and cream character, medium body, firm acidity and lean finish. 300 cases made. • $28 • (08/31/95) • **80**

Meursault Bouchères 1996: A polite wine, full in body, with good fruit, smooth texture, decent toasty oak and spice complexity—but it lacks in intensity, flavor definition and concentration. Drink now. 65 cases made. • $48 • (05/31/98) • **84**

Meursault Les Charmes 1993: Very intense earthy, ripe fruit character, medium body, high acidity and long finish. 100 cases made. • $45 • (08/31/95) • **84**

Meursault Les Charmes 1992: Simple, lean and a bit hollow, with a mint, herb and wet earth character; seems a bit diluted. 250 cases made. • $NA • (08/31/94) • **79**

Meursault Les Criots 1992: Mature, tastes tired on the palate, with stale apple and earthy flavors. 250 cases made. • $38 • (08/31/94) • **73**

Meursault Les Genevrières 1996: Well made but fairly delicate, showing subtle nuances of toasty oak, honey and pear. Medium-bodied, it lacks intensity of fruit, but it's smooth on the finish, and certainly makes for a balanced Meursault that will drink nicely around 2000. 300 cases made. • $54 • (05/31/98) • **85**

Meursault Les Genevrières 1995: Smooth and supple, showing pretty pear, mineral, honey and marzipan flavors. Medium- to full-bodied, with toast notes lingering on the smoky finish. Drink now. 250 cases made. • $50 • (05/31/97) • **91**

Meursault Les Narvaux 1996: Fairly straightforward and neutral, showing decent fruit and mineral character, but also a slight dilution despite the full body, firm acidity and rather silky texture. A bit dry and chewy on the finish. Try in 1999. 125 cases made. • $39 • (05/31/98) • **82**

Meursault Les Narvaux 1995: Well made, relatively ripe, with a supple core of fruit and spice flavors, medium body, moderately intense finish. Smells a bit reductive, but it sure has a lovely rich, full mouthfeel. Drink now through 2000. 100 cases made. • $40 • (05/31/97) • **87**

BALMONT, JEAN

Cabernet Sauvignon Vin de Pays d'Oc 1995: Good richness to balance the herb and cherry flavors, which linger even after the moderate tannins kick in. • $7 • (12/15/96) • **84**

Chardonnay Vin de Pays du Jardin de la France 1995: Apple flavors dominate this basic white. Finishes with nice touches of butter and spice. • $7 • (06/15/97) • **80**

Merlot 60% Cabernet Sauvignon 40% Vin de Pays d'Oc 1995: A fruity, cherry flavored wine, with hints of tobacco and a crisp, firm finish. • $7 • (12/15/96) • **81**

Merlot Vin de Pays d'Oc 1995: A tough customer, this has earthy aromas followed up by astringent flavors. Just a smidgeon of plum flavor. • $7 • (12/15/96) • **76**

Syrah Vin de Pays d'Oc Rosé 1997: Has an off-putting, sweaty character that is quite overpowering. Very funky for a rosé. 1,000 cases made. • $6 • (07/31/98) • **73**

BARA, PAUL

Brut Champagne 1989: Fresh, lively and nicely rounded out by bright lemon and vanilla flavors. This light-style Champagne is velvety in texture and

FRANCE

long on the finish. Showing better than last year. Drink now through 2000. • $40 • (12/31/97) • **90**

Brut Champagne 1988: Powerfully fruity, boasting apple and honey aromas, tight, tart flavors and ample acidity to keep it lively. • $45 • (11/30/95) • **90**

Brut Champagne 1982: Snappy and crisp. A straightforward Brut at first that develops some nice buttery and more complex touches in the glass. Fruity aromas with a good dose of peach. • $34 • (12/31/88) • **89**

Brut Champagne Comtesse Marie de France 1985: Attractive and still vibrant. Toasty, slightly nutty aromas and firm fruit flavors. Crisp texture and a lingering, spicy finish. • $55 • (12/31/96) • **88**

Brut Champagne Grand Cru 100% 1986: Vividly fruity, with peach and apricot flavors, but it clamps down on the finish. Seems a bit awkward, but has interesting cheese aromas and good complexity. 1,000 cases made. • $36 • (12/31/94) • **86**

Brut Champagne Spécial Club Grand Cru 100% 1988: Elegant, crisp and stylish. Aromas are slightly toasty, flavors are lean, lemony and nutty. The texture and acidity is refreshing and appetizing. 500 cases made. • $49 • (12/31/94) • **85**

BARANCOURT

Brut Champagne Cuvée de Fondateurs 1985 • $NA • (12/31/90) • **90**

BARAT, MICHEL

Chablis 1996: Pleasant. Has some fine fruit flavors, with butter and mineral notes adding interest. Medium-bodied. Drink now. • $12 • (08/31/97) • **85**

Chablis 1995: A bulldozer of a Chablis. Big, thick, and packed with flavors and character—perhaps at the expense of finesse. Lingers on the finish, with notes of pear, apple, honey and smoke. Try now. • $15 • (08/31/96) • **87**

Chablis 1994 • $14 • (08/31/95) • **86**

Chablis Côte de Léchet 1996: Fabulous Chablis, especially if you look for mineral, wet earth and wet stone. Full-bodied and subtle, with tropical and pear flavors in the background, this is not for everyone, but if you are an aficionado of mineral-laden character, go for it. Hold until 2005. • $15 • (05/31/98) • **94**

Chablis Côte de Léchet 1995: This *premier cru* is lovely. Its rich, sweet-fruit character is hidden by sharp acidity now, but it's nicely balanced, with bounteous citrus, honey, grassy herb and ripe fruit flavors. Medium- to full-bodied; long, long finish. Best after 1999. • $15 • (06/15/97) • **89**

Chablis Côte de Léchet 1994 • $16 • (05/31/96) • **83**

Chablis Côte de Léchet 1993 • $NA • (08/31/95) • **83**

Chablis Les Fourneaux 1994 • $16 • (05/31/96) • **80**

Chablis Mont de Milieu 1996: Fantastic. Its greatness already shows in the shy and reserved nose, which tantalizes with hints of floral, honey, mineral, wet earth and gunsmoke. At first sip this full-bodied liquid that has the texture of extra-virgin olive oil delivers great acidity and a burst of fresh fruit. Wonderful harmony on the long finish. Tempting now, better from 2005 to 2010. • $15 • (05/31/98) • **94**

Chablis Mont de Milieu 1995: Super-ripe, lush, and almost kirshlike in taste, this cherry flavored wine seems heavy, but delivers plenty of flavors, with a mineral, citrus, kiwi, almost tropical character. Full-bodied. Ready now through 2000. • $15 • (06/15/97) • **86**

Chablis Mont de Milieu 1994 • $16 • (05/31/96) • **87**

Chablis Mont de Milieu 1993 • $NA • (08/31/95) • **86**

Chablis Vaillons 1996: Big, rich, buttery and full-bodied, but showing a wonderful, vibrant, clean core of lemon zest, mandarin orange, pineapple and apple skin notes. Balanced, a bit spicy and honeyed, it's hard to ask more from a Chablis. Fabulous intensity from the midpalate on to a long, long finish. Tempting around 2002 through 2010. • $15 • (05/31/98) • **93**

Chablis Vaillons 1995: An exotic *premier cru* that's never seen any oak, packed with grassy floral, quince jam and wet stone notes. Medium- to full-bodied, crisp and round at the same time. Lengthy finish. Better in 1999 to 2002. • $15 • (06/15/97) • **87**

Chablis Vaillons 1994 • $16 • (05/31/96) • **87**

Chablis Vaillons 1993 • $NA • (08/31/95) • **82**

Key: SS—Spectator Selection CS—Cellar Selection HR—Highly Recommended BB—Best Buy $NA—Price not available Ⓐ—Auction Price (BT)—Barrel Tasting
Dates in parentheses indicate the issues in which the ratings were published.

BAREFOOT

Merlot Vin de Pays 1995: An average-quality red. Its modest fruit flavors dominated by sweet oak, it's a bit awkward. Moderately tannic. From Corsica. • $6 • (07/31/97) • **78**

BARET, CHÂTEAU

Pessac-Léognan 1997: Some dried cherry character on the nose. Light-bodied, with light tannins and a watery finish. • $NA • (06/15/98) (BT) • **75-79**

Pessac-Léognan 1996: Blackberry and mineral aromas and flavors. Medium-to-full body, with firm, silky tannins and a mineral and stone finish. Sleek wine. Very good for this producer. • $19 • (06/15/98) (BT) • **85-89**

Pessac-Léognan 1995: Very floral, with violets, roses and hints of fruit. Medium-bodied, with well-integrated tannins and a medium aftertaste. Needs some time to come together. Try after 1999. • $18 • (01/31/98) • **86**

Pessac-Léognan 1992: A little bit of berry and plum flavor, but still diluted and very light. • $12 • (04/15/95) • **73**

Pessac-Léognan 1991: A wine with focused black cherry and earthy aromas and flavors. Light body and silky texture. • $12 • (03/31/94) • **81**

Pessac-Léognan 1989 • $18 • (03/15/92) • **93**

Pessac-Léognan White 1995: A slightly funky; candied white with apple, marzipan aromas and flavors. Medium-bodied, with a light finish. Drink if you must. • $20 • (04/30/98) • **78**

Pessac-Léognan White 1993 • $19 • (05/31/95) • **78**

BARGE, GILLES

Côte-Rôtie 1991: A muscular wine, with firm tannins and straightforward fruit, but it's rather simple and short on the finish. Drinkable now. • $NA • (05/31/94) • **83**

Côte-Rôtie 1990: Still evolving; a traditional-style wine, showing game, pepper and spice flavors. The tannins are still firm; try now. • $NA • (05/31/94) • **86**

Côte-Rôtie 1989 • $30 • (04/15/93) • **83**

BARGE, PIERRE

Côte-Rôtie 1988 • $42 • (07/31/91) • **84**

BAROLET, DR.

Aloxe-Corton Villamont 1952 • $59 Ⓐ • (08/31/90) • **92**

BARONNE, CHÂTEAU DE LA

Montagne d'Alaric Corbières 1991 • $10 • (03/15/94) • **81**

Montagne d'Alaric Corbières 1990 • $NA • (03/15/94) • **83**

BARRABAQUE, CHÂTEAU

Canon-Fronsac 1997: Dark-colored, with interesting mineral and berry character. Medium body, with silky tannins and a light finish. • $NA • (06/15/98) (BT) • **80-84**

BARRADIS, CHÂTEAU LE

Monbazillac 1990: An interesting mix of apricot and maple flavors, finishing slightly dry. Has some nice acidity, with a touch of overripeness. 5,000 cases made. • $15 • (08/31/97) • **86**

Monbazillac 1988 • $20 • (07/15/91) • **76**

BARRAL, DOMAINE LEON

Faugères 1994: Delicious and smooth, almost like a mature Burgundy. Beautiful cherry and spice flavors are wrapped inside a silky texture, and an interesting beefy note adds to its character. Drink now. • $10 • (06/15/98) • **86**

BARRAUD, DANIEL

Mâcon 1996: Balanced at first, with lime, lemon, honey and spice flavors, this full-bodied white turns slightly hot and burning on the palate. Drink now. 400 cases made. • $16 • (05/31/98) • **82**

Pouilly-Fuissé Cuvée Vieilles Vignes 1994: Somewhat mature already, featuring butterscotch and buttery flavors that seem heavy. Rich, fat, lacking a bit of freshness on the finish. Drinkable now. 416 cases made. • $28 • (05/31/96) • **80**
Pouilly-Fuissé Cuvée Vieilles Vignes 1993: The austere quality softens and delivers some lovely, ripe pear, butter and spice flavors. Quite fresh, even tart on the finish. 417 cases made. • $28 • (05/15/95) • **84**
Pouilly-Fuissé La Roche 1996: Fruit and oak clash a bit in this full-bodied Pouilly. Ripe and sweet-tasting, with lime, honey and spice, but the wood makes it a tough drink. May be better after 1999. 400 cases made. • $26 • (05/31/98) • **83**
Pouilly-Fuissé La Roche 1994: Quite tight, offering a hint of complexity—butter, fig, pear and green apple. Fresh but slightly tart on the finish. 141 cases made. • $24 • (05/31/96) • **80**
Pouilly-Fuissé La Verchère 1996: Lovely; packed with acidity and honey, blending the spice, lime and sweet-tasting fruit in a balanced whole. For now, it's racy and acidic, but give it time and it will deliver lots of mineral. Very clean, pure finish. Try after this year. 1,200 cases made. • $25 • (05/31/98) • **90**
Pouilly-Fuissé La Verchère 1994: Very pretty and attractive, a light- to medium-bodied white putting all the pieces together, from ripe tropical aromas to the citric crispness on aftertaste that keeps going, titillating the palate. 416 cases made. • $21 • (05/31/96) • **87**
Pouilly-Fuissé Vieilles Vignes 1996: Decent fruit and oak complexity, but the wood accents dominate for now. The floral, honey and lime aromas and flavors are nice, though. Drink through 2000. 200 cases made. • $30 • (05/31/98) • **81**
St.-Véran En Crêches 1996: Fairly elegant, with wood-flavored spice, grilled meat and butter notes. A bit tart and green on the finish. Light- to medium-bodied. Drink now or hold until 1999. 800 cases made. • $17 • (05/31/98) • **81**

BARRÉ, DOMAINE

Muscadet de Sèvre et Maine 1993 • $9 • (10/31/94) • **82**
Muscadet de Sèvre et Maine Le Muscadet de Barré 1995: Light-bodied yet round on the palate, this pleasant white offers delicate flavors of citrus and almond that linger on the clean finish. • $9 • (04/30/97) • **84**
Muscadet de Sèvre et Maine Le Muscadet de Barré 1994 • $9 • (11/15/95) • **79**

BARREYRES, CHÂTEAU

Haut-Médoc 1995: A young, robust Bordeaux with ample fruit flavor backed by a firmly tannic texture and significant oak influence. It has the depth, complexity and balance to improve with age. Drink from 1999 to 2004. 42,000 cases made. • $12 • (01/31/98) • **88**
Haut-Médoc 1986 • $8 • (06/30/89) • **78**

BARROT, DOMAINE LUCIEN

Châteauneuf-du-Pape 1994: A bit tough—firmly tannic and with a crisp, acidic core—but it also shows well-defined, complex flavors of black cherries, tobacco, anise and herbs. Though a bit austere, it has potential; try in 1999. • $21 • (09/15/97) • **88**
Châteauneuf-du-Pape 1989 • $20 • (10/15/91) • **88**
Châteauneuf-du-Pape 1988 • $18 • (10/15/91) • **87**
Châteauneuf-du-Pape 1986 • $18 • (10/15/91) • **89**
Châteauneuf-du-Pape 1981 • $16 • (09/30/87) • **87**

BARRYES, CHÂTEAU

Haut-Médoc 1989 • $10 • (07/15/92) • **75**

BARTET, G.

Gevrey-Chambertin Clos St.-Jacques 1995: Well made, supple and succulent, deliciously flavored with pure, clean red and blackberry notes, with a hint of wet earth and a wonderfully subtle spicy quality. Medium-bodied, with firm but ripe tannins and distinctive *goût de terroir*. Tempting now, better in 1999. 158 cases made. • $71 • (11/15/97) • **87**
Gevrey-Chambertin Le Clos St.-Jacques 1994: A beauty, with lovely pure, clean black currant flavors and aromas and a supple texture. Delicate finish suggests a deft winemaker at work. Ends with a wisp of tannins that make it attractive to drink now. • $NA • (11/15/96) • **86**

BARTHOD, GHISLAINE

Bourgogne 1990: Well-crafted but somewhat austere, showing good texture and character and modest rose petal, tarragon and strawberry flavors. Has a chewy finish. Drinkable now. • $23 • (12/15/92) • **83**
Bourgogne 1988 • $20 • (03/31/91) • **82**
Chambolle-Musigny 1990: This solid red offers a round texture, perfumed aromas, a core of earth, tobacco and plum flavors and firm tannins. Drinkable now. • $25 • (12/15/92) • **87**
Chambolle-Musigny 1988 • $50 • (03/15/91) • **88**
Chambolle-Musigny Aux Beaux Bruns 1994: Has some delicious fruit flavors, but kicks in a bit too much gritty tannin to qualify as delicate. Might grow into itself by 1999 to 2000. • $NA • (11/15/96) • **81**
Chambolle-Musigny Aux Beaux Bruns 1990: Like a piece of art; this wine grows on you as it ripples across the palate, showing increasing plum, blackberry and smoke aromas and flavors and a silky texture. Very fine. Drink now to 1999. • $50 • (12/15/92) • **93**
Chambolle-Musigny Aux Beaux Bruns 1988 • $45 • (02/28/91) • **83**
Chambolle-Musigny Les Charmes 1994: Crisp and chewy with grainy tannins. A beam of currant and anise flavors shine through on the finish. • $NA • (11/15/96) • **85**
Chambolle-Musigny Les Charmes 1990: Exquisite, well structured and firm. Underneath the hard, tannic surface is a lovely core of lush berry, violet, plum and earth flavors that show breeding. Drink now. • $50 • (12/15/92) • **90**
Chambolle-Musigny Les Charmes 1984 • $27 • (10/31/87) • **82**
Chambolle-Musigny Les Cras 1990: Charming and supple. The pretty raspberry and cherry flavors make this pleasant enough to drink now, but it will improve with age. • $50 • (12/15/92) • **87**
Chambolle-Musigny Les Cras 1988 • $45 • (02/28/91) • **87**
Chambolle-Musigny Les Cras 1985 • $37 • (07/31/88) • **88**
Chambolle-Musigny Les Véroilles 1990: Extremely firm, restrained and understated, with plum, cherry and forest underbrush notes that should show beautifully after a few years in the cellar. Drink now. • $50 • (12/15/92) • **90**
Chambolle-Musigny Les Véroilles 1988 • $45 • (02/28/91) • **81**

BARTON & GUESTIER

Beaujolais St.-Louis 1995: Fresh flavors of black cherries and plums. Light-bodied, but firm enough to drink with food. Finishes on a pleasant spicy note. • $7 • (09/15/96) • **82**
Beaujolais St.-Louis 1994 • $7 • (10/31/95) • **82**
Beaujolais St.-Louis 1993 • $7 • (06/30/94) • **82**
Beaujolais-Villages 1995: Spicy cinnamon and sandalwood aromas lend personality. Firm and a bit gamy on the palate, it's rather austere for Beaujolais; try with grilled meats. • $9 • (09/15/96) • **82**
Beaujolais-Villages 1993 • $7 • (06/15/95) • **72**
Cabernet Sauvignon Vin de Pays d'Oc 1996: Good, but a little tough, with dried cherry and herbal flavors. 90,000 cases made. • $7 • (10/31/97) • **80**
Cabernet Sauvignon Vin de Pays d'Oc 1995: A straightforward, medium-bodied red with simple berry and blackpepper flavors and a firm texture. • $8 • (07/31/97) • **80**
Cabernet Sauvignon Vin de Pays d'Oc 1994 • $6 • (10/31/95) • **80**
Chardonnay Vin de Pays d'Oc 1996: A bit dull-tasting, with modest apple and lemon flavors. Turns earthy on the finish. 125,000 cases made. • $7 • (10/31/97) • **78**
Chardonnay Vin de Pays d'Oc 1995: This has a dried out flavor to it, and little else. • $8 • (06/30/97) • **71**
Chardonnay Vin de Pays d'Oc 1994 • $9 • (12/15/95) • **82**
Châteauneuf-du-Pape 1992: Rustic game and barnyard aromas and flavors, with hints of chocolate and prunes and tough tannins. Lacks finesse and already mature. For fans of the traditional style. • $17 • (11/15/95) • **79**
Châteauneuf-du-Pape 1990: Tough and earthy; a rough-textured wine with austere, barklike flavors, offering little in the way of generosity. Try now. • $16 • (10/31/93) • **71**
Châteauneuf-du-Pape 1983 • $11 • (09/30/87) • **74**
Gevrey-Chambertin 1985 • $21 • (04/30/88) • **89**
Margaux 1985 • $12 • (04/30/88) • **75**
Merlot Bordeaux Founder's Collection 1725 1995: Plenty of spice and a ripe, plummy character denote this simple Bordeaux. There's some tannin, so drink with meats or cheeses. 16,000 cases made. • $10 • (08/31/97) • **81**
Merlot Vin de Pays d'Oc 1996: This well-focused French red shows black cherry, meaty and herbal notes typical of the varietal, in a round, soft package that has just enough grip to accompany food. Fresh and flavorful, it's made for drinking now, at a price that invites you to imbibe freely. Tasted

twice, with consistent notes. 225,000 cases made. • $7 • (11/15/97) BB • **85**

Merlot Vin de Pays d'Oc 1995: A mixture of plum, spice and earth flavors, with a gamy finish. A bit soft, though within bounds. • $8 • (12/15/96) • **82**

Merlot Vin de Pays d'Oc 1994 • $6 • (10/31/95) • **82**

Merlot Vin de Pays d'Oc 1993 • $6 • (02/28/95) • **81**

Mâcon St.-Louis 1993: Rather rich and weighty. The creamy pear, apple and hazelnut character turns a bit harsh and dull on the short finish. Slight dilution. 1,666 cases made. • $7 • (08/31/95) • **78**

Pommard 1985 • $21 • (11/30/87) • **81**

Pouilly-Fuissé 1992: Time in the bottle has lent attractive smoky, toasty notes, but it's soft, lacking firmness and depth. 25,000 cases made. • $16 • (03/31/95) • **79**

St.-Julien 1985 • $13 • (02/15/88) • **83**

Sauternes 1985: Attractively earthy, chalky and moderately rich, but it's balanced toward softness. Good quality, but not for special occasions. • $12 • (05/31/88) • **75**

Sauvignon Blanc Bordeaux Founder's Collection 1725 1995: Crisp and quite herbal in character, with good body and structure, it's a firm and flavorful white for those tired of Chardonnay. 8,000 cases made. • $10 • (07/31/97) • **83**

Sauvignon Blanc Vin de Pays du Jardin de la France 1993 • $6 • (10/31/94) • **76**

Syrah Vin de Pays d'Oc 1995: Delivers decent ripe cherry and berry flavors, but it's astringent as well, with a green note on the finish. 5,000 cases made. • $7 • (10/31/97) • **78**

Vouvray 1993 • $10 • (11/15/95) • **83**

BASQUE, CHÂTEAU DU

St.-Emilion 1995: Light, with berry and tobacco character, light body and tannins, and a fresh finish. Drink now. 6,500 cases made. • $20 • (01/31/98) • **79**

BASTIDE, CELLIER DE LA

Entre-Deux-Mers 1994 • $8 • (05/31/95) • **82**

BASTIDE BLANCHE, LA

Bandol Longue Garde 1993: A mature wine with some nice meaty flavors and good acidity, but it turns a bit pruney and coarse on the finish. Drink now. • $20 • (03/31/98) • **81**

Bandol Vieilles Vignes 1994: Lacks freshness and focus, with only modest berry and stewed tomato flavors. • $18 • (03/31/98) • **74**

BASTIDE DAUZAC, LA

Margaux 1996: A bit aggressive, with slightly metallic tannins and an herbal, berry character. • $NA • (01/01/97) (BT) • **75-79**

Margaux 1995: Shows some very good fruit, with plenty of berry and green tobacco character, but lacks a bit in the moderate finish. Medium- to full-bodied, with velvety tannins. Better after 1999. • $20 • (01/31/98) • **84**

Margaux 1994: Slightly lean, but has some attractive silky tannins and berry, tobacco flavors. Drink now or hold. • $18 • (01/31/97) • **79**

Margaux 1991: A good wine for this vintage with its silky mouthfeel, cherry flavors and slightly herbal character on finish. • $11 • (03/31/94) • **80**

BASTIDE DE SIRAN, LA

Margaux 1995: A well-proportioned, pretty wine, with crushed berries and violets. Full-bodied and velvety, with lovely spice, berry and chocolate flavors. Clean finish. Serious second label. Best after 2000. • $15 • (01/31/98) • **87**

Key: SS—Spectator Selection CS—Cellar Selection HR—Highly Recommended BB—Best Buy $NA—Price not available Ⓐ—Auction Price (BT)—Barrel Tasting

Dates in parentheses indicate the issues in which the ratings were published.

BASTOR-LAMONTAGNE, CHÂTEAU

Sauternes 1990: Impressively classy and focused; lemon, lime, dried apricot and toasty coconut flavors are presented in a seductive, velvety package. Drinkable now. • $25 • (04/15/95) • **92**

Sauternes 1989: Well made and concentrated, medium-bodied, built more for finesse than power, displaying lemon, honey and butterscotch flavors that offer zing and creaminess at the same time. • $33 • (04/15/95) • **88**

Sauternes 1988: Simple and light, offering modest lemon, honey and melon flavors, medium sweetness and a short finish. • $21 • (04/15/95) • **80**

Sauternes 1987: • $17 • (06/15/90) • **67**

Sauternes 1986: Rich and oily, yet racy, exhibiting terrific acidity along with wonderful sweetness, intense flavors and creamy character. A note of ash distracts slightly on the long finish. Try around 2000. • $NA • (04/15/95) • **88**

Sauternes 1985: Balanced toward lightnes and openness—not an extra-rich wine, possessing slightly herbal flavors. • $20 • (05/31/88) • **82**

Sauternes 1983: Balanced toward lightness and openness—not an extra-rich wine but nice nonetheless. Medium gold, clean and elegant, with ripe fig, apricot, tobacco and slightly herbal flavors. • $23 • (01/31/88) • **82**

BATACCHI, PHILIPPE

Clos de la Roche 1991: Very youthful, jammy and peppery, showing a dill edge to the anise, blackberry and currant aromas and flavors up front, turning crisp and lemony on the finish. Try now. 25 cases made. • $30 Ⓐ • (01/31/94) • **86**

Clos de la Roche 1990: A fruit bomb. Tastes like a barrel sample, with freshly crushed berry, lovely violet and vanilla notes and plenty of tannins to go along with the supple, delicious texture. Drink now. 83 cases made. • $59 • (12/15/92) • **93**

Côte de Nuits-Villages 1990: Shows the essence of Burgundy fruit flavor, with oodles of black licorice, raspberry and cherry nuances and fine tannins. A joy to drink now. 200 cases made. • $20 • (12/15/92) • **88**

Fixin 1990: Absolutely delicious, with loads of licorice and berry flavors and velvety tannins. Drinkable now. 125 cases made. • $23 • (12/15/92) • **87**

Gevrey-Chambertin Les Evosselles 1991: Strangely floral, brightly fruity and light. Try now. 110 cases made. • $30 • (01/31/94) • **79**

Gevrey-Chambertin Les Evosselles 1990: Like a polished diamond, this wine shines with bright color and a vivid texture. Razor sharp, well-made and satiny, offering ultra-clean raspberry, cherry, plum and vanilla flavors and racy acidity to lengthen the finish. Drinkable now. 250 cases made. • $32 • (12/15/92) • **91**

Gevrey-Chambertin Les Jeunes Rois 1991: Relatively dark in color and concentrated in flavor, offering bright cherry and currant aromas and flavors that linger on the finish. Drinkable now. 140 cases made. • $30 Ⓐ • (01/31/94) • **85**

Gevrey-Chambertin Les Jeunes Rois 1990: The essence of fruit, this tastes like a barrel sample it's so young and juicy, with full-throttle black cherry aromas and flavors and a beautiful round, fruity finish. An unusual wine. Drinkable now. 292 cases made. • $38 • (12/15/92) • **90**

Morey-St.-Denis Premier Cru 1991: Distinctive, almost bizarre, with odd, gamy, leathery notes. Drink now. 60 cases made. • $27 Ⓐ • (01/31/94) • **79**

Morey-St.-Denis Premier Cru 1990: Offers fruit, fruit and more fruit; this bubbles with raspberry flavors. So youthful and extracted it tastes like a barrel sample, but an underlying structure of fine tannins and lively acidity gives it a fresh finish. Drinkable now. 100 cases made. • $44 • (12/15/92) • **93**

BATAILLEY, CHÂTEAU

Pauillac 1997: Good ripe currant aromas. Medium-bodied, with light, velvety tannins and a medium finish with vanilla character. Clever winemaking. • $NA • (06/15/98) (BT) • **85-89**

Pauillac 1996: A solid red, with berry, mineral and spice aromas and flavors. Medium- to full-bodied, with well-knit tannins and a medium finish. Well made. Almost outstanding. • $25 • (06/15/98) (BT) • **85-89**

Pauillac 1995: A thick and compact wine, although slightly fat. Stunning aromas of violets, berries. Full-bodied and chunky, with lovely tobacco and cherry flavors and a long, velvet-textured finish. Best after 2002. • $22 • (01/31/98) • **89**

Pauillac 1992: Elegant, harmonious berry and light tobacco character, medium-to-light body, silky tannins and fresh finish. Try now. • $19 • (04/15/95) • **80**

Pauillac 1991: Some pretty tobacco, berry and herbal notes. Medium body with a very silky texture. • $19 • (03/31/94) • **83**

Pauillac 1989 • $39 Ⓐ • (03/15/92) • **81**
Pauillac 1988 • $29 Ⓐ • (04/30/91) • **90**
Pauillac 1982 • $32 Ⓐ • (08/31/92) • **86**
Pauillac 1970 • $30 Ⓐ • (05/15/93) • **88**
Pauillac 1961 • $53 Ⓐ • (04/30/96) • **84**
Pauillac 1945 • $200 • (11/30/95) • **78**

BATARD, SERGE

Muscadet-Côtes de Grandlieu Sur Lie Domaine Les Hautes Noëlles 1996: Lime-scented, with a soft, round texture that Muscadet achieves only in ripe vintages, but a core of citruslike acidity keeps it fresh and clean. Makes a pleasant apéritif. Drink now. • $9 • (05/31/98) • **83**

BATARDIÈRE, DOMAINE DE LA

Muscadet de Sèvre et Maine 1995: This light, crisp white has just enough pear and mineral flavors, and it's fresh and clean. • $8 • (06/15/97) • **82**
Muscadet de Sèvre et Maine 1994 • $8 • (12/15/95) • **74**

BAUBIAC, DOMAINE DE

Coteaux du Languedoc 1995: A good, solid red wine with appealing beefy and dried cherry flavors. Drink now. • $12 • (03/31/98) • **83**
Merlot Vin de Pays d'Oc 1996: An awkward wine with cloying berry and rhubarb flavors and an astringent finish. Past its prime. • $12 • (03/31/98) • **74**

BAUCHET PÈRE & FILS

Brut Champagne 1989: Simple in flavor and rustic in texture for Champagne. Not very much fun, it tastes overly mature, as if drying out. • $NA • (12/15/96) • **77**

BAUDRY, DOMAINE BERNARD

Chinon Les Granges 1996: Supple, yet firm. Chewy, with vivid black cherry, chocolate and light herb flavors. Has depth without heaviness. Drink now through 2001. • $14 • (02/28/98) • **87**
Chinon Les Granges 1995: Lush but light, with firm yet well-integrated tannins and ripe black cherry and plum flavors accented by a lovely gamy note. This exuberant red is delicious now. • $14 • (05/15/97) • **89**

BAUGET-JOUETTE

Brut Blanc de Blancs Champagne 1990: Powered by fruit, this is a bold, generous style of bubbly that combines toasty, earthy aromas with ripe citrus flavors and a mouthfilling texture. Gets better with each sip. • $52 • (11/30/96) • **91**
Brut Blanc de Blancs Champagne 1988: Rich, smooth and complex with layers of spice, ginger, pear and toasty flavors that are creamy and smooth, staying with you on a long, flavorful finish. Delicious now. 1,000 cases made. • $51 • (12/31/93) HR • **92**
Brut Blanc de Blancs Champagne 1985: Ripe, smooth and elegant, with lively, creamy pear, spice and honeyed notes that are intense and focused, picking up a hint of hazelnut on the aftertaste. Complex and stylish, with a long finish. Drink now. 825 cases made. • $59 • (12/31/92) • **90**
Brut Champagne 1985: Broad, ripe, rich and flavorful, with mouthfilling pear, spice, vanilla and toast flavors that are intense and concentrated. A smooth, substantive Champagne, with flavors that linger. Drinkable now. 1,400 cases made. • $55 • (12/31/92) HR • **90**
Brut Champagne Grande Réserve 1988: Smooth, rich, creamy and spicy with tiers of pear, ginger, vanilla and toast flavors that are focused and lively, finishing with excellent length. Tasty now but capable of aging. Drinkable now. • $47 • (12/31/93) • **93**

BAUMARD, DOMAINE DES

Anjou Logis de la Giraudière 1995: Light herb and spice aromas and flavors lend appeal, but overall it's rather light and simple. Pleasant for drinking now. 1,000 cases made. • $8 • (06/15/97) • **83**
Coteaux du Layon Carte d'Or NV: This sweet, honeyed white is seductive for its velvety texture and crème brûlée flavors, but it has only moderate concentration and intensity. Makes a nice apéritif. Drink now. • $12 • (05/31/98) • **83**
Coteaux du Layon Clos Ste.- Catherine 1996: Creamy coconut, dried orange and honey flavors are concentrated and sweet in this rich white. It has a velvety texture, and the fruit flavors are magnified by low alcohol and acidity. An intriguing wine that grows on you with every sip. Drink now through 2005. 500 cases made. • $25 • (05/31/98) • **90**
Coteaux du Layon Clos de Ste.- Catherine 1995: This lively white offers an intriguing interplay of sweet and tart, with coconut, vanilla and honey flavors balanced by pineapple, lime and peach notes. It's vibrant and refreshing, sweet yet crisp and clean. 500 cases made. • $22 • (05/15/97) • **92**
Coteaux du Layon Cuvée le Paon 1995: This sleek, racy white offers peach, pineapple and spice flavors, with crisp acidity offsetting modest sweetness now. Should be better in 1999 and beyond. 2,000 cases made. • $20 • (05/15/97) • **89**
Crémant de Loire 1992: Applelike and herbal in flavor, this bubbly is a bit simple in character but turns austere on the finish. 1,000 cases made. • $13 • (05/15/97) • **82**
Côteaux du Layon Clos de Ste.-Catherine 1988 • $11 • (04/15/90) • **81**
Côteaux du Layon White 1990 • $20 • (03/31/92) • **87**
Quarts de Chaume 1996: A real showstopper. When Loire whites combine great ripeness and complete botrytis, they develop a distinctive mineral note that complements and deepens the usual spice and honey flavors. This wine shows it beautifully, along with pineapple, crème brûlée and dried orange flavors. A superb follow-up to the classic '95 Quarts de Chaume. Drink now through 2025. 1,000 cases made. • $35 • (05/31/98) CS • **95**
Quarts de Chaume 1995: This gorgeous Loire white manages to be both extremely complex and utterly harmonious. Aromas of spice, crème brûlée and mango give way to mouthfilling flavors of honey, minerals, dried apricots and orange-peel, very sweet yet kept vivid by crisp, lime-scented acidity. Irresistable now, better—probably much better—in years to come. 1,000 cases made. • $35 • (05/15/97) CS • **98**
Quarts de Chaume 1993 • $27 • (12/15/95) • **88**
Quarts de Chaume 1990 • $45 • (03/31/92) • **89**
Quarts de Chaume 1988 • $20 • (04/15/90) • **82**
Savennières 1996: Alluring honey and spice aromas might lead you to think this white is sweet, but on the palate it's steely and dry, with flavors of minerals, almonds and dried fruits. It's powerful, food-friendly and will improve with age. Drink now through 2002. • $17 • (05/31/98) • **89**
Savennières 1995: Alluring aromas of honeysuckle and peaches give way to vivid flavors of peach, almond, grapefruit and minerals. Rich but nearly tart, it needs time to soften. Try now. 5,000 cases made. • $17 • (05/15/97) • **88**
Savennières 1993 • $14 • (12/15/95) • **85**
Savennières Clos de Saint Yves 1995: Austere and a bit lean, this very firm white offers delicate floral and peach aromas, but its structure dominates the light peach and mineral flavors. Try now. 1,000 cases made. • $20 • (06/15/97) • **87**
Savennières Clos du Papillon 1996: Delicate almond and floral aromas give way to a lean but muscular palate with almond, mineral and peach flavors. It's firm and crisp, but the ripe fruit notes on the finish are generous and long. Drink now through 2000. • $20 • (05/31/98) • **87**
Savennières Clos du Papillon 1995: Good ripeness and concentration give this a full-bodied, powerful character that is balanced and harmonious. Not showing much depth of flavor now, but that should come with time. 3,000 cases made. • $20 • (05/15/97) • **89**
Savennières Clos du Papillon 1993 • $14 • (12/15/95) • **88**
Savennières Trie Spéciale 1995: Distinctive smoky aromas lead to a richly textured white with round apple, toast and light earth flavors. It's a big wine, with integration as well as power, and an unusual character for the region. 2,000 cases made. • $27 • (05/15/97) • **88**

BAUME, DOMAINE DE LA

Cabernet Sauvignon France 1995: Medium-bodied, with plum and berry flavors and some herbal notes mixed in as well. Drink now. 30,000 cases made. • $6 • (06/15/98) • **79**
Chardonnay France 1996: A delicate white, with nice peach and green apple flavors. Finishes with a touch of sweetness. Sip it on a summer afternoon. 30,000 cases made. • $6 • (06/15/98) • **83**
Merlot France 1995: A straightforward mix of plum and herbal flavors, with a gamy touch. Drink now. 30,000 cases made. • $6 • (06/15/98) • **78**
Syrah France 1996: Packed full of berry, red plum and cherry flavors, with a good zip of acidity and leathery notes. Smooth and nicely concentrated, with a pleasing mouthfeel. Drink now through 2000. 30,000 cases made. • $6 • (07/31/98) • **84**

BEAUCASTEL, CHÂTEAU DE

Châteauneuf-du-Pape 1994: A nice mix of red fruit, herb and sweetly earthy flavors give appealing complexity, while soft tannins make it accessible now. The long finish promises improvement with age. • $23 Ⓐ • (02/28/97) • **87**

Châteauneuf-du-Pape 1993: The cherry, licorice and black pepper flavors are true to form, but dominated by firm tannins at this stage. Well made. Try now. • $37 • (11/15/96) • **86**

Châteauneuf-du-Pape 1992: A light, elegant version of Châteauneuf, with interesting leather and earth aromas, bright cherry and blackberry flavors and a lingering finish. Drink now. • $31 • (11/30/94) • **85**

Châteauneuf-du-Pape 1991: A solid wine, not as glorious as the top vintage, but still ripe and earthy. A leathery, barnyardlike component to the black cherry flavors, lingering on the finish. Try now. 10,000 cases made. • $8 Ⓐ • (03/31/94) HR • **89**

Châteauneuf-du-Pape 1990: Not as appealing as the '89, our Wine of the Year in 1991, but it's a generous, concentrated, intensely fruity Châteauneuf that blends mouthfilling flavors with complex cedar, spice and leather accents. Sturdy tannins and solid acidity. Drinkable now. Tasted twice. 17,000 cases made. • $40 • (03/15/93) HR • **92**

Châteauneuf-du-Pape 1989 • $84 Ⓐ • (10/15/91) CS • **97**

Châteauneuf-du-Pape 1988 • $58 Ⓐ • (10/15/91) • **90**

Châteauneuf-du-Pape 1987 • $17 • (09/30/89) • **86**

Châteauneuf-du-Pape 1986 • $11 Ⓐ • (10/15/91) • **91**

Châteauneuf-du-Pape 1985 • $53 Ⓐ • (10/15/91) • **91**

Châteauneuf-du-Pape 1984 • $22 • (11/30/89) • **89**

Châteauneuf-du-Pape 1983 • $65 Ⓐ • (10/15/91) • **90**

Châteauneuf-du-Pape 1982 • $30 • (11/30/89) • **92**

Châteauneuf-du-Pape 1981 • $64 Ⓐ • (10/15/91) • **96**

Châteauneuf-du-Pape 1980 • $38 • (11/30/89) • **83**

Châteauneuf-du-Pape White 1995: The deep gold color and butterscotch aromas are appealing but a bit extreme; this full-bodied wine is rich but flat, with almond, butter and minty notes. A bit rustic on the finish. Tough to match with food. Tasted twice, with consistent notes. • $45 • (10/15/97) • **81**

Châteauneuf-du-Pape White Vieilles Vignes 1995: Exotic and distinctive. The aromas call up fields of wild herbs and hot stones, the rich, thick flavors are ripe, concentrated and harmonious, with toast, mineral, herb, honey and smoke notes. Combines regional typicity with world-class winemaking. Delicious now and for years to come. • $82 • (10/15/97) • **95**

Côtes du Rhône White Coudoulet de Beaucastel 1993 • $22 • (11/30/94) • **84**

BEAUDET, PAUL

Mâcon-Berzé-le-Ville Château de Berzé 1995: Ripe and sweet-tasting, but a slight cardboardlike character detracts from the fruit flavors. • $NA • (08/31/96) • **76**

Mâcon-Viré 1995: Lean, crisp and refreshing, with well-defined notes of lime, fresh herbs, gooseberry and grass. Tart finish. Would go well with shellfish. Try now. • $NA • (05/31/97) • **85**

Pouilly-Fuissé Domaine des Trois Tilleuls Vieilles Vignes 1994: Tightly-wound earth, mineral, nutmeg and green apple notes. Quite lean and sharp on the finish, even a bit tough. Drinkable now. 1,000 cases made. • $NA • (05/31/96) • **83**

St.-Véran Domaine du Poète 1996: Supple and minerally, with distinctive matchstick, smoke, white pepper notes blending with pie crust, apple and pear. Fairly complex, intense and medium-bodied, it lasts on the finish. 830 cases made. • $14 • (05/31/98) • **85**

BEAULT-FORGEOT

Mazis-Chambertin Hospice de Beaune Cuvée Madeleine-Collig 1980 • $56 • (07/01/84) • **91**

Nuits-St.-Georges Les Plâteaux 1981 • $17 • (07/01/84) • **83**

Key: SS—Spectator Selection CS—Cellar Selection HR—Highly Recommended BB—Best Buy $NA—Price not available Ⓐ—Auction Price (BT)—Barrel Tasting
Dates in parentheses indicate the issues in which the ratings were published.

BEAUMET

Blanc de Noirs Champagne 1988: Very simple and dominated by the bubbles. It's clean but lacks much character other than apple. Drink now. • $35 • (12/31/93) • **78**

Brut Blanc de Blancs Champagne Cuvée Malakoff 1985: Vibrant and exotic. Lots of fresh and mysterious fruit in this, with orange, fig, and apple character, high acidity and loads of bubbles on the finish. Drinkable now. • $45 • (12/31/93) • **92**

Brut Blanc de Blancs Champagne Cuvée Malakoff 1979 • $30 • (05/31/87) • **89**

Brut Blanc de Noirs Champagne 1983: Firm, crisp and elegant, a flavorful wine centered around lemon and toast aromas and flavors, sharply focused, long and lively. White pepper and apple flavors are particularly appealing. A classy wine. • $30 • (12/31/89) • **89**

Brut Champagne 1988: Loads of foam and a large bead. Rather simple and short with some pear character, and fruity, but very light and thin. Tannic. Drink now. • $35 • (12/31/93) • **79**

Brut Rosé Champagne 1983: Firm and elegant, with spice and cherry aromas and flavors, a touch of smoke and a lively texture to make it interesting. One of the best of the vintage. 20,000 cases made. • $30 • (12/31/89) • **90**

Brut Rosé Champagne 1979 • $16 • (12/16/85) • **79**

BEAUMONT, CHÂTEAU

Haut-Médoc 1997: A delicate, well-made wine, with fine tannins and pretty fruit. 18,500 cases made. • $NA • (06/15/98) (BT) • **85-89**

Haut-Médoc 1996: Pretty red, with red currant, spice and berry aromas and flavors. Medium body, with well-integrated, fine tannins and a cool, fruity finish. 26,500 cases made. • $15 • (06/15/98) (BT) • **85-89**

Haut-Médoc 1995: Promises more on the nose than it gives on the palate, with gorgeous aromas of blueberries, vanilla and chocolate. Medium-bodied, with medium tannins a moderate finish. Best after 1999. 45,000 cases made. • $15 • (01/31/98) • **88**

Haut-Médoc 1994: A little hard and slightly one-dimensional. Dried cherry and wet earth aromas and flavors; medium body; firm tannins. Drink now. 27,500 cases made. • $14 • (01/31/97) • **82**

Haut-Médoc 1993: Some decent currant and black cherry, but it's awfully dry and has a whiff of paper that's distracting. Bottle sickness? Tasted twice, with consistent notes. 35,000 cases made. • $13 • (01/31/96) • **79**

Haut-Médoc 1992: Some cherry character but rather light and diluted. • $11 • (04/15/95) • **76**

Haut-Médoc 1991: Attractive and aromatic with herbal and vanilla character, but light and having a slightly dry finish. • $11 • (03/31/94) • **77**

Haut-Médoc 1990: Extremely ripe and raisiny, with baked fruit, coffee flavors and big, soft tannins. A little overdone for us. Drinkable now. 30,000 cases made. • $13 • (03/31/93) • **80**

Haut-Médoc 1989 • $14 • (03/15/92) • **82**

Haut-Médoc 1988 • $15 • (07/15/91) • **82**

Haut-Médoc 1986 • $12 • (06/30/89) • **84**

Haut-Médoc 1985 • $14 • (04/30/88) • **74**

Haut-Médoc 1982 • $18 • (08/31/92) • **87**

BEAUMONT DES CRAYÈRES

Brut Blanc de Blancs Champagne Nostalgie 1985: A big, open and welcoming Champagne with lots of vanilla, apple and pear aromas and flavors. Full-bodied and rather round with a long, flavorful finish. Drinkable now. • $NA • (12/31/93) • **88**

Brut Champagne Cuvée de Prestige NV: Full-bodied, ripe fruit flavor accented by mature toast, spice and nut nuances. This is rich, with a lush texture, but a bit heavy in style. Tasted twice, with consistent notes. 10,000 cases made. • $28 • (11/15/97) • **89**

Brut Champagne Cuvée de Réserve NV: Quite lively and refreshing, this unusually vivid Champagne blends fresh fruit flavors with attractive accents of butter and cream on a velvety texture. 25,000 cases made. • $22 • (10/31/97) • **89**

Brut Champagne Nostalgie 1990: Bright, lively and beautifully balanced Champagne that's dry, floral and honeylike in flavor, with a zingy, lingering finish. Distinctive for its elegance. Drink now through 2000. 4,000 cases made. • $32 • (11/30/97) • **90**

Brut Champagne Nostalgie 1987: Strong, muscular fizz with intriguing aromas and flavors of smoke and fruit; quietly foamy, good acidity and a long finish. Drink now. • $NA • (12/31/93) • **86**

Brut Rosé Champagne Privilège NV: A bright, lively, youthful rosé with subtle, fresh strawberry and cherry flavors and a clean, crisp finish. Drink now. • $28 • (11/30/97) • **86**

BEAUREGARD, CHÂTEAU

Pomerol 1997: Good berry and wet earth character, with a hint of new wood. Medium-bodied, with moderate, velvety tannins and a medium finish. • $NA • (06/15/98) (BT) • **85-89**

Pomerol 1996: A pretty, well-proportioned '96, with ripe berry and plum aromas and flavors, medium body and medium, velvety tannins. Almost outstanding. 5,500 cases made. • $80 • (06/15/98) (BT) • **85-89**

Pomerol 1995: A big, concentrated Pomerol. Impressive aromas of green tobacco, fresh and dried cherries and sweet fruit, with a hint of tar. Full-bodied, with well-integrated tannins and a long, velvety, tobacco aftertaste. Best after 2000. 5,000 cases made. • $21 Ⓐ • (01/31/98) • **91**

Pomerol 1994: Bountiful for the vintage. Plenty of black olive and fruit aromas and flavors. Full-bodied, with lovely velvety tannins and a very long finish. Drinkable now, but better in 1999. 5,000 cases made. • $26 • (01/31/97) • **89**

Pomerol 1993: Well made, delicious, medium-bodied, showing harmony between oak and fruit. Good amount of tannin and a sweet-tasting finish. Try now. 4,167 cases made. • $26 • (01/31/96) • **87**

Pomerol 1988 • $21 Ⓐ • (07/31/91) HR • **90**

Pomerol 1986 • $24 • (06/15/89) • **87**

Pomerol 1982 • $23 Ⓐ • (08/31/92) • **87**

BEAUREGARD, CHÂTEAU DE

Coteaux du Languedoc 1989 • $5 • (12/15/91) BB • **81**

Coteaux du Languedoc 1986 • $4 • (05/31/88) BB • **85**

BEAURENARD, DOMAINE DE

Châteauneuf-du-Pape 1996: Full-bodied but still lively, with black cherry, licorice, black pepper and gay flavors. Has good acidity and firm tannins, but it's still a bit raw. Try now. • $24 • (10/15/97) • **83**

Châteauneuf-du-Pape 1995: Ripe and lively, this vivid red offers bright cassis, licorice and black pepper flavors, with firm underlying tannins. It's velvety and delicious now, and should improve through 1999. • $24 • (10/15/97) • **87**

Châteauneuf-du-Pape 1994: A lush texture and sweet cherry flavor give this wine immediate appeal, though it has the underlying tannins to improve with age. Flavors of toast, clove and licorice add interest. 9,000 cases made. • $23 • (11/15/96) • **86**

Châteauneuf-du-Pape 1991: Rings true for Châteauneuf-du-Pape, with its leathery, earthy edge, but shows cherry and plum flavors underneath. Drink now. Tasted twice, with consistent notes. 9,500 cases made. • $19 • (06/15/93) • **82**

Châteauneuf-du-Pape 1990: Firm in texture, with focused black cherry, blackberry and black pepper aromas and flavors, well-integrated tannins and lots of fruit echoing on the finish. Balanced and flavorful; drinkable now. 9,500 cases made. • $19 • (11/15/92) HR • **90**

Châteauneuf-du-Pape 1989 • $21 • (10/15/91) • **86**

Châteauneuf-du-Pape 1988 • $20 • (10/15/91) • **89**

Châteauneuf-du-Pape 1986 • $24 • (10/15/91) • **88**

Châteauneuf-du-Pape 1985 • $20 • (10/15/91) • **87**

Châteauneuf-du-Pape 1983 • $20 • (10/15/91) • **87**

Châteauneuf-du-Pape 1982 • $9 • (04/01/85) BB • **85**

Châteauneuf-du-Pape 1981 • $20 • (10/15/91) • **88**

Châteauneuf-du-Pape White 1996: Fairly delicate, with lively, pure and clean flavors, showing mineral, pear, floral and citrus character that sings on the palate and goes on to a long, succulent finish. Drink now. • $24 • (10/15/97) • **87**

Côtes du Rhône 1996: Tart and sharp, it's a disappointing wine that's been overcropped and seems diluted. Herbal, green finish. • $10 • (10/15/97) • **75**

Côtes du Rhône 1994: Not much fruit here, with flavors of leather and copper, astringent tannins and a chocolaty finish. It's rich, but unbalanced. 12,000 cases made. • $10 • (10/15/96) • **79**

Côtes du Rhône Rosé 1996: Distinctive, with banana, fruit salad and cherry notes. Nice, but a bit muted and dull on the finish. • $10 • (10/15/97) • **79**

Côtes du Rhône Rosé 1995: Vibrant strawberry and watermelon aromas give way to lively citrus and berry flavors in this assertive rosé. Clean and dry, with a refreshing quinine note on the finish. 1,500 cases made. • $10 • (10/15/96) • **84**

BEAUSÉJOUR, CHÂTEAU

St.-Emilion 1997: Very short on the palate, with berry, earth and tobacco character and slightly dry tannins. Needs more fruit. • $NA • (06/15/98) (BT) • **80-84**

St.-Emilion 1996: Bubbling over with blackberry and cherry aromas. Full-bodied, with firm tannins and a medium finish. Well-structured. Almost outstanding. 5,000 cases made. • $36 • (06/15/98) (BT) • **85-89**

St.-Emilion 1995: Not quite outstanding but delicious all the same. Interesting berry, bark and porcini aromas. Medium-bodied, with lovely, velvety tannins and a savory tobacco, berry aftertaste. Best after 1999. • $35 • (01/31/98) • **89**

St.-Emilion 1994: Delicate, with strawberry, cherry and earth aromas and flavors. Medium-bodied, with firm tannins and a crisp finish. Drink now. • $38 • (01/31/97) • **86**

St.-Emilion 1993: A joy to drink. Plenty of pleasant berry and cherry aromas and flavors and a hint of cocoa. Medium body, fine tannins and a long, fresh finish. Drinkable now. • $30 • (01/31/96) • **87**

St.-Emilion 1992: Firm and crisp young red featuring dried cherry and berry aromas and flavors, medium-to-light body, medium tannins and light finish. Drinkable now. • $33 • (04/15/95) • **80**

St.-Emilion 1990: Wild, exciting and classy, with a round, polished texture and intense smoky, vanilla, grapey aromas and flavors. This property is really coming on strong. Drinkable now. 3,000 cases made. • $85 • (03/31/93) • **95**

St.-Emilion 1989 • $44 • (03/15/92) • **91**

St.-Emilion 1988 • $28 Ⓐ • (04/30/91) • **87**

St.-Emilion 1986 • $34 • (06/30/89) • **91**

St.-Emilion 1982 • $30 • (08/31/92) • **88**

St.-Emilion 1970 • $40 • (05/15/93) • **84**

St.-Emilion 1961 • $NA • (04/30/96) • **55**

St.-Emilion 1947: Has freshness and life, rich color and brilliant black cherry, exotic plum and spice flavors. It's nicely balanced, too, which allows the flavors to play out smoothly. Feels like it can still develop. • $110 • (05/31/97) • **88**

BEAU-SÉJOUR BÉCOT, CHÂTEAU

St.-Emilion 1997: Very woody, but with a solid core of fruit for the vintage. Medium-bodied, with moderate, velvety tannins. Wait and see. • $NA • (06/15/98) (BT) • **85-89**

St.-Emilion 1996: Extracted with berry, slightly smoky and burnt character. Medium-bodied, with medium tannins and short finish. • $NA • (01/01/97) (BT) • **85-89**

St.-Emilion 1995: Another firm wine, with dark chocolate and plum character, medium body and crisp acidity. • $30 • (01/01/97) (BT) • **85-89**

St.-Emilion 1993: Flavorful and quite firm, showing sweetness on the palate and some blackberry, roasted coffee bean, bark and tomato notes. Try now. • $25 • (01/31/96) • **86**

St.-Emilion 1988 • $21 • (06/30/91) • **87**

St.-Emilion 1986 • $22 • (07/31/89) • **79**

St.-Emilion 1982 • $25 • (05/15/89) • **85**

BEAU-SITE, CHÂTEAU

St.-Estèphe 1997: Medium-bodied, with cooked fruit character, moderate, slightly dry tannins and a short finish. Too bad. • $NA • (06/15/98) (BT) • **75-79**

St.-Estèphe 1996: Solid '96, with wonderful tannins woven into a delicious fruit structure. Medium- to full-bodied, with fine tannins and a refreshing finish. Almost outstanding. • $18 • (06/15/98) (BT) • **85-89**

St.-Estèphe 1995: An accessible '95. Pretty, delivering cherry and berry character on nose and palate. Medium-bodied, with medium tannins and a delicate finish. Try after this year. • $24 • (01/31/98) • **86**

St.-Estèphe 1992: Herbal and light with cut-grass character. Light-bodied, with a light finish. • $14 • (04/15/95) • **76**

St.-Estèphe 1991: Fresh and easy to drink with its cherry, spice and herb character. Light-bodied; light on the finish. • $13 • (03/31/94) • **78**

St.-Estèphe 1990: Attractive berry, spice and plum aromas and flavors, medium tannins and a long, silky finish. Drinkable now. 15,000 cases made. • $23 • (03/31/93) • **90**

St.-Estèphe 1989 • $20 • (03/15/92) • **90**

St.-Estèphe 1987 • $12 • (11/30/89) • **81**

St.-Estèphe 1986 • $18 • (11/30/89) • **86**

St.-Estèphe 1982 • $18 • (08/31/92) • **86**

St.-Estèphe 1970 • $36 • (05/15/93) • **82**

BEAU-SOLEIL, CHÂTEAU

Pomerol 1997: Decadent style. Gamy berry and leaf aromas and flavors. Lovely texture, with velvety round tannins and a fruity finish. A bit disjointed now, but should turn out very well. • $NA • (06/15/98) (BT) • **85-89**
Pomerol 1996: Dark in color, with smoke, berry and violet aromas and flavors. Medium-bodied, with velvety tannins and a fresh fruit finish. Almost outstanding. • $28 • (06/15/98) (BT) • **85-89**
Pomerol 1995: A bit simple, but with some good berry and tobacco aromas and flavors. Medium-bodied, with medium tannins and a soft finish. Better after this year. • $28 • (01/31/98) • **84**

BEAU-VALLON, CHÂTEAU DU

St.-Emilion 1990: There's a resinous quality in the aromas accompanied by sweet, plummy flavors and a robust, slightly alcoholic constitution. Drinkable now. • $14 • (08/31/95) • **83**
St.-Emilion 1987 • $10 • (05/15/90) • **81**
St.-Emilion 1986 • $10 • (09/30/89) • **84**
St.-Emilion 1985 • $8 • (09/30/88) • **82**

BEAUVOLAGE

Brut Blanc de Blancs Touraine Reserve 1989 • $24 • (01/31/92) • **83**
Brut Touraine Reserve 1989 • $24 • (01/31/92) • **84**
Brut Vouvray Suprême Cuvée Comtesse Anne 1985 • $39 • (01/31/92) • **80**
Cuvée Rouge et Noir Haut Poitou 1985 • $35 • (01/31/92) • **81**

BEL AIR, CHÂTEAU

Côtes de Castillon 1993: Dominated by dark cherry and currant flavors. Reasonably soft and ready to drink. 12,500 cases made. • $17 • (04/30/97) • **81**

BEL AIR, CHÂTEAU

Entre-Deux-Mers 1994 • $9 • (05/31/95) • **84**

BEL AIR, CHÂTEAU

Haut-Médoc 1994: A good, chunky '94 that delivers plenty of blackberry and dark chocolate character. Medium-bodied, with medium, chewy tannins and a long, fruity finish. Better after 1999. • $14 • (12/31/97) • **87**
Haut-Médoc 1988 • $15 • (04/30/91) • **85**
Haut-Médoc 1986 • $9 • (11/15/89) BB • **88**
Haut-Médoc 1985 • $5 • (03/15/88) BB • **80**
Haut-Médoc 1983 • $6 • (12/31/86) • **83**
Haut-Médoc 1981 • $6 • (05/01/84) • **72**

BÉLAIR, CHÂTEAU

St.-Emilion 1997: Slight notion of raisins, with plum character. Of medium body, with medium tannins and an abrupt finish. A bit overdone. • $NA • (06/15/98) (BT) • **80-84**
St.-Emilion 1996: Round and fruity, with straightforward berry, cherry and toasty oak character. Medium in body and tannins, with a light finish. • $NA • (01/01/97) (BT) • **80-84**
St.-Emilion 1995: Beautifully crafted, rich, unctuous vanilla, spice, chocolate and ripe fruit character. Full-bodied, adding loads of tannins. • $NA • (05/15/96) (BT) • **85-89**
St.-Emilion 1993: Soft and delicious, harmonious, quite light-bodied, showing anise, cherry and mocha flavors and supple tannins. Drinkable now. • $36 • (01/31/96) • **81**
St.-Emilion 1990: Offers plenty of floral, berry and rose aromas and flavors, medium-full tannins and a long, fresh finish. Drinkable now. 4,000 cases made. • $35 • (03/31/93) • **90**
St.-Emilion 1989 • $37 • (03/15/92) • **89**
St.-Emilion 1986 • $29 Ⓐ • (03/31/90) • **82**
St.-Emilion 1982 • $39 Ⓐ • (08/31/92) • **92**

Key: SS—Spectator Selection CS—Cellar Selection HR—Highly Recommended BB—Best Buy $NA—Price not available Ⓐ—Auction Price (BT)—Barrel Tasting
Dates in parentheses indicate the issues in which the ratings were published.

St.-Emilion 1970 • $49 • (05/15/93) • **88**
St.-Emilion 1961 • $68/1.5 liter • (04/30/96) • **87**

BEL-AIR, CHÂTEAU

Pomerol 1961 • $24 • (04/30/96) • **84**

BELCIER, CHÂTEAU DE

Côtes de Castillon 1990: Bright and vivid cherry and berry aromas and flavors are appealing in this light wine, with medium tannins and a silky finish. Drink now. • $NA • (03/31/93) • **84**
Côtes de Castillon 1985 • $5 • (06/30/88) • **76**

BEL EVÊQUE, CHÂTEAU

Corbières 1995: Full-bodied and concentrated, with nice dried cherry and plum flavors. A rustic but full-flavored style. Drink now. 8,000 cases made. • $10 • (04/30/98) • **82**
Corbières 1991 • $12 • (02/28/95) • **82**

BELGRAVE, CHÂTEAU

Haut-Médoc 1997: Dark in color, with grapey, spicy aromas. Medium-bodied, with chewy tannins and a medium finish. Well made but slightly austere. 25,000 cases made. • $NA • (06/15/98) (BT) • **80-84**
Haut-Médoc 1996: A rich wine, with lots of minty and cool fruit character and silky tannins. Medium- to full-bodied, with well-integrated tannins and a medium finish. Needs more of a center palate to be outstanding. 15,500 cases made. • $25 • (06/15/98) (BT) • **85-89**
Haut-Médoc 1995: A straightforward '95 with berry, cherry aromas and flavors, medium body and medium tannins. Best after 1999. • $25 • (01/31/98) • **85**
Haut-Médoc 1994: Tasty, with bitter chocolate and berry character. Medium-bodied, with firm tannins and a fruity finish. Drink now or hold. • $20 • (01/31/97) • **84**
Haut-Médoc 1993: Some simple, pleasant cherry and earth character, medium body and tannins and short finish. Drinkable now. • $20 • (01/31/96) • **81**
Haut-Médoc 1991: A lanky wine with very pretty black cherry and toasty oak flavors, couched in fine tannins. • $14 • (03/31/94) • **80**
Haut-Médoc 1988 • $28 • (07/31/91) • **79**
Haut-Médoc 1986 • $16 • (03/31/90) • **81**

BELIN, JULES

Nuits-St.-Georges Les St.-Georges 1943 • $NA • (08/31/90) • **91**

BELINGARD, CHÂTEAU

Bergerac Sec 1995: Starts off rather simple, but it gains some intensity with decent apple flavors. • $9 • (05/31/97) • **78**
Côtes de Bergerac 1994: Soft and spicy, with plummy, herbal flavors. Firm on the finish. • $9 • (05/31/97) • **82**
Monbazillac 1994: Fairly rich and ripe, with watermelon and honey flavors. It's exotic and intense, though a bit coarse on the finish. • $16 • (05/31/97) • **83**

BELLAND, ADRIEN

Corton Les Grèves 1982 • $17 • (09/01/85) • **87**
Santenay La Comme 1987 • $22 • (11/15/90) • **78**
Santenay La Comme 1982 • $25 • (08/01/85) CS • **91**

BELLAND, JEAN-CLAUDE

Santenay 1995: Solid and chunky, exhibiting earth and spice notes to complement the cherry flavor. Dry and a touch stemmy on the finish; maybe food would tame it. • $18 • (11/15/97) • **82**

BELLAND, ROGER

Chassagne-Montrachet Morgeot-Clos Pitois 1996: Good ripeness in this *premier cru*, but it's quite woody, with a malic, spicy, mocha blanket covering the pretty fruit. Full-bodied and tasting of intense toasty bread, it has per-

FRANCE

sonality and a long finish. Better after 2000. 250 cases made. • $50 • (05/31/98) • **85**

Chassagne-Montrachet Morgeot 1994: A chewy, rich crème brûlée, toasty coconut, pear and citrus combination. Of medium-to-full body, this *premier cru* packs good flavors that stay on the lingering finish. Drinkable now. 250 cases made. • $NA • (05/31/96) • **86**

Criots-Bâtard-Montrachet 1996: Like a kiss, this caresses your senses with a lovely, supple texture, ripe fruit, spice, toasty oak and lively, fresh acidity. Full-bodied, it is very sleek and racy on the long, delicious, harmonious finish. A terrific wine to drink after 2005. 165 cases made. • $90 • (05/31/98) • **95**

Criots-Bâtard-Montrachet 1994: Soft, and mature already. Flavors and aromas of butterscotch, apricot, and burnt plastic, and lots of toasty oak on the finish. Tasted twice, with consistent notes. • $NA • (08/31/96) • **73**

Puligny-Montrachet Champ Gain 1994: Ripe and fat, delivering lots of apple, fig and date notes. Full in body and flavor, it tastes just a bit rough, caramelized and hot on the finish. Drink now. 200 cases made. • $NA • (05/31/96) • **85**

BELLE PÈRE & FILS

Crozes-Hermitage 1990 • $20 • (02/28/93) HR • **90**

Crozes-Hermitage Cuvée Louis Belle 1995: Ripe, a bit thick and rustic, medium- to full-bodied, with a raisiny, plum and cherry character. Generous, but lacks finesse on the finish; perhaps better after 1999. • $22 • (10/15/97) • **85**

Crozes-Hermitage Les Pierrelles 1995: Great dark-violet color, with some sharp, crisp cherry flavors, but it also reveals a vegetal, green side that is not attractive. Lacks a bit of ripeness. • $18 • (10/15/97) • **79**

Crozes-Hermitage Les Pierrelles 1991 • $17 • (05/31/94) • **84**

Hermitage 1991: Ripe berry, chocolate and meaty flavors mingle in this muscular yet gentle wine. This is concentrated and chewy. Drink now. Tasted twice. • $40 • (05/31/94) • **90**

Hermitage 1990: Broad, fleshy, spicy and seductive, this smooth-textured wine offers layers of currant, raspberry, plum, chocolate and violet aromas and flavors. Silky enough to drink now, but has enough stuffing to improve through to 2000. 200 cases made. • $46 • (04/15/93) • **93**

BELLEFONT-BELCIER, CHÂTEAU

St.-Emilion 1996: Decent, with some tobacco and cherry character and a hint of smoke. Medium-bodied, with medium tannins and short finish. Slight dilution. • $NA • (01/01/97) (BT) • **80-84**

St.-Emilion 1995: A bit raisiny, with intense character. Full-bodied, with medium tannins and a slightly hot finish. Overdone. • $NA • (01/01/97) (BT) • **80-84**

BELLEGARDE, CHÂTEAU

Margaux 1997: Good blackberry and plum aromas and flavors, with a hint of smokiness. Medium-bodied, with round tannins and a succulent finish. • $NA • (06/15/98) (BT) • **85-89**

Margaux 1996: A very clean and well-made '96, with everything in the right place. Not a blockbuster, but harmonious and fine. Medium- to full-bodied, with fine tannins and a fresh aftertaste. From the owners of Château Siran. Almost outstanding. • $22 • (06/15/98) (BT) • **85-89**

BELLEGRAVE, CHÂTEAU

Pomerol 1994: Attractive for its spicy qualities, complemented by dark cherry flavors. Good concentration and balance. Ready to drink. 400 cases made. • $38 • (04/30/97) • **84**

BELLEGRAVE-VAN DER VOORT, CHÂTEAU

Pauillac 1989 • $20 • (09/15/93) • **85**

Pauillac 1988 • $20 • (08/31/91) • **83**

Pauillac 1986 • $19 • (10/31/91) • **80**

BELLEVUE-FIGEAC, CHÂTEAU

St.-Emilion 1995: Slightly one-dimensional, with plum character, firm tannins and a delicate finish. • $NA • (01/01/97) (BT) • **80-84**

St.-Emilion 1993: Light and fresh but rather weedy, offering dried herb and red fruit character. Soft and easy to drink now. • $28 • (01/31/96) • **79**

BEL-ORME-TRONQUOY-DE-LALANDE, CHÂTEAU

Haut-Médoc 1997: Good mineral and berry aromas and flavors. Medium-bodied, with medium tannins and a light finish. • $NA • (06/15/98) (BT) • **80-84**

Haut-Médoc 1996: Very well-crafted red that builds on your palate but then suddenly goes away. Alluring raspberry, mint and berry aromas and flavors. Medium-bodied, with moderate tannins and a medium finish. Almost outstanding. 11,670 cases made. • $22 • (06/15/98) (BT) • **85-89**

Haut-Médoc 1995: Lots of dried cherry and tobacco character. Medium-bodied, with fine tannins and a fresh, fruity finish. Delicious now, better after 1999. • $20 • (01/31/98) • **86**

Haut-Médoc 1994: Plummy and slightly earthy, with hints of fresh mushrooms on the nose. Medium-bodied and round, with fine tannins and a delicate finish. Drink now. 10,000 cases made. • $NA • (01/31/97) • **83**

BELVEZEL, DOMAINE DU

Vin de Pays des Côteaux de l'Ardèche Red 1995: Fresh and light, showing black cherry flavors with pleasant spice notes and just enough tannin for grip. Enjoy now. 800 cases made. • $9 • (10/15/96) • **83**

Vin de Pays des Côteaux de l'Ardèche White 1995: Lean and tart. It's firm, and offers some green apple flavors, but a vegetal note intrudes and the acidity is so sharp it's hard to enjoy. 300 cases made. • $9 • (12/15/96) • **77**

Viognier Vin de Pays des Côteaux de l'Ardèche 1995: Straightforward and simple, this round, well-balanced white offers floral and light apple flavors. Refreshing, and won't get in the way of food. 100 cases made. • $15 • (12/15/96) • **80**

BÉNAZETH, DOMAINE

Vin de Pays de l'Aude 1995: Not for the faint of palate. An extremely flavorful, challenging red, packed with fruit flavors and accented by wild game and earth notes that lend complexity. Full-bodied. Tannic but drinkable, with a lingering, earthy finish. Drink now through 2000. 950 cases made. • $10 • (07/31/98) • **88**

BENJAMIN DE BEAUREGARD, LE

Pomerol 1991: Light and herbal with a chocolate flavor, but very diluted on the finish. • $12 • (03/31/94) • **75**

BERARD PÈRE & FILS

Côte-Rôtie Cuvée Prestige 1986 • $29 • (08/31/92) • **80**

Crozes-Hermitage Cuvée Prestige 1989 • $15 • (08/31/92) • **71**

Hermitage Cuvée Prestige 1986 • $29 • (08/31/92) • **72**

BERGAT, CHÂTEAU

St.-Emilion 1997: Good berry character, but with a slight vegetal note. Light-to-medium in body, with a light finish. • $NA • (06/15/98) (BT) • **75-79**

St.-Emilion 1996: Lots of green olive and tobacco character. Medium-bodied, with a smoky tobacco aftertaste. Light finish. • $26 • (06/15/98) (BT) • **80-84**

St.-Emilion 1995: Attractive blackberry and floral aromas and flavors. Medium-bodied, with fine tannins and a smoky berry aftertaste. Best after 1999. • $25 • (01/31/98) • **87**

St.-Emilion 1991: Simple and attractive with a good core of fruit and silky tannins. • $13 • (03/31/94) • **80**

St.-Emilion 1990: A wine of moderation, with lovely earthy, tobacco, berry aromas and flavors and medium tannins. Drinkable now. 1,100 cases made. • $19 • (03/31/93) • **86**

BERGERIE, DOMAINE DE LA

Anjou White Les Pierres Girard 1996: A bit oxidized, but still drinkable. Honeyed aromas suggest sweetness, but it's dry on the palate, with dried peach, almond and a light, pleasant bitterness. Drink now. 1,100 cases made. • $11 • (06/30/98) • **78**

Coteaux du Layon Cuvée Fragrance 1995: An unctuous white showing raisin, date and caramel flavors. Moderately sweet with underlying acidity. Smooth and rich on the palate. Delightful on its own, but balanced enough

FRANCE

for rich foods. Drink now through 2002. 333 cases made. • $26/500ml • (06/15/98) • **88**

Coteaux du Layon Le Clos de la Bergerie 1995: Lovely botrytis aromas of spice, vanilla and honey give way to a voluptuous palate, with spicy caramel, orange-peel and pear flavors that are moderately sweet and beautifully balanced. Very appealing. Drink now through 2005. 1,400 cases made. • $13 • (06/15/98) • **89**

Quarts de Chaume 1995: This complex wine is beautifully focused, with rich orange-peel, honey, raisin and date flavors, pineapplelike acidity balancing moderate sweetness, full texture and a long finish. A wine that grows on you with every sip. Drink now through 2005. 200 cases made. • $31/500ml • (06/15/98) • **92**

BERLIQUET, CHÂTEAU

St.-Emilion 1997: Gorgeous concentration of violet and berry flavor, with currants. Full-bodied, with a velvety texture and a long, raspberry finish. Juicy wine. Slightly hollow center palate, but rich. • $NA • (06/15/98) (BT) • **85-89**

St.-Emilion 1996: A bit lean, but with good berry and floral character. Medium-bodied. Moderate, silky tannins. • $30 • (06/15/98) (BT) • **85-89**

St.-Emilion 1983 • $12 • (12/31/86) • **90**

BERNARD, DOMAINE MICHEL

Châteauneuf-du-Pape 1995: Bright and fruity, with lively berry and black pepper flavors and just enough tannin for grip. Harmonious and refreshing, it's delicious now, should hold through 1999. • $NA • (10/15/97) • **85**

Côtes du Rhône 1996: A crowd-pleaser of a young wine, with lovely crushed black pepper and licorice flavors and a bit more posh than many '96s. Surprisingly extracted for a standard Côtes du Rhône, with some firm tannins, but try chilled with grilled meats. Delicious. • $NA • (10/15/97) • **84**

Côtes du Rhône Les Domaniales 1993 • $6 • (12/31/95) • **68**

Côtes du Rhône-Villages 1996: Quite dark in color, showing ripe texture and the black pepper, chocolate, spice and blackberry character of a fine Côtes du Rhône. The finish is a bit simple, but with nice ripe tannins. Drink now. Labeled Domaine La Montagne d'Or. • $NA • (10/15/97) • **85**

BERNARD, GUY

Côte-Rôtie 1988 • $30 • (10/15/90) • **78**

BERNARD, JEAN

St.-Véran Château de Leynes Vieilles Vignes 1996: Zesty and vibrant, with a floral, citrus and green apple character. Light- to medium-bodied, it turns very crisp on the mouthpuckering finish. Drink now through 1999. 4,100 cases made. • $13 • (05/31/98) • **83**

St.-Véran Château de Leynes Vieilles Vignes 1995: Nice and clean, light-bodied and fresh, with green apple, hay, gooseberry, citrus and butter flavors. Crisp and fairly intense finish. • $NA • (08/31/96) • **83**

BERNARD, PAUL

Fleurie 1995: Bright black cherry and smoke flavors give a lift, and light tannins give grip for food, but an alcoholic finish leaves it a bit clumsy. 600 cases made. • $18 • (06/30/97) • **80**

BERNEAU, C.

Pouilly-Fumé Les Japeloups 1995: Austere yet subtly complex, this clean, concentrated white adds almond and beeswax notes to its classic flavors of herbs and pears. So pure it almost seems simple. A great complement to food. 1,000 cases made. • $12 • (05/15/97) • **90**

Sancerre Domaine de l'Orme 1995: Pear and melon flavors give this white a fuller profile than that of most Sancerre, but it still has plenty of acidity. Big enough for poultry dishes. 900 cases made. • $12 • (04/30/97) • **84**

Key: SS—Spectator Selection CS—Cellar Selection HR—Highly Recommended BB—Best Buy $NA—Price not available Ⓐ—Auction Price (BT)—Barrel Tasting
Dates in parentheses indicate the issues in which the ratings were published.

BERTAGNA, DOMAINE

Chambertin 1991: Light and chewy, a crisp, straightforward wine that offers modest strawberry and spice aromas and flavors. Try now. • $NA • (01/31/94) • **85**

Chambolle-Musigny Les Plantes 1994: Tries for delicacy and achieves a sort of modest gracefulness, with its pretty berry and spice flavors gliding along under a blanket of fine tannins. Best now. 83 cases made. • $51 • (11/15/96) • **85**

Clos de Vougeot 1994: Smooth and polished, with a strong leathery accent to its modest cherry and smoke flavors. Finishing with a tobaccolike edge. Almost ready to drink. 100 cases made. • $90 • (11/15/96) • **85**

Clos de Vougeot 1993: Lovely, rich plum, berry and vanilla aromas and flavors, medium body, fine tannins, good acidity and a long finish. Very good winemaking here. Try in 2000. • $90 • (05/15/96) • **88**

Clos de Vougeot 1991: Crisp and light; has a vaguely minty strawberry character and an austere, citrusy finish. • $NA • (01/31/94) • **77**

Clos St.-Denis 1994: Light in texture and modest in flavor, with some pleasant toasty berry flavors that fade quickly on the drying finish. 208 cases made. • $70 • (11/15/96) • **77**

Clos St.-Denis 1993: This shows loads of wild berry, mushroom and smoke character. Full- to medium-bodied, sporting fine tannins and a long, toasty oak finish. Better in 2000. • $71 • (05/15/96) • **90**

Nuits-St.-Georges Aux Murgers 1990: Compact but restrained, showing plenty of black cherry and tar aromas and flavors and round, ripe tannins. Try now. • $NA • (12/15/92) • **89**

Nuits-St.-Georges Aux Murgers 1985 • $41 • (02/28/89) • **85**

Vosne-Romanée Les Beaux Monts Bas 1985 • $35 • (10/15/88) • **82**

Vougeot Clos de la Perrière 1994: Medium-bodied, with some pretty fruit flavors, but a touch diluted and it turns a bit astringent on the finish. 833 cases made. • $56 • (11/15/96) • **79**

Vougeot Clos de la Perrière 1993: A bit lean but some good, clean berry and cedar aromas and flavors, fine tannins and fresh finish. Drink now. • $58 • (05/15/96) • **86**

Vougeot Clos de la Perrière 1991: Crisp, light and diluted. Drinkable now. • $NA • (01/31/94) • **78**

Vougeot Clos de la Perrière 1990: An attractive wine that gives lovely plum and cherry intensity and plenty of ripe tannins. Drinkable now. • $NA • (12/15/92) • **85**

Vougeot Clos de la Perrière 1985 • $40 • (04/15/89) • **87**

Vougeot Les Crâs 1985 • $30 • (03/31/88) • **85**

BERTHEAU, DOMAINE

Bonnes Mares 1987 • $55 • (06/15/90) • **89**

Chambolle-Musigny 1987 • $25 • (06/15/90) • **80**

Chambolle-Musigny Les Amoureuses 1987 • $50 • (06/15/90) • **84**

Chambolle-Musigny Les Charmes 1987 • $35 • (06/15/90) • **81**

BERTHET-RAYNE, DOMAINE

Côtes du Rhône-Villages Cairanne 1995: A ripe, round red layering plum and pretty smoke flavors over firm tannins. Try now. 1,500 cases made. • $9 • (02/28/97) • **86**

BERTINERIE, CHÂTEAU

Premières Côtes de Blaye 1988 • $10 • (07/15/90) • **85**

BERTOLLA, ALFRED GINO

Moulin-à-Vent Domaine du Granit 1995: Rich, firm and muscular, showing dark, vibrant color, aromas of coffee and dried fruits. Though the texture is polished, the underlying tannins are still powerful and the flavors are still muted. Needs food and perhaps another year of age to show its best. • $17 • (09/15/97) • **86**

Moulin-à-Vent Domaine du Granit 1994: Well structured, with firm tannins and enough acidity to give balance, but the plum and licorice flavors are subdued. May open up with food. • $14 • (09/15/96) • **83**

Moulin-à-Vent Domaine du Granit Cuvée Vieilles Vignes Réserve 1996: Firm yet approachable, this seductive red weaves flavors of smoke, toast, plum and black cherry into a sinuous, muscular harmony. A marriage of modern techniques with traditional style. Drink now through 2001. • $21 • (05/31/98) • **89**

BERTRAND, DOMAINE GEORGES

Corbières Domaine Ste.-Paule 1994: A good, full-bodied red with mint and tobacco flavors. Balanced, with some leathery notes on the finish. Ready to drink. • $12 • (05/31/97) • **84**

Corbières Rosé 1995: Loads of floral, spice and red berry aromas mark this pleasant, straightforward rosé. Great for summer sipping. • $12 • (05/15/97) • **83**

Gris de Gris Vin de Pays d'Oc 1995: A simple, dry rosé with very little flavor, but good balance. • $9 • (05/31/97) • **75**

BERTRAND, MAURICE

Montagny Les Coeres 1995: Quite fat and bold, a slightly rustic *premier cru* with marzipan, honey and oak shadings. Full-bodied, finishing on the heavy side. Drink now. • $NA • (05/31/97) • **79**

Montagny Premier Cru 1995: Well made, this is medium-bodied, with a nice lemon, mineral and fruit character. Drink now through 2003. • $NA • (05/31/97) • **85**

BESSIÈRE, DANIEL

Coteaux du Languedoc 1987 • $5 • (09/30/89) BB • **83**

Faugères 1987 • $6 • (09/15/89) • **73**

Minervois 1986 • $6 • (09/15/89) BB • **81**

St.-Chinian 1987 • $6 • (08/31/89) • **79**

BEYCHEVELLE, CHÂTEAU

St.-Julien 1997: Pretty use of new wood with mineral, berry and mint character. Medium-bodied, with well-integrated tannins. Well done. 40,000 cases made. • $NA • (06/15/98) (BT) • **85-89**

St.-Julien 1996: Attractive, well-perfumed wine. Raspberry and steel aromas and flavors. Medium-bodied, with fine tannins and a medium finish. A bit lean. 42,000 cases made. • $40 • (06/15/98) (BT) • **85-89**

St.-Julien 1995: Well-crafted red. Vivid blackberry and violet aromas and flavors. Full-bodied and very silky, with lovely tannins and a medium aftertaste of fruit and toasty oak. Best after 2000. • $22 Ⓐ • (01/31/98) • **89**

St.-Julien 1994: Offers some vanilla, spice and fruit character, but is slightly dry and lean on the finish. Drinkable now. 29,500 cases made. • $24 Ⓐ • (01/31/97) • **81**

St.-Julien 1993: Rather hollow '93, offering some decent berry, cherry and mint flavors and silky tannins but lacking in body. Slightly disappointing for this estate. Drinkable now. 25,000 cases made. • $21 Ⓐ • (01/31/96) • **80**

St.-Julien 1992: Well-presented Bordeaux, showing berry and cherry aromas and flavors, medium body, fine tannin and a long, delicious finish. Drinkable now. • $23 • (04/15/95) • **82**

St.-Julien 1991: A well-made, sexy wine that delivers lovely aromas of violet, smoke and blackberry. Stands out among the '91s with its silky texture and good intensity. • $25 • (03/31/94) • **85**

St.-Julien 1990: Beautifully integrated, with sweet fruit, silky tannins and crisp acidity. Lovely raspberry and tobacco character on the finish, but it's a little light. Drink now. 25,000 cases made. • $48 • (03/31/93) • **87**

St.-Julien 1989 • $50 Ⓐ • (03/15/92) • **95**

St.-Julien 1988 • $46 Ⓐ • (04/30/91) • **93**

St.-Julien 1987 • $25 Ⓐ • (05/15/90) • **79**

St.-Julien 1986 • $62 Ⓐ • (05/31/89) • **93**

St.-Julien 1985 • $49 Ⓐ • (10/15/94) • **91**

St.-Julien 1984 • $24 • (05/15/87) • **78**

St.-Julien 1983 • $51 Ⓐ • (03/01/86) • **88**

St.-Julien 1982 • $62 • (08/31/92) • **89**

St.-Julien 1981 • $33 Ⓐ • (10/15/94) • **81**

St.-Julien 1979 • $33 Ⓐ • (10/15/89) • **92**

St.-Julien 1978 • $26 Ⓐ • (12/31/89) • **86**

St.-Julien 1971 • $29 Ⓐ • (12/31/89) • **85**

St.-Julien 1970 • $21 Ⓐ • (05/15/93) • **90**

St.-Julien 1967 • $37 • (12/31/89) • **83**

St.-Julien 1962 • $64 Ⓐ • (11/30/87) • **95**

St.-Julien 1961 • $101 Ⓐ • (04/30/96) • **89**

St.-Julien 1959 • $108 Ⓐ • (10/15/90) • **80**

St.-Julien 1948 • $175 • (12/31/89) • **92**

St.-Julien 1947: Shows spicy, plummy flavors that turn a bit metallic and peppery on the crisp finish. • $79 • (05/31/97) • **83**

St.-Julien 1945 • $483 Ⓐ • (11/30/95) • **82**

St.-Julien 1929 • $232 Ⓐ • (12/31/89) • **95**

BEYER, LÉON

Gewürztraminer Alsace 1995: Smells like an Oriental spicebox, but the flat, dull flavors are disappointing. • $15 • (09/30/97) • **76**

Gewürztraminer Alsace 1993 • $15 • (11/15/94) • **86**

Gewürztraminer Alsace Cuvée Comtes d'Eguisheim 1993 • $32 • (09/15/95) • **87**

Gewürztraminer Alsace Réserve 1993 • $20 • (09/15/95) • **82**

Gewürztraminer Alsace Vendange Tardive 1994: Rather dull and flat. Sweet, but with simple, canned pineapple flavors. It's heavy but lacks liveliness and concentration. 100 cases made. • $55 • (10/15/96) • **82**

Pinot Blanc Alsace 1995: Seems a shade less than ripe due to its green peach flavors and underlying tart acidity. Still, the texture is appealing. Tasted twice, with consistent notes. • $11 • (09/30/97) • **77**

Pinot Blanc Alsace 1994 • $10 • (09/15/95) • **83**

Pinot Blanc Alsace 1993 • $10 • (11/15/94) • **87**

Riesling Alsace 1995: This Riesling has a slate and mineral expression, coupled with peach, apple and hazelnut nuances. Complex, with lively acidity and intensity that follows through to the dry finish. Try with food. • $15 • (09/30/97) • **87**

Riesling Alsace 1993 • $14 • (11/15/94) • **85**

Riesling Alsace Cuvée Comtes d'Eguisheim 1994: Polished and well integrated. Mineral and pine aromas are alluring and the flavors, though a bit closed now, are smooth and harmonious. 300 cases made. • $35 • (10/15/96) • **85**

Riesling Alsace Cuvée Comtes d'Eguisheim 1993 • $33 • (09/15/95) • **84**

Tokay Pinot Gris Alsace 1993 • $13 • (09/15/95) • **77**

Tokay Pinot Gris Alsace Cuvée Comtes d'Eguisheim 1994: Well-balanced and elegant for a Pinot Gris, this shows harmonious flavors of pears, pine nuts and pineapple, with firm acidity. A refreshing complement to food. 300 cases made. • $35 • (10/15/96) • **85**

Tokay Pinot Gris Alsace Sélection de Grains Nobles 1994: Thick and very sweet, with honeyed flavors of overripe apples and dried apricots. Turns more delicate on the lingering finish. Rich, but straightforward. 75 cases made. • $90 • (10/15/96) • **88**

Tokay Pinot Gris Alsace Vendange Tardive 1994: Pretty aromas of pear and vanilla give way to a sweet and rich, yet still delicate palate of orange-peel, caramel and coconut flavors. Not a powerhouse, but well-knit and complex. 100 cases made. • $55 • (10/15/96) • **89**

BIBIAN, DOMAINE

Madiran 1995: Supple and full-flavored, with pretty raspberry flavors and a finish that focuses on mineral notes. A concentrated wine with plenty of gusto. Drink now through 2001. 5,000 cases made. • $11 • (05/15/98) • **87**

Madiran Cuvée de Prestige 1993: Concentrated and rich, with loads of raspberry, plum and cherry flavors and a spicy note. Thick, powerful and well defined, finishing with a jolt of tannin and bright fruit flavors. Tempting now, but let it age to smooth out. Best from 1999 through 2003. 1,100 cases made. • $14 • (05/15/98) • **89**

BICHOT, ALBERT

Aloxe-Corton 1995: Lean, tough and tannic, showing diluted flavors of cherries and herbs. 1,500 cases made. • $20 • (11/15/97) • **74**

Aloxe-Corton 1983 • $18 • (11/30/86) • **68**

Beaune 1988 • $15 • (08/31/90) • **82**

Beaune Champs Pimont 1994: Lovely strawberry and floral aromas and flavors make this crisp, firm wine one to cellar. Best from 1999 to 2000. • $21 • (11/15/96) • **85**

Beaune Hospices de Beaune Cuvée Guigone-de-Salins 1989 • $68 • (01/31/92) • **83**

Beaune Les Bressandes 1986 • $24 • (07/31/88) • **80**

Beaune Les Teurons 1992: Shows very light, floral, stemmy flavors more than fruit. Drinkable now. • $NA • (12/15/94) • **77**

Bourgogne Château de Montpatey 1989 • $10 • (06/15/92) BB • **85**

Bourgogne Croix St.-Louis 1995: Light, and lacking fruit to match the structure. 15,000 cases made. • $12 • (11/15/97) • **76**

Bourgogne Croix St.-Louis 1989 • $9 • (06/15/92) BB • **83**

Bourgogne Croix St.-Louis White 1996: Not a showy wine, but clean and pure, with a distinct dried herb, gooseberry, floral and freshly cut grass character, unhindered by obvious oak. Drink upon release. 2,500 cases made. • $10 • (05/31/98) • **84**

Bourgogne Pinot Noir 1993: Quite satisfying for immediate consumption, sporting relatively ripe fruit flavors. A touch of burning on the finish keeps it from scoring higher. • $12 • (11/15/95) • **82**

Chablis 1996: A racy, medium-bodied village Chablis, with nice ripe pear and tropical fruit, pleasant lemon-tasting acidity and pretty honey notes, picking up a slight smoke and mineral character on the elegant finish. Tempting now, better after 2000. Excellent effort from this Beaune-based négociant. 26,650 cases made. • $22 • (05/31/98) • **88**

Chablis 1995: Light- to medium-bodied. Crisp and straightforward, with apple, pear, citrus, herb and vanilla flavors. Enjoy now. • $NA • (08/31/96) • **82**

Chablis Premier Cru 1994 • $21 • (05/31/96) • **84**

Chambolle-Musigny 1995: Lacking in fruit, with lifted aromas and astringent tannins. 916 cases made. • $27 • (11/15/97) • **72**

Chassagne-Montrachet 1994: Straightforward and lean. Some decent fruit flavors and good acidity, but it seems short and a bit diluted. 475 cases made. • $NA • (05/31/96) • **78**

Chassagne-Montrachet Premier Cru 1993: Clean and crisp vanilla, honey, cream and apple aromas and flavors. Slightly diluted finish. • $NA • (05/15/95) • **80**

Chassagne-Montrachet Red 1995: The modest fruit is overwhelmed by green, astringent tannins. 566 cases made. • $25 • (11/15/97) • **72**

Chassagne-Montrachet Morgeot Red 1992: Earthy, woody aromas and flavors never cut past the chewy tannins. This is lean, with a little currant sneaking in on the finish. • $NA • (12/15/94) • **77**

Châteauneuf-du-Pape 1988 • $13 • (09/30/90) • **84**

Châteauneuf-du-Pape 1987 • $10 • (03/15/90) • **82**

Châteauneuf-du-Pape 1986 • $9 • (11/30/88) • **86**

Châteauneuf-du-Pape 1985 • $12 • (11/15/87) • **86**

Corton 1995: Light and juicy. A light-bodied red of modest red berry flavor, but its non-challenging texture, easy tannins make it approachable now. A bit simple. Drinkable now. 208 cases made. • $43 • (11/15/97) • **79**

Corton Hospices de Beaune Cuvée Docteur-Peste 1989 • $100 • (01/31/92) • **88**

Côte de Beaune-Villages 1993: Some very light plum and tobacco character but light-bodied and drying on the finish. Drinkable now. • $15 • (11/15/95) • **74**

Côtes de Duras 1989 • $6 • (03/31/92) BB • **81**

Côte de Nuits-Villages 1993: Light and simple with some decent berry and cedar aromas and flavors but not much else. Drinkable now. • $15 • (11/15/95) • **77**

Gevrey-Chambertin 1995: Light-colored, tastes of strawberry and water. Diluted and astringent, despite a stab of sweetness at midpalate. Drink very chilled. 6,600 cases made. • $26 • (11/15/97) • **72**

Gevrey-Chambertin 1993: Fresh and easy, offering pleasant vanilla and dried cherry character, medium-to-light body, light tannins and fresh finish. Drink on release. • $30 • (11/15/95) • **81**

Latricières-Chambertin 1995: Shows the light color of rosé, is watery and diluted. Astringent finish. Very disappointing. 280 cases made. • $51 • (11/15/97) • **70**

Mâcon-Lugny 1994: Odd wine; tastes like cider. Has some fruit cocktail flavors and an astringent finish. Drink if you must. 2,166 cases made. • $NA • (05/31/96) • **72**

Mâcon-Villages 1994: Hard to cozy up to this green, hard, herbal and tough white. Too lean for us. 5,000 cases made. • $10 • (05/31/96) • **75**

Meursault 1994: Round and supple, but also a bit hollow from lack of fruit. Hints of chestnut, coffee and spice. Drinkable now. 1,000 cases made. • $25 • (05/31/96) • **78**

Meursault 1993: Steely apple, pear, melon character. Medium body; fresh acidity. Limited distribution. • $20 • (05/15/95) • **80**

Meursault Les Charmes 1993: Rather lean and light-bodied, demonstrating a strange character of mineral and peppermint; firm acidity. Limited distribution. • $30 • (05/15/95) • **77**

Monthélie Hospices de Beaune Cuvée Lebelin 1985 • $52 • (10/15/87) • **86**

Nuits-St.-Georges 1995: Herbal, with diluted flavors and a tough, astringent finish. 1,500 cases made. • $26 • (11/15/97) • **77**

Nuits-St.-Georges Aux Boudots Hospices de Nuits Cuvée Mesn 1986 • $36 • (03/31/90) • **77**

Nuits-St.-Georges Les Maladières Hospices de Nuits 1986 • $33 • (02/28/89) • **75**

Key: SS—Spectator Selection CS—Cellar Selection HR—Highly Recommended BB—Best Buy $NA—Price not available Ⓐ—Auction Price (BT)—Barrel Tasting
Dates in parentheses indicate the issues in which the ratings were published.

Nuits-St.-Georges Les Maladières Hospices de Nuits Cuvée Grangier 1986 • $30 • (03/31/90) • **80**

Nuits-St.-Georges Les Vignerondes Hospices de Nuits Cuvée 1986 • $40 • (02/28/89) • **85**

Pinot Noir Bourgogne Croix St.-Louis 1986 • $6 • (10/31/88) • **77**

Pinot Noir Bourgogne Le Bourgogne Bichot 1985 • $8 • (11/15/87) • **81**

Pommard 1993: Some pretty fruit character on nose and palate but slightly diluted, adding an herbal edge to the aftertaste. Astringent. • $26 • (11/15/95) • **78**

Pommard 1988 • $25 • (08/31/90) • **87**

Pommard 1986 • $20 • (09/15/89) • **79**

Pommard 1983 • $19 • (09/15/86) • **83**

Pommard Hospices de Beaune Cuvée Cyrot-Chaudron 1989 • $70 • (01/31/92) • **86**

Pommard Hospices de Beaune Cuvée Cyrot-Chaudron 1985 • $60 • (10/31/88) • **91**

Pouilly-Fuissé 1996: Quite earthy and pungent, but with decent fruit and a good weight on the palate. Turns a bit sour on the finish. Drink now. • $NA • (05/31/98) • **79**

Pouilly-Fuissé 1993: Green, herbal and tart, it tastes more like acidic juice than white Burgundy. Modest fruit; drinkable but uninteresting. 1,000 cases made. • $17 • (05/15/95) • **72**

Puligny-Montrachet 1994: Light and diluted, showing a cardboard, watery character. 1,000 cases made. • $26 • (05/31/96) • **70**

Puligny-Montrachet Les Folatières 1993: Clean and crisp green apple, pear and basil flavors; quite steely in texture. Medium body and tart finish. Limited distribution. • $32 • (05/15/95) • **83**

Rully White 1996: Crisp and fruity, with green apple, grapefruit and dried herb flavors, this medium-bodied white should make for nice drinking upon release. 1,660 cases made. • $13 • (05/31/98) • **83**

Santenay 1986 • $12 • (10/15/89) • **78**

Savigny-lès-Beaune 1995: Displays modest cherry character, is light and airy with moderate concentration, but turns a little tough on the finish. 630 cases made. • $18 • (11/15/97) • **80**

Savigny-lès-Beaune 1986 • $10 • (10/15/89) • **81**

Savigny-lès-Beaune Hospices de Beaune Cuvée Fouquerand 1988 • $39 • (01/31/92) • **78**

St.-Véran 1996: Distinctively smoky and slightly earthy, with matchstick, lime and green apple flavors. Some midpalate concentration in this light- to medium-bodied white. Drink now. • $NA • (05/31/98) • **80**

St.-Véran 1994: Straightforward white, showing tons of citrusy flavors but not enough fruit concentration. While lean, it should still be a good match with shellfish. Drinkable now. 1,083 cases made. • $NA • (05/31/96) • **80**

Vin Rouge NV • $3 • (08/31/89) • **75**

Volnay 1988 • $25 • (08/31/90) • **84**

Volnay 1986 • $25 • (07/31/88) • **84**

Volnay 1983 • $18 • (09/15/86) • **68**

Volnay Clos des Chênes 1992: Crisp and simple, showing enough berry flavor to balance the slightly chewy tannins. • $NA • (12/15/94) • **81**

Volnay Cuvée Blondeau Hospices de Beaune 1988 • $60 • (06/15/92) • **87**

Volnay Hospices de Beaune Cuvée Blondeau 1985 • $53 • (04/30/89) • **88**

Volnay Hospices de Beaune Cuvée Blondeau 1982 • $26 • (08/01/84) SS • **92**

Volnay Premier Cru 1993: Very clean, with fresh dried cherry, wet earth and mineral flavors, medium-to-light body and a light finish. Drinkable now. • $25 • (11/15/95) • **83**

Volnay-Santenots 1986 • $22 • (10/31/89) • **77**

Vosne-Romanée Aux Malconsorts 1994: Fresh and bursting with cherry and currant flavors at first, but this light-bodied wine turns slightly astringent on the finish. From Domaine du Clos Frantin. • $41 • (11/15/96) • **80**

Vosne-Romanée Les Beaux Monts 1988 • $34 • (07/15/90) • **87**

BIENFAISANCE, CHÂTEAU LA

St.-Emilion 1993: Exhibits a nice, tight core of pleasant red cherry flavor orbited by some spice notes. Well balanced and firm. Flavors linger on the finish. • $20 • (04/30/97) • **84**

BIEVILLE, DOMAINE DE

Chablis 1996: Supple and attractive, with ripe pear, lime and litchi flavors. Starts a bit dull, but offers a burst of acidity on the finish. Drink now. 2,500 cases imported. 6,488 cases made. • $15 • (08/31/97) • **83**

BILLARD-GONNET

Pommard Les Chaponnières 1995: Very pretty and elegant for Pommard, showing bright cherry and raspberry notes. Hard to predict if the delicate fruit will stand up to the tannins in 2000. • $45 • (11/15/97) • **85**

Pommard Les Charmots 1995: Herbal, lean and astringent. • $45 • (11/15/97) • **77**

Pommard Les Pezerolles 1995: Pretty violet, rose petal and black currant aromas flavor this medium-bodied, well-made Pommard. Shows the tough, angular tannins typical of '95 Pommards, but not their herbaceous character. Try after 2000. • $45 • (11/15/97) • **85**

Pommard Rugiens 1995: Emits lovely spicy cherry aromas, but turns lean and mean in the mouth and finishes with astringent tannins. • $54 • (11/15/97) • **82**

BILLAUD-SIMON

Chablis 1996: Ripe, yet fresh and lively, with gooseberry, grapefruit, kiwi, butter and cream flavors. Coats the palate with its smooth texture. Try now through 2000. 400 cases imported. 3,500 cases made. • $NA • (08/31/97) • **87**

Chablis 1995: Fresh, zingy and medium-bodied. Crisp lemon and honey flavors have a chalky note and are not overly tart. Drink now. • $NA • (08/31/96) • **85**

Chablis 1994 • $18 • (08/31/95) • **85**

Chablis Fourchaume 1996: Finesse and intensity mingle in this medium-bodied '96. Closed on the nose, but full of fruit and mineral, butter and toasty walnut notes, it's ripe but with a grip of lemon, grapefruit and apple character on the lingering finish. Hold until after 2000. • $26 • (05/31/98) • **90**

Chablis Fourchaume 1995: Unusually sweet-tasting for a '95 Chablis, this full-bodied wine falters a bit on the slightly rustic finish. Drink now. • $24 • (06/15/97) • **83**

Chablis Fourchaume 1994 • $NA • (05/31/96) • **89**

Chablis Fourchaume 1993 • $24 • (08/31/95) • **82**

Chablis Les Blanchots Vieilles Vignes 1996: It tastes of a new-oakish style of Chablis, but underneath has lovely lemon, ripe pear and honey flavors that burst with wonderful intensity. Compact, concentrated, velvety and minerally midpalate. Medium- to full-bodied, it takes off like a rocket on the searing finish. Try after 2000. • $60 • (05/31/98) • **92**

Chablis Les Blanchots Vieilles Vignes 1995: Ultra-rich and ripe, mingling honey, pear, kiwi, mineral, toast and vanilla flavors. Both ripe and crisp, it's beautifully made, though the wood tends to overwhelm the finish right now. Best after 2000. • $56 • (06/15/97) • **89**

Chablis Les Clos 1996: Great promise. A big but very balanced Chablis, with ripe pear and apple pie flavors on the nose, it turns up the volume on the palate, coating the taste buds with its lush texture, loads of mineral and firm citrus-acidity character. Full-bodied and reserved, it needs time. Try after 2005. • $NA • (05/31/98) • **94**

Chablis Les Clos 1994 • $45 • (05/31/96) • **92**

Chablis Les Clos 1993 • $43 • (08/31/95) • **83**

Chablis Les Preuses 1995: A serious *grand cru*; medium-bodied, round and supple, with a touch of honey balancing its lively citrus character, some nice mineral notes and a long finish. Try around 2000 to 2005. • $36 • (06/15/97) • **88**

Chablis Les Preuses 1994 • $NA • (05/31/96) • **60**

Chablis Les Preuses 1993 • $43 • (08/31/95) • **80**

Chablis Les Vaillons 1996: Thick, rich and ripe—and quite oaky—this full-bodied Chablis is as seductive as can be, with plenty of tropical, floral and pear flavors and a hint of mineral, but a slightly hot oak note on the finish distracts. Try after 2005. • $22 • (05/31/98) • **86**

Chablis Mont de Milieu 1996: Aerodynamic and wonderful, designed with laser-sharp flavors, it's reserved on the nose now, but shows wonderful balance, depth and richness on the palate, delivering sophisticated layers of white pepper, mineral, pear and spice with hints of honey. Fairly crisp but very long finish. Should flesh out after 2005. • $24 • (05/31/98) • **91**

Chablis Mont de Milieu 1995: Ripe, rich and full-bodied, this *premier cru* sparkles with life, offering fresh herb, citrus and honey aromas, toasty oak and mineral flavors and a classy, racy finish. Drink after 2000. 1,833 cases made. • $21 • (06/15/97) • **89**

Chablis Mont de Milieu 1994 • $24 • (05/31/96) • **90**

Chablis Mont de Milieu 1993 • $23 • (08/31/95) • **86**

Chablis Mont de Milieu Vieilles Vignes 1996: Well made Chablis in an oaky style. Full-bodied, offering layers of mocha, spice, chocolate and toasty bread along with pear and tropical notes. Smooth texture on the palate, leaving an intense feel on the finish. Tempting now, but hold until after 2000. • $27 • (05/31/98) • **91**

Chablis Mont de Milieu Vieilles Vignes 1995: A harmonious *premier cru*, showing a ripe, sweet-fruit character, plenty of lively, citrus, honey and mineral notes that burst with personality, and featuring a full body. Drink now to 2005. 292 cases made. • $25 • (06/15/97) • **89**

Chablis Montée de Tonnerre 1996: Intense and smooth. Velvety in texture and full in body, with wonderful lime, mineral, pear, pine and herbal notes, it shows wonderful balance. Tempting after 1999, good through 2005. • $24 • (05/31/98) • **93**

Chablis Montée de Tonnerre 1995: Honeyed Montée de Tonnerre, this medium-bodied *premier cru* bursts with lively citrus notes. Round, pure midpalate feel. Try around 2000. • $24 • (06/15/97) • **87**

Chablis Montée de Tonnerre 1994 • $23 • (05/31/96) • **87**

Chablis Montée de Tonnerre 1993 • $23 • (08/31/95) • **80**

Chablis Tête d'Or 1994 • $19 • (05/31/96) • **79**

Chablis Vaillons 1995: A firm, tightly built, ripe-tasting Chablis, of medium body, with lively citrus, Sauvignon Blanc-like grass and honey notes, crisp fruit flavors, and a slight mineral aroma. Try in 1999. • $21 • (06/15/97) • **85**

Chablis Vaillons 1994 • $22 • (05/31/96) • **86**

Chablis Vaillons 1993 • $23 • (08/31/95) • **80**

Chablis Vaudésir 1996: Polished and pretty, of medium body, with fresh citrus intensity, it delivers hints of honey, mineral and spice. A racy wine, but brace yourself for a vivid, crisp texture and finish. Tempting with oysters now, or hold through 2005. • $40 • (05/31/98) • **89**

Chablis Vaudésir 1995: Sensational *grand cru*—the sort of stuff Chablis lovers can't get enough of. Concentrated, harmonious and balanced, round and velvety, with ripe fruit, butter and mineral flavors. Drinkable now through 2005. 417 cases made. • $36 • (06/15/97) • **90**

Chablis Vaudésir 1994 • $38 • (05/31/96) • **90**

Chablis Vaudésir 1993 • $42 • (08/31/95) • **78**

BILLECART-SALMON

Brut Blanc de Blancs Champagne 1983: Tart, lean, crisp and well balanced, very intense and concentrated, sharp around the edges, and perhaps better with a year or two in the cellar to round out the edges. Drinkable now. • $50 • (12/31/89) • **88**

Brut Blanc de Blancs Champagne 1982: Nutty, floral style with medium body, nutty, appley flavors, which become stronger and deeper on the finish. More fruit than most, but very enjoyable. • $43 • (05/31/87) • **86**

Brut Champagne 1986: Well-proportioned yet muscular Champagne. This shows plenty of toasty, strawberry character, medium body and fresh acidity. Drink now. 6,000 cases made. • $45 • (12/31/93) • **88**

Brut Champagne 1983: Tart, crisp, lean and concentrated with sharply focused, well-balanced lemon, spice, cherry and vanilla-coconut notes that are quite pleasing. Full-bodied, with a sense of finesse. • $47 • (12/31/89) • **89**

BILLIOT, HENRI

Brut Champagne 1990: Generous, full-bodied and mouthfilling. This robust, fruit-centered bubbly is easy to like for its ample flavor and smooth texture. Drink now through 2000. • $39 • (11/30/97) • **90**

Brut Champagne Cuvée Laetitia NV: Made in a soft, creamy, luscious style, this has subtle apple and spice flavors and good acidity, but a light, frothy texture. Lingering finish. • $54 • (11/30/97) • **88**

Brut Champagne Réserve NV: A well-balanced, brightly flavored Champagne that's lively in texture. • $32 • (12/31/97) • **85**

BINET

Blanc de Blancs Champagne 1988: Rather light and simple, showing good apple and canned peaches character and a light foamy finish. Drinkable now. • $NA • (12/31/93) • **81**

Brut Champagne 1988: Develops on your palate as you taste it. Lots of character. Complex aromas and flavors of cinnamon, vanilla, and melons. Full-bodied yet refreshing. A good Champagne for food. Drinkable now. • $NA • (12/31/93) • **89**

BIROT, CHÂTEAU DE

Premières Côtes de Bordeaux 1990: Lean and herbal, with evolving spicy leather and cedar notes. It's well integrated and smooth, but lacks richness and breadth. Drinkable now. • $10 • (05/15/94) • **82**

FRANCE

BISTON-BRILLETTE, CHÂTEAU

Moulis 1995: Has lovely fruit and mineral aromas and flavors, with fine tannins and a silky finish. Lovely balance. • $NA • (05/15/96) (BT) • **85-89**

BITOUZET, PIERRE

Aloxe-Corton Les Valozières 1994: Light, soft and appealing for its berry and slightly leathery flavors that finish with a touch of tannin. 2,500 cases made. • $29 • (11/15/96) • **81**

Aloxe-Corton Les Valozières 1990: Young, hard and not giving much now, but shows promise with its black cherry, herbal and earthy complexity and tannic, muscular finish. Try now. • $NA • (12/15/92) • **88**

Aloxe-Corton Les Valozières 1989 • $28 • (11/30/92) • **82**

Aloxe-Corton Les Valozières 1986 • $19 • (08/31/90) • **78**

Bourgogne White 1995: A bit rustic; full-bodied but with a tart aftertaste. Some chestnut, spice and stemlike flavors. • $NA • (08/31/97) • **74**

Bourgogne White 1993: Sharp, tongue-twisting, citrusy white, revealing green-bean, earth and grapefruit character. Lean finish. Try with seafood. • $NA • (05/15/95) • **73**

Chablis Beauroy 1994 • $NA • (05/31/96) • **74**

Corton-Charlemagne 1995: A bit musty (but not corked). Dull and one-dimensional, somewhat lacking in fruit, with a chewy finish that's a bit dry. 150 cases made. • $NA • (05/31/97) • **75**

Corton-Charlemagne 1994: Balanced and supple, full-bodied and silky, coating the mouth with its fruit, honey and spice character. Of medium intensity, it lacks a touch of complexity for a *grand cru*. Drinkable now. 250 cases made. • $50 • (05/31/96) • **86**

Corton-Charlemagne 1993: Full-throttle, full-bodied wine, generous with tropical and ripe fruit flavors, mineral and spice. The color is already turning a bit gold, and this has a terrific, velvety finish. Try now. • $NA • (08/31/95) • **88**

Corton-Charlemagne 1992: Pure, focused, vivid and ripe, quite charming and fruity; offering excellent balance. Medium-bodied. 500 cases made. • $52 • (08/31/94) • **89**

Pommard La Platière 1994: A decent wine with solid flavors, but coarse tannins and stalky, floral accents bring it down a bit. Try in 1999. • $33 • (11/15/96) • **81**

Pommard La Platière 1993: Firm and tannic with a stout backbone, but rather lean in flesh. Medium body and finish, adding a lightly fruity aftertaste. Better in 1999. • $40 • (11/15/95) • **84**

Savigny-lès-Beaune 1994: Light and thin, this makes an attempt to be charming, but just remains hard. • $24 • (11/15/96) • **76**

Savigny-lès-Beaune 1993: Not big but fine and fresh, showing good dried cherry character and delicate tannins. Drinkable now. • $25 • (11/15/95) • **83**

Savigny-lès-Beaune Les Goudelettes White 1995: Well made but a bit short, with almond, shortcake, pear, grass and citrus flavors. Has enough concentration to improve with cellaring; try now. • $NA • (08/31/97) • **86**

Savigny-lès-Beaune Les Goudelettes White 1993: Ripeness balances refreshing citrus flavors. A light-to-medium-bodied white, offering delicate pear, orange-peel, apple and lime notes. Delicious finish. Drinkable now. • $NA • (05/15/95) • **83**

Savigny-lès-Beaune Les Goudelettes White 1992: Simple and straightforward, with the round texture of a good white, but so light on modest fruit flavors it seems diluted. 320 cases made. • $20 • (08/31/94) • **77**

Savigny-lès-Beaune Les Lavières 1994: Light, but firm in texture, with focused black cherry, spice and bitter-chocolate notes on the tart finish. Best now. • $27 • (11/15/96) • **85**

Savigny-lès-Beaune Les Lavières 1993: Light, rather simple, straightforward fruit and earth character. Short and slightly diluted on the finish. • $30 • (11/15/95) • **76**

Savigny-lès-Beaune Les Lavières 1990: This beautiful Savigny offers plenty of crushed raspberry flavors and earth notes against a relatively firm background of supple tannins. Drinkable now. • $NA • (12/15/92) • **88**

Savigny-lès-Beaune Les Lavières 1986 • $15 • (03/31/90) • **87**

Savigny-lès-Beaune Les Lavières 1985 • $19 • (03/15/88) • **67**

Savigny-lès-Beaune Les Talmettes White 1995: Quite rich and ripe, with excellent acidity, a citrus-spiked character, nice dried herb, honey and ripe fruit. Full-bodied, it turns a bit woody on the finish. Try now. • $NA • (08/31/97) • **88**

Savigny-lès-Beaune Les Talmettes White 1993: Very odd wine. A '93 *premier cru* that smells like oatmeal, earth and salted peanuts. Sharp and crisp. 250 cases made. • $NA • (05/31/96) • **73**

BITOUZET-PRIEUR

Meursault Les Corbins 1993: Racy and clean lemon, mineral, apple and cream aromas and flavors, medium body; very fruity and firm and a fresh finish. Drinkable now. 292 cases made. • $35 • (05/15/95) • **89**

Volnay Clos des Chênes 1987 • $36 • (12/31/90) • **80**

Volnay Pitures 1985 • $36 • (07/31/88) • **91**

BIZE & FILS, SIMON

Aloxe-Corton Le Suchot 1993. • $24 • (05/15/96) • **90**

Aloxe-Corton Le Suchot 1991: Earthy, gamy, minty aromas and flavors almost drown out blackberry finish. Drinkable now. 300 cases made. • $28 Ⓐ • (01/31/94) • **77**

Bourgogne Les Perrières 1990: Enticing, with pretty aromas and a seducive complexity of blackberry and black cherry notes. Has a smoky, toasty character and a fine texture. A joy to drink now. 100 cases made. • $17 • (12/15/92) • **87**

Savigny-lès-Beaune 1990: Very elegant, ripe, round and attractive, with plum, earth and currant notes and a medium-long finish. Drinkable now. 208 cases made. • $20 • (12/15/92) • **85**

Savigny-lès-Beaune Aux Fournaux 1993: Not deeply fruity, but cedary and woody in flavor and sturdy-textured. Firmly tannic on the finish. • $25 • (05/15/96) • **82**

Savigny-lès-Beaune Aux Fournaux 1991: Tough, earthy, leathery shoe polish aromas and flavors kill this for us. 250 cases made. • $25 • (01/31/94) • **60**

Savigny-lès-Beaune Aux Fournaux 1990: Brightly flavored, with plummy blueberry and cherry notes. Very closed in, but the firm finish is juicy and fruity. Drinkable now. 400 cases made. • $28 • (12/15/92) • **89**

Savigny-lès-Beaune Aux Fournaux Premier Cru 1992: Very rustic and earthy leather and barnyard aromas, tealike flavors and not much fruit. Dry texture; short finish. • $NA • (06/15/95) • **78**

Savigny-lès-Beaune Aux Grands Liards 1993: A lighter, leaner style of Burgundy, offering attractive herbal, smoky, cherrylike flavors, good balance and moderate tannins. Drink now while it's fresh. • $19 • (05/15/96) • **84**

Savigny-lès-Beaune Aux Grands Liards 1992: Mature, simple, revealing basic cherry and tea flavors and weak, watery texture. Drink now if you like this style. • $20 • (06/15/95) • **78**

Savigny-lès-Beaune Aux Grands Liards 1991: Light, earthy and modestly fruity. Drinkable now. 300 cases made. • $21 Ⓐ • (01/31/94) • **75**

Savigny-lès-Beaune Aux Grands Liards 1990: Pretty floral and spice notes and super-fine tannins. Should make for excellent drinking now. 417 cases made. • $22 • (12/15/92) • **87**

Savigny-lès-Beaune Aux Guettes 1991: Earthy, rubbery and slightly astringent; has little charm. 150 cases made. • $30 Ⓐ • (01/31/94) • **67**

Savigny-lès-Beaune Aux Guettes 1990: Juicy and ripe, with attractive cherry, plum and earth characteristics that won't overwhelm you, but the balance makes for a nice wine. Drinkable now. 170 cases made. • $33 • (12/15/92) • **86**

Savigny-lès-Beaune Aux Vergelesses 1992: Mature already, featuring almost sweet flavors of cherry, tea and brown sugar that linger on the finish. Light in tannins and acidity. Drinkable now. • $24 • (05/15/95) • **84**

Savigny-lès-Beaune Aux Vergelesses 1991: Light and simple; offers modest cherry notes and an earthy, slightly tannic finish. Drinkable now. 600 cases made. • $28 Ⓐ • (01/31/94) • **80**

Savigny-lès-Beaune Aux Vergelesses 1990: Very flattering, with attractive toast and smoke characteristics and masses of firm tannins, but feels a shade light in the middle and on the finish. Drinkable now. 125 cases made. • $29 • (12/15/92) • **90**

Savigny-lès-Beaune Aux Vergelesses 1989 • $27 • (01/31/92) • **87**

Savigny-lès-Beaune Les Bourgeots 1991: Simple, earthy and drying on the finish. 1,500 cases made. • $20 Ⓐ • (01/31/94) • **72**

Savigny-lès-Beaune Les Bourgeots 1989 • $19 • (01/31/92) • **85**

Savigny-lès-Beaune Les Marconnets 1993: Lots of fresh, lively fruit flavors in this smooth-textured, moderately tannic and well-balanced Burgundy. Hints of spice give it complexity. Drink now. • $25 • (05/15/96) • **86**

Savigny-lès-Beaune Les Marconnets 1992: Fruity and flavorful, yet also very tart. It's lively and crisp on the palate but finishes vegetal and leathery. • $24 • (06/15/95) • **82**

Key: SS—Spectator Selection CS—Cellar Selection HR—Highly Recommended BB—Best Buy $NA—Price not available Ⓐ—Auction Price (BT)—Barrel Tasting

Dates in parentheses indicate the issues in which the ratings were published.

Savigny-lès-Beaune Les Marconnets 1991: Gamy, toasty flavors overshadow the modest black cherry flavor in this meaty wine. Drinkable now. 180 cases made. • $30 Ⓐ • (01/31/94) • **80**

Savigny-lès-Beaune Les Marconnets 1990: Clever winemaking went into producing this delightful Savigny, where the toasty, smoky notes balance the berry flavors. Has fine tannins and a medium finish. Drinkable now. 300 cases made. • $33 • (12/15/92) • **90**

BLACHON, ROGER

St.-Joseph 1993 • $17 • (11/15/95) • **84**

St.-Joseph 1990 • $15 • (04/15/93) • **84**

BLAGUEURS, DOMAINE DES

Syrah Vin de Pays du Gard 1996: Quite focused, with berry flavors and leather and game notes. Firm and concentrated, with a nice crispness and power. May smooth out in another year or two; try from 1999. • $NA • (07/31/98) • **85**

BLAIN-GAGNARD

Bâtard-Montrachet 1996: Call in the palate damage patrol—this one digs a hole with enormous intensity. Incredibly opulent, thick and dense, yet also elegant and racy. To scream about, it packs in so much of everything, including loads of vibrant citrus-spiked acidity, creamy texture and ripe fruit. Cool silkiness on the long-as-can-be finish. Brilliant. Try around 2010. 200 cases made. • $110 • (05/31/98) CS • **97**

Bâtard-Montrachet 1994: Of medium body, soft and supple. With a well-balanced combination of citrus, honey, apricot and pear flavors, it's ready to drink. Tasted three times with consistent notes. • $NA • (08/31/96) • **83**

Bâtard-Montrachet 1992: Exotic, ripe and rich with fruit flavor, layered with peach, apricot and honey, almost like a late-harvest wine. It is bold and fruity, backing off a bit on the finish. Very good, but not our favorite style of white Burgundy. • $86 Ⓐ • (08/31/94) • **89**

Chassagne-Montrachet Caillerets 1996: Intense and on the oaky side, with toasty bread, grilled pineapple, freshly cut grass and dried herb notes mingling with some ripe fruit. Caressing in texture and full-bodied, it turns very crisp and a bit rough on the intense finish. Try after 2002. 325 cases made. • $45 • (05/31/98) • **85**

Chassagne-Montrachet Caillerets 1995: Super. Clean and pure, sparkling with lively acidity, yet coating the mouth with supple mineral, wet stone and light honey notes. Just lightly toasty, it's a graceful, medium- to full-bodied white. Better after 2000. • $45 • (05/31/97) • **91**

Chassagne-Montrachet Caillerets 1994: Very supple and seductive honey, cream, toasty coconut and mineral flavors. Full in body and delicious to drink now. Doesn't overwhelm us by its intensity, but who's complaining? 200 cases made. • $45 • (05/31/96) • **87**

Chassagne-Montrachet Caillerets 1992: Earthy, toasty aromas combine with vivid, aggressive fruit flavors for a lively but rangy white Burgundy. • $31 Ⓐ • (08/31/94) • **81**

Chassagne-Montrachet Clos St.-Jean 1996: A bit earthy, with smoke and mineral notes. Of medium-to-full body, with a creamlike midpalate texture, it tastes of green apple, pear, tropical and toasty oak. A bit angular now, with citrusy acidity on the juicy finish. Might improve by 2003. 125 cases made. • $45 • (05/31/98) • **88**

Chassagne-Montrachet Clos St.-Jean 1994: Round and smooth, soft, medium in body and intensity, offering some tropical fruit, citrus, apple and cream character. Fun and delicious now, but not much staying power on the relatively short finish. 125 cases made. • $45 • (05/31/96) • **85**

Chassagne-Montrachet La Boudriotte 1996: Full-bodied and dominated by wood, dried herbs, grass and a malic-milky, buttery, citrusy character, it turns a bit dry and sharp on the palate. Good *terroir*, so it might improve with age. Try after 2000. 360 cases made. • $45 • (05/31/98) • **83**

Chassagne-Montrachet La Boudriotte 1995: A racy and wonderful *premier cru*. Very intense, quite lactic and honeyed, showing some melon, mineral and floral character. Medium- to full-bodied, it's thick on the midpalate and vibrates with lively, citrus notes on the lingering finish. Try after 2002. 200 cases imported. • $45 • (08/31/97) • **93**

Chassagne-Montrachet La Boudriotte 1994: Elegant and almost delicate, this well-made, medium-bodied '94 shows substantial tropical fruit, grapefruit, mineral and lemon flavors. Lovely finish. 375 cases made. • $45 • (05/31/96) • **85**

Chassagne-Montrachet La Boudriotte 1993: Textbook Chassagne, exhibiting pineapple, chalk and mineral aromas and flavors; medium-bodied and crisp. Delicious to drink now. • $NA • (05/15/95) • **85**

Chassagne-Montrachet La Boudriotte 1992: Simple and straightforward, with coarse texture and some modest apple cider flavors. • $35 • (08/31/94) • **76**

Chassagne-Montrachet Morgeot 1996: Lovely, exotic, concentrated Chassagne, offering layers of violet, toasty oak, spice, pink grapefruit and pear, with hints of honey and pineapple. Full-bodied but too crisp on the finish to drink now, it has the stuffing to age and improve through 2005. 290 cases made. • $45 • (05/31/98) • **91**

Chassagne-Montrachet Morgeot 1994: Very balanced and supple, featuring some intense citrus, dried herb, honey and mineral quality. Fresh, focused, well-made and full-bodied. Silky finish. Needs until 1999 to show it all. 350 cases made. • $45 • (05/31/96) • **90**

Criots-Bâtard-Montrachet 1996: Classy, with a lovely honey-lime combination. Intense and showing good concentration, this full-bodied '96 has a lot of personality. Delicious and vibrant on the midpalate, hinting at the supple, minerally texture to emerge with age, the finish is balanced, supple and deftly imbued with toasty oak accents. Try around 2007. 100 cases made. • $110 • (05/31/98) • **95**

Criots-Bâtard-Montrachet 1994: Elegant yet very ripe, this medium- to full-bodied white delivers some rather intense citrus, honey and pear flavors. Rich but focused. 100 cases made. • $95 • (05/31/96) • **86**

BLANC, GEORGES

Mâcon-Azé Domaine d'Azenay 1993: Subtle, delicate touch of butter, mineral, spice, mint and nutmeg complexity and a very crisp, lemony, harmonious finish. Drinkable now. 3,542 cases made. • $12 • (08/31/95) • **85**

Mâcon-Azé Fleur d'Azenay 1993: Clean, crisp and straightforward Chardonnay-light, tight and austere. Green apple, citrus and a touch of butter character. 4,167 cases made. • $10 • (08/31/95) • **80**

BLANCHET, BERNARD

Pouilly-Fumé Les Champs des Plantes 1995: Light, crisp and refreshing, this clean, bright white shows lemon, light pear and light herb flavors, and is taut and lean. A nice apéritif. 2,000 cases made. • $20 • (04/30/97) • **85**

Pouilly-Fumé Les Champs des Plantes 1994 • $15 • (04/30/96) • **75**

BLANCHET, FRANCIS

Pouilly-Fumé 1993 • $12 • (11/15/95) • **87**

Pouilly-Fumé Cuvée Silex Très Vieilles Vignes 1996: Thick—almost chewy—on the palate. A distinctive style, marrying ripe fruit flavors of melons and apples with those of toast and bread dough. Displays richness, depth and balance. Drink now through 1999. 23 cases made. • $30 • (02/28/98) • **88**

BLANCK, DOMAINE PAUL

Gewürztraminer Alsace Altenbourg 1996: An understated style for Gewürz, displaying apple flavors, just a hint of roses and litchi, and a distinct bread dough character perhaps from lees aging. Still, there's no lack of body or concentration. Drink now. • $22 • (04/30/98) • **86**

Gewürztraminer Alsace 1995: Good concentration, with pear, melon and tropical notes, balanced on the soft side. A hint of bitterness on the finish. • $13 • (02/28/97) • **84**

Pinot Auxerrois Alsace Vieilles Vignes 1996: A lovely wine, very pure and balanced deftly between peach and nutty flavors, racy acidity and rich texture. Delicious at the table. Drink now through 1999. • $15 • (03/31/98) • **87**

Tokay Pinot Gris Alsace 1996: Soft and fleshy, this has stone-fruit aromas and flavors and quite a bit of refreshing acidity. Solid and appealing. Drink now through 2000. • $18 • (03/31/98) • **85**

Tokay Pinot Gris Alsace 1995: Broad and mouthfilling. A rich white with smoke- and spice-accented pear and rose flavors. Appealing, though short. • $13 • (02/28/97) • **84**

BLANCK FRÈRES

Gewürztraminer Alsace 1995: Reminiscent of a bouquet of roses, backed up by litchi and grapefruit accents. A soft, forward style of Gewürz that's ready to drink. • $10 • (02/28/97) • **83**

Gewürztraminer Alsace 1994 • $10 • (05/15/96) • **87**

Pinot Blanc Alsace 1995: Vibrant and refreshing, showing off citrus and almond flavors against a smooth texture. Crisp, clean finish. • $8 • (02/28/97) • **84**

Pinot Blanc Alsace 1994 • $10 • (05/15/96) • **78**

Riesling Alsace 1994 • $10 • (05/15/96) • **85**
Tokay Pinot Gris Alsace 1994 • $10 • (05/15/96) • **84**

BLASON D' ISSAN

Margaux 1995: Needs time to mellow a bit. Attractive cherry and wet soil aromas. Medium- to full-bodied, with firm, slightly angular tannins and a medium finish. Second label of Château d'Issan. Better after 2000. • $12 • (01/31/98) • **85**

BLEND STORMING

Vin de Table Français 1995: A smooth, softly fruity red, with little tannin and no harsh edges. Easy to enjoy. Drink now. 3,300 cases made. • $8 • (07/31/98) • **83**

BLOMAC, CHÂTEAU DE

Minervois Cuvée Tradition 1991 • $7 • (06/30/94) • **82**
Minervois Cuvée Tradition 1988 • $6 • (12/31/91) BB • **82**

BOCAGE, CHÂTEAU LE

Bordeaux Supérieur 1997: A bit diluted, with berry character and earthiness. Very light finish. • $NA • (06/15/98) (BT) • **75-79**
Bordeaux Supérieur 1996: Extremely light and watery. Light-bodied, with light tannins. Not much to it. • $16 • (06/15/98) (BT) • **75-79**

BOCARD, GUY

Bourgogne Aligoté 1996: Decent and clean, offering pure lime, apple, pear and wet earth character. Light-bodied, with a crisp finish. Drink now. 530 cases made. • $15 • (05/31/98) • **81**
Bourgogne White 1996: Wood, wet earth and marzipan character dominates in this medium-bodied white; too bad it's a bit empty on the midpalate. Drink now. 1,000 cases made. • $18 • (05/31/98) • **78**
Bourgogne White 1995: Woody and rustic, with some lactic, floral perfumes. Medium body and a short, tart finish. 1,300 cases made. • $17 • (08/31/97) • **72**
Meursault Charmes 1996: Odd, with a wet wood flavor. Medium-bodied and a bit acidic, it's slightly sour on the finish. 350 cases made. • $50 • (05/31/98) • **75**
Meursault Charmes Premier Cru 1992: Rich, ripe and luscious, a Meursault that's saturated with flavors of honey, almonds, pear and vanilla. Turns lighter on the finish. • $36 • (06/15/95) • **86**
Meursault Les Charmes 1995: Intense, with wonderful smoky, flinty spice notes mingling with pear, peach, apricot and tropical fruit flavors. Impressive balance. Full-bodied, with a hint of mineral that should emerge further with cellaring. Try after 2000. 350 cases made. 350 cases made. • $NA • (08/31/97) • **92**
Meursault Les Narvaux 1995: Disjointed, earthy and odd, tasting overripe like a melon gone bad. Bitter finish, with a matchstick note. 200 cases made. • $NA • (05/31/97) • **70**
Meursault Limozin 1996: Vibrant but crisp and fairly lean, this medium-bodied white offers decent fruit and a slightly green character. 500 cases made. • $38 • (05/31/98) • **79**
Meursault Limozin 1995: Subtle and closed now, but solidly structured, with good density and ripe fruit character and a fine mineral, wet earth and herb quality that adds complexity to the long, elegant finish. Try around 2000. 217 cases made. • $NA • (05/31/97) • **90**

BOILEAU, ETIENNE

Chablis 1996: This full-bodied Chablis is of medium intensity, shows decent balance and flavors of lemon, honey and pear. Drink now. • $16 • (08/31/97) • **84**
Chablis Mont de Milieu 1995: Starts out fine, with elegant aromas and flavors, but loses balance, turning slightly cooked in character. • $22 • (06/15/97) • **79**

> **Key:** SS—Spectator Selection CS—Cellar Selection HR—Highly Recommended BB—Best Buy $NA—Price not available Ⓐ—Auction Price (BT)—Barrel Tasting
> **Dates in parentheses indicate the issues in which the ratings were published.**

Chablis Montmains 1995: Opulent and unctuous, sweet, ripe and lush, this full-bodied Chablis sails with grace, carrying its generous honey, ripe pear, vanilla, dried herbs and smoke flavors to a long-lasting finish. Drink now to 2000. • $25 • (06/15/97) • **89**
Chablis Montée de Tonnerre 1996: Beautiful texture makes for a divine drinking experience, but be forewarned that this is oaky, with vanilla, butterscotch, toasty bread aromas and flavors. Full-bodied, it stays clean and fresh thanks to the excellent acidity of the '96 vintage. Much better than when previously reviewed. Best from 2000 through 2004. • $25 • (05/31/98) • **92**
Chablis Montée de Tonnerre 1995: Like liquid butter; palate-coating, with vibrant lemon and toasty spice notes. Finish is a bit hot. Seems disjointed overall. • $25 • (06/15/97) • **80**
Chablis Vaillons 1995: Rather crisp, showing dried herb, grass and pronounced green apple flavors. Medium-bodied, with a tart, green finish. Drink now to 2000. • $25 • (06/15/97) • **78**
Chablis Vaillons Domaine du Chardonnay 1996: Like a Sauvignon Blanc, this has gooseberry, floral and grassy notes, but after awhile it turns a bit hot and bitter. Medium-bodied. Drink now, chilled. • $NA • (05/31/98) • **85**
Chablis Vaugiraut 1995: Strange *premier cru*, showing mature colors, aromas and flavors. Slightly oxidized and rustic. Tasted twice, with consistent notes. • $23 • (06/15/97) • **75**
Petit Chablis 1996: Tastes unbalanced, with a buttery, green apple character and green tannins that are sharp. • $14 • (08/31/97) • **78**

BOILLOT, JEAN

Beaune Clos du Roi 1995: A high-toned, spicy style, showing concentration, elegance and sweet fruit to balance the firm tannins. • $44 • (11/15/97) • **86**
Beaune Clos du Roi 1994: Crisp and simple, with spicy strawberry flavors that echo lightly on the finish. • $41 • (11/15/96) • **80**
Beaune Clos du Roi 1992: Light, definitely tannic, but showing just enough berry and black cherry flavor to balance the tough edge. Drinkable now. • $29 • (12/15/94) • **79**
Beaune Clos du Roi 1991: Firm and almost fleshy, with a solid core of currant and berry aromas and flavors and a twang of vegetal, earthy notes to give it personality. Drinkable now. • $32 Ⓐ • (01/31/94) • **81**
Beaune Les Epenotes 1995: This is herbal, tough and hard to warm up to. • $44 • (11/15/97) • **78**
Beaune Les Epenotes 1994: Light in color and texture, with a modicum of spicy strawberry and leather flavors that persist on the delicate finish. • $41 • (11/15/96) • **80**
Beaune Les Epenotes 1992: Simple and chewy, a sturdy red with modest black cherry and spice flavors. Drinkable now. • $29 • (12/15/94) • **80**
Beaune Les Epenotes 1991: Light, firm and bright, with pretty raspberry, earth and mushroom aromas and flavors. Echoes fruit on the smooth, delicate finish. Drinkable now. • $32 Ⓐ • (01/31/94) • **83**
Nuits-St.-Georges Les Cailles 1995: A tough, sinewy '95, with woody, licorice and earthy notes that are lean in texture and astringent on the finish. Traditional style. Try in 2002. • $58 • (11/15/97) • **83**
Nuits-St.-Georges Les Cailles 1994: Offers buttery, spicy flavors and a warm finish, but it's short on freshness. Feels a bit thin next to the more successful Nuits-St.-Georges. Ready now. • $51 • (11/15/96) • **80**
Nuits-St.-Georges Les Cailles 1992: Light and herbal, with a floral component overshadowing the modest berry flavors. Drinkable now. • $38 • (12/15/94) • **77**
Nuits-St.-Georges Les Cailles 1991: Light and refreshing, with modest strawberry flavor and fine tannins. Drinkable now. • $48 Ⓐ • (01/31/94) • **81**
Puligny-Montrachet 1994: Some nice tropical and citrus flavors, but also somewhat one-dimensional and square. Leaves you hungry for a bit more complexity. Very drinkable now, though. • $49 • (05/31/96) • **83**
Puligny-Montrachet Clos de la Mouchère 1994: Supple and honey-flavored *premier cru*, sporting a whiff of lemon and ripe pear. Medium-bodied, attractive and drinkable now. Very soft finish. • $44 • (05/31/96) • **85**
Puligny-Montrachet Les Perrières 1994: Straightforward and a bit thin, showing some odd leesy notes and buttery, butterscotch, green apple character. • $45 • (05/31/96) • **77**
Puligny-Montrachet Les Pucelles 1994: Beautifully crafted, clean and crisp, boasting loads of honey, lemon, toasty oak and ripe pear complexity. Medium to full in body, it's elegant and restrained, classy, racy and long on the finish. Try in 1999. • $45 • (05/31/96) • **90**
Savigny-lès-Beaune Les Lavières 1992: Light and smooth, with a modest band of cherry and tobacco flavors coming through the fine tannins. Drinkable now. • $27 • (12/15/94) • **82**

Savigny-lès-Beaune Les Lavières 1991: A pretty wine that's bright and open in texture, offering berry, cherry and floral aromas and flavors. Drinkable now. • $30 Ⓐ • (01/31/94) • **84**

Volnay en Chevret 1992: Light and approachable, with modest black cherry and slightly gamy flavors. Drinkable now. • $34 • (12/15/94) • **80**

Volnay en Chevret 1991: Fresh, clean, simple and slightly toasty, showing a pleasant vanilla edge to the modest raspberry flavors. Delicate, graceful and stylish. Drinkable now. • $40 Ⓐ • (01/31/94) • **83**

Volnay Frémiets 1992: Firm, somewhat chewy, with modest black cherry flavors that finish a little sugary. Drinkable now. • $34 • (12/15/94) • **79**

Volnay Frémiets 1991: Lean and toasty, with a walnutty edge to the red cherry and raspberry flavors. An elegant wine that shows character in a modest frame. Drinkable now. • $40 Ⓐ • (01/31/94) • **84**

Volnay Les Caillerets 1995: Seductive and smooth, with new oak lending coffee and vanilla accents to the strawberry and cherry flavors. Lean yet balanced, with firm tannins. Try in 1999. • $59 • (11/15/97) • **86**

Volnay Les Caillerets 1994: Light and fresh, with appealing raspberry flavors on a delicate frame. • $51 • (11/15/96) • **80**

Volnay Les Caillerets 1992: Delicate but focused, delivering intense flavors. Notes of tea leaf and black cherry, with a touch of smoky, spicy oak character that lingers nicely on the finish. • $36 • (12/15/94) • **83**

Volnay Les Caillerets 1991: Very pretty, elegant, smooth and polished, showing bright raspberry, vanilla and spice aromas and flavors. Echoes fruit and violet notes on the light, long finish. Drinkable now. • $44 Ⓐ • (01/31/94) • **86**

Volnay Les Chevrets 1995: A light- to medium-bodied red that reveals toasty oak and cherry flavors marred by a strong, earthy character. Dry, tough finish. • $54 • (11/15/97) • **78**

Volnay Les Chevrets 1994: Light and watery, showing thin, vaguely berryish flavors. • $49 • (11/15/96) • **74**

Volnay Les Frémiets 1995: A wild gamy edge, plus a hint of licorice mark this lean, chewy Volnay. Rustic for the appellation, it ends with some astringent tannins. • $54 • (11/15/97) • **83**

Volnay Les Frémiets 1994: Light, almost rosèlike, with delicate strawberry flavors. • $49 • (11/15/96) • **80**

BOILLOT, JEAN-MARC

Bâtard-Montrachet 1996: Overtly oaky and spicy, this toasty wine turns a bit bitter on the palate. Medium-bodied, with pleasant grilled pineapple, hazelnut, butter and pear tart flavors. Fans of woody Chardonnay should try this upon release. 80 cases made. • $126 • (05/31/98) • **85**

Bâtard-Montrachet 1995: A full-bodied *grand cru*, wonderfully balanced, and rich, but refined. Tastes sweet and ripe, offering generous notes of honey, citrus and pear, and just a hint of spicy oak. Mouth-coatingly thick, but avoids getting heavy on the finish. Try after 2000. • $131 • (05/31/97) • **93**

Beaune Les Montrevenots 1995: A dark, intense, modern style, with aromas of freshly crushed berries. Medium- to full-bodied, it's impressive at first, but the tannins turn dry and hard on the woody finish. A gamble; hold until after 2000. Tasted twice, with consistent notes. • $33 • (01/31/98) • **83**

Beaune Les Montrevenots 1994: This stands out among the other '94s, with deep color and massive flavors. Sparkles with life and a beam of red berry, floral and wet earth flavors. Medium bodied, almost delicate on the very long, succulent, crisp finish. Needs till 2000 to let the rough edges of the tannins soften. • $27 • (11/15/96) • **90**

Beaune Les Montrevenots 1993: Nice and round, sporting good, ripe fruit character and medium body and tannins which come together harmoniously on the finish. A bit too tannic, so wait until 2000. • $30 • (11/15/95) • **85**

Beaune Les Montrevenots 1992: Riper than most in this appellation. Delivers some intense blackberry and raspberry flavors but peters out a bit on the finish. Still, a good effort for '92. • $29 • (12/15/94) • **85**

Beaune Les Montrevenots 1991: Supple and concentrated; shows a lot more density and vibrancy than most '91s. Scads of black cherry and blackberry flavors, shaded by earth and chocolate notes, make this cellar worthy. Try now. • $30 • (01/31/94) • **88**

Beaune Les Montrevenots 1990: So concentrated you can almost cut it with a knife, but though massive it manages also to be elegant. Shows excellent intensity of berry flavors and supple tannins. Drinkable now. • $39 • (12/15/92) • **92**

Beaune Les Montrevenots 1988 • $37 • (05/15/91) • **88**

Bourgogne 1994: Crisp and mildly tannic, with an earthy, underbrush note that tops the fruit flavor. Ready to drink. • $16 • (11/15/96) • **80**

Bourgogne 1993: Nice concentration of ripe plum, cedar and earth flavors. Very compact and muscular, yet fruity. Try now. • $17 • (11/15/95) • **86**

Bourgogne 1990: A wine with lots of personality and charm. Tightly reined-in, but delivers pretty raspberry, wet earth and spice notes. Drinkable now. • $19 • (12/15/92) • **88**

Chassagne-Montrachet 1994: Rich and thick, like cream, with a sweet core of ripe fruit, spice and honey. Full bodied, harmonious and seductive. A pleasure to drink now. • $NA • (08/31/96) • **88**

Givry White 1996: A true *terroir* wine that you either love or hate. Balanced and distinctive, with earthy, lead pencil, matchstick, pear, citrus and pineapple notes. Medium-bodied, it shows good intensity of fruit and acidity. Try from 1999 through 2002. 300 cases made. • $21 • (05/31/98) • **86**

Meursault 1996: Seductive village Meursault, with wonderfully ripe fruit and a velvety texture. Full-bodied, beautifully balanced and vibrant, it offers lime, honey, mineral, pear and tropical flavors along with just the right amount of spice and toasty oak accents. Long, clean finish. Try around 2002. 625 cases made. • $39 • (05/31/98) • **93**

Montagny Premier Cru 1996: Ripe yet racy, this impressive, full-bodied wine delivers layers of dried fruit, lime, kiwi, mineral and pineapple flavors. The long, intense finish is just delicious. Fine winemaking here. Tempting now through 2005. 915 cases made. • $20 • (05/31/98) • **91**

Pommard Les Jarolières 1994: This shows pure cassis and toast flavors that manage to push through the firm chewy tannins. Has a green edge. Try in 1999. • $44 • (11/15/96) • **85**

Pommard Les Jarolières 1993: Very harmonious now with cherry, earth, berry and meat character. Medium-to-full body, fine tannins and a long finish. Better in 1999. • $50 • (11/15/95) • **90**

Pommard Les Jarolières 1992: Succulent and complex, with interesting twists and turns. Layers of smoke, violet, spice and blackberry-boysenberry notes in a ripe, lovely wine with a firm, almost tart finish. Drink now. • $50 • (12/15/94) • **89**

Pommard Les Jarolières 1991: Tough in texture, but the blackberry and black cherry flavors are concentrated and dense enough to remain focused and show through the chewy tannins on the finish. Hold now through 2000. • $46 Ⓐ • (01/31/94) • **87**

Pommard Les Jarolières 1990: An exotic wine that seduces you with its multidimensional violet, red berry and plum flavors. Made in a full-bodied style that ends with loads of firm but fine tannins. Drinkable now. 50 cases made. • $67 • (12/15/92) • **94**

Pommard Les Rugiens 1994: Lovely, with good concentration; it's fresh, grapey, offering zingy currant, wild berry flavors. Talented vinegrowing and winemaking here. Needs until after 1999. • $68 • (11/15/96) • **86**

Pommard Les Saussilles 1991: Firm and focused, offering pleasingly dense berry flavors shaded by anise notes. Echoes fruit and spice on the finish. Drinkable now. • $NA • (01/31/94) • **85**

Pommard Les Saussilles 1990: So silky it melts in your mouth. Bright and lively, echoing raspberry and vanilla notes and ending with a long, smooth finish. Drink now. • $48 • (12/15/92) • **92**

Pommard Les Saussilles 1988 • $47 • (05/15/91) • **77**

Puligny-Montrachet 1996: Nice quality for a village wine, despite a slight volatile acidity. Otherwise, it shows lots of ripe fruit, citrus laced with honey and various layers of spice. Full-bodied but also elegant; drink around 2003. 1,250 cases made. • $42 • (05/31/98) • **89**

Puligny-Montrachet 1995: An extraordinary village wine, just wonderful to taste, with laser-sharp flavors of lime, honey and mineral, vibrant and succulent texture and character, medium-to-full body, and a long, delicious finish. Excellent now through 2005. • $41 • (08/31/97) • **92**

Puligny-Montrachet 1994: Seductively ripe and honeyed, this sweet-tasting, medium-bodied Burgundy makes for attractive drinking now, offering pear, apple pie and cream character. Holds together nicely on the medium-long finish. • $37 • (05/31/96) • **86**

Puligny-Montrachet 1993: This has the classic creamy, buttery, pearlike aromas and flavors, backed by crisp acidity. Tasted twice with consistent notes. Drinkable now. • $36 • (05/15/95) • **85**

Puligny-Montrachet 1992: Full-flavored and full-bodied, a ripe Burgundy with butter, butterscotch, citrus and spice flavors; quite supple, but the backbone of acidity keeps it together. Drink on release. • $NA • (08/31/94) • **87**

Puligny-Montrachet Champ Canet 1996: Classy and refined, showing lovely mineral, vanilla bean and buttery, croissantlike flavors. Sweet-tasting and ripe, with wonderful pear and tropical character, a silky texture and a vibrant, clean finish. Too bad there's a slightly distracting butterscotch, caramel note. Try around 2000 to 2002. 300 cases made. • $62 • (05/31/98) • **88**

Puligny-Montrachet Champ Canet 1995: Sensational, with a clean, pure aromatic profile. It seems to have it all: ripe and thick texture, vibrant and lively character, tropical fruit, dried herbs, peach, apricot, citrus and toasty spice complexity. Full-bodied, this *premier cru*'s finish explodes with flavors but remains balanced and seductive. Brilliant winemaking. Drink now through 2010. • $58 • (08/31/97) • **95**

Puligny-Montrachet Champ Canet 1994: Very ripe and nearly off-dry, its sweet apricot, pear and excessive honey flavors stand out. Full in body and unctuous almost to a fault; be prepared for something different here. Drinkable now. • $47 • (05/31/96) • **84**

Puligny-Montrachet Champ Canet 1993: This is rich in flavor and full-bodied with good depth and concentration. The pear, vanilla and hazelnut notes are supported by lively acidity, and they linger on the finish. Tasted twice with consistent notes. • $46 • (05/15/95) • **88**

Puligny-Montrachet La Truffière 1996: Simply fantastic *premier cru.* Densely textured and full-bodied, it packs in the ripest, sweetest fruit imaginable, with wonderful mineral, vanilla bean, honey and lime. The finish is like biting into a perfect fruit on a hot summer day. Buy, buy, buy! Best from 2000 through 2010. 105 cases made. • $72 • (05/31/98) • **96**

Puligny-Montrachet La Truffière 1995: Brilliant winemaking. Rather crisp and lively, but with good density of fruit, this full-bodied wine coats the palate, showing dried herb, honey, green apple and subtle, toasty oak accents that linger on the beautifully balanced, refreshing finish. Drink now through 2003. • $74 • (05/31/97) • **95**

Puligny-Montrachet La Truffière 1993: Bright, fruity and straightforward, with flavors that remind us of pineapple and tangerine. Drink now while it's fresh. • $50 • (05/15/95) • **83**

Puligny-Montrachet Les Combettes 1996: Exciting *premier cru.* Ripe, sweet-tasting, fresh and lively, this lovely '96 seduces you with its tropical, pear, mineral, butter and subtle toasty oak flavors. The well-defined lime-lemon notes weave a pattern through this medium-bodied, mouthfilling wine. Delightful around 2000 to 2002. 225 cases made. • $72 • (05/31/98) • **94**

Puligny-Montrachet Les Combettes 1995: Fabulous. Ripe and rich, with honey, ripe pear, tropical fruit and toasty coconut complexity. Full-bodied, highly toasty, seductive and with a supple but long finish. Drink now through 2005. • $75 • (08/31/97) • **94**

Puligny-Montrachet Les Combettes 1994: Amazing balance and concentration for a '94, showing both finesse and power, beckoning you back for another sip. Ripe-tasting, honey- and mineral-scented, lemon-spiked nectar. Shows a deft hand at keeping things on track from start to finish. Try now. • $62 • (05/31/96) • **93**

Puligny-Montrachet Les Combettes 1993: Fresh and lively honey, lemon and spice character. Medium in body and super clean; a lovely mineral, pear finish. • $54 • (05/15/95) • **86**

Puligny-Montrachet Les Folatières 1996: Striking silkiness and exciting ripe fruit make this a most delightful, harmonious and balanced '96 white Burgundy. Packed with lime, pear, vanilla, spice, pineapple and toasty coconut, this full-bodied wine is worth hunting down and stashing away through 2005. 275 cases made. • $56 • (05/31/98) • **93**

Puligny-Montrachet Les Folatières 1994: A Burgundy inspired by Sauternes, sporting loads of honey, apricot and apple. No subtlety here, but we love this full-bodied, rich and ripe white. Drinkable now or hold until 1999. • $51 • (05/31/96) • **90**

Puligny-Montrachet Les Pucelles 1996: Marvelous *premier cru.* Packed with fruit, acidity and judiciously toasty oak, this crafty wine is sensual and full-bodied, delivering layers of pear, floral, lime, mineral and spice notes in an oh-so-silky package. Difficult to ask for much more than this in a young Chardonnay. Very long, vibrant and chewy finish. Try after 2005. 125 cases made. • $62 • (05/31/98) • **94**

Puligny-Montrachet Les Pucelles 1994: Total seduction. A low-acidity, soft, supple and very honeyed *premier cru*, featuring fig, date, apricot and ripe pear flavors. Could use some more intensity, but what a fun, unctuous, full-bodied Chardonnay to drink now—and fast. • $58 • (05/31/96) • **90**

Puligny-Montrachet Les Referts 1996: Sensational *premier cru.* Thick, ripe and rich, full-bodied yet racy, it's still closed and backward on the nose, but the opulent texture envelops the palate with flavors ranging from butter to pie crust, spicy coconut, dried pineapple, pear tart and lemon. Great winemaking here. Best from 2000 through 2007. 415 cases made. • $62 • (05/31/98) • **95**

Puligny-Montrachet Les Referts 1995: Fresh, like lemonade, showing impressively clean and pure flavors, yet nicely ripe and opulent, too, this is elegant, but with some intense spice, green and dried fruit notes. The long finish is slightly toasty. Try now through 2005. • $58 • (05/31/97) • **92**

Key: SS—Spectator Selection CS—Cellar Selection HR—Highly Recommended BB—Best Buy $NA—Price not available Ⓐ—Auction Price (BT)—Barrel Tasting
Dates in parentheses indicate the issues in which the ratings were published.

Puligny-Montrachet Les Referts 1994: Sweet, honey-spiked white with apricot and peach character. Medium-to-full in body, it's delicious to drink now; may not have much staying power. • $47 • (05/31/96) • **87**

Puligny-Montrachet Les Referts 1993: A subtle, well-balanced white that keeps you coming back for more. Lightly fruity aromas lead to fresh and full fruit flavors accented by gorgeous butter and nutmeg on the finish. It's crisp and firm in texture. • $46 • (05/15/95) • **87**

Puligny-Montrachet Les Referts 1992: Ripe, round and generous, with oodles of pear, pineapple and lemon flavor, a smooth, creamy texture and a lingering, fruity finish. Very pure and focused, almost sweet, but with enough acidity to keep it fresh. Drinkable now. • $NA • (08/31/94) • **91**

Rully Grésigny White 1996: Wonderful rully. Lush and ripe, this full-bodied Chardonnay has plenty of acidity, fruit, oak and structure. Supple and harmonious in texture, with a distinctive smoky, woody, minerally complexity on the midpalate. Long finish. Attractive now but should age well through 2002. 750 cases made. • $21 • (05/31/98) • **90**

Volnay 1995: This deep-colored, grapey, cassis-driven red Burgundy has woody, hard tannins that lack finesse. Tough, oaky and medium-bodied, it seems overextracted. Try after 1999. • $32 • (01/31/98) • **83**

Volnay 1994: Chewy, coarse tannins wrap around the modest cherry candy flavors, but it has ripe fruit flavors in the middle that should save the day. • $27 • (11/15/96) • **80**

Volnay 1993: Amazing for a village wine. Unbelievable. Essence of wild raspberries added to a hint of earth. Full in body and lots of tannins, which the ripe fruit seems to soften somewhat. Drink now. 550 cases made. • $30 • (11/15/95) • **93**

Volnay 1992: Crisp and light, with enough ripe berry flavors to get past the firm tannins. Drinkable now. • $29 • (12/15/94) • **83**

Volnay 1991: A layer of coarse tannins takes away from the otherwise ripe, sweet fruit flavors. Light in structure, finishing with a bitter almond edge. Drinkable now. • $NA • (01/31/94) • **80**

Volnay 1990: Amazingly good for a village wine. Full-bodied, showing a beautiful combination of fruit and new wood nuances and tons of plum, cherry and earth flavors. Firm, elegant tannins play a nice supporting role to the long, violet-scented, refined finish. Drinkable now. 150 cases made. • $40 • (12/15/92) • **92**

Volnay Carelle Sous La Chapelle 1995: The first bottle was dominated by volatile acidity; the second sample was corky. • $47 • (01/31/98) • **59**

Volnay Carelle Sous La Chapelle 1994: Ripe, rich and lovely. A full-bodied, flavorful wine with plenty of cassis, black cherry and wet earth aromas and flavors. Sweet and ripe tasting. Drinkable now. • $39 • (11/15/96) • **88**

Volnay Carelle Sous La Chapelle 1993: Very fruity, showing good structure for medium-term aging. Attractive aromas of plums and melons are followed by medium body and tannin and a light finish. Better in 1999. • $42 • (11/15/95) • **89**

Volnay Carelle Sous La Chapelle 1992: Impressive structure for this vintage. Firm, youthful and vibrant, packed with ripe, sweet blackberry, boysenberry and violet flavors that lead to a tannic finish. Drinkable now. • $42 • (12/15/94) • **88**

Volnay Le Ronceret 1991: A solid beam of fresh currant and blackberry aromas and flavors shines through a light veil of fine tannins. Firm, focused, elegant and true to form. Drinkable now. • $NA • (01/31/94) • **86**

Volnay Pitures 1995: A deep-colored red, with an earth and nice red berry character. Shows some finesse despite the burly tannins, but it's dominated by a slightly dry finish. May improve by 1999. • $47 • (01/31/98) • **84**

Volnay Pitures 1994: Ripe, rich and flavorful. Full-bodied, it bursts with toasty oak, black cherry, anise, and dried herb flavors. Lots of hard tannins that need until at least 1999, and hope the fruit holds out. • $39 • (11/15/96) • **86**

Volnay Pitures 1993: Rich, ripe and lovely; quite solid, offering loads of well-defined red berry, plum and wet earth character and massive, supple tannins. Hold until at least 2000. • $42 • (11/15/95) • **92**

Volnay Pitures 1992: Crisp and focused, showing very pretty blackberry and floral aromas and flavors that echo nicely on the finish. • $NA • (12/15/94) • **85**

Volnay Pitures 1991: Crisp and lively, offering cedary currant flavors. Finishes chewy and a bit tannic. Try now. • $37 Ⓐ • (01/31/94) • **80**

Volnay Pitures 1990: Simply terrific, with toasty, smoky black cherry and earth aromas and flavors. Tastes almost sweet and offers almost everything you could want. Drink now. 75 cases made. • $55 • (12/15/92) • **94**

BOILLOT, LUCIEN

Bourgogne 1990: Focused and graceful, with fine violet, raspberry and cherry notes and even finer tannins. Drink now. 600 cases made. • $14 • (12/15/92) • **86**

Gevrey-Chambertin Cherbaudes 1994: Light, lean and diluted, showing some strawberry flavors. • $38 • (11/15/96) • **71**

Gevrey-Chambertin Cherbaudes 1993: Wonderful finesse and loads of dried cherry character here. Medium body, fine tannins and crisp acidity. Sweet fruit on the finish. Drink in 1999. • $40 • (11/15/95) • **88**

Gevrey-Chambertin Cherbaudes 1991: A sharp beam of raspberry and floral flavors shines through this light, lean wine. Crisply tannic. Drinkable now. • $34 Ⓐ • (01/31/94) • **82**

Gevrey-Chambertin Cherbaudes 1990: A firm wine, with pretty plum, cherry and herb flavors, medium body and a focused finish. Drinkable now. 175 cases made. • $35 • (12/15/92) • **85**

Gevrey-Chambertin Cherbaudes 1987 • $25 • (05/31/90) • **85**

Gevrey-Chambertin Les Corbeaux 1994: Firm in texture and bright with currant and berry flavors that ride smoothly over the fine-grained tannins. Finish is relatively light and pleasant. Drinkable now. • $35 • (11/15/96) • **82**

Gevrey-Chambertin Les Corbeaux 1993: Unusually full-bodied for this group, dark-colored with massive tannins and sensational currant, black cherry and wild berry flavors. Long, chewy finish. Definitely needs until after 2000. • $40 • (11/15/95) • **87**

Gevrey-Chambertin Les Corbeaux 1990: Vivid in color and flavor, this sharp-edged wine delivers focused raspberry, cherry, herb and earth characteristics and fresh acidity. Drinkable now. 156 cases made. • $33 • (12/15/92) • **88**

Nuits-St.-Georges Les Pruliers 1994: Under the firm tannins lurk some pretty currant, pepper and anise flavors, which extend into a spicy finish. Try in 1999. • $38 • (11/15/96) • **87**

Nuits-St.-Georges Les Pruliers 1993: Straightforward plum and cherry flavors, medium body and medium tannins. Try in 1999. • $40 • (11/15/95) • **85**

Nuits-St.-Georges Les Pruliers 1991: Pleasant strawberry and cherry flavors make this firm, mildly chewy wine pleasant and appealing. Finishes harmoniously. Drinkable now. • $36 Ⓐ • (01/31/94) • **83**

Nuits-St.-Georges Les Pruliers 1987 • $25 • (07/15/90) • **88**

Pommard Les Croix Noires 1991: Light and simple. The strawberry aromas have appeal, but the watery flavors fade quickly into astringency. • $30 Ⓐ • (01/31/94) • **75**

Pommard Les Fremiers 1994: A tender wine, supple and lush, of medium body, with a ripe core of fruit flavor. Attractive cherry, wild berry, rosemary character and a lovely finish. Drinkable now. • $35 • (11/15/96) • **85**

Pommard Les Fremiers 1993: Marvelous Pommard, featuring a nice concentration of clean, pure, beautiful red berry flavor that cascades on the palate. A bit of chocolate and mocha on the finish. Great now, but try after 2000. • $38 • (11/15/95) • **91**

Volnay Les Angles 1994: Light, almost watery, though a chocolate accent adds some richness to the narrow berry flavors. • $34 • (11/15/96) • **81**

Volnay Les Angles 1991: Light in color and lean; a layer of tannin allows only a glimpse of the cedary berry character underneath. Try now, but it will always be delicate. • $30 Ⓐ • (01/31/94) • **80**

Volnay Les Angles 1990: Layered with cherry, tobacco, plum and chestnut flavors, this well-crafted red is no blockbuster, but is quite elegant and refined, with a medium-long finish. Drinkable now. 600 cases made. • $32 • (12/15/92) • **87**

Volnay Les Angles 1985 • $33 • (07/15/88) • **86**

Volnay Les Brouillards 1993: Aromatic but could use a little more on the palate. Attractive plum, fruit, vanilla and leaf aromas and flavors, medium body and tannins and a short finish. Better in 1999. • $37 • (11/15/95) • **87**

Volnay Les Brouillards 1991: Crisp, light and modest in flavor. Raspberry and strawberry notes lurk under fine tannins. Drinkable now. • $28 Ⓐ • (01/31/94) • **81**

Volnay Les Brouillards 1990: Fun and interesting. Tastes like a bowl of raspberries, with a captivating texture and a firm, appealing finish. Drinkable now. 375 cases made. • $32 • (12/15/92) • **90**

Volnay Les Caillerets 1994: Fairly tannic and chewy considering the modest level of strawberry and floral flavors. • $35 • (11/15/96) • **79**

Volnay Les Caillerets 1993: Lots going on here, offering intense flavors of ripe raspberries and sliced plums. Medium-bodied with a solid core of fruit, medium-to-full tannins and a velvety texture. Try in 2000. • $38 • (11/15/95) • **91**

BOILLOT, PIERRE

Volnay-Santenots 1988 • $37 • (08/31/90) • **85**

Volnay-Santenots 1987 • $37 • (06/15/90) • **86**

BOIS DAUPHIN, DOMAINE DU

Châteauneuf-du-Pape Cuvée de Boisdauphin 1990: Firm and focused, with generous black cherry, blackberry and toast aromas and flavors and hints of chocolate on the smooth finish. Drinkable now. • $19 • (04/15/93) • **87**

BOIS DE LA GARDE, CHÂTEAU DU

Côtes du Rhône 1995: Lacks focus, with a cardboard edge to the berry aromas and stewed fruit flavors. Dry tannins on the finish. Drink now. 33,000 cases made. • $9 • (05/15/98) • **78**

BOISSAN, DOMAINE DE

Côtes du Rhône 1995: Earthy, lean and disappointing. Stewed flavors are unattractive. • $NA • (10/15/97) • **70**

Côtes du Rhône Clos de Fontvive Réserve 1994: Herbal and earthy notes dominate this light, dry red. There's not much flesh or fruit left, so drink up. • $NA • (10/15/97) • **74**

Côtes du Ventoux Le Montsegur Cuvée Speciale 1995: A soft, fruity red, this shows round berry flavors with hints of herbs and coffee. Has some grip, and will match well with simple, grilled foods. • $NA • (10/15/97) • **83**

Gigondas Vieilles Vignes 1995: Disappointing, with stewed tomato, herbal, bell pepper notes. Lean. • $NA • (10/15/97) • **75**

Vacqueyras 1995: Has some decent cherry notes, but it's lean and slightly metallic. One wishes for more concentration. Ends with some dilution. • $NA • (10/15/97) • **76**

BOISSET, CHÂTEAU

Bordeaux La Chapelle 1997: Stemmy, with some berry character, but light overall. • $NA • (06/15/98) (BT) • **75-79**

Bordeaux La Chapelle 1996: Weedy and very light, with silky tannins but not much else. • $16 • (06/15/98) (BT) • **75-79**

BOISSET, JEAN-CLAUDE

Beaujolais 1993 • $6 • (06/30/94) • **76**

Beaujolais-Villages 1993 • $7 • (06/30/94) • **83**

Bourgogne Confèrie des Chevaliers du Tastevin 1989 • $7 • (06/15/92) • **76**

Bourgogne Pinot Noir 1993: Very light. Some OK red berry and earth character, but it's a touch diluted and one-dimensional, adding an astringent finish. • $NA • (11/15/95) • **74**

Bourgogne Pinot Noir Charles de France 1993: Shows only modest cherry, raspberry and strawberry notes, light body and color and delicate finish. Drinkable now. • $NA • (11/15/95) • **75**

Bourgogne Tastevinage 1988 • $11 • (08/31/91) • **72**

Brouilly 1993 • $9 • (06/30/94) • **77**

Cabernet Sauvignon Vin de Pays d'Oc 1996: Has deep color, but the light texture and flavors make this a simple Cabernet. Herbal, earthy character, with a short finish. Drink now. 30,000 cases made. • $7 • (12/15/97) • **79**

Cabernet Sauvignon Vin de Pays d'Oc 1994 • $6 • (10/31/95) BB • **85**

Chablis 1994 • $14 • (06/30/95) • **82**

Chardonnay Bourgogne Charles de France 1993: A bit lean and green, yet showing pleasant mineral, chalk, pear and fig notes. It delivers good flavor intensity, but seems somewhat muted on the finish. • $10 • (08/31/95) • **81**

Chardonnay Bourgogne Charles de France 1992: Simple, refreshing, only a candied edge detracting from the lemony pear and spice flavors. Drink soon. 20,000 cases made. • $8 • (02/28/94) • **78**

Chardonnay Vin de Pays d'Oc 1996: A good, straightforward Chardonnay offering light tropical fruit flavors and a smooth texture. 30,000 cases made. • $7 • (12/15/97) • **82**

Chardonnay Vin de Pays d'Oc 1994 • $6 • (06/30/95) • **84**

Charmes-Chambertin 1993: Light and showing a sweet core of raspberry and strawberry notes, but it's somewhat diluted. Drink on release. 275 cases made. • $56 • (11/15/95) • **77**

Chassagne-Montrachet 1993: Some vanilla and dried apricot character but a diluted and light finish. Try now. 1,000 cases made. • $16 • (05/15/95) • **80**

Chassagne-Montrachet 1992: Lean and narrow with a musty, oaky edge that misses the mark. 5,000 cases made. • $17 • (02/28/94) • **73**

Chassagne-Montrachet Red 1993: Pleasant but light; deceptively seductive raspberry, cherry and wild berry flavors. Delicate texture, but the tannins are there to keep it going. 1,960 cases made. • $18 • (11/15/95) • **82**

Châteauneuf-du-Pape 1986 • $12 • (11/30/88) • **80**

Clos de Vougeot 1993: A rather light Pinot, offering some decent red berry flavor and dry, tannic structure. Try now. • $46 • (11/15/95) • **79**
Côte de Beaune-Villages 1982 • $5 • (07/01/85) BB • **86**
Côte de Nuits-Villages 1983 • $13 • (02/01/86) • **78**
Côtes du Ventoux 1988 • $4 • (10/15/90) • **75**
Gevrey-Chambertin 1993: Rather light and weedy, offering some fruit but also a metallic edge. Medium-to-light body and watery finish. 260 cases made. • $16 • (11/15/95) • **76**
Gevrey-Chambertin 1991: Displays nice cherry and anise aromas and flavors in a light, simple, chewy style. Drinkable now. • $NA • (01/31/94) • **82**
Gevrey-Chambertin 1990: A generously flavored Burgundy that's already losing its rough edges and getting ready to drink. It has earthy, plummy, mineral-like flavors, moderate tannins and a touch of astringency on the finish. • $17 • (01/01/94) • **82**
Gevrey-Chambertin 1982 • $9 • (06/01/85) • **74**
Mâcon Blanc-Villages 1994: Lavishly oaked, standing out with its full, ripe, sweet-tasting vanilla and toast notes. The wood may get tiring; the finish is slightly astringent. 10,000 cases made. • $8 • (08/31/95) • **80**
Mâcon Blanc-Villages 1993: This light, slightly fizzy wine with crisp acidity offers simple fruit cocktail flavors. Good for spritzers. • $6 • (01/01/94) • **77**
Merlot Vin de Pays d'Oc 1996: An interesting French red that goes for gusto, this wine has the light texture of a Beaujolais, but the deep color and smoky, dusky flavors of Merlot. A solid value for drinking now. 30,000 cases made. • $7 • (12/15/97) BB • **84**
Merlot Vin de Pays d'Oc 1994 • $6 • (10/31/95) • **75**
Meursault 1993: A bit one-dimensional, but it has some nice texture and a mineral note accompanying leaner citrusy, green and herbal flavors. Drink now. 3,500 cases made. • $16 • (05/15/95) • **81**
Meursault 1992: Ripe fruit in the aromas and flavors make this a generous, enjoyable, reasonably priced Meursault. Smells like pineapple and honey, feels smooth on the palate and leaves a lingering vanilla and honey finish. 2,000 cases made. • $15 • (05/31/94) • **87**
Morgon 1993 • $9 • (06/30/94) • **80**
Nuits-St.-Georges 1985 • $25 • (04/30/88) • **79**
Pinot Noir Bourgogne de Bourgogne 1992: A nicely balanced, modest style of Burgundy that's fruity and spicy in aroma, firm in texture and offers enough cherry and strawberry flavors. If only it didn't turn stemmy and murky on the finish. 1,500 cases made. • $9 • (11/30/94) • **82**
Pommard 1985 • $28 • (04/30/88) • **78**
Pommard Les Rugiens 1985 • $33 • (03/15/88) • **76**
Pouilly-Fuissé 1994: Earth, pear and hard-candy flavors keep this off-balance; though not flawed, it lacks harmony and varietal character. 6,500 cases made. • $14 • (06/30/95) • **75**
Pouilly-Fuissé 1993: There's a nice buttery aroma, but the flavors are lean and a bit diluted, finishing with an herbal tang. It's well-crafted, but lacks fruit. • $13 • (01/01/95) • **79**
Puligny-Montrachet 1993: A straightforward white; quite light, diluted and short. 450 cases made. • $18 • (05/15/95) • **74**
Puligny-Montrachet 1992: Simple and light, showing modest, stale fruit flavors. Drinkable now. • $25 • (08/31/94) • **78**
Rully Red 1992: This wine fails to balance its intensely ripe fruit and buttery oak flavors, and it turns coarse and tart on the finish. A top-heavy, simple wine that lacks an appealing core of flavors. • $8 • (01/01/94) • **76**
Rully White 1993: Clean and crisp, straightforward and easy to drink, presenting fresh apple and vanilla flavors and a slight metallic note. 3,500 cases made. • $11 • (06/30/95) • **81**
Rully White 1992: A pleasing, well-rounded Chardonnay from Burgundy, with toasty aromas and solid flavors of pear and nutmeg. Lively and well balanced through the lingering finish. 3,000 cases made. • $9 • (02/28/95) BB • **86**
Sauvignon Blanc Vin de Pays d'Oc 1996: A refreshing wine with pleasant citrus flavors that turn tart on the finish. 5,000 cases made. • $7 • (12/31/97) • **82**
Savigny-lès-Beaune 1993: Delicate and light-bodied, showing some pretty earth and sweet, ripe flavors and a slightly drying finish. Try in 1999. 4,600 cases made. • $12 • (11/15/95) • **82**
Syrah Vin de Pays d'Oc 1996: This robust Syrah has deep color and rich fruit aromas, but turns lean on the palate and dry on the finish. Fairly tannic. Drink now. 10,000 cases made. • $7 • (12/15/97) • **79**
Syrah Vin de Pays d'Oc 1994 • $6 • (10/31/95) • **80**

Key: SS—Spectator Selection CS—Cellar Selection HR—Highly Recommended BB—Best Buy $NA—Price not available Ⓐ—Auction Price (BT)—Barrel Tasting
Dates in parentheses indicate the issues in which the ratings were published.

Syrah Vin de Pays d'Oc 1993 • $6 • (02/28/95) • **77**
Viognier Vin de Pays d'Oc 1996: A lean, very dry white, with floral and herbal flavors. Simple and austere. 5,000 cases made. • $9 • (12/15/97) • **78**
Volnay Clos des Chênes 1985 • $28 • (04/15/88) • **86**

BOISSON, J.P.

Châteauneuf-du-Pape Domaine de Père Caboche 1994: This wine offers intensity without finesse, showing jammy cherry and cooked fruit flavors, thick tannins and a muddy finish. A slightly metallic note lingers on the finish. • $15 • (12/15/96) • **78**
Châteauneuf-du-Pape Elisabeth Chambellan Vieilles Vignes 1994: Firm tannins and a light body combine to make a lean wine, with light cherry and vanilla flavors that forge through the astringency. It's fresh and straightforward, but slightly clumsy. • $20 • (12/15/96) • **83**

BOIZEL

Brut Champagne 1988: This has an abundance of sliced apple character, lively acidity, and foam, but is too simple to be rated higher. Drink now. • $17 • (12/31/93) • **85**
Brut Champagne Joyau de France 1985: Gentle and delicious with a fine mousse and deep ripe apple and melon flavors. Crisp acidity, yet round and caressing. Drink now. • $26 • (12/31/93) • **89**

BOLLINGER

Brut Blanc de Noirs Champagne Vieilles Vignes Françaises 1989: A broadly flavored, full-bodied Champagne that's rich with buttery, appley, slightly nutty notes and a hint of cherry flavor. A real extrovert that tastes mature now. • $160 • (11/15/96) • **88**
Brut Blanc de Noirs Champagne Vieilles Vignes Françaises 1986: Tastes good but older than it is, showing slightly baked aromas, caramel and pineapple flavors and exuberant effervescence. May not be for everyone, but those who favor mature Champagne will love this. • $219 • (12/31/95) • **86**
Brut Champagne Grande Année 1989: Dry, distinctive and debonair, this outstanding Champagne is marked by toasty, slightly nutty, intriguing aromas and subtle, layered flavors of pear, honey and nutmeg. A soft but lively mousse and lingering finish add to its appeal. Even better than last year. Drink now through 2002. • $70 • (12/31/97) • **93**
Brut Champagne Grande Année 1988: A rich, mature, full-bodied, flavorful bubbly that has oodles of nutty, honeylike flavors, a broad, smooth texture and a spicy, buttery finish. Combines power and subtlety for a very attractive taste experience. Even better than in an earlier tasting. Try now. 16,667 cases made. • $60 • (07/31/96) CS • **93**
Brut Champagne Grande Année 1985: Classically styled; one of the all-time greats in standard vintage Champagne. Firm yet elegant, with plenty of smoke, apple and toast character, a fine, silky texture and great acidity. Drinkable now. Tasted three times; first two bottles were less good. 15,000 cases made. • $60 • (12/31/93) • **94**
Brut Champagne Grande Année 1983: Floral and grapefruit aromas and flavors make this crisp, medium-bodied wine lively and agreeable, but it's simple. A touch of ginger on the finish is especially appealing. • $43 • (12/31/89) • **86**
Brut Champagne Grande Année 1982: Rich, toasty and very assertive, high in extract and intensity with a heavy toasty flavor that complements the pear and cherry flavors. Smoky flavors carry the finish. It's a rich style that may be too powerful for some. • $30 • (07/15/88) • **93**
Brut Champagne Special Cuvée NV: A full-flavored, robust and mature style of Champagne that blends nutty, toasty aromas with rich honey and nut flavors. Shows fine depth, a great texture and a lingering finish. • $30 Ⓐ • (11/15/97) • **89**
Brut Rosé Champagne 1988: An elegant, dry rosé with sophisticated, complex flavors and a velvety texture that draws you back for another sip. The subtle, layered flavors of cherry, ginger, mineral and vanilla linger on the finish. Drink now through 2000. • $60 • (12/31/97) • **92**
Brut Rosé Champagne 1985: A boldly flavored, very mature-tasting bubbly with extravagant aromas, nutty flavors, a tart impression and a bit of astringency in the texture. Distinctive, but not for everyone. • $72 • (07/31/96) • **86**
Brut Rosé Champagne Grande Année 1985: Pale copper in color and delicate through and through, with modest cherry and bread dough aromas and flavors. Perhaps a bit metallic on the finish, but it would be enjoyable with food that isn't too rich. Drinkable now. • $60 • (11/15/91) • **85**

Brut Rosé Champagne Grande Année 1983: Rich, toasty and round, with a gentle structure, smooth texture, and subtle flavors of strawberry, smoke and a touch of cherry. A nip of crisp lime on the finish keeps it lively. • $50 • (12/31/89) • **89**

Brut Rosé Champagne Grande Année 1982: Toasty with cherry and spicy flavors but it lacks depth and finesse and the flavors lack persistence and depth. Still it's perfectly drinkable, finishing with a slightly metallic flavor. • $35 • (07/15/88) • **80**

Brut Rosé Champagne Grande Année 1979 • $40 • (12/16/85) • **94**

Extra Brut Champagne R.D. 1985: Full of character and complexity. A very dry, mature and intricate Champagne with earthy aromas, mushroom and smoke flavors and a tangy but lingering finish. Drink now through 1999. • $135 • (12/31/97) • **92**

Extra Brut Champagne R.D. 1982: Roasted almond and toast aromas turn tight and austere on the palate, where the mature grapefruit and citrus flavors turn to hints of sherry. Drink up. Tasted three times, with consistent notes. • $100 • (11/15/91) • **87**

Extra Brut Champagne R.D. 1979 • $79 • (12/31/89) • **94**

Extra Brut Champagne R.D. 1976 • $59 • (04/15/88) • **88**

Extra Brut Champagne R.D. 1975 • $64 • (05/16/86) • **89**

BONALGUE, CHÂTEAU

Pomerol 1994: Powerful toast and coffee aromas and flavors are evidence of new oak, but the tannins don't have enough fruit behind them. Try now. • $28 • (12/15/95) • **80**

Pomerol 1993: The deft combination of oak and fruit are appealing. Coffee flavors mingle with blackberry, floral and light truffle notes. Generous but not overly tannic. • $27 • (12/15/95) • **86**

BONGRAN, DOMAINE DE LA

Mâcon-Clessé Quintaine Cuvée Tradition 1996: Just lovely; packed with honey, lemon and lime. Full-bodied and ripe, it tastes slightly off-dry but remains deliciously balanced. Try with blue cheese, foie gras or something decadent. Very well-made, and silky-smooth on the clean finish. Drink now. 5,000 cases made. • $25 • (05/31/98) • **90**

Mâcon-Clessé Quintaine Cuvée Tradition 1995: Extraordinary winemaking. Off-dry, full-bodied, rich and ripe, this late-harvest Chardonnay is super-balanced and very flavorful. Brilliantly elegant aromas—reserved, and hinting of earth, white truffle and honey—follow through on the palate, which picks up toasty oak, dried fig, botrytislike peach and spice flavors. Incredibly complex. Long, clean finish. Drink on its own or with foie gras, a classic match, now and through 2002. 2,500 cases made. • $25 • (05/31/98) • **94**

BONHOMME, CHÂTEAU DE

Minervois 1991 • $8 • (03/15/94) • **83**

BONNAIRE

Brut Blanc de Blancs Champagne Cramant 1990: A very attractive Champagne with a rich, subtly layered blend of buttery, fruity flavors, a plush but bracing texture and a lingering finish. Drink now through 2000. • $40 • (12/31/97) • **90**

Brut Blanc de Blancs Champagne Cramant 1985: Attractive in a fresh, pleasant style. Tastes fruity and delicate, with direct flavors of pear and lemon. • $42 • (12/31/89) • **83**

Brut Blanc de Blancs Champagne Cramant 1983: Creamy and well-balanced with all the rough edges smoothed off. • $38 • (02/29/88) • **87**

Brut Blanc de Blancs Champagne Cramant 1979 • $40 • (05/31/87) • **86**

Brut Blanc de Blancs Champagne Special Club 1989: Luscious. Like a really nice, barrel-fermented Chardonnay with bubbles. Has rich and appealing pear and pineapple flavors and a soft texture. Drink now through 1999. • $48 • (12/31/97) • **90**

BONNAT, CHÂTEAU LE

Graves 1995: Pretty, medium- to full-bodied '95, showing a luscious red berry character with complex spice and oak flavors. You wish for a bit more complexity in the midpalate and length on the finish. • $NA • (05/15/96) (BT) • **80-84**

Graves 1989 • $18 • (04/30/92) • **81**

Graves 1988 • $18 • (12/31/90) • **87**

Graves 1987 • $12 • (04/15/90) • **83**

Graves White 1988 • $17 • (03/31/90) • **84**

BONNEAU DU MARTRAY

Corton 1995: Lovely aromas and flavors of pure, spicy cherries continue through the lingering finish. Tannins are ripe on the finish, and will need time to resolve. Try in 1999. 330 cases made. • $60 • (11/15/97) • **87**

Corton 1994: Ripe and harmonious, with sweet plum and wet earth aromas and flavors that pick up a spice note on the focused finished. Tannins are a bit tough, but should keep this developing well past 2000. • $55 • (11/15/96) • **89**

Corton 1993: Solid Corton offering lovely plum and red berry flavors and a hint of oak, medium body, firm tannins and a long, fresh finish. Better in 2000. • $45 • (11/15/95) • **88**

Corton 1985 • $62 • (10/15/88) • **91**

Corton-Charlemagne 1995: Delicious and superbly balanced, with ripe tropical fruit, spice and oak accents supported by a solid frame. The citrus flavors give this full-bodied wine zest, but it's still big and rich. Just wonderful to drink now through 2005. 4,000 cases made. • $70 • (08/31/97) • **93**

Corton-Charlemagne 1994: All-around finesse. Medium-bodied, with mineral, citrus and good fruit complexity. Lovely, balanced and refined on the finish. Try around 2000. 4,000 cases made. • $55 • (08/31/96) CS • **91**

Corton-Charlemagne 1993: Firm and elegant, with a solid, racy structure. Enticing smoke, spice, mineral and pear flavors turn to beautiful cream and mineral on the finish. 4,041 cases made. • $60 • (08/31/95) • **88**

Corton-Charlemagne 1992: Lush, soft and inviting; a generous, ready-to-drink Corton that tastes like honey, pear and apricot; has an attractive, clean finish laced with moderate lime flavors. Drinkable now. Tasted twice. 3,400 cases made. • $44 Ⓐ • (08/31/94) • **90**

BONNET, CHÂTEAU | BORDEAUX

Bordeaux 1997: Silky and fruity, with spice and cherry character, decent tannins and a light, fruity finish. Good, but needs a bit more fruit. • $NA • (06/15/98) (BT) • **80-84**

Bordeaux 1996: A black wine with a very grapey nose, but the palate is not as solid as you might think. Medium-bodied, with moderate, velvety tannins and a medium finish. Clever winemaking. Always a good value. • $7 • (06/15/98) (BT) • **85-89**

Bordeaux 1995: Firm and fruity. Dried cherry and floral aromas, with hints of vanilla and milk chocolate. Medium- to full-bodied, with firm tannins and a medium, silky finish. Best after this year. • $15 • (01/31/98) • **87**

Bordeaux 1994: Gamy and smoky aromas give way to ripe plum flavors in this firm, solid red. Try now. • $8 • (07/31/96) • **83**

Bordeaux Réserve 1996: Slightly linear and one-dimensional. Medium-bodied, with chewy tannins and a short finish. Better than the '95. • $NA • (01/01/97) (BT) • **80-84**

Bordeaux Réserve 1995: Lovely cherry, cassis and vanilla aromas and flavors. Medium body, with medium tannins. Delicious. Better than previous tasting. • $15 • (01/01/97) (BT) • **85-89**

Bordeaux Réserve 1994: Big and burly, with currant and berry aromas and flavors and generous, green herb accents. Full-bodied and tannic. Slightly dry finish. May be better in 1999. • $11 • (01/31/97) • **80**

Bordeaux Réserve 1993: Lovely, balanced plum, black cherry and vanilla aromas and flavors, medium body, fine tannins and a fresh finish. Try now. • $10 • (01/31/96) • **82**

Entre-Deux-Mers 1995: A fresh wine, offering grapefruit and apple with fresh, clean acidity. Hints of new wood. Medium-bodied, with a medium aftertaste. Drink now. • $10 • (04/30/98) • **85**

Entre-Deux-Mers 1994 • $8 • (03/31/96) • **84**

Entre-Deux-Mers 1993 • $10 • (05/31/95) • **85**

Graves 1985 • $5 • (04/15/88) BB • **84**

BONNET, CHÂTEAU | LANGUEDOC

Minervois 1995: A good, quaffable wine with appealing mineral, smoke and berry flavors. This is a nice introduction to Minervois. 1,650 cases made. • $7 • (03/31/98) • **84**

BONNIGAL, M.

Touraine Domaine la Prevote Sauvignon de Touraine 1993 • $7 • (10/31/94) • **83**

BON-PASTEUR, CHÂTEAU LE

Pomerol 1997: Interesting berry and mineral aromas. Medium-bodied, with velvety tannins but a watery finish. Shame. • $NA • (06/15/98) (BT) • **80-84**

Pomerol 1996: Chunky red, with firm tannins and a velvety texture. A bit tough, but it's got backbone with plenty of fruit behind it. Serious '96 for Pomerol. Better than last year. • $40 • (06/15/98) (BT) • **90-94**

Pomerol 1995: A bit rustic but very rich on the palate, with good doses of black cherry and dark chocolate. Medium- to full-bodied, with velvety tannins and a toasty oak and fruity aftertaste. Better after 1999. 3,500 cases made. • $38 • (01/31/98) • **90**

Pomerol 1994: A restrained, rather delicate Bon-Pasteur with attractive cherry and wet earth character and a fruity, fine palate. Medium body and tannins. Drink now or hold. 3,000 cases made. • $38 • (01/31/97) • **85**

Pomerol 1993: Elegant, enticing, subtle berry and dark chocolate aromas and flavors. Medium in body, soft tannins and a fresh, fruity finish. Drinkable now. 3,333 cases made. • $32 • (01/31/96) • **87**

Pomerol 1992: Pleasant, delicate vanilla, cherry and berry aromas and flavors, light body, silky tannins and a light finish. Drinkable now. • $21 • (04/15/95) • **81**

Pomerol 1990: Gorgeous; keeps you coming back for more. Has wonderful milk chocolate, roasted oak and fruit aromas and flavors and plenty of silky tannins. Drink now. 3,000 cases made. • $43 • (03/31/93) • **93**

Pomerol 1989 • $37 Ⓐ • (04/30/92) • **88**
Pomerol 1988 • $43 Ⓐ • (02/28/91) • **85**
Pomerol 1987 • $22 • (05/15/90) • **81**
Pomerol 1986 • $46 Ⓐ • (06/15/89) • **92**
Pomerol 1985 • $46 Ⓐ • (05/15/88) • **92**
Pomerol 1984 • $13 • (06/15/87) • **86**
Pomerol 1983 • $30 Ⓐ • (06/16/86) • **86**
Pomerol 1982 • $62 Ⓐ • (08/31/92) • **94**
Pomerol 1979 • $NA • (10/15/89) • **91**

BORD, CHÂTEAU DE

Côtes du Rhône-Villages Laudun 1995: Riper than most '95s, but also showing some raisin and plum flavors. Medium-bodied, with toasty oak notes on the firm, somewhat dry finish. 1,111 cases made. • $10 • (10/15/97) • **79**

Côtes du Rhône-Villages Laudun 1994: A silky red with pretty cherry and strawberry flavors, this is ripe and soft, with a pleasantly fruity finish. Drink now. 2,222 cases made. • $10 • (10/15/97) • **81**

Côtes du Rhône-Villages White Laudun 1996: Very shy and subtle. Still closed, but offers a lot of tart character in the mouth. Medium-bodied. Slightly green, and a touch bitter on the aftertaste. 555 cases made. • $10 • (10/15/97) • **79**

BORGEOT, DOMAINE

Bourgogne White 1996: Flavorful Bourgogne, with earth, citrus, pear, apple, mint and cigar-box flavors. Light- to medium-bodied, it's too bad it turns bitter on the finish. Drink now. 750 cases made. • $15 • (05/31/98) • **80**

Santenay Les Gravières White 1996: Simply brilliant Santenay *premier cru.* This full-bodied Chardonnay is amazingly thick and palate-coating. Imagine the texture of virgin olive oil, the coolness of homemade sorbet, the chiseled definition of a cut diamond, and you get an idea of its wonderous nature. It glides with great finesse, yet authoratively, to a long finish. Enjoy now through 2010. 125 cases made. • $26 • (05/31/98) • **93**

BORIE DE MAUREL, DOMAINE

Minervois Cuvée Sylla 1995: Voluptuous, with ripe, rich flavors of dark plum, dark cherry and nutmeg, with a bacony note thrown in for good measure. A nice mix of international-style plushness and traditional earth and mineral flavors. Drink now through 2000. • $18 • (03/31/98) • **90**

Syrah Minervois 1996: Solid and balanced, with plum and pepper flavors, and some leather notes on the finish. Smooth and fairly supple. Drink now. • $9 • (05/31/98) • **85**

Key: SS—Spectator Selection CS—Cellar Selection HR—Highly Recommended BB—Best Buy $NA—Price not available Ⓐ—Auction Price (BT)—Barrel Tasting
Dates in parentheses indicate the issues in which the ratings were published.

BORIE LA VITARÈLE

St.-Chinian 1995: Concentrated and intense, with an alluring smoke aroma that's backed up by dense flavors of plum, tobacco and blackberry. For all that, there's some nice, subtle spice notes and a rich, chocolaty finish. A jam-packed, powerful wine. Best from 1999 through 2005. 250 cases made. • $10 • (05/31/98) • **90**

BORNE, DOMAINE DE LA

Muscadet de Sèvre et Maine 1995: Clean, fresh and crisp, with a hint of the tang of the sea, this white cries out for shellfish, Muscadet's traditional accompaniment. It shows harmony and style. • $9 • (05/15/97) • **86**

BOSCQ, CHÂTEAU LE

St.-Estèphe 1997: Attractive, grapey aromas and flavors. Almost like grapeseed oil. Medium-bodied, with slightly dry tannins. A bit overdone. • $NA • (06/15/98) (BT) • **80-84**

St.-Estèphe 1996: Solid berry and mint aromas and flavors. Medium-bodied, with medium tannins and a vanilla and berry aftertaste. 6,200 cases made. • $22 • (06/15/98) (BT) • **85-89**

St.-Estèphe 1995: Pretty, elegant wine. Attractive berry, and cherry aromas. Medium-bodied, with silky tannins and a medium aftertaste of berry and vanilla. Best after 1999. • $20 • (01/31/98) • **88**

BOSCQ, CHÂTEAU LE

Médoc 1988 • $20 • (04/30/91) • **84**
Médoc 1986 • $10 • (06/30/89) • **75**
Médoc 1983 • $8 • (01/01/86) • **70**
Médoc 1982 • $6 • (10/01/85) BB • **76**

BOSQUET DES PAPES

Châteauneuf-du-Pape 1995: This chewy red has firm tannins, but the cherry and herbal flavors don't quite fill out its muscular structure. Perhaps a bit overextracted; try now. • $25 • (10/15/97) • **80**

Châteauneuf-du-Pape 1994: This elegant wine offers harmonious and pure flavors of violets, plums, minerals and licorice; well-balanced and accessible, with a long finish. Not a powerhouse, but beautifully made. Drink now through 2000. • $25 • (10/15/97) • **90**

Châteauneuf-du-Pape 1989 • $18 • (10/15/91) • **85**
Châteauneuf-du-Pape 1988 • $18 • (10/15/91) • **83**
Châteauneuf-du-Pape 1986 • $18 • (10/15/91) • **90**
Châteauneuf-du-Pape 1985 • $18 • (10/15/91) • **86**
Châteauneuf-du-Pape 1984 • $17 • (11/15/87) • **91**
Châteauneuf-du-Pape 1983 • $NA • (10/15/91) • **86**
Châteauneuf-du-Pape 1981 • $NA • (10/15/91) • **93**

Châteauneuf-du-Pape Cuvée Chantemerle 1995: This polished, harmonious red offers smooth flavors of black cherry and herb, and light earth notes. Tannins are firm on the finish, but the fruit lingers, too. It's accessible now, better in 1999. • $40 • (10/15/97) • **87**

Châteauneuf-du-Pape Cuvée Chantemerle 1994: Rustic, with good structure but not much fruit. Shows raisin, herbal, tobacco and earth flavors, chewy and full-bodied, then hard tannins shut down the finish. May soften with food or time; try in 1999. • $40 • (10/15/97) • **83**

Châteauneuf-du-Pape White 1995: A bit rustic, and already somewhat oxidized, with pie crust, cookie dough, honey, and spice flavors. Full-bodied. Harsh on the finish. Drink soon. • $24 • (10/15/97) • **75**

BOTT-GEYL, DOMAINE

Gewürztraminer Alsace Grand Cru Furstentum 1995: Has enough residual sugar to be a late-harvest Gewürz, yet it's brimming with honey, almond and orange-peel notes and enough tangy acidity to carry the flavors to a lingering finish. Drinkable now. • $27 • (09/30/97) • **87**

Gewürztraminer Alsace Grand Cru Sonnenglanz Vieilles Vignes 1995: A delicious white, sporting honey and rose petal aromas and flavors with a hint of bitter grapefruit. Moderately concentrated and on the soft side, so enjoy now. • $28 • (09/30/97) • **89**

Muscat Alsace Riquewihr 1995: The varietal character is muted here, though there are mineral and apricot flavors. Racy acidity lends an overall leanness and provides a crisp finish. • $16 • (09/30/97) • **83**

Pinot Blanc Alsace Beblenheim 1995: The ripe, tropical aromas and residual sweetness make a statement in this forward white, though the finish is crisp. Drink now. • $10 • (09/15/97) • **84**

Riesling Alsace Grafenreben 1995: Bold and rich, this medium- to full-bodied Riesling packs in aromas and flavors of baked apples, cinnamon and toasty almonds. Round and luscious. Enjoyable now, but should improve through 2000. • $20 • (09/30/97) • **89**

Sylvaner Alsace Beblenheim 1995: Vanilla custard and buttery notes aren't what you'd expect from Sylvaner, yet the texture is rich and there is modest depth and concentration here. Good length and harmony. Well made. • $10 • (09/15/97) • **85**

BOUACHON, HENRY

Châteauneuf-du-Pape La Tiare du Pape 1994: Balanced and accessible now, this velvety red offers modest black cherry, licorice and cinnamon flavors. Well-knit and easy to like. • $15 • (11/15/96) • **84**

Côtes du Rhône Chabrière 1994: Spice and caramel aromas are attractive, and the light berry and raisin flavors have some concentration. Not for aging, but shows a nice range of flavors now. • $8 • (10/15/96) • **82**

Côtes du Rhône-Villages Bellecombes 1994: Ripe, roasted flavors of smoked meat and figs are distinctive and rich. Though it will be a bit gamy for some, the concentration and character will appeal to many. • $9 • (10/15/96) • **84**

Crozes-Hermitage La Maurelle 1994: Matured, light and watery, with tea, leaf and light raisin flavors, and tannins that dry out on the short finish. Tasted twice with consistent notes. • $11 • (12/15/96) • **74**

BOUCHACOURT, ROLAND

Mâcon-Villages 1994: Light-bodied, with attractive flavors of pear and melon to offer a touch of ripeness, but it turns somewhat sour and diluted on the finish. 5,833 cases made. • $7 • (08/31/95) • **77**

Mâcon-Villages Château de Péronne 1994: A racy little white, showing some intensity of flavor including a pronounced grass and lime edge. Light-bodied, clean and very tart. Try with seafood. 4,583 cases made. • $7 • (08/31/95) • **80**

BOUCHARD, PASCAL

Chablis 1996: Solid, and sparkling with vivid flavors. Tastes ripe yet also firm and crisp, with earth, green apple, honey and ripe pear tones. Citrusy but balanced finish. Of medium body; it needs until the end of this year to '99 to show all. 200 cases imported. 33,333 cases made. • $21 • (08/31/97) • **86**

Chablis 1995: Interesting. Medium-bodied and fairly unctous, with nice fruit flavors, but a slight gluey, salty character on the finish. • $NA • (08/31/96) • **78**

Chablis 1994 • $18 • (05/31/96) • **71**

Chablis Beauroy 1994 • $NA • (05/31/96) • **80**

Chablis Blanchots 1996: Seductively opulent and flavorful. Quite oaky, with tropical, pear, wet earth, mineral, citrus, honey and toasty bread character. Full-bodied, delicious and pure, but hold until around 2000. 410 cases made. • $44 • (05/31/98) • **91**

Chablis Blanchots 1995: Dense and full-bodied, but lacks fruit intensity. Shows some decent pear, mineral and earth notes. Soft finish. 167 cases made. • $37 • (06/15/97) • **83**

Chablis Blanchots 1994 • $NA • (05/31/96) • **85**

Chablis Fourchaume 1996: A distinctively flinty, minerally Chablis that's quite earthy, with a pungent aroma. Medium-bodied with nice acidity and a vibrant character, but also a touch of bell pepper on the crisp finish. Try around 2005. Tasted twice, with consistent notes. 6,600 cases made. • $29 • (05/31/98) • **83**

Chablis Fourchaume 1995: Big and fat, but lacks elegance. It's full-bodied, with coarse flavors and texture and some ripe fruit notes. 2,500 cases made. • $24 • (06/15/97) • **75**

Chablis Fourchaume 1994 • $36 • (05/31/96) • **85**

Chablis Les Clos 1996: Very fresh, even a bit spritzy, with apple, floral and honey notes. Medium-bodied, with a slightly smoky finish. A fun '96 Chablis to drink now through 2000. 660 cases made. • $44 • (05/31/98) • **90**

Chablis Les Clos 1994 • $45 • (05/31/96) • **74**

Chablis Les Clos 1993 • $NA • (08/31/95) • **83**

Chablis Mont de Milieu 1996: Pure and racy Chablis, with an earth, smoke, citrus and green apple character softened by a dollop of honey, this medium-bodied '96 should come into its own around 2000 to 2002. Finishes a bit tart. 5,000 cases made. • $29 • (05/31/98) • **86**

Chablis Mont de Milieu 1995: Smells and tastes musty, as if it were corked. Dry finish. 2,500 cases made. • $23 • (06/15/97) • **65**

Chablis Mont de Milieu 1994 • $36 • (05/31/96) • **88**

Chablis Mont de Milieu 1993 • $NA • (08/31/95) • **84**

Chablis Montmains 1996: A very pretty wine; balanced, ripe and medium-bodied, with pear and green apple notes and a touch of honey. Supple and vibrant, with an attractive floral finish. Tempting now through 2002. 2,500 cases made. • $29 • (05/31/98) • **88**

Chablis Montmains 1995: A bit rustic, with some chewy wood, earth and lemon flavors that fail to harmonize on the slightly astringent finish. 1,667 cases made. • $23 • (06/15/97) • **73**

Chablis Montmains 1994 • $36 • (05/31/96) • **78**

Chablis Vaudésir 1996: Great white Burgundy that's atypical of Chablis yet fabulous. Clever winemaking mingles toasty new oak with clean, pure, well-defined lime, tropical, pear, mint and honeysuckle flavors that bounce around the mouth. Full-bodied. Supple texture turns a bit hard on the smoky, grilled meat, *very* long and exciting finish. Tempting now through 2005. 910 cases made. • $44 • (05/31/98) • **93**

Chablis Vaudésir 1994 • $NA • (05/31/96) • **72**

Petit Chablis 1996: Lively, with ripe pear, pineapple, floral aromas and flavors. Jolts the palate with its crisp texture and slightly green finish. Light-to-medium body. Drink now. 75 cases imported. 8,333 cases made. • $20 • (08/31/97) • **81**

BOUCHARD-AÎNÉ & FILS

Beaujolais-Villages La Vigneronne 1995: Lush blackberry flavor provides the appeal in this round, soft red. It lacks the structure for food, but can be enjoyed alone lightly chilled. • $12 • (04/30/97) • **84**

Bourgogne Les Vendangeurs White 1995: A good, fruity wine with apple and lemon flavors and just a touch of spice on the finish. Crisp and refreshing. • $14 • (01/31/97) • **83**

Chambertin Clos de Bèze 1959 • $NA • (08/31/90) • **84**

Chambertin Clos de Bèze Domaine Marion 1989 • $NA • (01/31/92) • **88**

Le Chardonnay de Chardonnay Bourgogne 1995: Simple and straightforward, with green apple, marzipan and woody flavors that taste a bit bitter. Medium-bodied. Drink chilled. Way overpriced. • $15 • (01/31/98) • **76**

Mâcon Pinot Chardonnay Dry Réserve 1995: A lean wine with modest green apple and pear flavors and an overly tart finish. • $12 • (01/31/97) • **78**

Mercurey White 1993: Mature and buttery, with nice flavors of honey and ripe pear and some good mineral and lemon notes. Nutty flavors linger on the finish. • $18 • (01/31/97) • **85**

Merlot Vin de Pays de l'Aude NV • $5 • (06/30/90) • **72**

Meursault 1995: Rather lean in flavor, showing oak-accented citrus and apple notes, but with a nice, smooth texture. A good Chardonnay. • $31 • (02/28/97) • **84**

Pouilly-Fuissé Dry Réserve 1995: Crisp, with flavors of apple and grapefruit and a nutty taste on the finish. Also has nice balance and texture. • $26 • (01/31/97) • **82**

Puligny-Montrachet 1995: Big and robust, with a smooth, thick texture and ample pear, vanilla and nutmeg flavors. Still a bit tough on the finish, but a good choice if you like full-bodied wines. Try now. • $36 • (02/28/97) • **84**

BOUCHARD PÈRE & FILS

Aloxe-Corton Domaines du Château de Beaune 1992: Simple and appealing, with a bright core of black cherry flavor that echoes on the finish. Drinkable now. • $30 • (12/15/94) • **82**

Aloxe-Corton Domaines du Château de Beaune 1991 • $30 • (01/31/94) • **84**

Aloxe-Corton Domaines du Château de Beaune 1990: So focused and pretty you want to drink it now—that is, until the firm tannins hit you on the finish. Offers plenty of blackberry and smoke characteristics to keep you tuned in. • $30 • (12/15/92) • **88**

Aloxe-Corton Domaines du Château de Beaune 1989 • $36 • (01/31/92) • **87**

Auxey-Duresses White 1996: Clean, pure and very pretty, this medium-bodied, floral '96 offers some lovely manderin orange, rose petal, peach, pear and lime notes that marry nicely. The mineral character comes through shyly now, but give this laser-sharp Chardonnay till 2000 to 2002. • $22 • (05/31/98) • **87**

Bâtard-Montrachet 1994: A medium-bodied Chardonnay showing pleasant fruit, toasty coconut and dried herb flavors. Picks up some intensity on the supple finish. • $96 • (05/31/96) • **87**

Beaujolais-Villages Le Chamville 1993 • $10 • (06/30/94) • **79**

BOUCHARD PÈRE & FILS

Beaune Clos St.-Landry White 1996: Wonderful finesse and harmony. Showing a round mouthfeel surrounded by spiky acidity, this full-bodied *premier cru* offers pear, mineral, dried herb and tropical flavors. The sweet-tasting finish is harmonious. Kept improving in contact with air so while tempting now, it's better after 2003. • $50 • (05/31/98) • **90**

Beaune Clos St.-Landry White 1995: Racy, full-bodied and rather concentrated, with ripe tropical character backed by mineral, citrus and honey notes. Crisp finish, but should smooth out after 2000. • $50 • (08/31/97) • **89**

Beaune Clos St.-Landry Domaines du Château de Beaune White 1994: Very elegant, subtle and quite creamy. Lots of spice, nutmeg, pear, toasty bread, mineral and vanilla flavors. Some intensity on the finish. Try in 1999. • $32 • (05/31/96) • **87**

Beaune Clos St.-Landry Domaines du Château de Beaune White 1993: Honey, pear and vanilla aromas and flavors, medium body, firm acidity and a good core of fruit. Drink now or hold. • $31 • (05/15/95) • **86**

Beaune Clos St.-Landry Domaines du Château de Beaune White 1992: Light but pleasant, simple and clean, with some modest apple, pear and mineral flavors. • $24 • (08/31/94) • **79**

Beaune Le Clos de la Mousse 1995: A juicy Pinot, showing a red currant accent to the silky cherry flavors. On the lean side, yet tasty. Ready in 1999. • $33 • (11/15/97) • **82**

Beaune Le Clos de la Mousse 1994: A strongly earthy, almost dirty note overshadows the modest fruit flavors in this light-textured wine. • $28 • (11/15/96) • **79**

Beaune Le Clos de la Mousse 1993: An extremely smooth, silky, young '93. Well-crafted plum, cherry and earth character, tannins sneaking up on the finish. Drinkable now, better in 1999. • $28 • (11/15/95) • **85**

Beaune Le Clos de la Mousse 1992: Firm in texture, chewy, with caramel and tobacco overtones to the modest berry flavor. Drink now. • $25 • (12/15/94) • **81**

Beaune Le Clos de la Mousse 1991: Tough, chewy and mature for the vintage. Drinkable now. 1,300 cases made. • $28 Ⓐ • (01/31/94) • **79**

Beaune Le Clos de la Mousse 1986 • $33 • (07/31/88) • **78**

Beaune Les Grèves Vigne de l'Enfant Jésus 1995: Well-concentrated and intense, it's black cherry and wild red berry flavors sparkle on the palate, unhindered by too much oak. Medium-bodied, with a lively mouthfeel that lingers on the fresh finish. Drink around 2000. • $63 • (11/15/97) • **86**

Beaune Les Grèves Vigne de l'Enfant Jésus 1994: A bit chewy, but the cherry, leather and floral flavors persist on the finish. Needs until 1999 to 2000 to soften the coarse tannins. • $49 • (11/15/96) • **85**

Beaune Les Grèves Vigne de l'Enfant Jésus Domaines du Château de Beaune 1993: Light and delicate, pleasant and accessible now, featuring some plum, cherry, chocolate character. Disappointing for this vineyard site. 1,500 cases made. • $50 • (11/15/95) • **82**

Beaune Les Grèves Vigne de l'Enfant Jésus Domaines du Château de Beaune 1992: Solid quality in a well-balanced Burgundy that has straightforward fruit flavors, good structure and acidity and a clean finish. 1,500 cases made. • $40 • (10/31/94) • **86**

Beaune Les Grèves Vigne de l'Enfant Jésus Domaines du Château de Beaune 1991: Youthful and polished, showing grace and finesse. Firmly tannic but plush underneath, with spicy, vanilla-scented berry and red plum flavor that persists on the finish. • $48 • (02/28/95) • **88**

Beaune Les Grèves Vigne de l'Enfant Jésus Domaines du Château de Beaune 1990: Smooth and generous, a supple, silky Beaune with caramel and tobacco notes playing against the polished raspberry and strawberry flavors. Delicious now. • $55 • (02/28/95) • **88**

Beaune Les Grèves Vigne de l'Enfant Jésus Domaines du Château de Beaune 1989 • $59 • (02/28/95) • **91**

Beaune Les Grèves Vigne de l'Enfant Jésus Domaines du Château de Beaune 1988 • $59 • (02/28/95) • **85**

Beaune Les Grèves Vigne de l'Enfant Jésus Domaines du Château de Beaune 1987 • $38 • (02/28/95) • **86**

Beaune Les Grèves Vigne de l'Enfant Jésus Domaines du Château de Beaune 1986 • $47 • (02/28/95) • **79**

Beaune Les Grèves Vigne de l'Enfant Jésus Domaines du Château de Beaune 1985 • $61 • (02/28/95) • **89**

Beaune Les Grèves Vigne de l'Enfant Jésus Domaines du Château de Beaune 1983 • $34 • (02/28/95) • **82**

Beaune Les Marconnets Domaines du Château de Beaune 1994: Firm, chewy and not much flavor to round it out, only touches of cherry and earth notes. • $29 • (11/15/96) • **79**

Key: SS—Spectator Selection CS—Cellar Selection HR—Highly Recommended BB—Best Buy $NA—Price not available Ⓐ—Auction Price (BT)—Barrel Tasting

Dates in parentheses indicate the issues in which the ratings were published.

Beaune Les Marconnets Domaines du Château de Beaune 1992: Crisp, a little tannic, only a modest level of cherry flavor sneaking through on the finish. • $27 • (12/15/94) • **79**

Beaune Les Marconnets Domaines du Château de Beaune 1991: Barnyardlike aromas and flavors . Nice vanilla- and spice-scented cherry flavor balances it relatively well. Drinkable now. 880 cases made. • $30 Ⓐ • (01/31/94) • **74**

Beaune Les Marconnets Domaines du Château de Beaune 1990: What a beauty. Solid as a rock and both firm and velvety, showing great complexity and tons of berry, plum and chocolate characteristics that come together on the almost sweet finish. Drink now. • $28 • (12/15/92) • **93**

Beaune Les Marconnets Domaines du Château de Beaune 1989 • $39 • (01/31/92) • **90**

Beaune Les Marconnets Domaines du Château de Beaune 1986 • $24 • (07/31/88) • **83**

Beaune Les Marconnets Domaines du Château de Beaune 1985 • $35 • (01/31/89) • **89**

Beaune Les Teurons Domaines du Château de Beaune 1993: Incredibly floral nose, medium body and tannins and a crisp finish. Open and delicious to drink now but will improve. 1,900 cases made. • $28 • (11/15/95) • **86**

Beaune Les Teurons Domaines du Château de Beaune 1991: Crisp and light, with focused blackberry and currant aromas and flavors that turn lean and slightly astringent on the finish. Try now. 900 cases made. • $29 Ⓐ • (01/31/94) • **80**

Beaune Les Teurons Domaines du Château de Beaune 1990: Quite forward and open for a '90. Light and pleasant, with clean, pretty chestnut and raspberry flavors. Drinkable now. • $30 • (12/15/92) • **84**

Beaune Les Teurons Domaines du Château de Beaune 1986 • $32 • (07/31/88) • **81**

Beaune Les Teurons Domaines du Château de Beaune 1985 • $35 • (01/31/89) • **85**

Beaune Les Teurons Domaines du Château de Beaune 1983 • $21 • (09/15/86) • **71**

Beaune Premier Cru White 1996: Prototypical mineral-driven '96 white Burgundy. Medium-bodied, with ripe-tasting fruit, its smooth texture is backed by a charging cavalry of acidity kept in check by a grip of mineral and earth notes. The balance comes through loud and clear on the long, harmonious finish. Tempting now, better after 2000 to 2010. Fantastic effort from négociant Bouchard and owner Joseph Henriot. • $38 • (05/31/98) • **92**

Beaune Premier Cru White 1995: Super for a *premier cru* village blend, full-bodied and silky as can be in texture, with mineral, honey, spice, tropical fruit character. Seductive and lovely from start to finish. Tempting now, but should improve through 2005. • $38 • (08/31/97) • **92**

Beaune Premier Cru White 1994: Subtle yet intense, elegant, and full in body. Lots of finesse at first, shouting its full-throttle tropical fruit, lime, earth and toasty bread flavors on the lovely, supple and silky finish. Drinkable now. • $28 • (05/31/96) • **87**

Bonnes Mares 1995: A sexy, distinctive, wild and savage red Burgundy. Packed with refined violet, rose petal aromas and wet earth, soil, *goût de terroir* and brooding blackberry flavors, this wine flexes its muscles. Good intensity, supple midpalate, firm tannins on the sweet-tasting finish. Try after 2000. • $89 • (11/15/97) • **92**

Bourgogne White 1996: Fairly lush and round, with some pear, vanilla and apple complexity. Crisp and balanced, albeit slightly bitter. Drink now with food. • $12 • (05/31/98) • **80**

Chambertin 1994: Where are the intensity, flavor and character expected from a *grand cru*? This is muted, with some minor-league red berry flavor and a slightly astringent finish. • $100 • (11/15/96) • **76**

Chambertin 1986 • $78 • (07/31/88) • **81**

Chambertin Clos de Bèze 1989 • $92 • (01/31/92) • **92**

Chambertin Clos de Bèze 1988 • $82 • (04/30/91) • **89**

Chambertin Domaines du Château de Beaune 1990: A bit lean and not showing much. Lacks flesh and depth, but delivers pleasant strawberry and cherry characteristics. Drinkable now. • $NA • (12/15/92) • **88**

Chambolle-Musigny 1994: Light and diffuse, this unfocused red offers only modest aromas and flavors. • $35 • (11/15/96) • **74**

Chambolle-Musigny 1993: Delicate, pretty, medium-bodied, offering well-defined floral, earth, rose petal and currant flavors. Good tannin structure yet very supple finish. Best in 2000. 310 cases made. • $36 • (11/15/95) • **88**

Chambolle-Musigny 1992: Middle-of-the-road Chambolle, with toasty, gamy, red berry flavors opening up to a firm-structured, tannic finish. • $32 • (12/15/94) • **79**

Chambolle-Musigny 1990: Focused and a bit austere now, but plenty of wet earth, forest underbrush and plum characteristics make it a promising wine for the cellar. Try now. • $NA • (12/15/92) • **86**

FRANCE

Chambolle-Musigny 1986 • $29 • (07/31/88) • **73**
Chardonnay Mâcon-Villages Le Chamville 1994: Subtle mineral, pear, apple and spice flavors develop in smooth little waves to a harmonious finish. Lacks a bit of intensity. • $11 • (08/31/95) • **82**
Chassagne-Montrachet 1996: Impressive and balanced village wine from Burgundy's comeback kid. Classy and subtle, with a good combination of ripe fruit, acidity and mineral character. Creamlike and velvety in texture, of medium body, with a juicy, toasty and smoky finish. Tempting now, best after 2000. • $39 • (05/31/98) • **90**
Chassagne-Montrachet Red 1993: The wood brings out smoky, toasty flavors that blend nicely with black cherry and licorice notes. Beautiful, silky, ripe mouthfeel and soft finish. Try now. • $25 • (11/15/95) • **87**
Chassagne-Montrachet Red 1990: A pleasant but straightforward wine that's quite light and one-dimensional, with cherry and herb flavors. Drinkable now. • $21 • (12/15/92) • **80**
Chassagne-Montrachet Red 1988 • $22 • (04/30/91) • **85**
Chevalier-Montrachet 1996: Enormously concentrated and intense, showing very ripe fruit underneath a hint of stemmy, earthy and herbal character that eventually disappears. An impressive oily subtext gives it a smooth texture in the midpalate, with tropical, toasty wood, mineral and dried herb flavors. Huge finish hints at a lovely, sweet future. Decant this if you drink it in the next decade, but better not to touch until around 2010. • $150 • (05/31/98) • **96**
Chevalier-Montrachet 1995: There's good intensity to this medium-bodied wine; a lovely combination of citrus, mineral, honey and ripe fruit flavors in a very harmonious package. Try after 2000. • $150 • (08/31/97) • **87**
Chevalier-Montrachet 1994: Very opulent, this is ultrathick, ultradense, oozing honey, lemon and ripe fruit flavors. Tempting now through 2000. • $125 • (05/31/97) • **92**
Chevalier-Montrachet 1993: Plenty of new wood here; shows firm acidity and lots of apple and mineral character. Medium-bodied, adding good fruit and a medium finish. Drink now. 1,900 cases made. • $93 • (08/31/95) • **86**
Chevalier-Montrachet 1992: It flies over the palate as delicately as a glider in the sky, leaving in its wake a trail of subtle, seamless flavors. Delicate with plenty of depth, offering focused lime, lemon, pear and toast flavors, with a creamy yet solid finish. 550 cases made. • $81 • (08/31/94) HR • **94**
Châteauneuf-du-Pape 1990: Bold and assertive, with cooked plum and smoke flavors and peppery accents. Full-bodied, tannic and well-balanced; drink now. • $16 • (04/15/93) • **83**
Châteauneuf-du-Pape 1985 • $11 • (09/30/87) • **82**
Clos de Vougeot 1995: Deep, robust and muscular, showing some wonderful red- and blackberry aromas and flavors with toasty oak, violet, rose petal, mocha, spice and coffee notes. Hard as nails now, one hopes its tannic shell will soften. Try after 2004. • $80 • (11/15/97) • **88**
Clos de Vougeot 1959 • $NA • (08/31/90) • **85**
Clos de la Roche 1989 • $NA • (01/31/92) • **89**
Corton Le Corton Domaines du Château de Beaune 1992: Nicely focused, fruity and smooth in texture, a young but promising red with firm tannins, great balance and just a touch of oak. Try now. 1,400 cases made. • $38 • (10/31/94) • **88**
Corton Le Corton Domaines du Château de Beaune 1991: Tough, astringent and thin, with modest fruit buried under the tannins. Unbalanced. 1,400 cases made. • $46 Ⓐ • (01/31/94) • **77**
Corton Le Corton Domaines du Château de Beaune 1990: Tightly knit, with loads of fruit and tannins, showing an impressive amount of black cherry and earth flavors and a round mouthfeel. • $50 • (12/15/92) • **91**
Corton Le Corton Domaines du Château de Beaune 1989 • $79 • (01/31/92) • **92**
Corton Le Corton Domaines du Château de Beaune 1988 • $77 • (03/31/91) • **91**
Corton Le Corton Domaines du Château de Beaune 1986 • $47 • (07/31/88) • **85**
Corton Le Corton Domaines du Château de Beaune 1983 • $37 • (09/15/86) • **83**
Corton-Charlemagne 1996: To die for—or almost. Deep on the nose but extremely backward, only hinting at the explosive stuff we find on the palate: honey, dried herbs, mineral, mocha and spices. As full-bodied and as smooth in texture as a Chardonnay can get, it still manages to kick in with amazing lime-spiked acidity on the long, long finish. Buy a case of this if you can find it and afford it. Tempting now through 2010. • $110 • (05/31/98) • **95**
Corton-Charlemagne 1995: Very nice. A well-made and opulent wine, full-bodied and concentrated, offering sweet tropical fruit, pear, green apple and citrus flavors. Better after 2000. • $110 • (08/31/97) • **90**
Corton-Charlemagne 1994: Skillful winemaking stands behind this lovely, fresh and intense '94. Packs lemon, pear and honey flavors in wonderful proportions. Seductively voluptuous and full-bodied, adding a focused, long finish. Drinkable now or hold until 1999. • $60 • (05/31/96) • **91**
Corton-Charlemagne 1993: Distinctive mushroom and cream aromas and flavors, medium body, firm acidity and delicious finish. Lovely to drink now. 1,000 cases made. • $61 • (08/31/95) • **87**
Corton-Charlemagne 1992: Well-rounded and creamy, with a beam of lemon to cut through the richness. A bit plain for a Corton, yet the complexity of the vanilla, pear, and lime flavors will make any wine-drinker happy. 1,000 cases made. • $50 • (08/31/94) • **89**
Côte de Beaune-Villages 1982 • $19 • (05/16/84) SS • **88**
Côte de Beaune-Villages Clos des Topes Bizot 1983 • $22 • (09/15/86) • **82**
Côte de Nuits-Villages 1990: Tastes like a pleasant, simple Beaujolais, with modest tannins and plenty of light fruit flavors. Drinkable now. • $NA • (12/15/92) • **78**
Côtes du Rhône Le Chamville 1993 • $10 • (11/15/95) • **78**
Echézeaux 1991: Tight, chewy and a lot more concentrated than most '91s, showing earthy rose petal and toast-scented currant and berry flavors. A chunky wine. Try now. 400 cases made. • $54 Ⓐ • (01/31/94) • **89**
Echézeaux 1990: Ripe, concentrated and complex, with tight currant, cherry and plum-tinged flavors that take on a pleasant, earthy edge on the finish, where the tight tannins kick in. Drinkable now. • $42 • (10/31/92) • **89**
Echézeaux 1989 • $62 • (01/31/92) • **88**
Gevrey-Chambertin 1993: Very good village wine. Lovely fruit and silky tannins. Medium-bodied, showing dark chocolate and berry character and a long, long aftertaste. Better in 1999. • $29 • (11/15/95) • **86**
Gevrey-Chambertin 1992: Delicate and verging on diluted. The wet earth, raspberry and black cherry character raises some interest. • $27 • (12/15/94) • **79**
Gevrey-Chambertin 1982 • $18 • (06/16/84) • **80**
La Romanée Château de Vosne-Romanée 1995: Extraordinary in its finesse, elegance and reserve, this velvety Burgundy subtly ambushes your palate with fantastic layers of toasty oak, ripe and exotic fruit flavors and masses of creamy, ripe tannins. The finish doesn't stop. Try around 2005 to 2010. • $210 • (11/15/97) • **95**
La Romanée Château de Vosne-Romanée 1994: Has brilliant flavors of violet-scented currant, berry and spice that open up beautifully with each sip. Elegant, pure and clear as a trumpet call, long and harmonious on the fruit-centered finish. Tempting now, but try to wait until 2002 to 2004. • $160 • (11/15/96) • **94**
La Romanée Château de Vosne-Romanée 1993: Refined but closed in now, showing some nice concentration of red berry flavor and tannins that clamp down on the finish. Of medium body, with lovely rose petal and currant notes. Try in 1999. 330 cases made. • $116 Ⓐ • (11/15/95) • **90**
La Romanée Château de Vosne-Romanée 1992: Under the coarse tannins lies a nice thread of spice, tobacco and berry flavor that lingers on the chewy finish. Try now. • $118 • (12/15/94) • **85**
La Romanée Château de Vosne-Romanée 1986 • $83 Ⓐ • (07/31/88) • **91**
Le Corton 1995: Displaying scrumptious cherry character, this red glides across the palate, yet it's firmly structured, with an astringent finish. Try in 2000. • $63 • (11/15/97) • **85**
Mâcon-Villages Le Chamville 1996: Quite supple, even soft, with an earthy ripe fruit character, but turns bitter on the finish. • $13 • (08/31/97) • **73**
Meursault 1996: A solid and muscular village Meursault, aromatically backward and reserved for now, but showing depth and a smooth, silky mouthfeel amid vibrant citrus, tropical, honey and spice flavors. Full-bodied, it has grip on the chewy finish. Try around 2005. • $35 • (05/31/98) • **90**
Meursault 1993: Crisp, smooth mineral character and citrusy, herbal notes. Long finish. Drinkable now. • $26 • (05/15/95) • **84**
Meursault 1992: Rather tight Meursault, light- to medium-bodied, with fresh and clean character from green apple, herb and citrus flavors. 630 cases made. • $20 • (08/31/94) • **83**
Meursault Les Genevrières 1995: Very impressive. Clean, pure, dense and full-bodied, unfolding its honey, toasty oak, spice and ripe fruit flavors in a silky package. Tempting now, should be great through 2005. • $66 • (05/31/97) • **91**
Meursault Les Genevrières 1994: Lovely, medium- to full-bodied, delivering a good amount of honey, apricot and ripe pear aromas and flavors. Lacks a bit of panache and intensity, but provides delicious drinking now. • $46 • (05/31/96) • **85**
Meursault Les Genevrières 1993: Relatively ripe and very delicious, featuring a polished, silky texture, zesty acidity and some attractive pear, honey and mineral flavors. Drink now. • $45 • (05/15/95) • **88**
Montrachet 1995: Beautiful harmony and balance in this wine, with flavors of spice, toasty oak, ripe fruit and citrus. Full-bodied, with a milky vanilla-

FRANCE

bean and mineral note that persists on the lingering finish. Try after 2000. • $320 • (08/31/97) • **92**

Montrachet 1994: Distinguished wine with a sense of class and mineral, honey, cream, vanilla, spice and ripe fruit flavors in the right proportions. Great elegande here and understated citrus intensity on the finish, which just builds and builds. Try after 1999. • $185 • (05/31/96) • **94**

Montrachet Domaines du Château de Beaune 1993: Intense, generously flavored, vibrant and well-made, offering floral, lime, dried herb character. Full-bodied. Needs time to soften its acidic edges; will be terrific. 300 cases made. • $181 • (08/31/95) • **88**

Nuits-St.-Georges 1983 • $21 • (09/15/86) • **68**

Nuits-St.-Georges Clos St.-Marc 1995: Herbaceous and astringent, with cherry and appleskin flavors. Medium-bodied, tart finish. • $53 • (11/15/97) • **72**

Nuits-St.-Georges Clos St.-Marc 1994: Tough, medicinal and already showing matured flavors, with prickly tannins on the finish. Try in 1999 to 2000. • $40 • (11/15/96) • **79**

Nuits-St.-Georges Clos St.-Marc 1993: Rather light in structure but chewy on the finish, inserting fresh red berry and earth character. Ends slightly dry; could use more ripe fruit. Try now. • $47 • (11/15/95) • **82**

Nuits-St.-Georges Clos St.-Marc 1992: Light and a little wimpy, barely offering any of its strawberry flavors. This is a *premier cru*? • $43 • (12/15/94) • **73**

Nuits-St.-Georges Clos St.-Marc 1991: Modest tobacco and plum flavors and hard tannins on the finish. Try now. • $45 • (01/31/94) • **75**

Nuits-St.-Georges Clos St.-Marc 1989 • $59 • (01/31/92) • **89**

Nuits-St.-Georges Clos St.-Marc 1985 • $53 • (02/28/89) • **87**

Nuits-St.-Georges Clos St.-Marc 1983 • $33 • (09/15/86) • **74**

Nuits-St.-Georges La Richemone 1989 • $NA • (01/31/92) • **89**

Nuits-St.-Georges Les Argillières 1990: A fruity style of Nuits, with ripe cherry and spice aromas and flavors and medium-hard tannins. Somewhat one-dimensional. Drinkable now. • $31 • (12/15/92) • **86**

Nuits-St.-Georges Les Cailles 1959 • $90 • (08/31/90) • **87**

Pinot Noir Bourgogne La Vignée 1992: Closer to water than wine, with a hint of strawberry character. • $NA • (12/15/94) • **70**

Pommard 1994: Light and simple, with some modestly complex fruit flavors and astringent tannins. • $27 • (11/15/96) • **75**

Pommard 1992: Crisp, simple, tasting modestly of black cherry. • $35 • (12/15/94) • **79**

Pommard 1988 • $37 • (04/30/91) HR • **90**

Pommard 1983 • $23 • (09/15/86) • **74**

Pommard Clos du Pavillon 1989 • $NA • (01/31/92) • **92**

Pommard Premier Cru Domaines du Château de Beaune 1990: For a blend of vineyards, this is unbelievable. Ripe, rich and firm, showing terrific breeding, with lovely, elegant, focused red berry flavors and super-fine tannins. Drinkable now. • $39 • (12/15/92) • **94**

Pommard Premier Cru Domaines du Château de Beaune 1988 • $53 • (03/31/91) • **89**

Pommard Premier Cru Domaines du Château de Beaune 1986 • $41 • (07/31/88) • **87**

Pouilly-Fuissé 1995: Medium-bodied, with nice, crisp, citrusy fruit flavors, it stands out for the way it picks up intensity on the lingering finish, kicking in with ripe flavors, honey and citrus shadings that linger long. Delicious now. • $22 • (05/31/97) • **86**

Puligny-Montrachet 1996: Lovely, smooth, sweet- and ripe-tasting, with a pronounced mineral, velvet feel on the midpalate. Lacking in complexity, yet satisfying for its harmony. Shows good length, with lime and ripe pear, touches of honey, tropical, vanilla bean and spice. Try around 2000. • $39 • (05/31/98) • **89**

Puligny-Montrachet 1993: Crisp and tart now, but it has the potential to evolve into a smoother, rounder wine, with some honey, lemon and mineral notes. Drinkable now. • $24 • (05/15/95) • **83**

Puligny-Montrachet Les Chalumeaux 1996: Clean and pure, this racy white Burgundy develops a lush, supple mouthfeel in contact with air, suggesting it will improve beautifully with age. Medium-to-full in body, offering ripe pear, floral, wet stone and spice notes. Quite chewy on the finish now; try around 2005 to 2007. • $50 • (05/31/98) • **91**

Puligny-Montrachet Les Folatières 1996: Outstanding. Totally closed on the nose now, but on the palate it shows some mineral, vanilla, butter, ripe pear, lime, honey and subtle toasty oak flavors in a combination that titillates the taste buds. Long, clean and pure finish. Try around 2005. • $55 • (05/31/98) • **90**

Puligny-Montrachet Les Folatières 1995: A full-bodied *premier cru* but it's rather firm, with oak overshadowing the fruit now. Slightly diluted and a bit dry on the finish. Bottle sickness? Try upon release. • $55 • (05/31/97) • **82**

Puligny-Montrachet Les Folatières 1994: Soft and supple, offering medium body and intensity, it tastes of vanilla ice cream, honey and apple. Could use more concentration. Drinkable now. • $38 • (05/31/96) • **84**

Puligny-Montrachet Les Folatières 1993: Some citric, mushroom character. Medium-bodied and crisp; slightly earthy finish. A bit dull overall. • $36 • (05/15/95) • **79**

Puligny-Montrachet Les Pucelles 1996: Impressively intense, with loads of mouth-coating mineral texture and lime, honey and ripe fruit. Full-bodied, with lovely personality on the long, toasty finish. Try around 2010. • $68 • (05/31/98) • **92**

Puligny-Montrachet Les Pucelles 1995: Very oaky in style, this tastes like a polished, high-tech wine. Has pear and vanilla notes but lacks depth and has some strange aromas. Perhaps suffers from recent bottling. • $68 • (05/31/97) • **72**

Puligny-Montrachet Les Pucelles 1994: Round and supple, balanced and harmonious honey, pear, vanilla and mineral character. Not very intense and quite soft on the finish, but makes for lovely drinking now. • $46 • (05/31/96) • **87**

Puligny-Montrachet Les Pucelles 1993: Fresh citric and mineral character, medium body, firm acidity and a clean finish. • $41 • (05/15/95) • **81**

Puligny-Montrachet Les Pucelles 1992: Subtly complex, still closed in aroma, but the flavors are clearly defined, and they grow on the finish. Reminds us of honey, hazelnut and pear, combined in a silky, seamless package. Drinkable now. 75 cases made. • $30 • (08/31/94) • **88**

Rully White 1996: Interesting dried fruit, fig, ripe pear and bread dough aromas and flavors. Intense acidity makes for a long, crisp, mouth-puckering taste sensation. Medium-bodied. Not very charming now; try after 1999. • $17 • (05/31/98) • **84**

Savigny-lès-Beaune Les Lavières Domaines du Château de Beaune 1990: Traditionally-styled, with mellow chestnut and cherry aromas and flavors and smooth tannins. Lacks intensity. Drinkable now. • $NA • (12/15/92) • **82**

Savigny-lès-Beaune Les Lavières Domaines du Château de Beaune 1989 • $29 • (01/31/92) • **82**

Savigny-lès-Beaune Les Lavières Domaines du Château de Beaune 1988 • $29 • (04/30/91) • **83**

Savigny-lès-Beaune Les Lavières Domaines du Château de Beaune 1986 • $25 • (07/31/88) • **78**

Volnay 1985 • $35 • (01/31/89) • **88**

Volnay Caillerets Ancienne Cuvée Carnot Domaines du Château de Beaune 1995: Lovely floral, cherry character and silky texture holds center stage until the curtain of tannins comes down. Try in 2000. • $44 • (11/15/97) • **85**

Volnay Caillerets Ancienne Cuvée Carnot Domaines du Château de Beaune 1994: A decent, medium-bodied '94, with some cherry, stemmy and herbal notes and slightly coarse tannins on the finish. • $37 • (11/15/96) • **78**

Volnay Caillerets Ancienne Cuvée Carnot Domaines du Château de Beaune 1993: Very fresh and straightforward, offering nice fruit character but not much more. Simple cherry aromas and flavors, high acidity, fresh finish. Drink now. 1,500 cases made. • $37 • (11/15/95) • **83**

Volnay Callierets Ancienne Cuvée Carnot Domaines du Château de Beaune 1992: A smooth and silky Burgundy with classic earthy, toasty, leathery aromas, polished fruit flavors and a good finish. Drinkable now. 1,500 cases made. • $29 • (10/31/94) • **85**

Volnay Caillerets Ancienne Cuvée Carnot Domaines du Château de Beaune 1991: Flavorful and smoky; this lean, firm-textured wine has flesh and style to frame the gamy, toasty, berryish aromas and flavors. Drinkable now. 1,500 cases made. • $37 • (01/31/94) • **85**

Volnay Caillerets Ancienne Cuvée Carnot Domaines du Château de Beaune 1990: Firm and tightly structured, with plenty of fruit to give it a velvety feel and intense, gamy cherry and tobacco flavors. The finish is loaded with tannins. Try now. • $37 • (12/15/92) • **90**

Volnay Caillerets Ancienne Cuvée Carnot Domaines du Château de Beaune 1989 • $52 • (02/29/92) CS • **94**

Volnay Caillerets Ancienne Cuvée Carnot Domaines du Château de Beaune 1986 • $34 • (07/31/88) • **83**

Volnay Chevret 1992: Light, but showing some ripe currant flavor that fades on the finish. Drinkable now. • $NA • (12/15/94) • **79**

Key: SS—Spectator Selection CS—Cellar Selection HR—Highly Recommended BB—Best Buy $NA—Price not available Ⓐ—Auction Price (BT)—Barrel Tasting
Dates in parentheses indicate the issues in which the ratings were published.

Volnay Frémiets-Clos de la Rougeotte Domaines du Château de Beaune 1994: Light and delicate, with some floral, cherry and minty flavors. A bit tannic for the lean structure. • $35 • (11/15/96) • **79**
Volnay Frémiets-Clos de la Rougeotte Domaines du Château de Beaune 1993: Light-to-medium body, showing some plummy, meaty flavors. A bit one-dimensional and dry on the finish. Try now. 590 cases made. • $35 • (11/15/95) • **84**
Volnay Frémiets-Clos de la Rougeotte Domaines du Château de Beaune 1992: Firm and a little chewy, with enough berry and currant flavor to keep it in balance. Drinkable now. • $38 • (12/15/94) • **82**
Volnay Frémiets-Clos de la Rougeotte Domaines du Château de Beaune 1990: An aromatic and open wine, with chestnut and cherry aromas and flavors that are not very intense, but show lovely balance. Try now or hold. • $NA • (12/15/92) • **86**
Volnay Frémiets-Clos de le Rougeotte Domaines du Château de Beaune 1985 • $44 • (01/31/89) • **87**
Volnay Taille Pieds Domaines du Château de Beaune 1992: Lean and crisply tannic, with a modest level of berry flavor that persists into the finish. Drinkable now. • $32 • (12/15/94) • **82**
Volnay Taille Pieds Domaines du Château de Beaune 1991: Earthy, almost muddy in flavor. A chewy wine that has little charm and is drying on the finish. Drinkable now. 450 cases made. • $34 • (01/31/94) • **78**
Volnay Taille Pieds Domaines du Château de Beaune 1990: Tight and hard as a rock when first tasted; packed with vanilla, chocolate, plum and black cherry elements. Try now. • $34 Ⓐ • (12/15/92) • **92**
Volnay Taille Pieds Domaines du Château de Beaune 1989 • $48 • (01/31/92) • **88**
Volnay Taille Pieds Domaines du Château de Beaune 1988 • $50 • (03/31/91) • **88**
Vosne-Romanée Aux Raignots Château de Vosne-Romanée 1994: Tries to be delicate, with a vibrant layer of raspberry and currant flavor, but the sandy tannins coat the mouth and show no signs of going away. Those who don't mind astringency will love it. • $48 • (11/15/96) • **85**
Vosne-Romanée Aux Raignots Château de Vosne-Romanée 1993: Firm and solid, muscular and full-bodied, featuring red berry, earth and mineral character. Some dryness on aftertaste makes us wonder how it will age. But try in 2006. • $51 • (11/15/95) • **88**
Vosne-Romanée Aux Raignots Château de Vosne-Romanée 1992: A beautifully perfumed but tightly wound red that will need until '96 or beyond to reach its peak. Has exotic leafy, earthy, meaty aromas, followed by tart cherry and plum flavors. Great finish, too. • $40 • (10/31/94) • **89**
Vosne-Romanée Aux Raignots Château de Vosne-Romanée 1991: Lean and simple, with a watery texture than cramps the modest berry flavors. Pleasant enough, but nothing special. Drinkable now. 750 cases made. • $51 • (01/31/94) • **80**
Vosne-Romanée Aux Raignots Château de Vosne-Romanée 1990: A more delicate Vosne, with game, berry and chestnut aromas and flavors and medium tannins. Drinkable now. • $53 • (12/15/92) • **85**
Vosne-Romanée Aux Raignots Château de Vosne-Romanée 1989 • $55 • (01/31/92) • **93**
Vosne-Romanée Aux Raignots Château de Vosne-Romanée 1986 • $50 • (07/31/88) • **89**
Vosne-Romanée Aux Raignots Château de Vosne-Romanée 1985 • $51 • (02/28/89) • **90**

BOUCHOTTE, VALENTIN

Savigny-lès-Beaune Les Jarrons 1988 • $31 • (02/28/91) • **83**

BOUGRIER, JEAN-CLAUDE

Vouvray 1996: This lively wine offers a nice mix of sweet and tart, with lime, pineapple and light honey flavors and a silky texture. It's balanced and clean. Drink now. 8,000 cases made. • $9 • (05/31/98) • **85**
Vouvray 1995: Soft and fresh, with bright floral and apple notes and just a hint of sweetness to round out the crisp, lemony acidity. A nice apéritif. 5,000 cases made. • $8 • (06/15/97) • **84**

BOUISSIÈRE, DOMAINE LA

Gigondas 1989 • $15 • (04/15/93) • **74**

BOUKANDOURA, HENRI

Merlot Vin de Pays de Coteaux de Murviel 1993 • $NA • (01/01/96) • **79**

BOULEY, JEAN-MARC

Pommard Les Rugiens 1987 • $34 • (11/15/90) • **63**
Pommard Les Rugiens 1985 • $30 • (10/31/88) • **92**
Volnay Clos des Chênes 1985 • $27 • (10/15/88) • **87**
Volnay Les Caillerets 1985 • $27 • (10/15/88) • **90**

BOUR, DOMAINE

Coteaux du Tricastin 1993 • $10 • (11/15/95) • **81**
Coteaux du Tricastin Red 1990 • $8 • (06/15/93) • **76**

BOURÉE PÈRE & FILS

Beaune Les Epenotes 1989 • $30 • (01/31/92) • **91**
Beaune Les Epenotes 1987 • $35 • (06/15/90) • **88**
Bonnes Mares 1985 • $85 • (05/31/88) • **91**
Bourgogne 1988 • $15 • (03/31/92) • **73**
Chambertin 1990: Not as concentrated as we would expect from a *grand cru*, but offers pleasant strawberry and earth characteristics and medium tannins nonetheless. Drinkable now. 125 cases made. • $85 • (12/15/92) • **84**
Chambertin 1987 • $100 • (05/31/90) • **90**
Chambertin 1985 • $81 Ⓐ • (05/31/88) • **92**
Chambolle-Musigny 1987 • $44 • (06/15/90) • **82**
Chambolle-Musigny Les Charmes 1987 • $56 • (06/15/90) • **82**
Charmes-Chambertin 1994: Almost orange in color, smelling and tasting cooked and oxidized. This wine is thin and unappealing. • $NA • (11/15/96) • **70**
Charmes-Chambertin 1988 • $75 • (03/31/91) • **89**
Charmes-Chambertin 1987 • $66 • (05/31/90) • **87**
Charmes-Chambertin 1985 • $68 • (05/31/88) • **88**
Clos de la Roche 1990: Graceful, with sumptuous earth, plum and cherry aromas and flavors and velvety tannins. Drinkable now. 125 cases made. • $70 • (12/15/92) • **90**
Clos de la Roche 1989 • $65 • (01/31/92) • **94**
Clos de la Roche 1988 • $85 • (03/31/91) • **91**
Clos de la Roche 1987 • $86 • (06/15/90) • **85**
Côte de Nuits-Villages 1994: A light wine that's oxidized and too tannic for its modest scope. • $NA • (11/15/96) • **77**
Gevrey-Chambertin 1989 • $35 • (01/31/92) • **85**
Gevrey-Chambertin La Justice 1988 • $54 • (03/31/92) • **78**
Gevrey-Chambertin La Justice 1985 • $51 • (05/31/88) • **85**
Gevrey-Chambertin Le Clos St.-Jacques 1990: Extremely firm, with fresh mushroom, wet earth and berry aromas and flavors and toasty chestnut notes. Try now. 75 cases made. • $60 • (12/15/92) • **90**
Gevrey-Chambertin Le Clos St.-Jacques 1987 • $56 • (05/31/90) • **86**
Gevrey-Chambertin Les Cazetiers 1994: Light, lean and vaguely spicy, offering tame tannins and a thin thread of berry flavor. Approachable now. • $NA • (11/15/96) • **80**
Gevrey-Chambertin Les Cazetiers 1987 • $66 • (05/31/90) • **80**
Gevrey-Chambertin Les Cazetiers 1985 • $67 • (05/31/88) • **91**
Latricières-Chambertin 1959 • $NA • (08/31/90) • **98**
Morey-St.-Denis 1987 • $35 • (05/15/90) • **74**
Nuits-St.-Georges Les Vaucrains 1985 • $68 • (05/31/88) • **93**
Santenay Les Gravières 1985 • $30 • (05/31/88) • **88**
Vosne-Romanée 1987 • $44 • (07/15/90) • **68**

BOURGEOIS, HENRI

Pouilly-Fumé 1996: Ripe and expressive. Displays the round, tropical fruitiness of a California Sauvignon Blanc, with lime, pineapple and mango notes. Almost sweet, but a core of acidity keeps it fresh. Distinctive. Drink now through 1999. 7,200 cases made. • $15 • (02/28/98) • **89**
Pouilly-Fumé 1995: Still firm, this crisp white offers well-defined flavors of lime, green apple and pear, with mineral and herbal accents. It's well-made in the traditional Loire style. Drink now. 6,500 cases made. • $15 • (01/01/98) • **87**
Pouilly-Fumé 1994 • $17 • (11/15/95) • **88**
Pouilly-Fumé La Demoiselle de Bourgeois 1995: Big and bold, yet classic in style, with beautifully defined mineral and herb notes framing ripe flavors of pear, almond and apple. Muscular, yet graceful. Remains refreshing through the long, clean finish. Drink now through 1999. 2,610 cases made. • $22 • (02/28/98) • **90**
Pouilly-Fumé La Demoiselle de Bourgeois 1993 • $22 • (11/15/95) • **88**

Sancerre d'Antan 1994: Mellowing now, this round white shows coconut and light honey notes accenting the apple and herbal flavors. Generous, with good depth, it's a good effort from a difficult vintage. Drink now through 1999. 222 cases made. • $25 • (03/31/98) • **87**

Sancerre Etienne Henri 1995: A beauty. Lush, honeyed, spicy aromas are atypical for Sancerre but nonetheless alluring in this powerful, distinctive white. The rich and bold flavors range from melon to walnut to herbs, but the classic, crisp mineral notes keep it rooted in the region. Drink now through 2000. 668 cases made. • $25 • (03/31/98) • **92**

Sancerre Grande Réserve 1996: Spicy pear flavors give this round white a ripe, distinctive character, generous and a bit softer than is typical. Clean, finishing with a pleasant nutmeg note. Drink now. 31,600 cases made. • $15 • (05/31/98) • **86**

Sancerre Grande Réserve 1995: Delicate yet racy, this light white stays crisp and clean, with lemon, grapefruit and light herb flavors. A lovely apéritif. • $15 • (04/30/97) • **85**

Sancerre Grande Réserve 1994 • $17 • (12/15/95) • **81**

Sancerre La Bourgeoise 1995: Generous and ripe, this round white offers pear, melon and toast flavors, with firm but not dominating acidity and a relatively soft texture. Harmonious, but a bit short. Drink now. 5,160 cases made. • $22 • (05/31/98) • **86**

Sancerre La Bourgeoise 1993 • $25 • (11/15/95) • **85**

Sancerre La Bourgeoise 1990 • $15 • (12/15/95) • **83**

Sancerre La Côte des Monts Damnés 1995: So well balanced it seems to defy gravity, this focused, vivid white shows fresh flavors of apples, minerals and herbs, somehow both delicate and intense. Still firm and young; great with food. Drink now through 1999. 1,055 cases made. • $22 • (03/31/98) • **90**

Sancerre La Côte des Monts Damnés 1994 • $24 • (04/30/96) • **83**

Sancerre Red La Bourgeoise 1995: Aromas of smoke and spice lead into flavors of black cherry, licorice and spice in this extracted red. It has good ripeness and concentration, but finishes a bit hot. Drink now through 2000. 2,385 cases made. • $22 • (05/31/98) • **84**

Sancerre Red La Bourgeoise 1990: Starting to mature, this red shows an amber rim and softening tannins, with cherry and raisin flavors and light earthy notes. Pleasant spice and mint notes linger on the finish. Drink now. 4,055 cases made. • $22 • (05/31/98) • **82**

Sancerre Rosé Les Bonnes Bouches 1996: This Pinot Noir rosé offers a pretty strawberry color and light strawberry flavors, with a crisp, acidic underpinning. It's light and simple. Drink now. 5,665 cases made. • $20 • (05/31/98) • **80**

BOURGEOIS, RICHARD

Pouilly-Fumé 1994 • $14 • (12/15/95) • **79**

Pouilly-Fumé 1993 • $15 • (10/31/94) • **79**

Sancerre 1995: This round white shows ripe flavors of apple and peach, with herbal notes and a clean finish. Lacks punch, but it's harmonious and easy to drink. 3,000 cases made. • $15 • (06/15/97) • **85**

Sancerre 1994 • $14 • (12/15/95) • **84**

Sancerre 1993 • $15 • (10/31/94) • **85**

BOURGEON, PAUL

Mâcon-Villages 1996: Tight and hard now, this medium-bodied wine yields little immediate pleasure. But give it time and you might taste the mineral, ripe pear, white pepper, stone and matchstick notes that make it distinctive. Has the balance to improve with cellaring. 1,250 cases made. • $11 • (05/31/98) • **86**

Mâcon-Villages 1995: Earthy, funky, acidic and tart. Unpleasant finish. • $NA • (08/31/96) • **71**

Mâcon-Villages 1993: Grassy like a Sauvignon Blanc, showing loads of green, almost asparagus flavors. Unbelievably tart. • $NA • (08/31/95) • **77**

BOURGEON, RENÉ

Bourgogne Les Pourrières 1995: A chewy Bourgogne, with modest cherry flavors. A touch hot and astringent. • $14 • (11/15/97) • **78**

Key: SS—Spectator Selection CS—Cellar Selection HR—Highly Recommended BB—Best Buy $NA—Price not available Ⓐ—Auction Price (BT)—Barrel Tasting
Dates in parentheses indicate the issues in which the ratings were published.

Givry Clos de la Brûlée White 1996: Perfumed and floral, this medium-bodied wine lacks a bit of class and turns sour on the finish. 1,000 cases made. • $NA • (05/31/98) • **75**

Givry Clos de la Brûlée White 1995: Racy, clean and crisp, medium- to full-bodied, with a subtle dose of oak accenting the pear, floral, mineral and honey character. Delicious and harmonious now, even better around 2000. 917 cases made. • $NA • (05/31/97) • **88**

Givry La Baraude 1995: A light red with confected flavors of strawberry and cherry. Tannic and dry on the finish. • $20 • (11/15/97) • **78**

Givry White 1995: Fresh and lovely, supple and fruity. Just a tad diluted on the midpalate, but succulent nonetheless, with raspberry and strawberry character. Try now through 2000. • $18 • (11/15/97) • **82**

BOURGNEUF, CHÂTEAU

Pomerol 1997: Strange aromas of salsa, tomato and grass. Medium-bodied and chewy, with lots of velvety tannins but a slightly grassy finish. • $NA • (06/15/98) (BT) • **75-79**

Pomerol 1996: Delicious flavors of berry and chocolate. Medium-bodied, with medium tannins and a slightly diluted midpalate, but it shows finesse. • $30 • (06/15/98) (BT) • **85-89**

Pomerol 1995: Impressive for this estate. Intense aromas of blackberries, cherries, pepper and tar. Full-bodied and very tannic, with a velvety texture and a long, intensely fruity, coffee-flavored aftertaste. Mouthpuckering. A big and powerful red. Best after 2002. • $30 • (01/31/98) • **92**

Pomerol 1994: Slightly overdone, with very herbal flavors. Full-bodied and very extracted with velvety, slightly hard tannins and a dry finish. • $20 • (01/31/97) • **82**

Pomerol 1993: Somewhat overdone green bean and berry aromas and flavors. Medium-bodied, medium-to-light tannins and an herbal, dry finish. Drinkable now. • $23 • (01/31/96) • **81**

Pomerol 1990: A solid, racy wine, with complex aromas of tar, licorice, violets and ripe fruit which follow through on the palate. Excellent tannin structure. Drinkable now. 5,000 cases made. • $23 • (03/31/93) • **94**

Pomerol 1989 • $32 • (03/15/92) • **90**

Pomerol 1988 • $19 • (06/30/91) • **90**

Pomerol 1985 • $28 • (11/30/88) • **86**

Pomerol 1982 • $NA • (05/15/89) • **83**

BOURILLON-DORLÉANS, DOMAINE

Vouvray Demi-Sec La Bourdonnerie 1995: Soft and light. Shows modest sweetness and balances citruslike acidity with light peach, herb and lemon flavors. Makes a nice apéritif. 3,000 cases made. • $15 • (06/15/97) • **84**

Vouvray Demi-Sec La Coulée d'Argent 1995: Herb and citrus flavors dominate this big-bodied but somewhat sharp white. It has concentration but lacks generosity. Drinkable now. 10,000 cases made. • $15 • (06/15/97) • **84**

BOUSCASSÉ, CHÂTEAU

Madiran 1995: A deep, brooding red, its smoke, plum and iron aromas turn to raspberry and cassis on the palate. The silky texture is enveloped in a cloak of tannins and the finish is lingering. Not for the faint of heart. Try in 1999. 16,500 cases made. • $15 • (09/30/97) • **89**

Madiran Vieilles Vignes 1995: Gorgeous aromas of roasted coffee and vanilla yield to flavors of cassis, chocolate and tobacco in this massive, backward wine. Its wall of tannin needs to be resolved, but the concentration and sweet fruit on the finish suggest it will come together in time. Try in 2001. 6,500 cases made. • $25 • (09/30/97) • **91**

Madiran Vieilles Vignes 1994: Silky mouthfeel and wild berry and game character are seductive, but due to a slight lack in depth and concentration, the tannins protrude somewhat. Should settle down by 1999. 6,600 cases made. • $26 • (09/30/97) • **87**

Madiran Vieilles Vignes 1990: Some development, showing rich, sweet, plummy flavors that kick in on midpalate. Loads of sweet fruit and glycerin, dried cherry, chocolate, tobacco and Provençal herbs. Complex, brawny and structured, with an immense finish. Buy this, if you can find it. 6,800 cases made. • $22 • (01/01/97) • **92**

Madiran Vieilles Vignes 1989: Combines brute strength with exotic aromatics. Showing its maturity, this is packed with sweet, gamy, decadent fruit, tobacco and a touch of manure. Ripe, luscious and just about ready to drink, the finish is long and firm. Needs to be decanted. 5,000 cases made. • $26 • (01/01/97) • **88**

Pacherenc du Vic-Bilh Le Calendrier des Pacherencs Doux 1995: Distinct pineapple and passion fruit notes ring through this light-bodied dessert wine, with a hint of earthiness. Moderately sweet finish. 1,250 cases made. • $19/500ml • (09/30/97) • **84**

BOUSCAUT, CHÂTEAU

Pessac-Léognan 1997: Rather light, with some berry and tobacco character, but lacks fruit on the finish. • $NA • (06/15/98) (BT) • **75-79**
Pessac-Léognan 1996: A bit lean, with some plum and berry flavor and firm tannins. Medium finish. Wait and see. • $18 • (06/15/98) (BT) • **85-89**
Pessac-Léognan 1995: Delicate and delicious. Pretty aromas of berries and milk chocolate follow through to a wine of medium body and silky palate, with fresh acidity and a medium finish. Best after 1999. 10,250 cases made. • $22 • (01/31/98) • **86**
Pessac-Léognan 1993: Straightforward tobacco and cherry character, medium-to-light body, light tannins and simple finish. Drinkable now. 10,833 cases made. • $25 • (01/31/96) • **82**
Pessac-Léognan 1990: Meaty and rich, with decadent smoky and berry aromas and flavors and velvety tannins. Drinkable now. 15,000 cases made. • $18 • (03/31/93) • **88**
Pessac-Léognan 1989 • $22 • (03/15/92) • **93**
Pessac-Léognan 1988 • $20 • (04/30/91) • **87**
Pessac-Léognan 1986 • $9 • (02/15/89) • **78**
Graves 1985 • $15 • (12/31/88) • **90**
Graves 1982 • $18 • (08/31/92) • **84**
Graves 1981 • $12 • (05/01/84) • **86**
Graves 1970 • $27 • (05/15/93) • **85**
Graves 1961 • $NA • (04/30/96) • **85**
Pessac-Léognan White 1995: Disappointing. Candied and rather oxidized, with some apple character but short on the palate. Drink if you must. Tasted twice, with consistent notes. • $24 • (04/30/98) • **78**
Pessac-Léognan White 1994 • $18 • (03/31/96) • **86**

BOUSQUET, CHÂTEAU DU

Côtes de Bourg 1995: A firm-textured, traditional style Bordeaux, with lean but attractive fruit flavors accented by cedar and tobacco, and a nicely tannic structure. Drink now through 2000. 15,000 cases made. • $9 • (01/31/98) • **85**

BOUSQUETTE, CHÂTEAU

St.-Chinian 1991 • $10 • (03/15/94) • **82**
St.-Chinian 1989 • $10 • (07/15/92) • **81**

BOUSQUETTE, DOMAINE DE LA

St.-Chinian 1986 • $8 • (03/31/90) • **82**

BOUSSAGOL, DOMAINE

St.-Chinian 1995: A fairly crisp red, with blueberry and cranberry flavors and a tart finish. Interesting, but could use more finesse. • $15 • (05/31/98) • **83**

BOUVERIE, LA

Costières de Nîmes 1995: Simple, with a diluted sweetness to the grape and cinnamon flavors that reminds us of fruit-juice drinks. 12,000 cases made. • $7 • (12/15/96) • **78**
Costières de Nîmes 1994 • $6 • (11/15/95) • **82**
Costières de Nîmes 1989 • $6 • (07/15/91) • **79**
Costières de Nîmes White 1995: Round and straightforward, it has a silky texture and good weight, but little in the way of distinctive flavors. 12,000 cases made. • $7 • (10/15/96) • **79**
Costières de Nîmes White 1994 • $6 • (09/30/95) • **82**
Merlot Vin de Pays d'Oc Cuvée Spéciale 1995: A balanced Merlot, with plenty of dried plum and herbal flavors. Ready to drink. 15,000 cases made. • $7 • (04/30/98) • **82**
Merlot Vin de Pays d'Oc Cuvée Spéciale 1994: Mature, with a nice herbal accent to the rich cherry and plum flavors. Solid, with moderate tannins. Try drinking this with roasted chicken. 8,000 cases made. • $8 • (12/15/96) BB • **85**
Merlot Vin de Pays d'Oc Cuvée Spéciale 1993 • $7 • (10/31/95) BB • **84**

BOUVET

Brut Saumur Saphir 1995: This sparkler shows unusual generosity for Saumur, with toast, cream and apple pie flavors that are round, soft and deep. It has a delicate, well-integrated mousse and a slightly spicy finish. Drink now. • $16 • (06/30/98) • **85**
Brut Saumur Saphir 1993: This rather austere, big-boned sparkler doesn't show much fruit, but maturity has given it pleasant toast and smoke flavors that linger on the finish. A good match for food. • $16 • (05/15/97) • **87**
Brut Saumur Saphir 1991 • $14 • (11/15/95) • **85**
Brut Saumur Saphir 1988 • $14 • (01/31/92) • **82**
Brut Saumur Saphir 1985 • $12 • (06/15/90) • **84**
Brut Saumur Vintage Saphir 1992 • $14 • (11/15/95) • **83**

BOUZEREAU & FILS, MICHEL

Bourgogne White 1996: Clean, smooth and pure, this is a lovely wine with impressive balance, although it's quite woody. Of medium body, with mineral, mint, pear and green apple flavors. A vanillalike, wet earth note on the silky finish draws you back for another sip. Buy a case and enjoy now through 2000. • $NA • (05/31/98) • **88**
Meursault Le Limozin 1996: Sleek and pretty, medium in body, with honey, pear, pink grapefruit, juicy pineapple, toasty coconut and carmelized hazelnut flavors balanced by fresh and vibrant limelike acidity. You only wish for a bit more weight in the midpalate. Drink around 2000. • $NA • (05/31/98) • **90**
Meursault Le Limozin 1995: Full-bodied and honeyed, delivering the standard oak accents, spice and pear notes and tasting hamonious on the finish, but it's a bit lacking in fruit concentration. Try upon release. • $NA • (05/31/97) • **87**
Meursault Le Tesson 1996: Rich but rustic, with floral, peach, tropical, earth and mineral character. Medium- to full-bodied, with lots of acidity blanketing the fruit. Slightly bitter finish. Try in 1999. • $NA • (05/31/98) • **80**
Meursault Le Tesson 1995: Delightful to smell and taste, this full-bodied, balanced wine marries toast, spice, honey, pear and other fruit flavors beautifully and has a lovely, sweet-tasting, smoke-accented finish. Drink now through 2000. • $NA • (05/31/97) • **88**
Meursault Le Tesson 1994: Attractive village wine; harmonious, supple and medium-bodied, offering lovely, focused ripe fruit character. A clean and authentic-tasting white Burgundy. Drinkable now. • $35 • (05/31/96) • **85**
Meursault Le Tesson 1992: Fairly ripe and rich, blending pear, hazelnut and vanilla flavors with an elegant, balanced finish. • $29 Ⓐ • (08/31/94) • **86**
Meursault Les Charmes 1994: Some exciting mineral and vanilla character in this medium-bodied white. Intense citrus, almond and butter character. Very well-made and voluptuous on the finish. Try now and through 2000. • $45 • (05/31/96) • **90**
Meursault Les Charmes-Dessus 1996: Seductive in a light and airy way, it lacks a bit of weight in the midpalate. Medium-bodied and quite racy, with ripe, tropical and citrus flavors, it's firmly structured, with a backbone of acidity. Turns a bit oaky on the finish, but the fruit mingles nicely. Try around 2000. • $NA • (05/31/98) • **90**
Meursault Les Charmes-Dessus 1995: Well made, this is supple and silky while at the same time offering a core of acidity and clean, pure notes of fresh lime, lemon, green apple, mineral and orange peel that balance the honeyed character. Full-bodied, with a lengthy finish. Try after 1999. • $50 • (05/31/97) • **92**
Meursault Les Genevrières 1996: A beauty; elegant, pure and racy, offering subtle accents of floral, honey, pear, tropical and toasty coconut notes. Full-bodied but refined. It lacks impressive midpalate concentration, but displays a silky texture enveloped in a minerally cocoon that should blossom around 2005. • $NA • (05/31/98) • **93**
Meursault Les Genevrières 1994: Super Chardonnay, full-bodied yet refined and classy. Quite toasty, beautifully supple and smooth, boasting a lovely honey and ripe fruit character. Concentrated and silky on the perfectly balanced finish. Drinkable now. • $45 • (05/31/96) • **95**
Meursault Les Genevrières 1992: Vividly fruity, lively with flavor and acidity, making the pear, apple and spice flavors last a long time on the finish. It's smooth, pure and refined. • $NA • (08/31/94) • **88**
Meursault Les Grands Charrons 1996: Lovely wine, showing mineral, wet stone, earth and ripe fruit character. Of medium-to-full body; elegant, vibrant, and bursting with lime-spiked acidity that takes it to a long, juicy finish. Hold until around 2005. • $36 • (05/31/98) • **91**
Meursault Les Grands Charrons 1995: A serious village wine; quite powerful, with a core of mineral, wet stone, dried herb and some honey flavors. It's hard and unyielding, closed on the nose and the palate now, but shows good potential; try after 2000. • $40 • (05/31/97) • **91**

FRANCE

Meursault Les Grands Charrons 1994: Soft and supple; very pleasant with honey, apricot, lemon and pear character. Seduces you with its sweet flavors and mineral texture. Delicious now. • $30 • (05/31/96) • **85**

Meursault Les Grands Charrons 1992: Pure, focused fruit, packed with intense pear, apple and grapefruit flavors that are laced with a touch of honey; lingers on the finish. More fruit intensity than most village Meursault. Try now. • $NA • (08/31/94) • **89**

Puligny-Montrachet Champ Gain 1996: Thick, dense, and full-bodied with a creamy feel on the midpalate, offering loads of mineral, vanilla, wet stone, toasty oak, bread dough, pear and apple pie character. Fresh, with vibrant acidity on the long, balanced finish. Tempting from 2000 through 2007. • $55 • (05/31/98) • **91**

Puligny-Montrachet Champ Gain 1995: Thick, dense and full-bodied, offering a mineral and wet stone character along with ripe pear and melon notes. The elegant finish, accented by toasty oak, leaves your palate clean. Drink now through 2000. • $50 • (05/31/97) • **95**

Puligny-Montrachet Champ Gain 1994: Magnificent. Restrained and yet full of flavor, it melts like whipped double cream in your mouth. The symphony of flavors—vanilla, mineral, hazelnut, coconut, pear and lemon—marry flawlessly in this tightly wrapped, medium- to full-bodied white. Drinkable now. • $45 • (05/31/96) • **94**

BOXLER, ALBERT

Gewürztraminer Alsace 1994: Luscious. Full-bodied and unctuous, this ripe wine is bursting with honey, spice and apricot flavors. Frankly sweet, with just enough acidity for balance. Hard to match with food, but great on its own. • $24 • (09/30/96) • **91**

Pinot Blanc Alsace 1994: This shows a bright personality, brimming with lemon, pineapple and mineral notes with an underlying fullness and good balance. It's still fresh, clean and refreshing. • $16 • (09/30/96) • **87**

Riesling Alsace Grand Cru Sommerberg 1993: As fresh and clean as a mountain stream. Aromas of wet stones and herbs make way for a racy palate of grapefruit and lime. Light but intense, it's a lively match for food. 1,000 cases made. • $28 • (09/30/96) • **88**

Tokay Pinot Gris Alsace 1994: Keeps drawing you back for another sip; not sweet, not dry. Ripe and concentrated, with alluring aromas of pears, coconut and roses, opulent flavors and a rich mouthfeel. • $24 • (09/30/96) • **91**

BOYD-CANTENAC, CHÂTEAU

Margaux 1997: Amazingly dark-colored. Loads of currants and ripe berry character. Medium-bodied, with full tannins but a very short finish. A wine with pretensions. • $NA • (06/15/98) (BT) • **85-89**

Margaux 1996: Impressive aromas of cassis and blackberry. Full-bodied, with firm tannins and a medium finish. A solid '96. Almost outstanding. • $30 • (06/15/98) (BT) • **85-89**

Margaux 1995: Pretty plum and berry aromas and flavors. Medium body, with some soft tannins and a fresh finish. • $25 • (01/01/97) (BT) • **85-89**

Margaux 1985 • $21 Ⓐ • (04/15/88) • **90**
Margaux 1983 • $22 Ⓐ • (04/16/86) • **86**
Margaux 1982 • $29 Ⓐ • (08/31/92) • **90**
Margaux 1961 • $31 • (04/30/96) • **84**

BRAC DE LA PERRIÈRE

Beaujolais-Villages Domaine de la Brasse 1996: Crisp, lively and bright, showing black cherry and lightly spicy flavors with an undercurrent of citrusy acidity. The tannins are soft, the texture supple. • $9 • (09/15/97) • **83**

Beaujolais-Villages Domaine de la Brasse 1995: Straightforward and pretty. A pleasant mix of cherry, spice and light banana notes gives this wine immediate appeal. It has enough structure to match with food. • $NA • (08/31/96) • **84**

Chiroubles Domaine des Gatilles 1996: Shows the crisp, light body typical of Chiroubles, but its black cherry flavors are deeper, more assertive than usual. Elegant and clean. • $13 • (09/15/97) • **86**

Juliénas Les Bucherats 1996: Shows weight on the palate, but the flavors are light and simple, the tannins modest but drying. A straightforward wine lacking charm. • $12 • (09/15/97) • **79**

Juliénas Les Bucherats 1995: Barnyard aromas and flavors can be characteristic of Beaujolais, but go to an unpleasant extreme in this earthy red. • $8 • (09/15/96) • **74**

Moulin-à-Vent Les Brigands 1996: Rustic, rather tough, with chocolate and earth aromas, black cherry, smoke and barnyard flavors. Try now. • $16 • (09/15/97) • **82**

Moulin-à-Vent Les Brigands 1994: Soft, spicy and round. The black cherry and slightly gamy flavors are balanced and supple and show a pleasant hint of kirsch on the finish. Drink now. • $16 • (09/15/96) • **85**

BRANAIRE-DUCRU, CHÂTEAU

St.-Julien 1997: Decent silky tannins with blackberry character, but short and rather light on the midpalate. • $NA • (06/15/98) (BT) • **80-84**

St.-Julien 1996: An impressive amount of violet and raspberry character, with firm, silky tannins behind. Medium-bodied, with medium tannins and a refreshing finish. • $30 • (06/15/98) (BT) • **85-89**

St.-Julien 1995: This shows a very good dose of ripe berry, smoke and vanilla aromas and flavors. Good tannins and a long finish. Almost outstanding. • $25 Ⓐ • (05/15/96) (BT) • **85-89**

St.-Julien 1994: Shows good finesse for the vintage. Cedar and berry aromas and flavors, with fine tannins and a silky finish. Better in 1999. • $20 Ⓐ • (01/31/97) • **87**

St.-Julien 1993: Attractive berry, wet earth aromas and flavors, medium body, medium silky tannins and a fresh finish. Try now. • $19 Ⓐ • (01/31/96) • **85**

St.-Julien 1991: Shows some good tobacco and vanilla flavors. Drinkable now. • $22 • (03/31/94) • **80**

St.-Julien 1990: Sleek and pretty, with floral, mint and plum aromas and flavors and lovely, silky tannins. Drinkable now. 20,000 cases made. • $38 • (03/31/93) • **90**

St.-Julien 1989 • $42 Ⓐ • (03/15/92) • **90**
St.-Julien 1985 • $30 Ⓐ • (06/30/88) • **89**
St.-Julien 1983 • $29 Ⓐ • (03/01/86) • **88**
St.-Julien 1982 • $41 Ⓐ • (08/31/92) • **90**
St.-Julien 1970 • $22 Ⓐ • (05/15/93) • **90**
St.-Julien 1961 • $89 Ⓐ • (04/30/96) • **80**
St.-Julien 1959 • $67 Ⓐ • (10/15/90) • **86**
St.-Julien 1945 • $175 • (03/16/86) • **67**

BRANE, CHÂTEAU BARON DE

Margaux 1994: Light in color and body, offering modest raspberry and strawberry flavors and tannic finish. Second label of Château Brane-Cantenac. • $NA • (06/30/95) • **70**

Margaux 1989 • $NA • (03/15/92) • **89**

BRANE-CANTENAC, CHÂTEAU

Margaux 1997: Pretty aromas of blackberries and minerals. Medium-bodied, with medium, velvety tannins but a very short finish. • $NA • (06/15/98) (BT) • **85-89**

Margaux 1996: The best Brane in years. Very minty, with berry and red fruit aromas. Full-bodied, with silky tannins and a long, caressing finish. A big, yet reserved wine. Shows great potential. Hard to believe it's the same wine I tasted last year. • $35 • (06/15/98) (BT) • **90-94**

Margaux 1995: Bright and fruity, with earthy berry aromas and flavors. Medium- to light-bodied, with fine tannins. • $NA • (05/15/96) (BT) • **80-84**

Margaux 1994: A no-nonsense claret with simple, fruity character, light body and silky tannins. Drink now. 9,600 cases made. • $19 Ⓐ • (01/31/97) • **81**

Margaux 1993: Some good berry and cherry character and a hint of black pepper. Medium-bodied, velvety tannins, polished finish. Try now. • $19 Ⓐ • (01/31/96) • **85**

Margaux 1991: Slightly diluted, but some pretty berry and raspberry flavors finding harmony in the fine tannins. • $24 • (03/31/94) • **80**

Margaux 1990: This is solid yet very appealing, with ripe fruit and vanilla character, fine, well-integrated tannins and a long, refreshing, jammy finish. Drinkable now. 29,000 cases made. • $28 • (03/31/93) • **91**

Margaux 1989 • $40 Ⓐ • (03/15/92) • **94**
Margaux 1988 • $42 • (08/31/91) • **76**
Margaux 1986 • $34 Ⓐ • (06/15/89) • **87**
Margaux 1985 • $23 Ⓐ • (06/30/88) • **89**
Margaux 1983 • $37 Ⓐ • (04/16/86) • **94**
Margaux 1982 • $29 Ⓐ • (08/31/92) • **88**
Margaux 1979 • $18 Ⓐ • (10/15/89) • **80**
Margaux 1970 • $26 Ⓐ • (05/15/93) • **87**

Key: SS—Spectator Selection CS—Cellar Selection HR—Highly Recommended BB—Best Buy $NA—Price not available Ⓐ—Auction Price (BT)—Barrel Tasting
Dates in parentheses indicate the issues in which the ratings were published.

Margaux 1962 • $34 Ⓐ • (11/30/87) • **60**
Margaux 1961 • $52 Ⓐ • (04/30/96) • **84**
Margaux 1947: Deep in color and rich in aroma, this is a healthy, robust wine with layers of cherry, black pepper, cedar and earthy spice flavors that remain supple up to the finish, where it turns a mite bitey. • $129 Ⓐ • (05/31/97) • **88**
Margaux 1945 • $NA • (03/16/86) • **87**

BRANGER, CLAUDE

Muscadet de Sèvre et Maine Sur Lie Domaine La Haute Févrie Excellence Vieilles Vignes 1996: This light, lively white offers lime, grapefruit and mineral notes. Quite crisp on the palate, with a hint of spritz that keeps it fresh. Makes a vibrant apéritif. Drink now. 1,500 cases made. • $13 • (06/30/98) • **83**

BRÉDIF, MARC

Chinon 1996: Alluring aromas of violets, smoke and blackberries follow through on the palate of this firm yet plushly textured red. Excellent definition, with bright flavors that linger on the finish. Drink now through 2000. • $16 • (06/15/98) • **87**
Chinon 1995: This vivacious red makes up in bright flavor what it lacks in power; it's balanced and clean, with raspberry, smoky and light herbal flavors and just enough tannin for grip. Drink now through 1999. • $16 • (06/15/97) • **88**
Chinon 1993 • $12 • (12/15/95) • **85**
Chinon 1992 • $12 • (10/31/94) • **84**
Vouvray 1995: Straightforward, with a nice balance of fruit and acidity. Light peach and herb flavors stay lively through the finish. Drink now. • $16 • (06/30/98) • **83**
Vouvray 1994: Solid and quite tight, with concentrated, crisp flavors of lemon, pineapple and herbs. Has good aging potential and should complement strong fish dishes. • $16 • (06/15/97) • **86**
Vouvray 1993 • $14 • (04/30/96) • **84**
Vouvray Vin Moelleux Nectar 1989 • $25/375ml • (04/30/96) • **90**
Vouvray Vin Moelleux Nectar 1985 • $16/375ml Ⓐ • (06/15/91) • **75**

BRÉGEON, ANDRE-MICHEL

Muscadet de Sèvre et Maine Sur Lie 1996: Round in texture and neutral in character, this soft white offers light apple and pear flavors and hints of minerals on the finish. Drink now. • $12 • (05/31/98) • **81**

BRÉTON, GUY

Morgon 1996: This ripe red shows an unusual mix of sweet berry and game flavors that stretch the traditional character of Gamay to extremes. Silky and deep on the palate. Rich enough to accompany strong meat dishes. Not typical for Beaujolais, but impressive. Drink now through 2001. 300 cases made. • $19 • (07/31/98) • **87**
Morgon 1994: Ripe and firm. Good concentration of spicy raspberry and black cherry flavors with gamy accents over solid tannins that give structure without getting in the way of the fruit. • $19 • (09/15/96) • **88**

BRETON, P.

Bourgueil Les Galichets 1993 • $15 • (05/15/96) • **84**

BRETONNIÈRE, YVES

Muscadet de Sèvre et Maine Domaine des 3 Versants, La Févrie 1993 • $8 • (10/31/94) • **77**

BREUIL, CHÂTEAU DU

Haut-Médoc 1992: Attractive, delicate currant, mint and cherry character, medium body, medium tannins and fresh, silky finish. Drinkable now. • $NA • (04/15/95) • **80**

BRICOUT

Brut Champagne 1985: Overflowing with strawberry and fruit cocktail aromas and flavors; there is medium acidity with intense caramel and brandy flavors on the finish. A bit coarse for us. Drinkable now. 500 cases made. • $48 • (12/31/93) • **80**
Brut Champagne Carte d'Or 1988: Buttery, spicy aromas and robust, rather sweet flavors. Fun to taste, but could be better balanced. 55,000 cases made. • $26 • (12/31/94) • **86**
Brut Champagne Carte d'Or Prestige 1986: Tart and lemony, this lean, crisp style zings across the palate, but may be too lean for some. Picks up pretty honey and vanilla notes on the finish. Drink now. • $40 • (12/31/91) • **86**
Brut Champagne Carte d'Or Prestige 1983: Very dry, with floral, nutty aromas and flavors, it's crisp and austere on the finish, not at all generous, deep or smooth. • $25 • (12/31/89) • **75**
Brut Champagne Cuvée Prestige 1991: This is wonderful. A daring and full-flavored Champagne that pushes the envelope of style—its concentrated, aggressive Chardonnay flavors accented by layers of toasty, spicy, earthy notes echo through a long finish. Drink now. 8,300 cases made. • $26 • (04/30/98) SS • **91**
Brut Champagne Elegance de Bricout 1985: • $NA • (12/31/90) • **85**
Brut Champagne Elegance de Bricout 1982: Simple but spicy, with pleasant ginger ale aromas and flavors, plus a nice touch of toast and vanilla. Smooth and tasty. • $50 • (12/31/88) • **90**

BRIDAY, MICHEL

Rully Champ Clou Red 1987 • $16 • (12/31/90) • **68**

BRIGANDS, DOMAINE DE

Moulin-à-Vent 1993 • $16 • (07/31/95) • **76**

BRILLETTE, CHÂTEAU

Moulis 1996: Has decent fruit flavors, but it's slightly diluted and has some herbal and metallic notes. 10,000 cases made. • $NA • (01/01/97) (BT) • **75-79**
Moulis 1995: More like Rioja than Bordeaux, but still good. Lots of wood (maybe too much) on this wine, with vanilla, cherry and toasty oak character. Medium-bodied, with a vanilla finish. Best after 2000. Tasted twice, with consistent notes. • $17 • (01/31/98) • **84**
Moulis 1990: Polished and deep, with smoke, roasted nut and cedar aromas and flavors, medium tannins and a crisp finish. Drinkable now. 6,700 cases made. • $18 • (03/31/93) • **87**
Moulis 1989 • $17 • (03/15/92) • **86**
Moulis 1988 • $15 • (08/31/91) • **81**
Moulis 1987 • $15 • (11/30/89) • **72**
Moulis 1986 • $14 • (11/30/89) • **78**
Moulis 1982 • $19 • (11/30/89) • **85**

BRISEBARRE, PHILIPPE

Vouvray Sec 1996: Anise and herbal flavors give distinctive character, but there's little fruit behind, and a light earthy note emerges on the tart finish. Drink now. 1,200 cases made. • $12 • (06/30/98) • **79**

BROCARD, JEAN-MARC

Bourgogne Domaine Ste.-Claire White 1994: Like biting into a lime. Amazing mouthpuckering intensity sears your palate with citrus and mineral notes. Tastes leesy and earthy now; could use more balance. Better in 1999. • $11 • (05/31/96) • **86**
Bourgogne sur Jurassique White 1995: Polished and racy, with toasty spice, mineral, pear and lovely honey flavors. Medium- to full-bodied, with good length and an elegant finish. Drink now through 2002. • $13 • (06/15/97) • **89**
Bourgogne sur Kimmeridjien White 1996: Wonderful. Clean and crisp, it shows plenty of honey, tropical fruit and wet soil and mineral aromas and flavors. Seductive from start to finish for its velvety texture, it delivers terrific intensity on the finish. Well crafted and impressive. Drink now through 2002. • $15 • (08/31/97) • **91**
Bourgogne sur Kimmeridjien White 1995: Excellent quality for a simple Bourgogne. Very polished, if oaky, it's full-bodied and seductive, offering lactic, pear and pie crust flavors, spiced oak notes, and a balanced, smoky finish. Drinkable now. • $14 • (06/15/97) • **88**
Bourgogne sur Portlandien White 1996: Very intense, with lime-lemon-grapefruit, herbal and freshly cut grass flavors that create a mouthpuckering sensation, yet it's fairly opulent and full-bodied. Drink now through

FRANCE

2003. Tasted twice, with similar notes. 7,500 cases made. • $8 • (05/31/98) • **88**

Chablis Beauregard 1996: Fantastic. Deep and complex, subtle and reserved on the nose, with a classy, creamy, silky texture on the palate. Lots of fruit and soil substance stimulate the senses and alert you that this is a serious Chardonnay. Long, subtle, oillike finish. Tempting now, but will improve through at least 2007. 2,500 cases made. • $25 • (05/31/98) • **95**

Chablis Beauregard 1995: Unctuous and seductive, full-bodied and balanced, its ripe pear, honey, mineral and lemon-shortcakelike flavors accented by spice. Long, flawless finish. Drink now through 2005. • $23 • (06/15/97) • **89**

Chablis Bougros 1996: Quite earthy and pungent in aroma, this is a beautifully crafted wine, full in body, supple in texture and packed with intense fruit and citrus character. Fans of distinctive Chablis won't be disappointed here. Very ripe finish. Tempting now through 2007. 1,250 cases made. • $45 • (05/31/98) • **93**

Chablis Bougros 1995: An opulent *grand cru* in a sweet-and-sour style, both powerful and racy. Dense, fat and ripe, with honey and tropical flavors accented with fresh, lemon-lime and dried herb notes. Full-bodied, supple, with an intense finish that lasts more than a minute. Try now through 2005. • $43 • (06/15/97) • **91**

Chablis Fourchaume 1996: Cutting-edge Chablis, sharp as a razor blade, with loads of lemon and lime but also a thick texture that hides beneath ripe fruit and mineral content. This full-bodied sprinter needs time to mature; try after 2005. 2,500 cases made. • $25 • (05/31/98) • **93**

Chablis Les Clos 1996: Supple, dense, opulent and full-bodied, this balanced Chablis shows loads of citrus and fruit character that's nicely softened by oak and honey accents. Long, satisfying and palate-cleansing finish. Served at room temperature, it's approachable now, but will improve through 2005. 1,250 cases made. • $45 • (05/31/98) • **93**

Chablis Les Clos 1994 • $NA • (05/31/96) • **76**

Chablis Malantes 1994 • $NA • (05/31/96) • **91**

Chablis Montée de Tonnerre 1995: Sings on the palate, vibrant and clean as it bursts with lemon, dried herbs, honey and ripe fruit flavors. Medium-to-full in body, it's ready now through 2000. • $23 • (06/15/97) • **86**

Chablis Montmains 1996: Fresh, intense, lively and vibrant, this mouthpuckering wine is also very sweet and succulent. Medium-bodied, with lovely balance, it shows freshly cut grass, wet earth, green apple and pineapple notes. The herbal finish is a bit rustic, but try with seafood. Better around 2005. 2,500 cases made. • $23 • (05/31/98) • **87**

Chablis Montmains 1995: Delightful, with succulent, fresh citrus notes that combine beautifully with the honeyed, ripe fruit character of this full-bodied, unctuous Chablis. Supple finish. Drink now through 2005. • $23 • (06/15/97) • **89**

Chablis Montmains 1994 • $NA • (05/31/96) • **87**

Chablis Vieilles Vignes 1996: What intensity. A gorgeous, pure Chablis, of medium body, that delivers lovely mineral, ripe fruit, cream and lemon character. It's quite subtle at first, but the finish rockets to amazing heights—exploding with flavors. Hunt down cases of this stuff. Enjoy now and in the near future. 139 cases made. • $21 • (08/31/97) • **91**

Chablis Vieilles Vignes Domaine Ste.-Claire 1994 • $NA • (05/31/96) • **85**

Petit Chablis 1996: A lovely, balanced, sweet-tasting and seductive Petit Chablis, with a swooning combination of flint, mineral, tropical fruit, pear, floral and lime flavors. Tempting now, but still a bit crisp on the finish, so could stand cellaring until 2000 or so. • $18 • (08/31/97) • **90**

Sauvignon de St.-Bris 1995: Flavorful and aromatic, with floral, earth, goosebery and pumpkin notes laced through subtle spice flavors. Medium-to-full in body. Drink now through 2000. • $12 • (06/15/97) • **86**

Sauvignon de St.-Bris Domaine Ste.-Claire 1994 • $NA • (05/31/96) • **87**

BROCHARD, HUBERT

Sancerre 1994 • $19 • (05/31/96) • **81**

BROTTE, LAURENT CHARLES

Châteauneuf-du-Pape White 1993: Ripe, fruity and satisfying, marked by apple and pear notes and delivered with a smooth, rounded texture. The flavors even linger on the finish. 1,900 cases made. • $17 • (10/15/94) • **84**

Côtes du Rhône-Villages Seguret 1990 • $5 • (04/15/93) • **79**

Côtes du Rhône-Villages Seguret 1986 • $6 • (09/30/89) BB • **80**

Gigondas 1990 • $10 • (03/31/94) • **86**

BROUSTET, CHÂTEAU

Barsac 1990: Chewy and intense, providing plenty of toasty oak, tropical fruit, dried apricot and honey flavors; the burning finish seems slightly aggressive. Drinkable now. • $23 • (04/15/95) • **83**

Barsac 1988: Ripe and rich, with lots of almond, honey and vanilla aromas and flavors that are sweet and concentrated without being cloying. A bit earthy or moldy on the finish. Drinkable now. • $4/375ml Ⓐ • (03/31/91) • **83**

BROWN, CHÂTEAU

Pessac-Léognan 1997: Balanced and fruity, it has a core of ripe berry and dried cherry character, with green tobacco underneath. Medium-bodied, with velvety tannins and a medium finish. • $NA • (06/15/98) (BT) • **85-89**

Pessac-Léognan 1996: You'll like the violet, berry and mineral aromas. Medium-bodied and balanced, with fine tannins and a long finish. Very harmonious. Rather impressive for the vintage from this producer. Almost outstanding. • $20 • (06/15/98) (BT) • **85-89**

Pessac-Léognan 1995: A bit coarse but with plenty of fruit. Give it time to come around. Very grapey, with berry and tobacco aromas. Full-bodied and very silky, with a long, ripe, almost raisiny aftertaste. Best after 2000. 6,600 cases made. • $18 • (01/31/98) • **88**

Pessac-Léognan 1994: Sleek, with aromas and flavors of dried cherry and mineral. Tannins are firm and slightly dry. Drink now. • $15 • (01/31/97) • **84**

Pessac-Léognan White 1995: This well-crafted white offers more on the nose than palate, with pretty aromas of apples, coconut and lemons. Medium-bodied, with fresh acidity and a slightly short aftertaste. Drink now. • $18 • (04/30/98) • **86**

BROWN-LAMARTINE, CHÂTEAU

Bordeaux Supérieur 1993: Some pretty red berry, anise and earth flavors but could use a bit more concentration. Herbaceous note on the slightly dry finish. • $NA • (01/31/96) • **79**

BRULLY, DOMAINE DE

Bourgogne White 1994: A bit green and herbal. Medium-bodied, tart and unripe. • $NA • (08/31/96) • **70**

Chassagne-Montrachet Les Vergers 1994: Woody, grassy and slightly rustic, with a drying finish. Not for everyone. • $NA • (08/31/96) • **74**

St.-Aubin Les Cortons White 1994: Supple and smooth, with mineral, vanilla bean and slightly herbal flavors and aromas. Drink now. • $NA • (08/31/96) • **84**

BRUN, JEAN-PAUL

Beaujolais Cuvée à l'Ancienne Domaine des Terres Dorées 1993 • $12 • (06/15/95) • **77**

Beaujolais Domaine des Terres Dorées Chardonnay 1995: Fresh and easy to drink. The crisp apple flavors and citrus and light vanilla notes clearly say Chardonnay. A lively, yet richly textured white. • $12 • (09/15/96) • **84**

Beaujolais Domaine des Terres Dorées Cuvée à l'Ancienne 1996: Soft and light, its ripe cherry and light spice flavors are slightly marred by a vegetal note. Drink now, chilled. • $10 • (09/15/97) • **79**

Beaujolais Domaine des Terres Dorées Cuvée à l'Ancienne 1995: The blackcherry flavors show a pleasantly bitter, smoky accent in this fresh, vivid wine. It's light-bodied and supple; drink lightly chilled. • $12 • (09/15/96) • **82**

Beaujolais Domaine des Terres Dorées Cuvée Tradition 1993 • $10 • (07/31/95) • **77**

Chardonnay Beaujolais Domaine des Terres Dorées 1996: Crisp, with bright, citrusy flavors of grapefruit and lemon, yet it still feels round on the palate. A clean, modest complement to food. • $11 • (09/15/97) • **82**

Chardonnay Beaujolais Domaine des Terres Dorées 1993 • $14 • (07/31/95) • **87**

Key: SS—Spectator Selection CS—Cellar Selection HR—Highly Recommended BB—Best Buy $NA—Price not available Ⓐ—Auction Price (BT)—Barrel Tasting

Dates in parentheses indicate the issues in which the ratings were published.

BRUN LABRIE, CHÂTEAU

Bordeaux 1994: Light vanilla, cherry and herbaceous notes mingle in this light, yet firm, red. 5,000 cases made. • $6 • (07/31/96) • **78**

BRUNET, PATRICK

Fleurie Domaine de Robert 1993: Light and simple, showing tea, tobacco and some cherry flavors in a thin texture. Turns dry on the finish. Drink now. • $15 • (09/15/96) • **77**

BRUSSET, DANIEL

Gigondas Les Hauts de Montmirail 1991 • $18 • (03/31/94) • **87**
Gigondas Les Hauts de Montmirail 1990 • $28 • (04/15/93) • **89**
Gigondas Les Hauts de Montmirail 1989 • $22 • (11/15/91) HR • **91**
Gigondas Les Hauts de Montmirail 1988 • $19 Ⓐ • (09/30/90) • **90**

BRUSSET, DOMAINE

Côtes du Rhône-Villages Cairanne 1995: The first bottle was corked, but the second bottle showed ripe, fairly deep currant flavors, crisp, fresh and lively texture and a lingering, somewhat tart, finish. Try now. 7,500 cases made. • $11 • (10/15/97) • **84**
Côtes du Rhône-Villages Cairanne Coteaux des Trabers 1990 • $11 • (04/15/93) • **71**
Côtes du Rhône-Villages Cairanne Côteaux des Trabers 1988 • $7 • (12/15/90) BB • **86**
Côtes du Rhône-Villages Cairanne Coteaux des Trabers 1986 • $7 • (06/15/89) • **61**
Gigondas Les Hauts de Montmirail Elevé en Fûts de Chène 1994: An alluring red with plenty of black cherry and ripe plum flavors, along with notes of toasty oak, mocha and spice, this is rich yet focused, with the backbone to age. Drink now through 2000. 2,000 cases made. • $24 • (10/15/97) • **90**

BRUT DARGENT

Brut Blanc de Blancs Côtes du Jura 1984 • $10 • (03/31/88) • **82**
Brut Blanc de Blancs Côtes du Jura Chardonnay 1988 • $11 • (06/15/90) • **83**
Brut Côtes du Jura 1992 • $11 • (12/31/94) • **76**
Brut Rosé Côtes du Jura 1984 • $10 • (03/31/88) • **86**
Brut Rosé Côtes du Jura Pinot Noir 1990 • $11 • (12/31/94) • **80**
Côtes du Jura Méthode Traditionnelle 1994: Solidly built, with obvious fruit and nut flavors. Full-bodied but smooth enough. • $13 • (05/31/97) • **80**

BUCY, MAISON JOSEPH DE

Mâcon-Clessé 1996: Straightforward Pouilly, with lime and pear notes but not much length. Light-to-medium in body, it seems a tad diluted. Drink now. 500 cases made. • $10 • (05/31/98) • **77**

BUFFET, FRANÇOIS

Pommard Les Rugiens 1985 • $40 • (10/15/88) • **88**
Volnay Champans 1995: Blacker in color than Syrah and full-bodied, this expresses pure blueberry, blackberry and cassis flavors. Too bad the tannins are a bit dry. Should settle down by around 2000. • $30 • (11/15/97) • **89**
Volnay Clos de la Rougeotte 1995: This cherry- and cassis-scented red imparts a purity; then the green, harsh tannins take over. Questionable whether the fruit will outlive the tannins. • $30 • (11/15/97) • **84**
Volnay En Champans 1985 • $35 • (10/15/88) • **91**

BUNAN, DOMAINES

Bandol Château La Rouvière 1995: Warm and spicy-tasting with ripe flavors of plum, cherry and berry. A nice meaty note marks the finish. Drink now. • $NA • (05/31/98) • **83**
Bandol Château La Rouvière 1989 • $19 • (03/31/95) • **83**
Bandol Mas de la Rouvière 1995: A little gamy-tasting, with some lovely plum and berry flavors. This is a good articulation of Bandol. Drink now. 5,000 cases made. • $14 • (05/31/98) • **85**
Bandol Mas de la Rouvière 1990 • $15 • (03/31/95) • **87**
Bandol Rosé Château La Rouvière 1996: There are some nice cherry and berry flavors in this straightforward and quaffable rosé. Balanced and medium-bodied. Drink now. 2,000 cases made. • $14 • (05/31/98) • **84**
Bandol Rosé Mas de la Rouvière 1993 • $14 • (08/31/95) • **78**
Bandol White Mas de la Rouvière 1996: A quaffable and well-focused white with good apple and lime flavors, some spicy notes on the finish. Drink now. 2,000 cases made. • $14 • (05/31/98) • **83**

BURGAUD, BERNARD

Côte-Rôtie 1995: Alluring and distinctive. The spicy, gamy aromas are very expressive of Syrah; the palate is rich and concentrated, with ripe black cherry flavor accented with mineral, licorice and game notes, then very tannic on the finish. A terrific example of the traditional style. Drink beginning in 1999. 1,083 cases made. • $38 • (10/15/97) • **92**
Côte-Rôtie 1994: With alluring aromas of wild game and bitter herbs followed by bold flavors of black cherries, smoke, licorice and herbs, this lively and fresh red is buttressed by firm but balanced tannins. Though not a blockbuster—and already drinking well—it's a fine example of its appellation. 1,080 cases made. • $38 • (10/15/97) • **90**
Côte-Rôtie 1992: Gamy, earthy aromas and flavors are enticing, and wrap around a core of ripe cherry flavor that adds balance. An excellent effort in a difficult vintage. • $30 • (12/15/96) • **89**
Côte-Rôtie 1991: Fresh and focused, offering ripe black cherry flavors and an undercurrent of smoky roasted meat. It's smooth and accessible; drinkable now. • $36 • (05/31/94) • **87**
Côte-Rôtie 1990: Ripe, rich and balanced, with refreshing, citrusy acidity and all the ripe berry, wildflower and game aromas and flavors you could want. Smooths itself out on the finish, and the tannins are well-integrated. Best now. 1,000 cases made. • $37 • (04/15/93) • **91**
Côte-Rôtie 1989 • $32 • (01/31/92) • **84**
Côte-Rôtie 1988 • $40 • (03/31/91) • **87**
Côte-Rôtie 1987 • $29 • (02/28/90) • **85**
Côte-Rôtie 1986 • $31 • (01/31/89) • **93**
Côte-Rôtie 1984 • $22 • (10/15/87) • **90**
Côte-Rôtie 1983 • $18 • (05/01/86) • **92**

BURGUET, ALAIN

Bourgogne 1992: Light and simple, a little chewy around the fine thread of raspberry that persists into the finish. • $15 • (12/15/94) • **82**
Bourgogne 1990: Firm and straightforward, displaying modest strawberry and vanilla aromas and flavors and an herbal touch on the tough finish. Drinkable now. • $18 • (12/15/92) • **84**
Gevrey-Chambertin 1992: Extremely floral and distinctive with a modicum of fruit to keep it in balance. • $26 • (12/15/94) • **80**
Gevrey-Chambertin 1991: Well defined; youthful berry and plum aromas and flavors show a moderate level of intensity and finish with a tobacco edge. Drinkable now. • $30 Ⓐ • (01/31/94) • **83**
Gevrey-Chambertin 1990: A vivid expression of Pinot Noir that's focused and charming. Not a blockbuster, but quite subtle, showing a range of cherry, currant, vanilla and earth flavors that come together to create an exciting, concentrated finish. Try now. • $NA • (12/15/92) • **89**
Gevrey-Chambertin Vieilles Vignes 1991: A disappointment. Very crisp and tannic; almost green and stemmy. • $39 Ⓐ • (01/31/94) • **75**
Gevrey-Chambertin Vieilles Vignes 1990: Excellent quality for a Gevrey village wine. Offers lovely, bright, vivid cherry, blackberry and earth aromas and flavors and a solid core of well-integrated tannins and fruit. Drinkable now. • $43 • (12/15/92) • **90**
Gevrey-Chambertin Vieilles Vignes 1988 • $45 • (12/31/90) • **88**
Gevrey-Chambertin Vieilles Vignes 1986 • $33 • (07/15/89) • **84**

BURIER, JACQUES

Pouilly-Fuissé Château de Beauregard 1996: Exotic, with a lovely balance of oak and fruit. It smells of apple blossoms and tastes of kiwi, lime, pineapple and juicy ripe pear. Crisp yet also very smooth in texture, this medium-bodied Pouilly turns smoky and toasty on the lingering finish. Hunt for it. Drink now through 2000. 10,000 cases made. • $21 • (05/31/98) • **91**
Pouilly-Fuissé Château de Beauregard 1995: Ripe and rich, but a bit overdone, with marzipan, hazelnut, honey, pear and apple character. Full-bodied, it finishes a bit heavily. Drink now. 1,000 cases made. • $21 • (05/31/97) • **81**
Pouilly-Fuissé Château de Beauregard 1994: Fat, rich and somewhat unfocused, showing a truffle, buttery and honeyed character that is seductive

but doesn't quite pull together on the short finish. Drink now. 2,416 cases made. • $23 • (05/31/96) • **80**

Pouilly-Fuissé Château de Beauregard 1993: A middle-of-the-road Pouilly, offering modest fruit and a diluted finish. Drink now. • $18 • (05/15/95) • **74**

Pouilly-Fuissé Château de Beauregard Cuvée Prestige 1996: Racy and wonderfully balanced. Deftly marries the lively, fresh tropical, pear and citrus aromas with subtle oak notes. Medium-bodied, it coats the palate with a mineral-laden texture, delivering sweet-tasting ripples as it cascades to a succulent, long finish. You'll want to have at least a case. Drink now through 2005. 2,000 cases made. • $21 • (05/31/98) • **92**

St.-Véran Les Perriers 1996: Fairly intense and compacted, with lime and a whiff of honey, as well as pear, tropical and apple character. Medium-bodied, it's clean but simple on the finish. Drink now through 1999. Tasted twice, with consistent notes. 3,500 cases made. • $14 • (05/31/98) • **83**

BURN, ERNEST

Gewürztraminer Alsace Grand Cru Goldert Clos St.-Imer La Chapelle 1995: A deeply colored, botrytized style that packs in plenty of honey and apricot notes yet retains a sense of balance, though the finish is a bit hot. Nice with desserts or cheeses. • $40 • (09/30/97) • **88**

Riesling Alsace Grand Cru Goldert Clos St.-Imer La Chapelle 1995: A rich, fat *grand cru* with a creamy, leesy character augmenting the apple and peach. Delicious and satisfying, but lacking the complexity and length of the best '95s. • $40 • (09/30/97) • **89**

Tokay Pinot Gris Alsace Grand Cru Goldert Clos St.-Imer Vendanges Tardives 1995: An assertive white, full of personality, with up-front flavors of apricot, pear and honey that are immediately appealing. The moderate acidity suggests it's drinkable, but may improve by 2000. • $50 • (11/15/97) • **87**

BURRIER, GEORGES

Chardonnay Mâcon-Villages 1994: Rich and honeyed with plenty of spice and ripe apple flavors. Lacks intensity and depth, but has some nice fennel and licorice notes. 2,000 cases made. • $10 • (05/31/96) • **84**

Pouilly-Fuissé 1994: Rich and flavorful, sporting loads of honey and spice. It also has very good green apple and citrus flavors wrapped together in an elegant style. Crisp and delicious. 2,400 cases made. • $18 • (05/31/96) • **86**

CABANNE, CHÂTEAU LA

Pomerol 1991: More like water than wine. Clean and fruity, but very light. • $15 • (03/31/94) • **73**

Pomerol 1990: Restrained, early-maturing Pomerol, with pretty, silky tannins and fresh smoky, chocolate, black cherry character. Drinkable now. 5,000 cases made. • $27 • (03/31/93) • **87**

Pomerol 1989 • $20 Ⓐ • (03/15/92) • **92**

Pomerol 1982 • $23 • (08/31/92) • **84**

Pomerol 1961 • $NA • (04/30/92) • **77**

CABASSE, DOMAINE DE

Côtes du Rhône-Villages Seguret Le Rosé de Marie Antoinette 1996: Crisp and lacks a bit of fruit, with some toasty oak, cinnamon, butter and light red berry notes. Medium-bodied; turns a bit lean on the finish. Rather simple; quaffable. Drink chilled. • $14 • (10/15/97) • **80**

CABOCHE, DOMAINE DU PÈRE

Châteauneuf-du-Pape 1989 • $20 • (10/15/91) • **84**

Châteauneuf-du-Pape 1988 • $20 • (10/15/91) • **87**

Châteauneuf-du-Pape 1986 • $20 • (10/15/91) • **81**

Châteauneuf-du-Pape 1985 • $20 • (10/15/91) • **85**

Châteauneuf-du-Pape 1983 • $18 • (10/15/91) • **77**

Châteauneuf-du-Pape 1981 • $30 • (10/15/91) • **87**

Key: SS—Spectator Selection CS—Cellar Selection HR—Highly Recommended BB—Best Buy $NA—Price not available Ⓐ—Auction Price (BT)—Barrel Tasting
Dates in parentheses indicate the issues in which the ratings were published.

CABRIAC, CHÂTEAU DE

Corbières 1992 • $9 • (03/15/94) • **87**

Corbières Cuvée Marquise de Puivert 1995: Game and tobacco are the predominant aromas, followed by flavors of cherry and dried herbs. The tannins are tough in this medium-bodied red, yet the finish lingers nicely. 12,000 cases made. • $10 • (12/15/97) • **85**

CABRIÈRES, CHÂTEAU

Châteauneuf-du-Pape 1995: This red offers alluring flavors of ripe plums, chocolate and herbs; fleshy yet just firm enough for food. Drinkable now. • $23 • (09/15/97) • **84**

Châteauneuf-du-Pape 1994: Light, yet generous with spicy berry flavors over well-integrated tannins. Unobtrusive yet supportive, this would be pleasant with dinner. Drink now. 3,200 cases made. • $23 • (12/15/96) • **85**

Châteauneuf-du-Pape 1988 • $17 • (11/30/90) • **82**

CACHEUX, JACQUES

Echézeaux 1992: Lean and chewy, offering a modest level of berry and cigar-box flavors that finish narrow and with some finesse. • $NA • (12/15/94) • **83**

Vosne-Romanée Les Suchots 1992: A bit chewy, but the plum and currant flavors jump out of the glass. A hint of tea and tobacco on the finish. Drinkable now. • $NA • (12/15/94) • **83**

CADEAUX

Brut Blanc de Blancs France Royal Crown Cuvée Privée NV: An inviting nonvintage sparkling wine—fresh, fruity and dry with it's clean flavors, crisp texture and a bracing finish. Ready for cork-popping now, it's an opportunity to enjoy very good bubbly at a bargain price. 10,000 cases made. • $10 • (12/31/97) BB • **85**

CADET-BON, CHÂTEAU

St.-Emilion 1997: Exotic aromas of spices, flowers and ripe berries, with a hint of raisins. Full-to medium-bodied, with velvety tannins but a slightly hollow midpalate. Impressive. • $NA • (06/15/98) (BT) • **85-89**

St.-Emilion 1996: Enticing aromas of violets, minerals and blackberries. Medium- to full-bodied, with very silky tannins and a medium finish. Shows classy soil. Almost outstanding. 2,000 cases made. • $29 • (06/15/98) (BT) • **85-89**

St.-Emilion 1995: Firm and muscular. Strong aromas of dried cherry and wet earth, with a hint of gravel. Medium- to full-bodied, with firm tannins and an aftertaste of stones and dried herbs. Best after 2000. 1,600 cases made. • $28 • (01/31/98) • **87**

St.-Emilion 1994: Good concentration of berry flavor, but it's also slightly herbal, especially on the finish. Medium-bodied, with firm tannins. Try now. • $NA • (01/31/97) • **82**

CADET-PIOLA, CHÂTEAU

St.-Emilion 1988 • $20 • (07/15/91) • **89**

St.-Emilion 1982 • $23 • (05/15/89) • **88**

CADY, DOMAINE

Coteaux du Layon St.-Aubin Les Varennes 1995: Good concentration and great balance mark this impressive white, with its round sweetness, spicy botrytis notes and firm underlying acidity. Though not showy, it has classic structure. Drink now through 2010. • $20 • (05/31/98) • **90**

CAILBOURDIN, DOMAINE A.

Pouilly-Fumé Cuvée de Boisfleury 1996: Alluring pear and melon aromas carry through on the palate of this rich yet taut white. It has fine concentration and a firm backbone of acidity, suggesting the flavors will bloom with time. Drink now through 2001. • $15 • (05/31/98) • **88**

Pouilly-Fumé Cuvée de Boisfleury 1995: Round and tender for Pouilly-Fumé, this white shows ripe pear and light hazelnut flavors, with clean but discreet acidity. Would make a nice apéritif. • $18 • (05/15/97) • **86**

Pouilly-Fumé Cuvée de Boisfleury 1993 • $17 • (10/31/94) • **81**

FRANCE

Pouilly-Fumé Les Cris 1996: Rustic in style, this big-boned white shows earthy and light cheesy flavors, with strong herbal and grassy accents. Drink now through 1999. • $17 • (05/31/98) • **83**

Pouilly-Fumé Les Cris 1995: Alluring aromas of smoke and herbs draw you in, then crisp, steely flavors hold your interest. It's a bit austere, but has the balance and concentration to complement food. • $20 • (06/15/97) • **87**

Pouilly-Fumé Les Cris 1994 • $19 • (06/15/96) • **80**

Pouilly-Fumé Les Cris 1993 • $19 • (11/15/95) • **89**

CAILLOT, ROGER

Bâtard-Montrachet 1995: Impressive. Big, rich, thick and intense, it's full-bodied and offers a generous toasty oak, pear tart, spice and vanilla character. So concentrated it takes off like a rocket on the finish. Cellar until at least 2006. • $92 • (08/31/97) • **95**

Bourgogne 1995: Light, yet expresses sappy strawberry and licorice flavors. Ready now. • $13 • (11/15/97) • **81**

Bourgogne Les Herbeux White 1995: Ripe yet elegant, with seamless texture and loads of peach, raspberry and pineapple flavors, this full-bodied beauty is a delight. Drink now through 2000. • $16 • (08/31/97) • **89**

Meursault Clos du Cromin 1995: Lovely, with floral, honey, almond biscuit and ripe pear flavors. Full-bodied, the crisp, citrusy character keeps it clean and gives length to the delicious finish. A real food wine. Try from 1999 to 2005. • $32 • (08/31/97) • **89**

Meursault en la Barre Clos Marguerite 1995: Wonderful. Rich and sweet-tasting, this full-bodied wine is packed with tropical fruit, pear, fresh fig and melon flavors that ripple through to a finish accented by subtle oak notes. A smooth, creamlike texture makes it appealing now, but it should be better after 2000. • $32 • (08/31/97) • **92**

Meursault Le Limozin 1995: A dream wine. Hedonistic and seductive, but very classy. Still closed on the nose, hinting only at flowers and honey, but on the palate it explodes with lime, grapefruit, mango, raspberry, pineapple and spice. Leaves the palate clean, and the ultralong finish is pure and sparkling with life. Fantastic now through 2005. • $32 • (08/31/97) • **94**

Meursault Le Tesson 1995: Rich and intense, with loads of toasty oak, spice and ripe fruit aromas and flavors. Medium-to-full in body, it's well balanced, with citrus notes kicking in at the end for a fresh, long finish. Drink after 2000. • $31 • (08/31/97) • **90**

Monthélie 1995: Disjointed and herbaceous, it smells diluted, then turns sweet on the palate before astringent tannins kick in on the finish. • $17 • (11/15/97) • **76**

Pommard 1995: Herbal but also sweet, like red beets, this medium-bodied wine strives for balance but turns astringent. • $27 • (11/15/97) • **77**

Pommard 1987 • $35 • (09/15/89) • **79**

Pommard Epenots 1995: Deep-colored and full-bodied, it looks better than it tastes. Turns herbal and green, with tart tannins. What a shame. • $30 • (11/15/97) • **79**

Puligny-Montrachet Les Folatières 1995: Hard as nails, it gives little now, but there's lots of stuffing here, with a wet earth, citrus, stemmy, appleskin character softened by some honey notes. Full-bodied, long and rich, it should be a beauty around 2005. (Recent bottling may have shocked the wine, says winemaker Michel Caillot.) • $45 • (08/31/97) • **93**

Puligny-Montrachet Les Pucelles 1995: Ripe and fairly opulent, with tropical fruit, toasty oak and spice tones, this full-bodied '95 offers wonderful balance and length. Delicious now, and should hold through 2005. • $68 • (08/31/97) • **90**

Santenay White 1995: An impressive village wine. Almost yellow in color, this ripe, thick, flavorful white also offers a classy crisp structure and excellent balance. Youthful-tasting, with lovely honey, ripe fruit, lactic-vanilla and spice flavors. Harmonious finish. Try now through 2000. • $18 • (08/31/97) • **88**

Volnay Clos des Chênes 1995: Intense, beautiful blackberry and cassis bush character is very impressive. Excellent concentration in this medium-bodied red, but the tannins are extremely tough now. Perhaps better after 2000. • $27 • (11/15/97) • **86**

CAILLOU, CHÂTEAU

Barsac 1991: Some appealing butterscotch, nut, lemon, pear and vanilla flavors. Not much depth, but it'll do as an apéritif. Drink now. • $NA • (04/15/95) • **83**

Barsac 1990: Fabulously balanced and fully botrytised, it shows alluring complexity, creamy texture, zippy acidity, caramel, honey and lemon flavors and an extremely long finish. • $NA • (04/15/95) • **92**

Barsac 1989: Fresh, medium-bodied white demonstrating attractive mineral notes and a lemon, honey character. Very creamy finish is supported by good acidity. Drinkable now. • $40 • (04/15/95) • **87**

Barsac 1988: Distinctive and straightforward, promoting some wet earth, mushroom, cedar and honey flavors. Drinkable now. • $39 • (04/15/95) • **84**

Barsac 1987: • $32 • (06/15/90) • **85**

Barsac 1983: Firmly balanced between sugar and acidity, it just lacks the focused flavors for excellence. Medium-gold, sugary tobacco flavors; not very concentrated. • $22 • (01/31/88) • **76**

Barsac Private Cuvée 1986: Powerful, yet exquisitely balanced, featuring toast, hazelnut, pineapple, apricot and cream flavors. Medium in body and sweetness. Try in 1999. • $NA • (04/15/95) • **92**

Barsac Private Cuvée 1983: Balanced, medium sweetness, with good intensity. The toasty, smoky flavors and dried apricot, honey and spice notes come together on the silky finish. Should improve with age. • $NA • (04/15/95) • **89**

CAILLOU, DOMAINE DU

Châteauneuf-du-Pape 1990: Dense, concentrated and deeply colored, packing in plenty of fruit flavors and adding layers of gamy, earthy, woodsy accents to give it extra interest. Solid berry, plum and prune flavors carry it on the finish. Lots of fine tannins and great balance. Try now. • $19 • (04/15/93) • **89**

Châteauneuf-du-Pape 1988 • $22 • (03/31/91) • **86**

CAILLOU BLANC DU CHÂTEAU TALBOT

Bordeaux 1995: Delivers some very good apple, honey and white pepper aromas and flavors. Medium-bodied, with fresh acidity and a short aftertaste. Drink now. • $21 Ⓐ • (04/30/98) • **86**

Bordeaux 1994 • $23 • (03/31/96) • **90**

CAILLOUX, LES

Châteauneuf-du-Pape 1990: A generous, spicy, berry-flavored wine with flavors that expand as you sip. Gentle for a Châteauneuf, with plenty of soft tannins and an easy texture. Great for drinking now. 1,500 cases made. • $24 • (04/15/93) • **88**

Châteauneuf-du-Pape 1988 • $18 • (10/15/91) • **88**

Châteauneuf-du-Pape 1986 • $18 • (10/15/91) • **79**

Châteauneuf-du-Pape 1985 • $16 • (10/15/91) • **82**

Châteauneuf-du-Pape 1983 • $55 • (10/15/91) • **88**

Châteauneuf-du-Pape 1981 • $30 • (10/15/91) • **76**

Châteauneuf-du-Pape Cuvée Centenaire 1990: Big, muscular, ripe and velvety, this seductively smooth, many-layered wine offers plum, currant, cherry, toast and chocolate flavors in turn and finishes soft and exotic, with impressive length. A distinctive style. 350 cases made. • $24 • (04/15/93) • **93**

Châteauneuf-du-Pape Sélection Reflets 1986 • $18 • (05/31/89) • **89**

CAIRANNE, CAVE DES COTEAUX

Côtes du Rhône-Villages 1988 • $6 • (02/28/90) BB • **81**

Côtes du Rhône-Villages Cairanne 1988 • $6 • (06/30/90) • **76**

CALAGE, CHÂTEAU DE

Coteaux du Languedoc 1991 • $7 • (03/15/94) • **80**

CALISSANNE, CHÂTEAU

Coteaux d'Aix-en-Provence Clos Victoire 1995: Starts off ripe and fairly rich-tasting, but assertive tannins blunt its appeal. Good berry and cherry flavors close down on the finish. Tasted twice, with consistent notes. Drink now through 2000. 500 cases made. • $30 • (03/31/98) • **83**

Coteaux d'Aix-en-Provence Clos Victoire 1994: This explosive wine shows the exuberant fruit flavors and toasty oak accent of a California red with its blackberry, cassis, licorice and spice flavors. Delicious, in the international style. Drinkable now. 200 cases made. • $28 • (10/15/96) • **90**

Coteaux d'Aix-en-Provence Cuvée Prestige 1995: Fresh, fruity and appealing, with plum, cherry and berry flavors. Finishes with notes of spice and pepper. 2,000 cases made. • $15 • (02/28/98) • **85**

FRANCE

Coteaux d'Aix-en-Provence Cuvée Prestige 1994: Ripe and smooth, with rich flavors of plums, chocolate and coffee and a buttery texture that hides the firm tannins. Compact and well-integrated. Try now. 1,000 cases made. • $16 • (10/15/96) • **87**
Coteaux d'Aix-en-Provence Cuvée Prestige 1990 • $15 • (06/15/93) • **79**
Coteaux d'Aix-en-Provence Cuvée Prestige 1988 • $12 • (08/31/91) • **78**
Coteaux d'Aix-en-Provence Cuvée du Château 1995: Lively and assertive, with delicious licorice, dark cherry and berry flavors. Has some nice herbal and tobacco notes on the finish. Drink now through 2000. 5,000 cases made. • $10 • (03/31/98) BB • **85**
Coteaux d'Aix-en-Provence Cuvée du Château 1994: Straightforward, with good berry and plum flavors. Some nice clovelike flavors linger on the finish. 5,000 cases made. • $10 • (02/28/98) • **85**
Coteaux d'Aix-en-Provence Rosé Cuvée du Château 1996: A dry rosé, with good dried cherry, melon and mineral flavors and a nice touch of acidity. Drink with salmon. 5,000 cases made. • $10 • (12/31/97) • **84**
Coteaux d'Aix-en-Provence White Clos Victoire 1996: Tries to put a lot up front but it fades in the end. Has decent pear and spice flavors, with floral notes on the finish. 300 cases made. • $30 • (03/31/98) • **80**
Coteaux d'Aix-en-Provence White Clos Victoire 1995: A spicy-tasting wine, with floral notes as well. Finishes on a buttery note that lingers appealingly. Smooth and mature-tasting. 300 cases made. • $30 • (12/31/97) • **84**
Coteaux d'Aix-en-Provence White Clos Victoire 1994: Tasting more of oak than of fruit, with almost bitter, toasty, smoky flavors dominating the modest melon. Tasted twice with consistent notes. 500 cases made. • $30 • (12/15/96) • **78**
Coteaux d'Aix-en-Provence White Cuvée Prestige 1996: Rough and diluted-tasting, with modest pear and honey flavors. Finishes on a coarse note. 1,000 cases made. • $15 • (03/31/98) • **75**
Coteaux d'Aix-en-Provence White Cuvée Prestige 1995: Thick and polished, this wine makes a firm impact then stays with you, offering melon, lemon, bread dough and nutmeg flavors that linger on the finish. Distinctive and well-integrated. 1,000 cases made. • $16 • (10/15/96) • **86**
Coteaux d'Aix-en-Provence White Cuvée du Château 1996: A coarse, uninspired white wine that has only the faintest hint of fruit flavors. 1,000 cases made. • $10 • (03/31/98) • **73**

CALON-SEGUR, CHÂTEAU

St.-Estèphe 1997: A light- to medium-bodied wine, with pretty toasty oak and berry character and a smoky, silky finish. • $NA • (06/15/98) (BT) • **85-89**
St.-Estèphe 1996: A wonderful velvety texture, with plenty of spice and berry character. Full-bodied, with full tannins and a long finish. Not as great as the '95, but close. • $40 • (06/15/98) (BT) • **90-94**
St.-Estèphe 1995: Greatest Calon-Segur ever made. An absolutely amazing red, this third-growth Bordeaux is remarkable for its layers of berry, violets and perfume. It's full-bodied and very velvety on the palate, with masses of character and an ultralong finish. Best after 2004. • $75 • (01/31/98) SS • **96**
St.-Estèphe 1993: Good '93 featuring sweet berry and tobacco character, medium body, firm tannins and slightly dry finish. Try now. • $25 • (01/31/96) • **84**
St.-Estèphe 1991: A bit lean, but some very nice tobacco and fruit aromas and flavors. Medium body and a short finish. • $21 • (03/31/94) • **82**
St.-Estèphe 1989 • $27 Ⓐ • (03/15/92) • **95**
St.-Estèphe 1988 • $25 Ⓐ • (07/15/91) • **85**
St.-Estèphe 1986 • $26 Ⓐ • (05/31/89) • **86**
St.-Estèphe 1985 • $25 Ⓐ • (05/31/88) • **88**
St.-Estèphe 1983 • $21 Ⓐ • (10/31/86) • **83**
St.-Estèphe 1982: Has very strong cedarlike aromas and flavors, with just enough berry flavor to balance. • $100 • (07/31/97) • **85**
St.-Estèphe 1970 • $23 Ⓐ • (05/15/93) • **83**
St.-Estèphe 1962 • $NA • (11/30/87) • **70**
St.-Estèphe 1961 • $146 • (04/30/96) • **86**
St.-Estèphe 1959 • $NA • (10/15/90) • **82**
St.-Estèphe 1947: Shows spicy caramel and slightly metallic aromas, metallic flavors as well, never enriching. Tasted from magnum. • $360 • (07/31/97) • **84**
St.-Estèphe 1945 • $475 • (11/30/95) • **90**

Key: SS—Spectator Selection CS—Cellar Selection HR—Highly Recommended BB—Best Buy $NA—Price not available Ⓐ—Auction Price (BT)—Barrel Tasting
Dates in parentheses indicate the issues in which the ratings were published.

CALOT, DOMAINE

Morgon Cuvée Unique Vieilles Vignes Réserve 1996: Far from typical for Beaujolais, this intense red offers loads of sweet, concentrated fruit, like a cherry liqueur, with a thick texture and firm underlying tannins. Impressive if not quite harmonious. Best from 1999 through 2001. • $19 • (07/31/98) • **88**

CAMENSAC, CHÂTEAU DE

Haut-Médoc 1996: A well-made '96, with solid fruit and firm tannins. Medium body. A bit one-dimensional now. • $NA • (01/01/97) (BT) • **85-89**
Haut-Médoc 1995: Clean and fresh, with plenty of ultrafine tannins and a lovely complement of cherry and mineral notes. Very fresh finish. Almost outstanding. • $NA • (05/15/96) (BT) • **85-89**
Haut-Médoc 1989 • $16 • (03/15/92) • **86**
Haut-Médoc 1986 • $14 • (06/30/89) • **83**
Haut-Médoc 1979 • $22 • (10/15/89) • **82**
Haut-Médoc 1970 • $35 • (05/15/93) • **87**

CAMPEROS, CHÂTEAU

Sauternes 1995: This moderately sweet white shows some spicy notes of botrytis and some concentration of overripe grapes, but mostly it just seems cloying. 1,000 cases made. • $27 • (11/30/97) • **78**

CAMPLAZENS, CHÂTEAU

Coteaux du Languedoc La Clape Séléction 1990 • $7 • (03/15/94) • **83**

CAMPREDON, CHÂTEAU DE

St.-Chinian 1993: An earthy, herbal and cherry profile sets the tone for this red that ends up lean and tannic. 5,000 cases made. • $7 • (07/31/96) • **79**
St.-Chinian 1990 • $7 • (06/30/94) • **78**

CANARD-DUCHENE

Brut Champagne Patrimoine 1983: Ripe and intense, somewhat alcoholic and soft in a style that manages to correct itself and find a modest equilibrium. After a glass or so the style begins to wear on you. • $42 • (12/31/89) • **80**

CANET, CHÂTEAU

Minervois Cuvée Elevée en Futs Grande Réserve 1988 • $6 • (05/31/90) • **69**

CANET VALETTE

St.-Chinian 1995: Focused, ripe and fruity, with a lovely floral component as well. Offers loads of raspberry, cherry and cassis flavors, with notes of chocolate and spice on the finish. Drink now through 1999. 2,000 cases made. • $10 • (01/01/98) • **88**

CANON, CHÂTEAU

Canon-Fronsac 1995: Solid and chunky Bordeaux offering lots of dark chocolate and berry character, velvety tannins and a very good finish. • $27 Ⓐ • (05/15/96) (BT) • **85-89**
Canon-Fronsac 1990: A pretty wine, with loads of blackberry and licorice character and supple round tannins on the finish. Drinkable now. 4,000 cases made. • $18 • (03/31/93) • **85**
Canon-Fronsac 1989 • $49 Ⓐ • (03/15/92) • **82**
Canon-Fronsac 1983 • $45 Ⓐ • (10/15/94) • **86**

CANON, CHÂTEAU

St.-Emilion 1997: Pretty milk chocolate and berry aromas and flavors. Medium in body, with light, velvety tannins and a fruity finish. • $NA • (06/15/98) (BT) • **85-89**
St.-Emilion 1996: Good concentration, but slightly herbal in character. Medium- to full-bodied, with vanilla and tobacco flavors and a medium finish. • $38 • (06/15/98) (BT) • **85-89**

St.-Emilion 1995: A difficult wine to figure out; I have tasted very good bottles and really poor ones. Here's a good one: Slightly coarse, but with good concentration. Very smoky and fruity, with hints of grilled meats and funky earth. Full- to medium-bodied and chunky, with chewy tannins and a long, fruity finish. Best after 2000. • $27 Ⓐ • (01/31/98) • **86**

St.-Emilion 1993: Delicious, succulent chocolate, berry and cherry aromas and flavors. Medium- to light-bodied, adding delicate tannins and a fresh finish. Drinkable now. • $28 Ⓐ • (01/31/96) • **85**

St.-Emilion 1992: A bit austere and simple, revealing cherry, green pepper character, light body and a hard finish. Drinkable now. Tasted twice, with consistent notes. • $32 • (04/15/95) • **76**

St.-Emilion 1990: One of the best modern-day vintages of Canon. Everything is in just the right proportions. Medium- to full-bodied with fascinating, velvety earth and berry notes. Try now. • $54 Ⓐ • (04/30/95) • **91**

St.-Emilion 1989 • $49 Ⓐ • (04/30/95) • **90**
St.-Emilion 1988 • $52 Ⓐ • (04/30/95) • **88**
St.-Emilion 1987 • $22 Ⓐ • (04/30/95) • **86**
St.-Emilion 1986 • $63 Ⓐ • (04/30/95) • **90**
St.-Emilion 1985 • $48 • (04/30/95) • **91**
St.-Emilion 1983 • $45 Ⓐ • (04/30/95) • **84**
St.-Emilion 1982 • $111 Ⓐ • (04/30/95) • **93**
St.-Emilion 1981 • $30 • (10/15/94) • **89**
St.-Emilion 1980 • $27 Ⓐ • (04/30/95) • **79**
St.-Emilion 1979 • $40 • (04/30/95) • **90**
St.-Emilion 1978 • $50 • (04/30/95) • **91**
St.-Emilion 1977 • $18 • (04/30/95) • **74**
St.-Emilion 1976 • $25 • (04/30/95) • **81**
St.-Emilion 1975 • $31 Ⓐ • (04/30/95) • **86**
St.-Emilion 1974 • $20 • (04/30/95) • **62**
St.-Emilion 1973 • $27 Ⓐ • (04/30/95) • **72**
St.-Emilion 1972 • $20 • (04/30/95) • **79**
St.-Emilion 1971 • $49 Ⓐ • (04/30/95) • **85**
St.-Emilion 1970 • $62 Ⓐ • (04/30/95) • **88**
St.-Emilion 1969 • $25 • (04/30/95) • **74**
St.-Emilion 1967 • $26 Ⓐ • (04/30/95) • **83**
St.-Emilion 1966 • $67 Ⓐ • (04/30/95) • **84**
St.-Emilion 1964 • $81 Ⓐ • (04/30/95) • **90**
St.-Emilion 1962 • $175 • (04/30/95) • **91**
St.-Emilion 1961 • $129 Ⓐ • (04/30/95) • **95**
St.-Emilion 1960 • $75 • (04/30/95) • **79**
St.-Emilion 1959 • $101 Ⓐ • (04/30/95) • **86**
St.-Emilion 1958 • $80 • (04/30/95) • **89**
St.-Emilion 1957 • $75 • (04/30/95) • **82**
St.-Emilion 1955 • $61 Ⓐ • (04/30/95) • **90**
St.-Emilion 1953 • $125 • (04/30/95) • **91**
St.-Emilion 1952 • $95 • (04/30/95) • **79**
St.-Emilion 1950 • $44 Ⓐ • (04/30/95) • **76**
St.-Emilion 1949 • $375 • (04/30/95) • **92**
St.-Emilion 1948 • $97 Ⓐ • (04/30/95) • **90**
St.-Emilion 1947 • $550 • (04/30/95) • **93**
St.-Emilion English Bottling 1947 • $623 Ⓐ • (04/30/95) • **90**
St.-Emilion 1945 • $348 Ⓐ • (11/30/95) • **84**
St.-Emilion 1943 • $125 • (04/30/95) • **86**
St.-Emilion 1942 • $200 • (04/30/95) • **80**
St.-Emilion 1937 • $150 • (04/30/95) • **81**
St.-Emilion 1934 • $175 • (04/30/95) • **50**
St.-Emilion 1933 • $160 • (04/30/95) • **77**
St.-Emilion 1929 • $250 • (04/30/95) • **89**
St.-Emilion 1928 • $300 • (04/30/95) • **87**
St.-Emilion 1926 • $225 • (04/30/95) • **79**
St.-Emilion 1923 • $175 • (04/30/95) • **90**
St.-Emilion 1920 • $200 • (04/30/95) • **86**
St.-Emilion 1916 • $175 • (04/30/95) • **79**

CANON-DE-BREM, CHÂTEAU

Canon-Fronsac 1997: Impressive level of ripe fruit, with blackberry and raspberry aromas and flavors. Medium-bodied, with chunky tannins and fruit structure. Almost outstanding. • $NA • (06/15/98) (BT) • **85-89**

Canon-Fronsac 1996: Soft and round, with dried cherry, berry character, medium body and a soft, succulent finish. • $NA • (01/01/97) (BT) • **80-84**

Canon-Fronsac 1995: Very good '95, with silky tannins and a good amount of berry and tobacco character. Medium-bodied, with medium tannins and finish. Drink now or hold. • $18 • (01/31/98) • **86**

Canon-Fronsac 1994: Very light and forward in style, with aromas and flavors of tobacco, tomato and herb. • $17 • (01/31/97) • **74**

Canon-Fronsac 1993: Rather simple herbal, berry and cherry character, medium-to-light body, light tannins and finish. Drinkable now. • $14 • (01/31/96) • **80**

Canon-Fronsac 1992: Light and fruity, revealing watery, mineral, cherry character. Drinkable but uninviting. • $13 • (04/15/95) • **75**

Canon-Fronsac 1990: Rich and opulent wine with plenty of attractive chocolate, berry character, round tannins and a long aftertaste. Drinkable now. 8,000 cases made. • $17 • (03/31/93) • **89**

Canon-Fronsac 1989 • $23 • (03/15/92) • **84**
Canon-Fronsac 1986 • $15 • (03/31/90) • **86**
Canon-Fronsac 1982 • $NA • (08/31/92) • **91**

CANON-LA GAFFELIÈRE, CHÂTEAU

St.-Emilion 1997: Dark in color, with mineral and berry character. Medium-bodied, with medium tannins and a velvety texture. Pretty '96. • $NA • (06/15/98) (BT) • **85-89**

St.-Emilion 1996: A very good, chunky '96, if not quite as good as I remember. Smoke and berry aromas and flavors. Medium- to full-bodied, with good tannins and a medium finish. Almost outstanding. • $55 • (06/15/98) (BT) • **85-89**

St.-Emilion 1995: One of the greatest wines ever produced by this estate. A wild and terrific red. Wonderful aromas of fruit, spices and chocolate (mole sauce!). Full-bodied and tannic, yet velvety and delightful. Masses of flavors on the finish. Best after 2001, but hard to resist now. • $60 • (01/31/98) • **95**

St.-Emilion 1994: Caresses with fine tannins, but it's slightly closed at the moment. Medium- to full-bodied, with a silky finish. Mineral and fruit define the character. Try in 1999. • $45 • (01/31/97) • **89**

St.-Emilion 1993: One of the great young wines we have tasted this year. A stupendous, silky, full-bodied red of great character and depth, deep color and tons of pure fruit. Layered with mineral, mint, blackberry and dried herb flavors. Long finish and well-integrated tannins make it tempting now, but try to wait until 2000. 6,600 cases made. • $30 • (01/31/96) HR • **92**

St.-Emilion 1992: Polished tobacco, fruit and smoke character; medium-bodied, silky and a flavorful finish. • $20 • (04/15/95) • **82**

St.-Emilion 1990: Combines power and elegance. It has the rich structure of a long-aging wine, yet the complexity is already elegant. Ripe fruit, cedar, licorice, violets, plums and minerals are all there. Tasted twice. Drinkable after 2000. 8,400 cases made. • $39 • (03/15/93) HR • **95**

St.-Emilion 1989 • $36 Ⓐ • (03/15/92) • **88**
St.-Emilion 1988 • $30 • (06/30/91) • **86**
St.-Emilion 1986 • $21 • (06/30/89) • **91**

CANON-MOUEIX, CHÂTEAU

Canon-Fronsac 1997: Medium-bodied, but with a slightly diluted midpalate. Light finish and fine tannins. • $NA • (06/15/98) (BT) • **80-84**

Canon-Fronsac 1996: Slightly thin, with some berry and cherry character, but dry and short on the finish. • $NA • (01/01/97) (BT) • **75-79**

Canon-Fronsac 1995: Slightly linear wine with good fruit concentration and medium tannins. Medium-bodied, with fine tannins and a medium, chocolate and berry aftertaste. Best after 1999. • $21 • (01/31/98) • **87**

Canon-Fronsac 1994: Light, simple and silky, with berry, tobacco and chocolate aromas and flavors. Firm tannins and a fresh, slightly herbal finish. Drink now or hold. • $21 • (01/31/97) • **80**

Canon-Fronsac 1993: Some decent fruit but slightly herbal. Medium in body, adding slightly aggressive tannins and a dried herb and berry finish. Drink now. • $18 • (01/31/96) • **81**

Canon-Fronsac 1992: Very light cherry and berry flavors, light tannins and a slightly weedy finish. • $14 • (04/15/95) • **78**

Canon-Fronsac 1990: An approachable wine, with an attractive berry, earthy character, round tannins and a soft finish. Drinkable now. 2,000 cases made. • $15 • (03/31/93) • **84**

Canon-Fronsac 1989 • $22 • (03/15/92) • **86**

CANORGUE, CHÂTEAU LA

Côtes du Lubéron 1990 • $10 • (04/15/93) • **84**

CANTELOUP, CHÂTEAU

Médoc 1995: Some fruit to this, but rather weedy and diluted. Light-bodied, with light tannins and a short finish. Drink now. • $10 • (01/31/98) • **78**

CANTELYS, CHÂTEAU

Pessac-Léognan 1997: Nice cherry aromas and flavors, but very light on the palate, with a short finish. • $NA • (06/15/98) (BT) • **75-79**
Pessac-Léognan 1996: Slightly simple, but it has good berry and cherry character. Medium-bodied, with medium tannins and a slightly short finish. • $35 • (06/15/98) (BT) • **80-84**
Pessac-Léognan 1995: Rather hard and tannic but shows some good clean fruit. Violet, berry and vanilla aromas. Full-bodied and chewy, with dark chocolate, berry and raspberry flavors. Plenty of character on the finish. Best after 2000. 2,500 cases made. • $30 • (01/31/98) • **88**
Pessac-Léognan White 1995: Captivating apple, grapefruit and light vanilla aromas, although it's less exciting on the palate. Medium-bodied, with good acidity and a short aftertaste. Drink now. • $NA • (04/30/98) • **86**
Pessac-Léognan White 1994 • $NA • (03/31/96) • **89**

CANTEMERLE, CHÂTEAU

Haut-Médoc 1997: Good concentration of blackberry, green tobacco and earth aromas and flavors. Medium-bodied, with a light finish. Very good for this estate. • $NA • (06/15/98) (BT) • **85-89**
Haut-Médoc 1996: Good fruit character, but with a slightly green note. Medium-bodied, with medium tannins and a one-dimensional finish. 20,000 cases made. • $25 • (06/15/98) (BT) • **85-89**
Haut-Médoc 1995: Extracted, with lots of rustic tannins and a light finish. Not up to much. 20,000 cases made. • $20 Ⓐ • (01/01/97) (BT) • **75-79**
Haut-Médoc 1991: Attractive, velvety wine with a fruit and dried-herb character, medium body and a medium finish. • $22 • (03/31/94) • **80**
Haut-Médoc 1990: A bit disappointing for this estate. Simple and fruity, with pleasant nutmeg, berry, grassy character and a light backbone of tannins. Drink now. 8,000 cases made. • $25 • (03/31/93) • **81**
Haut-Médoc 1989 • $48 Ⓐ • (03/15/92) • **91**
Haut-Médoc 1988 • $29 Ⓐ • (03/15/91) • **85**
Haut-Médoc 1987 • $21 • (05/15/90) • **87**
Haut-Médoc 1986 • $25 Ⓐ • (06/30/89) • **89**
Haut-Médoc 1984 • $17 • (06/15/87) • **85**
Haut-Médoc 1982 • $38 Ⓐ • (08/31/92) • **90**
Haut-Médoc 1981 • $15 Ⓐ • (05/01/84) • **70**
Haut-Médoc 1979 • $15 Ⓐ • (10/15/89) • **78**
Haut-Médoc 1970 • $25 Ⓐ • (05/15/93) • **88**
Haut-Médoc 1962 • $NA • (11/30/87) • **90**
Haut-Médoc 1961 • $87 Ⓐ • (04/30/96) • **84**
Haut-Médoc 1945 • $103 Ⓐ • (03/16/86) • **92**

CANTENAC-BROWN, CHÂTEAU

Margaux 1997: A lovely, velvety wine, with berry, cherry and vanilla aromas and flavors and very fine tannins. Impressive. • $NA • (06/15/98) (BT) • **85-89**
Margaux 1996: Beautiful cherry, raspberry and vanilla aromas, but slightly austere on the palate. Medium-bodied, with medium tannins and a fairly dry finish. Wait and see. Tasted twice, with consistent notes. • $25 • (06/15/98) (BT) • **80-84**
Margaux 1995: Slightly one-dimensional, but shows some very good fruit character. Dried berry and cherry aromas, with a hint of vanilla. Medium- to full-bodied, with medium, silky tannins and a fruity aftertaste. Best after 2000. • $25 • (01/31/98) • **88**
Margaux 1994: Velvety, with a good amount of berry and cherry character and hints of herb. Tannins are slightly hard; finish is short. Better in 1999. 15,000 cases made. • $16 Ⓐ • (01/31/97) • **85**
Margaux 1993: Intense blackberry flavor and a hint of violets. Medium-bodied, very firm tannins and medium finish. Try now. 15,000 cases made. • $23 • (01/31/96) • **85**
Margaux 1992: Delicate, beautiful, succulent, perfumed berry and raspberry aromas and flavors. Medium in body; a long aftertaste. Drinkable now. • $20 • (04/15/95) • **84**
Margaux 1991: Lots of fruit, with a hint of bell pepper. Medium-bodied and chewy, with a long aftertaste. • $23 • (03/31/94) • **82**
Margaux 1990: Big and powerful, with loads of tar, berry, chocolate character and velvety tannins. Drink now. 15,000 cases made. • $24 • (03/31/93) • **92**
Margaux 1989 • $30 Ⓐ • (03/15/92) • **89**
Margaux 1988 • $27 Ⓐ • (04/30/91) • **89**
Margaux 1987 • $18 • (02/15/90) • **78**
Margaux 1984 • $15 Ⓐ • (05/15/87) • **85**
Margaux 1982 • $45 Ⓐ • (05/01/85) • **91**
Margaux 1981 • $19 Ⓐ • (03/01/85) • **91**
Margaux 1970 • $26 Ⓐ • (05/15/93) • **83**
Margaux 1961 • $48 Ⓐ • (04/30/96) • **82**
Margaux 1959 • $NA • (10/15/90) • **89**
Margaux 1945 • $NA • (03/16/86) • **75**

CANTRIE, CHÂTEAU DE LA

Muscadet de Sèvre et Maine Sur Lie 1995: This austere, light white has very crisp acidity but little fruit, and the finish is a bit soapy. A weak effort in a strong vintage. • $8 • (05/31/97) • **75**

CANUET, CHÂTEAU

Margaux 1995: Thick and silky, with loads of berried-fruit and tannins. Full-bodied and very tannic, big and muscular. Serious red from Canuet, a second label of Château Cantenac-Brown. Best after 2001. • $20 • (01/31/98) • **90**
Margaux 1994: Some good berry character along with hints of rosemary and other dried herbs. Firm tannins and a very short finish. Drink now. 5,000 cases made. • $18 • (01/31/97) • **80**
Margaux 1993: Very herbal with green pepper, bush character and a slightly metallic edge. 5,000 cases made. • $13 • (01/31/96) • **74**
Margaux 1992: Some decent plum flavors, but lean and slightly dry on the finish. Tasted twice, with consistent notes. Drinkable now. • $12 • (04/15/95) • **74**
Margaux 1991: Like tasting overcooked strawberry jam. Also weedy and green. Not pleasant. Tasted twice. • $12 • (03/31/94) • **69**
Margaux 1990: This wine is thick yet balanced, with concentrated raspberry and cassis character, soft, ripe tannins and luscious fruit on the finish. Not quite as concentrated as the barrel sample. From Jean-Michel Cazes. Drinkable now. • $18 • (03/31/93) • **89**
Margaux 1989 • $18 • (03/15/92) • **82**
Margaux 1987 • $13 • (05/15/90) • **74**
Margaux 1986 • $15 • (11/30/89) • **88**

CAPBERN-GASQUETON, CHÂTEAU

St.-Estèphe 1991: Clean and fruity but very watery. • $13 • (03/31/94) • **74**
St.-Estèphe 1989 • $27 • (03/15/92) • **84**
St.-Estèphe 1986 • $20 • (11/30/89) • **76**
St.-Estèphe 1985 • $23 • (08/31/88) • **85**
St.-Estèphe 1983 • $19 • (02/15/88) • **66**
St.-Estèphe 1982 • $22 • (11/30/89) • **83**

CAP DE HAUT, CHÂTEAU

Haut-Médoc 1995: Very fine indeed. A silky, elegant red with chocolate and berry aromas and flavors. Medium-bodied, with subtle tannins and a fresh finish. • $NA • (01/01/97) • **88**

CAP DE MOURLIN, CHÂTEAU

St.-Emilion 1989 • $23 • (03/15/92) • **87**
St.-Emilion 1988 • $20 • (04/30/91) • **84**
St.-Emilion 1986 • $18 • (06/30/89) • **87**
St.-Emilion 1982 • $18 Ⓐ • (08/31/92) • **90**

CAPENDU, CHÂTEAU

Corbières Cuvée Elevée en Futs Grande Réserve 1988 • $6 • (05/31/90) • **77**
Vin de Pays d'Oc C Le Cabernet 1996: A solid red wine marked by cherry and herbal flavors, finishing on a spicy note. Drink now. • $12 • (04/30/98) • **82**
Vin de Pays d'Oc M Le Merlot 1996: Well focused, with bright cherry, berry and plum flavors and some nice spicy notes on the slightly tart finish. A polished and lively Merlot. Drinkable now. • $12 • (03/31/98) • **83**

Key: SS—Spectator Selection CS—Cellar Selection HR—Highly Recommended BB—Best Buy $NA—Price not available Ⓐ—Auction Price (BT)—Barrel Tasting
Dates in parentheses indicate the issues in which the ratings were published.

FRANCE

CARBONNIÈRES, DOMAINE DES

Côtes du Rhône-Villages Séguret 1996: Flavorful but a bit green, with some tart, drying tannins. Unripe fruit doesn't help. • $10 • (10/15/97) • **76**

Gigondas 1996: A dark, inky purple-colored '96, with firm structure and tannins. A bit herbal, with olive and stemmy notes, but shows good fruit. Medium-bodied, it turns a bit tough on the slightly rustic finish. Drinkable now. 1,800 cases made. • $15 • (10/15/97) • **85**

CARBONNIEUX, CHÂTEAU

Pessac-Léognan 1997: Rather lean, with berry character, but hard tannins and a slightly dry finish disappoint. • $NA • (06/15/98) (BT) • **75-79**

Pessac-Léognan 1996: Lots of toasty oak, with a plummy, slightly grassy character. Medium-bodied, with medium tannins and a light finish. • $25 • (06/15/98) (BT) • **80-84**

Pessac-Léognan 1995: Terrific aromas of blackberry and dark chocolate. Medium-bodied, with fine tannins and a long, succulent aftertaste. Delicious fruit and fine texture. Drinkable now. • $25 • (01/31/98) • **89**

Pessac-Léognan 1994: Light-bodied and smooth, with berry and vanilla aromas and flavors. Ready to drink. 20,000 cases made. • $29 • (01/31/97) • **80**

Pessac-Léognan 1993: Crisp, lively, firmly tannic, this delivers cassis, earth and plum flavors but also a slight herbal note. Somewhat dry on the finish. Drinkable now. • $23 • (01/31/96) • **82**

Pessac-Léognan 1992: Interesting, delicate tobacco, cedar and berry aromas and flavors; medium to light body with medium tannins and a succulent finish. • $17 • (04/15/95) • **84**

Pessac-Léognan 1991: Clean, lean and crisp with cherry character, light tannins and a refreshing finish. • $17 • (03/31/94) • **78**

Pessac-Léognan 1990: Subtle and balanced, with rich berry, mineral character, plenty of fruit and elegant tannins. This estate never makes showy wines, but they age well. Drinkable now. 22,000 cases made. • $19 • (03/31/93) • **87**

Pessac-Léognan 1989 • $26 • (03/15/92) • **85**

Pessac-Léognan 1988 • $19 Ⓐ • (02/28/91) • **86**

Pessac-Léognan 1987 • $15 • (05/15/90) • **80**

Pessac-Léognan 1986 • $19 Ⓐ • (09/15/89) • **87**

Graves 1985 • $20 Ⓐ • (11/30/88) • **87**

Graves 1982 • $26 • (08/31/92) • **83**

Graves 1970 • $33 • (05/15/93) • **84**

Graves 1961 • $72 Ⓐ • (04/30/92) • **85**

Pessac-Léognan White 1995: Solid Carbonnieux. Subtle aromas of lemon, melon and honey. Medium-bodied, with fine acidity and a fresh and fruity aftertaste. Drink now. • $25 • (04/30/98) • **86**

Pessac-Léognan White 1994 • $23 • (03/31/96) • **90**

Pessac-Léognan White 1993 • $18 • (05/31/95) • **87**

CARDONNE, CHÂTEAU LA

Médoc 1997: A good core of fruit for the vintage. Medium-bodied, with medium tannins and a smoky berry finish. Very good effort. • $NA • (06/15/98) (BT) • **85-89**

Médoc 1996: Interesting berry, violet and tar character. Medium-bodied, with medium, velvety tannins and a slightly hot finish. A little pumped up, but alluring. • $15 • (06/15/98) (BT) • **85-89**

Médoc 1995: A concentrated red. Best ever for La Cardonne and a superb value. Amazing for this château. Intense aromas of blackberries, mint and game. Full-bodied, with chunky tannins and fruit. Long finish. Best after 2001. • $18 • (01/31/98) • **90**

Médoc 1994: This ripe, chewy red offers generous flavors of plums, toast, tobacco and black pepper, with firm tannins and a long, licorice-scented finish. A well-crafted wine that's food-friendly now, and will be better in 2000. • $16 • (11/30/97) • **89**

Médoc 1986 • $10 • (02/15/90) • **84**

Médoc 1985 • $12 • (12/31/88) • **83**

Médoc 1983 • $13 • (10/15/86) • **79**

Médoc 1982 • $20 • (08/31/92) • **86**

CARDONNET, CHÂTEAU

Bordeaux 1994: Has an earthy, gamy character, with leathery and dried-plum flavors. Simple, lean and firm. 5,333 cases made. • $8 • (04/30/97) • **79**

CARDUS, CHÂTEAU

Médoc 1997: Decent fruit, but slightly grassy. Light-bodied, with light tannins. • $NA • (06/15/98) (BT) • **75-79**

Médoc 1996: Sleek and steely, with raspberry and herb aromas and flavors. Medium-bodied, with firm tannins and a short finish. • $14 • (06/15/98) (BT) • **80-84**

Médoc 1995: No-nonsense 1995. Good, dark color, with berry and dried herb aromas. Medium-bodied, with silky tannins and a minerally, slightly metallic aftertaste. Drinkable now. • $12 • (01/31/98) • **85**

CARILLON, CHÂTEAU DU

Fronsac 1994: This deeply colored red has an intriguing mix of black cherry, tobacco and herb flavors, but it's a bit diluted and finishes short. Clean and fresh, it's drinkable now. • $10 • (06/30/97) • **83**

CARILLON, LOUIS

Puligny-Montrachet 1995: Amazing quality for a village wine, with almost everything one hopes for in a great Chardonnay—generous fruit and acidity, pure, clean aromas and flavors with complex smoke and subtle oak accents, full body, opulent texture and a refreshing finish that just won't quit. Will improve until at least 2005. 1,667 cases made. • $40 • (05/31/97) • **92**

Puligny-Montrachet 1994: Solid, medium- to full-bodied, showing a core of grapefruit, ripe tropical fruit and lovely honey character. Very vivid and fresh yet ending in supple aftertaste. Drinkable now. 1,666 cases made. • $35 • (05/31/96) • **87**

Puligny-Montrachet 1993: Firm, medium-bodied; lemon, lime and mineral character. Pleasant aftertaste. 400 cases made. • $31 • (05/15/95) • **82**

Puligny-Montrachet 1992: Racy and well-made, a bracing Burgundy of medium body with vivid, distinct and refreshing grapefruit, fresh herb, and green apple flavors. Great intensity and length. Drinkable now. 2,500 cases made. • $33 • (08/31/94) • **90**

Puligny-Montrachet Champ Canet 1995: Balanced and subtle. Laced with honey, showing superb, silky texture, lots of ripe fruit and just a dollop of spicy oak, this full-bodied wine is a pleasure to drink. Long, clean finish. Try now through 2005. • $57 • (08/31/97) • **93**

Puligny-Montrachet Champ Canet 1994: Subtle aromas of lime and honey, and very concentrated. Vibrant core of zesty melon, honeysuckle, lime and cilantro flavors. Medium-bodied and beautifully balanced. Drinkable now. • $NA • (08/31/96) • **90**

Puligny-Montrachet Champ Canet 1993: Rich and opulent, featuring white truffle, honey and mineral aromas and flavors, medium body, fine acidity and long, tasty finish. Drinkable now. • $48 • (08/31/95) • **88**

Puligny-Montrachet Champ Canet 1992: A Puligny that will grow with age. Firm and flavorful, smelling of pears and peaches, tasting of vanilla and pear, with good balance and length on the finish. 340 cases made. • $43 • (08/31/94) • **90**

Puligny-Montrachet Les Perrières 1995: Well made, clean and pure. Its aromas and flavors are lovely; the wine is thick and rich, with good intensity, medium-to-full body. Ripe fruit and nice mineral character turns slightly toasty and smoky on the finish. Try after 2000. • $53 • (08/31/97) • **92**

Puligny-Montrachet Les Perrières 1994: A serious wine from one of the most reliable of the white Burgundy producers. Medium-bodied, with a solid backbone of honey and compacted fruit flavors, particularly lime. Very long, silky finish accented by toasty oak. Drinkable now. • $50 • (08/31/96) HR • **93**

Puligny-Montrachet Les Perrières 1993: Pretty lemon and toasty oak aromas and flavors. Medium body, good acidity and a long, fresh finish. • $50 • (08/31/95) • **86**

Puligny-Montrachet Les Perrières 1992: Ripe, smooth and flavorful, with pineapple and pear notes that really fill it out; round in texture, showing nice lingering fruit flavors on the finish. 575 cases made. • $41 • (08/31/94) • **90**

CARLES, CHÂTEAU DE

Fronsac 1995: Lovely and harmonious, fairly rich, full-bodied and complex, delivering impressive red berry, chocolate and earth character. • $NA • (05/15/96) (BT) • **85-89**

Fronsac 1993: Straightforward dried cherry and wet earth aromas and flavors, medium body, silky tannins and fresh finish. Drinkable now. • $10 • (01/31/96) • **81**

CARMES-HAUT-BRION, CHÂTEAU LES

Pessac-Léognan 1961 • $50 • (04/30/96) • **86**

CARONNE-STE.-GEMME, CHÂTEAU

Haut-Médoc 1997: Pretty black fruit character. Light- to medium-bodied, with medium tannins and a light finish. Well made. • $NA • (06/15/98) (BT) • **85-89**

Haut-Médoc 1996: Loads of cassis and mint. Full-bodied, with velvety, big tannins and a medium finish. Serious stuff. Amazing quality for this producer. Sleeper of the vintage. • $22 • (06/15/98) (BT) • **90-94**

Haut-Médoc 1995: Delicious wine. Not the biggest I've had, but wonderful to drink. Beautiful. Medium-bodied, with sweet berry, cherry flavors and a medium, silky finish. Got to love it. Drink now or hold. 23,000 cases made. • $20 • (01/31/98) • **89**

CARRUADES DE LAFITE ROTHSCHILD

Bordeaux White 1994 • $8 • (02/29/96) • **86**

Pauillac 1997: A pretty, balanced red, with tobacco and cherry aromas and flavors. Medium-bodied, with fine tannins. • $NA • (06/15/98) (BT) • **85-89**

Pauillac 1996: A wonderful, warming red, with tobacco and berry aromas and flavors and a fine tannin structure. Medium-bodied. Very pretty. • $27 • (06/15/98) (BT) • **85-89**

Pauillac 1995: Rich and decadent, an outstanding second wine. Earthy, with tobacco, cherry and bark aromas. Full- to medium-bodied, with velvety tannins and a medium aftertaste. Second label of Château Lafite-Rothschild. Best after 2000. • $30 • (01/31/98) • **90**

Pauillac 1994: Sleek, with refined tannins and lovely berry, mineral and mint aromas and flavors. A very good second wine. Drinkable now. • $26 • (01/31/97) • **86**

Pauillac 1993: Lively and crisp, medium- to light-bodied, offering some well-defined red berry flavors, but a bit one-dimensional and lean. Drinkable now. • $23 • (01/31/96) • **83**

Pauillac 1992: An attractive core of good fruit and spicy character, medium body and tannins and a short aftertaste. • $17 • (04/15/95) • **84**

Pauillac 1989 • $34 Ⓐ • (03/15/92) • **89**

Pauillac 1983 • $14 • (10/31/86) • **88**

Pauillac 1982 • $34 Ⓐ • (08/31/92) • **92**

Pauillac 1967 • $NA • (11/30/87) • **82**

Pauillac 1964 • $24 Ⓐ • (11/30/87) • **81**

Pauillac 1962 • $NA • (11/30/87) • **75**

Pauillac 1961 • $58 Ⓐ • (11/30/91) • **90**

Pauillac 1959 • $100 • (11/30/91) • **90**

Pauillac 1937 • $125 • (11/30/87) • **77**

Pauillac 1934 • $145 • (11/30/87) • **84**

Pauillac 1902 • $530 • (11/30/87) • **80**

CARSIN, CHÂTEAU

Premières Côtes de Bordeaux 1993: This vivid red offers attractive plum, floral and spicy aromas and flavors. Nicely balanced, with modest structure. Drinkable now. • $8 • (12/15/95) • **83**

CARTILLON, CHÂTEAU DU

Haut-Médoc 1997: Simple, clean and light-bodied, with light cherry flavors and a short finish. Could move up a notch next year. • $NA • (06/15/98) (BT) • **75-79**

Haut-Médoc 1996: Weedy and diluted. Light-bodied, with a light finish. Tasted twice, with consistent notes. 12,000 cases made. • $16 • (06/15/98) (BT) • **70-74**

Haut-Médoc 1995: Rather light, with some berry, herbal aromas and flavors. Light-bodied, with light tannins and a fresh finish. Drink now. • $15 • (01/31/98) • **78**

Haut-Médoc 1994: Very light and simple, with dried berry character, light tannins and a simple finish. Drink now. 20,400 cases made. • $NA • (01/31/97) • **77**

Haut-Médoc 1993: Very diluted with some spice and pepper character. • $12 • (01/31/96) • **76**

Haut-Médoc 1991: Very watery and light. Maturing quickly. • $10 • (03/31/94) • **74**

CASANOVA, LA

Muscat de Rivesaltes 1995: Rich and spicy. Flavors range from crème brûlée and orange-peel to a nice zip of white chocolate on the finish. Hard to resist. Would make a lovely end to any meal. 500 cases made. • $16 • (12/31/97) • **88**

CASENOVE, DOMAINE DE LA

Côtes du Roussillon 1995: The nose is a little high-toned, but there are raspberry and chocolate flavors beneath and it's almost sweet. An easy, enjoyable red. 5,000 cases made. • $11 • (09/30/97) • **84**

Côtes du Roussillon Cuvée François Jaubert 1995: Plentiful bacon-fat aromas are followed by deep plum and chocolate flavors. Verging on the style of a ruby Port, but it's well balanced and delicious. Enjoy now. 850 cases made. • $24 • (09/30/97) • **86**

Côtes du Roussillon Cuvée François Jaubert 1993: A darkly colored, intensely focused young wine displaying depth and harmony. Shows vanilla-accented flavors of chocolate, cherry and tobacco and a long, harmonious finish with plenty of grip. Hard to keep your hands off it now. 500 cases made. • $22 • (01/31/97) • **89**

Côtes du Roussillon La Garrigue 1994: Intense cherry and mint are the hallmarks of this soft, diffuse red. Tails off quickly on the finish. 3,500 cases made. • $10 • (09/30/97) • **82**

Côtes du Roussillon La Garrigue 1993: Straightforward and smooth, with a gamy accent to the berry and herb character. 1,600 cases made. • $10 • (01/31/97) • **83**

CASSAGNE-HAUT-CANON, CHÂTEAU

Canon-Fronsac La Truffière 1997: Dark-colored, with dried cherry and mineral aromas and flavors. Medium-bodied, with well-integrated tannins and a fruity finish. • $NA • (06/15/98) (BT) • **85-89**

CASSAN, DOMAINE DE

Côtes du Rhône-Villages Beaumes de Venise Cuvée St.-Christophe 1989 • $11 • (04/15/93) • **77**

CASTAGNIER, GUY

Bonnes Mares 1990: An alluring wine that shows remarkable harmony. Isn't as huge as some in this group, but the focused, packed berry, earth and smoke characteristics are seductive. Is almost sweet on the palate and velvety on the finish. Drinkable now. • $NA • (12/15/92) • **94**

Bonnes Mares 1989 • $67 • (01/31/92) • **91**

Bonnes Mares 1988 • $67 • (07/15/91) • **87**

Bonnes Mares 1986 • $50 • (04/15/89) • **91**

Chambolle-Musigny 1990: Aromatic and supple, with plenty of pretty raspberry, plum and earth flavors that form a harmonious texture on the firm finish. Drinkable now. • $NA • (12/15/92) • **87**

Chambolle-Musigny 1989 • $39 • (01/31/92) • **88**

Chambolle-Musigny 1986 • $31 • (07/15/89) • **84**

Charmes-Chambertin 1990: Offers beautiful fruit flavors, but is more one-dimensional than some others wines in this group. Still, it shows a solid structure of tannins, acidity and fruit. Drinkable now. • $NA • (12/15/92) • **89**

Charmes-Chambertin 1989 • $62 • (01/31/92) • **90**

Clos de Vougeot 1990: Very fruity, with medium tannins, pleasant plum, cherry, vanilla and chocolate notes and firm tannins. Drinkable now. • $NA • (12/15/92) • **87**

Clos de Vougeot 1989 • $64 • (01/31/92) • **85**

Clos de Vougeot 1988 • $65 • (08/31/91) • **86**

Clos de la Roche 1990: Not a huge wine, but the racy structure, fresh acidity and elegant plum, berry and earth flavors offer plenty of pleasure. Drinkable now. • $NA • (12/15/92) • **90**

Clos de la Roche 1989 • $62 • (01/31/92) • **90**

Clos de la Roche 1988 • $63 • (07/15/91) • **91**

Clos de la Roche 1986 • $43 • (07/15/89) • **75**

Key: SS—Spectator Selection CS—Cellar Selection HR—Highly Recommended BB—Best Buy $NA—Price not available Ⓐ—Auction Price (BT)—Barrel Tasting
Dates in parentheses indicate the issues in which the ratings were published.

FRANCE

Clos St.-Denis 1990: Graceful and balanced, a refined *grand cru*, with a fine tannin and fruit structure and lots of flavors, including earth, plum and raspberry. Drinkable now. • $NA • (12/15/92) • **93**

Clos St.-Denis 1989 • $62 • (01/31/92) • **91**

Clos St.-Denis 1988 • $63 • (07/15/91) • **89**

Clos St.-Denis 1986 • $43 • (07/15/89) • **84**

Gevrey-Chambertin 1990: Smooth and round, with interesting forest underbrush and wet earth notes complementing the berry and cherry flavors on an elegant framework. Drinkable now. • $NA • (12/15/92) • **87**

Latricières-Chambertin 1990: Not as intensely fruity as others in this group, but shows a generous amount of earthy, ripe berry aromas and flavors and medium tannins. Drinkable now. • $NA • (12/15/92) • **89**

Latricières-Chambertin 1989 • $62 • (01/31/92) • **93**

Latricières-Chambertin 1988 • $63 • (07/15/91) • **93**

Mazis-Chambertin Mazy-Chambertin 1990: An elegantly made Mazis that displays good class and balance, with ripe cherry, blackberry and tobacco aromas and flavors. The finish shows fantastic harmony. Drinkable now. • $NA • (12/15/92) • **94**

Mazis-Chambertin Mazy-Chambertin 1989 • $62 • (01/31/92) • **93**

Mazis-Chambertin Mazy-Chambertin 1988 • $63 • (07/15/91) • **91**

Morey-St.-Denis 1990: The crisp strawberry and raspberry aromas and flavors are bright and lively and the tannins are supple in this delicious wine that's drinkable now. • $NA • (12/15/92) • **85**

Morey-St.-Denis 1989 • $NA • (01/31/92) • **86**

Morey-St.-Denis 1986 • $28 • (07/15/89) • **66**

CASTELLANE, DE

Brut Blanc de Blancs Champagne 1981 • $33 • (04/15/88) • **84**

Brut Blanc de Blancs Champagne 1980 • $22 • (05/31/87) • **91**

Brut Blanc de Blancs Champagne Chardonnay 1983: • $NA • (12/31/90) • **90**

Brut Champagne Cuvée Commodore 1981 • $50 • (04/15/88) • **87**

Brut Champagne Cuvée Florens de Castellane 1982: A tightly reined-in style. It's austere, with crisp lemony flavors that turn spicy and elegant and a subtle intensity that grows on you after the second and third sip. A tough astringency on the finish turns very dry. Drinkable now. • $59 • (12/31/90) • **88**

CASTELNAU DE SUDUIRAUT

Sauternes 1995: A medium-bodied Sauternes with lovely apple, honey, lemon and spice aromas and flavors. Medium-bodied, very sweet, with a fresh finish. Second label of Château Suduiraut. Drink now. • $30 • (04/30/98) • **86**

CASTELOT, CHÂTEAU LE

St.-Emilion 1995: Starts off better than it ends, with blackberry, tobacco and earth aromas and flavors, firm, slightly metallic tannins and a somewhat herbal finish. Drinkable now. 3,000 cases made. • $27 • (01/31/98) • **77**

CASTENET-GREFFIER, CHÂTEAU

Entre-Deux-Mers 1994 • $8 • (05/31/95) • **77**

CATHERINE DE ST.-JUERY

Coteaux du Languedoc 1993 • $8 • (03/31/95) • **84**

Coteaux du Languedoc 1992 • $8 • (03/15/94) BB • **87**

Coteaux du Languedoc 1991 • $8 • (06/15/93) • **80**

Coteaux du Languedoc 1990 • $8 • (10/31/92) BB • **85**

Syrah Coteaux du Languedoc 1995: Lovely flavors of cassis, coffee and smoke blend to form a well-focused and nicely polished French red, offering a smooth texture, good crispness and appealing notes of orange peel on the finish. A serious mouthful of wine for the price. Drinkable now. 5,500 cases made. • $9 • (03/31/98) BB • **86**

CATON, DOMAINE

Cabernet Sauvignon Vin de Pays de l'Hérault 1995: Its black cherry and cedar notes are overshadowed by a strong earthiness, followed by a tannic, woody character. • $6 • (12/15/96) • **76**

Cabernet Sauvignon Vin de Pays des Côtes de Thongue 1993: A rough-and-tumble country-red with plenty of assertive character. The gamy, leathery flavors have appeal; the tannins demand food. • $7 • (12/15/96) • **84**

Merlot Vin de Pays de l'Hérault 1995: The decent cherry and spice flavors are marred by a burnt-rubber taste. Crisp finish. • $6 • (12/15/96) • **77**

CATTIER

Brut Champagne Antique NV: Definitely something special. This Champagne has riper fruit, a richer texture and longer finish than most non-vintage bottlings, with a soft, lush mouthfeel and subtle, seductive flavors. Delicious, and reasonably priced at this score. 12,000 cases made. • $30 • (10/31/97) HR • **91**

Brut Champagne Chigny-Les-Roses Premier Cru 1988: A ripe style of Champagne with subtle apple, toasty, creamy character, medium body and a delicate finish. Drinkable now. • $35 • (12/31/93) • **87**

CAZAL-VIEL, CHÂTEAU

St.-Chinian 1990 • $8 • (03/15/94) • **83**

CAZANOVE, CHARLES DE

Brut Champagne 1990: What a combination of plush texture and lively, dry flavors in this elegant, subtle Champagne. Settle into this like an expensive leather sofa. The citrus and spice flavors expand as you sip, and linger on the long finish. Drink now through 2000. • $30 • (11/30/97) • **92**

Brut Champagne 1989: Has strong earthy, doughy aromas, mature, honeyed fruit flavors, a rather soft texture and a lingering finish. An unusual style that takes some getting used to. • $37 • (12/15/96) • **82**

Brut Champagne 1985: Good intensity of Pinot Noir character in this Champagne. It's full flavored with lots of character and good acidity. Drinkable now. 25,000 cases made. • $30 • (12/31/93) • **89**

Brut Champagne Magenta NV: Pretty basic bubbly, with tart but dull fruit flavors, a bit of a toasty accent and a short finish. Drink now. • $25 • (11/15/97) • **75**

Brut Champagne Millèsime 1989: A lush-textured, honey-flavored vintage Champagne that tastes smooth, creamy and fairly rich. Almost sweet, but not cloying; crisp acidity keeps it refreshing. 4,000 cases made. • $30 • (07/31/95) • **88**

Brut Champagne Stradivarius 1989: Buttery, smooth and generous style of Champagne that has a full texture, ample fruit flavors and nice touches of complexity. Very appealing. 2,000 cases made. • $50 • (02/28/95) • **89**

Brut Champagne Stradivarius 1985: This wine locks in the flavors on your palate. Well defined with excellent structure, there's loads of creamy, pear, apple flavors and ripe acidity. Much better than when we tasted it in December 1991. Drinkable now. 20,000 cases made. • $50 • (12/31/93) • **91**

Brut Rosé Champagne NV: A bright-colored, spicy smelling rosé that's lively and fresh in flavor, smooth in texture and tangy on the finish. • $30 • (12/31/97) • **85**

CAZES, DOMAINE

Muscat de Rivesaltes 1995: This dessert wine has broad flavors of clove and ripe peach; soft on the finish. 15,000 cases made. • $12 • (08/31/97) • **84**

Rivesaltes 1989: Smooth and a bit oxidized, with caramel and foxy flavors. 1,000 cases made. • $12 • (08/31/97) • **80**

Rivesaltes Ambré 1988: A ripe dessert wine, with intense orange and maple syrup flavors. It's vibrant and fairly crisp, with a long finish. 1,000 cases made. • $10 • (08/31/97) • **83**

Rivesaltes Cuvée Aimé Cazes 1975: Outstanding. Rich, medium-bodied, focused and quite intense, with delicious apricot, caramel and spice flavors and, on the finish, lingering nuances of hazelnut. 150 cases made. • $29 • (08/31/97) • **90**

Rivesaltes Tuilé 1982: A lovely stickie with plenty of character. Broad and generous, with harmonious flavors of dried apricot, orange and caramel, finishing on a honeyed note. 600 cases made. • $14 • (08/31/97) • **87**

Vin de Pays des Côtes Catalanes Le Credo 1994: Dead-ringer for a good Crozes-Hermitage. Meaty, peppery, blackberry flavors meld in this broad-shouldered red; only the dusty tannins give away its less noble heritage. Well done. Ready now. 2,000 cases made. • $12 • (09/30/97) • **87**

CAZIN, FRANÇOIS

Cheverny 1995: This light, crisp white has vivid grass and grapefruit flavors. A bit lean, and it needs food to soften the citrusy acidity. 600 cases made. • $12 • (05/31/97) • **82**

Cheverny Le Petit Chambord 1994 • $12 • (05/15/96) • **84**

CECI, DOMAINE

Chambolle-Musigny Aux Echanges 1988 • $33 • (07/15/91) • **91**
Chambolle-Musigny Aux Echanges 1987 • $20 • (03/31/90) • **72**
Clos de Vougeot 1988 • $48 • (07/15/91) • **93**
Clos de Vougeot 1987 • $40 • (03/31/90) • **82**

CÈDRE, CHÂTEAU DU

Cahors 1989 • $11 • (10/31/92) • **82**
Cahors 1988 • $10 • (08/31/91) • **83**
Cahors 1987 • $11 • (08/31/91) • **81**
Cahors Le Prestige 1988 • $14 • (08/31/91) • **84**
Cahors Le Prestige 1987 • $14 • (03/15/90) • **75**
Cahors Le Prestige 1985 • $9 • (12/31/88) • **80**

CELLIER DES BARONNIES

Côtes du Lubéron 1993 • $NA • (11/15/95) • **81**
Vacqueyras 1990 • $NA • (09/30/95) • **87**

CERTAN DE MAY, CHÂTEAU

Pomerol 1997: Absolutely delicious. Draws you back for another sip. Medium-bodied, with moderate, very fine tannins and a long, plum and berry aftertaste. • $NA • (06/15/98) (BT) • **90-94**

Pomerol 1996: Shows considerable richness. Full-bodied and chewy with tobacco, chocolate and toasty oak character, it's a big wine for the vintage. • $NA • (05/15/97) (BT) • **90-94**

Pomerol 1995: Powerful and rich, packed with everything you can expect in a top '95: loads of tannins, fruit, spice and toasty oak complexity. One to lay down for years. Very exciting. • $NA • (05/15/96) (BT) • **95-99**

Pomerol 1994: Powerful and ripe for the vintage. Lovely aromas of plums, berries and chocolate. Tannins are fine, finish is long and silky. Drink now or hold. • $32 Ⓐ • (01/31/97) • **90**

Pomerol 1990: A big, ripe wine that maintains focus and complexity. It's chewy and firm, with notes of tobacco, black plums, meat and spice; the tannins are rich but not aggressive. Try now. 1,600 cases made. • $60 Ⓐ • (10/15/94) • **91**

Pomerol 1989 • $55 Ⓐ • (10/15/94) • **89**
Pomerol 1988 • $67 Ⓐ • (06/30/91) • **90**
Pomerol 1986 • $59 Ⓐ • (09/15/89) • **93**
Pomerol 1985 • $90 Ⓐ • (10/15/94) • **90**
Pomerol 1983 • $36 Ⓐ • (10/15/94) • **96**

Pomerol 1982: Soft and spicy, with layers of tobacco and plum, gentle cinnamon and nutmeg notes. Harmonious, complex, elegant. • $252 Ⓐ • (07/31/97) • **90**

Pomerol 1981 • $45 Ⓐ • (10/15/94) • **95**
Pomerol 1979 • $68 Ⓐ • (10/15/89) • **90**

CERTAN-GIRAUD, CHÂTEAU

Pomerol 1988 • $23 • (02/28/91) • **89**
Pomerol 1986 • $22 • (06/30/89) • **86**
Pomerol 1985 • $19 Ⓐ • (04/30/88) • **85**
Pomerol 1982 • $NA • (05/15/89) • **90**
Pomerol 1961 • $59 • (04/30/96) • **87**

Key: SS—Spectator Selection CS—Cellar Selection HR—Highly Recommended BB—Best Buy $NA—Price not available Ⓐ—Auction Price (BT)—Barrel Tasting
Dates in parentheses indicate the issues in which the ratings were published.

CHABLIS, CAVE DE

Chablis La Porte d'Or 1995: Extremely ripe apple flavors—almost ciderlike, and perhaps a little botrytis too—make this Chablis fat and atypical. • $16 • (06/15/97) • **78**

CHABLISIENNE, LA

Chablis 1996: A well-made, fairly supple village Chablis that delivers ripe fruit flavors and nice mineral notes. Of medium body and intensity, with a wet earth quality on the lemon-spiked finish. Try now through 2000. • $20 • (08/31/97) • **85**

Chablis 1994 • $NA • (08/31/95) • **85**

Chablis Beauroy 1995: A nice *premier cru*, full-bodied, with ripe fruit and toasty, sweet spice flavors, honey, pear, melon, marzipan and mineral notes. Excellent intensity on the delicate finish. Try around 2000. • $25 • (06/15/97) • **86**

Chablis Beauroy 1993 • $NA • (08/31/95) • **87**

Chablis Blanchot 1996: Not very clean. New oakish-style of Chablis, but it has a lot of round, silky character and some fine pear, honey and mineral flavors. Turns a bit tart and dry on the finish. Drink now through 2000. 500 cases made. • $42 • (05/31/98) • **79**

Chablis Blanchot 1995: Racy, intense and very complex, dishing out layers of lactic, spice, toasty bread and honey flavors that blend well with the clean, green apple and pear flavors. Full-bodied, with a long, smoky, lemony, flinty finish. Needs time, try after 2000. 625 cases made. • $25 • (06/15/97) • **89**

Chablis Blanchot 1993 • $NA • (08/31/95) • **81**

Chablis Bougros 1996: A closed, reserved '96 Chablis of great depth and concentration. Ripe, opulent and full-bodied, with tropical character balanced by a mouthful of compacted mineral and lime notes. The acidity kicks in on the almost tannic finish. Definitely hold this one until after 2005. 350 cases made. • $42 • (05/31/98) • **94**

Chablis Bougros 1995: A beautiful *grand cru*, showing subtle mineral, toasty oak, ripe fruit aromas and flavors. Full-bodied. Needs time to show it all; try after 1999. • $25 • (06/15/97) • **87**

Chablis Bougros 1993 • $NA • (08/31/95) • **82**

Chablis Côte de Léchet 1996: Very pretty, bursting with floral, honey, honeydew, melon and apricot aromas and flavors. Light- to medium-bodied, with a lemony, minerally finish, this is a delight to drink now. 4,000 cases made. • $25 • (05/31/98) • **87**

Chablis Côte de Léchet 1995: Ripe and fairly dense, this sweet-tasting, full-bodied Chablis delivers pretty butterscotch, vanilla extract and spice accents along with good, fresh fruit. Creamlike texture, quite chewy on the finish. Drink now through 2000. • $25 • (06/15/97) • **86**

Chablis Côte de Léchet 1993 • $NA • (08/31/95) • **84**

Chablis Cuvée L.C. 1994 • $23 • (05/31/96) • **81**

Chablis Fourchaume 1996: A beauty. Ultrarich but also very elegant, thanks to loads of fresh, citrusy acidity. Balanced and full-bodied, with marvelous pear, honey, mineral, spice and tropical character that you expect from '96. Tempting now, better after 2000. Tasted twice, with consistent notes. 10,000 cases made. • $27 • (05/31/98) • **94**

Chablis Fourchaume 1995: Supple, smooth and very ripe, this full-bodied wine coats the palate like thick cream yet remains elegant and vibrant through the long, slightly smoky finish. The lemon, ripe fruit, mineral and wet stone flavors mingle nicely. • $25 • (06/15/97) • **89**

Chablis Fourchaume 1994 • $30 • (05/31/96) • **84**

Chablis Fourchaume 1993 • $NA • (08/31/95) • **86**

Chablis Fourchaumes Les Vaulorents 1995: Distinguished. Supple and full-bodied, it oozes cream, mineral, pear and vanilla flavors. Very refined, with some good citrus nuances that keep it refreshing. Long finish. Tempting now, better around 2000. • $25 • (06/15/97) • **89**

Chablis Grenouilles Château Grenouilles 1993 • $NA • (08/31/95) • **86**

Chablis Les Clos 1996: This gentle Chablis behaves nicely, with some fine citrus, pear, honey, and floral aromas and flavors. Medium-bodied, it offers good ripeness but lacks a touch of acidity. Drink now through 2000. • $58 • (05/31/98) • **88**

Chablis Les Clos 1993 • $NA • (08/31/95) • **86**

Chablis Les Preuses 1993 • $NA • (08/31/95) • **86**

Chablis Mont de Milieu 1996: An oaky style of Chablis, nicely supple, with perfumed rose petal notes. Offers butter, butterscotch, caramel, spice and ripe pear flavors. Smooth finish. Drink now through 2005. 4,000 cases made. • $27 • (05/31/98) • **88**

Chablis Mont de Milieu 1995: A delight. Soft, supple and wonderfully rich for its butterscotch, toasty spice, mocha, coffee bean, honey, ripe pear and dried fig flavors. Full-bodied, it's a mouthful of silky texture. Citrusy finish ties it up with a bow. Drink now. 2,500 cases made. • $30 • (06/15/97) • **90**

Chablis Mont de Milieu 1994 • $30 • (05/31/96) • **83**

Chablis Mont de Milieu 1993 • $NA • (08/31/95) • **86**

Chablis Montmain 1996: Wonderful wine, elegant and full-bodied, with a terrific mineral character that gives it a thick, creamlike feel on the midpalate. Slight vanilla, spice and toasty oak accents marry nicely with the lime, tropical and floral notes. Balanced, with a very long finish. Tempting now (if you decant) or around 2002 to 2005. 2,000 cases made. • $25 • (05/31/98) • **93**

Chablis Montmain 1995: Racy, elegant *premier cru*, with clean, well-defined aromas and flavors of ripe fruiit, dried herbs, seashells and minerals. Full-bodied, with flawlessly smooth texture and a lime-spiked finish. • $25 • (06/15/97) • **88**

Chablis Montée de Tonnerre 1996: Great harmony in this generous, opulent, polished, full-bodied, ripe wine, lightly oaked and elegantly supported by firm, racy acidity and marvelous honey, pear and mineral character. Supple and velvety from start to slightly toasty bread-flavored finish. Drink from 2000 to 2005. 2,000 cases made. • $27 • (05/31/98) • **94**

Chablis Montée de Tonnerre 1995: A pleasant *premier cru* but quite chewy and slightly drying. Medium- to full-bodied, with floral, ripe pear and mineral flavors, some honey notes on the rather hard finish. • $25 • (06/15/97) • **85**

Chablis Montée de Tonnerre 1993 • $NA • (08/31/95) • **84**

Chablis Premier Cru 1996: Decent fruit, with wet hay, earth and buttery oak accents. Medium- to full-bodied, it's less racy than some. Intense, slightly sour finish. Drink now. 5,000 cases made. • $25 • (05/31/98) • **79**

Chablis Premier Cru Vieilles Vignes 1996: Wonderful wine, floral and fruity, with terrific, supple midpalate texture. Elegant, refined, medium-bodied, with a ripe pear, tropical, grapefruit and seductive mineral-laden character that makes it feel creamy and oily. Attractive, vibrant finish. Try after 2003. 2,000 cases made. • $25 • (05/31/98) • **93**

Chablis Premier Cru Vieilles Vignes 1995: Lovely floral, dried herb, honey, mineral complexity, all in finesse, with a silky texture accented by lively lemon notes on the subtle finish. The sort of wine you could drink lots of. Bravo. • $23 • (06/15/97) • **89**

Chablis Premier Cru Vieilles Vignes 1993 • $NA • (08/31/95) • **84**

Chablis Vaillon 1996: Seriously mineral-laden Chardonnay, tasting of wet stone and wet earth, etched with *terroir* and showing more soil than fruit. Balanced, medium-to-full in body, with a silky finish. Drink now through 2005. 3,000 cases made. • $25 • (05/31/98) • **93**

Chablis Vaillon 1995: A well made and fairly rich *premier cru*, of medium body, with a dried herb, green apple, honey and wet earth character that's refreshing and well-defined on the crisp but balanced finish. Try around 2000. • $25 • (06/15/97) • **86**

Chablis Valmur 1996: Complex and distinctive, with a wonderful mouthfeel of silky texture and full body. A lovely combination of mineral, earth, pear, dried herbs and lees flavors, with well-integrated wood and a long finish. Drink from 2000 to 2005. 50 cases made. • $42 • (05/31/98) • **94**

Chablis Valmur 1995: Deftly and elegantly made, with polished, dense texture, the vanilla, ripe fruit, spice, honey, mineral and smoke flavors of this full-bodied *grand cru* are well-integrated. Drink now to 2005. • $30 • (06/15/97) • **89**

Chablis Vaudésir 1996: Thick, with a good undertow of acidity but a bit overripe in flavor. Medium- to full-bodied, it ends on a slightly drying note. Drink now through 2000. 250 cases made. • $42 • (05/31/98) • **76**

Chablis Vaudésir 1995: Distinctive. Shaded by subtle oak, this medium-bodied *grand cru* is well made, offering some nice honey, lemon and pie crust flavors that follow through on the long finish. Try now. • $30 • (06/15/97) • **86**

Chablis Vaudésir 1993 • $NA • (08/31/95) • **85**

CHABOT, PATRICK

Pouilly-Fuissé 1996: A basic white, bland, watery and lacking character. Where are the earth and the *terroir*? Short finish. Disappointing. 2,500 cases made. • $15 • (01/31/98) • **74**

CHAINIER, DOMAINE

Bourgueil 1985 • $7 • (09/30/88) • **78**

Chinon 1985 • $7 • (09/30/88) • **83**

Chinon Moulin des Sablons Vieilles Vignes 1995: Ripe and plush, this lively, expressive red offers blackberry, tobacco and light herb flavors, with just enough tannin for grip. A lovely complement to lighter foods and drinkable now. 1,500 cases made. • $13 • (05/15/97) • **87**

Touraine Sauvignon Château de Pocé 1996: Bright flavors of green apples and limes give this light yet round white an appealing freshness. Would make a lively apéritif. 5,000 cases made. • $10 • (06/15/97) • **83**

Vouvray Meloterie Moelleux 1995: Moderately sweet, with a full body and good balance. Shows nice spice and light herb flavors, but the fruit is a bit muted. Drinkable now. 1,500 cases made. • $12 • (06/15/97) • **87**

CHAINTRÉ, CAVE DE

Mâcon-Chaintré 1995: Disapointing; a bit coarse and rustic, tasting of cedar and earth. • $NA • (08/31/96) • **74**

Mâcon-Fuissé 1995: Straightforward, of medium body and modest fruit intensity. Tinged with floral, hay, bitter almond and green apple notes. Tart finish. • $NA • (08/31/96) • **79**

Mâcon-Fuissé 1994: Round, smooth and quaffably pleasant, but it lacks fresh intensity. Already golden in color, with some banana, citrus, pear and almond flavors. Drinkable now. • $NA • (08/31/95) • **79**

St.-Véran 1995: Seems too mature for a '95. Shows some modest fruit, with a touch of caramel and a dull finish. • $NA • (08/31/96) • **74**

St.-Véran 1994: Lovely peach, apricot and almost Viognierlike flavors shine in this smooth, elegant, light- to medium-bodied white. It's slightly diluted, though. • $NA • (08/31/95) • **82**

CHAIS BAUMIÈRE

Chardonnay Vin de Pays d'Oc 1994 • $6 • (02/29/96) • **81**

Merlot Vin de Pays d'Oc 1993: It appears that some type of oak treatment was used here, but the flavors seem to lack focus and purity. 12,000 cases made. • $6 • (07/31/96) • **77**

Sauvignon Blanc Vin de Pays d'Oc 1994 • $6 • (02/29/96) • **81**

Syrah Vin de Pays d'Oc 1993 • $6 • (05/15/96) • **78**

Vin de Pays d'Oc Domaine de la Baume Cuvée Propriétaire 1994: Fruit and oak flavors provide interesting nuances, but the sweetness and tannin of wood is overpowering. Merlot and Grenache. 4,000 cases made. • $8 • (07/31/96) • **78**

CHAIZE, CHÂTEAU DE LA

Brouilly 1995: Smooth and well integrated. This wine offers a nice balance of blackcherry and licorice flavors and firm, harmonious tannins. Will stand up to food. 30,000 cases made. • $13 • (09/15/96) • **85**

Brouilly 1993 • $10 • (07/31/95) • **81**

CHALLON, DOMAINE

Bordeaux White 1995: Strives for a grand, oaky style, with smoky, buttery aromas and seemingly sweet flavors, but it's heavy and soft. • $13 • (05/31/97) • **79**

CHAMBERT-MARBUZET, CHÂTEAU

St.-Estèphe 1997: Lots of new wood, with vanilla, chocolate and some fruit on the nose. Medium-bodied, with medium tannins and a vanilla finish. Very short on fruit in the aftertaste. Wait and see. • $NA • (06/15/98) (BT) • **80-84**

St.-Estèphe 1996: Rather light, simple and diluted with some cherry character but very short. • $NA • (01/01/97) (BT) • **75-79**

St.-Estèphe 1995: Lacks some concentration, but shows pretty berry, vanilla and cherry aromas and flavors. Medium- to light-bodied, with a silky finish. Drink now. • $30 • (01/31/98) • **84**

St.-Estèphe 1994: Refined and delicious, with fine tannins and a caressing texture. Not big or concentrated, but enjoyable. Drink now or hold. 3,300 cases made. • $25 • (01/31/97) • **84**

St.-Estèphe 1993: Diluted, showing some decent wood, vanilla and plum character but very light. Drinkable now. 3,333 cases made. • $25 • (01/31/96) • **79**

St.-Estèphe 1992: Too much new wood; some decent fruit, but dominated and slightly dried out by the tannins. • $15 • (04/15/95) • **76**

St.-Estèphe 1991: Pretty, sexy aromas and flavors accompanied by lots of new wood and cherry notes. Medium body, silky texture and a light finish. Second label of Haut-Marbuzet. • $14 • (03/31/94) • **83**

St.-Estèphe 1990: A bit one-dimensional, but it offers beautiful aromas and flavors of berry, vanilla, and cherry, medium tannins and plenty of sweet fruit on the finish. Drinkable now. 3,800 cases made. • $25 • (03/31/93) • **86**

St.-Estèphe 1987 • $18 • (11/30/89) • **79**

St.-Estèphe 1986 • $25 • (05/31/89) • **81**
St.-Estèphe 1985 • $32 • (06/30/88) • **87**
St.-Estèphe 1983 • $15 • (09/30/86) • **77**
St.-Estèphe 1982 • $30 • (11/30/89) • **88**

CHAMFORT, BERNARD

Côtes du Rhône Cuvée de Rochedouble 1995: Almost jammy, with luscious plum and black cherry flavors, ripe and yet still fresh. Just enough tannin for balance; drink now. • $5 • (02/28/97) • **84**

CHAMIREY, CHÂTEAU DE

Mercurey 1991: Very crisp and moderately astringent, this tough little wine has charms that reveal themselves after several sips. Drinkable now. • $NA • (01/31/94) • **81**
Mercurey White 1994: Pleasant and sweet-tasting, it's round and a bit simple, showing apricot, peach and pear flavors. • $20 • (05/31/96) • **80**
Mercurey White 1992: Smooth-textured Burgundy, with some decent vanilla, butter, apple and pear flavors, and a fresh finish. From Antonin Rodet. • $17 • (08/31/94) • **83**

CHAMOUX, JEAN-PIERRE

Pouilly-Fumé Les Chantalouettes 1993 • $15 • (12/15/95) • **78**

CHAMPALOU

Vouvray 1995: Shows good concentration though it's somewhat austere. Flavors range from pineapple to lemon to creamy vanilla, and the firm acidity leaves only the faintest impression of sweetness. Should develop well. • $13 • (06/15/97) • **87**
Vouvray 1993 • $14 • (11/15/95) • **85**
Vouvray Cuvée Moelleuse 1994 • $20 • (05/15/96) • **83**

CHAMPAULT, DOMAINE

Sancerre 1996: Atypical for Sancerre, with its deep gold color, honeyed aroma and soft, round texture. Shows cooked apple and melon flavors, with a core of lemony acidity. Could be suffering from oxidation. Drink now. • $15 • (05/31/98) • **78**

CHAMPET, EMILE

Côte-Rôtie 1989 • $28 • (04/15/93) • **78**
Côte-Rôtie Côte Brune 1991: Rich and juicy, oozing with new oak. Classy, round and silky, with plenty of berry and plum flavors to balance the toast and vanilla. Drinkable now. • $32 • (05/31/94) • **87**
Côte-Rôtie Côte Brune 1990: Pure velvet, with extremely ripe raisin and prune flavors supported by full, round tannins. It's rich, but a bit rustic. Try now. • $33 • (05/31/94) • **89**

CHAMPS, JEANNE-MARIE DE

Corton Hospices de Beaune Cuvée Charlotte-Dumay 1985 • $76 • (10/15/88) • **87**
Nuits-St.-Georges Les Didiers Hospices de Nuits Cuvée Cabet 1988 • $26 Ⓐ • (09/30/90) • **83**
Nuits-St.-Georges Les Didiers Hospices de Nuits Cuvée Cabet 1985 • $53 • (03/15/88) • **96**
Nuits-St.-Georges Les Didiers Hospices de Nuits Cuvée Jacques Duret 1988 • $49 • (09/30/90) • **89**
Nuits-St.-Georges Les Terres Blanches 1988 • $39 • (07/15/91) • **90**

CHAMPS CLOS, LES

Sancerre 1996: Powerful, and rich with pear and spice flavors around a core of intense, citrusy acidity. Toast and smoky accents give depth, though it lacks some of the classic top notes. Distinctive, and should age well. Drink now through 2002. 10,000 cases made. • $14 • (03/31/98) • **88**
Sancerre 1995: Bold and intense, with full-bodied pear and herbal flavors amplified by racy, grapefruit acidity. Drinkable now. 5,000 cases made. • $14 • (04/30/97) • **88**
Sancerre Rosé 1997: This very crisp, pale rosé shows light cherry and spice flavors and a pleasant, silky texture. It's nearly neutral in style, but a hint of spice emerges on the finish. Drink now. 1,000 cases made. • $15 • (07/31/98) • **81**

CHANDON DE BRIAILLES

Aloxe-Corton 1983 • $25 • (09/15/86) • **84**
Corton Le Clos du Roi 1991: Tough, tannic and young, this Corton has smoky, earthy aromas, a tight texture laced with firm tannins, and tart, greenish flavors. You could admire it for its structure, but it's so light on fruit flavor that it becomes awkward and heavy handed. • $57 • (01/01/94) • **81**
Corton Le Clos du Roi 1986 • $27 Ⓐ • (02/28/90) • **85**
Corton Les Bressandes 1991: Smoky, earthy aromas and fairly generous fruit flavors make this an accessible, easy-drinking Burgundy from a difficult vintage. The flavors are plummy, beefy and generous, and the texture is smooth. The finish, lingers, too. Drinkable now. • $53 • (01/01/94) • **85**
Corton Les Bressandes 1988 • $75 • (02/28/91) • **89**
Corton Les Bressandes 1986 • $43 • (02/28/90) • **88**
Corton Les Maréchaudes 1991: A sturdy but refined Burgundy with just enough fruit flavor to fill out the basically tannic framework. It starts out with seductively spicy oak aromas, goes into solid cherry flavors and finishes with spice and smoke. Drinkable now. • $44 • (01/01/94) • **85**
Pernand-Vergelesses Ile des Vergelesses 1991: This has a good core of cherry and raspberry flavors balanced by firm acidity and tannins, making for a complete, well-rounded red Burgundy. Solidly built. Drink now. • $28 • (01/01/94) • **84**
Pernand-Vergelesses Ile des Vergelesses 1988 • $35 • (02/28/91) • **83**
Savigny-lès-Beaune 1991: A rather tight Burgundy with stiff tannins and tart acidity but enough cherry and raspberry flavor to fill it out. • $21 • (01/01/94) • **83**
Savigny-lès-Beaune Aux Fourneaux 1991: Fresh, flavorful and vibrant, with ample floral aromas, strawberry and cherry flavors and a clean, tannic finish. • $23 • (01/01/94) • **82**
Savigny-lès-Beaune Les Lavières 1991: A firm-textured, lean flavored Burgundy with raspberry and herbal accents and a touch of toasty oak. Moderate tannins and good acidity will make it a refreshing dinner time wine. • $26 • (01/01/94) • **84**
Savigny-lès-Beaune Les Lavières 1988 • $31 • (02/28/91) • **86**

CHANRION, NICOLE

Côte de Brouilly Domaine de la Voûte des Crozes 1996: Plush yet focused, this vibrant red exhibits ripe cherry and plum flavors, with notes of game and smoke that add character. Moderate tannins and good acidity. A fine food wine. Drinkable now. • $14 • (06/15/98) • **87**

CHANSON PÈRE & FILS

Beaune Clos des Fèves 1988 • $35 • (08/31/90) • **84**
Beaune Clos des Fèves 1987 • $23 • (07/31/89) • **85**
Beaune Clos des Fèves 1985 • $25 • (01/31/89) • **92**
Beaune Les Marconnets 1986 • $20 • (05/31/89) • **81**
Bourgogne Cuvée Alexis Chanson White 1994: Sweet-tasting and soft, showing distinctive mint, honey and ripe pear character. Light-bodied and ready to drink. • $10 • (05/31/96) • **79**
Chablis 1994 • $18 • (05/31/96) • **78**
Chablis Blanchots 1994 • $25 • (05/31/96) • **84**
Chablis Montmains 1994 • $29 • (05/31/96) • **83**
Corton 1986 • $30 • (04/30/89) • **90**
Givry 1988 • $13 • (12/31/90) • **78**
Montagny Premier Cru 1994: Nicely made and satisfying, a medium-bodied '94 featuring good concentration of ripe fruit flavors in an elegant package. Stands out for its chewy honey, pear, caramel character. • $13 • (05/31/96) • **84**
Pernand-Vergelesses Les Vergelesses 1988 • $24 • (08/31/90) • **85**
Pernand-Vergelesses White 1994: Straightforward and simple, cardboard character. Short on flavors. • $16 • (05/31/96) • **71**

Key: SS—Spectator Selection CS—Cellar Selection HR—Highly Recommended BB—Best Buy $NA—Price not available Ⓐ—Auction Price (BT)—Barrel Tasting
Dates in parentheses indicate the issues in which the ratings were published.

Pouilly-Fuissé St.-Vincent 1994: Lively, vibrant, juicy, lemony flavor. Tasty, light-bodied white of modest character. Try now with oysters or other seafood. • $19 • (05/31/96) • **84**

Vosne-Romanée Les Suchots 1988 • $55 • (09/30/90) • **87**

CHANTE-ALOUETTE, CHÂTEAU

St.-Emilion 1997: Very light for the vintage, with some berry and earth character, but rather short. • $NA • (06/15/98) (BT) • **75-79**

St.-Emilion 1996: Grape and violet aromas and flavors. Slightly lean on the palate, with medium, austere tannins and a minerally, grapey aftertaste. • $30 • (06/15/98) (BT) • **75-79**

St.-Emilion 1995: A bit tight and ungiving. Berry, mineral and stone aromas. Medium- to full-bodied, with medium tannins and finish. Best after 2000. • $28 • (01/31/98) • **87**

CHANTE CIGALE

Châteauneuf-du-Pape 1989 • $14 • (10/15/91) • **84**

Châteauneuf-du-Pape 1988 • $18 • (10/15/91) • **89**

Châteauneuf-du-Pape 1986 • $18 • (10/15/91) • **89**

CHANTE-PERDRIX, CAVE DE

St.-Joseph 1992 • $12 • (05/31/94) • **76**

St.-Joseph 1991 • $12 • (05/31/94) • **77**

St.-Joseph 1989 • $12 • (05/31/94) • **89**

CHANTE-PERDRIX, DOMAINE

Châteauneuf-du-Pape 1993: This is already old, showing flavors of dead leaves, earth and raisins. Thick and lifeless. • $17 • (12/15/96) • **76**

Châteauneuf-du-Pape 1990: Enjoyable but odd, with walnutty, honeylike, peppery aromas and similar flavors. Likable, but so unusual with its oxidized character that it throws you for a loop. Tasted twice, with consistent notes. • $20 • (04/15/93) • **79**

Châteauneuf-du-Pape 1989 • $20 • (08/31/92) • **82**

Châteauneuf-du-Pape 1988 • $17 • (05/31/91) • **82**

CHANTEFLEUR

Cabernet Sauvignon Vin de Pays d'Oc 1995: There's an earthy note that adds dimension to the band of cherry flavors, though not everyone will find it interesting. • $7 • (12/15/96) • **79**

Cabernet Sauvignon Vin de Pays d'Oc 1994 • $5 • (10/31/95) • **78**

Cabernet Sauvignon Vin de Pays d'Oc 1993 • $5 • (02/28/95) • **81**

Cabernet Sauvignon Vin de Pays de l'Ardèche 1991 • $5 • (06/15/93) BB • **81**

Cabernet Sauvignon Vin de Pays de l'Ardèche 1988 • $6 • (05/31/90) BB • **80**

Chardonnay Vin de Pays d'Oc 1994 • $5 • (06/30/95) • **73**

Merlot Vin de Pays d'Oc 1995: Well focused, with loads of cherry flavors and a touch of herbaceousness. Nice Merlot character. • $7 • (12/15/96) • **82**

Merlot Vin de Pays d'Oc 1994 • $5 • (10/31/95) • **76**

Merlot Vin de Pays d'Oc 1993 • $5 • (02/28/95) • **82**

Syrah Vin de Pays d'Oc 1993 • $5 • (02/28/95) • **80**

CHANTEGRIVE, CHÂTEAU DE

Graves 1991: Very watery with dried cherry, vanilla aromas and flavors. • $11 • (03/31/94) • **72**

Graves 1990: This is an angular, muscular wine with good, rich fruit and solid tannins. Drinkable now. • $14 • (03/31/93) • **87**

Graves 1989 • $20 • (03/15/92) • **88**

Graves 1982 • $20 • (08/31/92) • **88**

Graves Cuvée Edouard 1990: This wine shows aromas and flavors of cassis, smoke and a full yet fine tannin structure. Big and muscular. Drinkable now. • $16 • (03/31/93) • **88**

Graves Cuvée Edouard 1989 • $22 • (03/15/92) • **85**

Graves White 1993 • $10 • (05/31/95) • **83**

CHANTELEUSERIE, DOMAINE DE LA

Bourgueil Cuvée Alouettes 1996: Fresh and fruity, offering pretty flavors of black cherries, herbs and hints of dark chocolate. Clean and supple, with just enough tannin for grip. An easy match for lighter dishes. Drink now through 1999. • $11 • (02/28/98) • **85**

CHAPELLE, DOMAINE DE LA

Pouilly-Fuissé Vieilles Vignes 1995: Well made and seductive, with a silky texture and attractive cream, fruit, toasty bread and vanilla flavors. Medium-bodied, with a smooth, juicy finish. Ready to drink. From Catherine and Pascal Rollet. • $20 • (05/31/97) • **86**

CHAPELLE DE LA MISSION-HAUT-BRION, LA

Pessac-Léognan 1997: Rather herbal and slightly green, with tobacco and cherry characterbeneath. Medium-bodied, with medium tannins. • $NA • (06/15/98) (BT) • **80-84**

Pessac-Léognan 1996: Plenty of tobacco and cherry aromas and flavors. Medium-bodied, with medium tannins and a slightly diluted center palate. • $32 • (06/15/98) (BT) • **85-89**

Pessac-Léognan 1995: Plenty of red berry and cherry in this one. Medium-bodied, with elegant, well-integrated tannins and a long finish. • $25 • (01/01/97) (BT) • **85-89**

CHAPOUTIER, M.

Châteauneuf-du-Pape Barbe Rac 1995: Vivid, offering ripe fruit flavors of plums and blackberries with accents of licorice and tobacco. The tannins are full, but round and well balanced. Drinkable now, should improve through 2000. • $85 • (10/15/97) • **88**

Châteauneuf-du-Pape Barbe Rac 1994: Once you get through the tannins, this big red shows sweet, ripe flavors of plum and raisin, with cigar box and toast accents. Though firm, the core of fruit is rich enough to promise good drinking now to 2000. • $82 • (10/15/97) • **86**

Châteauneuf-du-Pape Barbe Rac 1992: Full-bodied, round in texture and marked by ripe, soft flavors of prunes and tomatoes, firm tannins and a lingering finish. • $44 Ⓐ • (10/15/95) • **84**

Châteauneuf-du-Pape La Bernardine 1994: Light, with pleasant cherry and milk chocolate flavors, but it's soft and simple for the appellation. Drinkable now. • $26 • (12/15/96) • **82**

Châteauneuf-du-Pape La Bernardine 1992: A full-bodied red with vague fruit flavors and pretty stiff tannins. Tastes a bit tired and watery in mid-palate, and turns astringent on the finish. • $26 • (11/15/95) • **77**

Châteauneuf-du-Pape La Bernardine 1990: Shows uncommon balance, proportion and finesse, offering lovely currant, cherry, chocolate and smoky oak flavors that are complex and luscious. The finish is long and complex, with soft but firm tannins. Tasty now. 8,000 cases made. • $16 • (08/31/92) SS • **90**

Châteauneuf-du-Pape La Bernardine 1989 • $12 Ⓐ • (08/31/91) • **84**

Châteauneuf-du-Pape La Bernardine 1988 • $17 • (12/31/91) • **81**

Châteauneuf-du-Pape La Bernardine 1985 • $14 Ⓐ • (03/15/90) • **89**

Châteauneuf-du-Pape La Bernardine 1983 • $15 • (09/30/87) • **89**

Châteauneuf-du-Pape White La Bernardine 1996: Clean and quite delicate, with good fruit. Medium-bodied, offering pear, almond and some mineral notes. Drink upon release with a light, summery dish or as an apéritif. • $29 • (10/15/97) • **85**

Châteauneuf-du-Pape White La Bernardine 1995: Rich butter and honey flavors give luscious depth, and pretty almond and vanilla notes linger on the finish. It's soft, though, and may not age well; enjoy the baby fat. • $29 • (09/15/97) • **85**

Châteauneuf-du-Pape White La Bernardine 1993: One of the more fruity, flavorful whites from Châteauneuf-du-Pape, showing fresh grassy, appley notes and a rich texture. Lingers on the finish, too. • $34 • (12/31/95) • **85**

Condrieu 1996: Perfumed aromas—flowers, musk and peach—are followed by peach and citrus flavors on a lean, crisply structured frame. Curt finish. Drink now through 1999. • $61 • (05/15/98) • **83**

Condrieu 1995: Silky and polished, this shows loads of toasty, oaky flavors, with spicy and floral notes beneath. There's ripe fruit, but it's an open question whether the wood will dominate as it ages. An ambitious wine with power and finesse. • $53 • (10/15/97) • **89**

Cornas 1995: Tight and restrained. Pretty strawberry and cherry aromas lead into a firm palate with cherry, currant and mineral flavors. The tannins are

firm but well integrated; the wine should begin to bloom in 2000. • $32 • (10/15/97) • **89**
Cornas 1991 • $32 • (05/31/94) • **86**
Cornas 1990 • $32 • (05/31/94) • **58**
Côte-Rôtie 1995: Thin, shallow, light in body, with herbal and light cherry flavors, light yet dry tannins. Spice and floral accents are pretty, but it lacks a ripe, solid core. Drinkable now. • $56 • (10/15/97) • **76**
Côte-Rôtie 1992: Fresh, with cherry and smoky flavors, but rather lean on the palate. Drinkable now. • $35 • (05/31/94) • **83**
Côte-Rôtie 1991: Smooth and youthful, a slightly chewy wine with fine tannins and a solid burst of leather-tinged cherry flavor. Drinkable now. • $37 • (10/31/93) • **85**
Côte-Rôtie 1990: An earthy style, with mulchy, green flavors-not quite ripe. Shows true Côte-Rôtie character—drink now. 5,000 cases made. • $27 Ⓐ • (05/31/94) • **80**
Côte-Rôtie 1989 • $30 • (07/31/91) • **86**
Côte-Rôtie 1988 • $27 • (11/15/91) • **84**
Côte-Rôtie Brune et Blonde 1992: From an off year in the Northern Rhône, but of interest and substance. Smoky, mineral accents and plummy, peppery flavors; good acidity, firm tannins and a lingering finish. • $48 • (12/31/95) • **87**
Côte-Rôtie Brune et Blonde 1990: Fresh and ebulliently flavorful, with lavishly black-pepper accented black cherry and raspberry aromas and flavors, hinting at vanilla and cedar on the finish. A solid wine, with a graceful sense of balance and refined tannins. 4,000 cases made. • $35 • (11/15/92) • **90**
Côte-Rôtie La Mordorée 1995: Riper and more concentrated than many wines of the vintage, this shows deep violet color, with expressive toasty aromas and dense, chewy flavors of cassis, blackberry and spice. It's a bit clumsy now, but should unwind and harmonize by 2000. • $105 • (10/15/97) • **90**
Côte-Rôtie La Mordorée 1992: Balanced but rather light, this marries smoky, earthy flavors with cherry and herbal notes. The tannins are firm and lean, offering some complexity for early drinking. • $73 Ⓐ • (10/15/95) • **83**
Côte-Rôtie La Mordorée 1991: Ripe and plump, with attractive flavors of plums, smoke and grilled meat. Full-bodied with silky tannins. Drinkable now. Tasted twice. • $158 Ⓐ • (05/31/94) • **86**
Côte-Rôtie La Mordorée 1990: A muscular wine that still achieves great elegance, with restrained ripe plum, tobacco and tar flavors. The tannins are huge, but the wine is balanced; try now. • $87 • (05/31/94) • **91**
Côtes du Rhône Belleruche 1994 • $10 • (12/31/95) • **82**
Côtes du Rhône Belleruche 1993 • $10 • (11/15/95) • **83**
Côtes du Rhône Rosé Belleruche 1996: A rosé that's a bit lean, with some crisp strawberry and raspberry flavors. Not much fruit intensity. • $10 • (10/15/97) • **79**
Côtes du Rhône White Belleruche 1996: A generous wine, this offers easy-drinking, mellow flavors of pear and melon. Drinks well now; better as an apéritif than with food. • $10 • (10/15/97) • **82**
Côtes du Rhône White Belleruche 1995: This full-bodied white stays light on its feet, kept fresh by lemony acidity and bright pear flavors. Herbal notes enliven the clean finish. Try with food. • $9 • (12/15/96) • **84**
Côtes du Rhône White Belleruche 1993 • $10 • (11/15/95) • **78**
Côtes du Rhône-Villages Rasteau 1990 • $14 • (04/15/93) • **79**
Côtes du Ventoux La Ciboise 1993 • $9 • (11/15/95) • **76**
Côtes du Ventoux La Ciboise 1990 • $7 • (04/15/93) • **76**
Crozes-Hermitage La Petite Ruche 1991 • $18 • (05/31/94) • **86**
Crozes-Hermitage Les Meysonniers 1995: Diluted. Has some decent red berry flavor, but it is hard, a bit green and vegetal, shows some tough tannins. • $20 • (10/15/97) • **80**
Crozes-Hermitage Les Meysonniers 1994: A middle-weight red, balanced and well-structured, but not very expressive now, with hints of licorice and black currants on the finish. Drinkable now. • $20 • (02/28/97) • **84**
Crozes-Hermitage Les Meysonniers 1993 • $22 • (12/31/95) • **85**
Crozes-Hermitage Les Meysonniers 1992 • $20 • (10/15/95) • **84**
Crozes-Hermitage Les Meysonniers 1991 • $17 • (05/31/94) • **80**
Crozes-Hermitage White Les Meysonniers 1995: Already browning, this rustic white shows oxidized flavors of cooked apples, earth and old butter. It's full-bodied, but tired. • $20 • (10/15/97) • **75**
Crozes-Hermitage Les Varonniers 1995: Well crafted, this is a hard, firm and tannic wine that shows impressive oak, currant, black cherry and spicy notes. Try now. • $60 • (10/15/97) • **88**

Key: SS—Spectator Selection CS—Cellar Selection HR—Highly Recommended BB—Best Buy $NA—Price not available Ⓐ—Auction Price (BT)—Barrel Tasting
Dates in parentheses indicate the issues in which the ratings were published.

Crozes-Hermitage Les Varonniers 1994: A voluptuous and seductive, sophisticated, international-style Rhône, velvety in texture, ripe in flavor, long on the finish, with sweet tannins that coat your mouth. Bursts with cassis, currant, spicy oak, mocha and chocolate flavors. Layered with complexity, you want to bite into this now through 2002. • $55 • (10/15/97) • **92**
Ermitage De l'Orée 1994: Great richness and concentration mark this ripe, deep white. The flavors run from vanilla to toast, melon and honey, with hints of anise, herbs and flowers. Harmonious and expressive, it's drinkable now, but will improve through 2000, at least. 200 cases imported. • $85 • (02/28/97) CS • **90**
Ermitage Le Pavillon 1995: Beautifully defined and characteristic flavors of black cherry, spice, licorice and violets shine through this medium-bodied, perfectly focused red. Not a blockbuster, but it's firm and crisp, and completely true to the appellation, marrying international-quality winemaking with authentic local character. Tempting now. • $118 • (10/15/97) • **94**
Ermitage Le Pavillon 1994: Elegant for Hermitage, this shows its balanced fruit, alcohol and tannin in a harmonious package. The flavors are all there: licorice, game, smoke; the wine is subdued yet complete. Should develop well through 2005. 200 cases imported. • $105 • (04/30/97) • **90**
Ermitage Le Pavillon 1992: Ambitious, offering plenty of ripeness, plenty of extraction and plenty of oak. Tough now, but cassis, smoke and bitter chocolate flavors promise to unwind after time in bottle. Try now. • $109 • (10/15/95) • **87**
Ermitage Le Pavillon 1991: Firm and focused, with concentrated black cherry, tobacco and spice aromas and flavors. Drinkable now. 450 cases made. • $102 • (05/31/94) • **87**
Ermitage Le Pavillon 1990: Dark, dense and concentrated. A firm-textured wine with a strong smoky character that threads through the powerful berry and spice flavors. The earthy notes are disturbing. Drinkable now. • $160 • (12/15/93) • **85**
Ermitage Le Pavillon NV • $60 • (01/31/89) • **88**
Gigondas 1995: Wonderful. Complex, well-crafted, full-bodied. Dark in color, concentrated in flavor, supple in texture, with ripe, rich and sweet tannins, it layers the palate with spice, smoke, toast, red- and black-cherry flavors. Drinkable now. 500 cases imported. • $22 • (10/15/97) • **90**
Gigondas 1994: Luscious flavors of ripe berries gain complexity from accents of black pepper and herbs. Firmly tannic yet neither heavy nor dull. Try with a beef stew on a cold night. • $22 • (02/28/97) • **87**
Hermitage La Sizeranne 1995: This firm, earthy wine leans towards the animal and mineral side of the varietal, lacking ripe fruit flavors. It's well structured and clean, though. Drinkable now. • $24 Ⓐ • (10/15/97) • **84**
Hermitage La Sizeranne 1994: This polished red has firm tannins, while the berry, herb, cedar and smoke flavors are all finesse. Though understated now, it has good balance, good aging potential and will marry beautifully with food. • $42 • (04/30/97) • **90**
Hermitage La Sizeranne 1992: Smooth and supple for Hermitage, showing plenty of ripe cherry flavors and appealing smoke and pepper notes. The tannins are firm, but well-integrated with the fruit. Drinkable now. • $45 • (11/15/95) • **87**
Hermitage La Sizeranne 1991: Chunky and tight, with a nice core of berry and spice flavors struggling to get past the fine tannins. Ends up balanced and promising fine things. Drinkable now. 10,000 cases made. • $42 Ⓐ • (05/31/94) • **86**
Hermitage La Sizeranne 1989 • $29 Ⓐ • (08/31/91) • **89**
Hermitage La Sizeranne 1988 • $25 • (12/31/91) • **85**
Hermitage La Sizeranne 1983 • $38 Ⓐ • (05/01/86) • **83**
Hermitage La Sizeranne 1981 • $26 Ⓐ • (11/01/84) • **88**
Hermitage La Sizeranne Grande Cuvée NV • $14 • (05/01/86) • **83**
Hermitage Monier de la Sizeranne Red 1990: Ripe, rich and complex, with deep currant, earth, oak and spice flavors that are finely woven together. The tannins are firm and rugged and clamp down on the finish. Drinkable now. 8,500 cases made. • $28 • (08/31/92) • **91**
Hermitage White Chante-Alouette 1995: Muscular, showing good concentration and ripeness, but it's somewhat rustic, and the buttery, pear and melon flavors turn a bit flat and earthy on the finish. Has power, but lacks finesse. Tasted twice, with consistent notes. • $49 • (10/15/97) • **84**
Hermitage White Chante-Alouette 1994: Distinctive tobacco and spicy aromas give way to expressive flavors of honey, spice and ripe melons in this elegant, sinuous white. It's clean, polished and harmonious, if not overly powerful, and should improve in the bottle. • $45 • (10/15/97) • **90**
Hermitage White de l'Orée 1995: Smooth and honeyed, this full-bodied white is lush and ripe, with melon, almond and white chocolate flavors. Generous and fresh, it's drinking well now but has the potential to gain complexity with age. • $99 • (10/15/97) • **90**
Muscat de Beaumes-de-Venise 1996: Lush and sweet, this full-bodied white offers orange peel, honey and spicy flavors, generous but with more sweet-

ness than fruitiness. The alcohol doesn't show at all. • $17/375ml • (10/15/97) • **84**

Muscat de Beaumes-de-Venise 1995: Bright orange-peel and clove aromas give way to candied orange and spice flavors. Silky, full-bodied, it has good intensity, moderate sweetness and a firm kick of alcohol. • $25 • (02/28/97) • **85**

Muscat de Beaumes-de-Venise 1993 • $13 • (10/15/95) • **86**

Muscat de Rivesaltes NV: Bold and distinctive, with white chocolate, spice, almond and marzipan flavors. Has that characteristic spirit character that gives a slightly hot, alcoholic note on the finish. • $NA • (10/15/97) • **85**

St.-Joseph Deschants 1995: Bright and fruity, sporting exuberant notes of cherries and cranberries, crisp and fresh, with firm tannins emerging on the finish. It's pure fruit, no oak, and should evolve well through 1999. • $23 • (10/15/97) • **87**

St.-Joseph Deschants 1994: Balanced and polished, this red offers pretty aromas and flavors of violets, raspberries and light toast, with well-integrated tannins and a clean, fresh finish. Drinkable now. • $22 • (11/30/96) • **87**

St.-Joseph Deschants 1992 • $20 • (05/31/94) • **88**

St.-Joseph Deschants 1991 • $20 • (05/31/94) • **79**

St.-Joseph Deschants 1990 • $20 • (04/15/93) • **83**

St.-Joseph Les Granits 1995: Voluptuous and relatively soft for the vintage, this generous red offers ripe plum flavors backed by toasty oak that adds chocolate and coffee notes. A polished wine that should drink well through 2000. • $56 • (10/15/97) • **89**

St.-Joseph White Deschants 1996: Toasty almond and ripe apple flavors are harmonious and lush in this smooth white. A touch of earth on the finish should smooth out with food. • $23 • (10/15/97) • **83**

St.-Joseph White Deschants 1994: Nutty, buttery aromas give way to round, somewhat dull flavors of ripe melons and cooked apples. Not lively, but there's enough weight to match with food. • $22 • (12/15/96) • **81**

St.-Joseph White Les Granits 1995: Buttery and butterscotch flavors dominate this blowsy white, but it's well concentrated, with pie crust and ripe apple flavors, and stays fresh on the finish. • $56 • (10/15/97) • **85**

Tavel Beaurevoir 1996: A wonderful dry rosé offering raspberry, spice and anise aromas and flavors. Medium-bodied and firm, balanced and long on the finish, it's perfect for lighter Mediterranean fare or straight sipping. Drink now. • $19 • (05/15/98) • **85**

CHARBAUT & FILS, A.

Brut Blanc de Blancs Champagne 1990: A vibrant, citrusy, lively style of bubbly with fresh lemon-lime flavors that linger on the finish. Crisp with acidity and very clean on the palate. Drink now. Tasted twice, with consistent notes. • $45 • (12/31/97) • **89**

Brut Blanc de Blancs Champagne 1988: Tight, rich and beautifully focused with spicy pear, lemon and cedary notes that turn elegant and complex on a long, rich finish. Picks up hints of honey and toast on the finish. Delicious now. 20,000 cases made. • $42 • (11/30/93) HR • **91**

Brut Blanc de Blancs Champagne 1987: Tastes off-dry, with perfumed, fruity aromas that turn soft and fleshy. Finishes with a coarseness and lack of finesse. Fails to impress, but it's certainly drinkable. Drink now. 10,000 cases made. • $42 • (08/31/92) • **76**

Brut Blanc de Blancs Champagne 1982: Deliciously rich and vivid, with layers of creamy cherry, toast, vanilla and spice flavors that are deep and concentrated. Plenty of pretty flavors on the aftertaste, too. Drink up. • $43 • (04/15/90) • **90**

Brut Blanc de Blancs Champagne 1979 • $34 • (05/31/87) • **96**

Brut Blanc de Blancs Champagne Certificate 1989: A vibrant example of vintage Champagne that accents its tight, crisp apple and lemon flavors with hints of vanilla and butter. A bit lean now, it opens up as you sip and should continue to develop complexity through 2000. • $80 • (11/30/96) • **89**

Brut Blanc de Blancs Champagne Certificate 1985: Refreshing wine with appley, young aromas and flavors and a hint of toasty oak. Medium-bodied with lovely acidity and a long finish. Better than when tasted in August 1992. Drink now. 4,000 cases made. • $88 • (12/31/93) • **88**

Brut Blanc de Blancs Champagne Certificate 1982: Broad, rich, well-defined pear, vanilla, apple and spice notes, a full-bodied style that's attractive; with time it may display more complexity and finesse, but for now those are modest shortcomings. • $82 • (12/31/89) • **87**

Brut Blanc de Blancs Champagne Certificate 1979 • $80 • (07/15/88) • **92**

Brut Blanc de Blancs Champagne Certificate 1976 • $63 • (05/31/87) • **87**

Brut Champagne 1987: Refined Champagne with bright ripe apple, lemon-lime and light toast character; excellent acidity and a long flavorful finish. Another lovely apéritif. Much better now with a little bottle age since we reported on it in August '92. Drink now. 6,000 cases made. • $42 • (12/31/93) • **88**

Brut Champagne 1985: • $49 • (12/31/90) • **94**

Brut Champagne 1979 • $23 • (02/01/86) • **74**

Brut Champagne NV: A hearty, fruity, straightforward Champagne with lots of apple and lemon flavors and a crisp texture. • $27 • (11/15/97) • **86**

Brut Rosé Champagne Certificate 1985: Soft, light and fruity, with pretty strawberry and watermelon flavors that turn delicate on the finish. Drinks well now. 4,000 cases made. • $85 • (08/31/92) • **85**

Brut Rosé Champagne Certificate 1982: Pretty orange salmon color, with plenty of Pinot Noir, strawberry and cherry flavors that show signs of complexity and nuance. • $82 • (12/31/89) • **88**

Brut Rosé Champagne Certificate 1979 • $80 • (07/15/88) • **89**

CHARBAUT FRÈRES

Brut Blanc de Blancs Crémant de Bourgogne 1986 • $15 • (01/31/92) • **80**

Brut Rosé Crémant de Bourgogne 1986 • $12 • (12/31/90) • **79**

CHARBONNIÈRE, DOMAINE DE LA

Châteauneuf-du-Pape Cuvée Mourre des Perdrix 1995: There's pretty cherry flavor on the palate, but the aromas are herbaceous and the finish is dry and bitter. A lean wine that may soften with food. Drink now. • $NA • (10/15/97) • **77**

Châteauneuf-du-Pape Cuvée Vieilles Vignes 1995: A disappointment in a strong vintage. This is light, green and dry on the finish, with hints of cherry lost in the mix. Drinkable now, though dry. 500 cases made. • $20 • (10/15/97) • **75**

CHARLEMAGNE, CHÂTEAU

Canon-Fronsac 1995: A solid '95, ripe and fruity, featuring wet earth, berry and cherry aromas and flavors, firm tannins and medium finish. • $NA • (05/15/96) (BT) • **85-89**

CHARLOPIN-PARIZOT, PHILIPPE

Bourgogne 1995: Quite oaky, with blackberry, vanilla and earth character. Firmly structured, but has good balance. Drinkable now. • $14 • (11/15/97) • **85**

Bourgogne Cuvée Prestige 1994: Light and a bit chewy, but the delicate currant and herb flavors balance well. Ready to drink. • $13 • (11/15/96) • **80**

Chambertin 1995: Excruciatingly intense to taste. Dominated by chocolate, bourbon and spicy new oak at this stage, with a core of sweet black cherry and cassis flavors. Incredibly concentrated and powerful, yet refined and classy at the same time, this is one of the more impressive wines of the vintage. Seamless finish. Give it until at least 2003. • $95 • (11/15/97) • **95**

Chambertin 1994: Shows a rich density for this vintage, offering pure, clear currant, blackberry, coffee and spice flavors that remain supple and focused through the long, harmonious finish. Tannins are smoothly integrated. Should keep growing well past 2000, even 2005. • $92 • (11/15/96) • **93**

Chambertin 1990: Firm in texture and bold in flavor, with complex cedar- and smoke-scented currant, plum and berry flavors, all tightly packed and long on the finish. The tannins are well integrated. At its best now. 100 cases made. • $90 • (08/31/92) • **94**

Chambertin 1989 • $35 • (11/15/91) • **91**

Chambolle-Musigny 1995: A bit traditional, with some chestnut, mocha and spice notes mingling nicely with the red- and blackberry character. It's ripe and fleshy, but with a slightly rustic, bourbonlike flavor. Chewy tannins. Drinkable now. • $37 • (11/15/97) • **84**

Chambolle-Musigny 1994: Showing a serious effort to outsmart the vintage odds, this wine delivers wet earth, plum, chocolate, spice and black cherry flavors with some intensity. A bit dry on the finish, though. Try now. • $36 • (11/15/96) • **84**

Charmes-Chambertin 1995: Like biting into a chocolate truffle. This '95 red Burgundy oozes with spicy, black chocolate, mocha, currant and red- and blackberry character. Lots of intensity below its sophisticated veneer of smooth tannins. Lovely, ripe, supple, and succulent, with a long and elegant finish. Tempting now through 2005. 125 cases made. • $87 • (11/15/97) • **96**

Charmes-Chambertin 1994: Has some delicious currant, spice and coffee flavors that pack themselves into a lovely beam, concentrated and elegant

FRANCE

through the open-textured finish. Balances the fruit and oak well, leaning toward fruit. Fine tannins need until 2000 to 2002. • $79 • (11/15/96) • **91**

Charmes-Chambertin 1993: A pure, clean, "serious" red Burgundy that coats the palate with its silky texture. Quite smoky and toasty in character, featuring lots of wild berry and currant flavors and complex aftertaste. Full-bodied, it seduces from start to finish. Delicious now but should age beautifully well into the next century. • $94 • (05/15/96) • **94**

Charmes-Chambertin 1990: Tight and focused, with a bright beam of toasty berry and plum aromas and flavors. Tannins wrap the flavors tightly on the finish, but the fruit persists and keeps echoing. Drinkable now. • $70 • (08/31/92) • **92**

Clos St.-Denis 1995: This showy red Burgundy will knock your socks off. Full-bodied, seductive, ripe, fleshy, it's a thick wine that's mega-oaky now, with loads of mocha, spice and meat flavors along with the red- and blackberry flavors. Fat, sweet tannins; long, intense, smoky finish. Try after 2002. • $80 • (11/15/97) • **93**

Clos St.-Denis 1994: Rich, pure and elegant, a shining beacon of clarity. Dark in color, full-bodied and redolent of currant, plum, spice and earth notes that swirl in a wonderful cloud of flavor that persists through the extraordinary finish. Should flesh out by 1999, and then keep going. • $79 • (11/15/96) • **95**

Clos St.-Denis 1993: Lovely clarity of berry and cherry character and a hint of mineral notes. Full, fine tannins and long, silky finish. Ultrafine Burgundy. Better in 2000. • $94 • (05/15/96) • **90**

Clos St.-Denis 1990: Tough in texture but beautifully focused, with elegant currant and berry flavors and floral and vanilla notes on the long finish. Drinkable now. • $76 • (08/31/92) • **89**

Fixin 1995: This sinewy red is masculine in style, with new oak providing a smoky, spicy character to the blackberry aromas and flavors. The tannnins are a touch astringent and need until 2000. • $NA • (11/15/97) • **88**

Fixin 1994: Decent black cherry and anise flavors, plus chunky tannins, make this a solid bet for drinking now. • $22 • (11/15/96) • **81**

Gevrey-Chambertin Cuvée Vieilles Vignes 1995: Beautiful toasty oak and lovely fruit tower in this seductive, well-balanced and supple wine. Full-bodied, it fans out on the palate but narrows a bit on the slightly lean finish. Needs until 2002 to show it all. • $37 • (11/15/97) • **90**

Gevrey-Chambertin Cuvée Vieilles Vignes 1994: Superior quality for a village Gevrey. Dark, with mineral, spice, currant and meatlike flavors. Quite chewy, but has the balance to suggest it will improve. Try now. • $35 • (11/15/96) • **85**

Gevrey-Chambertin Cuvée Vieilles Vignes 1993: Almost outstanding, featuring lovely plum, earth and berry character, velvety tannins and a medium finish. Drinkable now. • $NA • (05/15/96) • **88**

Gevrey-Chambertin Cuvée Vieilles Vignes 1990: Ripe, plush and generous, with a velvety smooth texture and beautifully articulated raspberry, black cherry and anise aromas and flavors intertwining through the long finish. Drinkable now. 150 cases made. • $40 • (04/30/92) • **90**

Gevrey-Chambertin Cuvée Vieilles Vignes 1989 • $75 • (11/15/91) • **88**

Gevrey-Chambertin Cuvée Vieilles Vignes 1988 • $31 • (12/31/90) • **79**

Gevrey-Chambertin La Justice 1995: A very pretty red that grows on you. This delicate, supple, elegant, medium-bodied '95 shows nice red berry, licorice and game flavors, ripe tannins and spicy, toasty oak notes. Enjoy now through 2000. • $NA • (11/15/97) • **86**

Gevrey-Chambertin La Justice 1994: Straightforward style with generous cherry and anise flavors. Ready to drink. • $33 • (11/15/96) • **81**

Marsannay En Montchenevoy Red 1995: Fat, ripe and rich, this sweet-tasting red has plenty of firm, chewy tannins, a burly texture, and some nice red- and blackberry flavor. Should make for satisfying drinking in 2000. • $20 • (11/15/97) • **87**

Marsannay En Montchenovoy Red 1990: Crisp and berrylike, but with enough flesh to bring out the smooth, polished texture. Balanced and appealing, with simple, refreshing flavors that are more like Beaujolais than Burgundy. Drinkable now. • $19 • (04/30/92) • **84**

Marsannay Red 1994: Light and vaguely flavorful, delivering a chunk of berry flavor before disapearing on the palate. • $20 • (11/15/96) • **79**

Morey-St.-Denis 1995: A solid, massive wine. Concentrated, with red cherry and spicy oak wrapped tightly in chewy tannnins. All the elements are present, including sweet, spicy fruit on the finish. Needs until 2000 to integrate. • $32 • (11/15/97) • **91**

Key: SS—Spectator Selection CS—Cellar Selection HR—Highly Recommended BB—Best Buy $NA—Price not available Ⓐ—Auction Price (BT)—Barrel Tasting
Dates in parentheses indicate the issues in which the ratings were published.

Morey-St.-Denis 1994: Fairly ripe, but sturdy with some prounounced oak character. Medium-bodied, with mocha, plum, cherry flavors and hard tannins. • $31 • (11/15/96) • **78**

Vosne-Romanée 1995: Beautifully refined Vosne. Graceful, elegant and transparent, with mocha, black cherry flavors and well-integrated oak notes. Long, subtle finish of spicy black fruits. • $37 • (11/15/97) • **90**

Vosne-Romanée 1994: Pure red cherry and raspberry flavors shine through the very firm tannins. Drinkable now. • $37 • (11/15/96) • **84**

CHARMAIL, CHÂTEAU

Haut-Médoc 1994: Full-bodied and very tannic, without much fruit flavor to back it up, this comes off as tough. • $14 • (02/28/98) • **78**

CHARME LABORY, LE

St.-Estèphe 1995: The second label of Château Cos-Labory combines beauty with power. Violet and berry aromas and flavors follow onto a full-bodied palate with velvety tannins. Best after 2001. 4,000 cases made. • $12 • (01/31/98) • **87**

CHARMES DE KIRWAN, LES

Margaux 1995: Impressive for a second label from Château Kirwan. Gorgeous aromas of wild raspberries and flowers. Medium- to full-bodied, with sleek, racy tannins and a long, silky finish. Drink now or hold. • $18 • (01/31/98) • **88**

CHARMES DE LIVERSAN, LES

Haut-Médoc 1995: Rather light, but has some good berry, tobacco and cedar flavors. Medium- to light-bodied, with light tannins, a fresh finish. A second label of Château Liversan. Drink now. 10,000 cases made. • $10 • (01/31/98) • **81**

CHARMES-GODARD, CHÂTEAU LES

Côtes de Francs 1995: A beautiful red that entices you to drink it. Alluring aromas of milk chocolate, raspberry, vanilla and fruit. Full-bodied, with velvety tannins and a long, fruity, chocolaty finish. Drinkable now. • $18 • (01/31/98) • **88**

Côtes de Francs 1989 • $NA • (03/15/92) • **86**

Côtes de Francs White 1995: Slightly candied, with celery and apple character, medium acidity, a short finish. Drink now. • $18 • (04/30/98) • **79**

Côtes de Francs White 1993 • $NA • (05/31/95) • **84**

CHARRON, CHÂTEAU DE

Bordeaux 1993: Herbaceous flavors dominate, with accents of black cherry and earth. Firm and straightforward. • $8 • (12/15/95) • **78**

Bordeaux White 1994 • $8 • (02/29/96) • **80**

CHARTOGNE-TAILLET

Brut Champagne Cuvée Fiacre Taillet NV: Generous fruit flavors and rather soft texture provide all-around appeal in this bright, easy-drinking Champagne. Tasted twice, with consistent notes. • $41 • (11/30/97) • **86**

Brut Champagne Cuvée Ste.-Anne NV: A nice mouthful of bubbly, from the crisp apple and vanilla flavors to the lively texture and clean finish. Everything's in proportion, and it keeps improving as you sip. • $30 • (11/30/97) • **90**

CHARTREUSE, CHÂTEAU DE LA

Sauternes 1987 • $NA • (06/15/90) • **77**

Sauternes 1983: A real find at this price. Deep gold, a bit shy on the nose, but rich, round, long and full on the palate with apricot, honey and spice, a wine with subtleties that grow on you. It keeps getting better with each sip. • $10 • (01/31/88) • **90**

CHARTRON, JEAN

Beaune Hospices de Beaune Cuvée Cyrot-Chaudron 1988 • $40 • (02/15/91) • **88**

Bourgogne Clos de la Combe 1990: Intense and firmly tannic, with ripe plum and currant flavors underneath. A bold, concentrated wine to drink now. • $11 • (03/31/92) • **85**

Bourgogne Clos de la Combe White 1996: Flavorful and ripe, though a bit earthy with a matchstick, pear and spice character. Medium-to-full in body, it has an attractively vibrant finish. Try now. 4,580 cases made. • $10 • (05/31/98) • **84**

Chevalier-Montrachet 1994: Sweet, rich and honeyed, this full-bodied wine offers plenty of fruit flavors, with vanilla bean, spice, toasty oak accents. Slightly hot and alcoholic on the finish. Try now. • $NA • (08/31/96) • **85**

Chevalier-Montrachet Clos des Chevaliers 1996: Call in the firefighters to chill the heat from this huge wine. Oaky but ripe, intense and concentrated, this full-bodied, muscular '96 white Burgundy overwhelms your palate with its fantastic ripe fruit, firm acidity, toasty wood and incredible thick and minerally midpalate. The finish doesn't stop until you drink a cool glass of water. Hold until 2010 or so. 175 cases made. • $170 • (05/31/98) • **97**

Chevalier-Montrachet Clos des Chevaliers 1993: Wonderful, creamy white Burgundy exhibiting loads of class. Pear, apple, toasty oak character, medium-to-full body, long finish. Drinkable now. • $112 • (05/15/95) • **90**

Chevalier-Montrachet Clos des Chevaliers 1992: This shows 1992 at its best—generous and harmonious. Extremely open and inviting with lots of flavors that mingle subtly and seamlessly and last a long time on the finish; blends pear, vanilla, nutmeg, toast and honey in a rich, seductive mix. The texture is wonderfully smooth, firmed up by fresh acidity, but thick enough to make the flavors really last. Drinkable now. 208 cases made. • $95 • (08/31/94) HR • **96**

Puligny-Montrachet Le Cailleret 1996: Impressive. Honey and lime combine in this full-bodied, toasty wine. Very balanced and appealing, with a long finish unveiling grilled pineapple, smoky meat and carmelized pear notes. Try around 2005. 630 cases made. • $60 • (05/31/98) • **90**

Puligny-Montrachet Le Cailleret 1994: Fairly rich tropical fruit, pear and coconut character and creamy texture. Medium-bodied, very round and supple. Nice vibrancy on the finish. • $42 • (05/31/96) • **85**

Puligny-Montrachet Le Cailleret 1993: Intense and lively, but quite tart and austere, showing green, herbal flavors and a lot of green-apple notes. Drinkable now. • $42 • (05/15/95) • **82**

Puligny-Montrachet Le Cailleret 1992: Extremely spicy and flavorful; full of generous pear, vanilla, nutmeg and cinnamon in a broad, appealing style. Has a long finish, too. Delicious to drink now. • $34 • (08/31/94) • **90**

Puligny-Montrachet Les Folatières 1996: Lovely, with deftly used toasty oak buttressing the butter, ripe pear, apple tart and mineral character of this full-bodied wine. Of medium intensity, it needs a bit of time to become supersilky. A bit short on the finish. Try around 2003. 4,000 cases made. • $55 • (05/31/98) • **88**

Puligny-Montrachet Les Folatières 1994: Opulent and rich, but there's a lot of toasty oak dominating whatever fruit is there. Too much for us. Still, the lemon, apple and honey notes show underneath. Drinkable now. • $42 • (05/31/96) • **81**

Puligny-Montrachet Les Folatières 1993: Chewy and showy, presenting a mouthful of vivid earth, honey, stone and fruit character; still tart on the finish. Drinkable now. • $37 • (05/15/95) • **84**

Puligny-Montrachet Les Folatières 1992: A well-balanced, well-made Puligny with bright, focused fruit flavors accented by toasty oak and vanilla aromas. Its flavors turn a bit earthy and smoky on the finish. 225 cases made. • $35 • (07/31/94) • **86**

Puligny-Montrachet Les Pucelles 1996: Vibrant, with a solid frame of oak, fruit and acidity, but lacking the finesse and harmony of the best '96s. Medium-bodied, it turns a bit harsh on the finish. Try now. 558 cases made. • $60 • (05/31/98) • **83**

Puligny-Montrachet Les Pucelles 1994: Supple, full-bodied and rather rich, sporting some lovely honey, pear, dried herb, toasty bread and lemon flavors. Good intensity from start to finish. Drinkable now. • $NA • (05/31/96) • **88**

Puligny-Montrachet Les Pucelles 1993: Interesting grapefruit, apple and mineral aromas which follow through on the palate. Medium body, high acidity and toasty oak finish. • $42 • (08/31/94) • **85**

Puligny-Montrachet Les Pucelles 1992: Beautifully balanced; combines seductively spicy aromas of nutmeg and cinnamon with ripe pear and vanilla flavors that linger nicely on the finish. Drinkable now. • $36 • (08/31/94) • **89**

CHARTRON & TRÉBUCHET

Auxey-Duresses White 1994: Theatrical white. Full in body, sporting bursts of toasty oak, pie crust and pear character. Delicious in an up-front way, it peters out a bit on the finish. Still, very seductive. Drinkable now. 833 cases made. • $14 • (05/31/96) • **85**

Auxey-Duresses White 1993: Some nice round and ripe character and modest fruit flavors; the finish seems a bit one-dimensional. • $19 • (05/15/95) • **79**

Auxey-Duresses White 1992: An oaky style, with enough pear and apple flavor to back up the toasty, buttery, spicy character obtained from aging in oak barrels. Has firm acidity, a smooth but restrained texture and a lingering finish. 250 cases made. • $18 • (07/31/94) • **85**

Bâtard-Montrachet 1994: A weak *grand cru*, even by '94 standards, with some simple butterscotch and green oak flavors. A bit one-dimensional, it lacks concentration and has an astringent finish. Tasted twice, with consistent notes. • $122 • (05/31/97) • **70**

Bâtard-Montrachet 1993: Ripe and rich, offering honey, pear, butter and tropical fruit flavors. Medium-bodied; good use of oak on the toasty finish. Try now. • $95 • (05/15/95) • **88**

Bâtard-Montrachet 1992: Delivers all the richness and viscosity you expect from this elite appellation. Buttery, spicy aromas and ripe pear, honey and hazelnut flavors make this seductive and intriguing to drink. It combines ripe, delicious fruit flavors with layers of complexity on the long finish. Drink now. 75 cases made. • $82 • (07/31/94) • **92**

Bourgogne Cuvée Jean Chartron Vieilles Vignes White 1995: Fresh and full-bodied, with good acidity keeping the toasty oak and spicy character in check. Nicely balanced, if slightly bitter on the finish, with wet hay, lime and bitter-almond character. Should go well with food. Drink now. 1,000 cases made. • $NA • (05/31/98) • **84**

Bourgogne White 1994: Wonderful for a simple Bourgogne. Fresher than many '94s, sporting juicy, succulent, mouthpuckering flavors of lime, pear and ripe apple and a long finish. Drinkable now. 6,666 cases made. • $10 • (05/31/96) • **87**

Chassagne-Montrachet 1996: Full-bodied and rich, but with a reserved aromatic profile, it kicks in on the palate with pleasant mineral, lime, vanilla bean, pie tart, pear and tropical flavors, all of medium intensity. A pretty wine to drink now through 2000. 3,000 cases made. • $40 • (05/31/98) • **86**

Chassagne-Montrachet Les Vergers Clos St.-Marc 1993: Crisp green apple, lime, mineral and stone flavors turn chewy and interesting on the tart finish. Drink now. • $33 • (05/15/95) • **85**

Chassagne-Montrachet Les Vergers Clos St.-Marc 1992: Toasty, oaky aromas blend well with the bright lemon and apple flavors in this smooth-textured, well-balanced Chassagne. Tastes clean, flavorful and complete. 875 cases made. • $30 • (07/31/94) • **85**

Chassagne-Montrachet Morgeot 1994: Impressive, very rich and ripe, packed with fig, apricot and honey flavors. Soft core, and very drinkable now. Not much length here, so better to consume it soon. 791 cases made. • $25 • (05/31/96) • **89**

Chassagne-Montrachet Morgeot 1992: Young and tight, but the array of toasty, honeyed, pearlike flavors is backed by firm acidity. Starts out subtly, but gains in complexity through the finish. Drinkable now. • $22 • (08/31/94) • **87**

Corton-Charlemagne 1994: Slightly odd, with overly pronounced oak and a burnt rubber character that detracts from the fruit. Medium-bodied, turns astringent on the finish. • $75 • (05/31/97) • **70**

Corton-Charlemagne 1993: A beautiful wine for the long term. Starts out very hard and crisp, but picks up cream, ripe pear and honey flavors on the palate and then sails to a long finish. Try now. • $58 • (05/15/95) • **90**

Corton-Charlemagne 1992: Light for a Corton-Charlemagne, but it is elegant in texture and long-lasting on the finish. We could ask for more ripeness and fullness to the lemon and apple flavors, but the balance and harmony are inviting. 50 cases made. • $56 • (07/31/94) • **88**

Côte de Beaune-Villages 1988 • $16 • (02/28/91) • **79**

Mâcon-Villages 1995: Medium-bodied, with modest flavors and a dull, flat and astringent finish. • $NA • (08/31/96) • **75**

Mâcon-Villages 1994: Pleasantly ripe for a '94 Mâcon, showing pear, butter, peanut and honey character that turns smooth and lovely on the finish. Light-to-medium body; good for drinking now. 642 cases made. • $12 • (08/31/95) • **81**

Mercurey White 1996: Chewy, almost tannic, with wet earth, floral, apple, white pepper and pear complexity. Of medium body, with a vibrant texture and lively acidity. A bit rustic and tart on the finish. Drinkable now. 630 cases made. • $20 • (05/31/98) • **84**

Mercurey White 1994: Clean, crisp and lively, showing some nice citrus, pear and apple flavors. A bit simple on the tart finish. 416 cases made. • $15 • (05/31/96) • **80**

FRANCE

Mercurey White 1992: An incredibly spicey and oaky wine. The flavors of butter, fig and maple are appealing for their intensity. Certainly exaggerated and lacking harmony, but still a good wine that's meant to be drunk with a hearty meal. Drink now. 105 cases made. • $15 • (01/01/95) • **84**

Meursault 1996: Lovely but quite oaky, in a heavily toasty way. Good intensity of ripe fruit plus a silky, creamy, buttery, minerally mouthfeel. Of medium body, with honey, citrus and spice notes on the finish. Try around 2000 to 2002. 2,330 cases made. • $35 • (05/31/98) • **87**

Meursault 1994: Appealing butter, peach, toast and pear flavors accompanied by zingy citrus components that give it lots of life on the finish. You wish for a bit more "volume" and density. Drinkable now. 2,500 cases made. • $22 • (05/31/96) • **85**

Meursault 1993: Straightforward and fruity, displaying apple, pear and light vanilla flavors, medium body and simple finish. Drinkable now. • $19 • (05/15/95) • **84**

Meursault Les Charmes 1993: Full-bodied and firm white Burgundy, featuring smoke, toast and pear flavors and lots of mineral character. It ends with a slightly herbal bite. 150 cases made. • $35 • (08/31/95) • **84**

Montagny Les Grandes Vignes 1996: Distinctive matchstick-like, smoky, earthy aromas and flavors add complexity to this crisp, well-made white. Medium-bodied, supple on the midpalate from good concentration, and intense on the finish. Drinkable now. 1,080 cases made. • $17 • (05/31/98) • **85**

Montrachet 1996: An overly woody and disappointing Montrachet. Offers caramel and toasty oak notes, pear, tart dough and yeast flavors. Medium-bodied, with a core of firm acidity. Try around 2000. 75 cases made. • $240 • (05/31/98) • **85**

Montrachet 1993: Round and attractive yet quite intense, delivering flavors of honey, toasty bread, marzipan, mango and spice. Drinkable now. 50 cases made. • $200 • (08/31/95) • **87**

Pernand-Vergelesses White 1994: A voluptuous, full-bodied '94 offering nice amounts of honey, peach and fig flavors. Lacks some length on the finish, but what's there is pleasant. 1,666 cases made. • $15 • (05/31/96) • **85**

Pernand-Vergelesses White 1993: Tart and very citrusy, displaying some pear notes. Extremely crisp, light finish. Drink now. • $19 • (05/15/95) • **79**

Pernand-Vergelesses White 1992: Buttery aromas, lean fruit flavors and a tight texture. Try now. 625 cases made. • $18 • (07/31/94) • **82**

Pommard Les Epenots 1988 • $45 • (02/28/91) • **87**

Pouilly-Fuissé Domaine de la Chapelle 1996: Quite lush, with spice, mocha and smoke character. Ripe and medium-bodied, with apple, grilled vegetable and pear notes. Drink now. 1,000 cases made. • $20 • (05/31/98) • **84**

Puligny-Montrachet 1996: Clean and pure '96, with wonderful, supple texture emerging as the mineral, wet stone and earth notes play background to the ripe fruit and firm acidity. Quite toasty from the oak, this medium- to full-bodied wine shuts down a bit on the tough finish, but try it around 2002. 1,541 cases made. • $45 • (05/31/98) • **87**

Puligny-Montrachet 1994: Seductive village wine, creamy and lush, full-bodied and fat, boasting layers of toasty coconut, pear, pie crust and spice. Yet for all its opulence, it remains elegant on the long finish. Worth seeking out. Drinkable now and through 2000. 2,083 cases made. • $26 • (05/31/96) • **90**

Puligny-Montrachet 1993: Fresh lemon, mineral, honey character, medium body, firm acidity and light, fruity finish. • $31 • (05/15/95) • **84**

Puligny-Montrachet 1992: Rich, complex aromas and smooth, ripe flavors add up to a generous, well-proportioned wine. This has pear, hazelnut and butter flavors, a silky texture and a long finish. Combines freshness, complexity and concentration. 1,050 cases made. • $25 • (07/31/94) HR • **90**

Puligny-Montrachet Les Referts 1994: Subtle and supple, showing nice fruit character, chewy, mineral, toasty flavors and medium body and intensity. Drinkable now. 250 cases made. • $29 • (05/31/96) • **84**

Puligny-Montrachet Les Referts 1992: For fans of a complex but restrained style. Very aromatic, but fairly tight in texture and restrained in fruit flavor, yet it opens up and lets the flavors linger on the finish. • $28 • (08/31/94) • **90**

Rully La Chaume White 1996: A distinctive Chardonnay, with a mint, earth, smoke, pear tart and lime aromatic profile. Of medium body, it's balanced, with a supple yet racy texture that ends on a crisp finish. Drink after 2000. 4,080 cases made. • $19 • (05/31/98) • **85**

Key: SS—Spectator Selection CS—Cellar Selection HR—Highly Recommended BB—Best Buy $NA—Price not available Ⓐ—Auction Price (BT)—Barrel Tasting

Dates in parentheses indicate the issues in which the ratings were published.

Rully La Chaume White 1994: Textbook honey and tropical fruit flavors of medium intensity. Medium- to light-bodied, this tastes a bit one-dimensional on the crisp and fresh finish. 3,083 cases made. • $14 • (05/31/96) • **83**

Rully La Chaume White 1993: Sharp and crisp, green, herbaceous character; a mouth-puckering experience, clean and firm. Drink now. • $16 • (05/15/95) • **78**

Rully La Chaume White 1992: Tastes like a single-malt Chardonnay, with an intense oak flavor and aroma. The ripe fig and apple flavors stand up well to the butter and toast flavors of the oak, but it is quite a mouthful of wood in the end. 2,200 cases made. • $15 • (01/01/95) • **84**

St.-Aubin La Chatenière White 1996: Lovely balance in this subtle, minerally, harmonious and medium-bodied '96. Clean and pure, with good weight on the palate, showing nice fruit (apple, pear and kiwi), oak-infused spice and excellent mineral potential. Toasty oak accents play nicely on the succulent, mile-long finish. Try after 2002. 2,330 cases made. • $25 • (05/31/98) • **90**

St.-Aubin La Chatenière White 1994: Balanced, harmonious pear, pie crust, cream and apple flavors topped by a touch of honey. Of medium body, this *premier cru* turns refreshingly lively on the finish. Drinkable now. 375 cases made. • $17 • (05/31/96) • **85**

St.-Aubin La Chatenière White 1993: Harmonious white. The slight herbal character is muted by a hint of ripe fruit, a touch of toastiness and some hazelnut and cream flavors. Tart aftertaste, though. • $23 • (05/15/95) • **83**

St.-Aubin La Chatenière White 1992: Fairly big-bodied and quite woody, it tastes of vanilla, spice and apple, and offers a round texture. Well made for those who enjoy an oaky style of Chardonnay. • $18 • (08/31/94) • **83**

St.-Romain White 1994: Some decent citrus, pear and apple flavors, but this medium-bodied white turns unfocused on the slightly sour finish. Drinkable now. 2,000 cases made. • $14 • (05/31/96) • **79**

St.-Romain White 1993: A certain suppleness. Quite tart but also showing pear, honey, grass and subtle grapefruit flavors. Drinkable now. • $NA • (05/15/95) • **80**

St.-Romain White 1992: A pleasantly aromatic and smooth-textured white Burgundy with buttery, appley flavors that are rather light. Light-bodied, too, with a short finish. Still, it's a good wine from a lesser district. 1,025 cases made. • $16 • (07/31/94) • **83**

St.-Véran Château de Chasselas 1996: Racy white, with firm acidity. Medium-bodied, with a slightly grassy, astringent character but also some nice fruit and oak flavors. Juicy finish. Drink now. 660 cases made. • $14 • (05/31/98) • **85**

St.-Véran Château de Chasselas 1994: Subtle oak shadings give it a vanilla bean flavor that marries nicely and smoothly with pear, melon, fig and spice notes. Atypical for St.-Véran, but pleasant. Drink now. 350 cases made. • $15 • (08/31/95) • **80**

Santenay White 1996: The wood dominates the fruit in this medium-bodied, spicy, smoky, chocolaty wine. Turns sour on the finish. A bit overdone. Drink chilled. 165 cases made. • $25 • (05/31/98) • **77**

Santenay White 1994: Understated and superelegant, featuring solid mineral, wet earth and spice character backed by some dried herb and pear flavors. Drinkable now. 175 cases made. • $15 • (05/31/96) • **89**

CHASSE-SPLEEN, CHÂTEAU

Bordeaux White 1994 • $20 Ⓐ • (03/31/96) • **85**

Bordeaux White 1993 • $22 Ⓐ • (05/31/95) • **80**

Moulis 1997: Showy and dark-colored, with rich blackberry and smoke aromas, but lacking in fruit. Medium-bodied, with medium tannins and an austere finish. Wait and see. • $NA • (06/15/98) (BT) • **85-89**

Moulis 1996: Solid for the vintage with berry, dark chocolate and floral aromas and flavors. Medium-bodied with compacted fruit, velvety tannins, medium finish. • $NA • (01/01/97) (BT) • **85-89**

Moulis 1995: Chunky and closed. Wonderful wild cherry and berry aromas with bark undertones. Medium- to full-bodied, with chewy tannins and a long, sweet fruit finish. A serious wine. Best after 2001. 41,000 cases made. • $26 • (01/31/98) • **90**

Moulis 1994: Delicate, with berry, chocolate and vanilla flavors. Medium-bodied, with fine tannins and a fresh finish. Drink now or hold. • $20 Ⓐ • (01/31/97) • **85**

Moulis 1993: Plenty of fruit in this one. Medium-to-full body, berry and cherry flavors, medium to full tannins and long finish. Drinkable now. 2,333 cases made. • $22 Ⓐ • (01/31/96) • **88**

Moulis 1992: Well made Bordeaux, exhibiting focused cassis and vanilla character, medium body, silky tannins and a fine finish. • $21 • (04/15/95) • **80**

Moulis 1991: Well crafted wine with smoky, berry and gamy aromas and flavors. Medium-bodied with round, soft tannins. • $21 • (03/31/94) • **84**

Moulis 1990 • $27 • (03/31/93) • **90**
Moulis 1989 • $58 Ⓐ • (03/15/92) • **95**
Moulis 1988 • $33 Ⓐ • (03/31/91) • **89**
Moulis 1987 • $15 • (02/15/90) • **78**
Moulis 1986 • $39 Ⓐ • (06/30/89) • **85**
Moulis 1985 • $41 Ⓐ • (05/15/88) • **86**
Moulis 1984 • $23 Ⓐ • (06/15/87) • **74**
Moulis 1983 • $38 Ⓐ • (10/15/94) • **90**
Moulis 1982 • $41 Ⓐ • (11/30/89) • **90**
Moulis 1981 • $26 Ⓐ • (10/15/94) • **88**
Moulis 1970 • $61 • (05/15/93) • **84**
Moulis 1961 • $52 • (04/30/96) • **82**

CHASSE, MARQUIS DE

Bordeaux Reserve 1994: Extremely tannic and tastes unripe, with only modest plum and cherry flavors. • $8 • (04/30/97) • **76**
Bordeaux Reserve 1993: Offers toast, coffee and tobacco aromas and flavors, with firm tannins and a chewy texture. Has concentration and a lingering finish. • $8 • (12/15/95) • **83**
Bordeaux White 1995: Along with ripe fruit and clean acidity, this round white offers apple, pear and floral notes and enough body to match with food. • $8 • (04/30/97) • **84**
Bordeaux White 1994 • $7 • (02/29/96) • **79**
Merlot-Cabernet Sauvignon Bordeaux Reserve 1995: A medium-bodied Bordeaux with simple Merlot-like flavors and rather tough tannins. Drink now. • $8 • (01/31/98) • **79**
Sauvignon Blanc-Sémillon Bordeaux Reserve 1996: Lean and crisp, simple in flavor but refreshing in balance. Drink now. • $7 • (02/28/98) • **79**

CHASTAN, CLAUDE

Châteauneuf-du-Pape Domaine de St.-Siffrein 1993: Straightforward and rather austere, yet well balanced, with cherry and raisin flavors, herb and tobacco accents. Drinkable now. • $16 • (02/28/97) • **85**

CHÂTEAU, DOMAINE DE

Côtes du Rhône-Villages Cairanne 1990 • $12 • (04/15/93) • **85**

CHATELAIN, JEAN-CLAUDE

Pouilly-Fumé 1996: Vibrant smoke and mineral notes show classic character in this bold white. On the palate, grapefruit and peach flavors are balanced and crisp. A clean, well-focused wine with rich varietal character. Drink now through 2000. 15,000 cases made. • $17 • (05/31/98) • **89**
Pouilly-Fumé 1995: A keen, lean white with alluring aromas of newly mowed grass and lemon zest, this is a bit tart on the palate but very refreshing. A good mate for shellfish. • $19 • (04/30/97) • **85**
Pouilly-Fumé Cuvée Prestige 1995: Quite lush for a Loire Valley Sauvignon Blanc, but still fresh, with lively acidity. It shows toast, melon and hazelnut flavors, with light herbal accents. A well-defined wine that will go well with fish or poultry. Drink now. 1,600 cases made. • $30 • (05/31/98) • **87**
Pouilly-Fumé Domaine de St.-Laurent-l'Abbaye 1996: This harmonious, well-defined white shows classic Loire Valley flavors of minerals, herbs and citrus, balanced and crisp, with a long, mouthwatering finish. Though not a showy wine, it's a fine partner for food. Drink now through 2000. • $17 • (05/31/98) • **89**
Pouilly-Fumé Domaine de St.-Laurent-l'Abbaye 1995: Ripe fruit and great balance make this white a delight. Vivid flavors of apple, pear and citrus are accented with herb and mineral notes, the acidity is bright but well integrated. A great food wine that should drink well through 2000. 12,000 cases made. • $15 • (06/15/97) • **90**
Pouilly-Fumé Les Charmes 1995: The ripe, sweet apple flavors are fresh and well defined in this round, firm white, and there's plenty of lime-scented acidity providing structure. It's harmonious and graceful, a fine complement to food. • $20 • (04/30/97) • **90**
Pouilly-Fumé Pilou 1996: This distinctive white dances to the beat of its own drummer. It's a vibrant, seamless marriage of oak and fruit that shows coconut, toasty almond, melon and vanilla flavors, with lively but restrained acidity and a rich, round texture. Not a classic Loire Sauvignon Blanc, but a beauty nonetheless. Drink now. 140 cases made. • $50/500ml • (05/31/98) • **92**

CHATENOY, DOMAINE DE

Menetou-Salon 1995: This light, lively white offers grass, green apple and lime flavors backed by firm acidity. It's well-focused and balanced, delicate yet vivid. Tasted twice, with consistent notes. 2,500 cases made. • $14/375ml • (06/15/97) • **86**
Menetou-Salon 1994 • $12 • (11/15/95) • **83**
Menetou-Salon 1993 • $11 • (08/31/94) • **85**
Menetou-Salon Red 1992 • $15 • (11/15/94) • **77**

CHAUVENET, F.

Auxey-Duresses Le Val Red 1989 • $NA • (01/31/92) • **79**
Auxey-Duresses White 1993: Simple and straightforward; some modest fruit character and plenty of citrus flavors on the tart finish. 800 cases made. • $19 • (05/15/95) • **76**
Beaune 1993: Simple, modest strawberry and earth character. Somewhat short and dry on the finish, ending on a paperish note. 2,170 cases made. • $24 • (11/15/95) • **70**
Beaune Hospices de Beaune Rosseau-Deslandes 1980 • $36 • (06/16/86) • **91**
Beaune Le Clos des Mouches 1986 • $27 • (12/31/88) • **82**
Beaune Les Grèves 1993: Pleasant, plummy earth and spice character, medium body, light tannins and cedary finish. Drink now. 300 cases made. • $29 • (11/15/95) • **80**
Beaune Les Grèves 1990: A charming wine that offers juicy currant, cinnamon and berry aromas and flavors and a supple texture that is enchanting. Drinkable now. • $35 • (12/15/92) • **89**
Beaune Les Grèves 1989 • $30 • (01/31/92) • **91**
Beaune Les Grèves 1986 • $25 • (12/31/88) • **79**
Beaune Les Teurons 1985 • $23 • (07/31/87) • **88**
Bienvenues-Bâtard-Montrachet 1993: Perfectly clear, lovely apple, mineral and chalk character, medium body, firm acidity and lemony finish. 100 cases made. • $115 • (08/31/95) • **86**
Bourgogne 1990: An easy-to-drink, easy-to-like Bourgogne, but not very deep. Offers nice balance, light tannins and decent cherry and strawberry flavors. • $NA • (12/15/92) • **80**
Cabernet Sauvignon Vin de Pays d'Oc 1994 • $9 • (10/31/95) • **84**
Chambolle-Musigny 1993: Light, modest fruit flavors. A bit diluted in the finish. Drink chilled on release. • $37 • (11/15/95) • **78**
Chambolle-Musigny 1990: Packs a lot of nice flavors into a medium-bodied wine. Offers subtle raspberry and plum flavors touched by fresh acidity and lively tannins. Drinkable now. • $45 • (12/15/92) • **85**
Chambolle-Musigny Les Charmes 1982 • $33 • (04/30/87) • **83**
Chardonnay Vin de Pays d'Oc 1994 • $8 • (12/15/95) • **86**
Charmes-Chambertin 1993: Unusually soft for the vintage, a medium-bodied red sporting cherry, earth and chocolate flavors and lush tannins. Already quite forward; tempting upon release. • $78 • (11/15/95) • **86**
Charmes-Chambertin 1986 • $65 • (07/31/88) • **90**
Charmes-Chambertin 1985 • $72 • (07/31/87) • **97**
Charmes-Chambertin 1983 • $24 • (09/15/86) • **88**
Chassagne-Montrachet 1993: Lean and steely Chassagne, displaying green, grassy, aggressive flavors and a tart finish. Try now. 1,000 cases made. • $32 • (05/15/95) • **83**
Clos de Vougeot 1990: Muscular, big and chewy, a complex Clos de Vougeot that shows plenty of currant, wet earth, mushroom and smoke aromas and flavors. Drink now through 2000. • $69 • (12/15/92) • **92**
Clos de Vougeot 1989 • $60 • (01/31/92) • **90**
Clos de Vougeot 1986 • $57 • (12/31/88) • **79**
Clos de la Roche 1990: Extremely ripe, with smoky cinnamon and brown sugar flavors that seem almost sweet on the delicious finish. Drinkable now. • $76 • (12/15/92) • **87**
Clos St.-Denis 1990: A stunning beauty. Velvety and multidimensional, offering unique character and texture, with cigar box, violet, cedar and blackberry aromas and flavors and a decadent finish. Drinkable now. • $65 • (12/15/92) • **95**
Clos St.-Denis 1989 • $60 • (01/31/92) • **87**
Clos St.-Denis 1986 • $50 • (02/28/89) • **90**
Clos St.-Denis 1985 • $67 • (07/31/87) • **94**
Corton 1993: Has some dried cherry and smoky character but tastes of cardboard too. Medium- to light-bodied, firm tannins, short, papery finish. 150 cases made. • $54 • (11/15/95) • **78**
Corton 1990: Like a marble sculpture; has solid tannins, masses of fruit and covers your palate with blackberry and toasty oak flavors. Drinkable now. • $60 • (12/15/92) • **94**
Corton 1989 • $50 • (01/31/92) • **93**

Corton 1986 • $50 • (07/31/88) • **87**
Corton 1985 • $53 • (07/31/87) • **96**
Corton Hospices de Beaune Docteur-Peste 1985 • $133 • (07/15/88) • **97**
Côte de Beaune-Villages 1985 • $16 • (07/31/87) • **84**
Echézeaux 1990: Closed and hard now, but underneath the tight structure lurk violet, red berry and currant flavors. Needs years to mold the steely tannins into something softer. Try now. • $62 • (12/15/92) • **91**
Echézeaux 1989 • $56 • (01/31/92) • **92**
Echézeaux 1985 • $47 • (07/31/87) • **89**
Gevrey-Chambertin Charreux 1985 • $33 • (10/15/87) • **88**
Gevrey-Chambertin Estournelles St.-Jacques 1990: While this is quite firm, it has more generosity and flesh than many Gevreys, offering enticing blueberry, black cherry and earth aromas and flavors and a focused finish. Drinkable now. • $56 • (12/15/92) • **89**
Gevrey-Chambertin Estournelles St.-Jacques 1989 • $40 • (01/31/92) • **91**
Gevrey-Chambertin Estournelles St.-Jacques 1986 • $35 • (07/31/88) • **89**
Gevrey-Chambertin Lavaut St.-Jacques 1991: Earthy and simple; a bright beam of raspberry and anise flavors pokes through a pervasive earthy character. • $NA • (01/31/94) • **79**
Gevrey-Chambertin Lavaut St.-Jacques 1990 • $56 • (12/15/92) • **90**
Gevrey-Chambertin Lavaut St.-Jacques 1989 • $45 • (01/31/92) • **88**
Gevrey-Chambertin Lavaut St.-Jacques 1986 • $35 • (07/31/88) • **86**
Gevrey-Chambertin Le Clos St.-Jacques 1989 • $45 • (01/31/92) • **89**
Gevrey-Chambertin Le Clos St.-Jacques 1986 • $35 • (07/31/88) • **85**
Mâcon Blanc-Villages Les Jumelles 1994: Ripe and firm fruit, almond and honey flavors. Light- to medium-bodied, adding an attractively bitter twist on the finish. Drink now. 4,000 cases made. • $8 • (08/31/95) • **83**
Merlot Vin de Pays d'Oc 1994 • $9 • (10/31/95) • **78**
Meursault Les Charmes 1993: A bit acidic, very crisp and tart, lean and hollow; could use more ripe fruit. • $47 • (05/15/95) • **77**
Monthélie 1990: Aromatic and flavorful in an elegant but light style, offering nice raspberry and Pinot Noir characteristics. Delicious, but a tad simple. Drinkable now. • $21 • (12/15/92) • **84**
Monthélie Les Champs Fulliot 1990: A bit hard now, but ripe and concentrated, coating your mouth with strawberry, earth, spice and plum flavors. The firm tannins should smooth out with a few years; drinkable now. • $NA • (12/15/92) • **87**
Monthélie Les Champs Fulliot 1989 • $20 • (01/31/92) • **81**
Nuits-St.-Georges 1994: Pretty berry and floral flavors make this lightish wine charming, despite grainy tannins on the finish. Drinkable now. • $30 • (11/15/96) • **83**
Nuits-St.-Georges 1993: Soft, silky vanilla, spice and plum aromas and flavors, medium body and tannins and crisp finish. Drinkable now. • $40 • (11/15/95) • **78**
Nuits-St.-Georges 1991: Very pretty raspberry and strawberry aromas turn light and astringent on the palate and barely peek through a veil of chewy tannins on the finish. Try now. • $NA • (01/31/94) • **81**
Nuits-St.-Georges Aux Chaignots 1990: Made in the old style, with chestnut, berry and spice aromas and flavors and round tannins. Slightly dry on the finish. Drinkable now. • $53 • (12/15/92) • **83**
Nuits-St.-Georges Aux Chaignots 1989 • $45 • (01/31/92) • **91**
Nuits-St.-Georges Aux Chaignots 1986 • $40 • (07/31/88) • **87**
Nuits-St.-Georges Les Perrières 1985 • $48 • (07/31/87) • **80**
Nuits-St.-Georges Les Plâteaux 1985 • $34 • (07/31/87) • **84**
Nuits-St.-Georges Les Plâteaux 1982 • $16 • (01/01/85) • **78**
Nuits-St.-Georges Les Pruliers 1990: An elegant Nuits, with beautiful fruit and fine tannins. Shows finesse and plenty of smoke, berry and earth aromas and flavors. Drinkable now. • $52 • (12/15/92) • **90**
Nuits-St.-Georges Les Pruliers 1989 • $45 • (01/31/92) • **88**
Pinot Noir Bourgogne Château Marguerite de Bourgogne 1993: Clean cherry, cedar and mocha aromas and flavors, medium to light body, soft tannins and fresh finish. One of the better wines from Chauvenet this year. Drink now. • $14 • (11/15/95) • **80**
Pinot Noir Bourgogne Château Marguerite de Bourgogne 1985 • $10 • (06/30/88) • **80**
Pommard 1990: This lovely, medium-bodied wine offers raspberry and chestnut aromas and flavors and a fine, long finish. • $45 • (12/15/92) • **86**
Pommard Hospices de Beaune Cuvée Dames-de-la-Cha 1982 • $36 • (02/01/85) CS • **91**

Key: SS—Spectator Selection CS—Cellar Selection HR—Highly Recommended BB—Best Buy $NA—Price not available Ⓐ—Auction Price (BT)—Barrel Tasting
Dates in parentheses indicate the issues in which the ratings were published.

Pommard Les Chanlins 1990: A bit tough at this stage and lacking finesse, but a distinctive wine, with smoky herbal and olive aromas and flavors. Drinkable now. • $59 • (12/15/92) • **87**
Pommard Les Chanlins 1989 • $45 • (01/31/92) • **86**
Pommard Les Chanlins 1986 • $40 • (07/31/88) • **90**
Pommard Les Epenots 1989 • $45 • (01/31/92) • **94**
Pommard Les Epenots 1985 • $48 • (07/31/87) • **95**
Puligny-Montrachet White 1993: Steely and balanced, showing a polished core of green apple, pear and melon flavors. Vibrant finish. Drinkable now. 800 cases made. • $35 • (05/15/95) • **86**
Puligny-Montrachet Red 1985 • $16 • (06/15/87) • **81**
St.-Romain White 1993: Very green and herbaceous, showing unpleasant, underripe character and a grassy finish. 1,000 cases made. • $19 • (05/15/95) • **70**
Santenay 1985 • $18 • (07/31/87) • **84**
Syrah Vin de Pays d'Oc 1994 • $9 • (10/31/95) • **74**
Volnay Clos de Chênes 1990: Focused and racy, with plenty of cherry, plum and tobacco flavors in an elegant, medium-bodied style. Drinkable now. • $58 • (12/15/92) • **86**
Volnay Clos de Chênes 1989 • $40 • (01/31/92) • **90**
Volnay Premier Cru 1989 • $36 • (01/31/92) • **88**
Vosne-Romanée Les Suchots 1985 • $46 • (07/31/87) • **92**

CHAUVENET, JEAN

Nuits-St.-Georges Aux Bousselots 1994: Has a brilliant beam of currant, plum and floral flavor that shines through the veil of fine tannins and echoes enticingly on the finish, promising to develop well. Try after 2000. • $44 • (11/15/96) • **87**
Nuits-St.-Georges Aux Bousselots 1985 • $49 • (05/31/88) • **88**
Nuits-St.-Georges Les Vaucrains 1994: There's a pretty wine under the sandy tannins, offering spicy currant and blackberry flavors that last on the finish. Bodes well for drinking now to 2000. • $44 • (11/15/96) • **87**

CHAUVENET-CHOPIN

Chambolle-Musigny 1994: Firm, with a round texture and good red berry and plum aromas and flavors. Drinkable now. • $40 • (11/15/96) • **83**
Côte de Nuits-Villages 1994: A light and simple wine that's vaguely earthy and floral in flavor. • $25 • (11/15/96) • **77**
Nuits-St.-Georges Aux Argillas 1995: Smooth and fat, wth subtle flavors of cherry and vanilla, this has weight and flesh but lacks the depth of fruit of the best wines of Nuits. Sweet oak lingers on the aftertaste. • $54 • (11/15/97) • **84**
Nuits-St.-Georges Aux Argillas 1994: A rather compacted wine, revealing little of itself. Medium body, with an earth and cherry character and a wall of tannins on the finish. Drinkable now. • $48 • (11/15/96) • **81**
Nuits-St.-Georges Aux Murgers 1995: Intense, with cassis, cranberry, blueberry, tar and cherry flavors. Starts out crisp, but smoothed by sophisticated oak treatment, it turns sophisticated and round on the palate, ending with a smoky, ripe finish. Well made. Try after 2000. • $54 • (11/15/97) • **89**
Nuits-St.-Georges Aux Murgers 1994: Sweet-tasting and ripe, this is a pleasant, medium-bodied wine that delivers plum, licorice and cherry flavors and manages to remain supple on the finish. Ready now. • $48 • (11/15/96) • **84**
Nuits-St.-Georges Vieilles Vignes 1994: Light in body, but jazzy, with pure raspberry flavors that finish with style. Ready now. • $40 • (11/15/96) • **82**

CHAUVIN, CHÂTEAU

St.-Emilion 1988 • $20 • (06/30/91) • **84**
St.-Emilion 1986 • $15 • (06/30/89) • **75**

CHAVE, BERNARD

Crozes-Hermitage 1994: The pungent gamy aroma says Syrah, but it's a bit one-dimensional on the palate, where light cherry and plum flavors are overmatched by earthy, gamy notes and tough tannins. It has concentration, though. Try now. 2,600 cases made. • $18 • (10/15/97) • **84**
Crozes-Hermitage 1991 • $45 • (06/15/93) • **85**
Crozes-Hermitage 1988 • $14 • (02/15/91) • **78**
Crozes-Hermitage 1985 • $12 • (11/30/88) • **86**
Hermitage 1994: Firm, showing good grip and attractive cherry flavors, but it's a bit clumsy and turns earthy on the finish. Drinkable now. 255 cases made. • $44 • (09/15/97) • **85**

Hermitage 1990: Firm and fleshy, with a nice array of grape, plum and earth aromas and flavors that extend into a rich finish. Drinkable now. • $45 • (04/15/93) • **87**
Hermitage 1989 • $40 • (12/31/91) • **91**
Hermitage 1986 • $32 • (11/30/88) • **86**

CHAVE, JEAN-LOUIS

Hermitage 1994: This Rhône red is intensely perfumed with the inky spiciness so unique to Syrah, then firm and concentrated on the palate, with loads of ripe blackberry, anise and smoke flavors. Rich yet polished, it marries traditional structure with modern fruit. Approachable now, but better with age. Drink now through 2014. 3,500 cases made. • $55 Ⓐ • (04/30/97) CS • **94**
Hermitage 1992: Balanced, even delicate aromas and flavors of cherry, game and eucalyptus, yet firm tannins promise long life. Not as muscular as Hermitage can be, but it covers all the bases. Drink now through 2000. • $27 Ⓐ • (10/15/95) • **88**
Hermitage 1991: Straightforward, with plenty of ripe, raisiny fruit. Has muscle and it's big. Drink now. • $44 Ⓐ • (05/31/94) • **85**
Hermitage 1990: Such rich fruit, jammed with plum, herb, licorice, meat, spice and tar flavors, that you almost overlook the muscular tannins and think you could drink it now. Don't. This wine is concentrated and built to age. Wild and distinctive, it's a beautiful representation of the northern Rhône at its best. Best now through 2007. 2,500 cases made. • $171 Ⓐ • (05/31/94) CS • **96**
Hermitage 1987 • $48 • (06/30/90) • **89**
Hermitage 1984 • $14 Ⓐ • (08/31/87) • **89**
Hermitage 1980 • $40 • (05/01/86) • **83**
St.-Joseph 1994: This is a chewy red, concentrated and expressive, delivering ripe raspberry, herbal and tobacco flavors and firm tannins. Drinkable now. • $25 • (11/30/96) • **89**
St.-Joseph 1992 • $NA • (05/31/94) • **76**

CHAVY, GÉRARD

Puligny-Montrachet 1995: Delicious from start to finish, this white Burgundy displays clean and pure flavors, lovely lemon, honey and tropical fruits, accented by distinct but not overdone toasty oak notes. Terrific now, should improve through 2005. 2,250 cases made. • $29 • (05/31/97) • **93**
Puligny-Montrachet Clavaillon 1995: Gorgeous. Very closed on the nose now, this full-bodied, deeply satisfying, well-crafted and concentrated wine is round, thick and dense, packed with crisp lemon and dried herb notes, ripe pear, honey and subtle oak flavors. Firm, long finish. Tempting now, fabulous after 2000. 375 cases made. • $35 • (05/31/97) • **93**
Puligny-Montrachet Les Folatières 1996: Great opulence in this wine, so it's too bad that it's overwhelmed, at least at this tasting, by a strong earthy character. Shows great intensity and concentration, with a mouthpuckering sensation of vibrant acidity, and marvelous minerally texture on the long finish. Try around 2000. 1,330 cases made. • $40 • (05/31/98) • **88**
Puligny-Montrachet Les Folatières 1995: Well made, with beautiful but subtle aromas of dried herb, honey and ripe fruit, a firm, tightly wound structure, clean, crisp citrus flavors. Rather thick and dense in texture, with a supercharged finish. Try after 2000. 1,050 cases made. • $35 • (05/31/97) • **91**
Puligny-Montrachet Les Perrières 1996: A super wine, well-crafted and full-bodied, offering a silky package despite vibrant acidity. Good concentration leads to a caressing, minerally textured midpalate that's very seductive. Displays layers of fruit, spice and lemon notes. Harmonious, long finish. Tempting from 2003. 208 cases made. • $40 • (05/31/98) • **92**
Puligny-Montrachet Les Perrières 1995: An ultrarich, thick and full-bodied wine, smooth almost to the point of being soft, with some honey, pear and marzipan flavors. A bit overdone, with a slightly bitter finish. Try now through 2000. 183 cases made. • $35 • (05/31/97) HR • **93**

CHAVY, PHILIPPE

Puligny-Montrachet Corvée des Vignes 1995: Some decent fruit, but the wood dominates and the overall feel is quite dull. Turns a bit dry on the slightly rustic finish. 125 cases made. • $35 • (05/31/97) • **78**
Puligny-Montrachet Corvée des Vignes 1994: Clean and pretty, bursting with lovely fig, pear and toasty bread aromas. Of light-to-medium body, it enchants by a focused delivery and long, lively finish. • $30 • (05/31/96) • **87**
Puligny-Montrachet Les Nosroyes 1994: Rather subtle yet well made, showing its stuff slowly. Starts a bit green and vegetal, but picks up some toasty oak, honey and cream flavors on the rather tight and crisp finish. Drinkable now. • $30 • (05/31/96) • **84**

CHAVY-CHOUET, CLAUDE & HUBERT

Meursault Les Casse-Têtes Vieille Vigne 1996: Fine intensity of fresh, vibrant citrus, pear, honey and spice. Of medium body, this mouthpuckering and slightly green Meursault delivers plenty of character but lacks some opulence. Steely finish makes it a good match with seafood. Drink through 2002. 150 cases made. • $45 • (05/31/98) • **84**
Puligny-Montrachet Hameau de Blagny Vieille Vigne 1996: Vibrant and lively. Compact, concentrated and well built, full of mineral tautness that creates a silky feel on the midpalate, supported by lots of citrus and ripe fruit. Of medium-to-full body, very elegant and ageworthy. Try around 2005 to 2008. 50 cases made. • $60 • (05/31/98) • **90**
Puligny-Montrachet Les Enseignères 1996: Thick and dense, with loads of acidity, this full-bodied, heavily toasty wine packs in the ripe, tropical, pear and spice notes effortlessly. Clean and pure like a mountain spring, it seems ageless. Long, graceful finish. Try around 2005 to 2010. 150 cases made. • $45 • (05/31/98) • **92**

CHAZELLES, DOMAINE DES

Mâcon-Viré 1996: Ripe and fairly rich, it seems a little overdone. Offers lemon, apple, floral and rosemary notes. Of medium-to-full body, it turns a bit chalky-dry on the finish. Drinkable now. 1,660 cases made. • $15 • (05/31/98) • **84**
Mâcon-Viré 1993: Balanced, attractive and subtle. The silky texture offers some almond, pear and apple tart flavors but it is a bit diluted. From Josette and Jean-Noël Chaland. • $12 • (08/31/95) • **80**

CHEFFIEUX, DOMAINE DE

St.-Joseph 1990 • $15 • (04/15/93) • **88**

CHÉNAS, CHÂTEAU DE

Moulin-à-Vent Red 1994 • $13 • (10/31/95) • **87**

CHENE, DOMAINE DU

St.-Joseph 1992 • $20 • (05/31/94) • **72**
St.-Joseph Anais 1992 • $20 • (05/31/94) • **79**
St.-Joseph Anais 1991 • $20 • (05/31/94) • **82**
St.-Joseph Anais 1989 • $20 • (05/31/94) • **82**

CHENONCEAU, CHÂTEAU DE

Touraine 1990 • $12 • (11/15/94) • **78**

CHÉREAU PERE & FILS, B.

Anjou Château de Pimpéan 1995: Smoky, toasty notes turn slightly bitter in this lean, cherry-scented red, and the tannins are dry on the finish. Drinkable now. 10,833 cases made. • $9 • (06/15/97) • **80**
Muscadet de Sèvre et Maine Cuvée des Ducs 1993 • $6 • (10/31/94) • **81**
Pouilly-Fumé Les Loges 1995: Bright and round, but a slightly candied, marzipan note detracts from the apple flavors. It's clean, but doesn't quite fit the varietal profile. 1,250 cases made. • $24 • (04/30/97) • **82**
St.-Nicolas de Bourgueil Domaine de la Rodaie 1996: Herbal and smoky flavors typical of the region dominate this light, silky red, but a core of sweet cherry keeps it balanced. A pretty wine for lighter dishes. Drink now. 7,800 cases made. • $16 • (06/15/98) • **84**
St.-Nicolas de Bourgueil Domaine de la Rodaie 1995: This light red offers berry and herb flavors, modest tannins and a pleasant, refreshing texture. Try with rich fish dishes. 2,500 cases made. • $17 • (06/15/97) • **83**
Sauvignon Blanc Touraine Domaine des Petits Faîteaux 1995: Crisp and light, veering toward the herbaceous end of the Sauvignon Blanc spectrum, without much fruit for balance. Still, it's clean and refreshing. 1,250 cases made. • $12 • (05/15/97) • **82**

CHÉREAU-CARRÉ

Muscadet Primeur Château du Coing de St.-Fiacre 1996: Grapefruit and lime flavors are the standouts in this very crisp white. Delivers good weight on the palate, and the finish is clean. 2,750 cases made. • $11 • (06/15/97) • **83**

Muscadet de Sèvre et Maine Les Vergers 1996: Full-bodied for Muscadet. Round, clean and firm, offering pear, almond and light banana flavors. Will stand up to most fish dishes. Drink now. 20,000 cases made. • $9 • (02/28/98) • **84**

Muscadet de Sèvre et Maine Les Vergers 1995: Distinctive, this Loire white exhibits unusual weight and concentration for Muscadet, yet it's still crisp and bright, with lime and light pineapple flavors. Will perk up a wide range of light dishes, at a price that will perk you up. 8,333 cases made. • $10 • (05/15/97) BB • **89**

Muscadet de Sèvre et Maine Sur Lie Château de Chasseloir Cuvée des Ceps Centenaires 1996: Fresh, clean and relatively soft on the palate, with ripe apple and citrus flavors. Refreshing, though basically neutral in character. Tasted twice, with consistent notes. Drink now. 2,800 cases made. • $14 • (05/31/98) • **83**

Muscadet de Sèvre et Maine Sur Lie Château de la Gravelle 1996: A snappy mix of lime and pear flavors gives a clean, refreshing fruitiness that stays crisp all the way through. A natural with shellfish. Drink now. 6,700 cases made. • $11 • (02/28/98) • **85**

Muscadet de Sèvre et Maine Sur Lie Château de la Gravelle 1995: Ripe, even plump, this is fruity and round for Muscadet, with ripe apple and pear flavors. Enough acidity to keep it refreshing. 6,667 cases made. • $15 • (06/15/97) • **83**

Muscadet de Sèvre et Maine Sur Lie Château du Coing de St.-Fiacre 1996: An attractive creamy almond aroma gives way to crisp citrus and pear flavors. Firm and clean, though a bit austere. A refreshing apéritif. Drink now. 18,750 cases made. • $11 • (02/28/98) • **84**

Muscadet de Sèvre et Maine Sur Lie Château du Coing de St.-Fiacre 1995: Big-boned and blunt, this rich white offers nut, pear and apple flavors over a metallic-tinged acidity. Clumsy on its own; try with food. 18,750 cases made. • $15 • (06/15/97) • **81**

Muscadet de Sèvre et Maine Sur Lie Château du Coing de St.-Fiacre Comte de St.-Hubert 1996: This big-boned white has unusual concentration for a Muscadet, with bold pear, melon and grapefruit flavors and real grip on the palate. Finishes with mineral and floral notes. Plenty big enough for food. Drink now through 2000. 2,800 cases made. • $14 • (05/31/98) • **87**

Muscadet de Sèvre et Maine Sur Lie Château du Coing de St.-Fiacre Comte de St.-Hubert 1995: A bold, firm white packed with orange, almond and spice notes that add interest to the basic apple flavor. Big enough to match with a wide range of foods. 1,250 cases made. • $17 • (04/30/97) • **86**

Muscadet de Sèvre et Maine Sur Lie Château du Coing de St.-Fiacre Grande Cuveé St.-Hilaire 1993: Toasty and a bit earthy in character, softened and darkened by maturity. The flavors are distinctive, but may show better with food than alone. 1,250 cases made. • $16 • (06/15/97) • **79**

Muscadet de Sèvre et Maine Sur Lie Château l'Oiselinière de la Ramée 1996: Lime and grapefruit aromas carry through on the palate in this crisp white, with accents of green apples and minerals. Makes a bracing accompaniment to shellfish. Drink now. 5,555 cases made. • $11 • (05/31/98) • **84**

Muscadet de Sèvre et Maine Sur Lie Grand Fief de la Cormeraie 1996: Mineral and floral notes add interest to this clean, crisp white. Pear and citrus flavors are focused and typical of the region, and the wine has a good attack and a fresh finish. Drink now. 2,800 cases made. • $13 • (05/31/98) • **85**

Muscadet de Sèvre et Maine Sur Lie Grand Fief de la Cormeraie 1995: Like biting into a ripe, juicy grapefruit, this is tart and refreshing, and the bold citrus flavors draw you back for another sip. A classic oyster-white. 2,750 cases made. • $15 • (05/15/97) • **86**

Muscadet de Sèvre et Maine Sur Lie Grand Fief de la Cormeraie Réserve du Commandeur 1995: Floral, spice and light honey notes give this light white a lively personality. Less assertive than many Muscadets, but stands out for its delicate flavors. • $16 • (04/30/97) • **84**

Muscadet de Sèvre et Maine Sur Lie Les Feux Barniers 1995: A balanced marriage of citrus and herbal notes give harmony and definition. It's firm but not tart, with good length. 8,333 cases made. • $12 • (05/15/97) • **86**

Muscadet de Sèvre et Maine Sur Lie Les Greniers du Moulin 1996: This clean, well-focused white has an appealing delicacy, with light floral and grapefruit flavors and a pleasant mineral note on the finish. Fine as an apéritif or with shellfish. Drink now. 20,000 cases made. • $10 • (05/31/98) • **84**

Key: SS—Spectator Selection CS—Cellar Selection HR—Highly Recommended BB—Best Buy $NA—Price not available Ⓐ—Auction Price (BT)—Barrel Tasting

Dates in parentheses indicate the issues in which the ratings were published.

Muscadet de Sèvre et Maine Sur Lie Réserve Numérotée 1996: This Muscadet is more complex than most, with bread-dough and floral notes accompanying the crisp green apple and grapefruit flavors. Very tart on the palate, needing food to come into balance. Drink now. • $NA • (05/31/98) • **84**

Saumur-Champigny Domaine des Elettes 1996: Alluring smoke, game and black pepper aromas carry though on the palate of this luscious red, joined by ripe plum flavors and hints of chocolate. Bigger than most Loire reds, it should benefit from age. Drink now through 2002. 6,000 cases made. • $16 • (05/31/98) • **87**

Sauvignon Blanc Touraine Fief de la Houssière 1996: Light herb and tart citrus flavors give personality, but it's light on the palate and short on the finish. Drink now. 6,700 cases made. • $10 • (05/31/98) • **78**

CHERET-PITRES, CHÂTEAU

Graves 1993: A lean red that offers smoky cherry and light earthy flavors, showing some firm but well-integrated tannins. Drinkable now. • $13 • (12/15/95) • **83**

CHERRIER & FILS, PIERRE

Sancerre Domaine de la Rossignole Cuvée Vieilles Vignes 1996: This very firm white has good weight on the palate, with clean, if subdued, flavors of pears and herbs. Refreshing, brings you back for another sip. Drink now. • $15 • (03/31/98) • **87**

Sancerre Domaine de la Rossignole Cuvée Vieilles Vignes 1995: A nice bridge between French and riper, New World styles, this white marries ripe flavors of melons and pineapple with crisp underlying acidity; it's both lively and lush. 1,000 cases made. • $20 • (04/30/97) • **88**

Sancerre Domaine de la Rossignole Cuvée Vieilles Vignes 1994 • $15 • (04/30/96) • **82**

CHESNAIE, CHÂTEAU DE LA

Muscadet de Sèvre et Maine Sur Lie 1993 • $8 • (10/31/94) • **83**

CHEVAL-BLANC, CHÂTEAU

St.-Emilion 1997: A harmonious, elegant '97, with beautiful cherry and chocolate aromas and flavors. Medium-bodied, with velvety tannins and a long finish. Different but very close in quality to the '96. Almost outstanding. • $NA • (06/15/98) (BT) • **85-89**

St.-Emilion 1996: All in finesse. Medium-bodied, with wonderfully integrated tannins and a long tobacco, berry and chocolate aftertaste. As close as it gets to outstanding. Wait and see after bottling. • $170 • (06/15/98) (BT) • **85-89**

St.-Emilion 1995: A beautiful Cheval-Blanc. Compacted and extremely fruity with gorgeous ripe fruit character. Highly perfumed with berry and floral aromas. Full-bodied, with velvety tannins and a lovely, fruity aftertaste. Best after 2002. • $220 • (01/31/98) • **94**

St.-Emilion 1994: Subtle aromas of fruit, grilled meat and cedar, yet it's a blockbuster on the palate. Full-bodied and tannic. Chewy. Better in 2000. 10,000 cases made. • $115 • (01/31/97) • **91**

St.-Emilion 1993: Gorgeous Cheval. Lovely, elegant plum, toasty oak, mineral and berry aromas and flavors give complexity to the medium body and silky tannins. The finish is fresh and lingering. Try now. • $75 • (01/31/96) CS • **90**

St.-Emilion 1992: Slightly underwhelming for this estate, but some beautiful oak complements good berry, meat and fruit character. Light- to medium-bodied, light tannins and crisp finish. • $65 • (04/15/95) • **80**

St.-Emilion 1990: Rich and racy, with toasty oak and nutty, ripe berry aromas and flavors, well-integrated tannins and a sweet fruit finish. Tasted twice. Drink from 1999. 12,000 cases made. • $182 Ⓐ • (03/31/93) • **91**

St.-Emilion 1989 • $114 Ⓐ • (03/15/92) • **90**
St.-Emilion 1988 • $63 Ⓐ • (12/31/90) CS • **93**
St.-Emilion 1987 • $42 Ⓐ • (02/15/91) • **82**
St.-Emilion 1986 • $122 Ⓐ • (02/15/91) • **93**
St.-Emilion 1985 • $105 Ⓐ • (10/15/94) • **92**
St.-Emilion 1984 • $69 • (02/15/91) • **78**
St.-Emilion 1983 • $166 Ⓐ • (10/15/94) • **97**
St.-Emilion 1982 • $373 Ⓐ • (08/31/92) • **95**
St.-Emilion 1981 • $72 Ⓐ • (10/15/94) • **91**
St.-Emilion 1980 • $56 • (02/15/91) • **84**
St.-Emilion 1979 • $119 Ⓐ • (02/15/91) • **88**
St.-Emilion 1978 • $105 Ⓐ • (02/15/91) • **94**

St.-Emilion 1977 • $20 • (02/15/91) • **74**
St.-Emilion 1976 • $77 Ⓐ • (02/15/91) • **88**
St.-Emilion 1975 • $177 Ⓐ • (02/15/91) • **91**
St.-Emilion 1974 • $36 • (02/15/91) • **83**
St.-Emilion 1973 • $60 • (02/15/91) • **83**
St.-Emilion 1972 • $40 • (02/15/91) • **82**
St.-Emilion 1971 • $79 Ⓐ • (02/15/91) • **89**
St.-Emilion 1970 • $151 Ⓐ • (02/15/91) • **88**
St.-Emilion 1969 • $NA • (02/15/91) • **75**
St.-Emilion 1967 • $57 Ⓐ • (02/15/91) • **85**
St.-Emilion 1966 • $137 Ⓐ • (02/15/91) • **87**
St.-Emilion 1964 • $251 Ⓐ • (02/15/91) • **85**
St.-Emilion 1962 • $98 Ⓐ • (02/15/91) • **85**
St.-Emilion 1961 • $413 Ⓐ • (04/30/96) • **93**
St.-Emilion 1960 • $74 Ⓐ • (02/15/91) • **81**
St.-Emilion 1959 • $316 Ⓐ • (02/15/91) • **90**
St.-Emilion 1958 • $200 • (02/15/91) • **86**
St.-Emilion 1955 • $230 Ⓐ • (02/15/91) • **94**
St.-Emilion 1953 • $359 Ⓐ • (02/15/91) • **87**
St.-Emilion 1952 • $360 • (02/15/91) • **91**
St.-Emilion 1951 • $150 • (02/15/91) • **76**
St.-Emilion 1950 • $280 • (02/15/91) • **89**
St.-Emilion 1949 • $936 Ⓐ • (02/15/91) • **84**
St.-Emilion 1948 • $450 • (02/15/91) • **97**
St.-Emilion 1947 • $NA • (05/31/97) • **90**
St.-Emilion 1946 • $470 • (02/15/91) • **87**
St.-Emilion 1945 • $296 Ⓐ • (11/30/95) • **95**
St.-Emilion 1943 • $139 Ⓐ • (02/15/91) • **85**
St.-Emilion 1941 • $175 • (02/15/91) • **71**
St.-Emilion 1940 • $520 • (02/15/91) • **83**
St.-Emilion 1938 • $150 • (02/15/91) • **75**
St.-Emilion 1937 • $280 • (02/15/91) • **93**
St.-Emilion 1936 • $280 • (02/15/91) • **81**
St.-Emilion 1934 • $450 • (02/15/91) • **93**
St.-Emilion 1933 • $270 • (02/15/91) • **88**
St.-Emilion 1931 • $230 • (02/15/91) • **72**
St.-Emilion 1930 • $280 • (02/15/91) • **82**
St.-Emilion 1929 • $350 • (02/15/91) • **90**
St.-Emilion 1928 • $480 • (02/15/91) • **92**
St.-Emilion 1926 • $400 • (02/15/91) • **85**
St.-Emilion 1924 • $300 • (02/15/91) • **69**
St.-Emilion 1923 • $200 • (02/15/91) • **65**
St.-Emilion 1919 • $500 • (02/15/91) • **70**
St.-Emilion 1917 • $500 • (02/15/91) • **70**
St.-Emilion 1916 • $300 • (02/15/91) • **71**
St.-Emilion 1915 • $500 • (02/15/91) • **72**
St.-Emilion 1908 • $500 • (02/15/91) • **71**
St.-Emilion 1905 • $600 • (02/15/91) • **70**
St.-Emilion 1899 • $1,200 • (02/15/91) • **90**

CHEVALIER DE RODILAN

Chardonnay Vin de Pays d'Oc 1994 • $6 • (12/15/95) • **77**
Merlot Vin de Pays d'Oc 1994 • $6 • (12/31/95) • **83**
Vin de Pays d'Oc 1994 • $6 • (12/31/95) BB • **84**

CHEVALIER, DOMAINE DE

Pessac-Léognan 1997: Pleasant chocolate and fruit aromas and flavors. Medium-to-light in body, with medium tannins and a short finish. • $NA • (06/15/98) (BT) • **80-84**
Pessac-Léognan 1996: A delicious red, with soft tannins and juicy fruit. Medium-bodied, with medium, fine tannins and a silky finish. Almost outstanding. 22,000 cases made. • $55 • (06/15/98) (BT) • **85-89**
Pessac-Léognan 1995: Offers more on the nose than the palate, yet it's delicious. Gorgeous aromas of berries and stones. Medium- to full-bodied, with well-integrated tannins and a berry and earth aftertaste. Drinkable now. • $25 Ⓐ • (01/31/98) • **87**
Pessac-Léognan 1994: Delicate and alluring, showing lovely aromas of berries, toasty oak and minerals. Light, fine tannins and a fresh finish. Drink now. 12,000 cases made. • $18 Ⓐ • (01/31/97) • **85**
Pessac-Léognan 1993: A very delicate style for this estate. Elegant, fresh and lively, offering plum and black cherry notes, fine tannins and crisp finish. Drinkable now. • $35 • (01/31/96) • **84**
Pessac-Léognan 1992: Lots of tobacco and some pretty plum, berry character. Medium in body, adding medium tannins and a cedary, mineral finish. • $23 Ⓐ • (04/15/95) • **80**
Pessac-Léognan 1991: Extremely well balanced wine with just enough fruit, toasty oak and fine tannins. Drinkable now. • $30 • (03/31/94) • **86**
Pessac-Léognan 1990: Rich and powerful, with meaty, smoky, earthy, berry character, tons of fruit and masses of soft, thick tannins. Drinkable now. 5,000 cases made. • $42 • (03/31/93) • **92**
Pessac-Léognan 1989 • $42 Ⓐ • (03/15/92) • **96**
Pessac-Léognan 1988 • $42 Ⓐ • (07/15/91) HR • **91**
Pessac-Léognan 1986 • $32 Ⓐ • (06/15/89) • **89**
Graves 1985 • $40 Ⓐ • (10/15/94) • **91**
Graves 1984 • $25 • (08/31/87) • **90**
Graves 1983 • $47 Ⓐ • (10/15/94) • **91**
Graves 1982 • $49 Ⓐ • (10/15/94) • **79**
Graves 1981 • $38 Ⓐ • (10/15/94) • **94**
Graves 1979 • $36 Ⓐ • (10/15/89) • **87**
Graves 1970 • $80 • (05/15/93) • **91**
Graves 1961 • $255 Ⓐ • (04/30/92) • **91**
Graves 1961 • $255 Ⓐ/1.5 liter (04/30/96) • **90**
Graves 1959 • $100 • (10/15/90) • **97**
Graves 1945 • $461 Ⓐ • (11/30/95) • **74**
Pessac-Léognan White 1995: Big and chunky, with plenty of apple, mango and vanilla. Full-bodied, with lots of fruit and wood. Drinkable now. • $25 Ⓐ • (04/30/98) • **90**
Pessac-Léognan White 1994 • $18 Ⓐ • (03/31/96) • **91**

CHEVALIER, GUY

Cabernet-Syrah Vin de Pays de l'Aude 1990 • $8 • (12/31/91) • **79**
Corbières La Coste 1990 • $9 • (03/15/94) • **81**
Corbières La Coste 1989 • $9 • (08/31/91) • **72**
Vin de Pays de l'Aude Le Texas 1989 • $9 • (07/15/91) • **74**

CHEVALIER PERE & FILS

Aloxe-Corton 1983 • $19 • (09/15/86) • **85**
Ladoix La Corvée 1992: Inviting aromas, complex but light flavors of cherry, tea and spice, moderate tannins and acidity and a short finish. Drink now. 200 cases made. • $25 • (05/15/95) • **84**

CHEVALIÈRE, DOMAINE LA

Chardonnay Vin de Pays d'Oc Réserve 1996: A good middle-of-the-road Chardonnay with pear, lemon and buttery flavors that linger on the finish. 30,000 cases made. • $10 • (10/31/97) • **84**
Syrah Vin de Pays d'Oc Chevalière Réserve 1996: Lively, with delicious berry, plum and leather flavors. A good, quaffable red. Drink now. • $NA • (07/31/98) • **84**
Syrah Vin de Pays d'Oc Réserve 1996: Quite peppery, with a nice dollop of spice. This is a full-flavored red wine that would complement food. Finishes with some pretty raspberry flavors. 500 cases made. • $10 • (10/31/97) • **85**
Vin de Pays d'Oc Red Première Cuvée 1995: Bursting with flavor, ripe and rich. Dominated by ripe plum and dark cherry components, augmented with appealing leathery and meaty notes. Balanced and nicely concentrated. Drink now through 2000. 5,000 cases made. • $13 • (04/30/98) • **88**
Vin de Pays d'Oc White Première Cuvée 1995: Light, lemony and fairly crisp, with an appealing buttery note on the finish. Elegant and enjoyable. 500 cases imported. • $13 • (10/31/97) • **84**
Viognier Vin de Pays d'Oc Réserve 1996: A neutral-tasting white wine with only modest peach and herbal flavors. 5,000 cases made. • $13 • (10/31/97) • **75**

CHEVILLON, DENIS

Nuits-St.-Georges Aux Chaignots 1987 • $33 • (07/15/90) • **87**
Nuits-St.-Georges Les Pruliers 1987 • $38 • (07/15/90) • **84**

CHEVILLON, ROBERT

Bourgogne 1989 • $16 • (01/31/92) • **77**
Nuits-St.-Georges 1992: Spicy, exotic aromas and flavors never quite lift off in this surprisingly mature-tasting but tannic wine. • $NA • (12/15/94) • **75**
Nuits-St.-Georges 1989 • $36 • (01/31/92) • **89**

FRANCE

Nuits-St.-Georges 1986 • $37 • (12/15/89) • **74**

Nuits-St.-Georges 1985 • $40 • (04/30/88) • **85**

Nuits-St.-Georges Aux Bousselots 1992: Delivers some sweet plum and black cherry flavors; a ripe-tasting Burgundy that is already appealing. • $NA • (12/15/94) • **84**

Nuits-St.-Georges Aux Chaignots 1992: Simple, light and watery, with a very modest strawberry flavor. • $NA • (12/15/94) • **70**

Nuits-St.-Georges Aux Chaignots 1991: Enough black cherry and currant flavors balance the firm tannins in this modest wine. Crisp and flavorful. 650 cases made. • $38 • (01/31/94) • **84**

Nuits-St.-Georges Les Cailles 1992: Medium-dark color, with nicely defined blackberry and currant flavors riding a layer of soft tannins to a gentle finish. Drink now. • $NA • (12/15/94) • **84**

Nuits-St.-Georges Les Cailles 1991: Ripe and perfumed, clean and crisp, with nicely defined currant and blackberry flavors that are stronger on the finish. Ends up crisp and juicy rather than broad. Drinkable now. 200 cases made. • $48 • (01/31/94) • **87**

Nuits-St.-Georges Les Perrières 1992: Lean, modest and simple, with straightforward strawberry notes and a sharp finish. Not much here. • $NA • (12/15/94) • **73**

Nuits-St.-Georges Les Pruliers 1992: Round and appealing, with a ripe core of plum, currant and black cherry. This light-textured wine stays with you. A good effort in this vintage. • $NA • (12/15/94) • **84**

Nuits-St.-Georges Les St.-Georges 1992: Starts off with some appealing strawberry, but it just dissipates on the chewy finish. • $NA • (12/15/94) • **78**

Nuits-St.-Georges Les St.-Georges 1991: Youthful and impressive. The floral, spicy vanilla aromas and balckberry flavor jump out of this elegant, lively Nuits. Fine tannins make it drinkable already. • $39 • (02/28/95) • **91**

Nuits-St.-Georges Les St.-Georges 1990: Ripe, chewy and concentrated, with densely packed violet, rose petal, black cherry, tobacco and floral notes; a great future ahead. • $62 Ⓐ • (02/28/95) • **92**

Nuits-St.-Georges Les St.-Georges 1989 • $53 • (02/28/95) • **86**

Nuits-St.-Georges Les St.-Georges 1988 • $59 • (02/28/95) • **90**

Nuits-St.-Georges Les St.-Georges 1987 • $43 • (02/28/95) • **88**

Nuits-St.-Georges Les St.-Georges 1986 • $55 • (02/28/95) • **82**

Nuits-St.-Georges Les St.-Georges 1985 • $75 • (02/28/95) • **89**

Nuits-St.-Georges Les St.-Georges 1983 • $NA • (02/28/95) • **84**

Nuits-St.-Georges Les Vaucrains 1992: Decent currant and cherry flavors and a crisp style. Youthful, fresh and pleasant for drinking now. • $NA • (12/15/94) • **80**

Nuits-St.-Georges Les Vaucrains 1991: Dense and expansive, with a slightly herbal edge to the chunky raspberry, blackberry and spice aromas and flavors, a powerful red buried under a thick layer of chewy tannins. Tightly wrapped now, it should be best from 2000. • $39 • (08/31/94) • **91**

Nuits-St.-Georges Les Vaucrains 1989 • $65 • (01/31/92) • **89**

Nuits-St.-Georges Roncière 1992: Light, crisp and a little tannic for the modest level of citrusy strawberry flavors. Try now. • $NA • (12/15/94) • **78**

Nuits-St.-Georges Roncière 1991: Firm in texture, densely flavorful; pours out its raspberry and currant flavors with vanilla and spice overtones. Harmonious and elegant, this has the right stuff to develop into 2000. • $34 • (08/31/94) • **91**

CHÈZE, DOMAINE

Condrieu Coteau de Brèze 1994: A seductive perfume, lush and floral, gives way to a round, soft palate with spice, floral and light herbal notes. For such an expressive wine, it shows uncommon delicacy. 500 cases made. • $33 • (12/15/96) • **87**

St.-Joseph 1991 • $NA • (11/15/95) • **78**

St.-Joseph Cuvée des Anges 1995: Well balanced and harmonious, this ripe wine has black cherry and blackberry flavors, tender and generous, with well-integrated tannins and appealing accents of toast and smoke. Drinkable now. 500 cases made. • $23 • (10/15/97) • **89**

St.-Joseph Cuvée Prestige de Caroline 1995: Chocolate and coffee flavors give this red an appealing sweetness, and while it may lack power, it offers silky elegance and vivid fruit. Not a long-ager; drink now. 950 cases made. • $17 • (10/15/97) • **87**

St.-Joseph Cuvée Prestige de Caroline 1994: Cherry and herbal flavors mark this lean wine, with astringent tannins dominating the fruit flavors on the palate. It's drinkable now, a bit simple and short. 850 cases made. • $23 • (11/30/96) • **82**

St.-Joseph Cuvée Prestige de Caroline 1992 • $18 • (05/31/94) • **76**

St.-Joseph Cuvée Prestige de Caroline 1991 • $18 • (05/31/94) • **81**

St.-Joseph Cuvée Ro-Rée 1995: Light berry and herbal flavors lack concentration, and the tannins are lean and dry. Toasty flavors add interest, but it's light for the vintage. Drink now. 1,800 cases made. • $13 • (10/15/97) • **81**

St.-Joseph White Cuvée Ro-Rée 1995: Assertive, with ripe fruit flavors, crisp acidity and notes of almond, herbs and apples, but it's a bit disjointed, and turns a bit harsh on the finish. 1,500 cases made. • $13 • (10/15/97) • **81**

CHEZEAUX, DOMAINE DES

Chambolle-Musigny Les Charmes 1985 • $75 • (06/15/88) • **91**

Griotte-Chambertin 1988 • $110 • (05/15/91) • **90**

Griotte-Chambertin 1985 • $150 Ⓐ • (06/15/88) • **91**

CHIDAINE, FRANÇOIS

Montlouis Clos du Breuil 1995: This well-balanced white is quite dry, but has good roundness on the palate. The fruit flavors are modest, with apple and green plum notes. 500 cases made. • $12 • (06/15/97) • **82**

Montlouis Clos du Breuil 1993 • $12 • (06/15/96) • **74**

Montlouis Clos Habert 1995: This light-bodied white shows modest sweetness, but there's plenty of acidity, too. An earthy note detracts slightly. 500 cases made. • $13 • (06/15/97) • **78**

Montlouis Les Tuffeaux 1995: Well balanced, showing off-dry honey and dried peach flavors and fresh acidity, clean and refreshing. Has some concentration, too. 500 cases made. • $13 • (06/15/97) • **84**

Montlouis Les Tuffeaux 1993 • $13 • (05/15/96) • **84**

Touraine Collection 1996: This light, fresh wine offers herb and hay flavors, but the simple apple and citrus notes fade quickly. Drink now. 2,000 cases made. • $10 • (05/31/98) • **78**

Touraine Collection 1995: Crisp and clean, this sprightly white offers well-balanced, mouthwatering flavors of lemon, herb and light pineapple. A good match for light foods. 500 cases made. • $13 • (05/15/97) • **87**

CHIGNARD, MICHEL

Fleurie Les Moriers 1995: Maturing, but it's still lively, with nice aromas and flavors of cherries and chocolate, and firm tannins for grip with food. • $20 • (09/15/97) • **83**

CHIQUET, GASTON

Brut Champagne 1989: A soft, ripe Champagne with a generous texture and mellow, honeyed flavors. Drink now. • $39 • (11/30/97) • **86**

Brut Champagne Special Club 1990: Powerful, full-bodied Champagne with robust aromas and flavors, a dry but plush texture, lively balance and long finish. Bold but sophisticated. Drink now through 2002. • $39 • (11/30/97) • **92**

Brut Champagne Tradition NV: A smooth, suave style of bubbly with attractive buttery flavors and a lingering finish. Drink now. • $31 • (11/30/97) • **86**

CHOBLET, LUC & ANDRÉE-MARIE

Muscadet-Côtes de Grandlieu Sur Lie Clos de la Sénaigerie 1996: Appealing, showing more fresh fruit flavors than many Muscadets, with apple, pear and peach notes and a good backbone of lemony acidity. Round and focused, with a pleasant, soft texture. Drink now. 10,000 cases made. • $10 • (05/31/98) BB • **86**

Muscadet-Côtes de Grandlieu Clos de la Sénaigerie 1995: This steely white isn't showing much fruit flavor now, but it has good concentration and bracing acidity. A bit austere on its own, it will bloom with food. 8,000 cases made. • $10 • (05/15/97) • **87**

CHOFFLET-VALDENAIRE

Givry 1995: Fruity and attractive, but a bit rustic. Medium-bodied, it delivers chewy, tough tannins along with nice intensity and concentration of soil, iodine, mineral, smoky spices and cherry character. A bit dry on the finish. Try with meat around 2000. • $15 • (11/15/97) • **83**

Key: SS—Spectator Selection CS—Cellar Selection HR—Highly Recommended BB—Best Buy $NA—Price not available Ⓐ—Auction Price (BT)—Barrel Tasting
Dates in parentheses indicate the issues in which the ratings were published.

FRANCE

Givry 1993: Ripe plum and black cherry notes mark this broadly textured, charming red. Nicely balanced, somewhat complex in flavor, moderately tannic. Drinkable now. 350 cases made. • $20 • (05/15/96) • **86**

Givry 1992: Flavors don't balance the nice bouquet. Expansive aromas of strawberry, cherry and spice are followed by lean, tough, unripe flavors and an astringent finish. 1,500 cases made. • $15 • (06/15/95) • **82**

Givry Clos de Choue 1995: Distinctive and pleasant, but slightly rustic, this offers bright raspberry and wild strawberry character and mineral notes. Unfortunately, it's a bit herbaceous. Try now through 2000. • $18 • (11/15/97) • **85**

Givry Clos Jus 1995: A very impressive, distinctive red with personality. A bit rustic, but who cares? It delivers loads of soil, iodine, mineral, iron, blood, and red berry notes accented with touches of toasty oak. A producer worth following. Try now with red meat; drink through 2002 or so. • $18 • (11/15/97) • **86**

CHON ET FILS, GILBERT

Muscadet de Sèvre et Maine Sur Lie Domaine de la Jousselinière 1995: Light and racy, with clean, crisp acidity and light grapefruit flavors, but it's tart and a bit green, with a short finish. • $10 • (06/15/97) • **79**

CHOPIN, A.

Côte de Nuits-Villages 1985 • $9 • (10/31/87) BB • **83**

Nuits-St.-Georges Aux Murgers 1988 • $28 • (07/15/90) • **91**

Nuits-St.-Georges Aux Murgers 1987 • $26 • (12/15/89) • **85**

Nuits-St.-Georges Aux Murgers 1986 • $29 • (10/15/88) • **78**

CHOPIN-GROFFIER

Chambolle-Musigny 1989 • $32 • (01/31/92) • **90**

Clos Vougeot 1995: Lean and sinewy, this is full of concentrated smoky, sappy blackberry flavor married to a masculine structure. Not many nuances yet in evidence, but all the elements are there. Try in 2002. • $92 • (11/15/97) • **92**

Clos Vougeot 1994: Chunky, youthful and aromatic, with ripe, full-bodied plum and floral flavors that still might lose the battle to the broad, drying tannins. Future is questionable. • $80 • (11/15/96) • **86**

Clos Vougeot 1993: Ah, attractive fruit flavors. Ripe, even fat, for the vintage, but also somewhat hot on the palate and finish that keeps it from scoring higher. Ripe plum and mint notes. Drinkable now. • $85 • (11/15/95) • **88**

Clos Vougeot 1992: Fresh and lively, a simple red with appealing currant and toasty, spicy notes that linger on the slightly chewy finish. Drink now. • $80 • (12/15/94) • **85**

Clos Vougeot 1991: This lean, sprightly, pretty wine shows modest cherry and berry flavors and hints of lime and anise on the finish. Has charm, but little depth. Drinkable now. 125 cases made. • $62 Ⓐ • (01/31/94) • **85**

Clos Vougeot 1990: What finesse. Despite the solid structure, it offers abundant black cherry, currant and plum flavors and manages to tame the massive, firm, long tannins. The finish is silky and enchanting. Drinkable now. • $70 • (12/15/92) • **94**

Clos Vougeot 1989 • $72 • (01/31/92) • **94**

Clos Vougeot 1988 • $70 • (05/15/91) • **87**

Côte de Nuits-Villages 1994: A straightforward, pleasant, early-drinking wine with a nice berry and mint character. • $22 • (11/15/96) • **80**

Côte de Nuits-Villages 1993: Pretty currant and cherry flavors. Quite tannic and firm. Medium in body, it seems a bit dry and tough on the finish now. Drinkable now. • $22 • (11/15/95) • **83**

Côte de Nuits-Villages 1992: Delicious, focused currant, black cherry and chestnut flavors; more concentrated than some *premiers crus*. Drinkable now. • $18 • (12/15/94) • **82**

Nuits-St.-Georges 1994: Ripe flavors make this charming and approachable, offering currant and berry flavors on a sturdy frame, and it's not too tannic. Ready now. • $35 • (11/15/96) • **84**

Nuits-St.-Georges 1993: Smooth and fruity, offering delicate aromas of rose petal, black cherry and earth and super, supple tannin structure. Drinkable now. • $45 • (11/15/95) • **79**

Nuits-St.-Georges 1991: Lean and tannic, but well defined, offering bright berry flavors at a modest level. Finishes a bit stemmy. Drinkable now. 250 cases made. • $33 Ⓐ • (01/31/94) • **83**

Nuits-St.-Georges 1990: A very elegant, very good village wine, with focused blackberry and chocolate aromas and flavors and very supple tannins. Drinkable now. • $43 • (12/15/92) • **89**

Nuits-St.-Georges 1989 • $32 • (01/31/92) • **91**

Nuits-St.-Georges Aux Chaignots 1995: Balanced, seductive and just lovely, with blackberry, cassis and wet earth character, and a slight peppery note sneaking into the firm but ripe texture. The finish is long and smooth, almost jammy. Very well made. Tempting now, better after 2000. • $56 • (11/15/97) • **88**

Nuits-St.-Georges Aux Chaignots 1994: Has lovely currant and spice aromas and flavors, but raspy tannins intrude a bit on the finish. Drink sooner, rather than later. • $50 • (11/15/96) • **85**

Nuits-St.-Georges Aux Chaignots 1993: Quite light and charming, delivering some earth, raspberry, cherry and rose petal notes. A bit dry on the lean finish. Drinkable now. • $60 • (11/15/95) • **82**

Nuits-St.-Georges Aux Chaignots 1992: Appealing, balanced and focused on toasty and currant flavors that lead to a juicy finish. Needs a bit more concentration. Drinkable now. • $45 • (12/15/94) • **84**

Nuits-St.-Georges Aux Chaignots 1991: A bit raw in texture and flavor, but comes together nicely on the palate, mixing smoke, toast and berry flavors harmoniously. Drinkable now. 125 cases made. • $40 Ⓐ • (01/31/94) • **86**

Nuits-St.-Georges Aux Chaignots 1990: An elegant wine, with excellent intensity. Offers plenty of smoke and raspberry aromas and flavors and firm tannins to back them up. Drinkable now. • $40 • (12/15/92) • **91**

Nuits-St.-Georges Aux Chaignots 1989 • $40 • (01/31/92) • **93**

Vougeot 1994: Light and diluted, with modest flavors. Very earthy and gamy. • $35 • (11/15/96) • **70**

Vougeot 1992: Smoky, toasty, gamy and quite interesting; a round-textured and flavorful 1992 that clamps down on the palate. Good complexity and length for this difficult vintage. • $35 • (12/15/94) • **84**

Vougeot 1991: Tough, astringent, cardboardy, possibly corky, especially because of the musty character on the finish. Has some nice raspberry and lemon flavors that belong to a good wine. • $NA • (01/31/94) • **79**

Vougeot 1990: It's hard to find a wine with better, brighter, livelier fruit than this, even in this vintage. The impressive toasty nut, plum, cherry and earth characteristics shine and there are plenty of firm tannins on the long finish. Drinkable now. • $44 • (12/15/92) • **93**

Vougeot 1988 • $32 • (05/15/91) • **92**

FRANCE

CHOPPIN, A.R.

Beaune Les Bressandes 1985 • $32 • (09/30/87) • **90**

Beaune Les Cents Vignes 1985 • $32 • (10/31/87) • **81**

Beaune Les Grèves 1985 • $32 • (09/30/87) • **79**

Beaune Les Teurons 1987 • $30 • (02/28/90) • **87**

Beaune Les Teurons 1985 • $32 • (10/31/87) • **87**

Beaune Les Toussaints 1987 • $30 • (02/28/90) • **83**

Savigny-lès-Beaune Aux Vergelesses 1987 • $32 • (02/28/90) • **79**

Savigny-lès-Beaune Aux Vergelesses 1985 • $25 • (10/31/87) • **87**

CINQUIN, PAUL

Régnié Domaine des Braves 1994: Aging well; attractive dried cherry, herb and toast flavors and still-fresh tannins. Finish is a bit dry, but a good food-wine. • $10 • (09/15/96) • **84**

CISSAC, CHÂTEAU

Haut-Médoc 1995: Attractive perfume characterizes this one, with flavors of red berry, vanilla and strawberry. Good tannins and lots of sweet fruit on the finish. • $NA • (05/15/96) (BT) • **85-89**

Haut-Médoc 1992: Delicate, fine, succulent berry, cherry and smoke aromas and flavors, medium tannins and a medium finish. • $14 • (04/15/95) • **81**

Haut-Médoc 1991: Slightly mature but pleasant and soft, with sweet berry fruit flavors. • $14 • (03/31/94) • **76**

Haut-Médoc 1990: This is a solid wine in a lovely aromatic style with black cherry, minty, vanilla character and medium-intense tannins. Drinkable now. 25,000 cases made. • $18 • (03/31/93) • **88**

Haut-Médoc 1989 • $23 Ⓐ • (03/15/92) • **85**

Haut-Médoc 1987 • $14 • (11/30/89) • **81**

Haut-Médoc 1986 • $26 Ⓐ • (11/30/89) • **79**

Haut-Médoc 1985 • $20 Ⓐ • (07/31/88) • **79**

Haut-Médoc 1982 • $38 Ⓐ • (11/30/89) • **81**

Haut-Médoc 1961 • $74 Ⓐ • (04/30/96) • **88**

CITRAN, CHÂTEAU

Haut-Médoc 1997: Unctuous aromas of graham crackers, berries and toasty oak. Medium-bodied, with fresh fruit flavors that quickly fade away on the finish. Too bad. • $NA • (06/15/98) (BT) • **80-84**

Haut-Médoc 1996: Wonderful ripe berry and raspberry aromas, with hints of new wood. Full-bodied and very velvety, with a long, sweet fruit finish. Chewy. Almost outstanding. • $22 • (06/15/98) (BT) • **85-89**

Haut-Médoc 1995: Not a big '95, but very pretty. Enticing cedar, tobacco and cherry aromas. Medium- to full-bodied, with fine tannins and a subtle aftertaste of tobacco and fruit. Best after 2001. 45,000 cases made. • $20 • (01/31/98) • **87**

Haut-Médoc 1994: Very fruity, medium- to full-bodied, with cassis and raspberry flavors. Firm, slightly dry tannins detract. Drinkable now. 20,800 cases made. • $20 • (01/31/97) • **82**

Haut-Médoc 1993: No-nonsense '93 featuring decent tobacco and cherry character. Medium to light in body, light tannins and fresh finish. • $20 • (01/31/96) • **80**

Haut-Médoc 1991: Surprisingly good considering the vintage. Velvety texture, delicate currant and toast notes, medium body and finish. • $13 • (03/31/94) • **84**

Haut-Médoc 1990: Not as great as the '89, but a seductive wine with attractive vanilla, black cherry aromas and flavors, medium tannins, lovely balance and a long, fresh finish. Drinkable now. 42,000 cases made. • $20 • (03/31/93) • **86**

Haut-Médoc 1989 • $20 • (03/15/92) • **93**

Haut-Médoc 1988 • $20 • (04/30/91) • **91**

Haut-Médoc 1983 • $12 • (04/01/86) • **82**

Haut-Médoc 1982 • $12 • (04/01/85) • **78**

Haut-Médoc 1961 • $22 • (04/30/96) • **77**

CLAIR, BRUNO

Chambertin-Clos de Bèze 1995: A supple, smooth and lovely Pinot Noir, medium-bodied but very racy, showing well-defined, pure and clean flavors of cassis, blackberry and black cherry, with just a hint of spicy oak. Firm tannins kick in on the finish, giving this '95 backbone. Drinkable now. 166 cases made. • $100 • (11/15/97) • **88**

Chambertin-Clos de Bèze 1994: Has some ripe flavors but never achieves intensity, playing out the currant and plum flavors, with a hint of toast, on the grainy finish. Drinkable now. • $97 • (11/15/96) • **86**

Chambertin-Clos de Bèze 1991: Ripe and elegant, a dark, dense wine in an airy frame, beaming its currant, black cherry and tobacco flavors right through the long finish. Drinkable now. 185 cases made. • $78 Ⓐ • (01/31/94) • **91**

Chambertin-Clos de Bèze 1990: Very complex, with a symphony of coffee, licorice, tobacco, plum, earth and cedar notes, a full-bodied structure and great intensity on the finish. Drinkable now. 188 cases made. • $70 • (12/15/92) • **93**

Chambolle-Musigny Les Véroilles 1995: Very ripe, full and fruity, with flavors bordering on kirsch, this is a round, fleshy red, unadorned by oak and balanced on the tannic side. Drinkable now. 391 cases made. • $33 • (11/15/97) • **87**

Chambolle-Musigny Les Véroilles 1994: Shows a serious effort to produce a concentrated wine. But, besides the red berry flavor, there is also an herbal accent and some hard tannins. • $35 • (11/15/96) • **80**

Corton-Charlemagne 1995: Ripe and flavorful, of medium body and intensity, this boasts plenty of citrus, honey, pear and melon character. Quite delicious. Drink after 2000. • $89 • (08/31/97) • **87**

Corton-Charlemagne 1994: Soft and supple, yet rich and full-bodied. Interesting chalk, earth and lemon aromas and flavors, with notes of pear, honey and dried herb. Drinkable now. • $NA • (08/31/96) • **83**

Corton-Charlemagne 1993: Very ripe mango and vanilla aromas and flavors. Full-bodied and quite rich. A lovely creamy, appley finish. Drinkable now. • $76 • (08/31/95) • **88**

Gevrey-Chambertin 1993: Really flavorful, smooth, easy to like, featuring cherry and strawberry notes accented by licorice. Attractive, medium-bodied and basically ready to drink. • $47 • (05/15/96) • **86**

Gevrey-Chambertin Clos du Fonteny 1995: A beautiful Pinot Noir, supple and subtle, with pretty cassis, currant and spice flavors. Medium-bodied, with a sweet-tasting, ripe, lingering finish. Drinkable now. 166 cases made. • $54 • (11/15/97) • **86**

Gevrey-Chambertin Clos du Fonteny 1994: Shows some very pretty currant and berry flavors on a firm frame. Somewhat drying tannins will always be present, but the flavors sneak in there. Drinkable now. • $54 • (11/15/96) • **80**

Key: SS—Spectator Selection CS—Cellar Selection HR—Highly Recommended BB—Best Buy $NA—Price not available Ⓐ—Auction Price (BT)—Barrel Tasting

Dates in parentheses indicate the issues in which the ratings were published.

Gevrey-Chambertin Clos du Fonteny Monopole 1992: Tart and tannic, displaying bright raspberry flavors accented by chocolate. Stays tight and closed through the finish; drink now, while it's still fruity. • $50 • (06/15/95) • **83**

Gevrey-Chambertin Fonteny 1991: Artfully expressed currant, black cherry and anise aromas and flavors persist on the finish of this crisp, lively, light wine. Drinkable now. 219 cases made. • $42 Ⓐ • (01/31/94) • **86**

Gevrey-Chambertin Fonteny 1990: This multidimensional, complex wine delivers superb intensity, with raspberry, earth and cigar box aromas and flavors. Shows a lot of elegance and the finish goes on and on. A great Gevrey. Drinkable now. • $45 • (12/15/92) • **92**

Gevrey-Chambertin Les Cazetiers 1995: Blackberry and plum flavors mingle with smoky oak notes in this appealing yet tightly knit '95 Pinot. Still, it has some rough-and-tumble tannins. Try in 2000. 91 cases made. • $66 • (11/15/97) • **82**

Gevrey-Chambertin Les Cazetiers 1994: Light and crisp, with pleasant raspberry and blackberry flavors that peak out nicely from under a layer of grainy tannins. Drinkable now. • $74 • (11/15/96) • **85**

Gevrey-Chambertin Les Cazetiers 1991: Ripe, pretty and delicate, showing an impressive concentration of currant, raspberry and floral aromas and flavors. Finishes firm and elegant. Drinkable now. 251 cases made. • $53 Ⓐ • (01/31/94) • **87**

Gevrey-Chambertin Les Cazetiers 1990: A solid wine, with ripe berry aromas and flavors and very firm acidity. Drinkable now. 200 cases made. • $55 • (12/15/92) • **89**

Gevrey-Chambertin Les Cazetiers 1989 • $61 • (01/31/92) • **89**

Gevrey-Chambertin Premier Cru 1994: Light and crisp, with a wisp of berry flavor wafting through the grainy tannins. • $41 • (11/15/96) • **78**

Marsannay 1994: Light and crisp, with modest red cherry and sweet-leather flavors. Drinkable now. • $20 • (11/15/96) • **80**

Marsannay 1992: Tastes just like a chocolate-raspberry dessert without the sweetness. Fascinating, but not what we look for in Burgundy. • $19 • (06/15/95) • **83**

Marsannay 1988 • $16 • (11/15/91) • **80**

Marsannay Les Grasses Têtes 1995: Slightly stemmy and unripe on the nose, same again on the dry, astringent finish. Otherwise, it's medium-bodied and decently concentrated with raspberry flavor. 358 cases made. • $21 • (11/15/97) • **82**

Marsannay Les Grasses Têtes 1994: Despite some slightly sandy tannins, this has charming, open currant and cherry flavors and a soft finish. Drink soon. • $24 • (11/15/96) • **80**

Marsannay Les Grasses Têtes 1993: Really ripe and flavorful, relatively soft in tannins, offering black cherry and chocolate notes, full body, smooth texture and a fruity finish. • $25 • (05/15/96) • **86**

Marsannay Les Grasses Têtes 1990: A light-styled, delicious wine, with straightforward plum and earth flavors and light tannins. Drinkable now. • $28 • (12/15/92) • **80**

Marsannay Les Longeroies 1995: Traditional in style, displaying licorice, cherry and wet leaf aromas and flavors, all borne upon a broad-shouldered frame. Wait until 2000 for the tannins to subside. 316 cases made. • $21 • (11/15/97) • **86**

Marsannay Les Longeroies 1994: Light, supple and appealing for its pure raspberry flavors. Drinkable now. • $24 • (11/15/96) • **81**

Marsannay Les Longeroies 1992: Firm-textured, tannic; lean but impressive. Attractive cherry and raspberry flavors fight through on the finish. Drinkable now. • $23 • (05/15/95) • **85**

Marsannay Les Longeroies 1990: Firm and one-dimensional, with vivid strawberry flavors and a touch of herbs. Drinkable now. • $18 • (12/15/92) • **83**

Marsannay Les Longeroies 1989 • $18 • (01/31/92) • **87**

Marsannay Les Vaudenelles 1995: Totally seductive, pure aromas of cassis and blackberries are presented in a silky, supple and elegant package. Has bright acidity and firm tannins, which need until 2000 to come together. Stunning for the appellation. 458 cases made. • $20 • (11/15/97) • **89**

Marsannay Les Vaudenelles 1994: Crisp in texture, with chewy tannins and light currant flavors. Drinkable now. • $22 • (11/15/96) • **78**

Marsannay Les Vaudenelles 1993: Quite rich, thick and chocolaty, delivering ripe fruit and herbal flavors and relatively soft tannins. Enjoy it now. • $22 • (05/15/96) • **85**

Marsannay Les Vaudenelles 1992: A sturdy, attractive Pinot Noir; tart, cranberry-flavored and accented by smoky oak. Not deep or concentrated; drinkable now. • $21 • (06/15/95) • **81**

Marsannay Les Vaudenelles 1989 • $18 • (01/31/92) • **81**

Marsannay Rosé Pinot Noir 1993 • $16 • (06/15/95) • **83**

Marsannay White 1996: A lovely, ripe white, with subtle floral, pear tart, bread dough and smoke aromas and flavors. Medium-bodied, racy and crisp, the weight on the midpalate suggests this will turn suppler with age. Great length on the balanced finish. Try now through 2005. 708 cases made. • $29 • (05/31/98) • **88**

Marsannay White 1995: Firm, sparkling with lemon, crisp fruit and subtle oak accents and showing some mocha, coffee bean and ripe pear notes, this is a well-structured, medium- to full-bodied white Burgundy that should improve through 2000. 650 cases made. • $21 • (05/31/97) • **85**

Marsannay White 1994: Ripe, rich and slightly heavy, with apricot, peach and quince jam flavors. Silky, full-bodied and sweet-tasting. Drink now. • $NA • (08/31/96) • **83**

Morey-St.-Denis 1985 • $20 • (05/15/88) • **73**

Morey-St.-Denis En la Rue de Vergy 1995: Pure red berry flavor shines through in this medium-bodied wine, accented with raspberry and wild berry notes. Not a blockbuster. Drinkable now. 283 cases made. • $34 • (11/15/97) • **86**

Morey-St.-Denis En la Rue de Vergy 1994: A chewy texture and stale flavors serve to derail this one. • $35 • (11/15/96) • **78**

Morey-St.-Denis En la Rue de Vergy 1991: Firm and focused. Lively blackberry and currant flavors bounce through this juicy wine. Drinkable now. 310 cases made. • $33 Ⓐ • (01/31/94) • **86**

Morey-St.-Denis En la Rue de Vergy 1990: This serious village wine offers tons of jammy raspberry, blueberry and spice flavors and is almost sweet on the palate, with ripe fruit and velvety tannins. Drinkable now. • $37 • (12/15/92) • **90**

Morey-St.-Denis En la Rue de Vergy 1989 • $36 • (01/31/92) • **90**

Morey-St.-Denis En la Rue de Vergy White 1996: Clean, pure, floral and fruity '96. Medium-bodied, with some pear, citrus and mineral notes. You wish for a bit more opulence, but it's fun to drink now. 280 cases made. • $55 • (05/31/98) • **85**

Morey-St.-Denis En la Rue de Vergy White 1995: A ripe and showy village wine, with loads of toasty oak, butterscotch, mineral, honey and lemon flavors that mingle in a powerful, full-bodied package that explodes on the finish. Impressive. Try now through 2005. 263 cases made. • $49 • (05/31/97) • **91**

Morey-St.-Denis En la Rue de Vergy White 1994: Solid core of fruit flavors, most notably lemon and melon, and some honey accents. Fairly firm and medium-bodied, with a clean, intense finish. Try now. • $NA • (08/31/96) • **87**

Savigny-lès-Beaune La Dominode 1995: A ripe, sweet red that begins on intense notes of pure raspberry, red cherry and vanilla. Elegant and stylish, yet structured, it concludes with a long finish. Wait until 2002 for it to reveal its charms. 433 cases made. • $40 • (11/15/97) • **91**

Savigny-lès-Beaune La Dominode 1994: Goes for flavor over finesse, with lots of anise and cherry notes, and hard tannins. A medium-bodied, solid wine. Drinkable now. • $40 • (11/15/96) • **83**

Savigny-lès-Beaune La Dominode 1991: More generous than most '91 Savignys. Black cherry and vanilla aromas and flavors keep singing on the finish. A soft wine; drinkable now. 399 cases made. • $32 Ⓐ • (01/31/94) • **86**

Savigny-lès-Beaune La Dominode 1990: A class act. Tastes like a raspberry reduction sauce and is so concentrated it nearly jumps out of the glass. A joy to taste, with rich raspberry and chocolate characteristics and tons of firm tannins. Drinkable now. • $32 • (12/15/92) • **92**

Savigny-lès-Beaune La Dominode 1989 • $24 Ⓐ • (01/31/92) • **89**

Savigny-lès-Beaune La Dominode 1985 • $24 • (03/15/88) • **80**

Vosne-Romanée Aux Champs Perdrix 1995: Light and simple, with some strawberry, raspberry and floral notes. Light-bodied, the tannins clamp down on the astringent, stripped finish. 200 cases made. • $38 • (11/15/97) • **75**

Vosne-Romanée Aux Champs Perdrix 1994: Light, and berryish in character, with a spicy accent to the minimal flavors. • $41 • (11/15/96) • **79**

Vosne-Romanée Aux Champs Perdrix 1991: Bright and flavorful. Earthy, decadent edge to the herbal black cherry character at the core and crisp, somewhat tart finish. Try now. 214 cases made. • $28 Ⓐ • (01/31/94) • **81**

Vosne-Romanée Aux Champs Perdrix 1989 • $30 • (01/31/92) • **91**

CLAIR, FRANÇOISE & DENIS

Puligny-Montrachet La Garenne 1994: If you think all '94s are soft and supple, think again. This one demonstrates a solid, incredibly intense core of lime, grapefruit and fresh pineapple flavors that are backed by earth and mineral complexity. Mouthpuckering yet elegant. Needs time. 125 cases made. • $44 • (05/31/96) • **89**

St.-Aubin Les Murgers des Dents de Chien White 1995: Ripe, rich, thick, full-bodied and very harmonious now, but where's the acidity to hold it together in the future? Soft, it offers decent citrus and apple notes that unfold on the pleasing finish. Drink upon release. 500 cases made. • $28 • (05/31/97) • **87**

St.-Aubin Les Murgers des Dents de Chien White 1994: Pure, clean and well-structured *premier cru*, showing crisp texture and ripe pear, citrus, mineral, ginger and dried herb complexity. Medium-bodied, smooth and silky on the vanilla- and spice-flavored finish. Drinkable now. Terrific accomplishment in this appellation. 333 cases made. • $27 • (05/31/96) • **90**

Santenay Clos de Tavannes 1990: Lean and tight, with a hint of vinegar in the sharply focused cherry flavors. Tight and tough on the finish. Drinkable now. • $29 • (02/15/93) • **83**

Santenay La Comme 1990: Light, earthy and flavorful, with woodsy, mushroomy overtones to the modest black cherry and raspberry flavors. Finishes soft and supple. Drinkable now. • $26 • (02/15/93) • **81**

Santenay La Comme 1988 • $25 • (06/15/92) • **85**

CLAIREFONT, CHÂTEAU DE

Margaux 1993: Sweet and fruity, offering modest licorice, currant and cherry flavors, rather light body and supple tannins. Second label of Château Prieuré-Lichine. Drink on release. • $15 • (01/31/96) • **79**

Margaux 1985 • $9 • (04/30/88) • **79**

CLAIRFONT, DOMAINE DE

Vin de Pays de Vaucluse 1995: Light and fresh, this has grape and light cherry flavors with almost no tannins. A simple quaff to try lightly chilled. 5,000 cases made. • $8 • (12/15/96) • **80**

Vin de Pays de Vaucluse 1994: Simple and tannic, with stewed rhubarb and cooked cherry flavors. 2,000 cases made. • $8 • (12/15/96) • **74**

Vin de Pays de Vaucluse 1991 • $6 • (10/31/92) BB • **82**

CLAPE, A.

Cornas 1995: A heavyweight bruiser of a wine, this is extremely oaky, inky purple-colored and incredibly concentrated. With a massive tannic structure that towers over the fruit, it has the impenetrable texture of a young Château Latour. So extracted it hurts the mouth. 1,250 cases made. • $36 • (10/15/97) • **91**

Cornas 1991 • $24 • (05/31/94) • **87**

Cornas 1990 • $26 • (04/15/93) • **87**

Cornas 1986 • $19 Ⓐ • (01/31/89) • **88**

Cornas 1984 • $13 • (08/31/87) • **78**

St.-Péray 1996: Clean and fresh white, delivering its light apple and herbal flavors in a straightforward style, with a crisp, apple-tinged finish. 83 cases made. • $18 • (10/15/97) • **84**

CLARKE, CHÂTEAU

Listrac 1995: A healthy dose of new oak gives this more polish than most Bordeaux AC can offer. Also has ripe plum and licorice flavors, firm tannins and the stuffing to improve through 2001. • $26 • (10/15/97) • **86**

Listrac 1992: Ambitious wine that shows plenty of flavor but falls short on harmony. Coffee, licorice and plum notes, a thick texture and big tannins need more polish. 20,000 cases made. • $18 • (07/31/96) • **81**

Listrac 1991: Puckers your mouth with wonderful strawberry, currant and toasty oak character, medium tannins and finish. Better with some more age. • $14 • (03/31/94) • **83**

Listrac 1990: A very ripe, somewhat rustic wine with raisin, leather and earthy flavors in an ample frame. It's chewy and rich, but drinkable now. 17,500 cases made. • $15 • (11/15/94) • **83**

Listrac 1989 • $16 • (03/15/92) • **85**

Listrac 1988 • $18 • (04/30/91) • **81**

Listrac 1986 • $17 • (11/15/89) • **90**

Listrac 1982 • $13 • (10/15/86) • **68**

CLAVEL, DOMAINE

Coteaux du Languedoc La Copa Santa 1995: Powerful and delicious. Leathery aromas, with plenty of plum and cherry flavors. A ripe, intense style, with a great deal of structure. A dead-ringer for a very good Châteauneuf-du-Pape. 100 percent Syrah. Drink now through 2000. • $15 • (02/28/98) • **91**

Coteaux du Languedoc La Méjanelle 7ème Printemps des Comédiens 1991 • $7 • (03/15/94) • **86**

Coteaux du Languedoc Terroir de la Méjanelle Les Garrigues 1995: A wine of power and depth, with a core of ripe plum, blackberry and dark cherry flavors that are wrapped inside a good dose of spice and licorice. Smoke and leathery notes persist on the finish. A blend of 50 percent Grenache and 50 percent Syrah. Drink now through 2000. 4,000 cases made. • $10 • (03/31/98) BB • **89**

Coteaux du Languedoc Terroir de la Méjanelle Mas de Clavel Vieilles Vignes 1995: Deep, rich and intense, with delicious raspberry flavors and an appealing dose of leather and smoke. A nice currantlike flavor chimes in on the finish. A chewy wine, drinkable now. 1,800 cases made. • $7 • (02/28/98) • **88**

CLAVERIE, CHÂTEAU LA

Côtes de Francs 1990: A light, everyday wine, with delicate, simple strawberry character and light, smooth tannins. Drinkable now. • $19 • (03/31/93) • **80**

Côtes de Francs 1989 • $21 • (03/15/92) • **88**

CLEMENT, ABEL

Côtes du Rhône 1993 • $8 • (11/15/95) • **77**

CLÉMENT, BERNARD & PIERRE

Sancerre 1994 • $14 • (12/15/95) • **80**

Sauvignon Blanc Vin de Pays du Jardin de la France 1996: Firm, with mineral and herbal flavors, hints of apples and peaches. Though a bit austere on its own, it has the body and acidity to match well with lighter dishes. Drink now. • $NA • (06/30/98) • **84**

CLÉMENT PICHON, CHÂTEAU

Haut-Médoc 1997: Shows berry and sweet fruit character and a long, vanilla aftertaste. A wine high on new wood. Too much? • $NA • (06/15/98) (BT) • **80-84**

Haut-Médoc 1996: A rather awkward, unbalanced wine with some concentrated fruit character, but earthy, aggressive tannins detract from the overall quality. • $NA • (01/01/97) (BT) • **75-79**

Haut-Médoc 1995: Big and coarse. Beautiful crushed red berry aromas. Full-bodied, and very velvety. Slightly dry on the finish. Drinkable now. • $15 • (01/31/98) • **86**

Haut-Médoc 1994: Already fading, this shows a tobacco, herbal, weedy character. Light-bodied, light finish. Not appealing. • $15 • (01/31/97) • **71**

Haut-Médoc 1993: Attractively smooth, showing some nice red berry flavor and a hint of gamy, earthy character, sweet-tasting finish and supple tannins. Drinkable now. • $15 • (01/31/96) • **80**

Haut-Médoc 1991: Weedy and diluted with strawberry flavor and grassy character. Tasted twice. • $12 • (03/31/94) • **68**

Haut-Médoc 1988 • $15 • (08/31/91) • **78**

Haut-Médoc 1987 • $14 • (11/30/89) • **73**

Haut-Médoc 1986 • $11 • (11/30/89) • **85**

CLERC, LAURENT

Puligny-Montrachet Les Charmes 1996: Pretty in a soft and easy way, but shows an unelegant cooked, canned pear character. Otherwise: good structure, firm acidity, toasty oak and spice and decent fruit flavors. Drink now or hold until 2000. From Henri Clerc. • $42 • (05/31/98) • **82**

Puligny-Montrachet Les Charmes 1995: Heavy-handed, with honey and late-harvest apricot flavors and a somewhat rustic, slightly bitter character. Buttery, appley and odd. • $NA • (08/31/97) • **71**

Puligny-Montrachet Les Charmes 1994: Sweet, lush and a bit overripe, with flavors and aromas of cooked fruit. Slightly dry finish. • $NA • (08/31/96) • **79**

CLERC & FILS, HENRI

Bâtard-Montrachet 1995: Almost overripe, with dried fig and date flavors, this full-bodied Chardonnay turns slightly raisinlike on the somewhat dry finish. Ready to drink. 65 cases made. • $100 • (05/31/97) • **76**

Key: SS—Spectator Selection CS—Cellar Selection HR—Highly Recommended BB—Best Buy $NA—Price not available Ⓐ—Auction Price (BT)—Barrel Tasting
Dates in parentheses indicate the issues in which the ratings were published.

Beaune Chaume Gaufriot 1995: Herbal, astringent, diluted, and sour on the finish. 156 cases made. • $27 • (11/15/97) • **70**

Beaune Chaume Gaufriot 1985 • $29 • (11/15/88) • **81**

Beaune Chaume Gaufriot White 1996: Woody and perfumed, with floral scents that aren't attractive, and sawdust notes. Full-bodied, it coats the palate, then turns slightly sour on the finish. Drinkable now. • $24 • (05/31/98) • **79**

Beaune Chaume Gaufriot White 1995: Lively and fresh up front, with some floral, melon and toasty chestnut character, but it turns dry on the overly woody finish. 50 cases imported. 80 cases made. • $35 • (08/31/97) • **77**

Beaune Chaume Gaufriot White 1994: A sweet-and-sour character (more sour than sweet), makes this a difficult wine to warm up to. • $NA • (08/31/96) • **70**

Bienvenues-Bâtard-Montrachet 1995: Rich and unctuous, but overripe and overdone, this extremely full-bodied wine leaves the impression of having already oxidized a bit. Lacks finesse and turns hot and burning on the finish. 188 cases made. • $95 • (05/31/97) • **73**

Bienvenues-Bâtard-Montrachet 1994: Impressive concentration in this full-bodied *grand cru*; oozing ripe fruit, honey, pie crust, tropical and toasty coconut flavors. Silky texture, but firm finish. Tempting to drink now. • $90 • (08/31/96) • **91**

Blagny Sous le Dos d'Ane 1995: Shows some minor fruit flavor, with an herbal, astringent character. Light-bodied, unripe. 325 cases made. • $NA • (11/15/97) • **73**

Bourgogne Les Riaux White 1995: Opulent and seductive, full in body and rich in texture, with a honey, pear and toasty almond character. Turns slightly hot on the finish, but a citrusy note saves the day. Drink now. 533 cases imported. 1,633 cases made. • $12 • (08/31/97) • **87**

Bourgogne White 1994: Exotic, ripe and full-bodied. Exploding with apricot, peach, tropical, cedar and mineral flavors. Too bad it turns coarse on the finish. • $NA • (08/31/96) • **80**

Chevalier-Montrachet 1996: Not for everyone with its overly ripe, cooked, and apple character. But there is classy *terroir*, and the wine is intriguing and exotic, with many facets, starting with a smoke, wet earth, spice, pine, toasty hazelnut and mineral character. Vibrant yet opulent finish. Try after 2005. • $120 • (05/31/98) • **92**

Chevalier-Montrachet 1995: Big and bold, exotic and seductive, with a wealth of toasty oak notes mingling with the peach, apricot, honey and spice flavors. Wonderful concentration, and the oak should be well integrated by around 2005. 77 cases made. • $110 • (05/31/97) • **93**

Clos de Vougeot 1995: Vibrant, ripe, forward flavors of cherries and plums fill this medium-bodied '95. Seems a bit stewed, with some coarse tannnins at the end. 127 cases made. • $NA • (11/15/97) • **86**

Meursault-Blagny Sous le Dos d'Ane 1995: A well-made *premier cru*, tightly structured, with a rich, thick mouthfeel. Full-bodied and nicely concentrated with flavors of dried herbs, honey and toasty coconut, and a lovely, citrus-spiked, crisp finish. Should settle down with age; try after 2000. 25 cases imported. 198 cases made. • $50 • (08/31/97) • **90**

Puligny-Montrachet 1996: Very woody, with an odd, burnt butter character. Medium-bodied, sour finish. Overly oaky for the amount of fruit. • $36 • (05/31/98) • **74**

Puligny-Montrachet 1995: Crisp and fresh, with vanilla-bean, honey and lemon flavors. Full-bodied, and a bit coarse and rustic. 576 cases made. • $35 • (05/31/97) • **80**

Puligny-Montrachet 1994: Fresh, but lean. Has exotic peach accents to the green apple, citrus and grass flavors. Light-to-medium-bodied, good length on the crisp finish. Try now. • $NA • (08/31/96) • **82**

Puligny-Montrachet Champs Gains 1996: Very ripe, rich and verging on tasting cooked, with an apple pie, bread dough, peach and floral character. Full-bodied, and so toasty it lacks elegance. Try around 2000. • $48 • (05/31/98) • **80**

Puligny-Montrachet Champ Gain 1995: A fun wine, with decent fruit, some apricot, peach, gooseberry, grass, toast and green apple flavors, nice texture and medium body. Crisp finish. Ready to drink. 186 cases made. • $45 • (05/31/97) • **82**

Puligny-Montrachet Champ Gain 1994: An exotic, *premier cru* that tastes like a Gewürztraminer. Rich, thick and full-bodied, with lovely spice, white pepper, tropical and honey flavors and a long, smoky finish. Delightful. Drink now. • $NA • (08/31/96) • **91**

Puligny-Montrachet Les Combettes 1996: Very ripe but hot and alcoholic, it tastes of peach, apricot and floral notes. Full-bodied and sweet, it seems a bit overdone in the oak department. Drink now. • $48 • (05/31/98) • **79**

Puligny-Montrachet Les Combettes 1994: Slightly herbal *premier cru*. Lots of toasty oak, spice, anise and lime flavors. Medium-bodied. Turns a bit bitter on the distinctively woody finish. Drinkable now. 249 cases made. • $45 • (08/31/96) • **79**

Puligny-Montrachet Les Folatières 1995: Delightful and exotic, with some peachy apricot flavors that are almost Viognierlike, and ripe fruit, dried herb, vanilla and mineral character. Full-bodied, with great balance and great length. Tempting now through 2005. (Shipped to the U.S. under the Laurent Clerc label.) 482 cases made. • $45 • (05/31/97) HR • **94**

Puligny-Montrachet Les Folatières 1995: An intense, compacted wine, with a crisp character and a nice, oily texture. Needs time; try after 2000. 60 cases imported. 104 cases made. • $38 • (08/31/97) • **87**

Puligny-Montrachet Les Folatières 1994: Like nectar. Seductive *premier cru*, with loads of fresh fruit, honey, spice and toasty oak flavors and aromas. Full-bodied. A bit hot and woody on the finish now, but it should calm down with age. Drink now to 2002. • $NA • (08/31/96) • **91**

Santenay Les Potets 1995: Modest cherry flavor and a hint of earth predominate in this light-bodied red, before the tough tannins take over. 362 cases made. • $NA • (11/15/97) • **78**

CLERC MILON, CHÂTEAU

Pauillac 1997: A very good '97, with plenty of berry and tobacco aromas and flavors. Medium in body, with medium tannins and a fruity finish. • $NA • (06/15/98) (BT) • **85-89**

Pauillac 1996: This has grown in the barrel into a big and rich wine, with lovely currant and lead pencil aromas and flavors. Full-bodied, with full tannins. Typically big Clerc. • $35 • (06/15/98) (BT) • **90-94**

Pauillac 1995: Like smelling a delicious raspberry sauce with hints of coffee and smoke, and the wine that follows is wonderfully structured, muscular and well toned. Full-bodied, with sleek and racy tannins and a long, characterful aftertaste. One of the top buys of the vintage from Bordeaux. Best after 2001. • $60 • (01/31/98) SS • **95**

Pauillac 1994: Complex aromas of spices, berries and plums, with fine, silky tannins and a caressing finish. Medium body. Hard not to drink it now, but better in 1999. • $40 • (01/31/97) • **89**

Pauillac 1993: Clerc Milon is a sure bet for a very good wine in any vintage. Impressive medium-to-full body, tobacco, cherry, tar and chestnut character, velvety tannins and medium finish. Try now. • $24 • (01/31/96) • **89**

Pauillac 1992: Solid yet very polished, exhibiting currant, berry and tobacco character, medium-to-full body, refined tannins and a long, velvety finish. • $22 • (04/15/95) • **88**

Pauillac 1991: A balanced, supple wine, with lovely blackberry, vanilla complexity, sweet and ripe. Tasted twice. • $22 • (03/31/94) • **85**

Pauillac 1990: A seamless wine with great character, offering cigar, tobacco, cedar, and rich plum flavors. Full-bodied yet well balanced, with lovely, full, silky tannins and a long finish. Drink after 2000. 13,000 cases made. • $30 • (03/31/93) • **94**

Pauillac 1989 • $44 • (03/15/92) HR • **96**

Pauillac 1988 • $26 • (04/30/91) SS • **94**

Pauillac 1986 • $38 Ⓐ • (05/31/89) • **97**

Pauillac 1985 • $47 Ⓐ • (05/15/88) • **91**

Pauillac 1984 • $18 • (06/15/87) • **78**

Pauillac 1983 • $17 • (10/15/94) • **87**

Pauillac 1982 • $41 Ⓐ • (08/31/92) • **90**

Pauillac 1981 • $27 • (10/15/94) • **88**

Pauillac 1961 • $NA • (04/30/96) • **76**

CLERGET, YVON

Bourgogne 1990: Nicely focused and fresh, but light, with bright strawberry notes. Drink on release. 250 cases made. • $15 • (12/15/92) • **82**

Pommard Les Rugiens 1990: Surprisingly light, showing simple strawberry and cherry aromas and flavors. Drinkable now. 200 cases made. • $48 • (12/15/92) • **79**

Volnay 1990: Nice, juicy and flavorful, offering berry and earth notes. Attractive in an elegant way. Drinkable now. 330 cases made. • $34 • (12/15/92) • **84**

Volnay Les Caillerets 1990: Elegance defines this Volnay. Lovely black currant, mint and chestnut aromas and flavors are presented in a subtle package, ending with round tannins. Drinkable now. 125 cases made. • $45 • (12/15/92) • **86**

Volnay Premier Cru 1990: Velvety and perfumed, with lovely black currant, mint and cherry notes, silky texture and a supple finish. Drinkable now. 225 cases made. • $37 • (12/15/92) • **87**

Volnay En Verseuilles 1990: Fresh but light, this medium-bodied wine offers good berry flavors and lively tannins. Drinkable now. 330 cases made. • $42 • (12/15/92) • **84**

CLIMENS, CHÂTEAU

Barsac 1991: Attractively sweet and lush, showing some zingy lemon, honey and spice flavors and a smooth finish. Drink as an apéritif. • $NA • (04/15/95) • **86**

Barsac 1990: Classy, both solid and seductive, featuring a velvety texture and subtle, spicy, toasty butterscotch, lemon and honey character. Hard to resist now. • $67 • (04/15/95) • **93**

Barsac 1989: High-wired, super-focused, seductively creamy and beautifully balanced. The beam of lemon, honey, spice, pear and melon flavor shines through to a fresh, long finish. Drinkable now. • $68 • (04/15/95) • **93**

Barsac 1988: Extremely polished and complex, showing beautiful dried herb, grass, honey and pine flavors. Has a long finish, medium body and just-so sweetness. Drinkable now. • $49 • (04/15/95) • **91**

Barsac 1986: Gorgeous, ripe, and rich, oozing with tropical, honey and mineral flavors that take off like a heat-seeking missile on the finish. Drinkable now. • $54 • (04/15/95) • **94**

Barsac 1983: Beautifully crafted, plump, very long and complex. Medium gold, lush and silky, with lemon, fig, apricot, pear, and a particularly elegant balance of acidity, fruit and wood. Power and finesse in the same package. • $54 Ⓐ • (01/31/88) CS • **95**

Barsac 1947: A very interesting wine. Dark in color, redolent of caramel and bark, with notes of spice and dried apricot sneaking in on the crisp finish. Slightly sugary, but not sweet. • $317 Ⓐ • (05/31/97) • **89**

CLINET, CHÂTEAU

Pomerol 1997: A velvety '97, with cinnamon and berry aromas and flavors. Medium-bodied, with medium tannins and a fruity, spicy aftertaste. • $NA • (06/15/98) (BT) • **85-89**

Pomerol 1996: Slightly diluted at the midpalate, but with very good berry, cherry and floral character. Medium-bodied, with fine tannins. • $125 • (06/15/98) (BT) • **85-89**

Pomerol 1995: Blockbuster. The essence of berry, cherry and tobacco character. Full-bodied and very tannic, yet incredibly opulent. Long aftertaste of smoke, game, chocolate and fruit. Best after 2002. • $140 Ⓐ • (01/31/98) • **95**

Pomerol 1994: Exotic aromas of violets, berry and toasty oak waft from this full-bodied wine. Packed to the brim with fruit and tannins and impressively long on the finish. Superb red from a producer known for opulence. Better in 2000. 3,900 cases made. • $72 Ⓐ • (01/31/97) HR • **93**

Pomerol 1993: Exciting and solid all the way through, showing super depth of color and character. Ripe, rich complexity and mineral, earth, currant and plum flavors. It's sweet-tasting and coats your mouth with supple and elegant tannins. A pleasure to drink now, but should improve for years. • $48 Ⓐ • (01/31/96) • **90**

Pomerol 1992: Clinet does it again in a weak year. Lots of new wood, cherry and raspberry aromas and flavors, medium body, firm tannins and slightly dry finish. Drinkable now. • $26 Ⓐ • (04/15/95) • **85**

Pomerol 1991: Consider it very good for this vintage: dark color, big and chewy, with vanilla and milk chocolate aromas and flavors, medium body and a clean finish. • $32 • (03/31/94) • **85**

Pomerol 1988 • $80 Ⓐ • (02/28/91) HR • **92**

Pomerol 1986 • $50 Ⓐ • (09/15/89) • **78**

Pomerol 1985 • $50 • (04/30/88) • **91**

Pomerol 1982 • $27 Ⓐ • (05/15/89) • **78**

Pomerol 1970 • $39 • (05/15/93) • **84**

Pomerol 1961 • $102 Ⓐ • (04/30/96) • **88**

CLOS BEAUREGARD

Pomerol 1993: Sweet cherry and vanilla flavors pop out of a soft, velvety texture. The tannins are light and well integrated, making it pleasant drinking now. 1,000 cases made. • $20 • (07/31/96) • **84**

CLOS CHAUMONT, CHÂTEAU

Premières Côtes de Bordeaux 1995: Racy little wine with earthy, spicy and berry aromas and flavors. Medium- to full-bodied, with plenty of fruit and just a touch of wood. Best after 2000. • $18 • (01/31/98) • **87**

CLOS DE L'EGLISE

Madiran 1988 • $13 • (08/31/91) • **79**

CLOS DE L'ESCANDIL

Minervois 1994: Well focused, with nice mineral flavors and good texture and structure. Good berry and cherry components and leathery notes. Balanced and harmonious. Tasted twice with consistent notes. Drink now through 2003. • $16 • (03/31/98) • **88**

CLOS DE L'ORATOIRE

St.-Emilion 1997: Dark-colored, with smoke, raspberry and blackberry aromas. Medium-bodied, with velvety tannins and a medium finish. Well made. 7,000 cases made. • $NA • (06/15/98) (BT) • **85-89**
St.-Emilion 1996: A lovely, velvety wine, with ripe berry, tobacco and vanilla aromas and flavors. Full-bodied and caressing, with a long, delicious finish. Better than the Canon-la-Gaffeliere from the same owner. 7,000 cases made. • $28 • (06/15/98) (BT) • **90-94**
St.-Emilion 1995: A chewy yet delicious young red, with plenty of ripe berry, chocolate and toasty oak character. Medium- to full-bodied, with velvety tannins and a medium aftertaste of chocolate and blackberry. Drinkable now. • $30 • (01/31/98) • **90**
St.-Emilion 1994: Silky and sexy with lovely berry, tobacco character and fine silky tannins. Medium-bodied, with a caressing texture and a succulent finish. From a château to watch. Drinkable now. • $29 • (01/31/97) • **90**
St.-Emilion 1993: Impressively ripe, featuring loads of raspberry, wet earth and dark chocolate character, medium-to-full body, velvety tannins and long finish. Not quite as great as we remember, but very good indeed. 4,654 cases made. • $25 • (01/31/96) • **88**
St.-Emilion 1992: Delicate chocolate, tobacco and fruit character, medium-to-light body and a succulent finish. • $19 • (04/15/95) • **81**
St.-Emilion 1990: Port-like, with masses of berry, chocolate and cedar aromas and flavors; thick and velvety, with an excellent tannin structure and a long, long finish. Drinkable now. 3,700 cases made. • $28 • (03/31/93) • **94**
St.-Emilion 1982 • $NA • (05/15/89) • **78**

CLOS DE LA ROILETTE

Fleurie 1995: This red shows balanced fruit and structure, with ripe black cherry, plum and light toasty notes harmonious over firm tannins. Drink now. • $15 • (07/31/97) • **86**
Fleurie Cuvée Tardive 1995: Quite rich and beautifully balanced, this ripe red offers firm flavors of black cherry, cola and chocolate, with firm acidity and ripe tannins. Drinkable now. • $20 • (07/31/97) • **88**

CLOS DE PAULILLES, LES

Banyuls Robert Doutres 1989 • $17 • (12/15/94) • **72**
Collioure 1989 • $20 • (12/15/94) • **80**

CLOS DE VILLEMAJOU

Corbières 1994: from the Languedoc-Roussillon region of France comes this silky-tasting red at a bargain price. Balanced and concentrated, it delivers its polished spice and ripe cherry flavors with a touch of elegance. Some nice smoky notes on the finish. Drink now. 10,000 cases made. • $8 • (04/30/98) BB • **85**
Corbières 1988 • $6 • (04/30/90) • **78**
Corbières 1985 • $7 • (05/31/90) • **71**

CLOS DES JACOBINS, CHÂTEAU

St.-Emilion 1997: Slightly herbal, with berry and cherry character. Medium in body, with light tannins and a light, fruity finish. • $NA • (06/15/98) (BT) • **80-84**
St.-Emilion 1996: A joy to taste. Medium to full in body, with violet, berry and vanilla character, silky tannins and a fresh finish. Very well-made. One of the sleepers of the vintage. • $25 • (06/15/98) (BT) • **90-94**
St.-Emilion 1995: Slightly rough and not giving much on the nose, but it shows a sensational finish. Loads of dried cherry and blackberry aromas, with a hint of wet earth. Full-bodied, with velvety, well-integrated tannins and an outstanding aftertaste. Drinkable now. • $30 • (01/31/98) • **90**
St.-Emilion 1994: Beautiful aromas of cherry, dried berry, and chocolate lead to a medium- to full-bodied wine with ultrafine tannins and a long, sweet, fruit finish. Enticing now, but better in 2000. 4,583 cases made. • $30 • (01/31/97) • **87**
St.-Emilion 1993: Smooth and round, offering delicious ripe tannins, toasty character and blackberry flavors. Medium body and intensity. Drinkable now. • $25 • (01/31/96) • **85**
St.-Emilion 1991: Rather weedy, smoky and herbaceous, with light body and astringent finish. Tasted twice with consistent notes. • $20 • (03/31/94) • **77**
St.-Emilion 1990: Light and simple, with stewed tomato and stemmy aromas and flavors and light tannins. Disappointing. Drinkable now. 3,500 cases made. • $35 • (03/31/93) • **77**
St.-Emilion 1989 • $45 • (03/15/92) • **85**
St.-Emilion 1988 • $26 • (04/15/91) HR • **90**
St.-Emilion 1987 • $24 • (05/15/90) • **73**
St.-Emilion 1986 • $34 • (06/30/89) • **94**
St.-Emilion 1985 • $31 • (09/30/88) • **89**
St.-Emilion 1984 • $20 • (05/15/87) • **83**
St.-Emilion 1982 • $NA • (08/31/92) • **82**
St.-Emilion 1981 • $16 • (06/01/84) • **81**

CLOS DES PAPES

Châteauneuf-du-Pape 1990: Thick and tannic, with lots of plum and pepper flavors and a chewy texture. Drinkable now. • $30 • (04/15/93) • **85**
Châteauneuf-du-Pape 1989 • $20 • (10/15/91) • **86**
Châteauneuf-du-Pape 1988 • $19 • (10/15/91) • **86**
Châteauneuf-du-Pape 1986 • $18 • (10/15/91) • **74**
Châteauneuf-du-Pape 1985 • $NA • (10/15/91) • **89**
Châteauneuf-du-Pape 1983 • $NA • (10/15/91) • **88**
Châteauneuf-du-Pape 1981 • $NA • (10/15/91) • **87**

CLOS DU CHÊNE, LE

Cahors 1994: Rich and smooth, with pleasant red plum and berry flavors that mesh well with the nice leathery component. Finishes on a mineral note. 100 percent Malbec. Drink now. • $9 • (05/15/98) • **85**

CLOS DU CLOCHER, CHÂTEAU

Pomerol 1994: Plum and black cherry aromas give way to more herbal and tobacco flavors. It's polished, but light-bodied and on the austere side, with firm tannins. Drinkable now. • $29 • (12/15/95) • **84**
Pomerol 1993: Fresh, open aromas of blackberry and vanilla give way to round flavors of ripe fruit and spices. A velvety texture adds appeal, while ripe tannins add structure. Drink now. • $28 • (12/15/95) • **86**
Pomerol 1985 • $20 • (02/29/88) • **88**
Pomerol 1982 • $33 • (05/15/89) • **83**

CLOS DU MARQUIS

St.-Julien 1996: Shows cool aromas and flavors of cassis bush minerals, a medium-to-full body, chewy tannins and a crisp, caressing finish. Impressive for a second wine in 1996, and almost as good as the '95. • $NA • (01/01/97) (BT) • **85-89**
St.-Julien 1995: Spicy and succulent, with fresh fruit character. Medium-to-full body, with elegant tannins and a fresh finish. Almost outstanding. • $25 • (01/01/97) (BT) • **85-89**
St.-Julien 1988 • $16 Ⓐ • (10/31/91) • **80**
St.-Julien 1987 • $12 • (05/15/90) • **79**
St.-Julien 1986 • $19 Ⓐ • (09/15/89) • **84**
St.-Julien 1985 • $89 Ⓐ • (09/30/88) • **84**

CLOS DU MONT-OLIVET

Châteauneuf-du-Pape 1990: Tight and complex, offering crushed pepper, plum and currant flavors that are a bit rough around the edges. Finishes with gripping tannins that hang on. Drinkable now. • $20 • (04/15/93) • **83**
Châteauneuf-du-Pape 1989 • $20 • (02/28/93) • **86**
Châteauneuf-du-Pape 1988 • $19 • (10/15/91) • **88**
Châteauneuf-du-Pape 1986 • $17 • (10/15/91) • **87**
Châteauneuf-du-Pape 1985 • $20 • (10/15/91) • **92**
Châteauneuf-du-Pape 1983 • $28 • (10/15/91) • **86**

Key: SS—Spectator Selection CS—Cellar Selection HR—Highly Recommended BB—Best Buy $NA—Price not available Ⓐ—Auction Price (BT)—Barrel Tasting
Dates in parentheses indicate the issues in which the ratings were published.

Châteauneuf-du-Pape 1982 • $12 • (03/16/86) • **91**
Châteauneuf-du-Pape 1981 • $30 • (10/15/91) • **87**

CLOS DU PAVILLON, DOMAINE DU

Aloxe-Corton Les Fournières 1995: A tough '95, its stemmy, cherry flavors overshadowed by astringent tannins. 192 cases made. • $34 • (11/15/97) • **79**
Beaune Les Epenottes 1995: A medium-bodied wine, showing chewy licorice and leather notes. Structured, but exhibits good balance. Try now. 408 cases made. • $24 • (11/15/97) • **80**
Pommard 1995: Earthy and gamy, with a licoricelike chewiness that appeals on the attack, then falls short, turning tough and astringent. 1,916 cases made. • $32 • (11/15/97) • **80**
Pommard 1994: Straightforward, with some decent cherry and spice character, but turns a bit astringent on the finish. From Domaine le Clos du Pavillon. • $36 • (11/15/96) • **75**

CLOS FOURTET

St.-Emilion 1997: Dark-colored, with blackberry and mint aromas. Medium-bodied, with medium tannins and a light finish. A bit hollow but well done. • $NA • (06/15/98) (BT) • **85-89**
St.-Emilion 1996: Wonderful blackberry and violet aromas. Full-bodied and silky, with fine tannins and a fresh finish. A serious '96 from St.-Emilion. • $40 • (06/15/98) (BT) • **90-94**
St.-Emilion 1995: Absolutely delicious. Impressive chocolate and spice aromas. Medium- to full-bodied, with well-integrated tannins and lots of chocolate and spice on the finish. Better after 2000. • $25 • (01/31/98) • **90**
St.-Emilion 1994: Aromatic, this shows a perfumed, dried herb and berry character. It's medium-bodied, with fine tannins and a light, caressing texture. Drink now. • $35 • (01/31/97) • **86**
St.-Emilion 1993: Light in color and body, showing plum, dried herb and toasty oak notes. Somewhat lean on the finish, but a pleasant glass of wine. Drinkable now. • $25 • (01/31/96) • **82**
St.-Emilion 1992: A decent core of plum, cherry and berry flavor, medium-to-light body, light tannins and a short finish. • $17 • (04/15/95) • **78**
St.-Emilion 1990: Rich and fleshy, with a bounty of black cherry and smoky tobacco character, velvety tannins and a long, long finish. Drink now. 5,000 cases made. • $30 • (03/31/93) • **90**
St.-Emilion 1989 • $28 • (03/15/92) • **89**
St.-Emilion 1988 • $25 Ⓐ • (10/31/91) • **86**
St.-Emilion 1986 • $41 • (06/30/89) • **80**
St.-Emilion 1982 • $20 Ⓐ • (08/31/92) • **83**
St.-Emilion 1970 • $29 • (05/15/93) • **85**
St.-Emilion 1961 • $45 • (04/30/96) • **84**
St.-Emilion 1945 • $280 • (11/30/95) • **81**

CLOS FRANTIN, DOMAINE DU

Chambertin 1989 • $73 • (01/31/92) • **88**
Chambertin 1986 • $63 • (02/28/89) • **90**
Clos de Vougeot 1995: On the herbal side of the flavor spectrum, with only moderate concentration of ripe fruit and a short finish. 258 cases made. • $55 • (11/15/97) • **84**
Clos de Vougeot 1994: Thin, stalky and ungenerous, rather like an astringent, old-fashioned Barolo gone wrong. • $50 • (11/15/96) • **73**
Clos de Vougeot 1992: Very light, almost watery, with just a touch of sweet plum flavor before the tannins kick in on the finish. Try now. • $NA • (12/15/94) • **77**
Clos de Vougeot 1989 • $56 • (01/31/92) • **91**
Clos de Vougeot 1987 • $56 • (07/15/90) • **85**
Clos de Vougeot 1986 • $37 • (11/30/88) • **87**
Corton 1990: Crisp, tart and earthy, with less breadth than Corton should have, offering tightly reined-in cherry and spice flavors that fade quickly behind a layer or two of tannin. Try now. • $53 • (11/30/92) • **81**
Corton 1989 • $58 • (01/31/92) • **86**
Corton-Charlemagne 1993: Polished and austere, delivering significant fruit and spice flavors in an elegant package. But it's as hard as nails now and could use a bit more generosity. • $NA • (08/31/95) • **85**
Echézeaux 1995: A crisp, straightforward Pinot Noir, fairly lean and angular. Light to medium in body, with an astringent finish. 416 cases made. • $55 • (11/15/97) • **80**
Echézeaux 1994: Earthy, coarse, mainly tannic and light in flavor. What fruit flavors it offers are ripe and sweet, but the tannins are troublesome. Try after 2000. • $50 • (11/15/96) • **81**
Echézeaux 1993: Intensely aromatic featuring dried fruit and plum character, medium body, fine tannins and fresh, crisp finish. Drinkable now. • $NA • (11/15/95) • **85**
Echézeaux 1992: A distinctive minty character runs through this firm-textured, nicely focused Echézeaux that echoes its berry and herb flavors on the tough finish. Drinkable now. • $NA • (12/15/94) • **87**
Echézeaux 1990: Firm in texture and focused in flavor, with generous plum, currant and blackberry aromas and flavors tightly wrapped in a moderate veil of tannin. Drinkable now. • $42 • (11/30/92) • **88**
Echézeaux 1989 • $45 • (01/31/92) • **93**
Echézeaux 1986 • $30 • (11/30/88) • **90**
Echézeaux 1985 • $37 • (09/15/87) • **96**
Gevrey-Chambertin 1995: A high-toned, spicy red that's on the herbal side, though some interesting licorice notes peek through. Astringent tannins dominate the finish. 758 cases made. • $30 • (11/15/97) • **79**
Gevrey-Chambertin 1992: Diluted and watery, with some modest red berry flavors. Short and tannic finish. • $NA • (12/15/94) • **78**
Gevrey-Chambertin 1990: Tart and lively, with a greenish streak running through the bright raspberry and toast aromas and flavors. Drinkable now. • $28 • (11/30/92) • **84**
Gevrey-Chambertin 1989 • $29 • (01/31/92) • **84**
Gevrey-Chambertin 1988 • $37 • (07/15/90) • **87**
Gevrey-Chambertin 1987 • $20 • (03/31/90) • **82**
Grands Echézeaux 1995: Medium-bodied, with some decent fruit, but it's also a bit herbal and lean, with dry tannins on the finish. 100 cases made. • $65 • (11/15/97) • **78**
Grands Echézeaux 1994: Chewy, chunky and not all that flavorful, with more tannin than the floral and berry notes lurking underneath can balance. Seems out of whack. • $60 • (11/15/96) • **79**
Grands Echézeaux 1993: Deep and ripe but also firm and hard at this stage, showing little charm. Tannic, but you can taste the sweetness of fruit underneath. Try after 2000. • $60 • (11/15/95) • **88**
Grands Echézeaux 1989 • $56 • (01/31/92) • **90**
Grands Echézeaux 1987 • $56 • (07/15/90) • **86**
Grands Echézeaux 1986 • $60 • (02/28/89) • **87**
Nuits-St.-Georges 1990: Light and fruity, with ripe plum and currant flavors that turn dry and leathery on the finish. A simple, pleasing wine, but doesn't have any extra dimensions. Drinkable now. • $29 • (11/30/92) • **81**
Nuits-St.-Georges 1989 • $29 • (02/29/92) • **91**
Nuits-St.-Georges 1986 • $20 • (11/15/88) • **82**
Nuits-St.-Georges 1983 • $18 • (02/01/86) • **83**
Richebourg 1989 • $117 • (01/31/92) • **95**
Richebourg 1986 • $100 • (08/31/89) • **88**
Vosne-Romanée 1990: Earthy, woody and stalky, with little aroma and flavors that show only a modest level of fruit. Drinkable now. • $28 • (11/30/92) • **78**
Vosne-Romanée 1989 • $30 • (01/31/92) • **89**
Vosne-Romanée 1986 • $19 • (12/31/88) • **80**
Vosne-Romanée 1985 • $29 • (10/15/87) • **91**
Vosne-Romanée Aux Malconsorts 1995: Light, fruity and simple, offering some raspberry, strawberry and cinnamon flavors. Light-bodied, slightly diluted. Short finish. 833 cases made. • $43 • (11/15/97) • **75**
Vosne-Romanée Aux Malconsorts 1993: Chewy, firm and tannic, delivering pretty currant, raspberry and licorice flavors, medium body and medium intensity. Should glow by 2000. • $NA • (11/15/95) • **87**
Vosne-Romanée Aux Malconsorts 1992: Lean, almost crisp, with little fruit to balance the hard tannins. The finish suggests it might improve. Try now. • $NA • (12/15/94) • **79**
Vosne-Romanée Aux Malconsorts 1990: A bit austere and reined in, but the moderate tannins are holding back lovely plum, berry and spice aromas and flavors. Remains subtle and elegant through the finish. Drinkable now. • $37 • (11/30/92) • **86**
Vosne-Romanée Aux Malconsorts 1987 • $30 • (07/15/90) • **88**
Vosne-Romanée Aux Malconsorts 1986 • $35 • (10/31/88) • **79**
Vosne-Romanée Aux Malconsorts 1985 • $55 • (09/30/87) • **95**

CLOS HAUT-PEYRAGUEY, CHÂTEAU

Sauternes 1990: Exotically charming, gingersnap flavors complementing the lemon, vanilla bean and wet earth character of this medium-bodied, very sweet, well-balanced Sauternes. Try now. • $NA • (04/15/95) • **90**

Sauternes 1989: A distinctive, earthy touch makes it a bit rustic; pretty orange-peel, honey and melon flavors come through on the balanced finish. Drink now. • $30 • (04/15/95) • **86**

Sauternes 1988: Very attractive, featuring a fresh, grassy edge to complement the tropical fruit and butterscotch flavors. Medium-bodied and accessible; try now. • $26 • (04/15/95) • **88**

Sauternes 1987 • $21 • (06/15/90) • **83**

Sauternes 1986: Ripe and thick, offering vanilla, spice and orange-peel flavors. The grassy, lime undertow keeps this full-bodied, very sweet Sauternes on track. • $23 • (04/15/95) • **89**

CLOS L'ABEILLEY

Sauternes 1990: Delicate and easy to drink, featuring vanilla, toast and pineapple flavors, medium body and sweetness and a rather hot finish. Second label from Château de Rayne-Vigneau. • $NA • (04/15/95) • **84**

CLOS L'EGLISE

Pomerol 1995: This wine has wonderful finesse and fruit. Lovely chocolate and raspberry aromas. Full-bodied, with beautiful silky tannins and lots of berry and milk chocolate on the aftertaste. Best after 2000. • $30 • (01/31/98) • **91**

Pomerol 1994: Shows some impressive ripeness, with cherry, raisin and tobacco aromas and flavors. Of medium body, with firm tannins and a fresh finish. Drinkable now. • $25 • (01/31/97) • **85**

Pomerol 1993: Muscular and slightly rustic, featuring loads of firm tannins and cherry, berry, dried fruit character. Full to medium in body and a long, somewhat dry finish. Drinkable now. • $25 • (01/31/96) • **85**

Pomerol 1988 • $26 • (06/30/91) • **83**

Pomerol 1986 • $33 • (02/15/90) • **86**

Pomerol 1982 • $43 Ⓐ • (05/15/89) • **88**

Pomerol 1961 • $75 • (04/30/92) • **68**

Pomerol 1947• $NA • (05/31/97) • **88**

Pomerol 1945 • $230 • (11/30/95) • **84**

CLOS LA COUTALE

Cahors 1995: Rich and concentrated, with lively red berry and cherry flavors. Focused and flavorful, with a lingering finish. A nice example of Cahors. A blend of 70 percent Malbec, 15 percent Merlot and 15 percent Tannat. Drink now through 2000. • $13 • (05/15/98) • **88**

CLOS LA FLEUR FIGEAC

St.-Emilion 1994: Expressive aromas of coffee and chocolate give way to rich coffee, cedar and plum flavors in this well-structured red. Drinkable now. 3,000 cases made. • $18 • (10/15/97) • **86**

CLOS LARCIS

St.-Emilion 1997: Simple, with clean berry flavors and light tannins. Light-to medium-bodied. • $NA • (06/15/98) (BT) • **80-84**

St.-Emilion 1996: Very light and watery. Some fruit character, but really lacking. Very disappointing. Tasted twice, with consistent notes. 3,300 cases made. • $20 • (06/15/98) (BT) • **75-79**

St.-Emilion 1995: Rather delicate for the vintage, with berry, tobacco character. Medium-to-light in body, with light tannins and a fresh finish. Drink now. • $15 • (01/31/98) • **82**

St.-Emilion 1994: Not a big wine, but a delicious one. Offers pretty aromas of berries and milk chocolate, fine tannins and a delicate, fruity finish. Drink now. 516 cases made. • $14 • (01/31/97) • **84**

St.-Emilion 1993: Light, simple, fruity and slightly diluted. A bit disappointing for this estate. Drinkable now. • $14 • (01/31/96) • **79**

St.-Emilion 1992: Better than expected. Elegant and drinkable, featuring cassis, berry and mint aromas and flavors, medium body, medium tannins and light finish. • $12 • (04/15/95) • **83**

St.-Emilion 1991: Rather lean, but has some interesting black olive and berry aromas and flavors. • $12 • (03/31/94) • **78**

Key: SS—Spectator Selection CS—Cellar Selection HR—Highly Recommended BB—Best Buy $NA—Price not available Ⓐ—Auction Price (BT)—Barrel Tasting

Dates in parentheses indicate the issues in which the ratings were published.

St.-Emilion 1990: A delicate and refined wine, with pretty vanilla and berry aromas and flavors and soft, refined tannins. Drinkable now. • $25 • (03/31/93) • **85**

St.-Emilion 1989 • $28 • (03/15/92) • **92**

CLOS MARSALETTE

Pessac-Léognan 1997: Light, with berry character but a rather stemmy and green aftertaste. • $NA • (06/15/98) (BT) • **75-79**

Pessac-Léognan 1996: Slightly herbal, with earth and berry character and a hint of grass. Medium-bodied, with moderate tannins and a medium finish. • $22 • (06/15/98) (BT) • **80-84**

Pessac-Léognan 1995: A solid, well-structured red, with plenty of cherry and floral character. Medium-bodied, with medium, firm tannins and a chewy, fruity finish. Best after 2000. • $20 • (01/31/98) • **88**

Pessac-Léognan 1994: Lovely, soft and chocolaty. Medium-bodied, with fine tannins and a long sweet, fruit finish. Drink now. • $18 • (01/31/97) • **85**

Pessac-Léognan 1993: Straightforward dark chocolate, berry and cherry aromas and flavors, medium body, firm tannins and a short finish. Drinkable now. • $NA • (01/31/96) • **84**

CLOS NAUDIN, DOMAINE DU

Vouvray Moelleux 1989 • $34 • (04/30/91) • **83**

Vouvray Moelleux Réserve 1989 • $54 • (03/31/91) • **89**

CLOS NOIR

Clos de la Roche 1992: Crisp, fresh, lightweight, like biting into a fresh bunch of currants; distinctive floral nuances add to the fruit. Drinkable now. • $NA • (12/15/94) • **86**

Côte de Nuits-Villages Préau 1994: Sour, stalky flavors kill this wine. • $NA • (11/15/96) • **74**

Côte de Nuits-Villages Préau 1992: A little tough in texture, with woodsy, toasty, slightly herbal flavors. • $NA • (12/15/94) • **79**

Fixin 1994: Earthy, mushroomy accents overpower the fruit flavors. • $NA • (11/15/96) • **77**

Gevrey-Chambertin Les Jeunes Rois 1992: Firm in texture but not too tannic, showing some nice floral and currant flavors that persist on the solid finish. Drinkable now. • $NA • (12/15/94) • **84**

Morey-St.-Denis 1992: Light and floral in aroma, a nice bead of raspberry flavor carrying through the smooth finish. Drinkable now. • $NA • (12/15/94) • **85**

CLOS RENÉ, CHÂTEAU

Pomerol 1988 • $24 • (04/30/91) • **88**

Pomerol 1986 • $22 • (06/15/89) SS • **94**

Pomerol 1985 • $17 • (03/15/88) • **92**

Pomerol 1983 • $17 • (03/16/86) • **91**

Pomerol 1982 • $32 Ⓐ • (05/15/89) • **87**

Pomerol 1962 • $35 • (11/30/87) • **60**

Pomerol 1959 • $50 • (10/15/90) • **88**

Pomerol 1945 • $175 • (11/30/95) • **88**

CLOS ROCHE BLANCHE

Sauvignon Touraine 1995 • $11 • (06/15/96) • **69**

Sauvignon Touraine 1994 • $9 • (12/15/95) • **80**

CLOS ST.-MARTIN

St.-Emilion 1997: Clean and well-made, with somewhat one-dimensional berry and violet character. Medium-bodied, with a light finish and firm tannins. Wait and see. • $NA • (06/15/98) (BT) • **80-84**

CLOS ST.-MICHEL

Châteauneuf-du-Pape 1990: Earthy, gamy, leathery flavors dominate the fruit in this medium-weight, problematic wine. Too gamy for us. • $16 • (11/15/92) • **76**

Châteauneuf-du-Pape Cuvée Réserve 1989 • $17 • (11/15/92) • **85**

CLOS ST.-PONCIAN

St.-Chinian 1990 • $NA • (03/15/94) • **80**

CLOS TRIGUEDINA

Cahors 1983 • $11 • (02/28/91) • **80**
Cahors Prince Probus 1985 • $17 • (02/28/91) • **82**
Cahors Prince Probus 1983 • $14 • (12/31/88) • **79**

CLOSEL, DOMAINE DU

Savennières Cuvée Spéciale 1995: This big wine is rather soft in acidity, but what it loses in focus it gains in flesh, with ripe peach, almond and dry, honey flavors. A bit rustic in style. 450 cases made. • $20 • (06/15/97) • **84**
Savennières Cuvée Spéciale 1994: Delicate floral and lanolin aromas are followed by ripe apple, lime and light herbal flavors in this harmonious white. Not powerful, but expressive. 450 cases made. • $20 • (06/15/97) • **86**
Savennières Cuvée Spéciale 1993 • $17 • (12/15/95) • **83**

CLUSEL ROCH

Côte-Rôtie 1994: Firm, clean and fresh, offering ripe black cherry, mineral, floral and spice notes, showing complexity despite the full, firm tannins. Not overextracted, it's harmonious and should develop well. Drinkable now. • $NA • (10/15/97) • **89**
Côte-Rôtie 1993: A pretty wine, with good varietal character but without serious concentration, this offers berry, mild game and spice flavors and moderate tannins. It's balanced, polished and drinkable now. 850 cases made. • $32 • (04/30/97) • **88**
Côte-Rôtie 1991: Lush and supple, with layers of ripe fruit, roasted meat and licorice, balanced with firm tannins. Drink now. • $40 • (05/31/94) • **85**
Côte-Rôtie Les Grandes Places 1994: Dense yet velvety, with toasty, ripe black cherry and emerging gamy flavors on the firm palate. Shows good balance and expressive varietal character; a slightly rustic quality adds to character. Drinkable now. • $NA • (10/15/97) • **89**
Côte-Rôtie Les Grandes Places 1991: Rich and smooth yet firm, offering flavors of crushed berries, spice and game. A solid wine; try now. Tasted twice. • $50 • (05/31/94) • **90**
Côte-Rôtie Les Grandes Places 1990: Powerful for this vintage. It's reserved, but shows plummy, gamy, spicy flavors with full tannins. Drinkable now. • $50 • (05/31/94) • **91**

CLUSEL, DOMAINE

Côte-Rôtie 1988 • $36 • (11/15/91) • **87**

CLUSIÈRE, CHÂTEAU LA

St.-Emilion 1997: Clean dried cherry and berry aromas and flavors. Medium-bodied, with light, fine tannins and a fresh finish. Not a big wine, but harmonious. • $NA • (06/15/98) (BT) • **85-89**
St.-Emilion 1996: Firm and racy, with currant, berry and mineral character. Medium- to full-bodied, with velvety tannins and a crisp aftertaste. Nicely made red. • $35 • (06/15/98) (BT) • **85-89**
St.-Emilion 1982 • $20 • (05/15/89) • **88**
St.-Emilion 1970 • $28 • (05/15/93) • **86**

COCHE-DURY, J.-F.

Auxey-Duresses Red 1987 • $30 • (02/28/90) • **87**
Corton-Charlemagne 1995: Brilliant and very intense. Wonderfully stony, minerally, very toasty from the grilled oak, showing thick weight on the midpalate. This is superimpressive, with a silky texture that's to die for, and all that oakiness will die down given the tight concentration in this full-bodied white Burgundy. Lots of ripe fruit, so no problem waiting for this wine to settle, around 2005. • $175 • (05/31/98) • **98**
Corton-Charlemagne 1994: A class act. This wonderful, silky-smooth wine is rich, sweet-tasting and very ripe yet also elegant and refined, packing in spice, mineral, mocha, coffee bean, smoke and ripe fruit flavors. A bit short on crisp acidity, it's ready now through 2000. • $312 Ⓐ • (05/31/97) • **95**
Corton-Charlemagne 1993: A blockbuster with the finesse to seduce the most demanding aficionados of top white Burgundy. Voluptuous, supple and intense as can be, this opulent crowd-pleaser delivers plenty of toasty oak, apple, citrus and mineral character. Brilliant winemaking at work here. Try in 2001. • $294 Ⓐ • (05/31/96) CS • **99**
Corton-Charlemagne 1992: Fabulous balance, showing rich, round and creamy texture, but it stays the course with racy acidity and elegance. Lots of depth and complexity, with honey, hazelnut, nectarine and smoke flavors. Drinkable now. • $748 Ⓐ • (08/31/94) • **93**
Meursault 1994: Ambitious winemaking at work here. Full-bodied, it at first shows lots of toasty oak, but then becomes silky smooth, balancing the fruit flavors against some distinctive milky, caramel, lemon and spice notes. Glides to a long finish. • $NA • (08/31/96) • **90**
Meursault 1993: Seductive white Burgundy, balanced, intense and full-bodied. Youthful-tasting, as tons of toasty oak, tropical fruit and grapefruit flavors go on and on. Try now. • $45 • (05/31/96) • **93**
Meursault 1992: Full-blown, flavorful and aromatic, with a rich texture, lots of honey accents and a lingering finish. Has a beautifully complex aroma of butter, toasty almonds and dried apricots. • $NA • (08/31/94) • **90**
Meursault Les Chevalières 1994: Classy. Full-bodied and flavorful, with some nicely balanced dried herb (particularly thyme and cilantro), honey and pear flavors. Silky, with a toasty finish. • $NA • (08/31/96) • **91**
Meursault Les Perrières 1995: Like virtual reality, this flawlessly harmonious wine makes you think any dream is within reach, with its perfect silkiness balanced by ripe fruit, well-integrated oak and the sensual sense of *terroir*. This one has just the right amount of honey, tropical, pear, toasty spice and wet earth notes. Extraordinary class on the long, smooth finish. Tempting now through 2010. • $130 • (05/31/98) • **97**
Meursault Les Perrières 1994: White Burgundy doesn't get much silkier and refined than this. As you sip this nectar, it glides over the palate like double cream. Full-bodied. Subtle toasty oak, honey, wet earth, spice and vanilla bean character. Classy, supple finish. Drinkable now. • $80 • (08/31/96) • **95**
Meursault Les Perrières 1993: Iron fist in a velvet glove, this powerful white caresses the palate despite its amazing fruit intensity. Silky and concentrated citrus, toasty bread and mineral complexity. Full in body, the finish keeps pounding it on. Try in 2000. • $80 • (05/31/96) • **95**
Meursault Les Perrières 1992: Complex, lovely, silky texture. It's a bit earthy, but also honey-flavored and ripe. Excellent backbone and a classy, racy finish. Drinkable now. • $83 • (05/15/95) • **93**
Meursault Les Rougeots 1995: Opulent, thick, dense and rich, this full-bodied, mouthfilling wine brings loads of ripe fruit along with notes of freshly squeezed lemon and deftly toasty oak. Very showy, it coats the palate and ends with a supersilky finish. Best after 2002. • $80 • (05/31/98) • **93**
Meursault Les Rougeots 1994: A typical Coche Meursault; silky yet firm, coating the mouth and leaving an impression of great concentration. Clean and well made, with lemon, honey and toasty oak flavors that mingle nicely on the finish. Drinkable now. • $NA • (08/31/96) • **90**
Meursault Les Rougeots 1993: Well crafted, intense and balanced, full in body, pumping out citrus, toasty oak, butter, honey and wet stone flavors in great intensity. Thick and fresh, very long on the slightly earthy finish. Drinkable now. • $60 • (05/31/96) • **92**
Meursault Les Rougeots 1992: A big wine, chewy yet polished, providing tons of butter, butterscotch, mineral, honey and chalk flavors and an earthy touch on the finish. The texture is smooth and silky. Try now. • $NA • (05/15/95) • **93**
Meursault Red 1987 • $30 • (02/28/90) • **80**
Pinot Noir Bourgogne 1987 • $25 • (02/28/90) • **79**

COING DE ST.-FIACRE, CHÂTEAU DU

Muscadet de Sèvre et Maine Sur Lie 1993 • $8 • (08/31/94) BB • **85**

COL DES VENTS

Corbières 1995: A bit thin and dried-out, with modest dried cherry flavors. Past its prime. 3,000 cases made. • $8 • (04/30/98) • **77**

COLBOIS, DOMAINE DANIEL

Chablis 1995: This firm white offers lean green apple and mineral flavors with crisp citrus undertones; light smoke and vanilla notes soften it on the finish. A clean, fresh Chardonnay. 4,167 cases made. • $20 • (06/15/97) • **84**
Chablis Premier Cru Cuvée Alexis 1993: Mature, showing apple cider, butter and nutmeg flavors that fan out on the finish. There's a bitter element, too. 217 cases made. • $25 • (06/15/97) • **78**

Chablis Premier Cru Cuvée Alexis 1992: A clean white, with some complexity. Softened with age, it's developed creamy butter and vanilla notes, but the melon and apple flavors still have snap. 500 cases made. • $25 • (06/15/97) • **85**

COLIN, MADAME FRANÇOIS

Puligny-Montrachet Les Demoiselles 1993: Well defined and ripe, exhibiting a beam of green apple, herb and citrus character and classy finish. Drinkable now. • $NA • (05/15/95) • **89**

COLIN, MARC

Bâtard-Montrachet 1996: Delicious, ripe '96. Elegant yet thick and dense, this full-bodied white Burgundy coats the palate with buttery, milky, creamy, minerally, spicy, toasty bread notes and tropical, lime, pear and apricot tart flavors. Harmonious finish. Tempting after 2003, earlier if you decant it for a couple of hours, but best around 2010. 45 cases made. • $130 • (05/31/98) • **97**

Chassagne-Montrachet 1994: A bit lean, but hinting at mint, butter, earth and cedar. Light- to medium-bodied, adding some richness on the ginger-flavored finish. • $35 • (05/31/96) • **84**

Chassagne-Montrachet 1993: A very clean white demonstrating freshly cut apple, light honey and spice character, medium-to-light body and crisp acidity. Drinkable now. • $32 • (05/15/95) • **82**

Chassagne-Montrachet 1992: Big and rangy, buttery in aroma, full of pear and orange flavors and backed by firm acidity. Very lively and straightforward. 210 cases made. • $20 • (08/31/94) • **84**

Chassagne-Montrachet Caillerets 1996: Delicious, well-made Chassagne, showing more depth and concentration than many '96s from this village. Mingles honey, freshly cut grass, dried herbs, ripe fruit and citrus with a dollop of toasty oak in a balanced package that is smooth in texture, full in body and long on the finish. Tempting now, better after 2000. 580 cases made. • $50 • (05/31/98) • **91**

Chassagne-Montrachet Caillerets 1994: Balanced, delicious, supple hazelnut, caramel and spice character. Shows some sparks, medium body and a lemony finish. Drinkable now. • $45 • (05/31/96) • **85**

Chassagne-Montrachet Caillerets 1993: A rich and buttery Chassagne, showing pedigree, and complex intensity from the dried-herb, honey and mineral notes. Long finish. Drinkable now. • $40 • (05/15/95) • **87**

Chassagne-Montrachet Caillerets 1992: Closed, tight and young, but underneath are great characteristics of lemon, pear, vanilla and spice that begin to open up on the finish. Drinkable now. • $32 • (08/31/94) • **86**

Chassagne-Montrachet Les Champs Gain 1995: Subtle and elegant, this yields its secrets slowly, turning up the intensity on the long finish. Full-bodied, with oak nuances and fresh fruit flavors, it's drinkable now through 2005. • $NA • (05/31/97) • **93**

Chassagne-Montrachet Les Champs Gain 1994: Straightforward and a touch green, of medium body and intensity, offering some dried herb, lemon and apple flavors. Drinkable now. • $40 • (05/31/96) • **85**

Chassagne-Montrachet Les Champs Gain 1993: Lean, decent honey, green apple and chalk character, medium body and a steely finish. • $40 • (05/15/95) • **84**

Chassagne-Montrachet Les Vide-Bourses 1996: Fairly lush and ripe for a '96 Chassagne, with a hint of menthol, honey, pear tart, lime and dried herb character. Of medium body, with some oak-infused spice, it turns a bit sour on the finish. Drinkable now. 130 cases made. • $45 • (05/31/98) • **80**

Chassagne-Montrachet Les Vide-Bourses 1994: Vibrant and lively honey, lemon, cream, mineral, spice and pie crust character. Of medium body, this *premier cru* is well structured and elegant. Drinkable now. • $38 • (05/31/96) • **90**

Montrachet 1996: Brilliant winemaking from a Montrachet master. Like a perfectly choreographed ballet, all the pieces are in the right place, with superlative finesse. Subtle and supple, intensely mineral, coating the palate with opulent, ripe fruit and vanilla bean, spice, tropical and deftly created toasty oak accents. Long, harmonious, silky finish. Tempting after 2000 through 2010. 50 cases made. • $250 • (05/31/98) • **99**

Montrachet 1995: Great class marks this intense, full-bodied beauty. Its honey, toasty oak, hazelnut and butterscotch flavors are superbly balanced, and despite its bold character it remains elegant and refined. Long finish of stupendous intensity and clarity. Try after 2000, preferably after 2005. • $250 • (05/31/97) • **98**

Montrachet 1994: A blockbuster with satiny mouthfeel, this full-bodied, full-throttled white Burgundy is a class act. Rich and thick, backed by toasty hazelnut, mineral, cedar, ripe fruit and long, restrained, citrus-spiked finish. Try in 2001. 47 cases made. • $200 • (05/31/96) • **96**

Montrachet 1993: Masses of fruit, tasting of lime, pineapple and honey as well as freshly crushed grapes. Medium-to-full body and a long, long finish. • $200 • (05/15/95) • **90**

Puligny-Montrachet Les Garennes 1996: Thick, dense and extremely rich, this full-bodied, smoky, toasty, spicy, oaky and muscular wine reveals its powerful structure in the midpalate, where it delivers large doses of silky, opulent texture. Hold until 2002. 130 cases made. • $50 • (05/31/98) • **90**

Puligny-Montrachet La Garenne 1995: Very round, supple and lush, this dense wine is smooth like cream and tastes of vanilla bean, whipped cream, mineral, lemon and pineapple. Subtle spice and oak accents add complexity to the lingering finish. Well made, it's delicious now through 2000. • $NA • (05/31/97) • **91**

Puligny-Montrachet La Garenne 1994: Tight and a bit hard now, medium-bodied, featuring some pear, floral and butterscotch flavors. Seems somewhat short and lacking in fruit. • $45 • (05/31/96) • **83**

Puligny-Montrachet La Garenne 1993: Bubbling with freshly crushed grape character. Medium body and medium richness; apple and cream notes on the finish. • $42 • (05/15/95) • **85**

Puligny-Montrachet Le Trézin 1996: Well made, with an attractively silky, minerally character on the palate, along with pear and green apple, but this medium-bodied white clamps down slightly on the finish. Drink upon release. 200 cases made. • $40 • (05/31/98) • **87**

Puligny-Montrachet Le Trézin 1994: Hard, unyielding and showing nothing on the nose right now, but on the palate are mineral, vanilla, cream and ripe pear flavors that are delightful. Drinkable now. • $40 • (05/31/96) • **85**

Puligny-Montrachet Le Trézin 1993: Sleek, clean mineral and honey character; medium-to-light bodied, adding crisp acidity. • $38 • (05/15/95) • **84**

St.-Aubin En Remilly White 1996: Wonderful. A clean, pure, zesty and vibrant wine, of medium body, with sweet and ripe fruit along with wet earth, spice, tropical, honey, mineral, and grass notes. Not lush or opulent, but well-built for aging. Try around 2005. 580 cases made. • $35 • (05/31/98) • **90**

St.-Aubin En Remilly White 1995: Soft, smooth and full-bodied, with a bite of *terroir* in the wet soil, spice and oak flavors, adding life to a wine otherwise dominated by a creamlike character. Long, toasty oak finish. Drink now through 2001. • $34 • (05/31/97) • **87**

St.-Aubin En Remilly White 1994: Lean and very tart, showing modest apple cider flavors and a short finish. • $24 • (05/31/96) • **73**

St.-Aubin En Remilly White 1993: Surprisingly smooth, ripe and velvety, butterscotch and toast flavors mingling with lime, chalk and citrus notes. Drinkable now. • $23 • (05/15/95) • **83**

St.-Aubin En Remilly White 1992: Interesting, but the smoky, earthy flavors dominate the modest apple and pear notes; for fans of a funky style. 410 cases made. • $14 • (08/31/94) • **80**

St.-Aubin La Chatenière White 1996: The distinctive smoky, minerally, matchsticklike character is accented by supple and elegant midpalate texture. Full-bodied, balanced and delicious, with some good fruit and loads of citrusy acidity. Turns a bit chewy and crisp on the mile-long finish now. Best from 2000 through 2005. 540 cases made. • $35 • (05/31/98) • **90**

St.-Aubin La Chatenière White 1995: A beauty. Harmonious, rich, ripe and thick-textured, full-bodied, with lovely pear, mineral, caramel and citrus flavors of moderate intensity. Subtle, mouthfilling finish. Drink now through 2005. • $33 • (05/31/97) • **89**

St.-Aubin La Chatenière White 1994: Tart and slightly paperish, as a cardboard taste takes away from whatever else might be in this *premier cru*, including its mineral, apple character. • $24 • (05/31/96) • **76**

St.-Aubin La Chatenière White 1993: Grassy style, but what's there shows finesse and class; sweet pea, green apple and lime flavors. A bit too tart and austere on the finish. • $24 • (05/15/95) • **83**

St.-Aubin Le Charmois White 1996: Elegant and racy St.-Aubin, showing a sensational mineral, vanilla bean and wet stone character. Flows over the palate with great purity, tiptoeing with grace to a long, succulent, ripe-tasting finish. Medium-to-full in body, with laser-sharp pear, mandarin orange, floral and peach notes. Try after 2000. 200 cases made. • $35 • (05/31/98) • **93**

St.-Aubin Le Charmois White 1995: Dense and thick, a bit short on class. Full-bodied, offering vanilla bean, pear and some lemon notes shaded by spice and oak. Finishes somewhat hot. Drink now through 2000. • $32 • (05/31/97) • **80**

Key: SS—Spectator Selection CS—Cellar Selection HR—Highly Recommended BB—Best Buy $NA—Price not available Ⓐ—Auction Price (BT)—Barrel Tasting
Dates in parentheses indicate the issues in which the ratings were published.

FRANCE

St.-Aubin Le Charmois White 1994: Soft, supple and pleasant *premier cru*, showing apricot, honey, apple and pear flavors, medium body and intensity and a touch of citrus keeping the finish alive. Drinkable now. • $24 • (05/31/96) • **85**

St.-Aubin Les Combes White 1996: Remarkable for its split personality of aromatic backwardness and open, lush texture. Smells of wet stone, mineral and little else, thus displaying a reserve that bodes well for the future, yet on the palate it's round and sweet-tasting, offering layers of ripe pear, tropical and honey flavors. Silky mouthfeel leads to a lingering, exciting, slightly smoky finish. Drink now through 2005. 290 cases made. • $35 • (05/31/98) • **93**

St.-Aubin Les Combes White 1995: Very elegant, with an impressive mineral character. Medium-bodied, with clean tropical fruit and pear flavors, and some lovely mineral, smoke and wet stone notes on the long, chewy finish. Drink now through 2002. • $33 • (05/31/97) • **89**

St.-Aubin Les Cortons White 1996: A tough but elegant and racy white. Pure and clean, with laser-sharp fruit and acidity, this medium-bodied Chardonnay spikes its way across the palate to a long, intense finish. Offers hints of smoke, mineral, hazelnut and spice. Try around 2005. 290 cases made. • $35 • (05/31/98) • **90**

St.-Aubin Les Cortons White 1994: Powerful but ungenerous. Somewhat too cedary and of medium body, it offers nice citrus, apple and honey flavors. Tough as nails on the finish. A good choice with seafood. • $24 • (05/31/96) • **85**

St.-Aubin Les Cortons White 1993: Pretty, approachable toasty oak, vanilla and pear character and a medium, slightly acidic finish. Drink now. • $24 • (05/15/95) • **81**

COLIN, PIERRE

Bâtard-Montrachet 1995: Very intense, thick, dense and ripe, with healthy portions of toasty oak and fruit, this has a lot going for it. A bit overdone and too oaky to score higher now. Drinkable now. • $NA • (05/31/97) • **86**

Bâtard-Montrachet 1994: Understated greatness. Very sharply focused and tightly wound. Give it time to fully deliver its mineral, stony, flinty, vanilla flavors. Super elegance. Very austere, but what pleasure in store for the patient collector! Try after 2000. • $NA • (05/31/96) • **94**

Bâtard-Montrachet 1993: Impressive mineral, spice and citric character. Medium-bodied and superfresh; crisp, tart finish. • $120 • (05/15/95) • **86**

Bâtard-Montrachet 1992: A real class act. It's generous and toasty in aroma, rich in flavor, expertly balanced and long on the finish. The pear, honey, vanilla and hazelnut flavors are vivid but blend subtly and gracefully for an overall effect of harmony. Drinkable now. • $50 • (08/31/94) • **95**

COLIN-DELÉGER, MICHEL

Chassagne-Montrachet 1993: Fresh, simple apple and honey aromas and flavors. Medium in body, some chalky character; rather short on the finish. • $NA • (05/15/95) • **83**

Chassagne-Montrachet En Remilly 1995: Opulent, ripe and very dense, this full-bodied *premier cru* brims with clean, pure fruit flavors. Yet despite its sheer volume, it remains elegant, with a finish so harmonious it flows like thick cream. The wood is subtle and complements the lovely honey, spice, melon and hazelnut notes. Delicious now through 2005. 400 cases made. • $50 • (05/31/97) • **94**

Chassagne-Montrachet En Remilly 1994: Seductive and charming, boasting tons of ripe pear and apple flavors. Rich honey, cream and dried herb complexity. Voluptuous mouthfeel and amazing silkiness. Drinkable now. 408 cases made. • $40 • (05/31/96) • **93**

Chassagne-Montrachet La Maltroie 1995: Closed on the nose, and though full-bodied and rich, it shows little now. Subtle honey, lemon, toasty oak, mineral and wet earth flavors turn chewy on the finish. 225 cases made. • $47 • (05/31/97) • **86**

Chassagne-Montrachet La Maltroie 1993: Well balanced, pretty pear, pineapple and nut flavors; silky texture. Rounder than most. Try now. • $44 • (05/15/95) • **84**

Chassagne-Montrachet Les Chaumées 1995: A seductive, fruit-driven, full-bodied wine with just enough oak lurking in the background to complement the hazelnut, honey, and citrus flavors. Harmonious finish is slightly smoky, very refined. Delicious now through 2005. 700 cases made. • $47 • (05/31/97) • **93**

Chassagne-Montrachet Les Chaumées 1994: Toasty, round, supple, ripe fig, melon and pear character. Would rate higher if it wasn't for a somewhat hollow midpalate. Drinkable now. 783 cases made. • $40 • (05/31/96) • **83**

Chassagne-Montrachet Les Chaumées 1992: Beautifully made, balanced and harmonious, showing some pretty, ripe honey, apple and pear flavors; it's got a lot going for it. • $45 • (08/31/94) • **87**

Chassagne-Montrachet Les Chenevottes 1995: Closed on the nose but forward on the palate, this packs in dried herb, crisp citrus, spice and tropical flavors. Balanced finish, with a nice mineral character. Try from 2000 to 2005. 550 cases made. • $50 • (05/31/97) • **91**

Chassagne-Montrachet Les Chenevottes 1994: Lovely elegance in this full- to medium-bodied white Burgundy. Melts in the mouth with silky mineral, vanilla, cream, pear and tropical fruit character. Very subtle finish. Drinkable now. 570 cases made. • $45 • (05/31/96) • **89**

Chassagne-Montrachet Les Chenevottes 1993: Focused and a bit green, apple mingling with asparagus flavors; slightly diluted finish. • $42 • (05/15/95) • **83**

Chassagne-Montrachet Les Chenevottes 1992: An expressive, balanced and medium-bodied white, with plenty of toasty, buttery and pear flavors backed by some mouth-puckering, lemon character that kicks in on the intense finish. • $36 • (08/31/94) • **88**

Chassagne-Montrachet Morgeot 1995: You can feel the concentration. Tight and solid, this racy wine has an intriguing stone, mineral and vibrant, citrusy character. Medium- to full-bodied, with a well-defined, ripe finish. Try after 1998. • $50 • (08/31/97) • **90**

Chassagne-Montrachet Morgeot 1994: Totally voluptuous and enchanting, oozing honey, ripe apricot and pear. Full in body and seductive. Drinkable now. 583 cases made. • $40 • (05/31/96) • **88**

Chassagne-Montrachet Morgeot 1993: Beautiful and subtle; focused apple, mineral and chalk flavors and the class you expect from fine white Burgundy. Drinkable now. • $44 • (05/15/95) • **89**

Chassagne-Montrachet Les Vergers 1995: Lush and fairly intense, with dried herbs, citrus, honey and mineral complexity. Full-bodied and very oily in texture, it needs time; try after 2000. • $50 • (08/31/97) • **91**

Chassagne-Montrachet Les Vergers 1994: Round, supple and flavorful, there is an interesting piney, resinous character mingling with the honey and pear notes. A bit tart on the finish. Drinkable now. 708 cases made. • $33 Ⓐ • (05/31/96) • **84**

Chassagne-Montrachet Les Vergers 1993: Fresh apple and cream flavors show a hint of mineral. Medium in body and lightly buttery; appley, coconut finish. Drink now. • $44 • (05/15/95) • **85**

Chassagne-Montrachet Les Vergers 1992: Good intensity, rather chewy, showing some lime, vanilla and butter notes backed with vibrant pineapple flavors. Lively and smooth, yet crisp; medium-bodied. • $47 Ⓐ • (08/31/94) • **86**

Chevalier-Montrachet 1993: Good concentration, displaying pineapple and vanilla character, medium body, plenty of fruit and well-integrated acidity. Drinkable now. • $83 Ⓐ • (05/15/95) • **88**

Puligny-Montrachet La Truffière 1995: This creamy-textured, minerally, full-bodied *premier cru* starts softly but ends with a bang. Harmonious, it's a pleasure to taste, with wet stone, pear and piecrust flavors, some lively lime and spice notes on the fresh finish. Seductive now and should improve through 2000. 275 cases made. • $70 • (05/31/97) • **92**

Puligny-Montrachet La Truffière 1994: Refined and classy, ripe and delicate. A full-bodied wine that delivers a lot of drinking pleasure with honey, marzipan, vanilla bean, mineral and pure fruit flavors. Drinkable now. • $NA • (08/31/96) • **93**

St.-Aubin En Charmois White 1993: A touch of mineral and lime and round texture make for appealing drinking in this well-made and focused white, but it's austere and short on the finish. • $24 • (05/15/95) • **80**

St.-Aubin Les Combes White 1993: Quite ripe, complex, lush and focused, showing lovely honey, floral, mineral and herb flavors. Drinkable now. • $NA • (05/15/95) • **87**

COLLET, JEAN

Chablis 1995: A showy, oak-aged style, with good fruit and citrus intensity. Full-bodied, with a chewy, green-wood finish. Better than an earlier sample. May improve after 2000. • $15 • (06/15/97) • **80**

Chablis 1994 • $NA • (08/31/95) • **85**

Chablis Mont de Milieu 1995: A crisp, citrusy Chablis, with honey and mineral notes. Medium in body, it should improve with age. Better around 2000. • $35 • (06/15/97) • **85**

Chablis Mont de Milieu 1994 • $25 • (05/31/96) • **75**

Chablis Montée de Tonnerre 1995: A well-made, balanced Chablis, fresh and pure, if quite oaky in style. Full-bodied and of medium intensity, with lovely honey and ripe fruit notes on the chewy, flinty, smoky finish. Drink now through 2005. • $35 • (06/15/97) • **87**

Chablis Montée de Tonnerre 1994 • $NA • (05/31/96) • **76**

Chablis Montée de Tonnerre 1993 • $NA • (08/31/95) • **82**
Chablis Montmains 1995: A bit overdone. Full-bodied, sweet, there's enough acidity to hold it together, for now, but drink before 2001. • $25 • (06/15/97) • **78**
Chablis Montmains 1994 • $20 • (05/31/96) • **85**
Chablis Montmains 1993 • $NA • (08/31/95) • **84**
Chablis Vaillons 1995: Distinctive combination of dried herbs, lactic, wet earth and pear flavors stand out. Supple in texture, medium- to full-bodied, with a fresh finish. • $25 • (06/15/97) • **85**
Chablis Vaillons 1994 • $20 • (05/31/96) • **81**
Chablis Vaillons 1993 • $NA • (08/31/95) • **85**
Chablis Valmur 1995: A slightly green, heavily oaked *grand cru*, full-bodied, with a long but clumsy finish. Tasted twice, with consistent notes. • $45 • (06/15/97) • **79**
Chablis Valmur 1994 • $50 • (05/31/96) • **87**
Chablis Valmur 1993 • $NA • (08/31/95) • **85**

COLLIN & BOURISSET

Pouilly-Fuissé Domaine Tranchand 1994: Quite a nice mouthfeel in this one, showing complex mineral and wet earth components that kick in on the finish and compensate for the lack of intense fruit. Drinkable now. 666 cases made. • $16 • (05/31/96) • **84**

COLLIN DU PIN

Bordeaux White 1995: Lots of fresh peach and honey aromas, but less character on the palate. Medium- to light-bodied, with fresh acidity and a light finish. Drink now. • $NA • (04/30/98) • **82**

COLLONGE, DOMAINE DE LA

Pouilly-Fuissé 1996: Rather fleshy and fat, showing a certain dilution, this wine turns tart on the finish. Offers modest fruit. Better after this year? 2,500 cases made. • $15 • (05/31/98) • **78**

COLOMBIER, DOMAINE DU

Crozes-Hermitage 1995: A lovely, concentrated, fruity wine, with supple texture, earthy, black currant and cassis bush character and lovely Syrahlike black pepper notes. The fruit and tannins are quite ripe. Medium-bodied, balanced and worth uncorking now through 2002. 417 cases made. • $12 • (10/15/97) • **88**
Crozes-Hermitage 1992 • $12 • (05/31/94) • **76**
Crozes-Hermitage Cuvée Gaby 1995: Earthy and reduced in aroma, with metallic, mineral, cassis bush and vegetal flavors. Excellent, deep color, and seemingly good concentration. Drinkable now. 667 cases made. • $18 • (10/15/97) • **75**
Crozes-Hermitage Cuvée Gaby 1992 • $15 • (05/31/94) • **80**
Crozes-Hermitage White 1996: Soft and quite generous, this round white has floral aromas and buttery flavors, smooth and harmonious. Not much fruit showing now, but the spicy, herbal and light earthy flavors are intriguing. 500 cases made. • $12 • (10/15/97) • **87**
Hermitage Non Filtré 1995: Focused and firm, of medium weight, offering pretty wild berry, floral and light mineral flavors, well-integrated tannins and a fresh, clean finish. Not a long-ager. Drinkable now. 417 cases made. • $54 • (10/15/97) • **88**
Hermitage 1991: Pretty, and accessible for Hermitage, with berry and coffee notes and supple tannins. Balanced, but lacks concentration; drinkable now. • $28 • (05/31/94) • **83**

COLOMBIER DE CHÂTEAU BROWN, LE

Pessac-Léognan 1996: Some decent berry, cherry and vanilla aromas and flavors, Light-to-medium body, light tannins and a short finish. Barely acceptable. 2,000 cases made. • $NA • (01/01/97) (BT) • **75-79**
Pessac-Léognan 1995: Rather weedy and slightly diluted, with some berry, stewed tomato character. Medium-bodied, with medium tannins, a short finish. Second label of Château Brown. Drink now. 2,000 cases made. • $15 • (01/31/98) • **78**

Key: SS—Spectator Selection CS—Cellar Selection HR—Highly Recommended BB—Best Buy $NA—Price not available Ⓐ—Auction Price (BT)—Barrel Tasting
Dates in parentheses indicate the issues in which the ratings were published.

Pessac-Léognan White 1995: Plenty of wood to this, with toffee and fruit aromas. Medium-bodied, with light acidity and a short aftertaste. Drink now. Second label of Château Brown. • $12 • (04/30/98) • **83**

COLOMBIER-MONPELOU, CHÂTEAU

Pauillac 1988 • $15 • (10/31/91) • **75**

COLOMBO, JEAN-LUC

Cornas Cuvée X 1994: A very pretty, very harmonious, very supple wine, quite exotic, with a lot of wood, but superbly round and showing terrific wild raspberry, currant, and light vanilla flavors. A modern style. Elegant yet full-bodied. • $NA • (10/15/97) • **90**
Cornas La Louvée 1994: A seamless marriage of ripe fruit and new oak, this polished red offers lively, youthful flavors without overbearing tannins. Lacks some traditional earthiness, but gains in freshness and balance. Drinkable now, should improve through 2002, at least. 200 cases made. • $51 • (10/15/97) • **89**
Cornas Les Ruchets 1993: Quite ripe for a difficult vintage, this traditional-style Syrah offers blackberry, black pepper and gamy flavors over moderate tannins. Accessible now. • $39 • (10/15/96) • **87**
Cornas Les Ruchets 1991 • $35 • (05/31/94) • **82**
Cornas Les Ruchets 1989 • $45 • (11/15/91) • **89**
Cornas Les Ruchets 1988 • $45 • (10/15/91) • **87**
Cornas Les Ruchets 1987 • $45 • (11/15/91) • **75**
Cornas Terres Brûlées 1993: Dense and unyielding now, this dark, tannic wine is full-bodied but not showing much fruit flavor, emphasizing coffee, tobacco and licorice flavors. Drinkable now. • $30 • (10/15/96) • **87**
Cornas Terres Brûlées 1992 • $30 • (10/15/95) • **89**
Côtes du Rhône Cuvée Syrah 1994: Generous yet balanced, this dark red offers ripe blackberry and licorice aromas and flavors. Full, yet fresh on the palate, with round, integrated tannins and a clean, spicy finish. Drinkable now. 1,400 cases made. • $13 • (10/15/96) HR • **88**
Côtes du Rhône Les Forots 1996: This round red offers ripe flavors of plums and blackberries, with notes of chocolate and black pepper. Generous but not too tannic, it's delightful now. 670 cases made. • $18 • (09/15/97) • **86**
Côtes du Rhône 1993 • $13 • (09/30/95) • **86**
Côtes du Rhône 100% Syrah 1993 • $18 • (09/30/95) • **86**
Crozes-Hermitage 1995: This light-bodied red is lively, well balanced and accessible, offering pretty cherry and berry flavors, with just enough tannin for grip. Drink now through 2000. 670 cases made. • $18 • (10/15/97) • **84**
Les Collines de Laure Vin de Table Français 1993 • $18 • (12/31/95) • **76**
St.-Joseph 1994: Bright fruit and tender tannins make this wine accessible now. Offers rich flavors of blackberries and raspberries, with smoky accents and some elegance. Drink now through 1999. • $17 • (11/30/96) • **85**
St.-Joseph Les Lauves 1994: Bright, crisp flavors of blackberries and black cherries give definition, while accents of chocolate and coffee give depth. Medium-bodied, vivid and fresh. Drinks well now; should hold through 2000 or so. 340 cases made. • $23 • (10/15/97) • **86**
Syrah Vin de Table Français Les Collines de Laure 1996: A juicy, blackberry-scented red that delivers ripe, round black-fruit character up front, finishes on the short side. Enjoy now. 1,000 cases made. • $16 • (09/30/97) • **82**
Viognier-Roussanne Côtes du Rhône 1994: Round, clean and silky, offering subdued flavors that hint of pineapple and almonds. Fresh on the palate, expanding on the finish. Well knit and balanced. • $16 • (10/15/96) • **86**

COLOUR VOLANT

Cabernet Sauvignon Vin de Pays d'Oc 1995: Freshly sawed wood and vanilla flavors dominate any fruit in this red, making it a little disjointed. Drinkable now. • $9 • (08/31/97) • **81**
Chardonnay Vin de Pays d'Oc 1995: An overtly oaky style of Chardonnay that stresses buttery, spicy, smoky flavors over the modest fruit component. Still, it's smooth and appealing. • $9 • (08/31/97) • **82**
Merlot Vin de Pays d'Oc 1995: American oak rounds out this red, giving it clove and vanilla flavors that overpower the simple cherry tones. Still, it's appealing. • $9 • (08/31/97) • **81**

COMBE, PIERRE

Côtes du Rhône-Villages Domaine des Richards 1990 • $7 • (10/15/91) BB • **89**
Côtes du Rhône-Villages Domaine des Richards 1987 • $4 • (01/31/89) • **78**

Vacqueyras Domaine des Richards Red 1989 • $9 • (10/15/91) • **86**

COMBEBELLE, CHÂTEAU DE

St.-Chinian Comte Cathare 1994: There's a nice chocolaty aroma to this wine, with good flavors of plum and raspberry. It finishes with brown sugar and cola notes. • $10 • (05/31/98) • **84**

COMBIER, DOMAINE

Crozes-Hermitage 1995: A bit simple, with crisp character, stewed tomato notes, a vegetal quality, but there's some ripeness underneath it all. • $18 • (10/15/97) • **78**
Crozes-Hermitage 1994: Round and supple, this approachable red offers black pepper, gamy and light black-cherry flavors, pleasant and straightforward. Drinkable now. 2,500 cases made. • $20 • (11/30/96) • **83**
Crozes-Hermitage 1992 • $14 • (10/15/94) • **85**
Crozes-Hermitage 1991 • $17 • (05/31/94) • **86**
Crozes-Hermitage Clos des Grives 1995: Well made, polished and international style Crozes, with well-integrated tannins, plenty of mocha, toasty spice, currant and black cherry character. A sexy, medium-bodied wine. Drinkable now. • $25 • (10/15/97) • **88**
Crozes-Hermitage Clos des Grives 1994: Concentrated and well integrated, this ripe wine offers bright plum and licorice flavors filled out nicely by toast and coffee flavors that suggest new-wood aging. Not typical for the region, but attractive and age worthy. 850 cases made. • $35 • (11/30/96) • **91**
Crozes-Hermitage Clos des Grives 1992 • $20 • (10/15/94) • **87**
Crozes-Hermitage Clos des Grives 1991 • $25 • (05/31/94) • **84**
Crozes-Hermitage Clos des Grives 1990 • $20 • (04/15/93) • **92**
Crozes-Hermitage White 1996: Generous, combining round flavors of pear, almond and spice with crisp, citrusy acidity. It's a bit short, but lively and clean. Should blossom with food. • $20 • (10/15/97) • **85**

COMMANDERIE, CHÂTEAU LA

Pomerol 1995: Solid, chunky, featuring firm and rich tannins, loads of berry, cherry flavor and long finish. • $NA • (05/15/96) (BT) • **85-89**
Pomerol 1991: Herbal and fruity, but rather watery. Tasted twice with consistent notes. • $15 • (03/31/94) • **72**
St.-Emilion 1997: Decent fruit, but a rather hollow midpalate. Light- to medium-bodied, with light tannins and a light finish. A bit lean. • $NA • (06/15/98) (BT) • **80-84**
St.-Emilion 1996: Pleasant fruit character in this medium-bodied wine, which doesn't try to do too much with what it has. Medium, velvety tannins and a refreshing finish. • $20 • (06/15/98) (BT) • **85-89**
St.-Emilion 1995: Vibrant, with plenty of crushed berry character and fresh acidity. Slightly one-dimensional. A wine for early drinking. • $NA • (01/01/97) (BT) • **85-89**
St.-Emilion 1994: Delivers more on the nose than on the palate, with it's lovely herb-accented aromas of chocolate and berry. Slightly green tannins and fruity finish. Drink now. 2,916 cases made. • $18 • (01/31/97) • **83**
St.-Emilion 1993: Elegant and quite firm, offering a decent core of plum, red berry, tobacco, cedar and chocolate notes. Of medium body, it's a bit one-dimensional. Drinkable now. • $15 • (01/31/96) • **83**
St.-Emilion 1989 • $19 • (03/15/92) • **92**
St.-Emilion 1988 • $15 • (10/31/91) • **79**
St.-Emilion 1983 • $11 • (01/01/86) • **79**

CONFURON, JEAN-JACQUES

Chambolle-Musigny 1994: Lithe but quite intense, this packs some nice raspberry, rose petal and plum flavors. Light-bodied, it's a touch sharp on the finish. Drinkable now. • $35 • (11/15/96) • **82**
Chambolle-Musigny 1989 • $35 • (11/30/92) • **81**
Chambolle-Musigny Premier Cru 1995: Awkward. The wood and tannins in this assertively oaky wine overwhelm whatever fruit there is. Drinkable now. • $62 • (11/15/97) • **84**
Chambolle-Musigny Premier Cru 1994: Ripe, open-textured and fresh, layered with berry, rose petal and chocolate flavors that keep singing on the generous finish. Drinkable now. • $50 • (11/15/96) • **90**
Chambolle-Musigny Premier Cru 1993: Amazing quality for a *premier cru*. A reserved and complex red Burgundy that opens up subltly. Full in body, offering chocolate, mineral and berry character, full tannins and a long finish. Superb. Try after 2000. 15 cases made. • $60 • (11/15/95) HR • **94**
Chambolle-Musigny Premier Cru 1991: Light in texture but ripe in flavor, showing floral, prune and currant aromas and flavors, finishing firm and crisp, almost with a lime edge. Drinkable now. • $37 Ⓐ • (01/31/94) • **86**
Clos de Vougeot 1994: Smooth, velvety and appealing for its layers of plum, currant and rose petal flavors against a firm backbone of beautifully balanced acidity. Nicely packaged with fine tannins and remarkable freshness. Should be an elegant charmer by 2000 or 2002. • $80 • (11/15/96) • **90**
Clos Vougeot 1993: Tough now, a wine with a future. Dried cherry and dried herb flavors, medium-to-full body, firm tannins and a long, spicy, tannic finish. Better in 2000. • $85 • (11/15/95) • **90**
Clos Vougeot 1991: Displays a firm texture, a moderate level of anise-scented raspberry flavor and a bit of chewiness on the finish. Drinkable now. • $60 Ⓐ • (01/31/94) • **85**
Côte de Nuits-Villages Les Vignottes 1994: A coating of drying tannins gets in the way of the modest raspberry flavors at first, but the flavors are intense enough to peek through on the finish. Try now. • $22 • (11/15/96) • **81**
Côte de Nuits-Villages Les Vignottes 1989 • $16 • (11/30/92) • **84**
Nuits-St.-Georges Aux Boudots 1995: For fans of oak. Aromas and flavors of black fruit, coffee and smoky oak. Smooth yet structured, with mouthpuckering tannins and vibrant acidity that need until 2000 to integrate. • $62 • (11/15/97) • **85**
Nuits-St.-Georges Aux Boudots 1989 • $32 • (11/30/92) • **81**
Nuits-St.-Georges Les Chaboeufs 1995: Soft, supple and a touch diluted, with nice subtlety that builds to sweet, ripe tannins and cherry, raspberry flavors. Medium-bodied, it's long but a bit hot on the finish. Tempting upon release through 2002. • $56 • (11/15/97) • **83**
Nuits-St.-Georges Les Chaboeufs 1994: Strives for elegance, weaving very pretty oaky vanilla notes through the currant and plum flavors and finishing with well-integrated tannins. Best now. • $45 • (11/15/96) • **88**
Nuits-St.-Georges Les Chaboeufs 1993: Firm and hard at this stage, medium-bodied, a mineral, earthy character blanketing the pretty currant and black cherry notes. Drinkable now. • $60 • (11/15/95) • **89**
Nuits-St.-Georges Les Chaboeufs 1989 • $32 • (11/30/92) • **83**
Nuits-St.-Georges Les Fleurières 1993: A well-made, fresh, medium-bodied Nuits, sporting enticing plum, currant, toast and spice character. Loads of tannins clamp down on the finish, so give it until 2000. • $45 • (11/15/95) • **90**
Nuits-St.-Georges Les Fleurières 1989 • $26 • (11/30/92) • **69**
Romanée St.-Vivant 1994: Round, silky and layered with mocha-scented plum, blackberry, spice and tobacco flavors that glow with the polish of refined tannins. The oak is a key component, but there is plenty of fruit character to carry it through 2001 to 2005, at least. • $120 • (11/15/96) • **91**
Romanée St.-Vivant 1993: Not as big as expected from this *grand cru*, but impressive. Very fresh citrus, berry and plum aromas and flavors, medium body and fine tannins. Drinkable now. • $150 • (11/15/95) • **89**
Romanée St.-Vivant 1989 • $113 • (10/31/92) • **90**
Vosne-Romanée Les Beaux Monts 1995: Blackberry and spicy oak flavors are wonderfully integrated in this full-bodied '95. The texture is like raw silk, and the acidity and tannin suggest waiting until 2000. Long, smoky finish. • $70 • (11/15/97) • **90**
Vosne-Romanée Les Beaux Monts 1993: Smelling this is like walking into a flower shop. Better than his Romanée-St.-Vivant. Lovely perfumes and fabulous concentration of fruit, adding loads of tannins and an ultralong, fruity finish. Superb potential. Better after 2000. • $63 • (11/15/95) • **94**

CONFURON-COTETIDOT, J.

Chambolle-Musigny 1993: Very flavorful, quite thick and rich, chunky texture. Lots of coffee, smoke, cassis and pepper notes and a chewy finish. Slightly rustic village wine. Try in 2000. • $NA • (05/15/96) • **88**
Chambolle-Musigny 1992: Light but smooth and supple, with an herbal edge to the modest berry notes. Finishes with a little more flavor than most 1992 Chambolles. • $38 • (12/15/94) • **83**
Chambolle-Musigny 1991: Simple and coarse, fruity enough to be pleasant, but has little Pinot or Chambolle character. • $41 Ⓐ • (01/31/94) • **74**
Chambolle-Musigny 1989 • $32 • (11/30/92) • **89**
Clos de Vougeot 1993: Very smoky, almost meaty, showing loads of berry, cassis and ripe fruit character, medium-to-full body, loads of velvety tannins and a long finish. Delicious now, but better in 2000. • $NA • (05/15/96) • **89**
Clos de Vougeot 1991: Supple and generous, this elegant wine features spicy, toasty chocolate, black cherry and blackberry aromas and flavors. Finishes smooth and delicate, echoing fruit and spice. Drinkable now. • $65 Ⓐ • (01/31/94) • **86**

FRANCE

Clos de Vougeot 1989 • $60 • (09/15/92) HR • **91**

Echézeaux 1993: Disappointing wine from this producer. Rather earthy and raisiny and a slightly watery finish. Disjointed. Drinkable now. • $NA • (05/15/96) • **81**

Echézeaux 1991: Looks and feels tired already; offers more gamy, toasty aromas and flavors than fruit. • $65 Ⓐ • (01/31/94) • **79**

Echézeaux 1990: A hard wine that needs time, but the texture and concentration are superb enough to provide a seductive, round mouthfeel. Has subdued raspberry and vanilla flavors and a long finish. Try now. • $65 • (12/15/92) • **91**

Echézeaux 1989 • $NA • (10/31/92) • **83**

Gevrey-Chambertin 1993: Deep-colored village wine, sporting pure cassis and black currant flavors. Sweet-tasting, as a wet earth component adds complexity. Don't expect showy opulence, just a beam of crisp, youthful, well-defined fruit. • $NA • (05/15/96) • **94**

Gevrey-Chambertin Lavaut St.-Jacques 1995: Distinctive, this medium-bodied red is a bit forward, with plum, cassis, prune and mocha flavors and soft texture. Kicks in with juicy intensity on the finish. Tempting upon release. • $70 • (11/15/97) • **85**

Nuits-St.-Georges 1995: Balanced, ripe and smooth, this Nuits is highly flavorful, sweet-tasting, fruity and round. Its wet earth, green- and black-olive, wild raspberry and dried herbs character seduces the senses. Full-bodied and silky, it has the compacted tannins to last through 2000 to 2002. • $50 • (11/15/97) • **89**

Nuits-St.-Georges 1993: Excellent village wine that bursts with vibrant cassis and currant flavors and a toasty, if slightly tart, finish. This medium-bodied Burgundy will be pretty but not showy in aging. Try around 2000. • $NA • (05/15/96) • **89**

Nuits-St.-Georges 1992: Unusual for its aromas that are difficult to describe. Has a cinnamon-scented, red berry character, with some spice notes and a tart, crisp finish. Appealing and drinkable now. • $38 • (12/15/94) • **84**

Nuits-St.-Georges Premier Cru 1993: Super personality, bursting with bright cassis and Syrahlike flavors. Very peppery, medium-to-full body, long, delicious finish. Try in 2000. • $NA • (05/15/96) • **89**

Nuits-St.-Georges Premier Cru 1991: Light and airy, showing pleasant currant and vanilla aromas and flavors. Drinkable now. • $47 Ⓐ • (01/31/94) • **77**

Nuits-St.-Georges Premier Cru 1990: Has a wonderful mouthfeel, with velvety tannins and concentrated, beautiful ripe plum and tobacco characteristics. Drinkable now. • $28 • (12/15/92) • **91**

Vosne-Romanée 1995: Wild and feral, showing plum and spice flavors, this should please fans of exotic red Burgundy. Solidly tannic finish. Try in 2000. • $48 • (11/15/97) • **87**

Vosne-Romanée 1993: What happened here? Rather light and weedy, showing some fruit cassis flavors, but medium-bodied at best and a weedy finish. Not very exciting. • $NA • (05/15/96) • **80**

Vosne-Romanée 1992: Sharp and tart, with floral, gamy, peppery notes that give it some character. Ends a bit short. • $34 • (12/15/94) • **78**

Vosne-Romanée 1990: Big and bulky, with loads of fruit and tannins. An impressive wine, but lacks a bit of finesse. Drinkable now. • $30 • (12/15/92) • **84**

Vosne-Romanée 1989 • $27 • (10/31/92) • **89**

Vosne-Romanée Les Suchots 1995: Very fruity, almost Port-like, showing cassis and plum flavors up front, yet the fat and richness don't follow through on the finish, and the tannnins are dry. Still, it's appealing. • $60 • (11/15/97) • **85**

Vosne-Romanée Les Suchots 1993: A middle-of-the-road '93, delivering some decent mocha, red berry and smoke flavors. Lacks a bit of depth and complexity. Quite crisp on the finish. Try now. • $NA • (05/15/96) • **84**

Vosne-Romanée Les Suchots 1991: A crisp, toasty, austere wine that features an anise tinge to the basic black cherry aromas and flavors. Turns herbal on the finish. Drinkable now. • $NA • (01/31/94) • **81**

Vosne-Romanée Les Suchots 1990: This light-textured Vosne is pleasant, offering modest cherry and strawberry flavors, but has a rather short finish. Sweet in flavor and round, but shows odd stewed tomato notes. Drinkable now. • $44 • (12/15/92) • **83**

Key: SS—Spectator Selection CS—Cellar Selection HR—Highly Recommended BB—Best Buy $NA—Price not available Ⓐ—Auction Price (BT)—Barrel Tasting
Dates in parentheses indicate the issues in which the ratings were published.

CONNÉTABLE DE TALBOT

St.-Julien 1995: Pretty, ready-to-drink '95. Attractive aromas of cream and raspberries. Medium- to light-bodied, with fine tannins and a light, fresh finish. Second label of Château Talbot. Drink now. • $18 • (01/31/98) • **84**

CONSEILLANTE, CHÂTEAU LA

Pomerol 1995: Fab red. Aromatic and elegant, with lovely violet, floral and fruity aromas and flavors. Full-bodied, with velvety tannins. Ripe fruit aftertaste has a hint of dark chocolate. Best after 2000. • $68 Ⓐ • (01/31/98) • **94**

Pomerol 1992: This entry has always been disappointing. Very light and fresh, diluted, offering floral and strawberry aromas and flavors. Tasted twice, with consistent notes. • $22 Ⓐ • (04/15/95) • **77**

Pomerol 1990: Pure fruit in this wine shows the true personality of the estate. Enticing aromas of nutmeg, cinnamon and fruit give way to rich, silky tannins. Drinkable now. 5,000 cases made. • $110 Ⓐ • (03/31/93) • **94**

Pomerol 1989 • $173 Ⓐ • (03/15/92) • **92**
Pomerol 1988 • $45 Ⓐ • (03/31/91) • **90**
Pomerol 1987 • $35 Ⓐ • (05/15/90) • **86**
Pomerol 1986 • $57 Ⓐ • (06/15/89) • **93**
Pomerol 1985 • $182 Ⓐ • (02/29/88) • **93**
Pomerol 1984 • $26 • (03/31/87) • **93**
Pomerol 1983 • $46 Ⓐ • (11/15/86) • **84**
Pomerol 1982 • $120 Ⓐ • (08/31/92) • **87**
Pomerol 1981 • $61 Ⓐ • (10/15/94) • **88**
Pomerol 1962 • $55 • (11/30/87) • **60**
Pomerol 1961 • $573 Ⓐ • (04/30/96) • **87**
Pomerol 1959 • $122 Ⓐ • (10/15/90) • **88**
Pomerol 1947 • $477 Ⓐ • (05/31/97) • **87**
Pomerol 1945 • $509 Ⓐ • (11/30/95) • **88**

CORBIN-MICHOTTE, CHÂTEAU

St.-Emilion 1995: Lovely soft wine with an abundance of cherry, berry and vanilla aromas and flavors. Medium body and velvety tannins on the finish. Harmonious. • $NA • (05/15/96) (BT) • **85-89**

St.-Emilion 1988 • $15 • (07/15/91) • **72**
St.-Emilion 1961 • $NA • (04/30/96) • **86**

CORCIA

Chambolle-Musigny 1992: Delicate with very pretty raspberry and spicy oak flavors on a frame that remains smooth and silky through the finish. Just a touch of tannin on the aftertaste. Drinkable now. • $22 • (12/15/94) • **83**

Clos de Vougeot 1992: Plummier than most, with a nice beam of currant and spice pushing through the firm tannins. Has richness, smokiness and style, then finishes a little short. Drinkable now. • $42 • (12/15/94) • **88**

Nuits-St.-Georges 1992: Lean and a little spicy, with modest berry and currant flavors that narrow down on the finish. • $22 • (12/15/94) • **79**

Vosne-Romanée 1992: Tough and chewy but finishing with enough finesse to be worth cellaring. Leathery in both texture and flavor, it only hints at currant on the finish. Try now. • $26 • (12/15/94) • **80**

CORDEILLAN-BAGES, CHÂTEAU

Pauillac 1995: Another elegant, seductive '95. Rich, ripe and balanced, with lovely red- and blackberry character backed by supple, sweet tannins and spicy, slightly smoky flavors. • $NA • (05/15/96) (BT) • **90-94**

Pauillac 1994: Shows plenty of new wood and concentrated fruit. Medium- to full-bodied with chocolate and berry flavors and a silky finish. Drinkable now. 1,000 cases made. • $20 • (01/31/97) • **88**

Pauillac 1992: Holds together beautifully on the palate, displaying plum, chocolate and light tobacco character, medium body and finish and medium, velvety tannins. • $18 • (04/15/95) • **85**

Pauillac 1991: Very nicely crafted. It has the character of tobacco, smoke and bitter chocolate, with medium body. Firm but slightly astringent on finish. • $16 • (03/31/94) • **83**

Pauillac 1990: A deep, dark giant, with smoky, cassis aromas and flavors and tons of fruit and tannins. Doesn't show much now but it's all there. Drinkable in 2000. 900 cases made. • $33 • (03/31/93) • **95**

Pauillac 1989 • $24 • (03/15/92) • **96**

CORDIER PÈRE & FILS

Mâcon 1995: Well made. Full-bodied, silky in texture, with a spicy, intense mouthfeel from the oak and tropical flavors. Lively, lemon-spiked acidity keeps it on track, delivering an opulent and fairly clean finish, with a note of burnt bread. Enjoy now through 2000. 1,250 cases made. • $12 • (05/31/98) • **86**

Mâcon Blanc-Villages 1995: A dependable white, fresh, clean and lively, with decent fruit flavors and medium body. Honey and floral aromas mingle with some grassy avocado notes on the pretty finish. Ready to drink. 1,000 cases made. • $12 • (05/31/97) • **84**

Mâcon-Fuissé 1996: A bit tart but with some ripeness of fruit, showing a butter, butterscotch, caramel, honey, lime character. Drinkable now. 400 cases made. • $12 • (05/31/98) • **83**

Pouilly-Fuissé Au Metertière 1996: Exploding with intensity, delivering loads of lime, tropical, grapefruit, pear and apple flavors that won't quit, all in a rich and full-bodied package that gives balance to this wonderful and exciting wine. Touches of honey, butter and spice on the complex, supple finish. Drinkable now. 400 cases made. • $32 • (05/31/98) • **90**

Pouilly-Fuissé Les Vignes Blanches 1996: Just wonderful. A lovely Pouilly, honeyed and lemony, showing a touch of spice, and oak accents. It cascades to a long finish that is a bit too toasty. Drinkable now. 500 cases made. • $32 • (05/31/98) • **88**

Pouilly-Fuissé Les Vignes Blanches 1995: Very ripe, slightly overdone, with oak and caramel flavors dominating. Turns bitter on the finish. Seems a bit oxidized. 583 cases made. • $33 • (05/31/97) • **76**

Pouilly-Fuissé Les Vignes Blanches 1994: Lots of character here, well made and smooth. Plenty of buttery, baked apple pie and herb flavors and a hint of toasty aromas. Balanced finish. Worth seeking out. Drinkable now. 500 cases made. • $34 • (05/31/96) • **87**

Pouilly-Fuissé Les Vignes Blanches 1993: Charming, ripe, seductively crisp pear, mango, apricot and pineapple flavors stay focused on the supple, chalky finish. 500 cases made. • $22 • (05/15/95) • **87**

Pouilly-Fuissé Lot No. 1 1995: Slightly overdone. Rather ripe and fat, with some buttery-accented fruit and honey flavors. Lacks intensity and focus. Heavy finish. Drink now. 1,000 cases made. • $25 • (05/31/97) • **77**

Pouilly-Fuissé Lot No. 1 1994: Serious Pouilly here. Focused and well constructed, showing earth, mineral, spice, fig and honey complexity. Good fruit intensity and finishing with smooth finesse. Buy a case and enjoy! 833 cases made. • $21 • (05/31/96) • **88**

Pouilly-Fuissé Lot No. 1 1993: Excellent concentration of fruit; medium-bodied, flavorful. Ripe pear, apple, honey and mineral notes turn to a lovely, fresh lime finish. Drinkable now. 833 cases made. • $19 • (05/15/95) • **87**

Pouilly-Fuissé Lot No. 2 1995: Fabulous. Tightly wound and firmly structured, with a silky mouthfeel, yet it's bursting with subtle honey and fruit, especially citrus, aromas and flavors, with some understated, oak shading. Long, long finish. Like being a five-year-old licking a lollipop, you can't stop drinking this one. Tempting now through 2000. 1,250 cases made. • $25 • (05/31/97) • **92**

Pouilly-Fuissé Lot No. 2 1994: Intensely crisp, citrusy and quite lean. Somewhat herbal, offering a touch of honey. Slightly one-dimensional. Should do well with shellfish. 1,666 cases made. • $21 • (05/31/96) • **82**

Pouilly-Fuissé Lot No. 2 1993: Super-intense, crisp and tart. Ripe yet vibrant palate showing pear, apple, honey and tropical fruit flavors. Medium-bodied; drinkable now. 500 cases made. • $19 • (05/15/95) • **86**

Pouilly-Fuissé Lot No. 3 1995: Wonderful, showing impressive concentration. medium-to-full body, with a honeyed thread running through; the citrusy fruit and toasty oak character kicks in with great intensity on the long, succulent finish. Drink now through 2000. 300 cases made. • $25 • (05/31/97) • **89**

Pouilly-Fuissé Vieilles Vignes 1996: Superb wine, smooth and supple, with a creamlike texture that caresses the palate. Sensual Chardonnay, cascading with lovely fruit, honeysuckle, spice and toasty oak accents. Full-bodied, it fills your senses. Long, clean, lemony finish. Tempting now through 2000. 1,000 cases made. • $29 • (05/31/98) • **94**

Pouilly-Fuissé Vieilles Vignes 1995: Sweet-tasting and full-bodied, but slightly overdone. Not as good as this producer's regular Pouilly. Drink now. 2,000 cases made. • $35 • (05/31/97) • **78**

Pouilly-Fuissé Vieilles Vignes 1994: Crisp, sharp and tart, in an uncompromisingly citrusy style. For those who love intense Chardonnay, sporting herbal and oregano flavors. Not for everyone, but delightful with mussels or oysters. 500 cases made. • $30 • (05/31/96) • **84**

Pouilly-Fuissé Vieilles Vignes 1993: Clean, crisp pear, green apple skin and honey flavors unfold almost sweetly on the finish. Medium in body. Try with seafood. 500 cases made. • $22 • (05/15/95) • **85**

Pouilly-Fuissé Vieilles Vignes 2ème Tri Sélection 1996: Surprisingly rich and ripe for a '96 Pouilly, offering gobs of honey, orange zest, pear, butter, oaky spice and butterscotch flavors. Full-bodied and well made, for people who love the fat sort of Pouilly. Has a lingering, lemony finish. Tempting now. 50 cases made. • $63 • (05/31/98) • **86**

Pouilly-Fuissé Vieilles Vignes Grapillage 1996: Lovely wine. Full-bodied and ripe, with multifaceted character, showing fine complexity of fruit and oak, with butter, orange zest, floral, mocha and honey notes. A long, clean and balanced finish, in a smoky, toasty style. Try around 2000. 50 cases made. • $63 • (05/31/98) • **88**

St.-Véran Clos à la Côte 1996: Ah! Ripe fruit character makes this stand out. Like biting into a ripe pear, plus dollops of honey, lime, spice and toasty bread from the oak. With lovely complexity and good balance, this is a delight to drink now through 2000. Buy a case and enjoy. 215 cases made. • $21 • (05/31/98) • **88**

CORMEIL-FIGEAC, CHÂTEAU

St.-Emilion 1988 • $20 • (04/30/91) • **85**

St.-Emilion 1986 • $12 • (06/30/89) • **75**

CORNEAU, DOMAINE PAUL

Pouilly-Fumé Tradition 1996: This firm wine isn't giving much right now, but its concentration is promising. Beneath the firm texture and fine acidity are hints of minerals, herbs and ripe fruit that should blossom with time. Best now through 2001. • $15 • (05/31/98) • **88**

CORNU, EDMOND

Aloxe-Corton 1995: The color of rosé, it tastes like wine cut with water. Some modest raspberry, spice and strawberry flavors. Tough finish. 625 cases made. • $29 • (11/15/97) • **75**

Aloxe-Corton 1994: Light, spicy and floral in character, but not much charm to it. • $26 • (11/15/96) • **77**

Aloxe-Corton 1991: Crisp and light, with a modest thread of black cherry flavor cutting through the citrus. Drinkable now. 500 cases made. • $24 Ⓐ • (01/31/94) • **78**

Aloxe-Corton Les Moutottes 1991 • $33 • (01/31/94) • **85**

Aloxe-Corton Les Moutottes 1987 • $35 • (12/31/90) • **83**

Aloxe-Corton Les Valozières 1995: A lovely '95, smooth and ripe, with the tannins wonderfully integrated but still present. Full-bodied, it offers plenty of depth, with flavors of blackberry, *griottes*, toasty spicy oak and mocha, and just a slight herbal hint. Cellar until 2000 for the tannins to soften. 125 cases made. • $40 • (11/15/97) • **87**

Bourgogne 1995: Light and diluted, there's not much here—a modest wine seemingly cut with water. 416 cases made. • $15 • (11/15/97) • **71**

Bourgogne 1990: Ripe and concentrated, with a lovely mouthfeel and a silky texture. Shows nice violet, strawberry and black cherry flavors and a focused, delicious finish. Drink and enjoy on release. 500 cases made. • $15 • (12/15/92) • **85**

Chorey-lès-Beaune Les Bons Ores 1995: Light, herbal, and barely tasting of Pinot Noir. 660 cases made. • $19 • (11/15/97) • **75**

Chorey-lès-Beaune Les Bons Ores 1994: This is drying, earthy and thin on the palate. • $22 • (11/15/96) • **73**

Chorey-lès-Beaune Les Bons Ores 1993: Crisp, odd, earthy, herbal character. May be at a strange phase now, only to improve later. Still quite lean and lacking some fruit. Drinkable now. 583 cases made. • $20 • (11/15/95) • **81**

Chorey-lès-Beaune Les Bons Ores 1992: Aromatic and attractive, with a minty, velvety currant character, good color and medium body. A pleasant, flavorful '92. Drinkable now. 150 cases made. • $17 • (12/15/94) • **85**

Corton Les Bressandes 1995: A core of sweet, raspberry and cherry flavor is waiting to emerge from behind the firm structure in this medium-bodied red. Drinkable now. 150 cases made. • $60 • (11/15/97) • **83**

Corton Les Bressandes 1994: An accessible style of Corton, molding its polished cherry and chocolate flavors into a smooth package. Narrows on the finish. Drinkable now. • $55 • (11/15/96) • **83**

Corton Les Bressandes 1993: Supple red of medium intensity and body, a bit closed now, but showing some pretty plum and red berry character. 183 cases made. • $57 • (11/15/95) • **87**

Corton Les Bressandes 1992: Lean and bright, with focused raspberry, spice and vanilla flavors that linger on the narrow finish. Try now. • $43 • (12/15/94) • **81**

FRANCE

Corton Les Bressandes 1991: Smooth, elegant and lovely; the beautifully defined black cherry and raspberry flavors are refined through the lithe finish. Drinkable now. 200 cases made. • $48 Ⓐ • (01/31/94) • **88**

Corton Les Bressandes 1990: A solid Corton, with smoky, earthy plum aromas and flavors and very firm tannins. A well-made wine to drink now. 200 cases made. • $60 • (12/15/92) • **89**

Corton Les Bressandes 1987 • $53 • (12/31/90) • **90**

Ladoix 1994: Very light, rosélike, with spicy cinnamon nuances to the thin strawberry flavors. • $24 • (11/15/96) • **79**

Ladoix 1993: Some sweet, pretty fruit character features light plum aromas and flavors, medium to light body, light tannins and a fresh finish. Drink now. 608 cases made. • $22 • (11/15/95) • **82**

Ladoix 1992: A pretty wine, with medium body, good fruit and a smooth finish. The raspberry and blackberry flavors are delicious. 38 cases made. • $18 • (12/15/94) • **80**

Ladoix 1991: Earth, anise and tar aromas and flavors turn tough and bitter on the finish. The fruit comes in to make it more appealing. Drinkable now. 583 cases made. • $18 Ⓐ • (01/31/94) • **81**

Ladoix 1987 • $18 • (02/28/91) • **78**

Ladoix La Corvée 1992: Flavorful currant, raspberry and violet notes. Dark color, but relatively light texture. Attractively built. Drink now. 38 cases made. • $25 • (12/15/94) • **84**

Ladoix La Corvée 1991: Light, smooth and simple, with appealing currant and cooked berry flavors. Drinkable now. 167 cases made. • $24 Ⓐ • (01/31/94) • **79**

Ladoix Les Carrières 1995: Light and diluted, this offers little in the way of fruit, and the tannins are dry. 300 cases made. • $25 • (11/15/97) • **75**

Ladoix Les Carrières 1994: Light and charming, more like a rosé, with delicate watermelon flavors. • $26 • (11/15/96) • **80**

Ladoix Les Carrières 1993: A beauty, showing supple texture and delicious complexity of smoke, earth, plum and currant, medium body, well-integrated tannins and good power on the finish. Try now. 375 cases made. • $27 • (11/15/95) • **89**

Ladoix Les Carrières 1992: Light but chewy, with the tannins and earthy-mineral notes more prominent than the prune flavor. Try now. 38 cases made. • $22 • (12/15/94) • **78**

Ladoix Les Corvées 1995: Somewhat murky flavors, light and astringent on the finish. 125 cases made. • $28 • (11/15/97) • **74**

Ladoix Vieille Vigne 1995: Red currants and strawberries are the dominant flavors in this elegant, light-bodied red. Moderate tannins. Drinkable now. 830 cases made. • $20 • (11/15/97) • **80**

Savigny-lès-Beaune 1995: Shows some decent, spicy strawberry notes, but this is lean and tough. 150 cases made. • $20 • (11/15/97) • **76**

Savigny-lès-Beaune 1994: Marked by green, minty aromas and flavors that lack charm. • $22 • (11/15/96) • **74**

Savigny-lès-Beaune 1993: Rather hard red does not give much on the palate of firm tannins and crisp acidity, but has some good fruit underneath. Medium-bodied, sweet fruit finish. Drinkable now. 375 cases made. • $22 • (11/15/95) • **85**

Savigny-lès-Beaune 1992: Light and simple, a modest level of black cherry and floral flavors giving it some class. Drinkable now. 50 cases made. • $18 • (12/15/94) • **81**

CORON PÈRE & FILS

Beaune 1995: Broad on the palate, this red offers cherry, blackberry and spice character. Oak aging adds roundness and a hint of vanilla on the finish. • $25 • (11/15/97) • **85**

Beaune Le Clos des Mouches 1995: Ripe cherry and plum flavors combine with toasty oak notes to provide a bit of richness. It's concentrated and intense but very tight, with austere tannins. Drinkable now. • $43 • (11/15/97) • **85**

Chassagne-Montrachet 1995: Interesting. Shows the viscous, creamlike velvetiness typical of the '95 vintage. Elegant at first, with pear, apple and hazelnut notes, it turns a bit odd with marzipan and a slight cardboard character that isn't totally clean. Drink now. • $33 • (01/31/98) • **84**

Clos de Vougeot 1995: Massive and backward. It's difficult to get a sense of this monolith, yet it's packed full of spicy cherry and earth character. Only the sweet oak and fruit notes on the long finish indicate its potential. • $63 • (11/15/97) • **90**

Key: SS—Spectator Selection CS—Cellar Selection HR—Highly Recommended BB—Best Buy $NA—Price not available Ⓐ—Auction Price (BT)—Barrel Tasting
Dates in parentheses indicate the issues in which the ratings were published.

Gevrey-Chambertin Lavaut St.-Jacques 1995: This has a lifted, acetone element on the nose in addition to the new oak, then turns weak and stemmy on the palate. Tasted twice, with consistent notes. • $53 • (11/15/97) • **77**

Mâcon-Loché Château de Loché 1995: New oak adds dimension and spice to the apple and mineral flavors. The finish is firm and chalky, with a buttery note. • $14 • (10/15/97) • **84**

Meursault 1995: Disappointing. Starts out with good finesse, but a tart, woody taste takes over and it turns bitter. Drink chilled, if you must. • $31 • (01/31/98) • **78**

Moulin-à-Vent Domaine de la Roche 1995: Want a traditional Moulin-à-Vent? Try this. It's firm and rather austere, with game and earth notes dominating the black fruit flavors and no new oak in sight. Not a blockbuster, but very well-made. 5,000 cases made. • $13 • (04/30/97) • **87**

Nuits-St.-Georges 1995: There's an earthy, vegetal edge to the plum and vanilla flavors. The dry tannins are prominent on the finish. Drinkable now. • $33 • (10/15/97) • **83**

Nuits-St.-Georges Les Cailles 1995: Good concentration and a velvety feel mark this savage and feral red. A firm, tannic style with cherry, plum, smoke and mint flavors that need until 2000 to resolve. • $52 • (11/15/97) • **86**

Pommard Les Epenots 1995: Beautiful aromas of black cherry and spice, accented by new oak, are followed by black fruit flavors and a rough-silk texture, all supported by a firmly tannic structure. Needs until 2000. • $54 • (11/15/97) • **87**

Pouilly-Fuissé 1995: Pleasant and simple, it offers light honey character but lacks concentration. • $24 • (10/15/97) • **79**

Pouilly-Vinzelles Château de Loché 1995: There's added depth to the honey, citrus and mineral flavors, along with richness. It finishes a bit short. • $19 • (10/15/97) • **84**

St.-Véran Domaine de Montagny 1995: An appealing St.-Véran, redolent of honey, vanilla and apple, all in a slightly rustic style. • $19 • (10/15/97) • **83**

Santenay 1995: The aromas and flavors are muted in this smooth red, and there's a chewy, licorice quality to it. Moderate tannins on the finish. • $22 • (11/15/97) • **77**

Vosne-Romanée Les Suchots 1995: Impressive winemaking. This subtle, reserved and well-made '95 displays a depth of cassis, blackberry and rose petal notes. The texture is fairly delicate, but the intensity kicks in on the balanced finish. Try after 2000. • $54 • (11/15/97) • **88**

CORSIN

Mâcon-Villages 1996: Just wonderful—sweet, ripe and balanced, smooth and round. Bursting with floral, citrus and succulent pear flavors, even touches of apricot and fig and, on the finish, notes of honey and melon. Unusually dense in texture for a Mâcon-Villages. Delicious. Buy a case, or two. 917 cases made. • $13 • (08/31/97) • **91**

Mâcon-Villages 1995: Impressively well-made village wine. Silky textured pear, honey, spice and toasty bread flavors. Fresh, citrusy finish with a note of hay. Tempting now. • $NA • (08/31/96) • **88**

Mâcon-Villages 1994: Delicious, racy, well-defined lime, hay, butter and honey notes. Round yet vibrant, it sparks with life and a long finish. Drink now. • $12 • (08/31/95) • **86**

Pouilly-Fuissé 1996: Lovely. Ripe, lush and quite generous, with sweet-tasting lime, honey, pear and tropical flavors. Balanced and just delicious, this medium- to full-bodied white turns elegant and long on the finish. Enjoy now through 2000. 1,375 cases made. • $23 • (05/31/98) • **92**

Pouilly-Fuissé 1995: Polished and subtle, with well-defined ripe fruit, especially citrus, character. Medium in body, it needs time to show more. Try now. 1,208 cases made. • $20 • (05/31/97) • **87**

St.-Véran 1996: Delicious. Shows ripe fruit character and good balance between the lime, honey, pear and pie tart flavors. Medium-bodied, complex and well-made, with a smoky, toasty, spicy-sweet taste and a clean, pure finish. Drink now through 2002. 1,650 cases made. • $16 • (05/31/98) • **88**

St.-Véran 1995: Oak flavors dominate at this point, but there is fruit beneath. Shows some vanilla, mineral, pear and apple notes, too. Try now. 1,500 cases made. • $15 • (05/31/97) • **84**

St.-Véran 1994: Impressively structured, silky-textured, showing depth and complexity and super layers of mineral, wet hay, pear, spice and melon. Very smooth, almond-flavored finish. • $15 • (08/31/95) • **87**

St.-Véran 1993: Youthful yet creamy-textured, with rich, buttery overtones. Provides some mineral notes on the somewhat astringent finish. • $15 • (08/31/95) • **83**

St.-Véran Tirage Précoce 1996: Clean, pure and flavorful, with lime and honey, also some tropical, pear, cream and mineral notes. Well made and fairly complex, of light-to-medium body, it's a delight to drink now. 1,590 cases made. • $15 • (05/31/98) • **86**

St.-Véran Tirage Précoce 1995: A big wine that needs time. Intense fruit, grass, mineral and citrus flavors. Full-bodied and slightly coarse on the finish. Try now. Tasted twice with consistent notes. • $NA • (08/31/96) • **88**

CORTON ANDRÉ, CHÂTEAU

Corton 1994: Earthy, muddy flavors dominate the palate and the finish is astringent. • $NA • (11/15/96) • **68**

COS-D'ESTOURNEL, CHÂTEAU

St.-Estèphe 1997: One of the wines of the vintage. Impressive berry and cherry aromas and flavors, with hints of spices. Medium- to full-bodied, with a solid core of fruit and velvety tannins. • $NA • (06/15/98) (BT) • **90-94**

St.-Estèphe 1996: Simply gorgeous, with seductive aromas of ripe berry and cherry highlighted with cinnamon and other sweet spices. Full- bodied, with full, velvety tannins and a long, long finish. Superb. • $75 • (06/15/98) (BT) • **95-99**

St.-Estèphe 1995: Spice rack of a wine, rather exotic. Concentrated aromas of tar, spices and currants. Full-bodied, with loads of velvety tannins and a long, ripe fruit aftertaste. Best after 2002. • $80 • (01/31/98) • **93**

St.-Estèphe 1994: Outstanding quality for the vintage. A full-bodied Bordeaux that offers wonderful aromas of tobacco, berry and cedar, loads of refined tannins and a long, flavorful finish. Better from 2000. 22,000 cases made. • $100 • (01/31/97) HR • **91**

St.-Estèphe 1993: Cos-d'Estournel never lets you down in a vintage. Pretty blackberry character hints of mocha and chocolate. Medium-bodied, adding velvety tannins and toasty oak finish. Drinkable now. • $33 • (01/31/96) • **88**

St.-Estèphe 1992: Impressive for the vintage, displaying a wonderful silky texture and plenty of blackberry and tobacco character. Drinkable now. • $26 • (04/15/95) • **87**

St.-Estèphe 1991: One of the best wines of the vintage. Well focused, with lots of chunky fruit. The vanilla, tobacco and chocolate flavors go on and on. Delicious now. • $31 • (03/31/94) • **88**

St.-Estèphe 1990: Like eating chocolate mousse; this wine delivers loads of chocolate, cherry and berry flavors and soft, round tannins. The '89 was better, however. Drinkable now. 30,000 cases made. • $72 Ⓐ • (03/31/93) • **90**

St.-Estèphe 1989 • $46 Ⓐ • (03/15/92) • **95**
St.-Estèphe 1988 • $36 Ⓐ • (07/15/91) CS • **95**
St.-Estèphe 1987 • $23 • (05/15/90) • **81**
St.-Estèphe 1986 • $62 Ⓐ • (05/31/89) • **93**
St.-Estèphe 1985 • $82 Ⓐ • (10/15/94) • **92**
St.-Estèphe 1984 • $29 • (03/31/87) • **93**
St.-Estèphe 1983 • $37 Ⓐ • (10/15/94) • **91**
St.-Estèphe 1982 • $112 Ⓐ • (08/31/92) • **93**
St.-Estèphe 1981 • $32 Ⓐ • (10/15/94) • **87**
St.-Estèphe 1980 • $33 • (05/15/90) • **83**
St.-Estèphe 1979 • $35 Ⓐ • (10/15/89) • **87**
St.-Estèphe 1978 • $38 Ⓐ • (05/15/90) • **93**
St.-Estèphe 1977 • $30 • (05/15/90) • **85**
St.-Estèphe 1976 • $43 • (05/15/90) • **84**
St.-Estèphe 1975 • $37 Ⓐ • (05/15/90) • **88**
St.-Estèphe 1973 • $31 • (05/15/90) • **82**
St.-Estèphe 1971 • $48 • (05/15/90) • **91**
St.-Estèphe 1970 • $51 Ⓐ • (05/15/90) • **89**
St.-Estèphe 1969 • $26 Ⓐ • (05/15/90) • **58**
St.-Estèphe 1967 • $22 Ⓐ • (05/15/90) • **82**
St.-Estèphe 1966 • $36 Ⓐ • (05/15/90) • **74**
St.-Estèphe 1964 • $65 • (05/15/90) • **84**
St.-Estèphe 1962 • $NA • (11/30/87) • **85**
St.-Estèphe 1961 • $154 Ⓐ • (04/30/96) • **89**
St.-Estèphe 1960 • $85 • (05/15/90) • **79**
St.-Estèphe 1959 • $230 • (10/15/90) • **90**
St.-Estèphe 1958 • $95 • (05/15/90) • **89**
St.-Estèphe 1956 • $60 • (05/15/90) • **79**
St.-Estèphe 1955 • $175 • (05/15/90) • **90**
St.-Estèphe 1954 • $80 • (05/15/90) • **81**
St.-Estèphe 1953 • $51 Ⓐ • (05/15/90) • **91**
St.-Estèphe 1952 • $90 • (05/15/90) • **95**
St.-Estèphe 1950 • $100 • (05/15/90) • **86**
St.-Estèphe 1949 • $195 Ⓐ • (05/15/90) • **80**
St.-Estèphe 1947 • $330 • (05/15/90) • **91**
St.-Estèphe 1945 • $278 Ⓐ • (5/15/90) • **77**
St.-Estèphe 1943 • $220 • (05/15/90) • **85**
St.-Estèphe 1942 • $110 • (05/15/90) • **78**
St.-Estèphe 1934 • $150 • (05/15/90) • **88**
St.-Estèphe 1929 • $390 • (05/15/90) • **92**
St.-Estèphe 1928 • $341 Ⓐ • (05/15/90) • **90**
St.-Estèphe 1926 • $300 • (05/15/90) • **77**
St.-Estèphe 1924 • $300 • (05/15/90) • **82**
St.-Estèphe 1920 • $350 • (05/15/90) • **93**
St.-Estèphe 1917 • $250 • (05/15/90) • **73**
St.-Estèphe 1899 • $700 • (05/15/90) • **87**
St.-Estèphe 1898 • $500 • (05/15/90) • **72**
St.-Estèphe 1870 • $1,250 • (05/15/90) • **90**
St.-Estèphe 1869 • $1,250 • (05/15/90) • **82**

COS-LABORY, CHÂTEAU

St.-Estèphe 1997: Attractive floral and berry aromas follow through on the palate. Medium-bodied, with fine tannins and a medium finish. Well crafted. 21,000 cases made. • $NA • (06/15/98) (BT) • **85-89**

St.-Estèphe 1996: Lovely berry, truffle and mushroom aromas and flavors. Medium- to full-bodied, with velvety tannins and a rich aftertaste. Almost outstanding. 22,000 cases made. • $25 • (06/15/98) (BT) • **85-89**

St.-Estèphe 1995: Slightly lean, but there are some beautiful aromas and flavors and racy tannins. Aromatic, with lovely perfumes of flowers and berries. Full-bodied, with very silky tannins and a fruity aftertaste. Best after 2001. 6,300 cases made. • $22 • (01/31/98) • **88**

St.-Estèphe 1994: A lovely, silky medium-bodied wine, with green tobacco, mint and berry aromas and flavors and fine tannins. Drinkable now. 5,700 cases made. • $25 • (01/31/97) • **86**

St.-Estèphe 1993: Nice and pleasant, a soft red that will make for pleasant drinking in the short term. Attractive chocolate, currant and mineral flavors. Drinkable now. 7,000 cases made. • $20 • (01/31/96) • **80**

St.-Estèphe 1992: Polished red berry and cedar character unfolds in a silky texture on your palate; medium-bodied. Drinkable now. • $20 • (04/15/95) • **85**

St.-Estèphe 1991: Very nice spice and fruit character for this vintage. Medium-bodied and velvety, but slightly diluted. • $20 • (03/31/94) • **83**

St.-Estèphe 1990: A textbook wine for the appellation, with spicy, meaty fruit character, full tannins and a long, juicy finish. Don't touch this for a decade. Drink in 2000. 6,700 cases made. • $25 • (03/31/93) • **94**

St.-Estèphe 1989 • $18 • (03/15/92) • **93**
St.-Estèphe 1988 • $20 • (04/30/91) • **85**
St.-Estèphe 1985 • $16 • (04/30/88) • **87**
St.-Estèphe 1984 • $12 • (06/15/87) • **73**
St.-Estèphe 1983 • $9 • (05/16/86) • **86**
St.-Estèphe 1982 • $NA • (08/31/92) • **86**
St.-Estèphe 1961 • $NA • (04/30/96) • **75**

COSTE, DOMAINE DE LA

Coteaux du Languedoc Cuvée Syrah 1994: A rough-hewn wine, with leather and game flavors, and some plummy notes. Not for everyone. 2,000 cases made. • $10 • (06/30/97) • **79**

Coteaux du Languedoc Cuvée Syrah 1993: A mélange of meaty blackberry and pepper flavors reminiscent of the Rhône. It's rich fruit stands up to the tannins for an enjoyable mouthful. Ready now. 2,000 cases made. • $10 • (01/31/97) • **87**

Coteaux du Languedoc Cuvée Sélectionnée St.-Christol 1993 • $7 • (03/31/95) • **82**

Coteaux du Languedoc Cuvée Sélectionnée St.-Christol 1991 • $8 • (12/15/94) • **85**

COSTE-CAUMARTIN

Beaune Les Chouacheux 1995: A bit diluted, light-bodied and slightly astringent. Shows some cherry and wet earth flavors. Drying finish. 250 cases made. • $36 • (11/15/97) • **74**

Bourgogne 1995: Modest red berry flavor mingles with modest spice notes in this dry and chewy, light-bodied red. Short finish. 416 cases made. • $13 • (11/15/97) • **75**

Bourgogne 1994: Earthy and bitter in flavor. • $15 • (11/15/96) • **72**

Bourgogne 1993: Lean but pretty, the tannins balanced by some nice red licorice, currant and earth flavors. Seems to clamp down on the finish. Drinkable now. • $18 • (11/15/95) • **83**

Bourgogne 1990: Big and broad shouldered, with chestnut, violet and black cherry aromas and flavors and a chewy texture. Drinkable now. • $16 • (12/15/92) • **88**

Bourgogne 1989 • $15 • (01/31/92) • **87**

Pommard 1995: Fruity and fairly smooth on the midpalate, offering some succulent black cherry flavors, but a bit diluted. It kicks in with unripe tannins. Try after 1999, chilled. 708 cases made. • $28 • (11/15/97) • **77**

Pommard 1994: Subtle and fairly well made, this shows some ripe plum and red berry flavors on the midpalate, but is somewhat weak on the slightly diluted finish. Drink soon. • $25 • (11/15/96) • **80**

Pommard 1993: Appealing but lighter than some of these Pommards, showing decent raspberry and cherry notes. A bit short on the finish. Drinkable now. 500 cases made. • $37 • (11/15/95) • **80**

Pommard 1991: Lean and flavorful, but an annoying streak of stalkiness. Try now. 1,083 cases made. • $30 Ⓐ • (01/31/94) • **79**

Pommard 1990: A monumental, fantastic Pommard that tastes like chocolate mousse with raspberry sauce. Extremely firm, tannic and full-bodied; will reward patient collectors. Try now. 1,250 cases made. • $28 • (12/15/92) • **94**

Pommard 1987 • $21 • (11/15/90) • **76**

Pommard Le Clos des Boucherottes 1995: Like a breath of fresh air, this bright, spicy cherry-flavored red is forward and enjoyable, if a bit simple and tough on the finish. 500 cases made. • $36 • (11/15/97) • **83**

Pommard Le Clos des Boucherottes 1994: Soft and supple, but also a touch diluted, this pleasant, light- to medium-bodied wine offers succulent cherry and anise flavors. Drink soon. • $35 • (11/15/96) • **82**

Pommard Les Boucherottes 1993: Pretty, freshly crushed raspberry, blueberry and blackberry flavors. Subtle and seductive, adding a delicious, smooth, juicy finish of massive, well-integrated tannins. Drinkable now. 716 cases made. • $42 • (11/15/95) • **90**

Pommard Les Boucherottes 1992: Ripe and generous, with some nice blackberry, tobacco and spice flavors and tannin on the finish. Drinkable now. 833 cases made. • $35 • (12/15/94) • **87**

Pommard Les Boucherottes 1991: Bright, lively and light in texture. Nicely balances the raspberry and toasty oak aromas and flavors and finishes light but harmonious. Drinkable now. 583 cases made. • $38 Ⓐ • (01/31/94) • **83**

Pommard Les Boucherottes 1990: Ripe but focused, this has a massive structure yet manages to remain elegant. A wine to put away for decades. From an exclusive vineyard owned only by Coste-Caumartin. Drinkable now. 650 cases made. • $37 • (12/15/92) • **95**

Pommard Les Boucherottes 1989 • $38 • (01/31/92) • **92**

Pommard Les Fremiers 1995: On the herbal side, with some licorice flavors and tough tannins. Hard to warm up to. 433 cases made. • $36 • (11/15/97) • **77**

Pommard Les Fremiers 1994: Crisp and fresh, but also quite light and simple, with modest cherry and strawberry flavors. Drink chilled. • $30 • (11/15/96) • **73**

Pommard Les Fremiers 1993: Not big but delicious. Wonderfully perfumed berry and dried cherry aromas and flavors. Medium in body, firm tannins and fruity finish. Drinkable now. • $NA • (05/15/96) • **88**

Pommard Les Fremiers 1992: Light and crisp, showing modest berry and floral flavors that persist on the finish. Drinkable now. 667 cases made. • $31 • (12/15/94) • **81**

Pommard Les Fremiers 1991: A light, appealing style that features modest raspberry and lemon aromas and flavors. Finishes with polish and style. Drinkable now. 500 cases made. • $33 Ⓐ • (01/31/94) • **85**

Pommard Les Fremiers 1990: This massive wine is bursting with everything; loaded with raspberry and earth characteristics and firm tannins. Drinkable now. 550 cases made. • $32 • (12/15/92) • **94**

Pommard Les Fremiers 1989 • $35 • (01/31/92) • **92**

Pommard Les Fremiers 1987 • $26 • (11/15/90) • **79**

Pommard Les Vignots 1992: Crisp in texture, with modest raspberry flavors that finish tight and slightly tannic. Drinkable now. 267 cases made. • $26 • (12/15/94) • **78**

COSTEAU, MADAME

Chardonnay Vin de Pays d'Oc 1996: Marked by an overriding earthiness, despite the butter and nutmeg notes. 10,000 cases made. • $8 • (10/31/97) • **72**

Key: SS—Spectator Selection CS—Cellar Selection HR—Highly Recommended BB—Best Buy $NA—Price not available Ⓐ—Auction Price (BT)—Barrel Tasting

Dates in parentheses indicate the issues in which the ratings were published.

Merlot Vin de Pays d'Oc 1995: Fairly bright and lively, with good, fresh cherry and berry flavors, a subtle herbal note. 7,000 cases made. • $7 • (11/15/97) • **81**

COSTIÈRES DE POMEROLS, LES

Picpoul de Pinet Coteaux du Languedoc Hugues Beaulieu 1996: A straightforward, well-made white wine with peach and apple flavors. Would make a good apéritif. 3,000 cases made. • $7 • (04/30/98) • **83**

COTAT, PAUL

Sancerre Chavignol Red 1989 • $21 • (09/30/92) • **79**

Sancerre Les Culs de Beaujeu 1995: Keen and elegant, this lively white marries bright citrus flavors with vivid herbal notes, while a buttery accent smooths out the long, crisp finish. A distinctive wine that draws you back for another sip. • $20 • (06/15/97) • **91**

Sancerre Réserve des Monts Damnés 1995: Herbal flavors dominate this crisp, lively white, but they're complex and appealing, ranging from mint to sorrel to fennel. Distinctive, and a bit eccentric. • $20 • (06/15/97) • **86**

CÔTE DE BALEAU, CHÂTEAU

St.-Emilion 1997: Decent berry and earth aromas and flavors. Medium- to light-bodied, with light tannins and a short finish. • $NA • (06/15/98) (BT) • **75-79**

CÔTE DE ROL, CHÂTEAU

St.-Emilion 1997: Fresh berry aromas with hints of green tea. Medium-bodied, with light tannins and a slightly stewed fruit character in the aftertaste. • $NA • (06/15/98) (BT) • **75-79**

St.-Emilion 1996: More like a dark-colored rosé. Light and fruity, with light tannins and a fresh finish. 5,000 cases made. • $17 • (06/15/98) (BT) • **75-79**

St.-Emilion 1995: A light and fruity red with delicate berry, chocolate and vanilla aromas and flavors. Light-bodied, with light tannins and a fresh, fruity finish. Drink now. 1,840 cases made. • $15 • (01/31/98) • **80**

CÔTE MONTPEZAT, CHÂTEAU

Côtes de Castillon 1994: This deep red offers a nice combination of ripe plum flavors, toasty oak notes, firm tannins and the concentration to match. Balanced enough to drink now or can age through 2000. • $15 • (06/30/97) • **86**

COTTIN, DOMAINE

Chambolle-Musigny 1990: Firm in texture, with a light stream of berry and spice flavors nosing through the tannins. Hints at stemminess on the finish. Drinkable now. • $22 • (06/15/93) • **83**

COUCHEROY, CHÂTEAU

Pessac-Léognan 1995: Has good concentration of fruit, but is slightly tough and mean with an herbal edge. Medium-bodied, with firm tannins and a dried herb aftertaste. Drinkable now. • $18 • (01/31/98) • **85**

Pessac-Léognan 1993: Subtle plum, milk chocolate, dried herb and berry character, medium body, soft tannins and long, succulent finish. Drinkable now. • $11 • (01/31/96) • **84**

Pessac-Léognan White 1995: Plenty of mineral and spice. Medium-bodied, with medium acidity and a medium, fruity aftertaste. Drinkable now. • $11 • (04/30/98) • **87**

Pessac-Léognan White 1994 • $10 • (03/31/96) • **83**

COUDERT, FERNAND

Fleurie Clos de la Roilette 1994: A year in the bottle has added notes of toast and coffee to the ripe plum flavors in this velvety wine. It's smooth and has good depth, drinking nicely now. • $16 • (09/15/96) • **84**

Fleurie Clos de la Roilette 1993 • $17 • (06/15/95) • **81**

COUËDIC, PAUL DU

Mercurey 1995: Weak, light and disappointing. Modest fruit. Chewy finish. • $18 • (11/15/97) • **71**

Mercurey Les Veleys 1995: This solid red shows very nice fruit, mineral and iron notes, lovely toasty oak and spice accents and tannins that are firm but ripe. A bit chewy, but should improve with cellaring. Try around 2000. • $20 • (11/15/97) • **85**

COUFRAN, CHÂTEAU

Haut-Médoc 1997: Aromas of prunes and raisins follow through onto the palate. Medium-bodied, with light tannins and a fluid finish. Overripe grapes? • $NA • (06/15/98) (BT) • **75-79**

Haut-Médoc 1996: Lots of mineral and spice. Full-bodied, with well-integrated tannins and a stone and raspberry aftertaste. Almost outstanding. • $20 • (06/15/98) (BT) • **85-89**

Haut-Médoc 1995: A bit earthy, but has good fruit character all the same, with intense currant bush and wet earth aromas and flavors. Full-bodied and chunky, with velvety tannins and a long, fruity finish. Drink after 2000. 41,000 cases made. • $25 • (01/31/98) • **87**

Haut-Médoc 1994: Good concentration of fruit flavor, with berry, tar and tobacco nuances. Medium- to full-bodied, with velvety tannins and a dried-berry finish. Drinkable now. • $20 • (01/31/97) • **85**

Haut-Médoc 1992: Fresh blackberry, slightly herbal aromas and flavors; light-bodied, light finish. • $12 • (04/15/95) • **81**

Haut-Médoc 1991: Pretty black cherry and spice aromas and flavors, but light-bodied and slightly dry on the finish. • $12 • (03/31/94) • **78**

Haut-Médoc 1990: Luscious and ripe. This is rich, almost Port-like, with loads of plummy, berry aromas and flavors and a long, ripe finish. Drinkable now. 34,000 cases made. • $17 • (03/31/93) • **88**

Haut-Médoc 1989 • $14 • (03/15/92) • **89**

Haut-Médoc 1988 • $15 • (04/30/91) • **84**

Haut-Médoc 1987 • $12 • (11/30/89) • **81**

Haut-Médoc 1986 • $13 • (06/30/89) • **85**

Haut-Médoc 1985 • $11 • (06/30/88) • **85**

Haut-Médoc 1982 • $NA • (08/31/92) • **85**

COUHINS-LURTON, CHÂTEAU

Pessac-Léognan 1994: Not for everyone, but this pungently earthy and herbal wine is distinctive. The aggressive aromas and vivid flavors are backed by a smooth texture and lingering finish. • $28 • (05/31/97) • **86**

COUILLAUD, LES FRÈRES

Chardonnay Vin de Pays du Jardin de la France Domaine La Morinière 1996: Light apple and citrus flavors mark this straightforward white. It's clean and fresh, fine as an apéritif. Drink now. 3,000 cases made. • $7 • (05/31/98) • **81**

Chardonnay Vin de Pays du Jardin de la France Domaine La Morinière 1995: Applelike and vegetal flavors mingle uneasily in this crisp white. Has the acidity for food, but lacks personality. 3,000 cases made. • $7 • (05/15/97) • **79**

Chardonnay Vin de Pays du Jardin de la France Domaine La Morinière 1994 • $7 • (11/15/95) • **77**

Chardonnay Vin de Pays du Jardin de la France Domaine La Morinière 1993 • $7 • (11/15/95) • **82**

Chardonnay Vin de Pays du Jardin de la France Domaine Trois Frères 1995: Soft and a bit cloying, with sweet, buttery flavors that overwhelm the modest apple flavor. It's smooth, but dull. 10,000 cases made. • $9 • (06/15/97) • **78**

Chardonnay Vin de Pays du Jardin de la France Domaine Trois Frères 1994 • $8 • (05/15/96) • **80**

Muscadet de Sèvre et Maine Sur Lie Château La Morinière 1996: Assertive, showing plenty of *sur lie* character, with bread-dough and spice notes, and delivering structure and concentration on the palate, with melon and almond flavors. A solid accompaniment to food. Drink now. 1,500 cases made. • $8 • (05/31/98) • **85**

Muscadet de Sèvre et Maine Sur Lie Château La Morinière 1995: This crisp wine verges on sourness but its round body and ripe pear flavors keep the balance. A bit austere, but should open with food. 1,500 cases made. • $8 • (05/15/97) • **85**

Muscadet de Sèvre et Maine Sur Lie Château La Morinière 1994 • $10 • (05/15/96) • **85**

Muscadet de Sèvre et Maine Sur Lie Château La Morinière 1993 • $10 • (11/15/95) • **85**

Muscadet de Sèvre et Maine Sur Lie Domaine La Morinière 1996: Shows marked *sur lie* flavors of bread dough and spices, but turns a bit soapy on the palate, with flavors of pears and apples. A distinctive, rustic style. Drink now. 2,500 cases made. • $8 • (05/31/98) • **80**

Muscadet de Sèvre et Maine Sur Lie Domaine La Morinière 1995: A muscular white, solid yet refreshing, this manages to balance concentration and liveliness. Has a firm core of acidity and flavors of pears and almonds that emerge on the finish. 2,500 cases made. • $8 • (05/15/97) • **86**

Muscadet de Sèvre et Maine Sur Lie Domaine La Morinière 1994 • $9 • (05/15/96) • **83**

Muscadet de Sèvre et Maine Sur Lie Domaine La Morinière 1993 • $9 • (11/15/95) • **81**

Muscadet de Sèvre et Maine Sur Lie Domaine Trois Frères 1995: Floral and grapefruit aromas are intriguing, but it turns simpler on the palate, a neutral mix of acid and alcohol. Refreshing, but bland. 4,000 cases made. • $9 • (06/15/97) • **81**

Vin de Pays du Jardin de la France Chardet Cuvée Prestige Couillaud 1996: Light, fresh and clean, but neutral in flavor, with light apple and citrus notes and a short finish. A blend of 50 percent Chardonnay, 50 percent Melon de Bourgogne. Drink now. 2,000 cases made. • $8 • (05/31/98) • **79**

Vin de Pays du Jardin de la France Chardet Cuvée Prestige Couillaud 1995: This light white offers crisp and simple apple and lemon flavors. An easy quaff but not distinctive. 2,000 cases made. • $8 • (05/15/97) • **80**

Vin de Pays du Jardin de la France Chardet White 1995 • $9 • (05/15/96) • **82**

Vin de Pays du Jardin de la France Chardet White 1994 • $9 • (11/15/95) • **84**

COUJAN, DOMAINE DE

Vin de Pays des Coteaux du Murviel 1990 • $7 • (03/15/94) • **86**

COULON & FILS, PAUL

Châteauneuf-du-Pape Boisrenard 1995: Voluptuous and seductive, showing violet, cassis, toast and chocolate flavors, sweet and long, with harmonious tannins and a long, sweet finish. A fine example of the international-style red today. Drink now through 2000. 1,000 cases made. • $45 • (10/15/97) • **92**

Châteauneuf-du-Pape Boisrenard 1994: This firm red offers elegant flavors of black cherry, toast, coffee and herbs, focused and harmonious. The tannins are ripe and well-integrated. A good match with food, it's drinkable now, will improve through 2000. 1,000 cases made. • $45 • (10/15/97) • **89**

Châteauneuf-du-Pape White Boisrenard 1995: An ambitious Châteauneuf, with loads of toasty oak, spice and mocha flavors along with pear notes and decent acidity. Tastes like a barrel-fermented white Burgundy. Medium to full in body, it hangs in on the finish thanks to fairly good concentration, but drink now. 500 cases made. • $50 • (10/15/97) • **86**

Châteauneuf-du-Pape White Boisrenard 1994: Alluring aromas of butter, honey and melons carry through on the palate of this well-structured, full-bodied white. A solid match for poultry or game. Expressive now but should age well, too. 80 cases made. • $40 • (11/15/96) • **90**

Côtes du Rhône-Villages Rasteau 1996: Fruity and rather crisp, but showing some cassis bush, stemmy, green flavors. A bit unripe and short on the finish. From Domaine de Beaurenard. 2,500 cases made. • $17 • (10/15/97) • **73**

COULY-DUTHEIL

Chinon Clos de L'Echo 1989 • $NA • (10/31/94) • **88**

Chinon La Diligence 1993 • $NA • (10/31/94) • **87**

Chinon Domaine Rene Couly 1993 • $12 • (10/31/94) • **84**

Chinon Domaine de Versailles 1981 • $13 • (03/15/87) • **86**

Chinon Les Gravieres d'Amador Abbe de Turpenay 1993 • $NA • (10/31/94) • **86**

Chinon Les Gravieres d'Amador Abbe de Turpenay 1986 • $10 • (04/30/88) • **72**

Chinon Les Gravieres d'Amador Abbe de Turpenay 1985 • $9 • (02/28/87) • **86**

Chinon Rosé René Couly 1993 • $NA • (10/31/94) • **83**

Saumur Champigny La Vigneronne Red 1985 • $10 • (02/15/87) • **87**

COUR PAVILLON, LA

Bordeaux 1994: A tough customer. Thin and somewhat dried out, with herbal flavors and aromas. • $10 • (04/30/97) • **77**

Bordeaux White 1995: Rich and full-flavored, with lovely peach, melon and herbal flavors. Well balanced and focused with nice acidity and texture. Finishes on a good, crisp note with a touch of honey to boot. • $10 • (04/30/97) • **87**

COURANCONNE, CHÂTEAU LA

Côtes du Rhône-Villages White Seguret 1996: Full-bodied and balanced, with some earth, grapefruit and lime flavors. Ripe and rich, it's quite zesty and vibrant on the chewy, crisp finish. Drinkable now. • $14 • (10/15/97) • **82**

COURBIS, MAURICE & DOMINIQUE

Cornas Champelrose 1995: Pretty violet and wild berry aromas bow to sweet cherry and blueberry flavors in this modestly structured yet harmonious red. It's firm on the finish. Drinkable now. 292 cases made. • $29 • (10/15/97) • **88**

Cornas La Sabarotte 1995: This polished red offers sweet fruit flavors of cassis and black cherry, with sophisticated toasty oak notes and full but ripe tannins. The structure is muscular, but the wine is so balanced there's no clumsiness at all. Reserved now, it will be delicious from around 2000. 292 cases made. • $29 • (10/15/97) • **93**

Cornas La Sabarotte 1994: Dense, and chewy with ripe fruit and sweet oak. Flavors of blackberry, coffee and licorice intertwine with firm tannins, assertive and well-defined. A modern style, made for drinking now. • $28 • (12/15/96) • **88**

St.-Joseph 1995: Herbal, vegetal aromas plump out on the palate, with ripe berry flavors and good concentration, but it finishes a bit tannic and dry. A rustic red that needs food to soften it. 2,917 cases made. • $19 • (10/15/97) • **80**

St.-Joseph Domaine des Royes 1994: Assertive cherry and black pepper aromas carry through on the firm, well-defined palate and long, smoky finish. Showing good balance and concentration, it's drinkable now through 2000. 290 cases made. • $20 • (11/30/96) • **87**

St.-Joseph White 1995: Fresh and well balanced, this shows good definition, with ripe pear, almond and light herbal flavors. There's plenty of fruit, expressive and satiny, and a long, crisp finish. Not a blockbuster, but a winner with food. 1,083 cases made. • $15 • (10/15/97) • **88**

COURCEL, DOMAINE DE

Pommard Clos des Epeneaux 1985 • $37 • (04/30/88) • **89**

Pommard Les Grands Epenots 1993: Lovely and distinctive, featuring tons of chocolate and mocha flavors. The smooth, round mouthfeel is followed by a supple, subtle, lasting finish. Drinkable now. • $33 • (11/15/95) • **88**

Pommard Les Rugiens 1993: Attractively lush and earthy, offering an intense, concentrated red berry, chocolate, mocha complexity. Smoky and toasty on the long finish. Drinkable now. • $42 • (11/15/95) • **90**

Pommard Les Rugiens 1985 • $32 Ⓐ • (04/30/88) • **92**

COURONNE, CHÂTEAU LA

St.-Emilion 1997: Grapey and simple, with some berry and stemmy character. Medium in body, with light tannins and a short finish. Good for the vintage. • $NA • (06/15/98) (BT) • **80-84**

St.-Emilion 1996: Slightly one-dimensional, but with good ripe berry character, medium tannins and a light finish. • $22 • (06/15/98) (BT) • **80-84**

St.-Emilion 1995: Offers some decent fruit, but it's rather light and weedy, with light tannins and a weedy aftertaste. Drink now. • $15 • (01/31/98) • **78**

St.-Emilion 1993: Sturdy and offers black cherry, toast and lightly earthy flavors over firm tannins. Not distinctive, but will match well with grilled meats. • $16 • (07/31/96) • **82**

St.-Emilion 1992: Notes of decaying leaves, mushrooms and earth dominate this dry red. Drink up. • $16 • (07/31/96) • **75**

Key: SS—Spectator Selection CS—Cellar Selection HR—Highly Recommended BB—Best Buy $NA—Price not available Ⓐ—Auction Price (BT)—Barrel Tasting
Dates in parentheses indicate the issues in which the ratings were published.

COUROULU, DOMAINE LE

Vacqueyras 1995: Vibrant and lively, with inky-dark color, it bursts with cassis, green olives, rose petal and ripe cherry flavors and Provençal notes. Light- to medium-bodied, it tingles with life on the palate. Try this delicious wine with pizza, pasta and Provençal foods. • $13 • (10/15/97) • **87**

Vacqueyras 1993: Maturing now, this round red has flavors of plum, raisin, cinnamon and smoke. The tannins are still firm and may outlive the fruit; drink now. 2,500 cases made. • $12 • (02/28/97) • **81**

Vacqueyras 1992 • $10 • (10/31/95) • **86**

Vacqueyras 1990 • $10 • (04/15/93) • **83**

Vacqueyras 1985 • $8 • (01/31/89) BB • **83**

COURSODON, PIERRE

St.-Joseph 1995: Lean, hard and chewy, with coffee and herbal flavors, a core of cherry. Drinkable now. 1,250 cases made. • $NA • (10/15/97) • **81**

St.-Joseph 1994: Lush and generous, this ripe red offers floral, cassis and licorice flavors, with firm but well-integrated tannins and a long finish of fruit and spices. Drinkable now. • $NA • (10/15/97) • **89**

St.-Joseph 1992 • $NA • (05/31/94) • **78**

St.-Joseph 1991 • $NA • (05/31/94) • **85**

St.-Joseph L'Olivaie 1995: Pretty black cherry aromas give way to cherry and light earth flavors in this firm, slightly rustic red. Has good concentration, but the finish is a bit dry. Try now. • $NA • (10/15/97) • **85**

St.-Joseph White 1996: Lively and citrusy, light- to medium-bodied, with some crisp acidity framing the mineral and pear notes. Drink now. • $NA • (10/15/97) • **85**

St.-Joseph White 1995: Big, lush, and yet well-knit, this distinctive white shows an intriguing mix of fruit and earth flavors, with herbal and almond notes emerging on the finish. • $NA • (10/15/97) • **85**

St.-Joseph White Le Paradis Saint Pierre 1996: Bold and big, yet still has finesse, with concentrated pear, vanilla and almond flavors, and a firm core of acidity to keep it lively. Drinkable now. • $NA • (10/15/97) • **88**

COURTADE, LA

Côtes de Provence Red 1990 • $24 • (06/15/93) • **76**

COURTAULT, JEAN-CLAUDE

Chablis 1996: Marvelous. Thick and dense, with a sophisticated vanilla, earth and ripe fruit complexity. Shows a lot of *terroir*, but it's sweet-tasting, and the concentration this small grower from Maligny near Chablis extracted from his vineyards in '96 is tangible. Extraordinary quality for a simple Chablis. Not imported into the U.S. • $NA • (08/31/97) • **92**

Chablis Montmain Domaine de la Tour 1996: Pretty Chablis, of medium body and intensity, showing lovely fruit and some mineral character. Tempting now through 2003. Not imported into the U.S. • $NA • (05/31/98) • **87**

Petit Chablis 1996: Lush and supple, medium-bodied, with lovely ripe pear, floral and ginger notes. Enjoy upon release. • $NA • (08/31/97) • **86**

COURTEILLAC, DOMAINE DE

Bordeaux Supérieur 1996: Rather light and fruity with very light tannins and a short finish. • $NA • (01/01/97) (BT) • **75-79**

Bordeaux Supérieur 1995: Sexy wine and amazingly good for this appellation. Loads of berry, mint and pomegranate aromas and flavors. Full- to medium-bodied, with lovely ripe, sweet fruit character. Red berries throughout. Fine tannins and a long, silky finish. Drinkable now. • $18 • (01/31/98) • **90**

Bordeaux Supérieur 1994: Pleasant, with ripe berry flavors and a hint of oak. Medium-bodied, with fine tannins, but slightly diluted. Drink now. • $15 • (01/31/97) • **84**

Bordeaux Supérieur 1993: Simple and fruity, showing some berry character but appearing slightly herbal on the finish. Drinkable now. • $NA • (01/31/96) • **79**

Bordeaux White Cuvée Antholien 1995: A very impressive white for the appellation. Shows lots of lemon, lime and toasty oak character, very smoky. Medium-bodied, with fresh acidity and a medium aftertaste. • $20 • (04/30/98) • **88**

Bordeaux White Cuvée Antholien 1994 • $NA • (03/31/96) • **88**

Bordeaux White Cuvée Antholien 1993 • $NA • (03/31/96) • **86**

COURTESSES, DOMAINE DE

Pouilly-Fuissé 1993: Oddly mature already, but silky and buttery on the palate. Sherry-like aromas; rose-petal, honey, mushroom flavors. 833 cases made. • $NA • (05/15/95) • **79**

Pouilly-Fuissé Cuvée Vieilles Vignes 1993: Floral notes border on eau-de-vie apricot character or sweet perfume; lean and hard in the mouth. 417 cases made. • $NA • (05/15/95) • **70**

COURTIAL, MICHEL

Cornas 1989 • $15 • (05/31/94) SS • **91**

Crozes-Hermitage 1991 • $8 • (05/31/94) • **83**

Crozes-Hermitage 1990 • $8 • (05/31/94) • **82**

Hermitage 1991: Elegant and broadens on the palate, showing black cherry, mint and licorice flavors, with firm tannins. Drink now. • $NA • (05/31/94) • **87**

St.-Joseph 1991 • $12 • (05/31/94) • **75**

COUSPAUDE, CHÂTEAU LA

St.-Emilion 1997: Good berry and spice aromas and flavors. Medium-bodied, with medium tannins and a light finish. • $NA • (06/15/98) (BT) • **80-84**

St.-Emilion 1995: Diluted and light, with some fruit showing, but it's earthy and strange. Barely acceptable. • $NA • (05/15/96) (BT) • **965**

COUSSERGUES, DOMAINE DE

Chardonnay Vin de Pays d'Oc 1996: A bit lumbering but fruity and pleasant. Peach and apple flavors, an herbal note on the finish. 7,000 cases made. • $8 • (04/30/98) • **82**

Merlot Vin de Pays d'Oc 1996: An herbal-style Merlot with plum and cherry flavors, a tobacco note on the finish. Drink now. 5,000 cases made. • $8 • (04/30/98) • **79**

Sauvignon Blanc Vin de Pays d'Oc 1996: Starts with good appley fruit, but clamps down and turns coarse on the finish. 10,000 cases made. • $8 • (04/30/98) • **78**

COUTET, CHÂTEAU

Barsac 1992: A pretty, medium-sweet white, showing attractive lemon, spice and wax character and an easy-to-like finish. • $NA • (04/15/95) • **81**

Barsac 1991: Lightly sweet; domineering oak flavors. Not really what we expect here, but it has some decent vanilla and toasty coconut character. Drink now. • $NA • (04/15/95) • **80**

Barsac 1990: Racy and elegant, quite floral, demonstrating some spicy, buttery, lime and juicy flavors that keep it fresh on the finish. Medium body and sweetness. Drinkable now. • $NA • (04/15/95) • **89**

Barsac 1989: Lush and viscous, very sweet, showing ripe tropical fruit and lemon flavors and a burning sensation on the finish that reflects good concentration. Drinkable now. • $29 • (04/15/95) • **90**

Barsac 1988: Extraordinary complexity and finesse are the hallmarks of this earth-scented, butter-laced, honeyed, lemon-flavored gem. The finish seems to never end thanks to all that great acidity. Drinkable now. • $47 • (04/15/95) • **91**

Barsac 1987 • $27 • (06/15/90) • **80**

Barsac 1983: Lighter than expected from this vintage, displaying medium intensity and sweetness and some decent honey, clove and dried fruit flavors. Try as an apéritif. • $27 Ⓐ • (04/15/95) • **83**

Barsac 1947: Feels thin and metallic compared to others; very citrusy. • $280 • (05/31/97) • **83**

Barsac Cuvée Madame 1989: Super-sweet, super-ripe, but not any better than the regular bottling. Dark color with a brilliant gold hue and very intense aromas of butterscotch, vanilla, honey and apricot. Tasted twice, with consistent notes. Drinkable now. • $190 • (04/15/95) • **90**

Barsac Cuvée Madame 1988: Lots of botrytis and spice character and ripe fruit here; quality is about the same as the regular bottling. Medium- to full-bodied, very sweet, round texture, butterscotch aftertaste. Drink now. • $175 • (04/15/95) • **91**

COUVENT DES JACOBINS

St.-Emilion 1989 • $28 • (04/30/92) • **89**

St.-Emilion 1988 • $28 • (03/31/91) • **81**

St.-Emilion 1985 • $27 • (03/31/88) • **84**

St.-Emilion 1983 • $27 • (03/16/86) • **95**

COYEUX, DOMAINE DES

Muscat de Beaumes-de-Venise 1993: Sweet and rather syrupy, this is subdued for a Muscat, but tangerine and vanilla flavors emerge on the finish. Rich, though a bit clumsy. • $20 • (10/15/96) • **83**

Muscat de Beaumes-de-Venise 1992 • $20 • (11/15/95) • **84**

CROCHET, GILLES

Sancerre La Grange aux Dimes 1995: A quicksilver wine. Light, intense, with tongue-tingling acidity and fresh flavors of herbs and citrus. Softens a bit on the finish, and would marry well with light, flavorful dishes. • $18 • (04/30/97) • **87**

CROCHET, LUCIEN

Sancerre 1995: Appealing floral and grass aromas in this white give way to bright citrus flavors with hints of spice and herbs. Tart on its own, but will marry beautifully with food. 1,000 cases made. • $17 • (06/15/97) • **88**

Sancerre 1994 • $16 • (06/15/96) • **87**

Sancerre 1993 • $15 • (12/15/95) • **82**

Sancerre La Croix du Roy 1995: This muscular white is clean and pure, with well-defined grass, citrus and light floral notes. Has very crisp acidity and the strength to improve with age. 300 cases made. • $19 • (05/15/97) • **89**

Sancerre La Croix du Roy 1994 • $18 • (06/15/96) • **86**

Sancerre Le Chêne 1995: This citrusy white has well-defined flavors of grapefruit, pears and herbs. A bit austere on its own, but should blossom with food. 800 cases made. • $20 • (05/31/97) • **87**

Sancerre Le Chêne 1994 • $19 • (05/15/96) • **88**

Sancerre Red La Croix du Roy 1994: Alluring aromas of smoke and spice give way to rather sharp, lean flavors of dried cherries, smoke and bitter herbs. Aggressive alone, but may soften with food. 150 cases made. • $23 • (06/15/97) • **83**

CROCK, CHÂTEAU LE

St.-Estèphe 1997: Decent berry and cherry character, but it falls short on the palate. Medium- to light-bodied, with light tannins. • $NA • (06/15/98) (BT) • **80-84**

St.-Estèphe 1996: A bit hard, with tough tannins, tar and cherry flavors. Medium-bodied. • $17 • (06/15/98) (BT) • **80-84**

St.-Estèphe 1995: A fresh and well-made *cru bourgeoise*. Bright berry and cherry aromas follow through on the palate. Medium-bodied, with firm tannins and a refreshing, zingy aftertaste. Drinkable now. • $16 • (01/31/98) • **87**

St.-Estèphe 1987 • $16 • (11/30/89) • **79**

St.-Estèphe 1986 • $21 • (11/30/89) • **92**

St.-Estèphe 1985 • $18 • (02/15/88) • **79**

St.-Estèphe 1983 • $9 • (12/16/85) • **81**

St.-Estèphe 1982 • $20 • (11/30/89) • **80**

CROIX, CHÂTEAU LA

Pomerol 1988 • $19 • (07/31/91) • **82**

Pomerol 1985 • $25 • (05/15/88) • **93**

Pomerol 1983 • $14 • (11/30/86) • **84**

Pomerol 1982 • $30 • (05/15/89) • **89**

Pomerol 1981 • $14 • (05/01/89) • **72**

Pomerol 1979 • $11 • (04/01/84) • **60**

CROIX CANON, CHÂTEAU LA

Canon-Fronsac 1997: Attractive blackberry and plum aromas and flavors. Medium-bodied, with well-integrated tannins and a fresh fruit aftertaste. Delicious. • $NA • (06/15/98) (BT) • **85-89**

Canon-Fronsac 1996: Perfumed and pleasant, but slightly diluted. Medium- to light-bodied, with light tannins and a cherry aftertaste. • $22 • (06/15/98) (BT) • **80-84**

CROIX DE FIGEAC, CHÂTEAU LA

St.-Emilion 1993: Light and herbaceous, featuring some red fruit and slightly aggressive tannins. • $NA • (01/31/96) • **76**

FRANCE

CROIX-DE-GAY, CHÂTEAU LA

Pomerol 1997: Rather light and slightly weedy, with berry and vanilla character, but light on the finish. Rather disappointing for this estate. • $NA • (06/15/98) (BT) • **75-79**
Pomerol 1996: Very light, with some good berry and cherry character and light tannins. Barely acceptable. • $NA • (01/01/97) (BT) • **75-79**
Pomerol 1995: A bit tough but should come around. Plenty of blackberry, cherry and tobacco aromas. Full-bodied, with velvety yet slightly astringent tannins. Medium finish. Needs time. Try after 2000. • $25 • (01/31/98) • **89**
Pomerol 1994: Enticing aromas of ripe berry, cherry and raspberry aromas. Medium-bodied, with fine tannins and a light, fruity finish. Drink now or hold. 3,750 cases made. • $30 • (01/31/97) • **87**
Pomerol 1993: Lovely, silky chocolate and berry character and smooth tannins. Medium body and finish. Delicious to drink now. • $20 • (01/31/96) • **85**
Pomerol 1992: Better than we remember from barrel. Subtle raspberry and toasty oak aromas; medium- to light-bodied, delivering firm fruit and slightly hard tannins and acidity. Succulent finish. • $17 • (04/15/95) • **82**
Pomerol 1991: A pleasing wine with roasted nut, cherry and tomato aromas and flavors. Medium body, silky texture and a quick finish. • $17 • (03/31/94) • **78**
Pomerol 1990: As usual, it's big, thick and rich with loads of nutmeg, berry and ripe fruit character. Long in the aftertaste, with extremely velvety tannins. Drinkable now. 5,000 cases made. • $28 • (03/31/93) • **94**
Pomerol 1989 • $27 • (03/15/92) • **88**
Pomerol 1988 • $30 • (06/30/91) • **89**
Pomerol 1985 • $22 Ⓐ • (03/15/88) CS • **91**
Pomerol 1983 • $16 • (07/01/86) CS • **94**
Pomerol 1982 • $27 Ⓐ • (05/15/89) • **91**
Pomerol 1961 • $NA • (04/30/96) • **82**
Pomerol 1945 • $NA • (03/16/86) • **70**

CROIX DU CASSE, CHÂTEAU LA

Pomerol 1997: Big and grapey, but with a slightly cooked character. Medium- to full-bodied, with velvety tannins and a medium finish. Slightly overdone. • $NA • (06/15/98) (BT) • **85-89**
Pomerol 1996: Violet and berry aromas, with a good dose of new wood. Medium-bodied, with moderate, velvety tannins and a medium finish. • $30 • (06/15/98) (BT) • **85-89**
Pomerol 1995: Decadent funkster of a wine. Dark, inky color. Masses of crushed raspberries and currants. Full-bodied and rather fat, with smoke, vanilla and gamelike flavors. A bit soft. Best after 2000. • $23 • (01/31/98) • **89**
Pomerol 1994: Wonderful. Smells of violet, berry and vanilla, and is full-bodied yet very refined, with long, silky tannins. An absolute joy to taste now, even better in 2000. • $25 • (01/31/97) • **89**
Pomerol 1993: Rather lean and hard, showing an earthy, slightly strange character. • $24 • (01/31/96) • **78**
Pomerol 1985 • $25 • (05/15/88) • **82**

CROIX-MILLORIT, CHÂTEAU DE LA

Côtes de Bourg 1986 • $9/375ml • (05/15/91) • **79**

CROIX ST.-GEORGES, CHÂTEAU LA

Pomerol 1995: A delicious Pomerol that will improve with age. Has lovely violet and berry aromas, and is medium-bodied, with velvety tannins and a medium to long, sweet-fruit aftertaste. Drink now or hold. 1,800 cases made. • $44 • (01/31/98) • **87**

CROIX SENAILLET, DOMAINE DE LA

St.-Véran 1994: Pleasant and well-made, light-bodied but balanced, featuring creamy yet fresh texture, some lovely fruit character and crisp finish. Nice as an apéritif. • $NA • (08/31/95) • **80**

Key: SS—Spectator Selection CS—Cellar Selection HR—Highly Recommended BB—Best Buy $NA—Price not available Ⓐ—Auction Price (BT)—Barrel Tasting
Dates in parentheses indicate the issues in which the ratings were published.

CROIZET-BAGES, CHÂTEAU

Pauillac 1997: Blackberries and raspberries on the nose. Medium-bodied, with light tannins and a fading finish. Good for this château. • $NA • (06/15/98) (BT) • **85-89**
Pauillac 1996: Not as good as I remember. Rather herbal and hard, with some sweet fruit. Medium-bodied, with a light finish. 12,500 cases made. • $22 • (06/15/98) (BT) • **80-84**
Pauillac 1995: Lovely, silky wine with boysenberry aromas and flavors, medium body and a fresh, fruity aftertaste. Best after this year. 11,670 cases made. • $20 • (01/31/98) • **86**
Pauillac 1994: Decent body, but overly herbal in character. Drink now. 12,000 cases made. • $25 • (01/31/97) • **75**
Pauillac 1993: More water than wine, this diluted Bordeaux tastes of stewed tomatoes and bell pepper. • $25 • (01/31/96) • **74**
Pauillac 1988 • $28 • (08/31/91) • **73**
Pauillac 1986 • $15 • (06/30/89) • **78**
Pauillac 1982 • $26 • (08/31/92) • **82**
Pauillac 1970 • $45 • (05/15/93) • **85**
Pauillac 1962 • $60 • (11/30/87) • **83**
Pauillac 1961 • $36 Ⓐ • (04/30/96) • **85**

CROS, DOMAINE

Minervois 1995: This has a nice gamy edge to it, with some plush flavors of plum and smoke, and a good dose of tannin and chocolate on the finish. Best now through 2003. • $7 • (05/31/98) • **85**

CRUCHET, RÉGIS

Vouvray Demi Sec 1995: Full-bodied and quite tart for an off-dry style. Offers pineapple, lemon and herb flavors, and a lively but short finish. 400 cases made. • $17 • (06/15/97) • **84**

CRUZEAU, CHÂTEAU DE

Pessac-Léognan 1997: Medium- to light-bodied, with good tannins but a slightly herbal tobacco character. • $NA • (06/15/98) (BT) • **80-84**
Pessac-Léognan 1996: A rather lean '96, with some berry, earth and raisin character, but slightly drying tannins on the finish. Tasted twice, with consistent notes. • $14 • (06/15/98) (BT) • **75-79**
Pessac-Léognan 1995: Loads of fruit in this wine. Wonderful aromas of berry, chocolate and tobacco, and similar flavors. Full-bodied, with a long, velvety finish. Best after 2000. • $15 • (01/31/98) • **90**
Pessac-Léognan 1994: Pretty, with violet, floral and vanilla character and a slight herbal accent. Well integrated tannins and a silky finish. Drinkable now. • $14 • (01/31/97) • **84**
Pessac-Léognan 1993: Pretty cherry, chocolate and berry aromas and flavors, medium body, medium-to-light silky tannins and a fresh finish. Drinkable now. • $14 • (01/31/96) • **83**
Pessac-Léognan 1992: Lean, short in fruit and tough in tannins. • $12 • (04/15/95) • **75**
Pessac-Léognan 1990: A wine with rich flavors of cassis, plum, blackberry and oak. There are masses of tannins to boot. Drinkable now. 15,000 cases made. • $16 • (03/31/93) • **91**
Pessac-Léognan 1989 • $14 • (03/15/92) • **86**
Pessac-Léognan 1988 • $14 • (02/28/91) • **87**
Pessac-Léognan 1986 • $10 • (06/30/89) • **87**
Graves 1985 • $9 • (06/15/88) BB • **85**
Graves 1982 • $20 • (08/31/92) • **91**
Pessac-Léognan White 1995: Attractive apple, lemon and lime aromas and flavors. Medium-bodied with fresh acidity and a light, refreshing aftertaste. Drink now. • $12 • (04/30/98) • **86**
Pessac-Léognan White 1994 • $12 • (03/31/96) • **86**

CUCKOO HILL

Chardonnay Vin de Pays d'Oc 1996: A fairly crisp wine with apple and honey flavors, an earthy finish. • $7 • (04/30/98) • **80**
Merlot Vin de Pays d'Oc 1996: Quite tart, with green plum and cherry flavors as well as a streak of dill. Has good focus, but it turns thin on the finish. Try with food. Drink now. • $6 • (03/31/98) • **81**
Viognier Vin de Pays d'Oc 1996: Not much here—only faint peach flavors and a drying finish. • $10 • (04/30/98) • **72**

CUILLERON, YVES

Condrieu Les Chaillets 1996: Tender in texture, almost sweet on the palate, this soft, round white offers floral, orange and apricot flavors that linger on the finish. It's harmonious, polished and true to the varietal. A beautiful meditation wine. • $58 • (10/15/97) • **93**

Condrieu Les Chaillets Vieilles Vignes 1995: Perfumed with intense and elegant aromas of lime, spice and flowers, this sophisticated white moves on to firm, polished flavors of apricot, honey, spice and citrus, pure and deep. It's classically proportioned, balanced and harmonious, with a long, exotic finish. 75 cases made. • $58 • (10/15/97) • **98**

Condrieu Les Chaillets Vieilles Vignes 1993 • $45 • (05/31/94) • **85**

Condrieu La Côte 1996: Vividly perfumed, firm and expressive, with clean, fresh acidity providing backbone for the floral, lime, vanilla and honey flavors. It's not opulent, but it's fresh and well focused. • $43 • (10/15/97) • **90**

Condrieu La Côte 1995: A lively and expressive white displaying focused flavors of peaches, spices and pretty floral notes, balanced and so light it dances on the palate. The finish is long and spicy. Polished and irresistible. • $40 • (10/15/97) • **92**

Condrieu Les Eguets 1996: Marked by great finesse, this is beautifully balanced, with peach, apricot, almond, tropical and spicy flavors. Clean and full-bodied, its silky texture coats the palate. Sweet but not cloying, with an elegant finish. Drink now. Selected harvest of botrytis-affected grapes. 150 cases made. • $60 • (10/15/97) • **95**

Condrieu Les Eguets Récoltes Tardives 1995: Powerful and expressive, with a bounteous botrytis-tasting character, it's thick but clean, with intense dried apricot, orange-peel, cigar box and smoke flavors simmering long on the back of the palate. Delicious. Full-bodied. Can age through 2005. • $60/500ml • (10/15/97) • **94**

Côte-Rôtie Côteau de Bassenon 1995: Toasty, smoky aromas give way to crisp flavors of cherries, herbs and coffee in this compact, dense red. The tannins are quite firm on the finish; this is lively and well-extracted. Drinkable now. • $35 • (10/15/97) • **86**

Côte-Rôtie Côteau de Bassenon 1994: This assertive red emphasizes the spicy, gamy side of Syrah, with plenty of black pepper and licorice flavors and very firm tannins. A solid wine. Drinkable now. 100 cases made. • $35 • (11/30/96) • **90**

St.-Joseph 1983 • $13 • (02/16/86) • **76**

St.-Joseph Cuvée de la Côte 1987 • $16 • (11/30/90) • **80**

St.-Joseph Cuvée Prestige L'Amarybelle 1994: Thick and chewy, this solid red offers cherry, raspberry, licorice and light herbal flavors, with firm tannins and a slightly gamy finish. Drinkable now. 150 cases made. • $22 • (11/30/96) • **86**

St.-Joseph Cuvée Prestige 1991 • $20 • (05/31/94) • **82**

St.-Joseph White Izeras 1996: An overblown style, rich and thick, loaded with butterscotch and vanilla flavors, hints of pear and melon, but it lacks the acidity for food. Still, it's seductive for those who like oaky whites. • $21 • (10/15/97) • **80**

St.-Joseph White Izeras 1995: Vibrant pear and pineapple aromas turn simple on the palate. Lively, fresh and tart, making up in zip what it lacks in depth. 125 cases made. • $22 • (12/15/96) • **82**

St.-Joseph White Le Bois Lombard Cuvée Prestige 1996: Ripe and round, this big white shows opulent butterscotch and honey flavors with hints of marzipan. Almost a late-harvest style. The acidity is low but the wine has personality and power. • $24 • (10/15/97) • **86**

CURÉ-BON, CHÂTEAU

St.-Emilion 1997: Dark-colored, with very ripe berry and spice aromas and flavors. Medium- to full-bodied, with silky tannins and a ripe berry aftertaste. Very good sample. Almost outstanding. • $NA • (06/15/98) (BT) • **85-89**

St.-Emilion 1996: Interesting aromas of tobacco, earth and berries. Full-bodied and tannic, with an outstanding balance on the palate. Impressive for this producer. Almost outstanding. • $28 • (06/15/98) (BT) • **85-89**

St.-Emilion 1995: Slightly one-dimensional, with blackberry and earth aromas and flavors. Medium-bodied, with firm tannins and a fresh finish. Drink now. 1,500 cases made. • $26 • (01/31/98) • **86**

CURÉ-BON-LA-MADELEINE, CHÂTEAU

St.-Emilion 1994: Straightforward, with good, fruity, dried cherry flavors and medium tannins. Drink now or hold. • $23 • (01/31/97) • **84**

CURSON, CHÂTEAU

Crozes-Hermitage 1989 • $17 • (07/15/91) • **89**

CUVÉE LES BASTIDES

Faugères 1990 • $NA • (03/15/94) • **87**

CUVÉE PIERRE ROUGE

Red 1990 • $7 • (06/30/92) • **78**

CYGNE BLANC DE FONRÉAUD, LE

Bordeaux White 1995: All dressed up with plenty of buttery and floral flavors, and an herbal note as well. A bit exaggerated overall, but tasty. 600 cases made. • $17 • (04/30/97) • **83**

Bordeaux White 1993 • $NA • (05/31/95) • **79**

CYPRÈS DE CLIMENS

Barsac 1992: Light and easy, featuring pine, pineapple, honey and grass flavors; quite pleasant as a clean and slightly sweet apéritif. Drink now. Second label from Château Climens. • $NA • (04/15/95) • **83**

CYRANO

Chardonnay Vin de Pays 1997: A soft, buttery component dominates, though there are appley flavors as well. Finish is a bit rough. 4,800 cases made. • $8 • (07/31/98) • **79**

DABIN, JEAN

Muscadet de Sèvre et Maine Sur Lie Sélection Ventois 1995: An earthy note on the finish detracts from the good concentration, almond and light pear flavors. Tasted twice, with consistent notes. • $9 • (06/15/97) • **78**

DAGUENEAU, DIDIER

Maudit 1990 • $50 • (09/30/93) • **84**

Pouilly-Fumé Buisson Menard 1993 • $40 • (11/15/95) HR • **92**

Pouilly-Fumé En Chailloux 1996: Unusually ripe and rich for the Loire, showing more of a Californian character in the melon, vanilla and honey flavors, but underlying acidity and hints of tarragon-scented herbs keep it close to home. Drinkable now. 4,000 cases made. • $26 • (05/31/98) • **87**

Pouilly-Fumé En Chailloux 1995: Lively aromas of pears, spice and smoke follow through on the palate in this round white, and firm acidity keeps it focused. Fresh and clean. 4,000 cases made. • $25 • (06/15/97) • **84**

Pouilly-Fumé En Chailloux 1994 • $26 • (05/15/96) • **83**

Pouilly-Fumé En Chailloux 1993 • $33 • (12/15/95) • **86**

Pouilly-Fumé Pur Sang 1996: Extraordinary in its richness, definition and depth, this Loire white is seamless and powerful, offering aromas and flavors of ripe melon, coconut, smoke, mineral and herb that will add dimensions of flavor to any dish. Delicious, from a rising star region. Drink now through 2001. 2,000 cases made. • $35 • (02/28/98) HR • **94**

Pouilly-Fumé Pur Sang 1995: Unique and delicious, this Loire Sauvignon Blanc is reminiscent of a great white Bordeaux, such as Haut-Brion, thanks to the vanilla and toast flavors of barrel fermentation. With enough acidity for balance and ripe fruit flavors that give it concentration and complexity, it's head and shoulders above the rest. 2,000 cases made. • $35 • (05/15/97) HR • **95**

Pouilly-Fumé Pur Sang 1993 • $38 • (11/15/95) • **89**

Pouilly-Fumé Silex 1996: Bold and ripe, offering powerful fruit flavors of melon, pineapple and fig, with notes of honey, vanilla and spice, kept lively by a vivid core of citrusy acidity. Rich yet harmonious, and food-friendly. Best from 2000 through 2003. • $50 • (02/28/98) • **93**

Pouilly-Fumé Silex 1995: Pow! Right in the kisser. Powerful and intense, this complex white marries nervy acidity, ripe fruit and toasty oak, well structured and distinctive. Drinkable now. • $50 • (06/15/97) • **92**

Pouilly-Fumé Silex 1994 • $49 • (05/15/96) • **88**

DAGUENEAU, JEAN-CLAUDE

Pouilly-Fumé Domaine des Berthiers 1995: This white offers powerful flavors of apples, smoke and earth. It has good structure but lacks balance; may smooth out with food. • $13 • (06/15/97) • **79**

DAGUENEAU, SERGE

Pouilly-Fumé 1995: An explosive wine, bursting with ripe fruit flavors of melon, pineapple and mango with accents of herbs, nuts, minerals and toast. Not classic for the region, but powerful and distinctive, big yet balanced. • $18 • (05/15/97) • **92**

DALEM, CHÂTEAU

Fronsac 1997: Very dark in color, with strong grape and floral aromas. Medium-bodied, with velvety tannins and a medium finish. Slightly hollow midpalate. • $NA • (06/15/98) (BT) • **85-89**

Fronsac 1990: This is a shapely, aromatic wine, with lovely flavors of black cherry and berry and silky tannins, but a little short on the finish. Drinkable now. • $20 • (03/31/93) • **86**

DALICIEUX

Beaujolais-Villages Leynes 1993: Fading now. Light and dry on the palate, this shows strawberry, vegetal and earthy flavors and dry tannins on the finish. • $11 • (09/15/96) • **77**

DAME, CHÂTEAU DE LA

Margaux 1988 • $15 • (02/15/91) • **86**

DAMOY, PIERRE

Chambertin 1994: Difficult to warm up to. Medium-bodied, with a stalky, herbal, earthy and astringent character. Thin and weak on the finish. • $70 • (11/15/96) • **74**

Chambertin 1993: A big Chambertin, medium- to full-bodied, delivering silky tannins and long finish that tastes of strawberry and raspberry jam. Try after 2000. • $69 • (11/15/95) • **91**

Chambertin-Clos de Bèze 1994: Light-weight, bordering on thin, and while some spicy oak notes make it interesting, the flavors never quite get going, even finishing a tad bitter. Drinkable now. • $75 • (11/15/96) • **78**

Chambertin-Clos de Bèze 1993: Elegant, attractive vanilla, plum and raspberry aromas, medium body, fine tannins and sweet, candied fruit finish. Better in 2000. • $55 • (11/15/95) • **91**

Chapelle-Chambertin 1994: Very chewy and tannic, with just a hint of plummy, meatlike flavor sneaking through the formidable tannins. Try in 2000. • $65 • (11/15/96) • **80**

Chapelle-Chambertin 1993: Can red Burgundy get silkier than this? A beauty to behold, featuring enormous concentration and superb currant and earth flavors. Massively tannic, but fruit supports the whole edifice. Try in 2000. • $57 • (11/15/95) • **91**

Gevrey-Chambertin Clos Tamisot 1994: Disappointingly light and diluted, an unfortunate trend with the '94s. • $35 • (11/15/96) • **70**

Gevrey-Chambertin Clos Tamisot 1993: Well crafted and silky, full in body. Earth and red berry flavors add some plum and mint. There is enough delicious fruit to balance the massive tannins. Cellar until past 2000. • $30 • (11/15/95) • **89**

DAMPIERRE, COMTE AUDOIN DE

Brut Blanc de Blancs Champagne 1985: So suave it practically melts in your mouth. Mellow, mature and subtle in flavor, smooth and soft in texture. Long-lasting finish. Probably at its most enjoyable now. • $97 • (12/31/96) • **93**

Brut Champagne Grande Année 1990: A grand Champagne that's suave in texture and quite flavorful, offering harmonious honey, butterscotch and citrus notes that expand on the palate and linger on the finish. Drink now through 2000. • $49 • (04/30/98) • **89**

Brut Champagne Grande Année 1983 • $32 • (12/31/90) • **89**

Brut Rosé Champagne Oeil de Perdrix 1990: A mature rosé. Its mellow, spicy, dried fruit flavors are subtle, and the texture is crisp, bordering on tannic. Think of it as a serious red wine. Drink now. • $49 • (04/30/98) • **85**

DARD & RIBO

Crozes-Hermitage 1990 • $17 • (04/15/93) • **86**

DARVIOT, YVES

Beaune Le Clos des Mouches White 1993: Pretty apple and cream aromas and flavors. Medium in body, showing loads of toasty coconut and vanilla character and a delicate, fruity finish. • $NA • (05/15/95) • **86**

Beaune Le Clos des Mouches White 1992: Rich and oily texture, toasty and smoky, with modest spice, vanilla and pear flavors and a subtle finish. • $43 • (08/31/94) • **84**

DASSAULT, CHÂTEAU

St.-Emilion 1996: Lots of earthy tobacco and coffee grind aromas that follow through on the palate. Medium-bodied, with good acidity but slightly aggressive, steely tannins. 9,500 cases made. • $NA • (01/01/97) (BT) • **75-79**

St.-Emilion 1995: A big wine, rich and plush, with lovely tar, berry and cedar and mineral flavors. Serious wine for this estate. 9,500 cases made. • $20 • (05/15/97) (BT) • **90-94**

St.-Emilion 1988 • $17 • (07/15/91) • **83**

St.-Emilion 1982 • $20 • (05/15/89) • **90**

DAUNY, NICOLE & CHRISTIAN

Sancerre Clos du Roy 1993 • $17 • (10/31/94) • **82**

DAUPHINE, CHÂTEAU DE LA

Fronsac 1997: A good level of raspberry and berry character. Medium-bodied, with medium tannins and a silky finish. • $NA • (06/15/98) (BT) • **85-89**

Fronsac 1996: Pretty and fruity, with pleasant berry and tobacco aromas and flavors. Medium-bodied, with a light, silky finish. • $20 • (06/15/98) (BT) • **85-89**

Fronsac 1995: Beautiful fruit marks this wine. Very grapey, with violet, floral and berry character. Full-bodied and velvety, with pretty tannins and a long, fresh fruit aftertaste. Drinkable now. • $20 • (01/31/98) • **89**

Fronsac 1994: Not much to it. Some good berry and dried herb notes, but it's light-bodied and short on the finish. Drink now. • $20 • (01/31/97) • **79**

Fronsac 1993: Enjoyable milk chocolate and berry character. Medium in body, delicate tannins and delicious finish. Drinkable now. • $22 • (01/31/96) • **82**

Fronsac 1992: Somewhat fruity, but slightly metallic and hard. Cherry, berry finish. • $17 • (04/15/95) • **75**

Fronsac 1990: A traditional-style Fronsac, with tomato and herbal character and hard, tight tannins. Drinkable now. 4,500 cases made. • $17 • (03/31/93) • **81**

Fronsac 1989 • $15 • (03/15/92) • **80**

Fronsac 1985 • $20 • (09/30/88) • **84**

DAUVISSAT, JEAN

Chablis 1996: Lovely, supple and silky, with a mineral, vanilla bean, wet stone, pear tart character that is very seductive. Full-bodied, this has harmony etched all over it, with plenty of fruit and crisp acidity as well as nice hints of honey and ripeness. A wine worth buying by the case. Tempting now through 2005. • $18 • (05/31/98) • **92**

Chablis Les Preuses 1996: Well made, round and ripe but also fresh, this medium- to full-bodied Chablis gives plenty of pleasure, with lemon, pear, grilled sausage and oyster aromas and flavors. Intense finish. Better in 2000. • $45 • (05/31/98) • **87**

Chablis Les Preuses 1995: This full-bodied, smooth *grand cru* is bit oaky now, with distinctive vanilla bean, toasty bread, mineral and ripe pear flavors. Try around 2000. • $45 • (06/15/97) • **86**

Chablis Les Preuses 1994 • $45 • (05/31/96) • **81**

Key: SS—Spectator Selection CS—Cellar Selection HR—Highly Recommended BB—Best Buy $NA—Price not available Ⓐ—Auction Price (BT)—Barrel Tasting
Dates in parentheses indicate the issues in which the ratings were published.

FRANCE

Chablis Montmain 1995: This *premier cru*, loaded with mineral and ripe fruit flavors, is chewy and full-bodied but maintains a racy complexity despite being rather heady. Drink now through 2000. • $NA • (06/15/97) • **87**

Chablis Séchet 1996: Clean and pure, with a lovely mouthfeel, it's the sort of supple, ripe, minerally Chardonnay that makes you swoon. Beautifully balanced and so sweet-tasting, with pear, pineapple, toasty oak, lime and lots of other stuff. Full-bodied, this should come into its own around 2005. • $23 • (05/31/98) • **92**

Chablis Séchet 1995: Harmonious *premier cru*. Medium to full in body, with a mineral, fruit and earth character that holds through the long, subtle finish. Delicious now, but will age beautifully through 2007. 250 cases made. • $23 • (06/15/97) • **89**

Chablis Séchet 1994 • $23 • (05/31/96) • **80**

Chablis Vaillons 1996: Distinctive, seductively steely '96 Chablis, with an intense and lovely lime-honey-spice combination that testifies to the purity of the minerally earth as well as to the crafty winemaking. Medium in body, superintense in texture, but balanced and so clean, vibrant and pure, you want to kiss this wine—or drink it now through 2007. • $25 • (05/31/98) • **94**

Chablis Vaillons 1995: Crisp, with lots of citrus and green apple flavors, but underneath is some sweet fruit. Medium-bodied. May be better in 1999 to 2000. • $24 • (06/15/97) • **84**

Chablis Vaillons 1994 • $24 • (05/31/96) • **90**

Chablis Vaillons Vieilles Vignes 1996: A bit showy, with lime and honey, showing some good mineral-laden and citrusy character, but it turns slightly burning on the finish. • $30 • (05/31/98) • **87**

Chablis Vaillons Vieilles Vignes 1995: A classy *premier cru*, tightly wound around impressively concentrated, palate-coating flavors. Full-bodied, with a long finish, it's tempting now but needs until after 2000 to fully develop. 500 cases made. • $30 • (06/15/97) • **89**

Chablis Vaillons Vieilles Vignes 1994 • $30 • (05/31/96) • **85**

DAUVISSAT, RENÉ & VINCENT

Chablis 1994 • $NA • (05/31/96) • **86**

Chablis La Forêt 1995: Notable for its ripe character, supported by crisp fruit flavors and a slight smoke and mineral component. Medium- to full-bodied. Can age, try in 1999 to 2000. • $32 • (06/15/97) • **87**

Chablis La Forêt 1994 • $NA • (05/31/96) • **87**

Chablis Les Clos 1994 • $60 • (05/31/96) CS • **93**

Chablis Les Clos 1993 • $61 • (08/31/95) • **87**

Chablis Les Preuses 1994 • $60 • (05/31/96) • **89**

Chablis Les Preuses 1993 • $61 • (08/31/95) • **89**

Chablis Séchet 1995: A fairly rich, classy *premier cru*, but firm and well structured, bursting with citrusy fresh fruit. Medium-bodied, with a harmonious finish laced with mineral notes. Hold until at least 2000. 500 cases made. • $32 • (06/15/97) • **90**

Chablis Séchet 1994 • $32 • (05/31/96) • **90**

Chablis Séchet 1993 • $32 • (08/31/95) • **86**

Chablis Vaillons 1995: A pure *premier cru*, crisp in character and well defined in flavor, offering honey, earth, mineral and green apple notes. Of medium body, it races to a long finish. 833 cases made. • $32 • (06/15/97) • **87**

Chablis Vaillons 1994 • $32 • (05/31/96) • **91**

Chablis Vaillons 1993 • $32 • (08/31/95) • **85**

DAUZAC, CHÂTEAU

Margaux 1997: Blueberry and mineral aromas, with plenty of vanilla character. Medium-bodied, with medium tannins and a vanilla finish. Lacks fruit. Too much wood? • $NA • (06/15/98) (BT) • **80-84**

Margaux 1996: Not as good as I remember. Has a strong herbal character and is a bit hard. Medium-bodied, with slightly coarse tannins and a medium finish. Wait and see. • $27 • (06/15/98) (BT) • **85-89**

Margaux 1995: Best Dauzac ever. Attractive berry and violet aromas follow through on the palate. Medium- to full-bodied, with racy tannins and a long, floral aftertaste. Very pretty indeed. Best after 2002. • $25 • (01/31/98) • **92**

Margaux 1994: Big and rich, delivering tobacco, berry, cherry and vanilla aromas and flavors. Medium- to full-bodied, with well-integrated tannins and a long finish. • $12 Ⓐ • (01/31/97) • **88**

Margaux 1993: More ripe fruit than in many '93s, offering red berry, plum, tobacco and chocolate flavors, medium body and nice, silky tannins. Try now. • $24 • (01/31/96) • **86**

Margaux 1992: Surprisingly ripe for the vintage, offering plum and currant character, medium body, silky tannins and a tobacco, cassis finish. • $17 • (04/15/95) • **84**

Margaux 1990: A plump wine, with an abundance of plum and berry flavors and soft, round tannins. Easy to drink; try now. 15,000 cases made. • $23 • (03/31/93) • **85**

Margaux 1989 • $22 Ⓐ • (03/15/92) • **90**

Margaux 1988 • $20 • (06/30/91) HR • **90**

Margaux 1985 • $21 • (09/30/88) • **87**

Margaux 1982 • $28 • (08/31/92) • **91**

DAUZAN LA VERGNE, CHÂTEAU

Haut-Montravel 1994: Smooth and tight with honey and pear flavors and a splash of citrus. A blowsy style. 500 cases made. • $11/500ml • (08/31/97) • **83**

DAVENAY, CHÂTEAU DE

Bourgogne 1994: Fresh, grapey and well made, with appealing anise and blackberry flavors and aromas. Medium-bodied. Ends with some complexity. Drinkable now. • $13 • (11/15/96) • **82**

Hautes Côtes de Beaune 1994: Light and crisp, with sufficient berry flavor to make it half-way pleasant. • $18 • (11/15/96) • **80**

Montagny Premier Cru 1993: Rich and ripe with nutmeg and green apple flavors. Well rounded and balanced, this is all up-front, delivering loads of acidity and moderate intensity. • $NA • (01/01/96) • **84**

DECELLE, CHÂTEAU LA

Coteaux du Tricastin 1989 • $7 • (07/15/91) BB • **82**

DEFAIX, BERNARD

Chablis 1996: Ripe and fairly smooth, with pear, apple and tropical fruit notes and a good, fresh finish. Drink now. 100 cases imported. 4,167 cases made. • $13 • (08/31/97) • **84**

Chablis Côte de Léchet 1996: For fans of steely Chablis. Very tight and tough now, but there's plenty of stuffing to this reserved, Iron Manlike Chablis. A thick mouthfeel coats the palate with a mineral-laden character, plenty of earth, citrus, dried herbs and sweet fruit notes. Cellar until around 2005 to 2007 and it should soften. 2,900 cases made. • $26 • (05/31/98) • **89**

Chablis Les Vaillons 1996: Distinctive Chablis, showing wet earth, mineral and good fruit, although it's a bit herbal. Medium-bodied, it turns a bit tough and drying on the finish. 830 cases made. • $26 • (05/31/98) • **84**

DEISS, DOMAINE MARCEL

Gewürztraminer Alsace Bergheim 1995: Pear and almond are the dominant themes, with floral accents. Medium-bodied. Vibrant acidity carries the flavors to a moderate finish. Enjoyable now. • $20 • (09/30/97) • **86**

Gewürztraminer Alsace Bergheim Vendanges Tardives 1994: Vibrant and bright, with a lanolin character to the honey and apple flavors. It's firm and compact right now, with some heat (alcohol) on the finish that upsets the balance. Still, it's impressive. • $35 • (11/15/97) • **89**

Gewürztraminer Alsace Grand Cru Altenberg de Bergheim Sélection de Grains Nobles 1994: Sweet and succulent, this Gewürz is surprisingly light on its feet, sporting pear, rose and honey flavors that turn to grapefruit on the lingering finish. Lacks power, but makes up for it with subtlety and finesse. • $79 • (10/15/97) • **90**

Gewürztraminer Alsace Grand Cru Altenberg de Bergheim Vendanges Tardives 1993: A bit coarse, and although the apple, pear and lanolin flavors come through, their intensity and concentration fail to match the structure. A mint or basil note appears just before the hot finish. • $45 • (11/15/97) • **87**

Gewürztraminer Alsace St.-Hippolyte 1995: Full-bodied and fat, exhibiting intense honey, orange and mineral flavors with a firm, sinewy framework. Still, it lacks the complexity and harmony of the best '95s. • $20 • (11/15/97) • **86**

Pinot Blanc Alsace Bergheim 1995: Textbook Pinot Blanc. Ripe and fat, full of juicy apple and citrus flavors and an accent of almond, followed by a fresh, mouthwatering finish. • $14 • (09/15/97) • **85**

Pinot Gris Alsace Beblenheim 1995: A substantial white that has everything in the right place, from the smoky floral and peach aromas to the almond

and citrus flavors on the aftertaste. Balanced, integrated and long, yet has the structure for aging. 500 cases made. • $20 • (10/15/97) • **90**

Riesling Alsace Beblenheim 1993: A maturing Riesling, revealing marzipan, apple, spice and mineral flavors, combined with concentration and depth. It's dry and steely, but the components are there, so wait until 1999. This would be great with a stuffed loin of pork or *choucroute garni*. • $19 • (01/01/97) • **90**

Riesling Alsace Bennwihr 1994: This white has loads of apple flavors and good concentration, but the dominant feature is searing acidity. Good length. • $19 • (09/30/97) • **85**

Riesling Alsace Burg 1993: The crisp acidity and honey, floral and apple flavors of this Riesling, which is hitting its stride now, have unified, but there's still a firm finish. Definitely a food wine. • $19 • (01/01/97) • **87**

Riesling Alsace Engelgarten 1994: A racy, taut Riesling sporting apple, spice and stone flavors. Still needs some time or a plate of sausages to bring it into its own. Try now. • $19 • (09/30/97) • **83**

Riesling Alsace Grand Cru Altenberg de Bergheim Vendanges Tardives 1994: A white that smells and tastes of pears and lime. It's simple and falls short on the finish. • $45 • (11/15/97) • **84**

Riesling Alsace Grasberg Vendanges Tardives 1994: Has a kerosene flavor that denotes maturing Riesling and apple and lime. There's a lot going on, all in a balanced, refreshing way. Well made. Drinkable now through 2003. • $35 • (11/15/97) • **88**

DELABY-GÉNOT, MARIE

Pommard Château Génot-Boulanger 1995: Medium in body and intensity, this lacks the fresh berry flavors we look for in a young Pinot Noir; has a muted nose and only decent fruit. Dry tannins. • $27 • (01/31/98) • **79**

DELAMOTTE

Blanc de Blancs Champagne 1982: Delicious and soft on the palate, but finishes tart and slightly astringent. Nutmeg and honey flavors are vivid. Enjoyable but slightly out of balance. • $28 • (04/15/88) • **84**

Brut Blanc de Blancs Champagne 1985: Wonderfully fresh and vibrant for an 11-year-old wine, this beautifully balanced bubbly combines lively lemon, apple and vanilla flavors in a creamy-smooth texture. Great to drink now. Has matured nicely since first reviewed in 1991. • $47 • (11/30/96) • **91**

DELAPORTE, DOMAINE VINCENT

Sancerre 1996: This beautifully balanced white begins with clean, pure aromas of citrus and mineral, then bursts with bright flavors of pears, minerals and herbs that linger on the finish. It's ripe yet crisp, rich yet keen, and a great match with food. Drink now through 2000. 2,500 cases made. • $23 • (03/31/98) • **90**

Sancerre 1995 • $23 • (04/30/96) • **83**

Sancerre 1993 • $NA • (10/31/94) • **82**

Sancerre Cuvée Maxime Les Galifards 1996: This lovely, distinctive white adds seductive new-oak flavors of vanilla and cream to the crisp mineral and citrus flavors of Sauvignon Blanc in a harmonious combination. Though hardly traditional, it's definitely a winner. Drink now through 2002. • $35 • (05/31/98) • **90**

DELARCHE PÈRE & FILS, MARIUS

Corton Les Renardes 1990: Pleasantly fruity, with tasty currant and black cherry-scented flavors that turn spicy. Finishes with firm tannins and a splash of vanilla from the oak. Drinkable now. • $49 • (06/15/93) • **87**

Corton-Charlemagne 1995: An explosive wine of amazing intensity. Firmly structured around a zesty core of fruit, mineral and citrus flavors, clean as a whistle, this steely Corton is a wine to hold until at least 2006, as its pale color, elegant aroma and muscular build suggest it will stay closed for years. • $NA • (05/31/97) • **96**

Corton-Charlemagne 1993: Distinctive beeswax, apple and lime character, medium body, plenty of new wood and a long, crisp finish. Aftertaste is rather candied. Drinkable now. • $NA • (08/31/95) • **81**

Pernand-Vergelesses 1989 • $15/375ml • (04/30/91) • **82**

Key: SS—Spectator Selection CS—Cellar Selection HR—Highly Recommended BB—Best Buy $NA—Price not available Ⓐ—Auction Price (BT)—Barrel Tasting

Dates in parentheses indicate the issues in which the ratings were published.

Pernand-Vergelesses Ile des Vergelesses 1990: Smells attractive, with a bouquet of fruit aromas, and turns elegant and spicy on the palate, with layers of plum and cherry flavors and a smooth, silky texture. Drinkable now. • $28 • (06/15/93) • **87**

Pernand-Vergelesses Ile des Vergelesses 1985 • $23 • (10/15/88) • **89**

Pernand-Vergelesses Les Vergelesses 1990: A pleasant wine that's crisp and focused, with bright cherry and strawberry-tinged flavors framed by toasty, cedary oak notes. Turns tannic on the finish. Drinkable now. • $25 • (06/15/93) • **84**

Pernand-Vergelesses White 1995: Great texture, but the flavors may not please everyone, leaning as they do toward citrus, dried herb, green appleskin, even lime. A rather tough drinking experience. Perhaps better after 2000. • $NA • (08/31/97) • **82**

DELAS

Châteauneuf-du-Pape 1985 • $17 • (10/31/87) • **91**

Châteauneuf-du-Pape 1983 • $18 • (10/15/91) • **72**

Châteauneuf-du-Pape Cuvée de Haute Pierre 1989 • $16 • (10/15/91) • **90**

Châteauneuf-du-Pape Cuvée de Haute Pierre 1988 • $17 • (10/15/91) • **86**

Châteauneuf-du-Pape Cuvée de Haute Pierre 1986 • $20 • (10/15/91) • **86**

Châteauneuf-du-Pape Cuvée de Haute Pierre 1985 • $20 • (10/15/91) • **86**

Châteauneuf-du-Pape Les Calcerniers 1995: A pretty wine, medium-bodied and delicate, with some ripe cherry, raspberry and pepper flavors. Fresh, and approachable now. 6,000 cases made. • $19 • (10/15/97) • **86**

Châteauneuf-du-Pape Les Calcerniers 1993: Chewy, with cassis, licorice and gamy flavors over firm tannins. Good focus in an accessible style. Drinkable now. • $20 • (11/15/95) • **84**

Condrieu 1994: Expressive, offering ripe peach and summery floral aromas and flavors, round and soft. A bit advanced for a '94, but still shows good varietal definition. 300 cases made. • $30 • (09/15/97) • **86**

Condrieu Clos Boucher 1995: New wood gives attractive sweet vanilla and butter flavors, but it tends to obscure the fruit. Still, the wine is ripe, rich and lush, and perhaps the coconut and spicy fruit flavors will emerge with time. Drinkable now. 333 cases made. • $48 • (10/15/97) • **85**

Cornas Chante-Perdrix 1991 • $28 • (05/31/94) • **86**

Cornas Chante-Perdrix 1990 • $28 • (09/30/93) • **88**

Côte-Rôtie Seigneur de Maugiron 1995: Light and rather soft on the palate, with black olive and herbal flavors, turning tougher on the finish, where an alluring gamy note emerges. It's delicacy may betray a lack of concentration, despite the rather rustic tannins. Drinkable now. 1,250 cases made. • $35 • (10/15/97) • **85**

Côte-Rôtie Seigneur de Maugiron 1994: Herbal and vegetal flavors crowd out the strawberry in this light-bodied, slightly diluted red. Lacks ripeness and concentration. Drinkable now. 2,100 cases made. • $35 • (10/15/97) • **78**

Côte-Rôtie Seigneur de Maugiron 1991: A supple wine with fresh cherry, chestnut and barnyard flavors. Accessible but not complex. Drinkable now. • $36 • (05/31/94) • **81**

Côte-Rôtie Seigneur de Maugiron 1990: Maturing well and showing better than an earlier tasting, this has good Syrah character in a traditional style, with its pepper, licorice and mineral notes thick yet fresh on the palate. It's balanced and firm and should hold through 2000, at least. • $30 • (11/30/96) • **89**

Côtes du Rhône Saint Esprit 1996: Shows the potential of '96. A bit earthy and reduced, but underneath is a ripe character and lots of interesting rosemary, dried herb, currant and tobacco flavors. Tastes better than it smells (at least now). Pretty concentrated for a standard Côtes du Rhône. Drink slightly chilled. 8,300 cases made. • $8 • (10/15/97) • **85**

Côtes du Rhône Saint Esprit 1995: This firm French red offers well-defined black cherry flavors, bright and crisp on the palate, with a light earthy note that adds complexity. The price is right, and it's drinkable now. 8,300 cases made. • $8 • (09/15/97) BB • **85**

Côtes du Rhône Saint Esprit 1994: The black cherry and meatlike flavors are light, but the underlying tannins are very firm. Fresh, but not quite balanced. Try with grilled meats. • $9 • (12/15/96) • **81**

Côtes du Rhône St.-Esprit 1993 • $9 • (11/15/95) • **83**

Côtes du Rhône White Saint Esprit 1995: Rich and ripe, almost thick on the palate, with round, soft flavors of honey and herbs blanketing the pear and almond notes. Distinctive and easy to drink, but could use more acidity for balance. 5,000 cases made. • $8 • (10/15/97) • **82**

Côtes du Rhône White Saint Esprit 1993: Maturing now, this amber-colored wine offers walnut, butterscotch and herbal flavors. Not much fruit flavor, but still holds together well. Drink now. • $9 • (12/15/96) • **80**

Côtes du Ventoux Val Muzols 1995: A light red, with spicy cherry and strawberry flavors and light tannins that turn firm on the finish. A good barbecue wine; try it slightly chilled. • $7 • (09/15/97) • **84**

Côtes du Ventoux Val Muzols 1994: Alluring aromas of spice and herbs carry over onto the palate where ripe plum flavors are suppported by firm yet unobtrusive tannins. Flavorful and harmonious, drink now. • $7 • (10/15/96) • **85**

Côtes du Ventoux Val Muzols 1993 • $8 • (11/15/95) • **76**

Crozes-Hermitage 1985 • $7 • (12/15/87) • **78**

Crozes-Hermitage Les Launes 1995: Smooth and supple, with strong anise, licorice and black cherry character. Medium-bodied, with a fresh underpinning of lime notes, it has some decent Syrah flavors. Drinkable now. 10,000 cases made. • $13 • (10/15/97) • **85**

Crozes-Hermitage Les Launes 1994: Subtle and understated, yet complex, it's a perfumy, lovely wine that just lets the fruit speak. Medium-bodied, not aggressively pumped up by oak at all, it's clean and pure, singing with rose petal and violet notes, sweet currant and blackberry flavors. A masterful job. Drink now through 2001. 2,100 cases made. • $13 • (10/15/97) • **91**

Crozes-Hermitage Les Launes 1992: Thick and simple, this offers herbal, stewed fruit and leather flavors over moderate tannins. Drinkable, but lacks freshness and fruit flavor. • $14 • (11/30/96) • **78**

Crozes-Hermitage Les Launes 1990 • $12 • (10/15/95) • **89**

Crozes-Hermitage White Les Launes 1995: Shows an intriguing intensity, with lively grapefruit flavors accented by almond, herb and spice notes. Not particularly subtle or sophisticated, but it sure wakes up the taste buds. 600 cases made. • $13 • (09/15/97) • **87**

Crozes-Hermitage White Les Launes 1993 • $12 • (11/15/95) • **83**

Hermitage Cuvée Marquise de la Tourette 1995: Vegetal, herbal flavors are a bit dull and rustic in this tart, firm red. Has some cherry notes, but overall it lacks ripeness and generosity. Drinkable now. 1,600 cases made. • $35 • (10/15/97) • **79**

Hermitage Cuvée Marquise de la Tourette 1994: Light and fruity, with strawberry and light spicy flavors, this is pleasant enough, but quite light for the appellation. Tannins are soft, finish is short; drink now. 1,600 cases made. • $35 • (10/15/97) • **80**

Hermitage Cuvée Marquise de la Tourette 1991: Almost overripe, with raisin flavors and tough tannins. Compact and a bit hard. Try now. • $35 • (05/31/94) • **84**

Hermitage Cuvée Marquise de la Tourette 1990: Alluring spice and ripe fruit aromas give way to ripe flavors of plum, chocolate and coffee in this dense, harmonious wine. It's firm, but not overly tannic, and just edging into the complexity of maturity. It's drinking well now, but has improved since an earlier tasting and will continue to improve through 2005. • $30 • (11/30/96) • **91**

Hermitage Les Bessards 1995: Jammy, even a bit cooked, with cooked cherries, mineral and earth flavors in a rustic style that's firmly tannic and slightly disjointed. It has some varietal expressiveness, and may come around in 1999. 250 cases made. • $65 • (10/15/97) • **82**

Hermitage Les Bessards 1994: This elegant red says Hermitage loud and clear with plenty of gamy, smoky and licorice accents to the core of firm, ripe fruit. The tannins are tender, but the wine is balanced and long. Drinkable now. 300 cases made. • $65 • (09/15/97) • **90**

Hermitage Les Bessards 1990: Thick and chewy, offering rich tar, leather and game flavors typical of Syrah, muscular tannins and ripe plum notes. Powerful and concentrated, but a bit rustic. Drinkable now. 291 cases made. • $20 Ⓐ • (10/15/95) • **89**

Merlot Vin de Pays d'Oc 1995: Herbal, with cherry and plum flavors. Nearly peters out on the finish. 2,700 cases made. • $7 • (11/15/97) • **78**

Merlot Vin de Pays d'Oc 1994: Stewed aromas and flavors dominate this over-ripe wine. Clamps down on the finish. 2,700 cases made. • $7 • (12/15/96) • **74**

Merlot Vin de Pays d'Oc 1993 • $9 • (07/31/95) • **83**

St.-Joseph Cuvée François de Tournon 1994: This ripe red shows good concentration and balance, with a lush texture, bold flavors of berries, smoke and herbs and a long, gamy finish. Drinks well now; should hold through at least 2005. 1,700 cases made. • $18 • (10/15/97) • **87**

St.-Joseph Cuvée François de Tournon 1991 • $NA • (05/31/94) • **79**

St.-Joseph Ste.-Epine 1994: Ripe, its plum, licorice and spicy flavors round and quite concentrated, turning a bit dry on the finish. Shows good varietal character. Drinkable now. 167 cases made. • $25 • (10/15/97) • **84**

Viognier Vin de Pays d'Oc 1994: An easy-drinking white, offering soft apple and mild floral flavors, clean and nearly sweet. It's fresh and light, but doesn't show much varietal character. 4,000 cases made. • $10 • (04/30/97) • **81**

Viognier Vin de Pays de la Drôme 1995: Earthy and rustic, showing dull flavors of cooked apples and canned fruit. Heavy and earthy. 4,000 cases made. • $10 • (10/15/97) • **74**

DELAUNAY, EDOUARD

Bourgogne Pinot Noir En Fleur 1993: Light, delicate, modest fruit flavors. Drink now. 5,000 cases made. • $15 • (11/15/95) • **78**

Clos de Vougeot 1993: Very light for this appellation, delivering a slightly weedy, metallic character, medium-to-light body, medium tannins and short finish. Drink now. 100 cases made. • $85 • (11/15/95) • **73**

Côte de Beaune-Villages 1993: Light, lean, modest strawberry and raspberry character, light tannins and rather short finish. Try now. • $18 • (11/15/95) • **79**

DELBECK

Brut Champagne 1990: A full-bodied, rather austere but powerful Champagne, with subdued fruit flavors and handsome spicy, earthy accents that linger on the finish. The dry, bold texture is compelling. Drink now through 2002. 1,800 cases made. • $34 • (04/30/98) • **90**

Brut Champagne Bouzy NV: Mature in style, this offers nutty, honeylike aromas and broad, apple cider flavors. Generous, but drink soon. 500 cases made. • $38 • (04/30/98) • **81**

Brut Champagne Cramant NV: A richly flavored, full-bodied sparkler with a deep-gold color, ample fruit notes accented by spicy, buttery nuances and a plush texture. Drink now. 500 cases made. • $38 • (04/30/98) • **86**

Brut Champagne Heritage NV: Very good for a non-vintage, this is well-made Champagne. It's vibrantly fruity, nicely crisp and assertive, turns mellow on the lingering finish. Drink now. 12,500 cases made. • $29 • (04/30/98) • **88**

DELESVAUX, PHILIPPE

Anjou Red 1996: Bright and chewy, showing typical character of black cherries, smoke and light herbs, with light but firm tannins and a fresh finish. Pleasant when served at room temperature or slightly chilled. Drink now through 2000. • $11 • (05/31/98) • **86**

Coteaux du Layon La Moque 1995: This unctuous, honeyed white has spicy, butterscotch notes adding dimension to the pear and pineapple flavors. Full-bodied, somewhat tannic. Quite evolved for a young wine; drink now. 65 cases made. • $30 • (05/31/97) • **89**

Coteaux du Layon Sélection de Grains Nobles 1996: Powerful botrytis aromas of spice and honey follow through on the rich, unctuous palate of this impressively concentrated white. It has the sweetness and creaminess of great crème brûlée, but with enough acidity to keep it lively. A long ager, too. Drink now through 2010. • $38/500ml • (05/31/98) • **92**

Coteaux du Layon Sélection de Grains Nobles 1995: This seriously sweet wine is bronze in color, with rich raisin, dried apple, coconut and honey flavors, yet lively acidity gives it good balance. One can really taste the concentration of the grapes, and it promises long life. 250 cases made. • $35/500ml • (05/15/97) HR • **94**

DELETANG, DOMAINE

Montlouis Demi-Sec Les Batisses 1996: Fruity and slightly sweet, offering peach, coconut and honey flavors in a rich, thick texture. Falling somewhere between a table wine and a dessert wine in character, it may be best as an afternoon meditation wine. Drink now through 2000. • $17 • (05/31/98) • **86**

Montlouis Les Batisses 1996: Pretty peach and dried apple aromas carry through on the round, velvety palate, with flavors of peach, honey and spice. Slightly sweet, but lively acidity keeps it in balance. Drink now through 2000. • $15 • (05/31/98) • **86**

Montlouis Les Batisses 1995: Quite dry, with firm acidity, this straightforward white offers light apple and green plum flavors. It's clean but short. Drink now. • $14 • (06/15/97) • **81**

Sauvignon Blanc Touraine 1996: Light, with pleasant hay and herb aromas, but sharp acidity mars the balance and dominates the simple apple flavors. Drink now. • $9 • (05/31/98) • **76**

Touraine Sauvignon de Touraine 1993 • $10 • (10/31/94) • **83**

DELMAS, Y. & D.

Cabernet Sauvignon Vin de Pays de l'Aude La Noble 1996: A bit thin and quite herbal-tasting. Lacks vigor. 3,300 cases made. • $6 • (05/15/98) • **75**

Chardonnay Vin de Pays de l'Aude La Noble 1996: Pretty apricot character is reminiscent of Viognier. Medium-bodied, fairly rich in texture. Flavors linger on the finish. 11,500 cases made. • $6 • (04/30/98) • **83**

Merlot Vin de Pays de l'Aude La Noble 1996: Workmanlike but unexciting, with dried cherry flavors and some brown sugar notes. Drink now. 3,800 cases made. • $7 • (05/31/98) • **77**

Sauvignon Blanc Vin de Pays de l'Aude La Noble 1996: Fairly blunt, with modest fig and herb flavors. Finishes on an astringent note. 2,200 cases made. • $6 • (05/15/98) • **75**

DEMERAULMONT, CHÂTEAU

St.-Estèphe 1988 • $10 • (08/31/91) BB • **82**

DEMESSEY

Bourgogne Cuvée Spéciale White 1996: Crisp and sharp, with green apple and citrus flavors. Light-bodied and steely. Drink now. 830 cases made. • $17 • (05/31/98) • **77**

Bourgogne Premier Tri Elevé en Fûts de Chêne White 1995: Full-bodied, oily-textured, with earth, wet stone, citrus, green apple and herbal flavors. Rather chewy finish, not totally harmonious. Drinkable now. 833 cases made. • $15 • (08/31/97) • **79**

Bourgogne White 1996: Oaky style, with vanilla, milk chocolate and chestnut notes. Light-bodied, it turns bitter on the finish. Drink now. 1,250 cases made. • $14 • (05/31/98) • **75**

Bourgogne White 1995: Medium-intense and medium-bodied, with butter, butterscotch and melon flavors. Tart and a bit rustic. Drink now. 667 cases made. • $14 • (08/31/97) • **72**

Chassagne-Montrachet Morgeot 1995: Very supple, ripe and lush, this full-bodied *premier cru* is lively, with a core of lemon, melon, wet earth, mineral and honey flavors. Some cooked fruit and slightly oxidized aromas disappeared after the bottle had been open two hours, and the wine seemed young and vibrant. Best to decant before serving now though 2005. 125 cases made. • $39 • (05/31/97) • **90**

Mâcon-Cruzilles Cuvée Spéciale 1996: Like a mini-Puligny-Montrachet. Sexy and distinctive, a heavily toasty, smoky, floral, citrusy wine, bursting with the intensity of its ripe flavors. Seems almost acidic, but leaves a long, mouthpuckering, grilled-bread finish. Try now. 4,167 cases made. • $14 • (08/31/97) • **87**

Mâcon-Cruzilles Les Avoueries 1996: Fruity and attractive, of medium body, showing nice apple and pear and touches of mineral and wet hay. Drink upon release, not too cold. 2,500 cases made. • $14 • (05/31/98) • **82**

Mâcon-Cruzilles Les Avoueries Oak Aged 1995: Very oaky, with mint, vanilla and cream aromas and flavors dominating. Medium-bodied. Slightly disjointed, time might smooth it out. Try now. 517 cases made. • $15 • (05/31/97) • **79**

Mâcon-Villages 1994: Straight-as-an-arrow style that grows on you as it warms up in the glass. Lean, crisp, well-defined citrus, gooseberry and grass character and a mouth-puckering finish. Try now. 1,666 cases made. • $12 • (08/31/95) • **83**

Meursault 1995: Attractive buttery notes up front, but then it falls apart as cardboard flavors emerge from the decent honey, spice and oak flavors. A bitter finish doesn't help. 416 cases made. • $32 • (05/31/97) • **72**

Montagny Les Resses 1995: Very fat and oily in texture, with some distinctive butterscotch, vanilla bean and biscuit flavors dominating the fruit. A bit heavy on the finish. 667 cases made. • $18 • (08/31/97) • **77**

Pernand-Vergelesses Sous le Bois de Noël et Belles Filles White 1996: A crisp '96 but with lots of finesse and elegance, offering vanilla bean, butter, toasty bread, mineral, bread dough and pear flavors. Medium-bodied, with a wonderful silky texture and a long, succulent finish. A seductive wine you can indulge in now through 2005. 330 cases made. • $19 • (05/31/98) • **90**

Pouilly-Fuissé 1996: Crisp and lively, of medium body, with lots of lime and grapefruit flavors. A touch minerally, but turns a bit short on the finish. Drink now. Tasted twice; first bottle was disappointing. 660 cases made. • $23 • (05/31/98) • **83**

Pouilly-Fuissé 1994: Rich and rather fat, it appears too mature for our taste, adding a cooked apple note that distracts from otherwise nice tropical fruit flavors. • $20 • (05/31/96) • **78**

Pouilly-Fuissé 1993: Intensely tart and crisp; fresh lime and herb flavors. The finish is lean and green. Drink now. 1,667 cases made. • $18 • (05/15/95) • **78**

Key: SS—Spectator Selection CS—Cellar Selection HR—Highly Recommended BB—Best Buy $NA—Price not available Ⓐ—Auction Price (BT)—Barrel Tasting
Dates in parentheses indicate the issues in which the ratings were published.

Puligny-Montrachet Le Cailleret 1995: Thick and heavy-handed, with butter, butterscotch and coffeelike notes overriding the fruit. Full-bodied, ready to drink. 100 cases made. • $49 • (08/31/97) • **77**

Puligny-Montrachet Les Pucelles 1995: Shows some lemon, cream and vanilla-bean flavors, but ends a bit tired and quite oxidized. 167 cases made. • $47 • (05/31/97) • **79**

St.-Aubin Les Frionnes White 1996: Vibrant though a bit rustic, with a slight grassy, milky-malic character mingling with the green apple and pear. Still, it's clean, pure and medium-bodied, with a long, succulent, wood-inspired, smoky finish. Drink now. 330 cases made. • $25 • (05/31/98) • **84**

St.-Véran 1995: Quite woody for the fruit available. Medium-bodied and silky in texture, a bit coarse on the finish. Drink now. 342 cases made. • $14 • (05/31/97) • **79**

DERVIEUX-THAIZE, A.

Côte-Rôtie Côte Blonde la Garde Cuvée Réservée 1988 • $42 • (08/31/91) • **79**

DESCHAMPS, DOMAINE CLAUDINE

Gevrey-Chambertin Bel-Air 1985 • $28 • (03/31/88) • **87**

DESCHAMPS, MARC

Pouilly-Fumé Les Champs de Cri Les Loges 1994 • $18 • (05/15/96) • **84**

Pouilly-Fumé Les Loges 1995: Assertive herbal aromas and flavors mark this as classic Loire Sauvignon Blanc, but though it's quite full-bodied it lacks the fruit for balance. May round out with food. • $17 • (06/15/97) • **86**

DESCHAUX, LUCIEN

Beaujolais Le Vieux Presbytère 1994: Light-bodied, even for Beaujolais. Mild cherry flavors have a hint of spice. Chill it for easy quaffing now. • $8 • (09/15/96) • **79**

Beaujolais-Villages Le Vieux Presbytère 1994: Well developed. Though not as fruity as many Beaujolais, a year in the bottle has added accents of chocolate and tea to the core of cherry flavors. • $10 • (09/15/96) • **84**

Cabernet Sauvignon Vin de Pays d'Oc 1996: The cassis and cherry notes are a bit candied, yet tasty, and it strikes a balance on the light side. • $6 • (12/15/97) • **82**

Cabernet Sauvignon Vin de Pays d'Oc 1994: Though the currant and berry notes lend some appeal, the flavors are on the light side. • $8/liter • (12/15/96) • **78**

Chardonnay Vin de Pays d'Oc 1996: Lively and fresh, with simple grapefruit-like flavors and crisp balance. • $6 • (12/15/97) • **81**

Chardonnay Vin de Pays d'Oc 1994: Simple and earthy-tasting, it's drinkable but nothing special. • $8/1 liter • (02/28/97) • **75**

Châteauneuf-du-Pape Le Vieux Abbe 1994: Light and supple, with strawberry and raspberry flavors, this wine is sweet but simple, with little structure or length. Drink now. • $14 • (12/15/96) • **80**

Châteauneuf-du-Pape Le Vieux Abbé 1992: A fruity, accessible, forward style of Châteauneuf, with cherry, raspberry and leather aromas, appealing fruit flavors and a smooth texture. Drink now. • $14 • (10/15/94) • **83**

Châteauneuf-du-Pape Le Vieux Abbé 1990: Soft and lighter than most Châteauneuf-du-Papes, almost Burgundian in style, with plenty of appealing strawberry, raspberry and spice aromas and flavors, finishing velvety. Drinkable now. • $13 • (11/15/92) • **86**

Châteauneuf-du-Pape Le Vieux Abbé 1987 • $10 • (12/31/91) • **82**

Côtes de Duras Blanc de Blancs 1995: Bizarre, with oniony flavors and aromas. Turns coarse and drying on the finish. Tasted twice, with consistent notes. • $8 • (04/30/98) • **69**

Côtes du Rhône 1995: A solid red, reticent on the nose but showing plum and dried cherry flavors, good concentration and stiff tannins. Best with food. Drink now through 2000. • $8 • (05/15/98) • **84**

Côtes du Rhône 1994: Light-bodied, with pleasant berry and spice aromas and flavors. Soft on the palate, if a bit tannic on the finish. Drinks well now. • $9 • (10/15/96) • **81**

Côtes du Ventoux La Cuvée du Chanoine 1990 • $5 • (01/31/92) • **75**

Côtes du Ventoux Le Vieux Presbytère 1989 • $6 • (12/31/91) BB • **80**

Haut-Médoc 1995: A reasonably good Bordeaux showing violet and berry character. Medium- to light-bodied, with a silky, light finish. Drink now. • $9 • (01/31/98) • **81**

Merlot Vin de Pays d'Oc 1996: Straightforward and appealing, with enough concentration for the plum and cherry candy notes to linger on the palate. Drink now. • $6 • (12/15/97) • **81**

Merlot Vin de Pays d'Oc 1995: Tastes candied and astringent, with modest raspberry flavors and a tannic finish. • $8/1 liter • (12/15/96) • **78**

Médoc 1990: A simple, sturdy red, with pruny aromas and flavors that turn toward cherry and toast on the finish. Drinkable now. 3,500 cases made. • $8 • (01/31/92) BB • **80**

Pouilly-Fuissé La Cuvée du Maître 1995: Maturing fast, with marzipan and spice notes. Bitter on the finish. Absurdly priced. • $16 • (01/31/98) • **70**

Rosé d'Anjou 1992 • $7 • (11/15/94) • **77**

Syrah Vin de Pays d'Oc 1996: A high-toned Syrah, dominated by leafy, black pepper and berry character without the bass notes. Appealing, though not very concentrated. • $6 • (12/15/97) • **83**

DESHENRYS, DOMAINE

Chardonnay Vin de Pays des Côtes de Thongue 1996: Simple and straightforward, with apple and watermelon flavors, it's decent, but not too exciting. 5,000 cases made. • $10 • (05/31/97) • **79**

Coteaux du Languedoc 1994: New oak predominates, with solid plum and cherry flavors underneath. Drinkable now. 5,000 cases made. • $11 • (05/15/97) • **84**

Merlot Vin de Pays des Côtes de Thongue 1995: Impressive though young. A lot of deep, black fruit character, with good concentration and balance. Drinkable now. 5,000 cases made. • $10 • (05/15/97) • **85**

Tradition Red Vin de Pays des Côtes de Thongue 1995: A blend of Cabernet, Merlot and Syrah, this is a serious, deeply colored French red of depth and structure, with intense aromas of freshly crushed plums and black cherries accented by new oak, black cherry flavors and a lingering finish. This is an impressive package showing real value. Drinkable now. 5,000 cases made. • $10 • (05/15/97) BB • **87**

DESMEURES, DOMAINE

Crozes-Hermitage Domaine des Remizières 1991 • $26 • (05/31/94) • **83**

Crozes-Hermitage Domaine des Remizières Cuvée Particulair 1986 • $8 • (05/31/89) BB • **84**

Hermitage Domaine des Remizières 1986 • $19 • (04/15/89) • **68**

DESMIRAIL, CHÂTEAU

Margaux 1994: Delicate, with pretty berry and vanilla nuances, fine tannins and a light, fruity finish. Drink or hold. • $23 • (01/31/97) • **83**

Margaux 1993: Good core of ripe berry, cherry and tobacco flavors. Medium body and tannins and a soft finish. Drinkable now. • $23 • (01/31/96) • **83**

Margaux 1991: Clean and easy to drink. Light body and cherry flavors; a slightly watery finish. • $16 • (03/31/94) • **78**

Margaux 1990: An excellent wine, with a beautiful core of plum and black cherry flavors, fine tannins and a firm backbone. Very pretty. From the owners of Château Brane-Cantenac. Drinkable now. 4,000 cases made. • $27 • (03/31/93) • **91**

Margaux 1989 • $27 • (03/15/92) • **86**

Margaux 1986 • $22 • (06/30/89) • **90**

DESSERRE, DOMAINE

Chinon 1987 • $9 • (12/31/88) • **86**

DESTIEUX, CHÂTEAU

St.-Emilion 1997: A silky red, with berry and mineral aromas and flavors. Medium-bodied, with fine tannins but a short finish. • $NA • (06/15/98) (BT) • **80-84**

St.-Emilion 1996: Lots of mineral and spice. Full-bodied, with well-integrated tannins and a stony, fruity, raspberry aftertaste. • $30 • (06/15/98) (BT) • **85-89**

St.-Emilion 1988 • $19 • (06/30/91) • **81**

St.-Emilion 1985 • $14 • (03/31/88) • **84**

DESVIGNES AÎNÉ & FILS

St.-Véran 1995: A bit odd in aroma and flavor, with notes of butterscotch, varnish and perfume. Turns bitter on the finish. • $NA • (08/31/96) • **72**

DESVIGNES, LOUIS-CLAUDE

Morgon Côte du Py 1993 • $16 • (07/31/95) • **83**

Morgon Javernières 1995: This polished red offers ripe black cherry and plum flavors, and an alluring gamy note characteristic of the appellation. Tannins are firm yet well-integrated, making it a good match for food. • $17 • (09/15/97) • **86**

Morgon Javernières 1993 • $17 • (07/31/95) • **79**

DEURRE, DOMAINE DE

Côtes du Rhône 1995: Dark and firmly structured, offering ripe plum and light herbal flavors. Hard tannins shut down the finish right now. Drinkable now. • $10 • (10/15/96) • **83**

Côtes du Rhône-Villages Vinsobres 1992: Light and silky, this shows pleasant but light flavors of cherries and raisins, with firm tannins emerging on the finish. 500 cases made. • $13 • (12/15/96) • **80**

Côtes du Rhône-Villages Vinsobres 1989 • $9 • (08/31/92) • **84**

DEUTZ

Brut Blanc de Blancs Champagne 1990: Wonderfully fruity and vibrant in flavor, although somewhat tight because of crisp apple, lemon and grapefruit notes. Tasty to drink now. • $33 Ⓐ • (11/30/95) • **89**

Brut Blanc de Blancs Champagne 1989: Rich and mouthfilling. A ripe, flavorful, distinctive Champagne that blends earthy-toasty aromas with full fruit flavors and accents of mineral and hazelnut. Drink now through 2002. • $45 • (12/31/97) • **92**

Brut Blanc de Blancs Champagne 1988: A broad-textured Champagne that's lively and intense, with toasty pear, pine and slightly vinegary flavors. Finishes crisp and lemony. Drink now. • $37 Ⓐ • (11/30/92) • **83**

Brut Blanc de Blancs Champagne 1985: • $53 Ⓐ • (12/31/90) • **83**

Brut Blanc de Blancs Champagne 1982: Full-bodied, toasty style, but elegant nonetheless. It has rich, mature Champagne flavors, with excellent depth and plenty of toasty-lemony flavors to keep your taste buds occupied. • $39 • (05/31/87) • **90**

Brut Champagne 1990: A generous, fruity, easy-going Champagne with lots of fruit character and good balance. Drink now. 5,000 cases made. • $35 • (12/31/97) • **89**

Brut Champagne 1988: Super-clean and powerful, yet elegant, showing subtle toasty, fruity character, medium body and a firm acid structure. Delicious. It's improved with bottle age since we last tasted it about a year ago. Drink now or hold. 10,000 cases made. • $35 • (12/31/93) • **89**

Brut Champagne 1985: • $40 • (12/31/90) • **83**

Brut Champagne Classic NV: A lean and tart Champagne with lemony flavors, a dry texture and buttery accents. For fans of austerity. • $27 • (11/15/97) • **82**

Brut Champagne Cuvée William Deutz 1988: The big easy. Rich, toasty flavors combine with a soft, nearly sweet character in this abundantly proportioned wine. Best now through 2000. • $85 • (12/31/97) • **89**

Brut Champagne Cuvée William Deutz 1985: This shows intense vanilla and apple aromas and flavors; it has a full body but is rather rough on the finish, with searing acidity. Needs time. Similar score given in December 1992. 3,500 cases made. • $60 • (12/31/93) • **85**

Brut Champagne Cuvée William Deutz 1982: Elegant and yeasty, with lemon, spice and toast flavors and a slightly coarse texture on the finish. • $61 • (12/31/89) • **85**

Brut Champagne Cuvée William Deutz 1979 • $47 • (07/16/85) • **90**

Brut Champagne Georges Mathieu 1982: Attractive for its pretty pear, cherry and vanilla notes; well balanced, deep and full-bodied, with plenty of richness and concentration and a full, fruity aftertaste. Ready now. • $40 • (12/31/89) • **89**

Brut Champagne Georges Mathieu Réserve 1985: Very firm and well-balanced, offering just enough crisp fruit flavor to back up the firmness. It has touches of earthy complexity, but stays basically straightforward in style. • $46 • (12/31/90) • **86**

Brut Rosé Champagne 1988: Tastes like it's already heading over the hill. Drink now. Tasted twice, with consistent notes. 3,500 cases made. • $40 • (12/31/92) • **74**

Brut Rosé Champagne 1985: A Rosé that's delicious and assertive. Firm, well structured and showing good Pinot Noir flavors of cherry and strawberry, with hints of spice for seasoning. • $46 • (12/31/90) • **88**

Brut Rosé Champagne 1982: • $35 • (12/31/87) • **86**

Brut Rosé Champagne Cuvée Marie-Damarisse NV: An appealing rosé in a straightforward style. Light pink in color, with spicy-earthy overtones and a rich texture. • $29 • (12/31/97) • **84**

Brut Rosé Champagne Cuvée William Deutz 1985: Still austere at 11-years-old, this rosé is extremely vibrant, well balanced—and in need of more aging. Its tight core of tart cherry flavor and crisp acidity renders it full of life and mouthwatering. The texture is just beginning to turn creamy. Try now through 2001. • $115 • (11/30/96) • **91**

DEUX ROCHES, DOMAINE DES

Mâcon-Davayé 1996: Like liquid honey poured over a cinnamon-baked pear. Pure, clean, ripe, rich—just delicious. As seductively thick as a late-harvest white, it's smooth and soft on the almond- and vanilla-infused finish. Buy a case and enjoy. • $14 • (08/31/97) • **89**

Mâcon-Villages 1995: Intense and very appealing ripe pear, apple and melon flavors. Medium-bodied, with a lush texture. Hints of honey and grass on the long finish. Delicious now. • $NA • (08/31/96) • **87**

Mâcon-Villages 1994: Richer than most '94 Mâcons, offering a smooth, buttery texture and picking up apple, pear, spice and melon flavors on the silky finish. 5,000 cases made. • $13 • (08/31/95) • **85**

St.-Véran 1995: Medium-bodied and balanced, with pear, citrus, honey, floral and spice flavors and aromas. Fairly ripe and sweet-tasting, but a tinge of bitter, haylike notes on the intense finish. Try now. Tasted twice with consistent notes. • $NA • (08/31/96) • **86**

St.-Véran 1994: Well crafted, balancing a touch of sweet-tasting wood with ripe melon, pear and fig flavors. At this stage it's woodier than most traditional St.-Vérans but finishes harmoniously. 6,250 cases made. • $15 • (08/31/95) • **85**

St.-Véran Les Terres Noires 1995: Worth seeking out. Intense, medium-bodied and beautifully balanced, it mingles tropical fruit, butter, toasty hazelnut, cream, citrus and floral flavors in a fresh and vibrant package. Lingering finish. Drink now. Tasted twice with consistent notes. • $NA • (08/31/96) • **88**

St.-Véran Les Terres Noires 1994: Tastes more like Meursault than St.-Véran with all the round, seductive pear, smoke and sweet vanilla character from wood. Turns slightly astringent on the finish. 1,666 cases made. • $17 • (08/31/95) • **82**

St.-Véran Vieilles Vignes 1995: Fancy winemaking. Toasty, smoky, honeyed flavors overwhelm, at least for now, the fruit flavors in this showy, medium-bodied wine. Drinkable now. 1,250 cases made. • $24 • (05/31/97) • **85**

DEVISE DE LILIAN, LA

St.-Estèphe 1995: Pretty balance of berry, chocolate and light vanilla aromas and flavors. Medium-bodied, with fine tannins and a fresh fruit aftertaste. A bit light on the finish. Best now. • $15 • (01/31/98) • **84**

DEVOY MARTINE, CHÂTEAU LE

Lirac White 1995: A muscular wine, firm and austere, offering light pear and herbal flavors over crisp acidity. Can stand up to rich foods but won't overwhelm them. 600 cases made. • $10 • (10/15/96) • **83**

DEYDIER & FILS, DOMAINE JEAN

Châteauneuf-du-Pape 1993: A tannic red wine with good but straightforward fruit flavors and a tough finish. Has more structure than flavor, but may just need cheese to balance it out. • $20 • (11/15/95) • **82**

Châteauneuf-du-Pape Les Clefs D'Or 1994: Herb, eucalyptus and tobacco flavors dominate the fruit flavors in this thin yet tannic red. It packs a punch. Drinkable now. • $25 • (12/15/96) • **82**

Châteauneuf-du-Pape Les Clefs d'Or 1983 • $16 • (10/31/87) • **78**

Côtes du Rhône 1993 • $13 • (09/30/95) • **85**

Côtes du Rhône Les Clefs D'Or 1995: An unsettled wine that shows funky aromas and some spritz on the palate. • $13 • (12/15/96) • **71**

DEYREM-VALENTIN, CHÂTEAU

Margaux 1995: Solid intensity of fruit with plenty of smoky, spicy berry character. Medium body, fine tannins and a long, silky finish. • $NA • (05/15/96) (BT) • **85-89**

Key: SS—Spectator Selection CS—Cellar Selection HR—Highly Recommended BB—Best Buy $NA—Price not available Ⓐ—Auction Price (BT)—Barrel Tasting

Dates in parentheses indicate the issues in which the ratings were published.

DIANE DE BELGRAVE

Haut-Médoc 1993: Weedy and unripe. Second label of Château Belgrave. Drink as soon as possible. • $NA • (01/31/96) • **75**

DICONNE, JEAN-PIERRE

Auxey-Duresses White 1995: Distinctive for its fresh, lively intensity. Offers citrus, pear, apple, vanilla and stone aromas and flavors and a fairly long, slightly toasty finish. A matchstick note keeps it from a higher score. Perhaps better around 2000. • $NA • (08/31/97) • **86**

Meursault Clos des Luchets 1995: A distinctive, full-bodied wine with a lot of fruit intensity, including some green apricot, white peach, ripe pear and grassy grape flavors that rocket across the palate, delighting with new sensations at each turn. This is no dull, silky-smooth experience; enjoy the ride now through 2004. • $NA • (05/31/97) • **90**

Meursault Les Luchets 1993: A bit simple but the flavors are quite tropical, featuring chalky, smoky, toasty, oaky notes, firm texture and vibrant, tart, lemony finish. • $NA • (08/31/95) • **84**

Meursault Les Narvaux 1993: Lean in texture, with intense citrus character; numbs your palate with acidity. Modest tropical fruit, green apple and pear flavors. • $NA • (08/31/95) • **83**

DIETRICH, DOMAINE ROBERT

Muscat Alsace Cuvée Exceptionelle 1994: A subtle version of this varietal, it has richness but lacks the flavor and depth to be anything more than a straightforward, pleasant white. • $16 • (11/15/97) • **80**

Pinot Blanc Alsace Cuvée Exceptionelle 1995: Fresh and lively with citrus and apple flavors, a slightly chalky texture and a note of almond on the finish. • $9 • (11/15/97) • **82**

Riesling Alsace Cuvée Exceptionelle 1995: Rich and soft for Riesling, this is already showing kerosene and marzipan aromas and flavors. There's a mineral character and the finish has a refreshing note of apple. Drinkable now. • $13 • (11/15/97) • **85**

Riesling Alsace Grand Cru Brand Kreutzfelder 1993: A harmonious, intense white whose maturing flavors of vanilla custard, almond, apple and minerals mingle with the medium-bodied texture. It's long, with an austere, minerally finish. Try with fish or pork dishes. • $20 • (11/15/97) • **89**

DILLON, CHÂTEAU

Haut-Médoc 1995: Quite impressive for its sheer intensity of pure cassis and dried herb character, but it's slightly lean in texture. The finish is a bit dry and slightly metallic. • $NA • (05/15/96) (BT) • **80-84**

DIMERIE, CHÂTEAU DE LA

Muscadet de Sèvre et Maine 1994 • $7 • (05/15/96) • **83**

DIOCHON, DOMAINE

Moulin-à-Vent Cuvée Vieilles Vignes 1995: Gorgeous. Lush, filling the mouth with blackberry and wild strawberry flavors, round and soft, but ripe tannins give firm support and tantalizing spice and vanilla notes emerge on the finish. Shows more international character than *terroir*, but it's delicious nonetheless. Tasted twice, with consistent notes. Drink now through 2000. • $16 • (07/31/97) • **89**

Moulin-à-Vent Cuvée Vieilles Vignes 1994: Attractive cherry and spice aromas turn straightforward on the palate, where they're dominated by firm tannins. It's clean and fresh, but still closed. • $19 • (09/15/96) • **85**

DIRLER

Gewürztraminer Alsace Grand Cru Saering 1996: Great expression of Gewürz. Spicy, with litchi and floral elements, rich yet not too fat or oily, and with just a hint of bitter grapefruit on the lingering finish. Drink now. • $28 • (03/31/98) • **88**

Pinot d'Alsace Alsace 1996: Like biting into a crisp, ripe apple with a little citrus thrown in for accent. Straightforward, with a diminutive finish; try as an apéritif. Drink now. • $16 • (03/31/98) • **83**

Sylvaner Alsace Cuvée Vieilles Vignes 1996: A rich Sylvaner full of apple and stony mineral character. Soft and enticing, it finishes on a lemony note. Drink now. • $14 • (03/31/98) • **84**

DOISY-DAËNE, CHÂTEAU

Bordeaux Dry 1993 • $15 • (05/31/95) • **82**

Sauternes 1991: Attractive and sharp, well made, light- to medium-bodied, but featuring pretty honey, almond, spice and pineapple flavors. Drinkable now. • $NA • (04/15/95) • **85**

Sauternes 1988: A bit grassy, medium-bodied and medium-sweet, but the vanilla bean, honey and pineapple flavors unfold harmoniously to a clean finish. Drinkable now. • $35 • (04/15/95) • **87**

Sauternes 1986: Elegant, polished and medium-sweet; spice, honey and lemon flavors give spark and finesse. Drinkable now. • $35 • (04/15/95) • **89**

Sauternes 1985: Tastes light and watery, more like a sweet Chenin Blanc than a classic Sauternes. It's sugary with a touch of apricot and tobacco flavors, but it's not very concentrated and lacks depth. • $24 • (05/31/88) • **73**

Sauternes 1983: A pleasant drink and there's even some complexity, but it's not cuddly. Light gold, waxy and sulfury on the nose, sugary sweet, with oak, honey, pear, and apricot on the palate. • $31 Ⓐ • (01/31/88) • **73**

DOISY-VÉDRINES, CHÂTEAU

Sauternes 1992: Sweet and sour, but interesting, offering orange-peel, marmalade, grapefruit and spice notes and a slightly bitter finish. Drink now. • $NA • (04/15/95) • **79**

Sauternes 1990: Intriguing lime, floral and tropical character; fresh and delicious, with medium weight and sweetness. Try now. • $38 • (04/15/95) • **88**

Sauternes 1989: This subtle white grows on you, showing lovely tropical, toasty coconut and lemon flavors that blend together harmoniously on the intense, long, sweet finish. Drink now. • $50 • (04/15/95) • **91**

Sauternes 1988: Supercharged, incredibly intense Sauternes, exploding with tons of dried apricot, tropical and lemon flavors whistling through your palate to a long, long finish. Bravo! Don't touch until after 2000. • $32 • (04/15/95) • **93**

Sauternes 1986: Ripe, round and honeyed, with a welcome touch of botrytis adding complexity. Spicy and toasty on the long finish. Drinkable now. • $52 • (12/31/89) • **86**

DOMINIQUE, CHÂTEAU LA

St.-Emilion 1997: Diluted, with a cherry, stemmy character. Light in body. • $NA • (06/15/98) (BT) • **75-79**

St.-Emilion 1996: Very grapey and juicy, with fine tannins and a flavorful finish. Medium-bodied, with a fresh aftertaste. Delicious. • $50 • (06/15/98) (BT) • **85-89**

St.-Emilion 1995: A bit rustic, but concentrated. Intense aromas of wet earth and bark, with a hint of fruit. Full-bodied, with full velvety tannins and a lovely, ripe berry and black olive flavor on the finish. Best after 2001. • $30 Ⓐ • (01/31/98) • **89**

St.-Emilion 1994: Shows impressive ripeness for the vintage, with a tobacco and berry character. Has a velvety texture, medium body and firm tannins. Try now. • $29 Ⓐ • (01/31/97) • **87**

St.-Emilion 1993: Firm and racy chocolate, berry and cherry aromas and flavors, medium body, fine tannins and a crisp finish. Try now. • $30 • (01/31/96) • **87**

St.-Emilion 1992: Soft and succulent; medium body and tannins and plenty of black olive, black cherry and vanilla character. • $15 Ⓐ • (04/15/95) • **83**

St.-Emilion 1991: A wine with refined tobacco and fruit flavors and an elegant tannin structure to harmonize with the fruit. • $18 • (03/31/94) • **80**

St.-Emilion 1990: Has loads of toasty new oak character, ripe fruit aromas and full, almost dry tannins. A little clumsy. Drinkable now. 7,000 cases made. • $60 • (03/31/93) • **88**

St.-Emilion 1989 • $65 Ⓐ • (03/15/92) • **91**

St.-Emilion 1988 • $25 • (06/30/91) • **86**

St.-Emilion 1986 • $43 Ⓐ • (06/30/89) • **95**

St.-Emilion 1985 • $28 Ⓐ • (03/31/88) • **83**

St.-Emilion 1983 • $31 Ⓐ • (05/16/86) • **88**

St.-Emilion 1982 • $41 Ⓐ • (08/31/92) • **79**

St.-Emilion 1979 • $20 Ⓐ • (10/15/89) • **81**

St.-Emilion 1961 • $NA • (04/30/96) • **85**

DONA, CELLIER DE LA

Côtes du Roussillon-Villages 1988 • $8 • (10/15/90) BB • **85**

DONA BAISSAS, CHÂTEAU

Côtes du Roussillon-Villages 1990 • $8 • (03/31/92) • **79**

Côtes du Roussillon-Villages 1988 • $7 • (10/15/90) • **77**

DONATS, CHÂTEAU LES

Premières Côtes de Blaye 1989 • $9 • (11/30/92) • **78**

DONJON, CHÂTEAU DU

Merlot Vin de Pays d'Oc 1995: A crisp red wine, with plummy flavors and aromas, also some dried cherry and spice notes. Drink now. 3,800 cases made. • $7 • (05/31/98) • **82**

Minervois Cuvée Prestige 1994: Shows loads of plum and dark cherry flavors, with a gamy note on the finish. Straightforward, with a nice richness. Drink now through 2001. 1,550 cases made. • $11 • (05/31/98) • **84**

Minervois Cuvée Tradition 1995: Some decent plum flavors, but ends up a bit murky-tasting, with a colalike note throughout and a drying finish. Past its prime. 6,600 cases made. • $8 • (05/31/98) • **79**

DOPFF & IRION

Gewürztraminer Alsace 1996: Austere, with white pepper aromas and an earthy, canned-fruit quality. Lacks depth and concentration. • $17 • (09/30/97) • **74**

Gewürztraminer Alsace 1995: Soft and delicate, this supple Gewürz has typically spicy aromas and flavors in a fruity, easy-drinking style. A pleasant apéritif. • $14 • (10/15/96) • **84**

Gewürztraminer Alsace Les Sorcières 1994: A seductive Gewürz that combines the trademark litchi, rose petal and spice character with finesse and harmony. Textured like taffeta, honey flavors take over midpalate, concluding with a grapefruit, almond-extract aftertaste that's as beguiling as it is long. • $23 • (09/30/97) • **91**

Gewürztraminer Alsace Sélection de Grains Nobles 1994: Offers the classic Gewürz flavors of rose and litchi, with a touch of honey and grapefruit, but it lacks the sheer intensity, expressiveness and length expected at this level. Ready now. • $99 • (11/15/97) • **89**

Muscat Alsace Les Amandiers 1996: A bright, floral white with hints of spice and grapefruit and just a touch of bitter almond on the finish. Try as an apéritif. • $18 • (09/30/97) • **84**

Pinot Blanc Alsace 1996: A straightforward Pinot Blanc, with a lemon and white peach character, smooth texture and refreshing finish. • $11 • (09/15/97) • **82**

Riesling Alsace 1996: A soft, rich Riesling with aromas and flavors evocative of spring blossoms and apples. Drinkable now. • $14 • (09/30/97) • **83**

Riesling Alsace 1995: Searingly tart, this lacks depth and varietal character. Tart green apple flavors, vegetal aromas, citrusy finish. • $12 • (09/30/96) • **76**

Riesling Alsace Grand Cru Schoenenbourg 1994: Perfumed like a pine forest, followed by marzipan and apple flavors supported by a complex, elegant structure. Firm and steely, with lively acidity on the finish, this would be terrific with pork roast or choucroute. • $27 • (09/30/97) • **90**

Riesling Alsace Les Murailles 1994: The lean, firm diesel and stone flavors are typical of this variety in certain soils, but there are apple notes and plenty of acidity, too. Tough on its own, but could blossom with food. • $20 • (09/30/97) • **86**

Riesling Alsace Vendanges Tardives 1994: Different flavors here—marzipan, honey and lime—that don't quite come together. There's more structure than flavor, and the finish is hot. • $67 • (11/15/97) • **83**

Sylvaner Alsace 1996: An assertive white sporting brisk acidity and earthy, apple-skin flavors on a frame that turns lean. • $11 • (09/15/97) • **79**

Sylvaner Alsace 1995: This refreshing, light-bodied wine shows bright herbal and almond notes with a backbone of lemony acidity. • $9 • (10/15/96) • **84**

Tokay Pinot Gris Alsace 1996: Red cherries come to mind when smelling and tasting this white, but there's an undercurrent of grapefruit that's bitter and doesn't quite mesh. • $16 • (09/30/97) • **79**

Tokay Pinot Gris Alsace 1995: Juicy, fruity and fresh with its ripe pear and apple flavors and vanilla notes. Accessible and food-friendly. • $13 • (11/15/96) • **86**

Tokay Pinot Gris Alsace Les Maquisards 1995: Not much going on in this white. It's simple, diluted and coarse. • $22 • (09/30/97) • **72**

DOPFF AU MOULIN

Gewürztraminer Alsace 1995: An opulent white displaying floral and apricot flavors that dissolve into grapefruit on the finish, where some heat makes it a bit coarse. • $14 • (06/30/97) • **82**

Riesling Alsace 1995: Delivers plenty of ripe peach and lime flavors, with racy acidity that pushes the fruit to a lingering finish. • $13 • (06/30/97) • **85**

DOUDET-NAUDIN

Aloxe-Corton Domaine Doudet 1994: Shows a more serious color than most simple wines of the vintage, and modest but appealing plum and cherry flavors without the coarse tannins. • $19 • (11/15/96) • **81**

Beaune Clos du Roi 1994: A sturdy wine with light cherry and anise flavors that linger on the finish. Drinkable now. • $18 • (11/15/96) • **83**

Chablis 1994 • $NA • (05/31/96) • **86**

Chablis Montmains 1994 • $NA • (05/31/96) • **90**

Corton Les Maréchaudes Vieilles Vignes 1994: Youthful, packing some power behind its plummy, spicy aromas and flavors. Nicely rounded and gleaming with polished tannins. Delicious now, but just wait until 2000 to 2003. • $60 • (11/15/96) • **91**

Corton Les Renardes 1945 • $NA • (08/31/90) • **86**

Nuits-St.-Georges Les Cailles 1994: Light and delicate, with some pretty red berry, vanilla and spice flavors. Slightly short finish. Drink upon release. • $39 • (11/15/96) • **79**

Savigny-lès-Beaune Aux Guettes Vieilles Vignes Dernière Récolte 1994: Light in texture, but has plenty of ripe cherry, currant and floral flavors that persist through the firm finish. Drinkable now. • $24 • (11/15/96) • **88**

Savigny-lès-Beaune Domaine Doudet 1993: A bit lean but offering some decent berry, mineral and plum character, medium to light body, firm, slightly dry tannins and a short finish. Drinkable now. • $18 • (11/15/95) • **80**

Vosne-Romanée Les Suchots 1993: Rather light and watery, delivering stewed tomato and weedy character, light body and tannins and a dry finish. • $36 • (11/15/95) • **76**

DOURTHE, PIERRE

Bordeaux Numero 1 1996: Diluted and weedy, with hints of tomato and berry. Light in body and finish. Surprisingly weak. Tasted twice, with consistent notes. • $9 • (06/15/98) (BT) • **970**

Bordeaux Numero 1 1995: Very good, straightforward Bordeaux with delicious fruit character. Crushed berries with a hint of chocolate. Medium-bodied, with well-integrated tannins and a medium, silky texture. Lovely now, but will improve with age. • $9 • (01/31/98) • **86**

Bordeaux Numero 1 1993: Plenty of cassis and berry character, medium-to-full body, silky tannins and a fruity finish. A serious merchant blend for the vintage. Drinkable now. • $9 • (01/31/96) • **83**

DOUTRES, ROBERT

Banyuls Les Clos de Paulilles 1995: Rich and expressive, with hints of walnut and butterscotch rounding out the plum and dried herb flavors. Lacks smoothness and shows dryness on the finish. 2,000 cases made. • $13/375ml • (06/30/97) • **85**

DOYENNÉ, CHÂTEAU LE

Premières Côtes de Bordeaux 1995: A generous, juicy, even complex wine that blends ripe plum and cherry flavors with toasty, mineral-like accents on a firm frame of moderate tannins and good acidity. • $14 • (01/31/98) • **86**

DOZON, DOMAINE

Chinon Clos du Saut au Loup 1995: Black cherry and light earth aromas introduce this big-boned wine with its aggressive tannins and flavors of tobacco, bitter almond and black cherry. It's concentrated but rustic. 3,800 cases made. • $13 • (06/15/97) • **83**

Chinon Clos du Saut au Loup Cuvée Alexandre 1991 • $15 • (10/31/94) • **75**

Chinon Rosé 1995: This strawberry-scented rosé is light and fairly neutral on the palate, but it's balanced and clean. A refreshing apéritif. 1,200 cases made. • $10 • (05/31/97) • **83**

DRACY, CHÂTEAU DE

Bourgogne 1995: Light and diluted, with crisp, citrusy strawberry aromas and flavors. Not a ripe wine. Astringent finish. 7,166 cases made. • $12 • (11/15/97) • **71**

Bourgogne 1989 • $9 • (06/15/92) • **82**

Bourgogne 1988 • $8 • (02/28/90) • **68**

Bourgogne 1986 • $7 • (12/31/88) • **76**

Bourgogne White 1996: Not overly complex, but nice. Full-bodied, vibrant from lots of acidity, and its ripe pear, tropical and mineral notes come together. A bit tart on the finish. From Albert Bichot. 1,580 cases made. • $11 • (05/31/98) • **82**

Monthélie 1993: Pretty black cherry flavor, medium body and a chewy texture on the finish. Drink on release. • $NA • (11/15/95) • **84**

Monthélie Baron de Charette 1995: The simple cherry flavor has an odd, dusty character, followed by a hollow midpalate and a dry finish. 200 cases made. • $18 • (11/15/97) • **77**

Pommard Baron de Charette 1995: The flavors are herbal and earthy, with a camphor note, though this sturdy, four-square red has decent concentration. Finishes on the tough side. 166 cases made. • $25 • (11/15/97) • **84**

DRAPPIER

Brut Blanc de Blancs Champagne Cuvée Signature NV: Generous in character and unusual for its vivid banana and pineapple flavors. Soft and plush in texture and easy to enjoy. 2,000 cases made. • $40 • (12/31/97) • **85**

Brut Champagne Carte Blanche NV: Refreshing, well balanced and well made. Light apple and lemon flavors, crisp acidity and a fine texture make it easy to like. 5,000 cases made. • $32 • (11/30/97) • **86**

Brut Champagne Carte d'Or 1990: Generous, full-bodied and broad-textured, this is a tempting, full-flavored and easy-drinking bubbly with toasty aromas and solid fruit flavors. Though relatively tight on the finish now, it should improve with time. Best after 1999. 2,000 cases made. • $45 • (12/31/97) • **91**

Brut Champagne Carte d'Or 1989: Flavorful and broad, with the spicy, fruity notes of an Alsace wine. Full-bodied, but basically straightforward. Has a smooth, full texture and good finish. 4,000 cases made. • $44 • (12/31/96) • **84**

Brut Champagne Carte d'Or 1988 • $44 • (11/30/92) • **86**

Brut Champagne Carte d'Or NV: A solidly made, well-balanced bubbly, with modest fruit flavors and a smooth but lively texture. 25,000 cases made. • $35 • (12/31/97) • **85**

Brut Champagne Collection Cuvée General Charles de Gaulle 1988 • $48 • (12/31/93) • **89**

Brut Champagne Collection Cuvée General Charles de Gaulle 1986 • $56 • (11/30/92) • **91**

Brut Champagne Grande Sendrée 1989: An intense, lively but rich-textured bubbly that combines vivid lemon and apple flavors with a soft, velvety texture and a lingering, crisp finish. Should improve in the cellar. Drink now through 2001. 2,000 cases made. • $76 • (12/31/97) • **91**

Brut Champagne Grande Sendrée 1988: Has an attractive, mouthfilling texture and straightforward fruit flavors. An appealing Champagne that goes right down the middle. 3,000 cases made. • $72 • (11/15/96) • **86**

Brut Champagne Grande Sendrée 1985 • $58 • (11/30/92) • **86**

Brut Rosé Champagne Grande Sendrée 1989: An immediately appealing rosé. Generous and fresh in flavor, with bright cherry accents, a mouthfilling texture and a lingering finish. Drink now. 200 cases made. • $72 • (11/30/97) • **88**

Brut Rosé Champagne Val des Demoiselles 1981 • $23 • (12/16/85) • **72**

Brut Rosé Champagne Val des Demoiselles NV: A charming, appealing rosé, fresh in flavor, crisp in texture, with a vivid pink hue and a lively mousse. Drink now. 2,000 cases made. • $40 • (11/30/97) • **86**

DROIN, JEAN-PAUL

Chablis Grenouille 1996: Hard to taste now. Austere and fairly woody, with toasty oak accents dominating the fruit. Offers a dry palate, along with pear, crème brûlée, pie tart and grilled pineapple flavors. Very open on the nose, with a lovely, silky mouthfeel but a hard finish. Great winemaker in a super *terroir*, so this should be better around 2005. • $45 • (05/31/98) • **85**

Key: SS—Spectator Selection CS—Cellar Selection HR—Highly Recommended BB—Best Buy $NA—Price not available Ⓐ—Auction Price (BT)—Barrel Tasting
Dates in parentheses indicate the issues in which the ratings were published.

FRANCE

Chablis Les Clos 1996: Fabulous harmony in this thick-textured, opulent, full-bodied and flavorful Chablis. The subtle oak accents are kept in check by the rich tropical, pear, citrus and honey character of this classy and supersmooth '96. So balanced it's tempting now, but has plenty of acidity for cellaring through 2005. • $40 • (05/31/98) • **96**

Chablis Les Clos 1994 • $45 • (05/31/96) • **85**

Chablis Les Clos 1993 • $40 • (08/31/95) • **86**

Chablis Montée de Tonnerre 1996: A good example of the spectacular quality of the '96 vintage in Chablis, this ripe and balanced *premier cru* delivers gorgeous mineral, lime, honey, tropical fruit, flint, stone and floral notes. Full-bodied, with smoky overtones on the long, succulent finish. Tempting now, but wait until after 2000, when the palate-coating mineral character should be fully developed. 1,000 cases made. • $18 • (08/31/97) • **94**

Chablis Montée de Tonnerre 1994 • $30 • (05/31/96) • **84**

Chablis Montée de Tonnerre 1993 • $26 • (08/31/95) • **85**

Chablis Montmains 1996: Round and full-bodied, it opens up with subtle oak flavors that move into lime, honey and a complex combination of fruit and dried herbs. Needs time to come together, but clearly very concentrated and well made. Refined, smooth yet lively finish. Try around 2003 to 2005. • $23 • (05/31/98) • **94**

Chablis Montmains 1994 • $28 • (05/31/96) • **91**

Chablis Montmains 1993 • $24 • (08/31/95) • **84**

Chablis Vaillons 1996: Grounded in the earth of Chablis with its minerally, wet soil character, it also shows intense lime, lemon, pink grapefruit, pear and apple concentration. Full-bodied and impressively silky on the midpalate, it explodes on the finish. Lively now, but better to wait until around 2002. • $23 • (05/31/98) • **94**

Chablis Vaillons 1995: Full-bodied, offering plenty of pear, lemon and honey flavors. Lacks freshness on the slightly flat finish. Drink up. • $NA • (08/31/96) • **84**

Chablis Vaillons 1994 • $28 • (05/31/96) • **85**

Chablis Vaillons 1993 • $24 • (08/31/95) • **81**

Chablis Valmur 1996: Thick and ultraopulent, full in body, quite muscular and toasty from much oak. Despite the wonderful midpalate and mineral-laden character, this a bit hard now, built for the long-term. Loads of fruit and acidity on the mouthpuckering finish. Try after 2005. • $40 • (05/31/98) • **95**

Chablis Vaudésir 1996: Classy and racy, this has almost all you can expect in a great Chardonnay. Blends finesse and opulence, with subtle flavors that grow on you, showing oak nuances, ripe fruit, honey and lime. Fabulous from the start, with a most sensual and caressing finish. Tempting now through 2005. • $40 • (05/31/98) • **95**

Chablis Vaudésir 1994 • $45 • (05/31/96) • **75**

Chablis Vaudésir 1993 • $40 • (08/31/95) • **85**

Chablis Vosgros 1996: Elegant, thick and full-bodied beauty. Silky as can be, with subtle toasty oak accents and flavors that range from gooseberry and buttery croissant to apple pie, whipped cream, ripe pear, cilantro and grilled pineapple. Cascades with amazing grace to a long, complex and herbal-flavored finish. Should improve through 2010. • $23 • (05/31/98) • **94**

Chablis Vosgros 1993 • $24 • (08/31/95) • **87**

DROUHIN, JOSEPH

Aloxe-Corton 1991 • $25 • (01/31/94) • **85**

Aloxe-Corton 1990: Firm and muscular, with intense, ripe cherry and dark chocolate flavors, medium body and a solid backbone of tannins. Drinkable now. • $33 • (12/15/92) • **88**

Aloxe-Corton 1989 • $27 • (01/31/92) • **89**

Aloxe-Corton 1986 • $25 • (04/30/89) • **83**

Aloxe-Corton 1985 • $23 • (11/15/87) • **90**

Bâtard-Montrachet 1994: Seductively toasty and smoky, and melts in the mouth like whipped butter. Medium- to full-bodied, the lovely lemon, honey, grass, pear, pineapple, and piecrust flavors stay the course. Delicious now. • $NA • (08/31/96) • **90**

Bâtard-Montrachet 1993: Crisp lime, honey and pear flavors in a vibrant package. Very clean finish. Drink now. • $105 • (05/15/95) • **86**

Bâtard-Montrachet 1992: Generous, supple, and charming, with creamy vanilla bean, peach, pear and toast flavors laced with some honey and hazelnut notes. Drinkable now. • $120 • (08/31/94) • **92**

Beaujolais-Villages 1994 • $NA • (06/15/95) • **77**

Beaune Clos des Mouches 1995: A balanced, lively, fruity wine, with a hint of earthy *terroir* and an elegant structure that reflects a deft touch. Medium in body and intensity, with ripe, well-integrated tannins and a supple finish. Drink now through 2002. • $45 • (01/31/98) • **88**

Beaune Clos des Mouches 1993: Good, straightforward Pinot, offering berry and cherry character, medium body, light tannins and a crisp finish. Drink now. • $50 • (11/15/95) • **86**

Beaune Clos des Mouches 1992: Quite tannic and rough, more like a 1991 than a '92, but has some sweet, ripe fruit below the tight, hard tannins. Fans of this wine know it ages well; try now. • $33 • (12/15/94) • **84**

Beaune Clos des Mouches 1991: Fresh and fruity, showing lots of attractive strawberry and red cherry aromas and flavors. Very bright and appealing for its beautifully defined fruit and substantial length. Drinkable now. • $37 Ⓐ • (01/31/94) • **86**

Beaune Clos des Mouches 1990: A joy to taste. Gorgeous, smooth, round, supple and full of crisp, focused raspberry, earth and currant aromas and flavors. Try now. 1,800 cases made. • $52 • (12/15/92) • **93**

Beaune Clos des Mouches 1989 • $42 Ⓐ • (02/29/92) • **92**

Beaune Clos des Mouches 1988 • $38 Ⓐ • (02/15/91) • **88**

Beaune Clos des Mouches 1987 • $29 Ⓐ • (06/15/90) • **83**

Beaune Clos des Mouches White 1996: Well made white that blends beautifully, with the overt emphasis on toasty oak with ripe fruit. Not for everyone (all this wood), but it works partly because of the lush, supple, mineral-driven texture and fresh, vibrant acidity. Seductive finish. Try after 2000. • $78 • (05/31/98) • **90**

Beaune Clos des Mouches White 1995: A pleasure to taste. Full-throttle, quite racy and backed by a core of citrus, well-integrated toasty bread and smoke flavors. The ripe and oily texture envelops the palate. Long, tartish finish. Drink now through 2000. • $70 • (08/31/97) • **90**

Beaune Clos des Mouches White 1994: Showing good intensity in its relatively lean package, this medium-bodied white offers ripe apple, lime and a touch of mineral character. Somewhat linear and one-dimensional. Try now. • $60 • (05/31/96) • **84**

Beaune Clos des Mouches White 1993: This fresh white Burgundy has honey, mineral and apple character. Medium-bodied and crisp, with a long, clean finish. • $48 • (05/15/95) • **85**

Beaune Clos des Mouches White 1992: Racy, with a lovely, silky texture and smoky, toasty, lemon and pear flavors, all in good proportions. Medium-bodied, focused and classy, with a gorgeous, minerally finish. Drinkable now. Tasted twice. • $55 • (08/31/94) • **90**

Beaune Grèves 1995: This has depth on the nose, followed by spicy red cherry flavor and a silky, juicy texture. Firm and balanced, with a lingering finish. • $35 • (11/15/97) • **84**

Beaune Grèves 1994: Polished but very light, offering modestly complex fruit flavor. Shows more character on the slightly chewy, green finish. Drink now. • $33 • (11/15/96) • **79**

Beaune Grèves 1992: Very light and crisp, with modest strawberry and floral notes. Drinkable now. • $25 • (12/15/94) • **80**

Beaune Grèves 1991: Light, firm and modestly flavorful, with a pleasant ring of toasty, cedary berry aromas and flavors that persist on the finish. Drinkable now. • $28 Ⓐ • (01/31/94) • **82**

Beaune Grèves 1989 • $47 • (01/31/92) • **88**

Beaune Grèves 1959 • $90 • (08/31/90) • **80**

Beaune Hospices de Beaune Cuvée Maurice Drouhin 1990: Focused and elegant, offering a nicely crafted texture, raspberry and earth aromas and a smooth, refined finish. Drinkable now. • $NA • (12/15/92) • **88**

Bonnes Mares 1995: Delicate and ripe, this is a balanced, sweet-tasting red Burgundy with lovely wild berry, raspberry and black cherry flavors. Supple on the palate, it turns a bit astringent on the finish. Better after 2000. • $100 • (11/15/97) • **87**

Bonnes Mares 1993: Vibrant, steely Burgundy sporting bright cherry and plum aromas, medium body, clean fruit flavors and fine tannins. Drink now. • $100 • (11/15/95) • **88**

Bonnes Mares 1992: Lithe, appealing berry and floral aromas and flavors; silky and generous on the palate right through the lean, supple finish. Try now. • $64 • (12/15/94) • **86**

Bonnes Mares 1991: Lean, almost delicate, with a minty, rose petal edge to the strawberry and raspberry fruit, which persists on the finish. A fragile wine with subtle flavors and substantial length. Tannins are beautifully integrated. • $76 Ⓐ • (01/31/94) • **89**

Bonnes Mares 1990: The lovely complexity grows on you, from the forest, wet earth and underbrush aromas to the silky blackberry flavors. Has an excellent backbone of tannins, and the intensity on the long finish is almost perfect. Drink now. • $91 • (12/15/92) • **93**

Bonnes Mares 1989 • $99 • (01/31/92) • **93**

Bourgogne Laforêt 1989 • $9 • (04/30/91) BB • **85**

Bourgogne Laforêt 1988 • $10 • (03/31/91) BB • **84**

Bourgogne Laforêt 1987 • $9 • (06/15/89) • **78**

Bourgogne Laforêt 1985 • $9 • (11/15/87) • **78**

Bourgogne Laforêt 1983 • $7 • (11/01/85) • **71**

Brouilly 1996: Soft, supple and light, neither the acidity nor the tannins are aggressive in the least. Offers cherry and strawberry flavors, with hints of cinnamon and vanilla. • $15 • (09/15/97) • **83**

Brouilly 1995: Silky and flush with fruit, showing lots of plum and black cherry flavors with attractive chocolate and banana accents. Just enough tannin for grip. • $16 • (08/31/96) • **86**

Brouilly 1994 • $13 • (06/15/95) • **82**

Brouilly 1993 • $12 • (06/30/94) • **86**

Chablis 1996: Distinctive, with a wet earth, underbrush and mineral character that's clean and pure, if not to everyone's taste. Medium-bodied, it doesn't show as much pure fruit flavor as some '96s, but still okay. Supple in texture, balanced finish. Drink now to 2000. • $19 • (08/31/97) • **87**

Chablis 1994 • $19 • (08/31/95) • **84**

Chablis Domaine de Vaudon 1994 • $24 • (08/31/95) • **85**

Chablis Les Clos 1996: Watch out Montrachets! This may burst with violet, spice and floral aromas from all that new oak, but the wood is balanced by the sweet core of ripe flavors (pineapple, pear, mango and mandarin). Opulent and lush, this full-bodied Chablis is at its best on the silky, mineral-laden midpalate, which is nearly flawless. Lovely, long finish. Tempting now; should improve through 2010. • $50 • (05/31/98) • **98**

Chablis Les Clos 1994 • $45 • (05/31/96) • **90**

Chablis Les Clos 1993 • $45 • (08/31/95) • **87**

Chablis Premier Cru 1996: Thick and dense, this ripe, full-bodied Chablis offers a superbly smooth, supple mouthfeel that is the epitome of harmony. Shows very nice mineral, tropical fruit and lemon complexity, with the citrus flavors kicking in on the long finish. Enjoy now through 2002. 2,000 cases made. • $25 • (08/31/97) SS • **90**

Chablis Premier Cru 1994 • $25 • (05/31/96) • **84**

Chablis Secher 1993 • $25 • (08/31/95) • **85**

Chablis Vaudésir 1996: Clean and racy, a bit woody, but with violet, rose petal, gooseberry and herbal notes. Very exotic in its toasty bread and grilled meat register. Medium- to full-bodied, it has excellent ripe fruit and lime acidity that promises a nice future. Try after 2000. • $48 • (05/31/98) • **89**

Chablis Vaudésir 1994 • $44 • (05/31/96) • **94**

Chablis Vaudésir 1993 • $45 • (08/31/95) • **83**

Chambertin 1995: A balanced, ripe, delicate, medium-bodied wine with wonderfully sweet tannins and lovely raspberry and wild berry flavors. A bit hot on the finish, but still nice. Drinkable now or hold until 2005. Not nearly as impressive as when tasted from barrel. • $100 • (11/15/97) • **86**

Chambertin 1994: Aims for elegance and achieves it, with lithe, beautifully focused raspberry, strawberry and rose petal flavors that show every sign of fleshing out if cellared until 1999. Tannins are smoothly integrated. • $94 • (11/15/96) • **91**

Chambertin 1993: Wonderful and well made, medium in body, with a full-throttle tannic structure and plenty of ripe fruit flavors. Drink in 2000. • $119 • (11/15/95) • **91**

Chambertin 1992: Lean and a little leafy-stemmy in character, but with enough strawberry flavor to save it. Drinkable now. • $74 • (12/15/94) • **79**

Chambertin 1991: Crisp and light, its rose petal-scented raspberry flavors bouncing through the delicate frame, picking up some smoky, meaty notes on the finish. Try now. • $84 Ⓐ • (01/31/94) • **86**

Chambertin 1990: Muscular yet harmonious, velvety and intense, with beautiful ripe plum, earth and cherry flavors and a hint of smoke. Drink now. • $113 • (12/15/92) • **91**

Chambertin 1989 • $114 • (01/31/92) • **90**

Chambertin 1988 • $83 • (02/15/91) • **94**

Chambertin 1986 • $80 • (02/28/89) • **90**

Chambertin 1985 • $53 Ⓐ • (11/15/87) • **95**

Chambolle-Musigny 1995: Lovely, silky and seductive. Full-bodied, with plenty of ripe red- and blackberry character and a supple texture. Medium-bodied, it's fresh and succulent, but turns a bit tough and astringent on the finish. Try after 1999, when the tannins will be softer. • $34 • (11/15/97) • **89**

Chambolle-Musigny 1992: Crisp and nicely focused, a lighter style with appealing raspberry and anise flavors that linger on the delicate finish. Drinkable now. • $25 • (12/15/94) • **82**

Chambolle-Musigny 1991: Light, almost watery, with extremely modest strawberry and citrus aromas and flavors. Drinkable now. • $29 Ⓐ • (01/31/94) • **75**

Key: SS—Spectator Selection CS—Cellar Selection HR—Highly Recommended BB—Best Buy $NA—Price not available Ⓐ—Auction Price (BT)—Barrel Tasting
Dates in parentheses indicate the issues in which the ratings were published.

Chambolle-Musigny 1990: Bright and vivid, with subtle leaf, plum, mushroom and wet earth flavors that grow into an interesting finish. Try now. • $36 • (12/15/92) • **87**

Chambolle-Musigny 1989 • $41 • (01/31/92) • **91**

Chambolle-Musigny 1986 • $27 • (07/31/88) • **88**

Chambolle-Musigny 1985 • $46 Ⓐ • (11/15/87) • **93**

Chambolle-Musigny Les Amoureuses 1995: Earthy, gamy, *sous-bois* aromas and flavors dominate this medium-bodied red. The intense fruit is disjointed from the tannins, which turn dry and astringent on the finish. • $85 • (11/15/97) • **79**

Chambolle-Musigny Les Amoureuses 1994: Light and refreshing, but several steps up from a rosé, this offers appealing raspberry and vanilla flavors that linger engagingly on the finish. • $67 • (11/15/96) • **84**

Chambolle-Musigny Les Amoureuses 1992: A good effort for '92. Smoky, gamy, red berry flavors blend with floral notes in a complex, supple, ripe wine. Has appealing concentration and a medium-long finish. Drink now. • $55 • (12/15/94) • **85**

Chambolle-Musigny Les Amoureuses 1991: Light, almost watery, with barely discernible currant flavors that sneak in on the finish. Drinkable now. • $67 Ⓐ • (01/31/94) • **77**

Chambolle-Musigny Les Amoureuses 1990: A classy, well-knit wine that's extremely seductive, with lovely vanilla, earth, smoke and berry aromas and flavors dancing across the palate and a beautiful, silky finish. Drinkable now. 250 cases made. • $80 • (12/15/92) • **93**

Chambolle-Musigny Les Amoureuses 1988 • $76 • (12/31/90) • **87**

Chambolle-Musigny Les Amoureuses 1955 • $230 • (08/31/90) • **65**

Chambolle-Musigny Les Baudes 1991: Delicate but flavorful and amazingly long on the finish, showing delicious currant, blackberry and anise aromas and flavors that remain silky and smooth through the finish. Drinkable now. • $39 Ⓐ • (01/31/94) • **86**

Chambolle-Musigny Les Baudes 1989 • $52 • (01/31/92) • **89**

Chambolle-Musigny Les Feusselottes 1989 • $55 • (01/31/92) • **92**

Chambolle-Musigny Les Hauts Doix 1990: Tight and elegant, with lovely, focused chocolate and berry flavors; medium-bodied. Drink now. • $53 • (12/15/92) • **88**

Chambolle-Musigny Les Sentiers 1989 • $55 • (01/31/92) • **92**

Chambolle-Musigny Premier Cru 1993: Somewhat hollow on the palate, showing decent plum and dried cherry character and medium body. It could use a bit more fruit on the finish. Perhaps better in 1999. • $45 • (11/15/95) • **87**

Chambolle-Musigny Premier Cru 1991: Light in texture, a pretty wine with appealing raspberry and vanilla aromas and flavors. Drinkable now. • $33 Ⓐ • (01/31/94) • **83**

Chambolle-Musigny Premier Cru 1989 • $50 • (01/31/92) • **89**

Charmes-Chambertin 1995: Deep, rich and spicy, this *grand cru* shows black cherry and licorice-tinged flavors, a fat midpalate and moderate tannins. Delicious. • $85 • (11/15/97) • **90**

Charmes-Chambertin 1994: A charming wine, light in color and body, but stringing some nice strawberry, anise, rose petal and vanilla flavors along a silky thread that weaves through the delicate finish. Approachable now. • $71 • (11/15/96) • **87**

Charmes-Chambertin 1993: Attractive berry and vanilla character, but it's still somewhat disappointing for a *grand cru*. Medium in body, delivering sweet fruit and a very delicate finish. Better in 1999. • $84 • (11/15/95) • **85**

Charmes-Chambertin 1991: Supple and elegant, a smooth-textured wine that offers a moderate level of blackberry and spice aromas and flavors that persist into a crisp finish, hinting at smoke and toast. Try now. • $59 Ⓐ • (01/31/94) • **87**

Charmes-Chambertin 1990: Opulent and sensational, with ripe fruit flavors that ooze from the glass. Not only does it have amazing fruit, but the tannins are equally impressive and are in near-perfect balance. Drink now. • $81 • (12/15/92) • **96**

Charmes-Chambertin 1989 • $80 • (01/31/92) • **92**

Charmes-Chambertin 1988 • $58 Ⓐ • (11/15/90) • **93**

Charmes-Chambertin 1986 • $60 • (02/28/89) CS • **91**

Charmes-Chambertin 1985 • $82 Ⓐ • (11/15/87) • **89**

Chassagne-Montrachet 1995: Very soft and round, an apéritif-style Chardonnay that offers good fruit and honey character along with smoky oak notes. Full-bodied, it's a bit disjointed on the less-than-elegant finish. • $46 • (05/31/97) • **76**

Chassagne-Montrachet 1994: Straightforward green apple, vegetal and dried herb notes. Tart finish. • $38 • (05/31/96) • **78**

Chassagne-Montrachet 1993: Chalky, fruity character and relatively rich texture, offering mineral and stone qualities and a clean finish. A laudable effort. Drinkable now. • $32 • (05/15/95) • **85**

Chassagne-Montrachet Marquis de Laguiche 1995: Very attractive, ripe and harmonious, with sweet-tasting honey and almond notes, dried herb and tropical fruit flavors, and toasty spice notes on the finish. Full-bodied and concentrated, it coats the mouth. Needs time; try after 2000. • $58 Ⓐ • (08/31/97) • **90**

Chassagne-Montrachet Marquis de Laguiche 1994: Some nice intensity in this fresh, medium-bodied white that delivers appealing, ripe fruit flavors. Harmonious and drinkable now. • $54 • (05/31/96) • **81**

Chassagne-Montrachet Marquis de Laguiche 1993: Green and tart apple, grapefruit and herb flavors and a crisp finish. Could use a bit more ripe fruit. Try now. • $44 Ⓐ • (05/15/95) • **84**

Chassagne-Montrachet Marquis de Laguiche 1992: A nicely fruity and fresh white Burgundy, with focused grapefruit, apple and lime flavors that give it life and zest. Clean and vibrant. • $42 • (08/31/94) • **85**

Chassagne-Montrachet Morgeot Red 1991: Light and spicy, showing a nice balance of strawberry and raspberry fruit with an overlay of sweet oak. Enjoyable to drink now. • $20 Ⓐ • (01/31/94) • **82**

Chassagne-Montrachet Red 1990: Straightforward Chassagne. Light and pleasant, with one-dimensional berry and earth aromas and flavors. Drinkable now. • $22 • (12/15/92) • **84**

Chassagne-Montrachet Red 1989 • $23 • (01/31/92) • **87**

Chiroubles 1996: Delicately spicy flavors of cinnamon and clove give personality and add nuance to the strawberry flavors. Light-bodied and quaffable. • $16 • (09/15/97) • **85**

Chiroubles 1995: Mouthwatering, with a nice balance of vivid plum and light chocolate flavors. Supple on the palate yet firm on the juicy finish. • $17 • (08/31/96) • **86**

Chiroubles 1993 • $12 • (06/30/94) • **83**

Chorey-lès-Beaune 1995: Faint kirsch notes highlight this delicate Pinot, which turns astringent on the finish. • $19 • (11/15/97) • **79**

Chorey-lès-Beaune 1993: Fine and clean, featuring zingy berry and plum character, light tannins and a fresh finish. Not big, but delicious. Drink now. • $20 • (11/15/95) • **83**

Chorey-lès-Beaune 1992: Light in body and texture, but showing a focused beam of clean, pure raspberry and currant. A good effort in a difficult vintage. • $16 • (12/15/94) • **83**

Clos de la Roche 1991: A succulent beam of spicy raspberry flavor picks up black pepper notes on the finish. Light, charming and a bit watery in texture. Drinkable now. • $49 Ⓐ • (01/31/94) • **85**

Clos de la Roche 1990: Pretty and delicate, with a bounty of raspberry flavors and refreshing acidity. Delivers a focused feeling along with ripe tannins. Try now. • $69 • (12/15/92) • **89**

Clos de la Roche 1989 • $77 • (01/31/92) • **88**

Clos de la Roche 1988 • $73 • (02/15/91) • **93**

Clos de la Roche 1986 • $53 • (07/15/89) • **83**

Clos de la Roche 1985 • $60 • (11/15/87) • **97**

Clos de Vougeot 1995: A ripe, medium-bodied Clos Vougeot with nice flavors of red- and blackberries and some tough tannins. Good intensity. Try after 2000. • $70 • (11/15/97) • **83**

Clos de Vougeot 1992: A delicate Burgundy with pretty raspberry and vanilla flavors that linger on the sweet finish. Tannins are very fine. Drinkable now. • $44 • (12/15/94) • **85**

Clos de Vougeot 1991: Light, elegant and soft in texture; very fine tannins and a bright beam of delicate raspberry and strawberry flavors runs through to the finish. Drink now to 1999. • $62 Ⓐ • (01/31/94) • **86**

Clos de Vougeot 1990: Opulent, with a hard-as-nails undertow that sweeps across the palate, then turns smooth and velvety on the focused finish, with lovely currant, raspberry, cherry and smoke notes. Drinkable now. • $71 • (12/15/92) • **91**

Clos de Vougeot 1988 • $85 • (02/15/91) • **90**

Clos de Vougeot 1986 • $55 • (04/15/89) • **86**

Clos de Vougeot 1985 • $38 Ⓐ • (11/15/87) • **94**

Clos St.-Denis 1995: A pretty wine in a delicate style, with some slight vanilla, red berry, currant and spice character. Light- to medium-bodied, it's nicely balanced and pleasant to drink. Ends with good refreshing acidity. Enjoy now through 1999. • $75 • (01/31/98) • **87**

Clos St.-Denis 1989 • $76 • (01/31/92) • **91**

Corton 1991: Tough, earthy and solid; pretty currant and plum flavors lurk behind a wave of gritty tannins and minerally, mushroomy notes. Try now. • $42 Ⓐ • (01/31/94) • **84**

Corton 1990: Very velvety, with plenty of attractive blackberry and earth aromas and flavors and firm, almost steely tannins. Drinkable now. • $58 • (12/15/92) • **88**

Corton 1985 • $48 • (11/15/87) • **92**

Corton Les Bressandes 1993: Delicious and beautifully crafted violet, vanilla and ripe fruit character, full body, silky tannins and a long, fresh finish. Better in 2000. • $70 • (11/15/95) • **93**

Corton Les Bressandes 1988 • $60 • (11/15/90) • **92**

Corton Les Bressandes 1986 • $45 • (04/30/89) • **90**

Corton-Charlemagne 1996: Beautiful, mixing ripeness with elegance. Not showing much aroma, but there's plenty of caressing, creamlike texture in the midpalate. Loads of lime, grapefruit, ripe pear and tropical flavors along with a hint of buttery mineral character. Of medium body, with a balanced and long finish. Try around 2002. • $92 • (05/31/98) • **92**

Côte de Beaune 1994: Light and simple, with whiffs of strawberry, raspberry and earth aromas and flavors. Delicate, slightly diluted finish. Drink chilled. • $23 • (11/15/96) • **76**

Côte de Beaune 1992: Light and crisp, but with a solid core of berry that keeps sailing through the finish to liven it up. • $18 • (12/15/94) • **81**

Côte de Beaune-Villages 1986 • $13 • (06/15/89) • **78**

Côte de Beaune-Villages 1985 • $14 • (11/15/87) • **85**

Côte de Nuits-Villages 1995: Red cherries are on display in this light-bodied, playful '95. Approachable now through 2002. • $22 • (11/15/97) • **82**

Côte de Nuits-Villages 1994: Chewy and spicy, with a minty, floral accent to the very light berry flavors. • $22 • (11/15/96) • **78**

Côte de Nuits-Villages 1990: Crisp and fresh, with attractive berry and earth aromas and flavors and a medium tannin structure. Drinkable now. • $20 • (12/15/92) • **82**

Côte de Nuits-Villages 1985 • $19 • (11/15/87) • **86**

Echézeaux 1994: Tough and stalky, with precious little fruit flavor or freshness to create balance. • $58 • (11/15/96) • **76**

Echézeaux 1991: A lithe, lively mouthful of anise-scented currant and blackberry flavors, which are much more appealing and distinctive than the earthy aromas. Drinkable now. • $49 Ⓐ • (01/31/94) • **87**

Echézeaux 1990: Effusively aromatic and flavorful, solid and seductive. The raspberry and earth characteristics are beautiful on the long finish. Drinkable now. 175 cases made. • $69 • (12/15/92) • **91**

Echézeaux 1988 • $60 • (11/15/90) HR • **93**

Echézeaux 1986 • $60 • (07/31/88) • **92**

Fleurie 1996: A pronounced herbal note gives personality but dominates the simple cherry flavor. Has enough tannin for grip. • $18 • (09/15/97) • **81**

Fleurie 1995: Smoky, gamy aromas give way to ripe plum flavors on the palate. Very firm tannins dominate the finish. A big wine that sacrifices balance for extraction. Try now. • $19 • (09/15/96) • **84**

Fleurie 1994 • $13 • (06/15/95) • **84**

Gevrey-Chambertin 1995: Light in color and body, it tastes stemmy and astringent. • $35 • (11/15/97) • **70**

Gevrey-Chambertin 1992: Light and fragrant, charming and delicate, emphasizing bright currant and strawberry flavors that linger nicely on the palate. Drinkable now. • $24 • (12/15/94) • **84**

Gevrey-Chambertin 1991: Crisp and lively, showing a nice streak of cherry and spice aromas and flavors. Drinkable now. • $25 Ⓐ • (01/31/94) • **81**

Gevrey-Chambertin 1990: Very attractive and seductive, with almost sweet flavors. Shows good intensity of berry, cherry and earth notes that develop into a focused beam on the finish. Drinkable now. • $36 • (12/15/92) • **88**

Gevrey-Chambertin 1986 • $27 • (02/28/89) • **83**

Gevrey-Chambertin 1985 • $33 • (11/15/87) • **91**

Gevrey-Chambertin Champeaux 1991: Light and spicy, featuring anise and earth overtones to the modest raspberry flavors. Finishes tough. Try now. • $37 Ⓐ • (01/31/94) • **80**

Gevrey-Chambertin Champeaux 1990: Boasts the quintessential, round, lush, ripe texture of many wines from this vintage. Elegant yet rich, with sweet berry, red licorice and black cherry flavors that are smooth and velvety on the long, flavorful finish. Drinkable now. • $70 • (12/15/92) • **91**

Gevrey-Chambertin Lavaut St.-Jacques 1989 • $70 • (01/31/92) • **86**

Gevrey-Chambertin Les Cazetiers 1989 • $70 • (01/31/92) • **91**

Grands Echézeaux 1994: Lean and open-textured, with floral and berry flavors plus a hint of wet earth. Ultimately, a delicate wine with a bit of astringency. Try now. • $92 • (11/15/96) • **82**

Grands Echézeaux 1992: Simple, sturdy and crisp, with tart berry and citrus notes that ring on the narrow, tannic finish. Try now. • $74 • (12/15/94) • **80**

Grands Echézeaux 1991: Oh, how seductive. Bright, youthful and focused, with delicious currant, vanilla and toast flavors and extremely well-integrated, smooth tannins. Bravo. • $85 • (02/28/95) • **93**

Grands Echézeaux 1990: Brilliant and youthful, featuring an intensity laced with vanilla, plum, spice and currant notes that shine through the tannic finish. Try now. • $100 • (02/28/95) • **91**

Grands Echézeaux 1989 • $114 • (02/28/95) • **90**

Grands Echézeaux 1988 • $85 • (02/28/95) • **88**

Grands Echézeaux 1987 • $40 • (02/28/95) • **90**
Grands Echézeaux 1986 • $55 • (02/28/95) • **84**
Grands Echézeaux 1985 • $75 • (02/28/95) • **86**
Grands Echézeaux 1983 • $NA • (02/28/95) • **79**
Griotte-Chambertin 1995: A fresh red that evokes aromas and flavors of red cherries, wet earth and spice. Concentrated, yet a bit lean with very big tannins, it has the requisite fruit to match. Wait until 2002. • $95 • (11/15/97) • **90**
Griotte-Chambertin 1994: Very light in color, with some spicy strawberry flavors that come to hint at rose petals on the long, crisply tannic finish. Try in 2000. • $73 • (11/15/96) • **78**
Griotte-Chambertin 1991: Very pretty, light and elegant, offering nicely focused black cherry, cola and coffee flavors that echo on the long finish. Stylish and drinkable now. • $63 Ⓐ • (01/31/94) • **88**
Griotte-Chambertin 1990: The essence of Burgundy, with enticing crushed fruit, berry, tea and cedar aromas and flavors, masses of ultrafine tannins and fresh acidity. Drinkable now. 250 cases made. • $84 • (12/15/92) • **94**
Griotte-Chambertin 1989 • $90 • (01/31/92) • **91**
Griotte-Chambertin 1988 • $81 • (11/15/90) • **91**
Griotte-Chambertin 1986 • $81 • (07/31/88) • **92**
Griotte-Chambertin 1985 • $68 • (11/15/87) • **95**
Juliénas 1996: Spicy notes add interest to this soft, simple red, with its straightforward cherry and light earth flavors, modest tannins and crisp, clean finish. • $14 • (08/31/97) • **83**
Juliénas 1995: Vivid, juicy cherry flavor and firm tannins balance each other nicely in this fresh, clean red. • $15 • (09/15/96) • **85**
Juliénas 1994 • $13 • (07/31/95) • **85**
Juliénas 1993 • $12 • (06/30/94) HR • **88**
Ladoix 1993: Very nicely made, delicate yet containing good ripe fruit. Unpretentious, neither opulent nor full-bodied, it tingles the palate with well-defined flavors. Drink now. • $20 • (11/15/95) • **81**
Ladoix 1991: Light and crisp; a decent level of currant flavor emerges nicely on the palate. Finishes soft and surprisingly generous. Drinkable now. • $17 Ⓐ • (01/31/94) • **83**
Latricières-Chambertin 1991: Lean, supple and delicate, displaying pretty currant and blackberry flavors, a smooth texture and a narrow finish. A bit short on finesse, but long on attractive flavors. Try now. • $59 Ⓐ • (01/31/94) • **85**
Latricières-Chambertin 1988 • $72 • (02/15/91) • **87**
Mâcon-Villages 1995: Ripe and crisp at the same time, with a firm structure yet a seductive, smooth mouthfeel. Medium-bodied, with clean lime, apple and mineral flavors. Drink now. • $NA • (08/31/96) • **85**
Maranges 1994: Very light, almost as light a rosé, but tannic enough to qualify as tough. • $20 • (11/15/96) • **77**
Maranges Premier Cru 1993: Straightforward Pinot showing cherry and light earth character and medium-fine tannins. Not much to talk about, but delicious all the same. Drinkable now. • $20 • (11/15/95) • **84**
Maranges Premier Cru 1990: A no-nonsense, simple Burgundy, with plummy, earthy aromas and flavors and medium tannins. Drinkable now. • $19 • (12/15/92) • **83**
Maranges Premier Cru 1989 • $20 • (01/31/92) • **85**
Mazis-Chambertin 1989 • $86 • (01/31/92) • **92**
Mercurey 1985 • $17 • (11/15/87) • **83**
Meursault 1995: Both round and compacted, this full-bodied Chardonnay delivers plenty of flavors, from citrus, fresh herbs, wet earth and mineral notes to toasty oak and honey, and has a pleasant, sweet-tasting finish. Drink now through 2000. • $42 • (05/31/97) • **87**
Meursault 1994: Appealing but light-bodied, offering citrus and pineapple flavors. Clean, crisp, not much complexity. Drinkable now. • $37 • (05/31/96) • **82**
Meursault 1993: A very good Meursault, showing toast, honey and citrus flavors. Built on a lean frame; lots of acidity. • $30 • (05/15/95) • **85**
Meursault Les Perrières 1995: What you wish all 1995s to be. Clean, pure, full-bodied, with a long life ahead, this wine is packed with honey, blanched almond, mineral, toasty bread and vibrant fruit flavors. A class act from start to finish. Should be best after 2000. • $60 • (05/31/97) • **94**
Meursault Les Perrières 1994: Focused mineral and lemon flavors give this a bit of subtlety. Of medium body, it's fresh and clean on the straightforward finish. • $52 • (05/31/96) • **84**

Key: SS—Spectator Selection CS—Cellar Selection HR—Highly Recommended BB—Best Buy $NA—Price not available Ⓐ—Auction Price (BT)—Barrel Tasting
Dates in parentheses indicate the issues in which the ratings were published.

Meursault Les Perrières 1993: A refined Meursault, not big, displaying well-defined fruit, acidity and structure; medium-bodied. • $38 • (05/15/95) • **85**
Meursault Les Perrières 1992: A well-made white that offers some lovely honey, toast, apple and pear notes along with a touch of coffee. Very delicate and gracious, with good acidity. Tasted twice. • $40 • (08/31/94) • **88**
Montagny 1995: Distinctive, ripe, rich and dense, with a silky texture and very intense flavors of mineral, grass and dried herbs, touches of honey and toasty oak. Long finish. Better wait until at least 2000. • $22 • (05/31/97) • **88**
Monthélie 1991: Firm in texture and spicy, with a toasty edge to the raspberry notes. A bit astringent. Try now. • $17 Ⓐ • (01/31/94) • **78**
Montrachet Marquis de Laguiche 1995: Subtle and classy, this wine is supple with near-perfect balance and spice, ripe fruit, toasty bread and mineral flavors that linger for minutes on the great, racy finish. Full-bodied; try around 2005. • $300 • (08/31/97) • **93**
Montrachet Marquis de Laguiche 1994: Rich and ripe, with lovely dried herb, fresh citrus and pineapple flavors. Balanced, not overly oaky, with a very elegant finish, it's a pleasure to taste now and should age gracefully, drinking well until 2000 to 2005. • $125 Ⓐ • (05/31/97) • **93**
Montrachet Marquis de Laguiche 1993: A crowd charmer: big, buttery and stylish. Oozes cream, toasty coconut, apple and spice notes. Full-bodied and tempting to drink now. • $179 Ⓐ • (08/31/95) • **90**
Montrachet Marquis de Laguiche 1992: Great finesse is the hallmark of this Montrachet. Well balanced, very supple and gorgeous; offers honey, nut, pear and grapefruit flavors, with a touch of mineral and vanilla notes on the lingering, subtle finish. Drink now. • $184 Ⓐ • (08/31/94) • **94**
Morey-St.-Denis 1993: A rather delicate Burgundy, showing Light-to-medium body, light, dry tannins and a light finish. Better in 1999. • $NA • (11/15/95) • **81**
Morey-St.-Denis 1990: Charms you with its effusive raspberry, cherry and strawberry aromas and flavors, delicious texture and smooth finish. Drinkable now. • $33 • (12/15/92) • **88**
Morey-St.-Denis Clos Sorbè 1993: A shining star that's delicate, offering loads of fine tannins and crisp fruit, medium body, lively acidity and a refreshing finish. Drink now. • $43 • (11/15/95) • **87**
Morey-St.-Denis Clos Sorbè 1989 • $45 • (01/31/92) • **86**
Morey-St.-Denis Monts Luisants 1988 • $38 • (02/28/91) • **92**
Morgon 1996: Firm and rather chunky, with smoky, spicy notes adding depth to the plum flavors. Firm tannins, good acidity. Drinkable now. • $15 • (09/15/97) • **84**
Morgon 1995: A generous wine with ripe cherry flavors, round tannins and a hint of vanilla. All the elements are attractive. Try now. • $16 • (09/15/96) • **86**
Morgon 1993 • $12 • (06/30/94) • **86**
Moulin-à-Vent 1996: A plump red, with round plum and black cherry flavors and accents of spice and licorice. Tannins are soft yet full, and the wine feels ripe and velvety on the palate. • $17 • (09/15/97) • **86**
Moulin-à-Vent 1995: Combining lively fruit and dense texture, this ageable red shows characteristic plum flavors with ripe tannins and good length. Ready to drink. • $18 • (09/15/96) • **87**
Moulin-à-Vent 1994 • $16 • (07/31/95) • **84**
Moulin-à-Vent 1993 • $13 • (06/30/94) • **85**
Musigny 1995: Sexy and racy, with wild raspberry, rose petal, violet, mocha and white chocolate character. Full-bodied, with ripe but firm tannins. Nice finesse. Tempting now through 2010. • $110 • (01/31/98) • **90**
Musigny 1994: Very firm and tannic, a bit drying, but it picks up some sweet berry flavor before ending a bit abruptly. Tannins may never recede, but the flavors could develop. Try in 2000. • $100 • (11/15/96) • **82**
Musigny 1993: A bit disappointing for such a renowned *grand cru.* Silky, well-structured red offering plum, raspberry and oak character but appearing a little too light. Medium in body, firm tannins and a light finish. Try in 1999. • $77 Ⓐ • (11/15/95) • **88**
Musigny 1991: Light, elegant, seductive and flavorful, displaying gorgeous currant, blackberry and floral aromas and flavors that are beautifully defined and delicate through the long finish. Try now. • $98 • (01/31/94) • **88**
Musigny 1990: A magical wine that's incredibly smooth. Has an abundance of plum, earth and chocolate aromas and flavors and a backbone of massive, velvety tannins. A pleasure to drink now. • $129 • (12/15/92) • **95**
Nuits-St.-Georges 1995: Delicate, pleasant and light-bodied, with ripe, easy tannins and raspberry, licorice and strawberry flavors. Well balanced. Drink upon release and through 2000. • $35 • (11/15/97) • **86**
Nuits-St.-Georges 1986 • $25 • (04/30/89) • **86**
Nuits-St.-Georges 1985 • $38 Ⓐ • (11/15/87) • **92**

Nuits-St.-Georges Aux Boudots 1990: Attractive, with cinnamon and berry aromas and flavors, silky tannins and a juicy finish. Drinkable now. • $57 • (12/15/92) • **88**

Nuits-St.-Georges Aux Boudots 1989 • $70 • (01/31/92) • **80**

Nuits-St.-Georges Roncière 1986 • $38 • (04/30/89) • **85**

Nuits-St.-Georges Roncière 1985 • $38 • (11/15/87) • **93**

Pernand-Vergelesses 1990: An eye-opener, with pretty, lively, bright fruit flavors on a supersupple framework that sing on the round finish. Drinkable now. • $21 • (12/15/92) • **87**

Pernand-Vergelesses 1985 • $17 • (11/15/87) • **91**

Pernand-Vergelesses White 1994: Crisp, even tart, this citrus-tasting white is attractively clean but lacks a bit of depth and interest. Should go well with shellfish, though. • $24 • (05/31/96) • **83**

Pommard 1995: A very raw wine, tough and chewy, showing red berry character and a lot of tannin. Not easy to warm up to, but this medium-bodied red, matched with a red meat dish around 2000, should offer some balance and pleasure. • $35 • (11/15/97) • **84**

Pommard 1992: Bright and fragrant, crisp on the palate and simple, with appealing strawberry flavor. Drinkable now. • $25 • (12/15/94) • **83**

Pommard 1991: Firm and chunky, showing solid yet delicate raspberry and black cherry aromas and flavors. Charming and satisfying. Drinkable now. • $27 Ⓐ • (01/31/94) • **84**

Pommard 1990: Pleasant but light for this appellation. Medium-bodied, with herbal, gamy flavors in an easy-to-drink style. Drinkable now. • $36 • (12/15/92) • **82**

Pommard 1989 • $43 • (01/31/92) • **85**

Pommard 1986 • $27 • (04/30/89) • **87**

Pommard 1985 • $34 Ⓐ • (11/15/87) • **93**

Pommard 1981 • $28 • (09/01/84) • **83**

Pommard Les Epenots 1993: Lovely, vivid raspberry and blackberry character, medium body and tannins and a clean finish. Drinkable now. • $35 • (11/15/95) • **85**

Pommard Les Epenots 1991: Light, charming and simple, with raspberry and lingonberry aromas and flavors. Has enough of a light tannic bite on the finish to try now. • $36 Ⓐ • (01/31/94) • **83**

Pommard Les Epenots 1990: Seductive and beautiful, with berry and earth flavors unfolding like soft waves. Offers a caressing texture on the firm finish and shows an appealing herbal character, too. Drinkable now. • $48 • (12/15/92) • **91**

Pommard Les Epenots 1989 • $56 • (01/31/92) • **89**

Pommard Les Epenots 1986 • $40 • (07/31/88) • **83**

Pommard Les Epenots 1985 • $41 • (11/15/87) • **95**

Pommard Les Rugiens 1989 • $56 • (01/31/92) • **87**

Pouilly-Fuissé 1996: Hard as nails, but with a bit of fruit peeking through, it offers solid structure, with an intense herbal, fresh grass, wet hay, bitter almond, wet earth, green apple character. Medium-bodied, it should soften by 2000. • $15 • (05/31/98) • **86**

Puligny-Montrachet 1995: Pretty, with some ripe fruit flavors and honey and floral notes. Full-bodied, it turns just a bit harsh on the finish, but it's still quite oily and seductive in texture—enough to warrant buying and drinking around 2000. • $47 • (08/31/97) • **87**

Puligny-Montrachet 1994: Lovely from first sip to last, both fresh and unctuous. Of medium body, it delivers some ripe apple, dried herb, cream and honey flavors. Crisp, slightly grassy finish. Drinkable now. • $39 • (05/31/96) • **87**

Puligny-Montrachet 1993: Clean and fresh, perhaps a bit modest on the palate, sporting tart acidity and a green apple finish. Drinkable now. • $32 • (05/15/95) • **81**

Puligny-Montrachet Clos de la Garenne 1996: Clean and pretty *premier cru* of pure, well-defined mineral character, showing wet stone and vanilla bean notes, with pear and fruit-pie notes thrown in. Medium to full in body, the texture is silky but also fresh thanks to a thread of lively citrus-spiked acidity. Needs at least until 2007. • $65 • (05/31/98) • **92**

Puligny-Montrachet La Garenne 1992: Refined, classy and tart, this slowly unfolds its secrets. Wonderful complexity, with good acidity and terrific apple, honey, hazelnut and mineral notes that seem so racy. Try with lobster or scallops. Drinkable now. • $43 • (08/31/94) • **92**

Puligny-Montrachet Les Folatières 1996: Distinctive, with a butter, butterscotch, spice, mineral and bread dough character accented by toasty oak, pear and tropical flavors. Full-bodied and very crisp and vibrant, this should settle down around 2003. • $65 • (05/31/98) • **87**

Puligny-Montrachet Les Folatières 1995: Shows some pleasant citrusy honey flavors, but lacks ripeness. It's fairly crisp in character, with a toast note. Full-bodied. Disappointing from Drouhin in this vintage. • $62 • (08/31/97) • **82**

Puligny-Montrachet Les Folatières 1994: A full-bodied white offering lots of personality and chewy, rich, mineral character. Clever winemaking here, and just the right proportions of toasty oak, honey and ripe fruit flavors. Sculpted with a deft hand from start to finish. Drinkable now. • $54 • (05/31/96) • **91**

Puligny-Montrachet Les Folatières 1993: Racy mineral, apple and honey character, medium body, firm acidity and a sleek finish. Drink now. • $42 • (05/15/95) • **84**

Puligny-Montrachet Les Pucelles 1993: Not bad for the vintage, providing some honey, herb and piecrust character, medium body, medium fruit and crisp acidity. • $50 • (05/15/95) • **84**

Romanée St.-Vivant 1992: Smooth and satisfying, spicy and ripe, displaying blackberry, black cherry and currant flavors that linger enticingly with a smoky edge on the finish. Tannins are a little drying; drinkable now. • $80 • (12/15/94) • **89**

Romanée St.-Vivant 1991: Crisp and polished, this lean, smooth-textured wine displays creamy raspberry, strawberry and vanilla aromas and flavors, but not exactly in profusion. Finishes a bit austere and citrusy. Drinkable now. • $90 Ⓐ • (01/31/94) • **86**

Romanée St.-Vivant 1989 • $94 • (01/31/92) • **92**

Rully White 1996: Delicious and balanced, offering ripe fruit in a tightly wound, high-acidity, juicy package. Medium-bodied, with a finish that is a bit tart now but should turn creamlike with some bottle age. Try now through 2002. • $21 • (05/31/98) • **86**

Rully White 1995: Nice quality for a Rully. It's a mouthful, very lush and ripe, oily in texture, with spice, pear, tropical fruit and dried herb complexity. Balanced, it's tempting now through 2002. • $22 • (08/31/97) • **87**

St.-Amour 1996: Round, even lush on the palate, this ripe red offers black cherry and blackberry flavors with hints of mincemeat spices. A generous wine, best on its own. • $18 • (09/15/97) • **85**

St.-Amour 1995: A well-made wine, with character. Strong spice and herb notes add interest to the black cherry flavors. Supple and fruity, supported by firm tannins. • $19 • (08/31/96) • **86**

St.-Aubin White 1996: Lively and vibrant—and a bit green and grassy—but it has tasty ripe fruit, too, with apple, pear and kiwi notes. Of medium body, it's delicious now with seafood. • $32 • (05/31/98) • **86**

St.-Aubin White 1995: Overripe, an almost late-harvest style of white Burgundy marked by toasty oak, butter, spice and cooked pear notes. Try upon release and through 2000. • $31 • (05/31/97) • **80**

St.-Aubin White 1994: Terrific quality for a simple village wine from this appellation. Ripe yet elegant, intense, full in body, delivering plenty of spice, citrus and pear flavors. Restrained, but drinkable now. • $22 • (05/31/96) • **90**

St.-Véran 1996: Rather dense and thick, full-bodied, with nice flavors of earth, wet hay, pear, honey and green apple. Fruity, clean and pure, with a creamlike, slightly grassy finish. Drink now. • $13 • (05/31/98) • **86**

St.-Véran 1995: Light-bodied and a bit diluted, with notes of ripe pear, citrus and fresh herbs. Drink now. • $23 • (05/31/97) • **80**

Santenay 1995: Savage in character, displaying modest fruit, medium body and dry tannins on the finish. Drinkable now. • $22 • (11/15/97) • **82**

Santenay 1990: Bright, lean and racy. Delivers nice black cherry and raspberry aromas and flavors, but turns a bit astringent and herbal on the finish. Drinkable now. • $22 • (12/15/92) • **83**

Santenay 1989 • $44 • (01/31/92) • **87**

Santenay 1985 • $17 • (11/15/87) • **88**

Santenay Beaurepaire 1991: Light and smooth; refreshingly straightforward, it shades its raspberry flavor with spice and tobacco overtones. A bit astringent on the finish. Drinkable now. • $17 Ⓐ • (01/31/94) • **81**

Savigny-lès-Beaune 1995: Herbaceous and diluted, with just a hint of ripe fruit and an astringent finish. • $23 • (11/15/97) • **73**

Savigny-lès-Beaune 1994: Light in color, crisp in texture, but the spicy berry flavors hang on pretty well. • $22 • (11/15/96) • **80**

Savigny-lès-Beaune 1993: Quite sweet-tasting, a light-bodied red to enjoy sooner rather than later. Delivers some nice raspberry, cherry and strawberry flavors. Try now. • $25 • (11/15/95) • **80**

Savigny-lès-Beaune 1992: Crisp and more than a little tannic, tight, with a narrow band of strawberry and spice. Try now. • $16 • (12/15/94) • **80**

Savigny-lès-Beaune 1991: Crisp, clean and lively, with a pretty thread of raspberry flavor. Drinkable now. • $18 Ⓐ • (01/31/94) • **83**

Savigny-lès-Beaune 1990: A straightforward fruit bomb. Very juicy, with ripe strawberry and earth flavors. A wine for early drinking. • $22 • (12/15/92) • **84**

Savigny-lès-Beaune 1989 • $23 • (01/31/92) • **87**

Savigny-lès-Beaune 1985 • $25 • (11/15/87) SS • **91**

Savigny-lès-Beaune 1981 • $16 • (09/01/84) • **79**

Volnay 1995: Middle-of-the-road Côte de Beaune, with some green, stemmy, cassis bush and red berry character. Medium-bodied, it turns a bit astringent on the finish; cellar until late this year. • $29 • (01/31/98) • **82**

Volnay 1991: Light and fragrant; modest raspberry and strawberry aromas and flavors persist on the simple finish. Drinkable now. • $26 Ⓐ • (01/31/94) • **81**

Volnay 1990: Solid as a rock, this distinctive Volnay delivers plenty of berry and earth aromas and flavors. Drinkable now. • $33 • (12/15/92) • **90**

Volnay 1985 • $29 • (11/15/87) • **88**

Volnay Clos des Chênes 1995: Delicate in style, with succulent cherry and red berry flavors that are cut short by aggressive tannins. Still, well made. • $37 • (11/15/97) • **84**

Volnay Clos des Chênes 1991: Floral and delicate, showing a violet edge to the currant and toast aromas and flavors. Finishes warm. Try now. • $32 Ⓐ • (01/31/94) • **81**

Volnay Clos des Chênes 1990: This classy Volnay offers loads of gamy, earthy berry characteristics and full, velvety tannins that explode on the finish. Drinkable now. • $42 • (12/15/92) • **93**

Volnay Clos des Chênes 1989 • $50 • (01/31/92) • **91**

Volnay Clos des Chênes 1988 • $45 • (02/15/91) • **85**

Volnay Clos des Chênes 1987 • $30 • (06/15/90) • **85**

Volnay Clos des Chênes 1986 • $31 • (04/30/89) • **80**

Volnay En Chevret 1994: Chewy tannins and modest currant flavors fight it out. Tannins win. • $32 • (11/15/96) • **77**

Volnay En Chevret 1993: Elegant for early drinking. Lovely, sweet and silky, featuring pretty violet flavors and a somewhat short finish. • $38 • (11/15/95) • **88**

Volnay En Chevret 1992: A light but appealing Volnay, with an oak-scented layer atop the floral raspberry flavors. Tart but satisfying finish. • $21 • (12/15/94) • **81**

Volnay En Chevret 1989 • $50 • (01/31/92) • **90**

Vosne-Romanée 1993: Totally ready to drink now. Decent plum, cedar and tobacco flavors, medium body and light tannins. • $38 • (11/15/95) • **82**

Vosne-Romanée Les Beaux Monts 1989 • $70 • (01/31/92) • **91**

Vosne-Romanée Les Beaux Monts 1988 • $46 Ⓐ • (03/31/91) • **80**

Vosne-Romanée Les Beaux Monts 1985 • $31 Ⓐ • (11/15/87) • **93**

Vosne-Romanée Les Petits Monts 1994: Light, a bit salty and with quite diluted fruit flavors. Short finish. • $52 • (11/15/96) • **77**

Vosne-Romanée Les Petits Monts 1990: Beautiful, showing round tannins and lots of pretty smoke, blackberry and cherry flavors. Drinkable now. 75 cases made. • $NA • (12/15/92) • **90**

Vosne-Romanée Les Suchots 1990: Substantially ripe and very appealing; not showy, but quite a mouthful, with black cherry and dark chocolate aromas and flavors and silky tannins on the long finish. Drinkable now. 225 cases made. • $58 • (12/15/92) • **86**

Vosne-Romanée Les Suchots 1989 • $70 • (01/31/92) • **89**

Vosne-Romanée Les Suchots 1988 • $57 • (02/28/91) • **90**

Vosne-Romanée Les Suchots 1985 • $42 • (11/15/87) • **94**

DROUHIN, ROBERT

Clos de Vougeot 1989 • $88 • (01/31/92) • **89**

DROUHIN-LAROZE

Bonnes Mares 1995: Traditional, with notes of licorice, strawberry and earth. Fairly smooth, but lacks the depth to rate higher. Medium-bodied, it turns a bit astringent on the slightly diluted finish. • $56 • (11/15/97) • **77**

Bonnes Mares 1993: Shockingly light for a Bonnes Mares. Some decent fruit flavors but rather diluted, showing light body and tannins and a slightly watery finish. Drinkable now. • $62 • (11/15/95) • **78**

Bonnes Mares 1992: Light, almost watery, with modest raspberry and cola notes that fade on the caramel-tinged finish. Drinkable already. 583 cases made. • $50 • (12/15/94) • **77**

Bonnes Mares 1988 • $81 • (12/31/90) • **93**

Bonnes Mares 1987 • $38 • (03/31/90) • **89**

Chambertin-Clos de Bèze 1995: Traditional style, but the heady perfume of rose petals and violets, grilled meat, Oriental spices and cassis, is enough to make red Burgundy aficionados swoon. Medium-bodied and supple on the midpalate, but firmly textured with chewy tannins on the lingering finish. Try after 1999. • $58 • (11/15/97) • **88**

Chambertin-Clos de Bèze 1994: Light, even bordering on diluted, with mild strawberry flavors. • $49 • (11/15/96) • **77**

Chambertin-Clos de Bèze 1993: Light and pleasant but also quite diluted, showing decent strawberry, raspberry and cherry notes. Drink up. • $68 • (11/15/95) • **81**

Chambertin-Clos de Bèze 1992: Very light and watery, with only a wispy character rising above the level of simple raspberry notes. Drink up. 416 cases made. • $60 • (12/15/94) • **78**

Chambertin-Clos de Bèze 1988 • $88 • (12/31/90) • **92**

Chambertin-Clos de Bèze 1987 • $40 • (03/31/90) • **90**

Chambertin-Clos de Bèze 1985 • $110 • (10/15/88) • **92**

Chambolle-Musigny Premier Cru 1994: Light in flavor but chewy with tannins, edging its modest strawberry flavors with an herbal accent. • $35 • (11/15/96) • **79**

Chapelle-Chambertin 1994: Tastes more like a dry Sangria than a *grand cru* Burgundy. Offers more orange peel and cinnamon flavors than Burgundian character, finishing light and soft. • $49 • (11/15/96) • **72**

Chapelle-Chambertin 1992: Very firm and chewy, with nicely focused strawberry and raspberry notes playing on a lean frame. The fruit persists on the mildly tannic finish. Try now. 83 cases made. • $45 • (12/15/94) • **84**

Chapelle-Chambertin 1988 • $68 • (12/31/90) • **88**

Clos de Vougeot 1995: Pretty blackberry and spicy oak flavors and a chewy texture mark this structured, slightly rustic wine. The long finish tastes of wild berry. • $56 • (11/15/97) • **88**

Clos de Vougeot 1994: Crisp and a bit chewy, with violet-petal and leafy overtones to the modest berry flavors. Tannins need until 1999 to 2000. • $46 • (11/15/96) • **82**

Clos de Vougeot 1993: Firm and lovely, showing excellent tannin structure. Unfolds red berry and mineral flavors nicely, offering a harmonious, lingering finish. Try in 2000. • $62 • (11/15/95) • **89**

Clos de Vougeot 1992: Sturdy, with lightish flavors of wild berry and anise, finishing a little coarse. Drinkable now. 333 cases made. • $50 • (12/15/94) • **78**

Clos de Vougeot 1988 • $81 • (12/31/90) • **89**

Clos de Vougeot 1987 • $38 • (03/31/90) • **79**

Clos de Vougeot 1985 • $60 • (10/15/88) • **88**

Gevrey-Chambertin 1994: Very light, with a raspberry-strawberry character. Short finish. • $36 • (11/15/96) • **73**

Gevrey-Chambertin Clos Prieur 1988 • $44 • (12/31/90) • **88**

Gevrey-Chambertin Lavaut St.-Jacques 1993: Straightforward and a bit tired, showing modest red berry and earth notes. Slightly drying on the diluted finish. • $38 • (11/15/95) • **77**

Gevrey-Chambertin Lavaut St.-Jacques 1988 • $44 • (12/31/90) • **80**

Latricières-Chambertin 1994: Light and lean. A crisp wine with modest red berry and cinnamon flavors that persist on the finish, picking up a hint of green. • $49 • (11/15/96) • **81**

Latricières-Chambertin 1993: Some simple, pleasant cherry and plum character and a hint of vanilla, but surprisingly light and diluted. Drink now. • $52 • (11/15/95) • **80**

Latricières-Chambertin 1992: Extremely light and watery, barely showing some raspberry notes that manage to linger on the simple finish. Drink up. 167 cases made. • $45 • (12/15/94) • **77**

Latricières-Chambertin 1988 • $68 • (12/31/90) • **91**

Latricières-Chambertin 1987 • $36 • (03/31/90) • **88**

Mazis-Chambertin 1985 • $47 • (10/15/88) • **90**

DROUIN, BÉATRICE & JEAN-MICHEL

Pouilly-Fuissé Domaine des Gerbeaux 1994: Clean, crisp, buttery, fruity character softens the hard edges. Of Light-to-medium body, this middle-of-the-road Pouilly should go well with food. Drinkable now. • $NA • (05/31/96) • **81**

Pouilly-Fuissé Domaine des Gerbeaux Cuvée Préstige 1994: Crisp Pouilly of wet hay, slight herbal, mineral and green apple character. Light to medium in body, it turns slightly tart on the finish. Try now. • $16 • (05/31/96) • **84**

DRUET, PIERRE-JACQUES

Bourgueil Les Cent Boissellées 1996: This approachable red offers a nice mix of cherry, smoke and light herb flavors, with light but firm tannins, a clean finish and regional character. Drink now. • $16 • (06/15/98) • **83**

Bourgueil Les Cent Boissellées 1995: Impressive power for a Loire red. This shows dark color, expressive blackberry and earth aromas and bold flavors

Key: SS—Spectator Selection CS—Cellar Selection HR—Highly Recommended BB—Best Buy $NA—Price not available Ⓐ—Auction Price (BT)—Barrel Tasting
Dates in parentheses indicate the issues in which the ratings were published.

of cassis, tobacco and herbs. The tannins are big but well integrated. Try now. 200 cases made. • $14 • (05/15/97) • **88**

DUBOEUF, GEORGES

Beaujolais Château de Buffavent 1996: Good stuffing for a simple Beaujolais, with bright cherry and light smoke flavors. It's soft and supple, but with a snap of acidity. • $8 • (09/15/97) • **81**
Beaujolais Flower Label 1994 • $7 • (06/15/95) • **81**
Beaujolais-Villages Château de la Grande Grange 1994 • $8 • (06/15/95) • **82**
Beaujolais-Villages Château de la Grande Grange 1993 • $7 • (06/30/94) • **73**
Beaujolais-Villages Château de Varennes 1996: Soft and supple, offering black cherry and cinnamon notes. A pleasant apéritif; try slightly chilled. • $9 • (08/31/97) • **83**
Beaujolais-Villages Château de Varennes 1995: Vivid, mouthfilling flavors of plums and cherries. Clean and fresh, it's round in texture but has a firm backbone of tannin. • $8 • (09/15/96) • **84**
Beaujolais-Villages Château de Varennes 1994 • $8 • (06/15/95) • **86**
Beaujolais-Villages Château de Varennes 1993 • $8 • (06/30/94) • **84**
Beaujolais-Villages Château des Vierres 1996: Balanced and true to type. Bright, spicy fruit flavors are lively in this round, supple red, and linger softly on the finish. • $9 • (08/31/97) • **84**
Beaujolais-Villages Château des Vierres 1995: Bright and fruity, with some depth. Ripe black cherry and grape flavors are appealing, and it has a nice balance of spice and tannin. • $8 • (09/15/96) • **84**
Beaujolais-Villages Château des Vierres 1994 • $8 • (06/15/95) • **83**
Beaujolais-Villages Château des Vierres 1993 • $7 • (06/30/94) • **82**
Beaujolais-Villages Domaine du Granit Bleu 1996: This chunky red offers good body for Beaujolais, with ripe cherry and light spice flavors. Can stand up to food. • $9 • (08/31/97) • **84**
Beaujolais-Villages Domaine du Granit Bleu 1995: Ripe fruit and round tannins give good texture on the palate. Plenty of plum flavors, accented with smoky, gamy notes. Crisp acidity keeps it lively. Drink now or hold. • $8 • (08/31/96) • **85**
Beaujolais-Villages Domaine du Granit Bleu 1994 • $8 • (06/15/95) • **84**
Beaujolais-Villages Domaine du Granit Bleu 1993 • $7 • (06/30/94) • **85**
Beaujolais-Villages Flower Label 1996: A balanced, well-structured red, with ripe plum flavors giving depth. Pretty spice notes emerge on the finish. • $9 • (08/31/97) • **84**
Beaujolais-Villages Flower Label 1995: Straightforward and sturdy, with balance and structure. Drinkable now. • $7 • (09/15/96) • **83**
Beaujolais-Villages Flower Label 1994 • $7 • (06/15/95) BB • **87**
Beaujolais-Villages Flower Label 1993 • $7 • (06/30/94) BB • **84**
Brouilly Château de Nervers 1996: Ripe yet lively, this well-balanced red offers bright black cherry, light chocolate and smoke flavors, with firm acidity and fine tannins. A nice match for food. • $11 • (07/31/97) • **86**
Brouilly Château de Nervers 1995: Round and quite rich, showing good concentration for a Brouilly, with flavors of ripe plum and chocolate. Delicious now. • $10 • (08/31/96) • **87**
Brouilly Château de Nervers 1994 • $10 • (06/15/95) • **85**
Brouilly Château de Nervers 1993 • $9 • (06/30/94) • **86**
Brouilly Château de Pierreux 1996: Full-bodied for a Brouilly, this ripe red shows plum and gamelike flavors and firm tannins. Try now. • $11 • (08/31/97) • **84**
Brouilly Château de Pierreux 1994 • $10 • (06/15/95) • **88**
Brouilly Château de Pierreux 1993 • $9 • (06/30/94) • **79**
Brouilly Château de Pierreux Comte de Toulgoët 1995: Alluring aromas of ripe fruit, toast and spice pave the way for ripe fruit and pleasantly gamy flavors and round tannins. Big and meaty, it shows the serious side of Beaujolais, but is drinkable now. • $10 • (08/31/96) • **87**
Brouilly Domaine de Combillaty 1996: Soft and ripe, this supple red offers plum and lightly earthy, spicy flavors on a smooth frame, with just enough tannin for grip. • $11 • (07/31/97) • **85**
Brouilly Flower Label 1995: Bright and fruity, perfumed with berry and floral aromas, this light, silky wine is perfect for summer afternoon quaffing. • $9 • (08/31/96) • **86**
Brouilly Flower Label 1994 • $9 • (06/15/95) • **86**
Brouilly Flower Label 1993 • $8 • (06/30/94) BB • **87**
Brouilly Grand Cuvée 1996: This ample red has generous plum, chocolate and spice flavors, round and full for a Brouilly, with firm yet integrated tannins. It's ripe yet balanced. • $11 • (07/31/97) • **86**
Chardonnay Vin de Pays d'Oc 1994 • $7 • (07/31/95) • **86**
Chardonnay Vin de Pays d'Oc Flower Label 1996: A good, quaffable Chardonnay, with apple flavors and spicy notes on the finish. Drink with poultry dishes. • $11/1.5 liter • (05/15/98) • **83**
Chasan Vin de Pays d'Oc 1994 • $6 • (07/31/95) • **80**
Châteauneuf-du-Pape 1990: Smoky and tannic but austere, showing prune, orange peel and leather flavors. Dry and astringent on the finish; drinkable now. • $12 • (04/15/93) • **82**
Chénas Domaine des Darroux 1996: A nice mix of ripeness and firmness creates clarity and balance, with cherry and black cherry flavors, and hints of spice on the finish. Good with food. • $10 • (07/31/97) • **86**
Chénas Domaine des Darroux 1995: Quite powerful for Beaujolais. This wine is dark in color, with intense plum aromas, and big tannins under ripe plum and cassis flavors. Drinkable now. • $8 • (09/15/96) • **88**
Chénas Domaine des Darroux 1994 • $9 • (07/31/95) • **79**
Chénas Domaine des Darroux 1993 • $8 • (06/30/94) BB • **88**
Chénas Flower Label 1996: Lively, its bright flavors of cherries and raspberries gaining complexity from spice and black pepper notes. Firm and fresh on the palate, a good match for food. • $10 • (07/31/97) • **86**
Chénas Flower Label 1994 • $9 • (06/15/95) • **85**
Chénas Flower Label 1993 • $7 • (06/30/94) • **84**
Chiroubles Château de Javernand 1995: Supple yet thick-textured, with spicy bright cherry and smoky flavors. Vivid and rich, it's a bit heavy for a Chiroubles, but shows good balance nonetheless. • $10 • (08/31/96) • **85**
Chiroubles Château de Javernand 1994 • $9 • (06/15/95) • **85**
Chiroubles Château de Javernand 1993 • $9 • (06/30/94) • **87**
Chiroubles Domaine Desmures 1996: Light and delicate, typical of Chiroubles, this pretty red shows bright cherry and strawberry flavors and lively acidity. • $10 • (07/31/97) • **85**
Chiroubles Domaine Desmures 1994 • $9 • (06/15/95) • **84**
Chiroubles Domaine Desmures 1993 • $9 • (06/30/94) • **86**
Chiroubles Flower Label 1996: Light yet firm, with an intriguing smoky note for extra dimension. Black cherry and spice flavors keep it true to the appellation. Clean and fresh. • $10 • (07/31/97) • **85**
Chiroubles Flower Label 1995: Typical Chiroubles—light, bright and pretty. Cherry, citrus and smoky flavors suffuse the palate then fade quickly, leaving somewhat dry tannins. • $9 • (09/15/96) • **83**
Chiroubles Flower Label 1994 • $9 • (06/15/95) • **79**
Chiroubles Flower Label 1993 • $8 • (06/30/94) • **85**
Côte de Brouilly Domaine de la Feuillée 1995: Juicy black cherry and plum flavors are bright and balanced in this typical Beaujolais. It's light enough to serve as an apéritif, but firm enough for food. • $9 • (08/31/96) • **85**
Côte de Brouilly Flower Label 1996: Light on the palate but firm on the finish, rather austere, with black cherry and spice flavors. Should soften and balance with food. • $11 • (08/31/97) • **84**
Côte de Brouilly Flower Label 1995: Polished and silky. Attractive floral and cherry aromas and flavors are a bit subdued right now, but show good balance. • $9 • (09/15/96) • **84**
Côte de Brouilly Flower Label 1994 • $9 • (06/15/95) • **80**
Côte de Brouilly Flower Label 1993 • $8 • (06/30/94) • **80**
Côte-Rôtie Domaine de la Rousse 1991: Vivid aromas of violets and berries, ripe and round on the palate, with a finish that echoes sweet vanilla. Rich and drinkable now. From Georges Duboeuf. • $NA • (05/31/94) • **87**
Côte-Rôtie Domaine de la Rousse 1989 • $24 • (02/28/93) • **82**
Côte-Rôtie Domaine de la Rousse 1988 • $18 • (07/31/91) • **87**
Côtes du Rhône 1994: Meaty, smoky aromas give way to flavors of black cherries and earth in this medium-bodied red. It's more friendly than complex; drink now. • $9 • (12/15/96) • **83**
Côtes du Rhône Domaine Agnès 1995: Ripe and jammy, this is lush on the palate, with plum and prune flavors that are simple but appealing. Shows enough tannin for food, but it's drinkable now. • $11 • (12/15/96) • **82**
Côtes du Rhône Domaine des Aires Vieilles 1994 • $6 • (06/15/95) • **78**
Côtes du Rhône Domaine des Moulins 1995: Smoky, almost charred-meat aromas give way to serious tannins and ripe, roasted flavors of bacon, plum and licorice. Ambitious, but lacks balance and harmony. Try now. • $11 • (12/15/96) • **84**
Côtes du Rhône Domaine des Moulins 1994 • $6 • (11/15/95) • **81**
Côtes du Rhône Domaine des Moulins 1993 • $6 • (11/30/94) • **82**
Côtes du Ventoux 1994 • $6 • (06/15/95) • **80**
Crozes-Hermitage 1990 • $8 • (04/15/93) • **83**
Crozes-Hermitage 1989 • $10 • (06/15/92) • **87**
Crozes-Hermitage 1988 • $9 • (01/31/91) • **85**
Fleurie Château des Bachelards 1996: Remarkable fruit intensity, with cassis, licorice and black pepper flavors that lean toward Grenache in character. It's chewy, ripe and long, an international style uncommon in Beaujolais. • $13 • (07/31/97) • **88**

Fleurie Château des Déduits 1996: Ripe black cherry and plum flavors, with herbal and licorice notes, mark this firm red. Concentrated but a bit clumsy; try now. • $13 • (08/31/97) • **84**

Fleurie Château des Déduits 1995: Quite rich, yet still elegant. Ripe plum and black cherry flavors with complementary notes of toast and smoke. Concentrated yet supple, it's a good choice with food. • $11 • (08/31/96) • **86**

Fleurie Château des Déduits 1994 • $12 • (06/15/95) • **87**

Fleurie Château des Déduits 1993 • $10 • (06/30/94) • **83**

Fleurie Clos des Quatre Vents 1994 • $12 • (06/15/95) • **88**

Fleurie Clos des Quatre Vents 1993 • $10 • (06/30/94) • **83**

Fleurie Domaine des Quatre Vents 1996: Ripe, delivering black cherry, plum and smoke flavors with enough grip for food. Firm and balanced, fresh and clean on the finish. Drinkable now. • $13 • (07/31/97) • **85**

Fleurie Domaine des Quatre Vents 1993 • $10 • (06/30/94) • **82**

Fleurie Flower Label 1996: Pretty spice and licorice aromas are alluring, clean black cherry flavors are ripe and balanced. Turns firm on the finish. Drinkable now. • $13 • (07/31/97) • **86**

Fleurie Flower Label 1995: Fresh and well-balanced marriage of black cherry, floral and spice flavors, firm tannins and clean acidity. Appealing and vibrant. Will drink well with food. • $11 • (08/31/96) • **86**

Fleurie Flower Label 1994 • $11 • (06/15/95) • **89**

Fleurie Flower Label 1993 • $9 • (06/30/94) BB • **88**

Fleurie Grand Pre 1993 • $10 • (06/30/94) • **86**

Fleurie La Madone 1994 • $12 • (06/15/95) • **88**

Gigondas 1989 • $12 • (01/31/92) • **84**

Gigondas 1988 • $10 • (09/30/90) • **79**

Juliénas Château de Poupets 1993 • $9 • (06/30/94) • **85**

Juliénas Domaine de la Seigneurie de Juliénas 1995: The plush velvety texture, bright berry and floral flavors and refreshing acidity combine to make this a soft, winning wine. Chill and enjoy. • $9 • (09/15/96) • **86**

Juliénas Domaine de la Seigneurie de Juliénas 1993 • $9 • (06/30/94) • **80**

Juliénas Flower Label 1996: A distinctive and seductive Beaujolais in an almost Californian style, this wine is ripe and fleshy, with jammy flavors of crushed blackberries and black-cherry syrup. Yummy. 16,000 cases made. • $10 • (07/31/97) BB • **86**

Juliénas Flower Label 1995: Pretty black cherry and floral aromas carry through to the palate in this fresh, fruity red. The tannins are firm, and light banana and herbal notes emerge on the finish. 25,000 cases made. • $9 • (09/15/96) • **85**

Juliénas Flower Label 1994 • $9 • (06/15/95) • **84**

Juliénas Flower Label 1993 • $8 • (06/30/94) • **79**

Mâcon-Lugny Fête des Fleurs 1994: Good concentration and clean, varietal fruit give this wine depth and appeal, which underscore its value. The fruit flavors run from apple to melon to pear, with just enough oak for structure and acidity for balance. Well made. 10,000 cases made. • $8 • (06/30/95) BB • **86**

Mâcon-Villages 1995: Creamy-textured, with ripe fruit flavors and a clean, grassy accent. Medium-bodied. Lightish finish has an earthy flavor. Ready now. • $8 • (08/31/96) • **83**

Mâcon-Villages 1994: Tart but fresh, showing some exotic banana and coconut flavors that marry nicely with the apple, pear and melon notes. Turns a bit green on the slightly drying finish. • $NA • (01/01/95) • **83**

Mâcon-Villages Domaine Lenoir 1996: Fairly tough and hard, with a green edge covering its nice tropical fruit flavors. Shows a certain elegance. A bit too chewy on the finish. • $9 • (08/31/97) • **82**

Mâcon-Villages Domaine les Chenevières 1996: Quite tart, clean and crisp, this linear, straightforward Mâcon offers a lot of citrusy and grasslike flavors. Try with food. • $9 • (08/31/97) • **82**

Mâcon-Villages Domaine les Chenevières 1994: Straightforward apple flavor and a fat palate-feel are strengths, but there's little complexity or depth. It's clean and offers easy drinking now. 13,000 cases made. • $8 • (06/30/95) • **81**

Mâcon-Villages Flower Label 1996: Clean, pure and crisp, with some lime and grapefruit flavors zinging along on the palate. A tart, but refreshing, light-bodied white. Drink with seafood. • $8 • (08/31/97) • **81**

Mâcon-Villages Flower Label 1994: Despite pleasant apple, herb and pear flavors, earthy aromas and a chalky texture pull this wine down. It has some richness but lacks finesse. 35,000 cases made. • $8 • (06/30/95) • **79**

Key: SS—Spectator Selection CS—Cellar Selection HR—Highly Recommended BB—Best Buy $NA—Price not available Ⓐ—Auction Price (BT)—Barrel Tasting

Dates in parentheses indicate the issues in which the ratings were published.

Merlot Vin de Pays d'Oc 1995: Fresh and fruity, with lively cherry and berry flavors. Finishes with hints of spice and vanilla. Delicious to drink now. • $7 • (12/15/96) • **85**

Merlot Vin de Pays d'Oc 1994 • $7 • (07/31/95) • **83**

Merlot Vin de Pays d'Oc Domaine de Bordeneuve 1997: A fresh, simple red with grapey flavors and leathery accents. Drink now. • $7 • (07/31/98) • **79**

Merlot Vin de Pays d'Oc Domaine de Bordeneuve 1994 • $7 • (07/31/95) • **84**

Merlot Vin de Pays d'Oc Domaine St.-Louis 1997: Extremely young-tasting, but very fruity and exuberant like Beaujolais nouveau. Has simple, grapey flavors and slightly yeasty accents. Drink now. • $7 • (07/31/98) • **79**

Merlot Vin de Pays d'Oc Domaine St.-Louis 1996: A fresh, bright red whose cherry and spice notes linger on the finish. Light-bodied, enjoyable now. • $7 • (08/31/97) • **82**

Merlot Vin de Pays d'Oc Domaine St.-Pierre 1997: Fresh, grapey flavors, a deep color and a smooth, soft texture make this appealing. Tannins are light, but the jammy fruit flavor is substantial. Drink now. • $7 • (07/31/98) • **84**

Merlot Vin de Pays d'Oc Flower Label 1997: Like fresh grape soda-pop. A simple, fruity, very young red wine in the style of Beaujolais Nouveau. Drink now. • $6 • (07/31/98) • **81**

Merlot Vin de Pays d'Oc Flower Label 1996: There's a cherry jam quality to this Merlot. Abrupt finish. • $7 • (08/31/97) • **79**

Morgon Domaine Bellevue 1996: Round and generous, this rich red shows deep color, ripe plum and meaty flavors and well-balanced tannins that make it a great match for food. A beautiful expression of the Gamay grape. Drink now. • $10 • (09/15/97) • **89**

Morgon Domaine Bellevue 1994 • $10 • (06/30/95) • **88**

Morgon Domaine Bellevue 1993 • $9 • (06/30/94) • **84**

Morgon Flower Label 1996: Straightforward, with modest black cherry and lightly spicy flavors on a leanish frame. Has enough grip for simple foods. • $10 • (08/31/97) • **83**

Morgon Flower Label 1995: A smoky note adds interest to this juicy, well-concentrated wine. The black cherry and light herbal flavors are fresh and linger on the finish. 30,000 cases made. • $9 • (09/15/96) • **85**

Morgon Flower Label 1994 • $9 • (06/30/95) BB • **87**

Morgon Flower Label 1993 • $8 • (06/30/94) • **83**

Morgon Jean Descombes 1996: Fresh and grapey, this marries a light, fresh, fruity character with a pleasant hint of bitter herbs that add complexity. A bit light for the appellation, but it's clean and well defined. Tasted twice, with consistent notes. Drink now. • $11 • (09/15/97) • **85**

Morgon Jean Descombes 1995: Kirsch and spice flavors are vivid in this unusually dense Beaujolais. Drinkable now. 14,000 cases made. • $10 • (09/15/96) HR • **88**

Morgon Jean Descombes 1994 • $11 • (06/30/95) • **88**

Morgon Jean Descombes 1993 • $9 • (06/30/94) • **85**

Moulin-à-Vent Domaine de la Tour du Bief 1996: The vanilla flavors of oak aging are a bit obvious but still well integrated in this ripe, fruity red; the tannins are firm. Drink now. • $13 • (09/15/97) • **87**

Moulin-à-Vent Domaine de la Tour du Bief 1994 • $12 • (07/31/95) • **86**

Moulin-à-Vent Domaine de la Tour du Bief 1993 • $10 • (06/30/94) • **87**

Moulin-à-Vent Domaine des Rosiers 1995: Seductive kirsch and chocolate aromas give this wine a distinct personality. The palate is velvety smooth with chocolate and cherry flavors and ripe tannins. Not a typical Beaujolais, but attractive nonetheless. • $11 • (09/15/96) • **87**

Moulin-à-Vent Domaine des Rosiers 1994 • $12 • (07/31/95) • **87**

Moulin-à-Vent Domaine des Rosiers 1993 • $10 • (06/30/94) BB • **89**

Moulin-à-Vent Flower Label 1996: Bright, showing vivid plum, chocolate and earth flavors, with crisp acidity over modest tannins. Light-bodied for the appellation, but has good definition. • $13 • (09/15/97) • **85**

Moulin-à-Vent Flower Label 1994 • $11 • (07/31/95) • **87**

Moulin-à-Vent Flower Label 1993 • $9 • (06/30/94) • **86**

Moulin-à-Vent Oak Aged 1993 • $11 • (07/31/95) • **85**

Pouilly-Fuissé 1996: Charming, delicate and elegant but also ripe, with lime, honey, pear and tropical flavors mingling nicely. The acidity is balanced by the ripe fruit. Succulent finish. Drink now through 2000. 20,000 cases made. • $19 • (05/31/98) • **87**

Pouilly-Fuissé 1995: Light in body, with some butter, vanilla and apple flavors, this is straightforward and rather lean. Short finish. Drink now. 44,400 cases made. • $16 • (05/31/97) • **78**

Pouilly-Fuissé 1994: Difficult to like, as matchstick and earth aromas and flavors dominate from start to finish. Where is the fruit? Tastes like it's just been bottled. 25,000 cases made. • $15 • (05/31/96) • **75**

Pouilly-Fuissé 1992: Pungent and earthy, but once those flavors blow off, pear and spice emerge. The earthy notes never quite disappear, but they fold in nicely on the finish. Drinkable now. • $11 • (09/15/93) • **84**

Pouilly-Fuissé Clos Reissier 1994: Attractive flavors of pineapple, lemon, cream and light earth run through this balanced, lively Mâcon. Not rich but still manages good intensity, displaying deft use of oak. 2,000 cases made. • $17 • (06/30/95) • **84**

Pouilly-Fuissé Clos Reissier 1993: A complex and flavorful, reasonably priced wine with toasty, smoky aromas, ripe flavors of fig, pear, butterscotch and walnut, followed by a long finish. This is seductive, smooth and distinctive. • $13 • (01/01/95) • **88**

Pouilly-Fuissé Domaine Béranger 1996: Thick and ripe, it bursts with lime and honey plus oak accents that turn a bit hot on the finish. But give this full-bodied Chardonnay time, perhaps until 1999, and you should be rewarded with a silky, still-fresh white. 3,300 cases made. • $20 • (05/31/98) • **88**

Pouilly-Fuissé Elevé en Fût de Chêne 1996: Well made, packed with fruit and citrus notes along with a mineral character. Medium- to full-bodied, it displays a supple texture. The oak accents offer some complexity on the finish, which is just a touch dry. Drink now through 2000. 5,000 cases made. • $20 • (05/31/98) • **87**

Pouilly-Fuissé Elevé en Fût de Chêne 1994: Ripe and sweet-tasting, almost late-harvest Chardonnay. Full-bodied, with heavily oaked flavors of ripe pear, apple pie and butter. A bit overdone, with a long, toasty finish. Drinkable now. • $15 • (05/31/97) • **82**

Pouilly-Fuissé Flower Label 1994: Rich and ripe, showing plenty of new oak and flavors of pineapple, mango, spice, sweet vanilla and hazelnut. Drinkable now. 35,000 cases made. • $16 • (06/30/95) • **86**

Pouilly-Fuissé Flower Label 1993: Rich but not flashy, this is a solidly built wine with slightly toasty aromas, pear and nutmeg flavors and a lasting finish. Well balanced, smooth-textured and appealing overall. • $12 • (01/01/95) • **84**

Pouilly-Fuissé Oak-Aged 1994: A showy Pouilly, as smoky, toasty notes from oak barrels give a buttery feel to this medium-bodied white. Nicely balanced citrus flavors maintain focus on the round finish. Drinkable now. 5,000 cases made. • $17 • (05/31/96) • **87**

Régnié 1995: Supple, yet shows good concentration and balance, with black cherry and smoke flavors and firm underlying tannins. Will bloom when drunk with food. • $8 • (08/31/96) • **85**

Régnié Château de Ponchon 1994 • $8 • (07/31/95) • **82**

Régnié Château de Ponchon 1993 • $8 • (06/30/94) • **82**

Régnié Domaine des Buyats 1996: Firm, well structured for Beaujolais, with straightforward black cherry flavors and hints of spice. Drinkable now. • $10 • (08/31/97) • **84**

Régnié Domaine des Buyats 1994 • $8 • (07/31/95) • **85**

Régnié Domaine des Buyats 1993 • $8 • (06/30/94) • **82**

Régnié Domaine du Potet 1995: Distinctive. Attractive floral and bell pepper aromas, ripe cherry and chocolate flavors. Thick on the palate, with solid tannins beneath. Juicy and rich. • $8 • (08/31/96) • **87**

Régnié Domaine du Potet 1994 • $8 • (07/31/95) • **86**

Régnié Domaine du Potet 1993 • $8 • (06/30/94) • **79**

Régnié Flower Label 1996: Behind the supple plum flavor there's a nice, chocolaty punch that lingers on the finish. It's ripe, balanced and can match with food. • $10 • (07/31/97) • **85**

Régnié Flower Label 1994 • $8 • (07/31/95) • **83**

Régnié Flower Label 1993 • $7 • (06/30/94) • **85**

St.-Amour Domaine de la Pirolette 1996: Smooth and quite full-bodied for Beaujolais, offering plum and sweet vanilla flavors, generous but with enough tannin for grip. Herbal notes add interest to the finish. • $13 • (07/31/97) • **86**

St.-Amour Domaine de la Pirolette 1995: Raspberry and floral aromas and flavors distinguish this from a typical Beaujolais and add interest to the cherry flavors. Tannins are firm but well integrated; try now. • $11 • (08/31/96) • **87**

St.-Amour Domaine de la Pirolette 1994 • $12 • (07/31/95) • **85**

St.-Amour Domaine de la Pirolette 1993 • $10 • (06/30/94) • **87**

St.-Amour Flower Label 1996: Soft and fleshy, with plum and black cherry flavors, ripe and straightforward. Fruity and easy to drink. • $13 • (07/31/97) • **85**

St.-Amour Flower Label 1995: Ripe and round, showing rich, smoke-touched plum flavors and well-integrated tannins that give polish to the texture. Not dramatic, but easy to like. • $11 • (09/15/96) • **84**

St.-Amour Flower Label 1994 • $11 • (07/31/95) • **84**

St.-Amour Flower Label 1993 • $9 • (06/30/94) BB • **87**

St.-Joseph 1988 • $11 • (11/30/90) • **76**

St.-Véran 1996: A bit simple but pleasant, with lime and honey flavors and a rather fruity character. Light- to medium-bodied. Some spice mingles in the citrusy finish. Drink now. 25,000 cases made. • $10 • (05/31/98) • **82**

St.-Véran 1995: Clean and well made. Light- to medium-bodied, with nicely balanced fresh melon, pear and lime flavors. Fairly intense, straightforward but nice finish. Enjoy now. • $9 • (08/31/96) • **84**

St.-Véran 1994: Tropical fruit and buttery flavors stand out in this exuberant white, which features crisp, citrusy acidity, harmony and even elegance. 25,000 cases made. • $9 • (06/30/95) • **86**

St.-Véran Domaine de la Bâtie 1996: Young and tight, with plenty of firm acidity. There's a midpalate richness, then it finishes lean. Not much fruit. Drink now. 5,000 cases made. • $10 • (08/31/97) • **78**

St.-Véran Domaine de la Bâtie 1993: Fresh, fruity and straightforward, on the light-bodied side, with a smooth texture and simple, grapey flavors. Uncomplicated. • $8 • (01/01/94) • **79**

St.-Véran Domaine de la Feuillarde 1995: Subtle yet fairly intense, fruity and satisfying. Delivers citrus, green apple, honey and blanched almond flavors. Medium-bodied, with a clean finish. Drink now. • $NA • (08/31/96) • **84**

St.-Véran Domaine St.-Martin 1995: Appealing, with nice fruit and good balance. More like a '94 than a '95; supple and creamy in texture, with honey, floral and apple notes. Enjoy now. • $NA • (08/31/96) • **82**

St.-Véran Domaine St.-Martin 1994: Smooth and round, light but well proportioned. Medium intensity and some decent fruit character. A bit diluted. 1,000 cases made. • $9 • (08/31/95) • **79**

Sauvignon Blanc Vin de Pays du Jardin de la France 1995 • $7 • (06/15/96) • **76**

Sauvignon Vin de Pays d'Oc 1994 • $6 • (07/31/95) • **81**

Syrah Vin de Pays d'Oc 1994 • $6 • (07/31/95) • **82**

Syrah Vin de Pays d'Oc Rosé 1994 • $6 • (08/31/95) • **85**

Vin de Pays d'Oc Domaine de Bordeneuve 1993 • $5 • (09/15/94) • **83**

Viognier Vin de Pays de l'Ardèche 1997: Smells like it's right out of the fermenting tank, with an overwhelming aroma of bananas. Soft, with simple but exuberant banana and peach flavors. Drink now. • $9 • (06/15/98) • **81**

DUBOIS, JEAN-LUC

Chorey-lès-Beaune 1990: Ripe and fruity, with rich black cherry and currant-scented flavors that pick up traces of mineral and spice on the finish. The tannins are fleshy and firm, making the wine drinkable now. • $30 • (06/15/93) • **87**

Ladoix La Combe 1990: Hard-edged and tannic, with an earthy lime- and currant-scented flavor profile. The tannins turn gritty and chewy. Drinkable now. • $19 • (06/15/93) • **84**

DUBREUIL-FONTAINE PÈRE & FILS, P.

Aloxe-Corton Les Vercots 1995: A tough wine with a chewy, licorice edge to the flavors and an herbal quality that turns lean and tart on the finish. 125 cases made. • $38 • (11/15/97) • **78**

Corton Le Clos du Roi 1993: Well made and harmonious, showing some lovely, complex mocha, spice and red berry notes. Sweet-tasting and flavorful, this medium-bodied *grand cru* is quite subtle and elegant. Try in 1999. • $NA • (05/15/96) • **87**

Corton Le Clos du Roi 1992: Lean and lithe, a little chewy from tannin, but the slightly gamy floral, blackberry and blueberry flavors persist into a solid finish. Harmonious and drinkable now. • $60 • (12/15/94) • **87**

Corton Le Clos du Roi 1991: Harmonious, seamless and elegant, displaying sparks of ripe currant, plum, berry, anise and mint notes and a bit of gaminess as well. Complex, showing more than the usual generosity on the finish. The tannins are present, but not harsh. Drinkable now. 450 cases made. • $52 Ⓐ • (01/31/94) • **90**

Corton Le Clos du Roi 1990: Pure fruit extract, with tons of raspberry, tobacco and vanilla flavors. Combines superb concentration of fruit and tannins. Drinkable now. • $61 • (12/15/92) • **93**

Corton Le Clos du Roi 1989 • $63 • (01/31/92) • **92**

Corton Le Clos du Roi 1987 • $34 • (12/31/90) • **85**

Corton Le Clos du Roi 1985 • $49 • (07/15/88) • **90**

Corton Le Clos du Roi 1982 • $25 • (09/16/85) • **86**

Corton Les Bressandes 1995: Modest flavors of cherry and toasty oak, with stemmy, herbal notes. The finish is slightly astringent. 150 cases made. • $57 • (11/15/97) • **80**

Corton Les Bressandes 1993: Plenty of ripe fruit here. Medium to full in body, featuring medium-velvety tannins and a long, spicy finish. Better in 2000. • $NA • (05/15/96) • **88**

Corton Les Bressandes 1992: Not a big wine but firm in texture, turning supple on the finish and echoing some very pretty raspberry, currant and floral flavors. • $57 • (12/15/94) • **85**

Corton Les Bressandes 1991: Clean and nicely focused, shining a beam of currant and blackberry flavors. Hints at anise and toast on the finish. A mini version of a fine Corton. Drinkable now. 250 cases made. • $50 Ⓐ • (01/31/94) • **88**

Corton Les Bressandes 1990: Very elegant, with ripe blackberry and earth aromas and flavors and firm tannins. Drinkable now. • $59 • (12/15/92) • **89**

Corton Les Bressandes 1985 • $50 • (01/31/89) • **86**

Corton Les Bressandes 1982 • $24 • (10/16/85) • **85**

Corton Les Perrières 1993: Delicious plum, berry and cherry flavors cascade to a long, velvety finish. Hard not to drink this one now. • $NA • (05/15/96) • **88**

Corton-Charlemagne 1995: Restrained yet powerful, this wine is racy and rich, yet elegant and subtle. Displays a symphony of pure, clean, fruity aromas, and its delicious ripe pear, pineapple, honey and wonderful mineral flavors are framed by unobtrusive toast accents. Brilliant winemaking. 208 cases made. • $74 • (05/31/97) • **98**

Corton-Charlemagne 1994: Delicate, and of medium concentration and body. Shows clean fruit, floral, honey and mineral flavors, and a touch of citrus on the very smooth finish. Drink now. • $NA • (08/31/96) • **83**

Corton-Charlemagne 1992: Full-bodied, heavy and a bit vague, with some hazelnut, pine nut and lemon flavors that lead to a clean finish. 250 cases made. • $61 • (08/31/94) • **84**

Pernand-Vergelesses 1993: Sprightly and clean, delivering refreshing acidity and firm tannins. Not generous, but shows some very good fruit and a delicious finish. Drinkable now. • $NA • (05/15/96) • **85**

Pernand-Vergelesses 1991: Lean and chewy; a small wine, with modest cherry flavors and well-modulated tannins. Drinkable now. 675 cases made. • $33 Ⓐ • (01/31/94) • **82**

Pernand-Vergelesses Clos Berthet Monopole White 1992: A bit earthy and quite woody; simple, with modest fruit flavors. • $30 • (08/31/94) • **79**

Pernand-Vergelesses Clos Berthet White 1996: Fairly minerally, with apple and some pear and earth notes. Not very ripe, but medium-bodied, with a steely backbone of acidity. Hopefully this will soften with age; try after 2000. 265 cases made. • $33 • (05/31/98) • **85**

Pernand-Vergelesses Clos Berthet White 1995: Slightly odd, with a flinty, matchstick quality, but it also has ripe fruit and citrus notes, honey, spice and mineral flavors. Full-bodied and racy on the finish. Try now through 2000. • $33 • (08/31/97) • **82**

Pernand-Vergelesses Côte de Beaune 1994: Firm in texture, with some coffee-scented currant flavors that turn herbal on the finish. • $20 • (11/15/96) • **77**

Pernand-Vergelesses Ile des Vergelesses 1995: Delicate, elegant and quite juicy and crisp. Light- to medium-bodied, it turns a bit dry on the finish. 250 cases made. • $38 • (11/15/97) • **79**

Pernand-Vergelesses Ile des Vergelesses 1993: Nice fruit, but it's a bit disjointed. Somewhat tart in texture, lacking focus and one-dimensional, with a slightly diluted finish. • $NA • (05/15/96) • **77**

Pernand-Vergelesses Ile des Vergelesses 1990: Firm and focused, with juicy, delicious berry and earth characteristics. Tightly built and succulent on the long finish. Drinkable now. • $37 • (12/15/92) • **88**

Pernand-Vergelesses Ile des Vergelesses 1989 • $40 • (01/31/92) • **84**

Pernand-Vergelesses Ile des Vergelesses 1982 • $18 • (10/16/85) • **78**

Pernand-Vergelesses White 1994: You can taste *terroir* in the wet earth and mineral notes, but it's rather lean, lacking a bit of ripe fruit. Drinkable now. 333 cases made. • $56 • (05/31/96) • **80**

Pernand-Vergelesses White 1992: Spicy flavor, lively texture and good acidity give this wine some presence. It's crisp and clean, and tastes of apples and nutmeg. • $21 • (11/15/94) • **82**

Pommard Les Epenots 1995: Full, ripe, with layers of sweet fruit and tannins, this offers plum, red- and blackberry flavors with a firm backbone. Good intensity on the slightly dry finish. Worth cellaring until 2000. 150 cases made. • $55 • (11/15/97) • **85**

Pommard Les Epenots 1990: Extremely silky, flowing over the palate and leaving a sense of lightness. A joy to drink, with lots of chocolate and raspberry nuances. Drinkable now. • $59 • (12/15/92) • **91**

Key: SS—Spectator Selection CS—Cellar Selection HR—Highly Recommended BB—Best Buy $NA—Price not available Ⓐ—Auction Price (BT)—Barrel Tasting
Dates in parentheses indicate the issues in which the ratings were published.

Savigny-lès-Beaune Aux Vergelesses 1993: Relatively light and straightforward, showing some cherry and strawberry flavors and earthy complexity. Good for everyday drinking. • $NA • (05/15/96) • **81**

Savigny-lès-Beaune Aux Vergelesses 1992: Firm and focused, turning supple on the finish. Shows slightly gamy black cherry and floral aromas and flavors. Drinkable now. • $25 • (12/15/94) • **81**

Savigny-lès-Beaune Aux Vergelesses 1991: Modest, showing pretty black cherry and raspberry flavors and a bit of toastiness to add an extra dimension. Try now. 667 cases made. • $22 Ⓐ • (01/31/94) • **82**

Savigny-lès-Beaune Aux Vergelesses 1990: Straightforward Savigny, with pleasant chestnut and strawberry notes. An early-maturing style, with medium tannins and a light finish. Drinkable now. • $25 • (12/15/92) • **81**

Savigny-lès-Beaune Aux Vergelesses 1985 • $24 • (01/31/89) • **88**

Volnay Les Brouillards 1994: Very pale in color and flavor, with a slightly gamy edge to the light berry flavors. • $27 • (11/15/96) • **78**

DUCLA, CHÂTEAU

Bordeaux Cœur de Cuvée 1995: Pretty berry and vanilla aromas give way to soft flavors of raspberries, cherries and herbs in this fleshy, supple red. Makes pleasant drinking now through 2001. 10,000 cases made. • $9 • (10/15/97) • **83**

Entre-Deux-Mers Cœur de Cuvée 1996: Aggressive herbal aromas and crisp, grapefruitlike flavors make this an assertive but tart white Bordeaux. Quite refreshing but lean. 4,400 cases made. • $8 • (09/30/97) • **81**

DUCLUZEAU, CHÂTEAU

Listrac 1993: Light and diluted, with tomato; weedy, with a hint of fruit on the palate. • $12 • (01/31/96) • **77**

Listrac 1987 • $7 • (11/30/89) • **79**

Listrac 1986 • $11 • (11/30/89) • **83**

Listrac 1982 • $16 • (08/31/92) • **81**

DUCRU-BEAUCAILLOU, CHÂTEAU

St.-Julien 1997: A pretty, balanced red, with plum, berry and cherry aromas and flavors. Medium-bodied, with medium tannins and a fruity finish. • $NA • (06/15/98) (BT) • **85-89**

St.-Julien 1996: A glorious, full-bodied wine. Silky and powerful, with loads of berry, cherry and mineral character and a long, long finish. Not as great as the '95 Ducru, but damn close. • $120 • (06/15/98) (BT) • **95-99**

St.-Julien 1995: The greatest Ducru produced this century. Breathtaking aromas of berries, violets, vanilla and blackberries set the stage for a wine that's full-bodied and tannic, yet very fine and long in the mouth. This has fabulous structure for aging and will be best after 2004. 18,000 cases made. • $48 Ⓐ • (01/31/98) CS • **97**

St.-Julien 1994: Offers a goodly amount of ripe fruit and dried cherry flavors, well balanced for the vintage, medium, round tannins and a fruity finish. Drink or hold. • $40 Ⓐ • (01/31/97) • **87**

St.-Julien 1993: Somewhat disappointing for this estate. Decent berry and plum flavors and firm tannins, although a slight tomato character takes away from the overall quality. Drinkable on release. • $26 Ⓐ • (01/31/96) • **81**

St.-Julien 1992: Lean, racy mint and berry character but very short on the finish. Tasted twice, with consistent notes. • $28 • (04/15/95) • **79**

St.-Julien 1991: Nice black cherry and tobacco flavors, quite velvety in the mouth. Drinkable now. • $31 • (03/31/94) • **83**

St.-Julien 1990: Tough and muscular, with loads of fruit hidden underneath the sharp tannins. A little clumsy now; needs time to mellow. Start drinking in 1999. Tasted twice. • $51 Ⓐ • (03/31/93) • **88**

St.-Julien 1989 • $26 Ⓐ • (10/15/92) • **91**

St.-Julien 1988 • $30 Ⓐ • (10/15/92) • **92**

St.-Julien 1987 • $27 Ⓐ • (10/15/92) • **83**

St.-Julien 1986 • $66 Ⓐ • (06/30/89) • **91**

St.-Julien 1985 • $76 Ⓐ • (10/15/94) • **90**

St.-Julien 1984 • $22 Ⓐ • (08/31/87) • **87**

St.-Julien 1983 • $49 Ⓐ • (10/15/94) • **87**

St.-Julien 1982 • $117 Ⓐ • (08/31/92) • **93**

St.-Julien 1981 • $50 Ⓐ • (10/15/94) • **89**

St.-Julien 1980 • $23 Ⓐ • (05/01/84) CS • **88**

St.-Julien 1979 • $37 Ⓐ • (10/15/89) • **87**

St.-Julien 1978 • $54 Ⓐ • (05/01/85) • **91**

St.-Julien 1962 • $79 Ⓐ • (11/30/87) • **80**

St.-Julien 1961 • $278 Ⓐ • (04/30/96) • **92**

St.-Julien 1959 • $214 Ⓐ • (10/15/90) • **90**

St.-Julien 1958 • $100 • (10/15/92) • **83**
St.-Julien 1957 • $85 • (10/15/92) • **77**
St.-Julien 1955 • $140 • (10/15/92) • **87**
St.-Julien 1953 • $240 • (10/15/92) • **88**
St.-Julien 1952 • $160 • (10/15/92) • **81**
St.-Julien 1949 • $220 • (10/15/92) • **90**
St.-Julien 1945 • $366 Ⓐ • (11/30/95) • **84**
St.-Julien 1934 • $190 • (10/15/92) • **82**
St.-Julien 1929 • $166 Ⓐ • (10/15/92) • **83**
St.-Julien 1928 • $250 • (10/15/92) • **88**
St.-Julien 1924 • $200 • (10/15/92) • **80**
St.-Julien 1898 • $450 • (10/15/92) • **97**
St.-Julien 1887 • $450 • (10/15/92) • **89**
St.-Julien 1867 • $950 • (10/15/92) • **92**

DUFOULEUR, LOIS

Beaune Champs Pimont 1991: Firmly tannic and tight enough to bury the otherwise appealing anise- and tar-scented currant flavors until the finish. Try now. • $NA • (01/31/94) • **85**

Beaune Clos du Roi 1991: Tough and chewy, but offers a mouthful of juicy currant, plum, mushroom and spicebox aromas and flavors. Finishes crisp and lemony. Try now. • $31 Ⓐ • (01/31/94) • **85**

Beaune Les Cents Vignes 1991: Velvety, refined and flavorful, offering a nice range of prune, coffee and currant aromas and flavors. Finishes soft and generous, with finely integrated tannins. Try now. • $34 Ⓐ • (01/31/94) • **86**

DUFOULEUR PÈRE & FILS

Beaune Champs Pimont 1991: A fruity Burgundy that's crisp and lively in balance and has plenty of black cherry flavor to keep it interesting. Turns lean on the finish. Drink now. • $17 • (05/31/95) • **84**

Bourgogne Cuvée Napoléon 1993: A pleasant-tasting, nicely balanced little Burgundy with a smooth texture and enough fruity, spicy flavor to satisfy. Drink now. 4,000 cases made. • $12 • (09/15/96) • **81**

Bourgogne Cuvée Napoléon White 1994: Very young and leesy. Rather green in taste, tart in flavor and lively in texture. Drink now. 5,000 cases made. • $12 • (09/15/96) • **77**

Fixin Clos du Chapitre 1993: A solid, ripe-tasting wine with a firm texture and good balance. Sturdy and straightforward. Drink now. 400 cases made. • $24 • (09/15/96) • **84**

DUGAT, CLAUDE

Charmes-Chambertin 1995: Just delicious. This succulent, fruity red is round, supple and loaded with sweet red- and blackberry flavors. It's medium- to full-bodied, and the firm tannins are well integrated. Balanced from start to finish. Give it until 2000 to show it all. • $110 • (11/15/97) • **93**

Charmes-Chambertin 1994: A bit odd, this is colorful and rather packed with plum, currant and earth flavors. Too bad about the stalky, herbaceous aromas and slightly astringent finish. • $75 • (11/15/96) • **82**

Charmes-Chambertin 1993: Lovely sweet fruit character here, offering medium body, plum, smoke and mineral flavors, medium tannins and a silky finish. Drinkable now. 25 cases made. • $90 • (11/15/95) • **90**

Gevrey-Chambertin 1995: Concentrated and sweet at first, then abruptly turns tannic and angular. The blackberry flavors return on the finish, so give it time. Try in 1999. • $48 • (11/15/97) • **88**

Gevrey-Chambertin 1994: Wonderfully concentrated fruit character marks this impressive village wine. Deep-colored, pure, richly flavored, medium- to full-bodied, with silky texture and loads of cassis bush, plum and mineral notes. Try in 1999. • $40 • (11/15/96) • **86**

Gevrey-Chambertin 1993: Great village wine! Beautifully made up, locating everything in the right place. Medium- to full-bodied, with loads of fine tannins, a hint of wood and an abundance of berry and cherry character. Try in 2000. • $40 • (11/15/95) • **90**

Gevrey-Chambertin Lavaux St.-Jacques 1995: Intense, concentrated and fresh, with cassis and blackberry flavors and tomato notes. Tough and chewy, it's difficult to judge now. Try after 2000. • $70 • (11/15/97) • **85**

Gevrey-Chambertin Lavaux St.-Jacques 1993: How to describe greatness? This is profound, ripe and rich, but shows restraint and elegance, too. As silky as it gets in this vintage, with a thread of currant, smoke, earth and plum flavors that marry seamlessly on the inspiring finish. Try in 2000. • $65 • (11/15/95) • **92**

Gevrey-Chambertin Premier Cru 1995: Slightly unripe, with stemmy, tomatolike aromas, this is full of fruit nonetheless. It's concentrated and dense, has a firm backbone and a wall of tannins on the finish. • $60 • (11/15/97) • **87**

Gevrey-Chambertin Premier Cru 1994: Smells a bit funky and smoky, but the flavors are true, centering around tart raspberry and red plum. Finish is crisp with tannins. Drinkable now. • $52 • (11/15/96) • **81**

Gevrey-Chambertin Premier Cru 1993: Impressive and showy Gevrey, featuring plenty of color, raspberry character, a hint of new wood, medium-to-full body, fine tannins and a long, long finish. Better in 2000. • $50 • (11/15/95) • **91**

DUGAT-PY, BERNARD

Gevrey-Chambertin Coeur de Roy Vieilles Vignes 1995: A huge, bold, superripe and thick style of red Burgundy. What it lacks in finesse this full-bodied '95 makes up for in power, with toasty oak, blackberry, cassis, raspberry, floral and spice, mocha and cappuccinolike flavors. Very supple tannins make it a delight now, but hold off until 2000. • $40 • (01/31/98) HR • **95**

Gevrey-Chambertin Coeur de Roy Vieilles Vignes 1994: A fruity, juicy Pinot Noir. Lacks a bit of ripeness; offers citrusy, tart character and a chewy finish. Drink now to 1999. • $38 • (09/30/97) • **81**

Gevrey-Chambertin Lavaux-St.-Jacques 1994: Well made, this '94 tries to make the best out of a difficult vintage, offering cherry and other red berry flavors and a layer of sophisticated spice and mocha for added complexity. Medium-bodied and quite ripe, it should be delicious around 1999. • $43 • (09/30/97) • **87**

Gevrey-Chambertin Petite-Chapelle 1994: Racy, packed with pure cassis, wild raspberry and earth flavors. Yet for all its power, this full-bodied '94 offers silky, sweet tannins. Flawless, long, succulent finish. Bravo! Drink after 2000. • $43 • (09/30/97) • **92**

Gevrey-Chambertin Vieilles Vignes 1994: Light in color and body, with some dilution. A bit green and tart. • $35 • (09/30/97) • **77**

DUHART-MILON ROTHSCHILD, CHÂTEAU

Pauillac 1997: Attractive, velvety texture, with a grapey, slightly herbal character. Medium-bodied, with a medium finish. • $NA • (06/15/98) (BT) • **85-89**

Pauillac 1996: A textbook claret for long-term aging. Full-bodied, with lots of slightly hard tannins and currant character. Long, long finish. Almost outstanding. • $25 • (06/15/98) (BT) • **85-89**

Pauillac 1995: Best Duhart in some time. Essence of blackberry and chocolate. Full-bodied and extremely velvety. Caressing and gorgeous to taste. Best after 2000. • $25 • (01/31/98) • **90**

Pauillac 1994: A well-crafted wine, this has berry, smoke and vanilla aromas and flavors, a caressing texture and fine tannins. Drink or hold. • $30 • (01/31/97) • **88**

Pauillac 1993: Nice, velvety texture, but slightly green bean and herbal in nature. Medium body and tannins, adding a long finish. Try now. • $25 • (01/31/96) • **80**

Pauillac 1992: Fresh, light, diluted, showing berry, cherry and vanilla aromas and flavors. Light-bodied, fruity finish. • $22 • (04/15/95) • **76**

Pauillac 1990: Black cherry and plum aromas leap from the glass and follow through on the palate with mint, tar and chocolate accents. It's focused, lively and firm, with plenty of concentration. Try now. 13,000 cases made. • $25 • (10/15/94) • **92**

Pauillac 1989 • $25 Ⓐ • (03/15/92) • **90**
Pauillac 1988 • $24 • (08/31/91) • **88**
Pauillac 1987 • $22 • (05/15/90) • **79**
Pauillac 1986 • $26 • (05/31/89) • **90**
Pauillac 1985 • $27 • (10/15/94) • **93**
Pauillac 1983 • $24 • (10/15/94) • **89**
Pauillac 1982 • $49 Ⓐ • (08/31/92) • **91**
Pauillac 1981 • $26 • (10/15/94) • **87**
Pauillac 1979 • $20 Ⓐ • (10/15/89) • **86**

DUJAC

Bonnes Mares 1987 • $31 Ⓐ • (03/31/90) • **91**
Bonnes Mares 1986 • $34 Ⓐ • (04/15/89) • **85**

Chambolle-Musigny 1993: Flavorful, complex and intriguing; the smoky, leafy, tealike notes invite you back for another sip. Open, generous, smooth and moderately tannic. Drinkable now through 2000. • $37 • (05/15/96) • **86**

Chambolle-Musigny Les Gruenchers 1987 • $47 • (03/31/90) • **93**
Chambolle-Musigny Les Gruenchers 1986 • $48 • (07/31/88) • **76**
Chambolle-Musigny Les Gruenchers 1985 • $43 • (03/31/88) • **74**

FRANCE

Charmes-Chambertin 1995: Advanced for a young wine, but with mature aromas of forest undergrowth, mushroom and wet earth and decent licorice, cinnamon, brown sugar and red berry notes. A disappointment, though. • $75 • (01/31/98) • **82**

Charmes-Chambertin 1991: Aromas are earthy and gamy, but flavors of currant and berry balance them, finishing lean and citrusy. Drinkable now. 300 cases made. • $71 Ⓐ • (01/31/94) • **83**

Charmes-Chambertin 1990: A luxurious wine, with impressive raspberry, violet and cedar aromas and flavors. Is in near-perfect harmony with the fruit and tannins. Drinkable now. 300 cases made. • $75 • (12/15/92) • **92**

Charmes-Chambertin 1989 • $72 • (01/31/92) • **90**

Charmes-Chambertin 1988 • $60 • (03/31/91) • **85**

Charmes-Chambertin 1986 • $50 • (07/31/88) • **85**

Charmes-Chambertin 1985 • $100 • (03/15/88) • **95**

Clos de la Roche 1991: Crisp in texture, with warm, earthy, gamy shades to the solid currant and cherry flavors, all of which play clearly across the palate. A bit shy in the middle, but has style and firmness. Try now. 500 cases made. • $77 Ⓐ • (01/31/94) • **88**

Clos de la Roche 1990: Clever winemaking brings you this distinctive, smoky, toasty, gamy Burgundy, with a satiny texture that packs in the firm tannins. Not big, but very rich. Drinkable now. 750 cases made. • $83 • (12/15/92) • **92**

Clos de la Roche 1989 • $80 • (01/31/92) • **89**

Clos de la Roche 1988 • $75 • (03/31/91) • **90**

Clos de la Roche 1987 • $53 • (03/31/90) • **86**

Clos de la Roche 1986 • $56 • (07/31/88) • **79**

Clos de la Roche 1985 • $85 • (03/15/88) • **95**

Clos St.-Denis 1993: Yummy, suave and plush-textured, as its fruity, spicy flavors seem sweet and really linger on the finish. Not too tannic to drink now and through 2000, and utterly delicious. • $79 • (05/15/96) • **91**

Clos St.-Denis 1992: A lush and broad-tasting Burgundy, with ample chocolate and vanilla flavors framing the core of plum and cherry. It's intriguingly toasty in aroma, and remains interesting through the finish. • $66 • (05/15/95) • **87**

Clos St.-Denis 1991: Toasty and earthy on the nose, but elegant berry, spice and game flavors persist into a lean finish. Seems a bit mature for a '91. Drinkable now. 233 cases made. • $77 Ⓐ • (01/31/94) • **86**

Clos St.-Denis 1990: A very distinctive wine that stands out with seductive, smoky, toasty bacon and game characteristics, but it's also surprisingly delicate for a '90 *grand cru*, showing plenty of solid tannins. Drinkable now. 350 cases made. • $83 • (12/15/92) • **90**

Clos St.-Denis 1989 • $80 • (01/31/92) • **91**

Clos St.-Denis 1987 • $58 • (03/31/90) • **85**

Clos St.-Denis 1986 • $56 • (07/31/88) • **89**

Clos St.-Denis 1985 • $89 • (03/15/88) • **91**

Echézeaux 1991: Light but ripe, offering a nice bead of currant and blackberry flavors shaded by anise, cedar and tobacco notes that keep ringing on the finish. Try now. 250 cases made. • $81 Ⓐ • (01/31/94) • **86**

Echézeaux 1990: Elegant, toasty and complex. Kicks in with nice tea, strawberry and roasted nut flavors on the delicate finish. Drinkable now. 850 cases made. • $88 • (12/15/92) • **91**

Echézeaux 1988 • $70 • (03/31/91) • **90**

Echézeaux 1987 • $56 • (05/15/90) • **82**

Echézeaux 1986 • $52 • (04/30/89) • **89**

Gevrey-Chambertin Aux Combottes 1995: Mature before its time. Light in color, with mushroom, truffle and plummy notes, it has a pleasant sweet core of cinnamon, clove, spice and licorice flavors, but falls down on the drying finish. Drink now. • $70 • (01/31/98) • **82**

Gevrey-Chambertin Aux Combottes 1993: Nicely fruity and easy in texture yet firmly tannic, this is elegant, almost soft in the middle, but has grip on the aftertaste. Try now to 2000. • $65 • (05/15/96) • **88**

Gevrey-Chambertin Aux Combottes 1991: Crisp and spicy, showing earthy, oaky overtones to the raspberry and currant aromas and flavors. Graceful; drinkable now. 267 cases made. • $63 Ⓐ • (01/31/94) • **84**

Gevrey-Chambertin Aux Combottes 1990: This distinctive red Burgundy is seductive despite the firm, hard core of tannins and fruit, showing chocolate, berry, smoke and spice flavors and a lovely, toasty finish. A well-made wine. Drinkable now. 350 cases made. • $67 • (12/15/92) • **92**

Gevrey-Chambertin Aux Combottes 1989 • $65 • (01/31/92) • **86**

Gevrey-Chambertin Aux Combottes 1988 • $54 • (03/31/91) • **86**

Gevrey-Chambertin Aux Combottes 1987 • $42 • (05/31/90) • **80**

Morey-St.-Denis 1995: Maturing fast, with a brown edge to the color, some earthy, mushroomy aromas and a dry tannic component. Tasted twice, with consistent notes. Drink now. • $40 • (01/31/98) • **78**

Morey-St.-Denis 1993: Very smooth, harmonious, mellow and rich in flavor, the ample fruit accented by spicy, woodsy notes. Tempting now for its silky texture, but can age through at least 1999. • $37 • (05/15/96) • **88**

Morey-St.-Denis 1992: Intriguing toasty aromas that flirt with funk followed by ripe, broad fruit flavors make this a distinctive and satisfying experience. Cherry and cranberry are smoothed over by lavish, oaky notes, all coming together in a lingering finish. Drink now. • $31 • (05/15/95) • **88**

Morey-St.-Denis 1991: Displays more citrusy lime aromas and flavors than red fruit, although it picks up light raspberry notes on the finish. Drinkable now. 775 cases made. • $38 Ⓐ • (01/31/94) • **84**

Morey-St.-Denis 1990: Raspberry, spice and earth aromas and flavors make this a pretty Pinot Noir to drink now. 1,400 cases made. • $41 • (12/15/92) • **87**

Morey-St.-Denis 1989 • $40 • (01/31/92) • **84**

DULONG

Cabernet Sauvignon Vin de Pays d'Oc 1996: A stout red with decent cherry flavors, but it's a little thin in the middle. 18,000 cases made. • $7 • (05/15/98) • **78**

Cabernet Sauvignon Vin de Pays d'Oc 1995: Plenty of spicy oak wraps around the plum and cherry flavors. It's rich and complex for this region, showing good length and a tobaccolike aftertaste. 11,000 cases made. • $7 • (12/15/96) BB • **86**

Chardonnay Vin de Pays d'Oc 1996: An attempt at a serious style that turns a bit awkward: the creamy flavors turn thin on the tart finish. Tasted twice, with consistent notes. Drink now. 8,000 cases made. • $7 • (05/31/98) • **78**

Chardonnay Vin de Pays d'Oc 1995: Low-key, subtly flavored, with modest fruit flavors and hints of oak. It's smooth and fairly full-bodied, with nice texture. 6,000 cases made. • $7 • (02/28/97) • **84**

Merlot Vin de Pays d'Oc 1996: What a deal on this well-concentrated French red, its delicious dark plum and cherry flavors wrapped inside some fairly serious tannins, finishing on a sweet cherry and spice note. Drink now through 2000. 15,000 cases made. • $7 • (05/15/98) BB • **85**

Merlot Vin de Pays d'Oc 1995: Pleasant and fruity, with good cherry and plum flavors and a bittersweet chocolate note. Turns ripe on the finish. 9,000 cases made. • $7 • (12/15/96) • **81**

DULUC, CHÂTEAU

St.-Julien 1996: Rather light and slightly weedy, with a diluted, dry finish. Wait and see. • $28 • (06/15/98) (BT) • **75-79**

St.-Julien 1994: Rather light and herbal in style, with medium body and a light finish. Drink now. • $NA • (01/31/97) • **76**

St.-Julien 1991: Feels supple in the mouth, but ends with an astringent finish and bell pepper flavors. Second label of Branaire. • $14 • (03/31/94) • **77**

St.-Julien 1989 • $NA • (03/15/92) • **84**

DUMANGIN, JEAN

Brut Champagne NV: Rather ripe fruit flavors distinguish this medium-bodied bubbly. Smooth in texture and a pleasure to drink. 7,000 cases made. • $30 • (10/31/97) • **86**

DUMAS, LAURENT

Fleurie 1996: Alluring aromas and flavors of berries, spice and smoke add complexity to the classic Beaujolais palette. Supple, lively and fresh. 2,000 cases made. • $17 • (09/15/97) • **85**

Fleurie 1995: All the elements are here: bright black cherry flavors, lush texture, firm backbone. Drink up. 2,000 cases made. • $17 • (01/01/97) • **84**

Fleurie 1993: This maturing red offers an uneasy combination of floral, candied fruit and vegetal flavors with drying tannins. Perhaps it's in a difficult phase, but it's not that pleasant now. • $18 • (01/01/97) • **74**

DUPLESSIS, CHÂTEAU

Moulis 1993: Light and watery, showing only modest fruit and dry tannins. • $11 • (01/31/96) • **76**

Key: SS—Spectator Selection CS—Cellar Selection HR—Highly Recommended BB—Best Buy $NA—Price not available Ⓐ—Auction Price (BT)—Barrel Tasting
Dates in parentheses indicate the issues in which the ratings were published.

DUPLESSIS-FABRE, CHÂTEAU

Moulis 1989 • $9 • (03/15/92) • **88**
Moulis 1987 • $7 • (11/30/89) • **71**
Moulis 1986 • $7 • (11/30/89) • **74**
Moulis 1982 • $10 • (11/30/89) • **79**

DUPUIS, ANDRÉ

Mâcon-Villages 1995: Well made and approachable now. Clean, with nice mineral, pear and apple flavors. Supple, balanced finish. • $NA • (08/31/96) • **83**

DURAND, NÖEL & JÖEL

Cornas 1994: Round and ripe, this is quite voluptuous for Cornas, with toasty oak, plum, cassis, tobacco and game flavors. It's generous and long, harmonious and expressive. Drinkable now. • $20 • (10/15/97) • **91**

St.-Joseph Les Côteaux 1994: Expressive and distinctive, this is earthy and spicy, deep and intense. It doesn't show easy fruit, but it's a serious, well-made wine that speaks of its *terroir*. For the connoisseur. Drinkable now. • $15 • (10/15/97) • **93**

DURBAN, DOMAINE DE

Muscat de Beaumes-de-Venise 1993 • $18 • (10/31/95) • **85**
Muscat de Beaumes-de-Venise 1988 • $15 • (03/31/91) • **86**

DURDILLY, PIERRE & PAUL

Beaujolais Les Grandes Coasses 1996: Bright black cherry and light smoke notes are vivid in this light-bodied yet plush red. It's fresh, but doesn't show much structure; drink now. • $10 • (06/30/97) • **81**

DURFORT-VIVENS, CHÂTEAU

Margaux 1993: Slightly one-dimensional but featuring some attractive mint, rosemary and cherry character. Medium body, firm tannins and a medium finish. Drink now. • $23 • (01/31/96) • **84**

Margaux 1991: A well-focused wine with a lovely mixture of smoke and berry notes, medium body and silky texture. • $20 • (03/31/94) • **83**

Margaux 1990: Delicate and sure-footed, with lovely cherry and vanilla aromas and flavors, silky tannins and sweet fruit on the finish. Drinkable now. 5,500 cases made. • $22 • (03/31/93) • **88**

Margaux 1989 • $28 • (03/15/92) • **92**
Margaux 1988 • $40 • (08/31/91) • **73**
Margaux 1986 • $25 • (06/15/89) • **90**
Margaux 1982 • $NA • (08/31/92) • **90**

DURIEU, DOMAINE

Châteauneuf-du-Pape 1989 • $17 • (10/15/91) • **85**
Châteauneuf-du-Pape 1988 • $16 • (10/15/91) • **86**
Châteauneuf-du-Pape 1986 • $16 • (10/15/91) • **89**
Châteauneuf-du-Pape 1985 • $14 • (10/15/91) • **79**
Châteauneuf-du-Pape 1984 • $13 • (11/15/87) • **78**
Châteauneuf-du-Pape 1983 • $NA • (10/15/91) • **82**
Châteauneuf-du-Pape 1981 • $NA • (10/15/91) • **90**
Côtes du Rhône-Villages 1988 • $6 • (03/15/91) • **78**

DUVAL-LEROY

Cuvée des Roys Champagne 1985 • $NA • (12/31/90) • **84**

DUVERGEY-TABOUREAU

Mâcon-Villages 1994: Well made, clean and crisp, offering pear, melon and fig flavors in a style rather ripe for the vintage. Pleasant and accessible now. 417 cases made. • $14 • (08/31/95) • **81**

St.-Véran 1993: Has buttery and mineral flavors, but it turns dry, herbaceous and tough on the palate and the clumsy, slightly burning finish. 1,000 cases made. • $16 • (08/31/95) • **79**

DUVERNAY

Rully Les Cloux Red 1988 • $18 • (12/31/90) • **82**

ECARD, MAURICE

Savigny-lès-Beaune Aux Serpentières 1993: This well-made '93 *premier cru* bursts with ripe red berry flavors and refined, smoky, toasty character. Supple mouthfeel, yet rich and complex. Full in body and very silky finish. Tempting now, but better in 1999. • $25 • (05/15/96) • **93**

Savigny-lès-Beaune Aux Serpentières 1989 • $25 • (11/15/91) • **88**
Savigny-lès-Beaune Aux Serpentières 1987 • $17 • (10/15/89) • **80**
Savigny-lès-Beaune Les Peuillets 1989 • $25 • (11/15/91) • **87**

ECU, DOMAINE DE L'

Muscadet de Sèvre et Maine Sur Lie Cuvée Hermine d'Or 1995: Crisp and clean. A well-focused, balanced white with modest but attractive notes of green apple, hyacinth and almond. A textbook Muscadet. Made from organically grown grapes. 2,200 cases made. • $10 • (04/30/97) • **87**

EGLISE CLINET, CHÂTEAU L'

Pomerol 1997: Firm and silky, with a solid core of berry and cherry flavor. Slightly reductive, but shows serious potential for the vintage. Medium- to full-bodied, with velvety tannins. • $NA • (06/15/98) (BT) • **90-94**

Pomerol 1996: Gorgeous aromas of blackberry, spice and chocolate. Full-bodied, with luscious fruit character and a long, silky, caressing finish. Superb quality for the vintage. Improving every month. Almost classic. • $140 • (06/15/98) (BT) • **90-94**

Pomerol 1995: A big and decadent wine that beckons you to taste it. Fabulous. Opulent aromas of fruit, game and tobacco. Full-bodied and supervelvety, with a lengthy autumnal aftertaste. Best after 2002. 1,600 cases made. • $275 • (01/31/98) • **96**

Pomerol 1994: Wonderful, dark color with a deep nose of olive, meat and fruit. Medium- to full-bodied, with loads of tannins and a fabulously long finish. From one of the hottest châteaus in Pomerol. Try in 1999. • $50 • (01/31/97) • **91**

Pomerol 1990: Soft and ripe, showing a definite ring of mintiness to complement the sweet currant and blackberry flavors. Remains solid through the finish. Try now. • $45 Ⓐ • (06/15/93) • **86**

Pomerol 1989 • $69 • (08/31/92) HR • **96**
Pomerol 1988 • $47 • (12/31/90) • **91**
Pomerol 1987 • $22 • (02/15/90) • **83**
Pomerol 1986 • $55 Ⓐ • (06/15/89) • **91**
Pomerol 1985 • $70 Ⓐ • (02/29/88) • **93**
Pomerol 1983 • $19 • (03/16/86) • **88**
Pomerol 1982 • $53 Ⓐ • (05/01/85) • **92**
Pomerol 1961 • $30 • (04/30/96) • **88**

EGLISE, CHÂTEAU DU DOMAINE DE L'

Pomerol 1997: Dried cherry character with hints of wet earth. Medium-bodied, with velvety tannins and a light, sweet fruit finish. Pretty. • $NA • (06/15/98) (BT) • **85-89**

Pomerol 1996: Good concentration, but slightly diluted on the finish. Medium-bodied, with good tannins and a fresh aftertaste. Pleasant wine for the short term. • $25 • (06/15/98) (BT) • **85-89**

Pomerol 1995: A cuddly and caressing wine. Plenty of crushed berries and chocolate in it. Full- to medium-bodied, with lots of soft tannins and a long, sweet fruit finish. Best after 1999. • $21 • (01/31/98) • **88**

Pomerol 1992: Delicate berry, cherry and strawberry aromas and flavors; light-bodied and firm, slightly thin. • $18 • (04/15/95) • **80**

Pomerol 1991: Soft and delicious. A tobacco and fruit character, medium body and a silky finish. • $18 • (03/31/94) • **82**

Pomerol 1990: A smooth and attractive wine, with lovely tobacco, chocolate and tomato aromas and flavors and a light, silky finish. Drinkable now. 3,500 cases made. • $37 • (03/31/93) • **87**

Pomerol 1989 • $49 Ⓐ • (03/15/92) • **93**
Pomerol 1961 • $NA • (04/30/96) • **87**

EGLY-OURIET

Brut Blanc de Noirs Champagne Cuvée Vieilles Vignes NV: A good but basic bubbly, with simple citrus flavors and a short finish. Drink now. • $36 • (04/30/98) • **80**
Brut Champagne Cuvée Spéciale NV: Nice depth and complexity. Mature and nicely layered flavors of toast, spice, citrus and mineral that linger on the finish make this intriguing and enjoyable. Drink now. • $40 • (04/30/98) • **89**
Brut Champagne Grand Cru Millesime 1986: Starts out bold and rich, with nut, almond and yeast aromas, but turns stylish and elegant on the palate, offering hints of almond, pear and spice flavors. Elegant, graceful and delicious to drink now. 4,100 cases made. • $40 • (06/15/93) • **90**
Brut Champagne Tradition NV: Like a mature Chardonnay, this offers a deep-gold color and mellow, nutty, buttery flavors that linger nicely on the finish. An enjoyable alternative to typical non-vintage Champagne. Drink now. • $30 • (04/30/98) • **89**
Brut Rosé Champagne NV: A serious rosé. Packed with cherry, mushroom and spice flavors, with vibrant acidity and a good, lingering finish. Great with dinner. Drink now through 2000. • $35 • (04/30/98) • **89**

FRANCE

ELGET, CHÂTEAU

Muscadet de Sèvre et Maine Sur Lie Cuvée Prestige 1994: Quite elegant. Attractive floral aromas, keen citrus and almond flavors, bright and well integrated. A good match for light-style fish dishes. • $6 • (04/30/97) • **85**

ENCLOS, CHÂTEAU L'

Pomerol 1989 • $27 Ⓐ • (04/30/92) • **82**
Pomerol 1988 • $20 • (03/15/91) • **85**
Pomerol 1986 • $20 • (06/15/89) • **92**
Pomerol 1984 • $20 • (03/31/87) • **83**
Pomerol 1982 • $29 Ⓐ • (05/15/89) • **86**
Pomerol 1945 • $100 • (03/16/86) • **78**

ENGARRAN, CHÂTEAU DE L'

Vin de Pays des Collines de La Moure 1990 • $7 • (03/15/94) • **84**

ENGEL, RENÉ

Clos Vougeot 1992: Behind a light burr of tannin there's a nice thread of black cherry, smoke and slightly pruny flavor that persists into an elegant finish. Drinkable now. • $NA • (12/15/94) • **86**
Clos Vougeot 1989 • $66 • (11/15/91) • **85**
Clos Vougeot 1988 • $37 Ⓐ • (03/15/91) • **91**
Clos Vougeot 1986 • $50 • (11/30/88) • **81**
Clos Vougeot 1985 • $75 Ⓐ • (10/15/87) • **85**
Clos Vougeot 1983 • $30 • (02/16/86) • **80**
Echézeaux 1992: More generous with its fruit than most '92s, but it's on a small scale and gets a little astringent on the finish. The currant and berry flavors carry through. Drinkable now. • $NA • (12/15/94) • **83**
Echézeaux 1989 • $47 • (11/15/91) • **89**
Echézeaux 1988 • $37 Ⓐ • (03/31/91) • **92**
Echézeaux 1986 • $38 • (11/30/88) • **78**
Echézeaux 1985 • $32 • (10/15/87) • **90**
Grands Echézeaux 1989 • $75 • (11/15/91) • **90**
Grands Echézeaux 1986 • $50 • (11/30/88) • **71**
Grands Echézeaux 1985 • $43 • (10/15/87) • **86**
Vosne-Romanée 1992: Lean and earthy, with very little fruit to balance. Drinkable, but charming only if you like such flavors. • $NA • (12/15/94) • **76**
Vosne-Romanée 1989 • $34 • (11/15/91) • **85**
Vosne-Romanée 1988 • $30 • (07/15/90) • **81**
Vosne-Romanée 1986 • $29 • (02/28/89) • **75**
Vosne-Romanée 1985 • $24 • (10/15/87) • **77**
Vosne-Romanée Les Brûlées 1989 • $35 • (11/15/91) • **87**
Vosne-Romanée Les Brûlées 1988 • $45 • (02/28/91) • **89**
Vosne-Romanée Les Brûlées 1986 • $32 • (10/31/88) • **68**
Vosne-Romanée Les Brûlées 1985 • $28 • (10/15/87) • **85**
Vosne-Romanée Les Brûlées 1983 • $22 • (03/16/86) • **78**

ENTRE NOUS

Vin de Pays d'Oc 1995: Light-bodied but fresh, with a modest berry and earth character. A bit chunky on the finish. Drink now. From Michel Chapoutier. • $NA • (10/15/97) • **81**

EPAYRIÉ, L'

Cabernet Sauvignon Vin de Pays d'Oc 1995: An herbal streak runs through this lean red. There's not much fruit flavor and the finish is tannic. 15,000 cases made. • $8 • (12/15/96) • **78**
Merlot Vin de Pays d'Oc 1995: This accentuates its spicier flavors. Shows herbal aromas, good concentration and a crisp finish. 15,000 cases made. • $8 • (12/15/96) • **83**

EPIRÉ, CHÂTEAU D'

Savennières Cuvée Spéciale 1994: Appealing peach and almond flavors lurk deep in this white, but earthy and smoky notes dominate and turn bitter on the finish. • $17 • (05/31/97) • **78**

ERMITAGE DE PIC ST.-LOUP

Coteaux du Languedoc Pic Saint Loup 1992 • $6 • (03/15/94) • **83**

ESMONIN, FRÉDÉRIC

Bourgogne Les Geneverières 1994: Light, and short on flavor, barely hinting at berry notes on the palate. • $15 • (11/15/96) • **79**
Gevrey-Chambertin Clos Prieur 1994: Very light color and thin flavors. • $27 • (11/15/96) • **77**
Gevrey-Chambertin Clos Prieur 1993: Like inhaling a Havana cigar, so strong are the tobacco flavors here. But thankfully it turns to currant and other red berry notes, and the structure is solid. Try in 2000. 830 cases made. • $30 • (11/15/95) • **86**
Gevrey-Chambertin Estournelles St.-Jacques 1995: Crisp and juicy, tasting of black cherry, cassis, green mango and grapefruit, but so acidic it's mouth-puckering. 375 cases made. • $35 • (11/15/97) • **76**
Gevrey-Chambertin Estournelles St.-Jacques 1993: Pretty plum and berry character, medium body, fine tannins and a fresh finish. Drinkable now. 350 cases made. • $40 • (11/15/95) • **84**
Gevrey-Chambertin Estournelles St.-Jacques 1990: Tart and juicy, with a narrow band of raspberry and cherry flavor that pulls your cheeks in. Firm and tight; drinkable now. • $39 • (10/31/92) • **84**
Gevrey-Chambertin Estournelles St.-Jacques 1989 • $42 • (03/31/92) • **86**
Gevrey-Chambertin Lavaut St.-Jacques 1990: Has a tart, green edge to the raspberry and cherry notes. The tight, narrow band of flavors has had time to evolve and develop. Drinkable now. • $39 • (10/31/92) • **83**
Gevrey-Chambertin Lavaut St.-Jacques 1989 • $42 • (03/31/92) • **88**
Gevrey-Chambertin Les Corbeaux 1990: This funky wine has flavors that stretch from herb, vegetal and olive notes to ripe currant. Clumsy, with a green touch to the flavors. Drinkable now. • $39 • (10/31/92) • **82**
Gevrey-Chambertin Les Corbeaux 1989 • $42 • (03/31/92) • **88**
Griotte-Chambertin 1989 • $80 • (03/31/92) • **92**
Mazis-Chambertin Hospices de Beaune Cuvée Madeleine Collignon 1995: Wine doesn't get much more seductive than this. Unbelievably supple, round, subtle, refined and elegant, with the smoothest, ripest tannins in the world. Offers layers of spice, chocolate, black currant, cassis and wet earth in a medium- to full-bodied package. Long, sexy finish. Drink now through 2005. 125 cases made. • $85 • (11/15/97) • **95**
Mazis-Chambertin Mazy-Chambertin 1990: A light, pleasantly fruity wine, with ripe plum and prune flavors framed by toasty oak notes. Finishes with light tannins. Drinkable now. 100 cases made. • $71 • (10/31/92) • **83**
Mazis-Chambertin Mazy-Chambertin 1989 • $80 • (03/31/92) • **89**
Ruchottes-Chambertin 1993: Beautiful tea leaf and berry aromas and flavors, medium body and tannins and a fresh finish. Try now. 200 cases made. • $65 • (11/15/95) • **90**
Ruchottes-Chambertin 1990: This smooth, fleshy wine has soft, ripe plum and cherry notes that are elegant and lively. Finishes with a lively aftertaste and firm but well-integrated tannins. Drinkable now. 100 cases made. • $71 • (10/31/92) • **86**
Ruchottes-Chambertin 1989 • $80 • (03/31/92) • **91**

Key: SS—Spectator Selection CS—Cellar Selection HR—Highly Recommended BB—Best Buy $NA—Price not available Ⓐ—Auction Price (BT)—Barrel Tasting
Dates in parentheses indicate the issues in which the ratings were published.

ESMONIN, MICHEL

Gevrey-Chambertin 1994: Firm tannins and modest berry and spice flavors. Try now. • $NA • (11/15/96) • **80**
Gevrey-Chambertin 1993: Light and pleasant, showing some decent sweet strawberry, raspberry and stewed tomato flavors, medium body and velvety texture. Try now. • $29 • (11/15/95) • **83**
Gevrey-Chambertin Estournelles St.-Jacques 1988 • $40 • (03/31/91) • **84**
Gevrey-Chambertin Le Clos St.-Jacques 1994: Quite oaky. Medium-bodied and silky, with more mocha-scented wood character than fruit flavor. Finishes with a bitter-chocolate, plum-flavored note. • $NA • (11/15/96) • **77**
Gevrey-Chambertin Le Clos St.-Jacques 1993: Seductive, beautiful plum, vanilla and berry flavors. Medium-bodied, offering ultrafine tannins and a long, succulent finish. Delicious now. • $64 • (11/15/95) • **89**
Gevrey-Chambertin Le Clos St.-Jacques 1987 • $44 • (03/31/90) • **87**
Mazis-Chambertin Mazy-Chambertin 1991: Ripe, generous and a little chewy, but showing enough smoky berry and tomato flavors to bode well. Try now. • $48 • (08/31/94) • **85**
Ruchottes-Chambertin 1991: Lean and distinctly herbal and leafy, a sturdy wine with a modest level of cherry to balance the earthy notes. Try now. • $48 • (08/31/94) • **82**

ESPÉRANCE, CHÂTEAU L'

Bordeaux Supérieur 1994: Light and spicy in style, with good cherry and plum flavors, an herbal note on the finish. • $10 • (06/30/97) • **81**

ESPIGOUETTE, DOMAINE DE L'

Côtes du Rhône Vieilles Vignes 1993 • $9 • (09/30/95) • **88**
Côtes du Rhône-Villages Plan de Dieu 1993 • $10 • (11/15/95) • **84**
Syrah Côtes du Rhône Vieilles Vignes 1993 • $10 • (11/15/95) • **79**

ESPRIT DE CHEVALIER

Pessac-Léognan 1996: Displays brilliant purple color and plum and floral character, but it's rather short and austere. Medium body. Second wine of Domaine de Chevalier. • $NA • (01/01/97) (BT) • **80-84**
Pessac-Léognan 1994: Cool and somewhat unripe, with cherry, leaf and herb aromas and flavors, firm tannins and a slightly hard finish. Drink now. • $NA • (01/31/97) • **80**

ESTIAC, BARON D'

Bordeaux White Première Grande Réserve 1994: Smells like apple juice and tastes like canned fruit. Not much fun. 37,500 cases made. • $8 • (04/30/97) • **71**

ESTOURNEL, MAITRE-D'

Bordeaux 1995: A simple, straightforward red wine that is dry, lean in flavor and short on the finish. • $12 • (01/31/98) • **78**
Bordeaux White 1995: Intense aromas of grass and flowers give way to crisp, lively flavors of citrus, green apple and herbs. A fresh, clean white with style and balance. • $10 • (04/30/97) • **86**
Bordeaux White 1993 • $9 • (02/29/96) • **84**

ESTREMIERES, DOMAINE DES

Côtes du Rhône 1996: Serious Côtes du Rhône. Lovely, offering ripe, vibrant wild raspberry, blueberry and floral notes and some velvety tannins that become quite firm but well integrated on the lingering finish. Drink now. From Jean Decherriäre. • $NA • (10/15/97) • **87**

ETANG DES COLOMBES, CHÂTEAU

Corbières 1991 • $8 • (03/15/94) • **80**
Corbières Bicentenaire Vieilles Vignes 1994: A soft red wine with modest flavors of plum and berry. Drink now. • $12 • (01/01/98) • **79**
Corbières Bicentenaire Vieilles Vignes 1993: A rich, mouthfilling red, displaying its wild berry and earth notes on a firm backbone. Has a touch of new oak for spice. Ready now. • $11 • (05/15/97) • **85**
Corbières Bicentenaire Vieilles Vignes 1991 • $10 • (03/15/94) • **80**
Corbières Bois des Dames 1993: Thick, rich and concentrated with loads of cherry, plum and pepper flavors. It's tannic, but not overpowering. Looking for a very good alternative to Cabernet? This is it. • $19 • (06/15/97) • **87**
Corbières Cuvée du Bicentenaire 1986 • $9 • (03/31/91) • **77**
Corbières Cuvée du Bicentenaire 1985 • $6 • (04/15/88) • **73**
Corbières Tradition 1993: A mature Corbières, with dried herb and cherry flavors underscored by a mineral component. Firm and flavorful, it begs for cheese or red meat to offset its tannins. • $9 • (05/15/97) • **85**

ETANG DU MOULIN

Minervois Réserve 1996: Smooth, with luscious blueberry and raspberry character. This exuberant, medium-bodied wine almost jumps out of the glass to be enjoyed. Finishes on a delicious spicy note. Drink now. 6,000 cases made. • $8 • (05/31/98) • **87**

EVANGILE, CHÂTEAU L'

Pomerol 1997: A wonderful solid core of ripe fruit. Medium- to full-bodied, with velvety tannins and a long, succulent aftertaste. Almost outstanding. • $NA • (06/15/98) (BT) • **85-89**
Pomerol 1995: Well-structured yet elegant and refined. Complex aromas of violets, berries and spice. Full-bodied and very velvety, with a smoke, berry and cherry aftertaste. • $115 Ⓐ • (09/15/98) • **94**
Pomerol 1993: Perhaps not as great as some people think, but it offers delicious berry, green tobacco and fruit aromas and flavors. Medium-bodied, firm tannins and a crisp finish. Tasted twice, with consistent notes. Try now. • $74 Ⓐ • (01/31/96) • **87**
Pomerol 1990: A beautifully polished wine, with well-integrated oak and fruit character and superfine tannins. A class act. Drink now. 4,500 cases made. • $110 Ⓐ • (03/31/93) • **92**
Pomerol 1989 • $70 Ⓐ • (03/15/92) • **92**
Pomerol 1988 • $50 Ⓐ • (06/30/91) • **87**
Pomerol 1986 • $54 Ⓐ • (09/15/89) • **88**
Pomerol 1985 • $137 Ⓐ • (02/29/88) • **92**
Pomerol 1984 • $75 • (02/15/87) • **79**
Pomerol 1983 • $81 Ⓐ • (10/15/94) • **92**
Pomerol 1982: Offers nice flavors, if a bit short and tight, with pruny, smoky notes, dried cherry on the finish. Hold until 2005. • $233 Ⓐ • (07/31/97) • **88**
Pomerol 1981 • $34 Ⓐ • (10/15/94) • **82**
Pomerol 1961 • $NA/1.5 liter (04/30/96) • **83**
Pomerol 1947: A graceful wine with mature earth, tobacco and berry flavors that finish with a touch of coarse tannin. • $NA • (05/31/97) • **87**
Pomerol 1945 • $1219 Ⓐ • (11/30/95) • **87**

FAIVELEY, J.

Beaune Champs Pimont 1989 • $34 • (01/31/92) • **90**
Beaune Champs Pimont 1985 • $36 • (03/15/88) • **86**
Bourgogne 1995: Delicious cherry flavors are not complex, but are direct and satisfying. Enjoy now for the fruit. • $13 • (11/15/97) • **85**
Bourgogne 1990: Well crafted, balancing nice spice and herbal notes against sweet black cherry and tobacco flavors. Ends with a gamy, sturdy finish. Drinkable now. 6,000 cases made. • $11 • (12/15/92) • **85**
Bourgogne 1989 • $12 • (01/31/92) • **84**
Bourgogne 1979 • $8 • (04/16/86) BB • **75**
Bourgogne White 1992: Firm and solid, with a focused band of ripe pear, spice, mineral and vanilla bean flavors. Light- to medium-bodied; subtle and attractive. • $16 • (08/31/94) • **85**
Chambertin-Clos de Bèze 1993: Thick, rich, smoky, exotic and packed with flavor. This is an all-out taste experience backed by firm tannins, chewy texture, lively acidity and a long finish. Needs until at least 1999 to show its best. • $113 • (05/15/96) • **91**
Chambertin-Clos de Bèze 1992: Very light and astringent, with a modest level of earthy, slightly gamy, vaguely berryish flavors. Try now. 542 cases made. • $92 • (12/15/94) • **78**
Chambertin-Clos de Bèze 1991: Thin, tough and tannic, although berry and currant flavors struggle through the astringent finish. An extreme style. 151 cases made. • $89 Ⓐ • (01/31/94) • **78**
Chambertin-Clos de Bèze 1990: Very appealing, with a sumptuous texture, tobacco, coffee and berry aromas and flavors and a smoky finish. An alluring wine. Drinkable now. 500 cases made. • $130 • (12/15/92) • **93**
Chambertin-Clos de Bèze 1989 • $63 Ⓐ • (01/31/92) • **90**
Chambertin-Clos de Bèze 1987 • $70 • (03/31/90) • **83**
Chambertin-Clos de Bèze 1986 • $58 Ⓐ • (07/15/89) • **88**

FAIVELEY, J.

Chambertin-Clos de Bèze 1985 • $105 • (03/15/88) • **96**
Chambolle-Musigny 1989 • $34 • (01/31/92) • **85**
Chambolle-Musigny 1985 • $45 • (05/15/88) • **89**
Chambolle-Musigny 1981 • $24 • (05/01/86) • **88**
Chambolle-Musigny La Combe d'Orveau 1995: Seductive aromas of smoke and vanilla from new oak give way to spicy black cherry notes in this structured '95. It's elegant, yet sports firm tannins that need until 1999 to soften. Long aftertaste of butterscotch and sweet fruit. • $61 • (11/15/97) • **89**
Chambolle-Musigny La Combe d'Orveau 1992: A chewy style of Chambolle that's a bit rough and tough. Has pleasant aromas and flavors, but finishes a bit green and dry. Try now. 125 cases made. • $56 • (12/15/94) • **77**
Chambolle-Musigny Les Fuées 1992: Light, smooth and floral, a little short on fruit, but the delicate berry flavors are pleasant and drinkable now. • $56 • (12/15/94) • **81**
Chambolle-Musigny Les Fuées 1991: Chewy, with juicy berry and plum flavors that never quite overcome the thick layers of tannin. Way out of balance, but may come around by 1998. 50 cases made. • $49 Ⓐ • (01/31/94) • **83**
Chambolle-Musigny Les Fuées 1990: Wonderful plum and black cherry flavors fold nicely into the earth and tobacco notes in this harmonious, medium-bodied, refined wine. Drinkable now. • $36 Ⓐ • (12/15/92) • **89**
Charmes-Chambertin 1992: Light and chewy, with some ripe currant and spice flavors sneaking into the lean, tannic finish. Drinkable now. 525 cases made. • $74 • (12/15/94) • **83**
Charmes-Chambertin 1991: A lean and elegant wine, firm and chewy, a bit earthy at first, but then the currant and blackberry flavors come coursing through and keep vibrating through the finish. Has enough intensity and finesse to age through 2000 at least. 75 cases made. • $75 Ⓐ • (01/31/94) • **92**
Clos de la Roche 1995: A wonderful expression of variety and site. Licorice and herb nuances accent the blackberry and smoke aromas and flavors in this silky, sexy Pinot that caresses the palate from start to finish. Drinkable now. • $93 • (11/15/97) • **90**
Clos de la Roche 1986 • $55 • (07/15/89) • **82**
Clos de la Roche 1985 • $105 Ⓐ • (03/15/88) • **78**
Clos de Vougeot 1992: Lean and tough, an astringent red that tastes more of forest underbrush than fruit, and it's too soon for that. 584 cases made. • $68 • (12/15/94) • **74**
Clos de Vougeot 1991: Crisp, flavorful and tightly wound, showing a lean core of blackberry and plum flavors and a layer of fine tannins. Drinkable now. 175 cases made. • $63 Ⓐ • (01/31/94) • **86**
Clos de Vougeot 1990: A graceful wine, with earth and berry characteristics, masses of fine tannins and a truly gorgeous finish. Try now. 500 cases made. • $50 Ⓐ • (12/15/92) • **92**
Clos de Vougeot 1989 • $41 Ⓐ • (01/31/92) • **85**
Corton Clos des Cortons 1992: Lean and tannic, with some pretty floral and berry flavors struggling to get past the layer of toughness. A roll of the dice, but try it in 1999. 967 cases made. • $62 • (12/15/94) • **85**
Corton Clos des Cortons 1991: Tough, tannic and drying on the palate, with a thin strand of juicy currant flavor. The tannins require cellaring until 1998. 250 cases made. • $63 Ⓐ • (01/31/94) • **83**
Corton Clos des Cortons 1990: Offers an enormous amount of fruit to back up the tannins, even though it's pretty hard on the palate. Drinkable now. 1,000 cases made. • $86 • (12/15/92) • **90**
Corton Clos des Cortons 1989 • $68 • (01/31/92) • **91**
Corton Clos des Cortons 1988 • $120 • (03/31/91) • **90**
Corton Clos des Cortons 1987 • $50 • (03/31/90) • **92**
Corton Clos des Cortons 1985 • $100 • (03/15/88) • **79**
Corton-Charlemagne 1992: Stylish, with lots of vibrant lemon, vanilla and toast flavors; shows excellent length. Not a grand, opulent style of Burgundy, but very fresh despite the oak. • $62 • (08/31/94) • **91**
Echézeaux 1993: Vividly fruity, distinctive and elegant, as a lively strawberry flavor runs from aromas through the lingering finish. Absolutely delicious and seductive. Drinkable now. • $56 • (05/15/96) • **91**
Echézeaux 1991: Tough, tannic and lean, with little to offset the tannins. Try now. 125 cases made. • $68 Ⓐ • (01/31/94) • **77**
Echézeaux 1990: Has a lovely structure and coats your mouth with silky red berry and plum flavors that echo on the firm finish with violet and earth notes. Try now. 350 cases made. • $71 Ⓐ • (12/15/92) • **91**
Echézeaux 1989 • $53 Ⓐ • (01/31/92) • **89**

Key: SS—Spectator Selection CS—Cellar Selection HR—Highly Recommended BB—Best Buy $NA—Price not available Ⓐ—Auction Price (BT)—Barrel Tasting
Dates in parentheses indicate the issues in which the ratings were published.

Echézeaux 1987 • $53 • (03/31/90) • **80**
Echézeaux 1985 • $74 • (03/31/88) • **89**
Fixin 1989 • $21 • (01/31/92) • **85**
Gevrey-Chambertin 1989 • $34 • (01/31/92) • **87**
Gevrey-Chambertin 1985 • $38 • (04/15/88) • **90**
Gevrey-Chambertin Combe au Moine 1989 • $47 • (01/31/92) • **87**
Gevrey-Chambertin Les Cazetiers 1992: Lean and spicy, a juicy red that keeps its anise and currant flavors coming on the narrow finish. Try now. • $NA • (12/15/94) • **80**
Gevrey-Chambertin Les Cazetiers 1991: Awkward, hard and a little bitter. Drinkable now. 175 cases made. • $33 Ⓐ • (01/31/94) • **79**
Gevrey-Chambertin Les Cazetiers 1990: Lovely rose petal, violet and raspberry aromas and flavors are charming, and fresh mushroom and wet earth notes emerge on the firm finish. Drinkable now. 900 cases made. • $49 • (12/15/92) • **89**
Gevrey-Chambertin Les Cazetiers 1989 • $47 • (01/31/92) • **89**
Gevrey-Chambertin Les Cazetiers 1988 • $57 • (03/31/91) • **89**
Gevrey-Chambertin Les Cazetiers 1985 • $53 • (03/31/88) • **92**
Gevrey-Chambertin Les Marchais 1992: Hats off to this village Gevrey for its focused, bright flavors that zero in beautifully on raspberry, black cherry and chestnut. Lingering finish. Try now. • $NA • (12/15/94) • **85**
Gevrey-Chambertin Les Marchais 1990: A great wine. This firm, tannic, racy red is full of berry, cherry and earth aromas and flavors. Not for the fainthearted. Drinkable now. 450 cases made. • $45 • (12/15/92) • **92**
Latricières-Chambertin 1992: Lean and tightly wound, with modest cherry and currant flavors struggling to get past the chewy tannins. Tough; needs until 2000. 584 cases made. • $70 • (12/15/94) • **81**
Latricières-Chambertin 1991: An earthy tobacco note drowns out the modest fruit character in this tough-textured, chunky wine. An echo of blackberry saves it on the finish. Give it until 2000. 125 cases made. • $69 Ⓐ • (01/31/94) • **87**
Latricières-Chambertin 1989 • $53 Ⓐ • (01/31/92) • **89**
Latricières-Chambertin 1985 • $77 • (03/15/88) • **88**
Mazis-Chambertin 1995: An explosive wine. Green gunsmoke tea, raspberry and clove greet the senses before transforming into black cherry and vanilla. Powerful, aristocratic and firmly structured, with a finish that goes on forever, this is stupendous Pinot Noir. Try in 2000. • $97 • (11/15/97) • **94**
Mazis-Chambertin 1991: A nice streak of currant, plum and violet aromas and flavors hangs on at the finish of this crisp, focused wine. Modest in tannins and drinkable now. 175 cases made. • $69 Ⓐ • (01/31/94) • **85**
Mazis-Chambertin 1990: Ripe and seductive, with rich plum, berry and tobacco aromas and flavors. Drinkable now. 500 cases made. • $52 Ⓐ • (12/15/92) • **91**
Mazis-Chambertin 1989 • $46 Ⓐ • (01/31/92) • **95**
Mazis-Chambertin 1985 • $91 Ⓐ • (03/15/88) • **92**
Mercurey Clos des Myglands 1995: The core of strawberry flavors is accented by a sage note, presumably from oak. Sweet fruit comes through on the finish, which is a little tough. • $23 • (11/15/97) • **84**
Mercurey Clos des Myglands 1985 • $20 • (04/30/88) • **75**
Mercurey Clos du Roy 1993: Rugged, full-bodied, cedary, mature flavors, good concentration and very firm tannins. Drinkable now. • $25 • (05/15/96) • **84**
Mercurey Clos du Roy 1988 • $22 • (03/31/91) • **84**
Mercurey Clos du Roy 1985 • $23 • (04/30/88) • **81**
Mercurey Domaine de la Croix Jacquelet 1988 • $18 • (03/31/91) • **81**
Morey-St.-Denis Clos des Ormes 1990: Impressively bright and delicious; the essence of a fine Pinot Noir. Very ripe and almost sweet, with plum and raspberry flavors and a succulent finish. Try now. • $12 Ⓐ • (12/15/92) • **92**
Morey-St.-Denis Clos des Ormes 1989 • $44 • (01/31/92) • **88**
Musigny Le Musigny 1949 • $NA • (08/31/90) • **92**
Nuits-St.-Georges 1990: Lacks extra dimension, but shows beautiful fruit flavors and firm tannins. Drinkable now. 1,500 cases made. • $36 • (12/15/92) • **85**
Nuits-St.-Georges 1989 • $33 • (01/31/92) • **83**
Nuits-St.-Georges 1985 • $40 • (03/15/88) • **90**
Nuits-St.-Georges Aux Chaignots 1992: Light and simple, with a bitter edge sneaking in past the modest berry flavors. Try now. • $NA • (12/15/94) • **76**
Nuits-St.-Georges Aux Chaignots 1990: Vibrant and well constructed, with lovely raspberry and berry aromas and flavors and velvety tannins. Drinkable now. 300 cases made. • $48 • (12/15/92) • **90**
Nuits-St.-Georges Aux Lavières 1992: Tough and tannic, hiding its modest black cherry and spice flavors under the tannins. • $NA • (12/15/94) • **78**

Nuits-St.-Georges Clos de la Maréchale 1992: Light and crisp, offering a nice thread of raspberry and strawberry flavors. Try now. • $NA • (12/15/94) • **80**
Nuits-St.-Georges Clos de la Maréchale 1991: Tough, astringent and dryingly tannic. Try now. 1,200 cases made. • $33 Ⓐ • (01/31/94) • **78**
Nuits-St.-Georges Clos de la Maréchale 1990: A sweet, solid red Burgundy from a pedigreed producer, with cinnamon, licorice and berry characteristics and round, ripe tannins. Drinkable now. 4,000 cases made. • $36 Ⓐ • (11/30/92) HR • **90**
Nuits-St.-Georges Clos de la Maréchale 1989 • $25 Ⓐ • (01/31/92) • **85**
Nuits-St.-Georges Clos de la Maréchale 1988 • $25 Ⓐ • (03/15/91) • **76**
Nuits-St.-Georges Clos de la Maréchale 1985 • $51 • (03/15/88) • **85**
Nuits-St.-Georges Clos de la Maréchale 1982 • $20 • (05/01/86) • **84**
Nuits-St.-Georges Les Damodes 1992: Bright, crisp and lively, with appealing strawberry and red cherry flavors that echo on the finish. Drinkable now. • $NA • (12/15/94) • **80**
Nuits-St.-Georges Les Damodes 1990: A vivid wine, with superfocused plum and spice aromas and flavors. The tannins are fine and elegant. Drinkable now. 300 cases made. • $45 • (12/15/92) • **91**
Nuits-St.-Georges Les Damodes 1989 • $45 • (01/31/92) • **90**
Nuits-St.-Georges Les Damodes 1988 • $52 • (03/31/91) • **85**
Nuits-St.-Georges Les St.-Georges 1992: Light and a little chewy, with extremely modest red cherry flavors lurking in the background. Try now. 150 cases made. • $62 • (12/15/94) • **77**
Nuits-St.-Georges Les St.-Georges 1991: Shows earthy raspberry character on a firm structure. The fruit fades. Drinkable now. 75 cases made. • $62 Ⓐ • (01/31/94) • **79**
Nuits-St.-Georges Les St.-Georges 1989 • $28 Ⓐ • (01/31/92) • **92**
Nuits-St.-Georges Porrets St.-Georges 1993: A big, assertive, promising Burgundy delivering lots of body, seemingly sweet fruit flavors, very firm tannins and a lingering aftertaste. Tough to drink now, but it should be excellent in time; try from 1998 to 2003. • $43 • (05/15/96) • **90**
Nuits-St.-Georges Porrets St.-Georges 1992: Tough and simple, with bitter, leafy accents playing off the modest black cherry flavor. Try now. • $NA • (12/15/94) • **79**
Nuits-St.-Georges Porrets St.-Georges 1991: Dull and flat; the earthy flavors fall short of full maturity. Finishes diluted. 200 cases made. • $37 Ⓐ • (01/31/94) • **76**
Nuits-St.-Georges Porrets St.-Georges 1990: Chewy and rich; manages to pack in a lot of fruit flavors, firm tannins and abundant spice, cherry and oak notes. Drinkable now. 800 cases made. • $45 • (12/15/92) • **90**
Nuits-St.-Georges Porrets St.-Georges 1989 • $42 • (01/31/92) • **84**
Nuits-St.-Georges Porrets St.-Georges 1985 • $47 Ⓐ • (03/15/88) • **76**
Pommard Les Chaponnières 1990: Truly elegant, with succulent fruit, vanilla, raspberry and earth aromas and flavors and an elegant finish. Drinkable now. 125 cases made. • $65 • (12/15/92) • **90**
Pommard Les Chaponnières 1989 • $50 • (01/31/92) • **90**
Rully Red 1986 • $18 • (06/15/89) • **83**
Vosne-Romanée 1989 • $35 • (01/31/92) • **88**

FAIZEAU, CHÂTEAU

Montagne-St.-Emilion Sélection Vieilles Vignes 1997: Bright berry and cherry character. Medium-bodied, with fine tannins and a long, fruity finish. Very good. • $NA • (06/15/98) (BT) • **85-89**
Montagne-St.-Emilion Sélection Vieilles Vignes 1996: A perfumed red with violet and floral aromas. Medium-bodied, with silky tannins and a sweet fruit aftertaste. Lovely. Almost outstanding. • $20 • (06/15/98) (BT) • **85-89**
Montagne-St.-Emilion Sélection Vieilles Vignes 1995: Big and juicy. Concentrated aromas of berries, flowers and currants. Full-bodied and tannic, yet velvety and quite fruity. A wonderful finish of berry, chocolate flavors. Best after 2000. • $18 • (01/31/98) • **90**
Montagne-St.-Emilion Sélection Vieilles Vignes 1994: Lovely and silky, this shows delicate berry, vanilla and chocolate aromas and flavors, fine tannins and a succulent, smooth finish. Delicious now, but should improve. • $15 • (01/31/97) • **86**
Montagne-St.-Emilion Sélection Vieilles Vignes 1993: Delicious now, showing chocolate, berry and cherry aromas and flavors, silky texture and a fruity finish. Not big, but offers some good fruit. Drinkable now. • $15 • (01/31/96) • **84**
Montagne-St.-Emilion Sélection Vieilles Vignes 1992: Aromatic mint, earth and cherry aromas and flavors, but light in body and finish. • $NA • (04/15/95) • **78**
Montagne-St.-Emilion Sélection Vieilles Vignes 1991: A nice little wine, with a core of light-bodied cherry, plum and tobacco notes. • $12 • (03/31/94) • **80**
Montagne-St.-Emilion Sélection Vieilles Vignes 1990: From the owners of Château La Croix-de-Gay. A decadent wine, with raspberry syrup, chocolate and cedar aromas and flavors, full, velvety tannins and a rich finish. Drinkable now. • $15 • (03/31/93) • **89**
Montagne-St.-Emilion Sélection Vieilles Vignes 1983 • $9 • (11/15/87) • **75**

FARAUD, MICHEL

Gigondas Domaine du Cayron 1994: This is packed with wild berry, herb and gamy aromas and flavors that marry well with the burly, tannic framework. Rich and powerful, this begs for cassoulet or braised lamb shank. Drink now through 2005. • $17 • (01/01/98) • **88**
Gigondas Domaine du Cayron 1988 • $14 • (10/15/91) • **89**
Gigondas Domaine du Cayron 1985 • $16 • (11/30/88) • **93**

FARGUES, CHÂTEAU DE

Sauternes 1990: This is really a wild wine. Emits wonderful aromas of orange peel, dried fruit and honey. Full-bodied and incredibly concentrated, with fine acidity and a long, zingy, sweet aftertaste. From the owner of Château d'Yquem. Better after 2000. • $85 • (01/31/97) • **94**
Sauternes 1988: Wonderfully spicy orange marmalade, cedar and pine-nut flavors; full-bodied and very sweet. Drinkable now. • $75 • (04/15/95) • **88**

FAUGÈRES, CHÂTEAU

St.-Emilion 1996: Impressive, with sweet berry and vanilla flavors. Medium-bodied, with well-integrated tannins and a sweet, fruity finish. A wine to watch. • $NA • (01/01/97) (BT) • **85-89**
St.-Emilion 1995: Intense, with blackberry, cherry and warm earth character, full body, full tannins and a long smoky finish. Where did this come from? Don't touch that dial. • $20 • (05/15/97) (BT) • **90-94**

FAURE, CHÂTEAU JEAN

St.-Emilion 1983 • $17 • (03/31/87) • **87**
St.-Emilion 1982 • $14 • (11/16/85) • **85**

FAURIE, BERNARD

Hermitage 1991: Bitter chocolate and berries burst out in this ripe wine. Very firm on the palate and long on the finish. Try now. • $26 • (05/31/94) • **88**
Hermitage 1990: This is velvety, with full, round tannins, black pepper, licorice and thick raisin flavors. It's concentrated; try now. • $30 • (05/31/94) • **89**

FAURY, PHILLIPPE

Condrieu 1993 • $28 • (11/15/95) • **78**
St.-Joseph White 1993 • $15 • (11/15/95) • **76**

FAUTERIE, DOMAINE DE

Cornas 1995: Lighter in body than many Cornas, this shows cherry, licorice and herbal flavors, with light but still slightly drying tannins. Will drink well by 1999. 417 cases made. • $23 • (10/15/97) • **83**
Cornas 1994: An assertive character, offering flavors of black cherry, herb, licorice and smoke, with firm yet fine tannins; quite fresh. Try now. • $24 • (12/15/96) • **88**
Cornas 1993: Notes of black cherry, licorice and light herbal flavors are attractive in this chewy wine. A bit light-bodied for the appellation, but makes pleasant drinking now. • $23 • (12/15/96) • **84**
Cornas 1991 • $NA • (05/31/94) • **84**
St.-Joseph 1995: A firm core of cassis flavor animates this otherwise rustic red, with its notes of leather and game and firmly tannic finish. An old-style wine with rustic power. Try now. 1,000 cases made. • $14 • (10/15/97) • **83**
St.-Joseph 1994: Chewy yet approachable, this shows ripe, fresh cherry and plum flavors, with chocolate and coffee notes that add depth. A well-made wine for early drinking. • $17 • (12/15/96) • **85**
St.-Joseph 1991 • $17 • (04/15/93) • **82**
St.-Joseph 1990 • $13 • (08/31/92) • **80**

St.-Péray 1995: Ripe yet quite fresh, this has plenty of butter flavors with enough pear and almond notes to balance, and a refreshing core of acidity. 667 cases made. • $15 • (10/15/97) • **85**

St.-Péray 1994: Assertive, this tastes like mulled wine, with spicy cinnamon and cooked-apple flavors and a hint of lemony acidity on the finish. Try as an apéritif. • $15 • (12/15/96) • **80**

FAUX FROG, LE

Chardonnay Vin de Pays d'Oc 1996: Tart and somewhat awkward, with lemony flavors and a strong herbal note on the finish. Drink now. • $8 • (05/31/98) • **77**

Merlot Vin de Pays d'Oc 1996: Pleasant, with dried cherry flavors and aromas. Finishes with some soft herbal notes. Drink now. • $8 • (05/31/98) • **80**

FAVRAY, CHÂTEAU DE

Pouilly-Fumé 1996: This crisp white shows flavors of pineapple and green apple, bright and accessible, with good balance and a soft finish. Works well as an apéritif or with lighter dishes. Drink now. 3,000 cases made. • $20 • (05/31/98) • **85**

FAVREAU, YANNICK

Pomerol 1993: Firm, interesting toasty oak, berry and dried herb character. Medium in body, with solid tannins and a medium finish. A négociant wine from a Belgian merchant. Mostly the second wine of Château Le Pin. Better in 1999. • $NA • (02/29/96) • **86**

FAYOLLE

Hermitage Les Diognières 1991: Concentrated but a bit rustic, with hard tannins and barnyard notes. Shows some berry and plum flavors. Try now. • $NA • (05/31/94) • **82**

Hermitage Les Diognières 1990: Closed with hard tannins, but shows some tar and berry flavors. Try now. • $NA • (05/31/94) • **84**

FENOUILLET, DOMAINE DE

Côtes du Rhône-Villages Beaumes-de-Venise 1995: Rather tart and crisp, with light cherry flavors. Stemmy character. Lacks charm. 167 cases imported. 500 cases made. • $13 • (10/15/97) • **71**

Côtes du Rhône-Villages Beaumes-de-Venise 1994: Crisp in style, a bit herbal and earthy, even bitter and tart. Slightly funky on the short finish. 1,667 cases made. • $13 • (10/15/97) • **72**

Côtes du Ventoux 1995: Herbal and earthy flavors run through this lean, somewhat dry wine. It lacks concentration for the vintage. Drink now. 250 cases imported. 1,667 cases made. • $10 • (10/15/97) • **76**

Côtes du Ventoux White 1996: An apéritif-like white, with some buttery pear notes. Medium-bodied, and slightly dull, buttery and herbal. 167 cases imported. 417 cases made. • $10 • (10/15/97) • **81**

Muscat de Beaumes-de-Venise 1996: A nice mix of honey, spice and orange flavors gives this sweet white zest and length. Though it's a bit spiritous on the palate, it finishes with pretty honey and spice notes. 250 cases imported. 2,916 cases made. • $17 • (10/15/97) • **83**

Muscat de Beaumes-de-Venise 1995: Fresh and fruity, overflowing with orange, honey and cream flavors. Quite sweet but not sticky, with full body and a powerful kick of alcohol. 100 cases made. • $23 • (10/15/96) • **86**

FERME ST.-MARTIN, DOMAINE DE LA

Côtes du Rhône-Villages Beaumes de Venise Cuvée Princesse 1995: Tart and simple, with some odd, stemmy, green, unripe flavors. • $NA • (10/15/97) • **70**

FERRAND, CHÂTEAU

Bordeaux 1995: Hard-edged, with only modest fruit flavors. Very herbal, with a dill-like character. • $7 • (04/30/97) • **79**

Key: SS—Spectator Selection CS—Cellar Selection HR—Highly Recommended BB—Best Buy $NA—Price not available Ⓐ—Auction Price (BT)—Barrel Tasting

Dates in parentheses indicate the issues in which the ratings were published.

Pomerol 1995: Decent balance of fruit and fine tannins, with herbal berry and earthy notes. • $NA • (05/15/96) (BT) • **80-84**

FERRANDE, CHÂTEAU

Graves 1995: A very appealing, inexpensive Bordeaux with a great mix of fruit, mineral and spice flavors on a silky texture that still has firm tannins. Tantalizing and complex from the first whiff to the lingering finish. Drink from 1999 to 2005. 25,000 cases made. • $12 • (01/31/98) • **90**

Graves 1981 • $7 • (03/16/85) • **75**

FERRATON, MICHEL

Crozes-Hermitage La Matinière 1995: Quite sweet, ripe and interesting, with mineral and cassis notes, but there's a funky, odd, rustic character that turns a bit vegetal on the crisp finish. • $18 • (10/15/97) • **76**

Crozes-Hermitage La Matinière 1994: Very modern style. Offers bright, ripe fruit flavors, almost jammy, with polished tannins and a clean, fresh finish of violets and plums. Well made, if a bit sterile now, it should improve through 2002. 400 cases made. • $18 • (11/30/96) • **87**

Crozes-Hermitage La Matinière 1990 • $16 • (04/15/93) • **89**

Crozes-Hermitage La Matinière 1988 • $14 • (06/30/90) • **85**

Hermitage Cuvée des Miaux 1994: Bright, fresh fruit flavors, running the gamut from plummy to grapey, with floral and even candied accents, but ironclad tannins run deep in this exuberant yet powerful wine. Expressive. Try now. 150 cases made. • $38 • (11/30/96) • **87**

Hermitage Cuvée des Miaux 1990: Polished and balanced, but lacking a bit in concentration. Black cherry and smoked-meat flavors, with soft tannins. Drinkable now. • $33 • (05/31/94) • **86**

FERRAUD & FILS, PIERRE

Mâcon-Fuissé 1996: A Mâcon with a perfumy, rose petal character, good acidity and medium body. Fresh, zingy finish, but turns green and bitter. Might deliver nicely with food. 667 cases made. • $9 • (08/31/97) • **75**

Mâcon-Villages 1996: A good Mâcon, dense, ripe and thick in texture, with a haylike quality and succulent, sweet melon, pear and apple flavors. Lacks a bit of class, but try with food for its crisp acidity on the finish. 1,000 cases made. • $9 • (08/31/97) • **84**

Mâcon-Villages 1995: Crisp and fresh. Light to medium in body, with a core of clean fruit and a zesty, slightly tart finish. Tasted twice, with consistent notes. • $NA • (08/31/96) • **80**

Mâcon-Villages 1994: Crisp, sharp and light-bodied, showing wet hay, lemon and green apple flavors of medium intensity. Good balance on the juicy finish. 667 cases made. • $9 • (08/31/95) • **79**

Pouilly-Fuissé La Chardonneraie 1995: A beautifully crafted, polished white Burgundy, with an excellent, ripe, sweet-tasting fruit character of great definition and a silky, minerally texture. Of medium body, it's a delight to drink now through 2000. 600 cases made. • $16 • (05/31/97) • **89**

St.-Véran 1995: Tart at first, mellows once aired. Medium-bodied, with ripe fruit flavors accented by lime, hay and vanilla bean notes. Ready now. • $NA • (08/31/96) • **81**

St.-Véran 1994: Sparkling with life and vibrant citrus character, this light- to medium-bodied white delivers intense lemon, grapefruit and pear notes. Could use a more complex finish. 1,083 cases made. • $10 • (08/31/95) • **84**

FERRET, J.-A.

Pouilly-Fuissé Les Clos 1995: Soft and supple, a rich, ripe Pouilly that tastes of buttered toast spread with quince jam, some marzipan, pear tart and oak accents. Very complex and harmonious, with a silky mouthfeel, but quite a punch on the slightly burning finish. Drink now through 2000. • $33 • (05/31/98) • **89**

Pouilly-Fuissé Les Ménétrières 1995: Beautiful mouthfeel. A bit too oaky at first but turning elegant, this full-bodied, ripe, rich yet classy wine delivers a seamless texture that coats the palate. It blends aromas and flavors reminiscent of vanilla, caramel, piecrust, honey, ginger snap and pear. Tempting now through 2000. • $41 • (05/31/98) • **91**

Pouilly-Fuissé Les Ménétrières 1993: Supple and honeyed, harmonious and enchanting, delivering some lovely mineral and wet earth character underneath the opulent pear and apple flavors. Long, lemony finish suggests it will hold until 1999. 150 cases imported. • $45 • (05/31/96) • **90**

Pouilly-Fuissé Les Moulins 1996: Soft and pretty, with a distinctive malic, buttery, spicy, toasty bread, mocha-oak character that plays along with the pear, honey and apple tart flavors. Of medium body and intensity, but comes across as a bit too oaky. Try around 1999 to 2000. • $25 • (05/31/98) • **85**

Pouilly-Fuissé Les Perrières 1995: A very rich style, with butter, honey, chocolate and burnt sugar character. Impressive for its ripe, full-bodied personality, but a bit overdone. Drink now. • $33 • (05/31/98) • **82**

Pouilly-Fuissé Les Scélés 1996: Gorgeous mouthfeel of compacted, mineral-laden, creamlike texture, yet there is plenty of tart acidity to move things along to a succulent finish. Add green apple skin, honey, toast, pie dough, fresh herb (thyme), vanilla bean and poppy seed flavors. Needs time; try in 2000. Tasted twice, with consistent notes. • $26 • (05/31/98) • **91**

Pouilly-Fuissé Les Vernays 1996: Surprisingly heavy-handed. Full-bodied but rustic, it jumps from the glass with butter, spice and caramel notes, and offers some fruit and honey. The midpalate texture is silky, but the finish burns a bit. Drink now. • $26 • (05/31/98) • **83**

Pouilly-Fuissé Les Vernays 1994: A lively, attractive combination of grass, mineral, green apricot, lime and honey flavors. Medium-bodied, with the citrus flavors peppering the crisp finish. Try now. • $NA • (08/31/96) • **87**

Pouilly-Fuissé Tournant de Pouilly 1994: Simply gorgeous. Rich, unctuous and supple, yet it's not overdone, boasting toasty coconut, spice, honey and hazelnut. Full body, electrifying flavors and a long finish. Try now through 1999. 100 cases imported. • $45 • (05/31/96) • **93**

Pouilly-Fuissé Tête de Cru 1994: A beautiful white, both thick and crisp, delivering a blend of honey and citrus character. Turns somewhat lean and green on the finish. Try now. 150 cases imported. • $40 • (05/31/96) • **85**

Pouilly-Fuissé Tête de Cuvée 1993: Impressively silky and creamy texture, with butterscotch, yeasty aromas and flavors. Lots of intense lemon, lime and pear character on the immensely pleasing, velvety finish that goes on and on. Drinkable now. • $35 • (05/15/95) • **90**

FERRIÈRE, CHÂTEAU

Margaux 1997: Some mineral, grape and vanilla character, but rather lacking in the midpalate. Short finish. • $NA • (06/15/98) (BT) • **80-84**

Margaux 1996: Gorgeous blackberry and cherry aromas and flavors are wrapped with pretty oak. Medium- to full-bodied, with silky tannins and a long finish. A beauty. Almost outstanding. 600 cases made. • $32 • (06/15/98) (BT) • **85-89**

Margaux 1995: What? Who? This is rich and powerful with masses of fruit, character and tannins. One of the sleepers of the vintage. Long, long finish. Best after 2002. 4,100 cases made. • $30 • (01/31/98) • **94**

Margaux 1994: Marked by its pretty, perfumy aromas, this is medium-bodied, with medium tannins and a delicate finish. Drinkable now. • $27 • (01/31/97) • **85**

Margaux 1993: Good sweetness of fruit here. Mint, dried herb and plum aromas and flavors, medium body and tannins and a silky finish. Drinkable now. 2,917 cases made. • $NA • (01/31/96) • **87**

Margaux 1992: Smooth and silky plum and cherry flavors, but slightly one-dimensional and short. Drink now. • $NA • (04/15/95) • **81**

FESLES, CHÂTEAU DE

Anjou Red Vieilles Vignes 1996: Deeply colored, showing expressive smoky, peppery aromas and plenty of gamy, smoky flavors under chewy tannins, but the extraction is at the expense of fruit. Best from 1999 through 2001. 1,200 cases made. • $12 • (05/31/98) • **83**

Anjou Red Vielles Vignes 1995: A light red, well balanced, with moderate tannins and light cherry flavors. Unobtrusive, it would make a modest accompaniment to lighter dishes. 3,333 cases made. • $13 • (06/15/97) • **82**

Bonnezeaux La Chapelle 1993: Lovely apricot, orange peel and spice aromas give way to ripe apricot and coconut flavors in this rich white. Not extremely sweet, shows good structure and balance. 833 cases made. • $36/500ml • (05/15/97) • **88**

Chardonnay Vin de Pays F de Fesles 1996: Thin and simple, with modest fig and herb flavors and a fairly astringent finish. 1,500 cases made. • $11 • (04/30/98) • **74**

Rosé de Loire Le Jardin 1995: Juicy and fresh, this rosé is simple yet vibrant, with clean berry flavors and a dry finish. Try it on a summer afternoon. 2,083 cases made. • $10 • (05/15/97) • **82**

FESSY, HENRY

Mâcon-Villages St.-Maurice de Sathonnay 1996: Toasty oak elements add nuance to the honeysuckle and peach flavors. A lean, elegant style that picks up a hint of vanilla on the finish. Drink now through 1999. • $9 • (05/31/98) • **84**

FESSY, SYLVAIN

Vosne-Romanée Maizières 1994: Light, with a swallow of mild currant flavor that echoes on the finish. Well-controlled tannins make this approachable now. • $NA • (11/15/96) • **83**

FEUILLATTE, NICOLAS

Brut Champagne Cuvée Palmes d'Or 1990: A mouthfilling, appetizing Champagne that balances deep fruit flavors with subtle hints of toast and spice that add complexity. Smooth in texture, with a lingering finish. Drink now through 2002. • $95 • (08/31/97) • **90**

Brut Champagne Cuvée Palmes d'Or 1985: Powerful, vibrant and intensely fruity. Has a broad array of flavors and a smooth texture. Well balanced and long on the finish. Great to drink now, but should gain complexity as it ages. Drink through 2000. Better than in an earlier tasting. 2,000 cases made. • $80 • (07/31/96) • **92**

Brut Champagne Premier Cru NV: A light, delicate Champagne that tastes lemony and smooth. Nothing out of place or out of proportion. • $25 • (10/31/97) • **87**

Brut Champagne Premier Cru Cuvée Spéciale 1988: A real standout. Full-bodied, concentrated and complex, it's a rewarding, nearly mature bottle of bubbly with depth of flavor, great breadth of texture and a long finish. Best now through 2000. • $50 • (11/30/97) • **93**

Brut Champagne Premier Cru Cuvée Spéciale 1986: Balanced on the tart side, tight in texture and lemony in flavor; a refreshing but rather austere style. • $40 • (11/15/96) • **85**

Brut Rosé Champagne NV: A very good, solid rosé Champagne with spicy aromas, lively cherry flavors and a touch of sweetness. • $27 • (11/30/97) • **86**

FÈVRE, WILLIAM

Chablis 1996: Rich and ripe if a bit rustic, with distinctive butter and butterscotch flavors, some grassy, green-apple notes. Turns a bit tart on the chewy finish. Drinkable now. • $NA • (08/31/97) • **84**

Chablis 1995: Young and zesty, but overoaked. Light-bodied, it tastes of wood, lemon, apple and honey. Good concentration of fruit. Try now. • $NA • (08/31/96) • **80**

Chablis 1994 • $16 • (05/31/96) • **79**

Chablis Bougros 1994 • $35 • (05/31/96) • **93**

Chablis Bougros 1993 • $35 • (08/31/95) • **85**

Chablis Grenouilles 1994 • $35 • (05/31/96) • **88**

Chablis Les Clos 1996: Quite woody, with the oak flavors dominating the fruit and structure of this otherwise lush Chablis. Mocha, spice and a burnt sugar character doesn't help. • $34 • (05/31/98) • **79**

Chablis Les Clos 1994 • $35 • (05/31/96) • **92**

Chablis Les Clos 1993 • $32 • (08/31/95) • **85**

Chablis Les Preuses 1994 • $35 • (05/31/96) • **87**

Chablis Montée de Tonnerre 1996: What opulence and amazing texture! Velvety as can be, this full-bodied, oak-aged Chablis coats your palate with lush, creamlike character. Lovely spice, mocha and butterscotch flavors combine with pear and apple tart flavors to make it smooth. Fairly forward; tempting now through 2005. • $22 • (05/31/98) • **92**

Chablis Montée de Tonnerre 1994 • $25 • (05/31/96) • **91**

Chablis Montmains 1994 • $22 • (05/31/96) • **83**

Chablis Montmains 1993 • $22 • (08/31/95) • **85**

Chablis Vaillons 1994 • $25 • (05/31/96) • **84**

Chablis Vaudésir 1995: An oaky *grand cru*, with butter, butterscotch and vanilla bean flavors dominating its fruit and *terroir*. Full-bodied, very ripe, as silky textured as any Chardonnay. Drink now through 2000. 725 cases made. • $32 • (06/15/97) • **86**

Chablis Vaudésir 1994 • $35 • (05/31/96) HR • **94**

FEYTIT-CLINET, CHÂTEAU

Pomerol 1995: A bit rustic but delivering some good fruit, earthy undertones, medium body and hard tannins. Wait and see how this evolves. • $NA • (05/15/96) (BT) • **80-84**

Pomerol 1985 • $30 • (04/30/88) • **88**

Pomerol 1983 • $13 • (07/16/86) • **70**

Pomerol 1982 • $37 Ⓐ • (05/15/89) • **91**

FIEFS DE LAGRANGE, LES

St.-Julien 1996: Intense aromas of grapes, minerals and wet earth, but slightly hollow on the palate. Full-bodied and very velvety, with a good finish. 35,108 cases made. • $NA • (01/01/97) (BT) • **80-84**

St.-Julien 1995: The quality of the tannins in this second label from Château Lagrange is wonderful. Sweet berry and floral aromas. Medium-bodied, with ultrafine tannins and a long, silky finish. Best after 2000. 12,500 cases made. • $19 • (01/31/98) • **88**

St.-Julien 1994: Decent fruit flavors, especially dried cherry, and slightly herbal aromas. Tannins are firm and slightly hard. A hint metallic. Better in 1999. 31,666 cases made. • $18 • (01/31/97) • **81**

St.-Julien 1993: Full of life and zingy character, a delicious, medium-bodied St.-Julien worth seeking out, featuring soft tannins and cassis, blackberry and mint flavors. Lovely to drink now. • $16 • (01/31/96) • **85**

St.-Julien 1991: A delicate wine that turns a bit astringent on the finish, delivering some alluring floral, red berry and tobacco flavors. • $13 • (03/31/94) • **79**

St.-Julien 1990: An elegant wine, with a lovely balance of blackberry and tobacco flavors and soft, silky tannins. Not a blockbuster, but well proportioned. Drinkable now. • $18 • (03/31/93) • **88**

St.-Julien 1988 • $17 • (04/30/91) • **92**

St.-Julien 1983 • $10 • (05/01/86) • **85**

FRANCE

FIEUZAL, CHÂTEAU DE

Pessac-Léognan 1997: Quite chunky for the vintage. Medium-bodied, with blackberry and cherry character, velvety tannins and a light to medium finish. Slightly hollow on the midpalate, but impressive. • $NA • (06/15/98) (BT) • **85-89**

Pessac-Léognan 1996: Good ripe fruit, with blackberry and currant aromas and flavors. Medium-bodied, with medium tannins and a silky finish. 7,000 cases made. • $35 • (06/15/98) (BT) • **85-89**

Pessac-Léognan 1995: A mouthful. Big and burly, full-bodied and very tannic, with a long finish. Dried berry and fresh mushroom aromas. This needs time. Try after 2002. • $30 • (01/31/98) • **91**

Pessac-Léognan 1994: Lovely, rich aromas of berries and dark chocolate rise from this medium-bodied wine, with firm tannins and zingy acidity. Drinkable now. • $16 Ⓐ • (01/31/97) • **87**

Pessac-Léognan 1993: Delicious raspberry and blackberry aromas and flavors. Medium-bodied and succulent, adding fine tannins and a sweet fruit finish. Drinkable now. • $25 • (01/31/96) • **87**

Pessac-Léognan 1992: Some good fruit but rather aggressive, showing gravel, meat and green bean character. Medium-bodied and slightly hard and dry. • $20 • (04/15/95) • **82**

Pessac-Léognan 1991: Not as good as expected. A lean wine with white pepper and cherry aromas and flavors, medium body and a light finish. Tasted twice. • $14 • (03/31/94) • **79**

Pessac-Léognan 1990: A powerful wine, with masses of tar, berry and earthy character, gripping tannins and sweet fruit on the finish. Drinkable now. 7,500 cases made. • $29 • (03/31/93) • **92**

Pessac-Léognan 1989 • $38 Ⓐ • (03/15/92) HR • **95**

Pessac-Léognan 1988 • $33 Ⓐ • (04/30/91) • **91**

Pessac-Léognan 1987 • $18 • (05/15/90) • **81**

Pessac-Léognan 1986 • $24 Ⓐ • (06/30/89) • **90**

Graves 1985 • $30 Ⓐ • (10/15/94) • **90**

Graves 1983 • $24 Ⓐ • (10/15/94) • **85**

Graves 1982 • $37 Ⓐ • (08/31/92) • **82**

Graves 1981 • $21 Ⓐ • (10/15/94) • **88**

Graves 1979 • $13 Ⓐ • (10/15/89) • **83**

Pessac-Léognan White 1995: Shows potential; needs time to develop. Intense mineral and cut-wood aromas with hints of fruit. Medium- to full-bodied, with appley fresh fruit character and a medium aftertaste. Better after 1999. • $30 • (04/30/98) • **89**

Pessac-Léognan White 1993 • $40 • (05/31/95) • **91**

FIGARO

Vin de Pays de l'Herault 1993 • $5 • (03/31/95) • **79**

Key: SS—Spectator Selection CS—Cellar Selection HR—Highly Recommended BB—Best Buy $NA—Price not available Ⓐ—Auction Price (BT)—Barrel Tasting

Dates in parentheses indicate the issues in which the ratings were published.

FIGEAC, CHÂTEAU

St.-Emilion 1997: Slightly lean but with pleasant berry, tobacco and cherry character. Light- to medium-bodied, with light tannins and a short finish. • $NA • (06/15/98) (BT) • **80-84**

St.-Emilion 1996: A medium-bodied '96 with earth, berry and cherry character. A pleasant, relaxed red. • $75 • (06/15/98) (BT) • **85-89**

St.-Emilion 1995: Best Figeac in years. Loads of blackberry, chocolate and stones. Full-bodied and concentrated with masses of tannins and fruit. Long, long finish. Needs time. Best after 2002. • $60 • (01/31/98) • **95**

St.-Emilion 1994: Beautiful. Good concentration, with a berry, tobacco and dried herb character. Medium-bodied, with fine tannins and a fruity finish. Better than anticipated now; best in 1999. • $50 • (01/31/97) • **88**

St.-Emilion 1993: Elegant and subtle, showing a good amount of toasty, vanilla-flavored new wood and a combination of herbal-scented Merlot character with cassis, earth and plum. Supple tannins. Drinkable now. • $24 Ⓐ • (01/31/96) • **87**

St.-Emilion 1990: Tantalizing, with beautiful aromas of chocolate, vanilla and berry that carry through to the long, clean finish. Round and juicy. Drinkable now. 12,500 cases made. • $105 • (03/31/93) • **92**

St.-Emilion 1989 • $49 Ⓐ • (03/15/92) • **93**

St.-Emilion 1988 • $46 Ⓐ • (06/30/91) HR • **93**

St.-Emilion 1987 • $35 • (10/31/91) • **83**

St.-Emilion 1986 • $78 Ⓐ • (10/15/94) • **84**

St.-Emilion 1985 • $64 Ⓐ • (10/15/94) • **90**

St.-Emilion 1984 • $20 Ⓐ • (03/31/87) • **83**

St.-Emilion 1983 • $62 Ⓐ • (10/15/94) • **91**

St.-Emilion 1982 • $118 Ⓐ • (08/31/92) • **90**

St.-Emilion 1981 • $43 Ⓐ • (10/15/94) • **87**

St.-Emilion 1980 • $20 Ⓐ • (05/01/85) • **90**

St.-Emilion 1979 • $37 Ⓐ • (10/31/91) • **88**

St.-Emilion 1978 • $48 Ⓐ • (10/31/91) • **89**

St.-Emilion 1976 • $48 Ⓐ • (10/31/91) • **87**

St.-Emilion 1975 • $77 Ⓐ • (10/31/91) • **78**

St.-Emilion 1971 • $27 Ⓐ • (10/31/91) • **84**

St.-Emilion 1970 • $73 Ⓐ • (10/31/91) • **92**

St.-Emilion 1966 • $79 Ⓐ • (10/31/91) • **85**

St.-Emilion 1964 • $110 • (10/31/91) • **93**

St.-Emilion 1962 • $90 • (10/31/91) • **85**

St.-Emilion 1961 • $192 Ⓐ • (04/30/96) • **90**

St.-Emilion 1955 • $250 • (10/31/91) • **96**

St.-Emilion 1953 • $82 Ⓐ • (10/31/91) • **86**

St.-Emilion 1952 • $48 Ⓐ • (10/31/91) • **85**

St.-Emilion 1950 • $220 • (10/31/91) • **91**

St.-Emilion 1949 • $271 Ⓐ • (10/31/91) • **99**

St.-Emilion 1947 • $509 Ⓐ • (10/31/91) • **93**

St.-Emilion 1945 • $300 • (10/31/91) • **96**

St.-Emilion 1943 • $150 • (10/31/91) • **90**

St.-Emilion 1942 • $125 • (10/31/91) • **85**

St.-Emilion 1939 • $125 • (10/31/91) • **83**

St.-Emilion 1937 • $125 • (10/31/91) • **69**

St.-Emilion 1934 • $160 • (10/31/91) • **79**

St.-Emilion 1929 • $400 • (10/31/91) • **98**

St.-Emilion 1926 • $300 • (10/31/91) • **87**

St.-Emilion 1924 • $350 • (10/31/91) • **88**

St.-Emilion 1911 • $400 • (10/31/91) • **78**

St.-Emilion 1906 • $350 • (10/31/91) • **78**

St.-Emilion 1905 • $430 • (10/31/91) • **95**

FIGEAT, COLETTE

Pouilly-Fumé Les Loges 1993 • $18 • (10/31/94) • **77**

FILHOT, CHÂTEAU

Sauternes 1991: Fresh and lively, revealing floral notes and vibrant, grassy, unripe apricot flavors; lightly sweet on the crisp finish. Drink as an apéritif. • $NA • (04/15/95) • **80**

Sauternes 1990: Pleasant, light-bodied, offering decent concentration of lemon, pear, melon and earth flavors; a bit short on the finish. • $29 • (04/15/95) • **81**

Sauternes 1989: A light style, supplying attractive lilac, honeycomb, butterscotch, lemon and grass flavors. Drinkable now. Good as an apéritif. • $27 • (04/15/95) • **85**

Sauternes 1988: Clean and fresh lemon and spice character; light and moderately sweet. Drink now. • $25 • (04/15/95) • **84**

Sauternes 1987 • $19 • (06/15/90) • **68**
Sauternes 1986: Has concentration and richness without a lot of fruit to balance the tobacco and toast aromas and flavors that dominate. Has a touch of caramel on the finish. Drinkable now. • $19 • (12/31/89) • **83**
Sauternes 1983: Distinctive, complex pine-nut, cedar, quince and fig flavors make you come back for another sip, but it also tastes woodier than most '83s. Drinkable now. • $33 • (04/15/95) • **87**
Sauternes 1980 • $11 • (05/01/84) • **80**
Sauternes Crème de Tête 1990: Unbelievably rich and unctuous, thick, ripe and creamy; quite sugary, sporting an orange flavor to accent the botrytis character. Drinkable now. • $NA • (04/15/95) • **90**

FILIPPI, JEANNE PAULE

Chablis Champs Royaux 1996: A pumped-up Chablis. Extremely viscous in texture, with very ripe vanilla custard and honey aromas and flavors, ending with the telltale mineral character. It's so ripe it almost covers the acidity at this point. Seems a little out of sorts today and difficult to judge. Could ultimately rate higher. Best from 2000 through 2005. 2,500 cases made. • $17 • (05/31/98) • **88**
Chablis Montée de Tonnerre 1996: Beautiful wine. Smells like a forest on a spring morning, with a hint of smoke and stone. Crisp, focused and lean, full of flint, honey and apple character, followed by some tannins on the finish. Best from 1999 through 2004. 300 cases made. • $25 • (05/31/98) • **89**
Chablis Vaillons 1996: Textbook Chablis aromas and flavors of smoke, mineral and apple, showing deft balance and a firm backbone, followed by a lingering aftertaste. It could use a touch more concentration. Best from 1999 through 2004. 500 cases made. • $25 • (05/31/98) • **89**

FILLIATREAU, L.

Saumur Champigny La Grande Vignolle 1995: Ripe flavors of plum, cinnamon and herbs provide depth, and it has a nice balance of fruit and moderate tannins. Drinkable now. 475 cases made. • $14 • (06/15/97) • **85**
Saumur Champigny La Grande Vignolle 1992 • $13 • (11/15/94) • **84**

FINES ROCHES, CHÂTEAU DES

Châteauneuf-du-Pape 1995: Chewy and concentrated, loaded with character from start to finish. Raspberry, cherry and licorice aromas turn to concentrated flavors of plum and dried herbs, picking up a leathery note on the long, slightly hot aftertaste. Drink now through 2005. 15,500 cases made. • $22 • (05/15/98) • **88**
Châteauneuf-du-Pape 1994: Black cherry, plum and black pepper flavors are well defined and appealing in this balanced, clean red. The tannins are firm but supportive. Try now. 5,000 cases made. • $20 • (11/15/96) • **85**
Châteauneuf-du-Pape 1989 • $20 • (05/31/92) • **81**
Châteauneuf-du-Pape 1986 • $14 • (09/30/90) • **85**
Châteauneuf-du-Pape 1985 • $12 • (10/31/87) • **80**
Châteauneuf-du-Pape 1984 • $12 • (09/30/87) • **89**

FLEUR, CHÂTEAU LA

St.-Emilion 1997: Pleasant plum and berry character, but slightly lean, with fine tannins and a short finish. Wait and see. • $NA • (06/15/98) (BT) • **80-84**
St.-Emilion 1996: Light and fruity, with berry and earth character, but slightly dry on the finish. • $20 • (06/15/98) (BT) • **80-84**
St.-Emilion 1995: Good backbone of tannins but slightly short on the finish. Loads of blackberry, mineral, pomegranate aromas. Medium-bodied, with medium tannins and a menthol, berry finish. Better after 1999. • $18 • (01/31/98) • **85**
St.-Emilion 1994: Slightly hard and one-dimensional, but shows some good, dried cherry character and a fresh finish. Drinkable now. • $19 • (01/31/97) • **82**
St.-Emilion 1993: Succulent and soft, featuring silky tannins and plenty of berry, plum and tobacco character. Medium body and finish. Drinkable now. • $17 • (01/31/96) • **85**
St.-Emilion 1992: Decent color but slightly weedy plum, dried herb character; light-bodied and lean. • $14 • (04/15/95) • **77**
St.-Emilion 1990: Decadent, with plenty of earth, tar, tobacco and cherry character and assertive tannins. A little rough around the edges. Drinkable now. 2,500 cases made. • $22 • (03/31/93) • **89**
St.-Emilion 1989 • $18 • (03/15/92) • **84**
St.-Emilion 1986 • $14 • (02/15/90) • **82**

FLEUR-CARDINALE, CHÂTEAU

St.-Emilion 1996: Attractive aromas of dark chocolate and berries, but the palate doesn't come through. Medium-bodied, with full tannins and a short finish. • $NA • (01/01/97) (BT) • **85-89**
St.-Emilion 1995: Ripe raspberry and cherry aromas, with a hint of earth. Full-bodied and velvety, with chocolate, berry flavors and a long, flavorful, toasty oak aftertaste. Best after 1999. • $22 • (01/31/98) • **87**
St.-Emilion 1994: An early-drinking wine, with fine tannins and medium body. Alluring aromas of strawberry, cherry and vanilla echo on the fresh finish. • $20 • (01/31/97) • **85**
St.-Emilion 1993: Well-proportioned '93, showing medium body, smooth tannins and attractive mineral, plum and cedar flavors. A Bordeaux that delivers finesse more than loads of character. Drinkable now. • $NA • (01/31/96) • **84**

FLEUR-PÉTRUS, CHÂTEAU LA

Pomerol 1997: Lovely and rich, with ripe berry, tobacco and fruit character. Medium-bodied, with medium, velvety tannins and a delicious finish. Almost outstanding. • $NA • (06/15/98) (BT) • **85-89**
Pomerol 1996: Attractive red berry character, with fine tannins and medium body. Silky texture. Not quite as exciting as I remember. • $45 • (06/15/98) (BT) • **85-89**
Pomerol 1995: Surprisingly ready, and delicious if a bit disappointing. Blackberries galore on the nose and palate. Medium-bodied, with well-integrated tannins and a medium aftertaste of fruit and tobacco. Better after this year. • $65 • (01/31/98) • **89**
Pomerol 1994: Pretty aromas of berries and wet earth and enticing flavors of fruit and vanilla. Medium-bodied, with silky tannins. Better in 1999. • $48 • (01/31/97) • **88**
Pomerol 1993: Nicely balanced. Medium- to light-bodied and elegant, with medium intensity and a very attractive core of sweet fruit. Supple tannins add to the pleasurable taste. Try now. • $39 • (01/31/96) • **86**
Pomerol 1992: Better than when tasted in barrel. Attractive leather, berry and light plum aromas and flavors, subtle, complex palate and light body. • $34 • (04/15/95) • **84**
Pomerol 1990: The flavors build on the palate with luscious cassis, olive and berry flavors and medium tannins. Drinkable now. 2,300 cases made. • $70 • (03/31/93) • **90**
Pomerol 1989 • $78 Ⓐ • (03/15/92) • **88**
Pomerol 1986 • $44 Ⓐ • (02/15/90) CS • **93**
Pomerol 1985 • $64 Ⓐ • (10/15/94) • **90**
Pomerol 1983 • $73 Ⓐ • (10/15/94) • **86**
Pomerol 1982 • $103 Ⓐ • (08/31/92) • **90**
Pomerol 1981 • $54 Ⓐ • (10/15/94) • **86**
Pomerol 1961 • $207 Ⓐ • (04/30/96) • **89**
Pomerol 1945 • $300 • (03/16/86) • **63**
Pomerol English Bottled 1959 • $226 Ⓐ • (10/15/90) • **92**

FLEUR-POURRET, CHÂTEAU LA

St.-Emilion 1995: Tightly knit, with a solid backbone of firm but ripe tannins, it delivers plenty of bitter chocolate, blackberry and red berry character. Long, tannic finish. • $NA • (05/15/96) (BT) • **85-89**
St.-Emilion 1992: Rather aggressive tobacco, herbal, stewed tomato character; medium in body and metallic on the finish. • $NA • (04/15/95) • **78**
St.-Emilion 1990: A very pretty, early-maturing wine, with tobacco, cedar, ripe fruit aromas and flavors and medium-light tannins. Drinkable now. 2,500 cases made. • $23 • (03/31/93) • **86**
St.-Emilion 1989 • $NA • (03/15/92) • **82**

FLEUR-ST.-GEORGES, CHÂTEAU LA

Lalande-de-Pomerol 1996: A bit weedy, with a slight metallic edge to the tannins. Medium body and tannins. • $NA • (01/01/97) (BT) • **75-79**
Lalande-de-Pomerol 1995: No-nonsense red, with berry, fresh tobacco aromas and flavors. Medium-bodied, with velvety tannins and a fruity finish. Best after 1999. 9,000 cases made. • $20 • (01/31/98) • **85**
Lalande-de-Pomerol 1994: Some decent fruit flavor, but slightly unripe. The berry and dried herb aromas and herbal, fruity flavors have a slight metallic note. Drink now. 8,000 cases made. • $18 • (01/31/97) • **78**
Lalande-de-Pomerol 1990: This is a slinky wine, with intense aromas and flavors of raspberries and ripe fruit, silky tannins and a slightly dry finish. Drink now. • $NA • (03/31/93) • **88**

FLEUR CRAVIGNAC, CHÂTEAU LA

St.-Emilion 1990: Ripe and concentrated, but overall it's simple and clumsy. Drink up. 2,000 cases made. • $18 • (08/31/95) • **76**

FLEUR DE GAY, CHÂTEAU LA

Pomerol 1997: Straightforward berry and cherry aromas and flavors. Medium-bodied, with delicate tannins. • $NA • (06/15/98) (BT) • **85-89**

Pomerol 1996: Good, ripe berry character with a hint of herbs, but it lacks concentration in the midpalate. Medium body, medium tannins and short finish. Not as good as hoped. • $NA • (01/01/97) (BT) • **85-89**

Pomerol 1995: Plenty of ripe fruit in this delicious red. Ripe berry, cherry and wet earth character. Full-bodied and chewy, with berry, vanilla and dark chocolate on the aftertaste. Best after 2000. • $80 • (01/31/98) • **90**

Pomerol 1994: Interesting, meaty, berry, fruity aromas and smoky, berry flavors, with medium tannins. Darned good, if not quite up to this estate's usual standard. Tasted twice, with consistent notes. Drinkable now. 1,250 cases made. • $38 Ⓐ • (01/31/97) • **88**

Pomerol 1993: An amazing '93. Gorgeous, full-bodied Pomerol of great intensity and harmony, bursting with pure fruit—from well-tuned, toasty flavors to mocha, blackberry, black olive, truffle and plum notes. A brilliant, seamless finish. Drinkable now but will age very well. 2,500 cases made. • $50 • (01/31/96) CS • **94**

Pomerol 1992: Impressive blackberry, tobacco and toasty oak aromas and flavors. Medium-bodied and rather chewy, offering medium, velvety tannins and a fruity, vanilla finish. • $40 • (04/15/95) • **85**

Pomerol 1991: Delicious and opulent, with toasty oak, plum and chocolate character, medium body and a long, velvety, flavorful finish. • $40 • (03/31/94) • **85**

Pomerol 1990: A brooding monster of a wine with great concentration of ripe fruit and fine tannins. The finish goes on and on. Drinkable now. 2,000 cases made. • $100 • (03/31/93) • **95**

Pomerol 1989 • $139 Ⓐ • (03/15/92) • **98**

Pomerol 1988 • $86 Ⓐ • (06/30/91) HR • **94**

Pomerol 1986 • $96 Ⓐ • (10/31/89) CS • **95**

Pomerol 1985 • $88 Ⓐ • (10/15/94) • **92**

Pomerol 1983 • $49 Ⓐ • (10/15/94) • **89**

Pomerol 1982 • $81 Ⓐ • (05/15/89) • **88**

FLEUR LARTIGUE, CHÂTEAU

St.-Emilion 1995: Rather light for a '95 St.-Emilion. Decent berry and tobacco character, but a slightly dry and diluted finish. Drink now. 3,000 cases made. • $20 • (01/31/98) • **78**

FOILLARD, JEAN

Morgon Côte du Py 1995: Morgon at its most expressive tastes like this: rich and ripe, round and deep, with layers of tobacco, spice and game flavors under the typical plum and licorice notes. Tannins are ripe and well integrated, the finish long and clean. Drinkable now. • $23 • (09/15/97) • **89**

Morgon Côte du Py 1994: This rich wine shows uncommon depth and complexity. Ripe, dark notes of coffee and chocolate swirl through the cassis and plum flavors, which turn exotic and spicy on the long finish. A big wine that's drinking well now. • $19 • (09/15/96) • **90**

FOLLIN-ARBELET, FRANCK

Aloxe-Corton Clos du Chapitre 1995: Light and fruity, with strawberry, cherry and licorice aromas and flavors. Light- to medium-bodied; the finish is slightly diluted and the tannins are drying. • $NA • (11/15/97) • **76**

Aloxe-Corton Les Vercots 1995: Light in color and body, with neutral flavors and an astringent finish. More like water than wine. • $NA • (11/15/97) • **70**

Key: SS—Spectator Selection CS—Cellar Selection HR—Highly Recommended BB—Best Buy $NA—Price not available Ⓐ—Auction Price (BT)—Barrel Tasting
Dates in parentheses indicate the issues in which the ratings were published.

FOMBRAUGE, CHÂTEAU

St.-Emilion 1994: This red starts off soft and friendly, with berry and licorice flavors, then turns tannic and harsh on the finish. May open with time, but it's a tough customer now. • $19 • (06/30/97) • **84**

St.-Emilion 1990: Round and spicy, with lots of earthy, gamy flavors that rob the wine of any charm or fruit. • $20 • (02/28/94) • **74**

St.-Emilion 1988 • $14 Ⓐ • (11/30/92) • **85**

St.-Emilion 1986 • $19 • (06/30/89) • **86**

St.-Emilion 1985 • $25 • (05/15/88) • **87**

FONBADET, CHÂTEAU

Pauillac 1995: Quite woody, offering medium-intense fruit flavors that seem for now to be dominated by oak. A bit dry on the finish. • $NA • (05/15/96) (BT) • **80-84**

Pauillac 1988 • $16 • (08/31/91) • **89**

Pauillac 1982 • $16 • (08/01/85) • **86**

FONNÉ, DOMAINE

Gewürztraminer Alsace Vogelgarten 1995: This tangy wine offers rich spice and bread dough aromas, flavors of orange peel and honey and a spicy finish. Delicious now, but amply concentrated for aging. • $NA • (09/30/96) • **89**

Pinot Blanc Alsace Vignoble de Bennwihr 1995: Concentrated and well balanced, this richly textured wine hints of lemon custard, creamy yet crisp, with a long finish of banana and pineapple. Well made and food-worthy. • $NA • (09/30/96) • **88**

Riesling Alsace Vignoble de Bennwihr 1995: Vibrant and flavorful, this light white is packed with grapefruit, mineral and peach flavors. A lively wine that should sing with food. • $NA • (10/15/96) • **85**

Tokay Pinot Gris Alsace 1995: Almond, melon and light coconut flavors channel through this juicy, ripe wine. Shows a nice balance of fruity sweetness and refreshing acidity. Drink now. • $NA • (09/30/96) • **87**

FONPLÉGADE, CHÂTEAU

St.-Emilion 1997: Slightly lean, with berry and cherry character, but rather light and hard on the finish. • $NA • (06/15/98) (BT) • **75-79**

St.-Emilion 1996: A silky wine, with fine tannins and a medium body. Slightly one-dimensional, but well made. 23,300 cases made. • $26 • (06/15/98) (BT) • **85-89**

St.-Emilion 1995: An abundance of berry, tobacco and cherry aromas and flavors. Medium- to full-bodied, with velvety tannins and a long, fruity chocolate aftertaste. Delicious now or hold. 6,000 cases made. • $24 • (01/31/98) • **88**

St.-Emilion 1992: Lean cherry, herbal character, medium to light in body and hard, metallic tannins. • $16 • (04/15/95) • **77**

St.-Emilion 1990: Rich and chunky, with loads of smoky, tobacco, sweet fruit character, soft tannins and a luscious cedar finish. Drinkable now. 7,500 cases made. • $25 • (03/31/93) • **90**

St.-Emilion 1988 • $18 • (06/30/91) • **85**

St.-Emilion 1982 • $NA • (05/15/89) • **77**

St.-Emilion 1961 • $NA • (04/30/96) • **86**

FONRÉAUD, CHÂTEAU

Listrac 1992: Pleasant plum and green bean flavors, light body and finish. • $15 • (04/15/95) • **76**

Listrac 1990: A no-frills wine, with focused tar and berry character and solid tannins. Drinkable now. 20,500 cases made. • $16 • (03/31/93) • **83**

Listrac 1988 • $15 • (04/30/91) • **82**

FONROQUE, CHÂTEAU

St.-Emilion 1997: Light and fruity, with fine tannins and a berry and cherry aftertaste. • $NA • (06/15/98) (BT) • **80-84**

St.-Emilion 1996: Some pretty berry and chocolate aromas, but the palate is lacking in fruit. Medium-bodied, with medium, firm tannins and a light finish. • $NA • (01/01/97) (BT) • **80-84**

St.-Emilion 1995: Racy berry, cherry and vanilla aromas and flavors, full body, fine tannins and a long, long finish. Impressive. Nearly outstanding. • $NA • (05/15/96) (BT) • **85-89**

St.-Emilion 1993: Pretty chocolate and berry character, medium to light in body and soft, silky tannins. Drinkable now. • $19 • (01/31/96) • **83**

St.-Emilion 1992: Fresh and crisp, more like a decent Loire red. Light-bodied; cherry, earth character. • $16 • (04/15/95) • **78**

St.-Emilion 1990: A real sleeper. Huge, with tons of tobacco, floral and berry character. It's thick yet agile, with very silky tannins and a long finish. Drinkable now. 6,500 cases made. • $28 • (03/31/93) • **94**

St.-Emilion 1989 • $24 • (03/15/92) • **88**

St.-Emilion 1982 • $6 Ⓐ • (08/31/92) • **89**

FONSALETTE, CHÂTEAU DE

Côtes du Rhône Réservé 1994: This solid red emits dark aromas of game and tar that follow through on the palate, along with black cherry and herbal notes, backed by muscular tannins. Drinkable now. • $25 • (10/15/97) • **86**

FONT D'ESTÉVENAS, LA

Côtes du Rhône-Villages Cairanne 1995: Nicely done, showing more harmony than some '95s in this category; medium-bodied, it delivers delicious ripe, sweet tannins and red berry and spice flavors. Turns a bit crisp on the finish, which is a bit short. Drink now. • $NA • (10/15/97) • **85**

Côtes du Rhône-Villages White Cairanne 1995: Thick, ripe and full-bodied, offering some honey-butter notes that, unfortunately, turn a bit tart on the finish. Fat style, but lacks elegance. • $NA • (10/15/97) • **76**

FONT DE MICHELLE, DOMAINE

Châteauneuf-du-Pape 1990: Tight and focused, with appealing black cherry and toast aromas and flavors, shaded by black pepper and bitter chocolate notes that persist on the finish. Try now. 2,000 cases made. • $17 • (04/15/93) • **82**

Châteauneuf-du-Pape 1989 • $18 • (10/15/91) • **83**

Châteauneuf-du-Pape 1988 • $21 • (10/15/91) • **86**

Châteauneuf-du-Pape 1986 • $20 • (10/15/91) • **89**

Châteauneuf-du-Pape 1985 • $20 • (10/15/91) • **84**

Châteauneuf-du-Pape 1983 • $25 • (10/15/91) • **85**

Châteauneuf-du-Pape 1981 • $20 • (10/15/91) • **88**

FONT DU LOUP, CHÂTEAU DE LA

Châteauneuf-du-Pape 1989 • $50 • (04/15/93) • **87**

FONT VILLAC

St.-Emilion 1989 • $14 • (11/30/92) • **81**

FONT-SANE, DOMAINE DE

Côtes du Ventoux 1990 • $8 • (04/15/93) • **80**

Gigondas 1990 • $15 • (04/15/93) • **82**

Gigondas 1985 • $13 • (01/31/89) • **86**

FONTAINE, CHÂTEAU LA

Fronsac 1993: A robust wine that combines good structure with plenty of flesh and spicy fruit. The finish is lingering. Drink now. 4,000 cases made. • $9 • (08/31/95) • **85**

FONTAINE-GAGNARD

Bâtard-Montrachet 1996: Vibrant and fresh, offering plenty of floral, lime and honey notes, it turns extremely silky and minerally on the palate, giving it an opulent mouthfeel. Full-bodied, with judiciously toasty oak accents, this is a showy wine with a long, succulent finish. Probably will deserve a higher score when it peaks around 2005 to 2010. 130 cases made. • $148 • (05/31/98) • **91**

Bâtard-Montrachet 1994: Fresh and lively, with fig, citrus, mineral, toast aromas and flavors. Focused and smooth on the finish. 141 cases made. • $90 • (05/31/96) • **86**

Bourgogne 1995: Lean, mean and astringent, with herbal flavors and very little fruit. Tough, dry finish. 316 cases made. • $10 • (11/15/97) • **70**

Bourgogne 1993: Nice concentration, offering currant, violet, mineral and wet earth flavors that make your palate pay attention. Long, well-balanced finish. Delicious now. • $14 • (11/15/95) • **88**

Chassagne-Montrachet Caillerets 1996: Subtle but pretty Chassagne, with a core of ripe pear, tropical and honey notes. Full-bodied, lush in texture, it has a minerally, silky mouthfeel that is superattractive. Crisp yet balanced finish. Try around 2002. 290 cases made. • $60 • (05/31/98) • **90**

Chassagne-Montrachet Caillerets 1994: This medium-bodied wine shows some tart, apple-cider flavors along with notes of dried herbs. Tasted twice, with consistent notes. 200 cases made. • $46 • (05/31/96) • **79**

Chassagne-Montrachet Clos St.-Jean Clos Les Murées 1996: Well made, finely tuned *premier cru*, showing a distinct malic, milky aroma but turning attractively complex, with toasty bread, lime, pear, dough and honey flavors that sail over the palate to a long, harmonious, silky finish. Better after 2002. 208 cases made. • $60 • (05/31/98) • **90**

Chassagne-Montrachet Clos St.-Jean Red 1995: Offers lovely cherry and wet earth flavors and enough flesh to stand up to the crisp acidity and tannins, with exotic oak adding complexity. It's long and well made. 95 cases made. • $36 • (11/15/97) • **85**

Chassagne-Montrachet Clos St.-Jean Red 1994: Light and simple, with a candied character of cherry and vanilla. Supple and ready to drink. • $36 • (11/15/96) • **78**

Chassagne-Montrachet Clos St.-Jean Red 1992: A lot of wine in a small frame, but it needs time for the ripe blackberry and anise flavors to poke through the fine tannins. Drinkable now. • $32 • (12/15/94) • **85**

Chassagne-Montrachet La Boudriotte 1996: Racy but a bit green, offering some green apples, dried herbs and freshly cut grass but also a minerally midpalate silkiness. Of medium body, steely and crisp, it turns a bit bitter on the finish. A vineyard site with a good track record for improving with age. Try after 1999. 325 cases made. • $60 • (05/31/98) • **84**

Chassagne-Montrachet La Boudriotte 1994: Attractively supple and relatively ripe, with a lovely honey, pear, piecrust, lemon and mineral character. Medium to full in body, it lacks intensity, but it's lush and silky on the finish. 308 cases made. • $46 • (05/31/96) • **86**

Chassagne-Montrachet La Grande Montagne 1994: Hard, lemony and tough to taste now, this *premier cru* shows little opulence. Well structured, with lots of lime, dried herb and mineral notes. A bit harsh on the finish. Drinkable now. 125 cases made. • $46 • (05/31/96) • **84**

Chassagne-Montrachet La Maltroie 1996: Tight and crisp but full in body, it has a compact, ripe fruit character and good concentration, with lots of mineral notes that bode well for the future. Intense and citrusy on the succulent, somewhat tart finish. Hold until about 2005. 240 cases made. • $60 • (05/31/98) • **89**

Chassagne-Montrachet La Maltroie 1994: You can taste the full Burgundian treatment in this. Fairly rich, with a chewy character and lots of toasty oak notes. Nicely balanced, with tropical fruit and lemon flavors on the finish. Enjoy now. 308 cases made. • $46 • (05/31/96) • **85**

Chassagne-Montrachet Les Chenevottes 1996: Vibrant and flavorful, medium to full in body, with a lush, ripe, even charming patina of toasty oak, pear, tropical and lemon-honey pie character. Sparkles with flavors on the juicy, succulent finish. Not very concentrated, so try in 1999 to 2002. 30 cases made. • $60 • (05/31/98) • **87**

Chassagne-Montrachet Les Chenevottes 1994: A distinctive white, both ripe and a bit tough, showing some pear, citrus and onion peel flavors. Full-bodied, with a vegetal, honeyed character on the rather intense finish. Try now. 30 cases made. • $46 • (05/31/96) • **84**

Chassagne-Montrachet Les Vergers 1996: Racy, clean and pure *premier cru* but also quite tart and crisp, it delivers knife-sharp green apple, earth, spice, lime, herb and toasty oak flavors. Medium-bodied, with supple mineral and honey notes that suggest it will soften with cellaring until around 2003. 208 cases made. • $60 • (05/31/98) • **86**

Chassagne-Montrachet Les Vergers 1994: Supple, round and distinctively appley, a focused but rather simple Chardonnay with a hint of mineral character on the crisp finish. 191 cases made. • $46 • (05/31/96) • **83**

Chassagne-Montrachet Morgeot 1996: This harmonious, full-bodied Chassagne is both ripe and racy, offering delightful honey, spice and succulent fruit flavors in a balanced package. Subtle yet flavorful finish. Try after 2003. 125 cases made. • $60 • (05/31/98) • **89**

Chassagne-Montrachet Morgeot 1994: Soft and supple, with a touch of honey and lime, this full-bodied but somewhat one-dimensional Chardonnay should be drunk now. 116 cases made. • $46 • (05/31/96) • **82**

Chassagne-Montrachet Morgeot Red 1995: Lovely, spicy black cherry aromas and flavors in this silky, light-textured red. Should come together in 2000. 158 cases made. • $36 • (11/15/97) • **87**

Chassagne-Montrachet Morgeot Red 1994: Easy to drink, light and supple, with a mingling of vanilla and cherry flavors, slightly earthy and herbal. Drink upon release. • $36 • (11/15/96) • **79**

Chassagne-Montrachet Morgeot Red 1993: A beauty from start to finish. Dishes out the pure, concentrated fruit flavors in buckets. Cassis, black cherry and earth aromas are amazing. Silky texture. Delicious now, but can hold for years. • $27 • (11/15/95) • **89**

Chassagne-Montrachet Red 1995: Shows modest berry flavors and herbaceous notes. This is light-bodied and straightforward, with a drying, astringent finish. 508 cases made. • $28 • (11/15/97) • **73**

Chassagne-Montrachet Red 1993: A big, burly, dark-colored, solid red Burgundy, offering medium tannins and smoky, earthy blackberry flavors. Impressive. Try now. • $23 • (11/15/95) • **87**

Chassagne-Montrachet Red 1985 • $16 • (12/31/88) • **85**

Chassagne-Montrachet White 1996: Crisp and medium-bodied Chassagne, lacking in charm but offering plenty of fresh, vibrant citrus and green apple flavors, with a fairly intense finish. Better after 1999. 500 cases made. • $51 • (05/31/98) • **84**

Chassagne-Montrachet White 1994: Simple and crisp, with apple cider flavors and a slightly green, astringent character. 550 cases made. • $40 • (05/31/96) • **74**

Criots-Bâtard-Montrachet 1996: This medium-bodied wine tastes sweet and wonderfully ripe, with lovely lime, honey, pineapple and ripe pear. Fabulous mineral character on the midpalate, but the finish is quite hot and burning with toasty oak. Very intense and concentrated. It may grow into a harmonious beauty; hold until 2005. 155 cases made. • $148 • (05/31/98) • **93**

Criots-Bâtard-Montrachet 1994: Very rich, thick and ripe, tasting of apricot, peach and ripe pear and oozing with honey character. Full-bodied and coats your mouth, but has a supple finish. Distinctive and delicious now. 166 cases made. • $90 • (05/31/96) • **88**

Montrachet 1996: Intense and compacted, hard to judge because it's closed and so woody, but offering layers of exotic Oriental spices and toasty oak, with a floral, violet and licorice character. Concentration is impressive in this full-bodied, very long wine, which almost burns the palate from all that intensity, especially on the hot-fuse kind of finish. Hold until around 2010. 37 cases made. • $336 • (05/31/98) • **93**

Pommard Les Rugiens 1995: Huge nose of sweet, ripe plum and spicy oak, a hint of barnyard, too. Though the tannins are mouthcoating, it's impressive and ambitious. 100 cases made. • $60 • (11/15/97) • **87**

Pommard Les Rugiens 1994: Tough, tannic and ungenerous with its barely discernable cherry flavors. Finishing mostly with stalky notes. • $56 • (11/15/96) • **77**

Volnay Clos des Chênes 1995: A weak, dry and astringent wine with a mouthpuckering finish. 183 cases made. • $60 • (11/15/97) • **76**

Volnay Clos des Chênes 1994: Lean, firm and chewy, showing a narrow beam of leafy berry flavors. Try in 1999. • $56 • (11/15/96) • **81**

Volnay Clos des Chênes 1993: Sleek and racy, sporting a solid core of fruit and steely tannins. Smoky, earthy character. Medium in body and tannins, with a fresh finish. This needs some cellaring; try in 2000. • $43 • (11/15/95) • **90**

Volnay Clos des Chênes 1992: A little more dense than most, with slightly gamy blackberry and currant flavors that persist on the solid finish. Drinkable now. • $48 • (12/15/94) • **85**

FONTAINE ST.-MARTIN, CHÂTEAU LA

Graves White 1995: A bit heavy and almost sweet, with floral aromas and flavors. Serviceable, but somewhat blunt. 5,000 cases made. • $10 • (04/30/97) • **78**

FONTANCHE, CHÂTEAU DE

St.-Chinian Cuvée Grand Veneur 1990 • $7 • (07/15/92) BB • **81**

FONTANELLES, DOMAINE DES

Merlot Vin de Pays d'Oc 1995: A rustic style with good cherry and berry flavors, but it's a bit dried out in the middle. • $7 • (11/15/97) • **80**

Merlot Vin de Pays d'Oc 1993: Modest black currant notes and some weedy elements and good depth add up to a flavorful quaff. • $7 • (07/31/96) • **83**

Sauvignon Blanc Vin de Pays d'Oc 1996: An attractive white wine, fresh, fruity and lively in texture, with vivid citrus and herb flavors. 2,500 cases made. • $8 • (05/31/97) • **85**

Shiraz-Syrah Vin de Pays d'Oc 1995: Heavy vanilla aromas and flavors dominate the modest fruit character, leaving the impression of a disjointed wine. • $8 • (12/15/97) • **77**

Shiraz-Syrah Vin de Pays d'Oc 1993: Very fruity, as grape, blueberry and cherry flavors end on a tannic, drying finish. Awkward. 4,000 cases made. • $7 • (07/31/96) • **77**

FONTENAY, HENRY DE

Sancerre Les Roysiers 1995: A smoky note adds interest to this round, herbal-scented white, while citrus and apple flavors keep it true to the varietal. It's lively yet not too sharp. 2,900 cases made. • $10 • (06/15/97) • **88**

FONTENIL, CHÂTEAU

Fronsac 1997: Dark violet in color, with floral and currant aromas. Medium-bodied, with medium tannins and a velvety finish. Pretty, unctuous wine. • $NA • (06/15/98) (BT) • **85-89**

Fronsac 1996: Pretty, cool red fruit aromas and flavors. Medium-bodied, with firm yet silky tannins and a slightly green character on the finish. • $18 • (06/15/98) (BT) • **85-89**

Fronsac 1995: Delicious, seductive wine. Gorgeous spicy, fruity and sweet aromas, with a hint of cinnamon. Medium to full in body, with lovely, silky tannins and a long, spicy, fruity finish. Drink now or hold. 3,500 cases made. • $15 • (01/31/98) • **90**

Fronsac 1994: Medium-bodied, with some impressive berry, chocolate and vanilla aromas and flavors, slightly diluted in the midpalate. Drink now. • $18 • (01/31/97) • **84**

Fronsac 1993: A bit rustic in style, offering some pretty ripe berry and raspberry aromas and flavors. Medium to light body, velvety tannins and a light finish. Drinkable now. 4,083 cases made. • $12 • (01/31/96) • **83**

Fronsac 1990: A classy red showing great winemaking. Fills your mouth with plum and black cherry flavors and silky tannins. From Michel Rolland. Drinkable now. 3,500 cases made. • $17 • (03/31/93) • **91**

Fronsac 1986 • $14 • (02/15/90) • **76**

Fronsac 1985 • $14 • (09/30/88) • **87**

FONTENILLE, CHÂTEAU DE

Bordeaux 1993: Spice and plum aromas lead to herbal-tinged berry flavors, all wrapped up in a concentrated yet balanced presentation. Drinkable now. • $10 • (08/31/95) • **84**

FONTJUN, DOMAINE DU

St.-Chinian 1990 • $5 • (07/15/92) • **76**

FONTSAINTE, DOMAINE DE

Corbières 1990 • $7 • (03/15/94) • **82**

Corbières Réserve la Demoiselle 1994: Nicely concentrated, with some good plum, cherry and tobacco flavors. Finishes with a good dose of spice and gamelike flavors. Distinctive and fairly rich. • $10 • (06/15/97) • **84**

Corbières Réserve la Demoiselle 1990 • $10 • (03/15/94) • **85**

Corbières Réserve la Demoiselle 1986 • $7 • (08/31/89) • **77**

Corbières Réserve la Demoiselle 1984 • $8 • (10/31/87) • **83**

FOREAU

Vouvray Demi-Sec 1995: Smoky, toasty notes add interest to this round yet firm white. Shows a nice balance of light sweetness and lively acidity, with pineapple and herb flavors. 100 cases made. • $23 • (05/15/97) • **87**

Vouvray Demi-Sec Domaine du Clos Naudin 1993 • $18 • (04/30/96) • **85**

Vouvray Moelleux 1995: Opulent aromas of dried peach and hazelnut give way to full-bodied flavors of ripe fruit, toast and spice in this voluptuous wine. Has enough acidity to stay lively. Should develop well. 200 cases made. • $38 • (05/15/97) • **89**

Vouvray Moelleux Réserve 1995: A blockbuster white from the Loire, this wine is rich and opulent, with extremely ripe aromas of dried fruit, nuts and toast; thick on the palate, with flavors of raisins, minerals, spice and

Key: SS—Spectator Selection CS—Cellar Selection HR—Highly Recommended BB—Best Buy $NA—Price not available Ⓐ—Auction Price (BT)—Barrel Tasting
Dates in parentheses indicate the issues in which the ratings were published.

toast. Quite sweet yet beautifully balanced, it's delicious now, but will improve as it ages; the older the better. 530 cases made. • $60 • (05/15/97) HR • **95**

Vouvray Sec Domaine du Clos Naudin 1994 • $16 • (04/30/96) • **81**

Vouvray Sec Domaine du Clos Naudin 1993 • $16 • (04/30/96) • **82**

FORÊT, CHÂTEAU LA

Sauternes 1991: Ripe, with pear and hazelnut flavors, this Sauternes is smooth and balanced, picking up honey and white chocolate flavors on the finish. 5,000 cases made. • $14 • (08/31/97) • **86**

FOREY PÈRE & FILS

Bourgogne 1993: Quite chewy at this stage, with decent fruit flavors. Square and tough, it turns a little dry on the one-dimensional finish. • $12 • (11/15/95) • **79**

Echézeaux 1994: Ripe and generous. An elegant wine layered with aromas and flavors of rose petal, currant, berry and violet. Velvety and graceful right through the well-defined finish. Try to keep hands off until 2001. • $60 • (11/15/96) • **92**

Echézeaux 1993: A super *grand cru* boasting loads of raspberry, plum and smoke character, medium-to-full body, fine tannins and a lovely, fruity finish. Better in 2000. • $45 • (11/15/95) • **91**

Echézeaux 1990: A rich, ripe, well-structured wine that's seductive, refined and powerful. Packs in concentrated raspberry, earth and smoke aromas and flavors that echo on the long finish. Drink now. 121 cases made. • $65 • (12/15/92) • **92**

Echézeaux 1989 • $NA • (01/31/92) • **90**

Nuits-St.-Georges 1994: Marked by chewy tannins that feel tough and taste bitter. • $28 • (11/15/96) • **78**

Nuits-St.-Georges 1993: Straightforward Pinot, showing light, modest structure and some decent licorice and black cherry flavors. A bit diluted on the finish. • $24 • (11/15/95) • **82**

Nuits-St.-Georges Les Perrières 1994: Earthy, gamy flavors intrude on the almost jammy berry flavors, but it finishes with an intriguing mix of the flavors. Tannins need until 1999 or 2000. • $36 • (11/15/96) • **82**

Nuits-St.-Georges Les Perrières 1993: Very firm and not giving much. Medium-bodied, sporting solid tannins and a long spicy, plummy finish. Needs time; try in 1999. • $33 • (11/15/95) • **85**

Nuits-St.-Georges Les Perrières 1990: A mellow Nuits, with attractive cherry, berry and chestnut aromas and flavors and medium tannins. Drinkable now. 162 cases made. • $40 • (12/15/92) • **79**

Nuits-St.-Georges Les Perrières 1989 • $NA • (01/31/92) • **89**

Nuits-St.-Georges Les Saint Georges 1994: Offers pure ripe currant and plum flavors with attractive mineral and leather shadings. Fine tannins are balanced for elegance. Drink now. • $40 • (11/15/96) • **87**

Vosne-Romanée 1994: This is light, and a bit crisp from tannins, but sings a nice little song of strawberry and raspberry flavors. Ready to drink. • $30 • (11/15/96) • **84**

Vosne-Romanée 1993: Wonderfully aromatic violets and plums follow through on the palate. Medium- to full-bodied, adding fine tannins and a fresh finish. Better in 2000. • $26 • (11/15/95) • **88**

Vosne-Romanée 1990: Quite straightforward, with game, strawberry and earth aromas and flavors, medium body and firm tannins. Drinkable now. 460 cases made. • $30 • (12/15/92) • **85**

Vosne-Romanée 1989 • $NA • (01/31/92) • **85**

Vosne-Romanée Les Gaudichots 1994: First impression is of coarse, drying tannins, but the pretty berry flavors are juicy enough to fight 'em to a draw. Try in 1999. • $NA • (11/15/96) • **85**

Vosne-Romanée Les Gaudichots 1993: Beautiful, well-defined fruit sets this one on fire, boasting lovely, ripe currant and black cherry character. Smoothly structured, it envelops the palate in seductive flavors. Tempting now; better after 2000. • $45 • (11/15/95) • **92**

FORGE, LA

Côtes du Lubéron 1989 • $7 • (11/15/91) • **79**

Morey-St.-Denis Premier Cru 1994: Tightly wound, medium-bodied, with loads of mocha, spice and oak flavors that are underscored by a good amount of ripe fruit flavor, leading to a supple finish. From Clos du Tart. • $NA • (11/15/96) • **84**

FORTANT DE FRANCE

Cabernet Sauvignon Vin de Pays d'Oc 1994: More reminiscent of Syrah, offering meaty, black cherry flavors and a tannic structure. Try now. • $7 • (07/31/96) • **79**

Cabernet Sauvignon Vin de Pays d'Oc 1993 • $7 • (02/28/95) • **83**

Cabernet Sauvignon Vin de Pays d'Oc Collection 1993: A woody, resinous note permeates this wine, making it difficult for the berry flavors to surface. If you like wood, this one's for you. • $11 • (12/15/96) • **78**

Chardonnay Vin de Pays d'Oc 1994 • $8 • (12/15/95) • **84**

Merlot Rosé Vin de Pays d'Oc 1994 • $7 • (09/30/95) • **78**

Merlot Vin de Pays d'Oc 1996: A tart wine, with only modest herbal flavors and a cloying quality. Kosher. • $NA • (03/31/98) • **77**

Merlot Vin de Pays d'Oc 1995: A firm French varietal red, with well-focused cherry and plum flavors and a dash of vanilla. It also has a nice, polished texture and a pleasant finish, making this a good value. 75,000 cases made. • $7 • (12/15/96) BB • **86**

Merlot Vin de Pays d'Oc 1994 • $7 • (10/31/95) • **83**

Merlot Vin de Pays d'Oc 1993 • $7 • (02/28/95) • **79**

Merlot Vin de Pays d'Oc Collection 1993: A fairly rich and nicely mature wine, with a solid core of ripe cherry and plum flavors and a pleasant herbal quality. Well structured. A good, spicy note marks the finish. • $11 • (12/15/96) • **85**

Sauvignon Blanc Vin de Pays d'Oc 1994 • $7 • (02/29/96) • **78**

Syrah Rosé Vin de Pays d'Oc 1994 • $7 • (09/30/95) • **80**

Syrah Rosé Vin de Pays d'Oc 1993 • $7 • (01/01/95) • **75**

FORTIA, CHÂTEAU

Châteauneuf-du-Pape 1989: Softening now, but still dense and dark, with coffee, prune and black pepper flavors that are rich and firm on the palate. A mature wine in the traditional style. • $20 • (11/15/96) • **86**

Châteauneuf-du-Pape 1988 • $22 • (06/15/93) • **78**

Châteauneuf-du-Pape 1985 • $22 • (05/31/92) • **81**

Châteauneuf-du-Pape 1983 • $14 • (12/31/87) • **87**

FORTNUM & MASON

Charmes-Chambertin English Bottling 1947 • $NA • (08/31/90) • **94**

FORTS DE LATOUR, LES

Pauillac 1997: Surprisingly soft and approachable, with delicious berry and chocolate character and a long, ripe fruit aftertaste. • $NA • (06/15/98) (BT) • **85-89**

Pauillac 1996: For a second wine, this is "the" wine of the vintage in this category. Full-bodied, with velvety tannins and a long, flavorful currant and berry finish. Gorgeous. • $50 • (06/15/98) (BT) • **90-94**

Pauillac 1995: A solid, well-built '95. Lovely chocolate, berry and tobacco aromas, with a hint of vanilla. Full-bodied, with velvety tannins and a long, flavorful finish. The best second label of Pauillac? Well, it is from Château Latour. Best after 2001. • $43 Ⓐ • (01/31/98) • **91**

Pauillac 1994: Plentiful plum and strawberry aromas and flavors mark this medium-bodied wine. Short on the finish. Drink now. • $39 Ⓐ • (01/31/97) • **82**

Pauillac 1993: Some good berry and cherry character, but rather lean and slightly hard with firm tannins. Try now. • $23 Ⓐ • (01/31/96) • **83**

Pauillac 1992: Pretty minty, berry, mineral character; medium-bodied, fine tannins and fresh finish. • $22 • (04/15/95) • **80**

Pauillac 1991: Simple and straightforward. The fruit is dominated by cherry; a light, slightly green finish. Second label of Latour. • $23 • (03/31/94) • **78**

Pauillac 1990: Draws you into the glass with enticing plum, blackberry, vanilla and coconut aromas and flavors. Full-bodied yet balanced, with an abundance of soft tannins, but not aggressive. Drinkable in 2000. • $75 • (03/31/93) • **94**

Pauillac 1989 • $42 Ⓐ • (03/15/92) • **91**

Pauillac 1985 • $54 • (08/31/91) • **87**

Pauillac 1983 • $29 Ⓐ • (10/15/90) • **85**

Pauillac 1982 • $87 Ⓐ • (08/31/92) • **93**

Pauillac 1979 • $14 Ⓐ • (10/15/89) • **87**

FORTUNE, DOMAINE

Beaujolais-Villages 1994 • $9 • (10/31/95) • **84**

FOUASSIER PÈRE & FILS

Sancerre Clos Paradis 1996: Unusual for the region but appealing, with soft, ripe flavors of apples, melon and even coconut. Silky, with just enough acidity to keep it balanced and lively with food. Drink now. 2,000 cases made. • $22 • (06/15/98) • **85**

Sancerre Les Romains 1996: Good intensity marks this firm, nervy white. Lively flavors of grapefruit and herbs are vivid and well defined, yet it's not tart, with hints of strawberry and pear on the long finish. Drink now through 1999. 1,500 cases made. • $20 • (06/15/98) • **87**

FOUGERAY, DOMAINE

Bonnes Mares 1991: Ripe in flavor and chewy in texture, a supple wine with concentrated black cherry and slightly gamy aromas and flavors. Nicely formed, if a bit shy on muscle or richness. An appealing wine; drinkable now. • $NA • (01/31/94) • **87**

Gevrey-Chambertin Les Leuvrées 1995: Diluted and light-colored, this offers just a whiff of red berries and a dry, astringent finish. • $26 • (11/15/97) • **73**

Marsannay St.-Jacques Red 1991: Tough in texture and light; the plummy flavors never quite get off the ground. Try now. • $NA • (01/31/94) • **77**

FOUGERAY DE BEAUCLAIR

Bonnes Mares 1995: Despite the new oak accents, there's an herbaceous element to this wine's aromas and flavors, along with astringent tannins. • $85 • (11/15/97) • **82**

Bonnes Mares 1994: Hard and chewy, but with enough berry freshness to battle the tannins and make this worth cellaring until 2000 to 2003 to see what develops. • $90 • (11/15/96) • **88**

Chambolle-Musigny 1995: Toasty oak dominates the modest cherry flavors in this short, simple red. The finish is rough and tannic. • $26 • (11/15/97) • **80**

Côte de Nuits-Villages 1995: Displays pretty cherry and licorice flavors and moderate structure. Drinkable now. • $18 • (11/15/97) • **80**

Fixin Clos Marion 1995: Pure Pinot flavors of red cherry, with hints of earth and spicy oak; lean and solidly tannic. A bit rustic, but honest and forthright. Drinkable now. • $27 • (11/15/97) • **83**

Fixin Clos Marion 1994: Shows an ugly, moldy streak that stops it in its tracks. • $27 • (11/15/96) • **73**

Marsannay Le Dessus des Longeroies Red 1995: Seems advanced at this stage, with rhubarb and tomato notes and green tannins. • $19 • (11/15/97) • **74**

Marsannay Les Favières Red 1995: Juicy, yet light in color and body, this wine offers modest fruit and a slightly astringent finish. • $19 • (11/15/97) • **75**

Marsannay Les Grasses Têtes Red 1995: Light, rosé-colored, stemmy and diluted. • $19 • (11/15/97) • **70**

Marsannay St.-Jacques Red 1995: The color of rosé, it's weedy-tasting and -smelling. What happened? Drink at your own risk. • $26 • (11/15/97) • **70**

Savigny-lès-Beaune Les Golardes 1995: Very light, with candied raspberry and strawberry aromas and flavors and an astringent finish. • $20 • (11/15/97) • **76**

Vosne-Romanée Les Damaudes 1995: There are decent red cherry and licorice notes and a chewy texture to this wine, but it's a little sour and tough. • $28 • (11/15/97) • **77**

FOURCAS-DUPRÉ, CHÂTEAU

Listrac 1995: A fruity '95 with wet earth, mineral and cassis character. Good tannins; slightly steely on the finish. • $NA • (05/15/96) (BT) • **80-84**

Listrac 1992: Displays some earth and black cherry character and mineral nuances, but a very short finish. • $15 • (04/15/95) • **79**

Listrac 1991: Astringent and angular. Interesting cherry flavor, but short, fading out too quickly. • $15 • (03/31/94) • **74**

Listrac 1990: A traditional-style wine, with earthy, smoky character, round tannins and a smoky finish. Drinkable now. 22,000 cases made. • $17 • (03/31/93) • **82**

Listrac 1989 • $25 • (03/15/92) • **86**

Listrac 1988 • $22 • (04/30/91) • **83**

Listrac 1983 • $9 • (10/31/86) • **89**

Listrac 1982 • $NA • (08/31/92) • **79**

FOURCAS-HOSTEN, CHÂTEAU

Listrac 1995: Flavorful. Rich, ripe, grapey and full-bodied, tasting of crushed wild berries, black currants and grapes. Very pure and vivid and judiciously oaked. Supple tannins. Needs a touch more elegance to be outstanding. • $NA • (05/15/96) (BT) • **85-89**

Listrac 1994: Polished and harmonious, displaying coffee, black cherry and licorice flavors with firm, ripe tannins and a long, smoky finish. Drinkable now. • $19 • (10/15/97) • **85**

Listrac 1992: Very one-dimensional, offering berried, slightly alcoholic character, medium body, soft tannins and a light finish. • $15 • (04/15/95) • **76**

Listrac 1991: Stylish and lean, but just average. Has a fruity, slightly herbal character. • $15 • (03/31/94) • **79**

Listrac 1990: A tough wine with a compact fruit and tannin structure but some rich berry and cherry flavors underneath. Drinkable now. 20,000 cases made. • $20 • (03/31/93) • **85**

Listrac 1989 • $19 • (03/15/92) • **87**

Listrac 1988 • $13 • (07/15/91) • **82**

Listrac 1986 • $14 • (11/15/89) • **79**

Listrac 1983 • $16 • (10/15/86) • **83**

Listrac 1982 • $18 • (08/31/92) • **90**

Listrac 1961 • $26 • (04/30/96) • **81**

FOURCAS-LOUBANEY, CHÂTEAU

Listrac 1988 • $17 • (02/28/91) • **83**

FOURNAS-BERNADOTTE, CHÂTEAU

Haut-Médoc 1988 • $18 • (06/15/91) • **76**

FRANC-BIGAROUX, CHÂTEAU

St.-Emilion 1988 • $24 • (07/31/91) HR • **91**

FRANC-JAUGUE-BLANC, CHÂTEAU

St.-Emilion 1995: Displays attractive autumnal aromas, with blackberry and leafy character. Medium- to light-bodied, with sweet fruit and fine tannins but a slightly diluted finish. Drink now. 3,200 cases made. • $20 • (01/31/98) • **82**

FRANC-MAYNE, CHÂTEAU

St.-Emilion 1995: Rather austere berry and earth character. Medium in body, with firm tannins and a sharp finish. • $NA • (05/15/96) (BT) • **80-84**

St.-Emilion 1993: A no-nonsense '93 featuring cherry, light dried herb and berry aromas and flavors, medium body, medium to light tannins and a fresh finish. Drinkable now. • $20 • (01/31/96) • **81**

St.-Emilion 1992: Firm, decent fruit but rather austere and herbal, light- to medium-bodied, delivering green pepper and slightly metallic character. • $17 • (04/15/95) • **79**

St.-Emilion 1991: Pleasant black cherry and bitter chocolate aromas and flavors, medium body and a silky texture. • $15 • (03/31/94) • **82**

St.-Emilion 1990: A succulent wine, with rich berry and white pepper aromas and flavors, firm tannins and a long, polished finish. From Jean-Michel Cazes. Drink now. 2,700 cases made. • $23 • (03/31/93) • **91**

St.-Emilion 1989 • $28 • (03/15/92) • **94**

St.-Emilion 1988 • $15 • (07/15/91) • **83**

FRANCE, CHÂTEAU DE

Pessac-Léognan 1992: Attractive cherry and vanilla aromas and flavors, but rather diluted. • $13 • (04/15/95) • **76**

Pessac-Léognan 1991: A wine with nice clean berry, fruit and tree bark flavors. Light tannins and a rather short, dry finish. • $13 • (03/31/94) • **78**

Pessac-Léognan 1990: Not a big wine, but enjoyable. Delicate in style, with spicy, cherry, autumnal aromas and flavors and silky tannins. Drinkable now. 16,000 cases made. • $20 • (03/31/93) • **85**

Pessac-Léognan 1989 • $22 • (03/15/92) • **89**

Pessac-Léognan 1988 • $18 • (02/28/91) SS • **92**

Key: SS—Spectator Selection CS—Cellar Selection HR—Highly Recommended BB—Best Buy $NA—Price not available Ⓐ—Auction Price (BT)—Barrel Tasting

Dates in parentheses indicate the issues in which the ratings were published.

Graves 1982 • $NA • (08/31/92) • **79**
Pessac-Léognan White 1993 • $NA • (05/31/95) • **85**

FRANK PHÉLAN

St.-Estèphe 1995: A balanced and delicious red. Dried cherry and earth aromas. Medium in body, with fine tannins and a medium, dried cherry, berry aftertaste. The second label of Château Phélan-Segur. Drinkable now. • $14 • (01/31/98) • **85**

FREJAU, DOMAINE LOU

Châteauneuf-du-Pape 1988 • $17 • (03/31/91) • **82**
Châteauneuf-du-Pape 1986 • $16 • (01/31/89) • **87**

FREYNELLE, CHÂTEAU LA

Bordeaux 1995: Great value. A hearty, dark-colored Bordeaux with ripe fruit flavors that seem to expand on the finish and firm tannins. • $8 • (01/31/98) • **86**
Bordeaux Clairet Rosé 1996: A dry, well-balanced rosé with a crisp texture and just enough fruity-meaty flavor to keep it interesting. Drink now. • $8 • (02/28/98) • **84**
Bordeaux White 1996: A crisp and juicy white, with vivid citrus flavors and a tangy finish. Drink now. • $8 • (02/28/98) • **84**

FRICK, PIERRE

Riesling Alsace Lerchenberg 1994: Ripe, almost honeyed, aromas belie crisp acidity. Green apples and grapefruit flavors are fresh but light; the finish is a bit tart. 800 cases made. • $18 • (10/15/96) • **83**
Tokay Pinot Gris Alsace 1994: Powerful spice aromas give way to full-bodied flavors of pear and blanched almond, with coconut and herbal accents. Concentrated and well integrated, it should improve with age. 675 cases made. • $19 • (09/30/96) • **89**

FUISSÉ, CHÂTEAU

Pouilly-Fuissé 1996: Ripe and pretty, with lovely pear, piecrust, lime and mineral notes. A pure, clean, flavorful, medium-bodied Pouilly that is balanced from start to finish. Drink now through 2000. 6,600 cases made. • $32 • (05/31/98) • **88**
Pouilly-Fuissé 1995: Smooth and subtle, medium-bodied, delivering pleasant fruit and floral character, with a lot of toasty flavors that linger on the finish. Drinkable now. • $16 • (05/31/97) • **85**
Pouilly-Fuissé 1994: Light to medium in body, with modest fruit flavors. Rather smooth and approachable, though it lacks a bit of character and turns slightly herbal on the finish. • $NA • (05/31/96) • **78**
Pouilly-Fuissé Le Clos 1995: Crisp and lean, of light to medium in body, with citrus, grass and some mineral notes. Turns a bit too tart on the finish. Lacks the dimension expected from this vineyard. Drinkable now. • $37 • (05/31/97) • **85**
Pouilly-Fuissé Le Clos 1994: If you like them silky, this is your type. Well crafted, with lots of fig, pear and butter flavors; it seduces you with its remarkable harmony. Enjoy now. • $34 • (05/31/96) • **89**
Pouilly-Fuissé Les Brûlées 1995: Well crafted, polished and delicious, this subtle, medium-bodied Pouilly delivers ripe fruit, honey and spice flavors shaded judiciously by toasty oak. Drinkable on release, but has a track record for aging well. • $37 • (05/31/97) • **87**
Pouilly-Fuissé Les Combettes 1996: Very pretty, clean and pure, with floral, mandarin orange, pear, honeydew and melon flavors. A supple, medium-bodied, fairly silky white that is a delight to drink now. Not complex, but still lovely. Tasted twice, with consistent notes. 330 cases made. • $37 • (05/31/98) • **88**
Pouilly-Fuissé Les Combettes 1994: Fairly opulent, fresh and lively, yet also smooth, offering some floral, honey and ripe apple flavors. Good concentration, with an unctuous mouthfeel; mineral, rose petal and apricot notes come out on the long, harmonious finish. Drinkable now. • $34 • (05/31/96) • **89**
Pouilly-Fuissé Vieilles Vignes 1996: Polished yet ripe, this elegant Pouilly glides over the palate with lots of finesse, leaving behind a trail of lime, pear, mocha, spice and toasty bread flavors. Lingering finish. Drink now through 2000. 2,080 cases made. • $49 • (05/31/98) • **91**
Pouilly-Fuissé Vieilles Vignes 1995: A balanced, subtle, fresh Chardonnay, silky-textured and impressively minerally. Very young, it's more lean than opulent, and light- to medium-bodied, with hints of honey, pineapple, citrus and toasty bread to its character. Pleasant to drink now, but with its track record, better wait until about 1999. • $48 • (05/31/97) • **91**
Pouilly-Fuissé Vieilles Vignes 1994: What a beauty. A well-sculpted wine built for finesse, charming you with its layers of citrus, honey and floral notes. It pulsates with complexity, showing good depth on the long, lovely finish. Drinkable now. • $44 • (05/31/96) • **90**
St.-Véran 1995: Polished, yet intense in character, with wet soil, orange peel, tobacco and tea-leaf notes mingling with the apple, pear and citrus flavors of Chardonnay. Finishes harmoniously, with whiffs of honey and spice. Drinkable now. • $15 • (05/31/97) • **87**

FUSSIACUS

Pouilly-Fuissé Vieilles Vignes 1993: Intense but tart; light to medium in body, plenty of citrus, green apple flavors and a touch of mineral character. Turns somewhat astringent on the finish. Drinkable now. • $NA • (05/15/95) • **80**

GAFFELIÈRE, CHÂTEAU LA

St.-Emilion 1997: A simple and fruity '97, with berry and wet earth character. Medium-bodied, with medium, dry tannins and a short finish. • $NA • (06/15/98) (BT) • **80-84**
St.-Emilion 1996: Silky and fine, with medium body, medium tannins and a supple texture. • $55 • (06/15/98) (BT) • **85-89**
St.-Emilion 1995: Perfumed and opulent, with blackberry, vanilla and mushroom aromas. Full-bodied and intensely tannic, with a velvety texture and a long, succulent aftertaste. Slightly astringent. Better after 2000. • $37 • (01/31/98) • **89**
St.-Emilion 1988 • $38 • (04/30/91) • **84**
St.-Emilion 1982 • $30 Ⓐ • (08/31/92) • **93**
St.-Emilion 1979 • $18 Ⓐ • (10/15/89) • **81**
St.-Emilion 1962 • $60 • (11/30/87) • **88**
St.-Emilion 1961 • $68 Ⓐ • (04/30/96) • **79**
St.-Emilion 1959 • $95 • (10/15/90) • **82**
St.-Emilion 1947: Very mature, but smooth and dark, with spicy flavors and some richness. • $NA • (05/31/97) • **87**
St.-Emilion 1945 • $200 • (11/30/95) • **85**

GAGNARD, JEAN-NOËL

Bâtard-Montrachet 1994: Opulent, and very woody at this stage. Full-bodied, cascading with honey, ripe fruit and caramel flavors. Long, oaky and powerful finish has hints of lemon, toasty bread and marzipan. Try now. • $NA • (08/31/96) • **90**
Bâtard-Montrachet 1993: One of the best wines of the vintage. Wonderful, fresh, classy vanilla, honey and cream aromas and flavors. Medium in body; lovely, long finish. • $100 • (05/15/95) • **90**
Bâtard-Montrachet 1992: Ripe, fruity and grand. Full of bold apricot, pineapple and pear flavors, with great intensity and a long, long finish. Drinkable now. • $100 • (08/31/94) • **94**
Chassagne-Montrachet Caillerets 1995: Supercharged and intense, concentrated and full of life, with a lactic, green quality overlapping the honey, citrus and mineral notes. Full-bodied, a flinty, minerally nuance adds to the long finish. It all makes for a wonderful and distinctive drinking experience. Best after 2000. • $65 • (08/31/97) • **93**
Chassagne-Montrachet Caillerets 1994: Silky, full-bodied and elegant—like sipping cream with melted honey. Pear, litchi, vanilla bean, and spice flavors are seductive. Nice, smoky, toasty bread notes on the finish. Drink now through 2000. • $NA • (08/31/96) • **93**
Chassagne-Montrachet Caillerets 1993: A bit green and hard, revealing fresh-cut apple and honey flavors and steely character. Medium-bodied; high acidity. • $50 • (05/15/95) • **82**
Chassagne-Montrachet Caillerets 1992: Youthful but very promising, with vanilla and hazelnut flavors held in tightly by a lemon and grapefruit acidity. Has mineral and earth accents and a long finish. • $47 • (08/31/94) • **87**
Chassagne-Montrachet Clos de la Maltroye 1995: Wonderful. Full-bodied, rich, ripe and thick, it manages to remain elegant and fresh. Offers loads of new oak, with spicy and smoky toasty bread accents and plenty of nicely ripe fruit flavors. Velvety structure carries through to a long, smooth finish. Try after 2000. 200 cases made. • $55 • (08/31/97) • **96**
Chassagne-Montrachet Clos de la Maltroye 1993: Perfumed apple, mineral and flint character, with the flavors following through on the palate. Steely and slightly hard finish. Drinkable now. • $33 • (05/15/95) • **85**
Chassagne-Montrachet Clos St.-Jean Red 1995: On the light side, with a stemmy, herbal character. Barely says Pinot Noir. • $55 • (11/15/97) • **74**

FRANCE

Chassagne-Montrachet Les Champs Gain 1995: Ripe and lush, but very oaky and more showy than classy, it delivers tons of spice, toasty bread and pear flavors, yet seems a bit overdone. Full-bodied, clean on the finish, with a nice citrusy-minty touch. Try after 2000. • $65 • (08/31/97) • **86**

Chassagne-Montrachet Les Champs Gain 1994: A supple and approachable full-bodied *premier cru*. Ripe fruit, toasty oak, and honey flavors abound, but intensity is lacking. • $NA • (08/31/96) • **85**

Chassagne-Montrachet Les Champs Gain 1993: Austere and tart, but offering some complexity; toasty, mineral flavors persist on the medium-long finish. • $33 • (05/15/95) • **80**

Chassagne-Montrachet Les Chenevottes 1995: Well made. Amazingly intense and concentrated, racy and tasting of sweet fruit and honey, it's layered with complexity. Has supple texture and a wonderful underpinning of crisp lime notes paving the way to a long, juicy finish. Drink now through 2005. • $65 • (08/31/97) • **93**

Chassagne-Montrachet Les Chenevottes 1994: Bravo! Exotic, ripe and oozing with tropical, fig, lemon and spice aromas and flavors. Full-bodied and balanced. Slightly smoky on the long finish. Drink now through 2000. • $NA • (08/31/96) • **91**

Chassagne-Montrachet Les Chenevottes 1993: Floral and lime flavors are grassy and tart, but it's clean and has a juicy finish. Try now. • $33 • (05/15/95) • **83**

Chassagne-Montrachet Les Chenevottes 1992: Subtle and pretty, a medium-bodied Chassagne with a toast, hazelnut and lemon character; offers appealing, lean and clean flavors. • $36 • (08/31/94) • **85**

Chassagne-Montrachet Les Masures 1994: Rich, ripe and seductive. Full-bodied, packed with toasty oak, raisin, tropical, citrus, vanilla and honey flavors. Delicious now. • $NA • (08/31/96) • **87**

Chassagne-Montrachet Les Masures 1993: Wonderfully put together, displaying vanilla, toasty oak and apple character, medium body, fresh fruit and a crisp finish. Drink now. • $30 • (05/15/95) • **85**

Chassagne-Montrachet Les Masures 1992: Crisp and lean in flavor, with green apple and citrus notes, backed by a fairly full body and a lively finish. • $30 • (08/31/94) • **82**

Chassagne-Montrachet Morgeot 1995: Old-style white Burgundy, with an unclean character. Tastes oxidized, like bad Sherry. Tasted twice, with consistent notes. • $55 • (05/31/98) • **70**

Chassagne-Montrachet Morgeot 1994: Ripe and rich, offering sweet-tasting milk, cream, honey and ripe fruit flavors. Full-bodied. Try now. • $NA • (08/31/96) • **87**

Chassagne-Montrachet Morgeot Red 1995: Light-bodied and pretty, with an herbal side and a touch of licorice. Well balanced. • $58 • (11/15/97) • **81**

Chassagne-Montrachet Morgeot Red 1994: An earthy, mushroomy character overshadows the modest berry flavors in this light, silky wine. Approachable now. • $25 • (11/15/96) • **79**

Chassagne-Montrachet Morgeot Red 1990: Light in texture, but firm and flavorful, with lively raspberry, red cherry and mineral aromas and flavors that remain smooth and silky through the finish. Drinkable now. Tasted twice. • $25 • (02/15/93) • **86**

Chassagne-Montrachet Morgeot Red 1989 • $25 • (11/15/91) • **87**

Chassagne-Montrachet Morgeot Red 1988 • $20 • (12/31/90) • **86**

Chassagne-Montrachet Morgeot Red 1985 • $18 • (11/30/87) • **79**

Chassagne-Montrachet Red 1995: Light and diluted, lean and astringent. Not much to it. • $35 • (11/15/97) • **70**

Chassagne-Montrachet Red 1994: Light and simple, with only modest fruit flavors and dry tannins. • $23 • (11/15/96) • **74**

Chassagne-Montrachet Red 1990: Ripe and fruity, with peppery berry flavors that run close to Beaujolais, but the finish shows a sturdy frame of oak and tannins. Drinkable now. • $50 • (11/30/92) • **84**

Santenay Clos de Tavannes 1995: A good, straightforward '95 red Burgundy, with spicy cherry flavors, lean texture and a firm finish. • $30 • (11/15/97) • **83**

Santenay Clos de Tavannes 1994: This is *premier cru* Burgundy? It has the color of rosé, but less complexity than a good one. Watery and thin. • $27 • (11/15/96) • **70**

Santenay Clos de Tavannes 1990: Light and zippy, with a bright beam of raspberry and tar aromas and flavors. Straightforward and nicely balanced; drinkable now. • $16 • (11/30/92) • **80**

Santenay Clos de Tavannes 1989 • $25 • (11/15/91) • **85**

Santenay Clos de Tavannes 1988 • $25 • (11/15/90) • **84**

GAGNEROT & FILS, FRANÇOIS

Corton-Charlemagne 1994: Soft and supple, a honeyed Chardonnay that is full-bodied and rather rich, with some nice pear, date and mineral notes. Very ripe finish bordering on sweet. Ready to drink now. • $36 • (05/31/96) • **84**

Ladoix Les Gréchons White 1994: A simple, straightforward, basic Chardonnay that delivers some pear, apple and citrus flavors without much complexity. Somewhat light-bodied; try with seafood or as an apéritif. • $NA • (05/31/96) • **80**

GAILLARD, PIERRE

Côte-Rôtie Côte Brune et Blonde 1990: Intense and focused, with tart cherry, earth and toast flavors that turn peppery on the finish. Soft and fleshy. Drinkable now. • $30 • (04/15/93) • **86**

Côte-Rôtie Côte Brune et Blonde 1989 • $28 • (10/15/91) • **89**

Côte-Rôtie Côte Brune et Blonde 1988 • $30 • (11/30/90) • **90**

Côte-Rôtie Côte Brune et Blonde 1987 • $24 • (08/31/89) • **82**

Côte-Rôtie Côte Brune et Blonde 1986 • $25 • (11/30/88) • **86**

St.-Joseph Clos de Cuminaille 1990 • $20 • (04/15/93) • **87**

St.-Joseph Clos de Cuminaille 1988 • $15 • (12/31/90) • **87**

St.-Joseph Clos de Cuminaille 1987 • $14 • (03/15/90) • **87**

GALET DES PAPES, DOMAINE DU

Châteauneuf-du-Pape 1995: Just lovely, packed with intense and sharp fruit. Terrific, lively core of crisp cherry, crushed black pepper and cassis. Extremely well done, the sort of wine you want to have a lot of around the house. Drink now. 2,167 cases made. • $25 • (10/15/97) • **85**

Châteauneuf-du-Pape 1989 • $21 • (08/31/92) • **88**

Châteauneuf-du-Pape Vieilles Vignes 1990: A strong current of ashy bitterness runs through this otherwise ripe, almost raisiny wine, making it a bit unpleasant. • $28 • (09/30/93) • **76**

Châteauneuf-du-Pape White 1996: Fresh, zesty and pure, medium-bodied, with some lovely grass, almond, pear and gooseberry flavors. Lacks the richness to score higher, but has good balance. Drinkable now. 200 cases made. • $22 • (10/15/97) • **86**

GALET VINEYARDS

Chardonnay Vin de Pays d'Oc 1996: A simple, fresh-tasting Chardonnay with banana flavor and medium body. 5,000 cases made. • $9 • (08/31/97) • **80**

Merlot Vin de Pays d'Oc 1996: Starts off smoothly, then turns astringent, with only modest fruit flavors. 5,000 cases made. • $9 • (08/31/97) • **78**

Merlot Vin de Pays d'Oc 1994: Any cherry aromas and flavors are reined in by the austere character. There's a minty note on the aftertaste. 5,000 cases made. • $9 • (07/31/96) • **80**

Syrah Vin de Pays d'Oc 1994: A little fruit and spice is peeking out from this otherwise modestly flavored red. Tough finish. 5,000 cases made. • $9 • (07/31/96) • **76**

GALICHETS, LES

Bourgueil 1992 • $NA • (10/31/94) • **75**

GALLIFFET, CHÂTEAU DE

Côtes du Rhône 1994: This well-structured red offers dark flavors of plum, coffee and tobacco, with firm tannins and a spicy finish. A great accompaniment to grilled beef. From Max Aubert. • $NA • (10/15/97) • **85**

GAMAGE, CHÂTEAU

Entre-Deux-Mers 1994 • $8 • (05/31/95) • **79**

GAMBIER, JEAN

Bourgueil Domaine del Galluches Cuvée Ronsard 1993 • $13 • (05/15/96) • **88**

GARAUDET, JEAN

Beaune Le Clos des Mouches 1990: Crisp and focused, with berry, cherry and currant flavors and nice toast and vanilla overtones. The modest, well-

Key: SS—Spectator Selection CS—Cellar Selection HR—Highly Recommended BB—Best Buy $NA—Price not available Ⓐ—Auction Price (BT)—Barrel Tasting
Dates in parentheses indicate the issues in which the ratings were published.

integrated tannins don't get in the way. Drinkable now. • $35 • (08/31/92) • **87**

Beaune Le Clos des Mouches 1989 • $32 • (11/15/91) • **91**

Beaune Le Clos des Mouches 1988 • $40 • (11/15/90) • **86**

Bourgogne Passe-tout-grains 1990: A very reasonably priced wine, with a strong beam of currant flavor running through its fruity-smelling nose and firm texture. Drinkable now. • $10 • (06/15/92) • **84**

Monthélie 1990: Tough and solidly built, offering plenty of tannins and generous currant and berry flavors. Drinkable now. • $25 • (08/31/92) • **85**

Monthélie 1989 • $22 • (11/15/91) • **86**

Monthélie 1988 • $23 • (11/15/90) • **88**

Pommard 1988 • $37 • (11/15/90) • **88**

Pommard 1987 • $25 • (09/15/89) • **88**

Pommard Les Charmots 1990: Fragrant and enticing, bursting with oak-scented, ripe currant, berry and plum aromas and flavors that turn spicy on the long finish. Tannins rush in on the palate, meaning this will need until 1999 to settle down, but the fruit intensity is there. 100 cases made. • $48 • (08/31/92) • **91**

Pommard Les Charmots 1988 • $46 • (11/15/90) • **90**

Pommard Les Charmots 1987 • $30 • (09/15/89) • **88**

Pommard Les Noizons 1990: Firm and focused, with generous currant and plum aromas and flavors that persist into a long, lively finish. Drink now. • $40 • (08/31/92) • **88**

Pommard Les Noizons 1989 • $34 • (11/15/91) • **91**

GARAUDET, PAUL

Bourgogne White 1996: Quite ripe and rich for a '96 Bourgogne Blanc, with a leesy, yeasty, ripe pear character, but also a cooked apple flavor that distracts. Medium-bodied; a bit sharp on the finish. Drink now. 750 cases made. • $15 • (05/31/98) • **84**

Bourgogne White 1995: A bit simple, with a rustic, woodsy, green and tart character. • $15 • (08/31/97) • **72**

Bourgogne White 1994: Has an interesting chalky, mineral character, but also a reductive, "ice box" flavor that's hard to like. Quite creamy in texture, with a crisp finish. 266 cases made. • $NA • (05/31/96) • **80**

Meursault Vieille Vigne 1995: Very rich and sweet-tasting, oozing with honey and piecrust flavors. The oak is subtle, making it easily drinkable now through 2000. • $NA • (05/31/97) • **85**

Meursault Vieille Vigne 1994: Well crafted and very exciting. Excellent concentration of fruit, mineral and earth notes that coat the mouth. Ripe and fresh; the silky texture is pure seduction. The intense, lingering finish needs time to soften; try in 1999. 570 cases made. • $26 • (05/31/96) • **89**

Meursault Vieilles Vignes 1996: Very pretty and elegant, with citruslike acidity mingling with floral, subtle toasty oak, mineral, pear and honey notes. Medium-bodied, it turns a bit dry and oaky on the finish, but it has the stuffing to age well through 2000 to 2005. 600 cases made. • $32 • (05/31/98) • **90**

Monthélie Les Champs Fulliot White 1996: The oak dominates the fruit, making this tough to review. Underneath all that spice and chestnut character is an appealing, medium-bodied, smooth-textured wine with mineral, lime and pear notes and roasted almonds. The oak accents burn on the finish. Perhaps better after 2000. 90 cases made. • $24 • (05/31/98) • **85**

Monthélie Les Champs Fulliot White 1995: Showing stunning quality for a village Monthélie, this gorgeous white Burgundy, full-bodied and thick, coats the palate with ripe fruit flavors, smoky, toasty oak accents and honey, mineral and spice nuances. Long finish. Drink now through 2005. • $23 • (05/31/97) • **91**

Monthélie Les Champs Fulliot White 1994: A middle-of-the-road '94 that's balanced but lacking in flavor. Somewhat lighter in body, it offers some modest lemon, earth and mineral flavors. A bit dull on the finish. 95 cases made. • $20 • (05/31/96) • **79**

Puligny-Montrachet 1996: Seductively silky, showing perhaps a bit too much butterscotch aroma, but delivering a lush mouthfeel packed with mineral, wet stone and vanilla bean notes along with good fruit. Full-bodied, the velvety, toasty finish is impressive. Try after 2000. 300 cases made. • $32 • (05/31/98) • **89**

Puligny-Montrachet 1995: Rich, thick and dense, as well as a bit hot and alcoholic. Full-bodied, with toasty, almost charred wood flavors and a slightly coarse finish. • $30 • (05/31/97) • **79**

Puligny-Montrachet 1994: Quite woody, with a hint of mineral, vanilla and butter. It's silky in texture, though lacking a bit in fruit flavors and somewhat short on the finish. 73 cases made. • $27 • (05/31/96) • **81**

GARDE, CHÂTEAU LA

Pessac-Léognan 1997: Some fruit, but rather diluted, with hints of earth and veggies. • $NA • (06/15/98) (BT) • **75-79**

Pessac-Léognan 1996: Velvety tannins, but slightly stewed character. Medium-bodied, with a cherry and mineral aftertaste. 1,000 cases made. • $18 • (06/15/98) (BT) • **80-84**

Pessac-Léognan 1995: Velvety and unctuous red. Attractive berry, porcini mushroom aromas and flavors. Full-bodied and very velvety, with a long aftertaste of chocolate and fruit. Delicious. Best after 2000, but who can wait? • $15 • (01/31/98) • **90**

Pessac-Léognan 1994: Warm and autumnal, with chocolate, berry and tobacco flavors. Medium- to full-bodied, with velvety tannins and a fruity finish. Delicious for the vintage. Drink now or hold. • $17 • (01/31/97) • **87**

Pessac-Léognan Réserve de Château 1993: Pretty, plummy Bordeaux showing plenty of vanilla and fruit character, medium body, fine tannins and fresh finish. Drinkable now. • $17 • (01/31/96) • **83**

Pessac-Léognan Réserve de Château 1991: A touch of green character, but plenty of plum and vanilla flavors. Medium body and velvety texture. • $13 • (03/31/94) • **78**

Pessac-Léognan White 1995: A very ripe white with lots of pineapple, honey and apple notes, piecrust and fruit flavors. Full-bodied, medium finish; needs a bit more on the finish to be outstanding, but quite impressive for the vintage. Drink now. • $15 • (04/30/98) • **88**

Pessac-Léognan White Réserve de Château 1994 • $16 • (03/31/96) • **87**

Pessac-Léognan White Réserve du Château 1993 • $14 • (05/31/95) • **86**

GARDINE, CHÂTEAU DE LA

Châteauneuf-du-Pape 1995: Balanced and ripe, with sweet-tasting black cherry, wild berry and spice flavors. Medium- to full-bodied, it's generous but lacks intense concentration; pleasant to drink now. • $31 • (10/15/97) • **87**

Châteauneuf-du-Pape 1994: Rather lean, with some herbal, coffee and spice flavors. Light- to medium-bodied, drying finish. Tasted twice, with consistent notes. • $28 • (10/15/97) • **75**

Châteauneuf-du-Pape 1990: Firm and fleshy, bursting with clearly articulated berry, cherry, tobacco and spice aromas and flavors, hinting at pepper on the solid finish. Drinkable now. • $24 • (09/30/93) • **87**

Châteauneuf-du-Pape 1989 • $25 • (10/15/91) • **95**

Châteauneuf-du-Pape 1988 • $33 • (10/15/91) • **85**

Châteauneuf-du-Pape 1986 • $17 • (10/15/91) • **90**

Châteauneuf-du-Pape 1985 • $15 • (12/31/87) • **87**

Châteauneuf-du-Pape 1984 • $15 • (12/31/87) • **78**

Châteauneuf-du-Pape 1983 • $25 • (10/15/91) • **89**

Châteauneuf-du-Pape 1981 • $NA • (10/15/91) • **86**

Châteauneuf-du-Pape Cuvée des Générations 1990: Rich, supple and smooth, with a wonderful band of spicy currant, berry and tobacco aromas and flavors. All of it remains in balance and finishes generous and fleshy. Drinkable now, but should be fine through 2000. • $38 • (09/30/93) • **89**

Châteauneuf-du-Pape Cuvée des Générations 1989 • $38 • (02/28/93) CS • **94**

Châteauneuf-du-Pape Cuvée des Générations 1985 • $NA • (10/15/91) • **92**

Châteauneuf-du-Pape Cuvée des Générations Gaston Philippe 1995: Gorgeous Châteauneuf. Lush, thick and ripe, with impressive, concentrated cassis flavors, notes of dried herbs, vanilla, spice and pepper. Full-bodied with a creamy texture, its mile-long finish is mind-blowing. Buy as much as your budget allows, then drink now or cellar through 2005. • $78 • (10/15/97) • **93**

Châteauneuf-du-Pape Cuvée des Générations Gaston Philippe 1994: Vivid and lush, this inky red explodes with crushed fruit flavors of blackberries, plums and black cherries, and buttresses them with toast, coffee and licorice notes. It shows great concentration and liveliness, with a long, spicy, black olive finish. Beautiful. • $60 • (10/15/97) • **91**

Châteauneuf-du-Pape White 1996: Fresh and zingy, with citrus, especially orange, and almond flavors. Crisp, but clean and flavorful. Well made, medium-bodied. Drink now. • $NA • (10/15/97) • **87**

Châteauneuf-du-Pape White Vieilles Vignes 1994: Sophisticated, showing a nice marriage of fruit and wood, this ripe wine offers butter and vanilla notes, melon, honey and light herbal flavors. It's delicious now, but has the structure and concentration to age. Tasted twice, with consistent notes. • $52 • (10/15/97) • **92**

Côtes du Rhône White 1996: A round white, offering pretty pear, herbal and mineral notes, soft and clean on the palate. Good regional character. Drink now. • $NA • (10/15/97) • **82**

Côtes du Rhône-Villages 1995: Light-bodied, with vegetal, herbal notes atop the plum and crushed cassis flavors. Has decent ripeness, but turns a bit crisp on the finish. Tasted twice, with consistent notes. • $18 • (10/15/97) • **81**

Côtes du Rhône-Villages Benjamin Brunel 1990 • $14 • (09/30/93) • **82**

GARENNE, DOMAINE DE LA

Mâcon-Azé 1995: A bit too woody for the fruit, with floral, hay, grass and citrus aromas and flavors. Light-bodied, turns a bit bitter on the finish. Drink now. 2,500 cases made. • $12 • (05/31/97) • **79**

Mâcon-Azé 1993: Mature, gold-colored, seems to be losing its fruit. Tart and astringent, with a bitter lime edge on the finish. From Perinet and Renoud-Grappin. • $NA • (08/31/95) • **74**

GARMONT

Sauvignon Bordeaux 1995: A pleasant, basic white with good melon and herb flavors. On the light side, but enjoyable. 35,000 cases made. • $10 • (04/30/97) • **82**

GARRIGUES, LES

Côtes du Rhône 1996: Straightforward, with some cherry and green flavors. Tastes a bit diluted. Herbal, tart finish. • $NA • (10/15/97) • **79**

GAUBY, DOMAINE

Côtes du Roussillon 1991 • $7 • (03/15/94) • **82**

Côtes du Roussillon Elevé en Fûts de Chêne 1996: Fresh-tasting, with fairly lush plum and berry flavors and a bittersweet chocolate note on the finish. Drink now. • $15 • (05/31/98) • **84**

Côtes du Roussillon-Villages Vieilles Vignes 1995: A serious red that exhibits a lot of pizzazz as well as concentration. New oak adds spice and roundness to the vibrant blueberry and cherry flavors. The structure is firm and the finish long, echoing the vanilla notes. • $21 • (12/15/97) • **88**

Côtes du Roussillon-Villages Vieilles Vignes 1991 • $9 • (03/15/94) • **85**

GAUDET, JEAN-FRANÇOIS

Régnié Domaine de la Grange-Barjot 1995: Soft, light and simple, with cherry and dried berry flavors over light tannins; the finish is clean but short. Quaffable now. • $11 • (09/15/97) • **80**

Régnié Domaine de la Grange-Barjot 1994: Light and diluted. Simple berry flavors with vegetal accents and a short, dry finish. • $12 • (09/15/96) • **76**

Régnié Domaine de la Grange-Barjot 1993 • $12 • (07/31/95) • **84**

GAUDRY, DOMAINE DENIS

Pouilly-Fumé 1996: A rich, nearly creamy texture carries flavors of coconut, pineapple and lime. Round and full-bodied. Crisp finish, with clean citrus and herbal notes. Drink now. • $19 • (02/28/98) • **87**

Pouilly-Fumé Coteaux du Petit Boisgibault 1995 • $19 • (04/30/96) • **85**

Pouilly-Fumé Coteaux du Petit Boisgibault 1993 • $NA • (10/31/94) • **87**

GAUNOUX, JEAN-MICHEL

Corton Les Renardes 1990: Simple and straightforward for a *grand cru*, with modest strawberry, earth and cherry aromas and flavors and a somewhat dull finish. Drinkable now. • $60 • (12/15/92) • **74**

Volnay Clos des Chênes 1990: Firm, fruity and medium-bodied, offering plenty of elegance in the raspberry and tea leaf aromas and flavors that echo on the lovely, long finish. Drinkable now. • $NA • (12/15/92) • **90**

GAUTHIER, PIERRE

Bourgueil Domaine du Bel Air Les Caillots 1995: This nicely balanced red marries round fruit flavors of cherry and plum with firm, well-integrated tannins and a spicy finish. Not showy, but very alluring. 2,500 cases made. • $12 • (05/15/97) • **87**

Bourgueil Domaine du Bel Air Les Grandmonts 1995: Toasty oak aromas and flavors and ripe, concentrated fruit flavors of plums and prunes set this powerful red apart from its peers. An extracted, jammy style that sacrifices typicity in pursuit of power. A bit overwhelming now, it should evolve into a smooth, deep wine. Best from 1999 through 2003. 600 cases made. • $21 • (06/15/98) HR • **90**

GAUTIER, BENOIT

Vouvray 1995: Quite lean and crisp for Vouvray, this offers herb and citrus flavors and sharp acidity. Needs food to soften and harmonize. • $12 • (06/15/97) • **80**

Vouvray Demi-Sec 1996: Crisp, quite dry, with light apple and peach flavors and a hint of spritz that keeps it lively. A nice match with light dishes. Drink now. • $18 • (06/30/98) • **82**

Vouvray Moelleux Clos La Lanterne 1996: This full-bodied white is quite dry, with smoky, toasty notes dominating the ripe apple flavors. Firm and balanced. Drinkable now. • $18 • (06/15/98) • **84**

Vouvray Sec Clos La Lanterne 1996: Apple and peach flavors are assertive, crisp and well defined in this lively white. A bit tart, but should soften with food. Drink now. • $15 • (06/30/98) • **82**

GAVOTY, DOMAINES

Côtes de Provence Cuvée Clarendon 1987 • $8 • (03/31/90) • **72**

GAY, CHÂTEAU LE

Pomerol 1997: Impressive balance and harmony. Medium- to full-bodied, with fine tannins and a medium finish. Very good. • $NA • (06/15/98) (BT) • **85-89**

Pomerol 1996: Simple and silky, with raspberry and watermelon aromas and flavors. Light-bodied, with a light finish. • $40 • (06/15/98) (BT) • **80-84**

Pomerol 1995: Sleek and racy Pomerol, boasting plenty of berry, cherry and mineral character and fine tannins. Wonderful Le Gay. • $NA • (05/15/96) (BT) • **90-94**

Pomerol 1993: Somewhat disappointing for Le Gay. Fresh and clean dried cherry and berry aromas and flavors. Medium in body, with sleek tannins and a crisp finish. Slightly one-dimensional. Drinkable now. • $29 • (01/31/96) • **80**

Pomerol 1992: Shockingly light. Clean, revealing some fruit, but really watery. Drinkable but uninviting. • $22 • (04/15/95) • **73**

Pomerol 1990: Absolutely massive, with tons of exotic ripe raspberry flavor and velvety tannins. Thick and rich, yet has great balance. Drink in 2000. 2,000 cases made. • $49 • (03/31/93) • **96**

Pomerol 1989 • $63 Ⓐ • (03/15/92) • **91**

Pomerol 1988 • $26 Ⓐ • (04/30/91) • **83**

Pomerol 1982 • $55 Ⓐ • (05/15/89) • **89**

Pomerol 1970 • $75 • (05/15/93) • **83**

Pomerol 1961 • $73/1.5 liter • (04/30/96) • **82**

GAZIN, CHÂTEAU

Pomerol 1997: This is a '97? A very ripe young wine, with tobacco, berry and cherry aromas and flavors. Full-bodied, with velvety tannins and a velvety texture at the long finish. Tasted twice, with consistent notes. • $NA • (06/15/98) (BT) • **90-94**

Pomerol 1996: Impressive ripe berry and grilled meat aromas and flavors. Medium-bodied, with medium, velvety tannins and a pleasant but slightly dry finish. • $60 • (06/15/98) (BT) • **85-89**

Pomerol 1995: Extremely attractive now, but will reward those with patience. Beautiful aromas of berries and chocolate. Medium- to full-bodied, with fine tannins and a lovely, berry-vanilla aftertaste. Best after 2000. • $45 • (01/31/98) • **90**

Pomerol 1994: Ripe, rich and powerful. Full-bodied, with plenty of velvety tannins and a long finish. Slightly coarse now, but will mellow with age. Try in 1999. • $43 • (01/31/97) • **90**

Pomerol 1993: Pretty Merlot character here, offering tobacco, cherry and olive aromas and flavors, medium-to-full body, good fruit and a medium-tannic finish. Try now. • $29 Ⓐ • (01/31/96) • **87**

Pomerol 1992: Slightly disappointing after various good barrel samples. Cherry, plum, tomato aromas and flavors, medium to light in body, slightly hard finish. Tasted twice. • $24 • (04/15/95) • **78**

Key: SS—Spectator Selection CS—Cellar Selection HR—Highly Recommended BB—Best Buy $NA—Price not available Ⓐ—Auction Price (BT)—Barrel Tasting
Dates in parentheses indicate the issues in which the ratings were published.

FRANCE

Pomerol 1991: Pretty aromas matched by cherry, toasty oak and good fruit flavors, but a little bitter on the finish. Drinkable now. • $24 • (03/31/94) • **81**

Pomerol 1990: An attractive, well-made wine. It shows rich plum, tar and berry aromas with ripe berry and chocolate flavors, medium-soft tannins and a light finish. Drinkable now. 8,500 cases made. • $60 • (03/31/93) • **88**

Pomerol 1989 • $37 Ⓐ • (03/15/92) • **91**

Pomerol 1988 • $40 Ⓐ • (06/30/91) • **87**

Pomerol 1985 • $29 Ⓐ • (09/30/88) • **90**

Pomerol 1982 • $49 Ⓐ • (08/31/92) • **93**

Pomerol 1970 • $10 Ⓐ • (05/15/93) • **80**

Pomerol 1961 • $63 Ⓐ • (04/30/96) • **84**

Pomerol 1945 • $220 • (11/30/95) • **83**

GEANTET-PANSIOT

Bourgogne Pinot Fin 1992: Attractively fruity in flavor, and well balanced for drinking now. Shows exuberant cherry and raspberry aromas and flavors, good freshness and acidity, and a bit of spice on the finish. Moderately tannic; drinkable now. 300 cases made. • $16 • (11/30/94) • **85**

Charmes-Chambertin 1993: Elegant, caressing, velvety texture. Medium- to full-bodied, adding a sweet berry, cherry, earthy, mineral finish. Seductive. Better in 2001. • $60 • (05/15/96) • **90**

Gevrey-Chambertin Poissenot 1993: Super *premier cru* boasting lots of depth and complexity. Chewy character, as tons of cassis and other red berry flavors fan out on the palate, adding a touch of wet earth. There's *terroir* written all over it from start to finish. A beauty. Try now through 2002. • $45 • (05/15/96) • **90**

GEISWELLER & FILS

Bourgogne 1990: A pleasant surprise from what used to be one of Burgundy's worst producers. A beautiful wine, with unique almond, leather, nutmeg and raspberry flavors. Distinctive in style, with a silky yet firm texture. • $NA • (12/15/92) • **86**

GENDRIER, MICHEL

Cheverny White 1996: Fresh, with ripe apple, crisp lemon and light almond notes, light-bodied but well balanced. Though tart on its own, it will complement shellfish and other light dishes. Drink now. • $11 • (05/31/98) • **82**

GENILLON, DOMAINE DE

Morgon Le Terrain Rouge 1994 • $10 • (10/31/95) • **82**

GENTAZ-DERVIEUX

Côte-Rôtie Côte Brune Cuvée Réservée 1990: Firm in texture, with earthy, barnyardy aromas and flavors and enough ripe blackberry and cherry notes to bring it around. A distinctive wine that lovers of old-style Rhônes will especially like. Drink now. Tasted twice. • $55 • (04/15/93) • **85**

Côte-Rôtie Côte Brune Cuvée Réservée 1987 • $40 • (06/30/90) • **73**

GEOFFROY, ALAIN

Chablis 1996: Delicious and seductive. Ripe, with pear, mango and apple flavors, round and supple, with a mineral and flinty quality. Harmonious, chewy, citrus-infused finish. Ready now. • $NA • (08/31/97) • **87**

Chablis 1995: Balanced, round, medium- to full-bodied, with a supple core of apple, hay, citrus and honey flavors. Perhaps a bit short on the finish. Delicious now. From Domaine Le Verger. • $NA • (08/31/96) • **84**

Chablis Beauroy 1996: Supple in comparison to some '96 Chablis, also nicely ripe, with tropical, peach and honey flavors. Medium-bodied, with good limelike acidity. Enjoy now through 2002. Only 10 cases imported. 3,875 cases made. • $20 • (05/31/98) • **86**

Chablis Beauroy 1995: A clean and classy *premier cru*, with a rich mouthfeel yet a sense of finesse. Enticing mineral flavors up front, wet stone and tart citrus flavors on the finish suggest holding until after 1999. 3,875 cases made. • $20 • (06/15/97) • **88**

Chablis Beauroy 1994 • $20 • (05/31/96) • **77**

Chablis Beauroy 1993 • $19 • (08/31/95) • **81**

Chablis Domaine le Verger Cuvée Vieilles Vignes 1996: Supple and well made, with some wet earth, lime and pear flavors. Quite smooth, medium-bodied, it's ready now through 1999. • $NA • (08/31/97) • **85**

Petit Chablis 1996: Distinctive, ripe and seductive, showing gooseberry, dried herb and ripe pear flavors accented by oak-inspired vanilla and butter tones that sparkle on the palate. Long finish. Drink now through 2000. • $NA • (08/31/97) • **86**

GEOFFROY, RENÉ

Brut Champagne Cuvée Prestige NV: Vivid fruit flavors, lively acidity and a silky texture give this bubbly a bright personality. On the light side, it's probably best as an apéritif. • $39 • (11/30/97) • **87**

Brut Champagne Cuvée Sélectionnée NV: An easy-going, melt-in-your-mouth Champagne, with mellow, mature fruit flavors and a soft mousse. Drink now. • $34 • (11/30/97) • **87**

GERARD, FRANÇOIS

Côte-Rôtie 1988 • $36 • (07/31/91) • **70**

Côte-Rôtie 1987 • $30 • (10/15/90) • **77**

GERIN, JEAN-MICHEL

Condrieu Côteau de la Loye 1995: Shows good varietal character, with floral, spicy and apricot notes, and pure fruit flavors, clean and fresh. It's balanced and long, subtle yet eminently drinkable. 475 cases made. • $47 • (10/15/97) • **89**

Condrieu Côteau de la Loye 1994: Classic Viognier aromas of peach and wildflowers pave the way for powerful flavors of peach, almond and spice; balanced, deep and long. Drinking well now, and should improve through 1999. 200 cases made. • $39 • (12/15/96) • **90**

Côte-Rôtie 1991: Rich yet supple, with vivid plum, game and spice flavors. This shows skillfull winemaking. Try now. • $NA • (05/31/94) • **88**

Côte-Rôtie Champin Junior 1995: Firm and harmonious, this medium-weight red shows smoke, pepper and licorice notes accenting the black cherry flavors. Should drink well now through 2005. 333 cases made. • $36 • (10/15/97) • **85**

Côte-Rôtie Champin Junior 1994: Ripe and lush, this shows deep raspberry flavors with lovely floral accents, elegant but with enough tannin to keep it firm. The finish is clean and long. Drinking well now, but should improve through 2002. 300 cases made. • $38 • (11/30/96) • **90**

Côte-Rôtie Champin le Seigneur 1995: This expressive red offers vibrant flavors of blueberry and blackberry, with accents of violets and licorice. The tannins are firm enough for balance, yet gentle and very well integrated. Shows the elegance of the appellation. It's approachable now, better in 1999. 1,250 cases made. • $40 • (10/15/97) • **90**

Côte-Rôtie Champin le Seigneur 1994: This broad-shouldered wine offers ripe fruit and muscular tannins, with flavors of plum, coffee, licorice and toast, and a dry but spicy finish. As powerful as many Hermitages. Drinkable now. 500 cases made. • $36 • (11/30/96) • **88**

Côte-Rôtie Champin le Seigneur 1993: This well-balanced wine marries ripe fruit and moderate tannins in a firm yet elegant structure; its raspberry and vanilla flavors are attractive and fresh. It's pleasant now but should drink well through 2003. • $33 • (11/30/96) • **88**

Côte-Rôtie Champin le Seigneur 1992: Solid and balanced, showing firm tannins wrapped around ripe berry and meaty flavors. Well made. • $32 • (05/31/94) • **88**

Côte-Rôtie Champin le Seigneur 1991: Solid, generous in its berry flavor, with a leathery edge, finishing broad and sturdy. Drinkable now. 2,200 cases made. • $27 • (05/31/94) • **84**

Côte-Rôtie Les Grandes Places 1995: Perfumed and expressive, elegant, rich with violet, rose petal, cassis and vanilla flavors. It shows great balance and finesse, is gentle yet beautifully focused and long on the finish. Drinkable now. 583 cases made. • $69 • (10/15/97) • **91**

Côte-Rôtie Les Grandes Places 1994: Powerful and expressive. Aromas of smoke, licorice and game leap from the glass and follow through on the rich, ripe palate. A dollop of new wood adds interest, but doesn't detract from the pure Syrah flavors. Delicious now. 100 cases made. • $56 • (11/30/96) • **92**

Côte-Rôtie Les Grandes Places 1993: Pretty floral and berry aromas and flavors give this wine a plush, delicate appeal; it has a smooth texture and moderate tannins. Not a long-ager, but attractive now. • $46 • (11/30/96) • **87**

GERMAIN, HENRI

Côte-Rôtie Les Grandes Places 1992: Well built but approachable. Elegant and offers chocolate, spice, blackberry and floral notes. The tannins are supple; drinkable now. • $45 • (05/31/94) • **86**

Côte-Rôtie Les Grandes Places 1991: A generous dose of new wood adds an extra dimension, but it's already rich with exotic berry, violet and smoke flavors. Lush, silky, irresistible; try now. • $45 • (05/31/94) • **92**

GERMAIN, HENRI | CHAMPAGNE

Blanc de Blancs Champagne 1988: This producer always makes excellent Chardonnay-based Champagnes. An uplifting wine that makes you want to take another sip. Fresh and clean with beautiful apple and cream character, medium body and a fresh finish. Drink now. • $NA • (12/31/93) • **90**

Brut Blanc de Blancs Champagne Président Grand Cru de Blanc 1988: Walks the tightrope between richness and delicacy. This is a distinctive, complex, flavorful Champagne that is as soft as velvet, yet persistent on the finish. Enjoy now. 2,000 cases made. • $60 • (12/31/96) • **91**

Brut Champagne 1990: Bold and well balanced, this is a vibrant, very dry, assertive Champagne with forceful acidity and ample citrus flavors that gain complexity and finesse as you sip. Drink now through 2000. 6,000 cases made. • $39 • (12/31/96) • **89**

Brut Champagne 1988: Ripe and fresh, with layers of fruit interspersed with toast and earth. Full-bodied and steely, with a crisp finish. Slightly coarse. Drink now. • $NA • (12/31/93) • **87**

Brut Champagne President Germain Grand Cru Chardonnay 1988: Combines ample fruit flavors with some nuances of age for a complex, intriguing wine with a smooth texture. Distinctive and harmonious, managing to blend opulent notes with an elegant mouthfeel. 3,000 cases made. • $60 • (12/15/95) • **90**

GERMAIN, HENRI | BURGUNDY

Chassagne-Montrachet Morgeot 1993: Delicious ripe apple, tropical fruit and vanilla character, medium to full in body, fine acidity and a toasty oak finish. Drinkable now. • $NA • (08/31/95) • **86**

Chassagne-Montrachet Morgeot 1992: Vivid and fruity in flavor, with crisp grapefruit and orange notes, a lively texture and good balance overall. Drinkable now. 260 cases made. • $39 • (08/31/94) • **85**

Meursault Le Limozin 1993: Rather thick and flavorful, showing apple, mango and cream character. Full-bodied and round, with well-integrated acidity but a rather short finish. Drink now. • $33 • (08/31/95) • **87**

Meursault Le Limozin 1992: A chewy, dense and racy Meursault with lots of personality; shows delicious fruit character, with focused toast, lime, mineral, grapefruit and honey notes. 150 cases made. • $33 • (08/31/94) • **90**

Meursault Les Charmes 1993: Impressive, classy mineral, apple, pineapple and toasty oak character, medium body, racy acidity and a long, solid, fresh and fruity finish. Drinkable now. • $43 • (08/31/95) • **89**

Meursault Les Charmes 1992: Earthy, herbal flavors and a rough texture make this less than exciting for us. It has some lemon and green apple notes, but a short finish. 270 cases made. • $40 • (08/31/94) • **77**

Meursault Les Chevalières 1993: Elegant and racy apple, cream and chalk character, medium body, fresh acidity and a flavorful finish. • $NA • (08/31/95) • **87**

GERMAIN, JACQUES

Beaune Aux Cras 1992: Light in texture, but the berry and spice flavors come together nicely on the finish for a delicate Beaune that is at its best now. • $NA • (12/15/94) • **83**

Beaune Aux Cras 1991: Crisp, focused and delicate, with brightly expressed raspberry and black cherry aromas and flavors that linger on the finish. Try now. 417 cases made. • $33 • (01/31/94) • **85**

Beaune Aux Cras 1990: Fleshy and quite impressive, delivering plenty of violet, vanilla, plum and cherry notes and a lot of ripe fruit flavors, but it's a little short on the finish to warrant an outstanding rating. Drinkable now. 417 cases made. • $46 • (12/15/92) • **89**

Beaune Aux Cras 1989 • $48 • (01/31/92) • **90**

Beaune Aux Cras Vieilles Vignes 1994: Wonderful aromas meld lovely berry and cherry nuances with spicy oak accents. Turns tight and chewy on the palate, a bit short on the finish. • $NA • (11/15/96) • **85**

Key: SS—Spectator Selection CS—Cellar Selection HR—Highly Recommended BB—Best Buy $NA—Price not available Ⓐ—Auction Price (BT)—Barrel Tasting
Dates in parentheses indicate the issues in which the ratings were published.

Beaune Les Boucherottes 1990: Cherry and strawberry flavors ripple across the palate and come together with silky tannins in this intense, bright, juicy wine. Drinkable now. 333 cases made. • $42 • (12/15/92) • **89**

Beaune Les Cents Vignes 1990: Big, chewy and muscular, with cinnamon and raspberry notes and ample fruit to balance the vanilla-scented new oak flavors. Has a solid tannic backbone. Drinkable now. 250 cases made. • $46 • (12/15/92) • **91**

Beaune Les Teurons 1992: A little more flavor from this vintage than most, centering around gamy black cherry and toasty, spicy notes on the finish. Drinkable now. • $NA • (12/15/94) • **84**

Beaune Les Teurons 1991: Light but chewy, with a modest level of ripe cherry flavor and an astringent finish. Try now. 583 cases made. • $33 Ⓐ • (01/31/94) • **79**

Beaune Les Teurons 1990: Classy and seductive, with just the right balance of concentrated fruit flavor to compensate for the vanilla-tinged new oak nuances. Plum and berry notes sail across the palate to a seductive, long finish. Drinkable now. 667 cases made. • $48 • (12/15/92) • **91**

Beaune Les Teurons 1989 • $50 • (01/31/92) • **92**

Beaune Les Teurons 1988 • $42 • (02/15/91) • **90**

Beaune Les Teurons 1986 • $33 • (07/31/88) • **70**

Beaune Les Teurons Vieilles Vignes 1994: Very closed now, but shows some solid character with a good amount of red berry, earth, vanilla, mocha aromas and flavors. Medium-bodied. • $NA • (11/15/96) • **80**

Beaune Les Vignes Franches 1994: Some plum, currant, rose petal and iris aromas. Quite polished and round, but a stalky, stemmy note takes away from the quality. Finish is a bit dry. • $NA • (11/15/96) • **80**

Beaune Les Vignes Franches 1992: Elegant, smooth and very light. Shows good berry and cherry flavors, but they turn short on the supple finish. Drinkable now. • $NA • (12/15/94) • **78**

Beaune Les Vignes Franches 1991: Lean and lively, showing nice raspberry and currant flavors underneath a layer of fine tannins and mineral notes. Drinkable now. 333 cases made. • $30 Ⓐ • (01/31/94) • **86**

Beaune Les Vignes Franches 1990: There's wonderful finesse in this wine, showing a concentrated core of sweet-tasting tar, spice and berry flavors, fine tannins and a long finish. Drinkable now. 333 cases made. • $46 • (12/15/92) • **91**

Beaune Les Vignes Franches 1989 • $45 • (01/31/92) • **91**

Chorey-Côte de Beaune Château de Chorey-lès-Beaune 1990: Firm and chewy, showing an elegant texture and lively raspberry characteristics. Drinkable now. 1,833 cases made. • $24 • (12/15/92) • **85**

Chorey-Côte de Beaune Château de Chorey-lès-Beaune 1989 • $24 • (01/31/92) • **84**

Chorey-lès-Beaune Château de Chorey-lès-Beaune 1992: Straightforward and a bit diluted, with modest strawberry and currant flavors and a short finish. • $NA • (12/15/94) • **76**

Chorey-lès-Beaune Château de Chorey-lès-Beaune 1991: Crisp and simple, a decent level of currant and vanilla flavor fading on the astringent finish. 1,250 cases made. • $20 Ⓐ • (01/31/94) • **78**

Chorey-lès-Beaune Château de Chorey-lès-Beaune 1986 • $16 • (07/31/89) • **80**

GERMAIN, MARIE-PIERRE

Aloxe-Corton Les Vercots 1989 • $NA • (01/31/92) • **88**

GERMAIN, THIERRY

Saumur Champigny La Marginale 1993: In a rustic style, firmly structured, with pungent earth and barnyard aromas and rich, deep flavors of plums, chocolate and toast. Drinkable now. 1,000 cases made. • $30 • (06/15/97) • **81**

Saumur Champigny Terres Chades Domaine des Roches Neuves Red 1992 • $13 • (01/01/95) • **86**

GIBALAUX, DOMAINE

Merlot Vin de Pays d'Oc 1996: A nicely concentrated wine, on the tart side, with a good dose of tannin and appealing cherry, tobacco and herbal flavors. Finishes with bittersweet chocolate notes. Drink now through 2000. • $7 • (03/31/98) • **84**

GILETTE, CHÂTEAU

Sauternes Doux 1947: On the dry side, with a prominent tobacco note amid the tight, citrusy fig flavors. Finishes with too much acidity. • $233 • (05/31/97) • **80**

GILLET, EMILIAN

Mâcon-Viré Quintaine 1994: Seductively opulent, very ripe and sweet-tasting, bordering on botrytis with all that honey, apricot and ripe pear, but interwoven with clean and fresh lime, mineral, wet stone and wet earth character. Gorgeously balanced, it coats the palate with silky texture and impressive flavors. Long finish. Slightly off-dry, so try as an apéritif or match with a slightly sweet dish like pumpkin soup. Drink now through 2005. 2,500 cases made. • $18 • (05/31/98) • **92**

GILOUX, ISABELLE & PATRICK

Beaujolais-Villages Clos de Creuse Noire 1995: Beginning to fade, this shows earthy and herbal flavors, soft on the palate but drying on the finish. • $10 • (09/15/97) • **78**

GIMONNET & FILS, PIERRE

Brut Blanc de Blancs Champagne NV: A Blanc de Blancs with substance, offering rich Chardonnay flavors, a mouthfilling texture and a crisp, citrusy finish. • $30 • (11/30/97) • **86**

Brut Blanc de Blancs Champagne Fleuron 1990: Full-flavored, full-bodied and rich in texture, this is a real mouthful of Champagne that shows ripe, buttery, mellow flavors and good balance. Drink now through 1999. • $40 • (11/30/97) • **89**

GINGLINGER, PAUL

Muscat Alsace Cuvée Caroline 1995: A lovely example of Muscat. Piquant and vibrant, its flavors of fresh flowers, dried spices, apricot and pine aren't too aggressive, have richness and linger on the finish. • $15 • (11/15/97) • **85**

Riesling Alsace Grand Cru Pfersigberg 1995: Full of mouthwatering, juicy peach and apricot flavors, this Riesling has richness and a firm acid structure for balance. The elements combine nicely on the lengthy finish. • $20 • (11/15/97) • **87**

Tokay Pinot Gris Alsace Cuvée des Prélats 1995: Its earthy, austere character doesn't quite mesh with the thick, opulent texture, and it's lacking in fruit. • $15 • (11/15/97) • **83**

GIRARD, DOMAINE

Sancerre La Garenne 1995: Mouthwatering and lively, with citrus, grass and lightly nutty flavors, lean and intense, and a lingering finish. Racy and crisp, it's a beautiful match for herb-flavored chicken or fish. 800 cases made. • $14 • (04/30/97) • **87**

Sancerre La Garenne 1994 • $17 • (05/15/96) • **87**

Sancerre La Garenne 1993 • $13 • (11/15/95) • **85**

GIRARD, ROBERT

Châteauneuf-du-Pape Cuvée du Belvedere Le Boucou 1990: Lean and earthy, with modest raspberry and spice aromas and flavors, bordering on chalky at the edges. Seems more mature than its actual age. Drink up. • $19 • (04/15/93) • **81**

GIRARDIN, ALETH

Beaune Le Clos des Mouches 1995: Modest fruit mingles with herbal flavors in this fairly tough, medium-bodied red. • $32 • (11/15/97) • **78**

Beaune Le Clos des Mouches 1993: Beautifullly crafted red offering wood, fruit and tannins in just the right proportions. Medium in body, medium silky tannins and a long, fresh finish. Try in 1999. • $48 • (11/15/95) • **90**

Beaune Le Clos des Mouches 1988 • $36 • (07/15/91) • **71**

Pommard 1995: A firm red, with earth, mineral, red- and blackberry flavors that balance the tannins. Solid and well made. Try in 1999. • $27 • (11/15/97) • **85**

Pommard Les Charmots 1995: Delivering decent blackberry, spice, banana and cinnamon flavors, a medium body, it starts out OK then turns dry on the finish. Slight dilution. Drinkable now. • $39 • (11/15/97) • **82**

Pommard Les Charmots 1988 • $44 • (07/15/91) • **87**

Pommard Les Epenots 1995: Offers plenty of nice plum and blackberry flavors to balance the ripe, supple tannins. A well-balanced Pommard, especially for the vintage. Should be ready by 2000. • $44 • (11/15/97) • **87**

Pommard Rugiens 1995: Round, ripe, unusually thick and seductive for a '95, this sophisticated, full-bodied Pommard offers delicious plum and blackberry flavors. A lush veneer of oak imparts spice, toasty bread, mocha and chocolate notes. Try after 2000. • $44 • (11/15/97) • **88**

GIRARDIN, ARMAND

Pommard Les Charmots 1993: Bold and wonderful berry, raspberry and vanilla character, full body and tannins, yet refined and caressing. Long aftertaste. Try in 2000. • $60 • (11/15/95) • **91**

Pommard Les Epenots 1993: Super concentration and structure, full body, loads of tannins, rich tobacco, gamy, meaty, fruity character and a long, long finish. Better after 2000. • $60 • (11/15/95) • **90**

GIRARDIN, JEAN

Santenay Clos Rousseau Château de la Charrière 1987 • $25 • (02/28/91) • **87**

Santenay La Comme Château de la Charrière 1987 • $25 • (02/28/91) • **83**

Santenay La Comme Château de la Charrière 1986 • $23 • (10/15/89) • **80**

GIRARDIN, VINCENT

Beaune Clos des Vignes Franches 1995: Lush and very supple, this is a juicy, succulent red with lovely red berry flavors and toasty oak notes. Medium-bodied and well balanced. Drinkable now. • $27 • (11/15/97) • **86**

Beaune Clos des Vignes Franches 1994: Ripe and succulent, delivering sweet red berry aromas and flavors, with toasty oak, spice and earth notes running beneath. Medium-bodied. Drinkable now. • $31 • (11/15/96) • **84**

Chassagne-Montrachet Clos de la Boudriotte Red 1995: A wine of great harmony and balance. The lovely nose of black cherries is followed by deep, substantial fruit flavor and subtle nuances of oak that continue through the finish. Drinkable now, it should improve through 2000. • $30 • (11/15/97) • **90**

Chassagne-Montrachet Clos de la Boudriotte Red 1994: A crisp Burgundy, light-bodied, with red berry aromas and flavors. Ready to drink. • $32 • (11/15/96) • **79**

Chassagne-Montrachet Le Cailleret 1996: Lovely and smooth, a full-bodied Chassagne that glides over the palate with lots of finesse, offering subtle layers of spice, pear, toasty oak, citrus and tropical flavors. Tempting now through 2003. 200 cases made. • $51 • (05/31/98) • **88**

Chassagne-Montrachet Morgeot Red 1995: Medium-bodied, with pure, clean cassis and blackberry flavors unhindered by much wood. A bit tough on the finish. Try after 1999. • $27 • (11/15/97) • **83**

Chassagne-Montrachet Morgeot Red 1994: Supple, silky and elegant, offering a lovely bead of simple strawberry and floral aromas and flavors. Try now. • $30 • (11/15/96) • **85**

Chassagne-Montrachet Morgeot Vieilles Vignes 1996: Full-bodied and ripe, yet subtle and caressing, with pear, toasty oak, spice and tropical flavors. Amazing creamlike texture. Sweet-tasting and delicious, with a lingering, smoky finish. Very balanced. Best from 2000 through 2005. 830 cases made. • $NA • (05/31/98) • **93**

Chassagne-Montrachet Morgeot Vieilles Vignes 1993: The wood, acidity and fruit are not very well integrated. Diluted; green finish. 417 cases made. • $34 • (05/15/95) • **75**

Corton-Charlemagne 1996: Powerful, almost tannic in its muscle structure, this big white Burgundy delivers some deep butter, honey, ripe fruit and oak accents. Fills every taste bud on the palate with a velvety, thick, oil-like texture. The high, citrusy acidity keeps this together. Long, long finish. Don't touch until around 2005. 200 cases made. • $83 • (05/31/98) • **94**

Corton Perrières 1995: Big, rich, fatter than most '95 red Burgundies, this is packed with cassis, blackberry, chocolate and toasty oak flavors, with just a hint of herb. Full-bodied, yet also juicy and succulent. Tough tannins on the finish suggest waiting until 2000. • $46 • (11/15/97) • **85**

Maranges Clos des Loyères Vieilles Vignes 1995: Displays spicy, succulent fruit flavors with some richness to balance the tannins. Still, it's intense and dry on the finish. • $20 • (11/15/97) • **84**

Maranges Clos des Loyères Vieilles Vignes 1994: Firm, maybe a bit too tannic for the modest strawberry flavors, but the density implies it can continue to grow through 2000 to 2001. • $23 • (11/15/96) • **86**

Meursault Les Narvaux 1996: Intense and impressive for its duality of crisp acidity and lush, ripe, sweet-tasting fruit. Loads of tropical, pear and citrus character, underlined by some toasty oak accents. This full-bodied Meursault will need time to show it all, but it has the seductive honey-and-fruit stuffing to hold for a decade. Long, vibrant, lime-flavored finish. Try around 2005. 500 cases made. • $42 • (05/31/98) • **93**

Meursault Les Narvaux 1993: Plenty of buttery, doughy, lemony aromas, but modest and fruity on the palate. Drink now. 417 cases made. • $29 • (05/15/95) • **81**

Meursault Les Perrières 1996: Magnificent. This to-die-for, full-bodied Meursault manages to be opulent and rich yet elegant and racy. The heavy toasty oak flavors are beautifully integrated into the vibrant lime, pear, honey and spice of this firmly structured, clean and pure wine. Long, long finish. Drink now through 2010. 100 cases made. • $65 • (05/31/98) • **95**

Pommard Clos des Lambots 1994: Shows a good effort to produce concentration. Darker and more flavorful than many in this appellation, it delivers a silky mouthfeel accented by black cherry, currant, earth and floral notes. Drinkable now. • $35 • (11/15/96) • **85**

Pommard Les Chanlins Vieilles Vignes 1995: Top notes of sweet, spicy oak are underscored by concentrated cherry and earth flavors that return on the aftertaste. Massive tannins need until 2002 to resolve. • $40 • (11/15/97) • **90**

Pommard Les Chanlins Vieilles Vignes 1994: One of *the* wines of the vintage in Côte de Beaune. It has balance and integrity, depth and complexity, supported by a lush, ripe, rich cassis, black cherry and earth character. Sweet-tasting tannins. Long, succulent finish. Try after 1999. • $43 • (11/15/96) • **92**

Pommard Les Rugiens Vieilles Vignes 1995: Delivers rich, chewy licorice and black cherry flavors up front, firm, mouthcoating tannins on the follow-through and an aftertaste that echoes with fruit. Needs until 2000 to harmonize. • $44 • (11/15/97) • **88**

Pommard Les Vignots 1995: Blackberry and sweet oak flavors mingle in this moderately rich Pommard. The fruit returns on the finish, so there's hope it will eventually balance the massive tannins. Wait until 2000. • $31 • (11/15/97) • **86**

Puligny-Montrachet Les Referts 1996: Pretty wine, quite intense, showing lovely, buttery, croissantlike flavors along with a touch of honey, toasty hazelnut and ripe fruit. Full-bodied and deftly smoky and toasty, with a minerally, silky texture that comes through on the lively finish. Try around 2002. 225 cases made. • $NA • (05/31/98) • **89**

Santenay Clos de la Confrérie 1994: A nice, lightish wine, with pretty black cherry flavors wrapped in a layer of grainy tannins. Drink it with cheese or juicy meats. • $25 • (11/15/96) • **82**

Santenay Clos de la Confrérie White 1993: Harmonious and crisp, with a round mouthfeel. Shows a caressing, creamy character as well as vibrant lime and grapefruit notes. Could use more fruit concentration; tart finish. Drinkable now. • $NA • (05/15/95) • **83**

Santenay Clos du Beauregard White 1996: Distinctive for its decadent combination of smoke, earth, mineral, wet soil and citrus aromas and flavors. Medium-bodied, with a crystaline acid character. Real *goût de terroir* in this *premier cru*. Well made and solid. Best after 2002. 100 cases made. • $NA • (05/31/98) • **87**

Santenay La Maladière 1995: A pretty, forward style that is soft and elegant. Destined for early consumption. • $25 • (11/15/97) • **83**

Santenay La Maladière 1994: Firm tannins, with sufficient intensity of flavor to balance them, make this a good bet for the cellar. It has lovely currant flavors and a hint of chocolate. Try in 1999. • $27 • (11/15/96) • **86**

Santenay Le Beaurepaire White 1996: Pretty as can be, with floral, citrus, pear and green apple notes accented by honey and some spice aromas and flavors. Medium-bodied, the mineral notes come through on the long, succulent finish. Laser-sharp and not showy, but a pleasure to taste. Tempting now through 2003. 500 cases made. • $33 • (05/31/98) • **88**

Santenay Les Gravières 1994: A straightforward Pinot Noir, but well made, with a lovely cassis bush and blackberry character. Quite crisp, but very pure in its expression. Try now. • $27 • (11/15/96) • **84**

Santenay Les Gravières White 1996: Lively, vibrant, medium-bodied *premier cru*, bursting with citrus, freshly cut grass, apple and tropical flavors. This exotic wine has a mineral component and a wonderful weight in the midpalate. Balanced, succulent finish. Tempting now, but better after 2002. 200 cases made. • $33 • (05/31/98) • **88**

Savigny-lès-Beaune Dessus les Vermots White 1996: A beauty that enthralls the palate, building its profile one layer at a time, each showing up on the gustatory radar screen like a delightful blip. Both ripe and racy, showing lovely fruit, judicious oak, opulent texture and succulent character. Medium to full in body, it has concentration and a long finish. Tempting now through 2005. 1,000 cases made. • $28 • (05/31/98) • **92**

Savigny-lès-Beaune Dessus les Vermots White 1993: Quite austere but clean and crisp, adding a hint of honey amidst the green-apple skin, lemon rind and grass flavors. Drink now. 917 cases made. • $23 • (05/15/95) • **80**

Savigny-lès-Beaune Les Vergelesses White 1996: Fairly thick and lush, with a pronounced smoke and toasty oak character. Supple, round mouthfeel despite the backbone of acidity, offering some pear, spice, mineral and hazelnut notes. Lovely finish. Drink now or hold until 2003. 250 cases made. • $32 • (05/31/98) • **87**

Volnay Clos des Chênes 1995: Great effort in this appellation. A delicious red that fills the mouth with rich black cherry flavors and spicy notes. The richness and concentration last through the lengthy finish. Give it until 2000 to integrate. 50 cases imported. 275 cases made. • $35 • (11/15/97) • **92**

Volnay Les Champans 1995: Marked by plenty of bright red berry aromas and flavors, moderate depth and concentration in the mouth and a lingering finish. Very elegant and well structured. • $35 • (11/15/97) • **85**

Volnay-Santenots 1995: Begins with pretty cherry aromas and flavors, follows with a sensation of richness on the palate, finishes with troublesome, drying tannins. Try in 1999. • $35 • (11/15/97) • **85**

Volnay-Santenots 1994: Decently balanced, this shows some finesse, with black cherry, wet earth and herbal flavors. Light-bodied, it turns a bit astringent on the finish. Drinkable now. • $38 • (11/15/96) • **82**

GISCOURS, CHÂTEAU

Margaux 1997: This black wine has rich raspberry and mineral aromas but falls short on the palate, with medium body and a lack of fruit. Tasted twice, with consistent notes. • $NA • (06/15/98) (BT) • **80-84**

Margaux 1996: An elegant red, with fine tannins and well-proportioned fruit. Medium-bodied, with medium tannins and a fruit, vanilla and chocolate aftertaste. 35,100 cases made. • $30 • (06/15/98) (BT) • **85-89**

Margaux 1995: A very refined red. One of the best Giscours in years. Wonderful aromas of crushed raspberries, blackberries and other fruits. Full-bodied, with very fine tannins and a long, caressing finish. All in finesse. Best after 2001. 20,000 cases made. • $24 Ⓐ • (01/31/98) • **92**

Margaux 1993: Sleek and racy, featuring some lovely cassis, cedar and black cherry flavors. Medium body, supple tannins. Drink now. 3,500 cases made. • $20 Ⓐ • (01/31/96) • **86**

Margaux 1991: A wine with an herbal berry character, medium body and a slightly diluted finish. • $24 • (03/31/94) • **78**

Margaux 1990: Complete and expressive, with intense black cherry, plum, tobacco character, fine silky tannins and a long, lively finish. Drink now. 33,000 cases made. • $12 Ⓐ • (03/31/93) • **92**

Margaux 1989 • $40 Ⓐ • (03/15/92) • **92**
Margaux 1988 • $30 Ⓐ • (04/30/91) • **89**
Margaux 1986 • $37 Ⓐ • (06/15/89) • **83**
Margaux 1985 • $40 Ⓐ • (09/30/88) • **86**
Margaux 1983 • $39 Ⓐ • (05/01/89) • **78**
Margaux 1982 • $50 Ⓐ • (08/31/92) • **88**
Margaux 1981 • $17 Ⓐ • (06/01/84) • **82**
Margaux 1980 • $NA • (01/01/84) • **80**
Margaux 1979 • $34 • (10/15/89) • **87**
Margaux 1978 • $51 Ⓐ • (01/01/84) • **87**
Margaux 1976 • $19 Ⓐ • (01/01/84) • **83**
Margaux 1970 • $79 Ⓐ • (01/01/84) • **81**
Margaux 1964 • $55 • (01/01/84) • **89**
Margaux 1962 • $51 Ⓐ • (11/30/87) • **68**
Margaux 1961 • $97 Ⓐ • (04/30/96) • **80**

GLANA, CHÂTEAU DU

St.-Julien 1997: Frozen red fruit on the nose. Medium-bodied, with some mineral character but slightly drying tannins. A bit overdone? • $NA • (06/15/98) (BT) • **80-84**

St.-Julien 1996: Interesting berry, cherry and vanilla character. Medium-bodied, with a slightly diluted midpalate and a clean finish. 8,000 cases made. • $15 • (06/15/98) (BT) • **80-84**

St.-Julien 1994: Clean and fruity, this shows a dried cherry and berry character, light to medium in body and a light finish. Drink now. • $15 • (01/31/97) • **80**

St.-Julien 1990: This thick, husky wine shows loads of tobacco, blackberry and redwood character, full, velvety tannins and a succulent finish. It lacks a bit of finesse, though. Drink now. 17,000 cases made. • $20 • (03/31/93) • **88**

Key: SS—Spectator Selection CS—Cellar Selection HR—Highly Recommended BB—Best Buy $NA—Price not available Ⓐ—Auction Price (BT)—Barrel Tasting
Dates in parentheses indicate the issues in which the ratings were published.

St.-Julien 1989 • $NA • (03/15/92) • **87**
St.-Julien 1987 • $NA • (11/30/89) • **81**
St.-Julien 1986 • $17 • (11/30/89) • **84**
St.-Julien 1982 • $NA • (11/30/89) • **85**
St.-Julien Vieilles Vignes 1996: Impressive concentration for this estate, with loads of tobacco, chocolate and berry aromas and flavors. Medium- to full-bodied, with medium, velvety tannins and a fresh finish. 8,000 cases made. • $NA • (01/01/97) (BT) • **85-89**
St.-Julien Vieilles Vignes 1995: A delicious, delicate red. Very perfumed, with chocolate-coated cherry character. Medium-bodied, with very fine tannins and a medium aftertaste. Best after 1999. 6,200 cases made. • $15 • (01/31/98) • **87**

GLEON MONTANIE, CHÂTEAU

Corbières Cuvée Spéciale 1990 • $11 • (03/15/94) • **87**
Corbières Cuvée Tradition 1990 • $9 • (03/15/94) • **85**

GLORIA, CHÂTEAU

St.-Julien 1997: Clean berry and violet aromas. Medium-bodied, with fine tannins and a caressing finish. Well made. • $NA • (06/15/98) (BT) • **85-89**
St.-Julien 1996: A beautiful '96, with just the right amount of ripe fruit and well-integrated, fine tannins. Medium-bodied, with a sweet fruit finish. Deft winemaking. Not overdone. Serious value. Just made outstanding. • $30 • (06/15/98) (BT) • **90-94**
St.-Julien 1995: Rather tough now, but with seriously good fruit concentration. Cherry and wet earth aromas. Medium-bodied, with full tannins and a tannic finish. Will improve with age. Best after 2002. • $22 Ⓐ • (01/31/98) • **90**
St.-Julien 1994: Chewy and tannic. Medium-bodied, with an almost raisiny character, a fluid midpalate and a tannic finish. Better in 1999. • $27 • (01/31/97) • **84**
St.-Julien 1992: Beautiful tobacco and currant aromas and flavors, a polished palate, medium to light in body and fine tannins. Much better than the '91. • $16 Ⓐ • (04/15/95) • **84**
St.-Julien 1991: Delicate red berry and raspberry aromas and flavors. This medium-bodied wine shows light tannins and a slightly drying finish. Tasted twice, with consistent notes. • $19 • (03/31/94) • **77**
St.-Julien 1990: Understated, with plum, vanilla and new oak flavors and silky, racy tannins. A firm and sleek wine. Drink now. 16,000 cases made. • $27 • (03/31/93) • **89**
St.-Julien 1989 • $22 Ⓐ • (10/15/92) • **89**
St.-Julien 1988 • $18 • (10/15/92) • **88**
St.-Julien 1987 • $15 • (11/30/89) • **84**
St.-Julien 1986 • $24 Ⓐ • (11/30/89) • **89**
St.-Julien 1985 • $35 Ⓐ • (10/15/92) • **90**
St.-Julien 1984 • $14 • (10/15/92) • **79**
St.-Julien 1983 • $41 Ⓐ • (10/15/92) • **83**
St.-Julien 1982 • $48 Ⓐ • (08/31/92) • **83**
St.-Julien 1981 • $17 Ⓐ • (10/15/92) • **83**
St.-Julien 1979 • $25 Ⓐ • (10/15/89) • **83**
St.-Julien 1978 • $24 Ⓐ • (10/15/92) • **74**
St.-Julien 1976 • $24 • (10/15/92) • **86**
St.-Julien 1975 • $24 Ⓐ • (10/15/92) • **83**
St.-Julien 1971 • $39 • (10/15/92) • **86**
St.-Julien 1970 • $33 Ⓐ • (10/15/92) • **88**
St.-Julien 1967 • $28 • (10/15/92) • **84**
St.-Julien 1966 • $55 • (10/15/92) • **87**
St.-Julien 1964 • $50 • (10/15/92) • **81**
St.-Julien 1962 • $55 • (10/15/92) • **79**
St.-Julien 1961 • $57 • (04/30/96) • **88**
St.-Julien 1960 • $NA • (10/15/92) • **71**
St.-Julien 1948 • $NA • (10/15/92) • **85**

GOBET, P.

Chiroubles La Fontenelle 1994 • $10 • (10/31/95) • **85**

GODEAU, CHÂTEAU

St.-Emilion 1994: A pleasant smoky aroma leads into a soft, fairly spicy and fruity wine, with good blackberry and plum flavors and a touch of earth. Ready to drink. 1,800 cases made. • $20 • (04/30/97) • **83**

GOERG, PAUL

Brut Champagne Millésimé 1989: Not sweet, but almost like a dessert in style. It has lovely vanilla, chocolate and banana notes carried on rich, creamy texture. Not long on the finish, but very flavorful and appealing. • $34 • (11/30/95) • **88**

GOISOT, GHISLAINE & JEAN-HUGUES

Bourgogne Aligoté 1996: Unbelievable quality for an Aligoté. Wonderful and lush, with a lime, butter and honey character, full in body and with an oily texture lurking underneath all that excellent acidity. Long, balanced finish. Tempting now with its gobs of fruit and floral notes; should be even better around 2000. 5,800 cases made. • $14 • (05/31/98) • **91**
Bourgogne Aligoté 1995: Thick and ripe, with sweet flavors, it's slightly candied, a bit overdone. Full-bodied, soft on the finish. Drink soon. • $NA • (06/15/97) • **79**
Bourgogne Aligoté 1994: Amazing quality for a Bourgogne Aligoté. An exciting and electrifying marriage of honey, lemon, earth and mineral flavors. Solidly structured, its texture is silky, and it's clean, fresh, slightly grassy and appealingly sweet on the finish. From Domaine du Corps de Garde. • $NA • (05/31/96) • **88**
Bourgogne Côtes d'Auxerre 1995: Pretty, quite sweet and ripe with flavors of berries, plum and smoke. Medium-bodied, quite tannic. Lacks a bit of balance. • $15 • (06/15/97) • **80**
Bourgogne Côtes d'Auxerre Corps de Garde White 1996: A beautifully made, balanced wine, with a lush, silky, creamlike texture. Full-bodied, it delivers marvelous mineral, stone and wet earth notes with decent tropical and pear flavors. A bit drying on the finish, yet still satisfying, hinting of toasty oak and honey. Tempting now but should hold through 2001 or so. 1,250 cases made. • $17 • (05/31/98) • **88**
Bourgogne Côtes d'Auxerre Corps de Garde White 1995: Stupendous. Silky in texture, full in body, with polished flavors, and a long finish, it's a seamless marriage of harmony and power. The spice, oak and fruit flavors show the smooth yet intense complexity of a *premier cru* Meursault. From one of Burgundy's rising stars in the field of white winemaking. Drink now through 2002. 1,500 cases made. • $15 • (06/15/97) • **91**
Bourgogne Côtes d'Auxerre Domaine du Corps de Garde White 1994 • $NA • (05/31/96) • **93**
Bourgogne Côtes d'Auxerre White 1996: Supple and honeyed, this ripe, charming and full-bodied white shows tropical, pear, toasty bread and spice notes. Kicks in with lime and crisp acidity on the balanced finish. Tempting now through 2000. 2,080 cases made. • $15 • (05/31/98) • **89**
Bourgogne Côtes d'Auxerre White 1995: Very pure, with some lovely honey, ripe pear and citrus flavors. Full-bodied, it's not showy, but rather subtle. Supple, refined finish. Drink now to 2000. • $13 • (06/15/97) • **88**
Chardonnay Bourgogne Côtes d'Auxerre 1994 • $NA • (05/31/96) • **87**
Chardonnay Bourgogne Côtes d'Auxerre Domaine du Corps de Garde 1994 • $NA • (05/31/96) • **92**
Sauvignon de St.-Bris 1996: Clean and very pretty, bursting with Sauvignon Blanc varietal aromas of freshly cut grass and gooseberry. Terrific thread of honey, quince, spice and butter. Medium-bodied and supple in texture, it kicks in with expected herbal notes on the long, smooth, ripe finish. Delicious now through 2000. 3,300 cases made. • $14 • (05/31/98) • **92**
Sauvignon de St.-Bris 1995: What a beauty! Ripe, rich and sweet-tasting, with full-blown tropical, honey, citrus, gooseberry and grass flavors delivered in a full-bodied, polished style with a long, succulent finish. Why wait? Buy a case or two and enjoy now. • $14 • (06/15/97) • **90**
Sauvignon de St.-Bris 1994 • $NA • (05/31/96) • **84**
Sauvignon de St.-Bris Corps de Garde Gourmand Fié Gris 1996: Distinctive Sauvignon Blanc, with gooseberry, freshly cut grass and herb notes. A bit sour, but very vibrant and fruity. Medium-bodied. Drink now. • $NA • (05/31/98) • **85**

GOMERIE, CHÂTEAU LA

St.-Emilion 1997: Good dark color, with berry, cherry and tobacco aromas and flavors. Medium-bodied, with a silky texture and a medium finish. Cool wine. • $NA • (06/15/98) (BT) • **85-89**
St.-Emilion 1996: Some berry, green tobacco and cherry character to this medium-bodied wine, with medium tannins and a delicate finish. • $NA • (01/01/97) (BT) • **85-89**
St.-Emilion 1995: Plummy and long, with vibrant fruit, medium body and silky tannins. Better than previous tasting. • $NA • (01/01/97) (BT) • **85-89**

GONET, MICHEL

Brut Blanc de Blancs Champagne Chardonnay Grand Crus 1988: A very rich style, almost too rich. It shows overripe apple and steely aromas and flavors, medium body and a tart finish. Drink now. • $NA • (12/31/93) • **82**

Brut Blanc de Blancs Champagne Club de Viticulteurs 1985: This is a very opulent, almost oxidized style with toasty nut and apple aromas and flavors. It's full-bodied and rich, with a long crisp finish. Perfect with fish or white meat dishes. Drink now. • $NA • (12/31/93) • **84**

GONON, PIERRE

St.-Joseph 1995: Fresh and fruity, this jammy red offers plenty of raspberry and blackberry flavors, with moderate, integrated tannins and lively acidity. It's modest but expressive; drink now through 1999. 1,500 cases made. • $NA • (10/15/97) • **85**

St.-Joseph 1994: Coffee and bitter chocolate aromas give way to round, ripe flavors of earth, prunes and spices. Tannins are firm and a bit heavy on the finish. Rich, it needs more fruit for balance. 1,333 cases made. • $NA • (10/15/97) • **83**

St.-Joseph White Les Oliviers 1995: A big-boned white showing ripe pear, butterscotch and vanilla flavors. A bit blowsy, but it pulls together on the finish. Ripe and almost sweet. • $NA • (10/15/97) • **84**

GOSSET

Brut Champagne Celebris 1988: Well balanced and nicely fruity, this firm-textured bubbly has vibrant flavors and a mouthwatering finish. Still slightly austere, it should improve through 2000. • $95 • (11/30/96) • **88**

Brut Champagne Grand Millésime 1989: A full-throttle, full-bodied, powerfully flavored Champagne that seems to show a lot of Pinot Noir character in its cherry and floral flavors and long, bold finish. Approachable now, but needs time to develop more complexity. Better through 2000. • $69 • (11/15/96) • **90**

Brut Champagne Grand Millésime 1985: Big and full-bodied, offering lots of honey and pear flavors, an exaggerated mousse and bracing acidity. Accents of spice, nut and vanilla come together on the lingering finish. 2,500 cases made. • $70 • (11/30/95) • **89**

Brut Champagne Grand Millésime 1983 • $75 • (12/31/93) • **90**

Brut Champagne Grand Millésime 1982 • $60 • (12/31/90) • **90**

Brut Champagne Grand Millésime 1979 • $45 • (07/15/87) • **96**

Brut Rosé Champagne 1982 • $75 • (12/31/88) • **88**

Brut Rosé Champagne Grand Rosé 1990: A fresh, nicely built rosé. Offers light cherry and strawberry aromas, a firm texture and lively fruit flavors that linger on the finish. Should improve through 2000. • $59 • (12/31/96) • **89**

Brut Rosé Champagne Grand Rosé 1988: There's plenty of fruit in this rosé, almost jammy flavors of cherries and plums, yet it's lively and fresh, with an attractive piecrust finish. Intense and focused. 1,250 cases made. • $60 • (12/15/95) • **90**

GOUBARD, MICHEL

Bourgogne White 1996: Overly buttery, with butterscotch and caramel aromas and flavors from the dominating wood, yet smooth and creamy in texture, full-bodied and balanced on the finish. For fans of oaky whites. Drink now. • $12 • (05/31/98) • **82**

Pinot Noir Bourgogne Côte Chalonnaise Mont-Avril 1989 • $10 • (03/15/93) • **77**

GOUBERT, DOMAINE LES

Côtes du Rhône-Villages Beaumes de Venise 1987 • $9 • (07/31/89) • **81**

Côtes du Rhône-Villages Beaumes de Venise 1985 • $9 • (04/30/88) • **80**

Côtes du Rhône-Villages Sablet 1985 • $8 • (04/30/88) • **76**

Gigondas 1994: A decent effort, straightforward, medium-bodied, with cherry and toasty oak flavors. Firm and slightly dry finish. Drink now. • $NA • (10/15/97) • **81**

Gigondas 1989 • $13 • (10/15/94) • **87**

Key: SS—Spectator Selection CS—Cellar Selection HR—Highly Recommended BB—Best Buy $NA—Price not available Ⓐ—Auction Price (BT)—Barrel Tasting
Dates in parentheses indicate the issues in which the ratings were published.

Gigondas 1986 • $13 • (03/15/90) • **81**

Gigondas 1985 • $11 • (04/30/88) • **89**

Gigondas Cuvée Florence 1994: Very polished, with a bounty of toasty oak, spice, mocha and coffee flavors accented by currant, black cherry, floral and mineral notes. Fairly balanced, and quite delicious now through 2000. • $NA • (10/15/97) • **87**

Gigondas Cuvée Florence 1989 • $23 • (10/15/94) • **87**

Gigondas Cuvée Florence 1986 • $24 • (04/30/88) • **92**

GOUGES, HENRI

Nuits-St.-Georges 1991: Firm and relatively fleshy for the vintage; has spicy cherry aromas and flavors and a tannic, slightly bitter finish. Drinkable now. 500 cases made. • $30 Ⓐ • (01/31/94) • **83**

Nuits-St.-Georges 1990: Round and rich, with attractive, spicy berry flavors and plenty of velvety tannins. Drinkable now. 100 cases made. • $40 • (12/15/92) • **88**

Nuits-St.-Georges 1986 • $30 • (07/31/88) • **84**

Nuits-St.-Georges Aux Chaignots 1986 • $40 • (07/31/88) • **90**

Nuits-St.-Georges Clos des Porrets St.-Georges 1991: Solid, straightforward, crisp and juicy. Try now. 625 cases made. • $40 Ⓐ • (01/31/94) • **81**

Nuits-St.-Georges Clos des Porrets St.-Georges 1990: Very intense, with loads of cherry, earth and plum aromas and flavors and a super tannin structure. The finish goes on and on. Drinkable now. 100 cases made. • $58 • (12/15/92) • **92**

Nuits-St.-Georges Clos des Porrets St.-Georges 1989 • $45 • (01/31/92) • **87**

Nuits-St.-Georges Clos des Porrets St.-Georges 1985 • $NA • (12/31/94) • **92**

Nuits-St.-Georges Clos des Porrets St.-Georges 1976 • $NA • (12/31/94) • **85**

Nuits-St.-Georges Clos des Porrets St.-Georges 1971 • $NA • (12/31/94) • **93**

Nuits-St.-Georges Clos des Porrets St.-Georges 1953 • $NA • (12/31/94) • **93**

Nuits-St.-Georges Clos des Porrets St.-Georges 1949 • $NA • (12/31/94) • **90**

Nuits-St.-Georges Clos des Porrets St.-Georges 1943 • $NA • (12/31/94) • **75**

Nuits-St.-Georges Les Pruliers 1991: Slightly decadent berry and currant flavors balance the earthy, citrusy notes that emerge on the moderately tannic finish. Try now. 625 cases made. • $40 Ⓐ • (01/31/94) • **81**

Nuits-St.-Georges Les Pruliers 1990: Extremely well toned, with hard tannins covering the lovely, ripe fruit flavors. Nonetheless, it shows pretty black cherry and earth notes. Drink now. 130 cases made. • $58 • (12/15/92) • **90**

Nuits-St.-Georges Les Pruliers 1989 • $45 • (01/31/92) • **86**

Nuits-St.-Georges Les Pruliers 1969 • $NA • (12/31/94) • **85**

Nuits-St.-Georges Les St.-Georges 1992: Soft and appealing at first, but turns a bit green on the finish, showing tough tannins. Has more character than many '92 red Burgundies. From a site known to produce long-aging wines of *grand cru* quality. Drinkable now. • $NA • (12/31/94) • **86**

Nuits-St.-Georges Les St.-Georges 1991: Beautiful intensity and character, but also a bit green and hard. Definitely needs until 1997 or beyond to soften. More concentrated than the '92. • $46 • (12/31/94) • **88**

Nuits-St.-Georges Les St.-Georges 1990: Very distinguished. A dense, rich Nuits, with raspberry, earth and spice characteristics and a wonderful velvety texture. Drinkable now. 75 cases made. • $60 • (12/15/92) • **92**

Nuits-St.-Georges Les St.-Georges 1989 • $49 • (01/31/92) • **89**

Nuits-St.-Georges Les St.-Georges 1985 • $45 • (02/15/88) • **68**

Nuits-St.-Georges Les St.-Georges 1983 • $NA • (12/31/94) • **81**

Nuits-St.-Georges Les St.-Georges 1972 • $NA • (12/31/94) • **84**

Nuits-St.-Georges Les St.-Georges 1964 • $NA • (12/31/94) • **92**

Nuits-St.-Georges Les St.-Georges 1959 • $NA • (12/31/94) • **81**

Nuits-St.-Georges Les St.-Georges 1955 • $NA • (12/31/94) • **93**

Nuits-St.-Georges Les St.-Georges 1937 • $NA • (12/31/94) • **79**

Nuits-St.-Georges Les St.-Georges 1926 • $NA • (12/31/94) • **68**

Nuits-St.-Georges Les Vaucrains 1991: Firm, spicy and straightforward, showing an aromatic currant and anise character. Finishes lean, simple and a bit tannic. Drinkable now. 375 cases made. • $44 Ⓐ • (01/31/94) • **80**

Nuits-St.-Georges Les Vaucrains 1990: A beautiful Nuits, with plummy, earthy characteristics and an excellent intensity of fruit and tannins. Well balanced and focused; drinkable now. 75 cases made. • $60 • (12/15/92) • **91**

Nuits-St.-Georges Les Vaucrains 1989 • $49 • (01/31/92) • **90**

Nuits-St.-Georges Les Vaucrains Premier Cru 1990: Silky and beautifully balanced. Has a quite round and supple texture. Try now. • $60 • (12/31/94) • **88**
Nuits-St.-Georges Les Vaucrains Premier Cru 1989 • $49 • (12/31/94) • **89**
Nuits-St.-Georges Les Vaucrains Premier Cru 1961 • $NA • (12/31/94) • **87**

GOULAINE, MARQUIS DE

Chardonnay Vin de Pays du Jardin de la France 1996: A hint of vanilla adds interest to the straightforward apple and citrus flavors in this clean, fresh white. It's balanced, but finishes short. Drink now. • $11 • (05/31/98) • **82**
Muscadet de Sèvre et Maine Sur Lie 1994 • $7 • (12/15/95) • **78**
Muscadet de Sèvre et Maine Sur Lie 1993 • $7 • (08/31/94) BB • **84**
Muscadet de Sèvre et Maine Sur Lie Cuvée du Millénaire 1995: Round flavors of juicy pears, with herb and light earth notes, are bolstered by firm acidity in this tasty, straightforward white. 3,000 cases made. • $15 • (06/15/97) • **85**
Muscadet de Sèvre et Maine Sur Lie Cuvée du Millénaire 1994 • $10 • (11/15/95) • **79**
Muscadet de Sèvre et Maine Sur Lie Cuvée du Millénaire 1993 • $10 • (10/31/94) • **77**
Sancerre 1996: It's mouthwatering just to sniff this vivid, juicy white. Aromas of lime, minerals and herbs give way to crisp apple and ripe pear flavors, lively and exuberant, with a clean, focused finish. Textbook style. Drink now through 1999. 4,000 cases made. • $17 • (03/31/98) • **88**
Vouvray 1996: This white begins with crisp, lemony aromas but turns slightly sweet on the palate—a nice mix of crisp and fruity, with pineapple and peach flavors. Lively and clean, it's a nice apéritif. Drink now. • $11 • (05/31/98) • **84**

GOULET, GEORGE

Blanc de Blancs Crémant Champagne 1982 • $30 • (07/31/88) • **86**
Brut Champagne 1982 • $30 • (07/31/88) • **90**
Brut Champagne Cuvée du Centenaire 1982 • $47 • (07/31/88) • **87**
Brut Rosé Champagne 1982 • $31 • (07/31/88) • **85**

GOUR DE CHAULE, DOMAINE DU

Gigondas 1993: Still fresh, this is firm and straightfoward, offering ripe plum, licorice and black tea flavors over firm tannins. Balanced and well integrated, with moderate concentration. Drink now. 750 cases made. • $18 • (10/15/96) • **86**
Gigondas 1986 • $13 • (09/15/90) • **90**

GOURGAZAUD, CHÂTEAU DE

Minervois 1994: Supple, with red berry and light smoky flavors, light tannins. A pleasant quaff, a bit diluted. Drinkable now. Tasted twice. • $9 • (12/15/97) • **78**
Minervois 1991 • $8 • (12/15/94) • **79**

GOUZOTTE D'OR, LA

Chablis 1996: Very seductive and sweet-tasting, this is a crowd pleaser. Balanced and attractively fruity, with loads of lemon, pear and honey, this full-bodied Chablis has a supple character and a gentle, if slightly hot, finish. Drink from 2002 to 2005. 450 cases made. • $18 • (05/31/98) • **87**
Mâcon-Villages 1996: Firm, fruity and flavorful, showing a slight grassy undertow along with green apple and bitter almond. Medium-bodied, with a crisp finish. Try now through 2000. 600 cases made. • $14 • (05/31/98) • **83**
Pouilly-Fuissé 1996: At first very fruity, this medium-bodied Chardonnay turns a bit hot and funky on the slightly unbalanced finish. Drink chilled. 500 cases made. • $22 • (05/31/98) • **76**
St.-Romain White 1996: Ripe, rich and medium-bodied, a bit rustic and grassy at first, it then opens to offer an enticing tropical and pear tart character. Harmonious, long, satisfying finish. Drink now or hold through 2002. A new négociant in Savigny-Lès-Beaune. 200 cases made. • $14 • (05/31/98) • **88**
St.-Véran 1996: A bit greenish, but rather thick and dense, this full-bodied wine has honey, pear, green apple and wet hay notes. Well made, but has a slightly bitter finish. Ripe enough to improve through 2000. 500 cases made. • $15 • (05/31/98) • **84**

GRAILLOT, ALAIN

Crozes-Hermitage 1995: Brilliant Crozes, so expressive, with a wonderful varietal character of freshly crushed black pepper, currant, iodine, mineral and lead-pencil complexity. So sexy. And, it's lush and polished on the palate, with massive but ripe tannins. Long finish. Best from 1999 through 2005. 5,500 cases made. • $15 • (10/15/97) • **92**
Crozes-Hermitage 1994: Pure, classic Syrah aromas of raspberry, licorice and game carry through on the rich palate, beautifully defined and balanced. Delicious now for its varietal character, it should improve through 2003. 4,000 cases made. • $15 • (11/30/96) HR • **92**
Crozes-Hermitage 1993 • $15 • (10/15/95) • **85**
Crozes-Hermitage 1992 • $14 • (05/31/94) • **84**
Crozes-Hermitage 1991 • $15 • (05/31/94) • **79**
Crozes-Hermitage 1990 • $17 • (04/15/93) • **88**
Crozes-Hermitage 1989 • $14 • (03/31/91) • **88**
Crozes-Hermitage 1986 • $9 • (04/15/89) • **88**
Crozes-Hermitage La Guiraude 1995: Intense and highly extracted, with a burst of crushed black pepper, currant and cherry character. Concentrated on the midpalate, it turns a bit tough on the finish, for now. But give the tannins until around 1999 to soften. 900 cases made. • $20 • (10/15/97) • **87**
Crozes-Hermitage La Guiraude 1994: Thick and chewy, this rich red offers black fruit, coffee and dark chocolate flavors, with thick tannins and a fruity but slightly bitter finish. Try now. • $20 • (11/30/96) • **90**
Crozes-Hermitage La Guiraude 1992 • $18 • (05/31/94) • **80**
Crozes-Hermitage La Guiraude 1991 • $18 • (05/31/94) • **84**
Crozes-Hermitage White 1996: This crisp white offers light pear, citrus and apple flavors, straightforward but lively. A good apéritif. Drink now. • $15 • (10/15/97) • **81**
Hermitage 1994: Beautiful Syrah flavors of raspberry, plum, black pepper and licorice are well balanced and bright in this round, sweet red. The tannins are firm yet well integrated, and linger with the fruit flavors on the finish. A fine example of the traditional style. Drink now. • $43 • (11/30/96) • **90**
Hermitage 1990: Muscular and powerful, with masses of plum, black cherry and spice flavors. The rich tannins are beautifully integrated and the wine has great balance. Drink now. • $45 • (05/31/94) • **90**
St.-Joseph 1995: Rich and concentrated, this sophisticated red combines toasty oak and ripe fruit flavors in a balanced, harmonious wine. A fine example of international-style winemaking that doesn't bury the local flavors. Try now. 800 cases made. • $19 • (10/15/97) • **91**
St.-Joseph 1994: Made in a lighter, elegant style, this offers raspberry and blackberry flavors with smoke and licorice accents. Though it's supple on the palate, firm tannins emerge on the finish. Drinkable now through 2000. • $NA • (11/30/96) • **87**
St.-Joseph 1993 • $17 • (11/15/95) • **80**
St.-Joseph 1992 • $18 • (05/31/94) • **80**
St.-Joseph 1991 • $18 • (05/31/94) • **86**

GRAMENON, DOMAINE

Côtes du Rhône La Sagesse 1995: An atypical style. Resiny aromas from new oak treatment lead into a menthol accent to the meager fruit character. This is hollow, with tannins and alcohol on the finish. Drink now. • $15 • (01/01/98) • **76**

GRAND BARRAIL LAMARZELLE FIGEAC, CHÂTEAU

St.-Emilion 1997: Pretty berry and plum aromas and flavors. Medium-bodied, with firm tannins and a short finish. • $NA • (06/15/98) (BT) • **85-89**
St.-Emilion 1996: A bit stewed in character, with plum and tomato flavors. Medium-bodied, with medium tannins and a short finish. • $32 • (06/15/98) (BT) • **80-84**
St.-Emilion 1986 • $15 • (06/30/89) • **72**
St.-Emilion 1982 • $25 Ⓐ • (05/15/89) • **85**

GRAND CAUMONT, CHÂTEAU DU

Corbières 1990 • $10 • (03/15/94) • **83**

GRAND CHARIOT

Corbières 1990 • $NA • (03/15/94) • **81**

FRANCE

GRAND CHEMIN, CHÂTEAU

Côtes de Bourg 1989 • $9 • (11/30/92) • **79**
Côtes de Bourg 1985 • $8 • (06/15/89) • **76**

GRAND CLARET, CHÂTEAU

Premières Côtes de Bordeaux 1988 • $7 • (07/31/91) • **78**

GRAND CRES, DOMAINE DU

Corbières 1990 • $10 • (06/15/93) • **82**

GRAND MAISON, DOMAINE DE

Pessac-Léognan 1986 • $8 • (04/15/90) • **80**

GRAND MONTMIRAIL, DOMAINE DU

Gigondas Cuvée Vieilles Vignes 1993: Offers promising smoky and herbal aromas, but turns a bit earthy on the palate despite some black cherry flavors. Light-bodied, with slightly drying tannins. 3,100 cases made. • $15 • (10/15/97) • **79**
Gigondas Cuvée Vieilles Vignes 1989: A ripe wine that's beginning to dry out. Round, roasted flavors of plums and prunes are jammy over hard tannins. Attractive but a bit muddled. Drink now. 6,000 cases made. • $15 • (10/15/96) • **82**

GRAND MOULAS, CHÂTEAU DU

Côtes du Rhône-Villages 1995: Straightforward, with strawberry and other red berry notes. Light body and soft tannins. A bit tart on the finish. Drink now, slightly chilled. 400 cases imported. 2,083 cases made. • $11 • (10/15/97) • **75**

GRAND MOULIN, CHÂTEAU

Corbières 1994: A well-sculpted wine, with ripe cherry and spice flavors and a lingering finish. Balanced and polished. Drink now. • $16 • (04/30/98) • **84**
Haut-Médoc 1983 • $6 • (04/16/86) • **63**

GRAND TINEL, DOMAINE DU

Châteauneuf-du-Pape 1989 • $15 • (10/15/91) • **88**
Châteauneuf-du-Pape 1988 • $17 • (10/15/91) • **87**
Châteauneuf-du-Pape 1986 • $20 • (10/15/91) • **86**
Châteauneuf-du-Pape 1985 • $23 • (10/15/91) • **75**
Châteauneuf-du-Pape 1983 • $25 • (10/15/91) • **87**
Châteauneuf-du-Pape 1981 • $27 • (10/15/91) • **89**

GRAND VILLAGE, CHÂTEAU

Bordeaux Supérieur 1995: Wonderful quality for a Bordeaux Supérieur. An elegant and well-made red. Plenty of floral and currant aromas, with a hint of grapes. Full- to medium-bodied, with well-integrated tannins and a long, silky finish. From the owners of Château Lafleur. Best after 2000. • $15 • (01/31/98) • **88**
Bordeaux White 1995: Plenty of apple, pineapple, lime and grass aromas and flavors. Medium-bodied, with lemon-lime flavors and a light, fresh finish that's slightly diluted. Drink now. • $15 • (04/30/98) • **85**

GRAND-CORBIN-DESPAGNE, CHÂTEAU

St.-Emilion 1961 • $14 • (04/30/96) • **84**
St.-Emilion 1945 • $NA • (03/16/86) • **70**

Key: SS—Spectator Selection CS—Cellar Selection HR—Highly Recommended BB—Best Buy $NA—Price not available Ⓐ—Auction Price (BT)—Barrel Tasting
Dates in parentheses indicate the issues in which the ratings were published.

GRAND-MAYNE, CHÂTEAU

St.-Emilion 1995: Rich, delicious blackberry, cherry, milk chocolate and tobacco character. Full-bodied and very velvety, showing intense fruit and round tannins. • $NA • (05/15/96) (BT) • **90-94**
St.-Emilion 1989 • $22 • (03/15/92) • **93**
St.-Emilion 1988 • $20 • (04/30/91) • **89**
St.-Emilion 1986 • $16 • (06/30/89) • **87**

GRAND-MOULINET, CHÂTEAU

Pomerol 1995: Classy in style, elegant in texture, this seems to melt in your mouth. The subtle flavors of black cherry and cinnamon grow on the palate and linger on the finish. Still firm enough to age. Drink now through 2005. 3,000 cases made. • $20 • (01/31/98) • **90**

GRAND-PONTET, CHÂTEAU

St.-Emilion 1997: Very smoky wine, like a chimney. Very ripe, with berry and mineral character, but falls away quickly. Where does it go? • $NA • (06/15/98) (BT) • **75-79**
St.-Emilion 1996: Slightly awkward now. Shows blackberry and dark chocolate on the nose, is medium-bodied, with firm tannins and a slightly burnt finish. May move up a notch next year. • $NA • (01/01/97) (BT) • **80-84**
St.-Emilion 1995: A delicious, multilayered red with chocolate and berry character and long, thickly silky tannins. Better than previous tasting. • $25 • (05/15/97) (BT) • **90-94**
St.-Emilion 1993: Big, solid peppery, gamy, tobacco aromas and flavors, full to medium in body, with hard tannins and a long finish. Try in 1999. • $22 • (01/31/96) • **86**
St.-Emilion 1988 • $21 • (07/15/91) • **86**
St.-Emilion 1961 • $NA • (04/30/96) • **82**

GRAND-PUY-DUCASSE, CHÂTEAU

Pauillac 1996: Dry and short, with some berry character but lacks balance. • $NA • (01/01/97) (BT) • **75-79**
Pauillac 1995: Some decent fruit in this—plenty of berry and cherry aromas and flavors. Moderate tannins and a slightly tough finish. Could move up a notch next year. • $NA • (05/15/96) (BT) • **80-84**
Pauillac 1989 • $29 Ⓐ • (04/30/92) • **86**
Pauillac 1988 • $24 Ⓐ • (04/30/91) • **89**
Pauillac 1986 • $24 Ⓐ • (06/30/89) • **85**
Pauillac 1985 • $22 Ⓐ • (02/29/88) • **90**
Pauillac 1961 • $45 Ⓐ • (04/30/96) • **87**

GRAND-PUY-LACOSTE, CHÂTEAU

Pauillac 1997: Plummy and fruity, with hints of vanilla. Medium-bodied, with light tannins and a fruity finish. Pleasant wine. • $NA • (06/15/98) (BT) • **85-89**
Pauillac 1996: Well crafted. The tannins are like cashmere. Elegant and fine, with wonderful currant, mint and berry character. Full-bodied, with a long finish. • $85 • (06/15/98) (BT) • **90-94**
Pauillac 1995: Wonderful dark chocolate and berry aromas. Full-bodied and concentrated, with lovely, velvety tannins and a long, chocolaty aftertaste. Another winning GPL. Drink after 2002. • $29 Ⓐ • (01/31/98) • **92**
Pauillac 1994: Vivid aromas of raspberries, licorice and cassis, hints of oak. Medium-bodied, with fine tannins and succulent fruit flavors that build on the palate. Better in 1999. • $21 Ⓐ • (01/31/97) • **88**
Pauillac 1993: Good fruit, some elegant currant notes, a slightly herbal character and well-integrated tannins. Drink now. • $23 Ⓐ • (01/31/96) • **85**
Pauillac 1992: Light and earthy, berry-flavored, but rather short and diluted. Tasted twice, with consistent notes. • $24 Ⓐ • (04/15/95) • **76**
Pauillac 1991: Straightforward green tobacco and fruit aromas and flavors, medium tannins and a very light finish. • $24 • (03/31/94) • **82**
Pauillac 1990: A big, up-front wine, with intense aromas of cedar, tobacco, cassis and berries that carry through on the palate and lots of tannins to back it all up. As big as the great '82. Drinkable now. 27,500 cases made. • $26 • (03/31/93) • **95**
Pauillac 1989 • $45 Ⓐ • (03/15/92) • **91**
Pauillac 1988 • $72 Ⓐ • (04/30/91) • **90**
Pauillac 1987 • $18 • (05/15/90) • **77**
Pauillac 1986 • $51 Ⓐ • (05/31/89) • **88**
Pauillac 1985 • $48 Ⓐ • (10/15/94) • **90**

Pauillac 1984 • $9 Ⓐ • (10/15/87) • **83**
Pauillac 1983 • $45 Ⓐ • (10/15/94) • **84**
Pauillac 1982 • $94 Ⓐ • (08/31/92) • **95**
Pauillac 1981 • $36 Ⓐ • (10/15/94) • **88**
Pauillac 1979 • $35 Ⓐ • (10/15/89) • **88**
Pauillac 1970 • $35 Ⓐ • (05/15/93) • **90**
Pauillac 1961 • $141 Ⓐ • (04/30/96) • **86**
Pauillac 1945 • $276 Ⓐ • (11/30/95) • **86**

GRAND-ROMANE, DOMAINE

Gigondas 1994: A bit light and soft, with muted cherry, raspberry, spice, anise and toasty oak flavors. Ready to drink. • $NA • (10/15/97) • **82**
Gigondas 1990 • $13 • (04/15/93) • **85**
Gigondas 1989 • $16 • (08/31/91) • **87**
Gigondas Medaille d'Argent 1990 • $16 • (01/31/92) • **85**
Gigondas Medaille d'Or 1990 • $16 • (01/31/92) • **87**

GRANDES MURAILLES, CHÂTEAU LES

St.-Emilion 1996: Rather simple, with plum and berry character. Light- to medium-bodied, with a light finish. • $32 • (06/15/98) (BT) • **80-84**
St.-Emilion 1989 • $NA • (03/15/92) • **88**
St.-Emilion 1982 • $NA • (05/15/89) • **81**

GRANDS CHÊNES, CHÂTEAU LES

Médoc Cuvée Préstige 1995: One of our discoveries of the vintage. Racy, rich and elegant, yet packed with intense, deep cassis and plum character and lots of toast, vanilla, mocha and oak flavors. Medium- to full-bodied, solid, ripe tannins. Almost outstanding. • $NA • (05/15/96) (BT) • **85-89**

GRANDS DEVERS, DOMAINE DES

Côtes du Rhône-Villages Valreas 1994: Light and thin, diluted, losing its modest fruit and exposing the bitter, dry tannic structure. Not a pretty sight. Drink up. 500 cases imported. 1,667 cases made. • $13 • (10/15/97) • **72**

GRANDS MARÉCHAUX, CHÂTEAU LES

Premières Côtes de Blaye 1997: Not a big wine, but grapey and fruity, with plum and green tobacco aromas and flavors. Light to medium in body, with a light, fruity finish. • $NA • (06/15/98) (BT) • **80-84**

GRANGE CLINET, CHÂTEAU LA

Premières Côtes de Bordeaux 1995: Flavorful and fruit-driven, dark in color, with moderate tannins, a smooth texture and ripe flavors. Drink now through 1999. 10,000 cases made. • $8 • (01/31/98) • **83**
Premières Côtes de Bordeaux 1993: Supple, showing off fresh berry flavors and hints of nutmeg. Has the polish of Bordeaux without much depth. 6,000 cases made. • $8 • (12/15/95) • **80**

GRANGE DE GRENET, CHÂTEAU LA

Bordeaux 1995: This balanced red shows ripe cherry flavors, light smoke notes and firm, integrated tannins. It's food-friendly and harmonious. Drinkable now. 800 cases made. • $8 • (06/30/97) • **85**

GRANGENEUVE, DOMAINE DE

Coteaux du Tricastin Cuvée de la Truffière 1995: This juicy red offers bright berry and cherry flavors, with modest tannins and a fresh, clean finish. It's lively and friendly, for drinking now. 667 cases made. • $15 • (10/15/97) • **83**

GRANGEOTTE, CHÂTEAU LA

Bordeaux 1993: Bright black cherry and firm underlying tannins give this good definition and balance. Drinkable now. • $9 • (12/15/95) • **81**

GRANGÈRE, CHÂTEAU LA

St.-Emilion 1997: Dark-colored, with interesting spice, cinnamon and berry aromas and flavors. Medium-bodied, with velvety tannins and a medium finish. • $NA • (06/15/98) (BT) • **85-89**
St.-Emilion 1996: Slightly stewed fruit character. Medium-bodied, with medium tannins and a light, rather dry finish. • $32 • (06/15/98) (BT) • **75-79**

GRANGES, CHÂTEAU LES

Haut-Médoc 1990: An appealing wine with straightforward cherry flavors and silky tannins. Drinkable now. • $NA • (03/31/93) • **83**

GRANGES, LES

Haut-Médoc 1991: Earthy and vegetal, with some concentration but not much appeal. 25,000 cases made. • $12 • (07/31/96) • **75**

GRANGES D'OR, CHÂTEAU DES

Médoc 1994: Tough in tannin and light in fruit, this rustic red might soften with food but probably won't improve with age. 9,500 cases made. • $12 • (11/30/97) • **76**

GRAS, ALAIN

Auxey-Duresses Red 1995: A vivid young red, showing spicy berry flavors that last through the finish. It's supple and lively, with just a hint of astringency at the end. • $23 • (11/15/97) • **85**
Auxey-Duresses Red 1993: More lean than opulent, with crisp acidity, firm texture and massive but round tannins. Offers plenty of fresh, red berry flavor, topped by mocha, chocolate and spice notes. • $20 • (11/15/95) • **86**
Auxey-Duresses Red 1992: A dark-colored '92, with attractive pepper, currant and blackberry flavors presented in a smooth package. Enjoy now. • $23 • (12/15/94) • **85**
Auxey-Duresses Red 1990: Focused but quite chewy, this medium-bodied wine offers a lot of tobacco and strawberry flavors and a smoky finish. Drinkable now. • $29 • (12/15/92) • **85**
St.-Romain Red 1995: Elegant, pure cherry and raspberry flavors distinguish this wine. Sadly, the astringent tannins detract from its overall appeal. • $23 • (11/15/97) • **84**
St.-Romain Red 1993: Nicely balanced, from fresh fruit character to smooth tannins. The round mouthfeel offers some crisp red berry flavors and an earthy touch on the finish. • $18 • (11/15/95) • **84**
St.-Romain Red 1992: Crisp in texture, with coarse tannins and modest currant flavors. • $21 • (12/15/94) • **78**
St.-Romain Red 1990: A firm wine, with plenty of intense characteristics. Shows a good dose of tobacco, black cherry and smoke flavors that lead to a finish supported by a solid backbone of tannins. Drinkable now. • $24 • (12/15/92) • **86**
St.-Romain White 1995: Nice texture, with pear, mint and tropical fruit flavors. A bit oily, with a citrus quality that gives it life and lifts its slightly tart finish. Drink now. • $20 • (08/31/97) • **81**
St.-Romain White 1994: Crisp and slightly herbal, with a reductive, "ice box" sort of character. Chewy and a bit tart on the finish, with a touch of a mineral, minty, earthy flavor. • $22 • (05/31/96) • **75**

GRATIEN, ALFRED

Brut Champagne 1988: Ripe peach and apple flavors and a smooth, soft texture make this easy to like. Drink now. 2,000 cases made. • $60 • (11/30/97) • **86**
Brut Champagne 1985 • $55 • (12/31/93) • **92**
Brut Champagne 1983 • $55 • (12/31/93) • **92**
Brut Champagne 1979 • $28 • (09/16/85) • **92**
Brut Champagne Classique NV: Wonderfully tasty, easy to drink and fresh, with lively fruit flavors accented by nutmeg and vanilla notes that linger on the finish. Nearly outstanding. 10,000 cases made. • $35 • (10/31/97) • **88**
Brut Champagne Cuvée Paradis NV: Something different and refreshing. Brightly fruity all the way through, with pear and pineapple aromas and flavors, crisp balance and a lingering finish. Drink now through 2000. 600 cases made. • $90 • (11/15/97) • **88**
Brut Rosé Champagne Cuvée Paradis NV: A distinctive, serious Champagne. Straw-colored, it initially emits strong earthy-toasty aromas, but then broadens and deepens to reveal layers of fruit, spice and honey that linger

FRANCE

on the finish. Drink now through 2000. 300 cases made. • $95 • (11/30/97) • **90**

GRATIEN & MEYER

Brut Saumur Cuvée Renaissance NV: Ripe apple and melon flavors are round and fruity in this generous sparkler, and a touch of toast adds depth. Lively bubbles keep it fresh. Drink now. 2,500 cases made. • $18 • (05/31/98) • **83**

Brut Saumur Fleur de Lys NV: Light and clean, its crisp peach and apple flavors kept lively by brisk bubbles. Simple, but makes a refreshing apéritif. Drink now. 25,000 cases made. • $14 • (05/31/98) • **82**

Saumur Demi-Sec Noir de Noirs Cardinal NV: Remember "cold duck"? This sparkling red wine offers slightly sweet, ripe plum and coffee flavors, with as much tannin as many still reds. Drink now. 10,000 cases made. • $14 • (06/30/98) • **79**

GRAVE, CHÂTEAU DE LA

Minervois 1990 • $7 • (03/15/94) • **82**

GRAVE À POMEROL, CHÂTEAU LA

Pomerol 1997: Gorgeous aromas of ripe plums. Full-bodied, with well-integrated tannins and a ripe fruit finish. Very impressive for the vintage. • $NA • (06/15/98) (BT) • **90-94**

Pomerol 1996: Rather thin and mean. Light to medium in body, with drying tannins and a short finish. • $35 • (06/15/98) (BT) • **75-79**

Pomerol 1996: Chewy and fruity with its tobacco, chocolate and berry character. Medium- to full-bodied, with thickly silky tannins. Almost outstanding. • $NA • (01/01/97) (BT) • **85-89**

Pomerol 1995: This offers some very good vanilla, spice, herb and red berry character. • $NA • (05/15/96) (BT) • **85-89**

Pomerol 1994: Pretty black olive and cherry aromas and flavors to match. Medium, fine tannins and a fresh, succulent finish. Drinkable now, better in 1999. • $35 • (01/31/97) • **88**

Pomerol 1993: Lovely black cherry and chocolate character, medium body, velvety tannins and a long cocoa, fruity finish. Drinkable now. • $28 • (01/31/96) • **87**

Pomerol 1992: At its peak, with pretty, velvety tobacco, chocolate and berry aromas and flavors, medium body and a soft finish. Not to hold; drink now. • $NA • (04/15/95) • **80**

Pomerol 1990: Extremely pretty, with coffee, berry aromas and flavors and rich, round tannins. Subtle and balanced in style. Drinkable now. 2,500 cases made. • $28 • (03/31/93) • **92**

Pomerol 1989 • $35 • (03/15/92) • **88**
Pomerol 1986 • $36 Ⓐ • (03/31/90) • **89**
Pomerol 1982 • $NA • (08/31/92) • **86**
Pomerol 1979 • $NA • (10/15/89) • **90**
Pomerol 1970 • $NA • (05/15/93) • **90**

GREFFET, DOMAINE

Pouilly-Fuissé 1993: Clean and flavorful, medium in body, presenting wet hay, green apple and lime tones and a tart finish. Drinkable now. 583 cases made. • $NA • (05/15/95) • **82**

St.-Véran 1995: Lean, mean, sharp and tart, with a bitter aftertaste. From Moillard. 1,542 cases made. • $14 • (05/31/97) • **72**

GREFFIÈRE, CHÂTEAU DE LA

Mâcon-la Roche Vineuse Vieilles Vignes 1993: Crisp and fresh, offering dried herb, green apple and cream flavors and a touch of mineral character on the tart finish. • $12 • (08/31/95) • **80**

GRENOUILLES, CHÂTEAU

Chablis Grenouilles 1995: Superb *grand cru*, delicate yet rich and full-bodied, displaying vibrant melon, grass and honeysuckle notes that complement the wet stone and mineral character on the toasty, smoky finish. Drink now through 2000. • $NA • (06/15/97) • **90**

GRESSIER-GRAND-POUJEAUX, CHÂTEAU

Moulis 1993: Loads of new wood, but the fruit also comes through. Ripe and delicious, sporting fine tannins and a slightly dry finish. Drinkable now. • $16 • (01/31/96) • **85**

Moulis 1961 • $NA • (04/30/92) • **84**

GREYSAC, CHÂTEAU

Médoc 1997: Decent concentration, but with a slightly grassy and metallic character. Medium-bodied, with light tannins and a short finish. • $NA • (06/15/98) (BT) • **75-79**

Médoc 1996: A plummy, grapey wine with a slightly earthy undertone. Medium-bodied, with medium tannins and a sweet fruit finish. Very satisfying. 35,000 cases made. • $15 • (06/15/98) (BT) • **85-89**

Médoc 1995: Good cherry and berry character with a medium body, medium tannins and a slightly short finish. 35,000 cases made. • $NA • (01/01/97) (BT) • **80-84**

Médoc 1994: Lean but firm, this sinewy red offers blackberry, licorice and tarlike aromas and flavors, with tannins that don't quite dominate the fruity finish. Give it until 1999 to come around. • $15 • (11/30/97) • **87**

Médoc 1990: A no-nonsense wine, with good character, nice ripe fruit flavors and round tannins. Drinkable now. 35,000 cases made. • $12 • (03/31/93) • **84**

Médoc 1989 • $12 • (03/15/92) • **79**
Médoc 1988 • $15 • (04/30/91) • **87**
Médoc 1986 • $10 • (11/30/89) • **85**
Médoc 1985 • $9 • (12/31/88) • **77**
Médoc 1983 • $8 • (07/31/87) • **65**
Médoc 1982 • $18 • (08/31/92) • **88**
Médoc 1981 • $8 • (06/01/84) • **77**

GRILLE, CHÂTEAU DE LA

Chinon 1987 • $18 • (08/31/91) • **77**

GRIPA, BERNARD

St.-Joseph 1992 • $NA • (05/31/94) • **77**
St.-Joseph Le Berceau 1992 • $NA • (05/31/94) • **83**

GRIPPAT, J.L.

St.-Joseph 1991 • $22 • (05/31/94) • **78**
St.-Joseph Vignes de l'Hospice 1991 • $NA • (05/31/94) • **83**
St.-Joseph Vignes de l'Hospice 1990 • $32 • (05/31/94) • **85**

GRIVAULT, ALBERT

Meursault 1995: A well-made, full-bodied, firmly structured white Burgundy, closed and minerally now, offering gobs of honey, hazelnut, fig, vanilla bean and ripe pear flavors. Delicious finish is clean, lemony and long. Try in 2000 to 2005. 666 cases made. • $28 • (05/31/97) • **88**

Meursault 1994: Talented winemaking. This creamy wine has aromas that seduce with their yeasty, piecrust and lemony character. Focused and tightly wound now, the citrus and honey notes should fully emerge by 1999. 633 cases made. • $25 • (05/31/96) • **88**

Meursault 1992: Quite showy for the vintage. Rich and flavorful, with lovely honey, peach and tropical flavors. Silky and balanced, with good acidity throughout. • $28 • (08/31/94) • **88**

Meursault Clos des Perrières 1996: A full-bodied Meursault with personality, showing an earthy component that may not be for everyone. But this *terroir* wine is superoily and opulent in texture, coating the palate with subtle honey, toasty oak, spice, tropical and pear accents. Very impressive, as the finish is balanced with good, fresh acidity. Tempting from 2000. 500 cases made. • $60 • (05/31/98) • **92**

Meursault Clos des Perrières 1995: Clean and pure, ripe and flavorful, this full-bodied '95 shows lovely mineral, pear, melon and honey character accented deftly by subtle oak, and a sweet-tasting finish that remains elegant. Tempting now, but it has the stuffing to age until after 2000. 358 cases made. • $62 • (05/31/97) • **90**

Key: SS—Spectator Selection CS—Cellar Selection HR—Highly Recommended BB—Best Buy $NA—Price not available Ⓐ—Auction Price (BT)—Barrel Tasting
Dates in parentheses indicate the issues in which the ratings were published.

Meursault Les Perrières 1996: Fabulous from start to finish, vibrating with complex, deep flavors, each adding resonance to the others as they twist and turn on the palate to a long finish. Honey, spice, pear, pineapple, toasty coconut—it runs the gamut—and it's all so fresh and lively. Of medium-to-full body, the silky mouthfeel is seductive. Tempting after 2000, but will hold at least until 2005. 760 cases made. • $50 • (05/31/98) • **94**

Meursault Les Perrières 1995: Dense, supple, rather palate-coating, this full-bodied wine unfolds gracefully to show lovely vanilla-bean, mineral, honey, pear and lemon flavors in moderate amounts. Try after 1999. 591 cases made. • $46 • (05/31/97) • **90**

Meursault Les Perrières 1994: Elegant and focused, with a good combination of mineral, vanilla, pear, honey and citrus flavors. Caresses the palate with its silky texture. A lovely wine that drinks well now, but should age. 716 cases made. • $39 • (05/31/96) • **90**

Meursault Les Perrières 1992: Soft, ripe and fat, showy and exuberant; offers exotic peach, dried apricot and honey flavors and a lush, mellow character. Tastes like botrytis. 400 cases made. • $80 • (08/31/94) • **87**

GRIVIÈRE, CHÂTEAU

Médoc 1997: Good velvety texture, with grape and berry aromas and flavors. Medium-bodied, with medium tannins but a very short finish and a hollow midpalate. • $NA • (06/15/98) (BT) • **85-89**

Médoc 1996: Intense berry, violet and fruit, but slightly rubbery. Medium-bodied and chewy. Wait and see. Tasted twice, with consistent notes. • $20 • (06/15/98) (BT) • **75-79**

Médoc 1995: A fat and rich red, with intense aromas of berries, mint and iodine. Full-bodied and very velvety, with lovely ripe fruit and a soft texture. Best after 1999. • $18 • (01/31/98) • **88**

Médoc 1993: Lacks flavor and concentration, tasting raw and unripe. • $16 • (04/30/97) • **73**

GRIVOT, JEAN

Chambolle-Musigny La Combe d'Orvaux 1987 • $60 Ⓐ • (06/15/90) • **85**

Clos de Vougeot 1995: Here are leafy, black-currant flavors, modest concentration and depth and severe tannins that leave an astringent feel in the mouth. Might smooth out by 2003. • $60 • (11/15/97) • **88**

Clos de Vougeot 1993: A powerful, delicious red Burgundy that features awesome black cherry and black currant flavors shaded by toasty, smoky oak. It's all wrapped in a firm but smooth texture and followed up by a lingering, fruity aftertaste. Has a great future ahead; try in 1999. 650 cases made. • $45 • (05/15/96) CS • **92**

Clos de Vougeot 1988 • $70 • (04/30/91) • **85**

Clos de Vougeot 1985 • $38 Ⓐ • (04/30/88) • **81**

Echézeaux 1995: A brilliant wine. Incredibly long and complex, yet so delicate and delicious. Subtle rose petal, violet, blackberry and cassis flavors build on the palate, pushed along by the most refined of tannins, mineral complexity and layers of exotic, toasty spice notes. Try after 2002. 250 cases made. • $60 • (11/15/97) • **94**

Echézeaux 1994: A powerhouse. Very impressive from the dark color and noble structure to the deep, rich red- and blackberry flavors and firm but harmonious tannins. Anise, wild berry, earth and mineral notes mingle in this ripe-tasting, masculine, muscular '94 red Burgundy. Tough finish for now, so don't touch until at least 2005. • $50 • (09/30/97) • **90**

Echézeaux 1993: An exotic and enticing Burgundy combining concentrated fruit with spicy, oaky accents that dance and linger on the finish. Reminiscent of cherry, berry, cinnamon and smoke, adding really firm tannins, lively acidity and fine overall balance. Drink in 1999. 200 cases made. • $45 • (05/15/96) • **92**

Nuits-St.-Georges Aux Boudots 1995: Big and bruising, this muscular Nuits is tightly locked behind a wall of tannins, but shows good depth of blackberry and cassis flavors. Try in 2002. • $45 • (11/15/97) • **88**

Nuits-St.-Georges Aux Boudots 1993: A handsome Burgundy that's stylish and sturdy at the same time. Offers solid fruit flavors, smoky, earthy accents, firm tannins and a lingering aftertaste. Has great balance and should be best in 1999. 300 cases made. • $32 • (05/15/96) • **90**

Nuits-St.-Georges Aux Boudots 1990: Mellow and slightly premature, showing pleasant roasted nut and berry aromas and flavors and medium tannins. Drinkable now. • $NA • (12/15/92) • **79**

Nuits-St.-Georges Aux Boudots 1989 • $NA • (01/31/92) • **77**

Nuits-St.-Georges Aux Boudots 1988 • $54 • (04/30/91) • **87**

Nuits-St.-Georges Les Charmois 1987 • $47 • (07/15/90) • **81**

Nuits-St.-Georges Les Pruliers 1988 • $53 • (04/30/91) • **89**

Nuits-St.-Georges Les Pruliers 1987 • $55 • (07/15/90) • **71**

Nuits-St.-Georges Roncière 1987 • $55 • (07/15/90) • **88**

Richebourg 1995: Dark and brooding, displaying loads of concentrated cassis and chocolaty fruit up front, but it seems lean and sinewy and turns very astringent on the finish. Try in 2002. • $150 • (11/15/97) • **90**

Richebourg 1994: Extremely well made. Rich and full-bodied, with ripe tannins. Firm in texture, dark in color, with a noble structure that shows good backbone of currant, black cherry, spice and subtle oak flavors. A muscular red Burgundy that has the stuffing to age until at least 2002—and shows *goût de terroir*. • $160 • (09/30/97) • **91**

Richebourg 1993: Intense, deep and smoldering, a young, powerful red that's closed in aroma but expansive and impressive in flavor. It has focused dried cherry, black cherry and currant flavors and extremely firm tannins, but enough fruit to balance them out. Aristocratic. Needs until at least 2000 to mellow. 100 cases made. • $128 • (05/15/96) • **96**

Richebourg 1990: Rather hard and austere, packing in plenty of black cherry, tea, herb and spice aromas and flavors and an iron backbone of tannins. A sour finish is slightly distracting. Needs time to come around; try from 1998. 150 cases made. • $NA • (12/15/92) • **84**

Richebourg 1989 • $178 Ⓐ • (01/31/92) • **93**

Vosne-Romanée 1995: Lush and pretty, this medium-bodied red shows violet, jasmine, rose petal and blackberry notes before the tannins clamp down on the finish. Try after 1999. • $35 • (11/15/97) • **80**

Vosne-Romanée 1993: Hearty, flavorful, tannic and well structured, delivering tastes of currant, pepper and cherry. Tightens up with tannins on the finish. Best in 1999. 300 cases made. • $22 • (05/15/96) • **88**

Vosne-Romanée 1990: Smells and tastes of old redwood, has high acidity and lacks freshness. Not recommended. • $NA • (12/15/92) • **69**

Vosne-Romanée 1985 • $31 • (04/30/88) • **87**

Vosne-Romanée Les Beaux Monts 1995: A subtle, understated style, its spicy blackberry flavors caress the palate before being supplanted by a healthy dose of tannin. The fruit comes through on the aftertaste. Try in 2000. • $45 • (11/15/97) • **89**

Vosne-Romanée Les Beaux Monts 1993: A deep, dark Burgundy that has concentrated, intense, ripe fruit notes, luscious oaky accents and a sense that it's still tight and youthful. Great balance between its firm acidity, tight tannins and ample hoard of flavors. Best to wait until 2000. 300 cases made. • $32 • (05/15/96) HR • **94**

Vosne-Romanée Les Beaux Monts 1990: An odd, disappointing wine that's prematurely aging, showing a brown edge. Medium-bodied, with modest caramel, chestnut and tomato flavors. • $NA • (12/15/92) • **76**

Vosne-Romanée Les Beaux Monts 1989 • $NA • (01/31/92) • **75**

Vosne-Romanée Les Suchots 1993: Slightly austere, showing firm tannins and some fruit, but could use a bit more concentration. Touches of acidity on the finish. Drinkable now. • $NA • (05/15/96) • **85**

GROFFIER, ROBERT

Bonnes Mares 1995: Stunning for its combination of deep fruit and classy structure. An extremely impressive, full-bodied, ripe and rich '95, filled with sweet tannins that coat the mouth, good acidity that leads to a lingering finish, and loads of well-integrated toasty oak, cassis and blueberry. Try after 2000. • $90 • (01/31/98) • **96**

Bonnes Mares 1989 • $79 • (01/31/92) • **81**

Bonnes Mares 1988 • $80 • (11/15/90) • **90**

Bonnes Mares 1987 • $67 • (07/31/89) • **89**

Bourgogne 1989 • $14 • (01/31/92) • **78**

Chambertin-Clos de Bèze 1987 • $45 • (07/31/89) • **88**

Chambolle-Musigny Les Amoureuses 1995: Stylish and nicely defined, with earth, smoky barbecue, grilled-meat, cassis and floral character. Medium-bodied, with full tannins that are firm on the finish and need until around 2000 to soften. • $75 • (01/31/98) • **90**

Chambolle-Musigny Les Amoureuses 1988 • $66 • (11/15/90) • **93**

Chambolle-Musigny Les Amoureuses 1987 • $51 • (08/31/89) • **86**

Chambolle-Musigny Les Amoureuses 1986 • $50 • (02/28/89) • **84**

Chambolle-Musigny Les Sentiers 1995: This seductive '95 red Burgundy leaves us nearly speechless. Deep in color, bursting with complex and exciting floral, violet, smoke, red- and blackberry aromas, it coats your palate with a swirl of flavors that remain vibrant on the long, velvety finish. Balanced, and tempting now through 2005. • $55 • (01/31/98) HR • **95**

Chambolle-Musigny Les Sentiers 1988 • $45 • (11/15/90) • **89**

Chambolle-Musigny Les Sentiers 1987 • $37 • (08/31/89) • **87**

Chambolle-Musigny Les Sentiers 1986 • $36 • (02/28/89) • **90**

Gevrey-Chambertin 1986 • $27 • (02/28/89) • **85**

GROLET, CHÂTEAU LA

Côtes de Bourg 1989 • $9 • (08/31/91) BB • **82**

Côtes de Bourg 1985 • $7 • (02/15/88) • **74**

GROLLE, PÈRE LA

Beaujolais 1996: This light, tart red has the straightforward simplicity of grape juice. Use it in a fruit-based punch. • $8 • (09/15/97) • **78**

Beaujolais Rosé 1996: An unusual rosé, pale pink, crisp but not tart, with light echoes of the cherry and smoke flavors found in red Beaujolais. It's irreproachable, but one wonders—why? • $8 • (09/15/97) • **82**

GROS, A.-F.

Clos Vougeot Le Grand Maupertuis 1989 • $NA • (01/31/92) • **90**

Echézeaux 1995: Very pretty, with nice blackberry and cassis flavors and floral notes. Medium-bodied, this starts out smoothly but turns diluted and chewy on the finish. Enjoy now through 2000. 25 cases made. • $85 • (11/15/97) • **86**

Echézeaux 1994: Light in body, with a thin veil of tannin around a tightly wound core of pure blackberry and black currant flavors, with shades of rose petal. Aproachable now, best from 1999. • $55 • (11/15/96) • **87**

Echézeaux 1993: Rather light and disapponting for this *grand cru* and producer. Elegant and fruity, adding fine tannins and racy acidity on the aftertaste. Try now. Tasted twice, with consistent notes. • $84 • (11/15/95) • **83**

Echézeaux 1992: Open-textured, with graceful berry, currant and floral aromas and flavors; a little touch of hay on the nose adds a distinctive note. Drinkable now. 108 cases made. • $106 • (12/15/94) • **83**

Echézeaux 1991: Light and crisp, with simple berry and cedar aromas and flavors and a citrusy finish. Try now. 100 cases made. • $70 Ⓐ • (01/31/94) • **76**

Echézeaux 1990: Ripe and rich, showing almost sweet fruit flavors. Offers hints of excellence. Drinkable now. 120 cases made. • $90 • (12/15/92) • **90**

Echézeaux 1988 • $84 • (02/15/91) • **91**

Hautes Côtes de Nuits 1995: Lean and mean, with little body or color but lots of astringency. 200 cases made. • $20 • (11/15/97) • **70**

Hautes Côtes de Nuits 1993: Already browning at the edges, it tastes of brown sugar and cooked fruit. Fat and ripe, leaving a hot, astringent mouthfeel. • $20 • (11/15/95) • **75**

Hautes Côtes de Nuits 1992: Light and fruity, nicely polished; offers a pleasant strawberry and spice character. Drinkable now. 1,042 cases made. • $22 • (12/15/94) • **81**

Hautes Côtes de Nuits 1989 • $19 • (06/15/92) • **78**

Hautes Côtes de Nuits 1988 • $22 • (03/31/91) • **80**

Richebourg 1992: An open and generous style, offering black cherry, root beer and toast aromas and flavors that linger on the supple finish. Approachable now. • $NA • (12/15/94) • **86**

Richebourg 1990: Exotic and very aromatic, with toast, smoked bacon and ginger aromas and flavors and a focused, long finish. Drink now. 90 cases made. • $180 • (12/15/92) • **94**

Richebourg 1989 • $130 • (01/31/92) • **97**

Richebourg 1988 • $190 • (02/15/91) • **97**

Savigny-lès-Beaune Clos des Guettes 1995: A confected, strawberry quality pervades this red, which has plenty of structure and a little heat on the finish, but lacks fruit. 50 cases made. • $38 • (11/15/97) • **78**

Vosne-Romanée Aux Réas 1995: Dense and chewy, redolent of blackberries and forest undergrowth, this is a bit rigid now, but the stiff tannnins should smooth out by 1999. 125 cases made. • $45 • (11/15/97) • **84**

Vosne-Romanée Aux Réas 1994: Light, crisp and firmly tannic, but delivers enough berry flavor to make it worth drinking through 1999. • $40 • (11/15/96) • **80**

Vosne-Romanée Aux Réas 1993: Enticingly sweet-tasting, featuring a ripe raspberry character that is quite soft at first, but with enough solid tannins below. Try this medium-bodied red around 1999. • $44 • (11/15/95) • **87**

Vosne-Romanée Aux Réas 1992: Has clean and focused fruit flavors with a smoky, red berry character, but it's diluted and short on the finish. 583 cases made. • $47 • (12/15/94) • **79**

Vosne-Romanée Aux Réas 1991: A light, pretty, anise-scented wine built around raspberry and vanilla flavors. Finishes with charm and echoes fruit. Drinkable now. 275 cases made. • $35 Ⓐ • (01/31/94) • **83**

Vosne-Romanée Aux Réas 1990: Light and delicate, with modest raspberry and cherry flavors and a light finish. An early-drinking wine; drink now. Tasted twice, with consistent notes. 200 cases made. • $40 • (12/15/92) • **79**

Vosne-Romanée Aux Réas 1988 • $41 • (02/28/91) • **71**

Vosne-Romanée Maizières 1993: Light, delicate chestnut, berry and cherry character, medium to light body, light tannins and a fresh finish. Try now. • $50 • (11/15/95) • **87**

GROS, ANNE

Bourgogne 1995: Kudos to this estate for a fresh, spicy cherry- and earth-flavored Bourgogne. Straightforward and tasty. Drink now through 2002. 625 cases made. • $19 • (11/15/97) • **83**

Chambolle-Musigny La Combe d'Orveau 1995: Herbal, astringent, medium-bodied, this tastes more of bell pepper than of fruit. Disappointing. 225 cases made. • $38 • (11/15/97) • **73**

Clos Vougeot Le Grand Maupertuis 1995: What the French call a *sauvage* wine, this will require years of cellaring before it's tame enough to serve. But it's serious red Burgundy, with deep, complex earth, violet, rose petal and blackberry aromas and flavors. Massively tannic on the palate and the finish. Try after 2005. 333 cases made. • $80 • (11/15/97) • **92**

Richebourg 1995: Seductive aromas and flavors of blackberries, toasty oak, grilled smoked meat and minerals pervade this wine. Full-bodied, thick and muscular, it coats your palate with fruit and firm tannins. Should be wonderful after 2005. 166 cases made. • $170 • (11/15/97) • **90**

Vosne-Romanée Les Barreaux 1995: Gorgeous, seductive, packed with the purest of cassis, blackberry and raspberry flavors and just enough spicy oak to add complexity. Thick, full-bodied and highly concentrated, this wine has an incredible, silky-smooth texture. Try after 2005. 125 cases made. • $55 • (11/15/97) • **93**

GROS, ANNE & FRANÇOIS

Bourgogne 1994: Fresh, grapey and crisp. Simple but attractive, beaming with sharp, citrusy flavors. Light-bodied. Drink now. • $17 • (11/15/96) • **80**

Bourgogne 1993: Very light, straightforward red berry flavor, a bit dry on the finish. You wish for more concentration. Drinkable now. • $13 • (11/15/95) • **81**

Bourgogne 1992: Relatively ripe and quite light. The flavors remain nicely focused on raspberry, currant and cherry. Drink young. 583 cases made. • $NA • (12/15/94) • **80**

Bourgogne 1990: Light but pretty, with delicate toast, leather, game and cherry notes. Made in a ripe style, but could use more concentration. Drink now. 750 cases made. • $17 • (12/15/92) • **84**

Chambolle-Musigny 1992: Lean in texture, with tightly focused raspberry and rose petal flavors that persist into a light finish. Drinkable now. 375 cases made. • $NA • (12/15/94) • **83**

Chambolle-Musigny La Combe d'Orveau 1993: Pretty Burgundy, offering some good tannic structure and currant and blackberry flavors in sizable amounts. Long finish. Needs time to smooth out; try in 2000. • $29 • (11/15/95) • **88**

Chambolle-Musigny La Combe d'Orveau 1990: A toasty wine that offers nice, sweetish fruit notes, but mostly shows distracting, odd gooseberry and citrus aromas and flavors that simply don't match the high quality we've come to expect from this fine producer. Tasted twice. Try now. • $40 • (12/15/92) • **72**

Clos Vougeot Le Grand Maupertuis 1994: Succulent berry, anise and mineral flavors jump out of the glass, heralding a wine of finely detailed clarity, build up to formidable richness and freshness, then finish with remarkable elegance and firm tannins. Tempting to drink, but should improve through 2001 to 2005. • $59 • (11/15/96) • **94**

Clos Vougeot Le Grand Maupertuis 1993: Laser-sharp definition of red berry flavor that zooms in with crystal clarity. As supple as the '93s come; medium-bodied, with fresh acidity carrying it on to a very long finish. Tempting now, but try after 2000. • $55 • (11/15/95) • **95**

Clos Vougeot Le Grand Maupertuis 1992: A ripe style that features plenty of currant, black cherry, vanilla and spicy oak flavors that flow together beautifully on the supple finish. Drinkable now. 333 cases made. • $NA • (12/15/94) • **88**

Clos Vougeot Le Grand Maupertuis 1991: Firm in texture but polished, showing off the modest black cherry and toast flavors to their best advantage. Drinkable now. 400 cases made. • $58 Ⓐ • (01/31/94) • **82**

Clos Vougeot Le Grand Maupertuis 1990: Magic grace and power embody this Clos Vougeot. Superbly concentrated, with tons of currant, cherry and

Key: SS—Spectator Selection CS—Cellar Selection HR—Highly Recommended BB—Best Buy $NA—Price not available Ⓐ—Auction Price (BT)—Barrel Tasting

Dates in parentheses indicate the issues in which the ratings were published.

smoke complexity and a stunning, velvety yet firm finish. Drinkable now. 350 cases made. • $75 • (12/15/92) • **95**

Richebourg 1994: Amazing concentration is its trademark. Its slight roasted chestnut and woody notes distract from the otherwise terrific currant, violet and floral character. Full-bodied, it fills the palate. A little tannic on the finish, but we trust this wine will be a smooth beauty by 2000. • $129 • (11/15/96) • **90**

Richebourg 1993: Extremely vivid and intoxicating plum and raspberry character, medium-to-full body, medium velvety tannins and a fresh finish. Try in 2000. • $100 • (11/15/95) • **91**

Richebourg 1992: Focused and flavorful, crisp-textured, with fresh currant, vanilla and spice overtones playing on the slightly tannic finish. Drinkable now. 208 cases made. • $NA • (12/15/94) • **86**

Richebourg 1991: Spicy, elegant and smoothly polished; the ripe currant, prune and spice flavors have chocolate and cream overtones. Graceful, harmonious and drinkable now, but has the goods to improve through 2000. 200 cases made. • $100 Ⓐ • (01/31/94) • **89**

Richebourg 1990: Amazingly rich, ripe and firm; the fruit just erupts like a volcano. Offers marvelous plum, currant and violet aromas and flavors and a touch of toasty bread and vanilla on the complex, supple finish. Drinkable now. 240 cases made. • $130 • (12/15/92) • **97**

Vosne-Romanée 1993: Lovely, elegant green tobacco and plum aromas and flavors, medium body, fine tannins and supple texture. Deliciously fruity finish. Drinkable now. • $40 • (11/15/95) • **88**

Vosne-Romanée 1992: Simple, charming and velvety, with appealing plum and currant flavors that linger on the soft finish. Drinkable now. 150 cases made. • $NA • (12/15/94) • **82**

Vosne-Romanée 1991: Firm and flavorful; a light, complex wine that paints an appealing profile of raspberry, black cherry, rose petal and anise aromas and flavors. Finishes toasty and spicy, with a lingering splash of fruit. Drinkable now. 200 cases made. • $32 Ⓐ • (01/31/94) • **86**

Vosne-Romanée Les Barreaux 1994: Packs a lot more flavor into its firm, lithe frame than most village Vosnes of the vintage, offering solid raspberry, mineral and floral flavors that hang on, echoing on the finish. Drinkable now. • $29 • (11/15/96) • **85**

GROS, JEAN

Bourgogne 1990: Delicate and pleasant, with a strawberry and butter component and a relatively light finish. 2,000 cases made. • $16 • (12/15/92) • **81**

Clos de Vougeot 1994: Light, but clear and delicate, with rose petal, raspberry and spice flavors. Very pretty, but also quite lean-bodied, and while it's nice to drink, it's definitely not *grand cru* quality. Drink now. • $89 • (11/15/96) • **82**

Clos de Vougeot 1992: Chunky in texture, somewhat overripe perhaps, with prune and anise flavors that pick up a little black cherry on the finish. Try now. • $NA • (12/15/94) • **83**

Clos de Vougeot 1991: Ripe, cedary and sturdy; the watery flavors manage to pick up berry and hazelnut tones on the finish. Not too tannic. Drinkable now. 75 cases made. • $80 Ⓐ • (01/31/94) • **81**

Nuits-St.-Georges 1994: Light and chewy, with anise-raspberry flavors that remain crisp on the finish. • $NA • (11/15/96) • **80**

Nuits-St.-Georges 1993: Tastes diluted, with vanilla, nail polish and slightly vegetal character, medium to light body and a short finish. Drink if you must. • $32 • (11/15/95) • **79**

Nuits-St.-Georges 1991: Excessively earthy, muddy, decadent aromas and flavors ruin this one for us. • $NA • (01/31/94) • **67**

Nuits-St.-Georges 1990: A fresh, bright Nuits, with attractive berry and earth characteristics and velvety tannins. Somewhat simple. Drinkable now. 192 cases made. • $30 • (12/15/92) • **85**

Nuits-St.-Georges 1989 • $39 • (01/31/92) • **87**

Nuits-St.-Georges 1988 • $22 Ⓐ • (02/28/91) • **81**

Nuits-St.-Georges 1985 • $36 • (07/31/88) • **85**

Richebourg 1994: Floral notes are fairly enticing, but it's also quite light and not that complex. Turns a bit bitter on the finish. Tasted twice, with consistent notes. Drink now. • $160 • (09/30/97) • **77**

Richebourg 1993: Vibrant fruit on the palate really impresses. Intense aromas of currant, mocha, game and plum. Very smooth, showing velvety texture, fine tannins and a long finish. Try in 2000. 83 cases made. • $160 • (11/15/95) • **94**

Richebourg 1992: Ripe, generous and supple, with spice, cinnamon and caramel overtones to the currant and raspberry flavors. Finishes smooth and sweet. Drinkable now. 83 cases made. • $78 Ⓐ • (12/15/94) • **88**

Richebourg 1991: An exotic wine, with dramatic wild berry, anise and coffee aromas. Spreads out on the palate to reveal more currant, plum and chocolate nuances. Smooth, polished, elegant and seductive; drinkable now. 140 cases made. • $149 Ⓐ • (01/31/94) • **92**

Richebourg 1990: Spellbinding, with smoke, ginger, spice and berry aromas and flavors. A full-bodied *grand cru*, with velvety texture and a firm, very long finish that's unforgettable. Drinkable now. 183 cases made. • $150 • (12/15/92) • **94**

Richebourg 1989 • $173 Ⓐ • (01/31/92) • **98**

Richebourg 1988 • $125 Ⓐ • (02/28/91) • **98**

Richebourg 1987 • $170 • (03/31/90) • **95**

Vosne-Romanée 1994: A lighter style that puts its modest currant and berry flavors ahead of its firm tannins. Drink now. • $NA • (11/15/96) • **81**

Vosne-Romanée 1993: Attractive, velvety texture is somewhat raisiny. Perhaps slightly overdone? Full-bodied with intense tar and fruit character and medium tannins. Drinkable now. 708 cases made. • $35 • (11/15/95) • **89**

Vosne-Romanée 1992: A delicate, soft Vosne-Romanée that brings out some oak-scented vanilla notes along with red berry flavors. Light-bodied and ready to drink. 667 cases made. • $35 • (12/15/94) • **78**

Vosne-Romanée 1989 • $39 • (01/31/92) • **90**

Vosne-Romanée 1988 • $29 Ⓐ • (02/28/91) • **90**

Vosne-Romanée 1987 • $32 • (04/30/90) • **89**

Vosne-Romanée Clos des Réas 1994: Packs some solid black cherry and currant flavors into a tart package, finishing with a curious citrusy character. Could smooth out by 1999 or 2000. • $63 • (11/15/96) • **83**

Vosne-Romanée Clos des Réas 1993: Alluring aromas of vanilla, currant and raspberry follow through on the palate. Medium- to full-bodied, with silky tannins and a fresh finish. Drink in 1999. • $60 • (11/15/95) • **91**

Vosne-Romanée Clos des Réas 1991: Distinctive, showing more cedar and earth than fruit. A bit diluted. Drinkable now. 720 cases made. • $53 Ⓐ • (01/31/94) • **78**

Vosne-Romanée Clos des Réas 1990: Very subtle, with gamy, roasted berry characteristics that build on the palate. Finely structured and finishes long and rich. From a vineyard exclusively owned by this producer. Drinkable now. 917 cases made. • $48 • (12/15/92) • **93**

Vosne-Romanée Clos des Réas 1989 • $70 • (01/31/92) • **92**

Vosne-Romanée Clos des Réas 1988 • $81 Ⓐ • (02/28/91) HR • **94**

Vosne-Romanée Clos des Réas 1987 • $44 • (04/30/90) • **93**

Vosne-Romanée Clos des Réas 1986 • $53 Ⓐ • (02/28/89) • **90**

Vosne-Romanée Clos des Réas 1985 • $83 Ⓐ • (07/31/88) • **87**

GROS, MICHEL

Bourgogne Hautes Côtes de Nuits 1993: Simple and bubbling with fruit. Medium body, plum and crushed strawberry flavors, light tannins and a fresh finish. Drink now. • $16 • (11/15/95) • **82**

Bourgogne Hautes Côtes de Nuits 1989 • $NA • (01/31/92) • **82**

Chambolle-Musigny 1994: Pretty and supple. An accessible, medium-bodied, juicy '94, with some attractive plum, floral and cherry aromas and flavors. Drink soon. • $38 • (11/15/96) • **83**

Chambolle-Musigny 1993: Amazing quality for a village wine, showing lovely elegance, solid structure, medium-to-full body, lots of mocha and red berry character, silky tannins and a long, fruity finish. One to age; try after 2000. 108 cases made. • $35 • (11/15/95) • **91**

Côte de Nuits-Villages 1990: Extremely elegant, with lovely, delicate berry, raspberry and earth aromas and flavors and silky tannins. Drinkable now. • $NA • (12/15/92) • **85**

Hautes Côtes de Nuits 1994: Fresh and grapey, but also quite stemmy and herbal, with only modest fruit flavor and some tart tannins. • $17 • (11/15/96) • **74**

Hautes Côtes de Nuits 1987 • $14 • (02/28/90) • **78**

Hautes Côtes de Nuits White 1994: An impressive white: compacted yet full of citrus, mineral and honey-glazed pear flavors as well as hints of the toasty hazelnut character that will develop with time. Full-bodied and balanced, it has a ripe aftertaste. Delicious now, but wait until after 2000. • $NA • (08/31/97) • **89**

Vosne-Romanée 1991: Tough, cedary and earthy, minimizing the fruit to show more toasty, spicy character. Drinkable now. 125 cases made. • $36 Ⓐ • (01/31/94) • **76**

Vosne-Romanée Clos de la Fontaine 1993: Fresh, lively mocha, coffee, cherry, earth and spice flavors. Balanced and crisp on the smoky, toasty, sweet-tasting finish. Drinkable now. • $NA • (05/15/96) • **87**

GROS FRÈRE & SOEUR

Clos Vougeot Musigny 1994: Smoothly polished and refined, with chocolate and coffee notes around a core of plum and berry flavors that persist into

FRANCE

the supple finish. Delicious to drink now, and could improve through 2000 or 2002. • $63 • (11/15/96) • **89**

Clos Vougeot Musigny 1992: Pretty, drinkable and flavorful, showing meaty, vanilla-scented blueberry and raspberry notes that never quite get revved up. • $NA • (12/15/94) • **85**

Clos Vougeot Musigny 1991: Crisp, austere and sharply focused. Lean raspberry, currant and black cherry flavors shade toward toastiness on the finish. An elegant wine. Drink now. 300 cases made. • $75 Ⓐ • (01/31/94) • **86**

Clos Vougeot Musigny 1990: Big and chewy; what impresses you first are all those smoky, toasty flavors. Packed with plum and cherry notes and loads of firm tannins. Drinkable now. 300 cases made. • $68 Ⓐ • (12/15/92) • **93**

Clos Vougeot Musigny 1989 • $80 Ⓐ • (01/31/92) • **91**

Clos Vougeot Musigny 1988 • $95 • (03/31/91) • **92**

Clos Vougeot Musigny 1985 • $102 Ⓐ • (03/31/88) • **75**

Côte de Nuits-Villages 1990: Shows very good density of fruit and medium tannins along with attractive, ripe plum and cedar notes on the finish. Drinkable now. • $18 • (12/15/92) • **86**

Grands Echézeaux 1994: Smooth and velvety. Elegant in its balance of sweet fruit and toasty oak, unfolding currant, plum and spice flavors that linger beautifully on the supple finish. Approachable now, but best from 1999 to 2000. • $83 • (11/15/96) • **91**

Grands Echézeaux 1993: A beautiful wine that sneaks up on you with its wonderful fruit character. Refreshing plum, berry and currant aromas follow through on the palate. Fine tannins. Better in 2000. • $69 • (11/15/95) • **93**

Grands Echézeaux 1992: Elegant, its silky texture supporting a nice beam of currant and blackberry flavor, shaded with touches of anise and mint around the edges. Drinkable now. • $NA • (12/15/94) • **87**

Grands Echézeaux 1991: Firm and crisp; this lighter, elegant style offers modest, tobacco-scented berry and currant aromas and flavors and a light, appealing finish. Drinkable now. 300 cases made. • $75 Ⓐ • (01/31/94) • **85**

Grands Echézeaux 1990: Very delicate and refined, well balanced and offering plenty of pretty strawberry, violet, vanilla and chocolate aromas and flavors. Quite supple. Drinkable now. 400 cases made. • $85 • (12/15/92) • **91**

Grands Echézeaux 1989 • $80 • (01/31/92) • **92**

Grands Echézeaux 1985 • $75 • (03/31/88) • **71**

Hautes Côtes de Nuits 1994: Its licorice and oak-scented vanilla, mocha and cherry flavors are appealing, but it ends with drying tannins. May be better after 1999. • $17 • (11/15/96) • **80**

Hautes Côtes de Nuits 1993: Some good berry flavor and a hint of cedar, but slightly short on the finish. Drinkable now. • $15 • (11/15/95) • **80**

Hautes Côtes de Nuits 1992: Light and crisp, with strawberry flavors clicking in delicately. • $NA • (12/15/94) • **79**

Hautes Côtes de Nuits 1989 • $NA • (01/31/92) • **82**

Hautes Côtes de Nuits White 1995: A straightforward, international style Chardonnay, showing some butter, butterscotch and vanilla notes atop ripe pear, cinnamon-apple tart character. Medium-bodied, and a bit astringent on the finish. • $NA • (08/31/97) • **81**

Richebourg 1994: Graceful '94 that plays to the vintage perfectly. Full-bodied, this aerodynamic wine delivers just enough extract without hitting a wall of hard tannins, finishing sleek and elegant. Superb winemaking at work here, delivering succulent violet, currant, floral and toasty oak notes. Tempting now through 2005. • $135 • (11/15/96) • **93**

Richebourg 1993: Beautifully crafted, opulent red, sporting fine tannins, succulent plum flavors and a long, silky finish. Better in 2000. • $110 • (11/15/95) • **94**

Richebourg 1992: Nuances of mocha and spice add to the fine, delicate thread of berry flavor, finishing creamy and smooth. Nicely fashioned; tasty to drink now. • $NA • (12/15/94) • **86**

Richebourg 1991: Polished and elegant. Bright raspberry and strawberry flavors shine through overtones of rose petal, vanilla and violet. Harmonious and supple; drink now. 300 cases made. • $100 Ⓐ • (01/31/94) • **90**

Richebourg 1990: A seductive wine, with tons of bright violet, licorice, black cherry, vanilla and earth characteristics. The finish is restrained and firm. Drinkable now to 2000. 350 cases made. • $51 • (12/15/92) • **96**

Richebourg 1989 • $81 • (01/31/92) • **95**

Richebourg 1988 • $192 • (02/28/91) • **91**

Key: SS—Spectator Selection CS—Cellar Selection HR—Highly Recommended BB—Best Buy $NA—Price not available Ⓐ—Auction Price (BT)—Barrel Tasting

Dates in parentheses indicate the issues in which the ratings were published.

Vosne-Romanée 1994: A light, pleasant, polished sort of wine, with modest raspberry and vanilla flavors. Ready now. • $33 • (11/15/96) • **81**

Vosne-Romanée 1993: Ripe and rich Burgundy, featuring wild chestnut, mocha, blackberry and plum character, medium-to-full body, fine tannins and a lovely, silky finish. Better in 1999. • $35 • (11/15/95) • **91**

Vosne-Romanée 1992: Light and spicy, smooth-textured, with a touch of chocolate on the finish. Drinkable now. • $NA • (12/15/94) • **80**

Vosne-Romanée 1991: Nicely articulated raspberry and cherry flavors persist on the finish, remaining delicate and appealing. Drinkable now. 450 cases made. • $35 Ⓐ • (01/31/94) • **84**

Vosne-Romanée 1989 • $39 • (01/31/92) • **91**

Vosne-Romanée 1988 • $46 • (03/31/91) • **89**

Vosne-Romanée 1985 • $35 • (04/15/88) • **70**

GROSSOMBRE, CHÂTEAU

Entre-Deux-Mers 1994 • $8 • (05/31/95) • **80**

GROSSOT, JEAN-PIERRE

Chablis 1996: Balanced and medium-bodied, with distinctive butter and butterscotch flavors that are a bit too much, but some lemon, grapefruit and honey notes save the day. Quite different from Grossot's normal, clean and pure style. Try now. • $18 • (08/31/97) • **86**

Chablis 1995: Plenty of honey and richness in this medium-bodied, tasty white, with an added mineral quality that lingers. Well balanced, it's drinkable now through 2000. 3,000 cases made. • $16 • (10/15/97) • **87**

Chablis 1994 • $17 • (05/31/96) • **89**

Chablis Les Fourneaux 1996: Beautiful balance between the mineral character and fresh acidity makes this Chablis a good cellar-candidate. Medium-bodied and crisp now, it should flesh out as it mellows, opening up with honey, floral, pear, toasty hazelnut and citrus and a chalky, flinty complexity. Try after 2000. • $22 • (05/31/98) • **90**

Chablis Les Fourneaux 1995: This *premier cru* has all the pieces. Firm structure yet velvet texture, medium-to-full body, subtle aromas of earth, forest and black truffles and notes of honey, crisp fruit and toast. Drinkable now; will improve through 2005. • $24 • (06/15/97) • **88**

Chablis Les Fourneaux 1994 • $22 • (05/31/96) • **91**

Chablis Les Fourneaux 1993 • $20 • (08/31/95) • **86**

Chablis Mont de Milieu 1994 • $25 • (05/31/96) • **88**

Chablis Mont de Milieu 1993 • $29 • (08/31/95) • **85**

Chablis Vaucoupin 1996: Lovely, thick and dense Chablis, showing lively vibrancy from the crisp apple, lemon and pink grapefruit notes that gain added complexity with some spice, mocha and toasty bread flavors. Well knit for the cellar, this full-bodied '96 should be in good drinking form around 2005. • $25 • (05/31/98) • **90**

Chablis Vaucoupin 1995: This full-bodied, rich *premier cru* has a lot going for it, packing plenty of tropical fruit, honey and toasty oak flavors into a classy package. Drinkable now. • $24 • (06/15/97) • **90**

Chablis Vaucoupin 1994 • $25 • (05/31/96) • **91**

Chablis Vaucoupin 1993 • $23 • (08/31/95) • **84**

GROTHÉ, CAVES JEAN

Pouilly-Fumé Acacia 1996: This bold white combines concentration and balance. Well-defined flavors of ripe apple, melon and vanilla are kept lively by notes of grapefruit and herbs. Bright and refreshing. Drinkable now. 1,200 cases made. • $15 • (05/31/98) • **87**

Pouilly-Fumé Acacia 1995: Herbal aromas and flavors are predominant, intensified by steely, citruslike acidity. It's admirably distinctive, but not everyone will enjoy it. 1,200 cases made. • $15 • (06/15/97) • **85**

Pouilly-Fumé Acacia 1994 • $16 • (05/15/96) • **84**

Pouilly-Fumé Acacia 1993 • $NA • (10/31/94) • **83**

Sancerre Acacia 1996: This beauty shows classic Sancerre character. It's keen and well focused, with lime, mineral and appealing herb flavors, but ripeness adds rich melon and cream notes. It's harmonious, clean and refreshing, and will make a perfect match with light but assertive dishes. Drink now through 2002. • $15 • (05/31/98) • **90**

Sancerre Acacia 1995: This delicate white offers pretty floral and light herbal aromas, with clean and crisp citrus and herbal flavors. Balanced; shows good typicity. 1,200 cases made. • $15 • (06/15/97) • **87**

Sancerre Acacia 1994 • $15 • (05/15/96) • **83**

Sancerre Acacia 1993 • $14 • (11/15/95) • **85**

GROUPEMENT DE PRODUCTEURS DE PRISSÉ

Mâcon-Villages 1996: Ripe and sweet, pure and clean, it offers nice balance and intensity, with lime, dried herb, green apple and tropical fruit flavors. Medium-bodied, too bad it turns a bit green on the finish. 16,667 cases made. • $11 • (08/31/97) • **85**
Mâcon-Villages 1995: A bit herbal but still appealing, with a grass, anise, basil and pine flavor combination that tastes almost like pesto. Medium-bodied, with a crisp finish. Drink now. • $NA • (08/31/96) • **83**
St.-Véran 1995: Straightforward, light-bodied Chardonnay. Pleasant but simple, with some pear, apple and melon notes. Drink now. • $NA • (08/31/96) • **78**

GRUAUD-LAROSE, CHÂTEAU

St.-Julien 1997: Plenty of grape and mineral aromas. Medium-bodied, with light tannins and a pleasant berry and vanilla aftertaste. • $NA • (06/15/98) (BT) • **85-89**
St.-Julien 1996: Wonderful berry, spice and cumin aromas and flavors. Full-bodied, with velvety tannins and a fresh finish. Outstanding. • $65 • (06/15/98) (BT) • **90-94**
St.-Julien 1995: Harmonious, but lacks a bit of concentration. Pretty, with delicious chocolate and berry aromas and flavors. Medium-bodied, with fine tannins and a medium finish. Best after this year. • $45 • (01/31/98) • **88**
St.-Julien 1994: Some good berry and tobacco notes, but it's slightly dry and lean compared to others. A bit disappointing for this estate. Drinkable now. • $40 • (01/31/97) • **82**
St.-Julien 1993: A seductive beauty. Medium in body, lovely, silky tannins and plenty of minty, cherry, berry character. Delicious now but will improve with age. • $30 • (01/31/96) • **88**
St.-Julien 1992: Tobacco, toasty oak and very fruity character; medium-bodied, medium tannins and a silky finish. Drinkable now. • $25 • (04/15/95) • **85**
St.-Julien 1991: Chewy and rich with a black cherry and currant character. Almost full-bodied, with a lovely supple texture. • $25 • (03/31/94) • **85**
St.-Julien 1990: A wine with lovely ripe fruit and an attractive tobacco and smoke character. It shows good tannin structure and a long finish. Well proportioned. Drinkable now. 32,000 cases made. • $35 • (03/31/93) • **90**
St.-Julien 1989 • $36 Ⓐ • (03/15/92) • **93**
St.-Julien 1988 • $27 Ⓐ • (03/31/91) • **84**
St.-Julien 1987 • $26 • (05/15/90) • **78**
St.-Julien 1986 • $59 Ⓐ • (05/31/89) • **93**
St.-Julien 1985 • $40 Ⓐ • (10/15/94) • **87**
St.-Julien 1984 • $21 • (05/15/87) • **88**
St.-Julien 1983 • $36 Ⓐ • (10/15/94) • **90**
St.-Julien 1982 • $83 Ⓐ • (08/31/92) • **94**
St.-Julien 1981 • $43 Ⓐ • (10/15/94) • **91**
St.-Julien 1980 • $251 • (02/28/91) • **83**
St.-Julien 1979 • $33 Ⓐ • (10/15/89) • **83**
St.-Julien 1978 • $36 Ⓐ • (02/28/91) • **91**
St.-Julien 1977 • $331 • (02/28/91) • **71**
St.-Julien 1976 • $NA • (02/28/91) • **85**
St.-Julien 1975 • $34 Ⓐ • (02/28/91) • **89**
St.-Julien 1974 • $281 • (02/28/91) • **63**
St.-Julien 1973 • $221 • (02/28/91) • **76**
St.-Julien 1971 • $311 • (02/28/91) • **85**
St.-Julien 1970 • $41 Ⓐ • (05/15/93) • **86**
St.-Julien 1969 • $16 Ⓐ • (02/28/91) • **50**
St.-Julien 1968 • $19 Ⓐ • (02/28/91) • **65**
St.-Julien 1967 • $331 • (02/28/91) • **78**
St.-Julien 1966 • $34 Ⓐ • (02/28/91) • **87**
St.-Julien 1964 • $701 • (02/28/91) • **88**
St.-Julien 1962 • $NA • (11/30/87) • **88**
St.-Julien 1961 • $279 Ⓐ • (04/30/96) • **90**
St.-Julien 1959 • $201 • (02/28/91) • **85**
St.-Julien 1957 • $65 • (02/28/91) • **78**
St.-Julien 1955 • $150 • (02/28/91) • **87**
St.-Julien 1953 • $195 • (02/28/91) • **88**
St.-Julien 1952 • $157 • (02/28/91) • **85**
St.-Julien 1950 • $145 • (02/28/91) • **83**
St.-Julien 1949 • $225 Ⓐ • (02/28/91) • **85**
St.-Julien 1947: Rich, complex and elegant, beautifully rounded and fine, almost sweet as it swirls its dark cherry, plum, earth and spicy vanilla flavors through the long finish. • $332 • (07/31/97) • **94**
St.-Julien 1945 • $365 Ⓐ • (11/30/95) • **88**
St.-Julien 1943 • $94 Ⓐ • (02/28/91) • **83**
St.-Julien 1937 • $150 • (02/28/91) • **87**
St.-Julien 1934 • $150 • (02/28/91) • **83**
St.-Julien 1929 • $550 • (02/28/91) • **85**
St.-Julien 1928 • $500 • (02/28/91) • **94**
St.-Julien 1926 • $180 • (02/28/91) • **95**
St.-Julien 1924 • $250 • (02/28/91) • **89**
St.-Julien 1921 • $250 • (02/28/91) • **87**
St.-Julien 1920 • $300 • (02/28/91) • **85**
St.-Julien 1918 • $323 Ⓐ • (02/28/91) • **78**
St.-Julien 1907 • $255 • (02/28/91) • **72**
St.-Julien 1906 • $300 • (02/28/91) • **85**
St.-Julien 1899 • $600 • (02/28/91) • **83**
St.-Julien 1893 • $500 • (02/28/91) • **78**
St.-Julien 1887 • $400 • (02/28/91) • **71**
St.-Julien 1878 • $500 • (02/28/91) • **83**
St.-Julien 1870 • $521 Ⓐ • (02/28/91) • **87**
St.-Julien 1865 • $NA • (02/28/91) • **65**
St.-Julien 1844 • $NA • (02/28/91) • **85**
St.-Julien 1834 • $NA • (02/28/91) • **83**
St.-Julien 1819 • $NA • (02/28/91) • **89**

GUÉRIN, ANDRÉ

Pouilly-Fuissé La Roche Cuvée No. 1 1994: An odd wine, packing tons of intense citrus flavors that lead to a long, long finish, but it's also excessively earthy, with a slight aroma of burnt matches. Drinkable now. • $NA • (05/31/96) • **83**

GUÉRIN, RENÉ

Pouilly-Fuissé La Roche 1994: Voluptous in texture and flavor, as expected from the low-acidity, very ripe, '94 vintage. Subtle on the nose, but tastes like a honey jar, with floral, caramel and toast notes thrown in. Full-bodied, with a slightly coarse finish. Drink soon. 267 cases made. • $22 • (05/31/97) • **85**
Pouilly-Fuissé La Roche 1993: Well made and solid, medium-bodied, displaying earth, wet straw and chalk character and some attractive lemon and pear flavors. Not for everyone. Drinkable now. 292 cases made. • $20 • (05/15/95) • **83**
Pouilly-Fuissé La Roche 1992: Smooth and complete, with lemon and pear flavors accented by a hint of toasty oak and balanced by a creamy texture. • $20 • (11/15/94) • **83**
Pouilly-Fuissé La Roche Cuvée No. 2 1994: Tart and odd-tasting—like onions—with some citrus and herbal flavors. Lean and not for everyone. 150 cases made. • $19 • (05/31/96) • **75**
Pouilly-Fuissé La Roche Sélection Vieilles Vignes Cuvée No. 1 1994: Well crafted, with a chewy, chalky character and mineral, honey, citrus and floral notes throughout. Try now. 200 cases made. • $NA • (05/31/96) • **86**
Pouilly-Fuissé La Roche Sélection Vieilles Vignes Cuvée No. 2 1994: Rich and clean, with good concentration of apricot, fig, citrus and pear flavors, along with a bitter almond note on the long, intense finish. Try now. 500 cases made. • $21 • (05/31/96) • **86**
Pouilly-Fuissé La Roche Vieilles Vignes 1996: Riper than some in this category, showing honey, spice, mocha and apple flavors. Medium-bodied, it turns a bit heavy on the finish. Too bad. Drink now or hold. 375 cases made. • $23 • (05/31/98) • **81**

GUÉRIN, THIERRY

Pouilly-Fuissé 1996: Both samples provided were reduced and stinky, with a rotten-egg character and sour finish. 660 cases made. • $23 • (05/31/98) • **65**
Pouilly-Fuissé Clos de France 1994: Fat and rich, with a lush character. Some nice honey, herb and green apple flavors, but this medium- to full-bodied white turns a bit herbaceous on the finish. Drink now. 150 cases made. • $22 • (05/31/96) • **82**
Pouilly-Fuissé Clos de France 1993: Medium body, revealing earth, wet straw, butter and herb notes. Drinkable now. 100 cases made. • $23 • (05/15/95) • **79**
Pouilly-Fuissé La Roche 1996: Once the odd aromas blow off, you find a medium-bodied, fairly concentrated and ripe wine. Minerally in structure, with chalky flavors and loads of lime, pear and green apple. A lot of personality. Try now through 2000. 750 cases made. • $24 • (05/31/98) • **88**
Pouilly-Fuissé La Roche 1995: Distinctive, yes, but impressive for its ripe flavors. Medium-bodied, it blends a Sauvignon Blanc-like grassy character

with the ripe pear, floral, earth and honey notes of Chardonnay. Drinkable now. 500 cases made. • $20 • (05/31/97) • **87**

Pouilly-Fuissé La Roche 1994: Tastes a bit odd, at least at this stage, with earthy, burnt-match aromas that detract from the citrus and green apple flavors. Light-to-medium body; lacks focus. 250 cases made. • $19 • (05/31/96) • **78**

Pouilly-Fuissé La Roche Vieilles Vignes 1994: Intense—in a word—summarizes this wine. Crisp and tart, with honeydew, pear, lemon and mineral flavors. It's focused from start to finish. Drinkable now. 250 cases made. • $22 • (05/31/96) • **85**

Pouilly-Fuissé Sélection Vieilles Vignes 1996: Smells like peanut butter and rotten eggs; tastes bitter and astringent. 250 cases made. • $25 • (05/31/98) • **70**

St.-Véran 1996: A bit earthy, with sauerkraut, wet wool, stone and matchstick flavors. Not very appealing, but perhaps it's the land that gave it this distinctive character. 1,080 cases made. • $16 • (05/31/98) • **77**

St.-Véran Clos des Pierres Brûlées 1995: Lavishly oaked and showy, but well made, offering toast, butter, butterscotch and pear flavors. Creamy texture, with complex earth notes creeping in on the lingering finish. Medium-bodied. Drinkable now. 1,000 cases made. • $16 • (05/31/97) • **86**

St.-Véran Clos des Pierres Brûlées 1994: A honeyed, sweet-tasting wine that is, in the end, pretty straightforward. Light-to-medium body, and delivers some earth and spice notes. But short on the finish. 833 cases made. • $13 • (05/31/96) • **79**

GUFFENS-HEYNEN

Mâcon-Pierreclos En Chavigne 1995: Stands out like a high-rise in a wheat field. Takes off with great intensity, unlike many '95 Pouilly, kicking into high gear with impressive concentration of sweet-tasting fruit and a long, succulent, citrusy finish shaded nicely by toasty oak. Well-crafted and a delight to taste. 300 cases made. • $20 • (05/31/97) • **91**

Mâcon-Pierreclos En Chavigne 1994: Distinctive. Full-bodied, with some pronounced milky aromas and flavors weaving through the ripe fruit, spice, chalk and lemon. Supple and smooth. Drink now. • $20 • (08/31/96) • **87**

Mâcon-Pierreclos En Chavigne Cuvée Bois Neuf Red 1990: Ripe, generous and decidedly toasty, with a sturdy backbone of acidity to balance the ripe currant and berry flavors. A toasty, smoky edge emerges on the finish. More complex than what you might expect from a red Mâcon. Drinkable now. • $18 • (08/31/92) • **82**

Pouilly-Fuissé 1995: Like a Meursault. Thick and dense, showing lovely oak, butter, honey, pear tart, caramel and citrus flavors. Clean and quite toasty, this full-bodied beauty is supple and elegant, and drinks wonderfully now. Try with white meat in a cream sauce with truffles. This is more balanced than his Premier Jus. • $34 • (05/31/98) • **90**

Pouilly-Fuissé Clos des Petits-Croux 1994: Deliciously seductive and offering substantial concentration. Shows silky texture and a lot of complexity, hinting at toasty bread, hazelnut, ripe pear, lemon and honey. Extremely flavorful now. • $34 • (05/31/96) • **92**

Pouilly-Fuissé Clos des Petits-Croux 1992: With its rich, ripe, powerful character, this could pass for a little Montrachet. Extremely toasty and buttery, the opulent texture coating your mouth; long, fresh, citrus-flavored finish. Drinkable now. • $NA • (05/15/95) • **93**

Pouilly-Fuissé Deuxième Tri 1993: Clever winemaking here. Seductively toasty, this chiseled white unfolds its butter, mineral, pear, apple and fresh herb notes, picking up intensity on the long, lemon-flavored finish. Drinkable now. • $43 • (05/15/95) • **90**

Pouilly-Fuissé Premier Jus 1995: Nice, maturing notes of honey, butter and toasty oak but, unfortunately, it comes across as rustic, herbal (as in green tannins) and tart on the finish. Drink now. • $40 • (05/31/98) • **79**

Pouilly-Fuissé La Roche 1994: A beauty, offering the full-blown white Burgundy treatment, as tons of ripe fruit flavors are backed by toasty hazelnut, smoke, honey, lemon, spice and butter characteristics that just keep going on the long finish. Full-bodied and silky, but it's somewhat more intense than the Clos des Petits-Croux, so try now. Tasted twice, with consistent notes. • $40 • (05/31/96) • **93**

Key: SS—Spectator Selection CS—Cellar Selection HR—Highly Recommended BB—Best Buy $NA—Price not available Ⓐ—Auction Price (BT)—Barrel Tasting
Dates in parentheses indicate the issues in which the ratings were published.

GUIBON, CHÂTEAU

Bordeaux 1994: Black cherry and tobacco flavors are appealing, but an underlying earthy note detracts. Firmly tannic, but may soften. • $5 • (07/31/96) • **78**
Entre-Deux-Mers 1994 • $6 • (05/31/95) • **82**

GUIGAL, E.

Châteauneuf-du-Pape 1994: Tastes sweet and sugary; full-bodied, it comes across as ripe, but then turns very tart on the finish. • $22 • (10/15/97) • **72**
Châteauneuf-du-Pape 1991: Dense, if a bit murky, this offers chocolate, plum and prune flavors, firm tannins and a spicy, bitter finish. Drink now. • $20 • (12/15/96) • **83**
Châteauneuf-du-Pape 1990: A solid, chunky style that packs in rich currant, earth, mineral and spicy flavors into a long, full, persistent finish. A lot of win, finishing with firm tannins. Best between now and 2002. 10,000 cases made. • $20 • (03/15/94) HR • **89**
Châteauneuf-du-Pape 1988 • $26 Ⓐ • (11/30/90) HR • **90**
Châteauneuf-du-Pape 1986 • $19 • (03/15/90) • **87**
Châteauneuf-du-Pape 1985 • $18 • (10/15/88) • **87**
Châteauneuf-du-Pape 1983 • $29 • (11/30/87) • **87**
Condrieu 1995: A big, bold white, with lively acidity and loads of pear, melon and honey flavors, though it lacks the indelible, spicy signature of Viognier. It's balanced and would be great with food. 8,000 cases made. • $33 • (02/28/97) • **88**
Condrieu 1994 • $45 • (12/31/95) • **88**
Condrieu La Doriane 1996: This striking white adds a robust smoky note to the characteristic peach, floral and honeyed flavors of Viognier. It's vivid and clean, with plenty of concentration and acidity to match with food, and a rich, long finish. • $60 • (10/15/97) • **92**
Condrieu La Doriane 1995: "This is what Viognier is supposed to taste like" seems to be what this gorgeous French white wine is telling you. Has well-defined aromas of apricot, flowers, and spices, firm spiciness on the palate, without a hint of sweetness or heaviness, and a long, long finish: Condrieu like this doesn't come around very often, so snap it up. 900 cases made. • $60 • (02/28/97) HR • **94**
Condrieu La Doriane 1994 • $50 • (09/30/95) • **89**
Côte-Rôtie Brune et Blonde 1990: Beautifully crafted, aromatic licorice and animal notes. Firm and concentrated, offering plenty of blackberry flavor. Drinkable now. • $162 Ⓐ • (11/15/95) • **90**
Côte-Rôtie Brune et Blonde La Pommière 1990: A special one-time bottling. Intense yet balanced, lush with oak and oozing with plum, licorice and gamy flavors. A real beauty. • $NA • (11/15/95) • **94**
Côte-Rôtie Côtes Brune et Blonde 1993: A terrific effort for the vintage. Firm and tight, this French red packs in ripe plum, vanilla, licorice and game flavors so ripe they're almost sweet. Neither showy nor overly powerful, this has great verve and allure. 20,000 cases made. • $33 • (04/30/97) HR • **91**
Côte-Rôtie Côtes Brune et Blonde 1992: Closed now but still fresh, this red offers good balance and moderate concentration, but isn't showing much fruit flavor. The finish is clean and long. Try now. • $33 • (11/30/96) • **87**
Côte-Rôtie Côtes Brune et Blonde 1991: Soft and pretty, packed with black cherry flavor; very lovely. Drinkable now through 2003. • $43 Ⓐ • (11/15/95) • **88**
Côte-Rôtie Côtes Brune et Blonde 1990: Made in a traditional style. Round and soft, with meaty, gamy, woodsy flavors. The tannins are soft; drink now or hold. Not as good as in an earlier tasting. • $29 • (11/15/95) • **88**
Côte-Rôtie Côtes Brune et Blonde 1989 • $38 Ⓐ • (11/15/95) • **88**
Côte-Rôtie Côtes Brune et Blonde 1988 • $35 Ⓐ • (11/15/95) • **89**
Côte-Rôtie Côtes Brune et Blonde 1987 • $28 • (11/15/95) • **84**
Côte-Rôtie Côtes Brune et Blonde 1986 • $345 Ⓐ • (02/28/90) • **90**
Côte-Rôtie Côtes Brune et Blonde 1985 • $34 Ⓐ • (03/15/90) • **91**
Côte-Rôtie Côtes Brune et Blonde 1984 • $28 • (11/15/95) • **79**
Côte-Rôtie Côtes Brune et Blonde 1983 • $63 Ⓐ • (11/15/95) • **90**
Côte-Rôtie Côtes Brune et Blonde 1982 • $33 Ⓐ • (11/15/95) • **87**
Côte-Rôtie Côtes Brune et Blonde 1980 • $40 • (11/15/95) • **81**
Côte-Rôtie Côtes Brune et Blonde 1979 • $45 • (11/15/95) • **83**
Côte-Rôtie Côtes Brune et Blonde 1978 • $115 Ⓐ • (11/15/95) • **84**
Côte-Rôtie Côtes Brune et Blonde 1976 • $38 Ⓐ • (11/15/95) • **85**
Côte-Rôtie Côtes Brune et Blonde 1971 • $75 • (11/15/95) • **72**
Côte-Rôtie Côtes Brune et Blonde 1969 • $100 • (11/15/95) • **78**
Côte-Rôtie Côtes Brune et Blonde 1966 • $125 • (11/15/95) • **83**
Côte-Rôtie Côtes Brune et Blonde 1964 • $100 • (11/15/95) • **83**
Côte-Rôtie Côtes Brune et Blonde 1962 • $NA • (03/15/90) • **89**

Côte-Rôtie Côtes Brune et Blonde 1961 • $100 • (11/15/95) • **90**

Côte-Rôtie Côtes Brune et Blonde Hommage à Etienne Guigal 1989 • $NA • (11/15/95) • **85**

Côte-Rôtie La Landonne 1993: This expressive red shows lush vanilla, ripe raspberry and dark chocolate notes that fill the mouth and linger on the finish, where well-integrated tannins kick in. Drinkable now, but should improve. • $120 • (12/15/97) • **87**

Côte-Rôtie La Landonne 1992: Toast and coffee flavors dominate the black cherry and plum notes in this big, firm red. It's very tannic and quite closed now, and though it shows impressive concentration, it may lack the balance to improve with age. • $136 Ⓐ • (11/30/96) • **85**

Côte-Rôtie La Landonne 1991: Deep and muscular, this is the most concentrated and tannic of the 1991s. It's meaty, smoky and spicy, with ripe plum flavors. Drink from 2000. • $283 Ⓐ • (11/15/95) • **95**

Côte-Rôtie La Landonne 1990: The richest of the crus in this monumentally rich vintage, offering ripe plum, smoke and game flavors and full, muscular tannins. Not as exuberant as La Mouline at this stage, but should last longer. Try in 2000. • $291 Ⓐ • (11/15/95) • **97**

Côte-Rôtie La Landonne 1989 • $230 Ⓐ • (11/15/95) • **94**

Côte-Rôtie La Landonne 1988 • $261 Ⓐ • (11/15/95) • **94**

Côte-Rôtie La Landonne 1987 • $187 Ⓐ • (11/15/95) • **89**

Côte-Rôtie La Landonne 1986 • $165 Ⓐ • (11/15/95) • **91**

Côte-Rôtie La Landonne 1985 • $396 Ⓐ • (03/15/90) • **90**

Côte-Rôtie La Landonne 1984 • $79 Ⓐ • (03/15/90) • **86**

Côte-Rôtie La Landonne 1983 • $244 Ⓐ • (03/15/90) • **94**

Côte-Rôtie La Landonne 1982 • $163 Ⓐ • (03/15/90) • **90**

Côte-Rôtie La Landonne 1981 • $108 Ⓐ • (03/15/90) • **82**

Côte-Rôtie La Landonne 1980 • $111 Ⓐ • (03/15/90) • **84**

Côte-Rôtie La Landonne 1979 • $140 Ⓐ • (03/15/90) • **91**

Côte-Rôtie La Landonne 1978 • $576 Ⓐ • (03/15/90) • **95**

Côte-Rôtie La Mouline 1993: This solid red is compact but muscular, with ripe flavors of plums, raisins and chocolate, and plenty of oak for backbone. Try now. • $120 • (12/15/97) • **87**

Côte-Rôtie La Mouline 1992: Thick and rich, this offers ripe plum and coffee flavors, almost sweet, with cinnamon and spice accents, velvety at first then powerful with tannin. It has real concentration and good balance. Try now. 500 cases made. • $136 Ⓐ • (11/30/96) CS • **91**

Côte-Rôtie La Mouline 1991: Sweet fruit flavors of raspberry and cherry are ripe and concentrated, while smoky and light herbal notes add interest. Beautifully focused; drink now. • $230 Ⓐ • (11/15/95) • **92**

Côte-Rôtie La Mouline 1990: Irresistible. This lush, concentrated wine is spilling over with gorgeous raspberry, floral, toast and smoky flavors; it's intense, lively and long. Delicious now, but better after 2000. • $233 Ⓐ • (11/15/95) • **98**

Côte-Rôtie La Mouline 1989 • $259 Ⓐ • (11/15/95) • **95**

Côte-Rôtie La Mouline 1988 • $288 Ⓐ • (11/15/95) • **95**

Côte-Rôtie La Mouline 1987 • $345 Ⓐ • (11/15/95) • **91**

Côte-Rôtie La Mouline 1986 • $143 Ⓐ • (11/15/95) • **94**

Côte-Rôtie La Mouline 1985 • $396 Ⓐ • (03/15/90) • **98**

Côte-Rôtie La Mouline 1984 • $75 Ⓐ • (11/15/95) • **87**

Côte-Rôtie La Mouline 1983 • $281 Ⓐ • (03/15/90) • **94**

Côte-Rôtie La Mouline 1982 • $173 Ⓐ • (03/15/90) • **92**

Côte-Rôtie La Mouline 1981 • $115 Ⓐ • (03/15/90) • **90**

Côte-Rôtie La Mouline 1980 • $245 Ⓐ • (11/15/95) • **83**

Côte-Rôtie La Mouline 1979 • $108 Ⓐ • (03/15/90) • **85**

Côte-Rôtie La Mouline 1978 • $544 Ⓐ • (03/15/90) • **96**

Côte-Rôtie La Mouline 1977 • $193 Ⓐ • (03/15/90) • **75**

Côte-Rôtie La Mouline 1976 • $290 Ⓐ • (03/15/90) • **87**

Côte-Rôtie La Mouline 1975 • $116 Ⓐ • (03/15/90) • **75**

Côte-Rôtie La Mouline 1974 • $NA • (03/15/90) • **89**

Côte-Rôtie La Mouline 1973 • $NA • (03/15/90) • **84**

Côte-Rôtie La Mouline 1972 • $NA • (11/15/95) • **75**

Côte-Rôtie La Mouline 1971 • $115 Ⓐ • (03/15/90) • **88**

Côte-Rôtie La Mouline 1970 • $219 Ⓐ • (03/15/90) • **74**

Côte-Rôtie La Mouline 1969 • $NA • (03/15/90) • **90**

Côte-Rôtie La Mouline 1968 • $NA • (03/15/90) • **82**

Côte-Rôtie La Mouline 1967 • $105 Ⓐ • (03/15/90) • **86**

Côte-Rôtie La Mouline 1966 • $NA • (03/15/90) • **88**

Côte-Rôtie La Turque 1993: Notes of chocolate, game and smoke emerge on the finish. Try now. It's true to the appellation in character. • $120 • (12/15/97) • **88**

Côte-Rôtie La Turque 1992: Fat and fruity, this offers ripe fresh blackberry and raspberry flavors with chocolate and licorice accents. There's plenty of fruit concentration and just enough tannin for grip. Lovely now through 2000. • $87 Ⓐ • (11/30/96) • **89**

Côte-Rôtie La Turque 1991: Complex and concentrated, this shows toast and vanilla oak flavors balanced by plenty of plum, berry and licorice notes; dense and long. Drink now. • $277 Ⓐ • (11/15/95) • **93**

Côte-Rôtie La Turque 1990: Beautiful and lush. The floral, vanilla and blueberry flavors are distinctive and concentrated; if the oak is dominant now, the fruit is ripe and lively. Drinkable now. • $380 Ⓐ • (11/15/95) • **95**

Côte-Rôtie La Turque 1989 • $341 Ⓐ • (11/15/95) • **91**

Côte-Rôtie La Turque 1988 • $238 Ⓐ • (11/15/95) • **92**

Côte-Rôtie La Turque 1987 • $345 Ⓐ • (11/15/95) • **89**

Côte-Rôtie La Turque 1986 • $229 Ⓐ • (11/15/95) • **92**

Côte-Rôtie La Turque 1985 • $552 Ⓐ • (03/15/90) • **98**

Côtes du Rhône 1994: Fairly ripe and quite lovely. Medium-bodied, with plum, coffee and spice notes. Fresh and harmonious; the tannins are a bit green, making the finish slightly tough. Drink now. • $10 • (10/15/97) • **83**

Côtes du Rhône 1993: A success for the vintage. Fresh, supple flavors of blackberries and licorice are backed by just enough tannin to keep them bright and clean. A spicy note lingers on the finish. • $10 • (10/15/96) • **85**

Côtes du Rhône Rosé 1996: Fresh and soft, this beguiling rosé doesn't show exuberant fruit, but it's balanced and refreshing. A pleasant quaffer. • $10 • (10/15/97) • **81**

Côtes du Rhône Rosé 1995: Bright aromas of strawberries and herbs fade to a fairly neutral palate, but it's fresh, clean and dry. A pleasant apéritif. • $10 • (10/15/96) • **81**

Côtes du Rhône Rosé 1994 • $11 • (09/30/95) • **80**

Côtes du Rhône White 1996: Crisp and clean, this lively white offers pure, well-focused flavors of lime, apple and herbs. More than assertive enough to match with food. • $10 • (10/15/97) • **85**

Côtes du Rhône White 1995: Pretty apple and pear aromas don't quite flesh out on the palate, but this straightforward white has enough body and acidity to match with food. • $10 • (10/15/96) • **81**

Côtes du Rhône White 1994 • $11 • (09/30/95) • **84**

Gigondas 1994: Luscious. This round, generous red is plush, with plum, licorice and spice flavors, and is full-bodied yet not overly tannic. Lovely now. 10,000 cases made. • $15 • (04/30/97) • **87**

Gigondas 1992: An expressive, ripe wine with a gamy edge. Shows raisin and smoke flavors, and is supple on the palate, though drying on the finish. • $15 • (10/15/96) • **79**

Gigondas 1991 • $16 • (11/15/95) • **83**

Gigondas 1990 • $15 • (03/15/94) • **84**

Gigondas 1988 • $15 • (03/31/91) • **85**

Gigondas 1986 • $17 • (11/30/90) • **87**

Gigondas 1985 • $17 • (09/30/88) SS • **91**

Gigondas 1984 • $15 • (11/30/87) • **86**

Gigondas 1983 • $18 • (07/31/87) • **91**

Hermitage 1993: Gamelike and coffee flavors are typical of Hermitage, and it shows a good core of cherry flavor for this difficult vintage. Balanced, and drinking well now. • $33 • (09/15/97) • **87**

Hermitage 1992: This offers a velvety texture with flavors of plum, raisins and cedar. Firm, underlying tannins emerge on the finish. Good with food, and drinkable now. • $33 • (11/30/96) • **86**

Hermitage 1990: Beautiful aromas of raspberry and cedar follow through on the lush, full palate. It's intense and well crafted, with a long, rich finish. Start drinking now. 5,000 cases made. • $61 Ⓐ • (05/31/94) CS • **93**

Hermitage 1989 • $33 • (04/15/93) CS • **91**

Hermitage 1988 • $36 Ⓐ • (12/31/91) • **83**

Hermitage 1987 • $29 • (01/31/91) • **86**

Hermitage 1986 • $30 Ⓐ • (02/28/90) CS • **92**

Hermitage 1985 • $81 Ⓐ • (04/15/89) CS • **92**

Hermitage 1983 • $40 Ⓐ • (04/30/87) • **87**

Hermitage 1982 • $24 Ⓐ • (05/01/86) • **91**

Hermitage 1980 • $50 • (09/01/84) CS • **91**

Hermitage 1978 • $75 Ⓐ • (03/15/90) • **91**

Hermitage 1976 • $32 Ⓐ • (03/15/90) • **80**

Hermitage 1969 • $100 • (03/15/90) • **84**

Hermitage 1966 • $100 • (03/15/90) • **90**

Hermitage 1964 • $100 • (03/15/90) • **93**

Rhône Hermitage 1991: A tight, tannic, unevolved red that needs time to develop. Good, deep color, lean fruit flavors, very firm tannins and a bit of a lingering finish. Try now. • $39 • (12/31/95) • **84**

Tavel 1996: Full in body yet thin in flavor, this deep salmon-colored rosé offers light herbal and spicy notes, quite hot on the finish. It's clumsy and dull. • $14 • (10/15/97) • **77**

Tavel 1995: Has the cherry flavors and mild tannins of a light red, is firm on the palate and shows a hint of spice on the finish. Would complement food. • $14 • (10/15/96) • **83**

Tavel 1994 • $11 • (12/31/95) • **85**

GUILBAUD, HERITIERS

Muscadet de Sèvre et Maine Clos de Beauregard Sur Lie 1993 • $8 • (11/15/95) • **79**

GUILLEMOT, PIERRE

Savigny-lès-Beaune Aux Serpentières 1994: Light and slightly astringent, with a thin layer of berry flavor peeking through the crisp finish. • $NA • (11/15/96) • **78**

Savigny-lès-Beaune Aux Serpentières 1990: Emphasizes the fruit more than the wood, with bright cherry and raspberry notes playing nicely against a subtle, toasty background. The finish is solid, with firm tannins. Drinkable now. 375 cases made. • $24 • (12/15/92) • **89**

Savigny-lès-Beaune Les Jarrons 1994: Light and youthful, with a cassislike flavor at the center, some floral grace notes and a hint of stalkiness. • $NA • (11/15/96) • **83**

Savigny-lès-Beaune Les Jarrons 1990: Offers plenty of good fruit flavors and tannins, but just doesn't have the concentration, length and class of its 1990 brethren. Drinkable now. 150 cases made. • $24 • (12/15/92) • **83**

GUILLOT-CLAUZEL, CHÂTEAU

Pomerol 1996: Pretty berry, citrus and floral aromas and flavors, a medium body, fine tannins and a light finish. Could move up. • $NA • (01/01/97) (BT) • **80-84**

Pomerol 1994: An exciting wine, especially aromatic, with violet, cherry, berry and vanilla aromas. Medium-bodied with lovely flavors and fine tannins. Delicate finish. Drink now or hold. • $NA • (01/31/97) • **88**

Pomerol 1993: One of the "finds" of the vintage. Delicious dark chocolate, berry and cherry character, medium body, firm tannins and long, succulent finish. Try now. • $NA • (01/31/96) • **88**

GUIMONIÈRE, CHÂTEAU DE LA

Anjou La Haie Frutière 1995: Black cherry and light herb flavors are fresh and round in this well-balanced red. Light tannins provide enough grip to match with food. 833 cases made. • $15 • (06/15/97) • **84**

Coteaux du Layon-Chaume Les Julines 1993: This sweet white is so alluring it's almost addictive. It offers spicy, honeyed aromas of botrytized grapes, then slides across the palate with lively orange-peel, vanilla, honey and spice flavors; a light but firm acidity keeps it fresh. A sunny, irresistible wine that's delicious, and should improve through 2000, at least. 2,500 cases made. • $14 • (08/31/97) • **91**

GUIRAUD, CHÂTEAU

Bordeaux Dry 1993 • $12 • (05/31/95) • **73**

Sauternes 1992: Rich and mouthfilling; offers bitter orange marmalade flavors and a hint of tropical notes and acidity. The finish is a bit heavy. Try now. • $NA • (04/15/95) • **84**

Sauternes 1990: Stunning Sauternes displaying great balance and smooth, creamy texture. Rich and ripe, it oozes dried apricot, almond, acacia, honey and spice flavors leading to a long, vibrant finish. Try now. • $56 • (04/15/95) • **96**

Sauternes 1989: This full-bodied Sauternes stretches the limits of botrytis. Offers loads of beeswax, almost moldy aromas, yet it is fresh and zingy with plenty of honey, spice, toast and lemon flavors. Try now. • $65 • (04/15/95) • **92**

Sauternes 1988: Elegant and well made, exhibiting medium body and sweetness. Nutmeg, clove and thyme flavors play against honey, melon and oak-scented vanilla notes. Ready to drink. • $52 • (04/15/95) • **87**

Sauternes 1987 • $NA • (06/15/90) • **72**

Sauternes 1986: A fabulous, exotic blockbuster of great balance and harmony, tasting of orange slices and chocolate, honey and cream, leading to an intense finish. Tempting now but built for aging. • $48 • (04/15/95) • **93**

Sauternes 1983: Perfect to drink now, the razor-sharp focus of citrus, dried fruit and almond flavors blending with honey, marzipan and spice. Excellent intensity on the long finish. • $38 Ⓐ • (04/15/95) • **89**

Sauternes Le Dauphin 1987: • $11 • (12/31/89) • **72**

Key: SS—Spectator Selection CS—Cellar Selection HR—Highly Recommended BB—Best Buy $NA—Price not available Ⓐ—Auction Price (BT)—Barrel Tasting

Dates in parentheses indicate the issues in which the ratings were published.

GUIRAUD-CHEVAL-BLANC, CHÂTEAU

Côtes de Bourg 1994: Lean, tough and herbal. Not much to fun to drink. • $8 • (04/30/97) • **74**

Côtes de Bourg 1989 • $6 • (11/30/92) • **77**

GUNES, CHÂTEAU DES

Haut-Médoc 1993: Light-bodied and rather dry, this rustic red offers cherry and herbal flavors that get shut down by tannins on the finish. Try now. 2,500 cases made. • $15 • (11/30/97) • **78**

GURGUE, CHÂTEAU LA

Margaux 1997: Looks and smells good, but lacks a bit of stuffing. Medium-bodied, with medium tannins and a short finish. • $NA • (06/15/98) (BT) • **80-84**

Margaux 1996: A lovely, silky red, with berry and floral aromas and flavors. Medium to full in body, with fine tannins and a fresh finish. Almost outstanding. 1,850 cases made. • $22 • (06/15/98) (BT) • **85-89**

Margaux 1995: Impressive quality for this wine. Loads of blackberry, mint and cherry aromas. Full-bodied and very balanced, with impressive fruit and tannin structure and a long, fruity aftertaste. Built for aging. Best after 2001. • $25 • (01/31/98) • **90**

Margaux 1994: A pretty, silky wine with fruit flavors of medium concentration and firm tannins. Medium-bodied. Try now. • $21 • (01/31/97) • **85**

Margaux 1993: Good concentration of fruit for the vintage, offering flavors of dried herb, plum and berry. Medium-bodied, medium tannins, fruity finish. From the owners of Château Chasse-Spleen. Try now. • $21 • (01/31/96) • **85**

Margaux 1991: A lovely, silky texture, and shows some refinement. Good raspberry notes, fruity, earthy aromas and flavors, followed up by a long finish. • $17 • (03/31/94) • **84**

Margaux 1990: A vivid, raffish, balanced Margaux, with sweet berry, spicy aromas and flavors, fine tannins and a lively finish. Drinkable now. 5,000 cases made. • $27 • (03/31/93) • **87**

Margaux 1989 • $30 • (03/15/92) • **92**

Margaux 1988 • $34 • (04/30/91) • **90**

Margaux 1987 • $23 • (11/30/89) • **82**

Margaux 1986 • $22 • (11/30/89) • **85**

Margaux 1985 • $19 • (02/15/88) • **90**

Margaux 1983 • $10 • (01/01/86) • **90**

Margaux 1982 • $24 • (11/30/89) • **85**

GUY, BERNARD

Côte-Rôtie 1992: Delicate and vivid berry and cherry flavors add light, smoky accents. Not a blockbuster but subtle and elegant. Drinkable now. 1,000 cases made. • $30 • (11/15/95) • **87**

Côte-Rôtie 1990: Lighter in color and texture than most Rhônes. This is a simple wine, with straightforward strawberry and currant flavors. Finishes modestly for such a good vintage. Drinkable now. Tasted twice, with consistent notes. • $30 • (04/15/93) • **80**

Côte-Rôtie 1987 • $25 • (08/31/89) • **87**

Côte-Rôtie 1986 • $29 • (09/30/88) • **89**

GUYARD, ALAIN

Vosne-Romanée Aux Réas 1987 • $29 • (07/15/90) • **71**

GUYON, ANTONIN

Corton-Charlemagne 1995: Gorgeous, one of the most vibrant '95s of the tasting. Wrapped in its lactic character are lively fruit flavors of quince, pineapple, mango and ripe pear—plus lime, cilantro and some deftly crafted toast accents. It's full-bodied, with a marathon-long finish that's chewy yet elegant. 275 cases made. • $65 • (05/31/97) • **96**

Corton-Charlemagne 1994: Fairly exotic and flavorful. Crisp, chewy, mineral notes and vibrant floral, citrus, toasty oak and apple flavors. Medium-to-full-bodied, with a long finish. Drinkable now. 258 cases made. • $65 • (08/31/96) • **87**

Meursault Les Charmes 1995: Very oaky in style, wood dominating now, but below are plenty of honey and lemon notes and the firm grip of deft winemaking to hold this full-bodied wine together. A creamlike flavor is present from start to long, juicy finish. Better after 2000. 250 cases made. • $40 • (05/31/97) • **89**

Meursault Les Charmes-Dessus 1994: Like a piece of great art, carefully constructed to deliver a harmonious whole. Very focused, full in body, intense and elegant. Drinkable now. Bravo! 350 cases made. • $32 • (05/31/96) • **92**

Pernand-Vergelesses White 1995: Lovely, oily and supple in texture, but with slightly green flavors of dried herbs and lime. Medium-bodied, it seems a bit dry and tart on the finish. Try now. 500 cases made. • $25 • (08/31/97) • **84**

Pernand-Vergelesses White 1994: A crisp, fresh, light-bodied white with a grassy, citrusy character and green apple flavors, showing real personality. Tastes almost like a Sauvignon Blanc on the clean, lingering finish. 375 cases made. • $20 • (05/31/96) • **82**

GUYOT, JEAN-CLAUDE

Pouilly-Fumé Les Loges 1994: The honey and vanilla aromas give a bit of a late-harvest character, and though the wine is dry they follow through on the rich palate, with orange-peel and almond notes. Distinctive and inviting. 200 cases made. • $18 • (04/30/97) • **88**

Pouilly-Fumé Les Loges 1993 • $17 • (04/30/96) • **84**

HAAG, DOMAINE JEAN-MARIE

Gewürztraminer Alsace Vallée Noble 1995: There's richness and flesh to this, but it's hollow, and the modest, bitter grapefruit flavors combined with high alcohol create imbalance. 700 cases made. • $14 • (09/30/97) • **79**

Pinot Blanc Alsace Vallée Noble 1995: Possibly reduced, nonetheless the texture is fat, with apple, herb and lemon flavors, but lacks a bit of concentration. 1,500 cases made. • $11 • (09/15/97) • **79**

Riesling Alsace Grand Cru Zinnkoepflé 1995: A laserlike beam of lime, fruit blossoms, apple and mineral greets the senses in this racy, elegant white. So delicate you may want to enjoy it all by itself, but the acid structure is perfect for food. 500 cases made. • $22 • (09/30/97) • **90**

HAEGELEN-JAYER

Chambolle-Musigny 1988 • $39 • (05/15/91) • **73**

Clos de Vougeot 1993: Lots of chewy, plummy, flavorful personality here; fresh, vibrant but also full-bodied. A wine to sink your teeth into. Tannic and somewhat rustic, but who cares? Try now. • $NA • (05/15/96) • **89**

Clos de Vougeot 1988 • $69 • (05/15/91) • **73**

Clos de Vougeot 1985 • $64 • (04/15/88) • **90**

Echézeaux 1988 • $61 • (08/31/91) • **67**

Nuits-St.-Georges Les Damodes 1988 • $39 • (05/15/91) • **89**

HAMELIN, E.A.R.L.

Chablis Beauroy 1995: Balanced, with crisp flavors but smooth texture, this medium-bodied *premier cru* has good concentration of fruit and mineral character, and a long finish. Good aging potential. Drink now through 2001. • $21 • (06/15/97) • **86**

HAMELIN, THIERRY

Chablis 1996: Pure and clean, with excellent concentration of fruit and good intensity. Mouthpuckeringly acidic now, with all that lime, but it's ripe and dense in texture. Drink around 2000. 1,200 cases made. • $17 • (08/31/97) • **90**

Chablis 1995: Crisp, medium-bodied and flavorful. Grassy, honey, pear, citrus and green apple flavors blend nicely through the fresh, smooth finish. Drink now. • $15 • (08/31/96) • **85**

Chablis Beauroy 1994 • $NA • (05/31/96) • **89**

Chablis Vau Ligneau 1995: Wonderful for its harmony. Full-bodied and ripe, clean and pure, mingling lovely tropical fruit, honey and ripe pear notes with characteristic mineral, wet stone and grass flavors. Drink now through 2005. • $21 • (06/15/97) • **88**

Chablis Vau Ligneau 1994 • $NA • (05/31/96) • **90**

Chablis Vieille Vigne 1996: Decent flavors, with lively lime, apple skin and herbal notes. Medium to full in body, with an undertow of wet earth, stone and pie dough. Slightly rustic finish. Try around 2000. 830 cases made. • $22 • (05/31/98) • **79**

Petit Chablis 1996: Amazingly classy and sophisticated for a simple Petit Chablis. Has silky texture and seductively ripe fruit flavors yet remains vibrant with lime, grapefruit and mineral notes that follow through on the lingering, fresh finish. Balanced and full-bodied. • $14 • (08/31/97) • **90**

HANTEILLAN, CHÂTEAU

Haut-Médoc 1991: Pleasant but short on the palate. Herbal, light and lean. • $15 • (03/31/94) • **75**

Haut-Médoc 1990: Traditional-style Bordeaux, with tomato and herbal aromas and flavors and soft, round tannins. Drinkable now. 35,000 cases made. • $17 • (03/31/93) • **81**

Haut-Médoc 1989 • $14 • (03/15/92) • **77**

Haut-Médoc 1987 • $13 • (11/30/89) • **75**

Haut-Médoc 1986 • $15 • (11/30/89) • **81**

Haut-Médoc 1982 • $18 • (08/31/92) • **86**

HAUT-BAGES-AVÉROUS, CHÂTEAU

Pauillac 1995: Delightful red with black cherry and berry aromas and flavors. Medium- to full-bodied, with fine tannins and a medium aftertaste. Second label of Château Lynch-Bages. Best after 2000. • $25 • (01/31/98) • **89**

Pauillac 1994: Some pretty floral and fruit aromas, but it's slightly hard on the palate, with firm tannins and a short finish. • $25 • (01/31/97) • **79**

Pauillac 1993: Nicely textured blackberry and vanilla character, but green-bean flavors detract from the overall quality. 10,000 cases made. • $19 • (01/31/96) • **79**

Pauillac 1992: Unripe grapes lend a dill, green-bean character. Drinkable but uninviting. • $17 • (04/15/95) • **71**

Pauillac 1991: Some decent ripe fruit, but a bit too herbal on the finish. • $16 • (03/31/94) • **79**

Pauillac 1990: Extremely well crafted, with mint, berry and cassis aromas and flavors and loads of velvety tannins. A spicy, juicy wine. Drink now. • $22 • (03/31/93) • **91**

Pauillac 1989 • $26 • (03/15/92) • **90**

Pauillac 1988 • $20 • (04/30/91) • **93**

Pauillac 1987 • $15 • (11/30/89) • **85**

Pauillac 1986 • $21 • (11/30/89) • **90**

Pauillac 1985 • $17 • (04/30/88) • **82**

Pauillac 1982 • $25 • (08/31/92) • **81**

Pauillac 1979 • $18 • (10/15/89) • **84**

HAUT-BAGES-LIBÉRAL, CHÂTEAU

Pauillac 1997: Simple and light, with berry and vanilla flavors, but falls short and is slightly dry on the finish. • $NA • (06/15/98) (BT) • **75-79**

Pauillac 1996: Rich berry and tobacco character. Medium-bodied, with medium tannins and a light finish. Not a particularly good sample; perhaps better than this? • $22 • (06/15/98) (BT) • **80-84**

Pauillac 1995: A bit coarse now, but massive. Sweet berry aromas with hints of citrus and smoke. Full-bodied, with big, velvety tannins and a long, long aftertaste. Best after 2001. 14,000 cases made. • $20 • (01/31/98) • **90**

Pauillac 1994: Plum, raspberry and oak notes peek through on the nose and carry through on the palate. Medium-bodied, with fine tannins and a crisp but slightly diluted finish. Try now. • $16 Ⓐ • (01/31/97) • **84**

Pauillac 1993: Lively cherry, berry and vanilla aromas and flavors, medium body, lovely tannins and a long, fresh finish. Try now. • $85 Ⓐ • (01/31/96) • **84**

Pauillac 1992: A bit one-dimensional, but offers currant and berry character, medium body, firm tannins and short finish. • $14 Ⓐ • (04/15/95) • **79**

Pauillac 1991: Supple and well made, with lovely fruity, tobacco character, medium body and fine tannins. • $17 • (03/31/94) • **84**

Pauillac 1990: Lean in texture but definitely ripe in flavor, with berry, black currant and herb aromas and flavors cutting right through the fine tannins. Finishes solid. Drinkable now. • $22 • (06/15/93) • **83**

Pauillac 1989 • $24 Ⓐ • (03/15/92) • **89**

Pauillac 1988 • $22 Ⓐ • (03/15/91) • **88**

Pauillac 1986 • $31 Ⓐ • (05/31/89) • **91**

Pauillac 1985 • $29 Ⓐ • (04/30/88) • **88**

Pauillac 1984 • $19 • (06/15/87) • **67**

Pauillac 1983 • $9 Ⓐ • (05/01/86) • **67**

Pauillac 1959 • $55 • (10/15/90) • **85**

HAUT-BAILLY, CHÂTEAU

Pessac-Léognan 1997: Decent grape and cherry character. Light to medium in body, with medium tannins and a short finish. Simple wine. • $NA • (06/15/98) (BT) • **80-84**
Pessac-Léognan 1996: Wonderful ripe berry and raspberry aromas and flavors. Full-bodied and velvety, with loads of ripe fruit and a lovely, caressing finish. Gorgeous wine for the vintage. • $35 • (06/15/98) (BT) • **90-94**
Pessac-Léognan 1995: A chewy, burly wine for aging. Big Haut-Bailly. Vivid berry and grape aromas. Full-bodied and tough, with masses of tannins and a long, wet earth and fruit aftertaste. Best after 2001. • $40 • (01/31/98) • **92**
Pessac-Léognan 1994: Chewy and big, this delivers bright plum, berry and cherry, with a hints of vanillla, on the nose and palate. Full-bodied, with tannins that build on the palate. Drinkable now. • $25 Ⓐ • (01/31/97) • **90**
Pessac-Léognan 1993: This shows some potential. Medium in body, medium-silky tannins and a long cherry, chocolate and black olive aftertaste. Drinkable now. 11,917 cases made. • $23 Ⓐ • (01/31/96) • **86**
Pessac-Léognan 1992: Solid and well balanced, exhibiting tobacco, mineral, berry and tar aromas and flavors. Full-bodied and firm yet not aggressive. Tasted twice, with consistent notes. Delicious now but will improve. • $25 • (04/15/95) • **87**
Pessac-Léognan 1990: A solid Cabernet character, with plenty of herbal cassis character, silky tannins and a smoky finish. Drinkable now. 11,000 cases made. • $28 • (03/31/93) • **88**
Pessac-Léognan 1989 • $40 Ⓐ • (03/15/92) • **92**
Pessac-Léognan 1988 • $34 Ⓐ • (04/30/91) • **94**
Pessac-Léognan 1986 • $30 Ⓐ • (06/15/89) • **91**
Pessac-Léognan 1983 • $38 Ⓐ • (10/15/94) • **91**
Graves 1985 • $37 Ⓐ • (10/15/94) • **91**
Graves 1984 • $19 • (06/15/87) • **87**
Graves 1983 • $38 Ⓐ • (10/15/94) • **91**
Graves 1982 • $33 Ⓐ • (10/15/94) • **84**
Graves 1981 • $20 Ⓐ • (10/15/94) • **87**
Graves 1979 • $29 Ⓐ • (10/15/89) • **84**
Graves 1961 • $160 Ⓐ • (04/30/96) • **88**
Graves 1947: Light, smooth and gentle, with tobacco and brown sugar flavors supported by just enough cherry to make it amiable. • $NA • (05/31/97) • **86**
Graves 1945 • $119 Ⓐ • (03/16/86) • **94**

HAUT-BATAILLEY, CHÂTEAU

Pauillac 1997: Ripe fruit character, but slightly diluted. Medium-bodied, with medium tannins and a fresh finish. • $NA • (06/15/98) (BT) • **80-84**
Pauillac 1996: Wonderful texture, with velvety, caressing tannins and a full body of ripe fruit. Extremely well-crafted. • $30 • (06/15/98) (BT) • **90-94**
Pauillac 1995: Offers more on the nose than on the palate at this stage, but delicious. Vivid aromas of crushed berries and grapes. Medium- to full-bodied, with full, fine tannins and a medium finish. Best after 2000. • $19 Ⓐ • (01/31/98) • **90**
Pauillac 1994: A harmonious wine with plum, berry and raspberry aromas and flavors, and fine tannins. Drinkable now. • $30 • (01/31/97) • **85**
Pauillac 1993: Attractive black cherry and currant aromas and flavors, medium body, firm tannins and a slightly simple finish. Drinkable now. • $17 Ⓐ • (01/31/96) • **84**
Pauillac 1992: Sleek, well-made Bordeaux offering cherry, plum and raspberry aromas and flavors, medium body, fine tannins and a medium finish. • $17 • (04/15/95) • **80**
Pauillac 1991: Light and slightly weedy but some pleasant berry fruit character and a light smoky finish. • $17 • (03/31/94) • **79**
Pauillac 1990: Weak for the vintage. What happened? 7,500 cases made. • $23 • (03/31/93) • **84**
Pauillac 1989 • $29 Ⓐ • (03/15/92) • **87**
Pauillac 1988 • $27 Ⓐ • (08/31/91) • **87**
Pauillac 1987 • $17 • (05/15/90) • **86**
Pauillac 1986 • $28 Ⓐ • (05/31/89) • **85**
Pauillac 1985 • $31 Ⓐ • (11/30/88) • **81**
Pauillac 1982 • $45 Ⓐ • (08/31/92) • **93**
Pauillac 1979 • $22 Ⓐ • (10/15/89) • **82**
Pauillac 1961 • $67 Ⓐ • (04/30/96) • **87**

HAUT-BEAUSÉJOUR, CHÂTEAU

St.-Estèphe 1997: Barrel sample. Not much to this. It has some berry and vanilla character and silky tannins, but fades very quickly. • $NA • (06/15/98) (BT) • **75-79**
St.-Estèphe 1995: Rich and full-bodied, as plenty of ripe tannins and chewy character make this a mouthful. Offers substantial earth, mocha, mineral, berry and floral complexity. Somewhat austere on the finish now. • $15 • (05/15/96) (BT) • **85-89**
St.-Estèphe 1994: Toasty oak aromas are enticing, then blend into a ripe, well-structured wine, with plum, licorice and chocolate flavors that linger on the finish. Drinkable now. • $15 • (01/01/97) • **88**
St.-Estèphe 1993: Attractive aromas of toast and coffee testify to oak maturation, and it has some nice black cherry flavors behind it. Drinkable now. • $15 • (07/31/96) • **85**

HAUT-BERGERON, CHÂTEAU

Sauternes 1992: Absolutely delicious, exhibiting loads of honey, spice and dried apricot character; full-bodied, sweet and very rich. Drinkable now. • $NA • (04/15/95) • **87**
Sauternes 1991: Already past its peak, but offers some decent dried-fruit, apricot and coconut character, full-bodied texture and a slightly dry and short finish. Drinkable now. • $NA • (04/15/95) • **83**
Sauternes 1990: A real star; exploding orange-peel, spice, dried apricot and honey flavors. Despite its rich, unctuous character, balance is impeccable, the long, cleansing finish going on forever. Try now. • $NA • (04/15/95) • **93**
Sauternes 1989: Big, powerful and rich, full-bodied; loads of sweet, thick honey character. Very spicy, leading to a honey and raisin finish. Drinkable now. • $NA • (04/15/95) • **90**
Sauternes 1988: Rather lean and austere, showing some interesting honey, spice, woody character. Disappointing. Sweet but slightly flat finish. • $NA • (04/15/95) • **79**
Sauternes 1987 • $NA • (06/15/90) • **81**
Sauternes 1986: Like digging a spoon into a great crème brûlée dessert. Medium-bodied, sweet, round and a long honey, vanilla, caramel aftertaste. Drink and enjoy. • $NA • (04/15/95) • **92**

HAUT-BERGEY, CHÂTEAU

Pessac-Léognan 1994: Decent fruit flavors, but rather lean and hard with a dry finish. Drink right away. • $NA • (01/31/97) • **79**

HAUT-BERNAT, CHÂTEAU

Puisseguin-St.-Emilion Vieilli en Fûts de Chêne 1992: Tastes like a decent Côtes du Rhône. Fruity, gamy, earthy, tomato character; medium in body and round. • $NA • (04/15/95) • **79**

HAUT BOMMES, CHÂTEAU

Sauternes 1987: • $NA • (06/15/90) • **74**

HAUT-BRIE-CAILLOU, CHÂTEAU

Médoc 1995: The texture is fleshy and round, but the flavors are on the herbal side and the tannins turn tough on the finish. May soften in a year or two. • $13 • (06/30/97) • **82**

HAUT-BRION, CHÂTEAU

Pessac-Léognan 1997: Impressively ripe and full of character for the vintage, with berry, tobacco, cedar and chocolate. Medium to full in body, with a long, fruity finish. Lovely. • $NA • (06/15/98) (BT) • **90-94**
Pessac-Léognan 1996: Slowly builds on your palate, then wows you with wonderful ripe fruit, earth and tobacco character. Full-bodied, with full tannins and a medium finish. Gorgeous. 12,500 cases made. • $180 • (06/15/98) (BT) • **90-94**
Pessac-Léognan 1995: A splendid Haut-Brion with wonderful elegance. Refined tannins. Dark-colored, with beautiful ripe berry, cherry and very smoky nuances. Full-bodied, with velvety tannins and a long, plush texture on the finish. Best after 2001. • $146 Ⓐ • (01/31/98) • **94**

Key: SS—Spectator Selection CS—Cellar Selection HR—Highly Recommended BB—Best Buy $NA—Price not available Ⓐ—Auction Price (BT)—Barrel Tasting
Dates in parentheses indicate the issues in which the ratings were published.

Pessac-Léognan 1994: Silky and unctuous, with aromas and flavors of violet, berry and vanilla, full body, fine tannins and long, flavorful finish. Very close in quality to Haut-Brion's '95. Tempting now, but best after 1999 and for many years thereafter. 16,000 cases made. • $92 Ⓐ • (01/31/97) CS • **93**

Pessac-Léognan 1993: Fabulous for the vintage. Wonderful aromas of violet, ripe fruit and toasty oak. Medium- to full-bodied, boasting loads of raspberry and vanilla flavors, medium tannins and a long, succulent finish. Drinkable now. • $70 Ⓐ • (01/31/96) • **91**

Pessac-Léognan 1992: Refined and delicious, offering mineral, berry, cherry and toasty oak flavors, medium-to-light body, fine tannins and a long finish. Drink now. • $78 Ⓐ • (04/15/95) • **87**

Pessac-Léognan 1991: Well-crafted, complex wine with classy use of oak, ripe fruit and a silky texture. Beautiful to drink now. • $65 • (03/31/94) • **87**

Pessac-Léognan 1990: The essence of Graves, with great concentration but no rough edges. The fruit and tannins are rich yet fully integrated, and the tobacco and cedar notes are classic for this estate. Drink after 2000. 12,000 cases made. • $190 Ⓐ • (04/30/93) CS • **96**

Pessac-Léognan 1989 • $352 Ⓐ • (03/15/92) • **97**

Pessac-Léognan 1988: Firm, youthful and disarming with its bright, richly delicious currant, berry and tobacco flavors. Perhaps a bit uncharacteristic of Haut-Brion, but beautifully balanced and elegant. • $105 Ⓐ • (04/30/97) • **92**

Pessac-Léognan 1987 • $48 Ⓐ • (10/15/90) • **90**

Pessac-Léognan 1986 • $122 Ⓐ • (06/30/89) • **92**

Graves 1985 • $128 Ⓐ • (10/15/94) • **95**

Graves 1984 • $38 Ⓐ • (07/31/87) • **80**

Graves 1983 • $93 Ⓐ • (10/15/94) • **88**

Graves 1982 • $249 Ⓐ • (08/31/92) • **99**

Graves 1981 • $78 Ⓐ • (10/15/94) • **82**

Graves 1980: Soft, light and elegant, with lots of smoke and tar notes and a delicate thread of berry flavor at the core. • $42 Ⓐ • (04/30/97) • **83**

Graves 1979 • $105 Ⓐ • (11/15/91) • **92**

Graves 1978 • $140 Ⓐ • (11/15/91) • **96**

Graves 1976: Slightly off-balance, with prickly tannins, but the light cherry flavors make it pleasant to drink. • $70 Ⓐ • (04/30/97) • **81**

Graves 1975 • $97 Ⓐ • (11/15/91) • **92**

Graves 1974 • $36 Ⓐ • (11/15/91) • **74**

Graves 1971 • $54 Ⓐ • (11/15/91) • **85**

Graves 1970 • $111 Ⓐ • (11/15/91) • **94**

Graves 1967: At its optimal maturity level, with a nice balance of tarry, earthy notes over a thread of berry and currant flavor hiding at the center. • $67 Ⓐ • (04/30/97) • **86**

Graves 1966 • $165 Ⓐ • (11/15/91) • **94**

Graves 1964: Mature, a bit woodsy, but with a sense of elegance and harmony that shows off the wisps of black cherry and tobacco flavor. Seems to be fading. • $96 Ⓐ • (04/30/97) • **85**

Graves 1962 • $77 Ⓐ • (11/15/91) • **93**

Graves 1961: Very mature, with a smoky, even slightly burnt nuance, but powerful with ripe cherry, toast and tobacco flavors that linger on the solid, smooth finish. A glorious mouthful of wine, at its best now. • $612 Ⓐ • (04/30/97) • **96**

Graves 1959 • $540 Ⓐ • (11/15/91) • **98**

Graves 1958: Light, a bit acidic, but showing enough spicy, tarry notes to make it interesting. • $64 Ⓐ • (04/30/97) • **79**

Graves 1957: Showing a lot of character and depth, this is still firmly tannic but generous with its tobacco, hot brick, woodsy and caramel flavors, finishing a bit drying. • $NA • (04/30/97) • **86**

Graves 1955: Firm and remarkably fresh for its age, it's a bit tannic but bright with spicy raspberry and blackberry flavors. • $249 Ⓐ • (04/30/97) • **90**

Graves 1953: Very mature, with a gamy nuance, this is smooth and appealing for its polished feel and harmony. Nice caramel and toast overtones add dimension. • $307 Ⓐ • (04/30/97) • **91**

Graves 1950: Light but beautifully sweet, floral and berrylike, an elegant wine with delicacy and vibrant flavor. Finishes nicely, too. A lovely example of the gentler side of Haut-Brion in full maturity. • $124 Ⓐ • (04/30/97) • **88**

Graves 1949 • $460 Ⓐ • (11/15/91) • **95**

Graves 1948: Light, earthy, really mushroomy notes around a light core of raspberry flavor. Very nice, still youthful. • $460 Ⓐ • (04/30/97) • **87**

Graves 1947: Ripe, warm and rich in texture, with lots of caramel, spice, berry and floral flavors swirling through, elegant and long. • $480 Ⓐ • (04/30/97) • **92**

Graves 1945 • $805 Ⓐ • (11/15/91) • **99**

Graves 1937: Has a Port-like aspect that brings some richness to the smoky, tarry aromas and flavors. Feels light but complete, if fading. • $140 Ⓐ • (04/30/97) • **83**

Graves 1934: Earthy, barky flavors predominate in this modest wine with lots of forest-floor character and a bit of roughness. • $185 Ⓐ • (04/30/97) • **77**

Graves 1929: Magnificent. Complex, powerful and deep, juicy and totally alive with beautifully focused, vibrant flavors of black cherry, citrus, red plum and anise, with a firm backbone. • $747 Ⓐ • (04/30/97) • **97**

Graves 1928: Less harmonious at this time than the 1926 or '29, but still feels youthful and alive. Shows some nice wild berry character over earthy, mushroom notes. • $522 Ⓐ • (04/30/97) • **87**

Graves 1926: Ripe, prunelike flavors in a warm, complete package. Not profound, but has lovely blackberry notes still vibrating at the core. • $498 Ⓐ • (04/30/97) • **89**

Graves 1924: On its last legs, but it has a wonderful thread of spicy, tobacco-scented mushroom and truffle character that finishes a bit tough. • $259 Ⓐ • (04/30/97) • **83**

Graves 1920: Past due, showing more metallic, sour flavors than anything else. • $NA • (04/30/97) • **72**

Pessac-Léognan White 1995: Haut-Brion always does it right. This enticing white Bordeaux shows full body, medium acidity and is simply brimming with gorgeous aromas and flavors of coconut, lemon and papaya. A long vanilla and apple pie aftertaste completes the package. Drink now or hold. 650 cases made. • $146 Ⓐ • (04/30/98) CS • **92**

Pessac-Léognan White 1994 • $92 Ⓐ • (03/31/96) CS • **96**

Pessac-Léognan White 1993 • $70 Ⓐ • (05/31/95) • **92**

HAUT-CORBIN, CHÂTEAU

St.-Emilion 1997: Slightly simple, but with good berry and tobacco character. Light- to medium-bodied, with a light finish. • $NA • (06/15/98) (BT) • **80-84**

St.-Emilion 1996: A solid '96 with good fruit and well-integrated tannins. Medium- to full-bodied, with silky texture and a medium mineral and fruit aftertaste. 46,000 cases made. • $22 • (06/15/98) (BT) • **85-89**

St.-Emilion 1995: Soft and generous, with round and velvety tannins and a ripe fruit finish. 8,000 cases made. • $20 • (01/01/97) (BT) • **85-89**

St.-Emilion 1991: A bit weedy and stewed, but some sweet fruit shows through. Medium body and astringent finish. • $16 • (03/31/94) • **76**

St.-Emilion 1990: A gorgeous wine with a beautiful mix of exotic fruit and earth flavors on the nose and palate. The tannins are fine and well proportioned. Drinkable now. 2,500 cases made. • $18 • (03/31/93) • **91**

St.-Emilion 1989 • $26 • (03/15/92) • **89**

HAUT DE LA BÉCADE, CHÂTEAU

Pauillac 1994: A sturdy, tannic Bordeaux with handsome but austere fruit flavors, a rather tough texture and spicy finish. Should improve with time. Drink now through 2000. 1,500 cases made. • $16 • (02/28/98) • **84**

HAUT DES TERRES BLANCHES, DOMAINE DU

Châteauneuf-du-Pape 1989 • $16 • (05/31/92) • **84**

Châteauneuf-du-Pape 1988 • $16 • (07/15/91) • **85**

Châteauneuf-du-Pape Réserve du Vatican 1983 • $12 • (09/30/87) • **88**

HAUTERIVE LE HAUT, CHÂTEAU

Corbières 1993 • $10 • (10/31/95) • **85**

Corbières 1990 • $10 • (03/15/94) • **88**

HAUT FAUGÈRES, CHÂTEAU

St.-Emilion 1988 • $17 • (04/30/92) • **84**

HAUTE GALINE, DOMAINE

Minervois 1991 • $7 • (03/15/94) • **83**

HAUT-GARDÈRE, CHÂTEAU

Pessac-Léognan 1997: Perfumed wine with violet and floral aromas. Medium-bodied, with a velvety texture and a medium finish. Well made for the vintage. • $NA • (06/15/98) (BT) • **85-89**
Pessac-Léognan 1996: Slightly earthy, with prune notes on the nose and palate. Medium-bodied, with medium tannins and a short finish. • $18 • (06/15/98) (BT) • **80-84**
Pessac-Léognan 1995: A drink-me Pessac. Exquisite blackberry, truffle and earth aromas. Medium- to full-bodied, with very fine tannins and a clean, fruity aftertaste. Best after 2000. • $15 • (01/31/98) • **89**
Pessac-Léognan 1986 • $11 • (09/30/89) • **81**
Graves 1985 • $15 • (07/31/88) • **77**
Pessac-Léognan White 1995: Good mineral and lemon aromas and flavors, with hints of green apple-peel. Medium-bodied, with crisp acidity and a light finish. Drink now. • $15 • (04/30/98) • **85**

HAUT-LAGRANGE, CHÂTEAU

Pessac-Léognan 1997: Weedy and light. Not much on the palate. Light-bodied, with light tannins. • $NA • (06/15/98) (BT) • **75-79**
Pessac-Léognan 1996: A slightly raisiny '96 with austere tannins and a hollow midpalate. Needs more fruit. • $22 • (06/15/98) (BT) • **75-79**
Pessac-Léognan 1995: Another sleek, exciting red. Lovely perfumes of berry, violet and cherries. Full-bodied and very well-structured, with fine tannins and a long, refreshing finish. Best after 2000. • $20 • (01/31/98) • **90**
Pessac-Léognan 1994: Rather simple, but with some good, berry, cherry and earth notes. Medium-bodied, with a short finish. Drink now. • $NA • (01/31/97) • **79**
Pessac-Léognan 1993: Rather simple tobacco, slightly herbal, fruity aromas, medium to light body, light tannins and short finish. Drinkable now. 2,166 cases made. • $17 • (01/31/96) • **81**
Pessac-Léognan 1992: A mouthful but rather herbal, displaying medium-to-full body, medium tannins and a flavorful tobacco, cherry and bell pepper finish. Drinkable now. • $14 • (04/15/95) • **81**
Pessac-Léognan 1991: Very silky and caressing wine. Cherry, strawberry aromas and flavors and fine tannins. • $14 • (03/31/94) • **83**
Pessac-Léognan White 1994 • $NA • (03/31/96) • **85**
Pessac-Léognan White 1993 • $NA • (05/31/95) • **83**

HAUT-LARIVEAU, CHÂTEAU

Canon-Fronsac 1997: Grape and violet aromas and flavors. Medium in body, with fine tannins and a light, vanilla finish. • $NA • (06/15/98) (BT) • **85-89**
Canon-Fronsac 1996: A pretty '96 with mineral, green tobacco and tea aromas and flavors. Medium- to full-bodied, with firm tannins and a fresh finish. 31,000 cases made. • $20 • (06/15/98) (BT) • **85-89**
Canon-Fronsac 1995: Ripe and decadent, well polished. Wild berry, milk chocolate, pepper and spice notes. Full-bodied and silky, with beautiful ripe fruit and chocolate character and a long, caressing finish. Best after 2001. • $20 • (01/31/98) • **89**

HAUT-MAILLET, CHÂTEAU

Pomerol 1990: A pretty wine, with lovely berry and chocolate aromas and flavors, medium tannins and a flavorful, fruity, cedary finish. Drinkable now. • $25 • (03/31/93) • **88**

HAUT-MARBUZET, CHÂTEAU

St.-Estèphe 1997: A minerally '97 with light to moderate fruit concentration, medium, fine tannins and a short finish. • $NA • (06/15/98) (BT) • **85-89**
St.-Estèphe 1996: Wonderful aromas of cassis, violets. Medium-bodied, with well-integrated tannins and a mineral, violet finish. Almost outstanding. • $NA • (01/01/97) (BT) • **85-89**
St.-Estèphe 1995: Sexy thing. Exhibits blackberries and violets, with toasty hints of new barrels. Medium-bodied, with lovely, silky tannins and a balance of ripe berry and raspberry flavors. Best after 2001. • $22 Ⓐ • (01/31/98) • **91**
St.-Estèphe 1994: Bright and fruity, with lots of spice, cherry and vanilla flavors, fine tannins and a fruity finish. Medium-bodied. Better in 1999. 25,000 cases made. • $15 Ⓐ • (01/31/97) • **87**
St.-Estèphe 1993: Delicious fresh cherry, berry and vanilla aromas and flavors, medium body and round tannins. Drinkable now. 23,077 cases made. • $33 • (01/31/96) • **85**
St.-Estèphe 1992: Currant, thyme and vanilla flavors, medium body, fine tannins and a delicate finish. • $17 • (04/15/95) • **83**
St.-Estèphe 1991: Pleasing and supple, with a spicy, vanilla and fruit character, medium body and a soft finish. • $16 • (03/31/94) • **84**
St.-Estèphe 1990: An extremely pretty, perfumed wine with velvety tannins and rich spicy, blueberry flavors. Not a huge wine, but it's gorgeous. Drink now. 18,500 cases made. • $33 Ⓐ • (03/31/93) • **92**
St.-Estèphe 1989 • $35 Ⓐ • (03/15/92) • **90**
St.-Estèphe 1988 • $29 Ⓐ • (12/31/90) SS • **91**
St.-Estèphe 1987 • $20 • (11/30/89) • **82**
St.-Estèphe 1986 • $41 Ⓐ • (11/30/89) • **92**
St.-Estèphe 1985 • $34 Ⓐ • (10/15/94) • **88**
St.-Estèphe 1983 • $22 Ⓐ • (10/15/94) • **90**
St.-Estèphe 1982 • $103 Ⓐ • (08/31/92) • **90**
St.-Estèphe 1981 • $24 • (10/15/94) • **90**
St.-Estèphe 1979 • $30 • (10/15/89) • **85**
St.-Estèphe 1962 • $50 • (11/30/87) • **70**
St.-Estèphe English Bottled 1959 • $60 • (10/15/90) • **83**

HAUT-MAZIÈRES, CHÂTEAU

Bordeaux 1993: Attractive berry and spicy aromas give way to fresh fruit flavors backed by a pleasant toasty accent. It's light but balanced and firm enough for food. • $9 • (12/15/95) • **83**
Bordeaux White 1993 • $10 • (02/29/96) • **87**

HAUT-NOUCHET, CHÂTEAU

Pessac-Léognan 1993: Rather light, offering some dried cherry and berry character and a hint of herbs. Light-bodied, light tannins and short finish. Drinkable now. • $NA • (01/31/96) • **78**
Pessac-Léognan White 1994 • $NA • (03/31/96) • **85**
Pessac-Léognan White 1993 • $NA • (03/31/96) • **83**

HAUT-REDON, CHÂTEAU

Bordeaux 1994: Bordeaux flavors and Beaujolais structure. The fresh plum and grape flavors have herbal and smoky accents. 4,000 cases made. • $9 • (12/15/95) • **83**

HAUT-RIAN, CHÂTEAU

Entre-Deux-Mers 1995: A fresh-tasting, vinous wine dominated by herbal flavors and aromas. Straightforward, very dry and firm. 2,000 cases made. • $8 • (04/30/97) • **82**
Entre-Deux-Mers 1994 • $8 • (05/31/95) • **80**
Entre-Deux-Mers 1993 • $8 • (05/31/95) • **80**
Premières Côtes de Bordeaux 1988 • $7 • (05/15/90) BB • **81**

HAUT SARPE, CHÂTEAU

St.-Emilion 1995: Round and soft for a '95, with lead-pencil, berry and fresh mushroom character. Medium-bodied, with medium tannins and a light finish. Try now. 10,000 cases made. • $37 • (01/31/98) • **82**
St.-Emilion 1988 • $19 • (06/30/91) • **83**
St.-Emilion 1982 • $20 • (05/15/89) • **87**
St.-Emilion 1979 • $12 Ⓐ • (04/01/84) • **78**
St.-Emilion 1970 • $30 • (05/15/93) • **89**

HAUTE-SERRE, CHÂTEAU DE

Cahors 1993: Dominated by an earthy character, with dried cherry and red plum flavors. Appealing despite the rough edges. Drink now. • $12 • (05/15/98) • **82**
Cahors 1990: Lovely. Delicious flavors of dried cherry, plum and spice and a long finish, with a note of brown sugar. Smooth and ready to drink. • $17 • (05/15/98) • **85**

Key: SS—Spectator Selection CS—Cellar Selection HR—Highly Recommended BB—Best Buy $NA—Price not available Ⓐ—Auction Price (BT)—Barrel Tasting
Dates in parentheses indicate the issues in which the ratings were published.

FRANCE

Cahors Géron Dadine de Haute-Serre Cuvée Prestige 1990: Firm and focused, with flavors of dried cherry, spice and herb. Finishes on an almost resinous note, with a little touch of orange peel. For fans of older, mature wines. Drink now. • $20 • (05/15/98) • **85**

HAUT-SURGET, CHÂTEAU

Lalande-de-Pomerol 1995: An exotic, flavorful, ripe and satisfying wine at a reasonable price. Its concentrated cassis and black cherry flavors are supported by firm tannins and a touch of spicy oak. Drink now through 2002. 3,000 cases made. • $15 • (01/31/98) • **87**

HAUT-VIGNEAU, CHÂTEAU

Pessac-Léognan 1996: Rather simple, with interesting berry and earth aromas and flavors. Medium-bodied, with light tannins and a fresh finish. • $20 • (06/15/98) (BT) • **80-84**

Pessac-Léognan 1995: Rather stinky, with an earthy cabbage quality. Medium-bodied, with funky flavors and a short finish. Drink if you must. • $18 • (01/31/98) • **74**

HAUTES OUCHES, DOMAINE DES

Anjou Villages 1992: Age has added alluring notes of spice and nuts to this red, but also earthy, vegetal notes. The tannins are still very firm, suggesting it may not improve. 500 cases made. • $10 • (06/15/97) • **78**

Vin de Pays du Jardin de la France Grolleau Gris 1995: Straightforward, clean and crisp, with light apple and caramel notes that dance on the palate, then disappear. 300 cases made. • $8 • (06/15/97) • **83**

HAUTS-CONSEILLANTS, CHÂTEAU LES

Lalande-de-Pomerol 1993: Spice, tobacco and plum flavors give this appeal and balance; firm tannins lend structure. Drinkable now. • $19 • (12/15/95) • **84**

HAUTS DE BRAME, CHÂTEAU LES

St.-Estèphe 1986 • $22 • (03/31/91) • **80**

HAUTS DE PLAISANCE, CHÂTEAU LES

Bordeaux Cuvée Alix 1995: Supple, with vivid, appealing red berry character and light tannins that make it easy to drink, though a smoky note turns bitter on the finish. Drink now through 2003. 2,000 cases made. • $17 • (10/15/97) • **79**

Bordeaux Cuvée Alix White 1996: A serious style of white Bordeaux that owes a lot of its buttery, caramel-like aromas and flavors to oak barrels. It's smooth and seemingly sweet on the palate. 500 cases made. • $17 • (09/30/97) • **84**

Premières Côtes de Bordeaux Alix 1995: A bit hard, with berry and cherry and dried herb character. Medium-bodied, with medium tannins and finish, and slightly metallic. • $NA • (01/01/97) • **79**

HAUTS DE PONTET, LES

Pauillac 1996: Silky and cool, but slightly metallic on the short finish. Medium-bodied, with medium tannins. • $NA • (01/01/97) (BT) • **80-84**

Pauillac 1995: Intense aromas of flowers and berries. Medium-bodied, with straightforward fruit and a short finish. • $NA • (01/01/97) (BT) • **80-84**

HAUTS DE SMITH, LES

Pessac-Léognan 1995: A good second label from Château Smith-Haut-Lafitte, showing blackberry, dried herbs and cherry. Full-bodied and tannic, with lots of Cabernet Sauvignon character. Drinkable now. 2,500 cases made. • $18 • (01/31/98) • **85**

Pessac-Léognan 1994: A wine with no pretensions, it's just fruity and drinkable. Of medium body, with light tannins. Drink now. • $16 • (01/31/97) • **79**

Pessac-Léognan White 1995: Too good to be a second label. Interesting character of grass, celery and fruit. Medium- to full-bodied, with fresh acidity and a good amount of fruit in the aftertaste. Drink now. • $18 • (04/30/98) • **88**

HAUX, CHÂTEAU DE

Bordeaux White 1994 • $10 • (02/29/96) • **84**

HÉBRART, MARC

Brut Champagne Special Club 1990: An intensely flavorful, vibrantly crisp Champagne that may need time to mellow. Has an appealing array of toasty, vanillalike, citrusy flavors that last from the first whiff to the finish. Drink now through 2001. • $47 • (04/30/98) • **90**

HEIDSIECK, CHARLES

Brut Blanc de Blancs Champagne Blanc des Millénaires 1985: A rich, ample, plush-textured Champagne that melts in your mouth. Combines toasty-earthy aromas, lively fruit flavors and a creamy mousse. Drink now. • $70 • (11/30/97) • **94**

Brut Blanc de Blancs Champagne Blanc des Millénaires 1983: A quiet, subtle Champagne offering lightly smoky aromas and modest fruit and nut flavors on a rather light frame of acidity. Smooth in texture and light on the finish. • $70 • (12/31/96) • **85**

Brut Blanc de Blancs Champagne Brut de Chardonnay 1981 • $30 • (05/31/87) • **78**

Brut Champagne 1990: An attractive, well-balanced, soft-textured, easy-drinking Champagne with charming, light fruit and spice flavors that linger on the finish. • $48 • (08/31/97) • **88**

Brut Champagne 1985: Suave, satisfying and flavorful, blending wonderful toasty, earthy aromas with mellow and mature fruit flavors that linger on the long finish. Hard to think of a more powerful and enticing Champagne to drink tonight. Even better than in earlier tastings. • $48 • (12/31/96) • **93**

Brut Champagne 1983: A Champagne with uncommon character, this mature wine is round, creamy and generous on the palate, with all sorts of honey, toast and earth aromas and flavors. A rich, full-bodied, heady style of Champagne. • $41 • (03/31/91) • **90**

Brut Champagne 1982: Powerful, rich and memorable. Extremely intense with toasty, smoky and nutty flavors (walnuts come to mind). Long, yeasty finish that is wonderful. A surprisingly fine Champagne at half the price of the prestige cuvées. • $40 • (12/31/88) SS • **93**

Brut Champagne Blanc des Millénaires 1983: A beautifully rich, creamy, expansive Champagne with abundant pear and apple flavors accented by vanilla and toast. This is a great example of a vintage Champagne at its peak: mature but still lively, generous and long on the finish. 3,000 cases made. • $55 • (12/31/95) HR • **92**

Brut Champagne Millésime 1983: Beautiful flavors of rich, toasty, pear, apple and spice, with a fine structure that keeps the flavors lingering on the finish. An impressive package that's ready to drink now. • $38 • (12/31/89) • **87**

Brut Champagne Réserve NV: Luxurious and inviting in style, this has toasty, vanilla aromas, compelling and complex fruit flavors, a creamy smooth texture and a lingering finish. Drink now. • $34 • (05/31/98) • **91**

Brut Rosé Champagne 1985: Pale salmon color and intricate aromas mark this as a fully mature, complex Champagne. The flavors reveal subtle cherry, toast, mushroom and spice nuances that grow and mingle on the finish. Lush and expansive in texture, too. Drink now. • $55 • (12/31/97) • **95**

Brut Rosé Champagne 1983: Pale, delicate and creamy in texture, with lots of toasty overtones to the modest berry and vanilla aromas and flavors. Smooth and flavorful without sacrificing delicacy. • $49 • (03/31/91) • **89**

Brut Rosé Champagne 1982: Hangs together wonderfully well. Prominent Pinot Noir character mingles nicely with toasty, assertive and crisp flavors. Balanced, complex, lush and clean. • $40 • (12/31/88) • **91**

HEIDSIECK MONOPOLE

Brut Champagne Blue Top NV: A nice, ripe-tasting Champagne with fairly full flavors and good balance. It has nuances of apple, earth and nuts, and a lingering finish. • $28 • (07/31/97) • **85**

Brut Champagne Diamant Bleu 1989: Seamless. If a wine can be graceful, this one is. Has intriguing apricot, ripe apple and spice flavors, vibrant acidity, a smooth but refreshing texture and a long, lively finish. Drink now through 2000. 10,000 cases made. • $60 • (11/15/96) HR • **91**

Brut Champagne Diamant Bleu 1985: So smooth, so fine, it's a joy to drink. There are layers of tropical fruit, smoke and coconut with medium body and firm acidity. Drink now. • $85 • (12/31/93) • **92**

Brut Champagne Diamant Bleu 1982 • $70 • (11/30/87) • **89**

FRANCE

Brut Champagne Diamant Bleu 1979 • $39 • (05/16/86) • **93**
Brut Champagne Diamant Rosé 1982 • $85 • (11/30/87) • **90**
Brut Champagne Dry Monopole 1985 • $NA • (12/31/90) • **90**
Brut Champagne Dry Monopole 1982 • $43 • (12/31/88) • **88**
Brut Rosé Champagne 1983: Dry and cherryish, but lacks the richness and texture one expects from a Rosé Champagne, leaving it coarse and simple. • $40 • (12/31/89) • **75**
Brut Rosé Champagne 1982: Good balance with distinctive earthy style. Meaty flavors with hint of cherries. Crisp finish. • $43 • (12/31/88) • **84**
Brut Rosé Champagne 1979 • $27 • (12/16/85) • **72**
Brut Rosé Champagne Diamant 1988: Dry, subtle and delicate, this is for fans of understatement. It has very light cherry aromas and flavors, a firm, crisp texture and lively, fruity finish. Outstanding quality. 2,000 cases made. • $60 • (12/31/96) • **90**

HÉLÈNE, CHÂTEAU

Corbières Cuvée Hélène de Troie 1994: Starts with some attractive minty and peppery flavors, but dries out on the finish. Past its prime. • $20 • (04/30/98) • **80**
Corbières Cuvée Tradition 1990 • $7 • (03/15/94) • **83**
Corbières White Cuvée Penelope 1995: Quite distinctive, with floral and spice flavors, and a good wollop of earthiness as well. Has a nice mineral note on the finish. • $7 • (03/31/98) • **82**

HENRIOT

Brut Blanc de Blancs Champagne NV: A lemon meringue of a Champagne. It's light in body, almost sweet, with creamy, buttery flavors and a frothy texture. 7,000 cases made. • $36 • (07/31/97) • **85**
Brut Champagne 1988: This is really expressive with distinctive raspberry and cream aromas and flavors, medium body and acidity and a flavorful finish. Drink now. • $39 • (12/31/93) • **88**
Brut Champagne Cuvée des Enchanteleurs 1985: A sophisticated, mature Champagne from a great year. It's understated in flavor, elegant in texture, still lively in balance. Graceful and distinctive. 5,000 cases made. • $70 • (08/31/97) • **89**
Brut Champagne Cuvée Baccarat 1983: You can't not like the intense toasty, apple character in this one. It's got very good acidity, slight tannin pucker, and rich fruit. Drink now. • $NA • (12/31/93) • **88**
Brut Champagne Millésimé 1989: Complex and mature in style, this is a full-bodied but appealingly austere-tasting Champagne that expands on the finish. The perfect bubbly for those who value reserve and maturity. 23,000 cases made. • $40 • (08/31/97) HR • **91**
Brut Champagne Souverain NV: A solid, quality Champagne with a firm, vibrant texture and ample, crisp fruit flavors that carry through the finish. Completely refreshing and appealing. 33,000 cases made. • $29 • (07/31/97) • **89**
Brut Rosé Champagne 1981 • $28 • (07/01/86) • **93**

HERBEAUX, CHÂTEAU DES

Chambertin 1990: Rich, ripe and concentrated without losing a sense of lightness and deftness, melding the spicy, toasty nuances of oak with a supple beam of blackberry, currant and black cherry flavors. Showing a lot of complexity already. Drinkable now. • $75 • (02/15/93) • **89**
Chambertin 1988 • $75 • (12/31/90) • **87**
Clos Vougeot 1988 • $65 • (11/30/90) • **86**
Musigny 1988 • $75 • (12/31/90) • **83**
Volnay-Santenots 1988 • $36 • (11/30/90) • **88**

HERESZTYN, BERNARD

Gevrey-Chambertin Les Goulots 1988 • $44 • (07/15/91) • **90**

HERESZTYN, STANISLAS

Gevrey-Chambertin 1987 • $25 • (03/31/90) • **83**
Gevrey-Chambertin Les Champonnets 1988 • $37 • (12/31/90) • **82**

Key: SS—Spectator Selection CS—Cellar Selection HR—Highly Recommended BB—Best Buy $NA—Price not available Ⓐ—Auction Price (BT)—Barrel Tasting
Dates in parentheses indicate the issues in which the ratings were published.

HÉRITIER-GUYOT, L'

Auxey-Duresses White 1994: An odd wine that has a perfumy, floral, butterscotch character that is somewhat balanced by a nice chewy, chalky texture and mineral notes. It turns rather lean on the finish, though. 125 cases made. • $18 • (05/31/96) • **80**
Bourgogne White 1994: Some modest fruit flavors, but mostly quite tart and lean. 300 cases made. • $12 • (05/31/96) • **77**
Chambolle-Musigny 1994: Light and diluted, with less than ample fruit aromas and flavors. • $28 • (11/15/96) • **73**
Chambolle-Musigny 1993: Diluted and light, tasting like it was cut with water, showing a filter-pad, cardboard flavor on the finish. Drink if you must. • $30 • (11/15/95) • **74**
Chassagne-Montrachet 1995: Opulent but slightly overripe, with not-so-attractive butter and cooked apple notes; the texture is smooth and thick, however. Try now through 2000. 125 cases made. • $33 • (08/31/97) • **79**
Chassagne-Montrachet 1994: It's Burgundian, with a toasty, honeyed complexity, but it lacks fruit concentration. Short and a bit diluted despite the full body and texture. Tastes a little candied on the finish. 125 cases made. • $28 • (05/31/96) • **80**
Clos de Vougeot 1994: Light, bordering on thin, with modest strawberry and cocoa flavors that do a diminuendo on the finish. Aproachable already. • $49 • (11/15/96) • **79**
Clos de Vougeot 1993: Rather lean and hard, showing game, leather and fruit aromas and flavors, medium body and tough tannins. Try now. • $35 • (11/15/95) • **84**
Clos de Vougeot 1988 • $51 • (03/15/93) • **76**
Corton-Charlemagne 1995: Thick, rich and opulent; quite hedonistic, with nicely blended notes of toasty coconut and spicy wood. Full-bodied, even massive, turning a bit rustic on the finish. Try after 2000. 96 cases made. • $50 • (08/31/97) • **85**
Corton Les Renardes 1993: Rather straightforward plum, berry and light cedar character, medium body, light tannins and a fresh finish. • $60 • (11/15/95) • **86**
Côte de Nuits-Villages 1993: Rather firm, tannic and quite dry; medium-bodied. Hopefully currant and black cherry flavors will balance tannins in the future. Try now. • $15 • (11/15/95) • **83**
Echézeaux 1994: Disappointing. Green and astringent, with herbal aromas and flavors. Some ripe character in the midpalate, but finishes with dry tannins. • $47 • (11/15/96) • **76**
Gevrey-Chambertin Les Cazetiers 1993: Tannic and structured on the palate, featuring a good core of red berry flavor. Quite tasty and ripe, medium-bodied, rather hard at this stage. Try now. • $45 • (11/15/95) • **84**
Hautes Côtes de Nuits White 1994: Very fresh and intense, with a nice lemony, zesty character. Some green apple, grapefruit and dried herb flavors and somewhat short on the finish. 551 cases made. • $13 • (05/31/96) • **79**
Mâcon-Villages 1996: Slightly woody, but the oak treatment gives this a roundness that some '96 Mâcons lack. Butter, pear, apple pie and walnut flavors. Drink now. 1,000 cases made. • $12 • (05/31/98) • **80**
Mâcon-Villages 1995: Clean, crisp and fruity. Light- to- medium-bodied, with lime, apple, pear and spice notes. Drink now. • $NA • (08/31/96) • **83**
Meursault 1995: Interesting, full-bodied and with a slightly tart texture, this is extremely ripe, almost overly so, with apricot, peach and cooked apple flavors. Drink now. • $NA • (08/31/97) • **77**
Puligny-Montrachet Les Chalumaux 1995: Ripe and full-bodied but rustic, with an old-wood, chestnut, mocha character that's unappealing, followed by a burning taste on the finish. • $45 • (08/31/97) • **78**
St.-Romain White 1994: A sharp, vibrant, assertive white that tastes like a delicious Sauvignon Blanc—a bit grassy and herbal, with a tangy note on the long, fruity, lively finish. 175 cases made. • $16 • (05/31/96) • **86**
Santenay 1994: A roséiike red Burgundy that tastes of strawberry juice. Diluted and slightly astringent on the finish. • $18 • (11/15/96) • **70**
Vougeot Clos Blanc de Vougeot White 1995: Full-bodied and quite ripe, with opulent flavors of honey, citrus, mineral and spice that linger on the sophisticated finish. Delicious now, should only get better through 2005. 403 cases made. • $43 • (08/31/97) • **88**
Vougeot Clos Blanc de Vougeot White 1994: Very pretty and nicely balanced, with apricot, floral, honey and lemon notes. Focused on the clean, fresh finish. A lively wine to enjoy now. 786 cases made. • $40 • (05/31/96) • **89**
Vougeot Les Crâs 1994: Brown-colored and diluted, with minor-league flavors of brown sugar and cherry. Light and disappointing. • $42 • (11/15/96) • **71**
Vougeot Les Crâs 1993: Lean and tannic, with some fruit, but it's hot and burning on the palate. Out of balance. Drink if you must. • $35 • (11/15/95) • **77**

HERMITAGE, CHÂTEAU L'

St.-Emilion 1997: Strong blackberry and cherry aromas, with hints of new wood. Medium-bodied, with velvety tannins and a medium finish. Almost outstanding. But is it St.-Emilion? • $NA • (06/15/98) (BT) • **85-89**

HERON

Merlot Vin de Pays d'Oc 1995: A concentrated wine with dark plum and dark cherry flavors. Fairly rich, with notes of clove and chocolate, some cedary notes on the finish. 18,000 cases made. • $9 • (11/15/97) • **84**

Merlot Vin de Pays d'Oc 1994: Too much heavy-handed oak lends an overly vanilla character to the lush Merlot fruit. 7,600 cases made. • $9 • (07/31/96) • **79**

HERZOG

Cabernet Sauvignon Vin de Pays d'Oc 1996: Modest cherry, dill and bell pepper flavors denote this red. An underlying crispness gives it a tough edge. Kosher. 6,000 cases made. • $7 • (12/15/97) • **76**

Cabernet Sauvignon Vin de Pays d'Oc NV • $7 • (03/31/91) BB • **88**

Chardonnay Vin de Pays du Jardin de la France 1996: Straightforward, offering basic apple and citrus flavors, with just enough weight on the palate to stand up to lighter dishes. Kosher. Drink now. 6,000 cases made. • $7 • (05/31/98) • **81**

Merlot Vin de Pays d'Oc 1996: Flavors of cherry and tomato and spicy-earthy accents provide good varietal character. It's light- to medium-bodied, with light tannins. Kosher. 12,000 cases made. • $7 • (12/15/97) • **82**

Merlot Vin de Pays d'Oc NV • $7 • (03/31/91) • **75**

Muscadet de Sèvre et Maine 1995: Shows oxidized character, with not enough fruit for balance. The finish is pinched and astringent. Kosher. Tasted twice, with consistent notes. Drink now. 3,000 cases made. • $8 • (05/31/98) • **74**

HORTE, CHÂTEAU DE L'

Corbières Réserve Spéciale 1991 • $9 • (03/15/94) • **83**

HORTUS, DOMAINE DE L'

Coteaux du Languedoc Pic St.-Loup Grande Cuvée 1995: A well-polished wine with appealing toasty flavors and luscious berry notes. Medium-bodied, with a minty quality on the finish. Drink now. • $16 • (03/31/98) • **85**

Coteaux du Languedoc 1991 • $8 • (03/15/94) • **83**

HUËT, S.A.

Vouvray Cuvée Constance 1995: This luscious white pours like oil into the glass. Complex aromas of honey and spices, rich, soft, sweet flavors of dried fruits, honey, vanilla and butterscotch. Though very sweet, it has lively acidity. Drink now through 2025. • $60/500ml • (06/15/97) • **93**

Vouvray Demi-Sec Clos du Bourg 1995: Not showy, rather it's endowed with a subtle complexity that grows on you. Full-bodied, with light sweetness and fine acidity, and flavors of cream, rose petals, hazelnuts and toast. Drink now through 2000. • $20 • (05/15/97) • **89**

Vouvray Moelleux Clos du Bourg Première Trie 1995: Rich yet refreshing, like a deep-dish lemon-custard pie in a glass, this Loire white is sweet yet crisp and clean, with bright lemon and cream flavors. A clean and harmonious white. Drink now through 2004. • $35 • (05/15/97) CS • **94**

Vouvray Le Mont 1995: Ripe yet dry. Tastes more like Savennières than Vouvray, with mineral, smoke and citrus flavors. Crisp, yet muscular on the palate. Try now. • $18 • (05/15/97) • **88**

Vouvray Sec Clos du Bourg 1993 • $18 • (12/15/95) • **85**

HUGEL

Alsace Gentil 1996: Here's a vibrant white displaying floral, citrus and peach character and ending in a lip-smacking tanginess. Delicious now. • $10 • (11/15/97) • **85**

Alsace Gentil 1995: Quaffable, showing round melon and creamlike flavors with hints of spice, and a pleasantly creamy texture. Not complex, but would make a good apéritif. • $9 • (10/15/96) • **83**

Alsace Gentil Hugel 1993 • $10 • (11/15/94) • **86**

Gewürztraminer Alsace Jubilée Réserve Personnelle 1995: A sleek, firm Gewürztraminer with pure aromas of pear and rose petals, leaning toward white pepper and mineral on the palate. Drinkable now. Tasted twice. • $30 • (11/15/97) • **90**

Gewürztraminer Alsace 1993: The aromas are textbook Gewürz—spice, litchi, rose petals—and these notes carry through on the straightforward, dry palate. It's well balanced and clean. • $16 • (11/15/96) • **83**

Gewürztraminer Alsace Sélection de Grains Nobles 1989: Very fresh and young for its age, this vivid Gewürz offers the signature spice and litchi flavors with good focus and moderate sweetness. There's plenty of pineapple and banana flavors to pair up with desserts and enough depth to enjoy this on its own. Much better than a previous sample. • $124 • (11/15/96) • **93**

Gewürztraminer Alsace Sélection de Grains Nobles 1983 • $NA • (04/30/87) • **95**

Gewürztraminer Alsace Sélection de Grains Nobles 1981 • $NA • (04/30/87) • **93**

Gewürztraminer Alsace Sélection de Grains Nobles 1976 • $NA • (04/30/87) • **90**

Gewürztraminer Alsace Sélection de Grains Nobles 1961 • $NA • (04/30/87) • **98**

Gewürztraminer Alsace Vendange Tardive 1989 • $60 • (01/01/96) • **89**

Pinot Blanc Alsace Cuvée Les Amours 1993: Firm and still fresh, this offers flavors of pear, lime and banana. Crisp acidity balances its round body. Try as an apéritif or with lighter dishes. • $11 • (11/15/96) • **85**

Pinot Noir Alsace Jubilee Réserve Personnelle 1995: Exhibits good color and a wonderful scent of pure Pinot Noir fruit. Raspberries, strawberries and cherries mingle in this sprightly red that begs drinking now. Best slightly chilled. • $35 • (11/15/97) • **87**

Pinot Noir Alsace Jubilee Réserve Personnelle 1990 • $29 • (11/15/94) • **81**

Riesling Alsace 1994: Beginning to develop some mature flavors, this rich, firmly structured white has apple, marzipan and kerosene notes. It's full-bodied and well balanced to match freshwater fish or pork dishes. Drinkable now through 2000. • $15 • (11/15/97) • **87**

Riesling Alsace 1993: Clean and solid, this offers characteristic mineral, petroleum and lime flavors, with very firm acidity and good structure. It needs food, or another year in the bottle, to soften and open. • $14 • (11/15/96) • **85**

Riesling Alsace Sélection de Grains Nobles 1976 • $NA • (04/30/87) • **98**

Tokay Pinot Gris Alsace Jubilée Hugel Réserve Personnelle 1993: Showing its maturity with a marzipan and hazelnut character, this has a fat, glycerinlike texture in the middle, but never gets heavy or cloying. Good length. Delicious now. Tasted twice. • $31 • (11/15/97) • **87**

Tokay Pinot Gris Alsace Sélection de Grains Nobles 1989: Still very young and fresh, with great concentration and balance. Opens with discreet but rich aromas of crème brûlée and coffee, then moves to sweet honey and spice flavors backed by firm acidity. Finishes long and with a teasing bitterness that draws you back for more. Irresistible now, but should only improve with time in the bottle • $162 • (08/31/95) • **97**

Tokay Pinot Gris Alsace Sélection de Grains Nobles 1976 • $NA • (04/30/87) • **87**

Tokay Pinot Gris Alsace Tradition Hugel 1993: A white with structure but no fruit and flesh to fill it out. Shows some marzipan flavors. Try now. • $20 • (11/15/97) • **83**

Tokay Pinot Gris Alsace Vendange Tardive 1989: Opulent yet balanced, and benefiting from bottle age, this marries butter, pastry dough and honey flavors with a clean, underlying acidity. Hints of walnuts and white truffles add interest. Understated yet seductive, it's delicious now but has a long future ahead. Much better than a previous sample. • $81 • (11/15/96) • **92**

HUNOLD, DOMAINE BRUNO

Brut Crémant d'Alsace Cuvée du Paradis NV: Floral and lemon aromas highlight this delicate, lively sparkler. It's soft and creamy in texture, with a lingering, crisp finish which makes it a perfect apéritif. 1,500 cases made. • $15 • (09/15/97) • **86**

Gewürztraminer Alsace 1995: Ripe and fat, promising litchi and honey and a slight pungency due to botrytis, this full-bodied white turns a little simple on the finish. 5,000 cases made. • $11 • (09/30/97) • **82**

Gewürztraminer Alsace Grand Cru Vorbourg 1995: A beautiful Gewürz that's ripe, spicy and exotic without being overbearing. The luscious texture coats the mouth, while offering honey and rosewater flavors. Though full-bodied, a touch of bitterness on the finish keeps it in check. 900 cases made. • $15 • (11/15/97) • **89**

Pinot Blanc Alsace 1995: Broad, ripe and powerful, cutting a swath across the palate with its apple, mango and nutlike flavors. It's all reigned in by a lemony acidity on the finish. 6,000 cases made. • $9 • (09/15/97) • **86**

FRANCE

Riesling Alsace 1995: Ripe and exotic, showing apricot and mango flavors and just a hint of sweetness to round it all out. Falls short on the finish. 4,000 cases made. • $10 • (09/30/97) • **84**

Tokay Pinot Gris Alsace Grand Cru Vorbourg 1995: Appealing for its texture and richness, but there's a canned-fruit character that detracts. Not up to *grand cru* level. 700 cases made. • $17 • (09/30/97) • **79**

HYOT BEAUSÉJOUR, CHÂTEAU

Côtes de Castillon 1993: There are some candied-cherry flavors but not much else. Still very tannic. • $8 • (04/30/97) • **76**

ILE, DOMAINE DE L'

Côtes de Provence Rosé Porquerolles 1996: An interesting, mature-tasting wine with flavors of herb and mineral and a lingering note of dried cherry on the finish. Try it when in the mood for something different. 4,000 cases made. • $13 • (12/31/97) • **85**

ISSAN, CHÂTEAU D'

Margaux 1997: Typical blackberry and green tobacco aromas and flavors. Medium-bodied, with medium to light tannins and a short finish. • $NA • (06/15/98) (BT) • **80-84**

Margaux 1996: Good concentration of fruit and tannins. Medium-bodied, with medium tannins and a delicious aftertaste. • $25 • (06/15/98) (BT) • **85-89**

Margaux 1995: Needs time to come together, but impressive. The grapey, berry and violet aromas follow through. Full-bodied and chewy, with an impressive mouthfeel. Slightly hollow midpalate. Puckers your mouth first, but caresses it in the end. Best after 2001. • $20 Ⓐ • (01/31/98) • **89**

Margaux 1994: Intense aromas of plums, pickles and tar. Full-bodied, with lots of tannins and a slightly dry finish. A bit overdone. Try now. 12,000 cases made. • $25 • (01/31/97) • **83**

Margaux 1993: Nicely made, smooth, showing anise, currant and black cherry character. Enjoy now, but it lacks some length on the finish. • $25 • (01/31/96) • **83**

Margaux 1990: Impressive concentration but lacks finesse. A big, burly wine, with prune, raisin and earth character, rich, round tannins and a long finish. Drinkable now. 12,000 cases made. • $25 • (03/31/93) • **86**

Margaux 1989 • $34 Ⓐ • (03/15/92) • **84**

Margaux 1988 • $29 Ⓐ • (04/30/91) • **88**

Margaux 1987 • $20 • (05/15/90) • **76**

Margaux 1986 • $35 Ⓐ • (06/15/89) • **83**

Margaux 1985 • $37 Ⓐ • (04/15/88) • **88**

Margaux 1984 • $32 Ⓐ • (03/31/87) • **86**

Margaux 1983 • $36 Ⓐ • (04/16/86) • **91**

Margaux 1982 • $27 Ⓐ • (08/31/92) • **88**

JABOULET AÎNÉ, PAUL

Châteauneuf-du-Pape 1983 • $10 • (10/15/91) • **85**

Châteauneuf-du-Pape Les Cèdres 1995: This chewy wine shows ripe fruit flavors and a pleasantly round texture. Less muscle and intensity than expected from the appellation, but sturdy. Drink now. 10,000 cases made. • $30 • (12/15/96) • **86**

Châteauneuf-du-Pape Les Cèdres 1994: This round, generous red offers plum, black pepper, licorice and meaty flavors with an underpinning of modest tannins. Attractive now. 1,108 cases made. • $25 • (11/15/96) • **87**

Châteauneuf-du-Pape Les Cèdres 1990: Big and oaky, with layers of rich chocolate, oak and currant flavors seasoned by hints of spice. Drink now. • $63 Ⓐ • (08/31/92) • **87**

Châteauneuf-du-Pape Les Cèdres 1989 • $36 Ⓐ • (07/15/91) HR • **91**

Châteauneuf-du-Pape Les Cèdres 1988 • $13 Ⓐ • (10/15/91) • **86**

Châteauneuf-du-Pape Les Cèdres 1986 • $17 Ⓐ • (10/15/91) • **87**

Châteauneuf-du-Pape Les Cèdres 1985 • $34 Ⓐ • (10/15/91) • **88**

Châteauneuf-du-Pape Les Cèdres 1981 • $NA • (10/15/91) • **86**

Cornas 1995: Though supple for Cornas, this polished red offers bright plum, chocolate and licorice flavors. It's clean and well defined, with good acidity to keep it lively. Drink now through 2002. • $33 • (10/15/97) • **85**

Key: SS—Spectator Selection CS—Cellar Selection HR—Highly Recommended BB—Best Buy $NA—Price not available Ⓐ—Auction Price (BT)—Barrel Tasting
Dates in parentheses indicate the issues in which the ratings were published.

Cornas 1990 • $29 • (11/30/92) • **82**

Côte-Rôtie Les Jumelles 1995: Black cherry and gamelike aromas and flavors are expressive and alluring in this tender red, which shows good concentration yet soft tannins that make the wine accessible now. It's clean and fresh. • $44 • (10/15/97) • **88**

Côte-Rôtie Les Jumelles 1991: Not a blockbuster, but pretty, with subtle berry, game and licorice flavors; balanced and soft. Drinkable now. • $35 • (05/31/94) • **86**

Côte-Rôtie Les Jumelles 1989 • $38 • (02/28/93) • **81**

Côte-Rôtie Les Jumelles 1985 • $35 • (09/30/88) • **93**

Côtes du Rhône Parallèle 45 1996: A delicious Côtes du Rhône at a more than reasonable price, this red is rich and concentrated, displaying raspberry, cherry and dried herb notes, light tannins and a lengthy aftertaste. Drink now through 2000. 60,000 cases made. • $10 • (05/15/98) BB • **87**

Côtes du Rhône Parallèle 45 1995: Round and ripe, this offers attractive black cherry, licorice and light herbal flavors, with firm but unobtrusive tannins that add backbone. It's nicely balanced and drinking well now. 53,000 cases made. • $9 • (12/15/96) • **86**

Côtes du Rhône Parallèle 45 1994: Clean and firm. This offers aromas and flavors of smoke, black cherry, licorice and earth, straightforward but well knit. Drink now. 25,400 cases made. • $8 • (11/15/96) BB • **84**

Côtes du Rhône Parallèle 45 1993 • $9 • (11/30/94) • **83**

Côtes du Rhône-Villages 1995: This light-bodied red has plenty of flavor, with notes of cherries, game, pepper and spice. Light tannins make it accessible now. Try with chicken or paté. 4,000 cases made. • $15 • (11/15/96) • **86**

Côtes du Ventoux 1993 • $7 • (09/30/95) • **85**

Côtes du Ventoux 1990 • $18 • (04/15/93) BB • **82**

Crozes-Hermitage Domaine de Thalabert 1995: Closed up slightly today, yet there's plenty of sweet blackberry and plum character along with hints of vanilla, all cloaked in a shroud of ripe, mouthcoating tannins. A modern expression of Syrah that will develop well. Best from 2000 through 2008. • $25 • (01/01/98) • **90**

Crozes-Hermitage Domaine de Thalabert 1994: Delicious aromas of crushed raspberries and kirsch, followed by a mouthful of velvety textured fruit, licorice, mint and chocolate flavors. This Rhône red has firm tannins to match its generous fruit flavor, and should improve through 2000. 16,226 cases made. • $24 • (12/15/96) • **90**

Crozes-Hermitage Domaine de Thalabert 1992 • $22 • (10/15/95) • **85**

Crozes-Hermitage Domaine de Thalabert 1991 • $16 • (05/31/94) • **88**

Crozes-Hermitage Domaine de Thalabert 1989 • $18 • (07/15/91) • **90**

Crozes-Hermitage Domaine de Thalabert 1988 • $15 • (10/15/90) • **83**

Crozes-Hermitage Domaine de Thalabert 1987 • $10 • (03/31/90) • **83**

Crozes-Hermitage Domaine de Thalabert 1986 • $16 • (09/30/88) • **88**

Crozes-Hermitage Domaine de Thalabert 1985 • $22 • (09/30/88) • **85**

Crozes-Hermitage Les Jalets 1995: A lively red, with vivid raspberry and herbal flavors, hints of licorice and tar. Light-bodied, with soft, rather supple tannins, it's attractive now, lacks the stuffing to age. Drink now. • $14 • (10/15/97) • **84**

Crozes-Hermitage Les Jalets 1994: A bright burst of raspberry flavor gives this wine panache, and it has the concentration to back it up, with pretty chocolate and floral notes on the finish. It's monolithic now, but should develop more complexity with age. 27,000 cases made. • $14 • (11/30/96) HR • **91**

Crozes-Hermitage Les Jalets 1992 • $14 • (10/15/95) • **84**

Crozes-Hermitage Les Jalets 1990 • $14 • (03/31/94) HR • **88**

Gigondas 1989 • $18 • (07/15/91) • **84**

Hermitage La Chapelle 1995: A vivid, lush, international-style Syrah from the Rhône Valley, polished and lavishly oaked, stuffed with ripe flavors of plums, prunes, chocolate and toast. Firm tannins dominate the texture now, but this wine should smooth out and gain in complexity given some time in the cellar. Try soon. 5,800 cases made. • $75 • (10/15/97) • **93**

Hermitage La Chapelle 1994: Ripe and lush, this rich red shows loads of jammy plum flavors graced by mineral, black pepper and dark chocolate flavors. The texture is as thick as that of young Port. Attractive now, it needs until 2002 to show its stuff. 7,500 cases made. • $62 • (11/30/96) CS • **91**

Hermitage La Chapelle 1991: Voluptuous, smooth, intriguing, offering the smoky, toasty notes of new wood and ripe cherry and plum flavors. Polished yet concentrated; try now. • $50 • (05/31/94) • **90**

Hermitage La Chapelle 1990: Bold, ripe and powerful, with a solid, rich core of mineral, currant, plum and cedar flavors that are remarkably complex, smooth and polished, with fine but firm tannins. Elegant, refined and tasty to drink now, but sure to age. 9,400 cases made. • $62 • (08/31/92) HR • **95**

Hermitage La Chapelle 1989 • $55 • (08/31/91) CS • **93**

Hermitage La Chapelle 1988 • $45 • (03/31/91) • **92**
Hermitage La Chapelle 1986 • $35 • (11/15/89) • **89**
Hermitage La Chapelle 1985 • $50 • (12/31/87) • **90**
Hermitage La Chapelle 1984 • $31 • (11/15/89) • **80**
Hermitage La Chapelle 1983 • $90 • (11/15/89) • **94**
Hermitage La Chapelle 1982 • $64 • (11/15/89) • **89**
Hermitage La Chapelle 1981 • $44 • (11/15/89) • **83**
Hermitage La Chapelle 1980 • $59 • (11/15/89) • **79**
Hermitage La Chapelle 1979 • $62 • (11/15/89) • **86**
Hermitage La Chapelle 1978 • $180 • (11/15/89) • **98**
Hermitage La Chapelle 1976 • $65 • (11/15/89) • **87**
Hermitage La Chapelle 1975 • $50 • (11/15/89) • **81**
Hermitage La Chapelle 1974 • $90 • (11/15/89) • **85**
Hermitage La Chapelle 1973 • $70 • (11/15/89) • **89**
Hermitage La Chapelle 1972 • $150 • (11/15/89) • **90**
Hermitage La Chapelle 1971 • $140 • (11/15/89) • **85**
Hermitage La Chapelle 1970 • $175 • (11/15/89) • **93**
Hermitage La Chapelle 1969 • $200 • (11/15/89) • **92**
Hermitage La Chapelle 1967 • $150 • (11/15/89) • **83**
Hermitage La Chapelle 1966 • $270 • (11/15/89) • **95**
Hermitage La Chapelle 1964 • $220 • (11/15/89) • **93**
Hermitage La Chapelle 1962 • $250 • (11/15/89) • **91**
Hermitage La Chapelle 1961 • $725 • (11/15/89) • **100**
Hermitage La Chapelle 1959 • $500 • (11/15/89) • **77**
Hermitage La Chapelle 1955 • $330 • (11/15/89) • **88**
Hermitage La Chapelle 1953 • $550 • (11/15/89) • **90**
Hermitage La Chapelle 1952 • $480 • (11/15/89) • **77**
Hermitage La Chapelle 1949 • $450 • (11/15/89) • **77**
Hermitage La Chapelle 1944 • $800 • (11/15/89) • **93**

Hermitage Le Chevalier de Sterimberg White 1994: Surprisingly delicate for white Hermitage, marrying melon, citrus and vanilla flavors in a well-balanced, clean package. Though not exuberantly fruity, it matches with poultry and meaty fish. • $37 • (10/15/95) • **87**

Hermitage Le Pied de la Côte 1995: Ripe berry fruit makes a vivid first impression in this exuberant, almost jammy red. The gamy, tarry notes of Syrah are present but in the background. The texture is thick but still lively, with full, ripe tannins. Big and bold, if somewhat lacking in elegance now. Try soon. Tasted twice with consistent notes. • $33 • (10/15/97) • **90**

Hermitage Le Pied de la Côte 1991: Alluring spice, berry and smoke aromas lead to firm, focused flavors of ripe fruit, licorice and black pepper. Clean, vibrant and concentrated, adding firm tannins and a long, fruity finish. A very traditional style. Drinkable now. • $30 • (10/15/95) • **90**

Muscat de Beaumes-de-Venise Vin Doux Naturel 1995: Perfumy orange and tea aromas give way to a ripe, heavy-textured wine with sweet orange marmalade flavors braced by bitter almond notes. A great wine for a lingering sunset. 3,800 cases made. • $22 • (12/15/96) • **86**

Muscat de Beaumes-de-Venise Vin Doux Naturel 1993 • $22 • (10/15/95) • **90**

Muscat de Beaumes-de-Venise Vin Doux Naturel 1986 • $17 • (10/15/88) • **84**

St.-Joseph Le Grand Pompée 1994: Expressive, concentrated and youthful, this rich wine offers ripe aromas of plums, game and tobacco, deep flavors to match the firm tannins and a long finish. It shows more sophistication than most St. Josephs, and promises a long life. 16,725 cases made. • $21 • (11/30/96) • **91**

St.-Joseph Le Grand Pompée 1992 • $15 • (05/31/94) • **84**
St.-Joseph Le Grand Pompée 1985 • $12 • (10/15/88) • **86**

Vacqueyras 1995: Though quite supple, this shows pretty blackberry and black pepper flavors; ripe but light-bodied. Ready to drink. 2,800 cases made. • $16 • (12/15/96) • **86**

Vacqueyras 1990 • $14 • (09/30/95) • **90**

JACOB, ROBERT & RAYMOND

Corton-Charlemagne 1994: A big, serious and distinctive '94 that's smoky and intense. Tightly structured, this full-bodied, racy wine shows at this stage only a bit of its powerful mineral, floral, fruit and toast flavors. Try in 2000. • $NA • (05/31/96) • **93**

JACQUART

Brut Champagne 1983: Charming flavor and finesse, with toast, ginger, pear and spice flavors and a long, lingering aftertaste. Drink now. • $43 • (04/15/90) • **88**

Brut Champagne 1982: Crisp, toasty and delicate with spicy pear, yeast and fruity flavors, fine structure and lively acidity that carries the flavors. • $39 • (12/31/88) • **90**

Brut Champagne La Cuvée Renommée 1982: Creamy and delicate, more vanilla and toast than fruit, but there's enough of a thread of concentration to carry through to a long, lovely finish. • $64 • (12/31/88) • **90**

Brut Rosé Champagne La Cuvée Renommée 1982: Salmon color, delicate texture, soft structure, with nuances of tea, berry and toast, dry and clean. Flavorful. • $74 • (12/31/88) • **88**

JACQUES, CHÂTEAU DES

Chardonnay Beaujolais-Villages 1994: A basic white wine, refreshing but simple. Light in body, crisp in texture and lean in flavor. Purchased by Louis Jadot in late 1996. • $16 • (04/30/97) • **79**

Moulin-à-Vent 1994: Straightforward, marked by fresh blackberry flavor and firm tannins. Tasty, but lacks the depth of Moulin-à-Vent at its best. Purchased by Louis Jadot in late 1996. • $18 • (04/30/97) • **84**

JACQUES-BLANC, CHÂTEAU

St.-Emilion Cuvée du Maitre 1988 • $23 • (04/30/91) • **78**

JACQUES DE MERIAL

Vin de Pays des Bouches du Rhône 1993 • $NA • (11/15/95) • **79**
Vin de Pays des Bouches du Rhône White 1993 • $NA • (11/15/95) • **79**

JACQUESON, DOMAINE RENÉ

Gevrey-Chambertin Fonteny 1990: Smells okay, but turns leathery and bitter on the palate, finishing with little grace or charm. Drinkable now. 308 cases made. • $24 • (06/15/93) • **72**

JACQUESON, H & P

Rully Grésigny White 1994: Oak flavors dominate in this medium-bodied *premier cru*. Offers some fruit and spice flavors of moderate intensity. • $NA • (08/31/96) • **79**

Rully La Pucelle White 1996: Deceptively wonderful Rully that keeps improving when open for hours, making it a long ager. Offers loads of mineral, earth and *terroir* character, plus vanilla, pear, peach, almond and floral notes that are exotic. Let the wood integrate with the fruit; try after 2000. • $20 • (05/31/98) • **90**

JACQUESSON

Brut Blanc de Blancs Champagne 1990: An austere, extremely dry and crisp wine that may mellow with time. Has spare citrus and walnut flavors, a bracing texture and a fine, tangy mousse. Worth cellaring to see what happens. Drink after 1999. 6,500 cases made. • $35 • (12/31/97) • **86**

Brut Champagne Degorge Tardive 1975 • $64 • (12/31/93) • **90**

Brut Champagne Perfection 1988: A creamy, light delicate vintage Champagne with a fine structure. Medium-bodied, with elegant acidity, light frothy foam and a long lightly toasty finish. Drink now. • $35 • (12/31/93) • **89**

Brut Champagne Perfection 1985: • $33 • (12/31/90) • **84**

Brut Champagne Perfection NV: Light, crisp and refreshing, with clean fruit flavors and a lively texture. 21,000 cases made. • $25 • (11/15/97) • **85**

Brut Champagne Signature 1989: A mellow, mature Champagne with ample buttery, nutty nuances to complement the rich fruit flavors. Smooth in texture, and lingering on the finish. Much better than last year. Drink now. 1,900 cases made. • $55 • (12/31/97) • **90**

Brut Champagne Signature 1985: Not giving you much now, but with time it will. A very firm wine with super clean apple aromas and flavors and a hint of toast, medium body and fine acidity on the finish. Drink now. • $50 • (12/31/93) • **88**

Brut Champagne Signature 1979 • $34 • (07/31/87) • **93**

Brut Rosé Champagne Perfection NV: Hearty red-wine flavors seep through in this bold, dry rosé. Fairly generous in texture, too, but turns lean on the finish. 2,500 cases made. • $32 • (11/30/97) • **86**

Brut Rosé Champagne Signature 1989: Ripe in flavor, generous and broad in texture, packing in lots of plummy, cherrylike flavors accented by notes of toast and spice. The mature blend of flavors lingers on the finish, too. 830 cases made. • $65 • (11/30/96) • **89**

FRANCE

JADOT, LOUIS

Auxey-Duresses Duc de Magenta White 1993: Tart and citrusy, tasting like a Chablis, showing green apple, toast, spice and honey flavors that come together nicely on the crisp finish. Drink now. • $18 • (05/15/95) • **86**
Bâtard-Montrachet 1993: Racy and impressively mineral in character. Velvety and medium in body; toast, pear and honey flavors linger on the finish. Tempting now but will last for years. • $47 Ⓐ • (05/15/95) • **88**
Beaujolais Jadot 1993 • $8 • (01/01/95) • **77**
Beaujolais-Villages 1996: An easy-drinking wine, balanced, bright and fruity, round and soft, with straightforward flavors of black cherries and cinnamon that mingle pleasantly. 150,000 cases imported. • $9 • (08/31/97) BB • **83**
Beaujolais-Villages 1995: Brawny for a Beaujolais. The meaty texture and firm tannins show promise, but the fruit flavors are obscured. A bit clumsy; try now. • $10 • (09/15/96) • **81**
Beaujolais-Villages 1994 • $10 • (06/15/95) • **84**
Beaune Clos des Couchereaux 1994: Crisp in texture, with mild black cherry and floral flavors that linger gently on the finish. Try now. • $22 • (11/15/96) • **82**
Beaune Clos des Couchereaux 1993: Good intensity of dried herb and plum aromas and flavors. Medium in body, adding firm tannins and a slightly one-dimensional finish. Drinkable now. • $25 • (11/15/95) • **87**
Beaune Clos des Couchereaux 1992: Smells ripe and generous but gets tight and tannic enough to overshadow the black cherry and toast flavors. Try now. • $19 • (12/15/94) • **81**
Beaune Clos des Couchereaux 1991: Tough and astringent; a modest wine, with weak anise and berry aromas and flavors. Shows more earthy notes than fruit on the finish. Try now. • $17 Ⓐ • (01/31/94) • **78**
Beaune Clos des Couchereaux 1988 • $35 • (03/31/91) • **90**
Beaune Clos des Couchereaux 1985 • $34 • (03/15/88) • **91**
Beaune Clos des Ursules 1995: Very pretty and nicely balanced, this racy, elegant, succulent red offers a good dose of *terroir*, wet earth, bitter chocolate, red- and blackberry character. Medium-bodied, tempting to drink now, but should improve through 2000. • $35 • (11/15/97) • **88**
Beaune Clos des Ursules 1994: A serious wine; youthful, deep in both color and concentration of fruit. Well made but extremely firm at this stage, it bursts with currant, black cherry and wild berry flavors, then fans out in a crisp finish. Try now. • $31 • (11/15/96) • **88**
Beaune Clos des Ursules 1993: More elegant than chunky, this is a delight to taste now, showing its core of plum, cedar and red berry flavors. Turns slightly chewy on the finish. Drink now. • $35 • (11/15/95) • **88**
Beaune Clos des Ursules 1992: Flavorful and solid, kicking in on the finish with a layer of tannins and red berry flavors. Drinkable now. • $29 • (12/15/94) • **85**
Beaune Clos des Ursules 1991: A big disappointment. Usually among the best Beaune *premier crus*, this is thin and mildly astringent. • $23 Ⓐ • (01/31/94) • **75**
Beaune Clos des Ursules 1990: Very seductive, with lovely intensity, super berry flavors and nicely integrated tannins. Drinkable now. • $44 • (12/15/92) • **91**
Beaune Clos des Ursules 1989 • $73 Ⓐ • (02/29/92) • **91**
Beaune Clos des Ursules 1988 • $43 Ⓐ • (03/31/91) • **91**
Beaune Clos des Ursules 1987 • $30 • (06/15/90) • **81**
Beaune Clos des Ursules 1986 • $33 • (03/15/89) • **88**
Beaune Clos des Ursules 1985 • $62 Ⓐ • (03/15/88) SS • **95**
Beaune Clos des Ursules 1983 • $25 Ⓐ • (03/15/89) • **93**
Beaune Clos des Ursules 1980 • $26 • (03/15/89) • **83**
Beaune Clos des Ursules 1978 • $47 Ⓐ • (03/15/89) • **89**
Beaune Clos des Ursules 1976 • $29 Ⓐ • (03/15/89) • **85**
Beaune Clos des Ursules 1973 • $40 • (03/15/89) • **86**
Beaune Clos des Ursules 1971 • $70 • (03/15/89) • **78**
Beaune Clos des Ursules 1969 • $120 • (03/15/89) • **90**
Beaune Clos des Ursules 1966 • $41 Ⓐ • (03/15/89) • **90**
Beaune Clos des Ursules 1964 • $90 • (03/15/89) • **86**
Beaune Clos des Ursules 1962 • $90 • (03/15/89) • **79**
Beaune Clos des Ursules 1961 • $125 • (03/15/89) • **88**
Beaune Clos des Ursules 1959 • $160 • (03/15/89) • **98**
Beaune Clos des Ursules 1957 • $110 • (03/15/89) • **89**
Beaune Clos des Ursules 1954 • $75 • (03/15/89) • **81**

Key: SS—Spectator Selection CS—Cellar Selection HR—Highly Recommended BB—Best Buy $NA—Price not available Ⓐ—Auction Price (BT)—Barrel Tasting
Dates in parentheses indicate the issues in which the ratings were published.

Beaune Clos des Ursules 1952 • $100 • (03/15/89) • **87**
Beaune Clos des Ursules 1949 • $175 • (03/15/89) • **86**
Beaune Clos des Ursules 1947 • $175 • (03/15/89) • **95**
Beaune Clos des Ursules 1945 • $250 • (03/15/89) • **84**
Beaune Clos des Ursules 1937 • $175 • (03/15/89) • **92**
Beaune Clos des Ursules 1933 • $200 • (03/15/89) • **80**
Beaune Clos des Ursules 1928 • $200 • (03/15/89) • **97**
Beaune Clos des Ursules 1926 • $200 • (03/15/89) • **88**
Beaune Clos des Ursules 1923 • $175 • (03/15/89) • **78**
Beaune Clos des Ursules 1919 • $300 • (03/15/89) • **90**
Beaune Clos des Ursules 1915 • $400 • (03/15/89) • **95**
Beaune Clos des Ursules 1911 • $300 • (03/15/89) • **81**
Beaune Clos des Ursules 1906 • $NA • (03/15/89) • **92**
Beaune Clos des Ursules 1904 • $NA • (03/15/89) • **88**
Beaune Clos des Ursules 1895 • $NA • (03/15/89) • **80**
Beaune Clos des Ursules 1887 • $NA • (03/15/89) • **90**
Beaune Hospices de Beaune Cuvée Dames-Hospitalier 1985 • $85 • (03/15/88) • **90**
Beaune Hospices de Beaune Cuvée Nicolas-Rolin 1985 • $85 • (03/15/88) • **92**
Beaune Les Avaux 1990: Lively and fresh, with lovely plum and cherry aromas and flavors. Behind the subtle texture lurks nice concentration and a large dose of refined tannins. Drinkable now. • $28 • (12/15/92) • **87**
Beaune Les Boucherottes 1989 • $38 • (01/31/92) • **90**
Beaune Les Boucherottes 1988 • $33 • (03/31/91) • **92**
Beaune Les Boucherottes 1985 • $30 • (03/15/88) • **91**
Beaune Les Bressandes 1986 • $28 • (05/31/89) • **90**
Beaune Les Bressandes 1985 • $35 • (03/15/88) • **87**
Beaune Les Chouacheux 1986 • $24 • (05/31/89) • **85**
Beaune Les Chouacheux 1985 • $30 • (03/15/88) • **91**
Beaune Les Grèves White 1995: Lush and ripe, generous with its toasty oak notes and honey, spice, mineral and fruit flavors. Full-bodied, slightly burning and bitter on the finish. Drink now through 2000. • $40 • (08/31/97) • **83**
Beaune Les Grèves White 1994: Tasty, flavorful, full-blown style, with ripe pear, butter and spice galore. It gives you lots of wine for your buck. Verges on being overdone, but lovely all the same. • $38 • (05/31/96) • **86**
Beaune Les Grèves White 1993: A mouthful but somewhat dull on the palate; vanilla, apple and chalk aromas and flavors. Medium in body. Drink now. • $36 • (05/15/95) • **82**
Beaune Les Teurons 1991: Light and green, with an astringent edge to the earthy flavors. Drinkable now. • $NA • (01/31/94) • **76**
Beaune Premier Cru 1991: A firm, tannic, solidly built Burgundy whose enticing aromas remind us of cedar and tobacco and whose flavors are like black cherry and spices. But it turns tannic and tight on the finish, with a green, astringent taste. Drinkable now. • $19 • (01/01/94) • **84**
Beaune Premier Cru 1988 • $26 • (06/15/93) • **83**
Beaune Premier Cru 1987 • $28 • (09/15/92) • **81**
Bonnes Mares 1995: Velvetlike on the palate, it shows some good red- and blackberry flavor but lacks the concentration to fend off drying tannins on the finish. Try now. • $90 • (11/15/97) • **83**
Bonnes Mares 1994: Crisply tannic, marked by exotic plum and leather aromas and flavors that set it apart from most other Burgundies. Drying finish; tannins want until 2000. • $61 • (11/15/96) • **89**
Bonnes Mares 1991: Firm and focused, a layer of fine tannins framing a core of currant, black cherry and toast flavors that persist into a generous finish. Drinkable now. • $51 Ⓐ • (01/31/94) • **87**
Bonnes Mares 1990: Big and chewy, this muscular monster of a wine has plenty of earth, chocolate, berry and cherry aromas and flavors and a firm backbone of tannins. Try now. • $75 • (12/15/92) • **91**
Bonnes Mares 1988 • $46 Ⓐ • (03/15/91) • **88**
Bonnes Mares 1987 • $52 • (06/15/90) • **91**
Bonnes Mares 1986 • $57 • (04/15/89) • **89**
Bonnes Mares 1985 • $90 Ⓐ • (03/15/88) • **95**
Bourgogne 1995: A solid, medium-bodied red with cherry and earth flavors and a firm finish. • $14 • (11/15/97) • **81**
Bourgogne 1994: Crisp and a bit green, delivering some cassis-bush character and a citrusy finish. Light-bodied. Drink now. • $12 • (11/15/96) • **79**
Bourgogne 1992: Good for a basic red Burgundy. Ripe and spicy in aroma, plummy and cherrylike in flavor and firm and moderately tannic in texture. • $11 • (11/30/94) • **83**
Bourgogne 1990: Very light and watery compared to many Bourgognes from this vintage, with very modest strawberry, cherry and milk-chocolate notes. Drink now. • $12 • (12/15/92) • **77**
Bourgogne 1989 • $12 • (06/15/93) • **76**
Bourgogne 1985 • $11 • (04/30/88) • **78**

Bourgogne White 1996: A basic white with simple citrus character. • $14 • (10/15/97) • **77**

Brouilly 1996: Crisp, well balanced, showing good weight on the palate, but the black cherry and spice flavors are subdued, and fade quickly on the firmly tannic finish. Drink now. • $14 • (09/15/97) • **86**

Brouilly 1995: A well-balanced, understated wine that's supple and fresh. Black cherry flavors are subdued but clean and are offset by firm, discrete tannins. • $16 • (08/31/96) • **84**

Brouilly 1993 • $10 • (07/31/95) • **78**

Chambertin-Clos de Bèze 1995: Here's a harmonious, beautifully integrated Pinot Noir from a solid producer. This red Burgundy displays good color and delivers aromas and flavors of chocolate and black cherry, with a powerful structure and a lengthy finish. Try after 2000. • $90 • (11/15/97) • **92**

Chambertin-Clos de Bèze 1994: Fresh and youthful, vibrant with its currant, berry and mineral flavors, but the tannins really clamp down, making the finish dry and biting. Needs until 2001 to 2004 to sort the tannins; may turn out to be elegant. • $72 • (11/15/96) • **91**

Chambertin-Clos de Bèze 1993: Sleek and racy Burgundy. Vivid black cherry, mineral character. Medium-bodied, adding an abundance of fine tannins and a long, fresh finish. Better in 2000. • $87 • (11/15/95) • **90**

Chambertin-Clos de Bèze 1992: A solid Burgundy offering smoke, berry and floral flavors and a chalky edge that ends up feeling chunky and tannic. Drinkable now. • $70 • (12/15/94) • **86**

Chambertin-Clos de Bèze 1991: Brilliantly focused, with currant, violet and raspberry flavors packed into a lean and elegant frame, finishing long and seductive. Try now. • $60 • (02/28/95) • **91**

Chambertin-Clos de Bèze 1990: Supple, concentrated and classy, with plum, currant and prune flavors. Tannins clamp down on the finish, but time will make for great drinking in a few years. • $105 • (02/28/95) • **92**

Chambertin-Clos de Bèze 1989 • $100 • (02/28/95) • **88**

Chambertin-Clos de Bèze 1988 • $90 • (02/28/95) • **88**

Chambertin-Clos de Bèze 1987 • $68 • (02/28/95) • **88**

Chambertin-Clos de Bèze 1986 • $63 • (02/28/95) • **85**

Chambertin-Clos de Bèze 1985 • $113 • (02/28/95) • **88**

Chambertin-Clos de Bèze 1983 • $NA • (02/28/95) • **83**

Chambolle-Musigny 1993: Some good red fruit character, but could use a little more concentration. Light-to-medium body, medium tannins and slightly dry finish. Drink now. • $28 • (11/15/95) • **84**

Chambolle-Musigny 1992: Very light and stalky, only modest raspberry flavors sneaking in to add a little charm. Drinkable now. • $26 • (12/15/94) • **77**

Chambolle-Musigny 1991: Crisp and citrusy, with modest raspberry fruit poking through the fine layer of tannins, echoing berry and cherry on the light finish. Drinkable now. • $22 Ⓐ • (01/31/94) • **84**

Chambolle-Musigny 1990: Elegant, beautiful and extremely aromatic, with lovely plum, raspberry and chocolate notes. Shows a ripe, almost sweet character, firm tannins and a long finish. Drinkable now. • $30 • (12/15/92) • **91**

Chambolle-Musigny 1986 • $30 • (07/15/89) • **78**

Chambolle-Musigny 1985 • $38 Ⓐ • (05/15/88) • **91**

Chambolle-Musigny Les Baudes 1994: Ripe in flavor and relatively dense, with currant and plum character packed into the cracks between the chewy tannins. Delicious now. • $35 • (11/15/96) • **89**

Chambolle-Musigny Les Feusselottes 1991: Delicate, aromatic, a noseful of berry, floral and gamy aromas, adding a bit more ripeness in the flavors to offset the layer of fine tannins. Drink now. • $31 Ⓐ • (01/31/94) • **83**

Chapelle-Chambertin 1994: Impressively rich and ripe for the '94 vintage, this wine is thick and dense, muscular and massive, and packed with red- and blackberry flavors, mineral notes and hard, tough tannins. All that power needs time to be tamed, so don't touch until 2005 or so. Tasted twice, with consistent notes. • $56 • (09/30/97) • **92**

Chapelle-Chambertin 1988 • $75 • (03/15/91) • **93**

Chapelle-Chambertin 1985 • $54 • (03/15/88) • **90**

Chassagne-Montrachet 1995: Lush, with dried fig, toasty oak, melon, spice and pear aromas and flavors. Full-bodied, with a somewhat heavy-handed finish. Try now. • $35 • (08/31/97) • **84**

Chassagne-Montrachet 1992: Nice and harmonious, with a lovely flavor spectrum, showing some vanilla, apple tart and honey notes that make it a fine, if not very complex, drink. • $23 • (08/31/94) • **86**

Chassagne-Montrachet Morgeot Clos de la Chapelle Duc de Magenta 1995: Thick and rich, with a new oak character peppered by spice and fruit, this seems a bit overdone. Full-bodied, it turns a bit heavy on the finish. Drink now. • $40 • (08/31/97) • **80**

Chassagne-Montrachet Morgeot Clos de la Chapelle Duc de Magenta 1994: Full-bodied, with a fat texture that coats your mouth. Caramel, fig and ripe pear flavors. Mature, slightly short, bitter and heavy finish. Drink now. • $NA • (08/31/96) • **78**

Chassagne-Montrachet Morgeot Clos de la Chapelle Duc de Magenta 1993: Some pretty vanilla, toasty oak and green apple character. Medium-bodied and slightly sharp but well crafted. Drink now. • $30 • (05/15/95) • **82**

Chassagne-Montrachet Morgeot Clos de la Chapelle Duc de Magenta Red 1988 • $20 • (03/31/91) • **85**

Chassagne-Montrachet Morgeot Clos de la Chapelle Duc de Magenta Red 1986 • $18 • (10/31/89) • **77**

Chassagne-Montrachet Morgeot Clos de la Chapelle Duc de Magenta Red 1985 • $19 • (04/15/88) • **83**

Chevalier-Montrachet Les Demoiselles 1995: Lush and very pretty, balanced and smooth, showing some tropical fruit, pear and toasty bread flavors. Full-bodied, it's delicious now but has the acidic backbone to last through 2005. • $170 • (08/31/97) • **92**

Chevalier-Montrachet Les Demoiselles 1994: Well made and silky, supple and full-bodied. Ripe with tropical fruit, honey and toasty oak flavors. Delicious. Drink now. • $NA • (08/31/96) • **91**

Chevalier-Montrachet Les Demoiselles 1993: Classy and round, promoting some green apple, mineral and dried-herb flavors and good intensity on the finish. Drinkable now. • $72 Ⓐ • (05/15/95) • **89**

Chevalier-Montrachet Les Demoiselles 1992: Good concentration. Tight and restrained, it holds back now and tastes somewhat woody and closed-in. Medium-bodied, with vanilla, pear and apple flavors, and some excellent mineral notes on the finish. Drinkable now. • $108 Ⓐ • (08/31/94) • **91**

Clos St.-Denis 1994: Dark colored and flavorful, distinctive and interesting, with a good amount of spice, currant, plum and wet earth character. Quite generous, medium- to full-bodied, and showing more concentration than many *grands crus*. Try now. • $55 • (11/15/96) • **91**

Clos St.-Denis 1993: Surprisingly light for a *grand cru*. Delicate Pinot offering cherry, vanilla and tobacco aromas and flavors, medium-to-light body, fine tannins and fruity finish. Drink now. • $62 • (11/15/95) • **82**

Clos St.-Denis 1992: Light and crisp, with a smoky, gamy edge to the modest black cherry flavors, finishing with a wee touch of bitterness. Drinkable now. • $58 • (12/15/94) • **80**

Clos Vougeot 1995: This tough, angular Clos Vougeot is quite woody and somewhat dry, but there is ripe and exuberant plum and blackberry character beneath. Full-bodied. Drink now. • $60 • (11/15/97) • **84**

Clos Vougeot 1994: Hard as nails but extremely impressive for its brooding, dark color and amazing concentration. Not for the faint of heart, but dig into it and you'll find layers of mineral, currant and dried herb flavors. Tannic, but should smooth out after 2000. • $42 • (11/15/96) • **90**

Clos Vougeot 1993: A big wine in a beautiful package. From the deep color, through the perfumy spice, mint and game aromas, to the rich plum fruit, sweet oak and full tannins, this promises pleasure for the future. It's balanced and deep, already showing some complexity. • $NA • (11/15/95) • **92**

Clos Vougeot 1992: Firm and chewy, lean, with modest tobacco and berry flavors, hinting at spice on the finish. Drinkable now. • $42 • (12/15/94) • **80**

Clos Vougeot 1991: Only modest berry and anise aromas and flavors. Light and astringent, turning stemmy on the finish. • $37 Ⓐ • (01/31/94) • **77**

Clos Vougeot 1990: Long and flavorful, like a fine cigar; this is full of classy tobacco, plum and current flavors that echo on an extremely solid finish. Drinkable now. 175 cases made. • $55 • (12/15/92) • **91**

Clos Vougeot 1989 • $74 • (01/31/92) • **87**

Clos Vougeot 1988 • $68 • (11/15/91) • **73**

Clos Vougeot 1986 • $50 • (04/15/89) • **87**

Clos Vougeot 1985 • $73 Ⓐ • (03/31/88) • **82**

Corton Les Pougets 1995: Elegant but fairly lean, this is a spear of crisp cassis, black cherry, spicy oak and currant. Medium-bodied, with enough firm tannins to warrant cellaring until 2000. Not nearly as impressive as when tasted from barrel. • $54 • (11/15/97) • **85**

Corton Les Pougets 1994: A racy wine with sharp acidity to support the mineral-scented currant and wild berry flavors. Finishing with some finesse. Drinkable now. • $40 • (11/15/96) • **86**

Corton Les Pougets 1993: Balanced and deeply satisfying, a full-bodied red that's both delicate and ripe, showing pretty red berry and earth flavors. Try in 2000. • $46 • (11/15/95) • **92**

Corton Les Pougets 1992: Smooth and balanced, with a nice core of caramel-tinged berry flavors. Drinkable now. • $40 • (12/15/94) • **83**

Corton Les Pougets 1991: Richly aromatic, but the tannins tend to overshadow the modest wild berry flavor until the finish, where the fruit echoes nicely. Drink now. • $34 Ⓐ • (01/31/94) • **86**

JADOT, LOUIS

Corton Les Pougets 1990: A fruit bomb, with a refined structure of cherry and earth flavors and a spicy, smoky, firm, long finish. Drinkable now. • $50 • (12/15/92) • **90**

Corton Les Pougets 1989 • $64 • (01/31/92) • **93**

Corton Les Pougets 1988 • $61 • (03/31/91) • **93**

Corton Les Pougets 1987 • $41 • (06/15/90) • **87**

Corton Les Pougets 1986 • $42 • (04/30/89) • **86**

Corton Les Pougets 1985 • $52 • (03/15/88) • **89**

Corton-Charlemagne 1995: Beautifully balanced, with texture as thick as olive oil. Still shy on the nose and subtle in its flavors, it will be sometime after 2000 before it plays at full volume its various tropical fruit, peach, mineral, pear and spice notes. Full-bodied, its finish is the definition of harmony. • $54 Ⓐ • (08/31/97) • **94**

Corton-Charlemagne 1994: Well made and harmonious, with aromas and flavors of smoke, toasty oak, anise and fruit. Medium-bodied, with an attractive, smooth texture. Fresh finish. Enjoy now. • $NA • (08/31/96) • **86**

Corton-Charlemagne 1993: Seductive, creamy, silky texture, sporting nice pear, fig and mineral flavors and a very elegant finish. Drink now. • $41 Ⓐ • (05/15/95) • **89**

Corton-Charlemagne 1992: Terrific. Both smooth and chewy, delivering tons of character and flavor. The butter, caramel, hazelnut and pear flavors fold into a cream-accented finish that's topped by a smoky accent and goes on and on. 725 cases made. • $74 Ⓐ • (08/31/94) HR • **93**

Côte de Beaune-Villages 1994: Not much fruit in this astringent, underripe red. • $16 • (01/01/97) • **77**

Côte de Beaune-Villages 1990: Smooth and supple, with plum, cherry and smoke flavors bringing out the classic Pinot Noir structure of this round, elegant wine. Drinkable now. • $15 • (12/15/92) • **87**

Côte de Beaune-Villages 1989 • $19 • (08/31/92) • **84**

Côte de Beaune-Villages 1986 • $15 • (06/15/89) • **78**

Côte de Beaune-Villages 1985 • $17 • (04/15/88) • **79**

Criots-Bâtard-Montrachet 1995: A serious wine: lots of new oak, an angular structure, hard as nails. This needs time, but it has the stuffing to keep, with mineral, wet earth, spice and ripe fruit complexity. Full-bodied, it will be at its best around 2005. • $135 • (08/31/97) • **93**

Echézeaux 1995: This is big and burly, with a pruny character to the fruit. Seems disjointed now, and sports severe tannins, so perhaps better in 1999. • $90 • (11/15/97) • **85**

Fixin 1993: Sleek and well made. Great for a wine from this rather obscure appellation. Ripe plum and mineral aromas and flavors, medium body, fine backbone of tannins and fresh finish. Drink now. • $18 • (11/15/95) • **87**

Fixin 1990: Lovely, with attractive, smoky, meaty licorice and fruit aromas and flavors and fresh tannins and acidity. Drinkable now. • $15 • (12/15/92) • **85**

Fixin 1989 • $21 • (01/31/92) • **88**

Fleurie 1996: Fresh berry and spice aromas are enticing, but the palate delivers liveliness rather than depth, with simple fruity flavors and light tannins. A pleasant picnic wine. • $14 • (09/15/97) • **84**

Fleurie 1994 • $13 • (10/31/95) • **85**

Fleurie 1993 • $11 • (07/31/95) • **81**

Gevrey-Chambertin 1995: A round, supple Gevrey that displays cassis and red berry notes and a lingering finish. The moderate tannins suggest waiting, but drink soon. • $30 • (11/15/97) • **85**

Gevrey-Chambertin 1986 • $25 • (07/15/89) • **77**

Gevrey-Chambertin Estournelles St.-Jacques 1994: Rich color is promising, but the drying tannins rain on the parade. • $39 • (11/15/96) • **78**

Gevrey-Chambertin Estournelles St.-Jacques 1993: Full-bodied, featuring plenty of tannin structure and nice blackberry and wet earth character. Just short of outstanding because it's a bit one-dimensional. Drink now. • $48 • (11/15/95) • **89**

Gevrey-Chambertin Estournelles St.-Jacques 1988 • $50 • (03/15/91) • **91**

Gevrey-Chambertin Estournelles St.-Jacques 1986 • $40 • (07/15/89) • **87**

Gevrey-Chambertin Estournelles St.-Jacques 1985 • $41 • (03/31/88) • **86**

Gevrey-Chambertin Le Clos St.-Jacques 1995: Some pretty spicy oak and red- and blackberry flavor is on display in this elegant package, but it lacks a bit of generosity and flesh. The firm tannins build up on the finish, so try after 2000. • $60 • (11/15/97) • **86**

Gevrey-Chambertin Le Clos St.-Jacques 1994: Fresh and remarkably lively. A raucous wine that packs in plenty of wild berry and mineral flavors on a rough frame. Needs until 1999 to 2000 to settle down. • $44 • (11/15/96) • **86**

Key: SS—Spectator Selection CS—Cellar Selection HR—Highly Recommended BB—Best Buy $NA—Price not available Ⓐ—Auction Price (BT)—Barrel Tasting
Dates in parentheses indicate the issues in which the ratings were published.

Gevrey-Chambertin Le Clos St.-Jacques 1992: A polished wine with character and complexity. Very well crafted, with smooth tannins and gorgeous black cherry flavors. Just short of outstanding because it lacks the extra dimensions on the finish. • $44 • (12/15/94) • **88**

Gevrey-Chambertin Le Clos St.-Jacques 1991: Offers Bardolinolike strawberry and cherry aromas and flavors and a nice burst of fruit on the finish. Light, simple and drinkable now. • $80 Ⓐ • (01/31/94) • **80**

Gevrey-Chambertin Le Clos St.-Jacques 1990: Round, smooth and quite decadent, with lots of flavors—earth, mushroom, berry and cedar—adding excitement to this medium-bodied, elegant wine. Drinkable now. • $48 • (12/15/92) • **90**

Gevrey-Chambertin Le Clos St.-Jacques 1989 • $22 Ⓐ • (01/31/92) • **90**

Gevrey-Chambertin Le Clos St.-Jacques 1988 • $52 • (03/15/91) • **88**

Gevrey-Chambertin Le Clos St.-Jacques 1986 • $44 • (07/15/89) • **84**

Gevrey-Chambertin Le Clos St.-Jacques 1985 • $75 Ⓐ • (03/31/88) • **94**

Griotte-Chambertin 1990: Powerful yet refined, with beautiful raspberry and spice aromas and flavors and a silky tannin mouthfeel. Drinkable now. • $70 • (12/15/92) • **91**

Griotte-Chambertin 1988 • $75 • (03/15/91) • **94**

Griotte-Chambertin 1987 • $50 • (07/15/90) • **80**

Mâcon Blanc-Villages Château des Jacques 1996: Crisp and a bit herbal, with bracing green apple and lime flavors, but as it opens up in the glass and warms up in temperature, it becomes softer. Light- to medium-bodied, with a clean finish. Try with seafood. 750 cases made. • $12 • (05/31/98) • **82**

Mâcon-Lugny Les Petites Pierres 1996: A rich, broad wine, a bit shy on the nose, but possesses apple and citrus flavors and moderate concentration, finishing with a touch of earthiness. Drink now. • $13 • (05/31/98) • **82**

Mâcon-Lugny Les Petites Pierres 1993: Dominated by earth and mineral flavors, adding some honey, green apple and spice notes as well. Fairly intense, showing good depth and a modest finish. Drink now. • $9 • (01/01/96) • **83**

Mâcon-Villages 1996: A leesy quality adds some depth and richness up front, but the finish is austere and a touch earthy. • $12 • (10/15/97) • **78**

Mâcon-Villages Domaine de la Grange Magnien 1995: Light-bodied. Some good intensity, but turns a bit sour on the palate and the finish and has a slight cardboard aroma. • $NA • (08/31/96) • **77**

Marsannay Red 1994: Tough and tannic, marshalling little fruit flavor to battle the roughness. • $15 • (11/15/96) • **76**

Marsannay Red 1986 • $11 • (06/15/89) • **77**

Marsannay White 1992: Quite intense but also bulky and a bit disjointed now; it needs a year or so to come around. Good acidity, with some toast, grapefruit and lime flavors. Tasted twice. • $NA • (08/31/94) • **83**

Mazis-Chambertin 1990: A massive wine built for aging, with tons of hard tannins, but has plenty of ripe plum, berry and earth notes underneath the tough surface. Try now. • $70 • (12/15/92) • **90**

Mazis-Chambertin 1987 • $50 • (05/31/90) • **92**

Meursault Les Charmes 1992: Delicious and quite subtle, with vivid and bright pear, vanilla and mineral flavors; below the seductive creamy texture, this reveals good backbone and structure. Not showy, just classy. • $35 • (08/31/94) • **89**

Meursault Les Perrières 1995: Round and ripe, fairly opulent and of good intensity and concentration, showing honey, spice, pear and sconelike flavors. Full-bodied, well balanced. Drink now through 2005. • $51 • (08/31/97) • **88**

Meursault Les Perrières 1994: Both supple and crisp, playing on contrasts in its attractive, ripe, smooth and creamy package. Honey, dried herb and ripe pear notes. Delicous now. • $38 • (05/31/96) • **89**

Meursault Les Perrières 1993: Subtle Meursault boasting a lovely palate that unfolds with toasty coconut, apple, mineral and cream character. Medium-bodied and very long on the finish. Good now, but wait a couple of years. • $37 • (05/15/95) • **90**

Monthélie 1990: This well-crafted wine is chewy yet elegant, with attractive strawberry and earth aromas and flavors and supple tannins. Drink now. • $18 • (12/15/92) • **86**

Monthélie 1989 • $21 • (01/31/92) • **87**

Morgon 1996: Gamy, smoky notes give this smooth, firm red an almost Burgundian profile; black cherry flavor is well defined but rather muted. Try now. • $14 • (09/15/97) • **85**

Morgon 1995: Straightforward, with a nice balance of plum flavors and firm tannins give this wine a place at the dinner table. • $15 • (09/15/96) • **84**

Moulin-à-Vent 1996: Well structured, with a nice balance of firm tannins and bright acidity, and ripe flavors ranging from blackberry to game to tobacco. Try now. • $16 • (09/15/97) • **86**

Moulin-à-Vent 1995: Balanced and well structured, showing meaty, cherry and chocolate flavors over firm yet polished tannins. It's smooth but slightly dull. • $17 • (09/15/96) • **84**

Moulin-à-Vent 1994: Polished, with its meaty and plum flavors softening now but still tannic underneath. A nice chocolate note on the finish. At its best now. • $14 • (09/15/96) • **86**

Moulin-à-Vent 1993 • $11 • (07/31/95) • **82**

Moulin-à-Vent Château des Jacques 1996: This firm wine shows impressive structure. The muscular tannins and firm acidity are well balanced, and there are hints of ripe fruit, game and toast flavors, but it's a bit closed. Should improve given time. Best now through 2005. 4,000 cases made. • $19 • (05/31/98) HR • **90**

Moulin-à-Vent Château des Jacques Clos de Champ de Cour 1996: This bright red shows clean, fresh black cherry flavors deepened by notes of game and minerals and kept vivid by crisp acidity. It has moderate tannins and a lingering, fruity finish. From a new line of Beaujolais from Jadot that are not yet imported into the U.S. Drink now. • $NA • (01/01/98) • **86**

Moulin-à-Vent Château des Jacques Clos des Thorins 1996: Lots of character here. Gamy and mineral notes underpin ripe, dark fruit flavors of cassis and licorice; it's firm yet juicy, concentrated yet clean. A beautiful example of the traditional style. From a new line of Beaujolais from Jadot that are not yet imported into the U.S. Drink now through 2002. • $NA • (01/01/98) • **88**

Moulin-à-Vent Château des Jacques Clos du Grand Carquelin 1996: Very traditional and utterly beguiling, this big red is packed with gamy, plum, coffee and mineral flavors, with firm tannins and fresh acidity. It's muscular in the mouth but tender on the finish, a beautiful match with hearty foods. From a new line of Beaujolais from Jadot that are not yet imported into the U.S. Drink now through 2002. • $NA • (01/01/98) • **89**

Moulin-à-Vent Château des Jacques Clos la Roche 1996: Rich yet firm, this big-boned red shows very ripe plum, spice and even raisin flavors, yet has a firm backbone of acidity that keeps it fresh. Full tannins still need time to soften. From a new line of Beaujolais from Jadot that are not yet imported into the U.S. Best from now through 2004. • $NA • (01/01/98) • **88**

Musigny Le Musigny 1986 • $70 • (04/15/89) • **77**

Musigny Le Musigny 1985 • $74 • (03/31/88) • **88**

Nuits-St.-Georges 1985 • $30 • (04/15/88) • **91**

Nuits-St.-Georges Aux Boudots 1991: Firm and flavorful. Features simple currant and toast aromas and flavors and a balanced, harmonious finish. Drinkable now. • $26 Ⓐ • (01/31/94) • **84**

Nuits-St.-Georges Aux Boudots 1988 • $49 • (02/28/91) • **88**

Nuits-St.-Georges Aux Boudots 1986 • $38 • (04/30/89) • **85**

Nuits-St.-Georges Aux Boudots 1985 • $42 • (03/15/88) • **75**

Nuits-St.-Georges Clos des Corvées 1994: Has a distinctly sour edge that renders it less than charming. • $31 • (11/15/96) • **76**

Nuits-St.-Georges Clos des Corvées 1992: Straightforward, with modest strawberry and raspberry flavors. Light but also offers a hint of ripe currant on the smooth finish. • $28 • (12/15/94) • **80**

Nuits-St.-Georges Clos des Corvées 1990: An elegant Nuits, with pleasant black cherry and plum characteristics, medium tannins and a fresh finish. Drinkable now. • $36 • (12/15/92) • **85**

Nuits-St.-Georges Clos des Corvées 1989 • $56 • (01/31/92) • **85**

Nuits-St.-Georges Clos des Corvées 1988 • $49 • (02/28/91) • **89**

Nuits-St.-Georges Clos des Corvées 1987 • $35 • (04/30/90) • **84**

Nuits-St.-Georges Clos des Corvées 1986 • $37 • (04/30/89) • **83**

Nuits-St.-Georges Clos des Corvées 1985 • $46 • (03/15/88) • **96**

Pernand-Vergelesses 1985 • $18 • (04/15/88) • **85**

Pernand-Vergelesses Clos de la Croix de Pierre 1995: Fairly elegant, but also a bit lean. Light- to medium-bodied, with red berry and herbal character accented by spicy mocha and toast notes. Try now. • $24 • (11/15/97) • **81**

Pernand-Vergelesses Clos de la Croix de Pierre 1994: A charming wine with light currant and berry flavors, this is lovely—except for a chalky texture. • $20 • (11/15/96) • **79**

Pernand-Vergelesses Clos de la Croix de Pierre 1993: Easygoing red sporting delicate floral, berry character and medium-fine tannins. Drinkable now. • $19 • (11/15/95) • **84**

Pernand-Vergelesses Clos de la Croix de Pierre 1992: Bright, generous and a little chewy, but there's a solid core of silky berry underneath that persists into the finish. • $18 • (12/15/94) • **84**

Pernand-Vergelesses Clos de la Croix de Pierre 1991: A bit raw in texture but youthful and lively, displaying concentrated red currant and raspberry flavors and a chewy finish. Fresh and appealing. Drinkable now. • $15 Ⓐ • (01/31/94) • **83**

Pernand-Vergelesses Clos de la Croix de Pierre 1990: Just lovely, with plenty of pretty cherry, strawberry and wet earth notes on the palate. Has round tannins. Nothing big or terribly complex but fun to drink now. • $18 • (12/15/92) • **88**

Pernand-Vergelesses Clos de la Croix de Pierre 1989 • $21 • (01/31/92) • **86**

Pernand-Vergelesses Clos de la Croix de Pierre 1988 • $17 • (03/31/91) • **86**

Pernand-Vergelesses Clos de la Croix de Pierre 1987 • $15 • (11/15/90) • **79**

Pernand-Vergelesses Clos de la Croix de Pierre 1986 • $17 • (07/31/89) • **85**

Pernand-Vergelesses Clos de la Croix de Pierre 1985 • $18 • (04/15/88) • **83**

Pernand-Vergelesses White 1995: Fat and quite buttery, thick and ripe but lacking a bit of elegance. Offers lots of clean citrus, pear and oak accents. Full-bodied, the finish seems a bit shorter than many '95s. Drink now through 2005. • $21 • (08/31/97) • **85**

Pommard 1995: A pretty Pommard, yet it seems meager and lacking in rich fruit. Finishes tough. • $30 • (11/15/97) • **80**

Pommard 1988 • $36 • (03/31/91) • **83**

Pommard Clos des Poutures 1994: Firm and quite deep but also a bit rustic, with a chestnut nose that may not be for everyone. Also offers some floral and red berry flavors. Full-bodied with some dry tannins. Try now. • $30 • (11/15/96) • **81**

Pommard Les Arvelets 1990: So closed now that it doesn't yield much at first but kicks in near the finish, with tons of fine tannins and sweet, ripe fruit flavors that go on and on. Try now. • $42 • (12/15/92) • **90**

Pommard Les Chaponnières 1985 • $39 • (03/15/88) • **91**

Pommard Les Grands Epenots 1989 • $50 • (01/31/92) • **88**

Pommard Les Grands Epenots 1988 • $38 • (03/31/91) • **86**

Pouilly-Fuissé 1996: Enticing aromas of honey and butter yield to citrus and vanilla flavors in this crisp, straightforward white. Enjoy now. • $21 • (10/15/97) • **81**

Pouilly-Fuissé 1993: Quite buttery and appealing, sporting some lemon and pear notes. Turns slightly herbal on the finish. Too bad because it started out so nicely. • $18 • (05/15/95) • **81**

Pouilly-Fuissé Cuvée Réserve Spéciale 1996: A woody style, showing smoke, toast and floral character, but the structure is fairly supple and there might be enough fruit to carry it. Drinkable now. 3,000 cases made. • $32 • (05/31/98) • **82**

Pouilly-Fuissé Cuvée Réserve Spéciale 1995: Straightforward, with toasty oak-tinged apple and citrus character. Light to medium in body, it's a touch diluted in midpalate. Tart finish. Drink now. • $32 • (05/31/97) • **79**

Pouilly-Fuissé Cuvée Réserve Spéciale 1993: Showy butter and sweet vanilla flavors boast of oak influence, but the wine underneath is modest, with light lemon and green apple notes. • $23 • (03/31/95) • **82**

Puligny-Montrachet 1995: Ripe, even overripe, which gives it a sweetish, burnt-wood character and a heavy, slightly hot finish. Medium- to full-bodied. Offers some fruit and spice flavors. Drink now. • $35 • (08/31/97) • **79**

Puligny-Montrachet 1994: What went wrong? A disappointing wine from a normally solid négoçiant. It tastes odd, with a grassy, astringent character, and finishes short. Not recommended. Tasted twice, with consistent notes. • $NA • (05/31/97) • **65**

Puligny-Montrachet 1993: Sharp and solid, this crystallike wine seduces with its challenging, tightly-wound core of citrus, lime and dried herb character. Nice concentration of mineral and honey flavors on the long finish. • $30 • (08/31/95) • **86**

Puligny-Montrachet 1992: The exotic toasty, figgy aromas in this wine aren't backed up by much fruit or body. Starts big, but fades fast on the finish. • $29 • (06/15/95) • **81**

Puligny-Montrachet Clos de la Garenne Duc de Magenta 1995: Extraordinary. Blending finesse with great intensity, it caresses the palate yet retains an iron-fist-in-a-velvet-glove kind of character. Shows harmony and succulent fruit, spice and toasty oak complexity. Ripe, minute-long finish. Drink now through 2005. • $58 • (08/31/97) • **94**

Puligny-Montrachet Clos de la Garenne Duc de Magenta 1992: Seductive, gorgeous, smooth and creamy texture that coats your mouth. The vanilla, mineral and pear flavors, laced by a touch of smoke and hazelnut, are full-bodied and elegant. • $33 • (08/31/94) • **92**

Puligny-Montrachet Les Folatières 1995: Nicely balanced and very flavorful, with tropical, melon, floral and wet earth flavors. Full-bodied and a delight to taste, with a long, lemony-sweet finish. Drink now through 2005. • $51 • (08/31/97) • **92**

Puligny-Montrachet Les Folatières 1993: Lively mineral, apple and lime aromas and flavors, medium body and fresh acidity. • $33 • (05/15/95) • **86**

Puligny-Montrachet Les Perrières 1994: Thick, rich and almost oily in texture, though it still manages to remain elegant and structured. Tons of ripe fruit, including pear, apricot and ripe apple, adding a touch of honey, mineral and chalk. Somewhat tart on the finish now, but give it time. • $38 • (05/31/96) • **91**

Régnié 1994 • $12 • (10/31/95) • **78**

Régnié 1993 • $9 • (07/31/95) • **78**

Romanée St.-Vivant 1993: Very fine fruit and tannin structure. Not a big wine but significant for its sleek and racy style. Try now. • $135 • (11/15/95) • **88**

Ruchottes-Chambertin 1988 • $48 Ⓐ • (03/15/91) • **91**

St.-Aubin White 1995: Sensational quality for a simple St.-Aubin. Has the texture of satin, and is ripe, rich and flavorful, its fruit character supported by subtle oak, vanilla bean and spice accents. Full-bodied, with great balance and a wonderful finish. Try now through 2005. • $21 • (08/31/97) • **90**

St.-Aubin White 1994: Very accessible, with a round, smooth texture and a touch more intensity than many other village wines. Has grapefruit, apple, almond and herbal notes. Drink now. • $19 • (05/31/96) • **83**

St.-Véran Domaine de Curis 1995: Balanced and pleasant, with green apple, lemon, dried herb and haylike flavors. Slightly diluted finish. Drink now. • $NA • (08/31/96) • **80**

St.-Véran La Chapelle 1993: A smooth, soft texture and light buttery flavors make this an agreeable if simple wine. Tasted twice, with consistent notes. Drink now. • $13 • (11/15/94) • **80**

Santenay Clos de Malte 1993: Both delicate and firm, sporting earth and nicely defined Pinot Noir fruit flavors ranging from cherry to raspberry. Sizable amount of tannins. Good to drink now. • $16 • (11/15/95) • **85**

Santenay Clos de Malte 1990: Juicy and flavorful, offering focused black cherry, earth and plum characteristics and an elegant, fruity finish. Drinkable now. • $18 • (12/15/92) • **87**

Santenay Clos de Malte White 1995: Pretty, with honey, toasty almond, chocolate brownie, pear and apple flavors. Medium-bodied and moderately intense, with a smooth texture. Enjoyable now through 2000. • $22 • (08/31/97) • **87**

Santenay Clos de Malte White 1994: Straightforward and crisp, with some decent green apple flavors. But tart on the finish. • $17 • (05/31/96) • **78**

Savigny-lès-Beaune La Dominode 1995: Shows deep color and appealing herbal and berry aromas, but this red lacks flesh and depth. The tannins are dry. • $24 • (11/15/97) • **79**

Savigny-lès-Beaune La Dominode 1992: Focused and firm, with a modest undercurrent of black cherry flavor that expands a bit on the finish. Drinkable now. • $16 • (12/15/94) • **82**

Savigny-lès-Beaune La Dominode 1990: A delightful wine that's not huge by any stretch of the imagination but crafted in just the right proportions, evolving from cherry and berry flavors to chocolate and earth notes. Has firm, supple tannins. Drinkable now. • $23 • (12/15/92) • **88**

Savigny-lès-Beaune White 1994: Soft and pleasing, with some toasty coconut, pineapple and spice flavors. It caresses the palate with its silkiness but could use just a bit more intensity and concentration. Drinkable now. • $20 • (05/31/96) • **84**

Volnay 1992: Crisp and aromatic, showing enough spicy black cherry flavors to finish nicely. Drinkable now. • $26 • (12/15/94) • **83**

Volnay 1990: This solid wine offers fresh, focused raspberry and strawberry flavors that are full and rich along with caressing tannins. Drink now. • $28 • (12/15/92) • **87**

Vosne-Romanée 1991: Fresh and crisp, offering a nice core of black cherry flavor and pleasant rose petal and walnut shadings. Fresh and smooth on the finish. Drinkable now. • $21 Ⓐ • (01/31/94) • **83**

Vosne-Romanée 1990: Displays stunning balance in a village wine, with alluring violet, berry and chocolate flavors, fine tannins and a long, delicious finish. Drinkable now. • $30 • (12/15/92) • **92**

Vosne-Romanée 1989 • $40 • (01/31/92) • **89**

Vosne-Romanée 1985 • $33 • (03/31/88) • **86**

Vosne-Romanée Les Suchots 1993: Not quite as great as when tasted from barrel in spring of 1995. Still lovely and elegant, showing attractive plum character, delicate tannins, medium body and medium-silky texture. Better in 2000. • $46 • (11/15/95) • **88**

Vosne-Romanée Les Suchots 1991: Lean, crisp and modest, centered around a thread of raspberry flavor and hints of chocolate and cedar on the finish. Drinkable now. • $34 Ⓐ • (01/31/94) • **81**

Vosne-Romanée Les Suchots 1990: Well made and pretty. More open and accessible than some wines, offering lovely cherry, strawberry and earth aromas and flavors and good intensity on the finish. Drinkable now. 225 cases made. • $49 • (12/15/92) • **88**

Key: SS—Spectator Selection CS—Cellar Selection HR—Highly Recommended BB—Best Buy $NA—Price not available Ⓐ—Auction Price (BT)—Barrel Tasting

Dates in parentheses indicate the issues in which the ratings were published.

JAFFELIN

Aloxe-Corton 1993: What a shame. Starts out fruity, but then turns very papery and dry. Drink in 2000. • $20 • (11/15/95) • **74**

Aloxe-Corton 1992: Interesting floral and rhubarb overtones to strawberry and watermelon flavors. A lean and lively village Aloxe. • $19 • (12/15/94) • **81**

Aloxe-Corton 1989 • $27 • (01/31/92) • **89**

Auxey-Duresses Red 1993: Disappointing, lean and herbal, showing asparagus and metallic character. Not much wine here. Light color, watery. • $12 • (11/15/95) • **74**

Auxey-Duresses Red 1991: Light and simple, with appealing currant flavor to cut through the firm tannins. Drinkable now. • $12 Ⓐ • (01/31/94) • **79**

Auxey-Duresses Red 1990: Fresh and lively, with crushed raspberry characteristics. Elegant and rather light, but the violet, smoke and cherry flavors are attractive. Drinkable now. 200 cases made. • $16 • (12/15/92) • **84**

Auxey-Duresses Red 1989 • $16 • (01/31/92) • **85**

Auxey-Duresses White 1992: Lively, showing a subtle and focused band of apple, pear and peach flavors backed by some mineral and crisp citrus notes. • $13 • (08/31/94) • **82**

Bâtard-Montrachet 1993: Classy, racy and quite delicate, delivering good complexity of honey, chalk and pear notes. Wonderfully silky on the palate. Drinkable now. • $70 • (08/31/95) • **88**

Beaujolais-Villages Domaine de Riberolles 1994 • $8 • (06/15/95) • **76**

Beaujolais-Villages Domaine de Riberolles 1993 • $7 • (06/30/94) • **84**

Beaune Champs Pimont 1993: Simple and one-dimensional, delicate but also a bit diluted. Short finish. • $19 • (11/15/95) • **73**

Beaune Champs Pimont 1992: Light and lean, with a bead of bright berry flavor that shines through to the finish. Drinkable now. • $22 • (12/15/94) • **82**

Beaune Champs Pimont 1991: Light, floral and distinctive, with blackberry and black cherry flavors at the core, plus shades of iris, jasmine and lime adding zing to the finish. Drinkable now. • $22 Ⓐ • (01/31/94) • **85**

Beaune Champs Pimont 1990: A succulent, ripe style of Beaune, packed with ripe plum, cherry and earth notes. Seduces you with its velvety texture and supple tannins. Drinkable now. 200 cases made. • $25 • (12/15/92) • **90**

Beaune Champs Pimont 1989 • $27 • (01/31/92) • **89**

Beaune du Châpitre 1986 • $18 • (12/31/88) • **77**

Beaune Hospices de Beaune Cuvée Clos des Avaux 1986 • $65 • (12/31/88) • **85**

Beaune Les Bressandes 1990: Flavorful and juicy, showing pretty plum, raspberry, cherry and earth aromas and flavors. All the parts are very much in balance in this supple, medium-bodied wine. Try now. 300 cases made. • $27 • (12/15/92) • **87**

Beaune Les Bressandes 1989 • $28 • (01/31/92) • **85**

Bourgogne Hautes-Côtes de Beaune 1993: Simple Burgundy showing floral, strawberry aromas and flavors and a slightly dry finish. Drink now. • $12 • (11/15/95) • **79**

Bourgogne Hautes-Côtes de Beaune 1992: Light in texture, but a fine thread of raspberry and currant jam flavors show through and persist into the finish. • $13 • (12/15/94) • **80**

Bourgogne du Chapitre 1993: Starts out round and pretty, light in body, medium intensity, but then turns slightly forward, diluted and vegetal on the finish. Drinkable on release. • $10 • (11/15/95) • **78**

Bourgogne du Châpitre 1990: Delicate and pretty, with floral, strawberry and nut characteristics that make for easy drinking now. 1,000 cases made. • $11 • (12/15/92) • **82**

Bourgogne du Châpitre White 1993: Fruity and straightforward, quite light, revealing modest pear, apple and a hint of honey-tropical character. Drinkable now. • $10 • (05/15/95) • **77**

Brouilly 1994 • $12 • (07/31/95) • **78**

Brouilly 1993 • $12 • (06/30/94) • **77**

Chambertin Le Chambertin 1986 • $65 • (12/31/88) • **89**

Chambertin Le Chambertin 1983 • $48 • (04/16/86) • **93**

Chambolle-Musigny 1993: One-dimensional with some attractive fruit character but rather light and diluted on the finish. Drink now. • $24 • (11/15/95) • **78**

Chambolle-Musigny 1989 • $28 • (01/31/92) • **89**

Chambolle-Musigny 1988 • $32 • (12/31/90) • **88**

Chambolle-Musigny 1983 • $21 • (03/16/86) • **81**

Charmes-Chambertin 1990: Port-like, with an abundance of ripe berry flavors, full tannins and a superlong finish. The ripe fruit keeps you coming back for more. Try now. 100 cases made. • $55 • (12/15/92) • **92**

Charmes-Chambertin 1989 • $66 • (01/31/92) • **87**

Charmes-Chambertin 1986 • $45 • (12/31/88) • **77**

Chassagne-Montrachet Les Vergers 1992: Clean, with pear, spice and apple flavors, showing a touch of vanilla and toast notes on the fresh, zesty finish. • $30 • (08/31/94) • **84**
Chassagne-Montrachet Red 1992: A well-knit core of solid red berry and supple tannins. Drinkable now. • $16 • (12/15/94) • **83**
Chassagne-Montrachet Red 1990: Smooth and round in the mouth and firm on the finish, this balanced wine offers attractive toast and berry aromas and flavors. Drinkable now. 200 cases made. • $16 • (12/15/92) • **85**
Chassagne-Montrachet Red 1989 • $18 • (01/31/92) • **86**
Chorey-Côte de Beaune 1989 • $13 • (01/31/92) • **75**
Clos St.-Denis 1989 • $53 • (01/31/92) • **94**
Clos de Vougeot 1990: This pleasant, chocolate-scented Clos de Vougeot delivers more finesse than power, but seems a bit frugal with the fruit. Medium-bodied, with a medium finish. Try now. 150 cases made. • $55 • (12/15/92) • **86**
Clos de Vougeot 1989 • $60 • (01/31/92) • **89**
Clos de Vougeot 1986 • $45 • (12/31/88) • **77**
Clos de Vougeot 1985 • $49 • (06/15/88) • **96**
Corton 1989 • $54 • (01/31/92) • **91**
Corton 1986 • $45 • (12/31/88) • **87**
Corton 1983 • $45 • (04/01/86) CS • **91**
Côte de Beaune-Villages 1989 • $14 • (01/31/92) • **82**
Côte de Nuits-Villages 1989 • $15 • (01/31/92) • **84**
Echézeaux 1989 • $60 • (01/31/92) • **91**
Echézeaux 1986 • $45 • (12/31/88) • **86**
Echézeaux 1983 • $30 • (05/01/86) • **90**
Fixin 1993: Very light and weedy, with stewed tomatoes and beans. • $17 • (11/15/95) • **76**
Fixin 1989 • $18 • (01/31/92) • **85**
Fleurie 1993 • $15 • (06/30/94) • **81**
Gevrey-Chambertin 1992: Light overall, with a smooth texture and a pleasant thread of black cherry and tobacco flavors. Drinkable now. • $24 • (12/15/94) • **82**
Gevrey-Chambertin 1989 • $30 • (01/31/92) • **88**
Gevrey-Chambertin 1988 • $25 • (08/31/91) • **88**
Gevrey-Chambertin 1986 • $49 • (02/28/89) • **85**
Gevrey-Chambertin 1983 • $17 • (10/01/85) • **77**
Gevrey-Chambertin Lavaut St.-Jacques 1990: Wonderfully intense fruit flavors lend class and charm to this solid wine. Has a great backbone of acidity and tannins. Drinkable now. 100 cases made. • $42 • (12/15/92) • **91**
Gevrey-Chambertin Lavaut St.-Jacques 1989 • $40 • (01/31/92) • **81**
Ladoix Côte de Beaune 1989 • $13 • (01/31/92) • **85**
Mâcon-Villages 1994: Looks and tastes as if aging quickly. Chocolate, bark and caramel flavors mingle with pear and apple. Drink fast, if you have some. 1,666 cases made. • $9 • (08/31/95) • **75**
Meursault 1993: Clean and tart, tightly wrapped around citrus, green apple and herb flavors. Very crisp, mouth-puckering finish. Where is the opulence of Meursault? • $18 • (05/15/95) • **82**
Meursault Les Cras 1992: Intense and concentrated, with grapefuit and pineapple flavors accented by mineral and earth notes on the finish. Has lots of fruit, good balance and a tightly knit texture. Try now. • $34 • (08/31/94) • **88**
Meursault Les Genevrières 1993: Round and silky texture adding lively honey, citrus and floral aromas and flavors. Some mineral character surfaces on the tart finish. Drinkable now. • $25 • (05/15/95) • **85**
Montagny 1992: A crisp, grassy style, refreshing, with some apple and citrus notes. Still, it's quite light. • $12 • (08/31/94) • **80**
Monthélie 1991 • $13 • (01/31/94) • **85**
Monthélie 1990: Beautiful and well balanced, showing both finesse and intensity in the cherry and smoke characteristics and racy tannins. Drinkable now. • $17 • (12/15/92) • **88**
Monthélie 1989 • $19 • (01/31/92) • **87**
Monthélie 1986 • $15 • (06/15/89) • **79**
Morey-St.-Denis Les Ruchots 1989 • $30 • (01/31/92) • **86**
Morgon 1994 • $11 • (07/31/95) • **81**
Morgon 1993 • $12 • (06/30/94) • **88**
Nuits-St.-Georges 1993: Very light, both in color and body, offering very modest strawberry and raspberry flavors. Lacks fruit and tastes dry on the short finish. • $25 • (11/15/95) • **74**
Nuits-St.-Georges 1992: More Beaujolais than Nuits-St.-Georges, with tart raspberry and strawberry flavors on a very light frame. • $25 • (12/15/94) • **79**
Nuits-St.-Georges 1989 • $27 • (01/31/92) • **83**
Nuits-St.-Georges 1986 • $28 • (02/28/89) • **80**
Nuits-St.-Georges 1983 • $19 • (09/15/86) • **72**
Nuits-St.-Georges Les Damodes 1989 • $36 • (01/31/92) • **90**
Pernand-Vergelesses 1993: Delicious for early drinking, showing berry, cedar and earth aromas and flavors. Medium-bodied, with smooth texture and a caressing finish. Can age. • $14 • (11/15/95) • **82**
Pernand-Vergelesses 1991: Light and crisp; has appealing strawberry flavor and a fresh, tart finish. Drinkable now. • $13 Ⓐ • (01/31/94) • **80**
Pernand-Vergelesses 1990: Pleasant in a down-to-earth sort of way, with good cherry, herb and chocolate flavors complementing the firm tannins. Try now. 200 cases made. • $16 • (12/15/92) • **85**
Pernand-Vergelesses 1989 • $19 • (01/31/92) • **86**
Pinot Noir Bourgogne 1989 • $10 • (01/31/92) • **83**
Pommard 1991: Behind the chunky tannins lies a core of ripe currant and black cherry flavors shaded by floral and cedar notes. Try now. • $20 Ⓐ • (01/31/94) • **83**
Pommard 1990: Seductive, with lots of raspberry and earth characteristics, lovely, silky tannins and a flavorful finish. Drinkable now. 200 cases made. • $30 • (12/15/92) • **89**
Pommard 1989 • $33 • (01/31/92) • **85**
Pommard 1986 • $26 • (04/30/89) • **79**
Pommard 1985 • $38 • (03/15/88) • **89**
Pommard 1983 • $19 • (09/15/86) • **81**
Puligny-Montrachet 1993: Clean and racy mineral and spice character, medium body and fresh acidity. • $20 • (05/15/95) • **84**
Romanée St.-Vivant 1990: Harmony is the code word here. Supple and focused, with a racy character and tons of lovely raspberry, cherry and earth aromas and flavors. Is smooth and just great on the finish. Drinkable now. 150 cases made. • $75 • (12/15/92) • **93**
Romanée St.-Vivant 1989 • $80 • (01/31/92) • **91**
Rully Red 1986 • $13 • (06/15/89) • **77**
Rully White 1992: Tart and lean, the narrow band of grapefruit, lemon and floral notes lively and focused. Overall, pleasant and straightforward. • $14 • (08/31/94) • **81**
St.-Aubin Premier Cru White 1992: Light but balanced, offering a good harmony of toasty, vanilla-flavored wood notes and decent apple and citrus flavors. • $13 • (08/31/94) • **81**
St.-Aubin 1989 • $14 • (01/31/92) • **84**
St.-Romain White 1993: Straightforward and clean, delivering modest fruit flavors on a tart, crisp, light frame. Drink now. • $12 • (05/15/95) • **77**
St.-Véran 1994: Distinctive, offering more fruit intensity than some St.-Vérans but showing a rustic, drying character on the rough finish. 833 cases made. • $10 • (08/31/95) • **76**
Santenay Clos Rousseau 1993: Elegant, refined, silky texture. Subtle earth, red berry and mocha flavors lead to a ripe finish. Try now. • $17 • (11/15/95) • **84**
Santenay 1990: Jammy, chewy and pretty, with raspberry, cherry and earth aromas and flavors and round tannins. Drinkable now. 300 cases made. • $16 • (12/15/92) • **85**
Santenay 1989 • $17 • (01/31/92) • **85**
Santenay La Maladière 1990: Nicely structured, with lively raspberry, vanilla and cherry aromas, silky tannins and a racy finish. 400 cases made. • $19 • (12/15/92) • **84**
Santenay La Maladière 1989 • $20 • (01/31/92) • **82**
Santenay La Maladière 1988 • $21 • (08/31/91) • **84**
Santenay La Maladière 1985 • $22 • (03/15/88) • **84**
Savigny-lès-Beaune 1989 • $18 • (01/31/92) • **85**
Volnay 1993: One of the few good wines from Jaffelin this year. Juicy cherry and chestnut aromas and flavors, medium to light body, slightly dry tannins and fresh finish. Drink now. • $24 • (11/15/95) • **86**
Volnay 1992: Simple and a little chewy, generous with its rustic berry and slightly candied flavors. • $20 • (12/15/94) • **79**
Volnay 1991: The light thread of raspberry and spice aromas and flavors is marred only by a greenish tinge on the finish. Lean and crisp; drinkable now. • $20 • (01/31/94) • **81**
Volnay 1990: Pretty, elegant and seductive, with subtle notes that kick in with sweet, ripe cherry and plum flavors on the silky finish. Drinkable now. 200 cases made. • $24 • (12/15/92) • **85**
Volnay 1989 • $29 • (01/31/92) • **89**
Volnay 1988 • $30 • (08/31/91) • **88**
Volnay 1986 • $27 • (04/30/89) • **86**
Volnay 1985 • $30 • (03/15/88) • **88**
Volnay 1983 • $17 • (10/16/85) • **92**
Vosne-Romanée 1989 • $29 • (01/31/92) • **86**
Vosne-Romanée 1986 • $30 • (02/28/89) • **79**

JAMELLES, LES

Cabernet Sauvignon Vin de Pays d'Oc 1994 • $7 • (10/31/95) • **84**

Cabernet Sauvignon Vin de Pays d'Oc 1993 • $7 • (02/28/95) • **82**
Chardonnay Vin de Pays d'Oc 1994 • $7 • (12/15/95) • **80**
Cinsault Vin de Pays d'Oc 1994 • $7 • (01/01/95) • **81**
Cinsault Vin de Pays d'Oc 1993 • $7 • (01/01/95) • **80**
Merlot Vin de Pays d'Oc 1995: Ripe and firm, with tart cherry, plum and spice flavors that linger on the finish. Well balanced and still fairly tannic. Try now. 48,000 cases made. • $7 • (12/15/96) • **85**
Merlot Vin de Pays d'Oc 1994 • $7 • (10/31/95) • **82**
Merlot Vin de Pays d'Oc 1993 • $7 • (02/28/95) • **77**
Mourvèdre Vin de Pays d'Oc 1993 • $7 • (10/31/95) • **75**
Muscat Sec Vin de Pays d'Oc 1994 • $8 • (02/29/96) • **78**
Rolle Vin de Pays de l'Ile de Beauté 1994 • $8 • (02/29/96) • **75**
Syrah Vin de Pays d'Oc 1994 • $7 • (10/31/95) • **84**
Viognier Vin de Pays d'Oc 1994 • $12 • (02/29/96) • **78**

JAMET, JEAN-PAUL & JEAN-LUC

Côte-Rôtie 1994: Marked by expressive aromas and solid texture, this rich, dense red is also bursting with cassis, spice, licorice and mineral flavors. It's hard now, but well knit, and promises fine development. Try in 2000. • $NA • (10/15/97) • **91**
Côte-Rôtie 1991: Concentrated yet balanced, with ripe raspberry and tar flavors on a solid frame and a rich, smoky finish. A combination of intensity and poise. Drinkable now. • $39 • (05/31/94) • **90**
Côte-Rôtie 1990: Try this rich and luscious wine with roast lamb studded with rosemary; the flavors will marry beautifully. It's big and expressive, but still needs time to open. • $39 • (05/31/94) • **92**
Côte-Rôtie 1988 • $49 • (06/15/93) • **78**

JANASSE, DOMAINE DE LA

Châteauneuf-du-Pape 1995: This well-defined red combines firm tannins with layered flavors of cassis, black peppers and herbs, ripe and fresh. Drinkable now. • $30 • (10/15/97) • **87**
Châteauneuf-du-Pape Chaupin 1995: Ripe fruit plus traditional style equals distinctive character in this hearty red. The flavors mingle dried fruits, earth and smoke, well balanced and long. It's firm, even chewy, but has the richness to match with food and develop in the bottle. Drink now. • $22 • (10/15/97) • **88**
Châteauneuf-du-Pape Chaupin 1994: Pleasant silky texture, and ripe with flavors of dried cherries, tomatoes and herbs. Firm tannins. A bit blunt and rustic. Try now. 667 cases made. • $20 • (02/28/97) • **84**
Châteauneuf-du-Pape Vieilles Vignes 1994: Lush, with ripe plum and sweet cherry flavors, concentrated yet not tough. The tannins stay integrated through the long finish, good acidity keeps it fresh. An easy-drinking wine that's food-friendly. Drink now. 500 cases made. • $40 • (10/15/97) • **89**
Châteauneuf-du-Pape White 1996: Very pretty, delicate and fairly crisp, offering pear, apple and melon flavors. Seems like it has had some sophisticated oak-aging, so its texture is smooth. Delicious now. 333 cases made. • $28 • (10/15/97) • **84**
Châteauneuf-du-Pape White 1995: Vivid and exuberant yet full-bodied and rich. Layered with very subtle thyme, rosemary, almond, pear, mineral and toasty bread flavors. Delicate and balanced, this impressive, still lively '95 ends with a succulent finish. Drink now. 417 cases made. • $NA • (10/15/97) • **90**
Châteauneuf-du-Pape White 1994: If you're looking for a mature Châteauneuf, try this. Full-bodied, with almond, butter, butterscotch and ripe pear flavors. Delicious, supple texture, with a lingering, lively finish. Drink now. 333 cases made. • $NA • (10/15/97) • **85**
Châteauneuf-du-Pape White Cuvée Spéciale 1996: Quite traditional, with some buttery, oaky, almond flavors weighing on the fresh fruit. Medium to full in body, it's a stab at a serious wine, but the oak takes over and the finish seems a touch bitter. Try now. 50 cases made. • $40 • (10/15/97) • **83**
Côtes du Rhône 1995: Slightly herbal, with a crisp, rather lean structure, but some vivid cherry and wild berry character carries this through to a succulent, fairly intense finish. Drink now. 2,500 cases made. • $10 • (10/15/97) • **80**
Côtes du Rhône Les Garrigues 1996: Lovely, with more body than some '96 Côtes du Rhône, offering appealing licorice, coffee, mocha and berry. Exuberant, without much breeding, but who cares? Enjoy now with pizza and pasta. 333 cases made. • $20 • (10/15/97) • **83**
Côtes du Rhône Les Garrigues 1995: Pretty currant, cherry, lead-pencil and earth character gives this wine much personality. *Vin de terroir*. Has ripe, delicious fruit and an intense finish. Medium-bodied. Drink now. 500 cases made. • $20 • (10/15/97) • **86**
Côtes du Rhône Les Garrigues 1994: Sweet berry and herbal flavors mingle in this round, spicy red. The tannins are soft on the palate but turn a bit dry on the finish. Drink soon, with food. 292 cases made. • $NA • (10/15/97) • **80**

JANIN, PAUL

Beaujolais-Villages Domaine des Vignes des Jumeaux 1994: Smoky, gamy aromas give way to flavors of plum, bitter chocolate and a light earthiness in this tannic red. Not as fruity as a typical Beaujolais, but has good concentration. Try with grilled meats. • $10 • (09/15/96) • **84**
Moulin-à-Vent Domaine des Vignes du Tremblay 1993: Earthy and metallic notes dominate this maturing, still tough red, which even hints of the taste of blood. It's muscular but not too friendly. • $10 • (09/15/97) • **78**

JANODET, JACKY

Moulin-à-Vent Domaine Les Fines Graves 1996: Cinnamon and smoke aromas and ripe cherry and prune flavors are lush in this velvety red, but it's a bit soft and blowsy. Appealing now, but not an ager. 2,000 cases made. • $19 • (05/31/98) • **85**
Moulin-à-Vent Domaine les Fines Graves 1994: The pretty floral and blackberry flavors are a bit overpowered by the firm tannins, but that may be beneficial when drunk with food. • $14 • (09/15/96) • **83**

JASMIN, ROBERT

Côte-Rôtie 1995: Concentration comes at the cost of elegance in this chewy red. It shows raisin, toast and coffee flavors with rustic, drying tannins. Drinkable now. • $NA • (10/15/97) • **82**
Côte-Rôtie 1994: Jammy and rustic, this straightforward red shows cooked cherry, vegetal and spicy vanilla flavors. Has personality, but lacks harmony. Tart finish. • $NA • (10/15/97) • **79**
Côte-Rôtie 1992: Pretty and silky, but isn't showing much yet. The berry, chocolate and spice flavors come out on the finish. Try now. • $42 • (05/31/94) • **84**
Côte-Rôtie 1991: A bit lean, but some pretty spice and black pepper notes are hiding under the tannin. • $43 • (05/31/94) • **82**
Côte-Rôtie 1990: Not big, but elegant and balanced, with spicy cherry and raspberry flavors and soft tannins. Try now. Tasted twice. • $45 • (05/31/94) • **86**
Côte-Rôtie 1988 • $32 • (12/31/90) • **89**
Côte-Rôtie 1987 • $30 • (06/30/90) • **90**

JAU, CHÂTEAU DE

Côtes du Roussillon White 1996: A fresh, crisp, straightforward white with almond and peach flavors, ending with an earthy note. Drinkable now. 3,500 cases made. • $10 • (09/30/97) • **82**
Côtes du Roussillon-Villages 1995: Soft and harmonious, displaying its pepper, raspberry and herb notes in a relaxed, easy-going style. Drinkable now, especially with grilled meat or fowl. 4,000 cases made. • $10 • (09/30/97) • **85**
Côtes du Roussillon 1988 • $6 • (08/31/91) • **75**
Muscat de Rivesaltes 1995: A new dimension in Muscat, this is extravagantly fruity, with its sweetness balanced by crisp acidity. Long-lasting finish. 3,000 cases made. • $11/375ml • (05/31/97) • **90**
Vin de Pays d'Oc Le Jaja de Jau Black Label 1996: A fruity red with grapey, cherry flavors. Simple and drinkable; try with food. A blend of 60 percent Syrah and 40 percent Grenache. 4,000 cases made. • $7 • (10/31/97) • **80**
Vin de Pays d'Oc Le Jaja de Jau Blue Label 1996: A crowd-pleaser, offering flavors of cherry and chocolate, a soft texture and refreshing acidity balanced by light tannins. Drink now. A blend of 60 percent Cabernet and 40 percent Merlot. 3,000 cases made. • $7 • (12/15/97) • **83**
Vin de Pays d'Oc Le Jaja de Jau Green Label 1996: Honeysuckle aromas and modest citrus flavors mark this simple but refreshing wine. 3,000 cases made. • $7 • (10/31/97) • **80**
Vin de Pays d'Oc Rosé Le Jaja de Jau Purple Label 1996: Light and refreshing for its simple strawberry and bright cherry flavors. Serve well-chilled as an apéritif. 1,000 cases made. • $7 • (09/15/97) • **82**
Vin de Pays des Côtes Catalanes Le Jaja de Jau 1993 • $7 • (09/15/94) • **83**

Key: SS—Spectator Selection CS—Cellar Selection HR—Highly Recommended BB—Best Buy $NA—Price not available Ⓐ—Auction Price (BT)—Barrel Tasting
Dates in parentheses indicate the issues in which the ratings were published.

FRANCE

JAUMIER, DENIS

Quincy 1995: This bold, brassy white shows almond and lanolin aromas and flavors, with melon and licorice notes. Has character and some concentration, but is atypical. Drink now. • $13 • (05/31/98) • **81**

JAVILLIER, PATRICK

Bourgogne Cuvée Oligocène White 1995: A bit heavy, but it offers plenty of honey, ripe pear and toasty oak flavors. Full-bodied; try upon release. • $24 • (08/31/97) • **80**

Bourgogne Cuvée Oligocène White 1994: Fresh and crisp, with some apple and mineral flavors, but it doesn't really show much and even seems a bit hollow. Somewhat one-dimensional on the finish. 416 cases made. • $23 • (05/31/96) • **80**

Bourgogne Cuvée Oligocène White 1993: Solid and well made, showing supple texture yet a good backbone of lime, pear and green apple flavors and a long, slightly rough finish. Drinkable now. • $23 • (05/15/95) • **85**

Bourgogne Cuvée des Forgets White 1995: Ripe and rich but also very subtle. Full-bodied, packed with tropical, citrus and fresh herb character, there's a slight dilution in the midpalate, but its round, supple and satiny texture carries through the finish. Drink now. • $20 • (08/31/97) • **87**

Bourgogne Cuvée des Forgets White 1994: Full-bodied but slightly tart, with modest fruit and herb flavors. Turns a bit dry on the finish. • $NA • (08/31/96) • **78**

Bourgogne Cuvée des Forgets White 1993: Attractively ripe and supple, light- to medium-bodied, showing a vivid streak of lemon, apple and mineral character; juicy finish. Enjoy now. • $19 • (05/15/95) • **83**

Meursault 1995: Very ripe in style, this tastes a bit rustic but has plenty of honey, spice, pear and tropical fruit flavors. Full-bodied, with a velvety texture on the finish. Delicious now, should improve through 2000. • $35 • (08/31/97) • **86**

Meursault Au Murger de Monthélie 1995: Good intensity, with dried fig, spice, pear tart and toasty oak flavors. Medium-bodied, it would rate higher save for a slightly hot touch on the finish. Delicious now, better after 2000. • $45 • (08/31/97) • **86**

Meursault Au Murger de Monthélie 1994: Well crafted, and as round, smooth and silky as white Burgundy gets. Medium-bodied, with pronounced milk, vanilla bean and clean fruit aromas and flavors. Finish is accented by notes of honey and toasty oak. Drink now through 1998. • $NA • (08/31/96) • **88**

Meursault Clos du Cromin Cuvée Spéciale Mise Tardive 1995: Excellent quality for a village wine. Rich, hedonistic, seductive yet solid as a rock, it's superbly crafted. All the pieces come together in the right, subtle proportions to form a lovely, full-bodied wine with honey, pear, flint and stone character. A beautiful finish, albeit a bit bitter now, ends the fireworks. Try after 2005. • $40 • (08/31/97) • **91**

Meursault Clos du Cromin 1993: The minerally, creamy texture delivers fine toast, hazelnut and butter character on a narrow frame. Drinkable now. • $38 • (05/15/95) • **87**

Meursault Les Casse-Têtes 1995: Very ripe, even overly so (some cooked apple flavors), with a tartish texture. Medium-bodied and a bit disjointed. • $45 • (08/31/97) • **75**

Meursault Les Casse-Têtes 1994: Solid, fresh and well balanced from start to finish. Pure peach, mango, pear and apple flavors are well integrated with mineral, honey and toasty oak notes. Medium-bodied. Try now through 1999. • $NA • (08/31/96) • **92**

Meursault Les Casse-Têtes 1993: Quite racy; lovely balance between vibrant acidity and toast, honey, hazelnut and pear flavors. Medium in body; crisp finish. Drinkable now. • $38 • (05/15/95) • **86**

Meursault Les Casse-Têtes 1992: Nice, smooth and moderately intense, with some ripe-tasting honey, coffee and vanilla bean flavors; ends with a tangy touch of citrus. • $30 • (08/31/94) • **85**

Meursault Les Charmes 1995: Thick, rich and ripe. A bit rustic, but when held overnight in an open bottle it gained finesse and complexity. Wonderful, zesty, citrusy character with spice and oak accents. This *premier cru* needs until 2005. • $50 • (08/31/97) • **90**

Meursault Les Clous 1994: Beautifully balanced and concentrated, with mineral, green apple, prune and honey flavors. Thick and full-bodied, but not overdone. Try now; may want to decant hours before serving. • $NA • (08/31/96) • **90**

Meursault Les Clous 1993: A fruit bomb of a wine, ripe and lush, sporting tiers of tropical fruit, mineral, smoke and toasty oak flavors and a chalky finish. Great complexity. • $40 • (08/31/95) • **85**

Meursault Les Narvaux 1995: Seemed overly oaky at first, but then this village wine opened up—showing fruity and floral pear, quince, mineral and vanilla-bean flavors. Medium-bodied, sweet tasting and ready to drink upon release, but worth decanting before serving. 125 cases made. • $NA • (05/31/97) • **90**

Meursault Les Narvaux 1992: Big and rich, showy and full-bodied; has plenty of toast, pineapple and grapefruit flavors, all backed by a core of good acidity. Long-lasting finish; drinkable now. • $35 • (08/31/94) • **92**

Meursault Les Tillets 1995: Ripe, thick and fat in texture and in character, with some lactic, mineral, pear and honey flavors. A lovely wine of medium body and moderate intensity. Drink now. • $39 • (08/31/97) • **89**

Meursault Les Tillets 1994: Balanced to perfection; backs up its pear, peach and apricot flavors with subtle oak and spice nuances. Has a silky texture and is seductive on the palate. Superb. Drinkable now. • $NA • (08/31/96) • **90**

Meursault Les Tillets 1993: Polished and sophisticated, this wonderfully smooth, full-bodied and complex Meursault has loads of mineral, tropical fruit and citrus flavors. Honey and hazelnut emerge gracefully on the finish. Try now. 300 cases made. • $38 • (08/31/95) • **89**

Meursault Les Tillets 1992: Full-bodied, flavorful Meursault; it hits you with its baked pear, toast and honey flavors that are broad, lush and ripe. Tasted twice, and drinkable now. 833 cases made. • $33 • (08/31/94) • **89**

Puligny-Montrachet Les Levrons 1994: Rich, ripe and full-bodied, oozing caramel, spice, mineral, toasty coconut and ripe pear flavors. Not too intense, but who is complaining? Silky and well made. Drinkable now. 100 cases made. • $NA • (05/31/96) • **90**

Puligny-Montrachet Les Levrons 1993: Distinctive and seductive, displaying a lush, creamy texture and lime, butterscotch, toast, hazelnut, honey and pear flavors. Supple and ripe; round mouthfeel. Drinkable now. • $38 • (05/15/95) • **87**

Savigny-lès-Beaune Dessus de Montchenevoy White 1995: Ripe and fresh at the same time, quite hard now, and distinctive for a slight cooked apple note. Full-bodied, with citrus, apple tart and melon flavors, and a hint of mineral on the long, lime-flavored finish. • $25 • (08/31/97) • **87**

Savigny-lès-Beaune Dessus de Montchenevoy White 1994: Impressive Savigny village wine from one of Meursault's best growers. Ripe, but firmly structured, full-bodied and quite intense. Beautiful mineral, fruit, and spice flavors. Sort of chalky and very toasty on the slightly hard finish. Try now. • $NA • (08/31/96) • **90**

Savigny-lès-Beaune Dessus de Montchenevoy White 1993: Tart and crisp, with a mineral, lime and spice character that makes it attractive. The tartness intensifies on the lean finish, but should go well with shellfish. 350 cases made. • $29 • (05/31/96) • **82**

JAYER, HENRI

Echézeaux 1988 • $59 Ⓐ • (05/15/91) • **94**
Echézeaux 1987 • $115 • (05/15/91) • **87**
Echézeaux 1986 • $160 • (05/15/91) • **88**
Echézeaux 1985 • $264 Ⓐ • (05/15/91) • **96**
Echézeaux 1982 • $150 • (06/16/86) CS • **94**
Echézeaux 1981 • $100 • (05/15/91) • **82**
Echézeaux 1980 • $220 • (05/15/91) • **89**
Echézeaux 1979 • $175 • (05/15/91) • **92**
Echézeaux 1978 • $440 • (05/15/91) • **91**
Echézeaux 1976 • $400 • (05/15/91) • **90**
Echézeaux 1972 • $300 • (05/15/91) • **81**
Echézeaux 1970 • $300 • (05/15/91) • **80**
Echézeaux 1969 • $550 • (05/15/91) • **91**
Richebourg 1987 • $280 • (05/15/91) • **87**
Richebourg 1986 • $350 • (05/15/91) • **93**
Richebourg 1985 • $625 • (05/15/91) • **99**
Richebourg 1980 • $300 • (05/15/91) • **88**
Richebourg 1979 • $290 • (05/15/91) • **93**
Vosne-Romanée Aux Brûlées 1987 • $100 • (05/15/91) • **85**
Vosne-Romanée Aux Brûlées 1986 • $105 • (05/15/91) • **90**
Vosne-Romanée Aux Brûlées 1985 • $300 • (05/15/91) • **93**
Vosne-Romanée Aux Brûlées 1980 • $185 • (05/15/91) • **88**
Vosne-Romanée Aux Brûlées 1979 • $150 • (05/15/91) • **88**
Vosne-Romanée Aux Brûlées 1978 • $310 • (05/15/91) • **92**
Vosne-Romanée Aux Brûlées 1976 • $250 • (05/15/91) • **81**
Vosne-Romanée Aux Brûlées 1972 • $250 • (05/15/91) • **87**
Vosne-Romanée Cros Parantoux 1988 • $180 • (05/15/91) • **93**
Vosne-Romanée Cros Parantoux 1987 • $85 • (05/15/91) • **86**
Vosne-Romanée Cros Parantoux 1986 • $105 • (05/15/91) • **87**
Vosne-Romanée Cros Parantoux 1985 • $230 • (05/15/91) • **95**

Vosne-Romanée Cros Parantoux 1980 • $175 • (05/15/91) • **89**
Vosne-Romanée Cros Parantoux 1978 • $310 • (05/15/91) • **94**
Vosne-Romanée Les Beaux Monts 1988 • $160 • (05/15/91) • **89**

JAYER, J.

Echézeaux 1988 • $65 Ⓐ • (03/15/91) • **91**
Nuits-St.-Georges Aux Lavières 1985 • $38 • (03/15/88) • **88**
Vosne-Romanée Les Rouges 1985 • $44 • (03/15/88) • **80**

JAYER-GILLES, ROBERT

Bourgogne Aligoté 1996: Clean and pure yet straightforward Aligoté. Good citrus and green apple notes. Light-bodied, a bit short on the finish. Quaffable now. 915 cases made. • $14 • (05/31/98) • **80**

Bourgogne Aligoté 1995: Crisp and tart, a lean wine with little complexity or depth. A bit sour on the finish. • $14 • (08/31/97) • **74**

Bourgogne Aligoté 1994: A taut, crisp, but intensely herbal wine. Dried herb, green apple and mineral flavors. Rather green and simple finish. • $13 • (08/31/96) • **79**

Bourgogne Hautes-Côtes de Nuits 1993: Full-blown, earthy, ripe, rich, plummy red berry character. Seductive now, featuring lots of personality in a rustic way. Quite chewy as it adds peppery notes on the finish. Try now through 2000. • $22 • (05/15/96) • **88**

Côte de Nuits-Villages 1995: Impressive. Very oaky in style, with toasty, vanilla accents to the blackberry flavors. Firm finish. Shows what can be done with less-than-great *terroir* if you have commitment. • $40 • (11/15/97) • **88**

Côte de Nuits-Villages 1994: Light, earthy, simple, with pretty strawberry flavors. Drinkable now. • $30 • (11/15/96) • **80**

Côte de Nuits-Villages 1993: Gorgeous, melts in the mouth, like a reduced blackberry and wine sauce. It delivers the essence of flavors in a silky, medium-bodied package. Ripe tannins make this drinkable now. • $36 • (11/15/95) • **90**

Côte de Nuits-Villages 1992: Immediately attractive for its aromatic, spicy, currant and berry character, but turns simple in flavor and light in texture. Drinkable now. • $28 • (12/15/94) • **82**

Côte de Nuits-Villages 1991: Marked by spicy, sweet oak, this offers enough ripe currant and blackberry flavors to keep it in balance. Try now. 300 cases made. • $29 Ⓐ • (01/31/94) • **82**

Côte de Nuits-Villages 1990: A superb, massive wine for this appellation, offering tons of smoky berry and earth characteristics and silky tannins. Drinkable now. 650 cases made. • $34 • (12/15/92) • **90**

Echézeaux 1994: Lushly aromatic and deep in flavor. A gorgeous wine with impressive length. The exotic rose petal, currant and beefy aromas are the best element now, but the flavors of spicy currant have much to grow on. Best from 2000 to 2002. • $115 • (11/15/96) • **93**

Echézeaux 1992: Has the ripe fruit and rich texture that are missing in so many '92s, layering the berry, spice and delicate herbal flavors. Drinkable now. • $110 • (12/15/94) • **89**

Echézeaux 1989 • $101 • (01/31/92) • **94**

Echézeaux du Dessus 1995: This velvety, seductive '95 exhibits perfumed, complex aromas of roses, savage black fruits and spice. It's medium- to full-bodied, deep and concentrated, with a structure that will develop over the next six to eight years. Long, harmonious finish. 200 cases made. • $150 • (11/15/97) • **95**

Echézeaux du Dessus 1993: Superb concentration of exotic blackberries and raspberries and a good dose of smoky oak. Full in body with velvety tannins and long, wild-fruit finish. Try after 2000. • $135 • (11/15/95) • **95**

Echézeaux du Dessus 1991: Smooth, polished, silky and elegant, unfolding raspberry, smoke, toast, game and plum flavors that persist into a long, luscious finish. Has scratchy tannins to lose, but the goods to age through 2000. 200 cases made. • $85 Ⓐ • (01/31/94) • **91**

Echézeaux du Dessus 1990: Superintense and gorgeous in texture, this powerful wine is also delicate, with violet, game, berry and earth nuances that are so well integrated they feel like cream on the palate. Drinkable now. 200 cases made. • $100 • (12/15/92) • **97**

Hautes Côtes de Beaune 1995: This displays toasty oak aromas and spicy black cherry flavors, then clamps down on the finish. It's awkward at this stage, but seems to have all the elements to come together in 1999. • $30 • (11/15/97) • **87**

Hautes Côtes de Beaune 1994: Has an earthy accent, but the pleasant strawberry and chocolate flavors keep it flying nicely. • $25 • (11/15/96) • **82**

Hautes Côtes de Beaune 1993: Exciting, vibrant, medium-bodied red, featuring perfumy, rose petal, currant, smoky flavors folded into the wood and impressive tannin structure. Try in 2000. • $22 • (11/15/95) • **90**

Hautes Côtes de Beaune 1990: Shows impressive concentration, with a deep color and violet and vanilla flavors. A clever wine that feels smooth at first, but has too much new oak for our taste, giving the wine an astringent finish. Drinkable now. 700 cases made. • $24 • (12/15/92) • **80**

Hautes Côtes de Beaune 1989 • $24 • (01/31/92) • **84**

Hautes Côtes de Beaune 1988 • $26 • (05/15/91) • **88**

Hautes Côtes de Beaune White 1996: Honeyed and woody style of regional Bourgogne, with lime, smoked oak and caramel. Lacks concentration. Try with food upon release. 715 cases made. • $24 • (05/31/98) • **79**

Hautes Côtes de Beaune White 1995: Earthy and odd, tart and crisp with a lean frame. Not pleasant. Difficult to recommend. • $27 • (08/31/97) • **70**

Hautes Côtes de Beaune White 1994: Pretty, with a nice concentration of honey, pineapple, green apricot and grass flavors. Medium-bodied, crisp finish. Try now. • $25 • (08/31/96) • **82**

Hautes Côtes de Nuits 1995: Lovely aromas of rose petal, violet, cassis and toasty oak pump up this medium-bodied, slightly diluted but succulent and seductive '95 red. Lacks just a bit of ripeness, but the flavors are delicious. Drink now through 2000. • $30 • (11/15/97) • **84**

Hautes Côtes de Nuits 1994: Light and refined, with a pretty beam of raspberry and spice flavors that get little competition from the soft tannins. Ready now. • $25 • (11/15/96) • **82**

Hautes Côtes de Nuits 1992: Light and fruity, with a tantalizing overlay of spicy oak to the currant and plum flavors. Simple and inviting; drinkable now. • $23 • (12/15/94) • **82**

Hautes Côtes de Nuits 1989 • $24 • (01/31/92) • **86**

Hautes Côtes de Nuits White 1996: Nice wine. Fairly ripe and rich, with kiwi, pineapple and pear, yet also loads of palate-cleansing citrus notes. Medium-bodied. Smooth texture. Quite oaky. Drink now through 2000. 830 cases made. • $24 • (05/31/98) • **85**

Hautes Côtes de Nuits White 1995: A nice wine, with satiny texture and, although it's slightly herbal, some mineral and green apple notes. • $27 • (08/31/97) • **85**

Hautes Côtes de Nuits White 1994: Well-crafted. Oozes clean, fresh citrus aromas and subtle, toasty oak and honey flavors. Medium-bodied and lushly textured. Drinkable now through 2000. • $25 • (08/31/96) • **90**

Hautes Côtes de Nuits White 1993: Smooth and sophisticated; lovely mineral, chalky, lemony character. A little closed up and difficult to judge now, finishing somewhat rough, but give it the benefit of the doubt. • $20 • (05/15/95) • **87**

Nuits-St.-Georges Les Damodes 1994: With its spicy, buttery accent, this feels smooth and graceful, offering ripe plum, spice and currant flavors, integrated tannins and generous length. Drink now to 2000. • $70 • (11/15/96) • **90**

Nuits-St.-Georges Les Damodes 1993: An explosion of currant and berry aromas and flavors. Full-bodied, with toasty oak and fruit, velvety tannins and long finish. Better in 2000. • $85 • (11/15/95) • **92**

Nuits-St.-Georges Les Damodes 1992: Lithe, very pretty spicy oak aromas and blackberry and currant flavors are settling nicely into a firm framework. The lingering finish shows more spice notes. • $70 • (12/15/94) • **85**

Nuits-St.-Georges Les Damodes 1991: Smooth, round and generous, offering spicy, toasty new oak, currant and blackberry aromas and flavors. Captures the maximum of this vintage for this appellation. Drinkable now. 50 cases made. • $55 Ⓐ • (01/31/94) • **88**

Nuits-St.-Georges Les Hauts Poirets 1995: International in style, this is loaded with mocha, violet and spice character from new wood, yet underneath is sweet black cherry flavor. Supple and soft with fine tannins, this should drink well by 2000. • $85 • (11/15/97) • **92**

Nuits-St.-Georges Les Hauts Poirets 1994: Generous, supple and spicy with new-oak nuances to the fresh currant and raspberry flavors. Finishes gracefully with well-integrated tannins. Ready to drink. • $65 • (11/15/96) • **87**

Nuits-St.-Georges Les Poirets 1993: Breathtaking wine. Amazing concentration of wild fruit. Full-bodied, adding full, velvety tannins and a finish that lingers for minutes. Hold this until 2005. • $70 • (11/15/95) • **93**

Nuits-St.-Georges Les Poirets 1992: Packs a lot of spicy, tobacco-scented fruit on a modest frame. Warm and toasty, but finishing austerely as the fine tannins clamp down. Try now. • $58 • (12/15/94) • **84**

Nuits-St.-Georges Les Poirets 1991: Distinctively toasty and spicy, this ripe, round wine has a generous component of black cherry, currant and prune

Key: SS—Spectator Selection CS—Cellar Selection HR—Highly Recommended BB—Best Buy $NA—Price not available Ⓐ—Auction Price (BT)—Barrel Tasting
Dates in parentheses indicate the issues in which the ratings were published.

flavors that extends into a polished finish. Drinkable now. 125 cases made. • $48 Ⓐ • (01/31/94) • **86**

Nuits-St.-Georges Les Poirets 1990: Unbelievable structure in a Nuits. A giant wine, with a huge amount of fruit and tannins, but shows elegance and refinement at the same time. Made for long-term aging; try now to 2000. 125 cases made. • $48 • (12/15/92) • **97**

JEAN, PIERRE

St.-Emilion 1988 • $10 • (06/30/91) BB • **85**

JENARD

Cabernet Sauvignon Vin de Pays d'Oc 1994: A pretty wine, displaying cherry and herbal flavors with straightforward appeal. Modest finish. • $7 • (12/15/96) • **81**

Merlot Vin de Pays d'Oc 1994: Mellow and cleanly made. Appealingly ripe and spicy, with ripe plum and prune flavors. Still a bit tannic on the finish. • $7 • (12/15/96) • **83**

JESSIAUME PÈRE & FILS

Santenay Les Gravières 1988 • $21 • (03/31/91) • **86**

JOBARD, CHARLES & REMI

Chardonnay Bourgogne 1994: A standout for its different flavors. Intense butterscotch, toast and citrus flavors. Very round and silky on the long finish. Excellent quality for a simple Bourgogne. • $20 • (05/31/96) • **85**

Meursault Les Charmes 1995: Ripe, rich and thick, offering lots of cinnamon, apple tart, honey and melon flavors. A bit heavy, but full-bodied and seductive. Drink now. • $50 • (08/31/97) • **84**

Meursault Les Chevalières 1995: Clean, pure and vibrant, a testimonial to excellent winemaking. Of medium-to-full body, with nice, sweet-and-ripe fruit character, this shows class as it deftly balances slightly toasty oak with lemon, honey and appley pear flavors. Good harmony on the long, racy finish. Best from 2005 through 2010. 128 cases made. • $35 • (05/31/97) • **90**

Meursault Les Chevalières 1994: Clean and fresh, with good intensity, likeable citrus and melon flavors and youthful finish. Drinkable now. • $32 • (05/31/96) • **84**

Meursault Les Genevrières 1995: Racy and distinctive, with beautiful, pure, clean fruit and subtle toasty oak flavors. Supple in texture and full-bodied, with citrus, orange peel, dried herb, tropical and mineral notes that provide life on the long but subtle finish. Drink now through 2005. 144 cases made. • $47 • (05/31/97) • **93**

Meursault Les Genevrières 1994: Very seductive, very honeyed and very balanced. Elegant and understated grapefruit and ripe pear flavors. Amazing fullness and harmony, with a mineral component to die for. Super-long finish. Drinkable now through 2000. • $45 • (05/31/96) • **93**

Meursault Le Porusot-Dessus 1995: Superb. You can taste the earth, the *terroir*, of this remarkable *premier cru*. It has the smooth texture of thick cream, with wonderful mineral, spice, wet stone, pear and dried herb flavors. Some honey notes kick in on the toasty finish, for good measure. Drink now through 2005. 185 cases made. • $45 • (05/31/97) • **94**

Meursault Sous la Velle 1995: Lovely, with a compacted mineral, lemon, floral and fruit character. Full-bodied, it's shaded by subtle, toasty oak notes and has a long, juicy, sweet-tasting, toasty finish. Best from 2000 through 2005. 138 cases made. • $33 • (05/31/97) • **90**

JOBARD, FRANÇOIS

Bourgogne White 1993 • $NA • (05/31/96) • **80**

Meursault 1993: A lovely, well-made and nicely balanced white that marries its ripe fruit and sweet honey character to the citrus and mineral notes. This is delicious now. • $NA • (05/31/96) • **88**

Meursault Le Porusot 1993: Lots going on here, with spice, pineapple, toasty oak and a good amount of citrus flavor. Rich but not overdone to make a very focused and lively wine. Try now. • $NA • (05/31/96) • **89**

Meursault Le Porusot 1992: Honey, hazelnut, chalk, almond character, silky-textured, showing ripe flavors on the long finish. Should improve with age given this producer's track record. Tasted twice, with consistent notes. • $50 • (05/15/95) • **89**

Meursault Les Genevrières 1993: Very rich and ripe, with tons of tropical fruit, apricot, peach and floral aromas and flavors. A bit rustic, turning a little coarse on the finish, but this full-bodied wine certainly isn't boring. Drinkable now. Tasted twice, with consistent notes. • $NA • (05/31/96) • **85**

Meursault Les Genevrières 1992: Fat and ripe, quite silky, exhibiting spicy, honeyed character and a lovely blend of toasty hazelnut and pear flavors. Drinkable now. • $50 • (05/15/95) • **87**

JOBARD, RÉMI

Bourgogne White 1996: Super quality for a Bourgogne. Clean, pure and classy, this medium-bodied white offers plenty of midpalate silkiness and a lovely combination of dried herbs, wet earth, butter, honey and ripe fruit, all in a firmly structured package. Long, seductive finish. Drink now through 2003. • $20 • (05/31/98) • **90**

Meursault En Luraule 1996: Lush, smooth and full-bodied; shy in aroma but showing good mineral, wet stone, earth and fruit character on the palate. The oily mouthfeel is very attractive, and it deftly balances its different parts on the long finish. Best from 2000 through 2005. • $37 • (05/31/98) • **89**

Meursault Le Poruzot-Dessus 1996: Delicious Meursault, showing both lively acidity and deftly toasty oak-flavored spice. Vibrant and full of personality, it's medium-to-full in body and rather sleek and silky, with mineral and ripe fruit. Best from 2000 through 2005. • $52 • (05/31/98) • **90**

Meursault Les Genevrières 1996: Brilliant. Elegant and seductively decadent, offering loads of everything, from the clean and pure lime, lemon and other citrus flavors, including a touch of mandarin and bitter orange marmalade, to the grilled pineapple, toasty coconut, spicy oak and pear tart. Full-bodied, firmly structured and exotic, this one is tough to beat for sheer pleasure. Best from 2002 through 2007. • $55 • (05/31/98) • **93**

Meursault Sous La Velle 1996: Nice village Meursault, firmly structured, backward and reserved on the nose but hinting at much depth, then kicking in with ripe and rich but elegant fruit texture. Mineral, pear, spice and vanilla bean notes and loads of reined-in acidity bring this full-bodied wine to a harmonious, creamlike, satisfying finish. A wine to lay down. Domaine formerly called Charles & Rémi Jobard. Best from 2005 through 2010. • $35 • (05/31/98) • **91**

JOBLOT

Givry Clos de la Servoisine 1994: Dark in color and complex in character, this firmly structured wine is a pleasure. Woody now, it shows impressive concentration of fruit flavors. Medium-bodied. Impressive for the appellation. Try now. • $NA • (11/15/96) • **85**

Givry Clos de la Servoisine 1989 • $25 • (01/31/92) • **88**

Givry Clos du Cellier-aux-Moines 1994: Nice, but with a rather oaky accent to the licorice, earth, spice and red berry flavors. Tempting now. • $NA • (11/15/96) • **82**

Givry Clos du Cellier-aux-Moines 1989 • $25 • (01/31/92) • **90**

Givry Clos du Cellier-aux-Moines 1988 • $26 Ⓐ • (12/31/90) • **84**

JOGUET, CHARLES

Chinon Clos de la Cure 1996: This slightly lean red offers coffee, toast and herb flavors, with light cherry notes and firm, slightly drying tannins. Better with food. Drink now. • $17 • (06/15/98) • **83**

Chinon Clos de la Cure 1995: A luscious red packed with ripe cherry and blackberry flavors, velvety and rich on the palate, with alluring smoke notes that add depth. Textbook Chinon. Delicious now. 1,500 cases made. • $17 • (05/15/97) • **90**

Chinon Clos de la Dioterie Vieilles Vignes 1995: Ripe and round yet fresh and clean, this beautifully defined red marries blackberry and toast flavors with herbal and spice accents in a balanced package that's all the more alluring for its restraint. Drinkable now. • $27 • (08/31/97) • **90**

Chinon Clos de la Dioterie Vieilles Vignes 1993 • $26 • (12/15/95) • **82**

Chinon Clos de la Dioterie Vieilles Vignes 1992 • $25 • (10/31/94) • **88**

Chinon Clos du Chêne Vert 1995: Elegant. Beautiful texture, fresh yet firm, silky and smooth, showcasing well-defined flavors of currants, fresh herbs, coffee and licorice. Fruit flavors are a bit muted now, but the wine has good grip and should show more in 1999. • $28 • (08/31/97) • **88**

Chinon Clos du Chêne Vert 1993 • $24 • (12/15/95) • **88**

Chinon Cuvée Terroir 1996: Plump, rich and soft. Alluring aromas of smoke and game give way to a velvety texture with flavors of ripe cherries and plums. Supple yet deep. Will match well with food. Drink now through 2000. • $14 • (02/28/98) • **87**

Chinon Cuvée des Varennes du Grand Clos 1986 • $15 • (04/30/88) • **82**

Chinon Cuvée du Clos de la Dioterie 1986 • $21 • (12/31/88) • **89**

Chinon Jeunes Vignes 1996: Smoky, gamy and meaty flavors are deep and rich in this firm, concentrated red. Plum, raisin and coffee notes add depth and promise to develop well. Best now through 2002. • $15 • (06/15/98) • **87**

Chinon Jeunes Vignes 1995: Lively, emphasizing the herbal and meaty aspects of Cabernet Franc, with fainter black cherry and licorice notes. Clean and fresh, with moderate tannins. Drinkable now. • $19 • (08/31/97) • **84**

Chinon Les Varennes du Grand Clos 1995: Ripe and rich, this shows deeper flavors than most Loire reds, with notes of plum, meat, smoke and light herbs. It's balanced, firmly structured but not clumsy. Drinkable now. • $20 • (06/15/97) • **90**

Chinon Les Varennes du Grand Clos 1993 • $24 • (12/15/95) • **85**

Chinon Rosé 1996: This fruity rosé offers cherry and berry flavors with good acidity and a slight tannic grip. Has enough structure to match with light dishes. Drink now. • $14 • (06/15/98) • **82**

Chinon Rosé 1995: Light strawberry aromas fade on the palate in this neutral rosé. Offers citrusy acidity, but it's simple and straightforward. • $18 • (08/31/97) • **78**

JOLIESSE

Merlot Vin de Pays d'Oc Reserve 1995: Softly textured, with plum, vanilla and strawberry flavors, finishing on an herbal note. • $NA • (04/30/97) • **80**

JOLIETTE, DOMAINE

Côtes du Roussillon-Villages Cuvée Romain Mercier 1995: Firm and well focused, with plum and berrylike flavors shadowed by some sweetly spicy notes. Drink now through 2000. • $7 • (05/31/98) • **83**

JOLIVET, PASCAL

Pouilly-Fumé 1995: Flavors of herbs, pear and pineapple emerge on the palate of this well-focused and firmly structured white, after an initial dose of acidity. Surprisingly delicate and elegant. • $17 • (05/15/97) • **89**

Pouilly-Fumé 1994 • $17 • (05/15/96) • **86**

Pouilly-Fumé La Grande Cuvée 1994 • $22 • (06/15/96) • **88**

Pouilly-Fumé La Loge Aux Moines 1995: This round white offers ripe pear and apple flavors, with herbal accents and enough acidity to keep it firm. Balanced, clean and a bit tight; it may improve with time. • $23 • (06/15/97) • **87**

Pouilly-Fumé La Loge Aux Moines 1994: Honey and hazelnut notes add complexity to this round, yet extremely dry white. It shows pear and herb flavors, with good structure and firm acidity. Not a show-stopper, but seductive and enjoyable. Time in the bottle has improved it. • $23 • (05/15/97) • **90**

Sancerre 1996: Alluring aromas of herbs, pears and light toast give way to lively but subtle flavors of toast, melon, minerals and herbs in this complex white. Beautifully balanced and a great match with food. Drink now through 2000. 2,200 cases made. • $17 • (03/31/98) • **90**

Sancerre 1995: Rich texture and ripe fig flavors give this unusual weight for the style, but the herb and citrus flavors are clean and classical. Try now. 9,500 cases made. • $17 • (05/15/97) • **90**

Sancerre 1994 • $17 • (04/30/96) • **80**

Sancerre Château du Nozay 1996: This round white shows vanilla and butter aromas and has a firm, almost tannic weight on the palate. It offers pear and apple flavors, with clean acidity and good balance. Should bloom with food. Drink now through 2000. • $21 • (06/15/98) • **88**

Sancerre Château du Nozay 1995: This well-knit white shows ripe pear and pineapple flavors, with racy acidity to keep it lively and fresh. Offers more fruit than herbal flavors, and finishes with real zest. • $20 • (06/15/97) • **88**

Sancerre Château du Nozay 1994: A '94 that's improved with time. Toasty, smoky notes add interest to this full-bodied white, complementing the firm acidity and ripe apple and herb flavors. Not typical of this style, but complex and intriguing. • $20 • (05/15/97) • **90**

Sancerre La Grande Cuvée 1995: This powerful Loire white shows a well-defined character of intensity and depth, perfectly true to the regional style with concentrated herb, pear, apple and mineral flavors that are rich and long. A beautiful wine that marries typicity and individuality. Drink now through 2003. • $42 • (06/15/98) HR • **93**

Sancerre La Grande Cuvée 1994: Powerful and distinctive. An unusual Sancerre, from the deep gold color to the rich, toasty aromas to the full, even tannic, mouthfeel. Yet the well-defined herbal and spiced-pear flavors are beautifully typical of Loire Sauvignon Blanc. This is an unyielding wine, with none of the easy fruitiness of New World Chardonnay, but it rewards attention with complexity and style. Much better than previously reviewed. • $30 • (08/31/97) • **93**

JOLY, N.

Savennières Becherelle 1995: Intense and expressive, this wine starts softly with honeysuckle and ripe peach aromas, hits the palate with a keen acidity, then expands with rich peach, lime, mineral and spice flavors that build to the finish. It's young and tight but should gain considerably with age. • $20 • (05/15/97) • **91**

Savennières Becherelle 1994: Quite powerful and very austere, this big white offers apple, smoke and mineral flavors over searing acidity. It's impressive, in a way, but not much fun. 100 cases made. • $16 • (01/01/97) • **84**

Savennières-Coulée de Serrant Clos de la Coulée de Serrant 1994: A distinctive wine with real class, this has smoky, spicy aromas and subtle yet complex flavors of apple, mineral, toast and spice, firm but not overly acidic. 2,000 cases made. • $41 • (05/15/97) • **89**

Savennières-Roche aux Moines Clos de la Bergerie 1994: Powerful and distinctive. Rich, toasty aromas give way to toast, melon and hazelnut flavors in this big, dry white. Bold yet well defined, it has the muscle to improve with age. • $26 • (06/15/97) • **89**

Savennières-Roche aux Moines Clos de la Bergerie 1993: Good concentration, with deep color, smoky aromas and ripe apple and mineral flavors, but though it's solid, it's a bit short. Muscular, but rustic. • $24 • (06/15/97) • **85**

JOLYS, CHÂTEAU

Jurançon 1996: Distinctive-tasting, with flavors of clove, cream and a hint of green peach. Balanced and fairly crisp, with a good finish. • $13 • (04/30/98) • **85**

Jurançon Sec 1995: Simple and straightforward, with appley flavors and a slightly milky taste. • $10 • (04/30/98) • **77**

Jurançon Vendanges Tardives 1995: Fairly complex, with bitter almond, maple and honeylike flavors, and a luscious white chocolate note on the sumptuous finish. Rich and well balanced. 50 cases made. • $38/375ml • (04/30/98) • **88**

JONQUEYRES, CHÂTEAU

Bordeaux Supérieur 1995: Attractive, blending ripe-enough fruit flavors with interesting accents of spice, cedar and tobacco that linger on the finish. Moderate tannins. Drink now through 2000. 10,000 cases made. • $12 • (01/31/98) • **85**

Bordeaux Supérieur 1994: Attractive aromas and flavors of black cherry and smoke give this immediate appeal. Though light-bodied, it has firm tannins. Drink now. • $NA • (07/31/96) • **84**

Bordeaux White Les Comtes de Jonqueyres 1995: Vivid grassy, grapefruit-like flavors and a crisp, tangy texture give this considerable pizzazz. A blend of 65 percent Sauvignon Blanc, 30 percent Sémillon and 5 percent Muscadelle. 2,500 cases made. • $10 • (02/28/98) • **84**

JONQUIÈRES, CHÂTEAU

Corbières 1991 • $7 • (03/15/94) • **81**

JONQUIÈRES, DOMAINE DES

Côtes du Rhône 1995: Quite lush and pretty, with soft, smooth tannins, some intense fruit. Turns slightly tart on the finish but still a good wine. • $NA • (10/15/97) • **81**

Key: SS—Spectator Selection CS—Cellar Selection HR—Highly Recommended BB—Best Buy $NA—Price not available (A)—Auction Price (BT)—Barrel Tasting

Dates in parentheses indicate the issues in which the ratings were published.

FRANCE

JOSMEYER

Gewürztraminer Alsace Cuvée des Folastries 1994: Spice, orange-peel and tea flavors are bold and clean in this full-bodied, rich yet dry Gewürz. Fresh and balanced; try with spicy foods. • $19 • (09/30/96) • **88**

Pinot Auxerrois Alsace "H" Vieilles Vignes 1994: Round and generous, with ripe tropical flavors of pineapple and coconut, soft yet with sufficient acidity and a honeyed finish. Like a blowsy summer afternoon. • $23 • (09/30/96) • **86**

Pinot Blanc Alsace 1995: Soft and simple, this shows juicy flavors of pear, banana and lemon. It's agreeably light and finishes clean. • $13 • (10/15/96) • **83**

Riesling Alsace Grand Cru Hengst 1993: Racy and intense, packed with bright grapefruit and mineral flavors that attack the palate. Clean and well-knit; drinkable now. • $35 • (09/30/96) • **88**

Riesling Alsace Le Kottabe 1994: Tart, tight and lean, with mineral and grapefruit flavors and mouth-puckering acidity. • $18 • (09/30/96) • **78**

Riesling Alsace Vendanges Tardives 1991: Mineral and floral aromas give way to more generous pineapple and apricot flavors, with a nice play of slight sweetness and refreshing acidity. It has good weight and balance, and should age well. • $58 • (10/15/96) • **88**

Tokay Pinot Gris Alsace Cuvée du Centenaire Vieilles Vignes 1993: Silky and alluring, it's unusually supple and elegant for Pinot Gris, with grilled hazelnut and dried pear flavors. Dry, but still opulent and the finish is clean and long. • $34 • (09/30/96) • **88**

Tokay Pinot Gris Alsace Le Fromenteau 1994: Rich but very dry, with apple, lemon and herb flavors, full body, thick texture and a clean finish. Drink now with food. • $20 • (10/15/96) • **84**

JOUBERT, C. & M.

Juliénas 1996: Leafy and earthy notes are more prominent than the cherry flavors in this round, soft red. It's fresh, and has just enough grip for food, with a pleasantly peppery finish. Drink now. • $10 • (05/31/98) • **84**

JOUGLA, DOMAINE DES

St.-Chinian 1995: Crisp and sinewy, with astringent tannins that are destined to outlive the modest sweet plum and herb-tinged flavors. Still, the lasting impression is one of sweet fruit. Drink now. 15,000 cases made. • $9 • (12/15/97) • **84**

St.-Chinian 1990 • $9 • (03/15/94) • **84**

St.-Chinian 1986 • $7 • (05/15/89) • **76**

JUGE, MARCEL

Cornas 1986 • $23 • (11/30/90) • **83**

Cornas Coteaux 1986 • $21 • (02/10/91) • **78**

Cornas Cuvée C 1986 • $25 • (06/15/89) • **85**

Cornas Cuvée S C 1986 • $30 • (06/15/89) • **87**

JUILLOT, EMILE

Mercurey La Cailloute 1994: Pure fruit flavor shines though this straightforward and quite tart wine. A bit green, with an herbaceous tannic edge. Light- to medium-bodied. • $NA • (11/15/96) • **80**

Mercurey Les Combins 1995: A wine of depth and character. Spicy black fruits are displayed on a chewy, solid framework, but there is no lack of concentration. Give it until 2000 to soften. 458 cases made. • $NA • (11/15/97) • **88**

Mercurey Les Combins 1994: Impressive color and crisp, well-defined flavors. Lovely, pure red berry aromas and flavors and tannins that are a touch dry on the finish. Medium-bodied, fresh and grapey. • $NA • (11/15/96) • **85**

Mercurey Les Croichots 1995: Less focused than the best of this appellation, yet there's decent cherry flavor and modest concentration. The finish turns dry and astringent. 291 cases made. • $NA • (11/15/97) • **85**

JUILLOT, MICHEL

Bourgogne Côte Chalonnaise Red 1990: Simple, straightforward red Burgundy, with an earthy edge to the modest cherry and spice flavors. Finishes dry and a bit austere. Drinkable now. 800 cases made. • $13 • (10/31/92) • **80**

Bourgogne Côte Chalonnaise White 1995: Tart and slightly bitter, a somewhat herbal, astringent character dominates this lean wine. 250 cases imported. 1,600 cases made. • $12 • (08/31/97) • **74**

Bourgogne White 1994: Light and straightforward, showing modest fruit flavors. Seems a bit diluted. 1,500 cases made. • $14 • (05/31/96) • **74**

Corton-Charlemagne 1996: Wonderful richness in this full-bodied, velvety, ripe, supple and creamlike '96. A grand wine, opulent without being showy, delivering pretty floral, lime, ripe pear and vanilla bean notes, then a mineral component that floats along on the long, harmonious finish. Clean and pure, so be patient; it should improve without getting heavy through 2010. 250 cases made. • $95 • (05/31/98) • **94**

Corton-Charlemagne 1995: Clean, flavorful and full-bodied *grand cru.* Nice and quite soft, it lacks a bit of vibrancy, but remains very seductive and harmonious, offering pear, citrus and well-integrated oak flavors. Try now through 2005. 275 cases made. • $95 • (05/31/97) • **88**

Corton-Charlemagne 1994: Ripe, supple and fairly rich, with honey, caramel and fruit flavors. Full-bodied, but a bit too woody. Tasted twice, with consistent notes. • $NA • (08/31/96) • **79**

Corton Les Perrières 1994: Modest in scope for a Corton, with lighter, berrylike flavors that veer toward mineral and anise notes on the chewy finish. Try in 2000. • $48 • (11/15/96) • **80**

Corton Les Perrières 1988 • $54 • (08/31/92) • **75**

Mercurey 1994: Somewhat floral in character, but also a bit herbal and stemmy. Supple tannins, drinkable now. • $26 • (11/15/96) • **75**

Mercurey 1989 • $21/375ml • (08/31/92) • **75**

Mercurey Clos Tonnerre 1994: A sweet tasting but straightforward Burgundy, with a brown-sugar character and supple tannins. Drink now. • $25 • (11/15/96) • **77**

Mercurey Clos Tonnerre 1989 • $24 • (08/31/92) • **85**

Mercurey Clos des Barraults 1995: There are mint and cherry flavors, light-bodied, with a tough, tannic ending. Disappointing for this producer. 580 cases made. • $30 • (11/15/97) • **80**

Mercurey Clos des Barraults White 1996: Straightforward. Medium-bodied, with some decent fruit, supple on the midpalate. Lacks a bit of intensity on the finish; drink now. 500 cases made. • $30 • (05/31/98) • **79**

Mercurey Les Champs Martins 1989 • $24 • (08/31/92) • **84**

Mercurey Les Champs Martins White 1996: Elegant, distinctive and well made. A lush, ripe and thick white, with a supple texture, wonderful sweet-tasting fruit and gobs of citrus. Offers an extra dimension with a mineral, matchstick, earth component that lasts on the long and intense finish. Racy and impressive. Enjoy now through 2005. 250 cases made. • $30 • (05/31/98) • **89**

Mercurey White 1995: Fairly ripe, with pear, tropical fruit and butter aromas. Full-bodied, lacks a bit of elegance, and the wood tastes green. Drink now. 250 cases imported. 1,667 cases made. • $19 • (08/31/97) • **79**

Mercurey White 1994: Rich and unctuous, with a lot of character. Full-bodied, with honey, toasty oak and a chalky, chewy character. Could use a bit more fruit, but it's definitely ready now. 1,583 cases made. • $23 • (05/31/96) • **86**

JUNOT, RENÉ

Vin de Table Français Red NV: An exuberant red, well-balanced and filled with delicious cherry and berry flavors. Plenty of cinnamon and spice as well. Drink now. • $5/1.5 liter • (05/15/98) • **84**

JURAT, CHÂTEAU LE

St.-Emilion 1997: Slightly herbal, with a cut grass and tomato character. Light-bodied, with astringent tannins. • $NA • (06/15/98) (BT) • **75-79**

St.-Emilion 1996: Good berry and tobacco aromas and flavors in this young wine. Medium-bodied, with medium tannins and a chocolaty finish. Medium-term. 4,000 cases made. • $15 • (06/15/98) (BT) • **85-89**

St.-Emilion 1995: A very light '95, with simple berry and cherry character. Light finish. 4,000 cases made. • $NA • (01/01/97) (BT) • **75-79**

St.-Emilion 1994: Fresh, with dark chocolate and berry aromas that echo on the finish. Medium-bodied with fine tannins. Delicious now. 4,083 cases made. • $18 • (01/31/97) • **87**

St.-Emilion 1991: A decent wine with a cherry and berry character, smooth texture and light finish. • $14 • (03/31/94) • **76**

JUSTICES, CHÂTEAU LES

Sauternes 1991: Features some good body and sweetness with honey and lemon character, but appears slightly herbal on the finish. Drinkable now. • $NA • (04/15/95) • **81**

Sauternes 1990: An impressive balance of toasty oak, honey and lemon aromas and flavors, medium-bodied and sweet with a fresh finish. Drink now. • $NA • (04/15/95) • **87**

Sauternes 1989: Plenty of ripe fruit character, showing powerful raisin aromas and flavors of orange, vanilla, cream and honey; long, long finish. Drinkable now. • $23 • (04/15/95) • **91**

Sauternes 1988: Plenty of ripe pear and pineapple flavors and hints of tobacco and almond. Drinkable now. • $9 Ⓐ • (11/15/91) • **87**

Sauternes 1987 • $24 • (06/15/90) • **75**

Sauternes 1986: Light and easy to drink, showing lime and vanilla aromas and flavors, medium sweetness and a light finish. Drinkable now. • $20 • (04/15/95) • **79**

Sauternes 1983: Always a disappointment. Flat and unbalanced. Not very pleasant. Tasted twice, with consistent notes. • $18 • (04/15/95) • **65**

KIENTZLER, ANDRÉ

Pinot d'Alsace Alsace 1993 • $11 • (09/15/95) • **84**

Riesling Alsace Réserve 1993 • $13 • (08/31/95) • **86**

KIRWAN, CHÂTEAU

Margaux 1997: Very well made, with mineral, berry and spice aromas and flavors. Medium-bodied, with a medium finish. • $NA • (06/15/98) (BT) • **85-89**

Margaux 1996: Lots of blackberry and mineral aromas and flavors, with an underlying woodiness. Medium-bodied, with moderate tannins and a medium finish. Clever winemaking. Almost outstanding. • $30 • (06/15/98) (BT) • **85-89**

Margaux 1995: A big, voluptuous red. Best Kirwan ever. Dark ruby in color, with intense blackberry and wet earth aromas. Full-bodied, with luscious ripe fruit and big velvety tannins. Best after 2002. • $30 • (01/31/98) • **93**

Margaux 1994: Enticing aromas of cherries, violets and vanilla. Medium-bodied, with fine tannins and a sweet, fruity, silky finish. Drink now or hold. 10,400 cases made. • $35 • (01/31/97) • **85**

Margaux 1993: One of the better Kirwans in quite a while. Wonderfully aromatic tobacco, earth and red fruit character and hints of smoky oak. Medium in body, medium-fine tannins and fresh finish. Drink now. • $20 • (01/31/96) • **86**

Margaux 1992: Weedy, artichoke flavors, rather simple tobacco and chocolate character; medium tannins and finish. Drinkable now. • $22 • (04/15/95) • **78**

Margaux 1990: A vivacious wine, with lots of ripe fruit, tobacco and cedar character, well-integrated tannins and a long finish. A vast improvement over the '89. Drinkable now. 11,300 cases made. • $28 • (03/31/93) • **90**

Margaux 1989 • $20 Ⓐ • (03/15/92) • **87**

Margaux 1988 • $21 Ⓐ • (04/30/91) • **87**

Margaux 1986 • $25 • (06/30/89) • **82**

Margaux 1985 • $28 Ⓐ • (02/15/89) • **90**

Margaux 1983 • $37 Ⓐ • (07/16/86) • **86**

Margaux 1970 • $50 • (05/15/93) • **86**

Margaux 1945 • $175 • (11/30/95) • **82**

KLUG

Cabernet Sauvignon Merlot Vin de Pays d'Oc Selection des Grands Chais 1994 • $7 • (12/31/95) • **78**

Cabernet Sauvignon Merlot Vin de Pays d'Oc Selection des Grands Chais 1993 • $7 • (07/31/95) • **79**

Chardonnay-Sauvignon Blanc Vin de Pays d'Oc Sélection des Grands Chais 1994 • $7 • (02/29/96) • **81**

Chardonnay Vin de Pays d'Oc Sélection des Grands Chais 1994 • $7 • (02/29/96) • **82**

Merlot Vin de Pays d'Oc Selection des Grands Chais 1994 • $7 • (12/31/95) • **75**

Key: SS—Spectator Selection CS—Cellar Selection HR—Highly Recommended BB—Best Buy $NA—Price not available Ⓐ—Auction Price (BT)—Barrel Tasting
Dates in parentheses indicate the issues in which the ratings were published.

KREYDENWEISS, MARC

Riesling Alsace Andlau 1994: Well balanced and quite full-bodied, this shows ripe peach, mineral and floral flavors with very firm acidity and a fresh finish. Try with spicy fish dishes. • $18 • (09/30/96) • **86**

Riesling Alsace Grand Cru Andlau 1993 • $18 • (02/29/96) • **81**

Riesling Alsace Grand Cru Kastelberg 1993 • $34 • (02/29/96) • **78**

Riesling Alsace Grand Cru Wiebelsberg 1994: Soft and round, with spicy vanilla and cream flavors in a late-harvest style. Tighter mineral and grapefruit flavors emerge on the finish. Not one for long-term aging but seductive now. • $28 • (10/15/96) • **85**

Riesling Alsace Grand Cru Wiebelsberg 1993 • $28 • (05/15/96) • **82**

Tokay Pinot Gris Alsace Grand Cru Moenchberg 1993 • $32 • (02/29/96) • **85**

Tokay Pinot Gris Alsace Lerchenberg 1994: Intense and ripe. Assertive flavors of spice, honey and chocolate are rich and dark, polished and long. Though not overly sweet, this would make a delicious after-dinner treat. • $22 • (09/30/96) • **89**

KRUG

Brut Blanc de Blancs Champagne Clos du Mesnil 1985: Classic in balance, harmony and flavor. Displays a fantastic combination of mature flavors and plush texture, with a sense of freshness and vibrancy that elevates it well above the outstanding level. Drink now through 2000. Far better than when tasted last year. • $210 • (12/31/97) • **96**

Brut Blanc de Blancs Champagne Clos du Mesnil 1983: Good example of a mature Champagne. Full-bodied, assertive flavor and intriguingly nutty in character, showing lingering walnut, cider and mushroom notes. Some will love this, but it's not for everyone. • $229 • (11/30/95) • **88**

Brut Blanc de Blancs Champagne Clos du Mesnil 1982: • $150 • (12/31/90) • **84**

Brut Blanc de Blancs Champagne Clos du Mesnil 1981 • $140 • (12/31/90) • **87**

Brut Blanc de Blancs Champagne Clos du Mesnil 1980 • $100 • (05/31/87) • **80**

Brut Champagne 1989: Rich in texture and character, elegant in balance and long on the finish, this vintage bubbly is its own cause for celebration. A unique spicy quality adds complexity to the already deep, persistent flavors. Enjoy now through 2000. Tasted twice, with consistent notes. • $125 • (11/30/97) CS • **94**

Brut Champagne 1985: A seductive, fully mature, spicy-flavored Champagne that's rich in texture, full in body, still quite firm in balance and long on the finish. What a satisfying taste experience! Ready to drink now. • $120 • (12/31/96) • **94**

Brut Champagne 1982: If you like your Champagne very mature, drink this. Superbly rich, with bread dough and vanilla and ripe fruit aromas and flavors. Full bodied yet fine with mature and rich flavors. Drink now. • $130 • (12/31/93) • **90**

Brut Champagne 1981 • $105 • (08/31/92) • **88**

Brut Champagne 1979 • $120 • (08/31/92) • **84**

Brut Champagne 1976: Proudly shows its age in the honeyed, nutty, smoky flavors, but retains freshness and is crisp in texture, letting the complex flavors last and linger on the long finish. Complete, harmonious and distinctive. Even better than when tasted in 1992. • $280 • (12/31/96) • **93**

Brut Champagne 1973 • $530 • (08/31/92) • **92**

Brut Champagne 1971 • $200 • (08/31/92) • **87**

Brut Champagne 1969 • $370 • (08/31/92) • **89**

Brut Champagne 1966 • $210 • (08/31/92) • **89**

Brut Champagne 1964 • $230 • (08/31/92) • **95**

Brut Champagne 1962 • $250 • (08/31/92) • **96**

Brut Champagne 1961 • $210 • (08/31/92) • **82**

Brut Champagne 1959 • $280 • (08/31/92) • **92**

Brut Champagne 1955 • $260 • (08/31/92) • **92**

Brut Champagne 1953 • $300 • (08/31/92) • **89**

Brut Champagne 1952 • $300 • (08/31/92) • **91**

Brut Champagne 1949 • $330 • (08/31/92) • **85**

Brut Champagne 1947 • $450 • (08/31/92) • **98**

Brut Champagne 1945 • $500 • (08/31/92) • **93**

Brut Champagne 1942 • $500 • (08/31/92) • **90**

Brut Champagne 1938 • $500 • (08/31/92) • **91**

Brut Champagne 1937 • $950 • (08/31/92) • **96**

Brut Champagne 1929 • $1500 • (08/31/92) • **94**

Brut Champagne 1928 • $1500 • (08/31/92) • **95**

Brut Champagne Collection 1976: A rare, old gem of a Champagne with subtle, sophisticated, mature flavors and a light, delicate texture. Very dry but not austere, it seems to expand with each sip, and the finish lingers for minutes. Best now. • $249 Ⓐ • (12/31/97) • **93**

Brut Champagne Grande Cuvée NV: An unusually mature style of non-vintage Champagne that blends nutty, buttery aromas with crisp, lemony flavors. Full-bodied and creamy in texture. Tasted twice, with consistent notes. • $100 • (11/15/97) • **87**

Brut Champagne Private Cuvée 1947: Shows earthy, toasty, complex flavors, with some freshness, but it's an old bottle of a mature Champagne, with all the complexity and richness one could want. • $NA • (07/31/97) • **92**

Brut Rosé Champagne NV: A rosé of exceptional character and finesse. Beautifully integrated layers of subtle ginger, orange zest, toast and vanilla give it complexity and depth, and the rich but light texture makes it sublime to sip. A long, long finish completes the seamless package. 1,250 cases made. • $150 • (12/31/97) • **95**

KUENTZ-BAS

Pinot Blanc Alsace 1995: A subtle, understated style, with modest apple and lemon character. Vibrant and appealing, with a mouth-watering finish. • $15 • (09/15/97) • **83**

L DE LA LOUVIÈRE

Pessac-Léognan 1996: Good plum, berry and vanilla aromas highlight this medium-bodied wine, with slightly odd, earthy berry flavors and a short finish. • $NA • (01/01/97) (BT) • **75-79**

Pessac-Léognan 1995: A fresh, easy-to-drink red, with cherry, berry and a hint of herbs. Medium-bodied, medium tannins. Second label of Château La Louvière. Drink now or hold. • $15 • (01/31/98) • **82**

Pessac-Léognan 1994: This is pretty, with chocolate and berry flavors and silky tannins. Shows good fruit, and has a fresh, slightly herbal finish. Drink now or hold. • $15 • (01/31/97) • **84**

Pessac-Léognan 1993: Fresh and vibrant, sporting a feeling of juicy, grapey fruit on the palate and ending in nice, crisp acidity. Shows some tomato, herb, plum and mocha aromas and flavors. Drinkable now. • $15 • (01/31/96) • **80**

Pessac-Léognan White 1995: Promises more on the nose than it gives on the palate, with subtle apple, grass and mineral aromas. Medium-bodied, with lovely cut apple flavors. Slightly simple aftertaste. Drink now. • $15 • (04/30/98) • **84**

Pessac-Léognan White 1994: An honest, wonderfully fruity white wine with a lively texture, bright citrus flavors and a lingering finish. Refreshing and enjoyable. • $14 • (05/31/97) • **89**

Pessac-Léognan White 1993 • $15 • (05/31/95) • **86**

LABAT, CHÂTEAU

Haut-Médoc 1997: Dried cherry aromas and flavors. Medium-bodied, with a hollow midpalate and a slightly hard finish. • $NA • (06/15/98) (BT) • **80-84**

Haut-Médoc 1996: Raspberry and mineral aromas and flavors through and through. Medium-bodied, with fine tannins and a medium finish. Shows finesse. • $23 • (06/15/98) (BT) • **85-89**

Haut-Médoc 1995: Loads of fruit in this, but slightly one-dimensional. Alluring aromas of raspberries and currants. Medium- to full-bodied, with velvety tannins and caressing texture. Second label of Château Caronne-Ste.-Gemme. • $22 • (01/31/98) • **87**

Haut-Médoc 1981 • $7 • (04/01/85) • **72**

LABÉGORCE, CHÂTEAU

Margaux 1995: Thick, rich, ripe, concentrated and seductive. Balanced and full-bodied, delivering tons of red berry, tar and earth character. Melts like butter, but it has a lot of sweet fruit and solid tannins. Almost outstanding. • $NA • (05/15/96) (BT) • **85-89**

Margaux 1991: Light and diluted, with tobacco and tomato aromas and flavors. • $14 • (03/31/94) • **74**

Margaux 1990: A wine made from overripe grapes with a rather stewed fruit character. Full-bodied and raisiny, with full tannins. Drinkable now. 11,000 cases made. • $20 • (03/31/93) • **82**

Margaux 1987 • $13 • (03/31/91) • **77**

Margaux 1986 • $15 • (02/15/90) • **86**

Margaux 1982 • $20 • (08/31/92) • **88**

LABÉGORCE-ZÉDÉ, CHÂTEAU

Margaux 1995: A compact, lively '95, showing stunning blackberries, violets and fruit. Full-bodied, yet quite hemmed-in. Racy tannins on the finish. Best after 2001. • $22 • (01/31/98) • **89**

Margaux 1992: A polished Bordeaux providing good color and berry and raspberry aromas, but slightly diluted on the finish. Drink now. • $14 • (04/15/95) • **79**

Margaux 1991: A solid wine with a refined berry and smoke character, medium body and velvety tannins. • $14 • (03/31/94) • **84**

Margaux 1990: Subtle, with aromas of cinnamon, tobacco, and plums that follow through to the palate. Ultrafine tannins. Drinkable now. 9,500 cases made. • $22 • (03/31/93) • **89**

Margaux 1989 • $20 • (03/15/92) • **86**

Margaux 1988 • $20 • (04/30/91) • **83**

Margaux 1987 • $16 • (11/30/89) • **84**

Margaux 1986 • $22 • (11/30/89) • **91**

Margaux 1985 • $38 Ⓐ • (02/29/88) • **84**

Margaux 1983 • $15 • (10/15/86) • **88**

Margaux 1982 • $21 • (11/30/89) • **87**

LABET, PIERRE

Beaune Aux Coucherias 1995: Dry and astringent, lacking in fruit, with some lifted, volatile aromas. • $37 • (11/15/97) • **75**

Beaune Aux Coucherias 1993: Convoluted style, showing ripe, slightly raisiny character and a dry, tannic finish. Perhaps better in time • $26 • (11/15/95) • **73**

Beaune Aux Coucherias 1992: Light and pleasant, with some attractive licorice, smoke, spice and red berry flavors around a tannic core that needs time to smooth out. • $26 • (12/15/94) • **80**

Beaune Aux Coucherias 1991: Woody and harsh, with little roundness of fruit to relieve the tough texture. Finishes mercifully short. • $32 Ⓐ • (01/31/94) • **66**

Beaune Aux Coucherias 1990: An elegant Beaune that's supple and lovely, with plenty of earthy plum characteristics and well-integrated tannins. A joy to drink now. • $35 • (12/15/92) • **88**

Beaune Clos des Monsnières 1995: Lacking in elegance but distinctive in style, with aromas of earth and red licorice. Tastes ripe and sweet, with red berry flavors packed in. Loads of tannins, slightly astringent. Try after 2000. • $34 • (11/15/97) • **83**

Beaune Clos des Monsnières 1994: Already showing an orange-tint to its color, this very light Burgundy has a roséIike texture and is extremely diluted. • $29 • (11/15/96) • **70**

Beaune Clos des Monsnières White 1996: Full-bodied, reserved and backward on the deep nose, but bursting with honey, ripe fruit and acidity on the palate, which it coats with a silky, creamlike texture. Try now through 2010. Nice effort for a communal appellation. 500 cases made. • $33 • (05/31/98) • **90**

Beaune Les Monsnières White 1994: A bit odd, with a perfumy, floral character. Modest fruit intensity and some cardboard notes. • $26 • (05/31/96) • **70**

Beaune Les Chouacheux 1994: Despite some interesting plum and dried herb flavors, the mouthfeel is one of dilution. Drink chilled. • $35 • (11/15/96) • **73**

Beaune Les Monsnières 1993: Lovely ripe strawberry character in this slightly simple but well-structured red that features firm tannins and a medium body of fruit. Try now. • $20 • (11/15/95) • **87**

Beaune Les Monsnières 1991: Extremely earthy, with anise and mud aromas and flavors; never becomes charming or shows much fruit. • $25 Ⓐ • (01/31/94) • **70**

Beaune Les Monsnières 1990: Stylish, aromatic and beautiful, with ripe, appealing plum, earth and chocolate flavors lingering on the firm but round finish. Drinkable now. • $30 • (12/15/92) • **89**

Bourgogne 1995: Licorice, smoke and earth are the main components of this rustic red. Try now. • $10 • (11/15/97) • **78**

Bourgogne 1994: Some appealing, sweet-tasting character in this otherwise light wine. Rather crisp finish. • $21 • (11/15/96) • **77**

Pinot Noir Bourgogne 1993: Pleasantly juicy and vibrant, showing some plum, currant and earth flavors. Tannins creep up on the finish. Try now. • $14 • (11/15/95) • **84**

Savigny-lès-Beaune Aux Vergelesses White 1994: Attractive, pleasant, moderate intensity, with a nice tropical character in its banana, pear and apple flavors. Lacks concentration, but nice all the same. • $34 • (05/31/96) • **84**

LABET & N. DECHELETTE, J.

Clos Vougeot Château de la Tour 1991: Light and affable, showing a decent level of berry flavor and an overlay of earthy, stalky notes. Tries hard to be likable, and mostly succeeds. Drinkable now. • $60 Ⓐ • (01/31/94) • **84**
Clos Vougeot Château de la Tour 1988 • $50 • (11/30/90) • **91**
Clos Vougeot Château de la Tour 1987 • $50 • (02/15/91) • **84**
Clos Vougeot Château de la Tour 1985 • $60 • (06/15/88) • **90**

LABOROTTE, LA

Cornas 1991 • $NA • (05/31/94) • **82**

LABOURÉ-ROI

Beaujolais-Villages 1995: Light and crisp, offering tart cherry and light herb flavors. A hint of spritz keeps it lively but amplifies the tartness. • $9 • (09/15/97) • **78**
Bonnes Mares 1990: What a disappointment for a *grand cru*. Firm in texture, with a modest level of cherry and toast flavors peeking through the veil of tannin. Try now. 106 cases made. • $56 • (06/15/93) • **78**
Bonnes Mares 1989 • $55 • (08/31/92) • **92**
Bourgogne 1993: A bit earthy but some decent berry and cherry aromas and flavors, medium body and dry tannins. • $9 • (11/15/95) • **80**
Bourgogne 1991: Fresh and fruity, offering appealing strawberry, black cherry and spice aromas and flavors that persist on the soft finish, where it echoes a touch of stemminess. Drinkable now. 1,500 cases made. • $8 • (06/15/93) BB • **83**
Bourgogne 1989 • $8 • (08/31/92) • **83**
Bourgogne 1988 • $12 • (03/31/91) • **83**
Bourgogne White 1993: Seems advanced for its age, presenting oaky, drying, grassy flavors. • $8 • (05/15/95) • **70**
Bourgogne White 1992: Ripe, with exaggerated varietal flavors of sweet apple and fig. It lacks freshness and turns flat on the finish. A dull wine that has little concentration. 7,500 cases made. • $8 • (01/01/95) • **76**
Chablis 1994 • $19 • (08/31/95) • **84**
Chablis Fourchaume 1993 • $17 • (08/31/95) • **82**
Chablis Les Clos 1993 • $NA • (08/31/95) • **80**
Chambertin 1989 • $55 • (08/31/92) • **88**
Chambertin Clos de Bèze 1989 • $60 • (08/31/92) • **84**
Chambolle-Musigny 1991: A healthy dose of oak adds attractive vanilla and brown-sugar notes to the cherry and strawberry flavors in this silky wine. It's harmonious, lean and tannic. Drinkable now. • $30 • (01/31/95) • **85**
Chambolle-Musigny 1990: Light in texture but generous in flavor, with appealing raspberry, earth and spice aromas and flavors that persist into a firm, focused finish. Drinkable now. 1,600 cases made. • $20 • (06/15/93) • **84**
Chambolle-Musigny 1988 • $35 • (02/28/91) • **86**
Chambolle-Musigny Domaine Cottin 1989 • $30 • (03/31/92) • **76**
Charmes-Chambertin 1993: Crisp, well-defined, lovely red berry flavors, medium body and massive but nicely integrated tannins. Try now. • $59 • (11/15/95) • **86**
Charmes-Chambertin 1990: Ripe, generous and flavorful, with an odd anise edge to the basic berry and cherry flavors. Smooth and round, turning a bit soft and watery on the finish. Drinkable now. 125 cases made. • $45 • (06/15/93) • **85**
Chassagne-Montrachet 1993: Subtle green apple, honey and toasty oak aromas and flavors. Medium-bodied and fresh with a honeyed finish. Slight dilution. Drink now. • $23 • (05/15/95) • **85**
Chassagne-Montrachet 1992: An oaky, stiff-textured white with appley and buttery aromas, woody-buttery flavors and vanilla on the finish. • $NA • (08/31/94) • **81**
Chassagne-Montrachet Caillerets 1993: Sort of showy, lots of toasty oak character mingling with the lemon and apple flavors. Rather lean and tart; a bit too woody for us. • $25 • (05/15/95) • **84**
Clos de Vougeot 1993: Good, silky texture with medium and fine tannins but slightly herbal and weedy on the finish. Disappointing for this appellation. Try now. • $57 • (11/15/95) • **80**
Clos de Vougeot 1990: A firm, focused wine that's lighter in style and elegant, offering strawberry, orange-peel and cherry aromas and flavors. Finishes tight and a bit astringent. Drinkable now. 165 cases made. • $44 • (06/15/93) • **83**
Corton-Charlemagne 1993: Tart, firm and muscular, showing a tight core of mineral, lime and green apple flavors and elegance on the finish. Try now. • $52 • (05/15/95) • **82**
Crozes-Hermitage 1991 • $9 • (06/15/93) • **86**
Echézeaux 1993: Fresh and crisp, medium-bodied, showing lively, vivid flavors and silky texture. A touch of chocolate and mocha adds complexity to the raspberry and currant notes. Try now through 2000. • $54 • (11/15/95) • **89**
Echézeaux 1990: This is an Echézeaux? Light, simple and firm in texture, with little intensity. Drinkable now but boring. 210 cases made. • $36 • (06/15/93) • **80**
Gevrey-Chambertin 1993: Amazingly refined for a simple village wine, offering vibrant plum, currant and earth aromas. Medium in body, solid fruit and long, silky finish. • $22 • (11/15/95) • **87**
Gevrey-Chambertin 1991: There's plenty of fruit here, ripe blackberry and plum flavors in a round, almost jammy structure, with spicy oak and chocolate notes. Lacks subtlety, but has good concentration. Drinkable now. • $22 • (01/31/95) • **85**
Gevrey-Chambertin 1990: Firm in texture, with solid black cherry and currant flavors that try to get past the gravelly tannins and succeed in part. Drinkable now. 1,600 cases made. • $20 • (06/15/93) • **83**
Gevrey-Chambertin 1988 • $35 • (12/31/90) • **81**
Mâcon Blanc-Villages 1994: Interesting roasted pine-nut, grapefruit and pear flavors. Crisp, but slightly diluted and astringent finish. 9,000 cases made. • $10 • (08/31/95) • **79**
Mazis-Chambertin 1990: Tough and tannic, with more earthy, stemmy flavors than fruit, although hints of nice strawberry and spice come through on the finish. Drinkable now. 106 cases made. • $29 • (06/15/93) • **79**
Meursault 1993: Plenty of mineral, apple, floral, citrus character. Medium in body, tart acidity and herbal finish. • $22 • (05/15/95) • **82**
Meursault 1992: Rich, ripe and well-made Meursault, delivering a lush character, with toast, butter, hazelnut and wet earth flavors that all add up to fine complexity. • $NA • (08/31/94) • **87**
Meursault Red 1993: Not a big wine, but this delicate, perfumy Burgundy is pleasurable to taste. Light in color and body, offering sweet-tasting raspberry and cassis flavors. Enjoy on release. • $22 • (11/15/95) • **83**
Montagny 1993: Nice, lush and supple. Offers some ripe pineapple, pear and green apple flavors and turns lemony and crisp on the finish. • $NA • (05/15/95) • **83**
Nuits-St.-Georges 1993: Simple and very light with some fruit, but rather weedy and dry on the finish. • $27 • (11/15/95) • **75**
Nuits-St.-Georges 1991: An attractive wine with flavors that blend smoky oak and spicy fruit. It's on the light side, stylish and smooth, with a fresh, lingering finish. Drinkable now. • $28 • (01/31/95) • **86**
Nuits-St.-Georges 1990: Tight and firm, but a floral, plummy cherry edge and crisp tannins remind you that this a young, unevolved wine. Drinkable now. 1,500 cases made. • $20 • (06/15/93) • **86**
Pommard 1993: Crisp and fresh, showing good intensity of blackberry flavor on a relatively lean frame. Clean as can be, but you wish for some more concentration. Try on release. • $24 • (11/15/95) • **84**
Pommard 1991: Solid and a bit rustic, this wine shows ripe black cherry and attractive earthy flavors, with fair concentration leading to a lingering but slightly dry finish. Drinkable now. • $24 • (01/31/95) • **85**
Pommard 1990: Young, tight and compact, with spicy plum and cherry aromas. Firm and tannic, too, but the core of fruit flavor needs time to evolve. Drinkable now. 1,000 cases made. • $20 • (06/15/93) • **85**
Pommard Les Bertins 1993: Captivating fruit, tasting like freshly crushed raspberries and cherries and adding a light mineral character. Medium in body, tannins and finish. Try now. • $29 • (11/15/95) • **86**
Pommard Les Bertins 1985 • $29 • (03/15/88) • **79**
Puligny-Montrachet 1993: Vivid golden color, vibrant; demonstrates mostly grapefruit flavors and a hint of honey. Elegant, juicy finish. • $24 • (05/15/95) • **84**
Puligny-Montrachet Les Chalumaux 1993: Medium-bodied; quite green, grassy and aggressive, offering some lime, green apple and herb flavors. Drinkable now. • $30 • (05/15/95) • **81**
Richebourg 1990: Light in color and intensity, this is pleasant enough, but simple and fruity. The strawberry and spice notes are nice, but it's more like a simple Chassagne than an exalted Richebourg. 180 cases made. • $71 • (06/15/93) • **84**
St.-Véran 1994: Too oaky, tasting more of freshly cut wood boards than wine, but the sweet vanilla shadings and pear and citrus flavors finish nicely. 25,000 cases made. • $8 • (08/31/95) • **77**

Key: SS—Spectator Selection CS—Cellar Selection HR—Highly Recommended BB—Best Buy $NA—Price not available Ⓐ—Auction Price (BT)—Barrel Tasting
Dates in parentheses indicate the issues in which the ratings were published.

St.-Véran 1993: Gentle, nicely balanced, presenting lime, earth, wet straw and green apple flavors and a lively, fresh finish. • $9 • (01/01/95) • **83**

Vosne-Romanée 1991: This gentle, mellow wine offers attractive cherry, spice and toast flavors. Soft and subtle, it's easy to drink now, but shouldn't be held. • $23 • (01/31/95) • **83**

LABRY, A. & B.

Auxey-Duresses Red 1995: Good expression of Pinot Noir in this polished, modern-style red. The black-fruit flavors are concentrated, if not very complex. Drinkable now. 1,000 cases made. • $17 • (11/15/97) • **84**

Auxey-Duresses Red 1992: Pretty, floral aromas and bright cherry and strawberry flavors distinguish this red of firm texture and medium body. Drink now, while it's charming and delicious. 1,500 cases made. • $16 • (05/15/95) • **87**

LACAUSSADE-ST.-MARTIN, CHÂTEAU

Premières Côtes de Blaye 1996: A bit funky in flavor, but with decent grape and berry. Medium- to light-bodied, with a short finish. • $22 • (06/15/98) (BT) • **75-79**

LACHESNAYE, CHÂTEAU

Haut-Médoc 1992: Light and earthy, with a tobacco, watery, cherry character. • $18 • (04/15/95) • **70**

Haut-Médoc 1990: Well crafted, with rich, earthy, cherry aromas and flavors and a wonderful balance of silky tannins. The finish is long. Drinkable now. • $17 • (03/31/93) • **88**

LACHETEAU

Vouvray 1996: Cooked apple and cinnamon flavors are soft and a bit sweet. Lacks focus, but would make a nice apéritif, on ice with soda. Drink now. 4,000 cases made. • $12 • (06/30/98) • **79**

LACLAVERIE, CHÂTEAU

Côtes de Francs 1997: OK berry and earth aromas and flavors, but a bit lacking in fruit on the palate. • $NA • (06/15/98) (BT) • **75-79**

Côtes de Francs 1996: Rather light and diluted, with tobacco, weed and berry character, but lacks a consistent palate. Tasted twice, with consistent notes. • $20 • (06/15/98) (BT) • **75-79**

LACOMBE-NOAILLAC, CHÂTEAU

Médoc 1997: Weedy and grassy, with an earthy chestnut aftertaste. • $NA • (06/15/98) (BT) • **75-79**

Médoc 1996: Lovely, with red berry and cassis aromas and flavors. Medium-bodied, with medium tannins and a light aftertaste. 1,600 cases made. • $17 • (06/15/98) (BT) • **80-84**

Médoc 1995: Rather light and weedy, with some berry, tomato character, Light-to-medium body and a fresh finish. Drink now. 14,000 cases made. • $15 • (01/31/98) • **79**

Médoc 1994: Pretty plum and earth aromas, but it could use a greater concentration of fruit on the palate. Medium-bodied and lean, with hard tannins. Try now. 15,000 cases made. • $15 • (01/31/97) • **79**

LACOSTE-BORIE

Pauillac 1993: Medium-bodied but rather diluted plum, herbal, metallic character. • $19 • (01/31/96) • **75**

Pauillac 1990: Plenty of smoky, ripe raspberry aromas and fruit and a smooth texture with integrated tannins. A wine for early drinking. • $18 • (03/31/93) • **87**

Pauillac 1989 • $15 • (03/15/92) • **89**

Pauillac 1988 • $19 • (04/30/91) • **89**

Pauillac 1986 • $15 • (06/30/89) • **84**

Pauillac 1983 • $7 • (06/15/87) • **75**

LADAU, CHÂTEAU DE

Coteaux du Languedoc 1991 • $NA • (03/15/94) • **82**

LADOUCETTE, DE

Pouilly-Fumé 1995: Round and ripe, this offers more fruit than most in its category, with pear, apple and melon notes, but still has crisp acidity for balance. Has more weight than intensity, but makes a fine match with food. Drink now. • $29 • (06/15/98) • **87**

Pouilly-Fumé 1994: Muscular, showing firm acidity and enticing, smoky flavors. It's quite tart, and not showing much fruit, but should open with food. • $29 • (04/30/97) • **85**

Pouilly-Fumé 1993 • $25 • (04/30/96) • **87**

Sancerre Comte Lafond 1996: This keen white has a lovely balance of grapefruit, mineral and herbal flavors, lively and well defined. Not rich, but graceful and long. Drink now. • $28 • (06/15/98) • **87**

Sancerre Comte Lafond 1995: Complex yet well balanced, this alluring white marries steely acidity with ripe, almost lush fruit flavors and light smoke notes. Irresistible. • $28 • (05/15/97) • **90**

LAFARGE, MICHEL

Meursault 1992: Simple and straightforward. Shows plenty of lime, grapefruit and green apple flavors, but overall it seems rather dull. Tasted twice, with similar results. 180 cases made. • $NA • (08/31/94) • **78**

Pinot Noir Bourgogne 1992: Modest and straightforward, with some strawberry and plum flavors. • $20 • (12/15/94) • **72**

Pinot Noir Bourgogne 1990: Light and simple, but we love those smoky, toasty, gamy flavors that complement the strawberry notes. Drink now. 540 cases made. • $18 • (12/15/92) • **82**

Pinot Noir Bourgogne 1989 • $19 • (01/31/92) • **85**

Volnay 1992: Crisp and lively, with modest berry and floral flavors kicking in on the finish. • $35 • (12/15/94) • **80**

Volnay 1991: Crisp, light, simple and straightforward. An earthy, drying note takes the edge off the fruit. Drinkable now. 333 cases made. • $38 Ⓐ • (01/31/94) • **77**

Volnay 1990: Well made and subtle, with a sense of elegance despite the intensity from the deeply concentrated earth, ripe black cherry and plum flavors. The finish is beautiful and smooth. Drinkable now. • $43 • (12/15/92) • **90**

Volnay 1989 • $41 • (01/31/92) • **88**

Volnay Clos des Chênes 1994: Silky as can be yet powerful and concentrated, this complex, deep, flavorful and classy wine amazes the senses with all its subtle toasty oak, mocha, red- and blackberry and earth character. Displays real *goût de terroir*. Wonderful quality for this difficult vintage, from an old Volnay master. Tempting now, better after 2003. 250 cases made. • $70 • (09/30/97) • **92**

Volnay Clos des Chênes 1993: Not quite as exciting as his Clos du Château des Ducs yet lovely, fruity and intensely flavored nonetheless. medium-to-full body, zingy acidity; turns silky on the finish. Approachable now, but probably will improve. • $94 • (05/15/96) • **88**

Volnay Clos des Chênes 1992: Very pretty, with polished blackberry and black cherry character, turning spicy and crisp on the finish. Drinkable now. • $65 • (12/15/94) • **85**

Volnay Clos des Chênes 1991: Delicious and supple, with superbly focused floral, raspberry and strawberry flavors and fine tannins. Ready to enjoy now. • $62 • (02/28/95) • **92**

Volnay Clos des Chênes 1990: Ripe and rich, bursting with currant and blackberry, then becoming a little chewy on the finish. Youthful, exuberant and flavorful without being heavy. Drinkable now. • $75 • (02/28/95) • **94**

Volnay Clos des Chênes 1989 • $67 • (02/28/95) • **93**

Volnay Clos des Chênes 1988 • $72 • (02/28/95) • **89**

Volnay Clos des Chênes 1987 • $52 • (02/28/95) • **88**

Volnay Clos des Chênes 1986 • $39 • (02/28/95) • **87**

Volnay Clos des Chênes 1985 • $75 • (02/28/95) • **89**

Volnay Clos des Chênes 1983 • $NA • (02/28/95) • **82**

Volnay Clos du Château des Ducs 1994: Firm and flavorful, of medium body and succulent, with lovely flower, currant and wild berry character. Quite tannic and hard to warm up to now, but let the oak settle, the fruit flavors integrate, and try around 2000. 200 cases made. • $70 • (09/30/97) • **87**

Volnay Clos du Château des Ducs 1993: Vibrant and lovely cherry and plum flavors and a hint of bark. Medium in body, adding soft tannins, sweet fruit and succulent finish. Try now. • $65 • (11/15/95) • **93**

Volnay Clos du Château des Ducs 1992: Light, a little chewy, but the ripe black cherry flavors and tobacco and earth overtones persist into the finish. Drinkable now. • $65 • (12/15/94) • **83**

Volnay Clos du Château des Ducs 1991: A firm, chunky, solid wine that features generous raspberry, anise and currant aromas and flavors. Finishes

FRANCE

with depth, a sense of refinement and elegance. Drinkable now. 333 cases made. • $62 Ⓐ • (01/31/94) • **86**

Volnay Clos du Château des Ducs 1990: Just gorgeous, with startling violet, tobacco, red berry and earth aromas that are echoed on the palate. The tannins are refined and it's drinkable now. This vineyard site is a monopole, meaning that only Lafarge makes wine from it. 325 cases made. • $75 • (12/15/92) • **95**

Volnay Clos du Château des Ducs 1989 • $67 • (01/31/92) • **94**

Volnay Clos du Château des Ducs 1988 • $65 • (07/15/91) • **90**

Volnay Premier Cru 1988 • $44 • (07/15/91) • **87**

Volnay Vendanges Sélectionées 1992: Bright and aromatic, but it turns crisp and not very generous in flavor. Try now. • $40 • (12/15/94) • **81**

Volnay Vendanges Sélectionées 1991: Light and tart; displays pretty raspberry and floral aromas and flavors and a bite of tannin on the finish. Try now. 415 cases made. • $40 Ⓐ • (01/31/94) • **82**

LAFAURIE-PEYRAGUEY, CHÂTEAU

Sauternes 1995: A Sauternes for early drinking. Lovely aromas of coconut and honey with hints of dried apricot. Medium-bodied and sweet, with a lemon pie aftertaste. Drink now. • $30 • (04/30/98) • **87**

Sauternes 1992: Very impressive for the vintage. Medium-bodied and medium- sweet, showing tropical, mineral, lemon and honey flavors that offer plenty of pleasure on the pretty finish. Drinkable now. • $NA • (04/15/95) • **86**

Sauternes 1991: Very sweet and soft, displaying an opulent texture and some cedar, caramel and butterscotch flavors. Drinkable now. • $NA • (04/15/95) • **80**

Sauternes 1990: Gorgeous, classy, appealing creamy texture, lemon, honey and dried apricot flavors, medium body and sweetness and a long finish. Drink now or hold through the decade. • $43 • (04/15/95) • **90**

Sauternes 1989: Unforgettable; packs it in and doesn't pull punches, displaying chewy, bold, toasty oak character and honey, spice, dried apricot and pineapple flavors that end in a fresh finish. Drinkable now. • $50 • (04/15/95) • **94**

Sauternes 1988: Elegant yet intense, medium-bodied; offers plenty of refined toast, vanilla, butter, honey, lemon-pie and spice flavors and a long, long finish. Try now. • $45 • (04/15/95) • **89**

Sauternes 1987 • $27 • (06/15/90) • **87**

Sauternes 1986: Creamy and buttery with custard, spice and oaky flavors that are very sweet and rich. Drinkable now or in the next three to five years. • $30 • (12/31/89) • **86**

Sauternes 1985: Rich and complex, with hazelnut, ginger and orange overtones to the classic fig and tobacco Sauternes flavors. Earthy and sophisticated, long and elegant. Easily one of the best Sauternes of this vintage. • $32 • (09/30/88) • **92**

Sauternes 1983: A vibrant, beautifully balanced wine, lingering on the finish, with good acidity to keep you coming back for more. Medium-gold, with lots of ripe apple, pear, spice, delicacy, depth and a fair amount of wood. • $40 • (01/31/88) • **91**

LAFERRERE, HUBERT

Mâcon 1996: Racy but a bit lean, with lemon and pear character. A slight herbal note takes over on the drying finish. Drink now. 1,160 cases made. • $17 • (05/31/98) • **81**

Mâcon-Chardonnay Hand Picked 1995: A decent Mâcon with a fresh, fruit character. Straightforward, light-bodied, crisp on the finish. Drink now. 1,083 cases made. • $19 • (05/31/97) • **80**

LAFITE ROTHSCHILD, CHÂTEAU

Pauillac 1997: Harmonious, with plenty of tobacco and cherry character and a full-bodied core of fruit and tannins. Long finish. Has the clarity of Margaux fruit with the richness and complexity of Haut-Brion. The best of the first growths and perhaps the wine of the vintage. • $NA • (06/15/98) (BT) • **90-94**

Pauillac 1996: It was outstanding last year—now it's great. Massive, rich red with wild tobacco and berry character. Full-bodied, with velvety tannins and a long, long finish. Stunning. One of the wines of the vintage. • $190 • (06/15/98) (BT) • **95-99**

Pauillac 1995: Here's the best Lafite in ages. It's a polished Bordeaux, extremely sophisticated and harmonious, with blackberry, dark chocolate and olive aromas. Full-bodied and very silky, with a lovely fruity chocolate aftertaste. Best after 2000, but who can wait? • $275 • (01/31/98) CS • **97**

Pauillac 1994: A luscious Lafite that is silky and elegant with layers of wonderful violet, berry, cherry and chocolate flavors. It's full-bodied, with racy, refined tannins and good length. Drinkable now, but best from 1999 and through another decade. 18,750 cases made. • $200 • (01/31/97) CS • **93**

Pauillac 1993: Very polished and well-crafted black cherry, toast, earth and mineral flavors, all in nice proportions. Medium body, supple tannins. Slightly disappointing for Lafite. Drinkable now. Tasted twice, with consistent notes. • $72 • (01/31/96) • **86**

Pauillac 1992: A real achievement for the vintage, boasting plenty of fruit, tobacco and dark chocolate character. Full-bodied and velvety; impressive richness of ripe tannins. Drinkable now. • $65 • (04/15/95) • **89**

Pauillac 1991: A balanced, supple wine, with lovely blackberry, complex vanilla and ripe sweetness. Tasted twice with consistent notes. • $60 • (03/31/94) • **85**

Pauillac 1990: The great first-growth estate produced a wine with amazing length in this new vintage. Goes on and on, with mint, plum and cassis aromas and flavors and ultrafine tannins. A superb Bordeaux. Drinkable now. • $550 • (03/31/93) • **97**

Pauillac 1989 • $113 Ⓐ • (03/15/92) • **95**

Pauillac 1988 • $104 Ⓐ • (11/30/91) • **94**

Pauillac 1987 • $46 Ⓐ • (11/30/91) • **88**

Pauillac 1986 • $141 Ⓐ • (11/30/91) • **96**

Pauillac 1985 • $101 Ⓐ • (10/15/94) • **95**

Pauillac 1984 • $39 Ⓐ • (11/30/91) • **87**

Pauillac 1983 • $90 • (10/15/94) • **91**

Pauillac 1982 • $243 Ⓐ • (08/31/92) • **97**

Pauillac 1981 • $73 Ⓐ • (10/15/94) • **88**

Pauillac 1980 • $38 Ⓐ • (11/30/91) • **86**

Pauillac 1979 • $88 Ⓐ • (11/30/91) • **92**

Pauillac 1978 • $92 Ⓐ • (11/30/91) • **94**

Pauillac 1977 • $29 Ⓐ • (11/30/91) • **87**

Pauillac 1976 • $152 Ⓐ • (11/30/91) • **88**

Pauillac 1975 • $139 Ⓐ • (11/30/91) • **71**

Pauillac 1974 • $NA • (11/30/91) • **89**

Pauillac 1973 • $30 Ⓐ • (11/30/91) • **87**

Pauillac 1972 • $31 Ⓐ • (11/30/91) • **82**

Pauillac 1971 • $52 Ⓐ • (11/30/91) • **87**

Pauillac 1970 • $138 Ⓐ • (11/30/91) • **92**

Pauillac 1969 • $25 Ⓐ • (11/30/91) • **80**

Pauillac 1968 • $19 Ⓐ • (11/30/91) • **61**

Pauillac 1967 • $42 Ⓐ • (11/30/91) • **80**

Pauillac 1966 • $120 Ⓐ • (11/30/91) • **84**

Pauillac 1965 • $45 • (11/30/91) • **73**

Pauillac 1964 • $101 Ⓐ • (11/30/91) • **87**

Pauillac 1963 • $50 • (11/30/91) • **69**

Pauillac 1962 • $124 Ⓐ • (11/30/91) • **93**

Pauillac 1961 • $713/1.5 liter • (04/30/96) • **94**

Pauillac 1960 • $90 • (11/30/91) • **92**

Pauillac 1959 • $489 Ⓐ • (11/30/91) • **94**

Pauillac 1959 • $NA/1.5 liter • (11/30/91) • **98**

Pauillac 1958 • $59 Ⓐ • (11/30/91) • **77**

Pauillac 1957 • $150 • (11/30/91) • **87**

Pauillac 1956 • $83 Ⓐ • (11/30/91) • **85**

Pauillac 1955 • $173 Ⓐ • (11/30/91) • **94**

Pauillac 1954 • $85 Ⓐ • (11/30/91) • **82**

Pauillac 1953 • $314 Ⓐ • (11/30/91) • **94**

Pauillac 1953 • $NA/1.5 liter • (11/30/91) • **96**

Pauillac 1952 • $185 • (11/30/91) • **90**

Pauillac 1951 • $150 • (11/30/91) • **78**

Pauillac 1950 • $177 Ⓐ • (11/30/91) • **91**

Pauillac 1949 • $357 Ⓐ • (11/30/91) • **87**

Pauillac 1949 • $NA/1.5 liter • (11/30/91) • **90**

Pauillac 1947: Classic Lafite elegance; lean but vibrant, with cherry, herb and chocolate flavors layered with hints of earth and tobacco. • $240 Ⓐ • (05/31/97) • **92**

Pauillac 1946 • $214 Ⓐ • (11/30/91) • **79**

Pauillac 1945 • $710 Ⓐ • (11/30/95) • **90**

Pauillac 1944 • $380 • (11/30/91) • **63**

Pauillac 1943 • $320 • (11/30/91) • **87**

Pauillac 1943 • $NA/1.5 liter • (11/30/91) • **85**

Key: SS—Spectator Selection CS—Cellar Selection HR—Highly Recommended BB—Best Buy $NA—Price not available Ⓐ—Auction Price (BT)—Barrel Tasting
Dates in parentheses indicate the issues in which the ratings were published.

Pauillac 1942 • $320 • (11/30/91) • **80**
Pauillac 1941 • $500 • (11/30/91) • **69**
Pauillac 1940 • $700 • (11/30/91) • **85**
Pauillac 1938 • $225 • (11/30/91) • **83**
Pauillac 1937 • $300 • (11/30/91) • **81**
Pauillac 1934 • $420 • (11/30/91) • **90**
Pauillac 1933 • $200 • (11/30/91) • **80**
Pauillac 1931 • $550 • (11/30/91) • **77**
Pauillac 1929 • $725 Ⓐ • (11/30/91) • **87**
Pauillac 1929 • $NA/1.5 liter • (11/30/91) • **88**
Pauillac 1928 • $674 Ⓐ • (11/30/91) • **66**
Pauillac 1926 • $400 • (11/30/91) • **89**
Pauillac 1926 • $NA/1.5 liter • (11/30/91) • **69**
Pauillac 1925 • $200 • (11/30/91) • **56**
Pauillac 1924 • $474 Ⓐ • (11/30/91) • **88**
Pauillac 1923 • $300 • (11/30/91) • **75**
Pauillac 1922 • $325 • (11/30/91) • **64**
Pauillac 1920 • $700 • (11/30/91) • **94**
Pauillac 1919 • $254 Ⓐ • (11/30/91) • **76**
Pauillac 1918 • $238 Ⓐ • (11/30/91) • **80**
Pauillac 1917 • $500 • (11/30/91) • **75**
Pauillac 1916 • $350 • (11/30/91) • **71**
Pauillac 1916 • $NA/1.5 liter • (11/30/91) • **89**
Pauillac 1913 • $500 • (11/30/91) • **82**
Pauillac 1911 • $443 Ⓐ • (11/30/91) • **83**
Pauillac 1910 • $460 Ⓐ • (11/30/91) • **69**
Pauillac 1909 • $500 • (11/30/91) • **73**
Pauillac 1908 • $600 • (11/30/91) • **86**
Pauillac 1907 • $700 • (11/30/91) • **64**
Pauillac 1906 • $350 • (11/30/91) • **90**
Pauillac 1905 • $500 • (11/30/91) • **88**
Pauillac 1904 • $660 • (11/30/91) • **84**
Pauillac 1903 • $352 Ⓐ • (11/30/91) • **68**
Pauillac 1902 • $950 • (11/30/91) • **80**
Pauillac 1901 • $700 • (11/30/91) • **74**
Pauillac 1900 • $2500 • (11/30/91) • **79**
Pauillac 1900 • $NA/1.5 liter • (11/30/91) • **70**
Pauillac 1894 • $1500 • (11/30/91) • **71**
Pauillac 1892 • $1300 • (11/30/91) • **72**
Pauillac 1891 • $797 Ⓐ • (11/30/91) • **70**
Pauillac 1887 • $1500 • (11/30/91) • **67**
Pauillac 1886 • $299 Ⓐ • (12/15/88) • **88**
Pauillac 1881 • $750 • (11/30/91) • **66**
Pauillac 1875 • $608 Ⓐ • (12/15/88) • **91**
Pauillac 1875 • $NA/1.5 liter • (12/15/88) • **97**
Pauillac 1870 • $3500 • (11/30/91) • **92**
Pauillac 1870 • $NA/1.5 liter • (11/30/91) • **62**
Pauillac 1869 • $3500 • (11/30/91) • **87**
Pauillac 1868 • $3500 • (11/30/91) • **91**
Pauillac 1865 • $400 Ⓐ • (11/30/91) • **50**
Pauillac 1832 • $9000 • (11/30/91) • **78**

LAFLEUR, CHÂTEAU

Pomerol 1997: Fruity, with just the right amount of new wood. Shows wonderful finesse. Medium-bodied, with medium tannins and a pretty finish. Real wine. A beauty. • $NA • (06/15/98) (BT) • **90-94**
Pomerol 1996: Very fine tannins, with just the right amount of fruit to balance. Racy and silky. 1,000 cases made. • $275 • (06/15/98) (BT) • **90-94**
Pomerol 1995: Compact, and fabulously concentrated. Subtle yet powerful. Intense aromas of blackberries, black cherries and fresh mushrooms. Full-bodied, with masses of well-integrated, fine tannins and fabulously ripe fruit. Long, sweet fruit finish. Best after 2002. 1,000 cases made. • $250 • (01/31/98) • **95**
Pomerol 1993: Bracing wine for the vintage, featuring firm tannins and ripe berry and cherry aromas and flavors. Medium- to full-bodied, closed finish. Drinkable now. • $94 Ⓐ • (01/31/96) • **88**
Pomerol 1992: Refined currant and tobacco flavors, medium body, silky texture and a medium, fruity finish. Drinkable now. • $91 Ⓐ • (04/15/95) • **88**
Pomerol 1990: Dense, sweet and rich, with several layers of chewy tannins to shed, but plenty of opulent cherry, currant and tobacco flavors showing through. Wait until 2005 or 2010. • $424 Ⓐ • (05/15/94) • **95**
Pomerol 1989 • $303 Ⓐ • (03/15/92) • **96**
Pomerol 1988 • $194 Ⓐ • (05/15/94) • **91**
Pomerol 1986 • $244 Ⓐ • (10/31/89) • **90**
Pomerol 1985 • $365 Ⓐ • (10/15/94) • **91**
Pomerol 1983 • $96 Ⓐ • (05/15/94) • **94**
Pomerol 1982 • $622 Ⓐ • (08/31/92) • **90**
Pomerol 1981 • $88 Ⓐ • (10/15/94) • **92**
Pomerol 1979 • $345 Ⓐ • (10/15/89) • **96**
Pomerol 1978 • $163 Ⓐ • (05/15/94) • **82**
Pomerol 1975 • $636 Ⓐ • (05/15/94) • **78**
Pomerol 1973 • $94 Ⓐ • (05/15/94) • **78**
Pomerol 1971 • $128 Ⓐ • (05/15/94) • **85**
Pomerol 1970 • $167 Ⓐ • (05/15/94) • **86**
Pomerol 1967 • $275 • (05/15/94) • **67**
Pomerol 1966 • $498 Ⓐ • (05/15/94) • **85**
Pomerol 1964 • $230 Ⓐ • (05/15/94) • **87**
Pomerol 1962 • $261 Ⓐ • (05/15/94) • **86**
Pomerol 1961 • $3280 Ⓐ • (04/30/96) • **93**
Pomerol 1959 • $550 • (05/15/94) • **87**
Pomerol 1955 • $557 Ⓐ • (05/15/94) • **50**
Pomerol 1953 • $650 • (05/15/94) • **85**
Pomerol 1952 • $361 Ⓐ • (05/15/94) • **87**
Pomerol 1950 • $2000 • (05/15/94) • **91**
Pomerol 1949 • $2100 • (05/15/94) • **80**
Pomerol 1947: Magnificent. Sweet, ripe and beautiful with its plum, perfumed berry, black cherry, herb and spice flavors that glide and swirl elegantly. A wine of one piece, it's harmonious, long and endlessly delicious. • $2240 Ⓐ • (05/31/97) • **99**
Pomerol 1945 • $NA • (11/30/95) • **80**
Pomerol English Bottling 1952 • $361 Ⓐ • (05/15/94) • **79**

LAFLEUR-GAZIN, CHÂTEAU

Pomerol 1997: Delicious berry and plum character. Medium-bodied, with medium tannins and a refreshing aftertaste. Well balanced. • $NA • (06/15/98) (BT) • **85-89**
Pomerol 1996: Racy and silky, with plenty of good fruit flavors and fine tannins. Medium body. • $NA • (01/01/97) (BT) • **85-89**
Pomerol 1995: A pretty, harmonious red with tobacco, berry and cherry aromas and flavors, medium-to-full body, and a balance of silky tannins. Best after 2000. • $30 • (01/31/98) • **90**
Pomerol 1994: Perfumed aromas of dried cherries and dried herbs, make way for fresh fruit flavors, with a slightly green edge. Refreshing and easy to drink now. • $25 • (01/31/97) • **83**
Pomerol 1993: Delicious milk chocolate, berry and cherry aromas and flavors, medium body, delicate tannins and fresh finish. Drinkable now. • $24 • (01/31/96) • **85**
Pomerol 1990: Round and generous, with an abundance of rich fruit and soft tannins. The character goes from earthy to licorice. Drinkable now. 3,500 cases made. • $30 • (03/31/93) • **90**
Pomerol 1989 • $NA • (03/15/92) • **87**
Pomerol 1945 • $300 • (11/30/95) • **80**

LAFON, DOMAINE DES COMTES

Meursault 1995: Sexy village Meursault that blows you away with its intriguing, exotic composition of deftly toasty oak accents married flawlessly to honey, spice, tropical and botrytislike dried fruit flavors. Full in body, silky and seductive. Hunt down as many bottles as you can, then horde them until around 2002 to 2010. • $50 • (05/31/98) • **93**
Meursault 1994: Starts better than it ends. Shows nice aromas of vanilla, cream and honey, but it's a bit empty on the palate, picking up new wood notes along way. Short finish. • $NA • (05/31/97) • **78**
Meursault 1993: A chewy wine, medium-bodied, it begins hard but turns charming after a few hour's aeration, smoothing out to show lots of toasty oak, lactic, roasted peanut and almond-cookie flavors, along with some lemon-apple-pear character. A wine for aging; try after 2005. • $60 • (05/31/97) • **88**
Meursault 1992: Showy, ripe and almost sweet, with layers of butter, honey, vanilla and pear flavors that expand on the finish. Has good acidity and a smooth texture, too. Drink now. • $48 • (05/15/95) • **88**
Meursault Clos de la Barre 1995: Fantastic. A grand village Meursault of great complexity, elegant yet full-bodied and opulent, cascading with suave grace over the palate, delivering dollops of honey, smoke, spice, tropical, pear and lemon and a hint of botrytislike dried fruit character. Buttery, silky finish tops it off. Try around 2002 to 2007. • $55 • (05/31/98) • **94**
Meursault Clos de la Barre 1994: Round, supple, almost soft, this full-bodied wine oozes cream, vanilla-bean and mineral flavors, with some pear, honey and toasty notes, finishing with a lovely kick of lemon. Delicious now. • $60 • (05/31/97) • **89**

Meursault Clos de la Barre 1993: Great winemaking. With its full-blown Burgundian treatment, this seems very oaky at first, but underneath are clearly defined, compacted, pure fruit, spice and herb flavors—pear, mango, lemon, lime, cilantro—that build to a powerful, refreshing, silky finish. Tempting now, but try to wait until after 2000. • $75 • (05/31/97) • **92**

Meursault Clos de la Barre 1992: A silky, smooth Burgundy that's full-bodied and plays variations on its carmel, butterscotch, coffee and spice notes. It also delivers some refreshing lemon character and a chalky, mineral quality that gives it depth and interest. Drinkable now. • $55 • (01/01/96) • **90**

Meursault Désirée 1995: Complex and balanced, deep and satisfying, this is packed with flavors, such as butter, almond-filled croissant, toasty coconut, grilled pineapple and pear tart. Full-bodied yet elegant, with good acidity, it caresses the palate and ends on a long, melodious, silky-as-can-be finish. Try in 2000 to 2007. Not available in the U.S. • $NA • (05/31/98) • **93**

Meursault Désirée 1994: Very round and lush in the mouth, this full-bodied village Meursault is opulent and ripe tasting, with honey and mineral notes shaded by toasty oak and a medium-intense fruit character. Very balanced, albeit quite oaky on the finish. Try now. • $75 • (05/31/97) • **87**

Meursault Désirée 1993: Brimming with rich, ripe, sweet flavors and lots of oak, honey and spice notes, this is a silky, full-bodied beauty that is flavorful and long on the supple finish. Drink now through 2005. • $75 • (05/31/97) • **93**

Meursault Goutte d'Or 1995: A thick and ripe *premier cru*, with toasty oak flavors that try to overwhelm the fruit, this chewy Meursault lacks a bit of elegance but offers a mouthful. Full-bodied. Velvety feel on the midpalate, turning tough on the finish. Should come together by 2002. • $65 • (05/31/98) • **89**

Meursault Les Charmes 1995: Wonderful Meursault, as caressing and silky as they get. Refined yet extremely flavorful, silky but also vibrant, with deft use of toasty oak to give it a smoky, grilled character atop the pear, bread dough, butter and tropical flavors. Full-bodied, with an elegant, medium-intense finish that's not as oaky as Lafon's 1995 Perrières. • $80 • (05/31/98) • **97**

Meursault Les Charmes 1994: Quite oaky now, with lots of spice, mocha and toasty bread flavors, plenty of honey and cream notes. A full-bodied, rich, ripe and delicious white Burgundy that should gain in depth after 2000. • $90 • (05/31/97) • **90**

Meursault Les Charmes 1993: Passionate, savage and attractive, this is very oaky but also quite honeyed, with some truffle and cream flavors. Full-bodied, with good balance; you can taste the richness and lively acidity. Delicious now through 2000. • $NA • (05/31/97) • **92**

Meursault Les Charmes 1992: What a beauty! Brilliant winemaking here. It pushes the envelope with seductive toasty hazelnut, pear, pie crust, honey and earth flavors in perfectly balanced proportions. This is what white Burgundy is all about. Awesome now, but should taste great for years. • $109 Ⓐ • (01/01/96) • **93**

Meursault Les Genevrières 1994: Lovely, full-bodied, silky, ripe and exciting, packing lemon, toasty oak, coffee bean, mocha and ripe fruit flavors into a seductive package. Has a smoky finish that goes on for minutes. Drinkable now through 2005. • $NA • (05/31/97) • **90**

Meursault Les Genevrières 1993: A tightly structured wine, quite oaky now, with some lovely vanilla, spice, mocha and toasty bread aromas, but also some honey, lemon and ripe fruit notes. Full-bodied, it impresses with a mineral concentration. Hard as nails now, but give it until 2000 and serve decanted. • $180 • (05/31/97) • **94**

Meursault Les Genevrières 1992: Showy and unctuous, full-throttled, full-bodied white Burgundy that's amazingly ripe, rich and fat. Delivers tons of honey, toasty coconut, spice, pear and apricot flavors, but stays fresh and vibrant on the finish. Drinkable now. • $75 • (01/01/96) • **94**

Meursault Les Perrières 1995: Incredibly powerful. Thick and rich, with loads of toasty oak that tastes a bit hot, burning and bitter. A wine with a great track record (just try the Lafon's 1989 Perrières, which drinks beautifully), this offers almost botrytislike flavors (honey, dried fruit, fig and date character) along with a thick midpalate. Full in body but medium in acidity, it's very concentrated. Definitely hold until around 2005. • $90 • (05/31/98) • **95**

Meursault Les Perrières 1993: Classy white Burgundy, boasting a leesy character that's bursting with exciting lemon, honey, toasty bread and pie-crust flavors. Extremely well made, tightly wrapped, focused and concentrated, right through the long, searing finish. Better in 2000. • $80 • (05/31/96) • **93**

Meursault Les Perrières 1992: A full-blown, full-bodied, ripe and rich white Burgundy that's packed with toasty oak, pear, spice and caramel flavors. For those who love this fat style. Turns to truffle and mushroom flavors on the chewy, intense finish. Drink now. • $80 • (01/01/96) • **90**

Monthélie Les Duresses 1992: A stylish red from a lesser village in Burgundy. It has attractive spicy, cedary, chocolaty aromas, good cherry and berry flavors and a lean, tart, rather tannic finish. Drinkable now. • $25 • (05/31/95) • **84**

Montrachet 1995: Monumental, racy wine built for the cellar. Very complex, elegant and firmly structured, with fresh, pure and clean acidity playing against the lovely fruit. Compacted, with tropical, honeydew, ripe pear and apple notes mixing with the deftly toasty character. Full-bodied, with a long and delicious finish that never seems to end. Try around 2005. • $400 • (05/31/98) • **98**

Montrachet 1994: A wonderful Burgundy, dominated by lactic aromas, with some spicy vanilla, cream and toast flavors and plenty of cinnamon, lemon and apple-tart notes. Would rate classic save for a slight hollowness that's very atypical of Lafon's Montrachets. Accessible now on through 2000. • $403 Ⓐ • (05/31/97) • **94**

Montrachet 1993: Mind-boggling, full-throttle white Burgundy that not only delivers amazing toast, butterscotch, honey and ripe fruit complexity, but also kicks in on the finish with awesome intensity. Creamy, silky texture and overall balance are simply magical. Drinkable now or age until the next century. 100 cases made. • $403 Ⓐ • (05/31/96) HR • **98**

Puligny-Montrachet Champ-Gain 1995: Impressively built. Thick and dense in body, but also reserved and tough. Quite oaky, with grilled pineapple, pear tart and lime flavors. It has some years to go before turning silky, but there is a lot of fresh, citrusy acidity to keep the wood in check. Definitely don't touch until around 2005 to 2008. Not available in the U.S. • $NA • (05/31/98) • **93**

Volnay 1992: Lively and approachable, with raspberry and strawberry flavors on a lean frame; slightly candied finish. Drinkable now. • $NA • (12/15/94) • **85**

Volnay Champans 1994: A delicate, floral style, light in color and body but supple and pretty. Offers medium intensity and character, and supple, ripe tannins. Enjoy upon release. 160 cases made. • $55 • (09/30/97) • **83**

Volnay Clos des Chênes 1994: A terrific '94. Dark in color, deep and enticing in flavor, with a silky, supple and harmonious texture. Quite reserved on the nose now, but it fans out its ripe, rich fruit on the palate to a long finish. Try after 2000. 125 cases made. • $55 • (09/30/97) • **90**

Volnay Clos des Chênes 1993: Interesting '93, as some earthy, minty, red berry notes marry into an elegant package. Of medium body, it's flavorful and sweet-tasting, adding a long, exuberant finish. Try in 2000. • $NA • (05/15/96) • **88**

Volnay En Champans 1993: A bit simple for the vintage, delivering black cherry and wet earth aromas and flavors. Medium-bodied, light tannins, light finish. Drinkable now. • $NA • (05/15/96) • **85**

Volnay En Champans 1991: Earthy, smoky aromas and flavors characterize this light, slightly astringent wine. Shows a touch of berry and a bit more complexity than most. Drinkable now. • $54 Ⓐ • (01/31/94) • **83**

Volnay-Santenots Les Santenots du Milieu 1994: A beauty. Elegant and refined, a delicate '94 that then kicks in with power on the finale. It's supple, intense and flavorful, with crisp, freshly crushed red berry, violet, rose petal and toasty spice notes; the tannins are firm, should soften by 2000. 700 cases made. • $55 • (09/30/97) • **92**

Volnay-Santenots Les Santenots du Milieu 1993: A red of distinction. Loads of fruit but also fascinating mineral and spice character. Full body, fine tannins and long, long finish. Needs time; better in 2001. • $53 Ⓐ • (05/15/96) • **93**

Volnay-Santenots Les Santenots du Milieu 1992: A sweet-tasting beauty, packed with red berry, earth and mineral character, remaining tight now but should improve and soften upon aging until 2001. Somewhat dry on the finish. Massive tannins and long, long finish. One of the best red Burgundies we've tasted from the difficult '92 vintage. • $NA • (01/01/94) • **90**

Volnay-Santenots Les Santenots du Milieu 1991: Offers chewy tannins and pleasant currant and berry aromas and flavors in a firm, fragrant, modest package. Drinkable now. • $54 Ⓐ • (01/31/94) • **84**

LAFON-ROCHET, CHÂTEAU

St.-Estèphe 1997: A bit raisiny and grassy, with berry and violet character beneath. Medium-bodied, with slightly drying tannins. Slightly overdone? Wait and see. • $NA • (06/15/98) (BT) • **80-84**

Key: SS—Spectator Selection CS—Cellar Selection HR—Highly Recommended BB—Best Buy $NA—Price not available Ⓐ—Auction Price (BT)—Barrel Tasting
Dates in parentheses indicate the issues in which the ratings were published.

St.-Estèphe 1996: Lafon-Rochet is on a roll with this vintage. Pretty mineral and berry aromas and flavors. Medium- to full-bodied, with solid yet refined tannins and a long, silky finish. • $30 • (06/15/98) (BT) • **90-94**

St.-Estèphe 1995: The best wine ever produced at this estate. So sexy, so wonderful now—but be patient. Dark in color, ruby, inky. Blueberries, cream and vanilla character. Full-bodied, with full yet fine tannins. It literally massages your palate. Best after 2001. • $33 • (01/31/98) • **93**

St.-Estèphe 1994: Fruity, with berry, cherry and tobacco aromas and flavors. Medium-bodied, chewy on the finish. Drinkable now. 24,166 cases made. • $18 Ⓐ • (01/31/97) • **88**

St.-Estèphe 1993: Attractive and quite beefy, showing loads of tobacco, cassis and wet earth character. Full in body, it coats your mouth with massive but supple tannins. This one needs time; try in 2000. 15,200 cases made. • $23 • (01/31/96) • **88**

St.-Estèphe 1992: Bright and vivid, interesting currant character. Medium in body with firm tannins but slightly astringent on the finish. Drinkable now. • $18 • (04/15/95) • **84**

St.-Estèphe 1991: Simple, light and fruity, with pleasant berry and cherry flavors and a slightly dry finish. • $18 • (03/31/94) • **78**

St.-Estèphe 1990: Traditional St.-Estèphe, with spicy, earthy and berry aromas and flavors, firm tannins and a rich finish. No frills but well made. Drinkable now. 12,000 cases made. • $21 • (03/31/93) • **89**

St.-Estèphe 1989 • $34 Ⓐ • (03/15/92) • **92**

St.-Estèphe 1982 • $86 Ⓐ • (08/31/92) • **90**

St.-Estèphe 1945 • $100 • (03/16/86) • **75**

LAFONT MENAUT, CHÂTEAU

Pessac-Léognan White 1995: Serious wine for the vintage. Pretty melon, apple and cream aromas and flavors. Medium- to full-bodied, with lots of character. Long finish. A newcomer to watch. Drink now or hold. • $NA • (04/30/98) • **88**

LAGRANGE, CHÂTEAU

Pomerol 1997: Good berry and fruit character. Medium-bodied, with moderate, chewy tannins and a medium finish. Not easy to taste now, but shows good texture. • $NA • (06/15/98) (BT) • **85-89**

Pomerol 1996: Decent fruit here, with berry, cherry and chocolate character, but could use a little more concentration. 23,333 cases made. • $NA • (01/01/97) (BT) • **80-84**

Pomerol 1995: Tight and muscular with big tannins and well-integrated fruit flavors, this is built for aging. Long finish. Better than previous tasting. 24,166 cases made. • $21 Ⓐ • (05/15/97) (BT) • **90-94**

Pomerol 1994: Pretty and elegant, with perfumed aromas of berries and minerals and a pleasant combination of toasty oak and berry flavors. Medium-bodied, with medium, fine tannins. Drinkable now. • $25 Ⓐ • (01/31/97) • **86**

Pomerol 1993: Delicious and round, showing gamy, earthy, red berry character. Medium in body, medium-velvety tannins and a fruity finish. Drinkable now. • $21 Ⓐ • (01/31/96) • **83**

Pomerol 1992: Evolving more quickly than we thought. Light in body and diluted, showing dried-herb and berry flavors. • $24 • (04/15/95) • **75**

Pomerol 1990: Dense and powerful, with a breathtaking aftertaste of blackberries, chocolate and earth. Superb wine with harmonious structure to easily take you into the next century. Drinkable in 2000. 3,000 cases made. • $30 • (03/31/93) • **95**

Pomerol 1989 • $39 Ⓐ • (03/15/92) • **87**

Pomerol 1982 • $41 Ⓐ • (05/15/89) • **84**

LAGRANGE, CHÂTEAU

St.-Julien 1997: Smart winemaking, reflecting good use of wood and extraction of fruit. Fine tannins. Lacks a bit of fruit on the midpalate but still very good. • $NA • (06/15/98) (BT) • **85-89**

St.-Julien 1996: Elegant and well crafted. Very fine indeed. Rather minerally and fruity, with lots of mint. Medium-bodied, with firm tannins. Seductive finish. 9,580 cases made. • $40 • (06/15/98) (BT) • **90-94**

St.-Julien 1995: Wonderfully crafted, with mint, blackberry and chocolate aromas. Full-bodied, with loads of berry flavor and velvety tannins. Best after 2001. • $21 Ⓐ • (01/31/98) • **91**

St.-Julien 1994: Balanced and harmonious for the vintage with a cherry, plum and tobacco character, fine tannins and a fresh finish. Delicious now. 25,000 cases made. • $25 Ⓐ • (01/31/97) • **88**

St.-Julien 1993: A very good St.-Julien from this consistent property, really caressing your palate in velvety tannins. Medium body and pretty berry, vanilla, toasty oak character. Drinkable now. • $21 Ⓐ • (01/31/96) • **89**

St.-Julien 1992: Extremely well made, exhibiting a lovely balance of round, supple tannins and vivid berry and cherry flavor. Medium body and tannins and a fruity finish. Drinkable now. • $20 • (04/15/95) • **87**

St.-Julien 1991: A lovely wine for this vintage, with smoky blackberry and tobacco flavors. An elegant, medium-bodied wine that delivers velvety texture with its fine tannins. • $24 • (03/31/94) • **86**

St.-Julien 1990: Like a Rodin sculpture: rugged yet well-defined. It shows concentrated cassis, berry and dark chocolate flavors, rich tannins and a long, opulent finish. Drink now. 22,500 cases made. • $30 • (03/31/93) SS • **95**

St.-Julien 1989 • $39 Ⓐ • (03/15/92) • **95**

St.-Julien 1986 • $37 Ⓐ • (02/15/90) • **86**

St.-Julien 1985 • $48 Ⓐ • (10/15/94) • **91**

St.-Julien 1983 • $28 Ⓐ • (10/15/94) • **88**

St.-Julien 1982 • $36 • (08/31/92) • **89**

St.-Julien 1981 • $19 Ⓐ • (10/15/94) • **85**

St.-Julien 1961 • $48 Ⓐ • (04/30/96) • **86**

LAGREZETTE, CHÂTEAU

Cahors 1994: Deep and polished, showing blackberry, currant and spice flavors that follow through to the firmly structured finish. Drinkable now. 8,500 cases made. • $19 • (08/31/97) • **87**

Cahors 1993: Sweet coconut aromas, courtesy of new oak, float above cherry and woodsy notes. Moderate depth and intensity. Drinkable now. 6,500 cases made. • $19 • (01/31/97) • **87**

Cahors 1992 • $12 • (03/31/95) • **86**

Cahors 1990 • $10 • (09/15/94) • **83**

Cahors 1989 • $10 • (09/15/94) • **88**

Cahors Chevaliers Lagrezette 1994: Fairly mature, showing red plum and cherry flavors with a dash of pepper. Solid, it would do well with grilled meats. A blend of 85 percent Malbec, 13 percent Merlot, 2 percent Tannat. Drink now. 5,200 cases made. • $13 • (05/15/98) • **84**

Cahors Chevaliers Lagrezette 1992: Very herbal, with faint plum flavors, notes of smoke and chocolate. Still quite tannic. 5,000 cases made. • $14 • (02/28/97) • **79**

Cahors Cuvée Dame Honneur 1994: Thick and rich, with loads of ripe plum and spice flavors and a note of leather. Smooth, with an intriguing thread of clove woven into its suppleness. Lovely finish. A blend of 90 percent Malbec, 10 percent Merlot. Drink now through 2000. 860 cases made. • $21 • (05/15/98) • **88**

Cahors Moulin Lagrezette 1995: Quite a mouthful, with focused flavors of cherry and red plum. A well-defined wine that finishes on a spicy note. A blend of 70 percent Malbec, 30 percent Merlot. 6,000 cases made. • $11 • (05/15/98) • **85**

LAGUNE, CHÂTEAU LA

Haut-Médoc 1997: Slightly lean, but with some good berry and vanilla aromas and flavors. Medium- to light-bodied, with a light finish. Tasted twice. • $NA • (06/15/98) (BT) • **80-84**

Haut-Médoc 1996: Good violet and raspberry character on the nose and palate. Medium-bodied, with moderate tannins and a medium finish. Plenty of berries and vanilla in the aftertaste. • $30 • (06/15/98) (BT) • **85-89**

Haut-Médoc 1990: A wine to linger over. The aromas are opulent with new oak and ripe fruit; a rich, concentrated palate offers cherry, current, cedar and licorice flavors. It's full-bodied yet graceful, beautifully structured and seamless, with a long fruity finish. Drinkable now. 25,000 cases made. • $52 Ⓐ • (10/15/94) • **95**

Haut-Médoc 1989 • $41 Ⓐ • (10/15/94) • **87**

Haut-Médoc 1988 • $34 Ⓐ • (04/30/91) • **91**

Haut-Médoc 1987 • $20 • (05/15/90) • **89**

Haut-Médoc 1986 • $40 Ⓐ • (06/30/89) • **89**

Haut-Médoc 1985 • $47 Ⓐ • (10/15/94) • **89**

Haut-Médoc 1984 • $26 Ⓐ • (03/31/87) • **86**

Haut-Médoc 1983 • $45 Ⓐ • (10/15/94) • **91**

Haut-Médoc 1982 • $62 Ⓐ • (08/31/92) • **94**

Haut-Médoc 1981 • $32 Ⓐ • (10/15/94) • **91**

Haut-Médoc 1979 • $26 Ⓐ • (10/15/89) • **86**

Haut-Médoc 1962 • $70 Ⓐ • (11/30/87) • **80**

Haut-Médoc 1961 • $125 Ⓐ • (04/30/96) • **88**

Haut-Médoc 1945 • $200 • (03/16/86) • **87**

LAISSUS, CHÂTEAU

Côte de Brouilly Vieilles Vignes 1994: Polished, yet still firm. Bottle-aging has given nice tea and tobacco notes to the ripe black cherry flavors that linger on the finish. • $13 • (09/15/96) • **84**

LALANDE, DOMAINE DE

Mâcon-Chaintré 1995: Rather fat and ripe, but slightly bitter on the finish and a bit short on class despite its attractive, full-bodied mouthfeel. From Dominique Cornin. Not imported into the U.S. Drink now. • $NA • (05/31/97) • **80**

Pouilly-Fuissé Clos Reyssié 1996: Rich, ripe and full-bodied, with impressive oak accents, it delivers plenty of spice, mocha, toasty bread, pear tart character, but it turns slightly heavy on the finish. Not imported into the U.S. Drink now. • $NA • (05/31/98) • **87**

Pouilly-Fuissé Clos Reyssié 1995: Supple, smooth and quite delicious, with notes of smoke and toast mingling with honey, spice and fruit flavors. Medium-bodied, with a creamy, citrus-spiked finish. Harmonious. From Dominique Cornin. Not imported into the U.S. Drink now. • $NA • (05/31/97) • **86**

LALANDE-BORIE, CHÂTEAU

St.-Julien 1993: Vivid, polished '93 offering mint, berry and vanilla aromas and flavors, medium body, sleek tannins and long, silky finish. Delicious. • $18 • (01/31/96) • **85**

St.-Julien 1991: Decent texture and a lean structure, with red berry and stewed tomato flavors. • $14 • (03/31/94) • **77**

St.-Julien 1990: This delivers plenty of plummy tobacco character and velvety tannins with an attractive smoky, fruity finish. Drinkable now. • $19 • (03/31/93) • **90**

St.-Julien 1989 • $17 • (03/15/92) • **88**

St.-Julien 1988 • $17 • (04/30/91) • **87**

St.-Julien 1987 • $15 • (11/30/89) • **81**

St.-Julien 1986 • $17 • (11/30/89) • **91**

St.-Julien 1982 • $17 • (08/31/92) • **91**

LALEURE-PIOT

Bourgogne Passe-tout-grains 1993: Vibrant red featuring sliced plum and citrus character, medium body, crisp acidity and light tannin structure. Drinkable now. • $15 • (11/15/95) • **84**

Chorey-lès-Beaune Les Champs Longs 1995: An oddball. Closed up today, with barely a hint of strawberry, followed by dry, astringent tannins and heat. • $22 • (11/15/97) • **74**

Chorey-lès-Beaune Les Champs Longs 1993: Brilliant, vivid dried cherry, raspberry and wet earth character, medium body and tannins and a long, crisp finish. Try now. • $17 • (11/15/95) • **87**

Corton Le Rognet 1995: A pretty Pinot Noir, with crisp, clean and pure currant, cassis and black cherry flavors accented by smoky, toasty oak notes. Light- to medium-bodied, with refined tannins. Try now. • $59 • (11/15/97) • **87**

Corton Le Rognet 1994: Has plenty of charm, with its raspberry and red plum flavors, supple texture and fine tannins. Approachable now. • $NA • (11/15/96) • **85**

Corton Le Rognet 1993: Nicely balanced between plum, earth and red berry notes. Medium in body, well-integrated tannins. The finish is ripe and long but a touch alcoholic. Try now. • $47 • (11/15/95) • **89**

Corton Les Bressandes 1995: A lovely, delicate and elegant wine that typifies the feminine side of the '95 red Burgundy vintage. Supple and charming, with delicious red- and blackberry flavor and a velvety texture, it doesn't assault the palate with harsh tannins. Delivers a caress rather than a blow. Medium-bodied, ready now through 2000. • $62 • (11/15/97) • **87**

Corton Les Bressandes 1994: Firm, focused and forward. Appealing for its chunky plum, smoke and sweet oak flavors that finish with a touch of astringency. Try now. • $66 • (11/15/96) • **82**

Corton Les Bressandes 1993: Tight and not giving much at this stage, yet featuring some fine tannins and ripe fruit. medium-to-full body and a short finish. Give it time; try after 2000. • $51 • (11/15/95) • **91**

Key: SS—Spectator Selection CS—Cellar Selection HR—Highly Recommended BB—Best Buy $NA—Price not available Ⓐ—Auction Price (BT)—Barrel Tasting
Dates in parentheses indicate the issues in which the ratings were published.

Corton Les Bressandes 1990: Voluptuous, with loads of smoky black cherry aromas and flavors and velvety tannins. Drinkable now. • $NA • (12/15/92) • **90**

Corton-Charlemagne 1996: Beautiful and exciting '96, full-bodied and racy, with a ripe fruit character mingling nicely with smoky, earthy, minerally notes. Medium-toasty, the oak accents give it a slight cigar and mocha flavor. Good concentration shows in the velvety midpalate; finishes long. Tempting now, better 2000 to 2010. 100 cases made. • $96 • (05/31/98) • **93**

Corton-Charlemagne 1994: Decent apple and toasty oak flavors. Very tart and a bit short on the finish. • $70 • (05/31/96) • **75**

Côte de Nuits-Villages 1990: Extremely high in volatile acidity, with aromas of paint thinner and nail-polish remover. What a shame, since it also shows an amazing amount of rich fruit flavor. Not recommended. • $NA • (12/15/92) • **65**

Côte de Nuits-Villages Les Bellevues 1995: Fresh, sappy, lively and well defined, with lovely red berry, blueberry and floral notes. Light- to medium-bodied, its firm tannins should soften by around 2000. • $22 • (01/31/98) • **86**

Pernand-Vergelesses 1995: Light and simple, with a somewhat supple midpalate, but turning very astringent. A bit hot and alcoholic on the finish. • $25 • (11/15/97) • **74**

Pernand-Vergelesses Ile des Vergelesses 1995: Supple and charming, with a core of fruit and firm tannins, it offers some pretty cassis bush, blackberry, bitter chocolate and toasty oak flavors. Slight dilution, a bit astringent on the finish. Try now. • $40 • (11/15/97) • **84**

Pernand-Vergelesses Ile des Vergelesses 1994: Earthy, almost woodsy aromas and flavors overshadow the modest berry flavors in this lean, chewy wine. • $NA • (11/15/96) • **79**

Pernand-Vergelesses Ile des Vergelesses 1993: Soft at first, offering a currant, vanilla and smoke character before tannins tighten on the palate and finish. Medium body and good concentration. Try in 2000. • $33 • (11/15/95) • **85**

Pernand-Vergelesses Ile des Vergelesses 1990: Offers loads of fruit; a very round texture with glorious currant, cherry and earth notes. Drinkable now. • $NA • (12/15/92) • **90**

Pernand-Vergelesses Les Vergelesses 1995: A refined, harmonious Pinot Noir, light- to medium-bodied, with very pretty cassis, blackberry and black cherry flavors. Accented by lightly toasty, spicy notes, it's a joy to taste now. • $31 • (11/15/97) • **86**

Pernand-Vergelesses Les Vergelesses 1994: Earthy, musty flavors detract from some pretty mulberry notes, but it finishes with some charm. • $43 • (11/15/96) • **79**

Pernand-Vergelesses Les Vergelesses 1993: Some good floral, dried cherry aromas but rather muted in the palate, adding hard tannins and short aftertaste. Perhaps better after a year or two of bottle age. • $24 • (11/15/95) • **84**

Pernand-Vergelesses Les Vergelesses 1992: Open-textured, with appealing wild berry and plum flavors. Rustic in style but generous enough. Drinkable now. • $27 • (12/15/94) • **83**

Pernand-Vergelesses Les Vergelesses 1990: Juicy and ripe, combining lovely black cherry, herb and tar notes and fine tannins. The finish goes on and on. Drinkable now. • $NA • (12/15/92) • **89**

Pernand-Vergelesses Premier Cru White 1996: Quite diluted. Light- to medium-bodied, showing oak and earth along with clean and pure pear and apple flavors. Drink now. 500 cases made. • $35 • (05/31/98) • **79**

Pernand-Vergelesses Premier Cru White 1994: A solid, muscular, full-bodied floral white that has tons of flavors—oak, cedar, apple, pear and mineral. A bit rough-and-tumble, like a hammer hitting you over the head, but it has personality. Try now. • $34 • (05/31/96) • **88**

Pernand-Vergelesses Premier Cru 1993: Lively acidity and fresh fruit but rather one-dimensional. Medium to light body and firm tannins. Drinkable now. • $22 • (11/15/95) • **84**

Pernand-Vergelesses White 1996: Balanced, it blends nicely ripe fruit with good acidity in a harmonious, full-bodied package. Supple texture makes this wine a joy to taste, as the mineral, dried herb, pear and other intriguing notes flow to a long, vibrant finish. Tempting now through 2007. 1,000 cases made. • $27 • (05/31/98) • **89**

Pernand-Vergelesses White 1994: Lean and crisp, with only modest fruit flavors and little length. • $28 • (05/31/96) • **78**

Savigny-lès-Beaune Aux Vergelesses 1993: Not a big wine, but has lovely bright fruit character. Medium-bodied, adding firm tannins and medium aftertaste of dried cherries and minerals. Drinkable now. • $25 • (11/15/95) • **86**

FRANCE

LAMARCHE, FRANÇOIS

Clos de Vougeot 1995: Bright cassis flavors are the highlight of this elegeant Clos de Vougeot. Not a blockbuster, but very appealing despite tannins that are firm and dry on the finish. 316 cases made. • $64 • (11/15/97) • **88**
Clos de Vougeot 1987 • $55 • (09/30/90) • **86**
Clos de Vougeot 1985 • $48 • (10/15/88) • **90**
Echézeaux 1995: Thick and dense, but also rather angular and pumped up, this muscular red Burgundy offers loads of impressive red- and blackberry character, massive firm tannins and a monolithic structure. A bit disjointed now, try after 2000. 300 cases made. • $61 • (11/15/97) • **89**
Echézeaux 1987 • $48 • (09/30/90) • **87**
La Grand Rue 1995: This has lovely spice-accented cherry flavor, elegance, moderate structure and a very smoky aftertaste. A little drying on the finish. Drinkable now. 500 cases made. • $98 • (11/15/97) • **90**
Vosne-Romanée La Grande Rue 1987 • $68 • (09/30/90) • **91**
Vosne-Romanée La Grande Rue 1985 • $60 • (10/15/88) • **89**
Vosne-Romanée Les Suchots 1985 • $36 • (10/15/88) • **91**
Vosne-Romanée Malconsorts 1995: Displays expressive aromas of ripe plum and wild berries, accented by spicy oak. Moderately concentrated, yet turning quite dry and woody on the finish. 191 cases made. • $56 • (11/15/97) • **83**
Vosne-Romanée Aux Malconsorts 1985 • $44 • (10/15/88) • **84**

LAMARQUE, CHÂTEAU DE

Haut-Médoc 1997: Light and diluted, with some berry and cherry character and fine tannins, but not enough structure to be more than average in quality. • $NA • (06/15/98) (BT) • **75-79**
Haut-Médoc 1992: Very light and diluted with cherry, earthy character and a light finish. • $13 • (04/15/95) • **74**
Haut-Médoc 1991: Elegant yet simple. Delivers ripe fruit in a lean-structured wine. • $13 • (03/31/94) • **80**
Haut-Médoc 1990: A firm and well-structured wine, with a solid tannin backbone and fresh cherry and herbal character. Drinkable now. 25,000 cases made. • $18 • (03/31/93) • **86**
Haut-Médoc 1989 • $26 • (03/15/92) • **89**
Haut-Médoc 1988 • $20 • (04/30/91) • **86**
Haut-Médoc 1987 • $10 • (11/30/89) • **74**
Haut-Médoc 1986 • $18 • (11/30/89) • **75**
Haut-Médoc 1982 • $18 • (08/31/92) • **82**

LAMARTINE, CHÂTEAU

Cahors Cuvée Particulière 1994: Crisp and tannic, with plum and cherry flavors and an earthy finish. 2,000 cases made. • $15 • (07/31/98) • **81**

LAMARZELLE, CHÂTEAU

St.-Emilion 1997: Dark in color, with a velvety texture, but needs a bit more fruit on the palate. Medium-bodied, with moderate tannins. • $NA • (06/15/98) (BT) • **80-84**
St.-Emilion 1996: Firm and fruity, with pleasant berry character, silky tannins and a straightforward finish. • $32 • (06/15/98) (BT) • **80-84**

LAMBLIN & FILS

Bourgogne White 1995: Citrusy flavors of green apple and lemon dominate this crisp and zingy wine, carrying through to the tart finish. • $9 • (01/31/97) • **80**
Chablis 1996: Very pretty, with personality. Fat and spicy, it has a grilled sausage, white pepper and sweet apple character. Medium to full in body, it offers great intensity for a village Chablis, with mineral, stone and lemon notes on the long, ripe finish. • $NA • (08/31/97) • **90**
Chablis Fourchaume 1996: Lush, ripe and sweet-tasting, a full-bodied *premier cru* that has soul and an earthy character with lots of tropical fruit, pear, apple and mineral tones. Amazingly distinctive, with a sharply focused finish. Tempting now through 2007. • $NA • (08/31/97) • **92**

LAMBRAYS, DOMAINE DES

Clos des Lambrays 1993: Very classy *grand cru*, showing lively raspberry, wild berry, cassis and toasty oak flavors that marry nicely with firm tannins. Rather sweet and ripe, chewy. Long finish. Try now. • $50 • (05/15/96) • **89**

LAMOTHE, CHÂTEAU

Sauternes 1988: Light and fruity, with appealing nectarine and earth aromas and flavors that are a bit grassy, smoothing out on the finish. Drinkable now. • $16 • (03/31/91) • **84**
Sauternes 1986: Has complexity and subtlety in a medium-weight framework, ripe and round without being overblown. Smooth and well balanced for drinking now. • $29 • (12/31/89) • **85**

LAMOTHE DE HAUX, CHÂTEAU

Bordeaux White 1994 • $8 • (02/29/96) • **78**

LAMOTHE-DESPUJOLS, CHÂTEAU

Sauternes 1987 • $NA • (06/15/90) • **84**

LAMOTHE-GUIGNARD, CHÂTEAU

Sauternes 1992: Smooth but slightly unbalanced, showing some spicy apricot and honey flavors and a somewhat alcoholic finish. Drinkable now. • $NA • (04/15/95) • **78**
Sauternes 1990: Impressively unctuous, powerful and exotic, good acidity backing up the ripe, rich marmalade, spice, honey and dried apricot flavors. A mouth-filling Sauternes that should age for decades, but is tempting now. • $30 • (04/15/95) • **92**
Sauternes 1989: Flashy and enticing, round, thick and velvety, offering full-throttle tropical flavors backed by some vanilla and lemon notes. Lacks a bit of acidity. Drinkable now. • $25 • (04/15/95) • **88**
Sauternes 1988: Quite mature already and very sweet. Ripe, rich and thick, displaying dried apricot, honey and butterscotch character, though falling a bit short on the finish. • $35 • (04/15/95) • **87**
Sauternes 1987: • $23 • (06/15/90) • **77**
Sauternes 1986: Wonderfully balanced, presenting a grassy, lime edge that cuts through the ripe, rich, oily texture. Distinctive and harmonious, yet serious enough to postpone drinking until after 2000. • $30 • (04/15/95) • **92**
Sauternes 1983: A racy, clean-as-a-whistle Sauternes that graciously unfolds its spice, clove, honey and smoke flavors. Needs another five to ten years to show it all. • $NA • (04/15/95) • **92**

LAMY, HENRY

St.-Aubin En Remilly White 1995: Very pretty, full-bodied, ripe but also elegant, showing a bounty of honey, tropical fruit and pear flavors that melt together beautifully on the palate. A silky-smooth but fairly long finish renders this wine drinkable now through 2000. • $22 • (05/31/97) • **90**

LAMY, HUBERT

Chassagne-Montrachet Les Macherelles 1996: Very satisfying, this full-bodied, lush, flavorful *premier cru* offers plenty of tropical, lime, ripe pear and deftly toasty oak flavors that integrate nicely. Clean and pure, it vibrates over the palate to a long, succulent, minerally finish. Tempting now, but should improve through at least 2005. 75 cases made. • $38 • (05/31/98) • **92**
Chassagne-Montrachet 1995: Fresh, clean, crisp and lively, this wine stresses fruit over oak, with well-defined pear, apple and mineral flavors. Full-bodied. A pleasure to drink now, but should improve through 2000 to 2005. 50 cases made. • $NA • (05/31/97) • **88**
Criots-Bâtard-Montrachet 1995: Full-bodied and quite intense, but a bit overdone with coarse, burnt caramel and toasty oak flavors. 25 cases made. • $NA • (05/31/97) • **84**
St.-Aubin Clos de la Chatenière White 1996: Full-bodied *premier cru*, offering loads of honey, mineral and floral notes, ripe fruit and acidity in a splendid, balanced package. The smooth yet succulent texture fills the palate. Delicious from start to finish. Tempting now, but better to wait until after 2002. 390 cases made. • $22 • (05/31/98) • **92**
St.-Aubin Clos de la Chatenière White 1995: Disappointing and a bit odd, this medium-bodied wine has some strange perfumes and a slightly bitter, drying, short finish. 300 cases made. • $22 • (05/31/97) • **74**
St.-Aubin En Remilly White 1996: Wonderful '96, full-bodied and rich, showing an excellent marriage of oak shadings, ripe fruit and acidity. Supple and seductive texture, multidimensional and well made. Long, full, deeply

FRANCE

satifying finish. Tempting now, better around 2002. 550 cases made. • $22 • (05/31/98) • **92**

St.-Aubin La Princée White 1996: Fairly tough and lean, this steely 1996 shows some ripe fruit character but mostly green apple and grass aromas and flavors. Try with seafood. 550 cases made. • $16 • (05/31/98) • **83**

St.-Aubin La Princée White 1995: A bit rustic, with some distracting icebox flavors, but below those there are some nice mineral notes and ripe fruit flavors. Drink now through 2000. 375 cases made. • $17 • (05/31/97) • **83**

St.-Aubin Les Cortons White 1996: Lovely, medium-bodied wine, a bit earthy and quite crisp, but with ripe fruit and racy acidity all in fine balance. Despite the fruit-acid intensity, it has a supple, minerally middle and a long, harmonious finish. Drink now through 2005. 150 cases made. • $22 • (05/31/98) • **87**

St.-Aubin Les Cortons White 1995: A full-bodied, ripe, rich '95, showing some caramel, spice, tropical fruit and coffee notes. Turns creamy smooth on the finish. Try now. 150 cases made. • $22 • (05/31/97) • **87**

St.-Aubin Les Frionnes White 1996: Big and bulky, this rich, ripe, thick and full-bodied white offers loads of *terroir* in the form of wet stone and mineral character. Fine fruit and acidity galore give you plenty of wine for your buck. The honey, spice and pear notes are pretty on the finish. Drink now through 2005. 380 cases made. • $20 • (05/31/98) • **91**

St.-Aubin Les Murgers des Dents de Chien White 1996: Extraordinary, both supple and concentrated, with ripe tropical pear, bread dough, butter, vanilla bean and mineral flavors. The smooth, velvety texture is to die for, and the sweet-tasting character and fresh acidity make for a terrific *premier cru*, harmonious and long on the finish. Drink now through 2006. 75 cases made. • $28 • (05/31/98) • **92**

St.-Aubin Les Murgers des Dents de Chien White 1995: Well structured for a '95, with a compacted fruit-and-mineral character. Decent grip on the palate, with lemon, apple, pear and some subtle, toasty oak notes. Turns silky on the finish. Drink now. 50 cases made. • $NA • (05/31/97) • **88**

LANCELOT-ROYER, P.

Brut Blanc de Blancs Champagne Cuvée des Chevaliers NV: A light, almost delicate style of Champagne that starts with complex toasty, spicy aromas, then shows lively fruit flavors and a tangy finish. Appealing. Tasted twice, with consistent notes. Drink now. • $33 • (04/30/98) • **87**

LANÇON PÈRE & FILS

Châteauneuf-du-Pape Domaine de la Solitude 1994: This rustic, vivid red offers raspberry, black pepper and bacon flavors wrapped in firm tannins. Finishes with a kick of alcohol. Try now. • $20 • (11/15/96) • **87**

Côtes du Rhône Domaine de la Solitude 1995: Herbal and peppery notes overshadow the mild cherry flavors. Light-bodied but tannic, it's clean but not very generous. • $9 • (10/15/96) • **80**

Côtes du Rhône White Domaine de la Solitude 1994: Smooth and round, with a marked vanilla note to the flavors of pear and coconut. Soft and clean, with a light herbal finish. • $9 • (10/15/96) • **84**

LANCYRE, CHÂTEAU DE

Coteaux du Languedoc Pic St.-Loup Grande Cuvée 1995: Smooth and supple, with dark cherry and plum flavors and a good leathery note. This has plenty of stuffing to back up the flavors, and a lingering finish. Drink now through 2000. 1,300 cases made. • $22 • (05/31/98) • **87**

Coteaux du Languedoc Pic St.-Loup Vieilles Vignes 1995: A fresh, fruity wine, with good plum and berry flavors. Drink now. 4,000 cases made. • $12 • (05/31/98) • **80**

Coteaux du Languedoc White La Rouvière 1996: A rich and full-bodied white, with lovely cream and almond flavors, and some spicy elements on the finish. An interesting mix of flavors and texture that needs some rich food to stand up to it. Drink now. 1,650 cases made. • $15 • (06/15/98) • **87**

LANDE, DOMAINE DE LA

Bourgueil Cuvée Prestige 1993: Maturity has polished this elegant red and added lovely spice and cedar notes to the ripe cherry and chocolate flavors. A good effort in a difficult vintage. 1,000 cases made. • $17 • (05/15/97) • **88**

LANDIRAS, CHÂTEAU DE

Graves 1996: Rather steely and slightly hard, but displays good berry and earth character and a fresh finish. • $NA • (01/01/97) (BT) • **80-84**

Graves 1995: Medium-bodied, with tomato, berry and grasslike aromas and flavors. Rather mature at this stage; drink now. • $15 • (01/31/98) • **80**

Graves Cuvée Suzanne 1996: All finesse, with beautiful berry, cherry and floral character. Medium in body, with medium, fine tannins and a medium finish. Not trying to be more than it is. Very good indeed. • $NA • (01/01/97) (BT) • **85-89**

Graves White 1995: A rich and exotic wine for the vintage. Loads of mineral, spice and honey. Medium- to full-bodied, with honey and maple flavor, lovely fruit. Slightly heavy, but you have to like it. Very underrated. Drink now. • $15 • (04/30/98) • **90**

LANDRAT-GUYOLLOT, DOMAINE

Pouilly-Fumé La Rambarde 1996: Not for the fainthearted. Assertive grassy and herbal aromas and flavors show classic regional style, but there's not much ripe fruit to soften the tart varietal character. Drink now through 2000. 5,000 cases made. • $19 • (06/15/98) • **86**

LANESSAN, CHÂTEAU

Haut-Médoc 1992: Some decent body but just too unripe, presenting stewed tomato, green-bean character. Drinkable but uninviting. • $15 • (04/15/95) • **73**

Haut-Médoc 1990: Polished and smooth, with lovely aromas and flavors of cherry and earth and very velvety tannins. Drinkable now. 3,000 cases made. • $16 • (03/31/93) • **86**

Haut-Médoc 1989 • $20 • (03/15/92) • **85**

Haut-Médoc 1988 • $20 • (07/31/91) • **80**

Haut-Médoc 1985 • $22 Ⓐ • (04/30/88) • **87**

Haut-Médoc 1982 • $23 Ⓐ • (08/31/92) • **91**

LANGE, CHÂTEAU

Sauternes 1987 • $NA • (06/15/90) • **78**

LANGLOIS-CHÂTEAU

Chinon Château de Rivière 1995: Smoky, toasty notes are alluring, but dominate the light cherry flavors, and the tannins are a bit aggressive. Drinkable now. • $13 • (06/15/97) • **84**

Chinon Château de Rivière 1992 • $11 • (10/31/94) • **77**

Pouilly-Fumé Les Pierrefeux 1994 • $18 • (04/30/96) • **78**

Sancerre Château de Fontaine-Audon 1995: Alluring aromas of newly mowed hay make way for grassy, herbal and citruslike flavors in this tart, intense, textbook Sauvignon Blanc. • $18 • (04/30/97) • **89**

Sancerre Château de Fontaine-Audon 1994 • $18 • (04/30/96) • **78**

Saumur Red 1993 • $11 • (05/15/96) • **84**

Saumur White 1994 • $11 • (05/15/96) • **85**

Vouvray Château de Valmer 1995: Full-bodied, with a muscular core to balance its round softness and an appealing smoky note along with sweet peach and pineapple flavors. A generous wine with noticeable sweetness. • $13 • (06/15/97) • **86**

LANGOA BARTON, CHÂTEAU

St.-Julien 1997: Soft and velvety texture, with vanilla and berry aromas and flavors. Attractive and easy to like. • $NA • (06/15/98) (BT) • **85-89**

St.-Julien 1996: A lovely, balanced red, with berry, mineral and vanilla aromas and flavors. Medium- to full-bodied, with fine tannins and a long, silky textured finish. Fine winemaking. 2,500 cases made. • $40 • (06/15/98) (BT) • **90-94**

St.-Julien 1995: This big and powerful red has an iron backbone of tannins, aromas and flavors of black cherry, vanilla and hints of spice. Full-bodied, and though very tannic, it's velvety and fine. Try after 2002. • $30 • (01/31/98) • **93**

St.-Julien 1994: Excellent dark color and a brooding character marked by plum, raspberry, licorice and vanilla notes. Medium- to full-bodied, with fine tannins and a lovely, sweet fruit finish. Try now. 7,500 cases made.

Key: SS—Spectator Selection CS—Cellar Selection HR—Highly Recommended BB—Best Buy $NA—Price not available Ⓐ—Auction Price (BT)—Barrel Tasting
Dates in parentheses indicate the issues in which the ratings were published.

• $30 • (01/31/97) • **88**
St.-Julien 1993: Very good berry and cherry flavor and a hint of new wood. Medium in body, with medium-firm tannins and light finish. Try now. • $22 Ⓐ • (01/31/96) • **86**
St.-Julien 1991: Soft, simple and fruity, with black cherry and chocolate notes. A bit dry. • $18 • (03/31/94) • **77**
St.-Julien 1990: A balanced, refined wine with everything in the right proportions. Vanilla, cherry and plum character and fine tannins are all there. Drinkable now. 7,000 cases made. • $27 • (03/31/93) • **91**
St.-Julien 1989 • $39 Ⓐ • (03/15/92) • **94**
St.-Julien 1988 • $35 Ⓐ • (07/15/91) • **86**
St.-Julien 1985 • $38 Ⓐ • (06/15/88) • **91**
St.-Julien 1982 • $30 • (08/31/92) • **91**
St.-Julien 1961 • $115 • (03/16/86) • **63**
St.-Julien 1945 • $300 • (11/30/95) • **86**

LANGOUREAU, SYLVAIN

Meursault La Pièce sous le Bois 1992: Quite soft and harmonious, it delivers some pleasant butter, vanilla and pear flavors, ending with a toasty note on the finish. • $32 • (08/31/94) • **85**
St.-Aubin En Remilly White 1992: Crisp and simple, with modest apple, pear and spice notes. Seems a bit advanced for such a young wine. • $17 • (08/31/94) • **77**

LANSON

225th Anniversary Cuvée 1981 • $43 • (10/15/88) • **89**
225th Anniversary Spècial Cuvée 1980 • $43 • (11/30/86) • **95**
Brut Blanc de Blancs Champagne 1983: Not for everyone, this well-aged Champagne has intriguing aromas of ripe Brie, and flavors of toast, fig, vanilla and apple, followed by a tart finish. • $NA • (01/01/95) • **85**
Brut Champagne 1990: A vibrant texture and vivid fruit flavors light up this dry, crisp, electric-style Champagne. Refreshing now, but should gain complexity with age. Drink now through 2002. • $30 • (11/30/97) • **89**
Brut Champagne 1989: A generous, flavorful style, from the golden color to the ripe fruit and nut flavors to the rich texture and lasting finish. Shows all the welcoming character of the vintage. 64,916 cases made. • $27 • (12/31/96) • **89**
Brut Champagne 1988: Tastes like a fresh, lively, concentrated Chardonnay with bubbles. Has good acidity and a lingering finish. Drinkable now. Tasted twice. • $39 • (12/31/94) • **89**
Brut Champagne 1985: A super Champagne. Wonderfully focused and well balanced, with focused lemon and apple aromas, sweet, ripe lemon flavor and hints of dough. Medium-bodied, with a creamy mouthfeel. 40,000 cases made. • $37 • (12/31/90) HR • **93**
Brut Champagne 1983: Young, intense, rich and lively, with good depth of flavor and lemon, spice and ginger nuances in an agressive style that needs food to offset some of the coarseness. Drink now. • $30 • (12/31/89) • **85**
Brut Champagne 1982: Toasty, rich and concentrated, offering elegance and finesse, complexity and suppleness, yeasty and with just a hint of Pinot Noir fruit. Finish is long and tasty. • $27 • (10/15/88) • **92**
Brut Champagne Black Label NV: Good, solid Champagne that blends ripe fruit flavors, a round but lively texture and modest toasty, yeasty notes for a pleasant taste experience. Drink now. • $25 • (11/15/97) • **85**
Brut Champagne Noble Cuvée 1988: A solid, satisfying, brassy Champagne with a blast of crisp fruit flavor and a tangy, crisp texture. Has enough maturity to keep your interest. Drink now. • $70 • (12/31/97) • **87**
Brut Rosé Champagne 1982: A nicely made, light and delicate rosé. Shy nose that reveals just a touch of cherry and spice. It feels elegant and smooth on the palate. Subtle wine with some smokiness on the finish. • $35 • (12/31/88) • **88**
Brut Rosé Champagne NV: Crisp and fresh, a zingy, moderately fruity rosé of very good quality. Drink now. • $28 • (11/30/97) • **86**
Extra Dry Champagne Ivory Label NV: A bright, vibrant Champagne with snappy fruity flavors, fine balance and a smooth but tangy texture. The lingering finish makes it special. Drink now. • $22 • (11/15/97) • **89**

LAPELLETRIE, CHÂTEAU

St.-Emilion 1990: Lean and earthy, a simple wine with modest flavors and some nice spicy, toasty notes on the finish. Drinkable now. • $19 • (02/28/94) • **79**
St.-Emilion 1989 • $19 • (07/15/92) • **82**

LAPIERRE, M.

Morgon 1995: This firmly structured red mingles ripe plum and distinctly gamy notes, concentrated enough to balance the big tannins. A dinner wine; try with wild game. • $22 • (08/31/97) • **87**
Morgon 1994: Berry and vanilla aromas are attractive, but the flavors are muted on the firm palate, and tannins dominate the finish. May show more balance with food. • $18 • (09/15/96) • **84**

LAPLACE, DOMAINE FLEURY

Madiran 1994: On the light side, with berry and plum flavors. Finishes on a slightly herbal note. • $10 • (06/30/97) • **82**

LAPLACE, DOMAINE FRÉDÉRIC

Madiran 1994: Delicious and rich, but still quite tannic. Has good, ripe plum and berry flavors, with some tobacco notes. Try now. • $12 • (06/15/97) • **85**

LAPORTE, DOMAINE

Sancerre Domaine du Rochoy 1996: Crisp, showing lively aromas of citrus and herbs, with an appealing fennel note; stays lean and citrusy on the palate, with mineral and herbal accents. Good with shellfish. Drink now. • $20 • (06/30/98) • **86**
Sancerre Domaine du Rochoy 1994 • $15 • (04/30/96) • **84**
Sancerre Domaine du Rochoy 1993 • $17 • (11/15/95) • **88**

LARCIS-DUCASSE, CHÂTEAU

St.-Emilion 1997: Raisiny, with coffee grind aromas and flavors. Diluted finish. • $NA • (06/15/98) (BT) • **75-79**
St.-Emilion 1996: A bit rustic, with prune, berry and cherry character and velvety tannins. Slightly diluted. Tasted twice, with consistent notes. 6,000 cases made. • $22 • (06/15/98) (BT) • **80-84**
St.-Emilion 1995: Harmonious. A wine with pretty fruit and velvety tannins. Medium- to full-bodied, with chocolate, berry character and a fruity finish of medium length. Try now. • $20 • (01/31/98) • **88**
St.-Emilion 1994: Slightly metallic and weedy overall, despite some decent fruit flavor. Aggressive on the finish. Drink now, if you must. • $18 • (01/31/97) • **78**
St.-Emilion 1991: Simple and light, with notes of chive and berry. • $16 • (03/31/94) • **74**
St.-Emilion 1990: Harmonious and well proportioned, with lovely berry and cassis character, firm tannins and a crisp finish. Drinkable now. 5,000 cases made. • $25 • (03/31/93) • **90**
St.-Emilion 1989 • $28 • (03/15/92) • **91**
St.-Emilion 1988 • $20 • (04/30/91) • **82**
St.-Emilion 1982 • $27 • (08/31/92) • **85**

LARGE, A.

Côte-de-Brouilly 1994 • $10 • (10/31/95) • **84**

LARMANDE, CHÂTEAU

St.-Emilion 1997: Shows raisin, spice and tar with some prunes. Medium-bodied, with medium tannins and a short finish. A bit overdone. Wait and see. • $NA • (06/15/98) (BT) • **80-84**
St.-Emilion 1996: Violet and berry aromas and flavors. Medium- to full-bodied, with silky tannins and a mineral and violet aftertaste. Harmonious. Almost outstanding. 9,500 cases made. • $30 • (06/15/98) (BT) • **85-89**
St.-Emilion 1995: This wine sneaks up on you to deliver loads of fruit and tannins. Intense aromas of berries and minerals with hints of tobacco. Full-bodied, very velvety, with lovely fruit and tannins. Long, minty-fruity aftertaste. Best after 2000. 9,500 cases made. • $20 Ⓐ • (01/31/98) • **93**
St.-Emilion 1994: Subtle violet, berry and mineral aromas and layers of lovely, ripe berry flavors. Medium-bodied, with fine tannins. Delicious now, but will improve. 10,000 cases made. • $35 • (01/31/97) • **88**
St.-Emilion 1993: Polished raspberry, toasty oak character, medium body, fine tannins and fresh finish. Drinkable now. • $29 Ⓐ • (01/31/96) • **87**
St.-Emilion 1992: Succulent and fruity, offering vanilla, cherry and mineral aromas and flavors, medium-to-light body, light tannins and fresh finish. • $20 • (04/15/95) • **84**

FRANCE

St.-Emilion 1990: This dances across your palate with floral, vanilla, blackberry and black cherry flavors and superbly silky tannins. Exciting. Drink now. 8,000 cases made. • $24 • (03/31/93) • **94**

St.-Emilion 1989 • $18 Ⓐ • (03/15/92) • **95**

St.-Emilion 1988 • $46 Ⓐ • (04/30/91) • **86**

St.-Emilion 1986 • $43 Ⓐ • (06/30/89) • **91**

St.-Emilion 1985 • $27 Ⓐ • (10/15/94) • **89**

St.-Emilion 1983 • $33 Ⓐ • (10/15/94) • **88**

St.-Emilion 1982 • $29 Ⓐ • (08/31/92) • **82**

St.-Emilion 1981 • $34 Ⓐ • (10/15/94) • **89**

LARMANDIER-BERNIER

Brut Blanc de Blancs Champagne NV: This elegant bottling has what we look for in Blanc de Blancs: a vivid, lively blend of deep fruit and vanilla flavors, soft but ample mousse and a lingering finish. • $30 • (11/30/97) • **88**

Brut Blanc de Blancs Champagne Special Club 1992: A good, solid Champagne but on the lean side, showing doughy aromas, narrow lemon and apple flavors and a crisp finish. Drink now. • $40 • (11/30/97) • **86**

Brut Champagne Tradition NV: A very good, solid Champagne that offers a combination of toasty, mature flavors and lively fruit. Well balanced, with a lingering finish. • $25 • (10/31/97) • **87**

Extra Brut Blanc de Blancs Champagne Vieilles Vignes de Cramant NV: A cream-puff of a bubbly that's light and airy, with a soft texture and modest lemon and vanilla flavors. • $32 • (12/31/97) • **85**

LAROCHE

Chablis 1995: Zesty, crisp and even a bit tart. Light-bodied, and delivers fresh apple, pear and lemon flavors. Rather simple, but enjoyable. • $NA • (08/31/96) • **83**

Chablis 1994 • $15 • (05/31/96) • **81**

Chablis Beauroy 1993 • $19 • (08/31/95) • **84**

Chablis Blanchots 1995: A lovely *grand cru* with the texture of extra-virgin olive oil, flavors of cream, vanilla bean, wet stone, mineral and pear. As full-bodied as Chardonnay gets, it maintains structure on the finish. Drink now through 2005. • $32 • (06/15/97) • **89**

Chablis Blanchots 1994 • $40 • (05/31/96) • **92**

Chablis Blanchots 1993 • $37 • (08/31/95) • **85**

Chablis Blanchots Réserve de l'Obédiencerie 1994 • $56 • (05/31/96) • **92**

Chablis Blanchots Réserve de l'Obédiencerie 1993 • $56 • (08/31/95) • **81**

Chablis Les Clos 1996: Sexy, racy Chablis that shows this wonderful '96 vintage at its best. Full-bodied yet elegant, it packs loads of mineral, honey, ripe pear, tangerine and wet earth flavors in a subtle, round, seductive package that should only get better with cellaring. Long, multilayered finish. Tempting now, but this monument will hold through 2010 and perhaps beyond. 800 cases made. • $82 • (05/31/98) CS • **99**

Chablis Les Clos 1994 • $50 • (05/31/96) • **91**

Chablis Les Clos 1993 • $47 • (08/31/95) • **85**

Chablis Cuvée Première 1994 • $NA • (05/31/96) • **83**

Chablis Cuvée Première 1993 • $17 • (08/31/95) • **79**

Chablis Les Fourchaumes 1996: Polished like a diamond, this full-bodied, full-throttle, bold '96 Chablis invades the palate like an unstoppable army, firing salvos of lemon, pear, honey, mineral and flinty flavors that keep rippling to a long and harmonious finish. Great stuff. Drink now through 2010. • $40 • (05/31/98) • **94**

Chablis Les Fourchaumes 1995: Lively, nicely balanced and refreshing, with lemon, mineral, vanilla bean and spice flavors. Of medium body, the finish is clean and slightly chewy. Try now. 3,700 cases made. • $32 • (06/15/97) • **85**

Chablis Les Fourchaume 1993 • $23 • (08/31/95) • **86**

Chablis Les Fourchaumes Vieilles Vignes 1994 • $25 • (05/31/96) • **84**

Chablis Réserve de l'Obédience 1996: This clever wine extracts maximum mileage from heavily toasty, violet-scented, fancy new oak, yet remains ethereal in its balance, supple in texture and enormously ripe, with luscious, almost late-harvest flavors. Full-bodied and sweet-tasting, this delicious young Chardonnay is a ringing effort even by the high level of the vintage. Decant and serve at room temperature now, or try after 2005. 400 cases made. • $110 • (05/31/98) • **98**

Key: SS—Spectator Selection CS—Cellar Selection HR—Highly Recommended BB—Best Buy $NA—Price not available Ⓐ—Auction Price (BT)—Barrel Tasting

Dates in parentheses indicate the issues in which the ratings were published.

Chablis St.-Martin 1996: With wonderful ripe fruit, good acidity and a sweet character, this full-bodied village wine delivers plenty of butter and spice flavors. Slightly spritzy, with a pure, clean and long finish. Try after 2003. 3,500 cases made. • $23 • (05/31/98) • **88**

Chablis St.-Martin 1995: Well structured, medium-bodied. Lemon and honey notes mingle nicely with the ripe pear, apple tart, fig and spice flavors. Complex, long, sweet-tasting finish. Try now. • $19 • (08/31/96) • **86**

Chablis St.-Martin Vieilles Vignes 1995: Soft, supple, honeyed—a delight to taste young. Just shy of full-bodied, it blends citrus, earth and ripe fruit flavors into a balanced whole. Creamy-textured finish. Enjoy now. • $NA • (08/31/96) • **87**

Chablis St.-Martin Vieilles Vignes 1994 • $16 • (05/31/96) • **81**

Chablis Vaillons 1995: Rich, ripe and distinctive, tasting of wet earth, mineral and fruit, this *premier cru* has a creamlike texture accented by crisp citrus and dried herb flavors. Long finish. Try after 2000. • $30 • (06/15/97) • **89**

Chablis Vaillons 1994 • $21 • (05/31/96) • **81**

Chablis Vaillons 1993 • $21 • (08/31/95) • **82**

Chablis Vaudevey 1995: Sweet tasting, with honey, mineral and salted peanut character. Medium-bodied, crisp finish. Try now. • $NA • (06/15/97) • **84**

Chablis Vaudevey 1994 • $18 • (05/31/96) • **85**

Chablis Vaudevey 1993 • $18 • (08/31/95) • **81**

Mâcon-Lugny 1994: Clean but simple. The green, tart and grassy character turns sour on the diluted finish. 1,200 cases made. • $10 • (08/31/95) • **75**

Mâcon-Villages 1994: Straightforward and attractive butter, wet hay and almond character. Light-bodied and a bit diluted. Drink now. 6,000 cases made. • $9 • (08/31/95) • **77**

Nuits-St.-Georges 1988 • $28 • (11/15/90) • **87**

LAROSE-PERGANSON, CHÂTEAU

Haut-Médoc 1996: A surprisingly opulent wine for the vintage. Has intense aromas of blackberries, flowers and earth, and is full-bodied and compacted, with a ripe berry and cassis finish. • $NA • (01/01/97) (BT) • **85-89**

LAROSE-TRINTAUDON, CHÂTEAU

Haut-Médoc 1997: Velvety texture, but slightly green, with black currant and leaf character and a fading finish. Good effort. • $NA • (06/15/98) (BT) • **80-84**

Haut-Médoc 1996: Grapey, with black licorice aromas. Medium in body, with with soft tannins and a round texture. An attractive, friendly wine. Could move up. • $NA • (01/01/97) (BT) • **80-84**

Haut-Médoc 1995: Smoky, earthy and fruity. Medium-bodied, with pointed tannins and an earthy, slightly funky finish. Drinkable now. 90,000 cases made. • $18 • (01/31/98) • **84**

Haut-Médoc 1994: Simple and fruity. Offers a pretty plum and berry character on nose and palate. Medium-bodied, with light tannins and a light finish. Drink now. 80,000 cases made. • $18 • (01/31/97) • **84**

Haut-Médoc 1990: This wine is rather dull and slightly metallic in character with stemmy, earthy flavors and a light finish. Drinkable now. 80,000 cases made. • $12 • (03/31/93) • **75**

Haut-Médoc 1989 • $12 • (03/15/92) • **87**

Haut-Médoc 1988 • $9 • (04/30/91) • **84**

Haut-Médoc 1987 • $9 • (11/30/89) • **71**

Haut-Médoc 1986 • $10 • (11/30/89) • **78**

Haut-Médoc 1985 • $8 • (11/30/88) BB • **84**

Haut-Médoc 1983 • $13 • (10/15/86) • **73**

Haut-Médoc 1982 • $16 • (11/30/89) • **79**

Haut-Médoc 1979 • $15 • (10/15/89) • **76**

LARRIVET, DOMAINE DE

Pessac-Léognan 1995: A velvety yet slightly closed wine, this needs time to open. Dark chocolate, blackberry and cherry aromas. Full-bodied and chewy, with lots of ripe tannins and a medium, flavorful finish. Best after 2000. This is the second label of Château Larrivet-Haut-Brion. 1,000 cases made. • $20 • (01/31/98) • **89**

Pessac-Léognan White 1995: A bit candied, with apple, marzipan and white pepper aromas and flavors. Medium- to light-bodied, with a light aftertaste. Drink now. 800 cases made. • $18 • (04/30/98) • **79**

LARRIVET-HAUT-BRION, CHÂTEAU

Pessac-Léognan 1997: Good concentration of fruit, with mint and chocolate aromas and flavors. Medium in body, with medium tannins and a short finish. • $NA • (06/15/98) (BT) • **85-89**

Pessac-Léognan 1996: Inky in color, with cacao, fruit and smoke character on the nose. Full-bodied, with chewy tannins and a quickly fading finish. Impressive color and nose, but needs more on the finish to be outstanding. • $22 • (06/15/98) (BT) • **85-89**

Pessac-Léognan 1995: A smoky, fruity and richly aromatic wine. Medium-bodied, with fine tannins and a long, flavorful finish. Delicious now. • $20 • (01/31/98) • **86**

Pessac-Léognan 1994: Attractive aromas of ripe berry, raspberry and vanilla introduce this medium-bodied wine, with ultrafine tannins and a long, delicate, fruit finish. Drink now or hold. • $12 Ⓐ • (01/31/97) • **88**

Pessac-Léognan 1993: Pretty tobacco, smoke and toasty oak character. Medium in body, medium-soft tannins and medium aftertaste of red berries and chocolate. Delightful. • $19 • (01/31/96) • **86**

Pessac-Léognan 1992: Subtle and silky tobacco, tar and berry character; a good core of fruit and tannins, but short on the finish. • $15 • (04/15/95) • **79**

Pessac-Léognan 1989 • $22 Ⓐ • (03/15/92) • **89**

Pessac-Léognan 1988 • $25 • (04/30/91) • **94**

Pessac-Léognan 1986 • $17 • (06/15/89) • **82**

Pessac-Léognan White 1995: A subtle white, showing pretty apple, peach and honey aromas and flavors. Medium-bodied, with fresh acidity and a delicate, fruity aftertaste. Drink now. • $NA • (04/30/98) • **85**

Pessac-Léognan White 1994 • $12 Ⓐ • (03/31/96) • **83**

Pessac-Léognan White 1993 • $17 • (05/31/95) • **87**

LASCAUX, CHÂTEAU DE

Coteaux du Languedoc 1994: A bit simple, with modest plum and berry flavors, and a gamy note on the finish. • $10 • (06/30/97) • **78**

Coteaux du Languedoc 1991 • $9 • (03/15/94) • **84**

Coteaux du Languedoc 1990 • $9 • (03/15/94) • **85**

Coteaux du Languedoc Pic St.-Loup Les Nobles Pierres 1994: An odd mix of cola and mint aromas and flavors, with a drying finish. • $15 • (01/01/98) • **74**

LASCOMBES, CHÂTEAU

Margaux 1997: Pleasant. Medium-bodied, with raspberry and pepper character, light tannins and a light finish. • $NA • (06/15/98) (BT) • **80-84**

Margaux 1996: Very aromatic, with vanilla, spice and berry aromas and flavors. Medium- to full-bodied, with fine tannins and a medium aftertaste. Slightly hollow center palate. 20,000 cases made. • $40 • (06/15/98) (BT) • **85-89**

Margaux 1995: Slightly tight now, but shows impressive berry, smoke and meat character. Full-bodied and very tannic, with masses of fruit. Give this some time. Best after 2001. • $30 • (01/31/98) • **92**

Margaux 1994: A wine of wonderful finesse, offering lovely, dense aromas of berries, licorice and black currants, very fine tannins and a long, silky finish. Drink now or hold. • $20 Ⓐ • (01/31/97) • **88**

Margaux 1993: Simple blackberry and cherry flavors and a delicate tannin structure. 20,000 cases made. • $26 • (01/31/96) • **80**

Margaux 1990: A rich wine, with leathery, berry, milk chocolate character, fine tannins and a long finish. Drinkable now. 26,500 cases made. • $22 • (03/31/93) • **86**

Margaux 1988 • $30 Ⓐ • (08/31/91) • **82**

Margaux 1983 • $40 Ⓐ • (02/15/88) • **84**

Margaux 1982 • $20 Ⓐ • (08/31/92) • **81**

Margaux 1981 • $39 Ⓐ • (05/16/85) • **85**

Margaux 1979 • $24 Ⓐ • (10/15/89) • **84**

Margaux 1961 • $95 Ⓐ • (04/30/96) • **86**

LASSALLE, J.

Brut Blanc de Blancs Champagne 1987: A nicely mature and enjoyable Champagne from a not-so-great year. Like a rich, aged Chardonnay with bubbles, it has butter, pear and vanilla aromas and flavors and a lingering finish. Drink soon. • $40 • (12/31/96) • **87**

Brut Blanc de Blancs Champagne 1986: Fresh and youthful for its age, but harmonious and subdued. Its crisp citrus flavors blend well with the buttery and toasty notes. A creaminess gives it a nice subtlety and the finish is firm. Drinkable now. 500 cases made. • $40 • (12/15/94) • **90**

Brut Champagne 1987: Nicely mature aromas clash with tight, sharp, acidic texture, making this an intriguing but lean taste experience. Drink now before it develops further. • $39 • (11/30/95) • **83**

Brut Champagne Cuvée Angeline 1987: Has abundant acidity, good citrus flavors and a tart finish. Tight and crisp, but enjoyable. Better than expected from this off-year. • $45 • (12/31/96) • **85**

Brut Champagne Special Club 1992: Showy in style, open and fruity in flavor and slightly sweet, this is pleasant and frothy. Drink now. • $50 • (11/30/97) • **86**

Brut Champagne Special Club 1989: A fully mature, soft-textured Champagne. It has aromas of vanilla custard and similarly rich, soft flavors. Mellow and ready to drink, enjoy it now. • $50 • (12/31/96) • **90**

Brut Champagne Special Club Premier Cru 1985: Gorgeously rich and almost fat in flavor, with butterscotch, pear and vanilla notes and a creamy, smooth texture. This is showy, round, easy to like and ready to drink. Melts in your mouth. 300 cases made. • $46 • (12/31/94) HR • **91**

Brut Rosé Champagne Réserve des Grandes Années NV: A serious, full-bodied rosé Champagne with a deep salmon color, spicy-toasty aromas and generous, mature fruit flavors that linger on the finish. It improves with each sip. Drink now through 2000. • $40 • (11/30/97) • **91**

LASSARAT, ROGER

Pouilly-Fuissé Clos de France 1994: Crisp and tart, a lean-textured wine with some green apple and lime flavors. Very hard to enjoy now. 704 cases made. • $NA • (05/31/96) • **79**

Pouilly-Fuissé Clos de France 1993: Effusively fruity; crisp green apple, grapefruit and fresh herb flavors and a hint of pineapple. Austere at this stage but refreshing; clean finish. Drinkable now. 833 cases made. • $13 • (05/15/95) • **84**

Pouilly-Fuissé Cuvée Prestige 1994: Straightforward and extremely crisp, with lots of citrus flavors but not quite enough complexity. A bit lean and simple on the finish, but should make a good match with seafood. Try now. 381 cases made. • $NA • (05/31/96) • **81**

Pouilly-Fuissé Cuvée Prestige 1993: Seems quite advanced for a 1993, demonstrating meat, lemon, hazelnut, marzipan, honey and dried-fruit flavors. Quite toasty and silky; somewhat hot on the very long finish. Drink now. • $NA • (05/15/95) • **84**

Pouilly-Fuissé Cuvée Prestige Vin Non Filtré 1993: Chalky, chewy Pouilly, offering a silky mouthfeel but also some cedary, woody, earthy components and more elegant spice and fruit flavors. Big finish. Drinkable now. • $NA • (05/15/95) • **85**

LASSERRE DU HAUT, DOMAINE

Merlot-Tannat Vin de Pays des Côtes de Gascogne 1996: A quaffable, light-bodied red with grapey flavors and just enough tannin to keep it honest. Drink now. • $7 • (03/31/98) • **79**

LASSIME, MARQUISE DE

Cabernet Sauvignon Vin de Pays des Côtes de Gascogne 1996: A tough customer. Its modest fruit never surmounts the acidic hardness and astringent tannins. 9,000 cases made. • $6 • (12/15/97) • **78**

Cabernet Sauvignon Vin de Pays des Côtes de Gascogne 1995: Herb and chocolate notes run through this modestly flavored red, sporting decent varietal character. 8,500 cases made. • $6 • (07/31/96) • **80**

Merlot Cépage Côtes de Gascogne 1991 • $5 • (10/31/92) • **76**

Merlot Vin de Pays des Côtes de Gascogne 1996: Nice and juicy, with delicious berry and cherry flavors and decent concentration. Good pepper and chocolate notes mark the finish. 10,000 cases made. • $6 • (11/15/97) • **84**

Merlot Vin de Pays des Côtes de Gascogne 1995: There's good weight and concentration to back up the blackberry flavor here. Still, it's modest in proportion. 9,000 cases made. • $6 • (07/31/96) • **80**

Vin de Pays des Côtes de Gascogne White Réserve 1996: On the tart side, with a floral and citrus character, this white is simple and short. 5,000 cases made. • $6 • (09/30/97) • **78**

LASTOURS, CHÂTEAU

Gaillac 1995: A bit dried out and stewy-tasting, with modest plum and cherry flavors. A blend of Fer, Syrah, Merlot and Tannat. Past its prime. • $8 • (04/30/98) • **78**

LATHAM, CHÂTEAU

Corbières 1995: Light and peppery, with some plumlike flavors, too. A simple-tasting red wine. 6,000 cases made. • $6 • (06/30/97) • **79**

LATHAM, COLLECTION ERIC

Corbières Les Hauts de Mandourelle 1993: Wild, dried cherry and green olive aromas and flavors turn extremely dry and astringent. Tough to warm up to. 8,000 cases made. • $6 • (07/31/96) • **77**

LATOUR, CHÂTEAU

Pauillac 1997: Firm and rich, with plenty of currant and berry character. Medium- to full-bodied, with velvety tannins and a slightly short finish. The weakest of the first growths, but it should improve with barrel age. • $NA • (06/15/98) (BT) • **90-94**

Pauillac 1996: A *wunderkind*. Greatest Latour since 1990. Stunning clarity of currant and mineral character. Full-bodied, with full, velvety tannins and a long finish. One of the wines of the vintage. • $250 • (06/15/98) (BT) • **95-99**

Pauillac 1995: An outstanding Latour, offering marvelous character on the nose and palate with its complex layers of blackberry, tobacco, cedar and berries. This first-growth Bordeaux is full-bodied and velvety, with a long fruit and tobacco aftertaste. Best after 2002. • $150 Ⓐ • (01/31/98) CS • **94**

Pauillac 1994: Vivid aromas of cassis and vanilla, followed by a bounty of fruit flavors and fine, silky tannins, all building on the palate. A fine, elegant Latour that's unusually approachable now, though better in 1999. • $107 Ⓐ • (01/31/97) • **90**

Pauillac 1993: Powerful and extremely balanced, a wine with guts and character, delivering seamless texture and mint, lead-pencil, currant, chocolate and slightly toasty character. Deep and full-bodied, yet the tannins are incredibly supple. Great soil and winemaking here. Try in 2000. • $84 Ⓐ • (01/31/96) • **91**

Pauillac 1992: Star of the vintage. Absolutely delicious vanilla, berry and currant flavors; very good intensity, medium body and medium-firm tannins. Very silky with a long finish. Drinkable now. • $77 Ⓐ • (04/15/95) • **89**

Pauillac 1991: Stretching the limits of this vintage. A complex wine with a major dose of new wood. Very silky and fine. Better after a little more time in the cellar. • $50 Ⓐ • (03/31/94) • **89**

Pauillac 1990 • $425 Ⓐ • (03/15/93) CS • **100**

Pauillac 1989 • $147 Ⓐ • (03/15/92) • **97**

Pauillac 1988 • $118 Ⓐ • (04/30/91) • **93**

Pauillac 1987 • $64 Ⓐ • (10/15/90) • **80**

Pauillac 1986 • $134 Ⓐ • (05/31/89) • **93**

Pauillac 1985 • $132 Ⓐ • (10/15/94) • **94**

Pauillac 1984 • $63 Ⓐ • (03/31/87) • **92**

Pauillac 1983 • $104 Ⓐ • (10/15/94) • **89**

Pauillac 1982 • $446 Ⓐ • (08/31/92) • **94**

Pauillac 1981 • $96 Ⓐ • (10/15/94) • **89**

Pauillac 1979: Pretty and still lively, this medium-bodied wine is focused and balanced, with spicy and woodsy accents to its black cherry flavors. Drink now through 2005. • $97 Ⓐ • (12/15/97) • **89**

Pauillac 1978: An old-style wine, with hard tannins and ripe, slightly raisiny flavors. The mineral, cigar box and mint notes are appealing, but the wine is still quite tough. Drink now or hold; it may soften. • $155 Ⓐ • (12/15/97) • **88**

Pauillac 1976: Rather light and nearing full maturity, this offers cigar box, herbal and woodsy aromas and flavors. Supple on the palate, yet firm on the finish. Drink now. • $72 Ⓐ • (12/15/97) • **87**

Pauillac 1975: Famously tough, this monster is finally beginning to soften. Dark flavors of coffee, raisins, tobacco and earth are emerging through the tannins. Drinkable now, but may improve through 2000. • $137 Ⓐ • (12/15/97) • **91**

Pauillac 1971: Shows mature color and aromas, with tobacco, mint and herb notes, but it's still very firm on the palate, and the fruit may dry out before it softens. Drink now. • $92 Ⓐ • (12/15/97) • **82**

Pauillac 1970: Controversial. Many tasters praised it, but I found it a bit tough. Still, there's a core of sweet fruit, with spice, mineral and tobacco notes on the long finish. Drink now or hold. • $390 Ⓐ • (12/15/97) • **90**

Pauillac 1967: Mature now, this silky wine offers raisin, tobacco, mineral and slightly gamy flavors, and turns a bit dry on the finish. A good effort for the vintage, but needs drinking now. • $94 Ⓐ • (12/15/97) • **87**

Pauillac 1966: Still quite young, this ripe, lively wine is rich with plum, cedar, spice and roasted flavors, fresh and balanced. A jeroboam served at dinner had the inky color of the '90—and even younger flavors. Beautiful now, but will hold for a decade. • $304 Ⓐ • (12/15/97) • **95**

Pauillac 1965 • $55 Ⓐ • (03/31/90) • **74**

Pauillac 1964: Considered the best from a difficult vintage, this wine is mature now, with open smoke, mineral and gamelike aromas and fading but still elegant flavors of cedar and chocolate. Drink now. • $184 Ⓐ • (12/15/97) • **88**

Pauillac 1963 • $135 Ⓐ • (03/31/90) • **77**

Pauillac 1962: Overshadowed by the '61 but worth seeking out. Firm yet round, with cherry, raisin, chocolate and licorice flavors that show real intensity. Drink now through 2005. • $262 Ⓐ • (12/15/97) • **91**

Pauillac 1961: This bottle lived up to expectations: full-bodied, rich and firm, still very lively, packed with plum, chocolate and tobacco flavors, with an extraordinarily long, sweet finish. Hard to resist now, but should improve through 2005, at least. • $805 Ⓐ • (12/15/97) • **99**

Pauillac 1960: Still lively, despite the poor reputation of the vintage, this offers cherry, raisin, chocolate and earthlike flavors. Balanced, with firm tannins. Best now, but can hold through 2000. • $70 Ⓐ • (12/15/97) • **89**

Pauillac 1959: Not a perfect bottle, with a crumbling cork, lots of sediment and a slightly browning color. Still, it was silky and firm, fragrant and enticing, with cherry, cedar and mineral notes. Drink now or hold. • $650 Ⓐ • (12/15/97) • **89**

Pauillac 1958 • $125 Ⓐ • (03/31/90) • **81**

Pauillac 1957: A disappointment in this lineup. The color is still deep, but the flavors are tough and a bit vegetal, with brown sugar and earth notes. Drink up. • $185 Ⓐ • (12/15/97) • **81**

Pauillac 1956 • $134 Ⓐ • (03/31/90) • **62**

Pauillac 1955: A generous wine with gorgeous, open flavors of sweet fruit, minerals, coffee and chocolate. It's still firm enough to handle food, and the finish is very long. Drink now through 2000. • $243 Ⓐ • (12/15/97) • **92**

Pauillac 1953: Unusually elegant, even delicate, for Latour, but beautiful nonetheless, with supple, refined flavors of sweet cherries, raisins, tobacco, spices and minerals. A favorite among the tasters. Drink now through 2000. • $192 Ⓐ • (12/15/97) • **90**

Pauillac 1952: Still quite powerful, this displays dark color and mature, generous aromas and flavors of minerals, dried cherries and tobacco. Tannins are firm, but not dry. Mature now, but will hold through 2005. • $296 Ⓐ • (12/15/97) • **88**

Pauillac 1950 • $270 Ⓐ • (03/31/90) • **79**

Pauillac 1949: A real beauty, still vibrant and intense, yet utterly harmonious, with mineral, dried cherry, raisin and cassis flavors that linger on the long finish. It's perfect now, but will likely hold for at least another decade. • $620 Ⓐ • (12/15/97) • **94**

Pauillac 1948: Assertive, but less harmonious than nearby vintages, this firm, medium-bodied wine offers earth, iodine and cherry flavors. Eccentric but interesting. Drink now. • $348 Ⓐ • (12/15/97) • **85**

Pauillac 1947: A big wine that's beginning to lose its grip, with noticeable volatile acidity and drying tannins. It's vivid with prune and chocolate flavors, but lacks harmony. Drink now. • $561 Ⓐ • (12/15/97) • **84**

Pauillac 1945: Utter perfection. Deep ruby in color, it's bursting with rich fruit and dark chocolate aromas. On the palate it's full and opulent, with ripe fruit, cedar and tobacco flavors that linger and expand on the finish. An exceptional bottle of an exceptional wine. Still has plenty of life ahead. • $1600 Ⓐ • (12/15/97) • **100**

Pauillac 1944 • $287 Ⓐ • (03/31/90) • **70**

Pauillac 1943 • $253 Ⓐ • (03/31/90) • **67**

Pauillac 1942 • $418 Ⓐ • (03/31/90) • **59**

Pauillac 1940 • $260 Ⓐ • (03/31/90) • **64**

Pauillac 1937 • $288 Ⓐ • (03/31/90) • **89**

Pauillac 1936 • $119 Ⓐ • (03/31/90) • **75**

Pauillac 1934: The vintage of the decade is still showing well, at least in this bottle. The wine is brick-colored, with fragrant mineral and dried cherry aromas, and is silky on the palate, a bit dry but still vibrant. May still evolve, but it's hard to believe it can get better than this. • $233 Ⓐ • (12/15/97) • **92**

Pauillac 1929 • $180/1.5 liter Ⓐ• (03/31/90) • **95**

Key: SS—Spectator Selection CS—Cellar Selection HR—Highly Recommended BB—Best Buy $NA—Price not available Ⓐ—Auction Price (BT)—Barrel Tasting

Dates in parentheses indicate the issues in which the ratings were published.

Pauillac 1928: Still vivid in color and flavor, this famously tannic wine has become supple and expressive, with mineral, iodine and brown sugar flavors. Fading, but slowly; it may not improve, but it still has life ahead. • $1350 Ⓐ • (12/15/97) • **90**

Pauillac 1926: Fully mature now, this is brick-colored, with earthy aromas and firm, slightly dry flavors of raisin, cedar and dried cherries. Drink up. • $660 Ⓐ • (12/15/97) • **83**

Pauillac 1924 • $633 Ⓐ • (03/31/90) • **91**

Pauillac 1920 • $658 Ⓐ • (03/31/90) • **50**

Pauillac 1918: Delicate and sweet, fading but elegant, this suple wine has alluring aromas of violets and cherries, with light earth and raisin flavors. • $168 Ⓐ • (12/15/97) • **91**

Pauillac 1908: Assertive and distinctive, if not perfectly balanced, this is quite perfumed, with aromas of prunes, cloves and cedar. Sweet and supple on the palate, it's perked up by a slight touch of volatile acidity. • $259 Ⓐ • (12/15/97) • **89**

Pauillac 1900 • $525 Ⓐ • (03/31/90) • **90**

Pauillac 1899: Extraordinary purity. This ethereal wine is light rose-colored, with elegant rose petal, chocolate and coffee aromas and silky, supple flavors of raisin and cedar. Still shows a firm backbone on the finish. • $2850 Ⓐ • (12/15/97) • **90**

Pauillac 1892: Still lively and even fleshy, this offers a bright brick color, chocolate and light barnyard aromas, and supple well-integrated flavors of raisins and cedar that linger long on the finish. • $460 • (12/15/97) • **92**

Pauillac 1875 • $NA • (03/31/90) • **77**

Pauillac 1874 • $NA • (03/31/90) • **97**

Pauillac 1870 • $NA • (03/31/90) • **94**

Pauillac 1865 • $NA/1.5 liter • (03/31/90) • **94**

Pauillac 1847 • $NA/1.5 liter • (03/31/90) • **93**

LATOUR, LOUIS

Aloxe-Corton 1992: Light and sweet tasting, supple and lean, with some modest raspberry and plum flavors. Seems a bit hot on the finish. Ready now. 1,800 cases made. • $19 • (12/15/94) • **80**

Aloxe-Corton 1955 • $NA • (08/31/90) • **85**

Aloxe-Corton Domaine Latour 1995: Shows herbal aromas and flavors, but there appears to be some fatness midpalate, then severe tannins and heat. Unbalanced. 6,000 cases made. • $26 • (11/15/97) • **77**

Aloxe-Corton Domaine Latour 1993: Delicate plum, berry and vanilla character, medium to light body, fine tannins and a fresh finish. Drink now. 2,500 cases made. • $21 • (11/15/95) • **82**

Aloxe-Corton Domaine Latour 1991: Light and crisp, with a narrow beam of raspberry flavor that remains through the finish. Drinkable now. 250 cases made. • $18 Ⓐ • (01/31/94) • **82**

Aloxe-Corton Domaine Latour 1990: Pleasant and delicate, a wine that will give lots of pleasure relatively early thanks to its creamy vanilla, milk chocolate and bright strawberry flavors. Try now. 2,000 cases made. • $22 • (12/15/92) • **84**

Aloxe-Corton Domaine Latour 1989 • $24 • (01/31/92) • **84**

Aloxe-Corton Les Chaillots 1995: A *premier cru* with the color of a rosé, flavors of strawberry and cherry, an astringent finish. Not exactly what one expects to find in a bottle of red Burgundy. 3,000 cases made. • $32 • (11/15/97) • **75**

Aloxe-Corton Les Chaillots 1985 • $37 • (04/15/88) • **76**

Auxey-Duresses White 1995: Slightly tart, with citrus, green apple, pear, melon and honey flavors. A touch of grassiness gives this fresh, medium-bodied wine a distinct personality. Satiny texture and smooth finish; tempting now through 2005. 100 cases imported. 333 cases made. • $19 • (08/31/97) • **88**

Bâtard-Montrachet 1995: Big, showy, heavily toasty and enormously flavorful, with great intensity and power on the finish. Delicious ripe pear flavors, along with cinnamon, nutmeg, orange-peel and dried fig notes. Needs time; try around 2005. 167 cases imported. 500 cases made. • $134 Ⓐ • (08/31/97) • **95**

Bâtard-Montrachet 1994: Exotic and well made. Rich, ripe and velvety, with honey, mint, apricot jam, fig, mango and tobacco flavors. Full-bodied, for delicious drinking now. • $120 • (08/31/96) • **88**

Beaune Domaine Latour 1995: Light in color and body, offering some sweet-tasting cherry, licorice, spice and strawberry notes in a soft package. Pretty finish. Drink slightly chilled. 1,000 cases made. • $28 • (11/15/97) • **75**

Beaune Domaine Latour 1993: Rather light but enjoyable to drink, featuring soft tannins, delicate berry, cherry character and fresh finish. Drink now. 1,000 cases made. • $22 • (11/15/95) • **80**

Beaune Domaine Latour 1991: Crisp texture, modest flavor, with watered-down berry aromas and flavors. Drinkable now. 42 cases made. • $17 Ⓐ • (01/31/94) • **77**

Beaune Domaine Latour 1990: Elegant and well made, this round, smooth wine has perfumed, delicate aromas, medium body and chocolate, cedar and earth flavors. Drinkable now. 500 cases made. • $21 • (12/15/92) • **87**

Beaune Domaine Latour 1989 • $22 • (01/31/92) • **91**

Beaune Domaine Latour White 1993: Pretty apple, cream and honey flavors and a hint of oak on the nose and palate. Medium-bodied, firm acidity and a long, long finish. Impressive for the appellation. Drink now. 250 cases made. • $30 • (08/31/95) • **86**

Beaune Les Vignes Franches 1993: Delicate, easy-to-drink '93 that caresses your palate with fine tannins, although it's slightly light. Drinkable now. 583 cases made. • $26 • (11/15/95) • **80**

Beaune Les Vignes Franches 1992: Very light and floral, an appealing red that finishes with a stemmy edge. 250 cases made. • $20 • (12/15/94) • **76**

Beaune Les Vignes Franches 1985 • $51 Ⓐ • (03/15/88) • **90**

Beaune White 1994: Ripe, rich and a bit overdone, with a slight cardboardy flavor. • $NA • (08/31/96) • **77**

Bonnes Mares 1989 • $60 • (01/31/92) • **93**

Bourgogne 1992: Crisp in texture but watery in flavor, showing only modest strawberry accents on the light finish. 4,000 cases made. • $10 • (12/15/94) • **74**

Bourgogne 1990: Light and simple, with cherry and strawberry flavors. Pleasant to drink now, but seems a bit diluted. 4,000 cases made. • $10 • (12/15/92) • **79**

Bourgogne Cuvée Latour 1990: Lovely and harmonious, with pretty floral, wet earth and rose petal aromas that echo on the palate and on the silky, cherry-tasting finish. Drink now. 6,000 cases made. • $11 • (12/15/92) • **86**

Bourgogne Cuvée Latour 1989 • $NA • (01/31/92) • **80**

Bourgogne White 1993: Quite hard and tart. Light-to-medium in body, some decent fruit character; bitter almond, acidic finish. 5,833 cases made. • $10 • (05/15/95) • **73**

Chablis 1995: Medium-bodied and woody, with honey, pear, citrus and green apple flavors. Mouthpuckering finish has minerally, chalky accents. • $NA • (08/31/96) • **85**

Chablis 1994 • $18 • (05/31/96) • **76**

Chablis Beauroy 1996: Fresh and zesty, packed with fruit, mineral, earth and honey. Direct, frank and full-bodied, this is lovely, clean and pure, with a smooth finish. Drink now through 2005. 1,100 cases made. • $27 • (05/31/98) • **89**

Chablis Fourchaume 1996: Fairly thick, but also a bit easy, lacking the structure of a top Chablis. Some ripe pear and tropical character, but it turns a bit sour on the finish. Drink now. 1,400 cases made. • $30 • (05/31/98) • **77**

Chablis Montmains 1996: Supple and especially gentle for a '96 Chablis, with some melon, honeydew and lemon flavors. Medium-bodied. Drinkable now to 2001. 1,900 cases made. • $28 • (05/31/98) • **85**

Chablis Montmains 1995: Fairly rich, medium-bodied *premier cru.* Crisp and zesty, with complex fruit flavors and touches of honey, spice and cream on the long, balanced finish. Ready now. • $NA • (08/31/96) • **86**

Chablis Montmains 1994 • $25 • (05/31/96) • **76**

Chambertin 1993: Surprisingly weak dried cherry and wet earth character. Medium-bodied, fine tannins and a sweet fruit finish. Drinkable now. 200 cases made. • $102 • (11/15/95) • **84**

Chambertin Cuvée Hèritiers Latour 1989 • $90 • (01/31/92) • **78**

Chambertin Cuvée Hèritiers Latour 1985 • $76 • (03/15/88) • **95**

Chardonnay Grand Ardèche Vin de Pays des Coteaux de l'Ardèche 1995: Rich and smoky, with an earthy aroma and pear and spice flavors. A distinctive style, but not for everyone. • $12 • (06/30/97) • **78**

Charmes-Chambertin 1985 • $50 • (03/15/88) • **85**

Chassagne-Montrachet 1995: Elegant and lovely, with clean, pure fruit aromas, richness and density on the palate. Pear, tropical and toasty coconut flavors, fairly supple, picking up intensity on the finish. Drink now through 2005. 2,833 cases made. • $38 • (05/31/97) • **88**

Chassagne-Montrachet 1994: Focused and lively, with an assertive vegetal component. Light-to-medium body, with hints of honey, spice, dried herb and wet earth. Good intensity and richness on the finish. Drinkable now. 3,333 cases made. • $34 • (05/31/96) • **82**

Chassagne-Montrachet 1993: Clean citrus and apple character; light and delicate on the palate, adding a crisp vanilla finish. 1,750 cases made. • $32 • (05/15/95) • **82**

Chassagne-Montrachet 1992: Mellow and tasty, with nut and honey flavors, good balance and smooth texture. Solid and satisfying. 2,400 cases made. • $26 • (08/31/94) • **82**

LATOUR, LOUIS

Chassagne-Montrachet Les Chenevottes 1994: Focused and somewhat angular, offering little right now, but there are some interesting mineral, toasty oak, ripe pear and apple flavors. 500 cases made. • $37 • (05/31/96) • **85**

Chassagne-Montrachet Les Chenevottes 1993: Attractive cream, apple and honey aromas and flavors, medium body, firm acidity and long, toasty oak and fruit finish. • $35 • (05/15/95) • **86**

Chevalier-Montrachet Les Demoiselles 1995: A legend in the making—fabulous from start to finish. More food than wine, this full-bodied, massive, ripe wine requires chewing, not sipping, to enjoy. Rich and ripe yet totally harmonious, this beauty cascades with complex oak, honey, peanut butter, melon and all sorts of exotic spices. Creamy in texture, with an ultralong finish. Drink now through 2005. 67 cases imported. 167 cases made. • $134 Ⓐ • (08/31/97) • **98**

Chevalier-Montrachet Les Demoiselles 1994: Medium-bodied and quite delicate, with ripe, sweet-tasting pear, apricot and honey flavors underscored by a minerally note. Try now. • $160 • (08/31/96) • **86**

Chassagne-Montrachet Morgeot 1995: Splendidly balanced, with ripe fruit and spice flavors mingling beautifully. Full-bodied. If serving at room temperature, it's drinkable now through 2005. 250 cases imported. 625 cases made. • $43 • (08/31/97) • **90**

Clos Vougeot 1995: Light in color, it tastes diluted and astringent. Not much there. Pretty sad for this to be sold as a *grand cru*. 250 cases made. • $74 • (11/15/97) • **71**

Corton Château Corton Grancey 1995: Light in color, this delivers some brown sugar, spice, cinnamon, black cherry and toasty bread complexity on the palate. Hot, slightly alcoholic finish. Drink now. 1,250 cases made. • $49 • (11/15/97) • **78**

Corton Château Corton Grancey 1993: Sleek and racy berry, plum and vanilla character. Very fresh on the palate with fine tannins. Drink now. 1,250 cases made. • $43 • (11/15/95) • **88**

Corton Château Corton Grancey 1992: Light in color and flavor, with appealing strawberry and mint aromas and taste notes. Simple and drinkable. • $NA • (12/15/94) • **80**

Corton Château Corton Grancey 1990: Not made in a big style, but the intensity is there, with mint and milk chocolate notes, a very creamy, supple mouthfeel and a smooth, round finish. Develops in the glass. Tasted twice. Drinkable now. 800 cases made. • $43 • (12/15/92) • **89**

Corton Château Corton Grancey 1989 • $48 • (01/31/92) • **89**

Corton Château Corton Grancey 1985 • $90 Ⓐ • (03/15/88) • **89**

Corton Château Corton Grancey 1959 • $NA • (08/31/90) • **89**

Corton Château Corton Grancey 1953 • $NA • (08/31/90) • **91**

Corton Château Corton Grancey 1947 • $NA • (08/31/90) • **85**

Corton Clos de la Vigne au Saint 1985 • $43 • (03/15/88) • **89**

Corton Domaine Latour 1991: Basic cherry flavors have an anise edge in this light, spicy wine. Finishes on the crisp side, echoing fruit. Drinkable now. 117 cases made. • $29 Ⓐ • (01/31/94) • **84**

Corton Domaine Latour 1990: Incredibly light for this appellation, with a weak color, premature aromas and flavors and a diluted finish. Drinkable now. • $35 • (12/15/92) • **70**

Corton Domaine Latour 1985 • $38 • (03/15/88) • **90**

Corton-Charlemagne 1995: Impressive for its balance, sweet-tasting fruit flavors and lingering, oak-spiced finish. Full-bodied, showing excellent intensity on the supercharged finish, this vigorous *grand cru* white Burgundy is drinkable now through 2000. 1,250 cases imported. 3,750 cases made. • $71 Ⓐ • (08/31/97) CS • **93**

Corton-Charlemagne 1994: Distinctive and a bit rustic. Very intense, with excellent concentration of lime, dried herb, smoke, cream and honey notes. Try now. 4,166 cases made. • $96 Ⓐ • (05/31/96) • **90**

Corton-Charlemagne 1993: Muscular, honey, toasty oak and mineral aromas and flavors, medium-to-full body, fine acidity and long, tasty finish. • $67 Ⓐ • (08/31/95) • **88**

Corton-Charlemagne 1992: Very seductive but also quite earthy now and difficult to assess. But we love the honeyed, ripe richness and racy, tight beam of hazelnut, toffee, vanilla and fruit flavors. There is a toasty, smoky and complex finish. 2,200 cases made. • $77 Ⓐ • (08/31/94) • **90**

Côte de Beaune-Villages 1990: Simple and a little green, falling short of the overall quality of this vintage. 4,000 cases made. • $16 • (12/15/92) • **78**

Côte de Nuits-Villages 1995: Soft, watery and very disappointing. Roséllike color and body, neutral flavors, dry finish. This is wine? 150 cases made. • $15 • (11/15/97) • **70**

Key: SS—Spectator Selection CS—Cellar Selection HR—Highly Recommended BB—Best Buy $NA—Price not available Ⓐ—Auction Price (BT)—Barrel Tasting

Dates in parentheses indicate the issues in which the ratings were published.

Criots-Bâtard-Montrachet 1994: If you like chocolate milk shakes, this is for you. Thick, ripe and lush, with mocha, spice, chocolate and ripe fruit flavors. Full-bodied and a bit tired already; drink soon. • $NA • (08/31/96) • **82**

Echézeaux 1985 • $49 • (03/15/88) • **87**

Gevrey-Chambertin 1995: A lean, firm red, with an earthy accent to the black cherry flavors. Accessible now. 3,000 cases made. • $34 • (11/15/97) • **75**

Gevrey-Chambertin 1992: Balanced and pretty, offering some complexty, with tar, rose petal, raspberry and cherry flavors. It's light, but also silky and appealing. Ready now. 900 cases made. • $27 • (12/15/94) • **84**

Gevrey-Chambertin 1990: Straightforward and earthy, with wet earth, hay and barnyardy notes underneath the modest cherry flavors. Drinkable now. 2,000 cases made. • $32 • (12/15/92) • **78**

Gevrey-Chambertin 1989 • $35 • (01/31/92) • **87**

Gevrey-Chambertin 1985 • $36 • (10/15/88) • **77**

Mâcon-Lugny Les Genièvres 1993: Expressive and vibrant, this light-bodied, bone-dry Mâcon titillates the palate using clean flavors—lemon, lime, apple and spice—that end on a juicy finish. Drink with seafood. 33,333 cases made. • $11 • (08/31/95) • **83**

Mercurey 1995: Chalonnaise rosé. Diluted, lean and astringent, with candied fruit flavors. 1,600 cases made. • $18 • (11/15/97) • **72**

Meursault 1995: A beautiful village white that coats the palate with its rich, creamlike texture. Full-bodied, with nice mineral, pear, toasty coconut, hazelnut and honey flavors, it glides to a graceful, sweet-tasting finish. Tempting now through 2005. 6,750 cases made. • $30 • (05/31/97) • **90**

Meursault 1994: Vibrant, zesty, with a grassy, green apple character but rather lean on the finish. 7,500 cases made. • $30 • (05/31/96) • **79**

Meursault 1993: A medium-bodied white demonstrating mineral, apple and some asparagus flavors; crisp, lightly fruity finish. 4,166 cases made. • $27 • (05/15/95) • **83**

Meursault-Blagny 1995: Extremely well made, and a good reflection of its minerally *terroir*. It's vibrant yet full-bodied and firmly structured with subtle honey, fresh herbs, citrus and green apple flavors, well concentrated, with that mineral overtone. Hold until 2000 or so. 2,083 cases made. • $42 • (05/31/97) • **90**

Meursault-Blagny Château de Blagny 1993: Ready to drink, showing apple and mushroom aromas and flavors, medium body and simple finish. 2,900 cases made. • $34 • (08/31/95) • **81**

Meursault Les Charmes 1995: Smooth; the full Burgundian treatment. Medium- to full-bodied, shows some fried pineapple, toasty coconut notes and a crisp edge of dried herbs and toast and smoke flavors that give character. Try after 2000. 75 cases imported. 250 cases made. • $52 • (08/31/97) • **90**

Meursault Les Gouttes d'Or 1995: Ripe and rich, its sweet-tasting fruit character mingling nicely with stony, flinty notes. Full-bodied, it offers great intensity and a long finish. Drink after 2000. 125 cases imported. 375 cases made. • $49 • (08/31/97) • **90**

Meursault Les Gouttes d'Or 1994: Distinctive chestnut and cedar flavors mingle with a touch of honey and lime in this rather straightforward Chardonnay. Try now. 500 cases made. • $40 • (05/31/96) • **80**

Meursault Les Gouttes d'Or 1993: Rich and smooth, supple, delivering some nice mineral, tropical fruit and pear flavors and a hint of honey and toasty oak on the sweet-tasting finish. Drinkable now. 500 cases made. • $37 • (08/31/95) • **86**

Meursault Les Gouttes d'Or 1992: Lush, exotic and ripe in flavor, generous and silky in texture and very long-lasting on the finish. Has fine balance, but it leans toward the fat and full-blown style. 350 cases made. • $31 • (08/31/94) • **89**

Montagny La Grande Roche 1995: A lush, round, dense Chardonnay, with some lovely lemon, mineral and ripe fruit character. Medium- to full-bodied, it's vibrant and long on the finish. Drink now. 15,000 cases made. • $14 • (05/31/97) • **85**

Montagny La Grande Roche 1994: A vibrant and exciting *premier cru* from a minor appellation, with intense flavors of dried herb, fresh basil, honey and grapefruit. Juicy, though it turns a bit herbal and short on the finish. 11,666 cases made. • $13 • (05/31/96) • **84**

Montrachet 1993: Massive, rich and ripe—surprisingly opulent for the vintage. Loads of coconut, tropical fruit and smoke flavors. Extremely silky on the palate, adding a long, long finish. • $195 • (08/31/95) • **90**

Montrachet 1992: Builds on a solid base of flavors and adds layers as you drink it. Quite lively and exotic; has some inviting flavors of ginger, hazelnut, pear, coconut and pineapple. Ripe and full-bodied; delicious to drink now. 150 cases made. • $206 Ⓐ • (08/31/94) CS • **95**

Nuits-St.-Georges 1993: Delivers some ripe fruit character but remains sligthly diluted in texture. Drink now. 500 cases made. • $31 • (11/15/95) • **78**

Nuits-St.-Georges 1991: Hints of cherry and spice liven up this light, elegant style. Finishes clean and modestly tannic, echoing fruit and spice. Drinkable now. 42 cases made. • $28 Ⓐ • (01/31/94) • **84**

Pernand-Vergelesses White 1995: Tight, closed, it delivers some dried herb, citrus, spice and mineral flavors. Pretty, but not very concentrated. Succulent, well-balanced finish. Medium- to full-bodied. Try after 2005. 50 cases imported. 833 cases made. • $21 • (08/31/97) • **85**

Pernand-Vergelesses White 1994: Oaky and fat, with some modest honey, pear and pie-crust aromas and flavors. Could use some more fruit. 383 cases made. • $20 • (05/31/96) • **78**

Pommard 1995: It's light, delicate and quite sweet, and you don't taste much *terroir* or definition, but this traditional-style, light- to medium-bodied wine offers some spice, cinnamon, plum and strawberry. 1,100 cases made. • $32 • (11/15/97) • **82**

Pommard 1993: Delicate and delicious now. Medium in body, featuring game and berry character, medium tannins and fresh finish. 500 cases made. • $28 • (11/15/95) • **82**

Pommard Les Epenots 1992: Crisp and nicely focused, showing more flavor than aroma at this point, echoing raspberry and spice on the finish. 50 cases made. • $32 • (12/15/94) • **83**

Pommard Les Epenots 1991: Youthful color, light and fragrant, with pleasant strawberry and floral notes on the finish. A little citrusy but lively. A bit less ripeness than the '90. • $32 • (02/28/95) • **85**

Pommard Les Epenots 1990: Shows very pretty, spicy vanilla, strawberry and raspberry flavors that persist on the finish. Delicious. Try now. • $37 • (02/28/95) • **88**

Pommard Les Epenots 1989 • $38 • (02/28/95) • **85**

Pommard Les Epenots 1988 • $38 • (02/28/95) • **81**

Pommard Les Epenots 1987 • $30 • (02/28/95) • **81**

Pommard Les Epenots 1986 • $NA • (02/28/95) • **82**

Pommard Les Epenots 1983 • $NA • (02/28/95) • **84**

Pouilly-Fuissé 1995: Nice, clean and pure '95 white Burgundy, showing a firm structure and lots of good acidity to hold up the ripe fruit. Medium-bodied and well made. Drink now. • $15 • (05/31/98) • **85**

Pouilly-Fuissé 1994: Good fruit but one-dimensional. Offers plenty of pear, apple and even a touch of tropical fruit character. It's round and sweet-tasting, but turns slightly herbal on the finish. 12,500 cases made. • $21 • (05/31/96) • **81**

Pouilly-Fuissé 1993: A clean and straightforward Pouilly, offering some wet earth, green apple character and good acidity. Medium body, medium length. Drink now. 16,667 cases made. • $15 • (05/15/95) • **80**

Puligny-Montrachet 1995: A bit crisp and stemmy, despite some honeyed ripe fruit character and spicy oak accents. Medium-bodied; drink chilled. 2,416 cases imported. 4,500 cases made. • $39 • (08/31/97) • **79**

Puligny-Montrachet 1994: Sharp and tart, with a green, earthy character. Modest fruit. 5,000 cases made. • $35 • (05/31/96) • **72**

Puligny-Montrachet 1993: Impressive village wine offering good concentration of toasty oak, apple and pear character, medium body and richness and a lovely coconut finish. 4,250 cases made. • $34 • (05/15/95) • **84**

Puligny-Montrachet 1992: Supple and generous village wine, with ripe pear and a hint of honey laced with mineral and vanilla flavors. Drinkable now. 4,000 cases made. • $27 • (08/31/94) • **87**

Puligny-Montrachet La Garenne 1995: Opulent, thick but also laser sharp in flavor, with citrus, tropical fruit and spice notes. Balanced, well made, full-bodied, it's a pleasure to taste. Delicious now, should improve through 2005. 167 cases imported. 500 cases made. • $49 • (08/31/97) • **90**

Puligny-Montrachet La Garenne 1994: Fresh and impressively crisp and vibrant for a 1994. Slightly herbal and even grassy, with ripe pear, green apple and honey flavors. Medium-bodied, and has good intensity. Drink now. • $NA • (08/31/96) • **85**

Puligny-Montrachet La Garenne 1993: Delicious mineral, apple and spice aromas and flavors. Medium body, well-integrated acidity and a long finish. 750 cases made. • $36 • (08/31/95) • **87**

Puligny-Montrachet Les Folatières 1995: Very seductive, full-bodied and amazingly silky, it fans out on the palate with rose petal, honey, mineral, spice, tropical fruit and toasty bread notes. Try now through 2005. 333 cases imported. 500 cases made. • $56 • (08/31/97) • **92**

Puligny-Montrachet Les Folatières 1994: Round and smooth, with a mineral and green apple character. Somewhat lighter in body and a bit short and simple. Tasted twice, with consistent notes. 750 cases made. • $29 Ⓐ • (05/31/96) • **79**

Puligny-Montrachet Les Folatières 1993: Extremely fresh apple, truffle and honey aromas and flavors. Full-bodied, fine acidity and a long, tasty finish. Drinkable now. 500 cases made. • $39 • (08/31/95) • **86**

Puligny-Montrachet Les Folatières 1992: Distinctively earthy, nutty and buttery in style. Solid and firm in texture, complex in flavor and very long-lasting on the finish. Drinkable now. 780 cases made. • $34 • (08/31/94) • **89**

Puligny-Montrachet Les Referts 1994: Very ripe and open, full-bodied and honeyed. Herbal, tropical fruit and spice flavors are a bit simple but make for fun drinking. Ready now. • $27 Ⓐ • (08/31/96) • **84**

Romanée St.-Vivant Les Quatre Journaux 1995: Light and simple, looking and tasting more like rosé than Vosne-Romanée. Has a certain sweetness on the palate but absolutely zero *goût de terroir*. Just a straightforward red, at Burgundylike prices. Shame on the producer for bottling this Pinot under the name of this famed appellation. 250 cases made. • $160 • (11/15/97) • **74**

Romanée St.-Vivant Les Quatre Journaux 1993: Elegant, delicious cassis and berry aromas and flavors, medium body, silky tannins and a long, fruity finish. Better in 2001. • $NA • (05/15/96) • **89**

Romanée St.-Vivant Les Quatre Journaux 1992: Delicate, with floral, slightly herbal overtones to the focused thread of raspberry and green tobacco flavor. Finishes a little chewy. Drinkable now. 200 cases made. • $120 • (12/15/94) • **81**

Romanée St.-Vivant Les Quatre Journaux 1990: Very pleasing, with a lot of milk chocolate, raspberry and vanilla aromas and flavors. A very delicate style, with good intensity on the soft finish. Try now. 300 cases made. • $139 • (12/15/92) • **89**

Romanée St.-Vivant Les Quatre Journaux 1989 • $140 • (01/31/92) • **93**

Romanée St.-Vivant Les Quatre Journaux 1985 • $99 • (03/15/88) • **98**

Romanée St.-Vivant Les Quatre Journaux 1953 • $NA • (08/31/90) • **94**

St.-Véran 1995: Sturdy, with flavors of earth, honeydew and beeswax. Somewhat rustic finish. Slightly diluted. Drink now. 2,500 cases made. • $12 • (05/31/97) • **79**

St.-Véran 1994: Smooth and round, tasting ripe and sweet, offering pear, melon and cream flavors. Lacks a bit of vibrancy. Enjoy now. 2,500 cases made. • $11 • (08/31/95) • **83**

Santenay 1989 • $NA • (01/31/92) • **80**

Savigny-lès-Beaune 1992: Light, crisp and simple, with modest raspberry and tobacco flavors. Drinkable now. 1,200 cases made. • $13 • (12/15/94) • **78**

Savigny-lès-Beaune 1991: Light, simple and pleasant. Drinkable now. 100 cases made. • $13 Ⓐ • (01/31/94) • **79**

Savigny-lès-Beaune 1989 • $NA • (01/31/92) • **84**

Vosne-Romanée Les Beaux Monts 1985 • $36 • (03/15/88) • **86**

LATOUR, PIERRE

Volnay 1953 • $NA • (08/31/90) • **86**

Volnay 1952 • $NA • (08/31/90) • **90**

LATOUR À POMEROL, CHÂTEAU

Pomerol 1997: A well-balanced and elegant '97 with plum, toasty oak and berry character. Medium-bodied, with medium tannins. Delicious. • $NA • (06/15/98) (BT) • **85-89**

Pomerol 1996: Pleasant chocolate and berry aromas and flavors, with undertones of toasty oak. Medium-bodied, with medium, velvety tannins and a short finish. • $55 • (06/15/98) (BT) • **85-89**

Pomerol 1995: A pretty, elegant Pomerol, but a big disappointment since it scored 95-100 points in barrel tastings. Beautiful aromas of blackberries and porcini mushrooms. Full-bodied, with silky tannins and a lovely, smooth finish. Better after 2000. • $55 • (01/31/98) • **89**

Pomerol 1994: Very fine, this has attractive aromas of fruit and dried herbs, fine tannins and a long finish of vanilla, mineral and mint character. Drinkable now. • $47 • (01/31/97) • **89**

Pomerol 1993: Disappointing for this estate. Appealing now, showing crisp, light-bodied texture and some cherry, olive, dried herb and blackberry notes. Somewhat diluted. A barrel sample tasted earlier was much better. • $40 • (01/31/96) • **81**

Pomerol 1992: Firm and steely, showing cherry, raspberry and wet earth aromas and flavors, medium-to-light body, good tannins and a fresh finish. 3,000 cases made. • $30 • (04/15/95) • **80**

Pomerol 1990: Muscular yet harmonious, showing tar, licorice and currant aromas and flavors. The firm tannins are well integrated; the flavors are ripe yet fresh and well balanced. Drink now. • $60 • (10/15/94) • **90**

Pomerol 1989 • $55 • (05/15/94) • **93**

Pomerol 1988 • $29 Ⓐ • (10/15/94) • **90**

Pomerol 1986 • $50 • (10/15/94) • **86**

Pomerol 1985 • $40 Ⓐ • (05/15/94) • **90**

Pomerol 1983 • $75 • (10/15/94) • **92**

Pomerol 1982 • $144 Ⓐ • (08/31/92) • **97**

Pomerol 1981 • $50 • (10/15/94) • **88**
Pomerol 1979 • $45 • (05/15/94) • **85**
Pomerol 1976 • $75 • (05/15/94) • **87**
Pomerol 1975 • $70 • (05/15/94) • **80**
Pomerol 1971 • $80 • (05/15/94) • **82**
Pomerol 1970 • $115 Ⓐ • (05/15/94) • **91**
Pomerol 1966 • $175 • (05/15/94) • **79**
Pomerol 1964 • $87 Ⓐ • (05/15/94) • **82**
Pomerol 1962 • $200 • (05/15/94) • **86**
Pomerol 1961 • $1800/1.5 liter • (04/30/96) • **94**
Pomerol 1959 • $NA • (10/15/90) • **90**
Pomerol 1955 • $200 • (05/15/94) • **82**
Pomerol 1953 • $350 • (05/15/94) • **88**
Pomerol 1952 • $300 • (05/15/94) • **85**
Pomerol 1949 • $1500 • (05/15/94) • **72**
Pomerol 1947: A solid wine, dense with generous leather- and tobacco-scented berry flavors that persist. • $NA • (05/31/97) • **91**
Pomerol 1945 • $978 Ⓐ • (05/15/94) • **74**

LATOUR-GIRAUD

Meursault Clos du Cromin 1994: Fat and ripe, with some honey and floral notes. Tastes a bit overdone. Also slightly simple and astringent on the finish. • $NA • (05/31/96) • **75**
Meursault Le Limozin 1995: Voluptuous, but slightly odd, with a combo of varnish, apricot and peach flavors that won't please everyone. Quite intense but also quite crisp. Medium-bodied. • $NA • (08/31/97) • **70**
Meursault Le Porusots 1995: Rich, dense and full-bodied, this is a mouthful of Chardonnay flavors, with mineral, grass, honey and toast notes in balanced amounts. Stays the course, with an elegant structure to its sweet-tasting, lemony and fairly intense finish. Try now. • $NA • (05/31/97) • **88**
Meursault Les Genevrières 1995: Class act for a *premier cru*. Extremely clean and pure in flavor, it sparkles with intense, ripe fruit and spice concentration, titillating the palate from start to finish. Full-bodied. Shows great potential as it glides with crisp definition to a long, flawless, subtle and elegant finish. Bravo! Drink now through 2010. • $NA • (08/31/97) • **97**
Meursault Les Genevrières 1994: Quite elegant and rather tightly built, with mineral, grapefruit and vanilla aromas and flavors, but it needs a bit more length and concentration. • $NA • (05/31/96) • **84**
Meursault Les Narvaux 1994: Some decent apple, pear and honey notes, adding chalky, chewy character on the finish. • $NA • (05/31/96) • **81**
Meursault Les Perrières 1995: Dense yet subtle and charming, this wine grows on you. It's full-bodied, layered with lemon, crisp fruit, a good dose of toasty oak and a chewy mineral character that all come together on the wonderful, lingering, smoky finish. A class act that's tempting now, but best to wait until after 2000. • $NA • (05/31/97) • **93**
Meursault Les Perrières 1993: Polished and austere, showing some floral, honey and mineral flavors; good concentration. Drinkable now. • $NA • (05/15/95) • **85**
Puligny-Montrachet Champ Canet 1995: A scorching wine, with toasty oak almost burning up the palate. Lots of ripe flavors, too, with plenty of tropical character, but the overall impression is that it's slightly inelegant and overdone. May smooth out with time. • $NA • (05/31/97) • **83**
Puligny-Montrachet Champ Canet 1994: Voluptous and rich, thick and full-bodied. This unctuous wine delivers some nice honey, toast and caramel flavors. A touch hard on the finish, though. • $NA • (05/31/96) • **85**
Puligny-Montrachet Champ Canet 1993: Some pear, appley, steely character. Medium-bodied, slightly candied. • $NA • (05/15/95) • **78**

LAUNAY, CHÂTEAU

Entre-Deux-Mers 1994 • $9 • (05/31/95) • **79**

LAURENS

Blanc de Blancs Blanquette de Limoux Clos des Demoiselles 1986 • $11 • (12/31/90) • **81**
Brut Blanc de Blancs Blanquette de Limoux Tête de Cuvée 1988 • $15 • (11/30/92) • **82**

Key: SS—Spectator Selection CS—Cellar Selection HR—Highly Recommended BB—Best Buy $NA—Price not available Ⓐ—Auction Price (BT)—Barrel Tasting
Dates in parentheses indicate the issues in which the ratings were published.

LAURENS, DOMAINE J.

Brut Blanc de Blancs Blanquette de Limoux 1988 • $10 • (11/30/92) • **80**

LAURENT, DOMINIQUE

Beaune Premier Cru 1994: More mature than some in this category, it tastes of mineral, plum, woodsy underbrush and truffle. Medium-bodied, silky and ready to drink. • $38 • (09/30/97) • **85**
Beaune Premier Cru Vieilles Vignes 1993: Pretty, plummy red featuring velvety tannins and a hint of vanilla on aftertaste. Medium in body and tannins and an easy finish. Drinkable now. • $NA • (05/15/96) • **86**
Bonnes Mares 1994: Gorgeous. The aromas speak of poetry and rose petals, violets, jasmine. The flavors entice with succulent cassis, earth and subtle oak notes. Everything is in the right place in this harmonious, sexy, rounded, balanced beauty. More silky than powerful. Tempting now through 2010. • $160 • (09/30/97) • **96**
Bonnes Mares 1992: Very ripe, smooth, generous and supple with gorgeous violet, currant and berry flavors that persist on the long finish, accented by a touch of spicy oak. • $NA • (12/15/94) • **90**
Bourgogne Cuvée No. 1 1994: A simple Bourgogne Rouge of amazing quality, this is packed with spice, mineral, floral, currant and plum complexity. Seductive with supple, ripe tannins, the finish is a bit hard now so try around 2000. • $18 • (09/30/97) • **89**
Chambertin-Clos de Bèze 1994: Impressively dark in color and thick in texture, it tastes strongly of oak now, but it's also quite rich and ripe. The fruit has to struggle to get through, though. Offers lovely ripe tannins, with sweet plum and red berry, spicy mocha, fresh coffee and bitter chocolate flavors. A complex wine from a sophisticated winemaker. Try after 2005. • $150 • (09/30/97) • **93**
Chambertin-Clos de Bèze 1992: A laudable effort, ripe and delicate, supple and stylish, unusual for this vintage. It carries focused blackberry, black cherry, mint and toasty oak flavors, finishing with a satisfying silkiness. Drink now. • $125 • (12/15/94) • **91**
Chambolle-Musigny Les Sentiers 1994: Sexy and hedonistic, with aromas and flavors to die for. Imagine licorice, violet, rose petal and cassis flavors, subtle oak accents, all presented in a delicate, supple, harmonious and balanced wine. Seductive, ripe, sweet tannins. It doesn't hit you with a big statement, but grows on you with fascinating complexity. Tempting now through 2005. Decant before serving. • $95 • (09/30/97) • **94**
Charmes-Chambertin 1992: Starts off ripe and generous, offering lovely raspberry, cedar and toast flavors that become rich and seductive on the finish. Gets somewhat tannic. Try now. • $62 • (12/15/94) • **87**
Clos Vougeot 1993: What can we say? Packed to the rim with fruit. Full body and tannins and a kaleidoscope of black cherry and red berry flavors. Long finish. Give this time; better in 2003. • $NA • (05/15/96) • **94**
Echézeaux 1994: Ripe, rich and full-bodied, packed with intense earth, black cherry and cassis character, it bursts with explosive flavors and shows amazing supple, ripe tannins. A pure and clean, mouthcoating, immensely extracted Pinot Noir, especially for this difficult vintage. Great length. Almost the perfect red Burgundy. Wine of the vintage? • $75 • (09/30/97) • **97**
Gevrey-Chambertin Lavaux St.-Jacques 1994: Brilliant winemaking. Displays amazing extraction of flavors for this difficult vintage. Pure, clean aromas are followed by concentrated and vivid black- and red berry flavors that marry nicely with earthy tones and sophisticated oak-infused mocha, coffee and chocolate notes. Supple, ripe tannins. So sweet we had it analyzed for residual sugar, but none was found. Long finish that won't stop. Tempting now, better from 2000 to 2005. • $80 • (09/30/97) • **93**
Gevrey-Chambertin Vieilles Vignes 1993: Profound, caressing and superbly crafted, boasting tons of red berry, spice and wood-scented character. Cascades through your palate to a long, exquisite, delicate, toasty, smoky finish. Supple and silky; amazing quality for a village wine. Tempting now but better in 2000. • $NA • (05/15/96) • **95**
Grands Echézeaux 1994: Impresses more with its finesse than its power. Emits beautiful aromas so charming and sexy you'll swoon, and the combination of violet, rose petal and cassis flavors make it quite distinctive. Supple, ripe tannins. Drink after 2000. • $125 • (09/30/97) • **90**
Mazis-Chambertin 1993: Wine of the vintage? From very old vines, this is a monumental red Burgundy of superb length. Amazingly complex aromas of black and red berries, mineral and cedar. Full in body and packed with tannins, it might be approachable around 2002 and then should age for two decades. • $117 • (05/15/96) • **98**
Nuits-St.-Georges La Richemone 1994: Distinctive, with real wet earth, *goût de terroir*, mineral character along with cassis notes. Surprisingly subtle on

the oak for a Laurent wine. Supple, sweet tannins. Long, ripe finish is impressive. Try after 2000. • $75 • (09/30/97) • **92**

Nuits-St.-Georges Les Vaucrains 1993: Thick, rich and packed with flavors, it's more like Cabernet than Pinot. Impressive mint, berry and plum aromas and flavors, full body and tannins and long finish. Needs time; try in 2003. • $NA • (05/15/96) • **89**

Pommard Les Epenots 1994: A supercharged, full-bodied and full-flavored wine, showing seductive character of deep complexity from mineral, currant, toasty oak and black cherry flavors. Long, delightful finish with impressively supple and ripe tannins. Try after 2000. • $95 • (09/30/97) • **94**

Pommard Les Epenots 1993: An electrifying *premier cru* packed with personality. Very chewy and full-bodied, it delivers tons of harmony and delicious mocha, cassis and wild berry flavors. Given time this should offer gobs of pleasure. Long, crisp finish. Try in 2000. • $85 • (05/15/96) • **93**

Pommard Vieilles Vignes 1993: This beautiful '93 combines crisp aromas of cassis and black currant typical of the vintage with a slight toast, mocha, coffee complexity. Seductive, chewy, minerally, earthy, spicy character. Long, flavorful finish. Try in 2000. • $48 • (05/15/96) • **93**

Ruchottes-Chambertin 1993: A big mouthful here: full-bodied and loads of fruit. Berry, plum, pineapple, the flavor sensations go on and on. Velvety tannins and long finish. Amazing. Better in 2006. • $117 • (05/15/96) • **96**

Volnay 1993: Dark colored, brooding, difficult to taste. Overly vibrant and crisp cassis and black cherry flavors. Seems a bit tart and rustic, but it has substantial fruit concentration. Better in 2000? • $NA • (05/15/96) • **86**

Vosne-Romanée 1994: Decent fruit creeps in, but it's also a bit green and lacks the sort of balance you want in red Burgundy. Medium-bodied, drying finish. • $46 • (09/30/97) • **79**

Vosne-Romanée 1993: Rather lean, but very good plum and berry character. Medium body, somewhat one-dimensional flavors and hard tannins. Drinkable now. • $NA • (05/15/96) • **86**

LAURENT, JEAN

Brut Blanc de Blancs Champagne NV: Rich, nicely mature aromas and flavors make this distinctive. Will appeal to those who want to go beyond mere fruit flavor and bubbles. Full-bodied. Drink now. 1,300 cases made. • $27 • (04/30/98) • **88**

Brut Blanc de Noirs Champagne NV: A seductive combination of bright fruit flavor and a smooth, buttery texture makes this very attractive. Grabs your attention and holds it through the lingering finish. Drink now. 4,000 cases made. • $25 • (04/30/98) • **88**

Brut Champagne Millésime 1989: Austere in style, this distinctive Champagne offers lemony, chalky flavors and a slightly astringent texture. It grows on you, and seems to expand as you sip. Should improve with time. Drink now through 2000. 800 cases made. • $35 • (04/30/98) • **88**

Brut Rosé Champagne NV: Like an elegant Pinot Noir, with bubbles. Has the classic cherry, spice and earth flavors of Pinot, with the lively, exuberant texture of Champagne. Shows real character and length. Drink now through 2000. 1,000 cases made. • $29 • (04/30/98) • **90**

LAURENT-PERRIER

Brut Champagne 1988: Toasty, smoky aromas, clean, lively fruit flavors and a touch of maturity complement its depth, elegance, good acidity and lingering finish. Very stylish and easy to like. • $42 • (11/30/95) • **90**

Brut Champagne 1985 • $40 • (12/31/90) • **87**

Brut Champagne 1983: Shows the maturity you might expect from a 1983, but this was an excellent vintage for Champage and this one offers a rich and earthy core of toasty pear and pineapple, finishing with a long, flavorful finish. Packs in lots of flavor. A special drinking experience. Drink now. 50,000 cases made. • $40 • (11/30/93) HR • **93**

Brut Champagne 1982: Just lovely. A subdued elegance gives way on the finish to a lively, creamy and complex aftertaste that lingers on. Lots of attractive dough and yeast aromas and flavors, it's both creamy and crisp. A class act all the way. • $95 • (12/31/88) • **93**

Brut Champagne Brut L.P. NV: An all-around good sparkler with fresh fruit flavors, a smooth texture and lively balance. • $25 • (10/31/97) • **84**

Brut Champagne Grand Siècle 1985: Incredibly fine and intense, with grapefruit, vanilla, toast aromas and flavors and all perfectly integrated. An absolute joy to drink today. Continues to improve in the bottle. Given 91 points in October 1993. • $109 • (12/31/93) • **92**

Brut Champagne Grand Siècle 1982: Sophisticated, youthful and complex. A lovely wine in the lighter style. Smooth and creamy, ripe and concentrated, it is intense without being heavy. Layers of honey, vanilla, and pear. • $72 • (12/31/88) • **92**

Brut Champagne Grand Siècle 1979 • $87 • (02/15/88) • **90**

Brut Rosé Champagne NV: Light, fresh and nearly sweet, this is a good but relatively simple rosé with strawberry flavors and a short finish. • $40 • (12/31/97) • **84**

Brut Rosé Champagne Grand Siècle Alexandra 1988: Quite interesting. A distinctive but austere rosé that features aromas of mushroom and mineral, mature flavors of brown sugar and cherry but a dry, smooth texture that carries over on the lingering finish. Drink now. • $110 • (04/30/98) • **88**

Brut Rosé Champagne Grand Siècle Cuvée Alexandra 1982: Pretty salmon color, with rich, toasty, elegant and complex spice, cherry, toast and nutmeg flavors that are broad and expansive, finishing with a cherry and spice aftertaste. • $125 • (12/31/89) • **91**

LAUZE, COMTE DE

Châteauneuf-du-Pape 1993: Simple cherry, raisin and coffee flavors are light and dull, and firm tannins take over the palate. Try now. • $NA • (12/15/96) • **80**

Châteauneuf-du-Pape White 1993: The pear, lime and herbal flavors are attractive in this firm white, but an intrusive, sweet buttery note mars the balance. • $NA • (12/15/96) • **79**

LAVABRE, CHÂTEAU

Coteaux du Languedoc Pic St.-Loup 1995: Beautiful and finely crafted, with layer upon layer of fruit, spice and chocolate flavors. Offers delicious plum, smoke and clovelike components as well, with fine tannins and a lingering finish. Lively, ripe and well balanced, it's simply delicious. Drink now for its youthfulness or try in 2000. 1,500 cases made. • $13 • (02/28/98) HR • **92**

LAVILLE BERTROU, CHÂTEAU

Minervois 1991 • $9 • (03/15/94) • **82**
Minervois 1990 • $9 • (06/15/93) • **77**
Minervois 1988 • $8 • (08/31/91) • **76**

LAVILLE HAUT BRION, CHÂTEAU

Pessac-Léognan 1995: Solid Laville. Plenty of toasty oak and ripe fruit. Full-bodied and very rich, with apple, coconut and fresh fruit on the aftertaste. Surprisingly zingy, good acidity. Best from late this year. • $55 • (04/30/98) • **91**

Pessac-Léognan 1994 • $62 Ⓐ • (03/31/96) • **86**
Pessac-Léognan 1993 • $55 • (05/31/95) • **89**

LEBEGUE-BICHOT

Chambertin Clos de Bèze 1945 • $305 • (08/31/90) • **96**

LEBEGUE & CO., J

Merlot Vin de Pays d'Oc 1995: A bright, fresh, young red wine with lively cherry and raspberry flavors, light body and smooth texture. • $6 • (08/31/97) • **84**

LÉCHENEAUT

Chambolle-Musigny 1995: A fleshy, chunky style of Chambolle, moderately structured, showing ripe plum and blackberry flavors and smoky oak nuances. Try now. 125 cases made. • $40 • (11/15/97) • **88**

Chambolle-Musigny 1993: Compact Chambolle showing plenty of thick fruit but also slight barnyard character. Medium- to full-bodied, adding silky tannins and a pretty plum, berry finish. Try in 2000. • $48 • (11/15/95) • **88**

Chambolle-Musigny Premier Cru 1995: Superb. Both finesse and power play out dramatically in this ripe, rich, thick, velvety and seductive red. It has depth and complexity, layers of red- and blackberry flavors, fat tannins and sweet fruit that just wraps around the palate. Drink now through 2010. 75 cases made. • $60 • (11/15/97) • **96**

Chambolle-Musigny Premier Cru 1994: Light, but pleasantly fruity, with nice strawberry and floral flavors. Finishing with coarse tannins. Try now. • $50 • (11/15/96) • **83**

Chambolle-Musigny Premier Cru 1993: A beautiful, full-bodied red Burgundy to dream about. Ripe yet full of finesse, its well-defined plum,

FRANCE

currant, earth and rose petal flavors unfold graciously. Firm structure of supple tannins. Don't touch until 2004. • $68 • (11/15/95) • **93**

Clos de la Roche 1995: Chunky, with deep black cherry flavors that take on a savage edge. The tannins are a bit burly. It's satisfying, although lacking the length of the best '95s. 37 cases made. • $100 • (11/15/97) • **89**

Clos de la Roche 1993: Round and sweet tasting, a lovely, medium-bodied wine with currant, raspberry and black cherry flavors. Great, crisp intensity on the long, chewy finish. Try now. • $90 • (11/15/95) • **91**

Clos de la Roche 1992: Striving for delicacy and grace, this pretty wine shows floral, spicy oak nuances to the fine thread of raspberry flavor that extends into the finish. • $70 • (12/15/94) • **88**

Nuits-St.-Georges 1992: Crisp, light and modestly fruity, with just a hint of currant flavor to brighten it. Drinkable now. • $26 • (12/15/94) • **78**

Nuits-St.-Georges Les Cailles 1995: Fresh, crisp and spicy, with mocha, chocolate, white pepper and cassis flavors struggling with some tough tannins for now. Medium-bodied, it has the stuffing and acidity to live on and improve through 2000. 141 cases made. • $60 • (11/15/97) • **86**

Nuits-St.-Georges Les Cailles 1994: Crisp texture and bright currant flavors make up this light, attractive wine. Tannins present, but not overpowering. Try now. • $55 • (11/15/96) • **82**

Nuits-St.-Georges Les Cailles 1992: Soft and medium-bodied, delivering some enticing cinnamon, toast, vanilla, plum and black cherry flavors that last on the finish. Ready now. • $39 • (12/15/94) • **82**

Nuits-St.-Georges Les Damodes 1995: Beautiful aromas of blackberries and roses are followed by a firmly structured, crisp-tasting wine. Plenty of dry tannins in evidence, so wait until 2000. 300 cases made. • $53 • (11/15/97) • **85**

Nuits-St.-Georges Les Damodes 1994: A lean wine, and chewy, with a slightly sour edge. • $45 • (11/15/96) • **79**

Nuits-St.-Georges Les Damodes 1993: Sleek and exciting, it bursts with fresh floral, currant, spice, black cherry and lightly toasty flavors. Medium- to full-bodied, adding an underpinning of acidity and a long, chewy finish. Try in 2000. • $68 • (11/15/95) • **93**

Nuits-St.-Georges Les Damodes 1992: Smooth and appealing, with a spicy edge to the currant flavor and a slightly astringent finish. Tasty now. • $35 • (12/15/94) • **83**

Nuits-St.-Georges Premier Cru 1993: Big, chunky Nuits delivering spice, vanilla and fruit notes, full body, medium tannins and long, tasty finish. Try in 2000. • $60 • (11/15/95) • **90**

LECHERE

Brut Blanc de Blancs Champagne 1990: An inviting Champagne with compelling flavors and a velvety mousse. Almost sweet, it's well-rounded, well-balanced and attractive. Drink now through 2000. • $40 • (11/30/97) • **89**

Brut Blanc de Blancs Champagne 1985: Intense and earthy, with ripe pear and fruit cocktail flavors that turn slightly bitter on the finish. Drink now. Tasted twice. • $44 • (05/15/92) • **78**

Brut Blanc de Blancs Champagne Grand Cru 1983: A complex, focused wine, with more style than charm. Firm and concentrated, featuring earthy lemon, nutmeg and cedar flavors that extend into a long finish. An austere style, with character and complexity. 500 cases made. • $90 • (05/15/92) • **92**

Brut Champagne Orient Express Cuvée Speciale NV: Bold but sophisticated. Enticing toasty-earthy aromas, wonderfully complex flavors of pear, almond, vanilla and nutmeg, a fine mousse, plush texture and a long finish make this special. • $50 • (11/30/97) • **91**

Brut Rosé Champagne NV: A pleasant and refreshing rosé that is straightforward, fruity and slightly sweet. Drink now. • $35 • (12/31/97) • **83**

LECLERC, PHILIPPE

Bourgogne Les Bons-Bâtons 1994: Smoky, toasty, spicy aromas and flavors make this orange-tinted wine taste more inviting than it looks. Drink soon, though. • $NA • (11/15/96) • **80**

Bourgogne Les Bons-Bâtons 1992: Firm, ripe and spicy, marked by new oak nuances around a generous core of ripe currant and black cherry. Drinkable now. • $18 • (12/15/94) • **80**

Bourgogne Les Bons-Bâtons 1988 • $22 • (08/31/91) • **64**

Key: SS—Spectator Selection CS—Cellar Selection HR—Highly Recommended BB—Best Buy $NA—Price not available Ⓐ—Auction Price (BT)—Barrel Tasting
Dates in parentheses indicate the issues in which the ratings were published.

Chambolle-Musigny Les Babillères 1994: The color of old sherry or melted milk chocolate, this looks, smells and tastes mature for such a young wine. • $NA • (11/15/96) • **70**

Chambolle-Musigny Les Babillères 1992: Light and delicate, carrying a pound of oak and more barrel flavors than fruit, finishing with a wash of spice and vanilla. Try now. • $45 • (12/15/94) • **79**

Gevrey-Chambertin 1994: Tired and oxidized flavors, brown-colored, significantly tannic. • $NA • (11/15/96) • **72**

Gevrey-Chambertin 1984 • $26 • (07/15/87) • **90**

Gevrey-Chambertin Champeaux 1994: Old, tired, caramelized and oxidized flavors that finish with a brown-sugar sweetness. • $NA • (11/15/96) • **74**

Gevrey-Chambertin Champeaux 1991: Ripe, pruny and definitely woody, this frankly oaky style has enough chocolaty plum and spice flavors to balance the toastiness. Try now through 2000. • $65 Ⓐ • (01/31/94) • **84**

Gevrey-Chambertin Champeaux 1990: Rich and oaky; isn't everyone's glass of wine, but offers loads of cedar, tobacco box, plum and leather flavors in a tightly wrapped package that contains extremely firm tannins. From a producer who prides himself on aging his wines for about two and a half years in new oak barrels before bottling them unfiltered. Drink now. • $50 • (12/15/92) • **91**

Gevrey-Chambertin Champeaux 1985 • $55 • (10/31/88) • **79**

Gevrey-Chambertin Combe au Moine 1994: Very odd. It's the brownish color of chocolate and it tastes of spice and oak, with little fruit flavor, dry tannins. Like an old, oxidized wine. • $NA • (11/15/96) • **68**

Gevrey-Chambertin Combe au Moine 1992: Spicy, chewy and a little drying from too much tannin, but the toast and prune notes manage to be heard over the din. Drinkable now. • $72 • (12/15/94) • **82**

Gevrey-Chambertin Combe au Moine 1991: Firm, oaky, spicy and pruny, with a tough, tannic finish. Not very likable. • $83 Ⓐ • (01/31/94) • **73**

Gevrey-Chambertin Combe au Moine 1990: Fleshy and rich, with bold plum, berry and oak characteristics and a sweet aftertaste of ripe fruit. Has a lot of power. Drinkable now. 375 cases made. • $70 • (12/15/92) • **92**

Gevrey-Chambertin Combe au Moine 1988 • $72 • (07/15/91) • **82**

Gevrey-Chambertin Combe au Moine 1987 • $68 • (05/31/90) • **76**

Gevrey-Chambertin Combe au Moine 1985 • $70 • (10/15/88) • **92**

Gevrey-Chambertin Combe au Moine 1984 • $42 • (08/31/87) • **82**

Gevrey-Chambertin Cuvée Vieilles Vignes 1994: Brown colored, and seemingly oxidized; nothing but barklike flavors. • $NA • (11/15/96) • **73**

Gevrey-Chambertin En Champs 1992: Those who like oaky Burgundies will like the clean character in this. It shows enticing violet, blueberry, black cherry flavors. Drinkable now. • $42 • (12/15/94) • **84**

Gevrey-Chambertin En Champs 1991: Shows a bit more oak than the light cherry flavor might warrant, but finishes with nice, ripe sweetness. Firm and chewy. Drinkable now. • $40 • (01/31/94) • **80**

Gevrey-Chambertin La Platière 1992: Light and simple, with modest strawberry and raspberry flavors, and a short, drying, oaky finish. • $39 • (12/15/94) • **76**

Gevrey-Chambertin La Platière 1991: Thin and woody. Drink now. • $43 Ⓐ • (01/31/94) • **72**

Gevrey-Chambertin La Platière 1990: Big and chewy, with plenty of everything in the chocolate, plum, berry and oak aromas and flavors. Elegance isn't this wine's speciality, but if you want character, this is for you. Drinkable now. • $35 • (12/15/92) • **90**

Gevrey-Chambertin La Platière 1989 • $44 • (10/31/92) • **81**

Gevrey-Chambertin La Platière 1988 • $40 • (07/15/91) • **74**

Gevrey-Chambertin La Platière 1987 • $35 • (05/31/90) • **81**

Gevrey-Chambertin La Platière 1985 • $38 • (10/15/88) • **90**

Gevrey-Chambertin Les Cazetiers 1994: Looks and smells like a 10-year-old wine—all brown sugar and coffee in character, getting a bit thin on the finish. • $NA • (11/15/96) • **73**

Gevrey-Chambertin Les Cazetiers 1992: Oak-dominated, with drying tannins and modest fruit flavors. Too much oak for such a light vintage. Drinkable now. • $68 • (12/15/94) • **73**

Gevrey-Chambertin Les Cazetiers 1991: An oaky style that works in enough pruny currant flavors to stay balanced. Drink now to 2000. • $75 Ⓐ • (01/31/94) • **79**

Gevrey-Chambertin Les Cazetiers 1990: Very traditional in style and a bit woody, with chestnut, cedar and plum aromas and flavors and a chunky texture. Aged for about two and a half years in oak casks and not filtered. Drinkable now. 375 cases made. • $65 • (12/15/92) • **85**

Gevrey-Chambertin Les Cazetiers 1988 • $73 Ⓐ • (07/15/91) • **82**

Gevrey-Chambertin Les Cazetiers 1987 • $63 • (05/31/90) • **85**

Gevrey-Chambertin Les Cazetiers 1985 • $91 Ⓐ • (10/15/88) • **89**

Gevrey-Chambertin Les Cazetiers 1984 • $29 Ⓐ • (08/31/87) • **83**

LECLERC, RENÉ

Gevrey-Chambertin Combe au Moine 1985 • $41 Ⓐ • (10/31/88) • **82**

LECLERC-BRIANT

Brut Blanc de Blancs Champagne NV: A light sty!e of Champagne with a soft mousse and crisp, green apple flavors. Refreshing, but could be more harmonious. • $29 • (12/31/97) • **83**

Brut Champagne 1979 • $31 • (03/15/88) • **85**

Brut Champagne Cuvée de Réserve NV: An easy-to-like style that blends ripe, slightly sweet fruit flavors with lively acidity and a fresh feel. • $24 • (10/31/97) • **84**

Brut Champagne Cuvée Wolfgang Mozart 1983: Has nice, mature, nutty, spicy and toasty aromas and similar flavors that dance around a central thread of lemon and vanilla, making this an interesting wine, but it could show a little more finesse. • $60 • (12/31/91) • **85**

Brut Champagne Divine 1989: Enticing and luxurious. Full-flavored, full-bodied and nearly mature, this shows a rich blend of honey and walnut notes on a soft but firm texture, and echoes mellow flavors on the finish. Drink now through 2000. 2,000 cases made. • $55 • (11/30/97) • **92**

Brut Champagne Divine 1988: Combines subtlety and power for an elegant, lively, flavorful Champagne. Complex aromas of lemon, vanilla and bread dough are followed by solid fruit notes and a seductive echo of the aromas on aftertaste. 2,000 cases made. • $50 • (11/30/95) • **92**

Brut Champagne Divine 1985: Crisp and elegant, with lively lemon, vanilla and butter aromas and flavors with hints of pear, all held together in a neat package that focuses the flavors on the finish. • $45 • (12/31/91) • **89**

Brut Champagne Le Clos des Champions NV: A good but lean-tasting bubbly that's very dry, almost austere in flavor. 415 cases made. • $36 • (10/31/97) • **82**

Brut Champagne Les Chèvres Pierreuses NV: Drinkable, but simple and grapey, with almost none of the finesse you expect. Tasted twice, with consistent notes. 415 cases made. • $36 • (12/31/97) • **72**

Brut Champagne Les Crayères NV: A nice bottle of bubbly with green-apple flavors and a smooth texture. Good, but simple. 415 cases made. • $36 • (10/31/97) • **84**

Brut Champagne Spécial Club 1983: Full-bodied, goes down easy, with plenty of fruit and a touch of coarseness. But overall it's balanced, with lemon, apple and toast notes. Young and lively, ready to drink. 1,800 cases made. • $35 • (12/31/89) • **83**

Brut Rosé Champagne Rubis Rosé de Noirs 1989: This has the crimson color of Cold Duck, and nearly the same grapey fruitiness, though finishing crisp and dry. Exuberant fruit, lacking sophistication and depth. • $29 • (12/15/95) • **83**

LEFLAIVE, DOMAINE

Bâtard-Montrachet 1994: Like sipping cream. Oily-textured and full-bodied, with pear, piecrust, vanilla bean, peach and toasty bread flavors. Appealingly round, supple, harmonious finish. Tempting now through 2000. • $NA • (08/31/96) • **94**

Bienvenues-Bâtard-Montrachet 1994: Soft and honeyed, with the mouthfeel of double cream, this full-bodied wine is a pleasure to drink. Vanilla bean, mineral, bread dough, piecrust, apple and pear flavors. Drink now. • $NA • (08/31/96) • **92**

Bienvenues-Bâtard-Montrachet 1993 • $125 • (05/31/96) • **89**

Chevalier-Montrachet 1993: Brilliant winemaking here. A gorgeous, full-bodied white Burgundy that manages to deliver tons of lemon, honey and pear flavors in a seductive package, yet it's fresh and draws you back for more. Intense finish. Delicious now, but could age for years. • $90 Ⓐ • (05/31/96) • **95**

Chevalier-Montrachet 1992: A clearly outstanding wine that's chock full of flavor and liberally spiced with toasty oak. This is a full-bodied, white Burgundy. The lingering, expanding aftertaste is a hallmark of quality. • $241 Ⓐ • (05/15/95) • **93**

Puligny-Montrachet 1992: Very subtle in flavor, but firm and smooth in texture, with hints of pear and toasty oak coming out on the lingering finish. Not obvious, but it grows in interest as you sip. • $53 Ⓐ • (05/15/95) • **87**

Puligny-Montrachet Clavoillon 1994: Elegant double-cream texture and full body. Wonderful vanilla bean, mineral, stone and honey flavors. Refined finish. Delightful now, and through 2000. • $48 Ⓐ • (08/31/96) • **90**

Puligny-Montrachet Clavoillon 1993: A beauty from start to finish. Standing out for its amazingly vibrant character, this superbly focused white needs to age a few years to fully integrate the layers of citrus, mineral and toasty oak that tantalize the palate. Long aftertaste. • $37 Ⓐ • (05/31/96) • **92**

Puligny-Montrachet Clavoillon 1992: A flamboyant, ripe and seductive style of Chardonnay with plenty of fruit flavor accented by intriguing notes of butter, vanilla, nutmeg and toast. Firm with acidity, full-bodied and long on the finish. Drinkable now. 300 cases made. • $73 Ⓐ • (05/15/95) CS • **92**

Puligny-Montrachet Les Combettes 1994: Melts in the mouth, building on the palate to a smoky finish. Soft, ripe and silky-textured, offering creamy vanilla and pineapple flavors that end with strong accents of toasty oak. Drinkable now. • $NA • (08/31/96) • **90**

Puligny-Montrachet Les Combettes 1992: This river runs deep and wide. The aromas are peachy and pearlike, the flavors full of apricot, nutmeg and hazelnut that linger and expand on the finish. It's expansive and concentrated, smooth as velvet, and hard to resist. Drink now. • $115 Ⓐ • (05/15/95) • **91**

Puligny-Montrachet Les Folatières 1994: Round, supple and medium-bodied. Super creamy texture that seductively coats your palate. Tastes of vanilla bean, spice, lemon, honey, ripe pear and apple pie flavors. Seamless finish. Delicious to drink now. • $NA • (08/31/96) • **90**

Puligny-Montrachet Les Folatières 1993: Beautiful, distinctive, amazing chalk and mineral character, sporting notes of citrus and wet earth. Thick but fresh, this full-bodied white coats your palate while remaining structured and focused. Delicious now, but better in 2000. • $95 • (05/31/96) • **91**

Puligny-Montrachet Les Pucelles 1994: Seductive and subtle, this refined *premier cru* melts on the palate; tastes of honey, cream, and apricot. Medium- to full-bodied. Delicious now and through 1999. • $NA • (08/31/96) • **88**

Puligny-Montrachet Les Pucelles 1993: A class act. Full-bodied and ripe, but also fresh and vibrant, with a silky, creamy mouthfeel and complex honey, oregano, basil, vanilla and mineral notes. Clear, clean and wonderfully focused; this has a smooth, supple finish that goes on and on. • $58 Ⓐ • (05/31/96) • **92**

Puligny-Montrachet Les Pucelles 1992: A stylish wine with a nice buttery, nutty character and subtle fruit flavors of apple and lime. The texture is smooth and silky and the flavors seem to expand on the finish. Drinkable now. • $115 Ⓐ • (05/15/95) • **89**

LEFLAIVE FRÈRES, OLIVIER

Bâtard-Montrachet 1995: Quite intense but not as harmonious as many great '95 whites. Offers lots of toasty oak complexity atop the ripe fruit, and a rich texture, but it seems overly oaky. May be better after 2000. 50 cases made. • $130 • (08/31/97) • **89**

Bâtard-Montrachet 1994: Almost like a late-harvest Chardonnay. Full-bodied, ripe and rich, oozing honey, floral, basil and anise flavors. Citrus notes come through on the long, marzipan-tasting finish. Drink now through 1999. • $NA • (08/31/96) • **89**

Bâtard-Montrachet 1993: Crystal clear, offering apple and cream aromas and flavors and a hint of coconut on the finish. Medium body and fine acidity. Well made. Drinkable now. 75 cases made. • $100 • (08/31/95) • **88**

Bâtard-Montrachet 1992: Immensely pleasing and well crafted, boasting a silky texture and freshly cut mushroom, ripe pear and butter notes. Drinkable now. • $100 • (05/15/95) • **92**

Bienvenues-Bâtard-Montrachet 1992: Seductive and silky, all the pieces in the right places, showing complex white truffle and honey flavors that are so enchanting. Long, polished finish. Drinkable now. • $85 • (05/15/95) • **92**

Bonnes Mares 1987 • $50 • (09/30/90) • **88**

Bourgogne Aligoté 1996: Light and quaffable, a bit sharp with some citrus and green apple notes and a slightly paperish character that distracts. Drink now. 205 cases made. • $15 • (05/31/98) • **77**

Bourgogne Aligoté 1995: Odd and slightly sour. Crisp and a bit grassy, with an earthy character. Medium-bodied, tart finish. 500 cases made. • $16 • (08/31/97) • **72**

Bourgogne Aligoté 1994: Straightforward and a bit green, with an odd, slightly metallic, earthy character. 200 cases made. • $12 • (01/01/96) • **70**

Bourgogne Les Sétilles White 1996: Decent ripeness in this otherwise straightforward Burgundy, but a bit lightish on the midpalate, picking up a slight paperish note amid the pear, apple and pineapple character. A bit sour on the finish. Drink now. 415 cases made. • $17 • (05/31/98) • **81**

Bourgogne Les Sétilles White 1995: Rustic, slightly hot. Full-bodied, with some disjointed, burnt butter, green apple notes. 5,000 cases made. • $13 • (08/31/97) • **70**

Bourgogne Les Sétilles White 1994: Tart, hard and simple, with very modest fruit flavors. 1,500 cases made. • $14 • (01/01/96) • **70**

LEFLAIVE FRÈRES, OLIVIER

Bourgogne Les Sétilles White 1993: Straightforward and simple, offering modest fruit flavors and slight dilution. Drink now. • $NA • (05/15/95) • **72**

Bourgogne White 1996: Fairly nice Bourgogne. Ripe pear mingles with a matchstick and earth character. Of medium body, it has a lush texture for a regional wine. Well made. Drink now or hold until 1999. 500 cases made. • $11 • (05/31/98) • **80**

Charmes-Chambertin 1989 • $60 • (01/31/92) • **88**

Charmes-Chambertin 1986 • $50 • (07/31/88) • **88**

Chassagne-Montrachet 1995: Lovely for its tropical, grapefruit and floral notes. Medium-bodied, it's a delicious, if not complex, drink. A bit short on the slightly flinty finish. Tempting now, should improve through 2003. 3,000 cases made. • $41 • (08/31/97) • **87**

Chassagne-Montrachet 1994: Ripe and honey-sweet. Medium-bodied, with some attractive fruit, grassy and toasty oak flavors. A bit one-dimensional, though. Drink now. • $NA • (08/31/96) • **84**

Chassagne-Montrachet 1993: Pretty little wine offering creamy, appley character, medium body and firm acidity. Try now. • $NA • (05/15/95) • **81**

Chassagne-Montrachet Morgeot 1995: Ripe and flavorful, with good balance and impressive complexity of flavors: mineral, spice, toasty bread and something akin to fried pineapple sprinkled with toasty coconut. Full-bodied, it caresses the palate yet ends with a bang. Try now. 400 cases made. • $52 • (08/31/97) • **90**

Chassagne-Montrachet Morgeot 1994: Intensely toasty, with hazelnut, piecrust, apple, citrus, caramel and pear flavors. Medium-bodied and elegant. Crisp finish. Drink now. • $NA • (08/31/96) • **84**

Chassagne-Montrachet Morgeot 1993: Appealing and ready to drink, this smoky, toasty and lush Burgundy offers some modest chalk, mineral and fruit flavors. 75 cases made. • $38 • (08/31/95) • **84**

Chassagne-Montrachet Morgeot 1992: Clean-tasting, well-balanced and harmonious. Its pear, orange, vanilla and spice flavors are lean but complex. Tight and well-knit. Drink now. 26 cases made. • $45 • (08/31/94) • **85**

Chassagne-Montrachet Morgeot Red 1993: Lean and meager, the crisp, fresh texture delivering little pleasure. Modest cherry, earth notes. Firm tannins don't help. • $34 • (11/15/95) • **79**

Chassagne-Montrachet Red 1992: Light-bodied, with a delicate raspberry, floral and smoky character. A bit diluted on the finish. Drink now. • $NA • (12/15/94) • **77**

Chassagne-Montrachet Red 1991: Perhaps a bit on the oaky side, but the ripe black cherry and raspberry flavors shine through. May always be lean. Drinkable now. 700 cases made. • $15 Ⓐ • (01/31/94) • **84**

Chassagne-Montrachet Red 1990: Firm and aromatic, delivering a subtext of barklike, herbal, vegetal, vanilla and cinnamon flavors. Very distinctive, but a bit lean. Drinkable now. 600 cases made. • $17 • (12/15/92) • **85**

Chassagne-Montrachet Red 1986 • $26 • (02/29/88) • **89**

Chassagne-Montrachet Red 1985 • $32 • (10/31/88) • **83**

Chevalier-Montrachet 1994: Delicious for its ripe peach, apricot and pear flavors, the low acidity makes it already a bit burning on the palate, but there is sweetness galore with notes of honey, spice and chocolate and it's thick and rich. This has improved since last tasted. Drink now. • $181 • (05/31/97) • **90**

Clos St.-Denis 1989 • $56 • (01/31/92) • **93**

Clos de la Roche 1989 • $63 • (03/15/93) • **82**

Corton Les Bressandes 1986 • $45 • (07/31/88) • **88**

Corton-Charlemagne 1993: Clean and fresh, offering zingy acidity, medium body, toasty oak, lime and apple flavors and crisp finish. Not big, but delicious. 75 cases made. • $75 • (08/31/95) • **85**

Corton-Charlemagne 1992: Firm and tart, hinting of honey and hazelnut; rather lean, displaying green apple, pear and a touch of mineral on the finish. Drinkable now. Tasted twice, with consistent notes. • $65 • (05/15/95) • **85**

Criots-Bâtard-Montrachet 1995: Well balanced, with some intense tropical fruit, toasty oak, spice and citrus flavors. Satiny in texture and full in body, it kicks in for a long finish. Has the stuffing to improve through 2002. 400 cases made. • $125 • (08/31/97) • **92**

Givry 1988 • $16 • (10/31/92) • **76**

Mercurey White 1996: Pure and stylish, a well-made white with a pronounced earthy, matchsticklike character. Of medium body, it offers nice fruit with good length. Tempting now but better in 1999 to 2001. 40 cases made. • $23 • (05/31/98) • **86**

Key: SS—Spectator Selection CS—Cellar Selection HR—Highly Recommended BB—Best Buy $NA—Price not available Ⓐ—Auction Price (BT)—Barrel Tasting
Dates in parentheses indicate the issues in which the ratings were published.

Mercurey White 1995: Impressive for the Mercurey appellation. Smooth and round, with nice citrusy-lime flavors, along with touches of honey and earth. Full-bodied and quite harmonious, it offers some nice dried herb complexity on the lovely finish. Try after 2000. 500 cases imported. 1,100 cases made. • $16 • (08/31/97) • **90**

Mercurey White 1994: Green and herbal, with modest fruit. Very tart. 200 cases made. • $20 • (05/31/96) • **74**

Mercurey White 1993: Lively and vibrant, light-bodied, featuring zingy acidity and green apple, citrus and herb character. The finish is lean but juicy. Drink now. • $NA • (05/15/95) • **80**

Meursault 1995: Lovely from start to finish. Ripe in character but with a fresh underpinning of citrus notes. Smooth in texture, full in body, it delivers a wonderful taste sensation, with apple tart, pear, vanilla-bean and spice flavors. Tempting now, best after 2000. 2,300 cases made. • $41 • (08/31/97) • **90**

Meursault 1994: Good intensity, and nice concentration of fruit flavors accented by notes of toasty oak, honey and floral. Medium-bodied, with a seductive finish. Drinkable now. • $NA • (08/31/96) • **86**

Meursault 1993: Lean, but offering good mineral, pear and apple character and citrusy notes. Drinkable now. • $NA • (05/15/95) • **85**

Meursault 1992: Delicate and elegant, with moderate fruit flavors and a silky texture; but you wish it had more intensity. Drinkable now. 550 cases made. • $32 • (08/31/94) • **82**

Meursault Les Charmes 1995: Opulent and hedonistic, this seductive, full-bodied beauty delivers loads of ripe fruit, along with some honey and spice complexity, in a seamless package. Long, elegant finish. Difficult to ask for a nicer Chardonnay to drink tonight through 2005. 300 cases made. • $62 • (08/31/97) • **91**

Meursault Les Perrières 1995: Nice concentration, with butter, butterscotch, spice, pear, citrus, mineral and apple tart complexity, full body. But the finish is slightly dry and very chewy. Maybe age will make it more harmonious. Try after 2000. 250 cases made. • $58 • (08/31/97) • **88**

Meursault Les Perrières 1994: Supple and delightful, with honey, mineral and vanilla bean complexity. Medium- to full-bodied, and the silky texture is impressive. Long finish has cigar box and toasty oak character. Try now. • $NA • (08/31/96) • **91**

Meursault Les Perrières 1993: Stylish, offering plenty of ripe lemon and pineapple character, medium-to-full body and fine acidity. 125 cases made. • $42 • (08/31/95) • **88**

Meursault Les Perrières 1992: Nicely balanced, with subtle spice, vanilla and pear flavors braced by good acidity. The sort of wine you want to drink a lot of. 128 cases made. • $45 • (08/31/94) • **87**

Montagny Les Bonneveaux 1996: Crisp and intense, of Light-to-medium body, with loads of citrus and green apple character. You wish for riper fruit, but it's clean and pure, with a racy, steely finish. Try after 1999. 40 cases made. • $NA • (05/31/98) • **84**

Monthélie 1991: Crisp and a bit astringent. A decent beam of currant flavor pokes through. Drinkable now. 175 cases made. • $19 Ⓐ • (01/31/94) • **80**

Monthélie Premier Cru 1990: Light and simple, with cherry and strawberry flavors and light tannins. Drinkable now. 100 cases made. • $19 • (12/15/92) • **82**

Montrachet 1995: Remarkably harmonious. Full-bodied, velvety and sweet-tasting, with loads of ripe fruit and spice flavors. Finishes with a dose of toasty oak that needs until at least 2005 to fold nicely into the wine. 60 cases made. • $270 • (08/31/97) • **92**

Montrachet 1994: Rich, ripe, soft and lush. Coats the mouth and sends ripples of flavor across the palate. Very silky and loaded with tropical fruit, honey and toasty coconut. Sweet and flavorful, with a smooth finish. Enjoy now. • $NA • (08/31/96) • **90**

Montrachet 1993: A beauty, featuring pie crust, apple and citrus aromas and flavors, medium body, fine acidity and finish shaded by toasty oak. Drinkable now. 25 cases made. • $180 • (08/31/95) • **89**

Montrachet 1992: Quite fat, demonstrating a rich texture and lots of pear, mineral and honey flavors. Medium-bodied; perfect to drink now. • $175 • (05/15/95) • **87**

Morey-St.-Denis 1989 • $30 • (01/31/92) • **87**

Pinot Noir Bourgogne 1992: Modest plum and strawberry aromas, matched with smoky, spicy flavors and a dry, tannic finish add up to a typical, solid Burgundy. Drink now while the fruit lasts. • $9 • (11/30/94) • **82**

Pommard 1993: A bit lean but some vivid cherry and mineral character. Medium-bodied with fine tannins and a long, crisp finish. Better in 1999. • $32 • (11/15/95) • **84**

Pommard 1992: A delicate Pommard, with a tannic underpinning that makes it last on the finish. Light in texture and offering only modest strawberry, raspberry and cherry flavors. Try now. • $NA • (12/15/94) • **84**

Pommard 1990: A concentrated village wine that's rich, ripe and supple, packed with wild raspberry, leaf and earth aromas and flavors. Coats your mouth and leaves a lasting impression on the elegant finish. Drinkable now. 500 cases made. • $30 • (12/15/92) • **92**

Pommard 1989 • $32 • (01/31/92) • **84**

Pommard Les Epenots 1993: A lean '93 with some berry, herbal character. Medium-bodied with firm tannins and a light fruity finish. Leflaive's village Pommard is better. • $46 • (11/15/95) • **82**

Pommard Les Epenots 1990: A delight to smell, this toasty wine offers terrific smoke, game and plum aromas and flavors that come across gracefully on the lovely, supple finish. Drinkable now. 125 cases made. • $35 • (12/15/92) • **90**

Pommard Les Epenots 1989 • $40 • (01/31/92) • **88**

Pommard Les Rugiens 1993: Tough red, offering loads of tannins and hot fruit, full body, substantial raspberry and cherry character and a hint of earth. Slightly overdone. Needs time to mellow; try in 2000. • $48 • (11/15/95) • **86**

Pommard Les Rugiens 1992: Nicely focused, medium-bodied, with pretty blackberry, boysenberry and violet notes. Firm but slightly lean on the finish. Drinkable now. • $NA • (12/15/94) • **84**

Pommard Les Rugiens 1991: Tough, astringent and very lean. Try now. 200 cases made. • $37 Ⓐ • (01/31/94) • **77**

Pommard Les Rugiens 1990: A class act. Muscular yet supple and well constructed, oozing with intense, concentrated black cherry, fleshy, ripe fruit flavors and smoky, chocolaty undertones that come together on the firm but supple finish. Drinkable now. 100 cases made. • $35 • (12/15/92) • **91**

Puligny-Montrachet 1995: Quite forward for a '95, with spice, oak and burnt caramel flavors that seem a bit heavy-handed. Full-bodied it also offers pear tart, apple and tropical notes. Try now through 2000. 3,800 cases made. • $41 • (08/31/97) • **85**

Puligny-Montrachet 1994: Nicely balanced, lush and honeyed village wine. Gains complexity as it airs, showing pear, green apple, caramel and toasty oak flavors in good proportions. Try now. • $NA • (08/31/96) • **86**

Puligny-Montrachet 1993: Very clean and fresh Chardonnay displaying apple, mineral character, fresh acidity and a medium, creamy finish. • $NA • (05/15/95) • **85**

Puligny-Montrachet 1992: Solid and straightforward, firm, medium-bodied, with good balance and moderate fruit intensity; delivers some honey and pear flavors and a moderate-long finish. Drinkable now. 600 cases made. • $38 • (08/31/94) • **84**

Puligny-Montrachet Champ Canet 1995: Supple, round and flavorful. Lacks a bit of intensity, but what's there is balanced and delicious, with spice, honey and ripe pear flavors. Full-bodied. Drink now through 2000. 400 cases made. • $52 • (08/31/97) • **87**

Puligny-Montrachet Champ Canet 1994: Thick, rich, ripe and seductive, with loads of toasty oak and honeyed-tropical fruit flavors. Full-bodied and very silky, it coats the palate and glides to a smooth, slightly chalky finish. Drink now. • $NA • (08/31/96) • **90**

Puligny-Montrachet Champ Canet 1993: Ripe and lush style, quite smoky and toasty, offering dried herb, mineral and pear flavors. A bit heavy-handed on the finish. 100 cases made. • $40 • (08/31/95) • **81**

Puligny-Montrachet Champ Canet 1992: A very good white that features toast, butter and vanillalike flavors that are nicely supported by firm acidity. The texture is full but a bit tight, and the finish is lingering. Drinkable now. 100 cases made. • $50 • (08/31/94) • **86**

Puligny-Montrachet Champ Gain 1995: Powerful but balanced, with the rich, thick and opulent texture expected from a top '95 white Burgundy. Full-bodied, it has loads of ripe fruit and spice character. Try after 2000. 500 cases made. • $52 • (08/31/97) • **91**

Puligny-Montrachet Champ Gain 1994: Masterfully done. Seductive, with beautifully balanced, full-bodied layers of lemon, honey, tropical fruit and cigar-box flavors. Long, subtle and toasty finish. Enjoy now through 1999. • $41 • (08/31/96) HR • **92**

Puligny-Montrachet Champ Gain 1993: Very lively, sporting honey, mineral and cream character, medium body, fine acidity and a zingy finish. Drinkable now. 125 cases made. • $35 • (08/31/95) • **86**

Puligny-Montrachet Les Folatières 1995: A delight to drink. Opulent, rich and seductive, a thick wine that's harmonious and full-bodied, with tropical, pear, spice and lemon complexity. Has supple texture but retains its elegance on the long finish. Drink now through 2003. 350 cases made. • $62 • (08/31/97) • **90**

Puligny-Montrachet Les Folatières 1994: Delicate and silky textured. Honey, floral, apricot, pear and very toasty oak flavors. Finish has smoky notes and a creamy texture. Drink now through 1999. • $NA • (08/31/96) • **88**

Puligny-Montrachet Les Folatières 1993: Well made Burgundy in a relatively lean package. What's there is quite delicious, offering mineral, pear and lightly toasty bread flavors. Smooth finish and ready to drink. 225 cases made. • $42 • (08/31/95) • **86**

Puligny-Montrachet Les Folatières 1992: A distinctively oaky, smoky aroma and tightly-wound flavors of apple, grapefruit and mint make for a big, bold, square-jawed wine. Has good fruit concentration and a lingering aftertaste. Drinkable now. 100 cases made. • $52 • (08/31/94) • **90**

Rully Premier Cru White 1996: Fairly ripe and quite racy, with a distinctive matchstick, pear and earth complexity. Of medium body, it delivers nice mineral character. Very crisp finish, so might be better to cellar until 1999 to 2000. 80 cases made. • $23 • (05/31/98) • **84**

Rully Premier Cru White 1994: An ager. Amazing concentration of mineral, citrus, tropical fruit and pear flavors that are exciting to taste. Appears "reductive" at first (like stale ice), but after a while it reveals great depth and length. Don't touch till after 2000. 400 cases made. • $19 • (05/31/96) • **91**

Rully Red 1990: Crisp in texture, with a definite woody, spicy character that obscures the modest core of fruit. Drinkable now. Tasted three times. • $20 • (11/30/92) • **80**

St.-Aubin En Remilly White 1996: Sophisticated and elegant, a racy '96, crisp but also packed with fruit and mineral character. Of medium body, it grips the palate with its intense fruit-acid combination and ends on a long finish. Needs until 2000 to settle down. 125 cases made. • $29 • (05/31/98) • **88**

St.-Aubin En Remilly White 1995: Seductive and supple at first, it turns a bit harsh on the finish, making this dense wine seem a bit disjointed, at least for now. Of medium-to-full body and firm texture, it shows subtle honey, mineral and wet stone notes ending on a chewy finish that might turn great after 2000. 400 cases made. • $26 • (05/31/97) • **87**

St.-Aubin En Remilly White 1994: A fat, supple wine that oozes ripe fruit and honey. Full-bodied and chalky, this *premier cru* delivers some toast, pear and pie crust flavors. Nice, long finish. Try now. 300 cases made. • $22 • (05/31/96) • **87**

St.-Aubin En Remilly White 1993: Attractive mineral, spice and toasty oak character, medium body and a light, fruity finish. • $NA • (05/15/95) • **83**

St.-Romain White 1994: Crisp and lively, with sharp, earthy flavors of dried herbs and green apple. Rather lean. 200 cases made. • $18 • (05/31/96) • **79**

St.-Romain White 1993: Crisp, citrusy white Burgundy, offering green apple, orange-peel and cream flavors. A bit green on the finish. Drink now. • $NA • (05/15/95) • **76**

Santenay 1993: A lean machine, light-bodied and somewhat odd at this stage, tasting of sausage, cherry and spice flavors. Drink now. • $20 • (11/15/95) • **79**

Santenay 1986 • $17 • (07/31/88) • **81**

Santenay Les Gravières 1990: Bright and clean, with an elegant texture and nice plum, tobacco and black cherry flavors. A bit short on the finish. Drinkable now. 300 cases made. • $17 • (12/15/92) • **85**

Volnay 1992: Light and supple, showing a nice core of smoky berry flavors that just make it to the finish. • $NA • (12/15/94) • **81**

Volnay 1987 • $27 • (08/31/90) • **78**

Volnay Clos de la Barre 1991: Light, bright and polished. Vanilla-scented raspberry and anise aromas and flavors persist delicately on the finish. Drinkable now. 150 cases made. • $36 Ⓐ • (01/31/94) • **84**

Volnay Clos de la Barre 1990: An exquisite wine, with finesse and a silky texture. It's thick and light, yet also supple and tannic, oozing with toasty currant, cherry and game aromas and flavors. Drinkable now. 125 cases made. • $36 • (12/15/92) • **92**

Volnay Clos de la Barre 1989 • $38 • (01/31/92) • **92**

Volnay Clos de la Barre 1986 • $28 • (07/31/88) • **89**

Volnay Frémiets 1993: Beautiful, vivid and ripe, sporting a gorgeous core of plum and red berry flavors and silky texture. Tannins creep up on the finish, so should need until 2000 to show it all. • $42 • (11/15/95) • **93**

Volnay Frémiets 1991: Smells pretty, with appealing raspberry, vanilla and toast aromas, but turns crisp, almost astringent on the finish, showing more citrus flavor than anything else. Best now. 150 cases made. • $33 Ⓐ • (01/31/94) • **82**

Volnay Frémiets Premier Cru 1990: What a mouthful. Stands out with well-integrated, distinctive, toasty, smoky bacon and black cherry aromas and flavors. Very classy, with an excellent tannin structure. Drinkable now. 125 cases made. • $35 • (12/15/92) • **92**

LÉGER-PLUMET, BERNARD

Pouilly-Fuissé Domaine des Gerbaux Fût de Chêne 1992: Sensational Pouilly, featuring earthy, buttery, lime-flavored, mineral character, a solid backbone that turns remarkably harmonious on the palate and a long, intense and fresh finish. Drinkable now. • $NA • (05/15/95) • **90**

Pouilly-Fuissé Les Chailloux 1993: Fresh and clean; steely texture and wet hay, green apple, chalky flavors. Could provide more round opulence on the finish. Drink with seafood. 2,033 cases made. • $20 • (05/15/95) • **82**

St.-Véran 1996: Oak-aged St.-Véran, fairly straightforward but shows balance and polish. Long, with spice, toasty bread, pear and apple flavors. Tart finish. Drink now. 660 cases made. • $10 • (05/31/98) • **81**

LÉGLAND, BERNARD

Chablis 1996: Fruity and pleasant, light- to medium-bodied, with some mineral, vanilla, butter and pear flavors. Crisp finish. Drink now. • $NA • (08/31/97) • **82**

Chablis Montmains 1996: Oaky in a very nice way, quite silky and opulent, with vanilla bean, pear tart, apple pie and buttered croissant flavors. Despite the woody character, there is enough citrus and fruit to bring this into wonderful balance around 2005. • $24 • (05/31/98) • **91**

Chablis Montmains 1995: Clean, sweet- and ripe-tasting, packing in honey, pear, apple and mineral flavors. Medium to full in body, this *premier cru* is as crisp as they come. Try after 2000. 1,667 cases made. • $22 • (06/15/97) • **88**

Petit Chablis 1996: Ripe and sweet-tasting, but a bit funky, with almond, meat and lemon flavors. Tart finish. Tasted twice, with consistent notes. From Bernard Légland. • $NA • (08/31/97) • **74**

LEGRAS, R & L

Brut Blanc de Blancs Champagne Cuvée St.-Vincent 1976 • $33 • (05/31/87) • **85**

Brut Blanc de Blancs Champagne Présidence 1982 • $29 • (05/31/87) • **85**

LEGROS, FRANÇOIS

Chambolle-Musigny Les Noirots 1990: Firm and tight, with a core of black cherry, earth, cedar and currant flavors that is focused and complex. Drinkable now. • $40 • (03/15/93) • **88**

Chambolle-Musigny Les Noirots 1989 • $30 • (11/15/91) • **92**

Nuits-St.-Georges Aux Bousselots 1990: Dry, chewy and tannic, with a solid core of cherry and raspberry flavors that is stiff with tannins and tightly wound. The finish offers a glimpse of hope and complexity, with spicy oak and fruit nuances. Drinkable now. • $39 • (03/15/93) • **87**

Nuits-St.-Georges Les Perrières 1990: Shows lots of currant and black cherry-scented flavors up front, but turns tart and lean on the finish, where the tannins become more evident. Drinkable now. • $39 • (03/15/93) • **88**

Nuits-St.-Georges Les Perrières 1989 • $29 • (11/15/91) • **87**

Vougeot Les Crâs 1990: Starts out with generous black cherry and currant-scented flavors, but then the tannins kick in and it tightens up. Can try it now. • $45 • (03/15/93) • **87**

LEJEUNE

Bourgogne 1994: Soft and a bit simple, with a spicy, chocolate note along with the red berry flavors. Slightly dull finish. • $NA • (11/15/96) • **74**

Bourgogne 1993: Tight and dry, tannins being outplayed by the fruit. Lacks ripeness. Very hard finish. Better in 2000? • $14 • (11/15/95) • **76**

Bourgogne 1990: Rather intense and focused, with solid, ripe berry flavors and firm tannins. Drinkable now. 460 cases made. • $18 • (12/15/92) • **85**

Bourgogne Passe-tout-grains 1994: Shows a stalky edge to the modest cherry flavors. Simple and easy to drink. • $NA • (11/15/96) • **78**

Bourgogne Passe-tout-grains 1993: Crisp, decent core of plum, cherry and currant flavors and a silky, ready-to-drink mouthfeel. Somewhat hot and raisiny on the finish. Try now. • $13 • (11/15/95) • **80**

Pommard 1994: Light, supple, and straightforward, with some modest red berry, vanilla and spice flavors. Short finish and slightly dry tannins. • $NA • (11/15/96) • **75**

Pommard 1993: Rather light and fruity, offering an interesting aroma and flavors of pineapple and berry, fine tannins and a delicate fruit finish. Drinkable now • $NA • (05/15/96) • **84**

Pommard Les Argillières 1994: Light in color, almost orange, with little freshness. • $NA • (11/15/96) • **72**

Pommard Les Argillières 1993: Superbly crafted, with a deft touch of wood. Offers some mocha, chocolate and spice notes that distinguish it from many others. Delicious on release. 667 cases made. • $36 • (11/15/95) • **88**

Pommard Les Argillières 1991: Tough and drying, showing sweet cherry and currant notes. 400 cases made. • $36 Ⓐ • (01/31/94) • **77**

Pommard Les Argillières 1990: So huge and tannic we wonder if it's not overdone. Offers substantial fruit, but also a lot of new wood, with impressive vanilla, milk chocolate and fruit characteristics. Let the monster tannins sort themselves out; uncork around 2000. 580 cases made. • $40 • (12/15/92) • **88**

Pommard Les Poutures 1994: As light as a rosé, with some spice and vanilla notes. Drink chilled. • $NA • (11/15/96) • **70**

Pommard Les Poutures 1993: Wonderfully rich and decadent smoke, game and berry character. Full-bodied and velvety in texture, adding firm tannins and long finish. Drinkable now. 583 cases made. • $31 • (11/15/95) • **85**

Pommard Les Poutures 1991: Cherry flavor, but is watery at the core and finishes with more oak than fruit. Drinkable now. 450 cases made. • $32 Ⓐ • (01/31/94) • **75**

Pommard Les Rugiens 1994: Has a sweet, pruny accent with a hint of sour candy. More supple than most '94s, but it falls off on the finish. • $NA • (11/15/96) • **81**

Pommard Les Rugiens 1993: Delicious flavors. Not the biggest of wines, but some fine tannins, medium body and a tasty gamy and berry finish. Drink now. 125 cases made. • $65 • (11/15/95) • **83**

Pommard Les Rugiens 1991: Woody, spicy notes characterize this firm-textured, dryingly tannic wine. 80 cases made. • $52 Ⓐ • (01/31/94) • **79**

Pommard Les Rugiens 1990: If you are a chocoholic, this is for you. Smells and tastes like chocolate mousse, with smoky raspberry and sweet fruit flavors. The firm but refined tannins take over on the long finish. Drinkable now. 150 cases made. • $49 • (12/15/92) • **92**

LEMENICIER, JACQUES

Cornas 1990 • $16 • (04/15/93) • **75**

LENOBLE, A.R.

Brut Blanc de Blancs Champagne NV: Combines rich flavors and a plush texture for a truly complete and satisfying Champagne. Dreamy, mouthfilling bubbles and deep fruit flavors are balanced by fine acidity. • $30 • (11/30/97) • **90**

Brut Champagne 1988: A buttery, smooth, almost sweet Champagne that's soft and mouthfilling, with lingering fruit and spice flavors. Drink now. • $35 • (11/15/97) • **88**

Brut Champagne Gentilhomme 1988: Imagine a late-harvest Champagne. Ripe, peachy, honeylike flavors and a generous texture make this melt in your mouth. Soft, and almost sweet. Drink now. • $42 • (11/30/97) • **87**

Brut Champagne Réserve NV: On the austere side of the spectrum, this is nevertheless quite agreeable, with earthy, spicy flavors backed by modest fruit. Quite dry. • $25 • (10/31/97) • **84**

LÉONARD DE ST.-AUBIN

Beaujolais-Villages 1995: A bit more sophisticated than many Beaujolais-Villages. Supple, with understated cherry and citrus flavors, accented by spicy, smoky notes. Flavors bloom on the finish. 1,200 cases made. • $9 • (08/31/96) • **85**

Chambolle-Musigny 1993: Solid, flavorful, fairly fruity, rather soft and easy on the tannins. A modestly proportioned red that's pleasant but closed in. 500 cases made. • $30 • (05/15/96) • **84**

Chassagne-Montrachet 1994: An exaggerated style, the ripe honey and spice notes almost overpowering this white. It tastes a bit candied, but still pleasant. Flavors soften somewhat on the finish. 600 cases made. • $26 • (05/31/96) • **84**

Gevrey-Chambertin 1993: A stiff-textured, tightly structured Burgundy showing flavors that tend toward the lean, herbal side. Intense but not expansive. Drink now. 1,250 cases made. • $26 • (05/15/96) • **84**

Meursault 1995: Sweet oak flavors are appealing in this round, soft wine, but there's not enough fruit and it finishes with a hint of Bourbon flavor. Not typical of its appellation. 1,750 cases made. • $26 • (06/30/97) • **77**

Meursault 1992: A basic white Burgundy that tantalizes you with spicy aromas, but turns rather thin and lean on the palate. • $21 • (11/15/94) • **78**

Key: SS—Spectator Selection CS—Cellar Selection HR—Highly Recommended BB—Best Buy $NA—Price not available Ⓐ—Auction Price (BT)—Barrel Tasting
Dates in parentheses indicate the issues in which the ratings were published.

Nuits-St.-Georges 1993: Tight, tannic and not especially fruity at this stage, showing lean, slightly green flavors and tough texture. 1,400 cases made. • $26 • (05/15/96) • **78**

Nuits-St.-Georges 1985 • $25 • (11/30/87) • **71**

Pommard 1995: This simple red has little concentration, most of what's there is in the form of astringent tannins, with light flavors of raspberries and vanilla. 975 cases made. • $28 • (06/30/97) • **77**

Pommard 1993: Firmly textured, almost tough; difficult to enjoy now, but may not mellow with age. The aromas are resinous, oaky and earthy and the flavors slightly herbal. Try in 1999. 1,200 cases made. • $27 • (05/15/96) • **85**

Pouilly-Fuissé 1993: A hard white, with mineral and asparagus flavors but not much fruit, fading quickly. 8,000 cases made. • $12 • (03/31/95) • **76**

Puligny-Montrachet 1995: Heavy and dull, this full-bodied white shows toasty flavors but little fruit, and it lacks in acidity. A disappointment for the appellation. 2,100 cases made. • $28 • (06/30/97) • **78**

Puligny-Montrachet 1994: A stylish, well-constructed white that's fairly rich, sporting ripe apple and spice flavors. It has modest intensity and an aftertaste loaded with vanilla. 1,750 cases made. • $27 • (05/31/96) • **86**

Puligny-Montrachet 1992: If a wine can be suave, this is. It has toasty, spicy, oaky aromas, a smooth texture and long, buttery aftertaste. Not overtly fruity, but with plenty of nut, coffee and honey flavors. 1,250 cases made. • $24 • (11/15/94) • **87**

Volnay 1993: Intriguing, spicy-smelling, smooth and supple, featuring ripe fruit flavors and exotic nuances of cinnamon and smoke. Nicely concentrated and long on the finish, firmly tannic but impeccably balanced. Drinkable now. 650 cases made. • $26 • (05/15/96) • **89**

LÉOVILLE BARTON, CHÂTEAU

St.-Julien 1997: A well-crafted red, with silky tannins and pretty berry, mineral and spice character. Medium in body, with a medium finish. As usual, Barton does his wine the right way. Almost outstanding. • $NA • (06/15/98) (BT) • **85-89**

St.-Julien 1996: Rich and tannic, yet reserved and well structured. Medium- to full-bodied, with velvety tannins and a caressing finish. Léoville Barton is a sure thing almost every vintage these days. • $75 • (06/15/98) (BT) • **90-94**

St.-Julien 1995: Tantalizing red, with violet, berry and blackberry aromas and hints of earth. Full-bodied and chewy, with lots of fruit and flavors. Long, velvety finish. Best after 2001. • $50 • (01/31/98) • **93**

St.-Julien 1994: A mouthful for the vintage, with its lovely berry, chocolate and tobacco aromas and flavors, medium-to-full body and chewy tannins. Fresh finish. Drinkable now. 21,700 cases made. • $45 • (01/31/97) SS • **90**

St.-Julien 1993: Léoville Barton continues to move up. Bright berry flavor and a lovely, silky tannin structure. Wonderful ripe fruit and long, delicious finish. Very well made. • $30 • (01/31/96) • **88**

St.-Julien 1991: Supple and pretty, showing soft plum and currant notes that end with a velvety finish, though it's a bit short. Drinkable now. • $23 • (03/31/94) • **84**

St.-Julien 1990: Sleek and racy, with plum, raspberry and earth aromas and flavors, silky tannins and a wonderfully long finish. Drinkable now. • $48 • (03/31/93) • **93**

St.-Julien 1989 • $33 Ⓐ • (03/15/92) • **94**
St.-Julien 1988 • $29 Ⓐ • (03/31/91) HR • **91**
St.-Julien 1987 • $20 • (05/15/90) • **80**
St.-Julien 1986 • $36 Ⓐ • (05/31/89) • **90**
St.-Julien 1985 • $44 Ⓐ • (10/15/94) • **90**
St.-Julien 1983 • $29 Ⓐ • (10/15/94) • **90**
St.-Julien 1982 • $58 Ⓐ • (08/31/92) • **90**
St.-Julien 1981 • $31 • (09/15/94) • **88**
St.-Julien 1962 • $80 • (11/30/87) • **70**
St.-Julien 1961 • $139 Ⓐ • (04/30/96) • **87**
St.-Julien 1959 • $125 • (10/15/90) • **85**
St.-Julien 1945 • $340 • (03/16/86) • **73**

LÉOVILLE LAS CASES, CHÂTEAU

St.-Julien 1996: Classy juice. This full-bodied wine shows delectable floral, spice and violet aromas and flavors, fine, well-integrated tannins, and finishes with length. Impressive. • $NA • (05/15/97) (BT) • **90-94**

St.-Julien 1995: Superb. Exotic aromas of spices, smoke and berries introduce this full-bodied wine, with its big, luscious tannins and long, long finish. A monster. • $75 • (05/15/97) (BT) • **95-99**

St.-Julien 1992: Slightly disappointing at this juncture. Berry, vanilla and earth character, medium body, soft tannins and light finish. Drinkable now. • $35 • (02/29/96) • **84**

St.-Julien 1991: A mouthful of fruit in this full-bodied red, featuring masses of mint, berry and cherry flavors, velvety tannins and long finish. One of the best '91s. Really delicious for the Médoc in an off-year. Drinkable now. • $38 • (02/29/96) • **89**

St.-Julien 1990: A lovely, harmonious wine with subtle aromas and flavors of cedar, tobacco and cherry. Medium- to full-bodied with ultrafine tannins and a long finish; all done with finesse. Drinkable now, but better after 2001. • $73 • (09/15/96) • **91**

St.-Julien 1988 • $46 Ⓐ • (02/15/92) • **95**
St.-Julien 1987 • $NA • (02/15/90) • **84**
St.-Julien 1986 • $86 Ⓐ • (02/15/90) • **96**
St.-Julien 1985 • $46 Ⓐ • (10/15/94) • **94**
St.-Julien 1984 • $33 • (02/15/90) • **82**
St.-Julien 1983 • $49 Ⓐ • (10/15/94) • **87**
St.-Julien 1982 • $168 Ⓐ • (08/31/92) • **94**
St.-Julien 1981 • $39 Ⓐ • (10/15/94) • **88**
St.-Julien 1980 • $NA • (02/15/90) • **84**
St.-Julien 1979 • $36 Ⓐ • (02/15/90) • **90**
St.-Julien 1978 • $55 Ⓐ • (02/15/90) • **94**
St.-Julien 1977 • $20 • (02/15/92) • **78**
St.-Julien 1976 • $28 Ⓐ • (02/15/92) • **83**
St.-Julien 1975 • $60 Ⓐ • (02/15/92) • **88**
St.-Julien 1971 • $66 • (04/01/86) • **76**
St.-Julien 1970 • $41 Ⓐ • (02/15/90) • **89**
St.-Julien 1966 • $61 Ⓐ • (02/15/92) • **86**
St.-Julien 1964 • $53 Ⓐ • (02/15/92) • **88**
St.-Julien 1962 • $41 Ⓐ • (11/30/87) • **85**
St.-Julien 1961 • $151 Ⓐ • (04/30/96) • **85**
St.-Julien 1959 • $127 Ⓐ • (10/15/90) • **96**
St.-Julien 1955 • $190 • (02/15/92) • **81**
St.-Julien 1953 • $225 • (02/15/92) • **87**
St.-Julien 1952 • $165 • (02/15/92) • **73**
St.-Julien 1950 • $165 • (02/15/92) • **73**
St.-Julien 1948 • $165 • (02/15/92) • **65**
St.-Julien 1947 • $141 Ⓐ • (02/15/92) • **86**
St.-Julien 1945 • $600 • (11/30/95) • **89**
St.-Julien 1928 • $450 • (02/15/92) • **90**

LÉOVILLE POYFERRÉ, CHÂTEAU

St.-Julien 1997: Dark in color, with intense violet and berry aromas and a hint of green tobacco. Medium-bodied, with medium tannins, but it quickly melts away on the palate. • $NA • (06/15/98) (BT) • **85-89**

St.-Julien 1996: Silky and elegant, with a slight dilution on the midpalate. Medium-bodied, with fine tannins. Wait and see after bottling. • $55 • (06/15/98) (BT) • **85-89**

St.-Julien 1995: Best Léoville Poyferré ever. Big, mouthpuckering wine. Bubbling over with mint, blackberry and currant character. Full-bodied, with extremely full yet finely textured tannins and a long, silky texture. Try after 2002. • $36 • (01/31/98) • **93**

St.-Julien 1991: Some fine complexity here, with beautiful smoky, red berry and vanilla flavors, but it doesn't have much length. Drinkable now. • $23 • (03/31/94) • **81**

St.-Julien 1990: A chewy wine, with impressively rich aromas and flavors of ripe plums, tobacco, cedar and earth and attractive velvety tannins. Drinkable now. 18,500 cases made. • $64 • (03/31/93) • **92**

St.-Julien 1989 • $42 • (03/15/92) • **90**
St.-Julien 1988 • $21 Ⓐ • (07/15/91) • **81**
St.-Julien 1987 • $24 • (05/15/90) • **86**
St.-Julien 1986 • $24 • (05/31/89) • **86**
St.-Julien 1985 • $25 Ⓐ • (04/30/88) • **92**
St.-Julien 1984 • $25 • (10/15/87) • **85**
St.-Julien 1983 • $28 Ⓐ • (03/01/86) • **83**

St.-Julien 1982: Ripe, generous and typical of the vintage for its lively fruit character that lasts on the long finish. Needs cellaring until 2005 or 2010 in order to spread out a bit and settle down, but it's a comer. Tasted from magnum. • $53 Ⓐ • (07/31/97) • **90**

St.-Julien 1981 • $25 • (06/01/84) • **88**
St.-Julien 1961 • $64 Ⓐ • (04/30/96) • **85**
St.-Julien 1945 • $210 • (03/16/86) • **80**

LEPITRE, ABEL

Brut Champagne 1986 • $NA • (12/31/93) • **84**
Brut Champagne 1985 • $NA • (12/31/93) • **84**

LEQUIN-ROUSSOT

Chassagne-Montrachet Morgeot Red 1985 • $24 • (05/31/88) • **86**
Corton Les Languettes 1985 • $39 • (07/15/88) • **86**
Nuits-St.-Georges 1985 • $39 • (04/15/88) • **75**
Santenay 1987 • $15 • (11/15/90) • **76**
Santenay 1985 • $18 • (05/31/88) • **78**
Santenay La Comme 1985 • $24 • (05/31/88) • **85**

LEROY

Auxey-Duresses Les Clous Red 1988 • $52 • (05/15/91) • **85**
Bourgogne d'Auvenay 1988 • $15 • (04/30/91) • **87**
Bourgogne d'Auvenay 1985 • $12 • (03/31/88) • **73**
Bourgogne Leroy 1990: Chunky and earthy, with spice and berry flavors and a good concentration of fruit and tannins on the finish. Drinkable now. • $18 • (12/15/92) • **86**
Bourgogne Leroy 1989 • $18 • (01/31/92) • **85**
Bourgogne Leroy White 1992: Light and tart, offering very crisp texture and some straightforward citrus, floral, wet hay and apple flavors. Very firm on the finish. Drinkable now. Tasted twice with identical results. 8,000 cases made. • $19 • (08/31/94) • **80**
Bourgogne White 1993: Delicious, easygoing white, offering apple, cream and mineral character, medium body and pretty finish. • $15 • (08/31/95) • **83**
Chambertin 1993: Wonderfully sexy, soft and silky, featuring pretty plum and vanilla character, medium body, ultrafine tannins and sweet fruit finish. Better in 1999. 72 cases made. • $690 Ⓐ • (11/15/95) • **95**
Chambertin 1992: Lean, accessible, nicely focused, a sharp beam of black cherry, toast and spice flavors shining through. Smooth tannins make it drinkable already. • $187 Ⓐ • (12/15/94) • **88**
Chambertin 1991: An extreme wine, lean in structure but silky and polished, exotic in flavor, featuring an array of spices both sweet and sharp around a fine thread of floral berry and black cherry fruit. A stylish wine to drink now, or hold until 2000. Tasted three times. 75 cases made. • $257 Ⓐ • (01/31/94) • **88**
Chambertin 1990: Remarkably balanced and harmonious, this is complex, tightly knit, big and massive, with tons of toasty, roasted wood and game characteristics. Also delivers tobacco box, smoke, plum and cherry flavors on the ripe, very elegant finish. Drinkable now. 169 cases made. • $456 Ⓐ • (12/15/92) • **96**
Chambertin 1989 • $264 Ⓐ • (01/31/92) • **93**
Chambertin 1985: Closed and compact, this is still hard, but it offers plenty of sweet fruit character graced by a mineral and spicy complexity. Better around 2000. • $383 Ⓐ • (12/15/96) • **93**
Chambertin 1978: Harsh, rustic, acidic, earthy and murky. Another showed celery overtones. • $468 Ⓐ • (12/15/96) • **70**
Chambertin 1969: A deep, complex *grand cru*, of pure fruit. Seductive and powerful, with black currant, wet earth and mineral notes that reflect the Chambertin *terroir* perfectly. This outstanding vintage is known for balanced, long-lived wines, and here is the evidence. Drink now through 2010. • $383 Ⓐ • (12/15/96) • **98**
Chambertin 1961: Although not considered a great vintage in Burgundy, there were some notable successes. This full-bodied Chambertin is gorgeous and packed with complexity, from the earthy, mineral notes, to the cedar, mint and black currant flavors. A touch drying on the finish, but it's deeply satisfying nonetheless. Drink now through 2000. • $220 • (12/15/96) • **94**
Chambertin 1959: From a great vintage that benefited from near-perfect weather, Leroy produced a classic Chambertin. Ripe, rich, thick and almost Port-like, with lovely plum, chocolate and spice accents that are superbly complex. Sweet-tasting and lush, with a few good years ahead of it yet; drink now through 2005. • $599 Ⓐ • (12/15/96) • **95**
Chambertin 1955: Has a sweet fruit character that is overlaid with a complex of smoky, earthy flavors along with notes of mineral, faded roses and tea leaf. Bottle variation made this wine difficult to evaluate, though. One sample was a bit dry. Drink now through 2000. • $506 Ⓐ • (12/15/96) • **88**
Chambertin 1949: Rich, deep and very complex, this offers layers of lovely black currant and earth character. "Masculine" in style, opposed to the "feminine" and near-perfect Musigny from this vintage. It's also a bit leaner and shorter on the finish. Drink now through 2005. • $NA • (12/15/96) • **94**
Chambertin-Clos de Bèze 1959: Starts out rich, thick, sweet and lush, but not as much class as the '59 Chambertin. There is some nice mineral flavor but tart on the finish. The oak dominates over the fruit, suggesting it has already peaked. • $98 • (12/15/96) • **84**
Chambertin-Clos de Bèze 1955: Sweet and lush, with a silky mouthfeel, but it also shows some oak and chestnut character. Some red berry, plum,chocolate and spice flavors, but a bit dry on the finish. Must have been terrific 10 years ago. • $94 • (12/15/96) • **86**
Chambolle-Musigny Les Charmes 1993: Lovely, elegant berry, vanilla and spice character, medium body, fine tannins and light, fresh finish. Drinkable now. 24 cases made. • $200 • (11/15/95) • **90**
Chambolle-Musigny Les Charmes 1992: Sweet and ripe at first, but it ends a bit diluted. Modest raspberry and currant notes with a gamy, smoky edge. Drink soon. • $NA • (01/01/94) • **79**
Chambolle-Musigny Les Fremières 1993: Generous and seductively flavorful, offering ripe plum, currant, black cherry and chocolate. Same quality level as a barrel sample tasted in the spring of 1995. Tempting now, but hold until 2000. 24 cases made. • $125 • (11/15/95) • **88**
Chambolle-Musigny Les Fremières 1992: Decidedly gamy, but backed up with a decent quotient of black cherry flavor, all of which lingers on the smooth finish. Drinkable now. • $NA • (01/01/94) • **83**
Chambolle-Musigny Les Fremières 1991: A lithe, lean wine that seems earthy at first, but the blackberry and currant fruit comes bursting through as the flavors emerge wrapped in a blanket of fine tannins. Try now. 48 cases made. • $74 Ⓐ • (01/31/94) • **87**
Chambolle-Musigny Les Fremières 1990: Has everything in unbelievable amounts: concentration, fruit, color, tannins and suppleness. Stands out with its rich character of grilled, toasty oak, violet, raspberry and chocolate aromas and flavors. Will need years before the new oak and fruit flavors melt together harmoniously. Drinkable in 1999 or 2000. 143 cases made. • $79 • (12/15/92) • **94**
Chambolle-Musigny Les Fremières 1989 • $80 • (01/31/92) • **94**
Chapelle-Chambertin 1964: In this vintage of full-bodied, rich red Burgundies, Leroy turned out some superlative wines, as this *grand cru* demonstrates. This is sweet and round, medium-to-full body, with lovely red berry and licorice character. Very smooth finish. Quite pleasant and at its peak. Enjoy it now. • $118 • (12/15/96) • **90**
Clos de la Roche 1993: Big and beautiful, boasting voluptuous blackberry and vanilla character, full body, silky tannins and long, sweet finish. Better in 2000. Rated just a notch below a barrel sample earlier this year. 72 cases made. • $498 Ⓐ • (11/15/95) • **94**
Clos de la Roche 1992: A good red Burgundy that is fruity, moderately tannic and tart. Medium-bodied; lively cherry and raspberry flavors. Drinkable now. • $125 Ⓐ • (05/15/95) • **84**
Clos de la Roche 1991: Earthy, floral and flavorful, offering a core of solid blackberry and currant underneath a layer of slightly gamy, musty, smoky violet character. Tough and chewy on the finish, but juicy at the core. Drinkable now. 237 cases made. • $124 Ⓐ • (01/31/94) • **90**
Clos de la Roche 1990: Leaves you speechless. Shows such concentration, grace and beauty, it's obviously the work of an artist. Complex vanilla, violet, plum and blackberry flavors are cut with razor-sharp acidity, and it shows a smoky, toasty aftertaste. The considerable fruit balances new oak. Drinkable in 1999 or 2000. 218 cases made. • $289 Ⓐ • (12/15/92) • **97**
Clos de la Roche 1989 • $148 Ⓐ • (01/31/92) • **94**
Clos de Vougeot 1993: Stupendous. So balanced it's difficult not to drink this one now. Lovely spice, mocha and fruit character. Full-bodied, adding velvety tannins and a long, savory finish. Better in 2000. • $403 Ⓐ • (11/15/95) • **96**
Clos de Vougeot 1992: Not flashy, but it packs a lot of flavor into a lean frame, showing ripe blackberry, currant, anise and floral character that maintains its balance and focus through the lingering finish. Best now. • $100 Ⓐ • (12/15/94) • **90**
Clos de Vougeot 1991: Highly distinctive, offering layers of earthy flavors. Mineral and mushroom notes shade the core of black cherry, currant and blackberry that extends into a rich, finely tannic finish. Best now. 75 cases made. • $181 • (01/31/94) • **90**
Clos de Vougeot 1990: A full-blown Clos de Vougeot that's been given the full-blown new oak treatment. Stands out in this group, with its violet, raspberry and plum characteristics and massive, hard tannins. Drinkable in 1999. 400 cases made. • $155 Ⓐ • (12/15/92) • **97**

Key: SS—Spectator Selection CS—Cellar Selection HR—Highly Recommended BB—Best Buy $NA—Price not available Ⓐ—Auction Price (BT)—Barrel Tasting
Dates in parentheses indicate the issues in which the ratings were published.

Clos de Vougeot 1989 • $173 Ⓐ • (01/31/92) • **95**

Clos de Vougeot 1988 • $177 Ⓐ • (04/30/91) • **89**

Corton Les Renardes 1993: A Corton with finesse. Pretty blackberry, toasty oak and smoke flavors, solid fruit, firm tannins and long, succulent finish. Better in 2000. Same quality and score as a barrel sample tasted earlier this year. 169 cases made. • $185 • (11/15/95) • **92**

Corton Les Renardes 1992: Ripe, chewy and distinctive, packing a fair amount of blackberry and currant flavors into a solid frame. Has overtones of anise and earth that echo on the tannic finish. Best now. • $83 • (12/15/94) • **91**

Corton Les Renardes 1991: A crisp, sharply pleated wine that folds in raspberry, violet, vanilla and anise aromas and flavors and coats your mouth with fruit and tannins on the finish, while remaining elegant, classy and focused. Try now. 121 cases made. • $100 Ⓐ • (01/31/94) • **90**

Corton Les Renardes 1990: If you like the violet and vanilla flavors from masses of new oak and fruit, this is for you. Refined, with enough fruit to back up the tannins. Drinkable now, or hold until 2000. 167 cases made. • $111 • (12/15/92) • **92**

Corton Les Renardes 1989 • $117 • (01/31/92) • **95**

Corton-Charlemagne 1993: Solid and muscular, turning silky on the finish, delivering pear, vanilla bean and coconut flavors edged between smoky, toasty oak shadings. • $150 • (08/31/95) • **88**

Gevrey-Chambertin Aux Combottes 1993: Provides lots of strawberry, vanilla and cherry character, medium body and tannins and soft finish. Drinkable now. Same quality as we remember in a barrel sample earlier this year. 24 cases made. • $220 • (11/15/95) • **89**

Gevrey-Chambertin Aux Combottes 1992: Has a little more distinction than most, folding its violet, berry and currant flavors into a nice package. Drinkable now. • $83 • (12/15/94) • **86**

Gevrey-Chambertin Aux Combottes 1991: Distinctively earthy and floral. Violet and rose petal aromas and flavors and a lively array of berry and passion fruit swirl across the palate and into the firm finish. Drink now. 48 cases made. • $100 Ⓐ • (01/31/94) • **88**

Gevrey-Chambertin Aux Combottes 1990: A beautiful Gevrey, with great concentration and elegant, toasty raspberry and vanilla characteristics. Like many from this appellation, it's very firm but offers more flesh than most on the finish. Drinkable now. 144 cases made. • $111 • (12/15/92) • **92**

Gevrey-Chambertin Aux Combottes 1989 • $68 Ⓐ • (01/31/92) • **93**

Gevrey-Chambertin Les Cazetiers 1971: This *premier cru* has aged beautifully. Smells amazingly seductive with its ethereal scents of iris and rose petal. Good intensity on the palate, bringing out nuances of mineral, chalk and tar in a medium-bodied frame. The fruit flavors fade a bit, but the subtle finish is persistent. Enjoy now. • $NA • (12/15/96) • **89**

Gevrey-Chambertin Les Cazetiers 1969: Like an ugly duckling next to the sensational Chambertin 1969, but it still holds its own. Lovely black currant and floral aromas and flavors. Medium body and turns a bit tart on the finish. Drink up. • $180 • (12/15/96) • **87**

Gevrey-Chambertin Les Cazetiers 1962: Beautifully balanced and full-bodied, with a pleasant, round mouthfeel. Has coffee bean aromas and plenty of sweet fruit character. A slight tartness on the finish suggests now is the time to drink this. • $78 • (12/15/96) • **87**

Gevrey-Chambertin Les Cazetiers 1961: A *premier cru* of amazing quality, still showing at this mature age. It's multi-dimensional and balanced, with delicious ripe fruit, black currant and roasted chestnut flavors. A lingering finish, too. A treat to drink now. • $NA • (12/15/96) • **92**

Grands Echézeaux 1945: Has probably seen better days, since the vintage is known for highly concentrated wines. This has attractive aromas, accented by subtle but very pretty violet and other floral notes. Some decent fruit, but fading a bit. Medium-bodied and slightly dry, but the fruit got a boost with food. Drink now. • $633 • (12/15/96) • **87**

Latricières-Chambertin 1993: Loads of personality. Full in body, offering a core of earth, currant, chocolate, leather and plum. Slightly rough finish. Drinkable now. As good as a barrel sample from the spring of '95. 48 cases made. • $325 • (11/15/95) • **91**

Latricières-Chambertin 1992: Crisp and chewy, with enough body to deliver some complexity; gamy currant notes predominate now. Flavors echo nicely on the finish, but this doesn't quite live up to its name. Drinkable now. • $155 • (12/15/94) • **86**

Latricières-Chambertin 1991: Earthy notes keep peering through the currant and berry aromas and flavors in this chewy, hard-textured wine. Offers a real mouthful of as-yet unfocused flavor; has the stuff to be worth cellaring until 1999 or 2000. Tasted twice. 73 cases made. • $181 Ⓐ • (01/31/94) • **89**

Latricières-Chambertin 1990: Pure fruit, with laser-guided flavors that engulf your taste buds. Offers masses of violet, fruit and berry characteristics and ultrafine tannins and acidity. Superb. Try now. 195 cases made. • $204 • (12/15/92) • **96**

Latricières-Chambertin 1989 • $151 Ⓐ • (01/31/92) • **93**

Mazis-Chambertin 1985: Superbly sweet and ripe, offering broad fruit flavors and a distinctive mineral-and-earth character. Lots of class, full-bodied and robust. Ready to drink now through 2000. • $359 Ⓐ • (12/15/96) • **91**

Mazis-Chambertin 1978: A bit funky on the nose, developing into mature tea leaf, earth and spice aromas. Has a salty character but a certain sweetness prevails in the end. It does show some nice currant flavors, but the overall impression is that it's a bit dry and oaky. • $350 Ⓐ • (12/15/96) • **83**

Mazis-Chambertin 1971: Quite powerful but slightly sharp, with nice mineral, chalk, earth, tea leaf and cherry flavors. Medium body, with chewy texture. Slightly drying on the finish. Drink now through 2000. • $364 Ⓐ • (12/15/96) • **86**

Mazis-Chambertin 1964: What great Burgundy is all about. Complex and wonderfully balanced, with a round texture, fragrant aromas, ripe fruit flavors and a mineral character. Predictions that '64s would be long-lived, especially from Maison Leroy, prove correct. Drink now through 2000. • $275 • (12/15/96) • **95**

Mazis-Chambertin 1959: Quite magical, with a distinctive *goût de terroir* typical of this *grand cru*, with lots of mineral and earthy notes. Silky texture, deep and complex, it rivals the 1959 Chambertin, but is less sweet. Full-bodied and still very fresh, drink now through 2005. • $385 • (12/15/96) • **94**

Mazis-Chambertin 1955: Simply fabulous. From a difficult vintage full of rather simple wines, Leroy stands out with a great red Burgundy like this. Ripe and sweet, with flavors of cedarwood, mint and currant that fan out on the palate. Keeps growing more complex in in the glass. Start uncorking, if you're lucky enough to have some lying around. • $450 • (12/15/96) • **95**

Mazis-Chambertin Hospices de Beaune Cuvée Madeleine Collignon 1985: Sweet-tasting, ripe and extremely seductive. Full-bodied and complex in its earthy currant flavors, with wonderful balance. As delicious as it is, though, it's more showy than elegant; a brown sugar character keeps it from scoring higher. Soft finish, drink now. • $495 • (12/15/96) • **91**

Musigny 1993: An explosive and superbly crafted Burgundy that packs black currant, plum, earth and toast flavors. Full-bodied and has enormous intensity and concentration. Needs until 2005 to show it all. 72 cases made. • $690 Ⓐ • (11/15/95) CS • **97**

Musigny 1992: Light and supple, with a nice range of berry and smoked bacon notes finishing with a little grip of fine tannin. Best to drink now. • $183 Ⓐ • (12/15/94) • **89**

Musigny 1991: Earthy up front, featuring fine tannins, nicely articulated blackberry, wild berry and game aromas and flavors and a crisp, refined finish. Very firm in texture. Drinkable now. 50 cases made. • $439 Ⓐ • (01/31/94) • **91**

Musigny 1985: This Leroy Musigny, from such a highly-rated vintage, never won over the critics. It does show some nice aromas of vanilla, chocolate and earth, with red berry flavors. Oddly though, it's full-bodied but not very dense on the palate and a bit drying on the finish. Drink now through 2000. • $455 Ⓐ • (12/15/96) • **87**

Musigny 1969: More delicate than the '66 Chambertin, with some vanilla and floral aromas. Lovely fruit complexity on the palate, but not as long on the finish as expected. Good finesse, though. Drink now through 2002. • $183 • (12/15/96) • **88**

Musigny 1966: Lots of ripe, rich and sweet fruit flavors, but a dominant brown sugar character makes it less elegant than the '69. Drink now through 2000. • $144 Ⓐ • (12/15/96) • **87**

Musigny 1961: A bad bottle, a bit oxidized. Rustic and tart, with plummy notes and a drying finish. • $498 • (12/15/96) • **83**

Musigny 1949: Ethereal scents, a lush and silky texture and intense flavors of ripe, rich, sweet fruit. Powerful and youthful, the plum, cherry and mineral character are incredibly balanced. At its pinnacle and perfect to drink now, but should last until 2000 at least. • $750 Ⓐ • (12/15/96) • **98**

Nuits-St.-Georges 1993: Excellent, intense aromas and flavors of spice, plum and berry. Medium in body, firm tannins. Less than outstanding because of a somewhat short finish. Drinkable now. 267 cases made. • $110 • (11/15/95) • **89**

Nuits-St.-Georges 1945: This is simply a curiosity, with some vanilla and maderized-oxidized flavors. Lean and thin, with more acidity than fruit. • $NA • (12/15/96) • **75**

Nuits-St.-Georges Au Bas de Combe 1992: A full-blown style that stretches the boundaries of Burgundy with coffee, raisin and chocolate flavors that are practically sweet. Appealing, if unusual. Drink now. • $63 • (06/15/95) • **82**

Nuits-St.-Georges Au Bas de Combe 1991: A firm, chewy mouthful of anise- and tobacco-scented currant and wild berry flavors. Tighter and earthier than most, yet seems youthful and exuberant. Drinkable now, or hold until 2000. Tasted twice. 24 cases made. • $58 Ⓐ • (01/31/94) • **90**

Nuits-St.-Georges Au Bas de Combe 1990: Shows clever winemaking; a pretty Burgundy, with plum, spice and toasty oak aromas and flavors and a fine tannin structure. Not as big as some, but very well balanced. Drinkable now. 48 cases made. • $58 • (12/15/92) • **88**

Nuits-St.-Georges Aux Allots 1992: Stylish, concentrated and flavorful, unfolding its delicious currant and smoky tobacco character into a long and appealing finish. Drinkable now. • $55 • (12/15/94) • **87**

Nuits-St.-Georges Aux Allots 1991: Firm and focused, offering a lovely streak of ripe currant, blackberry and spicy oak aromas and flavors. Drink now. Tasted twice. 121 cases made. • $40 Ⓐ • (01/31/94) • **85**

Nuits-St.-Georges Aux Allots 1990: Spectacular, with amazing concentration of fruit and tannins. A smoky, toasty violet and spice component surfaces from the glass, and it shows wonderful harmony. Drink now. 142 cases made. • $67 • (12/15/92) • **95**

Nuits-St.-Georges Aux Allots 1989 • $45 Ⓐ • (01/31/92) • **92**

Nuits-St.-Georges Aux Allots 1988 • $49 Ⓐ • (04/30/91) • **89**

Nuits-St.-Georges Aux Boudots 1993: Just as we remember a barrel sample earlier this year. Wonderfully aromatic nutmeg and fruit character, medium body, supple tannins and spicy aftertaste. Better in 2000. 217 cases made. • $185 • (11/15/95) • **91**

Nuits-St.-Georges Aux Boudots 1992: Tight and beautifully structured; packs spicy, violet-scented blackberry, currant and vanilla flavors onto a lithe and racy frame. Sweet tannins. Drinkable now. • $79 • (12/15/94) • **90**

Nuits-St.-Georges Aux Boudots 1991: Oddly aromatic, offering plenty of barnyard, mineral and currant aromas and flavors. Drinkable now. Tasted three times. 219 cases made. • $93 Ⓐ • (01/31/94) • **83**

Nuits-St.-Georges Aux Boudots 1990: A huge wine, with tons of spice, violet and berry flavors and masses of full tannins. Appears to be built to last for decades. Drinkable now. 460 cases made. • $108 • (12/15/92) • **94**

Nuits-St.-Georges Aux Boudots 1989 • $117 • (01/31/92) • **95**

Nuits-St.-Georges Aux Boudots 1988 • $230 • (04/30/91) • **93**

Nuits-St.-Georges Aux Lavières 1992: Dark-colored, plush in texture, toasty-earthy in aroma and nicely accented by vanilla and chocolate from oak aging. Fruit is modest but clean; a rich, round package. • $63 • (05/15/95) • **87**

Nuits-St.-Georges Aux Lavières 1991: A narrow beam of violet-scented currant and berry flavors is shaded by smoky, toasty, earthy notes. Crisp and focused; drinkable now. 121 cases made. • $59 Ⓐ • (01/31/94) • **83**

Nuits-St.-Georges Aux Lavières 1990: Shows great breeding, with tons of ripe, spicy fruit flavors, ripe tannins and toasty oak notes. Extremely well made. Drink now. 168 cases made. • $59 • (12/15/92) • **94**

Nuits-St.-Georges Aux Lavières 1989 • $75 • (01/31/92) • **89**

Nuits-St.-Georges Aux Lavières 1988 • $84 • (04/30/91) • **82**

Nuits-St.-Georges Aux Vignerondes 1993: Defines harmony. Purple-colored and thick with currant, spice and lightly toasty flavors. Tastes sweet, ripe and supple, showing restraint and elegance. As good as a barrel sample tried earlier this year. Drink now. 24 cases made. • $185 • (11/15/95) • **95**

Nuits-St.-Georges Aux Vignerondes 1992: Smooth, well made and dark in color. Tastes of currant and black cherry and has an appealing balance and toasty character. • $79 • (12/15/94) • **85**

Nuits-St.-Georges Aux Vignerondes 1991: Dark and dense, this peppery, spicy, cedary wine has enough intense currant and blackberry flavors to carry it through 1998 to 2000, when it should be at its best. Tasted twice. 73 cases made. • $93 • (01/31/94) • **87**

Nuits-St.-Georges Aux Vignerondes 1990: A gorgeous Nuits that's extremely concentrated and firm, boasting beautiful, gamy plum and black cherry characteristics along with masses of charred, toasty new oak notes that will need time to soften. Amazingly balanced for such a big wine. Tasted twice. Drinkable now. 150 cases made. • $100 • (12/15/92) • **95**

Nuits-St.-Georges Aux Vignerondes 1989 • $53 Ⓐ • (01/31/92) • **92**

Nuits-St.-Georges La Richemone 1989: Ripe, plummy and round, quite generous and spicy, with a complement of sweet fruit. Also has some meaty, peppery notes and a hint of tomato. A bit tough on the slightly dry finish. Drink now through 2000. • $NA • (12/15/96) • **85**

Nuits-St.-Georges La Richemone 1938: Hard and harsh, ending up a bit tart. Past its peak. • $NA • (12/15/96) • **75**

Key: SS—Spectator Selection CS—Cellar Selection HR—Highly Recommended BB—Best Buy $NA—Price not available Ⓐ—Auction Price (BT)—Barrel Tasting

Dates in parentheses indicate the issues in which the ratings were published.

Pommard Grands Epenots 1964: Some decent fruit character, fairly round and pleasant, but it shows its age with the rustic, tart tannins on the finish. Medium body. A *premier cru* that's beginning to fade, so drink soon. • $92 • (12/15/96) • **84**

Pommard Les Vignots 1993: Exuberant, lovely, freshly crushed grape flavors. Tight and firm now, boasting an intriguing blend of pure cassis and some earthy notes. Long finish. Try after 2000. Even better than barrel sample tasted earlier this year. 437 cases made. • $128 Ⓐ • (11/15/95) • **92**

Pommard Les Vignots 1992: A lovely Pommard: blackberry and boysenberry flavors laced with violet and a hint of minty, gamy complexity. Medium-bodied, satisfying, with supple tannins. Try now. • $77 Ⓐ • (12/15/94) • **85**

Pommard Les Vignots 1991: Earthy, barnyardy aromas and flavors hit you first, but rich currant and blackberry flavors come through and keep singing through the long, rich finish. Remarkably intense for the vintage. Drinkable now. Tasted twice. 292 cases made. • $44 Ⓐ • (01/31/94) • **89**

Pommard Les Vignots 1990: Exotically seductive, with amazing violet, rose petal, raspberry and currant aromas. The essence of fruit blooms in this wine and the flavors linger on the remarkably classy finish. This defines great Burgundy. Drinkable now or in the next century. 262 cases made. • $74 • (12/15/92) • **97**

Pommard Les Vignots 1989 • $60 Ⓐ • (01/31/92) • **96**

Pommard Les Vignots 1988 • $125 Ⓐ • (04/30/91) • **88**

Pommard Trois Follots 1990: A sensual wine that oozes with concentrated raspberry extract and more than a hint of wood. The intense flavors ripple across the palate to a long, impressive finish. Drinkable now. 24 cases made. • $69 • (12/15/92) • **95**

Richebourg 1993: Elegantly fine and classy—the epitome of silkiness. Full-bodied yet reserved and firmly structured, delivering loads of red berry and vanilla character and a long finish. Will be even better in 2000 or later. • $989 Ⓐ • (11/15/95) CS • **96**

Richebourg 1992: Bright, generous and supple, with layers of berry, mineral and subtle spice nuances; concentrated and remarkably approachable. Has a wonderful clarity of flavor. • $265 Ⓐ • (12/15/94) • **91**

Richebourg 1991: Firmly tannic and tough, showing undercurrents of cherry and currant bubbling beneath a layer of tannins and stalky, floral violet notes, but the breeding is evident. Needs until at least 2000 or 2001. 146 cases made. • $267 Ⓐ • (01/31/94) • **90**

Richebourg 1990: Massive and gorgeous, with tons of violet, plum and raspberry aromas and flavors and so many toasty, smoky, vanilla-flavored new oak nuances that it almost masks the fruit now. Very firm and solid despite its perfumed, immediate appeal. Don't touch until the turn of the century. 240 cases made. • $299 • (12/15/92) • **98**

Richebourg 1989 • $287 Ⓐ • (01/31/92) • **96**

Richebourg 1949: Not as impressively lush as expected for a Richebourg from this celebrated vintage. Full-bodied, rich and still very solid, with spice, roasted chestnut and plum flavors. Very good, but a distracting woody aroma, somewhat dry finish and lack of supple sweetness keeps it out of the outstanding ranks. • $700 Ⓐ • (12/15/96) • **89**

Romanée St.-Vivant 1993: Exotic and thick, featuring wild berry, floral, mint and spice character, full body, masses of fruit and a long, vanilla-spice finish. Better after 2000. 72 cases made. • $500 • (11/15/95) • **95**

Romanée St.-Vivant 1992: A lot of violet and spice character runs through the subtle aromas and flavors, glowing with sweet blackberry and currant notes on the supple finish. Drinkable now. • $210 • (12/15/94) • **91**

Romanée St.-Vivant 1991: Dramatic, earthy and elegant, packed with blackberry and currant flavors shaded by truffle and violet overtones. The fruit persists on the supple finish. Drink now. Tasted twice. 175 cases made. • $267 Ⓐ • (01/31/94) • **91**

Romanée St.-Vivant 1990: Wild, beautiful and classy; a wine that stands out for its deep color. The refined violet, vanilla, blueberry and raspberry flavors burst out of the glass, delivering a lot of character in a restrained, supple package. Drinkable in 2000. 240 cases made. • $299 • (12/15/92) • **97**

Romanée St.-Vivant 1989 • $197 Ⓐ • (01/31/92) • **95**

Romanée St.-Vivant 1988 • $431 Ⓐ • (04/30/91) • **95**

Savigny-lès-Beaune Les Narbantons 1993: Nice fruit here but also an earthy component that gives it character and may not be for everyone. Still, the currant, plum and wet earth flavors are well integrated. Drinkable now. 169 cases made. • $70 • (11/15/95) • **89**

Savigny-lès-Beaune Les Narbantons 1992: Light and supple, with complex gamy, earthy berry and black cherry flavors that hint at anise on the finish. Drinkable now. • $40 • (12/15/94) • **85**

Savigny-lès-Beaune Les Narbantons 1991: Delicate and subtle, yet impressively concentrated, featuring plenty of brilliantly articulated black cherry, currant and toast aromas and flavors that echo on the supple finish. Drinkable now. 194 cases made. • $44 Ⓐ • (01/31/94) • **89**

Savigny-lès-Beaune Les Narbantons 1990: Big, well-crafted and muscular, lacking in finesse what it makes up in power, with loads of new oak and tannins and plenty of roasted coconut, vanilla and raspberry flavors. Drinkable now. 288 cases made. • $138 Ⓐ • (12/15/92) • **92**

Savigny-lès-Beaune Les Narbantons 1989 • $65 • (01/31/92) • **91**

Volnay-Santenots 1993: Like great sex: exciting at first and relaxing in the end. Full-bodied and very voluptuous, boasting loads of berry, smoky, chocolate character. Full, velvety tannins and a long finish. Better after 2000. 97 cases made. • $138 Ⓐ • (11/15/95) • **96**

Volnay-Santenots 1992: Crisp in texture but plays out its ripe berry and slightly gamy flavors nicely. Drinkable now. • $62 Ⓐ • (01/01/94) • **83**

Vosne-Romanée 1969: Fairly fruity, with some modest red berry aromas and flavors. A bit astringent on the finish; it has seen better days. • $60 • (12/15/96) • **80**

Vosne-Romanée Aux Genaivrières 1992: This emphasizes oak over fruit flavors, showing vanilla, chocolate and maple syrup overtones and some black cherry underneath. Enticing and rich, but balanced for drinking now before the fruit dries up. • $61 • (05/15/95) • **84**

Vosne-Romanée Aux Genaivrières 1991: Very firm and chewy; earthy at first, turning smooth and relatively fruity beneath several layers of chunky tannins. Shows blackberry, currant and plum flavors and finishes tight and polished. Tasted twice. Drinkable now. 121 cases made. • $57 Ⓐ • (01/31/94) • **90**

Vosne-Romanée Aux Genaivrières 1990: Like a slow-burning fuse on your palate: the ripe fruit, firm tannins and toasty oak characteristics build to the finish. Shows great winemaking. Drinkable now. 364 cases made. • $61 • (12/15/92) • **95**

Vosne-Romanée Aux Genaivrières 1989 • $75 • (01/31/92) • **91**

Vosne-Romanée Aux Réas 1990: Out of this world. A kaleidoscope of aromas and flavors, offering red berry, toasty oak, chocolate, spice and fully integrated tannins. Will improve for decades. Drinkable now. 48 cases made. • $58 • (12/15/92) • **97**

Vosne-Romanée Les Beaux Monts 1993: An extremely refined yet full-bodied and very powerful red. Bold aromas of licorice, berry, vanilla and currant follow through on the palate. Silky tannins, but it remains rather closed: try after 2000. 362 cases made. • $392 Ⓐ • (11/15/95) • **94**

Vosne-Romanée Les Beaux Monts 1992: A little coarse in tannins, but the plummy, grapey flavors are good. Drinkable now. • $98 Ⓐ • (12/15/94) • **85**

Vosne-Romanée Les Beaux Monts 1991: Tough and chewy; this earthy, gamy wine emerges with a distinctive violet scent, a solid core of currant and berry flavors and a tight, hard finish. Drinkable now. 292 cases made. • $100 Ⓐ • (01/31/94) HR • **91**

Vosne-Romanée Les Beaux Monts 1990: What else do you want in a Burgundy? It's both powerful and delicate, with lovely, enchanting spice, plum, vanilla and black currant flavors that cascade across the palate, showing endless complexity. Drinkable now. 775 cases made. • $200 Ⓐ • (12/15/92) HR • **95**

Vosne-Romanée Les Beaux Monts 1989 • $142 Ⓐ • (01/31/92) • **92**

Vosne-Romanée Les Beaux Monts 1988 • $81 Ⓐ • (04/30/91) • **93**

Vosne-Romanée Les Brûlées 1993: The essence of fruit, featuring loads of plum, cherry and strawberry character, full body, substantial velvety tannins and a long, long finish. Better after 2000. 24 cases made. • $185 • (11/15/95) • **93**

Vosne-Romanée Les Brûlées 1992: More flavorful than most Vosne-Romanées, delivering some interesting gamy, smoky flavors to enhance the lovely, focused boysenberry and blackberry flavors. Ready now. • $83 • (12/15/94) • **85**

Vosne-Romanée Les Brûlées 1989 • $111 Ⓐ • (01/31/92) • **94**

LEROY, DOMAINE

Chambertin 1994: Very appealing and well made, showing good concentration. Dark-colored and medium-bodied, with flavors of plum and currant. Fine-textured tannins on the finish, though you wish for a bit more intensity. Try in 2001 to 2002. • $448 • (11/15/96) • **86**

Chambertin 1993: An amazing full-bodied wine. The supple character of the ultrafine tannins, the richness of the sweet, cassis-scented fruit are dreamy. Red Burgundy doesn't get much better than this. Tempting now, but better hold off until 2005. • $500 • (12/15/96) • **98**

Chambertin 1991: Lush, ripe, balanced and profound, loaded with ripe fruit and tannins, its flavors centered on chocolate, spice, wet earth and mineral. This should come together nicely by 2000 to 2005. • $311 • (12/15/96) • **94**

Chambertin 1990: Powerful and youthful, thick, full-bodied and rich—lots of depth here. Still very youthful and closed, with loads of plum and currant flavors. Don't touch before 2000; it should improve for a couple of decades. • $481 • (12/15/96) • **96**

Chambertin 1989: Ripe and complex, with intense floral, violet, currant, blackberry and black cherry flavors. Full-bodied and seems surprisingly closed for a '89. Should have the stuffing to last a few more years, but not as deep and complex as the '91 Chambertin. • $310 • (12/15/96) • **91**

Chambertin 1988: Seems disjointed compared with the '90, '91 and '93, which offer impressive harmony despite their different stages of development. This one hasn't come together yet. Plenty of plum and blackberry, and a fresh character, but it turns astringent and chewy on the finish. When it will be ready is anybody's guess. • $480 • (12/15/96) • **88**

Chambolle-Musigny Les Charmes 1994: Remarkable for its purity of flavor, this has a delicate, almost fragile frame filled to the brim with raspberry, mulberry, rose petal and mineral flavors that glow on the silky finish. Drink now through 2001. • $165 • (11/15/96) • **89**

Chambolle-Musigny Les Fremières 1994: Bright and flavorful. A crisp-textured wine with a fine layer of tannins around the juicy core of pure currant and berry flavors. Best now. • $80 • (11/15/96) • **88**

Clos de Vougeot 1994: Powerful, packing a lot of flavors into a tight bud that needs until around 2000 to open up. Full-bodied and dark-colored, this shapely wine shows some lovely plum, earth, mocha, spice, mineral and currant complexity. Quite tannic. • $205 • (11/15/96) • **88**

Clos de la Roche 1994: The unusually cedary and spicy aromas don't quite prepare you for the plummy, citrus-peel flavors that evolve as the finish plays out. Has some style and grace. Drinkable now. • $286 • (11/15/96) • **86**

Clos de la Roche 1993: A wine for the next century. Dense, thick and ripe, this intense *grand cru* displays a searing intensity of flavors and aromas. It blends nicely smoky, toasty oak and sweet fruit. Very youthful, closed and hard now. The firm tannins need until at least 2005 to soften. • $325 • (12/15/96) • **94**

Clos de la Roche 1991: A beautiful wine that has much in common with the grand '90 Clos de la Roche, albeit not as broad and powerful. Medium-bodied, with pure, ripe fruit flavors, punctuated by notes of wet earth and cedar. Rich and silky on the palate, it keeps growing richer in the glass. Firm tannins on the finish still, so better try around 2000. • $124 • (12/15/96) • **90**

Clos de la Roche 1990: Powerful, with great depth and length. Shows the darkest color of the domaine's four Clos de la Roche presented at this tasting. Pure fruit character, with hints of violet and currant. It's still very closed and firm; try from 2000 to 2010. • $413 • (12/15/96) • **94**

Clos de la Roche 1989: Medium-bodied, with expressive aromas. Like many '89 red Burgundies, this is beginning to show some maturity with its woodsy, earthy aromas, but there are plenty of currant and other good fruit notes as well. Nice for drinking now. • $147 • (12/15/96) • **85**

Corton Les Renardes 1995: A ripe, lovely, full-bodied '95, offering a soothing velvety texture, and good balance between the sweet tannins and lovely currant, blackberry, coffee and black cherry flavors. The finish is succulent and seductive. Try after 2000. • $250 • (11/15/97) • **90**

Corton Les Renardes 1994: Youthful and pure in flavor. Showing impressive length, clarity and a solid core of plum and spice flavors accented by a layer of toasty oak, hinting at mineral and mocha on the finish. Fine tannins want until 1999 to 2002. • $145 • (11/15/96) • **90**

Gevrey-Chambertin Aux Combottes 1995: A touch reduced on the nose at the time of this tasting, with smoky, earthy notes, but the flavors of coffee, wet earth, black currant and Asian spices are unique and compelling. Firm and moderately tannic, this should drink beautifully from 2000. • $NA • (11/15/97) • **90**

Gevrey-Chambertin Aux Combottes 1994: Dense and impressive for its well-packed black cherry and spice flavors. Fades a bit on the finish, but tames the tannins into semi-smooth velvet. Best from 1999 to 2000. • $145 • (11/15/96) • **86**

Latricières-Chambertin 1995: This solidly structured *grand cru* is traditional in style, with incredible aromas of blackberries, wood-smoke, earth and game, followed by deep black cherry and plum notes. Rich in power and concentration, if lacking in finesse. Try in 2000. • $600 • (11/15/97) • **91**

Latricières-Chambertin 1994: Spicily aromatic, with gorgeous roasted chestnut, violet and red berry flavors that swirl nicely on the delicate frame, hinting at wet earth on the finish. Has some firm tannins, but the flavors come through nicely enough to promise good things by 2001-2002. • $286 • (11/15/96) • **90**

Latricières-Chambertin 1993: An exotic, beautiful wine that's ripe, rich, full-bodied and packed with extremely fine tannins. Bursts with fresh grapey, floral, currant and violet flavors. Ample acidity on the back of the palate carries this to a long finish. Great balance from beginning to end. Tempting now, but should last for decades. • $325 • (12/15/96) • **95**

FRANCE

Latricières-Chambertin 1990: Great power and intensity, rich and ripe with loads of currant flavor and an earthy character. Oakier than the '93 Latricières, and less racy and subtle, but the finish is longer, suggesting that this youthful '90 needs until at least 2000 to blossom. • $250 • (12/15/96) • **93**

Musigny 1994: A supple, sculpted wine that plays out its spicy, floral plum and coffee flavors in a gentle, elegant stream. Fine tannins can use until 1999 to 2000. • $448 • (11/15/96) • **85**

Musigny 1993: Unbelievably exotic, it bursts with currant, violet, spice and floral aromas and flavors that are simply sensational. Tremendous, very silky texture. The toasty oak needs some time to fold into the explosive fruit character. Full-bodied and long on the finish. Tempting now and should last for decades to come. • $500 • (12/15/96) • **98**

Musigny 1991: Racy and silky yet powerful and brooding, a deep, savage wine that shows a lot of class. Impressively ripe tannins, with mineral, earth, spice and currant flavors. It continues to grow, and should improve with more cellaring. Try from 2000 to 2005. • $439 • (12/15/96) • **94**

Musigny 1990: Big, thick, rich and full-bodied. More muscular, powerful and aggressive on the palate than the '93 Musigny and just as impressive. Very youthful, with lovely black currant and chocolate character. This will need lots of time yet to open up; don't touch until 2000. • $NA • (12/15/96) • **98**

Musigny 1989: Bursts with deep, rich fruit flavors against a backdrop of vanilla, spice and coffee. Compared with many '89s, this fresh Musigny appears to have good acidity and should stand the test of time. Full-bodied and silky. Drinkable now. • $225 • (12/15/96) • **91**

Musigny 1988: Typical '88, with lots of rich, ripe and sweet fruit character, but also some coarse tannins. Full-bodied, with spicy, earthy notes, but its very aggressive and sharp finish makes it unappealing now. The jury is still out as to its future. • $480 • (12/15/96) • **88**

Nuits-St.-Georges 1994: A finely focused bead of pure currant flavor, shaded with notes of mineral and earth, carries the day, despite a final layer of chewy tannins in this medium-bodied, elegant wine. Give it until 1999 to 2001. • $95 • (11/15/96) • **88**

Nuits-St.-Georges Aux Allets 1994: Firm in texture, with a tightly packed but narrow bead of currant and mineral flavors that gain some momentum on the finish, but never quite get revved-up. Drinkable now. • $80 • (11/15/96) • **83**

Nuits-St.-Georges Aux Boudots 1995: In a class by itself. Earthy and a bit funky at first sniff, it fans out on the palate like no other Nuits '95 we tasted, delivering a rich, ripe, supple mouthfeel that's to die for. Layered with wet earth, dried flower, black cherry, violet and mineral notes. It kept improving in the glass. Bravo! Great now through 2010. 242 cases made. • $250 • (11/15/97) • **93**

Nuits-St.-Georges Aux Lavières 1994: An earthy, volatile character puts a question mark on this soft, simple red. • $80 • (11/15/96) • **78**

Nuits-St.-Georges Aux Vignerondes 1994: Has some ripe cherry and currant flavors on an open-textured frame. Tannins are a bit drying. Try now. • $145 • (11/15/96) • **82**

Pommard Les Vignots 1995: Extremely earthy, possibly reduced, yet this is a meaty, structured Pommard packed with sweet, chewy fruit. The tannins run roughshod on the finish, but it wraps around the palate. Don't touch until 2002. 194 cases made. • $110 • (11/15/97) • **92**

Pommard Les Vignots 1994: Impressively perfumed, with charming violet and floral scents. Shows a slightly rustic, woody chestnut character that's unusual for Leroy's wines, but there is plenty of concentration and ripe sweet fruit flavors, too. Drinkable now. • $80 • (11/15/96) • **87**

Richebourg 1995: Traditional in style, full-bodied and fleshy, this offers earthy, cherry and smoky flavors, a concentrated midpalate, ripe, fat fruit and a tannic finish. Needs until 2003 to really show its stuff. • $600 • (11/15/97) • **95**

Richebourg 1994: Dark-colored, lush and thick, with violet and currant flavors that fan out impressivlely on the midpalate. Delivers a great deal of elegance, but it ends with a bang, with a lot of chewy and rather hard tannins. But there is enough fruit to expect a good future here. Try after 2000. • $367 • (11/15/96) • **90**

Richebourg 1993: Not as dense and complex as the '90 Richebourg, but perhaps better balanced. Seductively exotic, with complex interplay of violet, dried herb, floral and cassis notes. Loads of sweet, ripe, pure fruit balancing the fine tannins. Try in 2000 or later. • $500 • (12/15/96) • **95**

> **Key:** SS—Spectator Selection CS—Cellar Selection HR—Highly Recommended BB—Best Buy $NA—Price not available Ⓐ—Auction Price (BT)—Barrel Tasting
> **Dates in parentheses indicate the issues in which the ratings were published.**

Richebourg 1991: A beauty of deep and dark color, sweet and ripe flavors, this has tons of fruit balancing nicely against the firmly structured tannins. Delicious currant, spice and ginger flavors go into a lush finish. Tempting now, but it should be even more harmonious around 2000. • $220 • (12/15/96) • **94**

Richebourg 1990: Just as a Leroy '90 *grand cru* should be: big, boisterous, deep, thick, rich and powerful. Beautiful aromas, ripe fruit flavors and wonderful mineral and earth notes that add complexity. Supple and velvety in texture, but so intense, it should age until after 2000 before opening. • $575 • (12/15/96) • **96**

Richebourg 1989: Disappointing and a far cry from the wine we rated classic four years ago. Has some good red berry, gingerbread and spice flavors and fine tannins, but lacks focus and seems a bit flat. The finish was shorter than expected. If it's in your cellar, try a bottle. • $206 • (12/15/96) • **85**

Richebourg 1988: Difficult to evaluate now. Lovely in many regards—a fresh jolt of acidity on the palate and impressive plum, black cherry and earthy flavors—but it's slightly tart and astringent, too. Will it smooth out? Try around 2000. • $345 • (12/15/96) • **87**

Romanée St.-Vivant 1995: One of the great wines of the vintage—you'll think it's from another planet. Decadent stuff, this red Burgundy is full-bodied, ripe and sweet-tasting, with savage earth, petrol, tar, cassis, mocha, chocolate and coffee flavors. It boasts incredible concentration and superbly integrated tannins that blanket your palate like velvet. Drinkable now, but will improve through 2020. • $600 • (11/15/97) CS • **98**

Romanée St.-Vivant 1994: Refined winemaking. Lovely, sweet and ripe, very harmonious and balanced, almost delicate in its structure although it has plenty of firm tannins to keep it together. Offers lovely floral and red- and blackberry notes that aren't buried by heavy-handed use of oak. The supple, smooth finish is a palate-pleaser. Tempting now, better after 2002 to take full advantage of the emerging aromas. • $475 • (09/30/97) • **93**

Romanée St.-Vivant 1993: Incredibly exotic. This is elegant and racy, with an explosion of flavors, layers of violet, currant, and cassis. Great finesse, too. The aromas are simply out of this world and very similar to what the wine tasted like in-barrel. Much more expressive than when we tasted it blind last year (a few months after bottling), when it may have been in "shock" and we rated it "only" 95 points. Classy, ultrafine tannins. This has always been Lalou Bize-Leroy's favorite among her '93 reds. Try in 2006 and over the subsequent 10 to 20 years. • $500 • (12/15/96) • **99**

Romanée St.-Vivant 1991: A sensational 1991 from Domaine Leroy. It has loads of ripe fruit and tannins. Balanced and silky, with a hint of mineral and a strong wet earth character that makes this somewhat savage. Needs time to show it all; try in 2000 or later. • $219 • (12/15/96) • **95**

Romanée St.-Vivant 1990: Like other '90 red Burgundies, it has taken on a Rhône-like, peppery, plummy character. Full-bodied, ripe and powerful, but it seems a bit awkward compared with impressions from a tasting four years ago. Could be going through an odd phase now. Try in 2000 or later. • $405 • (12/15/96) • **92**

Romanée St.-Vivant 1989: Lovely fruit, full-bodied and fresh, with good acidity and firmly structured tannin. It's hard to complain about this fine wine. But it did rate much better in a tasting four years ago. It lacks a bit of intensity now in comparison with the '90, '91 and '93. • $197 • (12/15/96) • **89**

Romanée St.-Vivant 1988: Some vanilla, cherry, and oak flavors battle it out with what taste like dry, astringent tannins. Medium-bodied and rather hard in texture. Will it achieve balance with time? Try in 2000 later. • $431 • (12/15/96) • **88**

Savigny-lès-Beaune Les Narbantons 1995: Ripe and supple, this is a sweet-tasting Pinot Noir with spice, mocha, toasty oak, blackberry and cassis flavors. Medium-bodied, with some chewy tannins for now, it ends with a delicate finish. Try now to 2000 with lighter foods. • $80 • (11/15/97) • **85**

Savigny-lès-Beaune Les Narbantons 1994: Drying tannins battle fairly ripe black cherry and spice flavors, which manage to maintain their poise. Drink now. • $56 • (11/15/96) • **81**

Volnay Santenots 1994: Complex floral and berry aromas and flavors ride nicely on a crisp texture, finishing with a strawberry kick and a load of tannins. Will need until 2000, at least. • $92 • (11/15/96) • **85**

Vosne-Romanée Aux Brûlées 1994: In a difficult vintage, this still manages to capture the fragile elegance of Vosne-Romanée, offering plenty of ripe currant and plum flavors shaded with spicy, rose petal nuances. Tannins are very fine. Best from 1999 to 2000. • $145 • (11/15/96) • **89**

Vosne-Romanée Aux Genaivrières 1994: Earthy aromas and flavors predominate in this relatively dense, mineral-scented wine, finishing tight and chewy. Drinkable now. • $80 • (11/15/96) • **84**

Vosne-Romanée Les Beaux Monts 1995: Stylish and aristocratic yet down-to-earth, this full-bodied, exciting red starts out with great subtlety, then builds in intensity, concentration and complexity as it unfolds its wet earth, red- and blackberry and toasty coffee flavors in a big, burly, tannic but long finish. A wine that comes across as very natural. Try after 2002. 340 cases made. • $250 • (11/15/97) • **92**

Vosne-Romanée Les Beaux Monts 1994: Ripe and sturdy, this is generous with its delicious sweet oak-scented plum and currant flavors. A deep layer of formidable tannins is troublesome, but it could evolve through 2002 to 2003. • $145 • (11/15/96) • **87**

LES HAUTS DE SMITH

Pessac-Léognan 1993: Some attractive black cherry and berry character but slightly diluted in the midpalate. Medium to light in body, light tannins and rather short finish. Drinkable now. • $NA • (01/31/96) • **79**

Pessac-Léognan White 1994 • $NA • (03/31/96) • **89**

LESCURE, CHANTAL

Beaune Les Chouacheux 1995: Nicely made. Already a bit ruby-colored, this turns up the volume on the midpalate with a lush, round mouthfeel and red berry character. Falls a bit short on the slightly dry finish. 210 cases made. • $32 • (01/31/98) • **85**

Beaune Les Chouacheux 1989 • $19 • (08/31/92) • **88**

Chambolle-Musigny Les Mombies 1995: Showing signs of early maturity, this medium-bodied red is browning at the edges, with leafy, spicy and oaky notes, mushroom and red berry flavors and dry tannins. Drink very soon. 24 cases made. • $37 • (01/31/98) • **79**

Clos de Vougeot 1995: Dried out, tough and hard. Already browning, it smells a bit funky, and tastes lean, mean and ugly, with bitter tannins. A disgrace to the appellation. 22 cases made. • $72 • (01/31/98) • **71**

Clos de Vougeot 1990: Light, watery and simple, with little flavor other than a touch of strawberry and earth. Drinkable now. 110 cases made. • $44 • (06/15/93) • **76**

Clos de Vougeot 1989 • $45 • (08/31/92) • **82**

Côte de Beaune La Grande Chatelaine 1995: A solid Pinot, with well-integrated red berry, spice and chocolate flavors. Medium-bodied, with ripe tannins, good color and structure. Drink now through 2000. 406 cases made. • $23 • (01/31/98) • **85**

Nuits-St.-Georges Les Damodes 1995: Thin and very oaky, lacking fruit. Light- to medium-bodied, it turns very dry on the finish, coating the palate with astringency. 146 cases made. • $38 • (01/31/98) • **78**

Nuits-St.-Georges Les Damodes 1990: Lean, tough and leathery, with currant and cherry flavors buried beneath. Time may benefit this wine, but it may always retain its chewy edge. Drinkable now. 226 cases made. • $25 • (06/15/93) • **80**

Pommard Les Bertins 1995: A delicate, pretty Pinot Noir with little power or impressive fruit. Round and balanced, with licorice, red berry and slightly toasty oak character and a smooth finish. Enjoy now through 2000. 170 cases made. • $46 • (01/31/98) • **85**

Pommard Les Bertins 1990: Thin and hollow, disappointing for a 1990, lacking richness and flavor. A narrow band of plum and leather flavors turns green and tannic on the finish. Drinkable now. 497 cases made. • $22 • (06/15/93) • **76**

Pommard Les Bertins 1989 • $25 • (08/31/92) • **87**

Pommard Les Bertins 1988 • $22 Ⓐ • (11/30/90) • **88**

Pommard Les Vaumuriens 1995: Quite flavorful and bold, but also elegant, it shows its earth, lime and black cherry flavors in a medium-bodied, rather hard package. Drinkable now. 265 cases made. • $36 • (01/31/98) • **85**

Vosne-Romanée Les Suchots 1995: Tastes like an old wine, with vanilla, mocha and spice notes but little fruit. Medium-bodied, it turns green and harshly tannic on the finish. 49 cases made. • $49 • (01/31/98) • **75**

Vosne-Romanée Les Suchots 1990: Lean and focused, with a bright, sharp beam of currant and berry flavors reined in by hard-edged tannins and acidity. A simple wine that's drinkable now. 381 cases made. • $26 • (06/15/93) • **81**

Vosne-Romanée Les Suchots 1989 • $25 • (08/31/92) • **89**

LESTAGE, CHÂTEAU

Listrac 1990: A perky wine, with complex aromas and flavors of chocolate, cherry, spice and cedar; it has lively tannins and fresh acidity. Drinkable now. • $18 • (03/31/93) • **88**

Listrac 1988 • $20 • (08/31/91) • **82**

LESTAGE-SIMON, CHÂTEAU

Haut-Médoc 1987 • $13 • (11/30/89) • **74**

Haut-Médoc 1986 • $13 • (11/30/89) • **85**

Haut-Médoc 1982 • $15 • (11/30/89) • **84**

LEVET, B.

Côte-Rôtie La Chavaroche 1992: Tough and clumsy. Stewed fruit and vegetal flavors lack freshness, and the tannins are hard and dry on the finish. May improve, but don't bet on it. 125 cases made. • $30 • (11/30/96) • **77**

LEYRAT

Pineau des Charentes Grande Réserve Sélection Robert Hass NV • $23 • (03/31/91) • **82**

LIAISON, LA

Chardonnay Vin de Pays d'Oc 1996: A rich and flavorful blend of Chardonnay and Viognier that's a fine value, too. Has a smooth, inviting texture and enough fruit concentration for a lingering finish. Drink now. • $10 • (10/31/97) • **86**

Merlot Vin de Pays d'Oc 1995: Medium-bodied, with good berry and cherry flavors and herbal notes. A lively wine with an appealing earthiness on the finish. • $10 • (11/15/97) • **83**

LIBARDE, DOMAINE DE

Bergerac 1993: A thin, weedy offering that doesn't give much pleasure. • $5 • (07/31/96) • **74**

LICHINE, ALEXIS

Bordeaux Premier de Lichine 1993: A bit of a leafy-berry character reminiscent of Cabernet Franc, but the finish is tough and tannic. • $6 • (08/31/95) • **77**

Cabernet Sauvignon Vin de Pays d'Oc 1993 • $6 • (07/31/95) • **80**

Merlot Vin de Pays d'Oc 1993 • $6 • (07/31/95) • **78**

LIGER-BELAIR

Beaune Les Avaux 1947 • $NA • (08/31/90) • **87**

LIGNIER, GEORGES

Bonnes Mares 1987 • $75 • (03/31/90) • **92**

Chambolle-Musigny 1987 • $32 • (06/15/90) • **77**

Clos St.-Denis 1987 • $49 • (05/15/90) • **89**

Clos St.-Denis 1985 • $54 • (03/15/88) • **91**

Clos de la Roche 1987 • $55 • (03/31/90) • **90**

Clos de la Roche 1985 • $106 Ⓐ • (03/15/88) • **85**

Gevrey-Chambertin 1987 • $29 • (05/31/90) • **84**

Gevrey-Chambertin Aux Combottes 1987 • $34 • (05/31/90) • **87**

Morey-St.-Denis 1987 • $25 • (05/15/90) • **82**

Morey-St.-Denis 1985 • $23 • (03/15/88) • **82**

Morey-St.-Denis Clos des Ormes 1987 • $32 • (05/15/90) • **88**

Morey-St.-Denis Clos des Ormes 1985 • $28 • (03/15/88) • **86**

LIGNIER, HUBERT

Clos de la Roche 1994: Crisp and nicely focused, its earthy currant and plum flavors piercing a layer of persistent tannins. Needs cellaring until 2001 to 2002 to see which side wins. • $95 • (11/15/96) • **87**

Clos de la Roche 1990: Round, velvety, stylish and wonderful, with gorgeous wild strawberry and raspberry flavors and hints of wood. Drinkable now. 250 cases made. • $90 • (12/15/92) • **92**

Gevrey-Chambertin 1994: Medium-bodied , with nice raspberry, currant and floral notes. Balanced and delicate. Drinkable now through 1999. • $NA • (11/15/96) • **83**

Morey-St.-Denis 1994: Light, with some strawberry and raspberry flavors. A bit short and astringent on the finish. • $38 • (11/15/96) • **73**

Morey-St.-Denis 1990: Focused, distinctive and pleasant, with menthol, cedar and black currant flavors that come across as sharp and lively. Drinkable now. • $36 • (12/15/92) • **86**

Morey-St.-Denis Premier Cru 1990: Subtle and ripe, with round flavors making it succulent. Has red licorice, smoke and raspberry aromas and flavors and a juicy finish. Drinkable now. • $36 • (12/15/92) • **88**

Morey-St.-Denis Premier Cru Vieilles Vignes 1994: Deep, rich, concentrated, a wine packed with plum, currant and earth flavors. Well made and full-bodied, and has a lot of nicely integrated tannins. Hands off until after 1999 to 2000. • $50 • (11/15/96) • **89**

LILIAN LADOUYS, CHÂTEAU

St.-Estèphe 1997: Simple blackberry character, with medium to light body and a light finish. Good, but nothing special. • $NA • (06/15/98) (BT) • **80-84**
St.-Estèphe 1996: Plenty of red currant and berry character. Medium- to full-bodied, with velvety tannins. Slightly dry on the finish. • $20 • (06/15/98) (BT) • **85-89**
St.-Estèphe 1995: A bit clumsy and simple now. Medium-bodied, with bright berry aromas and flavors, velvety tannins and a cherry, berry aftertaste. Drinkable now. 18,000 cases made. • $18 • (01/31/98) • **85**
St.-Estèphe 1994: Rather light, but with some nice fruit and vanilla flavors and a refined, tannic texture. Tasted twice with consistant notes. Drink now or hold. 13,333 cases made. • $15 • (01/31/97) • **81**
St.-Estèphe 1993: Some decent red berry flavor on a rather lean frame, drawing a slight toasty character from the oak. Elegant tannins make it pleasant drinking now. • $NA • (01/31/96) • **82**

LIONNET, JEAN

Cornas 1987 • $23 • (03/31/90) • **90**
Cornas 1986 • $23 • (01/31/89) • **87**
Cornas Domaine de Rochepertuis 1994: Already showing some brick hue, with a cedary, camphor note to the plum aroma. There's a core of fruit but it's a tough, sinewy red, with unforgiving tannins. Best now through 2006. 500 cases made. • $NA • (01/01/98) • **86**
Cornas Domaine de Rochepertuis 1993: A wall of tannins surrounds the sweet, plum and menthol flavors in this muscular red. It shows good concentration and character for a difficult vintage. Drink now through 2003. 500 cases made. • $NA • (01/01/98) • **85**
Cornas Domaine de Rochepertuis 1992: Full-bodied, with a lush texture that's appealing, and there are attractive plum, prune and tobacco flavors, but a vegetal note and a dry finish detract a bit. 500 cases made. • $12 • (10/15/96) • **83**
Cornas Domaine de Rochepertuis 1991 • $23 • (05/31/94) • **80**
Cornas Domaine de Rochepertuis 1990 • $23 • (05/31/94) • **89**
Cornas Domaine de Rochepertuis 1988 • $28 • (01/31/91) • **83**

LIOT, CHÂTEAU

Sauternes 1993: A light-and-easy Sauternes displaying lemony, lightly sweet character. Drinkable now. • $NA • (04/15/95) • **82**
Sauternes 1990: Pretty apéritif-styled Sauternes displaying creamy, pear character. Light in body and medium sweet, leading to a light finish. Drinkable now. • $23 • (04/15/95) • **81**
Sauternes 1989: Lively character and polished flavors of honey, cream and spice; medium sweetness and a fresh finish. Drinkable now. • $29 • (04/15/95) • **84**
Sauternes 1988: Fresh, straightforward pear, apple and honey aromas and flavors, medium-to-light body, medium sweetness and a light finish. Drinkable now. • $50 • (04/15/95) • **86**
Sauternes 1986: Rich and fairly concentrated, showing lots of toast and spice notes gracing the pear and honey aromas and flavors, long and elegant on a medium-weight frame. Try now. • $22 • (12/31/89) • **87**
Sauternes 1985: A good value with vivid flavors, even if not quite as magnificent as the big names. Medium gold with a sugary nose, simple honey, tobacco and slightly earthy flavors. Balance keeps it from being cloying. • $9 • (05/31/88) • **84**

LIQUIERE, CHÂTEAU DE LA

Faugères 1992 • $8 • (03/15/94) • **85**

Key: SS—Spectator Selection CS—Cellar Selection HR—Highly Recommended BB—Best Buy $NA—Price not available Ⓐ—Auction Price (BT)—Barrel Tasting
Dates in parentheses indicate the issues in which the ratings were published.

LIVERSAN, CHÂTEAU

Haut-Médoc 1997: Clean berry and cherry aromas, with hints of wet earth. Medium-bodied, with firm tannins and a fresh fruit finish. Well made. • $NA • (06/15/98) (BT) • **85-89**
Haut-Médoc 1996: A bit lean, with firm tannins and a smoke and vanilla aftertaste. Medium-bodied, with a medium finish and rather simple fruit character. 16,500 cases made. • $16 • (06/15/98) (BT) • **80-84**
Haut-Médoc 1995: Some good berry aromas and flavors with a dried herb undertone, but lacks a bit of fresh fruit concentration. Medium-bodied, with fine tannins, a short finish. Better after this year. 15,000 cases made. • $15 • (01/31/98) • **85**
Haut-Médoc 1994: A rather lean and slightly diluted offering, with some berry and herb notes. Drink now. 16,666 cases made. • $15 • (01/31/97) • **76**
Haut-Médoc 1993: Some very good berry, cherry and almond flavors, medium body and tannins and a firm, slightly short finish. Drink now. • $15 • (01/31/96) • **85**
Haut-Médoc 1990: This is very rich and fruity, with alluring aromas and flavors of tobacco, cassis and vanilla and a fine tannin structure. Drinkable now. 15,000 cases made. • $19 • (03/31/93) • **89**
Haut-Médoc 1989 • $18 • (03/15/92) • **87**
Haut-Médoc 1988 • $15 Ⓐ • (07/31/91) • **87**
Haut-Médoc 1985 • $11 Ⓐ • (04/30/88) • **90**
Haut-Médoc 1982 • $24 • (08/31/92) • **85**
Haut-Médoc 1961 • $29 • (04/30/96) • **84**

LOGIS DE LA GIRAUDIÈRE

Cabernet Anjou Rouge de Cépage 1989 • $8 • (08/31/91) • **80**

LOISEAU, YVES

Chinon Rosé Domaine du Colombier 1996: This pale rosé offers light flavors of cherry and herb. Clean and soft on the palate, with enough acidity to keep it fresh. Simple but harmonious. Drink now. 500 cases made. • $13 • (07/31/98) • **82**

LONES, DOMAINE DES

Côteaux du Tricastin 1988 • $11 • (05/31/91) • **84**
Côteaux du Tricastin 1986 • $7 • (10/15/88) • **82**

LONG-DEPAQUIT, A.

Chablis 1996: Nicely made, offering lots of lime, lemon, hay and green apple flavors of good length and intensity. Makes for pleasant drinking now. From Albert Bichot. • $NA • (08/31/97) • **85**
Chablis 1995: Lovely, ripe and very supple. Medium-bodied, with a gorgeous balance of floral, honey and mineral flavors and a creamy smooth texture that caresses the palate. Drink now. From Albert Bichot. • $NA • (08/31/96) • **86**
Chablis 1994 • $NA • (08/31/95) • **81**
Chablis Blanchots 1994 • $NA • (05/31/96) • **88**
Chablis Les Beugnons 1996: Pretty wine, with a sweet, tropical, ripe pear character, accented by smooth mineral notes on the midpalate. Medium-bodied and very pleasant, with a lingering, chewy finish. Drink around 2003. 1,250 cases made. • $25 • (05/31/98) • **90**
Chablis Les Clos 1994 • $30 • (05/31/96) • **90**
Chablis Les Clos 1993 • $NA • (08/31/95) • **85**
Chablis Les Lys 1996: Supple and ripe, dense and full-bodied, with some wet earth mingling with fruit cocktaillike ripe pear, tropical and apple character along with a floral note. Turns chewy on the minerally finish, suggesting that it would be better to hold until after 2002. 1,150 cases made. • $25 • (05/31/98) • **89**
Chablis Les Preuses 1996: A grand '96 Chablis, with the hallmark sensations of the vintage: floral, pear, honey, citrus and tropical aromas and flavors that overtake your senses. Full-bodied and very intense, with great freshness, it offers a wonderful creamy texture and sails to a long, harmonious finish. Tempting now, but better to hold until after 2000. 125 cases made. • $35 • (05/31/98) • **95**
Chablis Les Vaillons 1996: Very pretty, seductive and delicious. A full-bodied Chablis that's not showy but stresses floral, pure and clean pear, tropical, lime and mineral character. Balanced, it's open enough to try now through 2005. 2,500 cases made. • $25 • (05/31/98) • **92**

Chablis Les Vaillons 1995: A bit tart, with slightly green, herbal and gluelike flavors that lack elegance. Medium-bodied, short finish. • $22 • (06/15/97) • **73**
Chablis Les Vaillons 1994 • $23 • (05/31/96) • **80**
Chablis Les Vaucopins 1996: A mellow and sweet-tasting '96, with lots of ripe pear, mandarin, floral and honeydew character, this medium-bodied package makes for a delicious drink now through 2002. 2,400 cases made. • $25 • (05/31/98) • **88**
Chablis Les Vaucopins 1995: Lots of distinctive character and intensity here, with wet earth, salty, minerally flavors, but when aerated it turns a bit rustic, rough in texture. Try now through 2005. • $21 • (06/15/97) • **85**
Chablis Les Vaudésirs 1995: Bursting with citrus intensity, like chewing on a lime, but also offers some honey, spice and smoke flavors. Medium-bodied, crisp finish. Try with shellfish, now to 2000. Tasted twice. • $29 • (06/15/97) • **85**
Chablis Moutonne 1995: A mouthful, supple and palate-coating, with lovely mineral- and cream-tinged texture joined by subtle honey, ripe pear and wet stone notes on the clean, full-bodied finish. Drink now to 2000. Tasted twice. • $36 • (06/15/97) • **89**

LORENTZ, GUSTAVE

Gewürztraminer Alsace 1994: Clean and fresh. Offers enticing aromas of honey and peach, round flavors of coconut and almond in a generous, rather soft texture. • $15 • (09/30/96) • **86**
Pinot Blanc Alsace 1995: Seems a little simple and a touch on the sweet side. 5,000 cases made. • $11 • (09/15/97) • **78**
Pinot Blanc Alsace 1994: Simple, yet pleasingly crisp. Shows a mingling of herbal and light pear flavors and a short, but clean, finish. • $12 • (10/15/96) • **82**
Riesling Alsace 1994: Made in a delicate style, with restrained grapefruit and floral notes, this is light and lively. • $14 • (10/15/96) • **82**
Tokay Pinot Gris Alsace Réserve 1993: A clean, austere style with dry, even lean, herbal and pear flavors. Some tartness keeps it refreshing. • $15 • (10/15/96) • **84**

LORIEUX, ALAIN

Chinon 1995: Round and full, with chocolate, plum and light herb notes over firm tannins. It's a big wine, muscular and a bit clumsy, but a good match for food. 2,500 cases made. • $12 • (06/15/97) • **86**

LORNET, FREDERIC

Arbois Ploussard 1996: This red is roséelike in color, with an earthy aroma but good flavors of cherry and spice, and a resinous note on the finish. • $13 • (04/30/98) • **82**
Arbois Vin de Paille 1994: Quite aggressive. Drying, bitter walnut flavors override the faint butterscotch notes. A major disappointment. • $50/375ml • (04/30/98) • **75**
Brut Rosé Arbois NV: Simple but appetizing. A sparkling rosé with light, lean, earthy, berrylike flavors and a dry finish. Drink now. • $17 • (05/15/98) • **82**
Chardonnay Arbois 1995: A rough-hewn wine with some smooth edges. Has interesting ripe apple and spice flavors, some creamy elements as well. Try it for a change of pace. • $13 • (04/30/98) • **83**
Chardonnay Arbois Les Messagelins 1995: A wine of character and solid richness, with appealing and somewhat delicate flavors of ripe apple and cinnamon, and an herbal note on the finish. Try with cheese fondue. • $20 • (04/30/98) • **86**
Pinot Noir Arbois 1996: Light and a bit astringent, with some faint cherry and berry flavors. • $15 • (04/30/98) • **78**

LOUDENNE, CHÂTEAU

Bordeaux White 1993 • $13 • (05/31/95) • **75**
Médoc 1996: Very grapey aromas waft from this medium bodied wine. Has light to medium tannin structure and a light finish. • $NA • (01/01/97) (BT) • **80-84**
Médoc 1995: Simple and grapey, with decent fruit and tannins. Not much to get excited about. • $15 • (01/01/97) (BT) • **80-84**
Médoc 1992: Very light and watery; some decent strawberry, tobacco character finishes rather green and unripe. 10,000 cases made. • $15 • (04/15/95) • **73**
Médoc 1991: Earthy character to the currant flavor, with a lean, light-bodied structure. Pleasant to drink now. • $12 • (03/31/94) • **80**
Médoc 1990: A very ripe wine, with mature fruit aromas and flavors that verge on raisins; well-integrated, medium tannins; long finish. Drinkable now. 25,000 cases made. • $17 • (03/31/93) • **87**
Médoc 1989 • $13 • (03/15/92) • **81**
Médoc 1988 • $10 • (08/31/91) • **82**
Médoc 1987 • $10 • (11/30/89) • **75**
Médoc 1986 • $12 • (11/30/89) • **74**
Médoc 1985 • $14 • (11/30/88) • **75**
Médoc 1982 • $NA • (08/31/92) • **88**
Médoc 1981 • $11 • (09/01/84) • **84**

LOUVIÈRE, CHÂTEAU LA

Pessac-Léognan 1997: A grapey red with tobacco and earth character. Medium-bodied, with medium, velvety tannins and a simple finish. • $NA • (06/15/98) (BT) • **85-89**
Pessac-Léognan 1996: Very silky, with lovely fruit character and a solid backbone of ripe tannins. A wine that doesn't try to be too much. Harmonious. • $25 • (06/15/98) (BT) • **85-89**
Pessac-Léognan 1995: A firm, well-made red, with pretty cherry and berry aromas. Medium in body, with finely knit tannins and a long, silky, fruity aftertaste. • $25 • (01/31/98) • **87**
Pessac-Léognan 1994: Big and chewy, this shows vivid cherry, mineral and meat aromas and flavors, with a too-herbal accent. Full-bodied, with slightly dry and coarse tannins. Drinkable now. • $25 • (01/31/97) • **83**
Pessac-Léognan 1993: Medium-bodied, pretty red, offering anise, currant and plum flavors and a fresh, crisp finish. There are some firm tannins. Drinkable now. • $12 Ⓐ • (01/31/96) • **85**
Pessac-Léognan 1992: Plenty of body, offering spice, dried herbs, tobacco and berry on the nose and palate. Drinkable now. • $20 • (04/15/95) • **80**
Pessac-Léognan 1991: Another disappointment. Surprisingly sweet, ripe fruit for this vintage, with black cherry and tobacco notes and an herbaceous finish. • $20 • (03/31/94) • **79**
Pessac-Léognan 1990: Seductively powerful, with tons of lovely oak and ripe fruit, full tannins and a long, luscious finish. Drinkable now. 18,750 cases made. • $21 • (03/31/93) • **94**
Pessac-Léognan 1989 • $22 • (03/15/92) HR • **91**
Pessac-Léognan 1988 • $24 • (08/31/91) SS • **92**
Pessac-Léognan 1986 • $30 • (06/15/89) • **91**
Graves 1985 • $16 • (06/30/88) • **87**
Graves 1983 • $16 • (11/30/86) • **78**
Graves 1982 • $23 Ⓐ • (08/31/92) • **91**
Pessac-Léognan White 1995: A fresh and zingy white with lemongrass and lime aromas and flavors. Medium-bodied, with lively acidity and a light finish. May be better after this year. • $30 • (04/30/98) • **86**
Pessac-Léognan White 1994: A solid, flavorful white Bordeaux, smooth in texture, showing fine balance between its vivid fruit and herb notes and their oaky undertones. • $22 • (05/31/97) • **88**
Pessac-Léognan White 1993 • $12 Ⓐ • (05/31/95) HR • **90**

LUC, CHÂTEAU DE

Corbières 1990 • $5 • (07/15/92) BB • **84**

LUDEMAN-LA-CÔTE, CHÂTEAU

Graves 1995: This straightforward red is well balanced but not very expressive, with light black cherry and cedar flavors. Drinkable now. 4,500 cases made. • $14 • (11/30/97) • **84**

LUGNY, CAVE DE

Chardonnay Mâcon-Villages Pierres Blanches 1995: Flat, dull and has a pronounced paperlike character. What happened here? • $11 • (08/31/96) • **70**
Mâcon-Chardonnay Chardonnay de Chardonnay Vieilles Vignes 1995: medium-to-full body, offering a whiff of hazelnut accented by pear, lemon, honey and lightly toasty oak. Rich, ripe and round on the palate. Drinkable now. • $NA • (08/31/96) • **81**
Mâcon-Lugny Chardonnay Les Charmes 1995: A bit funky, with earthy overtones. It offers some decent fruit and spice flavors, but turns bitter on the finish. • $NA • (08/31/96) • **74**
Mâcon-Lugny Les Charmes 1996: Ripe and fairly rich, but somewhat dull, with supple and soft tropical fruit flavors. Kicks in with vivid lemon acidity on the midpalate, but it's a bit flat in the finish. Drink now. 70,800 cases made. • $12 • (08/31/97) • **80**

Mâcon-Lugny Les Charmes 1994: Vibrant and fresh, this balanced white offers layers of green apple, pear and honey flavors in a medium-bodied package. Slightly fizzy. 80,000 cases made. • $9 • (08/31/95) • **84**

Mâcon-Villages Pierres Blanches 1996: Fairly dense in texture, but with some distinctive green, stemmy, earthy flavors. Quite ripe and rich. Try with food. 2,500 cases made. • $11 • (08/31/97) • **80**

LUMPP, FRANÇOIS

Givry Petit Marole White 1995: An elegant and rather racy white, medium-bodied, with wet earth, stone and mineral notes mingling with citrus and other fruit flavors. Subtle oak adds a touch of complexity. Try after 2000. 150 cases made. • $20 • (05/31/97) • **88**

LUNEAU-PAPIN, PIERRE

Muscadet de Sèvre et Maine Sur Lie Clos des Allées 1995: Light and clean, with citrus flavors and light floral accents. An easy quaff that makes a refreshing apéritif. 750 cases made. • $12 • (05/15/97) • **83**

LUPÉ-CHOLET

Aloxe-Corton 1985 • $18 • (03/15/88) • **84**

Beaune Les Avaux 1986 • $NA • (07/31/88) • **89**

Bourgogne Clos de Lupé 1993: Light and hard with a slightly veggie character. Not much joy here. • $12 • (11/15/95) • **73**

Bourgogne Clos de Lupé 1992: Tart, sharp and lean, with a lemony, herbal character. • $NA • (12/15/94) • **77**

Bourgogne Clos de Lupé 1985 • $15 • (03/31/88) • **79**

Bourgogne Clos de la Roche 1986 • $10 • (07/31/88) • **78**

Bourgogne Comte de Lupé 1989 • $8 • (01/31/92) • **86**

Bourgogne Comte de Lupé 1988 • $9 • (02/28/90) BB • **83**

Bourgogne Comtesse de Lupé White 1994: Light, tart, slightly diluted, with modest fruit flavors. • $NA • (05/31/96) • **73**

Chablis Château de Viviers 1994 • $NA • (08/31/95) • **82**

Chablis Château de Viviers 1993 • $NA • (08/31/95) • **83**

Chambolle-Musigny 1992: Soft, light and charming, with smooth, appealing licorice, currant and raspberry flavors. A slightly stemmy edge on the finish. Ready now. • $NA • (12/15/94) • **83**

Chambolle-Musigny 1986 • $20 • (07/31/88) • **81**

Chassagne-Montrachet 1994: Crisp and tightly built, not showing much now in terms of fruit, but the chalky, mineral character is appealing and suggests it might age well. It shows some good concentration, with almond, pear and pie crust flavors. Drinkable now. • $NA • (05/31/96) • **85**

Côte de Nuits-Villages 1992: Pleasant but a bit simple, modest currant and cherry flavors peeking through the cedar and chestnut. Short finish and a bit diluted. • $NA • (12/15/94) • **79**

Crozes-Hermitage 1987 • $8 • (03/31/90) BB • **83**

Gevrey-Chambertin 1994: Has an earthy, stalky character and drying tannins. • $17 • (11/15/96) • **74**

Hautes Côtes de Beaune 1987 • $10 • (04/15/90) • **78**

Mâcon-Villages 1994: A white with modest spicy, creamy fruit flavors. Shows some crisp, citrusy notes on the finish, too. Drinkable now. • $NA • (05/31/96) • **77**

Meursault 1994: Slightly tart and lean, with a hint of ripe pear and honey. • $NA • (05/31/96) • **79**

Nuits-St.-Georges Château Gris 1994: Very light in color and in structure, with some red berry flavors and a short finish. • $25 • (11/15/96) • **72**

Nuits-St.-Georges Château Gris 1993: A little meager, but showing some pretty spice, berry and vanilla character, medium to light body, fine tannins and short finish. Better in 1999? • $35 • (11/15/95) • **82**

Nuits-St.-Georges Château Gris 1992: Very firm and tannic for such light flavors. It falls short on the fruit until the berry note on the finish. Drinkable now. • $NA • (12/15/94) • **78**

Nuits-St.-Georges Château Gris 1987 • $38 • (03/31/90) • **84**

Nuits-St.-Georges Château Gris 1986 • $33 • (07/31/88) • **86**

Nuits-St.-Georges Château Gris 1985 • $39 • (02/15/88) • **88**

Nuits-St.-Georges Château Gris 1983 • $24 • (06/16/86) • **77**

Nuits-St.-Georges Les Vignerondes Hospices de Nuits 1986 • $NA • (07/31/88) • **91**

Key: SS—Spectator Selection CS—Cellar Selection HR—Highly Recommended BB—Best Buy $NA—Price not available Ⓐ—Auction Price (BT)—Barrel Tasting

Dates in parentheses indicate the issues in which the ratings were published.

Pommard Les Boucherottes 1983 • $19 • (06/16/86) • **86**

Puligny-Montrachet 1994: A pleasant surprise from Lupé-Cholet. Light-to-medium body, offering up a touch of vanilla, spice and honey. Elegant and subtle. Drinkable now. Tasted twice, with consistent notes. • $NA • (05/31/96) • **84**

Savigny-lès-Beaune Aux Serpentières 1994: Pleasant, rather light in body and structure, with a beam of black cherry, earth and spice flavors. Chewy finish. Try now. • $16 • (11/15/96) • **80**

Savigny-lès-Beaune Aux Serpentières 1985 • $17 • (03/15/88) • **83**

Volnay 1986 • $NA • (07/31/88) • **91**

LUQUET, ROGER

Mâcon Clos de Condemine 1996: Clean and pure, with a lively lemon, orange zest, mineral and wet stone character. A balanced Mâcon that comes through with a long finish. Medium-bodied. Enjoy upon release. 2,900 cases made. • $11 • (05/31/98) • **86**

Mâcon Clos de Condemine 1995: Starts out OK, with a smooth texture and some nice flavors, but it turns astringent, slightly hot and alcoholic on the finish. • $NA • (08/31/96) • **73**

Mâcon Clos de Condemine 1994: Round and smooth. Shows some decent fruit but lacks panache, despite its almond, pear and green apple character. Needs more intensity. 2,916 cases made. • $9 • (08/31/95) • **79**

Pouilly-Fuissé 1996: A bit earthy, but those stinky notes blow off after a while. Slightly tart, with green apple, almond and mineral notes. 2,500 cases made. • $19 • (05/31/98) • **80**

Pouilly-Fuissé 1994: Odd and flat, with earthy, funky, almost cheesy flavors. It shows some ripe fruit underneath, with a fine, fresh finish. Perhaps in an awkward stage now. 2,083 cases made. • $16 • (05/31/96) • **81**

Pouilly-Fuissé 1993: Light, tangy and refreshing. This fresh white Burgundy has lively acidity, simple fruit flavors and hints of spice on the finish. 2,500 cases made. • $12 • (11/15/94) • **81**

Pouilly-Fuissé Clos du Bourg 1994: Attractive and earthy, with pear, pineapple and citrus flavors touched by a white pepper note that adds some spice. The sweet-tasting finish gives it a touch of richness. 708 cases made. • $19 • (05/31/96) • **85**

Pouilly-Fuissé Clos du Bourg 1993: Delivers intense earthy flavors of lime, orange blossom and wet straw. It's round, supple oily texture is impressive, leading to a long, vibrant finish. Drinkable now. 708 cases made. • $20 • (05/15/95) • **86**

St.-Véran 1996: Rather full-bodied, it's like biting into a lemon. Offers some green apple, herb and mineral notes. Nicely balanced finish, but steely in structure. Drinkable now. 3,300 cases made. • $12 • (05/31/98) • **83**

St.-Véran 1995: With its appealing, vibrant, grassy character, this is more like a Sauvignon Blanc than a Chardonnay. Light-to-medium in body, fresh and crisp, offering some green apple and citrus flavors. • $NA • (08/31/96) • **82**

St.-Véran 1994: Interesting but not exciting. Offers slightly earthy truffle, citrus and pear character. Quite chalky and dry on the finish. 4,166 cases made. • $10 • (08/31/95) • **80**

LURTON, J. & F.

Chardonnay Vin de Pays d'Oc 1996: Simple and straightforward, with apple and citrus flavors. Drink with food. • $7 • (09/15/97) • **81**

Grenache Vin de Pays d'Oc Domaine de Bachellery 1995: A big red with good concentration, offering raspberry flavors, some leathery notes as well. Textbook Grenache flavors. Try now. 1,000 cases made. • $6 • (10/31/97) • **86**

Merlot Bordeaux 1996: Light-bodied yet firmly tannic, this simple red offers cherry and herbal flavors and a short finish. Drinkable now. • $7 • (11/30/97) • **78**

Merlot Bordeaux 1995: Light-bodied and rather simple, this straightforward red shows cherry and herbal flavors with light tannins, short finish. Drinkable now. 10,000 cases made. • $8 • (10/15/97) • **79**

Merlot Vin de Pays d'Oc 1996: A pleasant core of cherry and berry flavors in this wine, but it turns a bit tannic in the middle. Drink with food. 25,000 cases made. • $7 • (11/15/97) • **83**

Merlot Vin de Pays d'Oc Domaine des Salices 1996: Flavorful, mellow, rich and satisfying. Cedar and cinnamon accents lend complexity to the warm cherry and plum flavors. Medium-bodied, light in tannin. Drink now. 2,200 cases made. • $7 • (07/31/98) • **86**

Pinot Noir Vin de Pays d'Oc Domaine d'Antugnac 1996: Cherry flavors dominate this fairly light red. It's simple, with an herbal note on the finish. 1,500 cases made. • $8 • (10/31/97) • **79**

Sauvignon Blanc Bordeaux 1996: This lean, angular white hits the herbaceous side of Sauvignon Blanc. Focused, but perhaps a bit short on fruit, it will make a clean, crisp complement to shellfish. • $7 • (11/15/97) • **83**

Sauvignon Blanc Vin de Pays d'Oc Domaine des Salices 1996: Tangy, with bright citrus and herbal flavors, but despite its crisp acidity, it's soft and round on the palate. 1,500 cases made. • $7 • (11/15/97) • **80**

Sauvignon Blanc Vin de Pays d'Oc Les Fumées Blanches 1996: Check out the price tag on this sharp, crisp and well-defined French white. It offers appealing citrus and spice flavors, the grapefruit notes linger on the finish. A fairly serious effort, that would pair well with fish or fowl. 20,000 cases made. • $6 • (12/31/97) BB • **85**

Sauvignon Blanc Vin de Pays d'Oc Les Fumées Blanches 1995: Pleasant and spicy, with interesting, mature flavors of orange-peel and herbs that taste almost sweet. • $7 • (10/31/97) • **84**

Syrah Vin de Pays d'Oc Domaine de Serame 1995: A medium-bodied red with the raspberry and black pepper flavors of the varietal and a horsey note that will endear some, alienate others. Drink now. 1,500 cases made. • $7 • (12/15/97) • **84**

Syrah Vin de Pays d'Oc Domaine des Salices 1996: A luscious and well-concentrated red, with a beautifully ripe fruit aroma and rich flavors of plum, berry and raspberry. There's plenty of stuffing as well, and a nice lively acidity. Finishes with plenty of chocolate and spice. Drink now through 2002. 2,500 cases made. • $7 • (07/31/98) • **87**

Syrah Vin de Pays d'Oc des Rives de l'Argent Double 1995: Unusual. The color is impressive, but the wine is dominated by a harsh smoky quality right through to the tannic finish. 500 cases made. • $10 • (12/15/97) • **73**

Vin de Pays d'Oc Domaine de Bachellery 1994: Shows good complexity, from the tobacco, blackberry and vanilla bouquet to the ripe, smooth texture. Some tannins protrude on the finish, but it's a delicious wine overall. Drink now. A blend of 50 percent Syrah and 50 percent Merlot. 2,000 cases made. • $6 • (12/15/97) • **87**

Viognier Vin de Pays d'Oc Domaine des Salices 1996: A zippy Viognier with good peach and spice flavors. Has a nice herbal note to it as well. 2,500 cases made. • $10 • (10/31/97) • **84**

LUSSEAU, CHÂTEAU

St.-Emilion 1997: A delicious wine, with tobacco, berry and chocolate aromas and flavors. Medium-bodied, with a rather short finish. • $NA • (06/15/98) (BT) • **80-84**

St.-Emilion 1996: Lovely smoky oak and berry flavors and medium-bodied on the attack, but light and diluted on the finish. • $NA • (01/01/97) (BT) • **75-79**

St.-Emilion 1995: Not a big wine, but delicious. Extremely attractive berry, floral, citrus aromas, with a hint of new wood. Medium-bodied, with silky tannins and medium finish. Best after 1999. • $24 • (01/31/98) • **86**

LYNCH, MICHEL

Bordeaux 1993: A light, herbal '93 showing tomato and berry character. • $10 • (01/31/96) • **76**

Bordeaux White 1994 • $8 • (03/31/96) • **84**

Bordeaux White 1993 • $8 • (05/31/95) • **78**

Merlot Bordeaux 1995: Plump and soft, showing gentle flavors of raspberries and herbs, with light tomato and vanilla accents. Has just enough grip for food and is drinking well now. • $9 • (10/15/97) • **83**

Sauvignon Blanc Bordeaux 1996: A fine white to drink either before or with a meal, and especially nice with seafood entrées. It's tangy and vivid in taste, but fairly ripe and round in texture and lasting on the finish. A very drinkable wine at an attractive price. 25,000 cases made. 25,000 cases made. • $9 • (09/30/97) BB • **89**

LYNCH-BAGES, BLANC DE

Bordeaux White 1994 • $40 • (03/31/96) • **90**

Bordeaux White 1993 • $28 • (05/31/95) • **88**

LYNCH-BAGES, CHÂTEAU

Pauillac 1997: Good berry and mineral character. Medium-bodied, with fine tannins and a light, sweet fruit finish. Tasted twice. • $NA • (06/15/98) (BT) • **85-89**

Pauillac 1996: Mint, blackberry and cherry aromas and flavors. Medium-bodied, with medium, fine tannins and a fresh finish. Very fine indeed. • $55 • (06/15/98) (BT) • **90-94**

Pauillac 1995: Much better than I ever remember. Complex aromas of currants, berries and mint. Full-bodied, very tannic, but velvety and caressing. Getting better all the time. Best after 2002. • $48 Ⓐ • (01/31/98) • **94**

Pauillac 1994: Gorgeous. Medium- to full-bodied, with well-integrated tannins and nuances of violet, berry, toasty oak and mineral. Long, caressing finish. Drinkable now. 35,000 cases made. • $36 Ⓐ • (01/31/97) • **89**

Pauillac 1993: Not big, but a lovely, harmonious Lynch-Bages featuring blackberry, cherry and vanilla aromas and flavors, medium body, fine tannins and fresh finish. Drinkable now. 35,000 cases made. • $33 Ⓐ • (01/31/96) • **87**

Pauillac 1992: Attractive, modest plum and cherry character, medium body and tannins and a firm finish. Drinkable now. • $30 Ⓐ • (04/15/95) • **81**

Pauillac 1991: Like silk in your mouth with its cassis and fruit flavors. Medium-bodied with a fine finish. Drinkable now. • $25 • (03/31/94) • **86**

Pauillac 1990: Big-boned, with plenty of flesh, this wine shows loads of plum, tar and smoke character and full, velvety tannins. Highly extracted. Drinkable now. 35,000 cases made. • $58 Ⓐ • (03/31/93) • **94**

Pauillac 1989 • $99 Ⓐ • (03/15/92) • **98**

Pauillac 1988 • $64 Ⓐ • (10/15/94) • **97**

Pauillac 1987 • $36 Ⓐ • (02/15/90) • **86**

Pauillac 1986 • $75 Ⓐ • (10/31/89) • **94**

Pauillac 1985 • $105 Ⓐ • (10/15/94) • **97**

Pauillac 1984 • $30 Ⓐ • (10/31/89) • **87**

Pauillac 1983 • $60 Ⓐ • (10/15/94) • **90**

Pauillac 1982 • $130 Ⓐ • (08/31/92) • **91**

Pauillac 1981 • $42 Ⓐ • (10/15/94) • **90**

Pauillac 1980 • $24 • (10/31/89) • **88**

Pauillac 1979 • $40 Ⓐ • (10/15/89) • **91**

Pauillac 1978 • $54 Ⓐ • (10/31/89) • **92**

Pauillac 1977 • $25 • (10/31/89) • **78**

Pauillac 1976 • $45 Ⓐ • (10/31/89) • **70**

Pauillac 1975 • $55 Ⓐ • (10/31/89) • **90**

Pauillac 1973 • $15 Ⓐ • (10/31/89) • **82**

Pauillac 1971 • $26 Ⓐ • (10/31/89) • **67**

Pauillac 1970 • $129 Ⓐ • (10/31/89) • **90**

Pauillac 1967 • $23 Ⓐ • (10/31/89) • **79**

Pauillac 1966 • $71 Ⓐ • (10/31/89) • **90**

Pauillac 1964 • $25 Ⓐ • (10/31/89) • **76**

Pauillac 1962 • $61 Ⓐ • (10/31/89) • **94**

Pauillac 1961 • $191 Ⓐ • (04/30/96) • **88**

Pauillac 1960 • $55 • (10/31/89) • **76**

Pauillac 1959 • $230 Ⓐ • (10/15/90) • **95**

Pauillac 1958 • $60 • (10/31/89) • **79**

Pauillac 1957 • $95 • (10/31/89) • **88**

Pauillac 1955 • $73 Ⓐ • (10/31/89) • **92**

Pauillac 1954 • $75 • (10/31/89) • **74**

Pauillac 1953 • $73 Ⓐ • (10/31/89) • **77**

Pauillac 1952 • $140 • (10/31/89) • **83**

Pauillac 1949 • $184 Ⓐ • (10/31/89) • **84**

Pauillac 1947 • $350 • (10/31/89) • **90**

Pauillac 1945 • $477 Ⓐ • (11/30/95) • **85**

Pauillac Danish Bottled 1945 • $477 Ⓐ • (10/31/89) • **80**

LYNCH-MOUSSAS, CHÂTEAU

Pauillac 1997: Berry, plum and cherry aromas and flavors. Medium in body, with velvety tannins. Very good for the vintage. • $NA • (06/15/98) (BT) • **85-89**

Pauillac 1996: Good silky tannins, but slightly astringent. Medium-bodied, with firm tannins and a short finish. Wait and see. • $26 • (06/15/98) (BT) • **80-84**

Pauillac 1995: Fat and round with rich fruit character, but slightly flabby. Intense aromas of violets, currants and berries. Full-bodied and thick, with velvety tannins, a medium finish. Best after 2001. • $22 • (01/31/98) • **87**

Pauillac 1991: Very herbal character with brown sugar aromas and flavors. A little overchaptalized. • $16 • (03/31/94) • **73**

Pauillac 1990: A wine with spicy tobacco and chocolate character and medium fruit and tannins. Not one to lay down for too long. Drinkable now. 12,500 cases made. • $18 • (03/31/93) • **87**

Pauillac 1989 • $18 • (03/15/92) • **90**

Pauillac 1988 • $25 • (08/31/91) • **85**

Pauillac 1986 • $18 • (06/30/89) • **86**

Pauillac 1982 • $22 Ⓐ • (08/31/92) • **81**

Pauillac 1961 • $21 • (04/30/96) • **84**

Pauillac 1959 • $115 • (10/15/90) • **86**

M & G

Côte de Beaune-Villages 1987 • $20 • (03/31/91) • **73**
Gevrey-Chambertin 1987 • $40 • (03/31/91) • **73**
Vouvray Moelleux 1988 • $10 • (03/31/91) • **81**

MACHARD DE GRAMONT

Aloxe-Corton Les Morais 1985 • $34 • (07/15/88) • **80**
Beaune Aux Coucherias 1993: This has personality. A good balance of bright flavors, lively texture and herbal aromas, with a lingering finish. Drinkable now. • $28 • (09/15/96) • **84**
Beaune Les Chouacheux 1993: Attractive, well balanced and well rounded, with ample fruit, spice and oak flavors that linger on the finish. Moderately tannic. Drinkable now. • $28 • (09/15/96) • **85**
Beaune Les Chouacheux 1985 • $34 • (05/31/88) • **89**
Beaune Les Epenotes 1993: Sturdy, with very subtle fruit flavors, firm tannins and acidity. Not concentrated, but fine at the dinner table. • $28 • (09/15/96) • **82**
Chorey-lès-Beaune Les Beaumonts 1993: Cherry and smoke-scented, moderately tannic and slightly bitter on the finish. • $18 • (09/15/96) • **79**
Chorey-lès-Beaune Les Beaumonts 1985 • $22 • (07/31/88) • **84**
Nuits-St.-Georges Aux Allots 1987 • $30 • (07/15/90) • **82**
Nuits-St.-Georges Aux Allots 1985 • $35 • (05/31/88) • **86**
Nuits-St.-Georges Les Damodes 1990: Smoky and spicy aroma, leading to generous fruit tones, very firm tannins and tough but flavorful finish. Fine depth and concentration. Drinkable now. • $48 • (05/31/95) • **89**
Nuits-St.-Georges Les Hauts Poirets 1993: Rich and alluring chocolaty, herbal, plummy and spicy flavors, with a soft but firm texture and a great finish. Delicious. Drinkable now. • $34 • (09/15/96) • **89**
Nuits-St.-Georges Les Poirets 1985 • $41 • (06/15/88) • **84**
Nuits-St.-Georges Les Hauts Pruliers 1993: Nicely balanced with candied cherry aromas, solid fruit flavors accented by spice and a lingering finish. Firm in texture. Drinkable now. • $34 • (09/15/96) • **87**
Nuits-St.-Georges Les Pruliers 1988 • $37 • (07/15/91) • **88**
Nuits-St.-Georges Les Pruliers 1987 • $32 • (04/30/90) • **85**
Nuits-St.-Georges Les Pruliers 1986 • $22 • (12/15/89) • **77**
Nuits-St.-Georges Les Pruliers 1985 • $36 • (02/15/88) • **90**
Nuits-St.-Georges Les Vallerots 1985 • $47 • (05/31/88) • **78**
Nuits-St.-Georges en la Perrière Noblot 1985 • $41 • (05/31/88) • **89**
Pinot Noir Bourgogne Domaine de la Vierge Romaine 1985 • $13 • (06/30/88) • **81**
Pommard Clos Blanc 1993: A solid, vibrant Pommard with a nice core of cherry and berry flavors, firm tannins and a distinctive aroma of rosemary. Drink now through 2000. • $40 • (09/15/96) • **85**
Savigny-lès-Beaune Aux Guettes 1993: Modest, smooth and drinkable now. Has herbal aromas and a bit of cherry flavor. • $25 • (09/15/96) • **82**
Savigny-lès-Beaune Aux Guettes 1985 • $25 • (07/31/88) • **89**
Vosne-Romanée Les Réas 1988 • $32 • (07/15/91) • **89**

MACMAHON, MARQUIS DE

Chassagne-Montrachet Abbaye de Morgeot 1992: Tough and tight, with an odd earthy note along with some apple, mineral and vanilla flavors. Seems astringent on the finish. • $NA • (08/31/94) • **77**
Meursault Les Meix Chavaux 1992: Mellow, smooth and supple; a bit earthy, with nice but modest pear, vanilla and grapefruit flavors. Ready to drink. • $NA • (08/31/94) • **83**
Puligny-Montrachet La Garenne 1992: Too earthy to our taste, but it also displays some hazelnut, smoke and apple flavors. Quite tart and almost sour on the finish; perhaps time will smooth out the rough edges. • $NA • (08/31/94) • **79**

MAGDELAINE, CHÂTEAU

St.-Emilion 1997: An aromatic wine with floral and fruit character. Medium-bodied, with moderate, velvety tannins and a medium finish. Well made for the vintage. • $NA • (06/15/98) (BT) • **85-89**
St.-Emilion 1996: Slightly thin, but there's a pretty, silky texture to this young red. Light- to medium-bodied, with cherry flavors and a simple finish. • $42 • (06/15/98) (BT) • **80-84**
St.-Emilion 1995: The tannins and fruit are wound-up like a knot. Alluring violet and blackberry aromas. Full-bodied, compact in structure, with racy tannins and a long, fruity finish. Best after 2001. • $40 • (01/31/98) • **91**
St.-Emilion 1994: A Bordeaux lover's wine, all finesse. Fabulous aromas of violets, cherry, and rasberry, with a hint of oak. Medium-to full-bodied, with supersilky tannins and a long, ripe fruit finish. Wonderful now. • $39 • (01/31/97) • **90**
St.-Emilion 1993: Wonderful, vibrant perfumes of roses, flowers and fruit. Medium-bodied, medium to light tannins and crisp finish. Drinkable now. • $24 Ⓐ • (01/31/96) • **85**
St.-Emilion 1992: Soft and drinkable, presenting tobacco, berry and plum character, medium body, gentle tannins and a slightly herbal finish. • $32 • (04/15/95) • **80**
St.-Emilion 1990: A big, extracted wine, with loads of fruit and full tannins. Drinkable now. 3,800 cases made. • $36 Ⓐ • (03/31/93) • **90**
St.-Emilion 1989 • $49 Ⓐ • (03/15/92) • **88**
St.-Emilion 1988 • $37 Ⓐ • (10/31/91) • **81**
St.-Emilion 1986 • $58 Ⓐ • (02/15/90) • **94**
St.-Emilion 1985 • $50 Ⓐ • (06/30/88) • **90**
St.-Emilion 1982 • $68 Ⓐ • (08/31/92) • **91**
St.-Emilion 1979 • $24 Ⓐ • (10/15/89) • **89**
St.-Emilion 1961 • $125 Ⓐ • (04/30/96) • **90**
St.-Emilion 1959 • $150 • (10/15/90) • **89**
St.-Emilion 1947: Elegant, smooth and seductive, very mature, with underbrushlike and coffee flavors that linger on the finish. • $NA • (05/31/97) • **87**
St.-Emilion 1945 • $115 Ⓐ • (11/30/95) • **76**

MAGE, DOMAINE DU

Merlot-Tannat Vin de Pays des Côtes de Gascogne 1996: A firm and flavorful wine with nice cherry and berry flavors. Does a good imitation of Beaujolais. Finishes on an herbal note. • $7 • (11/15/97) • **83**
Ugni Blanc-Colombard Vin de Pays des Côtes de Gascogne 1996: A great value in French wine. Fresh, lively and packed with fruit flavor, this well-balanced white is quite refreshing. Drink now. • $7 • (10/31/97) • **85**

MAGNEAU, CHÂTEAU

Graves 1987 • $12 • (05/15/90) • **78**

MAGNI, DOMAINE

Châteauneuf-du-Pape 1990: Tough and earthy, a big, hearty wine, with more green olive and cedar flavors than fruit. Finishes astringent and slightly bitter. Try now. • $17 • (08/31/92) • **73**

MAGNIEN, HENRI

Gevrey-Chambertin 1985 • $25 • (10/15/87) • **81**
Gevrey-Chambertin 1982 • $12 • (07/01/85) • **89**
Gevrey-Chambertin Les Cazetiers 1985 • $40 Ⓐ • (10/15/87) • **88**
Gevrey-Chambertin Les Cazetiers 1983 • $20 Ⓐ • (12/16/85) • **72**
Gevrey-Chambertin Les Cazetiers 1982 • $16 • (05/01/84) • **80**
Gevrey-Chambertin Premier Cru 1985 • $29 • (10/15/87) • **80**

MAGNOL, CHÂTEAU

Haut-Médoc 1993: Moderately rich, with some pretty plum, cherry and spice flavors. Finishes with a chocolate note. Try now. From Barton & Guestier. • $19 • (04/30/97) • **84**
Haut-Médoc 1983 • $9 • (07/31/87) • **77**
Haut-Médoc 1981 • $8 • (08/31/87) • **69**

MAHLER BESSE & CO.

Bordeaux Monocle 1993: Beginning to fade. Tea and earthy berry flavors turn dry on the finish. Already at its peak. • $9 • (07/31/96) • **76**

Key: SS—Spectator Selection CS—Cellar Selection HR—Highly Recommended BB—Best Buy $NA—Price not available Ⓐ—Auction Price (BT)—Barrel Tasting
Dates in parentheses indicate the issues in which the ratings were published.

MAILLARD PÈRE & FILS

Corton-Charlemagne 1995: Full-bodied and very fruity, with ripe pear, hazelnut, mineral and marzipan character. A bit hot and burning at the end. Would score higher but for the somewhat heavy finish. • $50 • (05/31/97) • **87**

Corton White 1994: Hard and a bit unyielding, with decent fruit flavors and a mineral background, but a touch one-dimensional on the finish. • $NA • (05/31/96) • **81**

MAIRE, JEAN

Blanc de Blancs Champagne Cuvée Elysée 1985 • $33 • (12/31/93) • **88**
Brut Blanc de Noirs Champagne 1988 • $43 • (12/31/93) • **87**
Brut Champagne 1988 • $33 • (12/31/93) • **87**
Brut Champagne 1985 • $NA • (12/31/90) • **75**

MAISON BLANCHE, DOMAINE DE

Chablis Blanchots Vielles Vignes 1994 • $NA • (05/31/96) • **84**
Chablis Mont de Milieu Vieilles Vignes 1994 • $NA • (05/31/96) • **80**
Chablis Mont de Milieu Vieilles Vignes 1993 • $NA • (08/31/95) • **86**

Quincy 1995: More floral than herbal, this soft white lacks typical Sauvignon Blanc character, but it's round and fruity, with pear and melon flavors and a clean, delicate finish. Drink now. 40,000 cases made. • $10 • (05/31/98) • **85**

Quincy 1993 • $15 • (12/15/95) • **82**

MAISON CHARME

Cabernet Sauvignon Vin de Pays de l'Hérault 1993: Black currant and bitter chocolate flavors marry well with the somewhat lean, medium-bodied structure. 10,000 cases made. • $5 • (07/31/96) • **81**

Merlot Vin de Pays de l'Hérault 1993: Extremely earthy, with no fruit flavors left, it's dirty-tasting and overly gamy. Tasted twice, with consistent notes. 10,000 cases made. • $5 • (12/15/96) • **67**

MAISON DE LAMARTINE

Beaujolais-Villages 1993 • $10 • (01/31/95) • **71**
Moulin-à-Vent 1993 • $15 • (01/31/95) • **83**

MALAGAR, CHÂTEAU

Bordeaux White 1993 • $NA • (05/31/95) • **78**

Premières Côtes de Bordeaux 1994: Light and weedy. Not much there. Drink it if you must. 2,416 cases made. • $14 • (01/31/97) • **70**

Premières Côtes de Bordeaux 1992: Interesting black pepper, spice, green bean character; medium body, medium tannins and light finish. • $NA • (04/15/95) • **78**

MALAIRE, CHÂTEAU

Médoc 1997: Tar and berry aromas and flavors. Light-to-medium in body, with light tannins and a slightly citrusy finish. • $NA • (06/15/98) (BT) • **75-79**

Médoc 1996: Big and tannic. Plenty of fruit character, but with an underlying notion of slightly green, leafy things. Medium- to full-bodied, with full, firm tannins. Wait and see. • $17 • (06/15/98) (BT) • **80-84**

Médoc 1995: A slightly mean little wine. Lots of berry character, but a bit metallic. Medium-bodied, with firm tannins and an earthy mineral finish. Drink now or hold. • $15 • (01/31/98) • **79**

Médoc 1993: Characteristically Bordeaux in aroma, with cedar, spice and herbal notes. A balanced wine that borders on the herbal side. Drink now. • $13 • (04/30/97) • **83**

MALANDES, DOMAINE DES

Chablis Côte de Léchet 1996: The flavors are very thick, opulent, rich and deeply satisfying. You'll enjoy this full-bodied Chardonnay for its lush, thick, velvety texture and ripe, tropical, earthy flavors. What a subtle, silky finish! Tempting after 2000 through 2010. 750 cases made. • $17 • (05/31/98) • **94**

Chablis Montmains 1993 • $NA • (08/31/95) • **83**

MALARTIC-LAGRAVIERE, CHÂTEAU

Pessac-Léognan 1997: Violet and spice aromas and flavors. Medium-bodied, with fine tannins and a fresh fruit aftertaste. Well done for the vintage. • $NA • (06/15/98) (BT) • **85-89**

Pessac-Léognan 1996: Plummy and fruity, with hints of oak. Medium-bodied, with velvety tannins and a fresh aftertaste. 4,000 cases made. • $25 • (06/15/98) (BT) • **85-89**

Pessac-Léognan 1995: Harmonious, pretty red. Extremely floral in character, with hints of berries. Medium-bodied and quite fruity, with a lovely, silken texture and a lengthy, fruity aftertaste. Best after 2000. 5,000 cases made. • $25 • (01/31/98) • **88**

Pessac-Léognan 1994: Some good berry and chocolate aromas and flavors, but overall it's a rather delicate wine, with fine tannins and a light finish. Drink now or hold. • $25 • (01/31/97) • **81**

Pessac-Léognan 1993: A bit lean but some good tobacco and cherry character, medium body, firm tannins and medium finish. Drinkable now. 833 cases made. • $25 • (01/31/96) • **83**

Pessac-Léognan 1989 • $24 • (03/15/92) • **85**
Pessac-Léognan 1988 • $32 • (07/15/91) • **84**
Pessac-Léognan 1986 • $18 • (06/15/89) • **90**
Graves 1982 • $34 Ⓐ • (08/31/92) • **92**

Pessac-Léognan White 1995: Interesting but slightly rough. Aromas of dried coconut with hints of fruit. Medium-bodied, with woody, chalky flavors and a short finish. Drinkable now. • $25 • (04/30/98) • **85**

Pessac-Léognan White 1994 • $25 • (03/31/96) • **90**

MALESCASSE, CHÂTEAU

Haut-Médoc 1997: Pleasant berry and cherry aromas and flavors open to a light- to medium-bodied palate, with firm tannins and a short finish. • $NA • (06/15/98) (BT) • **80-84**

Haut-Médoc 1996: A well-structured, cool wine with silky tannins and a lovely texture. Not a blockbuster, but showing lovely harmony for the vintage. Almost outstanding. • $20 • (06/15/98) (BT) • **85-89**

Haut-Médoc 1995: Thick and grapey, with loads of berry and tobacco character. Full-bodied and velvety, with a long, ripe fruit finish. Close to outstanding. Better than previous tasting. • $20 • (01/01/97) (BT) • **85-89**

Haut-Médoc 1994: Big and slightly simple, with sweet berries, flowers and spice on the nose and palate. Medium-bodied, with ripe fruit accents and medium, silky tannins. Try now. 13,000 cases made. • $23 • (01/31/97) • **85**

Haut-Médoc 1993: Some vanilla, dried herb and berry character, slightly lean. Fine tannins, medium body and short finish. Drink now. • $17 • (01/31/96) • **83**

Haut-Médoc 1991: Herbal, diluted and seems rather advanced in age for this vintage, but has pretty mint notes. • $13 • (03/31/94) • **78**

Haut-Médoc 1989 • $13 • (03/15/92) • **84**
Haut-Médoc 1987 • $9 • (11/30/89) • **74**
Haut-Médoc 1986 • $9 • (11/30/89) • **88**
Haut-Médoc 1982 • $18 • (11/30/89) • **82**

MALESCOT-ST.-EXUPERY, CHÂTEAU

Margaux 1997: Pleasant violet and berry aromas with mineral undertones. Medium-bodied, with fine tannins and a light finish. • $NA • (06/15/98) (BT) • **80-84**

Margaux 1996: Lovely smoke, berry and cherry aromas and flavors, with velvety tannins and a fresh aftertaste. A pretty wine. • $35 • (06/15/98) (BT) • **85-89**

Margaux 1995: Extremely well-made. Beautifully aromatic, with nutmeg and berry aromas. Medium- to full-bodied, with well-integrated tannins. Coffee, vanilla and fruit on the aftertaste. Best after 2001. • $35 • (01/31/98) • **91**

Margaux 1994: Plenty of plum, spice and fruit character here, with fine tannins and a long and silky finish. Medium- to full-bodied. Drinkable now. 9,700 cases made. • $33 • (01/31/97) • **86**

Margaux 1990: Despite a definite gamy edge, this meaty wine has a silky texture and a nice range of currant, coffee and cedar flavors to its credit. Best now through 2000. • $24 • (02/28/94) • **87**

Margaux 1989 • $27 • (03/15/92) • **87**
Margaux 1988 • $20 • (04/30/91) • **89**
Margaux 1986 • $29 • (06/15/89) • **88**
Margaux 1985 • $25 Ⓐ • (09/30/88) • **87**
Margaux 1983 • $39 Ⓐ • (09/30/86) • **82**
Margaux 1981 • $14 Ⓐ • (05/01/89) • **87**

Margaux 1962 • $80 • (11/30/87) • **65**
Margaux 1961 • $85 Ⓐ • (04/30/96) • **85**
Margaux 1959 • $150 • (10/15/90) • **87**
Margaux 1945 • $200 • (11/30/95) • **79**

MALESTROIT, COMTE DE

Muscadet de Sèvre et Maine Sur Lie Château la Noë 1995: Muscular but slightly clumsy, mingling tart acidity, pear, almond and light earth flavors and a firm texture. May round out with food. 8,000 cases made. • $8 • (05/15/97) • **84**

MALIGNY, CHÂTEAU DE

Chablis 1996: Fairly ripe yet a bit crisp and tart, delivering grassy, green apple and leafy aromas and flavors. Medium-bodied, the finish a bit chewy. Drink now. • $18 • (08/31/97) • **85**

Chablis Fourchaume 1996: A *premier cru* that's (nearly) to die for. Offers that distinctive and unique Chablis-like mineral and wet earth character mingled with magnificently rich, ripe tropical flavors. A seductive combination in a full-bodied, balanced wine with a long finish. Great quality. Enjoy now through 2005 and beyond. • $25 • (08/31/97) • **93**

Chablis Fourchaume 1995: A well-built, oddball wine, it's smooth, with clean flavors of honey, lime and herbs, medium body and a fairly crisp finish. Drink now through 2000. 8,333 cases made. • $22 • (06/15/97) • **85**

Chablis L'Homme Mort 1995: A clean and sweet-tasting *premier cru*, offering ripe pear, piecrust and vanilla flavors. Supple in texture, full in body, with a citrus-spiked finish. 1,667 cases made. • $22 • (06/15/97) • **86**

Chablis Montmain 1995: An earthy, slightly odd wine, with lactic, cardboard, toasty oak flavors. Medium-bodied, but not very clean. 333 cases made. • $22 • (06/15/97) • **70**

Chablis Montée de Tonnerre 1995: Pure and well defined, sweet and unctuous, with ripe fruit, honey and mineral notes. Too bad it's a bit dry and rustic on the finish. Drink now through 2005. 833 cases made. • $22 • (06/15/97) • **85**

Chablis Vau de Vey 1996: Chablis fans will enjoy this wondeful wine, with its distinctive matchstick, mineral, flinty notes accented by firm lemon and lime and a mouthpuckering finish. Medium-bodied, this has personality. Try after 2002 when it settles down. 10,000 cases made. • $25 • (05/31/98) • **89**

Chablis Vau de Vey 1995: A bit rustic for a *premier cru*, with some tart, drying wood and wet cardboard flavors, modest fruit and a short finish. 7,500 cases made. • $22 • (06/15/97) • **77**

Petit Chablis 1996: A good, decent Petit Chablis, with a slightly rustic edge, showing some hay, earth and mineral notes along with apple and lemon character. Drink now. • $NA • (08/31/97) • **83**

MALLE, CHÂTEAU DE

Sauternes 1991: Rich and ripe for the vintage, offering date, fig and orange notes, creamy texture and a seductively tart, marzipan-flavored finish. • $NA • (04/15/95) • **85**

Sauternes 1990: Electrifying spice, tropical and dried apricot flavors deliver lots of pleasure. Very sweet, yet a long, fresh finish. What can we say? Buy it and try after 2000, but waiting is difficult. • $30 • (04/15/95) • **95**

Sauternes 1989: Fresh and floral style; appealingly focused vanilla, honey and toast character. Good balance, medium body and sweetness. Drinkable now. • $28 • (04/15/95) • **88**

Sauternes 1988: Elegant, focused and well balanced, offering finesse, medium sweetness and body and lovely citrus, honey and quince flavors. Drinkable now. • $23 • (04/15/95) • **88**

Sauternes 1987 • $15 • (06/15/90) • **81**

Sauternes 1986: Electrifying, seductive and focused, ripe, rich, thick and luscious; creams your mouth with honey, apricot, cedar and spice flavors. Racy and balanced, it's tempting now but should improve through 2010. • $43 • (04/15/95) • **94**

Sauternes 1981 • $13 • (08/31/86) • **84**

Key: SS—Spectator Selection CS—Cellar Selection HR—Highly Recommended BB—Best Buy $NA—Price not available Ⓐ—Auction Price (BT)—Barrel Tasting
Dates in parentheses indicate the issues in which the ratings were published.

MALLERET, CHÂTEAU DE

Haut-Médoc 1991: Soft and smooth, with attractive herb and light bell pepper aromas and flavors, light tannins and soft finish. • $13 • (03/31/94) • **79**

Haut-Médoc 1989 • $NA • (03/15/92) • **90**
Haut-Médoc 1981 • $6 • (03/01/85) • **77**

MALMAISON, CHÂTEAU

Moulis 1991: Rather lean and watery despite some pleasant fruit and almond notes. Tasted twice. • $14 • (03/31/94) • **71**

Moulis 1990: A property on the rise. This is a thick wine with elegance; it has focused berry and plum aromas and flavors and a velvety tannin structure. Drinkable now. • $14 • (03/31/93) • **89**

Moulis 1989 • $16 • (03/15/92) • **85**

MALROME, CHÂTEAU

Bordeaux Supérieur 1993: Offers ripe fruit flavor, but there's a barnyard streak. Will appeal to some, alienate others. 20,000 cases made. • $11 • (08/31/97) • **79**

MALTROYE, CHÂTEAU DE LA

Bâtard-Montrachet 1996: Smooth-textured at first, but it has quite a green and earthy character, and the finish turns tart. An odd wine that's rather unbalanced. 30 cases made. • $95 • (05/31/98) • **75**

Chassagne-Montrachet Boudriottes Red 1985 • $17 • (10/15/88) • **86**
Chassagne-Montrachet Clos St.-Jean Red 1985 • $19 • (10/15/88) • **89**

Chassagne-Montrachet Clos du Château de la Maltroye 1996: Subtle flavors unfold in this crisp *premier cru* of medium body. Not particularly ripe, and the finish is steely, with a hint of wet paper. 540 cases made. • $40 • (05/31/98) • **78**

Chassagne-Montrachet Clos du Château de la Maltroye 1994: Subtle, appealing, ripe and elegant, with nice vanilla, honey, mineral, and citrus flavors. A harmonious *premier cru*. Drink now. • $NA • (08/31/96) • **86**

Chassagne-Montrachet Grandes Ruchottes 1996: Very distinctive, even exotic with its floral perfume. Surprisingly oily in texture, opulent in body and ripe in character for a '96 Chassagne. Earthy at first, it opens up in the glass, showing ripe fruit, smoke and toasty aromas and a full-bodied mouthful of tropical, honey and wet stonelike flavors that perk up the taste buds. Tempting now, but better after 2000. 130 cases made. • $50 • (05/31/98) • **92**

Chassagne-Montrachet Grandes Ruchottes 1993: Straightforward, modest fruit flavors and a diluted finish. 167 cases made. • $40 • (05/15/95) • **77**

Chassagne-Montrachet Morgeot Vieille Vigne 1993: Tart, tight and ungenerous, presenting lime, citrusy flavors and lean texture. Not much there. 417 cases made. • $35 • (05/15/95) • **78**

Chassagne-Montrachet Morgeot Vigne Blanche 1996: Sour and odd, with a swampy, grassy, herbal character. Diluted and unripe. 330 cases made. • $40 • (05/31/98) • **73**

MANCIAT, JEAN

Mâcon 1996: This vibrant wine manages to present loads of citruslike acidity yet also a full-bodied, ripe, supple mouthfeel. Mineral notes dominate the fruit. Balanced, with minimum oak fuss. Pure, clean finish. Tempting now through 1999. 1,080 cases made. • $12 • (05/31/98) • **88**

Mâcon-Villages Franclieu 1993: Tart and crisp, showing loads of citrus flavors. Austere and difficult to warm up to. A bit simple. 583 cases made. • $13 • (08/31/95) • **74**

Mâcon-Villages Franclieu Cuvée Spéciale 1993: A round, lemony note and Light-to-medium body Plenty of wet hay, green pea and green apple flavors. Austere finish. 75 cases made. • $14 • (08/31/95) • **79**

MANCIAT-PONCET

Pouilly-Fuissé Les Crays 1994: A prototype for '94 white Burgundy: laced with a thread of pretty honey and fruit, nicely fresh and crisp on the finish. Lovely and light-bodied; drinkable on release as an apéritif or with light dishes. 2,500 cases made. • $18 • (05/31/96) • **84**

Pouilly-Fuissé Les Crays 1993: Crisp lemon and pear flavors blend together nicely, adding a hint of honey and floral notes on the juicy finish. A touch diluted; drinkable now. 2,550 cases made. • $17 • (05/15/95) • **83**

MANDAGOT, CHÂTEAU

Coteaux du Languedoc Montpeyroux 1995: Awkward, with a stewed character. It finishes on a slightly bitter herbal note. Past its prime. 2,000 cases made. • $10 • (05/31/98) • **77**

MANN, ALBERT

Gewürztraminer Alsace 1995: This is what Gewürz is all about: aromas of roses and litchi, a lush, soft texture and an easy-drinking style, a hint of grapefruit peel on the finish. Ready now. • $19 • (09/15/97) • **85**

Gewürztraminer Alsace Grand Cru Furstentum 1994: This dense, somewhat shy white shows varietal character in its spice and honey flavors, and good balance, with enough acidity to match a bit of sweetness. Not flamboyant, but a good wine for food. • $28 • (10/15/96) • **86**

Gewürztraminer Alsace Grand Cru Furstentum Cuvée Victoria 1993 • $36 • (09/15/95) • **86**

Gewürztraminer Alsace Grand Cru Steingrubler 1994: Honey, spice and rose petal notes are true to Gewürz, and a bit of sweetness smooths its passage. A pleasant, well-made wine with clear varietal character. Tasted twice with consistent notes. • $27 • (10/15/96) • **85**

Riesling Alsace Grand Cru Schlossberg 1994: Firm and still a bit closed, but mineral and peach flavors emerge on the long finish. Try now, with food. • $25 • (09/30/96) • **86**

Tokay Pinot Gris Alsace Grand Cru Hengst 1994: Generous, and true to its varietal character. A rich wine, so ripe it hints at sweetness. Shows pineapple, coconut and vanilla flavors with firm underlying acidity for balance. • $28 • (10/15/96) • **88**

Tokay Pinot Gris Alsace Grand Cru Hengst 1993 • $22 • (09/15/95) • **87**

MANUEL, DOMAINE RÉNE

Bourgogne White 1993: Toast, hazelnut, honey and pear aromas are well defined—and echoed on the palate—but the wine turns hard, tart and herbal on the finish. • $11 • (05/15/95) • **84**

Meursault Clos de la Baronne 1993: Clean and well defined but tart and lacking in body, offering some modest fruit and herbal character. • $25 • (05/15/95) • **79**

Meursault Clos de la Baronne Red 1988 • $18 • (03/31/91) • **79**

Meursault Les Bouchères 1993: Vivid and well defined, rather steely, offering mostly lime, lemon and grapefruit flavors and also hints of mineral and honey on the vibrant finish. Try now. • $44 • (05/15/95) • **85**

Meursault Les Bouchères 1992: Rich in aroma, full-bodied and ripe in flavor, with loads of pineapple, honey and peach notes, layered with butter, toast and hazelnut. Very long-lasting on the finish. Tasted twice; drinkable now. From Labouré-Roi. • $NA • (08/31/94) • **91**

MARBUZET, CHÂTEAU

St.-Estèphe 1997: A rich and delicious red, with blackberry and dried herb aromas and flavors. Medium in body, with silky tannins and a long, long finish. • $NA • (06/15/98) (BT) • **85-89**

St.-Estèphe 1995: Rather coarse, but there's some ripe fruit character and an underlying herbal, slightly metallic quality. Full- to medium-bodied, with firm tannins, a long finish. Drinkable now. • $26 • (01/31/98) • **85**

St.-Estèphe 1994: Good concentration, but the slightly herbal, green character detracts. Slightly coarse tannins and a fruity finish. Drinkable now. • $24 • (01/31/97) • **80**

St.-Estèphe 1993: Some good concentration of fruit but rather herbal and grassy with a metallic edge. • $20 • (01/31/96) • **78**

St.-Estèphe 1992: Tobacco and cassis aromas and flavors, medium body, firm tannins and a stone, berry, slightly herbal finish. Drinkable now. • $16 • (04/15/95) • **78**

St.-Estèphe 1990: Full-bodied and tannic, with loads of currant and black cherry flavors, rich, spicy notes, plenty of stuffing and a long, flavorful finish accented by chocolate and coffee. Drinkable now. • $19 • (09/15/93) • **86**

St.-Estèphe 1989 • $21 • (03/15/92) • **89**
St.-Estèphe 1988 • $17 • (07/15/91) SS • **92**
St.-Estèphe 1987 • $14 • (11/30/89) • **80**
St.-Estèphe 1986 • $16 • (11/30/89) • **86**
St.-Estèphe 1985 • $21 • (06/30/88) • **87**
St.-Estèphe 1983 • $22 • (10/15/86) • **91**
St.-Estèphe 1982 • $22 • (11/30/89) • **86**

MARCHAND, CLAUDE

Chambolle-Musigny 1986 • $32 • (07/15/89) • **85**
Charmes-Chambertin 1986 • $50 • (07/15/89) • **92**
Gevrey-Chambertin 1987 • $22 • (07/15/90) • **81**
Gevrey-Chambertin 1986 • $28 • (07/15/89) • **89**
Morey-St.-Denis 1987 • $30 • (09/30/90) • **80**
Morey-St.-Denis Clos des Ormes 1986 • $33 • (07/15/89) • **85**

MARCHAND, DOMAINE JEAN-PHILIPPE

Charmes-Chambertin 1987 • $60 • (12/31/90) • **76**
Gevrey-Chambertin Aux Combottes 1987 • $30 • (07/15/90) • **82**

MARCHAND, JEAN

Châteauneuf-du-Pape Clos des Pontifes 1994: A mingling of earthy, gamy and smoky flavors, characteristic of the region, in a round, yet rather supple wine. Accessible now. • $NA • (12/15/96) • **84**

Châteauneuf-du-Pape Clos des Pontifes 1993: Jammy and flavorful, if rather simple, this offers cherry and strawberry flavors in a thick, sweet structure, with ample yet unaggressive tannins. Accessible now. • $26 • (11/15/96) • **84**

MARCHAND-GRILLOT & FILS

Gevrey-Chambertin 1990: Firm and aromatic, offering a beam of raspberry, red cherry and tobacco aromas and flavors. Smooth in texture, finishing with a nice touch of herb. Try now. • $20 • (06/15/93) • **84**

Gevrey-Chambertin Petite Chapelle 1986 • $30 • (10/15/89) • **76**

MARCHE-CANON, CHÂTEAU LA

Canon-Fronsac 1996: A bit pumped up with new wood, but with silky tannins and fresh fruit character. Medium-bodied. Slightly sweet on the medium finish from the new oak, like a Rioja. Too much. • $20 • (06/15/98) (BT) • **75-79**

MARCHIVE, LYNE & JEAN-BERNARD

Chablis 1996: A lovely Chablis, lush and ripe. Of medium body and intensity, this balanced wine displays loads of lime and lemon flavors, some dried herbs and ripe fruit flavors. Try now. From Domaine des Malandes. • $NA • (08/31/97) • **86**

Chablis 1994 • $NA • (08/31/95) • **85**

Chablis Côte de Léchet 1995: A fresh *premier cru* with well-defined fruit flavors, medium body, chewy finish. Ready now. 1,000 cases made. • $20 • (06/15/97) • **85**

Petit Chablis 1996: Quite appealing, with wonderfully clean, pure, well-defined flavors and structure. Medium to full in body, it offers lime, mineral, pear and fresh coconut flavors, and a lime-tasting finish that won't quit. Balanced, but should improve with cellaring. From Domaine des Malandes. • $NA • (08/31/97) • **87**

MARCOUX, DOMAINE DE

Châteauneuf-du-Pape 1988 • $24 • (10/15/91) • **82**
Châteauneuf-du-Pape 1986 • $20 • (10/15/91) • **84**
Châteauneuf-du-Pape 1983 • $25 • (10/15/91) • **87**
Châteauneuf-du-Pape 1981 • $30 • (10/15/91) • **85**

Châteauneuf-du-Pape Special Cuvée 1990: Smells ripe and jammy, with lots of cherry and plum-scented characteristics that come through on the palate. Big, firm and tannic; a rustic style. Try now. 200 cases made. • $22 • (08/31/92) • **88**

Châteauneuf-du-Pape Vieilles Vignes 1989 • $30 • (10/15/91) • **95**

MARDON, DOMAINE

Quincy 1995: A strong, toasty, smoky note veers toward earthy, nearly overwhelming the ripe apple and quince flavors. Drink now. • $13 • (05/31/98) • **77**

MARES, ROGER

Cabernet-Syrah Mas des Bressades 1988 • $11 • (10/31/90) • **81**

FRANCE

MARGAINE, A.

Brut Blanc de Blancs Champagne Special Club 1989: Plush in texture but firmly balanced with refreshing acidity, this is a mouthfilling, flavorful Champagne with subtle spicy accents and a lingering finish. Should gain in complexity with age. Drink now through 2000. • $43 • (11/30/97) • **90**

Brut Champagne NV: Fresh but delicate fruit flavors and a velvety texture make this light-bodied bubbly very appealing. Drink now. • $29 • (11/30/97) • **86**

MARGAUX, CHÂTEAU

Margaux 1997: Very, very fine indeed, with wonderful mineral, blackberry and raspberry character and an underlying vanilla and floral note. Medium-to full-bodied, with sweet, ripe fruit and ultrafine tannins. A benchmark for 1997. • $NA • (06/15/98) (BT) • **90-94**

Margaux 1996: Fabulous harmony in this young wine, with aromas of roses, cherries and blackberries. Full-bodied, with fine tannins and a long, silky texture. Almost classic. • $311 Ⓐ • (06/15/98) (BT) • **90-94**

Margaux 1995: Wine of the vintage and the greatest Château Margaux ever produced. A stunning red. The essence of raspberry, violet and berry, with hints of vanilla and toasty oak. Full-bodied and thick, yet racy, with masses of tannins and a harmonious structure. Long, long finish. At its best after 2005. 18,000 cases made. • $145 Ⓐ • (01/31/98) CS • **100**

Margaux 1994: Not a big Margaux, this is all in refinement. Pretty aromas of berries, raspberries and toasty oak and warm flavors that build on your palate. Medium-bodied, with fine, well-integrated tannins and a caressing finish. Drinkable now. • $98 Ⓐ • (01/31/97) • **90**

Margaux 1993: Château Margaux is back after a weak '92. Big for the vintage, featuring loads of new oak to provide a smoky, toasty taste. Attractive currant, black cherry and rose petal character. Medium-bodied, exotic and ripe. Somewhat hard now, and you wish for a bit more concentration, but time should turn it into a lovely wine. Drinkable now. • $102 Ⓐ • (01/31/96) • **90**

Margaux 1992: Elegant but light for Château Margaux. Fresh and delicious black cherry and raspberry aromas and flavors, medium-to-light body, firm tannins and light finish. Tasted three times, with consistent notes. • $89 Ⓐ • (04/15/95) • **81**

Margaux 1991: A little disappointing, but a pretty wine to smell and taste. Impressive fruit and wood accented by silky tannins, but slightly dry and herbaceous on the finish. • $41 Ⓐ • (03/31/94) • **85**

Margaux 1990: A seductive, tantalizing wine with gorgeous aromas and flavors of tobacco, cedar, berry and cassis, superb soft tannins and a long, long finish. Drinkable now. 25,000 cases made. • $253 Ⓐ • (03/31/93) • **96**

Margaux 1989 • $173 Ⓐ • (03/15/92) CS • **99**
Margaux 1988 • $133 Ⓐ • (03/31/91) CS • **97**
Margaux 1987 • $61 Ⓐ • (05/15/90) • **87**
Margaux 1986 • $231 Ⓐ • (06/15/89) CS • **98**
Margaux 1985 • $181 Ⓐ • (10/15/94) • **95**
Margaux 1984 • $53 Ⓐ • (02/28/87) CS • **93**
Margaux 1983 • $221 Ⓐ • (10/15/94) • **98**
Margaux 1982 • $405 Ⓐ • (08/31/92) • **95**
Margaux 1981 • $126 Ⓐ • (10/15/94) • **95**
Margaux 1980 • $69 Ⓐ • (05/01/84) CS • **90**
Margaux 1979 • $131 Ⓐ • (12/15/89) • **91**
Margaux 1978 • $161 Ⓐ • (12/15/89) • **92**
Margaux 1977 • $52 Ⓐ • (07/15/87) • **75**
Margaux 1976 • $63 Ⓐ • (07/15/87) • **81**
Margaux 1975 • $77 Ⓐ • (07/15/87) • **88**
Margaux 1971 • $63 Ⓐ • (07/15/87) • **77**
Margaux 1970 • $103 Ⓐ • (07/15/87) • **70**
Margaux 1967 • $46 Ⓐ • (07/15/87) • **84**
Margaux 1966 • $152 Ⓐ • (07/15/87) • **90**
Margaux 1964 • $69 Ⓐ • (07/15/87) • **86**
Margaux 1962 • $97 Ⓐ • (12/15/89) • **86**
Margaux 1961 • $547/1.5 liter Ⓐ • (04/30/96) • **92**
Margaux 1959 • $309 Ⓐ • (10/15/90) • **93**
Margaux 1957 • $68 Ⓐ • (07/15/87) • **90**
Margaux 1955 • $253 Ⓐ • (07/15/87) • **79**

Key: SS—Spectator Selection CS—Cellar Selection HR—Highly Recommended BB—Best Buy $NA—Price not available Ⓐ—Auction Price (BT)—Barrel Tasting
Dates in parentheses indicate the issues in which the ratings were published.

Margaux 1953 • $666 Ⓐ • (12/15/89) • **84**
Margaux 1952 • $251 Ⓐ • (07/15/87) • **85**
Margaux 1950 • $600 • (07/15/87) • **89**
Margaux 1949 • $311 Ⓐ • (07/15/87) • **95**

Margaux 1947: Lean, lithe, almost delicate in structure, with lovely plum, spice and earth notes gliding through nicely. Tasted from magnum. • $863 Ⓐ • (07/31/97) • **89**

Margaux 1945 • $868 Ⓐ • (11/30/95) • **90**
Margaux 1943 • $176 Ⓐ • (07/15/87) • **78**
Margaux 1937 • $181 Ⓐ • (07/15/87) • **82**
Margaux 1934 • $418 Ⓐ • (07/15/87) • **88**
Margaux 1929 • $293 Ⓐ • (07/15/87) • **83**
Margaux 1928 • $863 Ⓐ • (07/15/87) • **84**
Margaux 1926 • $300 • (07/15/87) • **77**
Margaux 1924 • $325 Ⓐ • (07/15/87) • **73**
Margaux 1923 • $168 Ⓐ • (07/15/87) • **81**
Margaux 1920 • $187 Ⓐ • (07/15/87) • **79**
Margaux 1918 • $87 Ⓐ • (07/15/87) • **80**
Margaux 1917 • $300 • (07/15/87) • **62**
Margaux 1916 • $NA • (07/15/87) • **63**
Margaux 1909 • $480 • (07/15/87) • **65**
Margaux 1908 • $402 Ⓐ • (07/15/87) • **85**
Margaux 1905 • $800 • (07/15/87) • **64**
Margaux 1900 • $9000 Ⓐ • (07/15/87) • **93**
Margaux 1899 • $NA • (07/15/87) • **94**
Margaux 1898 • $NA • (07/15/87) • **75**
Margaux 1893 • $444 Ⓐ • (07/15/87) • **95**
Margaux 1892 • $457 Ⓐ • (07/15/87) • **80**
Margaux 1887 • $517 Ⓐ • (07/15/87) • **81**
Margaux 1870 • $NA • (07/15/87) • **89**
Margaux 1868 • $1035 Ⓐ • (07/15/87) • **69**
Margaux 1865 • $NA • (07/15/87) • **97**
Margaux 1864 • $NA • (07/15/87) • **98**
Margaux 1848 • $NA • (07/15/87) • **95**
Margaux 1847 • $NA • (07/15/87) • **96**
Margaux 1791 • $NA • (07/15/87) • **97**
Margaux 1771 • $NA • (07/15/87) • **99**

MARGON, DOMAINE DE

Chardonnay Vin de Pays des Côtes de Thongue Delphine de Margon 1996: Tastes mature and almost resinous, with flavors of fig, green apple and a hint of butterscotch. Distinctive, with a rich texture and spicy finish. 5,000 cases made. • $11 • (04/30/98) • **83**

MARILYN MERLOT

Merlot Vin de Pays de l'Aude 1987 • $6 • (03/15/90) • **77**

MARIS, DOMAINE

Minervois Carte Noire 1995: Thick and intense, brimming with superripe flavors of plum, cherry and leather, this rich red has just enough underlying firmness to keep it honest. Finishes on a delicious chocolate note. A great buy from France's Languedoc region. 10,000 cases made. • $9 • (02/28/98) BB • **88**

Minervois Carte Noire 1990 • $9 • (03/15/94) • **80**
Minervois J. Maris Cuvée Prestige 1990 • $9 • (03/15/94) • **86**

MARJOSSE, CHÂTEAU

Bordeaux 1997: Looks interesting, with good color and mildly fruity aromas, but rather light with a delicate finish. • $NA • (06/15/98) (BT) • **80-84**

Bordeaux 1996: A simple and fruity red, with light, silky tannins and a fresh, fruity finish. • $18 • (06/15/98) (BT) • **80-84**

Bordeaux 1995: Simple and fruity, with some berry and cherry character, medium body and a light finish. • $NA • (01/01/97) (BT) • **80-84**

Bordeaux 1994: Very light and diluted, with some pleasant dried cherry notes. • $NA • (01/31/97) • **77**

Bordeaux 1993: Light and slightly dry, showing some cherry, dried herb and earth flavor and a hint of tomato. Drinkable now. • $NA • (01/31/96) • **80**

Entre-Deux-Mers 1995: An elegant white with impressive character. Lots of grapefruit and honey aromas and flavors, plenty of mineral and apple flavors. Medium-bodied, medium finish. Drink now. • $NA • (04/30/98) • **85**

Entre-Deux-Mers 1994 • $NA • (03/31/96) • **85**

MAROSLAVAC-LEGER

Bourgogne La Combe White 1996: Clean, pure and attractively smoky, with woody accents and toasty bread, pear and hazelnut character. Light to medium in body, with a crisp, grapefruit- and kiwi-flavored finish. Enjoy on release through 2000. 165 cases made. • $17 • (05/31/98) • **84**

Bourgogne White 1995: Strange, gluelike aromas and flavors distract from the fruit concentration in this full-bodied wine. Too bad. 625 cases made. • $12 • (08/31/97) • **70**

Chassagne-Montrachet Les Voillenots-Dessus 1995: Fairly rich, a bit oaky and hot, it seems slightly rustic. Full-bodied, with loads of flavors, a chewy finish. Drink now. 125 cases made. • $28 • (08/31/97) • **75**

Meursault Au Murger de Monthélie 1996: Wonderful village wine, full-bodied yet elegant, with lots of mineral, floral, honey and lime character. Sparkles with life on the palate, yet offers a palate-caressing, creamlike texture. Firmly structured, its laser-sharp flavors end on a long, succulent and subtle finish. Try in 2003 to 2007. 130 cases made. • $36 • (05/31/98) • **91**

Meursault Au Murger de Monthélie 1995: Gorgeously balanced and ripe, with a harmonious medley of honey, spice, toasty oak, mineral, pear and melon flavors. The citrus undertow keeps this full-bodied wine clean, leading to a delicious finish. Tempting now, better around 2000. 125 cases made. • $28 • (08/31/97) • **91**

Puligny-Montrachet Champs Gain 1996: Fruity, silky, ripe, delightful '96 whose full-bodied, opulent texture is backed by firm acidity and lots of vanilla, spice, pear and tropical notes. Well crafted, with a slight earthy note on the balanced finish. Try around 2003. 65 cases made. • $50 • (05/31/98) • **89**

Puligny-Montrachet Les Combettes 1996: A minerally '96, showing some good ripe fruit along with a spicy, buttery, toasty character. The oak is more toasty than in some wines, for a slightly burning aftertaste, but this medium-bodied white should drink nicely around 2003. 90 cases made. • $50 • (05/31/98) • **90**

Puligny-Montrachet Les Combettes 1995: Caresses the palate, like velvet. Shows remarkable finesse and grace, delivering its oak, fruit, citrus and spice accents in a cascade that ends in a long finish. Full-bodied, memorable for its amazing texture. Delicious now, better after 2000. 75 cases made. • $40 • (08/31/97) • **95**

Puligny-Montrachet Les Corvées des Vignes 1996: Full-bodied but a bit herbal, it delivers some decent fruit, citrus, mineral and spice flavors. Long, chewy, lime-flavored and slightly vegetal finish. Try around 2000. 500 cases made. • $40 • (05/31/98) • **85**

Puligny-Montrachet Les Corvées des Vignes 1995: Balanced and gentle. Full-bodied, it fans out its lovely, ripe honey, pear and tropical flavors, then kicks in with smoky, toasty notes on the slightly green finish. Delicious now, will hold through at least 2000. 500 cases made. • $30 • (08/31/97) • **88**

Puligny-Montrachet Les Folatières 1996: This well-sculpted creation shows refined fruit and mineral character, a silky palate feel and just the right amount of oak and acidity for balance. Full-bodied, it has marvelous length. Carafed for one hour or so, it's tempting now, but better after 2002. 130 cases made. • $50 • (05/31/98) • **93**

Puligny-Montrachet Les Folatières 1995: Exotic but hard as nails, showing little now. Delivers hints of its greatness with honey, mineral, apricot, peach, citrus and spice flavors. Full-bodied and intense; don't touch until after 2005. 125 cases made. • $40 • (08/31/97) • **93**

St.-Aubin Les Murgers des Dents de Chien White 1996: Clean but lean, a fairly straightforward white, showing only decent fruit complexity and lots of acidity. Try with seafood. 75 cases made. • $34 • (05/31/98) • **81**

MAROT, CHÂTEAU

Bergerac 1988 • $7 • (08/31/91) • **79**

MAROTTE, DOMAINE DE

Vin de Pays de Vaucluse Le Blanc de Marotte 1995: This ripe, juicy white offers flavors of pears and melons, with light herbal notes. It's full-bodied and fresh. • $11 • (12/15/96) • **84**

MARSAU, CHÂTEAU

Côtes de Francs 1997: Rather vegetal, with berry and leaf character. Light- to medium-bodied, with light tannins and a short finish. • $NA • (06/15/98) (BT) • **75-79**

Côtes de Francs 1996: Has pretty, tobacco, vanilla and chocolate flavors, but not quite enough concentration to score higher. 2,500 cases made. • $NA • (01/01/97) (BT) • **80-84**

Côtes de Francs 1995: Pretty and elegant. Wonderful aromas of chocolate mousse and berries. Full-bodied, with lovely, velvety tannins. Long and caressing fruit finish. Best after 2000. • $15 • (01/31/98) • **88**

Côtes de Francs 1994: Rather weedy and hard, with some berry flavor, but mainly it's green and metallic. • $NA • (01/31/97) • **75**

MARTIALIS, DOMAINE DE

St.-Emilion 1995: Watery and light, with weedy herbal and tomato character. Light body. Drink if you must. Second label of Clos Fourtet. Tasted twice, with consistent notes. • $18 • (01/31/98) • **72**

MARTIN, JEAN-JACQUES

Beaujolais-Villages 1993 • $NA • (06/15/95) • **80**

Juliénas 1993 • $14 • (07/31/95) • **72**

Pouilly-Fuissé Les Chevrières 1996: Crisp but with a nice ripe fruit character, it offers some pretty floral, pear, piecrust and mineral flavors. Of medium body, there is an attractive, balanced roundness on the finish. Drink or hold. 330 cases made. • $19 • (05/31/98) • **85**

Pouilly-Fuissé Les Chevrières 1994: Simply superb, with lots of crisp citrus flavors up front; turns silky and creamy as it glides to a smooth finish. Lovely apricot, lemon, honey and fig flavors from start to finish. Delicious now. • $NA • (05/31/96) • **89**

St.-Amour 1993 • $NA • (07/31/95) • **80**

St.-Véran 1996: Light and a bit candied, with pineapple juice, canned pear and kiwi notes mingling not so harmoniously. Crisp finish. 500 cases made. • $15 • (05/31/98) • **78**

St.-Véran 1995: Charming, ripe and sweet-tasting. Balanced honey, pear, vanilla bean, mocha, lemon and orange marmalade flavors. Medium-bodied, with a creamy-textured, delicious finish. Drink now. • $NA • (08/31/96) • **86**

MARTIN, ROBERT

Mâcon-Villages Domaine de la Denante 1995: Well-crafted and full-bodied. Ripe pear, melon, honey, fig, and spice flavors. Avoids greenness and remains restrained on the lemon flavored finish. Drink now. • $NA • (08/31/96) • **85**

St.-Véran Domaine de la Denante 1995: Beautifully crafted and full-bodied. Fairly opulent, then kicks in with intense fruit, particularly pure lime, and honey flavors that are exciting. Refreshing finish. Drink now. • $NA • (08/31/96) • **88**

MARTINE

Cabernet Sauvignon Vin de Pays d'Oc 1995: Harsh, with some plum flavors that turn astringent on the finish. Not much fun. 3,000 cases made. • $7 • (07/31/98) • **71**

Chardonnay Vin de Pays de l'Ile de Beauté 1996: A lumbering wine dominated by buttery flavors with an off-putting hint of geranium. 8,000 cases made. • $7 • (04/30/98) • **78**

Merlot Vin de Pays d'Oc 1995: Has rich Port-like aromas but it's a bit odd, with tart flavors of cherry and plum, bittersweet chocolate on the finish. 33,000 cases made. • $7 • (05/31/98) • **74**

MARTINOLLES, DOMAINE DE

Brut Blanquette de Limoux 1990 • $10 • (03/31/92) • **84**

Brut Blanquette de Limoux 1989 • $9 • (03/31/92) BB • **83**

Brut Blanquette de Limoux 1986 • $11 • (03/31/92) • **78**

Brut Crémant de Limoux 1989 • $10 • (11/30/92) • **81**

Chardonnay Vin de Pays d'Oc Cuvée Saint-Hilaire 1995: Bright fruit flavors make this lively and refreshing. The texture is crisp and tangy, and the finish is clean. 2,500 cases made. • $8 • (02/28/97) • **84**

Chardonnay Vin de Pays de l'Aude 1996: A bright, buttery Chardonnay that reminds us of Mâcon. Nothing fancy, but it's a good wine that's a good value. • $9 • (10/31/97) • **84**

MAS BLANC, DOMAINE DU

Banyuls Vendanges Tardives 1982 • $26 • (02/28/91) • **80**

Banyuls Vieilles Vignes 1982 • $27 • (02/28/91) • **82**
Banyuls Vieilles Vignes 1976 • $40 • (02/28/91) • **85**
Collioure Cuvée Cosprons Levants 1988 • $21 • (03/31/91) • **82**

MAS CHAMPART

Coteaux du Languedoc 1995: A fruit-bomb, but there's plenty of tannic framework to support it all. Wild berries and herbs lend a distinctive character. Try now. • $12 • (08/31/97) • **87**
Coteaux du Languedoc 1991 • $9 • (03/15/94) • **83**
St.-Chinian 1995: The deep color is misleading, as there are only pure raspberry and cherry flavors allied to a light structure, and just a hint of tannin on the finish. Not a blockbuster, but tasty. • $13 • (09/30/97) • **83**
St.-Chinian 1991 • $9 • (03/15/94) • **84**

MAS CREMAT, DOMAINE DU

Côtes du Roussillon 1995: A take-no-prisoners style of wine. Big aromas of sweet raspberry and cherry are followed by a mouthful of jammy, concentrated fruit. Full-bodied, rich and complex, bordering on alcoholic, with a long finish. Drink now through 2000. • $12 • (12/15/97) • **89**
Côtes du Roussillon 1991 • $10 • (03/15/94) • **83**

MAS DE DAUMAS GASSAC

Vin de Pays de l'Herault Haute Vallée du Gassac 1995: Shows ripe flavors of plums, tobacco and coffee, with firm tannins and a lingering, herbal finish. A well-made, straightforward wine for drinking now through 2000. • $24 • (09/30/97) • **84**
Vin de Pays de l'Herault Haute Vallée du Gassac 1994: A deeply colored, blockbuster red. Has effusive, oaky aromas, concentrated spicy currant flavors and massive tannins. Time will tell how it will mellow. Try after 2001. • $22 • (01/31/97) • **91**
Vin de Pays de l'Herault Haute Vallée du Gassac 1992 • $25 • (03/15/94) HR • **90**
Vin de Pays de l'Herault Haute Vallée du Gassac 1991 • $28 • (03/15/94) • **87**
Vin de Pays de l'Herault Haute Vallée du Gassac 1990 • $28 • (10/31/92) • **87**
Vin de Pays de l'Herault Haute Vallée du Gassac 1989 • $28 • (03/15/94) • **93**
Vin de Pays de l'Herault Haute Vallée du Gassac 1987 • $23 • (10/31/89) • **85**
Vin de Pays de l'Herault Haute Vallée du Gassac 1986 • $25 • (12/15/88) • **81**
Vin de Pays de l'Herault White Haute Vallée du Gassac 1995: Exciting and exotic, with a smooth yet fresh texture, and sweet peach, pear and apricot flavors. Full-bodied. Drinkable now. • $32 • (01/31/97) • **90**

MAS DE GOURGONNIER

Coteaux des Baux de Provence 1995: Fleshy and plummy, with some good herbal notes. A solid, quaffable wine that should go well with food. • $9 • (02/28/98) • **84**
Coteaux des Baux de Provence 1990 • $11 • (03/15/93) • **80**
Coteaux des Baux de Provence 1988 • $9 • (04/30/91) • **79**
Coteaux des Baux de Provence 1984 • $5 • (03/15/87) BB • **82**
Coteaux des Baux en Provence 1983 • $4 • (12/16/85) • **70**
Coteaux des Baux de Provence Réserve du Mas 1994: Ripe, fleshy and chewy, showing leather, plum and cherrylike character. Firm, with nice focus and intensity. Flavors linger on the finish. Mature, ready to drink. • $12 • (02/28/98) • **87**

MAS DE LA DAME

Les Baux de Provence Cuvée Gourmande 1995: Freshly crushed raspberries are the order of the day, and this red displays a certain elegance and harmony as well. Try now. 5,000 cases made. • $11 • (09/30/97) • **87**

Key: SS—Spectator Selection CS—Cellar Selection HR—Highly Recommended BB—Best Buy $NA—Price not available Ⓐ—Auction Price (BT)—Barrel Tasting
Dates in parentheses indicate the issues in which the ratings were published.

Les Baux de Provence Réserve du Mas 1995: A spicy, warm, sweet plum- and raspberry-flavored red that sports medium body, lush texture and moderate structure. Delicious now. 1,500 cases made. • $14 • (09/30/97) • **87**

MAS DES BRESSADES

Cabernet-Syrah Vin de Pays du Gard 1990 • $13 • (04/15/93) • **83**

MAS DES CHIMÈRES

Coteaux du Languedoc 1994: This pleasant, chewy wine is dominated by dried cherry and berry flavors, with a fairly powerful gamy note and a spicy finish. Drink now. • $12 • (03/31/98) • **84**

MAS JULLIEN

Coteaux du Languedoc Les Cailloutis 1991 • $10 • (03/15/94) • **84**
Coteaux du Languedoc Les Depierre 1991 • $10 • (03/15/94) • **83**

MAS NEUF, CHÂTEAU

Costières de Nîmes 1996: Solid and hearty, with some good berry and pepper flavors, but a bit drying on the finish. Drink now. • $8 • (04/30/98) • **80**

MAS NEUF, DOMAINE DU

Muscat de Mireval NV: Sweet and luscious, with peach, apricot and ripe apple character. An appealing dessert wine with plenty of flavor. • $17 • (07/31/98) • **85**

MAS STE.-BERTHE

Coteaux d'Aix-en-Provence Cuvée Louis David 1990 • $16 • (07/15/92) • **81**
Coteaux d'Aix-en-Provence Cuvée Tradition 1993: Loads of exuberant, wild berry and spice flavors coat the palate, giving an impression of sweetness, but it's somewhat lacking in harmony overall. 3,000 cases made. • $11 • (01/31/97) • **84**
Coteaux d'Aix-en-Provence Cuvée Tradition 1992 • $10 • (03/31/95) • **80**

MASSON-BLONDELET, DOMAINE J.-M.

Pouilly-Fumé Les Bascoins 1994: Quite austere, this full-bodied white shows apple, lemon and light smoke notes, with very firm acidity. It's well focused, more a complement to food than an easy quaff on its own. • $16 • (04/30/97) • **84**
Pouilly-Fumé Les Bascoins 1993 • $15 • (11/15/95) • **90**

MATHIEU, DOMAINE

Châteauneuf-du-Pape 1990: A ripe, complex wine, with broad, rich, leathery plum, earth and spice flavors that are full-bodied and chocolaty on the finish. Has a good dose of alcohol, too, but is balanced and fun to drink now. 2,000 cases made. • $15 • (11/30/92) • **87**
Châteauneuf-du-Pape 1989 • $18 • (08/31/92) • **87**

MATHIEU, SERGE

Brut Blanc de Noirs Champagne Cuvée Tradition NV: Good, straightforward Champagne with a modestly fruity, slightly sweet profile and a smooth texture. 3,250 cases made. • $35 • (12/31/97) • **84**
Brut Champagne 1991: Fresh, fruity and lively, this is a light and attractive Champagne from a not-so-great year. 500 cases made. • $40 • (11/15/97) • **85**
Brut Champagne Cuvée Prestige NV: A lean, dry style of Champagne with modest apple flavors and a comparatively thin texture and finish. 2,750 cases made. • $35 • (11/15/97) • **82**
Brut Champagne Millésime 1990: Wonderfully balanced and subtly flavored, tasting seamless and harmonious. It's smooth all the way through, from the fresh fruit aromas to the vanilla-tinged flavors to the lengthy finish. Drink through 2000. • $39 • (12/15/96) • **90**
Brut Champagne Tête de Cuvée Select NV: A lively, fairly rich Champagne with unusual earthy, peppery aromas and simple apple flavors. 600 cases made. • $40 • (11/15/97) • **83**

Brut Rosé Champagne NV: A bold and flavorful rosé Champagne with a vivid coral color, attractive toasty aromas and generous fruit flavors. Has the body and presence of a still wine; should be great with dinner. Drink now. 500 cases made. • $37 • (11/30/97) • **90**

MATIBAT, DOMAINE DE

Chardonnay Vin de Pays d'Oc 1995: A one-note wine with plenty of buttery flavors. A bit coarse on the finish, but shows some nice spicy notes. 2,300 cases made. • $8 • (04/30/98) • **81**

Côtes de Malepère 1994: A bit stewy-tasting. Modest dried cherry flavors and some peppery notes on the drying finish. A blend of 50 percent Cabernet, 30 percent Merlot, 10 percent Malbec and 10 percent Syrah. Past its prime. 4,400 cases made. • $7 • (04/30/98) • **77**

Merlot Vin de Pays d'Oc 1995: Thin and a bit vegetal-tasting with only modest dried cherry and spice flavors. Past its prime. 6,475 cases made. • $6 • (05/31/98) • **73**

MATROT, JOSEPH

Meursault 1995: Thick, ripe, full-bodied and very flavorful, this wine is bursting with forward tropical fruit, honey, spice and slightly grassy flavors. A touch tart on the finish. Try now. • $32 • (08/31/97) • **85**

Meursault 1994: Strange, with a reductive flavor, like stale ice. Full-bodied, even elegant, but has a disturbing musty cardboard note. Tasted twice, with consistent notes. • $NA • (08/31/96) • **74**

Meursault 1993: Simple in flavor, slightly earthy even, turning dull on the finish. There's not much to get excited about. Tasted twice. • $26 • (05/15/95) • **74**

Meursault Les Charmes 1995: Supple in texture, odd in flavor, but with a marvelous mineral concentration. Overlook the orange-peel and gingerroot notes and concentrate on the honey and earth character. Full-bodied, it turns a bit tart and bitter on the finish; try after 2005. • $NA • (05/31/97) • **90**

Meursault Les Charmes 1993: Not much more than a generic white. Gets somewhat nice and spicy on the finish, but where's the fruit? • $37 • (05/15/95) • **77**

Meursault Les Charmes 1992: Ripe and lush, with texture like cream, and wonderful mineral, caramel, apple and pear flavors. Seductive, with excellent acidity; grows in complexity as it comes in contact with the air. From a producer known to make long-aged wines. Tasted three times. • $33 • (08/31/94) • **89**

Meursault Les Chevalières 1995: Very ripe and rich, a supercharged wine with a velvety mouthfeel. Very concentrated, so it's too bad it smells and tastes overripe, with a cooked apple note, some apricot jam and raisin character. If the rustic note doesn't bother you, here's a serious '95 that should be best around 2005. • $30 • (08/31/97) • **88**

Meursault Les Chevalières 1993: Hard at first but then begins to sing, flashing a distinctive mineral character that dominates from start to the seductively smooth finish. Drinkable now. 167 cases made. • $23 • (05/15/95) • **87**

Meursault Les Chevalières 1992: Round, ripe and intense, this is difficult to evaluate. Tastes reductive and a bit like cardboard, but the content of a bottle opened for hours turned seductive, silky and incredibly minerally. • $25 • (05/15/95) • **87**

Meursault-Blagny 1995: A ripe, rich and velvety package, distinctive for its minty, dried herb, fresh sage and mineral aromas, tropical fruit, pear and spicy toasty oak flavors. Lovely, with a core of intense fruit. One of Matrot's best wines in years. Try after 2000. • $46 • (08/31/97) • **93**

Meursault-Blagny 1993: Attractive Meursault showing lovely apple and pear aromas and flavors, medium body and firm acidity. Tasted twice. 567 cases made. • $34 • (05/15/95) • **83**

Puligny-Montrachet Les Chalumaux 1995: A full-bodied '95, rather closed now. Rich and ripe, it coats the palate with its harmonious texture, showing hints of the lovely honey, citrus, hazelnut and smoke flavors that should explode around 2000 to 2005. Long, beautiful, subtle finish. • $44 • (05/31/97) • **92**

Puligny-Montrachet Les Chalumaux 1992: Well-balanced and modestly flavored, with butter, green apple and vanilla flavors that linger a bit on the finish. May need some time for the tart fruit component to blend in. A wine with a good track record for improving with age. Tasted three times. • $30 • (08/31/94) • **85**

Puligny-Montrachet Les Combettes 1995: Almost too young to taste now, it at first seems disjointed, even rustic, with aromas of cooked apples. But underneath is one of the richest, most glorious wines of this tasting, with ripe pear, lime, honey and mineral notes that should come together nicely after 2005. • $50 • (05/31/97) • **90**

MATROT, PIERRE

Chardonnay Bourgogne 1994: A round, smooth, ready-to-drink Burgundy that has decent fruit flavors and toasty aromas. • $17 • (05/31/96) • **81**

Meursault 1992: Quite complex and very silky, exceptional finesse, with a solid core of pear, mineral, vanilla and white pepper flavors. Smooth and round finish. From a producer whose wines need time to show it all. • $20 • (08/31/94) • **88**

MAU, YVON

Cabernet Sauvignon Vin de Pays des Côtes de Gascogne 1996: A disjointed wine, with soft berry flavors that never quite mesh with the astringent tannins. May be better in 1999. 15,000 cases made. • $6 • (12/15/97) • **80**

Merlot Vin de Pays des Côtes de Gascogne 1996: A red with personality. Quite peppery in character, with good cherry and berry flavors, some interesting cedary nuances, too—all nicely integrated and lingering on the finish. 20,000 cases made. • $6 • (11/15/97) • **85**

Merlot Vin de Pays des Côtes de Gascogne 1994: An appealing richness underlies flavors of strawberry and red currant, but there's not much depth. Drink now. 5,000 cases made. • $6 • (07/31/96) • **81**

Sauvignon Blanc Bordeaux 1996: A soft and simple white wine, watery and vague in flavor. 20,000 cases made. • $6 • (09/30/97) • **75**

MAUCAILLOU, CHÂTEAU

Moulis 1996: Decent character of berry and cherry, and firm tannins, but lacks a center palate. • $NA • (01/01/97) (BT) • **80-84**

Moulis 1992: Light and diluted, with strawberry, tobacco, herbal character. • $14 • (04/15/95) • **73**

Moulis 1988 • $14 • (07/31/91) • **82**

Moulis 1985 • $18 • (08/31/88) • **88**

Moulis 1983 • $16 • (03/15/87) • **87**

Moulis 1982 • $25 • (11/30/89) • **90**

Moulis 1981 • $14 • (10/01/85) • **88**

MAUCOIL, CHÂTEAU

Châteauneuf-du-Pape Réserve Suzeraine 1994: Light and simple. Shows light berry and tobacco flavors and lean tannins, with a licorice note on the finish. Not an ager. • $20 • (02/28/97) • **82**

Châteauneuf-du-Pape Réserve Suzeraine 1985 • $13 • (11/15/87) • **86**

MAUME

Charmes-Chambertin 1988 • $60 • (07/15/91) • **86**

Gevrey-Chambertin 1993: Seductive and distinguished, showing lots of pure, lively cassis, black cherry and wild berry character. It expands on the palate, adding coffee, spice, mocha and cedar notes. Very complex and full-bodied. Try in 2000. • $NA • (05/15/96) • **90**

Gevrey-Chambertin 1987 • $25 • (03/31/90) • **77**

Gevrey-Chambertin En Pallud 1994: Sweet and ripe-flavored, this tastes a bit syrupy. Turns a bit dry on the finish. • $28 • (11/15/96) • **75**

Gevrey-Chambertin En Pallud 1987 • $36 • (03/31/90) • **80**

Gevrey-Chambertin Lavaut St.-Jacques 1993: Very pure and vibrant cassis and currant character, lovely floral, rose petal complexity, medium body, wet earth notes and lingering finish. Could use a bit more opulence and body. Slightly drying aftertaste. • $NA • (05/15/96) • **86**

Gevrey-Chambertin Lavaut St.-Jacques 1991: Lean and tight, with a fine beam of raspberry and cherry flavor poking through the layer of tannins. Drinkable now. • $40 • (08/31/94) • **84**

Gevrey-Chambertin Premier Cru 1994: Tough and tart, hinting at nice fruit flavors under it all. Drinkable now. • $40 • (11/15/96) • **82**

Gevrey-Chambertin Premier Cru 1991: Ripe and generous, with an open texture; floats across the palate, showing plum, black cherry and spice with an herbal edge on the finish. Tannins are not obtrusive. Drinkable now. • $28 • (08/31/94) • **87**

Mazis-Chambertin 1994: Fresh and bright, offering a crisp mouthful of currant, blueberry and rose petal flavors that are integrated nicely with the firm tannins. Has plenty of room to grow; give until 1999 to 2000. • $63 • (11/15/96) • **88**

Mazis-Chambertin 1991: Lean and chewy, showing a lot of tea leaf and herbal notes around a tannic core of dark fruit and spice. Remains astringent on the finish. Try now. • $59 • (08/31/94) • **82**

FRANCE

Mazis-Chambertin 1987 • $56 • (03/31/90) • **74**

MAVETTE, DOMAINE DE LA

Gigondas 1995: A tough customer right now, not showing very much in the way of aromas or flavors, but the texture is rich and the structure firm, with plenty of fine tannins. Could ultimately score higher. Best from 2000 through 2007. • $15 • (05/15/98) • **84**

MAYARD, JEAN-LUC

Châteauneuf-du-Pape Domaine du Galet des Papes 1993: Light-bodied, with more tannin than fruit, showing light cherry, earthy and vegetal flavors and an anise-scented finish. May improve with food. 500 cases made. • $23 • (12/15/96) • **79**

Châteauneuf-du-Pape Domaine du Galet des Papes 1992: Aging fast, showing mature and complex aromas of earth, leather and spice, with decent fruit flavors underneath, full body and a good finish. • $23 • (10/15/95) • **82**

Châteauneuf-du-Pape Domaine du Galet des Papes Vieilles Vignes 1994: Black pepper, prune and some vegetal flavors fight their way through drying tannins in this muscular yet clumsy red. Drinkable now. 200 cases made. • $31 • (12/15/96) • **78**

Châteauneuf-du-Pape Domaine du Galet des Papes Vieilles Vignes 1993: Traditional in style, this shows cherry, tea and black pepper flavors, somewhat diluted, with firm underlying tannins and a decent finish. Drink now. 200 cases made. • $28 • (12/15/96) • **82**

Châteauneuf-du-Pape Domaine du Galet des Papes Vieilles Vignes 1992: Decent flavor, soft in balance, offering prune and herb accents. Drinkable now. • $32 • (10/15/95) • **81**

FRANCE

MAYNE, CHÂTEAU DU

Sauternes 1995: Pretty wine from Mayne. Subtle, spicy and sweet with a lovely vanilla and smoke finish. Medium-bodied, very sweet, with a long thick-textured finish. Drink now or hold. • $NA • (04/30/98) • **88**

MAYNE DES CARMES, CHÂTEAU

Sauternes 1989: An earthy character influences the fig, honey and walnut flavors in this medium-weight wine. Good if you don't mind a little funkiness. The finish is modest and slightly bitter. • $20 • (06/30/92) • **83**

MAZERIS, CHÂTEAU

Canon-Fronsac 1997: Medium-bodied red, with plenty of ripe fruit character and velvety tannins. • $NA • (06/15/98) (BT) • **85-89**

Canon-Fronsac 1996: Zingy and lively with focused, dried cherry and berry aromas and flavors. Medium-bodied, with firm tannins and a earthy, rich finish. Delicious. • $NA • (01/01/97) (BT) • **85-89**

Canon-Fronsac 1995: Firm, rich fruit contributes to smoky, earthy, black cherry aromas and flavors and a solid tannin backbone. • $NA • (05/15/96) (BT) • **85-89**

Canon-Fronsac 1994: An herbal wine with a slightly metallic, unripe edge. Firm tannins and light finish. • $20 • (01/31/97) • **75**

Canon-Fronsac 1993: Some berry and chocolate flavors, yet too light and diluted to be anything but average. Drinkable now. • $19 • (01/31/96) • **78**

Canon-Fronsac 1990: Very ripe—perhaps too ripe—with meaty raisin and plum flavors and a dry, tannic finish. Has rich flavors, but the structure won't hold it for long. Drink now. • $18 • (05/15/94) • **80**

MAZERIS-BELLEVUE, CHÂTEAU

Canon-Fronsac 1990: This wine is extremely firm, with full tannins and exotic cassis, berry and earth aromas and flavors. Drinkable now. 5,000 cases made. • $15 • (03/31/93) • **88**

Key: SS—Spectator Selection CS—Cellar Selection HR—Highly Recommended BB—Best Buy $NA—Price not available Ⓐ—Auction Price (BT)—Barrel Tasting

Dates in parentheses indicate the issues in which the ratings were published.

MÉDITÉO

Cabernet Sauvignon Vin de Pays d'Oc 1996: Modern in style, with mint and black currant aromas and flavors. It's of medium weight and well balanced. Drinkable now. • $7 • (12/15/97) • **84**

Chardonnay Vin de Pays d'Oc 1996: Quite vibrant and flavorful, with juicy apple, citrus and green peach. There's a refreshing purity to the fruit flavors; spicy notes linger on the finish. • $7 • (09/15/97) • **85**

Merlot Vin de Pays d'Oc 1996: There's a nice, fruity richness to this wine, with its alluring kirschlike aroma and jammy flavors. Polished and lively. • $7 • (11/15/97) • **85**

Syrah Vin de Pays d'Oc 1996: Look at all this French red offers for so few dollars. It shows good length, with plenty of peppery, jammy blackberry flavors, starting out soft and round, revealing tannic strength on the finish. Drinkable now. 10,000 cases made. • $7 • (12/15/97) BB • **86**

MELLOT, DOMAINE ALPHONSE

Sancerre Domaine La Moussière 1996: Makes an impact but lacks balance, with citrus flavors and a smoky, slightly earthy note. Has good concentration; may harmonize over time. Tasted twice, with consistent notes. Best from 1999 through 2002. • $18 • (05/31/98) • **84**

Sancerre Domaine La Moussière 1995: Acidity dominates fruit in this crisp white. Offers light citrus and green apple flavors with herbal accents. Showing good structure, it should blossom with food. • $18 • (06/15/97) • **86**

Sancerre Domaine La Moussière 1994 • $20 • (04/30/96) • **83**

Sancerre Domaine La Moussière Cuvée Edmond Vieilles Vignes 1995: A racy, lively white with vanilla and coconut notes suggestive of new oak treatment. The mineral and herbal notes are clean and fresh, but there are deep, ripe fruit flavors, too. An exuberant wine that needs time to show its best. Drink now through 2002. • $38 • (03/31/98) • **91**

MELOTERIE, DOMAINE DE LA

Vouvray Demi-Sec 1989 • $9 • (06/15/91) • **87**

MÉO-CAMUZET

Bourgogne 1990: Throws a lot of fruit at you, with pretty berry, cherry and raspberry flavors and a slight citrus edge. Ripe and balanced; a tasty mouthful of Pinot Noir. Ready now. • $20 • (06/15/93) • **85**

Bourgogne 1989 • $23 • (11/15/91) • **83**

Bourgogne Passe-tout-grains 1992: Hats off to this exotic wine packed with floral, violet and boysenberry flavors. Refreshes the palate with more pure, clean fruit than many other '92s. • $NA • (12/15/94) • **83**

Bourgogne Passe-tout-grains 1990: A ripe, bold style that gushes with raspberry, cherry and currant flavors framed by smoky oak and firm, drying tannins. Still, on the finish you taste a rich core of fruit. Drinkable now. • $17 • (03/31/92) • **86**

Bourgogne Passe-tout-grains 1989 • $17 • (07/15/91) • **84**

Clos de Vougeot 1995: Wonderfully ripe and sweet-tasting, this yummy, full-bodied Clos Vougeot starts out subtle and reserved, then makes its case with terrific elegance and refinement. The super cassis, blackberry and mineral character is enchanting. Long finish. Try after 2000. Falls short of expectations based on barrel tasting. • $70 • (11/15/97) • **92**

Clos de Vougeot 1994: Dense and chewy, with exotic herb and bitter chocolate grace notes to the main melody of sweet plum and currant flavors. Firm tannins want until 2000. • $NA • (11/15/96) • **90**

Clos de Vougeot 1993: Perhaps not as concentrated as expected from this top winery. Sleek and silky mocha, fruit, vanilla and spice character, medium body, fine tannins and long, crisp finish. Drinkable now. • $55 • (11/15/95) • **88**

Clos de Vougeot 1992: Very pretty ripe flavors on a supple frame, the blackberry and spice hinting at chocolate on the smooth finish. Drinkable now. • $57 • (12/15/94) • **88**

Clos de Vougeot 1990: Serves up nice supple berry and currant flavors, but they're not as bright and lively as we've found in most 1990s. Tannins are smooth and easy on the finish. Ready now. Tasted twice. • $77 • (09/30/93) • **84**

Clos de Vougeot 1989 • $91 • (11/15/91) CS • **94**

Clos de Vougeot 1988 • $95 • (11/30/90) • **92**

Clos de Vougeot 1986 • $55 • (11/30/88) • **91**

Clos de Vougeot 1985 • $105 • (03/31/88) • **93**

Corton 1992: Manages to focus its generous beam of blackberry and currant flavors through layers of spicy oak and very fine-grained tannins. Supple and beautifully crafted, it rises above the vintage. Drinkable now. • $57 • (12/15/95) • **91**

Corton 1989 • $76 • (11/15/91) • **93**

Corton 1986 • $50 • (10/31/88) • **89**

Corton Le Rognet 1995: A bit simple, this medium-bodied red is still rather elegant. Shows some pretty toasty bread, game and red- and blackberry flavors. A bit dry on the finish. Drinkable now. • $70 • (11/15/97) • **79**

Corton Le Rognet 1990: Elegant and spicy, with a pretty core of ripe black cherry and raspberry flavor that turns smooth and silky on the finish. Delicious now. 150 cases made. • $68 • (06/15/93) • **89**

Nuits-St.-Georges 1992: Gorgeous fruit unfolds with a cascade of violet, currant and black cherry flavors. Elegant, smooth and drinkable. Could only use a bit more concentration. Drinkable now. • $33 • (12/15/94) • **86**

Nuits-St.-Georges 1990: Ripe and spicy, with a definite touch of new oak to add complexity to the ripe plum and black cherry flavors. Has a smooth, elegant finish. Drinkable now. • $38 • (02/15/93) • **88**

Nuits-St.-Georges 1989 • $52 • (11/15/91) • **92**

Nuits-St.-Georges 1988 • $50 • (11/30/90) • **91**

Nuits-St.-Georges 1987 • $42 • (12/15/89) • **86**

Nuits-St.-Georges 1986 • $32 • (11/15/88) • **90**

Nuits-St.-Georges Aux Boudots 1994: Refined, elegant, impeccably balanced to show off the sweet, spicy plum, rose petal and caramel flavors that linger appealingly on the finish. Approachable now, best through 1999 to 2000. • $NA • (11/15/96) • **88**

Nuits-St.-Georges Aux Boudots 1993: Pretty Burgundy, sporting loads of peppery, spicy, fruity character, although slightly short on the finish. Medium in body, fine tannins. Try in 2000. • $60 • (11/15/95) • **90**

Nuits-St.-Georges Aux Boudots 1992: Firm, chewy and solid, with dark berry and spicy prune flavors lurking underneath a layer of fine tannins. Drinkable now. • $54 • (12/15/94) • **85**

Nuits-St.-Georges Aux Boudots 1991: Firm in texture and modest in intensity, serving up appealing aromas and flavors that emerge harmoniously on the finish. 175 cases made. • $62 Ⓐ • (01/31/94) • **84**

Nuits-St.-Georges Aux Boudots 1990: A balance of rich, plummy flavors and spicy, toasty oak notes gives this wine finesse, intensity and complexity. Lively and luscious on the finish. Drinkable now. 250 cases made. • $68 • (02/15/93) • **91**

Nuits-St.-Georges Aux Boudots 1989 • $81 • (11/15/91) • **90**

Nuits-St.-Georges Aux Boudots 1988 • $80 • (11/30/90) • **92**

Nuits-St.-Georges Aux Boudots 1987 • $56 • (12/15/89) • **88**

Nuits-St.-Georges Aux Boudots 1986 • $46 • (11/15/88) • **92**

Nuits-St.-Georges Aux Murgers 1993: Lots of wood in this brooding, dark-colored Burgundy. Plenty of plum, chestnut and currant flavors, full body, a fresh core and solid tannins. Drinkable now. • $60 • (11/15/95) • **93**

Nuits-St.-Georges Aux Murgers 1992: Pretty berry and vanilla flavors rise past the chewy tannins in this medium-bodied, deep-colored wine. Drinkable now. • $54 • (12/15/94) • **86**

Nuits-St.-Georges Aux Murgers 1991: Smooth in texture and attractive, showing fresh currant and wild berry flavors that keep echoing on the finish, nicely shaded by spicy oak. Drinkable now. 275 cases made. • $62 Ⓐ • (01/31/94) • **88**

Nuits-St.-Georges Aux Murgers 1990: A firm wine that offers generous, clear black cherry, raspberry and spice aromas and flavors. Solid, with pure, focused flavors balanced by enough acidity and tannin. Drinkable now. 375 cases made. • $68 • (02/15/93) • **90**

Nuits-St.-Georges Aux Murgers 1989 • $81 • (11/15/91) • **94**

Nuits-St.-Georges Aux Murgers 1988 • $80 • (11/30/90) • **91**

Nuits-St.-Georges Aux Murgers 1987 • $56 • (12/15/89) • **93**

Nuits-St.-Georges Aux Murgers 1986 • $48 • (11/15/88) • **92**

Nuits-St.-Georges Aux Murgers 1985 • $73 • (04/15/88) • **90**

Richebourg 1993: Simply fabulous. Like an iron fist in a velvet glove, this seduces yet displays a firm side. Very sweet-tasting and ripe, boasting superb currant, mint and black cherry flavors. Goes on and on. Bravo! Try after 2000. • $175 • (11/15/95) • **94**

Richebourg 1992: Supple, stylish, generous and bursting with delicious currant and raspberry notes layered under violet and spicy oak tones. It keeps pouring out the flavor on a long, polished finish. Delicious now. • $NA • (12/15/94) • **91**

Richebourg 1990: A stunning 1990 that packs in a wonderful range of ripe, delicious fruit and combines it with elegance, finesse and grace. Deeply colored, with tiers of black cherry, currant and raspberry-scented flavors that pick up spicy anise and cedar notes. Impeccably balanced, long, rich and concentrated. A sheer joy to drink now, but should age through the decade with ease. 125 cases made. • $242 • (06/15/93) • **97**

Richebourg 1989 • $270 • (11/15/91) • **97**

Richebourg 1988 • $253 • (11/30/90) • **96**

Richebourg 1987 • $165 • (12/15/89) • **96**

Richebourg 1986 • $160 • (10/31/88) • **90**

Richebourg 1985 • $235 • (03/31/88) • **97**

Vosne-Romanée 1994: A lithe, gentle wine with a strong, peppery floral accent to the light strawberry flavors. Ready to drink. • $30 • (11/15/96) • **80**

Vosne-Romanée 1992: Sharp and tart. The pretty rose petal, black currant and smoky, toasty flavors are clean and pure, but it could use a bit more concentration. • $33 • (12/15/94) • **80**

Vosne-Romanée 1990: Long and lavish, with many threads of nutmeg- and vanilla-scented blackberry, plum and currant aromas and flavors weaving together through the elegant finish. A polished wine that's flavorful and generous without weight. Drinkable now. • $36 • (02/15/93) • **93**

Vosne-Romanée 1989 • $47 • (11/15/91) • **91**

Vosne-Romanée 1988 • $50 • (12/31/90) • **87**

Vosne-Romanée 1987 • $35 • (12/15/89) • **90**

Vosne-Romanée 1986 • $30 • (10/31/88) • **88**

Vosne-Romanée Aux Brûlées 1995: A very solid, chewy red that's angular at this stage, with firm tannins and alcohol prominent on the finish. Licorice, plum and smoke are the flavors. • $70 • (11/15/97) • **87**

Vosne-Romanée Aux Brûlées 1994: Impressively ripe and sweet-tasting, generously supported by oak and spice accents, this delivers plenty of plum and black cherry aromas and flavors. Thick, supple and lingering finish. More harmonious than Méo's Cros-Parantoux. Drinkable now. • $35 • (11/15/96) • **89**

Vosne-Romanée Aux Brûlées 1993: Beautifully crafted red offering crushed raspberry and plum character. Full-bodied yet silky and sophisticated, caressing your palate. Try in 2000. • $75 • (11/15/95) • **93**

Vosne-Romanée Aux Brûlées 1992: With more density and color than most '92s, this is almost exuberantly fruity and generous, showing bright currant, berry and spicy oak aromas and flavors. Drinkable now. • $72 • (12/15/94) • **85**

Vosne-Romanée Aux Brûlées 1991: Silky and flavorful; an earthy edge to the pretty blackberry and cherry flavors and shades of chocolate and cedar add extra dimensions. An elegant wine, with impressive length. Drinkable now. 137 cases made. • $73 Ⓐ • (01/31/94) • **89**

Vosne-Romanée Aux Brûlées 1990: Supple, forward and fruity, with an amazing range of spicy cherry, raspberry and currant flavors that are pure and delicious, picking up toasty oak notes in the background. Complex, concentrated, young and vibrant. The tannins barely show on the long, full finish. Drinkable now. 225 cases made. • $81 • (06/15/93) • **93**

Vosne-Romanée Aux Brûlées 1989 • $91 • (11/15/91) • **94**

Vosne-Romanée Aux Brûlées 1988 • $84 • (11/30/90) • **89**

Vosne-Romanée Aux Brûlées 1987 • $63 • (12/15/89) • **95**

Vosne-Romanée Cros Parantoux 1994: Seductive, smooth and polished. Impressive for its ripe red berry, plum, earth and spice character, it has a touch of dilution, but its round texture makes it a pleasure to drink now. • $70 • (11/15/96) • **87**

Vosne-Romanée Cros Parantoux 1992: Well-defined fruit, focusing on raspberry and currant, in a smooth wine with supple tannins and toasty character. It's good, but doesn't approximate the *grand cru* character as it usually does. Tasted twice. • $73 • (12/15/94) • **85**

Vosne-Romanée Cros Parantoux 1991: Subtle and elegant, showing plenty of blackberry, vanilla and toast aromas and flavors up front and on the finish, although it takes a dip in the middle. Drinkable now. 75 cases made. • $73 Ⓐ • (01/31/94) • **88**

Vosne-Romanée Cros Parantoux 1990: A tremendous wine for this price. Amazingly ripe, complex and elegant, with tiers of black cherry, currant, raspberry and spice aromas and flavors. Shows tremendous balance between elegance and concentration, suppleness and structure, intensity and finesse. Picks up toasty oak notes and fine tannins on the finish. Drinkable now. 100 cases made. • $81 • (06/15/93) • **99**

Vosne-Romanée Cros Parantoux 1989 • $91 • (11/15/91) • **95**

Vosne-Romanée Cros Parantoux 1988 • $84 • (11/30/90) • **94**

Vosne-Romanée Cros Parantoux 1987 • $63 • (12/15/89) • **95**

Vosne-Romanée Cros Parantoux 1986 • $60 • (07/31/88) • **93**

Vosne-Romanée Les Chaumes 1994: Has a fresh, salty aroma and a nice bead of rose petal-scented currant flavor that lingers over a modest level of tannin. Best now. • $35 • (11/15/96) • **85**

Vosne-Romanée Les Chaumes 1993: Magnificent. Supple yet full of vibrant currant, raspberry and violet notes and a touch of earth. Quite ripe and sweet, but it needs time. Try in 2004. • $70 • (11/15/95) • **93**

Vosne-Romanée Les Chaumes 1992: Richer than most in this vintage, with a smoky, toasty character to the currant and black cherry. Flavors persist on the finish and the tannins are in balance. • $43 • (12/15/94) • **86**

Vosne-Romanée Les Chaumes 1990: Ripe, focused, generous, supple, spicy and complex, with currant, raspberry, chocolate and spice aromas and flavors. Drinkable now. 240 cases made. • $55 • (02/15/93) • **94**

Vosne-Romanée Les Chaumes 1989 • $62 • (01/31/92) • **91**

Vosne-Romanée Les Chaumes 1986 • $38 • (12/31/88) • **83**

Vosne-Romanée Les Chaumes 1985 • $80 • (03/31/88) • **92**

MERIC, CHÂTEAU

Graves 1989 • $16 • (07/15/92) • **77**

Graves 1988 • $17 • (04/30/91) • **76**

MERIC, DE

Brut Champagne NV: A mature Champagne that features nutty, figgy flavors and a smooth, easy texture. 6,000 cases made. • $30 • (10/31/97) • **84**

MÉRODE, PRINCE FLORENT DE

Aloxe-Corton 1994: Has an earthy mushroom accent to its soft berry flavors, finishing coarsely. Lacking in definition. • $26 • (11/15/96) • **78**

Aloxe-Corton 1987 • $30 • (02/28/91) • **87**

Aloxe-Corton Premier Cru 1995: Dill aromas are followed by a diluted, tough red wine with dry tannins. 107 cases made. • $24 • (11/15/97) • **74**

Aloxe-Corton Premier Cru 1990: Fresh and pleasant, with gamy cherry and toast notes making it interesting. Not a big wine, but one that will be enjoyable earlier than most from this vintage. Drinkable now. 130 cases made. • $37 • (12/15/92) • **86**

Corton Le Clos du Roi 1995: Disappointing. A bit green and diluted, offering modest ripe berry flavor. Medium-bodied, with some forest underbrush, mushroom notes. Dry finish. 238 cases made. • $38 • (11/15/97) • **79**

Corton Le Clos du Roi 1994: Relatively light, and balanced toward plummy flavors. Layered with chewy tannins that pick up a chocolaty accent on the finish. Best from 2000. • $42 • (11/15/96) • **78**

Corton Le Clos du Roi 1993: Very solid and closed. Knocks you over the head. Full body, medium tannins and a muscular finish. Give it time; try after 2000. 220 cases made. • $44 • (11/15/95) • **88**

Corton Le Clos du Roi 1992: Ripe and chewy, with fresh, youthful berry and currant flavor that lingers on the supple finish. Try now. 242 cases made. • $42 • (12/15/94) • **86**

Corton Le Clos du Roi 1990: As velvety as wines get in Corton; melts in your mouth, with lovely chocolate, raspberry and cherry aromas and flavors and a smoky, toasty, vanilla-flavored finish that is supple and delicious. Should be great sooner than most; try now. 95 cases made. • $38 • (12/15/92) • **90**

Corton Le Clos du Roi 1987 • $44 • (03/31/90) • **87**

Corton Le Clos du Roi 1986 • $49 • (08/31/89) • **80**

Corton Les Bressandes 1994: Light-bodied, thinly flavored, and drying on the finish thanks to swarms of bitter tannins. • $36 • (11/15/96) • **76**

Corton Les Bressandes 1993: Pretty Corton, not for long aging but very pleasant now. Shows plum, cedar and cream character, medium body, soft tannins and medium finish. 457 cases made. • $37 • (11/15/95) • **86**

Corton Les Bressandes 1992: A little chewy, but the berry and spice flavors slide in on the chunky finish. Best now. 500 cases made. • $35 • (12/15/94) • **81**

Corton Les Bressandes 1990: Not as concentrated in fruit as some, but shows a solid backbone of tannins and pleasant fruit characteristics. Try now. 200 cases made. • $54 • (12/15/92) • **85**

Corton Les Bressandes 1989 • $56 • (11/30/92) • **84**

Corton Les Bressandes 1987 • $45 • (03/31/91) • **92**

Corton Les Bressandes 1986 • $38 • (08/31/89) • **84**

Corton Les Bressandes 1985 • $52 • (02/15/88) • **93**

Corton Les Maréchaudes 1995: Light and woody. A simple wine with an astringent finish and dill pickle juice aromas. Where is the fruit? 204 cases made. • $34 • (11/15/97) • **71**

Key: SS—Spectator Selection CS—Cellar Selection HR—Highly Recommended BB—Best Buy $NA—Price not available Ⓐ—Auction Price (BT)—Barrel Tasting
Dates in parentheses indicate the issues in which the ratings were published.

Corton Les Maréchaudes 1994: Lean, but focused, with a relatively modest level of black cherry flavor and an herbal accent to the finish. Short of *grand cru* quality, but nice to drink. • $32 • (11/15/96) • **80**

Corton Les Maréchaudes 1993: Firm, vibrant and fruity, featuring lots of cherry character and fresh acidity. Rather lean but delicious. Drinkable now. 194 cases made. • $32 • (11/15/95) • **87**

Corton Les Maréchaudes 1992: Relatively light and pleasant, with a decent level of berry flavor sneaking in on the chewy finish. Best now. 216 cases made. • $32 • (12/15/94) • **82**

Corton Les Maréchaudes 1990: Fruity and flavorful; the blend of earth, strawberry and cherry notes makes for pleasant drinking. Not as big as the best, but offers enough depth to please most Burgundy lovers. Drinkable now. 250 cases made. • $49 • (12/15/92) • **86**

Corton Les Maréchaudes 1987 • $36 • (08/31/90) • **88**

Corton Les Maréchaudes 1986 • $33 • (08/31/89) • **82**

Corton Les Maréchaudes 1985 • $49 • (03/15/88) • **81**

Corton Les Renardes 1994: Builds a big structure with its tannins and acidity, but the herbal, wet earth flavors never flesh out enough to fill in the frame. Finishes with a touch of bitterness. • $36 • (11/15/96) • **76**

Corton Les Renardes 1993: Light, pleasant, delicate red berry and floral notes and a crisp but fresh and lively finish. Try now. 194 cases made. • $37 • (11/15/95) • **85**

Corton Les Renardes 1992: Supple and nicely focused, with raspberry and blackberry notes that keep singing on the smooth finish. Not powerful but showing nice flavors. Best now. 212 cases made. • $35 • (12/15/94) • **82**

Corton Les Renardes 1990: How much more refined can a Corton get? You can taste the finesse. The violet, raspberry and earth characteristics just go on and on at the end, when the supple but long finish kicks in. Try whenever you've got a chance. 90 cases made. • $54 • (12/15/92) • **94**

Corton Les Renardes 1987 • $36 • (03/31/90) • **92**

Corton Les Renardes 1986 • $38 • (08/31/89) • **76**

Ladoix Les Chaillots 1995: Light wine, both in color and body, offering merely decent fruit. A bit herbal and astringent. Short finish. 658 cases made. • $15 • (11/15/97) • **75**

Ladoix Les Chaillots 1994: A light quaff, with thin strawberry and leather flavors growing grainy on the finish. • $17 • (11/15/96) • **74**

Ladoix Les Chaillots 1993: A surprise from this rather unheralded village. Marvelous pure fruit from start to finish, boasting an excellent tannin structure, medium body and currant, vanilla and cream flavors. Try after 2000. 631 cases made. • $17 • (11/15/95) • **90**

Ladoix Les Chaillots 1992: Light and tight, hinting at currant at first, but fading quickly. A small wine with small flavors. 658 cases made. • $21 • (12/15/94) • **76**

Ladoix Les Chaillots 1991: Crisp in texture, but a nice beam of currant and spice flavors opens up on the finish. Drinkable now. 1,100 cases made. • $28 Ⓐ • (01/31/94) • **81**

Ladoix Les Chaillots 1990: Shows the essence of fruit, and so refined that the flavors linger. Ripe without being overblown, seducing you with its focused black cherry, blackberry and plum aromas and flavors. Drinkable now. 550 cases made. • $23 • (12/15/92) • **88**

Ladoix Les Chaillots 1987 • $18 • (11/15/90) • **77**

Ladoix Les Chaillots 1986 • $18 • (08/31/89) • **74**

Pommard La Platière 1995: Light and disappointing, more water than wine, with a dry, astringent texture and stewed tomato flavors. 563 cases made. • $27 • (11/15/97) • **74**

Pommard La Platière 1994: Light and slightly diluted, with a stalky, unripe character. Some unaggressive red berry and plum flavors do little to help balance this wine. • $31 • (11/15/96) • **74**

Pommard La Platière 1993: Chunky Pommard, offering plenty of thick fruit and tannins, medium to full in body, excellent backbone and long finish. Drinkable now. 583 cases made. • $31 • (11/15/95) • **88**

Pommard La Platière 1992: Crisp in texture, with modest black cherry flavor poking through the firm tannins. Drinkable now. 542 cases made. • $31 • (12/15/94) • **79**

Pommard La Platière 1990: Full of finesse despite the concentrated character and solid tannins. Focused and well made, delivering plenty of red berry, violet and smoke aromas and flavors and refined tannins. Drinkable now. 475 cases made. • $48 • (12/15/92) • **90**

Pommard La Platière 1989 • $48 • (11/30/92) • **86**

Pommard La Platière 1987 • $36 • (08/31/90) • **76**

Pommard La Platière 1986 • $35 • (07/31/89) • **86**

Pommard La Platière 1985 • $45 • (03/15/88) • **94**

Pommard La Platière 1984 • $23 • (02/15/88) • **71**

FRANCE

MESTRE-MICHELOT

Chardonnay Bourgogne 1993: Lean, hard and a bit green, displaying decent citrus and apple flavors. Bitter, herbal notes kick in on the finish. Drink if you must. • $NA • (05/15/95) • **74**
Meursault Genevrières 1993: Very attractive mineral, apple and pineapple notes and a touch of toasty oak. Medium-bodied, exhibiting solid fruit and flinty aftertaste. Drink now. • $NA • (05/15/95) • **89**
Meursault Le Limozin 1993: A tart Meursault that tastes quite green but also shows some decent lime, honey and grapefruit flavors. Try now. • $NA • (05/15/95) • **82**
Meursault Le Limozin 1992: Lovely and complex, medium-bodied, shows toast, butter, peach and mineral flavors, all in a smooth and vibrant package; deliciously lingering finish. Drinkable now. • $38 • (08/31/94) • **89**
Meursault Le Porusot 1992: Ripe and opulent in style, luxurious and flavorful, piling honey and pineapple on top of hazelnut, toast and butter. Lush in texture, but not too fat. A forward style that is very enjoyable now. • $NA • (08/31/94) • **89**
Meursault Sous la Velle 1993: Quite tight and hard now but shows excellent potential. Toast, dried-herb and green-apple flavors come together refreshingly on the finish. Drinkable now. • $NA • (05/15/95) • **85**

MÉTAIREAU, LOUIS

Muscadet de Sèvre et Maine Sur Lie Cuvée One 1995: Very crisp and refreshing, with clean lemon and light herb flavors. On the lean side, but has some concentration and would complement shellfish. 2,760 cases made. • $20 • (06/15/97) • **85**
Muscadet de Sèvre et Maine Sur Lie Cuvée One 1993 • $14 • (06/15/96) • **80**

METAIRIE, LA

Corbières 1989 • $7 • (12/15/91) • **78**

MEULIERE, CHÂTEAU DE LA

Premières Côtes de Bordeaux 1988 • $9 • (02/28/91) • **76**

MEUNIER ST.-LOUIS, CHÂTEAU

Corbières 1991 • $NA • (03/15/94) • **87**

MEURSAULT, CHÂTEAU DE

Beaune Les Cents Vignes 1985 • $31 • (02/28/90) • **87**
Beaune Premier Cru 1992: On the light side, presenting pleasant flavor and smooth texture. Hints of smoke and mineral add to currant and cherry notes; the finish lingers nicely. Drinkable now. • $26 • (05/15/95) • **83**
Pinot Noir Bourgogne du Château 1992: A sturdy, rather simple red Burgundy that is medium-bodied, moderately tannic and greenish in flavor. Best to drink now. • $13 • (06/15/95) • **82**
Pinot Noir Bourgogne du Château 1988 • $16 • (01/31/92) • **82**
Savigny-lès-Beaune Savigny du Domaine 1992: Simple and mature tasting, offering plum, honey and apricot flavors, mild tannins and a sense of sweetness. Drink now. • $20 • (06/15/95) • **79**
Volnay Clos des Chênes 1992: Heavy oak makes this supple and overdone. Tasting almost sweet: vanilla, maple syrup and butter flavors. Not our style. • $30 • (06/15/95) • **78**
Volnay Clos des Chênes 1988 • $47 • (07/15/91) • **87**

MEYER-FONNÉ

Edelzwicker Alsace Katzenthal 1996: Round and quaffable, the spicy, floral notes stand out in this white blend. Rich and balanced, but it finishes short. • $10/liter • (11/15/97) • **83**
Edelzwicker Alsace Katzenthal 1994: Bold, if a bit confused, this blend offers orange, spice and mineral flavors in a light, crisp package. Easy to like, especially for beginners. • $9/liter • (10/15/96) • **82**
Extra Brut Crémant d'Alsace NV: A lively sparkler that offers a toasty nose followed by apple and honey flavors. Rich and round, this makes a great apéritif. • $18 • (11/15/97) • **86**
Gewürztraminer Alsace Grand Cru Wineck-Schlossberg Vendange Tardive 1994: A nice balance of racy acidity and sweet pineapple flavor gives this wine liveliness and harmony. Crème brûlée and spice notes emerge on the finish. 140 cases made. • $33/500ml • (10/15/96) • **88**
Gewürztraminer Alsace Réserve Particulière 1996: Beguiling aromas of pear, rose petal and hops are followed by the taste of rosewater, all with an elegant yet luscious texture. Reflects the winemaker's deft touch with Gewürztraminer, and delicious now. • $14 • (11/15/97) • **88**
Gewürztraminer Alsace Réserve Particulière 1995: A lush, exotic style, full of litchi, mango and apricot flavors that persist to the grapefruit-peel finish. Balanced on the soft side, so enjoy it now. 1,800 cases made. • $16 • (09/30/97) • **84**
Gewürztraminer Alsace Réserve Particulière 1994: This lively Gewürz marries zesty lime and ripe pineapple flavors in a big body with plenty of acidity. It's rich and refreshing at once. 1,800 cases made. • $16 • (09/30/96) • **87**
Gewürztraminer Alsace Réserve Particulière 1993 • $18 • (09/15/95) • **85**
Gewürztraminer Alsace Réserve St.-Urbain 1995: Sweet and rich, but the honey flavors play a one-note song. 400 cases made. • $20 • (09/30/97) • **84**
Gewürztraminer Alsace Réserve St.-Urbain 1993 • $20 • (09/15/95) • **87**
Muscat Alsace Sur Lie 1995: Orange-peel and lime are the prominent flavors in this bright, very crisp white. Lively and refreshing, a good apéritif. 900 cases made. • $14 • (09/30/96) • **84**
Muscat Alsace Sur Lie 1994: Tanky flavors with hints of cheese and barely discernible notes of orange peel. 800 cases made. • $14 • (09/30/96) • **74**
Muscat Alsace Tiré Sur Lie 1995: The piney character of this modest white is overwhelming, and leaves a soapy aftertaste. 90-94 cases made. • $14 • (09/30/97) • **74**
Pinot Blanc Alsace 1993 • $10 • (07/31/95) • **86**
Pinot Blanc Alsace Vieilles Vignes 1996: Extremely rich, showing some peach flavors and bread dough elements (perhaps from lees contact), this is a concentrated, young Pinot Blanc. Drinkable now. • $10 • (11/15/97) • **87**
Pinot Blanc Alsace Vieilles Vignes 1995: Has ripe, fruit-salad aromas that segue into floral, citrus and earthy notes on the palate. It's well balanced, with moderate concentration and length. 2,800 cases made. • $11 • (09/30/97) • **84**
Pinot Blanc Alsace Vieilles Vignes 1994: Light-bodied, yet rich in honey, melon and creamy flavors. Though there's not quite enough acidity for balance, the floral sweetness has its own appeal. 3,000 cases made. • $10 • (10/15/96) • **84**
Pinot Noir Alsace 1994: Crisp and fruity, offering pretty strawberry and light herbal flavors with light tannins and fresh acidity. Try lightly chilled. 600 cases made. • $14 • (10/15/96) • **83**
Riesling Alsace Grand Cru Kaefferkopf 1994: Clean, crisp and vibrant. Fragrant, with floral and grilled nut aromas, then bright and juicy on the palate, with firm, lemony acidity. 120 cases made. • $23 • (09/30/96) • **86**
Riesling Alsace Grand Cru Wineck-Schlossberg 1995: A beautifully structured Alsace white, its grace and inner strength setting off the complex red berry, almond and apple flavors. It's densely textured and exhibits remarkable length, with a haunting aftertaste of cassis. An impressive example of its type, and affordable, too. 300 cases made. • $25 • (11/15/97) • **93**
Riesling Alsace Grand Cru Wineck-Schlossberg 1993: True to traditional Alsace style, this is lean and clean, with lime, mineral and light floral notes and firm acidity. A refreshing wine that will marry well with food. 240 cases made. • $24 • (09/30/96) • **87**
Riesling Alsace Kaefferkopf 1993 • $25 • (09/15/95) • **84**
Riesling Alsace Réserve Particulière 1996: Stunning aromas reveal the purity and aristocracy of this Riesling. Exhibits a complex array of flowers, apple, peach, black currant and mineral flavors, precision balance and a seamless texture. 1,400 cases made. • $14 • (11/15/97) • **90**
Riesling Alsace Réserve Particulière 1995: Like a tropical fruit mélange, here's a fat, voluptuous white that retains enough acidity to avoid being flabby. Delicious now. 1,200 cases made. • $14 • (09/30/97) • **85**
Riesling Alsace Réserve Particulière 1994: Crisp, even austere, showing pear and mineral flavors underscored by firm acidity. It has intensity; try now. 1,000 cases made. • $14 • (10/15/96) • **85**
Riesling Alsace Vignoble de Katzenthal 1993 • $18 • (09/15/95) • **82**
Sylvaner Alsace 1993 • $10 • (09/15/95) • **85**
Tokay Pinot Gris Alsace Hinterberg de Katzenthal Vendange Tardive 1994: Honeyed and spicy, it's rich and sweet, offering creamy apricot and pear flavors in a thick texture with enough acidity to keep it fresh. Harmonious, straightforward, powerful. 100 cases made. • $35/500ml • (10/15/96) • **90**
Tokay Pinot Gris Alsace Réserve Particulière 1996: This is a soft, easy, delicious Pinot Gris, full of apple and spice flavors and just enough acidity to balance it all. Drinkable now through 2000. • $15 • (11/15/97) • **87**
Tokay Pinot Gris Alsace Réserve Particulière 1995: Botrytis gives an exotic, mushroom accent to this ripe, plush, tropical fruit-flavored white. There's

plenty of acidity beneath and the finish is a bit hot. 1,200 cases made. • $15 • (09/30/97) • **82**

Tokay Pinot Gris Alsace Réservée Particulière 1993 • $17 • (08/31/95) • **87**

MEYNEY, CHÂTEAU

St.-Estèphe 1997: Simple berry and spice aromas and flavors. Light- to medium-bodied, with light tannins and a fresh finish. • $NA • (06/15/98) (BT) • **75-79**

St.-Estèphe 1996: Lovely, balanced St. Estèphe, with spice, tobacco and nutmeg aromas and flavors. Medium-bodied, with fine tannins and a long, silky aftertaste. Delicious. • $30 • (06/15/98) (BT) • **85-89**

St.-Estèphe 1995: Slightly disappointing for Meyney, but still a pretty wine. Aromas of roses and berries follow through onto a medium-bodied palate. Tannins are medium-to-light; finish is short. Drink now. • $21 Ⓐ • (01/31/98) • **85**

St.-Estèphe 1994: A wonderfully silky wine, with lovely cherry, raspberry and plum aromas and flavors. Medium-bodied, with fine tannins and a fresh, fruity finish. A joy to taste. Drinkable now. • $22 Ⓐ • (01/31/97) • **87**

St.-Estèphe 1993: Meyney is always a winner. Lovely mint, berry, cherry and vanilla aromas and flavors, medium body, silky tannins and fresh finish. Drinkable now. • $11 Ⓐ • (01/31/96) • **86**

St.-Estèphe 1992: Very polished and silky tobacco, mint, currant and vanilla aromas and flavors. Medium in body. • $15 • (04/15/95) • **83**

St.-Estèphe 1991: A fruity wine with a hint of herbs and bell pepper. Medium-bodied with a light finish. • $15 • (03/31/94) • **79**

St.-Estèphe 1990: A beautiful wine, with cassis, berry and citrus aromas and flavors, medium tannins and a long, crisp finish. Drinkable now. 25,000 cases made. • $25 • (03/31/93) • **90**

St.-Estèphe 1989 • $40 Ⓐ • (03/15/92) HR • **93**

St.-Estèphe 1987 • $14 • (05/15/90) • **87**

St.-Estèphe 1986 • $41 Ⓐ • (11/30/89) • **88**

St.-Estèphe 1985 • $27 Ⓐ • (08/31/88) • **92**

St.-Estèphe 1984 • $11 • (05/15/87) • **79**

St.-Estèphe 1983 • $34 Ⓐ • (10/15/86) • **92**

St.-Estèphe 1982 • $42 Ⓐ • (08/31/92) • **91**

St.-Estèphe 1979 • $19 Ⓐ • (10/15/89) • **87**

St.-Estèphe 1961 • $78 Ⓐ • (04/30/96) • **83**

MÉZIAT, PIERRE

Chiroubles Domaine Marquis des Pontheux Sélection Vieilles Vignes 1995: Firm on the palate, with earth and dried cherry flavors, this lean red has the grip for food but isn't much fun. • $15 • (09/15/97) • **77**

MIAUDOUX, CHÂTEAU

Bergerac 1995: A full-bodied, tannic, ripe-flavored red that seems to stress spicy oak over its black cherry and plum notes. Hearty and robust, and in need of a little more time. Best from 1999 through 2001. • $7 • (07/31/98) • **84**

Saussignac Réserve 1994: Offers nice smoky, toasty flavors, some honey and apricot notes as well. Flavors linger on the finish. 400 cases made. • $11/500ml • (08/31/97) • **84**

MICHAUD, ALAIN

Brouilly Cuvée Sélectionnée 1995: Smooth, polished, maturing but still well knit, with cherry, coffee and spice flavors, light tannins and a floral finish. Combines traditional flavors with skillful winemaking. • $14 • (09/15/97) • **85**

Brouilly Cuvée Sélectionée 1994: Polished, with a balanced structure. The black cherry flavors are smooth and still fresh, and the tannins are sufficient to stand up to food. • $15 • (09/15/96) • **84**

Brouilly Prestige de Vieilles Vignes 1994: Rich and ripe. This hefty red is well-integrated and still fresh, with deep plum and chocolate flavors and firm tannins for balance. Developing nicely, it is drinking well now but can be held. • $18 • (09/15/96) • **88**

Brouilly Prestige de Vieilles Vignes 1993 • $17 • (06/15/95) • **79**

Key: SS—Spectator Selection CS—Cellar Selection HR—Highly Recommended BB—Best Buy $NA—Price not available Ⓐ—Auction Price (BT)—Barrel Tasting

Dates in parentheses indicate the issues in which the ratings were published.

MICHAUD, J.F.

Beaujolais Le Toléron 1994 • $8 • (10/31/95) • **83**

MICHEL, LOUIS

Chablis 1995: Tart and rather simple, with a slightly woody character. Somewhat green and unripe. Tasted twice with consistent notes. • $NA • (08/31/96) • **78**

Chablis 1994 • $20 • (05/31/96) • **80**

Chablis Grenouilles 1996: Very ripe and opulent, full-bodied, with intense green apple, pear and lime flavors. A bit heavyhanded. Try after 2000. 200 cases made. • $48 • (05/31/98) • **88**

Chablis Grenouilles 1995: Mouthfilling and very rich, this full-bodied white blends power and subtlety into a balanced whole, showing some lovely spice, toasty bread, honey, mineral and wet stone flavors that come together on the silky, long finish. Drink now through 2010. 292 cases made. • $46 • (06/15/97) • **91**

Chablis Grenouilles 1994 • $45 • (05/31/96) • **93**

Chablis Grenouilles 1993 • $42 • (08/31/95) • **86**

Chablis Les Clos 1996: Subtle style, full-bodied, silky as can be, with the ripe fruit balanced by good acidity. Excellent mineral, earth, pear and pie tart complexity. Bursting with intensity, it ends with a bang, delivering a long finish. Bravo! Drink after 2000. 250 cases made. • $46 • (05/31/98) • **94**

Chablis Les Clos 1994 • $45 • (05/31/96) • **74**

Chablis Les Clos 1993 • $40 • (08/31/95) • **83**

Chablis Montmains 1995: A seductive, hedonistic Chablis that pumps out the honey, ripe pear, mineral and lemon flavors, and is full-bodied and unctuous in texture yet elegant, with a fresh, mineral- and vanilla-flavored finish. Drink now through 2005. • $26 • (06/15/97) • **89**

Chablis Montmains 1994 • $24 • (05/31/96) • **86**

Chablis Montmains 1993 • $23 • (08/31/95) • **80**

Chablis Montée de Tonnerre 1996: Crafty winemaking here. Lovely, silky mouthfeel, a concentrated wine with excellent acidity, ripe fruit flavors and some walnut notes on the finish. Voluptuous and full-bodied, it seduces the senses now, but should keep improving through 2005 and perhaps beyond. 800 cases made. • $30 • (05/31/98) • **93**

Chablis Montée de Tonnerre 1995: Racy, yet rich and thick-as-oil, with plenty of well-defined flavors including spice, honey, ripe pear, apple tart, piecrust and mineral notes. Long, chewy finish. Tempting now through 2005. 2,500 cases made. • $27 • (06/15/97) • **89**

Chablis Montée de Tonnerre 1994 • $28 • (05/31/96) • **86**

Chablis Montée de Tonnerre 1993 • $23 • (08/31/95) • **81**

Chablis Vaillons 1996: Both samples provided were corky. 400 cases made. • $29 • (05/31/98) • **55**

Chablis Vaillons 1995: A thick, ripe *premier cru*, full-bodied and supple, with sweet-tasting fruit character plus spice, peanut butter and toasty bread notes. Elegant, flinty finish. Try now through 2005. • $26 • (06/15/97) • **87**

Chablis Vaillons 1994 • $24 • (05/31/96) • **93**

Chablis Vaudésir 1996: Intense but in a crisp style, showing an earth, salt, iodine and mineral character and a slighty herbal, drying finish. Medium-bodied. Drink now. 400 cases made. • $45 • (05/31/98) • **84**

Chablis Vaudésir 1995: Impressively full-bodied and balanced, with flavors of pear tart, melon and tropical fruits, and some lemon, mineral and spice notes. Tempting now, better after 1999. • $44 • (06/15/97) • **89**

Chablis Vaudésir 1994 • $42 • (05/31/96) • **90**

Chablis Vaudésir 1993 • $40 • (08/31/95) • **82**

MICHEL, ROBERT

Cornas Cuvée des Coteaux 1991 • $16 • (05/31/94) • **89**

Cornas La Geynale 1991 • $20 • (05/31/94) • **82**

MICHELE, ROBERT

Muscadet de Sèvre et Maine Les Trois Fils 1995: Simple and soft. The apple flavor is fresh, but one-dimensional, and the finish is a bit cloying. 3,500 cases made. • $7 • (06/15/97) • **78**

Muscadet de Sèvre et Maine Les Trois Fils 1994 • $7 • (05/15/96) • **77**

Muscadet de Sèvre et Maine Les Trois Fils 1993 • $NA • (10/31/94) • **84**

Vouvray Les Trois Fils 1995: Appealing and well balanced, with light peach and citrus flavors, slight sweetness and crisp acidity, all in harmony. 4,000 cases made. • $9 • (06/15/97) • **84**

Vouvray Les Trois Fils 1993 • $7 • (11/15/95) • **82**

MICHEL FRÈRES

Brut Blanc de Blancs Crémant de Bourgogne 1992: Forward, fruity, slightly sweet bubbly with good balance and fruity, earthy flavors. Drink now. • $15 • (12/31/97) • **83**

MICHELOT, ALAIN

Nuits-St.-Georges 1988 • $39 • (07/15/91) • **91**
Nuits-St.-Georges 1982 • $17 • (05/01/84) • **86**
Nuits-St.-Georges Aux Chaignots 1988 • $56 • (05/15/91) • **90**
Nuits-St.-Georges Aux Champs Perdrix 1986 • $30 • (12/15/89) • **81**
Nuits-St.-Georges La Richemone 1988 • $54 • (05/15/91) • **89**
Nuits-St.-Georges Les Cailles 1988 • $54 • (05/15/91) • **83**
Nuits-St.-Georges Les Cailles 1982 • $19 • (07/16/85) • **90**
Nuits-St.-Georges Les Vaucrains 1988 • $56 • (05/15/91) • **87**
Nuits-St.-Georges Les Vaucrains 1986 • $30 • (12/15/89) • **88**
Nuits-St.-Georges Porrets St.-Georges 1988 • $56 • (05/15/91) • **83**

MICHELOT, C.

Meursault Les Charmes 1993: A bit too woody for us, but some decent fruit and crisp acidity underneath it all. • $NA • (05/15/95) • **78**
Meursault Les Grands Charrons 1992: Seductive and as smooth-textured as a Chardonnay gets, with exotic tangerine, mineral and pear flavors backed by well-integrated acidity. Great length. Drinkable now. • $NA • (08/31/94) • **90**
Puligny-Montrachet 1993: Odd wine, revealing some strange, volatile, paint thinner flavors that seem unappealing. Very woody. • $NA • (05/15/95) • **70**

MICHELOT, G.

Meursault 1994: Attractive from start to finish, with seductive lemon, piecrust, toasty bread and ripe pear flavors. It's full-bodied yet also manages to be elegant and refreshing. Long finish. Amazing quality for a simple village wine. • $NA • (05/31/96) • **90**
Meursault 1993: Showy and toasty, smooth, sporting a lively edge and lean frame. Somewhat short; could use more fruit concentration. Drinkable now. • $NA • (05/15/95) • **83**
Meursault Clos du Cromin 1993: Honey, nut, pear and earth character, medium body, substantial crispness and a long, fresh finish. Try now. • $NA • (05/15/95) • **86**
Meursault Le Cromin 1992: Gorgeous, jumping with complexity and beautiful aromas; rich and elegant, with fig, vanilla, pear and honey notes, each flavor more distinctive than the last. Delicious now. • $38 • (08/31/94) • **91**
Meursault Les Grands Charrons 1993: Delicious honey, nut and floral aromas and good taste, but this is still quite austere; grassy, herbal finish. Drinkable now. • $NA • (05/15/95) • **84**

MICHELOT, DOMAINE

Bourgogne White 1995: Straightforward, with some odd aromas of glue and earth. Full-bodied, the structure lacks a bit of elegance, the finish is slightly heavy. Try now. • $18 • (08/31/97) • **76**
Meursault Clos St.-Félix 1995: A distinctive Meursault, with some wood, citrus and grape character. A cardboard note sticks out after the wine has been opened awhile; drink now. • $35 • (05/31/97) • **79**
Meursault Clos St.-Félix 1994: Elegant and subtle, with some mineral, pear and tropical flavors. It's pleasant to drink now, but seems a touch short on the finish. • $35 • (05/31/96) • **83**
Meursault Clos du Cromin 1994: A well-crafted, supple Burgundy, showing a seductive core of toasty oak, pineapple, coconut and spice flavors. The silky texture carries through on the finish. Drinkable now. • $38 • (05/31/96) • **85**
Meursault Genevrières 1995: A distinctive wine, with dried herb and wet earth accents. Odd, but quite intense. Medium-bodied, and a bit hot, as well as rustic, on the finish. Try now through 2000. • $65 • (05/31/97) • **78**
Meursault Genevrières 1994: An oaky style of Burgundy with lots of toasty bread, apple and pear flavors. Quite thick and fat, but the cedar notes dominate. Where is the fruit? • $55 • (05/31/96) • **78**
Meursault Le Limozin 1995: A fruit-driven white Burgundy, slightly rough around the edges, but it has plenty of life, with a lime and fresh herb quality that complements and refreshes the creamy vanilla character. Try now. • $40 • (05/31/97) • **87**
Meursault Le Porusot 1994: A full-bodied wine in a forward, opulent style, offering pleasing doses of honey, fig, and almond. The finish is supple and very round but a touch short. • $40 • (05/31/96) • **83**
Meursault Les Charmes 1995: Very odd, gluelike aromas and flavors distract from the pear, honey and floral notes. Full-bodied, it's bitter on the finish. A disappointing *premier cru* from this grower. • $65 • (05/31/97) • **70**
Meursault Les Charmes 1994: Smooth and supple, a light- to medium-bodied '94 that's ready to drink, with pleasant pear, spice, vanilla, honey and toasty hazelnut flavors. • $50 • (05/31/96) • **85**
Meursault Les Grands Charrons 1995: A bit overdone with oak; bitter chocolate, spice and new wood character dominate the fruit. Tightly built, quite firm, you can guess at some honey and ripe fruit underneath the sawdust flavors. Drinkable now. • $40 • (05/31/97) • **83**
Meursault Les Grands Charrons 1994: Round, supple and toasty. An attractive Chardonnay that shows some apple and spice flavors and a smooth finish. Lacks complexity, though. • $38 • (05/31/96) • **81**
Meursault Les Narvaux 1995: A racy wine, exhibiting distinctive flavors of dried herbs, wet earth and minerals—and a lot of toasty oak. A burning, slightly hot finish detracts. Try now through 2000. • $45 • (05/31/97) • **87**
Meursault Les Narvaux 1994: As smooth as cream, this full-bodied Burgundy caresses the palate with its lush character. Overflowing with flavors—honey, vanilla, spice, toasty pine nuts and piecrust—it shows staying power on the long, balanced finish. Drinkable now. • $40 • (05/31/96) • **87**
Meursault Les Perrières 1995: Full-bodied, silky in texture, racy and vibrant, with plenty of lime, toasty oak, mineral and spice flavors. Short of outstanding because the long, smoky finish turns quite hot, with a bitter aftertaste. Drink upon release. • $75 • (05/31/97) • **88**
Meursault Les Perrières 1994: Supple and creamy, with ripe pear, mineral and loads of honey flavors. A full-bodied, showy Chardonnay, with notes of toasty bread on the finish. Drinkable now. • $60 • (05/31/96) • **85**
Meursault Les Tillets 1995: A tough wine, with some herb, honey and mineral notes. Quite intense. A bit alcoholic and hot on the finish. • $45 • (05/31/97) • **82**
Meursault Sous la Velle 1995: Hard and a bit closed, this full-bodied wine shows mostly oak now, but you can also taste some honey, spice, mocha, piecrust and pear flavors. Burns a bit on the slightly hot finish. • $33 • (05/31/97) • **85**
Meursault Sous la Velle 1994: Supple and elegant, a round, silky Burgundy with tons of toasty bread and coconut flavors along with some pear and apple notes. Could use a bit more fruit concentration. Still, very seductive and pleasant now. • $30 • (05/31/96) • **85**
Puligny-Montrachet 1995: Slightly hard now, but full-bodied and concentrated, showing a rather firm character and some crisp green apple and citrus flavors. Drink with seafood. • $NA • (08/31/97) • **82**
Puligny-Montrachet La Garenne 1995: Very fruity, with a core of lively citrus, dried herb and honey notes. A bit herbal on the finish, but this fresh, medium-bodied *premier cru* should be great around 2000, if not a bit earlier. • $50 • (05/31/97) • **86**

MICHELOT, JEAN

Pommard 1987 • $33 • (08/31/90) • **78**
Pommard 1985 • $29 • (04/30/88) • **87**
Pommard 1983 • $21 • (06/16/86) • **78**

MICHELOT-BUISSON

Meursault Clos St.-Felix 1993: Well-defined mineral, spice and honey aromas and flavors, medium body, firm acidity and a long, fresh, fruity finish. • $NA • (05/15/95) • **87**
Meursault Les Charmes 1992: Bold with lots of personality; the winemaker is stretching here, putting the pedal to the floor. Chewy and flavorful, it tastes somewhat tough, youthful and even a bit coarse now, but it turns supple and gracious after a while in the glass, revealing a tight core of vanilla, cedar, pear and earth flavors. Drinkable now. • $57 • (08/31/94) • **91**
Meursault Les Narvaux 1993: Interesting use of wood here; loads of green apple character. Medium body and a slightly dull, tart finish. • $NA • (05/15/95) • **80**
Meursault Les Perrières 1993: Fine, delicate cream, apple and pear aromas and flavors, medium body and smooth texture. Crisp finish. Drinkable now. • $NA • (05/15/95) • **84**

MILHAU-LACUGUE, CHÂTEAU

St.-Chinian 1990 • $8 • (03/15/94) • **83**

MILLEGRAND, CHÂTEAU

Minervois 1988 • $5 • (04/30/90) • **77**

MILLET-DOUCET, DOMAINE

Sancerre 1996: A crisp white with herbal, mineral and slightly earthy flavors over tart, citrusy acidity. Assertive but a bit harsh; perhaps food will soften its edges. Drink now. 300 cases made. • $19 • (06/15/98) • **84**

MILLOT, JEAN-MARC

Echézeaux 1993: Clean and fresh, offering very good intensity of berry, cherry and cedar character. Medium body, fine tannins, medium finish. Drinkable now. • $NA • (05/15/96) • **86**

MINET, RÉGIS

Pouilly-Fumé Vieilles Vignes 1996: Expressive lime and mineral flavors give this crisp white a lively character, and while it remains elegant on the palate, it has good concentration. Nice with food. Drink now through 2000. • $18 • (05/31/98) • **88**

Pouilly-Fumé Vieilles Vignes 1995: There's good intensity in this bold white, with its ripe fruit flavors, firm acidity, melon, almond and smoke notes that linger on the finish. A good match with food. Should improve in the bottle. Drink now through 2000. • $15 • (05/31/97) • **89**

Pouilly-Fumé Vieilles Vignes 1993 • $14 • (12/15/95) • **84**

MIOLANE, CHRISTIAN

Beaujolais-Villages Cuvée des Chasseurs 1995: Cinnamon and nutmeg aromas give way to soft, black cherry flavors. Round and ripe, with just enough tannin for food. • $12 • (09/15/97) • **84**

MIQUEL, CHÂTEAU

St.-Chinian 1994: Lovely violet, cherry and lavender aromas and flavors greet the senses. Rich and fleshy, there's tannin underneath, but it all comes together well. Drinkable now. • $7 • (07/31/96) • **85**

MIQUEL, DOMAINE

Syrah Vin de Pays d'Oc 1995: Ripe, rich and full of dark plum, berry and jammy flavors. This is a young, firm Syrah with plenty of power and some finesse as well. Finishes with good jolt of chocolaty flavor. • $12 • (10/31/97) • **87**

MIREFLEURS, CHÂTEAU

Bordeaux Supérieur 1995: Goes for an assertive style, full-bodied, firmly tannic and with hints of spicy oak, and has just enough cherry and berry flavor to fill out the frame. 20,000 cases made. • $8 • (01/31/98) • **85**

MISSEREY, P.

Nuits-St.-Georges Les Vaucrains 1988 • $35 • (08/31/92) • **83**

MISSION-HAUT-BRION, CHÂTEAU LA

Pessac-Léognan 1997: Very fine for La Mission—slightly too fine. Medium-bodied, with a very good tannin structure and lots of berry and wet earth character. Needs a richer center palate to be outstanding. • $NA • (06/15/98) (BT) • **85-89**

Key: SS—Spectator Selection CS—Cellar Selection HR—Highly Recommended BB—Best Buy $NA—Price not available Ⓐ—Auction Price (BT)—Barrel Tasting

Dates in parentheses indicate the issues in which the ratings were published.

Pessac-Léognan 1996: Harmonious, with tobacco, chocolate and berry character. Medium to full in body, with integrated tannins and a medium finish. Could move up next year. • $115 • (06/15/98) (BT) • **85-89**

Pessac-Léognan 1995: Textbook red from this appellation, with plum, blackberry and hints of fresh mushrooms. Full-bodied, with lovely smoke, berry and cherry flavors. Very velvety. Best after 2001. • $130 • (01/31/98) • **93**

Pessac-Léognan 1993: Superbly elegant, supple and lush, featuring mineral, mint, cassis, dried herb, cedar and plum complexity, soft tannins and a seductive finish. Drinkable now. • $45 Ⓐ • (01/31/96) • **89**

Pessac-Léognan 1992: Slightly disappointing, yet good nonetheless. Focused core of dried cherry and berry character; medium-bodied and fruity, demonstrating silky texture. Drinkable now. • $44 • (04/15/95) • **84**

Pessac-Léognan 1991: Fine, firm, and elegant wine with tobacco, red berry aromas and flavors, medium body and tannins, long finish. • $45 • (03/31/94) • **85**

Pessac-Léognan 1990: Excellent winemaking is evident here. A big wine with wonderful wet stone, berry and leafy aromas and flavors and ultrafine tannins. Drinkable now. 7,000 cases made. • $63 Ⓐ • (03/31/93) • **95**

Pessac-Léognan 1989 • $237 Ⓐ • (03/15/92) • **96**
Pessac-Léognan 1988 • $68 Ⓐ • (11/15/91) • **90**
Pessac-Léognan 1987 • $51 Ⓐ • (11/15/91) • **84**
Pessac-Léognan 1986 • $85 Ⓐ • (11/15/91) • **97**
Graves 1985 • $111 Ⓐ • (10/15/94) • **90**
Graves 1984 • $55 • (11/15/91) • **85**
Graves 1983 • $83 Ⓐ • (10/15/94) • **93**
Graves 1982 • $191 Ⓐ • (08/31/92) • **97**
Graves 1981 • $78 Ⓐ • (11/15/91) • **87**
Graves 1980 • $36 Ⓐ • (11/15/91) • **86**
Graves 1979 • $91 Ⓐ • (11/15/91) • **86**
Graves 1978 • $162 Ⓐ • (11/15/91) • **94**
Graves 1975 • $395 Ⓐ • (11/15/91) • **90**
Graves 1974 • $53 Ⓐ • (11/15/91) • **87**
Graves 1973 • $40 Ⓐ • (11/15/91) • **80**
Graves 1972 • $50 • (11/15/91) • **77**
Graves 1971 • $87 Ⓐ • (11/15/91) • **91**
Graves 1970 • $155 Ⓐ • (11/15/91) • **83**
Graves 1969 • $28 Ⓐ • (11/15/91) • **84**
Graves 1968 • $60 • (11/15/91) • **67**
Graves 1967 • $35 Ⓐ • (11/15/91) • **89**
Graves 1966 • $217 Ⓐ • (11/15/91) • **93**
Graves 1965 • $92 Ⓐ • (11/15/91) • **76**
Graves 1964 • $242 Ⓐ • (11/15/91) • **91**
Graves 1963 • $100 • (11/15/91) • **78**
Graves 1962 • $132 Ⓐ • (11/15/91) • **90**
Graves 1961 • $722 Ⓐ • (04/30/96) • **96**
Graves 1960 • $140 • (11/15/91) • **84**
Graves 1959 • $780 Ⓐ • (11/15/91) • **94**
Graves 1958 • $180 • (11/15/91) • **83**
Graves 1957 • $165 • (11/15/91) • **85**
Graves 1956 • $210 • (11/15/91) • **87**
Graves 1955 • $616 Ⓐ • (11/15/91) • **89**
Graves 1954 • $375 • (11/15/91) • **86**
Graves 1953 • $256 Ⓐ • (11/15/91) • **93**
Graves 1952 • $310 • (11/15/91) • **98**
Graves 1950 • $350 • (11/15/91) • **79**
Graves 1949 • $882 Ⓐ • (11/15/91) • **95**
Graves 1948 • $600 • (11/15/91) • **98**

Graves 1947: Still firm and chewy, with a solid core of slightly raisiny cassis flavors, and finishing dark, with hints of caramel. • $1414 Ⓐ • (05/31/97) • **90**

Graves 1946 • $700 • (11/15/91) • **85**
Graves 1945 • $767 Ⓐ • (11/30/95) • **96**
Graves 1944 • $350 • (11/15/91) • **78**
Graves 1943 • $450 • (11/15/91) • **88**
Graves 1942 • $275 • (11/15/91) • **83**
Graves 1941 • $250 • (11/15/91) • **81**
Graves 1940 • $330 • (11/15/91) • **82**
Graves 1939 • $126 Ⓐ • (11/15/91) • **87**
Graves 1938 • $253 Ⓐ • (11/15/91) • **81**
Graves 1937 • $200 • (11/15/91) • **88**
Graves 1936 • $200 • (11/15/91) • **62**
Graves 1935 • $575 • (11/15/91) • **85**
Graves 1934 • $173 Ⓐ • (11/15/91) • **86**
Graves 1933 • $475 • (11/15/91) • **74**
Graves 1931 • $375 • (11/15/91) • **70**
Graves 1928 • $407 Ⓐ • (11/15/91) • **84**

Graves 1926 • $375 • (11/15/91) • **59**
Graves 1924 • $550 • (11/15/91) • **89**
Graves 1921 • $437 Ⓐ • (11/15/91) • **85**
Graves 1919 • $600 • (11/15/91) • **85**
Graves 1918 • $322 Ⓐ • (11/15/91) • **83**
Graves 1916 • $350 • (11/15/91) • **82**
Graves 1914 • $500 • (11/15/91) • **65**
Graves 1904 • $600 • (11/15/91) • **85**
Graves 1899 • $850 • (11/15/91) • **92**
Graves 1895 • $700 • (11/15/91) • **99**
Graves 1888 • $NA • (11/15/91) • **95**
Graves 1877 • $NA • (11/15/91) • **93**

MISTRAL, CAVE DU

Sauvignon Blanc Vin de Pays de l'Herault Gallerie 1996: A good, fairly well-structured white with nice flavors of pear, honey and spice. Finishes on a citrus note. Drink now. 6,000 cases made. • $8 • (03/31/98) • **83**
Viognier Vin de Pays de l'Herault Gallerie 1996: A simple white, with basic citrus flavors and a slight floral quality. 4,800 cases made. • $10 • (12/15/97) • **79**

MOC ET BARIL

Cabernet d'Anjou 1994 • $7 • (09/30/95) • **76**
Cabernet d'Anjou Rosé 1992 • $7 • (10/31/94) • **78**

MOCERI

Cabernet Sauvignon Vin de Pays de l'Aude 1987 • $4 • (06/30/90) BB • **77**
Merlot Vin de Pays de l'Aude 1987 • $4 • (06/30/90) BB • **78**

MOËT & CHANDON

Brut Champagne Cuvée Dom Pérignon 1990: Toasty, earthy aromas and an expanding mousse make this an unusually assertive Champagne. Creamy in texture, ripe and fruity in flavor, it's distinctive but not for everyone. Best now. Tasted twice, with consistent notes. • $110 • (11/30/97) • **89**
Brut Champagne Cuvée Dom Pérignon 1988: Beautiful. Offers great toasty, earthy aromas, lively but mellow fruit flavors and a lingering finish. Seems suave and sophisticated, even better than when reviewed earlier. Tempting to drink now, but should improve through 2000. • $89 • (12/31/96) • **93**
Brut Champagne Cuvée Dom Pérignon 1985: Excellent finesse in this wine that is still fresh with lime and citrus, but it also hints at lovely hazelnut, nutmeg and coffee bean notes. A very long orange-peel-scented finish. A touch lighter than the '82. Drinkable now. • $110 • (10/31/95) • **90**
Brut Champagne Cuvée Dom Pérignon 1983: Has oodles of Champagne complexity in a creamy, smooth package. Rich, toasty, creamy and elegant, with delicious nutty flavors that linger on the finish. Enormously concentrated; shows the full benefit of long-term aging on the yeast. • $79 Ⓐ • (05/15/92) • **95**
Brut Champagne Cuvée Dom Pérignon 1982: Seductive and wonderfully balanced, crisp yet it caresses the palate. Has a very complex toasty bread and buttery croissant character along with some nutmeg, spice, chocolate and vanilla notes. At its peak, so drink and enjoy. • $150 • (10/31/95) • **93**
Brut Champagne Cuvée Dom Pérignon 1980 • $135 • (10/31/95) • **88**
Brut Champagne Cuvée Dom Pérignon 1978 • $190 • (10/31/95) • **90**
Brut Champagne Cuvée Dom Pérignon 1976 • $150 • (10/31/95) • **87**
Brut Champagne Cuvée Dom Pérignon 1973 • $175 • (10/31/95) • **90**
Brut Champagne Cuvée Dom Pérignon 1969 • $225 • (10/31/95) • **89**
Brut Champagne Cuvée Dom Pérignon 1966 • $250 • (10/31/95) • **85**
Brut Champagne Cuvée Dom Pérignon 1962 • $200 • (10/31/95) • **79**
Brut Champagne Cuvée Dom Pérignon 1959 • $300 • (10/31/95) • **84**
Brut Champagne Impérial 1992: An attractive earthy-toasty flavor gives personality to this rather light, dry and crisp bubbly. Drink now. • $48 • (12/31/97) • **85**
Brut Champagne Impérial 1990: Really alive and kicking, with fresh, lively citrus and honey flavors, crisp acidity and good depth. A mouthful of refreshing flavor now, and should improve through at least 2000. Better than when reviewed in 1995. • $40 • (12/31/96) • **91**
Brut Champagne Impérial 1988: So slick and clean. The best standard vintage Moet we have had in years. A solid wine. This wine perfectly marries the ripe fruit and toasty character. Full-bodied and refined with a long silky texture. A perfect Champagne for drinking now but will age for years to come. • $35 • (12/31/93) SS • **91**
Brut Champagne Impérial 1986 • $40 • (03/31/92) • **77**
Brut Champagne Impérial 1985 • $57 • (12/31/90) • **87**
Brut Champagne Impérial 1983 • $42 • (12/31/89) • **69**
Brut Champagne Impérial 1982 • $52 • (04/15/88) • **84**
Brut Champagne Impérial 1980 • $58 • (03/16/85) • **91**
Brut Champagne Impérial NV: Crisp apple and grapefruit flavors make this bright and lively, but it's fairly simple in structure and appeal. Tasted three times, with consistent notes. • $40 • (12/31/97) • **82**
Brut Rosé Champagne Cuvée Dom Pérignon 1986: A wonderfully flavorful, well-balanced and harmonious Champagne with intriguing toasty aromas, firm fruit flavors and a crisp but lingering finish. Drink now. • $190 • (11/30/97) • **91**
Brut Rosé Champagne Cuvée Dom Pérignon 1985: This rosé shows elements of fine, matured still wines with its spicy, smoky, even gamy flavors, yet wraps them in a soft, full mousse that gives structure and firmness. Elegant yet subtle, it's a wine for meditation. This is significantly better than an earlier sample. • $150 • (04/30/97) • **89**
Brut Rosé Champagne Cuvée Dom Pérignon 1982: A beautifully mature, mellow Champagne that has lots to offer the serious connoisseur. Almost Burgundian in flavor, with mushroom, spice and almond accents to the core of honey and cherry. The flavors linger and blend on the finish. • $130 • (12/31/94) • **92**
Brut Rosé Champagne Cuvée Dom Pérignon 1978 • $89 • (10/15/86) • **90**
Brut Rosé Champagne Cuvée Dom Pérignon 1975 • $85 • (12/16/85) • **93**
Brut Rosé Champagne Impérial 1992: This generous, mature-tasting rosé is salmon in color, easy in texture and has tart cherry and mushroom flavors. Could substitute for a red Burgundy at dinner. Drink now. • $55 • (11/30/97) • **88**
Brut Rosé Champagne Impérial 1990: The copper color, nutty aromas and vanilla and earthy flavors suggest an older wine. Not much fruit or depth here. • $47 • (12/15/95) • **82**
Brut Rosé Champagne Impérial 1988: Pale salmon in color and soft and fleshy in texture, with smoke and spicy cherry flavors that turn mature on the finish. Balanced and easy to drink for those who like dry, mature rosés. Drink now. Tasted twice. • $34 • (06/15/93) • **85**
Brut Rosé Champagne Impérial 1986: Tart and clean, with a cherry edge to the crisp flavors. Dry and a bit rough in texture, but charming and agreeable. Drinkable now. • $43 • (03/31/92) • **83**
Brut Rosé Champagne Impérial 1983 • $40 • (12/31/89) • **88**
Brut Rosé Champagne Impérial 1982 • $36 • (04/15/88) • **90**
Brut Rosé Champagne Impérial 1978 • $55 • (12/16/85) • **70**
Brut Rosé Champagne Impérial NV: With a beautifully deep coral color and bold Pinot Noir flavors, this could easily substitute for red dinner wine. A generous rosé with a lingering finish. • $40 • (11/30/97) • **89**
Demi-Sec Champagne Nectar Impérial NV: Sweet, soft and honey-flavored, this is an easy-to-drink, dessert-style Champagne. • $38 • (12/31/97) • **84**

MOILLARD

Aloxe-Corton Les Affouages 1989 • $NA • (01/31/92) • **83**
Bâtard-Montrachet 1994: Deliciously rich and concentrated, intensely spicy, boasting loads of clove and nutmeg notes supported by ripe apple and pear flavors. It has a lingering finish of vanilla and butterscotch. 118 cases made. • $85 • (05/31/96) • **90**
Beaujolais-Villages Domaine de Reyssiers 1995: Quite austere for Beaujolais, with black cherry flavors and gripping tannins. Lacks the exuberance typical of Gamay. • $12 • (09/15/97) • **74**
Beaune 1990: Ripe and firm, showing plum and red berry flavors and a good backbone, but lacking a bit of flesh despite the mouth-coating tannins that strike on the finish. Drinkable now. 1,100 cases made. • $26 • (12/15/92) • **87**
Beaune Hospices de Beaune Cuvée Clos des Avaux 1988 • $80 • (08/31/91) • **88**
Beaune Les Grèves Domaine Thomas-Moillard 1990: Impressive concentration and length make this a wine that stays with you for a long time. Tastes like freshly sliced plums, with intense flavors, firm tannins and a very long finish. Drinkable now. 400 cases made. • $40 • (12/15/92) • **91**
Beaune Les Grèves Domaine Thomas-Moillard 1989 • $28 • (01/31/92) • **89**
Beaune Les Grèves Domaine Thomas-Moillard 1986 • $14 • (12/31/88) • **80**
Beaune Les Grèves Domaine Thomas-Moillard 1985 • $25 • (03/15/87) • **89**
Beaune Les Grèves Domaine Thomas-Moillard 1984 • $12 • (02/15/87) • **87**
Bonnes Mares Domaine Thomas-Moillard 1986 • $45 • (11/15/88) • **86**
Bonnes Mares Domaine Thomas-Moillard 1984 • $35 • (05/31/87) • **92**
Bourgogne Hautes-Côtes de Beaune Les Alouettes 1990: Very light and simple, with pleasant earth and cherry flavors and light tannins on the rather short finish. Drinkable now. 450 cases made. • $16 • (12/15/92) • **79**

FRANCE

Bourgogne Hautes-Côtes de Beaune Les Alouettes 1989 • $17 • (01/31/92) • **83**

Bourgogne Hautes-Côtes de Beaune Les Alouettes 1988 • $15 • (07/15/91) • **83**

Bourgogne Hautes-Côtes de Beaune Les Alouettes White 1994: Crisp, featuring some nice honey and spice flavors, good richness and a straightforward finish. 3,000 cases made. • $15 • (05/31/96) • **82**

Bourgogne Hautes-Côtes de Nuits Les Hameaux 1986 • $11 • (12/31/88) • **81**

Bourgogne Hautes-Côtes de Nuits Les Vignes Hautes 1989 • $NA • (01/31/92) • **84**

Bourgogne Passe-tout-grains Notre Dame des Ceps 1990: Light and simple, with modest cherry and tobacco aromas and flavors, hinting at stemminess on the finish. • $9 • (08/31/91) • **75**

Chablis Communaux d'Aronce 1994 • $22 • (05/31/96) • **85**

Chambertin 1984 • $42 • (05/31/87) • **76**

Chambertin Clos de Bèze 1984 • $42 • (05/31/87) • **80**

Chambertin Clos de Bèze 1983 • $60 • (09/16/85) CS • **93**

Chambolle-Musigny 1984 • $15 • (11/30/86) • **89**

Chardonnay Bourgogne Hautes-Côtes de Nuits 1994: Modest depth and decent acidity, offering good grapefruit and gooseberry flavors. It has a nice touch of spice on the finish. 2,530 cases made. • $14 • (05/31/96) • **81**

Chardonnay Bourgogne Tradition 1994: Simple, smelling and tasting of apple juice, adding a slightly bitter finish. 3,800 cases made. • $12 • (05/31/96) • **78**

Chardonnay Vin de Pays d'Oc Pavillon St. James 1995: An international-style Chardonnay with lots of spice and ripe pear flavors. Has a nice smoky edge and plenty of butter and spice notes on the finish. 8,600 cases made. • $8 • (08/31/97) • **84**

Charmes-Chambertin 1990: Ripe and chewy, with an earthy streak running through the plum and berry flavors, which echo on the finish. Drinkable now. • $35 • (12/31/93) • **84**

Charmes-Chambertin 1985 • $55 • (05/31/88) • **94**

Chassagne-Montrachet Morgeot Red 1985 • $15 • (05/31/87) • **84**

Chénas Les Mélardières 1995: Herbal, woodsy flavors dominate the fruit in this tannic but slightly lean red. May soften with food. 250 cases made. • $14 • (09/15/97) • **80**

Chiroubles Domaine Plaforet 1994: Bottle age has added a pleasant spicy note to this light, silky red. Berry and cherry flavors are still fresh, however, and the wine slips down nicely. Drink now. 1,100 cases made. • $15 • (09/15/97) • **84**

Clos de Vougeot 1984 • $32 • (05/31/87) • **90**

Clos de Vougeot 1983 • $45 • (10/16/85) CS • **95**

Corton-Charlemagne 1994: Extremely buttery-tasting, sporting very good acidity and concentration. It has tropical notes of banana and melon and a spicy finish. Falls slightly short, but still packs plenty of flavor. 194 cases made. • $60 • (05/31/96) • **87**

Corton Clos des Vergennes 1990: Supple and rich, with round, ripe red berry, chocolate and earth characteristics. Drinkable now. 500 cases made. • $53 • (12/15/92) • **89**

Corton Clos des Vergennes 1989 • $40 • (01/31/92) • **89**

Corton Clos des Vergennes 1985 • $36 • (05/31/87) • **92**

Corton Clos des Vergennes 1983 • $19 • (10/01/85) • **88**

Corton Le Clos du Roi Domaine Thomas-Moillard 1989 • $41 • (01/31/92) • **85**

Corton Le Clos du Roi Domaine Thomas-Moillard 1984 • $24 • (05/31/87) • **87**

Côte de Beaune-Villages 1995: Modest cherry and strawberry flavors and hints of rhubarb and tomato carry through to the tannic finish. Drinkable now with food. 9,200 cases made. • $15 • (11/15/97) • **81**

Côte de Beaune-Villages 1994: Disappointing, with a light body, modest flavors and a slightly astringent finish. 6,300 cases made. • $20 • (11/15/96) • **72**

Côte de Brouilly Château de la Perrière 1994: Tough and rustic, with an aggressive, earthy character, firm tannins. Shows character, but not the friendliness typical of Beaujolais. 1,350 cases made. • $15 • (06/30/97) • **78**

Côte de Nuits-Villages 1994: A bit green and somewhat diluted. Lacks character. 4,050 cases made. • $21 • (11/15/96) • **73**

Key: SS—Spectator Selection CS—Cellar Selection HR—Highly Recommended BB—Best Buy $NA—Price not available Ⓐ—Auction Price (BT)—Barrel Tasting
Dates in parentheses indicate the issues in which the ratings were published.

Côtes du Rhône Les Violettes 1996: Fresh and fruity, this shows some of the grapey softness of Beaujolais, with the herbal and brambly notes of southern France. Generous, and easy to drink. 20,000 cases made. • $9 • (09/15/97) • **83**

Côtes du Rhône Les Violettes 1995: Flavors of plum, black cherry and chocolate are fresh and focused in this round red. It's soft on the palate, yet has a firm tannic core. Drinkable now. 8,000 cases made. • $7 • (12/15/96) • **83**

Echézeaux 1990: Tough and tannic, a very ripe wine that gets soft in the middle and never quite allows its flavors to open up. Finishes with a bite of prune and smoke. Drinkable now. • $45 • (12/31/93) • **81**

Echézeaux 1985 • $47 • (04/15/88) • **94**

Echézeaux 1984 • $30 • (11/15/86) SS • **96**

Fixin 1989 • $NA • (01/31/92) • **88**

Fixin Clos d'Entre Deux Velles 1989 • $28 • (01/31/92) • **86**

Fixin Clos d'Entre Deux Velles 1985 • $16 • (05/31/87) • **79**

Fixin Clos d'Entre Deux Velles 1984 • $11 • (11/30/86) • **78**

Fixin Clos de la Perrière 1990: A lively wine, with focused fruit flavors, well-integrated tannins and plenty of attractive berry, earth and spice nuances. Drinkable now. 900 cases made. • $30 • (12/15/92) • **85**

Fixin Clos de la Perrière 1986 • $18 • (02/28/89) • **85**

Fixin Clos de la Perrière 1983 • $12 • (10/16/85) • **78**

Fixin Confrérie des Chevaliers du Tastevin 1988 • $19 • (08/31/91) • **84**

Gevrey-Chambertin 1995: Shows wonderfully sweet, concentrated fruit, black cherry, raspberry and a gamy note. It's firm, as you would expect from this commune, yet it has finesse and style. 5,300 cases made. • $26 • (01/31/98) • **88**

Gevrey-Chambertin 1994: Light and diluted, with some brown sugar, licorice and herblike aromas and flavors. 7,600 cases made. • $34 • (11/15/96) • **73**

Gevrey-Chambertin 1990: Pleasant and smooth, with a pretty berry and milk chocolate component. Medium-bodied and rather soft. Try now. 4,125 cases made. • $33 • (12/15/92) • **85**

Gevrey-Chambertin 1987 • $20 • (03/31/90) • **66**

Grands Echézeaux 1984 • $39 • (05/31/87) • **90**

Hautes Côtes de Beaune Les Alouettes 1994: Green, stalky aromas never become charming. 17,700 cases made. • $17 • (11/15/96) • **77**

Hautes Côtes de Nuits 1983 • $6 • (11/01/85) • **76**

Ladoix Côte de Beaune 1989 • $NA • (01/31/92) • **85**

Maranges Les Clos Roussots 1994: Lean and chewy, with a lively core of anise-scented berry flavor that persists through the focused finish. 1,950 cases made. • $23 • (11/15/96) • **84**

Meursault 1994: Powerful, tightly wound, featuring exotic flavors of mineral and orange peel, pear and apple. The finish is fairly restrained. 1,500 cases made. • $29 • (05/31/96) • **85**

Meursault Clos du Cromin 1994: An overripe style, as honey and spice notes wrap around a decent core of apple and pear flavors. Finishes on a sharp, cheesy note. 545 cases made. • $28 • (05/31/96) • **82**

Meursault Les Charmes 1994: Rich and aromatic, boasting good length and body. Ripe pear and apple flavors are highlighted by buttery and spicy notes. It has a firm backbone of acidity and the butterscotch lingers on the finish. 52 cases made. • $37 • (05/31/96) • **89**

Moillard Rouge NV • $4 • (05/31/88) BB • **81**

Monthélie 1995: Pretty berry notes and an earthy character combine with an angular profile. Straightforward and appealing, if a bit weak on the finish. Drinkable now. 1,400 cases made. • $20 • (11/15/97) • **79**

Morey-St.-Denis Monts Luisants 1995: A medium-bodied, silky Pinot redolent of cherry, beef bouillion and earth. Lacks intensity midpalate, with some firm tannins at the end. 575 cases made. • $26 • (11/15/97) • **86**

Morey-St.-Denis Monts Luisants 1994: A straightforward, herbal wine that lacks a bit of everything. 580 cases made. • $31 • (11/15/96) • **74**

Morey-St.-Denis Monts Luisants 1991: Lean, austere, almost stemmy in flavor, with just enough spicy, earthy fruit-tinged flavor to make it drinkable. Drink up. 900 cases made. • $30 • (03/15/94) • **76**

Morey-St.-Denis Monts Luisants 1990: Racy and lively, with focused vanilla, tobacco and berry notes that offer plenty of concentration. Has nice intensity on the firm finish. Drink now. 500 cases made. • $33 • (12/15/92) • **90**

Morey-St.-Denis Monts Luisants 1989 • $28 • (01/31/92) • **89**

Morey-St.-Denis Monts Luisants 1988 • $30 • (12/15/90) HR • **91**

Morey-St.-Denis Monts Luisants 1985 • $21 • (05/31/87) • **87**

Morgon Tastevinage 1993: Lean, with the herbal, barnyard flavors of a maturing Pinot Noir, but not much grace or harmony. Drink now. Tasted from half-bottle. • $16 • (09/15/97) • **75**

Moulin-à-Vent Les Joies 1994: Mature aromas of spice and tea give way to ripe black cherry and spice flavors in this firm red. It's a bit chunky, but will show well with food. 1,900 cases made. • $18 • (09/15/97) • **84**

Musigny 1984 • $38 • (05/31/87) • **92**

Nuits-St.-Georges Clos de Thorey Domaine Thomas-Moillard 1990: Rather austere and aggressive in an old style. Harsh and slightly acidic, with drying tannins on the finish. Try now. 2,150 cases made. • $50 • (12/15/92) • **79**

Nuits-St.-Georges Clos de Thorey Domaine Thomas-Moillard 1989 • $35 • (01/31/92) • **89**

Nuits-St.-Georges Clos de Thorey Domaine Thomas-Moillard 1988 • $50 • (12/31/90) • **89**

Nuits-St.-Georges Clos de Thorey Domaine Thomas-Moillard 1987 • $27 • (12/15/89) • **88**

Nuits-St.-Georges Clos de Thorey Domaine Thomas-Moillard 1986 • $28 • (11/15/88) • **78**

Nuits-St.-Georges Clos de Thorey Domaine Thomas-Moillard 1985 • $38 • (05/31/87) • **89**

Nuits-St.-Georges Clos de Thorey Domaine Thomas-Moillard 1984 • $24 • (05/31/87) • **84**

Nuits-St.-Georges Clos de Thorey Domaine Thomas-Moillard 1983 • $19 • (09/16/85) • **84**

Nuits-St.-Georges Hospices de Nuits Cuvée Jacques Duret 1988 • $68 • (08/31/91) • **89**

Pinot Noir Bourgogne 1985 • $7 • (03/31/88) • **78**

Pinot Noir Vin de Pays d'Oc Hugues le Juste 1994 • $9 • (01/01/96) • **77**

Pinot Noir Vin de Pays d'Oc Pavillon St.-James 1994: There's ripe raspberry and cherry flavor and a firm structure that turns astringent, but drink it now while the fruit lasts. 2,400 cases made. • $9 • (07/31/96) • **79**

Pommard Clos des Epeneaux 1985 • $45 • (06/30/88) CS • **92**

Pommard Les Rugiens 1994: Has some density to the color and to the chunky black cherry, gamy and spice flavors, making for a chewy wine. Best now. 250 cases made. • $45 • (11/15/96) • **82**

Pommard Les Rugiens 1990: An attractive and elegant wine that lacks the concentration of many Pommards, yet it's delicious, with raspberry and smoke aromas and flavors. Can be drunk earlier than many from this vintage; drinkable now. 200 cases made. • $50 • (12/15/92) • **86**

Pommard Les Rugiens 1985 • $40 • (06/30/88) • **85**

Pommard Murchaux 1994: This light, but pleasantly supple, wine shows some decent anise and red berry flavors. Drink now. 6,500 cases made. • $38 • (11/15/96) • **79**

Pouilly-Fuissé Domaine Greffet 1994: Well-balanced grapefruit and licorice flavors characterize this fairly rich white that finishes with a touch of honey. 1,720 cases made. • $22 • (05/31/96) • **84**

Puligny-Montrachet 1994: Buttery and full-bodied, offering spicy flavors and aromas. Lots of ripe pear, apple and honey notes lead to a finish of butterscotch and vanilla that is not overpowering. 860 cases made. • $30 • (05/31/96) • **86**

Puligny-Montrachet Les Perrières 1994: Bright pear and apple flavors are framed by some nice, toasty notes. Restrained, but still packs plenty of punch. The crisp finish should prove a good match for a cream sauce. 139 cases made. • $39 • (05/31/96) • **87**

Romanée St.-Vivant 1984 • $42 • (05/31/87) • **87**

Rully Red 1989 • $14 • (08/31/91) • **82**

St.-Joseph 1988 • $15 • (08/31/91) • **85**

St.-Véran Domaine de la Verchère 1994: Stylistically akin to American Chardonnay in its ripe apple and pear flavors. This white has a nice, honeyed quality that runs throughout, but could be richer and more concentrated. 1,910 cases made. • $12 • (05/31/96) • **82**

Santenay 1994: Marked by earthy, dirty flavors that are most unappealing. 2,700 cases made. • $25 • (11/15/96) • **69**

Savigny-lès-Beaune Domaine Thomas-Moillard 1990: Very perfumed, with lovely berry nuances. Almost sweet on the palate, adding a ripe, firm, supple finish. Drinkable now. 450 cases made. • $20 • (12/15/92) • **88**

Syrah Vin de Pays d'Oc Hugues le Juste 1994 • $7 • (05/15/96) • **79**

Syrah Vin de Pays d'Oc Pavillon St.-James 1995: A focused wine with dark cherry and beef-bouillonlike flavors. Closes down on the finish, but still flavorful. 10,000 cases made. • $7 • (10/31/97) • **83**

Vacqueyras 1989 • $9 • (10/15/91) • **77**

Volnay 1994: Firm in texture, with a nice core of black cherry flavor to go against the chewy tannins. Best now. 1,520 cases made. • $29 • (11/15/96) • **81**

Volnay Clos des Chênes 1985 • $32 • (07/15/88) • **89**

Volnay Clos des Chênes 1983 • $15 • (12/01/85) • **75**

Vosne-Romanée Aux Malconsorts Domaine Thomas-Moillard 1989 • $60 • (01/31/92) • **93**

Vosne-Romanée Aux Malconsorts Domaine Thomas-Moillard 1988 • $50 • (03/31/91) • **88**

Vosne-Romanée Aux Malconsorts Domaine Thomas-Moillard 1987 • $30 • (08/31/89) • **91**

Vosne-Romanée Aux Malconsorts Domaine Thomas-Moillard 1986 • $29 • (10/31/88) • **88**

Vosne-Romanée Aux Malconsorts Domaine Thomas-Moillard 1985 • $47 • (07/31/88) • **95**

Vosne-Romanée Aux Malconsorts Domaine Thomas-Moillard 1984 • $28 • (05/31/87) • **80**

MOINGEON

Savigny-lès-Beaune 1992: Light and crisp, a simple red with distinct floral overtones to the light strawberry flavors. • $NA • (12/15/94) • **80**

Vosne-Romanée Les Suchots 1992: A little earthy or gamy around the edges, but the forceful berry flavors finish with some grace. • $NA • (12/15/94) • **80**

Vougeot Les Crâs 1992: Simple and light, with modest currant and cherry flavors. A bit short on the finish. Drinkable now. • $NA • (12/15/94) • **77**

MOMMESSIN

Aloxe-Corton 1995: Black cherries mingle with the flavor of new oak in this well-integrated, classy wine. Smooth and rich, it has a lingering finish with spicy accents. Try in 2000. Very impressive from Mommessin. 733 cases made. • $26 • (11/15/97) • **89**

Aloxe-Corton 1994: Soft and appealing for its modest cherry and lightly herbal flavors, chipping in its slightly bitter tannins at the end. 750 cases made. • $29 • (11/15/96) • **77**

Aloxe-Corton 1991: Firm and austere, with only a modest level of black cherry and floral aromas and flavors. Drinkable now. 200 cases made. • $16 Ⓐ • (01/31/94) • **80**

Aloxe-Corton 1990: Wow! Packed with berry, cherry and earth characteristics and huge tannins; this is solid, firm, concentrated and balanced, with impressive structure. Drinkable now. • $20 • (12/15/92) • **91**

Aloxe-Corton Les Valozières 1989 • $28 • (01/31/92) • **88**

Auxey-Duresses Red 1989 • $13 • (01/31/92) • **82**

Beaujolais-Villages 1996: Exuberant, with assertive black cherry and spice aromas, bright fruit and firm acidity on the palate. Having some concentration, it should be better later this year. 55,000 cases made. • $9 • (08/31/97) • **84**

Beaujolais-Villages 1995: Pretty berry and spice aromas give way to fresh cherry flavors and a meaty texture, with bright acidity and firm tannins. This has punch. Drinkable now. • $9 • (09/15/96) • **84**

Beaujolais-Villages 1994 • $8 • (06/15/95) • **83**

Beaujolais-Villages Château de Montmelas 1996: Lively bright cherry flavors, but notes of chocolate and citrus give a slightly candied character. Tastes made, more than grown. 14,100 cases made. • $8 • (09/15/97) • **79**

Beaujolais-Villages Château du Carra 1994 • $8 • (06/15/95) • **83**

Beaune 1993: Clean and well-defined red berry, floral, plummy character. Solid and perhaps a bit dry on the finish, but the tannins should soften with time. Try now. 683 cases made. • $23 • (11/15/95) • **85**

Beaune 1989 • $18 • (01/31/92) • **90**

Beaune Les Cents Vignes 1995: Appealing aromas of black cherries and spicy oak are followed by a roundness in the mouth, culminating in a firm finish. Drinkable now. 283 cases made. • $26 • (11/15/97) • **86**

Beaune Les Cents Vignes 1994: Light in structure, but appealing for its modest spicy anise-scented black cherry flavors. Finishing with firm tannins. Drinkable now. 325 cases made. • $31 • (11/15/96) • **83**

Beaune Les Cents Vignes 1993: Well-crafted red showing a charming use of new wood, medium body and tannins and ripe fruit. Delicious now. 316 cases made. • $30 • (11/15/95) • **89**

Beaune Les Cents Vignes 1992: Tannins are somewhat coarse but the black cherry flavor tastes ripe. Toasty, aniselike overtones add a nice touch. Drinkable now. 625 cases made. • $26 • (12/15/94) • **83**

Beaune Les Cents Vignes 1990: Wonderfully balanced, refined and smooth, with gorgeous plum and earth aromas and flavors and firm, supple tannins. Drinkable now. • $20 • (12/15/92) • **90**

Beaune Les Cents Vignes 1989 • $23 • (01/31/92) • **86**

Beaune Premier Cru 1995: A tough customer. Lacks fruit for the vintage. Shows an herbal note, an astringent finish. • $21 • (11/15/97) • **80**

Bonnes Mares 1993: Well-defined cherry, vanilla and tobacco flavors and a hint of tea leaf. Medium-bodied, adding velvety tannins and long, sweet fruit finish. Drinkable now. • $80 • (11/15/95) • **89**

Bourgogne 1995: What fruit there is shows a currant and spice character, but this wine is tart and tannic. • $9 • (11/15/97) • **74**

Bourgogne White 1995: Fresh and zesty, with carbon dioxide in the wine that makes it almost bubbly. But it offers lots of nice flavors—quince, pear, apple. A lovely alfresco white Burgundy to drink upon release.750 cases imported. 6,667 cases made. • $12 • (08/31/97) • **85**

Brouilly 1996: Expressive, exhibiting vivid black cherry, coffee and spice flavors, harmonious and balanced, with bright acidity and light, firm tannins. 17,700 cases made. • $11 • (07/31/97) • **86**

Brouilly 1995: A combo of sweet cherry and dried cherry flavors give this light, firm wine a slightly candied character, but vibrant acidity keeps it fresh. Tannins are a bit dry on the finish. • $14 • (09/15/96) • **82**

Brouilly 1994 • $10 • (06/15/95) • **82**

Brouilly Château de Briante 1996: Distinctive. Floral and vanilla aromas add interest to this supple yet lively wine. Shows cherry, berry and spice flavors, with crisp acidity, vivid and subtle at once. 9,500 cases made. • $12 • (07/31/97) • **86**

Brouilly Château de Briante 1995: Shows personality in a rustic style. Light, with an earthy edge to the simple cherry flavors. Drying tannins emerge on the finish. • $14 • (09/15/96) • **81**

Brouilly Château de Briante 1994 • $11 • (06/15/95) • **82**

Cabernet Sauvignon Vin de Pays d'Oc 1993 • $6 • (10/31/95) • **82**

Chablis 1994 • $20 • (05/31/96) • **70**

Chablis Fourchaume 1996: Austere, mineral-like aromas flesh out in the mouth, revealing apple and lemon flavors that are pure, if one-dimensional. • $22 • (10/15/97) • **83**

Chablis Fourchaume 1994 • $24 • (05/31/96) • **82**

Chambolle-Musigny 1992: Supple and accessible, with some modest red berry flavors, but watery and dry on the finish. Try now. 667 cases made. • $32 • (12/15/94) • **77**

Chambolle-Musigny 1990: Pleasant but slightly one-dimensional, with lots of pretty raspberry, plum and earth aromas and flavors. Drinkable now. • $22 • (12/15/92) • **86**

Chambolle-Musigny Premier Cru 1993: Beautiful plum, dried cherry and mineral character, medium-to-full body, silky tannins and fresh, fruity finish. Better in 2000. • $45 • (11/15/95) • **88**

Chardonnay Vin de Pays d'Oc 1994 • $6 • (12/15/95) • **84**

Charmes-Chambertin 1994: Light in body, with straightforward flavors of currant and earth that get tangled-up in the tannins on the finish. Drinkable now. 183 cases made. • $70 • (11/15/96) • **83**

Charmes-Chambertin 1993: Light perhaps for a *grand cru*, but some very firm tannins and mineral, dried cherry character run through and through. Medium-bodied. Try in 1999. • $68 • (11/15/95) • **85**

Charmes-Chambertin 1992: Lean, crisp and chewy, but there's a nice core of raspberry and floral character that persists into the modest finish. Try now. • $NA • (12/15/94) • **82**

Charmes-Chambertin 1990: Overflowing with raspberry, strawberry and other fruit flavors and has all the tannins you expect with such great concentration. Drinkable now. • $45 • (12/15/92) • **96**

Charmes-Chambertin 1985 • $45 • (02/15/88) • **83**

Chassagne-Montrachet 1994: Overdone, and almost over-the-hill. Full-bodied and rich but it also has some off notes that don't bode well for the future. • $NA • (08/31/96) • **71**

Chassagne-Montrachet 1993: Lovely, balanced apple, toasty oak and mineral aromas and flavors. Medium- to full-bodied; fresh acidity and medium finish. 550 cases made. • $24 • (05/15/95) • **85**

Chassagne-Montrachet 1992: A toasty, buttery aroma, backed by crisp, reasonably appley flavors add up to a complete, satisfying white. The flavors linger nicely on the finish, too. 500 cases made. • $26 • (08/31/94) • **84**

Chassagne-Montrachet Morgeot 1994: Very rich, opulent and showy. Loads of fig, date, raisin, spice, mocha and almond flavors. Seems a bit advanced though, so drink it soon. • $NA • (08/31/96) • **80**

Chassagne-Montrachet Morgeot 1993: Elegant apple, coconut and pear aromas and flavors. Medium in body, fine acidity and fresh finish. 250 cases made. • $25 • (05/15/95) • **85**

Châteauneuf-du-Pape 1995: Aromatic, perfumed with cassis, game and chocolate aromas, and full in body, with ripe, soft tannins and plenty of ripe fruit. A bit rustic, it's lively and appealing. Accessible now. • $17 • (10/15/97) • **84**

Key: SS—Spectator Selection CS—Cellar Selection HR—Highly Recommended BB—Best Buy $NA—Price not available Ⓐ—Auction Price (BT)—Barrel Tasting

Dates in parentheses indicate the issues in which the ratings were published.

Châteauneuf-du-Pape 1994: Though this shows admirable structure, it's not giving much fruit flavor yet. It's fresh and well balanced, with solid tannins and a clean finish. Drinkable now. • $19 • (11/15/96) • **88**

Châteauneuf-du-Pape Clos des Brusquières 1994: Straightforward, this firm red offers cherry, licorice and coffee flavors with some rustic tannin underneath a supple texture. 2,000 cases made. • $20 • (11/15/96) • **85**

Châteauneuf-du-Pape Clos des Brusquières 1993: Good, but on the lean side, featuring smoky aromas, tart cherry flavors and a slightly unripe sensation on the finish. Moderately tannic. • $17 • (11/15/95) • **80**

Clos de Tart 1995: A delicious 1995. Notes of violets, blackberries and toasty oak are silky-smooth on the palate. It's quite delicate, yet has enough firm tannins to warrant waiting until 1999. Tasted twice, with consistent notes. 1,800 cases made. • $103 • (11/15/97) • **89**

Clos de Tart 1994: Supple at first, with some currant, spice and toasty oak character up front, this heads into a chewy finish that makes its future development something of a question mark; may be better after 1998. 1,833 cases made. • $99 • (11/15/96) • **82**

Clos de Tart 1993: Distinctively smoky and toasty, sporting lovely, silky texture and nice wood. The finish is a bit diluted and alcoholic. Could use more fruit concentration. Drinkable now. • $86 • (11/15/95) • **84**

Clos de Tart 1992: Lean and spicy, delicate, exhibiting cedar and vanilla grace notes to the basic currant flavor; finishes with a sweet edge. Drinkable now. • $99 • (12/15/94) • **85**

Clos de Tart 1991: Strikingly earthy and spicy on the nose, picking up black cherry and currant on the palate. The tannins give a drying walnut character on the finish. Drinkable now. 700 cases made. • $73 Ⓐ • (01/31/94) • **87**

Clos de Tart 1990: Unique, fascinating and well structured, offering crushed black pepper aromas and flavors that run like a thread through the bright berry and smoke characteristics. A beauty of a wine. Drinkable now. • $96 • (12/15/92) • **95**

Clos de Tart 1989 • $52 • (01/31/92) • **92**

Clos de Tart 1985 • $77 Ⓐ • (02/15/88) • **91**

Clos de Tart 1950 • $125 • (08/31/90) • **78**

Corton 1985 • $28 • (02/15/88) • **91**

Corton-Charlemagne 1992: Dense, round and ripe, with pronounced tropical and honeyed flavors coating your mouth; it gains complexity with lush, sweet fruit and some mineral, apple and citrus notes. Drinks almost like a dry dessert wine. 200 cases made. • $70 • (08/31/94) • **89**

Corton Les Grèves 1989 • $45 • (01/31/92) • **91**

Côte de Beaune-Villages 1985 • $13 • (02/15/88) • **85**

Côte de Nuits-Villages 1985 • $17 • (07/31/88) • **85**

Côtes du Rhône 1994: Light and silky, but rather dull and the light cherry flavors are marred by vegetal notes. 65,000 cases made. • $9 • (10/15/96) • **77**

Côtes du Rhône Château de Domazan 1996: Not up to the quality of some other '96 Côtes du Rhône wines in this category, showing an odd, sweet character and an herbal finish. Lacks balance. • $7 • (10/15/97) • **77**

Côtes du Rhône Château de Domazan 1995: Black cherry flavors are straightforward but rich in this round red. Well-knit tannins and a slightly bitter note on the finish keep it firm enough to drink with food. 19,000 cases made. • $8 • (10/15/96) BB • **84**

Côtes du Rhône Château de Domazan 1993 • $7 • (11/15/95) • **78**

Côtes du Ventoux 1996: Round and slightly rustic, with sweet fruit and herbal flavors. It's soft and generous, but lacks backbone. Drink now. • $7 • (10/15/97) • **79**

Côtes du Ventoux 1994: Round and fleshy. Flavors of black cherry, game and raisin are ripe and soft. It's sweet on the palate, a bit rustic and dry on the finish. 40,000 cases made. • $NA • (10/15/96) • **81**

Côtes du Ventoux 1993 • $6 • (11/15/95) • **84**

Crozes-Hermitage 1994: Fresh and fruity, this supple red offers bright raspberry and light herbal flavors, with soft tannins and a clean, short finish. Enjoy it now. 3,100 cases made. • $13 • (11/30/96) • **83**

Crozes-Hermitage 1992 • $11 • (11/15/95) • **79**

Echézeaux 1979 • $18 • (02/16/86) • **86**

Fixin 1989 • $15 • (01/31/92) • **87**

Fleurie 1996: Good weight and grip on the palate, with more polish than the usual Beaujolais. Flavors of fresh plums, light chocolate and herbs. Should complement food and last through 1999. 11,200 cases made. • $14 • (08/31/97) • **87**

Fleurie 1995: Lighter than most Fleuries, but the black cherry and spice flavors are appealing. Drink now. • $16 • (09/15/96) • **82**

Fleurie 1994 • $12 • (06/15/95) • **87**

Fleurie Clos de la Roilette 1995: Chunky, with firm tannins. Gamy and earthy flavors dominate the fruit, and the finish is a bit dry. Might soften with food. • $17 • (09/15/96) • **81**

Fleurie Clos de la Roilette 1994 • $12 • (06/15/95) • **84**
Fleurie Domaine de la Presle 1996: Lush, tender and round, with deep black cherry and coffee flavors, soft tannins and a spicy finish. Has enough acidity to stay fresh; drinkable now. 4,800 cases made. • $15 • (08/31/97) • **84**
Gevrey-Chambertin 1995: On the herbal side, and light for a Gevrey. Tough finish. Not very impressive. • $22 • (11/15/97) • **78**
Gevrey-Chambertin 1991: Light-textured, with gamy currant aromas and somewhat watery flavors. Drinkable now. 500 cases made. • $22 Ⓐ • (01/31/94) • **78**
Gevrey-Chambertin 1985 • $25 • (02/15/88) • **90**
Gevrey-Chambertin Lavaut St.-Jacques 1990: Rather complex, with fresh mushroom, vanilla and berry flavors that are tightly wrapped around firm tannins now, but it should grow into a subtle, velvety wine with age. Try now. • $45 • (12/15/92) • **90**
Gevrey-Chambertin Lavaut St.-Jacques 1989 • $45 • (01/31/92) • **85**
Gevrey-Chambertin Premier Cru 1995: Stewed, vegetal and diluted, with an astringent finish. 591 cases made. • $35 • (11/15/97) • **72**
Gevrey-Chambertin Premier Cru 1994: Spicy, new-oak character adds charm and depth to this medium-weight, vaguely cherry-scented wine. Drinkable now. 333 cases made. • $47 • (11/15/96) • **83**
Gevrey-Chambertin Premier Cru 1993: An attractive core of raspberry and cherry notes. Fresh and relatively light, it offers nice pleasure now. • $45 • (11/15/95) • **83**
Gevrey-Chambertin Premier Cru 1992: Lean and chewy, a strong anise component running through the modest currant flavors. Drinkable now. 792 cases made. • $42 • (12/15/94) • **81**
Gigondas 1995: Light and rather simple, with raspberry and herbal flavors, light but firm tannins and a short, dry finish. Drinkable now. • $12 • (10/15/97) • **79**
Gigondas 1993 • $14 • (11/15/95) • **87**
Juliénas 1996: Fresh grape and cherry flavors give bright appeal; crisp acidity and moderate tannins give the structure to match with simple foods. 9,800 cases made. • $11 • (09/15/97) • **86**
Juliénas Domaine de la Conseillère 1996: A crisp edge of acidity gives this red good definition, while ripe black cherry and chocolate flavors give it richness. It's balanced and fresh, a nice accompaniment to food. 2,700 cases made. • $12 • (09/15/97) • **86**
Mâcon Villages 1994 • $11 • (05/31/96) • **70**
Maranges 1989 • $13 • (01/31/92) • **87**
Merlot Vin de Pays d'Oc 1994: Not distinctively Merlot-like, but there are some nice herb and tobacco flavors. Straightforward and simple. • $6 • (12/15/96) • **80**
Merlot Vin de Pays d'Oc 1993 • $6 • (10/31/95) • **83**
Meursault 1994: Vibrant and powerful, delivering plenty of herbal, mineral, cedar and ripe fruit flavors and aromas and lots of toasty oak flavors on the long, crisp finish. Drink now. • $NA • (08/31/96) • **86**
Meursault 1993: Lovely pineapple and coconut aromas and flavors, medium-to-full body, fine acidity and fresh finish. Delicious. 850 cases made. • $24 • (05/15/95) • **85**
Meursault 1992: Quite ripe and rich, with fruit all over the place, and a round texture packed with grapefruit, lemon, pineapple and butter-toast flavors. Delivers character, if not much finesse. 750 cases made. • $25 • (08/31/94) • **88**
Meursault-Blagny 1994: A rich *premier cru* with an attractive mineral note. Honeyed, full-bodied, and bursting with slightly coarse toasty oak and dried herbs. Quite sweet on the finish. Drink now. • $NA • (08/31/96) • **84**
Meursault Les Charmes 1992: Broad, ripe and quite aromatic, this gold-colored wine shows some floral, honey and pear flavors that are appealingly rich but seem to peter out a bit on the finish. Drinkable now. 208 cases made. • $34 • (08/31/94) • **87**
Meursault Les Criots 1993: Wonderful tropical fruit and toasty oak character, medium-to-full body, fresh acidity and long, flavorful finish. 200 cases made. • $25 • (05/15/95) • **88**
Meursault Premier Cru 1993: Open and rich but also a bit heavy-handed, showing ripe melon, pear, green apple, mineral, and wet earth flavors. Harmonious on the finish. Drinkable now. 300 cases made. • $40 • (05/15/95) • **85**
Morey-St.-Denis La Forge 1995: Smoky, blackberry flavors and a touch of wet earth are framed nicely by the firm structure of this medium-bodied red. Subtle oak and fruit notes mingle on the finish, which is slightly astringent. 466 cases made. • $52 • (11/15/97) • **87**
Morey-St.-Denis La Forge 1993: Light and a bit diluted, featuring modest red berry, tobacco and earth flavors and short finish. Drink now. • $57 • (11/15/95) • **81**
Morgon 1996: This distinctive Beaujolais offers real value, showing a strong note of kirsch that lends an exotic appeal and good concentration that provides backbone, and a dense yet polished texture. Drink now. 14,000 cases made. • $11 • (08/31/97) BB • **88**
Morgon 1994 • $10 • (07/31/95) • **84**
Morgon Domaine de Lathevalle 1996: Offering attractive crushed raspberry and blueberry flavors, it's so full of fruit it's almost sweet, but bright acidity keeps it lively. Not typical Beaujolais, but eminently drinkable. 5,100 cases made. • $12 • (08/31/97) • **84**
Morgon Domaine de Lathevalle 1995: A meaty flavor characteristic of Morgon dominates, backed by firm tannins. Drink now. • $14 • (09/15/96) • **83**
Morgon Domaine de Lathevalle 1994 • $10 • (07/31/95) • **88**
Moulin-à-Vent 1996: Shows good concentration from the rich texture to the firm tannins to the ripe cherry and kirsch flavors. Try now. 10,300 cases made. • $13 • (08/31/97) • **87**
Moulin-à-Vent 1995: Black cherry and black pepper are the dominant flavors in this firm wine. It's fresh and clean, but could use more fruit to balance the hard tannins. Drink now. • $15 • (09/15/96) • **84**
Moulin-à-Vent 1994 • $12 • (07/31/95) • **85**
Moulin-à-Vent Domaine de Champ de Cour 1996: Concentrated, closed right now, but promises good things to come. Shows dark color, muscular structure and ripe flavors of plums and blackberries with meaty, toasty accents. Drink now. 4,500 cases made. • $14 • (08/31/97) • **89**
Moulin-à-Vent Domaine de Champ de Cour 1995: Lively black cherry and spice flavors run riot through this exuberant wine, and the tannins are just firm enough for food. Not complex, but quite likeable. • $16 • (09/15/96) • **87**
Moulin-à-Vent Domaine de Champ de Cour 1994 • $12 • (07/31/95) • **89**
Nuits-St.-Georges 1995: Rich and smoothly textured, showing muted flavors of chocolate and spicy oak. Full and fat through to the end, which is a bit dry with tannins. 1,158 cases made. • $30 • (11/15/97) • **85**
Nuits-St.-Georges Aux Boudots 1994: Medium-bodied but lithe, with enticing, pretty rose petal, violet and currant aromas and flavors. The tannins are chewy, but don't overwhelm. Try now. 233 cases made. • $43 • (11/15/96) • **80**
Nuits-St.-Georges Aux Chaignots 1993: Pretty rose petal, raspberry and currant notes. Medium-bodied, well crafted, adding a sweet-tasting, delicious finish. Drinkable now. • $57 • (11/15/95) • **87**
Nuits-St.-Georges Aux Chaignots 1992: Lean and firm, with a nice thread of currant and vanilla flavors weaving through the fine tannins. Drink now or hold. 400 cases made. • $45 • (12/15/94) • **82**
Nuits-St.-Georges Aux Chaignots 1990: Rich as olive oil, with beautiful fruit. This viscous red has loads of raspberry and cedar characteristics and fine, silky tannins. Drinkable now. • $29 • (12/15/92) • **90**
Nuits-St.-Georges Les St.-Georges 1995: A burly Nuits packed with red- and blackberry fruit and tannins, but turns chewy, even a bit dry, on the finish. Try after 1999. 216 cases made. • $39 • (11/15/97) • **81**
Nuits-St.-Georges Les Vaucrains 1989 • $45 • (01/31/92) • **90**
Nuits-St.-Georges Premier Cru 1991: Firm, tannic and aromatic, offering peppery, spicy currant and chocolate flavors that sneak in at a modest level. Drinkable now. 150 cases made. • $28 Ⓐ • (01/31/94) • **83**
Pommard 1995: Here's a rough-and-tumble, burly type of Pinot, true to its appellation, full of chewy, licorice-tinged cherry flavors and a hefty dose of tannins. Drinkable now. 816 cases made. • $30 • (11/15/97) • **83**
Pommard 1994: Shows red berry, anise and toasty oak aromas and flavors, but the finish is a bit hard and the tannins fairly dry. 1,000 cases made. • $34 • (11/15/96) • **79**
Pommard 1993: Relatively soft and accessible Pommard, showing a sweet- and ripe-tasting character. Clean and pure Pinot Noir flavors on the medium-long finish. 1,083 cases made. • $35 • (11/15/95) • **84**
Pommard 1989 • $28 • (01/31/92) • **88**
Pommard Premier Cru 1993: Diluted and watery with some berry character, but rather metallic and weedy. 375 cases made. • $40 • (11/15/95) • **76**
Pouilly-Fuissé 1996: A subtle white that shows modest richness combined with apple and clove notes. • $15 • (10/15/97) • **79**
Pouilly-Fuissé 1995: Very odd, showing a varnish and cooked fruit character. • $15 • (05/31/98) • **70**
Pouilly-Fuissé 1994: Excellent effort from this négociant. Intensely citrusy, with a backdrop of mineral notes that adds nice complexity. This full-bodied Burgundy packs a wallop of pear, honey and apricot flavors. Drinkable now. 4,416 cases made. • $25 • (05/31/96) • **88**
Pouilly-Fuissé 1993: Youthful and flavorful, a light- to medium-bodied white presenting plenty of lime, grapefruit and butter notes. Clean and crisp finish. 5,833 cases made. • $18 • (05/15/95) • **84**
Pouilly-Fuissé Château Pouilly 1993: Simple and straightforward, showing modest grapefruit and apple notes and a somewhat minerally finish. Drink now. 1,917 cases made. • $20 • (05/15/95) • **76**

Puligny-Montrachet 1994: Soft, round and ripe, with a chalky, chewy, mineral character underlying some nice pear and apple flavors. Medium- to full-bodied, it turns a bit dry on the finish. • $NA • (08/31/96) • **82**

Puligny-Montrachet 1993: A bit hard, but some good fruit and nut character on the nose and palate; medium in body, good acidity, nutty finish. 700 cases made. • $27 • (05/15/95) • **84**

Puligny-Montrachet 1992: A flavorful, well-made Chardonnay; delivers lovely tropical, citrus, pear and apple flavors. Tastes more like an international-style Chardonnay than distinctive Burgundy, but it makes for nice drinking all the same. Drinkable now. 625 cases made. • $27 • (08/31/94) • **85**

Puligny-Montrachet La Garenne 1992: Austere, earthy and green-tasting, with tons of super-tart apple flavors. Sharp, but the acidity, at least, makes it fresh. 166 cases made. • $36 • (08/31/94) • **77**

Puligny-Montrachet Les Folatières 1993: Delicious apple pie and tropical fruit character. Medium-bodied, good acidity and loads of fruit on the finish. 350 cases made. • $40 • (05/15/95) • **86**

Puligny-Montrachet Premier Cru 1994: A bit overdone and woody, and the distinctive butterscotch, mint and caramel flavors dominate the fruit. Full-bodied, but slightly hollow in the midpalate. Drink now. • $NA • (08/31/96) • **79**

St.-Amour 1996: Balanced and firm, but very straightforward in character, with hints of cherries and spice. 7,800 cases made. • $14 • (08/31/97) • **83**

St.-Amour Domaine de Monrève 1996: Though light-bodied for a St.-Amour, it's lively and fresh, with pretty black cherry and spice flavors, good underlying acidity. 2,200 cases made. • $14 • (08/31/97) • **84**

St.-Aubin 1990: A light style that's a bit harsh, with stemmy, vegetal aromas and flavors and brown sugar and cinnamon notes on the finish. Drinkable now. • $NA • (12/15/92) • **77**

St.-Aubin En Remilly White 1994: Middle-of-the-road *premier cru*. Has a silky palate and some butter, apple tart, cream and toasty oak flavors on the finish. Medium-bodied. Drink now. • $NA • (08/31/96) • **81**

St.-Véran Domaine de l'Evèque 1994: Decent and simple, with the fresh taste of lemonade. This light-bodied white makes for a quaffable drink on a hot summer day. 3,333 cases made. • $14 • (05/31/96) • **79**

Santenay Clos Rousseau 1995: Seems tired and dull, with modest licorice and cherry flavors and a vanilla note. 680 cases made. • $22 • (11/15/97) • **76**

Santenay Clos Rousseau 1994: Soft, supple and a bit simple, this delivers a decent vanilla, red berry character. Light-bodied. Drink upon release. 708 cases made. • $25 • (11/15/96) • **74**

Santenay Clos Rousseau 1993: Dark-colored and firm, this chewy red features cherry pit, earth and wild berry flavors. Try now. 800 cases made. • $26 • (11/15/95) • **84**

Santenay Clos Rousseau 1992: Crisp in texture and aromatic, with cherry flavor that tightens a little on the finish. Tasty now. 792 cases made. • $23 • (12/15/94) • **80**

Santenay Clos Rousseau 1990: You can taste the soil in this one; wet earth and mineral components play nicely against plum and red berry flavors. Has lovely balance and a round mouthfeel. A wine with character. • $14 • (12/15/92) • **86**

Savigny-lès-Beaune 1995: Already showing some brown color, but the flavors aren't bad, with herbal and earthy nuances to the berry flavors. Finish is astringent. • $15 • (11/15/97) • **78**

Savigny-lès-Beaune 1994: Sturdy and chewy, with modest cherry flavors and a stalky edge. 1,000 cases made. • $20 • (11/15/96) • **79**

Savigny-lès-Beaune 1993: Impressive concentration yet a bit overextracted on the finish. Nice plum and red berry character, but the lean, tannic texture makes you wonder how it will age. Try in 2000. 1,160 cases made. • $21 • (11/15/95) • **87**

Savigny-lès-Beaune 1992: Lean in texture, modest in flavor, featuring more black cherry than anything else. Has a sugary edge. Drinkable now. 1,330 cases made. • $19 • (12/15/94) • **78**

Savigny-lès-Beaune 1991: Has a firm texture, herbal and floral overtones to the crisp, green plum character. Drinkable now. 500 cases made. • $16 Ⓐ • (01/31/94) • **79**

Savigny-lès-Beaune 1990: Wild and exotic, bursting at the seams with tons of round fruit flavors, loads of wild berry characteristics, hints of violets, earth and blueberries and well-integrated tannins to boot. Worth seeking out. Drinkable now. • $14 • (12/15/92) • **90**

Savigny-lès-Beaune 1985 • $17 • (07/31/88) • **80**

Syrah Vin de Pays d'Oc 1993 • $6 • (10/31/95) • **79**

Key: SS—Spectator Selection CS—Cellar Selection HR—Highly Recommended BB—Best Buy $NA—Price not available Ⓐ—Auction Price (BT)—Barrel Tasting

Dates in parentheses indicate the issues in which the ratings were published.

Volnay 1985 • $80 • (03/15/88) • **91**

Volnay Taille Pieds 1995: Pleasant and fairly balanced, relatively light and tasting of cherry and strawberry with a touch of earth. Quite ripe and sweet, but a bit simple. Drinkable now. 275 cases made. • $28 • (11/15/97) • **84**

Volnay Taille Pieds 1994: Earthy, green and astringent, with little charm to balance those attributes. 333 cases made. • $33 • (11/15/96) • **77**

Volnay Taille Pieds 1993: Juicy cherry, mushroom and plum character, medium body and tannins and a dry finish. Delicious now. 316 cases made. • $40 • (11/15/95) • **80**

Volnay Taille Pieds 1992: Crisp in texture, ripe and generous, centering around smoky berry flavor and a floral note on the finish. Drinkable now. 542 cases made. • $29 • (12/15/94) • **84**

Volnay Taille Pieds 1991: Ripe and focused, with a tarry, anise edge to the concentrated currant and berry aromas and flavors. Shaded on the finish by a nice hint of mint. Has character and style; drinkable now. 150 cases made. • $23 Ⓐ • (01/31/94) • **85**

Volnay Taille Pieds 1990: Incredibly concentrated, with phenomenal amounts of fruit extract. Needs time to show it all, but the plum, tobacco and black cherry aromas and flavors stay with you for a long time on the firm finish. Drinkable now. • $23 • (12/15/92) • **92**

Vosne-Romanée 1995: Ripe and sweet-tasting, medium- to full-bodied, but a bit alcoholic. Offers supple tannins, nice red berry flavors, excellent acidity, good balance and a long finish. Tempting now through 2005. 433 cases made. • $30 • (11/15/97) • **86**

Vosne-Romanée 1993: Attractive berry, chestnut and almond character but slightly meager in structure. Light- to medium-bodied, light tannins. Drink now. • $40 • (11/15/95) • **81**

Vosne-Romanée 1992: Light and simple, with modest strawberry and cherry aromas and flavors that offer a touch of ripe, sweet notes on the finish. 483 cases made. • $49 • (12/15/94) • **80**

Vosne-Romanée Aux Brûlées 1989 • $38 • (01/31/92) • **89**

Vosne-Romanée Les Suchots 1995: Just smelling its pure, spicy red and blackberry makes your mouth water for this succulent, textured Pinot. Structured for a Vosne, and it offers grainy but fine tannins and a long finish. 200 cases made. • $45 • (11/15/97) • **88**

Vosne-Romanée Les Suchots 1994: Crisp, medium-weight style threads the needle with pretty raspberry and spice flavors that linger gently on the grainy tannic finish. Drink sooner rather than later. 208 cases made. • $49 • (11/15/96) • **81**

Vosne-Romanée Les Suchots 1990: This concentrated Vosne is bursting with plum, cherry and vanilla flavors and is round and supple on the intense finish. Drinkable now. • $35 • (12/15/92) • **91**

Vosne-Romanée Premier Cru 1993: Exuberantly plummy character, medium body, fine tannins and a long, fruity finish. Drinkable now. • $46 • (11/15/95) • **87**

MONARDIÈRE, DOMAINE LA

Côtes du Rhône Cuvée des Calades 1996: Quite pretty, but in an herbal style, with some cassis bush and red berry notes. A bit lean on the finish, but still fresh and pleasant. Drink chilled. 183 cases imported. 833 cases made. • $9 • (10/15/97) • **80**

Côtes du Rhône Cuvée des Calades 1994: This tannic red lacks generosity and ripeness. Its flavors are stemmy and earthy, and the tannins are aggressive on the finish. • $10 • (12/15/96) • **78**

Vacqueyras 1994: A generous red, this shows plenty of ripe plum flavors, with notes of tobacco and cedar. Firm tannins provide structure. Drink now. • $15 • (12/15/96) • **85**

Vacqueyras Réserve des 2 Monardes 1995: Light in color and aroma, with a slight dilution, but it's a supple wine, with floral, cherry and toasty oak flavors. Delicate finish. 2,333 cases made. • $13 • (10/15/97) • **82**

Vin de Pays de Vaucluse 1996: Clean and pure, with lovely black pepper, red berry and mineral flavors. Light-bodied and made for drinking young, slightly chilled and with simple foods, this red has enough ripeness to make anyone smile. Drink now. 1,167 cases made. • $8 • (10/15/97) • **84**

MONBADON, CHÂTEAU

Côtes de Castillon 1994: This light, straightforward red offers black cherry flavors and firm tannins, with grip but not much depth. It's fresh and clean, but finishes short. • $10 • (06/30/97) • **83**

MONBOUSQUET, CHÂTEAU

St.-Emilion 1997: Pleasant berry and tobacco aromas and flavors. Medium in body, with medium tannins. A bit diluted on the finish. Tasted twice, with consistent notes. • $NA • (06/15/98) (BT) • **80-84**

St.-Emilion 1996: Dark and concentrated, with toasty oak, berry and violet aromas and flavors. Full-bodied and chewy, with velvety tannins and a long finish. Impressive but slightly one-dimensional. Tastes like Napa Cab. Almost outstanding. • $45 • (06/15/98) (BT) • **85-89**

St.-Emilion 1995: Immediate gratification in a bottle. Dark in color, with loads of coffee, tobacco, grilled meat and fruit aromas. Full-bodied and very velvety, with a long, smoky berry aftertaste. Gorgeous now, best after 2000. • $30 • (01/31/98) • **92**

St.-Emilion 1993: Caresses your palate. Impressive color, concentration and fruit, full- to medium-bodied, round tannins and a long aftertaste of toasty oak, chocolate and berries. Drinkable now. • $23 • (01/31/96) • **88**

MONBRISON, CHÂTEAU

Margaux 1997: Inky in color, with mineral and spice aromas and hints of red fruit. Medium-bodied, with light tannins and a fading finish. Promises more on the nose than it delivers on the palate, but very good. • $NA • (06/15/98) (BT) • **85-89**

Margaux 1996: Decent aromas and flavors of grapes, berries and earth, medium body and fine tannins, but it's slightly diluted on the finish. • $NA • (01/01/97) (BT) • **80-84**

Margaux 1995: A straightforward, well-made red. Bright berry aromas, with a hint of citrus. Medium-bodied, with firm tannins and a silky, sweet fruit finish. Best after this year. • $22 • (01/31/98) • **87**

Margaux 1994: A bit meager, but does show some nice berry and dried herb notes. Medium-bodied, dry tannins. Tasted twice with consistent notes. Drink now. • $25 • (01/31/97) • **79**

Margaux 1993: A bit disappointing. Short and herbal, adding some blackberry and green bean character. Drinkable now. • $26 • (01/31/96) • **75**

Margaux 1992: Perfumed, mineral and grassy character; light-bodied and light finish. • $21 • (04/15/95) • **77**

Margaux 1991: Simple, straightforward, with cherry flavors and aromas that have a toasty oak character; medium body. • $14 • (03/31/94) • **81**

Margaux 1990: Luscious and elegant, with a bounty of ripe blackberry, licorice and tobacco character and well-integrated tannins. One of the very best *cru bourgeois*. Drinkable now. 5,500 cases made. • $22 Ⓐ • (03/31/93) • **91**

Margaux 1989 • $27 Ⓐ • (03/15/92) • **93**
Margaux 1988 • $24 Ⓐ • (02/28/91) HR • **92**
Margaux 1987 • $20 • (11/30/89) • **86**
Margaux 1986 • $26 Ⓐ • (11/30/89) • **92**
Margaux 1985 • $25 Ⓐ • (10/15/94) • **90**
Margaux 1984 • $15 • (05/15/87) • **78**
Margaux 1983 • $20 • (10/15/94) • **86**
Margaux 1982 • $22 • (11/30/89) • **90**
Margaux 1981 • $19 • (10/15/94) • **82**

MONCONTOUR, CHÂTEAU

Brut Touraine Tête de Cuvée 1993 • $13 • (06/15/96) • **77**
Brut Vouvray 1994 • $16 • (06/15/96) • **83**
Vouvray 1993 • $12 • (06/15/96) • **82**

MONDOT

St.-Emilion 1995: Elegant, and attractive to drink now. Aromatic, with an earthy, cherry character. Medium-bodied, with velvety tannins and a medium, caressing finish. Second label of Château Troplong-Mondot. Drink now or hold. • $25 • (01/31/98) • **86**

MONDOTTE, CHÂTEAU LA

St.-Emilion 1997: Amazing for the vintage. Inky in color. Beautiful violet, wet earth and fruit aromas. Medium-bodied and velvety, with violet and berry character. • $NA • (06/15/98) (BT) • **90-94**

St.-Emilion 1996: Ink-colored, with lovely blackberry, spice, cumin and vanilla aromas. Full-bodied, with velvety tannins and a caressing finish. A sexy wine. 4,150 cases made. • $210 • (06/15/98) (BT) • **90-94**

MONGEARD-MUGNERET

Bourgogne 1994: Green and chalky, with little fruit flavor. • $14 • (11/15/96) • **74**

Bourgogne 1993: Harmonious, with fruit balancing the tannins nicely. Fresh, pretty floral and cherry flavors. Try now. • $16 • (11/15/95) • **83**

Bourgogne 1992: Light and crisply tannic, only a modest level of strawberry sneaking in. 875 cases made. • $14 • (12/15/94) • **79**

Bourgogne 1989 • $9 • (01/31/92) • **85**

Clos de Vougeot 1994: Youthful, but already complex with berry, currant, mocha and mineral flavors swirling through the firm structure. Finishing with a strong hint of rose petal and fine tannins that can use until 1999 or 2000. • $61 • (11/15/96) • **88**

Clos de Vougeot 1993: Like eating chocolate mousse. Full in body, delivering loads of velvety tannins and a long aftertaste of mocha, chocolate and fruit. Somewhat earthy, but delicious. Better after 2000. • $60 Ⓐ • (11/15/95) • **93**

Clos de Vougeot 1992: Light and chewy with tannin and a greenish edge to the berryish flavors. Try now. 308 cases made. • $61 • (12/15/94) • **80**

Clos de Vougeot 1991: Crisp, light and a bit more astringent than we'd like in such a delicate wine. Herbal, floral berry flavors extend into a long but fragile finish. Drinkable now. • $45 Ⓐ • (01/31/94) • **83**

Clos de Vougeot 1989 • $41 Ⓐ • (01/31/92) • **87**
Clos de Vougeot 1987 • $25 Ⓐ • (05/15/90) • **81**
Clos de Vougeot 1986 • $38 Ⓐ • (07/31/89) • **87**

Echézeaux 1995: There's plenty of decadent black fruit character in this round, medium-bodied wine, yet it has an herbal, stemmy quality that detracts. Very dry finish. 608 cases made. • $47 • (11/15/97) • **84**

Echézeaux 1993: Seductive and elegant, sporting alluring plum, raspberry and mineral aromas and flavors. Medium- to full-bodied with fine tannins and a sweet, really fine fruit finish. Try in 2000. • $50 • (11/15/95) • **91**

Echézeaux 1992: A little green around the edges, tart and astringent enough to take the charm away from the modest berry flavors. Try now. 1,058 cases made. • $44 • (12/15/94) • **78**

Echézeaux Vieille Vigne 1993: Amazing intensity of vivid flavors. Ripe plum, black cherry, minty taste. Of medium body, it shows finesse despite the massive, supple tannins. Long and flavorful finish. Try after 2000. • $50 Ⓐ • (11/15/95) • **92**

Echézeaux Vieille Vigne 1991: Ripe and gamy; has a toasty edge to the supple plum and wild berry aromas and flavors and hints at vanilla bean and coffee on the spicy finish. Smooth and round. Drinkable now. • $43 Ⓐ • (01/31/94) • **90**

Echézeaux Vieille Vigne 1989 • $43 Ⓐ • (01/31/92) • **93**
Echézeaux Vieille Vigne 1988 • $67 Ⓐ • (02/15/91) • **88**
Echézeaux Vieille Vigne 1987 • $46 Ⓐ • (05/15/90) • **86**
Echézeaux Vieille Vigne 1986 • $53 Ⓐ • (08/31/89) • **90**

Fixin 1995: Pungent and herbal, this has intensity, but ultimately comes across lean and astringent. 408 cases made. • $20 • (11/15/97) • **79**

Fixin 1994: Drying tannins and medicinal flavors throw this out of whack. • $20 • (11/15/96) • **78**

Fixin 1992: Straightforward and tart, a bit herbal and fresh-tasting. A light-bodied Burgundy ends on a zesty raspberry note. Drinkable now. 533 cases made. • $20 • (12/15/94) • **79**

Fixin 1991: Earthy, a bit jammy and simple. The flavors are decent, but the texture is watery. Drinkable now. • $18 Ⓐ • (01/31/94) • **77**

Fixin 1990: Light in color, with weedy dill and earthy strawberry flavors that thin out on the finish. Turns barnyardy on the aftertaste. Drinkable, but there are better 1990s. 500 cases made. • $7 Ⓐ • (03/15/93) • **77**

Fixin 1989 • $25 • (01/31/92) • **83**
Fixin 1986 • $12 Ⓐ • (10/15/89) • **84**

Grands Echézeaux 1995: Traditional in style, round and fleshy, with a tomatolike element along with the blackberry flavors. It's spicy and lively in the mouth, with a firm, slightly astringent finish. 454 cases made. • $83 • (11/15/97) • **89**

Grands Echézeaux 1994: Light in color, and though it tries to pack some prune, spice and tobacco flavors, the finish is astringent, almost chalky. • $73 • (11/15/96) • **76**

Grands Echézeaux 1993: Not as good as its two Echézeaux, but delivers very good concentration of ripe plum and mint flavor and firm tannins. Medium in body, a bit forward. Drinkable now. • $83 Ⓐ • (11/15/95) • **87**

Grands Echézeaux 1992: Earth and barnyard aromas predominate in this tough-textured red; barely fruity enough to balance. Might improve by 1997. 633 cases made. • $75 • (12/15/94) • **80**

Grands Echézeaux 1991: Ripe and elegant, offering a generous array of gamy, toasty, rose petal-scented currant, black cherry and plum aromas and

FRANCE

flavors that extends into a chewy finish. Needs until 1998 or 2000 to sort out the tannins. 600 cases made. • $68 Ⓐ • (01/31/94) HR • **91**
Grands Echézeaux 1989 • $82 Ⓐ • (01/31/92) • **93**
Grands Echézeaux 1987 • $48 Ⓐ • (05/15/90) • **85**
Grands Echézeaux 1986 • $43 Ⓐ • (08/31/89) • **92**
Grands Echézeaux 1955 • $NA • (12/31/94) • **82**
Grands Echézeaux 1953 • $NA • (12/31/94) • **87**
Hautes Côtes de Nuits 1994: As light as a rosé in color and texture, with some modest strawberry flavors and dry tannins. • $15 • (11/15/96) • **71**
Hautes Côtes de Nuits 1993: Lots of personality here. Medium to light in body, ripe, silky tannins and very good red berry, earthy concentration. Pretty finish. Drinkable now. • $17 • (11/15/95) • **85**
Hautes Côtes de Nuits 1992: Crisp, light and simple, with modest strawberry flavors. 358 cases made. • $15 • (12/15/94) • **76**
Hautes Côtes de Nuits 1989 • $16 • (01/31/92) • **77**
Nuits-St.-Georges Aux Boudots 1989 • $49 • (01/31/92) • **84**
Nuits-St.-Georges Aux Boudots 1987 • $32 • (04/30/90) • **81**
Nuits-St.-Georges Aux Boudots 1984 • $23 • (02/15/88) • **78**
Richebourg 1994: Firm and flavorful, with ripe currant and plum flavors, hints of mineral and a touch of earth. A delicious wine that offers everything but a glorious finish. Nicely balanced and the tannins are fine. Drinkable now. • $138 • (11/15/96) • **88**
Richebourg 1993: Lush and velvety, sporting well-defined currant, plum and tobacco character and firm finish. A well-made, medium-bodied Burgundy that should last and improve until around 2000. • $110 • (11/15/95) • **88**
Richebourg 1992: Lean and earthy, a watery red showing only simple underbrush and cherry flavors that fade on the finish. Try now. 117 cases made. • $134 • (12/15/94) • **77**
Richebourg 1991: A strong, earthy anise streak runs through the berry and toast aromas and flavors in this crisp, firm, focused Burgundy. Nicer on the palate than on the nose. Drinkable now. • $117 Ⓐ • (01/31/94) • **88**
Richebourg 1989 • $63 Ⓐ • (01/31/92) • **92**
Richebourg 1987 • $34 Ⓐ • (08/10/90) • **90**
Richebourg 1985 • $123 • (03/15/88) • **92**
Savigny-lès-Beaune 1994: Unappealing, with a taste that brings to mind furniture polish. • $20 • (11/15/96) • **72**
Savigny-lès-Beaune 1993: Better than the winery's *premier crus* due to the use of less wood in aging. Medium body, silky tannins and a long finish of sweet, ripe red berries. Drink now. • $22 • (11/15/95) • **87**
Savigny-lès-Beaune Les Narbantons 1995: Has elegance, a midpalate sweetness and good fruit concentration. Cherry and tomato flavors hold court, with a hint of spicy oak on the finish. 360 cases made. • $23 • (11/15/97) • **85**
Savigny-lès-Beaune Les Narbantons 1994: Modest in scale. A lighter wine with some nice spice and cherry sour-candy notes, finishing with an earthy accent. • $24 • (11/15/96) • **80**
Savigny-lès-Beaune Les Narbantons 1993: Lightly smoky, a delicate style of Pinot Noir, offering some toast, leather and cherry flavors. Light- to medium-bodied, nicely balanced. Drink now. • $26 • (11/15/95) • **83**
Savigny-lès-Beaune Les Narbantons 1992: A touch of sweet, ripe fruit peeks through in this light-bodied, lively wine. A bit short on the finish. 617 cases made. • $23 • (12/15/94) • **80**
Savigny-lès-Beaune Les Narbantons 1991: Narrow and lean, but has pretty cherry and spice aromas and flavors. Finishes a touch earthy. Drinkable now. • $21 Ⓐ • (01/31/94) • **81**
Savigny-lès-Beaune Les Narbantons 1990: A good but bizarre wine that's marred by dry, bitter tannins that overshadow the modest plum and cherry flavor profile. Drinkable now. 550 cases made. • $33 • (06/15/93) • **80**
Savigny-lès-Beaune Les Narbantons 1989 • $28 • (01/31/92) • **78**
Vosne-Romanée 1995: Shows loads of spicy, brambly fruit, juicy acidity and tannic structure. While it lacks the depth and concentration of the best in this appellation, it's very impressive, with a smoky, bacon fat finish. 745 cases made. • $29 • (11/15/97) • **87**
Vosne-Romanée 1992: Lean and chewy, tightly tannic, with only modest currant flavors hovering in the background; features tobacco and tea on the finish. 983 cases made. • $29 • (12/15/94) • **79**
Vosne-Romanée 1991: A firm, flavorful, crisp-textured wine, with toasty berry and spice aromas and flavors that echo nicely on the finish. Drinkable now. • $26 Ⓐ • (01/31/94) • **84**
Vosne-Romanée 1989 • $34 • (01/31/92) • **85**
Vosne-Romanée 1986 • $26 • (08/31/89) • **79**

Key: SS—Spectator Selection CS—Cellar Selection HR—Highly Recommended BB—Best Buy $NA—Price not available Ⓐ—Auction Price (BT)—Barrel Tasting
Dates in parentheses indicate the issues in which the ratings were published.

Vosne-Romanée Les Orveaux 1995: A "Vosne-Romanée rosé" that is light, simple and already maturing. Pale in color, with some bitter chocolate, earth and game flavors. 291 cases made. • $42 • (11/15/97) • **74**
Vosne-Romanée Les Orveaux 1994: Crisp, gritty tannins overshadow the lightish strawberry and floral flavors. • $36 • (11/15/96) • **78**
Vosne-Romanée Les Orveaux 1993: Relatively light, showing some modest red berry flavor and tannin structure. Serve chilled upon release. • $40 • (11/15/95) • **82**
Vosne-Romanée Les Orveaux 1992: A modest Vosne-Romanée, with some cherry and banana flavors complemented by light toasty notes. Very simple. 475 cases made. • $36 • (12/15/94) • **78**
Vosne-Romanée Les Orveaux 1991: This crisp-textured wine offers a fascinating range of blackberry, leaf and lime aromas and flavors and more citrus than anything else on the finish. Smells better than it tastes. Drinkable now. • $32 Ⓐ • (01/31/94) • **82**
Vosne-Romanée Les Orveaux 1989 • $43 • (01/31/92) • **94**
Vosne-Romanée Les Orveaux 1987 • $35 • (07/15/90) • **62**
Vosne-Romanée Les Orveaux 1986 • $34 • (08/31/89) • **82**
Vosne-Romanée Les Orveaux 1985 • $32 • (03/15/88) • **82**
Vosne-Romanée Les Petits Monts 1987 • $35 • (04/30/90) • **74**
Vosne-Romanée Les Suchots 1987 • $18 Ⓐ • (06/15/90) • **82**
Vougeot Les Crâs 1989 • $NA • (01/31/92) • **93**

MONMOUSSIN

Brut Touraine Etoile 1986 • $13 • (12/31/90) • **82**
Brut Touraine Monmousseau 1983 • $11 • (02/15/88) • **79**
Extra Dry Vouvray 1985 • $13 • (12/31/90) • **81**

MONNIER, RENÉ

Beaune Les Cents Vignes 1985 • $25 • (10/31/87) • **89**
Meursault Les Charmes 1995: Quite thick and ripe, with a woodsy, slightly heavy character that's a bit overdone, but it's full-bodied and flavorful, with pear, honey and almond notes. Try upon release. • $NA • (08/31/97) • **81**
Meursault Les Charmes 1994: Lush and ripe, tasting of spice, dates, figs and melons. Full-bodied and supple, but somewhat one-dimensional for this famous *premier cru* producer. Ready now. • $NA • (08/31/96) • **83**
Meursault Les Charmes 1992: A core of focused, pure fruit flavor makes this refreshing and tasty to drink. It layers subtle vanilla and honey accents on top of generous pear and pineapple for a satisfying mixture that lingers on the finish. Drinkable now. 408 cases made. • $40 • (08/31/94) • **89**
Meursault Les Chevalières 1995: A thick, ripe and rich village Meursault, balanced and compacted, with dried herbs and mineral flavors, honey notes. Full-bodied, it's delicious now through 2005. • $NA • (08/31/97) • **90**
Meursault Les Chevalières 1994: Lush, seductive village wine, showing some pretty floral, honey, and ripe pear flavors. Medium- to full-bodied, with a touch of toasty oak on the lingering finish. Drink now. • $NA • (08/31/96) • **85**
Meursault Les Chevalières 1992: Beautiful intensity in this steely, vibrant white; has appealing mineral, lime and apple flavors. Drinkable now. • $25 • (08/31/94) • **86**
Pommard Les Vignots 1985 • $30 • (11/15/88) • **89**
Pommard Les Vignots 1982 • $17 • (07/01/85) • **81**
Puligny-Montrachet Les Folatières 1994: A sweet, ripe *premier cru* that's medium-bodied and coats the mouth with lush apricot, peach, pineapple and honey flavors. Hazelnut and toasty oak flavors mark the smooth finish. Drink now. • $NA • (08/31/96) • **89**
Puligny-Montrachet Les Folatières 1992: Earthy, toasty aromas and tart, citrus flavors; a chewy texture and a short, clean finish. Solid, but nothing special. • $40 • (08/31/94) • **82**

MONPERTUIS, DOMAINE DE

Châteauneuf-du-Pape 1995: Lively, with ripe cherry and plum flavors, black pepper and licorice accents, and firm, slightly intrusive tannins. Drinkable now. 2,500 cases made. • $23 • (10/15/97) • **85**
Châteauneuf-du-Pape 1994: Tough and dry. Earthy, dried fruit aromas give way to earthy and metallic flavors, with drying tannins. Drinkable now. 2,917 cases made. • $23 • (10/15/97) • **76**
Châteauneuf-du-Pape 1993: Focused black cherry and spice flavors give this polish, while firm tannins help it match with food. It's discreet and fairly light, but well crafted. 100 cases made. • $23 • (11/15/96) • **85**
Châteauneuf-du-Pape 1990: Ripe and intense, with spicy, peppery plum and black cherry-tinged flavors that turn a bit leathery on the finish. Tasted

three times, with significant bottle variation. Drinkable now. 2,000 cases made. • $16 • (04/15/93) • **83**

Châteauneuf-du-Pape 1987 • $14 • (06/30/90) • **83**

Châteauneuf-du-Pape 1986 • $18 • (09/30/89) • **73**

Châteauneuf-du-Pape Tradition 1994: Fresh cherry flavor shines through, with lively black pepper and licorice notes lingering on the finish. It's supple and balanced, with no hard edges; drink now through 2000. 417 cases made. • $35 • (10/15/97) • **84**

Châteauneuf-du-Pape White 1994: Over the hill, with apple cider, oxidized character. 833 cases made. • $23 • (10/15/97) • **73**

Côtes du Rhône Vignoble de la Ramière 1996: Dark-colored and ripe, with herbal, black olive and currant flavors. Medium-bodied, the tannins are a bit tough and rustic. Still, it's a nice wine for simple foods. Drink now. Made from Counoise grapes. 833 cases made. • $12 • (10/15/97) • **81**

Côtes du Rhône Vignoble de la Ramière 1995: Vivid blackberry and black pepper aromas give way to round, soft, black fruit flavors that are thick on the palate. Good concentration makes for fine drinking now. 350 cases made. • $12 • (10/15/96) • **86**

Counoise Vin de Pays du Gard Vignoble de la Ramière 1995: Light but round, this soft red offers grape and plum flavors marred slightly by a burnt, earthy note. 900 cases made. • $9 • (10/15/96) • **78**

MONT BELAIR, CHÂTEAU

St.-Emilion 1989 • $12 • (11/15/91) • **81**

MONT CLAIR

Chardonnay Vin de Pays d'Oc 1995: A rather full-bodied, smooth textured white wine with an abundance of ripe fruit flavors. • $8 • (05/31/97) • **83**

Chardonnay Vin de Pays d'Oc 1993: A smooth, fruity, slightly sweet white wine that's pleasant but simple. 25,000 cases made. • $7 • (02/28/97) • **80**

MONT ROSE, DOMAINE

Merlot Vin de Pays d'Oc 1995: A pleasantly fruity red wine with medium body and light tannins. Ready to drink. 4,000 cases made. • $6 • (06/30/97) • **83**

MONT ST.-MICHEL

Cabernet Sauvignon Vin de Pays d'Oc Unfiltered 1995: Modest black currant and cherry flavors are underscored by a firm backbone in this balanced, pleasant red. Drinkable now. 10,000 cases made. • $8 • (12/15/96) • **82**

Merlot Vin de Pays d'Oc Unfiltered 1995: Solid and fairly rich, with good plum and black cherry flavors. Finishes with a nice tobacco note. Drinkable now. 10,000 cases made. • $8 • (12/15/96) • **85**

MONT TAUCH, LES PRODUCTEURS DU

Corbières 1991 • $7 • (03/15/93) • **81**

Fitou 1990 • $8 • (04/15/93) • **74**

Fitou 1985 • $6 • (04/15/89) • **79**

Vin de Pays du Torgan Le Sanglier 1991 • $6 • (04/15/93) BB • **83**

MONT-REDON, CHÂTEAU

Châteauneuf-du-Pape 1994: Maturing now, this chewy red has cherry, vanilla and light earth flavors that turn a bit dry on the finish but should shine with food. • $24 • (10/15/97) • **80**

Châteauneuf-du-Pape 1992: Maturing now, this shows dried cherry and gamy aromas that will appeal to fans of the traditional style. Well integrated, drinkable now. • $20 • (11/15/96) • **85**

Châteauneuf-du-Pape 1990: Fleshy and lively, a complex wine with a generous range of spicy, peppery overtones wrapped around solid cherry and plum flavors. A delicious wine that keeps itself in balance while showing plenty of muscle. Try now. • $23 • (09/30/93) • **91**

Châteauneuf-du-Pape 1989 • $31 Ⓐ • (08/31/92) • **79**

Châteauneuf-du-Pape 1988 • $22 • (10/15/91) • **83**

Châteauneuf-du-Pape 1986 • $17 • (10/15/91) • **85**

Châteauneuf-du-Pape 1985 • $25 • (10/15/91) • **90**

Châteauneuf-du-Pape 1984 • $11 • (09/30/87) • **92**

Châteauneuf-du-Pape 1983 • $25 • (10/15/91) • **88**

Châteauneuf-du-Pape 1981 • $30 • (10/15/91) • **90**

Châteauneuf-du-Pape White 1996: A well-made, distinctive white worth hunting down as an alternative to oaked Chardonnays. Shows good concentration and is full-bodied, offering a burst of ripe fruit and honey, and mineral notes. Smooth in texture with a lingering finish. Drinkable now. • $26 • (10/15/97) • **88**

Châteauneuf-du-Pape White 1995: Rich and thickly textured, yielding deep flavors of hazelnut, herbs, melon and vanilla that persist and expand on the finish. It's muscular, even austere, but has the structure and balance for long life. • $27 • (02/28/97) • **89**

Châteauneuf-du-Pape White 1993: Simple and funky in character, with earthy aromas, a bit of fruit flavor and medium body. • $23 • (11/15/95) • **76**

Côtes du Rhône 1995: Soft yet generous, this round red offers plum, chocolate and light herbal flavors. Fresh, and accessible now. • $11 • (09/15/97) • **83**

Côtes du Rhône 1993 • $10 • (11/15/95) • **78**

MONTAUDON

Brut Champagne 1988 • $25 • (12/31/93) • **84**

Brut Champagne NV: A most distinctive Champagne, from the marked toasty-doughy aromas to the expansive but dry flavors of fig and walnut to the rich texture that carries the flavors through a lingering finish. And, it's made in a quantity that suggests availability. Tasted twice, with consistent notes. 12,500 cases made. • $30 • (11/30/97) SS • **91**

MONTBAYON, DOMAINE DE

Côtes du Rhône-Villages Roaix 1996: Very soft and quite appealing, it tastes like a low-acidity wine. Medium-bodied, and offers flavorful spice, crushed black pepper, wild berry character and a succulent, toasty oak finish. Drink now. From D. Chastan. • $NA • (10/15/97) • **85**

Vacqueyras 1996: A beautifully balanced red, deep purple in color, lush and rich in texture, with satiny, ripe tannins. Medium-bodied and seductive, not too serious, it offers layers of fresh red- and blackberry flavors, crushed black pepper and dried herb notes. Smooth finish. Drink now. • $NA • (10/15/97) • **87**

Vacqueyras 1995: Very pretty and balanced, a tender and gentle wine that has floral and red berry notes. Medium-bodied and balanced, well-knit with smooth tannins. Delicious now. • $NA • (10/15/97) • **85**

MONTESQUIEU, DOMAINES H. DE

Bordeaux Baron de Montesquieu Le Secondat 1993: A firm, earthy wine with leathery aromas and flavors. Lean and rustic on the finish. • $11 • (04/30/97) • **79**

Bordeaux M de Montesquieu 1993: An earthy, brawny style, offering plum and spice flavors. Turns astringent on the finish. • $9 • (04/30/97) • **78**

Bordeaux White Baron de Montesquieu Le Secondat 1994: Quite lean and firm, with flavors of melon and green peach. Finishes on the tart side. • $11 • (04/30/97) • **77**

Bordeaux White M de Montesquieu 1994: A smoky, peachy-tasting wine with some good mineral notes. Finishes on the light side. • $9 • (04/30/97) • **82**

Graves Supérieur Moelleux 1993: A dessert wine in a rich style, with exuberant aromas and flavors of peach, almond and honey on a firm texture with good acidity. Nicely balanced, not too sweet, with a long finish. • $17/500ml • (04/30/97) • **86**

MONTFORT, CHÂTEAU DE

Vouvray 1996: This blowsy white shows slightly sweet and earthy flavors with modest apple notes and a tart finish. Drink now. • $10 • (05/31/98) • **78**

Vouvray 1995: Enticing aromas of walnuts and dried apples give way to crisp yet rich flavors of apples, honey, tea and minerals in this lively white. It's crisp, yet hints at sweetness. A delicious apéritif. • $8 • (06/15/97) • **89**

Vouvray 1994 • $9 • (12/15/95) • **77**

MONTGUERET, CHÂTEAU DE

Rosé d'Anjou 1996: This pale pink wine is soft on the palate, with slightly sweet strawberry pie flavors and an edge of citrusy acidity. Drink now, well chilled. • $13 • (06/15/98) • **79**

Saumur White 1996: Creamy, buttery aromas lead to lively tropical fruit flavors in this atypical yet attractive white. It's quite full-bodied, shows significant oak, yet maintains a refreshing acidity. Drink now. • $13 • (06/30/98) • **86**

MONTHÉLIE-DOUHAIRET

Bourgogne Aligoté 1996: A delicious Aligoté. Distinctive, with lots of matchstick, wet earth and game character. Decent fruit and citrus notes. Light-bodied, with a supple texture, balanced finish. Drink through 2000. 250 cases made. • $17 • (05/31/98) • **84**
Bourgogne Aligoté 1995: Tart with sulfurlike and rotten-egg aromas that may all blow away; some decent citrus flavors lurk beneath. • $17 • (08/31/97) • **70**
Bourgogne Aligoté 1994: Crisp and a bit green, even a bit disjointed, but it's fresh, with decent herb, citrus and green apple flavors. Should go well with oysters or grilled fish. 300 cases made. • $14 • (05/31/96) • **80**
Meursault 1995: Delicious, with a ripe fruit character that harmonizes with the spice and honey nuances. Full-bodied and balanced, it's silky and smooth on the palate, though one wishes for a bit more concentration. Drink now. • $41 • (05/31/97) • **86**
Meursault 1994: A hard wine that doesn't show much now, but there is a chalky, chewy mineral character that signals depth and good aging potential. Could use a bit more fruit. Try now. 100 cases made. • $34 • (05/31/96) • **84**
Meursault Les Cras 1996: Starts out with a slightly green aroma that follows through on the palate. Offers some decent fruit but lacks harmony. Try after 1999. 100 cases made. • $40 • (05/31/98) • **77**
Meursault Les Cras 1992: Very thin in texture, light on flavor, leaning toward sour. Basic white wine that could be from almost anywhere. • $37 • (11/15/94) • **74**
Meursault Les Santenots 1996: Intense and concentrated, bursting with lively aromas and flavors (kiwi, wet earth, honey, dried herbs, freshly cut grass, pear, lime, cilantro and parsley), it's most impressive for its full body and caressing, silky texture. Long, vibrant, palate-cleansing finish. Try around 2000 to 2005. 165 cases made. • $53 • (05/31/98) • **93**
Meursault Les Santenots 1995: Ripe yet solid, this full-bodied white Burgundy has a lot of fig, spice, honey and toasty coconut flavors that create personality-plus. One might wish for more fruit, but the silky texture is mouth-coating, the finish is smooth. Drink now through 2000. • $50 • (05/31/97) • **89**
Meursault Les Santenots 1994: Shows some personality. A bit coarse, but it delivers decent tropical fruit, apple and pear flavors. 175 cases made. • $34 • (05/31/96) • **82**
Monthélie 1994: Light and spicy, with a pleasant berry note that almost balances the chewy tannins. • $26 • (11/15/96) • **79**
Monthélie 1985 • $16 • (06/30/88) • **81**
Monthélie Clos le Meix Garnier 1995: A light red with modest concentration of cherry and strawberry flavors. • $30 • (11/15/97) • **79**
Monthélie Clos le Meix Garnier 1994: The chewy tannins more than temper the modest cherry flavors. • $22 • (11/15/96) • **79**
Monthélie Clos le Meix Garnier 1992: Tough and awkward, starting out nice with cherry and strawberry aromas, but tannic and rather bitter on the finish, with tobacco and smoke flavors. • $23 • (10/31/94) • **76**
Monthélie Le Meix Bataille 1995: Goes for extraction over finesse, judging from the fruity aromas, black cherry flavors and stiff tannins. Lacks a bit of flesh. • $30 • (11/15/97) • **84**
Monthélie Le Meix Bataille 1994: The crisp, juicy structure gives the lightish berry flavors a boost. Tasty now. • $26 • (11/15/96) • **82**
Monthélie Les Duresses 1995: Light and fresh, this crisp red Burgundy is racy, succulent and fun to drink young. Shows delicious blackberry, black cherry, earth and spice flavors, and is light-bodied, but well made and balanced. Drink now through 2000. • $27 • (11/15/97) • **84**
Monthélie Les Duresses 1994: Straightforward, with red berry aromas and flavors. Slightly herbal and astringent on the finish. • $31 • (11/15/96) • **77**
Monthélie Les Duresses White 1996: Hard and steely, it's very closed on the nose. It tastes of grapefruit, pear and apple, with a buttery and green undertow, in a medium-bodied package that vibrates with intensity. The midpalate is somewhat supple. Try after 2000. 100 cases made. • $35 • (05/31/98) • **85**
Monthélie Les Duresses White 1995: Silky smooth *premier cru*, full-bodied yet elegant, with a pure, clean fruit character, some nice mineral and vanilla notes and a slightly toasty finish. Drink now or can hold through 2000. • $37 • (05/31/97) • **88**
Monthélie Les Duresses White 1994: Subtle and balanced, showing some chalky lime, mineral and honey flavors, but a hint of a green, herbal character detracts from it. We wish for more harmony and length on the finish. Try now. 125 cases made. • $31 • (05/31/96) • **84**
Monthélie Les Duresses White 1992: An exotic flavor of anise accents the modest pear and apple notes in this smooth-textured, nicely balanced white Burgundy. Complete and harmonious. • $34 • (11/15/94) • **84**
Monthélie White 1995: A subtle, well-made, rather sweet-tasting wine, with a clean, firm structure. Closed on the nose now, but silky textured, offering some nice pear, mineral and wet stone flavors. A touch short on the finish. Drink now. • $30 • (05/31/97) • **86**
Monthélie White 1994: Quite round but straightforward, with some caramel, butter and pear flavors. Harmonious and crisp on the delicate finish. 125 cases made. • $20 • (05/31/96) • **83**
Pommard Les Chanlins 1995: Honest and forthright, this is fresh and a little stiff right now from the new oak, yet appears to have a core of cherry flavor. Tough finish. • $50 • (11/15/97) • **84**
Pommard Les Fremiers 1995: Some balance shines through in this medium-bodied Pommard. Offers decent fruit and tannins that aren't too harsh, but it's still a bit herbal and dry on the finish. • $50 • (11/15/97) • **80**
Pommard Les Fremiers 1994: Light and lively. Appealing for its bright strawberry and raspberry notes, finishing a bit tight. Drinkable now. • $42 • (11/15/96) • **83**
Volnay Champans 1995: Fresh and chewy, displaying a licorice component and a chunky texture, with rough, harsh tannins. • $40 • (11/15/97) • **82**
Volnay Champans 1994: Light in texture, but firm enough in structure to add some zip to the off-key cherry flavors. • $35 • (11/15/96) • **80**
Volnay Champans 1993: Full-blown currant juice; a reduction of fruit. Wonderfully concentrated layers of raspberry character. Full-bodied with velvety tannins, sweet fruit and very long finish. Try in 2000. • $44 • (11/15/95) • **93**
Volnay Champans 1992: Crisp, tart and fruity, with cherry and cranberry flavors, firm tannins and a dry finish. A sturdy, well-structured wine. Drinkable now. • $38 • (10/31/94) • **82**
Volnay Champans 1985 • $25 • (07/15/88) • **87**

MONTMIRAIL, CHÂTEAU DE

Gigondas Cuvée de Beauchamp 1990 • $13 • (04/15/93) • **75**
Gigondas Cuvée de Beauchamp 1985 • $14 • (09/30/88) • **78**
Gigondas Cuvée de Beauchamp 1983 • $11 • (11/30/86) • **90**
Vacqueyras Cuvée de L'Ermite Red 1990 • $11 • (04/15/93) • **82**

MONTPATEY, CHÂTEAU DE

Bourgogne White 1996: A full-bodied wine that seems a bit greenish and stemmy, underneath some fine pear, mineral, apple and oak complexity. Too bad. From Albert Bichot. 1,500 cases made. • $11 • (05/31/98) • **77**
Chardonnay Bourgogne 1994: More water than wine. Diluted and thin, tasting a bit of cardboard. 1,667 cases made. • $10 • (05/31/96) • **70**
Chardonnay Bourgogne Marquis d'Espiès 1993: Odd, lean, extremely citrusy and high in acidity. Shows modest green apple skin and lime flavors. Drink now. • $10 • (05/15/95) • **72**

MONTROSE, CHÂTEAU

St.-Estèphe 1997: An attractive clarity of currant and berry flavor combined with a silky tannin structure makes for a harmonious, medium-bodied '97. A very good red for early drinking. • $NA • (06/15/98) (BT) • **85-89**
St.-Estèphe 1996: The greatest Montrose I have ever tasted. An amazing balance between ripe, crystal-clear fruit and fine yet rich tannins. Full-bodied, with full tannins and concentrated fruit. A textbook claret that defines greatness in reds from this area. • $80 • (06/15/98) (BT) • **95-99**
St.-Estèphe 1995: Perhaps not the best Montrose, but very good. Blackberry and dried cherry aromas have bark undertones. Medium- to full-bodied, with well-integrated tannins. Slightly alcoholic on the medium finish. Needs time to come together. Tasted twice, with consistent notes. Best after 2000. 18,000 cases made. • $33 Ⓐ • (01/31/98) • **88**
St.-Estèphe 1994: Rather lean for Montrose, but has some attractive berry, vanilla, spice and redwood aromas and flavors. Slightly dry finish. Tasted twice with consistent notes. Drinkable now. 18,000 cases made. • $38 Ⓐ • (01/31/97) • **84**
St.-Estèphe 1993: Fabulous for a '93. Montrose continues to make excellent wines regardless of the vintage. Rich and elegant tobacco, cherry, smoke,

Key: SS—Spectator Selection CS—Cellar Selection HR—Highly Recommended BB—Best Buy $NA—Price not available Ⓐ—Auction Price (BT)—Barrel Tasting
Dates in parentheses indicate the issues in which the ratings were published.

FRANCE

toasty oak character, medium-to-full body, fine tannins and long, flavorful finish. Drinkable now. 21,250 cases made. • $24 Ⓐ • (01/31/96) • **90**

St.-Estèphe 1992: Well crafted and nicely textured, offering cassis, tobacco and cherry character. Medium-bodied and soft; a fruity finish. Drinkable now. • $25 Ⓐ • (04/15/95) • **86**

St.-Estèphe 1991: Soft, supple and pretty. A harmonious wine with berry, cherry and spice notes and an attractive finish. Tasted twice with consistent notes. • $28 • (03/31/94) • **85**

St.-Estèphe 1990: A polished, concentrated wine, with intense cherry, raspberry, vanilla and tobacco aromas and flavors, velvety tannins and a long, rich finish. Drinkable now. 22,000 cases made. • $96 Ⓐ • (03/31/93) • **94**

St.-Estèphe 1989 • $67 Ⓐ • (03/15/92) • **95**

St.-Estèphe 1988 • $42 Ⓐ • (03/31/91) • **87**

St.-Estèphe 1987 • $26 Ⓐ • (02/15/90) • **80**

St.-Estèphe 1986 • $49 Ⓐ • (05/15/89) SS • **96**

St.-Estèphe 1985 • $44 Ⓐ • (10/15/94) • **89**

St.-Estèphe 1984 • $27 Ⓐ • (03/31/87) • **88**

St.-Estèphe 1983 • $31 Ⓐ • (10/15/94) • **85**

St.-Estèphe 1982 • $82 Ⓐ • (08/31/92) • **92**

St.-Estèphe 1981 • $35 Ⓐ • (12/01/84) • **90**

St.-Estèphe 1979 • $26 Ⓐ • (10/15/89) • **81**

St.-Estèphe 1970 • $89 Ⓐ • (04/01/86) • **80**

St.-Estèphe 1962 • $100 • (11/30/87) • **90**

St.-Estèphe 1961 • $269 Ⓐ • (04/30/96) • **85**

St.-Estèphe 1959 • $157 Ⓐ • (10/15/90) • **90**

St.-Estèphe 1947: One bottle was very smooth, gentle and appealing for its spicy cherry and other lively flavors. Delicious, if a bit less imposing than expected from Montrose. Another bottle had turned acidic. • $200 Ⓐ • (05/31/97) • **89**

St.-Estèphe 1945 • $186 Ⓐ • (11/30/95) • **79**

MONTROSE, LA DAME DE

St.-Estèphe 1995: Plenty of berry, raspberry and fruit aromas. Medium-bodied, with velvety tannins and a medium-to-light finish. Very good second label of Château Montrose. Drink now or hold. 6,600 cases made. • $30 • (01/31/98) • **85**

St.-Estèphe 1994: Exhibits a caressing texture of silky tannins, but it's slightly lacking in fruit concentration. Medium-bodied, with a light midpalate. Drink now or hold. 7,250 cases made. • $30 • (01/31/97) • **78**

MONT-TANA

Merlot Vin de Pays d'Oc 1996: A lean wine with decent plum and berry flavors, but it doesn't flesh out as nicely as it should. • $7 • (11/15/97) • **80**

Sauvignon Blanc Vin de Pays d'Oc 1996: A fresh and fruity Sauvignon with ripe fruit flavors and a touch of buttery complexity. Drink now. • $8 • (10/31/97) • **84**

MONTUS, CHÂTEAU

Madiran 1995: Muscular, showing the very firm tannins typical of the Tannat grape, but there's enough fruit flavor for balance, and tar and licorice notes add interest. Try now. 12,500 cases made. • $20 • (09/30/97) • **86**

Madiran 1985 • $10 • (04/15/89) • **79**

Madiran Cuvée Prestige 1995: This is a big wine, muscular not fat, with deep color, very firm tannins and concentrated plum, tobacco and earth flavors that are closed right now. Has style and personality, but needs patience; try in 2000. 5,000 cases made. • $38 • (09/30/97) • **90**

Madiran Cuvée Prestige 1994: Beautifully displayed flavors of blackberry and plum make a sweet entry, then the tannins take over. Very astringent on the back palate and finish. It's doubtful that the fruit will survive the tannins. 7,000 cases made. • $36 • (09/30/97) • **85**

Madiran Cuvée Prestige 1990: Now almost 8 years old, this red is still young and tight, with very deep color, very firm tannins and excellent concentration. The still-fresh, still-closed flavors range from plum to raisin to chocolate. Deserves your patience; try in 2000. 5,600 cases made. • $35 • (01/01/97) • **92**

Madiran Cuvée Prestige 1989 • $30 • (07/15/92) • **85**

Madiran Elevée en Fûts de Chêne 1989 • $17 • (07/15/92) • **77**

Pacherenc du Vic-Bilh Sec 1995: Like a rustic version of white Bordeaux. Vanilla and clove accents dominate this white, which picks up notes of gooseberry and melon. Rich in texture and sporting some tannin, it makes an impression. • $19 • (09/30/97) • **84**

MONTVAC, DOMAINE DE

Vacqueyras 1993: Showing its age, this light-bodied wine combines lean, herbal flavors with dry tannins. Drink up. 6,000 cases made. • $12 • (02/28/97) • **76**

MONTVIEL, CHÂTEAU

Pomerol 1996: An elegant wine with sweet berry flavors, slightly earthy overtones. Medium in body, with medium tannins and a sweet fruit finish. Pretty. • $NA • (01/01/97) (BT) • **85-89**

Pomerol 1995: A pretty '95, with crushed berry character, medium-to-light body and fine tannins. Early drinker. Not as good as last year. • $30 • (01/01/97) (BT) • **80-84**

MOREAU, BERNARD

Chassagne-Montrachet 1996: Lively and vibrant, with mineral, honey, pear, toasty oak and lots of citrus flavors, this crisp, medium-bodied Chassagne is delicious. Give it time and the texture will turn smooth. Try around 2000. • $30 • (05/31/98) • **87**

Chassagne-Montrachet 1995: A tough wine to taste. Square and hard, with an herbal backdrop to some wonderfully sweet fruit, honey, lactic, spice and nut character. Well made, with good concentration. Should develop into something lovely around 2000. • $30 • (08/31/97) • **88**

Chassagne-Montrachet La Maltroie 1995: Bold, rich but rather hard, showing some candied flavors, with oak, quince, tropical fruit, mineral and lemon notes. Full-bodied, but a touch dry on the finish. Try now. • $35 • (05/31/97) • **84**

Chassagne-Montrachet Les Chenevottes 1996: Lovely ripe fruit character—more so than in many '96 Chassagnes. The ripe pear, spice, mineral, honey and toasty hazelnut mingle beautifully in this medium-bodied, racy wine. Wonderful balance of fruit, acidity and oak. Nice now, better after 2000. • $38 • (05/31/98) • **88**

Chassagne-Montrachet Les Chenevottes 1995: Wonderful, from start to finish, with a lively core of lime, cilantro and dried herb accented by sweet-tasting ripe fruit, spice and earth. Balanced and full-bodied, with a firm finish that will need time. Try after 2000. • $35 • (05/31/97) • **90**

Chassagne-Montrachet Les Grandes Ruchottes 1995: Very impressive but hard as nails, it's idiosyncratic and distinctive, full-bodied and superintense, with zingy acidity and some toasty oak, tropical fruit, honey and mineral notes. Like a lit fuse on the finish; don't touch until 2005. • $39 • (08/31/97) • **89**

Chassagne-Montrachet Morgeot 1996: Racy and well made, medium-bodied, with a lush, round, creamlike mouthfeel. Delivers subtle apple, mineral, dried herb, toasty oak and grass aromas and flavors to a steely but vibrant finish. Will soften and improve with age. Try after 2002. • $38 • (05/31/98) • **88**

Chassagne-Montrachet Morgeot 1995: Super. Ripe and rich, with a happy marriage of tropical, dried herb and mineral notes. Full-bodied, with great length on the finish. Try from 2000 to 2010. • $35 • (05/31/97) • **92**

MOREAU, LOUIS

Chablis 1996: Ripe in character, and well balanced, with some nice butter, lemon and apple flavors. Medium-bodied, it turns a bit sharp on the finish. Try now. 2,000 cases imported. 6,610 cases made. • $17 • (08/31/97) • **80**

Chablis Domaine de Bieville 1995: Fun. Like lemonade; lots of lemon and fruit character and a bit spritzy. Fresh and light-bodied. Tart finish. Drink now. • $NA • (08/31/96) • **82**

Chablis Les Fourneaux 1996: Ripe yet elegant, fat yet crisp, with honey, mineral, pear, mocha and spice flavors. Silky at first, it turns up the toasty, slightly burning notes on the intense finish. Needs time. Try around 2000. 640 cases made. • $25 • (05/31/98) • **87**

Chablis Les Fourneaux 1995: Clean, well-defined and tightly built, with lots of mouthpuckering citrus flavors—a crisp character that's unusual for '95 Chablis but refreshing. A bit one-dimensional, but delicious now. 511 cases made. • $NA • (06/15/97) • **86**

Chablis Premier Cru 1995: Tight and tart, but with a good minerally, chewy core and some ripe, sweet-tasting litchi, pear and pineapple flavors. Medium-bodied. Try now. • $NA • (06/15/97) • **85**

Chablis Vaulignot 1996: Ripe and vibrant, this well-made and balanced '96 Chablis is fairly refined and very flavorful, with a silky character. Medium-bodied, it delivers earth, apple, pear and mineral notes. Try around 2003. 2,080 cases made. • $22 • (05/31/98) • **87**

Chablis Vaulignot 1995: Distinctive and racy, with flinty, matchstick, smoke and mineral notes, ripe and elegant, too, it also delivers lovely pear, floral and melon notes. Full-bodied. Try after 2000. 2,044 cases made. • $NA • (06/15/97) • **89**

Petit Chablis 1996: Fairly ripe, but also crisp and acidic. Shows lime and grapefruit flavors, touches of honey and mineral. A bit grassy and chewy on the finish. Drink now. 650 cases imported. 1,978 cases made. • $NA • (08/31/97) • **84**

MOREAU & FILS, J.

Chablis 1996: Fairly soft, with ripe pear, melon and tropical fruit flavors. Medium-bodied, slightly chewy and dry on the finish. • $NA • (08/31/97) • **78**

Chablis 1995: Medium-bodied, with an intense burst of lemon and apple flavors followed by a slightly green, bitter almond note that lingers on the chewy finish. • $15 • (08/31/96) • **83**

Chablis 1994 • $13 • (08/31/95) • **82**

Chablis Les Clos 1996: Sensational quality defines this racy yet generous, opulent, full-bodied white. A mineral streak weaves itself through the creamy, silky structure, offering an ethereal experience of wet stones, flinty notes and a real sense of *terroir*. Add the fresh citrus, honey, floral and pear flavors and you get a divine complexity. Pure, clean, chewy finish. Try after 2000. • $47 • (05/31/98) • **98**

Chablis Les Clos 1994 • $40 • (05/31/96) • **92**

Chablis Les Clos 1993 • $47 • (08/31/95) • **85**

Chablis Les Clos des Hospices 1994 • $48 • (05/31/96) • **89**

Chablis Les Clos des Hospices 1993 • $55 • (08/31/95) • **84**

Chablis Moreau 1994 • $15 • (05/31/96) • **79**

Chablis Vaillons 1996: Minerally but also quite herbal and slightly drying, this medium-bodied wine is tough, even tart. Try around 2000. • $25 • (05/31/98) • **78**

Chablis Vaillons 1995: *Premier cru* in a crisp, firm style. Medium-bodied, with a flavorful balance of spicy earthiness and sweet ripeness. Attractive, chewy and chalky long finish. Drink now. • $22 • (08/31/96) • **88**

Chablis Vaillons 1994 • $22 • (05/31/96) • **83**

Chablis Vaillons 1993 • $25 • (08/31/95) • **83**

Chablis Vaillons Cuvée Préstige Guy Moreau 1995: Very classy. This *premier cru*, with a tightly knit structure, shows depth of flavor, its supple texture accented by salt, lemon, mineral, ripe pear, honey and apple notes. Full-bodied. Drink now through 2005. From 60-year-old vines. • $27 • (06/15/97) • **88**

Chablis Vaillons Cuvée Préstige Guy Moreau 1994 • $25 • (05/31/96) • **74**

Chablis Valmur 1996: Wonderful '96 Chablis in a very earthy, wet-soil kind of style, showing a real *goût de terroir*. Loads of mineral mingle with pear, honey and dried herb flavors. Lush, opulent and distinctive, it ends on a seamless, superlong finish. Bravo! Tempting now through 2005. • $46 • (05/31/98) • **93**

Chablis Valmur 1995: Rich, with some mineral and spice flavors, but too earthy and slightly dry on the palate. Not elegant. Tasted twice, with consistent notes. • $43 • (06/15/97) • **72**

Chablis Valmur 1994 • $39 • (05/31/96) • **91**

Chablis Valmur 1993 • $47 • (08/31/95) • **81**

Chablis Vaudésir 1996: This thick, round Chablis seems a bit forward. Full-bodied and silky, with a mocha, mineral, honey and pear pie character. Burns a bit on the slightly hot finish. Try now through 2000. • $45 • (05/31/98) • **82**

Chablis Vaudésir 1995: This full-bodied *grand cru* is both crisp and supple, showing lively fruit flavors but also grass, dried herbs, flint, wet stone, mineral and honey notes. Pure and clean, a wine for drinking now through 2005. • $43 • (06/15/97) • **87**

Chablis Vaudésir 1994 • $39 • (05/31/96) • **88**

Chablis Vaudésir 1993 • $47 • (08/31/95) • **85**

Merlot Vin de Pays de Cassan 1992 • $6 • (02/28/95) • **83**

MOREUX, PATRICE

Pouilly-Fumé La Loge aux Moines 1995: Big-boned for a Sauvignon Blanc, this shows ripe pear and melon flavors with attractive spice and smoke notes. It's concentrated yet still refreshing, with a long, citrus-accented finish. 700 cases made. • $19 • (05/15/97) • **90**

MOREUX, ROGER

Sancerre 1995: Hazelnut and light earthy flavors give this big white a distinctive character. A bit rustic, but has good concentration. 1,800 cases made. • $17 • (06/15/97) • **84**

Sancerre Les Monts Damnés 1995: Bright grasslike and floral aromas give way to round flavors of apple and peach in this soft but lively white. Pretty, and easy to drink. 500 cases made. • $19 • (06/15/97) • **85**

MOREY, ALBERT

Bâtard-Montrachet 1992: Strikes a nice balance between ripe, spicy pear and vanilla flavors, but it doesn't have all the extra dimensions. Young and awkward, still it's a nice glass of Bâtard. • $114 • (02/28/94) • **85**

MOREY, BERNARD

Chassagne-Montrachet Caillerets 1993: Clean and well-made mineral and honey aromas and flavors, medium body and good texture. Drink now. • $35 • (05/15/95) • **86**

Chassagne-Montrachet Caillerets 1992: Doesn't quite taste ripe. It's a crisp and lean style with tart acidity and a narrow band of pear and spice flavors; clipped on the finish. Drinkable now. • $33 • (02/28/94) • **81**

Chassagne-Montrachet La Maltroie 1996: Full-bodied, supple and tempting, with more ripe, intense fruit than many '96 Chassagnes. Offers a smooth, creamlike texture and a pear, bread dough, spice and toasty oak character. Pretty finish. Drink now through 2002. • $45 • (05/31/98) • **88**

Chassagne-Montrachet Les Baudines 1993: Lean mineral and apple aromas and flavors, light body, crisp finish. 75 cases imported. • $35 • (05/15/95) • **81**

Chassagne-Montrachet Les Baudines 1992: Tight and crisp with vanilla, pear and apple notes that are intense and lively, but it lacks body and depth. Drinkable now. • $33 • (02/28/94) • **87**

Chassagne-Montrachet Les Embazées 1993: Superbly crafted, exhibiting a subtle mineral, apple and melon character and lovely, silky texture. Drinkable now. • $35 • (05/15/95) • **89**

Chassagne-Montrachet Les Embazées 1992: A low-key style with muted spice and pear flavors that come up short on the finish. Drinkable now. • $33 • (02/28/94) • **84**

Chassagne-Montrachet Morgeot 1993: Honey, lemon and mineral character galore and a slight grassiness. Medium body and finish; high acidity. Drinkable now. • $35 • (05/15/95) • **83**

Chassagne-Montrachet Morgeot 1992: Ripe and supple with spicy pear, honey and nutmeg flavors that run deep and complex. Has the depth and concentration to age. Drinkable now. • $33 • (02/28/94) • **89**

Chassagne-Montrachet Red 1990: Crisp and firm, with tight, ripe strawberry, oak and spice flavors and anise and currant notes that linger on the finish. Drinkable now. 130 cases made. • $28 • (06/15/93) • **85**

Chassagne-Montrachet Red 1989 • $23 • (11/30/92) • **81**

Chassagne-Montrachet Red 1987 • $20 • (10/31/89) • **75**

Chassagne-Montrachet Vieille Vigne 1993: Toast, apple, pear and chalk flavors are quite tight and hard now, but show a round mouthfeel. Lovely, steely. Try now. • $NA • (05/15/95) • **86**

Chassagne-Montrachet Vieille Vigne 1992: A wine with uninteresting, simple flavors that don't taste ripe or intense. Watery finish. Drink now. • $29 • (02/28/94) • **80**

St.-Aubin Le Charmois White 1992: Smooth and creamy, with intense, focused spice, hazelnut and pear flavors. Finishes with good length; drinkable now. • $23 • (02/28/94) • **83**

Santenay Grand Clos Rousseau 1987 • $24 • (10/15/89) • **87**

MOREY, MARC

Bâtard-Montrachet 1993: Impressive concentration. Layers of ripe fruit and fresh acidity, full-bodied, wonderful cream, apple and mineral flavors and extremely long aftertaste. Drinkable now. 15 cases made. • $110 • (08/31/95) • **89**

Bâtard-Montrachet 1992: Big-volumed Burgundy, with gorgeous, complex honey, pear, peach, lemon and toast character in extremely well-proportioned amounts; subtle yet deep, it melts like butter in the palate and picks up intensity on the finish. • $92 • (08/31/94) • **93**

Beaune Les Paules 1988 • $24 • (08/31/90) • **85**

Beaune Les Paules 1985 • $15 • (12/31/88) • **84**

Key: SS—Spectator Selection CS—Cellar Selection HR—Highly Recommended BB—Best Buy $NA—Price not available Ⓐ—Auction Price (BT)—Barrel Tasting

Dates in parentheses indicate the issues in which the ratings were published.

Chassagne-Montrachet 1996: Lovely, well made, concentrated and silky village wine. Offers a creamlike, minerally, supple mouthfeel backed by intense flavors. Elegant yet with plenty of ripe fruit. Balanced by fresh acidity, this is a joy now, but should improve. Drink now through 2005. 205 cases made. • $32 • (05/31/98) • **90**

Chassagne-Montrachet 1994: Quite supple and attractive, backed by vanilla, apple, pear, cream and mineral flavors. The oak flavors are a bit too pronounced, but it's nicely round on the finish. 79 cases made. • $33 • (05/31/96) • **85**

Chassagne-Montrachet 1992: Woody, buttery flavors dominate this clean, solidly-built Chassagne. Drinkable now. • $30 • (08/31/94) • **83**

Chassagne-Montrachet Caillerets 1995: Shows lovely ripe fruit, along with some dried- and fresh-herb, delicious tropical fruit, pear and mineral notes. Medium- to full-bodied, it coats the palate. Intense finish needs until after 2000 to soften. • $50 • (08/31/97) • **89**

Chassagne-Montrachet Caillerets 1993: Fat and rich, harmonious, sporting a chalk, mineral, pineapple, vanilla and ripe fruit character. Almost outstanding. • $35 • (05/15/95) • **89**

Chassagne-Montrachet En Virondot 1996: Distinctive, very intense and balanced Chassagne, full-bodied and flavorful, with ripe fruit and an earthy, almost gamy white truffle, vanilla bean, mineral and citrus character. Supple on the midpalate and steely on the finish. Best from 2002 through 2005. 950 cases made. • $44 • (05/31/98) • **90**

Chassagne-Montrachet En Virondot 1995: This *premier cru* is silky-smooth, full-bodied, creamy-textured, with mineral, pear, piecrust, vanilla bean, honey and butter flavors and a seductive finish. It's a lovely wine that tastes great now but should improve through at least 2000. 916 cases made. • $45 • (05/31/97) • **90**

Chassagne-Montrachet En Virondot 1994: Like eating a waffle with maple syrup. Soft, sweet and fun to drink now. Lots of honey, pear, piecrust and doughy flavors. 1,083 cases made. • $40 • (05/31/96) • **85**

Chassagne-Montrachet En Virondot 1993: Fresh and zesty, a vibrant, straightforward white that bubbles with life but little depth. Shows some pear, melon and salty flavors. Drink now. • $35 • (05/15/95) • **80**

Chassagne-Montrachet En Virondot 1992: Seductive, full-bodied and silky with excellent balance; the flavors wrap around a tight core of pear, grapefruit and honey. It remains fresh and crisp on the finish. Drinkable now. • $35 • (08/31/94) • **90**

Chassagne-Montrachet Les Chenevottes 1996: Subtle, subdued and reserved, this classy, minerally, full-bodied Chassagne offers a slick, seductive smoothness of texture, caressing ripe fruit and a wonderful balance between all parts, including acidity and oak. The finish could be a bit more intense. Drink now through 2006. 660 cases made. • $44 • (05/31/98) • **91**

Chassagne-Montrachet Les Chenevottes 1995: Subtle yet flavorful. A rich, thick and ripe wine that keeps its balance, harmony and elegance. Drinkable now. • $42 • (08/31/97) • **89**

Chassagne-Montrachet Les Chenevottes 1994: Thick and opulent, this showy, full-bodied white Burgundy delivers lots of toasty coconut, caramel, pear and butter flavors. Turns very oaky on the rich finish. Drinkable now. Tasted twice, with consistent notes. 500 cases made. • $40 • (05/31/96) • **86**

Chassagne-Montrachet Les Chenevottes 1992: Rather bold and gold-colored Chassagne, with butterscotch, butter and pear flavors; it's round and ready to drink, with a silky, somewhat mature texture. • $35 • (08/31/94) • **84**

Chassagne-Montrachet Les Vergers 1996: A pure, racy *premier cru* of great personality, layered with grass, honey, lime and mineral intensity that makes you pay attention. Serious stuff here—full-bodied, long, deep and very interesting. Balanced finish. Drink now through 2003. 540 cases made. • $48 • (05/31/98) • **93**

Chassagne-Montrachet Les Vergers 1994: Round and supple yet fresh. Approachable now, it's seductive without being overdone. Enjoy the lovely, unctuous mix of honey, lime, butter, cream and mineral flavors that caress your palate. Whoa! 516 cases made. • $40 • (05/31/96) • **90**

Chassagne-Montrachet Morgeot 1996: A very pretty, full-bodied, smooth, creamy Chassagne. Delicious vanilla, milk, pear, spice and bread dough flavors. Decent intensity, and while quite oaky, it manages to deliver a balanced package with a clean, long finish. Best from 2000 through 2005. 150 cases made. • $50 • (05/31/98) • **91**

Chassagne-Montrachet Morgeot 1995: Round and supple, with subtle citrus, toasty hazelnut, pear and biscuit flavors. Medium to full in body, with a ripe note, but turns a bit tart on the finish. Needs time; try after 2000. • $50 • (08/31/97) • **89**

Chassagne-Montrachet Morgeot 1994: Rich yet elegant, with loads of honey, fresh fig and date flavors, but also enough lemon and grapefruit notes to give this full-bodied wine a sense of balance. The nutmeg and spice add complexity to the finish. 141 cases made. • $48 • (05/31/96) • **87**

Chassagne-Montrachet Morgeot 1993: Lovely, very showy young white presenting nut, apple and pear aromas and flavors, medium body, ripe fruit and round finish. Drink now. • $35 • (05/15/95) • **86**

Chassagne-Montrachet Morgeot 1992: Ripe and buttery in flavor, rich and smooth in texture, yet lively and well-balanced with acidity. • $36 • (08/31/94) • **85**

Puligny-Montrachet Les Pucelles 1995: Fantastic. This unique '95 is vibrant yet dense, full-bodied and elegant, fresh like dawn yet amazingly complex. It delivers a symphony of pure, clean, well-defined lemon, toasty oak and spice notes along with all sorts of fresh fruit flavors that persist on the long finish. Should only gain complexity after 2000. 167 cases made. • $45 • (05/31/97) • **95**

Puligny-Montrachet Les Pucelles 1994: Distinctive for its attractive, chewy, chalky texture; a mouthful of a wine, with mineral and floral qualities in its honey and pear flavors. Full-bodied and a bit soft. Drinkable now. 166 cases made. • $60 • (05/31/96) • **86**

Puligny-Montrachet Les Pucelles 1993: Quite young, exhibiting very good concentration of fruit and fresh acidity, medium body and earthy mineral finish. • $50 • (05/15/95) • **87**

Puligny-Montrachet Les Pucelles 1992: A seductively rich, fat style with abundant, ripe flavors of pear, honey, cream and vanilla. If richness is your goal, you can't do much better than this. Full-bodied; drinkable now. • $53 • (08/31/94) • **90**

MOREY, PIERRE

Bourgogne White 1992: Simple and lean, clean but neutral, showing just a hint of apple, smoke and lemon flavors. • $19 • (08/31/94) • **78**

MOREY-BLANC

Meursault Les Charmes 1992: Modestly-proportioned white, with some pear, vanilla, butter and toast notes. Well-balanced but on a modest scale. • $57 • (08/31/94) • **83**

Meursault Les Narvaux 1992: A bit traditional and rustic, showing straightforward fruit and a touch of butter. It's sturdy and lacks finesse. • $40 • (08/31/94) • **79**

MOREY-COFFINET, MICHEL

Chassagne-Montrachet 1996: Successful village wine. Lovely and reserved in aroma, it delivers a mouthful of ripe fruit and spice, smoke and earth complexity. Silky and creamlike, it weighs on the midpalate, with caressing texture. A bit crisp, even rustic, on the finish. Try around 2002. 300 cases made. • $35 • (05/31/98) • **89**

Chassagne-Montrachet 1995: Intense and concentrated—the hallmarks of the outstanding '95 white Burgundies—this offers a generous dried herb, honey and wet stone character. A marvelous, medium- to-full-bodied wine, with a crisp finish that needs until after 2000 to be tamed. • $32 • (08/31/97) • **90**

Chassagne-Montrachet 1994: More cardboard and paper than fruit, and old already. Tasted twice with consistent notes. • $NA • (08/31/96) • **70**

Chassagne-Montrachet 1992: Ripe, buttery aromas give way to simple, earthy flavors and an earthy finish, making this an awkward, old-fashioned style. • $25 • (07/31/94) • **78**

Chassagne-Montrachet Caillerets 1996: A subtle and caressing Chassagne, showing lots of finesse and balance, with pear, tropical, mineral, apple and pronounced toasty oak accents. Medium-bodied, it's just a touch hollow on the midpalate, but good for drinking now. 250 cases made. • $45 • (05/31/98) • **82**

Chassagne-Montrachet Caillerets 1994: Ripe and rich, with a caramel, baked apple, cinnamon and spice character. The toasty oak notes dominate the fruit now, but this is a full-bodied and rather showy white with a very long finish. A wine to enjoy now. 225 cases made. • $34 • (05/31/96) • **88**

Chassagne-Montrachet Caillerets 1992: Straightforward simple style of white Burgundy that doesn't have much fruit in the aromas or flavors. It tastes diluted; only a lingering lemon and mineral character gives it life. • $36 • (07/31/94) • **78**

Chassagne-Montrachet La Romanée 1996: Subtle yet quite opulent, well made and silky in texture, this full-bodied Chassagne delights with its pure, clean fruit and citrus, mineral, honey and toasty oak accents. Balanced but not very long or intense. Buy a case to enjoy now through 2005. 265 cases made. • $47 • (05/31/98) • **91**

Chassagne-Montrachet La Romanée 1995: A smooth *premier cru* indeed, rather accessible upon release, with butterscotch, vanilla, toasty oak flavors dominating the fruit, but this full-bodied wine turns on the power on the long finish. Has more voluptuous body than the regular Chassagne, though the latter has more muscled youth. Drink now through 2005. • $45 • (08/31/97) • **92**

Chassagne-Montrachet La Romanée 1994: A beautifully crafted, medium- to full-bodied white that's incredibly supple and creamy in texture, with a solid mineral character. Has some hints of basil and oregano, wet earth and apple flavors. Harmonious and elegant, it beckons for another sip. Terrific. 233 cases made. • $37 • (05/31/96) • **88**

Chassagne-Montrachet La Romanée 1992: This rich, satisfying white Burgundy has butterscotch and custard aromas followed by lemon, apple and floral flavors that expand and linger on the finish. Nicely balanced. Drinkable now. • $39 • (07/31/94) • **87**

MORILLEAU, MICHEL

Chardonnay Vin de Pays du Jardin de la France Prieuré Royal Saint-Laurent Réserve 1995: Light vanilla notes add interest to this crisp white, and the apple and lemon flavors are bright and clean. A good apéritif. 10,000 cases made. • $8 • (05/15/97) • **83**

Muscadet-Côtes de Grandlieu Prieuré Royal Saint-Laurent 1995: Though firm acidity is the dominant element in this refreshing white, rounder flavors of pear, almond and herb emerge on the finish. Deceptively simple, it's quite enticing. 5,000 cases made. • $9 • (05/15/97) • **87**

MORIN, GÉRARD

Sancerre Le Manoir 1993 • $14 • (11/15/95) • **87**

Sancerre Vieilles Vignes 1996: Offers vivid grapefruit and mineral aromas, then turns simpler on the palate, with apple and citrus flavors and a light soapy note that diminishes its crispness and focus. Drink now. • $15 • (05/31/98) • **82**

Sancerre Vieilles Vignes 1995: This lean white shows some herb and green apple flavors, but a strong earthy note undermines its meager pleasures. • $15 • (06/15/97) • **75**

MOROT, ALBERT

Beaune Les Bressandes 1990: Very mellow, with nice, subtle toast and smoke notes bracketed between earth, chestnut and cherry flavors. Round and supple on the finish. Drinkable now. • $38 • (12/15/92) • **86**

Beaune Les Bressandes 1988 • $30 • (03/31/91) • **87**

Beaune Les Cents Vignes 1991: Tough, astringent, earthy and bitter with little freshness or charm. • $28 Ⓐ • (01/31/94) • **73**

Beaune Les Cents Vignes 1988 • $30 • (04/30/91) • **91**

Beaune Les Grèves 1988 • $32 • (07/15/91) • **86**

Beaune Les Marconnets 1990: A bit simple but good, showing modest strawberry, earth, wet hay and plum aromas and flavors, medium body and supple tannins. Drinkable now. • $38 • (12/15/92) • **84**

Beaune Les Teurons 1991: Gamy, ashy aromas and flavors add a layer of complexity to the modest cherry flavors. Finish is tough and earthy. • $28 Ⓐ • (01/31/94) • **78**

Beaune Les Teurons 1990: Ripe and juicy, with pretty plum and berry notes that don't offer much length, but certainly give a lot of pleasure. Drinkable now. • $39 • (12/15/92) • **85**

Beaune Les Teurons 1988 • $20 Ⓐ • (07/15/91) • **80**

Beaune Les Toussaints 1991: A quiet wine, offering modest berry and chocolate aromas and flavors and a bite of tannin on the light finish. Drinkable now. • $28 Ⓐ • (01/31/94) • **79**

Beaune Les Toussaints 1990: Pleasant and approachable, with nice chestnut and berry notes and a light, velvety finish. Drinkable now. • $38 • (12/15/92) • **84**

Savigny-lès-Beaune Aux Vergelesses 1991: Bright raspberry flavor enlivens this modest, sharply focused wine. Crisp and light; drinkable now. • $26 • (01/31/94) • **82**

Savigny-lès-Beaune Aux Vergelesses La Bataillère 1988 • $26 • (03/31/91) • **86**

MORTET, CHARLES

Bourgogne 1989 • $14 • (01/31/92) • **87**

Key: SS—Spectator Selection CS—Cellar Selection HR—Highly Recommended BB—Best Buy $NA—Price not available Ⓐ—Auction Price (BT)—Barrel Tasting

Dates in parentheses indicate the issues in which the ratings were published.

Bourgogne 1986 • $15 • (06/15/89) • **79**

Chambertin 1989 • $68 • (01/31/92) • **94**

Chambertin 1987 • $69 • (03/31/90) • **87**

Chambertin 1986 • $62 • (02/28/89) • **91**

Chambertin 1985 • $64 • (06/15/88) • **90**

Chambolle-Musigny Aux Beaux Bruns 1989 • $34 • (01/31/92) • **89**

Clos de Vougeot 1989 • $47 • (01/31/92) • **86**

Clos de Vougeot 1986 • $43 • (04/15/89) • **84**

Gevrey-Chambertin 1989 • $25 • (01/31/92) • **88**

Gevrey-Chambertin 1988 • $35 • (02/15/91) • **89**

Gevrey-Chambertin 1987 • $28 • (03/31/90) • **86**

Gevrey-Chambertin 1986 • $24 • (02/28/89) • **87**

Gevrey-Chambertin Champeaux 1989 • $34 • (01/31/92) • **90**

Gevrey-Chambertin Champeaux 1988 • $46 • (03/15/91) • **87**

Gevrey-Chambertin Champeaux 1987 • $36 • (03/31/90) • **81**

Gevrey-Chambertin Champeaux 1986 • $33 • (02/28/89) • **86**

Gevrey-Chambertin Clos Prieur 1989 • $30 • (01/31/92) • **88**

Gevrey-Chambertin Clos Prieur 1988 • $41 • (02/15/91) • **91**

Gevrey-Chambertin Clos Prieur 1987 • $32 • (03/31/90) • **83**

Gevrey-Chambertin Clos Prieur 1986 • $30 • (02/28/89) • **84**

Gevrey-Chambertin Clos Prieur 1985 • $29 • (07/31/88) • **92**

MORTET, DENIS

Bourgogne Les Charmes au Châtelain 1994: Ambitious winemaking lets the oak dominate, but there is also good concentration of red berry flavor. Medium-bodied. Impressive for a basic Burgundy. • $18 • (11/15/96) • **83**

Bourgogne Les Charmes au Châtelain 1993: Like freshly crushed raspberries and black cherries. Full- to medium-bodied, adding firm tannins and a long, fresh finish. Try now. • $15 • (11/15/95) • **88**

Bourgogne Les Charmes au Châtelain 1992: Delicious, with a ripe core of currant and black cherry flavors and a touch of vanilla, all presented in a sophisticated package. • $NA • (12/15/94) • **83**

Chambertin 1995: Utterly beguiling, with deep aromas and flavors of cassis, black cherry and exotic oak, an elegant mouthfeel, a subtle vanilla finish. Forward, and approachable in 1999. • $115 • (11/15/97) • **93**

Chambertin 1994: Firm in texture, offering currant and berry flavors with nice hints of anise and other spices. A pretty wine with a freshness that needs until 2000 or so to fan out. • $90 • (11/15/96) • **87**

Chambertin 1993: Super well-crafted Burgundy, offering lovely wild berry, plum and currant character and a hint of vanilla. Medium in body, loads of tannins and long, sweet fruit finish. Better in 1999. • $115 • (11/15/95) • **94**

Chambertin 1992: Very pretty, with an appealing rose petal accent to the blackberry and raspberry flavors up front; fades a little on the finish. Charming; drinkable now. • $NA • (12/15/94) • **85**

Chambertin 1991: Lean and focused, a spicy wine with a fine thread of black cherry and earth aromas and flavors, sharply focused and elegant on the finish. Try now. • $91 Ⓐ • (01/31/94) • **86**

Chambolle-Musigny Aux Beaux Bruns 1995: With its beautiful, deep, brooding Pinot Noir character, this red Burgundy has it all. The remarkably vibrant raspberry and blackberry flavors are framed softly by floral and vanilla nuances, and the structure is solid. Balanced by finely integrated tannins, its power is matched only by its finesse. Try in 2002. 110 cases made. • $59 • (11/15/97) HR • **97**

Chambolle-Musigny Aux Beaux Bruns 1994: Combines pure fruit character with an elegant structure and a supple texture to create a lithe, delicious wine whose elements do curlicues on the long, enchanting finish. Approachable now. • $46 • (11/15/96) • **90**

Chambolle-Musigny Aux Beaux Bruns 1993: Seductive ripe fruit, tobacco and toasty oak notes, medium-to-full body, silky tannins and long, flavorful aftertaste. Better in 2000. • $43 • (11/15/95) • **91**

Chambolle-Musigny Aux Beaux Bruns 1992: Charming and delicate, with enough currant and red berry flavors to make it interesting. Supple and elegant finish. Try soon. • $NA • (12/15/94) • **84**

Chambolle-Musigny Aux Beaux Bruns 1991: A delicate wine that shows little distinction. Drinkable now. • $46 Ⓐ • (01/31/94) • **78**

Clos Vougeot 1995: A stunning Clos Vougeot, packed with ripe blackberry flavor matched by a beautifully balanced structure and a sense of harmony. Just needs until 2003 to hit its stride. Brilliantly done. • $81 • (11/15/97) • **95**

Clos Vougeot 1994: Complex, rich and perfumy, layering focused and racy flavors of anise, fresh mushroom, violet and berry. Crisp on the finish, but balanced by the solid flavors. • $63 • (11/15/96) • **88**

Clos Vougeot 1993: Blockbuster Burgundy featuring complex aromas and flavors of plum, vanilla and spice. Super fruity, followed by a super finish. Great backbone of tannins. Try after 2000. • $80 • (11/15/95) • **94**

Clos Vougeot 1992: Impressive for its pure fruit, tightly structured with firm, fine tannins and a beam of lovely currant and berry flavor that lingers on the finish. Try now. • $NA • (12/15/94) • **88**

Clos Vougeot 1991: Light, fragrant, simple and direct, offering a narrow beam of raspberry and earth aromas and flavors. Drinkable now. • $63 Ⓐ • (01/31/94) • **81**

Gevrey-Chambertin 1995: A brooding, deep, complex and darkly colored red Burgundy offering loads of blackberry character, wonderfully integrated spicy oak and firm tannins. Presented in a balanced package. Try after 2000. 1,125 cases made. • $42 • (11/15/97) • **91**

Gevrey-Chambertin 1994: Fresh as dawn, a remarkable village wine sparkling with life. Full of beautifully defined cassis bush, black cherry and black currant flavors. Medium-bodied and very juicy, with nicely integrated tannins and a long finish. Worth holding until 1999. • $33 • (11/15/96) • **91**

Gevrey-Chambertin 1993: An impressive village wine that's wonderfully floral and fruity. Medium-bodied, with fine tannins and a long, succulent finish. Delicious to taste, but will age for many years to come. Try in 2000. • $42 • (09/15/96) • **90**

Gevrey-Chambertin 1992: Light but quite delicious, with a sweet core of clean raspberry and cherry flavors and a supple, crisp finish. Well made and juicy. • $NA • (12/15/94) • **84**

Gevrey-Chambertin 1991: Light, fresh and agreeable, showing earthy strawberry aromas and flavors. Finishes earthy. Drinkable now. • $33 Ⓐ • (01/31/94) • **78**

Gevrey-Chambertin Au Vellé 1995: Brilliant, racy and sexy. A sip of this medium- to full-bodied, pure-tasting beauty transports you to the highest levels of winedom, as the layers of cassis, blackberry, earth, violet, rose petal and toasty, smoky and spicy oak meld in a wonderful whole with firm tannins, crisp acidity and succulent, ripe fruit. Long finish. Tempting around 2000, best after 2005. 575 cases made. • $47 • (11/15/97) • **92**

Gevrey-Chambertin Au Vellé 1994: Relatively supple and sweet tasting, with raspberry, currant and earth flavors. Medium-bodied. Drinkable now. • $37 • (11/15/96) • **80**

Gevrey-Chambertin Au Vellé 1993: A lovely, silky red featuring very good color and plenty of dried cherry, plum, chocolate character, medium body, fine tannins and crisp finish. Better in 2000. • $46 • (11/15/95) • **88**

Gevrey-Chambertin Champeaux 1993: Well-crafted cherry and vanilla aromas and flavors, medium body, fine tannins and sweet, fruity finish. Drinkable now. • $58 • (11/15/95) • **90**

Gevrey-Chambertin Champeaux 1992: A sturdy red with straightforward currant and floral flavors that persist into a chunky finish. Best now. • $NA • (12/15/94) • **83**

Gevrey-Chambertin Champeaux 1991: Light, refreshing and charming, serving up spicy raspberry and strawberry flavors and a hint of anise on the smooth finish. Drinkable now. • $46 Ⓐ • (01/31/94) • **84**

Gevrey-Chambertin Clos Prieur 1991: Smooth, supple, flavorful and medium in weight, displaying appealing currant and blackberry flavors. Drinkable now. • $40 Ⓐ • (01/31/94) • **85**

Gevrey-Chambertin En Champs Vieille Vigne 1995: An exotic, seductive Pinot from the spicy, blackberry, violet and coffee aromas to the long supple finish. Loads of blackberry, cassis and smoky oak flavors. Shows great class and finesse, with fine tannins and a dense mouthfeel. Should hit its stride around 2000. 204 cases made. • $55 • (11/15/97) • **93**

Gevrey-Chambertin En Champs Vieille Vigne 1993: Impressively dark-colored, sporting a lovely ripe berry, plum character on the nose. Surprisingly delicate finish. Medium in body, adding silky tannins and vanilla, cherry aftertaste. Try in 1999. • $50 • (11/15/95) • **90**

Gevrey-Chambertin En Motrot 1995: Gorgeous purity of clean, scrumptious red- and blackberry flavor shines through in this full-bodied, ripe, seductive, perfumy and racy red Burgundy. Notes of spice, mocha, chocolate, toasty and smoky oak play subtly in the background, giving depth to a complex wine. Near perfect finish. Tempting now through 2010. 240 cases made. • $47 • (11/15/97) • **95**

Gevrey-Chambertin En Motrot 1994: Fresh and flavorful, with well-defined black currant, toasty oak and plum flavors. Medium-bodied, ripe and sweet-tasting, it strives for concentration but has a tannic streak—might soften by 1998. • $37 • (11/15/96) • **86**

Gevrey-Chambertin En Motrot 1993: A silky, medium-bodied Gevrey, bursting with fresh, grapey and ripe red berry flavors. Touches of earth persist on the finish. Well-defined structure and beautiful texture should make this a delight to drink in 2000. • $46 • (11/15/95) • **90**

Gevrey-Chambertin Lavaut St.-Jacques 1995: A brilliant wine. Captures the grace, elegance and inner strength of a Gevrey *premier cru*. Fresh, ripe and opulent, sporting complex cassis, black cherry and spice flavors and a solid structure that will need until 2002 to strut its stuff. • $59 • (11/15/97) • **93**

Gevrey-Chambertin Lavaut St.-Jacques 1994: Bright, fresh and lively, delivering a racy mouthful of raspberry flavor that gets some zing from crisp acidity and non-competitive tannins. Best now. • $46 • (11/15/96) • **84**

Gevrey-Chambertin Lavaut St.-Jacques 1993: Intensely fruity, featuring dried cherry and mineral character, medium body, fine tannins and a long, fruity finish. Better in 1999. • $58 • (11/15/95) • **90**

Gevrey-Chambertin Les Champeaux 1994: Crisply textured, with wonderful wild plum and currant flavors in a narrow beam that cuts right through the fine tannins. Finishing with style and grace. Best now through 1999. • $46 • (11/15/96) • **88**

Marsannay Les Longeroies Red 1994: Light in body, but generous with its cherrylike flavors, making it enchanting to drink. Ready now. • $24 • (11/15/96) • **85**

Marsannay Les Longeroies Red 1993: Impressive red from this village, sporting lovely, ripe berry, smoke, mint and vanilla aromas and flavors. Medium-bodied and very silky. Drink now. • $30 • (11/15/95) • **89**

MORTET, THIERRY

Bourgogne 1995: Bright, juicy and medium-bodied, with pretty floral and red berry character. The tannins are a bit chewy, but it's nice to drink slightly chilled now. 325 cases made. • $19 • (11/15/97) • **80**

Bourgogne 1994: Crisp and straightforward, but fresh and grapey, with a herbal undertone. Light-bodied. Drink now. • $18 • (11/15/96) • **79**

Bourgogne 1993: Beautifully fruity, offering firm acidity and moderate tannins. Drinkable now. • $NA • (05/15/96) • **84**

Chambolle-Musigny 1995: Fairly pale in color, it tastes light and a bit diluted on the palate. Drink chilled. 100 cases made. • $39 • (11/15/97) • **79**

Chambolle-Musigny Aux Beaux Bruns 1995: A pretty wine full of lovely cassis and blackberry flavors. It's fresh and succulent, of medium body and moderate intensity, with a lively, albeit slightly chewy, finish. Try after 1999. 100 cases made. • $62 • (11/15/97) • **85**

Chambolle-Musigny Aux Beaux Bruns 1994: Offers some decent plum and red berry aromas and flavors, but this medium-bodied Pinot Noir lacks freshness and definition. Also a bit diluted. Drink now. • $47 • (11/15/96) • **79**

Chambolle-Musigny Aux Beaux Bruns 1993: Vivid, bright and lively, featuring moderate tannins, smooth texture and fresh fruit flavors lightly accented by spice. Very good example of an elegant Chambolle. Drinkable now. • $58 • (05/15/96) • **87**

Gevrey-Chambertin 1995: Rich and round, full of sweet, ripe blackberry flavor augmented by a wild herb element. Coarse tannins protrude on the finish. Drinkable now. 550 cases made. • $39 • (11/15/97) • **84**

Gevrey-Chambertin 1994: Marked by earthy, dirty flavors. • $34 • (11/15/96) • **74**

Gevrey-Chambertin 1993: A wonderfully fruity wine that's pure in flavor, beautifully balanced and smooth. The ripe black cherry notes linger on the finish. It's concentrated and delicious. Drink now through 2001. Tasted twice with consistent notes. • $42 • (09/15/96) • **92**

Gevrey-Chambertin Clos Prieur 1995: Medium-bodied and showing some good fruit, but also a bit earthy, with a slightly astringent character. 125 cases made. • $48 • (11/15/97) • **78**

Gevrey-Chambertin Clos Prieur 1994: Light in texture and showing pretty strawberry flavor, but drying tannins might make it a problem. Try in 1999. • $40 • (11/15/96) • **81**

Gevrey-Chambertin Clos Prieur 1993: A medium-rich red offering lovely, velvety texture and lots of cherry, berry and cedar character. Better in 2000. • $50 • (05/15/96) • **88**

MORTET & FILS

Bourgogne Les Charmes au Châtelain 1990: A rather rich wine for this category, displaying dark chocolate mouse, vanilla and coffee notes that make it interesting. Has good concentration on the elegant finish. Drink now. • $NA • (12/15/92) • **87**

Chambertin 1990: Sleek, beautiful and extremely pretty, with sweet cherry and wild berry aromas and flavors and fine tannins, but could be more concentrated on the finish. Drinkable now. 75 cases made. • $92 • (12/15/92) • **86**

Chambolle-Musigny Aux Beaux Bruns 1990: Supple and balanced, with plenty of cherry, raspberry and chocolate flavors. Shows finesse on the finish. Drinkable now. • $45 • (12/15/92) • **90**

Clos de Vougeot 1990: Wonderfully intense, with smoke, plum and earth characteristics. The ripe, rich flavors lead to a focused, firm and extremely seductive finish. Drinkable now. 175 cases made. • $NA • (12/15/92) • **94**

Gevrey-Chambertin 1990: Effusively aromatic and starts out firm on the palate, but the violet, cherry and chocolate flavors open up and come together nicely on the flavorful finish. Try now. • $NA • (12/15/92) • **90**

Gevrey-Chambertin Champeaux 1990: A seductive wine that bursts with pure raspberry, bright cherry and spice flavors. Smooth tannins. Drinkable now. • $45 • (12/15/92) • **91**

Gevrey-Chambertin Clos Prieur 1990: Shows good depth and great class, with beautiful blackberry, black cherry and spice flavors that stay with you on the intense, firm finish. Drinkable now. • $38 • (12/15/92) • **93**

MORTON, CHÂTEAU

Bordeaux Supérieur 1993: Thin and tart, already aging, with drying tannins and meager flavors of dried berries and stewed vegetables. 4,000 cases made. • $11 • (10/15/97) • **74**

MOSNIER, SYLVAIN

Chablis 1996: Very earthy, with a wet soil, sour character that is not attractive. An odd wine. 1,000 cases made. • $17 • (05/31/98) • **73**

Chablis Beauroy 1996: Quite a fruit salad—citrus, pear, peach, tropical—all in a medium-bodied, juicy package. Lacks a bit of class and concentration. Slightly drying and herbal on the finish. Drink now. 250 cases made. • $24 • (05/31/98) • **80**

Chablis Beauroy 1995: Clean and vibrant *premier cru*. Medium-bodied and rather lean, with plenty of mineral and wet stone notes well-integrated into the honeyed, ripe fruit flavors. A beautiful Chablis that should age well and be best around 2000. 667 cases made. • $NA • (06/15/97) • **86**

Chablis Côte de Lechet 1996: For hardcore Chablis fans. Distinctively flinty and earthy, with wet stone and matchstick aromas that follow through on a fairly silky, mineral-laden palate. Full in body, it has a prune, cherry pit and raspberry character to it. Lemony, a bit tart and bitter on the finish. Try in 2002 to 2007. 250 cases made. • $24 • (05/31/98) • **87**

Chablis Côte de Léchet 1995: Good intensity, with citrus, dried herbs and lemon flavors to balance the rich texture of this full-bodied *premier cru*. Fresh and lively, while also delivering cream, butter and mineral notes in generous amounts. Long finish. Try now through 2005. 375 cases made. • $NA • (06/15/97) • **87**

Chablis Vieilles Vignes 1996: A bit earthy, with a slightly herbal, drying character. Of medium body, it's quite lemony. Not as balanced as some. 1,000 cases made. • $20 • (05/31/98) • **79**

MOTTE, DOMAINE DE LA

Coteaux du Layon Rochefort 1996: This thick, sweet white is packed with honey, spice and vanilla flavors, and notes of orange-peel add a pleasant, bracing bitterness to the finish. Good concentration and balance. Drink now through 2004. • $12 • (05/31/98) • **87**

MOUCHET, CHÂTEAU DE

Montagne-St.-Emilion 1961 • $NA • (04/30/96) • **87**

MOUEIX, CHRISTIAN

Merlot Bordeaux 1995: Good and sturdy, in a lean style. It has fresh fruit aromas, rather austere cedar and tobacco flavors, light tannins and a nicely dry finish. • $10 • (01/31/98) • **83**

Merlot Bordeaux 1994: Some good cherry flavors highlight this fairly lean wine. It's a bit green tasting, but balanced. Turns tannic on the finish. • $10 • (04/30/97) • **80**

Merlot Bordeaux Christian Moueix 1993: Not much on the nose and the fruit flavors lack depth. A smooth texture punctuated by a hint of spice and plum on the finish. • $10 • (08/31/95) • **79**

Key: SS—Spectator Selection CS—Cellar Selection HR—Highly Recommended BB—Best Buy $NA—Price not available Ⓐ—Auction Price (BT)—Barrel Tasting

Dates in parentheses indicate the issues in which the ratings were published.

MOUEIX, JEAN-PIERRE

St.-Emilion 1995: Considerable style to its plum, herb and flashy oak flavors. It's smooth, well balanced and has a lingering finish. Drink now through 2002. • $16 • (01/31/98) • **87**

St.-Emilion 1993: Light and simple cherry and tea flavors, with lightly vegetal notes and some tannin on the short finish. • $14 • (07/31/96) • **79**

St.-Emilion 1989 • $13 • (06/15/93) • **74**

St.-Emilion 1988 • $13 • (04/30/92) • **82**

MOULIN BOUSQUET, CHÂTEAU

Corbières 1990 • $NA • (03/15/94) • **82**

MOULIN DE BEL-AIR, CHÂTEAU

Médoc 1989 • $NA • (03/15/92) • **77**

MOULIN DE CITRAN, CHÂTEAU

Haut-Médoc 1991: Decent cherry, currant and tobacco flavors, but light and simple. • $13 • (03/31/94) • **78**

Haut-Médoc 1989 • $14 • (03/15/92) • **80**

MOULIN DE DUHART

Pauillac 1995: A little funky, with earthy berry and smoky aromas. Medium-bodied, yet very tannic with a slightly dry finish. Coarse. Wait and see. Second label of Château Duhart-Milon-Rothschild. Perhaps better after 2000. • $18 • (01/31/98) • **81**

Pauillac 1994: Shows some good concentration, but the slightly green, vegetal character detracts from the overall quality. Drink now. • $18 • (01/31/97) • **78**

Pauillac 1993: Some decent fruit yet also lacking definition. Offers plum, blackberry and wet earth notes, but tastes slightly diluted on the finish. Drinkable now. • $16 • (01/31/96) • **79**

Pauillac 1990: Horsy, gamy flavors dominate this wine, but if you don't mind that, it's drinkable. • $14 • (02/28/94) • **75**

Pauillac 1989 • $20 • (12/31/92) • **84**

MOULIN DE LA GARDETTE

Gigondas 1995: Charming and very beautiful. Not a big wine, but tender and pure, with clean floral, rose petal, earth and cherry flavors. Complex, with a long finish, and delicious to revel in. Drinkable now. • $NA • (10/15/97) • **88**

Gigondas 1994: Distinctive, with lovely cassis, coffee, crushed black cherry and wild berry flavors. Quite lush and smooth on the palate, medium-bodied, it shows length on the lingering finish. Drinkable now. • $NA • (10/15/97) • **86**

MOULIN DE LAUNAY, CHÂTEAU

Entre-Deux-Mers 1993 • $8 • (05/31/95) • **80**

MOULIN DU CADET, CHÂTEAU

St.-Emilion 1995: Lovely, solid spice, toasty oak and red berry flavors mingle harmoniously. Lots of ripe tannins. • $NA • (05/15/96) (BT) • **85-89**

St.-Emilion 1993: Light, simple, attractive berry flavor and delicate, sweet fruit character on the finish. Drinkable now. • $NA • (01/31/96) • **79**

St.-Emilion 1992: Light color and a mint, cedar, fruit aroma. Like a weak Rioja. • $NA • (04/15/95) • **70**

St.-Emilion 1990: There's plenty of fruit in this wine, with intense raspberry and berry aromas and flavors, silky tannins and a long finish. Drinkable now. 1,800 cases made. • $NA • (03/31/93) • **91**

St.-Emilion 1989 • $NA • (03/15/92) • **86**

MOULIN DU PONT, LE

Mâcon-Fuissé Vendanges Manuelles 1995: Straightforward and attractively smooth, with an undertow of lime, honey and green apple. Overly herbal and tart on the finish, though. • $NA • (08/31/96) • **78**

St.-Véran Vendanges Manuelles 1995: Well made, ripe and crisp, with lively citrus, green apple and honey flavors. Some grassy notes and a balanced finish. A fresh quaff for a hot summer day. • $NA • (08/31/96) • **85**

MOULIN HAUT-LAROQUE, CHÂTEAU

Fronsac 1990: A big, rich wine, with beautiful aromas and flavors of toasty oak and raspberries and round, velvety tannins. Drink now. 6,000 cases made. • $14 • (03/31/93) • **89**
Fronsac 1986 • $11 • (11/15/89) • **78**

MOULIN PEY-LABRIE, CHÂTEAU

Canon-Fronsac 1997: Marked by coffee, spice, cumin and vanilla. Full-bodied and rich, with velvety tannins and a medium finish. Very impressive. Seriously good for the vintage. • $NA • (06/15/98) (BT) • **85-89**
Canon-Fronsac 1996: Decent fruit and tannins, but slightly diluted on the palate. Medium-bodied, with medium tannins and a light finish. 7,500 cases made. • $18 • (06/15/98) (BT) • **75-79**
Canon-Fronsac 1995: A subtle wine that hides its impressive fruit concentration; a bounty of blackberry, raspberry and wet earth. Full-bodied, with masses of tannins and a long, fruity finish. Best after 2000. 3,000 cases made. • $18 • (01/31/98) • **90**
Canon-Fronsac 1990: Rich and thick, with smoky, cherry, earthy character, full, silky tannins and a long, flavorful finish. Drinkable now. • $16 • (03/31/93) • **88**

MOULIN RICHE, CHÂTEAU

St.-Julien 1997: Interesting mineral and berry aromas and flavors. Light- to medium-bodied, with a light finish. • $NA • (06/15/98) (BT) • **80-84**
St.-Julien 1996: Wild berry and cherry aromas and flavors. Medium-bodied, with moderate tannins and a medium finish. A good wine. • $25 • (06/15/98) (BT) • **85-89**
St.-Julien 1995: A very good, silky red, with dried cherry and berry aromas. Medium-bodied, with medium, velvety tannins and moderate finish. Best after 2000. • $25 • (01/31/98) • **85**
St.-Julien 1987 • $18 • (11/30/89) • **79**
St.-Julien 1986 • $20 • (11/30/89) • **88**
St.-Julien 1985 • $20 • (06/15/88) • **83**
St.-Julien 1982 • $22 • (11/30/89) • **90**

MOULIN ROUGE, CHÂTEAU DU

Haut-Médoc 1987 • $12 • (11/30/89) • **74**
Haut-Médoc 1986 • $14 • (11/30/89) • **87**
Haut-Médoc 1983 • $10 • (07/31/87) • **83**
Haut-Médoc 1982 • $13 • (11/30/89) • **80**

MOULIN-ST.-GEORGES, CHÂTEAU

St.-Emilion 1997: Violet and raspberry aromas. Medium- to full-bodied, with a good core of fruit and a slightly simple finish. • $NA • (06/15/98) (BT) • **85-89**
St.-Emilion 1996: From the owner of Ausone, and very serious. Black-ink color. Chocolate and berry aromas, with loads of fruit. Full-bodied, with big, velvety tannins and a long, caressing finish. A delicious, voluptuous wine. • $30 • (06/15/98) (BT) • **90-94**
St.-Emilion 1995: Voluptuous, upfront red. Gorgeous aromas of red berries, milk chocolate and vanilla. Full-bodied and very velvety, with lovely soft, ripe tannins and a long, sweet fruit finish. Best after 2000. • $24 • (01/31/98) • **92**

MOULIN-TACUSSEL, DOMAINE

Châteauneuf-du-Pape 1990: Buttery oak and ripe blueberry and blackberry flavors combine for a sweet-seeming, rich-tasting wine, with a full, chocolaty finish. Full-bodied and moderately tannic. Drink now. • $19 • (04/15/93) • **88**

MOULINE, CHÂTEAU LA

Moulis 1988 • $20 • (02/15/91) • **81**

MOULINET, CHÂTEAU

Pomerol 1997: Well-integrated tannins mesh with a fruity palate. Medium-bodied. Not complex, but well made. • $NA • (06/15/98) (BT) • **85-89**
Pomerol 1996: A very pretty red, with cassis, berry and violet character. Medium-bodied, with medium, velvety tannins and a fresh finish. A beauty. Almost outstanding. 5,000 cases made. • $30 • (06/15/98) (BT) • **85-89**
Pomerol 1995: Not a big wine but a gorgeous one, with vanilla, cherry and berry on nose and palate, and ultrafine tannins. 6,083 cases made. • $NA • (05/15/97) (BT) • **90-94**
Pomerol 1992: A steely Pomerol, displaying earth, mineral and cherry aromas and flavors; light-bodied, firm, short finish. • $16 • (04/15/95) • **79**
Pomerol 1988 • $17 • (07/31/91) • **88**
Pomerol 1982 • $10 • (05/15/89) • **87**

MOULINIER, G.

St.-Chinian Cuvée des Sigillaires 1996: Delicious, polished and supple, with lovely cassis, cherry and raspberry flavors that linger on the finish with a nice dose of chocolate, spice and tobacco. Drink now through 2000. • $13 • (03/31/98) • **87**
St.-Chinian Les Terrasses Grillées 1995: A ripe, concentrated and supple wine that rolls across the palate, this is filled with roasted, ripe fruit and meaty flavors that combine seamlessly and glide into a silky finish. Luscious, finishing on a chocolaty note. 98 percent Syrah, 2 percent Grenache. • $20 • (03/31/98) • **89**
St.-Chinian Les Terrasses Grillées 1994: A well-structured red wine with plenty of dark cherry, cassis and spice flavors and some appealing leathery notes on the finish. An easy to drink but powerful wine that is a good representative of what the Languedoc has to offer. A blend of 98 percent Syrah and 2 percent Grenache. Drink now. • $20 • (01/01/98) • **88**

MOURGUE DU GRES, CHÂTEAU

Costières de Nîmes Terre d'Argence 1996: Solid. Plenty of gusto, with berry and plum flavors and a good wallop of tannin and spice on the finish. Shows a nice leathery note as well. Drink now. • $11 • (04/30/98) • **84**

MOUSSET, LOUIS

Châteauneuf-du-Pape 1982 • $6 • (12/16/84) • **75**
Gigondas 1983 • $6 • (12/01/84) • **75**
Vin de Table Français Le P'tit Bistrot NV: A serviceable red that shows modest berry and leafy flavors in a light, simple presentation. 12,000 cases made. • $5 • (12/15/97) • **75**

MOUTON D'ARMAILHACQ, CHÂTEAU

Pauillac 1945 • $300 • (11/30/95) • **70**

MOUTON-BARONNE-PHILIPPE, CHÂTEAU

Pauillac 1988 • $32 Ⓐ • (04/30/91) • **90**
Pauillac 1986 • $38 Ⓐ • (05/31/89) • **93**
Pauillac 1985 • $26 Ⓐ • (05/15/88) SS • **91**
Pauillac 1984 • $18 • (06/15/87) • **64**
Pauillac 1983 • $27 Ⓐ • (03/01/86) • **88**
Pauillac 1982 • $37 • (08/31/92) • **88**
Pauillac 1981 • $20 Ⓐ • (06/01/84) • **81**
Pauillac 1970 • $31 Ⓐ • (05/15/93) • **86**
Pauillac 1961 • $111 Ⓐ • (04/30/96) • **88**
Pauillac 1945 • $390 • (03/16/86) • **80**

MOUTON-CADET

Bordeaux 1995: Straightforward, offering cherry and herbal flavors. Well balanced, with brisk tannins and a clean finish. A modest wine that will show better with food. Drink now through 2002. • $8 • (10/15/97) • **82**
Bordeaux White 1996: Crisp and focused, with a nice touch of richness, straightforward and appealing lemon, herb and grass flavors. Drink now. • $9 • (06/15/98) • **83**
Bordeaux White 1995: This round-textured white Bordeaux offers solid fruit flavors, accented by moderately herbal notes, and a soft finish. • $8 • (09/30/97) • **84**

MOUTON-ROTHSCHILD, CHÂTEAU

Pauillac 1997: This has weight for a '97, with velvety tannins and a full body. Long berry and cherry aftertaste. Very well made. • $NA • (06/15/98) (BT) • **90-94**
Pauillac 1996: Full-bodied, with ripe berry and currant character and a velvety tannin structure. Wait and see after the bottling, but outstanding now. • $190 • (06/15/98) (BT) • **90-94**
Pauillac 1995: This classic wine is only showing a portion of what it's got to offer, but it's excellent even so. Inky in color, with masses of berry, violet, mint, mineral and cherry character, and full in body, with tons of velvety tannins and a moderate finish. Needs time to open. Best after 2004. • $180 Ⓐ • (01/31/98) CS • **96**
Pauillac 1994: Dark-colored, with intense aromas of blackberries, tar and spice, and toasty oak notes as well. Full-bodied, with very silky tannins and a chewy, ripe fruit-accented finish. An impressive Mouton. Better in 1999. • $91 Ⓐ • (01/31/97) • **91**
Pauillac 1993: Mouton comes through again. Impressive '93, deep in color and full-bodied, boasting plenty of currant, black cherry, mint and toast character. Well crafted, showing depth for this vintage. Give the tannins some time to mellow. Try in 2000. • $84 Ⓐ • (01/31/96) • **90**
Pauillac 1992: Impressive. Beautiful plum, berry, tobacco, cedar and toasty oak aromas and flavors, medium body and tannins and a succulent finish. Drinkable now. • $65 Ⓐ • (04/15/95) • **88**
Pauillac 1991: Incredibly fine and subtle for the vintage with tobacco, black currant and berry aromas and flavors, medium body and a long flavorful, silky finish. Drink or hold. • $49 Ⓐ • (03/31/94) HR • **89**
Pauillac 1990: Seductive, with plum, smoke and vanilla aromas and flavors, full, silky tannins and a long, rich finish. Still quite backward; needs time to unwind. Drink now. 25,000 cases made. • $96 Ⓐ • (05/15/93) CS • **95**
Pauillac 1989 • $150 Ⓐ • (03/15/92) • **99**
Pauillac 1987 • $71 Ⓐ • (05/15/90) • **89**
Pauillac 1986 • $335 Ⓐ • (05/31/89) CS • **98**
Pauillac 1985 • $172 Ⓐ • (10/15/94) • **96**
Pauillac 1984 • $57 Ⓐ • (03/31/87) • **92**
Pauillac 1983 • $110 Ⓐ • (10/15/94) • **94**
Pauillac 1982 • $482 Ⓐ • (05/15/91) • **93**
Pauillac 1981 • $97 Ⓐ • (10/15/94) • **91**
Pauillac 1980 • $56 Ⓐ • (06/16/86) • **67**
Pauillac 1979 • $89 Ⓐ • (10/15/89) • **96**
Pauillac 1978 • $109 Ⓐ • (05/15/91) • **92**
Pauillac 1977 • $61 Ⓐ • (06/16/86) • **68**
Pauillac 1976 • $75 Ⓐ • (06/16/86) • **85**
Pauillac 1975 • $100 Ⓐ • (05/15/91) • **89**
Pauillac 1974 • $56 Ⓐ • (06/16/86) • **67**
Pauillac 1973 • $84 Ⓐ • (06/16/86) • **75**
Pauillac 1972 • $88 Ⓐ • (06/16/86) • **65**
Pauillac 1971 • $77 Ⓐ • (06/16/86) • **78**
Pauillac 1970 • $147 Ⓐ • (05/15/91) • **84**
Pauillac 1969 • $100 Ⓐ • (06/16/86) • **78**
Pauillac 1968 • $300 Ⓐ • (06/16/86) • **64**
Pauillac 1967 • $61 Ⓐ • (06/16/86) • **87**
Pauillac 1966 • $140 Ⓐ • (05/15/91) • **88**
Pauillac 1965 • $179 Ⓐ • (06/16/86) • **61**
Pauillac 1964 • $122 Ⓐ • (06/16/86) • **84**
Pauillac 1963 • $410 Ⓐ • (06/16/86) • **77**
Pauillac 1962 • $216 Ⓐ • (11/30/87) • **98**
Pauillac 1961 • $2864 Ⓐ/1.5 liter • (04/30/96) • **92**
Pauillac 1960 • $156 Ⓐ • (06/16/86) • **84**
Pauillac 1959 • $767 Ⓐ • (10/15/90) • **99**
Pauillac 1958 • $289 Ⓐ • (06/16/86) • **68**
Pauillac 1957 • $124 Ⓐ • (06/16/86) • **86**
Pauillac 1956 • $748 Ⓐ • (06/16/86) • **85**
Pauillac 1955 • $353 Ⓐ • (05/15/91) • **95**
Pauillac 1954 • $661 Ⓐ • (06/16/86) • **81**
Pauillac 1953 • $532 Ⓐ • (05/15/91) • **94**
Pauillac 1952 • $306 Ⓐ • (06/16/86) • **90**
Pauillac 1951 • $283 Ⓐ • (06/16/86) • **84**
Pauillac 1950 • $291 Ⓐ • (06/16/86) • **83**
Pauillac 1949 • $769 Ⓐ • (05/15/91) • **87**
Pauillac 1948 • $600 Ⓐ • (06/16/86) • **87**
Pauillac 1947: Texture has turned coarse, but the cedar, mint and tobacco flavors are vibrant. Not much fruit left, but it's still a real mouthful of wine. • $1125 Ⓐ • (05/31/97) • **89**
Pauillac 1946 • $2114 Ⓐ • (06/16/86) • **77**
Pauillac 1945 • $2585 Ⓐ • (11/30/95) • **94**
Pauillac 1944 • $562 Ⓐ • (06/16/86) • **86**
Pauillac 1943 • $523 Ⓐ • (06/16/86) • **78**
Pauillac 1940 • $337 Ⓐ • (06/16/86) • **77**
Pauillac 1939 • $488 Ⓐ • (06/16/86) • **55**
Pauillac 1938 • $622 Ⓐ • (06/16/86) • **73**
Pauillac 1937 • $262 Ⓐ • (05/15/91) • **91**
Pauillac 1936 • $475 Ⓐ • (06/16/86) • **63**
Pauillac 1934 • $687 Ⓐ • (05/15/91) • **90**
Pauillac 1933 • $341 Ⓐ/375ml • 06/16/86) • **78**
Pauillac 1929 • $353 Ⓐ • (05/15/91) • **75**
Pauillac 1928 • $792 Ⓐ • (05/15/91) • **89**
Pauillac 1926 • $543 Ⓐ • (06/16/86) • **65**
Pauillac 1925 • $472 Ⓐ • (06/16/86) • **55**
Pauillac 1924 • $457 Ⓐ • (06/16/86) • **69**
Pauillac 1921 • $500 • (05/15/91) • **80**
Pauillac 1920 • $581 Ⓐ • (06/16/86) • **75**
Pauillac 1919 • $600 • (05/15/91) • **79**
Pauillac 1918 • $1125 Ⓐ • (05/15/91) • **83**
Pauillac 1916 • $431 Ⓐ • (06/16/86) • **67**
Pauillac 1914 • $550 • (06/16/86) • **65**
Pauillac 1912 • $400 • (06/16/86) • **62**
Pauillac 1910 • $400 • (05/15/91) • **76**
Pauillac 1905 • $875 Ⓐ • (05/15/91) • **88**
Pauillac 1900 • $NA • (05/15/91) • **90**
Pauillac 1899 • $282 Ⓐ • (06/16/86) • **82**
Pauillac 1881 • $926 Ⓐ • (06/16/86) • **74**
Pauillac 1878 • $521 Ⓐ • (05/15/91) • **99**
Pauillac 1874 • $1087 Ⓐ • (05/15/91) • **95**
Pauillac 1870 • $NA • (05/15/91) • **87**

MUGNERET, GEORGES

Chambolle-Musigny Les Feusselottes 1992: Light and fruity, pleasant raspberry and strawberry flavors echoing on the simple finish. Drinkable now. • $NA • (12/15/94) • **83**
Chambolle-Musigny Les Feusselottes 1989 • $47 • (04/30/92) • **87**
Chambolle-Musigny Les Feusselottes 1988 • $54 • (11/15/90) • **86**
Chambolle-Musigny Les Feusselottes 1987 • $41 • (10/15/89) • **92**
Chambolle-Musigny Les Feusselottes 1986 • $45 • (11/15/88) • **90**
Clos Vougeot 1994: Lithe and lively, with nicely packaged plum and tobacco flavors, hinting at herb at the edges, finishing with refined tannins. Approachable now. • $NA • (11/15/96) • **84**
Clos Vougeot 1991: Very light and delicate, with a bright beam of raspberry flavor. Simple and easy to drink, echoing the lively fruit on the long finish. • $90 Ⓐ • (01/31/94) • **83**
Clos Vougeot 1990: Crisp and sharp, with intense berry characteristics that deliver plenty of focused cherry, smoke and toast flavors and a mouth-puckering finish. Drinkable now. 150 cases made. • $89 • (12/15/92) • **91**
Clos Vougeot 1988 • $90 • (11/15/90) • **84**
Clos Vougeot 1987 • $68 • (10/15/89) • **91**
Clos Vougeot 1986 • $73 • (11/30/88) • **90**
Nuits-St.-Georges Aux Chaignots 1994: Its stalky, stemmy, green aromas and flavors are a turn-off. • $NA • (11/15/96) • **70**
Nuits-St.-Georges Aux Chaignots 1993: A bit earthy but solid, offering loads of cherry and blackberry character, medium-to-full body, fine tannins and long, fresh finish. Better in 2001. • $NA • (05/15/96) • **88**
Nuits-St.-Georges Aux Chaignots 1992: Light in color, light in aroma and light in flavor, with only a touch of raspberry flavor on the finish. Drinkable now. • $NA • (12/15/94) • **79**
Nuits-St.-Georges Aux Chaignots 1991: Crisp and almost austere. Pleasant strawberry and milk chocolate flavors struggle to rise above a modest level. Drinkable now. • $50 Ⓐ • (01/31/94) • **80**
Nuits-St.-Georges Aux Chaignots 1990: Elegant and round, with pretty raspberry, chestnut and berry aromas and flavors, medium tannins and a charming finish. Drinkable now. 325 cases made. • $45 • (12/15/92) • **88**
Nuits-St.-Georges Aux Chaignots 1989 • $43 • (04/30/92) • **86**
Nuits-St.-Georges Aux Chaignots 1988 • $47 • (11/15/90) • **80**
Nuits-St.-Georges Aux Chaignots 1987 • $41 • (10/15/89) • **87**
Nuits-St.-Georges Aux Chaignots 1986 • $40 • (11/15/88) • **89**
Nuits-St.-Georges Aux Chaignots 1984 • $26 • (03/15/87) • **89**

Key: SS—Spectator Selection CS—Cellar Selection HR—Highly Recommended BB—Best Buy $NA—Price not available Ⓐ—Auction Price (BT)—Barrel Tasting
Dates in parentheses indicate the issues in which the ratings were published.

Ruchottes-Chambertin 1994: A gentle, flavorful wine that lets its pure currant and plum flavors unfold and grow in intensity, on the palate and beyond. Fresh, youthful and unblemished by tannins. Lovely now, but can improve through 2000. • $65 • (12/31/96) HR • **92**
Ruchottes-Chambertin 1992: Lean and tight, showing some cherry flavor at the core, but the overlay of herbal, stalky character is too much. Drinkable now. • $NA • (12/15/94) • **74**
Ruchottes-Chambertin 1990: An impressive *grand cru*, with delicate, sweet berry and earth aromas and flavors and a finish that goes on and on. The tannin and fruit structure is truly beautiful, with great balance and harmony. Drinkable now. 300 cases made. • $78 • (12/15/92) • **93**
Ruchottes-Chambertin 1989 • $66 • (04/30/92) • **91**
Ruchottes-Chambertin 1988 • $69 • (11/15/90) • **92**
Ruchottes-Chambertin 1987 • $44 • (10/15/89) • **93**
Ruchottes-Chambertin 1986 • $45 • (11/15/88) • **91**
Ruchottes-Chambertin 1985 • $150 • (02/15/88) • **92**
Ruchottes-Chambertin 1984 • $34 • (03/15/87) • **83**
Ruchottes-Chambertin 1982 • $26 • (09/01/85) SS • **92**

MUGNERET, GÉRARD

Nuits-St.-Georges Aux Boudots 1988 • $48 • (02/28/91) • **76**
Nuits-St.-Georges Aux Boudots 1987 • $40 • (07/15/90) • **88**
Vosne-Romanée 1988 • $37 • (02/28/91) • **86**
Vosne-Romanée 1987 • $32 • (07/15/90) • **79**
Vosne-Romanée Les Suchots 1988 • $57 • (02/28/91) • **84**
Vosne-Romanée Les Suchots 1987 • $42 • (07/15/90) • **82**

MUGNERET, RENÉ

Vosne-Romanée 1985 • $27 • (04/30/88) • **90**
Vosne-Romanée 1983 • $16 • (11/16/85) • **73**
Vosne-Romanée 1982 • $17 • (07/16/85) • **86**

MUGNERET-GIBOURG

Bourgogne 1994: Crisp in texture, with a small bead of currant flavor sneaking through. • $NA • (11/15/96) • **79**
Bourgogne 1992: An overlay of sweet oak gives this a little extra class, with berry and currant notes threaded through the fine texture. • $NA • (12/15/94) • **80**
Bourgogne 1990: A serious Bourgogne Rouge that's powerful enought to require aging. Clever winemaking has produced lovely violet, smoke and raspberry aromas and flavors. Drinkable now. 275 cases made. • $18 • (12/15/92) • **86**
Bourgogne 1989 • $17 • (06/15/92) • **82**
Echézeaux 1994: Slightly thin and astringent, and lacks balance, its stemmy notes mingling with red berry, salty, fishy flavors. Tart finish. • $NA • (11/15/96) • **79**
Echézeaux 1992: Firm and chewy, almost crisp, with smoke and toast notes adding some extra dimension to the strawberry and raspberry flavors. Drinkable now. • $NA • (12/15/94) • **82**
Echézeaux 1991: Firm and crisp, featuring pretty rose petal-scented currant and raspberry aromas and flavors and hints of smoke on the finish. Has style, but seems a bit watery. Try now. • $68 Ⓐ • (01/31/94) • **85**
Echézeaux 1990: Like satin, this wine caresses the palate with intense red berry, violet and earth flavors, yet has a real iron backbone that leads to a sophisticated, supple finish. Shows wonderful finesse. Drinkable now. 250 cases made. • $66 • (12/15/92) • **93**
Echézeaux 1989 • $62 • (04/30/92) • **88**
Echézeaux 1988 • $70 • (11/15/90) • **89**
Echézeaux 1987 • $50 • (10/15/89) • **93**
Echézeaux 1986 • $55 • (11/30/88) • **83**
Echézeaux 1985 • $57 • (02/29/88) • **93**
Echézeaux 1984 • $32 • (03/15/87) • **85**
Vosne-Romanée 1994: This is a light wine, with chewy tannins and berryish flavors that don't linger very long on the palate. • $NA • (11/15/96) • **78**
Vosne-Romanée 1993: Simple, rather light and clean berry, cherry and almond aromas and flavors, medium-to-light body, light tannins and diluted finish. Drinkable now. • $NA • (05/15/96) • **83**
Vosne-Romanée 1992: Light color, light body and some decent red berry flavors. Delicate and easy to drink, but a bit diluted. • $NA • (12/15/94) • **79**
Vosne-Romanée 1991: Crisp, focused and lively, showing toasty, anise-scented berry flavors and a juicy, fresh finish. Drinkable now. • $400 Ⓐ • (01/31/94) • **83**
Vosne-Romanée 1989 • $34 • (04/30/92) • **81**
Vosne-Romanée 1988 • $34 • (12/31/90) • **64**
Vosne-Romanée 1987 • $30 • (10/15/89) • **90**
Vosne-Romanée 1986 • $33 • (12/31/88) • **81**
Vosne-Romanée 1985 • $33 • (02/29/88) • **85**

MUGNERET-GOUACHON, B.

Echézeaux 1985 • $29 • (12/31/88) • **91**

MUGNIER, JACQUES-FRÉDÉRIC

Bonnes Mares 1993: Gorgeous—a joy to drink. Ample, seductive, rich in dark fruit flavors including black cherry and currant, plush-textured and long on the finish. Firm tannins, lively acidity, wonderful balance. Drink now. • $90 • (05/15/96) • **92**
Chambolle-Musigny 1993: Rich, ripe fruit and ample, rounded texture make this an appealing, broad, generous Burgundy. Try now. • $39 • (05/15/96) • **88**
Chambolle-Musigny 1989 • $41 • (01/31/92) • **91**
Chambolle-Musigny 1988 • $96 Ⓐ • (05/15/91) • **86**
Chambolle-Musigny Les Amoureuses 1993: Rather closed, offering only medium concentration of black cherry, red berry and currant flavors. Still, quite an elegant structure although at this stage the tannins seem dry. Better in 2000. • $100 • (05/15/96) • **85**
Chambolle-Musigny Les Amoureuses 1989 • $62 • (01/31/92) • **90**
Chambolle-Musigny Les Amoureuses 1988 • $80 • (05/15/91) • **86**
Chambolle-Musigny Les Fuées 1993: A purely luscious, plush-textured, young red boasting generous fruit flavors, moderate tannins and lingering finish. Pleasurable to drink through 1999. • $69 • (05/15/96) • **89**
Chambolle-Musigny Les Fuées 1988 • $60 • (05/15/91) • **89**
Musigny 1989 • $125 • (01/31/92) • **88**

MUMM, G.H.

Brut Blanc de Blancs Champagne Mumm de Cramant NV: Light and fresh, delicate in texture and subtle in flavor. A fine apéritif. • $40 • (12/31/97) • **84**
Brut Champagne Cordon Rouge 1989: An alluring, up-front Champagne, with buttery, vanillalike aromas, ripe flavors and a rather soft, easy texture. Delicious, in a forward, winey style. • $32 • (12/15/96) • **89**
Brut Champagne Cordon Rouge 1988: Bold in flavor and creamy in texture. It has assertive toasty, doughy aromas, ripe pear and lemon flavors and a lingering finish. Ready to drink. Improved since earlier tastings. • $30 • (12/31/96) • **89**
Brut Champagne Cordon Rouge 1985: A fruit bomb. Tastes like chocolate covered cherries. Full-bodied with a velvety texture. Excellent acidity and a long flavorful finish. Would work well with dessert. Much better than we remembered from other tastings. Drinkable now. • $35 • (12/31/93) • **90**
Brut Champagne Cordon Rouge 1982 • $37 • (12/31/88) • **85**
Brut Champagne Cordon Rouge 1979 • $55 • (02/16/86) • **93**
Brut Champagne Cordon Rouge NV: A most distinctive Champagne with an extra dimension that makes it stand out from the pack. It offers pungent earthy, toasty aromas that melt on the palate into opulent, creamy flavors that linger with richness on the finish. Tasted twice, with consistent notes. • $25 • (11/15/97) SS • **90**
Brut Champagne Grand Cordon 1985: Not giving much now. Wonderfully structured with lots of fruit, firm acidity and a long aftertaste. Beautifully integrated mousse. Drinkable now. • $100 • (12/31/93) • **91**
Brut Champagne René Lalou 1985: A delectable Champagne—from the bouquet of honey, spice and almond through the creamy texture, bold flavors and lingering finish. Shows complexity of age while retaining the vibrant acidity and freshness of youth. Drink now through 2001. • $50 • (12/31/96) • **92**
Brut Champagne René Lalou 1982: Lots of toasty, yeasty complexity in a delicate, medium-bodied wine, soft around the edges but firmly anchored by a streak of lemony acidity. Beautifully balanced. • $55 • (09/30/88) • **90**
Brut Champagne René Lalou 1979 • $56 • (05/16/86) • **95**
Brut Rosé Champagne Cordon Rosé 1988: Mature and dry in style, with toasty aromas and earthy, mineral flavors that turn astringent and lean on the finish. 5,000 cases made. • $35 • (12/31/94) • **83**
Brut Rosé Champagne Cordon Rosé 1985: A colorful wine, both literally and in the flavor department, with hints of walnut, toast, orange peel, cherry and earth. A bit tart on the finish. • $100 • (01/31/92) • **86**
Brut Rosé Champagne Cordon Rosé 1983: Earthy, tart and tangy, with lime-tinged cherry aromas and flavors and earthy overtones that keep it from

being delicious; but essentially it's correct and drinkable. • $30 • (12/31/89) • **81**

Brut Rosé Champagne Cordon Rosé 1982: Full of character, rough-hewn, but rich and assertive, with woody, earthy, nutty flavors and a smoky finish. Will go well with lots of flavorful dinner dishes. • $30 • (12/31/88) • **83**

Champagne Carte Classique Extra Dry NV: Toasty aromas, fine balance and delicate fruit flavors combine to make this an appealing Champagne that's light on its feet. • $25 • (11/15/97) • **85**

MURÉ

Gewürztraminer Alsace Grand Cru Vorbourg Clos St.- Landelin 1993 • $21 • (08/31/95) • **91**

Gewürztraminer Alsace Grand Cru Vorbourg Clos St.-Landelin Sélection de Grains Nobles 1994: Honey is the dominant theme in this dessert wine. Comes off as straightforward and immediate. Ready now. 38 cases made. • $51/375ml • (02/28/97) • **83**

Gewürztraminer Alsace Grand Cru Vorbourg Clos St.-Landelin Vendanges Tardives 1994: Plenty of appeal. Rich, fat, moderately sweet, displaying honey, almond and a touch of grapefruit to reign in the flavors on the lingering finish. Enjoy now. 100 cases made. • $33/500ml • (02/28/97) • **86**

Muscat Alsace Grand Cru Vorbourg Clos St.-Landelin 1994 • $26 • (05/15/96) • **85**

Muscat Alsace Grand Cru Vorbourg Clos St.-Landelin 1993 • $15 • (09/15/95) • **84**

Muscat Alsace Grand Cru Vorbourg Clos St.-Landelin Sélection de Grains Nobles 1994: Pungently spicy aromas, backed by rich, moderately sweet flavors of citrus peel and honey with a touch of crème brûlée thrown in. Try with light desserts. 38 cases made. • $100/500ml • (02/28/97) • **85**

Muscat Alsace Grand Cru Vorbourg Clos St.-Landelin Vendanges Tardives 1994: There's no denying the honey, orange and bergamot flavors in this delicate wine; it says Muscat from start to finish. Great apéritif. 100 cases made. • $40/500ml • (02/28/97) • **85**

Pinot Blanc Alsace Clos St.-Landelin 1995: New oak makes this version an anomaly, but it's tasty. Tropical, buttery flavors are supported by a rich texture, an applelike acidity and a hint of coconut on the finish. • $18 • (09/15/97) • **85**

Pinot Blanc Alsace Clos St.-Landelin 1993 • $14 • (09/15/95) • **82**

Pinot Blanc Alsace Côte de Rouffach 1995: Starts out soft and lush, like a lemon meringue pie, but then the vibrant acidity takes over. Moderate concentration, but the finish is a bit metallic. • $11 • (09/15/97) • **80**

Pinot Noir Alsace Clos St.-Landelin 1994: Attractive aromas of cherries and toasty oak give way to a silky mouthful of cherry and spice flavors and, unfortunately, a marked bitter note. • $21 • (11/15/96) • **81**

Pinot Noir Alsace Clos St.-Landelin Viellie en Pièces de Chêne 1993 • $25 • (09/15/95) • **84**

Riesling Alsace Côte de Rouffach 1995: Pure apple and peach notes resonate through this elegant, rich white. Vibrant acidity keeps it humming to a lingering aftertaste of spring flowers and lemony freshness. • $13 • (09/30/97) • **88**

Riesling Alsace Grand Cru Vorbourg Clos St.-Landelin 1995: Disjointed now, this Riesling begins with soft, ripe tropical fruit aromas and a rich mouthfeel, then becomes dominated by searing acidity. Not for those with sensitive teeth, but time should smooth it out. • $23 • (09/30/97) • **88**

Riesling Alsace Grand Cru Vorbourg Clos St.-Landelin 1994 • $19 • (05/15/96) • **86**

Riesling Alsace Grand Cru Vorbourg Clos St.-Landelin 1993 • $15 • (09/15/95) • **85**

Riesling Alsace Grand Cru Vorbourg Clos St.-Landelin Vendanges Tardives 1994: Aromas of a pine forest on a rainy day are brought to mind by this soft Riesling with a touch of sweetness. Ready now. 16 cases made. • $36/500ml • (02/28/97) • **84**

Sylvaner Alsace Clos St.-Landelin Cuvée Oscar 1994 • $12 • (05/15/96) • **84**

Sylvaner Alsace Clos St.-Landelin Cuvée Oscar 1993 • $12 • (09/15/95) • **83**

Tokay Pinot Gris Alsace Grand Cru Vorbourg Clos St.-Landelin 1995: Honey, citrus and spice play off each other in this ripe, soft white. It's slightly sweet, yet everything comes into balance by the lingering finish. • $24 • (09/30/97) • **86**

Tokay Pinot Gris Alsace Grand Cru Vorbourg Clos St.-Landelin 1994 • $23 • (05/15/96) • **88**

Key: SS—Spectator Selection CS—Cellar Selection HR—Highly Recommended BB—Best Buy $NA—Price not available Ⓐ—Auction Price (BT)—Barrel Tasting

Dates in parentheses indicate the issues in which the ratings were published.

Tokay Pinot Gris Alsace Grand Cru Vorbourg Clos St.-Landelin Vendanges Tardives 1994: A step up in sweetness puts this white in the dessert course. Honey, hazelnuts and a hint of orange-peel provide the attraction. Drinkable now. 78 cases made. • $27/375ml • (02/28/97) • **85**

MURETTES, DOMAINE DES

Minervois Clos de l'Olivier 1995: Ripe, rich and well concentrated with luscious flavors of plum, berry and spice that intensify on the finish. A smooth red with a leathery note on the finish. A blend of 69 percent Syrah, 19 percent Carignan and 12 percent Grenache. Drink through 1999. • $11 • (03/31/98) • **87**

MURISALTIEN, LE MANOIR

Bourgogne White 1995: A bit cooked and rustic, with some perfumy, flowery, apricotlike flavors. Lacks finesse, and tastes quite tart. • $NA • (08/31/97) • **73**

Mâcon-Cruzilles 1996: A fairly oaky style, with butterscotch, butter, mocha and spicy character, honey, smoke and toasty notes. Complex and attractive for those who like this style. Drink now. 1,250 cases made. • $10 • (05/31/98) • **85**

Mâcon-Fuissé 1996: Lovely balance between the fruit, acidity and mineral character. Very impressive for all that complexity (lime, pear, apple, wet earth and slight smoky, toasty notes). The superintense finish remains pure and clean. Buy a case and enjoy now through 2000. • $12 • (05/31/98) • **89**

Pouilly-Fuissé 1996: What Pouilly should be. This chalky, minerally style should come into its own around 1999 to 2000. For now, nice ripe pear, lime and spice flavors give it an attractive complexity, with *terroir* dominating. Medium-bodied. 330 cases made. • $18 • (05/31/98) • **88**

Puligny-Montrachet Les Pucelles 1995: Thick and ripe, a full-bodied wine that shows some mineral, toasty bread, honey and ripe pear flavors. Seems a bit dry on the finish. Drink now. 100 cases made. • $44 • (05/31/97) • **84**

MUSSY

Beaune Les Epenottes 1995: Very light, with the color of strawberry juice. Tastes herbaceous and lean on the finish. Not much wine here. • $38 • (11/15/97) • **73**

Beaune Les Epenottes 1994: Best to drink this Burgundy slightly chilled, as it is very light. Modest anise, floral, strawberry, cherry and herb flavor notes and crisp finish. • $38 • (11/15/96) • **77**

Beaune Les Epenottes 1993: Some decent plum and berry flavor, but rather light and slightly diluted on the finish. Drinkable now. • $26 • (11/15/95) • **78**

Beaune Les Epenottes 1992: Simple, modest and diluted, with some decent raspberry and strawberry flavors. Drink up. • $32 • (12/15/94) • **74**

Beaune Les Epenottes 1991: Firm, focused and sturdy, with youthful plum, currant and tar aromas and flavors and echoes of ripe plum on the spicy finish. Supple and rich. Drinkable now. • $34 Ⓐ • (01/31/94) • **88**

Beaune Les Epenottes 1986 • $28 • (05/31/89) • **86**

Beaune Les Montrevenots 1995: Rustic, light and stemmy, this green and unripe Pinot Noir has chewy tannins and herbaceous character. Light-bodied and diluted. • $38 • (11/15/97) • **75**

Beaune Les Montrevenots 1994: Disappointing. Thin, light and diluted, but with modest fruit flavors and aromas. Drinkable now. • $38 • (11/15/96) • **72**

Beaune Les Montrevenots 1993: Lovely rose petal and berry character with a medium body and firm tannins. Not big but deliciously fresh. Drink now. • $26 • (11/15/95) • **84**

Beaune Les Montrevenots 1992: Firm in texture, with just enough raspberry and currant flavor to balance the tannins. Finish is a little sugary. Drinkable now. • $32 • (12/15/94) • **79**

Beaune Les Montrevenots 1991: Sturdy and flavorful, with an exotic cigar, tobacco and mineral edge to the currant and plum flavors. Finishes earthy and a bit chewy. Drinkable now. • $34 Ⓐ • (01/31/94) • **86**

Beaune Les Montrevenots 1990: Elegant, but unyielding and rather lean and mean, with pretty berry and cherry aromas and flavors and a hint of herb. Lacks flesh. Drinkable now. • $45 • (12/15/92) • **87**

Beaune Les Montrevenots 1986 • $28 • (05/31/89) • **86**

Bourgogne 1994: Crisp and fresh, with aromas and flavors of red berries. A bit herbal on the finish. • $18 • (11/15/96) • **78**

Pommard 1994: An understated Pommard with some fruit flavors and a bit of an herb accent. Tannins are slightly astringent. • $42 • (11/15/96) • **75**

Pommard 1993: Distinctive style—gamy and barnyardy, adding some odd salami notes. A bit drying on the finish. • $34 • (11/15/95) • **82**

Pommard 1992: Supple and generous, with raspberry and toast flavors that linger on the finish. Drinkable now. • $38 • (12/15/94) • **84**

Pommard 1991: Chunky and simple; a nice, curranty wine that veers off toward lime on the finish. Drinkable now. • $41 Ⓐ • (01/31/94) • **81**

Pommard 1985 • $35 • (10/15/88) • **86**

Pommard Les Epenots 1995: Light and herbaceous, with a stewed tomato character. Light-bodied, with astringent tannins. • $61 • (11/15/97) • **74**

Pommard Les Epenots 1994: Light in structure, but firm and almost astringent. Offers modest cherry and floral flavors for balance. • $58 • (11/15/96) • **80**

Pommard Les Epenots 1993: Medium- to light-bodied red that lacks depth and complexity. Some raspberry and strawberry flavors and a short, slightly dry finish. • $45 • (11/15/95) • **79**

Pommard Les Epenots 1992: A supple Pommard that gains some complexity as the blackberry, prune and raspberry flavors unfold into a rather short finish. Drinkable now. • $49 • (12/15/94) • **82**

Pommard Les Epenots 1991: Tries to be elegant, but comes up a little short. The unripe berry flavors never quite smooth out. Try now. • $54 Ⓐ • (01/31/94) • **80**

Pommard Les Epenots 1990: Very well made in a subtle, refined style, with round, supple cherry characteristics graced by silky tannins. Drinkable now. • $50 • (12/15/92) • **86**

Pommard Les Pézerolles 1995: Light and simple, with rosélike color. Herbal and astringent. • $61 • (11/15/97) • **74**

Pommard Les Saussilles 1995: Fleshy and chewy, with some richness in the midpalate, but leaves the impression of unripe fruit and tannins. • $52 • (11/15/97) • **79**

Pommard Les Saussilles 1994: Light and pleasant, with little *oomph* behind the berry and floral flavors but a fair level of tannin. Try now. • $50 • (11/15/96) • **80**

Pommard Premier Cru 1993: Smells somewhat like a barnyard but rich fruit lies under it all. Medium body and tannins, and peppery finish. Tastes more like Rhône than Burgundy. • $38 • (11/15/95) • **79**

Pommard Premier Cru 1991: Tough in texture, offering a broad array of prune, mushroom and berry aromas and flavors. Finishes softer than many '91s. Tannic, but drinkable now. • $NA • (01/31/94) • **83**

Pommard Premier Cru 1986 • $35 • (04/30/89) • **86**

Volnay 1993: Rather earthy and funky showing some good red fruit character, but it's light-bodied with a slightly bitter finish. Drinkable now. • $NA • (11/15/95) • **79**

Volnay 1992: Balanced but on the light side, showing some decent red berry flavors and a tannic edge on the finish. Drinkable now. • $NA • (12/15/94) • **77**

Volnay 1991: Ripe and exotic, with a violet and spicebox edge to the thick, concentrated plum and currant aromas and flavors. Offers a real mouthful of flavor on the finish. Try now. • $34 Ⓐ • (01/31/94) • **86**

MUTS, CHÂTEAU LES

Côtes de Bergerac 1983 • $6 • (11/15/86) • **80**

MUZARD & FILS, LUCIEN

Pommard Les Cras Vieilles Vignes 1995: Tough and earthy, showing an herbal side to the modest fruit. Dry tannins dominate the finish. 150 cases made. • $20 • (11/15/97) • **78**

Santenay Clos de Tavannes 1995: An unripe, green 1995 red Burgundy. Slight dilution doesn't help the crisp texture. 350 cases made. • $20 • (11/15/97) • **76**

Santenay La Maladière 1995: Fairly dense, but herbal and tart. Medium-bodied, it leaves an astringent mouthfeel as the herbaceous notes kick in on the finish. 2,500 cases made. • $20 • (11/15/97) • **77**

Santenay Les Gravières 1995: Straightforward, showing some spice, cinnamon and cherry. Turns a bit sour on the finish. Drink now, slightly chilled. 580 cases made. • $20 • (11/15/97) • **76**

MYLORD, CHÂTEAU

Entre-Deux-Mers 1994 • $8 • (05/31/95) • **78**

Entre-Deux-Mers 1993 • $8 • (05/31/95) • **79**

MYRAT, CHÂTEAU DE

Barsac 1991: A bit earthy, offering lemon, spice and mineral character; quite crisp, moderately sweet and rich, but somewhat flat on the finish. Drinkable now. • $NA • (04/15/95) • **80**

NADDEF, PHILIPPE

Gevrey-Chambertin 1988 • $25 • (07/15/91) • **80**

Gevrey-Chambertin 1987 • $19 • (03/31/90) • **86**

Gevrey-Chambertin 1985 • $25 • (04/15/88) • **94**

Gevrey-Chambertin Champeaux 1987 • $28 • (03/31/90) • **90**

Gevrey-Chambertin Champeaux 1985 • $29 • (03/31/88) • **80**

Gevrey-Chambertin Les Cazetiers 1987 • $35 • (03/31/90) • **88**

Mazis-Chambertin 1988 • $60 • (07/15/91) • **69**

Mazis-Chambertin 1987 • $22 Ⓐ • (03/31/90) • **89**

Mazis-Chambertin Vieilles Vignes 1991: Firm and chewy, with anise and mint flavors dominating the chunky berry and currant flavors. Drink now to 2000. • $48 • (08/31/94) • **89**

NAGES, CHÂTEAU DE

Costières de Nîmes Cuvée Joseph Torrès 1995: Ripe and sturdy, this fruity red offers plum, licorice and minty notes, fresh and clean on the palate. The tannins are ripe and round; the wine is exuberant and easy to drink. • $11 • (10/15/97) • **84**

Costières de Nîmes Réserve du Château 1996: Berry and herbal flavors are lively and fresh in this straightforward red. It has a lively regional accent. Drink now. • $9 • (10/15/97) • **82**

Costières de Nîmes Réserve du Château 1995: There are some nice berry and plummy flavors in this wine, but they turn a bit coarse and dry on the finish. Drink now. 15,000 cases made. • $9 • (01/01/98) • **79**

Costières de Nîmes Réserve du Château White 1996: A decent, medium-bodied white, with a lemony, pearlike touch. A bit heavy-handed and lacks some finesse. • $9 • (10/15/97) • **79**

Merlot Vin de Pays d'Oc 1995: Firm and focused, with cherry and plum flavors, and some nice spicy notes on the finish. This wine has a good edge, making it a good foil for a hearty stew. Drink now through 2000. 5,000 cases made. • $8 • (05/31/98) • **83**

Vin de Pays du Gard Les Cigales 1995: Rather rustic and mature in character, offering herb, plum and smoke flavors on a tannic texture. A blend of 75 percent Carignan and 25 percent Alicante. Drink now. 3,000 cases made. • $6 • (07/31/98) • **78**

NAIGEON-CHAUVEAU

Mâcon-Villages 1995: Initially seductive—full-bodied and laced with ripe fruit and honey—but went downhill after it was open for a while. Turned tart and dry on the finish. • $NA • (08/31/96) • **79**

St.-Véran Les Monts 1995: Nice as an apéritif or with light dishes. Light- to medium-bodied, with pretty citrus, honey, pear, peach and grassy flavors, and a hay accent to the finish. Drinkable now. • $NA • (08/31/96) • **84**

NAIRAC, CHÂTEAU

Barsac 1992: Sweet, yet tasting like bitter orange liqueur. Some may like it, but not us. • $NA • (04/15/95) • **75**

Barsac 1991: A serious effort, providing dried apricot, honey and fig flavors that continue nicely on the finish. Drink now. • $NA • (04/15/95) • **84**

Barsac 1990: An intense, medium-to-full bodied sweet wine with real grip, showing off its apricot, orange-peel, honey, toast and butter flavors accompanied by lots of panache. Explodes on the finish. Drink now. • $31 • (04/15/95) • **90**

Barsac 1989: Fresh and elegant, lavishly oaked and toasty, showing vanilla, chocolate and honey flavors; medium-bodied, medium-sweet, relatively austere. • $38 • (04/15/95) • **87**

Barsac 1988: Full-bodied, balanced, well-made Barsac, with just the right amount of new wood, ripe fruit and botryitis character. Try now. • $30 • (04/15/95) • **91**

Barsac 1987 • $31 • (06/15/90) • **81**

Barsac 1986: Simple, fruity and ripe, smooth in texture and showing hints of honey and spice on the finish. Drinkable now. • $31 • (12/31/89) • **77**

Barsac 1983: Dominated by oak-scented vanilla now, but incredibly fresh and youthful, with spice, floral and honey character. Medium-sweet, fresh finish. Drinkable now. • $33 • (04/15/95) • **87**

FRANCE

NARDIQUE LA GRAVIÈRE, CHÂTEAU

Entre-Deux-Mers 1994 • $8 • (05/31/95) • **72**
Entre-Deux-Mers 1993 • $8 • (05/31/95) • **79**

NATTER, HENRY

Sancerre Cuvée François de la Grange de Montigny 1995: Ripe, showing round aromas and flavors of melon and vanilla, with accents of herbs and citrus. It's still firm, but seems to be developing rapidly. Drink now. 2,000 cases made. • $20 • (03/31/98) • **85**
Sancerre Domaine de Montigny 1996: Both firm and rich, with an almost creamy texture that carries flavors of lime, pear, minerals and herbs. Has the concentration to develop with age. Drink now through 2000. 4,000 cases made. • $16 • (03/31/98) • **87**
Sancerre Domaine de Montigny 1995: Elegant and well defined, this clean, fresh white offers floral, light grass and peach aromas and flavors with firm yet unobtrusive acidity and great balance. Not a powerhouse, but shows character. 3,000 cases made. • $16 • (05/15/97) • **90**
Sancerre Domaine de Montigny 1993 • $15 • (12/15/95) • **83**
Sancerre Domaine de Montigny Red 1995: This light, tender red offers sweet cherry and spice flavors, with bright acidity and very light tannins. A quaffable wine that will match well with light dishes. Drink now. 4,000 cases made. • $16 • (05/31/98) • **83**
Sancerre Domaine de Montigny Red 1990 • $15 • (10/31/94) • **84**

NAUDIN-FERRAND, HENRI

Bourgogne Aligoté 1994: Crisp and straightforward, with modest fruit flavors and a tart finish. 2,916 cases made. • $NA • (05/31/96) • **76**
Bourgogne Hautes-Côtes de Beaune White 1994: Zingy acidity holds it together, and the peach, apricot, mineral, wet earth and pear flavors are lovely. No oak character, but it's subtle, elegant and delicious. A great effort for this appellation. 845 cases made. • $NA • (05/31/96) • **88**
Côte de Nuits-Villages Le Clos de Magny 1995: Some modest fruit coexists with chewy, fairly dry tannins in this light- to medium-bodied, rustic red. Drink chilled. • $16 • (11/15/97) • **76**
Côte de Nuits-Villages Le Clos de Magny 1994: Light and crisp, with an appealing glow of raspberry and floral aromas and flavors that echo through the finish without interference from excessive tannin. Approachable now. • $15 • (11/15/96) • **84**
Côte de Nuits-Villages Vieilles Vignes 1995: Fairly soft, with decent red berry flavor. Turns a bit chewy, but still kicks in with some good flavors on the succulent finish. Try now. • $18 • (11/15/97) • **82**
Hautes Côtes de Nuits 1994: Light, diluted and simple, with a grassy, herbal note. • $18 • (11/15/96) • **71**
Hautes Côtes de Nuits White 1996: Impressive. Ripe and rich for an Hautes Côtes, very lively and vibrant, bursting with lime, mineral, lemon, honey and apple flavors. The medium-bodied, balanced, superclean finish goes on and on. Drink on release through 2000. 494 cases made. • $14 • (05/31/98) • **87**
Hautes Côtes de Nuits White 1995: Ripe, rich and lush, with good intensity, the fruit mingling nicely with the oak, but it ends a bit abruptly. Full-bodied, with appealing lime, honey, and grapefruit flavors. Drink now. • $18 • (08/31/97) • **86**
Hautes-Côtes de Beaune White 1996: Good ripeness and balance in this medium-bodied white. Offers ripe pear, apple, honey and citrus flavors and supple texture from start to finish. Delicious. Try in 1999. 876 cases made. • $14 • (05/31/98) • **87**
Hautes-Côtes de Beaune White 1995: Sparkles with life, offering some grass, ripe fruit and toasty spice flavors. Quite succulent and medium in body. Approachable now. • $15 • (08/31/97) • **84**

NEGLY, CHÂTEAU DE LA

Syrah-Grenache Coteaux du Languedoc 1995: Fruity, with opulent jammy, berry, briary flavors that roll across the palate. Polished, concentrated and fresh-tasting, with pleasant leather and mineral notes. Delicious now, but should gain with age. Drink now through 2002. 1,000 cases made. • $10 • (03/31/98) • **87**

Key: SS—Spectator Selection CS—Cellar Selection HR—Highly Recommended BB—Best Buy $NA—Price not available Ⓐ—Auction Price (BT)—Barrel Tasting
Dates in parentheses indicate the issues in which the ratings were published.

NENIN, CHÂTEAU

Pomerol 1990: A pretty, restrained wine, with plum, tobacco and berry notes and silky tannins. Drinkable now. 10,000 cases made. • $25 Ⓐ • (03/31/93) • **88**
Pomerol 1986 • $24 Ⓐ • (06/30/89) • **84**
Pomerol 1982 • $40 Ⓐ • (05/15/89) • **89**
Pomerol 1970 • $24 Ⓐ • (05/15/93) • **84**
Pomerol 1961 • $47 • (04/30/96) • **91**
Pomerol 1959 • $61 Ⓐ • (10/15/90) • **88**
Pomerol 1947: Sturdy, alive and dense, but not very elegant. • $37 • (05/31/97) • **85**
Pomerol 1945 • $250 • (11/30/95) • **71**

NERTHE, CHÂTEAU LA

Châteauneuf-du-Pape 1995: This polished red is tender and quite accessible for its youth, with flavors of toast, black cherry and licorice over moderate tannins and bright acidity. Well balanced and made in a modern style. It's delicious now through 2000. 19,580 cases made. • $30 • (10/15/97) • **85**
Châteauneuf-du-Pape 1994: Assertive and distinctive. This ripe, sinuous red shows well-defined aromas and flavors of ripe cherry, smoke, mineral and black pepper. Drinkable now. 2,083 cases imported. 13,750 cases made. • $29 • (10/15/97) • **89**
Châteauneuf-du-Pape 1993: The ripe plum flavors, accented by notes of chocolate and licorice, are attractive in this round, expressive red. Enough tannin to match with food, but accessible now. • $25 • (11/15/96) • **88**
Châteauneuf-du-Pape 1990: Deep, intense and finely polished, with loads of plum, spice and leather flavors. Rich, chewy and well balanced. Dried cherry and chocolate flavors linger on the long finish. Drink now. • $25 • (10/15/94) • **89**
Châteauneuf-du-Pape 1989 • $25 • (10/15/91) • **87**
Châteauneuf-du-Pape 1988 • $25 • (10/15/91) • **88**
Châteauneuf-du-Pape 1986 • $18 • (10/15/91) • **87**
Châteauneuf-du-Pape 1985 • $17 • (10/15/91) • **86**
Châteauneuf-du-Pape 1983 • $25 • (10/15/91) • **88**
Châteauneuf-du-Pape 1981 • $30 • (10/15/91) • **94**
Châteauneuf-du-Pape Cuvée des Cadettes 1994: Generous and sophisticated. This ripe, well-integrated red offers polished flavors of toasty oak, ripe cassis, plum and chocolate in a velvety texture. An international-style wine with elegance and allure. Drink now through 2005. 750 cases made. • $50 • (10/15/97) • **92**
Châteauneuf-du-Pape Cuvée des Cadettes 1993: Here's a Châteauneuf in the international style, with deep color, toasty oak aromas and round, soft flavors of plums and chocolate. It's attractive, if atypical, and drinkable now. • $48 • (11/15/96) • **88**
Châteauneuf-du-Pape Cuvée des Cadettes 1990: Ripe and rich on the palate, more flavorful than aromatic, offering cedary, toasty notes in the aromas and focused plum and currant flavors on a round, smooth texture. Drink now. • $50 • (04/15/93) • **89**
Châteauneuf-du-Pape Cuvée des Cadettes 1989 • $30 • (10/15/91) • **88**
Châteauneuf-du-Pape Cuvée des Cadettes 1988 • $30 • (10/15/91) • **89**
Châteauneuf-du-Pape White 1996: Seductive white, offering subtle layers of oak mingling with the tangerine, citrus, bright floral and almond notes. Medium-bodied and concentrated, the clean, pure character entices you to sip. Buy a case and enjoy now with a fresh water fish, like trout. 1,250 cases made. • $30 • (10/15/97) • **91**
Châteauneuf-du-Pape White 1995: Traditional style Châteauneuf, but rather well done, and it's held up OK. Ripe, rich, full-bodied and quite buttery, with toasty oak, almond, pear notes. The finish is pretty convincing, and long. 500 cases imported. 2,167 cases made. • $30 • (10/15/97) • **86**
Châteauneuf-du-Pape White 1994: Spice and herbal flavors of anise, white pepper and clove stand out in this silky white. Distinctive and expressive, it's a world away from fruit-basket Chardonnays. • $28 • (12/15/96) • **83**
Châteauneuf-du-Pape White Clos de Beauvenir 1994: Fairly traditional style. Rich, full-bodied, yellow in color, with overly ripe fruit flavors and dried fig, brandy and raisin character. Turns a bit oxidized and slightly firm on the finish. Drink now. 417 cases made. • $50 • (10/15/97) • **83**

NICOLAS

Beaujolais-Villages Réserve 1995: Big for a Beaujolais, this has tannin and body, but it's a bit hollow in the middle, with modest cherry and gamelike flavors. Might blossom with food. 150,000 cases made. • $9 • (04/30/97) • **84**
Bonnes Mares 1959 • $NA • (08/31/90) • **75**

Cabernet Sauvignon Vin de Pays d'Oc Maison Nicolas Réserve 1995: On the herbal side of the flavor spectrum, exhibiting dill and cedar notes, a firm finish. Drinkable now. 32,000 cases made. • $7 • (05/15/97) • **78**

Cabernet Sauvignon Vin de Pays d'Oc Maison Nicolas Réserve 1994: Delicious red currant flavors play off the earth and woodsy accents. Moderately tannic. Drinkable now. 32,000 cases made. • $7 • (07/31/96) • **82**

Cabernet Sauvignon Vin de Pays d'Oc Maison Nicolas Réserve 1993 • $6 • (10/31/95) • **78**

Chardonnay Vin de Pays d'Oc Maison Nicolas Réserve 1996: Fresh and slightly sweet-tasting with nice mineral, peach and citrus flavors. Serve well chilled. 32,000 cases made. • $7 • (09/15/97) • **83**

Chardonnay Vin de Pays d'Oc Maison Nicolas Réserve 1994 • $6 • (12/15/95) • **83**

Merlot Vin de Pays d'Oc Maison Nicolas Réserve 1996: Straightforward and simple, with dried cherry flavors and a little spice. 32,000 cases made. • $7 • (11/15/97) • **80**

Merlot Vin de Pays d'Oc Maison Nicolas Réserve 1995: Cherry and spice flavors highlight this easy-drinking red. A little tannin pulls it all together on the finish. Ready now. 32,000 cases made. • $7 • (05/15/97) • **83**

Merlot Vin de Pays d'Oc Maison Nicolas Réserve 1994: A severely flawed wine with extremely volatile aromas and strong vinegar flavors. Tasted twice with consistent notes. 15,000 cases made. • $6 • (01/31/97) • **53**

Merlot Vin de Pays d'Oc Maison Nicolas Réserve 1993 • $6 • (10/31/95) BB • **84**

Pouilly-Fumé 1993 • $9 • (12/15/95) • **81**

Sancerre Les Champs Clos 1993 • $9 • (12/15/95) • **77**

Vouvray 1993 • $6 • (11/15/95) • **83**

NICOLE, CUVÉE

Puligny-Montrachet 1992: An extreme style of white Burgundy that tastes like honey and nectarine in a full-bodied package. It tastes sweet and thick like a dessert wine, then finishes on the tart side. 200 cases made. • $40 • (06/15/95) • **84**

NIELLON, MICHEL

Bâtard-Montrachet 1994: Almost like a late-harvest wine; thick, rich, ripe and oozing with tropical fruit, honey, and caramel flavors. Full-bodied, with structure provided by a nice thread of lemon flavor that runs through the finish. Simply delicious. Drink now. • $135 • (08/31/96) • **91**

Bâtard-Montrachet 1993: Lovely, well crafted and smoother than most '93s, boasting honey, butter and vanilla flavors; medium-bodied, balanced, delicious and quite ripe. Drinkable now. • $122 • (05/15/95) • **88**

Chassagne-Montrachet 1994: Well made and seductive, with pure, clean fruit flavors that caress your palate. Light-to-medium body, with mineral, vanilla and pear notes. It shows a round and supple yet fresh finish. • $45 • (05/31/96) • **88**

Chassagne-Montrachet 1993: A touch of complexity emerges shyly; some grassy notes mingle attractively with honey, almond, and lime flavors. Hard now, but has an artist's signature all over it. Drinkable now. • $38 • (05/15/95) • **86**

Chassagne-Montrachet 1992: A full and rich white Burgundy, with bacon and pear aromas and smooth, generous texture along with good fruit on the finish. Lively and vibrant. • $32 • (08/31/94) • **86**

Chassagne-Montrachet Clos St.-Jean 1994: A rich, voluptuous and distinctive *premier cru*, with complex flavors of dried herb, honey and tropical fruit. Lovely, full-bodied and very ripe in character. Drinkable now. • $NA • (05/31/96) • **89**

Chassagne-Montrachet Clos St.-Jean 1993: Pretty fresh pear and delicate chalky character. Medium-to-light body; fresh acidity. Try now. • $NA • (05/15/95) • **84**

Chassagne-Montrachet Clos St.-Jean 1992: A Chassagne with character and personality, showing plenty of silky spice, nutmeg, toast, pear, and butter flavors that marry well on the sophisticated finish. Deft winemaking here. • $NA • (08/31/94) • **88**

Chassagne-Montrachet Clos de la Maltroie 1995: Sparkles with excellent concentration of fruit, but it's also a bit green as can be expected from a youthful Chassagne. Give it time to blend the honey, spice and tropical fruit notes. Full-bodied; try after 2000. • $50 • (08/31/97) • **90**

Chassagne-Montrachet Clos de la Maltroie 1994: Beams out a focused ray of lemon and honey, presented in a solid, full-bodied frame that beckons you for another sip. Fresh, vibrant and well crafted. Enjoy now. • $NA • (05/31/96) • **90**

Chassagne-Montrachet Clos de la Maltroie 1993: Green, grassy, honey notes blend nicely with lime and citrusy flavors and a hint of mineral on the finish. Drinkable now. • $NA • (05/15/95) • **88**

Chassagne-Montrachet Clos de la Maltroie 1992: Appealing, fat and ripe, with hazelnut and marzipan flavors; a bit soft and definitely ready to drink. • $NA • (08/31/94) • **87**

Chassagne-Montrachet Les Champs Gain 1995: Fabulous. Distinctive and concentrated, with aromas of dried herbs bursting from the glass. Full-bodied and opulent, it coats the palate. Hints of wet earth, dried flowers and honey make the lingering finish very interesting. Delicious now through 2005. • $50 • (08/31/97) • **95**

Chassagne-Montrachet Les Champs Gain 1994: Rather rich and ripe, with supple, lush honey, lemon, toast, and apricot aromas and flavors. This full-bodied '94 is a mouthful. Clean, focused and has a lovely round finish. Drinkable now. • $55 • (05/31/96) • **85**

Chassagne-Montrachet Les Champs Gain 1993: Interesting nut, toasty oak and fruit aromas and flavors, but slightly short on the finish. Drinkable now. • $46 • (05/15/95) • **83**

Chevalier-Montrachet 1995: Shows great class. A superconcentrated wine, subtle, racy, and loaded with mineral, wet stone, and vanilla-cream flavors—both powerful and subtle. Remarkable harmony. Full-bodied and a pleasure to taste now, but clearly better after 2005. • $130 • (08/31/97) • **95**

Chevalier-Montrachet 1994: A blockbuster that delivers tons of flavor. Rich coconut, citrus, cream, honey, and ripe fruit strike the palate in this full-bodied, very concentrated and intense wine. Well-crafted and generous on the long finish. Tempting now, but should age through 2000. • $135 • (05/31/96) • **92**

Chevalier-Montrachet 1993: Very good concentration for the vintage, with enticing mineral, apple and pear character, medium body and a fresh finish. Try now. • $122 • (05/15/95) • **88**

NOBILIS

Minervois 1990 • $NA • (03/15/94) • **87**

NOBLE, DOMAINE LA

Merlot Vin de Pays de l'Aude 1991 • $7 • (06/15/93) • **77**

Merlot Vin de Pays de l'Aude 1990 • $7 • (03/31/92) • **73**

NOUVEAU, CLAUDE

Maranges 1994: Light and diluted, with some decent raspberry and cherry aromas and flavors. Tannins are a bit raspy and hard. • $NA • (11/15/96) • **73**

Maranges La Fussière 1994: Earthy, stalky flavors make this tough wine particularly unpleasant, with only a sharp edge of berry flavor detectable. • $NA • (11/15/96) • **77**

Santenay Grand Clos Rousseau 1994: With lots of tannin for the very light flavors, this is chewy but not generous. • $NA • (11/15/96) • **74**

Santenay Les Charmes Dessus 1994: Biting tannins and earthy, stalky flavors do this one in. • $NA • (11/15/96) • **71**

Santenay White 1995: Very flavorful and distinctive, but a bit too crisp and rather lean on the first sip. Medium-bodied, it offers some nice citrus, pineapple, honey and mango flavors. Long, crisp finish. Drink with shellfish. • $NA • (08/31/97) • **83**

Santenay White 1994: Straightforward, crisp and light-bodied, with green apple, rose petal and herbal flavors. Refreshing and quite intense. Clean and tart on the finish. 500 cases made. • $NA • (05/31/96) • **78**

NUMERO 2 DE LAFON-ROCHET, LE

St.-Estèphe 1996: A medium-bodied wine with good tannins and a fruity, straightforward finish. • $NA • (01/01/97) (BT) • **80-84**

OGEREAU, DOMAINE

Anjou-Villages 1990 • $NA • (10/31/94) • **85**

OGIER, MICHEL

Côte-Rôtie 1990: Firm and tannic, with appealing black cherry and violet aromas and flavors. Subtle, with nuances of toast, hazelnut and vanilla. Drinkable now. 350 cases made. • $42 • (04/15/93) • **88**

Côte-Rôtie 1988 • $38 • (11/15/91) • **87**

FRANCE

OGIER & FILS, A.

Châteauneuf-du-Pape Grande Cuvée 1985 • $22 • (06/15/93) • **76**

OLEK-MERY

Chinon Cuvée des Tireaux 1993 • $18 • (05/15/96) • **87**

OLIVIER, CHÂTEAU

Pessac-Léognan 1997: Fresh floral aromas with grapey undertones. Medium-bodied, with silky tannins and a short finish. • $NA • (06/15/98) (BT) • **80-84**
Pessac-Léognan 1996: A well-crafted red. Impressive wild berry and mineral aromas follow through on the palate. Full-bodied, with firm tannins and a medium finish. Almost outstanding. 7,500 cases made. • $28 • (06/15/98) (BT) • **85-89**
Pessac-Léognan 1995: Builds on the palate. Attractive floral and berry aromas, with hints of tomato. Medium- to full-bodied, with chunky tannins and a long, fruit and vanilla aftertaste. Give it time. Best after 2000. 10,000 cases made. • $25 • (01/31/98) • **89**
Pessac-Léognan 1994: Slightly simple, this has dried cherry, berry and herb aromas and flavors. Medium-bodied, with fine tannins and a fresh finish. Drink or hold. 10,000 cases made. • $23 • (01/31/97) • **84**
Pessac-Léognan 1993: Very grapey, offering wet earth, berry and cherry aromas and flavors, medium body and tannins and a slightly coarse finish. Drinkable now. 9,333 cases made. • $23 • (01/31/96) • **85**
Pessac-Léognan 1992: A good amount of cherry and violet character; firm tannins and vibrant fruit. • $18 • (04/15/95) • **83**
Pessac-Léognan 1990: Firm, focused and elegant; this is a solid wine, with a wide band of cherry, spice, tobacco and olive aromas and flavors. Finishes smooth in texture. Drinkable now. 8,500 cases made. • $20 • (12/31/92) HR • **90**
Pessac-Léognan 1989 • $23 • (03/15/92) SS • **95**
Pessac-Léognan 1988 • $25 • (02/15/91) HR • **91**
Graves 1985 • $20 • (02/15/89) SS • **93**
Graves 1983 • $23 • (05/01/89) • **92**
Graves 1982 • $21 • (08/31/92) • **90**
Graves 1981 • $14 • (10/16/85) • **86**
Pessac-Léognan White 1995: Subtle apple, honey and chalk aromas and flavors. Medium-bodied, with fresh acidity and a short finish. Drink now. • $16 • (04/30/98) • **85**
Pessac-Léognan White 1994 • $16 • (03/31/96) • **90**
Pessac-Léognan White 1993 • $16 • (05/31/95) • **85**

OLLIEUX, CHÂTEAU LES

Corbières 1988 • $5 • (11/30/90) BB • **80**

ORATOIRE ST.-MARTIN, DOMAINE DE L'

Côtes du Rhône-Villages Haut-Coustias Cairanne 1993: Berry and spice flavors are appealing, and still fresh for the wine's age, but drown in the astringent tannins that take over the finish. Drinkable now. • $16 • (12/15/96) • **83**
Côtes du Rhône-Villages Réserve des Seigneurs Cairanne 1994: Earthy on the nose and harsh on the palate, this wine has more extract than balance. It's rustic and a bit coarse. • $12 • (12/15/96) • **78**

ORMES-DE-PEZ, CHÂTEAU LES

St.-Estèphe 1997: Rather diluted, with wet soil and berry character, firm tannins and a short finish. • $NA • (06/15/98) (BT) • **75-79**
St.-Estèphe 1996: Rather grapey and slightly minty, with firm tannins. Medium-bodied. Nicely crafted. • $25 • (06/15/98) (BT) • **85-89**
St.-Estèphe 1995: Vibrant, with violet, floral and berry aromas and flavors. Medium-bodied, with fine tannins and a fresh finish. • $25 • (01/01/97) (BT) • **85-89**

Key: SS—Spectator Selection CS—Cellar Selection HR—Highly Recommended BB—Best Buy $NA—Price not available Ⓐ—Auction Price (BT)—Barrel Tasting
Dates in parentheses indicate the issues in which the ratings were published.

St.-Estèphe 1994: Fairly tough, with loads of slightly dry tannins and moderately concentrated fruit flavors. Lacks balance. May be better in 1999. 17,000 cases made. • $25 • (01/31/97) • **79**
St.-Estèphe 1993: Wonderful polish to this red, adding a core of ripe, red berry flavor. Medium-bodied, harmonious mouthfeel and an extremely elegant, supple finish. Delicious now. 15,000 cases made. • $19 • (01/31/96) • **87**
St.-Estèphe 1992: Decent licorice, spice and cedar character, with a light body and light tannins. • $17 • (04/15/95) • **78**
St.-Estèphe 1991: Very fruity and pleasant with berry and cherry aromas and flavors, medium tannins and a light finish. • $15 • (03/31/94) • **82**
St.-Estèphe 1990: A monstrous wine, with huge amounts of cherry and toasty oak flavors and velvety tannins. Quite hard on the palate, but the very long finish suggests greatness. From Jean-Michel Cazes. Drink now. 12,500 cases made. • $22 • (03/31/93) • **93**
St.-Estèphe 1989 • $24 • (03/15/92) • **86**
St.-Estèphe 1988 • $21 • (04/30/91) • **88**
St.-Estèphe 1987 • $15 • (05/15/90) • **83**
St.-Estèphe 1986 • $22 Ⓐ • (11/30/89) • **87**
St.-Estèphe 1985 • $27 Ⓐ • (04/30/88) • **89**
St.-Estèphe 1983 • $17 • (10/15/86) • **86**
St.-Estèphe 1982 • $43 Ⓐ • (08/31/92) • **84**
St.-Estèphe 1961 • $55 • (04/30/96) • **87**

ORMES-SORBET, CHÂTEAU LES

Médoc 1988 • $20 • (04/30/91) • **84**

ORMIERES, CHÂTEAU

Minervois 1991 • $7 • (03/15/94) • **83**

ORSCHWIHR, CHÂTEAU D'

Pinot Blanc Alsace Cuvée Drachenfels 1995: Ripe and assertive in character, with a little sweetness offset by a tangy combination of apricot and citrus flavors. 450 cases made. • $16 • (06/30/97) • **83**

ORVAL, L'

Merlot Vin de Pays d'Oc 1994: An ambitious wine that, while well-oaked, still has a delicious fruitiness. Ripe plum, clove and spice flavors dominate. Finishes with a splash of cherry flavor. • $NA • (12/15/96) • **86**

OSTANGE, DOMAINE D'

Mâcon 1993: Good, straightforward Chardonnay, light in body and bone-dry, showing well-defined, crisp lime, mineral and green apple flavors and a fresh finish. From Noël Perrin. • $NA • (08/31/95) • **82**

OSTERTAG, DOMAINE

Gewürztraminer Alsace Epfig 1996: A little residual sweetness and what seems like a touch of botrytis add an element of exoticism to this fruit bomb. Very lively and light on its feet, with good concentration and intensity. The finish lingers. Drink now. • $20 • (04/30/98) • **86**
Gewürztraminer Alsace Fronholz 1995: So lush you could spread it on toast. Full of honey, this viscous white coats the mouth, coming together neatly at the end with a fillip of grapefruit peel. Enticing. • $25 • (09/30/97) • **89**
Muscat Alsace Fronholz 1995: Vivid and fresh, this wine is atypical for the style. It exhibits ripe apple and peach flavors, but there are floral and grapefruit notes on the finish. Very appealing. • $22 • (09/30/97) • **85**
Pinot Blanc Alsace Barriques 1995: Simple, light and lemony, with a buttery note at the end. • $14 • (09/15/97) • **75**
Pinot Blanc Alsace Barriques 1994: Heavy aromas and flavors of smoke and oak dominate, overwhelming the modest fruit flavors. • $15 • (09/30/96) • **77**
Pinot Gris Alsace Barriques 1995: Pretty nondescript, except for the vanilla from new oak. Shows just a little floral and peach flavor, with an astringent finish. • $22 • (09/30/97) • **78**
Pinot Gris Alsace Barriques 1994: Straightforward and balanced. An easy-drinking wine, with its round, sweet pear and refreshing lemon flavors and an intriguing herbal note that lingers on the finish. • $23 • (10/15/96) • **86**
Riesling Alsace Epfig 1995: A fruit bomb, with firm acidity that carries the seductive peach, apricot and honeysuckle flavors to a lovely ending.

Impeccably balanced and seamless, this white should marry well with rich fish or pork dishes. • $18 • (09/30/97) • **89**

Riesling Alsace Grand Cru Muenchberg 1995: A joy to taste. This Riesling needs time, but the high acidity is balanced by loads of apricot, smoke and mineral flavors. Very intense, complex and long; brimming with acidity for the long haul. Try after 2000. • $33 • (09/30/97) • **90**

OTT, DOMAINES

Bandol Cuvée Marine 1993 • $20 • (08/31/95) • **81**
Côtes de Provence 1989 • $25 • (07/15/92) • **84**
Côtes de Provence 1987 • $22 • (05/31/91) • **78**
Côtes de Provence Clair de Noirs 1993 • $25 • (08/31/95) • **81**
Côtes de Provence La Déesse 1993 • $20 • (08/31/95) • **77**

OUDINOT

Brut Blanc de Blancs Champagne 1988: Extremely fruity style of *blanc de blancs*. The nose and palate is dominated with apple, lime and banana character, full-bodied with steely acidity. Drinkable now. • $29 • (12/31/93) • **88**

Brut Blanc de Noirs Champagne 1988: A rich, muscular, more ripe style yet very fruity vintage Champagne with ripe flavors, good acidity and a long toasty, butterscotch finish. Drink now. • $29 • (12/31/93) • **88**

Brut Champagne 1985 • $28 • (12/31/90) • **90**

Brut Rosé Champagne 1983: Floral cherry and strawberry aromas and flavors are especially appealing in this simple, elegant wine. The fruit and toast balance neatly for easy sipping. • $25 • (12/31/89) • **88**

OUPIA, CHÂTEAU D'

Minervois 1995: Shows some good plum and cherry flavors, but it clamps down on the finish with assertive tannins. Lacks freshness and comes off as unbalanced in the end. Drink now. • $8 • (03/31/98) • **81**

PABIOT, J.A.D.

Pouilly-Fumé Domaine des Chantebines 1993 • $16 • (11/15/95) • **86**
Pouilly-Fumé Prestige de Vieilles Vignes 1993 • $23 • (11/15/95) • **85**

PABIOT, DIDIER

Pouilly-Fumé 1995: A vibrant wine, this mingles fresh herb and floral notes with ripe apple and melon flavors, then finishes clean and fresh. Will match well with assertive, light dishes. • $15 • (04/30/97) • **87**

PABIOT, DOMINIQUE

Pouilly-Fumé Les Cerisottes 1993 • $15 • (12/15/95) • **78**

PABIOT & FILS, JEAN

Pouilly-Fumé Domaine des Fines Caillottes 1996: The deep golden color and sweet vanilla notes are atypical for the region, but the wine is attractive, with ripe melon and almond flavors that leave a hint of sweetness on the finish, and just enough acidity to match with food. Drink now. • $17 • (05/31/98) • **86**

Pouilly-Fumé Prestige des Fines Caillottes 1995: This intriguing white tastes like a late-harvest wine, with its golden color, honeyed aromas and round, soft texture. The flavors lean toward melon, almond and figs. Though atypical, it's concentrated and distinctive. Drink through 1999. • $25 • (05/31/98) • **87**

PADERE, CHÂTEAU DE

Buzet 1994: A solid, hearty red for everyday drinking. The cherry notes take on a wild, almost gamy edge and it's chewy and satisfying. Good length, too. Enjoy now. • $11 • (12/15/97) • **85**

Buzet 1990: Rich and round, the green olive flavor balanced by plum, ending moderately tannic. • $10 • (07/31/96) • **83**

Buzet 1986 • $5 • (12/15/88) • **79**

PAGODES DE COS, LES

St.-Estèphe 1995: Berry aromas, with a mushroom and slightly grassy character. Medium- to full-bodied, with velvety tannins and a smoky tobacco aftertaste. A second label from Château Cos-d'Estournel, and damn good. Best after 2000. • $27 • (01/31/98) • **87**

PAILLARD, BRUNO

Brut Blanc de Blancs Champagne 1983 • $40 • (05/31/87) • **94**
Brut Blanc de Blancs Champagne 1975 • $42 • (05/31/87) • **70**

Brut Blanc de Blancs Champagne Réserve Privée NV: A down-to-earth Champagne that contrasts a light, foamy texture with pungent earth and mineral-like flavors. Not for everyone. Drink now. • $45 • (04/30/98) • **78**

Brut Champagne 1989: Serious, ripe and robust, with rich, nutty, spicy flavors, a plush texture and a lingering finish. Appealing. Drink now through 2001. • $50 • (04/30/98) • **89**

Brut Champagne 1985: An expressive, serious wine with lovely aromas of chocolate and berries that follow though on the palate. Full-bodied yet balanced with well-integrated acidity and long finish. Drinkable now. • $35 • (12/31/93) • **93**

Brut Champagne Première Cuvée NV: A classy Champagne from the toasty aromas to the zesty fruit flavors to the lingering, spicy finish. Firm in texture and bright in flavor. Drink now. • $27 • (04/30/98) • **89**

Brut Rosé Champagne Première Cuvée NV: Very pretty. A complete package—from the light, spicy aromas to the light cherry flavors backed by lively acidity to the lingering, juicy finish. Drink now. • $38 • (04/30/98) • **88**

PAILLAS, CHÂTEAU

Cahors 1993: Dusty tobacco notes accent the cherry flavors in this firm, dry red. Flavors expand on the finish. Try with food. • $13 • (05/15/97) • **85**

Cahors 1992: Shows interesting, mature aromas of Earl Grey tea and red fruits, but the drying tannins say drink up. • $14 • (05/15/97) • **79**

PAILLET-QUANCARD, CHÂTEAU DE

Première Côtes de Bordeaux 1990: Tart, earthy and unpleasant; a wine with very little meat on its bones. For those who like austere Bordeaux only. 11,000 cases made. • $14 • (06/15/93) • **76**

PALLIERES, DOMAINE LES

Gigondas 1988 • $20 • (08/31/92) • **79**
Gigondas 1986 • $21 • (11/15/91) • **79**
Gigondas 1984 • $14 • (09/30/89) • **86**
Gigondas 1983 • $15 • (01/31/89) • **88**
Gigondas 1982 • $11 • (05/31/87) • **89**
Gigondas 1981 • $11 • (03/15/87) • **90**

PALME, CHÂTEAU LA

Côtes du Frontonnais 1988 • $7 • (07/31/91) • **63**

PALMER, CHÂTEAU

Margaux 1997: Very pretty aromas of minerals and black fruits. Medium-bodied, with medium tannins and a fresh fruit finish. All in finesse. Outstanding. • $NA • (06/15/98) (BT) • **90-94**

Margaux 1996: A sleek and silky wine, with fine tannins and fresh fruit. Medium-bodied, with a medium finish. Very well made. A real beauty, as always. • $70 • (06/15/98) (BT) • **90-94**

Margaux 1995: Elegant and beautiful. Outstanding Palmer. Extremely pretty aromas of black cherries and vanilla. Full-bodied, with velvety tannins and a long, cherry, vanilla aftertaste. A delightful wine. Best after 2000. 14,500 cases made. • $67 • (01/31/98) • **94**

Margaux 1994: Exuberant aromas of new wood, chocolate and tobacco. Medium- to full-bodied, yet wonderfully refined with cedar, tobacco, cherry and berry flavors. Really a joy to taste. Drink or hold. 14,000 cases made. • $40 Ⓐ • (01/31/97) • **89**

Margaux 1993: Supersilky wine featuring toasty oak, berry and cherry character, medium body, fine tannins and delicate finish. Drinkable now. • $30 Ⓐ • (01/31/96) • **88**

FRANCE

Margaux 1992: Light and fruity, offering some pretty cherry and plum character, but straightforward and short on the finish. • $24 Ⓐ • (04/15/95) • **80**
Margaux 1991: This estate is always very good in a mediocre vintage. Lovely character of vanilla, cherry and berry, firm tannins and a long, silky finish. Drinkable now. • $38 • (03/31/94) • **87**
Margaux 1990: Gives more in flavor than in aroma at the moment, but excellent. It's chunky for a Margaux, with loads of plummy cedar flavors and full, soft tannins. Drinkable now. 16,000 cases made. • $42 Ⓐ • (03/31/93) • **91**
Margaux 1989 • $105 Ⓐ • (03/15/92) • **95**
Margaux 1988 • $68 Ⓐ • (02/28/91) CS • **96**
Margaux 1987 • $44 Ⓐ • (05/15/90) • **84**
Margaux 1986 • $72 Ⓐ • (06/15/89) • **94**
Margaux 1985 • $69 Ⓐ • (10/15/94) • **91**
Margaux 1984 • $25 Ⓐ • (10/15/87) • **84**
Margaux 1983 • $141 Ⓐ • (10/15/94) • **90**
Margaux 1982 • $33 Ⓐ • (08/31/92) • **92**
Margaux 1981 • $54 Ⓐ • (10/15/94) • **89**
Margaux 1980 • $32 Ⓐ • (05/01/85) • **86**
Margaux 1979 • $53 Ⓐ • (10/15/89) • **90**
Margaux 1978 • $72 Ⓐ • (05/01/85) • **81**
Margaux 1970 • $88 Ⓐ • (05/15/93) • **91**
Margaux 1962 • $98 Ⓐ • (11/30/87) • **80**
Margaux 1961 • $1663 Ⓐ/1.5 liter • (04/30/96) • **93**
Margaux 1959 • $619 Ⓐ • (10/15/90) • **98**
Margaux 1945 • $567 Ⓐ • (11/30/95) • **91**

PALMER & CO.

Brut Blanc de Blancs Champagne 1988: Sumptuously ripe and enticing. Gorgeous fruit and spice flavors are woven into a plush but lively texture, and a fine mousse keeps them vibrating on the finish. Better showing than last year. Drink now through 2000. Tasted twice, with consistent notes. • $40 • (12/31/97) • **93**
Brut Champagne 1989: Beautifully balanced and complete, it's a crisp but creamy textured, full-flavored Champagne. Drink now through 2000. • $40 • (12/31/97) • **89**
Brut Champagne NV: A straightforward, crisply balanced Champagne with apple and lemon flavors and subtle doughy accents. Drink now. • $29 • (11/15/97) • **83**
Brut Rosé Champagne NV: An elegant style of rosé, from the light coral color to the crisp, elegant texture and subdued cherry flavors that seem to grow and accelerate as you sip. Beautifully balanced and a pleasure to drink. • $34 • (11/30/97) • **90**

PALOUMEY, CHÂTEAU

Haut-Médoc 1994: Lean and tannic, with some modest plum and spice flavors, finishing on a harsh note. • $15 • (04/30/97) • **79**

PANNIER

Brut Champagne Cuvée Louis Eugène NV: Acceptable quality, but awkward in style, with fat, buttery flavors but a lean, hard-edged texture. • $43 • (10/31/97) • **78**
Brut Champagne Egérie 1990: What a generous, indulgent style of Champagne. Caramel aromas, full fruit flavors and lush nutmeg and vanilla accents blend seamlessly on a luxurious, rich texture. Long on the finish, too. Drink now through 2002. • $49 • (11/15/97) • **91**
Brut Champagne Sélection NV: Bright and bold, an assertive, full-bodied style with butterscotch aromas, lively fruit flavors and a lingering finish. • $25 • (10/31/97) • **87**

PANNIER, REMY

Cabernet Franc Rosé Vin de Pays du Jardin de la France 1997: Fresh and crisp, this pale, dry rosé has a vibrant texture and a vivid core of strawberry flavor. Enjoy it for the exuberance of youth. Drink now. 18,000 cases made. • $7 • (07/31/98) • **83**

Cabernet Franc Rosé Vin de Pays du Jardin de la France 1996: Here's an appealing, dry rosé with bright cherry and strawberry flavors, a zingy texture and a lingering finish. An attractive example of an unusual style, at a price that invites trying a change of pace. Drink now. 30,000 cases made. • $6 • (12/15/97) BB • **86**
Cabernet Sauvignon Vin de Pays d'Oc 1997: A fresh, easygoing red, with light, simple fruit flavors and very little tannin. Drink now. 9,400 cases made. • $7 • (07/31/98) • **80**
Cabernet Sauvignon Vin de Pays d'Oc 1996: The cherry flavor begins softly in this simple red, then disappears, and the finish turns tough. 4,000 cases made. • $6 • (12/15/97) • **78**
Chardonnay Vin de Pays d'Oc 1996: A simple, bland white that's drinkable but has little Chardonnay character. 3,000 cases made. • $6 • (12/15/97) • **77**
Merlot Vin de Pays d'Oc 1997: Light, smooth and appealing, with fresh strawberry and cherry flavors and very little tannin. Drink now. 8,000 cases made. • $7 • (07/31/98) • **83**
Merlot Vin de Pays d'Oc 1996: A light, cherry-flavored red with a hint of spice. Finishes slightly astringent. 3,000 cases made. • $6 • (12/15/97) • **78**

PAPE, CHÂTEAU LE

Pessac-Léognan 1996: Very light and slightly weedy, with berry and cherry undertones. Light- to medium-bodied, with light tannins and a fresh finish. • $26 • (06/15/98) (BT) • **75-79**
Pessac-Léognan 1990: An elegant austerity pervades this wine. It blends ripe black currant aromas and flavors with a lean texture. Drinkable now. • $16 • (08/31/95) • **83**

PAPE CLEMENT, CHÂTEAU

Pessac-Léognan 1997: Rich and beautiful for the vintage, with tobacco and cherry aromas and flavors. Medium-bodied, with velvety tannins and a medium finish. Almost outstanding. • $NA • (06/15/98) (BT) • **85-89**
Pessac-Léognan 1996: Decadent aromas of berry, tobacco and mushroom. Medium-bodied, with full, velvety tannins and a succulent finish. A beauty. • $45 • (06/15/98) (BT) • **90-94**
Pessac-Léognan 1995: Brillant violet, berry and black-truffle aromas. Full-bodied and very chewy, with loads of berry, tobacco and earthlike flavors. Medium finish. Only in fourth-gear now, wait for fifth and sixth. Best after 2002. • $40 • (01/31/98) • **92**
Pessac-Léognan 1994: Shows decent fruit flavor, but is slightly dry and herbal and the finish is short. Medium-bodied. Drink or hold. Tasted twice, with consistent notes. • $50 • (01/31/97) • **80**
Pessac-Léognan 1993: Elegant and light- to medium-bodied, showing some nice fruit and meaty, gamy character that's quite appealing. Drink now. • $38 • (01/31/96) • **84**
Pessac-Léognan 1992: Subtle aromas of berry, tobacco and stones follow through on the palate; light-bodied. Tasted twice, with consistent notes. • $26 • (04/15/95) • **79**
Pessac-Léognan 1990: No holds barred on this wine. It's packed with decadent, earthy fruit aromas and flavors and loads of tannins. Drink now. 11,000 cases made. • $47 • (03/31/93) • **92**
Pessac-Léognan 1989 • $43 • (03/15/92) • **88**
Pessac-Léognan 1988 • $40 • (12/31/90) HR • **93**
Pessac-Léognan 1987 • $24 • (05/15/90) • **84**
Pessac-Léognan 1986 • $36 • (06/30/89) • **92**
Graves 1985 • $44 • (06/30/88) • **83**
Graves 1983 • $20 • (03/31/87) • **89**
Graves 1982 • $33 • (02/01/85) • **84**
Graves 1981 • $17 • (06/01/84) • **77**
Graves 1979 • $20 • (10/15/89) • **84**
Graves 1970 • $66 • (05/15/93) • **84**
Graves 1962 • $120 • (11/30/87) • **90**
Graves 1961 • $560 • (04/30/96) • **88**
Graves 1959 • $100 • (10/15/90) • **80**
Pessac-Léognan White 1994 • $60 • (03/31/96) • **96**
Pessac-Léognan White 1993 • $50 • (05/31/95) • **88**

PAPES, CAVES DES

Châteauneuf-du-Pape 1993: Voluptuous but already quite mature. This shows round cedar, raisin and leather flavors, with hard underlying tannins. It's rustic, but it has heart. Drinkable now. 20,000 cases made. • $17 • (04/30/97) • **83**

Key: SS—Spectator Selection CS—Cellar Selection HR—Highly Recommended BB—Best Buy $NA—Price not available Ⓐ—Auction Price (BT)—Barrel Tasting
Dates in parentheses indicate the issues in which the ratings were published.

Châteauneuf-du-Pape 1988 • $14 • (10/31/93) • **83**

Châteauneuf-du-Pape Les Closiers 1994: Harmonious for its appealing flavors of raspberries, cherries, black pepper and tobacco, complex yet well integrated, with firm yet unobtrusive tannins and fresh acidity. Not a powerhouse, but food-friendly, and should improve through 1999. • $19 • (10/15/97) • **86**

Crozes-Hermitage 1990: A traditionally styled Syrah. Maturing, it offers a mix of game and barnyard flavors, silky but still firm, with raisin and coffee notes on the finish. Lacks fruit, but not character. Drink now. 3,000 cases made. • $11 • (02/28/97) • **86**

Côtes du Rhône 1993 • $7 • (11/15/95) • **83**

Côtes du Rhône White 1996: Very crisp and quite lean, this lively white offers citrus and mineral flavors. Not showy, but a great match with food. • $7 • (10/15/97) • **85**

Côtes du Rhône White 1993 • $7 • (11/15/95) • **74**

Côtes du Rhône Domaine des Jonquiers 1993: Vivid blackberry and licorice flavors, but a volatile acidic edge brings a note of instability to this ripe, firm wine. 3,000 cases made. • $8 • (10/15/96) • **78**

Côtes du Rhône Heritage Elevé en Foudre de Chène 1995: Delivers very pretty blackberry and cherry flavors, and more body than many in this category, showing supple character and texture, and good balance. Rather impressive for this appellation. Drink now. • $11 • (10/15/97) • **84**

Gigondas 1990: Ripe and fleshy, delivering plenty of flavors—from cassis and raisins to chocolate and smoked meats. The tannins are softening, but still give backbone. A well-made wine at its peak now. 5,000 cases made. • $14 • (10/15/96) • **88**

Gigondas 1988 • $13 • (10/31/93) • **78**

Gigondas Réserve des Fustiers 1994: Light and supple, this offers light cherry, herb and floral notes. The tannins are a bit dry on the finish. Drink now. • $15 • (10/15/97) • **79**

PAQUET, FRANÇOIS

Mâcon Blanc-Villages Cépage Chardonnay 1994: A pleasant, fresh, sharp and tart character, mingling quince, pear and apple notes. Juicy, clean and vibrant finish. 3,000 cases made. • $9 • (08/31/95) • **79**

Mâcon Blanc-Villages Cépage Chardonnay 1993: Light and straightforward, showing grapefruit, hay and a slight salty, fishy and cardboard taste on the finish. Diluted. 3,000 cases made. • $9 • (08/31/95) • **70**

Mâcon-Lugny Cépage Chardonnay Cuvée St.-Denis Tradition 1993: Clean, crisp wet hay, green apple and citrus are quite tart and unyielding, but light, fresh and dry. 1,916 cases made. • $9 • (08/31/95) • **78**

PAQUET, JEAN-PAUL

Pouilly-Fuissé Domaine de Fuissiacus Vieilles Vignes 1994: What happened? Dull-tasting, quite diluted, showing a cardboard note and only modest fruit flavors. • $15 • (05/31/96) • **72**

Pouilly-Fuissé Domaine Les Vieux Murs 1994: A round, straightforward white, with pleasant smoky aromas and soft, simple flavors of apple and spice, a bit hollow at the center. 1,100 cases made. • $23 • (06/30/97) • **81**

PARAN-JUSTICE, CHÂTEAU

St.-Emilion 1995: An autumnal red with berry, mushroom and leaf character. Medium-bodied, with chocolate and berry flavors, medium tannins and a slightly short finish. Drink now. 6,000 cases made. • $20 • (01/31/98) • **80**

PARAZA, CHÂTEAU DE

Minervois 1985 • $6 • (02/29/88) • **80**

Minervois Cuvée Spéciale 1996: Fresh, fruity and fairly chewy, with good berry, cherry and plum flavors and a nice tobacco note on the finish. 20,000 cases made. • $6 • (02/28/98) • **83**

Minervois Cuvée Spéciale 1986 • $6 • (10/15/88) • **76**

PARCE, DOCTEUR

Collioure Domaine du Mas Blanc Cuvée Cosprons Levants 1991 • $21 • (12/15/94) • **81**

Domaine du Mas Blanc Rimage Banyuls 1991 • $27 • (12/15/94) • **78**

PARDE DE HAUT-BAILLY, LA

Pessac-Léognan 1995: A wonderful, sleek and harmonious wine. Gorgeous aromas of bright berries, vanilla, tobacco, and chocolate. Full-bodied, with super well-integrated tannins and a long, long, silky finish. Second label of Château Haut-Bailly. Best after 2000. • $15 • (01/31/98) • **88**

PARENT

Beaune Les Epenottes 1995: Light and quaffable, with strawberry and cherry flavors. Chewy, slightly dry tannins. 150 cases made. • $38 • (11/15/97) • **76**

Beaune Les Epenottes 1994: Light and a bit tight in texture, showing understated cherry and herb flavors. • $33 • (11/15/96) • **80**

Beaune Les Epenottes 1993: A delicate '93 that won't knock your socks off but is fun to drink now, featuring silky tannins, medium body of fruit and fresh finish. Drink now. 416 cases made. • $57 • (11/15/95) • **85**

Beaune Les Epenottes 1991: Extremely light and medicinal in aroma, tasting watery and musty. Tasted twice with consistent notes. 833 cases made. • $NA • (01/31/94) • **69**

Beaune Les Epenottes 1990: This pretty wine wraps nicely around a core of spice, chestnut, cinnamon and berry flavors and offers a ripe, almost sweet nuance and a silky finish. Drinkable now • $NA • (12/15/92) • **85**

Bourgogne 1995: Smells overly earthy and tastes dilute. 250 cases made. • $18 • (11/15/97) • **70**

Bourgogne 1994: Light, green in character and basically uninviting except for a nice hint of berry flavor on the finish. • $17 • (11/15/96) • **78**

Corton Les Renardes 1994: Light, and more matured than many, showing more game and leather notes than fruit flavors. Finish is lean and relatively simple. Try in 1999. • $57 • (11/15/96) • **78**

Corton Les Renardes 1993: Elegant, distinguished Corton featuring lovely cedar, berry and plum character. Not a big wine but really pretty. Smooth tannins and fresh finish. Drink in 1999. 125 cases made. • $62 • (11/15/95) • **90**

Corton Les Renardes 1992: Has light, grapey, peppery and herbal flavors, but seems diluted. Not very interesting. 125 cases made. • $76 • (12/15/94) • **74**

Corton Les Renardes 1990: Smells and tastes of strawberries, but where is the beef? Lacks character, but makes for pleasant *grand cru* drinking. Drinkable now. • $NA • (12/15/92) • **83**

Monthélie Les Champs Fulliot 1992: Very pretty, spicy berry and currant flavors open up a little just before the coarse tannins clamp down on the finish. Try now. • $NA • (12/15/94) • **81**

Pommard 1982 • $18 • (11/01/85) • **83**

Pommard La Croix Blanche 1995: Delicate but balanced, traditional, with some decent fruit, licorice aromas and flavors, and dry tannins. 100 cases made. • $45 • (11/15/97) • **80**

Pommard Les Chanlins 1993: Soft and gentlemanly, somewhat light but pleasant, offering plum and red berry flavor and a dry finish. Tasted twice, with consistent notes. 10 cases imported. 10 cases made. • $47 • (11/15/95) • **78**

Pommard Les Chaponnières 1995: Traditional, but decent fruit makes for a pleasant, medium-bodied wine. Sweet and ripe in the midpalate, it offers plum, black cherry and fig flavors. A bit dry on the finish, but should smooth out by 1999. 60 cases made. • $45 • (11/15/97) • **83**

Pommard Les Chaponnières 1994: Balanced and flavorful, with flavors of cherry, licorice, spice and vanilla. Slightly short and drying on the finish. Try in 1999. • $46 • (11/15/96) • **80**

Pommard Les Chaponnières 1993: Succulent and soft chocolate, berry and tobacco character and medium tannins. Delicious now. 375 cases made. • $50 • (11/15/95) • **86**

Pommard Les Chaponnières 1992: Crisp and spicy, with a gamy edge to the lean blackberry flavor. 375 cases made. • $50 • (12/15/94) • **80**

Pommard Les Chaponnières 1991: This solid wine has a chewy texture, chunky tannins and nicely defined black cherry and earth aromas and flavors. Try now. 292 cases made. • $NA • (01/31/94) • **82**

Pommard Les Chaponnières 1990: A traditional style, with distinctive, earthy leaf, mushroom and chestnut aromas and flavors, but an unexciting finish. Drinkable now. • $NA • (12/15/92) • **81**

Pommard Les Epenots 1994: A bit funky and earthy, with some decent red berry flavors in a light-bodied frame. Slight dilution marks the finish. • $51 • (11/15/96) • **75**

Pommard Les Epenots 1993: Delightful aromas of raspberries and strawberries, with well-integrated, smooth tannins. Good acidity. Drinkable now. Not as good as a barrel sample tasted earlier. 833 cases made. • $57 • (11/15/95) • **87**

FRANCE

PARIGOT PÈRE & FILS

Pommard Les Epenots 1992: Ripe yet delicate, medium-bodied, with decent strawberry, raspberry and red licorice flavors that turn sweet on the supple finish. Drinkable now. 417 cases made. • $70 • (12/15/94) • **83**

Pommard Les Epenots 1991: Nicely defined blackberry and black cherry aromas and flavors make this smooth, polished and supple. Drinkable now. 333 cases made. • $NA • (01/31/94) • **83**

Pommard Les Epenots 1990: Well-crafted and silky, with raspberry and cherry characteristics. Try now. • $NA • (12/15/92) • **89**

Pommard Les Epenots 1959 • $NA • (08/31/90) • **94**

Pommard Les Rugiens 1992: Lean in structure but supple enough to show its generous blackberry and raspberry flavor nicely, echoing toast and spice as well. Drinkable now. • $NA • (12/15/94) • **86**

PARIGOT PÈRE & FILS

Beaune Les Grèves 1987 • $26 • (02/28/90) • **88**

Pommard Les Charmots 1987 • $28 • (07/31/89) • **87**

Pommard Les Charmots 1985 • $34 • (06/15/87) CS • **93**

PASCAL, JEAN

Pommard La Chanière 1986 • $30 • (10/15/88) • **78**

PASCAUD-VILLEFRANCHE, CHÂTEAU

Sauternes 1986: Tobacco and toasty aromas and flavors frame the fairly ripe but not-too-concentrated fruit. Sweet and simple. • $24 • (12/31/89) • **78**

PASSAT, ANDRE

Côte-Rôtie 1985 • $25 • (10/15/87) • **88**

PASTOU, PAUL & JEAN-MARC

Sancerre Les Boucaults 1995: This steely, rather unyielding white offers light menthol and herb flavors and very firm acidity. Drink now. Tasted twice, with consistent results. 1,200 cases made. • $15 • (06/15/97) • **85**

PATACHE D'AUX, CHÂTEAU

Médoc 1997: Pretty berry and cherry aromas and flavors. Medium to light in body, with light tannins. • $NA • (06/15/98) (BT) • **80-84**

Médoc 1996: Highly extracted, with loads of smoke, berry and dark chocolate character. Full-bodied and velvety, with a long, delicious finish. A slightly hollow center palate. Wait and see. 10,000 cases made. • $14 • (06/15/98) (BT) • **85-89**

Médoc 1995: Slightly simple, with some good dried cherry character and hints of mineral and iron. Medium-bodied, with medium tannins and a light finish. Drink now. 21,000 cases made. • $12 • (01/31/98) • **83**

Médoc 1994: Slightly diluted, but shows an attractive berry and cherry character, fine tannins and a refreshing finish. Drinkable now. 21,666 cases made. • $NA • (01/31/97) • **80**

Médoc 1988 • $17 • (04/30/91) • **80**

Médoc 1982 • $20 • (05/01/85) • **83**

PATISSIER, G.

St.-Amour Vignoble Les Poulets 1994 • $13 • (10/31/95) • **81**

PATISSIER, P.

Juliénas 1994 • $10 • (10/31/95) • **88**

PATRIARCHE PÈRE & FILS

Bourgogne-Hautes-Côtes de Nuits Cuvée Varache 1989 • $11 • (01/31/92) • **81**

Côtes du Rhône-Villages Cuvée Leblanc-Vatel 1985 • $5 • (08/31/89) • **77**

Key: SS—Spectator Selection CS—Cellar Selection HR—Highly Recommended BB—Best Buy $NA—Price not available Ⓐ—Auction Price (BT)—Barrel Tasting
Dates in parentheses indicate the issues in which the ratings were published.

Mâcon-Villages Cuvée Pierre Bontemps 1995: Straightforward Mâcon, crisp and light-bodied. Clean and lean, with whiffs of honey and ripe pear. Drink now. 2,500 cases made. • $11 • (05/31/97) • **80**

PATRICK, BARON

Chablis Premier Cru 1995: Perfumed, floral aromas are followed by ripe peach notes. Low acidity for this appellation; ready to drink. • $32 • (06/15/97) • **82**

PAUILLAC DE CHÂTEAU LATOUR

Pauillac 1997: Good cherry and berry character, with a medium body and soft tannins. For early drinking. • $NA • (06/15/98) (BT) • **80-84**

Pauillac 1996: For the third wine of Latour, very good indeed. Medium-bodied, with lovely berry and cherry character and a medium finish. Delicious. • $25 • (06/15/98) (BT) • **85-89**

Pauillac 1995: Rich and round, with luscious berry and tobacco character. Full-bodied, moderately tannic, with a slightly tough finish. Pretty darned good for a third wine. • $20 • (01/01/97) (BT) • **85-89**

Pauillac 1990: Shows interesting decadent aromas and flavors of earth, berries, and chocolate, with round and soft tannins. A big, rustic style. Try in 1999. • $29 Ⓐ • (03/31/93) • **89**

PAVELOT, JEAN-MARC

Pernand-Vergelesses Les Vergelesses 1991: Fresh and aromatic, showing nice raspberry flavor and hints of spices and earth on the finish. Drinkable now. • $NA • (01/31/94) • **81**

Savigny-lès-Beaune 1993: Lovely high acidity, freshly crushed fruit character, medium body and a long, delicate finish. Drinkable now. • $22 • (11/15/95) • **85**

Savigny-lès-Beaune 1992: Sparkling with bright raspberry, floral and cherry flavors presented in a tight package. A bit bitter on the lean finish, but the aromas are enchanting. • $NA • (12/15/94) • **84**

Savigny-lès-Beaune 1991: Crisp and light; the modest berry flavors fade into citrus on the finish. Drinkable now. • $20 Ⓐ • (01/31/94) • **80**

Savigny-lès-Beaune 1990: Firm, ripe and juicy; this is immediately appealing for its fine raspberry flavors, lively tannins and good acid balance. Try now. • $22 • (12/15/92) • **89**

Savigny-lès-Beaune 1986 • $18 • (10/15/89) • **84**

Savigny-lès-Beaune White 1994 • $NA • (05/31/96) • **79**

Savigny-lès-Beaune Aux Gravains 1994: A delicate wine that is supple, generous and elegantly polished to show nicely defined currant, cherry and violet aromas and flavors that linger persistently on the finish. • $20 • (11/15/96) • **89**

Savigny-lès-Beaune Aux Gravains 1993: Solid Pinot fruit, strawberry, currant and cherry aromas and flavor. Medium body, firm tannins and long finish. Drinkable now. • $30 • (11/15/95) • **89**

Savigny-lès-Beaune Aux Gravains 1992: Crisp and tight, focused berry flavors pushing through the firm tannins. Drinkable now. • $NA • (12/15/94) • **80**

Savigny-lès-Beaune Aux Gravains 1991: This crisp, flavorful style displays a greenish, lemony edge to the basic currant and plum aromas and flavors. Finishes tight and tannic. Try now. • $24 Ⓐ • (01/31/94) • **81**

Savigny-lès-Beaune Aux Guettes 1993: Well made, lively and vibrant, offering delicious currant, plum and earth character, medium body, massive, supple tannins and a juicy, high-acidity finish. Try after 2000. • $28 • (11/15/95) • **90**

Savigny-lès-Beaune Aux Guettes 1992: Smooth and velvety, with a generous beam of black cherry and toasty spice flavors shining through. Drinkable now. • $NA • (12/15/94) • **85**

Savigny-lès-Beaune Aux Guettes 1991: Light, fruity and silky, showing attractive raspberry, blackberry and delicate spice character. Finishes smooth and refined. Drinkable now. • $24 Ⓐ • (01/31/94) • **86**

Savigny-lès-Beaune Aux Guettes 1990: A stunning wine. Focused and concentrated, with blueberry, violet and currant flavors in perfect harmony with the supple tannins. The finish is seductive. Worth the hunt. Drinkable now to 2000. • $33 • (12/15/92) • **92**

Savigny-lès-Beaune Aux Guettes 1985 • $20 • (02/15/88) • **89**

Savigny-lès-Beaune La Dominode 1994: Lively flavors and a rather crisp texture. Offers cherry, spice and earth notes but is a bit herbaceous on the finish. Try in 1999. • $22 • (11/15/96) • **80**

Savigny-lès-Beaune La Dominode 1993: Very harmonious core of lovely plum, blackberry and smoke character and a succulent finish. Medium body, high acidity, medium tannins. Tempting now, but should improve past 1999. • $28 • (11/15/95) • **90**

Savigny-lès-Beaune La Dominode 1992: Light, crisp and simple, with appealing raspberry flavor that lingers nicely on the finish. • $NA • (12/15/94) • **86**

Savigny-lès-Beaune La Dominode 1991: Crisp and citrusy. A modest level of currant tries to sneak in on the finish. Drinkable now. • $27 Ⓐ • (01/31/94) • **78**

Savigny-lès-Beaune Les Narbantons 1994: Well made and attractive, in a delicate and smooth style. Showing some nice red berry and earth flavors. Try in 1999. • $18 • (11/15/96) • **82**

Savigny-lès-Beaune Les Narbantons 1993: Vivid, lively, crisp, medium-bodied red sporting lovely acidity and a long, slightly woody but flavorful finish. Drinkable now. • $29 • (11/15/95) • **87**

Savigny-lès-Beaune Les Narbantons 1992: Crisp and somewhat earthy, with a gamy streak running through the floral cherry flavors. Drinkable now. • $NA • (12/15/94) • **82**

Savigny-lès-Beaune Les Narbantons 1991: A nice beam of raspberry and strawberry flavors shines on into the delicate finish of this light, pleasant wine. Drinkable now. • $24 Ⓐ • (01/31/94) • **84**

PAVIE, CHÂTEAU

St.-Emilion 1997: A caressing texture, but very little fruit. Medium-bodied, with medium tannins but very little flavor. Hollow. Wait and see. • $NA • (06/15/98) (BT) • **80-84**

St.-Emilion 1996: Lots of fruit, mineral and floral aromas and flavors. Medium- to full-bodied, with lots of silky tannins and a long, long finish. Almost outstanding. • $45 • (06/15/98) (BT) • **85-89**

St.-Emilion 1995: Elegant and refined. Floral and fruity, with roses and blackberries. Medium-bodied, with fine tannins and a fruity, chocolate aftertaste. Best after 1999. • $30 Ⓐ • (01/31/98) • **88**

St.-Emilion 1994: Some pretty cherry and mineral aromas and flavors, but slightly diluted and short on the palate. Drink now. • $45 • (01/31/97) • **82**

St.-Emilion 1993: Full-bodied and delicious from start to finish, showing good depth of fruit and lovely harmony. Exciting flavors of black olive, wet earth and blackberry. Smoky, silky finish. Drinkable now. • $27 Ⓐ • (01/31/96) • **88**

St.-Emilion 1992: Delicate and delicious, pretty and silky, offering toasty oak, light coffee and raspberry aromas and flavors, medium body and tannins and firm finish. Drinkable now. • $30 • (04/15/95) • **82**

St.-Emilion 1990: A steamroller of a wine with tons of extract. The toffee, floral and plum aromas and flavors keep coming. Superb tannin structure. Better than the '89. Try in 1999. 12,000 cases made. • $38 • (03/31/93) • **94**

St.-Emilion 1989 • $36 Ⓐ • (03/15/92) • **90**

St.-Emilion 1988 • $45 Ⓐ • (03/31/91) • **89**

St.-Emilion 1987 • $35 • (05/15/90) • **82**

St.-Emilion 1986 • $48 Ⓐ • (06/30/89) • **93**

St.-Emilion 1985 • $66 Ⓐ • (10/15/94) • **91**

St.-Emilion 1983 • $47 Ⓐ • (10/15/94) • **90**

St.-Emilion 1982 • $54 Ⓐ • (08/31/92) • **94**

St.-Emilion 1981 • $36 Ⓐ • (10/15/94) • **89**

St.-Emilion 1979 • $28 Ⓐ • (10/15/89) • **86**

St.-Emilion 1970 • $26 Ⓐ • (05/15/93) • **89**

St.-Emilion 1961 • $119 Ⓐ • (04/30/96) • **78**

St.-Emilion 1947: Crisp at the center, with some lovely berry flavors oozing through the earthy, tobaccolike flavors at the core. • $232 Ⓐ • (05/31/97) • **86**

PAVIE-DECESSE, CHÂTEAU

St.-Emilion 1997: Dark-colored and grapey, with plenty of oak. Medium- to full-bodied, with velvety tannins and a medium finish. Needs more fruit on the midpalate to be outstanding. • $NA • (06/15/98) (BT) • **85-89**

St.-Emilion 1996: Slightly simple and lean, but with a good concentration of berry character and firm tannins. Medium finish. • $30 • (06/15/98) (BT) • **80-84**

St.-Emilion 1995: Really delicious, with crushed blackberries and raspberries. Full-bodied and chunky, with lots of fruit and velvety tannins. Impressive finish—very long. Best after 2002. • $28 • (01/31/98) • **91**

St.-Emilion 1994: Some good berry and cherry aromas and flavors, with a slightly herbal accent. Medium-bodied, with firm tannins and a short finish. Rather disappointing for this estate. Drink now. • $25 • (01/31/97) • **80**

St.-Emilion 1993: A pleasant, lively core of plum, cassis, mineral and dried herb flavors; medium body and firm tannins. Try now. • $24 • (01/31/96) • **85**

St.-Emilion 1992: Well made. Beautiful perfumes of violets and raspberries, a medium body and very round tannins; gorgeous fruit character. Drinkable now. • $19 • (04/15/95) • **84**

St.-Emilion 1990: A chunky wine, with loads of strawberry, earth, toasty oak, and mint aromas and flavors. Velvety tannins and a long finish. Drink now. 4,800 cases made. • $22 • (03/31/93) • **93**

St.-Emilion 1989 • $29 • (03/15/92) • **90**

St.-Emilion 1988 • $16 Ⓐ • (03/31/91) HR • **94**

St.-Emilion 1986 • $21 Ⓐ • (06/30/89) • **93**

St.-Emilion 1985 • $22 • (10/15/94) • **91**

St.-Emilion 1983 • $26 • (10/15/94) • **91**

St.-Emilion 1982 • $30 • (08/31/92) • **89**

St.-Emilion 1981 • $22 • (10/15/94) • **88**

St.-Emilion 1961 • $51 • (04/30/96) • **87**

PAVIE-MACQUIN, CHÂTEAU

St.-Emilion 1997: Dark in color, with violet, berry and mineral aromas. Medium-bodied, with silky tannins. Clever winemaking. Needs a bit more fruit on the short finish. • $NA • (06/15/98) (BT) • **85-89**

St.-Emilion 1996: So velvety and fine, it draws you back for another sip. Medium-bodied, with lovely ripe fruit and a smoke and berry finish. Delicious. 8,000 cases made. • $45 • (06/15/98) (BT) • **90-94**

St.-Emilion 1995: Greatest wine ever made at this estate. A breathtaking wine to drink now, but please wait. Lots of fruit, spice and tomato character. Full-bodied and very velvety, with a long, flavorful finish. Now or later, it's hard to resist. • $35 • (01/31/98) • **93**

St.-Emilion 1994: Superbly aromatic, with violets, berries and toasty oak character. Medium-bodied, with sleek tannins and a long, fruity finish. A racy and exciting wine from a property on the rise in St.-Emilion. Best in 1999. • $40 • (01/31/97) • **90**

St.-Emilion 1993: Pretty St.-Emilion. Medium in body, featuring lovely cassis, wild berry and black cherry notes. Lots of fruit here. Drink now. • $18 • (01/31/96) • **86**

St.-Emilion 1991: A floral, fresh wine with a light body and a refreshing finish; simple and straightforward. • $15 • (03/31/94) • **78**

St.-Emilion 1982 • $NA • (05/15/89) • **89**

PAVILLON BLANC DU CHÂTEAU MARGAUX

Bordeaux White 1995: Big, fat and slightly flat. Full-bodied and lacking in acidity, with an apple, pineapple and marzipan character. Short aftertaste. Disappointing considering the price. Drink now. • $60 • (04/30/98) • **84**

Bordeaux White 1994: Something special happens in the seamless blending of subtle spicy, buttery notes with the solid, crisp citrus flavors in this beautifully balanced and vibrant white wine. Drink now through 2000. • $40 • (09/30/97) BB • **91**

Bordeaux White 1993: Oak aging adds roundness and flavors of vanilla and honey to this lush white, but fruit flavors of apple, pear and melon are still fresh, and there's enough acidity to keep it in balance. Though restrained, it's a wine of substance and style. • $42 • (04/30/97) • **89**

PAVILLON LA CROIX FIGEAC, CHÂTEAU

St.-Emilion 1995: Very pretty cassis bush, plum and herb flavors, adding firm, slightly dry tannins. • $NA • (05/15/96) (BT) • **80-84**

PAVILLON LA GRANGE

Margaux 1994: Alluring aromas of tobacco and herbs give way to less expressive but clean flavors of black cherries, herbs and toast in this modest but balanced red. The tannins are quite firm; try in 1999. 4,200 cases made. • $22 • (11/30/97) • **86**

PAVILLON-MERCUROL, DOMAINE DU

Crozes-Hermitage 1991 • $NA • (05/31/94) • **85**

Crozes-Hermitage 1990 • $NA • (05/31/94) • **88**

Crozes-Hermitage 1989 • $45 • (05/31/94) • **85**

FRANCE

PAVILLON ROUGE DU CHÂTEAU MARGAUX

Margaux 1997: Pretty, perfumed wine, with cherry, berry and light vanilla aromas and flavors. Medium-bodied, with sweet berry flavor and a long finish. Delicious. • $NA • (06/15/98) (BT) • **85-89**
Margaux 1996: A zingy red with good tannins and plenty of ripe berry, smoke character. Medium body and medium tannins. • $NA • (01/01/97) (BT) • **85-89**
Margaux 1995: Lots of violet and berry in this wine, lively toasty oak character, too. Full-bodied, with silky tannins and a medium, smoky finish. An amazing second label from a top estate. Best after 2002. • $22 Ⓐ • (01/31/98) • **91**
Margaux 1994: Bright berry and cherry aromas with a citrus note beneath. Light- to medium-bodied, with light tannins and a short finish. Not much to it. Drink now. • $32 Ⓐ • (01/31/97) • **80**
Margaux 1989 • $28 Ⓐ • (04/30/92) • **87**
Margaux 1988 • $37 Ⓐ • (04/30/91) • **88**
Margaux 1987 • $19 • (05/15/90) • **79**
Margaux 1986 • $30 Ⓐ • (06/30/89) • **84**
Margaux 1985 • $33 Ⓐ • (04/15/88) SS • **93**
Margaux 1983 • $36 Ⓐ • (06/30/87) • **80**
Margaux 1982 • $60 Ⓐ • (07/15/87) • **85**
Margaux 1981 • $26 Ⓐ • (07/15/87) • **87**
Margaux 1980 • $20 • (07/15/87) • **76**
Margaux 1979 • $30 Ⓐ • (07/15/87) • **78**

PAYSAGE

Merlot Vin de Pays d'Oc Caillou Vineyards 1994: Rich plum, blackberry and spice flavors are wrapped up in a juicy texture. It's concentrated with medium tannins, but drinkable now. 10,000 cases made. • $10 • (07/31/96) • **84**
Merlot Vin de Pays d'Oc Caillou Vineyards 1993 • $10 • (03/31/95) • **73**
Vin de Pays d'Oc Galet Vineyards 1993 • $10 • (10/31/95) • **80**

PECH DE JAMMES, CHÂTEAU

Cahors 1989 • $8 • (09/30/94) • **81**
Cahors 1988 • $10 • (09/30/92) • **81**
Cahors 1987 • $9 • (06/30/90) • **78**
Cahors 1983 • $9 • (10/15/88) • **77**

PECH REDON, CHÂTEAU DE

Chardonnay Vin de Pays d'Oc 1995: Focused and flavorful, also fairly intense. Good apple and fig flavors finish with a touch of spice. A bit wild tasting in the end. • $11 • (05/31/97) • **84**
Coteaux du Languedoc La Clape 1994: Generous and flavorful, full of spice and ripe fruit. Smooth, with a nice, dark chocolate note on the finish, it's ready to drink. • $12 • (05/31/97) • **84**
Coteaux du Languedoc La Clape 1991 • $10 • (03/15/94) • **84**
Coteaux du Languedoc La Clape Cuvée Réservée 1995: Very Rhône-like, from the violet and raspberry aromas to the blackberry and meatlike flavors. Ready to drink. A blend of Grenache, Syrah and Cinsaut. • $10 • (05/15/97) • **84**
Coteaux du Languedoc La Clape Cuvée Réservée 1991 • $10 • (03/15/94) • **81**
Coteaux du Languedoc La Clape White 1995: Fairly rich with some good tropical fruit flavors that linger, with spice notes, on the finish. • $11 • (05/31/97) • **84**

PÉDAUQUE, LA REINE

Chassagne-Montrachet 1993: Rather straightforward, green and diluted, revealing modest fruit flavor. 25 cases made. • $26 • (05/15/95) • **76**
Chassagne-Montrachet 1992: Lively, crisp and well-balanced, showing lime, mineral and creamy vanilla flavors. Solid and straightforward. 260 cases made. • $22 • (08/31/94) • **82**
Corton-Charlemagne 1993: Some nice fruit underneath, but not showing optimally at this point. Seems a bit flat and dull, although a well-knit texture carries the wine. Try now. 25 cases imported. • $55 • (05/15/95) • **83**
Corton-Charlemagne 1992: Straightforward and rather simple, with modest apple, lemon and earth flavors; offers a crisp taste but also some stale fruit flavors that distract. • $52 • (08/31/94) • **83**
Corton Les Renardes 1993: Starts out rather lean and crisp, showing a hint of wet earth, cedar, plum and red berry flavor, and picks up ripe character on the smooth but slightly hot finish. • $50 • (11/15/95) • **83**
Gevrey-Chambertin 1993: A bit lean on the palate but some pretty berry, cherry character. Medium-bodied, medium tannins and a lean finish. Drink now. • $25 • (11/15/95) • **79**
Mâcon-Villages Coupées 1994: Already showing gold color and mature flavors, this is aging quickly and ungraciously. Flat, dull and uninteresting flavors dominate. 1,667 cases made. • $9 • (08/31/95) • **70**
Meursault Les Charmes 1992: Round and supple, this well-made Meursault delivers pretty pear, peach, vanilla, and cream flavors, and the finish is long, but it lacks a bit of volume and concentration in the middle. Drinkable now. 200 cases made. • $29 • (08/31/94) • **85**
Nuits-St.-Georges 1993: Light and diluted, showing only modest red berry flavor. Not much here. Disappointing. • $25 • (11/15/95) • **75**
Pommard 1993: Pretty crushed raspberry and a hint of earth but it's slightly light, adding firm tannins and delicate finish. Drink in 1999. • $30 • (11/15/95) • **80**
Pouilly-Fuissé Griselles 1993: Rather round and supple, revealing grapefruit and green apple flavors, but a bit one-dimensional. 600 cases made. • $15 • (05/15/95) • **79**
Puligny-Montrachet Les Folatières 1993: Interesting green apple skin and cream notes, medium body and a tart finish. Drinkable now. 25 cases made. • $32 • (05/15/95) • **80**

PÉDESCLAUX, CHÂTEAU

Pauillac 1996: Always an underachiever. Overextracted, with a rubbery, metallic character and hard tannins. • $NA • (01/01/97) (BT) • **965**
Pauillac 1995: Pretty, with cherry and floral aromas and flavors, medium body and medium tannins; crisp finish. • $NA • (01/01/97) (BT) • **85-89**
Pauillac 1986 • $18 • (02/15/90) • **79**

PÉGAU, DOMAINE DU

Châteauneuf-du-Pape Cuvée Réservée 1994: This firm red marries alluring black cherry flavors with a pleasing hint of bitter coffee in a well-balanced and generous frame. Try now. 5,500 cases made. • $27 • (09/15/97) • **88**
Châteauneuf-du-Pape Cuvée Réservée 1991: Plum and berry notes are accented by spice, mint and leather nuances lingering on the firmly tannic finish. Drink now. 4,000 cases made. • $20 • (10/15/95) • **89**
Châteauneuf-du-Pape Cuvée Réservée 1989 • $22 • (04/15/93) • **85**
Châteauneuf-du-Pape Cuvée Réservée 1988 • $17 • (11/15/91) • **88**

PÉLAQUIÉ, DOMAINE

Côtes du Rhône-Villages Laudun 1995: Straightforward, with stemmy, herbal, green notes. Shows a slight dilution, making it a bit dry and unfocused on the finish. • $11 • (10/15/97) • **74**
Côtes du Rhône-Villages Laudun White 1996: Impressively full in body, with an oily, ripe texture, offering some almond, stone, citrus, and honey flavors. Kicks in with a lingering, lime-spiked, nicely toasty finish, but remains ripe-tasting and harmonious. Delicious now. • $12 • (10/15/97) • **89**
Côtes du Rhône-Villages Laudun White 1995: Firm and full-bodied, this white is rather austere at the start, but ripe pear and melon flavors emerge on the finish. Can stand up to pork or veal dishes. • $12 • (12/15/96) • **85**
Lirac 1995: Fairly round in the midpalate, this red has a rather thick texture, but it's a bit herbal. Medium-bodied, it also offers rose petal, plum and cherry notes. Drink now. • $11 • (10/15/97) • **84**
Tavel 1996: A delicate and elegant rosé, offering some decent red berry flavors. Balanced. Serve chilled. • $13 • (10/15/97) • **81**
Tavel 1995: Light strawberry and herbal flavors float through this full-bodied, rather alcoholic rosé. It has punch, but lacks balance. • $13 • (12/15/96) • **81**

PELLÉ, DOMAINE HENRY

Menetou-Salon Morogues 1995 • $16 • (05/15/96) • **87**
Menetou-Salon Morogues 1994 • $15 • (11/15/95) • **84**
Menetou-Salon Morogues 1993 • $15 • (08/31/94) • **87**
Menetou-Salon Morogues Clos des Blanchais 1995 • $19 • (05/15/96) • **85**
Menetou-Salon Morogues Clos des Blanchais 1994 • $17 • (11/15/95) • **82**

Key: SS—Spectator Selection CS—Cellar Selection HR—Highly Recommended BB—Best Buy $NA—Price not available Ⓐ—Auction Price (BT)—Barrel Tasting
Dates in parentheses indicate the issues in which the ratings were published.

Menetou-Salon Morogues Clos des Blanchais 1993 • $19 • (11/15/95) • **87**
Menetou-Salon Morogues Red 1994 • $15 • (12/15/95) • **81**
Menetou-Salon Morogues Red 1987 • $11 • (07/15/89) • **85**
Sancerre La Croix au Garde 1995 • $18 • (05/15/96) • **85**
Sancerre La Croix au Garde 1994 • $18 • (12/15/95) • **81**
Sancerre La Croix au Garde 1993 • $17 • (10/31/94) • **86**
Sancerre La Croix au Garde Red 1994 • $18 • (12/15/95) • **80**

PELLETIER & FILS, M.

Nuits-St.-Georges 1994: Tart and juicy, a lively wine centered around raspberry and bitter-almond flavors that turn citrusy on the finish. As ready as it will ever be. • $NA • (11/15/96) • **82**
Nuits-St.-Georges Clos des Argillières 1994: Firm, chewy and modestly endowed with flavors of plum and tobacco that manage to match the tannins blow for blow. Try in 1999. • $NA • (11/15/96) • **83**

PELOUX, DU

Châteauneuf-du-Pape 1986 • $12 • (04/15/89) • **85**
Côtes du Rhône-Villages 1986 • $5 • (05/15/89) • **78**

PEÑA, CHÂTEAU DE

Côtes du Roussillon-Villages 1995: A tightly wound red, showing berry, cherry and mineral flavors with herb and chocolate notes on the finish. Inviting now, should evolve with age. A blend of Syrah, Carignan, Grenache, and Mourvèdre. Best from 1999 through 2001. 6,600 cases made. • $9 • (05/31/98) • **85**
Muscat de Rivesaltes 1996: Effusively fruity and sweet. Appealing flavors of orange peel, melon and clove. Good concentration and a lingering finish. • $9/375ml • (04/30/98) • **85**
Vin de Pays des Pyrénées-Orientales Cuvée de Peña 1996: Straightforward and fruity, with berry and black cherry flavors and a touch of cinnamon on the finish. Drink now. 16,500 cases made. • $6 • (04/30/98) • **81**

PENNAUTIER, CHÂTEAU DE

Cabardès 1989 • $7 • (12/15/91) • **75**

PENSEES DE LAFLEUR

Pomerol 1997: All in finesse. Pretty berry and plum aromas and flavors. Medium-bodied, with medium tannins and a light finish. • $NA • (06/15/98) (BT) • **85-89**
Pomerol 1996: Almost as good as the first wine by Lafleur. Wonderful velvety tannins and loads of pure fruit character. Long finish. 250 cases made. • $80 • (06/15/98) (BT) • **85-89**
Pomerol 1995: Concentrated and impressive. Gorgeous aromas of fruit, tobacco and olives. Full-bodied and chewy, with loads of fruit and velvety tannins. Long, long finish. Second wine of Lafleur; best second label of a top estate in Bordeaux. Needs time. Try after 2002. • $75 • (01/31/98) • **93**

PÉPIÈRE, DOMAINE DE LA

Muscadet de Sèvre et Maine Sur Lie 1995: A bracing white with classic Muscadet character—from the firm acidity to the pear, light herb and spice flavors to the fresh, clean finish. It's muscular yet balanced, and very refreshing. 1,000 cases made. • $9 • (05/15/97) • **88**
Muscadet de Sèvre et Maine Sur Lie Clos des Briords 1995: Creamy vanilla notes add interest to this firm, lemon-scented white, but there's pear and melon flavors at the core. Fresh and clean. 250 cases made. • $12 • (05/15/97) • **85**

PÉRENNE, CHÂTEAU

Premières Côtes de Blaye 1989 • $9 • (03/31/91) • **78**
Premières Côtes de Blaye 1986 • $7 • (06/30/89) • **82**
Premières Côtes de Blaye 1985 • $7 • (02/15/88) • **80**
Premières Côtes de Blaye 1982 • $5 • (11/16/85) BB • **79**

PÉRILLIERÈ, DOMAINE DE

Côtes du Rhône-Villages 1995: Very pretty, with some sweet-tasting berry flavors and good toasty oak and black pepper flavors. Fresh and fairly long, but slightly crisp finish. Enjoy now. From Cave de Vignerons. 2,500 cases made. • $10 • (10/15/97) • **85**

PERNOT, PAUL

Beaune Les Teurons 1990: Crisp and focused, with bright, vibrant black cherry, wild berry and toast aromas and flavors that remain intense and elegant right through the long finish. Has the raw material to develop well through 2000. 85 cases made. • $33 • (04/30/92) • **90**
Beaune Les Teurons 1988 • $33 • (03/31/91) • **86**
Blagny La Pièce sous le Bois 1990: Tart, thin and woody, with a spurt of fruit at the very end that lifts it into the respectable range. • $33 • (04/30/92) • **79**

PERON, JULES

Saumur Red 1993 • $6 • (11/15/94) • **83**

PEROUSE, LA

Chardonnay Vin de Pays d'Oc 1995: A good, if rather heavy, Chardonnay with simple fruit flavors and some apparent oak aging. • $8 • (12/15/97) • **82**
Chardonnay-Viognier Vin de Pays d'Oc 1996: A straightforward white, offering some decent peach and appley flavors. A blend of 81 percent Chardonnay and 19 percent Viognier. • $8 • (07/31/98) • **81**
Merlot Vin de Pays d'Oc 1995: Distinctive, with tomato and spice flavors and a fleshy texture wrapped up in some light but dusty tannins. Should pair well with food. Drink now. • $8 • (12/15/97) • **84**
Merlot Vin de Pays d'Oc 1994: Deep, dark colors and black fruit flavors to match, accented by toasty oak. It's firmly structured and monolithic at this stage. Drinkable now. 11,000 cases made. • $8 • (07/31/96) BB • **86**
Syrah-Cabernet Vin de Pays d'Oc 1996: A rough-hewn red, with plummy flavors and a herbal edge. A bit tough around the edges now, it needs some time to integrate. A blend of 52 percent Syrah and 48 percent Cabernet. Best from 1999 through 2000. • $8 • (07/31/98) • **83**
Vin de Pays d'Oc Cuvée Blanc 1995: A lively white with good pear and honey flavors. Smooth and somewhat elegant, with spicy notes on the finish. Juicy tasting, quite quaffable. Drink now. 1,000 cases made. • $8 • (03/31/98) BB • **85**
Vin de Pays d'Oc Cuvée Rouge 1995: Good, expressive Cabernet flavors of black currant in this firmly structured red give way to a lean finish with a bit of sweet fruit. Try with food. • $8 • (12/15/97) • **84**
Vin de Pays d'Oc Cuvée Rouge 1994: A blast of black cherries marks this solid, chunky red. The tannins are moderate, leading to a modest finish. 3,600 cases made. • $8 • (07/31/96) • **82**

PERRACHON, PIERRE-YVES

Chénas Domaine de la Croix Marzelle 1994: Rich, yet a bit clumsy, this ripe red offers bitter chocolate, licorice and black cherry flavors that battle to emerge from beneath drying tannins. Drinkable now. • $13 • (09/15/96) • **81**

PERRET, ANDRÉ

St.-Joseph Les Grisières 1992 • $13 • (05/31/94) • **77**

PERRIER, JOSEPH

Brut Champagne 1985 • $37 • (12/31/90) • **82**
Brut Champagne 1979 • $22 • (10/01/85) • **87**
Brut Champagne Cuvée Josephine 1982: Rich and gingery, with toasty vanilla, cherry and lemony flavors that are intense, complex, lively and enticing. Packed with flavor and full of finesse, this is a wonderful 1982 that goes well beyond the average. Drinkable now. • $100 • (12/31/90) • **93**
Brut Champagne Cuvée Joséphine 1985: A wonderful antique with a lacy texture and beautifully mature flavors. Mouthfilling and generous, yet delicately balanced and long on the finish. • $96 • (12/31/97) • **90**
Brut Champagne Cuvée Royale 1989: An easy-drinking, lightly fruity Champagne that has a pillowy mouthfeel and bright flavors. Drinkable now. 3,300 cases made. • $40 • (12/31/97) • **87**
Brut Champagne Cuvée Royale 1985: Enjoyable vintage bubbly with pleasant cookie dough and apple aromas and flavors, good acidity and a long fla-

FRANCE

vorful finish. Slightly better than in fall 1990. Drinkable now. • $38 • (12/31/93) • **86**

Brut Champagne Cuvée Royale 1982: Very attractive. Extremely flavorful, fruity and figgy tasting, yet light in body and lively on the palate. Creamy and supple in texture. • $32 Ⓐ • (12/31/89) • **89**

Brut Champagne Cuvée Royale NV: A flash of candy-apple flavor makes this a showy but likeable bubbly. On the soft side in texture. 50,000 cases made. • $19 • (10/31/97) • **85**

Brut Rosé Champagne Cuvée Royale NV: Definitely mature in character, this amber-colored rosé has nutty, sherry-like aromas, lean fruit flavors and a lingering finish. Full of personality, but not for everyone. 1,500 cases made. • $45 • (11/30/97) • **86**

PERRIER, PASCAL

St.-Joseph Domaine de Gachon 1990 • $19 • (04/15/93) • **90**

PERRIER-JOUËT

Brut Champagne 1955 • $NA • (10/15/87) • **90**

Brut Champagne 1947 • $NA • (10/15/87) • **85**

Brut Champagne 1928 • $NA • (10/15/87) • **97**

Brut Champagne 1911 • $104 Ⓐ • (10/15/87) • **95**

Brut Champagne 1900 • $NA • (10/15/87) • **97**

Brut Champagne 1893 • $NA • (10/15/87) • **80**

Brut Champagne 1825 • $NA • (10/15/87) • **95**

Brut Champagne Fleur de Champagne 1988: One of the best 'flower bottle' vintages in years. Textbook top notch Champagne with fruity, light toasty aromas and flavors, full body yet a fine underlying acidity. Very long finish. • $80 • (12/31/93) • **91**

Brut Champagne Fleur de Champagne 1985 • $75 • (12/31/90) • **86**

Brut Champagne Fleur de Champagne 1983: A fresh, crisp wine in a light, somewhat austere style that turns more generous on the palate with bright, lemon-apple flavor and a pleasant touch of spice on the finish. • $65 • (12/31/89) • **88**

Brut Champagne Fleur de Champagne 1982: Light, clean and delicate with creamy, smooth texture. Vanilla and doughy tones in nose and mouth, with delicious light fruit flavors. • $65 • (12/31/88) • **88**

Brut Champagne Fleur de Champagne 1979 • $50 • (02/01/86) • **93**

Brut Champagne Fleur de Champagne Belle Epoque 1989: Creamy-textured, ripe and slightly sweet, this mouthfilling cream puff of a Champagne is easy to enjoy. Drink now. • $100 • (12/31/97) • **87**

Brut Champagne Grand Brut 1989: A lean but graceful Champagne with tangy citrus flavors, a lively texture and dry finish. Drink through 1999. Tasted twice, with consistent notes. • $35 • (12/31/97) • **86**

Brut Champagne Grand Brut NV: Rich in texture and full-flavored, this packs more punch than the usual Champagne. Combines bright fruit flavors with an attractive buttery character that lingers on the finish. • $28 • (11/15/97) • **87**

Brut Champagne Reserve Cuvée 1988: A fresh vintage Champagne with vibrant aromas and flavors of lemons, pears, and shortbread cookies; medium body and a refreshing finish. Large bead and foamy texture. Drinkable now. • $35 • (12/31/93) • **87**

Brut Rosé Champagne Fleur de Champagne 1986: Wonderfully mature and distinctive, reminding us of a well-aged Burgundy, but with a refreshing effervescence that keeps it light and lively. Dry, and elegant. For special occasions. • $90 • (12/15/94) • **92**

Brut Rosé Champagne Fleur de Champagne 1985: Distinctive for its mature, smoke and earth notes that complement the spicy cherry and Pinot Noir flavors that are crisp, rich and deep. Flavors linger on the finish. • $70 • (12/31/89) • **88**

Brut Rosé Champagne Fleur de Champagne 1982 • $57 • (11/15/87) • **89**

Brut Rosé Champagne Fleur de Champagne 1978 • $55 • (12/16/85) • **90**

Brut Rosé Champagne Fleur de Champagne Belle Epoque 1988: A lean, dry rosé with modest cherry and spice flavors, lively acidity and a crisp finish. The flavors are light, pleasant and mature. Drink through 1999. • $110 • (12/31/97) • **88**

Key: SS—Spectator Selection CS—Cellar Selection HR—Highly Recommended BB—Best Buy $NA—Price not available Ⓐ—Auction Price (BT)—Barrel Tasting

Dates in parentheses indicate the issues in which the ratings were published.

PERRIÈRE, DOMAINE

Vin de Pays de l'Aude Les Amandiers 1990 • $5 • (10/31/92) BB • **80**

Vin de Pays de l'Aude Les Amandiers 1988 • $4 • (04/15/90) • **77**

PERRIÈRE, DOMAINE DE LA

Coteaux du Languedoc Cuvée Prestige 1994: Dominated by cherry and spice, with a fairly potent gamy note in the middle and on the finish. Needs food. A blend of 85 percent Syrah and 15 percent Grenache. Drink now. • $10 • (05/31/98) • **80**

Merlot Vin de Pays d'Oc 1995: Not your typical Merlot, this is a distinctive red with rich flavors of dried cherry, bittersweet chocolate and dark plum. Has a nice crispness and balance to it as well. Drink now through 2001. 10,000 cases made. • $7 • (05/31/98) • **84**

PERRIN RÉSERVE

Côtes du Rhône 1996: Very pretty, with hints of herb and cherry, this is a succulent, light-bodied wine to drink with easy foods like pasta, pizza, quiche, salad, etc. Well made, unpretentious. Buy a case and serve chilled. 40,000 cases made. • $10 • (10/15/97) • **85**

Côtes du Rhône 1995: Seductive, amazingly balanced, this is a full-bodied Côtes du Rhône, deep-purple in color, with plum, cassis and roasted coffee flavors. The ripe, sweet tannins just melt in the mouth. And, it has *terroir* personality. You want to drink this by the case; buy, buy and buy some more. 40,000 cases made. • $10 • (10/15/97) • **88**

Côtes du Rhône 1994: The ripe plum and gamy flavors of Syrah shine through this rich red, a new offering from the owners of Château de Beaucastel. Firm yet generous, it's tannic enough to age yet balanced enough to drink now. A good value all around. 37,500 cases made. • $10 • (10/15/96) BB • **86**

Côtes du Rhône White 1996: A lively mix of floral, citrus and almond flavors gives this wine freshness and typicity. Crisp and clean, it's a pleasant apéritif. • $10 • (10/15/97) • **83**

Côtes du Rhône White 1995: Notes of grilled almonds and vanilla add interest to this firm, spicy white. Clean and well balanced, with apple and melon flavors. 6,000 cases made. • $10 • (10/15/96) • **84**

PERROT-MINOT, HENRI

Chambolle-Musigny 1990: Crisp and austere with red cherry and earthy notes. Drinkable now. 460 cases made. • $32 • (03/15/94) • **82**

Chambolle-Musigny La Combe d'Orveau 1991: Austere, with rubbery, acrid flavors that mar what little black cherry fruit exists. 250 cases made. • $45 • (03/15/94) • **74**

Charmes-Chambertin 1991: Aromatic, with spicy, toasty, chocolate nuances to the core of black cherry and berry fruit. Drink now. 800 cases made. • $50 • (03/15/94) • **85**

Morey-St.-Denis En la Rue de Vergy 1992: The fruit flavors really come out as you sip this solid, ripe, firmly textured Burgundy. It is focused, with well-balanced acidity and moderate tannins, and the fruit lingers on the finish. Drinkable now. 600 cases made. • $27 • (05/15/95) HR • **89**

Morey-St.-Denis En la Rue de Vergy 1990: Dark in color, rich in flavor with spicy black cherry, plum and raspberry fruit, picking up a floral note with the oak and tannins a little heavy handed. Drinkable now. 580 cases made. • $25 • (03/15/94) • **87**

Morey-St.-Denis La Riotte 1990: Light and smooth, offering a range of plum, cola and herb aromas and flavors that finish with a ring of fruit. Drinkable now. 200 cases made. • $40 • (12/31/93) • **86**

Morey-St.-Denis La Riotte Premier Cru 1992: Supple, broad and easygoing, featuring soft tannins, good acidity and fairly bright cherry and berry flavors. Appealing to drink now. • $35 • (05/15/95) • **86**

PESQUIER, DOMAINE DU

Gigondas 1990 • $15 • (04/15/93) • **86**

Gigondas 1989 • $15 • (04/15/93) • **83**

Gigondas Ancien Vignoble des Princes d'Orange 1993: Ripe, roasted aromas are attractive but promise a generosity the wine doesn't deliver with its black pepper and herbal flavors and dry, tannic finish. Drinkable now. 3,500 cases made. • $18 • (10/15/96) • **82**

PETIT CHEVAL, LE

St.-Emilion 1988 • $35 • (03/31/91) • **89**

PETIT-FAURIE-DE-SOUTARD, CHÂTEAU

St.-Emilion 1988 • $20 • (04/30/91) • **82**
St.-Emilion 1986 • $15 • (06/30/89) • **80**

PETIT-FIGEAC, CHÂTEAU

St.-Emilion 1995: Firm, fruity but slightly austere. Medium-bodied, offering firm tannins and a slightly green finish. • $NA • (05/15/96) (BT) • **80-84**
St.-Emilion 1993: Pretty, focused red berry, currant and tobacco aromas and flavors, medium body, medium-silky tannins and a fresh finish. Drinkable now. • $22 • (01/31/96) • **83**
St.-Emilion 1992: Some good fruit tinged with wet earth. Medium-bodied and very firm; a decent finish. • $18 • (04/15/95) • **80**
St.-Emilion 1990: Seductive, with everything in proportion: black cherry and berry aromas and flavors with soft yet firm tannins. Beautiful. Drinkable now. • $24 • (03/31/93) • **90**
St.-Emilion 1989 • $21 • (03/15/92) • **90**

PETIT-PUCH, CHÂTEAU DU

Entre-Deux-Mers 1994 • $8 • (05/31/95) • **79**

PETIT-VILLAGE, CHÂTEAU

Pomerol 1997: Chocolate and cinnamon aromas. Medium-bodied, with fine tannins and a medium, sweet fruit finish. • $NA • (06/15/98) (BT) • **85-89**
Pomerol 1996: Enticing aromas of blackberry and violet. Medium-bodied, with high acidity, new wood and a medium finish. A bit disjointed now, but it will come around. • $50 • (06/15/98) (BT) • **85-89**
Pomerol 1995: Sleek and refined. Pretty berry and mineral aromas and flavors. Medium- to full-bodied, with silky tannins and a berry, vanilla aftertaste. Best after 2001. Tasted twice, with consistent notes. • $40 • (01/31/98) • **88**
Pomerol 1994: Alluring aromas of violet, berry and vanilla make way for a medium-bodied mouthful of berry and dried herb flavors, silky tannins. Drinkable now, but better in 1999. 4,500 cases made. • $55 • (01/31/97) • **88**
Pomerol 1993: Sleek and well-crafted Pomerol offering red berry, toasty oak and a hint of smokiness. Medium in body, fine tannins and fresh finish. Drinkable now. 4,500 cases made. • $24 Ⓐ • (01/31/96) • **86**
Pomerol 1992: Velvety chocolate, cedar and fruit character; medium in body, impressive texture and medium finish. Drinkable now. • $34 • (04/15/95) • **84**
Pomerol 1991: A bit aggressive with its berry, chocolate and herb character and hard tannins. Tasted twice, with consistent notes. • $22 • (03/31/94) • **75**
Pomerol 1990: A showy wine with velvety-textured tannins and rich fruit. This has no rough edges. Drinkable now. 3,900 cases made. • $47 • (03/31/93) • **92**
Pomerol 1982 • $78 Ⓐ • (05/15/89) • **92**
Pomerol 1959 • $NA • (10/15/90) • **86**

PETITE EGLISE, LA

Pomerol 1986 • $15 • (09/15/89) • **78**

PETITS QUARTS, DOMAINE DES

Bonnezeaux Le Malabé 1995: This big white has all the trimmings: rich texture, ripe sweetness, firm acidity and classic flavors of apricots, orange peel and spice. Drink now. 175 cases made. • $24 • (05/15/97) • **90**
Coteaux du Layon 1er Tri 1995: This rich, somewhat blowsy white is big and sweet, with apricot, honey, orange peel and light mineral flavors and just enough acidity for balance. 100 cases made. • $15 • (06/15/97) • **87**

PÉTRUS, CHÂTEAU

Pomerol 1997: A complex wine marked by mineral, berry and dried cherry. Full-bodied and very balanced, with perfectly integrated tannins and a long, silky finish. One of the wines of the vintage. • $NA • (06/15/98) (BT) • **90-94**
Pomerol 1996: A chewy and flavorful young red with plenty of chocolate and plum character. Medium- to full-bodied, with moderate, velvety tannins. Harmonious. • $450 • (06/15/98) (BT) • **90-94**
Pomerol 1995: A magnificent Pétrus. A virtual spicerack of a wine, this Bordeaux features exotic, spicy aromas, with nuances of cinnamon, strawberries and raspberries. Full-bodied and tannic, with an amazing wild berry, sweet fruit and spice aftertaste. Best after 2002. • $900 • (01/31/98) CS • **98**
Pomerol 1994: Wonderfully rich and concentrated, with milk chocolate, berry and floral aromas, loads of fruit flavors and soft, round tannins. Full-bodied and has good length. A great wine for the vintage, but then, what do you expect from Pétrus? Better from 1999 on, but inviting now. 3,200 cases made. • $350 Ⓐ • (01/31/97) CS • **93**
Pomerol 1993: A truly classic Pétrus and comparable to the '88, '86 and '82. Showy and impressive with excellent use of new oak. It delivers loads of toasty coconut and chocolate flavors balanced by plum and blackberry notes. Incredible concentration for the vintage. Supple, long finish. Try after 2000. • $310 Ⓐ • (01/31/96) CS • **95**
Pomerol 1992: Not great but very good. Lovely finesse and good backbone of tannins and fruit. Medium-bodied and silky, featuring a berry, tobacco and mineral finish. • $180 Ⓐ • (04/15/95) • **88**
Pomerol 1990: An aristocratic wine, almost as good as the awesome '89. Expressive and sophisticated, with wonderful aromas of ripe fruit and vanilla and a palate of extremely silky tannins and superb fruit concentration. Drink after 1999. 4,000 cases made. • $228 Ⓐ • (03/31/93) • **98**
Pomerol 1988 • $355 Ⓐ • (08/31/91) • **94**
Pomerol 1987 • $206 Ⓐ • (02/15/91) • **85**
Pomerol 1986 • $369 Ⓐ • (02/15/91) • **96**
Pomerol 1985 • $449 Ⓐ • (10/15/94) • **93**
Pomerol 1984 • $161 Ⓐ • (02/15/91) • **83**
Pomerol 1983 • $285 Ⓐ • (10/15/94) • **93**
Pomerol 1982 • $622 Ⓐ • (08/31/92) • **94**
Pomerol 1981 • $292 Ⓐ • (10/15/94) • **89**
Pomerol 1980 • $268 Ⓐ • (02/15/91) • **86**
Pomerol 1979 • $303 Ⓐ • (02/15/91) • **90**
Pomerol 1978 • $325 Ⓐ • (02/15/91) • **89**
Pomerol 1976 • $295 Ⓐ • (02/15/91) • **86**
Pomerol 1975 • $543 Ⓐ • (02/15/91) • **93**
Pomerol 1973 • $177 Ⓐ • (02/15/91) • **78**
Pomerol 1971 • $565 Ⓐ • (02/15/91) • **94**
Pomerol 1970 • $764 Ⓐ • (02/15/91) • **92**
Pomerol 1968 • $157 Ⓐ • (02/15/91) • **79**
Pomerol 1967 • $308 Ⓐ • (02/15/91) • **87**
Pomerol 1966 • $613 Ⓐ • (02/15/91) • **93**
Pomerol 1964 • $929 Ⓐ • (02/15/91) • **94**
Pomerol 1962 • $605 Ⓐ • (02/15/91) • **94**
Pomerol 1961 • $8050 Ⓐ/1.5 liter • (04/30/96) • **93**
Pomerol 1959 • $1125 Ⓐ • (02/15/91) • **96**
Pomerol 1958 • $275 Ⓐ • (02/15/91) • **85**
Pomerol 1955 • $430 Ⓐ • (02/15/91) • **91**
Pomerol 1953 • $633 Ⓐ • (02/15/91) • **92**
Pomerol 1952 • $437 Ⓐ • (02/15/91) • **89**
Pomerol 1950 • $697 Ⓐ • (02/15/91) • **99**
Pomerol 1949 • $1969 Ⓐ • (02/15/91) • **98**
Pomerol 1948 • $1150 Ⓐ • (02/15/91) • **91**
Pomerol 1947 • $1529 Ⓐ • (02/15/91) • **97**
Pomerol 1945 • $2328 Ⓐ • (11/30/95) • **88**

PEU DE LA MORIETTE, DOMAINE LE

Vouvray Moelleux Cuvée Exceptionelle 1989 • $19 • (06/15/91) • **80**

PEYBONHOMME-LES-TOURS, CHÂTEAU

Premières Côtes de Blaye 1994: A good, round, simple wine, made in a fleshy style, with good plum and herbal flavors. Ready to drink. 2,000 cases made. • $10 • (04/30/97) • **83**

PEYRADE, LA VICOMTE DE LA

Muscat de Frontignan NV: Quite lively and fruity, with good honey, spice and orange flavors, and rich, with a nice white chocolate note on the finish. Well balanced with firm acidity throughout. Delicious. 350 cases made. • $10/500ml • (08/31/97) • **88**

FRANCE

PEYRAUD, CHÂTEAU

Premières Côtes de Blaye 1993: Soft and light, showing light berry and green pepper flavors on a modest frame. Drinkable now. • $9 • (12/15/95) • **79**

Premières Côtes de Blaye 1989 • $8 • (03/31/91) • **80**

PEYRE ROSE, DOMAINE

Coteaux du Languedoc Clos des Cistes 1993: Impressive. Huge, ripe and well focused, with plum, chocolate, spice, cherry and herb flavors that meld seamlessly. A nice, gamy aroma, fine tannins and plenty of stuffing, with olivelike flavors throughout. Finishes with some sweet currant and cassis flavors. Drink now through 2002. • $27 • (02/28/98) • **92**

Coteaux du Languedoc Clos Raphaël 1993: A rustic wine with tarry flavors and aromas. It's mature-tasting and ready to drink. • $19 • (03/31/98) • **84**

Syrah Coteaux du Languedoc Clos Léone 1993: Lively for its vivid flavors of berries, herbs and cola with firm tannins and a spicy finish. Trades harmony for exuberance. Drinkable now. • $26 • (10/31/97) • **85**

PEYROS, CHÂTEAU

Madiran 1994: Tough and herbal-tasting, with modest plum and berry flavors. Past its prime. • $12 • (05/15/98) • **79**

PEYROU, CHÂTEAU

Côtes de Castillon 1995: A generous and harmonious Bordeaux that's a good value. Has light tannins and a smooth texture. Blends plum, herb and mineral flavors. Drink now. • $10 • (01/31/98) • **84**

PEZ, CHÂTEAU DE

St.-Estèphe 1997: Frozen raspberry character. Medium-bodied, with light tannins and a short finish. Attractive. Could move up in 1999. • $NA • (06/15/98) (BT) • **80-84**

St.-Estèphe 1996: Compact and racy, with firm tannins and chunky fruit character. Slightly one-dimensional, but with plenty of plum flavor and a caressing finish. • $24 • (06/15/98) (BT) • **85-89**

St.-Estèphe 1995: A reserved style. Wonderfully elegant tannins, medium-to-full body and plenty of blackberry and cherry flavors on the finish. • $NA • (05/15/96) (BT) • **85-89**

St.-Estèphe 1994: This balanced red offers ripe cherry and cassis flavors with hints of chocolate and licorice, round tannins and a pleasant, spicy finish. Drinkable now but should improve. • $15 • (01/01/97) • **87**

St.-Estèphe 1990: A wine overflowing with berry and raspberry flavor. Structurally it's elegant and fine, with firm tannins and excellent length. Drink now. 12,000 cases made. • $20 • (03/31/93) • **93**

St.-Estèphe 1989 • $27 Ⓐ • (03/15/92) • **89**

St.-Estèphe 1988 • $19 Ⓐ • (06/15/91) • **83**

St.-Estèphe 1986 • $21 Ⓐ • (06/30/89) • **90**

St.-Estèphe 1985 • $15 • (06/30/88) • **90**

St.-Estèphe 1982 • $35 Ⓐ • (04/01/86) • **90**

St.-Estèphe 1961 • $NA • (04/30/96) • **85**

PHÉLAN-SÉGUR, CHÂTEAU

St.-Estèphe 1997: Berry and mineral character. Medium-to-light body, with medium tannins and a light finish. • $NA • (06/15/98) (BT) • **80-84**

St.-Estèphe 1996: Silky, pretty and well crafted. Medium-bodied, with fine tannins and a light finish. Elegant. • $30 • (06/15/98) (BT) • **85-89**

St.-Estèphe 1995: Lovely balance to this wine, with fruit and tannins in the right proportion. Medium-bodied, with fine tannins and a fruity aftertaste. Best after 2000. • $25 • (01/31/98) • **88**

St.-Estèphe 1994: Interesting floral aromas, especially violets, and a hint of fruit. Medium-bodied, with ripe fruit flavors and ultrafine tannins. Delicate finish. Better in 1999. • $18 Ⓐ • (01/31/97) • **86**

Key: SS—Spectator Selection CS—Cellar Selection HR—Highly Recommended BB—Best Buy $NA—Price not available Ⓐ—Auction Price (BT)—Barrel Tasting
Dates in parentheses indicate the issues in which the ratings were published.

St.-Estèphe 1993: Elegant cherry, berry and milk chocolate aromas and flavors, medium body, fine tannins and a delicate finish. Drinkable now. • $15 Ⓐ • (01/31/96) • **84**

St.-Estèphe 1992: A lovely core of fruit, with a medium body, velvety tannins and a succulent finish. Drinkable now. • $17 • (04/15/95) • **85**

St.-Estèphe 1991: A classy wine with a subtle character of berry and wet earth. It is medium-bodied with firm tannins and has a good core of fruit flavors. • $15 • (03/31/94) • **85**

St.-Estèphe 1990: A wine with rich, spicy vanilla, berry and chocolate aromas and flavors and round, rich tannins. Better than the '89. Drinkable now. 24,000 cases made. • $27 • (03/31/93) • **91**

St.-Estèphe 1989 • $29 Ⓐ • (03/15/92) • **85**

St.-Estèphe 1988 • $29 Ⓐ • (07/15/91) • **87**

St.-Estèphe 1987 • $16 • (11/30/89) • **82**

St.-Estèphe 1986 • $29 Ⓐ • (11/30/89) • **86**

St.-Estèphe 1982 • $43 Ⓐ • (11/30/89) • **88**

St.-Estèphe 1982 • $34 Ⓐ • (08/31/92) • **91**

St.-Estèphe 1970 • $26 Ⓐ • (05/15/93) • **84**

St.-Estèphe 1961 • $42 • (04/30/96) • **84**

PHILIPPE, JEAN

Brut Blanquette de Limoux 1986 • $11 • (06/15/90) • **80**

PHILIPPONNAT

Brut Blanc de Blancs Champagne 1980 • $26 • (05/31/87) • **92**

Brut Blanc de Blancs Champagne Cuvée Première 1980 • $39 • (12/31/88) • **89**

Brut Blanc de Blancs Champagne Grand Blanc 1985 • $40 • (12/31/90) • **87**

Brut Champagne Clos des Goisses 1988: Plush-textured and tasty, this very classy Champagne shows mouthfilling fruit flavors, a soft but persistent mousse and hints of nutty, toasty maturity on the lingering finish. Drink now through 2002. • $99 • (11/30/97) • **91**

Brut Champagne Clos des Goisses 1986: From a fabled vineyard, but still rather austere and mineral-like in flavor. Hard to say if this will open up and become a complex, mature vintage Champagne. Scored higher in 1994. • $116 • (11/30/96) • **84**

Brut Champagne Clos des Goisses 1985: Bold and assertive, with great aromas of toast, nutmeg and walnut, and lots of apple, fig and nut flavors. Very dry, firmly acidic, full-bodied, but nicely balanced out by the generous fruit. Utterly plush in texture. Drinkable now. 1,500 cases made. • $90 • (12/31/94) • **92**

Brut Champagne Clos des Goisses 1982: Crisp, youthful and tart. Not your creamy style of vintage Champage, but it is solidly built, distinctively spicy, with intriguing nutmeg and cedary flavors on top of citrus fruit and floral touches. • $89 • (12/31/88) • **84**

Brut Champagne Grand Blanc 1989: Bold and full-bodied, from the heady aromas to the powerful flavors to the lingering finish. A toasty, earthy, rich but dry character makes this Champagne distinctive. Best now through 2000. • $50 • (11/30/97) • **93**

Brut Champagne Grand Blanc 1988: A crisp, refreshing, almost austere Blanc de Blancs with vibrant lemon and green-apple flavors and a tart texture. Expands on the finish, though, so should improve through 1999. • $50 • (11/30/96) • **87**

Brut Champagne Grand Blanc 1986: Unctuous and concentrated, with strong, toasty aromas and beautifully mature flavors dominated by almond and smoke. Very assertive and bold, with a finish that comes off a bit astringent. 4,000 cases made. • $49 • (12/31/94) • **89**

Brut Champagne Grand Blanc 1982: Toasty and nutty with crisp, clean austere flavors and a touch of spicy saltiness. Lacks finesse and elegance. • $38 • (12/31/88) • **84**

Brut Champagne Le Reflet NV: A classy, generously flavored Champagne that blends toasty, floral aromas with ripe fruit flavors and a creamy smooth texture that keeps things going on the finish. Drink now. • $40 • (11/15/97) • **89**

Brut Champagne Royale Réserve NV: Fresh and lively in character, this is a really vibrant Champagne with good acidity. Fine as an apéritif or with a meal. • $25 • (10/31/97) • **88**

Brut Rosé Champagne Réserve NV: A slightly tired tasting rosé with spicy aromas followed by earthy flavors and touch of bitterness on the finish. • $36 • (12/31/97) • **78**

PIADA, CHÂTEAU

Barsac 1991: Wonderfully harmonious and elegant, buttery, creamy and slightly honeyed; to drink, not just to sip. Try as an apéritif. • $NA • (04/15/95) • **86**

Barsac 1990: Super-ripe and unctuous botrytis character. Extremely sweet without being cloying, offering tons of spicy, dried apricot, lemon and honey flavors which thickly coat your mouth. Try to keep for the next century. Tasted twice, with consistent notes. • $NA • (04/15/95) • **93**

Barsac 1989: Creamy and wonderfully harmonious, you can't go wrong here; marzipan, honey, nut and lemon flavors add up to a great drink. Drink now. Tasted twice, with consistent notes. • $NA • (04/15/95) • **91**

Barsac 1988: Nicely focused intensity, offering medium body and sweetness and caramel, wet earth, fig, dried apricot and toast flavors in satisfying amounts. Drinkable now. • $NA • (04/15/95) • **87**

Barsac 1987: There's true Sauternes character in this kosher wine. Has toasty, ripe aromas marked by botrytis and rich, nutty flavors. Full-bodied and sweet, with a long, full finish. • $35 • (03/31/91) • **86**

Barsac 1986: Straightforward Sauternes, displaying some decent cream, honey and lemon flavors, light-to-medium body and medium sweetness. Could use more concentration. • $NA • (04/15/95) • **83**

Barsac 1983: Rather delicate and fully mature, demonstrating nice aromas of dried apricot and pineapple, but a bit rustic. Drink now. • $11 • (04/15/95) • **84**

PIALADE, LA

Côtes du Rhône 1994: Light and supple, offering cherry, raspberry and cinnamon flavors, simple yet appealing. A pretty wine for drinking now. From Château Rayas. • $NA • (12/15/96) • **82**

PIAUGIER, DOMAINE DE

Côtes du Rhône 1995: Smooth and round, but also diluted, with a pepperish, cherry, strawberry character. Turns herbal on the finish. 1,250 cases made. • $10 • (10/15/97) • **77**

Côtes du Rhône-Villages Sablet Montmartel 1994: Nicely balanced, this chewy red has enough cherry and raspberry flavors to fill out the firm tannins. Still lively and fresh. 583 cases made. • $16 • (10/15/97) • **83**

Côtes du Rhône-Villages Sablet Montmartel 1990 • $10 • (04/15/93) • **84**

Côtes du Rhône-Villages Sablet Briguières 1994: There's a core of cherry flavor in this very firm red, but it's overwhelmed by earthy, gamy flavors and drying tannins. Drink up. 833 cases made. • $16 • (10/15/97) • **79**

Côtes du Rhône-Villages Sablet Ténébi 1994: Pretty spicy aromas give way to a lean-bodied wine with flavors of cherries and berries and light earthy notes. Drinks well now. 250 cases made. • $17 • (10/15/97) • **82**

Gigondas 1994: Slightly dry and herbal, with some stewed tomato notes. Supple and drinkable now, but a bit diluted. 833 cases made. • $19 • (10/15/97) • **76**

Gigondas 1990 • $15 • (04/15/93) • **88**

PIBARNON, CHÂTEAU DE

Bandol 1995: A focused wine, with dried cherry and leather flavors and a nice touch of gaminess. Crisp, bright and vivid, with a smooth finish that shows hints of orange peel and spice. Will blossom further with age. Tasted twice, with consistent notes. Drink now through 2005. • $25 • (05/31/98) • **88**

Bandol 1994: This red combines personality and structure. The flavors range from tar to tarragon, with ripe plum and date notes, the tannins are firm and well integrated. Drink now. • $24 • (06/30/97) • **87**

Bandol 1990 • $23 • (04/15/93) • **80**

Bandol 1987 • $17 • (03/15/90) • **75**

Bandol 1985 • $17 • (10/15/88) • **79**

Bandol 1984 • $NA • (08/31/86) • **70**

Bandol 1982 • $9 • (10/01/85) • **75**

Bandol Rosé 1995: A delicious rosé. Round, rich and spicy, displaying raspberry and cherry flavors and a refreshingly dry finish. Perfect with salads and other light foods. • $21 • (05/15/97) • **85**

PIBRAN, CHÂTEAU

Pauillac 1997: Exotic aromas of cumin, vanilla and sugar. Medium-bodied, with good fruit but very exaggerated toasty wood character and raisiny flavor. Slightly overdone. • $NA • (06/15/98) (BT) • **80-84**

Pauillac 1996: Bright violet and cherry aromas and flavors. Medium-bodied, with fine tannins and a fresh finish. Well made. • $22 • (06/15/98) (BT) • **85-89**

Pauillac 1995: Elegant and harmonious. Charming aromas of currants, berries and flowers. Medium- to full-bodied, with fine tannins and a long, caressing finish. Best after 2000. • $20 • (01/31/98) • **88**

Pauillac 1994: Striking concentration, with loads of fruit and chewy tannins, but verging on overly herbal. Full-bodied, full tannins and a dry finish. Slightly over extracted. 4,500 cases made. • $19 • (01/31/97) • **83**

Pauillac 1993: Some decent concentration but rather herbal and green, showing bell pepper character. Disappointing. Drinkable now. • $19 • (01/31/96) • **78**

Pauillac 1992: Some decent fruit and grassy flavors, but rather hard and tannic. • $15 • (04/15/95) • **75**

Pauillac 1991: Rich and quite powerful for this vintage with its good tannins. But slightly herbaceous on the finish. • $15 • (03/31/94) • **82**

Pauillac 1990: Incredibly rich yet elegant. It overflows with ripe blackberries, tobacco and chocolate, backed up with velvety tannins. Drinkable in 2000. 4,000 cases made. • $25 • (03/31/93) • **93**

Pauillac 1989 • $25 • (03/15/92) • **95**

Pauillac 1987 • $16 • (11/30/89) • **85**

Pauillac 1986 • $18 • (11/30/89) • **88**

Pauillac 1982 • $18 • (11/30/89) • **90**

PICARD, CHÂTEAU

St.-Estèphe 1997: Rhubarb and cooked fruit aromas and flavors. Medium-bodied, with medium, velvety tannins and a moderate finish. Overdone. • $NA • (06/15/98) (BT) • **75-79**

St.-Estèphe 1996: Decent fruit, but slightly diluted, with fine tannins and a light finish. • $24 • (06/15/98) (BT) • **80-84**

PICARD, JEAN-PAUL

Sancerre 1995: This big white offers full-bodied texture and green apple flavors, but a vegetal note lingers on the finish. 5,000 cases made. • $15 • (06/15/97) • **79**

Sancerre Cuvée Prestige 1993 • $17 • (11/15/95) • **86**

PICARD, MICHEL

Cabernet Sauvignon Vin de Pays d'Oc 1996: An easy-drinking Cabernet with good plum, cherry and tobacco flavors, good concentration and a clean finish. • $10 • (12/31/97) • **83**

Chablis 1996: Well made, in a typically austere style, offering fat, ripe fruit character, with lime and apple and a touch of honey. Supple on the mid-palate, but turns crisp on the finish. Drink now through 2000. 2,000 cases made. • $22 • (01/31/98) • **85**

Chardonnay Vin de Pays d'Oc 1996: A straightforward Chardonnay with butter, pear and spice flavors that linger on the lively finish. Better than when previously reviewed. Drink now. • $10 • (05/31/98) • **82**

Châteauneuf-du-Pape 1996: A stylish Châteauneuf-du-Pape, displaying plenty of cherry, plum, chocolate and herbal aromas and flavors and a glycerin-like texture. All knees and elbows today, with high alcohol, firm but ripe tannins and moderate length. Needs time to integrate. Best from 2000 through 2007. • $23 • (05/15/98) • **87**

Côtes du Rhône 1996: Just a touch of sulfur on the nose, but it dissipates quickly to reveal a moderately concentrated, modern Côtes du Rhône with pretty cherry, berry and plum flavors and firm tannins. Drink through 1999. • $11 • (05/15/98) • **83**

Mâcon-Villages 1996: An attractive little white, nothing complicated, but clean, pure and sharp. Offers a bouquet of honeysuckle, wet grass, green apple and hints of honey. Well made, tight and lingering on the finish. Drink through 1999. • $12 • (01/31/98) • **83**

Merlot Vin de Pays d'Oc 1996: Plenty of fruit, with nice cherry, dark plum and currant flavors. Quite straightforward, though a bit tart. Finishes with hints of tobacco and herb. • $10 • (12/31/97) • **82**

Pouilly-Fuissé 1996: Well made Pouilly-Fuissé. Shows nice earth and fruit complexity and excellent crisp acidity in a medium-bodied, balanced package. Worth hunting down for drinking through 1999. 3,000 cases made. • $24 • (01/31/98) • **87**

Syrah Vin de Pays d'Oc 1996: A well-crafted wine that's loaded with flavor. Has layers of pretty cherry, berry and spice notes that mesh seamlessly with earthy and leathery notes to give it some punch. Drink through 1999. 18,000 cases made. • $10 • (04/30/98) • **86**

Vouvray 1996: Light and quite crisp, this is in the dry style, with apple, peach and almond flavors and firm acidity. Straightforward and refreshing. Drink now. • $12 • (05/31/98) • **83**

PICCININI, DOMAINE

Minervois 1996: Appealing for its freshness and fruitiness, with delicious flavors of plum, berry and spice. Well balanced, with a soft texture and a lingering finish of chocolate and orange peel. Drink now through 2000. • $10 • (05/31/98) • **87**
Minervois 1995: Shows decent plum and cherry flavors, but it also has a dull, earthy streak through the middle. • $10 • (06/30/97) • **78**
Minervois 1992 • $8 • (06/30/94) • **75**
Minervois Clos l'Angély 1994: Plum, berry and pepper flavors dominate this focused red. Drinkable now. • $12 • (06/15/97) • **84**

PICHON

Chardonnay Domaine Gibalaux Vin de Pays d'Oc 1995: Simple and crisp, with green apple and citrus flavors. 25,000 cases made. • $8 • (06/30/97) • **79**
Merlot Vin de Pays d'Oc Domaine Gibalaux 1995: Smoky black cherry aromas and flavors have some depth yet the finish winds up on the astringent side. Try with food. 25,000 cases made. • $8 • (08/31/97) • **82**

PICHON, CHÂTEAU

Haut-Médoc 1985 • $13 • (08/31/88) • **85**

PICHON, PHILIPPE

St.-Joseph 1988 • $22 • (11/15/91) • **76**

PICHON-LONGUEVILLE-BARON, CHÂTEAU

Pauillac 1997: Grape and tar aromas. Medium-bodied, with slightly rustic tannins and a short finish. May be better in 1999. Tasted twice, with consistent notes. • $NA • (06/15/98) (BT) • **80-84**
Pauillac 1996: A well-balanced '96, with good berry and green tobacco character. Medium-bodied, with velvety tannins and a fruity finish. Almost outstanding. • $55 • (06/15/98) (BT) • **85-89**
Pauillac 1995: A balanced, early-drinking red. Beautiful blackberry and mineral aromas. Medium- to full-bodied, with fine tannins and a medium finish. Best after 1999. • $39 Ⓐ • (01/31/98) • **88**
Pauillac 1994: Plenty of dried cherry and plum aromas and flavors, hints of toasty oak. Medium-bodied, with fine tannins and a light finish. Slightly disappointing for this estate. Drink or hold. • $36 Ⓐ • (01/31/97) • **86**
Pauillac 1993: Stylish, well-defined red berry, mineral, smoke, and toast flavors, adding some herbal notes. Medium-body, well balanced, with a crisp but satisfying and lingering finish. Try now. 25,000 cases made. • $31 Ⓐ • (01/31/96) • **85**
Pauillac 1992: Impressive violet and berry aromas precede a polished, smooth texture and chocolate, toasty oak character on the finish. Very tannic; perhaps too much? Drinkable now. • $29 Ⓐ • (04/15/95) • **84**
Pauillac 1991: Solid as rock. Well-structured and very balanced with lovely reserved violet, berry character, firm tannins and a long, slightly herbaceous finish. Drinkable now. • $27 • (03/31/94) • **84**
Pauillac 1990: Not as great as expected. It's thick and viscous with loads of fruit flavors. Full-bodied and oily textured with plenty of tannins and a long, smoky, chewy finish. Better after 2002. • $96 Ⓐ • (09/15/96) • **91**
Pauillac 1989 • $87 Ⓐ • (03/15/92) • **98**
Pauillac 1988 • $55 Ⓐ • (03/31/91) SS • **95**
Pauillac 1987 • $25 Ⓐ • (10/15/90) • **88**
Pauillac 1986 • $42 Ⓐ • (05/31/89) • **97**
Pauillac 1985 • $42 Ⓐ • (10/15/94) • **90**
Pauillac 1984 • $23 • (09/30/88) • **78**
Pauillac 1983 • $35 Ⓐ • (10/15/94) • **85**
Pauillac 1982 • $39 Ⓐ • (08/31/92) • **92**
Pauillac 1981 • $34 Ⓐ • (10/15/94) • **85**
Pauillac 1980 • $17 • (09/30/88) • **79**
Pauillac 1979 • $38 Ⓐ • (10/15/89) • **88**
Pauillac 1978 • $38 Ⓐ • (09/30/88) • **80**
Pauillac 1977 • $13 • (09/30/88) • **76**
Pauillac 1976 • $21 Ⓐ • (09/30/88) • **73**
Pauillac 1975 • $32 Ⓐ • (09/30/88) • **74**
Pauillac 1974 • $15 • (09/30/88) • **78**
Pauillac 1973 • $27 • (09/30/88) • **78**
Pauillac 1972 • $13 • (09/30/88) • **68**
Pauillac 1971 • $34 Ⓐ • (09/30/88) • **71**
Pauillac 1970 • $29 Ⓐ • (09/30/88) • **83**
Pauillac 1969 • $21 • (09/30/88) • **78**
Pauillac 1967 • $15 Ⓐ • (09/30/88) • **80**
Pauillac 1966 • $34 Ⓐ • (09/30/88) • **80**
Pauillac 1964 • $37 Ⓐ • (09/30/88) • **88**
Pauillac 1962 • $65 • (09/30/88) • **88**
Pauillac 1961 • $100 Ⓐ • (04/30/96) • **85**
Pauillac 1960 • $50 • (09/30/88) • **81**
Pauillac 1959 • $85 Ⓐ • (10/15/90) • **94**
Pauillac 1958 • $95 • (09/30/88) • **79**
Pauillac 1957 • $45 Ⓐ • (09/30/88) • **76**
Pauillac 1955 • $73 Ⓐ • (09/30/88) • **81**
Pauillac 1954 • $64 Ⓐ • (09/30/88) • **80**
Pauillac 1953 • $150 • (09/30/88) • **80**
Pauillac 1952 • $120 • (09/30/88) • **84**
Pauillac 1950 • $150 • (09/30/88) • **83**
Pauillac 1949 • $127 Ⓐ • (09/30/88) • **87**
Pauillac 1947 • $114 Ⓐ • (09/30/88) • **80**
Pauillac 1945 • $400 • (11/30/95) • **82**

PICHON-LONGUEVILLE-LALANDE, CHÂTEAU

Pauillac 1997: Good level of mineral and berry aromas and flavors, but lacking a bit in concentration and structure. Medium-bodied, with moderate tannins. Finishes slightly short. Wait and see. • $NA • (06/15/98) (BT) • **85-89**
Pauillac 1996: Excellent concentration of fruit, with rosemary, berry and cherry aromas and flavors. Full-bodied, with well-integrated tannins and a long finish. Sleek and steely. • $130 • (06/15/98) (BT) • **90-94**
Pauillac 1995: A megawine, with layers of fruit and various levels of character. This exceptional Bordeaux is full-bodied and very tannic, with masses of rich fruit, berry and tobacco. Very velvety. This powerhouse needs time. Best after 2003. • $160 • (01/31/98) CS • **96**
Pauillac 1994: An extremely well-balanced and well-crafted wine. Shows impressive dried cherry, cassis and dried herb character. Medium-bodied, with silky tannins and a mineral, cassis aftertaste. Better after 2000. • $58 Ⓐ • (11/15/97) • **88**
Pauillac 1993: Slightly disappointing: a bit too much herbal character. Medium-bodied, with cassis and green bean flavors, medium tannins and a slightly dry finish. Drink now or hold. • $41 Ⓐ • (11/15/97) • **80**
Pauillac 1992: Rather overtly herbal and oaky, but shows some good plum and earth character. Medium-bodied, with medium tannins and a decent finish. Drink up. • $28 Ⓐ • (11/15/97) • **83**
Pauillac 1991: Very good for a 1991. Satisfying and delicious, this shows pretty cherry, chocolate and tobacco flavors and aromas. Medium-bodied, with firm tannins, plenty of toasty oak and a medium finish. Drink or hold. • $41 Ⓐ • (11/15/97) • **86**
Pauillac 1990: Wonderful and concentrated, with intense, complex aromas of chocolate and berries. Full-bodied, with very ripe fruit and well-integrated, velvety tannins. Better after 2002. • $86 Ⓐ • (11/15/97) • **94**
Pauillac 1989: Not giving all that much at the moment, but this is a compacted, thick, classic-quality wine. Full-bodied, chunky and rich with berry, chocolate and pepper character. Full tannins and a medium finish. This is a brutish wine. Better after 2002. • $96 Ⓐ • (11/15/97) • **95**
Pauillac 1988: Despite slightly strange aromas (plum-skin, berry, stewed tomato), this is pretty to taste. Medium-to-full body, with round, silky tannins and a tobacco, berry character on the finish. Drink now or hold. • $77 Ⓐ • (11/15/97) • **87**
Pauillac 1987: Still showing well, with caressing tannins and lovely fruit. Displays chocolate, berry and dried herb character. Medium-bodied, with soft, velvety tannins. Flavors echo on the finish. Drink now. • $58 Ⓐ • (11/15/97) • **87**
Pauillac 1986: Superbly structured, with breathtaking aromas of plums, chocolate and berries that follow through on the palate. Full-bodied, with full tannins and a long, alluring finish. Needs time; better after 2002. • $124 Ⓐ • (11/15/97) • **97**

Key: SS—Spectator Selection CS—Cellar Selection HR—Highly Recommended BB—Best Buy $NA—Price not available Ⓐ—Auction Price (BT)—Barrel Tasting
Dates in parentheses indicate the issues in which the ratings were published.

Pauillac 1985: Still incredibly youthful. Exhibits fabulous aromas of fresh fruit, minerals and chocolate with a hint of spice. Full-bodied and concentrated, with loads of fruit and tannins. Better after 2000. • $94 Ⓐ • (11/15/97) • **96**

Pauillac 1984: Impressive quality for such a dreadful vintage. Shows attractive dried plum and dark chocolate aromas and flavors. Full-bodied, with full tannins that are slightly dry, but has a good concentration of fruit. • $34 Ⓐ • (11/15/97) • **88**

Pauillac 1983: This wine has always been underrated. Shows wonderful aromas of chocolate, berry and earth. Full-bodied, with full, velvety tannins and a sweet berry finish. Drink now or hold. • $94 Ⓐ • (11/15/97) • **92**

Pauillac 1982: No surprises here—this is always a stunner. Showing wonderful aromas of berries, spice, earth and ripe fruit, it's full-bodied, with silky tannins and a multi-dimensional array of flavors on the finish. Built for aging, but why wait? • $248 Ⓐ • (11/15/97) • **97**

Pauillac 1981: Harmonious and delicious. Entices with aromas of spice and fruit. Medium in body, with medium, velvety tannins and a tobacco, berry aftertaste. Drink now. • $65 Ⓐ • (11/15/97) • **89**

Pauillac 1980: Still holding on, but slightly one-dimensional. Medium-bodied, with firm, slightly dry tannins and a plummy aftertaste. Drink now. • $34 Ⓐ • (11/15/97) • **80**

Pauillac 1979: A surprise, showing plenty of ripe and exotic fruit for the vintage. Dark-ruby in color, with ripe plum and earth character. Full-bodied, with a long chocolate, berry finish. Drink now or hold. • $68 Ⓐ • (11/15/97) • **93**

Pauillac 1978: A joyous bottle of red, emitting aromas of flowers, plums and a hint of earth. Medium-bodied, with medium, velvety tannins and a long, fresh finish. Drink now. • $113 Ⓐ • (11/15/97) • **88**

Pauillac 1976: Holding on very well for a '76, and delicious to boot. Brick-ruby in color, with rose petal and plum aromas and flavors, a hint of mushroom. Medium body, smooth texture. • $49 Ⓐ • (11/15/97) • **87**

Pauillac 1975: Slightly tough, but a damn nice glass of red. Ruby-garnet in color, with tobacco, cedar and fruit aromas and flavors. Medium- to full-bodied with full, velvety tannins and ripe fruit. Will improve with age. • $63 Ⓐ • (11/15/97) • **89**

Pauillac 1970: Fresh and complex, generous in character, with lovely dried cherry and spice aromas that follow through on the palate. Full-bodied, with concentrated fruit and firm tannins, this has a long life ahead. • $97 Ⓐ • (11/15/97) • **94**

Pauillac 1966: Elegant and soft for what is usually described as a tough vintage, this shows light tobacco and cherry aromas. Medium-bodied, with fine tannins and a chocolate, berry finish. • $62 Ⓐ • (11/15/97) • **85**

Pauillac 1964: Solid wine for the vintage, exhibiting lovely aromas of mocha and berries. Full-bodied, with sweet berry and milk chocolate character. Impressive, considering the rain that fell during the harvest. Drink now. • $41 Ⓐ • (11/15/97) • **89**

Pauillac 1962: Slightly disappointing for the vintage, displaying mushroom and earth character. Acidic and dry. Perhaps a bad bottle? • $88 Ⓐ • (11/15/97) • **78**

Pauillac 1961: Outstanding, but not as stunning as some think. Slightly dry on the finish. Dark-ruby in color, with a garnet edge. Full- to medium-bodied, with silky tannins and flavors of mushroom, plum and cedar. • $207 Ⓐ • (11/15/97) • **90**

Pauillac 1959: Complex and delicious, with wonderful aromas of cassis and cedar. Full-bodied, with caressing tannins and a long berry, bark and earth aftertaste. • $195 Ⓐ • (11/15/97) • **92**

Pauillac 1957: Not much to it, really. Slightly soapy and fruity on the nose, full-bodied, with strange flavors, and it's dry. Barely drinkable. • $NA • (11/15/97) • **72**

Pauillac 1955: Racy and sleek, with an interesting character. Bright ruby-red in color, with dried cherry, spice and tobacco aromas. Full-bodied, with an abundant wild berry and cedar character and firm tannins. Slightly one-dimensional. • $67 Ⓐ • (11/15/97) • **86**

Pauillac 1953: Promises more on the nose than it delivers on the palate, emitting lovely plum, mineral and mint aromas. Medium in body, with fine tannins and a slightly acidic finish. • $76 Ⓐ • (11/15/97) • **86**

Pauillac 1950: Harmonious and light but verging on being thin. Ruby-garnet in color, with tea, cedar and berry aromas. Medium in body, with vanilla and plum flavors and a smooth finish. • $87 Ⓐ • (11/15/97) • **83**

Pauillac 1949: A pretty wine with lovely perfumes and fruit, but it's slightly disappointing on the palate. Medium in body, with firm tannins and a moderately milky, plummy aftertaste. • $261 Ⓐ • (11/15/97) • **86**

Pauillac 1947: A beautifully proportioned antique of a wine. Brick-red, with cherry and spice on the nose and palate. Full-bodied and velvety, it has a slightly acidic finish but shows plenty of ripe fruit. • $489 Ⓐ • (11/15/97) • **91**

Pauillac 1945: Powerful yet refined, with delicious aromas and flavors. Dark brick-red in color, with tobacco, berry and cherry character. Full-bodied, with excellent concentration and a long, soft, caressing finish. • $698 Ⓐ • (11/15/97) • **93**

Pauillac 1942: Impressive for such a weak, war-vintage, although it's drying out now. Exhibits aromas of milk chocolate, plum and earth. Medium-bodied, with ripe fruit and mushroom character, silky texture and a dry finish. • $70 Ⓐ • (11/15/97) • **82**

Pauillac 1940: Ancient history. A mummy of a wine.• $NA • (11/15/97) • **50**

Pauillac 1937: Displays ripe fruit character, but it's dry. Offers meat, berry and earth aromas, with berry flavor and a hint of cedar on the palate, but it's dry on the finish. • $NA • (11/15/97) • **81**

Pauillac 1928: More like an old Burgundy, with nutlike, leather, fruit and brown sugar character. Hints of earth and oranges. Medium-bodied. • $503 Ⓐ • (11/15/97) • **80**

Pauillac 1922: Another wine on its way to the crypt. Amber-garnet in color, with tea, cherry and geranium character. Medium-bodied, with some berry and almond notes. Dry finish. • $NA • (11/15/97) • **80**

Pauillac 1920: Dead on arrival. Nothing left. • $NA • (11/15/97) • **50**

Pauillac 1914: There's a sense of ripeness in this skeleton of a wine. Dark-garnet in color, with mushroom, spice and earth character. Medium-bodied, with fine tannins and an acidic finish. • $NA • (11/15/97) • **82**

PICHOT, J.-C.

Vouvray Demi-Sec Domaine Le Peu de la Moriette 1995 • $13 • (05/15/96) • **87**

Vouvray Domaine Le Peu de la Moriette 1996: Toasty, earthy aromas give way to a sweet and fruity palate, with melon, toasty almond and coconut flavors. It's moderately sweet, but has enough acidity for balance. A muscular wine that can age. Drink now through 2000. • $8 • (05/31/98) • **86**

Vouvray Les Larmes de Bacchus 1996: Pretty spice and honey aromas give way to a thick, seriously sweet palate that stays lively thanks to crisp acidity. It offers honey, dried pineapple, lemon and cream flavors—complex yet harmonious. Well-knit and concentrated, yet not overblown, it will improve with age. Drink now through 2010. • $30/375ml • (05/31/98) • **92**

Vouvray Moelleux Domaine Le Peu de la Moriette 1996: This lively white is sweet yet crisp, with floral, pineapple and honey character. It's both intense and slightly disjointed; harmony may come with time. Drink now through 2001. • $19 • (05/31/98) • **84**

Vouvray Molleux Domaine Le Peu de la Moriette 1995 • $18 • (06/15/96) • **75**

PICO, GEORGES

Chablis Montmains Domaine de Bois d'Yver 1995: A racy *premier cru* with plenty of fruit, zingy acidity and some earth character. Medium-bodied, with a velvety feel at midpalate, long finish. Has the stuffing to age past 1999. • $NA • (06/15/97) • **86**

PICQ, GILBERT

Chablis 1996: Ripe, medium-bodied yet crisp and vibrant. Very flavorful, with tropical, grapefruit, kiwi, lime and herb character. Balanced and long on the attractively smoky finish. Tempting now, better around 2000. • $19 • (08/31/97) • **89**

Chablis Vaucoupin 1995: Charming, with ripe fruit, mineral, earth, vanilla bean, cream and toasty oak flavors. Medium- to full-bodied, this *premier cru* is tempting now but will be better after 1999. 292 cases made. • $17 • (06/15/97) • **87**

Chablis Vosgros 1996: Ripe and lively, with pear, pineapple, lemon and wet earth marrying beautifully in this pure, clean, full-bodied Chardonnay. Balanced, vibrant finish. Drink around 2005. 700 cases made. • $22 • (05/31/98) • **90**

Chablis Vosgros 1995: A soft and pleasant *premier cru* Chablis, with pear, honey and citrus flavors. Of medium body, it's ready to drink. • $17 • (06/15/97) • **82**

PICQUE-CAILLOU, CHÂTEAU

Pessac-Léognan 1993: Fairly intense and concentrated with lovely spice and fruit elements. Lean but firm, with plenty of cherry and cassis flavors for balance, as well as some olive and tobacco notes. • $25 • (04/30/97) • **85**

Graves 1982 • $NA • (08/31/92) • **78**

FRANCE

PIERRIERE, CHÂTEAU LA

Côtes de Castillon 1986 • $6 • (12/31/88) • **77**

PIGNAN

Châteauneuf-du-Pape Réserve 1989 • $27 • (08/31/92) • **83**
Châteauneuf-du-Pape Réserve 1988 • $30 • (10/15/91) • **82**
Châteauneuf-du-Pape Réserve 1986 • $29 • (10/15/91) • **83**
Châteauneuf-du-Pape Réserve 1985 • $38 • (08/31/87) SS • **95**
Châteauneuf-du-Pape Réserve 1983 • $38 • (10/15/91) • **85**
Châteauneuf-du-Pape Réserve 1981 • $35 • (10/15/91) • **94**
Châteauneuf-du-Pape Réservé 1980 • $30 • (10/15/86) • **87**

PIGUET-GIRARDIN

Santenay La Comme 1994: Lean and chewy, with a layer of coarse tannins that envelopes the modest berry flavors. • $23 • (11/15/96) • **81**

PILLOT, FERNAND

Chassagne-Montrachet 1994: Good power and decent concentration, giving a rich feel in the mouth, but the slightly vegetal flavors of this well-structured white may not be quite everyone's taste. • $NA • (05/31/96) • **85**
Chassagne-Montrachet Les Grandes Ruchottes 1994: Rather intense and nicely creamy, with some dried herb, fresh basil, pear and honey flavors. It's crisp, with a floral character. Try now. • $NA • (05/31/96) • **88**
Chassagne-Montrachet Les Grandes Ruchottes 1993: Lovely pear, honey and chalk aromas and flavors, medium body and a mineral, glycerin texture. • $37 • (05/15/95) • **84**
Chassagne-Montrachet Les Vergers 1994: Beautiful, round, supple, full-bodied and seductive, with a dried herb character that adds complexity to the honey and ripe fruit flavors. More powerful than elegant, with a long finish. Solid. • $NA • (05/31/96) • **90**
Chassagne-Montrachet Les Vergers 1993: A good amount of almond, spice and honey character. Medium- to full-bodied; straightforward yet fairly rich fruit flavors. Drink now. • $30 • (05/15/95) • **85**
Chassagne-Montrachet Morgeot 1994: Ripe yet very fresh, with a green, dried herb character along with honey, butterscotch and pear flavors. Long, intense and exotically sweet-tasting on the mouth-puckering finish. Drinkable now, but can age. • $NA • (05/31/96) • **85**
Chassagne-Montrachet Morgeot 1993: Fresh and clean mineral, spice and honey flavors. Medium-bodied with a lightly fruity, crisp finish. • $33 • (05/15/95) • **84**
Chassagne-Montrachet Vide Bourse 1994: Unctuous, overflowing with ripe, rich honey, herb and lime flavors. Seductive from start to finish, this full-bodied *premier cru* remains fresh on the long finish. A beauty. • $NA • (05/31/96) • **90**
Chassagne-Montrachet Vide Bourse 1993: Vibrant, lemony and honeyed, pleasant, delivering plenty of zest but not much depth. Try now. • $32 • (05/15/95) • **85**
Puligny-Montrachet 1994: Pulls no punches. Extremely intense, hinting at green apricot, with wonderful floral and mineral notes that tantalize the palate. A searing, slightly vegetal finish. • $NA • (05/31/96) • **88**

PILLOT, FERNAND & LAURENT

Chassagne-Montrachet Vieilles Vignes 1995: This light, lean red has drying tannins around a lean core of cherry flavor, with hints of spice on the finish. Try now. 250 cases made. • $39 • (06/30/97) • **80**
Volnay 1995: This pale, light red offers firm tannins, light spice flavors, and almost no fruit. It's a disgrace to the appellation. 250 cases made. • $39 • (06/30/97) • **75**

PILLOT, JEAN

Chassagne-Montrachet 1995: Very rich and ripe, this is full-bodied and sparkling with life from lemon-spiked acidity. It offers nice honey, ripe pear, cream and mineral flavors, ending a bit dry. Drink now through 2002. • $28 • (05/31/97) • **88**
Chassagne-Montrachet 1994: Distinctive, even slightly odd, honeysuckle, varnish, rose petal and perfume flavors. Thick and ripe, but a bit overdone. Ready now. Tasted twice, with consistent notes. • $NA • (08/31/96) • **79**
Chassagne-Montrachet 1992: A bit too funky for our tastes, with smoky-earthy aromas, mineral, honey and grapefruit flavors and a crisp finish. • $NA • (08/31/94) • **80**
Chassagne-Montrachet Caillerets 1996: A bit odd and swampy, showing good structure of acidity, wood and fruit, but the distinctive aromas and flavors distract. 200 cases made. • $50 • (05/31/98) • **76**
Chassagne-Montrachet Caillerets 1994: Silky and delicious at first, it offers sweet-tasting pear, honey and honeydew melon flavors. Round and a bit unfocused on the finish. 83 cases made. • $42 • (05/31/96) • **85**
Chassagne-Montrachet Caillerets 1993: Some subtle apple, cream and toasty oak character. Lean style. • $50 • (05/15/95) • **80**
Chassagne-Montrachet Les Champs Gain 1996: Some sweet-tasting richness peeks through in this attractive, balanced, medium-bodied, flavorful, minerally wine. Offers Chassagnelike characteristics of dried herbs and slightly grassy, cilantro notes along with honey, pear and pink grapefruit flavors. Hints at a supple, smoky and toasty finish that should improve with cellaring through 2000 to 2003. 165 cases made. • $38 • (05/31/98) • **90**
Chassagne-Montrachet Les Champs Gain 1995: Beautiful wine, sparkling with life, unfolding its arsenal of lemon, spice, butter, honey and crisp fruit flavors and gunning for a long finish. Medium- to full-bodied, silky yet firm, it plays on contrasts and leaves you totally enraptured. Drinkable now, but try to wait until after 2000. 300 cases made. • $35 • (05/31/97) • **94**
Chassagne-Montrachet Les Champs Gain 1994: Lively and crisp, mingling citrus, wet earth and honey flavors in a rather tight package. Charming from start to finish, with a very fresh finish. Drink now. 150 cases made. • $32 • (05/31/96) • **85**
Chassagne-Montrachet Les Champs Gain 1992: Ripe and rich, with a lush texture that's kept in check with a good backbone of acidity; offers a mouthful of pear, vanilla, honey and grapefruit flavors. Worth the search; drinkable now. • $32 • (08/31/94) • **90**
Chassagne-Montrachet Les Chenevottes 1996: Subtle and ripe, with an underpinning of delicious, sweet-tasting pear, tropical and honey flavors. Of medium-to-full body, the spicy, toasty bread notes add complexity, showing lovely, supple texture as the wine warms up in the glass and opens with contact with air. Best after 2003. 200 cases made. • $35 • (05/31/98) • **90**
Chassagne-Montrachet Les Chenevottes 1995: Clean, deep and complex, with mineral, vanilla bean, pear and tropical fruit flavors, and oak notes that stay subtly in the background. Lovely mouthfeel, supple and full-bodied, this is a thick-textured Chassagne with excellent intensity. Delicious now, but should improve through 2005. • $33 • (05/31/97) • **92**
Chassagne-Montrachet Les Chenevottes 1994: Rich and creamy, with lush hazelnut and tropical fruit flavors. Full-bodied and has lots of personality; this puts on quite a show. Drink now. 175 cases made. • $30 • (05/31/96) • **87**
Chassagne-Montrachet Les Chenevottes 1993: Relatively light and very tart, austere, delivering some green apple, dried-herb character. • $35 • (05/15/95) • **81**
Chassagne-Montrachet Les Chenevottes 1992: Charming Chassagne, quite thick in texture, showing an unctuous lime and honey character that seduces you and begs for another sip. Balanced and vibrant with a pear and toasty note on the finish. • $30 • (08/31/94) • **89**
Chassagne-Montrachet Les Macherelles 1994: A well-crafted and highly focused *premier cru*, delivering its gorgeous lemon, honey and mineral flavors with digital clarity. Somewhat fuller in body, it has more intensity than most '94s. Should improve with age. • $NA • (05/31/96) • **88**
Chassagne-Montrachet Les Macherelles 1993: Harmonious, smooth texture; good mineral, chalk and class. A lovely Chassagne, tart and hard but with enough concentration. Bravo! Drinkable now. • $NA • (05/15/95) • **87**
Chassagne-Montrachet Les Vergers 1996: This has a seductive mouthfeel and a lush, creamlike texture, but it's also overly oaky, with loads of butter and butterscotch aromas and flavors that dominate the fruit. Full-bodied, the sweet fruit comes through on the crisp, citrusy but succulent finish. Needs time. Try after 2001. 165 cases made. • $38 • (05/31/98) • **88**
Chassagne-Montrachet Les Vergers 1994: Gorgeous, silky, elegant, a little fuller in body, offering a cascade of mineral, vanilla, pear and earth flavors. Subtle yet powerful, it tastes as smooth as double cream. Try this in 2000. 175 cases made. • $32 • (05/31/96) • **93**
Chassagne-Montrachet Morgeot 1996: Gorgeous. Starts out with lots of reserve in the aromas, but tantalizes with its depth, following through on

Key: SS—Spectator Selection CS—Cellar Selection HR—Highly Recommended BB—Best Buy $NA—Price not available Ⓐ—Auction Price (BT)—Barrel Tasting
Dates in parentheses indicate the issues in which the ratings were published.

the palate with ripe, sweet-tasting pear, honey and tropical flavors along with a dollop of smoke and mineral character. Full-bodied, balanced and silky-smooth, it turns subtle on the harmonious finish. Tempting now, better after 2003. 175 cases made. • $40 • (05/31/98) • **93**

Chassagne-Montrachet Morgeot 1995: Distinctive aromas of dried herbs and a bit of grass follow through to the supple, well-built palate, mingling there with spice, mocha and wood flavors. There is good concentration of fruit in this full-bodied Chardonnay, and the finish is refreshing and long. Try in 1999. • $38 • (05/31/97) • **90**

Chassagne-Montrachet Morgeot 1994: A lovely, full-bodied '94, bursting with honey, pear and apple pie flavors. Stays the course with a lemony character that gives it structure. Fabulous drinking now. 200 cases made. • $NA • (05/31/96) • **89**

Chassagne-Montrachet Morgeot 1992: Vivid and ripe in flavor, showing the peach and honey notes of botrytis. Full-bodied and technically dry, but seems to be sweet. An enjoyable but noticeably different style. Drinkable now. • $37 • (08/31/94) • **83**

Chevalier-Montrachet 1996: Lovely, thick and opulent, showing very toasty oak accents along with pie tart, apple and pear character. Full-bodied, with a supersilky and round mouthfeel, it turns up the toasty notes on the burning finish. Try around 2003. 25 cases made. • $150 • (05/31/98) • **94**

Puligny-Montrachet 1996: Impressively thick and dense, this oily, full-bodied '96 delivers plenty of citrus, honey, floral and mineral character, but turns a bit drying and astringent on the finish. Drink now. 250 cases made. • $30 • (05/31/98) • **85**

Puligny-Montrachet 1995: Thick and rich, but also very lively, with a core of dried herbs, mineral, honey and fresh fruit flavors that offer real zest on the long, slightly toasty finish of this full-bodied village wine. • $30 • (05/31/97) • **90**

Puligny-Montrachet 1994: Crisp, fresh and mineral, with a ripe mouthfeel. Very well built for a village wine. Could use a bit more fruit concentration, but it has finesse. 250 cases made. • $NA • (05/31/96) • **85**

Puligny-Montrachet 1993: Clean and fresh steel, mineral and spice character, medium body, firm acidity and a racy finish. • $30 • (05/15/95) • **82**

Puligny-Montrachet 1992: Earthy but elegant, of medium body; chewy and mouth-puckering, and packing plenty of grapefruit, pineapple, pear, and mineral flavors. Fresh and delicious now. • $26 • (08/31/94) • **87**

PILLOT, JEAN-MARC

Puligny-Montrachet Le Caillerets 1996: A mouthfilling '96, with mineral, floral and toasty oak character. Medium-bodied, with the potential to grow smooth and supple with age. Lacks a bit of fruit intensity. Try around 2003. 125 cases made. • $NA • (05/31/98) • **86**

PILLOT, PAUL

Chassagne-Montrachet Clos St.-Jean Red 1986 • $23 • (02/28/90) • **84**
Chassagne-Montrachet Clos St.-Jean Red 1985 • $24 • (11/15/88) • **86**

PIN, CHÂTEAU LE

Pomerol 1997: Pretty, fruity wine with a soft texture and attractive blackberry and vanilla character. Medium-bodied, with a delicate, fruity finish. • $NA • (06/15/98) (BT) • **85-89**

Pomerol 1996: Plenty of plum and chocolate character in this one. Medium in body, and tannins are medium, but the finish is slightly disappointing. Wait and see. • $NA • (01/01/97) (BT) • **85-89**

Pomerol 1995: Wild thing. Extremely ripe fruit, with nutmeg, cumin and berry aromas, ripe and exotic flavors. Really exotic. Full-bodied, and very velvety. Almost raisiny. Not as outstanding as the 1994, but excellent nonetheless. Am I spliting hairs over quality? Best after 2001. • $955 Ⓐ • (01/31/98) • **93**

Pomerol 1994: A classic Le Pin that's absolutely gorgeous. Has beautiful, accentuated aromas of roasted coffee, fruit and oak. Full-to-medium body with a sleek tannin structure and a long, silky finish. Very fine indeed. Hard not to drink this now, but will improve with cellaring through at least 2004. 500 cases made. • $289 Ⓐ • (01/31/97) CS • **95**

Pomerol 1993: Delicious Le Pin. Exotic and flashy, sporting lots of new wood which lends a smoky, toasty oak character to the berry notes. Medium in body, delicate tannins and fruity finish. Drinkable now. • $211 Ⓐ • (01/31/96) • **90**

Pomerol 1992: The biggest disappointment of the vintage. Why bottle such a wine? Very light and watery with milk chocolate, berry and vanilla character. Tasted twice. • $164 Ⓐ • (04/15/95) • **74**

Pomerol 1990: Irresistible. Sexy and exciting with exotic aromas and flavors of vanilla, chocolate, earth, and berries and an incredibly long aftertaste of sweet, ripe fruit. Try in 1999. 500 cases made. • $479 Ⓐ • (03/31/93) • **97**

Pomerol 1989 • $680 Ⓐ • (05/15/94) • **94**
Pomerol 1988 • $497 Ⓐ • (05/15/94) • **95**
Pomerol 1986 • $441 Ⓐ • (06/15/89) • **95**
Pomerol 1985 • $749 Ⓐ • (10/15/94) • **98**
Pomerol 1983 • $825 Ⓐ • (10/15/94) • **91**

Pomerol 1982: Sensational. Extraordinarily plush and fuzzy, with great, fat intensity of currant and berry flavors, nuanced with hints of chocolate, spice and iris. • $2172 Ⓐ • (07/31/97) • **98**

Pomerol 1981 • $651 Ⓐ • (10/15/94) • **91**
Pomerol 1979 • $672 Ⓐ • (05/15/94) • **90**

PINARD, VINCENT

Sancerre Cuvée Florès 1995: Rich and round for Sancerre, this big white offers ripe pear, melon and apple flavors and plenty of acidity to keep it lively. An appealing almond note comes out on the long finish. 3,000 cases made. • $15 • (05/15/97) • **89**

Sancerre Red 1995: Spicy, toasty aromas are alluring, and the wine is fresh and well defined, with cherry, toast and light herb flavors. Try with salmon or veal. 1,250 cases made. • $18 • (06/15/97) • **85**

PINEDE, DOMAINE DE LA

Châteauneuf-du-Pape 1990: Spicy, earthy, gamy flavors tend to dominate this robust wine, but sweet, raisiny notes sneak through on the finish. An interesting wine that may not improve with age. 3,500 cases made. • $15 • (04/15/93) • **78**

PINEY, CHÂTEAU

St.-Emilion 1995: A friendly, easy-to-drink St. Emilion. Soft and earthy, with berry, chocolaty, leafy character. Medium-bodied, with light tannins and a sweet fruit finish. Drink now. 5,400 cases made. • $20 • (01/31/98) • **81**

PINS, CHÂTEAU LES

Côtes du Roussillon-Villages 1995: Rich, ripe and lush, this full-throttle wine shows gorgeous flavors of plum, dark cherry and spice. It's balanced, for all its flavor, and has lovely spicy aromas. A smooth, supple wine. A blend of 40 percent Syrah, 30 percent Grenache, and 30 percent Mourvèdre. Drink now through 2000. 1,500 cases made. • $11 • (05/31/98) • **87**

PINSON, LOUIS

Chablis 1996: Sauvignon Blanc? No, Chardonnay. Showing lovely cut-grass, gooseberry and floral notes, it's ripe and pretty, with pronounced lemon, lime and herb notes. Medium-bodied and a bit drying on the intense finish. Nice now, should improve through 2002. 830 cases made. • $19 • (05/31/98) • **85**

Chablis Les Clos 1996: A cult wine among some Chablis aficionados, very distinctive and intense. A bit earthy, with honey and wet stone notes that give this great personality. Full-bodied, opulent and minerally, it shows good concentration and, above all, ripe fruit. The superlong finish is a bit tough, even slightly herbal. Don't touch until 2005 to 2007. 910 cases made. • $33 • (05/31/98) • **90**

Chablis Mont de Milieu 1996: Wonderful midpalate, both concentrated and minerally. Distinctive, this medium-bodied Chablis tastes almost like salted crackers, with an interesting seaweed, iodine, mineral, pear crust and citrus character and a hint of honey. This has the racy structure to age, so don't touch until after 2000. 2,080 cases made. • $22 • (05/31/98) • **93**

Chablis Mont de Milieu 1995: Fantastic. Round, velvety textured and packed with mineral character, this full-bodied beauty also offers subtle fruit, earth, wet stone and honey notes, and a refreshing, citrusy finish. Drink now through 2000. 1,250 cases made. • $23 • (06/15/97) • **90**

PIPER-HEIDSIECK

Brut Champagne 1982: Distinctive floral overtones. Spicy and tart, it is pleasantly ripe and earthy. • $32 • (12/31/88) • **86**

Brut Champagne NV: Straightforward Champagne that's toasty in aroma, lean and a bit tart in flavor. • $28 • (10/31/97) • **83**

Brut Champagne Rare 1988: Deep and pure, displaying classic Chardonnay flavors of melon, fig and almond, with plenty of acidity for structure, then adding nutmeg and toast flavors on the long finish. Balanced, with great structure for aging. • $66 • (04/30/97) • **93**

Brut Champagne Rare 1985: Amazing balancing act between richness and freshness. Shows mature flavors but it has the structure to age. Intense aromas and flavors of smoke, fruit and nuts. Medium-bodied with great acidity and long flavorful finish. Much, much better than in the past. 20,600 cases made. • $80 • (12/31/93) • **93**

Brut Champagne Rare 1985: A fully mature Champagne with earthy, nutty flavors, a texture that's almost soft and a lingering, nutty finish. Nearly over the hill, it could use more stuffing and liveliness. • $66 • (12/31/96) • **81**

Brut Champagne Rare 1979 • $34 Ⓐ • (03/15/87) • **89**

Brut Champagne Rare 1976 • $66 • (08/01/85) • **88**

Brut Champagne Sauvage 1985: Beautifully integrated and mature tasting, with roasted and toasty aromas. It's full-bodied, with vanilla and lemon flavors and a finish full of honey. Stylish and satisfying. 20,062 cases made. • $35 • (11/30/94) • **90**

Brut Rosé Champagne 1982: Nice, creamy texture. Lush and soft, with tart cherry aromas. Off-dry rosé with mature Pinot Noir character and some touches of smoke and oak. The finish is rather pleasant and long. • $38 • (12/31/88) • **84**

Brut Rosé Champagne NV: Here's a mellow, mature rosé that's luxurious in texture, rich in nutty-toasty flavors and long on the finish. A wonderfully deep salmon color and well-integrated bubbles also make it special. • $48 • (11/30/97) • **89**

Extra Dry Champagne NV: Delicious, refreshing and elegant, from the toasty aromas to the fresh fruit flavors and subtle, lingering finish. • $28 • (10/31/97) • **89**

PIQUE-SÈGUE, CHÂTEAU

Bergerac Rosé 1996: Extreme vegetal notes and aromas make for a rough-tasting rosé. • $6 • (06/15/98) • **73**

PIQUEMAL, DOMAINE

Côtes du Roussillon 1995: This is a powerful and well-balanced red, packed with blueberry, raspberry and cherry flavors that linger on the finish. It starts out with gamy, leathery aromas, but give it some air and they dissipate. Drink now through 2002. 5,000 cases made. • $10 • (05/31/98) • **87**

Côtes du Roussillon Elevé en Fûts de Chêne 1994: Powerful and smooth, with vibrant flavors of dark cherry, smoke and spice. Wrapped inside the concentrated flavors is an alluring peppery note that gives this wine a special verve. Tempting now, but best to let the tannins smooth out. Best from 2000 through 2004. • $16 • (05/31/98) • **89**

PIRLET, LUC

Chardonnay Vin de Pays d'Oc Les Grandes Vallées 1995: Unbalanced and raw tasting; only modest apple flavors exist that unfortunately turn harsh on the finish. 2,000 cases made. • $10 • (05/31/97) • **72**

Merlot Vin de Pays d'Oc Les Grandes Vallées 1995: Plenty of cherry flavor, and a touch of vanilla, combined with a viscous texture. Turns a little astringent on the finish. 2,000 cases made. • $10 • (05/15/97) • **81**

PITRAY, CHÂTEAU DE

Côtes de Castillon 1992: Spicy cherry and plum flavors are framed by firm tannins. It's medium-bodied, straightforward and simple, but balanced and rich enough for food. • $8 • (11/15/94) • **80**

Côtes de Castillon 1990: Rough, straightforward and tannic, with modest spice and anise flavors. Pleasant plum and cherry notes partially offset its basic austerity. May have smoothed out by now. 5,000 cases made. • $9 • (03/15/93) • **80**

Côtes de Castillon 1988 • $7 • (02/28/91) BB • **83**

Côtes de Castillon 1986 • $6 • (09/30/89) BB • **81**

Key: SS—Spectator Selection CS—Cellar Selection HR—Highly Recommended BB—Best Buy $NA—Price not available Ⓐ—Auction Price (BT)—Barrel Tasting
Dates in parentheses indicate the issues in which the ratings were published.

PIZAY, CHÂTEAU DE

Beaujolais 1995: Smoky, herbal notes add interest to black cherry flavors, and there's some grip on the finish. Drink soon. • $9 • (09/15/97) • **80**

Morgon 1995: Maturing now, this smooth red shows dried cherry, cedar and spice flavors, with polished tannins that turn a bit dry on the finish. Well knit and balanced for food. • $11 • (09/15/97) • **85**

Régnié 1995: Muscular for a Régnié, showing deep color, game and plum aromas and flavors and a firm tannic backbone. A bit lean but still fresh, and will blossom with food. • $11 • (09/15/97) • **86**

PLACE D'ARGENT

Cabernet Sauvignon Vin de Pays de l'Aude 1985 • $5 • (04/15/89) • **78**

Merlot Vin de Pays de l'Aude 1987 • $5 • (04/30/90) • **77**

Merlot Vin de Pays de l'Aude 1985 • $5 • (12/15/88) BB • **80**

PLAGNAC, CHÂTEAU

Médoc 1997: Barely acceptable, with stewed tomato and grassy character. • $NA • (06/15/98) (BT) • **970**

Médoc 1996: A medium-bodied wine with a slightly herbal, weedy character under the fruit. Slightly diluted finish. • $14 • (06/15/98) (BT) • **75-79**

Médoc 1995: Light and watery, featuring modest fruit and weak tannin structure. Disappointing. • $NA • (05/15/96) (BT) • **75-79**

Médoc 1994: Very light and watery, with a weedy, tobacco, stewed tomato character. Barely acceptable. • $15 • (01/31/97) • **70**

Médoc 1993: Why bottle this? Smells and tastes of stewed tomatoes and bell pepper; watery and short. • $11 • (01/31/96) • **70**

Médoc 1991: Bell pepper character dominates this wine, but some decent sweet fruit and its round texture show through. • $11 • (03/31/94) • **78**

Médoc 1989 • $12 • (03/15/92) • **88**

Médoc 1988 • $8 • (04/30/91) • **79**

Médoc 1987 • $8 • (11/30/89) • **77**

Médoc 1986 • $9 • (11/30/89) • **82**

Médoc 1985 • $9 • (08/31/88) • **68**

PLAIMONT

Colombelle Vin de Pays des Côtes de Gascogne White Colombelle 1994 • $6 • (02/29/96) • **76**

PLAISANCE, CHÂTEAU

Premières Côtes de Bordeaux Cuvée Spéciale 1989 • $13 • (01/31/92) • **86**

PLANELS, CHÂTEAU DES

Minervois Cuvée Unique 1995: Ripe and fairly powerful, with peppery and plummy flavors and good focus. Nice leathery notes on the finish. Drink through 1999. 275 cases made. • $8 • (03/31/98) • **84**

PLANERES, CHÂTEAU

Côtes du Roussillon 1989 • $7 • (04/15/93) • **78**

Côtes du Roussillon White 1994 • $8 • (02/29/96) • **82**

PLANTEY, CHÂTEAU

Pauillac 1989 • $NA • (03/15/92) • **78**

PLANTIERS DU HAUT-BRION, LES

Graves 1974 • $24 • (03/31/89) • **80**

PLINCE, CHÂTEAU

Pomerol 1997: Shows a slight notion of raisins, but some good berry and cherry flavors beneath. Medium-bodied, with medium tannins and a light finish. Perhaps better than this tasting indicates. • $NA • (06/15/98) (BT) • **80-84**

Pomerol 1996: Chewy and rich for the vintage. Full-bodied, with plush tannins and a long, delicious finish. Not a blockbuster, but well balanced. • $NA • (01/01/97) (BT) • **85-89**

Pomerol 1995: Beautiful, delivering tons of sweet fruit, spice, mocha and earth complexity. Full in body, solid, rich, ripe tannins and a long, silky finish. Almost outstanding. • $NA • (05/15/96) (BT) • **85-89**

Pomerol 1993: Some decent body but the stewed tomato and herbal nature takes away from the quality. • $24 • (01/31/96) • **78**

Pomerol 1990: This is rich and concentrated, but a bit overripe and overoaked, with plum and cherry flavors accented by bitter chocolate, coffee and prune notes. Drinkable now. • $25 • (01/01/94) • **82**

Pomerol 1982 • $NA • (05/15/89) • **92**

PLOYEZ-JACQUEMART

Brut Blanc de Blancs Champagne 1988: An insider's wine. Ultrafine Champagne with great acidity and wonderful appley, vanilla fruit; it's medium-bodied and superfirm with a creamy texture. Drink now or age. 670 cases made. • $42 • (12/31/93) HR • **93**

Brut Champagne Leisse d'Harbonville 1989: Exotic wine that bombards your palate with exotic fruit character. A big wine but not heavy. Mango, papaya, and pineapple aromas and flavor, full body, rich foam, full acidity, and a long flavorful finish. Drink now. 450 cases made. • $65 • (12/31/93) • **90**

Brut Champagne Leisse d'Harbonville 1985: A very dry and lively style with fresh lemon, apple and light toasty character, medium body and long refreshing finish. Fine texture. Excellent apéritif. Drink now. Tasted twice. 225 cases made. • $65 • (12/31/93) • **89**

PLUMET HÉRITIERS, HENRI

Pouilly-Fuissé Clos du Chalet Pouilly 1995: Pretty, its ripe fruit notes complementing its crisp, citrus flavors. Medium in body, gaining some lush honey, pear, vanilla and apple notes on the chewy finish. Drink now. 2,083 cases made. • $24 • (05/31/97) • **85**

Pouilly-Fuissé Clos du Chalet Pouilly 1994: Both fat and crisp, this mouthful of a wine delivers plenty of character with its pineapple, salted peanut and citrus flavors. Try now. • $NA • (05/31/96) • **85**

Pouilly-Fuissé Clos du Chalet Pouilly 1993: Surprisingly brownish color for a 1993. Shows some cacao, cedar, green apple aromas and flavors; slightly short finish. Drink now. • $NA • (05/15/95) • **79**

St.-Véran Les Cornillauds 1995: Wood-city, with cardboardlike flavors. Turns bitter on the finish. • $12 • (05/31/97) • **74**

POCÉ, CHÂTEAU DE

Brut Crémant de Loire 1982 • $12 • (07/31/88) • **84**

POINTE, CHÂTEAU LA

Pomerol 1997: Good berry, tobacco, earth character. Medium-bodied, with medium tannins and a light finish. • $NA • (06/15/98) (BT) • **85-89**

Pomerol 1996: Quite a chewy '96, with berry and tobacco aromas and flavors. Medium-bodied, with velvety tannins and medium finish. A bit more fruit in the center palate would make it outstanding. • $25 • (06/15/98) (BT) • **85-89**

Pomerol 1995: Gorgeous Pomerol. One of the best values in the region. Coffee, tobacco and fruit aromas. Full-bodied, with full yet velvety tannins and a long, sweet fruit finish. Best after 2001. • $25 • (01/31/98) • **93**

Pomerol 1994: Vibrant violet and berry aromas introduce this medium- to full-bodied offering, with its wonderfully intergrated tannins and long, silky finish. Really a fine wine, one of the sleepers of Pomerol. Better in 1999. 10,000 cases made. • $29 • (01/31/97) SS • **90**

Pomerol 1992: Interesting aromas and flavors of nutmeg, fruit and bread dough; medium- to light-bodied. • $19 • (04/15/95) • **78**

Pomerol 1990: Attractive cherry, raspberry character and firm tannins give this wine appeal, but it's a little short on the finish. Drinkable now. 9,000 cases made. • $27 • (03/31/93) • **86**

Pomerol 1989 • $23 Ⓐ • (03/15/92) • **95**

Pomerol 1988 • $13 Ⓐ • (07/31/91) • **83**

Pomerol 1986 • $19 Ⓐ • (06/15/89) • **90**

Pomerol 1982 • $31 Ⓐ • (08/31/92) • **84**

Pomerol 1970 • $29 Ⓐ • (05/15/93) • **88**

Pomerol 1962 • $35 • (11/30/87) • **80**

Pomerol 1961 • $39/1.5 liter • (04/30/96) • **85**

Pomerol 1945 • $149 Ⓐ • (11/30/95) • **80**

POIRON, HENRI

Muscadet de Sèvre et Maine Sur Lie Château des Grandes Noëlles 1995: Rounder and softer than many Muscadets, but has true, if slightly diluted, light pear and spice flavors. 800 cases made. • $10 • (05/15/97) • **79**

Muscadet de Sèvre et Maine Sur Lie Château des Grandes Noëlles 1993 • $9 • (08/31/94) BB • **84**

POL ROGER

Brut Blanc de Blancs Champagne Blanc de Chardonnay 1986: Even better than the very good 1985 *blanc de blancs* from Pol Roger. Super fresh and crisp like freshly cut pineapple. It's medium-bodied with vivacious, sparkling flavors. Drink now. • $63 • (12/31/93) • **90**

Brut Blanc de Blancs Champagne Blanc de Chardonnay 1985: A toasty, complex bubbly, with plenty of winey character, showing buttery, smoky overtones to the crisp apple and lemon flavors. Has layers of flavor wrapped in a tight package. A stylish wine that's drinkable now. • $62 • (01/31/92) • **89**

Brut Blanc de Blancs Champagne Blanc de Chardonnay 1982 • $50 • (12/31/90) • **91**

Brut Blanc de Blancs Champagne Blanc de Chardonnay 1979 • $41 • (12/31/90) • **84**

Brut Champagne 1988: Mature and full-bodied. The mushroomy aromas, buttery, hazelnut flavors and lingering finish are the benefits of its age. Fine to drink now. • $49 • (12/31/96) • **90**

Brut Champagne 1986: This Champagne shows a lovely nose of toast and apple but the palate seems slightly tired and short. For lovers of old Champagne. Drink now. Tasted twice. • $48 • (12/31/93) • **83**

Brut Champagne 1979 • $23 • (09/01/85) • **90**

Brut Champagne NV: Starts out with the rich, toasty aroma of well-aged Champagne, followed by floral, appley flavors and a soft texture that lets the flavors turn lean on the finish. • $35 • (11/15/97) • **85**

Brut Champagne Chardonnay 1988: A very likeable, elegant style of Champagne that's smooth and mouthfilling in texture, ample in its fruity, spicy flavors and has a lasting finish. • $62 • (11/30/96) • **89**

Brut Champagne Cuvée Sir Winston Churchill 1986: Flavorful yet dry, with lean citrus accents, lively acidity and a crisp, almost austere finish. Still has a great mouthfilling mousse after all these years on the yeast. Drink now. • $100 • (12/31/97) • **88**

Brut Champagne Cuvée Sir Winston Churchill 1985: Powerful, masculine style. Rich, and earthy wine with loads of flavor, fine acidity and a long smoky finish. Delicious. • $100 • (12/31/93) • **92**

Brut Champagne Cuvée Sir Winston Churchill 1982: Has uncommon depth, complexity and delicacy, with layers of honey, pear, toast and vanilla flavors that take on a rich, creamy texture and then glide across the palate. Long and full on the finish. 10,000 cases made. • $63 • (04/15/90) • **92**

Brut Champagne Extra Cuvée Réserve 1982: Toasty, buttery and perfumed aromas turn smoky and earthy on the palate, picking up complex mineral and pear flavors and a tannic texture, but it finishes OK. Not for everyone, but the style grows on you. Drink now. • $30 • (12/31/90) • **82**

Brut Champagne Extra Cuvée Reserve 1947: Silky and spicy, with a hint of earthy mushroom to the yeasty flavors. • $NA • (07/31/97) • **86**

Brut Champagne Réserve 1985 • $35 • (12/31/90) • **86**

Brut Rosé Champagne 1988: An elegant marriage of fruit and toast gives this vibrancy and depth. The flavors range from cherry and raspberry to smoke and toast, with a long, crisp finish. Delicious now, but should improve in the bottle. • $52 • (12/15/95) • **92**

Brut Rosé Champagne 1986: A complete, well-balanced, flavorful rosé that has fresh fruit flavors accented by spice. It's mouthfilling, vibrant and harmonious overall. • $53 • (12/15/94) • **88**

Brut Rosé Champagne 1985: A pale copper color and modest bread-dough aromas and flavors characterize this crisp, modestly intense bubbly. A lively wine that has some grace and elegance. Finishes with a touch of cherry. • $50 • (01/31/92) • **89**

Brut Rosé Champagne 1982: Good Champagne, but not for everyone. Mature, earthy and slightly astringent. Some cherry and apple cider flavors. • $34 • (12/31/88) • **80**

Brut Rosé Champagne 1979 • $28 • (12/16/85) • **88**

POMARÈDES, LES

Merlot Vin de Pays d'Oc 1996: A medium-bodied red with spice and dried cherry flavors and a leathery component. Drink now. 8,000 cases made. • $6 • (05/31/98) • **79**

FRANCE

POMMARD, CHÂTEAU DE

Pommard 1994: Light and thin, with a stalky, stemmy, herbal character. Some red berry flavors on the supple, slightly diluted finish. • $40 • (11/15/96) • **73**

Pommard 1993: Solid core of berry and raspberry flavor, full body, long tobacco and dried cherry finish and full yet fine tannins. Better in 2000. • $36 • (11/15/95) • **88**

Pommard 1992: Light and lean, with a nice strawberry and spice streak that echoes on the finish. Drinkable now. • $NA • (12/15/94) • **82**

Pommard 1991: Tough and astringent; a medium-weight wine with light-weight flavors. Picks up a touch of oak on the finish. Drinkable now. 3,500 cases made. • $40 Ⓐ • (01/31/94) • **82**

Pommard 1990: Bright, lively, juicy and extremely flavorful. Not as tannic as some Pommards in this vintage, but has plenty of pretty raspberry, cherry and earth flavors. Drinkable now. • $60 • (12/15/92) • **88**

Pommard 1989 • $65 • (01/31/92) • **86**

Pommard 1988 • $53 • (09/15/92) • **87**

Pommard 1979 • $49 Ⓐ • (09/01/85) • **88**

POMMERY

Brut Champagne 1989: A distinctly earthy bubbly with a rich texture and crisp apple flavors that turn lean on the finish. Drink now. • $35 • (12/31/97) • **85**

Brut Champagne 1985 • $40 • (12/31/90) • **87**

Brut Champagne 1982: Delicate style with plenty of charm and complexity. It's very toasty and creamy with rich honey and very delicate nuances. The finish is long and smooth with plenty of complexity. The price is a relative bargain. • $24 • (02/15/88) • **93**

Brut Champagne Brut Royal NV: Lively, fruity and fresh, an appetizing Champagne with attractive fruit flavors and fine balance. Subtle spice notes round it out and linger on the finish. • $21 • (07/31/97) • **87**

Brut Champagne Brut Royal Apanage NV: A nicely mature bottle of bubbly that shows distinctive character with its toasty aromas, refined-but-full fruit flavors and refreshingly dry texture. Add its lingering finish and you've got something special. 15,000 cases made. 15,000 cases made. • $27 • (07/31/97) HR • **90**

Brut Champagne Louise 1988: Beautifully complex aromas and assertive spicy, toasty, nutty flavors make this an exceptional Champagne. Beginning to show the rewards of age in the layers of flavor that unfold as you sip. Great before or during a meal. Best now through 2002. • $95 • (09/30/97) • **93**

Brut Rosé Champagne NV: An easy-to-drink, fruity, slightly sweet rosé Champagne with light cherry and strawberry flavors that linger on the finish. Best now. • $27 • (09/30/97) • **84**

Brut Rosé Champagne Louise 1990: This distinctive dry rosé features a light salmon color and austere but appetizing flavors of mushroom, dried cherry and mineral. This is worth cellaring, to let it mellow and improve. Drink now through 2002. • $119 • (11/30/97) • **90**

POMMIER, DENIS

Chablis 1996: Flavorful and ripe, but a bit disjointed, it delivers floral, butter and pear notes, then turns slightly tart on the somewhat heavy-handed, dull finish. Not currently imported into the U.S. Drink now. • $NA • (08/31/97) • **80**

Chablis Beauroy 1996: Racy and very intense, packed with lime, honey, spice and herb flavors, this medium- to full-bodied Chablis is elegant and steely. Needs time to soften its edges. Try around 2004. Not currently imported into the U.S. 280 cases made. • $NA • (05/31/98) • **87**

Petit Chablis 1996: Ripe and rich, with an oak-inspired vanilla, butter and butterscotch character. Offers some apricot and peach flavors, but turns slighty tart on the finish. Not currently imported into the U.S. Drink now. • $NA • (08/31/97) • **80**

Key: SS—Spectator Selection CS—Cellar Selection HR—Highly Recommended BB—Best Buy $NA—Price not available Ⓐ—Auction Price (BT)—Barrel Tasting

Dates in parentheses indicate the issues in which the ratings were published.

PONIATOWSKI, PRINCE

Vouvray Aigle - d'Or 1992: This applelike but earthy bubbly has rather pungent, mushroom aromas and a dry but mouthfilling texture. Not for everyone. • $12 • (05/31/97) • **77**

Vouvray Clos Baudoin 1993 • $16 • (12/15/95) • **85**

PONNELLE, DOMAINE

Côte de Beaune Les Pierres Blanches 1987 • $14 • (03/31/91) • **83**

PONNELLE, PIERRE

Beaune Les Grèves 1993: Attractive dried cherry and floral character, medium body, medium-firm tannins and crisp, lively finish. Drinkable now. • $21 • (11/15/95) • **82**

Bonnes Mares 1993: Light red, offering modest fruit character and structure and touches of ripe cherry and raspberry flavors. Amazingly bad for a *grand cru*. • $66 • (11/15/95) • **76**

Bonnes Mares 1990: Smooth in texture, moderately tannic and almost mature tasting, with black cherry and raspberry flavors accented by chocolate and cedar. It seems ready to drink now, before the fruit starts to fade. • $56 • (01/01/94) • **86**

Chambolle-Musigny Les Argillières 1991: Fragrant, with lovely floral raspberry aromas, but the flavors weaken and thin out. Drinkable now. • $NA • (01/31/94) • **79**

Clos de Vougeot 1993: Light and easy, offering some straightforward raspberry and strawberry notes. Quite diluted on the rather dry finish. What happened? • $57 • (11/15/95) • **77**

Clos de Vougeot 1991: Extremely earthy and barnyardy, although it's so crisp and narrow it hardly matters. • $NA • (01/31/94) • **72**

Clos de Vougeot 1990: Smooth, fruity and flavorful, well-balanced and appealing. It may not be the best Clos de Vougeot, but it's a spicy, nicely polished Burgundy that's astringent on the finish; ready to drink now. • $48 • (01/01/94) • **86**

Corton Le Clos du Roi 1993: Very fresh, crisp, vibrant cherry character and hints of earth, added to fine tannins and a citric finish. Could use some more fruit. • $43 • (11/15/95) • **82**

Corton Le Clos du Roi 1990: A full-flavored, cedary and earthy Burgundy that's assertive in aroma, tannic in texture and a bit dry on the finish. Mineral and chalk aromas mingle with coffee, cherry and spice flavors. Drinkable now. • $36 • (12/31/93) • **84**

Côte de Beaune Les Pierres Blanches 1992: A fresh, fruity red with lots of cherry and strawberry flavors, soft tannins and piney, herbal accents. Generous in flavor, easy in texture, ready to drink now. • $11 • (12/15/94) • **81**

Côte de Beaune Les Pierres Blanches White 1993: Fresh, vibrant, well-defined fruit flavors unhindered by woody notes. Extremely juicy; light- to medium-bodied. Drinkable now. • $14 • (05/15/95) • **83**

Fixin Les Hervelets 1959 • $NA • (08/31/90) • **94**

Mâcon-Villages 1993: Straightforward flavors of apple and grapefruit are lifted by crisp acidity in this easy-drinking wine. It has a few rough edges, but clean varietal character. • $8 • (01/01/94) • **80**

Mazoyères-Chambertin 1991: Earthy, mushroomy aromas and flavors almost mask the berry flavors, and the forest underbrush aromas and flavors will not appeal to many. • $NA • (01/31/94) • **82**

Musigny 1990: Earthy, bitter and thin, with a metallic edge that hurts the finish. 50 cases made. • $125 • (12/31/93) • **71**

Pouilly-Fuissé 1993: Aromatic and delicate, this silky, polished wine offers melon and smoky flavors with hints of apricots and herbs. Not a block-buster, but it has good integration and balance. • $14 • (05/31/94) • **86**

Vougeot Le Village Clos du Prieuré White 1993: Straightforward white, revealing only modest fruit flavors and a diluted finish. • $19 • (05/15/95) • **77**

PONSOT

Chambolle-Musigny Les Charmes 1988 • $58 • (04/30/91) • **92**

Chambolle-Musigny Les Charmes 1985 • $75 • (06/15/88) • **94**

Chapelle-Chambertin 1991: Smoky, gamy, barnyardy flavors pick up enough sweet fruit to balance this otherwise smooth wine better on the palate, but it's not for the faint of heart. • $65 • (08/31/94) • **80**

Clos de la Roche 1992: Firm in texture, but the sandalwood-scented currant flavor comes through, finishing tight and tannic. Try now. • $102 • (12/15/94) • **88**

Clos de la Roche 1984 • $48 • (02/15/88) • **73**
Clos de la Roche 1959 • $NA • (12/31/94) • **94**
Clos de la Roche Cuvée Vieilles Vignes 1990: Bold, rich, complex and concentrated; a tight, yet polished, highly extracted style. Packs in lots of currant, black cherry, toast and chocolate flavors that gently unfold on the long, full finish. Has rich tannins, but they're smooth and polished. Drinkable now. 500 cases made. • $150 • (03/15/93) • **92**
Clos de la Roche Cuvée Vieilles Vignes 1988 • $185 • (05/15/91) • **88**
Clos de la Roche Cuvée Vieilles Vignes 1985 • $200 • (06/15/88) • **90**
Clos de la Roche Cuvée William 1988 • $150 • (05/15/91) • **89**
Clos St.-Denis Cuvée Vieilles Vignes 1988 • $165 • (07/15/91) • **85**
Gevrey-Chambertin 1994: Charming all the way. Bright raspberry and spice flavors remain generous and supple through the lingering finish. Ready to drink. • $NA • (11/15/96) • **83**
Gevrey-Chambertin Cuvée de l'Abeille 1991: Lean and tannic, with notes of prune and black cherry flavor poking through the layer of chewiness. Hints at menthol and tobacco on the finish. A stylish red. Drink now. • $30 • (08/31/94) • **83**
Givry 1994: Light, and slightly syrupy, with brown sugar notes mingling with the cherry aromas and flavors. Like sipping candy. • $NA • (11/15/96) • **73**
Griotte-Chambertin 1991: Comes off as lean and simple, a spicy wine with cinnamon overtones to the modest currant and raisin flavors, smoky on the finish. Drink now. • $38 • (08/31/94) • **83**
Griotte-Chambertin 1988 • $150 • (05/15/91) • **89**
Hautes Côtes de Beaune 1994: Light and simple, with floral notes and pleasant strawberry flavors. • $NA • (11/15/96) • **80**
Hautes Côtes de Nuits Dame Huguette 1994: Light and bitter, with an astringent, herbal character. • $NA • (11/15/96) • **70**
Latricières-Chambertin 1988 • $150 • (05/15/91) • **91**
Mercurey Clos l'Evêque 1994: Crisp and fresh, a grapey style with plenty of lively cassis bush and red berry aromas and flavors. Medium-bodied, it has a lingering finish. Ready now. • $NA • (11/15/96) • **84**
Morey-St.-Denis 1990: Smells effusively fruity, with lots of plum, raspberry and black cherry aromas and similar flavors that follow through on the palate, picking up supple, generous floral notes. A wonderful array of fruit makes this delicious to drink now. 200 cases made. • $68 • (03/15/93) • **91**
Morey-St.-Denis Monts Luisants 1988 • $40 • (04/30/91) • **85**
Morey-St.-Denis Monts Luisants Vieilles Vignes White 1992: Tart and lean, the lemon-lime flavors cleanse and refresh the palate; a bit smoky and toasty on the finish. 520 cases made. • $59 • (08/31/94) • **81**
Pommard 1994: Fairly supple and pleasant, light- to medium-bodied, with a mild vanilla, spice, cherry character. Dry tannins cover the finish. Try from 1999. • $NA • (11/15/96) • **78**
Pommard Hospices de Beaune Cuvée Suzanne Chaudron 1994: Fairly extracted, offering flavorful, plump currant, dried herb and black cherry flavors. Shows good definition, offers ripe character and tastes delicious. Medium- to full-bodied. Firm tannins clamp down on the finish. Try in 1999 to 2002. • $NA • (11/15/96) • **86**

PONSOT, CHRISTINE

Coteaux du Tricastin 1994 • $NA • (11/15/95) • **79**
Coteaux du Tricastin 1993 • $NA • (11/15/95) • **83**
Côtes du Rhône 1994 • $NA • (11/15/95) • **81**
Côtes du Rhône-Villages 1994 • $NA • (11/15/95) • **79**

PONTAC-LYNCH, CHÂTEAU

Margaux 1993: Lean and austere with modest, red cherry flavors and a hint of spice. 10,000 cases made. • $26 • (04/30/97) • **79**

PONTET-CANET, CHÂTEAU

Pauillac 1997: Aromas of plums and grapes follow through onto a medium- to light-palate, with medium tannins and a short finish. Wait and see. • $NA • (06/15/98) (BT) • **85-89**
Pauillac 1996: Very good, almost outstanding. Violet and currant character, with velvety tannins and a medium aftertaste. • $40 • (06/15/98) (BT) • **85-89**
Pauillac 1995: This is the best Pontet-Canet I have ever tasted. Dark ruby-colored, offering berry, raspberry and dark chocolate character. Full-bodied and very fruity, with big, velvety tannins. A glorious red, this goes on and on on the palate, displaying wonderful structure and fruit. Best after 2002. • $22 Ⓐ • (01/31/98) SS • **94**
Pauillac 1994: Plenty of berry flavors, with spice notes and a mild, herbal undertone. Medium-bodied, with fine tannins and a fruity finish. Enjoy now. 48,000 cases made. • $29 Ⓐ • (01/31/97) • **88**
Pauillac 1993: One of the best Pontet-Canets in years. Lovely black cherry, raspberry, mint and mineral aromas and flavors, medium body, sleek, racy tannins and long, caressing texture. Enjoy now. 21,000 cases made. • $15 Ⓐ • (01/31/96) • **89**
Pauillac 1992: Straightforward, featuring cherry and berry aromas. Medium-bodied with some good tobacco character, medium tannins and a light finish. • $16 • (04/15/95) • **82**
Pauillac 1991: A pretty wine with bark, tobacco and fruit notes. Medium body and a velvety finish. • $16 • (03/31/94) • **80**
Pauillac 1990: This one tried to do too much; it's clumsy and out of balance. Intense aromas of blackberry and vanilla do not prepare you for the massive amount of astringent tannins. An interesting wine, but will it ever come around? 30,000 cases made. • $29 • (03/31/93) • **82**
Pauillac 1989 • $30 Ⓐ • (03/15/92) • **89**
Pauillac 1986 • $34 Ⓐ • (05/31/89) • **89**
Pauillac 1982 • $25 Ⓐ • (08/31/92) • **90**
Pauillac 1970 • $19 Ⓐ • (05/15/93) • **84**
Pauillac 1961 • $74 Ⓐ • (04/30/96) • **87**
Pauillac 1945 • $77 Ⓐ • (11/30/95) • **79**

PONTIFICAL, DOMAINE

Châteauneuf-du-Pape 1990: Compares to hot Texas chili in its smoky, meaty flavor and full body. Quite tannic and rustic in texture, with plenty of heat on the finish. Not for the faint of palate, but a good, solid wine to drink now. 600 cases made. • $22 • (04/15/93) • **83**

POTENSAC, CHÂTEAU

Médoc 1996: Charming cherry, violet and berry aromas and flavors. Medium-bodied, with well-integrated tannins and a crisp finish. Better than the '95. • $NA • (01/01/97) (BT) • **85-89**
Médoc 1995: Round and pretty, with cherry, berry and earth character. Medium body, with plush tannins. An early drinker. • $20 • (01/01/97) (BT) • **85-89**
Médoc 1988 • $19 Ⓐ • (10/31/91) • **80**
Médoc 1987 • $21 Ⓐ • (05/15/90) • **72**
Médoc 1986 • $26 Ⓐ • (11/30/89) • **86**
Médoc 1983 • $22 Ⓐ • (10/15/86) • **75**

POTHIER-EMONIN

Volnay 1986 • $24 • (04/30/89) • **85**

POTHIER-RIEUSSET

Beaune Les Boucherottes 1989 • $28 • (11/30/92) • **88**
Beaune Les Boucherottes 1988 • $35 • (11/30/90) • **88**
Beaune Les Boucherottes 1986 • $19 • (05/31/89) • **88**
Bourgogne 1986 • $10 • (06/15/89) • **79**
Bourgogne 1985 • $7 • (06/30/88) BB • **83**
Meursault Les Caillerets 1993: Lovely tropical fruit, fig and toasty oak aromas. Medium-bodied and firm with steely acidity and a touch of vanilla on the finish. Drinkable now. • $NA • (05/15/95) • **84**
Pommard 1989 • $32 • (11/30/92) • **82**
Pommard 1986 • $25 • (09/15/89) • **76**
Pommard Clos de Verger 1989 • $44 • (11/30/92) • **83**
Pommard Clos de Verger 1986 • $33 • (09/15/89) • **87**
Pommard Les Epenots 1989 • $49 • (11/30/92) • **82**
Pommard Les Rugiens 1989 • $49 • (11/30/92) • **84**
Pommard Les Rugiens 1986 • $35 • (09/15/89) • **72**
Volnay 1985 • $34 Ⓐ • (02/15/88) • **93**

POUGET, CHÂTEAU

Margaux 1997: Fairly well balanced for the vintage, with violet mineral aromas and flavors, medium body and a light finish. • $NA • (06/15/98) (BT) • **85-89**
Margaux 1996: A grapey, well-structured, medium-bodied '96 with a good level of fruit and medium tannins. • $30 • (06/15/98) (BT) • **85-89**

Margaux 1995: A pretty '95 with floral and plum aromas and flavors, medium body and medium tannins. Better than previous tasting. • $NA • (01/01/97) (BT) • **85-89**
Margaux 1990: Makes you want to dive into the glass. A beautiful wine, with sexy aromas and flavors of vanilla, raspberry and spice and fine tannins. Drinkable now. 3,500 cases made. • $22 • (03/31/93) • **91**
Margaux 1983 • $11 • (02/15/87) • **86**
Margaux 1970 • $NA • (05/15/93) • **84**

POUILLY, CHÂTEAU

Pouilly-Fuissé 1994: An uplifting wine, with a well-knit structure. Shows character, a good blend of citrus, honey, fig, spice and floral flavors. It's clean and well made. Drinkable now. From Canal Ducomet and Mommessin. 2,166 cases made. • $27 • (05/31/96) • **85**

POUJEAUX, CHÂTEAU

Moulis 1997: A soft, succulent wine with medium body, medium tannins and a light, fruity finish. Interesting mineral and raspberry character. Very good for the vintage. • $NA • (06/15/98) (BT) • **85-89**
Moulis 1996: Wonderful finesse. Full-bodied yet refined, with silky tannins and a long minty, mineral and berry aftertaste. A joyful wine. 24,000 cases made. • $25 • (06/15/98) (BT) • **90-94**
Moulis 1995: Best Poujeaux in decades. Fabulous richness and fruit, yet extremely refined in texture. Harmony through and through. Intense blackberry, cherry and violets, with a hint of oak. Full-bodied, with loads of ultrafine tannins. Goes on and on. Best after 2002. • $24 • (01/31/98) • **92**
Moulis 1994: Impressive aromas of cedar and ripe fruit. Full-bodied and very chewy with ripe, big tannins and a long, flavorful finish. Try in 1999. • $20 • (01/31/97) • **87**
Moulis 1992: Lean and slightly herbal, presenting stone, mineral and fruit character, medium body and firm tannins. Drinkable now. • $15 • (04/15/95) • **78**
Moulis 1991: Delicate and elegant, with ripe berry and chocolate aromas and flavors. Silky finish. • $15 • (03/31/94) • **83**
Moulis 1990: Round and rich, with a delicious smoky, earthy, berry character and velvety tannins. Drinkable now. 20,000 cases made. • $20 • (03/31/93) • **88**
Moulis 1989 • $21 • (03/15/92) • **90**
Moulis 1988 • $15 • (02/28/91) • **88**
Moulis 1987 • $15 • (05/15/90) • **74**
Moulis 1986 • $19 • (11/30/89) • **88**
Moulis 1985 • $18 • (09/30/88) • **87**
Moulis 1983 • $19 • (10/31/86) • **79**
Moulis 1982 • $22 • (08/31/92) • **85**

POUJOL, DOMAINE DU

Vin de Pays de l'Herault 1996: Forward and soft, with bright cherry flavors and a light, lively structure. Touches of game and tannin grace the finish. A blend of Merlot, Syrah, Cinsault, and Grenache. 450 cases made. • $10 • (12/15/97) • **84**

POUMEY, CHÂTEAU

Pessac-Léognan 1997: Chunky and slightly one-dimensional, but loaded with cherry character. Medium-bodied, with medium, chewy tannins. Better than the '95 or the '96. • $NA • (06/15/98) (BT) • **85-89**
Pessac-Léognan 1996: A very dark-colored wine, but slightly hollow in the center palate. Medium-bodied, with medium tannins and a short finish. • $25 • (06/15/98) (BT) • **85-89**
Pessac-Léognan 1995: Pretty dried cherry and perfumed aromas. Medium-bodied, with firm, slightly hard tannins and a green tobacco, tea and fruit aftertaste. Best after 1999. • $15 • (01/31/98) • **83**

POUSSE D'OR, DOMAINE DE LA

Pommard Les Jarolières 1995: Starting with pure elements of cherry and camphor on the nose, this racy '95 jazzes the palate with richness before being cut short by a firm, tannic finish. 532 cases made. • $60 • (11/15/97) • **88**
Pommard Les Jarolières 1994: Supple, but light and slightly diluted in character, with modest strawberry and red berry flavors. Ready to drink. • $62 • (11/15/96) • **76**
Pommard Les Jarolières 1993: Slightly disappointing for Pousse d'Or. Clean and fresh but somewhat lean in fruit. Medium-bodied, adding firm tannins and a fresh finish. Drink in 1999. • $65 • (11/15/95) • **85**
Pommard Les Jarolières 1992: Ripe, spicy and complex, rich and deep, with blackberry, vanilla and slightly herbal notes on the crisp finish. Drinkable now. 833 cases made. • $57 • (12/15/94) • **88**
Pommard Les Jarolières 1991: Crisp and distinctive, showing a streak of green stalkiness running through the modest blackberry flavors. Drinkable now. • $50 Ⓐ • (01/31/94) • **80**
Pommard Les Jarolières 1988 • $27 Ⓐ • (08/31/91) • **88**
Pommard Les Jarolières 1986 • $45 • (04/30/89) • **70**
Pommard Les Jarolières 1985 • $39 • (03/15/88) • **87**
Santenay Clos de Tavannes 1994: Beautiful, balanced and harmonious. Medium-bodied, this charmer is packed with anise, blackberry, cherry and toasty oak flavors. Ripe and sweet-tasting on the finish. • $30 • (11/15/96) • **87**
Santenay Clos de Tavannes 1993: Lovely rose petal and crushed raspberry aromas and flavors. Medium in body, long finish, delivering itself slowly while unfolding layers of pure, silky fruit. • $40 • (11/15/95) • **87**
Santenay Clos de Tavannes 1991: Firm in texture, but the solid band of currant and blackberry character finishes open and appealing. A real mouthful of flavor. Drinkable now. • $26 Ⓐ • (01/31/94) • **84**
Santenay Clos de Tavannes 1989 • $29 • (01/31/92) • **91**
Santenay Clos de Tavannes 1988 • $28 • (08/31/91) • **83**
Santenay Clos de Tavannes 1986 • $27 • (06/15/89) • **78**
Santenay Les Gravières 1992: Open-textured and showing nice nuances of smoke and toast on modest, dark berry flavors. Drinkable now. • $28 • (12/15/94) • **81**
Volnay Clos de l'Audignac 1989 • $45 • (01/31/92) • **92**
Volnay Clos de la Bousse d'Or 1995: Juicy and crisp, with decent, ripe red berry flavor. Medium-bodied, it has a mouthpuckering, citrusy character that provides a fresh jolt. Quite tannic. Try after 2000. 774 cases made. • $65 • (11/15/97) • **83**
Volnay Clos de la Bousse d'Or 1994: Extremely light, almost rosélike, with washed-out flavors. • $70 • (11/15/96) • **75**
Volnay Clos de la Bousse d'Or 1993: Fills your mouth with fruit and tickles your palate with tannins. Pretty Pinot, tasting of plums and sliced oyster mushrooms. Medium body, medium-fine tannins, silky finish. • $70 • (11/15/95) • **88**
Volnay Clos de la Bousse d'Or 1992: Lean but nicely focused, with ripe, smoky berry and tobacco flavors that linger on the crisp finish. Drinkable now. • $61 • (12/15/94) • **86**
Volnay Clos de la Bousse d'Or 1991: A bright, flavorful, smooth-textured wine, featuring modest tannins and a nice beam of blackberry and raspberry aromas and flavors. Hints at chestnut on the finish. Delicate and drinkable now. • $55 Ⓐ • (01/31/94) • **86**
Volnay Clos de la Bousse d'Or 1990: From a great vintage, this beautiful Burgundy almost has it all. Firm yet supple, packed with lovely raspberry, earth and chocolate aromas and flavors that end with a superlong finish. Drinkable now. 1,375 cases made. • $75 • (11/30/92) CS • **93**
Volnay Clos de la Bousse d'Or 1989 • $60 • (01/31/92) • **90**
Volnay Clos de la Bousse d'Or 1986 • $46 • (04/30/89) • **75**
Volnay En Chevret 1994: Chewy and tough, with modest berry flavors to balance. May be better in 1999. • $NA • (11/15/96) • **82**
Volnay Les Caillerets 1995: A wonderful Volnay for this vintage. Ripe and rich, with deep blueberry, blackberry and cassis flavors, it has layers of dense fruit that fold nicely into a long, lush, sweet-tasting finish. Tasty now, better after 1999. 923 cases made. • $52 • (11/15/97) • **89**
Volnay Les Caillerets 1993: Nice fruit here, but the finish is quite dry. Maybe it's just in an odd phase and needs quiet cellaring. Blackberry, plum and wet earth flavors. Hold until at least 1999. • $53 • (11/15/95) • **85**
Volnay Les Caillerets 1992: Nicely gamy, almost funky, backed by appealing boysenberry and black currant flavors. The aromas are spectacular but could use a bit more length on the crisp finish. Drinkable now. • $49 • (12/15/94) • **85**
Volnay Les Caillerets 1988 • $49 • (08/31/91) • **85**
Volnay Les Caillerets 1985 • $35 • (03/15/88) • **90**
Volnay Les Caillerets-Clos des 60 Ouvrées 1995: Lovely from start to finish. Ripe, succulent, bursting with blackberry character—it's seductive for all that juicy fruit. Medium-to-full body, with firm tannins that should smooth out by 2000. 825 cases made. • $55 • (11/15/97) • **89**

Key: SS—Spectator Selection CS—Cellar Selection HR—Highly Recommended BB—Best Buy $NA—Price not available Ⓐ—Auction Price (BT)—Barrel Tasting
Dates in parentheses indicate the issues in which the ratings were published.

FRANCE

Volnay Les Caillerets-Clos des 60 Ouvrées 1993: Succulent red, offering good concentration of fruit character. Medium in body, it has solid tannins but ends on a seductive, seamless finish. Try this charmer in 2000. • $60 • (11/15/95) • **89**

Volnay Les Caillerets-Clos des 60 Ouvrées 1992: Ripe and aromatic, a bit tight and crisp on the palate but generous with blackberry and black cherry notes. Drinkable now. • $53 • (12/15/94) • **86**

Volnay Les Caillerets-Clos des 60 Ouvrées 1990: A high-wire act of a wine that's elegant and firm, with loads of beautiful raspberry and earth flavors that gain depth on the gorgeous, supple finish. Drinkable now. 1,250 cases made. • $62 • (12/15/92) HR • **91**

Volnay Les Caillerets-Clos des 60 Ouvrées 1987 • $29 • (06/15/90) • **82**

Volnay Les Caillerets-Clos des 60 Ouvrées 1986 • $41 • (04/30/89) • **83**

Volnay Les Caillerets-Clos des 60 Ouvrées 1985 • $39 • (03/15/88) • **86**

POUSSIE, LA

Sancerre 1996: Crisp and a bit tart, this lively white shows grapefruit and green apple flavors with pretty spice and mineral accents. Light, clean and fresh, great with oysters. Drink now. • $25 • (06/15/98) • **87**

Sancerre 1995: A crisp, well-balanced white with good structure. Offers citrus and grass flavors, but the fruit is a bit muted. Should bloom with food. • $25 • (06/15/97) • **88**

Sancerre 1994 • $22 • (06/15/96) • **85**

Sancerre Red 1995: A ripe and flavorful red with smoke and plum aromas and rich flavors of tobacco, smoke and cherries. The firm tannins will soften with food. • $27 • (06/15/97) • **85**

Sancerre Rosé 1996: Pale pink in color, offering bright fruit flavors of raspberry and strawberry, with hints of spice, a nice balance of crisp acidity and light, fruity sweetness. Drink now. • $27 • (06/15/98) • **83**

PRADEAUX, CHÂTEAU

Bandol 1986 • $18 • (10/31/90) • **83**

PRATS, BRUNO

Cabernet Sauvignon Bordeaux 1995: Fresh and lively, this offers straightforward cherry and light herbal flavors, with modest tannins and a clean finish. Drinkable now. • $10 • (06/30/97) • **84**

Sauvignon Blanc Bordeaux 1995: Soft and light, this offers floral and apple flavors that turn slightly candied on the finish. An apéritif style. • $10 • (04/30/97) • **79**

PREISS-HENNY

Gewürztraminer Alsace Château de Mittelwihr 1994: A spicy, roasted note gives distinctive character, but overall it's broad and rather flat. Hints of vanilla and smoke linger on the palate. • $15 • (10/15/96) • **83**

Pinot Blanc Alsace 1994: Not complex, but a pleasure to drink with its clean pear and mineral flavors, vibrant acidity and light-bodied freshness. • $11 • (10/15/96) • **84**

Riesling Alsace Château de Mittelwihr 1994: Muscular and austere, this emphasizes the mineral and herbal aspects of Riesling, with tart grapefruit flavors. Would be perfect with a tarragon-scented chicken dish. • $13 • (10/15/96) • **84**

Sylvaner Alsace Château de Mittelwihr 1994: The firm acidity is appealing in this rather austere white, but earthy notes muddle the pear flavors. Big enough for food. • $10 • (10/15/96) • **79**

PRESIDENTE, DOMAINE DE LA

Merlot Vin de Pays d'Oc 1996: Clean and fairly crisp, with some well-defined berry, cherry and plum flavors and an herbal note that gives focus. A good, quaffable Merlot. Drink now. 18,000 cases made. • $6 • (04/30/98) • **84**

PREYS

Touraine Côte Cuvée Prestige 1989 • $9 • (01/31/92) • **75**

PRIEUR, JACQUES

Beaune Clos de la Féguine 1995: A very light Pinot Noir lacking complexity and depth. You wish for more of everything; tannins are a bit chewy on the finish. 258 cases made. • $43 • (11/15/97) • **77**

Beaune Clos de la Féguine 1994: Firm, almost chewy, but has some toasty, ripe cherry flavor, with a hint of chocolate, weaving through with some depth and length. Try in 1999. • $33 • (11/15/96) • **87**

Beaune Clos de la Féguine 1993: Ripe fruit but a tough wine, adding loads of tannins which verge on being dry. Medium in body and a solid core of fruit. Better in 1999. • $30 • (11/15/95) • **88**

Beaune Clos de la Féguine White 1995: Hints at its greatness with deep, honeyed aromas that follow through on the palate, mingling there with citrus, spice and ripe fruit flavors, even raspberry notes. This *premier cru* has the texture of a late-harvest wine, lovely balance and clean, crisp character on the floral finish. Drink now through 2010. 36 cases imported. 111 cases made. • $45 • (08/31/97) • **91**

Bourgogne White 1995: Fruity and smooth, with a chewy core of mineral, grapefruit, spice and pear flavors. Very zesty and fresh, full of life and good intensity, if lacking a bit of ripeness. Medium- to full-bodied, it needs time to soften. Try after 2005. 75 cases imported. 228 cases made. • $15 • (08/31/97) • **88**

Chambertin 1995: Old-fashioned in style, fairly weak in color and a bit astringent in texture, with green, stemmy, strawberry notes. Some ripeness struggles to get through. A disappointment from J. Prieur. 146 cases made. • $112 • (11/15/97) • **79**

Chambertin 1994: Plum and red berry flavors struggle to surface from an otherwise harsh, green tobacco leaf and mulchy character. Lean and tough finish. • $81 • (11/15/96) • **76**

Chambertin 1993: A retaste and still it doesn't stun us. Good amounts of stuffing with earth and berry aromas and flavors, velvety tannins and cedary finish. Drink now. • $90 • (05/15/96) • **89**

Chevalier-Montrachet 1995: Divine. Superrich and ripe. Supple in texture, with complex mocha, chocolate and spice accents, well-integrated oak. Full-bodied and concentrated, with excellent intensity, fresh acidity, flawless finish. Tempting now, or try in 2005 to 2010. 17 cases imported. 50 cases made. • $175 • (08/31/97) • **95**

Chevalier-Montrachet 1994: Satiny, balanced and attractive, a full-bodied white that delivers plenty of pear tart, peach, honey and toasty pine nut character. Like whipped cream in your mouth, but it shows a solid structure with plenty of lemon flavors on the long, refreshing finish. 45 cases made. • $150 • (05/31/96) • **93**

Chevalier-Montrachet 1993: Terrific potential shows in this handsome wine. Hard and closed now, it's still remarkably harmonious and delivers nice concentration, with mineral, vanilla, pear and spice flavors in fine proportions. Try now. 50 cases made. • $130 • (08/31/95) • **90**

Clos Vougeot 1995: Traditional in style, but this delicate, expressive, balanced Pinot Noir is not trapped in barbed tannins, offering a round, smooth and fruity mouthfeel. Medium-bodied, with raspberry, wild strawberry, cinnamon and licorice notes. Dries a bit on the lean finish. Drink in 1999. 274 cases made. • $80 • (11/15/97) • **83**

Clos Vougeot 1993: An absolute blockbuster, offering masses of fruit and tannins, full body and long, long finish. Needs time; better after 2000. • $54 • (11/15/95) • **92**

Clos Vougeot 1991: Firm, flavorful and light in texture, with crisp tannins and ripe, barnyard-scented berry and black cherry aromas and flavors. Has elegance. Try now. • $NA • (01/31/94) • **85**

Corton-Charlemagne 1995: Shows potential, but it's green, hard and unyielding now. The new oak, honey, spice and fruit character can't quite hide that it lacks a bit of balance, but it has thick texture, and stays clean and elegant on the long finish. Perhaps better after 2000. 28 cases imported. 86 cases made. • $90 • (08/31/97) • **90**

Corton-Charlemagne 1994: Fairly big and full-bodied. Offers lime, honey, and peach flavors in a firm structure, and a long, intense finish accented by toasty oak and herbal notes. Try now to 2002. • $NA • (08/31/96) • **86**

Corton-Charlemagne 1993: Vivid aromas of apple, cream, oak and hints of minerals. Medium-bodied and very crisp. Loads of new wood-perhaps a little too much. 83 cases made. • $68 • (08/31/95) • **84**

Corton Les Bressandes 1995: A solid, masculine '95, exhibiting plum and chocolate flavors on a firmly tannic structure. Sweet fruit and oak echo on the finish. Wait until 2000. 171 cases made. • $92 • (11/15/97) • **85**

Corton Les Bressandes 1994: Harmonious and rich, not a showy wine but generous with its coffee-scented plum, leather and red berry flavors. Fine tannins want until 1999. • $70 • (11/15/96) • **88**

Corton Les Bressandes 1993: Very woody, almost tasting like a Rioja with all that vanilla. But the flavors are ripe, delivering supple tannins. Try in 2000. • $70 • (11/15/95) • **88**

Corton Les Bressandes 1992: A chewy, flavorful, serious wine that packs pretty, violet-tinged blackberry and currant flavors onto a lean frame, with hints of gaminess around the edges. Drinkable now. • $NA • (12/15/94) • **89**

Corton Les Bressandes 1991: Ripe currant and toasty blackberry aromas and flavors pick up a touch of bark on the finish. Fresh, aromatic and supple; echoes fruit without the harsh tannins of some '91s. Drinkable now. • $NA • (01/31/94) • **87**

Meursault Clos de Mazeray 1995: Ripe, rich and opulent, with a pleasant mineral, pear, tropical fruit and honeydew melon character laced with hints of honey. Medium-to-full body, it's drinkable now, will hold through 2005. 138 cases imported. 420 cases made. • $42 • (08/31/97) • **90**

Meursault Clos de Mazeray 1994: Amazingly concentrated and elegant. This class act walks a tightrope between the intense citrus flavors and the subtle honey and toast character that comes through on the long, racy finish. Try now. 525 cases made. • $35 • (05/31/96) • **90**

Meursault Clos de Mazeray 1993: Delectable chalk, lemon and mineral aromas and flavors, medium body, fine acidity and long finish. Drink now. 625 cases made. • $34 • (08/31/95) • **85**

Meursault Clos de Mazeray 1992: A bit odd, simple, earthy and musty, with decent fruit in the middle. 833 cases made. • $32 • (08/31/94) • **75**

Meursault Clos de Mazeray Red 1993: Nice blend of wood and fruit, featuring nuances of mocha, spice and vanilla and red berry flavor. Plenty of tannins, but a bit lean. Try now. • $30 • (11/15/95) • **82**

Meursault Clos de Mazeray Red 1991: Simple, crisp, straightforward and light in weight, with modest earthy, spicy cherry character. Drinkable now. • $NA • (01/31/94) • **80**

Meursault Les Perrières 1995: What great texture. Lovely, with ripe, sweet-tasting Chardonnay character. Smooth as can be, it caresses the palate with its fruit, spice, toasty oak and honey notes. Supple, harmonious, lengthy finish. Try now through 2005. 24 cases imported. 72 cases made. • $80 • (08/31/97) • **96**

Meursault Les Perrières 1994: Nice and supple, with some pretty tropical fruit, fig and pear flavors. It's smooth and drinkable now. 83 cases made. • $70 • (05/31/96) • **85**

Meursault Les Perrières 1993: Wonderfully fresh and clean apple and cream aromas and flavors. Medium body, well-integrated acidity and a long, rich finish. 70 cases made. • $52 • (08/31/95) • **86**

Meursault Les Perrières 1992: Big and powerful, opulent and showy, it shows more muscle than most '92s. A bit woody now, but time should help smooth out the rough edges. Bursts with classy smoke, toast, floral, peach, honey and orange-peel flavors. Good acidity and a very long finish. Drink now to 2000. Tasted twice. • $45 • (08/31/94) • **92**

Montrachet 1995: Gorgeous and exotic, with the texture of thick cream, the flavors of a garden in bloom, aromas of orange, peach, apricot, and tropical fruit. Full-bodied, it glides over the palate to a long, sweet-tasting finale, with notes of spice and toasty oak adding complexity. The greatest Prieur Montrachet ever. Try after 2000. 48 cases imported. 150 cases made. • $290 • (08/31/97) HR • **99**

Montrachet 1994: Very ripe, rich, and elegant. Full-bodied, with a firm structure. Cream, vanilla bean, lightly toasty oak, honey and spice flavors. Quite appealing now. 150 cases made. • $200 • (08/31/96) • **92**

Montrachet 1993: Wine of the vintage? Vibrant and electrifying, boasting layers of ripe fruit. Shows wonderful freshness and harmony, full body and toasty oak, honey and tropical fruit character. The finish goes on and on. 167 cases made. • $208 • (08/31/95) • **92**

Montrachet 1992: A class act worth lining up around the block to taste. Massive, muscular and quite woody. Good acidity, formidable fruit concentration and a layer of toasty character make it a serious candidate for the wine of the vintage. Try now and beyond. Tasted twice with consistent scores. 200 cases made. • $200 • (08/31/94) HR • **97**

Musigny 1995: Very savage in character, displaying wild, bramble berry flavors on a rich, solid structure. The tannins are firm and dry on the moderate finish. 245 cases made. • $140 • (11/15/97) • **87**

Musigny 1994: Dark-colored and compacted, but a bit disjointed, with oak-shaded spice, mineral, red berry and plum flavors. Good intensity on the lingering, sharp finish. May be better after 1999. • $85 • (11/15/96) • **82**

Key: SS—Spectator Selection CS—Cellar Selection HR—Highly Recommended BB—Best Buy $NA—Price not available Ⓐ—Auction Price (BT)—Barrel Tasting
Dates in parentheses indicate the issues in which the ratings were published.

Musigny 1993: A blockbuster that's hard on the surface and full-bodied, revealing underneath a silky core of ripe plum, blackberry and mineral character that won't let go on the mile-long finish. It would be a waste to drink this before 2005. • $63 • (11/15/95) • **94**

Musigny 1992: Light and very pretty, with vanilla grace notes to the smooth-textured thread of raspberry, strawberry and mocha flavors. Graceful enough to drink already. • $NA • (12/15/94) • **85**

Musigny 1991: Distinctive and aromatic; earthy, gamy anise notes play over a chorus of currant and black cherry flavors. A complex wine, with a smooth texture and a good future. Try now. • $NA • (01/31/94) • **89**

Puligny-Montrachet Les Combettes 1995: Fantastic—so ripe, so balanced, so fresh—you just can't get enough. Brilliant success here, even by the high standards of this vintage. Offers loads of sweet-tasting tropical flavors, mingled with toasty coconut, mineral and pear tart notes. Perfect, velvety texture, with a long, clean finish. Tempting now through 2010. 87 cases imported. 268 cases made. • $60 • (08/31/97) • **97**

Puligny-Montrachet Les Combettes 1994: Oozing with voluptuous, unctuous honey, apricot and toasty hazelnut flavors. Full body, borders on nectar with a soft texture. Great to gobble up now. Stays quite fresh on the finish despite its richness. 375 cases made. • $50 • (05/31/96) • **90**

Puligny-Montrachet Les Combettes 1993: A bit lean, showing apple, mineral and lime character, medium body, tart acidity and medium finish. Drinkable now. 320 cases made. • $44 • (08/31/95) • **83**

Puligny-Montrachet Les Combettes 1992: Flawless, with unbelievable intensity yet great subtlety, this medium-bodied beauty is shining with pure, focused fruit, blending nicely into the toasty oak flavors. Try in 1999. Tasted twice. 500 cases made. • $44 • (08/31/94) • **92**

Volnay Clos des Santenots 1995: Diluted, weak, brick-colored, with hints of licorice and toasty oak. Dry tannins. 143 cases made. • $52 • (11/15/97) • **73**

Volnay En Champans 1995: A mixture of deep, red- and black-fruit flavors holds court in this elegant, structured Volnay. The tannins protrude, but the finish is long and the aftertaste fruity. Try in 2000. 98 cases made. • $50 • (11/15/97) • **89**

Volnay En Champans 1993: Pleasant mix of fruit, tobacco and cedar character. Medium-bodied with medium tannins and a crisp finish. Enjoy now. • $36 • (11/15/95) • **88**

Volnay En Champans 1992: Ripe and aromatic, with a stalky edge to the blackberry, currant and spice flavors. Drinkable now. • $NA • (12/15/94) • **85**

Volnay-Santenots 1993: Lovely clarity and finesse, medium body, fresh berry flavor, ultrafine tannins and long, long finish. Better in 1999. • $34 • (11/15/95) • **91**

Volnay-Santenots 1992: Beautifully aromatic, with a tannic underpinning. A vanilla-scented, lavishly oaked and solidly built Volnay that offers red berry notes and a lingering finish. • $NA • (12/15/94) • **85**

Volnay-Santenots 1991: Light, lively and especially attractive for its anise-scented currant and berry aromas and spicy flavors that extend into a polished finish. Drinkable now. • $NA • (01/31/94) • **85**

Volnay-Santenots Clos des Santenots 1993: Amazingly silky, boasting mouth-coating ripe tannins, medium body and beautiful mineral, earth, currant and plum flavors. The wood is surprisingly well integrated for a red wine from this estate. • $37 • (11/15/95) • **90**

PRIEUR-BRUNET

Beaune Clos du Roi 1991: Ripe currant flavor fights a losing battle against the coarse tannins in this chunky, straightforward wine. Try now. • $34 Ⓐ • (01/31/94) • **80**

Beaune Clos du Roi 1990: Light, smooth and supple, offering plenty of raspberry and cherry flavors, hints of spice and toast, smooth-textured tannins and a long finish. Drinkable now. • $32 • (02/15/93) • **86**

Beaune Clos du Roi 1988 • $30 • (12/31/90) • **82**

Bourgogne Cuvée Ste.-Jehanne de Chantal White 1995: Good texture from concentrated, ripe fruit, but it's a touch crisp, with some grass and green apple flavors. Medium body and nice intensity. Try chilled, with seafood. 250 cases imported. 1,080 cases made. • $13 • (08/31/97) • **83**

Chassagne-Montrachet Les Embazées 1995: Clean and pure, with rather crisp green apple and pear flavors, turning somewhat bitter on the finish. It's medium-bodied but should go well with food. Better after 2000. 50 cases made. • $45 • (08/31/97) • **80**

Chassagne-Montrachet Les Embazées 1994: Supple, medium-bodied *premier cru*, with nice citrus, pear and green apple flavors. Finish has notes of caramel, toasty oak and honey. Enjoyable now. • $NA • (08/31/96) • **85**

Chassagne-Montrachet Morgeot Red 1991: Coarse and chewy in texture, with a nice beam of raspberry-cherry fruit poking through the gravelly tannins. Drinkable now. • $29 Ⓐ • (01/31/94) • **82**

Chassagne-Montrachet Morgeot Red 1988 • $17 • (11/15/90) • **83**

Meursault 1995: Pretty, with a fresh, zingy character and smooth texture. Medium-bodied, it delivers marvelous spice, smoke and ripe fruit flavors that hold through a long, racy finish. Tempting now, better after 2000. 320 cases made. • $30 • (08/31/97) • **89**

Meursault 1994: Medium-bodied, with soft and pretty pear, chalk and lime flavors. Ready to drink. • $NA • (08/31/96) • **86**

Meursault Les Charmes 1995: Rich yet zesty in character, with citrus, stone, mineral and subtle toast accents. Medium-bodied and a bit lean on the slighty disjointed, crisp finish, but it has good intensity, ripe fruit complexity. Try after 2000. 344 cases made. • $40 • (08/31/97) • **89**

Meursault Les Charmes 1994: Elegant and fresh, with a sweet-tasting midpalate centered on honey, pear, dried herb, mineral and citrus flavors. Drinkable now. • $NA • (08/31/96) • **85**

Meursault Les Charmes 1993: Delicious and elegant *premier cru*, offering apple, cream and stone aromas and flavors, medium body, fine acidity and tasty finish. • $NA • (08/31/95) • **87**

Meursault Les Chevalières 1995: A wonderful '95 Meursault. Balanced and ripe, with terrific citrus, mineral, spice, pear and tropical fruit character. Thick and full-bodied, it coats the mouth yet stays clean and pure on the lingering finish. Drink now through 2005. 237 cases made. • $36 • (08/31/97) • **92**

Meursault Les Chevalières 1994: Crisp, with a modicum of fruit flavors and a touch of mineral character. Drinkable now. • $NA • (08/31/96) • **80**

Meursault Les Chevalières 1993: Some decent mineral and lemon character but it's slightly grassy, adding dried herbs and high acidity. Drink now. • $NA • (08/31/95) • **80**

Meursault Les Forges Dessus 1995: Diluted and paperish aromas and flavors distract in this medium-bodied wine. Bitter finish. • $35 • (01/01/98) • **74**

Meursault Les Forges Dessus 1994: Distinctive village wine. Has good concentration in the midpalate (particularly for a 1994), chalky, minerally, earthy flavors and a long, silky finish with notes of honey and toasty oak. Drink through 1999. • $NA • (08/31/96) • **89**

Pommard La Platière 1991: Generous, polished raspberry and strawberry flavors carry through to a smooth, delicate finish. A light, supple wine that is drinkable now. • $40 Ⓐ • (01/31/94) • **82**

Pommard La Platière 1990: Light and fruity, with generous strawberry and raspberry aromas and flavors that stay with you on the finish and remain smooth and velvety. Drinkable now. • $40 • (02/15/93) • **85**

Santenay Clos Rousseau White 1995: A satisfying, full-bodied '95, with honey, mineral and a good dose of crisp, citrusy lime flavor to keep it fresh and zesty. Best after 2000. 50 cases imported. 99 cases made. • $33 • (08/31/97) • **86**

Santenay Clos Rousseau White 1994: A well-made, medium-bodied *premier cru*. Supple, with nice pear, honey and cream aromas and flavors. Enjoy now. • $NA • (08/31/96) • **86**

Santenay En Boichot White 1995: Starts better than it finishes; has a slightly bitter aftertaste. Fairly well rounded, offering some spice, coffee and ripe fruit flavor, but loses it on the tough finish. Drink now. 75 cases imported. 258 cases made. • $24 • (08/31/97) • **83**

Santenay La Comme 1991: Earthy, jammy, tarry and slightly bitter, with only modest fruit poking through. Try now. • $21 Ⓐ • (01/31/94) • **78**

Santenay La Maladière 1991: A crisp, spicy wine that displays bright strawberry and vanilla flavors and smoky tobacco notes on the focused finish. Delicate; drinkable now. • $21 Ⓐ • (01/31/94) • **80**

Santenay La Maladière 1990: Light and delicate, with modest red cherry and spice aromas and flavors and an earthy, crisp finish. Drinkable now. • $23 • (02/15/93) • **77**

Santenay La Maladière 1988 • $20 • (11/15/90) • **80**

Volnay-Santenots 1990: Firm and focused, with dark cherry, currant and spice aromas and flavors. Finishes with significant but well-integrated tannins. Drinkable now. • $35 • (02/15/93) • **85**

Volnay-Santenots 1988 • $35 • (11/30/90) • **85**

Volnay-Santenots Clos des Santenots 1991: Spicy and oaky for such a lean, light wine. Polished to a gleam to show off modest berry and vanilla aromas and flavors. Drinkable now. • $NA • (01/31/94) • **83**

PRIEUR & FILS, PAUL

Sancerre La Croix du Perthuis 1996: Round yet firm, this straightforward white shows melon, apple and light mineral flavors, with crisp but not obtrusive acidity. Clean and fresh, a good mate for lighter dishes. Drink now. • $NA • (06/15/98) • **85**

PRIEURÉ, CHÂTEAU DE

Premières Côtes de Bordeaux 1985 • $4 • (05/31/88) • **71**

PRIEURÉ, CHÂTEAU DU

Côtes du Rhône 1993 • $8 • (11/15/95) • **82**

PRIEURÉ, CHÂTEAU LE

St.-Emilion 1995: Solid, tight blackberry, cherry and mineral aromas and flavors. Medium- to full-bodied, fine tannins and rich finish. Almost outstanding. • $NA • (05/15/96) (BT) • **85-89**

PRIEURÉ DE ST.-JEAN DE BEBIAN

Coteaux du Languedoc 1995: A young, powerful and concentrated wine loaded with flavors and beautiful aromas. Starts out monolithic, but unfolds to reveal smoky, meaty, tarry notes with a sweet, ripe edge. It also shows anise and chocolate flavors, along with supple tannins, on the lengthy finish. Approachable now, better in 2000. 4,000 cases made. • $20 • (10/31/97) • **92**

Coteaux du Languedoc 1994: Leather and game aromas dominate this concentrated, fairly tannic wine. It has rich, plummy flavors that explode on the palate. Try now. • $20 • (05/31/97) • **86**

Coteaux du Languedoc 1993: A ripe and and intense wine with loads and flavor and complexity. This is loaded with plum, cherry and spice flavors as well as delicious tobacco and cedar notes. Well-balanced with nice meaty aromas and a lingering finish. Drink now to 2000. • $20 • (01/01/97) • **90**

Coteaux du Languedoc 1991: Ripe and mature with dark plum and cherry flavors with some serious coffee notes as well. A well-rounded wine with good intensity and balance. Finishes with some nice cassis and tobacco flavors. • $20 • (01/01/97) • **89**

Coteaux du Languedoc 1989 • $23 • (06/30/92) • **77**

Coteaux du Languedoc White 1996: A powerful wine with a lots of richness and elegance. Has a definite mature flavor to it, with loads of spice, caramel and cream. Reminiscent of a white Hermitage. Flavors linger on the long finish, with some nice almond notes. Drink now through 2003. • $37 • (02/28/98) • **90**

Coteaux du Languedoc La Chapelle de Bébian 1995: Youthful, polished and well defined, with raspberry and blueberry character and nice nutmeg and chocolate notes. Flavors intensify on the finish. Drying tannins. Drink now. • $15 • (02/28/98) • **87**

PRIEURÉ DES MOURGES, CHÂTEAU DU

St.-Chinian 1991 • $10 • (03/15/94) • **86**

PRIEURÉ-LICHINE, CHÂTEAU

Margaux 1997: Impressive concentration of violet and berry aromas. Medium-bodied, with velvety tannins and a medium finish. Well made. • $NA • (06/15/98) (BT) • **85-89**

Margaux 1996: Slightly lean and dry on the palate, with medium body, medium tannins and a cherry, tobacco aftertaste. Wait and see. 27,000 cases made. • $40 • (06/15/98) (BT) • **85-89**

Margaux 1995: A wonderfully balanced and harmonious wine. Beautiful rose, floral and fruit aromas. Medium- to full-bodied, with velvety tannins and a long, fruity vanilla aftertaste. Best after 2000. 23,200 cases made. • $18 Ⓐ • (01/31/98) • **90**

Margaux 1994: Lichine is on a roll. Better than when tasted from barrel earlier this year, this is full-bodied, with wonderful floral and toasty oak aromas, chewy tannins and a long, fruit- and oak-accented finish. A really fine wine. Better in 2000. 20,475 cases made. • $19 Ⓐ • (01/31/97) • **88**

Margaux 1993: Fresh, simple black cherry and berry character. Medium-bodied, medium tannins and light finish. Drinkable now. • $18 Ⓐ • (01/31/96) • **81**

Margaux 1992: Elegant and silky tobacco, mint and cherry aromas and flavors; medium in body and fine tannins. Drinkable now. • $19 Ⓐ • (04/15/95) • **82**

Margaux 1991: An attractive, supple mouthful, with no-nonsense tobacco and red berry flavors, leading into a light finish. • $15 • (03/31/94) • **84**

FRANCE

Margaux 1990: A beautiful wine, with raspberry, cherry, plum and smoke aromas and flavors, medium tannins and a long finish. Drinkable now. 25,000 cases made. • $20 • (03/31/93) • **86**
Margaux 1989 • $36 Ⓐ • (03/15/92) • **86**
Margaux 1988 • $24 Ⓐ • (04/30/91) • **90**
Margaux 1987 • $15 • (02/15/90) • **78**
Margaux 1986 • $47 Ⓐ • (06/15/89) • **92**
Margaux 1985 • $55 Ⓐ • (02/15/88) • **82**
Margaux 1984 • $14 Ⓐ • (11/30/86) • **80**
Margaux 1983 • $41 Ⓐ • (04/16/86) • **96**
Margaux 1982 • $22 Ⓐ • (08/31/92) • **83**
Margaux 1981 • $17 Ⓐ • (11/01/84) • **86**
Margaux 1959 • $50 • (10/15/90) • **80**

PRIEURÉ-LICHINE, BLANC DU CHÂTEAU

Bordeaux White 1995: Some alluring mineral and pineapple aromas. Medium-bodied, with medium acidity and a slightly short aftertaste. Drink now. • $23 • (04/30/98) • **84**

PRIEURÉ-ROCH

Bourgogne Grand Ordinaire 1991: Light and spicy, with a bit of a sweaty, vegetal edge to the modest strawberry aromas and flavors. Finishes tart and lean. Drinkable, but not immediately appealing. • $16 • (06/15/93) • **74**
Clos de Vougeot 1990: Firm and focused, with a modest beam of raspberry and tobacco aromas and flavors. Lean and a bit tannic on the finish. Drinkable now. • $65 • (06/15/93) • **83**
Vosne-Romanée Hautes Maizières 1990: Light, lean and simple, showing a narrow range of raspberry and spice aromas and flavors. Silky in texture and finishes smoothly. Drinkable now. • $50 • (06/15/93) • **82**
Vosne-Romanée Les Clous 1990: Warm and spicy, with chocolaty, toasty plum and prune aromas and flavors. Full-bodied and moderately tannic, finishing with a slightly overripe edge. Could be fleshier, but has promise. Drinkable now. • $30 • (06/15/93) • **85**

PRIEURS DE LA COMMANDERIE, CHÂTEAU

Pomerol 1997: Good berry character here, but slightly diluted on the finish. Medium in body, with light tannins. • $NA • (06/15/98) (BT) • **75-79**
Pomerol 1995: Some decent fruit in this wine, with berry, herbal character. Medium-bodied, with firm tannins and a light finish. Drink now. • $18 • (01/31/98) • **81**
Pomerol 1985 • $27 • (09/30/88) • **93**
Pomerol 1983 • $25 • (09/30/86) • **79**

PRISSÉ, CAVE DE

Mâcon-Prissé Madame Costeau 1996: Displays ripe apple and honey nuances, moderate richness and a refreshing finish that lingers. 10,000 cases made. • $9 • (10/15/97) • **82**

PROSPER-MAUFOUX

Aloxe-Coton 1982 • $27 • (06/15/92) • **79**
Beaujolais-Villages 1995: Maturing now, this light red displays tea and cinnamon notes under soft cherry flavors. A bit dry on the finish. • $9 • (09/15/97) • **78**
Beaujolais-Villages 1994 • $10 • (06/15/95) • **74**
Beaujolais-Villages 1993 • $9 • (07/31/95) • **76**
Brouilly 1995: Light, supple, simple and quaffable, with cherry, herbal and light floral character. • $14 • (09/15/97) • **82**
Brouilly 1994 • $12 • (06/15/95) • **78**
Brouilly 1993 • $10 • (07/31/95) • **77**
Chassagne-Montrachet Les Chenevottes 1993: Interesting anise, grapefruit and grass flavors. The austere finish hints of mineral notes. • $30 • (05/15/95) • **82**
Chassagne-Montrachet Les Chenevottes 1992: Elegant and subtle, with a round texture that showcases some mineral, grapefruit, apple and pear flavors. 300 cases made. • $25 • (08/31/94) • **84**

Key: SS—Spectator Selection CS—Cellar Selection HR—Highly Recommended BB—Best Buy $NA—Price not available Ⓐ—Auction Price (BT)—Barrel Tasting
Dates in parentheses indicate the issues in which the ratings were published.

Châteauneuf-du-Pape 1988 • $16 • (05/31/92) • **81**
Côtes du Rhône White 1993 • $8 • (10/15/94) • **76**
Fleurie La Madone 1995: Tender, fleshy and round, showing black cherry and smoke flavors with an undercurrent of refreshing, crisp acidity. Tannins turn firm on the finish. Try now. • $16 • (09/15/97) • **84**
Pouilly-Fuissé 1995: This odd wine tastes of cardboard and varnish. Lean and lacking in fruit. 500 cases made. • $20 • (05/31/98) • **70**
Pouilly-Fuissé 1993: Balanced, with some richness on the palate, featuring light floral and mineral notes; but lacking ripe fruit and flavor intensity. • $16 • (03/31/95) • **79**
Puligny-Montrachet 1993: Very steely and fresh lemon, grass and apple character, medium body and a light finish. • $29 • (05/15/95) • **79**
Puligny-Montrachet 1992: Round and smooth, its butterscotch and buttery flavors are almost overwhelming. Also shows some honey, apple and spice notes. Drinkable now. 600 cases made. • $22 • (08/31/94) • **84**
Puligny-Montrachet Hameau de Blagny 1993: Nutty, strange-tasting; cardboard flavors. A bit heavy on the finish. • $30 • (05/15/95) • **70**
Puligny-Montrachet Les Folatières 1993: Slightly candied gingerbread and apple aromas and flavors, medium body, fruit cocktail notes and hard acidity. • $34 • (05/15/95) • **79**
Puligny-Montrachet Les Folatières 1992: Has an overripe, cidery aroma, nutty flavor and nutty, oxidized finish. Tastes as if something went wrong. Fully mature already. 150 cases made. • $30 • (08/31/94) • **70**
St.-Véran 1996: Starts out caressing the palate with an ultrathick, opulent, creamlike texture, but it turns burning and hot on the finish. Drink chilled. Tasted twice. 800 cases made. • $12 • (05/31/98) • **79**
Santenay Les Gravières 1985 • $17 • (10/15/89) • **85**

PROTHEAU & FILS, MAURICE

Mercurey Les Ormeaux White 1993: An earthy, minerally component runs through this fairly tight white. It has some very good apple and citrus flavors which linger on the finish and are joined by honey and spice. 2,500 cases made. • $17 • (01/01/96) • **85**
Rully La Chatalienne Red 1990: Lean and crisp, with drying tannins that barely allow the tart cherry and plum flavors to come out. Seems unbalanced. Drinkable now. • $14 • (06/15/93) • **74**
Rully Les Fromanges White 1995: Straightforward, with good body and balance, but lacks concentration and turns dull on the finish. 3,600 cases made. • $14 • (06/30/97) • **78**
Rully Les Fromanges White 1993: Intense, rich and flavorful, tasting of honeydew melon and a splash of citrus. Notes of clove and cardamom linger on the finish. 3,600 cases made. • $13 • (01/01/96) • **85**
Rully White 1992: A thick, buttery Chardonnay with broad, smooth texture, lots of vanilla and fig flavor and a lingering finish. Balanced on the soft, fat side. Drink now. • $8 • (02/28/95) • **84**

PRUNIER, MICHEL

Auxey-Duresses Clos du Val Red 1995: Light and a bit diluted, it tastes of dried herbs, strawberry and cherry. Light-bodied, the tannins turn a bit dry on the finish. Drink now. 250 cases made. • $40 • (11/15/97) • **75**
Auxey-Duresses Clos du Val Red 1994: Crisp and a bit simple. Of medium body with some red berry flavors and slightly coarse tannins, but a fun wine to drink. • $33 • (11/15/96) • **79**
Auxey-Duresses Premier Cru Red 1995: A chunky, solid Pinot, with an herbal quality to the modest fruit. Good concentration, if a bit rustic. Drink now through 2000. 416 cases made. • $36 • (11/15/97) • **82**
Auxey-Duresses Vieilles Vignes White 1996: Distinctive, with matchstick, earth, mineral, toasty oak, green apple and citrus flavors. Lacks a bit of the supple texture you expect, but still offers plenty of character. A bit short and burning on the finish. Drink now. 250 cases made. • $NA • (05/31/98) • **85**
Auxey-Duresses White 1994: Fairly rich and full-bodied, but short on backbone. Delivers plenty of tropical and honey flavors, but turns dry and heavy on the finish. • $NA • (08/31/96) • **77**
Beaune Les Sizies 1994: Firm and chewy in texture, but light in structure. Shows herbal, berry and anise flavors that turn dry on the finish. May be better after 1999. • $35 • (11/15/96) • **81**
Meursault Les Clous 1996: Fresh, clean and pure, with some lime mingling with honey, pear, tropical and toasty oak notes. Of medium body, it's quite crisp now, but give it till around 2000 to 2005 to soften and show its mineral, silky-textured potential. 125 cases made. • $NA • (05/31/98) • **89**
Volnay Les Caillerets 1995: Light and juicy, with some modest red berry flavor. The finish is astringent. 150 cases made. • $49 • (11/15/97) • **79**

Volnay Les Caillerets 1994: Astringent, green and unappealing for its lack of fruit flavors. • $39 • (11/15/96) • **74**

PRUNIER, VINCENT

Auxey-Duresses Clos du Val Red 1987 • $25 • (11/15/89) • **84**
Auxey-Duresses White 1994: Some intriguing floral and chalky aromas, a chewy texture and decent grapefruit and apple flavors. Rather lean, but focused. 279 cases made. • $NA • (05/31/96) • **80**
Chassagne-Montrachet Red 1990: Lean and earthy, with a metallic edge to the modest strawberry flavors. Comes off as simple and dull. • $16 • (06/15/93) • **77**
Meursault 1994: Round and fat, but lacks class, with slightly funky character. Harsh finish. 104 cases made. • $NA • (05/31/96) • **77**
Puligny-Montrachet La Garenne 1994: Opulent, showy and seductive. This is a lush, full-bodied white Burgundy with loads of toasty coconut, pineapple, spice and crème brûlée flavors that continue on long through the finish. 50 cases made. • $NA • (05/31/96) • **87**
St.-Aubin Premier Cru White 1994: Ripe and has a touch of honey and almond in it, but an odd note of varnish and overly butterscotchy character is surprising. Not for everyone. 291 cases made. • $NA • (05/31/96) • **78**

PUECH COCUT, DOMAINE

Cabernet Sauvignon Vin de Pays d'Oc 1994: Average-quality Cabernet. Has weak plummy flavors, a fairly stiff texture and a drying finish. • $6 • (12/15/97) • **76**
Chardonnay Vin de Pays d'Oc 1996: Firm and flavorful, and on the herbal side. Might be a bit extreme for some with its grassy aromas and flavors. • $6 • (09/30/97) • **78**
Merlot Vin de Pays d'Oc 1996: A chunky Merlot with a healthy dose of tannin, plummy and herbal flavors. Good with pizza. • $6 • (11/15/97) • **82**

PUECH-HAUT, CHÂTEAU

Coteaux du Languedoc St.-Drézéry 1995: A vibrant wine with delicious fruit and spice flavors: lovely notes of ripe plum and black cherry that mix well with clove and cinnamon overtones. Polished and high-toned. Drink through 1999. 5,000 cases made. • $10 • (03/31/98) BB • **86**

PUGET, DOMAINE DU

Cabernet Sauvignon Vin de Pays de l'Aude 1995: This has structure and vinosity, but lacks the fruit and flesh to fill out the bones. • $7 • (12/15/97) • **79**
Cabernet Sauvignon Vin de Pays de l'Aude 1991 • $6 • (06/30/94) • **78**
Cabernet Sauvignon Vin de Pays de l'Aude 1989 • $5 • (09/30/92) BB • **83**
Merlot Vin de Pays de l'Aude 1995: A medium-bodied wine of decent extraction, with cherry and plum flavors, but short on the finish. • $7 • (11/15/97) • **81**
Merlot Vin de Pays de l'Aude 1994: A sturdy, flavorful red with robust fruit flavors and firm texture. It's good and hearty, for simple meals. 7,500 cases made. • $7 • (07/31/97) • **83**
Merlot Vin de Pays de l'Aude 1991 • $6 • (06/30/94) • **73**
Merlot Vin de Pays de l'Aude 1990 • $6 • (06/15/93) • **78**
Merlot Vin de Pays de l'Aude 1989 • $5 • (06/30/92) • **77**
Merlot Vin de Pays de l'Aude 1988 • $4 • (06/30/90) • **76**

PULIGNY-MONTRACHET, DOMAINE DU CHÂTEAU DE

Bourgogne Clos du Château White 1996: Ripe and attractive, showing some honey, chocolate, floral and smoked wood character. A bit heavy handed, with a slightly bitter finish, but it has flavor. Medium-bodied. Drink now. 1,660 cases made. • $16 • (05/31/98) • **82**
Bourgogne Clos du Château White 1994: A bit rustic, with vanilla, pear, piecrust and green apple flavors. Fresh, though clumsy on the finish. • $NA • (08/31/96) • **77**
Côte de Nuits-Villages 1990: Lean and spicy, with more oak and nutmeg characteristics than the modest strawberry flavor can take. Could be livelier. • $21 • (08/31/92) • **78**
Côte de Nuits-Villages 1988 • $17 • (03/31/91) • **82**
Meursault 1996: What an exciting village Meursault! Full-bodied and charming yet firmly structured, with crisp acidity. The combination of lime, honey, toasty hazelnut, smoked oak, spice and pear tart flavors bursts from the glass, then follows through on the palate as the wine cascades to an explosive, long finish. Tempting now through 2010. 375 cases made. • $26 • (05/31/98) • **92**
Meursault 1994: Sophisticated in its oak nuances, and has some decent fruit and spice flavors, but doesn't quite balance them. Crisp finish. • $NA • (08/31/96) • **79**
Meursault Le Porusot 1995: Very showy. This monster of a '95 white Burgundy is like a rocket on the palate, blasting away with fruit, toasty oak and acidity. It's big, thick and ripe, but has a great future if you let time tame it. Try after 2000. Much better than when previously reviewed. 330 cases made. • $42 • (01/31/98) • **93**
Meursault Le Porusot 1994: Distinctive *premier cru*. Earth, herbal, pear and honey flavors. Slightly rough now; this medium-bodied wine turns a bit dry and hard on the finish. • $NA • (08/31/96) • **79**
Meursault Le Porusot 1993: Delicate and flavorful, a crisp Meursault that hints of honey, toasty coconut, pear and hazelnut notes and delivers a polished finish. Drinkable now. 192 cases made. • $30 • (05/15/95) • **88**
Meursault Le Porusot 1992: Flavorful and refined at the same time. Fruity and ripe, but not too showy, with ample pear, honey and mineral flavors that are held in nicely by the vibrant acidity and then expand on the finish. Drinkable now. 390 cases made. • $30 • (08/31/94) • **92**
Meursault Les Perrières 1995: A terrific '95 white Burgundy. Very ripe, showing tropical, lime and cilantro character and loads of toasty oak accents. Its creamlike texture is a delight, but the excellent acidity carries it along to a long, lively finish. Drink now through 2005. • $36 • (01/31/98) • **93**
Meursault Les Perrières 1994: Balanced and flavorful, fairly full-bodied and has nicely proportioned lemon, honey and pear flavors. No flaws, but it could be a bit punchier in its fruit. 166 cases made. • $16 • (05/31/96) • **84**
Monthélie 1990: Firm in texture and light in body, with modest tannins, cola-scented raspberry and strawberry flavors and a warm, spicy finish. Drinkable now. • $21 • (08/31/92) • **84**
Monthélie 1988 • $16 • (11/15/90) • **77**
Monthélie White 1996: Exciting, with a core of extremely vibrant, crisp, clean, pure citrus fruit, plus some mineral and wet stone flavors. Not much opulence, but fun to drink. Try around 2000. 250 cases made. • $22 • (05/31/98) • **89**
Monthélie White 1995: Wonderful, understated wine. Round, supple and concentrated, thick on midpalate, it delivers layers of slightly toasty oak, white chocolate, vanilla, pear and hazelnut. So smooth and velvety, it's a pleasure to sip. Try now through 2000. • $20 • (01/31/98) • **90**
Pommard 1990: The light color and tight texture keep the spicy rhubarb and strawberry flavors under wraps. A light, delicate style of Burgundy. Drinkable now. • $40 • (08/31/92) • **79**
Pommard 1988 • $34 • (08/31/90) • **83**
Puligny-Montrachet 1995: Well made, with a firm structure, offering fresh coconut, dried herb, tropical and green apple flavors. Quite intense but also quite crisp. Medium- to full-bodied, it has the midpalate concentration to gain complexity through 2000. Much better than when previously reviewed. • $32 • (08/31/97) • **90**
Puligny-Montrachet 1994: Ripe and full-bodied, loaded with honey and citrus flavors. Tastes round and flavorful, with an appealing toffee and toasty nut character. Lacks just a bit of punch on the finish. 750 cases made. • $16 • (05/31/96) • **86**
Puligny-Montrachet 1993: Clean and almost sweet-tasting, delivering honey, toast, fig and melon flavors that are delicious. Drinkable now. 667 cases made. • $26 • (05/15/95) • **84**
Puligny-Montrachet 1992: Broad and ripe flavors dominate in this round wine; shows some good pear, honey and coffee notes. 800 cases made. • $26 • (08/31/94) • **87**
Puligny-Montrachet Les Folatières 1995: Big, burly, rich and quite concentrated, coating the palate with creamy, velvety sensations and loads of baked apple, hazelnut, truffle and spice from fairly heavy oak treatment. A bit hot on the finish, but try after 2000. Much better than when previously reviewed. 135 cases made. • $48 • (01/31/98) • **90**
Puligny-Montrachet Les Folatières 1994: Fresh, crisp and flavorful, this clean Chardonnay provides some good apple, pear and citrus flavors. A touch diluted and short on the finish, though. 250 cases made. • $20 • (05/31/96) • **82**
Puligny-Montrachet Les Folatières 1993: Flavorful, medium-bodied white, featuring vibrant lime character and hints of honey and chalk on the finish. Drinkable now. 250 cases made. • $36 • (05/15/95) • **83**
Puligny-Montrachet Les Folatières 1992: A very stylistic white Burgundy that emphasizes buttery, creamy, hazelnut flavors accented by pear and honey on the finish. Rather lean and tight in the middle, but long on the aftertaste. 280 cases made. • $34 • (08/31/94) • **89**

FRANCE

Puligny-Montrachet Les Perrières 1993: Well-structured Puligny offering toasty oak and apple flavors, medium body, firm acidity and medium finish. Drinkable now. • $NA • (08/31/95) • **85**
St.-Aubin En Remilly 1990: Light and spicy, with a crisp texture and modest vanilla-scented strawberry and nutmeg aromas and flavors. • $25 • (08/31/92) • **79**
St.-Aubin En Remilly White 1995: A supple, easy-drinking wine, full-bodied and very soft. Nice flavors, but a bit too clumsy despite a smooth finish. Drink upon release. 283 cases made. • $25 • (05/31/97) • **79**
St.-Aubin En Remilly White 1994: A soft, supple, full-bodied and honey-scented *premier cru*, with ripe pear and toasty oak flavors. Creamy texture and delicious now. 333 cases made. • $11 • (05/31/96) • **85**
St.-Aubin En Remilly White 1993: Very distinctive toast, caramel, spice and honey aromas, turning incredibly tart and austere on the hard finish. Try now. 417 cases made. • $16 • (05/15/95) • **83**

PUY-BLANQUET, CHÂTEAU

St.-Emilion 1995: Big and tannic but a bit rustic with coarse tannins and raisiny flavors. Wait and see. • $NA • (05/15/96) (BT) • **80-84**
St.-Emilion 1994: This chewy red offers plum, earth and cedar flavors, muscular, mouthfilling tannins and plenty of body to stand up to food. Should improve with age; try in 1999. • $20 • (11/30/97) • **84**
St.-Emilion 1993: Some decent cherry and chocolate character, but slightly aggressive with a metallic edge. Drinkable now. • $15 • (01/31/96) • **78**
St.-Emilion 1990: Quite a jammy wine, with raspberry, blackberry and tobacco flavors, medium tannins and a short finish. Drinkable now. • $13 • (03/31/93) • **87**
St.-Emilion 1989 • $14 • (03/15/92) • **90**
St.-Emilion 1983 • $12 • (12/31/86) • **76**

PUYGUERAUD, CHÂTEAU

Côtes de Francs 1997: Dark, inky color. Plenty of violet, mineral and new wood. Medium-bodied, with velvety tannins and a medium finish. Lacks fruit midpalate. • $NA • (06/15/98) (BT) • **85-89**
Côtes de Francs 1996: Lovely berry, tobacco and spice aromas and flavors. Medium-bodied, with fine tannins and a spicy, fruity aftertaste. A seriously good value. • $17 • (06/15/98) (BT) • **85-89**
Côtes de Francs 1995: Plenty of blackberry, floral and earth character. Medium to full in body, with velvety tannins and a berry, chocolate and vanilla aftertaste. Better in 1999. • $16 • (01/31/98) • **87**
Côtes de Francs 1993: A light Bordeaux, showing strawberries and cherries, light tannins and light color. • $18 • (01/31/96) • **80**
Côtes de Francs 1990: A simple and fresh wine, with attractive tomato, herbal aromas and flavors and light tannins. Drinkable now. • $18 • (03/31/93) • **81**
Côtes de Francs 1989 • $18 • (03/15/92) • **83**
Côtes de Francs 1986 • $12 • (06/15/89) • **84**
Côtes de Francs 1985 • $9 • (06/30/88) • **83**
Côtes de Francs 1983 • $8 • (10/16/85) • **82**

PUZELAT, J.-M. & T

Touraine Sauvignon 1995: Cool mint and herb aromas give way to a palate of crisp, mostly neutral flavors. Would make a modest but supportive match for lighter dishes. 2,000 cases made. • $10 • (06/15/97) • **82**

QUANTIN, CHÂTEAU DE

Pessac-Léognan 1995: Rather light and slightly herbaceous. Light-bodied, with slightly metallic tannins and a short aftertaste. • $15 • (01/31/98) • **78**
Pessac-Léognan White 1995: A thick '95 with lots of apple, celery and honey. Medium-bodied, with medium acidity and a slightly coarse aftertaste. Better in 1999. • $15 • (04/30/98) • **84**

QUILLA, DOMAINE DE LA

Muscadet de Sèvre et Maine Sur Lie 1993 • $9 • (08/31/94) • **84**

Key: SS—Spectator Selection CS—Cellar Selection HR—Highly Recommended BB—Best Buy $NA—Price not available Ⓐ—Auction Price (BT)—Barrel Tasting
Dates in parentheses indicate the issues in which the ratings were published.

QUINAULT, CHÂTEAU

St.-Emilion 1995: Some decent fruit concentration to this, but it's slightly herbal and weedy, with medium tannins and aftertaste. Drink now or hold. • $15 • (01/31/98) • **80**
St.-Emilion L'Enclos 1997: Offers pretty berry and chocolate flavors, medium body, medium tannins and a fruity finish. Pleasing to the palate, but slightly one-dimensional. • $NA • (06/15/98) (BT) • **85-89**

R DE RIEUSSEC

Bordeaux Dry R de Rieussec 1993 • $8 • (05/31/95) • **79**
Bordeaux White 1994 • $10 • (03/31/96) • **84**

RABASSE CHARAVIN, DOMAINE

Côtes du Rhône-Villages Cairanne 1996: Shows fairly ripe fruit flavors, but the texture is harsh and the tannins green. Medium-bodied, with a tart, chewy finish. Difficult to cozy up to. 200 cases imported. 2,917 cases made. • $14 • (10/15/97) • **73**
Côtes du Rhône-Villages Cairanne White 1995: Very woody and rustic, this seems oxidized and almost over-the-hill. Tart finish. Drink soon. 150 cases made. • $12 • (10/15/97) • **71**
Côtes du Rhône-Villages Rasteau 1994: This chunky red offers cherry and herbal notes, with tough tannins and a vegetal finish. It's unbalanced and drying; drink up. 1,667 cases made. • $14 • (10/15/97) • **70**

RABAUD-PROMIS, CHÂTEAU

Sauternes 1991: Clean, delicate and attractive mineral, earth, pineapple and honey flavors, all presented in good proportions; not very sweet and quite light, but it's got some nice flavors. Drinkable now. • $NA • (04/15/95) • **82**
Sauternes 1990: Fresh and clean, quite light in this company but focused, revealing lively hay, earth, mineral and lemon flavors that offer good length but not much opulence. Drinkable now. • $NA • (04/15/95) • **88**
Sauternes 1989: Rich and ripe, exhibiting a creamy texture and lots of butter, lemon and wet hay flavors, but it lacks that something that comes from more botrytis. Medium length. • $30 • (04/15/95) • **86**
Sauternes 1988: Elegant and full-bodied, exhibiting a burst of botrytis character, impressive structure and spicy, dried apricot, honey, caramel and lemon flavors and a long finish. Drink now. • $35 • (04/15/95) • **93**
Sauternes 1987 • $22 • (06/15/90) • **83**
Sauternes 1986: Rather simple lemon, wax and honey flavors, offering medium sweetness and a delicate finish. Drinkable now. • $28 • (04/15/95) • **84**
Sauternes 1983: The honey, brown sugar, raisin, spice, dried apricot and cigar-box flavors are so intense they almost burn a hole in your palate. Medium sweetness, lots of complexity and a long finish. Try in 1999. • $51 • (04/15/95) • **91**
Sauternes 1947: Very dark, almost amber, with lots of honey and caramel flavors, touches of spice and orange peel. Long and fascinating, then finishing with crisp acidity against lightly sweet, honey flavors. • $NA • (05/31/97) • **85**

RAFFAULT, OLGA

Chinon Les Picasses 1990 • $16 • (10/31/94) • **77**

RAHOUL, CHÂTEAU

Graves 1988 • $18 • (08/31/91) • **80**
Graves 1986 • $18 • (12/31/90) • **83**

RAMAFORT, CHÂTEAU

Médoc 1997: Good berry and chocolate aromas and flavors. Medium-bodied, with soft tannins and a light finish. • $NA • (06/15/98) (BT) • **85-89**
Médoc 1996: Some good fruit here, with hints of dark chocolate and tar, but slightly herbal. Medium-bodied, with medium, hard tannins and medium finish. • $20 • (06/15/98) (BT) • **80-84**
Médoc 1995: Slightly one-dimensional, but very good indeed. Boysenberry and cherry aromas dominate, with similar flavors on the palate. Medium- to full-bodied, with silky tannins and a long finish. Best after 2000. • $18 • (01/31/98) • **87**

RAMAGE LA BATISSE, CHÂTEAU

Haut-Médoc 1990: Pretty raspberry and cherry aromas and flavors and light tannins. Drinkable now. 25,000 cases made. • $18 • (03/31/93) • **84**
Haut-Médoc 1989 • $15 • (03/15/92) • **88**
Haut-Médoc 1987 • $12 • (11/30/89) • **82**
Haut-Médoc 1986 • $14 • (11/30/89) • **82**
Haut-Médoc 1982 • $11 • (11/30/89) • **68**

RAME, CHÂTEAU LA

Ste.-Croix-du-Mont 1993: A ripe and luscious stickie, with nice pear and apricot flavors, finishing on a honeyed note. 3,000 cases made. • $11/500ml • (08/31/97) • **85**

RAMONET

Bâtard-Montrachet 1994: A refined Chardonnay. Supple and creamy-textured, with plenty of mineral, vanilla bean, piecrust, ripe pear, honey, lemon and spicy toasty oak notes, this drips with charm. Drink now through 2005. • $80 • (05/31/97) • **93**
Bâtard-Montrachet 1993: Distinctive menthol character, but it's subdued and balanced by concentrated fruit flavors. Thick, full-bodied, silky and harmonious. This is a delicious wine with great intensity and class. Try in 2000. • $140 • (05/31/96) • **94**
Bâtard-Montrachet 1992: A big wine with a lot going for it, quite rough and tumble now, but it should grow into a handsome gem. Shows plenty of mineral, toasty oak and honey flavors and a long, firm finish. Try after 1997. • $NA • (05/15/95) • **94**
Bienvenues-Bâtard-Montrachet 1994: Like biting into a brownie, this succulent, full-bodied white Burgundy shows plenty of spice, mocha and chocolate flavors from oak, but also some nice fruit character. Drink now. • $80 • (05/31/97) • **87**
Bourgogne Aligoté 1995: Amazing quality for Bourgogne Aligoté. Racy and stylish, with a wet soil, flinty, earthy, pear and sweet-tasting fruit character. Medium in body, it has the stuffing to age. Balanced on the toasty finish. A great success for Ramonet in this vintage. Best after 1998. • $20 • (08/31/97) • **89**
Chassagne-Montrachet 1995: Superb quality for a village wine. Distinctive and very intense, almost green, it bursts with grass, tropical fruit, butter, dried- and fresh-herb flavors, but the lush texture shows marvelous concentration of fruit. Full-bodied, with a long, ripe finish. Shows potential for cellaring; try after 2000. • $40 • (08/31/97) • **93**
Chassagne-Montrachet Caillerets 1995: Very showy, a smoky, toasty oak style of white Burgundy, but with amazing intensity that almost burns a hole in the palate. The toasty oak, spice, mocha and coffee bean flavors fold beautifully into the clean, pure ripe fruit. Full-bodied, the lively finish should last through the first part of the next century, so try after 2005. 200 cases made. • $45 • (05/31/97) • **95**
Chassagne-Montrachet Caillerets 1992: Exotic and quite minty, with floral, honey, acacia and pink grapefruit notes just bursting from the glass. Shows wonderful balance between acidity and the ripe flavors. Drinkable now. • $52 • (05/15/95) • **91**
Chassagne-Montrachet La Boudriotte 1995: Well crafted and interesting. A supple *premier cru*, complex and well balanced, with flavors of sage, oregano and other fresh herbs, notes of citrus and pineapple. Full-bodied, its rich texture tempts now, but it has the stuffing to last through 2005. • $50 • (08/31/97) • **93**
Chassagne-Montrachet Les Grandes Ruchottes 1995: A near-perfect *premier cru*, delivering sheer elegance and power. Amazing intensity, with spice, tropical fruit, smoke and toasty oak accents rippling over the palate to a long, clean and exciting finish that won't quit. Did I mention the silky texture? The thick, opulent body? Wait until it settles down, around 2005 or so. 300 cases made. • $70 • (08/31/97) • **97**
Chassagne-Montrachet Les Grandes Ruchottes 1994: Fabulous. Full-bodied, rich, ripe yet so balanced, the combination of power and refinement in this '94 white Burgundy stuns the senses. It coats the palate with its superthick oiliness but leaves it clean and fresh, while the subtle oak unobtrusively complements the pear, lemon, melon, spice and honey notes. Drink now through 2005. • $65 • (05/31/97) • **95**
Chassagne-Montrachet Les Ruchottes 1993: Distinctive and exotic, fat, rich and intense. It has notes of mint along with a floral, herbal, rose petal character and very ripe pear flavors. A full-bodied white that has a lot of personality. Try after 2000. • $75 • (05/31/96) • **90**
Chassagne-Montrachet Les Ruchottes 1992: Quite tart and austere, showing good fruit concentration and an exotic touch of spearmint. Flavorful, vibrant dried-herb and spice flavors; well-made finish. Try now. • $68 • (05/15/95) • **87**
Chassagne-Montrachet Les Vergers 1995: So intense, one fears it might burn a hole in the palate. Full-bodied, with masses of clean, pure, ripe fruit, it turns up the power on the finish. Try around 2005. • $50 • (05/31/97) • **92**
Chassagne-Montrachet Les Vergers 1992: Wonderful Chassagne, smelling of freshly crushed fruit and balanced with cream, lime and earth flavors. A beauty. Drinkable now. • $NA • (05/15/95) • **91**
Chassagne-Montrachet Morgeot 1992: Very flavorful and well crafted, showing chalk, mineral, green apple, smoke, toast and honey flavors. Good complexity leads to an earthy touch on the finish. Drinkable now. • $50 • (05/15/95) • **86**
Montrachet 1994: Amazingly classy and racy. Opulent yet extremely elegant, offering loads of beautifully toasty oak, lemon, ripe fruit and mineral flavors that coat the palate. Full-bodied, the texture is supple yet firm. Good intensity and good acidity on the long finish. Drink around 2005. • $250 • (05/31/97) • **96**
Montrachet 1992: A big, chunky, brooding white Burgundy, all muscle, offering tons of earth, mineral, mushroom, butter and honey flavors and a long, rich and unforgettable finish. Drinkable now. • $268 • (05/15/95) • **95**
Puligny-Montrachet Champ Canet 1995: Elegant and racy, full-bodied and very intense, showing great concentration of ripe fruit, spice and toasty bread flavors that linger on the long finish. A beauty. Enjoy now through 2005. • $70 • (08/31/97) • **92**
Puligny-Montrachet Champ Canet 1994: Clean and well made, the ripe fruit is overshadowed by the spicy, toasty oak now. Full-bodied and complex, it should turn more harmonious around 2000. • $50 • (05/31/97) • **89**
Puligny-Montrachet Champ Canet 1993: Distinctive and beautifully rich. An opulent wine that first comes across as very earthy and yeasty, then it opens up to full-throttle on the lemon, beef jerky and tropical fruit flavors. The freshness comes through on the long finish. Drinkable now. • $75 • (05/31/96) • **90**
St.-Aubin Les Charmois White 1995: A supple, creamy-textured, full-bodied white Burgundy of moderate fruit intensity, with well-integrated toasty oak. Smoky flavors linger on the fat, long finish. Enjoy upon release. • $35 • (05/31/97) • **87**

RAPET PÉRE & FILS

Aloxe-Corton 1995: Elegant, with crisp fruit and good intensity on the palate. Light to medium in body, it offers wet earth, black cherry, and spice flavors. Firm tannins linger on the finish, so try after 1999. 500 cases made. • $32 • (11/15/97) • **82**
Bourgogne en Bully 1988 • $19 • (03/31/91) • **80**
Corton-Charlemagne 1996: Very pretty wine, crisp and clean, with lovely floral, pear and citrus character. Tight and tough now, it offers ripe fruit that will develop with the mineral character into something delicious around 2005 to 2010. Nothing opulent, but lots of *terroir*. 415 cases made. • $79 • (05/31/98) • **90**
Corton-Charlemagne 1995: A most intriguing white Burgundy. Sheer nectar, yet this full-throttled wine stays elegant. Quite intense as the citrus, pear, spice and tropical flavors explode like little bombs on the palate, while the oak remains in the background. Full-bodied and dense, rich and harmonious, it's rather closed now, hinting at a grand future. Sublime now, even better after 2005. • $NA • (05/31/97) • **98**
Corton-Charlemagne 1994: Distinctively minty, with dried herb and pear flavors. Lots of intensity and a slightly vegetal note on the finish. Drinkable now. 250 cases made. • $70 • (05/31/96) • **86**
Corton Pougets 1995: Stemmy and dry, a disappointing Pinot that turns chewy on the finish. Lean. 165 cases made. • $50 • (11/15/97) • **78**
Pernand-Vergelesses 1988 • $31 • (02/28/91) • **79**
Pernand-Vergelesses Ile des Vergelesses 1995: This medium-bodied red hints at black cherry notes, with vanilla and coffee accents from new-oak aging. Hollow, with a tannic structure and dry finish. 250 cases made. • $34 • (11/15/97) • **78**
Pernand-Vergelesses Premier Cru White 1996: Quite lovely, fresh and vibrant, with floral, pear, mineral and wet earth character. Medium-bodied, it might flesh out with time as the sweet-tasting fruit peeks through on the juicy finish. Try around 2000 to 2002. 250 cases made. • $28 • (05/31/98) • **85**
Pernand-Vergelesses Premier Cru White 1994: Assertive, even aggressive, and the fruit flavors are modest. Hard to cozy up to this rather green wine. Drinkable now. 250 cases made. • $30 • (05/31/96) • **79**
Pernand-Vergelesses White 1994: Good intensity for a village wine, with vibrant fresh herb, grapefruit and apple flavors and an earthy character.

Somewhat lighter in body, but it kicks in on the long finish. A bit tart, but delicious now. 250 cases made. • $21 • (05/31/96) • **85**

RATEAU, JEAN-CLAUDE

Beaune Clos des Mariages 1988 • $25 • (01/31/92) • **77**
Beaune Les Reversées 1995: Light in color and quite oaky in character, this odd wine delivers some modest fruit character. Astringent finish. • $29 • (11/15/97) • **79**

RASPAIL-AY, DOMAINE

Gigondas 1990 • $20 • (04/15/93) • **80**
Gigondas 1989 • $19 • (04/15/93) • **83**
Gigondas 1988 • $19 • (11/15/91) • **79**
Gigondas 1986 • $15 • (01/31/89) • **92**
Gigondas Réserve 1994: Round and spicy, with candied plum and chocolate flavors that are distinctive, but atypical. Has the tannin to stand up to food, but tastes a bit like dessert. • $20 • (12/15/96) • **81**
Gigondas Réserve 1993 • $20 • (11/15/95) • **90**

RASPAIL, CHÂTEAU

Gigondas 1989 • $15 • (11/30/92) • **78**

RAUSAN-SEGLA, CHÂTEAU

Margaux 1996: Fabulous aromas of berries, raspberries, spice and plums. Full-bodied, with refined tannins and a medium, silky finish. Super well-crafted. • $55 • (06/15/98) (BT) • **90-94**
Margaux 1992: Extremely well made, blackberry, cherry and tobacco flavors unfolding on the nose and palate. Medium-bodied and very velvety in texture; fine tannins. Drinkable now. • $30 • (04/15/95) • **86**
Margaux 1990: A traditional-style Bordeaux, with redwood, tea and ripe plum aromas and flavors and plenty of soft, round tannins. Drinkable now. 16,000 cases made. • $38 • (03/31/93) • **87**
Margaux 1989 • $48 Ⓐ • (03/15/92) • **88**
Margaux 1988 • $51 Ⓐ • (03/15/91) HR • **92**
Margaux 1986 • $73 Ⓐ • (09/15/89) • **87**
Margaux 1985 • $45 Ⓐ • (05/31/88) • **92**
Margaux 1982 • $30 Ⓐ • (08/31/92) • **88**
Margaux 1981 • $29 Ⓐ • (10/16/84) • **86**
Margaux 1979 • $24 Ⓐ • (10/15/89) • **69**
Margaux 1970 • $37 Ⓐ • (05/15/93) • **89**
Margaux 1961 • $110 Ⓐ • (04/30/92) • **84**
Margaux 1947: Still lively, it's a bit acidic but rounded out with black cherry, floral and cedar flavors. Has some richness on the finish. • $NA • (05/31/97) • **86**
Margaux 1945 • $229 Ⓐ • (11/30/95) • **83**

RAUZAN, CHÂTEAU

Entre-Deux-Mers 1994 • $7 • (05/31/95) • **80**

RAUZAN-DESPAGNE, CHÂTEAU

Bordeaux 1994: Good, though a bit herbal, with cherry, tea and spice flavors. Ready to drink. • $10 • (06/30/97) • **83**
Entre-Deux-Mers 1994 • $8 • (05/31/95) • **82**

RAUZAN-GASSIES, CHÂTEAU

Margaux 1997: Good mineral, berry and mint aromas. Medium-bodied, with fine tannins and a medium finish. Well done. • $NA • (06/15/98) (BT) • **85-89**
Margaux 1996: Attractive berry, raspberry aromas. Full-bodied, with velvety tannins and a medium finish. Slightly hollow midpalate. 11,670 cases made. • $32 • (06/15/98) (BT) • **85-89**
Margaux 1995: Glorious aromas of violets and fruit, with hints of vanilla. Full-bodied, with fine tannins and an ultralong finish. Best after 2002. • $30 • (01/31/98) • **91**
Margaux 1994: Very light and simple, with some plummy notes and light tannins. Short and dry on the finish, however. 10,000 cases made. • $25 • (01/31/97) • **77**
Margaux 1993: Light and slightly diluted, offering some decent black cherry, earth and mineral flavors. A bit lean on the finish. Drinkable now. • $19 Ⓐ • (01/31/96) • **77**
Margaux 1988 • $35 • (08/31/91) • **85**
Margaux 1986 • $25 • (06/30/89) • **88**
Margaux 1982 • $32 Ⓐ • (08/31/92) • **84**
Margaux 1970 • $24 Ⓐ • (05/15/93) • **87**
Margaux 1961 • $43 Ⓐ • (04/30/96) • **85**
Margaux 1959 • $75 • (10/15/90) • **73**
Margaux 1945 • $300 • (03/16/86) • **91**

RAUZAN-SEGLA, CHÂTEAU

Margaux 1997: Lovely berry and violet aromas with hints of toasty oak. Medium-bodied, with medium tannins and a short finish. Well made. • $NA • (06/15/98) (BT) • **85-89**
Margaux 1996: A grapey, slightly one-dimensional wine, but it shows decent concentration for the vintage. • $NA • (01/01/97) (BT) • **80-84**
Margaux 1995: Best Rauzan-Ségla in modern times. Dark, inky color, intensely minty and smoky with an abundance of fruit. Full-bodied, very fruity, with a lovely minty berry and vanilla aftertaste. Best after 2002. • $48 • (01/31/98) • **94**
Margaux 1994: Fabulous aromas of vanilla, toasty oak and fruit, ultrafine tannins and a long, caressing finish. All in finesse. From a winery on the fast track to the top. Drink or hold • $50 • (01/31/97) • **90**
Margaux 1993: Lovely, elegant, medium-bodied '93. Well crafted, polished and delivering lots of finesse, showing its red fruit character and a touch of toasty oak notes. Drinkable now. • $33 • (01/31/96) • **87**
Margaux 1961 • $50 • (04/30/96) • **84**

RAVAUT, GASTON & PIERRE

Aloxe-Corton 1985 • $35 • (07/31/88) • **88**
Corton Hautes Mourottes 1985 • $46 • (07/31/88) • **92**
Ladoix La Corvée 1985 • $26 • (07/31/88) • **88**

RAVIER, OLIVIER

Brouilly Pisse-Vieille Domaine de la Grange Charton 1996: Supple and fresh, this light-bodied red offers cherry and light herbal flavors, with lively acidity and just enough tannin for grip. Good with grilled fish. Drink now through 1999. 250 cases made. • $11 • (06/15/98) • **84**
Côte de Brouilly Domaine de la Pierre Bleue 1996: Straightforward, showing black cherry and plum flavors with a slight metallic note, moderate tannins and balanced acidity. Pleasant fruit on the finish. Drink now. 1,200 cases made. • $10 • (06/15/98) • **84**
Fleurie La Madone 1996: This supple red shows black cherry, light meat and smoke flavors, with soft tannins and a fresh finish. A pretty wine, but a bit simple for a *cru*. Drink now. 500 cases made. • $12 • (06/15/98) • **84**
Juliénas Château de la Bottière 1996: Chewy, offering ripe flavors of plums and black cherries with hints of chocolate. Firm tannins don't get in the way of the exuberant fruit character. A solid match for food. Drink now through 2000. 300 cases made. • $10 • (05/31/98) • **86**
Morgon Côte du Puy 1996: Full-bodied and fleshy, yet with a firm backbone, this characteristic red offers ripe plum, meat, smoke and light herb flavors. Intense, yet still lively and approachable. Delicious with roasts and stews. Drink now through 2002. 400 cases made. • $10 • (07/31/98) • **89**
Moulin-à-Vent Château de Chénas 1996: Gamy and earthy flavors are strong in this traditionally styled red. Has a smooth texture and moderate tannins, with just enough black cherry flavor for balance. Drink now through 1999. 300 cases made. • $12 • (05/31/98) • **84**

RAVIER, SIMONE & OLIVIER

Côte de Brouilly Domaine de la Pierre Bleue 1994: Has mellowed with age, showing candied fruit and brown sugar flavors. Soft in texture, yet lightly tannic on the finish. • $9 • (09/15/96) • **79**

Key: SS—Spectator Selection CS—Cellar Selection HR—Highly Recommended BB—Best Buy $NA—Price not available Ⓐ—Auction Price (BT)—Barrel Tasting
Dates in parentheses indicate the issues in which the ratings were published.

RAYAS, CHÂTEAU

Châteauneuf-du-Pape Réservé 1994: Firm and fresh, this appealing red offers well-defined flavors of black cherries, tobacco and wild herbs, with firm tannins and a long finish. Drinkable now. • $65 • (10/15/97) • **90**

Châteauneuf-du-Pape Réservé 1993: Soft,round raspberry, chocolate and light herbal flavors. This lacks the concentration for aging but makes pleasant drinking now. Tasted twice with consistent notes. • $60 • (11/15/95) • **82**

Châteauneuf-du-Pape Réservé 1990: Dense and powerful, with a strange salty edge to the peppery, spicy black currant, raisin and black cherry aromas and flavors and hints of juniper and cedar on the finish. Seems raw and unformed at this stage, but has the pieces to come together into a full-bodied, muscular wine by 1997. 2,000 cases made. • $117 Ⓐ • (04/15/93) • **90**

Châteauneuf-du-Pape Réservé 1989 • $82 Ⓐ • (11/15/92) • **87**

Châteauneuf-du-Pape Réservé 1988 • $77 Ⓐ • (10/15/91) • **90**

Châteauneuf-du-Pape Réservé 1986 • $58 • (12/15/89) • **88**

Châteauneuf-du-Pape Réservé 1985 • $41 • (07/31/88) • **93**

Châteauneuf-du-Pape Réservé 1983 • $75 • (10/15/91) • **89**

RAYMOND-LAFON, CHÂTEAU

Sauternes 1991: Pretty and sweet. Delivers little length, tastes like an ice wine and shows some decent lemon, vanilla and honey. Try as an apéritif. • $NA • (04/15/95) • **80**

Sauternes 1990: Stands out in this crowd because of its stylish lilac, violet, floral, rose petal scents that delight from start to finish; medium to full in body and sweetness plus a long finish. Better in 1998. • $53 • (04/15/95) • **90**

Sauternes 1989: Pretty floral, lilac and lemon flavors, turning a bit short on the finish. • $52 • (04/15/95) • **87**

Sauternes 1988: Attractively balanced and distinctively floral, lilac notes marrying nicely with the orange-peel, melon and honey flavors. Medium-to full-bodied. Drinkable now. • $60 • (04/15/95) • **91**

Sauternes 1987: Very pretty and delicate, offering fresh and attractive spice, lemon, toast and orange-peel flavors; medium-bodied, medium sweet and ready to drink. • $58 • (04/15/95) • **86**

Sauternes 1986: Unusually tight and hard, showing distinctive floral and lilac notes and earth, soil, honey and violet flavors, all nicely focused. A bit rough. Drinkable now. • $53 • (04/15/95) • **87**

Sauternes 1983: Extremely harmonious, so complex it keeps you going back for another sip in a vain attempt to pick out the fruit flavors. Medium gold, unmabashedly lush and ripe, with complex sweet fruit, oak and tobacco. The finish echoes forever. • $58 Ⓐ • (01/31/88) • **93**

RAYNE, CHÂTEAU DE

Bordeaux White 1996: Clean and fresh in aroma, light in flavor and smooth in texture, this is a pleasant white Bordeaux. 3,500 cases made. • $6 • (02/28/98) • **83**

RAYNE-VIGNEAU, CHÂTEAU DE

Sauternes 1992: Attractive almond, apricot and lemon character and a relatively straightforward finish. Drinkable now. • $NA • (04/15/95) • **82**

Sauternes 1991: Lovely Sauternes, of medium sweetness and body, offering seductive, long-lasting honey, pear, floral and buttery flavors, carried by sharp acidity on the finish. Worth seeking out. • $NA • (04/15/95) • **85**

Sauternes 1990: Very fruity, zingy and racy, showing lovely lilac, floral and orange-peel flavors; medium in body and sweetness, quite fresh. • $30 • (04/15/95) • **88**

Sauternes 1988: Beautifully crafted and creamy-textured, displaying lovely pineapple, honey, mineral and wet earth character that unfolds its complexity to a long, balanced finish. Drinkable now. • $34 • (04/15/95) • **90**

Sauternes 1987 • $25 • (06/15/90) • **77**

Sauternes 1986: Wonderfully explosive, bursting with lime, honey, and dried apricot notes; it burns your palate with flavors that go on and on. Medium-to-full-bodied, very sweet, yet fresh and balanced. Drinkable now. • $49 • (04/15/95) • **91**

Sauternes 1983: Nice bright yellow color, rich, smooth herb, honey tobacco and vanilla flavors that are welded together. It's a bit sugary with some butterscotch flavors. • $27 Ⓐ • (01/31/88) • **77**

Sauternes 1947: Not sweet enough to conquer the abrasive acidity, finishing crisply and stingily. • $NA • (05/31/97) • **81**

REAL MARTIN, CHÂTEAU

Côtes de Provence 1990: Mature aromas of herb and sandalwood are followed by ripe, spicy fruit reminiscent of the Southern Rhône. Light, adding a dry, astringent finish. • $15 • (07/31/96) • **78**

RECTORIE, DOMAINE DE LA

Banyuls Cuvée Elisabeth NV: A vibrant dessert wine given distinction by its complex notes of oranges, raisins and nuts. Light and lively but builds to a lingering aftertaste of caramel. • $24 • (05/15/97) • **87**

Banyuls Cuvée Léon Parcé 1994: Driven by complex walnut and butterscotch flavors, followed by a tannic, hot finish. • $29 • (05/15/97) • **85**

Banyuls Cuvée Parcé Frères 1995: An intense aroma of fresh raspberries builds on the viscous palate to a firm, dry finish. Its appeal is all up front. • $20 • (05/15/97) • **82**

Collioure Cuvée I 1990 • $34 • (10/31/92) • **85**

REDDE, MICHEL

Pouilly-Fumé La Moynerie 1995: Round yet still firm, with ripe flavors of melon, pear and coconut. Showing some bottle development now, with slightly toasty, nutty flavors, but still has the backbone for food. Drink now. • $NA • (05/31/98) • **87**

Pouilly-Fumé La Moynerie 1994 • $16 • (11/15/95) • **85**

Pouilly-Fumé La Moynerie 1993 • $16 • (11/15/95) • **86**

Sancerre Les Tuilières 1995: Lush pineapple and floral aromas give way to flavors of ripe apples, fresh herbs and almonds in this full-bodied white. Firm acidity keeps it focused. A slight earthy note on the finish isn't out of character for the appellation but may detract from the pleasure for some. • $19 • (08/31/97) • **87**

Sancerre Les Tuilières 1993 • $17 • (08/31/94) • **88**

REIGNAC, CHÂTEAU DE

Bordeaux Supérieur Cuvée Prestige 1995: Firm, tannic and young; showing the spicy influence of new oak barrels. It has solid fruit and herb flavors and full body. May be even better with time. Best from 1999 through 2005. • $13 • (01/31/98) • **85**

Bordeaux Supérieur Cuvée Spéciale 1997: Very grapey, with a touch of stemminess. Medium-bodied, with medium tannins and a short finish. Hollow. • $NA • (06/15/98) (BT) • **80-84**

RELAIS DE PATACHE D'AUX, LE

Médoc 1995: Straightforward '95, with berry, toasty oak and mushroom aromas and flavors. Medium-bodied, with medium, fine tannins and medium finish. A second label of Château Patache d'Aux. Best after 2000. 4,100 cases made. • $14 • (01/31/98) • **83**

REMEJEANNE, DOMAINE DE LA

Côtes du Rhône Les Arbousiers 1996: Juicy, succulent, superbly fruity (cherry, currant, wild berry), light to medium in body, this is bursting with exciting fruit. Nothing complicated here, but what pleasure for what it is! Try with salads, pastas and pizzas now, drinking it slightly cool. From Quahi and Rémy Klein. 3,000 cases made. • $12 • (10/15/97) • **85**

Côtes du Rhône Les Arbousiers 1995: Rustic, in a traditional style, with earth and leather notes subduing the cherry flavors, and firm tannins dominant on the finish. Best with food. 3,000 cases made. • $11 • (09/15/97) • **80**

Côtes du Rhône Les Chevrefeuilles 1996: A fresh, juicy and succulent regional wine, with jammy fruit and light texture. You want to gobble it down without much pretense. Seek it out in restaurants and match with bistro food. Drink chilled. A producer to watch. From Quahi and Rémy Klein. 3,100 cases made. • $10 • (10/15/97) • **84**

Côtes du Rhône Les Chevrefeuilles 1995: Firm and well-structured. Has clean, black cherry flavors with earth and spice notes that add interest without getting too funky. It's sturdy, fresh and drinking well now. 3,300 cases made. • $9 • (09/15/97) • **85**

Côtes du Rhône Les Genèvriers 1996: A star of a regional wine. Sparkles with life, exuberant, ripe and sweet-tasting, packed with wildberry, currant and cherry notes. Mouthfilling, fresh and youthful, not complicated, soft and lively in structure. Buy a case, you won't be disappointed. Drink now,

FRANCE

chilled. From Quahi and Rémy Klein. 1,500 cases made. • $16 • (10/15/97) • **85**

Côtes du Rhône Les Genèvriers 1994: This coffee-scented red is earthy and tough on the palate, with very firm tannins and notes of blood and iron on the finish. Distinctive, but not for everyone. 1,400 cases made. • $14 • (09/15/97) • **84**

Côtes du Rhône Rosé Les Arbousiers 1995: A lovely, crisp, well-made rosé that still tastes of lots of fruit. Very lemony, rather medium-bodied, it delivers some nice, freshly crushed red berry flavors. Worth hunting down for summer meals and picnics. 300 cases made. • $10 • (10/15/97) • **85**

Côtes du Rhône White Les Arbousiers 1996: A seductive combination of lively acidity and appealing floral and mineral flavors. Well made, and shows good regional character. 830 cases made. • $11 • (10/15/97) • **85**

Côtes du Rhône White Les Arbousiers 1995: Fresh, offering light herbal and apple flavors, a smooth texture and enough acidity to keep it lively. Light enough for an apéritif, but can stand up to food. 415 cases made. • $11 • (09/15/97) • **84**

REMOISSENET PÈRE & FILS

Beaune Les Grèves 1988 • $38 • (11/30/90) HR • **90**
Bonnes Mares 1988 • $80 • (12/31/90) • **84**
Bonnes Mares 1985 • $88 • (03/15/88) • **82**
Chambertin 1985 • $100 • (03/15/88) • **91**
Clos de la Roche 1985 • $72 • (03/15/88) • **91**
Echézeaux 1985 • $73 • (03/15/88) • **75**
Givry du Domaine Thénard 1988 • $19 • (03/31/91) • **68**
Givry du Domaine Thénard 1985 • $18 • (04/30/88) • **77**
Mercurey Clos Fortoul 1988 • $17 • (03/31/91) • **83**
Nuits-St.-Georges Aux Argillas 1985 • $34 • (10/15/88) • **87**
Nuits-St.-Georges Aux Boudots 1964 • $70 • (11/10/90) • **70**
Richebourg 1985 • $138 • (03/15/88) • **91**
Vosne-Romanée Clos des Réas 1949 • $138 • (08/31/90) • **95**
Vosne-Romanée Les Suchots 1985 • $75 • (03/15/88) • **91**

REMPARTS DE BASTOR, LES

Sauternes 1991: Very light and moderately sweet, a decent apéritif, revealing a bitter almond, honey and wet-earth character. Tasted twice, with consistent notes. Second label from Château Bastor-Lamontagne. • $NA • (04/15/95) • **78**

RENAUDIE, CHÂTEAU LA

Bordeaux Supérieur 1995: Decent fruit but the slightly dry paper, reductive character detracts from the overall quality. • $NA • (01/01/97) • **77**

RENJARDE, DOMAINE DE LA

Côtes du Rhône-Villages 1991 • $10 • (04/30/94) • **85**
Côtes du Rhône-Villages 1990 • $11 • (11/15/92) • **87**

RENOIR, RENÉ

Cabernet Sauvignon Vin de Pays du Gard 1995: Attractive herb and cherry notes carry through to the crisp, almost tart, finish. Solid, and enjoyable now. 7,500 cases made. • $5 • (12/15/96) • **83**

Côtes du Rhône 1995: Supple and spicy, with cherry and berry flavors that are ripe, almost sweet. It doesn't have the structure to age, but it's appealing now. 3,500 cases made. • $7 • (10/15/96) • **83**

Côtes du Ventoux 1995: Soft and fruity, this shows both ripe and dried cherry flavors with a light, smoky accent. It's round with very little tannin—for drinking now. 3,500 cases made. • $6 • (10/15/96) • **82**

Merlot Vin de Pays du Gard 1995: A rather lean wine that combines cedary aromas, crisp cherry and plum flavors and a tannic texture. 7,500 cases made. • $5 • (01/31/97) • **83**

Tavel 1994: Lean and firm, with appealing berry, almond and light herb flavors, but it's already beginning to tire. 980 cases made. • $7 • (10/15/96) • **78**

Key: SS—Spectator Selection CS—Cellar Selection HR—Highly Recommended BB—Best Buy $NA—Price not available Ⓐ—Auction Price (BT)—Barrel Tasting
Dates in parentheses indicate the issues in which the ratings were published.

RÉSERVE DE LA COMTESSE

Pauillac 1995: Attractive blueberry and cherry aromas. Full- to medium-bodied, with silky, fine tannins and a long, embracing finish. Seriously good second label from Château Pichon-Lalande. Best after 2001. • $25 • (01/31/98) • **88**
Pauillac 1988 • $26 • (03/15/91) • **88**
Pauillac 1987 • $18 • (05/15/90) • **82**
Pauillac 1986 • $30 • (05/31/89) • **90**
Pauillac 1983 • $21 • (03/01/86) • **82**

RÉSERVE DE LÉOVILLE BARTON, LA

St.-Julien 1995: Beautifully aromatic red, with berry, currant and floral bouquet, and a hint of new wood. Medium-bodied, with good fruit flavors but a slightly short aftertaste. Delicious second label from Château Léoville Barton. Best from 2000. • $22 • (01/31/98) • **87**

RÉSERVE J.-J. DE BETHMANN

Pessac-Léognan 1995: A bit weedy, it has berry, chocolate aromas and flavors but is rather herbal in the aftertaste. Medium-bodied, with medium, velvety tannins. Second label of Château Olivier. Drink now or hold. 2,500 cases made. • $12 • (01/31/98) • **79**

RÉSERVE ST.-MARTIN

Cabernet Sauvignon Vin de Pays de l'Aude 1989 • $7 • (10/31/92) • **77**
Mourvèdre Minervois 1989 • $8 • (12/31/91) BB • **80**
Vin de Pays de l'Aude Sélection Rouge Cuvée No. 3 1990 • $4 • (09/30/92) • **78**

REVELETTE, CHÂTEAU

Coteaux d'Aix-en-Provence 1995: A wild red, brimming with raspberry, pepper and raw beef character. A little simple on the palate, with tannins that clamp down on the finish. 1,000 cases made. • $13 • (09/30/97) • **84**

Coteaux d'Aix-en-Provence 1993: Cherry and herbal flavors run through this lean, rather dry red. It's balanced, but light on the palate. Drink now. • $12 • (10/15/96) • **83**

Coteaux d'Aix-en-Provence Le Grand Rouge 1993: This velvety wine offers focused black cherry and blueberry flavors with sweet vanilla accents. Firm tannins are well integrated into the plush texture. Drink now or hold. • $20 • (10/15/96) • **87**

Coteaux d'Aix-en-Provence Le Grand Rouge 1992: This light red shows some blueberry flavors, but it's drying out now. Drinkable with food, but don't wait too long. • $20 • (10/15/96) • **78**

Coteaux d'Aix-en-Provence Rosé 1996: Firm and dry, with dried cherry and strawberry flavors. Turns a bit austere on the finish. • $9 • (09/15/97) • **82**

Vin de Pays des Bouches du Rhône Le Grand Blanc de Revelette 1995: This clean, lively white is bursting with fruit flavors—peach, pineapple and grapefruit—and shows intriguing floral notes, too. Ultimately a bit simple, but provides plenty of pleasure. 1,000 cases made. • $15 • (10/15/97) • **86**

Vin de Pays des Bouches du Rhône Le Grand Blanc de Revelette 1994: Aromatic of butter and honey, this is full-bodied, smooth and firm, with pretty floral notes on the finish. More solid than lively, it still has enough flavor to match with food. • $18 • (12/15/96) • **86**

REVERDY, BERNARD

Sancerre 1996: This bright, clean white marries ripe pear and fig flavors with a crisp backbone of lemony acidity. Fresh and light, a good match with shellfish. Drink now. 4,600 cases made. • $20 • (06/15/98) • **84**

REVERDY, HIPPOLYTE

Sancerre 1996: This vivid white has alluring mineral, herbal and citrus aromas that carry through onto the firm, rich palate. Muscular and a bit austere, but has good intensity and balance. Good with food and should improve with age. Drink now through 2002. • $21 • (06/15/98) • **90**

Sancerre 1995: Bright and expressive, this lively white offers grass, citrus and light floral notes on a delicate frame, with enough acidity to match with food. • $16 • (06/15/97) • **87**

Sancerre 1994 • $15 • (05/15/96) • **84**

Sancerre Red 1996: This light, crisp red shows true Pinot Noir character, with flavors of sour cherries, spices and light herbs. It has enough tannin to stand up to lighter dishes. Try lightly chilled. Drink now through 1999. • $NA • (05/31/98) • **84**

REVERDY, JEAN

Sancerre Vignoble de la Reine Blanche 1995: This steely white has great verve, with firm acidity and a clean, vivid mouthfeel, but there's plenty of fruit beneath, with flavors of green apples, herbs, citrus and minerals. Textbook Sancerre. • $15 • (06/15/97) • **89**

Sancerre Vignoble de la Reine Blanche 1994 • $16 • (04/30/96) • **88**

Sancerre Vignoble de la Reine Blanche 1993 • $17 • (10/31/94) • **84**

REVEREND, DOMAINE DU

Corbières 1990 • $NA • (03/15/94) • **82**

REYNARDIÈRE, DOMAINE DE LA

Faugères 1991 • $7 • (03/15/94) • **83**

REYSSAC, CHÂTEAU LE

Bergerac Sec 1996: Crisp and refreshing, tangy and lemony in flavor. A lively but straightforward white wine. Drink now. • $8 • (02/28/98) • **83**

RICHARD, CHÂTEAU

Bergerac White 1995: Quite earthy, though some richness and body support the green plum and almond flavors. Concentrated, with a moderate finish and firm acidity, it's a suitable companion to fresh-water fish or chicken. 1,000 cases made. • $9 • (09/30/97) • **85**

Côtes de Bergerac 1994: A wildness in this medium-bodied red adds dimension to the cassis and tobacco flavors. The firm structure and ample tannins will marry well with grilled meats. 1,000 cases made. • $12 • (09/30/97) • **85**

RICHAUD, DOMAINE

Côtes du Rhône Les Garrigues 1996: Has some good fruit, but a rather hard texture. Medium in body, it's a bit green, but may smooth out and deliver some peppery, red berry notes by 1998. 833 cases imported. 3,333 cases made. • $10 • (10/15/97) • **77**

Côtes du Rhône-Villages Cairanne 1996: A beauty. Full-bodied and rich in texture, with appealing complexity that plays on spice, mocha, pepper and red berry. Fresh and lively, yet with ripe, sweet tannins, it's a delight. The long, elegant finish will cut right through a rare steak. Delicious now. • $14 • (10/15/97) • **86**

Côtes du Rhône-Villages Cairanne 1995: Lively and flavorful, medium- to full-bodied, showing some nice, fairly ripe red berry notes along with crushed black pepper, toasty oak character. Ripe tannins and good, lush texture. Drinkable now. 5,833 cases made. • $14 • (10/15/97) • **86**

RICHEAUME, DOMAINE

Syrah Côtes de Provence 1988 • $15 • (10/31/90) • **73**

RICHEMONT

Cabernet Sauvignon Vin de Pays d'Oc Reserve 1995: Rich and nicely concentrated, with dark plum, cherry and an herbal note on the finish. A firm backbone of tannins gives some power. Finishes with a burst of berry and spice. Drink now through 2000. • $7 • (04/30/98) • **85**

Chardonnay Vin de Pays d'Oc 1994 • $6 • (12/15/95) • **85**

Chardonnay Vin de Pays d'Oc Reserve 1996: A good, straightforward Chardonnay with pleasant pear and apple flavors and a spicy note. Drink now. • $7 • (03/31/98) • **82**

Merlot Vin de Pays d'Oc 1993 • $6 • (10/31/95) • **81**

Merlot Vin de Pays d'Oc Reserve 1995: There are some nice spice and ripe plum flavors in this wine, but it finishes on a tart note. Drink now. • $7 • (03/31/98) • **79**

Sauvignon Blanc Vin de Pays d'Oc 1994 • $6 • (02/29/96) • **82**

Sauvignon Blanc Vin de Pays d'Oc Reserve 1996: A fairly tart, crisp Sauvignon Blanc with some nice citrus and herbal flavors. Drink now. • $7 • (03/31/98) • **82**

Syrah Vin de Pays d'Oc 1993 • $6 • (10/31/95) • **83**

Syrah Vin de Pays d'Oc Reserve 1995: Wow, check out the price and score on this ripe and rich French red. A lush-tasting wine in the international style, it offers an interesting mix of dark cherry and plum flavors complemented by a good dose of spice and mint. 5,000 cases imported. Drink now. • $7 • (04/30/98) BB • **87**

RIEUSSEC, CHÂTEAU

Sauternes 1993: Rich, ripe and sweet, like orange marmalade, yet exhibiting terrific acidity and exotic dry apricot, date, and chocolate flavors. Seductive and fabulously concentrated. Tempting now, but should be great through 2000. 2,000 cases made. • $NA • (04/15/95) • **92**

Sauternes 1992: Racy, well made and classy, quite light, but what's there is super, featuring pretty floral, honey, cream and nut flavors. • $NA • (04/15/95) • **85**

Sauternes 1991: Great for the vintage. Deep amber color, showing cedar, honey, orange-peel and spice character. Medium-bodied and quite sweet; long finish. Already perfect to drink. • $NA • (04/15/95) • **88**

Sauternes 1990: Richly textured and velvety, offering plenty of butterscotch, toasty oak, lime and tropical flavors that caress your palate. Great now, but should hold until 1999. • $58 • (04/15/95) • **92**

Sauternes 1989: Well proportioned and delicately built, delivering plenty of honey, spice and earth-mineral flavors. Drinkable now. • $62 • (04/15/95) • **89**

Sauternes 1988: Splendid, elegant, intensely spicy botrytized fruit character, rich and fat, kept in balance by an undertow of lemon-laced acidity. Drinkable now. • $55 • (04/15/95) • **91**

Sauternes 1987 • $32 • (06/15/90) • **89**

Sauternes 1986: Quite exotic and intense toasty coconut, honey and vanilla flavors, but the fruit seems buried by new oak character and it tastes a bit hot on the finish. Might improve with age. • $50 • (04/15/95) • **89**

Sauternes 1985: Pretty yellow straw color, elegant style with honey and buttery flavors that are of medium depth. Has some richness and length, finishing with a buttery, brown sugar flavor and honey. Decent length. • $38 • (05/31/88) • **86**

Sauternes 1983: Nectarlike if a bit on the sweet side, impressively complex, concentrated and focused. Deep gold, big, sweet and rich, with gobs of concentrated fig, brown sugar, butterscotch and oak flavor. A knockout. • $48 Ⓐ • (01/31/88) • **94**

Sauternes 1982 • $13 • (02/01/85) • **86**

Sauternes 1981 • $14 • (12/01/84) • **90**

RION PÈRE & FILS

Clos Vougeot 1987 • $48 • (11/15/90) • **86**

Nuits-St.-Georges Aux Murgers 1987 • $31 • (03/31/90) • **79**

RION, ARMELLE & BERNARD

Chambolle-Musigny Les Echésaux 1992: Where is the fruit? This is more water than wine, with light floral, raspberry, strawberry and cherry notes. Ready now. 225 cases made. • $24 • (12/15/94) • **75**

Nuits-St.-Georges 1992: Light and earthy, with a sour edge to the red berry flavors that turn musty on the finish. 195 cases made. • $32 • (12/15/94) • **74**

Nuits-St.-Georges Les Damodes 1992: Fresh and youthful, quite light, but with enough raspberry and cherry flavors to make it appealing. It's for drinking early. 216 cases made; 75 imported. 216 cases made. • $35 • (12/15/94) • **83**

Vosne-Romanée 1992: Light, earthy and herbal, with more tea leaf and tobacco flavors than fruit. Smooth texture though. Drinkable now. 325 cases made. • $24 • (12/15/94) • **77**

RION, DANIEL

Chambolle-Musigny Aux Beaux Bruns 1991: An odd but distinctive wine. Drinkable now. 100 cases made. • $43 Ⓐ • (01/31/94) • **76**

Chambolle-Musigny Aux Beaux Bruns 1989 • $45 • (01/31/92) • **89**

Chambolle-Musigny Aux Beaux Bruns 1988 • $37 • (01/31/91) • **87**

Chambolle-Musigny Aux Beaux Bruns 1986 • $39 • (04/15/89) • **86**

Chambolle-Musigny Aux Beaux Bruns 1985 • $33 • (03/31/88) • **88**

FRANCE

Chambolle-Musigny Les Charmes 1995: Superseductive, beautifully perfumed, intensely flavored. Quite minty and plummy, with some rose petal flavors. Turns a bit lean on the finish, but should smooth out around 1999. 150 cases made. • $82 • (11/15/97) • **87**

Chambolle-Musigny Les Charmes 1994: Crisp and sharply focused, shining a bright, clear beam of raspberry and strawberry flavors through the thin veil of fine tannin. Flavors echo beautifully on the finish. Delicious now and through 2000. • $58 • (11/15/96) • **88**

Chambolle-Musigny Les Charmes 1993: Elegant, perfumed red offering lovely vanilla, plum and berry aromas and flavors, medium body and tannins and soft, caressing finish. Better after 2000. • $63 • (11/15/95) • **92**

Chambolle-Musigny Les Charmes 1991: Floral and minty, almost menthollike overtones. Medium-weight, modestly tannic, ultimately simple and straightforward. Drinkable now. 120 cases made. • $70 Ⓐ • (01/31/94) • **84**

Clos Vougeot 1995: Wonderful aromas, fresh and deep. The spicy, red berry flavor takes on some vanilla and smoky notes from new oak, and the overall impression is elegant and stylish. Tough tannins. Try in 2000. 137 cases made. • $99 • (11/15/97) • **91**

Clos Vougeot 1994: Fresh, youthful and focused. A sturdy wine with bright currant, berry, mineral and spice flavors wrapped in a racy finish with a lingering echo of fruit and spice. Give until 1999 to 2002 to settle down, tame the firm tannins. • $76 • (11/15/96) • **92**

Clos Vougeot 1993: A giant of a wine. The greatest Clos Vougeot we have ever tasted. Mint, spice, dried herb and red berry flavors, full body, loads of tannins and a long, silky finish. An amazing wine, even for such a great vintage. Try in 2000 or later. 225 cases made. • $90 • (11/15/95) HR • **97**

Clos Vougeot 1992: Aromatic and more flavorful than most; packed with floral, mint, currant and blackberry notes, hinting at smoke on the chewy finish. Drinkable now. 150 cases made. • $90 • (12/15/94) • **89**

Clos Vougeot 1991: Offers a firm texture and a strong floral, minty tinge to the narrow band of jammy berry flavors. Well crafted for the vintage. Drinkable now. 90 cases made. • $85 Ⓐ • (01/31/94) • **87**

Clos Vougeot 1990: As classy as it gets in Burgundy. A great balancing act of power and elegance, boasting seductive black cherry, currant, smoke and earth flavors that take you for a memorable ride. Drinkable now. 100 cases made. • $100 • (12/15/92) • **97**

Clos Vougeot 1989 • $94 • (01/31/92) • **92**

Clos Vougeot 1988 • $53 Ⓐ • (01/31/91) • **92**

Clos Vougeot 1986 • $70 • (04/15/89) • **90**

Côte de Nuits-Villages 1993: Aromatic and seductive, offering rose petal, floral, perfumy, wet earth notes, medium body and tannins and excellent balance. Drinkable now. • $17 • (11/15/95) • **87**

Côte de Nuits-Villages 1990: Shows lots of class in the smoky berry and earth flavors and silky tannins. Drinkable now. 600 cases made. • $25 • (12/15/92) • **85**

Côte de Nuits-Villages 1986 • $15 • (07/31/88) • **81**

Nuits-St.-Georges 1986 • $31 • (04/30/89) • **85**

Nuits-St.-Georges 1985 • $28 • (03/15/88) • **85**

Nuits-St.-Georges Aux Lavières 1991: Firm, almost fleshy, with a generous beam of berry and minty oak flavors. Drinkable now. 250 cases made. • $35 Ⓐ • (01/31/94) • **86**

Nuits-St.-Georges Aux Lavières 1988 • $33 • (02/15/91) HR • **93**

Nuits-St.-Georges Aux Lavières 1987 • $21 • (04/30/90) • **87**

Nuits-St.-Georges Aux Vignerondes 1995: Very seductive, packed with rose petal, mint and cassis aromas and flavors. It smells so delicious you could just keep sniffing it, but it's a bit crisp and tough on the palate, and the tannins clamp down on the slightly drying finish. Too bad. May be better after 1999. 150 cases made. • $66 • (11/15/97) • **86**

Nuits-St.-Georges Aux Vignerondes 1994: Very aromatic, showing plenty of pretty rose petal, currant, mint and spice flavors. Of medium body, delicious, with a beam of pure fruit intensity that turns slightly crisp on the finish. See if it fleshes out by 1999. • $43 • (11/15/96) • **87**

Nuits-St.-Georges Aux Vignerondes 1993: Can Nuits get much better than this? The well-defined red berry flavors blend in spice and earth, unfolding beautifully to a long, refined but firm finish. A class act that's tempting now, but try to hold off until 2000. • $50 • (11/15/95) • **94**

Nuits-St.-Georges Aux Vignerondes 1992: Aromas and flavors with a minty underbrush character pervade this chewy, medium-weight wine. Pretty berry flavors finally emerge on the finish. Drinkable now. 200 cases made. • $NA • (12/15/94) • **84**

Key: SS—Spectator Selection CS—Cellar Selection HR—Highly Recommended BB—Best Buy $NA—Price not available Ⓐ—Auction Price (BT)—Barrel Tasting
Dates in parentheses indicate the issues in which the ratings were published.

Nuits-St.-Georges Aux Vignerondes 1991: Minty and exotic, showing distinctive herbal overtones to the basic berry flavors in a medium-weight, otherwise staightforward wine. Drinkable now. 200 cases made. • $52 Ⓐ • (01/31/94) • **84**

Nuits-St.-Georges Aux Vignerondes 1990: Superbly made, with great elegance. Has gorgeous flavors that show an array of mint, raspberry and cherry nuances, a fantastic tannin structure and great elegance. Drinkable now. 220 cases made. • $70 • (12/15/92) • **92**

Nuits-St.-Georges Aux Vignerondes 1989 • $63 • (01/31/92) • **93**

Nuits-St.-Georges Aux Vignerondes 1988 • $54 • (01/31/91) • **92**

Nuits-St.-Georges Aux Vignerondes 1987 • $35 • (04/30/90) • **95**

Nuits-St.-Georges Aux Vignerondes 1986 • $43 • (04/30/89) • **88**

Nuits-St.-Georges Aux Vignerondes 1985 • $40 • (03/15/88) • **91**

Nuits-St.-Georges Clos des Argillières 1995: This silky, medium-bodied red offers beautiful aromas of spicy Pinot fruit: red berries, licorice, violets and earth. Succulent and stylish, this should drink well from 1999. 180 cases made. • $66 • (11/15/97) • **90**

Nuits-St.-Georges Clos des Argillières 1994: Subtle and delicate, balanced on a small scale. Pushes the envelope of this vintage without turning too tannic. Medium-bodied and well made, with flavors of plum, currant and spice. Drinkable now. • $43 • (11/15/96) • **85**

Nuits-St.-Georges Clos des Argillières 1993: Lots of ripe fruit character, almost verging on raisins. Full in body, adding ripe, rich tannins and a long spicy, berry aftertaste. Try in 2000. • $50 • (11/15/95) • **88**

Nuits-St.-Georges Clos des Argillières 1992: Lean and crisp, bright but a little shy, with a minty component to the berry and currant flavors. Fine tannins. Drinkable now. 250 cases made. • $55 • (12/15/94) • **85**

Nuits-St.-Georges Les Argillières 1991: Light but nicely balanced, showing a pleasant range of raspberry, strawberry and mint aromas and flavors. Drinkable now. 300 cases made. • $52 • (01/31/94) • **82**

Nuits-St.-Georges Les Argillières 1990: A delicious wine, with gorgeous aromas of violets, rose petals and black currants. Medium-bodied, with sweet, ripe fruit flavors and a fine tannin structure. 600 cases made. • $52 Ⓐ • (12/15/92) • **93**

Nuits-St.-Georges Les Argillières 1989 • $63 • (01/31/92) • **91**

Nuits-St.-Georges Les Argillières 1988 • $48 • (01/31/91) HR • **91**

Nuits-St.-Georges Les Argillières 1987 • $36 • (04/30/90) • **92**

Nuits-St.-Georges Les Argillières 1986 • $47 • (04/30/89) • **90**

Nuits-St.-Georges Les Argillières 1985 • $75 • (03/15/88) • **94**

Nuits-St.-Georges Les Grandes Vignes 1995: The deep, black fruit aromas are impressive in this red, and the ripe flavors are accented by a mineral and earth component. It's round and supple, with firm tannins and a medium finish. Drink from 2000. 250 cases made. • $44 • (11/15/97) • **90**

Nuits-St.-Georges Les Grandes Vignes 1994: Light and crisp, with floral notes and a fine thread of berry flavor to carry it. • $30 • (11/15/96) • **80**

Nuits-St.-Georges Les Grandes Vignes 1993: Just super, and as good as a barrel sample earlier this year. Tight and silky, boasting solid fruit, firm tannins and plenty of alluring cherry, mineral character. Drinkable now. • $32 • (11/15/95) • **93**

Nuits-St.-Georges Les Grandes Vignes 1992: Light and a little chunky, but the grapey currant flavor makes it appealing. Drinkable now. 300 cases made. • $36 • (12/15/94) • **81**

Nuits-St.-Georges Les Grandes Vignes 1990: Extremely fruity, with gorgeous rose petal, berry and violet aromas and flavors, a refined tannin structure and long finish. Drinkable now. • $42 • (12/15/92) • **92**

Nuits-St.-Georges Les Grandes Vignes 1989 • $38 • (01/31/92) • **88**

Nuits-St.-Georges Les Hauts Pruliers 1995: A flatterer. This silky '95 shows off gorgeous blackberry and cherry notes. Round and medium-bodied, with fine tannins that should smooth out by 1999. 130 cases made. • $66 • (11/15/97) • **86**

Nuits-St.-Georges Les Hauts Pruliers 1994: The violet, rose petal, mint and currant aromas are seductive, and there is some pretty fruit flavor in this medium-bodied wine. Drinkable now. • $43 • (11/15/96) • **85**

Nuits-St.-Georges Les Pruliers 1993: Slightly one-dimensional in plum flavor but a solid red, delivering medium body, firm tannins and fruity finish. Drinkable now. • $50 • (11/15/95) • **88**

Nuits-St.-Georges Les Pruliers 1991: Light and fragrant; the lively currant and floral aromas and flavors remain fresh and crisp through the finish. Drinkable now. 200 cases made. • $54 Ⓐ • (01/31/94) • **84**

Nuits-St.-Georges Les Pruliers 1990: Not a big wine, but shows beautiful fruit aromas and flavors. Violet, floral and currant characteristics practically jump out of the glass. Drinkable now. 190 cases made. • $70 • (12/15/92) • **90**

Nuits-St.-Georges Les Pruliers 1989 • $63 • (01/31/92) • **92**

Nuits-St.-Georges Les Pruliers 1988 • $54 • (01/31/91) • **91**

Nuits-St.-Georges Les Pruliers 1987 • $35 • (04/30/90) • **91**

Nuits-St.-Georges Les Pruliers 1986 • $45 • (04/30/89) • **91**
Nuits-St.-Georges Les Pruliers 1985 • $43 • (03/15/88) • **88**
Vosne-Romanée 1995: Completely seductive. Pure, spicy berry and floral character cascades from the glass as the silky fruit glides across the palate. All the elegance and finesse one expects from this appellation are on display here. The flavors are intense and long, and need until 1999 to harmonize. 500 cases made. • $44 • (11/15/97) • **90**
Vosne-Romanée 1994: Shows some zingy currant flavor, flowing beneath the detached tannins. Ready to drink. • $30 • (11/15/96) • **81**
Vosne-Romanée 1993: Extremely rich raspberry and dried herb aromas and flavors. Medium- to full-bodied, silky tannins, long finish. Drinkable now. • $32 • (11/15/95) • **90**
Vosne-Romanée 1991: Crisp, focused, light and lean; has earthy anise-scented berry flavors along with nice rose petal shadings on the finish. Drinkable now. 650 cases made. • $35 Ⓐ • (01/31/94) • **83**
Vosne-Romanée 1990: This incredibly complex village wine shows wonderful rose, raspberry and oak aromas. Full-bodied, with silky, fine tannins and great finesse. Drinkable now. 500 cases made. • $42 • (12/15/92) • **91**
Vosne-Romanée 1989 • $37 • (01/31/92) • **89**
Vosne-Romanée 1987 • $21 • (04/30/90) • **89**
Vosne-Romanée 1986 • $31 • (04/30/89) • **87**
Vosne-Romanée 1985 • $28 • (02/29/88) • **78**
Vosne-Romanée Les Beaux Monts 1995: A symphony of seductive flavors, featuring violet, toasty bread, rose petal, jasmine, blackberry and cassis notes playing in harmony. This medium-bodied, succulent and delicious red Burgundy has supple, ripe tannins leading to a long finish. Tempting now through 2005. 350 cases made. • $66 • (11/15/97) • **92**
Vosne-Romanée Les Beaux Monts 1994: Fairly round, offering lovely currant, raspberry, mint and floral flavors. Medium-bodied, already seductive and supple on the finish. Drinkable now. • $43 • (11/15/96) • **87**
Vosne-Romanée Les Beaux Monts 1993: A princess of a wine, graceful and royal, showing plenty of class. Flavors are well-defined, quite ripe and sweet, offering black currant character that fans out on the palate. Pure, silky, long finish. Try after 2000. • $50 • (11/15/95) • **92**
Vosne-Romanée Les Beaux Monts 1992: Bright and flavorful, a little short on concentration, but shades its currant and berry tones with hints of rose petal and spice. Drinkable now. 400 cases made. • $56 • (12/15/94) • **86**
Vosne-Romanée Les Beaux Monts 1991: A narrow beam of blackberry and black cherry flavors runs through the veil of tannins in this decidedly fruity wine. Drinkable now. 420 cases made. • $52 Ⓐ • (01/31/94) • **84**
Vosne-Romanée Les Beaux Monts 1990: Aromatic, ripe and concentrated, showing superb, deep, rich plum, spice and berry flavors that are focused and elegant. Has a long, delicious finish. Drinkable now. 250 cases made. • $70 • (12/15/92) • **92**
Vosne-Romanée Les Beaux Monts 1989 • $63 • (01/31/92) • **90**
Vosne-Romanée Les Beaux Monts 1988 • $48 • (02/15/91) • **92**
Vosne-Romanée Les Beaux Monts 1986 • $43 • (04/30/89) • **91**
Vosne-Romanée Les Beaux Monts 1985 • $55 • (02/29/88) • **95**
Vosne-Romanée Les Chaumes 1995: Bursting at the seams with spicy, red cherry and raspberry flavors, this '95 red exhibits little new-oak character. Moderately structured and poised for early consumption. Lipsmacking. 150 cases made. • $66 • (11/15/97) • **87**
Vosne-Romanée Les Chaumes 1994: Succulent, medium-bodied, with pure, clean raspberry, currant and floral flavors. Sweet-tasting, but a touch crisp on the finish. Another successful 1994 from Patrice Rion. • $58 • (11/15/96) • **86**
Vosne-Romanée Les Chaumes 1993: Superfine, delivering classy plum, mint and mineral flavors and aromas, full body, fine tannins and a long, elegant finish. Superb. Try in 2000. • $50 • (11/15/95) • **93**
Vosne-Romanée Les Chaumes 1992: Firm in texture and brimming with floral, violet-tinged currant flavors. Drink now. 180 cases made. • $58 • (12/15/94) • **84**
Vosne-Romanée Les Chaumes 1991: Dense in texture and concentrated, pumping out ripe berry, currant and floral flavors and finishing with a distinct touch of mint. Drinkable now. • $54 • (02/28/95) • **91**
Vosne-Romanée Les Chaumes 1990: Powerful and beautifully structured, with a solid backbone of tannins; ripe, floral flavors run deep in this superbly crafted Burgundy. Drinkable now, or hold until 2000. • $70 • (02/28/95) • **93**
Vosne-Romanée Les Chaumes 1989 • $63 • (02/28/95) • **85**
Vosne-Romanée Les Chaumes 1988 • $54 • (02/28/95) • **91**
Vosne-Romanée Les Chaumes 1987 • $35 • (02/28/95) • **88**
Vosne-Romanée Les Chaumes 1986 • $54 • (02/28/95) • **84**
Vosne-Romanée Les Chaumes 1985 • $NA • (02/28/95) • **91**
Vosne-Romanée Les Chaumes 1983 • $36 • (02/28/95) • **82**

RION, MICHELE & PATRICE

Bourgogne Les Bons Bâtons 1993: Effusively aromatic, featuring vibrant currant, smoke and spice flavors that won't stop on the delicious, silky finish. Shows both finesse and power. Drinkable now. • $15 • (11/15/95) • **88**
Chambolle-Musigny Les Cras 1995: Controversial: You'll either love it or hate it. Overlook the earthy, horsey aromas, and dig into the superb blackberry, cassis, plum and wet soil character and you'll find yourself tasting something very intense, rich, ripe and long-lasting. Fat, sweet, ripe and seductive tannins are impressive, too. • $48 • (11/15/97) • **92**
Chambolle-Musigny Les Cras 1993: Vivid crushed berries through and through. Aromatic with a lovely rich palate of ripe fruit, rose and mint and firm tannins. A wine to age. Try in 2000. • $38 • (11/15/95) • **90**
Chambolle-Musigny Les Cras 1992: Extremely minty and floral, an aromatic Burgundy that's light and a little too tannic for the modest berry flavor. Try now. • $NA • (12/15/94) • **78**

RIPEAU, CHÂTEAU

St.-Emilion 1982 • $18 • (05/15/89) • **88**
St.-Emilion 1961 • $19 • (04/30/96) • **84**

RIVIÈRE, CHÂTEAU DE LA

Fronsac 1994: Though lean on the palate and slightly herbal in flavor, notes of sweet oak add appeal and it finishes soft and spicy. A pleasant red for drinking now. • $19 • (06/30/97) • **84**

ROALLY, DOMAINE DE

Mâcon-Viré 1995: An exotic Mâcon that baffles the senses. This voluptous, full-bodied elixir remains elegant as it combines white peach, apricot blossom, honey, citrus and tropical aromas. Swirls smoothly on the palate to a long, lively and flawless finish. Bravo! Drink or hold until after 2000. 500 cases imported. 1,208 cases made. • $23 • (05/31/97) • **93**
Mâcon-Viré 1994: Full-bodied, packing in ripe, sweet fruit flavors of pear, pineapple, mango, apple, along with honey notes. Round, harmonious and lingering finish. Drink now or hold until 2000. From Henri Goyard. 1,500 cases made. • $18 • (05/31/97) • **87**

ROBERT, DOMAINE

Brut Blanc de Blancs Blanquette de Limoux 1986 • $8 • (06/15/90) • **78**
Brut Blanc de Blancs Blanquette de Limoux 1983 • $8 • (01/31/88) • **77**

ROBERT, DOMAINE DE

Fleurie 1994: Maturing nicely, this soft yet vibrant red offers black cherry, smoke and spice flavors, with just enough tannin for grip. A bit hot on the finish, though. 835 cases made. • $17 • (06/30/97) • **81**
Morgon 1994: Maturing now, this shows concentration and integration, with plum, smoke and spice flavors, firm tannins. 835 cases made. • $16 • (06/30/97) • **83**

ROBERT, ALAIN

Brut Blanc de Blancs Champagne Le Mesnil 1985: An extremely solid and powerful Champagne, especially at 12 years old. It has a light, bright gold color and vivid fruit flavors accented by subtle smoky, nutty notes that linger on the finish. Drink now through 2002. 300 cases made. • $50 • (11/15/97) • **92**

ROBERT-DENOGENT

Pouilly-Fuissé Cuvée Claude Denogent 1994: Straightforward, with minor-league citrus and fruit aromas and flavors. A light wine that's fresh and should make a pretty good companion for seafood. • $28 • (05/31/96) • **80**
Pouilly-Fuissé Cuvée Claude Denogent Vieilles Vignes 1993: Showy, ripe and rich, displaying a chalky, chewy texture; honey and hazelnut flavors lack a bit of vibrancy. Drink now. 333 cases made. • $28 • (05/15/95) • **85**
Pouilly-Fuissé La Croix 1994: Lemony and crisp; a lean wine with green, herbaceous flavors and no fruit. • $23 • (05/31/96) • **75**
Pouilly-Fuissé Les Carrons 1994: Straightforward and a bit angular, with a cinnamon-spice character and green apple flavors. A bit one-dimensional on the finish. • $34 • (05/31/96) • **80**

Pouilly-Fuissé Les Reisses Vieilles Vignes 1994: Straightforward, with a lot of citrus and a touch of cinnamon and spice. Fairly lean and tart, but still enjoyable. • $24 • (05/31/96) • **80**

Pouilly-Fuissé Les Reisses Vieilles Vignes 1993: Some decent fruit but it's disjointed, with pronounced wet hay, herbal and asparagus flavors. Not very attractive. 500 cases made. • $25 • (05/15/95) • **74**

Pouilly-Fuissé Vieilles Vignes 1993: Lemon, herbal and wet earth character; medium-bodied, good acidity. A hint of cardboard on the finish is slightly distracting. Drinkable now. 667 cases made. • $NA • (05/15/95) • **79**

ROBIN, CHÂTEAU

Côtes de Castillon 1995: An exciting, sleek and wonderful wine, emitting milk chocolate, berry, violets and raspberries. Medium- to full-bodied, with raspberry, toffee and vanilla flavors, chewy tannins. Best after 2000. • $15 • (01/31/98) • **89**

Côtes de Castillon 1994: An impressive little wine, with sweet fruit and silky tannins that bring you back for more. It's finely textured and has a lovely, fruity finish. Drink now or hold. • $NA • (01/31/97) • **85**

Côtes de Castillon 1993: Light and plummy red showing light tannins and a hint of tomatoes. Drinkable now. • $NA • (01/31/96) • **79**

ROBLET-MONNOT, F.

Volnay Les Caillerets 1989 • $37 • (11/15/93) • **85**

ROBLIN & FILS, GEORGES

Sancerre Château de Maimbray 1996: Flinty mineral notes are textbook Sancerre in this firm, angular white. The fruit character is a bit lean, with lime and pine, but it should soften with food. Drink now through 1999. • $18 • (03/31/98) • **84**

ROCH, CLUSEL

Côte-Rôtie 1990: Gorgeous berry, vanilla and spice aromas and flavors wind themselves around your palate as this smooth, generous wine opens up and shows what it has. Elegant, ripe, rich and subtle, this keeps pumping out the berry and chocolate flavors on the supple finish. Drinkable now. 500 cases made. • $40 • (04/15/93) • **94**

ROCHEMORIN, CHÂTEAU DE

Pessac-Léognan 1997: Slightly overdone with a cooked fruit and raisin character. Medium-bodied, with rather dry tannins and a medium finish. • $NA • (06/15/98) (BT) • **75-79**

Pessac-Léognan 1996: Good chunky red with berry, tobacco aromas and flavors and a medium body. Finishes quickly. • $16 • (06/15/98) (BT) • **85-89**

Pessac-Léognan 1995: Slightly tough. Some decent fruit, but a bit herbal and weedy, with medium body, mean tannins and a hard finish. Better after 1999? Tasted twice, with consistent notes. • $15 • (01/31/98) • **81**

Pessac-Léognan 1994: Like biting into a cherry pie. A lovely, ripe wine for the vintage with medium body, fine tannins and a long, succulent finish. Delicious. Drink or hold. • $14 • (01/31/97) • **86**

Pessac-Léognan 1993: Subtle and elegant, medium- to light-bodied, featuring an appealing touch of cassis, wet earth and dried herbs. Delicious now. • $14 • (01/31/96) • **84**

Pessac-Léognan 1992: Extremely herbal and hard with aggressive tannins and vegetal character. • $13 • (04/15/95) • **72**

Pessac-Léognan 1991: Rather green with weak artichoke and tomato aromas and flavors. • $13 • (03/31/94) • **72**

Pessac-Léognan 1990: The earthy, meaty, mineral character and firm tannins make this a typical traditional Pessac-Léognan. Drinkable now. 4,000 cases made. • $12 • (03/31/93) • **89**

Pessac-Léognan 1989 • $16 • (03/15/92) • **88**

Pessac-Léognan 1986 • $15 • (06/15/89) • **84**

Graves 1985 • $14 • (06/15/88) • **85**

Graves 1982 • $22 • (08/31/92) • **90**

Key: SS—Spectator Selection CS—Cellar Selection HR—Highly Recommended BB—Best Buy $NA—Price not available Ⓐ—Auction Price (BT)—Barrel Tasting

Dates in parentheses indicate the issues in which the ratings were published.

Pessac-Léognan White 1995: A racy little white, with apple, mineral and chalk aromas and flavors. Medium-bodied, with medium acidity and a fresh finish. Drink now. • $15 • (04/30/98) • **86**

Pessac-Léognan White 1994 • $13 • (03/31/96) • **84**

ROCHER BELLEVUE FIGEAC, CHÂTEAU

St.-Emilion 1997: Plummy, cherry and berry aromas and flavors. Medium-bodied, with fine tannins and a fresh fruit finish. Attractive. • $NA • (06/15/98) (BT) • **85-89**

St.-Emilion 1996: Good tobacco, cherry character marks this medium-bodied wine, with good, silky tannins and a light finish. Well made, it could move up a notch next year. 5,000 cases made. • $NA • (01/01/97) (BT) • **80-84**

St.-Emilion 1995: Supple, ripe and sweet-tasting, quite silky and creamy, with grapey, red berry, cinnamon and spice character. Full-bodied with soft tannins, but a bit forward. • $NA • (05/15/96) (BT) • **85-89**

St.-Emilion 1994: Light, offering some fruit flavor, but it's weedy overall and rather metallic on the finish. Drink if you must. 5,833 cases made. • $17 • (01/31/97) • **72**

St.-Emilion 1991: Very odd aromas of salami and earth, but the palate is fresh and fruity. • $12 • (03/31/94) • **73**

St.-Emilion 1990: Obviously made from high-yield grapes. A wine with light grassy, berry, almost watery flavors and a light tannin structure. Drinkable now. 3,500 cases made. • $15 • (03/31/93) • **79**

St.-Emilion 1988 • $18 • (04/30/91) • **87**

ROCHES NEUVES, DOMAINE DES

Saumur Champigny 1992 • $13 • (11/15/94) • **81**

Saumur Red Champigny Terres Chaudes 1992 • $20 • (11/15/94) • **85**

ROCHEVINE, DOMAINE

St.-Joseph 1994: This firm, straightforward red shows good concentration and balance, but the black cherry and game flavors are dominated now by big, austere tannins. Hearty food—and another six months in bottle—should unlock its fruit. 5,500 cases made. • $17 • (10/15/97) • **85**

RODET, ANTONIN

Beaune Cave Privée 1994: Surprisingly deep-colored, with a velvety mouthfeel, ripe flavors and delicious violet, currant and toasty oak notes that finish with firm but well-integrated tannins. Unusual quality for this appellation. • $NA • (11/15/96) • **85**

Chambolle-Musigny 1993: Somewhat raisiny but an impressive concentration of ripe fruit. Medium- to full-bodied, adding chewy tannins and a tarry, berry-flavored aftertaste. Slightly overdone. Better in 2000. • $30 • (11/15/95) • **84**

Chassagne-Montrachet La Grande Montagne 1995: This pure and clean *premier cru* is thick, dense and intense, offering lots of lovely honey, ripe pear and spice flavors accented by toasty oak. Seems a bit dry, but that could be from recent bottling. This wine has a lot going for it. Enjoy now through 2002. • $54 • (05/31/97) • **90**

Chassagne-Montrachet La Grande Montagne 1994: A seductively ripe *premier cru* that's smooth and supple, but a touch unfocused in the aromas. Appealing apricot, ripe pear, mineral and honey flavors; it coats the mouth with its creamy, silky texture. 128 cases made. • $48 • (05/31/96) • **84**

Chassagne-Montrachet Morgeot 1994: A bit rustic, with some chestnut aromas. Modest grapefruit, honey and tropical notes. Tastes a bit diluted and short. 256 cases made. • $43 • (05/31/96) • **79**

Clos de Vougeot Cave Privée 1995: Odd—very ripe, verging on raisiny, with a dried fruit character. Full-bodied, plummy and rich, it turns strangely dry on the finish. What happened? Tasted twice, with consistent notes. 125 cases made. • $65 • (01/31/98) • **80**

Corton-Charlemagne 1995: Big, totally dominated by new oak flavors now, but there is plenty of excellent fruit concentration here, with an explosive, lemon-spiked character that carries the wine forward. So closed and tight now, it's difficult to rate, but it seems ready for a grand future. Try after 2005. • $75 • (05/31/97) • **93**

Corton-Charlemagne 1992: A superripe, supercharged style of Corton that comes across as thick, rich, almost cloying. A bit extreme for us, with all those butter, apple and honey flavors. Drinkable now. • $NA • (08/31/94) • **88**

Gevrey-Chambertin 1986 • $25 • (07/15/90) • **86**

Gevrey-Chambertin Estournelles St.-Jacques 1995: Rustic in style, this '95 goes for extraction and up-front fruit, but has more of a red berry, beetroot

FRANCE

and citrus character, finishing with tough tannins. Try in 2000. 76 cases made. • $50 • (11/15/97) • **85**

Gevrey-Chambertin Lavaut St.-Jacques 1982 • $35 • (06/30/87) • **92**

Gevrey-Chambertin Les Cazetiers 1993: Some good berry and fruit character but rather light, delivering elegant tannins and an easy finish. Drinkable now. • $45 • (11/15/95) • **84**

Mazis-Chambertin 1994: Deep, vibrant color and flavors, with fresh and focused notes of blackberry, violet and mineral. Picks up some drying tannins on the finish, but the flavors win out. Built to age, best from 2000-2001. • $NA • (11/15/96) • **92**

Mercurey Château de Chamirey White 1995: A superb Mercurey, and one of the great surprises of the vintage. Seductively mouthcoating, serious and full-bodied—and amazingly sweet and ripe. While opulent, it has a tight core of citrus, honey, dried herbs and ripe tropical fruit that keeps it on course through the long, vibrant and harmonious finish. Drink now through 2000. • $18 • (08/31/97) • **92**

Meursault Goutte d'Or Cave Privée 1995: Lovely Chardonnay, fresh and sweet-tasting, with nice, ripe fruit and honey character. Medium-bodied, it's juicy and not overoaked, leaving the palate refreshed on the delightful finish. Try upon release. • $54 • (05/31/97) • **87**

Meursault Les Perrières 1994: Seductively supple and honeyed, showing some buttery, pie crust flavors along with toasty hazelnut and pear. Creamy in texture, a little fuller in body, and harmonious for drinking now. 76 cases made. • $53 • (05/31/96) • **86**

Meursault Les Perrières 1992: The fruit flavors are bright and clean in this well-proportioned and modest Meursault. Elegant, creamy-textured and enjoyable, with a lingering, lightly toasty finish. Tasted twice. • $NA • (08/31/94) • **84**

Meursault Les Perrières Cave Privée 1995: Clean, pure, well-defined flavors zip along in this well-structured, full-bodied '95 *premier cru*, offering fresh fruit, citrus and oak notes in a chewy package. This one will need time, as it ends with a hard, woody finish now. Try after 2000. • $58 • (05/31/97) • **89**

Meursault Rodet 1992: Smells attractive, with rich butter, butterscotch, vanilla and peach flavors, and a round texture to go with it, but you are left wanting a bit more fruit in the midpalate. • $NA • (08/31/94) • **85**

Mâcon-Villages 1996: Ripe, supple, nearly sweet, this accessible white offers baked pear, piecrust, white pepper, tropical fruit and some chocolate-chip cookie flavors that linger pleasantly for a harmonious finish. A bit too soft, but try as an apéritif. • $14 • (08/31/97) • **87**

Mâcon-Villages 1995: Medium-bodied and fairly lush in texture. Delicate flavors of apple, citrus and pear. Try now. • $NA • (08/31/96) • **80**

Nuits-St.-Georges Les Porèts 1995: Seems a little oxidized and out of sorts. Very drying tannins. 177 cases made. • $50 • (11/15/97) • **70**

Nuits-St.-Georges Les Porèts 1994: Some pleasant, but modest, floral, rose petal, plum and leather aromas and flavors support this medium-bodied red. Tastes slightly coarse on the finish. Try now. • $59 • (11/15/96) • **79**

Nuits-St.-Georges Les St.-Georges 1995: On the crisp side, exhibiting leafy, tobacco accents to the black cherry flavors. Lean in style and astringent on the finish. 101 cases made. • $55 • (11/15/97) • **82**

Nuits-St.-Georges Roncière 1993: Chunky spice and plum aromas and flavors, medium-to-full body, firm tannins and long, succulent finish. Better in 1999. • $45 • (11/15/95) • **88**

Puligny-Montrachet Hameau de Blagny 1994: A bit lean and fruitless, offering only modest citrus, spice and honey flavors and a short finish. The wood dominates. 144 cases made. • $45 • (05/31/96) • **78**

Puligny-Montrachet Le Cailleret 1994: Rich, ripe and full-bodied, showing creamy, milky coconut aromas and flavors. May seem a bit overdone and too soft to some, but has its appeal. Good drinking now. 148 cases made. • $53 • (05/31/96) • **84**

Rully Château de Rully Red 1991: Lean and lively, offering a bright thread of wild berry and currant flavor that extends into a silky finish. Appealing to drink now. • $NA • (01/31/94) • **83**

Rully Château de Rully White 1992: It's maturing fast, with earthy, cheesy notes along with some modest apple and pear flavors. • $16 • (08/31/94) • **77**

Savigny-lès-Beaune 1995: Rather elegant and delicate, with a juicy, succulent undertow from the lovely wild berry, blueberry and cherry flavors, which are unhindered by much wood. Medium-bodied and balanced, this is nice and ripe. Drink around 2000. 252 cases made. • $25 • (11/15/97) • **86**

Volnay-Santenots 1993: Overdone, really. Concentrated but lacks finesse. Raisin, plum and mushroom aromas and flavors. Medium-bodied and a bit alcoholic. Drinkable now. • $35 • (11/15/95) • **84**

Vosne-Romanée 1993: Quite distinctive, showing mint, wet earth, plum and mineral flavors. A bit too raisiny to be truly classy, but it offers plenty of ripe character. Medium in body and tannins. Drinkable now. • $30 • (11/15/95) • **86**

ROEDERER, LOUIS

Brut Blanc de Blancs Champagne 1990: A vibrant young Champagne that's rich but tightly wound with citrus flavors and firm acidity. A mouthfilling mousse and fine balance make it tempting. Best from 2000. • $54 • (12/31/97) • **91**

Brut Blanc de Blancs Champagne 1983 • $45 • (12/31/90) • **83**

Brut Blanc de Blancs Champagne 1979 • $39 • (05/31/87) • **94**

Brut Champagne 1990: This has everything you want in a Champagne: bright, lively fruit flavors, intriguing accents of honey and spice, a smooth, creamy texture and a lingering finish. Tempting to drink now, but should improve through 2000 or so. 8,333 cases made. • $68 Ⓐ • (11/15/96) • **92**

Brut Champagne 1988: Powerfully fruity, lively in texture, featuring cherry and almond extract flavors and firm acidity. A bold Champagne that grabs you on the first sip, but fades a bit on aftertaste. • $38 • (11/30/95) • **85**

Brut Champagne 1985 • $50 • (12/31/90) • **85**

Brut Champagne 1982 • $47 Ⓐ • (12/31/88) • **93**

Brut Champagne Brut Premier NV: A crisp and appetizing Champagne that emphasizes lemon and apple flavors with accents of vanilla and cinnamon. Elegant in its completeness and smooth texture. Drink now. • $42 • (11/15/97) • **87**

Brut Champagne Cristal 1990: Combines open fruit flavors and vivid balance for a well-focused, citrus-flavored bubbly with a fresh texture and crisp finish. Drink now through 2000. 25,000 cases made. • $150 • (11/30/97) • **87**

Brut Champagne Cristal 1989: Rich and deep, ripe and full-bodied, this offers toasty, almond, spice and even white-chocolate flavors, emphatic yet harmonious. Has firm mouthfeel and a long finish; though the flavors are maturing, it will still evolve well. 25,000 cases made. • $119 Ⓐ • (04/30/97) • **92**

Brut Champagne Cristal 1988: Intriguing and complex, with enticing aromas of fig, butter and toast, backed by mouth-filling flavors of pear, cream and apple. Long on the finish, too. Gorgeous, refined and balanced. Drinkable now. 50,000 cases made. • $118 Ⓐ • (12/31/94) • **93**

Brut Champagne Cristal 1986 • $100 • (12/31/93) • **89**

Brut Champagne Cristal 1985 • $160 Ⓐ • (05/15/92) • **85**

Brut Champagne Cristal 1983 • $109 Ⓐ • (12/31/89) • **88**

Brut Champagne Cristal 1982 • $122 Ⓐ • (09/30/87) • **92**

Brut Champagne Cristal 1981 • $129 Ⓐ • (05/16/86) • **91**

Brut Rosé Champagne 1991: A delicate, well-balanced and intriguing rosé that keeps luring you back for another sip. It's light in color, tangy and citrusy in flavor and crisp in texture, with spicy nuances that linger on the finish. • $48 • (11/30/96) • **88**

Brut Rosé Champagne 1989: A lean, well-balanced, dry rosé, with a light salmon color and hints of cherry in the otherwise straightforward fruit flavors. 4,200 cases made. • $40 • (12/31/94) • **85**

Brut Rosé Champagne Cristal 1988: The color is barely rosé—deep gold with a hint of salmon—but the lively strawberry and honey flavors show a bright personality, fresh and clean, and the wine is firm on the palate. • $215 • (04/30/97) • **87**

ROGER, DOMAINE JEAN-MAX

Sancerre Cuvée G.C. 1995: Smoky and toasty notes add interest to this muscular white. It's full-bodied and has ripe apple flavors to balance the smokiness. • $18 • (06/15/97) • **87**

ROGUE, LA

Bandol 1987 • $11 • (11/30/90) • **83**

ROIS, CHÂTEAU DE

Muscadet de Sèvre et Maine Sur Lie 1995: Full and soft, this round white offers ripe apple and light toast flavors that will complement many foods without offending many palates. • $10 • (06/15/97) • **83**

ROLLAND, CHÂTEAU

Barsac 1987: • $NA • (06/15/90) • **77**

ROLLAND-MAILLET, CHÂTEAU

St.-Emilion 1995: Bright cherry and mineral aromas and flavors in this, though it's a little light on the finish and it could use a bit more fruit. • $NA • (05/15/96) (BT) • **80-84**

ROLLET, CATHERINE & PASCAL

Mâcon-Solutré-Pouilly 1995: Pure and clean, exactly what you would expect from traditional Mâcon, with floral, apple and pear notes unhindered by the taste of oak. Delicious, crisp, and drinkable now. 833 cases made. • $11 • (05/31/97) • **86**

Pouilly-Fuissé Au Coeur du Cru 1996: Lovely. Balanced, ripe and lush, yet very fresh and zingy. Medium-bodied, with pear, apple and pielike aromas and flavors. Coats the palate with fairly silky texture, and the finish is long. Drink now through 2000. • $NA • (05/31/98) • **89**

Pouilly-Fuissé Domaine de la Chapelle 1995: Ripe and fresh, with a mineral, wet stone character. Medium-bodied, it shows elegance, opulence and good balance, grilled pineapple, ripe pear and butter notes. Lush on the finish, although a bit too toasty. Drink now. 500 cases made. • $18 • (05/31/98) • **85**

Pouilly-Fuissé Domaine de la Chapelle 1994: Fairly rich, fresh tropical character, with pineapple, fig, coconut and pear flavors. Nicely balanced and very attractive now. 116 cases made. • $16 • (05/31/96) • **85**

Pouilly-Fuissé Domaine de la Chapelle 1993: Ripe and pleasant, with pear, floral, honey and fresh herb notes. A supple palate. Drinkable now. 125 cases made. • $15 • (05/15/95) • **85**

Pouilly-Fuissé Domaine de la Chapelle Vieilles Vignes 1996: Well made, lovely and balanced, with a lemon, mineral, apple pie, ripe pear, bitter almond and wet hay character. Medium-bodied, with a silky mouthfeel. Drink now through 1999. 500 cases made. • $20 • (05/31/98) • **87**

Pouilly-Fuissé Domaine de la Chapelle Vieilles Vignes 1994: Vibrant, lively and attractive, with spice, honey and wet hay notes. A little light and lacks power, but it's ready to drink now. 533 cases made. • $19 • (05/31/96) • **85**

Pouilly-Fuissé Domaine de la Chapelle Vieilles Vignes 1993: Remarkable; understated yet powerful. Unfolds its subtle lemon, honey, melon, pear and mineral character in one seductive wave after another. Lush, smooth texture creams your mouth; the finish is supple. Drinkable now. 400 cases made. • $19 • (05/15/95) • **90**

ROMANÉE-CONTI, DOMAINE DE LA

Echézeaux 1994: Succulent, juicy, elegant and satisfying. The lightest of the six DRC reds, but at least it's balanced and not astringent. Full-bodied and dark-colored, with lovely mix of mocha, rose petal, licoric and black cherry flavors, accented by toasty notes on the fine finish. Ripe, sweet tannins are impressive for this vintage. Tasted twice, with consistent notes. Drink now through 2000. 1,500 cases made. • $90 • (09/30/97) • **88**

Echézeaux 1993: Super vanilla, coffee, berry character, quite oaky and more like a Bordeaux than a Burgundy, but how can we fault it? Well structured and refined. Better in 2000. • $101 Ⓐ • (05/15/96) • **90**

Echézeaux 1992: Ripe but light-bodied, with pleasant spice, brown sugar, cinnamon and strawberry aromas and flavors. Light tannins and a tart finish. Disappointing. Drinkable now. • $77 Ⓐ • (05/15/95) • **79**

Echézeaux 1991: Smooth, ripe and opulent, layering the currant, black cherry and raspberry fruit with grace notes of spice and toast. Intense in flavor and refreshingly balanced with a thread of acidity, this is approachable now but should be at its best from 2000. 1,474 cases made. • $95 • (08/31/94) CS • **93**

Echézeaux 1990: Smooth, polished and velvety, a richly layered wine with marvelous plum, blackberry, vanilla, toast and spice aromas and flavors that linger on the finish. Graceful and deep. Perhaps best around 2000 to 2005. 1,446 cases made. • $182 Ⓐ • (12/31/93) CS • **94**

Echézeaux 1989 • $114 • (10/31/92) • **90**

Echézeaux 1988 • $124 Ⓐ • (04/30/91) • **92**

Echézeaux 1987 • $62 Ⓐ • (09/30/90) • **92**

Echézeaux 1986 • $91 Ⓐ • (08/31/89) • **92**

Echézeaux 1985 • $307 Ⓐ • (02/29/88) • **96**

Echézeaux 1984 • $60 Ⓐ • (02/28/87) • **90**

Echézeaux 1952 • $96 • (08/31/90) • **97**

Key: SS—Spectator Selection CS—Cellar Selection HR—Highly Recommended BB—Best Buy $NA—Price not available Ⓐ—Auction Price (BT)—Barrel Tasting
Dates in parentheses indicate the issues in which the ratings were published.

Grands Echézeaux 1994: Complex, its violet, licorice, dried herbs and wild raspberry character mingling with mocha, spice and oak accents. Like all '94 DRC reds, it seems at first sip a touch unripe, with green tannins on the lingering finish. But it grows fatter and more harmonious in the glass, so should improve with age. Try after 2000, to 2005. Tasted twice with consistent notes. 1,000 cases made. • $115 • (09/30/97) • **89**

Grands Echézeaux 1993: Solid and fairly tannic, featuring plum, black cherry and earth character. Rather lean, with mocha, spice and toast notes on the woody finish. Lacks the supple structure of some top '93s, and the color was a bit lighter. Time should soften its taut personality; try in 2005. • $135 • (05/15/96) • **88**

Grands Echézeaux 1992: Attractive and delicate berry, cherry, violet and vanilla aromas with brown sugar and cinnamon flavors. Medium to light body, with soft tannins and a light finish. Drinkable now. • $79 • (05/15/95) • **84**

Grands Echézeaux 1991: Firm in texture but it promises to become an opulent wine. The spicy, violet-scented black cherry and currant flavors roll across the palate in waves. Finishes ripe, smooth and gracefully balanced with refreshing acidity. 799 cases made. • $150 • (08/31/94) • **93**

Grands Echézeaux 1990: Smooth and polished, with jammy raspberry notes adding complexity and richness to the basic plum and currant flavors. Feels soft and generous. Drinkable now. 914 cases made. • $160 • (12/31/93) CS • **94**

Grands Echézeaux 1989 • $111 Ⓐ • (10/31/92) HR • **93**

Grands Echézeaux 1988 • $153 Ⓐ • (04/30/91) • **92**

Grands Echézeaux 1987 • $81 Ⓐ • (09/30/90) • **89**

Grands Echézeaux 1986 • $133 Ⓐ • (08/31/89) • **94**

Grands Echézeaux 1985 • $323 Ⓐ • (02/29/88) • **94**

Grands Echézeaux 1984 • $88 • (02/28/87) • **88**

Grands Echézeaux 1942 • $230 • (08/31/90) • **93**

La Tâche 1994: A muscular, tough young wine that's difficult to evaluate now. It smells delicious with violet, rose petal, toasty bread, mocha and spice notes, but a wall of green, astringent and dry tannins makes for a rough and hard-as-nails finish that seems unbalanced. This finish is crisp, ungenerous and somewhat short. Perhaps better after 2005. Three bottles tasted. 1,600 cases made. • $228 Ⓐ • (09/30/97) • **85**

La Tâche 1993: A superb tasting experience: this really builds on the palate. Elegant yet showing some richness, full of lovely plum, berry and vanilla notes. The tannins are refined in this medium- to full-bodied La Tâche, but the finish is still very tannic; try it in 2006. • $241 Ⓐ • (05/15/96) CS • **94**

La Tâche 1992: Smooth and supple in texture, medium to light in body. This delivers lovely cherry and strawberry aromas and a hint of earthiness in the spice and mocha flavors. Finishes light with fine tannins. Drinkable now. • $126 Ⓐ • (05/15/95) • **84**

La Tâche 1991: A gentle wine with seductive violet-scented currant, blackberry and spice flavors that swirl across the palate in profusion, echoing chocolate on the finish. Beautifully balanced and harmonious; concentrated enough to need at least until 1999 or 2000. 1,428 cases made. • $311 Ⓐ • (08/31/94) CS • **95**

La Tâche 1990: Tough and tight, an immensely concentrated wine, with plum and currant at the core plus shades of toast and exotic spices, all wrapped in a layer of tannin that will need until 2000 to open up. Until then, it's not showing enough to be able to predict where it's going. 2,005 cases made. • $428 Ⓐ • (12/31/93) • **91**

La Tâche 1989 • $368 Ⓐ • (10/31/92) • **91**

La Tâche 1987 • $198 Ⓐ • (09/30/90) • **92**

La Tâche 1986 • $140 Ⓐ • (08/31/89) CS • **98**

La Tâche 1985 • $616 Ⓐ • (02/29/88) • **98**

La Tâche 1984 • $96 Ⓐ • (02/28/87) • **95**

La Tâche 1947: From the better bottle came a remarkably subtle, many-layered wine with exotic spices, black cherry, cedar and mahogany notes lingering on the finish. Another bottle was disappointing; very tart, acidic, like chewing on an aspirin. • $690 Ⓐ • (05/31/97) • **93**

Richebourg 1994: Pure, clean and very intense, with toasty bread, grilled meat, blackberry and black cherry flavors. Full-bodied, it needs time to settle down, but has impressive structure, well-integrated tannins and a long, albeit slightly green, finish. It's the most complete and balanced of DRC's '94 reds. Try around 2005. Tasted two bottles, with similar notes. 1,000 cases made. • $156 Ⓐ • (09/30/97) • **90**

Richebourg 1993: Austere and tough in texture now, showing a dry, tannic edge. Offers compacted blackberry, dry cherry and vanilla character, accompanied by a somewhat green flavor. This is a closed wine that needs time to come together. Try in 2005. • $207 Ⓐ • (05/15/96) • **90**

Richebourg 1992: Elegant and light-bodied, the attractive berry, cherry and violet notes mingle with the cinnamon and brown sugar flavors. A pretty finish makes this quite smooth and seductive. Drinkable now. • $104 Ⓐ • (05/15/95) • **83**

Richebourg 1991: Lean in texture, modest in scope, with more tea leaf and underbrush flavors than fruit, although it finishes with a prune edge. Drinkable now. 1,187 cases made. • $141 Ⓐ • (08/31/94) • **80**

Richebourg 1990: Ripe and tannic, but smoothly polished, offering several layers of spice, fruit and toast, centered around a tight core of plum and currant flavor. Has richness and elegance to spare. Drinkable now. Tasted twice, with the first bottle showing a decidedly earthy edge. 1,315 cases made. • $310 Ⓐ • (12/31/93) • **91**

Richebourg 1989 • $214 Ⓐ • (10/31/92) • **90**

Richebourg 1988 • $238 Ⓐ • (04/30/91) • **94**

Richebourg 1987 • $153 Ⓐ • (09/30/90) • **93**

Richebourg 1986 • $126 Ⓐ • (08/31/89) • **94**

Richebourg 1984 • $94 Ⓐ • (02/28/87) • **91**

Richebourg 1954 • $175 • (08/31/90) • **88**

Romanée-Conti 1994: Surprisingly unimpressive and ungenerous when tasted blind against other '94 red Burgundies from top producers. It's rather crisp, accented by mocha, freshly ground coffee beans and other oak-supplied flavors, tasting of barely ripe cherry and raspberry flavors. Medium-bodied. Chewy finish. Start drinking in 1999. 700 six-bottle cases made. • $997 Ⓐ • (09/30/97) • **84**

Romanée-Conti 1993: Savage, muscular and tightly knit, this offers pure Pinot fruit. Has a full range of cassis, black cherry, mineral and vanilla notes, but it also shows an austere, underripe edge of spicy, tobacco and leafy flavors. With its tough tannins and good length, this is an outstanding "masculine" red Burgundy that has the power and potential to improve into the next century. • $1725 Ⓐ • (05/15/96) CS • **94**

Romanée-Conti 1992: A solid core of fruit and tannins in a medium-bodied wine. Plum, berry and mushroom aromas and flavors, with hints of violet, brown sugar and cinnamon. Drinkable now. • $1035 Ⓐ • (05/15/95) • **85**

Romanée-Conti 1991: Smooth, elegant and intense enough to keep the leafy, smoky berry and black cherry flavors rolling through the polished finish. Harmonious and concentrated, should be best from 2000. 420 cases made. • $1342 Ⓐ • (08/31/94) • **93**

Romanée-Conti 1990: Densely packed, with earthy, tarry and spicy overtones running through the powerful plum, currant and berry flavors, all wrapped in several layes of fine tannins. Give it until 2000. 620 cases made. • $750 • (12/31/93) CS • **93**

Romanée-Conti 1989 • $850 • (10/31/92) • **97**

Romanée-Conti 1987 • $978 Ⓐ • (09/30/90) • **89**

Romanée-Conti 1986 • $862 Ⓐ • (08/31/89) • **95**

Romanée-Conti 1985 • $3532 Ⓐ • (01/31/90) • **99**

Romanée-Conti 1984 • $747 Ⓐ • (01/31/90) • **94**

Romanée-Conti 1983 • $770 Ⓐ • (01/31/90) • **78**

Romanée-Conti 1982 • $700 Ⓐ • (01/31/90) • **85**

Romanée-Conti 1979 • $1136 Ⓐ • (01/31/90) • **90**

Romanée-Conti 1978 • $2731 Ⓐ • (01/31/90) • **95**

Romanée-Conti 1975 • $665 Ⓐ • (01/31/90) • **82**

Romanée-Conti 1964 • $1540 Ⓐ • (01/31/90) • **98**

Romanée-Conti 1953 • $805 Ⓐ • (01/31/90) • **93**

Romanée-Conti 1937 • $562 Ⓐ • (12/15/88) • **94**

Romanée St.-Vivant 1994: Tasted two bottles, the second of which was better, but both offered a backward, angular, medium-bodied wine that's very closed and tough. Interesting mocha, spice, licorice, red- and blackberry aromas follow through on the palate, but you wish the finish was more supple and balanced, and not dominated by green, dry and astringent tannins that are surprisingly rustic for such a glamorous wine. Given its track record, perhaps it will smooth out with several year of cellaring, but unlike some top '94 *grands crus*, it lacks harmony at this stage. Perhaps better after 2005. 1,600 cases made. • $135 • (09/30/97) • **80**

Romanée St.-Vivant 1993: Closed and tough, featuring tannic, austere character that's almost rustic. Offers plenty of redberry and blackberry flavors. Seems somewhat awkward and off-balance now, but it's a big wine and the potential is there. Try in 2005. • $135 • (05/15/96) • **92**

Romanée St.-Vivant 1992: Soft and supple, but very light and diluted. Offers modest fruit flavors with brown sugar and herbal accents. Not much to taste. A brownish edge signals that this is maturing quickly. Drink up fast. • $73 • (05/15/95) • **74**

Romanée St.-Vivant 1991: Ripe and generous, a fairly smooth-textured, with nicely integrated tannins and a smoky edge to the currant and berry flavors. Tasty and drinkable now. 1,548 cases made. • $120 • (08/31/94) • **88**

Romanée St.-Vivant 1990: Firm and flavorful, with a strong toasty-smoky edge to the earthy currant and plum aromas and flavors, finishing with a polished core of flavor poking through the veil of chewy tannins. Drinkable now. • $175 • (12/31/93) • **90**

Romanée St.-Vivant 1989 • $118 Ⓐ • (10/31/92) • **91**

Romanée St.-Vivant 1987 • $82 Ⓐ • (09/30/90) • **89**

Romanée St.-Vivant 1986 • $195 • (08/31/89) • **98**

Romanée St.-Vivant 1985 • $201 Ⓐ • (02/29/88) • **88**

Romanée St.-Vivant 1984 • $36 Ⓐ • (02/28/87) • **96**

ROMANIN, CHÂTEAU

Coteaux d'Aix-en-Provence Les Baux de Provence 1990 • $17 • (02/15/93) • **80**

ROMEFORT, CHÂTEAU

Médoc 1990: Smooth and supple, a polished wine with nicely rounded plum and cherry aromas and flavors, hinting at fresh leather on the finish. Drinkable now. • $10 • (02/28/94) • **84**

ROMER DU HAYOT, CHÂTEAU

Sauternes 1988: Drinkable, but flawed and flat tasting. Tasted twice. • $22/375ml • (04/30/91) • **72**

Sauternes 1986: Pleasant and showing some attractive fruit, but it finishes sugary and plain. Drinkable now. • $22 • (12/31/89) • **78**

Sauternes 1983: Sulfur and the tobacco-herbal aspects of the flavor cover the fruit, making this wine a gamble to cellar. Light gold, earthy, slightly cardboardlike, there's some ripe, honeyed fruit in there but you have to dig for it. • $19 • (01/31/88) • **72**

Sauternes 1982 • $13 • (10/16/85) • **82**

RONCÉE, DOMAINE DU

Chinon Clos de Marronniers 1993: Maturing now, this has seductive aromas of cedar, spice and tobacco, with dried cherry, spice and gamelike flavors. Still fresh, with bright acidity and firm tannins, it's distinctive and well made, especially for the vintage. • $20 • (05/15/97) • **88**

ROPITEAU FRÈRES

Bienvenues-Bâtard-Montrachet 1993: Vivid apple and mineral aromas and flavors. Medium body, racy acidity and chalky finish. Well constructed. • $105 • (08/31/95) • **86**

Bourgogne Hautes-Côtes de Nuits 1993: Light and short, this tastes like it was cut with water, offering only modest strawberry and earth flavors. • $12 • (11/15/95) • **72**

Chassagne-Montrachet 1993: Straightforward apple and mineral character; medium-bodied, medium finish. More like a Mâcon. Drinkable now. • $28 • (05/15/95) • **82**

Chassagne-Montrachet Red 1993: Soft and ripe, a bit light, but featuring enticing, sweet-tasting licorice and red berry flavors. Drink on release. • $17 • (11/15/95) • **80**

Criots-Bâtard-Montrachet 1993: Pretty mushroom, cream and apple aromas and flavors. Medium body and finish, with good acidity. Drink now. • $105 • (08/31/95) • **85**

Côte de Beaune-Villages 1993: Rather thin berry and tobacco character, but very light and dry on the finish. Drink now. • $13 • (11/15/95) • **75**

Côte de Nuits-Villages 1993: Delicate, sweet-tasting character and modest strawberry and cherry flavors. A bit light on the drying finish. • $14 • (11/15/95) • **77**

Gevrey-Chambertin 1993: Middle-of-the-road Burgundy with a slight dilution, showing only modest raspberry, cherry and strawberry flavors. Drinkable now. • $23 • (11/15/95) • **79**

Meursault 1993: Crisp and lean-framed, presenting a citrusy edge and dried herbs, honey, mineral and hints of hazelnut playing in the background. Drinkable now. Tasted twice, with consistent notes. • $27 • (05/15/95) • **85**

Meursault Les Perrières 1993: Vivid apple, mineral and cream aromas and flavors, medium body and a medium-long, fruity aftertaste. Tasted twice, with consistent notes. • $36 • (05/15/95) • **86**

Meursault Red 1993: Somewhat light and short, showing a lightish color. Decent Pinot Noir flavors, but vegetal notes appear on the diluted finish. Drink now. Serve chilled. • $16 • (11/15/95) • **78**

Mâcon-Villages Les Chanterelles 1994: Medium in body, round and silky, nicely ripe, hinting at wet earth, pear, melon and prosciutto ham. Astringent on the finish. 1,666 cases made. • $9 • (08/31/95) • **79**

Pinot Noir Bourgogne 1993: Light and a bit lean, delivering modest raspberry and cherry flavors. Drinkable now. • $9 • (11/15/95) • **79**

Pommard 1993: Good level of gamy fruit character but slightly green on the meaty finish. Medium in body and velvety tannins. Better in 2000. • $25 • (11/15/95) • **80**

Puligny-Montrachet Champ Gain 1993: Subtle and elegant, a medium-bodied Burgundy shaded by spice and vanilla flavors. Turns firm and chalky on the delicate but long finish. • $35 • (08/31/95) • **85**

Santenay 1993: Light- to medium-bodied, compacted and well defined, featuring delicious cherry, smoke and earth character. Drink slightly cool and enjoy this '93 for it's straightforward, fruity style. • $16 • (11/15/95) • **85**

St.-Véran 1994: Straightforward, fresh and pleasant, offering some pear, apple and wet hay flavors. Light-to-medium body. 833 cases made. • $11 • (08/31/95) • **80**

Viognier Vin de Pays d'Oc 1994 • $11 • (02/29/96) • **76**

Volnay Clos des Chênes 1993: Not very good. Has some fruit, but very papery and mushroomy. Better in 1999. • $30 • (11/15/95) • **75**

Vosne-Romanée 1993: Weedy, resembling cabbage. Light. Where's the fruit? • $26 • (11/15/95) • **74**

ROPITEAU-MIGNON

Meursault 1992: Seems mature, with some nutty, apple pie, vanilla notes, ending with a chewy, almost rustic finish. Bottled by Vaucher. • $NA • (08/31/94) • **79**

Meursault Les Gouttes d'Or 1993: Starts off well, showing mineral, apple and honey character but finishes slightly grassy. Medium body; tart acidity. Drinkable now. • $32 • (05/15/95) • **81**

ROQ DUR

Roussanne Vin de Pays d'Oc 1995: Quite mature, with a firm texture and flavors of almond and spice, a touch of Sherry on the finish. Impressive for its focus, but a bit hard around the edges. Drink now. 550 cases made. • $9 • (06/15/98) • **84**

Vin de Pays de la Vallée du Paradis Talairan 1995: A plain and simple red, with hardly any fruit flavor. Tastes stripped and boring. A blend of 40 percent Carignane, 40 percent Chenancon, 20 percent Merlot. Past its prime. 2,500 cases made. • $6 • (07/31/98) • **71**

ROQUE, CHÂTEAU DE LA

Bordeaux 1994: Black cherry and vanilla flavors float through this light-bodied yet still tannic red. Winds up tasting rather neutral, though. 5,000 cases made. • $6 • (07/31/96) • **80**

ROQUE, CHÂTEAU LA

Coteaux du Languedoc 1990 • $9 • (02/15/93) • **75**

Coteaux du Languedoc Pic St.- Loup 1991 • $7 • (03/15/94) • **82**

Coteaux du Languedoc Pic St.-Loup Cupa Numismae 1995: Focused and rich, with lush flavors of plum, dark cherry and blackberry sewn together with appealing spicy notes. It's polished, with a broad texture, and finishes on a subtle leathery note. Brooding and intense. A blend of 60 percent Syrah, 40 percent Mourvèdre. Drink now through 2004. 2,000 cases made. • $15 • (05/31/98) • **89**

Coteaux du Languedoc Pic St.-Loup Numismae 1990 • $10 • (03/15/94) • **86**

Coteaux du Languedoc White Pic St.-Loup 1996: Fresh and assertive, with plenty of punch. Quite appley, with crisp flavors of spice and citrus and some almond notes. Fairly rich. Finishes on an herbal note. 1,000 cases made. • $9 • (02/28/98) • **86**

ROQUEBRUN, CHÂTEAU

Coteaux du Languedoc White 1995: A full-blown style with plenty of buttery, spicy overtones. It's balanced, however, with attractive apple and pineapple flavors. • $15 • (05/31/97) • **85**

St.-Chinian Cave Les Vins de Roquebrun Cuvée Roches Noires 1994: Cherry and pepper flavors reign supreme in this fairly tannic wine. It has good concentration, some finesse as well. • $11 • (06/30/97) • **83**

Key: SS—Spectator Selection CS—Cellar Selection HR—Highly Recommended BB—Best Buy $NA—Price not available Ⓐ—Auction Price (BT)—Barrel Tasting

Dates in parentheses indicate the issues in which the ratings were published.

St.-Chinian Roquebrum Prestige 1994: Very peppery tasting, with some berry flavors mingling. Straightforward, flavors linger on the finish. • $7 • (06/30/97) • **81**

ROQUENEGADE, DOMAINE DE

Cabernet Sauvignon Vin de Pays de l'Aude 1991 • $8 • (03/15/94) • **87**

ROQUETAILLADE, CHÂTEAUFORT DE

Graves White 1996: Strong earthy, herbal aromas and flavors make this a distinctive, aggressive wine. Its concentration and lingering finish suggest it will improve with age. • $11 • (02/28/98) • **83**

ROQUETTE, DOMAINE DE LA | BORDEAUX

Pessac-Léognan 1995: Straightforward red. Dried cherry and light earth aromas and flavors. Medium-bodied, with fine tannins and a short finish. Drinkable now. • $NA • (01/31/98) • **85**

ROQUETTE, DOMAINE DE LA | RHÔNE

Châteauneuf-du-Pape 1995: Vivid and exuberant, a ripe red with black pepper- and licorice-accented raspberry and blackberry flavors. The tannins are ripe and firm, and don't get in the way. 4000 cases imported. • $25 • (10/15/97) • **89**

Châteauneuf-du-Pape 1993: Coffee, licorice and herb flavors run deeply through this thick, tannic wine. Has concentration, but lacks definition now; try in 1997. • $20 • (11/15/96) • **86**

Châteauneuf-du-Pape 1992: Smooth, mature and interesting to drink, from the woodsy aromas through the herb and currant flavors to the plush texture. • $20 • (10/15/95) • **85**

Châteauneuf-du-Pape 1990: Firm and flavorful, with roasted meat, earth and blackberry flavors and a solid dose of crisp tannins on the finish. Drinkable now. • $15 • (06/15/93) • **83**

Châteauneuf-du-Pape 1989 • $17 • (10/15/91) • **86**

Châteauneuf-du-Pape 1988 • $17 • (10/15/91) • **86**

Châteauneuf-du-Pape 1986 • $18 • (10/15/91) • **85**

Châteauneuf-du-Pape 1985 • $13 • (07/31/88) SS • **90**

Châteauneuf-du-Pape White 1996: Traditional in style, with nutty, rosemary and buttery notes; seems slightly woody and oxidized, and tastes a bit tart and crisp on the muted finish. • $25 • (10/15/97) • **79**

Vin de Pays de la Principauté d'Orange Le Pigeoulet 1996: An unpretentious Rhône red that will be just delicious with simple, Provençal foods. It shows ripe red berry, plum and anise flavors, is light to medium in body, clean and pure. A delight. 500 cases imported. • $10 • (10/15/97) • **86**

ROQUEVIGNAN, DOMAINE DE

Côtes du Rhône 1994: Light-bodied, with cherry and strawberry flavors, attractive spicy notes, light tannins that turn a bit dry on the finish. Drink now, while it's fresh. • $10 • (10/15/97) • **83**

ROSE FIGEAC, CHÂTEAU LA

Pomerol 1982 • $25 • (05/15/89) • **85**

ROSIERE, DOMAINE LA

Syrah Coteaux des Baronnies 1988 • $6 • (02/28/90) • **78**

ROSSI, G.

Chénas En Guinchay 1994 • $9 • (10/31/95) • **86**

ROSSIGNOL, MICHEL & MARC

Volnay 1995: Tough, hard and mean, this unripe red delivers brown sugar and licorice notes before turning dry and astringent on its sandpaperlike finish. • $22 • (01/31/98) • **77**

Volnay Les Pitures 1995: A delicate style. Shows some elegance and well-integrated oak, tannins and fruit. Not much of a bouquet, but its subtle red- and blackberry flavors should last, making this delightful now to 2000. • $33 • (01/31/98) • **86**

ROSSIGNOL, PHILIPPE

Bourgogne 1994: Thin, tart and a bit too tannic for the evanescent flavors. • $15 • (11/15/96) • **75**

Côte de Nuits-Villages 1994: Light, with drying tannins that almost smother the modest currant flavors. Drinkable now. • $20 • (11/15/96) • **79**

Côte de Nuits-Villages 1985 • $10 Ⓐ • (07/31/88) • **89**

Fixin En Tabeillion 1994: Light raspberry flavors ride on a beam of racy acidity, finishing with liveliness and charm. • $24 • (11/15/96) • **81**

Gevrey-Chambertin Cuvée Vieilles Vignes 1994: This has beautiful flavors, showing lovely currant, violet, and black cherry notes in a beam of pure fruit. Some firm tannins kick in at the end, but there's enough concentration to balance them. Drinkable now. • $28 • (11/15/96) • **85**

Gevrey-Chambertin Les Corbeaux 1993: Subtle and delicious, this harmonious *premier cru* coats your mouth with sweet-tasting, red berry flavors. Silky mouthfeel and wet earth, leather, plum, cedar, toast and spice character. It turns a bit tannic on the finish now, so don't touch until 2000. • $NA • (05/15/96) • **89**

Gevrey-Chambertin Les Corbeaux Cuvée Vieilles Vignes 1994: A wiry wine, crisp in texture, with fresh raspberry and spice flavors that echo lightly through the finish. Drinkable now. • $42 • (11/15/96) • **83**

Gevrey-Chambertin Les Corbeaux Cuvée Vieilles Vignes 1993: This shows a very refined style of elegant tannins, fresh fruit and long, lingering finish. Medium in body with plenty of fruit and perfume. Delicious now, but should improve well into the next century. • $NA • (05/15/96) • **90**

ROSSIGNOL-FEVRIER

Volnay 1988 • $32 • (03/31/91) • **92**

ROSSIGNOL-TRAPET

Beaune Teurons 1995: A delicate Pinot Noir, balanced but light in color and body, with pretty spice, cherry and wet earth character. Drinkable now. 458 cases made. • $30 • (11/15/97) • **82**

Beaune Teurons 1994: Light, crisp and fragrant with floral notes and spicy red-cherry flavors that linger delicately on the finish. • $NA • (11/15/96) • **82**

Beaune Teurons 1993: Plenty of currant character, medium body, firm tannins and long, sweet fruit finish. Drinkable now. 483 cases made. • $33 • (11/15/95) • **90**

Beaune Teurons 1992: Pleasant but light-bodied, with black cherry, fig and chocolate mousse flavors. Drinkable now. 416 cases made. • $30 • (12/15/94) • **83**

Beaune Teurons 1991: Firm and flavorful, with blackberry, anise and caramel aromas and flavors. Looks a bit mature, but tastes fine. Drinkable now. 267 cases made. • $27 Ⓐ • (01/31/94) • **81**

Beaune Teurons 1990: A well-crafted Burgundy that does justice to this fine vintage. So lively and young it practically jumps from the glass, with exciting, bright berry and toast characteristics. The finish is supple yet firm. Drinkable now. 30 cases made. • $46 • (12/15/92) • **91**

Chambertin 1995: A traditional, ripe style of '95, displaying licorice-tinged cherry flavors and a hint of gaminess. Structured and intense. Drinkable now. 458 cases made. • $68 • (11/15/97) • **90**

Chambertin 1994: Light in color and in body, with very pretty strawberry, rose petal and cinnamon aromas and flavors that linger on the crisp finish. Drinkable now. • $NA • (11/15/96) • **83**

Chambertin 1993: Pretty, focused plum and red berry character, medium body, firm tannins and medium fruity finish. Drinkable now. 541 cases made. • $77 • (11/15/95) • **90**

Chambertin 1992: Lean and silky, with a gamy edge to the cherry and tobacco flavors; a bit tannic, but the sweet flavors underneath bode well. Drinkable now. • $NA • (12/15/94) • **87**

Chambertin 1991: Delicate, elegant wine, silky and brimming with currant and berry flavors, finishing refined and adding a touch of spice to the fruit. Drinkable now. 1,058 cases made. • $58 Ⓐ • (01/31/94) • **87**

Chambertin 1990: A beauty of a wine that offers a mouthful of big, gorgeous flavors, rich texture and velvety finish. Packed to the brim with black currant, raspberry and toast characteristics. Wonderfully balanced and built for long aging. Drinkable in 1998 to 2000. 50 cases made. • $106 • (12/15/92) • **95**

Chapelle-Chambertin 1995: Light-colored and forward-tasting, with odd leather, plum, wet earth and mushroom flavors. Disappointing and astringent on the finish. 108 cases made. • $55 • (11/15/97) • **75**

Chapelle-Chambertin 1994: Delicate, a Burgundy made in an old-fashioned style, with some orange peel, rose petal and spice flavors. Light- to medium-bodied. Drink now. • $NA • (11/15/96) • **79**

Chapelle-Chambertin 1993: Very well-made dried cherry and earth aromas, medium body, full, almost dried tannins and a medium fruity finish. Drinkable now. 541 cases made. • $77 • (11/15/95) • **87**

Chapelle-Chambertin 1992: Lean and chewy with very little flavor to compensate, finishing with a bitter bite. Drinkable now. 167 cases made. • $56 • (12/15/94) • **79**

Chapelle-Chambertin 1991: Velvety and rich, an elegant wine that plays its complex flavors one card at a time, until the table is filled with plum, currant, blackberry, tobacco and coffee flavors piling up on one another. Everything comes together into a delicious finish. Drinkable now, or hold until 2000. 100 cases made. • $49 Ⓐ • (01/31/94) CS • **94**

Chapelle-Chambertin 1990: Has incredible harmony, a dense fruit and tannin structure and an amazing balance of refined smoke, berry, tobacco and raspberry characteristics. Drinkable now. 35 cases made. • $83 • (12/15/92) • **95**

Gevrey-Chambertin 1995: Savage character, with red fruits and touches of herbaceousness and new oak. Appealing, though angular and rustic. Drinkable now. 1,916 cases made. • $25 • (11/15/97) • **83**

Gevrey-Chambertin 1994: Light-bodied, with flavors a bit smoky and gamy and some dry tannins. • $NA • (11/15/96) • **77**

Gevrey-Chambertin 1993: Distinctive minty, lead-pencil, plummy character and medium body. Quite forward and accessible now, it's round yet intense. Drinkable now. 1,916 cases made. • $28 • (11/15/95) • **87**

Gevrey-Chambertin 1992: Simple, crisp and a little stemmy, but the modest berry flavors carry through on the finish. 2,083 cases made. • $26 • (12/15/94) • **79**

Gevrey-Chambertin 1991: Light, fruity and agreeable, with a lean structure and pretty floral, strawberry and red currant aromas and flavors. Drinkable now. 62 cases made. • $23 Ⓐ • (01/31/94) • **84**

Gevrey-Chambertin Petite Chapelle 1994: Earthy flavors and hard tannins overcome whatever charm this may have. • $NA • (11/15/96) • **77**

Gevrey-Chambertin Petite Chapelle 1993: Solid and fragrant, offering substantial dried cherry and plum character and a complement of fine tannins. Medium body and finish. Drinkable now. 191 cases made. • $43 • (11/15/95) • **88**

Gevrey-Chambertin Petite Chapelle 1992: Gamy, earthy aromas and flavors narrow down to a solid core of fruit that fades as the drying tannins clamp down on the finish. 208 cases made. • $39 • (12/15/94) • **82**

Gevrey-Chambertin Petite Chapelle 1991: Crisp and simple. Nice currant flavor comes in to save it on the tight, tannic finish. Drinkable now. 417 cases made. • $33 Ⓐ • (01/31/94) • **80**

Gevrey-Chambertin Petite Chapelle 1990: So intense it takes you aback, with earthy black cherry and violet aromas and flavors along with a stemmy, vegetal note and an extremely well-focused finish. Drinkable now. 25 cases made. • $21 Ⓐ • (12/15/92) • **90**

Latricières-Chambertin 1995: Tight and structured, with a core of concentrated fruit that builds to an intense finish. Red cherry flavor, with touches of spice and smoke. 175 cases made. • $55 • (11/15/97) • **86**

Latricières-Chambertin 1994: So light in color you can read through it. It even smells and tastes like a rosé, with delicate strawberry and spice flavors, but the tannins are a bit drying. • $NA • (11/15/96) • **77**

Latricières-Chambertin 1993: Fabulous Burgundy. Wonderful color and concentration of dried cherry and plum aromas. Full-bodied and very firm, featuring a solid core of fruit and fine tannins. Better in 2000. 191 cases made. • $64 • (11/15/95) • **92**

Latricières-Chambertin 1992: Light but balanced, with a modest level of earthy, slightly gamy black cherry flavor. Drinkable already. 250 cases made. • $56 • (12/15/94) • **86**

Latricières-Chambertin 1991: Lean, velvety and earthy, playing its mushroomy currant, berry and tobacco aromas and flavors over a chewy background. Nicely focused and long; has finesse and more muscle than most '91s. Drinkable now. 37 cases made. • $49 Ⓐ • (01/31/94) • **90**

Latricières-Chambertin 1990: Incredibly exciting, with violet, plum, earth and smoke aromas and flavors, loads of ripe fruit characteristics and velvety tannins. Drinkable now. 25 cases made. • $83 • (12/15/92) • **97**

ROSTAING, R.

Côte-Rôtie 1994: Supple and light-bodied, offering soft cherry, floral and light herbal flavors, with light but slightly drying tannins on the finish. Pretty but lacks substance. Drinkable now. • $35 • (10/15/97) • **83**

Côte-Rôtie 1990: Smooth and polished up front before the tannins weigh in. Hints of earth, mineral and black cherry flavors stay with you. Ready now. • $31 • (05/31/94) • **84**

Côte-Rôtie Côte Blonde 1987 • $40 • (06/30/90) • **86**

Côte-Rôtie La Landonne 1994: Classic Syrah character shines through this vivid, well-balanced red, with notes of plums, game, smoke and spice. Elegant and long, firm but not overbearing. Drinkable now. • $37 Ⓐ • (10/15/97) • **87**

Côte-Rôtie La Viaillere 1994: This polished red is supple in texture but well defined, with appealling cherry, spice and tobacco flavors and balanced tannins. Should make a harmonious match with game birds, and it's approachable now. • $41 • (10/15/97) • **85**

ROTHSCHILD, BARON PHILIPPE DE

Cabernet Sauvignon Vin de Pays d'Oc 1994 • $10 • (12/31/95) • **83**

Cabernet Sauvignon Vin de Pays d'Oc Cadet 1996: A straightforward, fruity red wine, with pleasant plum and berry flavors. Drink now. • $7 • (06/15/98) • **82**

Cabernet Sauvignon Vin de Pays d'Oc Cadet 1995: Fresh and full-flavored, with gobs of grapey blackberry flavor and moderate tannins. Drink now for the blast of fruitiness. • $7 • (08/31/97) • **84**

Chardonnay Vin de Pays d'Oc 1994 • $10 • (12/15/95) • **84**

Chardonnay Vin de Pays d'Oc Cadet 1995: Crisp, with citrus, especially grapefruit, flavors. Modest concentration. • $7 • (06/30/97) • **79**

Merlot Vin de Pays d'Oc 1994 • $10 • (12/31/95) • **82**

Merlot Vin de Pays d'Oc Cadet 1996: Firm and flavorful, with well-focused berry and cherry flavors, some spicy notes on the finish. Drink now. • $7 • (05/31/98) • **82**

Merlot Vin de Pays d'Oc Cadet 1995: A hearty, rustic-style red from France's Midi, this blends plummy, raspberrylike flavors with firm tannins and an earthy overtone. • $7 • (08/31/97) • **81**

Médoc 1995: A simple red, with an earthy aroma and decent plum and berry flavors. Drink now. • $12 • (06/15/98) • **80**

Médoc 1989 • $11 • (11/15/94) HR • **89**

Pauillac 1994: An appealing and well-rounded Bordeaux with pleasant flavors of plum and cherry, with a chocolaty note on the finish. Balanced, fresh and focused. Drink now. • $21 • (06/15/98) • **85**

Pomerol 1995: Has some structure and backbone, with simple, modest red plum and dried cherry flavors and a smooth finish. Drink now. • $23 • (06/15/98) • **81**

Sauternes 1994: Flabby, with only modest honey and pear flavors. • $27 • (06/15/98) • **74**

Sauternes 1991: Soft and easy to drink, with fresh fruit and herb flavors. Clean, if a bit lacking in concentration. Good value. • $25 • (11/15/94) • **85**

Sauvignon Blanc Vin de Pays d'Oc 1994 • $10 • (02/29/96) • **82**

Sauvignon Blanc Vin de Pays d'Oc Cadet 1995: Simple and straightforward, with good green apple and spice flavors. A refreshing and satisfying quaff. • $7 • (06/30/97) • **83**

St.-Emilion 1994: A rough-hewn and fairly earthy red, with red plum and herb flavors and a touch of cinnamon on the finish. Drink now. • $15 • (06/15/98) • **80**

St.-Emilion 1985 • $11 • (09/30/88) • **85**

ROTHSCHILD, BARONS EDMOND & BENJAMIN

Haut-Médoc 1987 • $24 • (03/31/91) • **75**

Haut-Médoc 1986 • $48 • (03/31/91) • **76**

ROTY, JOSEPH

Bourgogne Cuvée de Pressonier 1992: Light and juicy, with a minty raspberry and strawberry character. Has a fresh texture. Drinkable now. • $NA • (12/15/94) • **80**

Bourgogne Grande Ordinaire Cuvée Philippe Roty White 1992: Light and simple, with crisp tannins that are more than the fruit can absorb. • $NA • (12/15/94) • **73**

Key: SS—Spectator Selection CS—Cellar Selection HR—Highly Recommended BB—Best Buy $NA—Price not available Ⓐ—Auction Price (BT)—Barrel Tasting

Dates in parentheses indicate the issues in which the ratings were published.

Charmes-Chambertin Cuvée de Très Vieilles Vignes 1992: Firm in texture, with a narrow range of agreeable cherry and toast flavors that echo lightly on the finish. Drinkable now. • $135 • (12/15/94) • **82**

Gevrey-Chambertin Clos Prieur 1992: Firm in texture and solid in flavor, with smoky black cherry and currant flavors packed in. Aromatic and drinkable now. • $50 • (12/15/94) • **83**

Gevrey-Chambertin Cuvée des Champs-Chenys 1992: Firm in texture, with a nice thread of pure, ripe currant flavor running through the tannins. Tasted twice. Drinkable now. • $NA • (12/15/94) • **84**

Gevrey-Chambertin Fonteny 1992: Delicate, round and smooth. Has good character, showing roasted chestnut, toast and black cherry flavors and solid tannins. • $72 • (12/15/94) • **85**

Griotte-Chambertin 1992: Light in texture, showing more oak flavor than fruit, but the raspberry notes in the background suggest this will develop decently through 1997. • $200 • (12/15/94) • **83**

Marsannay Les Ouzeloy Red 1992: The oak dominates here, its toasty vanilla flavors mingling with some decent currant and black cherry notes. Drinkable now. • $NA • (12/15/94) • **80**

Mazis-Chambertin 1992: Has much more intensity and character than do most in this vintage, unfolding smoke, mint, currant and blackberry flavors through a veil of fine tannins. Drinkable now. • $200 • (12/15/94) • **88**

ROUGET, CHÂTEAU

Pomerol 1982 • $28 • (05/15/89) • **86**

Pomerol 1961 • $51 • (04/30/96) • **85**

Pomerol 1947: Remarkably fresh and alive, this is a gentle wine with delicious berry, currant, spice and lightly peppery flavors swirling through the finish. • $183 • (05/31/97) • **90**

Pomerol 1945 • $400 • (11/30/95) • **87**

ROUGET, EMMANUEL

Echézeaux 1993: Stunning from start to finish, seamless in its silky texture, exotic and bursting with rose, violet, toast and spice character. Big and full-bodied, it remains extremely racy. Sensational, really. Tempting now, but better in 2001. • $80 • (05/15/96) • **95**

Echézeaux 1991: Smooth and elegant, polished, with beautiful black cherry and berry flavors, plus a light herbal note on the finish. Tannins are deftly integrated. Drinkable now • $87 • (08/31/94) • **89**

Echézeaux 1988 • $81 • (11/15/90) • **96**

Echézeaux 1987 • $55 • (03/31/90) • **88**

Echézeaux 1986 • $55 • (12/31/88) • **87**

Nuits-St.-Georges 1995: Good fruit, clean and pure, with a hard edge. Medium-to-full in body, it may fan out in time, but for now it's unyielding. Slightly herbal on the finish. Try after 2000. • $35 • (01/31/98) • **88**

Nuits-St.-Georges 1993: Exuberant, ripe and delicious village wine, featuring lovely, sweet-tasting plum, spice and smoke flavors. Full-bodied, even chewy, adding supple tannins and a balanced finish. Well made. Try in 2000. • $NA • (05/15/96) • **90**

Nuits-St.-Georges 1989 • $48 • (11/15/91) • **86**

Nuits-St.-Georges 1987 • $32 • (03/31/90) • **86**

Savigny-lès-Beaune 1993: Crushed fruit flavors, wild berries and flowers point the way to wonderful character and medium tannins. Not a red of great class, but absolutely delicious. Better in 1999. • $NA • (05/15/96) • **89**

Vosne-Romanée 1995: Starts out better than it ends. Has some fat, sweet red berry character, but the tannins clamp down on the slightly herbal finish. Too bad. Drink now. • $35 • (01/31/98) • **82**

Vosne-Romanée 1993: Rather earthy and light, delivering some berry and cherry character and meaty highlights, but it's only medium- to light-bodied and lacks punch. Drinkable now. • $NA • (05/15/96) • **83**

Vosne-Romanée 1989 • $48 • (11/15/91) • **91**

Vosne-Romanée 1987 • $32 • (03/31/90) • **91**

Vosne-Romanée Cros Parantoux 1993: Racy, sleek *premier cru*, showing digital definition in every aspect of its flavor components. Loaded with sweet-tasting red berry character, and just a touch of wood and spice for added complexity. Very long, focused finish. Try in 2000. • $72 • (05/15/96) • **95**

Vosne-Romanée Cros Parantoux 1989 • $83 • (11/15/91) • **94**

Vosne-Romanée Les Beaux Monts 1993: Not giving it all at the moment but shows potential. Medium- to full- bodied, voluptuous, adding fine tannins and a long, flavorful finish. Better in 2001. • $55 • (05/15/96) • **91**

Vosne-Romanée Les Beaux Monts 1986 • $40 • (12/31/88) • **89**

ROULERIE, CHÂTEAU DE

Anjou Les Maronis 1995: A velvety, round red with smoke and chocolate aromas, rich flavors of plum, chocolate and spice. Firm tannins make it a match for food. Ready to drink. 2,083 cases made. • $13 • (06/15/97) • **85**

Coteaux du Layon Le Cerisier 1994: This off-dry white has good concentration on the palate, but the flavors lean toward the mineral and the vegetal, without much fruit or ripeness. Drink now. 500 cases made. • $29 • (06/15/97) • **82**

ROULOT, GUY

Bourgogne White 1995: Fabulous quality for a simple Bourgogne, from a white Burgundy master. Ripe, rich, minerally, this is a lovely, full-bodied, seductive wine showing compacted fruit character, honey and spice accents. Fresh, lively finish suggests it will age nicely through 2000, at least. 600 cases made. • $20 • (08/31/97) • **90**

Bourgogne White 1994: A quite fresh, light-bodied white with some crisp green apple flavors and pleasant chalky notes. • $19 • (05/31/96) • **80**

Bourgogne White 1993: A touch more ripeness than many generic Bourgognes; lightly flavored by pear and pink grapefruit notes. The finish is tart and lean, but balanced. Drink now. 750 cases made. • $19 • (05/15/95) • **80**

Meursault Le Tesson Clos de Mon Plaisir 1995: Impressive winemaking. Fabulous, restrained and thick-textured, packed with honey, fruit and spice complexity, plus refreshing lemon and mandarin flavors that give this full-bodied, silky, mouthfilling wine a refreshing lift on the succulent, deftly toasty finish. Try in 2000 to 2007. Tasted twice. • $50 • (05/31/98) • **94**

Meursault Le Tesson Clos de Mon Plaisir 1994: Lovely, round, ripe and supple, with lots of fresh tropical fruit, mineral and toasty flavors. Elegant on the lingering, near-flawless finish. Try now. • $43 • (05/31/96) • **91**

Meursault Le Tesson Clos de Mon Plaisir 1993: Complex and delicious, tart but harmonious, featuring flavors of dried herb, honey, lime and green apple. Drinkable now. 459 cases made. • $52 • (05/15/95) • **88**

Meursault Le Tesson Clos de Mon Plaisir 1992: Well made and tightly wound around a core of vibrant acidity and ripe flavors that peek through in this elegant, firm Meursault. Drinkable now. 460 cases made. • $40 • (08/31/94) • **87**

Meursault Les Charmes 1995: Gorgeous. Racy and classy, with subtle aromas of fruit, mineral, honey, spice and dried herbs, it kicks into high gear in the midpalate, turning rich, opulent, palate-coating. Seamless in texture, it's tempting now, but will be better after 2000. • $80 • (08/31/97) • **95**

Meursault Les Charmes 1994: Impressive, very muscular and tightfisted, with lots of fruit. Shows lovely mineral, earth, toasty bread and vanilla notes. Concentrated flavors linger on the finish. Try in 1999. • $63 • (05/31/96) • **92**

Meursault Les Luchets 1995: As polished as a diamond. Great winemaking has produced this vibrant, well-defined and well-structured '95 that bursts with clean, crisp lemon, honey and fresh fruit flavors, yet yields to the complex accents of spice and toasty oak. Medium to full-bodied, it's subtle and delicious from start to finish. Best after 2000. 400 cases made. • $45 • (05/31/97) • **93**

Meursault Les Luchets 1994: More intense than many other '94s, this balanced white delivers a citrus zing. Very pretty, focused and elegant, with pineapple, toasty pinenut and honey flavors. Try now. • $36 • (05/31/96) • **88**

Meursault Les Luchets 1992: Focused and intense, with toast, lime and pear flavors; elegant and keenly balanced, the steely finish needing time to show all it has. A sophisticated wine with everything in place. 500 cases made. • $32 • (08/31/94) • **90**

Meursault Les Meix Chavaux 1995: A supple '95, smooth and harmonious in texture, with some honey, pear and mineral character. Full-bodied, the finish is lively, with citrus notes giving it length. Try now. • $45 • (05/31/97) • **90**

Meursault Les Meix Chavaux 1994: A beautiful '94 that remains light on its feet, yet round and lush in texture. Medium-to-full-bodied and quite intense, with honey, ripe pear, and citrus flavors. Slightly grassy finish. Drink now through 1999. • $NA • (08/31/96) • **90**

Meursault Les Meix Chavaux 1993: Extremely steely and fresh style, featuring almond, apple and pear aromas and flavors. Medium in body and long, racy finish. Drink now. 250 cases made. • $37 • (08/31/95) • **87**

Meursault Les Perrières 1995: Beautiful. Stony and minerally, with wet earth character mixed with notes of pear and apple, this full-bodied wine offers subtle complexity as well as ripe, sweet flavors. Moderately intense and racy, it's delicious now, but will be more rewarding from 2000 to 2005. 300 cases made. • $80 • (08/31/97) • **95**

Meursault Les Perrières 1992: Vibrant yet seductively creamy, this supple but firm Meursault shows how good '92 is. Packed with pear, apple and grapefruit; you sense its future potential with the vanilla, butter and butterscotch character surfacing on the toasty finish. 116 cases made. • $58 • (08/31/94) • **91**

Meursault Les Vireuils 1995: Unusually solid and firm, even austere, for a '95 Meursault. It's medium- to full-bodied, with some dried herb, lemon and green apple flavors, and a chewy, minerally character on the finish. Should soften after 1999. • $45 • (05/31/97) • **90**

Meursault Les Vireuils 1994: Lush, ripe and very attractive. Solid showing of citrus and slightly grassy aromas and flavors keep it from turning heavy. Enjoy now. • $NA • (08/31/96) • **86**

ROUMIER, CHRISTOPHE

Charmes-Chambertin 1992: Tannins are a bit coarse but there is finesse behind them, showing notes of ripe currant and faded roses that linger on the finish. Drink now. • $55 • (12/15/94) • **88**

Charmes-Chambertin 1990: Offers loads of fruit and raspberry, pepper and earth characteristics. The superb depth is bolstered by a solid tannin structure. Drinkable now. 87 cases made. • $105 • (12/15/92) • **93**

Ruchottes-Chambertin 1992: Light and pretty, simple, with bright raspberry flavor and a mushroomy, toasty edge. Has some style and grace, folding its fine tannins in on the finish. Drinkable now. • $58 • (12/15/94) • **85**

Ruchottes-Chambertin 1991: Has a lot of flavor, but feels remarkably delicate and silky. The currant and anise aromas and flavors almost glow against the supple texture. Finishes long and delicately chewy. Drinkable now. 84 cases made. • $58 Ⓐ • (01/31/94) • **90**

Ruchottes-Chambertin 1990: An awesome wine, with amazing density of ripe fruit and tannins, yet it remains incredibly balanced and shows wonderful finesse. Don't touch this until the turn of the century. 87 cases made. • $80 • (12/15/92) • **97**

Ruchottes-Chambertin 1989 • $70 • (01/31/92) • **94**

ROUMIER, G.

Bonnes Mares 1992: Lean and tannic, squeezing just a bit of currant and blackberry flavor between the spicy, cedary notes. Best now. • $58 • (12/15/94) • **82**

Bonnes Mares 1991: Very firm and tannic, but the youthful flavors have the zing of blackberry, currant and anise flavors that remain lively through the finish, echoing currant. Has the stuff to age through 1999-2000 at least. 265 cases made. • $45 Ⓐ • (01/31/94) • **91**

Bonnes Mares 1990: Hard as granite, this is sculpted with an eye toward the 21st century. Packed to the brim with plum, blackberry, chocolate, smoke and earth aromas and flavors and burns with intensity on the extremely firm finish. Try around 2000. 550 cases made. • $100 • (12/15/92) • **96**

Bonnes Mares 1989 • $46 Ⓐ • (01/31/92) • **93**

Chambolle-Musigny 1992: Firm-textured but light in flavor, a tight little red that offers modest berry and toast notes lasting to the finish. Drinkable now. • $24 • (12/15/94) • **79**

Chambolle-Musigny 1991: Light and tart, with a nice beam of currant flavor running across a racy, citrusy streak. Drinkable now. 1,060 cases made. • $22 Ⓐ • (01/31/94) • **80**

Chambolle-Musigny 1990: Velvety and quite plummy, with dark chocolate and black cherry characteristics, medium body and a supple, ripe finish. Drinkable now. • $28 • (12/15/92) • **88**

Chambolle-Musigny 1989 • $38 • (01/31/92) • **90**

Chambolle-Musigny 1988 • $30 • (07/15/91) • **89**

Chambolle-Musigny 1985 • $26 • (02/15/88) • **87**

Chambolle-Musigny Les Amoureuses 1992: Charming and crisp in texture, its pretty raspberry and vanilla flavors lingering delicately on the finish. Approachable now. • $48 • (12/15/94) • **84**

Chambolle-Musigny Les Amoureuses 1991: Has beautifully defined currant and berry aromas and flavors that carry straight through the finish. A soft-textured wine that has some fine tannins. Drinkable now. 100 cases made. • $48 Ⓐ • (01/31/94) • **85**

Chambolle-Musigny Les Amoureuses 1990: Impressive intensity draws you into this remarkable wine that's closed now, but it offers excellent blackberry, cherry and earth flavors and a firm texture. Drinkable now. 225 cases made. • $55 • (12/15/92) • **92**

Chambolle-Musigny Les Amoureuses 1989 • $62 • (01/31/92) • **88**

Clos Vougeot 1992: A middle-of-the-road Burgundy that shows some nice currant and blackberry flavor and earthy, drying tannins; try now. • $48 • (12/15/94) • **79**

Clos Vougeot 1991: Light, fragrant, lean and somewhat austere, featuring a modest level of black cherry and toast aromas and flavors. Drinkable now. 62 cases made. • $45 Ⓐ • (01/31/94) • **84**

Clos Vougeot 1990: Just what you would expect from Clos Vougeot in an outstanding vintage, with lots of firm tannins and ripe berry and spice characteristics. Drinkable now. • $65 • (12/15/92) • **92**

Clos Vougeot 1989 • $62 • (01/31/92) • **87**

Morey-St.-Denis Clos de la Bussière 1992: A Burgundy that grows on you—slight in aroma, but offering some sweet, ripe black cherry flavors, a welcome tannic edge and a lingering finish. Drink now. • $24 • (12/15/94) • **84**

Morey-St.-Denis Clos de la Bussière 1991: Crisp and delicate, showing lovely raspberry and currant flavors that keep singing on the finish. Try now. 416 cases made. • $22 Ⓐ • (01/31/94) • **85**

Morey-St.-Denis Clos de la Bussière 1990: Shows plenty of intensity, with vivid raspberry, spice and smoke characteristics. A full-bodied wine, with a long finish built on firm tannins. Drinkable now. • $53 • (12/15/92) • **89**

Morey-St.-Denis Clos de la Bussière 1989 • $38 • (01/31/92) • **85**

Morey-St.-Denis Clos de la Bussière 1988 • $30 • (07/15/91) • **83**

Morey-St.-Denis Clos de la Bussière 1985 • $27 • (04/30/88) • **92**

Musigny 1992: Lean and tight, with plum and strawberry flavors that kick in with the spicy oak notes. A generous finish. Drink now. • $NA • (12/15/94) • **90**

Musigny 1991: Tough and chewy. Has modest blackberry and currant flavors, toasty, ashy overtones and a crisp but watery finish. A disappointment. Tasted twice. 37 cases made. • $85 Ⓐ • (01/31/94) • **78**

Musigny 1989 • $95 • (01/31/92) • **96**

ROUMIEU, CHÂTEAU

Barsac 1995: We have always liked wines from this underrated estate. This one is thick and medium-sweet, with spicy honey aromas and a hint of smoke. Medium-bodied, with a long vanilla aftertaste. Drink now. • $NA • (04/30/98) • **88**

ROUMIEU-LACOSTE, CHÂTEAU

Barsac 1990: A wine with a great future. Deceptively subtle, racy, exhibiting lemon, spice, orange, vanilla and butterscotch character. Full-bodied, sweet yet very compacted and firm; long, long finish. Try now. • $22 • (04/15/95) • **91**

ROUSSEAU, ARMAND

Chambertin 1995: What a sexy and exotic red Burgundy. Backward and unforgiving now, this wine is nonetheless packed with dense, ripe black cherry, plum and well-integrated oak flavors that fan out on the long finish. Very powerful, intense, and masculine, it will be drinkable from 2000. 483 cases made. • $195 Ⓐ • (11/15/97) • **96**

Chambertin 1994: Crisp but flavorful, with decent red berry character. Light bodied, it tastes fresh. Drink now. • $140 • (09/30/97) • **76**

Chambertin 1993: One for the cellar; has all the ingredients to age beautifully. Though tight in texture and closed in aroma now, its massive fruit flavors and near-perfect sense of balance are tip offs that it's a potentially great Burgundy. Drink after 2003. • $111 Ⓐ • (09/15/96) • **95**

Chambertin 1992: Delicate and appealing, with seductive, spicy, oak-scented raspberry, strawberry and rose petal aromas and flavors that linger on the supple finish. Tannins are submerged, making this drinkable already. • $69 Ⓐ • (12/15/94) • **88**

Chambertin 1991: A fairly big, chewy wine for the vintage, shading its ripe currant and plum fruit with a definite component of sweet, spicy oak, finishing with a pruny edge, a tannic bite and plenty of muscle. Drinkable now, but could stand cellering until 2000. • $130 • (01/31/94) • **91**

Chambertin 1990: A solid wine that's not giving much now. Has a satiny texture and fine, toasty, gamy violet and berry aromas and flavors. All the elements are in place for excellence; time will tell exactly how great it will be. Try now. 825 cases made. • $150 • (12/15/92) • **92**

Chambertin 1988 • $96 Ⓐ • (05/15/91) • **93**

Chambertin 1985 • $128 Ⓐ • (03/15/88) • **97**

Key: SS—Spectator Selection CS—Cellar Selection HR—Highly Recommended BB—Best Buy $NA—Price not available Ⓐ—Auction Price (BT)—Barrel Tasting
Dates in parentheses indicate the issues in which the ratings were published.

Chambertin-Clos de Bèze 1993: Bursting with fruit and oak flavors, this is a grand, opulent, concentrated Burgundy that will need time. It has oodles of cherry, berry, spice and cedar flavors that echo on the lingering finish. Firmly tannic, still backward. Drink after 1999. • $100 Ⓐ • (09/15/96) • **93**

Chambertin-Clos de Bèze 1992: Delicate and spicy, juicy enough, with lightish black cherry and rose petal flavors that reverberate on the finish. Tannins are nicely integrated, making it best now. • $NA • (12/15/94) • **88**

Chambertin-Clos de Bèze 1991: Light and elegant, featuring a smooth, polished beam of currant and plum aromas and flavors shaded with cola and coffee notes and a fresh youthful style. Drink now. • $135 • (01/31/94) • **88**

Chambertin-Clos de Bèze 1990: Impressively concentrated, packed with bright flavors. Shows ripe fruit, smoke and earth notes on the extremely long finish. An exciting wine that takes off like a rocket. Drinkable now. 450 cases made. • $135 • (12/15/92) • **95**

Chambertin-Clos de Bèze 1989 • $104 Ⓐ • (01/31/92) • **93**

Chambertin-Clos de Bèze 1988 • $188 • (05/15/91) • **95**

Charmes-Chambertin 1994: Light-colored, delicate and light-bodied, with nice rose petal and red berry character; lacking a bit of the complexity you expect from a top red Burgundy. Drink around 1999 to 2000. • $75 • (09/30/97) • **83**

Charmes-Chambertin 1985 • $86 Ⓐ • (10/15/88) • **86**

Clos de la Roche 1992: Smooth and delicate, with a nice core of blackberry and floral aromas and flavors that echo on the appealing finish. Harmonious and drinkable now. • $NA • (12/15/94) • **88**

Clos de la Roche 1991: Lithe, elegant and lean; lovely raspberry flavors up front edge toward currant and vanilla on the long, long finish. Not as concentrated as it could be, but stylish and persistant. • $75 • (01/31/94) • **89**

Clos de la Roche 1990: A round, rich, ripe and intense wine that delivers grace and pleasure, with plum, berry and smoke aromas and flavors. Drinkable now. • $78 • (12/15/92) • **92**

Clos de la Roche 1988 • $62 Ⓐ • (05/15/91) • **91**

Gevrey-Chambertin 1989 • $30 Ⓐ • (01/31/92) • **88**

Gevrey-Chambertin Le Clos St.-Jacques 1995: Silky and full of dense, chewy cherry and licorice flavors accented by spicy oak, this is a tasty, solid red for early drinking. 441 cases made. • $100 • (11/15/97) • **85**

Gevrey-Chambertin Le Clos St.-Jacques 1994: Tasty and fruity, lighter in color than many in this group, but holding its own in flavor, with cherry, citrus and wild berries. Light- to medium-bodied, with a crisp, slightly hot, finish. Try now. • $100 • (09/30/97) • **79**

Gevrey-Chambertin Le Clos St.-Jacques 1993: Beautifully fruity and vibrant in character, packed with lively cherry and berry flavors that are focused, lingering and accented by buttery oak. Tempting now. • $67 Ⓐ • (09/15/96) • **92**

Gevrey-Chambertin Le Clos St.-Jacques 1992: Firm and chewy, spicy, with a little ripe currant flavor lurking in the background. Drinkable now. • $41 Ⓐ • (12/15/94) • **78**

Gevrey-Chambertin Le Clos St.-Jacques 1991: A light, uncomplicated, lean mouthful of red raspberry and red currant flavors, with a light bite of tannin on the finish. Drinkable now. • $75 • (01/31/94) • **82**

Gevrey-Chambertin Le Clos St.-Jacques 1990: A supple 1990, with a firm core of solid tannins and enough fruit to compensate for the tannic backbone. A well-integrated wine, with lots of raspberry, mushroom and wet earth flavors. Drinkable now. • $85 • (12/15/92) • **90**

Gevrey-Chambertin Le Clos St.-Jacques 1989 • $72 Ⓐ • (01/31/92) • **90**

Gevrey-Chambertin Le Clos St.-Jacques 1985 • $81 Ⓐ • (10/15/88) • **92**

Mazis-Chambertin Mazy-Chambertin 1992: Very light and floral, with a touch of raspberry and strawberry flavor sneaking in on the palate. Drink now. • $NA • (12/15/94) • **82**

Mazis-Chambertin Mazy-Chambertin 1991: Supple and exotic; a mouthful of wild berry, black cherry, spice and earth notes comes together into an opulent, toasty finish. A graceful wine that cascades its flavors seductively, then hits the tannin mark on the finish. Drink now. • $75 • (01/31/94) • **90**

Mazis-Chambertin Mazy-Chambertin 1990: Ripe and chewy, with concentrated plum, black cherry and toast characteristics and a gorgeous finish. A monster wine that needs time to come around; try in 1999. • $75 • (12/15/92) • **93**

Mazis-Chambertin Mazy-Chambertin 1989 • $80 • (01/31/92) • **90**

Mazis-Chambertin Mazy-Chambertin 1985 • $63 • (10/15/88) • **85**

Ruchottes-Chambertin 1995: A straightforward, juicy '95 with a wild edge to the cherry and red berry flavors. It ends up slightly coarse; should drink well from 1999. 366 cases made. • $85 • (11/15/97) • **91**

Ruchottes-Chambertin Clos des Ruchottes 1993: Vibrant and delicious. Packed with fruit flavor and accented by spicy, floral notes. This is broad, mouth-filling, deep and concentrated. Firm tannins. Drink now through 2001. • $92 Ⓐ • (09/15/96) • **93**

Ruchottes-Chambertin Clos des Ruchottes 1992: Lean and very light with a pleasant ring of raspberry and hints of black cherry. Tannins are hardly present. Drinkable now. Tasted twice. • $NA • (12/15/94) • **84**

Ruchottes-Chambertin Clos des Ruchottes 1991: Lean and firm, opening out into a broad finish that rides a crescendo of currant, plum and blackberry flavors along with a few coffee and spice notes. Stylish and more intense than most '91s. • $NA • (01/31/94) • **89**

Ruchottes-Chambertin Clos des Ruchottes 1990: A well-toned monster, with a huge amount of ripe raspberry, cherry and earth aromas and flavors and tons of refined tannins. Goes on and on and on. A wine to welcome in the new century. • $80 • (12/15/92) • **96**

Ruchottes-Chambertin Clos des Ruchottes 1989 • $85 • (01/31/92) • **90**

ROUSSEAU, JEANNE

Beaujolais 1994 • $7 • (06/15/95) • **78**

Pouilly-Fuissé 1994: Solid white that offers lemon, apricot and pie-crust flavors in a crisp, delicate package. It's clean and tangy. • $13 • (06/30/95) • **83**

ROUSSELLE, CHÂTEAU LA

Fronsac 1996: Emits pretty berry and cherry aromas, but it's slightly diluted on the palate. Medium body, medium tannins, finishes short. • $NA • (01/01/97) (BT) • **80-84**

Fronsac 1995: Vivid and fruity, with plum, chocolate and violet flavors, finishing with freshness. Full-bodied, with fine tannins. • $NA • (01/01/97) (BT) • **85-89**

Fronsac 1990: Hard and steely; a wine with an excellent backbone of sharp tannins but a little thin in fruit. • $NA • (03/31/93) • **83**

ROUTAS, CHÂTEAU

Carignane Vin de Pays du Var Vieilles Vignes 1996: Peppery, with some nice flavors of cherry and spice. This is a lively and medium-bodied red wine that is imminently quaffable. Drink now. • $NA • (01/01/98) • **83**

Coteaux Varois 1993 • $7 • (11/30/94) • **82**

Coteaux Varois 1992 • $7 • (06/30/94) • **82**

Coteaux Varois Agrippa 1995: A generous, juicy, hearty red with lots of bright fruit flavors and spicy, cedary accents that linger on the finish. Has deep color, deep flavors and firm tannins. Drink now through 2000. A blend of 50 percent Syrah and 50 percent Cabernet Sauvignon. • $17 • (12/15/97) • **87**

Coteaux Varois Agrippa 1992: Slightly herbal and the fruit is dominated by excruciating tannins at the moment. May improve by 1999. 500 cases made. • $18 • (07/31/96) • **83**

Coteaux Varois Cyrano 1994: Loads of meaty, dark fruit mingle with aromas of violets and spicy oak. Rich, concentrated and structured. Try now. Made from Syrah. 390 cases made. • $18 • (07/31/96) • **86**

Coteaux Varois Infernet 1995: Firm and flavorful with cherry and plum notes, and good backbone of tannins. Finishes on a spicy note. A good hearty red wine that's meant for grilled meat. Drink now through 2000. 4,000 cases made. • $11 • (01/01/98) • **84**

Coteaux Varois Infernet 1994: Smooth and supple, delivering solid plum and blackberry flavors. Drink now. 2,500 cases made. • $10 • (07/31/96) • **84**

Coteaux Varois Infernet 1993 • $11 • (03/31/95) • **85**

Coteaux Varois Infernet 1992 • $8 • (06/30/94) • **83**

Coteaux Varois Luc Sorin 1994: Smooth and flavorful, boasting aromas and flavors of freshly crushed cherries, with accents of cedar and leather. Ample tannins provide structure, yet are polished. Drinkable now. • $15 • (01/31/97) • **87**

Coteaux Varois Luc Sorin 1993 • $15 • (03/31/95) • **87**

Coteaux Varois Luc Sorin 1992 • $11 • (06/30/94) • **87**

Coteaux Varois Mistral 1993: Amazing depth of color. Nose is completely undeveloped, but the palate exhibits plenty of ripe, black fruits set off by sweet, spicy oak. Loads of tannin. A Syrah-Cabernet blend. Try now. 400 cases made. • $20 • (07/31/96) • **88**

Coteaux Varois Rosé Rouvière 1996: A simple rosé that's dry and rather full-bodied, with grapey-earthy flavors. Made from Cinsault, Grenache and Syrah. 5,000 cases made. • $9 • (12/15/97) • **78**

Coteaux Varois Rouvière 1993 • $7 • (01/01/95) • **79**

Vin de Pays du Var Traditionel 1995: Fairly ripe, with dried cherry and plum flavors. A full-bodied red wine that finishes on a leathery note. A blend of 40 percent Cinsault, 40 percent Cabernet Sauvignon and 20 percent Carignan. Drink through 1999. 1,500 cases made. • $9 • (01/01/98) • **83**

Vin de Pays du Var White Coquelicot 1996: A buttery-tasting wine which, though it lacks finesse, is still tasty. Almond and pear flavors dominate. A blend of Chardonnay and Viognier. Drink now. 600 cases made. • $15 • (03/31/98) • **83**

ROUTIER, CHÂTEAU DE

Côtes de Malepère Cuvée Jean Lèzerat 1995: Interesting. Plush-tasting, with good dried cherry and berry flavors. Well focused, but it's hard to say if the fruit will outlast the substantial tannins. Drink now. 450 cases made. • $8 • (04/30/98) • **84**

ROUVIER SELECTIONS

Crozes-Hermitage 1991 • $12 • (05/31/94) • **85**

Côte-Rôtie 1990: Ripe, with floral, raspberry and vanilla flavors; it's full and long, firm and very well balanced. Try now. • $30 • (05/31/94) • **89**

ROUX, ARMAND

Coteaux du Languedoc Pic St.-Loup 1994: Floral aromas and raspberries are the hallmarks of this medium-bodied, firm red. A "dusty" character and chocolaty accents add interest and complexity. Drinkable now. 50,000 cases made. • $7 • (07/31/96) • **85**

Côtes du Lubéron La Forge 1989 • $6 • (04/15/93) BB • **80**

Côtes du Rhône La Berberine 1994 • $8 • (12/31/95) • **83**

Echézeaux 1959 • $110 • (08/31/90) • **94**

L'Epayrié Red Special Reserve NV: Pleasant, modest cherry flavor, but a resinous note detracts from the finish. 100,000 cases made. • $7 • (07/31/96) • **74**

Picpoul de Pinet Coteaux du Languedoc 1994 • $7 • (02/29/96) • **80**

Richebourg 1959 • $130 • (08/31/90) • **91**

Volnay Hospices de Beaune Général Muteau 1959 • $115 • (08/31/90) • **91**

ROUX, CHARLES

Côtes du Rhône-Villages Rasteau 1985 • $10 • (02/28/90) • **89**

ROUX PÈRE & FILS

Bourgogne White 1995: Firm, even a bit tart, but it has some ripe character and mineral, pear and tropical fruit notes. Medium-bodied; try now. 1,000 cases made. • $9 • (08/31/97) • **85**

Chardonnay Bourgogne 1994: Subtle yet intense. It's restrained but what's there is focused: spice, butter, melon and toasty pine nuts. Lovely, long, clean and focused finish. 3,333 cases made. • $NA • (05/31/96) • **87**

Chardonnay Bourgogne Les Genouvrées 1994: Ripe, honeyed and full-bodied, with tropical fruit, pear, mineral and slightly herbal notes. Just lacks concentration and seems flat on the finish. • $NA • (08/31/96) • **81**

Chassagne-Montrachet 1995: Smooth but of medium intensity, with citrus, some hazelnut and toasty spice flavors. A pretty wine. Try now. 375 cases made. • $31 • (08/31/97) • **85**

Chassagne-Montrachet 1994: Nicely toasty, with peach, citrus and green apple flavors. Crisp finish. Drinkable now. 375 cases made. • $NA • (08/31/96) • **80**

Chassagne-Montrachet 1993: Riper and richer than most, providing honey, woody, apple-tart flavors. Made in an accessible, creamy style, but could show more concentration. Drink now. 417 cases made. • $28 • (05/15/95) • **84**

Chassagne-Montrachet Clos St.-Jean Red 1983 • $13 • (09/16/85) • **86**

Chassagne-Montrachet Les Macherelles 1995: Well defined and clean, rich and supple, stressing its mineral and wet stone flavors. Great intensity and acidity here, as expected in this vintage, with a profusion of lemon and ripe pear notes and a long finish. Must cellar until after 2000. 250 cases made. • $35 • (05/31/97) • **93**

Corton-Charlemagne 1994: Very ripe and full-bodied, with more zesty, vibrant flavors than many '94 white Burgundies; a core of lime and citrus supports the gooey honey and tropical flavors. Nice toasty oak on the finish. Drink now through 1999. 75 cases made. • $NA • (08/31/96) • **88**

Meursault Clos des Porusots 1995: Harmonious, unctuous and rich, with subtle accents of toasty oak, lovely honey and ripe pear flavors. Full-bodied, it needs time—it's tough, almost tannic now. Try after 2000. 125 cases made. • $32 • (05/31/97) • **90**

Meursault Clos des Porusots 1994: Packed with reductive, dry ice aromas, it gets better as it airs, developing some vanilla and mineral notes that are

FRANCE

very seductive. Full-bodied and silky, with intense lime on the finish. Not for everyone, but enjoyable. 125 cases made. • $NA • (05/31/96) • **84**

Puligny-Montrachet Les Enseignères 1995: Amazingly supple, round and balanced, with a smooth, almost soft texture layered with mineral, honey, ripe pear and wet stone flavors. Closed on the nose, medium- to full-bodied, it is drinkable now but has the structure to improve through 2000. 208 cases made. • $38 • (05/31/97) • **91**

Puligny-Montrachet Les Enseignères 1994: Elegant, with some toasty bread, hazelnut, pear and pie crust flavors. Rather delicate finish. Tasted twice with consistent notes. • $NA • (08/31/96) • **82**

Puligny-Montrachet Les Enseignères 1993: Quite tough, but offering some decent, ripe honey, green apple and mineral notes. Long, earthy finish. Drinkable now. 333 cases made. • $28 • (05/15/95) • **85**

St.-Aubin La Chatenière White 1995: Ripe, rich and full-bodied, this wine features vibrant fruit and sweet-tasting, ripe pear and pineapple flavors, not overoaked, and very silky. Delicious finish, but a bit soft. Drink now. 275 cases made. • $29 • (05/31/97) • **87**

St.-Aubin La Chatenière White 1994: Round and smooth, with good fruit flavors and concentration. Medium-bodied. Drinkable now. • $NA • (08/31/96) • **83**

St.-Aubin La Chatenière White 1992: Rich and smooth, with some honey, walnut and apple flavors; quite lush in texture, but we could only wish for a bit more fruit intensity in this enjoyable white Burgundy. • $NA • (08/31/94) • **84**

St.-Aubin Les Cortons White 1994: Assertive and crisp, with some honey, almond and cedar aromas and flavors. Fresh and juicy, though it may strike some as a touch hollow in the midpalate. 833 cases made. • $NA • (05/31/96) • **83**

St.-Aubin Les Cortons White 1993: Candied, cooked apple taste and some toasty, wet hay character. Sour finish; oxidized? 667 cases made. • $21 • (05/15/95) • **77**

St.-Aubin Les Cortons White 1992: Nice, modest white Burgundy with subtle pear, vanilla, butter and walnut flavors and a very smooth, pleasant texture. • $NA • (08/31/94) • **82**

St.-Aubin Les Pucelles White 1994: Rustic, tart and simple, with modest fruit flavors and a lean finish. 2,000 cases made. • $NA • (05/31/96) • **73**

St.-Aubin White 1995: Round, thick and distinctive with some wet stone, earth, green apple and asparagus flavors. Rather firm, with a somewhat harsh finish. Try now through 2000. 1,083 cases made. • $25 • (05/31/97) • **79**

Santenay 1985 • $21 • (10/31/87) • **83**

Volnay En Champans 1988 • $35 • (03/31/90) • **86**

Volnay En Champans 1985 • $25 • (03/15/87) • **92**

ROUZÉ, JACQUES

Quincy 1996: Crisp, showing assertive Sauvignon Blanc aromas and flavors of herbs and minerals. Light but firm on the palate. Not particularly concentrated, but traditional in character. Drink now. 6,000 cases made. • $14 • (06/30/98) • **84**

ROY-THEVENIN, ALAIN

Montagny Les Burnins 1995: A relatively firm, concentrated Montagny, offering some sweet flavors among pronounced citrus notes. Medium- to full-bodied, it needs time. Try after 2000. From Château de la Saak. 208 cases made. • $19 • (05/31/97) • **88**

Montagny Premier Cru 1995: Clean and vibrant, with a grassy, Sauvignonlike character that plays nicely to the honey and subtle oak accents of this medium-bodied, balanced white. Try now through 2000. 2,500 cases made. • $17 • (05/31/97) • **87**

ROYES, DOMAINE DES

St.-Joseph 1995: Fleshy and generous with its round fruit flavors of plums and black cherries, accents of coffee and licorice. Not superconcentrated, but it's balanced and firm. Drink now through 2000. • $NA • (10/15/97) • **88**

St.-Joseph 1991 • $NA • (05/31/94) • **78**

Key: SS—Spectator Selection CS—Cellar Selection HR—Highly Recommended BB—Best Buy $NA—Price not available Ⓐ—Auction Price (BT)—Barrel Tasting
Dates in parentheses indicate the issues in which the ratings were published.

ROYLLAND, CHÂTEAU

St.-Emilion 1995: Delivers more on the nose than the palate but delicious. Pretty aromas of violets and crushed raspberries. Medium-bodied, with ripe red berry flavors, medium tannins and a fresh finish. • $NA • (01/01/97) • **86**

RUDEL, COMTE DE

Entre-Deux-Mers 1993 • $9 • (05/31/95) • **79**

RUET

Brouilly Cuvée Spéciale 1993 • $15 • (06/15/95) • **78**

Brouilly Vieilles Vignes 1996: A pretty red, offering plush black cherry and berry flavors with a hint of smoke, soft tannins and just enough acidity for liveliness. Makes a nice apéritif or try with lighter dishes. Drink now. • $15 • (06/15/98) • **85**

Brouilly Vieilles Vignes 1994: Smooth and firm, with a good texture and fresh, if slightly muted, plum and licorice flavors. Nicely spicy finish. A good food-wine. • $16 • (09/15/96) • **85**

RUINART

Brut Blanc de Blancs Champagne Dom Ruinart 1988: A fine example of blanc de blancs, this vivid, lively, lemon and butter-scented bubbly displays distinctive toasty accents and a crisp but lingering finish. Drink now through 2000. • $97 • (12/31/97) • **91**

Brut Blanc de Blancs Champagne Dom Ruinart 1986: Super rich and toasty Champagne in an elegant and refined style. Full bodied with apple, vanilla and lemon character, intense acidity and a medium finish. Drink now. • $83 • (12/31/93) • **90**

Brut Blanc de Blancs Champagne Dom Ruinart 1985: A gentle wine that gradually builds on your palate. Such finesse and elegance. Rich and beautiful with citrus, peach and vanilla character, full body and fresh acidity. This has greatly improved with bottle age since we tasted it in December 1991. Drinkable now but it will hold for years. • $83 • (12/31/93) • **95**

Brut Blanc de Blancs Champagne Dom Ruinart 1983 • $60 • (12/31/90) • **87**

Brut Blanc de Blancs Champagne Dom Ruinart 1982: Outstanding Champagne. Very rich, complex and mature, with a fascinating array of nutty, spicy aromas and ripe, satisfying fruit and smoke flavors. • $61 • (12/31/90) • **90**

Brut Blanc de Blancs Champagne Dom Ruinart 1981 • $61 • (12/31/89) • **90**

Brut Blanc de Blancs Champagne Dom Ruinart 1979 • $39 • (10/31/86) • **91**

Brut Blanc de Blancs Champagne Dom Ruinart 1978 • $40 • (05/16/86) • **87**

Brut Blanc de Blancs Champagne Dom Ruinart 1976 • $30 • (10/01/84) • **84**

Brut Champagne 1988: Seriously rich Champagne with structure and flavor of a Meursault. Fine bubbles and acidity and a long flavorful finish. Powerful and rich. Drinkable now. • $46 • (12/31/93) • **92**

Brut Champagne 1986: Another very rich and ripe wine with a fine foamy texture, toasty, vanilla, apple flavors, medium body and a long fresh finish. Tasted twice. Drink now. • $46 • (12/31/93) • **87**

Brut Champagne R de Ruinart 1992: Good balance, a refreshing texture and a lingering finish. On the austere side. A solid Champagne from a lesser vintage. Try with hors d'oeuvres and seafood. • $50 • (07/31/97) • **87**

Brut Champagne R de Ruinart 1990: Very aromatic and enticing. Full-bodied and full-flavored with nicely matured toasty aromas, butter and butterscotch flavors and a creamy smooth texture. Lingering finish, too. • $46 • (07/31/96) • **91**

Brut Champagne R de Ruinart 1988: This is wonderfully mature and complex, from the smoky, nutty aromas through the lingering, subtle finish. It's a bit austere in texture, but makes up for it in the intriguing, elegant blend of fruit and mature flavors—a rare quality and a pleasant find. Great to drink now. 500 cases made. • $50 • (11/30/95) HR • **94**

Brut Champagne R de Ruinart NV: A reserved but appetizing Champagne that combines toasty-earthy aromas, bright citrus flavors with spicy overtones and a dry but clean aftertaste. • $38 • (11/15/97) • **88**

Brut Rosé Champagne Dom Ruinart 1986: A subtle taste experience in a well-aged vintage rosé. It's mature and flavorful, but not aggressive, with lots of toasty, nutty accents to the solid core of mature fruit and spice flavors. Drink now. Tasted twice, with consistent notes. • $112 • (12/31/97) • **89**

Brut Rosé Champagne Dom Ruinart 1985: Easy-going, smooth and mouthfilling, with a creamy texture and flavors of pear, apple and cherry. It has the toasty, doughy, almond nuances that we look for in an aged bubbly. 200 cases made. • $96 • (12/15/94) • **89**

Brut Rosé Champagne Dom Ruinart 1979 • $80 • (09/30/88) • **92**

Brut Rosé Champagne Dom Ruinart 1978 • $40 • (09/30/86) • **91**

Brut Rosé Champagne R de Ruinart NV: A concentrated, lively rosé that's well-balanced, full-bodied and smooth-textured. Lots of bright fruit comes through on the palate and finish. Drink now. 200 cases imported. • $71 • (11/30/97) • **88**

RULLY, CHÂTEAU DE

Rully White 1995: Fairly elegant in style, with dried herb, pear and tropical flavors. A medium-bodied Chardonnay. Drink now. • $18 • (08/31/97) • **85**

Rully White 1994: A solid village wine with a crisp core of lemon, pear, wet earth and ripe apple flavors, though it seems a bit green on the finish. Drinkable now. • $20 • (05/31/96) • **81**

SABON & FILS, DOMAINE ROGER

Châteauneuf-du-Pape 1988 • $20 • (09/30/90) • **88**

Châteauneuf-du-Pape Cuvée Prestige 1988 • $23 • (09/30/90) • **85**

Châteauneuf-du-Pape Cuvée Réserve 1988 • $20 • (09/30/90) • **80**

SADE, MARQUIS DE

Brut Champagne Private Reserve 1988: Spicy and aromatic, with yeasty flavors and aromas. Aggressive at first, but it settles down, with pleasant butter, toast and almond notes. Firm and well balanced, with a citrusy finish. • $NA • (12/31/94) • **88**

Brut Champagne Private Reserve 1985: The simple, lemony aromas and flavors have intensity, but little finesse. There's rosemary on the finish, making the wine a little odd. • $48 • (03/31/92) • **79**

Brut Champagne Private Reserve 1981 • $56 • (12/31/90) • **89**

SAIER

Clos des Lambrays 1990: An earthy wine, with tart, leafy mineral and limestone flavors that dominate more than the black cherry notes. Tight and firm. Drinkable now. 1,750 cases made. • $73 • (03/15/93) • **80**

Clos des Lambrays 1989 • $68 • (11/15/91) • **85**

Clos des Lambrays 1988 • $75 • (03/31/91) • **91**

Clos des Lambrays Domaine des Lambrays 1985 • $55 • (02/15/88) • **78**

Mercurey Les Champs Martins 1988 • $17 • (08/31/91) • **80**

Mercurey Les Champs Martins 1985 • $20 • (03/31/88) • **83**

Mercurey Les Chenelots 1988 • $17 • (04/30/91) • **67**

ST.-ANDRÉ, CHÂTEAU

Châteauneuf-du-Pape 1988 • $16 • (11/30/90) • **87**

ST.-ANDRÉ-CORBIN, CHÂTEAU

St.-Georges-St.-Emilion 1997: A bit thin, with some mineral and berry character but a short rather dry finish. Wait and see. • $NA • (06/15/98) (BT) • **80-84**

St.-Georges-St.-Emilion 1996: A firm wine with good fruit, well-integrated tannins and a velvety finish. Slightly one-dimensional now. Could move up next year. • $NA • (01/01/97) (BT) • **80-84**

St.-Georges-St.-Emilion 1995: Very good '95, although slightly rustic. Dried cherry and mint aromas. Full-bodied, with well-integrated tannins and a mouthpuckering finish. Needs time. Try after 2001. • $14 • (01/31/98) • **87**

St.-Georges-St.-Emilion 1994: A firm wine, with plenty of dried cherry notes. Slightly one-dimensional, but the fruit flavors are ripe fruit and the tannins are good. Drink now. • $12 • (01/31/97) • **82**

St.-Georges-St.-Emilion 1993: Slightly rough red berry, metallic, steely character and a dry, lean finish. • $15 • (01/31/96) • **77**

St.-Georges-St.-Emilion 1990: A big, velvety wine, with loads of berry and cherry character, soft tannins and a lingering aftertaste of berries. Drinkable now. • $15 • (03/31/93) • **88**

St.-Georges-St.-Emilion 1989 • $15 • (04/30/92) • **91**

St.-Georges-St.-Emilion 1986 • $22 • (03/31/90) • **77**

STE.-ANNE, DOMAINE

Côtes du Rhône Cuvée Syrah 1994: A deep red showing the inky, gamy notes of ripe Syrah, with a polished yet chewy texture that should show well with grilled meats. Firm and polished, and should drink well through 2002. • $19 • (10/15/97) • **86**

Côtes du Rhône White Le Viognier 1995: Shows concentration and complexity, with well-defined, lively pineapple, vanilla and spice flavors that linger on the finish. Intriguing, and food-friendly. • $27 • (12/15/96) • **88**

Côtes du Rhône-Villages 1995: Berry and herbal flavors mingle in this light red. It's clean and fresh; a simple wine for drinking now. • $12 • (12/15/96) • **81**

Côtes du Rhône-Villages Cuvée Notre Dame des Cellettes 1995: This round, generous red offers lively flavors of strawberries, cinnamon and herbs, with just enough tannin for grip. Drink now, while it has the exuberance of youth. 1,067 cases made. • $16 • (10/15/97) • **84**

Côtes du Rhône-Villages Cuvée Notre Dame des Cellettes 1994: Round and fruity, yet with a firm underpinning of tannin, this is a generous wine with plum, berry and licorice flavors. Drinkable now. • $15 • (12/15/96) • **83**

Côtes du Rhône-Villages Cuvée Notre Dame des Cellettes 1987 • $8 • (01/31/89) • **80**

Côtes du Rhône-Villages Cuvée Saint-Gervais 1995: Lively, displaying a pretty combination of ripe fruit and firm structure, with plum, vanilla and appealing herbal flavors. Fresh and clean, it's drinkable now, but sturdy enough to improve through 2000. • $16 • (10/15/97) • **87**

Côtes du Rhône-Villages Cuvée Saint-Gervais 1994: Dark, spicy aromas give way to ripe flavors of plums, black pepper and licorice in this alluring red. Balanced and firm, it's appealing now, especially with food. • $16 • (12/15/96) • **87**

ST.-ANTONIN, DOMAINE

Faugères 1996: A powerful and crisp-tasting red, with dark plum, cherry and spice flavors and plenty of leather and game notes. Packs a punch and is well defined, though the flavors need time to meld. Best from 2000 through 2005. • $10 • (06/15/98) • **87**

ST.-DÉSIRAT, CAVE DE

St.-Joseph 1992 • $14 • (11/15/95) • **78**

Syrah Vin de Pays des Collines Rhodaniennes 1994: Tobacco and herbal aromas give a Provençal accent and follow through on the light-bodied, fruity palate. An early-drinking red without pretension, but it does offer a sense of place. 100,000 cases made. • $8 • (10/15/97) • **83**

Syrah Vin de Pays des Collines Rhodaniennes 1993 • $8 • (07/31/95) • **76**

ST.-ESTEVE D'UCHAUX, CHÂTEAU

Côtes du Rhône-Villages 1989 • $10 • (11/15/91) • **84**

STE.-EULALIE, CHÂTEAU

Minervois Cuvée Tradition 1995: A well-focused red, with lovely flavors of blackberry, plum and leather and a pleasant, though slightly drying, finish. Drink now. • $9 • (05/31/98) • **85**

Minervois 1994: Tastes of prunes, with some rhubarb flavors and a dull, root-beerlike finish. Past its prime. • $8 • (05/31/98) • **77**

Minervois 1992 • $8 • (06/30/94) • **78**

Minervois 1991 • $9 • (03/15/94) • **82**

ST.-FLORIN, CHÂTEAU

Entre-Deux-Mers 1995: Fairly rich, with a good backbone of acidity. Lacks some focus, however. With floral, melon and tropical flavors. • $8 • (04/30/97) • **81**

Entre-Deux-Mers 1993 • $7 • (02/29/96) • **75**

ST.-GEORGES, CHÂTEAU

St.-Georges-St.-Emilion 1990: Offers plenty of ripe, concentrated, stewed plum flavors in a style that is rustic and slightly astringent. The finish is long. • $23 • (08/31/95) • **86**

St.-Georges-St.-Emilion 1988 • $18 • (04/30/92) • **73**

St.-Georges-St.-Emilion 1986 • $14 • (07/15/90) • **87**

St.-Georges-St.-Emilion 1985 • $11 • (07/31/89) • **87**

ST.-GEORGES, DOMAINE

Corbières 1990 • $8 • (03/15/94) • **82**
Corbières Grand Millésime 1990 • $8 • (06/15/93) • **73**
Corbières Grand Millésime Elevé en Fûts de Chêne 1988 • $8 • (07/15/92) • **81**

ST.-GERMAIN, CHÂTEAU

Coteaux du Languedoc 1995: Beautifully complex, with incredibly concentrated and well-focused flavors of blackberry, currant, and ripe plum. Has a fragrant aroma and a lingering finish accented by leather and chocolate notes. Despite its impressive power, it comes off balanced and classy. Drink now through 2001. 2,800 cases made. • $12 • (03/31/98) • **91**

ST.-JACQUES, CHÂTEAU

Bordeaux Supérieur 1997: Very light and watery. Has some fruit but fades quickly. • $NA • (06/15/98) (BT) • **75-79**
Bordeaux Supérieur 1996: Some good violet and grapey character, but slightly diluted palate. Medium-bodied, with medium tannins and a light finish. Second wine of Château Siran. 15,000 cases made. • $13 • (06/15/98) (BT) • **80-84**
Bordeaux Supérieur 1995: Good '95, with a balance of ripe berry and dried cherry aromas and flavors and medium tannins. Best after 1999. • $15 • (01/31/98) • **83**
Bordeaux Supérieur 1993: Berry and cherry flavors dominate this wine. Still a bit tannic on the finish. • $13 • (06/30/97) • **82**

ST.-JAMES, CHÂTEAU

Corbières 1992 • $8 • (03/15/94) • **80**

ST.-LAURENT, CHÂTEAU

Corbières Réserve Privée 1994: Soft plum and cherry notes are augmented by spice in this nearly mature red. Dry, with moderate concentration and length, it needs food to smooth out the tannins. 10,000 cases made. • $7 • (12/15/97) • **84**
Corbières Réserve Privée 1991 • $7 • (06/15/93) • **78**
Corbières White Réserve Privée 1994: Subtle honey and nut flavors give this otherwise simple, but solid, wine a nice mature edge. • $7 • (10/31/97) • **80**

ST.-LAURENT-L'ABBAYE, DOMAINE DE

Pouilly-Fumé 1994 • $17 • (12/15/95) • **83**

ST.-LOUIS LA PERDRIX, CHÂTEAU

Costières de Nimes 1990 • $8 • (04/15/93) BB • **83**
Costières de Nimes Cuvée Marianne 1989 • $11 • (02/28/93) • **75**

ST.-LUC, DOMAINE

Coteaux du Tricastin 1993 • $8 • (12/31/95) • **84**
Coteaux du Tricastin 1989 • $7 • (12/31/91) BB • **83**
Coteaux du Tricastin 1988 • $11 • (08/31/91) • **77**
Coteaux du Tricastin White 1994 • $9 • (12/31/95) • **79**
Côteaux du Tricastin 1993 • $8 • (12/31/95) • **84**
Coteaux du Tricastin Syrah Elevé en Fût de Chêne 1993 • $14 • (12/31/95) • **85**

STE.-MAIRE, CHÂTEAU

Entre-Deux-Mers Cuvée Madlys 1993 • $10 • (05/31/95) • **80**

Key: SS—Spectator Selection CS—Cellar Selection HR—Highly Recommended BB—Best Buy $NA—Price not available Ⓐ—Auction Price (BT)—Barrel Tasting
Dates in parentheses indicate the issues in which the ratings were published.

ST.-MAURICE, CHÂTEAU

Côtes du Rhône 1995: Light in color and body, with only modest aromas. Dry, diluted and sharp finish. 50 cases imported. 20,833 cases made. • $8 • (10/15/97) • **70**
Côtes du Rhône-Villages Laudun Cuvée Vicomte Guillaue de Joyeuse 1995: Rather gentle, with licorice, plum, and cherry notes, it's appealing to drink now, with soft tannins and toasty oak accents on the finish. 12,500 cases made. • $8 • (10/15/97) • **81**

ST.-MICHEL, CHÂTEAU

Lussac-St.-Emilion 1995: A rustic Bordeaux with earthy aromas, modest fruit flavors and rather tough tannins. Might improve with time, but it's a gamble. 1,500 cases made. • $10 • (01/31/98) • **79**

STE.-PAULE, DOMAINE

Corbières 1990 • $9 • (03/15/94) • **83**

ST.-PIERRE, CHÂTEAU

St.-Julien 1997: Mineral and cherry aromas and flavors follow through onto the palate. Medium-bodied, with silky tannins and a light finish. • $NA • (06/15/98) (BT) • **85-89**
St.-Julien 1996: Plenty of licorice and spice character. Medium- to full-bodied, with medium tannins and a silky, caressing finish. Pretty wine. Got to like this. • $30 • (06/15/98) (BT) • **90-94**
St.-Julien 1995: Delicious, chewy wine with tobacco, chocolate and berry aromas and flavors. Full-bodied, with full, round tannins and a long, juicy aftertaste. Hard not to drink it now, but it will improve with age, probably best after 2000. • $30 • (01/31/98) • **90**
St.-Julien 1994: Darkly colored, emitting intense tar, asphalt and fruit aromas. Full-bodied and chewy, with round tannins. A straightforward, big Cab that will be better in 1999. • $32 • (01/31/97) • **86**
St.-Julien 1993: Pleasant red berry and cherry character, medium body, medium-to-light tannins and a fresh finish. Drinkable now. • $22 • (01/31/96) • **85**
St.-Julien 1992: Quite a mouthful of tobacco and plum flavor; medium-bodied and ripe, ending in a long, velvety finish. Drinkable now. • $18 • (04/15/95) • **87**
St.-Julien 1991: Well crafted, with a solid core of fruit. It doesn't show much now, but the blackberry flavor marries nicely with the oak. Drinkable now. • $17 • (03/31/94) • **84**
St.-Julien 1990: Made in a restrained style, but there's gorgeous fruit with chocolate, berry and plum character and compact, velvety tannins. Drinkable now. 8,000 cases made. • $26 • (03/31/93) • **92**
St.-Julien 1989 • $21 Ⓐ • (10/15/92) • **91**
St.-Julien 1988 • $27 • (10/15/92) • **88**
St.-Julien 1987 • $17 • (10/15/92) • **80**
St.-Julien 1986 • $24 • (10/15/92) • **90**
St.-Julien 1985 • $NA • (10/15/92) • **84**
St.-Julien 1984 • $12 • (10/15/92) • **79**
St.-Julien 1983 • $NA • (10/15/92) • **86**
St.-Julien 1982 • $28 • (10/15/92) • **83**
St.-Julien 1981 • $NA • (10/15/92) • **82**
St.-Julien 1979 • $24 • (10/15/92) • **77**
St.-Julien 1978 • $28 • (10/15/92) • **83**
St.-Julien 1975 • $20 • (10/15/92) • **72**
St.-Julien 1970 • $45 • (10/15/92) • **84**
St.-Julien 1969 • $15 • (10/15/92) • **70**
St.-Julien 1962 • $55 • (10/15/92) • **72**
St.-Julien 1961 • $NA • (04/30/92) • **82**
St.-Julien 1959 • $90 • (10/15/92) • **75**

ST.-PIERRE, LES CAVES

Châteauneuf-du-Pape Clefs des Prelats 1988 • $13 • (01/31/91) • **87**
Côte-Rôtie Marquis de Tournelles 1987 • $23 • (01/31/91) • **84**
Côtes du Rhône-Villages Les Lissandres 1988 • $7 • (12/15/90) BB • **84**
Hermitage Tertre des Carmes 1988 • $23 • (12/31/90) • **88**

ST.-ROBERT, CHÂTEAU

Graves 1996: Slightly one-dimensional, with earthy, berry character. Medium-bodied, with medium tannins and a rather diluted finish. 30,000 cases made. • $18 • (06/15/98) (BT) • **80-84**

Graves Cuvée Poncet-Deville 1996: Nice texture. Medium- to light-bodied, with fine tannins and a light berry, floral aftertaste. 10,160 cases made. • $30 • (06/15/98) (BT) • **80-84**

Graves Cuvée Poncet-Deville 1995: Enticing and complex, this elegant Bordeaux has toasty aromas, ample cherry, cedar and cinnamon flavors, a lingering finish and firm tannins. Best from 1999 through 2005. 1,200 cases made. • $25 • (01/31/98) • **89**

ST.-SAUVEUR, DOMAINE

Côtes du Ventoux 1990 • $6 • (08/31/92) • **79**

Côtes du Ventoux 1988 • $4 • (10/15/91) BB • **83**

Muscat de Beaumes-de-Venise Vin Doux Naturel 1988 • $17 • (03/31/91) • **80**

ST.-SULPICE, CHÂTEAU

Bordeaux 1994: Tea and dried fruit flavors make this supple red taste old before its time. Has a pleasant texture and some berry flavors, but needs drinking soon. • $9 • (10/15/97) • **78**

SAINT-YZANS, CHÂTEAU

Médoc 1995: Could use a little more flesh. Slightly one-dimensional, with lots of cherry character. Medium-bodied, with firm tannins and a slightly lean finish. • $NA • (01/01/97) • **85**

SALES, CHÂTEAU DE

Pomerol 1995: Lovely, soft tannins and plenty of chocolate and berry character. Fresh, subtle finish. • $NA • (05/15/96) (BT) • **85-89**

Pomerol 1986 • $18 Ⓐ • (06/30/89) • **86**

Pomerol 1985 • $37 Ⓐ • (06/30/88) • **87**

Pomerol 1982 • $49 Ⓐ • (05/15/89) • **88**

SALLE, DOMAINE DE LA

Beaune Champs Pimonts 1995: A disappointing '95 red Burgundy from the Côte de Beaune, offering some modest aromas and flavors, and some unripe herbal notes leading to a chewy, astringent finish. Drink chilled. • $NA • (11/15/97) • **74**

SALLE DE COEURS

Cabernet Sauvignon Vin de Pays d'Oc 1994 • $8 • (10/31/95) • **77**

Merlot Vin de Pays d'Oc 1994 • $8 • (10/31/95) • **81**

SALLE DE POUJEAUX, CHÂTEAU LA

Moulis 1989 • $15 • (03/15/92) • **85**

SALON

Brut Blanc de Blancs Champagne 1983: Distinctive and fully mature, layered with honey, almond, toast and fig flavors that are mellow and complex on a creamy texture. Lingering finish, too. Ready to drink. Scored higher in 1994. • $100 • (12/31/96) • **90**

Brut Blanc de Blancs Champagne Le Mesnil 1988: Fresh and lively in flavor, yet smooth in texture, here's a light but vibrant Champagne with citrus and spice flavors lingering on the finish. A bit unimpressive now, but has a track record for improving with time. Drink now through 2005. • $130 • (11/30/97) • **90**

Brut Blanc de Blancs Champagne Le Mesnil 1983: Elegant and firm, with lemon and grapefruit flavors that are balanced by a luscious, creamy texture. It's still crisp and lively for an aged Champagne and has a long, delicate finish. Drink now or cellar through 1997. • $NA • (11/30/94) HR • **93**

Brut Blanc de Blancs Champagne Le Mesnil 1982: Every time we taste this wine we love it even more. High volume and high intensity, they pulled out all the stops to get the most fruit and vanilla flavors, fine acidity and a long finish. A Cellar Selection in December 1991. At its peak. Drink now. 4,000 cases made. • $100 • (12/31/93) • **95**

Brut Blanc de Blancs Champagne Le Mesnil 1979 • $108 • (12/31/88) • **92**

Brut Blanc de Blancs Champagne Le Mesnil 1979 Disgorged Summer 1988 • $125 • (12/31/89) • **93**

Brut Blanc de Blancs Champagne Le Mesnil 1976 • $110/1.5 liter • (12/31/88) • **91**

SALVARD, DOMAINE DU

Cheverny 1993 • $9 • (12/15/95) • **82**

SALVAT, DOMAINE

Côtes du Roussillon Rosé Taïchac 1995: A fresh, flavorful, charming rosé with more than enough cherry and plum notes to give it substance and a lingering finish. • $11 • (05/31/97) • **86**

Côtes du Roussillon White Taïchac 1995: Lean and tart, with modest green apple and citrus flavors. Slightly bitter finish. • $11 • (05/31/97) • **77**

Muscat de Rivesaltes 1995: Extremely flavorful and deep, with assertive pear, spice and apricot flavors. A lively, powerful, sweet wine for the cheese course or after dinner. • $17 • (05/31/97) • **89**

Vin de Pays des Coteaux des Fenouillèdes Fenouill 1995: A jammy red with ripe flavors of plums, licorice and herbs, this is blunt but amiable. Drinkable now. • $8 • (06/30/97) • **81**

SANCERRE, CHÂTEAU DE

Sancerre 1995: Unusually vegetal and earthy, this is rich but lacks fruit and freshness. Drink now. • $15 • (03/31/98) • **75**

Sancerre 1994: Good structure in this white, but its flavors are a bit earthy and vegetal, without much fruit for balance. Tasted twice, with consistent notes. • $15 • (06/15/97) • **78**

SANG DES CAILLOUX, DOMAINE LE

Vacqueyras 1993 • $13 • (09/30/95) • **86**

Vacqueyras 1990 • $12 • (04/15/93) • **83**

SANTA DUC, DOMAINE

Gigondas 1990 • $21 • (04/15/93) • **80**

SANTÉ, BERNARD

Chénas 1994: Candied cherry and light chocolate flavors are soft and a bit dull in this round red. It's a bit ponderous for Beaujolais. • $15 • (06/30/97) • **79**

Moulin-à-Vent 1994: Not as big-boned as many Moulin-à-Vent, but shows attractive meaty, smoky flavors, lively black cherry notes and firm tannins. Should blossom with stews and roasts. • $18 • (04/30/97) • **86**

SARGET DE GRUAUD-LAROSE

St.-Julien 1995: A bit rustic, but shows good concentration. Attractive blackberry and game aromas. Tannic, with good berry and chocolate character and a mouthpuckering finish. A little alcoholic. Second label of Château Gruaud-Larose. Better after 2000. • $24 • (01/31/98) • **85**

SARRAU, ROBERT

Beaujolais-Villages 1996: A round red, lively and fresh, with clean, simple berry and grape flavors. Good weight on the palate, too. • $8 • (09/15/97) • **84**

Beaujolais-Villages 1995: Light and soft, this shows appealing black cherry and cinnamon flavors, with a hint of smoke on the finish. It has character, if not much depth. • $8 • (04/30/97) • **83**

Brouilly Clos Reissier 1995: Bright cherry and raspberry aromas give way to a silky palate with clean, ripe, red fruit flavors. It's soft, but has just enough tannin for grip. Lively. 2,800 cases made. • $10 • (04/30/97) • **85**

Fleurie Domaine du Grand Garant 1996: Polished, offering smooth texture and ripe flavors of blackberries, tobacco and licorice. Well balanced for drinking now, especially with food. 2,500 cases made. • $13 • (09/15/97) • **86**

Fleurie Grand Pré 1995: Ripe and round, yet slightly unfocused, with gamy, earthy flavors that tend to overwhelm the plum notes. Will stand up to food. 2,000 cases made. • $12 • (04/30/97) • **84**

Juliénas Château des Capitans 1996: Big, even for Juliénas, with chunky tannins and ripe, sweet flavors, but it lacks polish and balance now. Try now with food. 4,000 cases made. • $11 • (09/15/97) • **84**

Juliénas Château des Capitans 1995: Well made, harmonious and true to type, this appealing Beaujolais is plush yet firm, combining bright black cherry and plum flavors with smoky and gamy accents, firm tannins and bright acidity. 3,800 cases made. • $9 • (04/30/97) • **88**

Mâcon-Fuissé 1995: Unusual. Starts with buttery aromas, follows with orangelike flavors, then turns very dry and astringent on the finish. Awkward. 3,500 cases made. • $9 • (02/28/97) • **76**

Mâcon-Villages 1996: Hollow and on the tart side, showing meager fruit. Tasted twice, with consistent notes. • $9 • (08/31/97) • **76**

Merlot Vin de Pays d'Oc 1995: A slightly green-tasting wine, with minty and herbal flavors and aromas. The tart finish doesn't add much. • $7 • (12/15/96) • **79**

Morgon Domaine des Bouviers 1996: Light-bodied and tart for Morgon. Shows light ruby color, simple grapey aromas and lean flavors of cranberries and tart cherries. Lively and fresh. 4,000 cases made. • $11 • (09/15/97) • **83**

Moulin-à-Vent Domaine de la Tour du Bief 1995: Bright, spicy fruit flavors of black cherry and plum mingle with smoky and gamy accents. It's not as big as many Moulin-à-Vent, but is well defined and has enough tannin for food. 7,500 cases made. • $12 • (04/30/97) • **85**

Pouilly-Fuissé 1995: Mineral and lemon flavors and a smoky, almost matchsticklike aroma. 5,300 cases made. • $15 • (01/31/97) • **78**

St.-Véran 1996: An earthy-tasting wine, with some almond and fig tones. A bit heavy-handed and awkward. 7,500 cases made. • $10 • (08/31/97) • **78**

St.-Véran 1995: Somewhat coarse, with only modest green apple and vegetal flavors. Off-putting aromas. 6,500 cases made. • $8 • (01/31/97) • **72**

SARRY, DOMAINE DE

Sancerre 1997: This light white offers grapefruit and lemon flavors, with hints of herbs and minerals and a leesy character that adds a soft, almost soapy note. Drink now through 1999. 5,500 cases made. • $14 • (06/15/98) • **82**

SARTRE, CHÂTEAU LE

Pessac-Léognan 1997: A weedy, light red with light tannins and a diluted finish. • $NA • (06/15/98) (BT) • **75-79**

Pessac-Léognan 1996: A bit lean and tough. Medium-bodied, with firm tannins and a citrusy berry aftertaste. Wait and see. • $23 • (06/15/98) (BT) • **80-84**

Pessac-Léognan 1995: Offers pretty berry and milk chocolate aromas and flavors, medium body, soft tannins and a fresh aftertaste. Better after 1999. • $22 • (01/31/98) • **86**

Pessac-Léognan 1994: Light and weedy in character. Some fruit flavors, but it's not a wine to seek out. 8,000 cases made. • $NA • (01/31/97) • **74**

Pessac-Léognan 1993: Good cherry, berry and chocolate aromas and flavors, medium body and tannins and a crisp finish. Drink now. • $18 • (01/31/96) • **84**

Pessac-Léognan 1992: Short and lean but has a certain elegance, delivering berry, dried-herb and mineral flavor. • $14 • (04/15/95) • **79**

Pessac-Léognan 1991: Round and delicate, with black olive and herbal notes; medium body, but diluted on the finish. • $14 • (03/31/94) • **77**

Pessac-Léognan 1990: An elegant wine, with perfumed berry aromas and fine fruit and tannins. Drinkable now. 2,000 cases made. • $19 • (03/31/93) • **87**

Pessac-Léognan White 1995: Impressive richness to the flavors, which range from ripe apple to coconut, although slightly light in the aftertaste. Medium-bodied, with moderate acidity. Drink now. • $20 • (04/30/98) • **86**

Pessac-Léognan White 1994 • $18 • (03/31/96) • **90**

Pessac-Léognan White 1993 • $13 • (05/31/95) • **88**

Key: SS—Spectator Selection CS—Cellar Selection HR—Highly Recommended BB—Best Buy $NA—Price not available Ⓐ—Auction Price (BT)—Barrel Tasting
Dates in parentheses indicate the issues in which the ratings were published.

SAUGÈRE, LYLIANE

Côte-Rôtie La Colline d'Argent 1991: Nicely balanced and harmonious, smooth-textured and keeps the tannins well modulated, offering berry and spice flavors. Drinkable now. 1,100 cases made. • $27 • (05/31/94) • **86**

Hermitage 1992: Ripe and chunky, showing good ripeness for the vintage, sweet plum, earth and black pepper flavors and muscular tannins. Gutsy; will match well with grilled beef. Drinkable now through 1999. • $32 • (10/15/95) • **86**

Hermitage 1991: Ripe and luscious, this shows classic Syrah flavors of spice, licorice and game, plenty of ripe blackberry on the palate and a healthy dollop of new oak, which adds complexity. Try now. • $32 • (10/15/95) • **90**

Hermitage La Côte des Seigneurs 1990: A tough, sturdy and hard-edged young wine that's backward and closed, but once the spicy, leathery, black cherry and mineral flavors begin to emerge, it's gorgeous. The tannins are substantial, but also fine and balanced. Drinkable now to 2000. 660 cases made. • $26 • (04/15/94) HR • **91**

SAULT, DOMAINE DU

Corbières 1988 • $5 • (07/15/92) • **78**

SAUMAIZE, JACQUES

Pouilly-Fuissé Clos de La Roche 1994: Tasty and attractive, tasting almost like pear gelato, both creamy and fruity. Fresh and crisp, but not tart, on the lovely finish. Try now with oysters or shellfish. • $17 • (05/31/96) • **87**

Pouilly-Fuissé Vieilles Vignes 1994: Quite likeable and ready to drink, a straightforward white that has decent spice, citrus, apple and honey flavors. Turns creamy on the sweet-tasting finish. • $16 • (05/31/96) • **84**

Pouilly-Fuissé Vigne Blanche 1996: Ripe and round despite its massive citrus character, this wine shows layers of mineral, wet earth and stone notes along with the pear and pineapple flavors. Medium- to full-bodied, it remains a bit tart on the finish. Hold until 1999. Not imported into the U.S. • $NA • (05/31/98) • **89**

Pouilly-Fuissé Vigne Blanche 1994: Nicely made, with a round, citrus-honey character. It's crisp and enjoyable now. 1,000 cases made. • $NA • (05/31/96) • **85**

St.-Véran 1993: Maturing fast. Tastes woody. Vanilla bean and butterscotch flavors seem flat and dull on the finish. • $NA • (08/31/95) • **77**

St.-Véran Poncetys 1995: This incredible '95 could give many Côte de Beaune *premiers crus* a run for their money. The texture is super-dense and extra-opulent. Excellent balance between the concentrated fruit, limelike acidity, subtle toast, sweet honey flavor and mineral-laden character. Lingers on the palate as it meanders to a flawless finish that offers the smoothest of landings. The work of a master. Tempting now through 2005. Not imported into the U.S. • $NA • (05/31/98) • **94**

SAUMAIZE-MICHELIN

Mâcon-Villages Les Sertaux 1996: An ambitious Mâcon in which the wood is used to beef up the wine. Clean lemon, honey, apple tart and pear flavors, but the finish is dry. • $NA • (08/31/97) • **79**

Mâcon-Villages Les Sertaux 1993: Rather fat and heavy-handed, tasting of caramel, butter, pear, cream and lemon. Somewhat simple and dull on the finish. • $NA • (08/31/95) • **76**

Pouilly-Fuissé Clos de la Roche 1996: A medium- to full-bodied wine that hints at the silky texture it will provide with a bit of cellaring. Offers loads of honey and lime, with pear and tropical fruit thrown in. Very pretty, clean and pure finish. Drink now through 2000. 660 cases made. • $23 • (05/31/98) • **89**

Pouilly-Fuissé Clos de la Roche 1995: Polished and subtle, showing ripe fruit flavors and a lactic, cream and butterscotch character with good intensity on the crisp finish. Medium-bodied. Drink now through 1999. 667 cases made. • $28 • (05/31/97) • **86**

Pouilly-Fuissé Clos de la Roche 1994: An elegant white that has pineapple flavors mingling harmoniously with the creamy texture. Subtle and crisp on the finish. Try now. 750 cases made. • $NA • (05/31/96) • **84**

Pouilly-Fuissé Les Ronchevats 1995: A '95 Pouilly with personality. Medium-bodied, with smoky, toasty bread qualities shading the honey, spice, apple, pear and citrus flavors. Silky mouthfeel, polished finish. Try now. 167 cases made. • $29 • (05/31/97) • **87**

Pouilly-Fuissé Les Ronchevats 1994: Bursting with citrus and lime flavors, but it manages to stay nicely focused. An uncompromising, crisp style that should be wonderful with fish. A touch of mineral and honey on the finish. Drinkable now. 250 cases made. • $NA • (05/31/96) • **85**

Pouilly-Fuissé Vigne Blanche 1995: Decent fruit, but a distinctively lactic, toasty oak character dominates. Of medium body, with refreshing citrus flavors on the finish. Drink now. 750 cases made. • $23 • (05/31/97) • **83**

St.-Véran Les Crèches 1996: A bit lean, it bursts with acidity but not much ripe fruit. Light-bodied; a bit candied on the finish. Drink now. 400 cases made. • $15 • (05/31/98) • **78**

SAUTEREAU, DOMAINE

Sancerre Red Côtes de Reigny 1995: This silky red shows firm but well-integrated tannins under its tart cherry, smoke and herb flavors. Has good grip but could use more fruit. 1,000 cases made. • $15 • (06/15/97) • **83**

Sancerre Rosé Côtes de Reigny 1995: Shows deceptively neutral onion-skin color but offers spicy aromas, bright berry flavors and firm acidity. Best with food. 200 cases made. • $15 • (06/15/97) • **84**

Sancerre White Côtes de Reigny 1995: This beautiful white is both lush and pure, with clean apple, melon and herb flavors and firm, well-integrated acidity. Has remarkable balance and harmony. 8,000 cases made. • $14 • (05/15/97) • **89**

SAUVAGEONNE, CHÂTEAU LA

Coteaux du Languedoc Cuvée Prestige 1995: Well defined and straightforward, showing cherry, plum and pepper flavors and some leathery notes. 500 cases made. • $18 • (02/28/98) • **86**

SAUVANES, DOMAINE GUY DE

Faugères Cuvée Sarah 1995: Oozes with flavor and has nice concentration as well. Dominated by lovely berry, plum and cherry flavors with some hints of nutmeg on the finish. Drink now through 2000. 1,000 cases made. • $8 • (03/31/98) • **87**

SAUVION & FILS

Anjou 1996: Soft and fruity. Shows black cherry, light herb and smoke flavors, with light tannins and a clean, short finish. Try lightly chilled. Drink now. • $9 • (06/15/98) • **81**

Anjou 1995: Smoky, herbal flavors are appealing in this light red, and the tannins have grip, but there's not enough fruit to balance. Ready to drink. • $8 • (06/15/97) • **79**

Anjou Blanc 1995: Fresh apple character gives this wine personality; it has good body and balance. Not complex, but can stand up to light foods. • $7 • (06/15/97) • **82**

Chinon 1996: Black cherry, light herb and tobacco flavors mingle in this soft, round red. However, a slightly stemmy note detracts. Drink through 1999. • $9 • (06/15/98) • **78**

Chinon Les Roches Cachées 1995: Bold in flavor yet light in body, this red shows ripe raspberry, leaf, licorice and light metallic flavors, and finishes with firm tannins. • $9 • (06/15/97) • **87**

Muscadet de Sèvre et Maine 1996: This light, straightforward white is neutral in flavor, with light apple and mineral notes. It's tart and soft at once. Try as a spritzer or cooking wine. • $7 • (06/30/98) • **79**

Muscadet de Sèvre et Maine 1995: A clean and crisp white that's rich enough to stand up to food, with ripe pear and almond flavors energized by acidity. A balanced, focused wine. • $7 • (05/15/97) • **86**

Muscadet de Sèvre et Maine Sur Lie 1993 • $7 • (12/15/95) • **83**

Muscadet de Sèvre et Maine Sur Lie Carte d'Or 1995 • $7 • (05/15/96) • **84**

Muscadet de Sèvre et Maine Sur Lie Château du Cléray 1995: This snappy white offers crisp acidity and flavors of grapefruit and tart herbs. A bit short on fruit, but would make a lively match for lighter dishes. • $9 • (06/15/97) • **83**

Muscadet de Sèvre et Maine Sur Lie Château du Cléray Réserve du Cléray 1994 • $13 • (11/15/95) • **83**

Muscadet de Sèvre et Maine Sur Lie Sauvion du Cléray 1995 • $7 • (05/15/96) BB • **85**

Muscadet de Sèvre et Maine Sur Lie Sauvion du Cléray 1994 • $9 • (11/15/95) • **84**

Pouilly-Fumé 1995: This puts it all together: muscular acidity, firm structure, ripe flavors of pear and melon, alluring accents of herbs and smoke. Delicious. Drinkable now though a bit austere, but has the concentration to improve through 1999. 5,000 cases made. • $13 • (05/15/97) HR • **92**

Pouilly-Fumé Les Ombelles 1995: Rich and full-bodied for the region, but the flavors are a bit dull and it turns slightly vegetal on the finish. • $10 • (06/15/97) • **79**

Sancerre 1996: This rustic white mingles herbal and earthy flavors that lack freshness and definition. Metallic aftertaste. Drink now. • $13 • (06/15/98) • **77**

Sancerre 1995: Has lean grapefruit and lime flavors with grassy and herbal accents over very crisp acidity. A bit tart on its own, but should do nicely with food. Tasted twice, with consistent notes. • $13 • (06/15/97) • **84**

Sancerre Les Fondettes 1995: Good structure and very firm acidity provide this white with the muscle to match food; the flavors are discreet but harmonious, with citrus, herbal and mineral notes. Not a showboat, but rewards attention. • $11 • (06/15/97) • **87**

Saumur-Champigny 1996: A nice marriage of plum, smoke and meat flavors provides typical character in this Loire red. It's balanced and focused; the soft tannins make it approachable now, and the price tag invites you to imbibe freely. Drink now through 2000. • $9 • (06/15/98) BB • **85**

Saumur-Champigny Les Gravières du Roy 1995: This lively wine offers textbook flavors of Cabernet Franc: red berries, green herbs and tobacco. Though light on the palate, it's well balanced and should match well with food. • $10 • (06/15/97) • **88**

Sauvignon Blanc Vin de Pays du Jardin de la France 1995: Round yet crisp, with apple and lemon flavors, balanced and straightforward. • $6 • (06/15/97) • **83**

Touraine Les Genêtes 1995: This steely white has firm acidity but it's straightforward, almost neutral, in flavor. Clean and simple. • $7 • (06/15/97) • **79**

Vouvray 1995: Good structure and a luscious mouthfeel, but the flavors lean toward the herbal spectrum. Quite dry and a bit short. • $8 • (06/15/97) • **82**

SAUZET, ETIENNE

Bâtard-Montrachet 1995: Impressive for its intensity and well-defined flavors. Opulent and seductive, with an excellent underpinning of fresh, crisp, lime-tasting acidity, layers of mineral, wet earth, honey and spice. Full-bodied, with a chewy finish; try around 2005. 25 cases imported into the U.S. • $187 • (08/31/97) • **95**

Bâtard-Montrachet 1994: A crowd pleaser; charming, and delivers the goods. As smooth as they come, with silky texture and rich lemon, tropical, toasty oak, mineral and honey flavors. Full-bodied and ripe but still elegant. Ready to drink. • $177 • (08/31/96) • **92**

Bâtard-Montrachet 1993: Harmonious *grand cru*, with everything in the right place. Round, silky texture is backed up by firm acidity and nice amounts of honey, fruit and spicy-smoky flavors. Unusually ripe and honeyed for this vintage. Drink now. • $123 • (08/31/95) • **90**

Bâtard-Montrachet 1992: This is tight and subtle for a *grand cru*, revealing its pear, honey and hazelnut flavors slowly as you sip it. Very elegant, balanced and harmonious, with no sharp edges but with a sense of restraint. Drinkable now. • $127 • (08/31/94) • **91**

Bienvenues-Bâtard-Montrachet 1995: Deliciously well made. Full-bodied, tropical fruit-flavored and superbly balanced, it also boasts plenty of toasty bread and mineral notes. Thickly textured, it coats the mouth. Don't touch until around 2010, when it will have become a classically refined white Burgundy. • $185 • (08/31/97) • **96**

Bienvenues-Bâtard-Montrachet 1994: Pretty and full-bodied. Silky and ripe flavors—marzipan, honey, ripe pea and pie crust—with some peach and apricot notes. Ready to enjoy now. • $177 • (08/31/96) • **88**

Bienvenues-Bâtard-Montrachet 1993: Extremely well crafted, both subtle and powerful, the sort of wine that shows its pedigree from start to finish. Wonderfully concentrated, boasting a silky core and lots of mineral, pear and lightly toasty oak flavors. Superb. Can age for years. • $123 • (08/31/95) • **91**

Bienvenues-Bâtard-Montrachet 1992: All dressed up and ready for a night on the town. A very buttery, butterscotch-flavored white that's grand in scope, bold and rich in flavor and lingering on the finish. It's thick, almost sweet, yet balanced nicely with fruity, fresh acidity. Combines elegance and richness at the same time. • $127 • (08/31/94) • **94**

Bourgogne White 1995: Ripe and rich, with wonderful balance and supple texture, it's full-bodied and shows a panoply of honey, wild flower, mineral, spice and citrus flavors. Has a lingering, juicy finish hinting at good acidity; try after 2000. • $28 • (08/31/97) • **88**

Chardonnay Bourgogne 1994: Full-bodied, silky-textured Bourgogne, with earth, tropical, lime and honey flavors. Has a slight undertone of stale ice flavors and aromas at this stage. Try now. • $NA • (08/31/96) • **81**

Chassagne-Montrachet 1995: A great village wine, with a supple, ripe, well-balanced texture and character. Offers plenty of pineapple, citrus, pear and subtle oak shadings. Well made and of full body, it should be even better after 2000. • $53 • (08/31/97) • **92**

Chassagne-Montrachet 1993: Quite ripe, distinctive, silky texture. Mineral, pear and apple flavors come together nicely on the medium-long finish. Drinkable now. • $41 • (05/15/95) • **85**

Chevalier-Montrachet 1995: Impressive density that demonstrates it's a well-made *grand cru*. Opulent and succulent, it's full-bodied, sweet-tasting, ripe and wonderful, delivering a bounty of tropical fruit, toasty coconut and spice flavors. Quite intense but still subtle, it should age well past 2005. • $219 • (08/31/97) • **98**

Chevalier-Montrachet 1994: A beautifully honeyed, ripe and full-bodied white Burgundy. Plenty of tropical fruit, pear, mineral and floral notes here to please the palate. It should develop some nice complexity; try in 1999. • $NA • (08/31/96) • **90**

Chevalier-Montrachet 1993: Complex aromas and flavors of straw, apple and mineral and a hint of spice. Medium- to full-bodied; long finish. Try now. 15 cases made. • $159 • (05/15/95) • **88**

Chevalier-Montrachet 1992: Substantial and ripe-tasting, full-bodied and bold, with peach and pear flavors, firm acidity and a vanilla note that lasts on the finish. Drinkable now. • $114 Ⓐ • (08/31/94) • **92**

Montrachet 1994: Both showy and refined. This opulent wine offers tons of toasty oak, spice, ripe fruit, butter and mineral flavors. Full-bodied and harmonious, it cascades to a long, smoky finish. Drinkable now. • $278 • (08/31/96) • **96**

Montrachet 1993: Subtle yet rich apple, honey, vanilla and cream aromas and flavors, medium body, firm acidity and a long finish. • $220 • (05/15/95) • **90**

Puligny-Montrachet 1995: Magnificent—powerful, yet racy. A classy, full-bodied village wine that's worth collecting. Tightly wound and hard now, it shows little on the nose except citrus, spice and wood. Long, succulent and intense finish. This is a serious '95, with the depth to last for years; try it after 2005 when the minerally, ripe fruit character will express itself. • $55 • (08/31/97) • **92**

Puligny-Montrachet 1994: Full-bodied and complex, with some lovely fig, tropical, spice, honey and cigar box flavors. A touch hot and burning on the finish. Drink now. • $NA • (08/31/96) • **87**

Puligny-Montrachet 1993: Flavorful and quite ripe honey, hazelnut and earth flavors are knitted nicely together. Medium-bodied; vibrant, long finish. • $42 • (05/15/95) • **86**

Puligny-Montrachet 1992: Clean, crisp and flavorful, this straightforward, medium-bodied Burgundy delivers decent tart lime, apple, and honey flavors. Drinkable now. 2,150 cases made. • $46 • (08/31/94) • **84**

Puligny-Montrachet Champ Canet 1995: Flavorful, offering some bright floral, peach, apricot, almost Viognierlike flavors. Fairly crisp at first, it turned velvety with aeration, giving a lovely, silky feel on the palate. The toughest, greenest of the Sauzet Pulignys, try it after 2005. • $97 • (08/31/97) • **93**

Puligny-Montrachet Champ Canet 1994: A lovely wine, with toasty oak, ripe fruit, mineral and spice flavors. Subtle, yet full-bodied, with a silky, seductive texture. Try now. • $NA • (08/31/96) • **91**

Puligny-Montrachet Champ Canet 1993: Lots going on here: gorgeous texture of fruit and creamy acidity, medium-to-full body and honey, apple and mineral finish. • $68 • (05/15/95) • **88**

Puligny-Montrachet Champ Canet 1992: Bold and full of fruit flavor, this complex Puligny delivers a symphony of flavors, from pineapple and peach to vanilla, toast and hazelnut. Firm, almost chewy in texture, the richness lingering on the finish. Drinkable now. 560 cases made. • $68 • (08/31/94) • **93**

Puligny-Montrachet La Garenne 1995: A big, ripe, rich and thick *premier cru*, this ultra-full-bodied wine oozes with wet earth, floral, honey, salt, wet stone and butterscotch flavors. Sips like extra-virgin olive oil, but is kept clean by lime flavors on the slightly tart finish. Try after 2000. • $87 • (08/31/97) • **93**

Puligny-Montrachet La Garenne 1993: Lovely balance of lemon, mineral and honey character. Medium-bodied; fresh finish. • $63 • (05/15/95) • **85**

Puligny-Montrachet La Garenne 1992: Exotic and tropical, with pineapple, guava and mango flavors mingling with the lime and apple notes. This medium-bodied white is ripe, soft and very appealing, showing enough crisp flavors to hold it all together on the medium-intense finish. • $62 • (08/31/94) • **88**

Puligny-Montrachet Les Combettes 1995: Super. Well crafted, with a ripe texture and lush character, showing an undercurrent of fresh fruit and citrus notes that mingle with the honey, mineral, toasty almond and coconut flavors. Medium- to full-bodied. Try after 2000. • $112 • (08/31/97) • **94**

Puligny-Montrachet Les Combettes 1994: Beautiful *premier cru.* Rich and vibrant, with outstanding honey, spice and lemon aromas and flavors. Full-bodied and ripe, with a long, harmonious finish. Try through 1999. • $NA • (08/31/96) • **90**

Puligny-Montrachet Les Combettes 1993: Round and rather rich, but also quite oaky, showing herb, spice and vanilla flavors and some chalky notes on the finish. Try now. • $79 • (05/15/95) • **87**

Puligny-Montrachet Les Combettes 1992: Lively and rich, packed with ripe pineapple, pear and honey flavors. It makes for a deep, chewy-textured, fully ripe style of white Burgundy. Enjoy now for its opulence. 825 cases made. • $79 • (08/31/94) • **88**

Puligny-Montrachet Les Folatières 1993: Well-presented cream, apple and lemon character, medium-to-light body, firm acidity and a fresh finish. • $79 • (05/15/95) • **85**

Puligny-Montrachet Les Folatières 1992: Racy in character and built for aging. A firmly fruity and crisp Puligny with ample peach and pear flavors, a lively fresh finish and hints of butter and honey. • $68 • (08/31/94) • **91**

Puligny-Montrachet Les Perrières 1995: What class. Fresh and zesty as well as rich and opulent. Offers the spicy oak, tropical, pear and mineral flavors you find in many '95s. Full-bodied, with a long, slightly burning finish (from all that smoky oak). But cellar it until around 2005 and you'll be richly rewarded with an elegant, minerally, mature white Burgundy from one of the region's acknowledged masters. • $83 • (08/31/97) • **94**

Puligny-Montrachet Les Referts 1995: Big and ripe, bursting with seductive tropical fruit, pear tart, spice and honey flavors. Full-bodied, with wonderful acidity and elegance, it kicks in on the long finish. Drink now. • $83 • (08/31/97) • **93**

Puligny-Montrachet Les Referts 1994: A big, full-bodied *premier cru.* Pretty honey, lemon and tropical flavors and a surprising backbone of crisp-tasting citrus. Long, smoky finish. Drink through 1999. • $NA • (08/31/96) • **90**

Puligny-Montrachet Les Referts 1993: Rich coconut, pear and relatively ripe fruit character, medium to full in body and fresh acidity on the finish. • $NA • (05/15/95) • **86**

Puligny-Montrachet Les Referts 1992: Butter and nut flavors add complexity to the basic tart apple flavors, for this straightforward and enjoyable Puligny. Leans toward the green side. 725 cases made. • $62 • (08/31/94) • **85**

SAVARY, FRANCINE & OLIVIER

Chablis 1996: Exploding with lean and pure flavors, both ripe and crisp in texture, this beauty just beckons to be consumed. Wonderful balance between the acidity and the pear, apple, lemon and tropical fruit flavors. This domaine is a discovery for us. • $NA • (08/31/97) • **90**

SAVOYE, R.

Régnié 1994 • $9 • (10/31/95) • **81**

SCARAMOUCHE

Chardonnay Vin de Pays d'Oc 1996: Offers some decent buttery and citrus flavors, but it's a little hollow in the middle and finishes on a flat note. Tasted twice, with consistent notes. Drink now. • $9 • (05/31/98) • **79**

SCHLUMBERGER, DOMAINES

Alsace Schlumberger Réserve 1994: Rosewater and litchi flavors mingle in this exotic white. Finishes with grapefruit peel. • $15 • (06/30/97) • **85**

Gewürztraminer Alsace Fleur de Guebwiller 1993: Unusually elegant for a Gewürz—light-bodied yet intense, with alluring honey, smoke and dried peach aromas and flavors. The perfect balance of sweet and tart makes this a delicious accompaniment to assertive foods. 8,000 cases made. • $18 • (09/30/96) HR • **90**

Gewürztraminer Alsace Grand Cru Kitterlé 1994: Extremely subtle, showing red fruits such as cherry and cassis, as well as vanilla. Seamless and rich, with a touch of alcohol on the finish. Drinkable now. • $46 • (09/30/97) • **87**

Key: SS—Spectator Selection CS—Cellar Selection HR—Highly Recommended BB—Best Buy $NA—Price not available Ⓐ—Auction Price (BT)—Barrel Tasting
Dates in parentheses indicate the issues in which the ratings were published.

Pinot Blanc Alsace 1995: A lot of ripe apple and almond flavors and a rich yet elegant mouthfeel, all underscored by racy acidity. Serious stuff that begs for food. 80,000 cases made. • $13 • (09/15/97) • **88**

Pinot Blanc Alsace 1994: Rather austere in style, this shows flavors of herbs and lemons and finishes with a metallic note. • $11 • (10/15/96) • **79**

Pinot Blanc Alsace 1993 • $10 • (07/31/95) BB • **87**

Pinot Gris Alsace 1995: A complex fruit-cocktail nose introduces this firmly balanced, rich white marked by baked-apple and almond flavors. Full-bodied and satisfying. • $20 • (06/30/97) • **87**

Pinot Gris Alsace 1993: Round, firm and well structured, but it's still a bit closed, offering light pear and herbal flavors that are rich but dry. Exemplary character in a restrained style, it should improve with age. • $17 • (09/30/96) • **87**

Pinot Gris Alsace Grand Cru Kitterlé 1994: Looking like a Sauternes by the color, this honey, apricot and spice-flavored white is elegant and racy, with a mineral accent. Still, there's more framework than flesh. Try with Asian food. Showed better than an earlier sample. • $42 • (09/30/97) • **89**

Pinot Gris Alsace Les Princes Abbés 1995: Almond and coconut are up front in this white, which is ripe, sports some residual sugar and has an astringent finish. • $20 • (09/30/97) • **84**

Riesling Alsace Les Princes Abbés 1994: A distinctive, maturing Riesling with aromas of diesel and spice, flavors of apple and peach. The finish is a bit alcoholic. • $16 • (06/30/97) • **84**

Riesling Alsace Les Princes Abbés 1993: Typical Riesling aromas of pine and petrol give way to full yet crisp flavors of herbs, pear and minerals. Drink now. • $14 • (09/30/96) • **86**

Sylvaner Alsace 1995: A hint of residual sugar lends roundness to the apple and faint honey flavors, but the finish is tart. Needs light, simple food. 80,000 cases made. • $12 • (09/15/97) • **81**

SCHOFFIT, DOMAINE

Chasselas Alsace Cuvée Prestige Vieilles Vignes 1995: A medium-bodied, rich white, balanced on the soft side, exhibiting apple and pear flavors just slightly on the earthy side. Ready now. • $15 • (09/15/97) • **85**

Gewürztraminer Alsace Grand Cru Clos Saint-Théobald Rangen de Thann 1993 • $38 • (08/31/95) • **90**

Gewürztraminer Alsace Harth Cuvée Alexandre 1994: A Gewürztraminer that needs a spoon. A good example of the ripeness and opulence this grape variety can show. More complex and balanced than the '95s, this has honey, apricot, litchi and cardamom flavors that go on and on, finally reigned in by a grapefruit peel accent. And this isn't even Vendange Tardive! • $30 • (09/15/97) • **92**

Gewürztraminer Alsace Harth Cuvée Caroline 1995: More austere and minerally than usual for this grape variety, with acidity and a touch of bitter grapefruit as counterbalance. Beautifully displayed fruit and intensity. • $25 • (09/15/97) • **88**

Pinot Blanc-Auxerrois Alsace Cuvée Caroline 1995: Serious Pinot Blanc. Golden in color, and sporting loads of ripe apple, honey and butterlike flavors all wrapped up in a lush texture. There's some residual sugar, but it's balanced by citrusy acidity. Long finish. Well made. • $15 • (09/15/97) • **88**

Pinot Blanc-Auxerrois Alsace Cuvée Caroline 1994: Fresh and lively, with aromas and flavors of apple, citrus and baking bread. It's balanced and mouthfilling, with a firm finish. Drinkable now. • $15 • (09/15/97) • **85**

Pinot Blanc-Auxerrois Alsace Cuvée Caroline 1993 • $12 • (07/31/95) • **84**

Riesling Alsace Harth Cuvée Prestige 1994: This displays the classic apple, peach and spice character of Riesling from Alsace, allied with the austerity and firmness of this vintage. Well made; ready to drink. • $20 • (09/15/97) • **87**

Riesling Alsace Harth Cuvée Prestige 1993 • $16 • (07/31/95) • **88**

Tokay Pinot Gris Alsace Cuvée Prestige 1994: Lush, opulent and smoky, this is a soft, inviting Pinot Gris that you can relax into. Just off-dry, it's balanced and seductive. Drinkable now. • $20 • (09/15/97) • **88**

Tokay Pinot Gris Alsace Grand Cru Clos Saint-Théobald Rangen de Thann 1993 • $38 • (09/15/95) • **87**

SECOND DE CARNET, LE

Haut-Médoc 1995: Watery and very light, with some berry, vanilla character and a light finish. Second label of Château La Tour Carnet. • $12 • (01/31/98) • **71**

SEGIN-MANUEL

Bonnes Mares 1947: Not powerful or rich, but has delicacy and lots of floral character. • $NA • (07/31/97) • **81**

SÉGLA

Margaux 1996: Sweet and ripe, with good length, velvety tannins and a fresh finish. Harmonious. Very good for a second label from Rauzan-Segla. • $NA • (01/01/97) (BT) • **85-89**

Margaux 1995: Juicy, succulent and chunky, with loads of berry, tobacco and cherry aromas and flavors. Full-bodied and tannic, yet velvety and delicious. Almost too good for a second label. Needs time. Best after 2001. • $25 • (01/31/98) • **89**

Margaux 1994: Shows decent berry and cherry flavors, with a hint of dried herbs, and firm tannins. A short, slightly green finish. Second wine of Rauzan-Segla. Drink now or hold. • $NA • (01/31/97) • **82**

Margaux 1993: Polished black cherry and wet earth character on the nose and palate. Medium body, firm tannins and fresh finish. Drinkable now. • $NA • (01/31/96) • **83**

SEGUIN, HERVÉ

Pouilly-Fumé Le Bouchot 1995: There's ripe fruit in this fleshy white, but cheesy, earthy notes detract. Has Sauvignon Blanc character, but it's rustic and lacks freshness. 2,500 cases made. • $16 • (06/15/97) • **76**

SÉGUR, CHÂTEAU

Haut-Médoc 1988 • $15 • (12/31/90) • **82**

Haut-Médoc 1982 • $6 • (04/16/85) • **75**

SEIGNEURIE DE GICON

Côtes du Rhône-Villages Chusclan 1995: An odd wine for this category, quite light and a bit disappointing, with dried herbs and cherry pit character. Short, dry finish. • $NA • (10/15/97) • **72**

Côtes du Rhône-Villages Rosé Chusclan 1996: Wonderful, serious rosé. Full-bodied, with a rich, ripe and thick texture, it has a lovely mouthfeel, more big white than red, and fans out with delicious raspberry, spice and toasty oak flavors on the super-supple finish. Enjoy now. • $NA • (10/15/97) • **87**

SEIGNEURS DU PERIGORD

Bergerac 1996: A soft, light, inviting red bursting with leafy, spicy, berry flavors reminiscent of Merlot. Enjoyable now. 14,000 cases made. • $7 • (09/30/97) • **82**

Bergerac 1995: A soft, medium-bodied red that's fresh and straightforward. Good cherry flavor, then earthy accents on the finish. 6,000 cases made. • $7 • (07/31/96) • **80**

Bergerac White 1996: Enticing aromas of honey and spring flowers give way to lemon-accented apple flavors in this light-bodied, appealing white. Perfect for summer sipping. 6,500 cases made. • $7 • (09/30/97) • **84**

Monbazillac 1995: Sweet and thick in texture, but with earthy, nutty, tobaccolike flavors. A substitute for Sauternes, but it won't appeal to everyone. 5,000 cases made. • $15 • (10/31/97) • **78**

SELOSSE, JACQUES

Brut Blanc de Blancs Champagne 1986: A very popular, insiders' Champagne in France right now. A ripe, richly styled bubbly with intense flavors. Very intense ripe apple, apricot, dough, and yeast aromas and flavors, it's full bodied with a round and silky texture. Long finish. Drink now. • $NA • (12/31/93) • **89**

SENARD, DANIEL

Aloxe-Corton Les Valozières 1995: Fairly modest in aroma, it offers decent red berry flavor and some dry tannins. Should grow into an elegant red Burgundy around 1999. • $40 • (11/15/97) • **77**

Aloxe-Corton Les Valozières 1991: Lean and crisp, but has musty, medicinal flavors that aren't pleasant. • $38 Ⓐ • (01/31/94) • **68**

Corton En Charlemagne 1995: Delicate and elegant, ripe and succulent, this lovely red Burgundy is a pleasure to taste. Medium-bodied, with some rose petal, cherry and raspberry character, the well-integrated tannins balance well the lingering finish. Try around 1999. • $72 • (11/15/97) • **87**

Corton En Charlemagne 1994: Tough, stalky and rubbery, with a watery texture. • $61 • (11/15/96) • **75**

Corton En Charlemagne 1992: Firm in texture, with floral overtones to the currant and blackberry flavors. Gets a little chewy on the finish. Drinkable now. • $52 • (12/15/94) • **84**

Corton En Charlemagne 1991: Soft, supple and straightforward. The anise-scented wild berry flavors are a bit diluted when they get to the finish. Drinkable now. • $65 Ⓐ • (01/31/94) • **81**

Corton En Charlemagne 1990: Super-firm, but so full of beautiful fruit flavors that it coats the tannins. Beautifully crafted. Drink now. • $NA • (12/15/92) • **93**

Corton Le Clos du Roi 1995: There are more tough and under-ripe tannins than supple fruit in this Pinot. The flavors are cherry and chocolate. • $75 • (11/15/97) • **79**

Corton Le Clos du Roi 1994: Tries to be elegant, with light texture and delicate strawberry and floral flavors, but it just comes off as diluted. • $63 • (11/15/96) • **76**

Corton Le Clos du Roi 1992: A firm, ripe, chunky wine, with sweet black cherry and currant flavors that persist on the chewy finish. Drinkable now. • $52 • (12/15/94) • **85**

Corton Le Clos du Roi 1991: Chunky; ripe currant flavors struggle against a wall of earthy, tarry tannins. Finishes austere. Try now. • $65 Ⓐ • (01/31/94) • **79**

Corton Le Clos du Roi 1990: Extremely well made, with plenty of raspberry, earth and spice flavors and a lovely, supple structure. Compact and concentrated. Drinkable now. • $55 • (12/15/92) • **93**

Corton Les Bressandes 1995: Smooth and supple, with modest cherry flavors that disappear midpalate. Dry, tannic finish. • $75 • (11/15/97) • **79**

Corton Les Bressandes 1994: Has a burnt odor and a sour-tasting finish. • $63 • (11/15/96) • **73**

Corton Les Bressandes 1991: Light and floral almost to an extreme, showing more violet and irislike character than fruit. Finishes austerely. • $65 Ⓐ • (01/31/94) • **77**

Corton Les Bressandes 1990: A muscular wine, with lots of fruit aromas and flavors. Drinkable now. • $NA • (12/15/92) • **88**

Corton Les Meix 1995: Aromas and flavors of cherry and wet earth are wrapped up in a velvety texture that turns tannic on the finish. Moderately concentrated, lean in style. • $64 • (11/15/97) • **82**

Corton Les Meix 1992: Extremely minty and vegetal, bitingly tannic, with flavors of cedar and blackberry that can barely make themselves heard over the tannic din. Try in 1999. • $38 • (12/15/94) • **81**

Corton Les Meix 1990: Big, chewy and complex; this is a monster of a wine, filled with berry, spice and floral characteristics. Has a ripe, rich mouth-feel, firm tannins and a long, supple finish. Try now. • $NA • (12/15/92) • **93**

SENECHAUX, DOMAINE DES

Châteauneuf-du-Pape 1995: Cherry and strawberry flavors, accented with herb and game notes, are pleasant, but overall the wine is light and a bit dry. Drink now. 5,833 cases made. • $26 • (10/15/97) • **80**

Châteauneuf-du-Pape 1985 • $17 • (10/15/88) • **85**

Châteauneuf-du-Pape White 1996: Nicely subtle floral, mineral and nutty aromas, but turns a bit heavy, with buttery, ripe pear flavors. Quite sweet-tasting and pleasant for drinking upon release, but don't expect finesse. 100 cases imported. 583 cases made. • $30 • (10/15/97) • **84**

SÉNÉJAC, CHÂTEAU

Haut-Médoc 1988 • $14 • (04/30/91) • **78**

Haut-Médoc Artigue de Sénéjac 1995: Delivers some appealing cherry, berry and cedar flavors that show well through the finish. Try now. 500 cases made. • $11 • (04/30/97) • **83**

SENEZ, CHRISTIAN

Brut Champagne 1988: Decent, light and frothy, with modest candied pear character. Drink now. • $NA • (12/31/93) • **81**

Brut Champagne 1987: Decent, offering straightforward apple and melon aromas and flavors, but is rather aggressive and foamy in texture and very high in acidity. Drinkable now. • $NA • (12/31/93) • **84**

SEPTIMANIE

Maury Mascotte NV • $15 • (01/31/95) • **80**

SÉRAFIN PÈRE & FILS

Charmes-Chambertin 1995: A super Pinot Noir, this full-bodied, big '95 coats your palate with the silkiest of tannins, delivering layers of spicy oak, chocolate, mocha and loads of red- and blackberry flavor. Succulent, fresh, long finish. Tempting now, it should hit its stride after 1999. 100 cases made. • $95 • (11/15/97) • **96**

Charmes-Chambertin 1994: Light- to medium-bodied, a *grand cru* that's rather delicate, with some currant, plum, vanilla and mocha notes. Not much intensity, but a supple finish. Drink now. • $80 • (11/15/96) • **86**

Charmes-Chambertin 1993: Like an Olympic sprint champion: light on its feet yet very muscular, bursting out of the starting block with amazing grace. Tons of blackberry, floral and earth character. Don't even touch until the next century. Sensational! • $90 • (11/15/95) • **96**

Charmes-Chambertin 1992: Shows what could be done in 1992 with a little luck and hard work. Impressive intensity of spicy raspberry and juniper flavors persist into a pure, lively finish. Nicely-integrated tannins. Try now. • $50 • (12/15/94) • **89**

Charmes-Chambertin 1989 • $43 Ⓐ • (01/31/92) • **92**

Gevrey-Chambertin 1995: Clean and pure, exhibiting aromas and flavors of blackberry, plum and spicy oak. Elegant for the appellation, yet full of sweet sappy fruit, all wrapped up in firm tannins and bright acidity. Try in 2000. • $46 • (11/15/97) • **90**

Gevrey-Chambertin 1994: Light, but fragrant and flavorful with its small but generous beam of raspberry and spice flavors. • $40 • (11/15/96) • **82**

Gevrey-Chambertin 1990: An elegant, refined Pinot Noir, with terrific, toasty black currant and cherry flavors that echo on the vivid, silky finish. Drinkable now. • $45 • (12/15/92) • **89**

Gevrey-Chambertin 1988 • $35 • (03/31/91) • **92**

Gevrey-Chambertin Fonteny 1995: Soft in style for Gevrey, with evocative aromas of violets, blackberries and toasty oak yielding to cassis and damson plums on the palate. Ripe and velvety, yet firmly structured, with a lingering finish. Try in 1999. • $60 • (11/15/97) • **89**

Gevrey-Chambertin Fonteny 1993: Wonderful clarity of ripe fruit; fragrant and vivid. Medium-bodied, adding fine tannins and lovely vanilla flavors. Delicious now, but will age for many years to come. • $65 • (11/15/95) • **91**

Gevrey-Chambertin Fonteny 1992: Its spicy, earthy, tobacco, currant and plum flavors get revved up. Try now. • $40 • (12/15/94) • **85**

Gevrey-Chambertin Fonteny 1990: A focused Gevrey that's more elegant than generous, offering currant, black cherry and modest cinnamon flavors. Drinkable now. 150 cases made. • $63 • (12/15/92) • **87**

Gevrey-Chambertin Fonteny 1989 • $50 • (01/31/92) • **86**

Gevrey-Chambertin Fonteny 1988 • $50 • (05/15/91) • **92**

Gevrey-Chambertin Les Cazetiers 1995: A wonderful wine that stuns with its pure, refined cassis, violet, rose petal, blackberry and earth notes. It would score higher if not for its slight hint of stemmy, tomato character. Supple tannins, intense fruit. Give it time. Try in 2000. • $72 • (11/15/97) • **90**

Gevrey-Chambertin Les Cazetiers 1994: Very pretty, and aromatic, with rose petal, spice and violet-scented raspberry flavors. Mocha and wood notes follow through on the finish. Try now. • $60 • (11/15/96) • **86**

Gevrey-Chambertin Les Cazetiers 1993: Quite chunky layers of green tobacco, cherry and berry character, offering fine tannins, medium-to-full body and dried cherry, vanilla finish. Drink now. • $70 • (11/15/95) • **91**

Gevrey-Chambertin Les Cazetiers 1992: Good character and intensity prevail, with deep black cherry and raspberry flavors that turn chewy and tannic on the lingering, juicy finish. Try now. • $44 • (12/15/94) • **86**

Gevrey-Chambertin Les Cazetiers 1990: Beautifully aromatic, lively and vivid, with bright blackberry, violet, rose petal and mushroom flavors. Shows excellent intensity of well-balanced tannins and acidity. Drinkable now. 200 cases made. • $56 • (12/15/92) • **91**

Gevrey-Chambertin Les Cazetiers 1989 • $54 • (01/31/92) • **89**

Gevrey-Chambertin Les Cazetiers 1988 • $53 • (05/15/91) • **91**

Gevrey-Chambertin Vieilles Vignes 1994: Very light, but the rose petal, currant and cherry notes are pretty and its dry tannins don't overwhelm the delicate finish. • $40 • (11/15/96) • **80**

Key: SS—Spectator Selection CS—Cellar Selection HR—Highly Recommended BB—Best Buy $NA—Price not available Ⓐ—Auction Price (BT)—Barrel Tasting
Dates in parentheses indicate the issues in which the ratings were published.

FRANCE

Gevrey-Chambertin Vieilles Vignes 1993: Some good berry and plum character but slightly light on the finish. Medium in body with firm tannins. A bit one-dimensional. Drink now. • $55 • (11/15/95) • **85**

Gevrey-Chambertin Vieilles Vignes 1992: Shows some spicy new oak character and just barely enough berry and currant flavor to balance it. Drinkable now. • $35 • (12/15/94) • **84**

Gevrey-Chambertin Vieilles Vignes 1990: A bit ungenerous now on the palate, but the aromas are pretty, with cinnamon, earth, berry and slightly vegetal notes. Drinkable now. • $50 • (12/15/92) • **87**

Gevrey-Chambertin Vieilles Vignes 1989 • $45 • (01/31/92) • **92**

Gevrey-Chambertin Vieilles Vignes 1987 • $35 • (03/31/90) • **91**

SERGUE, CHÂTEAU LA

Lalande-de-Pomerol 1997: A no-nonsense red, with grape and mineral aromas and flavors. Medium-bodied. Short finish. • $NA • (06/15/98) (BT) • **80-84**

Lalande-de-Pomerol 1996: Violet and cassis almost jump out of the glass. Medium- to full-bodied, with velvety tannins and a fruity vanilla finish. More like California than Bordeaux, but very nice. • $20 • (06/15/98) (BT) • **85-89**

SERRE, CHÂTEAU LA

St.-Emilion 1997: Good dark color, with blackberry and cherry aromas and hint of milk chocolate. Medium-bodied, with soft texture and a light, fruity finish. Lovely. • $NA • (06/15/98) (BT) • **85-89**

St.-Emilion 1996: Good fruit for the vintage, and harmonious. Medium-bodied, with medium tannins and a refreshing finish. • $30 • (06/15/98) (BT) • **85-89**

St.-Emilion 1995: Just smell this and enjoy. Fabulous aromas of ripe berries and spices—cinnamon, allspice, ginger. Full-bodied, with full yet silky tannins and medium finish. An underrated estate. Best after 2002. • $28 • (01/31/98) • **91**

St.-Emilion 1990: It's easy to like this wine. Very attractive, with perfumed floral and rose aromas and an elegant, silky texture of sweet berry and floral flavors. Medium tannins hold it all together. Drinkable now. 3,000 cases made. • $22 • (03/31/93) • **88**

St.-Emilion 1988 • $18 • (06/15/91) • **80**

St.-Emilion 1985 • $15 • (05/15/88) • **91**

SERVEAU, BERNARD

Bourgogne 1989 • $10 • (01/31/92) • **83**

Bourgogne 1985 • $13 • (11/15/87) • **76**

Chambolle-Musigny 1989 • $27 • (01/31/92) • **83**

Chambolle-Musigny Les Amoureuses 1991: Soft and appealing, a bit watery at the center, but shows nicely defined blackberry, currant, vanilla and toast aromas and flavors that keep echoing on the finish. Drinkable now. 150 cases made. • $55 Ⓐ • (01/31/94) • **80**

Chambolle-Musigny Les Amoureuses 1990: Very closed and unyielding, showing excellent breeding and class. The vivid fruit and firm tannins are good guarantees that this will deliver great pleasure. Try now. 150 cases made. • $68 • (12/15/92) • **91**

Chambolle-Musigny Les Amoureuses 1989 • $50 • (01/31/92) • **85**

Chambolle-Musigny Les Amoureuses 1988 • $66 • (02/28/91) • **84**

Chambolle-Musigny Les Amoureuses 1985 • $75 • (06/15/88) • **91**

Chambolle-Musigny Les Chabiots 1991: Smooth and silky, with gamy, meaty overtones to the currant and berry fruit at the center. Fades a bit on the finish, but charming. 300 cases made. • $30 Ⓐ • (01/31/94) • **84**

Chambolle-Musigny Les Chabiots 1990: Light and pleasant, with pretty but modest strawberry, milk chocolate and cream aromas and flavors and a smooth, silky finish. Drinkable now. 250 cases made. • $35 • (12/15/92) • **85**

Chambolle-Musigny Les Chabiots 1989 • $30 • (01/31/92) • **79**

Chambolle-Musigny Les Chabiots 1988 • $39 • (02/28/91) • **86**

Chambolle-Musigny Les Chabiots 1987 • $30 • (06/15/90) • **78**

Chambolle-Musigny Les Chabiots 1985 • $39 • (06/15/88) • **90**

Chambolle-Musigny Les Chabiots 1984 • $23 • (04/15/87) • **91**

Chambolle-Musigny Les Sentiers 1991: Light, watery, stemmy and citrusy; not very likeable. 100 cases made. • $30 Ⓐ • (01/31/94) • **73**

Chambolle-Musigny Les Sentiers 1990: Bright, plummy and ripe, with hints of earth, strawberry and violet flavors and a smooth, focused texture. Drinkable now. 125 cases made. • $35 • (12/15/92) • **88**

Chambolle-Musigny Les Sentiers 1989 • $30 • (01/31/92) • **93**

Chambolle-Musigny Les Sentiers 1988 • $39 • (02/28/91) • **79**

Morey-St.-Denis Les Sorbès 1991: Tough, tannic and sturdy, offering simple currant flavors and chunky, drying tannins. Drinkable now. 500 cases made. • $30 Ⓐ • (01/31/94) • **82**

Morey-St.-Denis Les Sorbès 1990: Good but a bit simple, with modest strawberry and plum notes and a hint of chestnut on the finish. 50 cases made. • $35 • (12/15/92) • **80**

Morey-St.-Denis Les Sorbès 1989 • $30 • (01/31/92) • **86**

Morey-St.-Denis Les Sorbès 1988 • $35 • (02/28/91) • **88**

Morey-St.-Denis Les Sorbès 1987 • $30 • (05/15/90) • **83**

Morey-St.-Denis Les Sorbès 1985 • $39 • (06/15/88) • **88**

Morey-St.-Denis Les Sorbès 1984 • $22 • (03/15/87) • **87**

Nuits-St.-Georges Chaines Carteaux 1991: Firm in texture and modest in intensity, serving up appealing aromas and flavors that emerge harmoniously on the finish. 100 cases made. • $32 Ⓐ • (01/31/94) • **78**

Nuits-St.-Georges Chaines Carteaux 1990: Distinctive, rich and round, with impressive plum, berry and leaf aromas and plenty of round tannins. Tasted twice. Drinkable now. 83 cases made. • $46 • (12/15/92) • **91**

Nuits-St.-Georges Chaines Carteaux 1988 • $39 • (03/31/91) • **84**

Nuits-St.-Georges Chaines Carteaux 1985 • $39 • (06/15/88) • **86**

SERVIN

Chablis 1996: Ripe and fresh, with lemony butter, grilled almond and pecan pie flavors. Not your typical clean and pure Chablis. Very crisp finish. Drink now. • $17 • (08/31/97) • **83**

Chablis Bougros 1996: Distinctive, gun smoke, flinty character gives this an interesting twist. Full-bodied and rich, the smoky notes fan out on the palate and complement the honey, pear, fresh lime, lemon, herbal and walnut flavors on the long, harmonious finish. Tempting now, better around 2000. 100 cases made. • $42 • (05/31/98) • **90**

Chablis Les Clos 1996: Lovely, round, voluptuous texture leads into layers of wet earth, spice, white pepper, floral and toasty bread flavors. A bit honeyed, it has a lot of intensity on the slightly burning finish. Needs time. Try after 2000. 250 cases made. • $45 • (05/31/98) • **90**

Chablis Montée de Tonnerre 1996: Slightly earthy but opulent and polished, this elegant, velvety, flinty, full-bodied '96 Chablis is a mouthful of flavors—wet earth, mineral, pear, and cassis. Fresh and sinewy on the chalky, chewy finish, it will need time to show it all. Try around 2005. 1,100 cases made. • $26 • (05/31/98) • **90**

Chablis Montée de Tonnerre 1995: Chablis fanatics will die for this *premier cru*. Shows classic matchstick, earth and slightly smoky aromas, with tons of honey, mineral and ripe fruit flavors. Full-bodied, it's a smooth customer, flowing silkily over the palate to a long, hard-to-believe finish. Drink now through 2000. 7,500 cases made. • $17 • (06/15/97) • **90**

Chablis Vaillons 1996: A nice Chardonnay, with vanilla, grapefruit, lime and lots of fruit flavors. Medium-bodied and intense, this opens up nicely already, but drink around 2000. 400 cases made. • $24 • (05/31/98) • **88**

Chablis Vaillons 1995: A bit disappointing, showing a slightly rustic, diluted character, with caramel and burnt flavors. 485 cases made. • $18 • (06/15/97) • **72**

SIAURAC, CHÂTEAU

Lalande-de-Pomerol 1993: Light and weedy, slightly aggressive, showing some fruit but a very short aftertaste. Drinkable now. • $19 • (01/31/96) • **77**

Lalande-de-Pomerol 1990: Voluptuous and offers plenty of appealing ripe plum and cassis flavors, accented by smoke and herbs. It's a bit diluted, perhaps, but has freshness and firm tannins; enjoy now. • $19 • (05/15/94) • **84**

SIGALAS-RABAUD, CHÂTEAU

Sauternes 1986: Simple, sweet and fruity, with a touch of oxidation that takes away from the quality. • $42 • (12/31/89) • **77**

Sauternes 1985: Very smooth and honeylike but somewhat light compared to greater years. Has tasty pear and rich honey flavors and a long finish. Drink now. • $41 • (07/15/88) • **82**

Sauternes 1983: A bit rough around the edges, but all the elements are there to age into a great wine. Deep gold, with flavors that lean to pineapple and resin, framed with oak. Big and concentrated, like pineapple syrup magically transformed into wine. • $24 • (01/31/88) • **88**

SIGAUT, HERVÉ

Chambolle-Musigny 1992: Light, juicy and modest; more Beaujolais than Burgundy. This is almost washed out, with straightforward strawberry and raspberry flavors. • $NA • (12/15/94) • **82**

Chambolle-Musigny Les Sentiers 1995: Enticing aromas of cherries, spice and pure, crunchy Pinot fruit are the hallmarks of this elegant red. Straightforward and appealing. Drinkable now. 350 cases made. • $39 • (11/15/97) • **85**

Chambolle-Musigny Les Sentiers 1992: Very light and fragrant, more Beaujolais than Burgundy, with candied strawberry flavors echoing on the finish. Drinkable now. • $NA • (12/15/94) • **81**

Morey-St.-Denis Les Charrières 1995: Lovely, perfumed, and bursting with juicy raspberry and cherry flavors. Delicate and graceful, though not particularly complex or long. Drinkable now through 2000. 350 cases made. • $39 • (11/15/97) • **85**

SIGNATURES

Bordeaux 1995: Delicious red for early drinking. Medium in body, with delicate, silky tannins and a fresh, fruity finish. Drink now. • $NA • (01/31/98) • **82**

SILLAGE DE MALARTIC, LE

Pessac-Léognan 1995: Simple berry and vanilla aromas and flavors. Medium- to light-bodied, with light tannins and a simple fruity aftertaste. Second label of Château Malartic-Lagravière. Drink now. • $15 • (01/31/98) • **80**

Pessac-Léognan White 1995: Rather unpleasant, with funky flavors. Medium body, sour finish. Undrinkable. Tasted twice, with consistent notes. Second label of Château Malartic-Lagravière. • $15 • (04/30/98) • **68**

SILVER CLOUD

Brut Blanc de Blancs Blanquette de Limoux 1985 • $9 • (04/15/90) • **85**

SIMARD, CHÂTEAU

St.-Emilion 1970 • $NA • (05/15/93) • **84**

SIMIAN, CHÂTEAU

Châteauneuf-du-Pape 1989 • $19 • (08/31/92) • **84**

Châteauneuf-du-Pape 1988 • $20 • (07/15/91) • **86**

SIMONNET-FEBVRE

Chablis 1996: A supercharged village Chablis, with ripe flavors and a vibrant, fresh, citrus-spiked quality. Well balanced, this succulent Chardonnay oozes with tropical fruit, kiwi, banana, mineral and pear flavors. Full-bodied, with a very long finish. Drink now to 2000. • $15 • (08/31/97) • **91**

Chablis Fourchaume 1996: Exotic Chardonnay, almost like a Sauvignon Blanc, with gooseberry, floral, lime, kiwi and white pepper flavors, this medium-bodied white bristles with fresh acidity and clean fruit character. The chalky, mineral notes creep up on the lingering finish. Well made. Buy a case and hold it until 2000. 210 cases made. • $23 • (05/31/98) • **92**

Chablis Fourchaume 1995: Quite earthy, slightly rustic, with rich character and good acidity but insufficient class. Finishes a bit dry. 550 cases made. • $24 • (06/15/97) • **79**

Chablis Les Clos 1994 • $NA • (05/31/96) • **95**

Chablis Mont de Milieu 1996: Lovely aromas and flavors beneath a blanket of spritz and bubbles. Fresh, clean and pure. It sparkles (literally) with life and grapefruit, pear and apple flavors. Drink now. Tastes like a barrel sample. • $20 • (08/31/97) • **86**

Chablis Mont de Milieu 1995: Distinctive, a wine of *terroir*, its earth and mineral character blended with citrus and green apple flavors. Full-bodied and silky textured, with a nicely balanced finish. Try now to 2005. 2,300 cases made. • $22 • (06/15/97) • **86**

Chablis Mont de Milieu 1994 • $NA • (05/31/96) • **91**

Chablis Montée de Tonnerre 1996: Lovely, pure, clean Chardonnay with hints of floral, honey, stony earth and grapefruit flavors mingling nicely. Medium- to full-bodied, ripe and elegant, with a citrusy finish. Try around 2005. 410 cases made. • $20 • (05/31/98) • **89**

Chablis Preuses 1996: Rather intense, medium-bodied Chablis with, it seems, some wood that clamps down with a slightly drying mouthfeel. Also some apple, pear, and mineral. Might smooth out with time. • $36 • (05/31/98) • **82**

Chablis Preuses 1995: Very fresh at first, it turned a bit tired after aeration, suggesting it's best to drink it shortly after release. Full-bodied and rich, this is a mouthful of mineral, wet stone and cream. 60 cases made. • $40 • (06/15/97) • **84**

Chablis Vaillons 1996: Tight and quite hard at first, this medium-bodied '96 turns supple with a core of mineral-laden character on the palate. Has herbal, tropical, honeyed touches too, with a very lemony, vibrant and chewy finish. Best after 2002. 1,080 cases made. • $19 • (05/31/98) • **89**

Chablis Vaillons 1995: Odd, with white spirit flavors that detract from the otherwise pure lemon, honey and earth notes. Medium-bodied, with a toasty finish. 1,600 cases made. • $20 • (06/15/97) • **80**

Petit Chablis 1996: Delicate; very light and with a slight dilution. Offers modest fruit and mineral notes. Drink chilled. • $12 • (08/31/97) • **77**

Petit Chablis 1995: Clean, crisp, and very flavorful, delivering plenty of citrusy apple and pear flavors, and a hint of honey. Medium-bodied, with a harmonious, long finish. • $NA • (08/31/96) • **84**

SIRAN, CHÂTEAU

Margaux 1997: Harmonious for the vintage, with fine tannins and pleasant violet, mineral aromas and flavors. Commendable winemaking. • $NA • (06/15/98) (BT) • **85-89**

Margaux 1996: Plenty of plummy, grapey, berry aromas and flavors. Medium-bodied, with well-integrated fruit and tannin structure and a medium finish. Very fine indeed; almost outstanding. • $35 • (06/15/98) (BT) • **85-89**

Margaux 1995: Massive Margaux. Best Siran since the late 1920s. Bright currant and berry aromas, with hints of mushrooms and earth. Full-bodied, with big, velvety tannins and a long, long, fruity finish. Closed, but serious. Best after 2002. • $30 • (01/31/98) • **93**

Margaux 1994: Fairly straightforward, with dried cherry and earth aromas and flavors, and slightly dry tannins. Drink now or hold. • $25 • (01/31/97) • **79**

Margaux 1993: Very elegant black cherry, mint and berry aromas and flavors, medium body, fine tannins and a fresh finish. Best now. • $22 • (01/31/96) • **85**

Margaux 1991: Subtle complexity of berry, cherry and vanilla flavors and aromas, medium tannins and long aftertaste. • $15 • (03/31/94) • **84**

Margaux 1990: Rich and thick, this wine shows a restrained fruit and tannin structure but kicks in on the finish. Drinkable now. 10,000 cases made. • $22 • (03/31/93) • **90**

Margaux 1989 • $25 • (03/15/92) • **88**

Margaux 1988 • $19 • (06/30/91) • **88**

Margaux 1985 • $15 • (09/30/88) • **90**

Margaux 1982 • $30 • (08/31/92) • **89**

SIRÈNE DE GISCOURS, LA

Margaux 1995: Lovely aromas of blackberries and chocolate. Medium-bodied, with firm tannins and a fresh finish. Slightly short aftertaste. First appearance of a second label from Château Giscours. Try after 2000. 7,000 cases made. • $14 • (01/31/98) • **85**

SIRIUS

Bordeaux 1995: Impressive for a blended red. Attractively perfumed, with berries, flowers and wild raspberries. Medium- to full-bodied, with firm tannins and a long vanilla and berry aftertaste. Needs time. Best after 2000. 10,000 cases made. • $12 • (01/31/98) • **86**

Bordeaux White 1995: Very good for a merchant's blend. Interesting character of vanilla, apple, lime and kiwi. Medium-bodied, with medium acidity and a medium finish. Drink now. • $10 • (04/30/98) • **86**

Key: SS—Spectator Selection CS—Cellar Selection HR—Highly Recommended BB—Best Buy $NA—Price not available Ⓐ—Auction Price (BT)—Barrel Tasting
Dates in parentheses indicate the issues in which the ratings were published.

FRANCE

SIRUGUE & FILS, JEAN-LOUIS

Côte de Nuits-Villages Clos de la Belle Marguerite 1993: Light-bodied, pleasant and nicely balanced between dry, ripe tannins and black cherry and wet earth notes. Best now. • $15 • (11/15/95) • **83**

Côte de Nuits-Villages Clos de la Belle Marguerite 1990: An old style, with green, hard tannins that make the plum and currant-scented flavors taste tight and lean. Drinkable now. 2,000 cases made. • $10 • (06/15/93) • **82**

Côte de Nuits-Villages Clos de la Belle Marguerite 1988 • $16 • (03/31/91) • **83**

Gevrey-Chambertin 1993: Pretty, easy-to-drink Pinot delivering berry, cherry and chocolate character. Medium-bodied, with light, delicate fruit and medium-fine tannins. Try now. From Labouré-Roi. • $25 • (11/15/95) • **83**

Gevrey-Chambertin 1989 • $20 • (08/31/92) • **80**

SMITH-HAUT-LAFITTE, CHÂTEAU

Pessac-Léognan 1997: Alluring grape, spice and cinnamon aromas. Medium-bodied, with fine tannins and a short finish. Promises more on the nose than it delivers on the palate. • $NA • (06/15/98) (BT) • **85-89**

Pessac-Léognan 1996: Lots of new oak in this one, with spicy, vanilla and berry character. Medium-bodied, with medium, velvety tannins and a fruity finish. Too much new oak? 8,000 cases made. • $40 • (06/15/98) (BT) • **85-89**

Pessac-Léognan 1995: Big and tannic, this needs time. Lots of red berries and floral character on nose and palate. Full-bodied, with a slightly hollow midpalate at the moment. Very tannic, with an extracted, mouthpuckering finish. Try after 2002. 9,100 cases made. • $35 • (01/31/98) • **90**

Pessac-Léognan 1994: Highlighted by its delicate core of ripe fruit flavor, this is medium in body, with fine tannins and a fruity finish. Drink now or hold. • $21 Ⓐ • (01/31/97) • **86**

Pessac-Léognan 1993: Lots of great new wood here but just enough fruit to balance it out. Medium in body and tannins and a firm finish. Try now. • $25 • (01/31/96) • **86**

Pessac-Léognan 1992: Lovely berry, tobacco and chocolate character, medium body and medium, velvety tannins. Good finish. • $17 • (04/15/95) • **84**

Pessac-Léognan 1991: Very agreeable wine with ripe berry and smoky chocolate behind its fruit character. Medium body and a subtle finish. • $17 • (03/31/94) • **83**

Pessac-Léognan 1990: Superbly crafted. A wine with lush, velvety tannins and gorgeous plummy, earthy, vanilla notes. This estate is on the rise. Try now. 13,000 cases made. • $22 • (03/31/93) • **93**

Pessac-Léognan 1989 • $26 Ⓐ • (03/15/92) • **91**

Pessac-Léognan 1987 • $15 • (05/15/90) • **84**

Graves 1985 • $15 • (11/30/88) • **89**

Graves 1982 • $18 • (08/31/92) • **81**

Graves 1981 • $18 • (06/01/84) • **79**

Pessac-Léognan White 1995: An outstanding '95 with loads of character. Serious white. Extremely fresh aromas of apple, pineapple and honey, with hints of toffee. Medium-bodied, with fine acidity and a long aftertaste. Drink now or hold. • $40 • (04/30/98) • **91**

Pessac-Léognan White 1994 • $21 Ⓐ • (03/31/96) • **90**

Pessac-Léognan White 1993 • $30 • (05/31/95) • **86**

SOCIANDO-MALLET, CHÂTEAU

Haut-Médoc 1997: Dark-colored, with floral, fruit and currant bush aromas. Medium-bodied, with silky tannins and medium finish. Almost outstanding. • $NA • (06/15/98) (BT) • **85-89**

Haut-Médoc 1996: Quite amazing character in this wine. Fruity, with exotic spices like saffron and cumin. Medium- to full-bodied, with fine tannins and a silky finish. • $32 • (06/15/98) (BT) • **90-94**

Haut-Médoc 1995: A real fruit-bomb, with expressive aromas of currants, blackberries and vanilla. Full-bodied and chunky, with masses of fruit and well-knit tannins. Best after 2002. • $27 Ⓐ • (01/31/98) • **91**

Haut-Médoc 1994: An elegant balance of fine fruit flavors and well-integrated tannins. Medium in body, silky on the finish. Drink now or hold. • $20 Ⓐ • (01/31/97) • **86**

Haut-Médoc 1993: Polished and gorgeous, showing finesse and power, amazingly well-integrated tannins, full body and layers of currant, black cherry and plum flavors. Supple, tasty finish. Drink now. • $21 Ⓐ • (01/31/96) • **88**

Haut-Médoc 1992: So polished, so fine; this estate is nearly always producing fabulous wines. Medium body, delicate tannins and pretty berry and mint flavors; medium finish. Drinkable now. • $15 Ⓐ • (04/15/95) • **87**

Haut-Médoc 1991: A superbly crafted wine for this vintage. Supple in texture, but a little lean and short on the finish. • $17 • (03/31/94) • **85**

Haut-Médoc 1990: This estate nearly always makes outstanding wine. This one is vibrant, with vivid cherry and vanilla character and loads of tannins, yet it remains well balanced. Drink now. 18,500 cases made. • $29 Ⓐ • (03/31/93) • **91**

Haut-Médoc 1989 • $41 Ⓐ • (03/15/92) • **90**

Haut-Médoc 1988 • $34 Ⓐ • (03/31/91) • **87**

Haut-Médoc 1987 • $15 • (05/15/90) • **88**

Haut-Médoc 1986 • $37 Ⓐ • (11/30/89) • **94**

Haut-Médoc 1985 • $38 Ⓐ • (10/15/94) • **91**

Haut-Médoc 1984 • $11 • (03/31/87) • **84**

Haut-Médoc 1983 • $18 Ⓐ • (10/15/94) • **92**

Haut-Médoc 1982 • $60 Ⓐ • (11/30/89) • **92**

Haut-Médoc 1981 • $23 • (10/15/94) • **88**

SOCIANDO-MALLET, LA DEMOISELLE DE

Haut-Médoc 1995: Light and simple, with decent berry, cherry character, but somewhat lean and mean. Second label of Château Sociando-Mallet. • $15 • (01/31/98) • **79**

Haut-Médoc 1992: Pretty tobacco, cherry and berry aromas and flavors with modest body and firm, slightly green tannins. Amazing for a second label in such a weak year. • $17 • (04/15/95) • **80**

Haut-Médoc 1989 • $21 • (03/15/92) • **84**

SOLITUDE, DOMAINE DE LA | BORDEAUX

Pessac-Léognan 1993: Light and somewhat diluted, offering modest cherry, dried herb and chocolate flavors. Drink now. • $18 • (01/31/96) • **77**

Pessac-Léognan White 1995: Lovely, balanced white with vanilla, apple and coconut aromas and flavors. Medium-bodied, with medium tannins and a fresh aftertaste. Drink now. • $NA • (04/30/98) • **87**

Pessac-Léognan White 1994 • $15 • (03/31/96) • **90**

Pessac-Léognan White 1993 • $15 • (05/31/95) • **86**

SOLITUDE, DOMAINE DE LA | RHONE

Châteauneuf-du-Pape 1992: Spicy and smooth, but already about to go over the hill. Good, if you like tea, vanilla and brown sugar flavors with just a hint of fruit. • $22 • (11/15/95) • **79**

Châteauneuf-du-Pape 1990: Soft and generous, with fleshy plum, spice, tobacco and currant flavors and elegant earth shadings. Finishes long and smooth, with lush but firm tannins. Drinkable now. • $27 • (04/15/93) • **89**

Châteauneuf-du-Pape 1989 • $19 • (05/31/92) • **86**

Côtes du Rhône 1993 • $12 • (11/15/95) • **84**

SORIN, DOMAINE

Bandol 1995: A big, chewy red with ripe flavors of plum, cherry and berry, spicy notes on the finish and enough tannin to indicate it will smooth out with age. A hearty wine for a cold winter's day, with a rich chocolaty flavor throughout. Drink now through 2001. • $25 • (03/31/98) • **87**

Côtes de Provence 1994 • $13 • (10/31/95) • **86**

SORREL, H.

Hermitage 1991: Fresh and straightforward, with floral, berry and vanilla notes. It's pleasant and accessible now. Tasted twice. • $25 • (05/31/94) • **83**

Hermitage 1990: Crisp and unexpectedly earthy, with lime and citrus flavors and little richness or generosity. The tannins clamp down on the finish. Try now. • $35 • (04/15/93) • **82**

Hermitage 1985 • $29 • (07/31/88) • **87**

Hermitage Le Gréal 1991: Expressive aromas of dark chocolate, raisins and plums carry through the richness. Full-bodied, though the finish is a bit dry now. Try now. Tasted twice. • $45 • (05/31/94) • **88**

Hermitage Le Gréal 1990: Ripe, round and aromatic, loaded with generous currant, blackberry, spice and vanilla characteristics. Spicy and toasty on the solid finish, echoing cedar, tar and black pepper notes. Drinkable now. • $44 • (04/15/93) • **89**

Hermitage Le Gréal 1988 • $49 • (11/15/91) • **88**

Hermitage Le Gréal 1983 • $19 • (05/01/86) • **84**

Hermitage Le Gréal 1980 • $25 • (05/01/86) • **74**

Hermitage Le Vignon 1988 • $36 • (08/31/91) • **77**

SORREL, M.

Hermitage 1994: Pretty cherry and chocolate aromas are alluring, but it's simple on the palate and a bit diluted. For easy, pleasant drinking now. 1,000 cases made. • $40 • (12/15/96) • **83**
Hermitage Le Gréal 1994: Shows good Syrah character in its flavors of licorice, blackberry and tar, and it's balanced and well integrated, though not one for aging. Drink through 1999. 200 cases made. • $60 • (12/15/96) • **87**
Hermitage White 1994: Alluring aromas of hazelnut, herbs and smoke give way to fresh, ripe flavors of pear, honey and hazelnut. Elegant and complex, it gives more with every sip. 250 cases made. • $40 • (12/15/96) • **90**
Hermitage White Les Rocoules 1994: Lush and seductive. Rich with hazelnut, wildflower, pear and melon flavors, and firm acidity that pulls it beautifully into balance. In harmony from its vibrant aromas through its long, lingering finish, it's lovely now or will easily hold through 2000. 100 cases made. • $50 • (12/15/96) • **92**

SOUDARS, CHÂTEAU

Haut-Médoc 1997: Slightly odd vegetal note to the fruit character. Medium-bodied, and a bit syrupy. Disjointed; may be better in 1999. • $NA • (06/15/98) (BT) • **75-79**
Haut-Médoc 1996: Lots of wild berry and vanilla character. Medium-bodied, with lovely ripe fruit and a long, sweet fruit finish. Not a blockbuster, but delicious. • $17 • (06/15/98) (BT) • **85-89**
Haut-Médoc 1995: Some decent berry flavors, but rather weedy overall. Light-bodied, with light tannins and a simple finish. Drink now. Tasted twice, with consistent notes. 13,000 cases made. • $15 • (01/31/98) • **78**
Haut-Médoc 1994: Somewhat overextracted and dry, with green herb and tobacco nuances. Try now. • $NA • (01/31/97) • **79**
Haut-Médoc 1992: Good color, but very herbal and hard; somewhat aggressive finish. • $15 • (04/15/95) • **74**
Haut-Médoc 1991: A light, elegant claret, with black cherry flavors. Slightly diluted on the finish. • $15 • (03/31/94) • **79**
Haut-Médoc 1990: A pretty wine, with perfumed, spicy aromas, cherry and spice flavors and firm tannins, but it's slightly diluted. Drinkable now. 10,000 cases made. • $18 • (03/31/93) • **84**
Haut-Médoc 1989 • $15 • (03/15/92) • **85**
Haut-Médoc 1988 • $15 • (04/30/91) • **88**
Haut-Médoc 1987 • $12 • (11/30/89) • **77**
Haut-Médoc 1986 • $13 • (11/30/89) • **79**

SOUFRANDISE, DOMAINE DE LA

Mâcon-Fuissé 1995: A burst of aromas, with notes of roses, honey and quince, make this interesting. Smooth, well balanced and racy, it has a lot going for it. Try now. 375 cases made. • $16 • (05/31/97) • **86**
Mâcon-Fuissé 1993: Ripe pear, fig and mineral complexity. Light body, with a clean, crisp and delicious finish. • $NA • (08/31/95) • **84**
Mâcon-Fuissé Le Ronté 1996: Lovely, with more ripe fruit to balance the acidity than most '96 Mâcons have. Delivers lemon, pear, pineapple and a slightly smoky character. Medium-bodied, with a succulent finish. Try after 1999. Better than previous samples which were corky. 400 cases made. • $14 • (05/31/98) • **85**
Pouilly-Fuissé 1993: Refined and velvety, yet solid. Shows straightforward grapefruit, wet straw and green apple flavors. Drinkable now. 583 cases made. • $23 • (05/15/95) • **86**
Pouilly-Fuissé Clos la Soufrandise 1996: Very polished wine, some lovely mineral, compacted character that has yet to show all its elegance. For now, you get good floral, tropical and cream notes. An intriguing wine that needs time. 500 cases made. • $17 • (05/31/98) • **86**
Pouilly-Fuissé Domaine La Soufrandise Vieilles Vignes 1994: Quite civilized, with a smooth, round and lush texture, offering butter and pear notes. But the finish leaves a bitter, astringent lingering note. Starts better than it ends. • $25 • (05/31/96) • **78**
Pouilly-Fuissé Levrouté 1995: Well made, exhibiting a polished texture and a toasty oak, fruit and mineral character of nice intensity. Medium-bodied, with a lingering, chewy finish. Try now. 292 cases made. • $29 • (05/31/97) • **86**

Key: SS—Spectator Selection CS—Cellar Selection HR—Highly Recommended BB—Best Buy $NA—Price not available Ⓐ—Auction Price (BT)—Barrel Tasting
Dates in parentheses indicate the issues in which the ratings were published.

Pouilly-Fuissé Vieilles Vignes 1996: Well made in a super-intense style, with lovely lime, cilantro, mineral, tropical, avocado and apple character. Crisp and sharp now, but with plenty of ripe fruit to carry it in the future. Delicious long finish. Try in 1999. 1,300 cases made. • $21 • (05/31/98) • **89**
Pouilly-Fuissé Vieilles Vignes 1995: Delicious from start to finish. Fatter and fuller than many '95 Pouilly, this full-bodied late-harvest, dry white displays ripe fruit character accented by toasty bread and spice notes. Ready to drink. 1,250 cases made. • $25 • (05/31/97) • **87**

SOULEZ, PIERRE & YVES

Savennières Moelleux Clos du Papillon Cuvée d'Avant 1996: Savennières is rarely sweet, but this wine shows it can be a successful style for the region, with alluring honey and spicy aromas, flavors of melons, pears and honey, and enough acidity to keep it balanced. Unusual and intriguing. Drink now through 2003. • $24 • (06/15/98) • **88**
Savennières-Roche aux Moines Château de Chamboureau 1993: This white has good weight on the palate, yet its character is lush and delicate, with floral, almond and light peach flavors. Soft and charming. 2,000 cases made. • $31 • (06/15/97) • **85**

SOUMADE, DOMAINE LA

Côtes du Rhône-Villages Rasteau 1995: Seductive chocolate, mocha and spice flavors suggest lots of fancy oak in the aging of this rather sophisticated, full-bodied village Rhône wine. Distinctive, it stands out in this category for its supple international-style and smooth structure. Weighs in with good concentration on the toasty finish. A serious wine; drinkable now. 1,417 cases made. • $15 • (10/15/97) • **88**
Côtes du Rhône-Villages Rasteau 1986 • $11 • (02/28/90) • **82**

SOURS, CHÂTEAU DE

Bordeaux 1995: Intensely fruity, medium in body and featuring good cassis and wild berry backed by subtle oak flavors. A bit light, but providing firm tannins and juicy aftertaste. • $NA • (05/15/96) (BT) • **80-84**

SOUTARD, CHÂTEAU

St.-Emilion 1989 • $27 • (09/15/93) • **87**
St.-Emilion 1985 • $23 Ⓐ • (05/15/88) • **85**
St.-Emilion 1982 • $31 Ⓐ • (05/15/89) • **84**
St.-Emilion 1961 • $22 • (04/30/96) • **85**

SPARR, PIERRE

Brut Blanc de Blancs Marquis de Perlade NV: Serviceable but not exciting, an average quality bubbly with modest fruit flavor and cheesy, buttery overtones. 18,000 cases made. • $10 • (08/31/97) • **77**
Brut Blanc de Noirs Crémant d'Alsace Réserve NV: Brassy in color, this soft, rich sparkling wine has aromas of bread dough, ripe apples and red fruits, a creamy texture and a crisp finish. Drink now. 1,600 cases made. • $18 • (03/31/98) • **84**
Brut Crémant d'Alsace Dynastie 1993: A slight copper hue and a pronounced sweetness in this soft, mature Crémant. Honey, butterscotch and red fruits are the flavors. Enjoy now. 2,800 cases made. • $15 • (11/15/97) • **85**
Brut Crémant d'Alsace Pinot Gris 1992: Quite full-bodied for an Alsace sparkler, this is big enough for food. Marries ripe pear and earthy flavors with an exuberant mousse. 1,100 cases made. • $20 • (11/15/96) • **85**
Cuvée d'Alsace 1996: Crisp, floral and spicy, thanks to either the Gewürztraminer or Muscat in this blend. A lively apéritif with juicy acidity and baked apple flavors. Drink now. 6,500 cases made. • $10 • (03/31/98) • **82**
Gewürztraminer Alsace Carte d'Or 1996: A very soft Gewürz with floral notes augmented by honey and spice. The flavors are subtle and the texture lush enough to enjoy this on its own. 9,700 cases made. • $10 • (11/15/97) • **85**
Gewürztraminer Alsace Carte d'Or 1994: Broad and polished, this generous wine offers soft and slightly sweet ripe pineapple and coconut flavors. For drinking soon. 25,000 cases made. • $12 • (10/15/96) • **82**
Gewürztraminer Alsace Carte d'Or 1993 • $11 • (09/15/95) • **84**
Gewürztraminer Alsace Grand Cru Brand Sélection de Grains Nobles 1994: A soft, sweet white with vibrant acidity that carries the honey and litchi flavors to a bitter-almond finish. Good job in a tough vintage. Drink now through 2000. 265 cases made. • $48/500ml • (03/31/98) • **87**

Gewürztraminer Alsace Grand Cru Mambourg 1993: Succulent honey and toasty almond aromas are alluring, but it turns a bit heavy and flat on the palate. 2,600 cases made. • $26 • (10/15/96) • **79**

Gewürztraminer Alsace Grand Cru Mambourg Vendanges Tardives 1994: Intriguing. Distinctly spicy, with some raisin flavors, this is a well-balanced, expressive, late-harvest wine, its finish smacking of minerals. Drink now through 2000. 578 cases made. • $30 • (03/31/98) • **88**

Gewürztraminer Alsace Prestige 1994: Ripe, rich and slightly sweet, here's the Alsatian answer to Chardonnay but without the new oak. Appealing for its apricot and passion fruit flavors, it's best as an apéritif. 580 cases made. • $24 • (06/30/97) • **85**

Gewürztraminer Alsace Réserve 1996: Big, bold and flavorful. Honey, floral and litchi character galore in a fat texture that's not heavy or soft, all reigned in by the grapefruit-peel note on the finish. This would stand up to a ripe Muenster. 4,700 cases made. • $12 • (11/15/97) • **89**

Pinot Blanc Alsace Diamant d'Alsace Réserve 1996: A sleek white with apple, lemon and honey flavors packed into a lean frame. It's complex, focused and long. 17,000 cases made. • $8 • (11/15/97) • **87**

Pinot Blanc Alsace Diamant d'Alsace Réserve 1995: Aromas of spring flowers and lime herald this delicate white from France, brimming with green apple and mineral character. Poised and balanced, it's ready for summer sipping, at an affordable price. 30,000 cases made. • $9 • (06/30/97) BB • **85**

Pinot Blanc Alsace Diamant d'Alsace Réserve 1994: This has good body, but very little flavor, basically light citrus notes and alcohol. Try it in a spritzer. 28,000 cases made. • $10 • (11/15/96) • **78**

Pinot Blanc Alsace Hospices de Strasbourg 1995: Subtle and appealing, it's soft, lush and floral up front, followed by firm, lemony acidity that carries through to the finish. 1,823 cases made. • $15 • (06/30/97) • **84**

Pinot Gris Alsace Carte d'Or 1994: Rich, unctuous texture is appealing, though flavors are a bit muted in this full-bodied white. Light notes of pear and herb emerge on the finish. Try with food. 9,000 cases made. • $12 • (10/15/96) • **84**

Pinot Gris Alsace Carte d'Or 1993 • $11 • (09/15/95) • **83**

Pinot Noir Alsace Prestige 1995: A butterscotch element overshadows the pleasant berry and spice notes. A straightforward, light-bodied red. • $17 • (11/15/97) • **83**

Riesling Alsace Altenbourg Vendanges Tardives 1994: Petrol, mineral and spice are the dominant themes in this off-dry Riesling. Rich and full-bodied, it's already showing some mature character. Moderate length. Drink now through 2002. 575 cases made. • $30/500ml • (03/31/98) • **87**

Riesling Alsace Carte d'Or 1996: A little austere at this stage, but this Riesling shows concentration and depth married to flavors of apple, pear, minerals and just a hint of rosemary in the aroma. Try in 1999. 14,000 cases made. • $9 • (11/15/97) • **87**

Riesling Alsace Carte d'Or 1994: Restrained and delicate in style, this is crisp, clean and well balanced, but nearly neutral in flavor with light floral notes and hints of pear. 19,000 cases made. • $11 • (10/15/96) • **80**

Riesling Alsace Carte d'Or 1993 • $10 • (09/15/95) • **85**

Riesling Alsace Grand Cru Mambourg 1995: A Riesling of power and intensity whose peach, almond and mineral flavors build to a crisp, lemon-lime finish. Already shows some evolution, yet should improve over the next year. Best from 1999 through 2005. 450 cases made. • $24 • (03/31/98) • **89**

Riesling Alsace Grand Cru Mambourg 1993: Well made in a difficult vintage. Subtle yet complex, it's full of red berries, fruit blossom and almond aromas and flavors. There's firm, underlying acidity, but it's balanced and diaphanous. 1,200 cases made. • $25 • (06/30/97) • **87**

Riesling Alsace Grand Cru Schlossberg 1995: Rich, concentrated apple and floral aromas and flavors are underscored by gum-tingling acidity in this elegant Riesling. There's a lovely sense of harmony; should come together by 1999. Best from 1999 through 2005. 385 cases made. • $24 • (03/31/98) • **90**

Riesling Alsace Grand Cru Schlossberg 1993: Full-bodied and ripe, offering well-integrated melon, mineral and earth flavors that are austere and not very expressive now. Try now. 1,800 cases made. • $24 • (10/15/96) • **84**

Riesling Alsace Réserve 1995: Delicate, lively and intense, this white builds subtly to a glissando of apple, stone and spice notes. The firm acidity suggests pairing with food. Try now. 15,000 cases made. • $12 • (06/30/97) • **85**

Riesling Alsace Sélection de Grains Nobles 1989: Gorgeous. Medium-sweet and stuffed full of honey, petrol, dried fruit and mineral flavors as it nears maturity. Elegant, aristocratic and ethereal, this is a fine example of late-harvest Riesling from an excellent vintage. Drink now through 2002. 150 cases made. • $98 • (03/31/98) • **92**

Savagnin Rosé Klevener de Heiligenstein 1996: Tropical, passion fruit flavors combine with apple and peach in this crisply structured white (Savagnin Rosé is the name of the grape) that's delicious for sipping. Drink now. 640 cases made. • $15 • (03/31/98) • **84**

Savagnin Rosé Klevener de Heiligenstein 1995: Wet stone and forest aromas mark this white—it's more minerally than fruity. The aftertaste is tangy. An obscure novelty from Alsace. 650 cases made. • $14 • (06/30/97) • **83**

Tokay Pinot Gris Alsace Carte d'Or 1996: Vibrant, this Pinot Gris has blackberry, apple and smoky notes, all in a medium-bodied package structured for food. 7,800 cases made. • $10 • (11/15/97) • **86**

Tokay Pinot Gris Alsace Grand Cru Mambourg 1993: Rich yet restrained, compact yet concentrated. Firm and balanced, with clean and deep herbal and peach flavors that emerge on the long finish. Should improve with age; try now. 850 cases made. • $28 • (10/15/96) • **89**

Tokay Pinot Gris Alsace Réserve 1996: This beauty exemplifies the finesse of Pinot Gris. Packed with mineral and spicy elements, racy and complex, intense yet graceful. Long peach and apple aftertaste. Drinkable now through 2002. 4,500 cases made. • $12 • (11/15/97) • **91**

Tokay Pinot Gris Alsace Vendanges Tardives 1994: Slight mushroom aromas segue into honey and apple flavors in this diffuse, mature white. Pleasant, if not concentrated or complex. Drink now. 620 cases made. • $30/500ml • (03/31/98) • **84**

Tokay Pinot Gris Alsace Vendanges Tardives 1993: Made in a dry style, this offers nutty, pinelike aromas and clean, herbal flavors. Rich, yet balanced and refreshing. A good match for rich fish dishes. 350 cases made. • $45 • (10/15/96) • **89**

STRIFFILING, BERNARD

Morgon Domaine de Croix de Chèvre 1996: This lean, crisp red is rather light-bodied, but the flavors of cherry, spice and smoke show good intensity, and a core of acidity keeps it firm and lively. Drink now. 1,500 cases made. • $12 • (07/31/98) • **84**

SUDUIRAUT, CHÂTEAU

Sauternes 1995: Gorgeous Sauternes. Very ripe in style, with dried apricot and honey character. Medium- to full-bodied, sweet and spicy, with a dried apricot finish. Drink now or hold. • $45 • (04/30/98) • **90**

Sauternes 1990: Beautiful and alluring, harmonious and full-bodied, it caresses the palate with lovely dried fruit, toasty oak and vanilla flavors. Very sweet, but in balance. Delicious now. • $46 • (04/15/95) • **93**

Sauternes 1989: Exotically perfumed violet and rose petals burst on your palate, accompanied by dried apricot, lemon and honey flavors. Gorgeous and subtle, glowing on the finish. • $48 • (04/15/95) • **92**

Sauternes 1986: Ripe and golden, with buttered pear and pineapple aromas and long, honeyed fruit flavors. Lacks the roundness that should come with age. Drink now. • $35 • (12/31/89) • **85**

Sauternes 1985 • $20 Ⓐ • (11/30/88) • **81**

Sauternes 1984 • $22 • (11/30/88) • **81**

Sauternes 1983: Delicious and balanced, showing exciting earthy, white truffle flavors that add complexity to the honey and spice notes. Medium intensity. Drink now or hold until 2000. • $44 • (04/15/95) • **88**

Sauternes 1982 • $29 Ⓐ • (11/30/88) • **83**

Sauternes 1979 • $30 • (11/30/88) • **86**

Sauternes 1978 • $22 • (11/30/88) • **78**

Sauternes 1976 • $41 Ⓐ • (11/30/88) • **77**

Sauternes 1975 • $63 • (11/30/88) • **84**

Sauternes 1972 • $25 • (11/30/88) • **77**

Sauternes 1970 • $34 Ⓐ • (11/30/88) • **81**

Sauternes 1969 • $70 • (11/30/88) • **88**

Sauternes 1959 • $159 Ⓐ • (11/30/88) • **93**

Sauternes 1947: Has some welcome viscosity, but it also has incredibly high acidity, which takes away any majesty. It wants to be glorious, but who squeezed all the lemon in there? • $303 • (05/31/97) • **85**

Sauternes 1928 • $300 • (11/30/88) • **90**

Sauternes Crème de Tête 1989: An amazing, full-bodied Sauternes with the texture of double cream, cascading its exotic blend of orange-peel, thyme, dried-herb and honey flavors to a long finish. Drink now or hold. • $160 • (04/15/95) • **96**

Sauternes Cuvée Madame 1982 • $140 • (11/30/88) • **90**

SUNFLOWER VALLEY

Chardonnay Vin de Pays d'Oc 1996: Mineral and pear flavors mix well in this cleanly-made Chardonnay. Good for a big party. Drink now. • $7 • (03/31/98) • **83**

Merlot Vin de Pays d'Oc 1996: A simple, straightforward, plummy-tasting wine that will go well with food. Drink now. • $7 • (03/31/98) • **82**

Syrah Vin de Pays d'Oc 1996: Quite delicious. A smooth and well-rounded Syrah, on the light side, with bright cherry and berry flavors and an attractive silky quality to it as well. The spicy finish just goes on and on. Drink now. 800 cases made. • $7 • (04/30/98) • **85**

SURONDE, CHÂTEAU DE

Quarts de Chaume 1995: Vivid vanilla and orange aromas carry through to the palate in this intense white. It maintains a lively acidity, and has unusual cider and walnut notes. Never turns as sweet as many from this appellation and vintage, but it's characteristic nonetheless. Drink now through 2010. • $57 • (05/31/98) • **90**

Quarts de Chaume Trie Victor & Joseph 1995: A rich, unctuous marriage of sweet and tart, this golden white wine shows spice, raisin, pineapple and orange-peel flavors, thick and rich on the palate. It's powerful, yet not clumsy, and should improve for years in the bottle. Drink now through 2010. • $43/500ml • (05/31/98) • **93**

TABORDET, YVON & PASCAL

Pouilly-Fumé 1996: Muscular yet vibrant, this powerful white offers ripe pear and apple flavors, with bright notes of grapefruit, smoke and minerals. Balanced and well defined. Should age well. Drink through 2002. 4,000 cases made. • $14 • (06/15/98) • **89**

TAILHAS, CHÂTEAU

Pomerol 1988 • $20 • (04/30/91) • **91**

Pomerol 1982 • $15 • (05/15/89) • **82**

TAILLEFER, CHÂTEAU

Pomerol 1992: Rather lean and tart, sporting a berry, earthy, and slightly metallic character. Light-bodied; hard tannins. • $19 • (04/15/95) • **77**

Pomerol 1988 • $22 • (06/30/91) • **87**

Pomerol 1985 • $24 • (06/30/88) • **81**

Pomerol 1982 • $23 • (05/15/89) • **85**

TAILLEVENT

Brut Blanc de Blancs Champagne 1985: Floral and earthy, with a touch of bitterness on the finish. The pear, vanilla and spice flavors are elegant and balanced. Ready to drink now. • $49 • (11/15/91) • **84**

Brut Blanc de Blancs Champagne 1983: Lean and compact, it has lemon and spice flavors along with a coarse, metallic quality that detracts a bit. Nonetheless, there's good intensity and concentration of flavor. • $33 • (12/31/89) • **82**

TAIN L'HERMITAGE, CAVE DE

Cornas Michel Courtial 1986 • $11 • (07/31/89) • **89**

Crozes-Hermitage Les Nobles Rives 1995: Disappointing from start to finish, with light color, hollow midpalate, and an herbal, strawberry character that speaks little of Syrah. 41,667 cases made. • $11 • (10/15/97) • **75**

Crozes-Hermitage Michel Courtial 1986 • $6 • (05/15/89) • **77**

Crozes-Hermitage White Les Nobles Rives 1995: This big-boned white has bold flavors of honey, ripe pear and cooked apples, with some acidity for grip. A bit rustic in style, but may show better with food. 6,667 cases made. • $11 • (10/15/97) • **81**

Hermitage 1986 • $15 • (07/15/89) • **82**

Hermitage Michel Courtial 1986 • $15 • (03/31/90) • **89**

> **Key:** SS—Spectator Selection CS—Cellar Selection HR—Highly Recommended BB—Best Buy $NA—Price not available Ⓐ—Auction Price (BT)—Barrel Tasting
> **Dates in parentheses indicate the issues in which the ratings were published.**

Hermitage White Les Nobles Rives 1995: Ripe and rich, thick-textured and oily, with flavors of anise, pear, marzipan and loads of toasty oak. Super-smooth and super-full-bodied, it's for those who love mega-oaked wines, but it's a bit overdone for us. Long finish. Perhaps better after 1999. 417 cases made. • $29 • (10/15/97) • **85**

Hermitage White Les Nobles Rives 1994: Deep gold in color and quite evolved on the palate, this rustic white shows assertive flavors of spice, butterscotch and honey. It's big but a bit clumsy, yet is appealing in an earthy style. 417 cases made. • $29 • (10/15/97) • **86**

St.-Joseph Les Nobles Rives 1995: Light, lean and tart, with herbal and bell-pepper flavors and not much fruit. The tannins shut down the short finish. • $15 • (10/15/97) • **72**

St.-Joseph Michel Courtial 1986 • $8 • (07/31/89) • **79**

St.-Joseph White Les Nobes Rives 1995: Clean, firm and well balanced, with good acidity and concentrated, if subtle, fruit flavors that should develop nicely through 1999. A restrained style that shows real class. 833 cases made. • $15 • (10/15/97) • **89**

St.-Péray Les Nobles Rives 1995: Bright, vivid flavors of ripe apple, lime and mineral give liveliness and personality. It's pure, crisp and very refreshing. 2,500 cases made. • $11 • (10/15/97) • **87**

St.-Péray Les Nobles Rives 1994: Maturing now, this shows vegetal and earthlike flavors, with a bitter finish. A rustic wine that won't improve. 2,500 cases made. • $11 • (10/15/97) • **75**

TAITTINGER

Brut Blanc de Blancs Champagne Comtes de Champagne 1989: Bright and lemony, this vivid, well-balanced, youthful Champagne has a creamy texture and focused fruit flavors shaded by butter and vanilla. Drink now through 2002. • $113 • (11/30/97) • **89**

Brut Champagne Comtes de Champagne 1988: Crisp and lean, with pretty aromas and flavors of flowers, spices and peaches. Charming and light as an apéritif. Tasted twice. • $97 • (12/31/94) • **84**

Brut Blanc de Blancs Champagne Comtes de Champagne 1986: Opulent showy Champagne with grapefruit, marzipan aromas and flavors, medium body and fresh acidity. Tasted twice with consistent notes. Drink now. • $95 • (12/31/93) • **87**

Brut Blanc de Blancs Champagne Comtes de Champagne 1985 • $79 Ⓐ • (12/31/90) • **92**

Brut Blanc de Blancs Champagne Comtes de Champagne 1983 • $92 • (12/31/90) • **93**

Brut Blanc de Blancs Champagne Comtes de Champagne 1982 • $105 Ⓐ • (12/31/89) • **95**

Brut Blanc de Blancs Champagne Comtes de Champagne 1981 • $60 Ⓐ • (04/15/88) • **93**

Brut Blanc de Blancs Champagne Comtes de Champagne 1979 • $86 Ⓐ • (05/31/87) • **92**

Brut Blanc de Blancs Champagne Comtes de Champagne 1976 • $91 Ⓐ • (05/16/86) • **83**

Brut Champagne 1988: Smooth and elegant, with a tight, complex core of spice, pear, hazelnut and vanilla flavors that turns creamy and supple on the finish, where it delivers finesse and grace. Smells toasty and doughy. Drinkable now. • $48 • (09/30/93) • **89**

Brut Champagne 1985 • $50 • (12/31/90) • **89**

Brut Champagne 1983 • $38 • (12/31/89) • **84**

Brut Champagne Artist Collection Imai 1988: Solid, well-made, elaborately packaged Champagne with great balance, crisp texture and lively citrus fruit flavors. A bit of doughy complexity comes out on the finish. Drinkable now. • $150 • (02/28/95) • **88**

Brut Champagne Artist Collection Hartung 1986: Crisp, firm and elegant with a sharply focused beam of pear, spice, vanilla and ginger notes that are rich and concentrated. Finishes with a burst of flavor that stays with you on a long, full finish. Drinkable now. • $140 • (10/31/93) • **92**

Brut Champagne Artist Collection Lichtenstein 1985 • $150 • (05/15/92) • **89**

Brut Champagne Artist Collection Vieira da Silva 1983 • $120 • (05/15/92) • **94**

Brut Champagne Artist Collection Masson 1982 • $125 • (05/15/92) • **94**

Brut Champagne Artist Collection Arman 1981 • $87 • (05/31/87) CS • **92**

Brut Champagne La Française NV: A complete Champagne that pulls it all together: the vivid fruit flavors, the plush texture, the spicy-toasty nuances and the long finish. Even better than when last tasted. Drink now. • $38 • (11/30/97) • **89**

Brut Champagne Millésimé 1991: Assertive flavors and full body distinguish this serious Champagne. It has buttery, toasty nuances and a full texture. Drink now through 1999. • $52 • (11/30/97) • **87**
Brut Champagne Millésimé 1990: Quite elegant in texture, this is light and airy but has plenty of fruit flavors and complexity. Subtle and delicious in its combination of fruit and spice flavors. Best now through 1999. • $52 • (11/15/96) • **90**
Brut Champagne Millésimé 1989: Easy-going and smooth-textured, with spicy, doughy aromas. It's light, rather soft and has mellow citrus and vanilla flavors that linger on the finish. • $50 • (12/31/94) • **88**
Brut Champagne Millésimé 1986 • $47 • (08/31/92) • **85**
Brut Champagne Millésimé 1982 • $38 • (12/31/88) • **89**
Brut Rosé Champagne Comtes de Champagne 1993: Full of character and firm in texture, this rosé is very dry, quite full-bodied, marked by crisp cherry flavors and a firm finish. Quite good now, but should improve with age. Drink now through 2002. • $152 • (11/30/97) • **89**
Brut Rosé Champagne Comtes de Champagne 1991: A lean, crisp, bracing bubbly that, nevertheless, has enough depth to draw you back for another sip. It's dry almost to the point of austerity, but still appetizing. Drink through 2000. • $87 Ⓐ • (12/31/96) • **87**
Brut Rosé Champagne Comtes de Champagne 1986: Tight, firm and complex, with focused black cherry, smoke and vanilla flavors that are bright and pleasing. Turns elegant and crisp on the finish, inviting you back for another sip. Drinks well now. • $110 • (06/15/93) • **89**
Brut Rosé Champagne Comtes de Champagne 1985 • $119 Ⓐ • (05/15/92) • **88**
Brut Rosé Champagne Comtes de Champagne 1982 • $115 Ⓐ • (12/31/89) • **92**
Brut Rosé Champagne Comtes de Champagne 1981 • $43 Ⓐ • (04/15/88) • **94**
Brut Rosé Champagne Comtes de Champagne 1976 • $240 • (12/16/85) • **90**
Brut Rosé Champagne Cuvée Prestige NV: A plush, appealing, fresh rosé Champagne with a fine mousse and bright, light cherry and spice flavors. Drink now. • $48 • (11/30/97) • **87**

TALBOT, CHÂTEAU

St.-Julien 1997: Well-structured '97, with mineral and raspberry aromas and flavors, medium body, medium tannins and a ripe fruit finish. Seriously good. • $NA • (06/15/98) (BT) • **85-89**
St.-Julien 1996: Lovely chocolate and tobacco aromas and flavors. Medium- to full-bodied, with velvety tannins and a long aftertaste. Pretty as ever. Better than the '95. • $32 • (06/15/98) (BT) • **90-94**
St.-Julien 1995: Very good, but slightly disappointing. More on the nose than on the palate. Extremely pretty aromas of berry and tobacco, with hints of vanilla. Medium-bodied, with fine tannins and a fresh finish. A bit short. Drink now. • $21 Ⓐ • (01/31/98) • **87**
St.-Julien 1994: Solid Talbot, this wine shows layers of ripe fruit and tobacco on the nose. Medium-bodied, with medium tannins and good fruit flavors. Drink now or hold. • $28 Ⓐ • (01/31/97) • **87**
St.-Julien 1993: Ripe, lush red berry and plummy character. Medium-bodied, quite soft and delicious now, adding a seductive lead-pencil, mint, currant character and smooth finish. Drinkable now. 27,500 cases made. • $25 Ⓐ • (01/31/96) • **86**
St.-Julien 1992: Disappointingly lean and hard, revealing some decent plum and berry character but a rather metallic finish. Drinkable but uninviting. Tasted twice, with consistent notes. • $17 Ⓐ • (04/15/95) • **75**
St.-Julien 1991: A little disappointing. Decent chocolate, tobacco and black cherry flavors, but the finish is short and astringent. Tasted twice with consistent notes. • $22 • (03/31/94) • **78**
St.-Julien 1990: Like eating a reduced raspberry sauce. Rich and thick, With tons of fruit and velvety tannins, yet it's perfectly balanced. Drinkable now. 23,500 cases made. • $24 Ⓐ • (03/31/93) • **93**
St.-Julien 1989 • $62 Ⓐ • (03/15/92) • **90**
St.-Julien 1988 • $43 Ⓐ • (03/15/91) • **90**
St.-Julien 1987 • $19 • (05/15/90) • **85**
St.-Julien 1986 • $73 Ⓐ • (05/31/89) • **91**
St.-Julien 1985 • $47 Ⓐ • (10/15/94) • **90**
St.-Julien 1984 • $21 Ⓐ • (05/15/87) • **80**
St.-Julien 1983 • $48 Ⓐ • (10/15/94) • **90**
St.-Julien 1982 • $88 Ⓐ • (05/01/89) • **88**
St.-Julien 1981 • $41 Ⓐ • (10/15/94) • **85**
St.-Julien 1979 • $29 Ⓐ • (10/15/89) • **84**
St.-Julien 1962 • $43 Ⓐ • (11/30/87) • **55**
St.-Julien 1961 • $98 Ⓐ • (04/30/96) • **88**
St.-Julien 1959 • $167 Ⓐ • (10/15/90) • **86**
St.-Julien 1947: A very light-colored wine that's spicy, and almost silky until the citrusy acidity kicks in. • $165 • (05/31/97) • **83**
St.-Julien 1945 • $325 • (11/30/95) • **81**

TALMARD, DOMAINE

Mâcon-Villages Mâcon-Chardonnay 1995: Dull and flat, with vegetal aromas and flavors and a faint butter note on the finish. • $9 • (01/31/97) • **74**
Mâcon-Villages Mâcon-Chardonnay 1994: Well structured, ripe and mature with good pear and apple flavors and honey notes. Spicy and buttery on the finish. Full-bodied. • $9 • (01/31/97) • **84**
Mâcon-Villages Mâcon-Chardonnay 1993: Soft and simple, straightfoward and lacking interest; with light vanilla and clean apple and peach flavors. Drinkable now. • $10 • (06/30/95) • **78**

TALUAU, JOËL & CLARISSE

St.-Nicolas de Bourgueil Cuvée du Domaine 1995: This fleshy red shows black cherry, spice and herb flavors with firm tannins. It has good concentration. Drink now. 800 cases made. • $15 • (06/15/97) • **85**
St.-Nicolas de Bourgueil Cuvée du Domaine 1993 • $15 • (12/15/95) • **83**

TANESSE, CHÂTEAU

Premières Côtes de Bordeaux 1994: Already on the way out with it's strange, weedy, sundried-tomato character. Barely drinkable. 8,083 cases made. • $10 • (01/31/97) • **70**
Premières Côtes de Bordeaux 1992: Decent earthy, tobacco, fruity character and a slightly weedy finish. • $NA • (04/15/95) • **79**
Premières Côtes de Bordeaux White 1993 • $NA • (05/31/95) • **76**

TARDIEU-LAURENT

Châteauneuf-du-Pape 1995: A beautiful combination of tenderness and intensity, this ripe, international-style red offers well-defined and harmonious plum, chocolate and spice flavors, with smooth, firm tannins and great length. Delicious now, better with time; can age through 2003, at least. 175 cases made. • $40 • (10/15/97) • **93**
Cornas Vieilles Vignes 1995: Amazing for its polish, its class and its great rose petal, floral, cassis and spicy combination. It's so supple, ripe and rich, it has an ethereal quality to it, unfolding its refined, flowery and delicious fruit flavors into a long, seamless finish. Brilliant. Bravo! Tempting now, better after 2000. Tasted twice, with consistent notes. 75 cases made. • $53 • (10/15/97) • **95**
Côtes du Rhône Cuvée Guy Louis 1995: Very impressive, with black color and deep character. Thick, rich, and opulent, with supple, sweet and ripe tannins. Delivers a backbone of acidity and a character of currant, spice and smoke. Tempting now, better after 2000. 300 cases made. • $25 • (10/15/97) • **90**
Crozes-Hermitage Vieilles Vignes 1995: A serious, hard and firm, high-acidity, fresh Crozes. Purple-black in color, tough in texture, but oozing with currant, toasty oak, black cherry and mineral flavors. Medium- to full-bodied, it's impressive from start to finish, but don't touch it until around 2000. 50 cases made. • $23 • (10/15/97) • **90**
Gigondas Vieilles Vignes 1995: Blockbuster style. Very rich and thick, a showy and heady wine packed with lush plum, floral and toasty oak flavors. Full-bodied, stays balanced from start to supple finish. Try now. 50 cases made. • $40 • (10/15/97) • **92**
Hermitage 1995: Polished and lavishly oaked, this international-style red is ripe and generous, with toast, chocolate, plum and cassis flavors, and full but ripe and well-integrated tannins. Balanced and generous, it should start showing its stuff around 2000. 125 cases made. • $61 • (10/15/97) • **91**
St.-Joseph Vieilles Vignes 1995: This modern-style wine marries ripe fruit, with its lush flavors of plums, cassis and black cherries, with assertive, toasty oak notes of chocolate and coffee. It's polished and sophisticated, well integrated and long. Wait until 1999, then enjoy. 50 cases made. • $45 • (10/15/97) • **90**
Vacqueyras 1995: An irresistible, international-style Rhône, with a bounteous oak, plum, red- and blackberry, violet character. Polished and plush, big and full-bodied, but it has an undercurrent of marvelously crisp, lemon-spiked freshness that carries it to a lingering finish. Tempting now, better around 2000. 125 cases made. • $23 • (10/15/97) • **91**

FRANCE

TARENTE, DUC DE

Sancerre 1995: Keen herbaceous aromas and flavors scream Sauvignon Blanc in this clean, very crisp white. Not truly complex, but has good concentration, purity and definition. 8,500 cases made. • $22 • (06/15/97) • **88**

TARGÉ, CHÂTEAU DE

Saumur Champigny 1995: This alluring, elegant red delivers a soft, mouth-filling texture, ripe flavors of plums and berries and a smoky finish. Ready to drink. 3,000 cases made. • $15 • (06/15/97) • **86**

TARIQUET, DOMAINE DU

Chardonnay Vin de Pays des Côtes de Gascogne 1996: A bit coarse around the edges but still appealing, with pleasant fig, butter- and applelike flavors. Finishes on an almost salty note. • $9 • (04/30/98) • **80**

Gros Manseng Vin de Pays des Côtes de Gascogne Cuvée Tardive 1996: Off-dry, refreshing and vibrant, with some good peach flavors. Shows herbal notes on the finish. • $10 • (04/30/98) • **84**

Sauvignon Blanc Vin de Pays des Côtes de Gascogne 1996: A broad-shouldered white with herbal and onion character. Nicely concentrated, with appealing peachy notes on the finish. Drink with food. • $8 • (04/30/98) • **84**

Ugni Blanc-Colombard Vin de Pays des Côtes de Gascogne 1996: A ball of flavors dominated by peach, herbal and onion notes that lack focus in the end. • $7 • (04/30/98) • **79**

Vin de Pays des Côtes de Gascogne White 1995: Quite earthy, and it tastes slightly sweet, with modest apple flavors turning astringent on the finish. • $7 • (05/31/97) • **76**

Vin de Pays des Côtes de Gascogne White Cuvée Bois 1995: Has a nice aged quality to it, with buttery and toasty flavors and aromas, and fig and honey notes as well. Smooth, supple and harmonious, this is a wine meant to wash down a heavy cream sauce. Quite a mouthful. • $11 • (04/30/98) • **86**

TARLANT

Brut Champagne Cuvée Louis NV: Fresh, lively and full of fruit. An appealing, generous Champagne with bright apple, citrus and honey flavors. • $46 • (11/15/97) • **85**

Brut Champagne Dosage Zéro NV: Crisp and bracing, with light citrus flavors accented by spice. Stays tart and austere on the finish. • $33 • (11/15/97) • **82**

Brut Champagne Réserve NV: A bracing Champagne with vivid, crisp, grapefruit and lemon flavors and a slightly tannic texture. It may need until 1999 to soften. • $29 • (12/31/97) • **84**

TARTUGUIÈRE, CHÂTEAU

Médoc 1995: A good, everyday-style red wine with ripe, simple fruit flavors and an easy-going texture. Drink now. 10,000 cases made. • $9 • (01/31/98) • **84**

TATOUX, J.

Brouilly Garnache 1994 • $10 • (10/31/95) • **84**

TAUPENOT-MERME, DOMAINE

Chambolle-Musigny 1990: Fragrant, elegant and delightful to drink. This has pretty aromas of cherry, spice and roses, with flavors to match. Nicely balanced and drinkable now. 600 cases made. • $22 • (11/30/94) HR • **90**

Charmes-Chambertin 1990: Packed with flavor and firmly balanced with tannins and acidity. This offers ripe, focused cherry and currant flavors and meaty, earthy accents that keep it interesting through the long finish. 150 cases made. • $58 • (11/30/94) • **91**

Key: SS—Spectator Selection CS—Cellar Selection HR—Highly Recommended BB—Best Buy $NA—Price not available Ⓐ—Auction Price (BT)—Barrel Tasting
Dates in parentheses indicate the issues in which the ratings were published.

Gevrey-Chambertin Bel-Air 1990: A rustic, traditional wine, quite advanced for a 1990, with earthy, vegetal flavors and firm tannins. It could use more fruit character. Drink now. 150 cases made. • $30 • (01/31/95) • **81**

Morey-St.-Denis 1990: Lively, fruity and flavorful, starting with fresh berry and attractive brie aromas, followed by ripe cherry flavors and firm tannins. There's a bit of astringency on the finish, but the fruit lasts, too. 600 cases made. • $22 • (11/30/94) • **88**

TAYAC, CHÂTEAU

Côtes de Bourg 1990: Lean, toasty and austere, with a narrow band of currant and smoke aromas and flavors and a firm, tart finish. Drinkable now. • $12 • (06/15/93) • **78**

Côtes de Bourg 1988 • $10 • (01/31/92) • **78**

Côtes de Bourg Clos du Pain de Sucre 1995: A sturdy red, with black cherry, earth and licorice flavors of some concentration, but the firm tannins and rustic character keep it closed now. Drinkable now. 4,400 cases made. • $9 • (10/15/97) • **84**

Côtes de Bourg Rubis du Prince Noir 1993: This sturdy red shows better structure than flavor. Firm and balanced, with light plum and cola notes. Modest on its own, but should make a harmonious accompaniment to food. 7,500 cases made. • $12 • (10/15/97) • **83**

TELMONT, J. DE

Brut Champagne Grand Vintage 1988: Light and lacy, this is a smooth, delicate style of bubbly with subtle lemon and vanilla flavors. Tastes fine now, but won't go over the hill anytime soon. Drink through 2000. • $30 • (12/31/97) • **88**

TEMPIER, DOMAINE

Bandol 1995: A modern style. Aromas of crushed red berries and lively raspberry and cherry flavors mark this easy-drinking, light-bodied red. Uncomplicated and appealing. • $22 • (12/15/97) • **83**

Bandol 1994: Cigar-box and earthlike aromas give way to plum, tobacco and meat flavors that mesh seamlessly in this firm, fresh red. Distinctive and harmonious. Drink now through 2002. • $23 • (09/30/97) • **87**

Bandol 1984 • $15 • (12/15/87) • **79**

Bandol 1983 • $24 Ⓐ • (08/31/87) • **78**

Bandol 1981 • $13 Ⓐ • (08/31/86) • **73**

Bandol Cuvée Spéciale 1995: Meaty and wild, this shows more of the character of traditional Bandol. Intense, long notes of game, plum and wild herb are well balanced with medium-weight and tannins. Lingering finish. • $24 • (12/15/97) • **86**

Bandol Cuvée Spéciale 1994: Cherry and herbal flavors mingle in this light-bodied yet dryly tannic red. It has grip but lacks generosity; may fill out with food. Try now. • $25 • (09/30/97) • **83**

Bandol Cuvée Spéciale Cabassaou 1995: A wine with plenty of gusto and flavor, a well-structured combination of tradition and modernity. Ripe and well-rounded, with loads of chocolate, raspberry and cassis flavors. This is a big wine with ripe tannins that should only improve with age. 100 percent Mouvèdre. Drink now through 2005. • $45 • (03/31/98) • **91**

Bandol Cuvée Spéciale La Migoua 1995: A vibrant red with luscious red plum, sweet cherry and spice flavors. Clean and well-made, with coffee notes on the finish. A blend of 55 percent Mourvèdre, 25 percent Cinsault and 20 percent Grenache. Drink now through 2000. • $28 • (03/31/98) • **86**

Bandol Cuvée Spéciale La Migoua 1994: A light-bodied yet firm red, with bright cherry and herbal flavors that are fresh and well-defined, and a finish that mingles chocolate and tobacco notes. A pretty, balanced wine that's drinking well now. • $28 • (09/30/97) • **87**

Bandol La Migoua 1987 • $22 • (10/31/90) • **86**

Bandol Cuvée Spéciale La Tourtine 1995: Ripe-tasting and full-flavored, with plenty of plum, cherry and spice notes. A nice cedary streak through the middle lingers on the finish. A blend of 60 percent Mourvèdre, 30 percent Grenache and 10 percent Cinsault. Drink now through 2002. • $28 • (03/31/98) • **87**

Bandol Cuvée Spéciale La Tourtine 1994: This lively red offers fresh black cherry flavors with accents of tobacco and herbs. Harmonious and balanced, with just enough tannin for grip. Has international-style polish but maintains the character of Bandol. Drinkable now. • $28 • (09/30/97) • **89**

Bandol La Tourtine 1987 • $22 • (10/31/90) • **82**

TERME, CHÂTEAU MARQUIS DE

Margaux 1996: Pretty violet and berry aromas and some similar flavors, but lacks length on the finish. • $NA • (01/01/97) (BT) • **80-84**
Margaux 1988 • $23 • (04/30/91) • **92**
Margaux 1986 • $23 • (06/30/89) • **79**
Margaux 1961 • $NA • (04/30/96) • **82**

TERME, DOMAINE DU

Côtes du Rhône 1995: A bit herbal, but it shows modest cherry and earth flavors, too. Rather lean but also vibrant. • $NA • (10/15/97) • **78**
Gigondas 1994: This supple, fruity red offers pretty strawberry and cherry flavors, with notes of herbs and licorice that add depth. Ready now. • $17 • (10/15/97) • **84**
Gigondas 1993: Full-bodied and fleshy, this is ripe and concentrated with plum, currant, licorice and spice flavors. Not a powerhouse, but an elegant, harmonious wine with balance and length. Generous, it should improve in the bottle. • $17 • (10/15/96) • **89**

TERRASSE, CHÂTEAU LA

Bordeaux Supérieur La Terrasse sur la Rivière 1993: Pleasing black currant and plum flavors plus a dash of herbs and tobacco and medium body add up to a tasty wine for drinking now. • $9 • (08/31/95) • **85**

TERRASSES DE GUILHEM, LES

Merlot Vin de Pays de l'Herault 1995: Thick in texture, with meaty, plummy and herbal flavors that end on a slightly astringent note. Drink now. • $9 • (03/31/98) • **78**
Vin de Pays de l'Herault 1996: A young-tasting red, with plenty of berry, cherry flavors and a hint of spice. You could try it slightly chilled. Drink now. • $9 • (03/31/98) • **82**
Vin de Pays de l'Herault 1993 • $7 • (03/15/94) • **84**
Vin de Pays de l'Herault White 1996: Interesting, with chewy flavors of almond and green apple. Well balanced and crisp, with some nice citrus notes. Should match well with food. • $9 • (02/28/98) • **85**

TERRE FERME, DOMAINE DE

Châteauneuf-du-Pape 1989 • $20 • (08/31/92) • **88**

TERRES VINEUSES, DOMAINE DES

Corton Renardes 1995: Funky, this brown-colored wine tastes swampy, stemmy, green and herbaceous. Dry on the finish. 180 cases made. • $45 • (01/31/98) • **72**
Corton-Charlemagne 1995: Solid if not exciting, with a firm backbone of acidity. Medium-bodied, it lacks a bit of fruit, and the hints of paper, cardboard and sawdust are distracting. Try after 1999. 900 cases made. • $60 • (01/31/98) • **81**

TERRIÈRE, CHÂTEAU DE LA

Beaujolais-Villages Cuvée du Souzy Vieilles Vignes 1996: Light, fresh and fruity, with bright grape and cinnamon flavors and very little tannin. It's simple but quaffable; try slightly chilled. • $13 • (09/15/97) • **83**
Brouilly 1996: Bright fruit and lively texture give this red an exuberant appeal. It shows cherry, raspberry and lightly spicy flavors and just enough tannin for grip. • $16 • (07/31/97) • **85**
Brouilly Cuvée Jules du Souzy Vieilles Vignes 1995: Vanilla and toast aromas and flavors suggest oak aging, which is unusual for the appellation but appealing here; nicely balanced with bright raspberry and cherry notes. The texture is lush, yet firm enough for food. • $18 • (07/31/97) • **88**
Régnié 1996: This supple, harmonious red shows black cherry, spice and light herb flavors, is smooth on the palate, with just enough tannin for food. • $14 • (09/15/97) • **84**

TERROIR DE LAGRAVE

Gaillac 1994: A dry, lean red with a distinctive tang. Has peppery, cherrylike flavors and a firm, tannic texture. • $10 • (05/15/97) • **84**
Gaillac Cuvée Sigolène 1993: Tastes herbal, with green olive and black currant flavors. Starts off with a velvety texture, but the tannins build on the finish. • $12 • (04/30/97) • **81**
Gaillac Doux 1994: Somewhat simple, with modest lemon and kiwi flavors. A foxy flavor marks the finish. • $13 • (05/31/97) • **80**
Gaillac White Perlé 1995: Strong fruit flavors, mainly apple and pear, with some accents of butter. Dry and firm on the moderately long finish. Try with food. • $11 • (05/15/97) • **83**
Gaillac White Sec 1995: Broad and richly textured, with more flavors of almonds and straw than fruit. Rustic, yet appealing in its own way. • $10 • (05/15/97) • **82**

TERTRE, CHÂTEAU DU

Margaux 1997: Concentrated but slightly herbal. Medium-bodied, with medium tannins and a slightly dry finish. A bit overdone. Wait and see next year. • $NA • (06/15/98) (BT) • **80-84**
Margaux 1996: Some intense fruit character, but a little disjointed with a rather hollow texture. Medium-bodied, with full tannins and medium finish. Wait and see. • $20 • (06/15/98) (BT) • **85-89**
Margaux 1995: A rustic wine with decent fruit. Slightly weedy, with berry, earth and tobacco aromas and flavors. Medium-bodied, with velvety tannins and a medium finish. Try after 2000. 14,000 cases made. • $15 Ⓐ • (01/31/98) • **85**
Margaux 1991: A bit too herbal and diluted to rate higher, but there are some pretty cherry and chocolate flavors. • $17 • (03/31/94) • **77**
Margaux 1989 • $25 Ⓐ • (03/15/92) • **90**
Margaux 1988 • $35 Ⓐ • (06/30/91) • **86**
Margaux 1986 • $26 Ⓐ • (06/15/89) • **89**
Margaux 1985 • $29 Ⓐ • (06/30/88) SS • **93**
Margaux 1983 • $19 Ⓐ • (07/16/86) • **91**
Margaux 1982 • $29 Ⓐ • (08/31/92) • **80**

TERTRE DAUGAY, CHÂTEAU

St.-Emilion 1997: Fine texture to this wine, with berry, cherry aromas and flavors but a slightly diluted palate. Good color. • $NA • (06/15/98) (BT) • **80-84**
St.-Emilion 1996: A grapey and delicious young red. Medium-bodied, with velvety tannins and hints of red fruit and vanilla in the aftertaste. Not a blockbuster, but pretty. 6,000 cases made. • $50 • (06/15/98) (BT) • **85-89**
St.-Emilion 1995: Exotic and complex. Wonderful aromas of fruit, allspice, cinnamon and nuts. Full-bodied, with velvety tannins and an extended aftertaste. Best after 2000. 5,000 cases made. • $44 • (01/31/98) • **90**
St.-Emilion 1989 • $29 • (04/30/92) • **83**
St.-Emilion 1988 • $20 • (04/30/91) • **85**

TERTRE DE LAUNAY, CHÂTEAU

Entre-Deux-Mers 1995: A fresh-tasting white, smooth, rich and balanced, with good fig and herbal flavors and a nice touch of spice on the finish. • $8 • (05/31/97) • **85**

TERTRE ROTEBOEUF, CHÂTEAU LE

St.-Emilion 1990: Ripe and generous, with a streak of tannin that keeps the spicy, tobacco-scented black cherry flavors from showing well. Try now. • $76 Ⓐ • (06/15/93) • **83**
St.-Emilion 1989 • $79 Ⓐ • (03/15/92) • **93**
St.-Emilion 1988 • $56 Ⓐ • (06/15/91) • **90**
St.-Emilion 1987 • $25 • (02/15/90) • **83**
St.-Emilion 1986 • $39 • (06/30/89) • **90**
St.-Emilion 1985 • $61 Ⓐ • (06/30/88) • **89**
St.-Emilion 1983 • $35 • (05/16/86) • **81**
St.-Emilion 1982 • $30 • (09/16/85) • **85**

TÊTE, LOUIS

Morgon Les Charmes 1997: This fleshy red offers well-defined black cherry and smoke flavors. Though it's not as rich and tannic as the best Morgons, it has good fruit concentration and pleasant roundness on the palate. Drink through 1999. 6,000 cases made. • $13 • (07/31/98) • **84**

TÊTE, MICHEL

Beaujolais-Villages Domaine du Clos du Fief 1995: Round and supple, this fruity red offers black cherry, berry and smoky flavors. Just enough tannin to stand up to food. • $12 • (09/15/96) • **83**

Juliénas Domaine du Clos du Fief 1995: Ripe and supple, this velvety red offers black cherry and blackberry flavors and is fresh and harmonious. Makes for pleasant drinking now. • $16 • (09/15/96) • **86**

Juliénas Domaine du Clos du Fief Cuvée Prestige 1996: Ripe fruit and new oak marry well in this lush red. It offers floral, toasty and plummy aromas, with bright plum and vanilla flavors touched with spice and black pepper. Full tannins are well integrated; the wine is balanced, the pretty flavors linger on the finish. Drink now through 2000. • $20 • (05/31/98) • **90**

Juliénas Domaine du Clos du Fief Cuvée Prestige 1995: Impressively structured for Beaujolais, this dark red shows flavors of plum, game and chocolate, with firm but well-integrated tannins and a long finish. It's well made and distinctive. • $20 • (07/31/97) • **88**

Juliénas Domaine du Clos du Fief Cuvée Prestige 1993 • $20 • (07/31/95) • **83**

TEYSSIER, CHÂTEAU

Montagne-St.-Emilion 1997: Fresh blackberry and cherry aromas. Light-bodied, with fine tannins and lovely sweet fruit on the finish. Delicious. • $NA • (06/15/98) (BT) • **80-84**

Montagne-St.-Emilion 1996: Pretty aromas and flavors of violets, raspberries and minerals. Medium- to full-bodied, with racy tannins and medium finish. Well-constructed. 25,000 cases made. • $20 • (06/15/98) (BT) • **85-89**

Montagne-St.-Emilion 1995: A bit one-dimensional, but with plenty of ripe fruit. Good intensity of berry and raspberry aromas. Medium-bodied, with firm tannins and a medium aftertaste. Slightly hard and tannic. Best after 1999. • $NA • (01/31/98) • **86**

Montagne-St.-Emilion 1994: Slightly dry and tannic, with an herb and tomato character. Medium-bodied. Unappealing. • $NA • (01/31/97) • **77**

Montagne-St.-Emilion 1993: Rather one-dimensional, showing dark cherry character, medium body, high acidity and a fresh, slightly dry finish. • $NA • (01/31/96) • **78**

THÉVENET, JEAN

Mâcon-Clessé Domaine de la Bongran Quintaine Cuvée Tradition 1994: Brilliant. Seductive and exotic, a full-bodied, rich, ripe Chardonnay with flavors of peach, apricot, honey, almond, pear, mango and fresh herbs that build up to a formidable, intense, flawless finish that lasts for minutes. Amazing quality for a Mâcon. Drink or hold until past 2000. 1,667 cases made. • $25 • (05/31/97) • **93**

Mâcon-Clessé Domaine de la Bongran Quintaine Cuvée Tradition 1993 • $NA • (05/31/96) • **92**

Mâcon-Viré Domaine Emilian Gillet Quintaine 1993 • $20 • (05/31/96) • **89**

THÉVENET, JEAN-CLAUDE

Mâcon-Pierreclos 1996: Rich and ripe, with a real *terroir* character that makes it stand out. Smells earthy at first, then out come wonderfully ripe tropical fruit, sweet-tasting pear and rich honey flavors. Supple on the seductive, delicious, well-made finish. Drink now or hold until 1999. 2,500 cases made. • $13 • (08/31/97) • **90**

Mâcon-Villages 1994: Lively and vibrant lime, wet hay and grass notes carry over to the juicy, long finish. Somewhat tart, but seafood with a rich sauce should make a delicious match. 1,250 cases made. • $10 • (08/31/95) • **84**

St.-Véran Vieilles Vignes 1996: Quite intense, with lime and apple flavors, along with some nice honey, pear and tropical notes. Balanced and fairly ripe. Nice to drink through 1999. 1,080 cases made. • $18 • (05/31/98) • **85**

St.-Véran Vieilles Vignes Clos de l'Ermitage Cuvée 1994: Deep, intense, smooth, medium-bodied, round and minerally, offering crisp citrus flavors and pear and green apple notes. Drinkable now. 1,250 cases made. • $16 • (08/31/95) • **87**

Key: SS—Spectator Selection CS—Cellar Selection HR—Highly Recommended BB—Best Buy $NA—Price not available Ⓐ—Auction Price (BT)—Barrel Tasting
Dates in parentheses indicate the issues in which the ratings were published.

THÉVENET, JEAN-PAUL

Morgon Vieilles Vignes 1995: A real mouthful for Beaujolais, this is an ambitious red that hasn't yet achieved harmony. Offers rich game and earth flavors, with very firm tannins. Should round out with time; try in 1999. • $23 • (09/15/97) • **87**

THÉVENOT-MACHAL, JACQUES

Meursault 1995: An odd wine, with flavors something like glue and wax. Not pleasant. 100 cases made. • $26 • (05/31/97) • **70**

Meursault Le Porusot 1995: A bit hard now, perhaps due to shock from recent bottling. Medium-bodied, clean and crisp, with a distinctive matchstick, stone, flint, *goût de terroir* character. Good fruit intensity and lovely balance on the long, chewy finish. Should be better after 2000. 167 cases made. • $30 • (08/31/97) • **83**

Meursault Les Charmes 1995: A beauty. Incredibly thick and ripe, it still manages to be subtle and elegant, revealing little of itself except its class. Concentrated, the texture is like cream and caresses the palate, as do hints of tropical fruit, pear, mineral and spice. Balanced to a T, it tiptoes to a lovely finish. Tempting now through 2005. 125 cases made. • $30 • (08/31/97) • **96**

Puligny-Montrachet 1995: Distinguished and elegant, concentrated, full-bodied and balanced, showing good depth of aroma and flavor. Has an oily texture and grapefruit, mineral, spice, pear tart and toasty oak character. Long, smooth but vibrant finish. Try after 2000. • $25 • (08/31/97) • **90**

Puligny-Montrachet Les Folatières 1995: Superb, with palate-caressing texture, this wine oozes seduction. Full-bodied, with a yeasty-leesy vanilla, pear, mineral and citrus character. Very distinctive, delivering a long, chewy and mouthpuckering finish that suggests it should age until around 2000. 175 cases made. • $30 • (08/31/97) • **92**

Volnay-Santenots 1988 • $36 • (11/15/90) • **89**

THIBAULT, JEAN-BAPTISTE

Sancerre La Duschesne 1995: A well-structured white showing pleasant herb and citrus flavors, but a light earthy note detracts a bit. Crisp, but short. • $18 • (06/15/97) • **82**

THIBERT PÈRE & FILS

Mâcon-Fuissé 1996: Excellent balance and concentration, although the earthy tones might upset some. Shows personality and has tropical fruit, pear and apple notes. Good length. Medium-bodied, quite crisp on the finish. Try now. 2,500 cases made. • $19 • (08/31/97) • **85**

Pouilly-Fuissé 1994: Extremely well made, clean and focused, this sings with intense, nicely integrated spice and ripe fruit flavors. Terrific finish. 1,416 cases made. • $15 • (05/31/96) • **88**

Pouilly-Fuissé Vieilles Vignes 1994: Fresh, clean and well made. This is focused, medium-bodied and has citrus, green apple, honey and cream flavors. Very likeable. 466 cases made. • $16 • (05/31/96) • **86**

Pouilly-Fuissé Vignes Blanches 1994: Like biting into a slice of lime. Tart, crisp and unyielding, with just a hint of earth and butterscotch. It might work with the appropriate food. 350 cases made. • $14 • (05/31/96) • **79**

THIENPONT, FRANÇOIS

Lalande-de-Pomerol 1996: Light and fruity, with pretty plum and berry character. Light- to medium-bodied, with a succulent, fruity finish. • $18 • (06/15/98) (BT) • **80-84**

THIEULEY, CHÂTEAU

Bordeaux White 1995: Shows solid varietal character with appealing herbal and figlike flavors that linger on the finish. Also has decent depth, and is well balanced and focused. • $7 • (04/30/97) • **85**

Bordeaux White 1994 • $NA • (05/31/95) • **80**

Bordeaux White Cuvée Francis Courselle 1994 • $NA • (05/31/95) • **80**

THIVIN, CHÂTEAU

Côte de Brouilly 1995: Assertive but clumsy, this firmly tannic red tastes of plums, coffee and earth. Has concentration and character. Drinkable now. • $17 • (07/31/97) • **85**

Côte de Brouilly 1994: The sweet cherry and spicy strawberry flavors are vivid, but a bit candied. Light-bodied and supple, but shows faintly drying tannins on the finish. • $15 • (09/15/96) • **82**

THOMAS

Pouilly-Fuissé 1996: Tart and overly crisp; a lean wine, tough to warm up to, with lime all over the place and little ripe fruit. 830 cases made. • $18 • (05/31/98) • **76**

Pouilly-Fuissé 1994: Delicious for drinking now. Not very intense and somewhat diluted, it still provides lots of pleasure, as its honey touches make a perfect apéritif. Light-bodied and balanced, featuring some citrus, pear and apricot notes on the finish. 833 cases made. • $17 • (05/31/96) • **84**

Pouilly-Fuissé 1993: Extremely crisp, well-defined fruit; lots of wet hay, green apple, lime and fresh herb notes and a vibrant finish. Light to medium in body. 813 cases made. • $18 • (05/15/95) • **81**

Pouilly-Fuissé Vieilles Vignes 1996: Fruity yet full-bodied, with a good lemony core that brings an herbal note to this balanced white, with its creamy texture and crisp finish. Offers good fruit, wet earth complexity and a clean finish. Drink now. 290 cases made. • $25 • (05/31/98) • **86**

Pouilly-Fuissé Vieilles Vignes 1994: A beautiful, flavorful white, with plenty of ripe pear, toasty pine nut and butter notes along with a citrusy finish that is long and vibrant. Full-bodied and quite opulent, though it falls short of outstanding because it needs a tad more focus. 208 cases made. • $25 • (05/31/96) • **88**

St.-Véran 1995: Crisp and medium-bodied, with fairly intense fruit flavors, but has an oddly lactic, butterscotchy note, and turns sour on the finish. Tasted twice with consistent notes. • $NA • (08/31/96) • **78**

St.-Véran 1994: Fresh, elegant and fruity, delivering pretty citrus, pear and tropical fruit flavors. Buttery on the palate, smooth and creamy on the finish. 1,250 cases made. • $12 • (08/31/95) • **85**

St.-Véran Cuvée No. 2 1996: A bit earthy and a touch herbal, but caressingly full-bodied, with a lovely, supple midpalate; opulent, with a creamlike texture. Tastes fruity, with pear, lemon, kiwi and litchi accented by toasty, spicy oak. Balanced. Crisp finish. Drink now through 2000. 580 cases made. • $15 • (05/31/98) • **85**

St.-Véran Cuvée No. 718 1996: Clean, pure and attractive, its fairly supple mouthfeel, ripe pear and tropical character and a floral scent make for a nice wine, but don't expect much depth. Light-bodied; drink now. 2,080 cases made. • $12 • (05/31/98) • **84**

St.-Véran Vieilles Vignes 1996: A grassy, slightly herbal-style white, but there's also lovely floral and honey notes; medium-bodied, it has some minerally, opulent midpalate weight that gives it a rich, smooth character. Crisp finish, but open it for an hour or decant. Drink now through 2000. 580 cases made. • $18 • (05/31/98) • **87**

St.-Véran Vieilles Vignes 1995: Full-bodied, multi-layered and complex. Concentrated apple, melon, grapefruit and lees flavors. A bit earthy, but has good depth and a long finish. Try now. • $NA • (08/31/96) • **88**

St.-Véran Vieilles Vignes Cuvée Préstige 1994: St.-Véran of the vintage? Classy and sweet-tasting, featuring a creamy mouthfeel, delicious mineral, citrus, pear, chive and sweet pea flavors, medium body and long finish. 1,250 cases made. • $16 • (08/31/95) • **88**

THOMAS, CLAUDE

Sancerre Chavignol Les Monts Damnés 1994 • $20 • (06/15/96) • **78**
Sancerre Les Monts Damnés 1993 • $15 • (12/15/95) • **88**

THOMAS, LUCIEN

Sancerre Clos de la Crêle 1995: Light and lively. This is a clean, fresh white with textbook citrus and herbal flavors; not powerful, but it sings. 2,500 cases made. • $16 • (06/15/97) • **87**

THOMAS, PAUL

Sancerre Chavignol Les Comtesses Grande Reserve de Notre Vignoble 1994 • $19 • (06/15/96) • **88**

Sancerre Chavignol Les Comtesses Grande Reserve de Notre Vignoble 1993 • $21 • (11/15/95) • **86**

THOMAS-LABAILLE

Sancerre Chavignol Les Monts Damnés 1995: Grapefruit and green apple flavors have a hint of spicy herbs in this medium-weight white. Though rather restrained, it's well balanced for food. 400 cases made. • $20 • (04/30/97) • **87**

THOMAS-MOILLARD, DOMAINE

Beaune Grèves 1995: A dense, solid red, with black cherry, plum and tobacco notes and medium body. Balanced, it's drinkable now with food, or try in 1999. 930 cases made. • $28 • (11/15/97) • **85**

Beaune Les Grèves 1994: Lean, green and stalky in character, with harsh tannins and thin flavors. 920 cases made. • $33 • (11/15/96) • **74**

Clos Vougeot 1994: Polished and refined. Youthful berry and tobacco flavors weave together, and finish with a touch of mineral flavor and some astringency. Better after 2000. 250 cases made. • $65 • (11/15/96) • **83**

Corton Le Clos du Roi 1995: Serious red Burgundy. Brooding aromas of oak and black cherry are backed up by a tight, unevolved mouthful of dense blackberry, licorice and earth flavors. Long and complex, with an aftertaste of vanilla and sweet fruit; give this until 2002 to unfold. 320 cases made. • $43 • (11/15/97) • **91**

Corton Le Clos du Roi 1994: Packed with chewy texture and dense flavors, its a powerful wine showing high-gear black cherry, mineral and toasty flavors under a solid layer of tannins. Needs until 2001 to 2005 to soften tannins. 350 cases made. • $47 • (11/15/96) • **90**

Nuits-St.-Georges 1994: Ripe and tasty, with a solid beam of currant and blackberry flavors that extend into a nicely balanced finish. Has impressive length; should keep improving through 2000 or 2002. 532 cases made. • $35 • (11/15/96) • **84**

Nuits-St.-Georges Clos de Thorey 1995: This Pinot Noir notches it up a bit with some sweet, old-viney fruit. Also has plenty of tannins and a solid, rustic profile that seems a shade unripe on the finish. 1,458 cases made. • $39 • (01/31/98) • **85**

Nuits-St.-Georges Clos de Thorey 1994: Supple and round, with plum and cherry flavors folded nicely into the earth and oak notes. Medium-bodied, it ends a bit dry. • $42 • (11/15/96) • **82**

Vosne-Romanée Aux Malconsorts 1995: A core of cherry, accented by vanilla and earth, is shrouded in tannins and a backbone of acidity. There's a hint of rusticity, but the concentration and finish show promise if it's held until 1999. 1,200 cases made. • $43 • (03/31/98) • **85**

Vosne-Romanée Aux Malconsorts 1994: Light and more than a little funky, with earthy, leathery notes crowding the fine bead of berry flavors. Tannins are tight, too. Best from 1999. 1,317 cases made. • $47 • (11/15/96) • **80**

THORIN, MAISON

Beaujolais-Villages Château du Bost 1995: A vibrant Beaujolais with fruit and panache. Bright acidity helps focus the ripe blackberry flavor, and accents of spice and smoke give depth. A quaffing wine with style. • $9 • (04/30/97) • **86**

Bourgogne 1994: A light red Burgundy that's well balanced and agreeable, but simple in flavor. • $13 • (04/30/97) • **79**

Bourgogne White 1995: Light fruit flavors, a smooth texture and a rather watery finish define this basic white wine. • $12 • (04/30/97) • **78**

Brouilly Domaine de la Croix Briante 1995: Light and fruity, this offers cherry flavors with refreshing, tart acidity for liveliness. A simple, quaffable wine; soft on the palate. • $16 • (04/30/97) • **83**

Châteauneuf-du-Pape 1986 • $13 • (11/30/88) • **87**

Côtes du Rhône Les Antiques 1995: Light and fresh, marked by typical Grenache flavors of berries, licorice and herbs. Like a Beaujolais in style; drink now. • $10 • (12/15/96) • **83**

Côtes du Rhône White Les Antiques 1995: Full-bodied, showing flavors of almond, vanilla and lime; firm but without nuance. A good match with simple foods. • $10 • (02/28/97) • **83**

Fleurie Les Muriennes 1995: Very bold for a Beaujolais, with a rich, distinctive and appealing character. Packs in toasty, spicy accents to match the ripe plum and lightly gamy flavors and, though firm in structure, it's approachable. • $18 • (04/30/97) • **89**

Moulin-à-Vent Domaine des Pierres Roses 1995: Lively and enticing. Sweet vanilla flavors marry nicely with ripe, plummy ones, and toasty, new-oak

FRANCE

notes add pizzazz. Tannins are firm, yet balanced. Ready to drink. • $18 • (04/30/97) • **88**

Pommard 1986 • $24 • (02/28/90) • **75**

TIGNY, DE

Saumur Champigny Château de Chaintres 1992 • $10 • (11/15/94) • **79**

TIJOU, PIERRE-YVES

Coteaux du Layon-Chaume Château Soucherie 1995: Pretty spice notes shine through this round, moderately sweet white, with light apple and quince flavors that unfold on the finish. Well-structured. Try in a few years. 100 cases made. • $25 • (05/15/97) • **88**

Coteaux du Layon-Chaume Cuvée Clémentine 1993 • $20 • (05/15/96) • **89**

Savennières Clos des Perrieres 1995: This fresh white offers more purity than expressiveness, with mineral, citrus and light apple flavors. May open with time. 150 cases made. • $23 • (06/15/97) • **84**

Savennières Clos des Perrières 1993 • $17 • (05/15/96) • **85**

TIMBERLAY, CHÂTEAU

Bordeaux Supérieur 1997: Light and weedy, with a diluted palate, light tannins and a dry finish. • $NA • (06/15/98) (BT) • **75-79**

Bordeaux Supérieur 1996: A simple, fruity '96 with pretty berry flavors, light body and a soft finish. Very light but delicious. 3,000 cases made. • $13 • (06/15/98) (BT) • **80-84**

Bordeaux Supérieur 1995: A lighter-style '95, with tobacco, cherry and herbs on the nose and palate. Medium-bodied, with light tannins and a short finish. Drink now. 56,000 cases made. • $12 • (01/31/98) • **81**

Bordeaux Supérieur 1994: Rather lean, but has pleasant berry and mineral aromas and flavors, and fine tannins. Drink now. 39,500 cases made. • $10 • (01/31/97) • **79**

Bordeaux White 1995: A very lemony wine with hints of minerals. Medium-bodied, with fine acidity and a fresh aftertaste. Not the most powerful, but delicious now. • $7 • (04/30/98) • **84**

Bordeaux White 1993 • $8 • (05/31/95) • **73**

TINEL-BLONDELET, F.

Pouilly-Fumé Genetin 1995: Powerful aromas, herbal and astringent, give way to fruitier, but still sharp, flavors in this assertive white. It has personality, but it's rather extreme in style. Tasted twice, with consistent notes. 1,800 cases made. • $19 • (06/15/97) • **86**

Pouilly-Fumé Genetin 1993 • $17 • (05/15/96) • **86**

Pouilly-Fumé L'Arret Buffatte 1994: Distinctive. Notes of coconut and tropical fruit give this round white a unique profile, and there's enough acidity to balance its rich texture. Not your typical Pouilly-Fumé, but delicious. 1,000 cases made. • $19 • (04/30/97) • **90**

Pouilly-Fumé L'Arret Buffatte 1993 • $18 • (10/31/94) • **83**

TOLLOT-BEAUT & FILS

Aloxe-Corton 1995: Decent, straightforward red Burgundy, offering bark, wet earth and red berry flavors. Light-to-medium in body, with tannins that are a bit tough and a crisp finish. Try now. • $35 • (11/15/97) • **81**

Aloxe-Corton 1994: Crisp in texture, with delicate strawberry flavors and minty notes that finish lightly. • $37 • (11/15/96) • **82**

Aloxe-Corton 1993: Very good structure complements delicious floral, rose petal, currant and plum aromas and flavors. Drink now. • $29 • (11/15/95) • **86**

Aloxe-Corton 1992: Round and spicy, light and pleasant, showing peppery red berry notes in balance with a hint of oak. Ready to drink. 1,308 cases made. • $27 • (12/15/94) • **82**

Aloxe-Corton 1991: Firm and almost austere. A lean wine, with appealing plum and vanilla aromas and flavors in modest proportions. Drinkable now. 1,683 cases made. • $NA • (01/31/94) • **82**

Key: SS—Spectator Selection CS—Cellar Selection HR—Highly Recommended BB—Best Buy $NA—Price not available Ⓐ—Auction Price (BT)—Barrel Tasting
Dates in parentheses indicate the issues in which the ratings were published.

Aloxe-Corton 1990: A lively wine with a lot going on, from the cherry, toast and cedar aromas rising from the glass to the solid structure that carries the ripe, black cherry flavors and the lovely finish. • $38 • (12/15/92) • **93**

Aloxe-Corton 1989 • $60 Ⓐ • (01/31/92) • **90**

Aloxe-Corton 1985 • $29 Ⓐ • (03/15/88) • **89**

Aloxe-Corton Les Vercots 1995: This light *premier cru* offers modest aromas but delivers ripe fruit on the palate. Some nicely integrated spice and chocolate notes provide complexity on the moderate finish. • $40 • (11/15/97) • **80**

Aloxe-Corton Les Vercots 1994: Light, and floral in character, with a soft edge to the modest black cherry and spice flavors. • $40 • (11/15/96) • **83**

Aloxe-Corton Les Vercots 1993: Well-crafted, round and smooth, delicious, delivering mocha, vanilla and currant character. So supple it melts in the mouth, but has enough tannin structure to hold until 1999. • $37 • (11/15/95) • **89**

Beaune Clos du Roi 1995: Impressively intense *premier cru*. Balanced and ripe, yet elegant, it offers supple tannins and a velvetlike texture on the palate. With loads of fruit and oak, this full-bodied '95 is layered with mocha, spicy, red berry and blackberry flavors. Long, burning finish; try after 2000. • $40 • (11/15/97) • **90**

Beaune Clos du Roi 1994: Ripe and toasty, this wine is of modest scale, but features polished, spicy flavors that persist nicely on the velvety finish. Best now. • $40 • (11/15/96) • **87**

Beaune Clos du Roi 1993: Decent plum and berry character, but just slightly herbal. Medium-bodied with medium tannins and a silky finish. Try now. • $35 • (11/15/95) • **88**

Beaune Clos du Roi 1992: A pretty wine, with raspberry and cherry flavors playing against the chestnut and sweet-oak notes on the supple finish. Easy to drink. 525 cases made. • $30 • (12/15/94) • **85**

Beaune Clos du Roi 1991: A bright, flavorful, harmonious wine, with well-defined currant and blackberry flavors shaded by toast and vanilla notes and a touch of anise. Drink now. 517 cases made. • $30 Ⓐ • (01/31/94) • **87**

Beaune Clos du Roi 1990: A beauty of a wine; complex and refined, with bright violet, vanilla, tea and red berry aromas and flavors that grow and grow in the glass. Nicely structured, with firm tannins. Drinkable now. • $48 • (12/15/92) • **90**

Beaune Clos du Roi 1989 • $52 • (01/31/92) • **91**

Beaune Clos du Roi 1988 • $53 • (02/28/91) • **86**

Beaune Les Grèves 1995: A rich, round '95 Pinot, with lifted cherry flavors and hints of coffee and vanilla, but very tannic and hot on the finish. Disappointing for this appellation. • $35 • (11/15/97) • **79**

Beaune Les Grèves 1994: A delicate, medium-bodied Burgundy, offering mocha, spice, earth and red berry character that deepens toward the flavorful finish. Drink now or hold. • $30 • (11/15/96) • **83**

Beaune Les Grèves 1993: Very good chocolate, berry and raspberry character, medium body, velvety tannins and a fresh finish. Better in 1999. • $35 • (11/15/95) • **87**

Beaune Les Grèves 1992: Juicy and oak-scented, comes across as light and shows modest fruit flavors and a short, crisp finish. 283 cases made. • $30 • (12/15/94) • **79**

Beaune Les Grèves 1991: Lean and focused, with a delicate, bright beam of currant, blackberry and anise aromas and flavors that fade on finish. Drinkable now. 283 cases made. • $30 Ⓐ • (01/31/94) • **82**

Beaune Les Grèves 1990: Beautifully crafted, with wonderful plum, toast and berry characteristics and perfectly integrated tannins. Isn't enormously concentrated, but what it has is fantastic. Drinkable now. • $40 • (12/15/92) • **92**

Beaune Les Grèves 1989 • $44 • (01/31/92) • **90**

Bourgogne White 1995: Incredible quality for simple, regional Bourgogne. Very pretty, with super-silky texture and loads of apricot, peach, honey, citrus and toasty oak flavors. Marvelously balanced, this full-bodied, ripe wine almost smells late-harvest, but it stays the course with a racy yet supple finish. Best after 2000. • $20 • (08/31/97) • **90**

Bourgogne White 1994: Great quality for a Bourgogne; fresh and multi-dimensional. Medium-to-full-bodied, with cream, honey, citrus and green apple flavors. Seductive, buttery texture is thick and appealing. Drink now. • $NA • (08/31/96) • **87**

Bourgogne White 1993: Subtle and elegant, showing some nice mineral, lemon, vanilla, apple and chalk flavors shaded by sweet oak notes. Tart finish, but given time it may flesh out. 458 cases made. • $15 • (08/31/95) • **84**

Bourgogne White 1992: Vibrant acidity and seductive toasty, smoky and honeyed notes. Ends with some spice, pear and vanilla accents. A bit woody. Drinkable now. Tasted twice. • $15 • (08/31/94) • **85**

Chorey-Côte de Beaune 1993: Elegant and pure, a crystal-clear red offering plum, currant and touches of smoke on the crisp finish. Tempting now, but should hold until 1999. • $18 • (11/15/95) • **87**

Chorey-Côte de Beaune 1992: Light-texture, showing toast, raspberry and prune aromas and flavors, finishing a little earthy. Try now. 3,000 cases made. • $15 • (12/15/94) • **83**

Chorey-Côte de Beaune 1990: Well crafted and velvety, with plenty of action. Offers plum, redwood and vanilla flavors and tobacco and toast notes on the finish. Drinkable now. • $26 • (12/15/92) • **86**

Chorey-Côte de Beaune 1989 • $28 • (01/31/92) • **87**

Chorey-Côte de Beaune 1985 • $18 • (04/15/88) • **83**

Chorey-lès-Beaune 1995: An odd red that smells stemmy but tastes sweet and citrusy. Light- to medium-bodied, lean and astringent. • $22 • (11/15/97) • **77**

Chorey-lès-Beaune 1994: Tannins swarm a bit for this light a wine, but the black cherry and currant flavors manage to poke through. Drink now. • $20 • (11/15/96) • **80**

Chorey-lès-Beaune 1988 • $25 • (12/31/90) • **88**

Corton 1995: Oaky and smoky, international in style, this red Burgundy offers loads of spice, mocha and red- and blackberry flavors. Light in color, it seems a bit lean. One wishes for a bit more opulence in a *grand cru*, but this tastes pretty ripe on the finish. Try now. • $70 • (11/15/97) • **84**

Corton 1994: A solid wine that doesn't try to overwhelm, but fills in the niches with black cherry, anise and toast flavors that finish with some delicacy and harmony, and real flair. Approachable now, best from 1999. • $70 • (11/15/96) • **87**

Corton 1993: A well-crafted red boasting lovely vanilla, ripe berry and currant aromas and flavors, medium body, velvety tannins and fresh, long finish. Better in 2000. • $57 • (11/15/95) • **91**

Corton 1992: Light and fragrant, with appealing raspberry and strawberry flavors that fade a little on the sweet finish. A delicate style that is drinkable now. 250 cases made. • $45 • (12/15/94) • **82**

Corton 1990: Bubbling over the rim of the glass with fruit, this seductive, luscious wine has opulent blackberry and smoke characteristics. Drinkable now. • $56 • (12/15/92) • **94**

Corton 1989 • $67 • (01/31/92) • **90**

Corton 1986 • $45 • (08/31/89) • **87**

Corton 1985 • $75 • (03/15/88) • **97**

Corton Le Corton 1991: Beautifully articulated fruit flavors course through this elegant, brilliantly focused, supple wine. Much more generous than most '91s. A gorgeous mouthful that lingers. Drinkable now. 267 cases made. • $45 Ⓐ • (01/31/94) • **91**

Corton Les Bressandes 1995: Exhibits pure, spicy Pinot fruit, echoing cherry and red currant flavors, with hints of toasty oak. Juicy and rich, the oak notes pick up again on the lingering finish. • $70 • (11/15/97) • **87**

Corton Les Bressandes 1994: A refined style, with more to offer from the middle to the finish than up front. Flavors center around currant, black cherry and spice, with a finish that goes on and on. Best now. • $70 • (11/15/96) • **88**

Corton Les Bressandes 1993: Beautiful, fresh and crisp red Burgundy, showing lovely vanilla, plum, raspberry, currant flavors and an enticing earthy component. Hard now, but give it until 2000. • $57 • (11/15/95) • **90**

Corton Les Bressandes 1992: Relatively simple and direct, showing less oak than usual, but flavors focus nicely on raspberry, currant and vanilla. The finish is smooth and elegant. Approachable now. 400 cases made. • $45 • (12/15/94) • **85**

Corton Les Bressandes 1991: Youthful, exuberant flavors on a light frame, featuring a focused beam of berry and violet notes. Very seductive, with fine-textured tannins. • $48 • (02/28/95) • **89**

Corton Les Bressandes 1990: Red Burgundy doesn't get much better than this. Complex, ripe, lavish and dense, with deep black cherry, blackberry, vanilla and violet flavors that linger on the finish. Tempting now but will remain great for years. • $40 • (02/28/95) • **96**

Corton Les Bressandes 1989 • $58 • (02/28/95) • **94**

Corton Les Bressandes 1988 • $59 • (02/28/95) • **92**

Corton Les Bressandes 1987 • $33 • (02/28/95) • **86**

Corton Les Bressandes 1986 • $40 • (02/28/95) • **83**

Corton Les Bressandes 1985 • $NA • (02/28/95) • **88**

Corton Les Bressandes 1983 • $NA • (02/28/95) • **83**

Corton-Charlemagne 1995: Hard as nails, this well-concentrated white shows little now. Needs time to unfold its mineral, tropical fruit and spice flavors fully. Full-bodied, with a palate-coating texture that impresses. Difficult to score at this stage. Try after 2005. • $90 • (08/31/97) • **94**

Corton-Charlemagne 1994: Classy and well-crafted. Full-bodied, with some pretty flavors and aromas—mint, ripe pear, spice, and smoke. Long, silky finish with notes of mineral, toasty oak and lemon. Try now. • $NA • (08/31/96) • **90**

Corton-Charlemagne 1993: Impressive for the vintage. Extremely well-made, boasting cream, mineral, coconut and apple flavors, medium-to-full body and a long, crisp finish. 110 cases made. • $70 • (08/31/95) • **90**

Corton-Charlemagne 1992: A tart and firm style of Corton. Appealingly toasty and fresh, with bright and lively flavors accented by butter and ripe fruit notes; delivers a sharp, refreshing lime edge on the vanilla-scented finish. Be patient and hold off opening this until 2000. • $70 • (08/31/94) • **92**

Savigny-lès-Beaune Les Lavières 1995: Appealing currant and strawberry flavors take on spice notes from new oak. Medium-bodied, with decent concentration for early drinking. • $32 • (11/15/97) • **85**

Savigny-lès-Beaune Les Lavières 1994: Flavorful, with plenty of anise, succulent black cherry and toasty oak aromas and flavors. Sweet and ripe; medium-bodied with a lingering finish. Drinkable and worth seeking. • $30 • (11/15/96) • **84**

Savigny-lès-Beaune Les Lavières 1993: Extremely attractive. Vibrant aromas of cherry and tobacco follow through on the palate. Medium-bodied and a silky texture. Try now. • $25 • (11/15/95) • **90**

Savigny-lès-Beaune Les Lavières 1992: Firm in texture with nicely focused, spicy cherry flavor echoing on the slightly tannic finish. Drinkable now. 1200 cases imported. 9,000 cases made. • $24 • (12/15/94) • **84**

Savigny-lès-Beaune Les Lavières 1991: Light and crisp, offering simple raspberry and strawberry flavors in modest proportions. 983 cases made. • $22 Ⓐ • (01/31/94) • **82**

Savigny-lès-Beaune Les Lavières 1990: Delightfully complex, starting with raspberry, chocolate and plum flavors in a combination that beckons you back for more and ending with a toasty, refined finish. Drinkable now. • $35 • (12/15/92) • **90**

Savigny-lès-Beaune Les Lavières 1989 • $38 • (01/31/92) • **90**

TOMAZE, CHÂTEAU LA

Anjou Villages Cuvée des Lys 1990 • $10 • (12/15/95) • **83**

TONNELLE, CHÂTEAU LA

Haut-Médoc 1987 • $12 • (11/30/89) • **76**

Haut-Médoc 1986 • $11 • (11/30/89) • **70**

Haut-Médoc 1985 • $10 • (02/15/89) • **77**

TONNELLE, CHÂTEAU LA

Premières Côtes de Blaye 1990: A soft, simple, agreeable red that's full of herb and tomato flavors and shows hints of plum and cherry as well. Moderately tannic, smooth and drinkable now. 4,000 cases made. • $8 • (03/15/93) • **81**

TORTOISE CREEK

Chardonnay-Viognier Vin de Pays d'Oc Les Amoureux 1996: A sweet style with apple and peach flavors. Simple, with a taste of watermelon on the finish. 4,000 cases made. • $7 • (04/30/98) • **78**

Syrah-Mourvèdre Vin de Pays d'Oc Les Amoureux 1996: Rich and leathery-tasting, with plum and dried cherry flavors, and a good note of chocolate on the finish. Drink now through 1999. 3,000 cases made. • $6 • (04/30/98) • **83**

TOUMALIN, CHÂTEAU

Canon-Fronsac 1997: Delicious '97, with ripe berry, chocolate and fruit aromas and flavors. Medium-bodied, with velvety tannins and a ripe finish. Another very good Fronsac. • $NA • (06/15/98) (BT) • **85-89**

Canon-Fronsac 1996: Some decent fruit but slightly diluted, with tobacco, berry and earth character. Light, slightly dry finish. May move up after bottling. • $18 • (06/15/98) (BT) • **75-79**

Canon-Fronsac 1995: A well-made, racy little wine. Smells like a freshly baked cherry pie. Full-bodied, with velvety tannins and a medium finish. Best after 2000. • $18 • (01/31/98) • **88**

Canon-Fronsac 1990: Very light and simple for the vintage, with some cherry flavor but not much else. Drinkable now. 3,500 cases made. • $14 • (03/31/93) • **74**

TOUR, CHÂTEAU DE LA | BORDEAUX

Bordeaux Supérieur 1996: A goodly amount of floral—especially violet—character marks this medium-bodied wine. Short finish. 16,500 cases made. • $NA • (01/01/97) (BT) • **80-84**

Bordeaux Supérieur Réserve du Château 1995: Beautiful aromas of berry, raspberries and gravel. Full-bodied, with superfine tannins and a very long aftertaste echoing berries, gravel and raspberries. Best after 2000. • $16 • (01/31/98) • **88**

Bordeaux Supérieur Réserve du Château 1994: A sleek wine, with a pretty berry character accented by a hint of smoky, toasty oak. Tannins are fine and the finish is fresh. Drink now or hold. • $15 • (01/31/97) • **84**

Bordeaux Supérieur Réserve du Château 1993: Medium-bodied, tasting slightly herbaceous, with herbal and tomato flavors and some dry tannins. • $15 • (01/31/96) • **79**

TOUR, CHÂTEAU DE LA | BURGUNDY

Clos Vougeot 1995: Light and diluted, with some delicate strawberry and cherry aromas and flavors. A bit chewy on the finish. • $79 • (11/15/97) • **73**

Clos Vougeot 1994: Tries to get some cherry and anise flavors geared-up, but the finish is light and a bit astringent. May be pleasant by 1999. • $62 • (11/15/96) • **81**

Clos Vougeot 1993: Pleasant and already quite attractive. Mineral, earth and currant character makes this enticing. Rather tannic, sweet-tasting and well done. Lacks a bit of class and depth. Try in 1999. • $53 • (11/15/95) • **84**

Clos Vougeot 1992: Ripe and generous, with a spicy edge to the chunky currant and black cherry flavors which are nicely polished without discernible oak. Try now. • $51 • (12/15/94) • **87**

Clos Vougeot 1990: Overflowing with pure raspberry and cherry flavors; this has a very ripe texture, lots of velvety tannins and a long, beautiful finish. Try now. • $22 Ⓐ • (12/15/92) • **94**

TOUR-BALADOZ, CHÂTEAU

St.-Emilion 1995: Lively, vibrant cassis and wild berry notes, bracketed by subtle spice and smoky oak flavors, make this an appealing medium- to full-bodied Bordeaux. Lacks a bit of elegance on the slightly short finish. • $NA • (05/15/96) (BT) • **85-89**

St.-Emilion 1985 • $12 • (02/29/88) • **82**

TOUR BELLEVUE, CHÂTEAU

Haut-Médoc 1995: Earthy and herbal in flavor, simply sturdy in texture—disappointing for the vintage. 15,000 cases made. • $9 • (01/31/98) • **79**

TOUR BLANCHE, CHÂTEAU LA

Sauternes 1990: Delicious and drinkable now, offering spice, ginger and pepper flavors and attractive hints of pear, melon and honey that might go well with Asian food. • $56 • (04/15/95) • **88**

Sauternes 1989: Intense and exotic; ripe and rich botrytis flavors explode on the palate to a long finish. Very sweet and full in body, it packs in the spice, white pepper, cream, coffee, quince and dried apricot notes. • $49 • (04/15/95) • **92**

Sauternes 1988: Big and ripe, very sweet and full in body, with lots of tropical fruit, a lovely, creamy texture and some caramel, apricot and butter flavors. Long finish. Try now. • $32 • (04/15/95) • **89**

Sauternes 1987 • $23 • (06/15/90) • **82**

Sauternes 1986: Lacks a bit of tangy acidity to make you reach for another glass, but presents honey, milk and cream flavors and a simple finish. • $26 • (04/15/95) • **84**

Sauternes 1985: Sweet, luscious and distinctively toasty in aroma and flavor, showing the beginnings of complexity. Nicely structured, rich and long-lasting. • $32 • (07/15/88) • **85**

Sauternes 1983: Balanced and elegant, its subtle creamy character is tinged by vanilla and orange-peel flavors; medium in body and good acidity. Drink now. • $32 • (04/15/95) • **88**

TOUR BOISEE, DOMAINE LA

Minervois 1990 • $8 • (03/15/94) • **82**

Minervois Cuvée Marie-Claude 1990 • $11 • (03/15/94) • **88**

TOUR CALON, CHÂTEAU

Montagne-St.-Emilion 1990: There are some concentrated plummy, spicy, fruitcake aromas; however, the ripe, stewed flavors result in a dull, flat taste. • $13 • (08/31/95) • **82**

Montagne-St.-Emilion 1989 • $13 • (11/30/92) • **78**

Montagne-St.-Emilion 1986 • $10 • (09/30/89) • **81**

TOUR CARNET, CHÂTEAU LA

Haut-Médoc 1997: Impressive richness for the vintage, with spice, violet and berry character. Medium-bodied, with medium, velvety tannins and a slightly dry finish. Well done. • $NA • (06/15/98) (BT) • **85-89**

Haut-Médoc 1996: Lovely, velvety wine with plum, berry, cherry and vanilla aromas and flavors. Medium- to full-bodied, with caressing tannins and a flavorful finish. Almost outstanding. 8,330 cases made. • $20 • (06/15/98) (BT) • **85-89**

Haut-Médoc 1995: Pretty, with lovely berry, tobacco and vanilla aromas and flavors. Medium- to full-bodied, with well-integrated tannins and a medium aftertaste. Needs time to come around. Best after 2001. 18,000 cases made. • $15 • (01/31/98) • **87**

Haut-Médoc 1992: This has good body but is a bit too herbal and green to be better than average; medium tannins. • $17 • (04/15/95) • **76**

Haut-Médoc 1991: Very weak, but fair brown sugar and plum character. • $15 • (03/31/94) • **71**

Haut-Médoc 1989 • $24 • (03/15/92) • **92**

Haut-Médoc 1988 • $15 • (08/31/91) • **82**

Haut-Médoc 1985 • $22 • (12/31/88) • **71**

Haut-Médoc 1983 • $13 • (02/29/88) • **69**

Haut-Médoc 1945 • $130 • (03/16/86) • **88**

TOUR-DE-BESSAN, CHÂTEAU LA

Margaux 1989 • $NA • (03/15/92) • **87**

TOUR-DE-BY, CHÂTEAU LA

Médoc 1995: Plenty of bright cherry, berry and cassis aromas and flavors. Fine tannins and plenty of sweet fruit on the finish. Delicious. • $NA • (05/15/96) (BT) • **85-89**

Médoc 1992: Has a stewed tomato, herbal character. Diluted. • $11 • (04/15/95) • **73**

Médoc 1991: Very herbal, light and bitter. Astringent finish. • $11 • (03/31/94) • **74**

Médoc 1990: A traditional-style Bordeaux, with earth, leather, berry character and slightly overripe fruit on the finish. It has medium tannins with a soft texture. Drinkable now. 39,000 cases made. • $12 • (03/31/93) • **82**

Médoc 1989 • $19 • (03/15/92) • **85**

Médoc 1988 • $13 • (06/15/91) • **86**

Médoc 1987 • $10 • (11/30/89) • **79**

Médoc 1986 • $12 • (11/30/89) • **80**

Médoc 1983 • $18 • (10/16/85) • **78**

Médoc 1982 • $20 • (08/31/92) • **85**

Médoc Cuvée Prestige 1982 • $20 • (08/31/92) • **89**

Key: SS—Spectator Selection CS—Cellar Selection HR—Highly Recommended BB—Best Buy $NA—Price not available Ⓐ—Auction Price (BT)—Barrel Tasting
Dates in parentheses indicate the issues in which the ratings were published.

TOUR DE MIRAMBEAU, CHÂTEAU

Bordeaux Cuvée Passion 1995: Has some muscles to it. A rich and smoky red with tobacco, cherry and toasted oak aromas. Full-bodied and tannic, with chocolate and plum flavors. Needs time. • $NA • (01/01/97) • **87**

Entre-Deux-Mers 1994 • $NA • (05/31/95) • **82**

TOUR DE MONS, CHÂTEAU LA

Margaux 1992: Not much fruit here; some strawberry and cherry character, but very diluted. Drinkable now. • $15 • (04/15/95) • **75**

Margaux 1991: A simple and firm wine with medium body and tannins. A pleasant cherry character. Drinkable now. • $15 • (03/31/94) • **82**

Margaux 1990: A well-toned wine, with plenty of tobacco, cedar and plum aromas and flavors, loads of fruit extract and balanced silky tannins. Drinkable now. 10,000 cases made. • $20 • (03/31/93) • **89**

Margaux 1989 • $25 • (03/15/92) • **88**

Margaux 1986 • $19 • (11/30/89) • **90**

Margaux 1982 • $18 Ⓐ • (08/31/92) • **88**

Margaux 1945 • $200 • (03/16/86) • **89**

TOUR-DU-HAUT-MOULIN, CHÂTEAU

Haut-Médoc 1988 • $20 • (04/30/91) • **88**

Haut-Médoc 1987 • $15 • (11/30/89) • **80**

Haut-Médoc 1986 • $16 • (11/30/89) • **90**

Haut-Médoc 1985 • $15 • (02/15/89) • **84**

Haut-Médoc 1982 • $16 • (11/30/89) • **84**

TOUR DU MAYNE, CHÂTEAU

Haut-Médoc 1995: A solid, flavorful, hearty Bordeaux with plum and herbal notes, firm tannins. Full-bodied. Drink now through 2000. 10,000 cases made. • $9 • (01/31/98) • **85**

TOUR-DU-MIRAIL, CHÂTEAU

Haut-Médoc 1987 • $10 • (11/30/89) • **83**

Haut-Médoc 1986 • $12 • (11/30/89) • **79**

Haut-Médoc 1982 • $9 • (11/30/89) • **79**

TOUR-DU-PIN-FIGEAC, CHÂTEAU LA

St.-Emilion 1988 • $24 • (07/15/91) • **77**

St.-Emilion 1982 • $21 • (05/15/89) • **88**

TOUR-DU-PIN-FIGEAC-BELIEVIER, CHÂTEAU LA

St.-Emilion 1989 • $24 • (04/30/92) • **83**

St.-Emilion 1982 • $22 • (05/15/89) • **82**

TOUR-DU-ROC, CHÂTEAU

Haut-Médoc 1989 • $13 • (06/15/93) • **71**

Haut-Médoc 1987 • $10 • (11/30/89) • **74**

Haut-Médoc 1986 • $11 • (11/30/89) • **76**

Haut-Médoc 1982 • $12 • (11/30/89) • **84**

TOUR FIGEAC, CHÂTEAU LA

St.-Emilion 1997: Delicious chocolate and berry on the nose and palate. Medium- to light-bodied, with light tannins and a light, fruity finish. • $NA • (06/15/98) (BT) • **80-84**

St.-Emilion 1996: Lovely chocolate and berry aromas and flavors. Medium- to full-bodied, with velvety tannins and a succulent finish. • $22 • (06/15/98) (BT) • **85-89**

St.-Emilion 1982 • $22 • (05/15/89) • **89**

TOUR-HAUT-BRION, CHÂTEAU LA

Pessac-Léognan 1997: Very sweet cherry character and hints of stone on the nose and palate. Medium-bodied, with solid tannins and a delicious finish. • $NA • (06/15/98) (BT) • **85-89**

Pessac-Léognan 1996: A blast of delicious cherry, blackberry and stone on the nose and palate. Medium- to full-bodied, with silky tannins and a flavorful finish. Almost outstanding. • $35 • (06/15/98) (BT) • **85-89**

Pessac-Léognan 1995: Not quite as impressive as I remember. Slightly herbal, with dried cherry and berry aromas and flavors. Medium- to full-bodied, with firm tannins and a green tobacco-tasting, silky-textured finish. Best after 2000. Tasted twice, with consistent notes. • $35 • (01/31/98) • **88**

Pessac-Léognan 1990: Big and extracted, with earth, cassis and cedar character and muscular tannins. Weighty. Try now. 2,500 cases made. • $35 • (03/31/93) • **93**

Pessac-Léognan 1989 • $46 Ⓐ • (03/15/92) • **95**

Pessac-Léognan 1988 • $29 Ⓐ • (06/15/91) CS • **91**

Pessac-Léognan 1987 • $22 • (05/15/90) • **87**

Graves 1985 • $27 Ⓐ • (02/15/89) • **86**

Graves 1983 • $38 Ⓐ • (03/15/87) • **90**

Graves 1979 • $34 Ⓐ • (11/15/91) • **85**

Graves 1975 • $92 Ⓐ • (11/15/91) • **84**

Graves 1970 • $150 • (05/15/93) • **85**

Graves 1966 • $57 Ⓐ • (11/15/91) • **84**

Graves 1964 • $110 • (11/15/91) • **83**

Graves 1962 • $60 • (11/30/87) • **85**

Graves 1961 • $331 Ⓐ • (04/30/96) • **88**

Graves 1959 • $636 Ⓐ • (11/15/91) • **84**

Graves 1958 • $150 • (11/15/91) • **85**

Graves 1957 • $125 • (11/15/91) • **86**

Graves 1955 • $300 • (11/15/91) • **87**

Graves 1953 • $300 • (11/15/91) • **86**

Graves 1950 • $230 • (11/15/91) • **50**

Graves 1947 • $630 • (11/15/91) • **91**

Graves 1945 • $650 • (11/30/95) • **85**

Graves 1943 • $230 • (11/15/91) • **85**

Graves 1940 • $190 • (11/15/91) • **83**

Graves 1929 • $500 • (11/15/91) • **85**

Graves 1928 • $300 • (11/15/91) • **68**

TOUR HAUT-CAUSSAN, CHÂTEAU

Médoc 1992: Polished, lean and medium-bodied; fresh currant character and sleek texture. • $14 • (04/15/95) • **82**

Médoc 1991: An attractively aromatic wine with a cherry aroma and flavor, a smoky character, light body, mild tannins and a short finish. • $14 • (03/31/94) • **81**

Médoc 1990: A lively wine, with vivid aromas and flavors of tobacco, cherries and cinnamon and ripe, round tannins. Polished and well structured. Drinkable now. 10,500 cases made. • $17 • (03/31/93) • **89**

Médoc 1989 • $20 • (03/15/92) • **87**

Médoc 1988 • $13 • (07/15/91) • **79**

Médoc 1987 • $11 • (11/30/89) • **80**

Médoc 1986 • $14 • (11/30/89) • **88**

Médoc 1984 • $10 • (02/15/88) • **80**

Médoc 1982 • $16 • (08/31/92) • **90**

TOUR LÉOGNAN, CHÂTEAU LA

Pessac-Léognan 1996: Impressive for this producer. A cool fruit wine with frozen raspberry and strawberry character. Medium-bodied, with firm tannins and a fresh finish. • $26 • (06/15/98) (BT) • **85-89**

Pessac-Léognan 1995: A fresh and well-defined red, with violet, floral and fruit aromas, medium body, silky tannins and a long, fruity finish. Second label of Château Carbonnieux. Best after 1999. • $NA • (01/31/98) • **86**

Pessac-Léognan 1990: This shows good winemaking, with well-focused fruit and tannins. Drinkable now. • $21 • (03/31/93) • **87**

Pessac-Léognan 1986 • $11 • (02/15/89) • **85**

Pessac-Léognan White 1995: Very fresh, with pineapple and honey aromas and flavors. Medium-bodied, with lovely acidity and a pretty toffee, honey and fruit aftertaste. Drink now. • $NA • (04/30/98) • **86**

TOUR MARTILLAC, CHÂTEAU LA

Pessac-Léognan 1997: Very good dark color. Aromatic, with berry, mineral character. Medium-bodied, with medium, fine tannins and a light finish. Good for the vintage. • $NA • (06/15/98) (BT) • **85-89**

Pessac-Léognan 1996: Amazingly dark color and intense grape and berry aromas. Very concentrated and extracted. Slightly dry tannins. A bit unbalanced now, but wait and see. Better than the '95. • $NA • (01/01/97) (BT) • **85-89**

Pessac-Léognan 1995: Lovely, silky texture and quite delicate, almost light, with the fruit up front. It's a pleasure to taste now, but we wish for a bit more depth. Could move up to "very good" in our next tasting. • $NA • (05/15/96) (BT) • **80-84**

Pessac-Léognan 1993: Some nice ripeness in this medium- to full-bodied '93, as attractive plum, cherry and currant flavors linger on the palate. Supple tannins. Try now. • $18 • (01/31/96) • **83**

Pessac-Léognan 1992: Green tobacco, cedar and berry aromas and flavors, medium-to-light body, light tannins and a toasty oak finish. • $15 • (04/15/95) • **83**

Pessac-Léognan 1991: Elegant and aromatic, with a vanilla and cherry character, medium body and light, dry finish. • $15 • (03/31/94) • **78**

Pessac-Léognan 1990: Starts off slowly but then builds on the palate. It offers rich tar, berry and earth character and big tannins. Drinkable in 1999. 8,000 cases made. • $25 • (03/31/93) • **91**

Pessac-Léognan 1988 • $24 • (02/28/91) • **88**

Pessac-Léognan 1986 • $15 • (02/15/90) • **90**

Graves 1985 • $19 • (08/31/88) • **87**

Pessac-Léognan White 1994 • $30 • (03/31/96) • **89**

Pessac-Léognan White 1993 • $20 • (05/31/95) • **82**

TOUR-PRIGNAC, CHÂTEAU

Médoc 1995: A nicely balanced, harmonious Bordeaux at a great price, this blends ripe fruit and light spicy accents on a moderately tannic texture. Drink now through 2000. 50,000 cases made. • $10 • (01/31/98) • **86**

Médoc 1989 • $9 • (07/15/92) • **75**

TOUR-ST.-BONNET, CHÂTEAU LA

Médoc 1995: Very pretty, distinctive, sweet-tasting plum, red berry and somewhat minty character. Tannins are firm and the finish a bit harsh and inelegant now. • $NA • (05/15/96) (BT) • **80-84**

Médoc 1985 • $13 Ⓐ • (06/30/88) • **83**

TOURELLES, DOMAINE DES

Gigondas 1989 • $16 • (08/31/92) • **81**

TOURELLES DE LONGUEVILLE

Pauillac 1995: Marked by a combination of fruit and mushroom aromas and flavors. Medium- to full-bodied, with velvety tannins and a medium finish. Second label of Château Pichon-Longueville-Baron. Best after 2000. • $25 • (01/31/98) • **87**

Pauillac 1994: Slightly closed, this needs some time. With notes of berry and tobacco on the nose and palate, it's medium-bodied and moderately tannic. Finish is velvety. Good effort for a second wine. Try in 1999. • $25 • (01/31/97) • **85**

Pauillac 1993: Modest fruit but also a bit herbaceous; medium body, firm texture, and a somewhat dry finish. Try now. 10,000 cases made. • $20 • (01/31/96) • **78**

Pauillac 1992: Not bad texture but weedy, green and slightly metallic. Second label of Pichon-Longueville-Baron. Drinkable but uninviting. • $16 • (04/15/95) • **70**

Pauillac 1991: Loads of green peppers, medium-bodied with a velvety texture. • $16 • (03/31/94) • **78**

Key: SS—Spectator Selection CS—Cellar Selection HR—Highly Recommended BB—Best Buy $NA—Price not available Ⓐ—Auction Price (BT)—Barrel Tasting
Dates in parentheses indicate the issues in which the ratings were published.

Pauillac 1990: A well-knit wine, with ripe cassis, berry and tobacco character, lush tannins and an opulent finish. Drinkable now. • $24 • (03/31/93) • **90**

Pauillac 1989 • $27 • (03/15/92) • **94**

TOURETTE, CHÂTEAU LA

Pauillac 1995: Loads of blackberry, cherry and floral aromas. Full-bodied and very tannic, yet silky and caressing in texture, with a pretty aftertaste of sweet fruit and vanilla. Best after 2000. 1,500 cases made. • $22 • (01/31/98) • **89**

Pauillac 1994: A bit one-dimensional, but there's plenty of berry and cassis notes and the finish is fruity. Medium-bodied. Drink now or hold. 1,600 cases made. • $22 • (01/31/97) • **84**

TOURIER, PAUL

Puligny-Montrachet Champ Gain 1993: Tight and tart, showing modest pear and almond flavors. Not particularly rich or intense and turns a bit astringent on the finish. Try now. 1,295 cases made. • $26 • (01/01/96) • **82**

TOURNONS, CELLIER DES

Mâcon-Villages La Boisserolle 1995: Canned fruit flavors and aromas end in an earthy, dull finish. 2,000 cases made. • $9 • (01/31/97) • **75**

Pouilly-Fuissé Rocqenvert 1994: Good finesse here, showing a touch of wet earth, herb and smoke. Turns somewhat sharp and tart on the finish. Drinkable now. 166 cases made. • $19 • (05/31/96) • **83**

TOURS, CHÂTEAU DES

Brouilly 1996: Ripe and round, with characteristic meatlike notes to the black cherry flavors and spicy accents. With tannins round but firm, it's a good match with food. • $11 • (09/15/97) • **84**

Brouilly 1995: Rich and weighty for Brouilly. Plum and black cherry flavors are ripe and deep, though an earthy note detracts a bit. Needs food to soften the firm tannins. Drinkable now. 30,000 cases made. • $14 • (08/31/96) • **86**

Brouilly 1993 • $12 • (06/30/94) • **86**

Côtes du Rhône Réserve 1995: Shows pretty cherry, mocha and spice flavors, with green onion and olive notes. Light-bodied. You wish for more harmony and concentration. • $12 • (10/15/97) • **75**

Côtes du Rhône Réserve 1994: Offers berry and spice flavors that, for the most part, are dominated by the lean yet drying tannins. • $12 • (12/15/96) • **76**

Côtes du Rhône Réserve 1993 • $12 • (09/30/95) • **86**

Vacqueyras Réserve 1991 • $15 • (03/31/94) • **85**

Vacqueyras Réserve 1990 • $16 • (04/15/93) • **79**

Vacqueyras Réserve 1989 • $15 • (10/15/91) • **85**

TOURS, DOMAINE DES

Vin de Pays de Vaucluse 1994: A light and spicy style showing flavors of cinnamon, cedar and candied cherries, with light tannins and a slightly sweet finish. Ready to drink. • $8 • (12/15/96) • **78**

Vin de Pays de Vaucluse 1993 • $8 • (11/15/95) • **84**

Vin de Pays de Vaucluse 1990 • $7 • (04/15/93) BB • **82**

Vin de Pays de Vaucluse 1989 • $8 • (03/31/91) • **78**

TOUZOT, JEAN

Mâcon-Villages 1996: Tight, tart, crisp and citrusy, fresh and vibrant but lacks a bit of opulence. Still, the youthful character of this medium-bodied white has appeal. Drink now through 1999. 1,650 cases made. • $11 • (05/31/98) • **82**

Mâcon-Villages 1995: Fairly straightforward, with decent fruit flavors. Light-bodied and fresh on the palate, but lacks length. Drink now. • $NA • (08/31/96) • **77**

TRACY, CHÂTEAU DE

Pouilly-Fumé 1995: Well-focused with alluring smoke and grapefruit flavors. A natural for shellfish or dishes with lemony sauces. It's crisp, adding a muscular structure. • $18 • (04/30/97) • **84**

TRAPADIS, DOMAINE DU

Côtes du Rhône 1995: A big red, with exuberant plum, raisin and licorice flavors on a firmly tannic frame. Try now. • $11 • (09/15/97) • **85**

Côtes du Rhône-Villages Rasteau 1995: This beauty still has the grapey exuberance of a barrel sample, with bright fruit flavors, fresh firm tannins and pretty accents of chocolate and licorice. It's balanced and well structured, too. • $13 • (09/15/97) • **87**

Côtes du Rhône-Villages Rasteau Prestige 1995: A serious, hand-crafted red, made with ripe grapes, maximum extraction and a sense of place and history. It's still closed and tannic, but there's plenty of fruit beneath; should reward cellaring through 1999. • $17 • (09/15/97) • **90**

TRAPET, JEAN & JEAN-LOUIS

Chambertin 1995: An elegant, juicy, supple, fruit-laden wine packed with cassis bush, currant and black cherry flavors. Lovely, but also quite crisp, with tannins needing until around 2000 to soften. • $76 • (11/15/97) • **87**

Chambertin 1994: Earthy and astringent, maybe corky. • $NA • (11/15/96) • **55**

Chambertin 1993: Loads of lovely, ripe berry, cherry and earth aromas and flavors. Medium- to full-bodied, velvety tannins and a fresh finish. Needs time; better in 2000. • $NA • (05/15/96) • **92**

Chapelle-Chambertin 1995: A mellow and lovely, full-bodied wine, showing supersilky mouthfeel, and tobacco-box, toasty oak, chocolate, spice, cassis and plum flavors. A touch diluted. Tempting now, better after 1999. • $62 • (11/15/97) • **87**

Chapelle-Chambertin 1994: Tough, chewy texture with a solid beam of berry and anise flavor running through to the tannic finish. Tannins are troublesome, but there's a lot of fruit flavor for balance. • $NA • (11/15/96) • **85**

Chapelle-Chambertin 1993: Rich, ripe and flavorful red berry, plum and toasty oak notes, which turn somewhat tart on the finish. A bit tough now, but after 2000 it should be a joy to drink. • $NA • (05/15/96) • **87**

Gevrey-Chambertin 1993: Loads of cedar, spice and red berry character and long, chewy finish in this full-bodied red. Lacks a bit of class to rate higher because it's slighty rough on aftertaste. • $NA • (05/15/96) • **85**

Gevrey-Chambertin 1991: Crisp and lively, a tough-textured wine with ripe currant fruit sneaking in on the finish. • $23 • (03/15/94) • **80**

Gevrey-Chambertin Cuvée Vieilles Vignes 1995: Distinctive, with an earthy, soily, wet earth and blackberry character. Medium-bodied and supple at first sip, the firm tannins kick in on the crisp, chewy finish. A bit rough, but should smooth out around 2000. • $25 • (11/15/97) • **85**

Gevrey-Chambertin Petite Chapelle 1994: Polished and clean, with raspberry, cherry and cream flavors. Lacking a bit in intensity, but has relatively supple tannins. Try now. • $NA • (11/15/96) • **81**

Latricières-Chambertin 1995: The huge, smoky nose obscures cassis and black cherry flavors, which shine through on the palate in this backward, masculine red. Underneath are plenty of black fruit flavors that need until 2003 to harmonize with the massive structure. • $62 • (11/15/97) • **89**

Latricières-Chambertin 1993: Medium-bodied red showing vibrant, clean red berry flavors, earthy, chewy character and toasty, rather crisp finish. Try in 1999. • $NA • (05/15/96) • **86**

Latricières-Chambertin 1991: Soft and velvety, a ripe wine with a green streak running through it; probably best now. • $49 • (03/15/94) • **85**

TRAPET, LOUIS

Chambertin 1988 • $41 Ⓐ • (07/15/91) • **92**
Chambertin 1987 • $62 Ⓐ • (05/31/90) • **91**
Chambertin 1985 • $64 Ⓐ • (03/15/88) • **88**
Chambertin Cuvée Vieilles Vignes 1988 • $119 • (07/15/91) • **89**
Chapelle-Chambertin 1988 • $84 • (07/15/91) • **89**
Chapelle-Chambertin 1985 • $64 • (03/15/88) • **84**
Chapelle-Chambertin Réserve Jean Trapet 1987 • $62 • (03/15/91) • **79**
Gevrey-Chambertin 1988 • $24 Ⓐ • (07/15/91) • **81**
Gevrey-Chambertin 1987 • $30 • (07/15/90) • **74**
Gevrey-Chambertin 1985 • $40 • (05/31/88) • **79**
Latricières-Chambertin 1988 • $30 Ⓐ • (07/15/91) • **84**
Latricières-Chambertin 1987 • $62 • (05/31/90) • **88**
Marsannay Red 1987 • $17 • (03/31/91) • **78**

TREMBLAY, GÉRARD

Chablis 1994 • $14 • (05/31/96) • **79**

Chablis Fourchaume 1995: Quite eccentric for all its mineral and earth character. Not for everyone, but it's distinctive and tastes full-bodied and velvety. Try now through 1999. 3,333 cases made. • $NA • (06/15/97) • **85**

Chablis Fourchaume 1994 • $18 • (05/31/96) • **83**

Chablis Montmain 1995: Distinctively earthy, with an underbrushlike character. Seems disjointed. Medium body. 1,000 cases made. • $17 • (06/15/97) • **78**

TRENEL & FILS

Mâcon-Villages 1996: Fairly rich and ripe, with nice intensity of fruit, white pepper, melon and herbs (like basil) but also a slightly stemmy quality that gives personality. Medium in body, with a crisp finish and good acidity. Drink now with food. 1,083 cases made. • $NA • (08/31/97) • **85**

Mâcon-Villages 1995: Subtle and well made, showing mineral, citrus and apple notes in good balance, though quite astringent on the finish. • $NA • (08/31/96) • **80**

St.-Véran 1996: Very buttery and oaky, quite tart and bitter, this medium-bodied white seems a bit overdone. 1,775 cases made. • $12 • (05/31/98) • **76**

St.-Véran 1995: Fairly ripe and supple, with a good backbone of fresh citrus and fruit followed by a touch of hay and grassy flavors on the lingering finish. • $NA • (08/31/96) • **83**

TREVALLON, DOMAINE DE

Coteaux d'Aix en Provence Les Baux 1987 • $18 • (03/31/90) • **78**
Coteaux d'Aix en Provence Les Baux 1986 • $21 • (04/15/89) • **87**
Coteaux d'Aix en Provence Les Baux 1985 • $48 Ⓐ • (02/29/88) • **82**

TRIBUT, LAURENT

Chablis 1996: Complex and deep, but quite tart, bouncing spice, vanilla bean, toasty bread, pear and lime flavors all over the palate. Balanced yet intense, it's a medium-bodied package that's delicious but turns a bit tough on the very long, succulent finish. Better wait until after 2000. • $22 • (05/31/98) • **88**

Chablis 1994 • $22 • (05/31/96) • **82**

Chablis Beauroy 1995: Made in a style that's ready to drink now through 1999, this *premier cru* is rich, ripe and full-bodied, with the oak blended harmoniously into the chewy mineral, earth and ripe fruit flavors. • $30 • (06/15/97) • **87**

Chablis Beauroy 1994 • $30 • (05/31/96) • **78**

Chablis Côte de Léchet 1996: Quite ripe, with a supple texture and distinctive earthy, wet stone and *terroir* flavors. Medium- to- full in body, it's a bit sweaty on the slightly herbal, tart finish. • $30 • (05/31/98) • **79**

Chablis Côte de Léchet 1995: This *premier cru* Chablis shows mineral, earth, delicious ripe fruit and subtle wet stone character. Drinkable now. • $30 • (06/15/97) • **85**

Chablis Côte de Léchet 1994 • $30 • (05/31/96) • **84**

TRICON, OLIVIER

Chablis 1995: Polished, and elegantly medium-bodied. Shows nice green apple, pear and citrus flavors, and a creamy texture, accented by oak. Ready now. • $NA • (08/31/96) • **83**

TRIENNES, DOMAINE DE

Cabernet Sauvignon Vin de Pays du Var 1994: Toasty oak notes add another layer to the green olive and black currant flavors, giving dimension and complexity. It's firmly structured with a lingering finish. Attractive. • $15 • (12/15/96) • **86**

Chardonnay Vin de Pays du Var Clos Barry 1995: A full-blown, full-bodied style that has plenty of aromas but is a bit short on finesse. Has lots of oak, with moderate pear and spice flavors. • $18 • (02/28/97) • **84**

Merlot Vin de Pays du Var 1994: Round and fruity, offering plum and clove-like flavors. Still fairly tannic on the finish, but ready to drink. • $18 • (12/15/96) • **82**

TRIGNON, CHÂTEAU DU

Côtes du Rhône 1995: Light but pretty, with red- and blackberry flavors that are quite ripe and sweet. Shows a spicy note on the smoky, slightly dry finish. Drink slightly chilled. 1250 cases imported. 6,667 cases made. • $10 • (10/15/97) • **79**

Côtes du Rhône Blanc de Blancs 1996: Clean and crisp, this lively white offers pear, almond and floral notes, with good weight yet firm acidity. A fine accompaniment to lighter dishes. 250 cases imported. 1,250 cases made. • $10 • (10/15/97) • **84**

Côtes du Rhône Cuvée Viognier 1996: Very fresh and focused, this wine combines finesse and intensity, with loads of citrus, pear and mineral flavors. Vivid and well balanced, with a subtly spicy finish. It's not a blockbuster, but everthing is there and in place. 100 cases imported. 667 cases made. • $22 • (10/15/97) • **88**

Côtes du Rhône Viognier 1993 • $17 • (11/15/95) • **78**

Côtes du Rhône-Villages Rasteau 1995: Fairly green and crisp, and somewhat diluted, it offers only modest fruit flavors. Short finish. 417 cases imported. 2,500 cases made. • $15 • (10/15/97) • **72**

Côtes du Rhône-Villages Rasteau 1993 • $13 • (11/15/95) • **72**

Côtes du Rhône-Villages Rasteau 1986 • $9 • (12/15/90) • **80**

Côtes du Rhône-Villages White Sablet 1996: A bit woodsy, showing a rustic side and a tart, lean character. Short finish. 100 cases imported. 667 cases made. • $14 • (10/15/97) • **72**

Gigondas 1995: Rather firm and slightly herbal, but with wonderful cassis bush, black olive and cherry flavors. Medium-bodied, it turns a bit green on the somewhat drying finish. 667 cases imported. 5,000 cases made. • $20 • (10/15/97) • **85**

TRIMBACH

Gewürztraminer Alsace 1993: A soft, diffuse white that evokes roses and honey. It's balanced and generous, ready to drink. • $19 • (09/30/97) • **86**

Gewürztraminer Alsace Hors Choix Sélection de Grains Nobles 1989 • $NA • (11/15/90) • **97**

Muscat Alsace Réserve 1994: This lacks distinctive Muscat character, showing a lean and quite acidic structure and light flavors of apples and herbs. Unexpressive and rather dull. 1,000 cases made. • $17 • (09/30/96) • **77**

Pinot Blanc Alsace 1995: Starts off meekly, but turns quite rich in the mouth, showing a citrusy edge to the peach flavors before finishing with crisp acidity. • $14 • (09/30/97) • **82**

Pinot Blanc Alsace 1994: Big for a Pinot Blanc, showing a nice balance of ripe pear and crisp lime flavors that are clean and firm. It can stand up to food. A good value for what it offers. 15,000 cases made. • $10 • (09/30/96) BB • **85**

Pinot Gris Alsace Réserve Personelle 1993: Appealing for its nice balance of pear and nutty flavors. Firm acidity plays off ripe, spicy accents on the finish. Well made and harmonious. 1,500 cases made. • $29 • (10/15/96) • **86**

Pinot Noir Alsace Réserve 1993: Light, yet tough, with some berry and herbal flavors in the mix, but a strong vegetal note dominates. 8,000 cases made. • $15 • (10/15/96) • **76**

Pinot Noir Alsace Réserve Personnelle 1990: Ripe and round for an Alsace Pinot, this shows cherry and lightly spicy flavors with good concentration and some barnyard aromas. Holding up well for its age. 500 cases made. • $29 • (10/15/96) • **82**

Riesling Alsace 1994: There's a spartan quality here (typical of this producer), but also richness and ripe peach and stony flavors. Drinkable now. • $19 • (09/30/97) • **85**

Riesling Alsace 1993: Still young and quite austere, this offers tart, rather green acidity and mineral flavors. A lean, racy style that needs food to soften the tartness. 18,000 cases made. • $15 • (10/15/96) • **82**

Riesling Alsace Cuvée Frédéric Émile 1993: A complex array of pine forest, apple, lime and mineral aromas and flavors mingle in this fresh, racy white. Barely showing its age, it's balanced, steely and dry, with a long aftertaste. Drinkable now through 2003. • $35 • (11/15/97) • **88**

Riesling Alsace Cuvée Frédéric Émile Sélection de Grains Nobles 1989 • $NA • (11/15/90) • **90**

Tokay Pinot Gris Alsace Hors Choix Sélection de Grains Nobles 1989 • $NA • (11/15/90) • **99**

Tokay Pinot Gris Alsace Réserve Sélection de Grains Nobles 1989 • $NA • (11/15/90) • **90**

Key: SS—Spectator Selection CS—Cellar Selection HR—Highly Recommended BB—Best Buy $NA—Price not available Ⓐ—Auction Price (BT)—Barrel Tasting

Dates in parentheses indicate the issues in which the ratings were published.

TRIMOULET, CHÂTEAU

St.-Emilion 1990: Luscious fruit flavors are blended with a rich array of spicy notes. A seamless, supple texture adds to the complexity of the cherry, plum and blackberry flavors. Well balanced, with a touch of gaminess on the finish. Drinkable now. 8,000 cases made. • $20 • (09/15/93) • **86**

St.-Emilion 1988 • $16 • (06/15/91) HR • **91**

St.-Emilion 1982 • $15 • (05/15/89) • **81**

TRINQUEVEDEL, CHÂTEAU DE

Tavel 1995: A full-bodied, dry rosé, with flavors of strawberries, almonds and light herbs. Rather austere, it will show best with food. • $16 • (06/30/97) • **83**

TRIPOZ, DIDIER

Charnay-lès-Mâcon Clos des Tournons 1996: A beautiful, distinctive Chardonnay, full in body, supple in texture, yet with clean and vivid lime, butter and grapefruit aromas and flavors. Shows some minerally grip in the midpalate. Crisp finish. Try in 2000. 2,917 cases made. • $9 • (08/31/97) • **87**

Charnay-lès-Mâcon Clos des Tournons 1995: Ripe, sweet-tasting and medium-to-full-bodied. Offering a nice balance of honey and lemon, mineral and dried herb flavors that hold intensity on the finish. Drink now. • $NA • (08/31/96) • **86**

Mâcon-Villages 1996: Distinctive for its butter, butterscotch and bitter almond character, this dense, full-bodied Mâcon seems a bit overdone—despite an intense kick of fruit on the slightly dry finish. Try now. 833 cases made. • $15 • (08/31/97) • **78**

TROLLAT, RAYMOND

St.-Joseph 1994: Rustic in style, this shows good concentration, but the flavors are gamy and earthy and the tannins are harsh. There is ripe fruit flavor; try now. For fans of the old traditional style. • $NA • (11/30/96) • **87**

St.-Joseph 1992 • $15 • (05/31/94) • **83**

St.-Joseph 1991 • $15 • (05/31/94) • **88**

TRONQUOY-LALANDE, CHÂTEAU

St.-Estèphe 1997: Too herbal and grassy, although it's medium-bodied with medium tannins and a long aftertaste. • $NA • (06/15/98) (BT) • **75-79**

St.-Estèphe 1996: A bit fluid, but with some decent berry and tar character. Medium- to light-bodied, with light tannins and a fresh finish. • $22 • (06/15/98) (BT) • **80-84**

St.-Estèphe 1995: Slightly one-dimensional, but attractive, with plenty of violet, berry and vanilla character. Full-bodied, with well-integrated, full tannins that are long and silky. • $20 • (01/31/98) • **89**

St.-Estèphe 1994: Slightly one-dimensional, but offers some good, ripe berry flavors and a fruity finish. Moderate tannins. Drink now. • $18 • (01/31/97) • **82**

St.-Estèphe 1993: Clean, fresh, simple mint, berry and cherry aromas and flavors. More like a light Loire red. Drinkable now • $21 • (01/31/96) • **79**

St.-Estèphe 1991: Very fruity, but one-dimensional aromas and flavors of strawberry and cherry. Medium body, light tannins. • $17 • (03/31/94) • **79**

St.-Estèphe 1988 • $14 • (07/15/91) • **84**

St.-Estèphe 1987 • $13 • (11/30/89) • **84**

St.-Estèphe 1986 • $15 • (11/30/89) • **92**

St.-Estèphe 1982 • $20 • (11/30/89) • **86**

TROPLONG-MONDOT, CHÂTEAU

St.-Emilion 1997: Pretty berry and smoke aromas and flavors. Medium-bodied, with velvety tannins and a slightly hollow midpalate. Very pretty. • $NA • (06/15/98) (BT) • **85-89**

St.-Emilion 1996: Complex aromas of spices, tobacco and fruit follow through on the palate. Full-bodied yet refined, with silky tannins and a long finish. Well made. • $50 • (06/15/98) (BT) • **90-94**

St.-Emilion 1995: Clever winemaking. Modern and international in style. Not quite as exciting as I remember, but still outstanding. Inky-colored, with loads of vanilla, spice and meatlike aromas. Full-bodied and concentrated, with masses of berry, dark chocolate and vanilla flavors. Slightly astringent on the finish. Better after 2001. • $36 Ⓐ • (01/31/98) • **92**

St.-Emilion 1994: Best Troplong ever. Impressive dark color and loads of mineral, berry and spice aromas lead to a full-bodied and very tannic (though the tannins are fine) mouthfeel. Very closed and tight now, this needs time to come around. Try in 2000. • $43 Ⓐ • (01/31/97) • **92**

St.-Emilion 1993: One of the rising stars of the Right Bank. Sleek and racy, sporting fine tannins, plenty of beautiful currant and berry flavors, medium body, firm tannins and long finish. Better in 1998. • $29 Ⓐ • (01/31/96) • **88**

St.-Emilion 1992: Complex aromas of dark chocolate, tobacco and fruit. Very velvety vanilla, grape and chocolate flavors. Medium-to-full body; medium finish. Drinkable now. • $11 Ⓐ • (04/15/95) • **88**

St.-Emilion 1991: Beautiful, aromatic wine with a plum and chocolate character. Medium-bodied, but a very light finish. • $20 • (03/31/94) • **81**

St.-Emilion 1990: A showy wine, with appealing aromas and flavors of violets, vanilla and fruit and ultrafine tannins. If you like new wood, you will like this St.-Emilion. Drinkable now. 10,000 cases made. • $110 • (03/31/93) • **91**

St.-Emilion 1989 • $103 Ⓐ • (03/15/92) • **89**
St.-Emilion 1988 • $46 Ⓐ • (07/15/91) • **85**
St.-Emilion 1986 • $30 Ⓐ • (06/30/89) • **88**
St.-Emilion 1985 • $32 Ⓐ • (06/30/88) • **88**
St.-Emilion 1961 • $37 • (04/30/96) • **85**

TROTANOY, CHÂTEAU

Pomerol 1997: Gorgeous red fruit character with touches of new wood. Medium-bodied, with medium tannins and a fruity, velvety finish. Very good indeed—almost outstanding. • $NA • (06/15/98) (BT) • **85-89**

Pomerol 1996: A solid '96 with chewy fruit and tannins, and pretty aromas and flavors of chocolate and berries. Medium tannins. Harmonious structure. • $75 • (06/15/98) (BT) • **90-94**

Pomerol 1995: Lots of red berry character, with undertones of wet earth and fresh mushrooms. Full-bodied, with a bounty of fruit and loads of velvety tannins. Long, sweet fruit and caressing texture mark the finish. From the Moueix family of Château Pétrus fame. Best after 2002. • $160 • (01/31/98) HR • **97**

Pomerol 1994: Lovely. This is medium-bodied, firm and velvety, with berry, tobacco and herbal notes, firm, chewy tannins and a clean finish. Delicious now, but better in 1999. • $62 • (01/31/97) • **90**

Pomerol 1993: Complex and subtle with lots going on in the glass. Not a huge wine, but has wonderful berry, chocolate, earth and mineral character. Medium in body and tannins, adding a long, delicious finish. Better in 1999. • $50 • (01/31/96) CS • **91**

Pomerol 1992: Ultraclean raspberry and floral character, medium-to-light body, crisp acidity and a fresh finish. A little one-dimensional. • $42 • (04/15/95) • **82**

Pomerol 1990: Supple, generous and polished, with a slight tarry note adding interest to the ripe plum and cedar flavors. Has length and balance, but seems less powerful than in a tasting in Bordeaux last year. Best from 2000. • $80 Ⓐ • (05/15/94) • **92**

Pomerol 1989 • $124 Ⓐ • (05/15/94) • **90**
Pomerol 1988 • $52 Ⓐ • (08/31/91) • **89**
Pomerol 1987 • $26 Ⓐ • (10/15/88) • **88**
Pomerol 1986 • $43 Ⓐ • (05/15/94) • **82**
Pomerol 1985 • $70 Ⓐ • (05/15/94) • **81**
Pomerol 1983 • $41 Ⓐ • (10/15/94) • **86**
Pomerol 1982 • $254 Ⓐ • (08/31/92) • **96**
Pomerol 1981 • $45 Ⓐ • (10/15/94) • **94**
Pomerol 1980 • $37 Ⓐ • (10/15/88) • **83**
Pomerol 1979 • $51 Ⓐ • (10/15/89) • **88**
Pomerol 1978 • $87 Ⓐ • (10/15/88) • **83**
Pomerol 1976 • $49 Ⓐ • (10/15/88) • **86**
Pomerol 1975 • $186 Ⓐ • (10/15/88) • **84**
Pomerol 1970 • $230 Ⓐ • (10/15/88) • **95**
Pomerol 1967 • $NA • (10/15/88) • **84**
Pomerol 1966 • $220 Ⓐ • (10/15/88) • **92**
Pomerol 1964 • $173 Ⓐ • (05/15/94) • **83**
Pomerol 1962 • $139 Ⓐ • (10/15/88) • **88**
Pomerol 1961 • $289 Ⓐ • (04/30/96) • **90**
Pomerol 1959 • $108 Ⓐ • (10/15/88) • **92**
Pomerol 1955 • $245 Ⓐ • (10/15/88) • **94**
Pomerol 1953 • $300 • (10/15/88) • **86**
Pomerol 1952 • $NA • (10/15/88) • **83**
Pomerol 1949 • $1450 • (05/15/94) • **92**
Pomerol 1947 • $2156 Ⓐ • (10/15/88) • **80**
Pomerol 1945 • $1364 Ⓐ • (10/15/88) • **98**
Pomerol 1934 • $450 • (05/15/94) • **83**
Pomerol 1928 • $660 Ⓐ • (10/15/88) • **95**
Pomerol 1926 • $900 • (05/15/94) • **86**
Pomerol 1924 • $NA • (10/15/88) • **89**

TROTTEVIEILLE, CHÂTEAU

St.-Emilion 1997: Medium bodied with earthy, slightly herbal aromas and flavors and a light finish. Could use a bit more concentration. • $NA • (06/15/98) (BT) • **80-84**

St.-Emilion 1996: Slightly raisiny, but some good fruit character. Medium- to light-bodied, with fine tannins and a short finish. Pretty disappointing. • $30 • (06/15/98) (BT) • **80-84**

St.-Emilion 1995: Fresh and easy to drink now, with blackberry and milk chocolate aromas and flavors, medium body, a soft texture. Pretty disappointing for a top growth from St.-Emilion. Drink now. • $27 • (01/31/98) • **83**

St.-Emilion 1992: Light and slightly unripe herbal, berry, watery character. Drinkable but uninviting. • $18 • (04/15/95) • **71**

St.-Emilion 1991: Somewhat mature flavors, but a lovely tobacco and cherry character. Soft and round. • $18 • (03/31/94) • **82**

St.-Emilion 1990: Deceptive wine that starts out slowly on the palate but then kicks in on the finish with tobacco, cedar, vanilla and berry aromas and flavors and a long, velvety finish. Drinkable now. 4,500 cases made. • $29 • (03/31/93) • **91**

St.-Emilion 1989 • $44 • (03/15/92) • **90**
St.-Emilion 1988 • $51 • (04/30/91) • **85**
St.-Emilion 1982 • $24 Ⓐ • (08/31/92) • **89**
St.-Emilion 1962 • $30 • (11/30/87) • **75**

TRUCHOT, JACKY

Charmes-Chambertin Vieilles Vignes 1991: Firm, chewy and lean in texture, with a strong menthol note dominating the modest berry fruit. Try now. • $50 • (08/31/94) • **85**

TUILERIE, DOMAINE LA

Pouilly-Fumé 1997: Bright aromas and flavors of lime, grapefruit and mineral give a lively appeal. Light and crisp on the palate, with clean varietal character. Drink now. 3,500 cases made. • $14 • (06/15/98) • **84**

Vin de Pays des Côtes de Gascogne 1996: Distinctive, with oniony and herbal flavors and an earthy aroma. Drink with a rich poultry dish. A blend of Ugni Blanc, Sauvignon Blanc, Sémillon, Gros Manseng and Colombard. 16,650 cases made. • $6 • (05/15/98) • **82**

TUQUE, DOMAINE DE LA

Buzet 1992: Smells like tobacco and green olives, yet the black currant and cedar flavors are reminiscent of Cabernet Sauvignon. Fleshy, firmly structured, with some dry tannins on the finish. Drink now with food. • $10 • (12/15/97) • **84**

Buzet 1990: A powerful country red that combines sweet plum flavor and a rich texture. Tobacco and licorice accents add complexity. Try now. • $10 • (07/31/96) • **84**

TURCAUD, CHÂTEAU

Bordeaux 1994: Modest in flavor but nicely balanced for food, with harmonious flavors of cherries, vanilla and light herbs, firm but well-integrated tannins and a clean finish. Drink now through 2001. • $9 • (10/15/97) • **84**

Entre-Deux-Mers 1995: This full-bodied white has subtle flavors and a rich texture. It's solidly made and straightforward in style. • $9 • (10/15/97) • **81**

Entre-Deux-Mers 1994 • $8 • (05/31/95) • **80**
Entre-Deux-Mers 1993 • $8 • (05/31/95) • **78**

TURCKHEIM

Pinot Noir Alsace Cuvée Réserve 1989 • $15 • (10/31/91) • **80**

Pinot Noir Alsace Cuvée à l'Ancienne 1988 • $25 • (10/31/91) • **82**
Pinot Noir Alsace Rouge de Turckheim 1988 • $40 • (10/31/91) • **77**

TURGY, MICHEL

Brut Blanc de Blancs Champagne Le Mesnil Réserve Sélection NV: An easy-going, soft-textured, almost sweet bubbly with light, spicy fruit flavors. Tasty and straightforward. Drink now. • $25 • (04/30/98) • **85**

UNION CHAMPAGNE

Brut Blanc de Blancs Champagne Cuvée Orpale 1985: A plush texture combines with subtle, intricate flavors for a poised, extremely complex Champagne that's pure pleasure to drink. It shows the benefits of age in its mellow but still fresh fruit and spice flavors, and its luxuriously smooth mousse. Drink now through 2002. • $49 • (12/31/97) • **95**
Brut Blanc de Blancs Champagne de St.-Gall 1990: A grand but inviting Champagne with lots of ripe fruit flavors, a broad, smooth texture, plush bubbles and a lingering finish. Slightly sweet and definitely rich. Drink now through 1999. 8,500 cases made. • $34 • (12/31/97) • **91**
Brut Blanc de Blancs Champagne de St.-Gall NV: Nice and rich in flavor, round and full in texture, this satisfying glass of Champagne has ripe pear and vanilla notes that fill the mouth and linger on the finish. Drink now. 40,000 cases made. • $28 • (12/31/97) • **90**
Brut Champagne de St.- Gall NV: A good, functional brut that has simple flavors, fresh acidity and a clean finish. Drink now. 40,000 cases made. • $25 • (12/31/97) • **83**
Extra Dry Blanc de Blancs Champagne de St.- Gall NV: Refreshing, rather light and bright in flavor, with accents of lemon and vanilla and a creamy texture. Drink now. 8,500 cases made. • $30 • (12/31/97) • **86**

FRANCE

UNION DE PRODUCTEURS PLAIMONT, L'

Vin de Pays des Côtes de Gascogne White Colombelle Plaimont 1996: A fresh-tasting, vivid and lively white wine, refreshing for its zingy acidity and appealing fruit flavors. At this price, chill a few bottles—it's ready for summertime quaffing. 20,000 cases made. • $6 • (08/31/97) BB • **85**

UNION DE PRODUCTEURS DE ST.-EMILION, L'

St.-Emilion Cuvée Galius 1995: A pretty, well-made red with chocolate, raspberry and a hint of mint. Medium-bodied, with medium tannins and a fruity finish. Best now. 5,700 cases made. • $25 • (01/31/98) • **84**

USSEGLIO, PIERRE

Châteauneuf-du-Pape 1990: Bright and appealing. A light style of Châteauneuf-du-Pape that features spicy red plum, cherry and black pepper aromas and flavors. Drinkable now. • $16 • (04/15/93) • **85**

VACHERON, DOMAINE

Sancerre 1996: This tangy white shows searing acidity, with bright flavors of lemon and grapefruit that leave your teeth tingling. Green apple and herbal flavors are well defined, but a bit overshadowed by tartness. Drink now through 1999. • $18 • (03/31/98) • **86**
Sancerre 1995: This nervy white shows good intensity, with pure lime, herb and green apple flavors and very crisp acidity. Has excellent focus and definition. 600 cases made. • $18 • (05/15/97) • **89**
Sancerre Red 1995: Well focused and harmonious, showing bright cherry, toasty oak and light herb and spice flavors, with balanced tannins and a clean finish. A good representative of Sancerre Pinot Noir. Drink now through 2000. • $19 • (05/31/98) • **85**
Sancerre Red 1993: A tough, light red with tobacco, smoke and herb flavors embedded in dry tannins. Bitter finish. Some Pinot Noir character, but lacks generosity. 600 cases made. • $20 • (06/15/97) • **78**

Key: SS—Spectator Selection CS—Cellar Selection HR—Highly Recommended BB—Best Buy $NA—Price not available Ⓐ—Auction Price (BT)—Barrel Tasting
Dates in parentheses indicate the issues in which the ratings were published.

Sancerre Red Belle Dame 1995: Reflects prestige treatment: deluxe bottle, lavish oak, maximum extraction. Shows good concentration, with bitter cherry and toast flavors, but seems overdone. Let's see how it ages. Drink now through 2000. • $35 • (05/31/98) • **85**

VACHET-ROUSSEAU, G.

Gevrey-Chambertin 1988 • $30 • (12/31/90) • **85**

VAISSE, A.

Fleurie Grille-Midi 1994 • $12 • (10/31/95) • **87**

VAL D'ORBIEU

Cabernet Sauvignon Vin de Pays d'Oc Réserve St.-Martin 1996: A broad, fleshy red, sporting cherry and spice notes with a moderate structure. Supple and ready to drink. 70,000 cases made. • $8 • (06/30/97) • **84**
Chardonnay Vin de Pays d'Oc Réserve St.-Martin 1996: Straightforward and crisp, with good pear and ripe apple flavors and a nice, clean finish. 65,000 cases made. • $8 • (06/30/97) • **84**
Chardonnay Vin de Pays d'Oc Réserve St.-Martin 1994 • $8 • (12/15/95) • **81**
Corbières Les Deux Rives 1995: Shows some ripe plummy notes, but the overall impression is that of a diluted red that lacks focus. 12,000 cases made. • $7 • (09/30/97) • **77**
Corbières White Les Deux Rives 1996: A refreshing but simple white wine with modest flavors and a crisp-enough texture. 7,000 cases made. • $7 • (10/31/97) • **78**
Marsanne Vin de Pays d'Oc Réserve St.-Martin 1994 • $7 • (02/29/96) • **83**
Merlot Vin de Pays d'Oc Réserve St.-Martin 1996: Spicy red fruits and herbal flavors are the hallmarks of this young, simple red. 70,000 cases made. • $8 • (06/30/97) • **82**
Merlot Vin de Pays d'Oc Réserve St.-Martin 1993 • $7 • (11/30/94) • **77**
Mourvèdre Vin de Pays d'Oc Réserve St.-Martin 1995: A serious wine at a more-than-reasonable price, this red shows a bountiful wild herb and game character, with licorice notes for accent. Muscular and slightly rustic, yet full of personality. Drinkable now with food or hold until 1999. 20,000 cases made. • $8 • (06/30/97) BB • **87**
Muscat de St.-Jean-de-Minervois NV: A really nice, late-harvest style wine, with nutty, spicy, peachy aromas and flavors that linger on the finish. Quite sweet and smooth. 7,000 cases made. • $11/375ml • (05/31/97) • **86**
Muscat de St.-Jean-de-Minervois Petit Grains NV • $14 • (01/31/95) • **87**
Muscat Vin de Pays d'Oc Réserve St.-Martin 1996: An assertive white that smells sweet, floral and spicy, but tastes dry, peachy and full-bodied. An Alsace style from the south of France. 5,000 cases made. • $8 • (08/31/97) • **83**
Rosé de Syrah Vin de Pays d'Oc Réserve St.-Martin 1996: Lively and bright, this lavender-tinged rosé offers vivid berry and cherry flavors, and is clean, crisp and dry. A lovely apéritif. 20,000 cases made. • $8 • (06/30/97) • **85**
Sauvignon Blanc Vin de Pays d'Oc Réserve St.-Martin 1996: Fresh and crisp, with good herb and citrus flavors that linger on the finish. 40,000 cases made. • $8 • (06/30/97) • **81**
Syrah Vin de Pays d'Oc Réserve St.-Martin 1995: Soft and plush, with an underlying firmness, this red has dried cherry and herb flavors and a modest finish. 50,000 cases made. • $8 • (06/30/97) • **84**
Vin de Pays d'Oc La Cuvée Mythique 1994: Straightforward but solid, with black cherry and light herb flavors and mouthcoating tannins. It's clean and fresh, and should soften with food. 9,000 cases made. • $17 • (06/30/97) • **84**
Viognier Vin de Pays d'Oc Réserve St.-Martin 1996: This rich, French white is well made and affordable, too. It shows good varietal personality, with lovely floral, peach and almond flavors that are typical of Viognier and linger gracefully on the finish. 10,000 cases made. • $10 • (08/31/97) BB • **83**

VAL DES BRUYÈRES, DOMAINE

Merlot Vin de Pays d'Oc 1996: Green-tasting, with flavors of plum, cherry and rhubarb, and a cloying finish. • $7 • (03/31/98) • **77**

VAL JOANIS, CHÂTEAU

Côtes du Lubéron 1993: Flavors of dried cherries, herbs and mushrooms mingle in this straightforward wine. Food will soften the firm tannins. Drink now. 10,000 cases made. • $8 • (10/15/96) • **82**

Côtes du Lubéron 1992 • $8 • (11/15/95) • **84**

Côtes du Lubéron 1988 • $7 • (06/30/90) BB • **82**

Côtes du Lubéron Les Griottes 1992: Distinctive. This is expressive, with aromas and flavors of cassis, licorice, lemon and minerals. Not overly tannic, but solid and balanced. Intriguing, though not for everyone. • $16 • (10/15/96) • **85**

Côtes du Lubéron Les Griottes 1990 • $15 • (09/30/95) • **87**

Côtes du Lubéron Les Merises Fût de Chêne 1994 • $10 • (09/30/95) • **79**

Côtes du Lubéron Rosé 1995: Fresh, juicy and simple, this tangy rosé offers light strawberry and watermelon flavors with lemony acidity. 8,000 cases made. • $8 • (10/15/96) • **80**

Côtes du Lubéron Rosé 1993 • $8 • (08/31/95) • **85**

Côtes du Lubéron Rosé Les Merises Fût de Chêne 1995: Though light and dry, this is quite expressive, with strawberry and spice flavors that linger, fresh and clean, on the finish. A pleasant apéritif. 800 cases made. • $10/500ml • (10/15/96) • **84**

Côtes du Lubéron White 1995: This vibrant wine offers lemon and floral aromas and flavors, is bright on the palate and extremely tart on the finish. Needs food for balance. • $8 • (10/15/96) • **78**

Côtes du Lubéron White 1993 • $8 • (11/15/95) • **79**

VAL ST.-JEAN, DOMAINE

Merlot Vin de Pays des Côtes de Thongue 1994: A seriously stinky wine that smells swampy and tastes bitter and decayed. Tasted twice with consistent notes. 20,000 cases made. • $8 • (12/15/96) • **57**

VALANDRAUD, CHÂTEAU DE

St.-Emilion 1997: Chewy and velvety textured, with tobacco, cherry and chocolate aromas and flavors. Slightly herbaceous but rich for the vintage. • $NA • (06/15/98) (BT) • **85-89**

St.-Emilion 1996: Lovely. Remarkably deep in color, with plenty of grape and berry aromas, this wine is full-bodied with full, fine tannins, but lacks a bit in the midpalate. • $NA • (01/01/97) (BT) • **85-89**

St.-Emilion 1995: In-your-face red with lots of character. New wave Bordeaux. Best Valandraud yet. Dark in color, with complex aromas of berry, violet and new wood. Full in body, with velvety tannins and a long aftertaste of vanilla, coffee and cherries. Best after 2000. 950 cases made. • $300 • (01/31/98) • **93**

St.-Emilion 1994: Excellent concentration for the vintage, with seductive aromas and flavors of wild berry, mineral, mint and vanilla. Full-bodied, with fine, silky tannins and a caressing finish. Inviting now, but better in 1999. A rising star in St.-Emilion, and the best wine ever bottled from this estate. • $100 • (01/31/97) • **91**

St.-Emilion 1993: Newcomer to the Right Bank and making a lot of noise. Beautifully aromatic red berry, vanilla and tobacco character. Medium-bodied and very soft, featuring round tannins and medium finish. Drinkable now. 350 cases made. • $209 • (01/31/96) • **89**

VALCOMBE, CHÂTEAU

Côtes du Ventoux Cepage Syrah 1995: Attractive, delivering ripe, round flavors of plums, licorice and herbs with a firm tannic backbone. Will marry perfectly with grilled meats. • $10 • (12/15/96) • **85**

Côtes du Ventoux La Cerisaie 1995: Herbal flavors predominate in this round, rustic red. Cherry notes are pretty, but firm tannins shut down the finish. Try with food. 500 cases made. • $10 • (10/15/97) • **78**

Côtes du Ventoux La Cerisaie 1994: Assertive, but a bit clumsy. This shows a wild mix of raisin, stewed fruit, orange-peel and burnt coffee flavors, with a dry finish. 333 cases made. • $NA • (10/15/96) • **78**

Côtes du Ventoux White La Cerisaie 1996: A bit flabby, but has decent vanilla bean, pear, toasty almond and canned-pear flavors. Light-to-medium body. Drink chilled as a quaffable apéritif; oaky and sweet-tasting on the finish. 333 cases made. • $13 • (10/15/97) • **80**

VALENTIN, CHÂTEAU

Margaux 1994: Moderately rich and concentrated, with black cherry, mint and other herbal flavors. Still a bit tannic and lean, but well balanced. Finishes on a gamy note. 600 cases made. • $22 • (04/30/97) • **82**

VALETTE

Mâcon-Chaintré Vieilles Vignes 1994 • $15 • (05/31/96) • **91**

Mâcon-Chaintré Vieilles Vignes 1993 • $11 • (08/31/95) • **84**

Pouilly-Fuissé Clos Reyssié 1993: Smooth, round, spicy, silky— a solid frame. Grapefruit and tropical fruit notes emerge on the intense finish. Enjoy with fish. 333 cases made. • $26 • (05/15/95) • **88**

Pouilly-Fuissé Clos Reyssié 1992: Quite distinctive butterscotch aromas, with fresh lime and wet hay flavors. Creamy smooth texture and long finish offer a hint of honey and hazelnut. Mature complexity. Drinkable now. • $NA • (05/15/95) • **87**

Pouilly-Fuissé Clos Reyssié Réserve Particulière 1995: Late-harvest Chardonnay. Ripe yet not sweet (only off-dry), full-bodied yet structured, this is exotic, with loads of apricot, peach, quince jam, fresh herb and caramel flavors that surprise the palate. Try with spicy food, now through 2003. 250 cases made. • $40 • (05/31/97) • **92**

Pouilly-Fuissé Clos Reyssié Réserve Particulière 1993: Exquisite, silky and harmonious, fresh and fruity, showing creamy, pear tart, mineral flavors that caress the palate. Medium-bodied; faultless finish. Drinkable now. 167 cases made. • $33 • (05/15/95) • **89**

Pouilly-Fuissé Le Clos de Monsieur Noly 1993: Lots of buttery, toasty flavors play against citrusy, pineapple and other tropical notes. Medium-bodied; both velvety and firm. Drinkable now. 1,000 cases made. • $24 • (05/15/95) • **88**

Pouilly-Fuissé Le Clos de Monsieur Noly Vieilles Vignes 1993: Flavorful, fresh and supple, offering lemon, honey, pear and spice notes. Medium in body. Drinkable now. • $29 • (05/15/95) • **88**

Pouilly-Fuissé Tradition 1994: Distinctive and delicious, but a bit odd. Tastes off-dry like a botrytized Chardonnay, with peach, apricot, honey, caramel and cream flavors. Paired with spicy food, this full-bodied, rich and ripe Mâcon should be sublime. Drink now or hold till past 2000. 1,250 cases made. • $33 • (05/31/97) • **90**

VALLÉE, CHÂTEAU LA

Montagne-St.-Emilion 1995: A slightly lean red, this has pretty floral and nutty aromas and flavors, but it's light on the palate. Slightly dry finish. • $NA • (01/01/97) • **79**

VALLONGUE, CHÂTEAU DE

Coteaux d'Aix en Provence Les Baux 1988 • $11 • (12/15/91) • **73**

Coteaux d'Aix-en-Provence Les Baux Cuvée Murielle 1993: Declining now, showing tea, leather and light earth flavors, with drying tannins. Drink now. • $18 • (06/30/97) • **77**

VALLOUIT, L. DE

Châteauneuf-du-Pape 1989 • $16 • (12/31/91) • **77**

Côte-Rôtie 1989 • $30 • (01/31/92) • **89**

Côte-Rôtie 1985 • $20 • (10/15/87) • **75**

Gigondas 1989 • $13 • (01/31/92) • **89**

Hermitage 1983 • $12 • (05/01/86) • **79**

St.-Joseph Red 1989 • $13 • (01/31/92) • **76**

Vin de Pays des Collines Rhodanienn Les Sables 1989 • $6 • (12/31/91) BB • **81**

Vin de Pays des Collines Rhodanienn Les Sables 1988 • $4 • (06/30/90) BB • **78**

VARICHON & CLERC

Blanc de Blancs 1992 • $10 • (12/15/95) BB • **86**

Blanc de Blancs 1989 • $9 • (03/31/92) BB • **87**

Brut Blanc de Blancs 1991 • $10 • (12/31/94) BB • **87**

Brut Blanc de Blancs France Cuvée Privée 1995: Lively and fresh, fruity and well balanced, rather soft in texture. A good everyday bottle of bubbly. 15,000 cases made. • $12 • (05/31/97) • **84**

Brut Blanc de Blancs France Cuvée Privée 1994: A subtle, slightly sweet sparkling wine with solid fruit flavors accented by intriguing vanilla and spice notes that linger on the finish. 15,000 cases made. • $11 • (05/15/97) • **85**
Brut Rosé 1992 • $10 • (12/15/95) • **79**
Brut Rosé 1991 • $10 • (12/31/94) • **80**

VATAN, EDMOND

Sancerre Clos La Néore 1996: Displays more ripeness than many Sancerres of the vintage, with pear, spice and even vanilla flavors, backed with herbal notes. Round and appealing, but lacks the crispness typical of the region. Drink now. • $23 • (06/15/98) • **80**
Sancerre Clos La Néore 1994 • $NA • (06/15/96) • **76**
Sancerre Clos La Néore 1993 • $19 • (11/15/95) • **88**

VAUCHER

Corton-Charlemagne 1992: Great breeding in this does Corton proud. The butter, hazelnut, vanilla and pear flavors unfold in a subtle package that offers length. Try now. • $NA • (08/31/94) • **91**
Puligny-Montrachet 1992: Elegant and flavorful, with a ripe core of honey, pear, apple and citrus flavors; not very big or opulent, but a very attractive finish. • $NA • (08/31/94) • **88**

VAUDON, DOMAINE DE

Chablis 1996: This exciting wine is marvelously fruity, with a velvety, creamlike texture, delivering layers of ripe pear, buttery croissant, pineapple, white pepper, pink grapefruit, wheat cereal and dried coconut flavors. A great achievement in a communal appellation. • $20 • (05/31/98) • **93**

VELANGES, DOMAINE DES

Mâcon-Davayé 1996: Balanced and quite lovely. Fairly ripe, with apple, honey, tropical fruit and pear notes, hints of citrus and bitter almond. Turns a bit dry and tart on the finish. Drinkable now. From Michel Paquet. • $NA • (08/31/97) • **86**
Mâcon-Davayé 1995: Rather tough customer, delivering some decent fruit flavor, but also vanilla and tree bark flavors that turn bitter on the finish. Drink now. 833 cases made. • $9 • (05/31/97) • **76**
Pouilly-Fuissé 1996: Earth, mineral and fruit mingle nicely here. Medium-bodied, it turns a bit weak on the finish, with some candied notes. Drink now. 275 cases made. • $13 • (05/31/98) • **80**
St.-Véran 1996: Shows decent balance between fruit and acidity, with lime, pear and green apple flavors dominating. Light- to medium-bodied, it lacks ripeness. Drink now through 1999. 2,750 cases made. • $9 • (05/31/98) • **80**
St.-Véran 1995: Interesting, showing a coarse *terroir* character, with honey, floral and hay notes. Decent intensity, but the finish is short and rustic. Drink now. 3,333 cases made. • $10 • (05/31/97) • **80**
St.-Véran Cuvée Hors Classe 1996: Wood imposes itself on the fruit flavors in this medium-bodied white. Shows some decent pear and apple character, but also a slightly tart finish. Drink now or hold until around 1999. 580 cases made. • $11 • (05/31/98) • **80**
St.-Véran Cuvée Hors Classé 1995: Delicious. Medium- to full-bodied, its ripe, sweet-tasting fruit flavors seductively laced with honey, pear, pie crust, cream and fresh herb notes. Great now through 1999. From Michel Paquet. 583 cases made. • $12 • (05/31/97) • **88**

VENOGE, DE

Blanc de Blancs Champagne 1983 • $40 • (12/31/93) • **84**
Brut Blanc de Blancs Champagne 1990: What's not to like? There's a great combo of bright fruit flavors, plush texture and spicy finish in this broad, complex and totally agreeable bubbly. Drink now through 1999. 5,000 cases made. • $35 • (12/31/97) • **90**

Key: SS—Spectator Selection CS—Cellar Selection HR—Highly Recommended BB—Best Buy $NA—Price not available Ⓐ—Auction Price (BT)—Barrel Tasting
Dates in parentheses indicate the issues in which the ratings were published.

Brut Blanc de Noirs Champagne 1990: Truly fresh in its fruit flavors, zingy in texture and balance. Has a blast of grapefruit character that lasts from the aroma to the finish. 5,000 cases made. • $35 • (11/15/96) • **85**
Brut Champagne 1988 • $40 • (12/31/93) • **88**
Brut Champagne 1985 • $38 • (12/31/90) • **86**
Brut Champagne Cordon Bleu NV: This is special. A bold, mature style, with intriguing toasty, nutty aromas, rich and mellow flavors and a lingering finish. 80,000 cases made. • $27 • (10/31/97) • **89**
Brut Champagne des Princes 1990: Sophisticated, not showy, this intriguing, dry Champagne shows plenty of body and a handsome, mature character, yet it's still quite vibrant in balance and texture. Combines subtlety with power. Drink now through 2002. 3,000 cases made. • $79 • (12/31/97) • **94**
Brut Champagne Champagne des Princes 1985 • $60 • (12/31/93) • **92**
Brut Rosé Champagne Princesse NV: An atypical but delicious rosé that's like a fine Meursault with bubbles. There's almost no pink in the color, and the rich fruit flavors and lingering finish are reminiscent of ripe Chardonnay. 5,000 cases made. • $35 • (11/30/97) • **88**
Demi-Sec Champagne NV: Something different in a sweet Champagne. Has an attractive, toasty aroma and good acidity to back up the lush texture and indulgent, pastrylike flavors. 2,000 cases made. • $27 • (11/30/97) • **88**

VERDIGNAN, CHÂTEAU

Haut-Médoc 1997: Lovely perfumed young wine with violet, berry and cherry aromas. Medium-bodied, with medium, fine tannins and a fading finish. • $NA • (06/15/98) (BT) • **85-89**
Haut-Médoc 1996: A slightly mean '96 with green olive, mineral and fruit character. Medium-bodied, with medium tannins and a medium finish. • $16 • (06/15/98) (BT) • **75-79**
Haut-Médoc 1995: Impressive texture and plenty of berry character, but slightly herbaceous with an herbal, grassy undertone and finish. Medium-bodied, with fine tannins. Best after 1999. 25,000 cases made. • $15 • (01/31/98) • **83**
Haut-Médoc 1994: Delicious and silky, with green tobacco, berry and cherry notes, moderate tannins and a lithe finish. Try now • $15 • (01/31/97) • **85**
Haut-Médoc 1992: Clean and lightly fruity, showing firm tannins and a light, slightly herbal finish. Too diluted. • $14 • (04/15/95) • **75**
Haut-Médoc 1991: A wine with good silky texture, medium body and very light cherry flavor. • $14 • (03/31/94) • **80**
Haut-Médoc 1990: A very aromatic wine with attractive black cherry and roasted nut aromas and fruity flavors; the tannins are firm but the finish is light. Drinkable now. 30,000 cases made. • $17 • (03/31/93) • **85**
Haut-Médoc 1989 • $17 • (03/15/92) • **90**
Haut-Médoc 1988 • $15 • (04/30/91) • **86**
Haut-Médoc 1987 • $15 • (11/30/89) • **78**
Haut-Médoc 1986 • $15 • (11/30/89) • **76**
Haut-Médoc 1985 • $15 • (02/15/88) • **81**
Haut-Médoc 1983 • $13 • (04/01/86) • **69**
Haut-Médoc 1982 • $16 • (08/31/92) • **80**

VERDILLAC

Bordeaux 1993: Clumsy. The light berry and prune flavors are diluted and dominated by raspy tannins. Not much pleasure. 35,000 cases made. • $7 • (12/15/95) • **76**
Bordeaux White 1994 • $7 • (02/29/96) • **76**

VERGER, DOMAINE LE

Chablis 1994 • $NA • (08/31/95) • **84**

VERGET

Bâtard-Montrachet 1995: A wine to worship. Otherworldly; its different parts—structure, flavor, texture—are in total harmony. Super balance between the acidity, the fruit and the oak, with beguiling flavors of lemon, honey, pear and spice. Thick like a Sauternes yet elegant like a Montrachet, with the acidity of a fine Tokay—it's simply mind-boggling. 100 cases made. • $180 • (05/31/97) • **99**
Bâtard-Montrachet 1993: Quite ripe and forward, golden-colored, showing delicious apple, pear and grapefruit flavors. Very drinkable now. • $130 • (08/31/95) • **86**

Bâtard-Montrachet 1992: White Burgundy at its peak. Rich and seductive in flavor, broad in texture with a deep gold color, marked by toasty, smoky aromas, pear and nutmeg flavors and a spicy, long-lasting finish. • $125 • (08/31/94) • **93**

Bourgogne White 1996: A wonderful regional Bourgogne, balanced and sophisticated, showing a crisp, clean and pure flavor profile that's deceptive—let the wine breathe and it will open like a butterfly, turning supple, creamlike and velvety. Vanilla, wet earth, mineral, pear and apple flavors mingle. Medium-bodied. Try now (opening it one hour in advance) or, even better, hold until around 2000. 6,600 cases made. • $16 • (05/31/98) • **89**

Chablis 1996: Impressive communal Chablis. Super-seductive yet firmly built, with well-defined lime, butter, spice, eucalyptus and ripe fruit flavors. Full-bodied, thick and opulent in texture, this is a racy wine from start to finish that beckons you to take another sip. Tempting now through 2005. 860 cases made. • $20 • (05/31/98) • **91**

Chablis Fourchaume 1995: Ripe and soft, with a mineral, pear and spice character, but short on elegance and a bit tired already. Drink soon. • $29 • (06/15/97) • **80**

Chablis Montée de Tonnerre 1996: What a beauty. Tastes like a very mineral-ly Puligny-Montrachet. So intense you think your tastebuds may not survive this full-bodied Chablis with its concentrated lime, honey, spice, pear and tropical flavors. Oaky but in a balanced way, it's so thick it almost sticks to your palate, yet it rockets with grace to a trailing finish that won't end. Try from 2002 to 2010. 790 cases made. • $30 • (05/31/98) • **96**

Chablis Montée de Tonnerre 1995: A wild French white, with loads of personality and great class. Like a roller coaster, you can only hold on as it turns and twists your palate, with pure, elegant, well-knit flavors of lemon, fruit, toasty oak and flowers that hold on for a long, intense finish. Perhaps the best Chablis in 1995. Enjoy now through 2005. 300 cases made. • $29 • (06/15/97) • **92**

Chablis Montée de Tonnerre 1994 • $28 • (05/31/96) • **79**

Chablis Vaillons 1996: A godlike wine that might bring tears to the eyes of some Chardonnay aficionados. One of the most impressive white Burgundies of the '96 vintage. Balanced, full in body, supple in texture yet very intense, it builds its foundation with layer upon layer of fruit, spice, mineral, earth, butter and citrus notes. Stays in suspended animation in the midpalate for what seems like a good 60 seconds, almost vibrating with nervous agitation. Long and succulent finish. Decant if drinking now or cellar until 2005 for more mature complexity. 715 cases made. • $29 • (05/31/98) • **98**

Chablis Valmur 1995: Let this age or breathe and you will find some amazingly long flavors—citrus, toasty oak, ripe fruit, honey—that last for minutes on the finish. Has a great, lush, mouthfeel that any Chardonnay fan will love, but Chablis purists should stay away. Medium- to full-bodied, it's delicous now through 2005. • $142 Ⓐ • (06/15/97) • **91**

Chassagne-Montrachet 1996: Riper than most Chassagnes, with a buttery, cooked apple, tart character that lacks a bit of class, but the wine tastes very smooth. Medium-bodied, it offers vibrating, lively lime-honey notes on the midpalate and finish, but also turns slightly hot on the supertoasty finish. Drink now or hold. 425 cases made. • $35 • (05/31/98) • **87**

Chassagne-Montrachet 1993: Has the ripe fruit and buttery qualities we look for in a white Burgundy. Very aromatic, nicely flavorful and smooth, but turning tart and tight on the finish. Drinkable now. • $23 • (05/15/95) • **84**

Chassagne-Montrachet La Maltroie Cuvée Vieilles Vignes 1995: Like a three-flavored sorbet: pear, vanilla and lime. Clean, pure, vibrant yet full-bodied, this beauty is wonderfully balanced and flavorful. Straight as an arrow, medium- to full-bodied, with a long and racy, nicely toasty and spicy finish. Well done. Drink after 2000. • $44 • (08/31/97) • **94**

Chassagne-Montrachet La Romanée 1994: Excellent intensity for a '94. Mingles honey, lime, mineral and dried herb flavors. Great focus and clarity. A solid wine; try now. • $50 • (05/31/96) • **92**

Chassagne-Montrachet La Romanée 1993: Solid and deep yet also smooth, boasting mineral, apple and toast flavors. Drink now. Tasted twice. 375 cases made. • $30 Ⓐ • (05/15/95) • **88**

Chassagne-Montrachet La Romanée 1992: Vivid and vibrant, it's quite tart, with lemon, grapefruit and toast flavors. Try now. • $50 • (08/31/94) • **86**

Chassagne-Montrachet Les Champs Gain 1993: Dull-tasting and coarse in texture, this doesn't offer much pleasure. It has apple-skin flavors and a muddy finish. • $25 • (05/15/95) • **74**

Chassagne-Montrachet Morgeot Cuvée Vieilles Vignes 1995: What a great wine. The lime and honey combination is just delicious, not to mention harmonious, balanced and seductive. It caresses the palate, with the cool texture and clean, pure aromas of a sorbet, then kicks in with a dollop of spice. Medium-to-full in body; drink now through 2005. • $46 • (08/31/97) • **93**

Chassagne-Montrachet Morgeot Cuvée Vieilles Vignes 1993: Beautiful velvet texture and mineral undertones give it a lot of class. Solid backbone; grapefruit, hazelnut and honey character. Drinkable now. Tasted twice. • $39 • (05/15/95) • **89**

Chassagne-Montrachet Morgeot 1992: Combines a buttery, toasty aroma with bright pear and citrus flavors and accents of honey and vanilla. Tangy and long on the finish. Drinkable now. • $44 • (08/31/94) • **87**

Chassagne-Montrachet Premier Cru 1994: Nicely made, showing good balance. Somewhat fuller-bodied, with pear, dried herb, honey, lime, hazelnut and apple pie flavors. Lacks the intensity to climb into the outstanding category. Drinkable now, but can age, too. • $27 • (05/31/96) • **87**

Corton-Charlemagne Cuvée Vieilles Vignes 1994: Impressively intense, racy and sharply focused—like drinking nectar. Has a lovely honey, lime, pear and mineral character; unctuous while keeping a fresh mouthfeel. Drink now. Tasted twice, with consistent notes. • $57 • (05/31/96) • **92**

Ladoix White 1996: Straightforward and slightly dull, with green apple, citrus and pear flavors. Bitter finish. Disappointing. 495 cases made. • $24 • (05/31/98) • **79**

Mâcon-Villages Tête de Cuvée 1996: Pretty impressive if you want a greenish, slightly grassy but unctuous, full-bodied white Burgundy. Well-built, allowing the apple-skin, pear and citrus flavors to sing unhindered by too much oak, although you can taste the toasty, smoky wood-inspired character on the crisp finish. Very oily in texture, but a bit bitter on the finish. Needs time; try around 2000. 5,000 cases made. • $15 • (05/31/98) • **88**

Mâcon-Villages Tête de Cuvée 1995: A medium-bodied white of good intensity, this offers fine green-apple, pear and citrus flavors, all tightly wound, young and vibrant. Finish is nicely honeyed and intensely citrusy. Drink now. • $13 • (05/31/97) • **86**

Meursault 1993: Toasty, buttery accents lend extra interest to this crisp, lemon- and grapefruit-flavored Chardonnay. It is lean and elegant in texture, very bracing but not full-bodied. • $23 • (05/15/95) • **84**

Meursault Le Porusot 1995: Racy and classy. Shows more intensity than many '95 white Burgundies, with sparkling fruit, citrus, mineral and toasty oak flavors. Full-bodied, it's a fresh wine that coats the palate on the lingering, lemony, smoky finish. Try around 2003. • $50 • (05/31/97) • **93**

Meursault Le Porusot 1994: Decadent yet harmonious, balancing its ripe flavors nicely on the citrusy background to beckon you back for another sip. Well structured, it delivers its honey, grapefruit and toast flavors with great elegance. Enjoy it now through 2000. • $44 • (05/31/96) • **92**

Meursault Le Porusot 1993: Surprisingly silky for the vintage, showing apple, pear and mineral flavors and a touch of honey that kicks in on the refined finish. Drinkable now. 117 cases made. • $42 • (05/15/95) • **90**

Meursault Les Casse-Têtes 1995: A deep wine, with a solid core of mineral, dried herbs, spice and mocha flavors. A bit dry on the finish now, but there's plenty of fruit character and depth here. Try now to 2005. • $35 • (05/31/97) • **91**

Meursault Les Casse-Têtes 1993: Quite grassy and intense, offering dried-herb, citrus and lime flavors and a hint of honey. Try now. Tasted twice with consistent notes. 583 cases made. • $28 • (05/15/95) • **86**

Meursault Les Charmes Cuvée Vieilles Vignes 1995: A bold, sexy, strongly oaked, full-bodied *premier cru* with toasty coconut, butterscotch, a hint of honey, mineral and ripe pear flavors. May not be for everyone, but it's smooth and well made, with tons of lemony acidity that builds with aeration. Try after 2000. • $65 • (05/31/97) • **91**

Meursault Les Charmes Cuvée Vieilles Vignes 1994: Exemplifies '94, showing both the finesse and power of this vintage. Great lemon, honey and pie crust aromas and flavors. Medium-bodied and very clean, a well-crafted wine that kicks in with a long finish. • $52 • (05/31/96) • **91**

Meursault Les Genevrières Hospices de Beaune 1994: Fat, showy and almost overdone, oozing ripe and rich flavors. Full-bodied, this crowd-pleaser offers a symphony of toasty bread, butter, ripe fruit and citrus notes. Very creamy and silky in texture, adding honey-laced, ripe aftertaste. Enjoy now. Tasted twice, with consistent notes. • $35 • (05/31/96) • **90**

Meursault Les Genevrières 1992: Extremely buttery and oaky in aroma, but backed by firm fruit flavors and acidity. An ambitious, heavy style; drinkable now. • $50 • (08/31/94) • **87**

Meursault Les Rougeots 1994: Clean and crisp, with lively character, delivering some nice citrus, manderine orange and spice flavors. Fresh, vibrant and lovely from start to finish. Drinkable now. • $31 • (05/31/96) • **86**

Montrachet 1994: Racy, subtle and refined, it ends with a bang, delivering the whole scope of white Burgundy complexity, from very toasty hazelnut and bread flavors to ripe fruit, honey, mineral and lemon character.

Medium- to full-bodied, silky and seductive, adding a very long finish. Terrific now, but better in 2001. • $160 • (05/31/96) • **96**

Pouilly-Fuissé 1995: A lovely, medium-bodied Chardonnay, with well-defined fruit and spice flavors, quite crisp but also nicely ripe and sweet-tasting. Drink now. • $15 • (05/31/97) • **86**

Pouilly-Fuissé 1993: Distinctive butter, toast and butterscotch aromas, super-intense, citrusy flavors on the palate and a chalky, chewy, long finish. Drinkable now. 1,250 cases made. • $17 • (05/15/95) • **89**

Pouilly-Fuissé 1992: Rich, ripe and extremely attractive, delivering lots of toasty oak, hazelnut, lime and fresh pineapple flavors. A pleasure to drink now; seductive, long finish. 2,083 cases made. • $17 • (05/15/95) • **90**

Pouilly-Fuissé Tête de Cuvée 1996: A monster that you'll either hate or love. Overtly oaky, the toasty character is searingly intense on the palate. Full-bodied, thick, opulent, ripe, rich, it should become very silky with a bit of age. Has Verget's lime-honey signature flavors and a finish that won't quit. Hard to enjoy now, but if this beast calms down one day, it should make for a wonderful experience. Try around 2005. 1,400 cases made. • $15 • (05/31/98) HR • **93**

Pouilly-Fuissé Tête de Cuvée 1994: Creamy up-front, followed by notes of citrus, this is full of contrasts. Very appealing and you can feel the wine-making talent. Good concentration on the long finish. Try now. • $25 • (05/31/96) • **89**

FRANCE

Puligny-Montrachet Les Enseignères 1995: Takes off like a rocket on the palate, with amazing intensity of fruit, acidity and toasty oak. Wonderful mineral flavors, too. Don't touch until 2000 to 2010. 650 cases made. • $35 • (05/31/97) • **94**

Puligny-Montrachet Les Enseignères 1994: Focused, restrained and harmonious; shows spice, toasty oak, cream and nice fruit flavors. It all comes together on a fresh, seductive finish. Delicious now. • $33 • (05/31/96) • **89**

Puligny-Montrachet Les Enseignères 1993: Sharp and steely; toasty, buttery, pear flavors soften the hard edges somewhat. Medium-bodied, providing a touch of honey on the vibrant finish. Tasted twice. 625 cases made. • $29 • (05/15/95) • **86**

Puligny-Montrachet Les Pucelles 1993: A rather delicate Puligny, showing some lovely hazelnut, honey and apple flavors, light-to-medium body and a vibrant finish. Drink now. Tasted twice, with consistent notes. 367 cases made. • $33 Ⓐ • (05/15/95) • **85**

Puligny-Montrachet Sous le Puits 1995: Impressive for its tightly wound structure, offering some delicious honey, lime and mineral notes. A full-bodied *premier cru*. Drinkable now. • $43 • (08/31/97) • **88**

Puligny-Montrachet Sous le Puits 1994: Soft yet refreshing, providing a supple, delicious drinking experience. Mingles honey and pear flavors with citrus and ginger. Tasted twice, with consistent notes. • $38 • (05/31/96) • **86**

Puligny-Montrachet Sous le Puits 1992: Stylish, exuberant and lively, with tons of toast, butter and pear flavors. Its vibrant lime and lemon character keeps it in check, leading to a crisp finish that gives it length and promises a long life in the cellar. Try now. 600 cases made. • $38 • (08/31/94) HR • **93**

St.-Aubin Premier Cru White 1996: A lovely wine of great finesse, with mineral, vanilla bean, pear, apple pie and spices. Not exuberant, but this medium-bodied Chardonnay grows on you as it slides over the palate with its creamy texture. Ends with a long, supple and elegant finish. Delicious now, but should hold through 2005. 830 cases made. • $28 • (05/31/98) • **91**

St.-Aubin Premier Cru White 1994: Crisp and quite tart, light-to-medium body, with nicely focused citrus and green apple flavors, followed by a hint of honey and mineral on the finish. • $18 • (05/31/96) • **82**

St.-Aubin Premier Cru White 1993: Mineral, ripe fruit flavors are diminished only by a slight, cooked-apple quality. Drink now. Tasted twice. 1,125 cases made. • $19 • (05/15/95) • **84**

St.-Romain White 1996: Crisp and tough, showing milky, butter, butterscotch flavors. Light-to-medium in body, it lacks harmony. 1,450 cases made. • $21 • (05/31/98) • **76**

St.-Romain White 1994: Zingy and vibrant, with a core of lemon and green apple. Light-bodied and very crisp but clean and fresh on the somewhat grassy finish. • $17 • (05/31/96) • **80**

St.-Véran 1996: A bit of green in the flavor profile as is typical of '96 St.-Vérans, but its texture is seductive, opulent and rich, and caresses the palate with its creamy feel. Delightful citrus, ripe fruit, mineral-laden character makes for a wonderful wine now, but hold through 2000. 2,600 cases made. • $13 • (05/31/98) • **90**

St.-Véran 1995: Crisp in flavor but silky in texture, this ripe-tasting, medium-bodied white has plenty of fresh herb, gooseberry, citrus and ripe pear aromas and flavors. Chewy, lively finish. Drink now. • $13 • (05/31/97) • **84**

Santenay White 1996: Delicious, with good ripe character. Light- to medium-bodied, fairly crisp and sharp, but flavorful, with dried herbs, grass and some mineral notes. Not opulent or smooth, but try with seafood around 2000 to 2002. 460 cases made. • $24 • (05/31/98) • **87**

Key: SS—Spectator Selection CS—Cellar Selection HR—Highly Recommended BB—Best Buy $NA—Price not available Ⓐ—Auction Price (BT)—Barrel Tasting
Dates in parentheses indicate the issues in which the ratings were published.

VERGNES, CHÂTEAU DES

Bordeaux 1994: A decent quaff with flavors of plum, spice and blackberry, an earthy note and a pleasant finish. 28,000 cases made. • $10 • (04/30/97) • **81**

Sauvignon Blanc Bordeaux 1994: Smells sweet and tastes coarse, with only modest onion and canned-fruit notes. 16,500 cases made. • $10 • (04/30/97) • **75**

VERHAEGHE & FILS

Cahors Chateau du Cédre 1991 • $11 • (03/31/95) • **81**

VERNAY, GEORGES

Condrieu 1995: Dominated by oak, this heavy white shows vanilla and coconut flavors with little varietal character. It's simple and a bit dull. • $NA • (10/15/97) • **79**

Condrieu Côteau de Vernon 1995: Silky and fresh, this easy-drinking wine offers vanilla, citrus, apple and light spice flavors, smooth and pure, with a crisp finish. A delicious apéritif. 375 cases made. • $60 • (10/15/97) • **86**

Côte-Rôtie 1994: Delicate, light and straightforward, with strawberry and raspberry flavors, it's fruity, ready to drink. Lacks in concentration, but it's pretty and harmonious. 833 cases made. • $35 • (10/15/97) • **82**

Côte-Rôtie 1991: Ripe and luscious, with jammy cherry and smoke flavors in a supple, rustic style. Drinkable now. • $30 • (05/31/94) • **84**

VERNEDE, CHÂTEAU LA

Coteaux du Languedoc 1990 • $9 • (06/15/93) • **75**

VERSET, NOËL

Cornas 1994: Pungent, classic Syrah aromas of game, black olives and herbs follow through on the palate, where the game and leather flavors work to show through chewy tannins. It's concentrated but still closed. Drink now through 2004. • $35 • (10/15/97) • **89**

Cornas 1993 • $24 • (10/15/95) • **85**

Cornas 1987 • $23 • (03/31/90) • **88**

Cornas 1986 • $22 Ⓐ • (01/31/89) • **86**

VESSELLE, GEORGES

Brut Champagne Grand Cru 1986 • $NA • (12/31/93) • **85**

Brut Champagne Zero Grand Cru 1986 • $NA • (12/31/93) • **89**

VESSIGAUD PÈRE & FILS

Mâcon-Fuissé 1996: Balanced and silky, but also a bit showy, this is a full-bodied, ripe, generous Chardonnay that delivers some honey, citrus, marzipan, spice, pear, tropical and oak accents. A bit heavy on the finish. 1,160 cases made. • $16 • (05/31/98) • **87**

Pouilly-Fuissé Vieilles Vignes 1996: Elegant and refined, with supersilky texture. Closed on the nose but showing depth, with lime, honey, honeysuckle, spice and floral flavors generously endowing this medium- to full-bodied, racy Chardonnay. Restrained, clever winemaking. Delicious now through 2000. 500 cases made. • $27 • (05/31/98) • **90**

Pouilly-Fuissé Vieilles Vignes 1995: Crisp and flavorful, with citrus and green apple flavors, hints of toast and butter. Quite ripe. Juicy finish. Drink now. 333 cases made. • $14 • (05/31/97) • **84**

VEUVE CLICQUOT

Brut Champagne 1979 • $50 • (12/16/85) • **88**
Brut Champagne NV: Beautifully refreshing and fruity in character, creamy in texture and with a lingering toasty finish. Improved since our last tasting. Drink now. • $45 • (05/31/98) • **88**
Brut Champagne Gold Label Vintage Reserve 1985 • $52 • (09/30/93) HR • **92**
Brut Champagne Gold Label 1983 • $42 • (12/31/90) • **90**
Brut Champagne Gold Label 1982 • $37 • (12/31/88) • **85**
Brut Champagne La Grande Dame 1989: Full-bodied but sophisticated in both flavor and texture, this very dry but distinguished Champagne boasts appealing layers of toasty, doughy, smoky flavors, a mouthfilling mousse and a lingering finish. Ready now through 2002. • $100 • (11/30/97) HR • **94**
Brut Champagne La Grande Dame 1988: A big, generous Champagne with expansive aromas of butterscotch and satisfying flavors of almond, vanilla and apple. Mature and ready to drink. • $100 • (12/31/96) • **86**
Brut Champagne La Grande Dame 1985 • $100 • (12/31/93) • **94**
Brut Champagne La Grande Dame 1983 • $79 • (12/31/89) • **92**
Brut Champagne La Grande Dame 1979 • $61 • (05/16/86) • **96**
Brut Champagne Réserve 1989: Plush and mouthfilling in texture but modest in flavor, this is a pleasant glass of Champagne. Drink now. • $50 • (12/31/97) • **84**
Brut Champagne Réserve 1988: Bold and distinctive, with assertive aromas, a firm, slightly astringent texture and ample flavors of walnut, apple and spice. Drinkable now. • $50 • (07/31/95) • **89**
Brut Champagne Vintage Réserve 1985 • $50 • (12/31/93) • **90**
Brut Champagne 1982 • $47 • (05/31/87) SS • **93**
Brut Rosé Champagne 1983 • $47 • (12/31/89) • **86**
Brut Rosé Champagne La Grande Dame 1988: A class act. This rosé puts delicacy, flavor, complexity and balance together for a great taste experience. It is dry, firm in texture and full of subtle cherry and spice flavors that linger on the finish. Best now through 2002. 75-79 cases made. • $195 • (09/30/97) HR • **94**
Brut Rosé Champagne Réserve 1988: A very dry, restrained Champagne with a crisp, bracing texture, appealing flavors of cherry and a lively citrus finish. Tantalizing now, but may improve with time. Drink now through 2002. • $60 • (12/31/97) • **89**
Brut Rosé Champagne Réserve 1985 • $60 • (11/30/92) • **85**
Brut Rosé Champagne 1979 • $35 • (07/16/86) • **89**
Brut Rosé Champagne 1978 • $60 • (12/16/85) • **82**
Demi-Sec Champagne NV: Sweet and appealing in a straightforward way, with a rich texture and soft finish. • $45 • (12/31/97) • **84**

VIALE, DOMAINE GABRIEL

Crozes-Hermitage 1990 • $8 • (06/15/93) • **82**

VICHON MEDITERRANEAN

Cabernet Sauvignon Vin de Pays d'Oc 1995: Vibrant, rich, red cherry aromas and flavors up front, but it closes down pretty quickly on the finish. • $10 • (06/30/97) • **82**
Chardonnay Vin de Pays d'Oc 1995: Full-bodied, with butter and apple flavors. Straightforward, though turns a bit astringent on the finish. • $10 • (05/31/97) • **80**
Chasan Vin de Pays d'Oc 1995: A thickly textured white, rich in butter and pear flavors. Balanced on the soft side with plenty of up front fruit. Made from Chardonnay crossed with Listán varieties. • $12 • (06/30/97) • **85**
Merlot Vin de Pays d'Oc 1995: Fresh and fairly fruity with nice, dark cherry flavors and smoky notes. Medium-bodied with some tannins on the finish. • $9 • (05/31/97) • **82**
Sauvignon Blanc Vin de Pays d'Oc 1995: Vaguely floral in aroma, simple in flavor, smooth in texture, this is a bland white that bears little resemblance to Sauvignon Blanc. • $8 • (05/31/97) • **78**
Syrah Vin de Pays d'Oc 1995: Fruity, if a little lean in flavor and firm in texture, this is a straightforward red wine that will be fine at the table. • $10 • (07/31/97) • **84**
Viognier Vin de Pays d'Oc 1995: An exuberant white, exhibiting ripe apple and pear flavors of modest concentration. • $12 • (06/30/97) • **79**

VIDAL-FLEURY, J.

Châteauneuf-du-Pape White 1996: Clean but simple, offering light pear and vanilla flavors with herbal accents; crisp, then short on the finish. A disappointment for the vintage. 400 cases made. • $23 • (10/15/97) • **81**
Châteauneuf-du-Pape White 1993: Fruity and floral, this is uncharacteristic, but inviting nonetheless. Flavors of peaches, apples, roses and spice are balanced and lively. Try with meaty, grilled fish. 600 cases made. • $24 • (12/15/96) • **85**
Condrieu 1994: Full-bodied and intensely flavored, this is rich and very dry, with floral, spice and herbal flavors. Distinctive and expressive. 500 cases made. • $40 • (10/15/96) • **88**
Cornas 1990 • $27 • (05/31/94) • **80**
Cornas 1989 • $10 • (06/15/92) • **81**
Cornas 1988 • $20 • (01/31/91) • **85**
Côte-Rôtie 1990: Dense but not exuberant. Tastes like chocolate-covered raspberries. It's velvety and ripe. Try now. • $30 • (05/31/94) • **88**
Côte-Rôtie Côte Blonde La Chatillonne 1993: Coffee and raisin flavors struggle to emerge from beneath the very firm tannins in this medium-bodied yet highly-extracted red. Concentrated, but still may not have enough fruit to age with balance and grace. 250 cases made. • $42 • (11/30/96) • **84**
Côte-Rôtie La Chatillonne 1990: Powerfully aromatic, with lush raspberry, plum, vanilla and licorice flavors. Very concentrated and balanced. Try now. • $42 • (05/31/94) • **92**
Côte-Rôtie Côte Blonde La Chatillonne 1988: Expresive aromas of minerals, game and spice show maturity, but the wine is still fresh and quite elegant on the palate, with pepper, licorice and dried cherry flavors. A fine expression of Syrah in the traditional style. Drink now through 2000. 250 cases made. • $42 • (11/30/96) • **90**
Côte-Rôtie Côte Blonde La Chatillonne 1984 • $26 • (10/31/87) • **73**
Côte-Rôtie Côtes Brune et Blonde 1994: A nice marriage of elegance and concentration gives this verve and depth. It shows ripe raspberry and blackberry flavors, with smoky and gamy notes and firm, but unaggressive tannins. Drinkable now. 1,500 cases made. • $38 • (11/30/96) • **88**
Côte-Rôtie Côtes Brune et Blonde 1992: Maturing now, this offers coffee, raisin and dried cherry flavors, with cinnamon accents. There's moderate concentration on the palate, but tannins take over the modest finish. Drink now through 1999. 1,500 cases made. • $38 • (11/30/96) • **84**
Côte-Rôtie Côtes Brune et Blonde 1989 • $28 • (03/15/94) • **87**
Côte-Rôtie Côtes Brune et Blonde 1988 • $30 • (10/15/90) • **88**
Côte-Rôtie Côtes Brune et Blonde 1985 • $25 • (03/15/90) • **90**
Côte-Rôtie Côtes Brune et Blonde 1945 • $NA • (03/15/90) • **85**
Côte-Rôtie Côtes Brune et Blonde 1934 • $NA • (03/15/90) • **85**
Côtes du Rhône 1995: Ripe, sweet and supple, it's a lovely wine from start to finish, with plum, red berry and vanilla character. Has well-integrated tannins, and is seductive and lush on the lingering, fresh finish. Delicious now. Worth buying a case. 12,500 cases made. • $9 • (10/15/97) • **88**
Côtes du Rhône 1994: Supple and ripe, this makes up in rich plum, chocolate and cinnamon flavors what it lacks in concentration. Drink it now, while it still has enough tannin to stand up to food. 30,000 cases made. • $9 • (10/15/96) BB • **84**
Côtes du Rhône White 1996: Apple and banana flavors are lush and fresh. It's juicy and lively, and has enough body to match with food. Drink now. 2,000 cases made. • $10 • (10/15/97) • **83**
Côtes du Rhône White 1994: Dry and lean. Offers flavors of cooked apples and pastry dough, with lightly herbal and slightly bitter notes. Distinctive, though not harmonious. 1,500 cases made. • $10 • (10/15/96) • **79**
Côtes du Rhône-Villages 1994: An intense and rather muscular '94, pure and clean, with sweet, ripe berry character mixing with notes of cassis bush, dried herbs and chocolate, and a certain mineral flavor. Has personality but turns slightly tough on the finish. Still worth buying. 3,300 cases made. • $10 • (10/15/97) • **85**
Côtes du Ventoux 1994: Generous and round, this is soft and sweet. Flavors of ripe plum, chocolate and licorice, with just enough tannin for grip. Easy to like. 20,000 cases made. • $7 • (10/15/96) • **83**
Côtes du Ventoux 1990 • $7 • (06/30/94) BB • **84**
Crozes-Hermitage 1994: There's a distinctive personality here. This is a chewy wine with good structure behind vivid licorice, meat and berry flavors. Drink now. 10,000 cases made. • $14 • (11/30/96) • **88**
Crozes-Hermitage 1992: Light cherry, herbal and licorice flavors run close to the surface in this supple red, then recede as the tannins take over the finish. Clean but simple, it's drinkable now. 10,000 cases made. • $14 • (11/30/96) • **82**
Crozes-Hermitage 1990 • $10 • (05/31/94) • **87**

Crozes-Hermitage 1988 • $13 • (12/31/90) • **86**
Crozes-Hermitage 1986 • $10 • (05/31/88) • **78**
Crozes-Hermitage 1985 • $11 • (10/31/87) CS • **92**
Crozes-Hermitage White 1995: This blowsy white tastes of ripe apples, butter and hazelnuts. Generous, but lacking a bit in freshness and structure. Drink now. 400 cases made. • $14 • (10/15/97) • **79**
Gigondas 1990: Still fresh and well knit, this mingles plum, prune, licorice and light herbal flavors in a well-balanced and still tannic structure. Drink now. 2,000 cases made. • $19 • (10/15/96) • **84**
Gigondas 1985 • $13 • (10/31/87) • **86**
Hermitage 1985 • $22 • (10/31/87) • **89**
Hermitage 1945 • $NA • (03/15/90) • **80**
Hermitage 1937 • $NA • (03/15/90) • **91**
Muscat de Beaumes-de-Venise Réserve 1995: Full-bodied and unctuous on the palate, this is sweet but not cloying, with herbal accents to the ripe melon and orange flavors. The finish lingers like a Provençal sunset. 2,000 cases made. • $13 • 375ml • (10/15/96) • **87**
St.-Joseph 1994: Ripe and supple, this offers meaty and dried fruit flavors, with firm tannins kicking in on the finish. A traditional, somewhat rustic style. Drink now through 1999. 8,000 cases made. • $17 • (11/30/96) • **85**
St.-Joseph 1991: Still fresh, this is thick and sweet with fruit, with soft tannins and bright acidity. It's straightforward now, but could develop more complexity with age. Drink now through 1999. 8,000 cases made. • $17 • (11/30/96) • **86**
St.-Joseph 1990 • $14 • (05/31/94) • **85**
St.-Joseph 1988 • $14 • (01/31/91) • **84**
Vacqueyras 1994: Nice polish, with lead-pencil, coffee and plum notes. Light-to-medium in body, it has soft tannins and delicious red berry character. Drink now. 4,000 cases made. • $11 • (10/15/97) • **84**
Vacqueyras 1991: Black cherry, black pepper and light herbal notes combine nicely in this balanced, light-bodied offering. Not a blockbuster, but has personality. Try now. 10,000 cases made. • $13 • (10/15/96) • **86**
Vacqueyras 1990 • $9 • (03/31/94) BB • **86**
Vacqueyras 1988 • $14 • (12/15/90) • **89**

VIE-MAGNE, DOMAINE

Crozes-Hermitage 1990 • $10 • (11/15/95) • **84**

VIEILLE CURE, CHÂTEAU LA

Fronsac 1997: A silky wine with berry and green olive aromas and flavors. Medium-bodied, with medium tannins and a good finish. Serious Fronsac. • $NA • (06/15/98) (BT) • **85-89**
Fronsac 1996: An underrated producer. Plenty of plum, tobacco and smoke character. Full-bodied and chunky, with lots of fruit and velvety tannins. Medium finish. Almost outstanding. 6,600 cases made. • $20 • (06/15/98) (BT) • **85-89**
Fronsac 1995: Concentrated and juicy. Blackberry, gravel and earth aromas and flavors. Full-bodied, with lots of fruit and masses of tannins. Long and mouthpuckering. Needs time to mellow. Best after 2001. 8,000 cases made. • $20 • (01/31/98) • **89**
Fronsac 1994: A refined, silky wine with lovely berry, tobacco aromas and flavors and a fruity, dried herb finish. Better in 1999. • $19 • (01/31/97) • **87**
Fronsac 1993: Attractive cherry and cracked black pepper flavors, light-to-medium body, firm tannins and a light, slightly dry finish. Drinkable now. • $19 • (01/31/96) • **79**
Fronsac 1992: Deep red color and dried cherry and herb character; light-bodied and firm with some decent fruit but a short finish. Drink now and hurry. • $15 • (04/15/95) • **79**
Fronsac 1990: Tightly-knit. It's rich but not giving much with steely tannins. Try now. 7,000 cases made. • $19 • (03/31/93) • **88**
Fronsac 1989 • $16 • (03/15/92) • **88**
Fronsac 1988 • $19 • (10/31/91) • **81**
Fronsac 1987 • $14 • (05/15/90) • **82**
Fronsac 1986 • $15 • (05/15/91) • **81**
Fronsac 1985 • $15 • (12/31/88) • **88**
Fronsac 1982 • $15 • (08/31/92) • **84**

Key: SS—Spectator Selection CS—Cellar Selection HR—Highly Recommended BB—Best Buy $NA—Price not available Ⓐ—Auction Price (BT)—Barrel Tasting
Dates in parentheses indicate the issues in which the ratings were published.

VIEILLE FERME, LA

Côtes du Lubéron White 1995: Big-boned, with vibrant flavors of orange, orange-peel, anise and butter. A slight earthy note gives it a rustic aspect. A bit clumsy, but appealing. • $7 • (10/15/96) • **83**
Côtes du Lubéron White 1993 • $7 • (11/30/94) • **81**
Côtes du Rhône Reserve White 1993 • $10 • (11/30/94) • **81**
Côtes du Ventoux 1996: Gamelike and licorice notes show good Syrah character in this chewy, slightly rustic red. It shows good regional character, and has enough grip for food. • $8 • (10/15/97) • **84**
Côtes du Ventoux 1995: Lively and fresh, this fruity red is packed with raspberry and cherry flavors, with appealing accents of herbs and smoke. With just enough grip for food, it's drinking well now. • $8 • (10/15/97) • **85**
Côtes du Ventoux 1994: Fresh and fruity, this shows cherry and raspberry flavors with just enough tannin for grip. A supple, pleasant, easy-drinking wine. • $7 • (12/15/96) • **84**
Côtes du Ventoux 1992 • $7 • (11/30/94) • **84**
Côtes du Ventoux 1990 • $7 • (04/15/93) • **78**
Côtes du Ventoux 1988 • $8 • (06/30/90) • **78**
Côtes du Ventoux 1987 • $5 • (06/15/89) BB • **81**
Côtes du Ventoux 1986 • $6 • (10/15/88) BB • **83**

VIEILLE JULIENNE, DOMAINE DE LA

Châteauneuf-du-Pape 1994: Fruity and voluptuous, this ripe red offers cherry, plum and chocolate flavors, with a nice dollop of oaky flavors. It's tannic now, but there's enough fruit for balance. Drink now. • $20 • (09/15/97) • **87**
Châteauneuf-du-Pape 1990: A tight, tannic wine, with potential for aging. Already has a complex aroma, but the stiff texture and intense fruit will need time to open up for maximum enjoyment. Currant, black cherry, cedar, earth and spice flavors make it fascinating to sip. Try now. 6,000 cases made. • $17 • (04/15/93) • **91**

VIEILLES PIERRES, DOMAINE DES

Pouilly-Fuissé Vieilles Vignes Elevé en Fût de Chêne 1993: Well made, medium in body, showing supple texture, some butter, mushroom, wet earth, pear flavors and fresh lemon notes. Long finish. Drinkable now. • $NA • (05/15/95) • **87**
Pouilly-Fuissé Vieilles Vignes La Roche 1993: Very fresh, young and intense; light-bodied but bursting with floral, peach, pineapple, green apple and pear flavors. Juicy finish. Drink now. • $NA • (05/15/95) • **85**

VIENOT, CHARLES

Beaujolais-Villages 1993 • $8 • (06/30/94) • **77**
Bourgogne 1985 • $9 • (06/15/89) • **78**
Bourgogne 1983 • $6 • (12/16/85) • **75**
Bourgogne Clos Le Village White 1992: Fairly ripe and concentrated with some nice apple and fig flavors. This is a middle-of-the-road wine with some structure that indicates it may age well. It turns buttery on the finish. Drink now. • $9 • (01/01/95) • **82**
Chassagne-Montrachet Red 1991: Youthful, fruity and chewy, but the earthy, gamy aromas and flavors rob it of some charm. • $NA • (01/31/94) • **77**
Corton Les Maréchaudes 1985 • $57 • (07/15/88) • **84**
Côte de Nuits-Villages Cuvée Roi de Saxe 1993: Disappointing, showing light fruit character, a diluted midpalate and a short, paperish finish. • $15 • (11/15/95) • **71**
Gevrey-Chambertin 1985 • $32 • (04/30/88) • **87**
Hautes Côtes de Beaune 1992: A good, basic red Burgundy with solid cherry flavors, some smoky accents and good balance. Soft tannins and smooth texture make it drinkable now. • $11 • (10/31/94) • **83**
Mâcon-Villages 1993: A round wine with earthy, butter and fig flavors. More assertive than complex, it can stand up to grilled fish and birds. • $8 • (01/01/94) • **82**
Mercurey 1985 • $12 • (04/30/88) • **85**
Pommard 1985 • $33 • (04/30/88) • **81**
Pouilly-Fuissé 1993: Enticing aromas of smoke, toast and pears pull you into this wine, but there's not much fruit on the palate. Still, good acidity and deft use of wood give it verve and a pleasant, citrusy finish. • $13 • (01/01/95) • **83**

VIEUX-CHÂTEAU-CERTAN

Pomerol 1997: Solid '97, with violet, berry and earth aromas and flavors. Medium-bodied, with medium tannins and a slightly short finish. • $NA • (06/15/98) (BT) • **85-89**

Pomerol 1996: Delicious berry, cherry and tobacco aromas and flavors. Medium-bodied, with medium tannins and a delicious fruity finish. Almost outstanding. Wait and see. • $90 • (06/15/98) (BT) • **85-89**

Pomerol 1995: Wonderful fruit and texture. Dark-colored, and bubbling over with blackberry and raspberry character with undertones of chocolate, mint and vanilla. Full-bodied, with very velvety tannins and a long, flavorful finish. 3,800 cases made. • $80 • (01/31/98) • **95**

Pomerol 1994: Full-bodied, with a raisin and dried herb character and big tannins. A bit coarse, but with impressive concentration for the vintage, this needs time; try in 2000. • $70 • (01/31/97) • **89**

Pomerol 1993: Supple mocha, plum and red berry flavors and a slightly herbaceous character which detracts from the overall quality. Medium in body and tannins. Drinkable now. Tasted twice, with consistent notes. • $40 • (01/31/96) • **82**

Pomerol 1992: Disappointing; already at its peak. Some very soft plum and berry character. Tasted twice, with consistent notes. • $39 • (04/15/95) • **75**

Pomerol 1990: Lovely and ripe, with milk chocolate and plum flavors, soft, velvety tannins and a long, peppery finish. Still, we expected more after the strong '89. Drink now. 6,000 cases made. • $61 Ⓐ • (03/31/93) • **89**

Pomerol 1989 • $46 Ⓐ • (03/15/92) • **91**
Pomerol 1988 • $39 Ⓐ • (03/31/91) • **91**
Pomerol 1987 • $24 Ⓐ • (05/15/90) • **84**
Pomerol 1986 • $65 Ⓐ • (06/15/89) • **93**
Pomerol 1985 • $58 • (10/15/94) • **90**
Pomerol 1983 • $39 • (10/15/94) • **90**
Pomerol 1982 • $62 Ⓐ • (08/31/92) • **85**
Pomerol 1981 • $45 • (10/15/94) • **87**
Pomerol 1979 • $34 Ⓐ • (10/15/89) • **87**
Pomerol 1970 • $40 Ⓐ • (05/15/93) • **94**
Pomerol 1962 • $70 • (11/30/87) • **60**
Pomerol 1961 • $134 • (04/30/96) • **86**
Pomerol 1959 • $190 • (10/15/90) • **91**

Pomerol 1947: Supple, silky and decadent, with spicy prunelike notes that linger on the crisp finish. • $460 • (07/31/97) • **87**

Pomerol 1945 • $550 • (11/30/95) • **91**

VIEUX-CHÂTEAU-NÉGRIT

Montagne-St.-Emilion 1995: This deep-colored red shows ripeness and some concentration, but the plum and licorice flavors are dominated by earthy notes and dry tannins. Try now. 3,950 cases made. • $12 • (10/15/97) • **81**

VIEUX CHENE, DOMAINE DU

Côtes du Rhône-Villages 1995: Savage, slightly earthy, but packed with red berry, cassis bush, wild flower notes—what they might call *garrigue* in the south of France. Medium-bodied and a bit crisp, the tannins are rather ripe. Nice toasty, spicy notes on the finish. Drink now. • $NA • (10/15/97) • **85**

Côtes du Rhône-Villages White 1995: Showing maturity, with some butterscotch, spice and butterlike notes. Medium- to full-bodied, a bit rustic and heavy-handed on the finish. Drink now. 333 cases made. • $NA • (10/15/97) • **74**

Vin de Pays de Vaucluse 1990 • $7 • (01/31/92) • **77**

VIEUX DONJON, LE

Châteauneuf-du-Pape 1990: Warm, ripe and peppery-tasting, with leathery, earthy accents to the plum and currant flavors. Solid, flavorful and hearty; drink now or hold. 1,100 cases made. • $26 • (04/15/93) • **86**

Châteauneuf-du-Pape 1989 • $17 • (10/15/91) • **85**
Châteauneuf-du-Pape 1988 • $16 • (10/15/91) • **85**
Châteauneuf-du-Pape 1986 • $15 • (10/15/91) • **88**
Châteauneuf-du-Pape 1985 • $16 • (02/15/88) • **79**
Châteauneuf-du-Pape 1984 • $14 • (10/31/87) • **79**
Châteauneuf-du-Pape 1981 • $NA • (10/15/91) • **89**

VIEUX LAZARET, DOMAINE DU

Châteauneuf-du-Pape 1989 • $16 • (10/15/91) • **85**
Châteauneuf-du-Pape 1986 • $14 • (01/31/89) • **89**
Châteauneuf-du-Pape 1985 • $12 • (10/15/91) • **82**

VIEUX-ROBIN, CHÂTEAU

Médoc 1995: Steely and slightly tough, showing plenty of berry and earthy fruit nuances. Moderate tannins, but slightly coarse on the finish. • $NA • (05/15/96) (BT) • **85-89**

VIEUX ST.-SORLIN, DOMAINE DU

Mâcon-La Roche Vineuse 1995: Oak-aged Mâcon, lean and crisp, turning bitter on the finish. From Corinne and Olivier Merlin. 1,750 cases made. • $14 • (05/31/97) • **76**

VIEUX TÉLÉGRAPHE, DOMAINE DU

Châteauneuf-du-Pape 1990: Thick, chewy and full-bodied, with juniper, cedar and dried currant flavors. A muscular and focused Rhône, with an intriguing flavor profile, but too tough to warm up to at this young age. Everything is in balance, though. Drink now. 15,000 cases made. • $23 • (02/28/93) SS • **89**

Châteauneuf-du-Pape 1989 • $48 Ⓐ • (10/15/91) • **87**
Châteauneuf-du-Pape 1988 • $36 Ⓐ • (10/15/91) • **85**
Châteauneuf-du-Pape 1987 • $32 • (09/30/90) • **81**
Châteauneuf-du-Pape 1986 • $26 Ⓐ • (10/15/91) • **90**
Châteauneuf-du-Pape 1985 • $43 Ⓐ • (10/15/91) • **82**
Châteauneuf-du-Pape 1984 • $16 Ⓐ • (09/30/87) • **89**
Châteauneuf-du-Pape 1983 • $43 Ⓐ • (10/15/91) • **85**
Châteauneuf-du-Pape 1981 • $43 Ⓐ • (10/15/91) • **80**

Châteauneuf-du-Pape Vieux Mas des Papes 1993: Smells and tastes like cherries accented by herbs and spices. Full-bodied, rich, moderately tannic, and well balanced. Drink now. Second wine of Vieux Télégraphe. • $17 • (10/15/95) • **86**

Châteauneuf-du-Pape White 1996: Austere, with earthy overtones and hints of almonds and green apple. Seems lean on the finish. Needs food. 300 cases imported. • $33 • (10/15/97) • **78**

VIGNEAU-CHEVREAU

Vouvray Moelleux 1996: Cooked apple, cinnamon and herb flavors are moderately sweet and a bit dull in this soft, round white. Underlying acidity keeps it balanced. Drink now. 9,500 cases made. • $20 • (06/15/98) • **83**

Vouvray Moelleux Cuvée Château Gaillard 1996: Aromas of spice and honey carry through on the palate in this sweet, silky white. Shows concentration and balance, with peach and herb flavors that linger on the finish. Drink now through 2000. 7,500 cases made. • $25 • (06/15/98) • **86**

VIGNELAURE, CHÂTEAU

Coteaux d'Aix-en-Provence 1992: A mature, older wine with overripe fruit flavors that don't quite mesh in the end. Past its prime. • $12 • (01/01/98) • **80**

Coteaux d'Aix-en-Provence 1981 • $10 • (10/01/84) • **89**

Coteaux d'Aix-en-Provence Rosé 1996: A decent rosé with dried cherry and plum flavors. Drink well-chilled. • $9 • (09/30/97) • **79**

VIGNERONS DE BUZET, LES

Buzet Baron d'Ardeuil 1992: Showing its maturity, this red has cedar and spice notes, with cherry flavor receding into the background. Still holding up, so drink now. • $11 • (12/15/97) • **84**

Buzet Baron d'Ardeuil 1991: Still fresh and vivid, displaying cherry, blackberry, vanilla and cedar elements, all well-balanced and supported by firm tannins. Well integrated, with good length. • $11 • (12/15/97) • **87**

Buzet Baron d'Ardeuil 1990: Broad-shouldered, concentrated and wild, exhibiting a range of flavors—plum, leather, sage and a hint of oak. Try now. • $10 • (07/31/96) • **85**

Buzet Grand Réserve d'Après l'Original de César 1988: What a surprise. Shows incredibly deep color, a fabulous bouquet of roasted meat, black currant and spices, and rich, ripe fruit flavors. Showing amazing texture and balance, it remains very firm, fresh and long. Drinkable now through 2000. • $18 • (12/15/97) • **89**

Merlot Buzet Tradition 1995: This has candied aromas and dried-out cherry flavors. • $8 • (11/15/97) • **72**

Merlot Buzet Tradition 1993: Rich plum and blackberry notes are supported by a firm backbone and chewy texture. The finish suggests pairing this with food. • $7 • (07/31/96) • **82**

VIGNERONS DE MANCEY, CAVE DES

Bourgogne Cuvée Spéciale Vieille en Fûts de Chêne 1993: Rather lean-flavored, tight and tannic in texture, delivering earthy, herbal tones and an astringent finish. 3,000 cases made. • $9 • (05/15/96) • **79**

Mâcon-Villages 1995: Like lemonade—intense, fresh and quaffable. Slightly spritzy lime, green apple, and tropical flavors with a crisp, mouthpuckering finish. Drink now. • $NA • (08/31/96) • **82**

Mâcon-Villages 1994: Hard to embrace this funky, sour, tart white. Maybe it's just showing its character, but the earthy lime flavors are a bit too much. 467 cases made. • $7 • (08/31/95) • **75**

Mâcon-Villages Vieilles Vignes 1995: Crisp, even tart; has some sweet aromas and flavors, but citrus and acidity predominate. Medium-bodied. Drink now. • $NA • (08/31/96) • **76**

Mâcon-Villages Vieilles Vignes 1994: Intense but also quite sour. Lemon, lime and wet hay flavors turn grassy on the finish. 4,167 cases made. • $9 • (08/31/95) • **76**

VIGNERONS DE ST.-FÉLIX DE LODEZ

Coteaux du Languedoc La Cardabelle de St.-Felix 1995: A delicious, quaffable red, with dried cherry and cedar flavors and some white pepper notes as well. The flavors linger appealingly on the finish. Drink now. 3,000 cases made. • $NA • (05/31/98) • **85**

VIGNERONS DE ST.-GERVAIS

Syrah Côtes du Rhône-Villages 1996: With a little sulfur on the nose, it's perhaps suffering from bottling, yet the color is deep and there are black cherry, wild berry and mocha flavors allied to a firm structure and suave texture. Good grip on the finish. Needs time to integrate. Best from 1999 through 2005. 1,100 cases made. • $10 • (05/15/98) • **88**

VIGNERONS DE SAUMUR, CAVE DES

Saumur Red Cuvée Tradition 1996: This solid red mingles black cherry and game notes in a firmly tannic structure that is balanced and fresh. A juicy chewiness brings you back for another sip. Drink now through 2001. 10,000 cases made. • $7 • (05/31/98) • **86**

Saumur Red Cuvée Tradition 1995: The cherry, berry and spice flavors are bright and juicy but the tannins are soft—the combination makes for an attractive wine that's ready to drink. 10,000 cases made. • $7 • (06/15/97) • **84**

Saumur White Cuvée Tradition 1996: This straightforward white is a bit dull and rustic, with cooked flavors and a lean core of acidity. Drink now. 10,000 cases made. • $6 • (05/31/98) • **76**

Saumur White Cuvée Tradition 1995: This solid white has a good balance of acidity and roundness, with muted yet appealing melon and light peach flavors. Modest, but clean and focused. 10,000 cases made. • $6 • (06/15/97) • **84**

Saumur-Champigny Cuvée Tradition 1996: Black cherry, black pepper and leaf flavors run through this light but chewy red. It has moderate tannins, bright acidity and a clean finish. Drink now through 2000. 10,000 cases made. • $9 • (05/31/98) • **85**

Saumur-Champigny Cuvée Tradition 1995: A round, soft red with plum, chocolate and light herb flavors and modest tannins that show some grip on the finish. Ready to drink. 10,000 cases made. • $9 • (06/15/97) • **84**

Key: SS—Spectator Selection CS—Cellar Selection HR—Highly Recommended BB—Best Buy $NA—Price not available Ⓐ—Auction Price (BT)—Barrel Tasting
Dates in parentheses indicate the issues in which the ratings were published.

VIGNERONS DES COTEAUX DE ST.-JEAN, LES

Coteaux du Languedoc 1992 • $7 • (03/15/94) • **83**

Vin de Pays de l'Herault Cuvée des Capitelles NV • $6 • (03/15/94) • **84**

VIGNERONS D'IGE, LES

Mâcon-Igé 1995: Fresh, fruity and firm, with a lively, crisp finish. A complexity of floral, orange-peel, green apple and grassy notes. Drinkable now. • $NA • (08/31/96) • **84**

Mâcon-Igé 1994: Lovely Chardonnay. Medium in body and intensity, showing mineral, green apple and pear character. Balanced and delicious; smooth finish. • $NA • (08/31/95) • **84**

Mâcon-Igé Château London 1995: Interesting combination of floral, perfume, wax, mango and anise flavors. Medium-bodied, with some fruity intensity on the slightly tart finish. Drink now. • $NA • (08/31/96) • **77**

Mâcon-Igé Château London 1994: A rather neutral white, disclosing only bits of pear, apple and mineral character. Clean, light, short finish. Somewhat diluted. • $10 • (08/31/95) • **77**

Mâcon-Igé Château London 1993: Some decent ripe fruit blends nicely with a grassy, wet hay, bitter almond and citrus character. • $10 • (08/31/95) • **78**

St.-Véran 1996: Quite tart and green, with herbal, apple and citrus flavors. A tight, light- to medium-bodied wine with a steely finish. Drink now through 1999. 3,665 cases made. • $11 • (05/31/98) • **81**

St.-Véran 1995: Light-bodied and slightly bitter, with some modest fruit and honey flavors. Tart finish. • $NA • (08/31/96) • **77**

St.-Véran 1994: Flat and dull—no fruit. Bad from start to finish, showing a cardboard box character. Tasted twice, with consistent notes. • $NA • (08/31/95) • **62**

VIGNOBLES BARDE

Cabernet Sauvignon Bergerac Cuvée Angeline 1995: Well made and expressive. This shows hints of black currant, black cherry and vanilla flavors, and is focused and vibrant. Try now. 4,000 cases made. • $9 • (12/15/96) • **84**

Merlot Bergerac Cuvée Angeline 1995: A ripe style, with plum and cherry flavors and a distinctive mineral note that lingers on the finish. 6,000 cases made. • $9 • (12/15/96) • **80**

VIGOUROUX, GEORGES

Cahors Gouleyant 1996: Pleasant, fruity and well-defined, its berry and cherry flavors balanced by leather notes. A straightforward, well-rounded wine. Drink now through 1999. • $8 • (05/15/98) • **83**

VILLA BEL-AIR

Graves 1995: Rather weak effort for the vintage. Berry, herbal and earth aromas follow through to a medium-bodied palate with soft tannins and a medium finish. Drink now. • $12 • (01/31/98) • **79**

Graves 1994: Very light. Some strawberry flavors, but with a rather weedy, herbal accent. Drink now. • $12 • (01/31/97) • **75**

Graves 1993: Light, simple black olive and fruit character, medium body and slightly metallic tannins. Drinkable now. • $NA • (01/31/96) • **78**

Graves 1992: Very, very herbal, showing hard tannins and a slightly metallic character. • $NA • (04/15/95) • **70**

Graves White 1995: Better than expected. Rather chalky, with apple and dried apricot aromas. Full-bodied, with good acidity and a medium aftertaste. Drink now. • $12 • (04/30/98) • **84**

Graves White 1994 • $14 • (03/31/96) • **84**

Graves White 1993 • $NA • (05/31/95) • **84**

VILLAINE, A. & P. DE

Bouzeron La Digoine Red 1990: Stylish, forward and spicy, with generous blackberry, raspberry and currant flavors folded together with a nice touch of oak. Lean in texture, focused in flavor and drinkable now. A good value for '90 Burgundy. 2,000 cases made. • $16 • (11/30/92) • **87**

Bouzeron La Digoine Red 1989 • $17 • (11/15/91) • **84**

VILLAMONT, HENRI DE

Bourgogne 1989 • $11 • (03/31/91) • **78**

Chambolle-Musigny 1988 • $39 • (02/15/91) • **83**

Mâcon-Pierreclos 1996: Oaky style, showing honey, vanilla, butterscotch, caramel and spice. Lemony finish. Medium-bodied, with biting acidity. Drink now through 1999. 1,300 cases made. • $10 • (05/31/98) • **81**

Mâcon-Villages 1996: Green, herbal character mingles with apple and smoky notes in this lean but juicy Mâcon. Light- to medium-bodied. Drink now. 83,000 cases made. • $10 • (05/31/98) • **79**

Mâcon-Villages 1994: More water than wine in this disappointing, diluted white. Offers only modest fruit. • $NA • (08/31/95) • **70**

Pouilly-Fuissé 1996: Only modest fruit makes the scene. Light- to medium-bodied, it tastes a bit diluted, with a paper, cardboardlike character. 2,000 cases made. • $17 • (05/31/98) • **74**

Pouilly-Fuissé Domaine Carette 1996: Very perfumed. Medium-bodied, with lime, honey, floral, rose petal, violet notes. Fresh and lemony, it challenges the taste buds with bracing acidity. Drink now through 1999. 3,300 cases made. • $17 • (05/31/98) • **80**

St.-Véran 1996: Both samples provided were corky. 5,000 cases made. • $13 • (05/31/98) • **55**

St.-Véran Clos de l'Ermitage 1994: Good intensity, with vibrant citrus and green apple character, but it ends on a slightly sour note. • $NA • (08/31/95) • **79**

Savigny-lès-Beaune Le Village 1988 • $18 • (03/31/91) • **80**

VILLARD, FRANÇOIS

Condrieu Côteaux de Poncins 1995: Rich and smooth, it has the weight of a late-harvest wine yet it's dry and lively, with apricot, floral, coconut and spicy flavors. Marries concentration and balance in a firm, polished wine that should age well. 333 cases made. • $40 • (10/15/97) • **94**

Condrieu Les Terrasses du Palat 1995: Ripe fruit plus oak equals richness and roundness. This deep-colored, concentrated white offers marmalade, butter and spicy flavors, with just enough acidity for balance. A big wine with power and a distinctive character. 292 cases made. • $40 • (10/15/97) • **91**

Condrieu Quintessence 1996: Rich and thick, with honey, fig, tropical, orange-peel and vanilla flavors. Good intensity, and quite sweet, with an underpinning of citrus character. Drink now through 2000. 92 cases made. • $60 • (10/15/97) • **90**

Côte-Rôtie La Brocarde 1995: Exquisite. Generous with fruit and oak, offering well-knit flavors of cassis, blackberry and chocolate, finishing with appealing gamy notes. Round, dense yet supple, it's approachable now, but will be better around 1999. • $35 • (10/15/97) • **92**

St.-Joseph Côtes de Mairlant 1995: Toasty oak aromas leap from the glass, and draw you into this voluptuous red. The blackberry flavors are ripe and quite concentrated, and the tannins are well integrated. It's fresh and firm; try in 1999. 333 cases made. • $16 • (10/15/97) • **89**

St.-Joseph Reflet 1995: Ripe blackberry flavor shines through this generous red, both boosted and dominated by the sweet vanilla notes of heavily toasty oak. It's lush, round, and attractive in the international style. Drinkable now. 125 cases made. • $30 • (10/15/97) • **88**

VILLARS, CHÂTEAU

Fronsac 1997: Straightforward grapey, earthy aromas. Medium- to light-bodied, with fine tannins and a chocolate, berry aftertaste. • $NA • (06/15/98) (BT) • **80-84**

Fronsac 1996: Light and fruity, with some tobacco and berry character, light tannins and a light finish. Drink upon release. • $23 • (06/15/98) (BT) • **80-84**

Fronsac 1995: Silky, with chocolate, cassis bush character. Full body, full semi-soft tannins. A bit simple. • $NA • (01/01/97) (BT) • **85-89**

Fronsac 1990: A very aromatic wine, with a gamy, earthy, cherry character, medium tannins and short finish. Drinkable now. 11,000 cases made. • $17 • (03/31/93) • **83**

Fronsac 1989 • $16 • (06/15/93) • **78**

VILLEGEORGE, CHÂTEAU

Haut-Médoc 1993: Light and rather pleasant, but lacks concentration and tastes a bit diluted on the finish. Drink. • $NA • (01/31/96) • **79**

Haut-Médoc 1991: Lovely vanilla and fruit aromas and flavors, medium body and a silky finish. • $13 • (03/31/94) • **81**

Haut-Médoc 1989 • $14 • (03/15/92) • **79**

Haut-Médoc 1982 • $18 • (08/31/92) • **84**

VILLEMAURINE, CHÂTEAU

St.-Emilion 1997: Clean and fresh but very light, with cherry, berry character and a refreshing finish. • $NA • (06/15/98) (BT) • **80-84**

St.-Emilion 1996: A medium-bodied wine with lots of nice new wood and medium, silky tannins, but a bit lacking in fruit on the light, vanilla finish. Medium-bodied. 4,160 cases made. • $22 • (06/15/98) (BT) • **80-84**

St.-Emilion 1995: Simple, with some berry, tobacco and tomato aromas and flavors. Medium-bodied, with medium tannins and finish. Drink now or hold. Tasted twice, with consistent notes. • $20 • (01/31/98) • **82**

St.-Emilion 1994: A light wine—light-bodied and with light tannins—but offers some nice berry and strawberry nuances. Fresh finish. Drink now. 4,075 cases made. • $18 • (01/31/97) • **79**

St.-Emilion 1993: Bright, vibrant red berry character, light body and a fresh finish. More like a Loire red. • $16 • (01/31/96) • **79**

St.-Emilion 1992: Firm and lightly fruity showing toasty oak and cherry character, light-to-medium body, light tannins and a slightly diluted finish. • $13 • (04/15/95) • **79**

St.-Emilion 1991: Another delicate wine with plum and cherry flavors and a light finish. • $13 • (03/31/94) • **77**

St.-Emilion 1990: Understated but grand. A wine with floral, perfumed fruit aromas and flavors, lots of new oak character and fine, silky tannins. Drinkable now. 3,800 cases made. • $28 • (03/31/93) • **92**

St.-Emilion 1989 • $30 • (03/15/92) • **93**

St.-Emilion 1982 • $40 • (08/31/92) • **93**

VILLENEUVE, ARNAUD DE

Côtes du Roussillon-Villages 1991 • $9 • (03/15/94) • **85**

VILLERAMBERT, CHÂTEAU JULIEN

Minervois Cuvée Trianon 1989 • $15 • (12/15/91) • **73**

VILLOTTE, CHÂTEAU

Bordeaux 1993: Lean and supple, with light cherry flavors and a hint of chocolate. • $8 • (12/15/95) • **79**

Bordeaux White 1994 • $8 • (02/29/96) • **79**

VILMART

Brut Blanc de Blancs Champagne NV: Soft in texture and light in flavor, this creamy Champagne shows hints of citrus and vanilla. • $63 • (12/31/97) • **84**

Brut Champagne Coeur de Cuvée 1991: A light Champagne with lively citrus flavors, a smooth, mouthfilling texture and a tangy finish. Drink now through 1999. • $66 • (11/30/97) • **86**

Brut Champagne Cuvée du Nouveau Monde NV: This fruit-driven bubbly has a lot of table-wine character in its pear and butter flavors, and should be great with a meal. It's smooth, ripe-tasting and long on the finish. • $63 • (11/30/97) • **89**

Brut Champagne Grand Cellier NV: An openly fruity character makes this rather light, soft brut appealing if not complex. Short on the finish. • $63 • (12/31/97) • **81**

VIN DU SOLEIL

Merlot Vin de Pays d'Oc 1995: Nicely rich, with good plum and blackberry flavors and earthy aromas. A little tough on the finish. 5,000 cases made. • $8 • (04/30/97) • **79**

VINCENT & FILS, J.J.

Mâcon-Villages Domaine de Champ Brûlé 1996: Lean and a bit diluted, lacking fruit, it tastes of cardboard. Tart finish. 830 cases made. • $12 • (05/31/98) • **74**

Mâcon-Villages Pièce d'Or 1992: A good, ripe-tasting Mâcon with ample fruit flavors, smooth texture and plenty of body. It has good concentration and texture, but not much finesse. • $7 • (01/01/94) • **82**

Pouilly-Fuissé 1996: Like biting into a green apple. Clean and pure, but tough-as-nails, this medium-bodied, lean Pouilly stresses its citrus notes over all else, at least for now. If you dig, you unearth some mineral complexity. Better after 1999. 8,300 cases made. • $16 • (05/31/98) • **84**

Pouilly-Fuissé 1995: Plenty of flavor in this one with lemon, honey and pear overtones. Has good focus and concentration; little gets in the way of the fruit flavors. A mineral note lingers on the finish. • $15 • (01/31/97) • **84**

Pouilly-Fuissé 1993: Delicate and crisp, light-to-medium-bodied, offering clean green apple, grapefruit and butter flavors. Drink now. From the producer of Château Fuissé. 1,667 cases made. • $12 • (05/15/95) • **84**

Pouilly-Fuissé 1992: Intensely varietal with apple and fig flavors; this is a straightforward and obvious Chardonnay. It has a slight sweetness that gives it smoothness and a finish that comes on heavy with spice and butter. Flavorful, but not complex. Tasted twice with consistent notes. • $18 • (01/01/95) • **84**

Pouilly-Fuissé Château Fuissé 1993: A bit astringent and herbal but showing vibrant, well-defined Granny Smith apple and pear flavors. Drinkable now. 6,667 cases made. • $24 • (05/15/95) • **85**

Pouilly-Fuissé Château Fuissé 1992: Ripe and lively, with floral, buttery, orangelike flavors and a creamy texture. Stays interesting and satisfying on the finish. • $37 • (11/15/94) • **86**

Pouilly-Fuissé Château Fuissé Le Clos 1993: Polished and smooth, a creamy, medium-bodied white that delivers lightly toasty, honeyed, mineral, pear and grapefruit notes and a pretty, chalky finish. Drinkable now. 500 cases made. • $30 • (05/15/95) • **88**

Pouilly-Fuissé Château Fuissé Les Brûlés 1993: A lovely Pouilly, offering smooth texture and succulent, fruity, floral notes. It butters your mouth with mineral flavors and a long, solid finish. Drinkable now. 250 cases made. • $30 • (05/15/95) • **90**

Pouilly-Fuissé Château Fuissé Les Combettes 1993: Classy, rich and well balanced; supple, packing good concentration of fruit. The mineral, pear, honey, floral and light toast flavors are exquisite; subtle finish. Drinkable now. 250 cases made. • $30 • (05/15/95) • **90**

Pouilly-Fuissé Château Fuissé Vieilles Vignes 1993: Remarkably velvety, mineral character that you must taste to believe. Subtle, medium-bodied, fruity and firm, sporting toast, honey, pear and grapefruit flavors and a harmonious finish. Drinkable now. 1,667 cases made. • $35 • (05/15/95) • **90**

Pouilly-Fuissé Château Fuissé Vieilles Vignes 1992: Vividly fruity, lively and refreshing. It reminds us of grapefruit, pineapple and banana, rounded out by a creamy, lingering finish. Drinkable now. • $50 • (11/15/94) • **86**

St.-Véran 1992: A fairly full-bodied, smooth-textured wine marked by attractive vanilla and butter aromas that melt into the modest fruit flavors and linger on the finish. Good value, too. • $9 • (01/01/94) • **85**

St.-Véran Domaine des Morats 1996: Very woody, with pine, new oak, and vanilla flavors. Unbalanced. From Château Fuissé. 830 cases made. • $17 • (05/31/98) • **75**

VINET, GÉRARD

Muscadet de Sèvre et Maine Sur Lie Domaine de la Quilla 1995: This zippy white offers fresh lime and herbal flavors, but a soapy note on the palate detracts. 5,000 cases made. • $8 • (06/15/97) • **76**

VINIVAL

Rosé d'Anjou Vitrine du Monde 1997: This soft, lush rosé offers vibrant cherry and strawberry flavors in a round, off-dry style. A refreshing summertime quaff; drink very cold. Drink now. 1,200 cases made. • $6 • (07/31/98) • **83**

VINS DE ROQUEBRUN, CAVE LES

Cuvée Roches Noires Macération St.-Chinian 1991 • $9 • (03/15/94) • **85**

Prestige St.-Chinian 1991 • $8 • (03/15/94) • **80**

Key: SS—Spectator Selection CS—Cellar Selection HR—Highly Recommended BB—Best Buy $NA—Price not available Ⓐ—Auction Price (BT)—Barrel Tasting

Dates in parentheses indicate the issues in which the ratings were published.

Tradition St.-Chinian 1991 • $7 • (03/15/94) • **82**

VIOLET, CHÂTEAU

Sauternes 1987: • $NA • (06/15/90) • **79**

VIOLETTE, CHÂTEAU LA

Pomerol 1995: A bit tough, but there are some decent berry flavors and an earthy character to keep it interesting. Medium-to-light body, sleek tannins and a short finish. • $NA • (05/15/96) (BT) • **80-84**

Pomerol 1982 • $25 • (05/15/89) • **88**

Pomerol 1979 • $35 • (10/15/89) • **79**

VIORNERY, GEORGES

Brouilly 1995: Shows pretty black cherry and spice aromas and soft, ripe flavors of cherries and chocolate, with modest tannins emerging on the finish. Not a heavyweight, but has the grip for food. • $13 • (06/30/97) • **84**

Côte de Brouilly 1996: Smoky, meaty aromas add character to this muscularly structured red, with meaty, plum flavors and good balance. Though slightly rustic, it shows good concentration and typical flavors. Drink now through 2000. • $15 • (06/15/98) • **87**

VIRÉ, CAVE DE

Mâcon-Viré 1995: Smelled a bit fishy, tasted a bit salty and had a sour, cardboard character to the finish. • $NA • (08/31/96) • **73**

Mâcon-Viré 1994: Exotic and ripe, with some body and weight to it, with a grass, honey, pear and floral character. Extremely well-made and a pleasure to drink now. • $NA • (08/31/95) • **84**

Mâcon-Viré Cuvée Spéciale 1994: Wild Mâcon that's distinctively, intensely grassy, featuring gooseberry, raspberry and rose petal notes. Medium-bodied and rather ripe, spice and nutmeg on the finish adding complexity. Drink now. • $NA • (08/31/95) • **85**

Mâcon-Viré Fûts de Chêne Neufs 1992: Silky-textured, medium in body, a maturing wine with an impressively round and rich mouthfeel. An earthy component distracts from honey, hazelnut and butterscotch flavors. • $NA • (08/31/95) • **82**

Mâcon-Viré Grande Réserve 1994: Grassy, like a pure Sauvignon Blanc. Has mineral, herb and wet hay notes, but also good intensity of green apple and pear flavors. • $NA • (08/31/95) • **84**

Mâcon-Viré Les Charlottes 1995: Lively tropical fruit aromas don't follow through—the palate is round but simple, with light apple and herb flavors; clean and short. • $11 • (06/30/97) • **79**

VIRELY-ROUGEOT

Pommard 1992: An odd salty flavor and an astringent texture makes this difficult to like. 1,000 cases made. • $25 • (06/15/95) • **73**

VIRGINIE DE VALANDRAUD

St.-Emilion 1994: Fresh and fruity, with strawberry and toasty oak flavors, light tannins and a refreshing finish. Drink now or hold. • $NA • (01/31/97) • **82**

VISSOUX, DOMAINE DU

Beaujolais Cuvée Traditionnêlle 1995: A gentle red, with cherry and cinnamon flavors; supple and almost sweet. It's simple but drinks smoothly. • $13 • (09/15/97) • **83**

Beaujolais Cuvée Traditionnêlle Non Filtrée 1994: The black cherry flavors are complemented by a slightly bitter, smoky note in this light wine. It's still fresh; drink lightly chilled. • $NA • (09/15/96) • **83**

VITALLIS, CHÂTEAU

Pouilly-Fuissé 1996: Very buttery and supple, an oak-aged, ripe-tasting Pouilly that delivers caramel, spice, pear tart and butterscotch flavors. Medium-bodied, it's pleasant to drink now, with a chalky note for added complexity on the balanced finish. 415 cases made. • $15 • (05/31/98) • **85**

Pouilly-Fuissé Vieilles Vignes 1993: A bit too tart, offering substantial citrusy flavors, but it has a vibrant, juicy character. Lean and hard; steely finish lends itself to seafood. Drinkable now. 2,333 cases made. • $25 • (05/15/95) • **82**

VIVIER, CHÂTEAU LE

Médoc 1997: Some berry and cranberry character, with medium body and a light finish. Rather watery. • $NA • (06/15/98) (BT) • **75-79**

Médoc 1996: A bit diluted, with an herbal, slightly weedy character along with the red fruits. Medium-bodied, with medium tannins. Slightly diluted finish. Tasted twice, with consistent notes. • $16 • (06/15/98) (BT) • **80-84**

Médoc 1995: A winery new to me, and very good. Bubbling with blackberries and cherries, with a hint of herbs. Full-bodied and velvety, with lots of fruit character and a flavorful finish. Slightly hard. Best after 2000. • $15 • (01/31/98) • **87**

VIVIERS, CHÂTEAU DE

Chablis 1996: Serious village Chablis, holding your attention with all its parts in suspended animation. Fruit and what seem like oak accents play a deftly balanced duet, offering full body, smooth texture, ripe flavors and some mineral complexity. Reserved and classy from start to finish. Try around 2005. 8,750 cases made. • $18 • (05/31/98) • **92**

Chablis 1995: A bit simple and flat, but the thick, rich, lemony vanilla, caramel and cream flavors fill the palate. Drink now. From négociant Lupé-Cholet. • $NA • (08/31/96) • **80**

Chablis Blanchots 1996: Ripe but not over-ripe, rich but also elegant, flavorful with terrific pear, orange, mineral-laden and earth flavors. Full-bodied and very distinctive, with a rather elegant finish. Not as much *terroir* as some. Tempting now, better after 2000. 280 cases made. • $44 • (05/31/98) • **93**

Chablis Blanchots 1994 • $NA • (05/31/96) • **80**

Chablis Vaillons 1996: Subtle, chiseled like a stone and, indeed, the stony, minerally character comes through beautifully in this full-bodied, harmonious wine. Full of vanilla, pear, tropical and, again, mineral notes. Tempting now through 2010. 350 cases made. • $26 • (05/31/98) • **93**

Chablis Vaillons 1994 • $NA • (05/31/96) • **86**

Chablis Vaucopins 1996: Clean and pure, with lovely, sweet- and ripe-tasting fruit backed by honey, wet earth and mineral notes. With its lush and opulent texture, this is a crowd-pleaser. The seduction continues on the velvet-feeling finish with its lemony flavor. Try around 2005. 1,080 cases made. • $25 • (05/31/98) • **92**

Chablis Vaucopins 1994 • $NA • (05/31/96) • **84**

VOARICK, EMILE

Mercurey Clos de Paradis 1994: Light and straightforward, with some good earthy red berry character and supple tannins that make it a decent quaff. • $NA • (11/15/96) • **77**

Mercurey Clos du Roi 1994: Light and supple, with a brown-sugarlike character that doesn't linger. Short finish. • $NA • (11/15/96) • **72**

VOARICK, MICHEL

Aloxe-Corton 1993: Traditional; quite intense and full-bodied, featuring currant, spice and raisiny character. Some tough tannins will need until 2000 to come around. A bit overdone for us. • $30 • (01/01/95) • **82**

Aloxe-Corton 1990: Is juicy all right, but the light texture reminds us more of a Beaujolais. A rather approachable wine, with pretty cherry flavors. Drinkable now. • $26 • (12/15/92) • **79**

Corton Le Clos du Roi 1994: Firm in texture, with a solid core of licorice-scented blackberry flavors trying to poke through the gritty tannins, finishing with less than it starts with. May improve from 1999 to 2001. • $NA • (11/15/96) • **81**

Corton Le Clos du Roi 1993: Port-like masses of raisin, berry and tar, full body and tannins and a slightly alcoholic finish. Overdone? Better in 2000. • $60 • (11/15/95) • **85**

Corton Le Clos du Roi 1990: Quite disappointing. Tastes like cherry juice and lacks concentration and complexity, but does show pleasant sweetness and modest smokiness. Drinkable now. • $36 • (12/15/92) • **75**

Corton Les Bressandes 1990: Extremely traditional in style. Medium-bodied, with rather high acidity and a diluted finish. Not worth the price, but it's drinkable now. • $36 • (12/15/92) • **73**

Corton Les Languettes 1994: Smells of nail polish and tastes thin and hard. • $NA • (11/15/96) • **70**

Corton Les Renardes 1993: Loads of raisin, dried fruit and spice character. Could use a bit more finesse. Full in body, medium tannins and short finish. Needs time to open; try in 2000. • $60 • (11/15/95) • **86**

Pernand-Vergelesses 1993: Extremely ripe dried cherry, pepper and black cherry character verges on being raisiny. Full-bodied and slightly overdone, it could use more finesse. Drink now. • $20 • (11/15/95) • **85**

Romanée St.-Vivant 1990: An odd wine, with cherry, strawberry and earth aromas and flavors, but is a bit sour on the finish. Has good fruit, but lacks balance. The off-side of this wine is more obvious as it stays in the glass. Not recommended. • $76 • (12/15/92) • **69**

VOCORET & FILS

Chablis 1995: Bravo! Firm structure, medium body and a zesty lemon-honey flavor that makes sparks fly on the palate. Oily texture, yet crisp finish. Drink now. • $NA • (08/31/96) • **87**

Chablis 1994 • $14 • (05/31/96) • **78**

Chablis Blanchot 1995: Beautiful, rich and ripe *grand cru*, chewy and showing plenty of classic mineral character, along with honey, ripe pear, lemon and kiwi notes. Racy finish, with a nuance of toasty oak. Get a case, but don't drink any until after 2000. 1,000 cases made. • $40 • (06/15/97) • **90**

Chablis Blanchots 1994 • $42 • (05/31/96) • **92**

Chablis La Forêt 1994 • $19 • (05/31/96) • **84**

Chablis Les Clos 1994 • $NA • (05/31/96) • **83**

Chablis Montée de Tonnerre 1995: Lovely Chablis, very crisp. Medium-bodied, its flavors are well-defined, pure and subtle, with earth and truffle marrying honey and ripe fruit. Chewy, minerally, and slightly tart on the finish; try after 1999. 833 cases made. • $22 • (06/15/97) • **87**

Chablis Montée de Tonnerre 1994 • $20 • (05/31/96) • **84**

Chablis Vaillons 1994 • $20 • (05/31/96) • **86**

VOGE, ALAIN

Cornas 1991 • $25 • (05/31/94) • **86**

Cornas Cuvée Barriques 1990 • $25 • (04/15/93) • **87**

Cornas Cuvée Vieilles Vignes 1993: Quite accessible now, this balanced, fruity wine shows real elegance for a Cornas. Flavors of blackberry and cherry and a hint of smoke on the long, fruity finish. 100 cases made. • $34 • (10/15/96) • **86**

Cornas Cuvée Vieilles Vignes 1992: Polished and still fresh, this offers blackberry and sweet vanilla flavors over firm but unobtrusive tannins. Not powerful, but pleasurable. Drink now. 100 cases made. • $34 • (10/15/96) • **86**

Cornas Vieilles Vignes 1991 • $27 • (05/31/94) • **86**

Cornas Cuvée Vieilles Vignes 1990 • $27 • (05/31/94) • **83**

Cornas Cuvée Vielles Vignes 1989 • $32 • (04/15/93) • **83**

VOGÜÉ, COMTE GEORGES DE

Bonnes Mares 1995: Silky, beautiful and full-bodied, this is a rich and racy red Burgundy packed with intense blackberry, cassis and wet earth character that cascades to a very long, succulent finish. More fat and flesh in this wine than in most '95s. Try after 2002, once the firm tannins settle down. 500 cases made. • $175 • (11/15/97) • **91**

Bonnes Mares 1994: Light and supple, with more flavor than aroma, centering around notes of cherry, anise and coffee. Tannins remain crisp, requiring at least until 2000 to 2001. • $75 • (11/15/96) • **82**

Bonnes Mares 1993: A beauty, boasting clean, pure, subtle currant, black cherry and mint flavors. Elegant structure of silky tannins. Tight and closed in, it's not giving much now; try in 2000. 466 cases made. • $115 • (11/15/95) • **94**

Bonnes Mares 1992: Supple and generous, with gorgeous raspberry, currant and vanilla flavors, fine-textured tannins and a juicy finish. A stylish wine that is nice now. 583 cases made. • $85 • (12/15/94) • **88**

Bonnes Mares 1991: Deep in color and flavor, a wine that shows both power and elegance, muscular up front and more delicate on the finish. Flavors run toward ripe currant, chestnut and black cherry, echoing cherry on the finish, framed with fine tannins. Try now. 250 cases made. • $90 Ⓐ • (01/31/94) • **93**

Bonnes Mares 1990: A classy, monumental wine, with an impressive deep color and spellbinding complexity. The concentration takes your breath

FRANCE

away as the plum, blackberry, raspberry and vanilla flavors coat your palate. Try now. 500 cases made. • $110 Ⓐ • (12/15/92) • **99**

Bonnes Mares 1989 • $93 • (01/31/92) • **94**
Bonnes Mares 1988 • $65 Ⓐ • (03/31/91) • **89**
Bonnes Mares 1987 • $73 • (07/15/90) • **87**
Bonnes Mares 1979 • $48 • (11/16/84) • **88**
Bonnes Mares 1976 • $56 Ⓐ • (11/16/84) • **90**
Bonnes Mares 1972 • $125 • (11/16/84) • **79**
Bonnes Mares 1971 • $91 Ⓐ • (11/16/84) • **88**
Bonnes Mares 1959 • $179 • (11/16/84) • **83**
Bonnes Mares 1955 • $285 • (11/16/84) • **91**
Bonnes Mares 1949 • $500 • (11/16/84) • **90**
Bonnes Mares Avery Bottling 1959 • $NA • (11/16/84) • **87**
Bonnes Mares Grivolet 1934 • $NA • (11/16/84) • **82**

Chambolle-Musigny 1995: Solid for the appellation, this has smoky, underbrush notes to the blackberry flavors. Dusty tannins; moderate finish. Try in 1999. 750 cases made. • $75 • (11/15/97) • **85**

Chambolle-Musigny 1994: Supple and attractive, it's gentle and well-made with pretty currant, cherry, vanilla and milk chocolate flavors. Smooth, fine tannins. Light- to medium-bodied. Delicate finish. Ready to drink. • $50 • (11/15/96) • **82**

Chambolle-Musigny 1993: Sleek, fine, focused plum and fruit character, medium body and tannins and a crisp, lively finish. Better in 2000. 833 cases made. • $60 • (11/15/95) • **88**

Chambolle-Musigny 1992: Firm, chewy, and trying hard to show currant and spice flavors behind it all, but it comes up a little short. Drinkable now. 917 cases made. • $45 • (12/15/94) • **83**

Chambolle-Musigny 1991: Light and fragrant, a silky mouthful of lovely currant, blackberry and earthy flavors, which persist nicely on the finish. Drinkable now. 250 cases made. • $47 Ⓐ • (01/31/94) • **88**

Chambolle-Musigny 1990: Impressively structured, showing a lot of concentration, with masses of wood, plum, cherry and berry flavors. A serious Chambolle village wine. Try now. 917 cases made. • $45 • (12/15/92) • **90**

Chambolle-Musigny 1989 • $44 • (01/31/92) • **89**

Chambolle-Musigny Les Amoureuses 1995: A crowd-pleasing, classic Chambolle that dances on your palate like a ballerina, swooning with perfumed rose petal and violet, deep red- and blackberry flavors, and a touch of earthy, horsey character on the finish. The silky texture coats the palate like cream, and the finish is seamless. Full-bodied; tempting now through 2005. 200 cases made. • $175 • (11/15/97) • **94**

Chambolle-Musigny Les Amoureuses 1994: Crisp in texture, with delicate threads of blackberry, blueberry and a touch of anise flavor weaving through the slightly drying tannins. Drinkable now. • $75 • (11/15/96) • **85**

Chambolle-Musigny Les Amoureuses 1993: A blockbuster, dark in color, delivering beautiful cranberry, vanilla and plum aromas, full body and masses of fruit and tannins. Try after 2000. 200 cases made. • $125 • (11/15/95) • **94**

Chambolle-Musigny Les Amoureuses 1992: Light and fragrant, showing some ripe raspberry and currant flavors on the delicate framework. Finishes with a touch of tannin. Drinkable now. 250 cases made. • $85 • (12/15/94) • **83**

Chambolle-Musigny Les Amoureuses 1991: Has beautifully defined currant and berry aromas and flavors that carry straight through the finish. A soft-textured wine that has some fine tannins; drinkable now. 100 cases made. • $90 Ⓐ • (01/31/94) • **87**

Chambolle-Musigny Les Amoureuses 1990 • $66 • (12/15/92) • **94**
Chambolle-Musigny Les Amoureuses 1989 • $93 • (01/31/92) • **93**
Chambolle-Musigny Les Amoureuses 1988 • $93 • (02/28/91) • **89**
Chambolle-Musigny Les Amoureuses 1987 • $74 • (03/31/90) • **87**
Chambolle-Musigny Les Amoureuses 1971 • $85 • (11/16/84) • **86**
Chambolle-Musigny Les Amoureuses 1970 • $55 • (11/16/84) • **78**

Chambolle-Musigny Premier Cru 1995: This rather full, fleshy wine shows lovely, sappy cherry flavors augmented by spicy oak notes. Direct and satisfying, it's approachable now, but will be better in 1999. 666 cases made. • $100 • (11/15/97) • **88**

Musigny 1953 • $200 • (11/16/84) • **81**
Musigny 1952 • $200 • (11/16/84) • **85**
Musigny 1949 • $600 • (11/16/84) • **98**
Musigny 1945 • $2856 • (11/16/84) • **96**

Key: SS—Spectator Selection CS—Cellar Selection HR—Highly Recommended BB—Best Buy $NA—Price not available Ⓐ—Auction Price (BT)—Barrel Tasting
Dates in parentheses indicate the issues in which the ratings were published.

Musigny 1937 • $650 • (11/16/84) • **93**
Musigny 1934 • $600 • (11/16/84) • **95**

Musigny Cuvée Vieilles Vignes 1994: Crisp in texture, with spicy, floral and berry flavors that seem to grow, right into the mildly chewy finish. A delicious wine that needs until 1999 to 2001 to flesh out. • $120 • (11/15/96) • **88**

Musigny Cuvée Vieilles Vignes 1993: A tough-as-nails, assertive *grand cru* Burgundy. Full body and ripe fruit with loads of tannins that need time to open. Try in 2006. 1,000 cases made. • $140 • (11/15/95) CS • **96**

Musigny Cuvée Vieilles Vignes 1992: Tough and narrow, bright and floral, showing a nice thread of tart berry and spice character; finishes with tight, chalky tannins that will need until 1998 to 2000 to soften. 1,167 cases made. • $100 • (12/15/94) • **85**

Musigny Cuvée Vieilles Vignes 1991: Ripe and generous, shaded with nicely integrated, spicy oak, this great wine reveals many extra dimensions and oozes with anise, currant and blackberry flavors that go on and on, seemingly forever. • $116 • (02/28/95) • **96**

Musigny Cuvée Vieilles Vignes 1990: A monument. Brilliant, deep and stylish, delivering supple and intense currant, spice, vanilla and violet flavors. Firm finish. Drinkable now or hold until 2000. • $135 • (02/28/95) • **99**

Musigny Cuvée Vieilles Vignes 1989 • $134 • (02/28/95) • **93**
Musigny Cuvée Vieilles Vignes 1988 • $108 • (02/28/95) • **90**
Musigny Cuvée Vieilles Vignes 1987 • $105 • (02/28/95) • **87**
Musigny Cuvée Vieilles Vignes 1986 • $100 • (02/28/95) • **87**
Musigny Cuvée Vieilles Vignes 1985 • $206 • (02/28/95) • **87**
Musigny Cuvée Vieilles Vignes 1979 • $114 • (11/16/84) • **87**
Musigny Cuvée Vieilles Vignes 1976 • $74 Ⓐ • (11/16/84) • **86**
Musigny Cuvée Vieilles Vignes 1972 • $122 • (11/16/84) • **80**
Musigny Cuvée Vieilles Vignes 1971 • $150 Ⓐ • (11/16/84) • **90**
Musigny Cuvée Vieilles Vignes 1966 • $173 Ⓐ • (11/16/84) • **92**
Musigny Cuvée Vieilles Vignes 1962 • $550 • (11/16/84) • **90**
Musigny Cuvée Vieilles Vignes 1961 • $184 Ⓐ • (11/16/84) • **93**
Musigny Cuvée Vieilles Vignes 1959 • $440 • (11/16/84) • **89**
Musigny Cuvée Vieilles Vignes 1957 • $255 • (08/31/90) • **95**

Musigny Cuvée Vieilles Vignes 1947: Ripe, rich, deep and powerful on the nose, this is an excellent evocation of mature Burgundy, though excessive acidity on the palate throws the balance off a wee bit. • $180 • (05/31/97) • **91**

VOILLARD, JOËL

Côte de Nuits-Villages 1995: Light and simple, showing candied cherry and strawberry flavors. 650 cases made. • $19 • (11/15/97) • **78**

VOLPATO-COSTAILLE

Chambolle-Musigny 1988 • $34 • (02/28/91) • **78**

VOULTE GASPARET, CHÂTEAU LA

Corbières 1990 • $10 • (03/15/94) • **85**

Corbières Cuvée Réservée 1994: Elegant, though a bit simple, with plum and cherry flavors. Still quite tannic, with some gamy notes as well. 5,000 cases made. • $14 • (05/31/97) • **82**

VRAI CAILLOU, CHÂTEAU

Entre-Deux-Mers 1993 • $8 • (05/31/95) • **81**

VRANKEN

Brut Champagne Cuvée 21 NV: An appealing, light style of Champagne that features buttery, lemony flavors, a soft texture and a delicate aftertaste. Tasted twice, with consistent notes. • $100 • (09/30/97) • **85**

Brut Champagne Demoiselle Grande Cuvée NV: Pleasantly compact and elegant. A crisp and subtly concentrated wine that keeps improving as you sip. The flavors and texture turn creamy and linger on the finish. • $28 • (11/15/97) • **89**

Brut Champagne Demoiselle Tête de Cuvée 1990: A very solid, fruity-tasting, vibrant Champagne with fresh flavors, a crisp texture and a clean finish. Should open up with time. Best through 2002. • $60 • (09/30/97) • **89**

Brut Champagne Demoiselle Tête de Cuvée 1989: Big and bold, with exotic flavors, this is delightful—though it isn't classic Champagne. The flavors run from flowers to mangos to berries with hints of spice; the mousse is mouthfilling and beautifully integrated. Still very young. • $40 • (04/30/97) • **89**

Brut Champagne Demoiselle 1986 • $NA • (12/31/93) • **89**

Brut Rosé Champagne Tête de Cuvée NV: A fresh, fruity, clean-tasting rosé with enough cherry and plum flavor to give it life. Soft and agreeable in texture. Best now. • $40 • (09/30/97) • **85**

VRAYE-CROIX-DE-GAY, CHÂTEAU LA

Pomerol 1997: A bit lean and diluted. Medium-bodied, with medium tannins and a short finish. • $NA • (06/15/98) (BT) • **80-84**

Pomerol 1996: A medium-bodied wine with well-integrated tannins and a pleasant, dried cherry and chocolate character. • $NA • (01/01/97) (BT) • **85-89**

Pomerol 1995: Beautiful from start to finish. Elegant and powerful, a brooding, ink-colored, seamless '95 boasting well-defined, earthy red fruit and blackberry flavors. • $NA • (05/15/96) (BT) • **90-94**

WEINBACH, DOMAINE

Gewürztraminer Alsace Altenbourg Cuvée Laurence 1996: Exotic, tropical flavors are the dominant theme, and perhaps a touch of botrytis, in this ripe, yet balanced and persistent white. Captures the obvious flavors of the variety and the purity of the vintage. Well done. 50 cases imported. • $58 • (11/15/97) • **91**

Gewürztraminer Alsace Altenbourg Cuvée Laurence 1995: Big, full-bodied and voluptuous, this Gewürz offers exotic passion fruit, honey and orange-blossom character in a seemingly late-harvest style. Ripe and delicious. • $60 • (09/15/97) • **89**

Gewürztraminer Alsace Altenbourg Cuvée Laurence 1993 • $37 • (09/15/95) • **85**

Gewürztraminer Alsace Cuvée Laurence 1996: A floral-scented, lushly textured white full of rose and litchi flavors. Well balanced with a moderate finish, this is enjoyable now. 70 cases imported. • $48 • (11/15/97) • **87**

Gewürztraminer Alsace Cuvée Laurence 1995: A plush white, full of honey and orange-peel flavors, but it seems simple and on the sweet side. • $48 • (09/15/97) • **84**

Gewürztraminer Alsace Cuvée Théo 1996: This seems closed right now, but it shows some honey and mineral notes underscored by power and intensity. Strong finish. Try in 1999. 70 cases imported. • $35 • (11/15/97) • **86**

Gewürztraminer Alsace Cuvée Théo 1993 • $23 • (09/15/95) • **86**

Gewürztraminer Alsace Cuvée d'Or Quintessence de Grains Nobles 1994: Pure nectar. The sweetness is immediate, then the vibrant acidity buoys the honey, apricot and crème brûlée nuances to a long, lingering finish. Very young, this dessert wine needs time to unfold and develop its full complexity. 10 cases imported. • $165/375ml • (11/15/97) • **93**

Gewürztraminer Alsace Grand Cru Furstentum Cuvée Laurence 1996: The marriage of elegance and the honey, floral character here is unusual for this varietal. A firm mineral support provides length and intensity, while maintaining balance and harmony. Should drink well through 2002. 50 cases imported. • $67 • (11/15/97) • **92**

Gewürztraminer Alsace Grand Cru Furstentum Cuvée Laurence 1995: Almost thick enough to spread on toast. Lots of honey and apricot notes grace this fat, rich white. It's plush and forward, so don't wait to drink. • $60 • (09/15/97) • **88**

Gewürztraminer Alsace Grand Cru Furstentum Cuvée Laurence 1993 • $42 • (09/15/95) • **84**

Gewürztraminer Alsace Grand Cru Furstentum Sélection des Grains Nobles 1994: Classic Gewürztraminer aromas of roses, litchi and honey surround a core of stony, minerally flavors in this lavish white. Restrained and impeccably balanced, with a subtle length, this should develop beautifully over the next five years. Drinkable now through 2005. 40 cases imported. • $90/375ml • (11/15/97) • **95**

Gewürztraminer Alsace Réserve Personnelle 1996: A broad, easy-drinking white, full of honey and litchi flavors, with a touch of bitter almond adding character at the end. 40 cases imported. • $28 • (11/15/97) • **86**

Gewürztraminer Alsace Vendange Tardive 1994: An understated, honey-flavored white that shows wonderful harmony and a touch of sweetness. Would be the perfect accompaniment to a fruit tart or Muenster cheese. Spiced apple and honey linger on the aftertaste. 8 cases imported. • $90/375ml • (10/15/97) • **90**

Muscat Alsace Réserve 1996: A Muscat that combines the floral and spicy elements typical of this varietal. Richly textured, with lemony acidity that refreshes the palate while lingering on the finish. Enjoyable on its own. 75 cases imported. • $35 • (11/15/97) • **86**

Muscat Alsace Réserve 1995: Dry and spicy, redolent of orange blossoms and finishing with a citrusy tang, this is the style of Muscat that is rarely found outside Alsace. • $35 • (09/15/97) • **85**

Pinot Blanc Alsace Réserve 1996: An austere style. The palate is firm, dense and structured, with apple flavor and a hint of bitterness on the finish. Drinkable now. Tasted twice, with consistent notes. 400 cases imported. • $23 • (11/15/97) • **85**

Riesling Alsace Cuvée Ste.-Catherine 1996: Extremely ripe, exhibiting loads of butter, peach and apricot flavors. A bit disjointed, it starts out soft and rich, then turns lean and tart. Should come together by 1999. 85 cases imported. • $49 • (11/15/97) • **88**

Riesling Alsace Cuvée Ste.-Catherine 1995: Tastes like a late-harvest style with apricot aromas and flavors in spades, residual sugar and a lush, fat frame that suggests early drinking. Still, there's an underlying power and concentration. Unusual and delicious. • $45 • (09/15/97) • **89**

Riesling Alsace Cuvée Théo 1996: Lean and stony, the pure apple and mineral notes are very tightly wound now, and the acidity is prominent. Still, there's an underlying power and muscularity that suggests waiting until 1999 to try this young white. 150 cases imported. • $32 • (11/15/97) • **90**

Riesling Alsace Cuvée Théo 1995: Firm, rich and minerally, with power in reserve, this seems to be holding back now. With apple, honey and stone flavors. Try now. • $25 • (09/15/97) • **88**

Riesling Alsace Cuvée Théo 1993 • $23 • (07/31/95) • **89**

Riesling Alsace Grand Cru Schlossberg 1996: This is a hard, firm Riesling that displays plenty of mineral and herbal elements underscored by apple and almond. Unyielding at this point, it begs aging until 2000. Try with food. 200 cases imported. • $40 • (11/15/97) • **89**

Riesling Alsace Grand Cru Schlossberg 1995: Wow. A huge, backward wine, displaying top notes of mango, passion fruit and almond underscored by a massive, minerally structure. Concentrated, complex and long, give this giant until 2000 to open. Really exciting stuff. 200 cases imported. • $39 • (09/15/97) • **93**

Riesling Alsace Grand Cru Schlossberg 1994: Soft, yet refreshing. A ripe wine offering round flavors of grilled nuts, melons and hints of honey on the palate. Mineral, lime and apple flavors hover on the finish. • $25 • (09/30/96) • **87**

Riesling Alsace Grand Cru Schlossberg Cuvée d'Or Sélection des Grains Nobles 1995: Here's a racy, elegant dessert wine that combines apricot, honey and mineral notes with medium sweetness, firm structure and an airiness that almost seems ethereal, but the aftertaste is intense and goes on forever. Try in 2000. 2 cases imported. • $160/375ml • (11/15/97) • **93**

Riesling Alsace Grand Cru Schlossberg Cuvée Ste.-Cathérine 1996: Broad and rich, this Alsace Riesling serves up a generous ripe apple, honey and peach character on a racy, powerful structure. It's intense and deep, with a long, apple-flavored finish. Would make a nice complement to food, just needs until 1999. 360 cases made. • $61 • (11/15/97) • **92**

Riesling Alsace Grand Cru Schlossberg Cuvée Ste.-Cathérine 1995: Complex and satisfying, this shows the ripeness and richness of the vintage with its apricot, honey and almond flavors. But don't be fooled—there's a firm mineral and acid backbone that will allow this white to develop over the next 3 to 5 years. • $56 • (09/15/97) • **92**

Riesling Alsace Grand Cru Schlossberg Cuvée Ste.-Catherine 1993 • $38 • (09/15/95) • **86**

Riesling Alsace Grand Cru Schlossberg Vendange Tardive 1995: A luscious late-harvest white that displays the merest hint of kerosene before erupting in apricot, vanilla-custard and orange-peel flavors that are washed across the palate by the balancing, mouthwatering acidity. Very long finish. 8 cases imported. • $131/375ml • (11/15/97) • **92**

Riesling Alsace Réserve Personnelle 1996: A soft, ripe white with aromas of talc and roses that turn to apple and spice on the palate. This has power and an underlying firmness that should develop well over the next 3 to 5 years. 220 cases imported. • $24 • (11/15/97) • **88**

Sylvaner Alsace Réserve 1996: A young, fresh white reminiscent of apples, nuts and a hint of earth. Straightforward, with a citrusy acidity that refreshes on the finish. 100 cases imported. • $19 • (11/15/97) • **86**

Tokay Pinot Gris Alsace Altenbourg Cuvée Laurence 1996: Lovely Pinot Gris. Ripe, full and fleshy, the flavors range from peach and apricot to violets and vanilla custard—and never lose their intensity thanks to the racy acidity. Very long finish. Delicious now, it should gain complexity by 2000. 15 cases imported. • $65 • (11/15/97) • **90**

Tokay Pinot Gris Alsace Cuvée d'Or Sélection de Grains Nobles 1995: A dessert wine with elegance. The nectarine and honey flavors are accented by mandarin orange notes, and though it exhibits texture and richness, the overall impression is one of grace and delicacy. Subtle length. • $NA/375ml • (11/15/97) • **92**

Tokay Pinot Gris Alsace Cuvée Laurence 1996: Incredibly ripe, full-bodied and backward, this exhibits aromas and flavors of apricot, mineral and grilled nuts. Dense and powerful; wait until 1999. 70 cases imported. • $62 • (11/15/97) • **89**

Tokay Pinot Gris Alsace Cuvée Laurence 1995: On the sweet side, rich and round, with plenty of honey and pear flavors and balancing acidity. Try now with foie gras or cheese. • $60 • (09/15/97) • **87**

Tokay Pinot Gris Alsace Cuvée Ste.-Catherine 1996: Ripe and effusive, displaying apricot, nut and violet flavors. Full-bodied and rich in texture, with an appley finish. Drinkable now. 60 cases imported. • $52 • (11/15/97) • **88**

Tokay Pinot Gris Alsace Vendange Tardive 1996: Ripe and round, yet full of racy acidity, the nectarine, floral and smoke notes hold court up front before they are swept away by a refreshing citrus and apple character. This young, vivacious white is tempting now but better in 1999. 20 cases imported. • $83/375ml • (11/15/97) • **90**

WHEELER

Merlot Vin de Pays d'Oc 1995: Robust and fruity, with pepper, plum and currant flavors. Has a nice, gamelike note woven into its moderate structure. A blend of French and California grapes, made by a California winery. 4,000 cases made. • $15 • (04/30/97) • **81**

WILLM, ALSACE

Gewürztraminer Alsace 1994: Simple, round and soft on the palate, with some spice and melon flavors. A good quaff, but lacks marked Gewürz character. 7,500 cases made. • $12 • (10/15/96) • **81**

Gewürztraminer Alsace 1993 • $11 • (11/15/94) • **85**

Gewürztraminer Alsace Grand Cru Clos Gaensbrœnnel Willm Réserve Exceptionelle 1994: Slightly sweet, displaying subtle flavors of hazelnut and passion fruit. Seems a bit simple and one-dimensional overall. 3,500 cases made. • $30 • (02/28/97) • **81**

Pinot Blanc Alsace 1995: A crisp, firm white that offers bright citrus and mineral notes. It's a bit tart on its own, but a good foil for food and a bargain for all its Alsace character. It's clean and long on the finish, too. 12,000 cases made. • $8 • (09/30/96) BB • **87**

Pinot Blanc Alsace 1993 • $8 • (11/15/94) • **83**

Riesling Alsace 1993 • $10 • (11/15/94) • **78**

YON-FIGEAC, CHÂTEAU

St.-Emilion 1990: An understated wine, with ripe fruit and toasty nut aromas and flavors, medium tannins and a succulent finish. Drinkable now. 7,500 cases made. • $24 • (03/31/93) • **86**

St.-Emilion 1982 • $25 • (05/15/89) • **87**

YQUEM, CHÂTEAU D'

Sauternes 1990: Showing great class and depth, it's destined to be a classic. Full-bodied, compacted and rich, with intense aromas of vanilla, honey, and pears, loads of fruit flavors and a long, honeyed finish. Hard not to drink it now, but it will be better after 2000. 18,750 cases made. • $225 • (01/31/97) CS • **97**

Sauternes 1989: A majestic Yquem, exhibiting solid backbone and masses of toasty coconut, honey, spice and dried apricot character. Sweet but not very thick, with a long aftertaste. The new oak dominates now; try after 1999. • $200 • (04/15/95) • **97**

Sauternes 1988: Big and showy, rich and ripe, featuring sweet mango, pineapple and lime character. Full in body, with a long finish that reins in honey, dried apricot and toasty vanilla flavors. Drinkable now. • $200 • (04/15/95) • **94**

Sauternes 1987: Seductive and richly textured, demonstrating balanced honey, vanilla and lemon flavors; medium body and sweetness. Delicious, but a bit short and hot on the finish. Drinkable now. • $130 • (04/15/95) • **88**

Sauternes 1986: A beauty that's in almost perfect harmony. Full-bodied, exhibiting wet earth, honey, floral and ginger flavors that burn with intensity on the long, sweet finish. Better after 1999. • $310 • (04/15/95) • **95**

Sauternes 1985: Sweet, round and generous, with a nice twang of lemony citrus acidity to balance the decided honey-pear sweetness. What it lacks in extra dimensions in makes up for with richness and roundness. • $112 Ⓐ • (12/15/93) • **91**

Sauternes 1984: Racy and saucy, a brighter style of Yquem with a leaner profile, offering spicy, citrusy notes to complement the caramel and honey. Drinkable now, and should be fine through 2010. • $150 • (12/15/93) • **90**

Sauternes 1983: Super-intense and full-throttled, elegant and stylish. Dark amber in color and rich in complexity, this '83 coats your mouth with butterscotch, dried apricot, fig and spice flavors. Made to age for decades. • $260 • (04/15/95) • **98**

Sauternes 1982 • $118 Ⓐ • (12/15/93) • **91**
Sauternes 1981 • $240 • (12/15/93) • **87**
Sauternes 1980 • $143 Ⓐ • (12/15/93) • **84**
Sauternes 1979 • $317 Ⓐ • (12/15/93) • **85**
Sauternes 1978 • $80 Ⓐ • (12/15/93) • **80**
Sauternes 1976 • $261 Ⓐ • (12/15/93) • **92**
Sauternes 1975 • $339 Ⓐ • (12/15/93) • **97**
Sauternes 1971 • $275 Ⓐ • (12/15/93) • **90**
Sauternes 1970 • $173 Ⓐ • (12/15/93) • **84**
Sauternes 1967 • $543 Ⓐ • (12/15/93) • **81**
Sauternes 1966 • $208 Ⓐ • (12/15/93) • **84**
Sauternes 1962 • $284 Ⓐ • (12/15/93) • **85**
Sauternes 1961 • $351 Ⓐ • (12/15/93) • **83**
Sauternes 1959 • $637 Ⓐ • (12/15/93) • **93**
Sauternes 1958 • $330 Ⓐ • (12/15/93) • **88**
Sauternes 1957 • $489 Ⓐ • (12/15/93) • **85**
Sauternes 1955 • $553 Ⓐ • (12/15/93) • **78**
Sauternes 1953 • $902 Ⓐ • (12/15/93) • **80**
Sauternes 1950 • $395 Ⓐ • (12/15/93) • **88**
Sauternes 1949 • $803 Ⓐ • (12/15/93) • **91**
Sauternes 1948 • $593 Ⓐ • (12/15/93) • **92**

Sauternes 1947: Cloudy, even weird at first, seemingly nothing but acid and honey. But then the flavors fill in and it becomes a zingy mouthful of dried fruit, leather, tobacco and floral flavors around that core of honey, and the finish lingers gently and impressively. • $894 • (05/31/97) • **89**

Sauternes 1945 • $1200 • (12/15/93) • **95**
Sauternes 1943 • $538 Ⓐ • (12/15/93) • **83**
Sauternes 1942 • $452 Ⓐ • (12/15/93) • **87**
Sauternes 1937 • $974 Ⓐ • (12/15/93) • **94**
Sauternes 1934 • $643 Ⓐ • (12/15/93) • **88**
Sauternes 1928 • $775 Ⓐ • (12/15/93) • **92**
Sauternes 1924 • $678 Ⓐ • (12/15/93) • **86**
Sauternes 1921 • $2100 • (12/15/93) • **97**
Sauternes 1900 • $2200 • (12/15/93) • **97**
Sauternes 1893 • $2500 • (12/15/93) • **73**
Sauternes 1874 • $3000 • (12/15/93) • **98**
Sauternes 1870 • $4000 • (12/15/93) • **83**
Sauternes 1865 • $4000 • (12/15/93) • **73**
Sauternes 1847 • $15,000 • (12/15/93) • **99**

ZIND-HUMBRECHT, DOMAINE

Chardonnay Alsace Clos Windsbuhl Hunawihr 1993: An explosive combination of toasty oak and ripe fruit flavors gives this wine maximum aromatic impact. On the palate, searing acidity keeps the vanilla, toast and tropical fruit flavors in line. Idiosyncratic and expressive if not completely coherent, it suggests Chardonnay may have a future in Alsace. • $40 • (10/15/96) • **88**

Gewürztraminer Alsace Clos Windsbuhl Hunawihr 1995: Masses of honey and litchi dominate this full-bodied white, which is lively and rich but needs to settle down. A touch hot on the finish. Try now. • $75 • (09/30/97) • **89**

Gewürztraminer Alsace Clos Windsbuhl Hunawihr 1993 • $40 • (08/31/95) • **90**

Gewürztraminer Alsace Grand Cru Goldert 1993 • $35 • (08/31/95) • **92**

Gewürztraminer Alsace Grand Cru Goldert Vendange Tardive 1994: Though quite thick and sweet, this has exuberant acidity that makes it refreshing,

Key: SS—Spectator Selection CS—Cellar Selection HR—Highly Recommended BB—Best Buy $NA—Price not available Ⓐ—Auction Price (BT)—Barrel Tasting
Dates in parentheses indicate the issues in which the ratings were published.

even delicate. Pineapple and vanilla flavors are lively and fresh. Delicious now, or can easily age. • $72 • (10/15/96) • **91**

Gewürztraminer Alsace Grand Cru Hengst Wintzenheim 1995: Classic Gewürztraminer flavors of roses, litchi and grapefruit are amplified in this intense, full-bodied wine. Seems a little aggressive, however, with a burn on the finish. Try now. • $60 • (09/30/97) • **86**

Gewürztraminer Alsace Grand Cru Hengst Wintzenheim 1993 • $35 • (08/31/95) • **90**

Gewürztraminer Alsace Grand Cru Hengst Wintzenheim Vendange Tardive 1994: Very rich, yet quite dry. Despite alluring aromas of honey, litchi and hibiscus, this shows an intense mix of acidity and spice, with orange-peel and dried grapefruit flavors that attack the palate. Lots of character, but difficult to match with food. • $72 • (11/15/96) • **90**

Gewürztraminer Alsace Grand Cru Rangen de Thann Clos St.-Urbain 1995: Huge nose of botrytized fruit. Apricots, oranges, almonds and honey are punctuated by an intensity that puts this in a league of its own. Full-bodied, like a red wine in white-wine clothing, it displays bright acidity and a long finish. Forget dessert—drink this instead. • $95 • (09/30/97) • **93**

Gewürztraminer Alsace Grand Cru Rangen de Thann Clos St.-Urbain Sélection de Grains Nobles 1994: Almost orange in color, displaying the orange- and clove-scented nose from ultra-ripe grapes, this is dessert in a glass. Honey, apricot and spice flavors cascade across the palate, and it's beautifully balanced. The finish has a bitter grapefruit component. Drinkable now through 2002. • $225/375ml • (10/15/97) • **91**

Gewürztraminer Alsace Heimbourg Turckheim 1995: An intensely flavored white with a minty topnote to the orange, spice and honey flavors. It's concentrated, with a slightly hot finish. • $60 • (09/30/97) • **87**

Gewürztraminer Alsace Heimbourg Turckheim 1993 • $35 • (09/15/95) • **88**

Gewürztraminer Alsace Heimbourg Vendange Tardive 1994: Thick and rich, yet still vibrant and intense, this multi-layered wine marries racy grapefruit acidity with honeyed sweetness in a spicy, harmonious package with a lingering finish. Has the balance to match with food and the concentration to age. • $72 • (10/15/96) • **93**

Gewürztraminer Alsace Herrenweg Turckheim 1994: Lush and seductive, yet still firm and balanced, this concentrated white offers complex flavors of pineapple, grapefruit, honey and spice. Dry enough to go with food, yet rich enough to drink on its own. • $30 • (09/30/96) • **90**

Gewürztraminer Alsace Herrenweg Turckheim 1993 • $25 • (08/31/95) • **89**

Gewürztraminer Alsace Herrenweg Turckheim Vendange Tardive 1995: A huge white that explodes with honey, apricot, marmalade and white truffle, moderate sweetness and rich texture, yet retains vibrancy and freshness. A bitterness on the finish is characteristic of the varietal. 500 cases made. • $65 • (10/15/97) • **92**

Gewürztraminer Alsace Wintzenheim 1995: Intense, smoky and bursting with litchi, orange-peel and mineral notes, this Gewürz has an intensity of flavor that grips the palate. It's atypical, but its depth, balance and power can only come from low-yielding vines and meticulous, patient winemaking. Demands rich food or Muenster cheese. Drinkable now through 2000. 400 cases made. • $34 • (09/30/97) • **91**

Gewürztraminer Alsace Wintzenheim 1994: Big, muscular and firm on the palate, this mingles distinctive spice, almond, tea and rose petal flavors. Dry and quite bitter on the finish. • $22 • (09/30/96) • **87**

Gewürztraminer Alsace Wintzenheim 1993 • $20 • (08/31/95) HR • **90**

Muscat Alsace Grand Cru Goldert Gueberschwihr 1993 • $30 • (09/15/95) • **87**

Muscat Alsace Herrenweg Turckheim Vendange Tardive 1995: An attractive, perfumed Muscat that exhibits raisin, honey, rose and mineral aromas and flavors combined with a firm structure and a finish that's slightly hot. • $65 • (11/15/97) • **86**

Pinot Gris Alsace Clos Jebsal Turckheim Sélection de Grains Nobles 1994: Intense and expressive, brimming with flavors of honey, passion fruit, cardamom and an exotic note from botrytis, this is balanced on the soft side and delicious now. • $185/375ml • (10/15/97) • **90**

Pinot Gris Alsace Clos Jebsal Turckheim Sélection des Grains Nobles 1993: Extremely concentrated—so thick it's hard to swallow its spicy crème brûlée, dried coconut, ripe melon, even white truffle, flavors. Yet despite its ripe power, it's not cloyingly sweet; the balance is rock solid. Delicous now, but will improve for years. • $375 • (10/15/96) • **95**

Pinot Gris Alsace Clos Windsbuhl Hunawihr 1995: Massive, rich and thick, this white has a deep golden color and a sweet, tropical fruit character. Long fermentation (12 months) has enhanced exotic vanilla and butterscotch components that are absolutely stunning, from the honey and botrytis flavors to the exhausting finish. Like a chess grand master rather than an overpowering brute. • $75 • (09/30/97) HR • **93**

Pinot Gris Alsace Clos Windsbuhl Hunawihr Vendange Tardive 1994: Rich and viscous, this is powerful. Hits you in the face with ripe, sweet aromas and flavors of pears, coconut, crème brûlée and orange-peel. As thick as motor oil on the palate, but there's enough acidity to keep it refreshing. Delicious now, but can hold. • $80 • (10/15/96) • **92**

Pinot Gris Alsace Grand Cru Rangen de Thann Clos St.-Urbain 1995: An effusive white, full of ripe mango and passion fruit flavors, yet it's dry and spicy on the palate, with a firm structure. Displays lovely balance and harmony, suggesting it will improve through 2000. • $95 • (10/15/97) • **90**

Pinot Gris Alsace Grand Cru Rangen Thann Clos St.-Urbain Sélection de Grains Nobles 1993: One of a kind. From the mahogany color to the thick texture, walnut, tea and dried pineapple flavors and spicy, Sherry finish, this tastes like no other Alsace white we've tried. • $450 • (10/15/96) • **88**

Pinot Gris Alsace Grand Cru Rangen Thann Clos St.-Urbain Vendange Tardive 1994: Ripe, rich and sweet, like a banana-nut tart, with honey, hazelnut and dried fruit flavors that coat the palate and linger for minutes. Yet there's enough acidity to keep it lively, and the balance is impeccable. • $95 • (10/15/96) • **91**

Pinot Gris Alsace Heimbourg Turckheim Sélection de Grains Nobles 1994: Lush, ripe and powerful, you have to admire the concentration and subtle balance in this honeyed dessert wine, even though it lacks the complexity to be really exciting. Drinkable now. • $185/375ml • (10/15/97) • **90**

Pinot Gris Alsace Heimbourg Turckheim Sélection de Grains Nobles 1993: Alluring coconut and banana aromas promise a party, and the palate delivers with a sweet, yet spicy character that explodes with flavor. Though very sweet, it has balancing notes of dried pineapple acidity and rose petal bitterness that keep it focused and interesting. Enjoy it now or cellar for years. • $250/500ml • (11/15/96) • **95**

Pinot Gris Alsace Heimbourg Vendange Tardive 1994: Remember those vanilla ice cream bars covered with crushed, toasty almonds you loved as a kid? Here's the grown-up version, rich and sweet and long. Hard to match with food, but great on its own as dessert. • $72 • (10/15/96) • **90**

Pinot Gris Alsace Rotenberg Wintzenheim Sélection de Grains Nobles 1993: As sweet as honey, and almost as thick on the palate, this rich, unctuous wine offers honey, raisin, dried pear and dried apple flavors. The lengthy finish promises long-term development. • $250/500ml • (11/15/96) • **92**

Pinot Gris Alsace Rotenberg Wintzenheim Vendange Tardive 1995: Packed with botrytized flavors, apricot, grapefruit, orange-peel and honey coat the palate, the texture is lush, the acidity intense. A long, complex aftertaste completes the experience. Try now with food or wait until 1999. 100 cases made. • $80 • (10/15/97) • **94**

Pinot Gris Alsace Rotenberg Wintzenheim Vendange Tardive 1994: Rich and unctuous, this has a beam of bitterness that contrasts with the raisin and honey flavors, adding grapefruit and smoky notes to the mix. Try now. • $NA • (11/15/96) • **89**

Pinot Gris Alsace Vieilles Vignes 1995: Very ripe and fat, this is lush in texture and full of honey, apricot and passion fruit flavors. The finish is better than that of most '95s, but still a bit hot. • $60 • (09/30/97) • **87**

Pinot Gris Alsace Vieilles Vignes 1994: Ripe and powerful, this honeyed white offers rich flavors of melons, coconut and spices. Sweet, but with enough acidity for balance. Concentrated, clean and long on the finish. • $48 • (09/30/96) • **91**

Pinot d'Alsace 1995: A terrific Pinot Blanc from beginning to end, this wine has a smoky note that gives depth to the honey, peach, spice and orange-peel flavors. Displays firm structure, great harmony and good length. • $28 • (09/30/97) • **88**

Pinot d'Alsace 1994: An intriguing, if unusual, character for a Pinot Blanc. This is made in a late-harvest style with honey, apricot and nutty flavors and a noticeable sweetness on the palate. • $23 • (09/30/96) • **86**

Pinot d'Alsace 1993 • $17 • (07/31/95) • **91**

Riesling Alsace Clos Häuserer Wintzenheim 1995: A brooding white that oozes honey, botrytis and mineral flavors, wrapped in a racy, tightly wound structure. Intense and backward, with an incredibly long aftertaste. Try after 2000. • $45 • (09/30/97) • **91**

Riesling Alsace Clos Häuserer 1993 • $28 • (09/15/95) • **87**

Riesling Alsace Clos Windsbuhl Hunawihr 1995: This Riesling has honey and mineral flavors coating a gargantuan framework, followed by a long finish, but the overall impression is monolithic. Extremely closed and unevolved, it appears to be out-of-sorts today. Try after 2000. 100 cases made. • $65 • (09/30/97) • **92**

Riesling Alsace Clos Windsbuhl Hunawihr 1994: A powerful wine, oozing orange, pineapple and honey flavors. Big-bodied and ripe, yet there's enough underlying acidity to keep it fresh. Easy to like, but better alone than with food. • $50 • (09/30/96) • **90**

ZIND-HUMBRECHT, DOMAINE

Riesling Alsace Clos Windsbuhl Hunawihr 1993 • $40 • (09/15/95) • **86**

Riesling Alsace Grand Cru Brand Turckheim 1994: Opulent and showy, this ripe Riesling shows bright flavors of orange-peel and spices, with vibrant acidity and a clean finish. Luscious for drinking now. • $54 • (09/30/96) • **87**

Riesling Alsace Grand Cru Brand Turckheim 1993 • $40 • (07/31/95) • **89**

Riesling Alsace Grand Cru Brand Turckheim Vendange Tardive 1995: A wine that unfolds slowly on the palate, revealing flavors of baked apples, honey, apricots and lime. Its firm structure and tight finish suggest waiting until 1999 to unleash its charms. • $80 • (10/15/97) • **90**

Riesling Alsace Grand Cru Rangen de Thann Clos St.-Urbain 1995: Ripe and hedonistic, courtesy of apricot, orange-rind and botrytis flavors resting on an elegant, aristocratic framework, this Riesling is lacy but has an inner strength leading to a lingering, mineral finish. Powerful yet sublime. • $80 • (09/30/97) • **92**

Riesling Alsace Grand Cru Rangen de Thann Clos St.-Urbain 1994: Imagine a spicy, floral-scented honey that turns dry on the tongue. Alluring apricot and pineapple flavors mingle on the palate and linger on the finish; this wine is balanced and rich, yet subtle and restrained. • $70 • (09/30/96) • **91**

Riesling Alsace Grand Cru Rangen de Thann Clos St.-Urbain 1993 • $64 • (09/15/95) HR • **92**

Riesling Alsace Gueberschwihr 1995: Botrytis lends an exotic quality to this ripe, intense Riesling. The flavor spectrum includes honey, peach, apricot, apple, flint and lime, and the bright acidity is balanced by a hint of sweetness. The final impression is mouthwatering. Drinkable now through 2005. • $34 • (09/30/97) • **90**

Riesling Alsace Gueberschwihr 1994: Smoky mineral notes mingle with Granny Smith apple flavors in this medium-bodied, racy white. Alluring, but give it until 1999 or try with food. • $23 • (09/30/97) • **89**

Riesling Alsace Herrenweg Turckheim 1995: The huge, assertive aromas of baked apples, passion fruit and smoke become ripe apricots, spice and minerals on the palate in this complex and beguiling wine. It's structured, balanced and powerful, so wait until 1999 or enjoy now with rich food. 350 cases made. • $37 • (09/30/97) • **91**

Riesling Alsace Herrenweg Turckheim 1994: The deep color and spicy aromas indicate a late-harvest style, borne out by the honey and apricot flavors. But there's plenty of acidity for balance, and the wine finishes clean and long. • $30 • (09/30/96) • **88**

Riesling Alsace Herrenweg Turckheim 1993 • $25 • (07/31/95) • **88**

Riesling Alsace Herrenweg Turckheim Vendange Tardive 1995: A sleek thoroughbred that displays the honey, apricot and mandarin orange character of ripe fruit with botrytis, yet reigns it all in with a piquant, racy acidity. It's integrated, harmonious and long. Drinkable now through 2005. • $65 • (10/15/97) • **92**

Riesling Alsace Wintzenheim 1993 • $17 • (07/31/95) SS • **89**

Tokay Pinot Gris Alsace Clos Jebsal Turckheim 1993 • $55 • (07/31/95) • **92**

Tokay Pinot Gris Alsace Clos Windsbuhl Hunawihr 1993 • $55 • (07/31/95) • **89**

Tokay Pinot Gris Alsace Heimbourg Turckheim 1993 • $40 • (07/31/95) CS • **92**

Tokay Pinot Gris Alsace Vieilles Vignes 1993 • $34 • (07/31/95) • **89**

Key: SS—Spectator Selection CS—Cellar Selection HR—Highly Recommended BB—Best Buy $NA—Price not available Ⓐ—Auction Price (BT)—Barrel Tasting
Dates in parentheses indicate the issues in which the ratings were published.

Germany

In marked contrast to their tongue-twisting names and complicated official nomenclature, the sensory appeal of German wines is instantaneous. Combining abundant fruit with lively, refreshing crispness, German wines have a knack for charming the palates of novices and experts in equal measure.

Müller-Thurgau is the most widely planted German grape variety, but Riesling produces most of the country's greatest wines. Other very good, often great wines, are made from the Gewürztraminer, Scheurebe and Sylvaner grapes.

1. Mosel-Saar-Ruwer
2. Nahe
3. Rheingau
4. Rheinhessen
5. Pfalz

GERMAN WINE CLASSIFICATIONS

German wines are divided into several levels of quality based on ripeness and natural sugar levels. Kabinetts are the entry level of the so-called "QmP" wines, the respected category of German wines made from grapes that reach a minimum level of natural ripeness without chaptalization (the addition of sugar prior to fermentation). Most Kabinetts are moderately sweet and low in alcohol, with a tangy acidity at the finish. (Tasty wines are made in a similar style in the lower "QbA" category, but these are targeted at a less critical mass audience.)

The remaining categories are arranged by ascending order of natural sugar levels at harvest. Just above Kabinett is Spätlese, which means late harvest. Generally richer than Kabinett, Spätlese can be particularly successful when made in the very dry "trocken" style or the slightly less dry "halbtrocken" style. These are the German wines that are most similar to white table wines produced elsewhere, though they maintain a true distinctiveness.

Auslese, made from specially selected bunches of late harvest grapes, is almost always sweet. Beerenauslese is made from selected individual grapes, usually affected by "noble rot." Rarest of all is Trockenbeerenauslese, an intensely sweet wine made only from shriveled grapes affected by noble rot. The latter two types rank among the greatest sweet wines in the world, and can age for decades.

GERMAN WINE REGIONS

German wine regions produce distinctive styles of wines owing to their unique conditions of soil and climate. All of the important regions are located in what used to be called West Germany.

Rheingau. This is Germany's most aristocratic wine region, and historically its finest. For a period in the late 1980s and early 1990s a number of long-time estate owners were content to rest on their laurels; despite high prices, they didn't deliver a quality commensurate with the region's reputation. Fortunately, a younger generation of Rheingau producers is leading a quality revolution. And at its best, no region packs more vitality into its product: powerful wines noted for their longevity.

Mosel-Saar-Ruwer. One regional name encompasses all three vineyard areas, which produce Rieslings noted for their fruity acidity. The Middle Mosel (Mittelmosel) is perhaps the most famous wine region of Germany, and encompasses the familiar Piesporter Gold and Bernkasteler Doktor. Ruwer and Saar wines tend to be steelier and harder than Mosels, though in years of great ripeness they excel.

other light wines are less common.

Rheinpfalz. The southernmost of the well-known German regions and possibly the most exciting today. Its wines tend to be rich and earthy, with generous fruit. Many of the lighter wines are bottled in full liter bottles in the Rheinpfalz, often at very attractive prices.

CHOOSING GERMAN WINES

Vintage quality varies vastly from year to year in Germany. Also, since many great vineyards have several owners, consumers must look for growers who are meticulous about quality and who own the most favored sites of certain vineyards. No region can consistently be said to produce the best wines. Also, while the classifications that have been made in the German wine laws are useful, they are not infallible, and consumers must never rely on classification alone to make a buying decision.

A reliable path is to choose the wines according to the reputation of the producer. The best wines of Germany are reviewed each year in *Wine Spectator.* In addition, you can seek out shops where there are specialists with expertise in the sometimes arcane field of German wines. Developing a relationship with a reliable merchant or salesperson can be invaluable.

Courtesy of Weingut Robert Weil

The Weingut Robert Weil house in Kiedrich.

Nahe. Perhaps the best buy in Germany, the wines of the Nahe fall between the Rheingau and Mosel in style, with much of the power of the former and the raciness of the latter. Wines from famous vineyards in the Nahe can be undervalued compared to the better known Mosels and Rheingaus.

Rheinhessen. Nierstein has the best vineyards of Rheinhessen, and the wines have a distinctive flavor of smoked meat. Ripeness levels run high here compared with the rest of Germany, so Kabinetts and

BALBACH

Riesling Auslese Rheinhessen Nierstein Hipping 1996: Slightly light for an auslese, with tropical fruit and pineapple character and a hint of cream. Medium-bodied, medium-sweet and soft in texture. Drink now. • $NA • (11/30/97) • **84**

Riesling Eiswein Rheinhessen Nierstein Oelberg 1996: Displays amazing lemon and lime rind aromas and flavors. Thick and sweet, with tons of fruit, a long, lively finish and zingy acidity. Fun to taste, but slightly one-dimensional. Drink now. • $NA/375ml • (11/30/97) • **89**

Riesling Kabinett Rheinhessen Nierstein Pettenthal 1996: Impressive aromas of honey, cloves and fruit. Medium-bodied, off-dry, spicy, with a slight almond finish. Drink now. • $NA • (11/30/97) • **85**

BASSERMANN-JORDAN

Riesling Auslese Pfalz Deidesheimer Hohenmorgen 1996: Spicy and fruity with plenty of mineral character, this auslese offers an attractive balance of fruit, sweetness and fine acidity. Drink now. • $36 • (11/30/97) • **87**

Riesling Eiswein Pfalz Forster Ungeheuer 1996: An intensely sweet wine that impressively maintains the spicy, fruity character of Riesling. Spices, minerals and fruit melt together with citrus, sour eiswein characteristics. Medium-bodied and very sweet, with a long finish. Drink now. • $119/375ml • (11/30/97) • **90**

Riesling Kabinett Pfalz Deidesheimer Leinhöhle 1996: Shows pretty aromas and flavors of spice and honey, but slightly diluted on the palate. Medium to light in body, with light sweetness, a short finish. Drink now. • $16 • (11/30/97) • **83**

Riesling QbA Trocken Pfalz 1996: A Riesling with a pretty balance of spring-like aromas and flavors, crisp acidity and fruitiness. Medium-bodied and dry, with a fresh, fruity finish. Drink now. • $13 • (11/30/97) • **86**

Riesling Spätlese Pfalz Forster Jesuitengarten 1996: Despite very high acidity, this wine is a lot of fun to taste, showing pineapple, green apple and a hint of spice character. Medium-bodied, medium-sweet. Try now. • $26 • (11/30/97) • **87**

Riesling Spätlese Pfalz Forster Kirchenstück 1996: Young and tropical, with apricot and passionfruit aromas and flavors, this is full-bodied for a German Riesling with a fat, juicy texture. All comes together with some very ripe acidity on the finish. Drink now through 2000. • $20 • (04/30/98) • **86**

Riesling Spätlese Pfalz Ruppertsberger Nussbien 1996: Shows plenty of banana, apple and pineapple aromas and flavors. Medium-bodied with medium sweetness and a silky, clean finish. Drink now. • $26 • (11/30/97) • **87**

BIFFAR, JOSEF

Riesling Auslese Pfalz Deidesheimer Kalkofen 1996: Slightly unbalanced, but intense aromas of minerals and fruit follow through on the palate. Medium-bodied and medium-sweet, with a slight bitterness on the finish. Drink now. • $31 • (11/30/97) • **84**

Riesling Auslese Pfalz Deidesheimer Kalkofen 1995: A restrained style of auslese, offering pretty apple, honey and melon aromas and flavors. Ripe acidity and a fruity finish. Drink now or hold. • $33 • (11/30/96) • **86**

Riesling Auslese Pfalz Deidesheimer Kieselberg 1996: Delicious. Less sweet than some, but showing masses of fab ripe fruit. Full-bodied, with lively acidity and a long, long finish. Drink now. • $34 • (11/30/97) • **90**

Riesling Auslese Pfalz Wachenheimer Altenburg 1993 • $30 • (11/30/94) • **87**

Riesling Auslese Trocken Pfalz Deidesheimer Kalkofen 1993 • $25 • (11/30/94) • **84**

Riesling Eiswein Pfalz Deidesheimer Mäushöhle 1996: Delicious. A wine that lasts for minutes on the palate, showing nuances of spice, pie crust, crushed grapes, honey and citrus, with a hint of sweet-and-sour. Full-bodied, very sweet and thick. Drink now or hold. • $NA/375ml • (11/30/97) • **93**

Riesling Kabinett Pfalz Deidesheimer Kieselberg 1996: Fresh and spicy, with a lovely creamy texture and a long, fruity finish. Medium-bodied and off-dry, with flavors of apple and pear. Drink now. • $13 • (11/30/97) • **85**

Riesling Kabinett Pfalz Deidesheimer Kieselberg 1993 • $12 • (11/30/94) • **84**

Riesling Kabinett Pfalz Deidesheimer Kieselberg 1994 • $15 • (11/30/95) • **86**

Riesling Kabinett Trocken Pfalz Deidesheimer Mäushöhle 1996: A simple white with good citrus and pineapple aromas and flavors. Medium-bodied and dry, with fresh acidity and a light finish. Drink now. • $17 • (11/30/97) • **85**

Riesling Spätlese Halbtrocken Pfalz Deidesheimer Mäushöhle 1996: A medium-bodied Riesling with potential, exhibiting melon, toast and spice aromas and flavors. Medium-bodied and off-dry, with tart acidity and a fruity finish. Drinkable now. • $21 • (11/30/97) • **88**

Riesling Spätlese Pfalz Deidesheimer Grainhübel 1994 • $29 • (11/30/95) • **90**

Riesling Spätlese Pfalz Wachenheimer Altenburg 1993 • $18 • (11/30/94) • **87**

Riesling Spätlese Pfalz Wachenheimer Gerümpel 1996: Displays gorgeous aromas of honey, apricot and melon, but lacks a bit on the palate. Medium-bodied, medium-sweet, with dried-fruit flavors and a medium-crisp finish. Drink now. • $26 • (11/30/97) • **85**

Riesling Spätlese Pfalz Wachenheimer Gerümpel 1995: This has obvious appeal. Melon, talc and passion fruit flavors greet the senses. It's deceptively balanced and long, and vibrating with pure Riesling character. • $28 • (11/30/96) • **89**

Riesling Spätlese Pfalz Wachenheimer Goldbächel 1996: Abounds with crushed grape and melon character, with a hint of pear. Medium-bodied and sweet, with a silky texture and a fresh finish. Drink now. • $26 • (11/30/97) • **86**

Riesling Spätlese Pfalz Wachenheimer Goldbächel 1993 • $18 • (11/30/94) • **87**

Riesling Spätlese Trocken Pfalz Deidesheimer Grainhübel 1995: Lush, ripe, tropical notes highlight this lime- and apricot-scented Riesling. It's concentrated and intense, yet impeccably balanced and fresh. Complex and complete. Drinkable now or try in 2000. • $28 • (11/30/96) • **90**

Riesling Spätlese Trocken Pfalz Wachenheimer Gerümpel 1994 • $NA • (11/30/95) • **87**

Riesling Trockenbeerenauslese Pfalz Deidesheimer Kieselberg 1994 • $107 • (11/30/95) • **87**

BLUE NUN

Liebfraumilch Pfalz 1993 • $6 • (12/15/95) • **81**

BREUER, GEORG

Brut Rheingau 1991: A delicate, straightforward sparkler, displaying ripe flavors of apple and honey. Try as an apéritif. Made from a blend of 35 percent Pinot Noir, 30 percent Pinot Blanc, 30 percent Pinot Gris and 5 percent Riesling. 450 cases made. • $70 • (09/15/97) • **85**

Riesling Auslese Gold Cap Rheingau Rüdesheimer Bischofsberg 1993 • $NA • (11/30/94) • **86**

Riesling Auslese Gold Cap Rheingau Rüdesheimer Berg Schlossberg 1996: This elegant Auslese shows very good, focused character of spice, mineral and fruit, as well as sweetness. Medium-bodied, very sweet, lively finish. Drink now. • $100/375ml • (11/30/97) • **88**

Riesling Auslese Rheingau Rüdesheimer Berg Rottland Goldkapsel 1995: An attractive late-harvest Riesling that offers honeylike aromas, sweet peach and apricot flavors, rich texture and a relatively lean finish. Drinkable now, better after 2000. 10 cases made. • $80 • (04/30/97) • **88**

Riesling Beerenauslese Rheingau Rüdesheimer Bischofsberg 1993 • $NA • (11/30/94) • **86**

Riesling Beerenauslese Rheingau Rüdesheimer Bischofsberg Goldkapsel 1995: A super-rich and tasty late-harvest Riesling with a gorgeously thick texture and oodles of honey, peach and crème brûlée flavors that linger and intermingle on the finish. Tempting now, but try to wait until 2005 or beyond. • $43/375ml • (04/30/97) • **92**

Riesling Eiswein Gold Cap Rheingau Rüdesheimer Bischofsberg 1996: Lovely, elegant eiswein with loads of spice, mineral and lemon-lime aromas and flavors. Medium- to full-bodied, very sweet, with a lively, fresh finish. Complex and subtle. Drink now or hold. 8 cases made. • $300/375ml • (11/30/97) • **93**

Riesling QbA Halbtrocken Rheingau Rauenthaler Nonnenberg Charta 1993 • $NA • (11/30/94) • **82**

Riesling QbA Halbtrocken Rheingau Rüdesheimer Berg Schlossberg Charta 1993 • $NA • (11/30/94) • **82**

Riesling QbA Rheingau Montosa Charta 1996: Outstanding dry wine. Powerful, with lots of spicy, peppery and fruity aromas and flavors. Medium- to full-bodied and dry. Crisp and fruity finish. Drink now. 833 cases made. • $20 • (11/30/97) • **90**

Riesling QbA Rheingau Montosa Charta 1994: A distinctive and complex Riesling, dry, and marked by mineral, spice and lime flavors of good depth and length. Tempting now, but should improve through 2000. 500 cases made. • $19 • (04/30/97) • **88**

Riesling QbA Rheingau Rauenthal Nonnenberg Erstes Gewächs 1994: Serious and subtle, combining tangy fruit flavors and relatively full body with mineral accents and a very dry, crisp texture. Drinkable now, but should improve through at least 2000. • $36 • (04/30/97) • **88**

Riesling QbA Rheingau Rüdesheim Schlossberg Erstes Gewächs 1994: A delicate, tangy, light-bodied but intensely flavored Riesling that mates aromas of mineral and marzipan with subtle peach and lime flavors that linger on the finish. Drink now through 2004. 500 cases made. • $36 • (04/30/97) • **90**

Riesling QbA Rheingau Rüdesheim Estate 1995: A restrained but tangy Riesling with fine balance, refreshing peach, floral and mineral-like flavors and a lingering finish. • $15 • (04/30/97) • **86**

Riesling QbA Trocken Rheingau Rüdesheim Estate 1996: Delicate, well-crafted Riesling with flinty, mineral aromas and flavors. Medium-bodied, dry and lively, with a slightly short finish. Drink now. 291 cases made. • $15 • (11/30/97) • **86**

Riesling Qualitätswein Rheingau Rauenthal Nonnenberg 1995: Austere and bone dry, yet there's peach and apple character that's appealing, along with mineral and spice notes. Lean and tight, a candidate for the table. Best from 1999 through 2005. 500 cases made. • $38 • (03/31/98) • **88**

Riesling Qualitätswein Rheingau Rüdesheim Berg Schlossberg 1995: Beginning to show some petrol and marzipan flavors, typical of maturing Riesling. Powerful, vivid and dry, with a firm structure and a long aftertaste, this is a wine for food. Best from 1999 through 2005. 200 cases made. • $38 • (03/31/98) • **91**

Riesling Trockenbeerenauslese Rheingau Rüesheimer Bischofsberg 1993 • $NA • (11/30/94) • **87**

BUHL, REICHSRAT VON

Riesling Auslese Gold Cap Pfalz Forster Ungeheuer 1996: Pretty and seriously good Auslese with floral, lemon and tropical fruit aromas and flavors. Full-bodied, very sweet, and showing outstanding dry fruit, botrytis spice and fresh acidity on the finish. Super-intense aftertaste. Drink now or hold. • $27 • (11/30/97) • **90**

Riesling Auslese Pfalz Forster Ungeheuer 1996: Not as sweet as some, but bubbling over with crushed fruit on the nose and palate. Medium- to full-bodied, sweet, with a long melon, apple and grape aftertaste. Good acidity. • $27 • (11/30/97) • **87**

Riesling Eiswein Pfalz Forster Jesuitengarten 1996: Complex aromas of mineral, flint and fruit mingle with the lemon and lime undertones of an eiswein. Full-bodied and very sweet, with plenty of fresh acidity. Balanced and fine. Drink now or hold. • $89/375ml • (11/30/97) • **92**

Riesling Kabinett Pfalz Armand 1996: A wine packed with spicy, flinty character. Well-balanced, medium-bodied, medium-sweet, with a long flavorful finish and crisp acidity. Drinkable now, but will improve with age. • $15 • (11/30/97) • **88**

Riesling QbA Halbtrocken Pfalz Deidesheimer 1996: Racy and fresh, with intense aromas of melons, apples and peaches. Medium-bodied and off-dry, with loads of peach and spice character on the finish. Drink or hold. • $12 • (11/30/97) • **87**

Riesling Spätlese Halbtrocken Pfalz Forster Pechstein 1996: An elegant Riesling with a character of spice and pie crust, and a hint of apple. Medium-bodied and lightly sweet, with fresh acidity and slightly light finish. Drink now. • $19 • (11/30/97) • **85**

Riesling Spätlese Pfalz Forster Kirchenstück 1996: Shows good dried apricot and pineapple character, yet a hint of greenness creeps in. Medium-bodied, medium-sweet and very high in acidity, with a green apple skin finish. Try now. • $21 • (11/30/97) • **84**

Riesling Spätlese Trocken Pfalz Forster Ungeheuer 1996: A Riesling with very pleasing spicy and fruity character and a caressing texture. Medium-bodied and dry, with a medium finish. Drink now. • $20 • (11/30/97) • **87**

Riesling Trockenbeerenauslese Pfalz Forster Ungeheuer 1996: Outstanding harmony in an outstanding sweet wine. Displaying radiant aromas and flavors of tangerine, honey and spice, it's full-bodied and very sweet, with a long, lively finish. Drink now or hold. • $183/375ml • (11/30/97) • **93**

BÜRKLIN-WOLF, DR.

Muskateller Auslese Trocken Pfalz 1993 • $22 • (11/30/94) • **87**

Muskateller Trockenbeerenauslese Pfalz Wachenheimer Luginsland 1995: A bizarre mixture of orange peel and off flavors. Disjointed and not very appealing. • $89/375ml • (11/30/96) • **78**

Key: SS—Spectator Selection CS—Cellar Selection HR—Highly Recommended BB—Best Buy $NA—Price not available Ⓐ—Auction Price (BT)—Barrel Tasting
Dates in parentheses indicate the issues in which the ratings were published.

Riesling Auslese Pfalz Forster Pechstein 1995: Not a big auslese, but shows plenty of spicy, sweet, ripe fruit character with hints of peaches and melons. Medium-bodied. Sweet and very fresh finish. Drink now or hold. • $25/375ml • (11/30/96) • **88**

Riesling Beerenauslese Pfalz Wachenheimer Gerümpel 1996: Impressively balanced for a rare, sweet wine. Dark gold in color, with intense aromas of marmalade, citrus and maple-syrup. Full-bodied, very sweet and thick as honey, yet displays good acidity and plenty of fruit flavors. Drink now or hold. • $72 • (11/30/97) • **91**

Riesling Beerenauslese Pfalz Wachenheimer Goldbächel 1994 • $75 • (11/30/95) • **92**

Riesling Eiswein Pfalz Wachenheimer Gerümpel 1996: Not as flamboyant as some eisweins, though its citrus, spice character, tinged with underlying nuances of sweet and sour, is alluring. Medium-bodied and sweet, with a good finish. Drink now. • $185/375ml • (11/30/97) • **88**

Riesling Kabinett Pfalz 1993 • $13 • (11/30/94) • **83**

Riesling Kabinett Pfalz Ruppertsberger Gaisböhl 1995: Very rich, with loads of lemon, tropical fruit and pie crust aromas and flavors. Medium-bodied and lightly sweet, with a flavorful finish. A food-friendly kabinett. • $15 • (11/30/96) • **88**

Riesling Kabinett Pfalz Ruppertsberger Gaisböhl 1994 • $18 • (11/30/95) • **83**

Riesling Kabinett Pfalz Wachenheimer Rechbächel 1996: Delicious Kabinett. Very fresh wine with pear, light honey and spice aromas and flavors. Light-bodied, off-dry, with a light and refreshing finish. • $13 • (11/30/97) • **86**

Riesling Kabinett Pfalz Wachenheimer Rechbächel 1995: A full-blown, botrytized kabinett that delivers flavors ranging from dried apricot and honey to white pepper and tobacco. Quite full-bodied, complex and long. Interesting, if not typical. • $15 • (11/30/96) • **88**

Riesling Kabinett Pfalz Wachenheimer Rechbächel 1994 • $17 • (11/30/95) • **87**

Riesling QbA Pfalz 1993 • $12 • (11/30/94) • **76**

Riesling QbA Pfalz Forster 1996: Was a bit young and raw, but solid, with attractive ripe-fruit, spice and pineapple character. Medium-bodied, medium-sweet, with a very tart finish. Try now. • $9 • (11/30/97) • **85**

Riesling QbA Pfalz Forster 1995: Marked by its ripeness, this offers tropical fruit flavors and hints of hazelnut. Medium-bodied and lightly sweet. Fresh finish. • $20 • (11/30/96) • **86**

Riesling QbA Pfalz Forster 1994 • $14 • (11/30/95) • **85**

Riesling Spätlese Halbtrocken Pfalz Wachenheimer Gerümpel 1996: A wine with plenty of rich and spicy character. Medium-bodied, off-dry and refreshing. Long, spicy aftertaste. Drink now. • $16 • (11/30/97) • **87**

Riesling Spätlese Pfalz Forster Ungeheuer 1995: Wonderfully ripe and powerful with a bounty of spice, honey, lemon, smoke and tropical fruit character. Full-bodied and sweet with loads of flavor and a long, long finish. Drink now or hold. • $20 • (11/30/96) • **91**

Riesling Spätlese Pfalz Wachenheimer Altenburg 1995: Rich, ripe and ready to drink. Rather forward, showing aromas and flavors of apple, pineapple and earth. Medium- to full-bodied. Sweet, with a flavorful finish. • $20 • (11/30/96) • **86**

Riesling Spätlese Pfalz Wachenheimer Altenburg 1994 • $20 • (11/30/95) • **85**

Riesling Spätlese Pfalz Wachenheimer Gerümpel 1996: A very fresh wine with plenty of apple, cream and honey character. Medium-bodied, medium-sweet, with a long and lively spicy, fruit finish. Drinkable now. • $16 • (11/30/97) • **88**

Riesling Spätlese Pfalz Wachenheimer Gerümpel 1995: Rich in apple, mineral and honey flavors, balanced and fresh. The flavors are intense, harmonious and resonate on the palate. Drinkable now, but better in 2000. • $20 • (11/30/96) • **90**

Riesling Spätlese Pfalz Wachenheimer Gerümpel 1994 • $20 • (11/30/95) • **83**

Riesling Spätlese Pfalz Wachenheimer Gerümpel 1993 • $18 • (11/30/94) • **91**

Riesling Spätlese Trocken Pfalz Forster Kirchenstück 1996: Highly perfumed and abundant in mineral, flinty character. Medium to full in body, dry, with lots of flavors and a long spicy, crisp finish. Almost outstanding. Drink now. • $25 • (11/30/97) • **89**

Riesling Spätlese Trocken Pfalz Forster Kirchenstück 1995: A fragrant, exuberant Riesling with lots of lively peach, honey and grapefruit notes, fine acidity and a lingering finish. Clean, slightly sweet and well balanced. Drink now through 1999. 3,000 cases made. • $30 • (06/30/97) • **88**

Riesling Spätlese Trocken Pfalz Ruppertsberger Gaisböhl 1995: A solid, refreshing, slightly sweet Riesling with attractive peach flavors and lively acidity. Austere in flavor and on the finish. 3,100 cases made. • $30 • (06/30/97) • **86**

Riesling Spätlese Trocken Pfalz Ruppertsberger Reiterpfad 1994: A pretty basic Riesling, with vaguely green flavors, lemony acidity and a simple finish. 5,000 cases made. • $30 • (06/30/97) • **77**

Riesling Spätlese Trocken Pfalz Wachenheimer Altenberg 1993 • $19 • (11/30/94) • **84**

Riesling Spätlese Trocken Pfalz Wachenheimer Goldbächel 1994: Of average quality, with rather diluted flavors and a soft texture. Acceptable but simple. 2,000 cases made. • $30 • (06/30/97) • **78**

Riesling Trockenbeerenauslese Pfalz Forster Kirchenstück 1994 • $211 • (11/30/95) • **96**

Scheurebe Beerenauslese Pfalz Wachenheimer Gerümpel 1995: A strong petrol note pervades this wine, but it shows apple and honey flavors underneath. Has a lot of intensity, and the whopping acid level suggests hands off until 2000. • $49/375ml • (11/30/96) • **90**

Weissburgunder QbA Trocken Pfalz 1993 • $15 • (11/30/94) • **82**

White Pfalz Papageno 1995: An easy quaff. Soft and rather neutral, with restrained aromas of grapefruit and peach and rounder, off-dry flavors of peach and minerals. • $NA • (10/15/96) • **81**

CASTELL, FURST ZU

Kerner Kabinett Franken Schloss Castell QmP 1993 • $14 • (11/30/94) • **82**

Müller-Thurgau QbA Franken 1993 • $11 • (11/30/94) • **78**

Riesling Spätlese Franken Casteller Schlossberg QmP 1993 • $23 • (11/30/94) • **85**

CHRISTOFFEL, JOH. JOS.

Riesling Auslese Gold Cap Mosel-Saar-Ruwer Ürziger Würzgarten Five Stars 1994 • $NA • (11/30/95) • **87**

Riesling Auslese Gold Cap Mosel-Saar-Ruwer Ürziger Würzgarten Four Stars 1994 • $39 • (11/30/95) • **85**

Riesling Auslese Mosel-Saar-Ruwer Erdener Treppchen 1994 • $31 • (11/30/95) • **83**

Riesling Auslese Mosel-Saar-Ruwer Ürziger Würzgarten 1994 • $21 • (11/30/95) • **84**

Riesling Auslese Mosel-Saar-Ruwer Ürziger Würzgarten Two Stars 1994 • $NA • (11/30/95) • **83**

Riesling Beerenauslese Mosel-Saar-Ruwer Ürziger Würzgarten 1994 • $NA • (11/30/95) • **84**

Riesling Spätlese Mosel-Saar-Ruwer Erdener Treppchen 1994 • $17 • (11/30/95) • **83**

Riesling Spätlese Mosel-Saar-Ruwer Ürziger Würzgarten 1994 • $17 • (11/30/95) • **85**

CHRISTOFFEL ERBEN, JOH. JOS.

Riesling Auslese Mosel-Saar-Ruwer Erdener Treppchen 1993 • $22 • (11/30/94) • **87**

Riesling Auslese Mosel-Saar-Ruwer Erdener Treppchen Two Stars 1995: Lots of flinty mineral character in this wine but less than the expected concentration of fruit for an auslese. Medium-bodied, with a spicy finish. Ready to drink. • $29 • (11/30/96) • **85**

Riesling Auslese Mosel-Saar-Ruwer Ürziger Würzgarten 1996: Steely and fresh, with plenty of flinty character. Medium in body, medium-sweet and high in acidity. Crisp finish. Drink now. • $17 • (11/30/97) • **87**

Riesling Auslese Mosel-Saar-Ruwer Ürziger Würzgarten 1995: Offers alluring flavors and aromas of flint and spice, medium-sweet, yet it's rather light for a spätlese. Refreshing on the finish. Drink now. • $21 • (11/30/96) • **84**

Riesling Auslese Mosel-Saar-Ruwer Ürziger Würzgarten 1993 • $25 • (11/30/94) • **85**

Riesling Auslese Mosel-Saar-Ruwer Ürziger Würzgarten One Star 1996: Beautifully fresh and floral, with a lovely balance of sweet fruit and crisp acidity. Medium body, long finish. Drink now or hold. • $20 • (11/30/97) • **88**

Riesling Auslese Mosel-Saar-Ruwer Ürziger Würzgarten One Star 1995: A solid auslese with pretty crushed grape, lemon and earth aromas and flavors. Medium-bodied, sweet and refreshing on the palate. Give it time to come together, try in 2000. • $25 • (11/30/96) • **87**

Riesling Auslese Mosel-Saar-Ruwer Ürziger Würzgarten Three Stars 1996: A wine with an abundance of grapefruit and flinty character. Medium in body and sweetness. Crisp and racy on the finish. Drinkable now. • $32 • (11/30/97) • **87**

Riesling Auslese Mosel-Saar-Ruwer Ürziger Würzgarten Three Stars 1995: Delicious. Beautiful pear, slate and almond notes resonate from start to finish. Concentrated, intense and stylish, this is a racy, vivid wine. • $38 • (11/30/96) • **87**

Riesling Auslese Mosel-Saar-Ruwer Ürziger Würzgarten Three Stars 1993 • $31 • (11/30/94) • **86**

Riesling Auslese Mosel-Saar-Ruwer Ürziger Würzgarten Two Stars 1996: An almost outstanding Mosel Auslese with pretty floral, citrus character marked by a hint of flintiness. Medium-bodied and medium-sweet. Crisp finish. Drinkable now. • $23 • (11/30/97) • **89**

Riesling Eiswein Mosel-Saar-Ruwer Ürziger Würzgarten 1993 • $65 • (11/30/94) • **90**

Riesling Kabinett Mosel-Saar-Ruwer Erdener Treppchen 1996: Shows good intensity of mineral, floral character. Medium-bodied, medium-sweet, it's clean and fresh on the finish. Try now. • $11 • (11/30/97) • **87**

Riesling Kabinett Mosel-Saar-Ruwer Erdener Treppchen 1995: A zingy and fresh Riesling with extremely refined aromas of fruit and minerals. Light-bodied and off-dry, with crisp acidity and a mineral finish. Delicious now. • $14 • (11/30/96) • **87**

Riesling Kabinett Mosel-Saar-Ruwer Erdener Treppchen 1994 • $14 • (11/30/95) • **83**

Riesling Kabinett Mosel-Saar-Ruwer Ürziger Würzgarten 1995: A stony, mineral flavored wine that combines razor-sharp acidity with hints of peach and lime flavor for complexity. Fine balance. • $14 • (11/30/96) • **89**

Riesling Kabinett Mosel-Saar-Ruwer Ürziger Würzgarten 1994 • $NA • (11/30/95) • **82**

Riesling Kabinett Mosel-Saar-Ruwer Ürziger Würzgarten 1996: Displays clean, fresh aromas and flavors of lemons and minerals. Light- to medium-bodied, off-dry, with a crisp finish. Drink now. • $11 • (11/30/97) • **86**

Riesling Spätlese Mosel-Saar-Ruwer Erdener Treppchen 1996: Dominated by lemon, lime and grapefruit aromas and flavors and a touch of spice. Medium-bodied, medium-sweet, with medium acidity. Drink now. • $13 • (11/30/97) • **85**

Riesling Spätlese Mosel-Saar-Ruwer Erdener Treppchen 1995: A pretty wine with melons and flowers on the nose and palate. Medium-bodied, with a helping of acidity and a fresh finish. Ready to drink. • $17 • (11/30/96) • **87**

Riesling Spätlese Mosel-Saar-Ruwer Ürziger Würzgarten 1995: Clean and fresh with a melon and cream character. Medium-bodied, middling sweet, with zingy acidity and a fresh finish. Drink now or hold. • $17 • (11/30/96) • **86**

Riesling Spätlese Mosel-Saar-Ruwer Ürziger Würzgarten 1993 • $15 • (11/30/94) • **87**

CRUSIUS

Riesling Auslese Gold Cap Nahe Traiser 1995: Subtle auslese, very sweet-tasting. Sweet-and-sour in character with honey and melon flavors, a touch of straw and a hint of almond extract. Ready to drink. • $60/500ml • (11/30/96) • **86**

Riesling Auslese Nahe Schlossböckelheimer Felsenberg 1996: A perfumed Riesling with aromas of roses, dried herbs and honey. Medium-bodied. More like a good spätlese than an auslese. Drink now. 1,100 cases made. • $34 • (11/30/97) • **82**

Riesling Auslese Nahe Schlossböckelheimer Felsenberg 1995: An eccentric wine with a wild character. Wonderful intensity of pineapple and spice flavors, with a hint of smoke. Of medium body and sweetness, with a mighty spicy finish that lingers long on the palate. Drink now or hold. • $30 • (11/30/96) • **90**

Riesling Beerenauslese Nahe Traiser 1996: Plenty of botrytis in this one, but slightly dusty in aroma and flavor. Medium-bodied, sweet, with crisp acidity, a slightly sour finish. Drink now. 120 cases made. • $98/500ml • (11/30/97) • **85**

Riesling Eiswein Nahe Traiser 1996: Classic eiswein that's as thick as syrup yet lively and electrifying by virtue of its high acidity. Full-bodied and extremely sweet, with loads of citrus character ranging from tangerine to lemon-rind. Long finish. Drink now or hold. • $150/500ml • (11/30/97) • **95**

Riesling Kabinett Nahe Niederhäuser Felsensteyer 1996: Shows very good mineral and green-apple aromas and flavors but a slightly diluted finish. Medium-bodied, medium-sweet. Drink now. 1,900 cases made. • $19 • (11/30/97) • **82**

Riesling QbA Nahe Norheimer 1996: Strangely green and herbal, with a character verging on vegetable. Medium-bodied and medium-sweet, with a funky finish. Drink if you must. 2,500 cases made. • $12 • (11/30/97) • **78**

Riesling QbA Nahe Norheimer 1995: Fun and zingy, with its aromas and flavors of lemon, mineral and spice. Lightly sweet with a fresh, light finish. • $11 • (11/30/96) • **84**

Riesling Spätlese Nahe Niederhäuser Felsensteyer 1995: Shows some ripe fruit flavors and aromas, but slightly dull and disjointed overall, with candied finish. • $21 • (11/30/96) • **78**

Riesling Spätlese Nahe Traiser Bastei 1996: Shows exciting aromas of ripe tropical fruits, honey and almonds. Medium-bodied, medium-sweet, with a spicy, fruity aftertaste. Could use a bit more concentration. Drink now. 1,900 cases made. • $23 • (11/30/97) • **85**

Riesling Spätlese Nahe Traiser Bastei 1995: Appealing aromas of apple, clover honey and mineral lead the way into an elegant, graceful wine of subtle length. Seems more like a Mosel than Nahe. Drinkable now. • $22 • (11/30/96) • **88**

CRUSIUS & SOHN, HANS

Riesling Auslese Nahe Schlossböckelheimer Felsenberg 1994 • $NA • (11/30/95) • **87**

Riesling Auslese Trocken Nahe Traiser Bastei 1994 • $NA • (11/30/95) • **88**

Riesling Beerenauslese Nahe Traiser Rotenfels 1994 • $NA • (11/30/95) • **79**

Riesling Kabinett Halbtrocken Nahe Traiser Rotenfels 1994 • $NA • (11/30/95) • **84**

Riesling QbA Trocken Nahe Traiser Rotenfels 1994 • $NA • (11/30/95) • **80**

Riesling Spätlese Nahe Niederhäuser Felsensteyer 1994 • $NA • (11/30/95) • **85**

Riesling Spätlese Nahe Schlossböckelheimer Felsenberg 1994 • $NA • (11/30/95) • **87**

Riesling Spätlese Trocken Nahe Traiser Rotenfels 1994 • $NA • (11/30/95) • **81**

Riesling Trockenbeerenauslese Nahe Traiser Bastei 1994 • $NA • (11/30/95) • **80**

Weissburgunder QbA Trocken Nahe Traiser 1994 • $NA • (11/30/95) • **79**

DARTING, KURT

Huxelrebe Beerenauslese Pfalz Forster Schnepfenflug 1996: Not exactly from a noble grape, but impressive. Sweet and very intense, with sweet-and-sour, lemon-lime character throughout. Medium-bodied with lively acidity. Best after 2000. 250 cases made. • $22/500ml • (11/30/97) • **88**

Rieslaner Auslese Pfalz Dürkheimer Nonnengarten 1996: Fat and thick for auslese, with honeydew melon aromas. Medium- to full-bodied, with a clover honey finish. Slightly dull. Drink now. 333 cases made. • $21 • (11/30/97) • **84**

Rieslaner Beerenauslese Pfalz Ungsteiner Bettelhaus 1996: An electrified sweetie with a bounteous spicy lemon-lime and botrytis character. Full-bodied, very sweet and incredibly fresh. High acidity, long, long aftertaste. 204 cases made. • $23/500ml • (11/30/97) • **91**

Riesling Auslese Pfalz Ungsteiner Herrenberg 1996: Plenty of CO_2 in this bubbly auslese. It's lovely and delicate, showing crushed grapes, apple and pears on the nose and palate. Medium-bodied, medium-sweet and not as rich as others in this category, but delicious. Drink now. 200 cases made. • $18 • (11/30/97) • **85**

Riesling Kabinett Pfalz Ungsteiner Bettelhaus 1996: A real standout for this vintage, this shows lovely apricot and honey aromas and flavors, with a hint of spice and pie crust. Medium-bodied, medium-sweet, with a long, flavorful finish. Drink now. 233 cases made. • $11 • (11/30/97) • **90**

Riesling Spätlese Pfalz Dürkheimer Spielberg 1996: Enticing aromas and flavors of apple pie and cream. Medium-bodied, medium-sweet, with crisp acidity and a long, ripe fruit finish. Delicious. Drink now. 254 cases made. • $12 • (11/30/97) • **89**

Scheurebe Spätlese Pfalz Dürkheimer Spielberg 1996: This medium-bodied, medium-sweet wine exhibits alluring aromas of mango and cream and a silky texture. Drink now. 200 cases made. • $11 • (11/30/97) • **87**

DEINHARD

Riesling Auslese Mosel-Saar-Ruwer Bernkasteler Doctor 1995: A subtle wine that grows on the palate. Medium- to full-bodied and quite sweet, its zingy acidity and fresh fruit character kick in on the finish. Drinkable now. 210 cases made. • $40/500ml • (11/30/96) • **91**

Key: SS—Spectator Selection CS—Cellar Selection HR—Highly Recommended BB—Best Buy $NA—Price not available Ⓐ—Auction Price (BT)—Barrel Tasting

Dates in parentheses indicate the issues in which the ratings were published.

Riesling Auslese Mosel-Saar-Ruwer Wehlener Sonnenuhr 1995: Not as big as some, but a harmonious auslese with a good amount of spicy, flinty nutmeg character. Medium-bodied. Drink now or hold. 102 cases made. • $25/500ml • (11/30/96) • **87**

Riesling Auslese Rheingau Geisenheimer Rothenberg 1995: A textbook auslese, exhibiting almond, honey and spice flavors. Its power, mineral character, acidity and length suggest waiting until 2000 to try. 190 cases made. • $30 • (11/30/96) • **88**

Riesling Auslese Rheingau Oestricher Lenchen 1995: A pretty wine with peachy, spicy, flinty aromas and flavors. Medium-bodied and sweet, with a fresh and simple finish. 170 cases made. • $35 • (11/30/96) • **86**

Riesling Beerenauslese Mosel-Saar-Ruwer Bernkasteler Doctor 1995: Highly concentrated, with masses of spiced, honeyed and dried fruit aromas and flavors. Full-bodied and viscous. Incredibly sweet, with a long finish. Lively acidity holds it all together. Drink now. 10 cases made. • $70/375ml • (11/30/96) • **93**

Riesling Spätlese Mosel-Saar-Ruwer Wehlener Sonnenuhr 1995: Very ripe and tropical, sporting grapefruit, passionfruit and mineral flavors, highlighted by the botrytis accent. Drier than most, with plenty of acidic structure. Try now. 330 cases made. • $20 • (11/30/96) • **90**

Riesling Spätlese Rheingau Geisenheimer Rothenberg 1995: A drier style spätlese, but still packed with ripe, spicy, fruit aromas and flavors, off-dry, with crisp acidity. Long, smoky, spicy finish. Drink now or hold. 510 cases made. • $20 • (11/30/96) • **87**

Riesling Spätlese Rheingau Winkeler Hasensprung 1995: Delicious, with honey and spice flavors, a hint of earth. Medium-bodied and sweet, with a creamy texture and a refreshing finish. Perfect to drink now. 440 cases made. • $23 • (11/30/96) • **87**

White QbA Mosel-Saar-Ruwer Bereich Bernkastel 1993 • $13 • (11/30/94) • **78**

DIEL, SCHLOSSGUT

Riesling Auslese Gold Cap Nahe 1994 • $NA • (11/30/95) • **83**

Riesling Auslese Gold Cap Nahe 1993 • $86 • (11/30/94) • **92**

Riesling Auslese Nahe 1996: Fantastic for an auslese. Golden-colored, with aromas and flavors of very ripe pineapple and burnt almond. Full-bodied and very sweet, with an oily, thick texture and lots of zingy acidity and flavor. Wonderful wine. Drink or hold. • $41/375ml • (11/30/97) • **91**

Riesling Auslese Nahe 1995: Aromas of canned pears are followed by tart, thin flavors. Cloying finish. • $89/375ml • (11/30/96) • **78**

Riesling Auslese Nahe Dorsheimer Pittermännchen 1993 • $40 • (11/30/94) • **91**

Riesling Beerenauslese Gold Cap Nahe 1994 • $NA • (11/30/95) • **87**

Riesling Beerenauslese Gold Cap Nahe 1993 • $158 • (11/30/94) • **94**

Riesling Eiswein Gold Cap Nahe 1995: Very intense tropical fruit, especially pineapple, and petrol aromas which follow through on the palate. Full-bodied. Very sweet with a round texture, yet there's zingy acidity on the finish. Drink now or hold. • $NA/375ml • (11/30/96) • **92**

Riesling Eiswein Nahe 1995: Superclean. Wonderfully intense, sticky with lemon, honey and peach aromas. Medium-bodied and very sweet, with a honeylike texture and an oily yet refreshing finish. Drink now or hold. Better after 2000. • $260/375ml • (11/30/96) • **91**

Riesling Eiswein Nahe 1994 • $142 • (11/30/95) • **90**

Riesling Eiswein Nahe 1993 • $191 • (11/30/94) • **93**

Riesling Kabinett Nahe Dorsheimer Goldloch 1996: Spicy, flinty wine with a character of apple and melon. Medium in body, it's off-dry with a light, delicate finish. Drink now. • $20 • (11/30/97) • **87**

Riesling Kabinett Nahe Dorsheimer Goldloch 1995: A good example of kabinett, with a balance between the peach and passion fruit flavors and the citrusy acidity. Medium-bodied and showing a moderate finish, this should develop with age. • $24 • (11/30/96) • **86**

Riesling Kabinett Nahe Dorsheimer Goldloch 1994 • $23 • (11/30/95) • **87**

Riesling Kabinett Nahe Dorsheimer Goldloch 1993 • $21 • (11/30/94) • **89**

Riesling Kabinett Nahe Dorsheimer Pittermännchen 1996: A subtle yet complex white with floral, mineral and cream aromas and flavors. Medium-bodied and sweet, with a light, slightly short finish. Drink now. • $20 • (11/30/97) • **88**

Riesling Kabinett Nahe Dorsheimer Pittermännchen 1995: Plenty going on in this glass. Honey, melon, hazelnut and spice aromas and flavors, medium-bodied, off-dry. Wonderfully flavorful finish. Drink now or hold. • $24 • (11/30/96) • **89**

Riesling Kabinett Nahe Dorsheimer Pittermännchen 1994 • $NA • (11/30/95) • **84**

Riesling QbA Nahe 1996: Delicious, lively wine that's loaded with ripe melon and spice. Medium-bodied, off-dry, with lovely acidity and a fruity finish. Drink now. • $15 • (11/30/97) • **87**

Riesling QbA Nahe 1994 • $12 • (11/30/95) • **86**

Riesling Spätlese Nahe Dorsheimer Burgberg 1996: A typical and very good spätlese that shows complex aromas of flint and honeysuckle. Medium-bodied and lightly sweet, with a spicy, pineapple finish. Drink now. • $25 • (11/30/97) • **88**

Riesling Spätlese Nahe Dorsheimer Burgberg 1995: The seductive, vanilla and pie crust aromas lead to rich flavors of floral and peach. The texture is creamy, but the acidity keeps it all in check. Smoky finish. Try in 1999. • $28 • (11/30/96) • **88**

Riesling Spätlese Nahe Dorsheimer Goldloch 1996: Lovely perfumes of minerals, lemon and honey are on display in this medium-bodied, lightly sweet wine. Good apple flavors and a medium finish. Drink now. • $32 • (11/30/97) • **87**

Riesling Spätlese Nahe Dorsheimer Goldloch 1995: Fresh, vibrant and absolutely delicious. Delicate sense of harmony, with the lime, apple and talc flavors in perfect balance. Intense acidity suggests trying in 1999. • $32 • (11/30/96) • **89**

Riesling Spätlese Nahe Dorsheimer Goldloch 1994 • $30 • (11/30/95) • **80**

Riesling Spätlese Nahe Dorsheimer Pittermännchen 1996: An elegant, refined spätlese with a character of pears, apples and dried spices. Medium in body, sweetness and acidity. Round texture. Drink now. • $28 • (11/30/97) • **86**

Riesling Spätlese Nahe Dorsheimer Pittermännchen 1995: The nose is dominated by a burnt-match aroma, which sneaks onto the palate as well. • $24 • (11/30/96) • **72**

Riesling Spätlese Nahe Dorsheimer Pittermännchen 1994 • $30 • (11/30/95) • **83**

Riesling Spätlese Nahe Dorsheimer Pittermännchen 1993 • $28 • (11/30/94) • **90**

DÖNNHOFF, H.

Riesling Auslese Gold Cap Nahe Oberhäuser Brücke 1993 • $35 • (11/30/94) • **90**

Riesling Auslese Nahe Niederhäuser Hermannshöhle 1996: A beautifully balanced sweet wine with a creamy, silky texture and long, ripe fruit and honey flavors. Medium-bodied, with fine acidity and lots of mango and tropical fruit character. Drink now. • $27/375ml • (11/30/97) • **89**

Riesling Auslese Nahe Niederhäuser Hermannshöhle 1995: Quite dry and elegant, exhibiting a red berry character in addition to its almond and lemon custard flavors. Deft winemaking for this vintage. • $32 • (11/30/96) • **89**

Riesling Auslese Nahe Niederhäuser Hermannshöhle 1994 • $34 • (11/30/95) • **86**

Riesling Auslese Nahe Niederhäuser Hermannshöhle 1993 • $29 • (11/30/94) • **89**

Riesling Auslese Nahe Oberhäuser Brücke 1996: Lovely sweet, honeyed wine with subtle hints of spice and pineapple. Medium-bodied and sweet with a fresh finish. Drink now. • $26/375ml • (11/30/97) • **86**

Riesling Auslese Nahe Oberhäuser Brücke 1994 • $33 • (11/30/95) • **89**

Riesling Beerenauslese Nahe Oberhäuser Brücke 1995: A beauty, emitting fresh pear, apricot and honey aromas. Extremely youthful and undeveloped from the apple and pear flavors to the mouthwatering acidity. The finish is lingering and polished. Stunning from start to finish. • $49/375ml • (11/30/96) • **93**

Riesling Eiswein Nahe Oberhäuser Brücke 1996: Golden amber in color, this is slightly overdone with a bit of oxidation, but amazingly concentrated in its burnt almond, orange peel and smoky character. Full-bodied, very spicy, and a long, zingy finish. Already mature. Drink now. • $93/375ml • (11/30/97) • **90**

Riesling Eiswein Nahe Oberhäuser Brücke 1995: Everything is in the right place. Lovely, clean, thick with ripe fruit, honey and lemon aromas and flavors. Full-bodied and sweet, with a balancing acidity and a flavorful finish. • $129/375ml • (11/30/96) • **91**

Riesling Eiswein Nahe Oberhäuser Brücke 1994 • $127 • (11/30/95) • **94**

Riesling Eiswein Nahe Oberhäuser Felsenberg 1993 • $135 • (11/30/94) • **92**

Riesling Kabinett Nahe Niederhäuser Hermannshöhle 1993 • $13 • (11/30/94) • **88**

Riesling Kabinett Nahe Oberhäuser Leistenberg 1994 • $15 • (11/30/95) • **82**

Riesling QbA Nahe 1996: Fresh and floral with a lovely perfumed nose and palate. Medium-bodied and off-dry with an apple, creamy aftertaste. Drink now. • $12 • (11/30/97) • **85**

Riesling Spätlese Nahe Niederhäuser Hermannshöhle 1996: Elegant spätlese with pear, melon and honey aromas and flavors. Medium body, medium-sweet with a round texture and a fruity finish. Drink now. • $23 • (11/30/97) • **85**

Riesling Spätlese Nahe Niederhäuser Hermannshöhle 1995: Very good quality in a standard spätlese, with lemon and floral aromas and flavors, medium body, some sweetness and a light finish. Drink now. • $22 • (11/30/96) • **85**

Riesling Spätlese Nahe Niederhäuser Hermmanshöhle 1994 • $23 • (11/30/95) • **83**

Riesling Spätlese Nahe Niederhäuser Hermannshöhle 1993 • $19 • (11/30/94) • **88**

Riesling Spätlese Nahe Norheimer Kirschheck 1996: Subtle aromas of apple, cream and roses. Medium-bodied, medium-sweet with a lovely cut grapefruit and pineapple flavor. Crisp finish. Drink now or hold. • $21 • (11/30/97) • **87**

Riesling Spätlese Nahe Oberhäuser Brücke 1995: Subtle and well made. This offers lemon, honey, rose petal and spice aromas and flavors and a fresh, crisp finish. A harmonious wine of moderate sweetness. • $22 • (11/30/96) • **88**

Riesling Spätlese Nahe Oberhäuser Brücke 1994 • $23 • (11/30/95) • **85**

Riesling Spätlese Nahe Oberhäuser Brücke 1993 • $18 • (11/30/94) • **80**

Riesling Spätlese Nahe Schlossböckelheimer Felsenberg 1995: There's plenty to like in this flavorful spätlese, from the lime and apricot scents to the lingering honeyed finish. It's ripe and balanced, for drinking now or in 2000. • $26 • (11/30/96) • **87**

Riesling Trockenbeerenauslese Nahe Niederhäuser Hermannshöhle 1994 • $168 • (11/30/95) • **96**

EBERBACH, STAATSWEINGÜTER KLOSTER

Kabinett Rheingau Rauenthaler Baiken 1994 • $14 • (11/30/95) • **79**

Riesling Auslese Gold Cap Rheingau Erbacher Marcobrunn 1993 • $NA • (11/30/94) • **87**

Riesling Auslese Rheingau Erbacher Marcobrunn 1995: Offers muted fruit flavors, accented by honey notes, but lacks depth and finishes on an artificial note. Tasted twice, this second bottle scoring better than the first. 120 cases made. • $75 • (11/30/96) • **79**

Riesling Auslese Rheingau Rauenthaler Baiken 1996: Electrifyingly fresh, with apples and pears galore. Full-bodied and medium-sweet, with zingy acidity and a long, long finish. Best from 2000 through 2005. 110 cases made. • $18/375ml • (07/31/98) • **92**

Riesling Auslese Rheingau Steinberger 1993 • $NA • (11/30/94) • **84**

Riesling Beerenauslese Rheingau Rauenthaler Baiken 1993 • $NA • (11/30/94) • **92**

Riesling Beerenauslese Rheingau Rüdesheimer Schlossberg 1995: Moderately sweet, with a firm, acidic structure, yet it's a little raw and unformed at this stage. Hazelnut, honey and apricot are the dominant flavors. Should strut its stuff in 2000. 50 cases made. • $230/375ml • (11/30/96) • **90**

Riesling Eiswein Gold Cap Rheingau Erbacher Marcobrunn 1996: Aromas of blanched almonds and dried fruits with figs. Full-bodied, sweet and very thick, with loads of flavor and a long, long finish. Pralines and cream in a bottle. Amazing. Drink now through 2010. 10 cases made. • $320/375ml • (07/31/98) • **95**

Riesling Eiswein Rheingau Rauenthaler Baiken 1996: Pretty aromas of almond and pie crust, with honey and spice. Medium-bodied and medium-sweet, with fine acidity and a delicious finish. Elegant eiswein. Drink now. 20 cases made. • $130/375ml • (07/31/98) • **88**

Riesling Eiswein Rheingau Steinberger 1995: Beautiful, ripe fruit intensity in this wine, with vivid honey, lemon-curd and spice aromas and flavors. Full-bodied yet reserved, with a very sweet palate and a long, zingy finish. Drink now or hold. 15 cases made. • $NA/375ml • (11/30/96) • **91**

Riesling Kabinett Rheingau Erbacher Marcobrunn 1995: One of the best vineyards in the Rheingau and one of the best kabinetts of this vintage. Quite refreshing, with sliced apple, melon and mineral character throughout. Medium-bodied with fine acidity and loads of flavors on the finish. Drink now or hold. 120 cases made. • $75 • (11/30/96) • **89**

Riesling Kabinett Rheingau Rauenthaler Baiken 1996: Plenty of apple and peach in this young Riesling. Medium-bodied and lightly sweet, with a fresh finish. Slightly simple for this great vineyard. 1,000 cases made. • $16 • (07/31/98) • **85**

Riesling Kabinett Rheingau Rauenthaler Baiken 1994: On the tart side, with herbally apple flavors. A bit awkward and cloying on the finish. 2,000 cases made. • $14 • (08/31/96) • **79**

Riesling Kabinett Rheingau Rauenthaler Baiken 1993 • $NA • (11/30/94) • **81**

Riesling Kabinett Rheingau Steinberger 1996: Light flinty and mineral aromas and flavors. Medium to light in body, with strong acidity and a fresh finish. A bit young, but impressive. Best from 1999 through 2004. 8,000 cases made. • $17 • (07/31/98) • **87**

Riesling Kabinett Rheingau Steinberger 1995: A superb vineyard site and a very complete wine. Ripe and mouthfilling with apple, tropical fruit and grapefruit character. Medium-bodied and lightly sweet, with a clean and refreshing finish. 8,000 cases made. • $18 • (11/30/96) HR • **90**

Riesling Kabinett Rheingau Steinberger 1994: An austere, serious wine to be enjoyed with food. Well-structured, with mineral, apple and peach flavors and good acidity. 4,000 cases made. • $14 • (08/31/96) • **85**

Riesling QbA Rheingau Steinberger 1996: Attractive aromas of cream and apple, with floral undertones. Medium-bodied and off-dry, with lemon and apricot flavors and a fresh finish. Delicious. Drink now. 5,000 cases made. • $12 • (07/31/98) • **87**

Riesling Rheingau Steinberger 1994 • $14 • (11/30/95) • **85**

Riesling Spätlese Rheingau Erbacher Marcobrunn 1996: Outstanding intensity, with lots of apricot and apple aromas. Medium- to full-bodied. Medium-sweet, with a lively and flavorful finish. Super wine. Drink now through 2005. 310 cases made. • $24 • (07/31/98) • **91**

Riesling Spätlese Rheingau Erbacher Marcobrunn 1993 • $NA • (11/30/94) • **83**

Riesling Spätlese Rheingau Hochheimer Domdechaney 1996: Elegant aromas of tropical and citrus fruits. Medium-bodied, and off-dry, with a medium finish. Better on the nose than on the palate. Drink now. 1,000 cases made. • $18 • (07/31/98) • **85**

Riesling Spätlese Rheingau Hochheimer Domdechaney 1995: A spätlese with plenty of ripe fruit flavors and the searing acidity to match. Of moderate concentration and intensity, it's one for the cellar. 600 cases made. • $22 • (11/30/96) • **86**

Riesling Spätlese Rheingau Hochheimer Domdechaney 1993 • $NA • (11/30/94) • **86**

Riesling Spätlese Rheingau Rauenthaler Baiken 1996: Aromas of white peach and apple flow from the glass. Medium-bodied and off-dry, with crisp acidity and a medium finish. Slight dilution on the mid-palate. Drink now. 600 cases made. • $22 • (07/31/98) • **85**

Riesling Spätlese Rheingau Rauenthaler Baiken 1995: Sneaks up on you as its subtle aromas of mineral and spice unfold onto the palate. Medium-bodied and of medium sweetness, with a spicy mineral finish. Delicious now or can hold. 1,500 cases made. • $26 • (11/30/96) • **89**

Riesling Spätlese Rheingau Rüdesheimer Berg Rottland 1996: Intensely flavored wine, oozing with apricot tart aromas. Medium-bodied and lightly sweet, with lively acidity and a long aftertaste. Drink now. 800 cases made. • $18 • (07/31/98) • **90**

Riesling Spätlese Rheingau Steinberger 1995: Fairly dry for a spätlese, but nicely ripe and showing plenty of lemon, mineral character. Medium-bodied, off-dry with a fresh finish. Drink now or hold. 900 cases made. • $35 • (11/30/96) • **87**

EHLEN, STEPHAN

Riesling Kabinett Mosel-Saar-Ruwer Erdener Treppchen 1996: Lovely aromas and flavors of flowers and peaches are the main themes in this richly textured, soft Mosel. Deceptively balanced, with some lively acidity sneaking in on the finish. Drink now through 2001. • $12 • (04/30/98) • **85**

ESER, AUGUST

Riesling Kabinett Halbtrocken Rheingau Oestricher Lenchen 1993 • $15 • (11/30/94) • **73**

Riesling Kabinett Rheingau Oestricher Lenchen 1993 • $15 • (11/30/94) • **85**

Riesling Spätlese Halbtrocken Rheingau Oestricher Doosberg 1993 • $20 • (11/30/94) • **87**

Riesling Spätlese Rheingau Oestricher Lenchen 1993 • $20 • (11/30/94) • **85**

Riesling Spätlese Rheingau Rauenthaler Rothenberg 1993 • $21 • (11/30/94) • **87**

Key: SS—Spectator Selection CS—Cellar Selection HR—Highly Recommended BB—Best Buy $NA—Price not available Ⓐ—Auction Price (BT)—Barrel Tasting

Dates in parentheses indicate the issues in which the ratings were published.

FITZ-RITTER

Grauer Burgunder Kabinett Trocken Pfalz Wachenheimer Mandelgarten 1994 • $13 • (12/15/95) • **82**

Riesling Spätlese Pfalz Ungsteiner Herrenberg 1995: Beginning to show maturity, this is ripe and complex, offering nectarine, grapefruit and almond flavors with perhaps a touch of botrytis. Good, mouthwatering acidity keeps the flavors lively. Drink now through 2005. • $12 • (01/01/98) • **87**

FRANKHOF

Kabinett Rheingau Primus Classicus 1993: A ripe wine with some depth, this offers pine, dried apple and pear flavors and sufficient acidity to offset the light sweetness. • $NA • (10/15/96) • **83**

FRIEDRICH-WILHELM-GYMNASIUM

Riesling Spätlese Mosel-Saar-Ruwer Graacher Himmelreich 1994: Nice and fresh. Slightly spritzy and has a zippy acidity. Apple flavors are complemented by a touch of spice. • $12 • (08/31/96) • **82**

GALLAIS, LE

Riesling Auslese Gold Cap Mosel-Saar-Ruwer Wiltinger Braune Kupp 1996: Delicious sweet wine with a lovely harmony of spice, mineral and lemon-lime character. Medium-bodied and very sweet, with a long, crisp finish. Drink now. • $NA/375ml • (11/30/97) • **92**

Riesling Auslese Gold Cap Mosel-Saar-Ruwer Wiltinger Braune Kupp No. A 1995: This is exciting, offering mineral and pear flavors and some exotic, tropical notes (from botrytis). Firm acidity supports the complex flavors, brings them all together on the finish. • $NA • (11/30/96) • **90**

Riesling Auslese Gold Cap Mosel-Saar-Ruwer Wiltinger Braune Kupp 1994 • $NA • (11/30/95) • **91**

Riesling Auslese Mosel-Saar-Ruwer Wiltinger Braune Kupp 1994 • $75 • (11/30/95) • **84**

Riesling Auslese Mosel-Saar-Ruwer Wiltinger Braune Kupp No. E 1995: The pear flavor is beguiling, like Poire William, with a soft, round character that's a little simple. Finish is a bit cloying. • $NA • (11/30/96) • **84**

Riesling Beerenauslese Mosel-Saar-Ruwer Wiltinger Braune Kupp 1994 • $NA • (11/30/95) • **90**

Riesling Kabinett Mosel-Saar-Ruwer Wiltinger Braune Kupp 1996: This medium-bodied wine promises more on the nose than it delivers on the palate, with grapefruit, lemon and flint aromas. Off-dry and short on the finish. Drink now. • $21 • (11/30/97) • **83**

Riesling Kabinett Mosel-Saar-Ruwer Wiltinger Braune Kupp 1995: Emits exotic aromas of passionfruit and almond extract, but lacks the concentration and length to really sing. • $18 • (11/30/96) • **83**

Riesling Kabinett Mosel-Saar-Ruwer Wiltinger Braune Kupp 1994 • $22 • (11/30/95) • **79**

Riesling Spätlese Mosel-Saar-Ruwer Wiltinger Braune Kupp 1996: Some good concentration but a hint of greenness on the nose and palate. Green apple, lime and herbs. Medium-bodied, medium-sweet with a light finish. Drink now. • $33 • (11/30/97) • **81**

Riesling Spätlese Mosel-Saar-Ruwer Wiltinger Braune Kupp No. 15 1995: A seductive nose of lime and mineral turns tropical on the palate, showing hints of pineapple. Rich, ripe and balanced, with good length. • $NA • (11/30/96) • **87**

Riesling Spätlese Mosel-Saar-Ruwer Wiltinger Braune Kupp 1994 • $34 • (11/30/95) • **82**

GRAFF, CARL

Reisling Spätlese Mosel-Saar-Ruwer Erdener Treppchen 1994 • $9 • (12/15/95) • **84**

Riesling Kabinett Mosel-Saar-Ruwer 1994 • $6 • (12/15/95) • **84**

Riesling Kabinett Mosel-Saar-Ruwer 1993 • $8 • (11/30/94) • **83**

Riesling QbA Mosel-Saar-Ruwer Ürziger Schwarzlay 1993 • $7 • (11/30/94) • **81**

Reisling QbA Mosel-Saar-Ruwer Ürziger Schwarzlay 1994 • $5 • (12/15/95) • **81**

GRANS-FASSIAN

Riesling Auslese Mosel-Saar-Ruwer Trittenheimer Apotheke 1993 • $35 • (11/30/94) • **86**
Riesling Auslese Mosel-Saar-Ruwer Trittenheimer Apotheke Three Stars 1993 • $73 • (11/30/94) • **68**
Riesling Beerenauslese Mosel-Saar-Ruwer Trittenheimer Apotheke 1993 • $200 • (11/30/94) • **84**
Riesling Eiswein Mosel-Saar-Ruwer 1993 • $250 • (11/30/94) • **93**
Riesling Kabinett Mosel-Saar-Ruwer Trittenheimer Altärchen 1993 • $17 • (11/30/94) • **83**
Riesling Spätlese Mosel-Saar-Ruwer Piesporter Goldtröpfchen 1993 • $24 • (11/30/94) • **72**

GUNDERLOCH

Riesling Auslese Gold Cap Rheinhessen Nackenheimer Rothenberg 1996: An elegant auslese with lovely apple and melon aromas and flavors. Medium-bodied and sweet, with a fresh, delicate finish. Drink now. • $75 • (11/30/97) • **86**
Riesling Auslese Gold Cap Rheinhessen Nackenheimer Rothenberg 1995: Bold, ripe and exotic, full of apricot, almond and honey flavors. There's moderate acidity, but the sheer weight and richness of this wine overwhelm it. 50 cases made. • $62 • (11/30/96) • **88**
Riesling Auslese Gold Cap Rheinhessen Nackenheimer Rothenberg 1994 • $59 • (11/30/95) • **90**
Riesling Auslese Gold Cap Rheinhessen Nackenheimer Rothenberg 1993 • $48 • (11/30/94) • **92**
Riesling Auslese Rheinhessen Nackenheimer Rothenberg 1996: A bit disappointing for this producer. Gold-colored, with melon, passionfruit and honey aromas. Medium-bodied with syrup and applesauce flavors. A bit flat. Tasted twice, with consistent notes. Drink now. • $33 • (11/30/97) • **82**
Riesling Auslese Rheinhessen Nackenheimer Rothenberg 1995: There's loads of almond character in this fresh, well-balanced wine, yet it lacks concentration in the middle and the finish is slightly diluted. 300 cases made. • $32 • (11/30/96) • **85**
Riesling Auslese Rheinhessen Nackenheimer Rothenberg 1994 • $33 • (11/30/95) • **86**
Riesling Auslese Rheinhessen Nackenheimer Rothenberg 1993 • $30 • (11/30/94) • **91**
Riesling Beerenauslese Rheinhessen Nackenheimer Rothenberg 1996: Super sticky wine, with impressively rich aromas of ripe fruit, balanced with almond and a touch of spice. Full-bodied, very sweet and very thick, with loads of fruit and sweet-and-sour character, plus a long, fresh finish. Drinkable now, but will improve with age. • $99/375ml • (11/30/97) • **93**
Riesling Beerenauslese Rheinhessen Nackenheimer Rothenberg 1994 • $96 • (11/30/95) • **90**
Riesling Beerenauslese Rheinhessen Nackenheimer Rothenberg 1993 • $90 • (11/30/94) • **90**
Riesling Kabinett Rheinhessen Jean-Baptiste 1996: A wine that builds on your palate. Mineral, pear and melon aromas and flavors. Medium-bodied, medium-sweet with a lovely crisp acidity. Drink now. • $15 • (11/30/97) • **87**
Riesling Kabinett Rheinhessen Jean-Baptiste 1995: Ripe and exotic aromas of passionfruit and apricot are appealing, with firm acidity beneath, and end in a long finish. A beautiful expression of Riesling that's drinkable now. 800 cases made. • $15 • (11/30/96) • **89**
Riesling Kabinett Rheinhessen Jean-Baptiste 1993 • $14 • (11/30/94) • **89**
Riesling Kabinett Rheinhessen Nackenheimer Rothenberg Jean-Baptiste 1994 • $15 • (11/30/95) • **88**
Riesling QbA Trocken Rheinhessen 1994 • $12 • (11/30/95) • **84**
Riesling Spätlese Rheinhessen Nackenheimer Rothenberg 1996: Nicely balanced spätlese. Wonderful aromas of pineapple, honey and minerals. Medium-bodied, medium-sweet with a very fruity palate and a crisp, silky finish. Drink now. • $24 • (11/30/97) • **88**
Riesling Spätlese Rheinhessen Nackenheimer Rothenberg 1995: Sleek and fine with its lovely honey, mineral and floral character. Medium-bodied and lightly sweet, with a fresh, clean finish. Ready to drink, but can be held. 600 cases made. • $23 • (11/30/96) • **89**
Riesling Spätlese Rheinhessen Nackenheimer Rothenberg 1994 • $21 • (11/30/95) • **90**
Riesling Spätlese Rheinhessen Nackenheimer Rothenberg 1993 • $19 • (11/30/94) • **90**
Riesling Trockenbeerenauslese Gold Cap Rheinhessen Nackenheimer Rothenberg 1995: Bizarre juice. Slightly overdone, heavy and flat. Prematurely aged, it's dark amber in color with dried raisin, coffee and spice aromas and flavors. Full-bodied and very sweet, but slightly flat on the finish. 25 cases made. • $240/375ml • (11/30/96) • **84**
Riesling Trockenbeerenauslese Rheinhessen Nackenheimer Rothenberg 1996: Phenomenal German elixir. As thick as maple syrup, with mind-blowing sweetness and richness. Truly the essence of dried Riesling grapes. Full-bodied, outrageously sweet with marmalade, dried orange peel, honey, spice, burnt almond...it's more like fruit syrup than wine. Enjoy now. • $251/375ml • (11/30/97) HR • **100**
Riesling Trockenbeerenauslese Rheinhessen Nackenheimer Rothenberg 1994 • $NA • (11/30/95) • **95**

GUNTRUM, LOUIS

Müller-Thurgau Kabinett Rheinhessen Niersteiner Hölle 1993: Generous but clumsy, offering floral and pine aromas, a soft texture and sweet flavors, marred by a hint of sulfur. • $10 • (10/15/96) • **79**
Riesling Auslese Rheinhessen Oppenheimer Herrenberg 1993: Thick and sweet, tasting of candied pineapple and honey. Agreeable but without sophistication, balanced but simple. • $16 • (10/15/96) • **82**
Riesling Kabinett Halbtrocken Rheinhessen Oppenheimer Schützenhütte Villa Guntrum 1994: Pine and peach flavors are agreeable, but the wine feels a bit heavy until the acidity kicks in. • $14 • (10/15/96) • **78**
Riesling Rheinhessen 1994: Simple and a bit cloying, this tastes sweet and stale, like an apple cut and left on the counter too long. • $7 • (10/15/96) • **73**
White QbA Halbtrocken Rheinhessen Niersteiner 1994: Mineral and pine aromas and flavors keep this white on the austere side, though a hint of residual sugar rounds out the palate. Simple and clean. • $9 • (10/15/96) • **82**

HAAG, FRITZ

Riesling Auslese Mosel-Saar-Ruwer Brauneberger Juffer-Sonnenuhr 1994: Some developing aromas and flavors of marzipan, honey and apricot combine with a firm structure and moderate sweetness for a delicious presentation. Long aftertaste. Drink now through 2005. • $30 • (01/01/98) • **89**
Riesling Kabinett Mosel-Saar-Ruwer Brauneberger Juffer 1996: Delicate and subtle in its approach, yet there's substance and concentration to the honey and almond flavors, as well as plenty of verve. Drink now through 2002. • $15 • (04/30/98) • **88**
Riesling Spätlese Mosel-Saar-Ruwer Brauneberger Juffer-Sonnenuhr 1995: Terrific balance and reserve here, with mineral, petrol and honey characteristics, lovely ripeness and a searing intensity. Needs time to settle down. Best from 2000 through 2010. • $22 • (01/01/98) • **90**

HAART, JOHANN

Riesling Auslese Mosel-Saar-Ruwer Piesporter Goldtröpfchen 1996: Plenty of floral, apple and peach flavors to this delicate auslese. Everything's backed up by freshness and mineral character. Drink now through 2007. • $24/500ml • (04/30/98) • **88**
Riesling Spätlese Mosel-Saar-Ruwer Piesporter Goldtröpfchen 1996: A touch earthy on the nose, with soft, peachy flavors, a rich texture and enough acidity to keep everything lively. Drink now through 2000. • $16 • (04/30/98) • **83**

HAART, REINHOLD

Riesling Auslese Gold Cap Mosel-Saar-Ruwer Piesporter Goldtröpfchen 1995: A slate monster that's vibrant and intense, serving up flavors of peach and honey and a tropical note that kicks in toward the finish. A mouthwatering and pure expression of Mosel Riesling. 42 cases made. • $66 • (11/30/96) • **90**
Riesling Auslese Gold Cap Mosel-Saar-Ruwer Piesporter Goldtröpfchen 1993 • $81 • (11/30/94) • **94**
Riesling Auslese Mosel-Saar-Ruwer Piesporter Goldtröpfchen 1994 • $44 • (11/30/95) • **90**
Riesling Auslese Mosel-Saar-Ruwer Piesporter Goldtröpfchen AP No. 8 1996: Ripe for this vintage from this region, with pineapple and mineral character. Medium-bodied and medium-sweet, with a light, delicate finish. Delicious. Drink now. • $36 • (11/30/97) • **89**
Riesling Auslese Mosel-Saar-Ruwer Wintricher Ohligsberg 1993 • $28 • (11/30/94) • **89**
Riesling Beerenauslese Mosel-Saar-Ruwer Piesporter Goldtröpfchen 1996: A thick and racy BA with honey consistency and masses of tropical flavors. Zingy acidity. Classy wine. Drink now. • $162 • (11/30/97) • **93**

GERMANY

Riesling Beerenauslese Mosel-Saar-Ruwer Piesporter Goldtröpfchen 1994 • $NA • (11/30/95) • **94**

Riesling Kabinett Mosel-Saar-Ruwer Piesporter Goldtröpfchen 1996: Elegant and delicious, displaying beautiful aromas of melons and flowers. Medium-bodied and lightly sweet, with a long, fresh and fruity finish. Drink now or hold. • $19 • (11/30/97) • **90**

Riesling Kabinett Mosel-Saar-Ruwer Piesporter Goldtröpfchen 1995: Pure slate notes allied to a racy structure; this is for those who like dramatic tension between fruit flavor and acidity. Not for the timid. 217 cases made. • $18 • (11/30/96) • **88**

Riesling Kabinett Mosel-Saar-Ruwer Piesporter Goldtröpfchen 1994 • $18 • (11/30/95) • **88**

Riesling Kabinett Mosel-Saar-Ruwer Piesporter Goldtröpfchen 1993 • $16 • (11/30/94) • **87**

Riesling Spätlese Mosel-Saar-Ruwer Piesporter Domherr 1994 • $24 • (11/30/95) • **88**

Riesling Spätlese Mosel-Saar-Ruwer Piesporter Domherr 1993 • $22 • (11/30/94) • **86**

Riesling Spätlese Mosel-Saar-Ruwer Piesporter Goldtröpfchen 1996: A standout in this category, with extremely impressive concentration of ripe fruit ranging from pineapple to mango. Medium-bodied, lightly sweet and silky textured, it goes on and on and shows lovely acidity. Drink or hold. • $28 • (11/30/97) • **91**

Riesling Spätlese Mosel-Saar-Ruwer Piesporter Goldtröpfchen 1995: A solid wine, medium-bodied and sweet with flavors of honeydew melon, mineral and a hint of spices. Fresh, silky finish. Drink now. 108 cases made. • $26 • (11/30/96) • **87**

Riesling Spätlese Mosel-Saar-Ruwer Piesporter Goldtröpfchen 1994 • $27 • (11/30/95) • **87**

Riesling Spätlese Mosel-Saar-Ruwer Piesporter Goldtröpfchen 1993 • $25 • (11/30/94) • **86**

Riesling Spätlese Mosel-Saar-Ruwer Wintricher Ohligsberg 1995: Botrytis adds extra dimension to this very ripe spätlese. It's well balanced, but in the end, it's a little simple. 108 cases made. • $23 • (11/30/96) • **84**

Riesling Trockenbeerenauslese Mosel-Saar-Ruwer Piesporter Goldtröpfchen 1993 • $NA • (11/30/94) • **95**

HERRNSHEIM, HEYL ZU

Müller-Thurgau QbA Halbtrocken Rheinhessen 1995: Amazingly good for a Müller-Thurgau. Plenty of ripe, almost tropical, fruit character. Medium-bodied, off-dry, with dried apricot, honey and grapefruit flavors, a hint of earth. Fresh and smooth finish. 300 cases made. • $10 • (11/30/96) • **86**

Riesling Auslese Rheinhessen Niersteiner Pettenthal 1996: A subtle auslese with honey, floral and apricot aromas and flavors and a hint of spice. Medium-bodied and sweet, with plenty of fruity flavors and a crisp, balanced acidity. Drink now. • $22 • (11/30/97) • **88**

Riesling Auslese Rheinhessen Niersteiner Pettenthal 1994 • $26 • (11/30/95) • **80**

Riesling Auslese Rheinhessen Niersteiner Pettenthal 1993 • $20 • (11/30/94) • **88**

Riesling Kabinett Halbtrocken Rheinhessen Niersteiner Pettenthal 1995: Green apple, almond and honey notes mark this young Riesling. It's balanced with subtle yet intense flavors. Try now, with food. 300 cases made. • $18 • (11/30/96) • **86**

Riesling Kabinett Rheinhessen Niersteiner Oelberg 1995: A sweeter style of kabinett, this shows honey and green apple flavors, with just a hint of tropical fruit. Could be a bit more concentrated, but has immediate appeal. 120 cases made. • $14 • (11/30/96) • **85**

Riesling Kabinett Rheinhessen Schloss Mathildenhof 1996: Delicate, textbook kabinett. Wonderful Springlike aromas of flowers and minerals. Light-bodied and off-dry with crisp acidity and a subtle, fruity finish. Drink now. • $12 • (11/30/97) • **87**

Riesling Kabinett Rheinhessen Schloss Mathildenhof 1994 • $14 • (11/30/95) • **84**

Riesling Kabinett Rheinhessen Schloss Mathildenhof 1993 • $15 • (11/30/94) • **84**

Riesling Kabinett Trocken Rheinhessen Niersteiner Pettenthal 1996: Pretty, lively, dry white. Fresh and fruity with apple, melon and spice character. Medium-bodied and dry with lively acidity yet a round mouthfeel. Drink now or hold. • $12 • (11/30/97) • **87**

Key: SS—Spectator Selection CS—Cellar Selection HR—Highly Recommended BB—Best Buy $NA—Price not available Ⓐ—Auction Price (BT)—Barrel Tasting

Dates in parentheses indicate the issues in which the ratings were published.

Riesling QbA Rheinhessen Baron von Heyl 1994 • $10 • (11/30/95) • **84**

Riesling QbA Rheinhessen Baron von Heyl Niersteiner Spiegelberg 1996: Some melon and spice character but rather light and flat on the finish. Light-bodied, lightly sweet. Drink now. • $9 • (11/30/97) • **77**

Riesling QbA Trocken Rheinhessen 1995: Firm and vibrant, with green apple and honeydew melon flavors, this is a Riesling with balance and intensity. A dry wine that needs food. Drinkable now. 300 cases made. • $10 • (11/30/96) • **86**

Riesling QbA Trocken Rheinhessen Niersteiner 1996: Stylish white with peppery, spicy character. Medium-bodied, dry with a good round texture and a fresh finish. Try with food. Drink now. • $11 • (11/30/97) • **87**

Riesling Spätlese Halbtrocken Rheinhessen Niersteiner Pettenthal 1996: A crisp and clean off-dry white with delicate spicy and floral aromas and flavors. Light-bodied, with a delicate finish. Drink now. • $17 • (11/30/97) • **84**

Riesling Spätlese Halbtrocken Rheinhessen Niersteiner Pettenthal 1994 • $19 • (11/30/94) • **87**

Riesling Spätlese Mittelrhein Niersteiner Oelberg 1993 • $18 • (11/30/94) • **85**

Riesling Spätlese Rheinhessen Niersteiner Brudersberg 1996: A caressing spätlese with creamy, apple, pineapple and cookie character. Medium-bodied, medium-sweet with medium acidity. Quite thick in texture. Drink now. • $18 • (11/30/97) • **88**

Riesling Spätlese Rheinhessen Niersteiner Pettenthal 1993 • $17 • (11/30/94) • **82**

Riesling Spätlese Trocken Rheinhessen Niersteiner Pettenthal 1995: A classy, dry wine with floral, rose petal and biscuit aromas and flavors. Medium-bodied, it shows a pleasantly balanced acidity and a superclean finish. Delicious. Drink now. 120 cases made. • $18 • (11/30/96) • **89**

Riesling Spätlese Trocken Rheinhessen Niersteiner Pettenthal 1994 • $22 • (11/30/95) • **87**

Riesling Spätlese Trocken Rheinhessen Niersteiner Pettenthal 1993 • $19 • (11/30/94) • **76**

Silvaner QbA Rheinhessen Niersteiner Rosenberg 1993 • $12 • (11/30/94) • **80**

Silvaner QbA Trocken Rheinhessen Niersteiner Rosenberg 1996: Bone dry without much character. Light honey aromas with a hint of grassiness. Medium-bodied and very dry with a tart finish. Drink now. • $12 • (11/30/97) • **81**

Silvaner QbA Trocken Rheinhessen Niersteiner Rosenberg 1994 • $16 • (11/30/95) • **85**

Silvaner Trocken Rheinhessen Niersteiner Rosenberg 1995: A pretty Silvaner, showing lemon and honey flavors with a hint of allspice. Light- to medium-bodied, dry, with a round texture and clean finish. Drink now. 350 cases made. • $13 • (11/30/96) • **85**

HÖVEL, VON

Riesling Auslese Gold Cap Saar-Ruwer Oberemmeler Hütte 1993 • $90 • (11/30/94) • **90**

Riesling Auslese Saar-Ruwer Oberemmeler Hütte 1993 • $23 • (11/30/94) • **84**

Riesling Eiswein Saar-Ruwer Oberemmeler Hütte 1993 • $NA • (11/30/94) • **91**

Riesling Kabinett Mosel-Saar-Ruwer Oberemmeler Hütte 1996: Very ripe for a kabinett, this displays apple, pineapple and mineral aromas and flavors with a hint of spice. Medium-bodied, lightly sweet and creamy. Medium finish. Drink now. • $14 • (11/30/97) • **87**

Riesling Kabinett Mosel-Saar-Ruwer Oberemmeler Hütte 1995: Big for a Mosel, displaying vibrant green-apple flavor accented by mineral and tropical notes. Balanced and flavorful. • $13 • (11/30/96) • **88**

Riesling Kabinett Mosel-Saar-Ruwer Oberemmeler Hütte 1994 • $13 • (11/30/95) • **85**

Riesling Kabinett Mosel-Saar-Ruwer Scharzhofberger 1996: Clean and lively wine. Shows very good intensity of mineral, flinty aromas and flavors. Medium- to light-bodied, off-dry, with a long, fruity finish. Drink now. • $14 • (11/30/97) • **87**

Riesling Kabinett Mosel-Saar-Ruwer Scharzhofberger 1994 • $NA • (11/30/95) • **82**

Riesling Kabinett Saar-Ruwer Balduin von Hövel 1993 • $9 • (11/30/94) • **83**

Riesling Kabinett Saar-Ruwer Oberemmeler Hütte 1993 • $12 • (11/30/94) • **87**

Riesling QbA Mosel-Saar-Ruwer Balduin von Hövel 1996: Good, but nowhere near the quality of the amazing 1995. Very citrusy, with a hint of spice, medium-bodied and lightly sweet. Drink now. • $11 • (11/30/97) • **82**

Riesling QbA Mosel-Saar-Ruwer Balduin von Hövel 1995: One of the best QbA we have had in years. A mouthful for a simple Riesling with an abundance of tropical fruit, honey and mineral aromas and flavors. Medium-bodied and off-dry with fine acidity and a long flavorful finish. Very impressive. Try now. • $10 • (11/30/96) • **90**

Riesling Spätlese Mittelrhein Oberemmeler Hütte 1993 • $15 • (11/30/94) • **90**

Riesling Spätlese Mosel-Saar-Ruwer Oberemmeler Hütte 1995: Enticingly rich spätlese with lemon, peach and pie crust aromas. Medium- to full-bodied, moderately sweet, with loads of tropical fruit flavors and a long, ripe fruit finish. Drink now or hold. • $16 • (11/30/96) • **90**

Riesling Spätlese Mosel-Saar-Ruwer Oberemmeler Hütte 1994 • $16 • (11/30/95) • **81**

Riesling Spätlese Mosel-Saar-Ruwer Scharzhofberger 1995: In a sweeter style that makes it slightly thick and oily. Medium-bodied, with some mineral and honey flavors and a slightly short finish. Drink now or hold. • $16 • (11/30/96) RT • **85**

Riesling Spätlese Mosel-Saar-Ruwer Scharzhofberger 1994 • $16 • (11/30/95) • **84**

JOHANNISHOF

Riesling Auslese Rheingau Johannisberger Hölle 1995: Lime and mineral flavors are intense, augmented by a note of apricot (from botrytis), but right now the acidity dominates. Try in 2000. • $NA/375ml • (11/30/96) • **89**

Riesling Kabinett Rheingau Charta 1993 • $16 • (11/30/94) • **87**

Riesling Kabinett Rheingau Johannisberger Goldatzel 1993 • $14 • (11/30/94) • **87**

Riesling Kabinett Rheingau Johannisberger Vogelsang 1993 • $12 • (11/30/94) • **82**

Riesling QbA Rheingau Johannisberger Vogelsang 1995: A delicious sipper. Crisp, with straightforward melon and honey notes on the nose and palate, a medium body and a lightly sweet finish. • $NA • (11/30/96) • **85**

Riesling Spätlese Rheingau Johannisberger Goldatzel 1993 • $20 • (11/30/94) • **88**

Riesling Spätlese Rheingau Johannisberger Klaus 1993 • $18 • (11/30/94) • **85**

Riesling Spätlese Rheingau Winkeler Jesuitengarten 1995: Terrific spätlese, with mineral, apple and peach aromas and flavors. Medium-bodied and very sweet, with a crisp and fruity finish. Pure, with great intensity. Drink now or hold. • $NA • (11/30/96) • **91**

JOHANNISBERG, SCHLOSS

Riesling Auslese Rheingau 1996: Racy and spicy, with wonderful aromas and flavors. Medium in body and sweetness, with a finish that is ripe and fruity, long and flinty. Classy wine. Drink now or hold. • $74 • (11/30/97) • **91**

Riesling Auslese Rheingau 1995: A moderately intense auslese with honey and spice flavors and a hint of flintiness. Sweet, with medium body and light finish. Drink now or hold. 200 cases made. • $74 • (11/30/96) • **87**

Riesling Auslese Rheingau Rosalack 1993 • $90 • (11/30/94) • **68**

Riesling Beerenauslese Rheingau 1996: Emitting intense aromas of tropical fruit ranging from pineapple to mangoes, this full-bodied and very sweet wine shows racy acidity and long, long spicy, fruity flavors. A real beauty. Drink now or hold. • $NA • (11/30/97) • **92**

Riesling Eiswein Rheingau 1996: Closed and not giving as much as it will. Yet there's masses of flinty, spicy, honeyed, and sweet character. Full-bodied, very sweet and thick. Try after 2000. • $222 • (11/30/97) • **93**

Riesling Kabinett Rheingau 1996: Pretty aromas and flavors of apples, honey and cream predominate in this subtle Riesling. Medium-bodied, lightly sweet, with a long, spicy aftertaste. Drink now or hold. • $23 • (11/30/97) • **88**

Riesling Kabinett Rheingau 1995: Made in a fuller style, this offers mineral and almond aromas and flavors, lightly sweet. The short finish, with a bit of a bite, is a slight let down. 1,500 cases made. • $23 • (11/30/96) • **83**

Riesling Kabinett Rheingau Rotlack 1993 • $22 • (11/30/94) • **80**

Riesling QbA Rheingau 1996: Plenty of flint and spice aromas but slightly green on the finish. Medium-bodied, lightly sweet and extremely well-defined on the finish. Drink now. • $15 • (11/30/97) • **83**

Riesling QbA Rheingau 1995: The almond and green apple flavors are displayed in an off-dry style, but the finish is balanced on the tart side. Tasted twice, with consistent notes. • $19 • (11/30/96) • **81**

Riesling QbA Rheingau 1993 • $17 • (11/30/94) • **81**

Riesling Spätlese Rheingau 1996: A big, rich Riesling with a wonderfully long aftertaste of mineral, flint and fruit. Full-bodied, medium-sweet, with a crisp finish. Drink now or hold. • $28 • (11/30/97) • **90**

Riesling Spätlese Rheingau 1995: Subtle spätlese with aromas and flavors of lemon, earth and biscuit. Medium-bodied, with a round texture and a delicate finish. Ready to drink. 1,000 cases made. • $28 • (11/30/96) • **87**

Riesling Spätlese Rheingau 1993 • $NA • (11/30/94) • **79**

Riesling Spätlese Trocken Rheingau 1996: A great dry wine, showing intense mineral and flinty, spicy character. Medium- to light-bodied, dry, with a long, fruity, spicy finish. A classic Riesling. Perfect with light, delicate foods. Drink now. • $27 • (11/30/97) • **90**

Riesling Spätlese Trocken Rheingau 1995: As rich as many California Chardonnays, with its oily and spicy character. Medium- to full-bodied, with some acidity and a long flavorful finish. Simply delicious. 1,000 cases made. • $27 • (11/30/96) • **87**

Riesling Spätlese Trocken Rheingau Grunlack 1993 • $28 • (11/30/94) • **84**

Riesling Trockenbeerenauslese Rheingau Goldlack 1993 • $300 • (11/30/94) • **96**

JOST, TONI

Riesling Auslese Gold Cap Mittelrhein Bacharacher Hahn 1993 • $37 • (11/30/94) • **88**

Riesling Auslese Mittelrhein Bacharacher Hahn 1996: Lovely aromas of nectarines and honey, with a spicy element and tangy acidity on the palate. Builds to a long, lingering finish. Best from 2000 through 2010. • $37 • (04/30/98) • **90**

Riesling Auslese Mittelrhein Wallufer Walkenburg 1993 • $NA • (11/30/94) • **89**

Riesling Kabinett Mittelrhein Bacharacher Hahn 1996: A Riesling of wonderful grace and harmony, its peachy, minerally notes displaying clarity and definition thanks to racy acidity. Drink now through 2002. • $17 • (04/30/98) • **88**

Riesling Kabinett Mittelrhein Bacharacher Hahn 1993 • $14 • (11/30/94) • **87**

Riesling Spätlese Mittelrhein Bacharacher Hahn 1993 • $15 • (11/30/94) • **86**

Riesling Spätlese Mittelrhein Wallufer Walkenburg 1993 • $15 • (11/30/94) • **85**

Riesling Trockenbeerenauslese Mittelrhein Bacharacher Hahn 1993 • $NA • (11/30/94) • **90**

KARLSMUHLE

Riesling Auslese Long Gold Cap Saar-Ruwer Lorenzhofer 1993 • $31 • (11/30/94) • **88**

Riesling Auslese Saar-Ruwer Lorenzhofer 1993 • $22 • (11/30/94) • **84**

Riesling Eiswein Saar-Ruwer Lorenzhofer 1993 • $68 • (11/30/94) • **81**

Riesling Kabinett Saar-Ruwer Lorenzhofer Mäuerchen 1993 • $14 • (11/30/94) • **89**

Riesling Spätlese Halbtrocken Saar-Ruwer Lorenzhofer Felsay 1993 • $16 • (11/30/94) • **84**

Riesling Spätlese Saar-Ruwer Kaseler Nies'chen 1993 • $16 • (11/30/94) • **89**

KARTHÄUSERHOF

Riesling Auslese Mosel-Saar-Ruwer Eitelsbacher Karthäuserhofberg No. 30 1995: A searing, intense wine that vibrates with apple, peach and slate flavors. Laserlike focus, precision balance and fruity on the finish. For fans of a delicate style of auslese. 110 cases made. • $55 • (11/30/96) • **89**

Riesling Eiswein Mosel-Saar-Ruwer Eitelsbacher Karthäuserhofberg No. 33 1995: Crystal clear, with incredibly vivid aromas and flavors of crushed grapes, honey and flowers. Full-bodied and very sweet, with wonderfully refreshing acidity and a very long finish. Purity all the way. Better after 2000. • $92/375ml • (11/30/96) • **95**

Riesling Kabinett Halbtrocken Mosel-Saar-Ruwer Eitelsbacher Karthäuserhofberg 1996: A very crisp and lemony white. Light-bodied and dry, this has fresh, lively acidity but comes off a bit neutral. Try now. • $17 • (11/30/97) • **83**

Riesling Kabinett Mosel-Saar-Ruwer Eitelsbacher Karthäuserhofberg 1996: Young, austere and not giving much right now other than hints of apricot and slate. Concentrated though, with a stony taste and incredible length. Best from 2002 through 2012. • $17 • (01/01/98) • **90**

Riesling Kabinett Mosel-Saar-Ruwer Eitelsbacher Karthäuserhofberg 1995: Fresh and clean, offering lemon and mineral aromas and flavors. It's medi-

GERMANY

um-bodied, off-dry and has a light finish. Drink now. • $16 • (11/30/96) • **84**

Riesling QbA Mosel-Saar-Ruwer Eitelsbacher Karthäuserhofberg 1996: Extremely fresh Riesling with loads of lemon rind and mineral character. Medium-bodied, off-dry and flavorful. Citrus flavors go on and on. Drink or hold. • $14 • (11/30/97) • **88**

Riesling QbA Mosel-Saar-Ruwer Eitelsbacher Karthäuserhofberg 1995: Uninspiring, this has decent citrus character but it's rather light, lightly sweet—not showing much. Mundane. Tasted twice, with consistent notes. • $13 • (11/30/96) • **79**

Riesling Spätlese Mosel-Saar-Ruwer Eitelsbacher Karthäuserhofberg 1996: Very fresh, with lots of crushed grape and melon character. Medium-bodied, lightly sweet, crisp acidity and an earthy, fruity finish. Drink now. • $24 • (11/30/97) • **87**

Riesling Spätlese Mosel-Saar-Ruwer Eitelsbacher Karthäuserhofberg 1995: Taut and racy, this needs time to unravel its mineral, peach and floral flavors, complex and intense, dancing across the palate. Lingering finish. • $22 • (11/30/96) • **89**

KESSELER, AUGUST

Riesling Auslese Rheingau Rüdesheimer Bischofsberg 1996: Extremely honeyed and citruslike on the nose. Medium-bodied and sweet, with plenty of ripe fruit and a melon finish. Drink now. • $32/375ml • (11/30/97) • **87**

Riesling Auslese Rheingau Rüdesheimer Bischofsberg 1995: On the dry side for auslese, showing mineral and peach aromas and flavors, a bit difficult to taste for the carbon dioxide. • $36/375ml • (11/30/96) • **83**

Riesling Kabinett Rheingau 1996: Good intensity of pear, apple fruit in this kabinett with a lively acidity. Medium-bodied, off-dry and a long fruity finish. Delicious now through 2002. • $18 • (11/30/97) • **88**

Riesling Kabinett Rheingau 1993 • $NA • (11/30/94) • **86**

Riesling Kabinett Rheingau Rüdesheimer Berg Roseneck 1996: A pretty Riesling with green apple, pear and just a hint of spice. Medium-bodied, medium-sweet with a fruity finish. Slightly one-dimensional. Drink now. • $22 • (11/30/97) • **85**

Riesling Kabinett Rheingau Rüdesheimer Berg Rottland 1995: Decent, with vivid grape and lemon character, but it's very sweet and slightly cloying. A bit disappointing. Tasted twice, with consistent notes. • $29 • (11/30/96) • **79**

Riesling QbA Rheingau 1996: Like smelling a freshly baked apple pie. Medium-bodied, medium-sweet with crisp acidity and a fruity finish. Got to like it. Drink now. • $15 • (11/30/97) • **86**

Riesling QbA Rheingau 1993 • $NA • (11/30/94) • **85**

Riesling Spätlese Rheingau 1996: A good spätlese with honey, floral aromas and flavors. Medium-bodied, medium-sweet with a rather light finish. Drink now. • $25 • (11/30/97) • **85**

Riesling Spätlese Rheingau 1993 • $NA • (11/30/94) • **83**

Riesling Spätlese Rheingau Rüdesheimer Berg Rottland 1996: A live wire of a Riesling for the Rhine. Pretty melon, pear and cream aromas and flavors. Medium-bodied, medium-sweet with very lively acidity and ripe grapefruit on the finish. Almost outstanding. Drink now. • $36 • (11/30/97) • **89**

Riesling Spätlese Rheingau Rüdesheimer Bischofsberg 1995: Not the most complex spätlese, but showing some good lemon, spice and melon character. Medium-bodied and lightly sweet, with a refreshing finish. Drink now. • $40 • (11/30/96) • **85**

Riesling Spätlese Trocken Rheingau Rüdesheimer Berg Roseneck 1993 • $NA • (11/30/94) • **84**

KESSELSTATT, REICHSGRAF VON

Riesling Auslese Gold Cap Mosel-Saar-Ruwer Josephshöfer 1996: A balanced, sweet wine showing pineapple and lots of ripe fruit, along with a hint of spice. Medium-bodied, medium-sweet, with a long fresh finish. Delicious. Drink now or hold. 50 cases made. • $26/375ml • (11/30/97) • **88**

Riesling Auslese Gold Cap Mosel-Saar-Ruwer Piesporter Goldtröpfchen 1994 • $NA • (11/30/95) • **84**

Riesling Auslese Long Gold Cap Mosel-Saar-Ruwer Josephshöfer 1995: Firm and slightly dry for auslese, but delivers an inner strength that makes it attractive. Racy acidity and a mineral note add to the apple flavor. Approachable now. • $NA • (11/30/96) • **88**

Riesling Auslese Mosel-Saar-Ruwer Josephshöfer 1993 • $NA • (11/30/94) • **90**

Riesling Auslese Mosel-Saar-Ruwer Kaseler Nies'chen 1994 • $NA • (11/30/95) • **87**

Riesling Auslese Mosel-Saar-Ruwer Scharzhofberger 1995: A medium-weight auslese, showing a fresh fruit and honey character with a citrusy undertone, but still, it's slightly meager for this category. • $NA • (11/30/96) • **83**

Riesling Auslese Mosel-Saar-Ruwer Scharzhofberger 1994 • $NA • (11/30/95) • **82**

Riesling Auslese Mosel-Saar-Ruwer Wiltinger Braunfels 1993 • $NA • (11/30/94) • **86**

Riesling Beerenauslese Mosel-Saar-Ruwer Scharzhofberger 1996: A good example of the variety, with ripe fruit, mineral and blanched almond aromas and flavors. Medium- to full-bodied, very sweet and fresh on the finish. Drink now. 30 cases made. • $65/375ml • (11/30/97) • **90**

Riesling Beerenauslese Mosel-Saar-Ruwer Scharzhofberger 1995: Apple, peach and honey are the dominant flavors. Laserlike acidity on the finish tempers the thick texture. Best in 1999. • $NA • (11/30/96) • **90**

Riesling Eiswein Mosel-Saar-Ruwer Scharzhofberger 1996: Refined sweet wine. Honey, floral and apricot aromas. Mediu-to-full bodied, very sweet with a long, lively finish and a hint of spiciness. Drink now or hold. 20 cases made. • $107/375ml • (11/30/97) • **88**

Riesling Eiswein Mosel-Saar-Ruwer Scharzhofberger 1993 • $NA • (11/30/94) • **89**

Riesling Kabinett Halbtrocken Mosel-Saar-Ruwer Josephshöfer 1994: A bright, snappy wine showing some of the better traits of the varietal. Tastes of peaches, pine and lemon, with a good balance of sugar and acid and a light spritz to lend liveliness. • $NA • (10/15/96) • **84**

Riesling Kabinett Mosel-Saar-Ruwer Graacher Himmelreich 1996: Delicate and fruity, with melon, pear and apple aromas and flavors and a hint of flint. Light-bodied, lightly sweet. Fresh finish. Drink now. 300 cases made. • $14 • (11/30/97) • **86**

Riesling Kabinett Mosel-Saar-Ruwer Josephshöfer 1996: Lots of grapefruit and spice character here. Medium- to light-bodied, off-dry and fruity, with a balance of acidity. Delicious. Drink now. 500 cases made. • $15 • (11/30/97) • **86**

Riesling Kabinett Mosel-Saar-Ruwer Josephshöfer 1995: A subtle and fresh Mosel kabinett with mineral, floral and melon flavors and aromas. Light- to medium-bodied and lightly sweet. Crisp finish. Drink now or hold. • $NA • (11/30/96) • **87**

Riesling Kabinett Mosel-Saar-Ruwer Josephshöfer 1994 • $NA • (11/30/95) • **86**

Riesling Kabinett Mosel-Saar-Ruwer Ockfener Bockstein 1994 • $13 • (11/30/95) • **82**

Riesling Kabinett Mosel-Saar-Ruwer Piesporter Goldtröpfchen 1996: Delicious, solid kabinett with delicate floral, melon and apple character. Medium-bodied, off-dry, with a fresh finish. A joy to taste. Drink now. 500 cases made. • $15 • (11/30/97) • **88**

Riesling Kabinett Mosel-Saar-Ruwer Piesporter Goldtröpfchen 1995: The peach, slate and lime flavors are focused with laserlike acidity. A delicate wine that has intensity, too. Try as an apéritif. • $NA • (11/30/96) • **86**

Riesling Kabinett Mosel-Saar-Ruwer Piesporter Goldtröpfchen 1994 • $NA • (11/30/95) • **85**

Riesling Kabinett Mosel-Saar-Ruwer Piesporter Goldtröpfchen 1993 • $NA • (11/30/94) • **88**

Riesling Kabinett Mosel-Saar-Ruwer Scharzhofberger 1996: Delicious Mosel kabinett. Delicate yet intensely flavored, medium-bodied, off-dry, with loads of flinty, mineral and fruit character on the finish. Drink now or hold. 400 cases made. • $15 • (11/30/97) • **88**

Riesling Kabinett Mosel-Saar-Ruwer Scharzhofberger 1995: This has some depth and reserve, with an earthy element to the melon flavor. More body than most Mosel wines and it needs some time. Try now. • $NA • (11/30/96) • **86**

Riesling Kabinett Mosel-Saar-Ruwer Scharzhofberger 1994 • $NA • (11/30/95) • **86**

Riesling QbA Mosel-Saar-Ruwer Piesporter Goldtröpfchen 1994 • $NA • (11/30/95) • **85**

Riesling Spätlese Mosel Piesporter Goldtröpfchen 1993 • $NA • (11/30/94) • **86**

Riesling Spätlese Mosel-Saar-Ruwer Graacher Domprobst 1996: Sneaks up and finishes wonderfully. Showing subtle aromas of lemons and minerals, it's medium-bodied, lightly sweet and crisp, with a long apple, pie crust and fruit aftertaste. Drink now. 200 cases made. • $18 • (11/30/97) • **88**

Key: SS—Spectator Selection CS—Cellar Selection HR—Highly Recommended BB—Best Buy $NA—Price not available Ⓐ—Auction Price (BT)—Barrel Tasting
Dates in parentheses indicate the issues in which the ratings were published.

Riesling Spätlese Mosel-Saar-Ruwer Graacher Domprobst 1995: A fruit bomb that explodes with ripe melon, peach and mineral aromas and flavors. Delivers precision balance, but the finish trails off slightly. • $NA • (11/30/96) • **89**

Riesling Spätlese Mosel-Saar-Ruwer Josephshöfer 1996: Super-fresh, with plenty of melon and floral character. Medium-bodied and sweet, with a long, crisp finish. High in acidity. Drinkable now. 300 cases made. • $21 • (11/30/97) • **89**

Riesling Spätlese Mosel-Saar-Ruwer Josephshöfer 1995: Fresh and lively, it's medium-bodied with melon and mineral aromas and flavors, but could use more concentration as it doesn't leave much on your palate at the finish. • $NA • (11/30/96) • **84**

Riesling Spätlese Mosel-Saar-Ruwer Josephshöfer 1994 • $NA • (11/30/95) • **87**

Riesling Spätlese Mosel-Saar-Ruwer Kaseler Nies'chen 1996: Lots of lemon, peach and mineral character in this one. Medium-bodied, lightly sweet and fresh on the finish. Drink now. 200 cases made. • $18 • (11/30/97) • **88**

Riesling Spätlese Mosel-Saar-Ruwer Piesporter Goldtröpfchen 1996: Lacks a bit of concentration. Loads of green apple and flint character in this one. Medium-bodied and medium-sweet. Drink now. 500 cases made. • $15 • (11/30/97) • **84**

Riesling Spätlese Mosel-Saar-Ruwer Piesporter Goldtröpfchen 1995: A tightly wound Riesling that's full of nerve and ripe fruit intensity. The apricot flavors are refreshing, but a bit short on the finish. • $NA • (11/30/96) • **86**

Riesling Spätlese Mosel-Saar-Ruwer Piesporter Goldtröpfchen 1994 • $NA • (11/30/95) • **78**

Riesling Spätlese Mosel-Saar-Ruwer Scharzhofberger 1996: A very ripe wine with pineapple, honey and lemon character. Medium- to full-bodied, medium-sweet and crisp. Long and ripe on the finish. Serious spät. Drink now or hold. 400 cases made. • $19 • (11/30/97) • **90**

Riesling Spätlese Mosel-Saar-Ruwer Scharzhofberger 1995: Mineral notes on the nose give way to a zippy, high-wire act tasting of slate, green apple and peach. Drink now. • $NA • (11/30/96) • **88**

Riesling Spätlese Mosel-Saar-Ruwer Scharzhofberger 1994 • $NA • (11/30/95) • **85**

Riesling Spätlese Saar-Ruwer Scharzhofberger 1993 • $NA • (11/30/94) • **87**

Riesling Trockenbeerenauslese Mosel-Saar-Ruwer Scharzhofberger 1994 • $NA • (11/30/95) • **91**

KIMICH, JULIUS FERDINAND

Riesling Kabinett Pfalz Deidesheimer Herrgottsacker 1996: Has a minty topnote along with citrus and apricot flavors, but it's without the depth and intensity of the best Pfalz Rieslings. Appealing nonetheless. Drink now. • $13 • (04/30/98) • **83**

Riesling Kabinett Pfalz Forster Elster 1996: Exotic, tropical notes hold forth in this lively, medium-weight Riesling. On the dry side and has a little more body than usual for the variety. Citrus and hazelnut notes linger on the finish. Try with food. Drink now through 2002. • $13 • (04/30/98) • **86**

KNYPHAUSEN, BARON ZU

Kabinett Rheingau Erbacher 1994 • $11 • (12/15/95) • **80**

Riesling QbA Rheingau 1993 • $10 • (11/30/94) • **72**

Riesling Rheingau 1994 • $7 • (12/15/95) • **78**

Spätlese Rheingau Hattenheimer Wisselbrunnen 1994 • $18 • (12/15/95) • **82**

KNYPHAUSEN, FREIHERR ZU

Riesling Auslese Rheingau Kiedricher Sandgrub 1993 • $24 • (11/30/94) • **83**

Riesling Beerenauslese Rheingau Erbacher Michelmark 1993 • $88 • (11/30/94) • **90**

Riesling Eiswein Rheingau Erbacher Siegelsberg Baron zu Knyphausen 1996: Sweet and delicious eiswein with plenty of melon and lemon-lime flavors, but could use a little more concentration. Medium-bodied, very sweet, crisp finish. Drink now. 120 cases made. • $90/500ml • (11/30/97) • **86**

Riesling Kabinett Halbtrocken Rheingau Kiedricher Sandgrub 1995: Slightly one-dimensional but shows some pretty honeydew and melon aromas and flavors. Of medium body and dry, with a standard portion of acidity and a clean finish. • $13 • (11/30/96) • **84**

Riesling Kabinett Rheingau 1996: Attractive creamy, apple aromas and flavors. Medium-bodied, off-dry with spicy flavors and a crisp finish. Good with food. Drink now. 550 cases made. • $12 • (11/30/97) • **86**

Riesling Kabinett Rheingau 1995: A drier-style kabinett, with aromas and flavors of lemon and spice and a hint of mineral. Light- to medium-bodied with a crisp finish. Ready to drink. • $12 • (11/30/96) • **84**

Riesling Kabinett Rheingau Baron zu Knyphausen Erbacher Steinmorgen 1996: Pretty kabinett with green apple and floral character. Medium-bodied with lively acidity and a fresh finish. Drink now. 250 cases made. • $12 • (11/30/97) • **85**

Riesling Kabinett Rheingau Erbacher 1995: Austere, with green apple and almond flavors and a slightly earthy finish. Lacks verve and intensity. • $12 • (11/30/96) • **78**

Riesling Kabinett Rheingau Erbacher 1993 • $12 • (12/15/94) • **83**

Riesling Kabinett Rheingau Erbacher Marcobrunn 1993 • $NA • (11/30/94) • **74**

Riesling Kabinett Rheingau Erbacher Steinmorgen 1993 • $14 • (11/30/94) • **80**

Riesling Kabinett Trocken Rheingau Erbacher Steinmorgen 1996: Abounding with delicious aromas of apricots, roses and flowers. Medium-bodied and dry, with a round mouthfeel and a fresh, crisp finish. Drink or hold. 450 cases made. • $12 • (11/30/97) • **86**

Riesling Kabinett Trocken Rheingau Erbacher Steinmorgen 1995: Subtle aromas of peach, melon and honey. Light-bodied and off-dry, with light acidity but a diluted finish. Too bad. • $13 • (11/30/96) • **78**

Riesling QbA Rheingau 1996: Rather neutral with some decent apple, steely character but short on the finish. Drink now. 500 cases made. • $9 • (11/30/97) • **80**

Riesling QbA Rheingau 1995: Offers crushed grape, green fruit and raw honey flavors in a medium body, off-dry , with green apple-skin accent and a short finish. Not much to it. Tasted twice, with consistent notes. • $9 • (11/30/96) • **80**

Riesling QbA Rheingau 1993 • $10 • (11/30/94) • **72**

Riesling QbA Rheingau Baron zu Knyphausen Charta 1996: Fresh and lively with plenty of melon, apple flavors, medium to light body and a crisp and clean finish. Drink now. 300 cases made. • $12 • (11/30/97) • **85**

Riesling Spätlese Rheingau Baron zu Knyphausen Kiedricher Sandgrub 1996: Some decent fruit character with marzipan aromas and flavors. Medium-bodied, medium-sweet with a short finish. Drink now. 160 cases made. • $19 • (11/30/97) • **81**

Riesling Spätlese Rheingau Erbacher Marcobrunn 1995: This wine shows an intense mineral character with a hint of lime. Medium-bodied with firm acidity, but the short finish lets it down. • $25 • (11/30/96) • **84**

Riesling Spätlese Rheingau Hattenheimer Wisselbrunnen 1993 • $20 • (11/30/94) • **83**

Riesling Spätlese Trocken Rheingau Erbacher Steinmorgen 1996: A wine with good peach, fruit character and a fresh finish, but slightly simple. Medium-bodied and dry. Drink or hold. 100 cases made. • $18 • (11/30/97) • **82**

KOEHLER-RUPRECHT

Gewürztraminer Auslese Pfalz Kallstadter Steinacker 1994 • $NA • (11/30/95) • **78**

Muskateller Auslese Pfalz Kallstadter Saumagen 1996: Rich and slightly dry for an auslese, this stylish white exhibits spice, burnt almond and apricot character. Medium-bodied and off-dry, with a silky texture. Perfect with food. Drink now. • $NA • (11/30/97) • **88**

Muskateller Trockenbeerenauslese Pfalz Kallstadter Saumagen 1994 • $NA • (11/30/95) • **94**

Riesling Auslese Pfalz Kallstadter Saumagen 1996: Not as sweet as some in this category, but has an attractive spicy, honey and mineral character. Medium in body and sweetness, with medium acidity on the finish. Drink now. • $NA • (11/30/97) • **85**

Riesling Auslese Pfalz Kallstadter Saumagen 1995: Lively and fresh in a dry style, showing plenty of almond, apple, honey and touch of mineral aromas and flavors. Ready to drink; try with food. • $NA • (11/30/96) • **86**

Riesling Auslese Pfalz Kallstadter Saumagen 1994 • $NA • (11/30/95) • **88**

Riesling Auslese Pfalz Kallstadter Saumagen 1993 • $28 • (11/30/94) • **89**

Riesling Auslese Pfalz Kallstadter Saumagen Reserve 1995: This has richness and concentration balanced by high acidity, which offsets the nectarine and apricot flavors nicely. There's an impression that this wine is holding back. Wait until 2000. • $39 • (11/30/96) • **87**

Riesling Beerenauslese Pfalz Kallstadter Saumagen 1994 • $NA • (11/30/95) • **89**

Riesling Beerenauslese Pfalz Kallstadter Saumagen 1993 • $NA • (11/30/94) • **84**

Riesling Kabinett Halbtrocken Pfalz Kallstadter Steinacker 1996: Absolutely delicious. A ripe and juicy dry wine with melon, pie crust, cantaloupe

GERMANY

character. Full-bodied, off-dry, with loads of spicy, smoky fruit and a long, long finish. Drink or hold. • $NA • (11/30/97) • **89**

Riesling Kabinett Halbtrocken Pfalz Kallstadter Steinacker 1995: This is fresh and lively, with melon, grapefruit and a hint of earthy mineral character. It's medium-bodied, off-dry, with a crisp finish. Drink now or hold. • $NA • (11/30/96) • **85**

Riesling Kabinett Halbtrocken Pfalz Kallstadter Steinacker 1994 • $NA • (11/30/95) • **83**

Riesling Kabinett Pfalz Kallstadter Steinacker 1996: A very spicy wine with a hint of dried herbs on the finish. Medium-bodied, off-dry with lively acidity. Drinkable now. • $13 • (11/30/97) • **84**

Riesling Kabinett Pfalz Kallstadter Steinacker 1995: Very pretty kabinett with honey, apple and cream character. Rather silky and caressing in texture, with clean fruit flavor, light sweetness and crisp finish. Delicious. • $13 • (11/30/96) • **87**

Riesling Kabinett Pfalz Kallstadter Steinacker 1994 • $NA • (11/30/95) • **85**

Riesling Kabinett Pfalz Kallstadter Steinacker 1993 • $12 • (11/30/94) • **87**

Riesling Spätlese Halbtrocken Pfalz Kallstadter Saumagen 1996: A very intense wine loaded with ripe spice, tropical fruit and brown sugar aromas and flavors. Medium- to full-bodied, off-dry, with a long, spicy, honey finish. • $19 • (11/30/97) • **88**

Riesling Spätlese Halbtrocken Pfalz Kallstadter Saumagen 1994 • $NA • (11/30/95) • **86**

Riesling Spätlese Halbtrocken Pfalz Kallstadter Saumagen 1993 • $16 • (11/30/94) • **89**

Riesling Spätlese Pfalz Kallstadter Saumagen 1996: Good creamy, vanilla and candied pear aromas and flavors. Medium-bodied, medium-sweet, but slightly short and diluted on the finish. Tasted twice, with consistent notes. • $NA • (11/30/97) • **82**

Riesling Spätlese Pfalz Kallstadter Saumagen 1995: Oily, big spätlese with plenty of ripe, spicy fruit character. Only half-sweet. Medium- to full-bodied with creamy texture and a long, flavorful finish. Stylish. Drink now or hold. • $NA • (11/30/96) • **88**

Riesling Spätlese Pfalz Kallstadter Saumagen 1994 • $NA • (11/30/95) • **87**

Riesling Spätlese Pfalz Kallstadter Saumagen 1993 • $19 • (11/30/94) • **89**

Riesling Trockenbeerenauslese Pfalz Kallstadter Saumagen 1994 • $NA • (11/30/95) • **90**

Scheurebe Beerenauslese Pfalz Kallstadter Saumagen 1994 • $NA • (11/30/95) • **87**

KREUSCH, LEONARD

Riesling Auslese Mosel-Saar-Ruwer Piesporter Goldtröpfchen 1996: Not too sweet, even a bit on the tart side with some honey and earth flavors. A simple auslese. Drink now through 2005. • $15 • (04/30/98) • **83**

Riesling Auslese Mosel-Saar-Ruwer Piesporter Michelsberg 1996: Tastes like canned peaches with a sweet-and-sour component. Drink now. • $12 • (04/30/98) • **79**

Riesling Kabinett Mosel-Saar-Ruwer Piesporter Michelsberg 1996: Like a canned-fruit cocktail, simple and dilute. Drink now. • $8 • (04/30/98) • **76**

Riesling QbA Mosel-Saar-Ruwer Piesporter Goldtröpfchen 1996: Smells of apples and earth, the earthy note continuing onto the palate. Light, well balanced, just off dry. Moderate length. Drink now. • $9 • (04/30/98) • **79**

Riesling Spätlese Mosel-Saar-Ruwer Piesporter Michelsberg 1996: Shows artificial, concocted apricot flavors that turn weedy on the finish. • $10 • (04/30/98) • **73**

Riesling Spätlese Mosel-Saar-Ruwer Zeller Schwarze Katz 1995: Almond and honey notes mark this mature white, then turn candied at the end. Drink now. • $10 • (01/01/98) • **78**

White Mosel-Saar-Ruwer Piesporter Michelsberg 1993 • $8 • (08/31/94) • **79**

White Mosel-Saar-Ruwer Zeller Schwarze Katz 1993 • $8 • (08/31/94) • **78**

KRUGER-RUMPF

Riesling Auslese Nahe Münsterer Dautenpflänzer 1996: An elegant, lacy white with some tropical nuances and a hint of tapioca on the nose. Seductive and satisfying, slightly drier than most auslesen, with a kick of honey on the finish. Best from 2001 through 2012. • $20 • (04/30/98) • **89**

Riesling Spätlese Nahe Münsterer Dautenpflänzer 1996: A charmer. Exotic cherry and black currant notes distinguish this delicate spätlese. It's round and full of succulent fruit character, but there's plenty of zippy acidity too. Drink now through 2005. • $16 • (04/30/98) • **89**

KÜHLING-GILLOT

Riesling Spätlese Rheinhessen Oppenheimer Herrenberg 1996: Aromas of talc and vanilla custard turn to ripe peach and apricot in this rich, expansive spätlese. The acidity will need some time to integrate, as it leaves a tart impression now. Best from 2000 through 2007. • $18 • (04/30/98) • **85**

KÜNSTLER, FRANZ

Riesling Auslese Rheingau Hochheimer Hölle 1993 • $44 • (11/30/94) • **90**

Riesling Beerenauslese Rheingau Hochheimer Hölle 1996: Not much on the nose now, but smacks your palate with zingy acidity and exotic flavors. Full-bodied and very sweet, yet the lively acidity, ripe fruit and dried apricot give a lovely balance to the wine. Drink now. • $113/375ml • (11/30/97) • **91**

Riesling Beerenauslese Rheingau Hochheimer Hölle 1994 • $104 • (11/30/95) • **89**

Riesling Eiswein Rheingau Hochheimer Reichestal 1996: Nearly classic. Subtle yet powerful, with aromas and flavors of smoke, spice and citrus. Thick, oily and supersweet, this is a terrific eiswein. Drinkable now, but will age wonderfully. • $195/375ml • (11/30/97) • **94**

Riesling Kabinett Halbtrocken Rheingau 1993 • $13 • (11/30/94) • **85**

Riesling Kabinett Rheingau Hochheimer Herrenberg 1995: Very rich and concentrated, showing loads of spice and apple flavors, this is a big wine for a kabinett. Vibrant and balanced, with a clean, refreshing finish. 330 cases made. • $16 • (11/30/96) • **87**

Riesling Kabinett Rheingau Hochheimer Herrenberg 1994 • $17 • (11/30/95) • **77**

Riesling Kabinett Rheingau Hochheimer Herrenberg 1993 • $15 • (11/30/94) • **79**

Riesling Kabinett Rheingau Hochheimer Reichestal 1996: A delicious easy-to-drink kabinett with ripe apple and pear aromas and flavors. Medium-to-light bodied with a light finish. Drink now. • $18 • (11/30/97) • **84**

Riesling QbA Halbtrocken Rheingau 1995: Wonderfully fresh, with honeycomb, floral and grape aromas and flavors and, on the finish, a hint of burnt almonds. Medium-bodied, dry, with a clean finish. Ready to drink. 330 cases made. • $13 • (11/30/96) • **85**

Riesling QbA Halbtrocken Rheingau 1994 • $14 • (11/30/95) • **86**

Riesling Spätlese Rheingau Hochheimer Herrenberg 1994 • $30 • (11/30/95) • **90**

Riesling Spätlese Rheingau Hochheimer Herrenberg 1993 • $27 • (11/30/94) • **85**

Riesling Spätlese Rheingau Hochheimer Hölle 1995: A sweet-tart component is present in this wine, without the fruit to balance it. Still, it has redeeming notes of green apple and mineral and may be better with food. Tasted twice with consistent notes. 130 cases made. • $25 • (11/30/96) • **84**

Riesling Spätlese Rheingau Hochheimer Kirchenstück 1996: Superfresh and intensely flavored spätlese. Textbook wine. Subtle aromas of flowers, pineapple and spices which exploded on the palate. Medium-bodied, medium-sweet with a superlively finish. Best in a few months but who can wait? • $30 • (11/30/97) • **92**

Riesling Spätlese Trocken Rheingau Hochheimer Hölle 1996: A rich and alluring white with tropical fruit and spicy character. Medium-bodied and dry, with a lovely, silky ripe-fruit finish. Drink or hold. • $34 • (11/30/97) • **88**

Riesling Spätlese Trocken Rheingau Hochheimer Hölle 1994 • $30 • (11/30/95) • **88**

Riesling Spätlese Trocken Rheingau Hochheimer Stielweg 1996: A slightly simple wine, but with some good apple, lemon aromas and flavors. Medium-bodied, with fresh acidity and a light finish. Drink now. • $31 • (11/30/97) • **85**

Riesling Spätlese Trocken Rheingau Hochheimer Stielweg 1995: Subtle, with good complexity of character—cream, apple and earth aromas and flavors. Medium-bodied, off-dry with a crisp and flavorful finish. Drink now or hold. 180 cases made. • $29 • (11/30/96) • **86**

Riesling Spätlese Trocken Rheingau Hochheimer Stielweg 1994 • $30 • (11/30/95) • **87**

Riesling Spätlese Trocken Rheingau Hochheimer Stielweg 1993 • $28 • (11/30/94) • **84**

Riesling Trockenbeerenauslese Rheingau Hochheimer Hölle 1994 • $428 • (11/30/95) • **90**

Key: SS—Spectator Selection CS—Cellar Selection HR—Highly Recommended BB—Best Buy $NA—Price not available Ⓐ—Auction Price (BT)—Barrel Tasting

Dates in parentheses indicate the issues in which the ratings were published.

LAUERBURG

Riesling Spätlese Mosel-Saar-Ruwer Bernkasteler Bratenhöfchen 1993 • $17 • (12/15/95) • **83**

LEITZ, JOSEF

Riesling Auslese Rheingau Rüdesheimer Schlossberg 1994 • $38 • (11/30/95) • **88**

Riesling Kabinett Halbtrocken Rheingau Rüdesheimer Schlossberg 1993 • $20 • (11/30/94) • **87**

Riesling Kabinett Halbtrocken Rheingau Rüdesheimer Bischofsberg 1996: Elegant, balanced white with spicy, mineral aromas and flavors. Medium-bodied, lightly sweet, with a fresh, delicate finish. Drink now. • $15 • (11/30/97) • **86**

Riesling Kabinett Halbtrocken Rheingau Rüdesheimer Kirchenpfad 1995: Initially this wine seems too sweet for the style, but then the acidity kicks in and cleanses the palate. The ripe, almost tropical, fruit core creates great intensity of flavor. An intriguing wine. • $NA • (11/30/96) • **88**

Riesling Kabinett Halbtrocken Rheingau Rüdesheimer Kirchenpfad 1994 • $16 • (11/30/95) • **83**

Riesling Kabinett Halbtrocken Rheingau Rüdesheimer Kirchenpfad 1993 • $14 • (11/30/94) • **87**

Riesling Kabinett Rheingau Rüdesheimer Bischofsberg 1995: Ripe, racy and exotic. Refreshing acidity provides the perfect counterpoint to the melon and peach flavors in this vibrant young kabinett. Drinkable now. • $NA • (11/30/96) • **88**

Riesling Kabinett Rheingau Rüdesheimer Bischofsberg 1993 • $NA • (11/30/94) • **87**

Riesling Kabinett Rheingau Rüdesheimer Magdalenenkreuz 1996: Very fruity aromas with a hint of flowers and spices. Light-bodied and off-dry with intense fruit flavor and a high acidity. Should have mellowed; try now. • $15 • (11/30/97) • **87**

Riesling Kabinett Trocken Rheingau 1995: Rather simple and tart now, with lemon-lime aromas and flavors, dry, medium body and mouthpuckering finish. Drink now. • $14 • (11/30/96) • **80**

Riesling Kabinett Trocken Rheingau Rüdesheimer Klosterlay 1995: A well-made, dry Riesling with aromas and flavors of spice, honey and lemon, some acidity and a long, crisp finish. Delicious now. • $NA • (11/30/96) • **86**

Riesling Spätlese Halbtrocken Rheingau Rüdesheimer Berg Rottland 1995: Starts off well, with some attractive ripe apricot and melon character and light acidity, but it's slightly developed and dull, with a poor, short finish. • $20 • (11/30/96) • **80**

Riesling Spätlese Rheingau Rüdesheimer Berg Rottland 1995: A spätlese marked by crispness. Plenty of lemon and lime character, with a hint of licorice. Medium-bodied and moderately sweet, with a crisp finish. Drinkable now. • $NA • (11/30/96) • **87**

Riesling Spätlese Rheingau Rüdesheimer Berg Rottland 1994 • $NA • (11/30/95) • **84**

Riesling Spätlese Rheingau Rüdesheimer Berg Rottland 1993 • $20 • (11/30/94) • **89**

Riesling Spätlese Trocken Rheingau Rüdesheimer Berg Rottland 1993 • $NA • (11/30/94) • **88**

LIESER, SCHLOSS

Riesling Auslese Mosel-Saar-Ruwer Lieser Niederberg-Helden 1993 • $22 • (11/30/94) • **88**

Riesling Auslese Mosel-Saar-Ruwer Lieser Niederberg-Helden Two Stars 1993 • $30 • (11/30/94) • **89**

Riesling Kabinett Mosel-Saar-Ruwer 1996: Delicate and finely etched, with lime and slate flavors lurking behind a wall of firm acidity. Needs time to unfold, as the acidity is dominant now. Best from 2000 through 2005. • $14 • (04/30/98) • **86**

Riesling Spätlese Mosel-Saar-Ruwer Lieser Niederberg-Helden 1993 • $16 • (11/30/94) • **84**

LINGENFELDER

Riesling Auslese Halbtrocken Pfalz Freinsheimer Goldberg 1993 • $18 • (11/30/94) • **90**

Riesling Auslese Trocken Pfalz Freinsheimer Goldberg 1996: A delicious dry white from the Pfalz. Displays complex aromas of apples, spice and pie crust. Full-bodied and dry, with a long, fruity aftertaste. Drink now. 300 cases made. • $NA • (11/30/97) • **89**

Riesling Kabinett Halbtrocken Pfalz Freinsheimer Musikantenbuckel 1996: Delicious, subtle off-dry wine, emitting discreet aromas of cream, mango and apples. Medium-bodied, off-dry, with a pretty spicy, fruity finish. Drink now. 500 cases made. • $12 • (11/30/97) • **87**

Riesling Spätlese Halbtrocken Pfalz Grosskarlbacher Osterberg 1996: Why drink Chardonnay? Yellow in color, with clover honey and tropical fruit aromas and flavors, this is full-bodied and off-dry, with a lovely harmony of creamy, spicy and tropical fruit flavors. Long finish. Drink now. 500 cases made. • $14 • (11/30/97) • **90**

Riesling Spätlese Pfalz Grosskarlbacher Osterberg 1996: Smells like a big, rich Chardonnay—tropical fruit and cream galore. Full-bodied and medium-sweet, with beautiful fruity flavors and a round, soft texture. Drink now. 500 cases made. • $15 • (11/30/97) • **88**

Riesling Spätlese Pfalz Grosskarlbacher Osterberg 1993 • $15 • (11/30/94) • **87**

Riesling Spätlese Trocken Pfalz Freinsheimer Goldberg 1993 • $15 • (11/30/94) • **86**

Scheurebe Kabinett Trocken Pfalz Grosskarlbacher Burweg 1993 • $13 • (11/30/94) • **85**

Scheurebe Spätlese Pfalz Freinsheimer 1993 • $16 • (11/30/94) • **91**

Scheurebe Spätlese Pfalz Freinsheimer Goldberg 1996: Fat and rich wine with lots of grapefruit, spicy character. Medium to full in body, medium-sweet and oily. Medium finish. Drink now. 300 cases made. • $14 • (11/30/97) • **87**

Scheurebe Spätlese Trocken Pfalz Freinsheimer Musikantenbuckel 1996: A big, fat white, best for food. Very ripe, with loads of orange peel and spice character, this is full-bodied, dry and very oily, with a long spicy finish. Delicious. Drink now. 500 cases made. • $14 • (11/30/97) • **86**

LOOSEN, DR.

Riesling Auslese Gold Cap Mosel-Saar-Ruwer Erdener Prälat 1994 • $65 • (11/30/95) • **93**

Riesling Auslese Gold Cap Mosel-Saar-Ruwer Erdener Prälat 1993 • $61 • (11/30/94) • **94**

Riesling Auslese Gold Cap Mosel-Saar-Ruwer Ürziger Würzgarten 1994 • $47 • (11/30/95) • **91**

Riesling Auslese Gold Cap Mosel-Saar-Ruwer Wehlener Sonnenuhr 1995: A strong, mineral style that offers peach and honey flavors. It's solid, though a bit hollow. Ready to drink. • $43 • (11/30/96) • **86**

Riesling Auslese Long Gold Cap Mosel-Saar-Ruwer Erdener Prälat 1994 • $NA • (11/30/95) • **95**

Riesling Auslese Long Gold Cap Mosel-Saar-Ruwer Erdener Prälat 1993 • $225 • (11/30/94) • **96**

Riesling Auslese Mosel-Saar-Ruwer Erdener Prälat 1996: Extremely fresh and floral, with loads of sliced apple, melon and mineral character. Medium-bodied, medium-sweet, with a long crisp finish. Try now. • $49 • (11/30/97) • **91**

Riesling Auslese Mosel-Saar-Ruwer Erdener Prälat 1995: Deceptive and harmonious, delivering plenty of concentration and intense lime and apricot right through to the refreshing, fruity aftertaste. Not up to this producer's usual quality. • $45 • (11/30/96) • **89**

Riesling Auslese Mosel-Saar-Ruwer Erdener Prälat 1994 • $44 • (11/30/95) • **92**

Riesling Auslese Mosel-Saar-Ruwer Ürziger Würzgarten 1996: Bubbling over the rim of the glass with freshly cut apple, melon and fruit character. Medium-bodied and medium-sweet, it has a long, ripe fruit aftertaste with a hint of flint. Drink now. • $36 • (11/30/97) • **90**

Riesling Auslese Mosel-Saar-Ruwer Ürziger Würzgarten 1995: An extremely fresh auslese with lemon, tropical fruit and a hint of mineral flavor. Medium-bodied, with lively acidity and a fresh finish. Drink now. • $33 • (11/30/96) • **89**

Riesling Auslese Mosel-Saar-Ruwer Ürziger Würzgarten 1994 • $34 • (11/30/95) • **91**

Riesling Auslese Mosel-Saar-Ruwer Wehlener Sonnenuhr 1995: A tropical fruit salad of flavors sends a wakeup call to the senses in this ripe, seductive wine. It shows integration and the acidity to keep it all together. • $29 • (11/30/96) • **89**

Riesling Auslese Mosel-Saar-Ruwer Wehlener Sonnenuhr 1993 • $31 • (11/30/94) • **91**

Riesling Beerenauslese Mosel-Saar-Ruwer Erdener Treppchen 1996: An elegant BA with subtle honey, ripe fruit aromas and flavors. Medium-bodied and very sweet, with a long, crisp finish. Drinkable now. • $153/375ml • (11/30/97) • **90**

Riesling Kabinett Mosel-Saar-Ruwer Erdener Treppchen 1995: Ripe and lemony with some tropical fruit character that carries through the finish. Medium-bodied, rather dark-colored, deep yellow. Atypical for Mosel, but pleasant. • $16 • (11/30/96) • **84**

Riesling Kabinett Mosel-Saar-Ruwer Erdener Treppchen 1994 • $17 • (11/30/95) • **85**

Riesling Kabinett Mosel-Saar-Ruwer Erdener Treppchen 1993 • $15 • (11/30/94) • **88**

Riesling Kabinett Mosel-Saar-Ruwer Wehlener Sonnenuhr 1996: Subtle, serious kabinett, marked by intense character of lime, mineral, thistle, and earth. Medium-bodied and lightly sweet, this has a silky texture and a very high-acidity finish. Drink now. • $17 • (11/30/97) • **89**

Riesling Kabinett Mosel-Saar-Ruwer Wehlener Sonnenuhr 1994 • $16 • (11/30/94) • **88**

Riesling Spätlese Mosel-Saar-Ruwer Erdener Treppchen 1996: A very lemony wine with hints of minerals. Medium-bodied and off-dry, with a mineral and citrus finish. Slightly simple for Loosen. Drink now or hold. • $26 • (11/30/97) • **86**

Riesling Spätlese Mosel-Saar-Ruwer Erdener Treppchen 1995: Ripe peach and floral aromas segue into rich, mouthfilling fruit flavors. It's all held together with some firm acidity. Drinkable now. • $25 • (11/30/96) • **89**

Riesling Spätlese Mosel-Saar-Ruwer Erdener Treppchen 1994 • $27 • (11/30/95) • **90**

Riesling Spätlese Mosel-Saar-Ruwer Ürziger Würzgarten 1996: A wine with serious concentration of peach, apple and honey aromas and flavors. Medium-bodied, medium-sweet, with a silky texture and crisp acidity. Drink or hold. • $27 • (11/30/97) • **90**

Riesling Spätlese Mosel-Saar-Ruwer Ürziger Würzgarten 1995: A live wire of a spätlese, zingy with acidity yet very ripe with lemon, tropical fruit and mineral flavors. Medium-bodied, medium-sweet. Extremely fresh finish. Drink now. • $45 • (11/30/96) • **91**

Riesling Spätlese Mosel-Saar-Ruwer Ürziger Würzgarten 1994 • $29 • (11/30/95) • **89**

Riesling Spätlese Mosel-Saar-Ruwer Ürziger Würzgarten 1993 • $25 • (11/30/94) • **92**

Riesling Spätlese Mosel-Saar-Ruwer Wehlener Sonnenuhr 1996: Pretty apple, melon, lemon and flint aromas and flavors are on display in this medium-bodied, lightly sweet and extremely crisp and fresh spätlese. Still slightly effervescent. Try now. • $23 • (11/30/97) • **89**

Riesling Spätlese Mosel-Saar-Ruwer Wehlener Sonnenuhr 1995: Like freshly crushed berries on the palate. Medium-bodied, and medium-sweet with honey, grape, grapefruit and mineral flavors. Fresh, crisp finish. Drink now. • $21 • (11/30/96) • **89**

Riesling Trockenbeerenauslese Mosel-Saar-Ruwer Wehlener Sonnenuhr 1993 • $NA • (11/30/94) • **93**

Riesling Trockenbeerenauslese Mosel-Saar-Ruwer Ürziger Würzgarten 1994 • $NA • (11/30/95) • **96**

LOWENSTEIN, FÜRST

Riesling Beerenauslese Rheingau 1994 • $NA • (11/30/95) • **83**

MERKELBACH, ALFRED

Riesling Auslese Mosel-Saar-Ruwer Ürziger Würzgarten No. 11 1996: Lime blossom, chamomile, peach and apple intermingle in this lush-textured auslese, balanced on the soft side. Drink now through 2010. • $18 • (04/30/98) • **88**

Riesling Auslese Mosel-Saar-Ruwer Ürziger Würzgarten No. 12 1996: A fine minerally intensity underlies this medium-sweet auslese. Very pure flavors of lime, peach and slate are all perfectly balanced. Great finish. Best from 2002 through 2015. • $18 • (04/30/98) • **90**

Riesling Spätlese Mosel-Saar-Ruwer Erdener Treppchen No. 9 1996: Beautiful flavors of lime, apple and passionfruit mark this ethereal white of inner strength and harmony. The acidity sticks out a bit on the finish, so give it time to settle down. Best from 2000 through 2007. • $15 • (04/30/98) • **89**

Key: SS—Spectator Selection CS—Cellar Selection HR—Highly Recommended BB—Best Buy $NA—Price not available Ⓐ—Auction Price (BT)—Barrel Tasting
Dates in parentheses indicate the issues in which the ratings were published.

MÜLLER, EGON

Riesling Auslese Gold Cap Mosel-Saar-Ruwer Scharzhofberger 1994 • $NA • (11/30/95) • **90**

Riesling Auslese Gold Cap Mosel-Saar-Ruwer Scharzhofberger 1993 • $58 • (11/30/94) • **95**

Riesling Auslese Gold Cap Mosel-Saar-Ruwer Scharzhofberger No. D 1995: Super-ripe and concentrated, showing apricot, mango and pear notes that zip across the palate. Wonderful intensity of flavor, with a sweet-tart accent from the extra ripeness. Very long on the finish. • $400 • (11/30/96) • **93**

Riesling Auslese Mosel-Saar-Ruwer Scharzhofberger 1994 • $129 • (11/30/95) • **89**

Riesling Auslese Mosel-Saar-Ruwer Scharzhofberger Cask No. 103 1995: Unloads its fruit character on the finish: plenty of tropical fruit and lemon-lime aromas and flavors. Medium-bodied and moderately sweet with a zingy, crisp and fruity finish. Harmonious. Drink now or can hold. • $110 • (11/30/96) • **91**

Riesling Auslese Mosel-Saar-Ruwer Scharzhofberger Cask No. B 1996: Some serious effort here. Sweet and exciting, with lemon-lime and mineral aromas and flavors, this is medium-bodied, very sweet and incredibly lively on the finish. Best after 1999. • $NA/375ml • (11/30/97) • **94**

Riesling Beerenauslese Mosel-Saar-Ruwer Scharzhofberger 1994 • $NA • (11/30/95) • **93**

Riesling Beerenauslese Mosel-Saar-Ruwer Scharzhofberger 1993 • $NA • (11/30/94) • **98**

Riesling Eiswein Mosel-Saar-Ruwer Scharzhofberger No. 103 1996: Serious eiswein. The sirens go off with this one in your mouth. Golden colored lime, mineral and spice character. Full-bodied and thick yet very sweet and fresh. The intense acidity carries the flavors on and on on the palate. Best after 2000. • $NA • (11/30/97) • **95**

Riesling Kabinett Mosel-Saar-Ruwer Scharzhofberger 1996: Interesting for its lemon and chalk aromas and flavors. Medium-bodied, off-dry and crisp. High acidity. Long and flavor finish. Serve with light foods and salads. Drink now. • $27 • (11/30/97) • **87**

Riesling Kabinett Mosel-Saar-Ruwer Scharzhofberger 1995: Rather dull for a young kabinett with flat, floral aromas and flavors. Medium-bodied, moderately sweet and short on the finish. • $29 • (11/30/96) • **75**

Riesling Kabinett Mosel-Saar-Ruwer Scharzhofberger 1994 • $NA • (11/30/95) • **82**

Riesling Kabinett Mosel-Saar-Ruwer Scharzhofberger 1993 • $NA • (11/30/94) • **84**

Riesling QbA Mosel-Saar-Ruwer Scharzhofberger 1996: Serious QbA. Plenty of grapefruit and flint character in this off-dry wine. Medium-bodied and dry, with a round mouthfeel and a crisp finish. Needs food. Drink now. • $16 • (11/30/97) • **88**

Riesling QbA Mosel-Saar-Ruwer Scharzhofberger 1995: A crystal-clear white, with light spice, mineral and apple aromas and flavors. It's light-bodied and off-dry, with tart acidity and a crisp finish. Delicious to drink now. • $14 • (11/30/96) • **86**

Riesling QbA Mosel-Saar-Ruwer Scharzhofberger 1994 • $NA • (11/30/95) • **79**

Riesling Spätlese Mosel-Saar-Ruwer Scharzhofberger 1996: Crisp and quite rich for a spätlese. Medium-bodied and sweet, with mineral and citrus flavors and a long, zingy finish. Drinkable now. • $37 • (11/30/97) • **87**

Riesling Spätlese Mosel-Saar-Ruwer Scharzhofberger 1994 • $NA • (11/30/95) • **87**

Riesling Spätlese Mosel-Saar-Ruwer Scharzhofberger Cask No. 16 1995: The fruit just oozes out of the glass. In an extremely fresh style, it's like biting into a bunch of freshly picked grapes. Medium-bodied and of medium sweetness, with a lively, refreshing finish. Ready to drink. • $37 • (11/30/96) • **91**

Riesling Spätlese Mosel-Saar-Ruwer Scharzhofberger 1993 • $NA • (11/30/94) • **86**

MÜLLER-CATOIR

Muskateller Eiswein Pfalz Haardter Bürgergarten 1993 • $73/375ml • (11/30/94) • **92**

Muskateller Kabinett Halbtrocken Pfalz Gelber Haardter Bürgergarten 1994 • $23 • (11/30/95) • **87**

Muskateller Kabinett Trocken Pfalz 1996: Very pretty wine with lovely floral, spice aromas and flavors. Medium-bodied, off-dry with a very fruity, spicy, delicious finish. Drink or hold. • $23 • (11/30/97) • **88**

Rieslaner Auslese Pfalz Auslese Mussbacher Eselshaut 1994 • $30 • (11/30/95) • **93**

Rieslaner Auslese Pfalz Haardter Bürgergarten 1996: Solid auslese. Wonderful aromas of banana, mango and minerals. Full-bodied, sweet and honeyed with good acidity and a lovely fruity finish. Drink or hold. • $39/375ml • (11/30/97) • **89**

Rieslaner Auslese Pfalz Mussbacher Eselshaut 1996: A subtle yet very intense auslese with wonderful mango, tropical fruit character as well as honey. Medium-to-full bodied, very sweet with a long fresh finish. Drink now. • $37/375ml • (11/30/97) • **89**

Rieslaner Auslese Pfalz Mussbacher Eselshaut 1995: An auslese with loads of botrytis character. Intense apricot, honey and nectarine flavors, balanced by fresh acidity that carries the flavors to a moderate finish. Forward, very drinkable now, but better in 2000. • $40/375ml • (11/30/96) • **92**

Rieslaner Spätlese Pfalz Mussbacher Eselshaut 1996: Grabs your attention with electrified tastes of cream, mango and pie crust. Medium-bodied, sweet with lively acidity and a long pineapple, mango aftertaste. Drink now or hold. • $34 • (11/30/97) • **91**

Rieslaner Spätlese Pfalz Mussbacher Eselshaut 1993 • $26 • (11/30/94) • **89**

Rieslaner Trockenbeerenauslese Pfalz Mussbacher Eselshaut 1994 • $75 • (11/30/95) • **89**

Riesling Eiswein Pfalz Haardter Bürgergarten 1996: A very ripe and raisiny eiswein with zingy acidity and a long, long finish. Medium- to full-bodied and very sweet, with plenty of orange marmalade flavors. Drinkable now, better in a few years. • $94/375ml • (11/30/97) • **91**

Riesling Kabinett Halbtrocken Pfalz Haardter Herrenletten 1995: Loads of citrus character, as well as lots of lime and mineral flavors. Medium-bodied and almost dry, with a round texture. Slightly dull finish. • $21 • (11/30/96) • **83**

Riesling Kabinett Halbtrocken Pfalz Haardter Herrenletten 1994 • $21 • (11/30/95) • **82**

Riesling Kabinett Pfalz Haardter Bürgergarten 1994 • $21 • (11/30/95) • **87**

Riesling Kabinett Pfalz Haardter Bürgergarten 1993 • $17 • (11/30/94) • **85**

Riesling Kabinett Trocken Pfalz 1996: Emits interesting floral, apple and melon rind aromas. Medium-bodied, dry, with melon and lemon character, but a slightly diluted finish. Drink now. • $24 • (11/30/97) • **81**

Riesling Spätlese Halbtrocken Pfalz Haardter Herzog 1993 • $24 • (11/30/94) • **91**

Riesling Spätlese Pfalz Gimmeldinger Mandelgarten 1994 • $29 • (11/30/95) • **88**

Riesling Spätlese Pfalz Haardter Herzog 1996: A live wire of a wine. Fabulous aromas of pineapple, mango and spice. Medium-to-full bodied, medium-sweet with intense fruit flavors and a long, zingy finish. Best now. • $31 • (11/30/97) • **92**

Riesling Spätlese Trocken Pfalz Gimmeldinger Mandelgarten 1993 • $23 • (11/30/94) • **88**

Riesling Spätlese Trocken Pfalz Haardter Herrenletten 1996: Delicious and lively, with intense aromas of minerals and spices, this medium-bodied and dry wine has firm acidity and a zingy, spice aftertaste. Drink or hold. • $29 • (11/30/97) • **89**

Riesling Spätlese Trocken Pfalz Haardter Herzog 1995: A powerful wine loaded with flavors of honey, almond and minerals. Dry, rich and well balanced, with a hint of peach flavor on the finish. Drink now. • $29 • (11/30/96) • **87**

Scheurebe Eiswein Pfalz Haardter Mandelring 1996: Although less sweet and rich than some, this wine is marked by a beautiful balance of orange, honey and pineapple character, with crisp acidity. Medium- to full-bodied. Drink now. • $107/375ml • (11/30/97) • **88**

Scheurebe Kabinett Halbtrocken Pfalz Haardter Mandelring 1995: Lovely and mouthfilling, with honey, lemon and spice flavors, medium body and a crisp, dry finish. Drink now. • $24 • (11/30/96) • **85**

Scheurebe Kabinett Pfalz Haardter Mandelring 1996: Amazingly rich and wonderful kabinett with loads of tropical fruit, pineapple and pie crust character. Full-bodied, off-dry and super fruity on the finish. Try with food. Drink now. • $24 • (11/30/97) • **90**

Scheurebe Kabinett Pfalz Haardter Mandelring 1993 • $19 • (11/30/94) • **87**

Scheurebe Spätlese Pfalz Haardter Mandelring 1994 • $28 • (11/30/95) • **88**

NEIPPERG, GRAF VON

Lemberger Spätlese Trocken Württemberg Schwaigerner Ruthe 1990 • $20 • (03/31/95) • **77**

Rotwein QbA Württemberg 1993 • $10 • (03/31/95) • **80**

Schwarzriesling Kabinett Trocken Württemberg Neipperger Schlossberg 1992 • $14 • (03/31/95) • **78**

NEUHAUS, LUDWIG

Spätlese Rheinhessen 1995: A somewhat ripe wine with applelike and buttery flavors, a nice spicy note, too. Tasted twice, with consistent notes. 6,500 cases made. • $10 • (10/31/97) • **81**

NICOLAY, PETER

Riesling Auslese Mosel-Saar-Ruwer Erdener Prälat 1994 • $35 • (11/30/95) • **86**

Riesling Auslese Mosel-Saar-Ruwer Erdener Treppchen 1995: Thick and viscous in texture, showing honey, coconut and pineapple flavors that persist, concentrated and long. Very ripe and impressive, this is a big, bold auslese. • $30 • (11/30/96) • **91**

Riesling Auslese Mosel-Saar-Ruwer Ürziger Goldwingert 1996: A well-balanced auslese with creamy, apple and pineapple aromas and flavors. Medium-bodied, medium-sweet, with a delicate finish. Drink now. 100 cases made. • $30 • (11/30/97) • **87**

Riesling Auslese Mosel-Saar-Ruwer Ürziger Goldwingert 1995: Wonderful finesse in this sweet wine, with plenty of spicy, flinty character beneath the ripe and sweet fruit flavors. Fine acidity and a crisp finish. Drink now. • $119 • (11/30/96) • **88**

Riesling Auslese Mosel-Saar-Ruwer Ürziger Goldwingert 1994 • $NA • (11/30/95) • **84**

Riesling Kabinett Mosel-Saar-Ruwer Feinherb Ürziger Würzgarten 1996: Medium-bodied, off-dry and rich, with lemon, mineral and flinty character that goes on and on. Very high acidity on the finish. Try now. 500 cases made. • $17 • (11/30/97) • **86**

Riesling Spätlese Mosel-Saar-Ruwer Ürziger Goldwingert 1994 • $NA • (11/30/95) • **85**

Riesling Trockenbeerenauslese Mosel-Saar-Ruwer Ürziger Würzgarten 1996: Gorgeous, thick sweet wine with lemon, honey, pineapple and cream aromas and flavors. Full-bodied, wildly fresh with a long, long finish. Best after 1999. 10 cases made. • $500 • (11/30/97) • **93**

OTHEGRAVEN, VON

Riesling Auslese Mosel-Saar-Ruwer Kanzemer Altenberg 1993: A sweet, rich Riesling with nice honey and nut accents to the ripe peach flavors. Very fresh and fruity. 150 cases made. • $28 • (09/15/97) • **86**

Riesling Auslese Mosel-Saar-Ruwer Kanzemer Altenberg Cask No. 12 1996: An auslese in an austere style, yet there's plenty of appley, minerally flavors directed in a laserlike beam. Good balance and length add up to a delicate, ageworthy white. Best from 1999 through 2005. 100 cases made. • $30 • (03/31/98) • **88**

Riesling Kabinett Mosel-Saar-Ruwer Kanzemer Altenberg 1996: Fruit lovers beware: This Riesling is stuffed with stone and spice aromas and flavors, all matched to a racy, austere framework that needs time to knit together. Best from 2000 through 2010. 220 cases made. • $14 • (03/31/98) • **87**

Riesling Spätlese Mosel-Saar-Ruwer Kanzemer Altenberg 1996: Marked by pure slate and apple, concentrated and intense, with a finely etched backbone of acidity. Racy and long, this will match food well. Best from 2000 through 2006. 165 cases made. • $19 • (03/31/98) • **89**

Riesling Trockenbeerenauslese Mosel-Saar-Ruwer Kanzemer Altenberg 1994: Sweet, full of botrytis and zingy apricot, vanilla and honey flavors. Amazing concentration and verve. Just beginning to open and hit its stride. Fabulous finish. Big step up here to TBA level. Drink now through 2010. 7 cases made. • $450 • (03/31/98) • **94**

PAULY-BERGWEILER, DR.

Riesling Auslese Mosel-Saar-Ruwer Bernkasteler Lay 1996: Steely and flinty, with a hint of lime. Medium-bodied, with a fruity, sweet finish. Slightly dull. Drink now. 200 cases made. • $29 • (11/30/97) • **84**

Riesling Auslese Mosel-Saar-Ruwer Bernkasteler Lay 1994 • $21 • (11/30/95) • **86**

Riesling Auslese Mosel-Saar-Ruwer Bernkasteler Lay 1993 • $NA • (11/30/94) • **80**

Riesling Auslese Mosel-Saar-Ruwer Bernkasteler alte Badstube 1995: Shows some gorgeous aromas and flavors of flint and honey, but the palate is muted and slightly disjointed. • $30 • (11/30/96) • **81**

Riesling Auslese Mosel-Saar-Ruwer Bernkasteler alte Badstube am Doctorberg 1996: Attractive auslese with burnt almond, honey and fruit aromas and flavors. Medium-bodied, medium-sweet with a medium finish. Drink now. 100 cases made. • $30 • (11/30/97) • **86**

Riesling Beerenauslese Mosel-Saar-Ruwer Bernkasteler alte Badstube am Doctorberg 1993 • $55 • (11/30/94) • **85**

Riesling Beerenauslese Mosel-Saar-Ruwer Bernkasteler Badstube 1994 • $NA • (11/30/95) • **84**

Riesling Beerenauslese Mosel-Saar-Ruwer Bernkasteler Lay 1994 • $33 • (11/30/95) • **90**

Riesling Eiswein Mosel-Saar-Ruwer Bernkasteler Lay 1996: Very impressive. Golden colored with extremely ripe, almost raisin character. Dried apricot and dried pineapple aromas. Full-bodied, sweet with a long spicy, zingy acidity finish. Creamy, toffee flavors. Extremely lively. Drink now or hold. • $139 • (11/30/97) • **94**

Riesling Eiswein Mosel-Saar-Ruwer Bernkasteler Lay 1995: Fresh and clean, with a bracing acidity that offsets the sweetness. Flavors are honey and apricot, rich and concentrated, ending up in a sweet-tart finish common to eiswein. • $120 • (11/30/96) • **90**

Riesling Kabinett Mosel-Saar-Ruwer Bernkasteler alte Badstube am Doctorberg 1996: Shows interesting aromas of lemons, flowers and earth. Medium-bodied, off-dry and silky, it's a bit too sweet on the finish. Drink now. 600 cases made. • $19 • (11/30/97) • **85**

Riesling Kabinett Mosel-Saar-Ruwer Bernkasteler alte Badstube am Doctorberg 1995: A sweet and silky wine, medium-bodied, with ripe apple, lemon and spice flavors and aromas, and a crisp finish. Drink now. • $19 • (11/30/96) • **85**

Riesling Kabinett Mosel-Saar-Ruwer Bernkasteler alte Badstube am Doctorberg 1994 • $25 • (11/30/95) • **82**

Riesling Kabinett Mosel-Saar-Ruwer Bernkasteler alte Badstube am Doctorberg 1993 • $NA • (11/30/94) • **81**

Riesling Kabinett Mosel-Saar-Ruwer Wehlener Sonnenuhr 1994 • $NA • (11/30/95) • **83**

Riesling Spätlese Mosel-Saar-Ruwer Bernkasteler Alte Badstube am Doctorberg 1994 • $27 • (11/30/95) • **86**

Riesling Spätlese Mosel-Saar-Ruwer Bernkasteler Badstube 1996: The mineral character shows very well, especially on the palate, in this very flinty spätlese. Medium in body, sweetness and aftertaste. Slightly one-dimensional. Drink now or hold. 2,000 cases made. • $22 • (11/30/97) • **86**

Riesling Spätlese Mosel-Saar-Ruwer Bernkasteler Badstube 1994 • $24 • (11/30/95) • **85**

Riesling Spätlese Mosel-Saar-Ruwer Bernkasteler Doctor 1995: Offers straightforward apple and lime flavors and aromas, though it lacks the racy structure of higher scoring wines of the vintage. A soft, easy-drinking white that's ready now. • $35 • (11/30/96) • **83**

Riesling Spätlese Mosel-Saar-Ruwer Bernkasteler Doctor 1994 • $47 • (11/30/95) • **85**

Riesling Spätlese Mosel-Saar-Ruwer Bernkasteler Lay 1995: A rounder, fruitier style of spätlese. Aromas of melon, pineapple and other tropical fruits follow through onto the palate. Moderately sweet, with a long, creamy finish. Ready to drink. • $20 • (11/30/96) • **87**

Riesling Spätlese Mosel-Saar-Ruwer Bernkasteler alte Badstube am Doctorberg 1996: Slightly candied in style, with a steely, lime and honey character. Medium-bodied, very sweet for a spätlese. Rather simple. Drink now. 200 cases made. • $25 • (11/30/97) • **81**

Riesling Spätlese Mosel-Saar-Ruwer Bernkasteler alte Badstube am Doctorberg 1995: A spätlese whose ripe acidity, ripe fruit flavors and smooth, sweetish finish make it ready to drink now. Slightly simple. • $21 • (11/30/96) • **84**

Riesling Spätlese Mosel-Saar-Ruwer Wehlener Sonnenuhr 1996: Plenty of ripe fruit here: pineapple, apple and lemons. Medium-bodied, medium-sweet and high in acidity, it's a well-balanced and exciting wine. Drink now. 100 cases made. • $23 • (11/30/97) • **88**

Riesling Spätlese Mosel-Saar-Ruwer Wehlener Sonnenuhr 1995: The sweet fruit flavors and acidity lack integration, making this wine seem soft and unfocused. Disappointing for this category. • $20 • (11/30/96) • **82**

Riesling Trockenbeerenauslese Mosel-Saar-Ruwer Bernkasteler alte Badstube am Doctorberg 1993 • $70 • (11/30/94) • **84**

Riesling Trockenbeerenauslese Mosel-Saar-Ruwer Bernkasteler Badstube am Doctorberg 1994 • $NA • (11/30/95) • **86**

Key: SS—Spectator Selection CS—Cellar Selection HR—Highly Recommended BB—Best Buy $NA—Price not available Ⓐ—Auction Price (BT)—Barrel Tasting
Dates in parentheses indicate the issues in which the ratings were published.

PETERSHOF

Riesling Kabinett Mosel-Saar-Ruwer Eitelsbacher Marienholz 1994: A little on the sweet side. Nice peach and apple flavors finish with an earthy accent. 300 cases made. • $8 • (08/31/96) • **80**

Riesling Spätlese Mosel-Saar-Ruwer Eitelsbacher Marienholz 1994: Musty, sulfur aromas are unappealing, the wine is sickly sweet on the palate and vanishes on the finish. 400 cases made. • $10 • (10/15/96) • **72**

PFEFFINGEN

Riesling Auslese Pfalz Ungsteiner Hönigsäckel 1993 • $23 • (11/30/94) • **88**

Riesling Kabinett Halbtrocken Pfalz Pfeffo 1996: Citrus notes highlight the aromas, while the flavors range from herbs to nuts to minerals in this bold, rich Riesling. All the elements are here, from the ripe fruit to the tangy acidity, but it needs time to integrate. Good food wine. Best from 2000 through 2005. • $15 • (04/30/98) • **88**

Riesling Spätlese Pfalz Ungsteiner Herrenberg 1996: Plenty of ripe, exuberant tropical fruit and orange flavors, but not much substance to back them up. Drink now. • $20 • (04/30/98) • **81**

Riesling Spätlese Trocken Pfalz Ungsteiner Herrenberg 1993 • $18 • (11/30/94) • **83**

Scheurebe Auslese Pfalz Ungsteiner Herrenberg 1993 • $32 • (11/30/94) • **84**

PRÜM, JOH. JOS.

Riesling Auslese Gold Cap Mosel-Saar-Ruwer Wehlener Sonnenuhr 1995: Beautiful and balanced. Loads of pie crust and spice aromas. Medium-bodied and medium-sweet, with a lot of flavor on the finish. JJ does it again. Drink now. • $70 • (07/31/98) • **90**

Riesling Auslese Long Gold Cap Mosel-Saar-Ruwer Wehlener Sonnenuhr 1995: Dusty, lemony and fruity aromas. Medium- to full-bodied, with medium sweetness and an intensely spicy finish. Slightly too much petrol character. Best from 2000 through 2005. 25 cases made. • $315 • (07/31/98) • **87**

Riesling Auslese Mosel-Saar-Ruwer Wehlener Sonnenuhr 1995: A white with rosebush and citrus character. Medium-bodied and lightly sweet, with lively acidity and a long, flavorful finish. Delicious. Drink now. • $26 • (07/31/98) • **89**

Riesling Kabinett Mosel-Saar-Ruwer 1994: Intense aromas of lemon-lime, mineral and petrol. Medium-bodied and dry, with lots of lively acidity. Needs time. Best from 1999 through 2004. 600 cases made. • $17 • (07/31/98) • **88**

Riesling Kabinett Mosel-Saar-Ruwer Ürzinger Würzgarten 1993 • $12 • (11/30/94) • **83**

Riesling Kabinett Mosel-Saar-Ruwer Wehlener Sonnenuhr 1993 • $19 • (11/30/94) • **81**

Riesling Qba Mosel-Saar-Ruwer Dr. M. Prüm 1996: Perfumed aromas of citrus blossom, peach, honey and minerals lead into this luscious, deftly balanced young white with peach and lime flavors that linger subtly on the finish. Drink now through 2000. • $11 • (04/30/98) • **87**

Riesling Spätlese Mosel-Saar-Ruwer Wehlener Sonnenuhr 1995: Impressive aromas of fruit and earth. Medium-bodied and medium-sweet, with ripe fruit flavors and a moderate finish. A bit rustic. Drink now. • $23 • (07/31/98) • **86**

Riesling Spätlese Mosel-Saar-Ruwer Wehlener Sonnenuhr 1994: Plenty of lemon and mineral aromas. Medium-bodied and off-dry, with fine acidity and a medium, fruity finish. A bit reserved. Drink now. • $22 • (07/31/98) • **86**

Riesling Spätlese Mosel-Saar-Ruwer Wehlener Sonnenuhr 1993 • $27 • (11/30/94) • **86**

REINHARTSHAUSEN, SCHLOSS

Rheingau Chard Spätlese Trocken Erbacher Reinhell 1994 • $NA • (11/30/95) • **84**

Riesling Auslese Rheingau Erbacher Schlossberg 1993 • $NA • (11/30/94) • **85**

Riesling Auslese Rheingau Erbacher Siegelsberg 1996: Not a big auslese but some interesting aromas and flavors of spice, minerals and burnt almonds. Medium-bodied, medium-sweet with a slightly bitter finish. Drink now. • $31/375ml • (11/30/97) • **85**

Riesling Auslese Rheingau Erbacher Siegelsberg 1995: The character of this wine is so restrained that the light peach and mineral flavors come across as simple, one-dimensional. 100 cases made. • $69 • (11/30/96) • **87**

Riesling Beerenauslese Rheingau Erbacher Siegelsberg 1996: Displays a pretty balance of ripe pineapple, apple and honey character and intense sweetness. Medium- to full-bodied, with a texture like thick honey and a long sweet finish. Drink now. • $119/375ml • (11/30/97) • **87**

Riesling Beerenauslese Rheingau Erbacher Siegelsberg 1995: A young wine. Your first impression is of fresh melon and apricot, then the mouthwatering acidity kicks in, carrying the fruit flavors to a lingering finish. Intense, yet delicate. Drinkable now. 25 cases made. • $100/375ml • (11/30/96) • **91**

Riesling Beerenauslese Rheingau Hattenheimer Wisselbrunnen 1994 • $NA • (11/30/95) • **89**

Riesling Beerenauslese Rheingau Hattenheimer Wisselbrunnen 1993 • $NA • (11/30/94) • **83**

Riesling Eiswein Rheingau Erbacher Michelmark 1993 • $NA • (11/30/94) • **84**

Riesling Kabinett Halbtrocken Rheingau Kiedricher Sandgrub 1993 • $NA • (11/30/94) • **86**

Riesling Kabinett Rheingau Erbacher Schlossberg 1996: Attractive aromas of minerals, flint and fruit follow through on the palate. Light bodied, off-dry with a lovely silky finish. Drink now. • $17 • (11/30/97) • **86**

Riesling Kabinett Rheingau Erbacher Schlossberg 1995: Subtle notes of apple and mineral highlight this round wine. There's ripeness to the character, but the finish falls a bit short. 250 cases made. • $79 • (11/30/96) • **83**

Riesling Spätlese Rheingau 1993 • $NA • (11/30/94) • **82**

Riesling Spätlese Rheingau Erbacher Marcobrunn 1995: A powerful wine, restrained but concentrated, with a stony, spicy character and a dry, spicy finish. Medium-bodied. Try with food. 150 cases made. • $49 • (11/30/96) • **88**

Riesling Spätlese Rheingau Erbacher Marcobrunn 1994 • $NA • (11/30/95) • **85**

Riesling Spätlese Rheingau Erbacher Schlossberg 1995: Offers attractive peach and apple flavors, supported by zippy, citrusy acidity. Vibrant and mouthwatering. 250 cases made. • $39 • (11/30/96) • **87**

Riesling Spätlese Rheingau Erbacher Siegelsberg 1996: Pretty apple pie and honey character in this one. Medium- to light-bodied, medium-sweet with a light finish. Drink now. • $27 • (11/30/97) • **85**

Riesling Spätlese Rheingau Hattenheimer Wisselbrunnen 1994 • $NA • (11/30/95) • **86**

Riesling Spätlese Trocken Rheingau Erbacher Marcobrunn 1996: Fresh and lively, with a slightly herbal note, this is medium-bodied and dry, with a crisp finish. Drink now. • $40 • (11/30/97) • **83**

Riesling Spätlese Trocken Rheingau Erbacher Marcobrunn 1995: A nearly complete wine, with wonderful honey, spice and fruit aromas and flavors. Medium-bodied and dry, with fine acidity and a flavorful finish. Drink now or hold. 250 cases made. • $49 • (11/30/96) • **89**

Riesling Trockenbeerenauslese Rheingau Erbacher Siegelsberg 1996: Not as sweet as some TBAs, but maintains loads of spicy, Riesling character despite being so rich and sticky. Full-bodied, with a balance of acidity and flavor. A beauty. Drink now. • $NA/375ml • (11/30/97) • **89**

RESS, BALTHASAR

Riesling Beerenauslese Rheingau Oestricher Doosberg 1996: Another big and ripe BA, slightly over ripe. Surprizingly hot and slightly bitter. Full-bodied, medium-sweet with a spicy, burnt almond finish. Drink now. • $100/500ml • (11/30/97) • **82**

Riesling Eiswein Rheingau Hallgartener Hendelberg 1996: Big and ripe for the vintage—almost overripe. Full-bodied, sweet with a fat, oily texture. Long, spicy finish. Slightly dull. Drink now. • $NA/500ml • (11/30/97) • **86**

Riesling Kabinett Rheingau Hattenheimer Schützenhaus 1996: Floral, honey and mineral character throughout on this one. Medium-bodied, lightly sweet and plenty on the finish. Ripe fruit and mineral aftertaste. Delicious wine. Drink now. • $10 • (11/30/97) • **87**

Riesling Kabinett Rheingau Schloss Reichartshausen 1996: An odd, canned fruit salad character dominates. Medium-bodied, flat finish. Tasted twice with consistent notes. Drink now. • $13 • (11/30/97) • **76**

Riesling QbA Rheingau Hattenheimer 1996: Some good concentration in this wine but slightly too herbal in character. Medium-bodied, off-dry and oily with a herbal aftertaste. Drink now. • $9 • (11/30/97) • **79**

Riesling QbA Trocken Rheingau 1996: Clean and steely with some light tropical fruit and spice aromas and flavors. Medium-bodied, dry with a crisp finish. Very good with food. Drink now. • $8 • (11/30/97) • **86**

Riesling Spätlese Rheingau Oestricher Doosberg 1996: Creamy-textured, with lots of apple, pie crust and light tropical fruit character. Medium-bodied, medium-sweet, with a long, flavorful finish. Drink now. • $22 • (11/30/97) • **87**

RHEINART

Riesling Auslese Mosel-Saar-Ruwer Ayler Kupp 1994: Disjointed, with herbal with onion flavors and aromas. Too funky. 200 cases made. • $12 • (08/31/96) • **72**

Riesling Kabinett Mosel-Saar-Ruwer Ockfener Bockstein 1994 • $7 • (11/30/95) • **78**

Riesling Spätlese Mosel-Saar-Ruwer Ayler Kupp 1994 • $9 • (11/30/95) • **77**

Riesling Spätlese Mosel-Saar-Ruwer Ockfener Bockstein 1994: A bit awkard. Has an odd, nut and herb taste. 500 cases made. • $9 • (08/31/96) • **75**

RICHTER, MAX FERD.

Riesling Auslese Mosel-Saar-Ruwer Brauneberger Juffer 1994 • $NA • (11/30/95) • **85**

Riesling Auslese Mosel-Saar-Ruwer Graacher Domprobst 1993 • $28 • (11/30/94) • **87**

Riesling Auslese Mosel-Saar-Ruwer Veldenzer Elisenberg 1993 • $20 • (11/30/94) • **87**

Riesling Auslese Mosel-Saar-Ruwer Brauneberger Juffer-Sonnenuhr Two Stars 1994 • $NA • (11/30/95) • **79**

Riesling Auslese Mosel-Saar-Ruwer Veldenzer Elisenberg 1994 • $31 • (11/30/95) • **83**

Riesling Beerenauslese Mosel-Saar-Ruwer Brauneberger Juffer-Sonnenuhr 1993 • $140 • (11/30/94) • **93**

Riesling Beerenauslese Mosel-Saar-Ruwer Graacher Domprobst 1996: Dark gold in color, with an extremely ripe, almost raisiny character. Full-bodied and very sweet, it has an oily texture and pineapple finish. A bit fat for a Mosel BA. Drink now. 16 cases made. • $72/375ml • (11/30/97) • **88**

Riesling Eiswein Mosel-Saar-Ruwer Mülheimer Helenenkloster 1993 • $120 • (11/30/94) • **90**

Riesling Kabinett Mosel-Saar-Ruwer Brauneberger Juffer 1996: Bubbly and fresh kabinett with an abundance of mineral and fruit character. Medium-bodied, off-dry and lively on the finish. A joy. Drink now. 550 cases made. • $15 • (11/30/97) • **88**

Riesling Kabinett Mosel-Saar-Ruwer Brauneberger Juffer 1994 • $NA • (11/30/95) • **84**

Riesling Kabinett Mosel-Saar-Ruwer Graacher Himmelreich 1996: Fresh and bubbly kabinett with lemon, apple and mineral aromas and flavors. Medium-bodied, off-dry, with a silky texture. Drink now or hold. 500 cases made. • $15 • (11/30/97) • **87**

Riesling Kabinett Mosel-Saar-Ruwer Graacher Himmelreich 1994 • $NA • (11/30/95) • **85**

Riesling Kabinett Mosel-Saar-Ruwer Wehlener Sonnenuhr 1996: Pretty kabinett. Extremely flinty, with a balance of lemon and fruit character. Medium-bodied, off-dry and fruity, with a long aftertaste. Drink now or hold. 270 cases made. • $15 • (11/30/97) • **88**

Riesling Kabinett Mosel-Saar-Ruwer Wehlener Sonnenuhr 1993 • $15 • (11/30/94) • **82**

Riesling QbA Mosel-Saar-Ruwer 1996: Clean and steely, with some apple and mineral character. Medium- to light-bodied and off-dry, with a light finish. A bit simple. Drink now. 1,500 cases made. • $11 • (11/30/97) • **83**

Riesling Spätlese Mosel-Saar-Ruwer Brauneberger Juffer-Sonnenuhr 1996: Plenty of pineapple, mineral aromas and flavors. Medium in body, off-dry, with crisp acidity and an appley aftertaste. Drink now. 390 cases made. • $18 • (11/30/97) • **86**

Riesling Spätlese Mosel-Saar-Ruwer Brauneberger Juffer-Sonnenuhr 1994 • $NA • (11/30/95) • **86**

Riesling Spätlese Mosel-Saar-Ruwer Brauneberger Juffer-Sonnenuhr 1993 • $19 • (11/30/94) • **87**

Riesling Spätlese Mosel-Saar-Ruwer Graacher Domprobst 1996: Good ripeness in this wine but slightly short on the finish. Medium body, medium-sweet with plenty of pineapple and citric character. Light aftertaste. Drink now. 170 cases made. • $19 • (11/30/97) • **84**

Riesling Spätlese Mosel-Saar-Ruwer Graacher Domprobst 1994 • $NA • (11/30/95) • **86**

Riesling Spätlese Mosel-Saar-Ruwer Wehlener Sonnenuhr 1996: Very good indeed. A ripe and fruity spätlese with loads of pineapple, citrus and mineral character. Medium-bodied, lightly sweet and fresh on the finish. Drink now. 160 cases made. • $18 • (11/30/97) • **89**

Riesling Spätlese Mosel-Saar-Ruwer Wehlener Sonnenuhr 1994 • $NA • (11/30/95) • **86**

Riesling Trockenbeerenauslese Mosel-Saar-Ruwer Brauneberger Juffer-Sonnenuhr 1996: Not the sweetest wine but big and ripe with with loads of spicy, super ripe pineapple character with touches of smoky, burnt almond aromas and flavors. Full-bodied, sweet with a long, oily, fruity finish. Drink now. 15 cases made. • $142/375ml • (11/30/97) • **90**

ROCHE, YVES

Sparkling Germany Prestige Carte Noire NV: Sweet and simple, like lemon-lime soda pop. Drink now. • $7 • (12/31/97) • **77**

SAARSTEIN, SCHLOSS

Riesling Auslese Gold Cap Saar-Ruwer Serriger Schloss Saarsteiner 1993 • $96 • (11/30/94) • **90**

Riesling Auslese Saar-Ruwer Serriger Schloss Saarsteiner 1993 • $29 • (11/30/94) • **90**

Riesling Beerenauslese Saar-Ruwer Serriger Schloss Saarsteiner 1993 • $NA • (11/30/94) • **94**

Riesling Eiswein Saar-Ruwer Serriger Schloss Saarsteiner 1993 • $114 • (11/30/94) • **90**

Riesling Kabinett Saar-Ruwer Serriger Schloss Saarsteiner 1993 • $12 • (11/30/94) • **85**

Riesling Spätlese Saar-Ruwer Serriger Schloss Saarsteiner 1993 • $18 • (11/30/94) • **82**

ST. ANTONY

Riesling Auslese Rheinhessen Niersteiner Hipping 1993 • $46 • (11/30/94) • **90**

Riesling Spätlese Rheinhessen Niersteiner Orbel 1993 • $33 • (11/30/94) • **86**

Riesling Spätlese Saar-Ruwer Niersteiner Orbel 1993 • $NA • (11/30/94) • **86**

Riesling Spätlese Trocken Rheinhessen Niersteiner Olberg 1993 • $28 • (11/30/94) • **91**

Riesling Spätlese Trocken Saar-Ruwer Niersteiner Olberg 1993 • $NA • (11/30/94) • **91**

SALM-DALBERG, PRINZ ZU

Riesling Auslese Nahe Wallhauser Johannisberg 1993 • $29 • (11/30/94) • **87**

Riesling Eiswein Nahe Schloss Wallhausen 1993 • $110 • (11/30/94) • **91**

Riesling Kabinett Nahe Schloss Wallhausen 1994 • $13 • (11/30/95) • **84**

Riesling Kabinett Nahe Schloss Wallhausen 1993 • $13 • (12/15/95) • **89**

Riesling Spätlese Halbtrocken Nahe Schloss Wallhausen 1993 • $18 • (11/30/94) • **85**

Riesling Spätlese Nahe Schloss Wallhausen 1993 • $18 • (11/30/94) • **82**

Riesling Spätlese Nahe Wallhausen Johannisberg 1994 • $15 • (12/15/95) • **85**

White QbA Nahe 1994 • $7 • (12/15/95) • **80**

SCHAEFER, WILLI

Riesling Auslese Gold Cap Mosel-Saar-Ruwer Graacher Domprobst 1993 • $47 • (11/30/94) • **92**

Riesling Auslese Mosel-Saar-Ruwer Graacher Domprobst 1996: Sensational. Reserved on the nose, it begins to unfold on the palate and just keeps coming at you in waves. The peach, apricot and honey flavors are perfectly balanced, and there's intensity and power in reserve. Beautiful expression of both Riesling fruit and its German vineyard site. Best from 2002 through 2015. 55 cases made. • $55/375ml • (04/30/98) HR • **95**

Riesling Auslese Mosel-Saar-Ruwer Graacher Domprobst 1993 • $NA • (11/30/94) • **91**

Riesling Beerenauslese Mosel-Saar-Ruwer Graacher Domprobst 1993 • $43 • (11/30/94) • **94**

Key: SS—Spectator Selection CS—Cellar Selection HR—Highly Recommended BB—Best Buy $NA—Price not available Ⓐ—Auction Price (BT)—Barrel Tasting

Dates in parentheses indicate the issues in which the ratings were published.

Riesling Kabinett Mosel-Saar-Ruwer Graacher Domprobst 1993 • $13 • (11/30/94) • **82**

Riesling Spätlese Mosel-Saar-Ruwer Graacher Domprobst 1993 • $14 • (11/30/94) • **87**

Riesling Spätlese Mosel-Saar-Ruwer Graacher Himmelreich 1996: What a gorgeous Riesling. This German white has intensity, extract and length, with floral, lime and peach aromas and flavors that hang together beautifully on the sleek acid-and-mineral framework. Drink now through 2005. 112 cases made. • $17 • (04/30/98) HR • **91**

SCHMITGES

Riesling Auslese Mosel-Saar-Ruwer Erdener Treppchen 1996: Fruity and sweet, even sugary. Perfectly drinkable, but very simple. 250 cases made. • $24/375ml • (09/15/97) • **80**

Riesling Kabinett Mosel-Saar-Ruwer Erdener Treppchen 1996: Sweet, soft, fruity and clean, this is a good, basic Riesling. 300 cases made. • $12 • (09/15/97) • **80**

Riesling Qualitätswein Mosel-Saar-Ruwer 1996: This is enjoyably spicy and rich in flavor, and full-bodied for a Riesling. It's semi-sweet, with honey, almond and pear accents that linger on the finish. 200 cases made. • $10 • (09/15/97) • **86**

Riesling Spätlese Mosel-Saar-Ruwer Erdener Treppchen 1996: Sweet and simple, with peach flavors and soft texture. 200 cases made. • $18/375ml • (09/15/97) • **80**

Riesling Spätlese Trocken Mosel-Saar-Ruwer Erdener Treppchen 1996: A dry style, with grapefruit and apple flavors and firm acidity. Nice and crisp, but lean. 200 cases made. • $18 • (09/15/97) • **82**

SCHMITT SCHENK

Riesling Auslese Mosel-Saar-Ruwer Longuicher Maximiner Herrenberg 1994 • $14 • (11/30/95) • **83**

Riesling Kabinett Mosel-Saar-Ruwer Bernkasteler Badstube 1994 • $9 • (11/30/95) • **82**

Riesling Kabinett Mosel-Saar-Ruwer Graacher Himmelreich Spätlese 1994 • $12 • (11/30/95) • **82**

Riesling Kabinett Mosel-Saar-Ruwer Trittenheimer Altärchen 1994 • $9 • (11/30/95) • **81**

Riesling Kabinett Mosel-Saar-Ruwer Urziger Würzgarten 1994: Nicely smooth and ripe. Has balanced, well-defined apple and apricot flavors; would serve well as an apéritif. Finishes with a touch of honey. 250 cases made. • $9 • (08/31/96) • **85**

Riesling Spätlese Mosel-Saar-Ruwer Bernkasteler Badstube 1994 • $12 • (11/30/95) • **83**

Riesling Spätlese Mosel-Saar-Ruwer Erdener Treppchen 1994 • $12 • (11/30/95) • **87**

Riesling Spätlese Mosel-Saar-Ruwer Urziger Würzgarten 1994 • $11 • (11/30/95) • **83**

SCHMITT SÖHNE

Liebfraumilch Pfalz 1994 • $4 • (11/30/95) • **79**

Riesling Auslese Mosel-Saar-Ruwer 1993 • $9 • (08/31/94) • **79**

Riesling Kabinett Mosel-Saar-Ruwer 1994 • $6 • (11/30/95) • **73**

Riesling Kabinett Mosel-Saar-Ruwer Piesporter Goldtröpfchen 1993 • $7 • (08/31/94) • **81**

Riesling Kabinett Mosel-Saar-Ruwer Wehlener Sonnenuhr 1994 • $6 • (11/30/95) • **74**

Riesling Spätlese Mosel-Saar-Ruwer 1994 • $7 • (11/30/95) • **81**

Riesling Spätlese Mosel-Saar-Ruwer Piesporter Goldtröpfchen 1994 • $12 • (11/30/95) • **78**

Riesling Spätlese Mosel-Saar-Ruwer Piesporter Goldtröpfchen 1993 • $9 • (08/31/94) • **84**

White Mosel-Saar-Ruwer Bernkasteler Kurfürstlay 1993 • $9 • (08/31/94) • **81**

White Mosel-Saar-Ruwer Piesporter Michelsberg 1993 • $5 • (08/31/94) • **80**

White Mosel-Saar-Ruwer Zeller Schwarze Katz 1994 • $5 • (11/30/95) • **75**

White Mosel-Saar-Ruwer Zeller Schwarze Katz 1993 • $5 • (08/31/94) BB • **82**

White QbA Mosel-Saar-Ruwer Piesporter Michelsberg 1994 • $5 • (11/30/95) • **76**

White Niersteiner QbA Rheinhessen Gutes Domtal 1994 • $5 • (11/30/95) • **82**

White Spätlese Mosel-Saar-Ruwer Piesporter Michelsberg 1994 • $8 • (11/30/95) • **83**

SCHONBORN, SCHLOSS

Riesling Auslese Rheingau Erbacher Marcobrunn 1993 • $38 • (11/30/94) • **75**

Riesling Auslese Rheingau Rüdesheimer Berg Schlossberg 1993 • $25 • (11/30/94) • **77**

Riesling Beerenauslese Rheingau Rüdesheimer Berg Schlossberg 1996: Dark yellow-orange in color, with intense raisin, butterscotch and caramel aromas. Full-bodied, supersweet and as thick as syrup, it finishes with a jolt of grapefruit and dried apricot. Not currently available in the U.S. Drink now through 2010. • $NA/500ml • (07/31/98) • **94**

Riesling Kabinett Rheingau Hattenheimer Pfaffenberg 1996: Wonderfully fresh white. Aromas of mango and apple, with hints of pie crust that follow through on the palate. Medium-bodied and lightly sweet, with fresh acidity and a lively finish. Not currently available in the U.S. Drink now through 2005. • $NA • (07/31/98) • **89**

Riesling QbA Rheingau Erbacher Marcobrunn 1996: Beautiful aromas of pie crust and apple, with hints of peach. Medium-bodied and dry, with a short finish. Promises more on the nose than on the palate. Not currently available in the U.S. Drink now. • $NA • (07/31/98) • **85**

Riesling Spätlese Rheingau Erbacher Marcobrunn 1996: Light aromas of dried apricot and maple syrup. Medium-bodied and off-dry, with good fruit flavors and a medium finish. Not currently available in the U.S. Drink now. • $NA • (07/31/98) • **86**

Riesling Spätlese Rheingau Geisenheimer Rothenberg-Lothar Franz 1996: Superintense aromas of sliced peach and nectarine. Medium-bodied and lightly sweet, with ripe fruit flavors and a long finish. A beauty. Not currently available in the U.S. Drink now. • $NA • (07/31/98) • **90**

Riesling Spätlese Rheingau Hattenheimer Pfaffenberg 1996: A lovely, rich, peachy wine, with undertones of dough and crust. Medium-bodied and lightly sweet, with a soft texture and a long, flavorful aftertaste. Not currently available in the U.S. Drink now through 2000. • $NA • (07/31/98) • **88**

Riesling Spätlese Rheingau Hattenheimer Pfaffenberg 1993 • $NA • (11/30/94) • **85**

Riesling Spätlese Rheingau Rüdesheimer Bischofsberg 1993 • $21 • (11/30/94) • **78**

Riesling Trockenbeerenauslese Rheingau 1993 • $NA • (11/30/94) • **89**

SCHUBERT, C. VON

Riesling Auslese Gold Cap Mosel-Saar-Ruwer Maximin Grünhäuser Abtsberg Cask No. 83 1993 • $59 • (11/30/94) • **88**

Riesling Auslese Gold Cap Mosel-Saar-Ruwer Maximin Grünhäuser Herrenberg Cask No. 75 1993 • $52 • (11/30/94) • **88**

Riesling Auslese Mosel-Saar-Ruwer Maximin Grünhäuser Abstberg 1995: A racy wine, full of pear, mineral and marzipan flavors. Of moderate intensity and concentration, finishing on a positive, refreshing note. 200 cases made. • $35 • (11/30/96) • **87**

Riesling Auslese Mosel-Saar-Ruwer Maximin Grünhäuser Abstberg Cask No. 117 1995: Young and chewy with lovely, rich honey, floral and citrus aromas and flavors. Medium-bodied, with fine acidity and a sweet and fruity finish. Drink now. 90 cases made. • $63 • (11/30/96) • **89**

Riesling Auslese Mosel-Saar-Ruwer Maximin Grünhäuser Abtsberg 1994 • $45 • (11/30/95) • **85**

Riesling Auslese Mosel-Saar-Ruwer Maximin Grünhäuser Abtsberg Cask No. 55 1996: Pretty and fruity, with pear, apple and honey character. Medium-bodied, medium-sweet, with a delicate finish. Drink now. 100 cases made. • $28/375ml • (11/30/97) • **88**

Riesling Auslese Mosel-Saar-Ruwer Maximin Grünhäuser Abtsberg Cask No. 47 1994 • $67 • (11/30/95) • **84**

Riesling Auslese Mosel-Saar-Ruwer Maximin Grünhäuser Herrenberg 1995: Very young and backward but there's beautiful melon, honey and flint character to this wine. Of medium body and sweetness, with fine acidity and a lingering finish. Drink now. 200 cases made. • $30 • (11/30/96) • **89**

Riesling Auslese Mosel-Saar-Ruwer Maximin Grünhäuser Herrenberg 1994 • $NA • (11/30/95) • **80**

Riesling Auslese Mosel-Saar-Ruwer Maximin Grünhäuser Herrenberg Cask No. 91 1995: Very fresh, like a barrel sample. Medium in body and moderately sweet in character with plenty of crushed grape aromas and flavors. Drink now. 100 cases made. • $52 • (11/30/96) • **87**

Riesling Auslese Mosel-Saar-Ruwer Maximin Grünhäuser Herrenberg Cask No. 45 1994 • $58 • (11/30/95) • **87**

Riesling Eiswein Mosel-Saar-Ruwer Maximin Grünhäuser Abtsberg 1993 • $360 • (11/30/94) • **90**

Riesling Eiswein Mosel-Saar-Ruwer Maximin Grünhäuser Herrenberg 1996: Vivid wine with wonderful ripeness and sweetness yet an excellent intensity of mineral, spice character. Medium-bodied, very sweet with a long, crushed grape flavor. Best after 1999. 20 cases made. • $85/375ml • (11/30/97) • **90**

Riesling Eiswein Mosel-Saar-Ruwer Maximin Grünhäuser Herrenberg 1995: This seems more developed than most. The fruit flavors range from green apple to peach, with an attractive mineral note, and there's zingy acidity for support. Drinkable now, may improve with time. 50 cases made. • $144 • (11/30/96) • **90**

Riesling Eiswein Mosel-Saar-Ruwer Maximin Grünhäuser Herrenberg 1993 • $124 • (11/30/94) • **87**

Riesling Kabinett Mosel-Saar-Ruwer Maximin Grünhäuser Abstberg 1996: Slightly one-dimensional, but shows pretty melon, perfumed aromas. Medium-bodied, medium-sweet, with a fresh, fruity finish. Drink now. 650 cases made. • $19 • (11/30/97) • **86**

Riesling Kabinett Mosel-Saar-Ruwer Maximin Grünhäuser Abstberg 1995: Zingy acidity defines the apple and peach flavors, and there's a mineral component that adds dimension. A tightly wound, racy wine. Drinkable now. 1,000 cases made. • $21 • (11/30/96) • **87**

Riesling Kabinett Mosel-Saar-Ruwer Maximin Grünhäuser Abtsberg 1994 • $21 • (11/30/95) • **85**

Riesling Kabinett Mosel-Saar-Ruwer Maximin Grünhäuser Abtsberg 1993 • $22 • (11/30/94) • **87**

Riesling Kabinett Mosel-Saar-Ruwer Maximin Grünhäuser Bruderberg 1994 • $21 • (11/30/95) • **83**

Riesling Kabinett Mosel-Saar-Ruwer Maximin Grünhäuser Herrenberg 1996: Wonderfully fresh, with crushed grape, melon and lemon aromas and similar flavors last for a minute or two on the palate. Medium-bodied, off-dry, and crisp on the finish. Drinkable now. 500 cases made. • $18 • (11/30/97) • **90**

Riesling Kabinett Mosel-Saar-Ruwer Maximin Grünhäuser Herrenberg 1995: Lime, mineral and a note of pine accent the almond character in this rich, round wine. Seems a little dull and out of sorts. Tasted twice, with consistent notes. 850 cases made. • $19 • (11/30/96) • **78**

Riesling Kabinett Mosel-Saar-Ruwer Maximin Grünhäuser Herrenberg 1994 • $21 • (11/30/95) • **85**

Riesling Kabinett Mosel-Saar-Ruwer Maximin Grünhäuser Herrenberg 1993 • $20 • (11/30/94) • **83**

Riesling Kabinett Trocken Mosel-Saar-Ruwer Maximin Grünhäuser Abtsberg 1994 • $22 • (11/30/95) • **83**

Riesling QbA Mosel-Saar-Ruwer Maximin Grünhäuser 1994 • $16 • (11/30/95) • **82**

Riesling QbA Mosel-Saar-Ruwer Maximin Grünhäuser 1993 • $16 • (11/30/94) • **84**

Riesling QbA Mosel-Saar-Ruwer Maximin Grünhäuser Abstberg 1995: A finely balanced, elegantly wrought Riesling, showing lime, apple and slate aromas and flavors. Like a gymnast on the balance beam. 850 cases made. • $14 • (11/30/96) • **87**

Riesling QbA Mosel-Saar-Ruwer Maximin Grünhäuser Abtsberg 1994 • $16 • (11/30/95) • **87**

Riesling QbA Mosel-Saar-Ruwer Maximin Grünhäuser Bruderberg 1996: Elegant and balanced, with lemon, apple aromas and flavors and a hint of mineral. Medium to light in body, off-dry and fruity. Drink now. 200 cases made. • $12 • (11/30/97) • **86**

Riesling QbA Mosel-Saar-Ruwer Maximin Grünhäuser Herrenberg 1996: A slightly simple, off-dry white with lemon, floral aromas and flavors and a delicate finish. Drink now. 600 cases made. • $13 • (11/30/97) • **84**

Riesling QbA Trocken Mosel-Saar-Ruwer Maximin Grünhäuser Herrenberg 1994 • $17 • (11/30/95) • **80**

Riesling Spätlese Mosel-Saar-Ruwer Maximin Grünhäuser Abtsberg 1996: Displays extremely intense mineral and flinty character with pear undertones. Medium-bodied, medium-sweet and very crisp. Try now. 600 cases made. • $24 • (11/30/97) • **89**

Riesling Spätlese Mosel-Saar-Ruwer Maximin Grünhäuser Abstberg 1995: A sleek spätlese, with its mineral and flint character, medium body and light sweetness. 700 cases made. • $24 • (11/30/96) • **85**

Riesling Spätlese Mosel-Saar-Ruwer Maximin Grünhäuser Abtsberg 1994 • $27 • (11/30/95) • **89**

Riesling Spätlese Mosel-Saar-Ruwer Maximin Grünhäuser Abtsberg 1993 • $26 • (11/30/94) • **86**

Riesling Spätlese Mosel-Saar-Ruwer Maximin Grünhäuser Herrenberg 1995: High in acidity, the fruitiness is submerged at this point. Laserlike focus beams the mineral and lime flavors across the palate. Try now. 540 cases made. • $24 • (11/30/96) • **85**

Riesling Spätlese Mosel-Saar-Ruwer Maximin Grünhäuser Herrenberg 1994 • $25 • (11/30/95) • **82**

Riesling Trockenbeerenauslese Mosel-Saar-Ruwer Maximin Grünhäuser Abstberg 1995: Ripe and fat, this exhibits loads of botrytis character. It's full of honey and apricot flavors, balanced on the sweet side, and the acidity is refreshing on the finish. 20 cases made. • $390 • (11/30/96) • **89**

Riesling Trockenbeerenauslese Mosel-Saar-Ruwer Maximin Grünhäuser Abtsberg 1994 • $220 • (11/30/95) • **88**

SCHULZ, GERHARD

Riesling Spätlese Mosel-Saar-Ruwer Schweicher Annaberg 1996: Like a fruit juice that's been too long exposed to air. • $10 • (04/30/98) • **72**

SCHUMANN-NAGLER

Riesling QbA Rheingau Christopher Philipp 1995: On the austere side and already showing some mature marzipan and honey character. Softly textured, it lacks zing and persistence of flavor. Drink now. • $11 • (01/01/98) • **82**

Riesling Spätlese Rheingau Geisenheimer Kläuserweg 1995: There's ripeness to this, and also a firm underpinning of acidity. Nice peachy fruit with some mineral and spice typical of the Rheingau. The finish lingers. Drink now through 2002. • $16 • (01/01/98) • **84**

SEEBRICH, HEINRICH

Riesling Eiswein Rheinhessen Niersteiner Rosenberg 1996: An intense apricot character denotes this dessert wine, its sweetness countered by a zingy acidity. A honey note lingers on the finish. Only lacks a bit in concentration. • $38/375ml • (04/30/98) • **89**

SELBACH-OSTER

Riesling Auslese Mosel-Saar-Ruwer Lieser Niederberg-Helden Two Stars 1993 • $30 • (11/30/94) • **89**

Riesling Auslese Mosel-Saar-Ruwer Wehlener Sonnenuhr 1994 • $34 • (11/30/95) • **90**

Riesling Auslese Mosel-Saar-Ruwer Zeltinger Schlossberg 1994 • $37 • (11/30/95) • **87**

Riesling Auslese Mosel-Saar-Ruwer Zeltinger Sonnenuhr 1995: A very good auslese, offering aromas and flavors of honey, apricot and spice. Medium-bodied, sweet. Finishes with notes of crushed grape and spice. Fresh acidity gives solid structure. Drink now or hold. 110 cases made. • $32/375ml • (11/30/96) • **88**

Riesling Auslese Mosel-Saar-Ruwer Zeltinger Sonnenuhr 1993 • $25 • (11/30/94) • **88**

Riesling Auslese Mosel-Saar-Ruwer Zeltinger Sonnenuhr One Star 1996: A wine with lots of ripe Riesling character. Medium-bodied, medium-sweet with spicy, lemon and pear after taste. Drink now. • $36/375ml • (11/30/97) • **86**

Riesling Auslese Mosel-Saar-Ruwer Zeltinger Sonnenuhr One Star 1994 • $39 • (11/30/95) • **88**

Riesling Auslese Mosel-Saar-Ruwer Zeltinger Sonnenuhr Three Stars 1995: Honey is the dominant theme in this moderately sweet, medium-bodied white that offers direct appeal. Ready to drink. 50 cases made. • $57/375ml • (11/30/96) • **85**

Riesling Auslese Mosel-Saar-Ruwer Zeltinger Sonnenuhr Three Stars 1993 • $29 • (11/30/94) • **90**

Riesling Beerenauslese Mosel-Saar-Ruwer Zeltinger Sonnenuhr 1995: An elegant sticky, offering lemon, lime and flint aromas and flavors. Delivers good acidity and a clean, fresh finish. Not the richest or most intense sweetie, but delicious. Tasted twice with consistent notes. 30 cases made. • $91/375ml • (11/30/96) • **88**

Riesling Beerenauslese Mosel-Saar-Ruwer Zeltinger Sonnenuhr 1994 • $83 • (11/30/95) • **93**

Riesling Beerenauslese Mosel-Saar-Ruwer Zeltinger Sonnenuhr 1993 • $73 • (11/30/94) • **89**

Riesling Eiswein Mosel-Saar-Ruwer Bernkasteler Badstube 1996: A lively, tart, sweet wine with burnt almond, honey and marmalade character with an undertone of ripe tropical fruit. Medium- to full-bodied, very sweet with fresh finish. Drink now. • $NA • (11/30/97) • **90**

Riesling Kabinett Mosel-Saar-Ruwer Bernkasteler Badstube 1994 • $14 • (11/30/95) • **78**

Riesling Kabinett Mosel-Saar-Ruwer Graacher Domprobst 1996: Steely and crisp kabinett with a mineral and pear character. Medium- to light-bodied and off-dry, with a short finish. Drink now. • $13 • (11/30/97) • **84**

Riesling Kabinett Mosel-Saar-Ruwer Wehlener Sonnenuhr 1995: Young and undeveloped, showing a racy structure. Difficult to taste because of the carbon dioxide, but shows very good quality for kabinett. Try now. Tasted twice, with consistent notes. 220 cases made. • $16 • (11/30/96) • **85**

Riesling Kabinett Mosel-Saar-Ruwer Wehlener Sonnenuhr 1993 • $12 • (11/30/94) • **85**

Riesling Spätlese Mosel-Saar-Ruwer Wehlener Sonnenuhr 1996: A very good spätlese with lots of mineral, flint and fruit character. Medium-bodied and lightly sweet, with a silky texture and a long aftertaste. Drink now or hold. • $20 • (11/30/97) • **89**

Riesling Spätlese Mosel-Saar-Ruwer Wehlener Sonnenuhr 1995: Lovely slate and lime aromas complement the peachy flavors. Shows delicacy and ripe acidity, culminating in a subtle, lingering finish. Delicious now. 220 cases made. • $20 • (11/30/96) • **88**

Riesling Spätlese Mosel-Saar-Ruwer Wehlener Sonnenuhr 1994 • $18 • (11/30/95) • **78**

Riesling Spätlese Mosel-Saar-Ruwer Zeltinger Schlossberg 1994 • $NA • (11/30/95) • **83**

Riesling Spätlese Mosel-Saar-Ruwer Zeltinger Sonnenuhr 1995: A very mineral-flavored style of Riesling. Fresh, harmonious and lively, displaying notes of peach and apple. The finish is long and lingering. 220 cases made. • $20 • (11/30/96) • **89**

Riesling Spätlese Mosel-Saar-Ruwer Zeltinger Sonnenuhr 1993 • $16 • (11/30/94) • **88**

Riesling Trockenbeerenauslese Mosel-Saar-Ruwer Zeltinger Sonnenuhr 1996: Pretty and harmonious sweet wine with ripe fruit, honey and light flinty character. Medium-bodied, sweet with a long fruity finish. A delicate sweetie. Drink now. • $NA • (11/30/97) • **90**

Riesling Trockenbeerenauslese Mosel-Saar-Ruwer Zeltinger Sonnenuhr 1993 • $168 • (11/30/94) • **92**

SICHEL

Pinot Gris Pfalz 1993 • $8 • (12/15/95) • **82**
Pinot Noir Rotwein Pfalz Dornfelder 1992 • $6 • (03/31/95) • **77**
Riesling Pfalz 1993 • $8 • (12/15/95) • **80**
Riesling Rheingau Bereich Johannisberg 1993 • $8 • (12/15/95) • **82**
Riesling Spätlese Mosel-Saar-Ruwer Piesporter Goldtröpfchen 1994 • $14 • (12/15/95) • **82**
Trockenbeerenauslese Pfalz Kirschheimer Kreuz 1990 • $30/375ml • (12/15/95) • **84**
White Bereich Bernkastel Mosel-Saar-Ruwer 1993 • $8 • (12/15/95) • **78**
White Mosel-Saar-Ruwer Zeller Schwarze Katz 1993 • $8 • (12/15/95) • **81**
White Piesporter Michelsberg Mosel-Saar-Ruwer 1993 • $8 • (12/15/95) • **76**

SIMMERN, LANGWERTH VON

Riesling Auslese Rheingau Hattenheimer Nussbrunnen 1996: A big and delicious auslese, verging on beerenauslese in style. Full-bodied and sweet, with a delicious ripe fruit and spicy character. Long, long finish. Drink or hold. • $45 • (11/30/97) • **91**

Riesling Auslese Rheingau Hattenheimer Nussbrunnen 1993 • $NA • (11/30/94) • **87**

Riesling Kabinett Rheingau 1996: Lovely balanced Riesling with plenty of lemon, mineral and flinty character and fresh, clean acidity. Medium-bodied, lightly sweet with a fruity aftertaste. Drink now. • $11 • (11/30/97) • **86**

Riesling Kabinett Rheingau 1995: Bright and steely with a floral and light honey character. Light-bodied, semi-sweet and with fresh acidity, it's refreshing and lively to drink. • $13 • (11/30/96) • **86**

Riesling Kabinett Rheingau Eltviller Sonnenberg 1995: A clean, good quality Riesling with some lemon and mineral flavors and aromas. Medium-bodied, and just off-dry. Short finish. • $15 • (11/30/96) • **82**

Riesling Kabinett Rheingau Erbacher Marcobrunn 1996: Ripe and spicy kabinett with a hint of honey on the nose and palate. Medium-bodied, lightly sweet and fresh on the finish. Delicious now. • $14 • (11/30/97) • **88**

Riesling Kabinett Rheingau Erbacher Marcobrunn 1995: A zingy kabinett with sliced apple, melon and a hint of honey on the nose and palate.

Key: SS—Spectator Selection CS—Cellar Selection HR—Highly Recommended BB—Best Buy $NA—Price not available Ⓐ—Auction Price (BT)—Barrel Tasting
Dates in parentheses indicate the issues in which the ratings were published.

Medium-bodied, lightly sweet. Finish is long, fruity. Drink now. • $20 • (11/30/96) • **88**

Riesling Kabinett Rheingau Hattenheimer Mannberg 1996: Shows loads of lemon, floral and mineral aromas and flavors. Medium-bodied and lightly sweet, with a silky mouthfeel. Drink now. • $12 • (11/30/97) • **87**

Riesling Kabinett Rheingau Kiedricher Sandgrub 1993 • $NA • (11/30/94) • **82**

Riesling Kabinett Rheingau Rauenthaler Baiken 1996: A delicate, creamy-textured Riesling with pretty mineral and apple aromas and flavors. Medium- to light-bodied, lightly sweet and fresh. Drink now. • $13 • (11/30/97) • **87**

Riesling Kabinett Rheingau Rauenthaler Baiken 1993 • $NA • (11/30/94) • **70**

Riesling QbA Rheingau 1996: Attractive ripe pineapple with hints of spice and pie crust character. Medium-bodied, medium-sweet with a long flavorful finish. Drink now. • $10 • (11/30/97) • **86**

Riesling QbA Rheingau 1995: Bright and ripe fruit character—tropical fruit, honey and melon aromas and flavors. Medium-bodied and off-dry, with fresh yet light acidity and a silky finish. Exceptionally good for this category. • $10 • (11/30/96) • **87**

Riesling Spätlese Rheingau Erbacher Marcobrunn 1996: A lovely, flavor-intensive Riesling with lemon, spice and floral character. Medium-bodied and very sweet for a spätlese. Crisp finish. Drink now. • $25 • (11/30/97) • **87**

Riesling Spätlese Rheingau Erbacher Marcobrunn 1993 • $NA • (11/30/94) • **80**

Riesling Spätlese Rheingau Hattenheimer Mannberg 1995: Ripe and richly textured, but the finish leans toward marzipan flavors. A little dull and tired. • $NA • (11/30/96) RT • **77**

Riesling Spätlese Rheingau Hattenheimer Nussbrunnen 1993 • $NA • (11/30/94) • **81**

Riesling Spätlese Rheingau Rauenthaler Baiken 1996: An extremely fruity Riesling with mango and spice aromas and flavors. Medium-bodied, lightly sweet with a flavorful finish. Drink now. • $23 • (11/30/97) • **89**

Riesling Spätlese Rheingau Erbacher Marcobrunn 1995: Very dry, with firm acidity and a spicy mineral character. There's apple and almond flavors too, but they're light. • $30 • (11/30/96) • **83**

Riesling Trockenbeerenauslese Rheingau Hattenheimer Nussbrunnen 1993 • $NA • (11/30/94) • **90**

STICH DEN BUBEN

Kabinett Trocken Baden 1994: Firm, dry and austere, this offers light mineral and citrus flavors, with good body and a clean finish. Try with food. • $NA • (10/15/96) • **81**

THANISCH, DR. H.

Riesling Auslese Gold Cap Mosel-Saar-Ruwer Bernkasteler Doctor AP No. 6 1996: Very ripe in style, with an almost raisiny, dried fruit character to it. Medium to full in body and medium-sweet, with a long pineapple-flavored finish. Drink now. • $110/375ml • (11/30/97) • **88**

Riesling Auslese Gold Cap Mosel-Saar-Ruwer Bernkasteler Doctor 1993 • $211 • (11/30/94) • **85**

Riesling Auslese Long Gold Cap Mosel-Saar-Ruwer Bernkasteler Doctor AP No. 5 1996: Very sweet and intense for an auslese, with excellent concentration and fine acidity. Medium- to full-bodied, with a long lemon, mineral and spice finish. Drink now. • $163/375ml • (11/30/97) • **92**

Riesling Kabinett Mosel-Saar-Ruwer Bernkasteler Badstube 1996: Good for this appellation. Plenty of lemon, apple and flinty character. Medium-bodied, off-dry and very crisp. Drinkable now. 245 cases made. • $14 • (11/30/97) • **86**

Riesling Kabinett Mosel-Saar-Ruwer Bernkasteler Badstube 1993 • $NA • (11/30/94) • **85**

Riesling Spätlese Mosel-Saar-Ruwer Bernkasteler Badstube 1996: A lively wine with an abundance of mineral and fruit character for the vintage. Medium-bodied, medium-sweet and high in acidity. Try now. • $21 • (11/30/97) • **86**

Riesling Spätlese Mosel-Saar-Ruwer Bernkasteler Doctor 1996: Seriously good Doctor. Racy and sleek, with lemon, mineral and earthy character. Medium-bodied, medium-sweet, high in acidity. Long, powerful finish. Best after 1999. 230 cases made. • $51 • (11/30/97) • **89**

Riesling Spätlese Mosel-Saar-Ruwer Bernkasteler Doctor 1993 • $39 • (11/30/94) • **86**

THANISCH (MÜLLER-BURGGRAEF), DR. H.

Riesling Auslese Mosel-Saar-Ruwer Bernkasteler Doctor 1996: There is plenty of flavor in this wine, with its mineral, lemon, lime and spice character. Medium-bodied, medium-sweet, with a long, spicy finish. Drink or hold. • $NA • (11/30/97) • **88**

Riesling Auslese Mosel-Saar-Ruwer Bernkasteler Doctor 1994 • $NA • (11/30/95) • **84**

Riesling Auslese Mosel-Saar-Ruwer Bernkasteler Lay 1996: Promises more on the nose than it delivers on the palate, with honey, spice, almond and fruit notes. Medium-bodied, medium-sweet with spicy flavors, a short aftertaste. Drink now. 120 cases made. • $24 • (11/30/97) • **85**

Riesling Auslese Mosel-Saar-Ruwer Bernkasteler Lay 1995: Good crushed grape, melon and pear aromas and flavors mark the sweet, medium-bodied palate. Crisp finish. Drink now. 110 cases made. • $24 • (11/30/96) • **85**

Riesling Auslese Mosel-Saar-Ruwer Brauneberger Juffer-Sonnenuhr 1994 • $NA • (11/30/95) • **84**

Riesling Auslese Mosel-Saar-Ruwer Graacher Himmelreich 1996: Rather soft and fruity for the vintage with mineral and apple character. Medium in body, medium-sweet with a light aftertaste. Drink now. 60 cases made. • $24 • (11/30/97) • **85**

Riesling Auslese Mosel-Saar-Ruwer Graacher Himmelreich 1994 • $NA • (11/30/95) • **85**

Riesling Beerenauslese Mosel-Saar-Ruwer Bernkasteler Doctor 1995: Plenty of botrytis and spice character in this very sweet wine. Medium in body, with fresh acidity and a long, fruity finish. Not as concentrated as some wines in this category, but pretty. Drink now. 5 cases made. • $270/375ml • (11/30/96) • **88**

Riesling Beerenauslese Mosel-Saar-Ruwer Bernkasteler Doctor 1994 • $NA • (11/30/95) • **82**

Riesling Kabinett Mosel-Saar-Ruwer Bernkasteler Doctor 1996: Crisp and racy wine with flinty, steely aromas and flavors and hints of tropical fruit. Medium- to light-bodied, fresh acidity and a fruity finish. Drink now. 225 cases made. • $25 • (11/30/97) • **86**

Riesling Kabinett Mosel-Saar-Ruwer Bernkasteler Badstube 1995: Fine Mosel, with refined flavors and aromas of flint, fruit and spice. Medium-bodied, with fresh acidity. Drink now or hold. 250 cases made. • $14 • (11/30/96) • **85**

Riesling Kabinett Mosel-Saar-Ruwer Bernkasteler Badstube 1994 • $NA • (11/30/95) • **82**

Riesling Kabinett Mosel-Saar-Ruwer Bernkasteler Doctor 1995: A medium-bodied, medium-sweet kabinett with layers of ripe fruit flavor and mineral and spice notes on the fresh finish. One of this producer's better Doctors in a number of years. Drink now or hold. 110 cases made. • $25 • (11/30/96) • **89**

Riesling Kabinett Mosel-Saar-Ruwer Bernkasteler Doctor 1994 • $NA • (11/30/95) • **82**

Riesling Kabinett Mosel-Saar-Ruwer Lieserer Niederberg-Helden 1996: Displays good lemon, green apple character. Medium-bodied, off-dry and fresh with a light mineral aftertaste. Drink now. • $NA • (11/30/97) • **85**

Riesling Kabinett Mosel-Saar-Ruwer Wehlener Sonnenhur 1995: Clean and simple. Lemon, lime and a hint of mineral mark the character. Light-bodied and slightly sweet, with fresh acidity. Drink now. 110 cases made. • $13 • (11/30/96) • **85**

Riesling Kabinett Mosel-Saar-Ruwer Wehlener Sonnenuhr 1994 • $NA • (11/30/95) • **85**

Riesling Spätlese Mosel-Saar-Ruwer Bernkasteler Doctor 1996: Fresh and clean like a spring bouquet. Full of pretty floral, flint and pear aromas and flavors, it's medium-bodied and lightly sweet, with a crisp and delicate finish. Delicious now. 230 cases made. • $37 • (11/30/97) • **87**

Riesling Spätlese Mosel-Saar-Ruwer Bernkasteler Doctor 1995: A sleek and exciting spätlese with a flinty, spicy and fruity character. Medium-bodied, moderately sweet, with a long aftertaste. Textbook Doctor spät. Drink now or hold. 220 cases made. • $37 • (11/30/96) • **89**

Riesling Spätlese Mosel-Saar-Ruwer Bernkasteler Graben 1996: Exhibits good intensity of lemon, floral and mineral character. Medium-bodied, lightly sweet, with a long, fruity finish. Drink now. 115 cases made. • $21 • (11/30/97) • **86**

Riesling Spätlese Mosel-Saar-Ruwer Bernkasteler Graben 1994 • $NA • (11/30/95) • **82**

Riesling Spätlese Mosel-Saar-Ruwer Graacher Himmelreich 1995: A rather simple spätlese, with floral and apple aromas and flavors. Medium-bodied and moderately sweet, with a fruity finish. Drink now. 110 cases made. • $17 • (11/30/96) • **83**

Riesling Spätlese Mosel-Saar-Ruwer Wehlener Sonnenuhr 1994 • $NA • (11/30/95) • **82**

TYRELL

Riesling Auslese Gold Cap Mosel-Saar-Ruwar Eitelsbacher Karthäuserhofberg Cask No. 41 1994 • $NA • (11/30/95) • **90**
Riesling Auslese Gold Cap Mosel-Saar-Ruwer Eitelsbacher Karthäuserhofberg 1993 • $80 • (11/30/94) • **85**
Riesling Auslese Gold Cap Mosel-Saar-Ruwer Eitelsbacher Karthäuserhofberg Cask No. 19 1994 • $52 • (11/30/95) • **86**
Riesling Auslese Gold Cap Mosel-Saar-Ruwer Eitelsbacher Karthäuserhofberg Cask No. 43 1993 • $NA • (11/30/94) • **88**
Riesling Auslese Mosel-Saar-Ruwer Eitelsbacher Karthäuserhofberg 1994 • $35 • (11/30/95) • **85**
Riesling Auslese Mosel-Saar-Ruwer Eitelsbacher Karthäuserhofberg 1993 • $33 • (11/30/94) • **88**
Riesling Auslese Mosel-Saar-Ruwer Eitelsbacher Kathäuserhofberg Cask No. 30 1993 • $80 • (11/30/94) • **85**
Riesling Eiswein Mosel-Saar-Ruwer Eitelsbacher Karthäuserhofberg Cask No. 34 1993 • $NA • (11/30/94) • **83**
Riesling Kabinett Mosel-Saar-Ruwer Eitelsbacher Karthäuserhofberg 1994 • $17 • (11/30/95) • **85**
Riesling Kabinett Mosel-Saar-Ruwer Eitelsbacher Karthäuserhofberg 1993 • $15 • (11/30/94) • **88**
Riesling QbA Mosel-Saar-Ruwer Eitelsbacher Karthäuserhofberg 1994 • $14 • (11/30/95) • **83**
Riesling Spätlese Mosel-Saar-Ruwer Eitelsbacher Karthäuserhofberg 1994 • $23 • (11/30/95) • **84**
Riesling Spätlese Mosel-Saar-Ruwer Eitelsbacher Karthäuserhofberg 1993 • $20 • (11/30/94) • **86**

UNCKRICH

Riesling Spätlese Pfalz Kallstadter Saumagen 1995: A fruit bomb that's fresh, vivacious and flows across the palate like silk. Passion fruit and apricot flavors are accented by citrus, and the finish is mouthwatering. Drink now through 2002. • $13 • (01/01/98) • **87**

VALCKENBERG

Pinot Blanc QbA Rheinhessen 1994 • $6 • (12/15/95) • **83**
Pinot Blanc QbA Rheinhessen 1993 • $7 • (11/30/94) • **82**
Riesling Kabinett Rheinhessen 1994 • $6 • (12/15/95) • **79**
Riesling Kabinett Rheinhessen 1993 • $7 • (11/30/94) • **78**
White Kabinett Rheinhessen Bereich Wonnegau Madonna 1994 • $7 • (12/15/95) • **86**
White Kabinett Rheinhessen Bereich Wonnegau Madonna 1993 • $7 • (11/30/94) • **77**

VOLLRADS, SCHLOSS

Riesling Auslese Gold Cap Rheingau 1996: Funky aromas of white pepper and earth. Medium-bodied and very sweet, with some ripe fruit character and a slightly cloying finish. 200 cases made. • $38/500ml • (07/31/98) • **85**
Riesling Auslese Rheingau 1994 • $55 • (11/30/95) • **85**
Riesling Eiswein Gold Cap Rheingau 1996: One of the best wines from Vollrads in years. Thick and honeyed, with plenty of spicy lemon-lime aromas and flavors. Full-bodied and very sweet, with wonderfully vibrant acidity. Drink now. • $NA/500ml • (11/30/97) • **92**
Riesling Kabinett Halbtrocken Rheingau 1996: Shows good, clean and spicy character with undernotes of flowers and steel. Medium-bodied, lightly sweet, short on the finish. Drink or hold. • $16 • (11/30/97) • **83**
Riesling Kabinett Halbtrocken Rheingau 1995: Beautiful aromas of peach, apricot and honey make way for complexity and elegance on the palate and finish. It has length, depth and finesse. Drinkable now. • $17 • (11/30/96) • **88**
Riesling Kabinett Halbtrocken Rheingau 1994 • $17 • (11/30/95) • **77**
Riesling Kabinett Rheingau 1996: Superclean and subtle aromas of mineral and tropical fruit. Medium-bodied and lemony, with intense mineral character and a lively acidity. Needs time. Best from 2000 through 2005. 600 cases made. • $15 • (07/31/98) • **87**

Key: SS—Spectator Selection CS—Cellar Selection HR—Highly Recommended BB—Best Buy $NA—Price not available Ⓐ—Auction Price (BT)—Barrel Tasting
Dates in parentheses indicate the issues in which the ratings were published.

Riesling Kabinett Rheingau 1995: A harmonious wine, with lovely apple, peach and nutmeg notes on both nose and palate. Light- to medium-bodied, lightly sweet. Fresh, long and subtle finish. Textbook kabinett. • $17 • (11/30/96) • **88**
Riesling Kabinett Rheingau 1994 • $17 • (11/30/95) • **85**
Riesling Kabinett Trocken Rheingau 1996: Promises more on the nose than palate. Perfumed Riesling with melon, pie crust and honey aromas. Medium-bodied, dry, with melon and lemon flavors and a round mouthfeel. Slightly short finish. Drink now. • $17 • (11/30/97) • **85**
Riesling Kabinett Trocken Rheingau Blausilber 1993 • $13 • (11/30/94) • **79**
Riesling QbA Halbtrocken Rheingau Grunsilber 1993 • $9 • (11/30/94) • **77**
Riesling QbA Rheingau 1996: Tropical fruit aromas, with a light leafy character. Medium-bodied and off-dry, with fresh acidity and a fruity finish. Drink now. • $NA • (07/31/98) • **87**
Riesling QbA Rheingau 1995: Crisp and clean, light-bodied, offering a green apple, anise-seed character. Lightly sweet, with a refreshing finish. • $13 • (11/30/96) • **84**
Riesling QbA Rheingau 1994 • $13 • (11/30/95) • **75**
Riesling QbA Rheingau Grungold 1993 • $NA • (11/30/94) • **76**
Riesling QbA Trocken Rheingau 1996: Try this solid, weighty QbA with food. Emits good spicy, apricot aromas with a hint of earth. Medium-bodied and dry, it has a tropical fruit, orange-flavored finish. Drink now. • $14 • (11/30/97) • **85**
Riesling QbA Trocken Rheingau Grunsilber 1993 • $9 • (11/30/94) • **79**
Riesling QbA Trocken Rheingau Matuschka-Greiffenclau 1996: Creamy and appley, with fresh fruit aromas and flavors. Medium-bodied and very dry, with crisp acidity and a refreshing finish. Drink now through 2004. 600 cases made. • $13 • (07/31/98) • **86**
Riesling Rheingau Trocken 1994: Dry and lean, with refreshing lemony tartness but little flavor, just hints of minerals and herbs. It's clean but simple. • $NA • (10/15/96) • **78**
Riesling Spätlese Halbtrocken Rheingau 1996: A wine with a good intensity of mineral, steely character. Medium-bodied, off-dry and a clean, crisp finish. Drink now. 600 cases made. • $15 • (11/30/97) • **85**
Riesling Spätlese Halbtrocken Rheingau 1996: A fresh and minerally Riesling. Medium-bodied and lightly sweet, with a slightly short finish. More on the nose than on the palate. Drink now. 600 cases made. • $15 • (07/31/98) • **83**
Riesling Spätlese Halbtrocken Rheingau Rosasilber 1993 • $17 • (11/30/94) • **75**
Riesling Spätlese Rheingau 1996: Vollrads does superwell again. Very fresh, with sliced green apple and mineral. Medium-bodied and off-dry, with a velvety texture and a long, flavorful finish. Very good indeed. Drink now. 600 cases made. • $24 • (07/31/98) • **89**
Riesling Spätlese Rheingau 1996: Fresh and fruity with crushed grape and melon character. Medium- to light-bodied, light acidity and a clean finish. Drink now. 600 cases made. • $24 • (11/30/97) • **83**
Riesling Spätlese Rheingau 1995: A fairly dull spätlese, medium-bodied and lightly sweet, with a biscuit and honey character. Short finish. Tasted twice, with consistent notes. • $21 • (11/30/96) • **79**
Riesling Spätlese Rheingau Rosagold 1993 • $17 • (11/30/94) • **81**

WAGNER, DR. HEINZ

Riesling Auslese Saar-Ruwer Saarburger Rausch 1993 • $17 • (11/30/94) • **90**
Riesling Auslese Gold Cap Saar-Ruwer Saarburger Rausch Three Stars 1993 • $30 • (11/30/94) • **91**
Riesling Eiswein Saar-Ruwer Saarburger Rausch 1993 • $NA • (11/30/94) • **83**
Riesling Kabinett Saar-Ruwer Ockfener Bockstein 1993 • $11 • (11/30/94) • **87**
Riesling Kabinett Saar-Ruwer Saarburger Rausch 1993 • $11 • (11/30/94) • **78**
Riesling Spätlese Mosel-Saar-Ruwer Ayler Kupp 1996: Quite reserved, with hints of peach, honey and slate. Racy, balanced and well made, just lacks the stuffing to really sing. Best from 2000 through 2005. • $16 • (04/30/98) • **84**
Riesling Spätlese Saar-Ruwer Ockfener Bockstein 1993 • $13 • (11/30/94) • **82**

WEGELER ERBEN, J.

Riesling Auslese Rheingau Geisenheimer Rothenberg Geheimrat Wegeler 1996: Offers floral, lemon and lime aromas and flavors. Medium-bodied,

GERMANY

medium-sweet, with a fresh, delicate finish. Needs more concentration. Drink now. • $30/500ml • (11/30/97) • **83**

Riesling Eiswein Rheingau Oestricher Lenchen Geheimrat Wegeler 1996: A well-balanced, elegant eiswein. Golden in color, it shows loads of sweet and sour, tangerine and apricot aromas and flavors. Full-bodied and very sweet, with electrifying acidity. Drink or hold. • $NA/375ml • (11/30/97) • **90**

Riesling QbA Rheingau Rüdesheimer Schlossberg 1996: A fresh, clean and dry Riesling that displays honeydew, mineral and stone aromas and flavors. Medium-bodied and dry, with a crisp, clean finish. Drink now or hold. • $NA • (11/30/97) • **87**

Riesling QbA Trocken Rheingau 1996: Plenty of apple, honeydew and mineral aromas. Medium-bodied and dry, with green apple and melon flavors. Slightly short on the finish. Drink now. • $9 • (11/30/97) • **85**

Riesling Spätlese Mosel-Saar-Ruwer Bernkasteler Graben 1996: Interesting apple, earthy and slightly candied flavors. Medium in body and sweetness, flinty on the finish. Drink now. • $NA • (11/30/97) • **86**

Riesling Spätlese Rheingau Charta Geheimrat Wegeler Erben 1996: Big and spicy, with loads of mineral and fruit character. Full-bodied and dry, with petrol and fruit flavors. For lovers of dry German Rieslings. Needs food. Drink now. • $NA • (11/30/97) • **89**

Riesling Spätlese Rheingau Geisenheimer Rothenberg Geheimrat J. Wegeler Erben 1996: There are plenty of ripe fruit, apricot and spice aromas and flavors. Medium-bodied, medium-sweet, with a long, lively finish. Drink now. • $20 • (11/30/97) • **88**

Riesling Spätlese Trocken Rheingau Geheimrat J. 1996: An extremely attractive, delicate white with lovely perfumes of flowers and fruit that follow through on the palate. Medium-bodied and off-dry, with a fresh, fruity finish. Drink now. • $NA • (11/30/97) • **88**

Riesling Trockenbeerenauslese Rheingau Geisenheimer Rothenberg Geheimrat Wegeler 1996: More BA than TBA in weight, but it sneaks up on your palate and delivers loads of fruit and sweetness. Medium-gold in color, with honey, straw and citrus aromas. Full- to medium-bodied, very sweet and wonderfully long in the aftertaste. Best after 1999. • $NA/500ml • (11/30/97) • **89**

WEGELER-DEINHARD

Riesling Auslese Mosel-Saar-Ruwer Bernkasteler Doctor 1993 • $60 • (11/30/94) • **89**

Riesling Auslese Mosel-Saar-Ruwer Wehlener Sonnenuhr Geheimrat J. 1994 • $NA • (11/30/95) • **90**

Riesling Auslese Pfalz Forster Ungeheuer 1993 • $27 • (11/30/94) • **90**

Riesling Auslese Rheingau 1993 • $NA • (11/30/94) • **82**

Riesling Auslese Rheingau Oestricher Lenchen 1993 • $30 • (11/30/94) • **83**

Riesling Auslese Rheingau Winkeler Hasensprung Geheimrat J. 1994 • $NA • (11/30/95) • **91**

Riesling Beerenauslese Mosel-Saar-Ruwer Bernkasteler Doctor Geheimrat J. 1994 • $NA • (11/30/95) • **89**

Riesling Beerenauslese Rheingau Oestricher Lenchen 1993 • $75 • (11/30/94) • **78**

Riesling Beerenauslese Rheingau Oestricher Lenchen Geheimrat J. 1994 • $NA • (11/30/95) • **82**

Riesling Eiswein Mosel-Saar-Ruwer Kaseler Nies'chen 1993 • $NA • (11/30/94) • **89**

Riesling Kabinett Mosel-Saar-Ruwer Bernkasteler Graben Geheimrat J. 1994 • $13 • (11/30/95) • **84**

Riesling Kabinett Mosel-Saar-Ruwer Wehlener Sonnenuhr 1993 • $16 • (11/30/94) • **81**

Riesling Kabinett Pfalz 1993 • $12 • (11/30/94) • **89**

Riesling Kabinett Pfalz Forster Ungeheuer 1993 • $15 • (11/30/94) • **85**

Riesling Kabinett Rheingau Oestricher Lenchen Geheimrat J. 1994 • $13 • (11/30/95) • **86**

Riesling Kabinett Rheingau Rüdesheimer Berg Rottland 1993 • $15 • (11/30/94) • **75**

Riesling Spätlese Mosel-Saar-Ruwer Bernkasteler Doctor Geheimrat J. 1994 • $NA • (11/30/95) • **87**

Riesling Spätlese Mosel-Saar-Ruwer Bernkasteler Doctor 1993 • $55 • (11/30/94) • **78**

Riesling Spätlese Mosel-Saar-Ruwer Wehlener Sonnenuhr 1993 • $20 • (11/30/94) • **83**

Riesling Spätlese Mosel-Saar-Ruwer Wehlener Sonnenuhr Geheimrat J. 1994 • $NA • (11/30/95) • **88**

Riesling Spätlese Pfalz Forster Ungeheuer 1993 • $19 • (11/30/94) • **88**

Riesling Spätlese Rheingau Rüdesheimer Berg Rottland 1993 • $20 • (11/30/94) • **84**

Riesling Spätlese Rheingau Rüdesheimer Berg Rottland Geheimrat J. 1994 • $NA • (11/30/95) • **87**

Riesling Trockenbeerenauslese Pfalz Deidesheimer Herrgottsacker Geheimrat J. 1994 • $NA • (11/30/95) • **92**

WEHRHEIM, EUGEN

Riesling Kabinett Rheinhessen Niersteiner Rehbach 1994: Petrol aromas and flavors signal maturity, and there are honey and vanilla accents, too, in this easy-drinking white. Balanced and ready, with a lingering aftertaste of honey. Drink now. • $11 • (01/01/98) • **84**

WEIL, ROBERT

Riesling Auslese Gold Cap Rheingau Kiedricher Gräfenberg 1996: Outstanding balance in this wine. Superb concentration for an auslese. Rich, ripe fruit aromas with undertones of botrytis and minerals. Full-bodied and very sweet with excellent crisp acidity and a long intense finish. Drink now. 50 cases made. • $299/375ml • (11/30/97) • **92**

Riesling Auslese Gold Cap Rheingau Kiedricher Gräfenberg 1995: Exotic, showing pineapple and melon flavors that are delicately balanced. It's subtle yet lively, with a lingering finish. A wine that grows on you. 350 cases made. • $80/375ml • (11/30/96) • **90**

Riesling Auslese Gold Cap Rheingau Kiedricher Gräfenberg 1994 • $NA • (11/30/95) • **92**

Riesling Auslese Gold Cap Rheingau Kiedricher Gräfenberg 1993 • $NA • (11/30/94) • **94**

Riesling Auslese Rheingau Kiedricher Gräfenberg 1996: Harmonious sweet wine with lemon-lime and honey aromas and flavors. Medium- to full-bodied and very sweet, with a lively finish. Delicious. Drink now. 350 cases made. • $41/375ml • (11/30/97) • **89**

Riesling Auslese Rheingau Kiedricher Gräfenberg 1995: One of the sweeter auslesen of '95, its melon, peach and botrytis flavors are wrapped around a core of racy acidity. Concentrated and long. Drinkable now. 350 cases made. • $80/375ml • (11/30/96) • **89**

Riesling Auslese Rheingau Kiedricher Gräfenberg 1994 • $78 • (11/30/95) • **87**

Riesling Beerenauslese Rheingau Kiedricher Gräfenberg 1995: A stunning sticky. Big and rich, with loads of tropical fruit, honey and pineapple character. Full-bodied and very sweet with great flavors and a long, zingy finish. Drink now or hold. 67 cases made. • $150/375ml • (11/30/96) • **95**

Riesling Beerenauslese Rheingau Kiedricher Gräfenberg 1994 • $141 • (11/30/95) • **96**

Riesling Beerenauslese Rheingau Kiedricher Gräfenberg 1993 • $242 • (11/30/94) • **95**

Riesling Eiswein Rheingau Kiedricher Gräfenberg 1996: This classic, young eiswein shows little on the nose, but grabs you by the palate with super sweetness, intense citrus flavors and stirring acidity. Medium- to full-bodied and very sweet, with a spice, lemon and dried fruit finish. Best after 2000. 30 cases made. • $200/375ml • (11/30/97) • **96**

Riesling Kabinett Rheingau 1996: Plenty of apple, spice and mineral character in this wine. Medium-bodied, medium-sweet with a long flavorful finish. Tastes more like a spätlese. Drink now. 2,000 cases made. • $19 • (11/30/97) • **90**

Riesling Kabinett Rheingau 1995: A round and smooth kabinett, with plenty of ripe lemon and apple aromas and flavors, lightly sweet, with fresh acidity. Slightly simple now, but will improve with age. 1,167 cases made. • $19 • (11/30/96) • **85**

Riesling Kabinett Rheingau 1994 • $19 • (11/30/95) • **82**

Riesling Kabinett Rheingau 1993 • $17 • (11/30/94) • **85**

Riesling Spätlese Rheingau Kiedricher Gräfenberg 1996: A fantastic wine. Covers the range of flavors you expect in top class Riesling — honey, cloves, flowers and tropical fruit. Medium-bodied, medium-sweet with an intense fruity, spicy aftertaste and crisp acidity. Drink or hold. 500 cases made. • $41 • (11/30/97) • **92**

Riesling Spätlese Rheingau Kiedricher Gräfenberg 1995: With botrytis character, this is exotic and ripe. Dried fruit, almond and honey flavors mix with citrusy acidity in a concentrated, delicious presentation. Tempting now, but should age gracefully. 400 cases made. • $41 • (11/30/96) • **90**

Riesling Spätlese Rheingau Kiedricher Gräfenberg 1994 • $32 • (11/30/95) • **86**

Riesling Spätlese Rheingau Kiedricher Gräfenberg 1993 • $26 • (11/30/94) • **90**

Riesling Trockenbeerenauslese Rheingau Kiedricher Gräfenberg 1996: What can be said? Weil always makes stunning TBAs, and this is an amazing wine. Brilliant gold in color, showing concentrated honey, spice and burnt almond aromas, it's full-bodied, very sweet and abounds with honey, dried apricot and tropical fruit flavors. Thick as oil. Long, long finish. Drinkable now, best after 2000. 75 cases made. • $310/375ml • (11/30/97) CS • **97**

Riesling Trockenbeerenauslese Rheingau Kiedricher Gräfenberg 1995: Intense nose of apricot flan and toffee, followed by honey and butterscotch flavors. Thick and rich in texture and incredibly concentrated, finishing with a sweet-tart component. Impressive now, but should improve through 2001. 50 cases made. • $620/375ml • (11/30/96) • **94**

Riesling Trockenbeerenauslese Rheingau Kiedricher Gräfenberg 1994 • $291 • (11/30/95) • **95**

Riesling Trockenbeerenauslese Rheingau Kiedricher Gräfenberg 1993 • $250 • (11/30/94) • **95**

WERNER'SCHES, DOMDECHANT

Riesling Auslese Rheingau Hochheimer Domdechaney 1993 • $NA • (11/30/94) • **76**

Riesling Spätlese Halbtrocken Rheingau Hochheimer 1993 • $NA • (11/30/94) • **87**

Riesling Spätlese Trocken Rheingau Hochheimer Domdechaney 1993 • $NA • (11/30/94) • **82**

WURZBURG, STAATLICHER HOFKELLER

Kabinett Franken Hofkeller 1993 • $14 • (11/30/94) • **84**

Silvaner Kabinett Trocken Franken Würzburger Stein 1993 • $14 • (11/30/94) • **81**

Silvaner Kabinett Trocken Franken Würzburger Stein 1993: Dry, and moderately concentrated with nutty and earthy flavors and a hint of honey. Pungent to the nose. • $14 • (08/31/96) • **81**

White Kabinett Franken Hofkeller 1993: Firm, dry and flavorful with a nice concentration of apple, lime and mineral flavors and some earthy and spicy notes. 4,000 cases made. • $14 • (08/31/96) • **84**

ZILLIKEN

Riesling Auslese Gold Cap Mosel-Saar-Ruwer Saarburger Rausch 1993 • $NA • (11/30/94) • **91**

Riesling Auslese Long Gold Cap Mosel-Saar-Ruwer Saarburger Rausch 1993 • $114 • (11/30/94) • **93**

Riesling Auslese Mosel-Saar-Ruwer Saarburger 1995: More like a new-world Riesling, with its soft texture, abundance of ripe, tropical fruit aromas and flavors and less-than-lively acidity. Light finish. Drink now. 350 cases made. • $33 • (11/30/96) • **84**

Riesling Auslese Mosel-Saar-Ruwer Saarburger Rausch 1996: A stylish wine with intensely steely, mineral character. Medium-bodied and very sweet, with a medium finish that is slightly grassy. Drink now. 35 cases made. • $171/375ml • (11/30/97) • **87**

Riesling Auslese Mosel-Saar-Ruwer Saarburger Rausch 1994 • $34 • (11/30/95) • **84**

Riesling Auslese Mosel-Saar-Ruwer Saarburger Rausch 1993 • $35 • (11/30/94) • **90**

Riesling Beerenauslese Mosel-Saar-Ruwer Saarburger Rausch 1994 • $NA • (11/30/95) • **84**

Riesling Beerenauslese Mosel-Saar-Ruwer Saarburger Rausch 1993 • $NA • (11/30/94) • **93**

Riesling Kabinett Mosel-Saar-Ruwer Ockfener Bockstein 1996: Very good intensity of flint and mineral aromas and flavors. Medium-bodied, off-dry, very firm acidity. Needed time to develop in the bottle. However, should be drinkable now. 300 cases made. • $14 • (11/30/97) • **88**

Riesling Kabinett Mosel-Saar-Ruwer Saarburger Rausch 1996: Starts off slowly but finishes with lots of mineral and flinty character. Medium-bodied, off-dry. Silky texture. Drink now. 600 cases made. • $15 • (11/30/97) • **87**

Riesling Kabinett Mosel-Saar-Ruwer Saarburger Rausch 1995: Barely acceptable for its rather sour, green aromas and flavors. Not typical of this producer. Drink now, if you must. Tasted twice, with consistent notes. 110 cases made. • $14 • (11/30/96) • **71**

Riesling Kabinett Mosel-Saar-Ruwer Saarburger Rausch 1994 • $15 • (11/30/95) • **81**

Riesling Kabinett Mosel-Saar-Ruwer Saarburger Rausch 1993 • $13 • (11/30/94) • **87**

Riesling QbA Halbtrocken Mosel-Saar-Ruwer 1994: A model QbA: fresh and vibrant, with apple and mineral aromas and flavors. Medium-bodied and dry, with medium acidity and a crisp finish. • $10 • (11/30/96) • **85**

Riesling QbA Halbtrocken Mosel-Saar-Ruwer Zilliken Gutsriesling 1996: Surprisingly round and fruity for a relatively dry wine from this region. Delicious ripe fruit aromas and flavors, with lemon and light mineral undertones. Light- to medium-bodied, dry, with a fresh finish. Drink now. 400 cases made. • $11 • (11/30/97) • **86**

Riesling QbA Mosel-Saar-Ruwer Zilliken Gutsriesling 1996: Shows some good lemon, melon and spice aromas and flavors, but slightly boring. Medium-bodied, medium-sweet. Short finish. Drink now. 600 cases made. • $11 • (11/30/97) • **80**

Riesling Spätlese Mosel-Saar-Ruwer Ockfener Bockstein 1994 • $19 • (11/30/95) • **82**

Riesling Spätlese Mosel-Saar-Ruwer Saarburger Rausch 1996: A wine to age. This is a zingy Saar wine with loads of acidity, lemony fruit character and mineral flavors. Medium-bodied, medium-sweet, with a lively finish. Try now. 400 cases made. • $21 • (11/30/97) • **90**

Riesling Spätlese Mosel-Saar-Ruwer Saarburger Rausch 1995: Slightly dull, but shows some decent lemon, green apple and kerosene character. Lightly sweet with a short finish. Ready to drink. 660 cases made. • $19 • (11/30/96) • **84**

Riesling Spätlese Mosel-Saar-Ruwer Saarburger Rausch 1994: A very good Spätlese that delivers plenty of spicy and fruity aromas and flavors. Medium-bodied, not too sweet, with a fresh mineral finish. Drinkable now. • $20 • (11/30/96) • **86**

Riesling Spätlese Mosel-Saar-Ruwer Saarburger Rausch 1993 • $18 • (11/30/94) • **85**

Key: SS—Spectator Selection CS—Cellar Selection HR—Highly Recommended BB—Best Buy $NA—Price not available Ⓐ—Auction Price (BT)—Barrel Tasting

Dates in parentheses indicate the issues in which the ratings were published.

Italy

Italy makes more wine than any other country, but today its reputation rests not on quantity but on quality. Although Italy's greatest wines still come from the familiar regions of Piedmont and Tuscany, many other areas are emerging as serious wine producers. They include Umbria, Campania, Friuli, Trentino-Alto Adige, Sardinia, and Sicily, to name but a few.

Although Cabernet Sauvignon and Chardonnay are increasingly gaining favor throughout Italy, they still represent a relatively small portion of production. The soul of Italian wine is still found in its indigenous grape varieties, such as Nebbiolo, Barbera, Dolcetto, and Sangiovese for reds, and Trebbiano and Malvasia for whites. These native varieties allow Italy to offer an unparalleled breadth and variety of flavor profiles.

For many years white wine was an afterthought in this country of red-wine lovers. But that is changing rapidly as its whites improve. Indeed, Italy is rapidly improving the quality of its winemaking overall. When these improvements are combined with its fine vineyards and a favorable climate, it is easy to see why the Italians have now become formidable competitors in the world marketplace. Indeed, Italy's greatest wines are on a par with the best of France and the United States, and its everyday wines offer great value.

1. Piedmont: Barbera, Dolcetto
2. Veneto: Bardolino, Soave, Valpolicella
3. Trentino-Alto Adige
4. Friuli-Venezia
5. Tuscany
6. Umbria: Orvieto
7. The Marches: Verdicchio
8. Abruzzi: Montepulciano d'Abruzzo

THE DOC SYSTEM

Italy's appellation system is more complex than that of France or the United States. It has an older system of DOCs (*denominazioni di origine controllata*), over which has been superimposed a newer system of DOCGs (the G stands for *garantita,* and theoretically indicates a superior standard of wine quality). Over 250 different DOC and DOCG wines have been created, each with its own detailed rules and regulations covering such items as allowable grape varieties, acceptable yields, vineyard quality, soil type, geographic boundaries and minimum standards for aging.

Yet, too often, the ossified DOC rules have hindered rather than advanced the cause of Italian wine quality. While producers could get by simply by meeting the minimum standards of the DOC, creative winemakers found themselves stymied by rules that inhibited experiments with grape types, aging, the use of *barriques* (small wooden casks, typically made of French oak), and other winemaking techniques. The major consequence has been a plethora of so-called *vini da tavola,* unsanctioned wines that do not meet the official standards of the DOC/DOCG. At many estates, these wines surpass the level of the DOC wines in price and in quality. As a reflection of this trend and the growing dissatisfaction with the DOC system, a law was passed in 1992 establishing a new category entitled IGT (*indicazione geografica tipica*), intended as a rough equivalent of the French *vin de pays*. Ultimately this law may modify the existing system in favor of one that emphasizes geographic origin and wine quality above such formalities as grape blends, alcohol levels, and minimum aging requirements.

ITALIAN WINE REGIONS

It's been said that there's no such thing as Italian food, only Italian regional cuisines. Much the same can be said of Italian wine. The Piedmontese don't make wine like the Tuscans, who don't make wine like the Apulians, and so on. The key to sorting out the differences is understanding the unique climate and soils of Italy's many regions, ranging from the Alpine hills in the North to the bottom of the boot in the south. But winemaking philosophies and traditions play a large part.

Tuscany

Tuscany epitomizes in many ways the blend of art and science that characterizes Italian winemaking. Though the Tuscan landscape still looks like the background of the Mona Lisa, things are changing rapidly behind the graceful facades of her ancient *castelli* and wineries.

At the heart of Tuscany, in terms of both geography and importance is the Chianti zone, which produces one of the first five wines to have been accorded the rank of DOCG status. Chianti ranges in style from soft, fruity and quaffable to deeply colored, tannic and ageworthy. At the core of all Chianti is the incredibly adaptable Sangiovese grape. Although it is cultivated throughout much of Italy, only in Tuscany does it achieve its classic style: a delicate, aromatic wine of warmth and depth, with an almost ethereal astringency on the finish.

Chianti Classico, which can only come from the strictly defined Classico zone, is the most structured and ageworthy Chianti. The Classico Riserva designation is reserved for its best wines, which have been aged in oak for a minimum statutory period of 24 months. In the past, Chianti Classico tended to show amber highlights fairly early in its development, but this style is rapidly being displaced in favor of one that is more vigorously fruity and displays an almost Merlot-like red/purple glow when young. Among the top Chianti producers are Antinori, Ruffino, Poggerino, Felsina, Fontodi, San Felice, and Castello d'Ama.

On a level with Chianti Classico is the much smaller Chianti Rufina zone (not to be confused with the Ruffino Company, in Pontassiere), located in the hills east of Florence. Its most famous name is the Marchesi de' Frescobaldi, known for its Castello di Nippozano, Montesodi and Remole bottlings. Selvapiana is another top producer. The Rufina zone also borders the area called Pomino, an old DOC that was resurrected through the efforts of the Marchesi de' Frescobaldi, which owns all the vineyards. Pomino is a curiosity because, historically, it has relied heavily on French grapes for blends. The red Pomino made from Cabernet, Sangiovese and Merlot may be the best, but some excellent Chardonnay-based whites are made here as well.

The other Chianti zones—Colli Fiorentino, Pisani, Colli Senesi, Colli Aretini and Montalbano—offer distinct styles. The latter encompasses the Carmignano district, which like Pomino has a centuries old-history of blending in substantial portions of Cabernet Sauvignon. Capezzana and Ambra are well-known. The other Chianti regions are not generally *riserva* producers, but they do make appealingly soft and fruity everyday wines meant to be drunk very young.

From southern Tuscany comes Brunello di Montalcino, which along with Barolo, is Italy's most acclaimed—and often its most expensive—traditional red wine. The only permissible grape for this DOCG is the Sangiovese Grosso, a potent clone of the Sangiovese grape. Both a normal and a reserve Brunello are made by most producers in the area of Montalcino. But it's all a bit unsettled now, as no one seems quite sure whether the *riservas* (extra rich wines put out in the best years) will outlast the more classic, somewhat leaner *normale* bottlings. Certainly the wines of the top producers, such as Caparzo, Poggio Antico, Altesino, and others, seem to have the stuffing to age for decades. Note that for the budget-conscious or the impatient, Rosso di Montalcino, made from young vines and released in a fruitier style after minimal aging, may be the best choice from this region.

East of Montalcino, Vino Nobile di Montepulciano is trying to set itself out from the crowd. Also made from a local clone of the Sangiovese, it combines much of the austere power of a Brunello with the rounder fruitiness of a Chianti Riserva. But that makes it sound better than it is. At least for the time being, Vino Nobile di Montepulciano has yet to justify its premium asking price.

Tuscany is also the place that started the *vino da tavola* movement, and has consistently provided the most fertile hot-bed for experimentation, discovery, and the free borrowing of ideas and techniques from winemakers around the world. The wines that have resulted are known as Super Tuscans. The best of these are now considered in a class with the top *crus*

Harvey Steiman

The estate of established Piedmont producer Marchesi di Barolo.

of Burgundy, Bordeaux and California—and are priced accordingly. Two different approaches predominate, of which the most popular relies either partly or wholly on Cabernet Sauvignon vinified in a Bordelais style using small oak barrels. Examples of this type include Sassicaia, Salaia and Sammarco. The more original contributions are the super-Tuscans that have brought the indigenous Sangiovese to its ultimate expression, a supple core of warm fruit wrapped in an ethereal cloud of bright tannins. Made without the white grapes of traditional Chianti, and sometimes spiced up with a pinch or two of Cabernet, these extraordinary wines have no parallel outside of Tuscany. Some of the best are Fontalloro, Flaccianello, and Tignanello.

Piedmont

With its own dialect and a unique winemaking philosophy and style, Piedmont, in Northwestern Italy, is a world apart both culturally and oenologically. Yet it would be difficult to name a region where the art of the winemaker flourishes more profoundly than amidst its fog-draped hills. Like Burgundy, Piedmont's greatness flows from the precarious balance of nature, in which the threat of disaster always looms in even the greatest vintages. This is a northerly limit for the production of great red wine, and only in the years when nature's tempestuous moods are moderated do its greatest wines live up to their reputation.

Barolo, often called the king of Piedmont reds, is made from 100 percent Nebbiolo. The mist-shrouded hills of the Barolo region gave the Nebbiolo its name—from *nebbia*, meaning fog. Barolo is a wine of immense size and dimension, with masses of alcohol and tannins. Even more than the great wines of Bordeaux and Burgundy, it demands cellaring. When mature, Barolo is brick orange, with aromas of truffles, faded rose petals and smoke, and potent earth and tar flavors. Top producers include Aldo Conterno, Paolo Scavino, Bruno Giacosa, Pio Cesare, Mauro Sebaste, Sandrone, and Domenico Clerico.

Barbaresco is almost as long-lived and can be every bit as grand as Barolo. Not quite possessed of Barolo's immense strength, Barbaresco is more supple and elegant, making it ready to drink a bit sooner. The leading exponent of Barbaresco has been Angelo

Gaja, who until recently did not even produce Barolo. Spurred on by Gaja, other Barbaresco producers now also make fine wine, the best of which may be the single-vineyard bottlings of Produttori del Barbaresco.

Two other good choices include Nebbiolo d'Alba and Nebbiolo delle Langhe. The first is made outside the Barolo and Barbaresco zone of Langhe. Not subject to a long minimum-aging requirement, most Nebbiolo d'Alba is fruitier and less forbidding than Barolo or Barbaresco, and quite delicious. Nebbiolo delle Langhe, which is made in the zone, is usually declassified Barolo or Barbaresco. Both Nebbiolos can offer exceptional value. Look for wines made by leading Barolo and Barbaresco producers.

Gattinara is from the north of Piedmont, on the other side of Turin from Alba. The Novara-Vercelli hills are its home. This wine should rival Barolo and Barbaresco. Due to inconsistent winemaking, however, it rarely does. At its best, Gattinara is the Margaux of Piedmont, exquisitely delicate and deeply flavored, with a bouquet of truffles, black plum and violets. The producers Vallana, Travaglini, and Dessilani can be excellent.

Budget-conscious lovers of Gattinara should seek out the wines of the myriad villages around the Novara-Vercelli hills. The best is Spanna, taken from the local name for the Nebbiolo grape. Spanna can be superb, rivaling Gattinara at half the cost.

Barbera and Dolcetto are also excellent Piedmont reds. Deliciously fruity in their youth, most are intended for early consumption.

The Cortese may be Italy's finest native white grape. It is responsible for Gavi, Gavi di Gavi, and Cortese di Gavi. Another fine Piedmont white is made from the Muscat-like Arneis grape. It is finely scented and tart. And of course, Chardonnay is making its appearance here, sometimes in a full, oaky style that calls to mind a California Chardonnay.

UP-AND-COMING REGIONS

With prices of wines from Tuscany and the Piedmont on the rise, importers are increasingly turning to more obscure areas of Italy. Here are some of the most promising:

Apulia. On the heel of the Italian boot, Apulia is a sunny area that enjoys a moderating influence from the sea. Salice Salentino is a rich, often rustic red that can have real character—perhaps too much character for some palates. A lighter version called Rosso del Salento is also making a name for itself.

Valtellina. The Valtellina reds are a wholly different interpretation of Nebbiolo. Though complex, they are far lighter than the Piedmontese Nebbiolos. They shine with food; alone, they seem stingy. The leading wines are from the villages of Grumello, Inferno, Sassella, and Valgella. Perhaps the best is Sfursat, a potent wine made from dried grapes and eminently suitable as a replacement for Port with strong cheese. The leading producers are Rainoldi and Nino Negri.

Sicily. Sicily has proven its potential for bulk production of flavorful, if not terribly complex, red and white table wines. Corvo's top bottlings, as well as those of other producers such as Regaleali, suggest that there is also great quality potential here.

Sardinia. Another out-of-the-way island, Sardinia produces wines with a gentle ripeness and smooth fruit. The white, made from the exotic Vermentino grape, may have the potential to be the next Pinot Grigio, in terms of mass acceptance and sales.

Abruzzo. This promising region has been plagued by gross overproduction, which has obscured the potential for much better wines if yields are kept under control. Done well, Montepulciano d'Abruzzo (Montepulciano is the grape) can produce a sort of ripe, almost Rhône-like cousin of Chianti.

Veneto. The predominant red grape in this region is Corvina, which is typically blended with Rondinella, Molinara and Negrara to produce Valpolicella and Bardolino. The ultimate expression of the Corvina grape is Amarone, which requires extensive drying of the grapes on open racks to concentrate the must sufficiently to create a wine of monumental character. Bertani, Masi, Allegrini, and now even Bolla have shown that—aside from the traditional Amarones—there is a lot of unexploited potential for serious Valpolicella and Bardolino, made with far more intensity than the common versions, which are quite light. The same is true of Soave, made mostly from Garganega and Trebbiano.

Friuli. Although Cabernet Franc, with its distinctive peppery/herbal character, is best known as a major grape of the French districts St.-Emilion and Chinon, it has been cultivated in the Collio region of Friuli for well over a century. The Friuli interpretation emphasizes subtle aromatics allied with a complex, light body. Friuli also makes Merlots that have an abundance of bright fruit, a clean, dry finish and an herbal, almost grassy delicacy unique to this region. Adding Cabernet Sauvignon to the blend accents the herbal notes on the bouquet, and complements the round red-fruit notes of the Merlot grape.

Friuli also has shown a knack for producing refreshing, surprisingly complex white wines. Pinot Grigio has always been taken quite seriously in Friuli, although its huge commercial success has made it ubiquitous throughout Italy. Most are made in a dry, zesty style, often showing a distinctive smokiness on the nose. Sauvignon Blanc and Tocai Friulano (unrelated to the Tokay of Hungary), show more power and intensity. Some are vinified in wood casks, giving an even richer, firmer wine. Finally, the indigenous Ribolla Gialla should not be overlooked. Dry and quite lemony, its firm acidity makes it a perfect match with seafood.

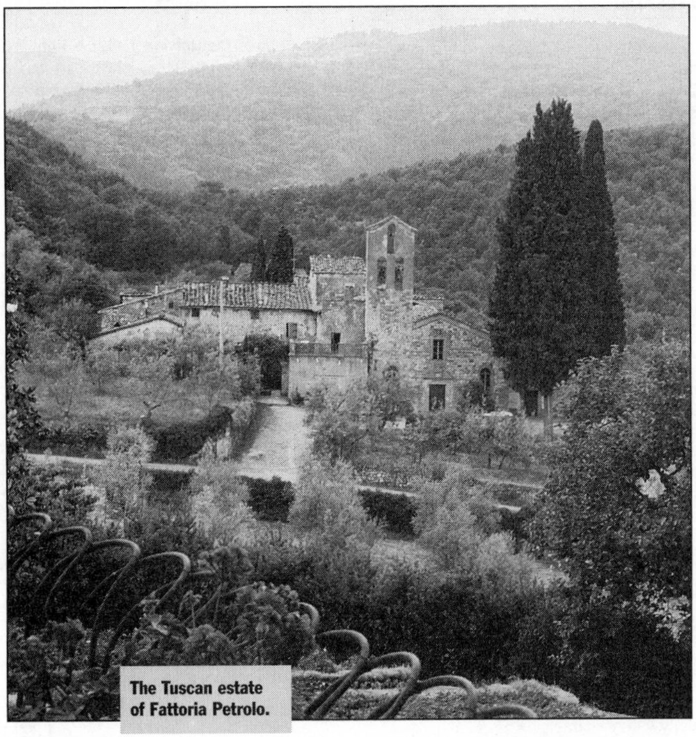
The Tuscan estate of Fattoria Petrolo.

James Suckling

Trentino-Alto Adige. The northeast region of Trentino-Alto Adige, spilling out of the Alps south of Austria, is known for its internationally acclaimed Pinot Grigio and Chardonnay. In addition, Pinot Bianco (Weissburgunder), Gewürztraminer and the German varietals Riesling, Sylvaner and Müller-Thurgau thrive in the cool, high-altitude vineyards found in these regions. Surprisingly, nearly three-quarters of the region's production is red wine, with Cabernet Sauvignon and Merlot capable of world-class quality; the indigenous varietals Teroldego and Lagrein also make wines of distinction.

ITALIAN VARIETAL WINES

Increasingly in Italy, as in France, grape varieties are getting top billing on wine labels. Below is a quick run-through of the leading types.

Sangiovese. Arguably Italy's most important grape, this mainstay of Chianti is becoming an important variety on its own. It tends to produce mid-weight, often quite fruity wines, with a characteristic tart, clean finish.

Pinot Grigio. This white grape is the same as Alsace's Pinot Gris, except that in Italian hands it sells like hot-cakes. Perhaps this is because Italy vinifies it in a light, fresh style with lots of soft fruit. Most of the best comes from Friuli, but it is increasingly being made successfully in other locales as well.

Merlot. Of all the classic Bordeaux varietals, Merlot appears to be the greatest commercial success. Often coupled with a regional name, such as Merlot del Piave, the Italians vinify it in a clean, fresh style so that it comes out something like a lightly herbal Chianti. Prices tend to be reasonable.

Chardonnay. Though a few very serious producers, such as Gaja, vinify a Chardonnay that tastes like a Meursault, most Italian Chardonnay is made in the style of a Pinot Grigio. This means little or no wood, and lots of cold-fermented, apple-like crispness up front.

Barbera. The best known examples of this red—from Alba and Asti in the Piedmont—can approach Barolo and Barbaresco in power, though rarely in finesse. Increasingly, experiments with low yields and new wood aging suggest star potential.

Dolcetto. Sometimes referred to as the Beaujolais of Italy, Dolcetto can be a very attractive wine when vinified in a grapey purple *nouveau* style. Like Barbera, its real future may lie in experiments with lower yields and barrel aging.

Trebbiano. Now beginning to make a name for itself as a single variety, this is the white grape that was once added to Chianti. It is also a component of many other popular Italian whites, such as Soave and Orvieto. With low yields and careful vinification, Trebbiano can be made into a potent wine that can even take barrel fermentation.

ABBONA, MARZIANO & ENRICO

Barolo 1986 • $30 • (12/15/92) • **81**
Barolo Vigneto Terlo Ravera 1990 • $25 • (07/31/95) • **85**
Barolo Vigneto Terlo Ravera 1989 • $23 • (06/15/94) • **89**
Dolcetto di Dogliani Papa Celso 1992 • $13 • (06/15/94) • **84**
Dolcetto di Dogliani Vigneto Doriolo 1993 • $11 • (07/31/95) • **83**
Nebbiolo d'Alba 1990 • $14 • (06/15/94) • **89**

ACCOMASSO & FIGLIO, GIOVANNI

Barolo Vigneto Rocchette 1985 • $24 • (01/31/92) • **75**
Nebbiolo delle Langhe 1982 • $14 • (07/31/89) • **65**

ACINUM

Amarone della Valpolicella 1990: Rich and lively, full of prune and leather notes combined with a viscous texture and tannic structure. A little one-dimensional. Drink now through 2002. • $30 • (05/31/98) • **86**

Valpolicella Classico Superiore 1995: Loads of ripe, succulent cherry and almond character. Buxom and lushly textured, with moderate tannins on the finish. Drink now. • $12 • (05/31/98) • **85**

AGOSTINA, PIERI

Rosso di Montalcino 1994: A solid rosso, with mineral, vanilla and licorice aromas and flavors and a gentle, silky finish. Medium-bodied. Good wine-making here. 250 cases made. • $NA • (11/30/96) • **85**

AIOLA

Chianti Classico 1993 • $13 • (10/31/95) • **80**
Chianti Classico 1991 • $NA • (10/31/93) • **85**
Chianti Classico 1990 • $11 • (09/15/92) • **81**
Chianti Classico Riserva 1988 • $18 • (09/15/92) • **79**
Logaiolo 1991 • $18 • (10/31/95) • **75**
Logaiolo 1990 • $NA • (10/31/93) • **83**

AJA, L'

Chianti Classico 1994: Not much to it. Diluted, with some berry flavor—but mostly leather—and water. Tasted twice with consistent notes. • $NA • (10/31/96) • **70**

Chianti Classico 1993 • $NA • (10/31/95) • **81**
Chianti Classico 1991 • $NA • (10/31/93) • **82**

Chianti Classico Riserva 1993: Rather meager compared to other Chianti Classico riserva, with a slightly weedy, berry character. • $NA • (10/31/96) • **77**

ALBOLA, CASTELLO D'

Acciaiolo 1993: A big, hearty, full-bodied but very tannic red wine, with attractive cedar and clove aromas, currant and cherry flavors. Needs time to soften, but the oaky tannins may still dominate. Try after 2000. • $40 • (05/31/97) • **86**

Acciaiolo 1990 • $35 • (07/31/95) • **84**
Acciaiolo 1988 • $40 • (09/15/91) • **88**

Chardonnay Toscana 1995: Dull and candied, this shows some almond and marzipan character but it's very short. Drink now. 500 cases made. • $25 • (09/30/97) • **75**

Chianti Classico 1995: A delicate and fruity Chianti with violet and dried cherry character, fine tannins and a medium finish. Slightly dry. 30,000 cases imported. Drink now. • $10 • (12/31/97) • **83**

Chianti Classico 1994: On the robust side and well made, with great balance, smooth texture, firm tannins and lots of focused fruit flavors. Drink now. 20,000 cases made. • $9 • (10/31/96) • **85**

Chianti Classico 1992 • $9 • (02/28/95) • **74**
Chianti Classico 1991 • $9 • (10/31/94) • **80**
Chianti Classico 1990 • $9 • (09/15/92) • **76**
Chianti Classico 1988 • $10 • (09/15/91) • **89**
Chianti Classico 1986 • $8 • (11/30/89) • **85**
Chianti Classico Riserva 1990 • $13 • (02/28/95) • **79**
Chianti Classico Riserva 1988 • $15 • (10/31/93) • **80**
Chianti Classico Riserva 1985 • $12 • (11/30/89) • **76**

Pinot Grigio Aquileia del Friuli 1995: A beautifully balanced wine. Fresh and lively with floral and peach aromas and flavors, and a delicate mineral flavor that adds dimension. Touches of honey and spice on the finish. 1,500 cases made. • $9 • (01/31/97) • **87**

Pinot Grigio Aquileia del Friuli 1993 • $9 • (12/15/94) • **77**

Pinot Grigio Umbria 1995: Essentially neutral, with barely perceptible flavors of pear and straw. Drink now. • $9 • (05/15/97) • **77**

ALERAMICI, MARCHESATO DEGLI

Brunello di Montalcino 1992: A light Brunello, yet a well-made one. Offers plenty of pretty berry, cherry aromas, a medium body, light tannins and a fresh finish. • $34 • (09/30/97) • **85**

Brunello di Montalcino 1991: A bit thin, with some decent berry and cherry flavors, but it turns cedary and even thinner on the finish. Already slightly tired. • $35 • (11/30/96) • **78**

Brunello di Montalcino 1990: Beautifully balanced Brunello featuring berry, rose and mineral aromas and flavors. Medium-bodied with fine tannins and a fresh finish. Delicious now. • $NA • (10/31/95) • **86**

Brunello di Montalcino Riserva 1991: A bit disjointed with its leathery berry character, slightly dry tannins and short finish. Drink now. • $40 • (09/30/97) • **78**

Il Galampio Rosso 1993: Some decent fruit flavors, but rather earthy with meaty, barky nuances to the character. Medium body, light tannins and too-short finish. Slightly acidic. • $18 • (10/31/96) • **79**

Rosso di Montalcino 1995: A Rosso with good berry and earth character, medium tannins and a simple finish. • $15 • (09/30/97) • **84**

Rosso di Montalcino 1994: Prematurely aged, this shows leather, cedar and spice flavors and a dry finish. Aged in old, slightly unclean wood? Disappointing for this producer. 1,333 cases made. • $15 • (11/30/96) • **79**

Rosso di Montalcino 1993 • $NA • (10/31/95) • **81**

ALESSANDRIA

Barolo 1993: International style of red, balanced, with sweet tannins. Offers plum, prune and red berry flavors and oak-infused spice, chocolate and toasty bread notes. A bit dry on the finish, though. Try after 1999. • $30 • (10/31/97) • **85**

ALESSI

Liuto 1995: Slightly oxidized and candied, it has some apple and honey character but it's dull and light on the finish. • $NA • (09/30/97) • **78**

ALESSIA, AGRICOLA

Calanchi di Vaiano 1995: A very good Tuscan white. Plenty of lemon and oak character. Medium-bodied with lemon, lime and vanilla flavors, a fresh finish. Drinkable now. • $15 • (09/30/97) • **85**

ALFIERI

Barbera d'Asti 1993: A mature Barbera, showing mushroom, forest underbrush and earth. The tannins are a bit dry on the finish. Drink now. • $27 • (10/31/97) • **80**

Barbera d'Asti La Tota 1995: Disappointingly light for a Barbera; smells and tastes diluted. Modest cherry and strawberry flavors mingle with odd, somewhat funky notes. • $17 • (10/31/97) • **75**

Monferrato Rosso Il Rosso dei Marchesi 1996: Light and diluted, with some strawberry and cherry notes. Short, astringent finish. • $12 • (10/31/97) • **72**

Monferrato Rosso San Germano 1994: A rustic wine, with grip: earth, mint, sage, dried herb, hot pepper—you name it. Medium- to full-bodied, the flavors explode on the palate and linger long on the finish. Try now through 2002 with spicy foods that will tame the tough tannins. • $32 • (10/31/97) • **84**

Key: SS—Spectator Selection CS—Cellar Selection HR—Highly Recommended BB—Best Buy $NA—Price not available Ⓐ—Auction Price (BT)—Barrel Tasting
Dates in parentheses indicate the issues in which the ratings were published.

ALLEGRINI

Amarone della Valpolicella Classico Superiore 1990: Tasting more like a young, Northern Rhône wine, this Italian red has barely evolved from its intense, young fruit stage. Packed with fresh raspberry, blackberry, cassis, and a butterscotch note, this Amarone will only gain complexity with time. Long finish, with ripe tannins. 5,416 cases made. • $31 • (06/15/97) • **94**
La Poja 1992: Rich and soft, yet full-bodied, this has hints of sweet vanilla and butterscotch along with intense cherry and chocolate notes and a dry, firm finish. Unique and appealing. 100 percent Corvina Veronese. Drink now through 2002. 833 cases made. • $22 • (06/30/98) • **88**
La Poja 1991: The very high-toned, almost floral aromas of this red suggest botrytis or dried fruit. It's thick and concentrated, with kirsch and chocolate flavors, lively acidity and medium tannins. A style that will appeal to fans of Amarone. • $25 • (06/15/97) • **86**
La Poja 1986 • $55 • (09/15/92) • **86**
Recioto della Valpolicella Amarone 1985 • $28 • (09/15/92) • **84**
Recioto della Valpolicella Classico Superiore Amarone 1991: Lean and compact, showing plum and fruitcake character and a tobacco note that turns dry and tannic on the finish. Tasted twice, with consistent notes. Drink now through 2002. 6,500 cases made. • $35 • (07/31/98) • **83**
Recioto della Valpolicella Classico Amarone Superiore 1980 • $13 • (12/31/87) • **85**
Valpolicella Classico 1996: A definite earthy note pervades the chocolate and cherry flavors in this smooth, light- to medium-bodied red. Cleansing finish. Tasted twice, with consistent notes. Drink now. 10,000 cases made. • $10 • (07/31/98) • **84**
Valpolicella Classico 1995: Banana aromas and some berry and cherry flavors are the hallmarks of this light, quaffable red. • $10 • (06/15/97) • **79**
Valpolicella Classico 1991 • $11 • (09/15/92) • **78**
Valpolicella Classico 1990 • $11 • (09/15/92) • **82**
Valpolicella Classico La Grola 1993: There's weight and concentration to this meaty red, and the chocolate and bitter cherry flavors suggests the *ripasso* method. The finish is rich and lingering. • $16 • (06/15/97) • **85**
Valpolicella Classico La Grola 1988 • $18 • (09/15/92) • **82**
Valpolicella Classico Superiore La Grola 1994: Not your ordinary Valpolicella. Expressive aromas of cherries and dried herbs take on a mushroom edge on the palate. Glycerinlike texture, medium-to-full body and some tannins on the long finish that need time to resolve. Drink now through 2003. 4,167 cases made. • $17 • (06/15/98) • **87**
Valpolicella Classico Superiore La Grola 1990 • $16 • (12/15/95) • **88**
Valpolicella Classico Superiore Palazzo della Torre 1990 • $13 • (12/15/95) • **84**
Valpolicella Classico Superiore Palazzo della Torre 1988 • $16 • (09/15/92) • **78**
Valpolicella Classico Superiore Palazzo della Torre 1986 • $16 • (09/15/92) • **85**
Valpolicella Classico Superiore Palazzo della Torre 1983 • $7 • (12/31/87) • **78**
Valpolicella Classico Superiore Palazzo della Torre Ripasso 1994: Huge color, still purple and opaque. Fresh, with cherry and chocolate nuances; elegant, with a crisp finish. Youthful, but not very expressive at this stage. May ultimately rate higher. Best from 1999 through 2004. 4,167 cases made. • $15 • (06/15/98) • **86**

ALMONDO, GIOVANNI

Roero Arneis Burigot 1993 • $14 • (02/28/95) • **84**

ALTARE, ELIO

Barbera d'Alba 1991 • $15 • (11/15/93) • **82**
Barbera d'Alba 1989 • $13 • (03/15/91) • **91**
Barbera d'Alba 1988 • $10 • (03/31/90) • **84**
Barbera d'Alba 1987 • $12 • (08/31/89) • **92**
Barolo 1992: A well-made wine. Has classic rose petal aromas backed by concentrated fruit flavors, firm texture and a lingering finish. Enough richness to age through 2000 or so. • $41 • (10/31/96) • **88**
Barolo 1991 • $30 • (10/31/95) • **85**
Barolo 1990 • $40 • (10/31/94) • **81**
Barolo 1988 • $32 • (10/31/93) • **85**
Barolo 1985 • $24 • (01/31/90) • **92**
Barolo 1982 • $13 • (06/30/87) • **88**
Barolo Vigneto Arborina 1990 • $45 • (10/31/94) • **93**
Barolo Vigneto Arborina 1989 • $45 • (10/31/93) • **85**
Barolo Vigneto Arborina 1988 • $42 • (10/31/93) • **88**
Barolo Vigneto Arborina 1982 • $15 • (09/15/87) • **87**
Cabernet Sauvignon Piedmont La Villa 1992 • $NA • (10/31/94) • **89**
Dolcetto d'Alba 1989 • $12 • (07/15/91) • **81**
Dolcetto d'Alba 1988 • $10 • (03/31/90) • **82**
Dolcetto d'Alba 1987 • $9 • (02/28/89) • **90**
Nebbiolo Piedmont Vigna Arborina 1987 • $32 • (09/15/90) • **84**
Nebbiolo Piedmont Vigna Arborina 1986 • $20 • (02/28/89) • **90**
Nebbiolo Piedmont Vigna Larigi 1987 • $28 • (05/31/90) • **89**
Nebbiolo delle Langhe 1989 • $12 • (07/15/91) • **85**
Nebbiolo delle Langhe 1988 • $10 • (03/31/90) • **81**
Nebbiolo delle Langhe 1987 • $9 • (07/31/89) • **85**
Vigna Arborina 1992 • $40 • (10/31/94) • **85**
Vigna Larigi 1992 • $40 • (10/31/94) • **91**

ALTESINO

Alte d'Altesi 1993: Slightly one-dimensional now, but there are loads of cherry, berry and jammy aromas and flavors in this wine. Medium-bodied, with a chewy texture. Drink now. Sangiovese and Cabernet Sauvignon. • $18 • (10/31/96) • **87**
Alte d'Altesi 1990 • $34 • (10/31/93) • **86**
Alte d'Altesi 1988 • $35 • (09/15/91) • **92**
Alte d'Altesi 1987 • $35 • (01/31/92) • **69**
Alte d'Altesi 1986 • $32 • (07/15/89) • **85**
Borgo d'Altesi 1993: Terrific aromas of chocolate, cassis and berries which follow through on the palate. Medium-bodied, with fine tannins and a light finish. Drink now. Cabernet Sauvignon. • $NA • (10/31/96) • **88**
Brunello di Montalcino 1992: A bit austere, but there's still some good fruit with berry, mineral character. Medium body, chunky tannins and moderate finish. Try now. 4,100 cases made. • $42 • (09/30/97) • **84**
Brunello di Montalcino 1991: Altesino excels in yet another vintage. This is a rich wine with flavors of cherry and berry, and a hint of cigar box. Medium- to full-bodied, with firm tannins and a long fresh finish. Try in 1999. 3,333 cases made. • $40 • (11/30/96) • **89**
Brunello di Montalcino 1990: Very perfumed tobacco and violet aromas. Medium body, adding fine tannins and a long, tobacco and cherry finish. Drink now. • $45 • (10/31/95) • **87**
Brunello di Montalcino 1988 • $28 • (04/30/94) • **91**
Brunello di Montalcino 1982 • $22 • (09/15/86) • **85**
Brunello di Montalcino 1981 • $22 • (09/15/86) • **80**
Brunello di Montalcino 1980 • $18 • (09/15/86) • **91**
Brunello di Montalcino 1979 • $20 • (09/15/86) • **82**
Brunello di Montalcino Montosoli 1990: One of "the" greatest Brunellos ever made. Very muscular with loads of polished tannins and fruit. Full-bodied and powerful, boasting gravel, mineral and berry character. Needs time; try after 2000. • $60 • (10/31/95) • **98**
Brunello di Montalcino Montosoli 1988 • $37 • (04/30/94) • **92**
Brunello di Montalcino Riserva 1990: Big and alcoholic. A full-bodied wine, with a mouthful of minty, spicy character and a long, fruity finish. Soft tannins. Slightly overdone. Drinkable now. 1,666 cases made. • $63 • (11/30/96) • **89**
Brunello di Montalcino Riserva 1988 • $50 • (10/31/94) • **90**
Brunello di Montalcino Riserva 1983 • $29 • (11/30/89) • **86**
Brunello di Montalcino Vigna Altesino 1985 • $32 • (09/30/90) • **91**
Brunello di Montalcino Vigna Altesino 1983 • $26 • (01/31/90) • **84**
Palazzo Altesi 1994: There's some raisiny-accented berry character to this medium-bodied, Burgundy-style red. Has light tannins and a short finish. Made from Sangiovese Grosso. • $18 • (10/31/96) • **80**
Palazzo Altesi 1993: Refreshing berry, plum and cherry aromas follow through on the palate. Medium-bodied, with slightly dry tannins but a fruity finish. Needs time to come together. Drink now. Sangiovese. • $18 • (10/31/96) • **87**
Palazzo Altesi 1990 • $26 • (10/31/93) • **89**
Palazzo Altesi 1988 • $26 • (09/15/91) • **90**
Palazzo Altesi 1987 • $25 • (01/31/92) • **78**
Palazzo Altesi 1985 • $23 • (10/31/90) • **82**
Palazzo Altesi 1983 • $17 • (02/15/88) • **88**
Rosso di Altesino 1989 • $8 • (01/31/92) BB • **86**
Rosso di Montalcino 1993 • $17 • (10/31/95) • **80**
Rosso di Montalcino 1992 • $15 • (04/30/94) • **81**
Rosso di Montalcino 1991 • $15 • (04/30/94) • **84**
Rosso di Montalcino 1988 • $15 • (07/15/91) • **73**
Rosso di Montalcino 1986 • $10 • (07/15/89) • **80**

AMA, CASTELLO DI

Chardonnay Toscana 1995: Delicious. Delivers almond and apple flavors with a hint of piecrust, and is of medium body with moderate acidity and a spicy finish. 2,900 cases made. • $18 • (09/30/97) • **87**
Chianti Classico 1995: Good, straightforward Chianti with plum and berry aromas and flavors. Medium body, with light tannins and a crisp finish. Easy to drink. 12,000 cases made. • $14 • (09/30/97) • **82**
Chianti Classico 1993 • $15 • (10/31/95) • **78**
Chianti Classico 1992 • $15 • (02/28/95) • **85**
Chianti Classico 1990 • $16 • (09/15/92) • **81**
Chianti Classico 1988 • $18 • (04/15/91) • **87**
Chianti Classico 1987 • $9 • (11/30/89) • **87**
Chianti Classico 1986 • $8 • (01/31/89) • **87**
Chianti Classico Bellavista 1993: Not as big as some Bellavista's but it's a refined red with blackberry and mineral aromas and flavors. Medium-bodied, with firm tannins and a silky texture. 1,900 cases made. • $40 • (09/30/97) • **87**
Chianti Classico Bellavista Riserva 1994: A fab Bellavista from Ama. Full-bodied and very, very long, it shows wonderful chocolate, berry and tobacco character and a fine backbone of tannins. Better after 2000. • $40 • (09/30/97) • **91**
Chianti Classico Bellavista Riserva 1993: A very good wine but perhaps not up to the normal excellence of this estate. Delivers good berry and earthy character, is full-bodied and tannic, but slightly high in acidity and austere at the finish. Drink now. • $40 • (09/30/97) • **87**
Chianti Classico Bellavista Riserva 1992 • $25 • (10/31/95) • **82**
Chianti Classico Bellavista Riserva 1991 • $25 • (02/28/95) • **87**
Chianti Classico Bellavista Riserva 1990: Greatest Chianti ever made. Inky in color, thick and powerful, emitting intense aromas of mineral, berry, and fruit. Full-bodied, with a huge backbone of tannin and a long, long finish. Better after 2000. • $NA • (09/30/97) • **95**
Chianti Classico Bellavista Riserva 1988: Breathtaking. This is a major league red. Full-bodied with velvety tannins and an outrageous character of crushed flowers and fruits. Drinkable now. • $NA • (09/30/97) • **94**
Chianti Classico Bellavista Riserva 1986 • $36 • (11/30/89) • **90**
Chianti Classico Bellavista Riserva 1985: Who says Chianti can't improve with age? This offers complex aromas and flavors of blackberries, cherries, violets and earth. Medium- to full-bodied, with firm tannins, fresh acidity and a long, long finish. Super wine. Drinkable now. • $NA • (09/30/97) • **92**
Chianti Classico Bellavista Riserva 1983 • $25 • (12/15/87) • **90**
Chianti Classico Bertinga 1990 • $34 • (02/28/95) HR • **93**
Chianti Classico Bertinga 1988 • $34 • (09/15/92) • **89**
Chianti Classico La Casuccia 1993: Aromatic, with a generous chocolate, chestnut and fruit character. Medium-bodied, with silky tannins and a light finish. Drink now. 1,900 cases made. • $40 • (09/30/97) • **86**
Chianti Classico La Casuccia 1992 • $25 • (10/31/95) • **82**
Chianti Classico La Casuccia 1991 • $25 • (02/28/95) • **86**
Chianti Classico La Casuccia 1990 • $38 • (02/28/95) • **93**
Chianti Classico La Casuccia 1986 • $40 • (11/30/89) • **87**
Chianti Classico La Casuccia 1985 • $40 • (09/15/91) • **89**
Chianti Classico San Lorenzo 1990 • $34 • (02/28/95) • **90**
Chianti Classico San Lorenzo 1988 • $34 • (09/15/92) HR • **91**
Chianti Classico San Lorenzo 1986 • $36 • (11/30/89) • **84**
Chianti Classico San Lorenzo 1985 • $32 • (11/30/89) • **86**
Vigna Il Chiuso 1993: Has some Burgundy character but it's slightly raisiny and cheesy. Medium-bodied, with medium tannins and a dry finish. Drinkable now. 1,000 cases made. • $28 • (09/30/97) • **81**
Vigna Il Chiuso 1992 • $25 • (10/31/95) • **73**
Vigna Il Chiuso 1991 • $25 • (02/28/95) • **88**
Vigna Il Chiuso 1990 • $34 • (10/31/93) • **85**
Vigna Il Chiuso 1988 • $25 • (09/15/91) • **90**
Vigna l'Apparita 1993: Powerful and exotic, this is the wine of the year from Tuscany. An outstanding Merlot displaying masses of currant and berry, hints of spice, it's full-bodied, with loads of velvety tannins and a long, long finish. Gives Château Pétrus a run for its money. Better after 2000. 1,000 cases made. • $100 • (09/30/97) HR • **96**
Vigna l'Apparita 1992 • $60 • (10/31/95) • **88**
Vigna l'Apparita 1991 • $60 • (02/28/95) • **92**
Vigna l'Apparita 1990 • $40 • (10/31/93) HR • **92**
Vigna l'Apparita 1988 • $NA • (09/15/91) • **93**
Vigna l'Apparita 1986 • $NA • (11/30/89) • **87**
Vigna l'Apparita 1985 • $NA • (11/30/89) • **92**

AMBRA

Barco Reale 1985 • $7 • (04/15/88) • **76**
Carmignano 1986 • $13 • (05/15/89) • **80**
Carmignano 1985 • $11 • (04/15/88) • **83**
Carmignano 1984 • $8 • (12/31/87) • **79**
Carmignano 1983 • $9 • (07/16/86) BB • **88**

AMBROSINI, LORELLA

Riflesso Antico 1994: Seriously oaky but seriously concentrated. A full-blown, full-bodied effort that's held back only by the overwhelming wood character. 100 percent Montepulciano d'Abruzzo and aged in *barrique*. Drink now. 170 cases made. • $29 • (04/30/98) • **84**
Val di Cornia Subertum 1994: Maturing quickly, its leathery, nutty aromas and smooth texture are still somewhat appealing. Drink now. A blend of 70 percent Sangiovese and 30 percent Merlot. 100 cases made. • $25 • (04/30/98) • **78**
Val di Cornia Tabaro 1995: Light and rather lean, with a crisp texture and fresh cherry and spice flavors. Refreshing, slightly tannic. A blend of 80 percent Sangiovese, 15 percent Ciliegolo and 5 percent Canaiolo. Drink now. 600 cases made. • $12 • (04/30/98) • **82**

AMERINI, CANTINA COLLI

Chardonnay Umbria Rocca Nerina 1995: Quite oniony-tasting, with some citrus flavors and an herbal, off-putting finish. • $19 • (06/15/98) • **74**
Sangiovese Umbria Torraccio 1995: A firm-textured, tannic red, with generous fruit flavors. The broad cherry and smoke flavors turn a bit tough on the finish. Drink now through 2000. • $25 • (06/15/98) • **84**

ANGELINI

Merlot Montello e Colli Asolani 1995: A resinous, slightly green note detracts from modest cherry flavors. Dry, nutty finish. • $9 • (05/31/98) • **76**
Pinot Grigio Veneto 1996: Smells just like those banana-marshmallow candies we ate as kids. Though pleasant, it seems concocted. • $9 • (05/31/98) • **78**
Syrah Toscana 1993: Deeply colored, with intense blackberry and violet aromas. Medium- to full-bodied, with fruity, gamy flavors, velvety tannins and a long, succulent, supple finish. An impressive wine from a newcomer to Syrah. Drinkable now. • $NA • (09/30/97) • **90**

ANGELO, DARIO D'

Montepulciano d'Abruzzo 1996: Light but flavorful, with herbal, jammy aromas and an almost effervescent texture. Not tannic. Drink now. 80,000 cases made. • $6 • (06/15/98) • **82**
Montepulciano d'Abruzzo 1993 • $4 • (03/31/95) • **82**

ANSELMI, ROBERTO

Cabernet Sauvignon Veneto Realda 1989 • $28 • (12/15/92) • **84**
Cabernet Sauvignon Veneto Realda 1988 • $28 • (09/15/92) • **78**
Recioto dei Capitelli 1988 • $34 • (09/15/92) CS • **95**
Recioto della Valpolicella 1985 • $19 • (06/30/91) • **86**
Recioto di Soave I Capitelli 1992 • $35 • (04/30/96) • **90**
Recioto di Soave I Capitelli 1989 • $35 • (09/15/92) HR • **94**
Soave Classico San Vincenzo 1993 • $9 • (05/31/95) BB • **86**
Soave Classico Superiore Capitel Croce 1994: Amazing. Mature flavors border on clove and orange peel, with a smoky note. Concentrated, with a rich texture, balancing acidity and a satisfying finish, all integrated with the new oak. Demonstrates what low yields and serious winemaking can do in a humble appellation. Drink now. • $15 • (04/30/98) • **88**
Soave Classico Superiore San Vincenzo 1996: Refreshing, beginning with white peach flavor and ending with a characteristic bitter-almond note, all on a light, balanced frame. Drink now. • $10 • (04/30/98) • **84**
Soave Classico Superiore San Vincenzo 1994 • $9 • (04/30/96) • **84**

Key: SS—Spectator Selection CS—Cellar Selection HR—Highly Recommended BB—Best Buy $NA—Price not available Ⓐ—Auction Price (BT)—Barrel Tasting
Dates in parentheses indicate the issues in which the ratings were published.

ANTARIO

Barolo Vigneto Castelletto 1993: Old-fashioned, rustic and stripped of fruit, with dry, astringent tannins. Already brown. Disappointing. 2,500 cases made. • $27 • (01/31/98) • **70**

Gavi Tenuta La Marchesa 1996: Clean, fresh citrus and melon flavors and lively acidity make this appetizing. Should complement a wide variety of foods. 1,000 cases made. • $15 • (08/31/97) • **85**

Pinot Grigio delle Venezie 1996: A clean but modestly flavored Pinot Grigio, refreshing but simple. 1,000 cases made. • $10 • (08/31/97) • **77**

ANTINORI

Bolgheri Guado al Tasso Tenuta Belvedere Red 1994: Slightly funky with barnyard aromas and flavors and hints of unripe fruit. Medium-bodied, with velvety tannins and a slightly dry finish. Tasted twice, with consistent notes. Drinkable now. • $42 • (09/30/97) • **81**

Bolgheri Rosato Scalabrone Tenuta Belvedere 1996: Juicy rosé with delicious strawberry aromas and flavors, medium-to-light body and a crisp finish. • $NA • (09/30/97) • **83**

Bolgheri Vermentino Tenuta Belvedere 1996: A stylish white, emitting aromas of apples, volcanic ash and cream. Of medium body, with a creamy texture and an attractive applelike aftertaste. • $NA • (09/30/97) • **85**

Borro della Sala 1993 • $13 • (10/31/94) • **77**

Cervaro della Sala 1995: The spice of new oak adds appeal to this rich-textured, herb-flavored wine, but it could be more harmonious. • $28 • (05/31/97) • **84**

Cervaro della Sala 1993: Oak dominates flavors of toast, butterscotch and vanilla, but there's enough sweet melon to keep it honest. A heavy wine that needs food. • $22 • (08/31/96) • **84**

Chardonnay Castello della Sala 1994 • $8 • (01/01/96) • **86**

Chardonnay Umbria Castello della Sala 1996: A wine with character. Shows almond, apple and volcanic ash aromas, and is medium-bodied with moderate acidity and a flavorful finish. Clean and interesting Chardonnay. • $12 • (10/15/97) • **85**

Chardonnay Umbria Castello della Sala 1995: Has some rough edges, but comes through with pear, lemon and apple flavors. Balanced, though it lacks depth. • $9 • (01/31/97) • **80**

Chianti Classico 1988 • $11 • (09/15/91) • **86**

Chianti Classico Badia a Passignano 1995: Chunky, with a generous cherry character. Of medium body, with light-to-medium tannins and a fruity finish. Drinkable now. • $13 • (09/30/97) • **86**

Chianti Classico Badia a Passignano 1994: A straightforward Chianti, this has cherry and berry aromas and flavors, a medium body and a slightly short finish. • $11 • (10/31/96) • **81**

Chianti Classico Badia a Passignano 1993 • $9 • (02/28/95) • **83**

Chianti Classico Badia a Passignano 1991 • $9 • (10/31/93) • **84**

Chianti Classico Badia a Passignano 1990 • $NA • (10/31/93) • **92**

Chianti Classico Badia a Passignano Riserva 1994: A lovely, velvety Chianti with soft texture and plenty of tobacco, cherry and berry character. Long finish. • $30 • (09/30/97) • **88**

Chianti Classico Badia a Passignano Riserva 1993: Subtle, and extremely well made. A wine with plenty of blackberry and dried cherry nuances, along with a hint of licorice. It's medium-bodied with fine tannins and a flavorful finish. Drinkable now. • $28 • (10/31/96) • **87**

Chianti Classico Badia a Passignano Riserva 1991 • $30 • (10/31/95) • **89**

Chianti Classico Badia a Passignano Riserva 1990 • $30 • (02/28/95) • **89**

Chianti Classico Badia a Passignano Riserva 1988 • $30 • (04/30/94) • **88**

Chianti Classico Peppoli 1995: Delivers berry, citrus and pepper character. Medium-bodied, with light tannins and a fresh finish. Drink now. • $19 • (09/30/97) • **82**

Chianti Classico Peppoli 1994: Slightly coarse, this is medium-bodied with light tannins and a dried berry and almost raisiny character. Finish is crisp. Drink now. • $18 • (10/31/96) • **84**

Chianti Classico Peppoli 1993 • $16 • (10/31/95) • **82**

Chianti Classico Peppoli 1991 • $NA • (10/31/93) • **82**

Chianti Classico Peppoli 1990 • $16 • (02/28/95) • **84**

Chianti Classico Peppoli 1988 • $19 • (09/15/91) • **88**

Chianti Classico Peppoli 1987 • $17 • (05/15/90) • **83**

Chianti Classico Peppoli 1986 • $17 • (07/15/89) • **90**

Chianti Classico Peppoli 1985 • $16 • (05/31/88) • **92**

Chianti Classico Riserva 1985 • $9 • (10/15/89) • **89**

Chianti Classico Riserva 1982 • $9 • (09/15/87) • **87**

Chianti Classico Tenute Marchese Antinori Riserva 1994: Harmonious. Has pretty aromas of dried cherries and mushrooms. Medium-bodied, with well-integrated tannins and a silky finish. • $33 • (09/30/97) • **87**

Chianti Classico Tenute Marchese Antinori Riserva 1993: A lovely, balanced wine with cherry and green tobacco aromas and flavors. Medium-bodied, with medium tannins and a sweet, ripe fruit aftertaste. Drink or hold. • $NA • (09/30/97) • **87**

Chianti Classico Tenute Marchese Antinori Riserva 1991 • $22 • (10/31/95) • **87**

Chianti Classico Tenute Marchese Antinori Riserva 1990 • $22 • (02/28/95) • **85**

Chianti Classico Tenute Marchese Antinori Riserva 1989 • $22 • (10/31/93) • **82**

Chianti Classico Tenute Marchese Antinori Riserva 1988: At its peak now. Offers attractive aromas and flavors of flowers, chestnuts and fruit, a medium body and a soft finish. Drink now. • $NA • (09/30/97) • **86**

Chianti Classico Tenute Marchese Antinori Riserva 1987 • $22 • (09/15/92) • **85**

Chianti Classico Tenute Marchese Antinori Riserva 1985: A delicious, balanced Chianti with loads of mushroom, berry and dried herb aromas and flavors. Medium-bodied, with medium, firm tannins and a succulent finish. Enjoy now. • $NA • (09/30/97) • **89**

Chianti Classico Tenute Marchese Antinori Riserva 1983 • $16 • (11/30/89) • **90**

Chianti Classico Tenute Marchese Antinori Riserva 1982 • $16 • (05/31/89) • **90**

Chianti Classico Tenute Marchese Antinori Riserva 1980 • $16 • (09/15/87) • **90**

Chianti Classico Villa Antinori Riserva 1994: Intriguing aromas of mushrooms, berry and earth. Medium body, with firm tannins, some new wood notes and a silky finish. Drink or hold. • $16 • (09/30/97) • **86**

Chianti Classico Villa Antinori Riserva 1993: Shows some pleasant berry and earth aromas and flavors, but the finish is on the light and dry side. A disappointment from this producer. • $13 • (10/31/96) • **80**

Chianti Classico Villa Antinori Riserva 1990 • $12 • (07/31/95) • **82**

Chianti Classico Villa Antinori Riserva 1989 • $12 • (01/01/94) • **82**

Chianti Classico Villa Antinori Riserva 1988 • $11 • (10/31/93) • **84**

Chianti Classico Villa Antinori Riserva 1987 • $11 • (11/30/91) • **82**

Chianti Classico Villa Antinori Riserva 1983 • $9 • (03/31/89) • **79**

Galestro Capsula Viola 1995: Very tart tasting, with grapefruit and lemon flavors and a biting finish. • $8 • (01/31/97) • **76**

Guado al Tasso 1993: Piero Antinori's answer to Ornellaia and Sassicaia. Pretty and delicious in this vintage. Plenty of crushed berry and dried herb aromas and flavors. Medium-bodied, with fine tannins. Drink now. • $68 • (10/31/96) • **87**

Guado al Tasso Tenuta Belvedere 1992 • $NA • (10/31/95) • **86**

Guado al Tasso Tenuta Belvedere 1990 • $NA • (02/28/95) • **89**

Muffato della Sala Umbria 1994: Smells like Sauternes with its peach, cream and lemon aromas. Medium-bodied and moderately sweet, with a lovely, intense, spicy, honeyed finish. Good, fresh acidity. Drink now. • $22/375ml • (10/15/97) • **88**

Orvieto Classico Campogrande 1996: A fresh, lively, thirst-quenching white. It's lean and crisp, with light citrus flavors. • $9 • (10/15/97) • **83**

Orvieto Classico Campogrande 1993 • $8 • (10/31/94) • **82**

Pinot Nero Umbria Consola 1990 • $NA • (10/31/93) • **84**

Pinot Noir Umbria Castello della Sala 1994: Good berry and cherry character with a hint of leather. Not bad for a Pinot Noir from Italy. Light-bodied, with light tannis and a silky finish. Drink now. • $NA • (10/15/97) • **83**

Rosso di Montepulciano Fattoria la Braccesca 1996: Straightforward and fruity with a pretty berry character and a soft texture. Drink now. • $NA • (09/30/97) • **85**

Rosso di Montepulciano La Braccesca 1993 • $11 • (10/31/95) • **80**

Santa Cristina 1995: Plenty of lovely berry and watermelon aromas and flavors in this Sangiovese-based wine. Medium- to light-bodied, light tannins, crisp finish. • $8 • (10/31/96) • **81**

Santa Cristina 1993 • $7 • (02/28/95) • **84**

Santa Cristina 1992 • $7 • (07/31/94) • **83**

Santa Cristina 1991 • $7 • (06/30/93) BB • **84**

Santa Cristina 1990 • $7 • (12/15/92) • **79**

Santa Cristina 1989 • $7 • (07/15/91) • **80**

Santa Cristina 1988 • $6 • (01/31/91) BB • **85**

Santa Cristina 1987 • $6 • (04/30/89) BB • **81**

Santa Cristina 1985 • $6 • (10/31/88) BB • **90**

Sauvignon Blanc Umbria Castello della Sala 1996: Fresh and fruity with lots of lemon and hints of celery and grass. Medium-bodied, with a refreshing, tart finish. • $11 • (10/15/97) • **83**

Sauvignon Blanc Umbria Castello della Sala 1995: Fresh and lively, with herbal and grassy flavors. Verges on being coarse, but it gets your attention. Finishes with an onionlike note. Good, though not for everyone. • $9 • (01/31/97) • **82**

Solaia 1994: A super red wine from a top Tuscan producer. Displaying inky color, intense aromas of blackberries, mint and currants, this vino da tavola is full-bodied, with full yet silky tannins and a long, long, fruity finish. Better after 1999. 800 cases made. • $69 Ⓐ • (09/30/97) CS • **93**

Solaia 1993: Could use a little more concentration for Solaia but very good nonetheless. Vivid blackberry flavors with raspberry undertones. Medium-bodied, with fine tannins and a fruity, delicate finish. Drink now. • $67 • (10/31/96) • **86**

Solaia 1991 • $60 Ⓐ • (10/31/95) CS • **90**

Solaia 1990 • $151 Ⓐ • (02/28/95) CS • **97**

Solaia 1989 • $134 Ⓐ • (11/15/93) • **88**

Solaia 1988 • $163 Ⓐ • (11/15/93) • **97**

Solaia 1987 • $60 Ⓐ • (11/15/93) • **88**

Solaia 1986 • $114 Ⓐ • (11/15/93) • **90**

Solaia 1985 • $240 • (11/15/93) • **94**

Solaia 1982 • $158 • (11/15/93) • **91**

Tignanello 1994: Delicious Tignanello. Rich aromas of chocolate, berry and tobacco. Medium- to full-bodied, with medium, firm tannins and a long succulent finish. Better after this year. • $42 Ⓐ • (09/30/97) • **89**

Tignanello 1993: Pretty ripe berry and cherry aromas and flavors with a wood note. Medium-bodied, with fine tannins and a silky finish. About the same quality as the '91 Tignanello. Drink now. • $42 • (10/31/96) • **86**

Tignanello 1991 • $64 Ⓐ • (10/31/95) • **86**

Tignanello 1990 • $139 Ⓐ • (02/28/95) CS • **92**

Tignanello 1989 • $33 • (10/31/93) • **87**

Tignanello 1988 • $144 Ⓐ • (11/15/93) • **95**

Tignanello 1987 • $42 Ⓐ • (11/15/93) • **87**

Tignanello 1986 • $86 Ⓐ • (11/15/93) • **87**

Tignanello 1985 • $144 Ⓐ • (11/15/93) • **88**

Tignanello 1983 • $61 Ⓐ • (11/15/93) • **88**

Tignanello 1982 • $115 Ⓐ • (07/15/87) CS • **91**

Toscana White 1996: A basic, slightly rough white, with aggressive earth and herbal flavors and an astringent texture. A blend of Trebbiano, Malvasia and Chardonnay. • $9 • (10/31/97) • **78**

Villa Antinori 1993 • $8 • (10/31/94) • **82**

Vino Nobile di Montepulciano La Braccesca 1994: Shows deep color, aromas of plum and dried cherry. Medium-bodied and tannic, with good fruit, but it's slightly diluted and austere on the finish. • $NA • (09/30/97) • **81**

Vino Nobile di Montepulciano La Braccesca 1993: Clever winemaking here. Plenty of new wood in this medium-bodied offering, along with silky tannins and a fresh fruit and vanilla aftertaste. • $NA • (10/31/96) • **85**

Vino Nobile di Montepulciano La Braccesca 1992 • $18 • (10/31/95) • **86**

ANTONIOLO

Gattinara 1988 • $18 • (10/15/94) • **83**

Gattinara Vigneto Castelle 1988 • $22 • (10/15/94) • **85**

AQUINO, GAETANO D'

Chianti Riserva 1988 • $10 • (09/15/92) • **82**

ARGIANO

Brunello di Montalcino 1992: A bit dry on the palate, with a slightly peppery character marring the sweet fruit. Tasted twice, with consistent notes. 3,300 cases made. • $35 • (09/30/97) • **75**

Brunello di Montalcino 1991: Elegant, delicious, and well made. Medium in body, with licorice, berry and cherry aromas and flavors, fresh finish. Silky tannins. 7,500 cases made. • $35 • (11/30/96) • **87**

Brunello di Montalcino 1990: Seductively round, full in body and flavorful, it bursts with floral, violet, red berry and milk chocolate notes. Excellent backbone of supple tannins. Drink now. • $35 • (10/31/95) • **90**

Brunello di Montalcino 1988 • $29 • (04/30/94) • **91**

Brunello di Montalcino 1979 • $11 • (09/15/86) • **77**

Brunello di Montalcino Riserva 1990: One of the biggest wines of this tasting, this should age for years to come. Full-bodied, with masses of fruit and tannins and flavors of berries, tobacco and cedar that go on and on. A monumental Brunello. Try after 2000. 1,500 cases made. • $52 • (11/30/96) CS • **95**

Brunello di Montalcino Riserva 1988 • $26 • (10/31/94) • **88**

Brunello di Montalcino Riserva 1985 • $42 • (12/15/92) • **88**

Rosso di Montalcino 1995: A firm and lively wine with blackberry and mineral aromas and flavors. Medium-bodied, with firm tannins and a crisp, long finish. 3,600 cases made. • $17 • (09/30/97) • **87**

Rosso di Montalcino 1994: A traditional style, with some nutty, cedary fruit flavors. Light tannins and a slightly dry finish. Old barrels? Rather disappointing for this producer. 4,166 cases made. • $17 • (11/30/96) • **79**

Rosso di Montalcino 1993 • $19 • (10/31/95) • **85**

Rosso di Montalcino 1992 • $13 • (10/31/94) • **77**

Rosso di Montalcino 1991 • $18 • (04/30/94) • **82**

Solengo 1995: A full-blown Italian red that knocks your socks off with exuberant fruit and wood. Shows wild aromas of berries, crushed raspberries and mint, with chocolate and toasty oak undertones and is soft and long, with gorgeous milk chocolate and berry flavors. Full-bodied, extremely velvety in texture. Better in 1999. • $50 • (12/31/97) HR • **94**

ARGIOLAS

Turriga 1989 • $22 • (05/31/95) • **89**

ARNALDO CAPRAI

Grechetto Grecante White 1993 • $12 • (10/31/94) • **85**

Montefalco 1991: Thick, with flavors of earth, spice and prunes. Sturdy, but lacks definition and grace. Drinkable now. 7,500 cases made. • $10 • (08/31/96) • **81**

Sagratino di Montefalco 1988: Smooth and thick, with dark flavors of chocolate, coffee and plums. Mature now, and a bit dry on the finish. It has more strength than grace; try with rich, meat dishes. 1,400 cases made. • $15 • (08/31/96) • **84**

ASCHERI, CANTINE GIACOMO

Barbaresco 1992 • $20 • (10/31/95) • **75**

Barbera d'Alba Vigna Fontanelle 1995: Impressively dark and loaded with fruit, this crisp, medium-bodied red offers lovely cherry, cassis bush, currant and citrus flavors that vibrate on the long, mouthpuckering finish. Needs food. Try now. 750 cases made. • $12 • (10/31/97) • **85**

Barolo 1993: Delicate and ripe, with lovely rose petal, plum, licorice and raspberry flavors. Medium in body, with supple tannins and smooth, silky-textured finish. Wonderful to drink now through 2000. 1,250 cases made. • $25 • (10/31/97) • **87**

Barolo Vigna Farina 1993: Nice and ripe, with a slightly herbal, green olive character atop the cassis bush and red berry notes. Medium-bodied, it's a pure, fresh, crisp Barolo that's accessible now, likely better in 1999. 625 cases made. • $35 • (10/31/97) • **88**

Barolo Vigna Farina 1992: An interesting, somewhat complex wine that's on the earthy side with good plummy flavors. Firm tannins and a rough texture detract. • $NA • (10/31/96) • **81**

Barolo Vigna Farina 1991 • $30 • (10/31/95) • **79**

Dolcetto d'Alba Vigna Nirane 1996: Delicate, pretty and well-balanced, this delivers seductive rose petal, strawberry and wild raspberry notes that are lovely. A joy to drink now. 708 cases made. • $14 • (10/31/97) • **84**

AVIGNONESI

Aleatico 1990 • $28 • (02/28/95) • **86**

Desiderio 1988 • $39 • (12/15/92) • **85**

Grifi 1994: Subtle. Enticing aromas of plums and spices waft from this medium-bodied wine. Has silky tannins and a spicy finish. 2,000 cases made. • $43 • (09/30/97) • **88**

Grifi 1993: Plenty of ripe fruit flavors with a barnyardy, earthy, spicy undertone. Medium-bodied, with fine tannins and a succulent, slightly short finish. Drinkable now. 2,500 cases made. • $45 • (10/31/96) • **87**

Grifi 1992: A slightly rustic wine, but shows some impressive, ripe Sangiovese character. Medium-bodied, with coarse tannins and a crisp finish. Drinkable now. 2,500 cases made. • $37 • (10/31/96) • **86**

Grifi 1990 • $36 • (02/28/95) CS • **91**

Grifi 1988 • $28 • (10/31/93) • **89**

Grifi 1987 • $NA • (11/15/93) • **87**

Grifi 1986 • $NA • (11/15/93) • **88**

Grifi 1985 • $NA • (11/15/93) • **90**

Grifi 1983 • $NA • (11/15/93) • **90**

Key: SS—Spectator Selection CS—Cellar Selection HR—Highly Recommended BB—Best Buy $NA—Price not available Ⓐ—Auction Price (BT)—Barrel Tasting

Dates in parentheses indicate the issues in which the ratings were published.

Grifi 1982 • $10 • (06/16/85) • **87**
Merlot 1994: A bit tough, but shows pretty dried herb, black currant and berry character. Medium-bodied, with racy tannins, a moderate finish. Drink now. 1,000 cases made. • $62 • (09/30/97) • **87**
Merlot 1993: Wonderfully aromatic with its truffle, berry, cherry and cedar nuances. Medium-bodied, with sleek and silky tannins and a fine finish. Great finesse and style in this wine. 2,500 cases made. • $32 • (10/31/96) HR • **90**
Merlot 1992: A very pretty wine with very good structure. Aromas and flavors of violet, berry and black cherry. Medium-bodied, with silky tannins. Drink now. 2,500 cases made. • $37 • (10/31/96) • **89**
Merlot 1991 • $36 • (10/31/95) • **88**
Merlot 1990 • $55 • (02/28/95) • **86**
Merlot 1989 • $36 • (10/31/93) • **82**
Merlot 1988 • $45 • (09/15/91) • **93**
Pinot Nero di Valdicapraia 1994: A simple Pinot Noir with spicy berry flavors, a light body, a silky texture. Drink now. 500 cases made. • $37 • (09/30/97) • **83**
Pinot Nero di Valdicapraia 1993: Pretty Pinot Noir with plum, earth and tea aromas and flavors. Medium-bodied, with a light, vanilla-accented finish. Drink now. 600 cases made. • $28 • (10/31/96) • **85**
Pinot Nero di Valdicapraia 1990 • $NA • (10/31/95) • **86**
Rosso 1994: A bit coarse with an earthy cherry character. Medium-bodied, with moderate tannins and slightly raised acidity on the finish. Drinkable now. • $NA • (10/31/96) • **80**
Rosso 1993 • $13 • (10/31/95) • **78**
Rosso di Montepulciano 1993 • $NA • (10/31/95) • **74**
Rosso di Montepulciano 1991 • $12 • (11/15/93) • **80**
Rosso di Montepulciano 1990 • $12 • (12/15/92) • **84**
Rosso di Montepulciano 1989 • $12 • (04/30/91) • **83**
Vin Santo 1984 • $75/375ml • (01/31/93) • **92**
Vin Santo 1977 • $18 • (10/01/85) • **92**
Vino Nobile di Montepulciano 1994: A wine with an interesting character of mushroom, chive and fruit. Medium-bodied, with soft tannins and a succulent finish. Drink now. 10,000 cases made. • $30 • (09/30/97) • **84**
Vino Nobile di Montepulciano 1993: Some good berry and leather aromas and flavors, medium body and a light finish. Drink very soon. Less than expected from this producer. Tasted twice with consistent notes. 11,000 cases made. • $25 • (10/31/96) • **80**
Vino Nobile di Montepulciano 1992 • $20 • (10/31/95) • **76**
Vino Nobile di Montepulciano 1990 • $22 • (02/29/96) • **85**
Vino Nobile di Montepulciano 1988 • $22 • (12/15/92) • **86**
Vino Nobile di Montepulciano 1985 • $12 • (02/15/88) • **86**
Vino Nobile di Montepulciano 1981 • $7 • (10/01/85) • **86**
Vino Nobile di Montepulciano 1980 • $6 • (07/01/85) • **85**
Vino Nobile di Montepulciano Riserva 1993: A lovely, fruity wine with dried cherry, floral and a hint of earth to its character. Medium body, with soft texture. 4,000 cases made. • $36 • (09/30/97) • **85**
Vino Nobile di Montepulciano Riserva Grandi Annate 1990 • $36 • (10/31/95) • **89**
Vino Nobile di Montepulciano Riserva 1988 • $24 • (11/15/93) • **87**

AZELIA

Barolo 1992: Powered by fruit flavors, this is concentrated and uncomplicated. Has a firm texture and plenty of tannins. Shows good potential for aging; try after 1999. From Luigi Savino. • $30 • (10/31/96) • **85**
Barolo 1991: Easy to like, with bright fruit and spice flavors, a smooth texture and lingering finish. Harmonious and complete. Drink now. • $NA • (10/31/96) • **85**
Barolo Bricco Fiasco 1993: Wonderful. The winemaker got lots of concentration into this one. Not too oaky, not too crisp, just the right balance. Ripe, rich and full-bodied, with marvelous red- and blackberry flavors, firm but ripe tannins and a long, deeply satisfying finish. Terrific now, better after 2000. From Luigi and Enrico Scavino. • $41 • (10/31/97) • **93**
Barolo Bricco Fiasco 1989 • $24 • (10/31/94) • **85**
Barolo Bricco Fiasco 1985 • $30 • (07/15/91) • **81**
Barolo Bricco Punta 1982 • $23 • (11/15/88) • **92**
Dolcetto d'Alba 1987 • $7 • (03/15/89) • **85**
Dolcetto d'Alba Bricco dell'Oriolo 1989 • $9 • (07/15/91) • **79**

BADIA A COLTIBUONO

Cancelli Red 1993 • $8 • (12/31/95) • **85**
Cancelli Red 1990 • $7 • (10/31/93) • **78**
Chianti Cetamura 1990 • $8 • (10/31/93) • **78**
Chianti Cetamura 1988 • $7 • (12/15/90) BB • **82**
Chianti Classico 1995: Has some berry character, with a hint of leather, but it's slightly dried out with an old-wood quality and a diluted structure. Tasted twice, with consistent notes. 10,800 cases made. • $18 • (09/30/97) • **79**
Chianti Classico 1994: A medium-bodied wine with an attractive, sweet, plum and strawberry character. Light tannins, crisp finish. Tasted twice with consistent notes. • $15 • (10/31/96) • **83**
Chianti Classico 1987 • $8 • (11/30/89) • **85**
Chianti Classico Riserva 1994: Has an attractive cherry, light earth and spice character, a medium body, fine tannins and a crisp finish. 10,000 cases made. • $20 • (09/30/97) • **85**
Chianti Classico Riserva 1993: A pretty, subtle riserva with aromas and flavors of plum and earth, a medium body and a soft finish. Drink now. • $28 • (10/31/96) • **86**
Chianti Classico Riserva 1990 • $25 • (02/28/95) • **85**
Chianti Classico Riserva 1988 • $20 • (07/31/95) • **84**
Chianti Classico Riserva 1987 • $15 • (09/15/92) • **84**
Chianti Classico Riserva 1985 • $16 • (09/15/91) • **90**
Chianti Classico Riserva 1983 • $15 • (11/30/89) • **78**
Chianti Classico Riserva 1982 • $13 • (07/31/88) • **88**
Sangioveto 1988 • $40 • (10/31/93) HR • **94**
Sangioveto 1985 • $NA • (11/30/89) • **85**
Sangioveto 1983 • $20 • (11/30/89) • **84**
Sangioveto 1982 • $21 • (09/15/88) • **83**
Sangioveto 1981 • $21 • (09/15/87) • **87**
Sangioveto di Coltibuono 1994: A wine with decadent and alluring autumnal aromas and flavors, medium body, chewy tannins and a rich finish. Drink now. • $35 • (09/30/97) • **88**
Trappoline White 1995: Plenty of toasty oak, almond and spice, with moderate acidity and a lemony, smoky finish. • $10 • (09/30/97) • **85**

BAGGIOLINO, FATTORIA

Chianti Colli Fiorentini 1994: Already past its prime, it's very light-colored with a slightly acidic, leathery character highlighting the fruit flavors. Not much to it. Tasted twice with consistent notes. • $NA • (10/31/96) • **74**
Chianti Colli Fiorentini 1993 • $NA • (02/28/95) • **72**
Chianti Colli Fiorentini 1992 • $NA • (02/28/95) • **83**
Chianti Colli Fiorentini 1990 • $NA • (10/31/93) • **86**
Chianti Colli Fiorentini Riserva 1993: In an old style, and already mature. Light-bodied with a fruity character, but it's rather dried out. Tasted twice with consistent notes. • $NA • (10/31/96) • **78**
Chianti Colli Fiorentini Riserva 1991 • $NA • (10/31/93) • **85**
Chianti Colli Fiorentini Riserva 1990 • $NA • (02/28/95) • **87**
Poggio Brandi 1993 • $NA • (10/31/95) • **85**
Poggio Brandi 1990 • $26 • (02/28/95) • **86**
Poggio Brandi 1986 • $19 • (08/31/91) • **86**
Poggio Brandi 1985 • $19 • (09/15/89) • **84**

BAGNOLI

Merlot Grave del Friuli 1996: A solid Merlot, showing cherry candy flavors and mouthwatering acidity that keeps everything fresh. Just a hint of tannin on the finish. Drink now. • $11 • (05/31/98) • **84**
Merlot Grave del Friuli 1995: Smoky, licorice flavors add complexity to cherry notes. Medium-bodied, with a hint of tannin on the finish, it's balanced and enjoyable. • $11 • (12/15/97) • **84**
Pinot Grigio Grave del Friuli 1996: Crisp and inviting, like biting into an apple. Shows accents of almond and lemon. Firm and lean, with decent length, this should accomodate light foods. Drink now. • $13 • (05/31/98) • **85**
Pinot Grigio Grave del Friuli 1995: Elegant, and delicately balanced. Plenty of apple and apricot flavors with hints of thyme and red fruits. A seductive white of depth and complexity. Well done. • $13 • (11/15/97) • **87**

BAIOCCHI, CANTINE

Vino Nobile di Montepulciano 1986 • $15 • (03/15/91) • **87**
Vino Nobile di Montepulciano Riserva 1985 • $10 • (11/30/89) • **85**

BANEAR

Cabernet Sauvignon Grave del Friuli 1995: Quite earthy, with black currant notes for support, all on a solid, burly framework that finishes with a bit of heat. Drink now. • $12 • (04/30/98) • **81**

Merlot Grave del Friuli 1995: Good, spicy fruitcake character in this light, fresh red. The acidity is lively, and it's balanced for early drinking. • $12 • (12/15/97) • **82**
Pinot Grigio Grave del Friuli 1996: A basic, almost neutral white showing a hint of apple flavor. • $12 • (11/15/97) • **75**
Sauvignon Blanc Grave del Friuli 1995: A dead ringer for a Loire Sauvignon Blanc with its stony, gooseberry and grassy aromas and flavors. Medium-bodied, showing good intensity and a hint of earth on the finish. • $12 • (11/15/97) • **85**

BANFI, CASTELLO

Belnero 1992 • $28 • (10/31/95) • **85**
Belnero 1990 • $30 • (07/31/94) • **83**
Brachetto d'Acqui 1995: Very sweet and very red in color. An exuberant, grapey, well-made sparkling wine. Try it at the end of the meal, with dessert or possibly with cheese. 1,400 cases made. • $13 • (01/31/97) • **84**
Brachetto d'Acqui 1992 • $16 • (05/15/93) • **87**
Brunello di Montalcino 1992: Good concentration for the vintage with berry and dried cherry aromas and flavors. Medium-bodied, with velvety tannins. Drink now. 25,000 cases made. • $38 • (09/30/97) • **86**
Brunello di Montalcino 1991: Rather light for this producer, this offers clean and simple berry, mineral and cherry flavors, with light tannins. Drink now. 20,000 cases made. • $NA • (11/30/96) • **84**
Brunello di Montalcino 1990: A wonderful Brunello boasting mineral, violet, berry and cherry character and a hint of new oak. Full-bodied and powerful, adding loads of tannins and a very long finish. Try in 1999. • $30 • (10/31/95) • **93**
Brunello di Montalcino 1986 • $32 • (12/31/92) CS • **91**
Brunello di Montalcino 1985 • $30 • (10/15/90) HR • **92**
Brunello di Montalcino 1982 • $28 • (12/15/87) • **89**
Brunello di Montalcino 1981 • $23 • (03/31/87) CS • **92**
Brunello di Montalcino 1980 • $20 • (09/15/86) • **90**
Brunello di Montalcino 1979 • $18 • (04/16/85) SS • **90**
Brunello di Montalcino Poggio all'Oro Riserva 1990: A gigantic wine, this delivers tons of fruit flavor and tannins, yet is superbly balanced. Full-bodied, with fully ripe tannins and a spicy, fruity aftertaste. Best wine ever from this winery. Better in 2001. 3,166 cases made. • $100 • (11/30/96) • **95**
Brunello di Montalcino Poggio all'Oro Riserva 1988 • $32 • (10/31/94) • **90**
Brunello di Montalcino Poggio all'Oro Riserva 1985 • $37 • (12/15/91) CS • **92**
Brut 1987 • $17 • (05/15/93) • **76**
Brut 1986 • $20 • (03/31/92) • **83**
Brut 1985 • $16 • (06/30/90) • **81**
Brut 1984 • $14 • (03/31/88) • **90**
Brut 1982 • $13 • (12/31/86) • **88**
Cabernet Sauvignon Tavernelle 1992 • $20 • (10/31/95) • **88**
Cabernet Sauvignon Tavernelle 1991 • $22 • (02/28/95) • **86**
Cabernet Sauvignon Tavernelle 1990 • $23 • (10/31/93) • **85**
Cabernet Sauvignon Tavernelle 1989 • $23 • (10/31/93) • **84**
Cabernet Sauvignon Tavernelle 1988 • $23 • (09/15/91) • **87**
Cabernet Sauvignon Tavernelle 1985 • $23 • (03/31/93) • **83**
Cabernet Sauvignon Tavernelle 1984 • $18 • (01/31/88) • **89**
Cabernet Sauvignon Tavernelle 1982 • $15 • (08/01/85) • **88**
Chardonnay Fontanelle 1993: This complex and distinctive Chardonnay blends toasty, spicy oak aromas with ample fruit and nutty nuances to make a concentrated, focused, nicely balanced whole. Long on the finish and thoroughly enticing. 1,200 cases made. • $17 • (02/29/96) HR • **91**
Chianti 1987 • $7 • (11/30/89) BB • **85**
Chianti Classico Riserva 1989 • $10 • (05/15/94) • **79**
Chianti Classico Riserva 1988 • $10 • (05/15/93) • **80**
Chianti Classico Riserva 1985 • $9 • (05/15/90) • **86**
Chianti Classico Riserva 1982 • $7 • (12/15/87) • **83**
Chianti Classico Riserva 1981 • $7 • (08/31/86) • **80**
Col di Sasso 1995: A pretty picnic wine with a fun, berry-cherry character and a fresh finish. Great served cold. Cabernet Sauvignon and Sangiovese. 40,000 cases made. • $7 • (10/31/96) • **83**
Col di Sasso 1994: This smooth red offers cola, chocolate and some cherry flavors, without much structure or complexity. It's polished, and drinking well now. 25,000 cases made. • $9 • (11/15/96) • **81**

Key: SS—Spectator Selection CS—Cellar Selection HR—Highly Recommended BB—Best Buy $NA—Price not available Ⓐ—Auction Price (BT)—Barrel Tasting
Dates in parentheses indicate the issues in which the ratings were published.

Colvecchio 1993: Fantastically perfumed, with floral, berry and mineral notes. Medium-bodied, with fine tannins and a light, delicate finish. Might be outstanding with a bit more concentration. Drink now. Syrah. 2,000 cases made. • $29 • (10/31/96) • **88**
Colvecchio 1992 • $25 • (02/28/95) • **78**
Colvecchio 1991 • $25 • (02/28/95) • **87**
Colvecchio 1990 • $30 • (10/31/93) • **85**
Dolcetto d'Acqui Argusto 1995: Peppery and licorice flavors bring some personality to this straightforward, light- to medium-bodied red. A bit dry on the finish. Drink slightly chilled. 1,200 cases made. • $13 • (01/31/98) • **79**
Excelsus 1993: A new wine from Banfi. Big and chewy and still not giving much on the nose or palate. Full-bodied, with chewy tannins and a hint of wild berry. Drink now. 2,000 cases made. • $45 • (09/30/97) • **90**
Fontanelle 1995: Well made. Shows subtle aromas of apple, honey and vanilla, with a hint of chalk, attractive honey and toasty oak flavors and a creamy texture. Medium-bodied. Drink now. 7,000 cases made. • $17 • (09/30/97) • **88**
Gavi Principessa Gavia 1996: Fruity and well balanced, with attractive banana and melon flavors and a lively texture. Very good quality. 5,200 cases made. • $13 • (08/31/97) • **85**
Mandrielle 1994: A serious red wine that combines smoky, chocolaty, cherrylike flavors with a firm, tannic texture and lingering finish. Having both depth and breadth, it should improve through 2000. 600 cases made. • $29 • (05/31/97) • **89**
Mandrielle 1993: A wine with plenty of berry aromas and flavors, but also a large dose of dried herbs on the nose. Medium-bodied, with fine tanins and a slightly dry finish. Drink now. Made from Merlot. 3,000 cases made. • $29 • (10/31/96) • **85**
Merlot Mandrielle 1992 • $25 • (02/28/95) • **89**
Merlot Mandrielle 1990 • $25 • (02/28/95) • **87**
Pinot Grigio-Chardonnay Toscana Le Rime 1997: Light and bright, fresh in fruit flavor, perfect for quaffing with any number of foods. Drink now. • $9 • (07/31/98) • **84**
Pinot Noir 1988 • $NA • (09/15/91) • **86**
Rosso di Montalcino 1995: Pretty plum and cherry character and a mushroomlike aftertaste. Medium body, medium firm tannins. 5,000 cases made. • $21 • (09/30/97) • **85**
Rosso di Montalcino 1992 • $9 • (10/31/94) • **80**
Rosso di Montalcino Centine 1994: A wonderful red for everyday drinking, this is fresh and clean, with a minty berry character and a light and fruity finish. Delicious now. 35,000 cases made. • $NA • (11/30/96) • **83**
Rosso di Montalcino Centine 1993 • $8 • (10/31/95) • **83**
Rosso di Montalcino Centine 1992 • $10 • (04/30/94) • **73**
Rosso di Montalcino Centine 1991 • $10 • (04/30/94) • **77**
Rosso di Montalcino Centine 1990 • $8 • (03/31/93) • **82**
Rosso di Montalcino Centine 1989 • $8 • (12/15/92) • **81**
Rosso di Montalcino Centine 1988 • $8 • (12/15/91) BB • **81**
Rosso di Montalcino Centine 1987 • $8 • (06/15/90) BB • **85**
Rosso di Montalcino Centine 1986 • $7 • (11/30/89) BB • **87**
Rosso di Montalcino Centine 1985 • $7 • (11/30/87) BB • **88**
Rosso di Montalcino Centine 1983 • $7 • (04/30/87) BB • **89**
San Angelo 1996: Smooth texture, buttery aromas and very little fruit flavor add up to a civilized but simple white wine. 23,000 cases made. • $13 • (05/31/97) • **82**
San Angelo 1995: Simple, with modest pear, peach and spice flavors. Turns slightly bitter on the finish. • $13 • (01/31/97) • **77**
San Angelo 1993 • $10 • (06/15/94) • **80**
Sant'Antimo Centine 1996: Fresh and fruity, with a good amount of strawberry and cherry flavor and a light and refreshing finish. Nice with simple foods. Try chilled. 30,000 cases made. • $9 • (09/30/97) • **82**
Summus 1994: Gorgeous to smell with its chocolate, berry and tobacco character, and just as good on the palate. Medium-bodied and very velvety, with lovely fruit flavors and a long, caressing finish. 4,000 cases made. • $40 • (09/30/97) • **90**
Summus 1993: Captivating to taste. Complex aromas and flavors of spices, dried herbs and fruit. Medium-bodied, with big tannins, yet silky and refined. Long, fruity finish. Drink now. 4,000 cases made. • $38 • (10/31/96) • **90**
Summus 1990 • $40 • (10/31/93) • **92**
Summus 1988 • $NA • (09/15/91) • **87**
Tavernelle 1994: Deep in color and flavor, rich in texture and long on the finish, this is an admirably concentrated, well-balanced red wine. Plum and raspberry, clove and vanilla notes lend complexity. Drink now through 2002. Cabernet Sauvignon. 800 cases made. • $27 • (05/31/97) • **90**

Tavernelle 1993: Very fine indeed, best Tavernelle in years. Gorgeous aromas of violets, cassis and berries with an underlying mineral note. Medium-bodied, with fine tannins and a sweet berry finish. Drink now. Cabernet Sauvignon. 3,000 cases made. • $25 • (10/31/96) • **89**

BARACCO DE BARACHO

Barolo 1988 • $26 • (06/30/93) • **77**

BARALE, FRATELLI

Barolo Castellero 1993: Distinctive and tasty, offering plum, red- and blackberry flavors. Medium-bodied, it weaves in a lovely mineral note that gives extra dimension. Fresh herbal notes on the firm but balanced finish. Try around 2000. • $NA • (10/31/97) • **87**

BARBI, FATTORIA DEI

Brigante dei Barbi 1994: Fruit, fruit, fruit. Medium-bodied, with round tannins and a fruity, dried cherry finish. Delicious. 1,850 cases made. • $40 • (09/30/97) • **87**
Brunello di Montalcino 1992: Offers a good amount of fruity, raisiny character and velvety tannins. Medium-bodied, with medium tannins and finish. Drink now. 8,300 cases made. • $35 • (09/30/97) • **86**
Brunello di Montalcino 1990: Wonderfully fresh and finely structured plum, violet and berry character. Full-bodied and silky and a crisp, refreshing finish. Drink now. • $26 • (10/31/95) • **88**
Brunello di Montalcino 1988 • $30 • (04/30/94) • **81**
Brunello di Montalcino 1981 • $20 • (09/15/86) • **85**
Brunello di Montalcino Blue Label 1986 • $28 • (08/31/91) • **84**
Brunello di Montalcino Blue Label 1981 • $20 • (01/31/91) • **81**
Brunello di Montalcino Riserva 1991: Concentrated and powerful, but slightly overdone. Full-bodied and tannic with a slightly raisiny character and a dry finish. Try after 2000? 2,750 cases made. • $49 • (09/30/97) • **87**
Brunello di Montalcino Riserva 1990: Barbi is in an ever improving mode. This is an intensely plummy wine, with fine tannins and acidity. Built for aging, it's full-bodied, yet compacted and solidly structured, with a silky texture. Drinkable now. 2,250 cases made. • $49 • (11/30/96) • **91**
Brunello di Montalcino Riserva 1988 • $35 • (10/31/94) • **85**
Brunello di Montalcino Riserva 1985 • $46 • (11/30/91) • **87**
Brunello di Montalcino Riserva 1977 • $20 • (09/15/86) • **86**
Brunello di Montalcino Vigna del Fiore Riserva 1991: Gives more on the nose than on the palate with its interesting aromas of bark and berries. Medium-bodied, with chewy tannins, moderate fruit and a slightly austere finish. Drink now. 1,100 cases made. • $65 • (09/30/97) • **85**
Brunello di Montalcino Vigna del Fiore Riserva 1990: A big mouthful here. This is full-bodied, with masses of velvety tannins and it's oozing with cherry, berry and tobacco flavors. Drink now. 2,250 cases made. • $68 • (11/30/96) • **91**
Brunello di Montalcino Vigna del Fiore Riserva 1988 • $48 • (10/31/94) • **90**
Brusco dei Barbi 1996: Very grapey and fruity on the nose, this vino da tavola is medium-bodied, with light tannins and a finish showing lots of sweet fruit, especially berries. A delicious red with a track record for yumminess, it's a real value at this price. Drink now or hold. 8,300 cases made. 8,300 cases made. • $10 • (09/30/97) BB • **87**
Brusco dei Barbi 1994: Bubbling with delicious, red fruit flavors, especially fresh raspberries, cherries and blackberries. Medium-bodied with soft tannins. Delicious now. 6,000 cases made. • $12 • (10/31/96) • **88**
Brusco dei Barbi 1992 • $10 • (02/28/95) • **83**
Brusco dei Barbi 1988 • $12 • (09/15/91) • **86**
Brusco dei Barbi 1986 • $9 • (04/30/89) • **79**
Brusco dei Barbi 1985 • $9 • (10/15/88) • **85**
Bruscone dei Barbi 1993: Oozing with berry, blackberry and cherry aromas. Medium- to full-bodied, with silky tannins and a long finish. Drink or hold. • $NA • (10/31/96) • **87**
Bruscone dei Barbi 1990 • $12 • (10/31/93) • **87**
Bruscone dei Barbi 1988 • $27 • (09/15/91) • **84**
Chianti Il Colle 1995: Attractive plum, raspberry and cherry aromas and flavors. Medium-bodied, with soft and ripe tannins and a long crisp finish. Already delicious, but will improve with age. • $NA • (10/31/96) • **85**
Rosso di Montalcino 1995: A solid Rosso with dried cherry and dried herb aromas and flavors. Medium-bodied, with firm tannins and a medium finish. Drink or hold. 3,800 cases made. • $15 • (09/30/97) • **85**
Rosso di Montalcino 1994: Delicious, long and fresh. Medium-bodied, with loads of berry and dried herb character and silky tannins. As always, a top Rosso from Barbi. 10,000 cases made. • $12 • (11/30/96) • **86**
Rosso di Montalcino 1993 • $14 • (10/31/95) • **85**
Rosso di Montalcino 1992 • $12 • (10/31/94) • **85**
Rosso di Montalcino 1991 • $9 • (04/30/94) • **80**

BAROLO, MARCHESI DI

Barbaresco 1990 • $18 • (10/31/93) • **88**
Barbaresco 1989 • $18 • (10/31/93) • **87**
Barbaresco Montestefano 1991 • $20 • (10/31/95) • **77**
Barbaresco Rio Sordo 1988 • $18 • (01/31/92) • **86**
Barbera d'Alba 1990 • $10 • (10/15/93) • **70**
Barbera d'Alba Paiagallo 1990 • $12 • (10/15/93) • **76**
Barbera del Monferrato 1985 • $5 • (09/15/87) BB • **82**
Barbera del Monferrato Le Lune 1988 • $6 • (07/15/91) • **78**
Barolo 1992: Has enough currant and herb flavors to hold interest, but it's modest in scope for a Barolo. Still firm and tannic in texture. Try now. 16,667 cases made. • $19 • (10/31/96) • **82**
Barolo 1991: Has a burst of peppery, plummy, spicy flavors, then fades on the finish. It's quite tannic, but ready to drink. 1,583 cases made. • $27 • (10/31/96) • **81**
Barolo 1990 • $15 • (10/31/94) • **79**
Barolo 1989 • $18 • (10/31/93) • **86**
Barolo 1988 • $18 • (10/31/93) • **88**
Barolo Brunate 1985 • $29 • (10/15/90) • **85**
Barolo Brunate 1982 • $14 • (02/15/89) • **89**
Barolo Cannubi 1989 • $30 • (10/31/94) • **91**
Barolo Cannubi 1988 • $30 • (10/31/93) • **85**
Barolo Cannubi 1985 • $29 • (10/15/90) • **88**
Barolo Castel la Volta 1987 • $20 • (01/31/92) • **89**
Barolo Castellena 1947: Old, caramel flavors are slightly sweet but pleasant enough, with some anise notes on the finish. • $NA • (05/31/97) • **80**
Barolo Coste di Rosé 1985 • $29 • (10/15/90) • **86**
Barolo Gran Riserva 1947: Bitter, sour; in a word, awful. • $NA • (05/31/97) • **67**
Barolo Riserva 1982 • $14 • (02/15/89) • **87**
Barolo Riserva 1978 • $20 • (02/28/89) • **86**
Barolo Sarmassa 1989 • $35 • (10/31/94) • **88**
Barolo Sarmassa 1988 • $30 • (10/31/93) • **83**
Barolo Valletta 1985 • $29 • (10/15/90) • **88**
Dolcetto d'Alba Madonna di Como 1995: Light, but pretty. Has wet earth, dried cherry and spice aromas and flavors and a slightly bitter, green finish. Ready to drink. 3,667 cases made. • $12 • (10/31/96) • **79**
Dolcetto d'Alba Madonna di Como 1990 • $10 • (01/31/92) • **77**
Dolcetto d'Alba Madonna di Como 1989 • $9 • (12/31/90) BB • **88**
Dolcetto d'Alba Madonna di Como 1987 • $8 • (02/15/89) • **87**

BARONE

Cabernet Piave 1993 • $5 • (01/31/96) • **78**
Chardonnay 1993 • $5 • (02/28/95) • **75**
Merlot Piave 1995: A basic, honest red with mild plum and herbal flavors, good balance and light tannins. 15,000 cases made. • $5 • (03/31/97) • **80**
Merlot Piave 1994 • $5 • (02/29/96) • **79**
Merlot Piave 1993 • $5 • (06/15/96) • **77**
Pinot Grigio 1995: Almost neutral in fruit flavor. Tart on the finish. A streak of buttery flavor seems out of place. 40,000 cases made. • $5 • (04/30/97) • **78**
Pinot Grigio 1994 • $5 • (04/30/96) • **78**
Pinot Grigio 1993 • $5 • (05/31/95) • **77**

BARTOLI, MARCO DE

Marsala Superiore Vigna La Miccia 1985 • $16 • (03/31/90) • **87**
Moscato di Pantelleria 1987 • $16 • (03/31/90) • **87**

BASCIANO, FATTORIA DI

Chianti Rufina 1995: Plenty of fruit, with berry, cherry and a hint of oak. Medium-bodied, with soft tannins and a long fnish. Delicious. 5,000 cases made. • $7 • (09/30/97) • **86**
Chianti Rufina 1994: Cleverly made, with blackberry, spice and vanilla aromas and flavors. Of medium body with solid tannins and a crisp, sweet fruit finish. • $NA • (10/31/96) • **86**
Chianti Rufina Riserva 1994: Wonderfully focused, with blackberry, licorice and fruit flavors. Medium-bodied, with moderate tannins and a long, fla-

ITALY

vorful finish. From a small producer on the upswing. Drink or hold. 2,000 cases made. • $11 • (09/30/97) • **88**

Chianti Rufina Riserva 1993: A Rufina producer to keep an eye on. Pretty and delicious, with an alluring plum, violet and blueberry character. Medium-bodied with gentle tannins and a lovely ripe fruit finish. Drink or hold. • $NA • (10/31/96) • **88**

Toscana I Pini 1995: Slightly simple, but with good concentration of berry, cherry and floral aromas and flavors. Medium-bodied, with medium tannins and a fruity finish. Drink now. 1,500 cases made. • $14 • (09/30/97) • **87**

Toscana I Pini 1994: Lively and well-defined flavors of black cherry, blackberry, toast and coffee give this wine depth and appeal. It's bright and harmonious, made in a crisp, fruity, international style. 500 cases made. • $13 • (11/15/96) • **88**

Toscana Vigna il Corto 1995: Excellent use of new wood in this New World-style red. Black currants and vanilla play wonderfully off one another. Medium- to full-bodied, with silky tannins and a long, flavorful finish. Needs a year or two to come together but shows potential. Drink now. 2,000 cases made. • $15 • (09/30/97) • **89**

BASSE, CASE

Soldera Intistiei 1987 • $68 • (01/31/92) • **87**

BATASIOLO, BENI DI

Barbaresco 1993: Bright and lively, medium to full-bodied, with sweet, ripe black cherry, currant and plum flavors. A fresh, crisp character on the finish. Drink now. • $23 • (10/31/96) • **84**

Barbaresco 1990 • $22 • (10/31/94) • **80**

Barbaresco 1989 • $18 • (10/31/94) • **72**

Barbera d'Alba 1994: Quite fruity, but extremely tart, lean and mouth-puckering in texture. Not for everyone. • $NA • (10/31/96) • **79**

Barbera d'Alba 1992 • $NA • (10/31/94) • **76**

Barbera d'Alba 1991 • $10 • (11/15/93) • **82**

Barbera d'Alba 1988 • $11 • (04/15/91) • **88**

Barbera d'Alba Sovrana 1994: Attractive, concentrated red in a traditional style that features ripe fruit, earth, chestnut and a good sense of *terroir*. Medium-bodied, with a supple frame and sweet tannins. Drink through 1999. 1,250 cases made. • $19 • (10/31/97) • **85**

Barbera d'Alba Sovrana 1993: Generous fruit flavors and stiff tannins distinguish this big, rough-textured Barbera. May soften with age. • $NA • (10/31/96) • **81**

Barbera d'Alba Sovrana 1990 • $18 • (10/31/94) • **79**

Barolo 1993: A superbly balanced, round and delicate '93 Barolo, with lovely, ripe fruit flavors, licorice and spice accents and a lingering finish. Of medium intensity and body, this is sheer pleasure to drink now through 2005. 16,667 cases made. • $20 • (10/31/97) • **89**

Barolo 1992: Rather light, but shows nice cedary aromas and cherry flavors. Firm and tannic in texture. Drink now. • $25 • (10/31/96) • **81**

Barolo 1991 • $22 • (10/31/95) • **82**

Barolo 1990 • $22 • (10/31/94) • **78**

Barolo 1989 • $18 • (10/31/93) • **81**

Barolo 1988 • $25 • (10/31/94) • **85**

Barolo 1985 • $15 • (03/31/90) • **84**

Barolo Bofani 1989 • $25 • (10/31/94) • **90**

Barolo Boscareto 1991: Aromatic and flavorful, with coffee, chocolate and spice accents to the cherry flavors. Almost soft, but stiff tannins kick in on the finish. Drink now. • $NA • (10/31/96) • **82**

Barolo Boscareto 1990 • $NA • (10/31/93) • **74**

Barolo Boscareto 1989 • $28 • (10/31/94) • **82**

Barolo La Corda della Briccolina 1991: Aromatic, with a rustic, earthy style that's interesting. Turns tough and dry on the finish, though. Drink now. • $60 • (10/31/96) • **80**

Barolo La Corda della Briccolina 1990 • $40 • (10/31/94) • **94**

Barolo La Corda della Briccolina 1989 • $38 • (10/31/93) HR • **94**

Barolo La Corda della Briccolina 1988 • $38 • (10/31/93) • **90**

Barolo La Corda della Briccolina 1987 • $35 • (01/31/92) • **84**

Barolo Riserva 1986 • $22 • (12/15/92) • **81**

Barolo Riserva 1982 • $17 • (03/31/90) • **79**

Key: SS—Spectator Selection CS—Cellar Selection HR—Highly Recommended BB—Best Buy $NA—Price not available Ⓐ—Auction Price (BT)—Barrel Tasting
Dates in parentheses indicate the issues in which the ratings were published.

Dolcetto d'Alba 1996: Smooth, silky, sweet and ripe style of Dolcetto, offering licorice, spice and black cherry flavors in a balanced and succulent package. Enjoy now. 8,333 cases made. • $11 • (10/31/97) • **85**

Dolcetto d'Alba 1995: Fresh, clean and vibrant—just what you expect from a young Dolcetto. Wet earth, cherry, pepper and grapey-leesy flavors. Drink now. • $13 • (10/31/96) • **85**

Dolcetto d'Alba 1990 • $13 • (10/31/92) • **77**

Dolcetto d'Alba 1989 • $12 • (02/15/92) • **84**

Dolcetto d'Alba 1988 • $11 • (12/31/90) • **85**

Moscato d'Asti 1991 • $15 • (05/15/93) • **83**

Moscato d'Asti 1989 • $14 • (07/15/91) • **85**

BAVA

Barbaresco 1982 • $23 • (04/30/91) • **83**

Barbera d'Asti 1985 • $13 • (03/15/91) • **87**

Barbera d'Asti Cocconato 1990 • $10 • (04/30/93) • **75**

Barolo 1985 • $19 • (04/30/91) • **83**

BEL COLLE

Barbaresco 1994: Quite funky, with earthy notes that overwhelm the wine. Dry, tannic, diluted and unbalanced. • $22 • (10/31/97) • **72**

Barbera d'Alba Le Masche 1995: Crisp, medium-bodied and fairly ripe, showing cherry, cassis bush and dried herb flavors. Should be pleasant with food. Drink now through 2000. • $20 • (10/31/97) • **83**

Barbera d'Alba Le Masche 1989 • $15 • (10/31/92) • **86**

Barbera d'Alba Vigneti in Verduno 1995: Clean, pure, and crisp, this offers cherry, raspberry and herbal flavors on a light- to medium-bodied frame. Should soften with food. Drinkable now. 650 cases made. • $13 • (10/31/97) • **80**

Barolo 1993: Very light and straightforward—more Dolcetto than Barolo—but a very succulent and fruity red, nonetheless. It's crisp and balanced, and should be drinkable upon release if chilled slightly. • $28 • (10/31/97) • **83**

Barolo Riserva 1982 • $15 • (03/31/90) • **85**

Barolo Vigna Monvigliero 1985 • $20 • (10/15/90) • **87**

Dolcetto d'Alba 1986 • $7 • (04/15/88) • **80**

Dolcetto d'Alba Altavilla 1990 • $12 • (10/31/92) • **81**

Dolcetto d'Alba Borgo Castagni in Verduno 1996: More supple than many Dolcettos, this offers plenty of ripe fruit flavors in a light- to medium-bodied frame. Has a balanced finish. Drink now. • $12 • (10/31/97) • **85**

Dolcetto d'Alba Madonna Como 1990 • $14 • (10/31/92) • **79**

BELLANOVA

Sicily Red 1995: Fresh fruit flavors give this medium-bodied red some zip. Good quality for everyday drinking and has a bargain price, too. 10,000 cases made. • $8/1.5 liter • (04/30/97) • **81**

Sicily White 1995: A simple, rather coarse-textured white wine with earthy aromas and basic citrus flavors. 10,000 cases made. • $8/1.5 liter • (05/31/97) • **76**

BELLAVISTA

Brut Gran Cuvée Franciacorta 1989 • $37 • (12/31/94) • **84**

Brut Gran Cuvée Franciacorta 1982 • $27 • (12/31/86) • **84**

Solesine 1994: Loads of toasty new oak and red berry aromas leap from the glass in this modern-style red. The sweet fruit has a spicy, sappy edge to it, with plenty of grip, and the flavors go on and on. It's youthful and should develop well over the year—if you can keep your hands off it. From Lombardy. A blend of 85 percent Cabernet and 15 percent Merlot. 800 cases made. • $45 • (12/15/97) HR • **91**

Solesine 1993: A full-bodied red with a sense of grace and refinement. Smooth and ripe, with delicious plum, cherry and spice flavors that echo on the finish, amplified by a nice chocolate note. Well balanced and ready to drink. • $43 • (03/31/97) • **90**

Solesine 1986 • $30 • (05/15/89) • **92**

Terre de Franciacorta 1994: Extremely supple and aromatic, with leafy, herbal-flavored accents to the blackberry and tobacco flavors that are reminiscent of Cabernet Franc. Well balanced, with a moderately firm structure, it's enjoyable now through 2000. • $17 • (12/15/97) • **86**

Terre de Franciacorta White 1995: A bold, distinctive white, full of honey and almond flavors. It's rich, concentrated and balanced for food. • $17 • (08/31/97) • **85**

ITALY

Terre de Franciacorta White 1994: A fruity wine with plenty of green peach and apricot flavors, but it turns earthy. • $17 • (03/31/97) • **79**
Terre de Franciacorta White Convento della Santissima Annunciata 1994: Quite mature-tasting, with interesting flavors of hazelnut, honey and almond that don't quite harmonize. Slightly candied finish. • $42 • (07/31/97) • **81**
Terre de Franciacorta White Convento della Santissima Annunciata 1993: Fairly rich and buttery, with good honey and tangerine flavors. A smooth, full-bodied white for drinking with food. • $41 • (03/31/97) • **85**
Terre de Franciacorta White Uccellanda 1994: Smooth and rich with honeyed and almondlike flavors. Interesting, with plenty of character. Chardonnay. Try with seafood. • $40 • (07/31/97) • **84**

BERA

Moscato d'Asti 1992 • $15 • (05/15/93) • **82**

BERETTA, CECILIA

Amarone della Valpolicella Classico Terre di Cariano 1990: Elegant and tightly wound, displaying tarry and stemmy notes and a hint of kirsch. Rich on entry, followed by a tannic finish with a distinct prune aftertaste. Not as concentrated as the best '90s. Drink now through 2005. • $40 • (05/31/98) • **88**
Amarone della Valpolicella Classico Terre di Cariano 1985 • $26 • (09/30/95) • **89**
Soave Classico Terre di Brognoligo 1995: Mature nuances of butter and nuts highlight the flavors in this charming Soave. Harmonious and moderately concentrated, with a lingering finish. Well done. Drink now. • $14 • (04/30/98) • **86**
Soave Classico Terre di Brognoligo 1993 • $8 • (04/30/96) • **80**
Valpolicella Classico Superiore Terre di Cariano 1993: Lovely. Fragrant aromas of cherry, cedar and vanilla are followed by well-integrated flavors, with harmonious structure and balance. Has aged gracefully and lingers on the palate. Drink now. • $15 • (04/30/98) • **87**
Valpolicella Classico Vigneti di Marano 1995: Fresh and vibrant, showing plenty of red cherry with accents of leather and earth, this red has a slightly chewy texture and a lingering finish. Drink now. 1,850 cases made. • $11 • (04/30/98) • **84**
Valpolicella Superiore Roccolo di Mizzole 1992 • $8 • (12/15/95) • **84**

BERETTA, GUSSALLI

Chardonnay Franciacorta Lo Sparviere 1993: A bit cloying, with some modest fig and almond flavors and a very strong earthlike accent. • $15 • (03/31/97) • **78**
Franciacorta Lo Sparviere Vino del Cacciatore Red 1991: Quite mature, with roasted flavors and aromas. Not much fruit flavor, but pleasant if you like a gamy edge. • $20 • (03/31/97) • **82**

BERGADANO, ENRICO

Barolo 1993: A soft and supple Barolo, offering red berry and spice flavors, with some dilution and some herbal notes. Turns a bit dry on the finish. • $NA • (10/31/97) • **83**

BERGAGLIO, NICOLA

Gavi Minaia 1995: Made in an herbal style, with appealing grassy and lemony flavors. Has some body to it and a good, clean finish. • $21 • (03/31/97) • **84**
Gavi Minaia 1994: Straightforward and flavorful, with tasty pear, lemon and spice flavors that linger on the finish. A solid wine with good varietal character. • $21 • (03/31/97) • **84**
Gavi Rovereto di Gavi 1994: A fairly rich, oaky style with lots of pear and ripe apple flavors. Reminiscent of Sauvignon Blanc, and has a nicely spicy finish. • $15 • (03/31/97) • **85**

BERSANO

Barbaresco 1993: Light Barbaresco, with modest fruit and a diluted midpalate. Some spice and toasty notes on the drying finish. • $30 • (01/31/98) • **73**
Barbaresco 1991 • $16 • (10/31/95) • **78**
Barbaresco 1983 • $7 • (01/31/89) • **79**
Barbaresco 1975 • $NA • (09/15/88) • **76**
Barbaresco 1971 • $NA • (09/15/88) • **78**
Barbaresco 1964 • $NA • (09/15/88) • **85**
Barbera d'Asti 1995: Light in color, a bit plummy and spicy, but lacking in intensity. A straightforward Barbera with a short, somewhat tough, dry finish. Drink now. 15,000 cases made. • $9 • (01/31/98) • **75**
Barbera d'Asti 1992 • $NA • (10/31/95) • **80**
Barbera d'Asti 1987 • $9 • (03/15/91) • **80**
Barolo 1993: Lush and ripe, of medium body and intensity, showing plum, red berry, tar and smoke character. Try now. 10,000 cases made. • $35 • (01/31/98) • **84**
Barolo 1991 • $18 • (10/31/95) • **78**
Barolo 1985 • $10 • (10/15/90) • **79**
Barolo 1983 • $9 • (11/15/88) • **81**
Barolo 1974 • $NA • (09/15/88) • **79**
Barolo 1971 • $NA • (09/15/88) • **77**
Barolo 1964 • $NA • (09/15/88) • **80**
Barolo Cascina Badarina 1990 • $30 • (10/31/95) • **87**
Castellengo Red 1986 • $16 • (04/15/91) • **88**
Dolcetto d'Alba 1994 • $12 • (10/31/95) • **78**
Gavi 1996: Pretty Gavi, offering harmony and some complexity, with flavors of lime, butter and vanilla. Fresh as a crisp apple, its length is fairly intense. Drink now as an apéritif or with appetizers. 15,000 cases made. • $12 • (01/31/98) • **83**

BERTANI

Bardolino Classico Superiore 1990 • $9 • (09/15/92) • **84**
Catullo Red 1990 • $12 • (11/15/94) • **79**
Catullo Red 1986 • $13 • (09/15/92) • **81**
Catullo Red 1984 • $9 • (02/15/89) • **86**
Catullo Red 1983 • $9 • (06/30/88) • **81**
Duè Uve White 1995: Good concentration, and the lively acidity provides a foil for the apple and almond character. 16,000 cases made. • $10 • (06/15/97) • **84**
Le Lave 1995: A mature element and oak treatment are the dominant themes in this lush white, accented by butter and apple flavors. It's balanced and the finish is long, ending with a pleasant astringency, but not overdone. Drink now. A blend of Chardonnay and Garganega. 3,200 cases made. • $19 • (04/30/98) • **87**
Le Lave 1994: A broad and rich white, with plenty of ripe apple, pear and fig flavors, spicy notes for complexity and a firm backbone. Try with grilled foods. 2,000 cases made. • $18 • (06/15/97) • **87**
Le Lave 1993 • $18 • (06/15/96) • **87**
Recioto Valpolicella Valpantena 1987: An unusual taste experience, but a great one. Try this bubbly Amarone-style red wine with cheese. It has intriguing, mature, red wine flavors, is slightly sweet but well-balanced, has a long finish. Drink now. 300 cases made. • $25 • (05/15/98) • **87**
Recioto della Valpolicella Amarone Classico 1986: Plenty of complex truffle, tobacco, dried cherry and butterscotch flavors, but it lacks fruit and the finish is dry and tannic. Drink soon. 2,000 cases made. • $46 • (06/15/97) • **85**
Recioto della Valpolicella Amarone Classico Superiore 1988: Beginning to mature, this is in the tobacco, leather and brown sugar phase, with a glycerinlike texture and rich, full-bodied structure. Still harboring fine tannins, but it's well integrated and long. Tasted twice, with consistent notes. Drink now through 2005. 4,200 cases made. • $59 • (05/31/98) • **88**
Recioto della Valpolicella Amarone Classico Superiore 1985 • $45 • (06/15/96) • **90**
Recioto della Valpolicella Amarone Classico Superiore 1983 • $40 • (11/15/94) • **87**
Recioto della Valpolicella Amarone Classico Superiore 1980 • $40 • (09/15/92) • **87**
Valpolicella Valpantena Secco-Bertani 1995: Here's a good value in a serious style of Valpolicella, from the *ripasso* method. Dried cherry and tobacco flavors combine with high acidity to give freshness and firm structure to this Italian red of good length. Drink now through 2000. 35,000 cases made. • $10 • (04/30/98) BB • **86**
Valpolicella Valpantena Secco-Bertani 1993: A very mature red, with cedary character and a dry finish. Drink soon. 22,000 cases made. • $10 • (06/15/97) • **79**
Valpolicella Valpantena Secco-Bertani 1992 • $10 • (06/15/96) BB • **87**
Valpolicella Valpantena Secco-Bertani 1988 • $9 • (11/15/94) • **76**
Valpolicella Valpantena Secco-Bertani 1987 • $9 • (09/15/92) • **73**

BERTELLI

Barbera d'Asti 1994: Funky, earthy, herbal and astringent. Not much there. • $NA • (10/31/97) • **72**

Barbera d'Asti Giarone 1993: Sweet, spicy oak flavors dominate the cherry flavors in this rather tannic and tough wine. Short on the finish. • $40 • (10/31/96) • **80**

Barbera d'Asti Giarone 1990 • $NA • (10/31/94) • **78**

Barbera d'Asti Montetusa 1994: An international-style Barbera. Sophisticated, supple, elegant, full-bodied, with toasty oak notes mingling nicely with the spice, red pepper, cassis, grilled bread and smoke flavors. Seductive and beautiful to taste, with good acidity holding the long finish together. Drink now through 2002. • $NA • (10/31/97) • **90**

Barbera d'Asti San Antonio Vieilles Vignes 1993: Shows some nice black cherry and raspberry flavors, but it's a bit one dimensional. Medium-bodied, with some drying tannins on the finish. 100% Barbera, from vines planted in 1944. • $40 • (10/31/96) • **79**

Giarone Red 1991 • $NA • (10/31/94) • **78**

I Fossaretti 1993: Distinctive and beautiful, with ripe, focused fruit flavors and spicy mint accents. Elegant and harmonious in texture. Dead ringer for a fine Bordeaux from the St. Julien district. Drink now or cellar through 2000. • $40 • (10/31/96) • **89**

I Fossaretti 1985 • $34 • (12/31/90) • **92**

Montetusa Red 1990 • $NA • (10/31/94) • **80**

St. Marsan 1995: A beautiful Syrah, dark in color, thick in texture, polished in structure. Offers lovely cassis, black currant, wild raspberry and various dried herb aromas and flavors. The oak doesn't stop the pure fruit from shining through. Cleanses the palate, providing a long, succulent finish. Drink now through 2002. • $45 • (10/31/97) • **90**

St. Marsan 1994: A beauty, with everything—an amazingly dark color, full body, velvety texture, black pepper, tar, spice, chocolate and gamy flavors, and a long finish. (100 percent Syrah.) • $38 • (10/31/96) • **91**

BIANCHI, A.

Chianti Classico Riserva Regina 1990: Lively and fruity, with a sweetness that gives it a candylike appeal, this round red shows cherry and raspberry flavors over soft tannins. The first glass is the best. 300 cases made. • $20 • (11/15/96) • **79**

BIBBIANO, TENUTA

Chianti Classico Montornello 1993 • $NA • (10/31/95) • **85**

Chianti Classico Vigna del Capannino 1990 • $NA • (02/28/95) • **86**

Chianti Classico Vigna del Capannino Riserva 1993: A delicate, light-bodied riserva showing aromas and flavors of berry and mushroom. Finish is crisp and flavorful. • $NA • (10/31/96) • **80**

BIGI

Orvieto Classico Secco Vigneto Torricella 1993: Light and refreshing, with character. Juicy apple and pear flavors with almond accents give substance; crisp acidity keeps it lively. A nice apéritif. 10,000 cases made. • $9 • (08/31/96) • **85**

Vino Nobile di Montepulciano 1985 • $12 • (11/30/90) • **81**

Vino Nobile di Montepulciano Riserva 1982 • $9 • (01/31/88) • **77**

Vino Nobile di Montepulciano Riserva 1980 • $8 • (09/01/85) • **84**

BINDELLA, RUDOLF

Vallocaia 1994: Lovely perfumes, with scents of violet, berries and flowers. Of medium body, with fine tannins and a light finish. Drink or hold. 500 cases made. • $30 • (09/30/97) • **86**

Vallocaia 1993: Shows a sweet berry and chocolate character, is medium-bodied and has soft, silky tannins and a light, fruity finish. Drink now. Sangiovese • $23 • (10/31/96) • **84**

Vallocaia 1990 • $23 • (11/30/94) • **82**

Vallocaia 1989 • $25 • (11/30/94) • **89**

Key: SS—Spectator Selection CS—Cellar Selection HR—Highly Recommended BB—Best Buy $NA—Price not available Ⓐ—Auction Price (BT)—Barrel Tasting

Dates in parentheses indicate the issues in which the ratings were published.

Vino Nobile di Montepulciano 1994: Crisp and fruity, with dried cherry and earth aromas and flavors. Medium-bodied, with light tannins and a tart finish. Drink now. 2,000 cases made. • $16 • (09/30/97) • **81**

Vino Nobile di Montepulciano 1990 • $14 • (02/29/96) • **83**

Vino Nobile di Montepulciano Riserva 1993: A delicate red with milk chocolate and berry character, medium body and a slightly short finish. Drink now. 4,000 cases made. • $23 • (09/30/97) • **82**

Vino Nobile di Montepulciano Riserva 1990 • $22 • (02/29/96) • **89**

Vino Nobile di Montepulciano Riserva 1985 • $27 • (10/31/90) • **68**

BIONDI-SANTI

Brunello di Montalcino 1990: A very good Brunello, in the old style, with slightly mature brick-red color and cedary, smoky, spicy character. There's a pretty richness to it, too, and a round, velvety texture. Drink now. • $58 • (11/30/96) • **87**

Brunello di Montalcino 1988 • $65 • (04/30/94) • **81**

Brunello di Montalcino Il Greppo 1990: Stiff and tannic, with its tough texture and modest fruit flavors a bit out of balance. • $50 • (10/31/96) • **79**

Brunello di Montalcino Il Greppo 1983 • $66 • (11/30/89) • **91**

Brunello di Montalcino Il Greppo 1982 • $45 • (10/15/88) • **92**

Brunello di Montalcino Il Greppo 1981 • $40 • (09/15/86) • **93**

Brunello di Montalcino Il Greppo 1980 • $40 • (09/15/86) • **88**

Brunello di Montalcino Il Greppo 1978 • $45 • (09/15/86) • **70**

Brunello di Montalcino Riserva 1990: A rich and powerful riserva, with plenty of berry, mineral character and a long silky finish. One of the best Biondi-Santi Brunellos in a long time, it's a wonderful, harmonious wine to drink now or age. 580 cases made. • $230 • (11/30/96) • **92**

Brunello di Montalcino Riserva 1988 • $145 • (10/31/94) • **87**

Brunello di Montalcino Riserva 1985 • $211 Ⓐ • (03/31/92) • **82**

Rosso di Montalcino Il Greppo 1984 • $22 • (01/31/90) • **82**

BIONDI-SANTI, JACOPO

Sassoalloro 1994: A joy to drink. A lovely, plummy wine with a caressing, velvety texture. Medium-bodied, with moderate tannins and a soft finish. • $28 • (09/30/97) • **88**

Sassoalloro 1991 • $NA • (02/28/95) • **87**

Schidione 1993: Absolutely delicious. Shows complex aromas of berries, plums and spices with hints of flowers. It's medium- to full-bodied, with velvety tannins and a long, finish. Drink now. • $107 • (09/30/97) • **90**

BISOL & FIGLI, DESIDERIO

Prosecco di Valdobbiadene Crede NV: Lovely Prosecco, just off dry, with peach aromas and flavors and a creamy midpalate. It's all wrapped up in a crisp, clean finish. Drink now. • $17 • (06/15/98) • **85**

BOATINA, LA

Merlot Collio 1993 • $11 • (06/15/96) • **75**

Pinot Grigio Collio 1996: Quite a mouthful of wine, the rich texture and concentrated apple and mineral flavors underscored by a mouthpuckering acidity. The finish is astringent. Still needs time and food. 3,200 cases made. • $16 • (06/30/98) • **86**

Pinot Grigio Collio 1994 • $12 • (04/30/96) • **87**

Verduzzo 1989 • $17 • (01/31/92) • **84**

BOCCE, FATTORIA LE

Chianti Classico 1995: A simple, fresh Chianti with a bright berry character. Light-bodied, with tart acidity and a fresh finish. Serve chilled. • $12 • (09/30/97) • **80**

Chianti Classico 1994: Enticing and delicious. Light tannins, and woodsy berry aromas and flavors. Has a medium body and a sweet, fruity finish. 20,000 cases made. • $11 • (10/31/96) • **83**

Chianti Classico 1993 • $9 • (10/31/95) • **84**

Chianti Classico 1992 • $9 • (02/28/95) • **80**

Chianti Classico 1991 • $13 • (10/31/93) • **81**

Chianti Classico 1990 • $11 • (09/15/92) HR • **90**

Chianti Classico Riserva 1993: Alluring aromas of fruit, wet earth and autumn. Medium-bodied, with well-integrated tannins and a slightly short finish. Drink now. • $16 • (09/30/97) • **86**

Chianti Classico Riserva 1991 • $14 • (10/31/95) • **84**

Chianti Classico Riserva 1990 • $15 • (02/28/95) • **85**

Chianti Classico Riserva 1988 • $16 • (09/15/92) • **86**

Vigna del Paladino Red 1990 • $NA • (10/31/93) • **84**

BOGLIETTI, ENZO

Barbera d'Alba 1993: Firm, with strawberry and currant flavors. It's mature and ready to drink, though it turns a little coarse on the finish. 500 cases imported. • $16 • (03/31/97) • **81**

Barbera d'Alba Vigna dei Romani 1993: Delicious, with an abundance of plum, dark cherry and spice flavors that are ripe and rounded, and an enticing, spicy aroma that echoes on the finish. Quite a mouthful: Enjoy it for its opulence. 100 cases imported. • $30 • (03/31/97) • **88**

Barolo Vigna delle Brunate 1992: Despite its age, it's still a green and stemmy tasting wine with modest game and cherry flavors, and leather on the finish. • $38 • (01/01/97) • **80**

Barolo Vigna delle Brunate 1991: This is a nicely textured wine with good plum and dried cherry flavors. Balanced, with a nice spicy note. • $32 • (01/01/97) • **83**

Dolcetto d'Alba 1995: A fresh young red with bold plum and pepper flavors and enough tannin to give firm grip on the palate. Ready to drink. • $17 • (05/31/97) • **85**

Nebbiolo delle Langhe 1993: Beautiful, complex aromas combine with lean, crisp fruit and herb flavors in this spare, tart, firm-textured wine. • $13 • (05/31/97) • **80**

BOLLA

Amarone della Valpolicella Classico 1990: Continues to improve. The plum and smoke notes have evolved to prune and leather, and it's a bit firmer than previously, with a tannic, chewy, sweet fruit finish. A solid effort, but not as good as the '89 or '88. Drink now through 2005. 8,000 cases made. • $30 • (05/31/98) • **89**

Amarone della Valpolicella Classico 1989: Roasted aromas and flavors are the hallmarks of this intense, inky wine, with its powerful and rich flavors of plum, prune, leather and chocolate that echo through the finish, accented by notes of orange peel and spice. Still quite young with plenty of body and tannins. Try in 2000. 13,000 cases made. • $20 • (01/31/97) SS • **91**

Amarone della Valpolicella Classico 1988 • $18 • (06/15/96) CS • **91**

Bardolino 1995: Simple and fruity, with berrylike flavors and aromas. A little dull around the edges. 128,000 cases made. • $8 • (01/31/97) • **77**

Bardolino 1990 • $8 • (01/31/92) • **79**

Bardolino 1982 • $5 • (10/31/88) • **74**

Bardolino Classico 1993 • $7 • (10/31/94) • **81**

Bardolino Classico 1991 • $8 • (09/15/92) • **81**

Cabernet Sauvignon Creso 1991: Fully mature, exhibiting loads of spice and sweet plum and cherry flavors, a smooth texture and a harmonious balance that turns a little drying on the finish. Good length and aftertaste. Well made. Drink now. 10,000 cases made. • $26 • (06/15/98) • **88**

Chardonnay 1996: Ripe, tropical notes of passion fruit are countered by almond and vanilla from new oak. Lacks harmony at this stage, but may come together this summer. 68,000 cases made. • $8 • (06/15/97) • **83**

Chardonnay 1994 • $6 • (02/29/96) • **73**

Chardonnay 1993 • $7 • (06/30/95) • **81**

Creso 1987 • $33 • (03/31/93) • **86**

Creso 1986 • $33 • (03/31/93) • **87**

Merlot Piave 1996: Spicy cherry marks this Merlot. It's fresh and lively for quaffing on its own or with hors d'oeuvres. 229,000 cases made. • $8 • (06/15/97) • **81**

Merlot Piave 1995: Flavors of plum and game dominate this angular wine. Turns a bit astringent on the finish. 170,000 cases made. • $8 • (01/31/97) • **77**

Merlot Piave 1994 • $8 • (01/31/96) • **82**

Merlot Piave 1993 • $7 • (10/31/94) • **83**

Merlot delle Venezie Colforte 1996: Plum and spice accents round out the bright cherry flavors in this light-bodied, easygoing Merlot. Drink now. 1,500 cases made. • $30 • (04/30/98) • **84**

Pinot Grigio 1996: An easy-drinking white with peach and apricot flavors and a hint of bitter almond. 166,000 cases made. • $7 • (06/15/97) • **82**

Pinot Grigio 1995: Tastes stripped and a bit oxidized, with dull, cloying flavors. Harsh and unappealing. 96,000 cases made. • $6 • (01/31/97) • **68**

Pinot Grigio 1994 • $6 • (10/31/95) • **78**

Pinot Grigio 1993 • $7 • (01/01/95) • **72**

Recioto della Valpolicella Amarone 1985 • $22 • (09/15/92) • **85**

Recioto della Valpolicella Amarone Classico 1986 • $18 • (10/31/94) • **85**

Recioto di Soave 1990 • $NA • (09/15/92) • **83**

Sangiovese di Romagna 1995: Straightforward and fairly fruity with some modest red plum, cherry and herb flavors. There's a slight spritziness to it as well. • $8 • (03/31/97) • **82**

Sangiovese di Romagna 1994 • $6 • (02/29/96) • **82**

Soave 1996: Fresh peach and banana flavors mark this simple, fruity white. It's soft and easy, perfect for summertime. 339,000 cases made. • $8 • (06/15/97) • **79**

Soave Classico 1993 • $7 • (10/31/94) BB • **85**

Soave Classico Tufaie Castellaro 1996: A Soave with marzipan and apple flavors that remain bright and focused on the crisp texture, finishing with an appealing lemon and almond aftertaste. Drink now. 10,000 cases made. • $15 • (06/30/98) • **85**

Valpolicella 1996: A nouveau-style Valpolicella, soft and supple, with banana and strawberry character, nutty finish. 511,000 cases made. • $8 • (06/15/97) • **78**

Valpolicella 1990 • $8 • (09/15/92) • **75**

Valpolicella 1986 • $6 • (12/15/89) • **71**

Valpolicella 1985 • $5 • (10/31/88) • **77**

Valpolicella Classico 1995: A soft, easy-drinking wine that's smooth and fruity, with strawberry and cherry flavors. 205,000 cases made. • $8 • (01/31/97) • **82**

Valpolicella Classico Le Poiano Jago 1994: Classic Valpolicella, exhibiting cherry and almond notes allied to a medium-bodied structure with a touch of bitterness on the finish. Drink now. 10,750 cases made. • $30 • (04/30/98) • **85**

Valpolicella Classico Vigneti di Jago 1987 • $13 • (09/15/92) • **81**

Valpolicella Classico Vigneti di Jago 1986 • $12 • (12/31/90) • **78**

Valpolicella Vigneti di San Vito 1990 • $NA • (09/15/92) • **78**

BOLLINI

Cabernet Sauvignon Grave del Friuli 1989 • $12 • (02/28/95) • **74**

Cabernet Sauvignon Grave del Friuli 1987 • $11 • (12/15/92) • **76**

Cabernet Sauvignon Grave del Friuli 1983 • $6 • (07/31/87) • **73**

Cabernet Sauvignon Trentino Reserve Selection 1989 • $15 • (04/30/94) • **80**

Chardonnay Trentino 1996: Opulent and generous, full of apple, butter and hazelnut notes that lose a bit of intensity on the finish. Still, well made. • $11 • (12/15/97) • **84**

Chardonnay Trentino 1995: Exhibits some depth and complexity, full of ripe peach, honey and spice accents, and finishes up with a bitter almond component. • $9 • (05/15/97) • **85**

Chardonnay Trentino 1993 • $8 • (01/31/95) • **78**

Merlot Trentino 1996: Here's a light-bodied, elegant Merlot with red cherry flavors. It's pleasant on its own, or try with light foods. Drink now. • $11 • (04/30/98) • **82**

Merlot Trentino 1992 • $8 • (02/28/95) • **77**

Merlot Trentino 1990 • $8 • (12/15/92) • **77**

Merlot Trentino Reserve Selection 1994: Hints of tar add to the spicy cherry flavors. Starts out nicely, turns astringent on the finish. Try with food. • $16 • (12/15/97) • **84**

Merlot Trentino Reserve Selection 1990 • $15 • (04/30/94) • **86**

Pinot Grigio Grave del Friuli Reserve Selection 1996: Floral and pear aromas and flavors are subtle yet evocative in this delicately structured Pinot Grigio. A fine, racy backbone of acidity keeps the flavors pulsing through the long finish. Drink now. • $15 • (05/15/98) • **86**

Pinot Grigio Grave del Friuli Reserve Selection 1994 • $8 • (06/15/96) • **84**

Pinot Grigio Grave del Friuli Reserve Selection 1993 • $13 • (07/31/95) • **80**

Pinot Grigio Trentino 1997: The ripe apple flavors are subtle yet there's very good concentration, as well as an almost viscous texture that's reigned in on the slightly bitter finish. Drink now. 21,000 cases made. • $11 • (05/31/98) • **85**

Pinot Grigio Trentino 1996: Light, refreshing and easy to drink, with fresh banana and crisp apple flavors. • $10 • (07/31/97) • **83**

Pinot Grigio Trentino 1995: An aromatic and rich white from Northeast Italy, smoothly textured, displaying a bountiful peach, flower and honey character and finishing with a pleasant touch of bitter almond. A lovely wine for so few dollars. 21,000 cases made. • $9 • (05/15/97) BB • **86**

Pinot Grigio Trentino 1993 • $9 • (12/15/94) • **81**

BOLOGNA, GIACOMO

Barbera Piedmont Bricco dell' Uccellone 1991 • $47 • (01/01/94) • **82**
Barbera Piedmont Bricco dell' Uccellone 1988 • $45 • (03/15/91) • **91**
Barbera Piedmont Bricco dell' Uccellone 1987 • $45 • (03/15/91) • **88**
Barbera Piedmont Bricco dell' Uccellone 1986 • $38 • (03/15/91) • **89**
Barbera Piedmont Bricco dell' Uccellone 1985 • $33 • (08/31/89) • **88**
Barbera Piedmont Bricco della Bigotta 1988 • $40 • (03/15/91) • **92**
Barbera Piedmont Bricco della Bigotta 1987 • $34 • (03/15/91) • **88**
Barbera Piedmont Bricco della Bigotta 1986 • $34 • (03/15/91) • **88**
Barbera d'Asti Ai Suma 1995: A lovely Barbera, with ripe cherry flavors and chocolate, mint and spice accents that cascade over the palate in multiple layers. Sweet, supple tannins make this fine to drink now through 1999. 1,500 cases made. • $48 • (10/31/97) • **87**
Barbera d'Asti Braida 1993: Interesting, with tea leaf, dried cherry and cranberry flavors. A bit lean and tart, but with the right food it might open up. Drink now. 1,000 cases made. • $38 • (10/31/96) • **82**
Barbera d'Asti Bricco della Bigotta 1994: An elegant wine that seems to have lost a bit of fruit. It's supple and medium-bodied, with fresh acidity weaving through the lean frame. Drinkable now. Tasted from magnum. 1,500 cases made. • $40 • (10/31/97) • **83**
Barbera d'Asti Bricco della Bigotta 1991 • $NA • (01/01/94) • **83**
Barbera di Rocchetta Tanaro Bricco dell'Uccellone 1993: Offers lots of mocha, spice and black cherry flavors, but smells of oak and turns a bit tannic and green on the finish. Tasted twice with consistent notes. 2,083 cases made. • $38 • (10/31/96) • **82**
Brachetto d'Acqui 1987 • $16 • (03/31/90) • **84**

BONCI, VALLEROSA

Verdicchio dei Castelli di Jesi Classico San Michele 1996: Soft and appealing, with good flavors of herbs, lemon and a touch of onion. Drink with food. • $10 • (10/15/97) • **83**

BONFIO, FEDERICO

Chianti Le Poggiolo Riserva 1985 • $11 • (03/31/90) • **76**
Chianti Le Poggiolo Riserva 1982 • $7 • (11/15/87) • **73**
Chianti Le Portine Riserva 1985 • $9 • (03/31/90) • **85**
Chianti Le Portine Riserva 1982 • $9 • (11/15/87) • **79**
Chianti Proprietor's Reserve 1985 • $15 • (03/31/90) • **85**

BORGO AL CASTELLO

Primitivo Tarantino Mother Zin 1996: Fresh and fruity, packed with blackberry and raspberry notes accented by smoke and herbs, and made in a practically nouveau style. Light in tannins, smooth in texture. Drink now. 4,000 cases made. • $10 • (01/01/98) • **85**

BORGO CONVENTI

Merlot Collio 1987 • $15 • (03/31/89) • **84**
Pinot Bianco Collio 1993 • $14 • (01/31/95) • **78**
Pinot Grigio Collio 1993 • $15 • (01/31/95) • **82**
Ribolla Gialla Collio 1993 • $14 • (01/31/95) • **80**
Sauvignon Collio White 1993 • $15 • (01/31/95) • **82**

BORGO DELLE ROSE

Pinot Grigio Grave del Friuli 1994 • $9 • (06/15/96) • **83**

BORGO MAGREDO

Cabernet Sauvignon Grave del Friuli 1994 • $8 • (06/15/96) • **82**
Cabernet Sauvignon Grave del Friuli 1990 • $NA • (02/28/95) • **72**
Chardonnay Grave del Friuli 1996: Already showing some marzipan and canned-fruit aromas and flavors, allied to a light structure that finishes short. Drink now. 10,000 cases made. • $9 • (05/31/98) • **78**

Key: SS—Spectator Selection CS—Cellar Selection HR—Highly Recommended BB—Best Buy $NA—Price not available Ⓐ—Auction Price (BT)—Barrel Tasting
Dates in parentheses indicate the issues in which the ratings were published.

Chardonnay Grave del Friuli 1995: Coarse, with candied flavors and aromas, finishing with some herb and onion flavors. Not much resemblance to Chardonnay. 10,000 cases made. • $9 • (01/31/97) • **75**
Chardonnay Grave del Friuli 1994 • $8 • (02/29/96) • **82**
Merlot Grave del Friuli 1996: A forward, soft, fruity style that smells and tastes like freshly crushed berries. Modest concentration and decent length. Delicious on its own. Drink now. 5,000 cases made. • $9 • (05/31/98) • **84**
Merlot Grave del Friuli 1995: Reminiscent of a young Beaujolais. Fresh and fruity, with plenty of berry and raspberry flavors. 5,000 cases made. • $9 • (03/31/97) • **83**
Merlot Grave del Friuli 1994 • $8 • (02/29/96) • **75**
Pinot Grigio Grave del Friuli 1996: Well constituted, with peach and almond flavors, medium body, good concentration and firm acidity. Drink now. 10,000 cases made. • $9 • (05/31/98) • **84**
Pinot Grigio Grave del Friuli 1995: A wine that goes in two distinct directions. Shows some nice, rich lemon and pear flavors, but also a tart dimension that intensifies on the finish. 10,000 cases made. • $9 • (01/31/97) • **81**
Pinot Grigio Grave del Friuli 1994 • $8 • (04/30/96) • **84**
Refosco Grave del Friuli 1994 • $8 • (04/30/96) • **77**
Sauvignon Grave del Friuli 1996: Plenty of personality in this bright, light-bodied white from the gooseberry, citrus and melon aromas and flavors. Crisply textured, it finishes with an earthy taste. Drink now. 4,000 cases made. • $9 • (06/15/98) • **84**
Sauvignon Grave del Friuli 1995: A lean and modestly flavored white wine, with earthy and herbal overtones. 4,000 cases made. • $9 • (01/31/97) • **78**
Sauvignon Grave del Friuli 1994 • $8 • (04/30/96) • **85**
Tocai Friulano Grave del Friuli 1996: A fleshier version of Tocai, this has richness and body along with herb and almond notes. It finishes with a touch of bitter almond. Drink now. 2,000 cases made. • $9 • (05/31/98) • **81**
Tocai Friulano Grave del Friuli 1995: Lively and straightforward, this offers a good amount of melon and citrus flavors backed up by a fairly rich texture. 2,000 cases made. • $9 • (01/31/97) • **82**
Tocai Friulano Grave del Friuli 1994 • $7 • (04/30/96) • **84**

BORGO SCOPETO, TENUTA

Chardonnay Toscana Violette 1996: Lovely aromas of cream and apples, with hints of piecrust. Medium-bodied, with medium acidity and an appley finish. • $NA • (09/30/97) • **85**
Chianti Classico 1994: Intense aromas of black cherries and violets. Medium-bodied with racy, silky tannins and a finish of blackberries. Better after this year. 2,500 cases made. • $12 • (09/30/97) • **86**
Chianti Classico 1993: Some fruit flavors are discerned, but they're rather diluted and light. 4,000 cases made. • $12 • (10/31/96) • **75**
Chianti Classico 1992 • $NA • (02/28/95) • **78**
Chianti Classico 1991 • $10 • (10/31/94) • **79**
Chianti Classico Riserva 1993: Elegant and well made. Aromas and flavors of cherry, berry, and violet, ultrafine tannins, medium body. Wonderful finesse in this wine. 3,500 cases made. • $23 • (10/31/96) • **86**
Chianti Classico Riserva 1990 • $22 • (10/31/94) • **83**

BORGO TINTOR

Chardonnay Isonzo Bortoluzzi 1996: A solid Chardonnay that exhibits crisp apple and citrus aromas and flavors on a firm, light-bodied frame. Drink through 1999. 500 cases made. • $14 • (06/15/98) • **83**
Chardonnay Isonzo Bortoluzzi 1994: Marked by mineral, lemon and almond flavors, with an earthy finish. Starts off strong, but fades. • $14 • (01/31/97) • **82**
Merlot Collio Bortoluzzi 1995: A lively Merlot, this has herbal accents to the cherry flavors, good richness and balance, yet it's one-dimensional. Moderate tannins on the finish. Drink through 1999. 1,000 cases made. • $14 • (06/15/98) • **84**
Pinot Grigio Isonzo Bortoluzzi 1995: This is mature, showing a lean, hard side from the acidity. Rich and concentrated, yet the fruit flavors are austere. Better with food. Drink now. 5,000 cases made. • $14 • (06/15/98) • **84**

BORGOGNO, LODOVICO

Barolo Preda Sarmassa 1993: A very pretty Barolo, with clean, pure floral and red berry flavors, medium body, good intensity on the palate and a subtle, supple finish. Well done. Delicious now. • $NA • (10/31/97) • **85**

BORGOGNO & FIGLI, GIACOMO

Barbaresco Riserva 1990: Classic Nebbiolo character of roses, tar and menthol. It's rich and mouthfilling, then the tannins take over, but the vintage is great, so give it until 2000. 1,000 cases made. • $22 • (06/15/97) • **86**

Barbaresco Riserva 1947: Thin, unappealing, asprinlike in flavor. • $NA • (05/31/97) • **65**

Barbera d'Alba 1990 • $10 • (06/15/94) BB • **88**

Barolo 1988 • $20 • (06/15/94) • **88**

Barolo Gran Riserva Speciale 1947: Crisp in texture, with modest earthlike, slightly medicinal and caramel flavors. • $NA • (05/31/97) • **79**

BORTOLUZZI

Chardonnay Isonzo 1994 • $15 • (06/15/96) • **84**

Pinot Grigio Isonzo 1994 • $15 • (06/15/96) • **82**

Sauvignon Isonzo 1994 • $15 • (06/15/96) • **83**

BOSCAINI, PAOLO

Amarone della Valpolicella Ca' de Loi 1988: Beginning to show maturity, from the truffle aromas to the prune and tobacco flavors. A glycerinelike texture and lingering but heady and tannic finish complete the profile. Drink now through 2005. 2,000 cases made. • $39 • (06/15/97) • **89**

Amarone della Valpolicella Classico Ca' de Loi 1993: Well done, in a traditional style. Prune, spice and coffee notes seem a bit advanced, but the wine shows some of the rich, supple texture and grip of Amarone. Drink now through 2000. • $45 • (07/31/98) • **84**

Amarone della Valpolicella Classico Marano 1994: Good richness, almost finding that slippery, glycerin groove on the palate to carry the coffee and plum flavors, but still finishes tannic. Drink now through 2002. • $29 • (07/31/98) • **85**

Amarone Recioto della Valpolicella Classico Marano 1988 • $23 • (09/15/92) • **83**

Bardolino Classico Superiore Le Canne 1985 • $6 • (07/31/88) BB • **82**

Chardonnay Colle dell'Imperatore Vigneti di Cornaiano 1994 • $11 • (06/15/96) • **82**

Pinot Grigio Castel Firmiano Vigneti di Cornaiano 1994 • $11 • (06/30/96) • **70**

Pinot Grigio Firmiano 1997: Delicate peach and apple flavors marry with a medium-bodied texture that turns firm on the finish, with an almond aftertaste. Drink now through 1999. • $15 • (07/31/98) • **81**

Pinot Grigio Valdadige La Cros 1997: Refreshing and lemony, this almond-flavored Pinot Grigio draws elegance from its firm acidity. Slightly bitter on the finish. Drink through 1999. • $12 • (07/31/98) • **81**

Santa Stefano de le Cane 1993: The cedar and tobacco notes suggest some maturity in this elegant red. There are drying tannins on the finish, so drink soon or try with food. 20,000 cases made. • $16 • (06/15/97) • **83**

Santo Stefano de le Cane 1988 • $15 • (09/15/92) • **80**

Santo Stefano Vino di Ripasso 1994: A complex wine whose cherry, woodsy and spicy aromas and flavors are muted today, and while it's concentrated and long on the finish, it seems to lack the extra focus and clarity to really stand out. May improve with time. Drink now through 2000. • $16 • (07/31/98) • **84**

Soave Classico Monteleone Vigneti di Costeggiola 1994 • $9 • (06/15/96) • **79**

Soave Classico Superiore Monteleone 1997: Aromas are mute in this young white, but there are quince and mineral notes, and body on the palate. Picks up a touch of honey on the finish. Drink through 1999. • $11 • (07/31/98) • **82**

Valpolicella Classico San Ciriaco 1997: A fresh, fruity, soft style of Valpolicella for early drinking. Its cherry flavor and gentle structure finish with a pleasant austerity. Drink now. • $14 • (07/31/98) • **82**

Valpolicella Classico San Ciriaco 1995: A simple, fruity red with bitter cherry flavors and an astringent, slightly alcoholic finish. 7,000 cases made. • $14 • (06/15/97) • **78**

Valpolicella Classico Superiore Marano 1996: On the lean side, this has decent concentration and balance, but finishes a little tough. Food should smooth it out. Drink now. • $11 • (07/31/98) • **81**

Valpolicella Classico Superiore Marano 1990 • $10 • (09/15/92) • **81**

Valpolicella Classico Superiore Marano 1985 • $6 • (09/15/88) BB • **81**

BOSCARELLI, PODERI

Chianti Colli Senesi 1993: All the pieces are here—plum and cherry flavors, a touch of spice—but it turns a little flat. Quite tannic on the finish. • $15 • (03/31/97) • **79**

Chianti Colli Senesi 1986 • $8 • (01/31/89) • **78**

Chianti Colli Senesi 1984 • $6 • (09/15/87) • **72**

Marchesi de Ferrari Corradi 1993: Sleek and racy, with a good concentration of berry and dried cherry character. Medium-bodied, with silky tannins and a long, delicious finish. Drink or hold. • $39 • (03/31/97) • **87**

Rosso di Montepulciano 1992 • $14 • (08/31/95) • **82**

Red 1985 • $30 • (02/15/89) • **92**

Red 1983 • $29 • (06/30/88) • **85**

Vino Nobile di Montepulciano 1994: A delicious red with plum, berry and cherry aromas and flavors, medium body and a soft, sweet fruit finish. Well made. Drink now. 500 cases made. • $25 • (09/30/97) • **86**

Vino Nobile di Montepulciano 1990 • $22 • (02/29/96) • **89**

Vino Nobile di Montepulciano 1981 • $10 • (07/01/86) • **71**

Vino Nobile di Montepulciano Riserva 1985 • $15 • (06/15/90) • **76**

Vino Nobile di Montepulciano Riserva 1981 • $11 • (10/31/86) • **70**

BOSCO, CASTIGLION DEL

Brunello di Montalcino 1991: A clean and well-made wine, with dried cherry and mint notes framed by fine tannins. Fresh finish. A good effort made. Drink now. 1,166 cases made. • $NA • (11/30/96) • **84**

Brunello di Montalcino 1990: Light and advanced, showing some leather and cedar character but very dry on the finish. Fading quickly. • $NA • (10/31/95) • **76**

Brunello di Montalcino 1979 • $14 • (04/30/87) • **93**

Brunello di Montalcino Riserva 1990: Exhibits vivid floral, berry and cherry aromas and flavors, with an impressively fresh acidity. Medium-bodied, with fresh, fine tannins and a succulent finish. Drinkable now. 555 cases made. • $NA • (11/30/96) • **87**

Rosso di Montalcino 1994: Old and oxidized, earthy in character, verging on cooked. Barely acceptable. 583 cases made. • $NA • (11/30/96) • **70**

Rosso di Montalcino 1988 • $11 • (07/15/91) • **82**

BOSCO, TENUTA IL

Pinot Nero Oltrepò Pavese 1988 • $9 • (06/30/91) • **81**

BOSSI, CASTELLO DI

Chianti Classico 1995: Dark-colored and bubbling over with fruit—blackberries, plums and cherries prevail. Medium-bodied, with light tannins and a very fresh, zingy finish. Crisp. 20,000 cases made. • $NA • (09/30/97) • **84**

Chianti Classico 1994: Already a little mature, offering aromas and flavors of leather, spice and dried cherry. Light and slightly dry on the finish. • $NA • (10/31/96) • **77**

Chianti Classico 1993 • $NA • (10/31/95) • **84**

Chianti Classico Berardo Riserva 1994: Good ripe fruit and lots of new wood—perhaps a bit too much. Medium in body, with slightly drying tannins. Drink now. 600 cases made. • $NA • (09/30/97) • **84**

Chianti Classico Riserva 1993: An interesting berry and dried herb character, with a medium body, light tannins and a crisp finish. Drink now. • $NA • (10/31/96) • **82**

Chianti Classico Riserva 1991 • $NA • (10/31/95) • **79**

Corbaia 1994: Dark purple color, with intense flavors of berry, cassis, mint and toasty oak. Of medium body, with very fine tannins and a caressing finish. Very good wine from this estate. Try now. 1,250 cases made. • $NA • (09/30/97) • **88**

Corbaia 1993: Expressive with its berry, black cherry and vanilla aromas and flavors. It's medium-bodied with light tannins and a lots of wood on the finish. Drink now. Sangiovese, Cabernet Sauvignon and Merlot. • $NA • (10/31/96) • **86**

Corbaia 1990 • $32 • (12/31/95) • **89**

Corbaia 1988 • $NA • (10/31/95) • **84**

BRANCAIA, PODERE LA

Brancaia 1995: A very good, easy-drinking red, it's fruity and delicious with cherry, berry character, a soft texture and a creamy finish. Drink now. • $NA • (09/30/97) • **85**

Brancaia 1993: Beautiful plum and berry character flowing out of the glass. Medium-bodied, with fine tannins and a crisp, fruit finish. Drink now. Bottled by Castello di Fonterultoli. • $NA • (10/31/96) • **87**
Brancaia 1991 • $NA • (02/28/95) • **86**

BRANDOLINI D'ADDA, CONTI

Merlot Grave del Friuli Vistorta 1995: A Merlot with character. Plum, berry and spice aromas are followed by plum and smoke flavors, all on a rich texture that shows concentration. Has firm tannins on the finish. Drink now through 1999. 2,600 cases made. • $17 • (05/31/98) • **86**
Merlot Grave del Friuli Visorta 1993: Here's a serious wine with jammy, cassis and smoky aromas and flavors that carry right through the rich, round palate. The light tannins suggest pairing with food. Enjoyable now. 1,000 cases made. • $14 • (01/01/97) • **86**
Merlot Grave del Friuli Vistorta 1992 • $14 • (04/30/96) • **88**

BREZZA & FIGLI, GIACOMO

Barbera d'Alba Cannubi 1993: A pure, elegant wine with an abundance of black currant and black cherry flavors. Has firm tannins and acidity, but the texture is smooth. Good to drink now. • $NA • (10/31/96) • **86**
Barbera d'Alba Cannubi 1991 • $NA • (10/31/94) • **77**
Barolo Cannubi 1991: Ripe, concentrated fruit flavors and a smooth, easy texture make this an opulent, generous Barolo. Tempting to drink now, but could be cellared through 2002. • $NA • (10/31/96) • **88**
Barolo Cannubi 1990 • $40 • (10/31/95) • **88**
Barolo Cannubi 1989 • $NA • (10/31/94) • **88**
Barolo Sarmassa 1993: A full-bodied style of Barolo, thicker than many '93s, with rich, ripe fruit flavors and firm but not drying tannins. Should be lovely around 2000. • $NA • (10/31/97) • **87**
Barolo Sarmassa 1991: Big, rich and expansive. Broad in texture, ripe and deep in flavor, mouthfilling and full-bodied. Plenty of fruit and anise aromas and flavors fill out the tannic frame. Drink now to 2007. • $NA • (10/31/96) • **90**
Dolcetto d'Alba San Lorenzo 1993 • $13 • (10/31/95) • **87**

BROLIO

Casalferro 1994: Pretty berry and floral aromas waft from this silky, medium-bodied wine. Lovely, fresh finish. Drink now. 5,580 cases made. • $28 • (09/30/97) • **86**
Casalferro 1993: Beautiful berry, cherry and plum aromas and flavors. Medium-bodied, with fine tannins and a long, sweet fruit finish. 100 percent Sangiovese. Drink now or hold. • $28 • (10/31/96) • **87**
Chianti Classico 1995: Brolio is back with quality. Loads of fruit for a '95 Chianti. Medium- to full-bodied, with fine tannins and a fruity, lightly wooded finish. Drink or hold. 70,000 cases made. • $13 • (09/30/97) • **86**
Chianti Classico 1994: A subtle wine, of medium body, showing berry and raspberry aromas and flavors with light and soft tannins and a ripe fruit finish. Delicious. 80,000 cases made. • $10 • (10/31/96) • **85**
Chianti Classico 1990 • $NA • (02/28/95) • **83**
Chianti Classico 1988 • $9 • (09/15/91) • **84**
Chianti Classico 1987 • $12 • (10/31/91) • **84**
Chianti Classico 1986 • $8 • (11/30/90) • **77**
Chianti Classico 1985 • $6 • (10/31/88) BB • **87**
Chianti Classico 1984 • $4 • (09/15/87) • **73**
Chianti Classico Riserva 1994: Brolio gets better and better. Plum, blackberry and wet earth character jumps out of the glass. Medium- to full-bodied, with well-integrated tannins and a long finish. Drink or hold. 15,000 cases made. • $17 • (09/30/97) • **88**
Chianti Classico Riserva 1993: A racy Chianti with a cherry-berry-minty character. Medium-bodied with fine tannins and a fresh, silky texture. Perfect to drink now. 15,000 cases made. • $14 • (10/31/96) • **86**
Chianti Classico Riserva 1990 • $13 • (01/01/95) • **87**
Chianti Classico Riserva 1988 • $13 • (10/31/94) • **87**
Chianti Classico Riserva 1985 • $12 • (09/15/91) • **86**
Chianti Classico Riserva 1983 • $10 • (05/15/90) • **80**
Chianti Classico Riserva del Barone 1983 • $11 • (11/30/89) • **85**
Chianti Classico Riserva del Barone 1983 • $26 • (10/31/94) • **81**
Chianti Classico Riserva del Barone 1978 • $11 • (06/01/85) • **90**
Sangiovese 1993 • $9 • (02/28/95) • **80**
Sangiovese 1991 • $9 • (07/31/94) BB • **85**
Torricella 1995: A slightly dull wine with some hazelnut and almond character but it's slightly candied on the finish. 1,340 cases made. • $19 • (09/30/97) • **78**
Torricella 1994: Very mature, with pineapple and honeylike flavors. A one-dimensional wine that lacks richness. • $19 • (01/31/97) • **77**
Vin Santo 1981 • $25 • (09/15/91) HR • **90**
Vin Santo 1977 • $13 • (03/31/90) • **85**

BROVIA, FRATELLI

Barbera d'Alba Sorí del Drago 1993 • $14 • (10/31/95) • **83**
Barolo 1990 • $NA • (10/31/95) • **83**
Barolo 1989 • $NA • (10/31/94) • **83**
Barolo Garblèt Sué 1991: A tough customer. Mineral and metallic flavors are wrapped in a drying, tannic texture. Interesting to smell, but difficult to drink. 375 cases made. • $34 • (10/31/96) • **79**
Barolo Monprivato 1990 • $44 • (10/31/95) • **88**
Barolo Monprivato 1989 • $NA • (10/31/94) • **80**
Barolo Rocche dei Brovia 1991: Light cranberry and cherry flavors, with tough tannins and a drying texture. 350 cases made. • $38 • (10/31/96) • **78**
Barolo Rocche dei Brovia 1989 • $NA • (10/31/94) • **87**
Barolo Rocche dei Brovia 1988 • $30 • (10/31/93) • **82**
Barolo Villero 1993: Well made, concentrated, and distinctive, with mineral, earth, and cherry flavors. Uncompromising style, medium-bodied and very elegant. The tannins, while well-integrated, need until 2000 or so to soften. 375 cases made. • $40 • (10/31/97) • **89**
Barolo Villero 1991: Elegant. On the lighter side for Barolo, with fresh cherry and anise flavors, a smooth texture and well-integrated tannins. Lingering finish, too. Drink now through 2000. 375 cases made. • $38 • (10/31/96) • **88**
Dolcetto d'Alba Vignavillej 1995: Quite tannic, but the fruit is decent. Medium-bodied, with mineral, cherry and spice flavors and a dry finish. Try in 1998. 667 cases made. • $15 • (10/31/97) • **79**
Dolcetto d'Alba Vignavillej 1993 • $13 • (10/31/95) • **80**
Nebbiolo d'Alba Valmaggione 1993: A fairly dark and fruity Nebbiolo, medium-bodied, delivering cherry, raspberry and spice flavors. Turns astringent on the finish though. Try with food. 267 cases made. • $18 • (10/31/97) • **79**
Roero Arneis 1994 • $14 • (01/01/95) • **80**

BRUGO

Gattinara 1986 • $15 • (07/31/95) • **86**
Spanna del Piemonte 1990 • $8 • (02/28/95) • **72**
Spanna del Piemonte 1987 • $NA • (10/31/96) • **67**

BUCCI

Verdicchio dei Castelli di Jesi Classico 1994: A good if simple white wine with modest aromas of honey and flavors of peach. • $14 • (04/30/97) • **82**

BUON DONNO

Chianti Classico 1994: Very light, with some dried cherry flavor but it's rather dry on the finish. Not much to this. • $NA • (10/31/96) • **78**
Chianti Classico 1993 • $NA • (10/31/95) • **79**
Chianti Classico 1992 • $NA • (02/28/95) • **70**
Chianti Classico Riserva 1993: Marked by pretty blackberry flavors with a floral undertone. Medium in body, with light, fine tannins and a fresh finish. Drink now. • $NA • (10/31/96) • **83**

BUONINSEGNA, LA

Villa Buoninsegna 1993: Has bright cherry and floral aromas and some good fruit on the palate, but it's slightly dry and short on the finish. Drink now. • $NA • (09/30/97) • **81**

Key: SS—Spectator Selection CS—Cellar Selection HR—Highly Recommended BB—Best Buy $NA—Price not available Ⓐ—Auction Price (BT)—Barrel Tasting
Dates in parentheses indicate the issues in which the ratings were published.

BURACCHI

Rosso di Montepulciano 1996: Fresh and lively with cherry and berry flavors, a hint of vanilla. Medium- to light-bodied, with light tannins and a crisp finish. Drink now. • $NA • (09/30/97) • **84**

Vino Nobile di Montepulciano 1994: A pretty red with floral, vanilla and cherry aromas. Medium-bodied, with light tannins and a silky, vanilla finish. • $NA • (09/30/97) • **83**

Vino Nobile di Montepulciano Riserva 1993: Lots of vanilla, oak character with hints of berry and cherry. Medium to light in body, with light tannins and a slightly dry finish. perhaps too much new wood. • $NA • (09/30/97) • **80**

BUZZINELLI, CARLO

Merlot Collio 1995: Good complexity here, with black cherry, spice, cedar and a hint of caramel in this mature, medium-bodied red. The tannins are still firm and the finish shows a combination of sweet fruit, acidity and tannins. Drink now through 2000. 1,000 cases made. • $13 • (06/30/98) • **85**

Pinot Bianco Collio 1996: Apple and almond are the main themes in this rich white, with a bitter citrus note on the finish. Drink now. 1,000 cases made. • $13 • (06/15/98) • **83**

Pinot Grigio Collio 1996: A delicious, mature Pinot Grigio, its peach and nut aromas and flavors, rich texture and acid structure well integrated. Hint of bitterness on the finish keeps it in focus. Drink now. 1,000 cases made. • $13 • (06/30/98) • **86**

Tocai Friulano Collio 1996: Loads of almond character in this crisp white that has both concentration and balance. Finishes with a hint of grapefruit peel. Drink now. 1,000 cases made. • $13 • (07/31/98) • **86**

CA' BIANCA

Barolo Cascina Denegri 1988 • $29 • (11/30/94) • **83**
Barolo Riserva Cascina Denegri 1985 • $30 • (06/15/94) • **88**

CA' BOLANI

Merlot Aquileia del Friuli 1996: Attractive berry, cherry and spice flavors grace this elegant, moderately concentrated red. Finishes on the crisp side. Drink now. • $12 • (07/31/98) • **83**

Sauvignon Aquileia del Friuli 1997: A pungent, herbal, gooseberry style of Sauvignon. Leaner than some '97s, yet still has body rather than crispness, with a touch of earthiness. Drink now. • $12 • (07/31/98) • **82**

Sauvignon Aquileia del Friuli Aristós 1997: Full of citrus, gooseberry and grass aromas and flavors, all well integrated with bright acidity and medium body. Drink now. • $19 • (07/31/98) • **85**

Venezia Giulia Opimio Aristós 1997: Light and dilute, showing modest grass and herb aromas and flavors and crisp acidity. Drink now. • $19 • (07/31/98) • **80**

CA' DE MONTE

Barolo 1990 • $16 • (02/28/95) • **88**
Dolcetto d'Alba 1993 • $8 • (07/31/95) • **83**
Gavi 1993 • $8 • (02/28/95) • **82**

CA' DEI GANCIA

Barolo 1993: A traditional Barolo, with cherry and chestnut flavors and dry tannins that shorten the finish. Medium-bodied, with little appeal now. A disappointing effort from this producer, whose first vintages were more modern. 583 cases made. • $75 • (10/31/97) • **78**

Barolo Cannubi 1992: Bright and fruity. Shows oaky aromas, vivid flavors and a lively texture. Tannic and somewhat tart. Drinkable now. • $NA • (10/31/96) • **83**

Barolo Cannubi 1990 • $65 • (10/31/94) • **93**
Barolo Cannubi 1989 • $65 • (10/31/93) • **96**
Il Defino Red 1991 • $NA • (10/31/95) • **81**

CA' DEL BOSCO

Brut Franciacorta 1992: An intriguing, dry sparkling wine with complexity of flavor and richness of texture. Mature flavors of toast, nuts and orange zest are balanced by lively acidity. Drink now. 13,000 cases made. • $46 • (04/30/98) • **88**

Brut Franciacorta NV: A hearty sparkling wine that's strong on apple and butter flavors, if short on elegance. Full-bodied and mouthfilling. 25,000 cases made. • $28 • (08/31/97) • **83**

Franciacorta Cuvée Annamaria Clementi 1990: A serious, sophisticated sparkling wine with the toasty, doughy aromas of aged Champagne backed by firm fruit and fresh acidity. Delicious now through 2000. 603 cases made. • $61 • (10/15/97) • **90**

Franciacorta Cuvée Annamaria Clementi 1989: Maturing nicely, this deep-gold sparkler is rich with toasty, honey and nutty flavors, yet maintains a bright, lemony acidity. It's bold and harmonious, and full-bodied enough to complement food. • $55 • (04/30/97) • **90**

Franciacorta Dosage Zero 1992: This elegant sparkler shows both delicacy and assertiveness, offering a complex mix of citrus, apple, honey and spice notes, well integrated and harmonious. Bright and lively, it's an excellent apéritif. • $45 • (04/30/97) • **88**

Franciacorta Red 1992 • $NA • (02/29/96) • **78**
Franciacorta Red 1988 • $11 • (01/31/92) • **81**
Franciacorta Red 1987 • $16 • (12/31/90) • **77**
Franciacorta Red 1985 • $11 • (09/15/88) • **83**

Franciacorta Rosé 1993: A dry, vivid rosé with subtle red wine flavors of cherry and herbs, and a fine, expansive mousse. Probably best during the meal. Drink now. 617 cases made. • $47 • (12/31/97) • **84**

Franciacorta Rosé 1991: A really nice, dry rosé that blends snappy acidity and a smooth texture with subtle cherry and spice flavors. Very good. 617 cases made. • $47 • (10/15/97) • **88**

Franciacorta Satèn 1992: An elegant, appealing sparkler that blends pleasantly toasty, doughy aromas with apple and vanilla flavors and smooth texture. Lingering finish, too. 1,688 cases made. • $53 • (08/31/97) • **90**

Maurizio Zanella 1991 • $40 • (02/29/96) • **88**
Maurizio Zanella 1990 • $34 • (07/31/93) • **85**
Maurizio Zanella 1988 • $32 • (09/30/91) HR • **93**
Maurizio Zanella 1987 • $40 • (12/31/90) • **88**
Maurizio Zanella 1985 • $38 • (09/15/88) • **92**
Pinot Nero Pinéro 1988 • $50 • (01/31/92) • **83**
Pinot Nero Pinéro 1987 • $69 • (06/15/90) • **82**

Terre de Franciacorta 1994: Bright and vibrant, a delicious red. Ripe cassis and raspberry combined with chocolate are followed by firm, yet fine tannins. The components need a little more time to come together, but the balance is there; try in 1999. 7,354 cases made. • $20 • (12/15/97) • **88**

Terre de Franciacorta Chardonnay 1994: There's a lot of character in this full-bodied, smooth and subtly flavored Chardonnay. It's restrained but satisfying as the citrus, vanilla and honey flavors mingle on the finish. Should improve through 2000. 1,000 cases made. • $59 • (08/31/97) • **91**

Terre de Franciacorta Pinéro 1994: Seductive and harmonious. Smoky, berry flavors and silky texture caress the palate all the way—until the finely-grained tannins take over on the finish. The sweet fruit and smoky notes echo on the aftertaste. 492 cases made. • $65 • (12/15/97) • **88**

Terre de Franciacorta White 1995: Subtle, displaying apple, herb and lemon flavors supported by vibrant acidity. Try with light seafood, especially shellfish. 8,083 cases made. • $20 • (08/31/97) • **84**

CA' DEL RE

Barbera d'Alba 1996: Beautiful fruit, jammy, ripe and concentrated. Medium-bodied and super well-balanced, it delivers loads of gorgeous raspberry, cherry, blueberry, violet, rose petal and wet earth notes that explode in one intense layer after another on the palate. Very fresh. Long finish. Drink now. From Mario Perrone. 400 cases made. • $10 • (10/31/97) • **90**

CA' NEUVA

Dolcetto di Dogliani 1990 • $16 • (10/31/92) • **81**

CA' ROMÉ DI ROMANO MARENGO

Barbaresco 1993: Good color and some fruity flavor, but it's pretty aggressive for the vintage with a green, herbal character. Medium-bodied, drying tannins. Try now. 1,083 cases made. • $39 • (10/31/96) • **81**

Barbaresco 1990 • $28 • (10/31/94) • **83**
Barbaresco 1989 • $30 • (10/31/93) • **85**
Barbaresco 1985 • $28 • (01/31/90) • **88**

Barbaresco Maria di Brun 1993: Lovely, succulent fruit is backed by layers of wet earth, violet, cassis and rose petal notes. Its supple tannin structure and medium body make it drinkable on release. Delicious. 371 cases made. • $50 • (10/31/97) • **86**

Barbaresco Maria di Brun 1990 • $40 • (10/31/94) • **89**

Barbaresco Maria di Brun 1989 • $43 • (10/31/93) • **86**

Barbaresco Maria di Brun 1985 • $37 • (01/31/90) • **92**

Barolo 1993: Light and simple, with strawberry, cherry and mint flavors, supple tannins and a short, somewhat green finish. Try chilled. 1,070 cases made. • $44 • (10/31/97) • **77**

Barolo 1985 • $35 • (10/15/90) • **89**

Barolo Rapet 1990 • $35 • (10/31/94) • **87**

Barolo Rapet 1989 • $32 • (10/31/94) • **82**

Barolo Rapet 1988 • $36 • (10/31/93) • **83**

Dapruvé 1993: Smells earthy and funky, with leathery, barnyardy aromas, but tastes of ripe fruit. Medium body, dry tannins; not the cleanest of wines. Drink now. 3,625 cases made. • $34 • (10/31/97) • **78**

Dapruvé 1989 • $24 • (04/15/94) • **80**

CA' RUGATE

Recioto di Soave La Perlara 1995: Smells like truffles and honey, then just melts in your mouth, all the while maintaining a sense of restraint and firmness, leaving an impression of butterscotch. Drink now through 2005. 100 cases made. • $19/500ml • (06/15/98) • **88**

Soave Classico 1996: A lean, compact style, showing a hint of carbon dioxide, keeping the toast and citrus flavors fresh. It's balanced, with some honey notes on the finish. Drink now. 8,000 cases made. • $12 • (06/15/98) • **85**

Soave Classico Monte Alto 1996: Deep-yellow color signals maturity and the smoky aromas and flavors confirm it. Overall, a well-made Soave that's still bright, balanced and offers apple, citrus and mineral flavors in a seamless presentation. Drink now. 200 cases made. • $13 • (06/15/98) • **87**

CA' VIT

Cabernet Sauvignon Trentino Riserva 1989 • $8 • (02/28/95) • **78**

Merlot Trentino 1997: Fresh black cherries and spices segue into a rich, plum- and fruitcake-flavored young red with seamless texture and balance. The finish shows good grip. Drink now through 2000. 58,000 cases made. • $8 • (06/30/98) • **84**

Merlot Trentino 1994: On the light side, with herb and smoke flavors but not much fruit. 28,000 cases made. • $9 • (06/15/97) • **78**

Merlot Trentino Riserva 1991 • $8 • (02/28/95) • **85**

Pinot Grigio delle Venezie 1997: Lovely fruit, peach and apricot, along with a smokiness and a floral component. Medium weight, rich and balanced, with a lingering aftertaste. Drink now. 378,000 cases made. • $8 • (06/30/98) BB • **86**

Teroldego Rotaliano Riserva 1991 • $8 • (02/28/95) • **77**

Vino Santo Trentino 1988: An appealing Vin Santo, displaying molasses and toffee aromas, honey and mushroom flavors and a nutty finish. A little cloying, yet the complex flavors win out. • $NA • (01/01/97) • **87**

CABUTTO

Barbera d'Alba Bricco delle Viole 1995: A crisp red, with earthy blackberry, cassis and herbal notes and light to medium body. Sadly, it tastes slightly unripe. Chill it slightly and drink with pizza. • $16 • (10/31/97) • **80**

Barolo Vigna La Volta 1993: Fruity and fairly intense, medium-bodied, with supple tannins, some mineral character and a crisp, chewy finish, this tasty Barolo is drinkable now through 2000. • $32 • (10/31/97) • **85**

Dolcetto d'Alba Vigna La Volta 1996: Impressive dark color, supple body and ripe fruit for a Dolcetto. Slightly earthy, but there's plenty of red berry, wet earth and spice flavors. Chewy finish should soften with pasta or pizza. Drink now. • $12 • (10/31/97) • **86**

Vendemmiaio 1994: Good everyday wine, with toasty oak, vanilla, chocolate, spice and cherry notes. Medium-bodied, though it could use more fruit. Drinkable now. • $30 • (10/31/97) • **81**

Key: SS—Spectator Selection CS—Cellar Selection HR—Highly Recommended BB—Best Buy $NA—Price not available Ⓐ—Auction Price (BT)—Barrel Tasting

Dates in parentheses indicate the issues in which the ratings were published.

CACCHIANO, CASTELLO DI

Chianti Classico 1994: Disappointing, considering the producer. Shows a decent berry character, but it's rather light and diluted. • $NA • (10/31/96) • **75**

Chianti Classico 1993 • $13 • (10/31/95) • **80**

Chianti Classico 1992 • $10 • (02/28/95) • **74**

Chianti Classico 1991 • $14 • (10/31/93) • **87**

Chianti Classico 1990 • $14 • (10/31/93) • **87**

Chianti Classico 1988 • $14 • (09/15/91) • **90**

Chianti Classico 1986 • $8 • (05/15/90) • **86**

Chianti Classico 1985 • $10 • (10/31/88) • **87**

Chianti Classico 1983 • $6 • (09/15/87) • **73**

Chianti Classico Millennio Riserva 1990 • $17 • (02/28/95) • **89**

Chianti Classico Millennio Riserva 1988 • $18 • (09/15/92) • **86**

Chianti Classico Millennio Riserva 1985 • $18 • (09/15/90) • **80**

RF 1993: Round and ripe, a soft-tasting wine that offers plenty of plum, blackberry and black cherry flavors. Firm finish. Drinkable now. • $25 • (10/31/95) • **84**

RF 1990 • $25 • (02/28/95) • **90**

RF 1988 • $20 • (09/15/91) • **90**

RF 1986 • $16 • (06/15/90) • **85**

RF 1985 • $15 • (08/31/88) • **91**

CALATRASI

Terrale 1996: Inviting aromas of cedar and spice combine with bright raspberry flavors and a lively texture for an appealing everyday-style red. Not tannic. Drink now. 26,000 cases made. • $6 • (02/28/98) • **84**

Terrale 1995: Rich and supple in texture, the blackberry and plum flavors have a minerally nuance. There's firmness underneath, but it's approachable now. • $6 • (01/01/97) • **85**

Terrale 1994 • $5 • (01/31/96) • **82**

Terrale 1993 • $5 • (05/31/95) BB • **84**

Terrale White 1996: A little rough around the edges, but there are some good flavors of lemon and a bit of green peach in this light white. • $6 • (10/31/97) • **83**

CALISSANO, LUIGI

Gavi Villa Meriggi 1994 • $10 • (02/29/96) • **81**

CALMASINO

Bardolino 1990 • $NA • (09/15/92) • **79**

CALO & SONS, MICHELE

Vigna Spano Red 1990 • $20 • (05/31/95) • **81**

CALONICA, LA

Girifalco Red 1995: Exotic aromas of fruits and spices follow through on the palate. Medium-bodied, with fine tannins and a fruity finish. Delicious. Drink now. 1,600 cases made. • $29 • (09/30/97) • **88**

Vino Nobile di Montepulciano 1993: A well-crafted red with pretty plum, vanilla and berry character, silky tannins and a fresh finish. Medium-bodied. Drink now. 4,100 cases made. • $16 • (09/30/97) • **85**

CAMERANO

Barolo 1993: Some rich, ripe fruit character, with fairly intense red berry flavor, some licorice and wet earth notes. Tannic and a bit dry on the finish, but give this medium-bodied red until 2000 to soften. • $NA • (10/31/97) • **83**

CAMIGLIANO, CASTELLO DI

Brunello di Montalcino 1992: Has some fruit with berry, tobacco character but it's slightly dry and austere. Medium-bodied, with dry tannins and a fresh finish. Drink now. • $NA • (09/30/97) • **82**

Brunello di Montalcino 1991: Slightly meager, with pretty minty, berry aromas, and similar flavors, but it falls away at the finish. Very short. 11,000 cases made. • $29 • (11/30/96) • **79**

Brunello di Montalcino 1990: Ripe and fresh smoky, leathery, cherry character. Medium in body. Delicious and supple, finishing crisply. Drink now. • $NA • (10/31/95) • **85**

Brunello di Montalcino 1988 • $NA • (04/30/94) • **89**

Brunello di Montalcino Riserva 1991: A perfumed red with floral, berry and citrus aromas. Medium-bodied, with light tannins and a crisp finish. Drink now. • $NA • (09/30/97) • **83**

Brunello di Montalcino Riserva 1990: Very good, in a traditional style. Slightly amber in color, but shows plenty of ripe berry flavor that holds through the long finish, where it picks up a tobacco note. Full-bodied, with full, silky tannins. Drink now or hold. 250 cases made. • $NA • (11/30/96) • **88**

Brunello di Montalcino Riserva 1977 • $11 • (08/01/85) • **85**

Chianti Colli Senesi 1985 • $3 • (12/15/87) • **77**

Chianti Colli Senesi 1983 • $2 • (05/16/85) BB • **82**

Rosso di Montalcino 1995: A chunky Rosso with a bounteous red berry, cherry character and a hint of minerals. Medium in body, with medium tannins and a fresh finish. • $NA • (09/30/97) • **86**

Rosso di Montalcino 1994: A little simple, but some clean, meaty berry aromas and flavors. Medium-bodied, with medium-soft tannins. Drink now. 4,166 cases made. • $NA • (11/30/96) • **79**

Rosso di Montalcino 1993 • $NA • (10/31/95) • **81**

Rosso di Montalcino 1991 • $NA • (04/30/94) • **80**

CAMPACCI

Chianti Classico 1993 • $NA • (10/31/95) • **79**

CAMPANILE

Pinot Grigio Grave del Friuli 1997: Peach, quince and floral notes are intriguing and mesh nicely with the broad, rich mouthfeel. Moderately concentrated with a grapefruit peel accent on the finish. Drink through 1999. • $11 • (06/30/98) • **85**

Pinot Grigio Grave del Friuli 1996: Rich and floral-scented, with apple and vanilla flavors that linger on the finish. Has balance, and it's ready now. • $11 • (06/15/97) • **85**

CAMPOGIOVANNI

Brunello di Montalcino 1992: Some berry and cherry character, but a slightly short finish. Medium to light in body, with light, austere tannins. Disappointing for this producer. Drink now. 4,750 cases made. • $30 • (09/30/97) • **80**

Brunello di Montalcino 1991: Just what a '91 Brunello should be. Delivers wonderful fruit flavor, soft tannins and a long, berry- and cherry-accented finish. Enjoy now. 65,000 cases made. • $30 • (11/30/96) • **89**

Brunello di Montalcino 1990: This producer goes from strength to strength. A sensational wine, fresh and vibrant, offering marvelous blackberry, blueberry and black cherry flavors that linger for a long, long time on the palate. Sophisticated, supple, smooth finish. Better after 1999. Tasted twice, with consistent notes. 5,500 cases made. • $33 • (10/31/95) • **95**

Brunello di Montalcino 1988 • $36 • (04/30/94) • **90**

Brunello di Montalcino 1986 • $28 • (11/30/91) HR • **92**

Brunello di Montalcino 1985 • $24 • (09/30/90) • **85**

Brunello di Montalcino 1982 • $22 • (07/31/88) CS • **92**

Brunello di Montalcino Vigna del Quercione Riserva 1990: Stunning concentration, with layers of berry, cherry and spice flavors. Full-bodied and very round, with loads of fruit and tannins. Drinkable now, but age it for decades to come. Even better than this producer's '90 norm, this is one of the greatest Brunellos ever made. 560 cases made. • $84 • (11/30/96) • **97**

CAMPRIANO

Chianti Colli Senesi 1994 • $NA • (10/31/95) • **83**

CANALE, TENUTA

Chianti Classico 1995: Lovely wine with elegant berry, cherry and raspberry aromas and flavors. Medium-bodied, with a nice balance of acidity. • $NA • (09/30/97) • **86**

Chianti Classico 1994: Simple and fruity, with dried cherry and light plum flavors. Finish is crisp. • $NA • (10/31/96) • **80**

Chianti Classico Riserva 1993: Barely holding its own—light-bodied and slightly acidic. • $NA • (10/31/96) • **74**

Poesia White 1995: Slightly oxidized with a creamy, milky character. Medium-bodied, with wood notes and a candied finish. • $NA • (09/30/97) • **79**

Sinfonia 1993: Very light for a super Tuscan red, with some berry aromas and flavors and a hint of pepper, but diluted. 90 percent Sangiovese and 10 percent Cabernet. • $NA • (10/31/96) • **78**

CANALETTO

Chardonnay 1994 • $6 • (06/15/96) • **83**

Chardonnay delle Tre Venezie 1995: A hint of banana adds to the applelike character of this simple white. Try as an apéritif. 50,000 cases made. • $7 • (06/15/97) • **79**

Chardonnay delle Tre Venezie 1993 • $6 • (12/15/94) • **82**

Merlot del Veneto 1995: Intense flavors of cherries and spice, in a red with a delicate, supple structure, finishing with a bitter-almond note. Drink now. 50,000 cases made. • $7 • (06/15/97) • **83**

Merlot del Veneto 1994 • $6 • (06/15/96) • **79**

Merlot del Veneto 1993 • $6 • (07/31/95) • **78**

Montepulciano d'Abruzzo 1993 • $6 • (03/31/95) • **83**

Pinot Grigio delle Tre Venezie 1994 • $6 • (07/31/95) • **80**

Pinot Grigio delle Tre Venezie 1993 • $6 • (12/15/94) • **79**

Pinot Grigio-Garganega Veneto 1996: The ripe, passion fruit flavors and crisp acidity in this white make it a delicious summertime sipper. 60,000 cases made. • $7 • (06/15/97) • **84**

CANALICCHIO DE SOTTO

Brunello di Montalcino Le Gode de Montosoli 1988 • $NA • (04/30/94) • **90**

Rosso di Montalcino 1991 • $NA • (04/30/94) • **85**

CANALICCHIO DI SOPRA

Brunello di Montalcino 1992: A bit lean with some berry, cherry, tobacco character and a medium-to-light body, but it's slightly dry on the finish. Drink now. • $NA • (09/30/97) • **80**

Brunello di Montalcino 1991: A ripe and supple wine, medium-bodied, with silky tannins. Pleasant, for drinking now. 583 cases made. • $NA • (11/30/96) • **83**

Brunello di Montalcino 1990: Elegant, firm, silky tannins and rich fruit. Medium- to full-bodied, sporting mineral, berry and cherry flavors and a fine finish. Drinkable now. • $45 • (10/31/95) • **88**

Brunello di Montalcino 1988 • $36 • (04/30/94) • **80**

Brunello di Montalcino Le Gode di Montosoli 1991: Light and rather tired, this shows aromas and flavors of leather, berry and cedar, turning dry on the finish. An unfortunate effort for this producer. Drink soon. • $NA • (11/30/96) • **76**

Brunello di Montalcino Le Gode di Montosoli Riserva 1988 • $35 • (10/31/94) • **88**

Brunello di Montalcino Riserva 1988 • $NA • (10/31/94) • **88**

Rosso di Montalcino 1995: A vibrant Rosso with strawberry, cherry character. Medium-bodied, with fine tannins and a long, fresh finish. Delicious. 1,000 cases made. • $22 • (09/30/97) • **85**

Rosso di Montalcino 1994: Slightly funky at first, but with just the slightest bit of air it opens, becoming a rich and fruity wine with an abundance of mineral, spice and dried cherry flavors. Fine tannins. Drink now. 750 cases made. • $NA • (11/30/96) • **85**

Rosso di Montalcino 1993 • $19 • (10/31/95) • **88**

Rosso di Montalcino 1991 • $NA • (04/30/94) • **82**

Rosso di Montalcino Le Gode di Montosoli 1994: A very perfumed, pretty wine with a character of violets, spice and dried herbs. Medium-bodied, with silky tannins and a long, flavorful finish. • $NA • (11/30/96) • **86**

CANDIDO, FRANCESCO

Salice Salentino Riserva 1988 • $8 • (07/31/93) BB • **84**

CANELLA

Prosecco di Conegliano NV: Floral and apple aromas and flavors mark this Prosecco, and a slight sweetness gives it a round, soft structure. Drink now. 10,000 cases made. • $12 • (07/31/98) • **82**

CANTAGALLO, TENUTA

Carleto 1996: Pleasant aromas of almonds and pears. Medium-bodied, with lovely pear and apricot flavors and a long, flavorful finish. Delicious. • $16 • (09/30/97) • **86**

Chianti Classico Riserva 1993: Interesting, with strawberry, cedar and a hint of vanilla. Medium-bodied, with silky tannins and a fruity finish. Drink or hold. • $17 • (09/30/97) • **86**

Chianti Montalbano 1995: Medium- to light-bodied, with berry and slightly smoky aromas and flavors, light tannins and a fruity finish. Drink now. • $10 • (09/30/97) • **81**

Gioveto 1995: Rather dull, with some berry character, but it's slightly earthy and cheesy on the finish. Light-bodied, with light tannins. Serve chilled. • $15 • (09/30/97) • **79**

CANTALUPO, ANTICHI VIGNETI DI

Ghemme Collis Breclemae 1985 • $25 • (01/31/92) • **81**

CAPACCIA, PODERE

Chianti Classico 1994: Zingy, dried cherry character on the nose and palate. Medium-bodied, with lively acidity and a long finish. • $NA • (09/30/97) • **85**

Chianti Classico 1990 • $NA • (10/31/93) • **84**

Chianti Classico 1988 • $NA • (09/15/91) • **89**

Chianti Classico Riserva 1993: Offers respectable berry and cherry aromas and flavors, but a rather lean and slightly dry finish. • $NA • (10/31/96) • **78**

Chianti Classico Riserva 1988 • $NA • (09/15/92) • **86**

Chianti Classico Riserva 1985 • $NA • (09/15/91) • **88**

Querciagrande 1994: Elegant, with dried cherry and berry aromas and flavors. Medium-bodied, with silky tannins and a fresh finish. Drink now. • $NA • (09/30/97) • **85**

Querciagrande 1993: Pretty blackberry and vanilla aromas and flavors. Medium-bodied with fine tannins and a silky finish. Drink now. • $NA • (10/31/96) • **85**

Querciagrande 1990 • $NA • (10/31/93) • **88**

CAPANNA

Brunello di Montalcino 1991: Tired, in look and in taste, with cedar, tar and dried berry denoting the character. Slightly funky and unclean. 1,500 cases made. • $30 • (11/30/96) • **74**

Brunello di Montalcino 1990: Round and easy berry, cherry and tobacco aromas and flavors, medium body and soft, light finish. Drink now. • $NA • (10/31/95) • **83**

Brunello di Montalcino 1988 • $NA • (04/30/94) • **84**

Brunello di Montalcino Riserva 1991: Some berry and cherry character, with cedar box aromas, but the dry tannins dominate this medium-bodied wine. 741 cases made. • $40 • (09/30/97) • **79**

Brunello di Montalcino Riserva 1990: Rather unforgiving and traditional in style, this is big and tannic, with a steely astringency. Medium-bodied, with good blackberry aromas and flavors, but hard texture. Try in 1999. 710 cases made. • $55 • (11/30/96) • **85**

Brunello di Montalcino Riserva 1988 • $NA • (10/31/94) • **90**

Rosso di Montalcino 1995: Has bright cherry, strawberry and earth aromas and flavors and is medium-bodied, with medium to light tannins. Short finish. 2,625 cases made. • $12 • (09/30/97) • **83**

Rosso di Montalcino 1994: Delicious. A medium-bodied rosso with a bountiful dried cherry character and a silky finish. 1,816 cases made. • $15 • (11/30/96) • **85**

Rosso di Montalcino 1993 • $NA • (10/31/95) • **82**

Rosso di Montalcino 1992 • $NA • (04/30/94) • **79**

Rosso di Montalcino 1991 • $NA • (04/30/94) • **80**

Key: SS—Spectator Selection CS—Cellar Selection HR—Highly Recommended BB—Best Buy $NA—Price not available Ⓐ—Auction Price (BT)—Barrel Tasting
Dates in parentheses indicate the issues in which the ratings were published.

CAPANNA FATTOI

Brunello di Montalcino 1991: Medium-bodied, showing good fruit flavors, with plenty of dried cherry notes. A slightly tomatolike, unripe fruit note on the finish. Drink now. 450 cases made. • $NA • (11/30/96) • **80**

Brunello di Montalcino Riserva 1990: Elegant, with its medium-bodied silky tannins and lovely, sweet, fruity vanilla, spice and cedar aftertaste. One of the more approachable riservas. Drink now. 83 cases made. • $47 • (11/30/96) • **85**

Brunello di Montalcino Riserva 1988 • $NA • (10/31/94) • **92**

Rosso di Montalcino 1994: Slightly mature already, with some berry flavors and and dried herb nuances. Light-bodied, light finish, too. 1,416 cases made. • $19 • (11/30/96) • **77**

CAPANNELLE

Barrique Red 1988 • $NA • (10/31/93) • **86**

Tuscany Red 1988 • $NA • (10/31/93) • **85**

CAPARZO

Brunello di Montalcino 1991: Fresh and lively with cherry, berry and licorice aromas and flavors. Medium-bodied, with fine tannins and a crisp finish. Drinkable now. 6,666 cases made. • $41 • (11/30/96) • **87**

Brunello di Montalcino 1990: Wonderful Brunello that's drinkable now. Beautiful and fruity, offering medium body, fine tannins and a long, caressing finish. • $64 Ⓐ • (10/31/95) • **91**

Brunello di Montalcino 1988 • $30 • (04/30/94) • **91**

Brunello di Montalcino 1985 • $34 • (07/15/91) • **83**

Brunello di Montalcino 1982 • $NA • (09/15/86) • **95**

Brunello di Montalcino 1981 • $18 • (09/15/86) • **90**

Brunello di Montalcino 1980 • $23 • (09/15/86) • **88**

Brunello di Montalcino La Casa 1991: Shows good concentration of bright and ripe fruit. Medium-bodied, with fine tannins and a fresh, smooth finish. Very good, but why make La Casa in this year? 1,500 cases made. • $76 • (11/30/96) • **86**

Brunello di Montalcino La Casa 1990: Big and thick, this powerhouse of a wine packs in a lot of flavors: plum, blackberry, earth and cedar. Impressive, seamless, with a silky texture and supple tannins. Tempting now, but better after 2000. 1,500 cases made. • $64 Ⓐ • (10/31/95) CS • **95**

Brunello di Montalcino La Casa 1988 • $60 • (04/30/94) • **94**

Brunello di Montalcino La Casa 1985 • $53 • (07/15/91) • **88**

Brunello di Montalcino La Casa 1982 • $50 • (11/30/89) • **67**

Brunello di Montalcino La Casa 1981 • $50 • (06/15/90) • **83**

Brunello di Montalcino La Casa 1979 • $27 • (09/15/86) • **89**

Brunello di Montalcino Rio Cassero 1992: A simple, light Brunello with berry and cherry aromas and flavors, light body and a light finish. Drink now. 3,400 cases made. • $50 • (09/30/97) • **82**

Brunello di Montalcino Riserva 1990: A wine built for aging with its solid tannins, silky yet powerful, and loads of fruit. Full-bodied, with a long, fruity finish. Impressive now, better after 2000. 750 cases made. • $68 • (11/30/96) • **93**

Brunello di Montalcino Riserva 1988 • $55 • (10/31/94) • **92**

Brunello di Montalcino Riserva 1981 • $23 • (06/15/90) • **70**

Ca' del Pazzo 1993: A silky and caressing Cabernet, of medium body, with tobacco, cherry and dried herb character and a medium finish. Drink or hold. 3,000 cases made. • $30 • (09/30/97) • **87**

Cà del Pazzo 1992 • $28 • (10/31/95) • **87**

Cà del Pazzo 1990 • $25 • (10/31/93) • **86**

Cà del Pazzo 1987 • $24 • (08/31/91) • **85**

Cà del Pazzo 1985 • $28 • (05/15/90) • **77**

Le Grance 1994: Very ripe, with apple, spice and piecrust aromas. It's medium-bodied, with moderate acidity and an almond and vanilla finish. Pleasant Chardonnay. 1,500 cases made. • $21 • (09/30/97) • **86**

Rosso di Montalcino 1995: A lovely, rich Rosso with berry, chocolate and vanilla aromas and flavors. Medium-bodied, with velvety tannins and a long, rich finish. Delicious. 10,000 cases made. • $15 • (09/30/97) • **86**

Rosso di Montalcino 1994: Caparzo makes solid wines, and this is no exception. It's medium-bodied and chunky, with lots of berry and mineral flavors, finishing with freshness. 10,000 cases made. • $20 • (11/30/96) • **85**

Rosso di Montalcino 1993 • $13 • (10/31/95) • **83**

Rosso di Montalcino 1991 • $15 • (04/30/94) • **85**

Rosso di Montalcino 1988 • $14 • (04/30/91) • **81**

Rosso di Montalcino 1986 • $10 • (09/30/89) • **86**

Rosso di Montalcino La Caduta 1995: A vibrant red with lovely floral and citrus aromas and flavors. Medium in body, with moderate tannins and a crisp finish. 2,400 cases made. • $20 • (09/30/97) • **87**

Rosso di Montalcino La Caduta 1994: A solid wine, offering dried berry and cherry flavors with hints of spice. Medium-bodied, with light tannins and a fresh finish. A treat to drink, as Caparzo's single-vineyard rossos typically are. 2,500 cases made. • $20 • (11/30/96) • **85**

Rosso di Montalcino La Caduta 1993 • $18 • (10/31/95) • **87**

Rosso di Montalcino La Caduta 1991 • $NA • (04/30/94) • **83**

CAPEZZANA

Barco Reale 1996: Alluring blackberry aromas follow through to a medium-bodied palate, light tannins and a light, slightly dry finish. Drink now. 8,400 cases made. • $12 • (09/30/97) • **81**

Barco Reale 1995: Medium-bodied with plenty of fresh and vivid berry and cherry aromas and flavors and a crisp finish. Serve slightly chilled. • $10 • (10/31/96) • **85**

Barco Reale 1994 • $NA • (10/31/95) • **75**

Barco Reale 1993 • $10 • (07/31/95) • **84**

Barco Reale 1987 • $12 • (07/15/91) • **78**

Carmignano 1994: A no-nonsense red with cherry, berry, almost raisiny, character. Medium-bodied with some austerity and a crisp finish. Drink now. • $17 • (10/31/96) • **80**

Carmignano Riserva 1985 • $25 • (07/15/91) • **83**

Carmignano Trefiano Vittorio Contini Bonacossi 1995: Has gorgeous plum and chocolate aromas, but a slightly reserved palate. Medium-bodied, with fine tannins and a fruity finish. Drink or hold. • $35 • (09/30/97) • **87**

Carmignano Trefiano Vittorio Contini Bonacossi 1994: Delivers some decent smoky-accented ripe fruit character, but it's slightly dry on the finish. Tasted twice with consistent notes. 1,083 cases made. • $35 • (10/31/96) • **78**

Carmignano Villa di Capezzana 1989 • $12 • (08/31/95) • **82**

Carmignano Villa di Capezzana 1986 • $15 • (07/15/91) • **81**

Carmignano Villa di Capezzana Riserva 1990: This tightly wound, distinctive red is tart and tannic, but the cherry and berry flavors are vivid and concentrated enough to keep the balance. Drink now through 2000. • $30 • (01/01/97) • **87**

Chardonnay Toscana Conti Contini 1996: Shows some appley Chardonnay character, but it's oxidized on the finish. Barely drinkable. Tasted twice, with consistent notes. 1,200 cases made. • $9 • (09/30/97) • **69**

Chianti Montalbano 1996: A refreshing Chianti with berry and cherry character, a medium-to-light body and crisp acidity. 8,800 cases made. • $10 • (09/30/97) • **83**

Chianti Montalbano 1995: Good, fruity aromas with a hint of herbal green bean. Some ripe fruit flavor but it turns herbal on the aftertaste, and astringent, too. • $10 • (10/31/96) • **79**

Chianti Montalbano Conte Contini Bonacossi 1994 • $8 • (10/31/95) • **81**

Chianti Montalbano Conte Contini Bonacossi 1993 • $8 • (07/31/95) • **84**

Chianti Montalbano Conte Contini Bonacossi 1990 • $9 • (09/15/92) • **81**

Chianti Montalbano Conte Contini Bonacossi 1988 • $8 • (10/31/91) • **79**

Chianti Montalbano Conte Contini Bonacossi 1983 • $6 • (09/15/86) BB • **83**

Ghiaie della Furba 1995: A solid Cabernet of berry, cherry and currant character, with a hint of dried herbs. Medium-bodied, with well-integrated tannins and a medium finish. Drink now. 1,500 cases made. • $39 • (09/30/97) • **87**

Ghiaie della Furba 1994: An opulent red with violet, berry and slightly herbal aromas and flavors. Full-bodied with plenty of fruit and a silky texture. Very well made. Try now. • $35 • (10/31/96) • **87**

Ghiaie della Furba 1990 • $NA • (10/31/95) • **86**

Ghiaie della Furba 1988 • $34 • (12/15/92) • **69**

Ghiaie della Furba 1987 • $30 • (12/15/91) • **79**

Ghiaie della Furba 1985 • $20 • (01/31/90) • **91**

Rosato di Carmignano Vin Ruspo 1996: Delicious rosé, with strawberry and raspberry aromas and flavors. Light-bodied, with fresh acidity and a fruity finish. • $NA • (09/30/97) • **86**

Sangiovese Toscana Conti Contini 1995: A simple, fruity Sangiovese with strawberry and dried cherry flavors, light tannins and a crisp finish. 15,000 cases made. • $10 • (09/30/97) • **82**

Sangiovese Toscana Conti Contini 1994: An easy-to-drink red with berry and plum flavors and a soft and fresh finish. • $9 • (10/31/96) • **82**

Sangiovese Toscana Conti Contini 1993 • $9 • (10/31/95) • **86**

Vin Santo di Carmignano Riserva 1991: Emits lovely aromas of almonds, honey and dried apricots, is full-bodied and moderately sweet with a thick and smooth texture. Long, long finish with a nutty, honey aftertaste. Unctuous. • $NA • (09/30/97) • **88**

CAPPELLANO, GIUSEPPE

Barbera d'Alba Vigneto Gabutti 1992 • $NA • (10/31/94) • **79**

Barolo 1992: Approachable and flavorful, with mature fruit flavors and hints of spice. Smoothly textured and not too tannic. Drink now through 2000. • $NA • (10/31/96) • **84**

Barolo 1991 • $NA • (10/31/95) • **78**

Barolo 1990 • $NA • (10/31/94) • **85**

Barolo 1989 • $NA • (10/31/94) • **86**

Barolo 1988 • $32 • (10/31/93) • **91**

Barolo Gabutti 1991 • $42 • (10/31/95) • **86**

Barolo Gabutti 1990 • $42 • (10/31/95) • **90**

Barolo Gabutti 1989 • $NA • (10/31/94) • **93**

Barolo Otin Fiorin Collina Gabutti 1993: An elegant wine in a lean package, offering ripe, sweet cherry flavor, firm tannins and wet earth, dried herb and mineral notes. Should drink nicely around 2000. 417 cases made. • $45 • (10/31/97) • **86**

Barolo Otin Fiorin Collina Gabutti 1992: Rich and luscious. Tannins are tamed, flavors are opulent and deep. Beautifully balanced and smooth in texture. Should improve through 2000. • $NA • (10/31/96) • **88**

CAPPUCCINA, LA

Recioto di Soave Arzìmo 1994: A delicious, amber-colored dessert wine. Caramel, honey and almond cookie notes predominate, with medium sweetness and lively acidity. The taste indicates new-oak treatment. Drink now through 2003. 165 cases made. • $25/500ml • (05/31/98) • **90**

Sauvignon Verona 1996: Tasty, though atypical. A distinct smokiness in the aroma carries to the palate, with some vanilla and nut flavors. Creamy in texture, rich, with a touch of bitterness on the finish. Drink now. 1,000 cases made. • $12 • (06/15/98) • **84**

Soave 1996: Full of character, this Soave is deeply colored, richly textured and shows ripe peach, lemon and bitter-almond flavors. Moderate finish. Drink now. 4,500 cases made. • $10 • (04/30/98) • **83**

Soave Superiore Fontégo 1996: More austere in style, with vibrant acidity that keeps the lemon and strawlike flavors lively. Has the structure for light seafood and fish. Made from Garganega, with 15 percent Chardonnay. Drink now. 1,300 cases made. • $12 • (04/30/98) • **83**

Soave Superiore San Brizio 1995: Showing maturity, this white has developed an intriguing butterscotch hard-candy element, finishing with a touch of bitter almond. Balanced, ready to drink. 500 cases made. • $17 • (04/30/98) • **85**

Verona Madégo 1996: There seems to be a serious red wine here, but the horsey, barnyard aromas and flavors dominate. Disappointing. Tasted twice, with consistent notes. A blend of 40 percent Cabernet Sauvignon, 40 percent Merlot and 20 percent Cabernet Franc. 1,200 cases made. • $12 • (07/31/98) • **69**

CARATELLO

Chianti Classico 1995: Rather chunky and a bit coarse, but has some solid berry character. Medium-bodied, with light tannins and a short finish. 5,000 cases made. • $14 • (09/30/97) • **82**

Chianti Classico 1991 • $9 • (10/31/93) • **79**

Chianti Classico 1988 • $9 • (12/15/90) • **77**

Chianti Classico 1983 • $4 • (08/31/86) • **70**

Chianti Classico 1982 • $3 • (03/01/86) BB • **85**

CARNASCIALE

Il Caberlot 1993: Rather weedy and unripe for a Cabernet, it has some currant flavor and velvety texture but the vegetal character detracts from the overall quality. • $NA • (09/30/97) • **81**

CARNEVALE, GIORGIO

Barbera d'Asti de la Rocchetta 1995: Light and lean, with some modest raspberry and strawberry character, a narrow band of flavors and tight, ungenerous tannins. Try with pasta. • $19 • (01/31/98) • **77**

Barbera d'Asti il Crottino 1994: Funky, herbal, lean and astringent. • $29 • (01/31/98) • **70**

Brachetto d'Acqui Dolce 1996: This is a lively, berry-scented sparkler that shows medium sweetness and strawberry notes, followed by a crisp finish.

Unpretentious and tasty. Try with light appetizers or fresh fruit and sorbets. • $28 • (12/31/97) • **86**

Dolcetto d'Alba 1996: Chewy, bulky and fairly thick on the palate for its type. Red berry and peppery notes are muddied a bit by a slightly unclean earthy nuance, but it's still good. Drink slightly chilled. • $17 • (01/31/98) • **83**

Gavi 1996: Clean, zesty and vibrant, with lime and grapefruit character. One-dimensional, but fresh and likeable as an apéritif. • $17 • (01/31/98) • **81**

Moscato d'Asti 1996: The aromas are pine and flowers, but it tastes like grapefruit and raisins, with moderate sweetness and a soft texture. Try on its own or with fresh fruit desserts. • $17 • (12/31/97) • **84**

Moscato d'Asti Sori' 1996: Grapefruit, flowers and honey are the dominant flavors in this discreet version of Moscato, which also has good zip. • $25 • (12/31/97) • **85**

CAROBBIO

Chianti Classico 1992 • $NA • (02/28/95) • **80**

Chianti Classico 1990 • $NA • (10/31/93) • **90**

Chianti Classico Riserva 1993: Plenty of fruit, with blackberry, cherry and tobacco aromas and flavors and a hint of new oak. Body is medium-to-full, with velvety tannins and a long succulent finish. Drink now. • $NA • (10/31/96) • **87**

Chianti Classico Riserva 1991 • $NA • (10/31/95) • **87**

Chianti Classico Riserva 1990 • $NA • (02/28/95) • **89**

Leone del Carobbio 1993: Slightly coarse and jammy, but impressively concentrated. Good ripe fruit flavors with a slightly meaty, baked-fruit accent. Full-bodied and very extracted with loads of fruit and tannins. Try now. • $NA • (10/31/96) • **87**

CAROSO

Montepulciano d'Abruzzo Riserva 1992: Quite a mouthful. Fairly rich and concentrated, if not particularly complex, with plum, cherry and coffee flavors. Drinkable now, though a bit tannic. • $12 • (07/31/97) • **84**

CARPENÈ MALVOLTI

Prosecco di Conegliano NV: Almond flavors combine with a rich texture in this balanced, slightly sweet bubbly that finishes on a crisp note. Drink now. 250,000 cases made. • $15 • (07/31/98) • **83**

CARPINETO

Chardonnay Farnito 1995: Marked by its lovely mix of smoky, toasty oak and ripe apple character. Medium-bodied, with medium acidity and finish. Delicious wine. 5,000 cases made. • $20 • (09/30/97) • **87**

Chianti Classico 1995: Succulent, with loads of chocolate, berry and cherry flavors. Of medium body, with velvety tannins and a finish of moderate length. 80,000 cases made. • $15 • (09/30/97) • **86**

Chianti Classico 1994: Rather disappointing for this producer. Simple and light, with some berry aromas and flavors and a light, slightly dry finish. Very herbal, like unripe Cabernet Sauvignon. • $14 • (10/31/96) • **78**

Chianti Classico 1993 • $10 • (10/31/95) • **82**

Chianti Classico 1992 • $9 • (02/28/95) • **83**

Chianti Classico 1988 • $12 • (09/15/91) • **87**

Chianti Classico Riserva 1994: Well crafted, with a pretty balance of berry, dried cherry and new wood. Medium-bodied, with medium, fine tannins and a long, flavorful finish. Try now. 60,000 cases made. • $18 • (09/30/97) • **87**

Chianti Classico Riserva 1993: Shows good color and fruit flavor, but on the herbal side. A bit too much unripe Cabernet? Nonetheless, it's medium-bodied, soft and fairly attractive. • $16 • (10/31/96) • **81**

Chianti Classico Riserva 1990 • $13 • (02/28/95) • **87**

Chianti Classico Riserva 1988 • $14 • (09/15/92) • **85**

Chianti Classico Riserva 1985 • $19 • (09/15/91) • **89**

Dogajolo 1996: Dark-colored with intense boysenberry and berry aromas. Medium- to full-bodied, with fine tannins and a peppery berry finish. A bit rustic but juicy. Try now. 15,000 cases made. • $11 • (09/30/97) • **85**

Key: SS—Spectator Selection CS—Cellar Selection HR—Highly Recommended BB—Best Buy $NA—Price not available Ⓐ—Auction Price (BT)—Barrel Tasting

Dates in parentheses indicate the issues in which the ratings were published.

Farnito 1994: Excellent Cabernet. Ink-colored, with intense flavors of currants, berries and a touch of dry herbs. Full-bodied, with fine tannins and a long, sweet fruit, vanilla, spicy finish. Drink now. 8,000 cases made. • $20 • (09/30/97) • **90**

Farnito 1991 • $18 • (02/28/95) • **87**

Farnito 1990 • $18 • (10/31/93) • **93**

Farnito White 1993: Simple in flavor and appeal, with some buttery, earthy notes. 1,000 cases made. • $20 • (02/29/96) • **76**

CARRETTA

Barbaresco Cascina Bordino 1993: Diluted; has a green edge to it. Turns crisp and short on the dry finish. 1,500 cases made. • $23 • (10/31/97) • **77**

Barolo Poderi Cannubi 1988 • $23 • (03/31/93) • **75**

Barolo Poderi Cannubi 1985 • $26 • (01/31/92) • **82**

Barolo Vigneti in Cannubi 1993: Light cherry and licorice flavors and aromas and medium body, but it's sour and sharp on the palate and the finish. Hard to like. 1,500 cases made. • $23 • (10/31/97) • **76**

Bianco del Poggio 1993 • $9 • (04/30/96) • **82**

Dolcetto d'Alba Vigna Tavoleto 1996: Juicy, light-bodied and succulent. Somewhat green, with funky, earthy aromas, it does offer decent raspberry and cherry notes and a straightforward finish. Drink chilled. 2,000 cases made. • $12 • (10/31/97) • **76**

Langhe 1995: Dark, polished, balanced and lovely, this impressive red offers well-defined black currant, cassis, wild raspberry and black cherry flavors and no oak. Good acidity is backed by supple tannins. Drink now through 2000. • $NA • (10/31/97) • **86**

Nebbiolo d'Alba Bric Paradiso 1990 • $19 • (04/30/93) • **82**

Nebbiolo d'Alba Bric Paradiso 1989 • $15 • (07/31/92) • **78**

Nebbiolo d'Alba Bric Tavoleto 1994: Stinky, funky aromas distract from the sweet fruit flavors, and the tannins are astringent. A rustic wine. 1,250 cases made. • $13 • (10/31/97) • **75**

Nebbiolo d'Alba Bric Tavoleto 1988 • $15 • (07/31/92) • **75**

Quercia Bric Red 1990 • $21 • (03/31/93) • **87**

Quercia Bric Red 1989 • $20 • (01/31/92) • **84**

CASA, LA

Chardonnay Piave 1995: Could be a generic white wine. Rather full in body, but it has very little flavor, just a touch of butter on the finish. • $8 • (02/28/97) • **78**

Merlot Piave 1995: A middle-of-the-road wine, with plum and berry flavors and some herb notes. • $9 • (03/31/97) • **78**

Pinot Grigio Piave 1995: Fresh and clean-tasting, with subtle, floral flavors and a relatively light body. • $8 • (04/30/97) • **83**

CASA EMMA

Chianti Classico 1995: Delicate, with berry and light earth aromas and flavors and a fresh and silky finish. • $15 • (09/30/97) • **81**

Chianti Classico 1994: Impressively rich for the vintage, this shows blackberry, cherry and chocolate aromas and flavors. Medium-bodied with gentle tannins and a long, rich finish. Drink now. • $NA • (10/31/96) • **86**

Chianti Classico 1993 • $NA • (10/31/95) • **85**

Chianti Classico 1992 • $NA • (02/28/95) • **77**

Chianti Classico 1991 • $NA • (10/31/93) • **83**

Chianti Classico Riserva 1994: Sexy and ripe, with a bounteous plum, berry and new wood character. It's medium- to full-bodied, with velvety tannins and a fruity, vanilla finish. Drink now. • $35 • (09/30/97) • **89**

Chianti Classico Riserva 1993: An elegant wine with aromas and flavors of mint, berry and cherry . Medium-bodied, with fine tannins and a crisp, fine finish. Drink or hold. • $NA • (10/31/96) • **87**

Chianti Classico Riserva 1990 • $NA • (02/28/95) • **87**

Soloìo 1994: Pretty aromas of berry, currants and flowers precede a medium-bodied wine with medium, fine tannins and a long, silky finish. Try now. • $NA • (09/30/97) • **88**

CASA FRANCESCO

Chianti Classico 1982 • $6 • (11/30/89) • **81**

Chianti Riserva 1988 • $8 • (12/15/92) • **80**

Chianti Riserva 1985 • $8 • (10/31/91) • **85**

CASA GIRELLI

Chardonnay Trentino i Mesi 1995: Rich and buttery, with apple, fig and toast flavors. New oak adds interest, as well as a hint of bitterness on the finish. Comes together nicely though. 2,500 cases made. • $9 • (06/15/97) • **83**

Chardonnay Trentino i Mesi 1994 • $9 • (06/15/96) • **85**

Chardonnay Trentino i Mesi 1993 • $9 • (12/15/94) • **84**

Moscato Rosa Trentino i Mesi 1991 • $29 • (06/15/96) • **84**

Müller Thurgau Trentino i Mesi 1993 • $9 • (12/15/94) • **82**

Pinot Grigio Trentino i Mesi 1996: Lean and crisp, with modest apple notes underscored by an earthy streak. Could use a bit more concentration. 2,400 cases made. • $10 • (12/15/97) • **79**

Pinot Grigio Trentino i Mesi 1995 • $9 • (06/15/96) • **85**

Pinot Grigio Trentino i Mesi 1993 • $NA • (01/31/95) • **78**

Pinot Nero Trentino i Mesi 1988 • $10 • (02/15/91) • **81**

Sangiovese delle Marche Fontella 1996: Soft in texture, plummy in flavor, this is an easy-going, non-tannic red. Drink now. 12,000 cases made. • $7 • (02/28/98) • **77**

CASA SOLA

Chianti Classico 1993 • $NA • (10/31/95) • **81**

CASAL THAULERO

Abbazia di Propezzano 1986 • $19 • (07/15/91) • **89**

Montepulciano d'Abruzzo 1993 • $6 • (02/29/96) • **82**

Montepulciano d'Abruzzo 1989 • $6 • (06/30/91) BB • **81**

Montepulciano d'Abruzzo 1988 • $5 • (05/31/90) BB • **80**

Montepulciano d'Abruzzo 1983 • $6 • (06/30/87) BB • **86**

CASALOSTE

Chianti Classico 1995: The plum and cherry character prevails, although it's very tart and high in acidity. Light- to medium-bodied, with a mouthpuckering finish. • $NA • (09/30/97) • **81**

Chianti Classico 1994: An alluring Chianti Classico with a goodly serving of dried cherry aromas and flavors, light tannins and a crisp finish. • $NA • (10/31/96) • **85**

Chianti Classico 1993: A clean and fresh riserva, light-bodied, berry and dried cherry in character. Crisp, clean finish. • $14 • (10/31/96) • **81**

Chianti Classico Riserva 1994: Loads of strawberry and cherry character in this medium-bodied wine. Has velvety tannins and a long, sweet fruit finish. • $NA • (09/30/97) • **86**

Chianti Classico Riserva 1993: Fresh, fruity and pretty, with strawberry and plum aromas and flavors and a medium-weight, silky texture. • $18 • (10/31/96) • **85**

CASALTE, FATTORIA LE

Vino Nobile di Montepulciano 1993: Decent ripe fruit flavors with a hint of funky, earthy undertones. Medium-bodied, with light tannins and a slightly dry finish. Drink now. • $NA • (09/30/97) • **80**

CASANOVA DI NERI

Brunello di Montalcino 1991: This medium-bodied wine delivers a goodly amount of fresh, ripe fruit character, especially on the flavorful finish, and its tannins are fine. Drink now or hold. 2,800 cases made. • $35 • (11/30/96) • **85**

Brunello di Montalcino 1990: Classy Brunello. Plenty of wonderful mineral, currant, berry and cherry character in this one. Full body, ultrafine tannins and succulent flavors that build on the finish. Drinkable now. • $33 • (10/31/95) • **90**

Brunello di Montalcino 1988 • $27 • (04/30/94) • **82**

Brunello di Montalcino Cerreto Alto Riserva 1990: Superripe raspberry and plum aromas and tons of fruity flavors. Full-bodied and incredibly chewy, this wine has all the requisites for aging—tannins, fruit and acidity. Amazing, coming from this producer. Try after 2000. 335 cases made. • $72 • (11/30/96) • **93**

Brunello di Montalcino Riserva 1988 • $NA • (10/31/94) • **92**

Rosso di Montalcino 1995: Pleasant and easy to like, with cherry and berry character, light tannins and a fresh finish. 4,700 cases made. • $13 • (09/30/97) • **83**

Rosso di Montalcino 1994: Simple and fruity, with some fun, funky aromas and flavors and a fresh finish. 6,300 cases made. • $14 • (11/30/96) • **81**

Rosso di Montalcino 1993 • $NA • (10/31/95) • **84**

Rosso di Montalcino 1991 • $14 • (04/30/94) • **84**

CASCINA BALLARIN

Barolo 1993: There's modest ripe fruit in this red, but it turns dry on the finish. • $NA • (10/31/97) • **79**

CASCINA BONGIOVANNI

Barolo 1993: Pure, clean and beautifully crafted, this gem shines with laser-sharp flavors of wild raspberry, cassis, currant and dried herbs. Full-bodied, with good underpinning of acidity, it lingers forever on the seductive finish. Drink now through 2005. 833 cases made. • $40 • (10/31/97) • **91**

Dolcetto d'Alba 1995: Impressive Dolcetto. Dark in color, with licorice, tar and rose petal complexity, this tastes like a mini-Barolo. Full-bodied, the tannins are ripe, sweet and well integrated with the blackberry character. Harmonious finish. Drink through 1999. 167 cases made. • $18 • (10/31/97) • **90**

CASCINA CASTLE'T

Barbera d'Asti 1995: Good intensity here, with cassis, currant, wild raspberry complexity along with—unfortunately—a slight metallic, herbal taste. Medium-bodied, it bursts with freshness and a crisp finish. Drink now. • $NA • (01/01/97) • **82**

Barbera d'Asti Policalpo 1994: Lovely, balanced, supple and complex Barbera, with roasted meat, toasty bread, licorice, tar, rose petals and wonderful blackberry concentration. Medium-bodied and silky-smooth, it's delicious to drink now. Long, elegant finish. Bravo! Drink now. • $NA • (01/01/97) • **88**

CASCINA GALLETO

Dolcetto d'Alba 1996: Well made, offering juicy cherry, cherry pit and wet earth flavors, with a slightly astringent finish. Drink now with pizza. From Mario Perrone. • $NA • (10/31/97) • **83**

CASCINA LA BARBATELLA

Barbera d'Asti 1994: Generous in style and ripe in flavor. Nicely balanced and easy to enjoy with its cherry and blackberry notes and moderate tannins. 333 cases made. • $9 • (10/31/96) • **85**

Barbera d'Asti Superiore Vigna dell'Angelo 1993: Enticing smoky, herbal aromas and hearty black cherry flavors. Firm-textured and moderately tannic with a lingering finish. Drink now. 417 cases made. • $16 • (10/31/96) • **86**

CASCINA LA PERTICA

Bianco Le Sincette 1996: A full-bodied white that's subtle in flavor and broad in texture. Modest butter, mineral and melon notes linger on the finish. Drink now. 2,000 cases made. • $12 • (02/28/98) • **83**

Riviera del Garda Bresciano Chiaretto Le Sincette 1996: Almost pungent in aroma, with herbal, smoky and black currant notes, this dry rosé is simple, but sports personality. 2,000 cases made. • $12 • (12/15/97) • **80**

Rosso Le Zalte 1994: Wow! What this wine lacks in opulence it makes up for in sheer density. The pure cassis and raspberry flavors keep coming, layer after layer, in this integrated, aristocratic red that builds in intensity to the finish. Soft enough to drink now, yet should develop through 2000. 500 cases made. • $18 • (12/15/97) • **90**

CASCINA LUISIN

Barbaresco 1993: Sweet-tasting and quite exotic. A pleasant wine, with an interesting touch of dried herbs. Medium body, supple tannins, rather fresh and crisp on the finish. Full of life. Good balance. Ready to drink. • $NA • (10/31/96) • **85**

Barbaresco Rabajà 1993: Green, herbal, bell pepper and unripe aromas and flavors. Medium body. • $NA • (10/31/96) • **70**

CASCINETTA

Moscato d'Asti 1992 • $11 • (05/15/93) • **81**
Moscato d'Asti 1991 • $11 • (05/15/93) • **81**
Moscato d'Asti 1987 • $9 • (12/31/90) • **80**

CASETTA

Barbera d'Alba Vigna Lazaretto 1990 • $10 • (12/15/94) • **77**
Barbera d'Alba Vigna Lazaretto 1987 • $9 • (03/15/91) BB • **89**

CASINA DI CORNIA

Chianti Classico 1994: Some good fruit character, but it's dry and slightly rubbery on the nose and palate. • $17 • (10/31/96) • **72**

L'Amaranto 1994: Plenty of good ripe fruit in this wine. Shows cassis, berry, raspberry and tar aromas and flavors. Medium-bodied, with fine tannins and a long, silky finish. Drinkable now. Made from Cabernet Sauvignon. • $17 • (10/31/96) • **88**

CASISANO-COLOMBAIO

Brunello di Montalcino 1990: Loads of rose petal and berry and a hint of tobacco. Medium in body, fine tannins and succulent finish. Drink now. • $NA • (10/31/95) • **87**

Rosso di Montalcino 1993 • $NA • (10/31/95) • **78**

CASÒN HIRSCHPRUNN

Casòn 1994: What a beauty. Exhibits cassis, cedar and roasted coffee and vanilla aromas and flavors, while its elegance and power are draped like a finely tailored Italian suit. So suave and supple it seduces you, yet it should get even better over the next few years. Best from 1999 through 2004. 1,100 cases made. • $30 • (07/31/98) • **89**

Contest 1994: Nice balance between oak and fruit in this elegant pear- and clove-flavored white. Intense and concentrated, with mouthcoating tannins and a smoky finish. A blend of mostly Pinot Grigio and Chardonnay. Drink through 1999. • $28 • (07/31/98) • **87**

Corolle 1994: Sporting herb and cherry, this has density, structure and moderate concentration. Cassis, cherry and cedar are the flavor highlights, lightly framed by oak and velvety tannnins. Drink now through 2001. • $17 • (07/31/98) • **86**

Mitterberg Bianco Contest 1995: Very oaky, showing more clove, vanilla and smoke notes than fruit. Finishes with both cleansing acidity and tannins. Needs time to integrate. Drink through 1999. • $29 • (07/31/98) • **85**

Mitterberg Bianco Etelle 1996: New oak provides most of the character in this delicately structured white. Overall, it's lean and slightly astringent on the finish. Drink through 1999. Tasted twice, with consistent notes. • $15 • (07/31/98) • **83**

Mitterberg Rosso Casòn 1995: A lovely red, full of cherry, black currant and smoky, spicy oak aromas and flavors set off by a firm, yet elegant structure and tangy acidity. Fruit and oak keep pulsing on the finish. Drink now through 2000. • $30 • (07/31/98) • **88**

CASTEL RUGGERO

Chianti Classico 1995: Delivers more on the nose than on the palate with its alluring aromas of blackberries and wet earth. Medium-bodied, with fine tannins and a light finish. Slightly diluted. • $NA • (09/30/97) • **82**

Chianti Classico 1994: A rising star in the region. Amazingly dark and rich for the vintage with berry, minty and wet earth aromas. Medium-bodied with soft tannins and a caressing finish. Drink now. • $NA • (10/31/96) • **88**

Chianti Classico 1993 • $NA • (10/31/95) • **85**
Chianti Classico 1988 • $NA • (09/15/91) • **86**

Chianti Classico Riserva 1993: Superb for the vintage. Gorgeous aromas and flavors of plum, mint and spices. Medium-bodied, with fine tannins and a fresh, zingy finish with a new-wood accent in the aftertaste. Drink now. • $NA • (10/31/96) • **89**

Key: SS—Spectator Selection CS—Cellar Selection HR—Highly Recommended BB—Best Buy $NA—Price not available Ⓐ—Auction Price (BT)—Barrel Tasting
Dates in parentheses indicate the issues in which the ratings were published.

CASTELGIOCONDO

Brunello di Montalcino 1992: Has good berry and mushroom aromas and flavors, and is medium-bodied, but the finish is slightly diluted and dry. Drink now. 10,000 cases made. • $40 • (09/30/97) • **80**

Brunello di Montalcino 1991: Slightly disappointing in that it's already on the way down. Shows some ripe fruit flavors, but rather dry and tannic on the finish. Slight amber hue to the ruby color. Drink soon. Tasted twice with consistent notes. From Frescobaldi. Tasted twice with consistent notes. 1,083 cases made. • $29 • (11/30/96) • **81**

Brunello di Montalcino 1990: Youthful violet, mineral and blackberry aromas and flavors. Full-bodied and very rich, adding velvety tannins and a long, minty finish. From Frescobaldi. Try now. • $30 • (10/31/95) • **92**

Brunello di Montalcino 1988 • $32 • (04/30/94) • **85**

Brunello di Montalcino Riserva 1990: Slightly coarse and rustic now, but this is a huge wine, full-bodied, with loads of ripe fruit flavors and chewy tannins. A bit too dry on the finish. Maybe it will evolve better than expected, try after 2000. 2,166 cases made. • $85 • (11/30/96) • **89**

Brunello di Montalcino Riserva 1988 • $NA • (10/31/94) • **90**

Rosso di Montalcino Campo ai Sassi 1996: There's an abundance of fruit in this Rosso, with berry, mineral and floral character. Has medium body, firm tannins, a refreshing finish. Drink or hold. 1,600 cases made. • $15 • (09/30/97) • **86**

Rosso di Montalcino Campo ai Sassi 1995: Has a cherry, earthy, farmyard character and a short finish. Slightly unclean, and very light for this producer. Disappointing. Tasted twice, with consistent notes. 8,300 cases made. • $15 • (09/30/97) • **74**

Rosso di Montalcino Campo ai Sassi 1993 • $15 • (10/31/95) • **83**
Rosso di Montalcino Campo ai Sassi 1992 • $15 • (10/31/94) • **79**
Rosso di Montalcino Campo ai Sassi 1991 • $15 • (04/30/94) • **77**

CASTELGREVE

Chianti Classico 1995: Displays lovely bright fruit, with berry and cherry aromas and flavors. Medium- to light-bodied, with light tannins and a fresh finish. Drink now. • $NA • (09/30/97) • **81**

Chianti Classico 1993 • $10 • (10/31/95) • **80**
Chianti Classico 1992 • $9 • (02/28/95) • **82**
Chianti Classico 1991 • $9 • (10/31/93) • **82**
Chianti Classico 1990 • $10 • (09/15/92) • **78**

Chianti Classico Riserva 1994: Round and velvety, with chocolate, berry and cherry aromas and flavors. Medium-bodied. Fruity finish. Delicious. • $NA • (09/30/97) • **86**

Chianti Classico Riserva 1993: Shows some decent fruit flavors, but is rather light and drying on the finish. 8,000 cases made. • $15 • (10/31/96) • **77**

Chianti Classico Riserva 1991 • $13 • (10/31/95) • **82**
Chianti Classico Riserva 1990 • $12 • (02/28/95) • **85**

CASTELL'IN VILLA

Chianti Classico 1990 • $NA • (10/31/93) • **84**
Chianti Classico 1988 • $13 • (09/15/91) • **88**
Chianti Classico 1986 • $13 • (09/15/90) • **79**
Chianti Classico 1985 • $12 • (06/30/89) • **86**
Chianti Classico 1983 • $7 • (09/15/87) • **87**
Chianti Classico Riserva 1988 • $NA • (10/31/93) • **79**
Chianti Classico Riserva 1985 • $NA • (09/15/91) • **83**
Chianti Classico Riserva 1982 • $18 • (11/30/90) • **86**
Santa Croce Red 1988 • $NA • (10/31/93) • **92**

CASTELLARE DI CASTELLINA

Canonico 1994: A slightly overripe Chardonnay with dried fruit character on the nose and palate. Medium-bodied, with medium acidity and a rich finish. Funky but fun. • $15 • (09/30/97) • **84**

Chianti Classico 1995: Delicate and fruity, with berry, cherry and plum aromas and flavors. Slightly diluted on the finish. 4,100 cases made. • $16 • (09/30/97) • **80**

Chianti Classico 1994: An attractive Chianti. Shows dried cherry and floral aromas and flavors, medium body, fine tannins and a crisp finish. Enjoy now. • $16 • (10/31/96) • **84**

Chianti Classico 1993 • $18 • (10/31/95) • **80**
Chianti Classico 1991 • $12 • (10/31/93) • **81**
Chianti Classico 1990 • $14 • (09/15/92) • **82**
Chianti Classico 1989 • $14 • (09/15/92) • **82**

Chianti Classico 1988 • $13 • (11/30/90) • **82**
Chianti Classico 1987 • $11 • (11/30/89) • **81**
Chianti Classico 1986 • $11 • (10/15/89) • **82**
Chianti Classico 1985 • $11 • (03/31/88) • **85**
Chianti Classico Riserva 1994: Straightforward, with good dried cherry flavors, medium-to-light body and a clean finish. 1,000 cases made. • $22 • (09/30/97) • **84**
Chianti Classico Riserva 1993: A bit simple but delivers some good dried cherry and cedar aromas and flavors. Light-bodied, with fresh acidity and a crisp finish. • $22 • (10/31/96) • **82**
Chianti Classico Riserva 1991 • $21 • (10/31/95) • **85**
Chianti Classico Riserva 1990 • $20 • (02/28/95) • **84**
Chianti Classico Riserva 1988 • $23 • (09/15/92) • **83**
Chianti Classico Riserva 1986 • $11 • (11/30/89) • **86**
Chianti Classico Riserva 1985 • $17 • (09/15/91) • **77**
Chianti Classico Riserva Il Poggiale 1993: Round and fruity, with lots of dried cherry flavors. Medium-bodied, with medium tannins and a fresh, fruity finish. Delicious now. 540 cases made. • $30 • (09/30/97) • **86**
Coniale di Castellare 1993: A delicious wine, bursting with fruit on the nose, with blackberry, plum and cherry throughout. It's medium-bodied, with lovely fruit and well-refined tannins. Drink now through 2001. 250 cases made. • $35 • (09/30/97) • **90**
Coniale di Castellare 1988 • $35 • (09/15/91) • **92**
Coniale di Castellare 1987 • $31 • (10/31/90) • **87**
I Sodi di S. Niccolò 1991 • $42 • (10/31/95) • **87**
I Sodi di S. Niccolò 1990 • $36 • (02/28/95) • **88**
I Sodi di S. Niccolò 1988 • $35 • (09/15/91) • **88**
I Sodi di S. Niccolò 1987 • $32 • (04/15/91) • **86**
I Sodi di S. Niccolò 1986 • $25 • (11/30/89) • **94**
I Sodi di S. Niccolò 1985 • $25 • (05/31/88) • **96**
I Sodi di S. Niccolò 1983 • $20 • (05/31/88) • **87**
I Sodi di S. Niccolò 1982 • $20 • (09/15/87) • **89**
I Sodi di S. Niccolò 1981 • $20 • (09/15/87) • **87**
Spartito 1994: Gold in color, with very ripe, dried apricot character. Medium-bodied and thick, with moderate acidity and a chewy finish. Slightly awkward, but interesting to taste. • $10 • (09/30/97) • **85**
Vin Santo 1984 • $28/375ml • (09/30/90) • **88**

CASTELLARIN

Cabernet Sauvignon Grave del Friuli 1995: A simple Cabernet with modest black currant and leaflike flavors, a light texture and a brief finish. Drink now. • $9 • (04/30/98) • **78**
Chardonnay Venezia Giulia 1996: Fresh and vibrant, with apple and faintly nutty flavors, though the overall impression is simple and one-dimensional. • $9 • (12/15/97) • **80**
Merlot Grave del Friuli 1995: A light, easy-drinking red that sports leafy, bell pepper and tobacco character. Drinkable now. • $9 • (12/15/97) • **79**
Pinot Grigio Venezia Giulia 1996: Stony and textured, more like Sauvignon than Pinot Grigio, yet attractive for its mineral, gooseberry and almond flavors. Rich, with moderate length. • $9 • (11/15/97) • **84**

CASTELLI MARTINOZZI

Brunello di Montalcino 1988 • $NA • (04/30/94) • **79**
Rosso di Montalcino 1991 • $NA • (04/30/94) • **84**

CASTELLUCCIO

Le More 1992 • $19 • (02/29/96) • **85**
Ronco dei Ciliegi 1990 • $35 • (02/29/96) • **77**
Ronco della Simia 1991 • $35 • (02/29/96) • **75**
Ronco delle Ginestre 1990 • $27 • (02/29/96) • **79**

CASTELVECCHIO

Cabernet Franc 1991 • $15 • (06/15/96) • **79**
Sauvignon Blanc 1993 • $13 • (06/15/96) • **77**

CATALDI MADONNA, TENUTA

Montepulciano d'Abruzzo 1995: More than you expect from Abruzzi. Shows deep color, concentrated, bright fruit flavors, a smooth texture and a lingering finish, without too much tannin. Drink now. • $14 • (02/28/98) • **86**
Trebbiano d'Abruzzo 1996: A slightly fizzy, spicy white wine with modest green apple flavors. • $13 • (12/31/97) • **78**

CAVALCHINA

Bardolino Chiaretto 1991 • $NA • (09/15/92) • **78**
Bianco di Custoza 1997: Fresh, crisp and pure, with concentrated flavors of apple and grass and mineral accents. Superbly balanced, the flavors linger on the finish. Shows what can be done in a less-than-famous appellation. Drink now. 5,500 cases made. • $10 • (07/31/98) BB • **86**
Bianco di Custoza 1993 • $10 • (01/31/95) • **80**
Bianco di Custoza Amadeo 1996: A touch of oak adds breadth and richness to this peach-flavored, deftly balanced, velvety-textured white that evokes honey and vanilla on the finish. Has the body and weight for light foods. Drink now. • $13 • (07/31/98) • **88**
Cabernet Sauvignon Vigneto del Falcone 1988 • $NA • (09/15/92) • **82**
Cabernet Sauvignon Vigneto del Falcone La Prendina 1989 • $NA • (09/15/92) • **88**
Le Pergole del Sole 1990 • $NA • (09/15/92) • **79**

CAVALLOTTO

Barbaresco Vigna San Giuseppe Riserva 1985 • $22 • (02/28/91) HR • **90**
Barbera d'Alba Bricco Boschis 1991 • $NA • (10/31/94) • **84**
Barbera d'Alba Bricco Boschis Vigna del Cuculo 1993: Shows good, sweet-tasting cherry and raspberry flavors and a juicy finish. Light-bodied, slightly herbaceous. Drink chilled. • $14 • (10/31/97) • **80**
Barolo 1991 • $29 • (10/31/95) • **82**
Barolo 1988 • $NA • (10/31/94) • **87**
Barolo Bricco Boschis Riserva 1990 • $39 • (10/31/95) • **87**
Barolo Vigna San Giuseppe 1988 • $15 • (10/31/93) • **77**
Dolcetto d'Alba Bricco Boschis 1996: Fresh and grapey, with cherry, wet earth and white chocolate flavors, chewy yet ripe tannins and a succulent finish. Drink now. • $14 • (10/31/97) • **82**
Dolcetto d'Alba Mallera 1987 • $10 • (03/15/89) • **83**

CAVAZZA

Cabernet Colli Berici 1996: On the herbal side, this is a solid, one-dimensional red showing modest cherry flavors. Drink now. 10,000 cases made. • $11 • (06/15/98) • **80**

CECCHI

Capitolare di Cardisco Spargolo 1991 • $29 • (10/31/95) • **89**
Chianti 1986 • $5 • (01/31/89) • **80**
Chianti Classico 1995: Firm in texture, moderately tannic, with appetizing black pepper and raspberry flavors, this Chianti will be a good match with many different dishes. 40,000 cases made. • $10 • (05/31/97) • **84**
Chianti Classico 1994: In a traditional, rather light style. Shows spicy, earthy aromas, delicate fruit flavors and a lingering finish. • $9 • (10/31/96) • **84**
Chianti Classico 1993 • $7 • (10/31/95) • **80**
Chianti Classico 1992 • $8 • (10/31/94) BB • **86**
Chianti Classico 1990 • $11 • (09/15/92) • **85**
Chianti Classico 1986 • $7 • (07/15/89) • **86**
Chianti Classico Masser Pietro di Teuzzo 1990 • $NA • (10/31/93) • **84**
Chianti Classico Teuzzo 1993 • $NA • (10/31/95) • **81**
Chianti Classico Teuzzo Riserva 1993: Rather simple and light, it shows some berry and tobacco flavors but is light and woody on the finish. Not as good as an earlier review. • $NA • (09/30/97) • **80**
Chianti Classico Villa Cerna Riserva 1990 • $15 • (02/28/95) • **76**
Sangiovese di Toscana 1995: Overflowing with strawberry character and spicy undertones. Medium-bodied, with soft texture and a fruity finish. Drink now. 30,000 cases made. • $8 • (09/30/97) • **85**
Sangiovese di Toscana 1993 • $6 • (07/31/95) • **82**
Spargolo Predicato di Cardisco 1988 • $36 • (10/31/93) • **89**
Spargolo Predicato di Cardisco 1985 • $36 • (01/31/92) • **78**
Spargolo Predicato di Cardisco 1983 • $25 • (03/15/91) • **75**
Spargolo Predicato di Cardisco 1982 • $12 • (09/30/89) • **68**
Vernaccia di San Gimignano 1996: Very fresh, with an apricot and dry ice character. Medium-bodied, with fresh acidity, a refreshing finish. 9,000 cases made. • $9 • (09/30/97) • **83**
Vino Nobile di Montepulciano 1991 • $12 • (02/29/96) • **83**
Vino Nobile di Montepulciano 1987 • $13 • (03/31/92) • **77**
Vino Nobile di Montepulciano 1983 • $9 • (05/15/89) • **77**

CELLOLE

Chianti Classico Riserva 1994: Wonderfully fresh, with blackberry and cherry aromas and flavors. Medium- to full-bodied, with firm tannins and a medium finish. Drink or hold. • $NA • (09/30/97) • **87**
Chianti Classico Riserva 1990 • $NA • (02/28/95) • **87**

CENNATOIO

Arcibalde 1994: Dark ruby in color, emitting mint, berry and black currant aromas. Medium- to full-bodied, with well-integrated tannins and a currant finish. Drink now. • $NA • (09/30/97) • **89**
Chianti Classico 1995: A pretty Chianti, with dried cherry and floral aromas and flavors. Medium- to light-bodied, with fresh acidity and a fruity finish. • $NA • (09/30/97) • **85**
Chianti Classico 1994: An elegant and silky wine with minty, blackberry aromas and flavors. Medium-bodied. The tannins are light and fine and the finish is crisp. 4,000 cases made. • $14 • (10/31/96) • **84**
Chianti Classico 1993 • $13 • (10/31/95) • **85**
Chianti Classico 1992 • $12 • (02/28/95) • **76**
Chianti Classico 1990 • $10 • (10/31/93) • **83**
Chianti Classico Riserva 1994: Big and voluptuous for its masses of fruit and velvety tannins. Full in body, with a round mouthfeel and wonderful, warm, ripe fruit on the finish. Drink or hold. • $NA • (09/30/97) • **90**
Chianti Classico Riserva 1993: Ambitious winemaking, but delivers slightly more on the nose than the palate with aromas of flowers, berries and a hint of new wood. Of medium body, with light tannins and a light finish. 800 cases made. • $21 • (10/31/96) • **85**
Chianti Classico Riserva 1990 • $17 • (02/28/95) • **87**
Etrusco 1994: Concentrated with berry, blackpepper and cherry aromas and flavors. Medium- to full-bodied, with medium tannins, high acidity on the finish. Slightly rustic. Drink now. • $NA • (09/30/97) • **87**
Etrusco 1993: Impressive harmony in this wine. Pretty, with plenty of ripe fruit, tobacco and vanilla aromas and flavors. Medium-bodied, showing fine tannins and a fruity finish. Drink or hold. Sangiovese. 1,200 cases made. • $32 • (10/31/96) • **89**
Etrusco 1991 • $26 • (02/28/95) • **88**
Etrusco 1990 • $11 • (10/31/93) • **89**
Mammolo 1994: This wine builds on your palate. It has good, deep color, flavors of berry and currant, a hint of wood. Medium-bodied, with very fine tannins and a long, fruity finish. Drink now. • $NA • (09/30/97) • **88**
Mammolo 1993: Well made, with its bright berry and vanilla aromas and flavors yet slightly light finish. Medium-bodied, with fine tannins. Drinkable now. 500 cases made. • $32 • (10/31/96) • **87**
Rosso Fiorentino 1994: Slightly tough, but there's very good berry character and a hint of mushrooms. Medium-bodied, with medium tannins and a short finish. Drink now. • $NA • (09/30/97) • **86**
Rosso Fiorentino 1993: Shows good ripe fruit, especially berry, character and a healthy dose of new wood. Medium-bodied, with fine tannins. Slightly high acidity on the finish. Try now. Cabernet Sauvignon. 650 cases made. • $32 • (10/31/96) • **84**
Rosso Fiorentino 1991 • $26 • (02/28/95) • **87**
Rosso Fiorentino 1990 • $10 • (10/31/93) • **83**

CERBAIA

Brunello di Montalcino 1988 • $NA • (04/30/94) • **82**
Rosso di Montalcino 1991 • $NA • (04/30/94) • **84**

CERBAIOLA

Brunello di Montalcino Salvioni 1986 • $60 • (12/15/92) • **93**

CERBAIONA

Brunello di Montalcino 1988 • $50 • (04/30/94) • **80**
Brunello di Montalcino 1985 • $60 • (11/30/91) • **71**
Rosso di Montalcino 1988 • $21 • (01/31/92) • **82**

Key: SS—Spectator Selection CS—Cellar Selection HR—Highly Recommended BB—Best Buy $NA—Price not available Ⓐ—Auction Price (BT)—Barrel Tasting
Dates in parentheses indicate the issues in which the ratings were published.

CERETTO, FRATELLI

Arneis Langhe Blange' 1996: Dry, lively and bracing, this fresh, straightforward, slightly spritzy wine should be drunk soon. • $15 • (08/31/97) • **84**
Arneis Langhe Blange' 1995: Fresh and lively, with a bit of spritziness. Juicy peach flavors pick up a touch of almond on the finish. • $17 • (03/31/97) • **82**
Barbaresco Asij 1993: Elegant and interesting. Fairly complex earth, tobacco, anise and berry flavors and ripe tannins in a medium body. Drink now. 2,000 cases made. • $25 • (10/31/96) • **86**
Barbaresco Asij 1991 • $23 • (10/31/95) • **74**
Barbaresco Asij 1990 • $23 • (10/31/94) • **80**
Barbaresco Asij 1989 • $23 • (10/31/93) • **85**
Barbaresco Asij 1988 • $23 • (10/31/93) • **77**
Barbaresco Asij 1987 • $22 • (07/15/91) • **86**
Barbaresco Asij 1985 • $15 • (01/31/90) • **64**
Barbaresco Asili 1994: This diluted, light-bodied red tastes like raspberries and strawberries marinated in water. Soft tannins. Drink chilled upon release. 517 cases made. • $65 • (10/31/97) • **75**
Barbaresco Asili 1993: This medium-bodied wine is at first velvety, round and supple, with intriguing tobacco, cedar, earth and vanilla flavors, but the finish turns tannic and hard. Try after 1999. 600 cases made. • $50 • (10/31/96) • **85**
Barbaresco Asili 1990 • $61 • (10/31/94) • **79**
Barbaresco Asili 1989 • $61 • (10/31/93) • **87**
Barbaresco Asili 1988 • $61 • (10/31/93) • **75**
Barbaresco Asili 1987 • $40 • (04/30/91) • **89**
Barbaresco Asili 1986 • $35 • (04/15/90) • **85**
Barbaresco Asili 1985 • $35 • (08/31/89) • **89**
Barbaresco Asili 1984 • $15 • (09/15/88) • **80**
Barbaresco Asili 1982 • $19 • (09/15/88) • **87**
Barbaresco Asili 1978 • $NA • (03/01/86) • **90**
Barbaresco Asili 1976 • $NA • (09/15/88) • **89**
Barbaresco Asili 1974 • $NA • (03/01/86) • **90**
Barbaresco Fasêt 1993: Well made, but somewhat angular. Fruit, spice, cedar, vanilla and chocolate flavors are rather complex. Medium-bodied, with well-integrated tannins. Try after 1999. 667 cases made. • $53 • (10/31/96) • **87**
Barbaresco Fasêt 1990 • $44 • (10/31/94) • **86**
Barbaresco Fasêt 1989 • $44 • (10/31/93) • **82**
Barbaresco Fasêt 1988 • $44 • (10/31/93) • **79**
Barbaresco Fasêt 1987 • $31 • (07/15/91) • **89**
Barbaresco Fasêt 1985 • $31 • (01/31/90) • **87**
Barbera d'Alba Piana 1995: Wonderfully ripe, complex and intriguing—although the aromas are rather earthy, even funky—and the flavors linger on the long, supple, satisfying finish. Should be a marvel to match this with mushroom or truffle dishes. 1,000 cases made. • $29 • (10/31/97) • **86**
Barbera d'Alba Piana 1993 • $17 • (10/31/95) • **83**
Barbera d'Alba Piana 1991 • $17 • (11/15/93) • **76**
Barbera d'Alba Piana 1990 • $17 • (04/30/93) • **70**
Barbera d'Alba Piana 1989 • $18 • (10/31/92) • **87**
Barolo Bricco Rocche 1990 • $100 • (10/31/94) • **88**
Barolo Bricco Rocche 1986 • $110 • (04/30/91) • **89**
Barolo Bricco Rocche 1985 • $56 • (03/31/90) • **86**
Barolo Bricco Rocche 1982 • $NA • (09/15/88) • **91**
Barolo Bricco Rocche 1980 • $NA • (03/01/86) • **90**
Barolo Brunate 1993: An intense style with rich, concentrated fruit, but the tannins are drying at this stage. Offers nice flavors of cherry, spice, chestnut, chocolate and bark, and it has good length on the finish. Should come into balance with time, as the tannins soften. Try around 2002. 1,967 cases made. • $49 • (10/31/97) • **88**
Barolo Brunate 1990 • $44 • (10/31/94) • **77**
Barolo Brunate 1989 • $44 • (10/31/93) • **86**
Barolo Brunate 1988 • $44 • (10/31/93) • **81**
Barolo Brunate 1986 • $40 • (04/30/91) • **80**
Barolo Brunate 1985 • $41 • (01/31/90) • **92**
Barolo Brunate 1983 • $27 • (07/31/89) • **85**
Barolo Brunate 1979 • $NA • (03/01/86) • **86**
Barolo Brunate 1978 • $39 Ⓐ • (09/15/88) • **86**
Barolo Brunate 1967 • $100 • (10/20/87) • **90**
Barolo Cannubi 1971 • $NA • (03/01/86) • **85**
Barolo Prapò 1993: Light-colored and made in a traditional style, this offers nice, ripe fruit. Too bad the tannins turn dry on the finish. Try after 2000. 1,167 cases made. • $50 • (10/31/97) • **83**
Barolo Prapò 1990 • $54 • (10/31/94) • **88**

Barolo Prapò 1989 • $54 • (10/31/93) • **82**
Barolo Prapò 1988 • $54 • (10/31/93) • **84**
Barolo Prapò 1986 • $50 • (02/28/91) • **91**
Barolo Prapò 1985 • $50 • (03/31/90) • **78**
Barolo Prapò 1983 • $31 • (07/31/89) • **86**
Barolo Prapò 1978 • $NA • (03/01/86) • **95**
Barolo Prapò 1976 • $80 • (09/15/88) • **82**
Barolo Prapò 1971 • $100 • (10/30/87) • **88**
Barolo Zonchera 1992: An old-fashioned Barolo with nutty, cedary aromas, tart cranberry and cherry flavors and a tannic texture. Drink now through 2000. 4,166 cases made. • $25 • (10/31/96) • **81**
Barolo Zonchera 1991 • $23 • (10/31/95) • **76**
Barolo Zonchera 1989 • $23 • (10/31/94) • **88**
Barolo Zonchera 1988 • $23 • (10/31/93) • **87**
Barolo Zonchera 1987 • $23 • (08/31/91) • **86**
Barolo Zonchera 1985 • $16 • (06/15/90) • **82**
Barolo Zonchera 1984 • $16 • (09/15/88) • **83**
Barolo Zonchera 1982 • $16 • (06/30/87) • **90**
Barolo Zonchera 1980 • $9 • (02/16/86) SS • **96**
Cabernet Sauvignon La Bernardina Da Uve 1991 • $26 • (02/28/95) • **93**
Chardonnay La Bernardina Da Uve 1993 • $24 • (02/29/96) • **87**
Dolcetto d'Alba Rossana 1996: A sweet-tasting, delicate red with good berry flavor and supple tannins. It's light-bodied, quaffable and harmonious on the finish. Drink now. 6,250 cases made. • $19 • (10/31/97) • **83**
Dolcetto d'Alba Rossana 1994 • $17 • (10/31/95) • **81**
Dolcetto d'Alba Rossana 1990 • $18 • (10/31/92) • **83**
Dolcetto d'Alba Rossana 1989 • $16 • (04/30/91) • **79**
Dolcetto d'Alba Rossana 1987 • $12 • (03/15/89) • **86**
Dolcetto d'Alba Rossana 1985 • $8 • (12/31/87) • **74**
La Bernardina Monsordo Red 1994: Thick, ripe, rich, loaded with personality, this warm and generous red may lack finesse but it's surely a mouthful of wine. Has layers of flavor—toasty, smoke, currant, red- and blackberry and spice. A bit of a hot-weather wine, but still impressive. Drink now through 2002. 500 cases made. • $36 • (10/31/97) • **89**
Moscato d'Asti I Vignaioli di Santo Stefano 1996: Quite sweet and slightly bubbly, with appealing aromas and smooth texture, it's simple and enjoyable as a dessert wine. Drink now. • $16 • (08/31/97) • **84**
Nebbiolo d'Alba Lantasco 1990 • $19 • (04/30/93) • **87**
Nebbiolo d'Alba Lantasco 1989 • $16 • (10/31/92) • **81**
Nebbiolo d'Alba Lantasco 1988 • $18 • (04/30/91) • **81**

CERRO, FATTORIA DEL

Chianti Colli Senesi 1987 • $5 • (07/31/89) • **74**
Rosso di Montepulciano 1996: Big and ripe for this category, it's full-bodied with lots of fruit and velvety tannins. A bit one-dimensional, but generous and fruity. Drink now. 9,100 cases made. • $11 • (09/30/97) • **86**
Rosso di Montepulciano 1992 • $9 • (07/31/94) • **83**
Vino Nobile di Montepulciano 1994: There's some solid fruit in this wine, but it's slightly diluted. Medium-bodied, with ripe berry, cherry and plum character, light tannins and a light finish. Drink now. 25,000 cases made. • $16 • (09/30/97) • **83**
Vino Nobile di Montepulciano 1990 • $14 • (05/31/95) • **74**
Vino Nobile di Montepulciano Riserva 1993: There's delicious fruit in this wine—plenty of berry, cherry and plum flavors. It's medium- to full-bodied, has soft tannins and a long, fruity finish. Drink or hold. 8,300 cases made. • $24 • (09/30/97) • **87**
Vino Nobile di Montepulciano Riserva 1988 • $16 • (07/31/94) • **85**
Vino Nobile di Montepulciano Vigneto Antica Chiusina 1993: Good, but slightly disappointing, dry finish. Has pretty berry, dried cherry aromas and flavors, a medium to light body. 1,600 cases made. • $25 • (09/30/97) • **82**
Vino Nobile di Montepulciano Vigneto Antica Chiusina 1990 • $19 • (02/29/96) • **87**

CERVETERI, CANTINA COOPERATIVA DI

Cerveteri Vigna Grande 1995: A snazzy, oak-aged red, with ample flavors of cherries and plums that are nicely rounded and lifted by accents of vanilla, cedar and nutmeg. Smooth and moderately tannic. Drink now through 2000. • $19 • (06/15/98) • **88**

CESARE, PIO

Arneis Langhe 1996: Interesting and fairly rich, with delicious flavors of pear and vanilla. A nicely concentrated wine meant for seafood or poultry. Finishes on a lovely spicy note. • $20 • (12/31/97) • **84**
Barbaresco 1993: The winemaker used so much oak with this wine it tastes like a strawberry-vanilla milkshake. Light body, soft tannins. Drink slightly chilled upon release. • $37 • (10/31/97) • **77**
Barbaresco 1992: Soft, supple, a bit diluted and ready to drink. Aromas and flavors of chocolate, spice and dried herbs. A bit harsh on the finish. • $33 • (10/31/96) • **77**
Barbaresco 1991 • $32 • (10/31/95) • **82**
Barbaresco 1990 • $28 • (10/31/94) • **89**
Barbaresco 1989 • $NA • (10/31/94) • **81**
Barbaresco 1988 • $34 • (10/31/93) • **83**
Barbaresco Il Bricco 1993: A light- to medium-bodied, easy-going red with milky, chocolaty, cherry flavors and soft tannins. Enjoy now through 2000. 50 cases made. • $49 • (10/31/97) • **83**
Barbaresco Il Bricco Riserva 1990 • $52 • (10/31/95) • **88**
Barbera d'Alba 1995: Crisp Barbera focusing on fresh, grapey, red berry flavors that explode on the palate. Very nice licorice, vanilla and spice notes. Almost citrusy, but should go well with food through 1999. 4,500 cases made. • $15 • (10/31/97) • **85**
Barbera d'Alba 1993: Subtle, elegant and well made, it plays to the vintage with generous fruit flavors and some spicy, mocha notes. A bit short on the finish. Drink upon release. • $13 • (10/31/96) • **86**
Barbera d'Alba 1991 • $10 • (10/31/94) • **86**
Barbera d'Alba 1989 • $17 • (10/15/93) • **83**
Barbera d'Alba 1987 • $12 • (04/15/91) • **81**
Barbera d'Alba 1985 • $12 • (11/15/88) • **78**
Barolo 1993: Smooth, round, and offering so much caramel and chocolate, it smells and tastes like a Mars candy bar. Supple tannins, spice and a hint of red berry flavor help balance it. Drink now through 2002. 6,000 cases made. • $34 • (10/31/97) • **86**
Barolo 1992: Alluring for its lush texture. Nice fruit and earth notes mingle with a slightly aggressive chestnut aroma. Medium-to-full body, with chocolate and plum flavors on the finish. Try now. 4,000 cases made. • $24 • (10/31/96) • **85**
Barolo 1990 • $28 • (10/31/94) • **88**
Barolo 1989 • $28 • (10/31/94) • **86**
Barolo 1988 • $28 • (10/31/93) • **83**
Barolo 1987 • $27 • (12/15/92) • **82**
Barolo 1985 • $38 • (05/15/91) • **89**
Barolo 1983 • $NA • (09/15/88) • **88**
Barolo 1982 • $NA • (09/15/88) • **91**
Barolo 1981 • $NA • (09/15/88) • **87**
Barolo 1978 • $42 Ⓐ • (09/15/88) • **85**
Barolo 1974 • $NA • (09/15/88) • **77**
Barolo 1971 • $NA • (09/15/88) • **80**
Barolo Ornato 1993: Smells like a chocolate milkshake, tastes of orange peel and roses, and has lovely notes of toasty oak and smoked meat. Full-bodied, velvety and very yummy. • $NA • (10/31/97) (BT) • **85-89**
Barolo Ornato 1990 • $41 • (10/31/94) • **95**
Barolo Ornato 1988 • $NA • (10/31/93) • **90**
Barolo Ornato Riserva 1985 • $48 • (05/15/91) HR • **91**
Barolo Riserva 1982 • $67 Ⓐ • (11/15/88) • **86**
Barolo Riserva 1980 • $19 • (02/15/87) • **72**
Barolo Riserva 1978 • $19 • (10/01/84) SS • **89**
Chardonnay Langhe Piodilei 1995: Big, fat, buttery and over-oaked, turning a bit bitter on the finish. Medium-bodied. Drink now. 400 cases made. • $35 • (01/31/98) • **77**
Chardonnay del Piemonte 1994 • $11 • (02/29/96) • **88**
Chardonnay del Piemonte 1993 • $10 • (02/28/95) • **84**
Cortese di Gavi 1994 • $17 • (02/29/96) • **84**
Cortese di Gavi 1993 • $16 • (02/28/95) • **87**
Dolcetto d'Alba 1996: Nice currant, sweet licorice and grapey red berry flavors mark this crisp wine. Slight dilution on the finish, with somewhat dry tannins. Drinkable now with food. 4,800 cases made. • $13 • (10/31/97) • **82**
Dolcetto d'Alba 1992 • $10 • (07/31/95) • **83**
Dolcetto d'Alba 1991 • $18 • (10/31/92) • **81**
Dolcetto d'Alba 1985 • $10 • (10/31/86) • **71**
Nebbiolo Piedmont 1983 • $8 • (02/16/86) • **88**
Ornato 1983 • $16 • (03/31/88) • **82**
Rosso del Piemonte 1989 • $12 • (01/31/92) • **83**

CESARI, UMBERTO

Albana di Romagna Colle del Re 1995: There's plenty of zip but not much fruit in this basic white. 10,000 cases made. • $10 • (05/15/97) • **75**
Albana di Romagna Colle del Re Passito 1993: A full-bodied, sweet and smoky-tasting dessert wine with an amber color and a strong but simple flavor profile. 1,000 cases made. • $27/500ml • (04/30/97) • **83**
Chardonnay Emilia Laurento 1995: Tired-tasting, with an overwhelming flavor of turned apple cider. Not recommended. Tasted twice, with consistent notes. 2,000 cases made. • $13 • (06/15/98) • **68**
Liano 1992: A rustic-style red with plum, prune and game flavors. Hearty and full-bodied, though still a bit tannic. Drink now. 2,500 cases made. • $12 • (03/31/97) • **84**
Sangiovese di Romagna Ca' Grande Superiore 1995: Already mature with roasted, herbal flavors. Very soft and easy-drinking, though one-dimensional. 25,000 cases made. • $8 • (03/31/97) • **80**
Sangiovese di Romagna Riserva 1995: A solid table-wine, with straightforward plum and spice flavors and moderate tannins. Drink now. 15,000 cases made. • $10 • (06/15/98) • **81**
Sangiovese di Romagna Riserva 1993: Slightly green tasting, with plum flavors and assertive tannins. Fairly well balanced, but gets a little tough on the finish. 15,000 cases made. • $10 • (03/31/97) • **79**
Sangiovese di Romagna Riserva 1992 • $10 • (02/29/96) • **83**

CESARI E FIGLI, FRANCO

Amarone della Valpolicella Il Bosco 1988 • $30 • (09/30/95) • **85**
Barolo Vigna Cerretta 1990 • $NA • (10/31/95) • **79**

CHERUBIN

Dolcetto d'Alba 1990 • $11 • (10/31/92) • **89**

CHIARLO, MICHELE

Asti Granduca Superiore 1989 • $10 • (02/15/92) • **84**
Barbaresco 1993: A class-act that caresses the palate. Full-bodied, yet elegant and subtle, with rich, ripe fruit flavors and good depth. Try after 2000. 3,333 cases made. • $28 • (10/31/96) • **89**
Barbaresco 1992 • $24 • (10/31/95) • **81**
Barbaresco 1990 • $25 • (10/31/94) • **85**
Barbaresco 1989 • $23 • (10/31/93) • **81**
Barbaresco 1988 • $23 • (10/31/93) • **85**
Barbaresco Rabajà 1993: Very high-toned floral aromas with red cherry and leather flavors. There's good concentration and a chewy texture to this structured red. Try now. • $57 • (06/15/97) • **85**
Barbaresco Rabajà 1990 • $48 • (10/31/94) • **90**
Barbaresco Rabajà 1989 • $48 • (10/31/93) • **91**
Barbaresco Rabajà 1988 • $48 • (10/31/93) • **90**
Barbera d'Asti 1995: Shows some richness, with delicious strawberry, dried cherry and spice flavors. Medium-bodied and fairly ripe. Would be a good alternative to a young Pinot Noir. 35,000 cases made. • $10 • (03/31/97) • **84**
Barbera d'Asti 1993 • $9 • (10/31/94) • **85**
Barbera d'Asti 1991 • $9 • (01/01/94) • **79**
Barbera d'Asti 1990 • $9 • (10/15/93) BB • **91**
Barbera d'Asti Superiore 1994: Fresh, fruity and light-textured; a charming wine that's ready to drink. 33,000 cases made. • $10 • (10/31/96) • **83**
Barbera d'Asti Superiore Valle del Sole 1994: Delicious earthy, lead pencil character and wonderful flavors of cassis, currant and black cherry. Excellent sense of *terroir*. Medium- to full-bodied, good concentration and firm tannins. Tempting now; better after 1999. 1,250 cases made. • $25 • (10/31/97) • **87**
Barbera d'Asti Superiore Valle del Sole 1993: An intriguing wine from 35-year-old vines. Rosemary, spice and toasty oak flavors mingle nicely with anise and ripe currant accents. Lush in texture. Turns fresh and crisp on the finish. Try now. 1,333 cases made. • $22 • (10/31/96) • **86**
Barbera d'Asti Superiore Valle del Sole 1990 • $20 • (07/31/95) • **90**
Barbera d'Asti Superiore Valle del Sole 1989 • $19 • (10/15/93) • **86**
Barbera d'Asti Superiore Valle del Sole 1988 • $19 • (10/31/92) • **83**

Key: SS—Spectator Selection CS—Cellar Selection HR—Highly Recommended BB—Best Buy $NA—Price not available Ⓐ—Auction Price (BT)—Barrel Tasting
Dates in parentheses indicate the issues in which the ratings were published.

Barbera d'Asti Superiore Valle del Sole 1987 • $19 • (02/15/92) • **84**
Barbera d'Asti Superiore Valle del Sole 1986 • $18 • (03/15/91) • **86**
Barilot 1994: A nice, lively, dark-colored, vibrant and fruity red. Decent amounts of currant and cassis mingle nicely with earth and mineral. Not a big wine, but fun to drink now. • $34 • (01/31/98) • **84**
Barilot 1993: Full-bodied, with good length, a fresh character and the stuffing to age. Tannic, but not overly so. A bit tart on the finish. 60 percent Barbera, 40 percent Nebbiolo. • $30 • (10/31/96) • **86**
Barilot 1991: More spice and wood accents here, the cherry flavor already receded into the background. Elegant, with moderate complexity, yet the tannins need until 1999 to smooth out. • $28 • (01/01/97) • **86**
Barilot 1990 • $25 • (10/31/94) • **85**
Barilot 1987 • $31 • (06/15/94) • **86**
Barilot 1986 • $31 • (12/15/92) • **73**
Barolo 1993: Attractive dried herb, mint and cherry pit flavors make this medium-bodied, fairly ripe Barolo distinctive. The tannins are firm on the toasty, smoky, slightly bitter finish. Best after 2000. 7,500 cases made. • $34 • (10/31/97) • **85**
Barolo 1992: Bright and lively, nicely balanced and elegant in texture. Has floral, cherrylike aromas and flavors, a solid structure of tannins and acidity and a lingering finish. Drink now. 10,833 cases made. • $28 • (10/31/96) • **85**
Barolo 1991 • $24 • (10/31/95) • **85**
Barolo 1990 • $25 • (10/31/94) • **85**
Barolo 1989 • $22 • (10/31/93) • **91**
Barolo 1988 • $23 • (10/15/93) SS • **92**
Barolo 1987 • $22 • (12/15/92) • **86**
Barolo Brunate 1990 • $47 • (10/31/94) • **92**
Barolo Brunate 1989 • $47 • (10/31/93) • **89**
Barolo Brunate 1988 • $47 • (10/31/93) • **89**
Barolo Cannubi 1993: Ripe, sweet fruit and better concentration than many '93s make this a delight. Medium-bodied and succulent, with wild raspberry, cherry and cassis flavors flowing through the clean, lush and smooth finish. Tempting now through 2002. 825 cases made. • $77 • (10/31/97) • **88**
Barolo Cannubi 1991 • $60 • (10/31/95) • **86**
Barolo Cannubi 1990 • $56 • (10/31/94) • **74**
Barolo Cerequio 1993: Light and succulent, with licorice, anise, cherry, and floral aromas that follow through on the chewy finish. Try now to 2000. 1,475 cases made. • $77 • (10/31/97) • **86**
Barolo Cerequio 1991 • $60 • (10/31/95) • **88**
Barolo Cerequio 1990 • $56 • (10/31/94) • **93**
Barolo Cerequio 1989 • $54 • (10/31/93) • **87**
Barolo Cerequio 1988 • $54 • (10/31/93) • **90**
Barolo Granduca 1985 • $20 • (02/28/91) • **89**
Barolo Riserva 1990: Full-bodied, big and ripe with violet aromas and plummy Port-like flavors. Rich, thick and fruity, it's well-balanced for drinking soon through 2001. 1,500 cases made. • $47 • (10/31/96) • **89**
Barolo Rocche di Castiglione 1990 • $47 • (10/31/94) • **85**
Barolo Rocche di Castiglione 1989 • $44 • (10/31/93) • **90**
Barolo Rocche di Castiglione 1988 • $44 • (10/31/93) • **89**
Barolo Rocche di Castiglione Riserva 1985 • $43 • (01/31/92) • **88**
Barolo Rocche di Castiglione Riserva 1983 • $30 • (02/28/91) • **78**
Barolo Vigna Cerequio 1988 • $57 • (03/31/93) • **88**
Barolo Vigna Rionda 1993: International style of red, with lots of fancy oak smoothing out the hard edges. Packed with mocha, spice and chocolate, it also shines with blackberry and currant flavors. Full-bodied, with well-integrated, ripe tannins that need until around 2000 to soften. Succulent finish. 340 cases made. • $64 • (10/31/97) • **90**
Barolo Vigna Rionda 1990 • $47 • (10/31/94) • **90**
Barolo Vigna Rionda di Serralunga 1989 • $47 • (10/31/93) • **89**
Barolo Vigna Rionda di Serralunga 1988 • $47 • (10/31/93) • **85**
Barolo Vigna Rionda di Serralunga Riserva 1986 • $45 • (12/15/92) • **84**
Barolo Vigna Rionda di Serralunga Riserva 1985 • $39 • (02/28/91) • **81**
Barolo Vigna Rionda di Serralunga Riserva 1983 • $36 • (02/28/91) • **87**
Barolo Vigna Rionda di Serralunga Riserva 1982 • $32 • (01/31/90) • **89**
Countacc! 1993: Shows abundant flavors of blackberry, cassis, spice and grilled meat, and hints of black olive. Lavishly oaked, medium in body, firm in structure. Tough tannins now. Wait until 2000; it has the acidity and vibrant length to hold until then. • $61 • (01/31/98) • **87**
Countacc! 1990 • $52 • (10/31/94) • **87**
Dolcetto d'Alba 1993 • $NA • (01/01/95) • **82**
Gavi 1996: Neutral wine, with a whiff of funky, earthy aromas that border on cardboard. Bitter, somewhat unclean finish. • $14 • (01/31/98) • **73**

Gavi Rovereto 1996: Slightly spritzy, but fresh, clean and straightforward. A bit neutral, showing some spice and lemon character. Drink now. • $23 • (01/31/98) • **78**

Gavi Rovereto 1995: Light and fresh, floral in aroma, subtly fruity in flavor, this is a simple, charming white wine. • $22 • (07/31/97) • **82**

Moscato d'Asti Nivole 1996: Delicate and peachy in character, with a lovely effervescence. Tasty and delicious. • $9/375ml • (07/31/97) • **86**

Moscato d'Asti Nivole 1995: A slightly bubbly, sweet and lively dessert wine with bright flavor and good balance. • $9/375ml • (05/31/97) • **86**

Moscato d'Asti Nivole 1994 • $9/375ml • (04/30/96) • **85**

CHIESA DI S. RESTITUTA, LA

Brunello di Montalcino 1988 • $32 • (04/30/94) • **85**

Brunello di Montalcino Vigna S. Pietro Riserva 1988 • $NA • (10/31/94) • **83**

Chiesa S. Restituta 1990 • $NA • (10/31/93) • **94**

Rosso di Montalcino 1992 • $NA • (10/31/94) • **83**

Rosso di Montalcino 1991 • $14 • (04/30/94) • **83**

Rosso di Montalcino 1986 • $9 • (05/31/88) • **83**

CHIONETTI & FIGLIO, QUINTO

Dolcetto di Dogliani Briccolero 1994: Round and supple, it's light- to medium-bodied, with a nice core of pepper, cherry and vanilla flavors. Drink upon release. 2,500 cases made. • $15 • (10/31/96) • **84**

Dolcetto di Dogliani Briccolero 1989 • $16 • (04/30/91) • **87**

Dolcetto di Dogliani San Luigi 1993 • $NA • (10/31/95) • **81**

CIABOT BERTON

Barbera d'Alba 1996: Very earthy in the aromas, with a lean, crisp, slightly green texture and an astringent finish. 167 cases made. • $18 • (10/31/97) • **73**

Barbera d'Alba Bricco San Biagio 1995: Lush and stylish, with plum, cassis and toasty oak. A ripe, sweet and lovely wine, presented in a medium-bodied package. Impressive concentration and length on the smoky finish. Drink now through 2002. 317 cases made. • $18 • (10/31/97) • **88**

Barbera d'Alba Bricco San Biagio 1994: Overly oaky now, this toasty, medium-bodied wine tastes of plum and dried cherry. Tannic and rough, it had just been bottled when tasted and should improve with some cellaring. • $NA • (10/31/96) • **80**

Barbera d'Alba Bricco San Biagio 1993: An uncompromising, savage wine with personality. Ripe, rich and packed with fruit, it shows plum, earth, cedar and mineral flavors. Full-bodied, with a long, rough and tannic finish. • $NA • (10/31/96) • **87**

Barolo 1993: Delicate and attractive, with the characteristic array of tar, rose petal and smoke aromas and flavors. Medium-bodied, it's rather lean, with drying tannins kicking in on the finish. Best from 2000 through 2002. 833 cases made. • $24 • (10/31/97) • **84**

Barolo 1991 • $NA • (10/31/95) • **71**

Barolo 1990 • $NA • (10/31/95) • **80**

Barolo 1988 • $28 • (12/15/92) • **85**

Barolo Roggeri 1993: Gorgeous, seductively ripe and opulent wine despite its medium body. Packed with sweet tannins and flavors. Well crafted, with violet, spice, licorice, cinnamon and plenty of cassis and blackberry flavors. Fairly delicate, with seamless texture and a smoky, toasty finish. Drink now through 2005. 333 cases made. • $28 • (10/31/97) • **92**

Dolcetto d'Alba 1996: Already maturing, with cassis, blueberry and cranberry flavors, crisp texture and some dry tannins. Drink now through 2000. 500 cases made. • $11 • (10/31/97) • **82**

Dolcetto d'Alba 1993 • $NA • (10/31/95) • **79**

Dolcetto d'Alba 1990 • $12 • (03/31/93) • **83**

Dolcetto d'Alba Rutuin 1993 • $NA • (10/31/95) • **84**

Nebbiolo delle Langhe 1988 • $12 • (03/31/93) • **82**

CIACCI PICCOLOMINI D'ARAGONA

Brunello di Montalcino 1990: Fabulous, traditional Brunello di Montalcino offering great color and masses of mint, berry, mineral and nut aromas and flavors. Full in body and tannins, huge. Needs time; try after 1999. • $35 • (10/31/95) • **93**

Brunello di Montalcino 1984 • $25 • (06/15/90) • **91**

Brunello di Montalcino Riserva 1988 • $50 • (10/31/94) • **91**

Brunello di Montalcino Vigna di Pianrosso 1988 • $40 • (04/30/94) • **88**

Rosso di Montalcino 1992 • $15 • (10/31/94) • **80**

Rosso di Montalcino 1988 • $16 • (04/30/91) • **82**

Rosso di Montalcino Vigna della Fonte 1993 • $17 • (10/31/95) • **87**

Rosso di Montalcino Vigna della Fonte 1991 • $16 • (04/30/94) • **81**

CIELO

Chardonnay Veneto 1996: On the leaner side, showing lively acidity, with almond and pear flavors and a hint of nutmeg. Austere on its own and chalky on the finish, it should perk up with food. Drink now. 25,000 cases made. • $6 • (04/30/98) • **82**

Chardonnay Veneto 1995: Subtly fruity, nicely balanced and refreshing, with light lemon and apple flavors that linger on the finish. • $6 • (04/30/97) • **84**

Cielogrigio 1995: Medium-bodied, with modest honey and toasty almond character, a smooth texture and a lingering finish. • $6 • (04/30/97) • **82**

Merlot Veneto 1996: The flavors are dilute in this simple, innocuous red. Drink now. 40,000 cases made. • $6 • (04/30/98) • **77**

Merlot Veneto 1995: Light and simple, with earthy aromas and basic fruit flavors. • $6 • (04/30/97) • **77**

Merlot Veneto 1992 • $5 • (10/31/94) • **82**

Pinot Grigio Veneto 1996: A medium-bodied white, with appealing, ripe apple flavors, but an overwhelmingly tannic, bitter note detracts. Drink now. 36,000 cases made. • $6 • (05/15/98) • **78**

Pinot Grigio Veneto 1993 • $5 • (05/31/95) • **83**

CIGLIUTI, FRATELLI

Barbaresco Serraboella 1994: An impressive '94, big, full bodied and rich. This has bold cassis, black cherry and berry flavors and nice wet-earth character. The crisp tannins give it a fresh sensation on the palate and on the long finish. Try around 2000. 375 cases made. • $45 • (10/31/97) • **87**

Barbaresco Serraboella 1986 • $20 • (08/31/89) • **86**

Barbera d'Alba Serraboella 1993 • $NA • (10/31/95) • **80**

Barbera d'Alba Serraboella 1989 • $15 • (11/30/91) • **87**

Dolcetto d'Alba Serraboella 1993 • $NA • (10/31/95) • **78**

CINCIOLE, LE

Chianti Classico 1995: Impressive ripeness on the nose, with just the right amount of new wood in maturation. Medium-bodied, with light tannins and a berry, vanilla finish. Drink now. • $16 • (09/30/97) • **83**

Chianti Classico 1994: Vivid, with lovely berry, cherry and plum aromas and flavors. Medium-bodied with light, soft tannins and a sweet, fruit finish that picks up a hint of vanilla. • $16 • (10/31/96) • **86**

Chianti Classico 1993 • $NA • (10/31/95) • **88**

Chianti Classico Valle del Pozzo 1994: Good concentration, lots of new wood. Medium-bodied, with loads of vanilla and a light finish. Perhaps a bit too much new wood? Tasted twice, with consistent notes. Drink or hold. • $26 • (09/30/97) • **83**

CISPIANO

Chardonnay 1995: Something went very wrong. This is amber-colored, with an odd, watery, beeswax character. Tasted twice, with consistent notes. • $NA • (09/30/97) • **65**

Chianti Classico 1993: This is fresh and silky, with aromas and flavors of plum, berry and vanilla, a medium-to-light body and a supple finish. Drink now. • $17 • (10/31/96) • **84**

Chianti Classico 1990 • $NA • (10/31/93) • **85**

Chianti Classico Riserva 1991: Fairly tight and austere, despite some good dried cherry and red plum flavors. Turns tart on the finish. • $28 • (03/31/97) • **81**

CLEMENTE & FIGLI, GUASTI

Barbaresco 1978 • $20 • (01/31/92) • **84**

Barbera del Monferrato 1990 • $8 • (04/30/93) • **79**

Barcarato 1989 • $27 • (03/31/93) • **88**

Barolo 1985 • $27 • (01/31/92) • **81**

Moscato d'Asti 1991 • $12 • (05/15/93) • **82**

CLERICO, DOMENICO

Arte 1992 • $26 • (10/31/94) • **86**

Arte 1989 • $30 • (12/15/92) • **89**

Arte 1988 • $26 • (02/28/91) • **90**

Arte 1987 • $22 • (01/31/90) • **78**
Arte 1986 • $22 • (02/15/89) • **88**
Arte 1985 • $22 • (01/31/88) • **91**
Barbera d'Alba 1991 • $15 • (11/15/93) • **80**
Barbera d'Alba 1990 • $14 • (12/15/92) • **84**
Barbera d'Alba 1988 • $12 • (03/15/91) • **84**
Barbera d'Alba 1987 • $8 • (08/31/89) • **85**
Barbera d'Alba 1985 • $8 • (11/30/87) • **84**
Barolo 1984 • $13 • (08/31/88) • **85**
Barolo Briccoto Bussia 1990 • $40 • (10/31/94) • **90**
Barolo Ciabot Mentin Ginestra 1993: Lovely wine, ripe and rich, with plum, black currant and wild raspberry character blended with some spice and toasty oak accents. It's fresh and succulent, with a lingering finish. Delicious now, better from 2000 to 2005. • $44 • (10/31/97) • **91**
Barolo Ciabot Mentin Ginestra 1992: Distinctive and powerful, from the vivid tobaccolike aromas to the rich core of fruit flavors to the lingering finish. Has depth, concentration, complexity and massive but well-integrated tannins that will help it age. Drink now to 2005. 283 cases made. • $32 • (10/31/96) • **92**
Barolo Ciabot Mentin Ginestra 1991 • $30 • (10/31/95) • **85**
Barolo Ciabot Mentin Ginestra 1989 • $45 • (10/31/93) HR • **92**
Barolo Ciabot Mentin Ginestra 1988 • $45 • (10/31/93) • **89**
Barolo Ciabot Mentin Ginestra 1985 • $27 • (04/15/90) CS • **92**
Barolo Ciabot Mentin Ginestra 1983 • $19 • (12/15/87) • **88**
Barolo Pajana 1993: Brilliant. Rich, ripe, sweet-tasting Barolo, with superbly smooth tannins, it offers layers of fabulous cassis, floral, violet, smoky toasty oak and plum flavors. Full-bodied and very dark in color, it's elegant but needs until around 2002 to give it all. • $44 • (10/31/97) • **93**
Barolo Pajana 1992: Concentrated, but still harmonious. Has a solid core of rich fruit flavors mingled with spicy, cedary accents that linger on the finish. Firm and tannic, but all is in balance. Needs until at least 2000. 200 cases made. • $32 • (10/31/96) • **90**
Barolo Pajana 1991 • $28 • (10/31/95) • **84**
Barolo Pajana 1990 • $40 • (10/31/94) • **90**
Barolo Vigna Bricotto della Bussia 1980 • $8 • (09/01/85) BB • **86**
Dolcetto d'Alba 1994 • $13 • (10/31/95) • **85**
Dolcetto d'Alba 1987 • $7 • (08/31/88) • **87**
Dolcetto d'Alba 1986 • $7 • (12/31/87) • **80**

COCCI GRIFONI

Falerio dei Colli Ascolani 1996: A solid-quality white wine with subtle citrus and mineral flavors and crisp acidity. A blend of Verdicchio, Trebbiano, Pecorino and Passerina. Drink now. 6,500 cases made. • $8 • (05/15/98) • **82**
Falerio dei Colli Ascolani Vigneti San Basso 1996: Refreshing in texture, aggressive in flavor, with bold grapefruit and celery flavors and crisp acidity. A blend of Trebbiano, Pecorino, Passerina and Verdicchio. Drink now. 1,250 cases made. • $10 • (05/15/98) • **82**

COCORA ORTONA

Montepulciano d'Abruzzo Farnese 1992 • $5 • (03/31/95) • **82**

COGNO, ELVIO

Barbera d'Alba Bricco del Merlo 1995: Full-bodied Barbera in the international style offering lovely toasty oak, violet, plum, red- and blackberry flavors. A slight greenness detracts from the otherwise seductive structure; chewy tannins call for cellaring. Drinkable now to 2002. • $23 • (10/31/97) • **87**
Barbera d'Alba Poggio Petorchino Bricco del Merlo 1991 • $15 • (07/31/95) • **85**
Barolo Ravera 1993: On the herbal side, tasting of green olive and pepperoni. Medium-bodied, with drying tannins on the finish. • $41 • (10/31/97) • **76**
Dolcetto d'Alba 1984 • $5 • (02/16/86) • **82**
Dolcetto d'Alba Vigna del Mandorlo 1996: Barrel sample. A super Dolcetto that stands out in its category. Deeper in color than most, lush in texture, medium to full in body, with good, ripe fruit and lovely licorice, spice and cassis flavors. Tannins clamp down on the finish; may be better in 1999, or try now with pasta or red meat. • $16 • (10/31/97) (BT) • **85-89**
Langhe Montegrilli 1995: A very impressive, super-dark red that bursts with fresh black currant, cassis and wild raspberry flavors, with a dollop of oak-infused spice. Medium-bodied, with just enough acidity, polished tannins and concentrated fruit to provide a lasting, balanced finish. Drink now through 2000. • $NA • (10/31/97) • **89**

COL D'ORCIA

Brunello di Montalcino 1992: Serious wine for the vintage, with berry, cherry, black cherry and a hint of spice. Medium-bodied, with velvety tannins and a long finish. Drink or hold. 8,300 cases made. • $35 • (09/30/97) • **88**
Brunello di Montalcino 1991: Rather traditional in style, this shows chestnut and berry notes on nose and palate, light tannins and a fresh finish. Light- to medium-bodied. A slight disappointment from this producer. Drink now. 12,666 cases made. • $NA • (11/30/96) • **80**
Brunello di Montalcino 1990: Elegant tobacco, berry and mineral aromas and flavors, medium body and tannins and a silky finish. Drinkable now. Slightly disappointing. Tasted twice, with consistent notes. • $NA • (10/31/95) • **87**
Brunello di Montalcino 1988 • $30 • (04/30/94) • **86**
Brunello di Montalcino 1985 • $23 • (11/30/90) • **88**
Brunello di Montalcino 1981 • $22 • (09/15/86) • **70**
Brunello di Montalcino 1979 • $15 • (09/15/86) CS • **94**
Brunello di Montalcino Poggio al Vento 1988 • $NA • (04/30/94) • **92**
Brunello di Montalcino Poggio al Vento Riserva 1990: Shows good berry, meat and leather character but it's a little dry and astringent for such a great vintage. Full-bodied, with dry tannins and finish. Disappointing. Tasted twice, with consistent notes. Drink now. • $64 • (09/30/97) • **84**
Brunello di Montalcino Poggio al Vento Riserva 1982 • $40 • (04/15/91) • **89**
Brunello di Montalcino Riserva 1991: A good quality, round-textured Brunello with cherr and wet earth character. Medium tannins, medium finish. Drink now. 1,450 cases made. • $48 • (09/30/97) • **86**
Brunello di Montalcino Riserva 1990: Not as big or powerful as some, but there are beautiful berry, cedar and spice aromas and flavors in this medium-bodied riserva. Fresh finish. Drink now or hold. 2,872 cases made. • $NA • (11/30/96) • **89**
Brunello di Montalcino Riserva 1988 • $27 • (10/31/94) • **90**
Brunello di Montalcino Riserva 1981 • $22 • (07/31/88) • **89**
Chianti Gineprone 1993: A decent, carafe-type Chianti that's simple in flavor and a bit tired. Dry, moderately tannic. Drink now. • $10 • (09/30/97) • **79**
Ghiaie Bianche 1995: Dull. Has some wood and apple character, but is slightly oxidized on the finish. Tasted twice, with consistent notes. • $NA • (09/30/97) • **76**
Moscadello di Montalcino Pascena 1993: Has aromas of apples, cream and syrup, is medium-bodied and medium sweet with honey, vanilla and melons on the finish. Fresh acidity. A lovely, sweet wine. • $NA • (09/30/97) • **88**
Olmaia 1993. Fabulous winemaking. Silky and caressing from start to finish. it's full-bodied, with blackberry, cherry and tobacco aromas and flavors and full yet polished tannins. Long finish. Drink now. • $39 • (09/30/97) • **91**
Olmaia 1992: A bit coarse now, but shows some promise. Intense aromas of fruit and grilled meat follow through on the palate. Medium-bodied, with chewy tannins and a short finish. Try now. Pure Cabernet Sauvignon. • $NA • (10/31/96) • **88**
Olmaia 1990 • $19 • (02/28/95) • **96**
Rosso degli Spezieri 1995: Bright and fruity Sangiovese with lovely dried cherry and berry character and a refreshing finish. Medium in body with straightforward flavors. Not for aging; enjoy now. • $NA • (03/31/97) • **85**
Rosso di Montalcino 1995: Good Rosso with a berry and cherry character, medium body, and a fresh finish. Drink now. 15,000 cases made. • $14 • (09/30/97) • **83**
Rosso di Montalcino 1994: More lively than many Rossos, this is medium-bodied with licorice, berry and mineral aromas and flavors, silky tannins and a flavorful finish. Drinkable now. 14,583 cases made. • $14 • (11/30/96) • **86**
Rosso di Montalcino 1993 • $NA • (10/31/95) • **74**
Rosso di Montalcino 1992 • $11 • (10/31/94) • **81**
Rosso di Montalcino 1991 • $11 • (04/30/94) • **78**
Rosso di Montalcino 1988 • $9 • (04/30/91) • **84**
Rosso di Montalcino 1985 • $7 • (06/30/88) • **80**
Rosso di Montalcino 1983 • $6 • (06/30/87) • **76**

Key: SS—Spectator Selection CS—Cellar Selection HR—Highly Recommended BB—Best Buy $NA—Price not available Ⓐ—Auction Price (BT)—Barrel Tasting
Dates in parentheses indicate the issues in which the ratings were published.

COLLA, PODERI

Barbaresco 1994: Clever winemaking mingles oak-infused mocha, chocolate and spice character with red berry flavor. Supple tannins and medium body. Lacks complexity but is pleasant to drink now. From Tenuta Roncaglia. 1,240 cases made. • $38 • (10/31/97) • **84**

Barbaresco 1993: Rich and full-bodied. Has smoky, meaty, berry and plum aromas and flavors, and a touch of mint. Smooth and supple, with a delicious finish. Try after 1999. From Tenuta Roncaglia. 583 cases made. • $37 • (10/31/96) • **88**

Barbera d'Alba 1995: Pretty licorice, cherry, and wild raspberry flavors, crisp texture and medium body. Should go well with pizza and simple foods. 933 cases made. • $18 • (10/31/97) • **83**

Barbera d'Alba 1994: Sturdy, and of medium body, with black cherry and toasty oak flavors. A bit hollow on the midpalate, but smooth and likeable on the short finish. 833 cases made. • $19 • (10/31/96) • **81**

Barbera d'Alba 1993: Lushly textured, with plum, cherry and tobacco aromas and flavors. Quite crisp and lean on the finish, though. Try now. • $17 • (10/31/96) • **79**

Barolo Dardi Le Rose Bussia 1993: Firm, even tough, but with lots of character and punch. A bit lean perhaps, this has good extraction of fruit, a long finish and layers of violet, dried herbs, spice, cassis, mineral and earth. Try around 2000 to 2005. 690 cases made. • $45 • (10/31/97) • **85**

COLLAVINI

Cabernet Sauvignon Collio Trebes 1993 • $12 • (05/31/96) • **86**

Cabernet Sauvignon Grave del Friuli 1984 • $8 • (04/15/90) BB • **85**

Cabernet Sauvignon Grave del Friuli Roncaccio 1993 • $9 • (06/15/96) • **82**

Cabernet Sauvignon Grave del Friuli Roncaccio 1991 • $8 • (02/28/95) • **82**

Chardonnay Grave del Friuli dei Sassi Cavi 1994 • $9 • (06/15/96) • **78**

Chardonnay Isonzo del Friuli dei Sassi Cavi 1996: Subtle, yet there's a minerally intensity, along with apple and lemon flavors and rich texture. Try with delicate seafood dishes. 10,000 cases made. • $12 • (12/15/97) • **83**

Colli Orientali del Friuli Romandolo 1993 • $17 • (05/31/96) • **84**

Merlot Collio Pubrida 1993 • $12 • (06/15/96) • **79**

Merlot Collio Riserva di Casa 1995: Light, yet there's a persistant, chewy, licorice component that begs to be noticed. On the right track, but needs a bit more depth and concentration. 10,000 cases made. • $12 • (12/15/97) • **80**

Merlot Grave del Friuli Campo Olivio 1993 • $9 • (06/15/96) • **78**

Merlot Grave del Friuli Campo Olivio 1991 • $7 • (02/28/95) • **80**

Picolit Colli Orientali del Friuli 1993 • $40 • (06/15/96) • **83**

Pinot Grigio 1994 • $9 • (06/15/96) • **80**

Pinot Grigio Collio Villa del Canlungo Vendemmia Tardiva 1996: Peach flavors and a hint of smokiness mark this richly textured white. Its balance and juicy fruit should have broad appeal. Drink now. 10,000 cases made. • $12 • (05/15/98) • **85**

Pinot Grigio Grave del Friuli Borgo Armenti 1993 • $7 • (12/15/94) • **82**

Refosco dal Peduncolo Rosso Grave del Friuli Pucino 1996: Don't let the light color fool you; there's plenty of herb-tinged berry flavors in this light-bodied, quaffable red. A pleasant earthy note adds dimension. Drink now. 10,000 cases made. • $10 • (04/30/98) • **83**

Refosco dal Peduncolo Rosso Grave del Friuli Pucino 1994 • $9 • (06/15/96) • **79**

Ribolla Gialla Colli Orientali del Friuli Turian 1994 • $15 • (06/15/96) • **82**

Schioppettino Colli Orientali del Friuli Turian 1993 • $20 • (06/15/96) • **83**

COLLE, IL

Brunello di Montalcino 1992: Dry and light; not much fruit left in the bottle. • $NA • (09/30/97) • **73**

Brunello di Montalcino 1991: Already past its time, this shows leather, tobacco and earth character. Dry and slightly acidic. Barely acceptable. • $NA • (11/30/96) • **71**

Brunello di Montalcino 1990: Nice complexity here, showing some mineral, truffle, mint, tobacco and floral notes that are enticing. Very approachable and lovely now, but on the light side. • $NA • (10/31/95) • **85**

Brunello di Montalcino Riserva 1990: Slightly old style, with its amber color and cedary, smoky, berry character. Medium-bodied, with silky tannins and a crisp finish. Drink now. • $NA • (11/30/96) • **85**

Rosso delle Colline Lucchesi 1986 • $7 • (03/31/90) • **81**

Rosso di Montalcino 1995: Very light and watery, clean and simple. Not much to it. • $NA • (09/30/97) • **75**

Rosso di Montalcino 1993 • $NA • (10/31/95) • **83**

COLLE BERETO

Chianti Classico 1994: Rather light and earthy with leather and berry notes. Light-bodied, with a light, slightly tart finish. • $17 • (09/30/97) • **78**

Chianti Classico Riserva 1994: Decent concentration, but there's a slight weediness to the plum character. Medium-bodied, a bit dry on the finish. • $24 • (09/30/97) • **80**

Chianti Classico Riserva 1993: A bodyless Chianti with some pleasant berry flavor, but no length on the palate. • $NA • (10/31/96) • **76**

Il Cénno 1990 • $27 • (12/31/95) • **91**

Il Tòcco 1993: A bit earthy and stinky, with ripe berry and cherry flavors and a hint of leather. Medium-bodied, with a dry finish. Slightly unclean. • $40 • (09/30/97) • **78**

Tuscany White 1996: Offers attractive lemon and mineral aromas and flavors, is of medium body, has fresh acidity and a medium finish. • $11 • (09/30/97) • **82**

COLLE DI TREQUANDA, IL

Chianti 1993 • $NA • (02/28/95) • **80**

Chianti 1990 • $NA • (10/31/93) • **86**

COLLEMATTONI

Rosso di Montalcino 1995: Lively, with floral, cherry and grape aromas and flavors. Medium in body, with light tannins and a fresh finish. • $NA • (09/30/97) • **85**

COLLOSORBO

Brunello di Montalcino 1991: Elegant and clean, its plum, berry, cherry and spice aromas and flavors carry through a fresh finish. Fine tannins. Drink now. • $NA • (11/30/96) • **85**

Rosso di Montalcino 1994: Fresh and straightforward, with berry and dried herb on the nose and palate and a crisp finish. • $NA • (11/30/96) • **82**

COLMELLO DI GROTTA

Chardonnay Isonzo del Friuli 1996: A pleasant Chardonnay that leans toward apple and almond flavors and racy acidity. Try with food. Drink through 1999. 500 cases made. • $13 • (06/15/98) • **82**

Chardonnay Isonzo 1994 • $13 • (06/15/96) • **83**

Pinot Grigio Isonzo del Friuli 1996: There's ripeness and straightforward peach flavors, but more concentration is needed. Drink now. 1,000 cases made. • $13 • (06/15/98) • **81**

Pinot Grigio Isonzo 1994 • $13 • (06/15/96) • **84**

Sauvignon Blanc Isonzo del Friuli 1996: Straightforward, showing modest apple, citrus and grass notes, moderately high acidity and a slightly bitter finish. Drink now. 500 cases made. • $13 • (06/15/98) • **81**

Sauvignon Blanc Isonzo 1994 • $13 • (06/15/96) • **79**

COLOGNOLE

Chianti Rufina 1995: Slightly diluted, with light fruit and crisp acidity. • $10 • (09/30/97) • **78**

Chianti Rufina 1994: This is delicate and slightly diluted. Has cherry, berry and lemon aromas and flavors and a crisp, light finish. • $NA • (10/31/96) • **78**

Chianti Rufina 1993 • $8 • (10/31/95) • **78**

Chianti Rufina Riserva 1993 • $12 • (10/31/95) • **85**

Chianti Rufina Riserva del Don 1994: Light and simple, with some berry and cherry flavors and a light, slightly diluted finish. Drink now. • $18 • (09/30/97) • **79**

Chianti Rufina Riserva del Don 1993: A soft and delicious, medium-bodied red with aromas and flavors of fresh mushrooms and berries and light, caressing tannins. • $NA • (10/31/96) • **83**

Quattro Chiacchiere 1995: Offers lovely, balanced aromas of almond, hay, minerals and spice, lovely flavors of ripe apple and mango. Medium-bodied, with a caressing texture. A well-made white. • $15 • (09/30/97) • **87**

COLOMBO, CANTINE

Rosso del Salento 1995: Very fruity in flavor and direct in style, this is a simple, fresh red with light tannins and a soft texture. Drink now. 10,000 cases made. • $7 • (01/01/98) • **80**

COLOSI

Malvasia delle Lipari Passito di Salina 1989 • $20/375ml • (03/31/92) • **81**

COLTERENZIO

Pinot Bianco Alto Adige Praedium Weisshaus 1996: Well made. Nothing fancy here, just plenty of peach and lemon flavors allied to richness and concentration, with vibrant acidity to support it all. Drink now. • $17 • (05/31/98) • **86**

Pinot Grigio Alto Adige Praedium Puiten 1996: Maybe just a touch corky. Otherwise, shows good richness and depth, full of fruit and vibrant acidity, with peach, quince and almond character and a lingering finish. Drink now. • $17 • (05/31/98) • **85**

COLUE, TENUTE

Barbaresco 1990 • $20 • (10/31/94) • **82**
Barbera d'Alba 1992 • $10 • (07/31/95) • **82**
Barolo 1989 • $20 • (10/31/94) • **83**

CONCADORO

Chianti Classico 1990 • $NA • (10/31/93) • **88**
Chianti Classico Riserva 1990 • $NA • (02/28/95) • **74**

CONTADI CASTALDI

Brut Franciacorta NV: A bold, dry style, with butterscotch, caramel and smoke flavors that make for a rough combination. Good, but lacks elegance. Drink now. 6,000 cases made. • $19 • (05/15/98) • **81**

Terre de Franciacorta White 1996: Very dry and crisp in character, with light vanilla accents over a core of bright lemon and apple flavors. Appealing in a restrained way. Drink now. 5,400 cases made. • $10 • (05/15/98) • **85**

CONTERNO-FANTINO

Barbera d'Alba Vignota 1995: Displays earthy, funky aromas and flavors and an astringent finish. 150 cases made. • $19 • (10/31/97) • **76**

Barbera d'Alba Vignota 1994: Medium-bodied and well balanced. Has an earthy aroma and lots of black cherry and raspberry flavors accented by notes of smoke and herb. Still fruity on the finish. 1,000 cases made. • $18 • (10/31/96) • **87**

Barbera d'Alba Vignota 1993 • $16 • (10/31/95) • **76**
Barbera d'Alba Vignota 1992 • $NA • (10/31/94) • **86**
Barbera d'Alba Vignota 1991 • $14 • (11/15/93) • **78**
Barbera d'Alba Vignota 1990 • $15 • (07/31/95) • **87**
Barbera d'Alba Vignota 1989 • $20 • (03/15/91) • **86**

Barolo Sorì Ginestra 1993: Firm and tannic, but has good depth and concentration of ripe fruit. A serious Barolo for this vintage, it's quite thick on the midpalate with flavors of red- and blackberries and well-integrated notes of oak and wet earth. Too bad the finish is astringent. 917 cases made. • $45 • (10/31/97) • **86**

Barolo Sorì Ginestra 1992: On the light side, with lean, green flavors and a tart, tannic finish. 458 cases made. • $37 • (10/31/96) • **76**

Barolo Sorì Ginestra 1991 • $32 • (10/31/95) • **84**
Barolo Sorì Ginestra 1990 • $40 • (10/31/94) • **96**
Barolo Sorì Ginestra 1989 • $31 • (10/31/93) • **83**
Barolo Sorì Ginestra 1988 • $30 • (10/31/93) • **80**
Barolo Sorì Ginestra Riserva 1982 • $24 • (01/31/90) • **84**

Barolo Vigna del Gris 1993: Herbal and sour, it tastes like unripe green olives and has a stemmy note on the tart finish. Disappointing. 375 cases made. • $45 • (10/31/97) • **77**

Barolo Vigna del Gris 1990 • $36 • (10/31/94) • **93**
Barolo Vigna del Gris 1989 • $29 • (10/31/93) • **88**
Barolo Vigna del Gris 1988 • $28 • (10/31/93) • **80**

Dolcetto d'Alba Bricco Bastia 1996: Typical Dolcetto of good quality: light to medium in body, with nice floral, cranberry and black cherry aromas and flavors and a crisp character. Drinkable now. 2,500 cases made. • $18 • (10/31/97) • **81**

Dolcetto d'Alba Bricco Bastia 1995: Well structured and agreably soft in texture. Displays lovely cherry, berry and floral flavors, with an earthy, barnyard note. Ready to drink. 1,917 cases made. • $17 • (10/31/96) • **84**

Dolcetto d'Alba Bricco Bastia 1994 • $15 • (10/31/95) • **85**

Langhe Monprá 1995: A wine with good concentration of fruit flavor and toasty, spicy notes. Full-bodied, dark-colored and ripe. It's certainly tannic, so give it until 1999 to 2000 to soften. 750 cases made. • $41 • (10/31/97) • **85**

Monprá 1993: Woody notes are the dominant theme, with black cherry and vanilla playing minor roles. Try now. • $36 • (01/01/97) • **84**

Monprá 1992 • $35 • (10/31/95) • **80**
Monprá 1991 • $35 • (10/31/94) • **86**
Monprá 1990 • $32 • (04/15/94) • **88**
Monprá 1989 • $30 • (10/31/92) • **87**
Monprá 1988 • $27 • (03/15/91) • **91**
Nebbiolo delle Langhe Ginestrino 1990 • $19 • (02/28/95) • **85**

CONTERNO, ALDO

Barbera d'Alba 1993 • $NA • (10/31/95) • **80**
Barbera d'Alba Conca Tre Pile 1990 • $22 • (04/30/93) • **91**
Barbera d'Alba Conca Tre Pile 1989 • $21 • (10/31/92) • **91**

Barolo 1993: Delicate, like a red Burgundy, with layers of toasty oak, violet, mint, cassis and toasty oak. Of medium body, it offers some well-integrated tannins. Drink now. 1,333 cases made. • $99 • (10/31/97) • **87**

Barolo 1991 • $62 • (10/31/95) • **81**
Barolo Bricco Bussia Vigna Cicala 1988 • $52 • (10/31/93) HR • **93**
Barolo Bricco Bussia Vigna Cicala 1985 • $67 Ⓐ • (06/15/90) • **90**
Barolo Bricco Bussia Vigna Cicala 1982 • $63 Ⓐ • (09/15/87) • **86**
Barolo Bricco Bussia Vigna Colonnello 1988 • $57 • (03/31/93) • **90**
Barolo Bricco Bussia Vigna Colonnello 1985 • $40 • (06/15/90) • **84**
Barolo Bussia Soprana 1989 • $42 • (10/31/93) • **86**
Barolo Bussia Soprana 1988 • $46 • (10/31/93) • **87**
Barolo Bussia Soprana 1985 • $40 • (09/15/90) • **87**
Barolo Bussia Soprana 1983 • $43 Ⓐ • (09/15/88) • **85**
Barolo Bussia Soprana 1982 • $18 • (09/15/87) • **85**
Barolo Bussia Soprana 1980 • $NA • (09/15/88) • **86**
Barolo Bussia Soprana 1978 • $83 Ⓐ • (09/15/88) • **92**
Barolo Bussia Soprana 1974 • $NA • (09/15/88) • **90**
Barolo Bussia Soprana 1971 • $NA • (09/15/88) • **87**

Barolo Cicala 1993: Barolo of the vintage. Beautifully balanced, from one of the region's finest vineyards, it sings with the purity of the Piedmont soil. Full-bodied but also elegant, with lots of ripe, sweet plum, jamlike currant and licorice flavors, and a superb minerally lead-pencil thread that gives extra dimension. As subtle as a top *grand cru* Burgundy, like Richebourg or perhaps Romanée St.-Vivant. Delicious now through 2005. 567 cases made. • $125 • (10/31/97) • **94**

Barolo Granbussia 1990 • $120 • (10/31/95) • **90**
Barolo Granbussia 1982 • $91 Ⓐ • (09/15/88) • **93**
Barolo Riserva Granbussia 1985 • $75 • (12/15/92) • **85**
Barolo Vigna Cicala 1990 • $NA • (10/31/94) • **83**
Barolo Vigna Colonello 1990 • $NA • (10/31/94) • **92**
Barolo Vigna Colonello 1989 • $52 • (10/31/93) • **89**
Barolo Vigna Colonello 1988 • $52 • (10/31/93) • **87**

Dolcetto d'Alba 1996: A compacted, rich, ripe, thick, dense, mineral- and cassis-scented Dolcetto. Full-bodied, it coats your mouth with layers of fruit and sweet, ripe tannins. Long, balanced and harmonious finish. • $22 • (10/31/97) (BT) • **90-94**

Dolcetto d'Alba 1995: Mature tasting and medium-bodied, with nice underbrush, truffle, butter and hazelnut flavors. Lacks the zippy freshness typical of Dolcetto, but might please fans of older wines. Drink now. • $22 • (10/31/97) • **84**

Dolcetto d'Alba 1987 • $12 • (09/15/90) • **84**
Dolcetto d'Alba 1985 • $10 • (05/15/87) • **77**
Dolcetto d'Alba Bussia 1993 • $20 • (10/31/95) • **85**
Dolcetto d'Alba Bussia Soprana 1990 • $18 • (10/31/92) • **84**
Il Favot 1992 • $NA • (10/31/94) • **89**
Il Favot 1988 • $32 • (03/31/93) • **89**
Nebbiolo Il Favot 1983 • $13 • (05/31/90) • **84**

Nebbiolo delle Langhe Il Favot 1995: The spicy, toasty oak treatment and ultrasweet, ultraripe character of this wine make it unique and distinctive for a Nebbiolo. Too bad the aromas are green and the tannins dry—perhaps they will soften after 1999. Serve with pasta. 583 cases made. • $60 • (10/31/97) • **83**

Key: SS—Spectator Selection CS—Cellar Selection HR—Highly Recommended BB—Best Buy $NA—Price not available Ⓐ—Auction Price (BT)—Barrel Tasting
Dates in parentheses indicate the issues in which the ratings were published.

ITALY

Nebbiolo delle Langhe Bussia Conca Tre Pile 1985 • $13 • (11/15/88) • **85**

CONTERNO, GIACOMO

Barbera d'Alba 1992 • $15 • (11/15/93) • **82**
Barbera d'Alba Cascina Francia 1991 • $15 • (11/15/93) • **81**
Barbera d'Alba Cascina Francia Serralunga d'Alba 1994: Fairly simple, but delivers a bit of charm with its strawberry and cherry flavors. A touch dry on the finish. Ready to drink. • $NA • (10/31/96) • **80**
Barolo 1985 • $23 • (04/15/90) • **87**
Barolo 1983 • $23 • (09/15/88) • **88**
Barolo 1982 • $57 Ⓐ • (09/15/88) • **90**
Barolo Bussia Munie 1993: Somewhat green and herbal, slightly diluted and short on the finish, this offers only modest fruit and licorice aromas and flavors. • $NA • (10/31/97) • **79**
Barolo Cascina Francia 1989 • $NA • (10/31/93) • **86**
Barolo Cascina Francia 1988 • $40 • (10/31/93) • **82**
Barolo Monfortino Riserva 1982 • $57 • (06/30/87) • **91**
Barolo Monfortino Riserva 1947: Very light, fino Sherry-like, almost gone. • $NA • (05/31/97) • **79**
Barolo Riserva Speciale 1978 • $NA • (09/15/88) • **83**
Barolo Riserva Speciale 1970 • $NA • (09/15/88) • **88**
Dolcetto d'Alba 1994 • $NA • (10/31/95) • **85**

CONTERNO, PAOLO

Barolo Ginestra 1993: Barrel sample. Impressive and uncompromisingly traditional. Fruity, rich, ripe and supple, full-bodied and intense. Has a lot of concentration and a lush, silky structure that lasts through the elegant finish. Tempting now, better after 2000. • $NA • (10/31/97) (BT) • **85-89**

CONTRATTO, GIUSEPPE

Barbera d'Asti Bricco della Fanciullaccia 1995: A young wine with strawberry and currant flavors. Simple, fairly fresh and fruity. • $NA • (03/31/97) • **80**
Barbera d'Asti Solus Ad 1994: Very sweet and ripe, a smooth red that is a pleasure to drink now. Medium-bodied and silky, this offers balanced doses of spice, chocolate, cherry and raspberry flavors and has sweet, supple tannins. Try now. 1,000 cases made. • $38 • (10/31/97) • **87**
Barbera d'Asti Tenuta Pian Del Re 1994: A well-rounded and full-bodied red with roasted flavors and aromas. Has a good dollop of spicy flavors that are woven into a good portion of dried cherry and plum flavors. Smooth finish. Drink now. • $NA • (03/31/97) • **86**
Barolo 1983 • $10 • (03/31/90) • **75**
Barolo 1979 • $9 • (09/30/86) • **76**
Barolo Cerequio 1993: • $NA • (10/31/97) • **79**
Barolo del Centenario Riserva 1978 • $18 • (05/16/86) • **86**

COPERTINO, CANTINA SOCIALE COOPERATIVA DEL

Copertino Riserva 1994: A broad, full-bodied, mature style of red that almost tastes sweet. Has lots of earthy, spicy, nutty flavors and light tannins. Drink now. 30,000 cases made. • $8 • (01/01/98) • **84**
Copertino Riserva 1993: For fans of mature Italian reds. This duplicates the interesting earthy, leathery aromas of age, while retaining some plummy flavors and a firm texture. • $10 • (04/30/97) • **79**

COPPO, LUIGI

Barbera d'Asti Camp du Rouss 1995: Lean, diluted and astringent, with only modest cherry flavors. • $19 • (10/31/97) • **75**
Barbera d'Asti Camp du Rouss 1993: A light, unchallenging wine whose modest fruity flavors taste diluted. • $15 • (10/31/96) • **77**
Barbera d'Asti Camp du Rouss 1991 • $13 • (10/31/94) • **75**
Barbera d'Asti Camp du Rouss 1990 • $13 • (10/31/94) • **85**
Barbera d'Asti Camp du Rouss 1988 • $21 • (03/15/91) • **88**
Barbera d'Asti Camp du Rouss 1986 • $19 • (03/31/90) • **87**
Barbera d'Asti Pomorosso 1994: Barbera at its best—ripe, rich, thick and seductive from start to finish. This super-exciting red is bursting with wild berry flavors and clean, clear earth notes, yet it's untouched by complicated oak notes. The supple tannic structure makes it a delight to drink through 1999, while the fruit is there, yet it's untouched by complicated oak notes. • $44 • (10/31/97) • **93**
Barbera d'Asti Pomorosso 1993: Generous and rather elegant, with vanilla, toasty oak, violet, currant and black cherry flavors. Mercifully, the oak doesn't overpower this lovely wine with its supple tannins. Long, luscious finish. Try now. • $43 • (10/31/96) • **89**
Barbera d'Asti Pomorosso 1990 • $33 • (10/31/94) • **90**
Barbera d'Asti Pomorosso 1989 • $30 • (10/31/94) • **79**
Barbera d'Asti Pomorosso 1987 • $41 • (03/15/91) • **90**
Barbera d'Asti Pomorosso 1986 • $41 • (03/15/91) • **84**
Barbera Le Taccole 1994 • $11 • (07/31/95) • **79**
Dolcetto d'Alba 1989 • $11 • (07/15/91) • **81**
Mondaccione 1994: A disjointed wine, light in color, medium-bodied, with earthy aromas but a polished texture. Tastes of cherry, wet earth, stones. Tannins are hard on the finish. • $NA • (10/31/97) • **76**
Mondaccione 1990 • $30 • (10/31/94) • **83**
Mondaccione 1988 • $34 • (01/31/92) • **73**
Mondaccione 1987 • $13 • (03/31/90) • **87**
Moscato d'Asti 1991 • $17 • (05/15/93) • **86**
Moscato d'Asti Moncalvina 1993 • $12 • (07/31/95) • **83**

CORDERO DI MONTEZEMOLO, PAOLO

Barbera d'Alba 1992 • $18 • (10/31/94) • **85**
Barolo 1990 • $40 • (10/31/94) • **82**
Barolo 1988 • $NA • (10/31/93) • **81**
Barolo 1980 • $16 • (12/15/87) CS • **91**
Barolo Enrico VI 1993: Has good color and starts out nicely, then turns sour on the finish. The red berry flavors are quite succulent, but it ends with a green, bell-pepper edge and drying tannins. 833 cases made. • $24 • (10/31/97) • **79**
Barolo Enrico VI 1990 • $40 • (10/31/94) • **91**
Barolo Enrico VI 1989 • $NA • (10/31/93) • **88**
Barolo Enrico VI 1988 • $NA • (10/31/93) • **78**
Barolo Enrico VI 1983 • $20 • (09/15/88) • **86**
Barolo Enrico VI 1982 • $20 • (09/15/88) • **88**
Barolo Enrico VI 1981 • $NA • (09/15/88) • **88**
Barolo Enrico VI 1980 • $NA • (09/15/88) • **85**
Barolo Monfalletto 1993: Light-bodied, crisp and fruity, but more like Dolcetto than Barolo. It does deliver some nice cherry, wild berry, orange peel, fresh fig, spice and chocolate flavors, and it's not bad. Drink slightly chilled. 2,500 cases made. • $30 • (10/31/97) • **81**
Barolo Monfalletto 1984 • $NA • (09/15/88) • **88**
Barolo Monfalletto 1983 • $17 • (02/28/89) • **85**
Barolo Monfalletto 1980 • $11 • (01/31/87) • **91**
Barolo Monfalletto 1979 • $NA • (09/15/88) • **82**
Barolo Monfalletto 1978 • $NA • (09/15/88) • **84**
Barolo Monfalletto 1975 • $NA • (09/15/88) • **77**
Barolo Monfalletto 1971 • $NA • (09/15/88) • **85**
Dolcetto d'Alba 1996: Pretty, with floral and red berry aromas that are seductive. Light- to medium-bodied, with good balance and supple tannins, the crisp finish is a bit rough. Drink now. 3,333 cases made. • $12 • (10/31/97) • **84**
Dolcetto d'Alba Monfalletto 1994 • $NA • (10/31/95) • **81**

CORINO

Barbera d'Alba Vigna Giachini 1989 • $14 • (11/30/91) • **91**
Barbera d'Alba Vigna Pozzo 1993: Darkly colored and exotic, with rose, earth, spice and berry aromas and flavors. Medium body. 250 cases made. • $28 • (10/31/96) • **85**
Barbera d'Alba Vigna Pozzo 1990 • $30 • (11/15/93) • **92**
Barolo Vigna Giachini 1993: A pretty, if straightforward, Barolo, with nice cherry and raspberry flavors, mint and floral notes and round, smooth tannins. Drink chilled. • $35 • (10/31/97) • **84**
Barolo Vigna Giachini 1992: Sturdy and straightforward, if on the lean side, with enough cherry and spice flavors to make it interesting. Drink now through 2000. 467 cases made. • $30 • (10/31/96) • **81**
Barolo Vigna Giachini 1991: Impressive. Full-bodied, with generous layers of cedar, currant, black cherry and vanilla flavors. Tempting to drink now, but has the stuffing to age through at least 2000. 267 cases made. • $30 • (10/31/96) • **88**
Barolo Vigna Giachini 1990 • $79 Ⓐ • (10/31/94) • **90**
Barolo Vigna Giachini 1988 • $45 • (10/31/93) • **93**
Barolo Vigneto Rocche 1993: Well made Barolo in the *barrique*, new-oak style. Lots of spice, mocha, toasty bread and violet notes overwhelm a bit the red- and blackberry flavors, but some plum and cassis notes manage to

ITALY

come through. Supple, well-integrated tannins. Drink now through 2005. • $35 • (10/31/97) • **90**

Barolo Vigneto Rocche 1992: Nicely mature and enjoyably exotic in flavor—nutty, spicy, meaty. A bit lean, but distinctive. Firmly tannic. Drink now. 250 cases made. • $28 • (10/31/96) • **86**

Barolo Vigneto Rocche 1991 • $NA • (10/31/95) • **79**

Barolo Vigneto Rocche 1990 • $45 • (10/31/94) • **91**

Dolcetto d'Alba Vigna Giachini 1990 • $14 • (03/31/93) • **84**

CORNACCHIA, BARONE

Montepulciano d'Abruzzo 1992 • $8 • (03/31/95) • **81**

Montepulciano d'Abruzzo 1988 • $5 • (12/31/90) • **78**

CORNAREA

Roero Arneis 1996: A rustic style, with sharp citrus and geraniumlike flavors. Not for everyone. • $18 • (12/31/97) • **78**

CORONCINO, FATTORIA

Verdicchio dei Castelli di Jesi Classico Il Coroncino 1995: Light in flavor, medium in body, crisp in texture, this is a refreshing white wine with a buttery finish. • $10 • (04/30/97) • **82**

CORREGGIA, MATTEO

Barbera d'Alba 1994: Wild, decadent aromas and compacted currant, blackberry, pepper and gamy flavors. Firmly tannic, but long on the finish. Ready to drink. 458 cases made. • $31 • (10/31/96) • **83**

Barbera d'Alba Bricco Marun 1994: Fabulous Barbera. Sophisticated, elegant and full bodied. Packed with fruit, spice, floral, chocolate, red berry and vanilla character, it's round, velvetlike, sweet and ripe; keeps you coming back for more. Drinkable now through 2000. • $28 • (10/31/97) • **90**

Barbera d'Alba Bricco Marun 1993: Medium-bodied, long and supple. Nice chocolate, mocha and raspberry flavors, but the oak takes over as the wine stands in the glass. Drinkable now. 200 cases made. • $30 • (10/31/96) • **84**

Barbera d'Alba Bricco Marun 1990 • $20 • (10/31/94) • **86**

Barbera d'Alba Marun 1991 • $29 • (10/31/94) • **83**

Bracchetto Langhe 1992 • $12 • (10/31/94) • **82**

Nebbiolo d'Alba La Val dei Preti 1993 • $28 • (10/31/95) • **85**

Nebbiolo d'Alba La Val dei Preti 1992 • $28 • (10/31/95) • **81**

Nebbiolo d'Alba La Val dei Preti 1991 • $19 • (10/31/95) • **86**

CORTACCIA, CANTINA SOCIALE DI

Chardonnay Alto Adige Anime 1997: Nutty, leesy aromas add an extra dimension to this crisp, appley white. A simple, easygoing style. Drink now. 10,000 cases made. • $10 • (05/31/98) • **81**

Pinot Grigio Alto Adige Anime 1997: Fresh Pinot Grigio, with peach, apple and floral accents, all nicely balanced. Lively acidity carries the flavors to a tasty conclusion. Drink now. 10,000 cases made. • $10 • (05/31/98) • **83**

CORTE PAVONE

Brunello di Montalcino 1991: Delicate and floral, with a light, fruity structure and delicate tannins. Delicious now. • $NA • (09/30/97) • **86**

Brunello di Montalcino Riserva 1990: Offers plenty of fruit with its delicious strawberry, cherry and toasty oak flavors. Velvety texture, long, long finish. Drink or hold. • $NA • (09/30/97) • **89**

CORTE SANT'ALDA

Amarone della Valpolicella 1992: Very solid Amarone. Offers dried fruit, butterscotch and nut character on a firm structure. Moderate length, with some tannins yet to resolve. Drink now through 2002. 800 cases made. • $42 • (05/31/98) • **85**

Amarone Recioto della Valpolicella 1986 • $19 • (09/15/92) • **85**

Amarone Recioto della Valpolicella Metius 1986 • $23 • (09/15/92) • **79**

Key: SS—Spectator Selection CS—Cellar Selection HR—Highly Recommended BB—Best Buy $NA—Price not available Ⓐ—Auction Price (BT)—Barrel Tasting
Dates in parentheses indicate the issues in which the ratings were published.

Recioto della Valpolicella 1995: Only a hint of sweetness on entry, where the dried cherry, prune and orange-peel flavors augment the rich, firm texture; finishing on a clean, dry, astringent note. Drink now through 2000. 100 cases made. • $16/375ml • (07/31/98) • **84**

Soave Campi Magri 1996: Straightforward, this white stays within the apple and straw flavor-range, with crisp texture and a bitter almond finish characteristic of the appellation. Drink now. 1,200 cases made. • $13 • (06/15/98) • **82**

Valpolicella 1996: A solid Valpolicella delivering the bitter cherry, slightly tart elements that marry well with tomato sauces. A hint of bitter almond on the finish. Drink now. 1,500 cases made. • $12 • (06/15/98) • **81**

Valpolicella 1991 • $9 • (09/15/92) • **83**

Valpolicella 1988 • $11 • (09/15/92) • **82**

Valpolicella Metius 1988 • $17 • (09/15/92) • **85**

Valpolicella Superiore 1994: Shows more of the black cherry, vanilla and leather side of Valpolicella, with bright acidity keeping it fresh and lively right to the mouthwatering finish. Drink through 1999. 700 cases made. • $15 • (06/15/98) • **85**

Valpolicella Superiore 1993 • $10 • (06/15/96) • **85**

Valpolicella Superiore Mithas 1994: A fresh, lush red in a modern style, with pure crushed cherry character and a chocolate accent, all on a medium-bodied framework. Good length. Drink through 1999. 700 cases made. • $21 • (05/31/98) • **87**

CORTE VECCHIA

Amarone della Valpolicella Classico 1990: Ripe and soft, with plum and tobacco flavors and a decent finish, this Amarone doesn't measure up to the best from this vintage. The tannins on the finish are astringent. Drinkable now. • $30 • (11/15/97) • **83**

Amarone Recioto della Valpolicella Classico 1985 • $19 • (09/15/92) • **83**

Valpolicella Classico 1988 • $9 • (09/15/92) • **83**

CORTESE, GIUSEPPE

Barbaresco 1982 • $19 • (12/15/88) • **85**

Barbaresco Rabajà 1986 • $19 • (09/15/90) • **89**

Barbaresco Rabajà 1983 • $18 • (01/31/90) • **75**

Barbaresco Rabajà 1981 • $12 • (08/31/89) • **72**

Barbera d'Alba 1995: Light and a bit disjointed, with a crisp character, some earth, cassis and cherry notes and a chewy, slightly astringent finish. 208 cases made. • $11 • (10/31/97) • **79**

Barbera d'Alba 1990 • $12 • (02/15/92) • **71**

Barbera d'Alba 1989 • $11 • (07/15/91) • **86**

Barbera d'Alba 1988 • $9 • (03/15/91) • **86**

Barbera d'Alba Morassina 1995: A well-made wine with fine red berry flavor, but a slightly herbaceous character interferes and renders this medium-bodied Barbera a bit astringent on the finish. Drink now. 267 cases made. • $16 • (10/31/97) • **82**

Dolcetto d'Alba 1991 • $15 • (12/15/92) • **84**

Dolcetto d'Alba 1989 • $9 • (12/31/90) • **83**

Dolcetto d'Alba Trifolera 1996: Impressive quality. Inky-black in color, full-bodied, this has blackberry, mineral and licorice flavors, fresh acidity and a backbone of firm tannins that clamp down on the finish. Drink with food, now through 2000. 833 cases made. • $11 • (10/31/97) • **88**

Nebbiolo delle Langhe 1990 • $15 • (07/31/92) • **83**

Nebbiolo delle Langhe Vigna in Rabajà 1988 • $13 • (02/28/91) • **80**

CORTI, LE

Chianti Classico 1995: Generous and fruity in character, crisp and lightly tannic in texture, this is a good, solid Chianti. Drink now through 2000. 5,000 cases made. • $15 • (10/31/97) • **84**

Chianti Classico 1994: Pleasant. Has dried berry and dried herb aromas and flavors, a medium body, silky tannins and a fresh finish. Drink now. • $20 • (10/31/96) • **82**

Chianti Classico 1993 • $NA • (10/31/95) • **81**

Chianti Classico 1992 • $11 • (10/31/95) • **79**

Chianti Classico 1990 • $14 • (10/31/93) • **85**

Chianti Classico Cortevecchia Riserva 1994: Ripe, rich and succulent, with lovely, velvety tannins and a long, fresh finish. A joy to drink. 1,200 cases made. • $25 • (09/30/97) • **88**

Chianti Classico Cortevecchia Riserva 1993: An extremely perfumed wine of medium body with violet, plum and vanilla aromas and flavors. Has light, soft tannins and a caressing finish. Drink now. • $NA • (10/31/96) • **87**

Chianti Classico Don Tommasso 1994: A solid Chianti with berry, minty and cherry aromas and flavors and firm tannins. Finish is long, silky. Drinkable now. 650 cases made. • $32 • (10/31/96) • **86**

Masso Tondo 1985 • $20 • (04/30/89) • **86**

CORTILE, IL

Chianti Colli Fiorentini 1990 • $NA • (10/31/93) • **79**

CORVO

Brio 1993 • $9 • (10/31/95) • **77**

Duca Enrico 1987 • $38 • (11/30/94) • **89**

Duca di Salaparuta Duca Enrico 1984 • $27 • (09/15/89) • **92**

Terre D'Agala 1989 • $11 • (05/31/95) • **80**

COSER, FABIO

Collio Bianco Vigna del Lauro 1996: A soft, fruity white, showing moderate peach, vanilla and lemon flavors with a hint of firmness on the finish. Drink now. 4,000 cases made. • $16 • (05/31/98) • **82**

Pinot Grigio Collio Vigna del Lauro 1996: Brisk, dry and minerally, here's a Pinot Grigio with lanolin and stony notes, intensity and verve that carry through to the lingering finish. Great with seafood. Tasted twice, with consistent notes. Drink now through 1999. 1,500 cases made. • $16 • (05/31/98) • **86**

Sauvignon Collio Vigna del Lauro 1996: Gooseberry, floral and citrus aromas and flavors remind one of the Loire, yet this is a softer, gentler version of Sauvignon Blanc, fresh and crisp on the finish. Drink now. 800 cases made. • $16 • (05/15/98) • **84**

Tocai Friulano Collio Vigna del Lauro 1996: Fresh and lively, showing straw, almond and lemon flavors in a balanced, pleasant package. Great as an apéritif. Drink now. 2,000 cases made. • $16 • (05/31/98) • **82**

COSI

Pinot Grigio Valdadige 1996: Very rich and concentrated, full of apple, peach and floral notes, with enough acidity for balance, this Pinot Grigio provides immediate gratification. 5,000 cases made. • $10 • (11/15/97) • **84**

Pinot Grigio Valdadige 1993 • $10 • (06/15/96) • **80**

COSIMI, RODOLFO

Bottaccio 1992: A smooth-textured, mature wine with concentrated plum- and prunelike flavors that linger on the finish. Moderately tannic. Drink now through 2000. 167 cases made. • $20 • (05/31/97) • **86**

Bottaccio 1990: Aromatic, with aromas and flavors of plum, berry and pepper. Of medium body, with velvety tannins. Finishes with a hint of new wood. Drinkable now. 167 cases made. • $NA • (10/31/96) • **86**

COSTANTI, CONTI

Brunello di Montalcino 1992: Rather disjointed, with raisiny character and dry tannins. Slightly diluted finish. Tasted twice, with consistent notes. • $49 • (09/30/97) • **79**

Brunello di Montalcino 1991: Beautifully crafted, with lively, bright berry, dried cherry and herb aromas and flavors. Medium-bodied, with some fine tannins and a fresh finish. Drink now or hold. • $48 • (11/30/96) • **87**

Brunello di Montalcino 1990: Best wine ever made by Costanti. It's bursting at the seams with fresh fruit. Layers of violet, rose petal and red berry are balanced by lovely oak. Drink now. • $54 • (10/31/95) • **93**

Brunello di Montalcino 1988 • $45 • (04/30/94) • **88**

Brunello di Montalcino 1987 • $40 • (12/15/92) • **88**

Brunello di Montalcino 1982 • $32 • (07/31/88) • **81**

Brunello di Montalcino 1980 • $17 • (09/15/86) • **89**

Brunello di Montalcino Riserva 1990: Wonderfully vivid, fruity character, with plum, raspberry and floral aromas and flavors. Of medium body, with moderate tannins. Finish is long and silky. Outstanding finesse in this wine. Costanti does it again. • $75 • (11/30/96) • **93**

Brunello di Montalcino Riserva 1988 • $NA • (10/31/94) • **89**

Rosso di Montalcino 1995: Good Rosso, with dried cherry and bubblegum character. Medium in body, with fine tannins. Drink now. • $26 • (09/30/97) • **85**

Rosso di Montalcino 1994: A flavorful wine, emitting alluring aromas of chocolate and berries and giving a mouthful of fruit and soft tannins. Not one to age long. Delicious now. • $22 • (11/30/96) • **86**

Rosso di Montalcino 1993 • $NA • (10/31/95) • **85**

Rosso di Montalcino 1991 • $21 • (04/30/94) • **81**

Vermiglio 1991 • $NA • (10/31/95) • **80**

D'ANGELO

Aglianico del Vulture 1991 • $15 • (01/31/96) • **84**

Aglianico del Vulture 1985 • $18 • (09/15/89) • **70**

Aglianico del Vulture Vigna Caselle Riserva 1990 • $20 • (01/31/96) • **85**

Canneto 1991 • $25 • (01/31/96) • **85**

D'ATTIMIS, CONTI

Brunello di Montalcino Ferrante 1983 • $35 • (09/30/90) • **88**

Chianti Classico Ermanno 1987 • $11 • (09/15/90) • **82**

Chianti Classico Ermanno Riserva 1985 • $13 • (09/15/90) • **84**

Chianti Classico Odorico 1988 • $10 • (11/30/90) • **78**

Vino Nobile di Montepulciano Varnero 1987 • $14 • (09/15/90) • **75**

DAL FORNO, ROMANO

Amarone Recioto della Valpolicella Vigneti del Monte Lodoletta 1987 • $47 • (09/15/92) • **89**

Recioto della Valpolicella 1988: A dessert wine of moderate intensity and sweetness, displaying complex flavors, though volatile acidity is predominant on the nose. Soft and rich, this is an Italian specialty. • $47 • (09/15/97) • **83**

Valpolicella Superiore 1987 • $20 • (09/15/92) • **86**

Valpolicella Superiore 1986 • $20 • (04/30/92) • **84**

DEI

Rosso di Montepulciano 1996: Fresh, fruity and forward with bright cherry aromas and flavors and a crisp finish. Nice chilled. 2,500 cases made. • $13 • (09/30/97) • **82**

Santa Caterina 1995: Interesting. Dark in color, with intense blackberry flavors and hints of herbs, a medium body, velvety tannins and a long finish. Needs another year to polish the rough edges. Try in 1999. 300 cases made. • $35 • (09/30/97) • **88**

Santa Caterina 1994: A full-bodied yet marvelously reserved wine, with fine tannins and a silky finish. Wonderful aromas and flavors of mint, eucalyptus and berry. All in finesse. Drink now. • $35 • (10/31/96) • **89**

Vino Nobile di Montepulciano 1994: Clean, ripe fruit character prevails, but it's slightly diluted. Medium to light in body, with a light finish. 2,100 cases made. • $20 • (09/30/97) • **81**

Vino Nobile di Montepulciano 1993: Shows some nice earthy, berry flavors, but is slightly short, slightly dry on the finish. Medium-bodied. Drink now. 2,200 cases made. • $25 • (10/31/96) • **84**

Vino Nobile di Montepulciano Riserva 1993: Displays wonderful richness and fruitiness for its type. Has complex aromas of berries, blackberries and fungi, is medium- to full-bodied, with velvety tannins. Long, flavorful finish. Drink or hold. 660 cases made. • $28 • (09/30/97) • **88**

Vino Nobile di Montepulciano Riserva 1991: A pretty Sangiovese, with cherry and berry aromas and flavors and fine tannins. Medium- to light-bodied. Crisp finish. Drink now. • $23 • (10/31/96) • **84**

Vino Nobile di Montepulciano Riserva 1985 • $13 • (04/15/90) • **85**

DELIZIA, LA

Le Delizie di Krizia Red 1989 • $18 • (12/15/94) • **75**

DESSILANI

Barbera Piedmont 1993: A well-balanced, ready-to-drink wine with plum and rhubarblike flavors and tobacco and herb notes that linger on the finish. • $9 • (03/31/97) • **84**

Barbera Piedmont 1990 • $8 • (10/31/92) BB • **83**

Barbera Piedmont 1986 • $7 • (03/15/91) BB • **87**

Caramino Riserva 1985 • $13 • (09/15/90) • **79**

Spanna 1990 • $9 • (02/28/95) • **79**

Spanna Riserva 1988 • $11 • (02/28/95) • **83**

DI MAJO NORANTE

Moscato Apianae da Uva Reale 1992: A lighter style, showing elements of pine and marmalade accented by citrus peel. Just slightly bitter on the finish. 1,000 cases made. • $16/500ml • (01/01/97) • **84**

DIEVOLE

Broccato 1994: Very fresh, with a generous floral and berry character. Of medium body, with light tannins and a fresh, fruity finish showing a hint of vanilla. Drink now. • $14 • (09/30/97) • **87**
Broccato 1987 • $19 • (12/15/91) • **86**
Chianti Classico 1995: Soft, silky and succulent, with aromas and flavors of chocolate, berry and cherry, medium body, fine tannins and a fresh finish. Delicious. Drink or hold. • $12 • (09/30/97) • **86**
Chianti Classico 1994: A core of ripe fruit flavors, lots of pretty berry, floral and violet aromas and flavors. Medium-bodied with some fine tannis and a refreshing finish. • $11 • (10/31/96) • **86**
Chianti Classico 1990 • $10 • (09/15/92) • **85**
Chianti Classico 1988 • $13 • (09/15/91) • **85**
Chianti Classico Dieulele 1990 • $24 • (10/31/93) • **84**
Chianti Classico Dieulele 1988 • $22 • (04/15/91) HR • **91**
Chianti Classico Rinascimento 1993: A drink-me Sangiovese, with plenty of berry and cherry flavors and soft, succulent tannins. Drink now. • $16 • (10/31/96) • **85**
Chianti Classico Riserva 1994: Firm and chunky, with blackberry and wet earth aromas and flavors. Medium-bodied, with medium tannins and a slightly short finish. Better after this year. • $18 • (09/30/97) • **86**
Chianti Classico Riserva 1993: Not a big wine but subtle and fresh, with dried cherry and violet aromas and flavors, a medium-to-light body and a refreshing finish. Drink now. • $18 • (10/31/96) • **84**
Chianti Classico Riserva 1988 • $18 • (09/15/92) • **88**
Chianti Classico Vigna Campi Nuovi 1988 • $15 • (04/15/91) • **82**
Chianti Classico Vigna Campi Nuovi 1987 • $10 • (11/30/90) • **84**
Chianti Classico Vigna Petrignano 1988 • $12 • (01/31/92) • **84**
Chianti Classico Vigna Sessina 1988 • $12 • (01/31/92) • **84**
Toscana Rinascimento 1994: Marked by its pretty blackberry and blueberry aromas, it's medium- to full-bodied, with round, ripe tannins and a long, fruity finish. A joy to drink. • $14 • (09/30/97) • **88**
Val d'Arbia 1996: Shows melon, apple and cream on the nose and is of medium body, with moderate acidity and a slightly candied finish. • $12 • (09/30/97) • **80**

DOSIO

Barolo Fossati 1993: Good fruit, supple texture, medium body and clean, pure flavors. Good intensity on the finish, though the tannins turn a bit dry. Try after 1999. • $NA • (10/31/97) • **85**

DRAGO, CASCINO

Bricco del Drago Vigna delle Mace 1987 • $17 • (01/31/92) • **75**
Bricco del Drago Vigna delle Mace 1986 • $22 • (01/31/92) • **81**
Bricco del Drago Vigna delle Mace 1985 • $22 • (01/31/89) • **79**
Bricco del Drago Vigna delle Mace 1982 • $14 • (11/30/87) • **84**
Campo Romano 1990 • $14 • (01/31/92) • **73**

DUCHI DI CASTELLUCCIO

Montepulciano d'Abruzzo 1994: From Italy comes this robust red, its vintage marking the producer's 20th. A good value for everyday drinking, it shows some rich plum flavors, a touch of mint and some herbal notes. 1,200 cases imported. • $13/1.5 liter • (03/31/97) BB • **84**

ECCO DOMANI

Pinot Bianco delle Venezie 1996: An elegant, focused white smelling of lemon custard, followed by citrus and apple flavors. Light-bodied, with a clean finish. Drink now. 25,000 cases made. • $10 • (05/15/98) • **85**

Key: SS—Spectator Selection CS—Cellar Selection HR—Highly Recommended BB—Best Buy $NA—Price not available Ⓐ—Auction Price (BT)—Barrel Tasting
Dates in parentheses indicate the issues in which the ratings were published.

Pinot Nero delle Venezie 1996: A fresh, vibrant red full of spicy berry character, soft and juicy in texture. Made for early consumption; drink now. 25,000 cases made. • $10 • (04/30/98) • **82**
Sangiovese Toscana 1996: A nicely balanced, medium-bodied red with ample raspberry flavors accented by black pepper. Good, uncomplicated, not tannic. Drink now. 25,000 cases made. • $10 • (04/30/98) • **83**

EINAUDI, LUIGI

Barbera 1995: Ripe and sweet, this medium-bodied red is very satisfying. Offers plenty of lovely cherry, licorice, black currant flavors. Balanced and long, with a slightly smoky, toasty finish. Delicious now through 2001. 583 cases made. • $15 • (10/31/97) • **88**
Barbera delle Langhe 1994: Sharp and crisp. A bit short on fruit, it has earthy accents and is tannic on the finish. • $16 • (10/31/96) • **77**
Barbera Langhe 1992 • $13 • (10/31/94) • **78**
Barolo 1993: Balanced between fruit, tannins and acidity, though fairly light-bodied, this has smooth tannins and straightforward flavors of cherry, mineral, chalk and smoke. Drinkable now through 2000. 1,050 cases made. • $41 • (10/31/97) • **83**
Barolo 1992: Fruity, ripe and supple. Its easy-going plum and cherry flavors and relatively soft tannins make it good to drink soon. • $41 • (10/31/96) • **82**
Barolo 1991 • $37 • (10/31/95) • **81**
Barolo 1989 • $43 • (10/31/94) • **71**
Barolo 1988 • $30 • (12/15/92) • **83**
Barolo 1982 • $23 • (06/30/87) • **81**
Dolcetto di Dogliani 1995: Mature notes of forest, mushroom and wet earth mix with the black cherry flavors in this soft red. Light-to-medium in body, a bit tart on the finish. Drink now. 6,667 cases made. • $14 • (10/31/97) • **79**
Dolcetto di Dogliani 1994: Quite aromatic, with some bottle bouquet. Spice, rose petal and tar flavors turn a bit dry on the leathery, slightly tired finish. • $14 • (10/31/96) • **78**
Dolcetto di Dogliani 1993 • $12 • (10/31/95) • **80**
Dolcetto di Dogliani 1990 • $11 • (10/31/92) • **87**
Dolcetto di Dogliani I Filari 1995: Medium-bodied, with cedar, black cherry and raspberry aromas and flavors. Slightly tannic. 275 cases made. • $20 • (10/31/96) • **83**
Dolcetto di Dogliani Vigna Tecc 1995: Ripe, sweet fruit makes this medium-bodied red fun to drink now. The mineral, spice and black cherry flavors come together on the crisp, slightly dry, finish. 2,083 cases made. • $18 • (10/31/97) • **82**
Dolcetto di Dogliani Vigna Tecc 1994: A firm-textured Barbera with aniselike aromas and focused fruit flavors to lend interest. Drinkable now. • $18 • (10/31/96) • **81**
Dolcetto di Dogliani Vigna Tecc 1993 • $16 • (10/31/95) • **84**
Nebbiolo Piedmont 1991 • $17 • (02/28/95) • **79**
Nebbiolo delle Langhe 1983 • $8 • (07/01/86) • **70**

ENDRIZZI

Pinot Grigio Trentino 1994 • $17 • (06/15/96) • **75**

ENO-FRIULIA

Cabernet Sauvignon Collio 1988 • $12 • (07/15/91) • **76**
Chardonnay Collio 1997: Apple aromas and flavors and a crisp structure are light and lacking in concentration. Drink now. • $12 • (07/31/98) • **78**
Chardonnay 1995 • $12 • (06/15/96) • **79**
Chardonnay Collio 1993 • $11 • (01/31/95) • **83**
Merlot Collio 1996: Not much aroma and the flavors are light, showing only modest herb and berry. Drink now. • $12 • (07/31/98) • **78**
Merlot Collio 1988 • $12 • (04/30/91) • **82**
Pinot Bianco Collio 1997: Beautifully displayed apple, peach, lemon and nut aromas and flavors typical of this varietal, with vibrant acidity and fine balance. Should be even better in about six months. Drink through 1999. • $12 • (07/31/98) • **86**
Pinot Bianco 1995 • $12 • (06/15/96) • **84**
Pinot Bianco Collio 1993 • $11 • (01/31/95) • **80**
Pinot Grigio Collio 1997: Delicious from start to finish. Tastes like quince and nuts, with a rich texture. Bright acidity keeps everything lively and fresh through the lingering finish. Drink through 1999. • $12 • (07/31/98) • **85**
Pinot Grigio 1995 • $12 • (06/15/96) • **78**
Pinot Grigio Collio 1993 • $11 • (01/31/95) • **81**

Sauvignon Isonzo del Friuli 1997: Broad and waxy in both aroma and flavor, this white shows richness and weight but isn't very expressive. Good, crisp finish. Drink through 1999. • $12 • (07/31/98) • **83**

Sauvignon Isonzo del Friuli 1995 • $12 • (06/15/96) • **83**

Tocai Friulano Collio 1997: Open and easygoing. Already rich and inviting. Low in acidity, showing banana and peach flavors, with a hint of almond peeking through. Drink through 1999. • $12 • (07/31/98) • **84**

Tocai Friulano Collio 1993 • $11 • (01/31/95) • **88**

ERBALUNA

Barolo 1993: Get past the earthy, funky aromas and you'll find a medium-bodied, ripe, sweet-tasting wine with layers of pretty red- and blackberry flavors. The tannins might soften with age. Try after 1999. • $NA • (10/31/97) • **81**

FALCHINI, RICCARDO

Campora 1991: A smooth-drinking, full-blown oak style. Rich and enticing, it offers blackberry, dark cherry, vanilla, spice and chocolate flavors. Gotta love it for its chutzpah. Drink now. 1,000 cases made. • $50 • (01/31/97) • **89**

Campora Toscana 1989: Mature; we wonder if it wasn't better four years ago. Has the cola and herb aromas from bottle aging but has lost most of its fruit. Little left but firm tannins and acidity. Past its prime. 1,000 cases made. • $50 • (01/01/98) • **77**

Chianti Colli Senesi Titolato Colombaia 1996: Nicely balanced, with bright fruit, hints of black pepper, lively acidity and modest tannins. Easy to enjoy. Drink through 1999. 6,000 cases made. • $9 • (07/31/98) • **85**

Chianti Colli Senesi Titolato Colombaia 1995: Fairly rich with appealing flavors of plum, chocolate and coffee that linger on the finish. Has a nice broad texture, making it taste smooth and well rounded. 13,000 cases made. • $9 • (03/31/97) BB • **86**

Paretaio 1993: A solid wine with floral aromas and dried cherry flavors. A roasted note lingers on the finish. 5,000 cases made. • $17 • (01/31/97) • **83**

Vernaccia di San Gimignano Abvinea Doni 1995: A dramatic version of Vernaccia (usually crisp and straightforward), that adds honey and butter nuances to the fresh peach flavors. Full-bodied, smooth-textured. Drink through 1999. 8,000 cases made. • $16 • (07/31/98) • **86**

Vernaccia di San Gimignano Vigna a Solatio 1996: Crisp in texture, lightly peachy and appley in flavor, this medium-weight white should be versatile with food. Drink now. 15,000 cases made. • $9 • (07/31/98) • **82**

Vernaccia di San Gimignano Vigna a Solatio 1995: This wine has richness, but also a strange, dried-herb flavor that turns somewhat bitter on the finish. 15,000 cases made. • $9 • (03/31/97) • **77**

Vernaccia di San Gimignano Vinea Doni 1994: A deliciously mature white, with appealing vanilla, pear and ripe apple flavors. Good depth, structure and body, with spicy notes that linger on the finish. It's quite intense, with good acidity and balance. 8,000 cases made. • $16 • (03/31/97) • **88**

Vin Santo di Caratello 1990: The aroma of this dessert wine is slightly muted, like walnut oil, but the intensity builds on the palate. Acidity keeps it lively, and the finish shows some tannins and a nutty character. 1,000 cases made. • $16/500ml • (05/31/97) • **85**

FALESCO

Merlot di Aprilia 1993 • $13 • (01/31/96) • **84**

Merlot Umbria 1996: For lovers of the smoky, spicy accent of oak. This tannic, monolithic red may smooth out with time, but right now the oak influence buries the fruit flavors. Drink through 2002. • $14 • (06/15/98) • **84**

Montiano Latium 1995: A luscious, layered, posh, international-style Italian red, with a beautifully oaky character that meshes well with the deep fruit flavors. Has great concentration and a long finish. Tannic, but well balanced. Drink now through 2001. 1,000 cases made. • $30 • (06/15/98) HR • **91**

Vitiano 1996: Polished and tasty, this fruit-driven Italian red offers sleek texture, nice cherry and raspberry flavors, spicy undertones and a lingering finish. Quite a nice bottle of wine for so few dollars. Ready now. 12,500 cases made. • $10 • (06/15/98) BB • **85**

FANTI

Brunello di Montalcino 1991: A solid '91, of medium body, with fresh berry and cherry aromas and flavors. Tannins are light and silky. Drink now. • $NA • (11/30/96) • **85**

Brunello di Montalcino 1990: Wonderfully perfumed strawberry, cassis bush character. Medium-bodied and soft with a fruity finish. Drink now. • $NA • (10/31/95) • **87**

Brunello di Montalcino 1988 • $NA • (04/30/94) • **79**

Rosso di Montalcino 1994: An attractive rosso with pretty, clean fruit and spice flavors over fine tannins. Fresh on the finish. • $NA • (11/30/96) • **84**

Rosso di Montalcino 1993 • $NA • (10/31/95) • **84**

Rosso di Montalcino 1991 • $NA • (04/30/94) • **82**

Rosso di Montalcino La Palazzetta 1995: Vibrant cherry and violet aromas announce a medium-bodied wine with focused fruit flavors, moderate tannins and a long finish. Drink now. • $NA • (09/30/97) • **87**

FANTINEL

Cabernet Franc Grave del Friuli F Sigillo Oro 1997: Lovely black currant and berry notes, with a touch of herbs in this slightly spritzy, vibrant red. Light and lively. Drink through 1999. • $12 • (06/15/98) • **85**

Cabernet Sauvignon Grave del Friuli 1996: A mixture of smoke, herbs and black currant greets the nose, followed by cedar and tobacco nuances on the palate in this smooth, integrated, medium-bodied Cabernet. The finish is crisp but lingering. Drink now through 2000. • $15 • (06/15/98) • **87**

Cabernet Sauvignon Grave del Friuli 1985 • $7 • (07/31/87) • **80**

Merlot Grave del Friuli Barone Rosso 1997: A mouthwatering Merlot from Italy at a price that's hard to beat. It's fresh and vivid, with cherry flavors that border on bittersweet chocolate and a focus and intensity that persist through the finish. Drink through 1999. • $9 • (06/15/98) BB • **86**

Pinot Bianco Grave del Friuli F Sigillo Oro 1997: Distinctive, showing nutty, smoky aromas followed by a rich, glycerinlike texture, earthy almond flavors and a hint of bitterness on the finish. Not for fans of fruit. Drink through 1999. • $12 • (06/15/98) • **82**

Pinot Grigio Collio 1997: Serious wine. Rich, nutty, bread-dough aromas from lees contact, which also adds a creaminess to the texture in this concentrated white. The floral, peach and almond flavors unfold nicely on the palate, and there's structure for aging. Drink now through 2000. • $15 • (06/15/98) • **88**

Pinot Grigio Grave del Friuli Montecristo 1996: Already seems mature, showing slightly oxidized, marzipan character and a sharp acidity. Drink now. • $9 • (07/31/98) • **78**

Sauvignon Grave del Friuli F Sigillo Oro 1996: Smells like marzipan and clove, with dilute, nonvarietal flavors on the palate. Finishes on the metallic side. • $12 • (07/31/98) • **76**

FARINA, REMO

Amarone della Valpolicella Classico 1993: Good, showing modest cherry and plum, but lacks the concentration of the best vintages. Drink now through 2002. 3,500 cases made. • $23 • (05/31/98) • **84**

Amarone Recioto della Valpolicella Classico 1983 • $13 • (03/31/90) • **70**

Bianco di Custoza 1996: Floral, perfumed aromas jump out of the glass in this boldly-flavored white. Apple and almond are the dominant notes leading into a crisp finish. Drink now. 3,000 cases made. • $8 • (05/15/98) • **82**

Soave Classico Superiore 1996: This has earthy, green olive notes, broadening on the palate with quince and almond notes. A dollop of bitterness lingers on the finish. Drink now. 5,000 cases made. • $8 • (06/15/98) • **84**

Valpolicella Classico Superiore 1995: Dried cherry and licorice aromas and flavors are the main themes in this light-bodied, balanced red. Drink now. 5,000 cases made. • $8 • (04/30/98) • **82**

FARINA, STEFANO

Barbaresco 1994: Weak, very diluted, with only modest fruit and a short, dry finish. 1,667 cases made. • $18 • (10/31/97) • **73**

Barbaresco 1993: Well made and well balanced. Of medium body, with earth, mineral and cherry flavors and a smoky, slightly salty finish. Tannins need time. Try after 1999. 1,000 cases made. • $19 • (10/31/96) • **88**

Barbaresco 1989 • $15 • (10/31/94) • **79**

Barbera d'Alba 1995: Interesting chalk and stone character mingles with toasty oak, plum and cherry flavors in this medium-bodied, ripe and satisfying red. Drink now. 8,333 cases made. • $9 • (10/31/97) • **85**

Barbera d'Alba 1994: Pretty and smooth, with plum, prune, currant and tar flavors and a fresh, crisp finish. Already showing bottle bouquet. Ready to drink. 4,167 cases made. • $9 • (10/31/96) • **84**

ITALY

Barolo 1993: Lots of plum and prune flavors, but it tastes overdone and lacks the lovely balance of many '93s. Medium-bodied, turns dry on the finish. Better after 2000? 4,167 cases made. • $24 • (10/31/97) • **78**
Barolo 1992: Wonderfully smooth and well balanced, with lots of bright plum and cherry flavors and polished tannins. Drink now through 2000. 3,333 cases made. • $22 • (10/31/96) • **86**
Barolo 1990 • $18 • (07/31/95) • **88**
Barolo 1989 • $16 • (06/15/94) HR • **90**
Chianti La Ginestra 1992 • $6 • (07/31/94) • **77**
Dolcetto d'Alba 1996: Lovely, ripe Dolcetto, offering plum, raspberry, and cassis notes. Medium in body, with well-integrated tannins and a supple finish. Enjoy now. 8,333 cases made. • $10 • (10/31/97) • **86**
Dolcetto d'Alba 1995: What Dolcetto should be. Like a barrel sample, it oozes luscious grape, crushed blackberry and raspberry flavors that remain clean and well defined. Supple texture. Enjoy upon release. 5,000 cases made. • $10 • (10/31/96) BB • **87**
Dolcetto d'Alba 1991 • $10 • (06/15/94) • **78**

FARNESE

Montepulciano d'Abruzzo 1996: Soft and supple, with plum and leatherlike flavors. Turns a bit herbal on the finish. 150,000 cases made. • $6 • (07/31/97) • **78**
Montepulciano d'Abruzzo 1993 • $5 • (02/29/96) BB • **85**
Sangiovese Abruzzi 1995: This vino da tavola shows remarkable intensity. It's ripe, smooth and full-flavored, with dried plum and cherry notes, dark and delicious—quite a mouthful of wine for so few dollars. 40,000 cases made. 40,000 cases made. • $6 • (07/31/97) BB • **85**
Trebbiano d'Abruzzo 1996: A generous, soft white wine with banana and fig flavors and a smooth texture. 75,000 cases made. • $6 • (05/31/97) • **83**

FARNETA, TENUTA

Chianti 1990 • $6 • (09/15/92) • **78**
Chianti Villa Farneta 1988 • $14 • (10/31/91) • **79**
Chianti di Collalto 1989 • $7 • (10/31/91) BB • **81**
Chianti di Collalto 1988 • $6 • (12/15/90) BB • **88**
Selezione di Bongoverno 1990 • $25 • (10/31/95) • **87**
Selezione di Bongoverno 1988 • $31 • (12/15/92) • **85**
Selezione di Bongoverno 1986 • $30 • (09/30/91) • **87**

FARNETE, LE

Carmignano Riserva 1993: Sweet, spicy oak flavors dominate, intriguing black cherry and plum flavors peek through on the finish. Full-bodied, tannic and fairly concentrated. A blend of 80 percent Sangiovese and 20 percent Cabernet Sauvignon. Drink now through 2000. 350 cases made. • $27 • (04/30/98) • **85**

FARNETELLA, CASTELLO DI

Chianti Colli Senesi 1995: Plenty of dried cherry, with a hint of herbal character, on the nose and palate. Medium-bodied, with fine tannins and a crisp finish. Drink or hold. 5,000 cases made. • $13 • (09/30/97) • **83**
Chianti Colli Senesi 1992 • $10 • (02/28/95) • **81**
Chianti Colli Senesi 1991 • $10 • (02/28/95) • **81**
Sauvignon Tuscany 1995: A good Sauvignon with mild grass and lime aromas. Medium-bodied, with lime and slightly earthy flavors and a light, fresh finish. 700 cases made. • $22 • (09/30/97) • **85**

FASSATI

Rocca delle Querce Red 1995: Very light, but fruity and fresh with good strawberry character. Pleasant chilled. • $NA • (09/30/97) • **80**
Rocca delle Querce White 1995: Lively and delicious, with enticing aromas of minerals, spice and volcanic rock. Medium in body, it has moderate acidity and a crisp, flavorful finish. • $NA • (09/30/97) • **85**
Rosso di Montepulciano Selciaia 1996: A bit simple, but fruity and soft with a pleasantly fresh aftertaste. Slightly rustic. Drink now. 5,000 cases made. • $8 • (09/30/97) • **81**
Rosso di Montepulciano Selciaia 1995: Nice use of new wood but not enough fruit to support it. Light- to medium-bodied, with light tannins and a cherry-vanilla finish. 4,000 cases made. • $8 • (09/30/97) • **80**
Rosso di Montepulciano Selciaia 1994: A hearty red, big on plummy, grapey, herbal flavors yet easy on the tannins so it's fairly smooth in texture. Drink now. • $8 • (01/01/97) • **83**
Vino Nobile di Montepulciano 1993: Bright and fruity, with dried cherry and floral aromas and flavors, medium body and a crisp finish. Drink now. 5,100 cases made. • $11 • (09/30/97) • **83**
Vino Nobile di Montepulciano 1991: Full-bodied, mature in flavor, showing earthy accents to the cherrylike flavors. Fairly smooth-textured and still firmly tannic. Drink now. • $20 • (01/01/97) • **79**
Vino Nobile di Montepulciano Riserva 1985 • $22 • (11/30/89) • **86**
Vino Nobile di Montepulciano Riserva 1978 • $8 • (07/01/86) • **73**
Vino Nobile di Montepulciano Salarco Riserva 1991: New wood prevails, but there's impressive ripe berry flavor through and through. Medium-bodied, with medium tannins and a light, woody finish. A bit overoaked? Drink now. 910 cases made. • $16 • (09/30/97) • **84**

FASTELLI

Brunello di Montalcino 1988 • $NA • (04/30/94) • **77**
Rosso di Montalcino 1991 • $NA • (04/30/94) • **76**

FATTOI

Brunello di Montalcino 1992: A delicate, fruity red with berry, tanned leather and cherry character. Has medium body, fine tannins. Drink now. • $45 • (09/30/97) • **84**
Rosso di Montalcino 1995: A Rosso with medium body, fresh acidity and a mineral and dried berry character. • $21 • (09/30/97) • **85**

FAUSTO GEMME

Gavi 1993 • $11 • (02/28/95) • **81**
Gavi La Merlina 1993 • $12 • (02/28/95) • **79**

FAZI-BATTAGLIA

Verdicchio dei Castelli di Jesi 1993 • $10 • (03/31/95) • **83**
Verdicchio dei Castelli di Jesi Classico 1995: A delicious Italian white, round and fruity, full of peach and apple flavors. Picks up a touch of bitter almond on the finish. It's ready to drink, fairly priced and widely available. 290,000 cases made. • $8 • (09/15/97) BB • **84**
Verdicchio dei Castelli di Jesi Classico Le Moie 1994: Juicy, like biting into a Golden Delicious apple. It also has plenty of spice notes and a touch of herb on the finish. Flavors linger. 5,000 cases made. • $12 • (10/15/97) • **85**
Verdicchio dei Castelli di Jesi Classico San Sisto 1993: A more serious white that has complexity from barrel aging in some new oak. Honey, butterscotch and baked-apple notes are well integrated in a rich texture that glides to a lingering conclusion. 2,900 cases made. • $14 • (09/15/97) • **87**

FELLUGA, LIVIO

Cabernet Franc Collio 1988 • $15 • (06/30/91) • **84**
Cabernet Franc Collio 1986 • $14 • (09/15/88) • **75**
Chardonnay Esperto 1995: If you like nutmeg, you'll love this. The spicy flavors and aromas are wrapped around some modest apple and honey flavors. Well made, with good texture. • $16 • (01/31/97) • **84**
Esperto Colli Orientali del Friuli 1994 • $14 • (10/31/95) • **80**
Merlot Colli Orientali del Friuli 1995: Plenty of herb and vanilla character, lively acidity and firm tannins. Starts off rich, then turns astringent on the finish, with a tobacco aftertaste. Drink through 1999. 3,300 cases made. • $23 • (06/15/98) • **84**
Merlot Colli Orientali del Friuli 1993 • $17 • (02/29/96) • **85**
Merlot Collio 1988 • $16 • (07/15/91) • **84**
Merlot delle Venezie Esperto 1995: High-toned and herbal, with an orange-chocolate note that's exotic but more at home in a box of candy than a glass of wine. Still, it's balanced and flavorful. 6,666 cases made. • $14 • (12/15/97) • **83**
Pinot Grigio Colli Orientali del Friuli 1996: Ripe and juicy, displaying apple and almond flavors, a rich texture and vanilla shadngs. The finish is crisp and refreshing, though not particularly long. Drink now. 18,000 cases made. • $19 • (05/31/98) • **84**

Key: SS—Spectator Selection CS—Cellar Selection HR—Highly Recommended BB—Best Buy $NA—Price not available Ⓐ—Auction Price (BT)—Barrel Tasting
Dates in parentheses indicate the issues in which the ratings were published.

Pinot Grigio Colli Orientali del Friuli 1995: Tastes mature for a young wine, with a strong floral aroma. It has richness and concentration, but the pear and apple flavors could be fresher. • $15 • (01/31/97) • **82**
Pinot Grigio Colli Orientali del Friuli 1994 • $15 • (10/31/95) • **85**
Pinot Grigio Collio 1993 • $15 • (01/31/95) • **76**
Pinot Grigio delle Venezie Esperto 1996: Ripe and broad, with flavors of honey and almond, this is balanced on the soft side. Almost viscous in texture, a slight astringency on the finish reigns it in. 12,500 cases made. • $14 • (12/15/97) • **83**
Terra Alte Colli Orientali del Friuli White 1995: Subtle and sophisticated, its aromas and flavors of red berries, apple and almond are displayed on a rich texture that's lively and fresh. Drink now. 4,000 cases made. • $33 • (06/15/98) • **85**
Terre Alte White 1994: A pleasant wine, with peach and apple flavors and the right acidity. Drink it up quickly. • $32 • (01/31/97) • **82**
Terre Alte White 1993 • $30 • (04/30/96) • **84**
Tocai Friulano Colli Orientali del Friuli 1996: Delightful, combining floral and almond flavors with freshness and elegance. Perfect as an apéritif. Drink now. 2,500 cases made. • $19 • (07/31/98) • **85**
Tocai Friulano Colli Orientali del Friuli 1993 • $18 • (04/30/96) • **87**

FELLUGA, MARCO

Carantan 1993: Extremely perfumed, showing notes of sandalwood and cardamom that turn to cherry and plum. Supple, beautifully balanced. It's toned and firmly structured, displaying firm yet ripe tannins. Drink now through 2001. 800 cases made. • $27 • (06/30/98) • **88**
Carantan 1990 • $20 • (06/15/96) • **78**
Carantan 1988 • $36 • (04/30/92) • **88**
Chardonnay Collio 1995: High acidity is the main component here, right to the tart finish, but it may soften with time allowing the apple flavors greater prominence. 6,700 cases made. • $13 • (06/15/97) • **81**
Merlot Collio 1993 • $11 • (06/15/96) BB • **82**
Molamatta 1996: Has verve and intensity, showing citrus and apple and a hint of carbon dioxide for freshness, on an elegant, laserlike framework. Drink now. 3,500 cases made. • $16 • (06/30/98) • **84**
Molamatta 1995: An unadorned, slightly spritzy white, showing fresh, green apple and lemon acidity that needs taming via food. A blend of Pinot Bianco, Tocai Friulano and Ribolla Gialla. 3,500 cases made. • $14 • (06/15/97) • **83**
Molamatta 1994 • $14 • (06/15/96) • **82**
Moscato Rosa del Friuli 1993 • $NA • (01/31/95) • **85**
Pinot Bianco Collio 1995: Deftly balanced and elegant, with the peach, melon and citrus flavors showing a finesse and raciness more common to Mosel Riesling. Perfect on its own or with light dishes. 3,000 cases made. • $13 • (06/15/97) • **86**
Pinot Grigio Collio 1995: Subtle in its appeal, fresh, balanced and elegant, this peach-flavored wine would be equally delightful as an apéritif or with light dishes. 23,500 cases made. • $13 • (06/15/97) • **85**
Pinot Grigio Collio 1994 • $11 • (06/15/96) • **82**
Tocai Friulano Collio 1995: A seductive, somewhat rich white, with lovely peach and floral aromas and flavors, modest depth. Best as an apéritif. 2,500 cases made. • $13 • (06/15/97) • **85**
Tocai Friulano Collio 1994 • $11 • (06/15/96) • **77**

FELSINA, FATTORIA DI

Chianti Classico 1995: Gobs of blackberry and mushroom character mark this medium-bodied wine. The tannins are well integrated, the finish is long. Great with grilled meats. 9,000 cases made. • $18 • (09/30/97) • **88**
Chianti Classico 1988 • $13 • (11/30/89) • **86**
Chianti Classico 1987 • $10 • (11/30/89) • **83**
Chianti Classico 1986 • $7 • (11/30/89) • **78**
Chianti Classico Berardenga 1994: A winner every time. Impressively dark and rich with plenty of berry and dried chocolate character and a good amount of structure to the firm tannins. Medium body, silky finish. Drink now. 10,000 cases made. • $14 • (10/31/96) • **88**
Chianti Classico Berardenga 1992 • $12 • (02/28/95) • **84**
Chianti Classico Berardenga 1990 • $12 • (09/15/92) • **91**
Chianti Classico Berardenga 1988 • $13 • (09/15/91) • **89**
Chianti Classico Berardenga 1987 • $8 • (05/15/90) • **83**
Chianti Classico Berardenga 1986 • $7 • (12/15/88) • **72**
Chianti Classico Berardenga Rancia Riserva 1990 • $28 • (02/28/95) SS • **93**
Chianti Classico Berardenga Rancia Riserva 1985 • $23 • (04/30/90) CS • **93**
Chianti Classico Berardenga Rancia Riserva 1983 • $17 • (12/15/88) • **91**
Chianti Classico Berardenga Riserva 1994: A serious red with superfine tannins and condensed fruit and earth aromas and flavors. Full-to-medium in body, with a medium finish. Drink now. 4,000 cases made. • $23 • (09/30/97) • **90**
Chianti Classico Berardenga Riserva 1993 • $NA • (01/31/96) • **87**
Chianti Classico Berardenga Riserva 1990 • $18 • (02/28/95) • **90**
Chianti Classico Berardenga Riserva 1988 • $17 • (09/15/92) • **92**
Chianti Classico Berardenga Riserva 1985 • $15 • (09/15/91) • **86**
Chianti Classico Berardenga Riserva 1983 • $12 • (11/30/89) • **87**
Chianti Classico Rancia Riserva 1994: This is a beautifully crafted Chianti with impressive berry, cherry and vanilla aromas and flavors. Full-bodied, with wonderfully integrated tannins, a long and silky finish. Drink now. 3,000 cases made. • $35 • (09/30/97) • **92**
Chianti Classico Rancia Riserva 1993: Round, ripe and voluptuous. Wonderful aromas and flavors of cherry, berry and minerals. Medium- to full-bodied with full, soft tannins and a long, velvety finish. Drink or hold. • $33 • (09/30/97) • **92**
Chianti Classico Rancia Riserva 1990: A beautifully aromatic wine with tobacco, grilled meat and berry character. Full-bodied, with full tannins and plenty of fruit. Slightly dry on the finish. Drink or hold. • $NA • (09/30/97) • **88**
Chianti Classico Rancia Riserva 1988: Great youth from a superb producer. Dark ruby-colored with grilled meat, porcino and fruit aromas and flavors. Full-bodied, with integrated tannins and loads of fruit. Slightly tough finish. Drink now. • $NA • (09/30/97) • **90**
Chianti Classico Rancia Riserva 1985: A powerful and aromatic wine with a generous wet earth and ripe fruit character. Medium- to full-bodied, with high acidity and a slightly hard finish. Drink now. • $NA • (09/30/97) • **87**
Chianti Classico Riserva 1993: Terrific winemaking here. Bubbling over with berry, raspberry and black cherry aromas. Medium-bodied and has fine tannins and a long silky, fruity finish. Drink or hold. • $19 • (10/31/96) • **89**
Fontalloro 1993: Superbly crafted. Displays bright cherry, dried berry and flowers on the nose and palate, a medium body, ultrafine tannins and a long, long, silky finish. Drink or hold. 2,400 cases made. • $40 • (09/30/97) • **90**
Fontalloro 1990 • $38 • (02/28/95) • **91**
Fontalloro 1988 • $NA • (11/15/93) • **93**
Fontalloro 1986 • $NA • (11/15/93) • **89**
Fontalloro 1985 • $24 • (09/15/88) • **91**
Fontalloro 1983 • $NA • (11/15/93) • **88**
Fontalloro 1982 • $NA • (11/15/93) • **92**
I Sistri 1995: Serious Chardonnay from Tuscany. Creamy and rich with flavors of apple and vanilla, a hint of pineapple. Medium-bodied, with moderate acidity and a fresh, flavorful finish. 2,000 cases made. • $25 • (09/30/97) • **88**
Maestro Raro 1989 • $38 • (10/31/93) • **83**
Maestro Raro 1988 • $38 • (10/31/93) • **91**

FERONIA

Bianco Capena 1995: Pungent aromas of apricot and marzipan are followed by bitterness—overall, a disjointed impression. 50,000 cases made. • $7 • (05/15/97) • **74**

FERRARI

Brut de Brut 1981 • $22 • (05/31/87) • **84**
Brut Giulio Ferrari Riserva del Fondatore 1988: Quite nice. This well-aged bubbly has generous Chardonnay-like flavors of pineapple, honey and butter. It's outgoing and expressive, with a fine, creamy texture and lingering finish. • $32 • (01/31/97) • **89**
Brut Perlé 1985 • $30 • (12/31/90) • **88**
Brut Rosé Metodo Classico 1988 • $28 • (12/15/95) • **89**
Perlé 1991: A dry, refreshing, sparkling wine that is light in style and smooth-textured. Subdued fruit flavors and clean on the finish. • $21 • (01/31/97) • **83**
Riserva del Fondatore 1982 • $66 • (06/30/93) • **85**
Sparkling Riserva del Fondatore 1989: Delicious sparkler. Bold flavors of toast, honey and hazelnut in this medium-bodied, creamy-textured brut, with a long aftertaste of butterscotch. An alternative to Champagne. Drink now through 2000. • $35 • (06/15/98) • **88**

FERRARI-CORRADI

Boscarelli 1994: Dark-colored, with intense berry, mushroom, bark and spice aromas. Medium-bodied, with chewy tannins and a slightly raisiny finish. Drink now. • $NA • (09/30/97) • **85**

FEUDI DI SAN GREGORIO

Falanghina 1995: A distinctly fruity and rich white, showing apple, nutmeg and just a hint of bitter almond on the dry and firm finish. • $NA • (05/31/97) • **84**
Fiano di Avellino 1993 • $20 • (03/31/95) • **87**
Greco di Tufo 1993 • $16 • (03/31/95) • **85**
Taurasi 1991 • $26 • (01/31/96) • **88**

FILIGARE, LE

Chianti Classico 1990 • $NA • (10/31/93) • **88**
Chianti Classico 1988 • $NA • (09/15/91) • **91**
Chianti Classico Riserva 1994: Really tasty. A pure, fruit-centered Chianti that's packed with raspberry and cherry flavors on a smooth and lightly tannic texture. Focused, deep and long-lasting. Drink now through 2000. 2,400 cases made. • $28 • (04/30/98) • **88**
Chianti Classico Riserva 1988 • $18 • (09/15/92) • **90**
Podere Le Rocce 1994: Generous and full-bodied, richly flavored, warm and lush in texture. A complex but supple wine with solid fruit flavor rounded nicely by oak. Drink now through 2000. 1,000 cases made. • $38 • (04/30/98) • **88**
Podere Le Rocce 1990 • $NA • (10/31/93) • **93**

FILIPUTTI, WALTER

Colli Orientali del Friuli White Poiesis 1996: Broad and waxy, with a dash of honey and almond, this is round and balanced on the soft side. Pleasant, if not very complex. A blend of 70 percent Tocai Friulano, 30 percent Pinot Bianco. Drink now. • $26 • (05/31/98) • **83**
Pinot Grigio Venezia Giulia 1996: Bright and appealing, but light, with modest apple and almond notes that finish short. Tasted twice, with consistent notes. Drink now. • $26 • (05/31/98) • **79**
Pinot Grigio 1995: Begins with soft, rich apple and herb flavors but turns a little tart on the finish. Try with food. 2,000 cases made. • $28 • (06/15/97) • **82**
Ribolla Gialla Colli Orientali del Friuli 1996: A fresh, crisp white, with peach and apple flavors that combine with a moderate richness midpalate, ending on a citrus note. Tasted twice, with consistent notes. Drink now. • $26 • (05/31/98) • **83**
Ribolla Gialla 1995: A crisp white, whose subtle fig and apple notes are accented by a hint of almond. 2,000 cases made. • $28 • (06/15/97) • **82**
Sauvignon Colli Orientali del Friuli 1996: A mature Sauvignon, this has aromas and flavors of baked apples and marzipan, with a hint of cherry, on a lean, firm structure. Curt finish. Drink now. • $26 • (06/15/98) • **83**
Sauvignon 1995: Aromas of peaches and apricots are followed by almond flavors in this moderately rich white. It ends up firm and crisp. 2,000 cases made. • $28 • (06/15/97) • **80**

FINI, BARONE

Cabernet Sauvignon Cabernello 1988 • $10 • (07/15/91) • **76**
Cabernet Sauvignon Cabernello 1985 • $9 • (04/15/88) • **85**
Pinot Grigio Valdadige 1995: A bit awkward, but has some nice peachy aromas and flavors. A slightly bitter note on the finish. • $9 • (01/31/97) • **80**
Pinot Grigio Valdadige 1993 • $10 • (07/31/95) • **77**

FIORIAE, LE

Chianti Classico 1994: Very light, and of a slightly weedy, peppery character. It's light-bodied with a diluted finish. • $NA • (10/31/96) • **76**
Chianti Classico 1992 • $NA • (02/28/95) • **75**
Chianti Classico Riserva 1990 • $NA • (02/28/95) • **80**

Key: SS—Spectator Selection CS—Cellar Selection HR—Highly Recommended BB—Best Buy $NA—Price not available Ⓐ—Auction Price (BT)—Barrel Tasting
Dates in parentheses indicate the issues in which the ratings were published.

FIORINA, FRANCO

Barolo 1982 • $22 • (05/31/88) • **79**
Dolcetto d'Alba 1990 • $14 • (10/31/92) • **83**
Dolcetto d'Alba 1989 • $13 • (04/30/91) • **83**
Dolcetto d'Alba 1987 • $8 • (07/31/89) • **76**
Freisa delle Langhe 1989 • $16 • (07/15/91) • **78**
Nebbiolo d'Alba 1985 • $9 • (08/31/88) • **80**

FIRESTEED

Barbera d'Asti 1995: Distinctively earthy, with some decent red berry character and spicy notes. Nice, supple texture turns a bit sharp on the finish. Medium-bodied. Drink now. 15,000 cases made. • $8 • (01/31/98) • **79**

FOLONARI

Merlot delle Venezie 1996: Aromas and flavors express the herbal, minty side of this grape. Finishes with astringency. Drink now. • $7 • (07/31/98) • **77**
Merlot Sangiovese Veneto 1997: An herbal-smellng, lean and crisp red showing moderate cherry and currant flavors and good balance. The acidity should match well with food. A blend of 60 percent Merlot and 40 percent Sangiovese. Drink now through 2000. • $7 • (06/15/98) • **83**
Pinot Grigio 1993 • $6 • (12/15/94) • **82**
Pinot Grigio Chardonnay delle Venezie 1997: Fresh and lively, with vanilla overtones to the apple and straw notes. Light-bodied and showing good concentration, it falls off a bit on the finish. A blend of 60 percent Pinot Grigio and 40 percent Chardonnay. Drink now. • $7 • (06/30/98) • **84**
Pinot Grigio delle Venezie 1997: Shows an apple and citrus character, light structure and diminutive finish. Drink now. • $7 • (06/15/98) • **79**
Valpolicella NV: A light red wine with appealing cherry flavors and nice spicy notes on the finish. Drink now. • $9/1.5 liter • (07/31/98) • **80**

FONTANA CANDIDA

Chardonnay 1995: Shows a nicely reduced aroma, but it's a bit severe, with biting acidity and lemon flavors. 10,000 cases made. • $6 • (01/31/97) • **77**
Chardonnay 1994 • $8 • (02/29/96) • **84**
Frascati Superiore 1996: A simple, basic white with a soft texture and clean flavors. • $6 • (10/15/97) • **78**
Frascati Superiore 1995: A straightforward, medium-bodied white, with good pear and herbal flavors and a hint of citrus on the finish. • $6 • (01/31/97) • **83**
Frascati Superiore 1993 • $9 • (10/31/94) • **79**
Merlot della Tre Venezie 1994 • $8 • (01/31/96) • **83**
Pinot Grigio 1995: Well focused, with ripe flavors of pear, apple, fig and spice that resonate on the finish. Lush and full-bodied, it's one of the better, and eminently affordable, varietal wines from Northern Italy. 50,000 cases made. • $6 • (01/31/97) BB • **86**
Pinot Grigio 1994 • $5 • (04/30/96) • **80**
Pinot Grigio 1993 • $7 • (12/15/94) • **82**
Pinot Grigio delle Venezie 1996: Soft and inviting, showing peach and floral aromas and flavors, all nicely balanced and in the right proportions. The finish is refreshing. • $7 • (12/15/97) • **85**
Villa Fontana 1993 • $6 • (05/31/95) • **82**

FONTANABIANCA

Barbaresco 1995: Lovely wine. Well made, with sophisticated, supple tannins. Delicious toasty oak-infused violet, spice and chocolate flavors, and some superb plum, cassis, and black cherry notes. Balanced from start to finish, it's medium-bodied and though not super-big nor super-complex, still a fine wine. 550 cases made. • $30 • (10/31/97) (BT) • **90-94**
Barbaresco Sorì Burdin 1993: Elegant and appealing, crisp and very fruity, an intense '93 that sparkles with cranberry, cassis and black cherry flavors. Medium-bodied, with supple tannins. Drink now through 2000. 650 cases made. • $30 • (10/31/97) • **85**
Dolcetto d'Alba Vigneto Bordini 1996: Pure, clean and juicy. Inky-purple in color, with grapey aromas and flavors that taste of freshly crushed fruit, hints of cherry and cassis. Light- to medium-bodied. Drink now. 1,000 cases made. • $14 • (10/31/97) • **84**

FONTANAFREDDA

Barbaresco 1989 • $18 • (10/31/94) • **79**
Barbaresco 1988 • $12 • (10/31/93) • **75**
Barbaresco 1983 • $12 • (09/15/88) • **80**
Barbaresco 1982 • $NA • (09/15/88) • **81**
Barbaresco 1978 • $NA • (09/15/88) • **86**
Barbaresco Coste Rubin 1993: Barrel sample. Oak mingles with herb flavors in this light-bodied, diluted wine. The finish is short and crisp. 1,000 cases made. • $21 • (10/31/97) (BT) • **75-79**
Barbera d'Alba 1994: Light and diluted, tasting like carrot juice with hints of strawberry and cherry. • $11 • (10/31/96) • **74**
Barbera d'Alba 1993 • $11 • (10/31/95) • **79**
Barbera d'Alba 1990 • $10 • (07/31/95) • **83**
Barbera d'Alba Raimonda 1995: Light in color, body and aroma, this innocuous red offers only modest cherry and strawberry flavors. Drink chilled. 5,000 cases made. • $14 • (10/31/97) • **77**
Barbera d'Alba Vigna Raimondo 1990 • $9 • (11/15/93) • **78**
Barolo 1992: The earthy, herbal aromas, metallic flavors and chalky texture make this difficult to enjoy. • $21 • (10/31/96) • **74**
Barolo 1990 • $16 • (10/31/94) • **89**
Barolo 1989 • $16 • (10/31/94) • **84**
Barolo 1988 • $13 • (10/31/93) • **85**
Barolo 1983 • $16 • (09/15/88) • **83**
Barolo 1982 • $16 • (09/15/88) • **84**
Barolo 1978 • $13 • (02/15/84) • **80**
Barolo Galarey 1993: Smoky cherry and bark notes struggle to be heard in this medium-bodied, rustic red, but the dry tannins ultimately overpower them. 3,750 cases made. • $27 • (10/31/97) • **76**
Barolo Lazarito 1982 • $42 • (09/15/88) • **90**
Barolo San Pietro 1982 • $42 • (09/15/88) • **85**
Barolo Serralunga d'Alba 1993: Modest fruit, spice and licorice flavors struggle to surface in this medium-bodied, crisp and green Barolo. Dry tannins on the finish. 8,250 cases made. • $33 • (10/31/97) • **77**
Barolo Vigna Gattinera 1990 • $39 • (10/31/95) • **81**
Barolo Vigna Gattinera 1989 • $NA • (10/31/94) • **67**
Barolo Vigna La Delizia 1989 • $39 • (10/31/94) • **90**
Barolo Vigna La Rosa 1989 • $39 • (10/31/94) • **81**
Barolo Vigna La Rosa 1982 • $40 • (02/15/88) CS • **90**
Barolo Vigna La Villa 1989 • $39 • (10/31/94) • **91**
Barolo Vigna La Villa Paiagallo 1990 • $39 • (10/31/95) • **85**
Barolo Vigna La Villa Paiagallo 1989 • $NA • (10/31/93) • **85**
Barolo Vigna Lazzarito 1990 • $39 • (10/31/95) • **87**
Barolo di Serralunga d'Alba 1992: Has ripe, almost sweet flavors and a fairly rich, not-too-tannic texture. Drink soon for its generous flavor. • $29 • (10/31/96) • **82**
Barolo di Serralunga d'Alba 1990 • $20 • (10/31/95) • **86**
Barolo di Serralunga 1989 • $20 • (10/31/94) • **89**
Barolo di Serralunga 1988 • $17 • (10/31/93) • **85**
Dolcetto d'Alba 1995: Light and watery, with modest strawberry and cherry aromas and flavors. Short finish. • $12 • (10/31/96) • **77**
Dolcetto d'Alba 1993 • $11 • (10/31/95) • **80**
Dolcetto d'Alba di Treiso 1996: Supple and ripe, with nice plum, black cherry, and wet earth character. Medium-bodied, the supple tannins make this a pretty wine to drink now. 6,250 cases made. • $13 • (10/31/97) • **82**
Dolcetto d'Alba di Treiso 1995: Lean in structure, modest in flavor, tart and green on the finish. 6,250 cases made. • $13 • (10/31/96) • **76**
Dolcetto d'Alba di Treiso 1993 • $NA • (10/31/95) • **84**
Dolcetto d'Alba di Treiso 1992 • $12 • (06/15/94) • **86**
Extra Brut Contessa Rosa 1990: A very light, crisp, green-tasting wine that's simple and tart. • $16 • (07/31/96) • **77**

FONTERUTOLI, CASTELLO DI

Brancaia 1994: Lovely combination of ripe fruit and new wood. Medium-bodied, with fine tannins and a berry, vanilla finish of moderate length. Delicious now. 35,000 cases made. • $35 • (09/30/97) • **87**
Brancaia 1990 • $24 • (10/31/93) • **91**
Chianti Classico 1995: A pretty, fruity wine with crushed berries on the nose and palate. Has medium body, light tannins and a crisp finish. Drink now. 210,000 cases made. • $17 • (09/30/97) • **85**
Chianti Classico 1994: Subtle, and well made. Some good berry aromas and flavors with firm tannins and a silky finish. Not giving much at the moment. Drinkable now. 18,000 cases made. • $13 • (10/31/96) • **85**
Chianti Classico 1993 • $13 • (10/31/95) • **81**
Chianti Classico 1992 • $13 • (02/28/95) • **85**
Chianti Classico 1991 • $13 • (10/31/93) • **88**
Chianti Classico 1990 • $13 • (09/15/92) • **89**
Chianti Classico 1988 • $14 • (11/30/90) • **85**
Chianti Classico 1987 • $11 • (11/30/89) • **90**
Chianti Classico 1986 • $11 • (01/31/89) • **85**
Chianti Classico 1985 • $11 • (11/30/89) • **88**
Chianti Classico Riserva 1995: Serious '95 Chianti here. Rich, with plenty of vanilla, berry and violet character. Medium-bodied, with medium velvety tannins and a fruity finish. • $NA • (01/01/97) • **89**
Chianti Classico Riserva 1983 • $15 • (11/30/89) • **88**
Chianti Classico Ser Lapo Riserva 1994: Big and chewy, generous with its blackberry, cherry and tobacco character. Medium- to full-bodied, with velvety tanins and a long finish. Drink now or hold. 80,000 cases made. • $32 • (09/30/97) • **89**
Chianti Classico Ser Lapo Riserva 1993: Cleverly made, this offers notes of plum and violet, and a hint of new wood, on the nose and palate. Medium-bodied, with light tannins and a fruity finish. Drink now or hold. • $31 • (10/31/96) • **87**
Chianti Classico Ser Lapo 1991 • $25 • (10/31/95) • **84**
Chianti Classico Ser Lapo Riserva 1990 • $26 • (02/28/95) • **86**
Chianti Classico Ser Lapo Riserva 1988 • $20 • (09/15/92) • **90**
Chianti Classico Ser Lapo Riserva 1986 • $25 • (11/30/90) • **88**
Chianti Classico Ser Lapo Riserva 1985 • $18 • (09/15/91) • **87**
Chianti Classico Ser Lapo Riserva 1983 • $15 • (01/31/89) • **88**
Concerto 1994: A solid red with chewy tannins and good fruit concentration. It's of medium body, with medium tannins and a fresh finish. Drink now or hold. 45,000 cases made. • $40 • (09/30/97) • **86**
Concerto 1993: Deeply colored and offers aromas and flavors of violet, raspberry and smoke. Medium-bodied with fine tannins and bright fruit character. Try now. A blend of 80 percent Sanigovese and 20 percent Cabernet Sauvignon. 4,000 cases made. • $38 • (10/31/96) • **88**
Concerto 1991 • $30 • (10/31/95) • **88**
Concerto 1990 • $27 • (10/31/93) • **88**
Concerto 1986 • $35 • (03/15/91) • **87**
Concerto 1985 • $25 • (02/15/89) • **84**
Concerto 1983 • $15 • (11/30/89) • **86**
Poggio alla Badiola Toscana 1996: A warm and velvety Tuscan red that seems to melt in your mouth. Attractive fruity, spicy flavors mingle on the smooth texture and linger on the finish. A blend of 94 percent Sangiovese, 3 percent Merlot, and 3 percent Cabernet Sauvignon. Drink now through 2000. • $14 • (04/30/98) • **88**
Poggio alla Badiola 1994: Simple, with an attractive dried berry character, medium body and a soft finish. Drink now, even slightly chillled. From the producers of Castello di Fonterutoli. • $NA • (10/31/96) • **80**
Siepi 1995: An up front style with satisfying fruit: lots of black currant and berry aromas and flavors. Medium-bodied, with medium, fine tannins. Drink now. 30,000 cases made. • $50 • (09/30/97) • **88**
Siepi 1994: A disappointment compared to 1993 and '92. Some good berry and cherry character, with a hint of vanilla, but also a large dose of green pepper. Light tannins and a light finish. A blend of Sangiovese and Merlot. • $47 • (10/31/96) • **81**
Siepi 1993: Like a top-growth Bordeaux. A monumental, exciting wine with purple-black color, full body and great concentration. Bursting with earthy cassis and mint flavors. Try now. A blend of Sangiovese and Merlot. Tasted twice, with consistent notes. 83 cases made. • $30 • (10/31/95) • **94**
Siepi 1992 • $30 • (10/31/95) • **90**

FONTEVINO

Brunello di Montalcino 1990: Slightly advanced, showing layers of flavor from berry to tobacco. Medium-bodied and silky with a long finish. Drink now. • $NA • (10/31/95) • **83**
Brunello di Montalcino Riserva 1988 • $NA • (10/31/94) • **79**
Brunello di Montalcino Villa dei Lecci 1992: Not a big wine but subtle, with cherry, berry and floral aromas and flavors. It's medium in body, has fine tannins and a complex aftertaste. 2,704 cases made. • $21 • (09/30/97) • **86**
Brunello di Montalcino Villa dei Lecci Riserva 1991: Shows some berry and cherry character, but it's slightly vegetal. Of medium body, with light tannins, light finish. 2,680 cases made. • $24 • (09/30/97) • **79**
Rosso di Montalcino 1993 • $NA • (10/31/95) • **85**

FONTI, FATTORIA LE

Chianti Classico 1995: A serious Chianti Classico that's dry and rather tannic, but has enough of the typical cherry, olive and herb flavors to make it quite appealing. Drink now. • $14 • (10/31/97) • **86**

FONTODI

Case Via 1995: Smelling this wine is like smelling a bouquet of flowers. It's medium-bodied, with a very good level of fruit, yet it's silky and refined in texture. Delicious now. 300 cases made. • $32 • (09/30/97) • **87**
Case Via 1994: Very good Syrah. Inky red, with berry, game, earth and a hint of spice on the nose. Full-bodied, with soft and silky tannins, lots of flavor and a medium finish. Drink or hold. 300 cases made. • $38 • (09/30/97) • **88**
Chianti Classico 1995: Delicious. Exhibits plenty of crushed berry character on the nose and palate, is medium body, has fine tannins and a crisp finish. Drink now. 7,000 cases made. • $18 • (09/30/97) • **88**
Chianti Classico 1994: Fontodi can do no wrong. Pretty and lively, with plummy, berry and violet aromas and flavors. Medium-bodied with silky, fine tannins and a flavorful finish. Drink now. 6,000 cases made. • $15 • (10/31/96) • **88**
Chianti Classico 1993 • $12 • (10/31/95) • **86**
Chianti Classico 1992 • $13 • (02/28/95) • **85**
Chianti Classico 1991 • $12 • (10/31/93) • **87**
Chianti Classico 1990 • $16 • (09/15/92) • **87**
Chianti Classico 1989 • $13 • (11/30/91) • **89**
Chianti Classico 1988 • $13 • (09/15/91) SS • **91**
Chianti Classico 1987 • $8 • (11/30/89) • **81**
Chianti Classico 1986 • $9 • (01/31/89) • **74**
Chianti Classico Al Sorbo 1990 • $27 • (02/28/95) • **91**
Chianti Classico Riserva 1994: A lovely wine of wonderful finesse, this is bubbling over with wild berry and plum character, has fine tannins and a long finish. Medium-bodied. Drink now or hold. 3,000 cases made. • $23 • (09/30/97) • **88**
Chianti Classico Riserva 1993: Ripe fruit perfumes this wine with a violet, floral undertone. Medium-bodied with fine tannins and a crisp, fresh finish. Not one to age, but delicious now. 3,000 cases made. • $19 • (10/31/96) • **89**
Chianti Classico Riserva 1991 • $18 • (10/31/95) • **90**
Chianti Classico Riserva 1990 • $20 • (02/28/95) • **89**
Chianti Classico Riserva 1988 • $18 • (10/31/93) • **89**
Chianti Classico Riserva 1985 • $16 • (09/15/91) • **93**
Chianti Classico Riserva 1983 • $8 • (09/15/87) • **87**
Chianti Classico Riserva 1982 • $7 • (09/15/87) • **87**
Chianti Classico Vigna del Sorbo Riserva 1994: Big and powerful, delivering masses of dried cherry, mineral and vanilla aromas. Full-bodied, with full tannins and a chewy finish. Needs time. Better after 2000. • $30 • (09/30/97) • **90**
Chianti Classico Vigna del Sorbo Riserva 1993: Round, ripe and voluptuous. Medium-bodied, with impressively ripe, round tannins, a bounteous cherry, berry and mineral character and a long, long finish. Drink now or hold. • $28 • (09/30/97) • **90**
Chianti Classico Vigna del Sorbo Riserva 1990: A bit too herbal and tough in tannin to be outstanding at this stage of its evolution. Inky-colored, with tobacco, cherry and Cabernet aromas and flavors. Full-bodied, with full tannins and a tough finish. Drink now or hold. • $NA • (09/30/97) • **89**
Chianti Classico Vigna del Sorbo Riserva 1988: A wonderfully vibrant red with cherry, plum and spices on the nose and palate. Medium in body, with fresh acidity and a lengthy, fruity finish. Drink now. • $NA • (09/30/97) • **90**
Chianti Classico Vigna del Sorbo Riserva 1985: Better on the nose than on the palate at this stage. Decadently rich aromas of truffles, earth and fruit. Medium-bodied, with good fruit, but it's slightly high in acidity and dry on the finish. Drink now. • $NA • (09/30/97) • **86**
Flaccianello 1994: Beautifully perfumed aromas of berries, currants and flowers. Medium-bodied, with medium, soft tannins and a long, fruity finish. Delicious. 2,200 cases made. • $40 • (09/30/97) • **88**

Key: SS—Spectator Selection CS—Cellar Selection HR—Highly Recommended BB—Best Buy $NA—Price not available Ⓐ—Auction Price (BT)—Barrel Tasting
Dates in parentheses indicate the issues in which the ratings were published.

Flaccianello 1993: Lots of blackberry and forestlike aromas in this wine. Medium-bodied, with very fine tannins and a silky finish. Try now. Sangiovese. • $35 • (10/31/96) • **89**
Flaccianello 1991 • $32 • (02/28/95) • **90**
Flaccianello 1990 • $NA • (11/15/93) • **90**
Flaccianello 1988 • $NA • (11/15/93) • **92**
Flaccianello 1987 • $NA • (11/15/93) • **88**
Flaccianello 1986 • $NA • (11/15/93) • **90**
Flaccianello 1985 • $NA • (11/15/93) • **90**
Flaccianello 1983 • $NA • (11/15/93) • **83**
Flaccianello 1982 • $NA • (11/15/93) • **85**
Pinot Nero Tuscany Case Via 1994: A pretty Pinot showing plenty of delicious strawberry, grape and raspberry aromas and flavors. Medium-bodied with fine tannins and a fresh finish. Drink or hold. 400 cases made. • $40 • (10/31/96) • **87**
Pinot Nero Tuscany Case Via 1993: One of the few Tuscan Pinots that emulates Burgundy. Elegant red with black cherry and red fruit character. Medium-bodied with firm tannins and a flavorful finish. Delicious now. 250 cases made. • $35 • (10/31/95) • **87**
Pinot Nero Tuscany Case Via 1992 • $30 • (02/28/95) • **83**
Pinot Nero Tuscany Case Via 1990 • $35 • (10/31/93) • **88**
Syrah Tuscany Case Via 1993: A big, chewy wine that's not giving much at the momen, though there are some berry, tar and meaty aromas and flavors coming through. Full-bodied, long finish. Try now. • $35 • (10/31/96) • **88**
Syrah Tuscany Case Via 1992 • $NA • (10/31/95) • **86**
Syrah Tuscany Case Via 1991 • $30 • (02/28/95) • **90**
Syrah Tuscany Case Via 1990 • $28 • (10/31/93) • **93**

FORADORI

Atesino Granato 1995: Black currant and woodsy notes are nicely framed by vanilla from new oak in this elegant, suave red. Medium-bodied, it has good concentration and a pleasant aftertaste with light tannins. 100 percent Teroldego. Drink now through 2002. • $45 • (06/30/98) • **87**
Atesino Karanar 1995: Gorgeous, internationally styled Cabernet showing smoky vanilla-tinged cherry flavors on a silky-smooth, elegant framework supported by firm tannins. Drink now through 2000. • $37 • (06/30/98) • **87**
Granato di Mezzolombardo 1988 • $33 • (01/31/92) • **86**
Pinot Bianco Trentino Sgarzon 1996: Attractive, but atypical. This is bright and full of apple and vanilla flavors that take on a smoky, buttery note on the finish. Drink now. • $33 • (05/31/98) • **83**
Pinot Bianco Trentino Sgarzon 1995: Exotic, toasty coconut accents make this atypical. Shows applelike and citrusy flavors, with a cacophony of acidity and tannin on the finish. Appealing, but may need food to settle it down. 500 cases made. • $30 • (06/15/97) • **84**
Teroldego Rotaliano 1996: A rich, succulent red from a grape variety indigenous to Trentino. Black cherry flavors are accented by licorice, with a supple but almost chewy density, vibrant acidity and a lingering finish. Drink through 1999. • $19 • (06/30/98) • **86**
Teroldego Rotaliano Sgarzon 1994: Impressive. Very deeply colored, this red exhibits lush cedar, black cherry and menthol aromas and flavors, a plush mouthfeel and medium weight, followed by silky tannins on the finish. Drink now through 2001. • $33 • (06/30/98) • **87**
Teroldego Rotaliano Vigneto Morel 1988 • $16 • (01/31/92) • **69**

FORMENTINI, CONTI

Cabernet Franc Collio 1994 • $13 • (05/31/96) • **86**
Merlot Collio 1996: On the lean, herbal side, showing only a modicum of red berry flavors. Drink now. • $13 • (04/30/98) • **75**
Pinot Grigio Collio 1995: Fresh and lively, with the peach and stone flavors, firm backbone and lingering finish composing a balanced and integrated whole. This needs food. Drink now. • $13 • (06/15/98) • **86**
Ribolla Gialla Collio 1994 • $13 • (06/15/96) • **79**

FORTUNA, LA

Brunello di Montalcino 1990: Delicious, soft, sweet fruit. Medium- to light-bodied, adding fine tannins and a lemony, berry finish. Drink now. • $NA • (10/31/95) • **84**
Rosso di Montalcino 1993 • $NA • (10/31/95) • **82**

FOSSI

Chianti 1990 • $8 • (04/30/92) • **83**

Chianti 1988 • $8 • (10/31/91) BB • **84**
Chianti Classico Riserva 1985 • $18 • (09/15/91) • **82**
Vanti 1992 • $8 • (07/31/95) • **83**

FRACASSI, UMBERTO

Barolo Vigneti di Ratti Mentone 1993: Very green and herbaceous, with little ripe fruit, sweet tannins. • $NA • (10/31/97) • **74**

FRANCESCO

Vino Nobile di Montepulciano Riserva 1990: A bit rough and rustic but broad and flavorful, tasting of fruit and herbs. 2,500 cases made. • $14 • (10/31/96) • **83**

FRANCO, NINO

Prosecco di Valdobbiadene Prosecco NV: More bread dough and almond than fruit in this rich, creamy sparkler, with a soft and just slightly cloying finish. Drink now. • $16 • (07/31/98) • **81**
Prosecco di Valdobbiadene Rustico NV: A fairly dry, refreshing, lemony sparkling wine, with just a hint of bread dough and a soft texture, finishing on an earthy note. Drink now. • $11 • (07/31/98) • **82**
Prosecco di Valdobbiadene Sassi Bianchi 1996: Yes, that's right, a dry Prosecco. An oddity, showing bitter almond and cherry notes, good richness and a structure that's both acidic and astringent. Drink now. • $10 • (07/31/98) • **79**

FRESCOBALDI, MARCHESI DE'

Albizzia Toscana White 1996: Shows very modest fruit flavors and an earthy, nutty accent. Drinkable, but simple. Ready now. A blend of 65 percent Chardonnay and 35 percent Trebbiano. • $8 • (04/30/98) • **76**
Brut 1985 • $12 • (12/31/90) • **86**
Chianti 1989 • $5 • (04/15/91) • **70**
Chianti 1988 • $5 • (11/30/89) BB • **85**
Chianti 1987 • $4 • (05/15/89) • **75**
Chianti 1986 • $3 • (12/15/87) • **75**
Chianti Rèmole 1996: A slightly diluted, earthy Chianti with some berry flavors, but rather meager overall. Drink now, slightly chilled. • $8/1.5 liter • (12/31/97) • **78**
Chianti Rèmole 1994 • $7 • (10/31/95) • **79**
Chianti Rèmole 1993 • $7 • (10/31/95) • **74**
Chianti Rufina Castello di Nipozzano Riserva 1994: Impressive perfumes of a violet, berry and floral character. Medium in body, with medium, fine tannins and a chocolate, berry finish. Delicious. Drink now or hold. 5,000 cases made. • $15 • (09/30/97) • **88**
Chianti Rufina Castello di Nipozzano Riserva 1993: Sleek and well made. Of medium body, with cherry and mineral aromas and flavors. Fine tannins mark the finish. Drink now. 30,000 cases made. • $15 • (10/31/96) • **86**
Chianti Rufina Castello di Nipozzano Riserva 1992 • $14 • (10/31/95) • **85**
Chianti Rufina Castello di Nipozzano Riserva 1991 • $NA • (10/31/93) • **88**
Chianti Rufina Castello di Nipozzano Riserva 1990 • $14 • (02/28/95) • **85**
Chianti Rufina Castello di Nipozzano Riserva 1989 • $14 • (05/15/94) • **80**
Chianti Rufina Castello di Nipozzano Riserva 1988 • $15 • (09/15/92) • **86**
Chianti Rufina Castello di Nipozzano Riserva 1986 • $11 • (09/15/90) • **82**
Chianti Rufina Castello di Nipozzano Riserva 1985 • $11 • (11/30/89) • **88**
Chianti Rufina Castello di Nipozzano Riserva 1983 • $10 • (11/30/89) • **89**
Chianti Rufina Montesodi 1995: A well-crafted wine with very good fruit and lots of new oak. it's medium-bodied, with fine tannins and a moderate finish. Try now. 410 cases made. • $33 • (09/30/97) • **89**
Chianti Rufina Montesodi 1993: Good structure with firm and well-integrated tannins but the green, unripe character detracts. Drink or hold. 5,000 cases made. • $34 • (09/30/97) • **79**
Chianti Rufina Montesodi 1991 • $32 • (10/31/95) • **86**
Chianti Rufina Montesodi 1990: Big and powerful, with masses of violet, floral and berry aromas and flavors. Full-bodied, with full tannins and lots of new wood. Thick and supple. Better after 2000. • $NA • (09/30/97) • **90**
Chianti Rufina Montesodi 1988: As stunning as the first time I tasted it. Full- to medium-bodied, with berry, truffle and tobacco aromas and flavors. Succulent, rich aftertaste. Drink or hold. • $NA • (09/30/97) • **90**
Chianti Rufina Montesodi 1985: Big and rich with sweet fruit and a round texture, but it's slightly herbal due to the high amount of Cabernet Sauvignon. Drink now. • $NA • (09/30/97) • **85**
Chianti Rufina Montesodi 1982 • $28 • (12/15/88) • **86**
Chianti Rufina Rémole 1993 • $7 • (02/28/95) • **78**
Chianti Rufina Rémole 1992 • $7 • (04/30/94) BB • **85**
Chianti Rufina Rémole 1991 • $7 • (10/31/93) • **81**
Chianti Rufina Rémole 1990 • $7 • (09/15/92) • **86**
Lamaione Toscana 1994: Bright and fruity, with berry, plum and tobacco aromas and flavors, medium body, medium tannins and a slightly short, tough finish. Not as good as past Lamaiones. Try now. 165 cases made. • $25 • (09/30/97) • **87**
Lamaione 1993: Impressive structure for the vintage. Complex aromas and flavors of berry, chocolate and pepper. Medium-bodied, with fine tannins. Drink now. Merlot made at Castelgiocondo in Montalcino. 600 cases made. • $21 • (10/31/96) • **90**
Lamaione Castelgiocondo 1992 • $18 • (02/28/95) • **89**
Lamaione Castelgiocondo 1991 • $18 • (02/28/95) • **90**
Mormoreto Toscana 1994: Deeply colored, with intense currant, mint and berry aromas, this wine is full-bodied, with lovely, silky, sexy tannins. A joy to taste now, but wait until 2000. 410 cases made. • $33 • (09/30/97) • **90**
Mormoreto 1993: A lovely, elegant wine with plenty of ripe fruit and vanilla aromas and flavors. Medium-bodied, with velvety tannins and fresh finish. Made from Cabernet Sauvignon. Drink now. 3,000 cases made. • $34 • (10/31/96) • **87**
Mormoreto 1988 • $NA • (11/15/93) • **94**
Mormoreto 1986 • $NA • (11/15/93) • **91**
Mormoreto 1985 • $NA • (11/15/93) • **90**
Mormoreto 1983 • $NA • (11/15/93) • **90**
Mormoreto Capitolare di Bitùrica 1991 • $32 • (02/28/95) • **90**
Mormoreto Capitolare di Bitùrica 1990 • $32 • (02/28/95) • **88**
Mormoreto Predicato di Bitùrica 1988 • $30 • (11/30/89) • **93**
Mormoreto Predicato di Bitùrica 1983 • $34 • (02/15/89) • **88**
Pomino Bianco 1997: Quite likable for its vibrant, fruity style. A fresh, lively white with banana and pineapple flavors, medium body and tangy finish. Drink now. • $17 • (07/31/98) • **85**
Pomino Bianco 1996: Attractive creamy apple aromas, with a hint of coconut, give way to a medium-bodied wine with moderate acidity and a creamy, fruit and vanilla finish. Drink now. 3,300 cases made. • $13 • (09/30/97) • **85**
Pomino Bianco Il Benefizio 1995: Aromas of toasty oak, honey and apple are inviting. It's medium-bodied, with pretty fruit and good acidity, but a slightly short finish. Try now. 580 cases made. • $22 • (09/30/97) • **86**
Pomino Rosso 1994: An elegant red with alluring floral and fruit tones on the nose and palate. Medium-bodied, with silky tannins and a fruity finish. Delicious, it's one of the best Pominos in a long time. Drink now. 1,100 cases made. • $18 • (09/30/97) • **87**
Pomino Castello di Pomino Red 1993: Offers some decent fruit flavors and silky tannins, but it's on the herbal, weedy side—too herbal to be anything save simply good. Drink now. 12,000 cases made. • $18 • (10/31/96) • **80**
Pomino Tenuta di Pomino 1992 • $17 • (10/31/95) • **83**
Pomino Tenuta di Pomino 1991 • $17 • (02/28/95) • **80**
Pomino Tenuta di Pomino 1988 • $17 • (10/31/93) • **82**
Pomino Tenuta di Pomino 1986 • $14 • (01/31/90) • **87**
Pomino Tenuta di Pomino 1985 • $12 • (09/15/88) SS • **93**
Sangiovese Toscana Pater 1996: Smooth and mellow. Medium-bodied. Offers solid cherry and spice flavors, firm acidity and just enough tannin. Should be versatile with food. Drink now. 20,000 cases made. • $9 • (04/30/98) • **84**
Sangiovese Toscana 1995: This velvety red offers candylike flavors of chocolate and brandied cherries, and shows very soft tannins. Attractive, if not typically Tuscan. Drink now. • $8 • (01/31/97) • **82**
Sangiovese di Toscana Pater 1994 • $NA • (10/31/95) • **81**
Vin Santo Tenuta di Pomino 1981 • $20 • (10/15/88) • **87**

FRIGGIALI, TENUTA

Brunello di Montalcino 1990: Vibrant fruity and milk chocolate character, full body, fine, powerful tannins and loads of fruit on the finish. Try now. • $NA • (10/31/95) • **88**
Brunello di Montalcino 1988 • $NA • (04/30/94) • **87**
Rosso di Montalcino 1995: A refreshing wine with cherry and watermelon character, medium body, light tannins and a crisp finish. • $NA • (09/30/97) • **82**
Rosso di Montalcino 1993 • $NA • (10/31/95) • **82**
Rosso di Montalcino 1991 • $NA • (04/30/94) • **78**

FRIMAIO

Chianti Classico 1994: Wonderfully rich with minty, blackberry aromas and flavors. Medium-bodied with silky tannins. • $NA • (10/31/96) • **85**

FUGA, TENUTA LA

Brunello di Montalcino 1991: Good concentration for this vintage, with black cherry, licorice and spice aromas and flavors. Medium-bodied with medium tannins. Drink now or can hold. 833 cases made. • $45 • (11/30/96) • **86**

Brunello di Montalcino 1990: Rustic and traditional Brunello. A lot of chestnut flavors here, but the texture is supple and it tastes quite ripe and sweet. Drink now. • $NA • (10/31/95) • **81**

Brunello di Montalcino Riserva 1991: A bit rustic, but shows good berry, cherry and tanned leather aromas and flavors. Medium-bodied, with plush tannins and a long finish. Drink now. • $51 • (09/30/97) • **86**

Brunello di Montalcino Riserva 1990: Loads of new wood and an intense vanilla character distinguish this ripe and fruity wine. It's full-bodied, with some hard tannins. Slightly overdone. May be better in 1999. 330 cases made. • $50 • (11/30/96) • **87**

Rosso di Montalcino 1995: Simple and fruity, with strawberry, cherry character, but it's slightly dry on the finish. • $17 • (09/30/97) • **79**

Rosso di Montalcino 1994: Slightly mature in color, with earthy berry aromas. Medium-bodied with velvety tannins, but a slightly funky, dry finish. Drink now. 1,166 cases made. • $20 • (11/30/96) • **78**

Rosso di Montalcino 1993 • $NA • (10/31/95) • **80**

Rosso di Montalcino 1992 • $NA • (04/30/94) • **79**

FULIGNI, EREDI

Brunello di Montalcino 1991: Pretty and elegant, with its mineral, berry and floral character and fresh finish. Medium-bodied, with fine tannins. Ready to drink. 965 cases made. • $46 • (11/30/96) • **86**

Brunello di Montalcino 1990: Perhaps not as great as this producer's 1988 Brunello, but it's supple and smooth and outstanding. Sweet- and ripe-tasting, offering coffee, blackberry and black cherry flavors. Full-bodied, soft tannins. Drinkable now. 850 cases made. • $46 • (10/31/95) • **90**

Brunello di Montalcino Riserva 1990: Muscular, with lots of ripe plum flavor, full yet elegant tannins and a smoky almond finish. Drink now or can hold. A beautiful Brunello from a producer with a track record for same. 286 cases made. • $75 • (11/30/96) • **91**

Brunello di Montalcino Riserva 1988 • $54 • (01/01/94) • **89**

Brunello di Montalcino Vigneti dei Cottimelli 1992: A simple, fruity Brunello with crisp acidity and fresh fruit flavors. Slightly disappointing for this producer. Drink now. • $45 • (09/30/97) • **83**

Brunello di Montalcino Vigneti dei Cottimelli 1989 • $39 • (11/30/94) • **88**

Brunello di Montalcino Vigneti dei Cottimelli 1988 • $NA • (04/30/94) • **91**

Brunello di Montalcino Vigneti dei Cottimelli Riserva 1988 • $NA • (10/31/94) • **95**

Rosso di Montalcino Ginestreto Vigneti dei Cottimelli 1995: A good Rosso that sneaks up on your palate and finishes with plenty of plum character. • $27 • (09/30/97) • **87**

Rosso di Montalcino Ginestreto 1994: The mineral and dried cherry aromas and flavors just jump out of the glass. Medium-bodied, with delicious fruitiness and a silky tannin structure that tickles your throat. Excellent winemaking, as is typical of this producer. Drink now or hold. 755 cases made. • $24 • (11/30/96) • **87**

Rosso di Montalcino Ginestreto Vigneti dei Cottimelli 1993 • $20 • (10/31/95) • **89**

Rosso di Montalcino Ginestreto Vigneti dei Cottimelli 1992 • $NA • (10/31/94) • **79**

Rosso di Montalcino Ginestreto Vigneti dei Cottimelli 1991 • $NA • (04/30/94) • **87**

FURLAN CASTELCOSA

Castelcosa Grigio 1996: A well-made white showing balance and harmony between the juicy apple and citrus flavors and the tangy acidity that brings everything to a lingering finish. Drink now. 6,000 cases made. • $12 • (05/15/98) • **85**

Castelcosa Grigio 1995: Showing its maturity, this medium-bodied white has an almond and peach character that broadens on the palate. Slightly astringent finish. Drink now. 6,000 cases made. • $10 • (12/15/97) • **84**

Chardonnay delle Venezie 1996: Fresh, appley Chardonnay character provides straightforward appeal and the broad, rich texture adds symmetry. Well balanced, with a clean finish that should match with food. Drink now. 2,000 cases made. • $12 • (04/30/98) • **85**

Merlot delle Venezie 1995: Badly marred by sweaty, cardboardy flavors. Not recommended. Tasted twice, with consistent notes. 2,000 cases made. • $15 • (04/30/98) • **61**

Merlot Friuli 1994: Rich flavors of cherry and cedar turn a bit lean on the finish. Try with food. 2,500 cases made. • $14 • (09/15/97) • **79**

Picolit Colli Orientali del Friuli 1992: A subtle dessert wine sporting orange and honey flavors and a hint of orange peel on the finish. It's delicate but concentrated; enjoy on its own or with light desserts. 183 cases made. • $39/500ml • (05/15/97) • **84**

Pinot Grigio Castelcosa 1994 • $10 • (06/15/96) • **80**

Tai 1995: Very aromatic and expressive. A lean, lively white displaying rose, ripe apple and vanilla custard flavors on a supple framework. Moderate finish. A blend of Tocai, Riesling and Traminer. 600 cases made. • $15 • (12/15/97) • **85**

Tai 1994 • $14 • (06/15/96) • **83**

GABBIANO, CASTELLO DI

Chianti 1996: Light, fresh, and plummy with hints of strawberries. Light-bodied, with light acidity, a light finish. 41,600 cases made. • $10 • (09/30/97) • **80**

Chianti Classico 1995: A bit dull, this has some berry and earth character and fresh acidity but it's nothing to get excited about. 25,000 cases made. • $12 • (09/30/97) • **80**

Chianti Classico 1990 • $9 • (04/30/94) • **81**

Chianti Classico 1987 • $7 • (11/30/89) • **81**

Chianti Classico 1986 • $7 • (05/31/89) BB • **82**

Chianti Classico 1985 • $7 • (02/15/88) • **72**

Chianti Classico 1983 • $6 • (05/31/87) BB • **85**

Chianti Classico Riserva 1993: Slightly meager, but shows some attractive cherry and tobacco aromas and flavors. Light-bodied, with light tannins, a flavorful finish. Drink now or hold. 6,250 cases made. • $15 • (09/30/97) • **83**

Chianti Classico Riserva 1990 • $15 • (02/28/95) • **86**

Chianti Classico Riserva 1985 • $19 • (04/30/94) • **82**

Chianti Classico Riserva 1983 • $19 • (09/15/92) • **78**

Chianti Classico Riserva 1982 • $11 • (07/31/88) • **84**

Chianti Classico Riserva Gold Label 1990 • $9 • (06/15/93) • **77**

Chianti Classico Riserva Gold Label 1988 • $12 • (06/15/93) • **87**

Chianti Classico Riserva Gold Label 1986 • $20 • (11/30/94) • **88**

Chianti Classico Riserva Gold Label 1985 • $20 • (06/15/93) • **82**

Chianti Classico Riserva Gold Label 1982 • $21 • (11/30/89) • **79**

Chianti Classico Riserva Gold Label 1981 • $18 • (02/15/88) • **81**

Il Cavaliere 1988 • $9 • (12/15/92) • **78**

Merlot Tuscany 1988 • $55 • (07/15/91) • **86**

perAnia 1990: Rich and powerful, with masses of plum, blackberry and earth flavor. Full-bodied and tannic. Perhaps too tannic? Needs time; try after 2000. 1,500 cases made. • $30 • (09/30/97) • **88**

perAnia 1988: A big wine that aging hasn't necessarily improved; woody flavors and tannic texture remain, while much of the fruit has faded. Aromatic, but rather stiff and mature. 100 percent Sangiovese. • $31 • (10/31/96) • **78**

perAnia 1986 • $30 • (12/15/92) • **72**

perAnia 1985 • $30 • (01/31/90) • **93**

perAnia 1983 • $25 • (07/15/87) • **83**

R & R 1986 • $38 • (01/31/91) • **90**

R & R 1985 • $30 • (03/31/90) • **91**

Toscana Galestro 1996: A simple white with citrus and mineral aromas and flavors. Medium-bodied, with fresh acidity, a refreshing finish. 10,000 cases made. • $8 • (09/30/97) • **81**

Toscana Red 1994: Tastes as tired as it looks, with a slightly amber hue, spice and leather flavors. Light body. Drink as soon as possible. • $8 • (09/30/97) • **76**

Vin Santo 1985 • $20 • (03/15/91) • **78**

Key: SS—Spectator Selection CS—Cellar Selection HR—Highly Recommended BB—Best Buy $NA—Price not available Ⓐ—Auction Price (BT)—Barrel Tasting
Dates in parentheses indicate the issues in which the ratings were published.

ITALY

GAGLIARDO, GIANNI

Barbera d'Alba La Matta 1995: Well made, balanced and satisfying, this full-bodied red offers ripe, sweet tannins, loads of elegant red- and blackberry flavors and a dollop of oak-infused spice and chocolate. The flavors cascade subtly through the long finish. Enjoy now through 2000. 10,000 cases made. • $14 • (10/31/97) • **89**
Barolo 1993: This light-bodied red offers cherry, raspberry and bitter chocolate flavors and soft tannins. Somewhat diluted, it's still fresh, clean and succulent enough to tempt you now through 2000. • $25 • (10/31/97) • **81**
Barolo 1992: A traditional style that unites spicy floral and tarry aromas with fresh cherry and currant flavors. Has great balance, an elegant texture and a lingering finish. Try now. 2,083 cases made. • $25 • (10/31/96) • **88**
Barolo Batié 1990 • $28 • (06/15/94) • **87**
Barolo La Serra 1989 • $26 • (06/15/94) • **85**
Barolo Preve 1993: Delicious, offering cranberry, blueberry, wild berry and mint flavors. Smooth tannins, medium body and just a touch of dilution. Should peak around 2000. 1,800 cases made. • $40 • (10/31/97) • **86**
Barolo Preve 1991: Quite bright and lively in flavor, tannic and firm in texture. Tastes like cedar and currants. Fairly tight on the finish but may mellow with age. Try after 1999. Tasted three times with consistent notes. 917 cases made. • $40 • (10/31/96) • **88**
Barolo Preve 1990 • $35 • (10/31/95) • **91**
Dolcetto d'Alba 1996: Distinctive and quaffable, with plum, licorice and floral notes. It's crisp, flavorful, light- to medium-bodied and ready to drink. 12,000 cases made. • $13 • (10/31/97) • **82**
Dolcetto d'Alba 1995: Fresh and straightforward, with cherry and strawberry flavors. Supple, light-bodied. Drink upon release. 2,667 cases made. • $13 • (10/31/96) • **79**
Dolcetto d'Alba 1994 • $13 • (10/31/95) • **82**
Dolcetto d'Alba Paulin 1995: A charmer. Bursts with fresh, grapey aromas and is extremely juicy, with soft tannins. Supple and sweet-tasting finish. Enjoy now. 500 cases made. • $20 • (10/31/96) • **86**
Langhe Casá Favorita 1996: Quite juicy and almost sweet, with a nice grapefruit flavor. Clean, fresh and delicious. Would serve well as an apéritif. • $13 • (12/31/97) • **84**
Langhe Casá Favorita 1995: Tastes sweet, with peach and apricot flavors, some lively citrus notes. Spicy nuance on the finish. Would serve well as an apéritif. 15,000 cases made. • $13 • (03/31/97) • **82**
Nebbiolo delle Langhe Batié 1993: Pretty VT Nebbiolo delle Langhe, fresh and lively, with a crisp core of succulent red berry, licorice, cassis and raspberry flavors. Medium-bodied, it sings on the vibrant finish. Not a complex wine, but should go well with pizza and other unpretentious foods. Drink slightly chilled. 3,000 cases made. • $30 • (10/31/97) • **85**
Nebbiolo delle Langhe Batié 1992: Has lots of fresh, bright fruit flavors and a juicy, firm texture. Drink now. 2,000 cases made. • $29 • (10/31/96) • **85**

GAIERHOF

Cabernet Sauvignon Trentino 1994: Oozes dark, smoky fruit with a tobacco note. Rich, concentrated and balanced, showing a velvety texture and firm backbone. Smoky plum flavors echo on the aftertaste. Drink now through 2002. • $13 • (05/31/98) • **88**
Maso Poli Sorni 1993 • $12 • (01/31/95) • **78**
Moscato Goldmuskateller Trentino 1995: A sweet and light dessert wine, with orange-peel, lime and floral flavors and aromas. • $13 • (10/31/97) • **83**
Nosiola Trentino 1993 • $15 • (01/31/95) • **74**
Pinot Grigio Maso Poli Atesino 1993 • $12 • (01/31/95) • **82**
Pinot Grigio Mosaico Torre di Luna Trentino 1993 • $10 • (01/31/95) • **81**
Pinot Grigio Trentino 1995: Ripe, tropical notes of mango and passion fruit hold sway in this rich, forward white. The finish is moderate and crisp. • $13 • (11/15/97) • **83**
Teroldego Rotaliano 1994: Mature and ready, the bright raspberry and strawberry flavors take on depth and richness in this smooth red that finishes with a slight astringency. Should pair well with food. Drink now. • $13 • (04/30/98) • **84**
Teroldego Rotaliano 1988 • $11 • (09/30/91) • **75**

GAJA

Barbaresco 1994: Gorgeous red, with attractive rose petal, violet, chocolate, spice and cassis flavors offered in an elegant and racy package. Sophisticated, well-integrated tannins, medium body, supple and has a long, delicious finish. Tempting now, better after 2000. Gaja made no single-vineyard *crus* this vintage, putting his best vats in this regular Barbaresco instead. 3,583 cases made. • $70 • (10/31/97) • **91**
Barbaresco 1993: Ripe, rich, supple and lush, this crowd pleaser has just the right amount of fruit and tannins. Full-bodied and balanced, it will need some time to show it all, but should not disappoint. Don't expect super elegance, this is more decadent pleasure. Try after 1999. • $70 • (10/31/96) • **87**
Barbaresco 1991 • $49 • (10/31/94) • **88**
Barbaresco 1990 • $66 • (10/31/93) • **94**
Barbaresco 1989 • $60 • (10/31/93) • **88**
Barbaresco 1988 • $38 Ⓐ • (10/31/93) • **87**
Barbaresco 1986 • $57 Ⓐ • (01/31/90) CS • **92**
Barbaresco 1985 • $149 Ⓐ • (12/15/88) CS • **95**
Barbaresco 1983 • $65 Ⓐ • (09/15/89) • **93**
Barbaresco 1982 • $106 Ⓐ • (09/15/89) • **93**
Barbaresco 1981 • $NA • (09/15/89) • **90**
Barbaresco 1980 • $14 • (07/01/85) • **88**
Barbaresco 1979 • $64 Ⓐ • (09/15/89) • **89**
Barbaresco 1978 • $111 Ⓐ • (09/15/89) • **93**
Barbaresco 1976 • $NA • (09/15/89) • **91**
Barbaresco 1974 • $NA • (09/15/89) • **89**
Barbaresco 1971 • $128 Ⓐ • (09/15/89) • **86**
Barbaresco 1967 • $55 Ⓐ • (09/15/89) • **83**
Barbaresco 1964 • $95 Ⓐ • (09/15/89) • **87**
Barbaresco 1961 • $132 Ⓐ • (09/15/89) • **92**
Barbaresco Costa Russi 1993: Impressively sculpted. The most tannic of Gaja's three single-vineyard *crus*. While closed on the nose now, it suggest lots of depth and, in the mouth, this full-bodied wine delivers a smooth ride, layered with flavors of pure fruit, wild berry and earth. • $140 • (10/31/96) • **93**
Barbaresco Costa Russi 1990 • $125 • (10/31/93) • **98**
Barbaresco Costa Russi 1989 • $125 • (10/15/93) CS • **96**
Barbaresco Costa Russi 1988 • $110 • (10/31/93) • **92**
Barbaresco Costa Russi 1986 • $74 Ⓐ • (01/31/90) • **89**
Barbaresco Costa Russi 1985 • $173 Ⓐ • (12/15/88) • **96**
Barbaresco Costa Russi 1982 • $203 Ⓐ • (09/15/88) • **91**
Barbaresco Sorì San Lorenzo 1993: The most perfumed and charming of Gaja's three Barbaresco *crus*. Beautiful, rich, medium to full-bodied and elegant, with multi-layered red berry and earth character. Fragrant aromas but turns on the power on the palate. Tempting now but best after 1999. • $140 • (10/31/96) • **92**
Barbaresco Sorì San Lorenzo 1990 • $139 • (10/31/93) • **96**
Barbaresco Sorì San Lorenzo 1989 • $139 • (09/15/93) HR • **98**
Barbaresco Sorì San Lorenzo 1988 • $125 • (10/31/93) • **93**
Barbaresco Sorì San Lorenzo 1986 • $110 Ⓐ • (01/31/90) • **91**
Barbaresco Sorì San Lorenzo 1985 • $268 Ⓐ • (12/15/88) • **96**
Barbaresco Sorì San Lorenzo 1983 • $111 Ⓐ • (09/15/88) • **90**
Barbaresco Sorì Tildìn 1993: The most complex and elegant of Gaja's three Barbaresco *crus*. Brooding, deep and multi-layered, this full-bodied wine only hints at its potential now. Still, its harmony is most impressive. Good backbone of supple tannins, with wonderful blackberry, currant, violet and wet earth notes. Try after 2000. • $140 • (10/31/96) CS • **94**
Barbaresco Sorì Tildìn 1990 • $139 • (10/31/93) • **100**
Barbaresco Sorì Tildìn 1989 • $139 • (10/15/93) CS • **96**
Barbaresco Sorì Tildìn 1988 • $125 • (10/31/93) • **93**
Barbaresco Sorì Tildìn 1986 • $98 Ⓐ • (01/31/90) • **93**
Barbaresco Sorì Tildìn 1985 • $214 Ⓐ • (12/15/88) • **97**
Barbaresco Sorì Tildìn 1983 • $177 Ⓐ • (09/15/88) • **89**
Barbaresco Sorì Tildìn 1982 • $203 Ⓐ • (09/15/89) • **94**
Barbaresco Sorì Tildìn 1981 • $144 Ⓐ • (09/15/89) • **87**
Barbaresco Sorì Tildìn 1979 • $144 Ⓐ • (09/15/89) • **89**
Barbaresco Sorì Tildìn 1978 • $263 Ⓐ • (09/15/89) • **90**
Barbaresco Sorì Tildìn 1973 • $NA • (09/15/89) • **88**
Barbaresco Sorì Tildìn 1971 • $NA • (09/15/89) • **91**
Barbaresco Sorì Tildìn 1970 • $NA • (09/15/89) • **78**
Barbera d'Alba 1992 • $42 • (10/31/95) • **81**
Barbera d'Alba Vignarey 1990 • $40 • (10/15/93) • **89**
Barbera d'Alba Vignarey 1987 • $35 • (04/15/91) • **88**
Barbera d'Alba Vignarey 1986 • $27 • (03/15/91) • **88**
Barbera d'Alba Vignarey 1984 • $13 • (02/15/87) • **82**
Barolo Sperss 1993: A sophisticated, well-made, balanced and pleasant red. Of medium body, it's dark in color, thick on the palate, with ripe fruit and sweet tannins; lacks only a bit of complexity and length to rate higher. Has a slight herbaceousness on the nose, which disappeared with aeration. Best decanted. • $100 • (10/31/97) • **88**
Barolo Sperss 1991 • $95 Ⓐ • (10/31/95) • **86**

Barolo Sperss 1989 • $60 • (10/31/93) • **96**
Barolo Sperss 1988 • $60 • (09/15/93) CS • **94**
Cabernet Sauvignon Piedmont Darmagi 1988 • $60 • (12/15/92) HR • **92**
Cabernet Sauvignon Piedmont Darmagi 1986 • $76 • (01/31/90) • **94**
Cabernet Sauvignon Piedmont Darmagi 1985 • $70 • (03/15/89) CS • **94**
Cabernet Sauvignon Piedmont Darmagi 1983 • $51 • (07/15/88) • **91**
Chardonnay Gaia & Rey 1994: A rich, thick-textured, Burgundian-style Chardonnay that's full-bodied, subtly fruity and amply accented with vanilla, nutmeg and hazelnut. Has a long, complex finish, too. Drinkable through 1999. 800 cases made. • $70 • (01/31/97) • **90**
Dolcetto Langhe 1994 • $22 • (10/31/95) • **88**
Nebbiolo d'Alba Vignaveja 1985 • $30 • (02/15/89) • **87**
Nebbiolo d'Alba Vignaveja 1983 • $16 • (02/15/87) SS • **94**
Sito Moresco 1991 • $30 • (10/31/94) • **88**
Sitorey 1993 • $45 • (10/31/95) • **84**
Sitorey 1991 • $35 • (10/31/94) • **85**

GALARDI, FATTORIA

Terra di Lavaro 1994: If a wine could be smoked, this would be. Strong smoky, ashy aromas and flavors dominate the otherwise ripe fruit in this deeply colored, full-bodied brute. May just need time, but it's a gamble. Drink now through 2002. • $29 • (06/15/98) • **84**

GANCIA

Rosso Spumante NV: A bright, red bubbly that's sweet, frothy in texture and lightly fruity, with cherry and strawberry notes. Drink now. • $10 • (05/15/98) • **81**

GAROFOLI

Classico Macrina Verdicchio dei Castelli di Jesi 1993 • $8 • (03/31/95) • **84**

GASTALDI

Dolcetto d'Alba Moriolo 1993 • $NA • (10/31/95) • **82**
Rosso Gastaldi 1988: Amazingly dark-colored and thick, it's very distinctive, but has some odd notes of herb, anise and burnt rubber. Turns herbal and rather dry on the finish. • $NA • (10/31/96) • **81**

GATTAVECCHI

Chianti Colli Senesi 1994: Tired and unclean. Fizzes in your mouth. Yuck. Tasted twice, with consistent notes. • $15 • (09/30/97) • **65**
Chianti Colli Senesi 1990 • $7 • (04/30/92) • **80**
Vino Nobile di Montepulciano 1994: Has some ripe fruit flavor, but it's slightly watery on the finish. • $19 • (09/30/97) • **78**
Vino Nobile di Montepulciano 1990 • $14 • (02/29/96) • **80**
Vino Nobile di Montepulciano 1988 • $14 • (12/15/92) • **83**
Vino Nobile di Montepulciano Riserva 1985 • $11 • (11/30/89) • **81**
Vino Nobile di Montepulciano Riserva dei Padri Serviti 1993: Attractive, with a character of berry and milk chocolate. Light-to-medium body, with light tannins and caressing texture. Drink now. • $22 • (09/30/97) • **82**

GEOGRAFICO

Brunello di Montalcino 1985 • $30 • (07/15/91) • **80**
Capitolare di Bitùrica 1994: A medium-bodied wine with lively berry and chocolate aromas and flavors, silky tannins and a medium finish. Drink or hold. 625 cases made. • $24 • (09/30/97) • **86**
Capitolare di Bitùrica Vigneti del Geografico 1990 • $NA • (02/28/95) • **88**
Chianti Classico 1995: A lean wine, this has some berry flavors but it's diluted and slightly dry on the finish. 50,000 cases made. • $13 • (09/30/97) • **77**
Chianti Classico 1994: A good fruity wine with firm tannins and notes of dried cherry on the finish. Medium-bodied, with light yet firm tannins. • $10 • (10/31/96) • **82**
Chianti Classico 1993 • $9 • (10/31/95) • **83**
Chianti Classico 1992 • $10 • (02/28/95) • **82**
Chianti Classico 1991 • $10 • (10/31/93) • **82**
Chianti Classico 1990 • $12 • (09/15/92) • **87**
Chianti Classico 1988 • $9 • (11/30/91) • **78**
Chianti Classico Castello di Fagnano 1991 • $12 • (10/31/93) • **75**
Chianti Classico Castello di Fagnano 1989 • $9 • (01/31/92) • **70**
Chianti Classico Castello di Fagnano 1988 • $9 • (10/31/91) • **86**
Chianti Classico Contessa di Radda 1988 • $14 • (09/15/92) • **88**
Chianti Classico Contessa di Radda 1987 • $11 • (10/31/91) • **80**
Chianti Classico Tenuta Montegiachi Riserva 1986 • $15 • (10/31/91) • **79**
Predicato di Bitùrica 1986 • $21 • (08/31/91) • **85**
Vernaccia di San Gimignano 1996: Delivers good citrus, honeydew melon and light spice aromas and flavors. Medium-bodied, with fresh acidity and a light finish. 25,000 cases made. • $10 • (09/30/97) • **83**
Vernaccia di San Gimignano Liberna Riserva 1994: Oxidized and slightly sweet, with a plasticlike character on the finish. Undrinkable. Tasted twice, with consistent notes. 2,000 cases made. • $NA • (09/30/97) • **65**
Vigneti del Geografico 1993: Slightly out of balance. Fresh, fruity aromas of raspberries with a hint of flowers. Medium-bodied, with slightly hard tannins and a fresh, slightly alcoholic finish. Drink or hold. • $NA • (10/31/96) • **84**
Vigneti del Geografico 1988 • $26 • (10/31/93) • **91**
Vino Nobile di Montepulciano Cerraia 1994: Rich, fruity and ripe, but with a heavy musty overtone. Tasted twice, with consistent notes. 2,000 cases made. • $17 • (10/31/97) • **68**
Vino Nobile di Montepulciano Vigneti alla Cerraia 1986 • $15 • (07/15/91) • **85**

GERLA, LA

Birba 1995: Not giving much on the nose at the moment, but the palate shows thick and chewy fruit structure, velvety tannins and grapey flavors. Drink now. • $NA • (09/30/97) • **86**
Birba 1994: A fairly chewy wine, showing tobacco, berry and wood aromas and flavors. Medium-bodied, with a velvety finish. Drink now. • $NA • (10/31/96) • **85**
Birba 1990 • $NA • (10/31/93) • **87**
Birbante 1989 • $NA • (10/31/93) • **84**
Brunello di Montalcino 1991: Fresh and fruity with its berry and mint aromas and flavors. Appealingly silky finish. Drink or hold. 1,000 cases made. • $30 • (11/30/96) • **85**
Brunello di Montalcino 1990: Light and easy-drinking Brunello, a bit diluted, offering some strawberry, mint and cherry flavors. Lean wine, and short finish. Disappointing for this producer. • $NA • (10/31/95) • **84**
Brunello di Montalcino 1988 • $30 • (04/30/94) • **86**
Brunello di Montalcino Riserva 1991: Some good earthy strawberry character here, but it's slightly diluted on the finish. Crisp acidity. Drink now. 400 cases made. • $44 • (09/30/97) • **83**
Brunello di Montalcino Riserva 1990: An almost perfectly proportioned wine, this is full-bodied, with full tannins, yet there's superb finesse to it all. Plenty of plum, licorice and mint aromas and flavors, too. 850 cases made. • $37 • (11/30/96) • **91**
Brunello di Montalcino Riserva 1988 • $NA • (10/31/94) • **89**
Rosso di Montalcino 1995: Simple yet fresh and lively, with dried cherry flavors and a light finish. 1,700 cases made. • $17 • (09/30/97) • **82**
Rosso di Montalcino 1994: Offers a lovely, velvety mouthfeel and succulent berry, cherry and spice flavors that hold through the finish. 1,500 cases made. • $13 • (11/30/96) • **84**
Rosso di Montalcino 1991 • $12 • (04/30/94) • **84**

GERMANO, ETTORE

Barolo Cerretta 1993: An international style, featuring new oak. Tastes of mocha, spice and chocolate, along with plum and red berry. Dry finish, with astringent tannins. • $NA • (10/31/97) • **76**
Barolo 1991 • $NA • (10/31/95) • **81**

GHISOLFI, ATTILIO

Barbera d'Alba 1990 • $18 • (10/15/94) • **86**
Barbera d'Alba Vigna Lisi 1994: Browning at the edges. Fast-maturing, and fairly lean, with modest ripe fruit and crisp lemon notes leading to a sharp, drying finish. • $20 • (01/31/98) • **76**
Dolcetto d'Alba 1991 • $12 • (10/15/94) • **84**

Key: SS—Spectator Selection CS—Cellar Selection HR—Highly Recommended BB—Best Buy $NA—Price not available Ⓐ—Auction Price (BT)—Barrel Tasting
Dates in parentheses indicate the issues in which the ratings were published.

GHIZZANO, TENUTA DI

Chianti 1996: Bright and fruity in flavor, this is easy to drink and enjoy. Just enough body to keep it balanced. Drink now. 2,300 cases made. • $10 • (04/30/98) • **85**

Veneroso 1994: A lovely, velvety wine with chocolate, berry and cherry aromas and flavors. Medium-bodied, with a pretty texture and a caressing finish. Delicious. A blend of 50 percent Cabernet, 35 percent Sangiovese and 15 percent Merlot. Drink now. • $22 • (09/30/97) • **86**

GIACOSA, BRUNO

Barbaresco 1985 • $42 • (08/31/89) • **84**

Barbaresco 1983 • $24 • (07/31/87) • **88**

Barbaresco Asili 1993: Beautiful, in a traditional style. Intense, complex and firmly structured, with a seductive, sweet-tasting, ripe fruit, dried herb, mineral and earth character. Long, silky finish. Try after 1999. • $NA • (10/31/96) • **90**

Barbaresco Asili 1990 • $NA • (10/31/94) • **92**

Barbaresco Gallina 1990 • $NA • (10/31/94) • **86**

Barbaresco Gallina 1989 • $NA • (10/31/93) • **79**

Barbaresco Gallina di Neive 1986 • $40 • (08/31/91) • **88**

Barbaresco Santo Stefano di Neive 1993: Traditional style, even slightly rustic, with chestnut aromas and complex, nutty, earthy red berry flavors that unfold on the palate. Full-bodied, with good concentration. Try after 1999. • $NA • (10/31/96) • **89**

Barbaresco Santo Stefano 1990 • $NA • (10/31/94) • **83**

Barbaresco Santo Stefano di Neive 1986 • $62 • (08/31/91) • **83**

Barbaresco Santo Stefano di Neive 1982 • $57 • (09/15/88) • **92**

Barbaresco Santo Stefano di Neive Riserva 1985 • $60 • (08/31/91) • **77**

Barbaresco Santo Stefano di Neive Riserva 1982 • $60 • (09/15/88) • **90**

Barbera d'Alba 1993 • $17 • (10/31/95) • **82**

Barbera d'Alba Altavilla 1990 • $18 • (10/15/93) • **77**

Barbera d'Alba Altavilla d'Alba 1987 • $12 • (03/15/91) • **73**

Barbera d'Alba Altavilla d'Alba 1986 • $12 • (03/15/91) • **77**

Barolo 1990 • $NA • (10/31/95) • **84**

Barolo 1980 • $19 • (09/15/87) • **78**

Barolo 1978 • $31 • (09/16/84) • **88**

Barolo Collina Rionda 1993: A bit earthy, but still lovely, round, rich and balanced. Features ripe red- and blackberry flavors, loads of *terroir*, well-integrated tannins and a long finish. Best from 2000 through 2002. 830 cases made. • $110 • (10/31/97) • **89**

Barolo Collina Rionda 1989 • $NA • (10/31/94) • **78**

Barolo Collina Rionda di Serralunga 1985 • $87 Ⓐ • (04/30/91) • **86**

Barolo Falletto 1993: Smells very funky and earthy, but offers lovely, ripe and sweet-tasting fruit that caresses the palate like few '93 Barolos. Light-to-medium body, it's tempting to drink now, but better around 2000. 1,602 cases made. • $90 • (10/31/97) • **87**

Barolo Falletto 1989 • $NA • (10/31/94) • **84**

Barolo Le Rocche di Castiglione Falletto 1982 • $38 • (07/31/89) • **80**

Barolo Riserva 1982 • $65 • (01/31/90) • **72**

Barolo Rocche 1982 • $41 • (09/15/88) • **90**

Barolo Villero 1989 • $NA • (10/31/94) • **81**

Barolo Villero 1988 • $39 • (10/31/93) • **70**

Barolo Villero di Castiglione 1983 • $29 • (01/31/89) • **85**

Dolcetto d'Alba 1989 • $12 • (02/28/91) • **88**

Dolcetto d'Alba Falletto 1996: A soft, full-bodied and supple Dolcetto, with plum, prune, fig and licorice flavors. Has a fresh, citrusy character that makes it lively on the lingering finish. Yummy to drink now. 1,167 cases made. • $14 • (10/31/97) • **84**

Dolcetto d'Alba Plinet di Trezzo Tinella 1985 • $8 • (12/31/87) • **77**

GIACOSA, CARLO

Barbaresco Montefico 1993: A bit lean and austere, lacking the flesh to accompany the floral and cherry flavors. Food may bring out more fruit. 100 cases imported. • $26 • (01/01/97) • **79**

Barbaresco Narin 1993: Elegant, supple and attractive for its licorice and cherry flavors. Drinkable now, with some tannins that suggest light meats or cheeses. • $26 • (01/01/97) • **82**

Barbaresco 1992: Already displaying some gamy notes, along with a lean texture and a good dose of tannin. Drinkable now. • $20 • (01/01/97) • **79**

Dolcetto d'Alba Vigna Cuchet 1995: There are some simple and pleasant cherry flavors in this wine, with a gamy aroma and a light finish. Tasted twice with consistent notes. • $14 • (01/01/97) • **77**

GIACOSA FRATELLI

Barbaresco 1987 • $16 • (03/31/93) • **78**

Barbaresco 1986 • $17 • (07/15/91) • **87**

Barbaresco Suri Secondine 1986 • $12 • (10/31/90) • **72**

Barbera d'Alba Maria Gioana 1987 • $24 • (03/31/93) • **83**

Barbera d'Alba Maria Gioana 1986 • $22 • (03/15/91) • **86**

Barolo 1985 • $20 • (03/31/93) • **70**

GINI

Chianti Classico 1994: A delicious, medium-bodied wine that shows pure fruit, with raspberry, cherry and mineral aromas and flavors. Silky tannins and a long, long aftertaste. Drink or hold. From Fattoria di Montecchio. • $NA • (10/31/96) • **86**

Col Foscarin 1989 • $22/375ml • (09/15/92) • **83**

Sauvignon Maciete Fumé 1993 • $NA • (01/31/95) • **87**

Soave Classico Superiore 1996: A well-made white that's vivid, with almond and mineral flavors, graceful presence, and a citrus peel note on the finish. Drink now. • $15 • (06/30/98) • **86**

Soave Classico Superiore La Froscà 1996: Good ripeness for the vintage, exhibiting peach and lemon aromas and flavors, a touch of minerals and a concentrated, rich texture. Characteristic bitter almond finish. Drink now. • $16 • (06/30/98) • **87**

GIOIOSA, LA

Merlot Veneto 1996: Plenty of menthol and spice notes in this moderately concentrated, medium-weight red that finishes slightly coarse. Drink now through 1999. • $5 • (07/31/98) • **83**

Pinot Grigio Veneto 1997: Light and slightly spritzy. A basic white with modest apple and almond flavors. Drink now. • $5 • (07/31/98) • **76**

GIOVELLO

Merlot Veneto 1996: An industrial wine with no Merlot character, just an artificial, slightly candied flavor. Not recommended. Tasted twice, with consistent notes. 45,000 cases made. • $7 • (04/30/98) • **68**

Merlot Veneto 1995: A soft, fruity red with aromas of crushed cherries followed by straightforward fruit that finishes up on the crisp side. Drinkable now. 12,500 cases made. • $6 • (01/01/97) • **81**

Pinot Grigio Veneto 1996: Woodsy, spicy accents add to the apple character of this medium-bodied Pinot Grigio. Finish turns a little metallic. Drink now. 90,000 cases made. • $7 • (05/15/98) • **79**

Pinot Grigio Umbria 1995: Fruity, bright flavors of green apple, peach and banana. Quite tart, and finishes with an earthy edge. 10,000 cases made. • $6 • (08/31/96) • **80**

GIRIBALDI, AZIENDA

Chardonnay delle Langhe Campo Fux Magna 1994 • $13 • (02/29/96) • **85**

GIUSTINIANA, LA

Gavi Lugarara 1995: Fruity, light and refreshing, with appealing peach and honey flavors and a crisp texture. 7,000 cases made. • $16 • (05/31/97) • **83**

Gavi Montessora 1995: This dry, appealing white is distinguished by lightly smoky, aniselike flavors and a clean, tangy, fruit character. 3,000 cases made. • $23 • (05/31/97) • **85**

Gavi Vignaclara 1994: Fairly rich, with a sagelike aroma, but it's quite oniony tasting, with herbal notes. A bit drying on the finish. Not for everyone. 2,000 cases made. • $25 • (03/31/97) • **78**

GLICINE, CANTINA DEL

Barbaresco 1985 • $27 • (08/31/91) • **75**

Dolcetto d'Alba 1989 • $13 • (11/30/91) • **79**

ITALY

GONDI, MARCHESE

Chianti Rufina 1990 • $NA • (10/31/93) • **85**
Chianti Rufina Tenuta di Bossi Riserva 1994: Pretty berry aromas, but it's too dry on the palate. Medium- to light-bodied, with dry tannins and an austere finish. What a shame. Tasted twice, with consistent notes. • $NA • (09/30/97) • **79**
Chianti Rufina Villa Bossi Riserva 1993: Good berry, mushroom and earth character, but a slightly dry, short finish. Medium-bodied. Drink now. • $NA • (09/30/97) • **79**
Colli dell'Etruria Centrale Tenuta di Bossi 1996: Simple, with some lemon and almond character. Medium-bodied, with a light finish. • $NA • (09/30/97) • **80**
Mazzaferrata 1993: A bit simple, but there's some good fruit, finishing with currant and berry. Body is medium, tannins are silky. Try now. • $NA • (09/30/97) • **86**

GORELLI

Brunello di Montalcino 1992: A balanced and silky red, with aromas and flavors of tobacco, cherry and berry. Medium-to-light in body. Fresh finish. Drink now. • $35 • (09/30/97) • **85**
Brunello di Montalcino 1991: Lots of wood in this wine, with intense wood and bark aromas and flavors mingling with the ripe fruit. Better in 1999. 125 cases made. • $32 • (11/30/96) • **86**
Brunello di Montalcino 1990: Elegant and minty, sporting fine tannins and fresh fruit. Medium-bodied and round with toasty oak and a clean finish. Drinkable now. • $NA • (10/31/95) • **87**
Brunello di Montalcino 1988 • $NA • (04/30/94) • **87**
Rosso di Montalcino 1995: Classy Rosso with an abundant red berry and cherry character. Medium-bodied, with fine tannins and a fruity finish. Drink or hold. • $20 • (09/30/97) • **89**
Rosso di Montalcino 1994: Caressing, offering berry and cherry flavors with hints of vanilla. Medium-bodied. Silky finish, with a slightly drying aftertaste. Drink now. 155 cases made. • $15 • (11/30/96) • **84**
Rosso di Montalcino 1993 • $NA • (10/31/95) • **86**
Rosso di Montalcino 1992 • $NA • (10/31/94) • **80**
Rosso di Montalcino 1991 • $NA • (04/30/94) • **82**

GORETTI MINIATI

Apoteosi 1990 • $NA • (10/31/93) • **87**
Chianti Classico Il Palagio 1991 • $NA • (10/31/93) • **86**
Chianti Classico Il Palagio 1990 • $NA • (10/31/93) • **86**

GRACCIANO DELLA SETA, TENUTA DI

Rosso di Montepulciano 1995: Absolutely delicious with its plum, berry and vanilla aromas and flavors. It's medium- to full-bodied, with soft tannins and a long, flavorful finish. Drink or hold. 1,300 cases made. • $10 • (09/30/97) • **87**
Vino Nobile di Montepulciano 1994: Lovely nose, with bright floral and fruit notes, but weak on the palate with a light finish. Medium- to light-bodied. Drink now. 1,750 cases made. • $14 • (09/30/97) • **81**
Vino Nobile di Montepulciano Riserva 1993: A weak wine, it has some fruit but is slightly weedy, diluted and unclean. Dry finish. Tasted twice, with consistent notes. 580 cases made. • $17 • (09/30/97) • **71**

GRASSO, ELIO

Barbera d'Alba Vigna Martina 1992 • $18 • (10/31/95) • **82**
Barbera delle Langhe Vigna Martina 1990 • $19 • (09/15/93) • **81**
Barolo 1991 • $24 • (10/31/95) • **81**
Barolo Casa Maté 1990 • $30 • (10/31/94) • **85**
Barolo Gavarini Vigna Chiniera 1990 • $30 • (10/31/94) • **87**
Barolo Gavarini Vigna Rüncot 1988 • $30 • (09/15/93) • **84**
Barolo Ginestra Vigna Casa Maté 1988 • $30 • (09/15/93) • **82**
Dolcetto d'Alba Gavarini Vigna dei Grassi 1989 • $18 • (07/15/91) • **76**
Gavarini 1989 • $20 • (07/15/91) • **83**

Key: SS—Spectator Selection CS—Cellar Selection HR—Highly Recommended BB—Best Buy $NA—Price not available Ⓐ—Auction Price (BT)—Barrel Tasting
Dates in parentheses indicate the issues in which the ratings were published.

GRASSO, SILVIO

Barolo 1993: A beautiful effort, clean, pure and unhindered by any taste of wood. What you get is fresh red- and blackberry flavors, nice mineral notes, good acidity and a lingering finish. Try after 2000. • $30 • (10/31/97) • **89**
Barolo Bricco Luciani 1993: Lovely, balanced and ripe. Medium-bodied, the cherry, raspberry, spice and licorice flavors fan out on the palate. Tannins are firm, even a bit green. Try in 2000. • $33 • (10/31/97) • **86**
Barolo Ciabot Manzoni 1993: Sophisticated and attractive. For the vintage, this is unusually dark in color, smooth in body, flavorful in character. Medium-bodied and very elegant, with cassis, violet, black cherry and blackberry flavors. Delicious now, but should gain in complexity with cellaring until 2000. • $35 • (10/31/97) • **90**

GRATTAMACCO

Bolgheri 1994: Distinctive for its intense red berry and redwood aromas, this has medium body, plummy flavors and chewy tannins. A bit rustic. Try now. • $NA • (09/30/97) • **86**
Bolgheri Bianco 1996: Light aromas of apricots and hints of grass. Medium-bodied, with ripe fruit flavors but a slightly short finish. Try now. • $NA • (09/30/97) • **84**
Tuscany Red 1990 • $NA • (10/31/93) • **93**
Tuscany Red 1989 • $NA • (10/31/93) • **86**
Tuscany Red 1988 • $NA • (09/15/91) • **87**
Tuscany Red 1986 • $25 • (12/15/92) • **72**

GRAVNER

Breg 1994: A northeast Italian white masquerading as a Burgundy. Shows impressive weight and spicy new-oak character, with an abundance of applelike flavors and citrusy acidity beneath. Slightly hot on the finish, yet fresh and lively. Try now. 1,000 cases made. • $65 • (06/15/97) • **89**
Chardonnay Collio 1994: Round and generous, displaying a hint of oak for accent, yet there's an underlying firmness that lingers on the finish. Well made, should be fine with grilled fish. 1,100 cases made. • $65 • (06/15/97) • **88**
Ribolla Collio 1994: New oak adds notes of clove and nutmeg to the concentrated fruit in this powerhouse, and the aftertaste has flavors of butterscotch and grilled nuts. Distinctive, and makes a statement for this region. 600 cases made. • $65 • (06/15/97) • **87**
Sauvignon Collio 1994: An extrovert, from the deep gold color to the toasty new-oak and butter nuances. Showing some mature elements, and tannins on the finish suggest drinking it soon. 1,000 cases made. • $65 • (06/15/97) • **85**

GREPPONE MAZZI, TENUTA IL

Brunello di Montalcino 1990: Silky and refined, featuring plenty of ripe fruit, mint and roasted new oak character, medium to full body, fine tannins and long, slightly dry finish. Try now. • $35 • (10/31/95) • **87**
Brunello di Montalcino 1982 • $30 • (09/15/86) • **90**
Brunello di Montalcino 1981 • $25 • (09/15/86) • **70**
Brunello di Montalcino Riserva 1988 • $40 • (10/31/94) • **85**
Brunello di Montalcino Riserva 1986 • $33 • (12/15/92) • **84**

GRESY, MARCHESI DI

Barbaresco Camp Gros 1990 • $63 • (10/31/94) • **83**
Barbaresco Camp Gros 1989 • $61 • (10/31/94) • **73**
Barbaresco Camp Gros Martinenga 1990 • $60 • (10/31/93) • **90**
Barbaresco Camp Gros Martinenga 1989 • $60 • (10/31/93) • **78**
Barbaresco Camp Gros Martinenga 1988 • $60 • (10/31/93) • **82**
Barbaresco Camp Gros Martinenga 1985 • $55 Ⓐ • (01/31/89) • **92**
Barbaresco Camp Gros Martinenga 1983 • $30 • (09/15/88) • **88**
Barbaresco Camp Gros Martinenga 1982 • $26 • (09/15/88) • **89**
Barbaresco Camp Gros Martinenga 1979 • $NA • (09/15/88) • **88**
Barbaresco Gaiun Martinenga 1990 • $63 • (10/31/94) • **83**
Barbaresco Gaiun Martinenga 1989 • $61 • (10/31/94) • **86**
Barbaresco Gaiun Martinenga 1988 • $60 • (10/31/93) • **83**
Barbaresco Gaiun Martinenga 1986 • $64 • (09/15/90) • **90**
Barbaresco Gaiun Martinenga 1985 • $55 • (01/31/89) CS • **95**
Barbaresco Gaiun Martinenga 1983 • $30 • (09/15/88) • **84**
Barbaresco Gaiun Martinenga 1982 • $26 • (09/15/88) • **87**

Barbaresco Martinenga 1994: Supple, medium-bodied and light, it does offer decent fruit flavor. Ready to drink. • $NA • (10/31/97) • **79**
Barbaresco Martinenga 1992 • $41 • (10/31/95) • **78**
Barbaresco Martinenga 1991 • $41 • (10/31/95) • **81**
Barbaresco Martinenga 1990 • $40 • (10/31/94) • **82**
Barbaresco Martinenga 1989 • $36 • (10/31/94) • **82**
Barbaresco Martinenga 1988 • $30 • (10/31/93) • **80**
Barbaresco Martinenga 1986 • $56 • (09/15/90) • **88**
Barbaresco Martinenga 1985 • $39 • (01/31/89) • **90**
Barbaresco Martinenga 1984 • $20 • (09/15/88) • **84**
Barbaresco Martinenga 1983 • $20 • (09/15/88) • **87**
Barbaresco Martinenga 1982 • $20 • (09/15/88) • **86**
Barbaresco Martinenga 1979 • $NA • (09/15/88) • **81**
Barbaresco Martinenga 1978 • $NA • (09/15/88) • **89**
Chardonnay Piedmont Gresy 1993 • $NA • (01/01/95) • **86**
Dolcetto d'Alba Monte Aribaldo 1996: Lively and fresh, this grapey, light-bodied, delicate and pretty Dolcetto sparkles with fruit. Enjoy now. • $NA • (10/31/97) • **84**
Dolcetto d'Alba Monte Aribaldo 1994 • $NA • (10/31/95) • **84**
Dolcetto d'Alba Monte Aribaldo 1993 • $NA • (10/31/95) • **80**
Dolcetto d'Alba Monte Aribaldo 1986 • $8 • (10/31/88) • **81**
Nebbiolo Martinenga 1986 • $11 • (10/15/88) • **82**
Sauvignon Langhe 1994 • $NA • (01/01/95) • **81**
Villa Martis 1994: Light and astringent, with simple strawberry and cherry flavors and a lean finish. Made from Nebbiolo and Barbera. • $NA • (10/31/97) • **75**
Virtus 1991 • $25 • (10/31/94) • **83**

GRETOLE, PODERI DI

Chianti Classico 1990 • $9 • (10/31/93) • **83**
Chianti Classico 1989 • $9 • (12/15/92) • **82**
Chianti Classico 1988 • $8 • (10/31/91) BB • **82**
Chianti Classico Riserva 1988 • $11 • (10/31/93) • **86**
Chianti Classico Riserva 1986 • $11 • (10/31/91) • **83**

GREVEPESA, CASTELLI DEL

Chianti Classico 1994: Already slightly mature, with an amber-hued edge and a leathery character. Light-bodied, with some fruit flavor and a light, slightly dry finish. • $NA • (10/31/96) • **76**
Chianti Classico Castelgreve Riserva 1988 • $9 • (09/15/92) • **79**
Chianti Classico Clemente VII 1995: Light and diluted, it has some plum and leather flavors but it's a weak wine in general. • $11 • (09/30/97) • **75**
Chianti Classico Clemente VII 1993 • $NA • (10/31/95) • **79**
Chianti Classico Clemente VII 1988 • $8 • (09/15/92) • **81**
Chianti Classico Clemente VII Riserva 1994: A bit weak, it's light-bodied with light tannins and a light finish. Some berry, cherry and leather flavors surface. • $18 • (09/30/97) • **78**
Chianti Classico Lamole 1990 • $NA • (10/31/93) • **76**
Chianti Classico Panzano 1988 • $11 • (09/15/92) • **84**
Chianti Classico Sant'Angiolo Vico Labate 1988 • $NA • (09/15/91) • **88**
Chianti Classico Vigna Elisa 1988 • $13 • (09/15/92) • **85**
Coltifredi Predicato di Cardisco 1988 • $21 • (10/31/93) • **85**
Gualdo al Luco 1993: Slightly leathery and dry, but shows some decent berry and tobacco flavors. Of medium body, with slightly high acidity. Drink now. • $NA • (09/30/97) • **82**
Gualdo alle Lame 1994: A delicious, rich white with an apple and almond character and a shot of new wood. Medium-bodied, showing good acidity and a flavorful finish. • $NA • (09/30/97) • **87**
Magiòlo 1990 • $NA • (10/31/93) • **84**

GROMIS

Barolo Conteisa Cerequio 1991: Quite tasty and unique. Gives a good blast of black pepper and currant flavors, though they fade on the finish. Drink now. • $NA • (10/31/96) • **84**
Barolo Conteisa Cerequio 1990: Ripe and distinctive from the deep color and tarry aromas to the black cherry and plum flavors. Broad, richly textured, and tannic but well balanced. Drink now through 2004. • $NA • (10/31/96) • **88**
Barolo Conteisa Cerequio 1989: Earthy, spicy aromas and flavors are distinctive and interesting. Has a bold, roasted character, full body, great concentration and a long finish. Drink now to 2005. • $NA • (10/31/96) • **90**

GUALDO DEL RE

Val di Cornia Suvereto 1996: An earthy, rustic flavor marks this smooth, broad-textured, low-tannin, easy-drinking red. Good, but not everyone's cup of tea. Drink now. 3,000 cases made. • $12 • (07/31/98) • **83**
Val di Cornia Suvereto 1995: Shows some berry and cherry aromas and flavors, but it's slightly coarse with a fruit character that verges on raisinlike, and a diluted finish. • $NA • (10/31/96) • **78**
Val di Cornia Suvereto Riserva 1994: A substantial red, full-bodied and full of character. Has deep color, firm tannins and a distinctive flavor profile that's earthy in an appealing way. Lingering finish. Drink now through 2001. 1,500 cases made. • $27 • (07/31/98) • **87**

GUERRA LUIGI

Pinot Grigio Colli Orientali del Friuli 1995: Smells and tastes oxidized. Tasted twice, with consistent notes. Past its prime. • $11 • (05/31/98) • **70**

GUICCIARDINI STROZZI

Millanni 1994: A voluptuous red with intense raspberry, chocolate and berry aromas. Full-bodied, with big, velvety tannins and a long, delicious finish. Drink now. 600 cases made. • $42 • (09/30/97) • **89**
Sòdole 1994: Perfumed and beautiful, with black cherry, berry and mineral aromas, chocolate and berry flavors with hints of vanilla. Medium-bodied, silky on the finish. Drink or hold. 1,200 cases made. • $26 • (09/30/97) • **88**
Vernaccia di San Gimignano Riserva 1995: Rather dull. Shows some lemon and hazelnut character, but it's somewhat oxidized, with a candied finish. 2,000 cases made. • $14 • (09/30/97) • **78**

GUICCIARDINI, CONTE FERDINANDO

Chianti Colli Fiorentini Il Cortile del Castello di Poppiano 1994: Generous and juicy, this medium-bodied Chianti has layers of floral, fruity and spicy flavors and a rich but not tannic texture. Drink now. • $9 • (10/31/97) • **86**
Chianti Colli Fiorentini Il Cortile del Castello di Poppiano 1993: A middle-of-the-road Chianti, with balsamic aromas, ripe fruit flavors and a soft texture. 25,000 cases made. • $10 • (10/31/96) • **77**
Chianti Colli Fiorentini Il Cortile del Castello di Poppiano 1990 • $8 • (05/15/95) BB • **88**
Chianti Colli Fiorentini Riserva Castello di Poppiano 1986 • $10 • (05/15/94) • **88**
Sangiovese Colli della Toscana Centrale Castello di Poppiano Tosco Forte 1995: A good, basic Sangiovese with smoky aromas and ripe, plummy flavors. It has smooth texture, medium body and soft tannins. Drink now. • $12 • (10/31/97) • **83**
Syrah Colli della Toscana Centrale Castello di Poppiano 1995: A seemingly warm, smooth, generous red with ripe fruit flavors and an easy-drinking texture. Drink now. • $12 • (10/31/97) • **84**
Syrah Toscana 1994: A hip style of super Tuscan wine, marked by oak. Shows buttery, cedary aromas and flavors, soft texture and a lingering finish with yet more oak. 3,000 cases made. • $15 • (10/31/96) • **84**
Tricorno 1990: Rich and broad-textured, with a smooth feel. Shows chocolaty flavors, good depth of fruit and a lingering finish. Drink now. 4,000 cases made. • $24 • (10/31/96) • **88**
Tricorno 1987 • $18 • (07/31/94) • **86**

HAAS, FRANZ

Chardonnay Alto Adige 1993 • $10 • (06/15/96) • **83**
Pinot Grigio Alto Adige Kris 1994 • $10 • (10/31/95) BB • **87**

HADERBURG

Brut Alto Adige/Südtirol 1993: Soft and off dry, with honey, vanilla and wax flavors and enough zip on the finish to keep everything in balance. Drink now. • $24 • (07/31/98) • **83**
Chardonnay Alto Adige/Südtirol Stainhauser 1996: Sweaty, earthy, cheesy aromas and flavors are dominant. Not recommended. Tasted twice, with consistent notes. • $15 • (07/31/98) • **65**

I DUE CIPRESSI

Brunello di Montalcino 1990: This is a lovely autumnal wine that has wild mushroom, tobacco and meaty aromas and flavors. Medium body, ripe fruit character, round tannins and a rich finish. Drinkable now. 600 cases made. • $28 • (10/31/95) • **87**
Brunello di Montalcino 1989 • $28 • (07/31/95) • **82**
Rosso di Montalcino 1993 • $14 • (10/31/95) • **84**
Rosso di Montalcino 1992 • $14 • (08/31/95) • **85**
Vino Nobile di Montepulciano 1992 • $11 • (10/31/95) • **76**
Vino Nobile di Montepulciano 1991 • $11 • (02/29/96) • **78**

I SELVATICI

Chianti Colli Aretini 1990 • $NA • (10/31/93) • **85**
Claresco Tuscany 1990 • $6 • (09/30/91) • **79**
Predicato di Cardisco 1985 • $25 • (08/31/91) • **81**
Vin Santo 1984 • $16/375ml • (04/30/91) • **89**

I SODI

Chianti Classico 1992 • $NA • (02/28/95) • **78**

I VERBI

Brunello di Montalcino 1990: Big and rich with tobacco, spice and dried berry aromas and flavors. Full-bodied, round, offering velvety tannins and long aftertaste. A bit rustic and rough. Drink now. • $NA • (10/31/95) • **86**
Rosso di Montalcino 1993 • $NA • (10/31/95) • **77**

IL GREPPONE MAZZI, TENUTA

Brunello di Montalcino 1991: Clean and crisp in style. Light tannins shore up cherry, berry and mint flavors that turn silky on the finish. Drink now. 2,776 cases made. • $35 • (11/30/96) • **83**
Brunello di Montalcino Riserva 1991: A light '92 Brunello, it has leather and berry character, a light and diluted finish. Drink now. • $50 • (09/30/97) • **78**
Brunello di Montalcino Riserva 1990: A great mouthful of concentrated fruit, absolutely delicious and succulent. Terrific aromas and flavors of spice, berries and violets. Full-bodied, with fine tannins and a long flavorful finish. Perhaps the greatest wine ever from this estate. 2,611 cases made. • $50 • (11/30/96) • **93**

ILLUMINATI

Montepulciano d'Abruzzo Zanna 1988 • $15 • (07/31/94) • **79**

INFERNOTTO

Barolo 1990 • $15 • (02/28/95) • **85**
Chianti 1992 • $4 • (07/31/95) • **78**
Chianti Classico 1992 • $5 • (07/31/95) • **77**
Pinot Grigio Grave del Friuli 1993 • $6 • (07/31/95) • **75**

INNOCENTI, VITTORIO

Acerone 1990 • $10 • (10/31/93) • **78**
Acerone 1988 • $13 • (07/15/91) • **80**
Acerone 1985 • $9 • (09/15/89) • **78**
Chianti 1990 • $9 • (10/31/93) • **81**
Chianti 1987 • $7 • (05/15/90) BB • **83**
Chianti 1986 • $7 • (03/31/90) • **77**
Vino Nobile di Montepulciano 1988 • $13 • (11/15/93) • **85**
Vino Nobile di Montepulciano 1985 • $10 • (03/31/90) • **77**

ISOLE E OLENA

Antiche Tenute 1989 • $6 • (08/31/91) • **80**
Antiche Tenute 1988 • $6 • (09/15/89) BB • **83**
Antiche Tenute 1987 • $4 • (01/31/89) BB • **81**
Antiche Tenute 1986 • $5 • (11/15/88) • **78**
Cabernet Sauvignon Tuscany Collezione de Marchi 1994: A chunky, delicious wine. Dark-colored, with rich aromas of black currants and wet earth. Full-bodied, with chewy tannins and a medium finish. Drink now. 1,200 cases made. • $32 • (09/30/97) • **90**
Cabernet Sauvignon Tuscany Collezione de Marchi 1993: A triumph for this vintage. Great, dark color and loads of berry, mint and eucalyptus aromas and flavors. Full-bodied, with fine tannins and a long, silky finish. Drink now. 400 cases made. • $32 • (10/31/96) • **91**
Cabernet Sauvignon Tuscany Collezione de Marchi 1991 • $30 • (02/28/95) • **90**
Cabernet Sauvignon Tuscany Collezione de Marchi 1990 • $30 • (10/31/93) • **95**
Cabernet Sauvignon Tuscany Collezione de Marchi 1988 • $40 • (09/15/91) • **94**
Cepparello 1995: Outstanding. The essence of raspberry and berry greets the nose, wonderful fruity flavors treat the palate. Full-bodied and really silky, with a long, long finish. Try now. 2,500 cases made. • $34 • (09/30/97) • **91**
Cepparello 1994: Subtle aromas and flavors of plum and tobacco. Medium-bodied, with medium tannins and slightly dry finish. Tasted twice, with consistent notes. Drinkable now. 2,500 cases made. • $32 • (09/30/97) • **87**
Cepparello 1993: Gorgeous berry, cherry, violet character to this medium-bodied and muscular wine, with loads of fine tannins and a long, slightly mouthpuckering finish. Drink now. Sangiovese. 2,500 cases made. • $32 • (10/31/96) • **91**
Cepparello 1991 • $28 • (02/28/95) • **86**
Cepparello 1990 • $30 • (10/31/93) • **93**
Cepparello 1989 • $NA • (11/15/93) • **85**
Cepparello 1988 • $NA • (11/15/93) • **92**
Cepparello 1986 • $NA • (11/15/93) • **85**
Cepparello 1985 • $NA • (11/15/93) • **90**
Cepparello 1983 • $NA • (11/15/93) • **90**
Cepparello 1982 • $NA • (11/15/93) • **94**
Chardonnay Tuscany Collezione de Marchi 1995: Plenty of toasty oak in this wine, as well with a hint of apple. Medium-bodied, with moderate acidity and a fresh, ripe fruit finish. 900 cases made. • $22 • (09/30/97) • **88**
Chardonnay Tuscany Collezione de Marchi 1994: Tastes oxidized with sherrylike flavors. Overdone and over the hill. • $18 • (01/31/97) • **68**
Chianti Classico 1995: Elegant, with pretty plum and cherry aromas and flavors. Medium- to light-bodied, with light tannins and a fresh finish. 12,000 cases made. • $13 • (09/30/97) • **85**
Chianti Classico 1994: Plenty of fruit and backbone in this Chianti. Dried berry with a hint of herbs on the nose and palate. Medium-bodied with light yet firm tannins and a fresh finish. Drink now. 12,000 cases made. • $14 • (10/31/96) • **87**
Chianti Classico 1993: Solid and hearty, with hints of oak and a nice bite of tannin to the focused cherry and spice flavors that linger on the finish. Drink now. • $12 • (10/31/96) • **86**
Chianti Classico 1992 • $12 • (02/28/95) • **79**
Chianti Classico 1991 • $13 • (10/31/93) • **82**
Chianti Classico 1990 • $12 • (09/15/92) • **90**
Chianti Classico 1988 • $9 • (11/30/90) BB • **89**
Chianti Classico 1987 • $9 • (09/15/89) • **88**
Chianti Classico 1986 • $7 • (07/31/88) • **86**
Chianti Classico 1985 • $196 Ⓐ • (05/31/88) BB • **89**
Chianti Classico 1983 • $5 • (12/15/86) BB • **85**
Collezione de Marchi l'Eremo 1990 • $NA • (10/31/93) • **89**
Collezione de Marchi l'Eremo 1988 • $NA • (09/15/91) • **90**
Syrah Tuscany Collezione de Marchi 1994: An excellent Syrah. Wonderfully spicy, with very good structure. Medium- to full-bodied, with berry, spicy and cinnamon flavors, medium tannins and a crisp finish. Drinkable now. 1,000 cases made. • $34 • (09/30/97) • **89**
Syrah Tuscany Collezione de Marchi 1993: Lovely Syrah. Concentrated and smoothly textured, with lovely ripe fruit and berry, cherry and spicy oak character; gushing with aromas and flavors of violet, berries and cherries. Drinkable now. 740 cases made. • $32 • (10/31/96) • **88**

JERMANN

Capo Martino in Ruttaris 1994 • $42 • (06/15/96) • **80**
Chardonnay 1994 • $23 • (06/15/96) • **75**
Chardonnay Where the Dreams Have no End... 1994 • $44 • (06/15/96) • **88**
Moscato Rosa Vigna Bellina 1993: Very delicate, from the salmon color to the rosewater finish, this strawberry-flavored sweet wine would serve

Key: SS—Spectator Selection CS—Cellar Selection HR—Highly Recommended BB—Best Buy $NA—Price not available Ⓐ—Auction Price (BT)—Barrel Tasting
Dates in parentheses indicate the issues in which the ratings were published.

equally well as an apéritif. Try on its own. 400 cases made. • $29 • (01/01/97) • **83**

Moscato Rosa del FVG Vigna Bellina 1989 • $26 • (03/15/91) • **81**

Moscato Rosa del FVG Vigna Bellina 1987 • $20 • (09/15/88) • **85**

Pinot Bianco Venezia Giulia 1996: Some earthy, minerally notes complement the lively structure and apple flavors, along with a hint of carbon dioxide for freshness. Drink now. 160 cases made. • $23 • (06/15/98) • **83**

Pinot Bianco 1994 • $21 • (06/15/96) • **79**

Pinot Bianco 1993 • $20 • (01/31/95) • **89**

Sauvignon Blanc Venezia Giulia 1996: Plenty of zip in this floral-scented Sauvignon, whose flavors lean toward the spicy side, with hints of peach and minerals. Balances subtlety and intensity. Drink now. 100 cases made. • $24 • (06/15/98) • **84**

Sauvignon 1994 • $23 • (06/15/96) • **85**

Sauvignon 1993 • $20 • (01/31/95) • **88**

Traminer Aromatico 1994 • $24 • (06/15/96) • **85**

Venezia Giulia Vinnae da Vinnaioli 1996: Lively, supple and well integrated, showing floral and lemon aromas and flavors, good concentration and length and a rich texture. Well made. Drink through 1999. 150 cases made. • $23 • (06/15/98) • **86**

Vinnae da Vinnaioli 1994 • $21 • (06/15/96) • **79**

Vinnae da Vinnaioli 1993 • $20 • (01/31/95) • **88**

Vintage Tunina 1994 • $35 • (06/15/96) • **84**

Vintage Tunina 1993 • $35 • (06/15/96) • **86**

KEBER, EDI

Merlot Collio Riserva 1995: Lovely and elegant, brimming with vibrant cherry and berry character and accents of vanilla, set off by a firm, balanced structure. The ripe but persistent tannins need either food or time. Best from 1999 through 2004. 600 cases made. • $26 • (05/31/98) • **87**

Merlot Collio Riserva 1993: Lovely, with loads of ripe plum, blackberry and spice flavors. It's full-bodied, rich and luscious, with a lingering finish. A concentrated wine that is ready to drink. • $22 • (03/31/97) • **88**

Pinot Grigio Collio 1996: Floral, talcum powder flavors are allied to a firm structure that ends up slightly astringent. Drink now. 800 cases made. • $23 • (07/31/98) • **77**

KRIS

Chardonnay Alto Adige 1996: A little carbon dioxide keeps this fresh and lively, and there are apple and earth notes, yet the impression is a straightforward one. Drink now. 2,080 cases made. • $9 • (06/15/98) • **79**

KRIZIA

Cabernet Franc Colli Orientali del Friuli 1994: Austere and tough, exhibiting a woody character and only a little black currant and mint. Drink now. • $21 • (04/30/98) • **79**

Pinot Grigio Colli Orientali del Friuli 1995: An attempt at a serious international style, with new oak treatment lending vanilla accents to the simple apple flavors. A bit overdone. • $21 • (11/15/97) • **81**

LAGARIA

Chardonnay Atesino 1996: Offers decent pear flavors with a touch of spice on the finish. Serve well-chilled. • $9 • (10/15/97) • **79**

Merlot Atesino 1996: Kirsch and spice are the dominant themes in this soft, easy-drinking red that lingers pleasantly on the finish. Slightly better than previously reviewed. Drink now. 20,000 cases made. • $8 • (06/15/98) • **82**

Pinot Grigio 1994 • $6 • (06/15/96) • **81**

Pinot Grigio delle Venezie 1996: Soft, with green-peach aromas and flavors. Simple, but satisfying. Drink now. • $9 • (10/15/97) • **82**

LAGEDER, ALOIS

Alto Adige Dornach 1996: An international style, displaying new oak aromas and flavors of vanilla and butter, well matched to the apple and pear in this richly textured white. Firm backbone and some tannins on the lengthy finish, suggest trying with food. Drink now. 550 cases made. • $19 • (06/30/98) • **86**

Alto Adige Tannhammer 1995: Heavily marked by new oak, yet still fresh and lively and exhibiting some ripe fruit on the palate. Difficult to pick up the Sauvignon characteristics, but fans of new oak will love it. 55 percent Chardonnay, 45 percent Sauvignon. Drink now. • $29 • (07/31/98) • **86**

Cabernet Alto Adige Löwengang 1994: Starts off with herbal, berry aromas; deeper plum and vanilla flavors emerge on the palate. Shows good concentration, depth and harmony, and a touch of astringency on the finish. Drink now through 2000. • $32 • (07/31/98) • **87**

Cabernet Riserva Alto Adige/Südtirol 1989 • $15 • (03/31/94) • **80**

Cabernet Sauvignon Alto Adige Cor Römigberg 1994: Gorgeous Cabernet Sauvignon from start to finish. Sweet, ripe cassis and black cherry are accented by toasty, vanilla-laced oak—the deep flavors supported by ample, ripe tannins and an intensity that persists long after the wine is swallowed. Drink now through 2004. 900 cases made. • $45 • (07/31/98) HR • **91**

Cabernet Sauvignon Alto Adige Cor Römigberg 1993: Fresh, deep and concentrated with black currant, spice and coffee aromas and flavors. Really hitting its stride. Well balanced, with firm tannins and a lengthy aftertaste. Drink now through 2002. 500 cases made. • $48 • (06/30/98) HR • **90**

Chardonnay Alto Adige 1994 • $11 • (06/15/96) • **84**

Chardonnay Alto Adige 1993 • $11 • (01/31/95) • **85**

Chardonnay Alto Adige Löwengang 1995: Plenty of spice and apple in this lean, oaky Chardonnay. It has the richness to bind all the elements. Still, it's fresh and tasty. Drink now. • $29 • (07/31/98) • **85**

Chardonnay Alto Adige Löwengang 1994: A spicy white, sporting clove, cinnamon and white pepper notes underscored by pear and fig. Firmly structured (thanks to new oak) and intense. Drink through 1999. 2,700 cases made. • $30 • (07/31/98) • **86**

Chardonnay Alto Adige Löwengang 1993 • $31 • (06/15/96) • **84**

Merlot Alto Adige 1994 • $13 • (06/15/96) • **81**

Merlot Alto Adige/Südtirol 1990 • $13 • (03/31/94) • **82**

Pinot Bianco Alto Adige Haberlehof 1995: A mature white, its broad apple and vanilla flavors moderately concentrated, turning lean and compact on the finish. The lasting impression is lightly tannic. Drink now. 1,100 cases made. • $17 • (06/30/98) • **85**

Pinot Bianco Alto Adige Haberlehof 1994 • $15 • (06/15/96) • **84**

Pinot Bianco Alto Adige 1993 • $10 • (01/31/95) • **78**

Pinot Grigio Alto Adige 1994 • $12 • (06/15/96) • **83**

Pinot Grigio Alto Adige 1993 • $10 • (01/31/95) • **82**

Pinot Grigio Alto Adige Benefizium Porer 1996: Bright and focused, showing concentrated apple, herb and vanilla notes augmented by firm structure and mineral detailing. Clove accentuates the aftertaste. Drink now. 2,750 cases made. • $18 • (07/31/98) • **86**

Pinot Grigio Alto Adige Benefizium Porer 1994 • $15 • (06/15/96) • **86**

Sauvignon Terlaner Alto Adige Lehenhof 1994 • $18 • (06/15/96) • **84**

Sauvignon Terlaner Alto Adige 1993 • $13 • (01/31/95) • **85**

LAMBERTI

Bianco di Custoza Orchidea Platino 1994 • $10 • (05/31/96) • **81**

Amarone Recioto della Valpolicella Corte Rubini 1993: Plenty of tobacco-scented plum flavors on a tight, compact frame that finishes up dry and astringent. Tasted twice with consistent notes. Drink now through 2000. 1,500 cases made. • $23 • (07/31/98) • **84**

Amarone Recioto della Valpolicella Corte Rubini 1990 • $20 • (06/15/96) • **87**

Amarone Recioto della Valpolicella Corte Rubini 1985 • $19 • (09/15/92) • **80**

Valpolicella Vigneti di Ca' Bolcana 1991 • $9 • (09/15/92) • **74**

LAMOLE DI LAMOLE

Chianti Classico 1995: A light and simple Chianti with bright cherry character and a light finish. 12,000 cases made. • $12 • (09/30/97) • **80**

Chianti Classico 1991 • $14 • (10/31/93) • **86**

Chianti Classico 1990 • $12 • (09/15/92) • **73**

Chianti Classico 1988 • $12 • (09/15/91) • **90**

Chianti Classico Affinato in Barriques 1994: Clean and simple, with tasty plum flavors and a soft texture. Drink now. 2,000 cases made. • $15 • (09/30/97) • **82**

Chianti Classico Riserva 1993: Slightly one-dimensional but fresh and fruity with blackberry aromas and flavors. Body is medium, tannins are fine, finish is light. Drink now. 9,000 cases made. • $17 • (09/30/97) • **85**

Chianti Classico Riserva 1988 • $17 • (09/15/92) • **82**

Chianti Classico Riserva di Campolungo 1993: An energetic red with an abundance of berry and blackberry aromas and flavors. Medium-bodied, with fine tannins and a lively, long finish. Delicious. 1,000 cases made. • $27 • (09/30/97) • **87**

Chianti Classico Vigneto di Campolungo 1985 • $20 • (04/30/90) • **90**

LANCIOLA

Chianti Classico Le Masse di Greve 1995: Quite young, with crushed berry and cherry aromas and flavors, a hint of farm yard. Medium-bodied, with slightly mouth-puckering acidity. 700 cases made. • $16 • (09/30/97) • **80**
Chianti Classico Le Masse di Greve 1991: Lots of gamy, stewed flavors which give good richness, but it lacks freshness and fruit flavors. • $16 • (03/31/97) • **79**
Chianti Classico Le Masse di Greve Riserva 1994: Intense aromas of blackberries and wet earth. Medium in body, with firm tannins and a long, velvety finish. Try now. 700 cases made. • $20 • (09/30/97) • **87**
Chianti Classico Le Masse di Greve Riserva 1993: Simple and slightly traditional, with leather and chestnut aromas and flavors and a light finish. Slightly tired. 550 cases made. • $20 • (09/30/97) • **81**
Chianti Colli Fiorentini 1995: Fairly generous, with plum, berry and cherry aromas and flavors. Medium-bodied, with light tannins and a round texture. 2,200 cases made. • $11 • (09/30/97) • **84**
Chianti Colli Fiorentini 1993: Good, if not complex, with plum and berry flavors and aromas. Finishes on a spicy note. • $11 • (03/31/97) • **82**
Chianti Colli Fiorentini Riserva 1994: Offers bright cherry and floral aromas, with similar flavors and a hint of oak on the finish. Medium- to full-bodied. A touch dry. Try now. 700 cases made. • $15 • (09/30/97) • **85**

LATINI, IL

Red Tuscany 1994: Some berry and cherry flavors come through but it's slightly austere and dry. Medium-bodied, with light tannis and light finish. Drink now. • $20 • (09/30/97) • **81**
Premium Red Tuscany 1994: Delivers a good amount of blackberry and black currant bush aromas and flavors. It's medium-bodied, with medium tannins and finish. Try now. • $NA • (09/30/97) • **87**

LECCIA, CASTELLO LA

Chianti Classico 1991 • $10 • (02/28/95) • **86**
Chianti Classico 1990 • $NA • (09/15/92) • **88**

LECCIAIA, LE

Brunello di Montalcino 1988 • $NA • (04/30/94) • **80**
Rosso di Montalcino 1991 • $NA • (04/30/94) • **78**

LENTO, CANTINE

Greco di Bianco 1996: Seductive and rich with delicious flavors of apple, butterscotch and vanilla. A bit chalky on the finish, but overall this a hearty and distinctive white wine. Try it if you're tired of Chardonnay. • $14 • (10/15/97) • **87**

LEONARDINI

Cabernet Sauvignon 1995: Lean and firm in texture, with modest flavors of cherry and mint, dove-tailing into a slightly astringent finish. Drinkable now with light food. • $8 • (01/01/97) • **82**
Cabernet Sauvignon Veneto 1991 • $6 • (11/15/94) • **78**
Merlot Piave 1995: Tastes a little green, with herbal and plum flavors. Medium-bodied, with a spice note on the finish. • $8 • (01/31/97) • **81**
Merlot Veneto 1991 • $6 • (11/15/94) • **74**
Montepulciano d'Abruzzo 1991 • $5 • (03/31/95) • **73**
Valpolicella 1990 • $5 • (04/30/92) BB • **81**

LEONARDO DA VINCI

Brunello di Montalcino 1991: Nicely crafted in a traditional style, this firmly tannic Brunello is spicy, cedary and cherrylike in flavor. Try now. 1,500 cases made. • $35 • (05/31/97) • **87**
Chianti 1995: Fresh, simple and fruity with decent berry and cherry flavors and a nice touch of smoke on the finish. Drinkable now. 25,000 cases made. • $6 • (03/31/97) • **80**

Key: SS—Spectator Selection CS—Cellar Selection HR—Highly Recommended BB—Best Buy $NA—Price not available Ⓐ—Auction Price (BT)—Barrel Tasting
Dates in parentheses indicate the issues in which the ratings were published.

Chianti Classico 1994: Robust, with roasted flavors and aromas. Good plum and black cherry flavors, but also a slightly bitter note that intensifies on the finish. 12,000 cases made. • $8 • (03/31/97) • **79**
Chianti Classico Riserva 1991: Interesting aromas of mushrooms and truffles, followed by dried cherry, herb and spice flavors. Mature, though still tannic, with a menthol-like note on the finish. 2,000 cases made. • $11 • (03/31/97) • **84**
Rosso di Montalcino 1994: On the light side, with jammy, fresh flavors and light tannins, this is ready to drink, like Beaujolais. 4,000 cases made. • $13 • (05/31/97) • **85**

LEONE DE CASTRIS

Copertino 1996: An agreeably mature character marks this medium-bodied, lightly tannic red. Earthy, spicy aromas and crisp fruit flavors keep it interesting. Drink now. 2,500 cases made. • $8 • (01/01/98) • **83**
Locorotondo White 1996: Looks and tastes a bit tired. Has a deep-gold color and earthy, nutty flavors. Drink now. 3,400 cases made. • $7 • (05/15/98) • **78**
Salice Salentino Maiana 1995: Hearty and full-bodied, packed with satisfying plummy, spicy flavors on a smooth, moderately tannic frame. Drink now through 2000. 2,500 cases made. • $8 • (01/01/98) • **85**
Salice Salentino Riserva 1994: Nicely balanced and focused, this is a very flavorful and smooth red wine that features bright berry flavors and spicy undertones, with a firm backbone of tannin and acidity. Drink now through 2001. 3,000 cases made. • $12 • (01/01/98) • **86**

LIBRANDI

Val di Neto Gravello 1989 • $20 • (05/31/95) • **87**

LILLIANO, CASTELLO DI

Anagallis 1994: A pretty, silky, medium bodied wine with plum, berry and mushroom aromas and flavors, silky tannins and a long finish. Delicious now. • $28 • (09/30/97) • **87**
Anagallis 1993: Alluring aromas of mint, violet and berries. Medium-bodied, this has well-integrated tannins and a fruity, delicate finish. Drink now. A blend of Sangiovese and Colorino. 1,460 cases made. • $28 • (10/31/96) • **87**
Anagallis 1990 • $25 • (02/28/95) • **88**
Anagallis 1987 • $25 • (12/15/92) • **85**
Anagallis 1985 • $34 • (03/31/90) • **86**
Chianti Classico 1995: Chewy for a Chianti, with plenty of ripe berry character. Medium-bodied, with medium tannins and a fresh finish. Drink now. • $11 • (09/30/97) • **87**
Chianti Classico 1994: Wonderful ripe fruit in this wine—raspberry, cherry and berry aromas and flavors and a hint of flowers. Medium-bodied, with soft tannins and a crisp, refreshing finish. 20,000 cases made. • $10 • (10/31/96) • **86**
Chianti Classico 1993 • $NA • (10/31/95) • **87**
Chianti Classico 1990 • $11 • (09/15/92) • **89**
Chianti Classico 1988 • $10 • (11/30/90) • **81**
Chianti Classico 1987 • $8 • (11/30/89) • **86**
Chianti Classico 1986 • $7 • (05/15/89) • **70**
Chianti Classico 1985 • $6 • (10/31/87) • **74**
Chianti Classico Riserva 1994: Interesting aromas of berries and mushrooms follow through on the palate. Medium-bodied, with medium, silky tannins and a medium finish. From a solid winery. Try now. • $25 • (09/30/97) • **88**
Chianti Classico Riserva 1993: A complex wine with aromas of berries, earth and fungi. Medium-bodied with gentle tannins and long, flavorful finish. A satisfying glass of wine. 1,875 cases made. • $24 • (10/31/96) • **88**
Chianti Classico Riserva 1990 • $22 • (02/28/95) • **86**
Chianti Classico Riserva 1988 • $NA • (09/15/92) • **89**
Chianti Classico Riserva 1985 • $14 • (11/30/89) • **89**

LISINI

Brunello di Montalcino 1991: Vivid and fresh, medium-bodied, with fairly chunky, ripe fruit flavors and notes of mint. Silky finish. Drink now or hold. 2,916 cases made. • $41 • (11/30/96) • **88**
Brunello di Montalcino 1988 • $36 • (04/30/94) • **80**
Brunello di Montalcino 1985 • $33 • (08/31/91) • **81**
Brunello di Montalcino 1983 • $22 • (07/31/89) • **73**
Brunello di Montalcino 1982 • $25 • (01/31/89) • **84**

Brunello di Montalcino 1975 • $30 • (09/15/86) • **78**

Brunello di Montalcino Riserva 1988 • $NA • (10/31/94) • **86**

Brunello di Montalcino Ugolaia 1991: Impressive for the vintage, this is juicy and velvety with an abundance of red- and black cherry aromas and flavors. Medium- to full-bodied, with a fruity finish. • $105 • (09/30/97) • **89**

Brunello di Montalcino Ugolaia 1990: A big and muscular wine with plenty of berry, cherry, mineral character and just the right amount of new wood as an accent. Full-bodied, with full tannins and a fresh finish. Better in 1999. 833 cases made. • $99 • (11/30/96) • **90**

Rosso di Montalcino 1995: Complex for a Rosso, with flavors of berry, notes of white pepper. Medium- to full-bodied, with firm tannins and a long, fresh berry finish. Drink now or hold. 1,500 cases made. • $23 • (09/30/97) • **87**

Rosso di Montalcino 1994: This is well made and fresh, with berry and licorice notes on the nose and palate, and fine, light tannins. Drink now. 1,000 cases made. • $15 • (11/30/96) • **85**

Rosso di Montalcino 1988 • $14 • (04/30/91) • **79**

LIVON

Chardonnay Collio Tre Clas 1995: Extremely minerally, like a Riesling from Alsace, this is lean and racy, full of floral, apple and almond character, followed by a vanilla-custard note. Should pair well with food. Drink now through 2000. • $20 • (05/31/98) • **87**

Pinot Grigio Collio Braide Grande 1995: A mature Pinot Grigio, showing lovely almond and vanilla character that combines with the rich palate, and a slightly astringent sensation on the lingering finish. Drink now. 1,500 cases made. • $20 • (05/31/98) • **85**

Refosco Colli Orientali del Friuli dal Peduncolo Rosso Riul 1988 • $11 • (01/31/92) • **79**

Schioppettino 1988 • $13 • (01/31/92) • **86**

Schioppettino 1987 • $18 • (04/15/90) • **81**

Tiareblù 1991: New oak sets the scene, with aromas of vanilla and butterscotch. Stiff tannins on the finish. Good depth to the black cherry and herbal notes, and it's lively and fresh, but the wood is strong. A blend of 50 percent Merlot, 35 percent Cabernet Sauvignon and 15 percent Cabernet Franc. Drink now through 2000. 300 cases made. • $35 • (05/31/98) • **84**

Tocai Friulano Collio 1996: A distinct minty character marks this crisp, light-bodied Tocai, as does a nervy intensity. Great apéritif. Drink now. • $13 • (06/15/98) • **84**

LOGGIA, FATTORIA LA

Chianti Classico Riserva 1990 • $17 • (02/28/95) • **85**

Nearco 1990 • $NA • (10/31/93) • **85**

LOMBARDO, ANTONINO

Chianti Colli Senesi 1996: A good, grapey red with watermelon and berry flavors, a medium to light body, light tannins and a fresh finish. Drink now. 5,000 cases made. • $11 • (09/30/97) • **82**

Rosso di Montepulciano 1996: A bit rustic, but shows a lot of obvious berry and green stemmy character. Medium-bodied, with light tannins and a crisp finish. Drink now. 830 cases made. • $13 • (09/30/97) • **83**

Vino Nobile di Montepulciano 1994: Attractive aromas of cherry, dried cherry and violets precede flavors of mineral, spice and a hint of oak. Silky finish. Medium body. Try now. 3,300 cases made. • $20 • (09/30/97) • **87**

Vino Nobile di Montepulciano Riserva 1993: Aromatic, with a blackberry character through and through. Medium in body, with medium to light tannins and a light finish. Drink now. 660 cases made. • $23 • (09/30/97) • **84**

LOSI, PAOLO & PIETRO

Chianti Classico Querciavalle 1990 • $10 • (07/31/94) • **85**

LUCE

Luce della Vite 1994: Deeply colored, emitting lovely blackberry, plum and spice aromas. Of medium body, very velvety, with lots of oak and a long and delicious finish. A serious debut wine. Drink now. • $55 • (09/30/97) • **89**

Luce della Vite 1993: Big and rich, concentrated and powerful, with masses of tobacco, berry and chocolate flavors and aromas. Full-bodied and very tannic with a tough finish. Built to age; it needs time. Try after 2000. • $55 • (09/30/97) • **90**

LUCIA, GALASSO

Don Giovanni di Giovanni Crosato Il Bianco 1994 • $25 • (06/15/96) • **77**

Don Giovanni di Giovanni Crosato Il Rosso 1994 • $25 • (05/31/96) • **85**

LUCIANI

Brunello di Montalcino 1991: A wonderfully warm and friendly wine with light, soft tannins and fresh fruit flavors that pick up a dried fruit note on the finish. Medium-bodied. Drinkable now. 416 cases made. • $39 • (11/30/96) • **86**

Brunello di Montalcino Riserva 1990: Ripe and powerful, yet reserved and impressive. It's full-bodied, with silky tannins and a minty, fruity, fresh finish. Better in 1999. 83 cases made. • $50 • (11/30/96) • **90**

LUNGAROTTI

Cabernet Sauvignon Lombardy 1983 • $18 • (05/15/91) • **85**

Cabernet Sauvignon Umbria 1979 • $11 • (02/15/87) • **79**

Chardonnay Torgiano I Palazzi 1994: Crisp and tangy. On the austere side, but quite refreshing. Interesting for its tightly focused lemon and grapefruit flavors. Drink through 1999. • $17 • (04/30/97) • **85**

Chardonnay Umbria 1995: A resinous wine, with pine and apple flavors. Simple, with spice notes on the finish. 25,000 cases made. • $12 • (01/31/97) • **80**

Chardonnay Umbria 1994 • $11 • (02/29/96) • **79**

Pinot Grigio Bianco dell'Umbria 1996: A simple, clean white wine that will wash down a meal, but little more. 12,000 cases made. • $12 • (08/31/97) • **78**

Pinot Grigio Umbria 1995: A ripe style, with pear and fig flavors. Well balanced, with a crisp finish that shows some nice notes of almonds and herbs. 8,000 cases made. • $11 • (01/31/97) • **84**

Pinot Grigio Umbria 1994: Lemony acidity and toasty flavors highlight this relatively neutral wine. It's quite crisp and firm. 8,000 cases made. • $13 • (08/31/96) • **82**

Pinot Grigio Umbria 1993 • $10 • (05/31/95) BB • **87**

San Giorgio 1986: Mature but still feisty. Tannic and full-bodied, with a stiff texture and nicely developed flavors of spice, fruit and meat. 4,000 cases made. • $30 • (04/30/97) • **86**

San Giorgio 1985 • $30 • (05/31/95) • **85**

San Giorgio 1982 • $34 • (07/15/91) • **77**

San Giorgio 1979 • $18 • (03/15/87) • **75**

San Giorgio 1978 • $19 • (04/16/85) • **84**

Sangiovese Umbria 1995: Young, vibrant and crisp-tasting, with flavors of plum and smoke, light tannins and medium body. Drink now, while it's fresh. • $8 • (04/30/97) • **84**

Torgiano Rubesco 1993: Soft and tasty. Cherry, berry and spicy flavors in a light, silky texture with just enough grip for food. Drinkable now. 80,000 cases made. • $11 • (08/31/96) • **84**

Torgiano Rubesco 1988 • $13 • (09/15/92) • **83**

Torgiano Rubesco 1987 • $11 • (05/15/91) • **83**

Torgiano Rubesco 1985 • $11 • (09/15/89) • **74**

Torgiano Rubesco 1979 • $8 • (01/01/86) • **77**

Torgiano Rubesco Monticchio Riserva 1982 • $25 • (09/15/92) • **71**

Torgiano Rubesco Monticchio Riserva 1980 • $27 • (07/15/91) • **84**

Torgiano Rubesco Monticchio Riserva 1978 • $23 • (09/15/89) • **82**

Torre di Giano Bianco di Torgiano 1995: Lean and crisp, its tart lemon and green apple flavors kept lively by a hint of spritz. Simple, but clean and refreshing. • $NA • (08/31/96) • **82**

Torre di Giano Bianco di Torgiano 1993 • $9 • (05/31/95) • **84**

Torre di Giano Red 1989 • $11 • (07/15/91) • **83**

Torre di Giano Torgiano White 1996: Tropical, passion fruit aromas combine with a hint of spritz in this fresh, lively and simple white. Try as an apéritif. 100,000 cases made. • $11 • (08/31/97) • **79**

Torgiano Vino Santo 1991: Silky and medium-sweet with appealing vivacity. Brown color reflects the honey, toffee and orange-peel flavors. Drink it well-chilled after supper. 10,000 cases made. • $13 • (08/31/96) • **88**

Torgiano Vino Santo 1985 • $7/375ml • (03/15/91) • **79**

Torgiano Vino Santo 1983 • $10 • (03/15/89) • **81**

Torgiano Vino Santo 1988 • $15 • (07/31/93) • **84**

MACCHIOLE, LE

Paleo 1993: Very green pepperlike aromas, with a hint of berries. Medium-bodied, with vanilla and spice notes and an herbal finish. A bit too herbal. Drink now. • $30 • (10/31/96) • **81**

MACHIAVELLI, ANTICA FATTORIA

Chianti Classico 1994: A very crisp Chianti, this has light body, light tannins and a refreshing finish. Vivid cherry and floral aromas and flavors. Delicious. • $NA • (10/31/96) • **82**
Chianti Classico Riserva 1986 • $16 • (10/31/91) • **84**
Chianti Classico Vigna di Fontalle Riserva 1993: A lively, medium-bodied Chianti. Offering lovely blackberry and cherry aromas and flavors, light tannins and a zingy finish. • $15 • (10/31/96) • **85**
Chianti Classico Vigna di Fontalle Riserva 1990 • $NA • (02/28/95) • **84**
Chianti Classico Vigna di Fontalle Riserva 1988 • $21 • (10/31/93) • **87**
Chianti Classico Vigna di Fontalle Riserva 1985 • $NA • (09/15/91) • **91**
Podere Solatio del Tani 1993: Loads of ripe berry, cherry and spice aromas and flavors. Medium-bodied, with rounded tannins and a gamy, earthy, succulent finish. Drink now or hold. Cabernet Sauvignon. • $NA • (10/31/96) • **85**

MACIOCHE, LE

Brunello di Montalcino 1992: A light Brunello with perfumed floral aromas and flavors and high acidity. Medium-bodied, with light tannins, and a crisp finish. Drink now. • $35 • (09/30/97) • **82**
Brunello di Montalcino 1991: A serious wine for the vintage, showing plenty of fruit flavor complemented by a skillful use of new wood. Medium-bodied, and the finish is long. Better in 1999. • $32 • (11/30/96) • **87**
Rosso di Montalcino 1995: Bitter, with a burnt rubber character. Something went wrong. Tasted twice with consistent notes. • $18 • (09/30/97) • **68**
Rosso di Montalcino 1994: Emits intense aromas of raspberries, which follow through onto the palate. Medium-bodied, with light tannins and a rich, fruity finish. An unctuous wine from a new name. • $17 • (11/30/96) • **86**

MACULAN

Breganze Brentino 1995: Reminiscent of a Bordeaux blend, with cedar and black currant, and a mushroom note indicating maturity. Smooth and balanced, it turns slightly astringent on the finish, with a lingering vanilla note. Contains 85 percent Merlot. Drink now through 1999. 2,950 cases made. • $14 • (06/15/98) • **85**
Breganze Brentino 1994: A somewhat mature red wine. Round, with roasted flavors of plum and cedar, integrated tannins and modest length. • $13 • (06/15/97) • **82**
Breganze Brentino 1990 • $12 • (09/15/92) • **79**
Breganze Brentino 1986 • $9 • (03/31/89) • **85**
Breganze di Breganze 1996: A combination of almond, straw and earth notes. Moderate richness and citrusy acidity make this an easy-drinking white. Drink now. 12,500 cases made. • $14 • (06/30/98) • **83**
Breganze di Breganze 1995: Broad, round and applelike, with its richness kept in check by a lemony finish with a hint of almond. • $13 • (06/15/97) • **83**
Breganze di Breganze Bianco 1993 • $5 • (01/31/95) • **79**
Cabernet Fratta Breganze 1990 • $39 • (09/15/92) • **92**
Cabernet Fratta Breganze 1986 • $29 • (03/31/89) • **92**
Cabernet Sauvignon Palazzotto Breganze 1990 • $24 • (09/15/92) • **77**
Cabernet Sauvignon Palazzotto 1987 • $30 • (01/31/92) • **82**
Cabernet Sauvignon Palazzotto 1986 • $19 • (03/31/89) • **71**
Cabernet Sauvignon Veneto 1994: A deeply colored, sophisticated red, full of character from the herb, cherry and vanilla notes, with concentration, balance and an elegant framework. There are still some solid tannins, so enjoy with food. Drink now through 2002. 2,500 cases made. • $20 • (06/15/98) • **88**
Cabernet Sauvignon Veneto 1993: There's a leafy, Cabernet character in this medium-bodied red, that shows black currant and herbal flavors and a hint of tannins. • $NA • (01/01/97) • **84**

Key: SS—Spectator Selection CS—Cellar Selection HR—Highly Recommended BB—Best Buy $NA—Price not available Ⓐ—Auction Price (BT)—Barrel Tasting
Dates in parentheses indicate the issues in which the ratings were published.

Cabernet Sauvignon Veneto Ferrata 1994: Light floral and plum aromas, with hints of cut wood and a slightly stemmy undertone. Medium-bodied, with very firm tannins and a short finish. A bit tough and dry. • $NA • (01/01/97) • **83**
Chardonnay Veneto Riale 1994: Nutmeg and smoke accents from new-oak work well with fig and apple flavors to provide depth and interest. The tannins should soften with food. • $22 • (06/15/97) • **87**
Dindarello 1993 • $14 • (01/31/95) • **87**
Dindarello 1991 • $28 • (09/15/92) • **84**
Dindarello 1989 • $24 • (07/15/91) • **84**
Merlot Breganze Marchesante 1995: A deeply-colored, polished red. Cherry, cedar, clove and vanilla aromas and flavors have depth and concentration, along with some solid tannins. Match with roasts or grilled meats. Drink now through 2000. 1,000 cases made. • $26 • (06/15/98) • **87**
Merlot Breganze Marchesante 1994: A well-crafted red. Light aromas of plum and milk chocolate open to a medium-bodied palate with medium soft tannins and a fresh finish. • $NA • (01/01/97) • **86**
Torcolato Breganze 1995: Brilliant Italian dessert wine, like a light-bodied Sauternes, full of botrytis and tropical fruit, vanilla and other spices. The acidity is moderately high, keeping it all vibrant, but it still needs time to integrate. Lovely concentration and expression, followed by a honeyed finish. Best from 2000 through 2005. 1,290 cases made. • $46 • (06/30/98) HR • **91**
Torcolato Breganze 1994: An elegant dessert wine sporting apricot, caramel and orange flavors. Balanced and fresh without being too sweet. • $47 • (06/16/97) • **85**
Torcolato 1990 • $19 • (01/31/95) HR • **92**
Torcolato 1988 • $35 • (04/15/91) • **91**
Torcolato 1985 • $15/375ml • (03/31/89) • **84**
Torcolato 1983 • $29 • (11/15/87) • **82**

MALPAGA

Chardonnay Trentino 1994 • $10 • (06/15/96) • **83**
Pinot Grigio Trentino 1994 • $10 • (06/15/96) • **84**

MANORA

Collezione 1994: Polished and fairly well-made in terms of texture, but the flavors are raisiny and the finish turns astringent. Disappointing. 700 cases made. • $24 • (10/31/97) • **76**
Paloalto 1994: Pleasant, balanced and smooth. Straightforward cranberry, raspberry and cherry flavors give it a kick of fresh acidity. Nicely integrated tannins make it drinkable now through 2002. A blend of Pinot Noir, Merlot, Cabernet and Barbera. 230 cases made. • $38 • (10/31/97) • **85**

MANZANO, FATTORIA DI

Podere Fontarca 1996: An enticing, exciting white offering subtle peaches-and-cream aromas, with a hint of lemons and similar flavors. Medium-bodied. Fresh and flavorful finish. 2,100 cases made. • $NA • (09/30/97) • **89**
Podere Il Bosco 1995: An amazing, stylish Syrah. The best in Italy at the moment. It's inky-colored, with intense aromas of cracked black pepper and fruit. Full-bodied, with full tannins and a long, long finish. Needs time in the bottle. Better after 1999. • $NA • (09/30/97) • **92**
Podere Il Bosco 1994: A nearly outstanding wine, from one of the hottest names in Syrah in Italy. Not as great as the '93, but wonderful. An exciting, modern wine with amazing aromas of crushed black pepper and raspberries. Medium-bodied with fine tannins. 700 cases made. • $32 • (10/31/96) • **89**
Podere Il Vescovo 1996: Medium- to light-bodied with berry and cherry flavors and a light, crisp finish. Similar to a good Beaujolais. 1,700 cases made. • $NA • (09/30/97) • **84**
Vigna del Bosco 1992 • $NA • (10/31/95) • **90**

MANZONE, GIOVANNI

Barbera d'Alba La Gramolere 1990 • $18 • (11/15/93) • **90**
Barolo La Gramolere 1991 • $28 • (10/31/95) • **82**
Barolo La Gramolere 1990 • $35 • (10/31/94) • **86**
Barolo La Gramolere 1989 • $35 • (10/31/93) • **89**
Barolo La Gramolere 1988 • $35 • (10/31/93) • **85**
Barolo La Gramolere 1993: Very elegant Barolo offering fresh, clean fruit flavors, floral notes, medium body, and smooth tannins. The pretty accents of cassis, tar and smoke make it delicious to drink now through 2002. Shows lots of finesse on the finish. • $33 • (10/31/97) • **88**

Dolcetto d'Alba La Gramolere 1990 • $14 • (03/31/93) • **76**

MARAI, FOSS

Cabernet Piave 1990 • $8 • (01/31/92) • **76**
Cabernet Sauvignon Piave Nono Gío 1992 • $38 • (06/15/96) BB • **82**
Prosecco di Valdobbiadene 1989 • $7 • (12/31/90) • **78**
Prosecco di Valdobbiadene 1986 • $7 • (12/31/88) BB • **83**

MARCA, LA

Cabernet Sauvignon Piave 1994: Pleasant, with cherry notes and a touch of herbs. Light in texture and body, with a hint of tannin on the crisp finish. Drink now. 70,000 cases made. • $6 • (06/15/98) • **83**
Cabernet Sauvignon Piave 1993 • $6 • (05/31/96) BB • **83**
Chardonnay Piave 1996: A basic white that shows a hint of apple flavor. Correct but simple. Drink now. 70,000 cases made. • $6 • (05/31/98) • **76**
Chardonnay Piave 1994 • $6 • (06/15/96) • **78**
Merlot Piave 1995: A simple, barely vinous red without much fruit flavor. Drink now. 70,000 cases made. • $6 • (05/31/98) • **76**
Merlot Piave 1993 • $6 • (06/15/96) • **78**
Merlot Piave Novello del Veneto 1995 • $6 • (02/29/96) • **80**
Merlot Piave Novello del Veneto 1994 • $6 • (01/31/96) • **83**
Pinot Grigio Veneto 1996: Simple and easygoing. Starts off with a nice peach aroma and flavor, but dissipates quickly. Drink now. 70,000 cases made. • $6 • (05/31/98) • **79**
Pinot Grigio Veneto 1994 • $6 • (06/15/96) • **80**

MARCARINI

Barbaresco Campo Quadro 1989 • $NA • (10/31/94) • **85**
Barbera d'Alba Ciabot Camerano 1988 • $18 • (03/15/91) • **90**
Barolo Brunate 1993: Sweet-tasting and pleasant, a medium-bodied, supple red with soft tannins and some licorice, cherry and raspberry flavors. Drink now, slightly chilled. 2,250 cases made. • $41 • (10/31/97) • **85**
Barolo Brunate 1992: Light for a Barolo, with tomatolike flavors and cedary, earthy accents. Tight and firm in texture. Try now. • $27 • (10/31/96) • **78**
Barolo Brunate 1991 • $26 • (10/31/95) • **77**
Barolo Brunate 1990 • $26 • (10/31/94) • **91**
Barolo Brunate 1989 • $25 • (10/31/93) • **91**
Barolo Brunate 1988 • $27 • (10/31/93) • **85**
Barolo Brunate 1985 • $35 • (03/31/90) • **90**
Barolo Brunate 1983 • $23 • (09/15/88) • **89**
Barolo Brunate 1982 • $18 • (09/15/88) • **90**
Barolo Brunate 1979 • $NA • (09/15/88) • **88**
Barolo Brunate 1978 • $NA • (09/15/88) • **80**
Barolo Brunate 1971 • $NA • (09/15/88) • **89**
Barolo Brunate 1964 • $100 • (09/15/88) • **96**
Barolo La Serra 1993: Clean and pure, with lovely, complex accents of earth, spice, bark and wood. Medium-bodied, it's more traditional than modern in style, with firm tannins that need until 1999 to soften. 1,000 cases made. • $41 • (10/31/97) • **86**
Barolo La Serra 1992: Modest fruit flavors against tough tannins make this a bit hollow on the midpalate. • $27 • (10/31/96) • **76**
Barolo La Serra 1991 • $26 • (10/31/95) • **77**
Barolo La Serra 1990 • $26 • (10/31/94) • **88**
Barolo La Serra 1988 • $27 • (10/31/93) • **77**
Barolo La Serra 1983 • $17 • (09/15/88) • **87**
Barolo La Serra 1982 • $18 • (09/15/88) • **91**
Barolo La Serra 1980 • $9 • (04/16/86) • **89**
Barolo La Serra 1978 • $18 • (09/16/84) • **79**
Dolcetto d'Alba Boschi di Berri 1989 • $23 • (04/30/91) • **89**
Dolcetto d'Alba Boschi di Berri 1988 • $17 • (03/31/90) • **86**
Dolcetto d'Alba Boschi di Berri 1987 • $13 • (03/15/89) • **89**
Dolcetto d'Alba Fontanazza 1996: An interesting, concentrated red that's harmonious and balanced. Has nice cherry flavors, smoky bacon notes and a complex, earthy character. Full-bodied and ripe, with a fresh, clean finish. Try around 2000. 2,500 cases made. • $13 • (10/31/97) • **89**
Dolcetto d'Alba Fontanazza 1995: Quite fresh and fruity, but tastes odd due to an ashy, earthy accent. Medium-bodied, but a bit short. • $13 • (10/31/96) • **75**
Dolcetto d'Alba Fontanazza 1991 • $12 • (07/31/95) • **84**
Dolcetto d'Alba Fontanazza 1990 • $13 • (10/31/92) • **85**
Dolcetto d'Alba Fontanazza 1989 • $13 • (04/30/91) • **84**
Dolcetto d'Alba Fontanazza 1988 • $11 • (03/31/90) • **87**
Dolcetto d'Alba Fontanazza 1987 • $9 • (03/15/89) • **78**
Dolcetto d'Alba Fontanazza 1985 • $7 • (02/15/87) • **82**
Nebbiolo delle Langhe 1988 • $10 • (03/31/90) • **84**
Nebbiolo delle Langhe Lasarin 1989 • $9 • (04/30/91) • **84**

MAREGA

Holbar Red 1993: Wow. Packed with sweet, ripe plum and raspberry flavors accented by a mature tobacco note, this red is concentrated, suave and complex. The tannins are still pretty stiff, but there's plenty of ripe fruit to balance them. Well done. A blend of 80 percent Merlot, 15 percent Cabernet and 5 percent Gamay. Drink now through 2002. 300 cases made. • $25 • (05/31/98) • **88**
Holbar Red 1991 • $22 • (04/30/96) • **85**
Pinot Bianco Collio 1996: There's a broad, waxy quality to this white, which combined with the apple and lemon flavors, rich texture and crisp finish, makes an appealing package. Drink now. 3,500 cases made. • $14 • (06/15/98) • **84**
Pinot Grigio Collio 1996: Distinctive aromas of almond, chamomile and honeysuckle segue into honey and beeswax flavors in this rich, yet subtly-nuanced wine. It's about as full-bodied as Pinot Grigio from Friuli can get, while remaining lively and focused. Drink through 1999. 2,500 cases made. • $14 • (05/31/98) • **87**
Pinot Grigio 1993 • $15 • (04/30/96) • **86**
Tocai Friulano Collio 1996: An herbal component in this white complements the apple flavors as a shiso leaf does sashimi. Solid, showing bright structure and moderate intensity. Drink now. 3,000 cases made. • $14 • (06/15/98) • **83**

MARENGO-MARENDA, PODERI E

Dolcetto d'Alba Le Terre Forti 1992 • $11 • (12/15/94) • **82**
Dolcetto d'Alba Le Terre Forti 1990 • $12 • (01/31/92) • **84**

MARLUNGHE

Colli Euganei Bianco 1994 • $10 • (06/30/96) • **79**
Fior d'Arancio Colli Euganei 1994 • $14 • (06/15/96) • **80**
Merlot Colli Euganei 1994 • $11 • (05/31/96) • **84**

MARRONETO, IL

Brunello di Montalcino 1988 • $NA • (04/30/94) • **80**

MARTINENGO

Barbera d'Asti 1991 • $11 • (07/31/95) • **84**

MARTINENGO, RINO

Barbera d'Asti 1991 • $12 • (06/15/94) • **87**
Barbera d'Asti Bricco del Donnaiolo 1991 • $35 • (06/15/94) • **88**

MARTINETTI, FRANCO

Barbera d'Asti Superiore Montruc 1994: From an up-and-coming Piedmont producer comes this ripe, sweet, crowd pleaser. Impressively fresh, grapey and youthful, with some spritziness. A fun, light-bodied, deep-colored, flavorful and fruity wine to drink upon release with pizza, pasta and grilled food. • $NA • (10/31/96) • **85**

MARTINI DI CIGALA

Chianti Classico San Giusto a Rentennano 1995: Rich and round, with berry and milk chocolate aromas and flavors, delicious on the finish. Medium-bodied. Drink now. • $NA • (09/30/97) • **86**
Chianti Classico San Giusto a Rentennano 1991 • $NA • (10/31/93) • **77**
Chianti Classico San Giusto a Rentennano 1990 • $16 • (10/31/93) • **85**
Chianti Classico San Giusto a Rentennano 1987 • $9 • (03/31/90) • **74**
Chianti Classico San Giusto a Rentennano 1986 • $8 • (01/31/89) • **79**
Chianti Classico San Giusto a Rentennano 1985 • $8 • (11/30/87) • **87**
Chianti Classico San Giusto a Rentennano 1983 • $6 • (09/15/87) • **80**
Chianti Classico San Guisto a Rentennano Riserva 1994: Lovely for its cherry, plum and floral aromas and flavors. Medium-bodied, with firm tannins and silky texture. Drink now or hold. • $NA • (09/30/97) • **87**

Chianti Classico San Giusto a Rentennano Riserva 1988 • $23 • (09/15/92) • **84**
Chianti Classico San Giusto a Rentennano Riserva 1985 • $17 • (11/30/89) • **91**
Chianti Classico San Giusto a Rentennano Riserva 1983 • $11 • (11/15/87) • **87**
Percarlo San Giusto a Rentennano 1993: A well-structured wine. Dark-colored, intense in aroma and flavor with its dried fruit, plum and raspberry character. Full-bodied with full tannins, but slightly dry on the finish. Drink now. • $NA • (09/30/97) • **88**
Percarlo San Giusto a Rentennano 1990 • $37 • (10/31/93) • **87**
Percarlo San Giusto a Rentennano 1989 • $21 • (10/31/93) • **81**
Percarlo San Giusto a Rentennano 1986 • $24 • (11/30/89) • **88**
Percarlo San Giusto a Rentennano 1985 • $25 • (02/15/89) • **92**
Percarlo San Giusto a Rentennano 1983 • $13 • (09/15/87) • **77**
Vin Santo San Giusto a Rentennano 1982 • $18/375ml • (12/31/88) • **96**
Vin Santo San Giusto a Rentennano 1981 • $25 • (12/31/87) • **89**

MARWOOD

Brut NV: Generous flavors and a lush texture make this nearly dry bubbly a pleasure to drink. Fresh citrus, spice and toast notes keep it interesting. Ready now. • $9 • (05/15/98) • **85**
Trentino Dolce Select NV: Quite sweet, appealing but simple in flavor, like spumoni in a bottle. Drink now. • $9 • (07/31/98) • **78**

MASCARELLO, BARTOLO

Barbera d'Alba 1993 • $10 • (10/31/95) • **81**
Barolo 1991 • $45 • (10/31/95) • **83**
Barolo 1989 • $NA • (10/31/94) • **76**
Barolo 1988 • $35 • (10/31/93) • **87**
Barolo 1983 • $27 • (05/31/88) • **88**
Dolcetto d'Alba 1993 • $10 • (10/31/95) • **81**

MASCARELLO & FIGLIO, GIUSEPPE

Barbaresco Marcarini 1988 • $32 • (10/31/93) HR • **94**
Barbaresco Marcarini 1985 • $30 • (08/31/89) • **85**
Barbera d'Alba Fasana 1987 • $10 • (03/15/91) • **80**
Barbera d'Alba Fasana 1985 • $9 • (11/30/87) • **85**
Barbera d'Alba Superiore Ginestra 1987 • $11 • (03/15/91) • **85**
Barbera d'Alba Superiore Santo Stefano di Perno 1987 • $13 • (09/15/90) • **83**
Barolo 1982 • $28 • (06/30/87) • **81**
Barolo 1978 • $19 • (09/16/84) • **91**
Barolo Belvedere 1985 • $35 • (06/15/90) CS • **93**
Barolo Bricco 1988 • $38 • (10/31/93) • **84**
Barolo Bricco Castiglione Falleto 1991: Tastes a bit earthy and oxidized; is very dry and tannic. Drinkable now. • $NA • (10/31/96) • **78**
Barolo Dardi 1982 • $18 • (09/15/87) • **87**
Barolo Monprivato 1991: Fruity and firm in texture, with lots of cherry and plum flavors, tight tannins and a lingering, if tannic, finish. Drink now. • $NA • (10/31/96) • **86**
Barolo Monprivato 1990 • $50 • (10/31/95) • **78**
Barolo Monprivato 1989 • $42 • (10/31/93) • **85**
Barolo Monprivato 1988 • $42 • (10/31/93) • **82**
Barolo Monprivato 1986 • $47 • (07/15/91) • **88**
Barolo Monprivato 1985 • $53 • (06/15/90) • **86**
Barolo Monprivato 1983 • $28 • (07/15/88) • **85**
Barolo Monprivato 1982 • $22 • (09/15/87) • **87**
Barolo Monprivato 1981 • $NA • (09/15/88) • **84**
Barolo Monprivato 1980 • $NA • (09/15/88) • **76**
Barolo Monprivato 1979 • $NA • (09/15/88) • **83**
Barolo Monprivato 1978 • $NA • (09/15/88) • **86**
Barolo Monprivato 1974 • $NA • (09/15/88) • **91**
Barolo Monprivato 1971 • $NA • (09/15/88) • **81**
Barolo Monprivato 1970 • $NA • (09/15/88) • **80**
Barolo Monprivato Falletto 1983 • $23 • (07/31/89) • **80**
Barolo Santo Stefano di Perno 1985 • $35 • (10/15/90) HR • **94**

Key: SS—Spectator Selection CS—Cellar Selection HR—Highly Recommended BB—Best Buy $NA—Price not available Ⓐ—Auction Price (BT)—Barrel Tasting
Dates in parentheses indicate the issues in which the ratings were published.

Barolo Villero 1983 • $17 • (10/15/88) • **77**
Dolcetto d'Alba Bricco 1993 • $12 • (10/31/95) • **79**
Dolcetto d'Alba Bricco Falletto 1987 • $9 • (03/15/89) • **88**
Dolcetto d'Alba Bricco Ravera 1988 • $10 • (09/15/90) • **82**
Dolcetto d'Alba Gagliassi 1989 • $13 • (07/15/91) • **85**
Dolcetto d'Alba Gagliassi 1987 • $10 • (03/31/90) • **80**
Dolcetto d'Alba Gagliassi Monforte 1987 • $9 • (03/15/89) • **82**
Dolcetto d'Alba Venora 1985 • $7 • (12/31/87) • **80**
Grignolino del Monferrato Casalese Besso 1988 • $9 • (01/31/90) • **75**
Nebbiolo d'Alba San Rocco 1988 • $16 • (07/31/92) • **82**
Nebbiolo d'Alba San Rocco 1986 • $15 • (09/15/90) • **85**

MASCIARELLI

Montepulciano d'Abruzzo 1995: A hearty, well-balanced red, with bright, fresh fruit flavors and light tannins. Drink now. 40,000 cases made. • $6 • (02/28/98) • **83**
Montepulciano d'Abruzzo 1993 • $6 • (02/29/96) BB • **85**
Montepulciano d'Abruzzo 1992 • $6 • (03/31/95) BB • **86**
Montepulciano d'Abruzzo Villa Gemma Riserva 1992: The mother of all Montepulcianos. A deep, dark, brooding, oak-aged monster of a wine with flavors of smoke, coffee, tobacco, cedar and blackberry. Over-oaked and overdone, but what a spectacle. Drink now through 2000. 1,000 cases made. • $30 • (02/28/98) • **88**

MASI

Amarone della Valpolicella Campolongo di Torbe 1990: Combines power and complexity in a formidable, full-bodied style. From the spicy, earthy aromas to the ripe, deep cherry and prune flavors and lingering finish, this stands well above the pack. • $47 • (04/30/97) • **92**
Amarone della Valpolicella Classico Campolongo di Torbe 1988 • $53 • (04/30/96) • **84**
Amarone Recioto della Valpolicella Campolongo 1983 • $26 • (04/15/88) • **85**
Amarone della Valpolicella Classico 1994: Cherry, menthol and vanilla hold court in this slim version of Amarone. Lacks the richness and fruit on the back of the palate to match the tannin and alcohol. Good effort in a difficult vintage. Better than previously reviewed. Drink now through 2000. • $28 • (07/31/98) • **84**
Amarone della Valpolicella Classico 1993: Agreeable. Ripe, raisinlike flavors, lots of body and alcohol, an appropriately thick, soft texture and a lingering finish. • $25 • (04/30/97) • **86**
Amarone della Valpolicella Classico 1991 • $28 • (04/30/96) • **85**
Amarone della Valpolicella Classico 1990 • $25 • (05/31/96) • **86**
Amarone della Valpolicella Classico 1989 • $28 • (11/15/94) • **85**
Amarone della Valpolicella Classico 1988 • $36 • (05/31/96) • **81**
Amarone della Valpolicella Classico 1981 • $15 • (10/31/88) • **84**
Amarone della Valpolicella Mazzano 1990: Beautiful Amarone. Truffle, prune, leather and chocolate character is matched by the silky texture and full-bodied structure. Just beginning to unwind, this is one for the future. The finish goes on and on. From one of the best *crus*. Drink now through 2010. 930 cases made. • $50 • (05/31/98) CS • **92**
Amarone della Valpolicella Classico Mazzano 1988 • $54 • (05/31/96) • **84**
Amarone Recioto della Valpolicella Classico Mazzano 1986 • $58 • (05/31/96) • **88**
Amarone Recioto della Valpolicella Classico Mazzano 1985 • $66 • (05/31/96) • **90**
Amarone Recioto della Valpolicella Classico Mazzano 1983 • $70 • (05/31/96) • **89**
Amarone Recioto della Valpolicella Mazzano 1980 • $26 • (10/31/88) • **88**
Amarone Recioto della Valpolicella Classico Mazzano 1979 • $91 • (05/31/96) • **88**
Amarone Recioto della Valpolicella Classico Mazzano 1977 • $99 • (05/31/96) • **89**
Amarone Recioto della Valpolicella Classico Mazzano 1976 • $99 • (05/31/96) • **87**
Amarone Recioto della Valpolicella Classico Mazzano 1974 • $133 • (05/31/96) • **89**
Amarone Recioto della Valpolicella Classico Mazzano 1971 • $NA • (05/31/96) • **84**
Amarone Recioto della Valpolicella Classico Mazzano 1969 • $NA • (05/31/96) • **91**
Amarone Recioto della Valpolicella Classico Mazzano 1964 • $290 • (05/31/96) • **92**

Amarone Recioto della Valpolicella Classico Mazzano 1958 • $NA • (05/31/96) • **92**
Amarone Recioto della Valpolicella Classico Mazzano 1941 • $NA • (05/31/96) • **88**
Amarone della Valpolicella Serègo Alighieri Vaio Armaron 1991: Starts off rich, with prune and chocolate, then this full-bodied red turns tannic, finishing on a hot (alcoholic) note. Good Amarone character without the fat and texture of the best vintages. Drink now through 2000. • $65 • (07/31/98) • **86**
Amarone della Valpolicella Serègo Alighieri Vaio Armaron 1990: Bold and silky, sporting complex prune, chocolate and mushroom character, this is beginning to enter its secondary phase of maturity. Great richness and structure and a lingering finish. Full, ripe, velvety tannins. Drink now through 2010. 1,500 cases made. • $57 • (05/31/98) • **90**
Amarone della Valpolicella Classico Serègo Alighieri Vaio Armaron 1988 • $55 • (05/31/96) • **90**
Bardolino 1994: A powerful aroma laced with spice and game notes is followed up by modest tea and plum flavors. • $9 • (01/31/97) • **78**
Bardolino 1993 • $15 • (04/30/96) • **78**
Bardolino Classico Superiore 1992 • $8 • (10/31/94) • **83**
Bardolino Classico Superiore 1990 • $8 • (09/15/92) • **78**
Bardolino Classico Superiore 1988 • $9 • (05/15/91) BB • **82**
Bardolino Classico 1985 • $5 • (05/31/88) • **77**
Bardolino Classico 1984 • $5 • (05/15/87) BB • **80**
Bardolino Classico Superiore La Vegrona 1990 • $15 • (04/30/96) • **79**
Campofiorin 1994: A rich, spicy, full-bodied red, showing prune and leather flavors, a smooth texture, lively acidity and mild tannins. A hearty, rustic style that finishes dry. Better with food. Drink now through 1999. • $17 • (05/31/98) • **85**
Campofiorin 1993: An extra measure of depth and richness lifts this full-bodied red above the ordinary. Shows a fruity, meaty, spicy flavor spectrum, firm tannins and good balance. • $15 • (04/30/97) • **86**
Campofiorin 1990: • $13 • (10/31/96) • **78**
Campofiorin 1988 • $15 • (09/15/92) • **79**
Campofiorin 1985 • $12 • (09/15/90) • **77**
Campofiorin 1983 • $7 • (05/15/89) BB • **81**
Campofiorin 1981 • $8 • (04/15/88) BB • **88**
Campofiorin "ripasso" 1991 • $14 • (05/31/96) • **84**
Campofiorin "ripasso" 1990 • $15 • (05/31/95) • **78**
Recioto della Valpolicella 1991 • $28 • (04/30/96) • **80**
Recioto della Valpolicella Recioto Amabile Serègo Alighieri 1994: Moderately sweet, packed with cherry, chocolate and violet character. Not unlike a young Port, yet less full-bodied and alcoholic. Packs a wallop, finishing slightly hot. Best from 1999 through 2005. • $50 • (05/31/98) • **88**
Serègo Alighieri Bianco 1996: An exuberant white that has weight and presence on the palate. Fruit flavors are subtle, finishing with a grapefruit peel note. A blend of 70 percent Garganega and 30 percent Sauvignon Blanc. Drink now. • $16 • (07/31/98) • **81**
Serègo Alighieri White 1995: Reminiscent of Sancerre, with its overtly tangy herb and grass aromas and crisp, lemony flavors. Quite dry, but lively and full of character. • $13 • (04/30/97) • **86**
Soave Classico Superiore 1997: Fresh and fruity, this Soave displays peach and almond aromas and flavors in a soft, easy-drinking style. Drink now. • $8 • (06/30/98) • **84**
Soave Classico Superiore 1995: A crisp, refreshing white with delicate flavors of almond and lemon, accented by a hint of earthiness on the finish. • $10 • (05/15/97) • **82**
Soave Classico Superiore 1994 • $9 • (06/15/96) • **79**
Soave Classico Superiore 1993 • $8 • (10/31/94) • **83**
Toar 1993: Aromatic, stylish, seductive. Shows ample oak-barrel influence in its spicy flavor profile. Solid fruit flavor fills out its tannic but smooth-textured frame, and the lingering finish is a good sign. • $20 • (04/30/97) • **88**
Toar 1992 • $15 • (04/30/96) • **89**
Toar 1991 • $20 • (05/31/95) • **86**
Valpolicella 1993 • $14 • (12/15/95) • **84**
Valpolicella Classico Superiore 1996: Shows more of the plum, leather and menthol flavors of Valpolicella in a slightly traditional style, with moderate concentration and structure and a baked-earth finish. Drink now. • $8 • (07/31/98) • **82**
Valpolicella Classico Superiore 1995: A basic, commercial style, showing modest red fruit flavors and a hint of astringency on the finish. Drink now. • $8 • (04/30/98) • **78**
Valpolicella Classico Superiore 1994: A fairly big wine with good flavors of game and plum. Plenty of backbone, and some nice dried cherry notes on the finish. • $9 • (01/31/97) • **84**
Valpolicella Classico Superiore 1992 • $8 • (11/15/94) • **80**
Valpolicella Classico Superiore 1991 • $8 • (10/15/94) BB • **86**
Valpolicella Classico Superiore 1989 • $8 • (09/15/92) • **82**
Valpolicella Classico Superiore 1987 • $7 • (12/31/90) • **78**
Valpolicella Classico Superiore 1985 • $5 • (05/31/88) • **76**
Valpolicella Classico Superiore Serègo Alighieri 1994: Showing maturity, from the licorice and leather character to the firm, chewy texture. Distinctive. Drink now. • $17 • (05/31/98) • **84**
Valpolicella Classico Superiore Serègo Alighieri 1993: Serious and structured, with enough gumption to match rich meat and poultry dishes. Full-bodied but not too tannic, focused on plum and tomato flavors that linger on the finish. • $15 • (04/30/97) • **87**
Valpolicella Classico Superiore Serègo Alighieri 1991 • $14 • (04/30/96) • **82**
Valpolicella Classico Superiore Serègo Alighieri 1988 • $18 • (09/15/92) • **82**
Valpolicella Classico Superiore Serègo Alighieri 1983 • $9 • (05/15/87) • **71**

MASI, RENZO

Chianti Paolo Masi 1991 • $6 • (06/15/93) • **79**
Chianti Rufina 1993 • $6 • (10/31/94) BB • **84**
Chianti Rufina Fattoria di Basciano 1991 • $9 • (10/31/93) • **78**
Chianti Rufina Fattoria di Basciano 1990 • $7 • (06/15/93) • **82**
Chianti Rufina Fattoria di Basciano 1990 • $8 • (10/31/93) • **88**

MASO CANTANGHEL

Pinot Nero Altesino Riserva 1988 • $33 • (02/15/91) • **84**

MASO POLI

Costa Erta Trentino White 1996: Very ripe, this has tropical notes of passion fruit and a touch of orange, but it diffuses quickly, without much of a finish. Drink now. • $19 • (05/31/98) • **80**
Pinot Grigio Trentino 1996: Starts out fresh and vibrant, with a ginger accent to the peach and quince flavors, but lacks concentration, finishing with a bitter almond note. Drink now. • $14 • (05/31/98) • **82**
Pinot Grigio Trentino 1995: Brisk and fruity with a touch of butterscotch but the finish is astringent. Firmness suggests trying with food or cellaring about six months. • $14 • (06/15/97) • **83**
Pinot Nero Trentino 1995: Overwhelmed by vanilla character, but it shows concentration and suppleness. Turns astringent on the finish. Lacks harmony. Drink now. • $19 • (06/30/98) • **80**
Pinot Nero Trentino 1994: Mature, with mint and spicy cherry aromas and flavors, modest concentration and a dry finish. Drink now. • $19 • (06/30/98) • **81**

MASSA, LA

Chianti Classico 1995: Focused blackberry character on the nose and palate. Medium-bodied, with crisp acidity and a tart, fruity finish. Drinkable now. • $20 • (09/30/97) • **84**
Chianti Classico 1994: Aromatic, with dried cherry and berry aromas and flavors in a medium body. Tannins are soft and finish is succulent. Try now. 4,300 cases made. • $15 • (10/31/96) • **85**
Chianti Classico 1993 • $14 • (10/31/95) • **82**
Chianti Classico 1992 • $12 • (02/28/95) • **84**
Chianti Classico 1990 • $NA • (10/31/93) • **89**
Chianti Classico Giorgio Primo 1994: Notable for its lovely bright berry character, it's of medium body, with fine tannins and a fresh finish. Drink now or hold. • $18 • (09/30/97) • **87**
Chianti Classico Giorgio Primo 1992 • $57 • (10/31/95) • **88**
Chianti Classico Giorgio Primo Riserva 1993: Beautiful, and very aromatic with floral, spices and dried herb aromas and flavors. Medium body, a portion of fine tannins and a silky finish. Subtle. Try now. 2,000 cases made. • $30 • (10/31/96) • **87**
Chianti Classico Riserva 1990 • $17 • (02/28/95) • **91**

MASSARA, FATTORIA

Barbera d'Alba 1990 • $12 • (12/15/92) • **86**
Barbera d'Alba 1987 • $7 • (09/15/90) • **74**
Barolo 1985 • $20 • (06/15/90) • **80**
Dolcetto d'Alba 1990 • $9 • (01/31/92) • **86**

MASSE DI GREVE, LE

Chianti Classico 1994: Spoiled with burnt rubber aromas and flavors. Why bottle this? Tasted twice, with consistent notes. • $NA • (09/30/97) • **65**
Chianti Classico 1990 • $11 • (04/30/94) • **89**
Chianti Classico 1988 • $13 • (04/30/91) • **87**
Chianti Classico 1985 • $12 • (07/15/89) • **92**
Chianti Classico Riserva 1988 • $20 • (09/15/92) • **90**
Chianti Classico Riserva 1985 • $20 • (09/15/91) • **89**

MASSOLINO

Barbera d'Alba 1993 • $NA • (10/31/95) • **84**
Barolo 1992: Sturdy and straightforward, with smoky aromas, cherry flavors, firm tannins and a rather short finish. Drinkable now. • $NA • (10/31/96) • **79**
Barolo 1990 • $30 • (10/31/95) • **77**
Barolo Vigneto Margheria 1991: A well-made wine that's young and closed right now. Floral aromas and solid cherry flavors bode well for the future. Tannic and tight in texture. Drink now. • $NA • (10/31/96) • **85**
Barolo Vigna Margheria 1990 • $37 • (10/31/95) • **78**
Barolo Vigna Parafada 1993: A racy Barolo. Medium-bodied, with *terroir* stamped all over its layers of mineral, lead pencil, floral, blackberry and black olive character, unhindered by any obvious taste of wood. Silky in texture, yet with an undertow of crisp acidity. Lingering finish. Drink now to 2003. • $45 • (10/31/97) • **89**
Barolo Vigna Parafada 1991: Nice balance of cherry, spice and floral flavors, firm tannins and acidity. Drink now through 2000. • $NA • (10/31/96) • **83**
Barolo Parafeda 1990 • $39 • (10/31/95) • **83**
Barolo Sorì Vigna Rionda 1991: Tight but flavorful, with earthy, floral aromas, solid fruit and spice flavors and a tannic texture. Has the fruit and depth to keep it interesting; try in 1999. • $NA • (10/31/96) • **84**
Barolo Vigna Rionda 1990 • $40 • (10/31/95) • **85**
Dolcetto d'Alba Vigna Barilot 1996 • $15 • • **87**
Dolcetto d'Alba Vigneto Barilot 1993 • $NA • (10/31/95) • **81**

MASTROBERARDINO

Avellanio 1992 • $10 • (07/31/94) • **77**
Avellanio 1991 • $12 • (03/31/93) • **83**
Avellanio 1989 • $11 • (07/15/91) • **87**
Fiano di Avellino Radici 1994: Not for the timid, this hearty, mature and distinctive white has vividly fruity, smoky flavors, full body, and a lingering finish. • $15 • (08/31/97) • **86**
Greco di Tufo 1995: Quite complex and intriguing. It's lean in texture, but chock full of interesting flavor nuances, from spicy, floral aromas to smoky, citrusy flavors that linger on the finish. • $20 • (04/30/97) • **87**
Lacryma Christi del Vesuvio 1991 • $15 • (07/31/93) • **84**
Lacryma Christi del Vesuvio 1989 • $14 • (07/15/91) • **89**
Lacryma Christi del Vesuvio White 1995: A distinctive, unusual and full-bodied white, with smoky, mineral-like flavors and a smooth texture. Worth a try. • $15 • (08/31/97) • **85**
Mastro Rosso 1994 • $10 • (01/31/96) • **79**
Taurasi Radici 1990: A good, solid red wine with pleasant black cherry, currant and tobacco flavors and a nice spicy note on the finish. Quite tannic, though balanced. • $22 • (03/31/97) • **85**
Taurasi Radici 1989 • $20 • (01/31/96) • **87**
Taurasi Radici 1988 • $21 • (07/31/94) • **88**
Taurasi 1987 • $19 • (09/15/92) • **80**
Taurasi 1986 • $18 • (07/15/91) • **87**
Taurasi 1982 • $13 • (07/15/87) • **75**
Taurasi Riserva 1987 • $18 • (07/31/94) • **78**
Taurasi Riserva 1985 • $22 • (06/30/91) • **84**
Taurasi Riserva 1981 • $21 • (02/15/89) • **78**
Taurasi Riserva 1980 • $15 • (09/15/89) • **75**
Taurasi Riserva 1977 • $28 • (10/16/84) CS • **92**

Key: SS—Spectator Selection CS—Cellar Selection HR—Highly Recommended BB—Best Buy $NA—Price not available Ⓐ—Auction Price (BT)—Barrel Tasting
Dates in parentheses indicate the issues in which the ratings were published.

MASTROJANNI

Brunello di Montalcino 1991: Ripe and rich for the vintage, with a berrylike, almost raisiny, character. Medium body, with silky tannins and a ripe finish. Slightly one-dimensional. Drink now or hold. • $33 • (03/31/97) • **85**
Brunello di Montalcino 1990: Big, ripe and full-bodied, this tannic monster still manages to show a lot of class. Offers tons of earth, red berry and black cherry notes. Drinkable now. • $27 • (10/31/95) • **94**
Brunello di Montalcino 1988 • $30 • (04/30/94) • **90**
Brunello di Montalcino 1982 • $17 • (06/15/90) • **87**
Brunello di Montalcino 1979 • $17 • (09/15/86) • **72**
Brunello di Montalcino Riserva 1990: An alluring Brunello with aromas and flavors of plum, berry, cherry and mint. Medium-bodied, with plenty of silky tannins and a fresh, succulent finish. Drink now or can hold. 583 cases made. • $90 • (11/30/96) • **91**
Brunello di Montalcino Riserva 1988 • $50 • (10/31/94) • **91**
Rosso di Montalcino 1995: A lovely, aromatic wine displaying floral and berry aromas and flavors. Medium in body and tannin, with a slightly dry finish. Drink now. 900 cases made. • $18 • (09/30/97) • **84**
Rosso di Montalcino 1991 • $13 • (08/31/95) • **84**
Rosso di Montalcino 1987 • $10 • (07/15/91) • **79**
San Pio 1992: A ripe wine with aromas and flavors of dried berry and plum. Of medium body, with soft tannins and a fruity, simple finish. Drink now. • $18 • (10/31/96) • **85**

MATRONÈO

Chianti Classico 1994: Lush and generous, with lots of fruit flavor accented by spicy oak and a smooth texture. Drink through 1999. 550 cases made. • $15 • (04/30/98) • **86**
Chianti Classico Riserva 1991: A mature and attractively complex Chianti from a so-so year. Age has added spicy, woodsy accents to the core of fruit flavor and firm tannins. Drink now. 350 cases made. • $26 • (04/30/98) • **86**

MATTA, JOHN

Ripa delle More 1993: Rather mature already with some leathery berry character, but relatively light for the vintage. Sangiovese. Tasted twice with consistent notes. • $NA • (10/31/96) • **76**

MAZZI

Amarone della Valpolicella Classico Punta di Villa 1994: Lovely dried fruit and floral aromas metamorphose into plum and butterscotch on the palate in this high-toned, elegant Amarone. Already showing some mature elements, it will develop quickly. Drink now through 2002. • $45 • (06/15/98) • **86**
Brunello di Montalcino Il Greppone Mazzi Riserva 1987 • $38 • (11/30/93) • **81**
Valpolicella Classico Superiore 1996: Light, showing cherry aromas and flavors bordering on acetone and a lean, crisp finish. Drink now. • $20 • (06/15/98) • **78**
Valpolicella Classico Superiore Poiega 1995: High-toned, focusing on the cherry and currant spectrum of aromas and flavors, yet attractive and elegant. The racy acidity and crisp finish cry out for food. Drink now. • $20 • (06/15/98) • **84**
Valpolicella Colle Crosetta 1988 • $17 • (09/15/92) • **82**
Valpolicella Poiega 1988 • $20 • (09/15/92) • **82**
Valpolicella Poiega 1986 • $20 • (09/15/92) • **86**
Valpolicella Superiore 1988 • $12 • (09/15/92) • **79**

MAZZOLINO, TENUTA

Barbera Oltrepò Pavese 1990 • $11 • (04/30/92) • **82**
Barbera Oltrepò Pavese 1989 • $10 • (04/15/91) • **82**
Noir 1987 • $45 • (09/30/91) • **86**
Oltrepò Pavese 1990 • $14 • (01/31/92) • **77**

MEDICI ERMETE

Concerto Lambrusco Reggiano 1994 • $14 • (12/15/95) • **81**

MELINI

Chianti Borghi d'Elsa 1992 • $13 • (07/31/95) • **74**
Chianti Borghi d'Elsa 1990 • $7 • (07/31/92) BB • **84**
Chianti Borghi d'Elsa 1989 • $6 • (10/31/91) • **81**
Chianti Classico Isassi 1995: Offers good plum, with a hint of earth, on the nose and palate; medium body, light tannins and a succulent but slightly diluted finish. • $13 • (09/30/97) • **80**
Chianti Classico Isassi 1994: Basically, it's light. Pretty, sweet fruit and orange peel aromas, with similarly light flavors, light-body and slightly dry, light finish. • $12 • (10/31/96) • **78**
Chianti Classico Isassi 1990 • $10 • (10/31/93) • **83**
Chianti Classico Isassi 1989 • $10 • (09/15/92) • **81**
Chianti Classico Isassi 1988 • $8 • (09/15/91) • **89**
Chianti Classico 1987 • $7 • (04/30/90) • **80**
Chianti Classico 1986 • $6 • (10/31/88) BB • **83**
Chianti Classico 1985 • $5 • (07/31/88) BB • **82**
Chianti Classico La Selvanella Riserva 1993: A decadent wine with smoky, meaty and fruity aromas and flavors. Medium-bodied, with soft tannins and a ripe fruit finish. Drink now. • $15 • (10/31/96) • **84**
Chianti Classico La Selvanella Riserva 1991: Nearly tired out, drinkable, but more of a curiosity than a pleasure. Has beefy flavors and dry, tannic finish. Drink now. • $20 • (04/30/98) • **78**
Chianti Classico La Selvanella Riserva 1990 • $13 • (02/28/95) • **79**
Chianti Classico La Selvanella Riserva 1988 • $14 • (10/31/93) • **85**
Chianti Classico La Selvanella Riserva 1987 • $13 • (09/15/92) • **83**
Chianti Classico La Selvanella Riserva 1985 • $7 • (09/15/91) BB • **87**
Chianti Classico La Selvanella Riserva 1982 • $6 • (06/30/88) BB • **85**
Chianti Classico Laborel Riserva 1990 • $11 • (02/28/95) • **78**
Chianti Classico Laborel Riserva 1987 • $11 • (12/15/92) • **85**
Chianti Classico Laborel Riserva 1986 • $10 • (10/31/91) • **83**
Coltri 1993: Simple and light with some dried cherry aromas and flavors, but not much else. 70 percent Sangioveto and 30 percent Cabernet Sauvignon. • $21 • (10/31/96) • **77**
I Coltri Vigna 1 1993: Concentrated but awkward. Smoky, coffeelike aromas and severe, tart cranberry flavors. A blend of 70 percent Sangioveto, 30 percent Cabernet Sauvignon. Drink now through 2000. • $24 • (04/30/98) • **78**
Coltri Vineyard 1 1990 • $20 • (12/31/95) • **85**
Coltri Vineyard 1 1988 • $19 • (11/30/94) • **86**
Coltri Vineyard 1 1986 • $20 • (12/15/92) • **85**
I Coltri Vigna 2 1994: Big, tannic and full-bodied, with robust flavors of black cherry, tobacco and coffee heavily accented by oak. An extreme style. A blend of 70 percent Cabernet Sauvignon, 30 percent Sangioveto. Drink now. • $24 • (04/30/98) • **82**
Coltri Due 1993: An attractive wine with floral and berry aromas and flavors, medium body and fine tannins. Delicious now, but will improve with age. 70 percent Cabernet Sauvignon and 30 percent Sangioveto. • $21 • (10/31/96) • **86**
Coltri Vineyard 2 1990 • $20 • (12/31/95) • **90**
Coltri Vineyard 2 1988 • $19 • (11/30/94) • **90**
Coltri Vineyard 2 1986 • $20 • (12/15/92) • **83**
Vernaccia di San Gimignano Le Grillaie 1996: Subtle aromas of apples, tangerines and vanilla give way to a medium-bodied wine with a lovely, creamy texture and fresh acidity. Drink now or hold. • $17 • (09/30/97) • **86**
Vino Nobile di Montepulciano 1985 • $10 • (04/15/90) • **82**
Vino Nobile di Montepulciano Riserva 1983 • $7 • (06/30/88) • **74**

MEZZACORONA, CANTINE

Cabernet Sauvignon Trentino 1995: Pleasant berry notes highlight this soft, lushly-textured red, complemented by vanilla accents. The firm tannins need some time to integrate, and there's impressive grip on the finish. A good value from Italy's Northeast. Try through 2000. 15,000 cases made. • $8 • (06/15/98) BB • **85**
Chardonnay Trentino 1997: A simple white with some apple flavor and a sharp finish. 15,000 cases made. • $8 • (06/15/98) • **77**
Merlot Trentino 1996: This soft, medium-bodied red adds just a hint of herbaceousness to the plum and cherry aromas and flavors characteristic of Merlot. Balanced and appealing. Drink now. 15,000 cases made. • $8 • (06/15/98) • **83**
Merlot Trentino 1993 • $8 • (06/15/96) • **81**
Merlot Trentino 1991 • $8 • (04/30/94) • **82**
Merlot Trentino 1990 • $8 • (09/15/92) • **81**
Pinot Grigio Trentino 1997: Plenty of peach and quince notes, with bright acidity and moderate concentration, followed by a modest finish. Solid Pinot Grigio. Drink now through 1999. 15,000 cases made. • $8 • (06/15/98) • **84**
Pinot Grigio Trentino 1995 • $8 • (06/15/96) • **82**
Pinot Grigio Trentino Vigneto Zablani 1994 • $15 • (06/15/96) • **85**
Pinot Grigio Trentino Vigneto Zablani 1993 • $17 • (12/15/94) • **83**
Pinot Noir Trentino 1995: Awkward. Starts out smooth and elegant, with straightforward cherry and herb flavors, but finishes with gum-coating tannins. Drink now through 1999. 15,000 cases made. • $8 • (06/30/98) • **79**
Teroldego Rotaliano Vigneto Sottodossi 1993 • $15 • (06/15/96) BB • **83**
Teroldego Rotaliano Vigneto Sottodossi 1992 • $17 • (02/28/95) • **84**

MICCINE, LE

da Gino 1994: A pretty red with floral and berry aromas and flavors. Medium-to-light in body, with a fresh, fruity finish. Drink now. • $NA • (09/30/97) • **85**
L'Aura 1996: Candied strawberry and peach aromas. Medium-bodied, with high acidity, a tart finish. Unbalanced. • $NA • (09/30/97) • **77**

MOCALI

Brunello di Montalcino 1992: An aromatic Brunello with a generous fresh cherry and light earth character. Medium-bodied, with crisp acidity and a light finish. Drink now. 580 cases made. • $29 • (09/30/97) • **84**
Brunello di Montalcino 1991: Some decent fruit flavors, though of rather meager richness, with light body, light tannins and simple finish. This estate's '94 rosso is better. 500 cases made. • $NA • (11/30/96) • **81**
Brunello di Montalcino 1990: Serious red featuring a solid backbone of tannins, accompanied by tobacco, black cherry and blackberry flavors. Stays fresh. Long, tannic finish. Drinkable now. • $NA • (10/31/95) • **88**
Brunello di Montalcino Riserva 1991: Very good riserva, with black cherry aromas of good intensity, a medium body, chewy tannins and a long finish. Drinkable now. 80 cases made. • $40 • (09/30/97) • **88**
Rosso di Montalcino 1995: Slightly one-dimensional, but with good intensity of dried cherry character on both the nose and palate. 410 cases made. • $15 • (09/30/97) • **85**
Rosso di Montalcino 1994: Good quality. It's a lovely, aromatic wine with dried berry and licorice aromas and flavors. Light- to medium-bodied, with light, silky tannins and a caressing finish. 500 cases made. • $NA • (11/30/96) • **85**

MOCCAGATTA

Barbaresco Basarin 1994: Tough, herbaceous and slightly diluted, with hard tannins accompanying the fruit. Medium body; it lacks in ripeness. Drink chilled. • $30 • (10/31/97) • **77**
Barbaresco Basarin 1993: New style, with the oak-induced flavors—vanilla, spice, mocha and mint—peeking through. Not harmonious at this stage, but time should balance the fruit and oak. Try after 1999. • $29 • (10/31/96) • **87**
Barbaresco Basarin 1992 • $26 • (10/31/95) • **79**
Barbaresco Basarin 1991 • $24 • (10/31/94) • **85**
Barbaresco Basarin 1990 • $26 • (10/31/93) • **90**
Barbaresco Basarin 1989 • $25 • (10/31/93) • **82**
Barbaresco Basarin 1987 • $23 • (07/15/91) • **86**
Barbaresco Bric Balin 1994: This supple, light- to medium-bodied wine offers decent red- and blackberry flavors, plus some dilution and an herbaceous edge. Drink chilled. • $33 • (10/31/97) • **77**
Barbaresco Bric Balin 1993: Quite lovely but also a bit rustic, offering flavors of cassis, violet, rose petal and toasty oak. Medium-bodied, the tannins clamp down on the slightly dry finish. Try after 1999. • $31 • (10/31/97) • **85**
Barbaresco Bric Balin 1992 • $28 • (10/31/95) • **83**
Barbaresco Bric Balin 1991 • $28 • (10/31/94) • **87**
Barbaresco Bric Balin 1990 • $31 • (10/31/93) • **93**
Barbaresco Bric Balin 1989 • $28 • (10/31/94) • **83**
Barbaresco Bric Balin 1988 • $28 • (10/31/93) • **89**
Barbaresco Bric Balin 1987 • $28 • (07/15/91) • **89**
Barbaresco Bric Basarin 1988 • $24 • (10/31/94) • **74**
Barbaresco Vigna Cole 1994: Light and supple, this balanced, well-made red blends chalky, chewy earth character with black cherry and blackberry flavors. The finish is long. Impressive for this vintage. The first bottle was corked. • $NA • (10/31/97) • **85**

Barbaresco Vigna Cole 1993: Flashy and seductive on the palate, but very oaky—the wood dominates the currant and black cherry flavors at this stage. Quite tannic, but should smooth out over time. Try after 1999. • $34 • (10/31/96) • **87**
Barbaresco Vigna Cole 1992 • $27 • (10/31/95) • **82**
Barbaresco Vigna Cole 1991 • $26 • (10/31/94) • **83**
Barbaresco Vigna Cole 1990 • $33 • (10/31/93) • **88**
Barbaresco Vigna Cole 1989 • $27 • (10/31/93) • **89**
Barbaresco Vigna Cole 1988 • $25 • (10/31/93) • **78**
Barbera d'Alba 1991 • $12 • (11/15/93) • **81**
Barbera d'Alba 1989 • $14 • (03/15/91) • **89**
Barbera d'Asti Basarin 1994: Delicious Barbera; international in style, inky black in color, offering layers of fruit, spice and toasty oak, all presented in a seductive, well-made and balanced package. Crisp acidity with ripe tannins. Long finish. Drink now through 2002. • $27 • (10/31/97) • **88**
Barbera d'Alba Basarin 1993: Wonderfully fruity. Generous ripe cherry and black currant flavors in a firm but not too tannic texture. Long and pleasant finish. • $23 • (10/31/96) • **89**
Barbera d'Alba Basarin 1991 • $NA • (10/31/94) • **80**
Barbera Piedmont Basarin 1990 • $25 • (11/15/93) • **84**
Dolcetto d'Alba Buschet 1996: A Dolcetto with some fat on it, this delivers dark color, ripe tannins and toasty spice, currant and cassis flavors. Of medium body, with good length on the finish and a more supple structure than most. Drink now. • $14 • (10/31/97) • **84**
Dolcetto d'Alba Buschet 1991 • $14 • (03/31/93) • **82**

MOLETTO

Cabernet Franc Lison-Pramaggiore 1995: Green olive, bell pepper and mint notes dominate this lean red that turns austere and astringent on the finish. Try with red meats. Drink now through 2000. 1,500 cases made. • $12 • (06/30/98) • **83**
Chardonnay Piave 1996: International in style, rich and buttery, forward and fruity. Lemon custard and apple flavors finish with a hint of vanilla. 2,000 cases made. • $11 • (12/15/97) • **83**
Merlot Piave 1995: Soft, plummy, fruitcake aromas are followed by plum and camphor flavors. The oak character doesn't mesh with the fruit. Tasted twice, with consistent notes. 10,000 cases made. • $13 • (11/15/97) • **77**
Pinot Grigio Piave 1997: Very ripe, smelling and tasting like apricot nectar with a dash of guava. There's tangy acidity beneath it all, and the two components need time to integrate. Drink now through 1999. 12,000 cases made. • $10 • (06/30/98) • **83**
Pinot Grigio Piave 1996: A hint of carbon dioxide livens up the herb and pear notes in this subtle, elegant white. Moderately concentrated and well balanced. Drink now. 5,000 cases made. • $11 • (05/15/98) • **83**
Veneto Colmello Rosso 1991: A ripe, harmonious red that reveals matured sweet plum and leather flavors with hints of licorice and spice. There's depth and dimension and a good finish, though still some tannins, so it's probably best with food. A blend of Cabernet Franc, Merlot, Malbec and Rosso Moletto. Drink now through 1999. 800 cases made. • $22 • (04/30/98) • **87**

MOLINO, FRANCO

Barolo Bricco Zuncai 1993: Very light in body and color, with only modest fruit flavor. It's sweet and oddly spritzy; a strange wine. • $NA • (10/31/97) • **74**

MOLINO, MAURO

Acanzio 1993: A full-flavored and richly-textured red wine with alluring spice aromas and generous cherry and blackberry flavors. Firmly tannic in texture. Try now through 2000. • $24 • (05/31/97) • **88**
Acanzio 1989 • $15 • (01/31/92) • **85**
Barolo Vigna Conca 1992: Light and spicy, with a prunelike flavor in the middle and a slightly dried edge to it. Drink now. • $35 • (01/01/97) • **81**
Barolo Vigna Conca 1986 • $29 • (02/28/91) • **87**
Barolo Vigna Conca 1985 • $25 • (03/31/90) • **82**
Dolcetto d'Alba 1989 • $14 • (02/28/91) • **87**
Dolcetto d'Alba 1988 • $12 • (03/31/90) • **82**
Nebbiolo delle Langhe 1989 • $12 • (07/31/92) • **83**
Nebbiolo delle Langhe 1988 • $12 • (03/31/90) • **84**
Pinotu 1989 • $20 • (08/31/91) • **84**

MONSANTO, FATTORIA

Chardonnay Fabrizio Bianchi 1994: An intriguing, substantive Chardonnay that blends bright fruit flavors with subtle nuances of honey, nutmeg and vanilla. It's complex and interesting, drawing you back for another sip. • $19 • (08/31/97) • **87**
Chardonnay Fabrizio Bianchi 1993 • $16 • (02/29/96) • **76**
Chianti Classico 1990 • $NA • (10/31/93) • **86**
Chianti Classico Riserva 1994: Beautiful chocolate, berry and earth aromas precede this medium-bodied wine with its round mouthfeel and medium finish. Drink now. 12,500 cases made. • $17 • (09/30/97) • **86**
Chianti Classico Riserva 1991 • $NA • (10/31/95) • **82**
Chianti Classico Riserva 1988 • $23 Ⓐ • (09/15/92) • **86**
Chianti Classico Riserva 1987 • $16 • (12/15/92) • **68**
Chianti Classico Riserva 1986 • $15 • (04/15/91) • **85**
Chianti Classico Riserva 1985 • $10 • (11/30/89) • **89**
Chianti Classico Riserva 1982 • $10 • (02/15/88) • **72**
Chianti Classico Riserva 1979 • $9 • (11/01/84) • **83**
Chianti Classico Riserva Il Poggio Vineyard 1985 • $25 • (03/31/90) • **80**
Chianti Classico Riserva Il Poggio Vineyard 1983 • $23 • (11/30/89) • **86**
Chianti Classico Riserva Il Poggio Vineyard 1982 • $23 • (06/30/89) • **88**
Chianti Classico Riserva Il Poggio Vineyard 1981 • $17 • (11/30/89) • **82**
Chianti Classico Riserva Il Poggio Vineyard 1979 • $16 • (09/15/87) • **93**
Fabrizio Bianchi Vigneto Scanni 1988 • $30 • (10/31/93) • **85**
Fabrizio Bianchi Vigneto Scanni 1985 • $33 • (12/15/92) • **74**
Nemo 1994: An opulent red that features toasty, chocolaty aromas, a soft texture and rich, oaky, ripe fruit flavors. Not too tannic. Best now through 2000. 1,500 cases made. • $33 • (10/31/97) • **88**
Nemo 1993: A lovely, caressing wine with fine tannins and an alluring berry, meaty, peppery character. Medium-bodied and has a succulent finish. Drink now or hold. Cabernet Sauvignon. • $30 • (10/31/96) • **87**
Nemo 1990 • $29 • (02/28/95) • **88**
Nemo 1988 • $30 • (09/15/91) • **91**
Nemo 1986 • $33 • (12/15/92) • **84**
Nemo 1983 • $28 • (09/15/90) • **87**
Sangiovese Fabrizio Bianchi 1993: A massive wine with loads of fruit and tannin, offering juicy plum and dried cherry flavors with herbal and spice notes on the finish. This structured, serious red is made in an international style that makes it approachable now, but it may be better in 1999. 2,000 cases made. • $26 • (07/31/97) • **90**
Tinscvil 1993: Good cherry, berry and earthy Sangiovese character. Medium-bodied, with a fruity finish. Drink now. A blend of 80 percent Sangiovese and 20 percent Cabernet Sauvignon. • $30 • (10/31/96) • **85**
Tinscvil 1990 • $21 • (02/28/95) • **81**
Tinscvil 1988 • $22 • (03/31/93) • **71**
Tinscvil 1986 • $32 • (01/31/93) • **83**
Tinscvil 1985 • $22 • (09/15/90) • **88**

MONSORDO

La Bernardina 1991 • $26 • (02/28/95) • **93**

MONTAGLIARI, FATTORIA DI

Chianti Classico La Quercia 1990 • $NA • (09/15/92) • **86**
Chianti Classico Riserva 1985 • $NA • (09/15/91) • **83**

MONTE ANTICO

Red 1991 • $9 • (12/31/95) • **89**
Red 1990 • $9 • (07/31/95) • **80**
Red 1985 • $6 • (06/30/88) • **85**
Red 1982 • $3 • (04/01/86) BB • **82**

MONTE BERNARDI

Chianti Classico 1995: A bit too much ripe fruit and new wood. Verging on a Rioja red in style. Medium-bodied, with soft tannins and berry with a vanilla character. Drink now. • $NA • (09/30/97) • **82**

Key: SS—Spectator Selection CS—Cellar Selection HR—Highly Recommended BB—Best Buy $NA—Price not available Ⓐ—Auction Price (BT)—Barrel Tasting
Dates in parentheses indicate the issues in which the ratings were published.

Chianti Classico 1994: Some pretty fruit flavor of a chocolate-berry character, but very (new French barrels) woody. Tastes more like Rioja than Chianti. Medium-bodied with light tannins and a long, vanilla finish. Drink now. • $25 • (10/31/96) • **80**

Chianti Classico 1993 • $NA • (10/31/95) • **80**

Chianti Classico Riserva 1994: Smells and tastes like Rioja. Very woody, with masses of vanilla right through the finish. Medium-bodied and soft. • $NA • (09/30/97) • **80**

Sa'Etta 1994: Fresh and fruity with strawberry, spice and vanilla aromas and flavors. Light-to-medium body with fine tannins and a fresh, slightly diluted finish. A little too much new wood. Drink now. • $32 • (10/31/96) • **80**

Sa'Etta 1993: An aroma and flavor of sweaty leather hovers over the ripe fruit flavors. • $32 • (10/31/96) • **76**

MONTECALVI

Rosso dell'Alta Valle della Greve 1995: One for the cellar. Concentrated, rich in flavor and full in body, it has an enticing spicy, chocolaty aroma, deep cherry and cranberry flavors and firm tannins. Drink after 1999. From Tuscany. • $36 • (10/31/97) • **90**

MONTECCHIO, FATTORIA DI

Chianti Classico 1995: Very aromatic with plums and berries. Medium-bodied, with light tannins and a slightly metallic, stemmy finish which detracts. 10,000 cases made. • $13 • (09/30/97) • **80Chianti Classico Riserva 1994:** Slightly simple for a riserva Chianti but it delivers clean and fresh fruit flavor with a raspberry finish of moderate length. 4,000 cases made. • $18 • (09/30/97) • **82**

Pietracupa 1995: Subtle and lovely. Floral, perfumed with raspberry and spice character. Medium-bodied, with fine tannins and a long, fruity, spicy finish. Drink now. 1,300 cases made. • $18 • (09/30/97) • **87**

Zefiro 1995: Pretty bright-blue bottle, but the wine doesn't taste like much. Light and fresh with a delicate bead. Slightly oxidized. 25,000 cases made. • $9 • (09/30/97) • **75**

MONTEGIACHI, TENUTA

Chianti Classico Riserva 1994: Delicate and fruity with its berry and cherry character, light tannins and fresh finish. Drink now. 1,200 cases made. • $20 • (09/30/97) • **83**

Chianti Classico Riserva 1993: A good Chianti with dried cherry and wet earth aromas and flavors, a medium body and a light finish. Drink now. • $20 • (10/31/96) • **82**

Chianti Classico Riserva 1990 • $NA • (02/28/95) • **83**

MONTEGROSSI, CASTELLO DI

Chianti Classico 1988 • $15 • (09/15/91) • **91**

Chianti Classico 1986 • $8 • (07/15/89) • **89**

Chianti Classico 1985 • $5 • (09/15/88) • **86**

Vin Santo 1982 • $19/375ml • (03/31/90) • **92**

MONTELLORI, FATTORIA

Chianti 1990 • $7 • (05/15/93) • **80**

Chianti Putto 1988 • $6 • (11/30/89) • **83**

MONTENIDOLI

Vernaccia di San Gimignano di Carato 1995: This very good white wine adds buttery, vanillalike nuances to the crisp fruit flavors and firm texture that are typical of Vernaccia. It works. Barrel fermented. Drink now. 1,250 cases made. • $20 • (10/31/97) • **85**

Vernaccia di San Gimignano Fiore 1995: There's an appealing herbal flavor to this characterful wine. Fairly rich and supple; distinctive with some nice citrus notes and earthy flavors. Quite tasty. Drink now. 1,600 cases made. • $9 • (10/31/97) • **85**

Vernaccia di San Gimignano Fiore 1994: The heavy, mature, nutty character of this wine might appeal to some, but seems tired to us. 1,600 cases made. • $9 • (01/01/97) • **77**

MONTESPERTOLI, CASTELLO DI

Chianti Colli Fiorentini Sonnino 1995: A pretty, well-crafted Chianti redolent of tobacco, cherry and vanilla. Medium-bodied, with silky tannins and a fruity finish. Delicious. Drink now or hold. • $NA • (09/30/97) • **86**

MONTEVERTINE

Il Novantuno di Sergio Manetti 1991 • $NA • (02/28/95) • **89**

Il Sodaccio 1994: Delicate and fruity, showing lovely berry, cherry and tobacco aromas and flavors. Medium- to light-bodied, with a silky finish. Drink now. 850 cases made. • $42 • (09/30/97) • **86**

Il Sodaccio 1990 • $32 • (10/31/93) • **83**

Il Sodaccio 1988 • $35 • (09/15/91) • **91**

Il Sodaccio 1987 • $32 • (01/31/91) • **87**

Il Sodaccio 1986 • $30 • (09/30/89) • **90**

Il Sodaccio 1985 • $25 • (03/15/89) • **91**

Il Sodaccio 1983 • $20 • (02/15/87) • **93**

Le Pergole Torte 1994: A wine of great finesse and polish. Chocolate, berry, tobacco and cedar aromas and flavors. Medium-bodied, with well-integrated tannins and a long, sweet fruit finish. Drink now or hold. 2,000 cases made. • $59 • (09/30/97) • **90**

Le Pergole Torte 1993: Sexy red. Can't get enough of it. Wonderfully elegant and fresh, this delivers plenty of cherry, berry and wild cherry aromas and flavors. Of medium body, with fine tannins and a fresh finish. Drink now or hold. • $49 • (10/31/96) • **90**

Le Pergole Torte 1992 • $46 • (10/31/95) • **86**

Le Pergole Torte 1990 • $45 • (10/31/93) • **91**

Le Pergole Torte 1988 • $NA • (11/15/93) • **93Le Pergole Torte 1987** • $NA • (11/15/93) • **86**

Le Pergole Torte 1986 • $NA • (11/15/93) • **86**

Le Pergole Torte 1985 • $NA • (11/15/93) • **91**

Le Pergole Torte 1983 • $NA • (11/15/93) • **86**

Le Pergole Torte 1982 • $17 • (07/16/86) • **90**

Le Pergole Torte 1981 • $12 • (07/16/85) • **87**

Le Pergole Torte Riserva 1990 • $58 • (10/31/93) • **92**

M 1993: Rich yellow in color, with ripe apple and tropical fruit character and a flavorful finish. Full-bodied, with medium tannins. Overdone, but delicious. 400 cases made. • $28 • (09/30/97) • **85**

Montevertine 1991 • $23 • (02/28/95) • **85**

Pian del Ciampolo 1993: A pretty, easy-to-drink wine. Pleasant and fruity with berry, strawberry and cedar flavors. Medium- to light-bodied with light tannins and a crisp finish. Drink now. Sangioveto and Canaiolo. • $21 • (10/31/96) • **83**

Riserva 1994: Emits beautiful berry, cherry and dried fruit aromas tinged with spicy wood. Medium-bodied, with fine tannins and a slightly dry finish. A bit disappointing. Drink now. Tasted twice, with consistent notes. 1,200 cases made. • $38 • (09/30/97) • **84**

Riserva 1993: Wonderful finesse and harmony to this wine. Beautifully aromatic, with notes of ripe raspberry, tea and violets. Medium-bodied, with some very fine tannins and a sweet fruit finish. Drink now. Sangioveto and Canaiolo. • $35 • (10/31/96) • **88**

Riserva 1990 • $30 • (10/31/93) • **86**

Riserva 1988 • $30 • (09/15/91) • **90**

Riserva 1987 • $30 • (03/15/91) • **91**

Riserva 1986 • $26 • (09/30/89) • **86**

Riserva 1982 • $18 • (02/15/87) • **84**

Riserva 1981 • $15 • (08/31/86) • **90**

Sangioveto 1985 • $17 • (08/31/88) • **89**

Sergio Manetti 1989 • $NA • (11/15/93) • **85**

MONTI, ANTONIO & ELIO

Montepulciano d'Abruzzo 1993 • $10 • (02/29/96) • **88**

Montepulciano d'Abruzzo 1989 • $7 • (09/30/91) • **75**

Montepulciano d'Abruzzo 1988 • $6 • (02/15/91) BB • **83**

MONTIVERDI

Chianti Classico 1990 • $NA • (10/31/93) • **87**

MONTORI, CAMILLO

Montepulciano d'Abruzzo 1991 • $6 • (03/31/94) • **82**

Montepulciano d'Abruzzo 1987 • $8 • (03/31/90) • **80**

MONTRESOR

Bianco di Custoza Fattoria di Cavalcaselle 1994 • $8 • (04/30/96) • **74**
Pinot Grigio la Colombaia Valdadige 1994 • $10 • (10/31/95) • **82**

MORASUTTI

Cabernet Sauvignon Grave del Friuli 1996: A light-bodied Cabernet Sauvignon showing aromas and flavors of cherry with accents of herbs and licorice. Balanced and lively, with a leafy texture. A great value at this price. Drink now. • $5 • (04/30/98) • **84**

Chardonnay Grave del Friuli 1996: Exuberant flavors of pear and almond mark this white that's softly-textured and finishes with a slightly candied aftertaste. Good value. Drink now. • $5 • (04/30/98) • **80**

Merlot Grave del Friuli 1995: Herbal and candied, this turns tough and dry on the finish. Drink now. • $5 • (04/30/98) • **74**

Pinot Grigio delle Venezie 1997: Floral and peach aromas and flavors are the hallmarks of this soft, inviting Pinot Grigio with straightforward appeal. Drink now. • $5 • (06/15/98) • **81**

MOSCA

Bardolino 1993 • $5 • (11/15/94) • **80**
Pinot Grigio 1993 • $5 • (10/31/94) • **75**
Valpolicella 1993 • $5 • (10/31/94) • **82**

MURAGLIA ESTATE, LA

Chianti Colli Senesi 1994: Vegetal flavors and harsh tannins dominate this rustic red. There are some cherry and vanilla flavors beneath the astringency, but the wine isn't giving much pleasure now. 6,200 cases made. • $9 • (03/31/97) • **79**

NADA, FIORENZO

Barbaresco 1994: Good fruit, appealing wet earth notes and well-integrated tannins in this fresh, medium-bodied and succulent red make it drinkable now through 2002. 417 cases made. • $44 • (10/31/97) • **86**

Barbaresco 1993: Bright and ripe, showing currant, berry and mineral flavors in a medium body. Well-structured, with a grip of firm tannins. Try now. 750 cases made. • $43 • (10/31/96) • **86**

NARDI, SILVIO

Brunello di Montalcino 1992: A very floral Brunello with berry and rose petal aromas and flavors, medium body and light, fine tannins. Drink now. • $28 • (09/30/97) • **86**

Brunello di Montalcino 1991: Some fruit flavor, but a little dried up already. Light-to-medium body, with dry tannins and a cherry, cedar aftertaste. Drink now. 6,000 cases made. • $26 • (11/30/96) • **79**

Brunello di Montalcino 1990: Exotic and ripe, with spicy aromas and plenty of sweet plum and cherry flavors. Fine texture, supple tannins and some roasted notes on the finish. 4,200 cases made. • $25 • (07/31/95) • **86**

Brunello di Montalcino 1988 • $33 • (04/30/94) • **86**
Brunello di Montalcino Riserva 1988 • $36 • (10/31/94) • **79**

Rosso di Montalcino 1995: Very good Rosso. Pretty and aromatic with its berry, cherry and truffle aromas and flavors. Medium-bodied, with chewy tannins and a succulent finish. Drink now through 2001. • $15 • (09/30/97) • **87**

Rosso di Montalcino 1994: Not a big wine, but pretty. Smells like freshly picked raspberries with a floral note. Light-bodied, with fresh acidity and a lively finish. Delicious served slightly chilled. 7,000 cases made. • $12 • (11/30/96) • **82**

Rosso di Montalcino 1993 • $13 • (10/31/95) • **84**
Rosso di Montalcino 1992 • $13 • (10/31/94) • **78**

Key: SS—Spectator Selection CS—Cellar Selection HR—Highly Recommended BB—Best Buy $NA—Price not available Ⓐ—Auction Price (BT)—Barrel Tasting
Dates in parentheses indicate the issues in which the ratings were published.

NEGRI, NINO

Valtellina 5 Stelle Sfursat 1994: Very rich and concentrated, this red displays prune, chocolate and walnut flavors accented by new oak. Full-bodied and moderately tannic; try with cheeses. 500 cases made. • $36 • (06/15/97) • **88**

Valtellina Superiore Inferno 1990 • $13 • (02/28/95) • **78**
Valtellina Superiore Inferno 1989: Nebbiolo • $NA • (10/31/96) • **77**
Valtellina Superiore Le Botti d'Oro 1989 • $13 • (02/28/95) • **77**
Valtellina Superiore Riserva 1986 • $20 • (02/28/95) • **86**

NEGRO

Barbera d'Alba Nicolon 1990 • $16 • (12/15/92) • **83**
Barbera d'Alba Nicolon 1989 • $12 • (03/15/91) • **88**

NEIRANO

Barbera d'Asti 1995: Simple, offering some decent red berry flavor, moderate intensity and a round finish. Could be riper. Drink slightly chilled. 2,917 cases made. • $10 • (10/31/97) • **80**

Barbera d'Asti 1994: Light and straightforward. Mildly fruity aromas and flavors with some leather and earth notes. A bit lean and slightly green on the finish. 4,167 cases made. • $7 • (10/31/96) • **77**

Barbera d'Asti Superiore Le Croci 1994: A pure and natural style that's supple in texture, light- to medium-bodied. Has red berry and blackberry aromas and flavors, and a toasty accent to the finish. Try now. 1,583 cases made. • $NA • (10/31/96) • **85**

Cantico Red NV: Light and simple, with strawberry and raspberry flavors plus a touch of vanilla. Light-bodied, with a short finish. Drink chilled. A blend of 80 percent Barbera, 20 percent Dolcetto. 20,000 cases made. • $6 • (01/31/98) • **76**

Gavi 1995: Fairly neutral, offering clean and modest lime, grapefruit and apple notes. • $9 • (01/31/98) • **79**

Gavi 1994 • $10 • (02/29/96) BB • **88**

Moscato d'Asti 1995: A lot of ripe fruit character here, and flavors that lean more towards nectarine and apricot. Soft and round, with a refreshing finish. • $10 • (12/31/97) • **86**

Pinot Grigio Oltrepò Pavese 1995: A zingy wine with peach and citrus flavors. Crisp and well-focused, with an earthy finish. • $8 • (12/31/97) • **83**

NEIVE, CASTELLO DI

Barbaresco Santo Stefano 1994 : Light in color and body, lacking a bit of fruit, this has some modest raspberry, strawberry and currant. A bit diluted and a bit dry on the short finish. 450 cases made. • $20 • • **76**

Barbaresco Santo Stefano 1990 • $20 • (10/31/94) • **88**
Barbaresco Santo Stefano 1989 • $20 • (10/31/93) • **90**
Barbaresco Santo Stefano 1988 • $23 • (10/31/93) • **77**
Barbaresco Santo Stefano 1987 • $20 • (12/31/90) • **79**
Barbaresco Santo Stefano 1982 • $27 • (09/15/88) • **86**
Barbera d'Alba Santo Stefano 1995 • $13 • • **70**
Barbera d'Alba Vigneto Messoirano 1988 • $11 • (07/15/91) • **83**
Dolcetto d'Alba Vigneto Basarin 1990 • $15 • (12/15/92) • **85**
Dolcetto d'Alba Vigneto Basarin 1989 • $12 • (02/28/91) • **80**
Dolcetto d'Alba Vigneto Basarin 1987 • $11 • (03/15/89) • **80**
Dolcetto d'Alba Vigneto Valtorta 1986 • $12 • (08/31/88) • **73**

NERVI, LUIGI & ITALO

Gattinara Vigneto Valferana 1983 • $15 • (05/31/90) • **77**
Spanna 1988 • $9 • (07/15/91) • **80**

NICCOLINI

Chianti 1990 • $6 • (04/30/92) BB • **84**

NICOLIS

Amarone della Valpolicella Classico Ambrosan 1992: A modern style, beginning to mature into caramel and nut aromas and flavors, accented by prune, vanilla and balsamic vinegar. Still on the lean, tough side, but the sweet fruit and warmth win out in the end. Drink now through 2000. 800 cases made. • $44 • (07/31/98) • **87**

Amarone della Valpolicella Classico 1991: A muddled wine that lacks definition despite some spicy elements; ripe, concentrated fruit and moderate length. Seems diluted and oxidized. • $27 • (11/15/97) • **79**

Valpolicella Classico Superiore Seccal 1993: Smoky aromas turn to plum and licorice in this mature Valpolicella; acidity and dry tannins make it rough around the edges. Good length though, and food should tame it. Drink now. 1,000 cases made. • $17 • (07/31/98) • **84**

NITTARDI, CASANUOVA DI

Biondo di Nittardi White 1996: Charming and fresh. Light, bright citrus flavors and a clean, tangy texture. A blend of Trebbiano and Malvasia. Drink now. 2,500 cases made. • $12 • (04/30/98) • **84**

Chianti Classico 1995: Chunky and rich for the vintage with a generous berry character. Medium in body, with velvety texture and a long, flavorful finish. Drink now or hold. 2,000 cases made. • $18 • (09/30/97) • **86**

Chianti Classico 1994: Attractive wild berry and wet earth aromas and flavors in this medium-bodied wine. Light tannins and a fresh finish. Drink now. 3,500 cases made. • $12 • (10/31/96) • **82**

Chianti Classico 1993 • $12 • (10/31/95) • **85**

Chianti Classico 1990 • $NA • (09/15/92) • **80**

Chianti Classico Casanuova di Nittardi 1992 • $NA • (02/28/95) • **82**

Chianti Classico Nittardi 1990 • $NA • (10/31/93) • **86**

Chianti Classico Nittardi Riserva 1990 • $NA • (02/28/95) • **86**

Chianti Classico Riserva 1994: Lovely and elegant, with dried cherry and blackberry aromas and flavors, medium body, fine tannins and a long, fresh finish. • $25 • (09/30/97) • **87**

Chianti Classico Riserva 1993: Attractive texture; very velvety. Berry, earthy and violet aromas and flavors, with well-integrated tannins, in a medium body. Drink now. • $NA • (10/31/96) • **86**

Chianti Classico Riserva 1988 • $NA • (09/15/92) • **80**

NOARNA, CASTEL

Cabernet Vallagarina Vigna Romeo 1989 • $22 • (12/15/92) • **72**

NOTTOLA

Vino Nobile di Montepulciano Vigna del Fattore 1994: Pure, vibrant black cherry flavor gives focus and life. Delicious, smooth, full-bodied, firm with acidity and tannin but accessible. Drink now through 2000. • $21 • (07/31/98) • **88**

NOVACELLA, ABBAZIA DI

Gewürztraminer Alto Adige Valle Isarco 1996: Rose, peach and quince aromas and flavors hold court, all on a rich, juicy texture and balanced structure. A modest finish with a distinct aftertaste of roses. Drink now. • $19 • (05/31/98) • **84**

Gewürztraminer Valle Isarco 1995: Fat and spicy, with plenty of fig and apple flavors and a pleasant, lingering finish. Best as an apéritif. 1,500 cases made. • $20 • (06/15/97) • **84**

Lagrein Alto Adige 1996: An appealing light-bodied red, mixing cherry candy, herb and earth flavors with a smooth texture and lingering finish. Drink now. • $16 • (06/30/98) • **84**

Moscato Rosa Alto Adige 1996: Fascinating. Orange-red in color, with floral, berry and orange peel aromas and candied berry flavors, all on a light, lacy structure. Some tannins on the finish. A unique style from Alto Adige. Drink now through 2003. • $19/375ml • (05/31/98) • **88**

Müller-Thurgau Alto Adige 1996: A more austere style, leaning toward verbena and mineral character, with good acidity and a bitter almond accent on the lingering finish. Drink now. • $16 • (05/31/98) • **83**

Müller-Thurgau Valle Isarco 1995: The aromas of this white are like a late-harvest Pinot Gris, smoky and rich, yet it's dry and spicy, with a firm and lingering aftertaste. 4,000 cases made. • $17 • (06/15/97) • **85**

Sylvaner Alto Adige Valle Isarco 1996: Plenty of floral, peach and citrus character here, with good acidity to keep it bright and lively. Still, it's balanced on the soft side and has a hint of bitterness on the finish. Drink now. • $15 • (05/31/98) • **84**

Sylvaner Valle Isarco 1995: Round, ripe melon and fig flavors have firm acidity that brings them into focus. Refreshing. 10,000 cases made. • $16 • (06/15/97) • **82**

NOZZOLE

Chardonnay Toscana Le Bruniche 1996: Starts out well, but finishes poorly; slightly candied. Has apple and meringue character, medium body, and medium acidity. • $12 • (09/30/97) • **79**

Chardonnay Tuscany Le Bruniche 1995: A modestly proportioned, pleasant but simple white wine with medium body and modest fruit flavor. • $11 • (05/31/97) • **79**

Chardonnay Tuscany Le Bruniche 1994 • $11 • (02/29/96) • **81**

Chianti Classico 1995: Well-crafted, this offers lovely crushed berry and raspberry aromas and flavors, a long and fresh aftertaste. Medium-bodied. Drink now. • $NA • (09/30/97) • **86**

Chianti Classico 1994: Light and simple, with cherry flavors and a hint of wood. Delicate and fruity, but short. • $NA • (09/30/97) • **80**

Chianti Classico 1990 • $13 • (10/31/93) • **88**

Chianti Classico La Forra 1995: Marked by new wood, it's medium-bodied, with round tannins and a fruity, vanilla finish. Good, but a bit too much wood. Drink now. • $NA • (09/30/97) • **83**

Chianti Classico La Forra Riserva 1994: A bit lean and woody, but has some good berry, cherry and earth aromas and flavors. Medium- to light-bodied, with a medium finish. Drink now. • $29 • (09/30/97) • **84**

Chianti Classico La Forra Riserva 1993: A chewy Chianti with berry and tobacco notes on the nose and palate. Medium-bodied with medium-to-light tannins and light finish. • $30 • (10/31/96) • **82**

Chianti Classico La Forra Riserva 1990 • $22 • (02/28/95) • **86**

Chianti Classico La Forra Riserva 1988 • $23 • (10/31/93) • **82**

Chianti Classico La Forra Riserva 1987 • $NA • (11/30/89) (BT) • **88**

Chianti Classico La Forra Riserva 1985 • $21 • (09/15/92) • **84**

Chianti Classico La Forra Riserva 1982 • $20 • (10/31/91) • **77**

Chianti Classico Riserva 1993: Disappointing, considering its producer. Shows some good, ripe fruit character with an earthy note, but it's rather dry and almost papery on the finish. Tasted twice with consistent notes. • $15 • (10/31/96) • **77**

Chianti Classico Riserva 1991 • $12 • (02/28/95) • **77**

Chianti Classico Riserva 1990 • $12 • (02/28/95) • **85**

Chianti Classico Riserva 1989 • $12 • (10/31/93) • **82**

Chianti Classico Riserva 1988 • $14 • (09/15/92) • **81**

Chianti Classico Riserva 1986 • $9 • (10/31/91) • **83**

Chianti Classico Riserva 1985 • $13 • (09/15/91) • **88**

Chianti Classico Riserva 1981 • $7 • (10/31/87) • **72**

Il Pareto 1993: Always a winner. Subtle aromas of blackberry, mint and lightly-toasty oak follow through to a terrific palate with refined tannins and medium body. Excellent potential. Made from Cabernet. Try now. • $45 • (10/31/95) • **92**

Il Pareto 1990 • $41 • (01/01/94) • **96**

Il Pareto 1989 • $30 • (10/31/93) • **85**

Il Pareto 1988 • $28 • (06/15/93) • **91**

OBERTO, ANDREA

Barbera d'Alba Giada 1993: A ripe style with good concentration. Offers loads of vanilla and spice notes, with inviting plum flavors beneath, and lively acidity. Still a bit tannic on the finish. Drink now. 50 cases imported. • $26 • (03/31/97) • **89**

Barbera d'Alba Giada 1992 • $24 • (10/31/95) • **84**

Barolo 1993: Balanced and succulent, this is fresh, lively and fruity. Light- to medium-bodied, it offers some interesting fruit and mineral flavors. Soft tannins make it accessible now through 2000. • $20 • (10/31/97) • **86**

Barolo 1992: There are some nice dried cherry and spice flavors in this wine. Turns tannic on the finish. • $32 • (01/01/97) • **79**

Barolo 1991: There's a prunelike element that runs through this wine. Not much on the finish. • $30 • (01/01/97) • **79**

Barolo Vigneto Rocche 1993: Spicy and vibrant, with fresh cherry and plum flavors and citrus notes. Medium-bodied, it has a smoky complexity on the crisp finish. Too bad the tannins are a bit dry. Try around 2000. • $22 • (10/31/97) • **80**

Barolo Vigneto Rocche 1992: Subtle, fruity flavors, firm tannins and not much length. Drink now through 2000. • $25 • (10/31/96) • **77**

Dolcetto d'Alba 1996: Quite ripe, showing vivid black cherry and wildberry character, but it's herbal as well. Light- to medium-bodied, the tannins clamp down on the finish. Drink now. • $11 • (10/31/97) • **79**

Dolcetto d'Alba Vigneto San Francesco 1994 • $15 • (10/31/95) • **75**

Nebbiolo delle Langhe Vigneto Albarella 1994: Light and nondescript, this red has a smooth texture but not much fruit character or focus. 300 cases imported. • $16 • (01/01/97) • **78**

ITALY

OBERTO, EGIDIO

Barolo La Serra 1993: A traditional Barolo, showing chestnut and earth flavors. Medium-bodied, the fruit is decent although the tannins are rustic. A drying finish doesn't bode well for the future, either. • $NA • (10/31/97) • **75**

OBERTO, LUIGI

Dolcetto d'Alba 1990 • $14 • (03/31/92) • **87**
Nebbiolo delle Langhe 1988 • $16 • (07/31/92) • **78**

ODDERO, FRATELLI

Barbaresco 1993: Appealing blackberry and red berry aromas and flavors. Not terribly complex, but it's well-made and shows nicely integrated tannins. Needs until after 1999. 1,333 cases made. • $19 • (10/31/96) • **86**
Barbaresco 1989 • $15 • (03/31/93) • **85**
Barbaresco 1982 • $15 • (09/15/88) • **84**
Barbera d'Alba 1995: Vivid, lively, zesty, packed with fresh red berry flavor, this dark-colored wine jolts your palate with its clean flavors. Medium-bodied but fairly lean, it's also tannic, so drink with food now through 1999. • $14 • (10/31/97) • **86**
Barbera d'Alba 1994: A fresh and fruity, easy-to-drink red with light tannins, a smooth texture and crisp acidity. • $NA • (10/31/96) • **83**
Barbera d'Alba 1985 • $9 • (07/15/88) • **77**
Barolo 1992: Very floral aromas and fresh cherry and cedar flavors. Light and soft for a Barolo. Ready to drink. 10,417 cases made. • $24 • (10/31/96) • **82**
Barolo 1991 • $17 • (10/31/95) • **79**
Barolo 1989 • $16 • (10/31/94) • **82**
Barolo 1983 • $15 • (09/15/88) • **85**
Barolo 1982 • $14 • (06/30/87) • **91**
Barolo 1980 • $7 • (05/16/86) • **73**
Barolo Mondoca di Bussia Soprana 1993: A beautiful wine that bespeaks the hand of a great traditional-style winemaker. Rich, ripe and concentrated, with a real sense of *terroir*, it delivers layers of wet earth, mineral, blackberry, spice and oak flavors. Intense but well-balanced, with a very long finish. Try around 2002. 653 cases made. • $29 • (10/31/97) • **90**
Barolo Mondoca di Bussia Soprana 1990 • $30 • (10/31/95) • **69**
Barolo Rocche dei Rivera di Castiglione 1993: Unusually full-bodied for a '93, yet elegant in structure. Coats your mouth with black cherry and anise flavors, and toasty, smoky, cigar-box accents. Chewy, tannic finish; cellar until 2000. • $58 • (10/31/97) • **85**
Barolo Vigna Rionda 1993: A rustic style, with the chestnut character turning dry and tough on the finish. Only modest fruit shows in this medium-bodied '93. • $58 • (10/31/97) • **74**
Barolo Vigna Rionda 1990 • $30 • (10/31/95) • **72**
Dolcetto d'Alba 1996: Sweet red- and blackberry character and ripe tannins highlight this medium-bodied red. It ends with a succulent, rather supple and sophisticated finish, but it's very earthy. • $14 • (10/31/97) • **83**
Dolcetto d'Alba 1995: Medium-bodied and very fresh, with bright, lean, cherry flavors. Slightly tart and tannic. 2,083 cases made. • $14 • (10/31/96) • **82**
Dolcetto d'Alba 1989 • $8 • (04/30/91) • **78**
Dolcetto d'Alba 1987 • $9 • (03/15/89) • **78**
Dolcetto d'Alba 1986 • $9 • (03/15/89) • **85**
Nebbiolo delle Langhe 1990 • $NA • (10/31/94) • **79**

OLIVETO

Chianti 1990 • $6 • (03/31/93) • **79**

OLMO, PODERE

Chianti Classico Riserva 1994: Rather simple, slightly earthy and short with some berry character. 415 cases made. • $18 • (09/30/97) • **79**

Key: SS—Spectator Selection CS—Cellar Selection HR—Highly Recommended BB—Best Buy $NA—Price not available Ⓐ—Auction Price (BT)—Barrel Tasting
Dates in parentheses indicate the issues in which the ratings were published.

ORNELLAIA, TENUTA DELL'

Le Volte 1995: An herbal-tasting red that turns a bit green in the end. Ripe and round, though not particularly complex. • $17 • (10/31/97) • **83**
Le Volte 1993 • $13 • (02/28/95) • **82**
Le Volte 1992 • $13 • (02/28/95) • **78**
Le Volte 1991 • $14 • (10/31/93) • **87**
Masseto 1994: Superb winemaking. Notable for its dark, inky color, intense cassis and berry aromas, this wine is full-bodied and very silky with a long, long finish. An outstanding Merlot, as usual from this producer. Better after 1999. • $NA • (09/30/97) • **92**
Masseto 1993: The Le Pin of Italy. Super-ripe berry, Merlot character, with aromas and flavors of violet, berry, cassis and a hint of dried herbs. Full-bodied, with full tannins, yet soft and velvety on the finish. Drink now. 1,500 cases made. • $117 • (10/31/96) • **91**
Masseto 1992 • $59 • (02/28/95) • **93**
Masseto 1991 • $59 • (02/28/95) • **91**
Masseto 1990 • $NA • (10/31/93) • **90**
Masseto 1989 • $60 • (10/31/93) • **83**
Masseto 1988 • $NA • (09/15/91) • **90**
Ornellaia 1994: A good backbone of tannins and fruit, but it's rather too herbal. Medium-bodied, with firm tannins and a green tobacco finish. Try now. Tasted twice, with consistent notes. • $56 • (09/30/97) • **85**
Ornellaia 1993: Not the biggest Ornellaia, but delicious. Pretty berry, cherry and dried herb character with a hint of new wood. Medium-bodied with soft tannins and a juicy finish. Not one for long aging; very good to drink now. • $50 • (10/31/96) • **88**
Ornellaia 1992 • $44 • (10/31/95) • **85**
Ornellaia 1991 • $38 • (02/28/95) • **86**
Ornellaia 1990 • $42 • (11/15/93) • **96**
Ornellaia 1989 • $NA • (11/15/93) • **87**
Ornellaia 1988 • $NA • (11/15/93) • **93**
Ornellaia 1987 • $NA • (11/15/93) • **88**
Ornellaia 1986 • $NA • (11/15/93) • **92**
Ornellaia 1985 • $NA • (11/15/93) • **87**
Poggio alla Gazze 1996: Has a subtle melon, honey and floral character, tinged with orange peel and tropical fruit. Medium-bodied, with well-integrated, lively acidity and a fresh finish. Delicious. • $NA • (09/30/97) • **88**

P.L.D. VITICOLTORI

Greco di Tufo Loggia della Serra 1996: A smooth and mellow white wine, buttery-tasting but still crisp, with good citrus and apple flavors. A bit obvious but quite tasty. • $20 • (12/31/97) • **84**

PACENTI, SIRO

Brunello di Montalcino 1991: Plenty of fruit flavors, with a firm backbone of tannins and just a hint of new wood on the nose and palate. Medium-bodied, with fine tannins and a long finish. Try now. • $36 • (11/30/96) • **89**
Brunello di Montalcino 1990: Really caresses your palate with tobacco, berry and cedar character. Full in body, wonderfully ripe and round, featuring velvety tannins and a long, flavorful finish. Drinkable now. • $36 • (10/31/95) • **92**
Brunello di Montalcino 1988 • $31 • (04/30/94) • **90**
Brunello di Montalcino Riserva 1990: Lovely, with mineral, berry and light spice flavors through and through. Medium-bodied, with silky tannins and a caressing texture. A tiny bit alcoholic, perhaps. Delicious now, but will improve with age. • $40 • (11/30/96) • **90**
Rosso di Montalcino 1995: Generous with its dried cherry, mineral and fruit character. Has a medium body, velvety tannins and a fruity finish. Drink or hold. • $12 • (09/30/97) • **88**
Rosso di Montalcino 1994: Firm and fresh, with a generous character of dried cherry and herbs. Medium-bodied, with silky tannins and a long, refreshing finish. Another winner from Pacenti. Drink now or hold. • $16 • (11/30/96) • **86**
Rosso di Montalcino 1993 • $18 • (10/31/95) • **90**
Rosso di Montalcino 1991 • $16 • (04/30/94) • **84**
Rosso di Montalcino 1989 • $14 • (04/30/92) • **87**

PACINA

Chianti Colli Senesi 1994: Slightly earthy, but offers some pretty, ripe fruit character. Medium in body. Tannins are fine, finish is light. Drink now. • $15 • (09/30/97) • **82**

PADAELECTI

Brunello di Montalcino Riserva 1988 • $NA • (10/31/94) • **83**

PADELLETTI

Brunello di Montalcino 1990: Delicate, almost meager cherry and raspberry flavor and a hint of leather on the nose and palate. Medium in body, fine tannins and a long finish. Drinkable now. • $NA • (10/31/95) • **85**
Brunello di Montalcino 1988 • $NA • (04/30/94) • **87**

PAGGIO

Pinot Grigio Alto Adige 1996: Assertive. Smells like flowers and tastes like baked apples with a hint of spice. Distinctive, vibrant and well-balanced, but not for everyone. 2,800 cases made. • $10 • (12/15/97) • **83**
Pinot Grigio Alto Adige 1994 • $8 • (06/15/96) • **86**

PAGLIARESE

Capitolare di Biturica Il Neri 1991 • $NA • (10/31/95) • **87**
Capitolare di Biturica Il Neri 1990 • $NA • (02/28/95) • **88**
Chianti Classico 1993 • $NA • (10/31/95) • **86**
Chianti Classico 1992 • $9 • (02/28/95) • **80**
Chianti Classico 1991 • $9 • (10/31/93) • **78**
Chianti Classico 1990 • $11 • (09/15/92) • **80**
Chianti Classico 1985 • $6 • (03/31/88) • **76**
Chianti Classico Boscardini Riserva 1981 • $9 • (05/31/88) • **82**
Chianti Classico Boscardini Riserva 1980 • $9 • (03/15/87) • **85**
Chianti Classico Riserva 1988 • $15 • (09/15/92) • **88**
Della Provincia di Siena Camerlengo 1991 • $NA • (10/31/95) • **85**

PAITIN

Barbaresco Sorì Paitin 1994: Light-bodied and quite juicy, but also herbaceous. Turns sour on the tannic finish. 1,000 cases made. • $29 • (10/31/97) • **72**
Barbaresco Sorì Paitin 1993: Bright and lively, with a solid core of fruit and tannin. Plenty of berry and herb flavors, but seems a bit simple and rough on the finish. Try with pizza or pasta. Drinkable now • $27 • (10/31/96) • **83**
Barbaresco Sorì Paitin 1991 • $20 • (10/31/95) • **85**
Barbera d'Alba Campolive 1995: A sweet, ripe, red, packed with lovely flavors of black cherry, blueberry and raspberry, plus hints of earth and chocolate. Light- to medium-bodied, it just lacks a bit of length. Drink slightly chilled now. 250 cases made. • $16 • (10/31/97) • **84**
Barbera d'Alba Campolive 1993: Seductive, ripe and sweet. Toasty oak, violet, spice, plum and blackberry flavors are appealing, though a touch diluted. Drink now. • $NA • (10/31/96) • **85**
Dolcetto d'Alba Sorì Paitin 1996: Fabulous wine, with great purple-red color, medium to full body, layers of rich wild berry, blueberry and cassis flavors. A dense Dolcetto worth hunting down. Has supple, well-integrated, ripe tannins, so enjoy now through 2000. 1,083 cases made. • $14 • (10/31/97) • **91**

PALAGIO, IL

Chardonnay Tuscany 1996: A medium-bodied wine, with aromas of apples and ash, light acidity and a chalky finish. A bit dull. Drink now. • $NA • (09/30/97) • **81**
Chianti Classico 1995: Wonderfully fruity with its raspberry and cherry aromas and flavors. Medium-bodied, with light tannins and a fresh, crisp finish. Drink now. • $NA • (09/30/97) • **83**
Chianti Classico 1994: A medium-bodied wine that shows a pretty berry and dried herb character, light tannins and a silky finish. • $NA • (10/31/96) • **83**
Chianti Classico 1993 • $NA • (10/31/95) • **82**
Chianti Classico 1992 • $NA • (02/28/95) • **79**
Chianti Classico Riserva 1991 • $NA • (10/31/95) • **86**
Chianti Classico Riserva 1990 • $NA • (02/28/95) • **86**

PALAZZETTA, LA

Brunello di Montalcino 1991: A pretty, plummy wine, with fine tannins and interesting dried herb and dried berry nuances. Medium-bodied, with fine tannins and a fresh finish. Ready to drink. 333 cases made. • $NA • (11/30/96) • **85**
Brunello di Montalcino 1988 • $NA • (04/30/94) • **84**
Rosso di Montalcino 1994: A simple no-nonsense Rosso. It's light-bodied, with dried cherry and berry aromas and flavors, hints of earth, and a light finish. 666 cases made. • $NA • (11/30/96) • **81**
Rosso di Montalcino 1991 • $14 • (04/30/94) • **83**

PALAZZINO, PODERE IL

Chianti Classico 1990 • $16 • (10/31/93) • **90**
Chianti Classico 1988 • $16 • (09/15/91) • **90**
Chianti Classico 1987 • $12 • (03/31/90) • **67**
Chianti Classico 1986 • $9 • (01/31/89) • **86**
Chianti Classico 1985 • $11 • (11/30/87) SS • **93**
Chianti Classico 1983 • $5 • (09/16/85) • **78**
Chianti Classico Riserva 1987 • $15 • (12/15/92) • **85**
Chianti Classico Riserva 1985 • $22 • (09/15/91) • **88**
Chianti Classico Riserva 1983 • $21 • (11/15/87) • **80**
Colli dell'Etruria Centrale La Rosa Bianca 1995: Flawed, with a bubbling palate and oxidized flavors. Tasted twice, with consistent notes. Not recommended. • $NA • (09/30/97) • **65**
Grosso Sanese Chianti Classico 1994: Has plenty of berry and cherry flavors, a hint of mushroom, light tannins and a light finish. Medium-bodied. Slightly short aftertaste. Drink now. • $35 • (09/30/97) • **84**
Grosso Sanese 1990 • $35 • (10/31/93) HR • **93**
Grosso Sanese 1988 • $29 • (03/15/91) • **88**
Grosso Sanese 1987 • $25 • (11/30/89) • **90**
Grosso Sanese 1986 • $22 • (02/15/89) • **87**
Grosso Sanese 1985 • $13 • (12/15/87) • **94**

PALAZZO VECCHIO, FATTORIA DI

Rosso di Montalcino 1993 • $NA • (10/31/95) • **84**
Vino Nobile di Montepulciano 1994: Delivers some good, ripe fruit but it's too dry and austere on the finish to score higher. Tasted twice, with consistent notes. • $15 • (09/30/97) • **77**
Vino Nobile di Montepulciano Riserva 1993: Offers some fruit and a hint of leather, but it's rather austere and dry on the finish. Drink now. • $23 • (09/30/97) • **79**

PALAZZONE, IL

Brunello di Montalcino 1991: A pretty wine with aromas and flavors of berry, cedar and leather. Medium body, with soft tannins and a fresh finish. • $NA • (09/30/97) • **86**
Brunello di Montalcino 1990: Smooth and elegant, showing well-defined flavors of blackberry, black cherry and flowers. Supple tannins make for nice drinking now. • $NA • (10/31/95) • **88**
Rosso di Montalcino 1995: Shows good dark color along with a mouthful of dried cherry, plum and violet flavors. Medium-bodied, with firm tannins. Drink now or hold. • $NA • (09/30/97) • **85**

PALLADINO

Barolo 1993: A traditional style of Barolo, going for earth and pure fruit, but picking up dry tannins and a rustic texture along the way. Medium-bodied, it seems far from ready to drink. Best from 2000 through 2003. • $NA • (10/31/97) • **83**

PALLAVICINI

Frascati Superiore 1995: Bland, with earthy aromas and flavors, and a finish that tastes of onion. • $9 • (01/31/97) • **75**
Frascati Superiore 1993 • $9 • (10/31/94) • **83**

PANCRAZI, MARCHESI

Pinot Nero Toscana Villa di Bagnolo 1994: A model for Italian Pinot Noir. It has breathtaking aromas of wild strawberries and raspberries with a hint of wet earth, a medium-to-full body with medium, velvety tannins and clean acidity. Lengthy, flavorful finish. Delicious now, but will improve. 1,000 cases made. • $32 • (09/30/97) • **90**

Toscana Tenuta di S. Donato 1995: Attractive strawberry and spice aromas and flavors mark this medium- to light-bodied wine, with light tannins and a fresh finish. Drink now. 1,000 cases made. • $17 • (09/30/97) • **85**

PANERETTA, CASTELLO DELLA

Chianti Classico 1993: Already at its peak. Shows a goodly amount of dried cherry and leather aromas and flavors. Medium body, light tannins, crisp finish. Drink now. • $NA • (10/31/96) • **79**
Chianti Classico 1992 • $NA • (02/28/95) • **79**
Chianti Classico 1991 • $NA • (10/31/93) • **85**
Chianti Classico 1990 • $NA • (10/31/93) • **84**
Chianti Classico 1988 • $NA • (09/15/91) • **79**
Chianti Classico Riserva 1990 • $NA • (02/28/95) • **86**
Chianti Classico Riserva 1988 • $NA • (09/15/92) • **80**
Chianti Classico Riserva 1985 • $NA • (09/15/91) • **92**
Terrine 1993: Lots of new wood, but also some impressive ripe berry and chocolate flavors. Medium-bodied, with fine tannins and a minty finish. Try now. • $NA • (10/31/96) • **88**
Terrine 1990 • $NA • (02/28/95) • **85**

PANIZZI, GIOVANNI

Vernaccia di San Gimignano 1996: Lively and brisk; a combination of crisp citrus and subtle mineral flavors in a totally refreshing white wine. Drink now. 3,750 cases made. • $15 • (04/30/98) • **87**
Vernaccia di San Gimignano Riserva 1995: A different style of Vernaccia, this strives for complexity. Has generous oak accents but we miss the lively fruit flavors and crisp acidity. Drink now. 580 cases made. • $24 • (04/30/98) • **84**

PANZANO

Chianti Classico Riserva 1985 • $NA • (09/15/91) • **86**

PAOLIS, CASTEL DE

Frascati Superiore Vigna Adriana 1995: A slightly sweet-tasting wine that turns coarse on the finish. The flavors and aromas are dominated by apples. 416 cases made. • $40 • (01/01/97) • **78**
I Quattro Mori 1994: A serious red, with lots of body and fruit flavor and a nice streak of spicy oak. Tannic but rich, with a lingering finish. Drink now through 1999. 333 cases made. • $45 • (04/30/97) • **88**

PARADISO, FATTORIA

Barbarossa 1983 • $6 Ⓐ • (03/15/89) • **80**
Sangiovese di Romagna Vigna delle Lepri Riserva Superiore 1987 • $16 • (07/15/91) • **85**

PARADISO, IL

Brunello di Montalcino 1990: No paradise here. Smelling a bit funky and tasting a bit odd. Hard to recommend. Lean and earthy. • $NA • (10/31/95) • **70**
Rosso di Montalcino 1993 • $NA • (10/31/95) • **82**
Rosso di Montalcino 1991 • $NA • (04/30/94) • **82**

PARUSSO, ARMANDO

Barbera d'Alba 1988 • $12 • (03/15/91) • **85**
Barbera d'Alba Bricco di Pugnana 1990 • $20 • (10/15/93) • **91**
Barbera d'Alba Bricco di Pugnana 1989 • $18 • (10/31/92) • **88**
Barbera d'Alba Ornati 1995: Lush and ripe, a sweet-tasting Barbera that delivers complex licorice, plum, prune, toast, chocolate, pepper and spice. Medium-to-full body, with a supple texture. Impressive. Delicious now through 2002. 517 cases made. • $17 • (10/31/97) • **88**
Barbera d'Alba Ornati 1994: Sharp, tart and green, this lacks opulence but offers herb, tea leaf and spice flavors. 667 cases made. • $17 • (10/31/96) • **77**

> **Key:** SS—Spectator Selection CS—Cellar Selection HR—Highly Recommended BB—Best Buy $NA—Price not available Ⓐ—Auction Price (BT)—Barrel Tasting
> **Dates in parentheses indicate the issues in which the ratings were published.**

Barbera d'Alba Ornati 1993: Fairly rich, with hints of spicy oak, chocolate, rose petal and black cherry flavors. Medium- to full-bodied and harmonious in texture. Just a bit short on the finish. Drink now. 517 cases made. • $18 • (10/31/96) • **87**
Barbera d'Alba Pugnane-Ornati 1992 • $17 • (10/31/94) • **75**
Barbera d'Alba Superiore 1989 • $11 • (10/31/92) • **84**
Barolo 1993: This light-colored red offers simple cherry aromas and ripe fruit flavor, then turns very dry and short on the finish. An odd wine. 583 cases made. • $28 • (10/31/97) • **76**
Barolo 1990 • $27 • (10/31/94) • **90**
Barolo 1985 • $27 • (04/30/91) • **84**
Barolo Bussia 1990 • $38 • (01/01/94) • **79**
Barolo Bussia 1989 • $38 • (10/31/94) • **92**
Barolo Bussia Vigna Munie 1993: Flavorful mineral, blackberry, and wet earth notes bespeak good *terroir*. It's fairly concentrated, with tannins that turn dry on the finish, so wait until 2000 or so before trying. 550 cases made. • $37 • (10/31/97) • **88**
Barolo Bussia Munie 1992: Bursting with fresh currant and cherry flavors backed by firm tannins and acidity. Drink now. 429 cases made. • $30 • (10/31/96) • **85**
Barolo Bussia Vigna Rocche 1993: Clean and elegant, with some earth, mineral and red berry flavor. Medium-bodied, it turns a bit lean and dry on the finish, but age might soften it. Try around 2000. 417 cases made. • $40 • (10/31/97) • **85**
Barolo Bussia Rocche 1992: Herbal flavors dominate in this tart, tannic Barolo. Lean in texture, not much fruit flavor. If you like crisp reds, try now. 304 cases made. • $35 • (10/31/96) • **77**
Barolo Bussia Rocche 1991: In a classic style, marked by mineral, floral and cherry flavors and a stiff texture. Melts in the mouth before toughening on the finish. Try now. 483 cases made. • $30 • (10/31/96) • **87**
Barolo Bussia Rocche 1988 • $35 • (10/31/93) • **87**
Barolo Mariondino 1990 • $32 • (10/31/94) • **68**
Barolo Mariondino 1989 • $30 • (10/31/93) • **87**
Barolo Mariondino 1988 • $25 • (10/31/93) • **90**
Barolo Mariondino 1986 • $23 • (04/30/91) • **83**
Bricco Rovella 1992 • $15 • (01/01/94) • **76**
Dolcetto d'Alba 1994 • $12 • (10/31/95) • **80**
Mariondino 1991 • $11 • (10/31/94) • **80**
Mariondino 1990 • $14 • (10/31/92) • **86**
Nebbiolo delle Langhe 1988 • $11 • (07/31/92) • **79**

PASINI, VOLPE

Merlot Colli Orientali del Friuli Villa Volpe 1993 • $11 • (06/15/96) • **80**
Pinot Bianco Colli Orientali del Friuli Zuc di Volpe 1994 • $20 • (06/15/96) • **77**
Pinot Grigio Colli Orientali del Friuli Villa Volpe 1994 • $11 • (06/15/96) • **84**
Pinot Grigio Colli Orientali del Friuli Zuc di Volpe 1994 • $20 • (06/15/96) • **84**
Refosco Colli Orientali del Friuli Zuc di Volpe 1990 • $20 • (06/15/96) • **81**
Sauvignon Colli Orientali del Friuli Villa Volpe 1994 • $11 • (06/15/96) • **76**

PASQUA, FRATELLI

Cabernet Sauvignon Marago 1989 • $13 • (09/15/92) • **83**
Recioto della Valpolicella Amarone Vigneti Casterna 1986 • $16 • (09/15/92) • **85**
Valpolicella Villa Borghetti 1989 • $7 • (09/15/92) • **79**

PASQUALE, VEGLIO

Barolo Vigna Batistot 1988 • $30 • (10/31/94) • **87**

PASQUERO, ELIA

Barbaresco Sorì Paitin 1985 • $14 • (03/31/90) • **88**
Barbera d'Alba Sorì Paitin 1989 • $10 • (11/30/91) BB • **88**
Barbera d'Alba Sorì Paitin 1988 • $8 • (03/15/91) • **83**
Dolcetto d'Alba Sorì Paitin 1991 • $11 • (09/30/93) • **80**

PATERNO, FATTORIA DI

Vino Nobile di Montepulciano 1994: Simple and spicy, medium- to light-bodied, with tobacco and berry character, light tannins and a crisp finish. Drink now. • $NA • (09/30/97) • **85**

Vino Nobile di Montepulciano Riserva 1993: Lovely, elegant Sangiovese with berry, tobacco and light earth tones. Medium-bodied, with light, silky tannins and a fresh finish. Very good. • $NA • (09/30/97) • **86**

PATERNOSTER

Aglianico del Vulture 1994: A distinctive red, sporting aromas and flavors of dried cherries, licorice and sage. It's soft and rich with good underlying structure and a lingering, cedary finish. Drinkable now. • $20 • (06/15/97) • **87**
Aglianico del Vulture 1987 • $16 • (01/31/92) • **82**
Aglianico del Vulture Don Anselmo Riserva del Foudatore 1985 • $32 • (09/15/92) • **81**

PECCHENINO, FRATELLI

Dolcetto di Dogliani Pizabo 1994 • $NA • (10/31/95) • **86**

PECORARI, FRANCESCO

Chardonnay Isonzo 1994: Aromas reminiscent of a well-used locker room give way to dull, earthy flavors. Too sweaty for us. • $NA • (06/15/97) • **68**
Isonzo Dom Pietro 1994: Stale and herbal with a cloying finish. 50 cases made. • $20 • (06/15/97) • **72**
Isonzo Lis Neris 1991 • $20 • (02/29/96) • **80**
Lis Neris 1990 • $20 • (10/15/94) • **89**
Pinot Grigio Gris 1994 • $12 • (06/15/96) • **81**
Pinot Grigio Isonzo 1994: Quite ripe with tropical aromas and flavors, and plenty of buttery notes to boot. A piney note runs through it, too. 5,000 cases made. • $12 • (01/31/97) • **83**
Sant' Jurosa Isonzo White 1994: A wine for extremists. From the lurid yellow color to the intense yet disjointed flavors, this is far from a typical Chard. 875 cases made. • $20 • (06/15/97) • **76**
Sauvignon Blanc Isonzo 1994 • $12 • (06/15/96) • **75**
Sauvignon Blanc Isonzo Picol 1994 • $12 • (06/15/96) • **83**
Tocai Friulano Isonzo 1994 • $12 • (06/15/96) • **81**
Verduzzo Friulano Tal Luc 1994 • $20 • (01/01/96) • **85**

PECORARI, PIERPAOLO

Chardonnay Isonzo 1993 • $16 • (01/31/95) • **83**
Merlot Isonzo del Friuli Baolar 1995: This has modest currant, herb and vanilla flavors but tastes muddled and finishes slightly astringently. Drink now. • $19 • (05/31/98) • **79**
Pinot Bianco Isonzo 1993 • $16 • (01/31/95) • **80**
Pinot Grigio Isonzo del Friuli 1996: Makes an impression on your palate. Racy, intense and minerally, reminiscent of an Austrian Riesling, with almond, peach flavors, a lean, sinewy structure and lingering finish. Drink now through 2000. 1,200 cases made. • $21 • (06/30/98) • **88**
Pinot Grigio Isonzo del Friuli Olivers 1996: Shows new-oak nuances of clove, nutmeg and vanilla that dominate the fruit character. There's richness, concentration and firm structure, though, so give it time. Drink now through 2000. • $19 • (05/31/98) • **83**
Pinot Grigio Isonzo 1994 • $18 • (06/15/96) • **75**
Pinot Grigio Isonzo 1993 • $16 • (01/31/95) • **78**
Sauvignon Isonzo del Friuli Kolàus 1996: Atypical. Deep yellow-green in color, with smoky, nutty, mature aromas that persist on the palate right through to the long finish. Rich and full-bodied, but oak is the dominant theme. Drink now. • $19 • (07/31/98) • **84**
Tocai Friulano Isonzo 1993 • $14 • (01/31/95) • **80**

PELISSERO

Barbaresco 1994: An exotic wine with flavors of thyme, sage, rosemary and cassis. Medium-bodied and lovely to taste, it covers the palate with round, supple tannins. Drinkable now through 2002. 664 cases made. • $32 • (10/31/97) • **86**
Barbaresco 1992 • $NA • (10/31/95) • **82**
Barbaresco Vanotu 1994: Exotic, elegant and succulent, showing rose petal, jasmine, violet, cassis, toasty oak and sweet-tasting licorice flavors. Medium-bodied and very supple. With just a touch of dilution, it is a delight to drink now. 500 cases made. • $42 • (10/31/97) • **86**
Barbaresco Vanotu 1993: Pinot Noir-like. Offers a core of tea, floral, cherry and strawberry flavors, but lacks harmony. Rather tart tannins on the crisp finish. Try now. 1,000 cases made. • $19 • (10/31/96) • **81**
Barbaresco Vanotu 1991 • $19 • (10/31/95) • **76**
Barbaresco Vanotu 1990 • $NA • (11/30/94) • **87**
Barbera d'Alba Piani 1995: Crisp, juicy and succulent. A fairly lean Barbera that needs food to soften it. Offers cherry, cassis bush and dried herb notes. Drink slightly chilled. 833 cases made. • $19 • (10/31/97) • **80**
Barbera d'Alba Piani 1994: A sturdy young red with a good balance of berry flavors and firm tannins. A bit rough on the finish, but the fruit lingers. • $NA • (10/31/96) • **84**
Barbera d'Alba Piani 1993 • $12 • (07/31/95) • **84**
Barbera d'Alba Ronchi 1990 • $11 • (04/30/93) • **87**
Dolcetto d'Alba Augenta 1994: Unusually hard for a Dolcetto; a bit rough in texture and tannic on the finish, but the exotic, floral, violet and currant flavors make it rather special. Ready to drink. 833 cases made. • $7 • (10/31/96) • **85**
Dolcetto d'Alba Augenta 1993 • $12 • (07/31/95) • **84**
Dolcetto d'Alba Munfrina 1996: A plummy Dolcetto, offering crisp cherry and dried herb flavors. Medium-bodied, acidic and slightly green, with dry tannins. 1,500 cases made. • $16 • (10/31/97) • **76**
Dolcetto d'Alba Munfrina 1994 • $NA • (10/31/95) • **84**
Dolcetto d'Alba Munfrina 1991 • $12 • (04/30/93) • **83**
Favorita Langhe 1993 • $11 • (07/31/95) • **76**

PERTIMALI

Brunello di Montalcino 1982 • $25 • (01/31/88) • **77**
Brunello di Montalcino Riserva 1985 • $41 • (11/30/90) • **83**
Rosso di Montalcino 1987 • $13 • (01/31/91) • **84**
Vigna dei Fili di Seta 1994: Slightly brown hue to the ruby color, and slightly sweaty aromas dominate the fruit flavors. Barely drinkable. Tasted twice with consistent notes. • $37 • (10/31/96) • **70**

PESCAIA, LA

Brunello di Montalcino 1990: Brownish-colored, simple and one-dimensional, like a weak Pinot Noir. Drink now. • $NA • (10/31/95) • **79**
Brunello di Montalcino 1988 • $NA • (04/30/94) • **80**
Rosso di Montalcino 1993 • $NA • (10/31/95) • **78**
Rosso di Montalcino 1991 • $NA • (04/30/94) • **77**

PESCATORI, CASA DI

Red 1993 • $5 • (01/31/96) • **80**

PETROGNANO

Pomino 1993 • $NA • (10/31/95) • **85**

PETROIO, FATTORIA DI

Chianti Classico 1995: Bubbling over with strawberry character, this is medium- to light-bodied with fresh acidity and a fruity finish. Drink now. 3,000 cases made. • $8 • (09/30/97) • **84**
Chianti Classico 1994: Lovely, soft and generous. Delivers nice plum and berry aromas and flavors and a succulent finish. Medium body. Drink now or hold. • $NA • (10/31/96) • **84**
Chianti Classico 1993 • $NA • (10/31/95) • **80**
Chianti Classico 1992 • $NA • (02/28/95) • **73**
Chianti Classico 1991 • $NA • (10/31/95) • **65**
Chianti Classico 1988 • $NA • (09/15/91) • **83**
Chianti Classico Cru Montetondo 1990 • $NA • (10/31/93) • **86**
Chianti Classico Cru Montetondo 1988 • $NA • (09/15/91) • **90**
Chianti Classico Riserva 1994: Wonderful intensity of blackberry, cherry character, but rather tough. Medium-bodied, with intense tannins and a slightly austere finish. Better after this year. 500 cases made. • $15 • (09/30/97) • **83**
Chianti Classico Riserva 1993: A big improvement over previous efforts from this property, this is a sleek and racy riserva with violet, berry and mineral aromas and flavors. Medium-bodied with very fine tannins and a refreshing finish. From Lenzi. • $NA • (10/31/96) • **86**
Chianti Classico Riserva 1990 • $NA • (02/28/95) • **79**
Chianti Classico Riserva 1988 • $17 • (10/31/93) • **84**
L'Unico di Petroio 1990 • $NA • (10/31/93) • **87**

PETROLO, FATTORIA

Chianti 1991 • $NA • (10/31/93) • **85**
Chianti 1990 • $NA • (10/31/93) • **80**
Chianti Colli Aretini 1995: A pretty, delicate and fruity Chianti with plum and berry character, soft texture and a fresh finish. 5,000 cases made. • $10 • (09/30/97) • **81**
Chianti Colli Aretini 1993: Very delicate, with pleasant berry aromas and flavors, but drying out slightly. Drink now. • $10 • (10/31/96) • **78**
Chianti Colli Aretini Riserva 1993: A leathery and light Chianti Classico with some fruit flavors, but a drying finish. Drink this one in a hurry. • $20 • (10/31/96) • **78**
Chianti Colli Fiorentini 1993 • $NA • (10/31/95) • **80**
Chianti Riserva 1991 • $NA • (02/28/95) • **84**
Galatrona 1994: A newcomer to Merlot—and red hot. This wine is dark-colored with the essence of blackberry, cherry and boysenberry marking its character. It's full-bodied and gushing with fruit, has full tannins, and is long and velvety. Better after 1999. 150 cases made. • $NA • (09/30/97) • **91**
Merlot Tuscany 1988 • $24 • (08/31/91) • **83**
Torrione 1994: A wonderfully aromatic red with blackberry, tobacco and cherry aromas. Medium-bodied, with silky tannins and a light, sweet fruit finish. Drink now or hold. 900 cases made. • $32 • (09/30/97) • **88**
Torrione 1993: A generous wine with mint, berry, and spice aromas and flavors. Medium-bodied, with firm tannins and a crisp finish. Drink now or hold. Sangiovese. • $NA • (10/31/96) • **87**
Torrione 1991 • $NA • (02/28/95) • **86**
Torrione 1990 • $NA • (10/31/93) • **90**

PIAN CORNELLO

Brunello di Montalcino 1992: Hard to believe it's really a '92. Shows plenty of bright berry, cherry and vanilla aromas and flavors, full-to-medium body, has fine tannins and a long finish. Drink now or hold. • $30 • (09/30/97) • **88**
Rosso di Montalcino 1995: Very fresh, with floral, violet and berry character, good structure. Medium-to-full body, with medium tannins and finish. Drink now or hold. • $14 • (09/30/97) • **86**
Rosso di Montalcino 1991 • $NA • (04/30/94) • **80**

PIANPOLVERE SOPRANO

Barbera d'Alba 1988 • $10 • (03/15/91) • **84**
Barbera d'Alba 1987 • $10 • (03/15/91) • **75**
Barbera d'Alba 1986 • $8 • (03/15/89) • **83**
Barbera d'Alba 1985 • $15 • (03/15/91) • **86**
Barolo 1991 • $32 • (10/31/95) • **84**
Barolo 1990 • $40 • (10/31/95) • **79**
Barolo 1988 • $30 • (10/31/93) • **80**
Barolo 1982 • $26 • (07/31/89) • **74**
Dolcetto d'Alba 1993 • $14 • (10/31/95) • **80**

PIAZZO, ARMANDO

Barolo 1993: Earthy, funky and a little horsey, this medium-bodied Barolo shows dry tannins that linger on the astringent finish. • $NA • (10/31/97) • **77**

PICCINI

Chianti 1991 • $6 • (06/15/93) • **75**
Chianti Classico 1995: Full of strawberry aromas and flavors, this is medium-bodied with fine, light tannins and a delicate finish. Drink now. • $NA • (09/30/97) • **83**
Chianti Classico 1994: Offers some ripe fruit aromas and flavors, but it's rather light and already showing some maturity. • $10 • (10/31/96) • **77**
Chianti Classico 1992 • $7 • (02/28/95) • **79**
Chianti Classico 1990 • $8 • (06/15/93) • **79**

Key: SS—Spectator Selection CS—Cellar Selection HR—Highly Recommended BB—Best Buy $NA—Price not available Ⓐ—Auction Price (BT)—Barrel Tasting
Dates in parentheses indicate the issues in which the ratings were published.

Chianti Classico Riserva 1994: Rather weak and mature, it has some berry character but leather and dryness dominate. Light-to-medium body; light finish. • $NA • (09/30/97) • **77**
Chianti Classico Riserva 1993: A bit funky with earth, tobacco and tomato aromas and flavors. Medium-bodied, with high acidity. • $13 • (10/31/96) • **73**
Chianti Classico Riserva 1990 • $10 • (02/28/95) • **79**

PICI, LE

Chianti Classico 1993 • $NA • (10/31/95) • **71**

PIEROPAN, LEONILDO

Recioto di Soave La Colombare 1994: Starts off nicely, with botrytis, apricot, mango and spice character that's grounded by the elegant structure and citrus-peel component. Finishes a bit short. Drink now through 2002. 150 cases made. • $23/500ml • (06/15/98) • **87**
Recioto di Soave La Colombare 1991 • $21 • (04/30/96) • **79**
Recioto di Soave La Colombare 1989 • $29 • (09/15/92) • **87**
Soave Classico Superiore 1996: Intense and expressive. Maturing bread-dough aromas are followed by flavors of lanolin and almonds, all on a rich, balanced structure. The aftertaste has mushroom notes and a light bitterness. Drink now. 3,000 cases made. • $13 • (06/15/98) • **87**
Soave Classico Superiore 1995: Shows a touch of marzipan in both aroma and flavor, as well as apple and grapefruit peel notes on the finish. Nicely integrated. Drink now. • $14 • (04/30/98) • **85**
Soave Classico Superiore 1994 • $12 • (06/15/96) • **80**
Soave Classico Superiore Vigneto Calvarino 1996: A racy style of Soave, with intense almond, white peach and mineral aromas and flavors, balance and concentration. Bitter grapefruit on the finish adds dimension and length. Drink now. 250 cases made. • $16 • (06/30/98) • **87**
Soave Classico Superiore Vigneto Calvarino 1995: Showing some maturity, with marzipan and baked-apple flavors, yet seems to have more freshness and verve to it than other '95s. It has a presence on the palate that persists, with a slight earthiness in the aftertaste. Drink now. • $17 • (04/30/98) • **87**
Soave Classico Superiore Vigneto Calvarino 1994 • $15 • (04/30/96) • **86**
Soave Classico Superiore Vigneto La Rocca 1995: Deeply colored and shy on the nose. Nevertheless, this mature Soave has plenty of personality. Smoke, baked apple and marzipan flavors are smooth and elegant and the finish lingers. Impressive. Drink now. 250 cases made. • $16 • (06/15/98) • **88**
Soave Classico Superiore Vigneto La Rocca 1993 • $15 • (04/30/96) • **83**

PIETROSO

Brunello di Montalcino 1988 • $NA • (04/30/94) • **89**

PIEVE SANTA RESTITUTA

Brunello di Montalcino Rennina 1990: Thick and ripe, still quite tannic, offering plum, cedar, tobacco, black cherry, earth and chocolate flavors. Somewhat drying on aftertaste. Angelo Gaja's debut vintage in Montalcino. Try now. • $NA • (10/31/95) • **85**

PIGHIN, FRATELLI

Chardonnay Grave del Friuli 1993 • $10 • (01/31/95) • **80**
Pinot Grigio Collio 1996: Round, rich and succulent. A crowd-pleaser whose apple, almond and lemon character is up-front, balanced and delicious. • $19 • (11/15/97) • **84**
Pinot Grigio Collio 1995: Moderately rich, this shows some apple and herb notes, with a touch of grapefruit-peel at the finish. • $18 • (05/15/97) • **79**
Pinot Grigio Collio 1993 • $16 • (01/31/95) • **80**
Pinot Grigio Grave del Friuli 1996: Very expressive, displaying floral top-notes followed by peach, hazelnut and smoke flavors, buoyed on a rich texture. Structured, with a lingering finish. • $12 • (11/15/97) • **86**
Pinot Grigio Grave del Friuli 1995: Clean and crisp with good lemon and melon flavors and a nice buttery note on the finish. This would be a good match for light seafood. • $12 • (01/31/97) • **84**
Pinot Grigio Grave del Friuli 1994 • $16 • (10/31/95) • **84**
Pinot Grigio Grave del Friuli 1993 • $11 • (12/15/94) • **83**
Sauvignon Blanc Collio 1993 • $16 • (01/31/95) • **81**

PIRA

Barolo 1993: Despite some dilution, this offers pleasant cherry, earth and mineral notes. The tannins are a bit drying and the frame is lean. Best around 2000. 500 cases made. • $45 • (10/31/97) • **84**
Barolo 1990 • $40 • (10/31/95) • **85**

PISTONE, LUIGI

Barolo Riserva 1947: Oxidized, tart, with some nice echoes of anise. • $NA • (05/31/97) • **80**

PLOZNER

Cabernet Sauvignon Grave del Friuli 1985 • $6 • (09/15/88) • **85**
Cabernet Sauvignon Grave del Friuli Bollini 1983 • $6 • (09/15/88) • **80**
Chardonnay Grave del Friuli 1996: Already mature, this Chardonnay shows more almond aromas and flavors than fruit, but it's concentrated and racy. Finishes a little lean and tart. Drink now. 1,000 cases made. • $11 • (07/31/98) • **81**
Chardonnay Grave del Friuli 1995: A good Chardonnay, with apple and pear flavors. It's crisp and clean, with a little spice on the finish. • $12 • (01/31/97) • **82**
Chardonnay Grave del Friuli 1994: Extremely buttery in character, with faint fruit flavors. All dressed up, but nowhere to go. • $18 • (01/31/97) • **78**
Chardonnay Grave del Friuli Barrique 1995: Ready to drink, the modest apple flavors competing with some oak nuances and a milky, leesy note. Drink now. 1,200 cases made. • $17 • (06/15/98) • **80**
Chardonnay Grave del Friuli Barrique 1993 • $17 • (06/15/96) • **87**
Merlot Grave del Friuli 1993 • $9 • (06/15/96) • **77**
Pinot Bianco Grave del Friuli 1993 • $10 • (01/31/95) • **82**
Pinot Grigio Grave del Friuli 1996: This has almond flavor and a moderately rich texture, but it's simple and finishes short. Drink now. 4,000 cases made. • $12 • (06/15/98) • **80**
Pinot Grigio Grave del Friuli 1995: Shows some solid fruit flavors, mostly apple and lemon, with nice, zingy acidity. • $12 • (01/31/97) • **82**
Pinot Grigio Grave del Friuli 1994 • $12 • (06/15/96) • **85**
Sauvignon Grave del Friuli 1993 • $10 • (01/31/95) • **78**
Tocai Friulano Grave del Friuli 1996: A rich, broad style of Tocai, showing appley flavors, all moderately concentrated and with everything in balance. Drink now. 750 cases made. • $10 • (06/15/98) • **83**
Tocai Friulano Grave del Friuli 1993 • $9 • (01/31/95) • **74**

PODERINA, LA

Brunello di Montalcino 1992: An unctuous red for such a weak vintage, showing good, deep ruby color, and vibrant berry, cherry and strawberry character. Medium-bodied, with velvety tannins and a medium finish. Drink now. 1,600 cases made. • $40 • (09/30/97) • **87**
Brunello di Montalcino 1991: Slightly mature, with a berry, cedar and cigar box character. Light- to medium-bodied, with light tannins and a light finish. Drink now. 3,583 cases made. • $NA • (11/30/96) • **79**
Brunello di Montalcino 1990: Elegant and succulent berry, floral and cherry aromas and flavors, medium body, fine tannins and sweet, crisp finish. Drink now. • $NA • (10/31/95) • **86**
Brunello di Montalcino 1988 • $32 • (04/30/94) • **91**
Brunello di Montalcino Riserva 1990: Pretty cedar and tobacco notes, with hints of fruit on the nose and palate. Medium-bodied, with a light finish. Not much to it for a riserva. Drink now. 416 cases made. • $NA • (11/30/96) • **83**
Brunello di Montalcino Riserva 1988 • $32 • (10/31/94) • **88**
Rosso di Montalcino 1994: Prematurely forward, this shows some dry, earthy, fruity flavors. 1,166 cases made. • $NA • (11/30/96) • **75**
Rosso di Montalcino 1983 • $6 • (12/01/85) BB • **87**

PODERUCCIO, IL

Brunello di Montalcino 1986 • $21 • (03/31/92) • **83**
Brunello di Montalcino I Due Cipressi 1985 • $22 • (04/15/91) HR • **91**
Rosso di Montalcino 1989 • $9 • (04/30/92) • **83**
Rosso di Montalcino I Due Cipressi 1988 • $9 • (04/30/91) • **83**

POGGERINO

Bugialla 1991 • $NA • (02/28/95) • **93**
Bugialla 1990 • $20 • (10/31/93) • **91**
Chianti Classico 1995: Bright fruit takes the spotlight here, via loads of wild cherry character. Medium- to light-bodied, with fresh acidity and a lively finish. 3,300 cases made. • $22 • (09/30/97) • **85**
Chianti Classico 1994: Consistently very good—here, lovely, with sweet, ripe fruit flavors of berry and cassis and a hint of herbs. Of medium body with gentle tannins and a fresh finish. Delicious to drink now. • $22 • (10/31/96) • **87**
Chianti Classico 1993 • $NA • (10/31/95) • **88**
Chianti Classico 1992 • $NA • (02/28/95) • **83**
Chianti Classico 1991 • $16 • (10/31/93) • **84**
Chianti Classico 1990 • $14 • (09/15/92) • **91**
Chianti Classico 1988 • $13 • (11/30/91) • **78**
Chianti Classico Bugialla Riserva 1994: Bright plum, berry, mineral and light oak aromas follow through on the palate of this full-bodied yet refined wine. Plenty of fine tannins for aging. A superlative Chianti from one of the region's leading estates. Try now or hold. 330 cases made. • $42 • (09/30/97) • **90**
Chianti Classico Bugialla Riserva 1993: Poggerino is an estate on the way up. This is seductive, with violet, berry and mint aromas and flavors, very silky tannins and a violet, spice finish. Drink now. • $28 • (10/31/96) • **88**
Chianti Classico Bugialla Riserva 1990: A racy and exciting Chianti. Dark-colored with minty, floral and raspberry aromas and flavors. Full-bodied, with fine tannins and a long finish. Superb now or can age. • $NA • (09/30/97) • **92**
Chianti Classico Bugialla Riserva 1988: Soft and pretty Chianti. with violet, berry and tobacco aromas and flavors, medium body, soft tannins and a subtle aftertaste. • $NA • (09/30/97) • **86**
Chianti Classico Riserva 1990 • $NA • (02/28/95) • **91**
Chianti Classico Riserva 1988 • $20 • (09/15/92) • **85**
Chianti Classico Riserva 1985: An old-style Chianti that has very little to do with the current quality of this fine producer. Light and simple, with some fruit and leather character, but it's fading fast. Drink yesterday. • $NA • (09/30/97) • **76**

POGGIO, CASTELLO DEL

Barbera d'Asti 1989 • $9 • (12/15/92) • **80**
Barbera d'Asti 1988 • $9 • (10/31/91) BB • **85**

POGGIO, IL

Albana di Romagna 1995: Quite dry and restrained, this is a solid, if simple, white wine with crisp acidity and fairly neutral fruit flavors. 25,000 cases made. • $10/1.5 liter • (04/30/97) • **81**
Sangiovese di Romagna Superiore 1995: Simple and satisfying, this offers some modest cherry and plum flavors, with good texture. • $NA/1.5 liter • (03/31/97) • **80**

POGGIO A 'FRATI

Chianti Classico Riserva 1985 • $NA • (09/15/91) • **84**

POGGIO AL SOLE

Chianti Classico 1992 • $NA • (02/28/95) • **84**
Chianti Classico 1988 • $NA • (09/15/91) • **91**
Chianti Classico Riserva 1990 • $NA • (02/28/95) • **86**
Chianti Classico Riserva 1988 • $NA • (09/15/92) • **81**
Chianti Classico Riserva 1985 • $NA • (09/15/91) • **88**

POGGIO AL SORBO

Chianti Classico 1995: A rustic, traditional-style Chianti that smells and tastes spicy and earthy, and feels tannic. Rather hard to warm up to. Drink now. 3,000 cases made. • $16 • (04/30/98) • **81**
Chianti Classico 1990 • $15 • (09/15/92) • **84**
Chianti Classico Riserva 1994: An earthy-tasting, rustic style of Chianti, drinkable but below par. Ready now. 1,200 cases made. • $21 • (04/30/98) • **73**
Chianti Classico Riserva 1990 • $15 • (02/28/95) • **79**
Le Robbiaie 1991 • $17 • (07/31/94) • **79**
Vin Santo Il Cavaliere 1986 • $24 • (07/31/94) • **91**

POGGIO AL VENTO

Chianti Colli Senesi 1990 • $NA • (09/15/92) • **85**

POGGIO ANTICO

Altero 1990 • $33 • (02/28/95) • **82**
Brunello di Montalcino 1992: A no-nonsense red with strawberry and cherry aromas and flavors and a hint of earth. Medium-bodied, with fine tannins and a crisp finish. Drink now. 2,800 cases made. • $50 • (09/30/97) • **85**
Brunello di Montalcino 1991: A pretty Brunello that's medium-bodied, with good velvety texture, berry, cherry and spice flavors and soft tannins. Caressing finish. Ready to drink. 5,416 cases made. • $46 • (11/30/96) • **86**
Brunello di Montalcino 1990: Delicious from start to finish; quite powerful. It's very ripe and very sweet-tasting and melts in the mouth, showing tons of plum, red berry and chocolate flavors. Drink now. 3,750 cases made. • $82 Ⓐ • (10/31/95) • **91**
Brunello di Montalcino 1989 • $42 • (11/30/94) • **90**
Brunello di Montalcino 1988 • $35 • (04/30/94) • **91**
Brunello di Montalcino 1987 • $45 • (12/15/92) • **87**
Brunello di Montalcino 1986 • $40 • (08/31/91) HR • **91**
Brunello di Montalcino 1985 • $58 Ⓐ • (11/30/90) CS • **95**
Brunello di Montalcino 1982 • $75 Ⓐ • (11/30/89) • **92**
Brunello di Montalcino 1979 • $13 • (09/15/86) • **72**
Brunello di Montalcino Riserva 1990: A blockbuster, with loads of fruit flavor, especially coconut, pouring out of the glass. Full-bodied and rich, with velvety tannins, yet slightly astringent on the finish. Try now. 1,500 cases made. • $75 • (11/30/96) • **93**
Brunello di Montalcino Riserva 1988 • $56 • (10/31/94) • **85**
Brunello di Montalcino Riserva 1986 • $62 • (12/15/92) • **89**
Brunello di Montalcino Riserva 1985 • $92 Ⓐ • (08/31/91) • **93**
Rosso di Montalcino 1993 • $25 • (10/31/95) • **83**
Rosso di Montalcino 1992 • $25 • (10/31/94) • **84**
Rosso di Montalcino 1991 • $24 • (04/30/94) • **83**
Rosso di Montalcino 1989 • $21 • (08/31/91) • **85**

POGGIO BONELLI

Chianti Classico 1993: Light and delicate, with some nice plum and cherry flavors but a slightly short finish. • $NA • (10/31/96) • **79**
Chianti Classico 1990 • $NA • (10/31/93) • **88**
Chianti Classico Tramonto D'Oca 1990 • $NA • (10/31/93) • **89**

POGGIO DEGLI ULIVI

Brunello di Montalcino 1988 • $NA • (04/30/94) • **88**
Rosso di Montalcino 1991 • $NA • (04/30/94) • **82**

POGGIO DI SOTTO

Brunello di Montalcino 1991: Impressive concentration for this vintage, but it's slightly disjointed. It has a medium body, very firm tannins and a raisiny note on the finish. Drink now. 833 cases made. • $45 • (11/30/96) • **82**
Rosso di Montalcino 1994: Slightly disjointed now, but this shows some promise. Plenty of strawberry and plum character, with a hint of oak. Medium-bodied, with fine tannins and a slightly astringent finish. Try now. 250 cases made. • $30 • (11/30/96) • **84**
Rosso di Montalcino 1993 • $NA • (10/31/95) • **83**
Rosso di Montalcino 1991 • $NA • (04/30/94) • **83**

POGGIO REALE

Chianti Rufina Riserva 1990 • $NA • (02/28/95) • **88**

Key: SS—Spectator Selection CS—Cellar Selection HR—Highly Recommended BB—Best Buy $NA—Price not available Ⓐ—Auction Price (BT)—Barrel Tasting
Dates in parentheses indicate the issues in which the ratings were published.

POGGIO SALVI

Brunello di Montalcino 1991: Plenty of dried cherry and herb aromas and flavors. Medium-bodied, with soft tannins and a fresh finish. Poggio Salvi makes beautiful wines; this one's delicious now. • $NA • (11/30/96) • **87**
Brunello di Montalcino 1990: Very ripe and full-bodied, featuring an abundance of rich berry, cherry and plum aromas and flavors and a long, silky finish. Drinkable now. • $45 • (10/31/95) • **91**
Brunello di Montalcino 1988 • $42 • (04/30/94) • **88**
Brunello di Montalcino 1985 • $30 • (11/30/90) • **83**
Brunello di Montalcino 1981 • $20 • (10/15/88) • **88**
Brunello di Montalcino 1979 • $15 • (03/15/87) • **88**
Brunello di Montalcino Riserva 1988 • $45 • (10/31/94) • **90**
Brunello di Montalcino Riserva 1981 • $35 • (11/30/90) • **85**
Lavischio 1995: This medium-bodied wine has enticing blackberry, cherry and blueberry aromas. The tannins are fine; the finish is silky. Drink now or hold. • $26 • (09/30/97) • **87**
Rosso di Montalcino 1994: Wonderfully fresh and fruity on the palate, with hints of spice and milk chocolate. Medium-bodied, with fine tannins and a refreshing aftertaste. It's hard not to drink this one now. • $15 • (11/30/96) • **86**

POGGIO SAN POLO

Brunello di Montalcino 1992: Shows simple aromas and flavors of berry and strawberry. Medium in body, with light tannins and a fresh finish. Drink now. 400 cases made. • $48 • (09/30/97) • **82**
Brunello di Montalcino 1991: A fresh and well-made '91, exhibiting good fruit flavors, some fine tannins and a silky finish. Drink now. 550 cases made. • $45 • (11/30/96) • **85**
Brunello di Montalcino 1989 • $24 • (07/31/95) • **91**
Brunello di Montalcino Riserva 1990: There are masses of fruit flavor and heaps of tannin in this gorgeous wine. It's full-bodied and the finish is long and fruity. Delicious now, or can hold. 116 cases made. • $70 • (11/30/96) • **91**
Rosso di Montalcino 1994: Fresh and lively, this offers simple flavors, especially notes of dried cherry, and a clean finish. 516 cases made. • $20 • (11/30/96) • **82**
Rosso di Montalcino 1990 • $15 • (08/31/95) • **88**
Rubio 1994: A serious wine with spicy, floral aromas, cherry and currant flavors and a firm, tannic texture. It's focused, flavorful and long on the finish. Drink now through 1999. 975 cases made. • $15 • (10/31/96) • **87**

POGGIO SCALETTE, PODERE

Il Carbonaione 1994: A gorgeous wine to drink or age. It has lively currant, berry and cherry aromas and flavors, is medium- to full-bodied and has firm tanins. Long finish. Drinkable now. 1,500 cases made. • $55 • (09/30/97) • **90**
Il Carbonaione 1993: Inky-colored, with intense blueberry and blackberry aromas and a hint of new wood. Full-bodied, and very concentrated with masses of fruit and tannins. One of the stars of the year from Tuscany. Needs bottle age; try after 1999. 1,500 cases made. • $55 • (09/30/97) • **93**
Il Carbonaione 1992: An almost black color and dense, nearly impenetrable flavors make this an imposing, monolithic wine. Has lots of oak and plenty of fruit concentration, too. Drink now. 150 cases made. • $40 • (10/31/96) • **90**

POGGIOLINO, IL

Chianti Classico 1994: Fine example of a traditional-style Chianti. Has subtle flavors of cedar, cranberry and spice that linger on the finish. Fine balance and firm tannins, too. Drink now through 2000. 850 cases made. • $14 • (04/30/98) • **87**
Chianti Classico 1993: A Chianti with some berry and cherry aromas and flavors, but a lack of body and structure. • $NA • (10/31/96) • **78**
Chianti Classico 1988 • $15 • (05/15/93) • **83**
Chianti Classico Riserva 1994: Wonderful to drink for its smooth texture, harmonious and rich fruit flavors and lingering finish. Not tannic. Drink now through 1999. 400 cases made. • $21 • (04/30/98) • **87**
Chianti Classico Riserva 1988 • $NA • (09/15/92) • **83**
Chianti Classico Riserva 1985 • $NA • (09/15/91) • **84**
Le Balze 1990: A hard, tight, tannic red wine whose aromas are opening up slightly to mellow, spicy notes, but it's still hard and tart in texture and tough on the finish—which doesn't bode well considering the age it has already. Drink now. 600 cases made. • $25 • (01/01/98) • **78**

POGGIOLO, IL

Brunello di Montalcino 1992: Delicate and fresh with its berry, mineral and wood character. Medium to light in body, with fine tannins and a slightly dry finish. Drink now. • $35 • (09/30/97) • **82**
Brunello di Montalcino 1991: Impressively solid for the vintage, this shows loads of fruit flavor and a firm backbone of excellent, silky tannins. Medium- to full-bodied. Long finish. Drink now. 500 cases made. • $30 • (11/30/96) • **88**
Brunello di Montalcino 1990: Brick-brownish color suggests a slightly fading Brunello. It lacks fruit and tastes of mushroom, brown sugar and truffle. Drinkable but not pleasant. • $NA • (10/31/95) • **77**
Brunello di Montalcino 1988 • $39 • (04/30/94) • **86**
Brunello di Montalcino 1985 • $34 • (11/30/90) • **93**
Brunello di Montalcino Beato 1992: There's a bounty of fruit in this Brunello with tobacco, vanilla and cherry aromas and flavors. Medium- to full-bodied, with soft tannins. Long finish. • $35 • (09/30/97) • **88**
Brunello di Montalcino Riserva 1990: Racy in style, with fabulous, ripe plum flavors underscored by complex, mineral and spice notes. Full-bodied with full, silky tannins and a long aftertaste. Deft winemaking. Try after 2000. 100 cases made. • $55 • (11/30/96) • **92**
Brunello di Montalcino Riserva 1988 • $NA • (10/31/94) • **75**
Brunello di Montalcino Sassello 1991: Delivers amazing quality for this vintage, with a bounty of fruit flavor, especially berry and cherry, and fine tannins. Medium- to full-bodied with a very silky finish. Drink now or hold. 160 cases made. • $39 • (11/30/96) • **89**
Brunello di Montalcino Sassello 1988 • $NA • (04/30/94) • **83**
Brunello di Montalcino Sassello Riserva 1991: An aromatic red, scented with violet, flowers and berries. Medium in body, with fine tannins, fresh acidity and a long, fresh finish. From a consistently good producer. • $55 • (09/30/97) • **87**
Brunello di Montalcino Sassello Riserva 1990: Very fine indeed. A solid, full-bodied wine, with generous berry, mineral and mint aromas and flavors, full tannins and a long, silky finish. 50 cases made. • $70 • (11/30/96) • **93**
Rosso di Montalcino 1991 • $NA • (04/30/94) • **78**
Rosso di Montalcino Sassello 1995: Displays amazing concentration of fruit for a Rosso. Oozes with red berries, is full-bodied, with a thick texture of ripe fruit and velvety, soft tannins. Long finish. Drink or hold. • $19 • (09/30/97) • **90**
Rosso di Montalcino Sassello 1994: A firm and fruity wine, with aromas and flavors of dark chocolate, berry and herb, supple tannins and a fruity finish. Medium-bodied. • $NA • (11/30/96) • **85**
Rosso di Montalcino Sassello 1993 • $NA • (10/31/95) • **65**
Rosso di Montalcino Sassello 1992 • $14 • (08/31/95) • **86**

POGGIONE, IL

Brunello di Montalcino 1992: Good balance for the vintage. Has lovely, fruity aromas of cherries and mushrooms, a medium body, fine tannins and a fresh finish. 4,250 cases made. • $40 • (09/30/97) • **85**
Brunello di Montalcino 1991: At its peak, with berry and cherry aromas and flavors and slightly drying tannins. Disappointing for this producer. Drink soon. 9,243 cases made. • $37 • (11/30/96) • **80**
Brunello di Montalcino 1990: Beautiful, very ripe plum and berry aromas and flavors. Medium-bodied and soft, adding medium-velvety tannins and a delicious finish. Drink now. • $38 • (10/31/95) • **87**
Brunello di Montalcino 1988 • $42 • (04/30/94) • **86**
Brunello di Montalcino 1982 • $30 • (09/15/88) • **88**
Brunello di Montalcino 1981 • $28 • (09/15/86) • **93**
Brunello di Montalcino Riserva 1990: Racy red with fine tannins and a minty, berry, cherry character. Medium- to full-bodied with medium-firm tannins and a fresh finish. Better after 1999 but drinkable now. 1,366 cases made. • $47 • (11/30/96) • **91**
Brunello di Montalcino Riserva 1988 • $48 • (10/31/94) • **90**
Brunello di Montalcino Riserva 1979 • $35 • (09/15/86) • **79**
Brunello di Montalcino Riserva 1978 • $35 • (07/01/84) SS • **92**
Rosso di Montalcino 1995: A subtle, complex Rosso with berry, earthy and fungi aromas and flavors. Medium body. Fine tannins. Drink now or hold. 10,000 cases made. • $18 • (09/30/97) • **87**
Rosso di Montalcino 1994: This has got some structure for a '94 Rosso. It's medium- to full-bodied, with firm tannins and a long, fruity finish. Drink now. 9,225 cases made. • $17 • (11/30/96) • **86**
Rosso di Montalcino 1993 • $17 • (10/31/95) • **79**
Rosso di Montalcino 1992 • $17 • (08/31/95) • **87**
Rosso di Montalcino 1991 • $18 • (04/30/94) • **82**
Rosso di Montalcino 1985 • $17 • (03/31/88) • **85**

POJER & SANDRI

Atesino Essenzia 1995: Intense and fragrant, the exotic citrus-peel, passion fruit and pineapple jump out of the glass. Elegant and racy, it might be better as an apéritif. Tasty, with tannins on the finish. Drink now through 2002. • $40/375ml • (07/31/98) • **88**
Atesino Faye 1994: Barrel aging adds a vanilla note to the mint, red berry and almond flavors in this elegant, balanced white. There's good concentration and toasty oak on the finish, so give it time to integrate. Made from Chardonnay and Pinot Bianco. Drink now through 2000. • $26 • (07/31/98) • **86**
Atesino Rosso Faye 1994: Deep color and gorgeous aroma, like a good St. Emilion. Roasted coffee and vanilla accent the plum and herb flavors. Medium-bodied; turns austere on the finish. 70 percent Lagrein. Drink now through 2000. • $32 • (07/31/98) • **87**
Chardonnay Trentino Di Faedo 1996: Displays body and concentration but the aromas and flavors remain submerged. Good length on the finish; may just need a few months to open. Drink now through 2000. • $16 • (07/31/98) • **84**
Müller-Thurgau Trentino 1996: Plenty of peach and mineral character in this rich, fruity white, underscored by lively acidity and a tangy finish. Shows what can be done with this grape. Drink through 1999. • $16 • (07/31/98) • **85**
Nosiola Trentino 1996: A clean, crisp, easy-drinking white, showing apple and herb flavors and a firm, mouth-watering finish. Good apéritif. Drink now. • $16 • (07/31/98) • **82**
Pinot Nero Trentino 1994: Shows some age in the color, with spicy balsamic vinegar, brown sugar and woodsy flavors, smooth texture and lightly tannic finish. Good effort with a difficult grape. Drink now. • $28 • (07/31/98) • **80**
Sauvignon Atesino 1996: Citrus and tropical notes abound in this rich, juicy white, its flavors lingering on the mouth-watering finish. Drink now. • $16 • (07/31/98) • **85**
Traminer Trentino 1996: The rose character is very pure, but a CO2 element initially masks both aroma and flavor in this racy white. Short aeration brings out more floral, spicy, tropical fruit. Best to decant. Drink through 1999. • $16 • (07/31/98) • **82**

POLIZIANO

Elegia 1995: Serious winemaking. Pretty aromas of blackberries and mint usher in this medium-bodied wine, with super well-integrated tannins and a long, silky finish. Drinkable now. 1,000 cases made. • $35 • (09/30/97) • **89**
Elegia 1994: An attractive character of dried herb and berry in this medium-bodied wine. Light, fine tannins and a pretty berry, vanilla finish. Drink now. • $NA • (10/31/96) • **85**
Rosso di Montepulciano 1990 • $10 • (12/15/92) • **83**
Vino Nobile di Montepulciano 1989 • $13 • (03/31/93) • **84**
Vino Nobile di Montepulciano 1988 • $12 • (12/15/91) • **81**
Vino Nobile di Montepulciano 1987 • $12 • (03/15/91) • **84**
Vino Nobile di Montepulciano 1985 • $13 • (09/15/88) • **89**
Vino Nobile di Montepulciano Vigneto Caggiole 1994: Very good effort. Caressing, with lovely, new wood-tinged berry and cherry flavors. Medium-bodied, with velvety tannins and a fruity finish. Drink now or hold. 1,500 cases made. • $27 • (09/30/97) • **87**
Vino Nobile di Montepulciano Vigneto Caggiole Riserva 1988 • $23 • (06/30/93) • **82**

PONTI, LANZA GINORI

Vigna di Bugialla Poggerino 1988 • $17 • (01/31/92) • **84**

PONTORMO

Chianti 1994: Hearty and simple, with ripe prune flavors and a firm, rather tannic texture. 500,000 cases made. • $6 • (10/31/96) • **80**

PORTA ROSSA, CANTINA DELLA

Barolo Riserva 1985 • $26 • (01/31/92) • **87**
Barolo Vigna Delizia Riserva 1982 • $25 • (08/31/91) • **87**
Diano d'Alba Vigna Bruni 1990 • $14 • (03/31/92) • **84**
Diano d'Alba Vigna Bruni 1988 • $25 • (02/15/91) • **85**

PRA, FRATELLI

Recioto delle Fontane 1990 • $NA • (09/15/92) • **77**
Recioto delle Fontane 1989 • $NA • (09/15/92) • **80**

PRA' DI PRADIS

Pinot Grigio Collio 1996: A pretty, elegant Pinot Grigio showing soft, peachy notes with a hint of spice. All the components are balanced and integrated. Drink through 1999. 500 cases made. • $18 • (05/15/98) • **84**
Pinot Grigio Collio 1994 • $16 • (06/15/96) • **84**
Stukara 1993: The dominant theme is herbal, yet there's decent complexity, though it turns tough. Not likely to improve. 411 cases made. • $23 • (09/15/97) • **80**
Tocai Friulano Collio 1996: A crisp, succulent white redolent of almond, citrus and pear flavors, displaying richness and texture midpalate. Well balanced and delicious. Drink now. 1,000 cases made. • $13 • (04/30/98) • **87**
Tocai Friulano Collio 1994 • $13 • (06/15/96) • **86**

PRATOLA, LE

Chianti Classico 1990 • $9 • (10/31/93) • **80**

PRAVINI

Merlot Trentino 1995: A lovely expression of Merlot, and a value for all it offers. Vibrant, concentrated and packed with spicy cherry and licorice flavors on a smooth texture. Well made. Drink through 1999. 10,000 cases made. • $9 • (04/30/98) BB • **86**

PRINCIC, DORO

Merlot Collio 1995: Rich, supple and concentrated, displaying black cherry and plum notes allied with a medium-bodied, lightly tannic structure. Moderate length. Drink through 1999. • $18 • (06/15/98) • **87**
Pinot Bianco Collio 1993: Ripe and full-bodied, sporting pear, almond and vanilla flavors, this is fully mature, with a hint of butterscotch on the finish. Best matched with food. • $7 • (06/15/97) • **85**
Pinot Grigio Collio 1995: Like a super-charged Mosel Riesling. Complex aromas of red berries mingle with apple and mineral notes, and it all comes together in a refreshing, balanced whole. Very beguiling, with a long aftertaste. • $14 • (06/15/97) • **88**
Tocai Friulano Collio 1996: Here's a delicate white that has citrus and grass notes and a firm structure, leaving an almond impression on the aftertaste. Drink now. • $15 • (06/15/98) • **85**
Tocai Friulano Collio 1995: This white starts off rich and concentrated, with a flavor of vanilla custard, but the finish shows firm acidity, pulling it all together. Ready to drink. • $12 • (06/15/97) • **83**

PRINCIPATO

Merlot-Cabernet Sauvignon Rosso della Vallagarina 1994: A soft style, with smoky accents adding dimension to the blackberry flavors. Could use more concentration and definition. 80,000 cases made. • $6 • (06/15/97) • **82**

PRINCIPE CORSINI

Chianti Classico Le Corti 1991 • $8 • (10/31/94) • **77**

PRODUTTORI DEL BARBARESCO

Barbaresco 1993: Some elegance here, but an herbaceous edge and dry finish dominate. Medium-bodied. Tough tannins. Disappointing. • $27 • (01/31/98) • **73**
Barbaresco 1991 • $21 • (10/31/95) • **79**
Barbaresco 1989 • $24 • (10/31/93) • **76**
Barbaresco 1988 • $24 • (10/31/93) • **84**
Barbaresco 1986 • $12 • (10/31/90) HR • **90**
Barbaresco 1984 • $12 • (09/15/88) • **80**
Barbaresco 1983 • $NA • (09/15/88) • **85**
Barbaresco 1982 • $NA • (09/15/88) • **87**
Barbaresco 1979 • $NA • (09/15/88) • **90**
Barbaresco Asili 1990 • $35 • (10/31/95) • **81**
Barbaresco Asili 1989 • $32 • (10/31/93) • **85**
Barbaresco Asili 1988 • $32 • (10/31/93) • **88**
Barbaresco Asili Riserva 1985 • $27 • (10/31/90) • **92**
Barbaresco Asili Riserva 1982 • $22 • (09/15/88) • **89**
Barbaresco Moccagatta 1989 • $29 • (10/31/94) • **87**
Barbaresco Moccagatta Riserva 1982 • $22 • (09/15/88) • **89**
Barbaresco Montefico Riserva 1982 • $22 • (09/15/88) • **85**
Barbaresco Montefico Riserva 1978 • $22 • (09/15/88) • **92**
Barbaresco Montestefano 1990 • $32 • (10/31/93) • **78**
Barbaresco Montestefano 1989 • $32 • (10/31/93) • **87**
Barbaresco Montestefano 1988 • $32 • (10/31/93) • **89**
Barbaresco Montestefano Riserva 1985 • $25 • (10/31/90) • **82**
Barbaresco Montestefano Riserva 1982 • $18 • (09/15/88) • **88**
Barbaresco Ovello 1989 • $29 • (10/31/94) • **85**
Barbaresco Ovello Riserva 1985 • $25 • (10/31/90) • **86**
Barbaresco Ovello Riserva 1982 • $22 • (09/15/88) • **86**
Barbaresco Paje Riserva 1982 • $22 • (09/15/88) • **91**
Barbaresco Pora 1989 • $29 • (10/31/94) • **84**
Barbaresco Pora Riserva 1982 • $18 • (09/15/88) • **91**
Barbaresco Pora Riserva 1979 • $24 • (09/15/88) • **91**
Barbaresco Rabajà 1990 • $35 • (10/31/95) • **86**
Barbaresco Rabajà 1989 • $33 • (10/31/94) • **82**
Barbaresco Rabajà Riserva 1982 • $22 • (09/15/88) • **89**
Barbaresco Rio Sordo 1990 • $35 • (10/31/95) • **82**
Barbaresco Rio Sordo 1989 • $29 • (10/31/94) • **88**
Barbaresco Rio Sordo Riserva 1988 • $30 • (04/15/94) • **76**
Barbaresco Rio Sordo Riserva 1982 • $22 • (09/15/88) • **87**
Barbaresco Selezione del Trentennio '30' 1988 • $28 • (04/30/92) HR • **91**
Nebbiolo Langhe 1995: A fairly supple, medium-bodied Nebbiolo with some decent earth, plum and spice notes. Drink now. • $14 • (01/31/98) • **80**
Nebbiolo Langhe 1990 • $10 • (07/31/92) • **83**
Nebbiolo Langhe 1988 • $9 • (02/28/91) • **82**

PRUNOTTO, ALFREDO

Barbaresco 1994: Supple, well-integrated tannins, lovely fruit and good acidity—all presented in a balanced package. Medium-bodied and not very complex, but it's ripe and ready to drink now through 2000. 2,340 cases made. • $29 • (10/31/97) • **85**
Barbaresco 1993: Distinctive, offering some earthy, herbal notes to the red berry flavors and a mocha-vanilla character on the slightly short finish. Medium-bodied and moderately tannic. Try now. 1,224 cases made. • $20 • (10/31/96) • **84**
Barbaresco 1991 • $25 • (10/31/95) • **79**
Barbaresco 1990 • $NA • (10/31/94) • **81**
Barbaresco 1989 • $21 • (10/31/94) • **85**
Barbaresco 1988 • $17 • (10/31/94) • **87**
Barbaresco 1987 • $27 • (03/31/92) • **70**
Barbaresco Montestefano 1993: Well made. Though closed and reserved now, it's seductive, with pretty red berry and blackberry aromas and flavors. Better after 1999. 1,230 cases made. • $30 • (10/31/96) • **88**
Barbaresco Montestefano 1990 • $NA • (10/31/94) • **85**
Barbaresco Montestefano 1989 • $35 • (10/31/94) • **85**
Barbaresco Montestefano 1987 • $37 • (03/31/92) • **76**
Barbaresco Montestefano 1986 • $37 • (12/31/90) • **86**
Barbaresco Montestefano 1985 • $29 • (03/31/90) • **87**
Barbaresco Rabajà Riserva 1982 • $19 • (07/31/87) • **81**
Barbera d'Alba 1993: Fruity, and nicely earthy in aroma, but it turns thin and dry on the tannic finish. • $NA • (10/31/96) • **77**
Barbera d'Alba 1991 • $11 • (11/15/93) • **74**
Barbera d'Alba 1987 • $9 • (03/31/90) • **85**
Barbera d'Alba 1985 • $8 • (07/15/88) • **81**
Barbera d'Alba 1983 • $6 • (07/15/87) BB • **89**
Barbera d'Asti Fiulot 1996: Pure, classy and racy. Unhindered by even a hint of oak, this wine is bursting with clean cassis, cherry and wild berry flavors. Nice spice notes on the supple, round and intense finish. Drink now through 2000. 12,580 cases made. • $11 • (10/31/97) • **89**
Barbera d'Alba Fiulot 1994: Attractively perfumed, with rose petal, violet, plum and cherry flavors in generous amounts. Toasty tannins that turn slightly tough on the finish. Drinkable now. • $NA • (10/31/96) • **85**
Barbera d'Alba Fiulot 1993 • $10 • (10/31/94) • **79**
Barbera d'Alba Fiulot 1992 • $8 • (11/15/93) • **80**

Key: SS—Spectator Selection CS—Cellar Selection HR—Highly Recommended BB—Best Buy $NA—Price not available Ⓐ—Auction Price (BT)—Barrel Tasting
Dates in parentheses indicate the issues in which the ratings were published.

ITALY

Barbera d'Alba Pian Romualdo 1994: A dark, brooding, fruity and solid Barbera with firm tannins and cherry, red berry, tree bark and wet earth notes. The crisp finish needs strong food. Best now through 2002. 1,708 cases made. • $18 • (10/31/97) • **86**

Barbera d'Alba Pian Romualdo 1993 • $22 • (10/31/95) • **85**

Barbera d'Alba Pian Romualdo 1991 • $19 • (10/31/94) • **77**

Barbera d'Alba Pian Romualdo 1990 • $19 • (10/31/94) • **81**

Barbera d'Alba Pian Romualdo 1989 • $19 • (07/31/95) • **85**

Barbera d'Alba Pian Romualdo 1988 • $19 • (11/15/93) • **80**

Barbera d'Alba Pian Romualdo 1987 • $14 • (09/15/90) • **81**

Barolo 1993: Lovely, balanced, delicate and sweet-tasting, this medium-bodied Barolo has ripe berry and plum flavors, good spice and floral notes. Ripe, well-integrated tannins make this tempting to drink now. It could hold until 2002, but why wait? 3,935 cases made. • $27 • (10/31/97) • **87**

Barolo 1992: Ripe, almost jammy; fruit flavors are enjoyable, despite the rather tannic texture. A good example of '92 Barolo. 2,000 cases made. • $27 • (10/31/96) • **82**

Barolo 1991 • $27 • (10/31/95) • **80**

Barolo 1990 • $29 • (10/31/94) • **86**

Barolo 1989 • $27 • (10/31/93) • **90**

Barolo 1988 • $27 • (09/30/93) HR • **93**

Barolo 1987 • $27 • (03/31/92) • **85**

Barolo 1985 • $31 • (03/31/90) • **82**

Barolo Bussia 1993: Lovely, delicate and aromatic Barolo, with enticing floral, wild berry and tar flavors that mingle attractively with the supple, well-integrated tannins. Medium- to full-bodied, it fills the palate with smooth, silky texture. Balanced, it's drinkable now to 2002. 2,833 cases made. • $50 • (10/31/97) • **90**

Barolo Bussia 1990 • $NA • (10/31/94) • **88**

Barolo Bussia 1989 • $37 • (10/31/94) • **89**

Barolo Bussia 1988 • $35 • (11/30/94) • **85**

Barolo Bussia 1986 • $39 • (03/31/92) • **78**

Barolo Bussia 1985 • $38 • (09/15/90) • **92**

Barolo Bussia 1983 • $NA • (09/15/88) • **88**

Barolo Bussia 1982 • $25 • (09/15/88) • **91**

Barolo Bussia 1978 • $NA • (09/15/88) • **86**

Barolo Bussia 1974 • $NA • (09/15/88) • **80**

Barolo Bussia 1971 • $52 Ⓐ • (09/15/88) • **90**

Barolo Bussia 1967 • $NA • (09/15/88) • **82**

Barolo Bussia 1964 • $NA • (09/15/88) • **80**

Barolo Bussia 1961 • $NA • (09/15/88) • **91**

Barolo Cannubi 1990 • $NA • (10/31/94) • **81**

Barolo Cannubi 1989 • $37 • (10/31/94) • **83**

Barolo Cannubi 1985 • $32 • (03/31/90) • **85**

Barolo Cannubi 1983 • $26 • (09/15/88) • **85**

Barolo Cannubi 1982 • $25 • (09/15/88) • **75**

Barolo Cannubi 1978 • $NA • (09/15/88) • **78**

Barolo Ginestra di Monforte d'Alba Riserva 1980 • $13 • (06/30/87) • **78**

Dolcetto d'Alba 1996: An elegant and delicate style, with very pretty ripe fruit presented in a medium-bodied and balanced package. Nice cassis-bush, citrus and orange-peel flavors, and a crisp finish. Ready to drink. 10,000 cases made. • $14 • (10/31/97) • **85**

Dolcetto d'Alba 1990 • $11 • (09/30/93) • **80**

Dolcetto d'Alba 1989 • $11 • (02/15/92) • **83**

Dolcetto d'Alba 1985 • $10 • (03/15/89) • **84**

Dolcetto d'Alba Mosesco 1990 • $15 • (09/30/93) • **82**

Nebbiolo d'Alba 1993 • $19 • (10/31/95) • **83**

Nebbiolo d'Alba Occhetti 1995: The fruit in this medium-bodied red is sweet, showing raspberry, black cherry and black currant, but the harsh tannins on the finish take some getting used to. Try in 1999. 3,083 cases made. • $21 • (10/31/97) • **80**

Nebbiolo d'Alba Occhetti 1994: A showy, full-bodied, dark-colored red with spicy oak, red berry, and smoky flavors and a fresh, crisp finish. Try now. 1,450 cases made. • $18 • (10/31/96) • **87**

Nebbiolo d'Alba Occhetti 1990 • $17 • (07/31/95) • **82**

Roero 1986 • $10 • (06/30/88) • **82**

Roero 1985 • $9 • (07/31/87) • **88**

PUGNANE

Barbera d'Alba 1993: Very fruity, with a pleasant, soft character. Offers plum, cherry and raspberry flavors and a juicy, smooth finish. • $NA • (10/31/96) • **83**

PUIATTI, GIOVANNI

Cabernet Franc Isonzo del Friuli 1997: Leafy, berry aromas and flavors mark this Cabernet Franc, reminiscent of Chinon, though softer in structure. Offers nice, sappy fruit, and it's well-balanced. Drink now through 2000. • $15 • (07/31/98) • **85**

Chardonnay Isonzo del Friuli 1997: Still youthful, displaying apple and nut flavors on a bright, elegant framework. Finishes short. Drink now. • $15 • (07/31/98) • **82**

Merlot Isonzo del Friuli 1997: Deeply colored, with a grapey character and soft texture. Appealing, and designed for early consumption. Drink now. • $15 • (07/31/98) • **82**

Pinot Grigio Isonzo del Friuli 1997: A lovely expression of Pinot Grigio, displaying peach, nut and smoke character, rich texture and vibrant acidity. Picks up a stoniness on the finish. Drink through 1999. • $15 • (07/31/98) • **85**

Sauvignon Isonzo del Friuli 1997: More emphasis on body and power than on aromatics, yet subtle gooseberry and melon flavors prevail in the end. May just need a few months to open up. Drink through 1999. • $15 • (07/31/98) • **84**

PUIATTI, VITTORIO

Chardonnay Collio 1995 • $18 • (06/15/96) • **78**

Chardonnay Collio 1993 • $15 • (01/31/95) • **83**

Merlot Collio 1989 • $26 • (01/31/92) • **78**

Pinot Bianco Collio 1995 • $18 • (06/15/96) • **82**

Pinot Bianco Collio 1993 • $15 • (01/31/95) • **87**

Pinot Grigio Collio 1997: Bubble-gum character is followed by a rich, stony palate. Soft in texture already; cellar only short-term. Drink through 1999. • $18 • (07/31/98) • **82**

Pinot Grigio Collio 1995 • $18 • (06/15/96) • **78**

Pinot Grigio Collio 1993 • $15 • (01/31/95) • **83**

Pinot Nero Collio 1989 • $26 • (09/15/92) • **70**

Sauvignon Collio 1997: Ripe peach aromas and flavors are married to a powerful structure and an almost viscous texture, yet there's just enough acidity—and a touch of bitterness at the end—to balance it all. Drink now. • $18 • (07/31/98) • **85**

Sauvignon Collio 1995 • $18 • (06/15/96) • **84**

Sauvignon Collio 1993 • $15 • (01/31/95) • **88**

Tocai Collio White 1995: A light wine with peach and grapefruit flavors. A bit astringent and milky on the finish. 4,000 cases made. • $18 • (06/15/97) • **78**

PUNSET

Barbaresco 1994: Light and unbalanced, tastes herbaceous and sour; smells funky. 856 cases made. • $20 • (10/31/97) • **71**

Barbaresco 1993: Fortunately, wet earth and *goût de terroir* save this wine because there's not much else except a few raspberry and cherry notes. Light-to-medium body; soft tannins. Drink now. 1,517 cases made. • $20 • (10/31/97) • **79**

Barbaresco 1989 • $17 • (06/15/94) HR • **90**

Barbaresco Campo Quadro 1994: Not well balanced, but it does offer ripe fruit, light-to-medium body and light tannins. Drink chilled. 2,885 cases made. • $29 • (10/31/97) • **80**

Barbera d'Alba 1994: The fruit is decent but the earthy, cheesy aromas aren't. Turns astringent on the finish. 1,944 cases made. • $12 • (10/31/97) • **76**

Barbera d'Alba 1990 • $14 • (04/30/93) • **87**

Dolcetto d'Alba Organically Grown 1995: Lovely, delicate and aromatic, with roses, violet, plum and raspberry notes. Light- to medium-bodied, with ripe, sweet-tasting tannins and a balanced structure, it's a pleasure to drink now. 2,206 cases made. • $12 • (10/31/97) • **85**

Dolcetto d'Alba 1991 • $11 • (04/30/93) • **76**

PUPILLE, FATTORIA LE

Morellino di Scansano 1996: Bubbling over with red fruit; berry character. Medium- to light-bodied, with light tannins and a long, fruity, silky finish. Drink now. 40,000 cases made. • $13 • (09/30/97) • **85**

Morellino di Scansano 1995: A little-known Tuscan producer on a roll. Seductive blackberry, cherry and vanilla aromas and flavors. Medium-bodied with fine tannins and a soft, round finish. Drinkable now. 2,900 cases made. • $10 • (10/31/96) • **89**

ITALY

Morellino di Scansano 1989 • $13 • (10/31/93) • **84**
Morellino di Scansano Riserva 1993: Well-crafted red with cherry, spice and berry aromas and flavors. Medium-bodied. Has fine tannins and a medium, silky finish. Better after this year. 33,000 cases made. • $20 • (09/30/97) • **87**
Morellino di Scansano Riserva 1988 • $NA • (10/31/93) • **85**
Morellino di Scansano Riserva 1986 • $16 • (06/30/91) • **86**
Saffredi 1994: Deep and dark in color, with intense tobacco, coffee and old-wood aromas. Medium-bodied, pleasantly soft-textured, but slightly dull on the finish. 15,000 cases made. • $46 • (09/30/97) • **84**
Saffredi 1993: Dark-colored with intense blackberry and cherry flavors, a hint of minerals. Medium-bodied. Velvety texture and a caressing finish. Try now. • $40 • (10/31/96) • **89**
Saffredi 1990 • $40 • (02/28/95) • **88**
Saffredi 1989 • $NA • (10/31/93) • **86**
Saffredi 1988 • $NA • (10/31/93) • **91**
Vin Santo Tuscany 1991: Mind-blowing Vin Santo. This wine offers nuances of honey, apricot, almond and fruitcake, with a hint of nuts. Full-bodied and sweet with thick, long and luscious flavors. Fantastic. Drink now or hold. 5,000 cases made. • $32 • (09/30/97) • **91**

QUERCE, FATTORIA LA

Chianti 1985 • $9 • (11/30/87) • **83**
Chianti Classico 1988 • $9 • (11/30/89) (BT) • **86**
Chianti Classico 1987 • $7 • (11/30/89) • **80**
Chianti Classico 1986 • $7 • (11/30/89) • **81**
Chianti Classico Caratello 1983 • $4 • (11/30/89) • **70**

QUERCECCHIO

Brunello di Montalcino 1990: Ripe but crisp with an interesting combination of black cherry, currant and tobacco flavors. Yet very hard and tannic, showing a funky chestnut character on the finish. Drink now. • $NA • (10/31/95) • **80**
Brunello di Montalcino 1988 • $NA • (04/30/94) • **79**
Brunello di Montalcino Riserva 1988 • $NA • (10/31/94) • **88**
Rosso di Montalcino 1993 • $NA • (10/31/95) • **77**
Rosso di Montalcino 1991 • $NA • (04/30/94) • **81**

QUERCETO, CASTELLO DI

Chianti Classico 1994: A pretty, silky wine with berry, tobacco and cherry aromas and flavors. Has fine tannins, medium body and finish. Drink now. • $12 • (09/30/97) • **86**
Chianti Classico 1992 • $9 • (10/31/95) • **82**
Chianti Classico 1990 • $14 • (10/31/93) • **85**
Chianti Classico 1989 • $15 • (09/15/92) • **84**
Chianti Classico 1988 • $14 • (09/15/91) • **86**
Chianti Classico Riserva 1990 • $14 • (02/28/95) • **87**
Chianti Classico Riserva 1988 • $19 • (09/15/92) • **86**
Chianti Classico Riserva 1985 • $16 • (11/30/89) • **91**
Chianti Classico Riserva Il Picchio 1990 • $27 • (10/31/95) • **88**
Chianti Classico Riserva Il Picchio 1988 • $NA • (09/15/92) • **83**
Cignale 1993: A refined, well-made red, with enticing aromas of berries, violets and dried cherries. Medium-bodied, with fine tannins and a long, silky finish. Drinkable now. • $NA • (09/30/97) • **89**
Cignale 1989 • $35 • (10/31/93) • **80**
Cignale 1988 • $40 • (02/28/95) • **87**
Cignale 1987 • $36 • (02/28/95) • **89**
Il Querciolaia 1988 • $40 • (09/15/91) • **88**
Il Querciolaia 1986 • $35 • (11/30/89) • **85**
Il Querciolaia 1985 • $30 • (02/15/89) • **85**
La Corte 1993: Lovely aromas of tobacco, fruit and mushrooms. Medium-bodied, with lovely, velvety texture and a spicy, fruity, tobacco finish. Drink now or hold. • $30 • (09/30/97) • **89**
La Corte 1988 • $30 • (07/31/95) • **80**
La Corte 1985 • $20 • (11/30/89) • **93**
La Corte 1983 • $17 • (11/30/89) • **83**

Key: SS—Spectator Selection CS—Cellar Selection HR—Highly Recommended BB—Best Buy $NA—Price not available Ⓐ—Auction Price (BT)—Barrel Tasting
Dates in parentheses indicate the issues in which the ratings were published.

QUERCIA AL POGGIO

Chianti Classico 1990 • $NA • (10/31/93) • **85**
Chianti Classico Riserva 1988 • $NA • (10/31/93) • **80**

QUERCIABELLA, FATTORIA

Batàr 1995: A well-made Chardonnay with interesting aromas of toasty oak and ripe fruit; a hint of honey, too. Medium-bodied, with moderate acidity and a toasty finish. Drink now or hold. • $55 • (09/30/97) • **88**
Camartina 1993: Good berry, tobacco character in this medium-bodied wine. Shows medium, chewy tannins and has a short finish. Try now. • $40 • (09/30/97) • **86**
Camartina 1991 • $NA • (10/31/95) • **85**
Chianti Classico 1995: Some good fruit flavors of berry and plum, with a mild stemmy note. Medium body, with medium, chewy tannins and a moderate finish.Drink now. • $17 • (09/30/97) • **85**
Chianti Classico 1994: Well made, with plenty of fruity, minty aromas and flavors, medium body, fine tannins, and a long silky finish. • $13 • (10/31/96) • **85**
Chianti Classico 1988 • $13 • (09/15/91) • **90**
Chianti Classico Riserva 1994: Opulent for a Chianti with its berry, grilled meat and fruits on the nose and palate. Medium-bodied, with fine tannins and a long, succulent finish. Delicious. • $25 • (09/30/97) • **88**
Chianti Classico Riserva 1993: Handsome aromas and flavors of licorice and fruit, with a woody note. Has a medium body and fine tannins, but a slightly austere finish. Drink now. • $NA • (10/31/96) • **83**
Chianti Classico Riserva 1991 • $NA • (10/31/95) • **84**
Chianti Classico Riserva 1988 • $20 • (09/15/92) • **90**
Chianti Classico Riserva 1985 • $17 • (09/15/91) • **89**

QUERCIAVALLE

Armonia 1995: Marked by intense aromas of fruit and meat with a hint of smoke. Medium-bodied, with medium, chewy tannins and a chocolate finish. Needs time in the bottle; try after 1999. • $35 • (09/30/97) • **87**
Chianti Classico 1995: Offers bright red cherry and strawberry aromas, and a medium-to-light body with high, crisp acidity. Citrusy finish. Drink now. • $15 • (09/30/97) • **82**
Chianti Classico 1994: Medium-bodied with light tannins and a slightly peppery, berry character. Fresh on the finish. First time tasted. 5,000 cases made. • $13 • (10/31/96) • **81**
Chianti Classico Riserva 1994: Very modern Chianti with an abundance of new wood. Medium- to full-bodied, it has big vanilla flavors and a medium, fruity finish. A bit too much new wood? Wait and see. • $22 • (09/30/97) • **84**
Chianti Classico Riserva 1993: Rather light, and its fruity character verges on tomatolike. Light-bodied, with light tannins. Short finish. 5,000 cases made. • $18 • (10/31/96) • **76**

QUINTARELLI, GIUSEPPE

Amarone della Valpolicella Classico 1991: Here's an example of why Amarone is unique in the world of wine. A beauty, from the deep, espressolike color and smoky, exotic aromas to the overripe berry and botrytis flavors. Glycerin-like in texture, yet muscular and high in alcohol, with a lingering finish. Drink now through 2005. • $98 • (06/15/98) • **92**
Valpolicella Classico Superiore 1991: An acquired taste. Mature, but still alive, displaying mushroom, fruitcake and woodsy aromas and flavors, a smooth texture and an elegant structure. Drink now. • $28 • (06/15/98) • **84**

RAGOSE, LE

Amarone della Valpolicella 1991: Beginning to show maturity, here's an elegant style of Amarone (very typical of this estate), with cherry, tobacco and leather notes and a lingering finish. Drink now through 2003. • $48 • (05/31/98) • **85**

RAJA, LA

Gavi 1995: A bit coarse, with modest pear and green apple flavors and a sightly astringent finish. 10,000 cases made. • $15 • (03/31/97) • **77**
Gavi 1993 • $13 • (06/15/94) • **77**

RAMPOLLA, CASTELLO DEI

Chianti Classico 1995: Plum and mushroom aromas open to a light palate of berries that is short and slightly dry. • $20 • (09/30/97) • **80**
Chianti Classico 1994: Rather traditional in style but delicious all the same. Pretty fruit flavors with a barky, earthy accent. Medium-bodied with light tannins and a crisp finish. 10,000 cases made. • $18 • (10/31/96) • **83**
Chianti Classico 1992 • $17 • (10/31/95) • **75**
Chianti Classico 1989 • $17 • (12/15/92) • **80**
Chianti Classico 1988 • $14 • (09/15/92) • **87**
Chianti Classico 1987 • $15 • (04/15/91) • **84**
Chianti Classico 1985 • $8 • (09/15/88) • **90**
Chianti Classico 1983 • $6 • (07/31/87) BB • **84**
Chianti Classico Riserva 1994: Reveals some herbal character but it's pleasantly fruity, with a sweet fruit finish. Body is medium; tannins are light. • $34 • (09/30/97) • **85**
Chianti Classico Riserva 1993: Slightly disappointing for this producer. Alluring berry, earth and bark aromas and flavors and soft tannins, but a slightly short and funky aftertaste. Old barrels? Drink now. 2,000 cases made. • $31 • (10/31/96) • **81**
Chianti Classico Riserva 1991 • $28 • (10/31/95) • **86**
Chianti Classico Riserva 1990 • $25 • (02/28/95) • **88**
Chianti Classico Riserva 1988 • $19 • (05/15/93) • **88**
Chianti Classico Riserva 1985 • $46 Ⓐ • (04/30/90) • **81**
Sammarco 1994: Outstanding. Dark, inky color, with intense cassis and blackberry aromas. Full-bodied, with full yet silky tannins and a long, long finish. Beautiful structure. Try after 2000. • $65 • (09/30/97) • **92**
Sammarco 1993: This estate continues to make great super Tuscan wines, even in tough vintages. Subtle yet complex aromas of berry, cedar, mint and violet. Medium-bodied, with fine tannins and plenty of fruit flavors. Drinkable now. A blend of Cabernet Sauvignon and Sangiovese. 3,000 cases made. • $58 • (10/31/96) CS • **90**
Sammarco 1991 • $58 • (10/31/95) • **87**
Sammarco 1990 • $77 Ⓐ • (10/31/95) • **91**
Sammarco 1986 • $46 • (03/15/91) • **76**
Sammarco 1985 • $163 Ⓐ • (11/30/89) • **90**
Sammarco 1983 • $28 • (09/15/88) • **88**
Trebianco 1995: A strange, stylish white, interesting to taste. Dark-yellow in color, with cooked pasta and floral aromas. Medium- to full-bodied, with moderate acidity and an almond and dried apricot finish. • $NA • (09/30/97) • **87**
Trebianco Vendemmia Tardiva 1995: A pretty, medium-sweet wine, with lemon, almond and apricot aromas. Medium-bodied. Unveils a hint of oak before the delicious, creamy honey finish. Try with strawberries and cream. • $NA • (09/30/97) • **86**

RAPITALA

Alcamo 1996: Delivers some decent lemon and herbal flavors, but it comes off somewhat coarse overall. • $NA • (10/15/97) • **79**

RATTI, RENATO

Barbaresco 1994: Nicely made Barbaresco for the vintage. Shows plum, spice, toasty bread and grilled meat flavors. Has the slightly lean finish one expects from a '94, but with the right food it will drink just fine now through 1999. 400 cases made. • $29 • (01/31/98) • **85**
Barbaresco 1990 • $26 • (10/31/94) • **85**
Barbaresco 1989 • $31 • (10/31/94) • **73**
Barbera Piedmont 1995: Funky and very earthy, with some plum and tar, this medium-bodied red turns a bit tough on the firm finish. Drink slightly chilled. 1,000 cases made. • $13 • (01/31/98) • **79**
Barbera d'Alba Torriglione 1994: International-style Barbera with flavors of toasty oak, plum, spice, chocolate and smoke. Ripe tannins fold into the sweet fruit in this medium-bodied red that has length, character and harmony. Drink now through 2002. 300 cases made. • $18 • (10/31/97) • **88**
Barolo 1993: Ripe and sweet-tasting, with plum, tar, mineral, smoky and gamy character. Medium-bodied, it has enough fruit to stand up to the tannins, so hold off opening until around 2001. 1,500 cases made. • $35 • (01/31/98) • **86**
Barolo 1990 • $31 • (10/31/94) • **85**
Barolo 1989 • $28 • (10/31/94) • **79**
Barolo 1985 • $23 • (09/15/90) • **85**
Barolo 1983 • $20 • (10/15/88) • **87**
Barolo 1982 • $17 • (06/30/87) CS • **93**
Barolo 1980 • $10 • (02/15/87) • **83**
Barolo 1979 • $8 • (01/01/86) • **89**
Barolo Conca 1993: Fairly crisp, despite the depth in this wine. Offers some butter, spice, plum, cherry and mocha flavors and chewy, tough tannins. Perhaps softer after 2000. 130 cases made. • $60 • (10/31/97) • **85**
Barolo Conca Marcenasco 1988 • $NA • (10/31/93) • **78**
Barolo Marcenasco 1993: Total seduction. Amazingly silky for a Barolo this young, with sweet, ripe tannins that coat the mouth. Medium-to-full body, it unfolds its ripe cherry, currant, dried herb, mint leaf and black olive flavors into a delicious, harmonious finish. A hint of toughness on the finish suggests holding it until around 2000. 2,100 cases made. • $40 • (10/31/97) • **90**
Barolo Marcenasco 1992: In a traditional style, from the dried herb and earthy flavors to the dry, tannic texture. Drink now. • $31 • (10/31/96) • **83**
Barolo Marcenasco 1991 • $33 • (10/31/95) • **84**
Barolo Marcenasco 1990 • $36 • (10/31/94) • **91**
Barolo Marcenasco 1989 • $40 • (10/31/94) • **87**
Barolo Marcenasco 1988 • $NA • (10/31/93) • **84**
Barolo Marcenasco 1985 • $37 • (10/15/90) • **82**
Barolo Marcenasco 1982 • $23 • (06/30/87) • **90**
Barolo Marcenasco 1981 • $15 • (06/30/87) • **84**
Barolo Marcenasco Rocche 1989 • $NA • (10/31/93) • **81**
Barolo Marcenasco Rocche 1988 • $NA • (10/31/93) • **79**
Barolo Marcenasco Rocche 1983 • $30 • (01/31/89) • **86**
Barolo Marcenasco Rocche 1981 • $19 • (06/30/87) • **88**
Barolo Rocche 1993: Crisp and fresh, this has nice mint, dried herb, wild raspberry and black cherry flavors, good intensity, good fruit and medium body. Drinkable now through 2000. 240 cases made. • $60 • (10/31/97) • **86**
Cabernet Sauvignon Piedmont 1989 • $25 • (06/15/94) • **83**
Dolcetto d'Alba 1996: A quaffable red with grapey, red berry flavors and herbal notes, but the fruit is lacking and it's slightly diluted. Disappointing for this normally good Dolcetto producer. Drink up. 6,000 cases made. • $14 • (10/31/97) • **78**
Dolcetto d'Alba 1995: Impressive. Dark-colored and medium-bodied, it bursts with cassis and black pepper flavors. Firmly structured, but the amazingly ripe tannins give a smooth, supple finish. Enjoy. 5,000 cases made. • $13 • (10/31/96) • **89**
Dolcetto d'Alba 1993 • $10 • (07/31/95) • **86**
Dolcetto d'Alba Vigna Colombé 1985 • $9 • (02/28/87) • **90**
Nebbiolo d'Alba 1993 • $18 • (10/31/95) • **82**
Nebbiolo d'Alba 1983 • $7 • (06/16/86) BB • **81**
Nebbiolo d'Alba Occhetti 1995: A rather ripe, full-bodied Nebbiolo delivering some cherry and licorice flavors, but it turns hard on the finish, which is soaked in dry tannins. Might soften by 1999. 2,500 cases made. • $16 • (10/31/97) • **79**
Villa Pattono IV 1994: Rich and ripe, with black currant, mint and cassis flavors. Full-bodied and supple, this delicious Piedmont red offers wonderfully smooth mouthfeel and a balanced finish. Enjoy now. 400 cases made. • $22 • (10/31/97) • **85**
Villa Pattono 1993: An experiment that didn't work. Spicy, chocolaty aromas are enticing, but the flavors are woody and tannic, the texture tough. Fades on the finish. A blend of 80 percent Barbera d'Asti, 15 percent Freisa, and 5 percent Uvalino. • $23 • (10/31/96) • **74**
Villa Pattono 1989 • $18 • (10/31/94) • **83**

REDI

Vino Nobile di Montepulciano 1994: Beautifully aromatic with plums, strawberries and cream. Medium-bodied, with medium, round tannins and a long, flavorful finish. Drinkable now. Not imported into U.S. • $NA • (09/30/97) • **87**

REGALEALI

Cabernet Sauvignon 1989 • $32 • (04/30/94) • **84**
Conte Tasca d'Almerita 1985 • $7 • (04/15/88) • **74**
Rosso 1987 • $11 • (12/15/89) • **77**
Rosso del Conte 1984 • $19 • (07/31/89) • **84**

RICASOLI, BARONE

Chianti 1996: Plenty of bright, grapey character to this wine. Medium-bodied, with light tannins and a fresh finish. 60,000 cases made. • $8 • (09/30/97) • **83**

Chianti 1995: Medium-bodied, and offers floral, berry and cherry aromas and flavors of good intensity, but it's slightly dry and astringent on the finish. 60,000 cases made. • $7 • (10/31/96) • **79**
Chianti 1994 • $7 • (10/31/95) • **80**
Chianti 1993 • $7 • (02/28/95) • **79**
Chianti 1990 • $6 • (11/30/91) BB • **81**
Chianti 1989 • $7 • (04/15/91) BB • **83**
Chianti 1987 • $6 • (11/30/89) • **79**
Chianti 1986 • $6 • (05/15/89) BB • **84**
Chianti Classico 1994: A succulent, fresh and impressively fruity wine. Wonderful aromas of dried berries and cherries with a hint of smoke. Of medium body with light tannins and a crisp finish. 45,000 cases made. • $8 • (10/31/96) • **85**
Chianti Classico 1993 • $8 • (10/31/95) • **81**
Chianti Classico Riserva 1994: A lovely plummy wine with soft tannnins and a fruity finish. Medium-bodied. Fruity palate. Drink now. 13,000 cases made. • $14 • (09/30/97) • **85**
Chianti Classico Riserva 1993: Very plummy, with a medium body and light tannins. Fresh and delicately fruity on the finish. 12,500 cases made. • $11 • (10/31/96) • **85**
Chianti Classico Riserva 1990 • $12 • (10/31/95) • **82**
Chianti Classico Riserva 1983 • $8 • (11/30/89) • **83**
Chianti Classico San Ripolo 1995: A lively Chianti with attractive crushed raspberry and cherry character. Medium body, light tannins, fresh on the finish. It's reasonably priced, with enough cases made to bolster availability. Enjoyable now, or can be cellared. 45,000 cases made. • $10 • (09/30/97) BB • **85**
Chianti Classico San Ripolo 1988 • $10 • (10/31/91) BB • **84**
Chianti Classico San Ripolo 1987 • $10 • (04/15/91) • **79**
Orvieto Classico 1996: Shows little on the palate. Has some citrus and earth character, but not much else. 20,000 cases made. • $8 • (10/31/97) • **78**
Orvieto Classico 1994: Creamy almond and vanilla aromas are attractive in this firm, round wine. The peach and light earthy flavors are well balanced and will stand up to food. • $7 • (08/31/96) • **84**
Toscana Formulae 1995: Slowly opens to reveal some nice plum, berry and spice flavors. Supple and full-bodied. Drink now. • $12 • (07/31/97) • **85**
Tremalvo 1987 • $18 • (12/15/91) • **87**

RIECINE

Chianti Classico 1995: A burst of fresh fruit on the nose leads into plummy berry flavors. Has fine tannins, a light, crisp finish and is medium-bodied. Drink now. • $20 • (09/30/97) • **87**
Chianti Classico 1994: A wonderfully perfumed wine of raspberry, plum and berry character. Medium-bodied with fresh, fruity flavors and a clean finish. Try now. 250 cases made. • $22 • (10/31/96) • **86**
Chianti Classico 1992 • $NA • (02/28/95) • **80**
Chianti Classico 1991 • $21 • (10/31/93) • **86**
Chianti Classico 1990 • $22 • (09/15/92) • **80**
Chianti Classico 1988 • $22 • (04/30/91) • **89**
Chianti Classico 1987 • $20 • (04/30/91) • **83**
Chianti Classico Riserva 1994: Beautifully balanced for a Chianti with its cherry and wet earth character and fine, well-integrated tannins. Medium-bodied, with a moderate finish. Drink now through 2002. 400 cases made. • $33 • (09/30/97) • **88**
Chianti Classico Riserva 1993: Elegant, all finesse. Gives subtle violet, berry and cherry aromas and flavors, with silky tannins and a long, crisp, caressing finish. Medium-bodied. Drink now or hold. 100 cases made. • $34 • (10/31/96) • **87**
Chianti Classico Riserva 1991 • $35 • (10/31/95) • **88**
Chianti Classico Riserva 1990 • $NA • (02/28/95) • **88**
Chianti Classico Riserva 1988 • $24 • (09/15/92) • **82**
Chianti Classico Riserva 1985 • $19 • (09/15/91) • **87**
La Gioia 1994: Elegance par excellence. This offers vivid dried berry and cherry aromas with a mineral undertone, carrying through to a long, mineral and berry finish. Medium-bodied, with sleek, racy tannins. Fine wine. Try now. 400 cases made. • $40 • (09/30/97) • **90**
La Gioia 1993: This wine is wonderfully classy for the vintage, harmonious and fine. Very grapey and fruity on the nose. Medium-bodied, with soft tannins and a fresh fruit finish. Drink now or hold. 100 cases made. • $41 • (10/31/96) • **89**
La Gioia 1991 • $42 • (10/31/95) • **89**
La Gioia 1990 • $45 • (10/31/95) • **90**
La Gioia 1988 • $65 • (09/15/91) • **91**
La Gioia 1987 • $45 • (04/30/91) • **82**

RIETINE

Chianti Classico 1995: Offers a lot of fruit and character for a '95 Chianti with its crushed blackberry and cherry aromas and flavors. Medium-bodied, with fine tannins and a fresh finish. Drink now or hold. • $NA • (09/30/97) • **86**
Chianti Classico 1994: Fresh and simple, with some pleasant berry and citrus aromas and flavors. Medium-to-light in body, with light tannins and a crisp finish. • $NA • (10/31/96) • **79**
Chianti Classico 1992 • $NA • (10/31/95) • **83**
Chianti Classico Riserva 1991 • $NA • (10/31/95) • **84**
Tiziano 1993: A big and powerful red for aging, this has unctuous aromas of berries, currants and mint, and is full-bodied and tannic with a very good backbone and a long finish. Try after 1999. • $NA • (09/30/97) • **88**
Tiziano 1990 • $NA • (10/31/95) • **85**
Tuscany White 1996: Medium body, with moderate acidity and a slightly short finish. Interesting ripe apricot and apple-skin aromas. • $NA • (09/30/97) • **82**

RIGHETTI, LUIGI

Amarone della Valpolicella Classico Capitel dé Roari 1991: Enjoyable now for its mushroom and leather aromas and flavors, this Amarone, with its medium weight and supple texture, still shows some sweet cherry and plum character but clamps down on the finish. Drink now through 2003. 3,000 cases made. • $20 • (06/15/98) • **85**
Amarone della Valpolicella Classico Capitel de Roari 1990 • $20 • (04/30/96) HR • **90**
Amarone Recioto della Valpolicella Capitel de Roari 1983 • $16 • (02/15/89) • **90**
Valcaia 1994: A rich, spicy, berry-scented red. Reminiscent of St.-Emilion, with its earthy, cherry flavors. Medium-bodied and supple. Just a hint of tannin on the lingering finish. Drink now. A blend of Corvina, Cabernet Sauvignon, and Sangiovese. • $17 • (05/31/98) • **86**
Valpolicella Classico Superiore Campolieti 1994: Herbal and grainy, smelling and tasting more like Bordeaux, but attractive nonetheless. Leafy, black currant and cedary notes on an elegant framework, moderate concentration and intense finish. Drink now through 2000. 5,000 cases made. • $11 • (06/15/98) • **84**
Valpolicella Classico Superiore Campolieti 1993 • $10 • (12/15/95) • **85**

RINALDI & FIGLI, FRANCESCO

Barbaresco 1985 • $23 • (09/15/90) • **87**
Barbaresco 1983 • $16 • (01/31/89) • **79**
Barbera d'Alba 1996: Light, pleasant, and straightforward, with cherry, plum, raspberry and cassis-bush character. Drink chilled. • $NA • (10/31/97) • **81**
Barbera d'Alba 1993 • $13 • (10/31/95) • **85**
Barbera d'Alba 1991 • $12 • (09/30/93) • **86**
Barbera d'Alba 1989 • $13 • (10/31/92) • **89**
Barbera d'Alba 1987 • $10 • (03/15/91) • **87**
Barbera d'Alba 1986 • $9 • (02/15/89) • **88**
Barolo 1988 • $22 • (09/15/93) • **79**
Barolo 1986 • $22 • (07/15/91) • **83**
Barolo 1983 • $NA • (09/15/88) • **84**
Barolo 1982 • $16 • (09/15/88) • **83**
Barolo 1978 • $12 • (09/16/84) • **89**
Barolo 1947: Light and acidic, this has lost it. • $NA • (05/31/97) • **74**
Barolo Brunate Riserva 1988 • $30 • (10/31/93) • **71**
Barolo Brunate Riserva 1985 • $24 • (07/15/91) • **89**
Barolo Brunate Riserva 1982 • $27 • (06/30/87) • **79**
Barolo Cannubbio 1988 • $30 • (10/31/93) • **83**
Barolo Cannubbio 1985 • $25 • (06/15/90) • **78**
Barolo Cannubbio 1982 • $16 • (10/31/87) • **75**
Barolo Cannubi 1990 • $NA • (10/31/94) • **89**
Barolo Cannubi 1989 • $NA • (10/31/94) • **79**
Dolcetto d'Alba 1989 • $12 • (07/15/91) • **80**
Dolcetto d'Alba Roussot 1991 • $12 • (09/30/93) • **76**
Dolcetto d'Alba Roussot 1990 • $13 • (10/31/92) • **78**
Dolcetto d'Alba Roussot 1988 • $10 • (07/15/91) • **78**

Key: SS—Spectator Selection CS—Cellar Selection HR—Highly Recommended BB—Best Buy $NA—Price not available Ⓐ—Auction Price (BT)—Barrel Tasting
Dates in parentheses indicate the issues in which the ratings were published.

ITALY

Dolcetto d'Alba Roussot 1987 • $9 • (03/31/90) • **86**

RINALDI, GIUSEPPE

Barolo 1992: Has spicy, chocolaty aromas and strongly fruity flavors, then turns dry and tannic on the finish. Perhaps overwhelmed by oak-aging. • $NA • (10/31/96) • **78**
Barolo Brunate 1991: Hearty, full-flavored and aromatic, blending earthy, spicy aromas with cherry and currant flavors that linger on the finish. Drink now to 2001. • $NA • (10/31/96) • **86**
Barolo Brunate Riserva 1989 • $38 • (10/31/94) • **80**

RIO GRANDE

Chardonnay Umbria Colle delle Montecchie 1996: A crisp white with lemon and herb flavors that turn just a tad vegetal on the finish. Drink now. • $8 • (06/15/98) • **79**
Umbria Casa Pastore 1995: Clean and fresh, simple and hearty, with a grapey flavor, medium body, and moderate tannins. Drink now. • $24 • (06/15/98) • **83**

RIPA, FATTORIA LA

Bianco della Lega 1996: Gives more on the nose, with its fresh melon, apple and peach aromas, than on the palate. Medium-bodied, with light acidity and a slightly earthy finish. • $12 • (09/30/97) • **82**
Chianti Classico 1995: Rather light and slightly diluted, this is light-bodied, with berry and dried cherry flavors and a light, dry finish. • $14 • (09/30/97) • **78**
Chianti Classico 1994: Light and fruity, with aromas and flavors of berry and watermelon, but they fade quickly on the palate. • $12 • (10/31/96) • **78**
Chianti Classico 1993 • $10 • (10/31/95) • **77**
Chianti Classico Riserva 1993: Has a decent core of fruit with a berry, leather character. Light-bodied, with a slightly dry finish. • $19 • (10/31/96) • **77**
Santa Brigida 1993: Like a pleasant glass of red Burgundy. Pretty berry, chocolate and leather aromas and flavors, with silky tannins and a slightly light finish. Drink now. A blend of Sangiovese and Cabernet Sauvignon. • $17 • (10/31/96) • **82**
Santa Brigida 1990 • $15 • (10/31/95) • **73**

RITRATTI

Pinot Nero Trentino 1991 • $12 • (02/28/95) • **78**

RIVETTI, FRATELLI

Barbera d'Alba Cairel 1990 • $12 • (06/15/94) • **82**
Nebbiolo d'Alba Vigneto Rainè 1990 • $14 • (06/15/94) • **86**

RIVETTI & FIGLI, GIUSEPPE

Moscato d'Asti La Spinetta Bricco Quaglia 1991 • $15 • (05/15/93) • **80**
Moscato d'Asti La Spinetta Vigneto Biancospino 1992 • $15 • (05/15/93) • **88**

RIZZARDI, GUERRIERI

Amarone della Valpolicella Classico 1990 • $22 • (06/15/96) HR • **90**
Amarone della Valpolicella Classico 1988 • $20 • (09/15/92) • **75**
Bardolino Tacchetto 1991 • $12 • (09/15/92) • **83**
Soave Classico 1994 • $8 • (06/15/96) • **82**
Soave Classico Costeggiola 1994 • $9 • (06/15/96) • **84**
Valpolicella Classico Poiega 1990 • $8 • (09/15/92) • **80**
Valpolicella Classico Poiega 1988 • $9 • (12/15/89) • **82**
Valpolicella Classico Superiore 1991 • $9 • (04/30/94) • **80**
Valpolicella Classico Superiore 1987 • $6 • (03/31/90) • **79**
Valpolicella Classico Superiore Villa Rizzardi Poiega 1993 • $7 • (06/15/96) • **85**

RIZZO, LUIGI

Barolo 1947: Very old flavors, but they're still alive, with some raspberry and anise flavors echoing on the chewy finish. • $NA • (05/31/97) • **84**

ROAGNA, ALFREDO & GIOVANNI

Barbaresco 1988 • $33 • (10/31/94) • **72**
Barbaresco 1986 • $26 • (07/15/91) • **86**
Barbaresco 1985 • $27 • (02/28/89) • **89**

ROCCA BERNARDA

Pinot Grigio Colli Orientali del Friuli 1996: A deeply colored, floral-scented style that's rich and vibrant, with modest apple flavors that finish short. Drink now. 2,500 cases made. • $14 • (05/31/98) • **83**
Sauvignon Blanc Colli Orientali del Friuli 1996: A lovely wine, bursting with peach, melon and floral elements, all beautifully balanced with vibrant acidity and a rich midpalate. The cleansing finish shows a hint of minerals. Drink through 1999. 4,700 cases made. • $14 • (06/15/98) • **87**
Tocai Friulano Colli Orientali del Friuli 1996: Aromas and flavors of pears, straw and nuts on an elegant framework with juicy acidity, all balanced to provide immediate pleasure. Drink through 1999. 4,500 cases made. • $13 • (06/15/98) • **83**

ROCCA DELLE MACIE

Chianti Classico 1995: Light, with some berry, plum character, but seems slightly watery on the finish. 60,000 cases made. • $10 • (03/31/97) • **79**
Chianti Classico 1994: Aromas and flavors of plum, coffee and black cherry, and good spiciness. Still tannic. Drink now. • $9 • (03/31/97) • **81**
Chianti Classico 1992 • $NA • (02/28/95) • **76**
Chianti Classico 1991 • $9 • (10/31/93) • **85**
Chianti Classico 1990 • $9 • (09/15/92) • **88**
Chianti Classico 1987 • $NA • (11/30/89) • **82**
Chianti Classico 1986 • $NA • (11/30/89) • **80**
Chianti Classico Riserva 1994: Starts slowly, but finishes nicely. Medium-bodied, with plum and mushroom flavors, fine tannins and a fresh finish. Drink now. 15,500 cases made. • $16 • (09/30/97) • **86**
Chianti Classico Riserva 1990 • $13 • (02/28/95) • **75**
Chianti Classico Riserva 1985 • $14 • (09/15/91) • **77**
Chianti Classico Riserva Tenuta di Fizzano 1994: A beautiful, velvety wine with berry, cherry and tobacco aromas and flavors, attractive tannins and a smooth finish. Medium-bodied. Drink now. 4,250 cases made. • $19 • (09/30/97) • **86**
Chianti Classico Riserva di Fizzano 1987 • $NA • (11/30/89) • **89**
Chianti Classico Riserva di Fizzano 1985 • $NA • (11/30/89) • **88**
Chianti Classico Riserva di Fizzano 1982 • $16 • (03/31/89) • **87**
Chianti Classico Tenuta di Sant' Alfonso 1995: Decent berry character and a hint of oak, but has a slightly stemmy and green aftertaste. Medium-bodied, with light tannins and a round texture on the finish. Drink now. 5,100 cases made. • $NA • (09/30/97) • **81**
Chianti Classico Tenuta Sant' Alfonso 1992 • $NA • (02/28/95) • **78**
Chianti Classico Tenuta Sant' Alfonso 1988 • $NA • (09/15/91) • **89**
Roccato 1994: Very good wine. Offers blackberry aromas dosed with new wood, silky tannins and a long, black currant and berry finish. Medium-bodied. Try now. 2,300 cases made. • $26 • (09/30/97) • **88**
Roccato 1993: A rich and flavorful wine with loads of plum, chocolate and black cherry flavors, as well as notes of vanilla and clove. Still a bit tannic on the finish, but likely at its best now, while fresh. • $18 • (01/31/97) • **87**
Roccato 1990 • $30 • (02/28/95) • **87**
Roccato 1988 • $NA • (09/15/91) • **90**
Rubizzo 1995: Soft and succulent, with berry, light spice and earth on the palate. Medium- to light-bodied, with light tannins and a fresh finish. Slightly short. Drink now. 8,800 cases made. • $10 • (09/30/97) • **85**
Rubizzo Sangiovese 1994: Thick, rich and juicy with plum and cherry flavors and tobacco notes on the finish. This is nicely focused, with good balance and structure. • $6 • (01/31/97) • **85**
Rubizzo 1993 • $10 • (02/28/95) • **77**
Ser Gioveto 1994: Cherry, leather and spices on the nose. Light-bodied, with light tannins and a light, fruity finish. A bit dull. 3,250 cases made. • $19 • (09/30/97) • **81**
Ser Gioveto 1990 • $16 • (02/28/95) • **82**
Ser Gioveto 1989 • $15 • (10/31/93) • **76**
Ser Gioveto 1987 • $NA • (11/30/89) • **90**
Ser Gioveto 1986 • $15 • (02/15/89) • **84**
Ser Gioveto 1985 • $15 • (11/30/89) • **88**

ROCCA DI CASTAGNOLI

Buriano 1993: Wonderfully elegant. Beautiful dried cherry, berry and floral aromas with a hint of spices. Medium-bodied, with fine tannins and a supple, silky finish. Delicious now. 165 cases made. • $NA • (09/30/97) • **89**
Buriano 1990 • $28 • (10/31/93) • **86**
Capraia 1990 • $22 • (10/31/93) • **82**
Chianti Classico 1995: There's wonderful fruit in this wine, boysenberry character through and through. Medium-bodied, it has fresh acidity and a fruity finish. 7,500 cases made. • $19 • (09/30/97) • **87**
Chianti Classico 1993: Shows aromas and flavors of dried cherry and an earthy note, but starting to dry out. Very delicate structure. • $NA • (10/31/96) • **78**
Chianti Classico 1991 • $17 • (10/31/95) • **80**
Chianti Classico 1990 • $14 • (02/28/95) • **86**
Chianti Classico Capraia Riserva 1993: Delicate. Offers a berry and cherry character in light body. Short finish. Drinkable now. • $20 • (10/31/96) • **78**
Chianti Classico Capraia Riserva 1988 • $NA • (09/15/92) • **84**
Chianti Classico Poggio A'Frati 1988 • $20 • (10/31/93) • **82**
Chianti Classico Poggio A'Frati Riserva 1993: Firm and fairly rich, with plum and dried cherry aromas and flavors. Medium-bodied, with a finish of moderate length. Drink now or hold. 3,300 cases made. • $27 • (09/30/97) • **87**
Chianti Classico Poggio A'Frati Riserva 1990 • $22 • (10/31/95) • **87**
Chianti Classico Poggio A'Frati Riserva 1988 • $21 • (09/15/92) • **87**
Le Pergoline 1996: Fresh, lemony aromas and the wine is medium-bodied with lots of lemony almond flavors. Lively finish. 1,000 cases made. • $13 • (09/30/97) • **83**
Poggio A'Frati 1990 • $18 • (10/31/93) • **89**
Stielle 1993: Attractive berry, tobacco and mushroom aromas and flavors. Medium-bodied, with fine tannins and moderate finish. Drink now. 1,800 cases made. • $33 • (09/30/97) • **86**
Stielle 1991 • $NA • (10/31/95) • **87**
Stielle 1990 • $33 • (10/31/95) • **90**
Stielle 1988 • $28 • (10/31/93) • **82**

ROCCA DI MONTEGROSSI

Chianti Classico 1995: Beautiful crushed berries and flowers mark the nose. Medium-bodied, with extremely high acidity and a fresh finish. Needs food. Drink now. • $15 • (09/30/97) • **83**
Chianti Classico 1994: Some decent berry and earth aromas and flavors, but slightly astringent and dry on the finish. Tasted twice with consistent notes. • $17 • (10/31/96) • **78**
Chianti Classico 1991 • $NA • (10/31/93) • **76**
Chianti Classico 1990 • $16 • (10/31/93) • **88**
Chianti Classico Riserva 1987 • $17 • (05/15/93) • **78**
Chianti Classico San Marcellino Riserva 1993: A wine with an abundance of cherry and mushroom. Medium-bodied, with firm tannins, and a slightly woody finish. Drink now or hold. • $NA • (09/30/97) • **83**
Geremia 1993: Beautiful Sangiovese aromas of tobacco, fruit and mushrooms. Medium-bodied, with fine tannins and a sizable dose of new wood. Try now. • $30 • (10/31/96) • **87**

ROCCA, ALBINO

Barbaresco Vigneto Brich Ronchi 1994: Light- to medium-bodied, with pleasant earthy, red- and blackberry flavors, it starts out supple and fruity, then firms up on the finish. Nicely crafted. Try around 2000. • $35 • (10/31/97) • **85**
Barbaresco Vigneto Brich Ronchi 1993: A beauty, with great, showy aromas and deep color. Harmonious, full-bodied, silky yet tightly wound. Rich but also elegant, with a beam of pure, grapey, red berry flavor carrying through from start to wonderful finish. Supple tannins. Tempting now, but try in 1999. • $30 • (10/31/96) • **91**
Barbaresco Vigneto Brich Ronchi 1991 • $23 • (10/31/94) • **83**
Barbaresco Vigneto Loreto 1994: Only modest fruit in this light-bodied, diluted red, and the tannins really clamp down on the finish. • $30 • (10/31/97) • **75**
Barbaresco Loreto 1993: A medium-bodied wine of medium intensity, with some crisp, lemony character. A bit harsh. Disappointing, given this estate's other nice '93s. • $25 • (10/31/96) • **75**
Barbaresco Loreto 1991 • $22 • (10/31/94) • **82**
Barbera d'Alba Gepin 1995: Lovely, balanced, fresh, medium-bodied, with plenty of ripe, sweet red berry character. Really delicious. Firm tannins and crisp acidity, but has the flesh to keep it all together. Drink now through 2002 with pasta, pizza or meats. • $16 • (10/31/97) • **87**
Barbera d'Alba Gepin 1994: Fresh, grapey and pure, bursting with wild berry and currant flavors. Quite sweet-tasting despite the acidity; medium body. Crisp, balanced finish. • $12 • (10/31/96) • **86**
Dolcetto d'Alba Vignalunga 1996: Serious juice. Inky-black in color, full-bodied, this powerful Dolcetto is still very backward on the nose, delivering just hints of earth, wild flowers and berries, but it packs it in on the palate, with mineral, ripe red and blackberry character. Loads of well-integrated tannins need until around 1999 to soften. Thicker and denser than Scavino's fruitier-styled and more elegant Dolcetto. • $15 • (10/31/97) • **92**
Dolcetto d'Alba Vignalunga 1993: Grapey, fresh, and full of life. An excellent, vibrant Dolcetto that's lovely to drink now, chock full of blueberry flavor and gentle tannins. Try with pizza; you won't regret it. Drink now. 250 cases made. • $11 • (10/31/96) • **85**

ROCCA, BRUNO

Barbaresco 1991 • $42 • (10/31/94) • **86**
Barbaresco Rabajà 1993: Exotic and modern, clearly a *barrique* style wine. Fancy and showy, but the oak mingles nicely with the deep, red berry flavors and the violet and rose petal aromas are appealing. Full-bodied and supple, with a long, fresh finish. 1,000 cases made. • $40 • (10/31/96) • **90**
Barbaresco Rabajà 1992 • $40 • (10/31/95) • **80**
Barbaresco Rabajà 1989 • $45 • (10/31/93) • **92**
Barbera d'Alba 1994: Nicely fruity, while subtly oaky. Plenty of currant and cherry flavors, moderate tannins and great balance. Smooth and inviting. 583 cases made. • $20 • (10/31/96) • **85**
Barbera d'Alba 1993 • $20 • (10/31/95) • **86**
Barbera d'Alba 1991 • $22 • (10/31/94) • **88**
Nebbiolo Fralù da Vigneto 1993 • $15 • (10/31/95) • **78**

ROCCADORO

Chianti 1991 • $9 • (03/31/93) • **73**
Chianti Classico 1990 • $10 • (05/15/93) • **74**
Chianti Classico Riserva 1988 • $14 • (03/31/93) • **80**

ROCCHE COSTAMAGNA

Barbera d'Alba 1995: Clean, pure and lovely from start to finish, this balances lively acidity with ripe, red- and blackberry flavors in a seductive, medium-bodied package. Perfect for food. Drink through 1999. 1,000 cases made. • $17 • (10/31/97) • **87**
Barbera d'Alba 1988 • $12 • (03/15/91) • **90**
Barbera d'Alba Rocche di La Morra 1993: Has interesting fruity, floral flavors, but the harsh, drying tannins make it difficult to drink. 1,000 cases made. • $16 • (10/31/96) • **75**
Barbera d'Alba Rocche di la Morra 1992 • $NA • (10/31/94) • **78**
Barbera d'Alba Rocche di la Morra 1991 • $14 • (04/30/93) • **84**
Barbera d'Alba Rocche di la Morra 1990 • $17 • (10/31/92) • **86**
Barolo Rocche dell'Annunziata 1993: A '93 that grows on you. Starts out with great finesse, then kicks in with sweet, ripe fruit flavors on the palate. Good concentration of mineral, plum, blackberry jam and spice notes. Better wait until around 2000 for the tannins to soften. • $32 • (10/31/97) • **87**
Barolo Rocche di La Morra 1991: Broad-textured, with some nice plummy, chalky flavors, but its very tannic and dry on the finish. 1,400 cases made. • $29 • (10/31/96) • **79**
Barolo Rocche di la Morra 1990 • $NA • (10/31/94) • **89**
Barolo Rocche di la Morra 1989 • $20 • (10/31/94) • **89**
Barolo Rocche di la Morra 1988 • $26 • (12/15/92) • **87**
Barolo Rocche di la Morra 1985 • $25 • (02/28/91) • **72**
Barolo Vigna San Francesco 1993: Nice and supple; fairly ripe, with sweet fruit flavors. A new-style Barolo with a cherry, currant, raspberry, spice, violet, rose petal and mocha character. Tannins turn chewy on the finish; try after 2000. 362 cases made. • $38 • (10/31/97) • **87**

Key: SS—Spectator Selection CS—Cellar Selection HR—Highly Recommended BB—Best Buy $NA—Price not available Ⓐ—Auction Price (BT)—Barrel Tasting
Dates in parentheses indicate the issues in which the ratings were published.

ITALY

Barolo Vigna San Francesco 1991: Full-bodied and tannic in texture, but with lots of spicy, fruity, mochalike flavors that linger on the finish. Good depth and intensity. Try now. • $37 • (10/31/96) • **87**

Barolo Vigna San Francesco 1990 • $NA • (10/31/94) • **90**

Dolcetto d'Alba 1996: A well-made Dolcetto with blackberry, spice and wet earth aromas and flavors, ripe tannins, plus some less attractive bell pepper and herbal notes. Still, it's balanced and tasty. Drink now. • $12 • (10/31/97) • **83**

Dolcetto d'Alba 1993 • $13 • (10/31/95) • **81**

Dolcetto d'Alba 1991 • $15 • (04/30/93) • **78**

Dolcetto d'Alba 1989 • $12 • (04/30/91) • **83**

Nebbiolo delle Langhe Roccardo 1989 • $13 • (04/30/91) • **85**

Rocche delle Rocche 1990 • $17 • (03/31/93) • **81**

ROCCHE DEI BROVIA

Barolo 1993: Straightforward Barolo, quite light but with an attractive toasty oak, cherry, mineral and wet earth character. Try around 2000, after the tannins soften. From Fratelli Brovia Azienda. 633 cases made. • $40 • (10/31/97) • **82**

ROCCHE DEI MANZONI, PODERI

Barbera d'Alba Vigna La Cresta 1995: Straightforward, mature, ripe and sweet fruit flavors mingle with notes of forest underbrush and spice. Medium-bodied and slightly diluted, the finish is a little dry. 1,642 cases made. • $25 • (10/31/97) • **81**

Barbera d'Alba Vigna La Cresta 1994: A spicy, medium-weight Barbera with solid fruit flavors, crisp texture and a lingering finish. • $16 • (10/31/96) • **84**

Barbera d'Alba Vigna La Cresta 1993 • $NA • (10/31/95) • **85**

Barolo Riserva 1990 • $35 • (10/31/95) • **89**

Barolo Riserva 1989 • $NA • (10/31/94) • **88**

Barolo Vigna Big 1993: An international-style red. A "modern" Barolo that smells like new oak, with chocolate, spice, toasty bread and violet notes blending nicely with red- and blackberry character. Medium-bodied, with a slight dilution, it tastes elegant and refined; has smooth tannins and it's not very rich. Oak dominates the finish. Best to wait until 2002. 686 cases made. • $25 • (10/31/97) • **86**

Barolo Riserva Vigna Big 1990 • $NA • (10/31/95) • **83**

Barolo Riserva Vigna Big 1989 • $NA • (10/31/94) • **87**

Barolo Vigna d'la Roul 1993: A light-bodied, light-colored Barolo that offers sweet-tasting licorice, spice, cherry and floral notes—almost like a maturing Pinot Noir. Tannins are a bit dry on the finish. Drink now to 2000. 808 cases made. • $25 • (10/31/97) • **83**

Barolo Riserva Vigna d'La Roul 1990 • $NA • (10/31/95) • **90**

Barolo Riserva Vigna d'La Roul 1989 • $NA • (10/31/94) • **92**

Barolo Vigna Rocche 1993: Modern-style Barolo, pushing the envelope with what seems like *barrique* treatment from the taste of the violet, spice and cassis flavors. Elegant, fairly lean, and medium-bodied. Should be a beauty around 2002. 2,708 cases made. • $22 • (10/31/97) • **88**

Bricco Manzoni 1994: Fairly polished, with some oak-infused spice, chocolate and vanilla notes adding complexity to the cherry and red berry flavors. Light- to medium-bodied, with good length. An attractive wine. Drink through 1999. 2,375 cases made. • $25 • (10/31/97) • **83**

Bricco Manzoni 1990 • $25 • (10/31/94) • **74**

Dolcetto d'Alba Vigna Rocche 1995: Fresh and young, tasting almost like Beaujolais, with peppery and cherry flavors. A touch watery, with some hard tannins on the slightly green finish. • $NA • (10/31/96) • **79**

Pinonero di Valentino 1994: Thick, ripe and rich, medium-bodied and very dark, but also very oaky, showing an interesting cinnamon, cumin, spice and blackberry character. Lacks a bit of finesse, though. Drink now through 2000. 470 cases made. • $22 • (10/31/97) • **83**

RODANO

Chianti Classico 1994: Very light, with stewed tomato and cut grass notes lurking under the fruit. • $15 • (10/31/96) • **71**

Chianti Classico 1993 • $13 • (10/31/95) • **78**

Chianti Classico 1990 • $10 • (10/31/93) • **87**

Chianti Classico Riserva Viacosta 1990 • $20 • (10/31/95) • **84**

Monna Claudia 1988 • $NA • (10/31/95) • **86**

ROMANDIOLA

Sangiovese di Romagna Il Pavone D'Oro Superiore 1993 • $7 • (02/29/96) • **84**

ROMITORIO, CASTELLO

Brio 1992 • $10 • (02/28/95) • **84**

Brunello di Montalcino 1988 • $30 • (11/30/94) • **91**

Romito del Romitorio 1993: In a modern, international style, this is amazingly dark in color and rich in fruit. Full body and tannins, with loads of oak. It needs time to mellow; try in 2000. Tasted twice, with consistent notes. • $25 • (10/31/95) • **91**

Romito del Romitorio 1992 • $20 • (11/30/94) • **88**

RONCADE, CASTELLO DI

Villa Giustinian 1988 • $13 • (10/15/94) • **85**

RONCO DEI TASSI

Bianco Collio 1994 • $18 • (06/15/96) • **77**

Bianco Collio 1993 • $17 • (01/31/95) • **84**

Pinot Grigio Collio 1993 • $15 • (01/31/95) • **85**

Sauvignon Collio 1994 • $17 • (06/15/96) • **83**

Tocai Friulano Collio 1994 • $18 • (06/15/96) • **80**

RONCO DEL GNEMIZ

Chardonnay Colli Orientali del Friuli 1995: Showing its maturity, this international-style Chardonnay has new oak accents that overshadow the apple and pear aromas and flavors. Tannic finish. Try with grilled fish and chicken. Drink now. 683 cases made. • $30 • (06/15/98) • **83**

Müller-Thurgau 1996: A light-bodied white, showing grapefruit and grassy aromas and flavors, nicely balanced with a firm structure and clean finish. Drink now. 433 cases made. • $19 • (06/15/98) • **84**

Picolit Colli Orientali del Friuli 1993 • $38 • (01/31/95) • **78**

Pinot Grigio Colli Orientali del Friuli 1996: More on the almond side of the Pinot Grigio flavor spectrum, with the flavors very tight and compact, finishing crisply. Drink now. 616 cases made. • $17 • (06/15/98) • **82**

Pinot Grigio Colli Orientali del Friuli 1995: Not for the meek. Bold and assertive, with plenty of intensity, from the straw, apple and almond flavors to the firm structure supporting it all. Its bracing acidity should complement food. • $16 • (06/15/97) • **86**

Pinot Grigio Colli Orientali del Friuli 1993 • $16 • (01/31/95) • **80**

Rosso 1986 • $15 • (03/31/89) • **80**

Rosso del Gnemiz 1988 • $28 • (09/15/92) • **85**

Tocai Friulano Colli Orientali del Friuli 1996: The subtle aroma is reminiscent of almonds, picking up grass and mineral flavors married to a rich, airy structure. Good intensity, with a subtle, lingering finish. Drink now. 358 cases made. • $17 • (06/15/98) • **84**

Tocai Friulano Colli Orientali del Friuli 1995: Straightforward, firm and dry, this white has straw and herb aromas, followed by rich peach flavors and a moderate finish. • $16 • (06/15/97) • **83**

Tocai Friulano Colli Orientali del Friuli 1994 • $18 • (06/15/96) • **82**

Tocai Friulano Colli Orientali del Friuli 1993 • $16 • (01/31/95) • **83**

ROSAZZO, ABBAZIA DI

Chardonnay Colli Orientali del Friuli 1993 • $19 • (01/31/95) • **79**

Pignolo 1987 • $36 • (06/30/91) • **85**

Pignolo 1985 • $22 • (09/15/88) • **86**

Pinot Grigio Colli Orientali del Friuli 1994: This full-bodied white displays flavors of apple, herbs and almond and a mature character. Rich enough to stand up to food. • $NA • (01/01/97) • **84**

Pinot Grigio Colli Orientali del Friuli 1993 • $19 • (01/31/95) • **79**

Ribolla Gialla Colli Orientali del Friuli 1993 • $19 • (01/31/95) • **75**

Ribolla Gialla Colli Orientali del Friuli 1990 • $21 • (01/31/92) • **76**

Ronco dei Roseti 1987 • $35 • (07/15/91) • **87**

Ronco dei Roseti 1986 • $22 • (03/15/89) • **85**

Ronco dei Roseti 1983 • $20 • (09/15/88) • **87**

Ronco della Abbazia 1988 • $11/375ml • (07/15/91) • **73**

Sauvignon Blanc Colli Orientali del Friuli 1993 • $18 • (01/31/95) • **83**

Verduzzo Colli Orientali del Friuli 1986 • $22 • (10/15/88) • **83**

ROSETI, DEI

Belconvento 1987 • $24 • (03/15/91) • **85**
Belconvento 1985 • $23 • (07/15/89) • **86**
Brunello di Montalcino 1982 • $20 • (07/31/89) • **89**
Brunello di Montalcino 1979 • $10 • (08/31/86) • **88**
Rosso di Montalcino 1988 • $13 • (01/31/91) • **87**
Rosso di Montalcino 1985 • $9 • (07/15/89) • **78**

ROSSO, CANTINA GIGI

Barbera d'Alba 1995: Crisp, light-bodied and fresh, with chewy tannins and some grassy, herbal notes. Seems unripe. 2,500 cases made. • $11 • (10/31/97) • **78**
Barbera d'Alba Vino del Buon Ricordo 1996 • $18 • • **86**
Barbera d'Alba Vino del Buon Ricordo 1995: A bit odd, with a gluelike, green aroma. Crisp and a bit unbalanced, with an astringent finish. 497 cases made. • $15 • (10/31/97) • **76**
Barbera d'Alba Vino del Buon Ricordo 1994: A very ripe, fruity, jammy wine. Rather soft for the type; ready to drink now. • $NA • (10/31/96) • **78**
Barolo Arione 1993: Light in body, color and aroma, this tastes and smells a bit rustic, with a chestnut, plum and earth character that lacks a bit of elegance. Turns quite ripe and nice on the finish, though. 1,567 cases made. • $23 • (10/31/97) • **80**
Barolo Arione Sorì dell'Ulivo 1990: Shows Barolo character in spades with its classic aromas of roses and tar, deep flavors laced with firm tannins, chewy texture and long finish. Drink now to 2005. • $NA • (10/31/96) • **92**
Dolcetto d'Alba Rocca Giovino 1995: Light, diluted and fairly one dimensional, with drying tannins on the finish. • $NA • (10/31/96) • **77**
Dolcetto di Diano d'Alba Moncolombetto 1996: Offers a fresh, grapey, cranberry character, with soft tannins. Light-bodied. Quite crisp and citrusy on the finish, but has some ripe fruit. Drink now. 2,010 cases made. • $12 • (10/31/97) • **80**
Dolcetto di Diano d'Alba Vigna Moncolombetto 1995: A treat. Bursting with vivid berry aromas and grapey flavors. Ripe tannins are impressive. Try with pizza and light foods. • $NA • (10/31/96) • **85**

ROTARI

Brut Trento Riserva 1993: Beautifully balanced and refreshing to drink. Rather rich in texture and fruit flavor, with bright acidity and a lingering finish. • $15 • (06/15/97) • **86**
Brut Trentino Riserva 1991 • $13 • (06/15/96) • **85**
Brut Trentino Riserva 1990 • $10 • (12/31/94) BB • **85**
Brut Trentino Riserva 1988 • $10 • (05/15/93) • **84**

RUBENTINO

Chianti 1990 • $6 • (04/30/92) • **78**
Chianti Classico 1989 • $8 • (04/30/92) • **81**

RUFFINO

Cabreo Il Borgo 1995: Big and powerful, it's ripe fruit aromas tinged with raisin, this is a full-bodied and velvety wine, with an abundance of fruit and tannins. Needs bottle age; try in 2000. • $28 • (09/30/97) • **90**
Cabreo Il Borgo 1994: A silky wine with berry, tobacco and a hint of wood on the nose and palate. Medium- to light-bodied, with fine tannins and a fresh finish. Drink now. • $28 • (09/30/97) • **87**
Cabreo Il Borgo 1993 • $NA • (10/31/95) • **87**
Cabreo Il Borgo 1990 • $NA • (10/31/93) • **92**
Cabreo Il Borgo Predicato di Bitùrica 1988 • $NA • (09/15/91) • **90**
Cabreo Il Borgo Predicato di Bitùrica 1987 • $27 • (12/15/92) • **82**
Cabreo Il Borgo Predicato di Bitùrica 1985 • $21 • (09/30/89) • **90**
Cabreo La Pietra 1995: Lively white peach, apple, floral and seabreeze aromas waft from this medium-bodied wine. Has a creamy texture and a moderate finish of vanilla and honey. Delicious. • $18 • (09/30/97) • **87**

Key: SS—Spectator Selection CS—Cellar Selection HR—Highly Recommended BB—Best Buy $NA—Price not available Ⓐ—Auction Price (BT)—Barrel Tasting
Dates in parentheses indicate the issues in which the ratings were published.

Chianti 1995: A pretty wine that's drinking well now. This is exuberant, delivering ripe cherry and plum flavors with spicy and smoky accents, moderate tannins and bright acidity. • $7 • (11/15/96) • **84**
Chianti 1994 • $NA • (10/31/95) • **80**
Chianti 1991 • $8 • (05/15/93) • **79**
Chianti 1990 • $8 • (01/31/92) • **77**
Chianti Classico 1987 • $7 • (04/30/90) BB • **83**
Chianti Classico 1984 • $5 • (11/30/86) • **78**
Chianti Classico Aziano 1995: A straightforward Chianti, light-bodied, with aromas and flavors of plum and strawberry. Clean finish. • $12 • (10/31/96) • **81**
Chianti Classico Aziano 1994: Light and simple, with some berry aromas and flavors and a lightly earthy, leathery finish. Not much here, really. • $12 • (10/31/96) • **78**
Chianti Classico Aziano 1992 • $10 • (02/28/95) • **72**
Chianti Classico Aziano 1991 • $11 • (10/31/93) • **78**
Chianti Classico Aziano 1990 • $10 • (09/15/92) • **88**
Chianti Classico Aziano 1989 • $10 • (04/30/92) • **79**
Chianti Classico Aziano 1988 • $11 • (09/15/91) • **83**
Chianti Classico Aziano 1986 • $8 • (05/31/89) BB • **85**
Chianti Classico Aziano 1985 • $8 • (08/31/88) • **80**
Chianti Classico Riserva Ducale 1995: Very grapey in character, with crushed berries and a hint of grass. Medium-bodied, with light tannins and a fruity finish. A little rustic. Drink now. • $16 • (09/30/97) • **81**
Chianti Classico Riserva Ducale 1993: Some pretty fruit flavors here, as well as hints of fresh mushroom and forestlike nuances. Medium- to light-bodied with light tannins and a light finish. • $15 • (10/31/96) • **82**
Chianti Classico Riserva Ducale 1990 • $15 • (02/28/95) • **84**
Chianti Classico Riserva Ducale 1989 • $14 • (04/30/94) • **83**
Chianti Classico Riserva Ducale 1988 • $15 • (09/15/92) • **82**
Chianti Classico Riserva Ducale 1987 • $14 • (09/15/92) • **86**
Chianti Classico Riserva Ducale 1986 • $16 • (10/31/91) • **89**
Chianti Classico Riserva Ducale 1985 • $13 • (09/15/91) • **90**
Chianti Classico Riserva Ducale 1979 • $16 • (09/16/85) • **80**
Chianti Classico Riserva Ducale Gold Label 1993: An impressive wine, with berry, cherry and wet earth character. Medium-bodied, with firm tannins and a mineral and fruit aftertaste. Drink now or hold. • $NA • (09/30/97) • **88**
Chianti Classico Riserva Ducale Gold Label 1990: Rather traditional in style and not showing as well as it should be. Offers pretty berry, cherry and chocolate aromas, with slightly raised, volatile acidity. Medium-bodied, with a soft texture and a simple aftertaste. Drink now. • $25 • (09/30/97) • **85**
Chianti Classico Riserva Ducale Gold Label 1988: Funky and disappointing, with a high level of volatile acidity and a cheesy character. Medium-bodied, with a succulent texture, but its full of chestnut and cheese flavors on the finish. • $NA • (09/30/97) • **79**
Chianti Classico Riserva Ducale Gold Label 1986 • $24 • (05/15/93) • **87**
Chianti Classico Riserva Ducale Gold Label 1985: Just at or slightly past its peak, but shows some pretty cigar, tobacco, dried cherry character. Full-bodied, with high acidity and a slightly dry finish. Drink up. • $NA • (09/30/97) • **86**
Chianti Classico Riserva Ducale Gold Label 1983 • $17 • (11/30/89) • **84**
Chianti Classico Riserva Ducale Gold Label 1982 • $20 • (05/31/89) • **80**
Chianti Classico Riserva Ducale Gold Label 1979 • $16 • (09/30/86) • **70**
Chianti Classico Riserva Ducale Gold Label 1978 • $NA • (11/30/89) • [illegible]
Chianti Classico Riserva Ducale Gold Label 1977 • $NA • (09/16/85 [illegible]
Chianti Classico Riserva Ducale Gold Label 1975 • $NA • (09/16 [illegible]
Chianti Classico Riserva Ducale Gold Label 1971 • $NA • ([illegible]
Chianti Classico Riserva Ducale Gold Label 1958 • $N [illegible] **82**
Chianti Classico Santedame 1995: Gorgeous and [illegible] ied cherry, mineral and fruit aromas and flavors. It' [illegible] has fine tannins and a fresh finish. Drink now or ho [illegible] /97) • **87**
Chianti Classico Santedame 1994: A p [illegible] with flavors of berry and plum, hints of earth and light [illegible]. Medium- to light-bodied. Finishes cleanly. • $12 • (10/3 [illegible]
Chianti Classico Santedame 1 [illegible] • (10/31/95) • **79**
Chianti Classico Santedam [illegible] 4 • (10/31/93) • **85**
Chianti Classico Santed [illegible] $14 • (10/31/93) • **87**
Chianti Classico Santedam [illegible] • $NA • (09/15/91) • **88**
Libaio 1996: Here's a bargain among quality Tuscan whites. It's medium-bodied, with inviting aromas of apple, cream and toast preceding the delicious apple, vanilla and toasty oak flavors. Fresh on the finish. • $10 • (09/30/97) BB • **87**

ITALY

Libaio 1995: Pleasant, with grapefruit and lemon flavors and a fruity aroma. Finishes with a touch of spice. Try with seafood. A blend of 90 percent Chardonnay and 10 percent Pinot Grigio. • $8 • (01/31/97) • **82**

Nero del Tondo 1995: Very fruity, with strawberry and spicy aromas and flavors, and hints of raisin. Medium-bodied, with light tannins and a ripe, fruity finish. Made from Pinot Noir. Drink now or hold. • $NA • (09/30/97) • **85**

Nero del Tondo 1994: Offers ripe plum aromas with hints of flowers and tea, lovely fruit flavors and velvety tannins. Medium-bodied. A rather atypical Pinot Noir, but delicious. • $NA • (09/30/97) • **87**

Nero del Tondo 1993 • $NA • (10/31/95) • **85**

Nero del Tondo 1988 • $18 • (09/15/91) • **88**

Orvieto Classico 1994: A little dull and cloying, with almond and butter flavors. Lacks focus, but it's serviceable. • $7 • (01/31/97) • **78**

Sangiovese Toscana Torgaio 1995: Light and fruity, this offers cherry, cola and lightly earthy flavors in a soft texture. For early drinking with simple food. • $8 • (01/31/97) • **83**

Sangiovese di Toscana Torgaio 1994 • $NA • (10/31/95) • **81**

Sangiovese di Toscana Torgaio 1992 • $10 • (10/31/93) • **83**

Vino Nobile di Montepulciano Lodola Nuova 1991 • $NA • (10/31/95) • **84**

Vino Nobile di Montepulciano Lodola Nuova 1989 • $12 • (07/31/94) • **82**

RUGGERI & C.

Prosecco di Valdobbiadene NV: Crisp and clean, with a floral character, finishing short. Drink now. 49,000 cases made. • $14 • (07/31/98) • **80**

Prosecco di Valdobbiadene Giustino B. 1996: Intriguing floral and almond aromas are followed by apple flavors, all richly interwoven with fine acidity that leaves a clean finish. Almond notes echo on the aftertaste. Drink now. 1,000 cases made. • $19 • (07/31/98) • **86**

Prosecco di Valdobbiadene S. Stefano NV: A tasty sparkler. The honey and citrus flavors are subtle, but the texture is rich, balanced by acidity that carries everything to a cleansing finish. Drink now. 6,000 cases made. • $15 • (07/31/98) • **84**

RUSSIZ SUPERIORE

Cabernet Franc Collio 1995: Broad-shouldered, showing cherry and plum; good concentration and weight, but it's a little rigid, lacking the nuance and complexity of the best. Drink through 1999. 1,100 cases made. • $20 • (07/31/98) • **86**

Collio Rosso Riserva Degli Orzoni 1993: Smooth and harmonious, full of coffee tones and spicy plum and cherry flavors. The richness is replaced by firm, silky tannins midpalate, but the sweet fruit echoes on the finish. A blend of 80 percent Cabernet Sauvignon, 10 percent Merlot and 10 percent Cabernet Franc. 800 cases made. • $30 • (06/30/98) • **89**

Collio Rosso Riserva Degli Orzoni 1990 • $30 • (06/15/96) BB • **83**

Merlot Collio 1993 • $18 • (05/31/96) • **86**

Pinot Bianco Collio 1993 • $NA • (01/31/95) • **84**

Pinot Grigio Collio 1995: Modest, with very delicate flavors of apple and lemon underscored by lively acidity. 4,500 cases made. • $18 • (06/15/97) • **83**

Pinot Grigio Collio 1994 • $16 • (06/15/96) • **83**

Pinot Grigio Collio 1993 • $NA • (01/31/95) • **78**

Riesling Italico Collio 1993 • $NA • (01/31/95) • **83**

Sauvignon Collio 1995: Fresh and lively, with floral and apple flavors. Modest, balanced and ready to enjoy. 6,000 cases made. • $18 • (06/15/97) • **83**

Sauvignon Collio 1993 • $NA • (01/31/95) • **83**

Tocai Friulano Collio 1993 • $NA • (01/31/95) • **81**

S. BIAGIO

Barolo 1993: Supple and fruity, but also a bit diluted. Offers woodsy, old-barrel aromas and flavors. A rustic wine with drying tannins. • $NA • (10/31/97) • **77**

S. STEFANO

Chianti Classico 1993: Already tasting a bit mature and forward, with an odd mushroom and earthy note. Turns dry and slightly herbal on the finish. • $NA • (10/31/96) • **72**

Prosecco di Valdobbiadene Ruggeri NV: An agreeably soft-textured, fruity-tasting sparkling wine that's satisfying and slightly sweet. • $15 • (10/15/97) • **84**

SACCARDI

Chianti Classico 1993: Solid and chewy, with plum and cherry flavors and a slightly herbal note. A juicy wine with loads of flavors, though little finesse. • $10 • (03/31/97) • **84**

Chianti Classico 1990 • $10 • (10/31/94) BB • **87**

Chianti Classico 1987 • $10 • (05/15/90) • **75**

Chianti Classico 1985 • $6 • (11/30/87) BB • **89**

Chianti Classico Riserva 1993: Flavorful, tasting plummy and herbal at once, with a spicy accent on the finish. A bit awkward. • $15 • (03/31/97) • **81**

Chianti Classico Riserva 1988 • $13 • (10/31/94) • **85**

Chianti Classico Riserva 1983 • $12 • (05/15/90) • **87**

Chianti Classico Riserva 1981 • $9 • (11/30/87) • **81**

SAFFIRIO, JOSETTA

Barolo 1992: Deep in color and quite aromatic. Tannic and full-bodied on the palate, with good fruit flavors accented by smoky oak, violet and citrus notes. Needs until at least 2000. • $NA • (10/31/96) • **85**

Barolo 1991: The ample fruit flavors are enveloped in a tight, tannic texture, but it's well built for aging. Should be excellent after 1999. • $NA • (10/31/96) • **88**

Barolo 1987 • $40 • (12/15/92) • **87**

SALA, LA

Campo All'Abero 1994: Delicious. Deep in color, with blackberry aromas and a hint of spice. Medium-bodied, with silky tannins and a long, sweet fruit finish. • $22 • (09/30/97) • **87**

Campo All'Abero 1993: Pretty aromas and flavors of cassis, berry and mint that carry through the finish. Medium-bodied, and the tannins are fine. Drink now or hold. • $22 • (10/31/96) • **85**

Campo All'Abero 1990 • $NA • (02/28/95) • **90**

Chianti Classico 1995: Some fruit to this, but it's slightly unripe, with a hint of dried herbs. Light finish. • $13 • (09/30/97) • **79**

Chianti Classico 1994: Pleasant character of plum, berry and earth. Medium body, silky tannins, short finish. • $13 • (10/31/96) • **80**

Chianti Classico 1993 • $NA • (10/31/95) • **79**

Chianti Classico 1991 • $NA • (10/31/95) • **81**

Chianti Classico 1990 • $NA • (10/31/93) • **84**

Chianti Classico Riserva 1994: Delivers more on the nose than on the palate, with gorgeous plum, berry, spice and cream aromas. It's medium-bodied, but falls short on the finish. Drink now. • $18 • (09/30/97) • **86**

Chianti Classico Riserva 1993: Simple and fruity with light tannins and a slightly pronounced acidity. Drink now. • $18 • (10/31/96) • **77**

Chianti Classico Riserva 1990 • $NA • (02/28/95) • **85**

Il Bianco 1996: A good, fresh white with lemon, apple and melon character, light mineral accents. Light-bodied and refreshing. • $8 • (09/30/97) • **84**

SALAPARUTA, DUCA DI

Bianca di Valguarnera 1994: Shows some maturity, and maybe a hint of botrytis, too. Toasty oak is well-integrated with tropical fruit and almond flavors, all wrapped in a rich, concentrated texture. Lingering finish. Ready now. 2,400 cases made. • $35 • (06/15/97) • **87**

Brio 1994: A fruit bowl of a white wine, with peach, apricot and pear flavors, but it's soft and fat in texture. • $8 • (05/31/97) • **78**

Colomba Platino Sicily 1995: Has a decidedly buttery element, as well as some vanilla and spice flavors. A fat, round wine with a short finish. • $10 • (01/31/97) • **81**

Duca Enrico 1992: Loads of spicy raspberry and kirsch flavors are the hallmarks of this fresh, appealing red. There are ripe tannins on the finish and a lasting impression of sweet, crushed raspberries. Well made; ready to drink. 4,580 cases made. • $45 • (06/15/97) • **89**

Duca Enrico 1990: A winner. Incredibly deep in color and youthful, bursting with vibrant blackberry, licorice and vanilla flavors that unfold gracefully. It has balance, concentration, harmony and a lingering finish with fine tannins. Well made and enjoyable now, but should be even better in 1999. 4,000 cases made. • $40 • (01/01/97) • **90**

Terre d'Agala 1993: Seductive all the way—from the raspberry, violet and spice flavors to the lingering finish. Balanced, structured and very modern in style, it's drinkable now through 2000. • $13 • (05/15/97) • **88**

ITALY

SALCETINO

Chianti Classico 1991 • $NA • (10/31/93) • **78**

SALETTE, LE

Amarone della Valpolicella Classico La Marega 1990: Quite high in acidity and still tannic on the finish, with some coffee and plum aromas and flavors, this shows a long aftertaste and plenty in reserve; needs time to unwind and strut its stuff. Difficult to assess today, it may rate higher in time. Best from 2000 through 2010. 900 cases made. • $29 • (06/15/98) • **87**

Amarone della Valpolicella La Marega 1988 • $25 • (09/15/92) • **81**

Valpolicella Ca' Carnocchio 1989 • $NA • (09/15/92) • **81**

Valpolicella Classico I Progni 1991 • $12 • (09/15/92) • **72**

Valpolicella Classico Superiore I Progni 1989 • $12 • (09/15/92) • **79**

SALLE, CASTELLO DI

Montepulciano d'Abruzzo 1995: A generous, quite fruity, dry red with enough tannin and body to go nicely with hearty main courses. Drink through 1999. • $17 • (02/28/98) • **85**

Montepulciano d'Abruzzo 1985 • $15 • (06/15/90) BB • **84**

SALVIANO

Orvieto Classico 1996: A fresh, floral-scented wine that's lively and crisp in texture and clean on the finish. Drink now. • $12 • (02/28/98) • **85**

SAMMICHELI

Chianti Classico 1990 • $9 • (03/31/93) • **78**

SAN FABIANO CALCINAIA

Cerviolo 1995: Delivers a vibrant character of crushed berries, medium body, fine tannins and lively fruit notes on the finish. Delicious. Drink now. 1,500 cases made. • $22 • (09/30/97) • **87**

Cerviolo 1993: Lovely and elegant. Medium-bodied, showing aromas and flavors of sweet berry and plum, fine tannins and a sweet fruit finish. Drink now. A blend of 70 percent Sangiovese and 30 percent Cabernet Sauvignon. • $18 • (10/31/96) • **87**

Cerviolo 1991 • $15 • (02/28/95) • **88**

Cerviolo 1990 • $13 • (10/31/93) • **89**

Cerviolo 1988 • $14 • (12/31/92) • **81**

Cerviolo 1986 • $19 • (03/31/90) • **82**

Chardonnay Toscana Cerviolo 1995: Nice apple, citrus and toasty oak character to this medium-bodied wine. Also has good acidity and a clean, refreshing finish. Drink now. 600 cases made. • $15 • (09/30/97) • **86**

Chianti Classico 1995: A beautiful, medium-bodied wine with pretty aromas of raspberries, strawberries and minerals, light tannins, and a fresh and silky finish. Drink now. 5,000 cases made. • $13 • (09/30/97) • **86**

Chianti Classico 1994: Vibrant aromas and flavors of strawberry and berry through and through. Medium-bodied with light, soft tannins and a crisp finish. Delicious to drink now. 5,000 cases made. • $13 • (10/31/96) • **83**

Chianti Classico 1992 • $11 • (02/28/95) • **76**

Chianti Classico 1991 • $12 • (10/31/93) • **84**

Chianti Classico 1990 • $9 • (10/31/93) • **85**

Chianti Classico 1988 • $12 • (09/15/91) • **84**

Chianti Classico Cellole 1990 • $11 • (10/31/93) • **86**

Chianti Classico Cellole 1988 • $15 • (09/15/91) • **83**

Chianti Classico Cellole Riserva 1993: More like a regular Chianti, with its fresh cherry and berry character and crisp acidity. Medium- to light-bodied and the finish is refreshing. Drink now. • $18 • (10/31/96) • **81**

Chianti Classico Cellole Riserva 1988 • $16 • (09/15/92) • **87**

Chianti Classico Cellole Riserva 1985 • $13 • (11/30/89) • **91**

Chianti Classico Riserva 1988 • $NA • (09/15/92) • **85**

Chianti Classico Riserva 1985 • $NA • (09/15/91) • **84**

Key: SS—Spectator Selection CS—Cellar Selection HR—Highly Recommended BB—Best Buy $NA—Price not available Ⓐ—Auction Price (BT)—Barrel Tasting

Dates in parentheses indicate the issues in which the ratings were published.

SAN FELICE

Ancherona 1995: Interesting orange-peel, apple and almond character marks this medium-bodied wine. Has moderate acidity; finishes short. • $17 • (09/30/97) • **82**

Belcaro 1996: Fresh and spicy, offering aromas and flavors of lemons and minerals, and a crisp finish of moderate length. Delicious. • $11 • (09/30/97) • **85**

Chianti Classico 1995: Loads of crushed berries and fruit in this. Medium-bodied, showing hints of earth and spice, light tannins and a crisp finish. Drink now. • $12 • (09/30/97) • **85**

Chianti Classico 1994: Light and simple, with berry and dried cherry aromas and flavors, a light body and a crisp finish. Drink now. • $12 • (10/31/96) • **80**

Chianti Classico 1993 • $11 • (10/31/95) • **80**

Chianti Classico 1992 • $10 • (02/28/95) • **80**

Chianti Classico 1991 • $13 • (10/31/93) • **80**

Chianti Classico 1990 • $11 • (09/15/92) • **87**

Chianti Classico Campo del Civettino 1990 • $NA • (10/31/93) • **83**

Chianti Classico Campo del Civettino 1988 • $NA • (09/15/91) • **84**

Chianti Classico Il Grigio Riserva 1994: Fresh and fruity, but slightly one-dimensional. Medium-to-light body, showing elegant flavors of berry and mushroom; a light finish. • $16 • (09/30/97) • **83**

Chianti Classico Il Grigio Riserva 1993: Light and straightforward with berry, cherry and earthy aromas and flavors and a light, sweet fruit finish. Drink now. 20,000 cases made. • $15 • (10/31/96) • **80**

Chianti Classico Il Grigio Riserva 1991 • $16 • (10/31/95) • **86**

Chianti Classico Il Grigio Riserva 1990 • $16 • (02/28/95) • **85**

Chianti Classico Il Grigio Riserva 1988 • $16 • (09/15/92) • **86**

Chianti Classico Il Grigio Riserva 1987 • $13 • (01/31/92) • **83**

Chianti Classico Il Grigio Riserva 1985 • $10 • (09/15/90) • **86**

Chianti Classico Il Grigio Riserva 1983 • $12 • (11/30/89) • **85**

Chianti Classico Il Grigio Riserva 1982 • $11 • (05/31/88) • **90**

Chianti Classico Poggio Rosso Riserva 1994: An intensely fruity riserva with gorgeous raspberry, berry and mineral character. Full- to medium-bodied, with velvety tannins and a delicious finish. Drink now or hold. • $27 • (09/30/97) • **90**

Chianti Classico Poggio Rosso Riserva 1993: Big and rich, with excellent, harmonious structure. Beautiful aromas and flavors of violet, berry and mineral. Full-bodied, with full tannins and balanced acidity. Better after 2000. • $30 • (09/30/97) • **90**

Chianti Classico Poggio Rosso Riserva 1990: A voluptuous red wine with an abundance of chocolate berry, tobacco and cherry character. Full body, with succulent fruit and tannins, and a delicious aftertaste. Gorgeous now, but will improve. • $NA • (09/30/97) • **92**

Chianti Classico Poggio Rosso Riserva 1988: Still young and vivacious with intense aromas of mint, mineral and berry which follow through on the palate. Medium-bodied, with racy tannins and a long finish. Fab now, better after 2000. • $NA • (09/30/97) • **89**

Chianti Classico Poggio Rosso Riserva 1987 • $23 • (06/30/93) • **68**

Chianti Classico Poggio Rosso Riserva 1986 • $24 • (01/31/92) • **86**

Chianti Classico Poggio Rosso Riserva 1985: A generous and rich Chianti Classico, offering pretty, ripe berry and plum aromas and flavors, with a hint of grilled meat. Full-bodied, with a velvety texture and a long, long finish. Drink now. • $NA • (09/30/97) • **89**

Chianti Classico Poggio Rosso Riserva 1983 • $17 • (11/30/89) • **87**

Chianti Classico Poggio Rosso Riserva 1982 • $15 • (09/15/90) • **81**

Chianti Classico Poggio Rosso Riserva 1981 • $15 • (08/31/88) • **87**

Chianti Classico Poggio Rosso Riserva 1978 • $14 • (03/15/87) • **73**

Predicato di Bitùrica 1985 • $28 • (12/15/91) • **82**

Predicato di Bitùrica 1983 • $22 • (11/30/89) • **87**

Predicato di Bitùrica 1982 • $19 • (01/31/88) SS • **92**

Vigorello 1994: A pretty, silky wine with pepper, spice and berry aromas and flavors. Medium-bodied, with fine tannins and a silky finish. Drink now or hold. • $24 • (09/30/97) • **89**

Vigorello 1993: Beautiful and elegant, with cherry, berry and vanilla aromas and flavors. Medium-bodied, with very fine tannins and a clean, crisp finish. Drink now or hold. • $27 • (10/31/96) • **88**

Vigorello 1990 • $NA • (10/31/93) • **91**

Vigorello 1988 • $NA • (11/15/93) • **88**

Vigorello 1987 • $25 • (06/15/93) • **87**

Vigorello 1986 • $NA • (11/15/93) • **91**

Vigorello 1985 • $18 • (09/15/90) • **89**

Vigorello 1983 • $NA • (11/15/93) • **91**

Vigorello 1982 • $NA • (11/15/93) • **92**

Vigorello 1981 • $13 • (01/31/88) • **84**

Vigorello 1980 • $12 • (02/28/87) SS • **95**

SAN FILIPPO

Brunello di Montalcino 1990: This shows finesse with silky tannins and gamy, smoky, tobacco character, medium body and a fresh finish. Drink now. • $NA • (10/31/95) • **85**

SAN GIORGIO

Brunello di Montalcino 1991: Rather thin and austere, with an atypical peppery cherry character. Dry finish. Hard to get excited about. • $NA • (09/30/97) • **78**

Brunello di Montalcino 1990: Fine and elegant, featuring silky tannins that tickle your palate and a wonderful cherry, mineral, salty character on the aftertaste. Long in the mouth. Drinkable now. • $28 • (10/31/95) • **89**

Brunello di Montalcino 1988 • $25 • (07/31/95) • **86**

SAN GIUSEPPE

Pinot Grigio Veneto 1997: An odd cinnamon aroma and flavor marks this crisp white, and it finishes short. Drink now. • $9 • (06/30/98) • **78**

Pinot Noir Veneto 1996: Light, showing modest cherry and herb flavors that wind up slightly astringent. Drink now. • $9 • (06/30/98) • **78**

SAN GUIDO, TENUTA

Bolgheri-Sassicaia 1994: Elegant for its pretty berry, cassis and dried herb aromas and flavors, this wine is of medium body, with medium, round tannins and a delicious finish. Try now. • $78 • (09/30/97) • **88**

Sassicaia 1993: Pretty cassis, berry and slightly herbal aromas which follow through on the palate. Medium-bodied, moderately tannic and has a light finish. A good, but not overly impressive, Sassicaia; slightly unripe nature of Cabernet Sauvignon detracts. Drink now or hold. • $67 • (10/31/96) • **85**

Sassicaia 1992: Relatively light, with sweet cherry, red berry character that improves in the glass. Somewhat diluted and a short finish. A difficult vintage in Tuscany. This will probably improve with cellaring; try in 1999. • $60 • (07/31/96) • **78**

Sassicaia 1991: Angular and quite hard now, with dried cherry, wet earth and black currant flavors. Lacks opulence and ripe fruit, turning slightly herbal and dry on the finish. Solidly built, it needs time for the tannins to soften. Try around 2002. • $57 • (07/31/96) • **81**

Sassicaia 1990: A sexy wine that has gained somewhat since 1993 when we rated it 90 points. Not as powerful as the '88, nor as rich as the '85, this is still prototypical Sassicaia for its great complexity. Offers mineral, lead pencil, tar, cassis and black olive notes, solid backbone and firm, elegant finish. • $90 • (07/31/96) • **93**

Sassicaia 1989: Pleasant example that makes for pretty drinking now and through 1998. Of medium body, it's supple and silky, with some tar, dried herb, mineral and cherry flavors. • $84 • (07/31/96) • **88**

Sassicaia 1988: The brute power of the '88 brings to mind Château Latour in top vintages. Full-bodied, it's firm and rock-solid yet tastes very silky thanks to sensational concentration of fruit. Loads of minerally, peppery character and blackberry and red berry flavors. Supercharged, intense, long finish. Try in 2003. • $99 • (07/31/96) • **97**

Sassicaia 1987: Delicate and clean, with pure, focused and direct raspberry, black cherry and black currant flavors. Quite elegant and of medium body, featuring some mineral and tar notes on the medium-intense finish. Drink now. • $92 • (07/31/96) • **86**

Sassicaia 1986: An interesting wine for aficionados of that lovely Sassicaia mineral, lead character coming from its unique *terroir* and microclimate. Nice dried cherry and dried herb notes, but it turns a bit dry on the slightly disjointed finish. Drinkable now. • $86 • (07/31/96) • **84**

Sassicaia 1985: Unreal for its sheer hedonistic quality. Oozes rich and ripe fruit and sweet wood character, but doesn't taste overripe. Loaded with cassis and mineral flavors backed by tar and spice. Much thicker and darker in color than the '88, which is more elegant. In its history the winery has made no other Sassicaia with such massive tannins, yet the texture of the wine is supple. Made from very small yields. Tempting now but better in 2005. • $220 • (07/31/96) • **99**

Sassicaia 1984: Pleasant surprise from a disastrous, rainy year in Tuscany. Some sweet fruit, mineral and licorice flavors charm the palate, but a touch of chestnut distracts. Medium-bodied, slightly drying finish. • $NA • (07/31/96) • **82**

Sassicaia 1983: Beautifully balanced and quite seductive, showing some lovely cassis, mineral and tar character. Very supple. Drinkable now through 2000. • $88 • (07/31/96) • **88**

Sassicaia 1982: Rather intense, in a fresh way, reflecting perhaps the relatively high acidity in this wine from the start. Of medium-to-full body, it bursts with cassis and black cherry flavors and a touch of Sassicaia's characteristic mineral persona. Drinkable now. • $125 • (07/31/96) • **90**

Sassicaia 1981: From a lesser vintage in Tuscany, it's slightly drying now, but still ripe, rich and lovely, delivering a tar, iron, mineral, red and black fruit character. Nice harmony and power. Drinkable now. • $120 • (07/31/96) • **89**

Sassicaia 1980: Light, watery and diluted vanilla and milk chocolate character. While smooth in texture and clean on the finish, this is a modest Sassicaia. Drinkable now. • $105 • (07/31/96) • **77**

Sassicaia 1979: Lovely and light, medium-bodied, caramel, mineral and black cherry character. From an average year in Tuscany, this '79 still shows that Sassicaia can age and turn out good wines even in difficult vintages. Drinkable now. • $102 • (07/31/96) • **83**

Sassicaia 1978: A huge red that should hold, even improve, for another decade. Deep, full-bodied, very ripe and complex. Tastes a bit savage, boasting earthy, dried herbal, salty, milky and red berry, dried fruit character. Still tannic and firm, adding a long, impressive finish. • $133 • (07/31/96) • **95**

Sassicaia 1977: Even though '77 was truly disappointing elsewhere in Tuscany, this Sassicaia is drinking nicely now, 19 years later. Very harmonious, offering soft texture, excellent blackberry character and a hint of tar. Somewhat lighter than the '75 and slightly short on the finish. • $NA • (07/31/96) • **85**

Sassicaia 1976: Even Sassicaia could not apparently escape the wet weather of this memorably bad vintage in Tuscany. It lacks harmony, having oxidized and developed a bitter orange character. Lean finish. • $79 • (07/31/96) • **65**

Sassicaia 1975: More than 20 years old, yet so intense you almost need an extinguisher to put out its fiery flavors. From a very good year in Tuscany, it's sweet, ripe and full-bodied, featuring complex mineral, earth and mint character. Impressively concentrated and silky-textured, revealing its age by a slight dryness on aftertaste. Drinkable soon. • $99 • (07/31/96) • **90**

Sassicaia 1974: From a year with excessive rainfall, it's quite soft yet still manages to offer pleasure, adding nice complexity of tobacco, wet earth, bitter chocolate, mineral and iron character. Drinkable now. • $NA • (07/31/96) • **83**

Sassicaia 1972: How Tenuta San Guido could produce such a delightful wine in a year that ranks among the most disastrous this century in Tuscany remains a mystery that goes to the heart of the Sassicaia legend. Inky, tarry, complex and medium-bodied; earthy, plummy and minty character and impressive finish. Would rate higher if not for a slight but distracting rustic chestnut aroma. • $NA • (07/31/96) • **85**

Sassicaia 1971: The first bottle showed hard, tough and lean character and a drying finish. The second was a more delicate wine, showing somewhat more fruit. Collectors should probably drink their '71s right away as they might be fading quickly. • $NA • (07/31/96) • **78**

Sassicaia 1970: A charmer that's supple, lush and silky, offering distinctive minty, red berry aromas and flavors and fresh character. Tuscany had good weather in 1970, yet this one tastes a touch diluted on the palate and finish. Drinkable now. • $NA • (07/31/96) • **83**

Sassicaia 1968: First bottle corked; second one medium-bodied, delicate and still fresh, showing a mineral, red berry, meat, spice character. Sassicaia's first commercial wine, this '68 (which includes some '67, '65 and '69) is a rare and expensive collector's item. • $550 • (07/31/96) • **88**

SAN LEONARDO, TENUTA

Merlot Trentino 1995: Shows more of the dill and tobacco side of Merlot, yet it's pleasant and round, finishing with a touch of astringency. Drink now. • $18 • (05/31/98) • **83**

Merlot Trentino 1994: Shows some weight and richness, which adds interest to the cedar and herb-scented fruit flavors. Lacks focus overall, but ready to drink. 1,500 cases made. • $18 • (06/15/97) • **84**

San Leonardo 1994: Delicious. New oak adds vanilla and clove nuances to the plum and black currant flavors in this rich red. It's balanced, exhibiting good depth of flavor and a sweet fruit finish. Drink now through 2000. • $47 • (06/16/98) • **87**

San Leonardo 1993: Fresh, marked by new oak, with more herb flavors than fruit, this red doesn't quite have the concentration to match its structure, but still, it's decently made. 2,500 cases made. • $47 • (06/15/97) • **84**

San Leonardo 1991: Deep and brooding, this red is easing into maturity, exhibiting woodsy flavors, but it's questionable whether the fruit will outlive the tannins. Drink now. 2,500 cases made. • $38 • (06/15/97) • **84**
San Leonardo 1990: Impressive. A fully mature red from a great vintage, it's beginning to show some brown but is packed with sweet, ripe fruit whose flavors now are mushroom, leather and spice. Powerful, full-bodied and concentrated, with a long finish, this shows what Northeast Italy is capable of when all the elements come together. A blend of Cabernet Sauvignon, Cabernet Franc, and Merlot. Drink now through 2000. • $40 • (01/01/98) • **89**
San Leonardo 1986 • $33 • (12/15/92) • **86**
San Leonardo 1985 • $35 • (12/15/92) • **82**
San Leonardo 1983 • $35 • (12/15/92) • **79**

SAN LEONINO, FATTORIA

Chianti Classico 1995: Some good berry notes, but it's rather woody on the nose and palate; slightly woody on the finish, too. Medium-bodied, with light tannins. Drink now. • $19 • (09/30/97) • **80**
Chianti Classico 1991 • $10 • (10/31/93) • **82**
Chianti Classico 1990 • $10 • (09/15/92) • **89**
Chianti Classico 1988 • $10 • (12/15/90) • **87**
Chianti Classico Riserva 1993: A very good Chianti with some stuffing for aging. Offers pretty perfumed aromas with hints of raspberries, a medium body, velvety tannins and a delicious fruit and bitter-chocolate aftertaste. Drink now or hold. • $25 • (12/31/97) • **87**
Chianti Classico Riserva 1988 • $19 • (09/15/92) • **85**

SAN LUIGI

Chianti Colli Senesi 1994: Light, charming and dry, offering subtle cherry and plum flavors that expand as you sip. Drink now. • $11 • (10/31/97) • **85**

SAN MICHELE

Chianti 1991 • $7 • (07/31/95) • **75**

SAN PIETRO

Bardolino 1991 • $18 • (09/15/92) • **81**
Cabernet Sauvignon Veneto Refolà 1988 • $NA • (09/15/92) • **80**
Gavi 1993 • $12 • (02/28/95) • **75**
Gavi Gazzaniga 1994 • $14 • (02/29/96) • **81**

SAN POLO IN ROSSO, CASTELLO DI

Cetinaia 1990: A ripe and delicious Sangiovese, with pleasant plum and chocolate aromas. Medium-bodied, with attractive tobacco and fruit character and a velvety, fresh finish. Drink now. • $NA • (03/31/97) BB • **86**
Cetinaia 1986 • $27 • (12/15/92) • **82**
Chianti Classico 1985 • $10 • (11/30/89) • **67**
Chianti Classico Riserva 1988 • $15 • (09/15/92) • **85**
Chianti Classico Riserva 1986 • $14 • (09/15/92) • **75**
Chianti Classico Riserva 1985 • $14 • (11/30/89) • **78**

SAN QUIRICO

Chianti Vecchione 1988 • $9 • (01/31/92) • **79**

SAN VINCENTI

Chianti Classico 1995: Pretty. Has vivid aromas of strawberries and raspberries, a medium body with silky tannins, crisp acidity and a flavorful finish. • $17 • (09/30/97) • **85**
Chianti Classico 1990 • $NA • (10/31/93) • **68**
Chianti Classico Podere di Stignano 1991 • $13 • (10/31/95) • **74**
Chianti Classico Riserva 1994: A lively, medium-bodied red with an attractive velvety texture and a fresh backbone of acidity. Plenty of berry, cherry and mineral character as well. Drink now or hold. • $18 • (09/30/97) • **86**
Chianti Classico Riserva Podere di Stignano 1988 • $17 • (10/31/95) • **81**
Colli dell'Etruria Centrale 1996: Medium-bodied, with some fruit but a slightly dull and candied finish. Melon and chalk aromas. • $13 • (09/30/97) • **78**

SANDRONE, LUCIANO

Barbera d'Alba 1994: Quite complete, with a supple texture and licorice, black cherry, plum, vanilla and caramel complexity. A ripe-tasting finish makes this delicious now. 500 cases made. • $24 • (10/31/96) • **86**
Barbera d'Alba 1991 • $22 • (11/15/93) • **77**
Barolo 1984 • $14 • (08/31/88) • **82**
Barolo 1983 • $20 • (12/15/87) • **90**
Barolo 1982 • $15 • (06/30/87) • **94**
Barolo Cannubi Boschis 1993: Very light strawberry, chocolate, vanilla, cherry flavors are underpinned by smoke. Tannins are smooth and it's pleasant, but what a disappointment from this famed grower. Drink chilled upon release. • $330 Ⓐ • (10/31/97) • **82**
Barolo Cannubi Boschis 1992: Fruity and pure in style. Not over-oaked, with luscious cherry, berry and currant flavors that mingle on the palate and linger on the long finish. Drink now. 667 cases made. • $45 • (10/31/96) • **87**
Barolo Cannubi Boschis 1991 • $NA • (10/31/95) • **84**
Barolo Cannubi Boschis 1990 • $256 Ⓐ • (10/31/94) • **96**
Barolo Cannubi Boschis 1989 • $50 • (10/31/93) CS • **95**
Barolo Cannubi Boschis 1988 • $50 • (10/31/93) • **92**
Barolo Cannubi Boschis 1986 • $34 • (12/31/90) • **89**
Barolo Cannubi Boschis 1985 • $182 Ⓐ • (01/31/90) • **92**
Barolo Le Vigne 1990 • $NA • (10/31/94) • **98**
Dolcetto d'Alba 1990 • $14 • (03/31/92) • **87**
Dolcetto d'Alba 1989 • $12 • (07/15/91) • **87**
Dolcetto d'Alba 1986 • $8 • (12/31/87) • **80**
Dolcetto d'Alba 1985 • $6 • (07/31/87) BB • **87**
Nebbiolo d'Alba Valmaggiore 1994: Charming, with appealing strawberry and raspberry flavors. Light- to medium-bodied, with a supple texture. Drink now. 750 cases made. • $NA • (10/31/96) • **84**

SANT'ANNA

Chianti Colli Senesi 1994: Good concentration of fruit, especially berry flavor, but rather herbal with a green bean accent. Medium body and a slightly austere finish. Drink now. 1,000 cases made. • $15 • (10/31/96) • **79**
Chianti Colli Senesi 1992 • $15 • (10/31/95) • **80**
Chianti Colli Senesi Riserva 1992: Berry flavors, accented by hints of bark and earth. Medium-bodied, with fine tannins. Slightly dry on the finish. Getting rather old. 5,000 cases made. • $16 • (10/31/96) • **80**
Vigna Il Vallone 1993: Clean and focused. Offers mint, berry and cherry flavors, with a hint of wet earth. Medium-bodied with fine tannis and a crisp finish. Drink now. 700 cases made. • $25 • (10/31/96) • **85**
Vigna Il Vallone 1992 • $23 • (10/31/95) • **86**

SANTA ANITA

Pinot Grigio Veneto 1996: This has alcohol and acid, with diluted, insipid flavors. • $9 • (05/15/98) • **75**

SANTA MARGHERITA

Merlot Lison-Pramaggiore Selva Maggiore 1990 • $12 • (12/15/92) • **79**
Pinot Grigio Alto Adige 1997: Shows some delicate citrus and mineral flavors, but overall this white is light and simple. Drink now. • $18 • (07/31/98) • **81**
Pinot Grigio Alto Adige 1994 • $13 • (06/15/96) • **80**

SANTA SOFIA

Amarone della Valpolicella Classico Gioé 1990: Showing its age, this is lean and lacking in concentration, with high-toned cherry flavors and a short finish. Given the vintage, one expects more. Drink now through 2000. 2,000 cases made. • $45 • (06/15/98) • **86**
Amarone della Valpolicella Classico Superiore 1988 • $30 • (09/30/95) • **85**
Amarone Recioto della Valpolicella Classico Superiore 1986 • $28 • (10/31/94) • **82**
Amarone Recioto della Valpolicella Classico Superiore 1984 • $29 • (09/15/92) • **86**

Key: SS—Spectator Selection CS—Cellar Selection HR—Highly Recommended BB—Best Buy $NA—Price not available Ⓐ—Auction Price (BT)—Barrel Tasting
Dates in parentheses indicate the issues in which the ratings were published.

Bardolino Classico 1996: A bracing, light red with modest cherry aromas and flavors and a crisp finish. Drink now. 5,000 cases made. • $9 • (07/31/98) • **79**

Bardolino Classico Superiore 1989 • $8 • (09/15/92) • **71**

Pinot Grigio Valdadige Vigneto Fratte 1996: Mature, lean and minerally, with a tangy structure that needs food. Apple, lemon and vanilla are the flavors, the finish is crisp. Drink now. 15,000 cases made. • $10 • (06/30/98) • **84**

Soave Classico Montefoscarino 1996: Balanced and typical of the appellation, but the almond flavors are shy and the finish short. Drink now. 10,000 cases made. • $9 • (06/30/98) • **82**

Soave Classico Superiore 1993 • $9 • (10/31/94) • **84**

Valpolicella Classico 1996: Leather and plum aromas and flavors suggest use of *ripasso* in this traditional Veronese red. Light-bodied, with a pronounced acidity that should match well with light foods. Drink now. 15,000 cases made. • $9 • (07/31/98) • **83**

Valpolicella Classico 1995: Lovely cherry, spice and coffee aromas and flavors are the hallmarks of this light-bodied, fruity red. An honest, pleasant sipper. • $10 • (09/15/97) • **82**

Valpolicella Classico Superiore 1992 • $8 • (12/15/95) • **80**

Valpolicella Classico Superiore 1989 • $8 • (09/15/92) • **78**

Valpolicella Classico Superiore Montegradella 1995: Rich and concentrated, displaying ripe, sweet cherry and menthol notes, and spicy accents on the finish. Some firm tannins provide support. Drink through 1999. 3,000 cases made. • $15 • (07/31/98) • **85**

SANTADI, CANTINA

Terre Brune 1992: A Bordeaux-style red exhibiting some maturity and coffee, caramel and cedar to complement the spicy plum flavors. Enjoyable now through 2000, try it with grilled red meats or game. • $35 • (01/01/97) • **88**

Terre Brune 1991: A concentrated red that's still very firm on the palate with an astringent finish. The plum flavors are overshadowed by cedar and vanilla, and further aging is a gamble. Try now with food. • $30 • (01/01/97) • **86**

SANTANGELO

Montepulciano d'Abruzzo Colli del Moro 1992 • $10 • (02/29/96) • **87**

SANTI

Amarone della Valpolicella 1993: Still firm and unyielding, with black cherry, plum and mineral aromas and flavors. Medium- to full-bodied, with mouthwatering acidity, this should develop nicely over the medium term. Best from 1999 through 2005. • $33 • (06/15/98) • **86**

Amarone della Valpolicella 1988 • $20 • (11/15/94) • **85**

Amarone Recioto della Valpolicella 1985 • $20 • (09/15/92) • **84**

Chardonnay Trentino Vigneto i Piovi 1995: Mature, exhibiting honey, lanolin and cooked apple notes and modest concentration. Past its prime. • $12 • (07/31/98) • **78**

Merlot Veneto 1995: Smells woody, with some sweet cherry, cedar and leather flavors that combine with a medium body and an astringent character, followed by a dry finish. Drink now. • $12 • (06/15/98) • **82**

Pinot Grigio Trentino Vigneto Sortesele 1996: Textbook Pinot Grigio, with quince and peach flavors, a hint of stoniness, a medium body with firm acidity and a lingering, minerally finish. Drink through 1999. • $12 • (06/15/98) • **85**

Pinot Grigio Trentino Vigneto Sortesele 1994 • $10 • (10/31/95) • **81**

Recioto della Valpolicella 1985 • $20 • (06/30/91) • **83**

Valpolicella Classico Solane 1993 • $8 • (12/15/95) • **86**

SANTO STEFANO

Moscato d'Asti 1991 • $17 • (05/15/93) • **88**

Moscato d'Asti 1990 • $17 • (01/31/92) • **88**

SARDELLI, A.

Chianti Bartenura 1989 • $8 • (05/15/93) • **73**

Chianti Classico Bartenura 1987 • $9 • (03/31/91) • **70**

SARTORI

Amarone della Valpolicella Classico 1993: Modest herb, cherry and leather aromas and flavors, but the overall impression is of a dull, tired wine. Tough tannins, too. Drink now. 2,000 cases made. • $31 • (07/31/98) • **79**

Amarone della Valpolicella Classico 1991: A medium-weight Amarone brimming with mouthwatering dried cherry and plum flavors. Doesn't have the complexity of the best, but satisfying nonetheless. 2,000 cases made. • $25 • (06/15/97) • **86**

Amarone della Valpolicella Classico 1990: A concentrated wine with plum, berry and bittersweet chocolate flavors, and a prune note that lingers on the finish. Still tannic, with a good acidity and balance. Try in 2000. 1,500 cases made. • $19 • (01/31/97) • **87**

Amarone Recioto della Valpolicella Classico Superiore 1982 • $11 • (11/15/88) • **79**

Amarone della Valpolicella Corte Bra 1991: Seems mature, with butterscotch and walnut nuances highlighting the cherry-chocolate flavors. Shows depth and complexity, but won't repay long keeping. Drink now through 2000. 500 cases made. • $37 • (06/15/97) • **87**

Bardolino Classico Superiore 1994: Cherry and spice flavors elevate this light, simple red. 3,000 cases made. • $7 • (06/15/97) • **77**

Chardonnay Grave del Friuli 1997: Smells and tastes like banana-marshmallow candies. Very young, with richness, but not a lot of depth. Drink through 1999. 600 cases made. • $9 • (06/15/98) • **81**

Chardonnay Grave del Friuli 1995: Well balanced, with moderate concentration, featuring apple and almond flavors, and an herbal note for accent. 1,000 cases made. • $8 • (06/15/97) • **83**

Merlot Grave del Friuli 1995: Vanilla and a hint of cherry are the main notes of this lean, firm red. Tannins dominate the finish. Drink now. 15,000 cases made. • $9 • (06/30/98) • **80**

Merlot Grave del Friuli 1994: Good concentration in this red. Its green olive and tobacco notes stretch the flavor range, yet its black currant flavors and elegance beg another glass. 10,000 cases made. • $8 • (06/15/97) • **84**

Merlot Grave del Friuli 1989 • $6 • (12/15/92) • **80**

Merlot Grave del Friuli 1986 • $6 • (11/15/88) • **80**

Pinot Grigio Grave del Friuli 1997: The peach and nut flavors are tasty in this forward, rich white that finishes on a slightly bitter note. Drink now. 22,000 cases made. • $9 • (06/30/98) • **83**

Pinot Grigio Grave del Friuli 1996: Aromatic and soft, showing apple and peach character. Clean and correct, though on the light side. 25,000 cases made. • $8 • (06/15/97) • **80**

Recioto di Soave 1995: Tasty Soave, exhibiting almond, caramel, butter and smoke aromas and flavors, elegantly presented and moderately sweet. Good aftertaste. Drink now through 2005. 200 cases made. • $26/375ml • (06/15/98) • **86**

Recioto di Soave 1994: A paradox of fresh, fruity elements and oxidative, nutty notes, this stickie starts out with peach and apricot flavors and finishes on a walnut theme. Tasty, but lacks concentration. 500 cases made. • $30/375ml • (06/15/97) • **85**

Regolo 1993: A broad-shouldered wine, its aromas and flavors leaning toward plum, licorice and leather. Medium body, supported by solid tannins. Made from Corvina and Rondinella. Drink now through 2000. 750 cases made. • $15 • (06/30/98) • **87**

Regolo 1992: A basic red that displays more structure than flavor, despite sweet oak notes on the finish. 2,000 cases made. • $20 • (06/15/97) • **79**

Soave Classico Superiore 1997: A modern style. Vibrant, focused, with a spicy nuances, adding vanilla and clove to the apple and almond flavors. Moderate finish. Drink now. 800 cases made. • $8 • (06/15/98) • **84**

Soave Classico Superiore 1995: A refreshing Soave that displays moderate depth and typical flavors of citrus, straw and almond. A good accompaniment to light seafood dishes. 3,000 cases made. • $7 • (06/15/97) • **84**

Valpolicella Classico Superiore 1996: Straightforward cherry character in this velvety red lends immediate appeal, followed by a crisp finish. Drink now. 2,000 cases made. • $8 • (07/31/98) • **83**

Valpolicella Classico Superiore 1994: Light and lively, displaying vibrant cherry flavors. Could use a bit more concentration. 3,000 cases made. • $7 • (06/15/97) • **80**

Valpolicella Classico Superiore 1990 • $6 • (09/15/92) • **80**

Valpolicella Classico Superiore 1985 • $4 • (11/15/88) BB • **80**

SASSETTI, LIVIO

Brunello di Montalcino 1991: A slightly rustic and old-style wine, with aromas and flavors of cedar, berry and bark, dry tannins and a short finish. 1,083 cases made. • $32 • (11/30/96) • **79**

Brunello di Montalcino 1988 • $48 Ⓐ • (04/30/94) • **86**

Rosso di Montalcino 1994: A stylish rosso, its character marked by raspberry, floral and mint notes. Medium-bodied, with light tannins and a racy, refreshing acidity. 916 cases made. • $16 • (11/30/96) • **85**
Rosso di Montalcino 1991 • $17 • (04/30/94) • **78**

SATTA, MICHELE

Bolgheri Bianco 1996: Simple and fruity, with sliced green-apple aromas and flavors. Light-bodied, with crisp acidity and a simple finish. • $NA • (09/30/97) • **83**
Bolgheri Rosato 1996: A fresh and simple rosé with almond and strawberry aromas and flavors and a crisp finish. • $NA • (09/30/97) • **82**
Bolgheri Rosso Piastraia 1995: Delivers berry and cherry character with a good dose of oak. Medium-bodied, with lots of vanilla flavors and a light to medium finish. Try now. 850 cases made. • $40 • (09/30/97) • **85**
Bolgheri Rosso Piastraia 1994: Smells like Burgundy with its berry, leather and tea aromas. It's of medium body, with delicate tannins and a silky texture. Slightly short finish. Drink now or hold. 600 cases made. • $38 • (09/30/97) • **85**
Bolgheri Vermentino Costa di Giulia 1996: Has decent white pepper and lemon character, but is a bit high in sulfur. Medium-bodied, with moderate acidity and a dull finish. 1,500 cases made. • $16 • (09/30/97) • **78**
Bolgheri Vermentino Costa di Giulia 1995: Offers more on the nose than on the palate, but still delicious. Emits alluring aromas of toasty oak, apple and straw, with a hint of spice. Medium-bodied, with moderate acidity and a light finish. Drink now. 1,200 cases made. • $16 • (09/30/97) • **85**
Diambra 1996: Good berry and white pepper aromas and flavors in this light-bodied wine. Moderate tannins and a spicy finish. • $NA • (09/30/97) • **82**
Vigna al Cavaliere 1994: A rather strange red, somewhat fruity in character but also quite harsh on the finish. • $35 • (09/30/97) • **78**

SAVIGNOLA PAOLINA

Chianti Classico 1995: Straightforward Chianti, with plenty of fresh, fruity character. Medium in body, with light tannins and a fresh finish. Drink now. • $13 • (09/30/97) • **83**
Chianti Classico 1994: Boasts some decent ripe fruit aromas and flavors, but with a slight leathery tinge. Dry finish. • $12 • (10/31/96) • **77**
Chianti Classico Riserva 1994: More like a regular Chianti. Light-bodied with light, bright cherry character and a light finish. • $20 • (09/30/97) • **79**
Chianti Classico Riserva 1993: This is medium- to light-bodied, with a sweet, fruity, berry character and a hint of cedar. Light tannins and a short finish. • $19 • (10/31/96) • **79**
Chianti Classico Riserva 1990 • $NA • (02/28/95) • **86**
Rosso di Savignola 1994: A very light, simple quaffer, more like a rosé. Serve chilled. • $10 • (09/30/97) • **79**

SCARLATTA

Montepulciano d'Abruzzo 1993 • $4 • (02/29/96) • **81**
Montepulciano d'Abruzzo Cerasuolo 1993 • $4 • (08/31/95) • **83**

SCARPA

Barbaresco 1981 • $20 • (09/15/88) • **84**
Barbaresco 1979 • $20 • (09/15/88) • **90**
Barbaresco 1978 • $NA • (09/15/88) • **90**
Barbaresco 1974 • $NA • (09/15/88) • **89**
Barbaresco I Tetti di Neive 1978 • $27 • (03/15/87) • **83**
Barbera d'Asti 1985 • $12 • (08/31/89) • **88**
Barolo 1985 • $NA • (09/15/88) • **90**
Barolo 1982 • $NA • (09/15/88) • **88**
Barolo 1978 • $NA • (09/15/88) • **89**
Barolo Le Coste di Monforte 1978 • $27 • (03/15/87) • **81**

SCAVINO, PAOLO

Barbera d'Alba 1992 • $13 • (10/31/95) • **88**
Barbera d'Alba 1991 • $30 • (10/31/94) • **87**
Barbera d'Alba 1990 • $40 • (10/15/93) • **89**
Barbera d'Alba Affinato in Carati 1994: Wonderful from start to finish. Super-ripe and sweet Barbera that's better than many Barolos. Full-bodied, made in a sophisticated style. Supple, and offering lovely, succulent red and blackberry flavors accented by lightly toasty oak, it's a pleasure to drink. Balanced, long finish. Try now through 2002. • $30 • (10/31/97) • **92**
Barbera d'Alba Affinato in Carati 1993: Offers smoky oak and ripe fruit aromas and flavors in equal measure. Dark-colored and tannic, with great concentration and good length on the finish. Try now. • $30 • (10/31/96) • **87**
Barolo 1985 • $21 • (10/15/90) • **88**
Barolo 1983 • $NA • (09/15/88) • **85**
Barolo 1982 • $NA • (09/15/88) • **88**
Barolo Bric dël Fiasc 1993: Modern style of Barolo. Dark in color, full in body, smooth in texture, with oak-infused violet, mocha, spice and lovely blackberry, cassis and floral character. Well balanced, with ripe tannins. Excellent concentration and intensity. Long finish. Worth waiting until after 2000 to drink. • $53 • (10/31/97) • **92**
Barolo Bric dël Fiasc 1990 • $50 Ⓐ • (10/31/94) • **93**
Barolo Bric dël Fiasc 1989 • $45 • (10/31/93) CS • **95**
Barolo Bric dël Fiasc 1988 • $45 • (10/31/93) • **87**
Barolo Bric dël Fiasc 1985 • $39 • (06/15/90) • **90**
Barolo Cannubi 1993: Modern-style, full-bodied Barolo that offers loads of pleasure. Impressive color and complexity; seduces with cigar-box, mineral, spice, blackberry, toasty oak and smoky flavors. Lush texture held together with wonderfully fresh acidity that contributes to a long finish. Best around 2005. • $53 • (10/31/97) • **92**
Barolo Cannubi 1992: Smoky, toasty notes accent the cherry and currant flavors in this big and tannic, yet well balanced and harmonious Barolo. Try in 1999. • $45 • (10/31/96) • **88**
Barolo Cannubi 1991 • $30 • (10/31/95) • **85**
Barolo Cannubi 1990 • $42 • (10/31/94) • **93**
Barolo Cannubi 1989 • $45 • (10/31/93) • **94**
Barolo Cannubi 1988 • $45 • (10/31/93) • **86**
Barolo Cannubi 1985 • $30 • (01/31/90) • **74**
Barolo Rocche dell'Annunziata Riserva 1990 • $65 • (10/31/95) • **90**
Dolcetto d'Alba Vigneto dël Fiasc 1996: Gorgeous Dolcetto from one of Piedmont's masters. Racy, with impressive concentration of vivid, sweet-tasting and ripe cassis and blackberry flavors, bursting with rose petal and violet aromas. Medium-bodied, the ripe, smooth tannins fold like silk on the palate, and the lively, well-defined flavors cascade to a deliciously balanced finish. We can only wish all Dolcettos were this beautiful. Drink now through 2000. • $17 • (10/31/97) • **90**
Dolcetto d'Alba Vigneto dël Fiasc 1995: Flavorful and impressive. Jammy, fresh tasting blackberry flavors are well balanced with oak and tannins. Full-bodied, and has a lovely inky-purple color. Drink now through 2000. 450 cases made. • $17 • (10/31/96) • **89**
Dolcetto d'Alba Vigneto dël Fiasc 1994 • $13 • (10/31/95) • **84**

SCHIOPETTO

Cabernet Franc Collio 1993: A solid, Bordeaux-style version, elegantly presented, with plenty of structure and concentration along with complex flavors of cedar, black currant and spice. Drinkable now. • $15 • (06/15/97) • **87**
Pinot Bianco Collio 1996: Flavors of apples, honey and pineapples are fresh and enticing in this moderately rich white. It's focused and lingers on the palate. Drink now. • $30 • (06/15/98) • **85**
Pinot Bianco Collio 1995: There are pretty apple and almond notes weaving throughout, and a subtle sense of balance, but the finish seems a little coarse. • $27 • (06/15/97) • **84**
Pinot Bianco Collio 1994 • $24 • (06/15/96) • **84**
Pinot Bianco Collio 1993 • $23 • (01/31/95) • **79**
Pinot Grigio Collio 1993 • $21 • (01/31/95) • **80**
Sauvignon Collio 1993 • $23 • (01/31/95) • **80**
Tocai Friulano Collio 1996: Starts off soft and appealing, exhibiting ripe peach notes in addition to grassy undertones, then firms up on the finish with a hint of bitter almond. This has power. Drink through 1999. • $29 • (06/15/98) • **86**
Tocai Friulano Collio 1995: A very suave, elegant white that weaves apple, melon and citrus notes through a velvety texture. A touch of bitter almond on the finish provides balance. Well made and ready to drink. • $27 • (06/15/97) • **86**
Tocai Friulano Collio 1994 • $24 • (06/15/96) • **79**

Key: SS—Spectator Selection CS—Cellar Selection HR—Highly Recommended BB—Best Buy $NA—Price not available Ⓐ—Auction Price (BT)—Barrel Tasting
Dates in parentheses indicate the issues in which the ratings were published.

SCRIMAGLIO

Barbaresco 1993: Stripped, lean, dry and astringent, with a browning color and neutral flavors. Disappointing from start to finish. Incredibly bad for a '93 Barbaresco. 1,000 cases imported. • $19 • (01/31/98) • **71**
Barbera d'Asti Superiore 1993: Ripe and fruity, with dried cherry and red plum flavors. Has a pleasant, roasted quality, and good spice notes that linger on the finish. Lively and enticing. Drink now. 5,000 cases made. • $10 • (03/31/97) • **84**
Barbera d'Asti Superiore Bricco Sant'Ippolito 1995: Wonderful Barbera—no, wonderful red wine, period. Dark ruby-colored, medium-bodied, with generous fruit, ripe tannins and layers of red berry, tar and spice notes. Clean, fruity finish. Drink now. 2,500 cases imported. • $13 • (01/31/98) • **86**
Barbera d'Asti Superiore Croûtin Riserva Personale 1995: Supple and delightful. Has a slight mature, plummy, earthy character, but its spice, licorice and toasty bread notes are delicious. Turns a bit sharp on the finish, but try now with a bowl of pasta. 200 cases imported. • $25 • (01/31/98) • **84**
Barbera d'Asti Superiore Croûtin Riserva Personale 1990: Ripe, and almost Port-like with dried plum and cherry flavors. Harmonious, balanced and rich, with a lingering finish. Definitely maturing in texture. Drink now. 1,200 cases made. • $36 • (03/31/97) • **87**
Barbera d'Asti Superiore Croûtin Riserva Personale 1989: Fairly tart, with an earthy aroma. Has dried cherry and currant flavors that don't quite mesh and becomes unbalanced on the finish. 1,100 cases made. • $32 • (03/31/97) • **81**
Barbera d'Asti Superiore Croûtin Riserva Personale 1988: Over-the-hill, but still intriguing. Fully mature and powerfully aromatic, this spicy, earthy red has barnyard aromas, nutty, meaty flavors, smooth texture and lingering finish. 1,100 cases made. • $32 • (05/31/97) • **78**
Dolcetto d'Alba 1996: Balanced and well made, with white pepper, spice and succulent red berry flavors, it's fresh, yet supple. This lovely Dolcetto is worth hunting down. Serve slightly chilled. Drink now. 1,500 cases imported. • $10 • (01/31/98) • **87**
Dolcetto d'Alba 1995: Tough for a Dolcetto, with pronounced herb and tomato flavors and a firm, tannic texture. 8,000 cases made. • $13 • (05/31/97) • **78**
Gavi 1996: Nice fruit—lime, apple, grapefruit—is followed by some chalky character, giving a nice edge to this light- to medium-bodied, clean and crisp wine. Enjoy now. 3,000 cases imported. • $10 • (01/31/98) • **84**
Roero Arneis 1996: Firm and fresh, with good green-apple and lemon flavors. Also has some nice spicy notes and a touch of richness on the finish. Enjoy with fish. 1,200 cases imported. • $13 • (10/15/97) • **84**

SEBASTE

Barolo 1985 • $NA • (09/15/88) • **90**
Barolo 1984 • $NA • (09/15/88) • **85**
Barolo 1983 • $NA • (09/15/88) • **86**
Barolo 1982 • $NA • (09/15/88) • **91**
Barolo 1979 • $NA • (09/15/88) • **85**
Barolo Bussia 1988 • $30 • (06/15/94) • **87**
Barolo Bussia 1987 • $25 • (06/30/93) • **78**
Barolo Bussia Riserva 1984 • $17 • (07/31/89) • **84**
Barolo Bussia Riserva 1982 • $15 • (11/15/87) • **90**
Bricco Viole 1993: Quite dark in color, with some crisp red berry flavors, this medium-bodied red turns a bit astringent on the finish. Good acidity, but seems a bit unripe. Drink chilled. • $16 • (10/31/97) • **78**
Bricco Viole 1989 • $20 • (06/15/94) • **86**
Bricco Viole 1988 • $19 • (06/30/93) • **79**
Bricco Viole 1986 • $16 • (01/31/89) • **89**
Bricco Viole 1985 • $13 • (10/31/87) • **91**
Dolcetto d'Alba Monrobiolo di Bussia 1992 • $16 • (06/15/94) • **83**
Langhe Passo delle Viole Red 1996: Starts better than it finishes. Displays a subtle nose, then delivers some nice, sweet and ripe fruit flavors before turning a bit dry and chewy on the rustic, astringent finish. • $13 • (10/31/97) • **79**

SEGHESIO, FRATELLI

Barbera d'Alba 1994: Light, lean and rather simple, with plummy, tomato-like flavors and a tannic finish. 417 cases made. • $14 • (10/31/96) • **79**
Barbera d'Alba 1989 • $12 • (11/30/91) • **81**
Barolo Bussia-Pianpolvere 1986 • $28 • (01/31/92) • **84**
Barolo Castelletto 1989 • $NA • (10/31/94) • **88**
Barolo Vigneto La Villa 1993: Firm tannins and interesting wild berry, dried herb, mineral and cherry flavors in this medium-bodied, elegant Barolo that needs until 2000 to soften. From Aldo and Riccardo Seghesio. • $40 • (10/31/97) • **83**
Barolo La Villa 1992: Nice balance of vivid fruit flavors and typical Barolo notes of smoke, anise and spice. Well-integrated tannins and a long finish. Try now. Tasted twice with consistent notes. 375 cases made. • $33 • (10/31/96) • **88**
Barolo La Villa 1991 • $NA • (10/31/95) • **81**
Dolcetto d'Alba 1989 • $12 • (11/30/91) • **77**
Dolcetto d'Alba Vigneto della Chiesa 1996: Succulent, medium-bodied Dolcetto with sweet tannins, ripe fruit, a good sense of balance and a supple finish. Fun to drink now. • $15 • (10/31/97) • **84**
Dolcetto d'Alba Vigneto della Chiesa 1995: Light- to medium-bodied with plum and cherry flavors and good length on the finish. Supple tannins. Try upon release with pizza and pasta. 542 cases made. • $14 • (10/31/96) • **84**
Dolcetto d'Alba Vigneto della Chiesa 1994 • $NA • (10/31/95) • **79**
Nebbiolo Piedmont Ruri 1989 • $14 • (01/31/92) • **84**

SELLA & MOSCA, TENUTE

Alghero Marchese di Villamarina 1990: Bordeaux-like in character, with black currant and cedar flavors, medium body and soft tannins. Drinkable now. Made from 100 percent Cabernet Sauvignon. • $36 • (06/15/97) • **84**
Vermentino di Sardegna La Cala 1996: A slight spritz adds freshness and keeps this floral, peach-flavored white lively. Soft and simple, it's perfect for a picnic or light summer meal. 60,000 cases made. • $9 • (09/15/97) • **82**

SELVA, TENUTA DELLA

Chianti 1995: Rather light and watery, with dried cherry character and light tannins. Drink if you must. • $NA • (01/01/98) • **74**
Selvin 1991: Slightly tired-tasting, but with some decent chocolate, tobacco and cedar aromas and flavors. Medium-bodied, with light tannins and a medium finish. Drink now. • $NA • (01/01/98) • **82**
Selvino 1994: Shows some good dried cherry and tar character, is medium-bodied, has firm tannins and a medium finish. Drink now. • $NA • (01/01/98) • **86**
Selvino 1990: Funky red with some good ripe fruit, but seems slightly old in character. Medium-bodied with hard tannins and a short finish. Drink now. • $NA • (01/01/98) • **78**
Usannella 1995: Watery and insipid. Barely acceptable as red wine. Tasted twice, with consistent notes. • $NA • (01/01/98) • **71**

SELVAPIANA

Chianti Classico 1986 • $5 • (11/30/89) • **82**
Chianti Classico Riserva 1985 • $11 • (11/30/89) • **89**
Chianti Classico Riserva 1983 • $10 • (11/30/89) • **86**
Chianti Classico Riserva 1982 • $10 • (11/30/89) • **87**
Chianti Rufina 1995: Rich and round, offering lovely violet and blackberry aromas with hints of oak. Medium-bodied, with velvety tannins. Rich on the finish. Very good Chianti. 4,200 cases made. • $14 • (09/30/97) • **88**
Chianti Rufina 1994: Notable for its delicious, delicate finish, it's an aromatic red with plum, berry and spice tones. Medium-bodied, round and smooth, with a light, spicy, fruity finish. 4,200 cases made. • $11 • (09/30/97) • **86**
Chianti Rufina 1992 • $10 • (02/28/95) • **82**
Chianti Rufina 1991 • $12 • (10/31/93) • **87**
Chianti Rufina 1990 • $13 • (09/15/92) • **92**
Chianti Rufina Bucerchiale 1990 • $20 • (02/28/95) • **92**
Chianti Rufina Bucerchiale Riserva 1994: Medium-bodied, with well-integrated tannins, but it seems slightly stemmy and green with berry, earthy character and a slight bite at the finish. Try now. • $NA • (09/30/97) • **86**
Chianti Rufina Bucerchiale Riserva 1993: Shows some gorgeous black cherry, violet and berry aromas and flavors, with a full body and full tannins, but it's slightly austere on the finish. Try now. • $NA • (09/30/97) • **88**
Chianti Rufina Bucerchiale Riserva 1990: A backward 1990 Chianti that needs time to develop. Full-bodied, with loads of tobacco, cherry and truffle character, full tannins and a long finish. Try after 2002. • $NA • (09/30/97) • **91**
Chianti Rufina Bucerchiale Riserva 1988: Fabulous nose, but a bit tough in the mouth. Attractive aromas of cherry, raspberry and truffles. Full in body, with firm tannins and a big backbone of acidity. Try after 2000. • $NA • (09/30/97) • **89**

Chianti Rufina Bucerchiale Riserva 1985: Amazing youth and class for a Chianti. Wonderfully perfumed, cherry and mineral aromas follow on the palate. Full-bodied, with firm tannins and fresh acidity. A little backward still. May be better after 2000. • $NA • (09/30/97) • **92**
Chianti Rufina Fornace Riserva 1993: A very good new wine from this producer. Plenty of flavors in this one—dried cherry, plum and a hint of vanilla. Medium-bodied with round tannins and a fruity, vanilla finish. Verging on too much new wood, but delicious. Needs time in the bottle to mellow. 450 cases made. • $35 • (10/31/96) • **87**
Chianti Rufina Riserva 1993: A pretty wine with fresh cherry and a hint of mint on the nose and palate. Medium-bodied. Light tannins and a light finish. Drink now. 3,000 cases made. • $17 • (10/31/96) • **85**
Chianti Rufina Riserva 1990 • $15 • (02/28/95) • **89**

SELVOLE

Barullo 1991 • $16 • (10/31/95) • **87**
Barullo 1990 • $15 • (02/28/95) • **78**
Chianti Classico 1994: A solid Chianti with straightforward cherry-berry character, medium body and solid tannins. Drink now. • $13 • (10/31/96) • **83**
Chianti Classico 1993 • $10 • (10/31/95) • **80**
Chianti Classico 1988 • $NA • (09/15/91) • **78**
Chianti Classico Lanfredini Castello di Selvole Riserva 1991 • $13 • (10/31/95) • **86**
Chianti Classico Lanfredini Riserva 1990 • $14 • (02/28/95) • **75**
Chianti Classico Lanfredini Riserva 1985 • $NA • (09/15/91) • **77**
Chianti Classico Riserva 1993: A solid core of berry and dried cherry flavors, with fine tannins and a fresh finish. Medium- to light-bodied. • $17 • (10/31/96) • **82**

SERAFINO

Barolo Riserva 1947: Shows some true Barolo character in its focus and concentration of tar, raspberry and floral flavors, but lacks the breadth on the finish. • $NA • (05/31/97) • **87**

SERENA, LA

Brunello di Montalcino 1988 • $NA • (04/30/94) • **89**

SERRISTORI, CONTI

Chianti Classico Riserva 1993: Fruity, with an interesting peppery character. Medium-bodied. Tannins are fine, finish is slightly short. From Cantine Gaggiano. • $NA • (10/31/96) • **80**

SESTA, TENUTA DI

Brunello di Montalcino 1988 • $42 • (04/30/94) • **79**
Brunello di Montalcino Campo della Spinaia 1992: Easy-going for a Brunello, but has enough character to hold your interest. It layers modest fruit and cedar flavors on an elegant, firm texture. 290 cases made. • $32 • (10/31/97) • **86**
Rosso di Montalcino 1991 • $NA • (04/30/94) • **75**

SETTEN, TENUTA

Cabernet Franc Piave 1994: Thyme and mint flavors jump out of the glass and the structure is firm, yet elegant. Fresh, lively and enjoyable now. • $11 • (06/15/97) • **84**
Pinot Grigio Piave 1995: Racy, displaying apple and earth flavors that culminate in a clean, refreshing finish. • $11 • (06/15/97) • **83**
Sauvignon Veneto 1995: Starts off rich, with nice apple and marzipan flavors, but turns bitter on the finish. • $11 • (06/15/97) • **79**

SETTIMO, AURELIO

Barolo Vigna Rocche 1993: Dark color, sweet flavor and supple texture make this a pleasure to taste. You can sense the earth, stones and *terroir* of the vineyard. Chalk, mineral and red berry flavors follow through on the rustic finish. Try after 1999. • $NA • (10/31/97) • **84**
Barolo Vigna Rocche 1982 • $19 • (05/31/88) • **83**
Barolo Vigna Rocche 1980 • $17 • (05/31/88) • **73**

SOLATIONE

Chianti Classico 1994: A hearty, tough-textured Chianti with ample fruit flavors, but very crisp acidity and tight tannins. Drink now. 1,800 cases made. • $13 • (04/30/98) • **79**
Chianti Classico Riserva 1993: Nice, compact, beautifully balanced and attractively fruity, this Chianti is a pleasure. Drink now through 2000. 200 cases made. • $20 • (04/30/98) • **88**

SOLDERA

Brunello di Montalcino Casse Basse 1990: A disappointment from this producer. Mature, seductive, sweet- and ripe-flavored red. Round and supple; quite advanced on the palate. Drink now. • $200 • (10/31/95) • **84**
Brunello di Montalcino Casse Basse 1988 • $200 • (04/30/94) • **92**
Brunello di Montalcino Casse Basse 1985 • $225 • (07/15/91) • **89**
Brunello di Montalcino Casse Basse Riserva 1990: Gorgeous; a glass full of cherries and flowers for the nose, succulent berry and cherry flavors for the mouth. Full-bodied, with full yet slightly soft tannins. Beautiful now, but will improve with age. 500 cases made. • $225 • (11/30/96) • **92**

SONNINO, FATTORIA

Cantinino Vigneto Fezzana 1993: A disappointing effort for this producer. Rather tired already with some plumminess, but mostly a musty, barky flavor and a dry finish. 1,444 cases made. • $NA • (10/31/96) • **75**
Cantinino Vigneto Fezzana 1990 • $NA • (10/31/93) • **85**
Cantinino Vigneto Fezzana 1988 • $NA • (10/31/93) • **83**
Chianti 1996: Simple and grapey, with fresh acidity and a crisp finish. Good chilled. • $NA • (09/30/97) • **81**
Chianti 1994: Fruity and rather light, this offers some plum and cherry aromas and flavors. Short on the aftertaste. 456 cases made. • $NA • (10/31/96) • **79**
Chianti 1993 • $NA • (02/28/95) • **79**
Chianti Castello di Montespertoli 1992 • $NA • (02/28/95) • **79**
Chianti Castello di Montespertoli 1991 • $NA • (10/31/93) • **80**
Chianti Castello di Montespertoli 1990 • $NA • (10/31/93) • **78**
Chianti Colli Fiorentini 1994: Some nice fruit flavors in this silky-textured wine, but it's rather short on the finish. • $NA • (10/31/96) • **78**
Chianti Colli Fiorentini 1993 • $NA • (10/31/95) • **85**
Chianti Colli Fiorentini Castello di Montespertoli 1994: An impressive amount of fruit and a hint of new wood mark this wine. Medium-bodied with fine tannins and a long, berry-vanilla finish. Good winemaking. Drink now or hold. 667 cases made. • $NA • (10/31/96) • **85**
Sanleone 1994: A pretty wine with mint, berry and blackberry aromas and flavors. Medium body with fine tannins and a flavorful finish. Made from Merlot and Sangiovese. 2,000 cases made. • $NA • (10/31/96) • **86**
Sanleone 1993 • $NA • (10/31/95) • **88**

SONVICO

Barbera d'Asti Vigna d'Angelo 1992 • $NA • (10/31/94) • **83**
La Vigna di Sonvico 1991 • $NA • (01/01/94) • **85**

SORAVAL

Chardonnay Trentino 1996: A smoky, oaked version of Chardonnay that stays crisp and lean, with enough concentration and apple flavors to support the oak. Good length. Drink now. 25,000 cases made. • $15 • (05/31/98) • **84**
Merlot Trentino 1996: An international style, marked by vanilla, smoke and plum notes, with good density and richness beneath. Sweet fruit is the lasting impression, but it needs time. Best from 1999 through 2004. 10,000 cases made. • $13 • (05/31/98) • **85**

SORTE, LA

Amarone della Valpolicella Classico Vigneti di Jago 1988: Full-throttle Amarone. A huge mouthful of plum, tar, tobacco and chocolate-tinged fruit, dense and chewy, followed by ripe tannins on the long finish. Not for

Key: SS—Spectator Selection CS—Cellar Selection HR—Highly Recommended BB—Best Buy $NA—Price not available Ⓐ—Auction Price (BT)—Barrel Tasting
Dates in parentheses indicate the issues in which the ratings were published.

the faint of heart. Drink now through 2010. 1,200 cases made. • $41 • (05/31/98) • **89**

Valpolicella Classico Superiore 1991 • $6 • (10/15/94) • **83**

SPALLETTI

Chianti 1996: A light, floral-scented, spicy-tasting Chianti that's perfectly enjoyable. Drink now. • $9 • (04/30/98) • **84**

Chianti 1995: Quite tart and still tannic, with currant and strawberry flavors. Finishes with a note of dark chocolate and a slight spritziness. Drink now. • $8 • (03/31/97) • **82**

Chianti 1993 • $7 • (07/31/95) • **82**

Chianti 1992 • $NA • (02/28/95) • **77**

Chianti Rufina 1993 • $NA • (10/31/95) • **83**

Chianti Rufina Riserva Poggio Reale 1993: Rather traditional in style, with chestnut, bark and some fruit on nose and palate. Medium-bodied, with soft tannins and a crisp finish. Drink now. • $19 • (09/30/97) • **81**

Chianti Rufina Riserva Poggio Reale 1990 • $NA • (10/31/95) • **80**

Palazzo al Campo 1994 • $NA • (10/31/95) • **82**

Sangiovese Toscana Palazzo al Campo 1995: Firm and light, aromatic, showing dried cherry and bark character and a mushroomy, fruity aftertaste. Medium-bodied, with firm tannins. Slightly dry. Drink now. • $13 • (12/31/97) • **79**

Vernaccia di San Gimignano 1996: Shows some apple and spice character, but it's rather dull and slightly candied overall. • $10 • (09/30/97) • **78**

Vernaccia di San Gimignano 1995: Fresh and lively, with appealing lemon, pear and grapefruit flavors. A good, solid white wine for the dinner table. • $10 • (03/31/97) • **83**

SPERI, FRATELLI

Amarone della Valpolicella Classico 1991: A full-blown Amarone, with prune, chocolate and tea flavors, all up front. It's thick and fairly rich, but the finish is a bit short. Drink now. • $34 • (01/31/97) • **85**

Valpolicella Classico Superiore Vigneto La Roverina 1994: A good, sturdy Valpolicella that's smooth, flavorful and dry, with spice-accented plum and tomato flavors. Moderate tannins supply some backbone. • $12 • (04/30/97) • **83**

Valpolicella Classico Superiore Vigneto La Roverina 1993 • $12 • (06/15/96) • **86**

Valpolicella Classico Superiore Vigneto La Roverina 1991 • $8 • (04/30/94) • **83**

SPESSA, CASTELLO DI

Pinot Grigio Collio 1995: A fully mature Pinot Grigio, with a coppery hue and smoky, pine forest aromas and flavors. Still spry and balanced, with a hint of butterscotch in the aftertaste. Drink now. 500 cases made. • $21 • (06/15/98) • **84**

Sauvignon Collio 1995: This has seen better days. Deepening in color, with sweaty, grapefruit character and a tinned-fruit finish. Past its prime. 500 cases made. • $21 • (07/31/98) • **77**

Tocai Friulano Collio 1995: Mature, displaying almond, straw and citrus notes, a rich texture and juicy acidity. Drink now. 300 cases made. • $21 • (06/15/98) • **84**

STIVAL

Chardonnay Veneto Le Rive 1995: A cardboard note pervades this mature white. Oak nuances of coconut and vanilla don't mesh with the fruit and structure. Drink now. 1,500 cases made. • $12 • (07/31/98) • **79**

Merlot Le Rive 1995: Menthol, cedar and tobacco notes share the spotlight in this lean, firmly textured Merlot. For fans of this style only. Drink through 1999. 5,000 cases made. • $12 • (06/30/98) • **79**

Merlot del Veneto Orientale 1993 • $6 • (01/31/96) • **72**

Pinot Grigio del Veneto 1993 • $6 • (10/31/95) • **75**

STRA & FIGLIO, GIOVANNI

Barolo 1993: Funky, rustic, disappointing. • $NA • (10/31/97) • **70**

STRACCALI

Chianti 1996: Deliciously fruity, just brimming with wonderful strawberry and cherry flavors. Light- to medium-bodied, with bright, lively acidity, this quaffable red is the perfect match for pizza. A bargain at this price and score. 26,700 cases made. 26,700 cases made. • $6 • (09/30/97) • **84**

Chianti 1994: Check this price for a good, hearty Chianti from a good-quality vintage. It displays a roasted character, along with dried cherry and red plum flavors. Tastes mature; though it's still somewhat tannic, it's ready now. 150,000 cases made. • $6 • (03/31/97) BB • **86**

Chianti 1993 • $7 • (02/28/95) • **73**

Chianti Classico 1992 • $NA • (02/28/95) • **79**

Chianti Classico 1991 • $NA • (10/31/93) • **83**

Chianti Classico 1990 • $6 • (09/15/92) • **79**

Chianti Classico Riserva 1990 • $NA • (02/28/95) • **71**

Chianti Classico Riserva 1988 • $NA • (09/15/92) • **81**

Chianti Vernaiolo 1991 • $6 • (10/31/93) BB • **83**

Sangiovese Toscana 1996: Fresh and fruity, with good acidity and a cherry and berry character throughout. Serve chilled. 10,830 cases made. • $6 • (09/30/97) • **81**

STURM

Pinot Grigio Collio 1995: Showing some maturity, with pine, marzipan and earth flavors. Still, it's vivid and focused, with good length and depth. • $15 • (11/15/97) • **85**

Pinot Grigio Collio 1994 • $14 • (06/15/96) • **77**

Refosco dal Peduncolo Rosso delle Venezie 1996: Delicious, from the fresh blackberry and raspberry character to the lush richness on the palate. Bright acidity keeps it lively. A perfect summer red. Drink through 1999. 600 cases made. • $15 • (07/31/98) • **87**

Refosco dal Peduncolo Rosso 1993 • $14 • (05/31/96) • **84**

Tocai Friulano Collio 1995: Straw and almond flavors mark this mature Tocai. It's concentrated and lively, with persistent flavors that are slightly underripe. Good finish. Drink now. 1,400 cases made. • $14 • (07/31/98) • **84**

Tocai Friulano Collio 1994 • $14 • (06/15/96) • **73**

SUBIDA DI MONTE

Pinot Grigio Collio 1994 • $11 • (06/15/96) • **85**

SVEVO

Saracento 1991 • $7 • (05/31/95) • **73**

TALENTI

Brunello di Montalcino 1992: Some berry and chocolate character to this, but it's rather lean and dry on the finish. Too much new oak. 330 cases made. • $NA • (09/30/97) • **77**

Brunello di Montalcino 1991: Shows pleasant aromas and flavors of cedar-accented berry and cherry, and silky tannins, but a short finish. At its peak now, so drink soon. 2,750 cases made. • $37 • (11/30/96) • **83**

Brunello di Montalcino Podere Pian di Conte 1990: A nicely maturing, ripe and sweet-tasting Brunello, showing very rich, plummy character and an almost Port-like texture. Somewhat rustic and tannic, so try now. • $NA • (10/31/95) • **88**

Brunello di Montalcino Podere Pian di Conte 1988 • $40 • (04/30/94) • **90**

Brunello di Montalcino Pian di Conte 1982 • $NA • (09/15/86) • **90**

Brunello di Montalcino Pian di Conte 1981 • $NA • (09/15/86) • **88**

Brunello di Montalcino Pian di Conte Riserva 1988 • $NA • (10/31/94) • **94**

Brunello di Montalcino Riserva 1990: Plenty of ripe fruit in this full-bodied offering, with silky tannins and a fresh finish. Slightly one-dimensional, however, with a nutty aftertaste. A bit disappointing for this producer. Try in 1999. 777 cases made. • $60 • (11/30/96) • **87**

Rosso di Montalcino 1994: Plenty of cedar-accented berry flavors and a fresh, crisp finish. Not the most complex wine, but sweet and succulent. Very enjoyable to drink now. 2,125 cases made. • $14 • (11/30/96) • **84**

Rosso di Montalcino Podere Pian di Conte 1995: Straightforward Rosso with a cherry and mineral character. Medium body, with light tannins and a fresh finish. 2,300 cases made. • $15 • (09/30/97) • **83**
Rosso di Montalcino Podere Pian di Conte 1993 • $NA • (10/31/95) • **79**
Rosso di Montalcino Podere Pian di Conte 1992 • $NA • (10/31/94) • **79**
Rosso di Montalcino Podere Pian di Conte 1991 • $18 • (04/30/94) • **81**

TALOSA

Chianti Colli Senesi 1988 • $8 • (11/30/90) BB • **88**
Rosso di Montepulciano 1989 • $11 • (01/31/92) • **79**
Vino Nobile di Montepulciano 1994: Light-bodied, with some fruit but a rather diluted finish. Drink now. 3,300 cases made. • $13 • (09/30/97) • **75**
Vino Nobile di Montepulciano Riserva 1993: Attractive dried cherry and berry aromas and flavors highlight this medium-bodied wine, with fine tannins and a crisp finish. Drink now. 4,100 cases made. • $17 • (09/30/97) • **84**
Vino Nobile di Montepulciano Riserva 1988 • $16 • (07/31/94) • **84**
Vino Nobile di Montepulciano Riserva 1986 • $15 • (07/15/91) • **84**
Vino Nobile di Montepulciano Riserva 1982 • $8 • (04/15/88) • **72**

TASSAROLO, CASTELLO DI

Gavi S 1994 • $14 • (02/29/96) • **76**
Gavi S 1993 • $14 • (02/29/96) • **82**

TAURINO, DR. COSIMO

Brindisi Patriglione 1981 • $14 • (12/31/90) • **85**
Brindisi Patriglione Riserva 1979 • $12 • (03/31/89) • **82**
Notarpanaro 1985 • $10 • (03/31/94) • **81**
Notarpanaro 1981 • $9 • (05/15/91) • **86**
Notarpanaro 1978 • $8 • (03/31/89) • **80**
Notarpanaro 1975 • $8 • (04/15/88) • **78**
Salice Salentino Riserva 1990 • $9 • (01/31/96) • **82**
Salice Salentino Riserva 1988 • $9 • (03/31/94) • **80**
Salice Salentino Riserva 1986 • $8 • (01/31/92) BB • **84**
Salice Salentino Riserva 1985 • $8 • (02/15/91) BB • **85**
Salice Salentino Riserva 1983 • $6 • (12/15/89) BB • **81**
Salice Salentino Riserva 1982 • $6 • (03/31/89) BB • **82**
Salice Salentino Riserva 1981 • $6 • (03/31/88) BB • **81**
Salice Salentino Riserva 1980 • $5 • (12/15/87) BB • **84**
Salice Salentino Rosato 1989 • $9 • (03/31/92) • **82**
Salice Salentino Rosato 1988 • $7 • (03/15/91) BB • **84**
Salice Salentino Rosato 1987 • $7 • (12/31/89) BB • **84**

TEDESCHI

Amarone della Valpolicella 1993: Plenty of structure here, but without the fruit to match. Muted aromas and flavors. Drink now. • $32 • (05/31/98) • **82**
Amarone della Valpolicella Capitel Monte Fontana 1988 • $NA • (09/15/92) • **85**
Amarone della Valpolicella Capitel Monte Olmi 1993: A high-toned style, showing floral and licorice character on a medium-bodied frame. Finishes short and a touch hot. Best from 1999 through 2005. • $24 • (05/31/98) • **83**
Amarone della Valpolicella Capitel Monte Olmi 1988 • $40 • (09/15/92) • **84**
Capitel San Rocco 1993: Smoke and tar aromas give way to cherry and wood flavors in this moderately structured red. Rustic. Drink now. • $16 • (05/31/98) • **82**
Capitel San Rocco 1988 • $NA • (09/15/92) • **78**
Capitel San Rocco 1983 • $11 • (02/15/89) • **84**
Valpolicella Capitel del Nicalò 1989 • $14 • (09/15/92) • **82**

TENAGLIA, TENUTA LA

Grignolino del Monferrato Casalese 1991 • $24 • (06/30/93) • **81**

Key: SS—Spectator Selection CS—Cellar Selection HR—Highly Recommended BB—Best Buy $NA—Price not available Ⓐ—Auction Price (BT)—Barrel Tasting
Dates in parentheses indicate the issues in which the ratings were published.

TERLANO, CANTINA SOCIALE

Pinot Bianco Alto Adige Vorberg 1995: A bright, lively Pinot Bianco bursting with ripe apple and peach character, finishing with a touch of bitterness. Try as an apéritif or with light foods. Drink through 1999. 1,500 cases made. • $17 • (05/15/98) • **86**
Pinot Bianco Alto Adige Vorberg 1994: A broad wine with some good texture. Delivers nice peach and fig flavors accented by spicy and nutty notes. • $20 • (01/31/97) • **84**
Pinot Grigio Alto Adige 1996: Butter and vanilla overtones mark this bold, up-front style. Though round, the flavors dissipate quickly, leaving the finish on the austere side. Drink now. 6,000 cases made. • $12 • (05/15/98) • **83**
Pinot Grigio Alto Adige Klaus 1995: Violet and apricot aromas and flavors combine with a soft, rich texture in this tasty Pinot Grigio that finishes with a dollop of citrus peel and a slightly alcoholic feel. Drink now. 1,500 cases made. • $17 • (05/15/98) • **84**
Pinot Grigio Alto Adige Klaus 1994: Redolent of honey and spice, turns buttery on the finish. This wine is rich, mature and ready to drink. • $20 • (01/31/97) • **84**

TERRABIANCA

Campaccio 1991 • $NA • (10/31/95) • **80**
Campaccio 1990 • $20 • (10/31/93) • **88**
Campaccio Barriques 1993: A bit tough and raisiny. Medium-bodied, with chewy tannins and a slightly dry finish. May improve with age; drink now or hold. 7,000 cases made. • $31 • (09/30/97) • **85**
Campaccio Barriques 1991 • $NA • (10/31/95) • **80**
Campaccio Barriques 1990 • $33 • (02/28/95) • **84**
Campaccio Barriques 1988 • $31 • (09/15/91) • **87**
Campaccio Barriques Speciale 1993: Serious wine. A racy and silky red with cherry and mineral aromas and flavors, a hint of wood. Medium-bodied, with a fresh, caressing finish. Drink now or hold. 2,000 cases made. • $58 • (09/30/97) • **90**
Chianti Classico Riserva 1991 • $NA • (10/31/95) • **84**
Chianti Classico Scassino 1992 • $12 • (02/28/95) • **78**
Chianti Classico Scassino 1991 • $16 • (10/31/93) • **85**
Chianti Classico Scassino 1990 • $13 • (09/15/92) • **90**
Chianti Classico Vigna della Croce Riserva 1993: A chewy Chianti with good, grapey floral character. Medium-bodied, with velvety tannins and a medium, fruity finish. Slightly simple but good. Drink now or hold. 2,000 cases made. • $27 • (09/30/97) • **85**
Chianti Classico Vigna della Croce Riserva 1990 • $17 • (02/28/95) • **87**
Chianti Classico Vigna della Croce Riserva 1988 • $25 • (09/15/92) • **88**
Chianti Classico Vigna della Croce Riserva 1985 • $NA • (09/15/91) • **87**
Piano del Cipresso 1993: Chewy, showing good berry character, with herb accents. Medium-bodied, with moderate tannins and finish. Try now. 3,750 cases made. • $31 • (09/30/97) • **88**
Piano del Cipresso 1990 • $20 • (10/31/93) • **86**
Piano del Cipresso 1988 • $29 • (09/15/91) • **83**
Piano del Cipresso Barriques 1991 • $NA • (10/31/95) • **87**
Piano della Cappella 1995: Subtle aromas of toasty oak and apple follow through to the palate. Medium-bodied, with good acidity but a slightly dull finish. 1,700 cases made. • $29 • (09/30/97) • **85**
Scassino 1994: Quite herbal and a bit thin, with modest plum and currant flavors. • $16 • (01/31/97) • **79**

TERRE DA VINO

Barolo Paesi Tuoi 1993: A funky, earthy and rustic '93 Barolo, offering modest fruit and dry tannins. • $NA • (10/31/97) • **77**

TERRE DEL BAROLO

Barolo 1993: A fresh, fruity-style Barolo, with crisp texture and tough tannins. Light- to medium-bodied, with spice, vanilla, chocolate and cherry flavors and a dry finish. • $29 • (10/31/97) • **78**

TERRE DEL PRINCIPE

Chianti Colli Senesi 1995: Distinctly gamy aromas and flavors dominate; not much fruit flavor. Somewhat drying on the finish. • $11 • (03/31/97) • **77**

Vernaccia di San Gimignano Perlato 1995: A wine of some depth and character. Ripe and rich, with charming peach, pear and melon flavors and some spicy notes that linger on the finish. • $19 • (03/31/97) • **85**

Vernaccia di San Gimignano San Biagio 1995: A good, middle-of-the-road white with modest peach and herb flavors, and pleasant notes of butter and bitter-almond. • $13 • (03/31/97) • **83**

Vin Santo 1991: Walnuts and maple are the predominant notes in this dessert wine. Thick and rich, with a long, lingering finish and an astringent quality. • $17/375ml • (05/31/97) • **83**

TERRE DI GINESTRA

Sicily Red 1995: Check out the price on this attractive Italian red, warm in appeal and broad in outline, with a soft texture that folds in mellow fruit and spice flavors. Nice for tonight. 10,000 cases made. • $9 • (06/15/98) BB • **85**

Red 1994: An inviting, hearty and complex red with an interesting array of fruity, earthy, spicy flavors. Fully mature, so drink soon. 10,000 cases made. • $9 • (04/30/97) • **86**

Sicily White 1996: A boldly flavored white sporting floral, nectarine and orange notes. Medium body, with a tangy finish. Drink now. 10,000 cases made. • $9 • (05/15/98) • **82**

TERRENO

Chianti Classico 1995: Rather green with its cut grass, herb and berry character. Medium in body, with a good, round texture, but the grassiness follows through on the finish. • $20 • (09/30/97) • **79**

TERRICCI

Antiche Terre de'Ricci 1994: Dry and astringent. Has some fruit, but too much iodine and new wood character. • $NA • (09/30/97) • **77**

Antiche Terre de'Ricci 1986 • $23 • (05/15/90) • **83**

Antiche Terre de'Ricci 1985 • $22 • (03/15/89) • **91**

Terricci 1986 • $20 • (09/30/91) • **67**

TERRICCIO, TENUTA DEL

Con Vento 1996: A satisfying, rich white with plenty of fruit. Interesting aromas of apple, cream and volcanic ash, and ripe fruit flavors. Medium-bodied, round in texture. Long finish. • $16 • (09/30/97) • **88**

Con Vento 1995: An assertive, flavorful, golden-colored white that's rich in texture and nicely tangy at the same time. The flavors, reminiscent of herbs, grapefruit and apricot, linger on the finish. Sauvignon Blanc. • $15 • (05/31/97) • **88**

Lupicaia 1993: A gentle beast of a red wine, with an inky color, concentrated plum and black cherry flavors accented by spicy oak, and a smoothly tannic texture. Balanced enough to be tempting now, but it should improve through at least 2002. • $58 • (05/31/97) • **93**

Rondinaia 1996: Lovely aromas of apples, cream and tropical fruit lead into apple pie, melon and fruit flavors. Medium-bodied, with a creamy texture and impressive balance. • $16 • (09/30/97) • **88**

Tassinaia 1995: Pretty and delicious, offering blackberries and spices on the nose and palate. Medium-bodied, with fine tannins and a silky texture. Drink now. • $29 • (09/30/97) • **87**

Tassinaia 1994: Firm and silky, with good berry and vanilla aromas and flavors and a supple, caressing texture, but slightly short. Somewhat disappointing compared to the '93. Drink now. Tasted twice with consistent notes. • $36 • (10/31/96) • **84**

Tassinaia 1993 • $NA • (10/31/95) • **90**

Tassinaia 1992 • $NA • (10/31/95) • **86**

TERUZZI & PUTHOD

Terre di Tufi 1995: A crisp and clean white with apple, mineral and citrus aromas and flavors, with hints of spice, too. Medium-bodied, with a clean finish. 16,500 cases made. • $24 • (09/30/97) • **88**

Vernaccia di San Gimignano 1996: A stylish Italian wine, with an almond and melon character. Medium-bodied, with fresh acidity and an almond-accented finish. 33,000 cases made. • $12 • (09/30/97) • **84**

Vernaccia di San Gimignano 1995: Fresh, and perfumed with honeysuckle aromas. Medium-bodied, with honey and mineral notes. Light finish. 25,000 cases made. • $12 • (09/30/97) • **83**

Vigna Peperino 1986 • $11 • (01/31/90) • **68**

Vigna Peperino 1985 • $11 • (10/31/88) • **92**

TIEFENBRUNNER

Cabernet Alto Adige Linticlarus 1992 • $13 • (02/29/96) • **83**

Cabernet Alto Adige 1987 • $9 • (03/31/89) • **84**

Chardonnay Alto Adige 1994 • $11 • (06/15/96) • **86**

Chardonnay Alto Adige 1993 • $8 • (01/31/95) • **82**

Chardonnay Alto Adige Castel Turmhof 1993 • $11 • (01/31/95) • **85**

Gewürztraminer Alto Adige Castel Turmhof 1993 • $15 • (01/31/95) • **87**

Pinot Bianco Alto Adige 1996: A little leesy, displaying more herb and nut character, yet the texture is supple and there's firm, lemony acidity. Drink now. 1,500 cases made. • $11 • (06/15/98) • **82**

Pinot Bianco Alto Adige 1993 • $8 • (01/31/95) • **78**

Pinot Grigio Alto Adige 1996: This has floral and peach character, along with richness and an appealing mineral note. Its firmness should marry well with food. Drink through 1999. 12,500 cases made. • $11 • (06/15/98) • **85**

Pinot Grigio Alto Adige 1995: Shows ripe peach and mineral notes, and maybe a touch of sweetness, though good acidity pulls everything together on the finish. • $11 • (06/15/97) • **84**

Pinot Grigio Alto Adige 1994 • $10 • (06/15/96) • **84**

Pinot Grigio Alto Adige 1993 • $9 • (01/31/95) • **84**

TIEZZI, ENZO

Brunello di Montalcino 1992: Pretty tobacco, vanilla and chocolate aromas and flavors. Medium-bodied, with medium, fine tannins and a slightly dry finish. Tasted twice, with consistent notes. Drink now. 600 cases made. • $32 • (09/30/97) • **84**

Brunello di Montalcino 1991: Pleasant, with aromas and flavors of berry, cherry and chocolate and light, silky tannins. Short finish. Drink now. • $30 • (11/30/96) • **80**

Brunello di Montalcino 1990: Round and delicious berry, cedar and meat character. Full-bodied and soft, leading to a simple finish. Drink now. • $NA • (10/31/95) • **85**

Cerrino 1994: Very simple and fruity, with some dried cherry flavor, but slightly coarse and short on the finish. • $NA • (10/31/96) • **76**

Rosso di Montalcino 1995: A very good Rosso, with a berry, violet, floral character. It's of medium body, has silky tannins and a medium finish. Delicious now. 500 cases made. • $12 • (09/30/97) • **86**

Rosso di Montalcino 1994: Soft and caressing to your palate. This wine shows aromas and flavors of berry and chocolate, and friendly tannins. Slightly short and diluted on the finish. • $12 • (11/30/96) • **82**

Rosso di Montalcino 1993 • $NA • (10/31/95) • **85**

TINAZZI

Bardolino Classico 1994: Dull and tired, this should have been drunk last year for its modest cherry and licorice flavors. • $9 • (11/15/97) • **74**

Soave Classico 1996: Soft and pleasant, with aromas and flavors of peaches and spring flowers, finishing with a hint of almond. Perfect with lunch or as an apéritif. Drink now. • $9 • (04/30/98) • **81**

Valpolicella Classico Superiore 1992: Still fresh, showing dried cherry, raspberry and the hint of oxidation one expects from an Amarone. Light-bodied, with some tannins on the finish. Enjoy now. • $9 • (11/15/97) • **82**

TOGATA, LA

Brunello di Montalcino 1991: A solid Brunello, of medium body, with minty, herbal berry character. The tannins are fine, the finish fresh. Drink now or can hold. From Tenuta Carlina. • $NA • (11/30/96) • **85**

TOMMASI

Amarone della Valpolicella Classico 1990: Full-bodied, full-flavored, smooth in texture and Port-like in character. Nicely mature. The chocolaty, gamy flavors match with rich meat dishes or after-dinner cheeses. Best now through 2000. 3,100 cases made. • $42 • (04/30/97) • **88**

Amarone della Valpolicella Classico 1989: Nicely aged, with gamy and nutty flavors, and loads of fruit flavors as well. Finishes with cinnamon, tobacco and chocolate notes. A big wine with plenty of power. Best in 1999. 900 cases made. • $23 • (01/31/97) • **88**

Amarone Recioto della Valpolicella Classico 1988: Compact, with plum, spice and dried cherry flavors up front and colalike flavors on the finish. A leaner version of Amarone. 3,000 cases made. • $23 • (01/31/97) • **86**

Amarone Recioto della Valpolicella Classico 1985: A mature Amarone, with aromas of mushrooms, leather and spice, and flavors to match. Supple and full-bodied, with a lasting finish. Not for the faint of heart. Drink now. 4,000 cases made. • $28 • (01/31/97) • **89**

Pinot Grigio Valdadige Le Rosse 1997: Subtle and complex, with hints of peach, grapefruit, tropical fruit and minerals that weave throughout this firm, concentrated yet delicately structured Pinot Grigio. Drink now through 1999. • $13 • (06/30/98) • **84**

Pinot Grigio Valdadige Le Rosse Vigneto del Campo 1995: Straightfoward, with almond and honey flavors and a crisp finish. Medium-bodied, and shows decent balance. 7,000 cases made. • $10 • (01/31/97) • **81**

Valpolicella Classico Vigneto del Campo Rafael 1993: Still fresh and fruity despite its age, this offers lovely strawberry and dark cherry flavors with a silky texture. Some nice cinnamon and spice notes on the finish. Drink now. 7,000 cases made. • $10 • (01/31/97) BB • **87**

TORRACCIA, LA

Chianti Classico 1995: A bit light and simple, but has a lively, crushed berry character and a crisp finish. • $NA • (09/30/97) • **80**

Chianti Classico 1994: Boasts a pleasant balance of ripe fruit, new wood and fine tannins. Medium-bodied, with moderate acidity and a round, slightly astringent mouthfeel. Drink now or hold. • $NA • (09/30/97) • **85**

Chianti Classico Il Tarocco 1993: A pretty Chianti to drink now, with chocolate and berry flavors and accents of leather. Medium-bodied, with well-integrated tannins and a succulent finish. 5,000 cases made. • $11 • (09/30/97) • **86**

Chianti Classico Il Tarocco Riserva 1993: Shows some fruit, but is lightly austere and dry on the finish. Medium-bodied, with hard tannins. Not going much farther in its evolution. 1,200 cases made. • $14 • (09/30/97) • **80**

Lucciolaio 1994: Lots of grapey aromas and flavors with notes of spice, but the dry, austere tannins detract. Wait and see. Tasted twice, with consistent notes. 800 cases made. • $25 • (09/30/97) • **79**

TORRE, LA

Brunello di Montalcino 1991: A beauty. This offers aromas and flavors of berry and chocolate, and is lovely and silky on the finish. For drinking now. 916 cases made. • $31 • (11/30/96) • **85**

Brunello di Montalcino 1990: Fruity, soft and a bit simple, offering pepper, tomato and cherry aromas and flavors, medium body and a succulent finish. • $NA • (10/31/95) • **85**

Brunello di Montalcino 1985 • $30 • (04/15/91) • **78**

TORRE DI LUNA

Pinot Grigio Trentino 1996: A fresh, floral and pear-scented white. Light-bodied, with apple and pear flavors and a hint of earthiness on the crisp finish. • $12 • (12/15/97) • **83**

TORRE ROSAZZA

Cabernet Sauvignon Colli Orientali del Friuli Ronco della Torre 1994: Minty, resinous aromas, followed by black currant, black cherry and rosemary. Medium-bodied. Astringent tannins on the finish. Drink now through 2002. 1,000 cases made. • $19 • (05/31/98) • **79**

Chardonnay Colli Orientali del Friuli 1996: A rich, apple-, almond- and clove-flavored Chardonnay with a firm structure and a finish that's like biting into a crisp apple. Drink now. 3,000 cases made. • $14 • (05/31/98) • **83**

Chardonnay Colli Orientali del Friuli 1994 • $11 • (04/30/96) • **81**

Merlot Colli Orientali del Friuli L'Altromerlot 1993: Rich and concentrated, with mature flavors of leather and licorice on a solid structure. Well balanced and firmly tannic on the finish, so try with food. Drink through 1999. 700 cases made. • $27 • (05/31/98) • **85**

Merlot Colli Orientali del Friuli L'Altromerlot 1992 • $20 • (02/29/96) • **88**

Key: SS—Spectator Selection CS—Cellar Selection HR—Highly Recommended BB—Best Buy $NA—Price not available Ⓐ—Auction Price (BT)—Barrel Tasting
Dates in parentheses indicate the issues in which the ratings were published.

Pinot Grigio Colli Orientali del Friuli 1996: Apple character predominates in this vibrant Pinot Grigio. Though well balanced, it's essentially one-dimensional. Drink now. 5,000 cases made. • $14 • (05/31/98) • **81**

Pinot Grigio Colli Orientali del Friuli 1994 • $11 • (04/30/96) • **87**

Pinot Nero Colli Orientali del Friuli 1993 • $13 • (04/30/96) • **83**

TORRE TERZA

Rosso di Montalcino 1991 • $9 • (04/30/94) • **84**

TORREGIORGI

Barbaresco 1990 • $NA • (10/31/95) • **82**

TORRESELLA

Cabernet Veneto 1996: A simple red, showing vegetal aromas and flavors, but there is a touch of cherry. Drink now. 20,000 cases made. • $8 • (06/15/98) • **78**

Chardonnay Veneto 1996: A basic white with canned-pear flavors that disappear quickly. 20,000 cases made. • $8 • (06/15/98) • **74**

Chardonnay Veneto 1995: Very dry, nearly austere in style, with simple fruit flavors. Refreshing, but lean and lacking in flavor. • $9 • (02/28/97) • **77**

Merlot 1996: A thin, weedy-tasting red with only a hint of Merlot character. Drink now. 20,000 cases made. • $9 • (05/31/98) • **74**

Merlot 1993 • $9 • (01/31/96) • **81**

Merlot Lison-Pramaggiore 1995: A good, middle-weight Merlot with decent herbal and dried cherry flavors. Turns tough on the finish. • $9 • (07/31/98) • **80**

Merlot Lison-Pramaggiore 1986 • $5 • (10/31/88) • **79**

Pinot Grigio Veneto 1996: This seems just slightly under-ripe, with some herb and green fruit notes and tart acidity in a straightforward presentation. Drink now. 80,000 cases made. • $8 • (05/31/98) • **79**

Pinot Grigio Veneto 1993 • $9 • (04/30/96) • **78**

TOSCOLO

Chianti Classico 1993: A rather hollow, watery-tasting wine that's short on fruit flavor. Dull. 8,850 cases made. • $10 • (10/31/96) • **74**

Chianti Classico 1990 • $8 • (04/30/94) BB • **85**

TRACOLLE

Chianti Classico 1993 • $NA • (10/31/95) • **71**

Chianti Classico 1988 • $NA • (09/15/91) • **69**

TRAVAGLINI

Gattinara 1993: Lean and modest wine, with only a hint of fruit. Turns dry on the finish. • $20 • (01/31/98) • **73**

Gattinara 1986 • $18 • (01/31/92) • **82**

Gattinara Numerata 1985 • $26 • (01/31/92) • **84**

Gattinara Riserva 1990: Ripe and plummy, with mineral, tar and spice, this medium-bodied wine is interesting, but the tannins are extremely dry. Too bad. • $29 • (01/31/98) • **80**

Spanna 1988 • $10 • (07/15/91) • **83**

TREROSE, TENUTA

Vin Santo 1986 • $33 • (07/31/93) • **89**

Vino Nobile di Montepulciano 1988 • $16 • (12/15/92) • **86**

Vino Nobile di Montepulciano 1986 • $16 • (07/15/91) • **80**

Vino Nobile di Montepulciano 1985 • $11 • (11/15/88) • **90**

Vino Nobile di Montepulciano Riserva 1993: A bit funky, but some decent fruit. Plenty of berry and mushroom character. Medium-bodied, with medium, velvety tannins and an earthy aftertaste. Drink now. • $60 • (12/31/97) • **81**

Vino Nobile di Montepulciano Riserva 1985 • $19 • (07/15/91) • **85**

Vino Nobile di Montepulciano Simposio 1988 • $40 • (12/15/92) • **88**

UCCELLIERA, FATTORIA

Brunello di Montalcino 1991: Slightly tired already, with smoke, cedar and berry aromas and flavors. Medium-bodied, smooth in texture. Drink now. 108 cases made. • $32 • (11/30/96) • **80**

Castellaccio 1994: A medium-bodied offering, with vanilla- and apple-accented almond and marzipan character. Moderate acidity. 290 cases made. • $25 • (09/30/97) • **81**
Castellaccio 1993: Impressive. Shows crushed blackberry and flower character a' plenty and is full-bodied, with well-integrated tannins and a long, long finish. Try now. 650 cases made. • $26 • (09/30/97) • **89**
Chianti 1995: Rather light and slightly diluted, but offers decent berry and vanilla aromas and flavors. • $18 • (09/30/97) • **80**
Rosso di Montalcino 1995: Dried cherry and earth character prevails in this medium-bodied, soft-textured red. 11,000 cases made. • $12 • (09/30/97) • **84**
Rosso di Montalcino 1994: Of a slightly traditional nature, but this shows some interesting aromas and flavors of game, earth and berry. Light bodied, with a light finish. 333 cases made. • $15 • (11/30/96) • **80**

UMANI RONCHI

Montepulciano d'Abruzzo 1994: A soft wine, offering some fruit and game-like flavors with a tannic finish. 30,000 cases made. • $6 • (03/31/97) • **78**
Montepulciano d'Abruzzo 1989 • $5 • (02/15/91) • **75**
Montepulciano d'Abruzzo Jorio 1995: Ripe, juicy, mouthfilling raspberry flavors and an easy-drinking texture make this a fine candidate for a red house-wine. Has good concentration and moderate tannins. Drink now through 2000. 3,000 cases made. • $11 • (06/15/98) • **86**
Pelago 1994: A modern-styled red, its berry, cedar and vanilla flavors well-balanced with the elegant structure and smooth texture. The lingering finish has some firm tannins. Drink now through 2000. 300 cases made. • $46 • (05/15/98) • **87**
Rosso Cònero 1995: A hearty but rustic-style red with strong, earthy aromas and spicy, herbal, cherrylike flavors. Not for everyone. 15,000 cases made. • $6 • (04/30/97) • **78**
Rosso Cònero Cúmaro 1994: A deep color, concentrated fruit flavors and firm tannins make this a seriously enjoyable wine that may improve with cellaring. Has both depth of flavor and a lingering finish. Drink now through 2001. 1,000 cases made. • $17 • (06/15/98) • **88**
Rosso Cònero Cúmaro 1988 • $22 • (09/15/92) • **83**
Rosso Cònero San Lorenzo 1994: A smooth, soft-textured red, with plenty of plummy, peppery flavors. Simple but tasty. Drink now. 8,000 cases made. • $10 • (06/15/98) • **81**
Rosso Cònero San Lorenzo 1993: Hearty in flavor and firm in texture, this is an attractive, well-balanced red with ample tannins. 8,000 cases made. • $9 • (03/31/97) • **84**
Verdicchio dei Castelli di Jesi Classico Superiore Casal di Serra 1995: A bold style from a little-known Italian district. Full-bodied and richly flavored, it has oaky, buttery aromas and peachy flavors backed by a firm, crisp texture. 6,000 cases made. • $9 • (04/30/97) • **86**
Verdicchio dei Castelli di Jesi Classico Casal di Serra 1993 • $9 • (03/31/95) • **85**
Verdicchio dei Castelli di Jesi Classico Superiore Villa Bianchi 1995: Rich, buttery aromas backed by crisp fruit flavors make for a well-balanced, complete white wine. It's dry, rather full-bodied and has a very smooth texture. 10,000 cases made. • $9 • (04/30/97) • **85**
Verdicchio dei Castelli di Jesi Classico Villa Bianchi 1993 • $8 • (03/31/95) • **81**

UNTEREBNERHOF, TENUTA

Pinot Grigio Alto Adige 1994 • $11 • (06/15/96) • **77**
Pinot Grigio Alto Adige Südtiroler Ruländer 1996: Slightly corky? A sour, earthy edge fights with the nutty, quince flavors. Otherwise rich, with a firm structure and astringent finish. This was the better of two bottles. 2,800 cases made. • $12 • (07/31/98) • **72**

UZZANO, CASTELLO DI

Chianti Classico 1988 • $NA • (09/15/91) • **87**
Chianti Classico Riserva 1985 • $NA • (09/15/91) • **85**

VADIAPERTI

Fiano di Avellino 1993 • $17 • (03/31/95) • **84**
Greco di Tufo 1993 • $14 • (03/31/95) • **74**

VAJRA, G.D.

Barbera d'Alba 1992 • $NA • (10/31/94) • **81**
Barbera d'Alba Bricco delle Viole 1993 • $35 • (10/31/95) • **82**
Barbera d'Alba Bricco delle Viole Riserva 1985 • $22 • (07/31/89) • **83**
Barolo 1990 • $28 • (10/31/94) • **64**
Barolo 1988 • $NA • (10/31/93) • **85**
Barolo 1982 • $14 • (03/15/87) • **91**
Barolo Bricco delle Viole 1982 • $19 • (08/31/88) • **91**
Barolo Fossati 1985 • $34 • (12/31/90) • **91**
Dolcetto d'Alba 1996: Fresh and grapey, even a bit earthy, with ripe fruit flavors and sweet tannins. Light-to-medium body; balanced, with a pretty, lingering finish. 2,700 cases made. • $13 • (10/31/97) • **84**
Dolcetto d'Alba Coste & Fossati 1996: A fabulous Dolcetto that has what you expect in a world-class red. Inky-black in color, full-bodied, with silky tannins and a sweet, ripe cassis, blackberry and black cherry character that coats your palate and lingers on the long, harmonious finish. What a beauty. Drink now and through 2000. 2,400 cases made. • $20 • (10/31/97) • **91**
Dolcetto d'Alba Coste & Fossati 1994 • $19 • (10/31/95) • **85**
Nebbiolo Langhe 1996: Fruity and clean, this is a straightforward red with a somewhat supple finish and acceptable tannins. 800 cases made. • $14 • (10/31/97) • **80**

VAL DI SUGA

Brunello di Montalcino 1992: Boasts lively strawberry and cut mushroom aromas and is medium- to light-bodied, with moderate acidity and a light finish. Drink now. 7,500 cases made. • $38 • (09/30/97) • **85**
Brunello di Montalcino 1991: Aromas and flavors of cedar, berry and game, with fine tannins. Turns a bit dry on the finish. There is a slightly mature-looking amber hue to the ruby color. Drink now. • $33 • (11/30/96) • **82**
Brunello di Montalcino 1990: Wonderfully perfumed violet, berry and light cedar character, medium body and firm tannins. Drinkable now. • $NA • (10/31/95) • **86**
Brunello di Montalcino 1988 • $26 • (04/30/94) • **78**
Brunello di Montalcino 1985 • $23 • (09/30/90) • **88**
Brunello di Montalcino Riserva 1991: A very woody wine with good berry and cherry character but a slightly dry finish. Medium body, medium tannins. Drink now. 500 cases made. • $48 • (09/30/97) • **82**
Brunello di Montalcino Riserva 1990: Old style. Pretty aromas of roasted meat and fruit. Medium body, with steely and austere tannins and a smoky, fruity finish. Drink soon, before it dries out. • $45 • (11/30/96) • **84**
Brunello di Montalcino Riserva 1988 • $NA • (10/31/94) • **87**
Brunello di Montalcino Riserva 1986 • $27 • (11/30/93) • **87**
Brunello di Montalcino Riserva 1982 • $20 • (11/30/89) • **89**
Brunello di Montalcino Vigna Spuntali 1990: An impressively rich and concentrated wine, with lots of new wood in evidence. Full-bodied, with healthy portions of both fruit and tannin, and a long, vanilla finish. Drink now or hold. • $70 • (11/30/96) • **89**
Brunello di Montalcino Vigna Spuntali 1988 • $52 • (07/31/95) • **88**
Brunello di Montalcino Vigna del Lago 1990: A big and burly Brunello, with masses of toasty oak flavor. Full-bodied, with full tannins and a long vanilla-accented finish. A bit too much perhaps. Drink now or hold. • $70 • (11/30/96) • **87**
Brunello di Montalcino Vigna del Lago 1988 • $52 • (04/30/94) • **90**
Brunello di Montalcino Vigna del Lago 1986 • $52 • (11/30/93) HR • **91**
Brunello di Montalcino Vigna del Lago 1985 • $52 • (07/15/91) • **90**
Rosso di Montalcino 1995: Light and simple, with plum and dried fruit character, and hints of earth and leather. Dry finish. 3,000 cases made. • $17 • (09/30/97) • **79**
Rosso di Montalcino 1994: There's a mouthful of fruit in this wine—plenty of berry and cherry flavors, with notes of cedar. Tannins are fine, finish is long. • $16 • (11/30/96) • **86**
Rosso di Montalcino 1993 • $NA • (10/31/95) • **77**
Rosso di Montalcino 1991 • $12 • (04/30/94) • **80**
Rosso di Montalcino 1988 • $10 • (04/30/91) • **87**
Rosso di Montalcino 1986 • $9 • (11/30/89) • **81**

VALDICAVA

Brunello di Montalcino 1991: A well-made, medium-bodied wine, with a silky texture and fine tannins framing flavors of fresh berries. Crisp finish. Drink now. 1,291 cases made. • $NA • (11/30/96) • **85**
Brunello di Montalcino 1990: Too bad its wet grass and mushroom character smells so funky, because the texture is smooth as can be, adding maturing berry, truffle and chestnut flavors. • $NA • (10/31/95) • **80**
Brunello di Montalcino 1988 • $28 • (04/30/94) • **86**
Brunello di Montalcino Madonna del Piano Riserva 1990: A terrific wine that caresses your palate with super-ripe berry and raspberry aromas and

ITALY

flavors, and a hint of new wood. Full-bodied, with soft tannins and a long finish. A joy to drink now, but will improve with age. • $NA • (11/30/96) • **93**

Brunello di Montalcino Madonna del Piano Riserva 1988 • $NA • (10/31/94) • **85**

Rosso di Montalcino 1995: A bounteous fresh strawberry character highlights this medium- to light-bodied red. Fresh on the finish. Not imported into U.S. • $NA • (09/30/97) • **83**

Rosso di Montalcino 1994: This gushes with fruit, especially plum and berry. Its tannins are harmoniously integrated and it finishes with a spicy vanilla note. Wonderful for the vintage. 2,166 cases made. • $NA • (11/30/96) • **87**

Rosso di Montalcino 1993 • $NA • (10/31/95) • **84**

Rosso di Montalcino 1991 • $15 • (04/30/94) • **78**

VALDIPIATTA, TENUTA

Rosso di Montepulciano 1995: Unclean and odd. Tastes like it's going through malolactic fermentation. Tasted twice, with consistent notes. • $13 • (09/30/97) • **68**

Trefonti 1994: Beautiful combination of smoky new wood and ripe fruit character. Medium body, with ripe berry and blackberry flavors and chocolate notes. Medium, full tannins. Try now. • $30 • (09/30/97) • **88**

Vino Nobile di Montepulciano Riserva 1993: A bit lean, there's some fruit character to it, but the finish is slightly acidic and earthy. • $27 • (09/30/97) • **78**

VALFIERI

Barbaresco 1989 • $16 • (04/15/94) • **77**

Barbaresco 1986 • $12 • (09/15/90) • **82**

Barbaresco 1985 • $8 • (07/31/89) • **70**

Barolo 1990 • $NA • (10/31/94) • **83**

Barolo 1985 • $13 • (10/15/90) HR • **90**

Dolcetto d'Alba 1988 • $8 • (12/31/90) • **81**

Dolcetto d'Alba 1987 • $5 • (03/15/89) • **78**

VALIANO

Chianti Classico 1994: Already a little mature with an amber edge and barky, earthy aromas. Old wood? Yet offers decent fruit flavors and a crisp finish. 1,000 cases made. • $11 • (10/31/96) • **78**

Chianti Classico 1992 • $8 • (02/28/95) • **79**

Chianti Classico Poggio Teo 1995: Rather dried out, it shows some fruit character but is short and unexciting on the finish. • $NA • (09/30/97) • **77**

Chianti Classico Riserva 1994: Delivers good, plummy character with accents of dried cherries. Medium- to light-bodied, with light tannins and a crisp, slightly short finish. • $NA • (09/30/97) • **83**

Chianti Classico Riserva 1993: Slightly one-dimensional, but there's a solid core of fruit and ripe tannins in this wine. Medium-bodied with firm tannins and a crisp finish. Drink now. 1,000 cases made. • $15 • (10/31/96) • **84**

VALLANA

Barbera Piedmont 1988 • $7 • (03/31/90) • **80**

Barbera Piedmont 1986 • $6 • (02/15/89) BB • **90**

Barbera del Piemonte 1990 • $9 • (10/31/92) • **79**

Barbera del Piemonte 1988 • $8 • (03/15/91) • **88**

Gattinara 1983 • $10 • (01/31/90) • **76**

VALLANIA

Cabernet Sauvignon Colli Bolognesi Terre Rosse Monte San Pietro 1986 • $18 • (09/30/91) • **66**

Terre Rosse 1985 • $9 • (03/31/90) • **70**

VALLAROM

Cabernet Sauvignon Trentino 1988 • $27 • (12/15/92) • **80**

Key: SS—Spectator Selection CS—Cellar Selection HR—Highly Recommended BB—Best Buy $NA—Price not available Ⓐ—Auction Price (BT)—Barrel Tasting

Dates in parentheses indicate the issues in which the ratings were published.

Chardonnay Trentino Riserva 1995: Delicious aromas and flavors of vanilla, nutmeg and apple, showing some maturity, yet well-balanced and harmonious, with richness and a firm acidity that keeps the flavors pumping through the finish. Drink now. • $20 • (05/31/98) • **85**

Pinot Nero Trentino 1990 • $25 • (07/31/93) • **74**

VALLE CHIARA, ABBAZIA DI

Dolcetto d'Ovada 1990 • $11 • (04/30/93) • **80**

Dolcetto d'Ovada 1989 • $13 • (07/15/91) • **79**

Torre Albarola 1988 • $24 • (01/31/92) • **87**

VALLE SELEZIONE ARALDICA

L'Araldo Collina Friulana 1985 • $20 • (05/15/91) • **84**

VALTELLINA, FATTORIA

Chianti Classico Giorgio Regni 1994: Good, deep color and concentration of fruit with plum and berry aromas and flavors. Medium bodied and soft, yet slightly short on the finish and simple overall. • $28 • (10/31/96) • **83**

Chianti Classico Giorgio Regni 1993 • $NA • (10/31/95) • **84**

Chianti Classico Giorgio Regni 1992 • $13 • (02/28/95) • **86**

Chianti Classico Giorgio Regni 1990 • $NA • (10/31/93) • **90**

Chianti Classico Giorgio Regni 1988 • $19 • (09/15/91) • **83**

Chianti Classico Giorgio Regni Riserva 1990 • $25 • (02/28/95) • **93**

Chianti Classico Giorgio Regni Riserva 1985 • $20 • (09/15/91) • **92**

Convivio Giorgio Regni 1991 • $30 • (02/28/95) • **91**

Convivio Giorgio Regni 1990 • $NA • (10/31/93) • **93**

VASELLI

Santa Giulia 1988 • $10 • (01/31/92) • **83**

Santa Giulia Rosso NV • $19 • (01/31/92) • **80**

VECCHIE TERRE DI MONTEFILI

Anfiteatro 1994: Bubbling over with plum, berry and ripe fruit aromas, the wine is medium- to full-bodied with velvety tannins and a long, fruity finish. Drinkable now. 250 cases made. • $50 • (09/30/97) • **89**

Anfiteatro 1993: A little jammy, but offers loads of berry, cherry and plum flavors. Full-bodied, with plush tannins and a long, fruity finish. Try now. 333 cases made. • $50 • (10/31/96) • **90**

Anfiteatro 1991 • $32 • (10/31/95) • **90**

Anfiteatro 1990 • $40 • (11/30/94) • **89**

Bruno di Rocca 1994: Well-integrated, mingling lovely, silky tannins and plenty of berry, spice and gamy flavors. Medium-bodied, moderate finish. Drink now or hold. 280 cases made. • $50 • (09/30/97) • **88**

Bruno di Rocca 1993: Super color and concentration, but very herbaceous with green bean, bell pepper character dominating the fruit flavors. Slightly overdone—too much unripe Cabernet character. Disappointing for this producer. 500 cases made. • $50 • (10/31/96) • **84**

Bruno di Rocca 1992 • $NA • (10/31/95) • **87**

Bruno di Rocca 1991 • $40 • (11/30/94) • **87**

Bruno di Rocca 1990 • $NA • (10/31/93) • **89**

Bruno di Rocca 1989 • $NA • (10/31/93) • **87**

Chianti Classico 1995: Quite ripe for the vintage, showing raisin, cracked black pepper and spice tones. Medium-bodied, with medium tannins and a spicy finish. Drinkable now. 1,500 cases made. • $23 • (09/30/97) • **85**

Chianti Classico 1994: Yet another solid Chianti from this estate. Character is intense for a simple Chianti, showing dried berry, mint and floral notes. Medium body, and a long minty, berry finish. Delicious now. 2,167 cases made. • $20 • (10/31/96) • **88**

Chianti Classico 1993 • $NA • (10/31/95) • **85**

Chianti Classico 1992 • $20 • (02/28/95) • **85**

Chianti Classico 1990 • $20 • (10/31/93) • **86**

Chianti Classico 1988 • $20 • (09/15/91) • **90**

Chianti Classico 1986 • $14 • (04/30/90) • **85**

Chianti Classico Anfiteatro Riserva 1988 • $24 • (09/15/92) • **89**

Chianti Classico Riserva 1985 • $NA • (09/15/91) • **90**

VENEGAZZÙ

Brut Loredan Gasparini 1988 • $14 • (12/15/92) • **78**

Brut Riserva 1988 • $16 • (05/15/93) • **83**

Brut di Venegazzu 1982 • $12 • (12/15/86) • **91**

Capo di Stato 1994: Delicious, from the smoky, black cherry aromas to the lingering, plummy aftertaste. This red has a glycerinelike texture, with all the components in harmony. Not a blockbuster, but balanced for drinking now. • $41 • (06/15/97) • **87**

Della Casa 1993: A serious red that has plenty of personality, but less finesse. Concentrated, with black cherry, tar and earth flavors and a long finish. Bold enough for grilled meats and aged, hard cheeses. • $23 • (06/15/97) • **87**

Della Casa 1990 • $15 • (09/15/92) • **85**

Della Casa 1985 • $25 • (03/31/90) • **91**

Della Casa 1983 • $25 • (02/15/89) • **86**

Della Casa 1982 • $15 • (07/15/87) • **82**

Della Casa 1980 • $10 • (02/15/87) • **72**

Loredan Gasparini 1990: • $NA • (10/31/96) • **83**

Loredan Gasparini Capo di Stato 1992 • $33 • (05/31/96) • **88**

Loredan Gasparini Capo di Stato 1990 • $33 • (05/31/95) • **83**

Loredan Gasparini Venegazzu della Casa 1992 • $20 • (06/15/96) • **83**

VENICA & VENICA

Bottaz 1993: A serious version of Refosco. Still deeply colored, with a whiff of acetone followed by vanilla and smoke nuances rounding out the red cherry flavor. It all works in this solid, medium-bodied red that shows light tannins on the lingering finish. Drink through 1999. 150 cases made. • $21 • (04/30/98) • **85**

Merlot Collio Perilla 1993: Deeply colored, with aromas of tar and spicy black fruit, followed by herbal-tinged black cherry flavors. It's fleshy and firm; mature enough to enjoy now with food. 400 cases made. • $21 • (12/15/97) • **86**

Pinot Bianco Collio 1996: Rich and juicy, there's plenty of apple, almond and lemon character in this fresh, appealing white. Delicious now. 800 cases made. • $15 • (11/15/97) • **84**

Tocai Friulano Collio 1996: Spicy, pungent aromas persist on the palate, where peach and a hint of apricot add to the mix. Ripe and rich, with just a slight bitter-almond note at the end. Drink now. 2,750 cases made. • $15 • (04/30/98) • **85**

Vignis 1994: Smells and tastes like Sauvignon Blanc, with its gooseberry and melon notes and a hint of new oak to round everything out. Medium-bodied and rich, with a lingering finish. Drink now. 300 cases made. • $20 • (12/15/97) • **87**

VERBENA

Brunello di Montalcino 1988 • $NA • (04/30/94) • **75**

Rosso di Montalcino 1991 • $NA • (04/30/94) • **83**

VERDUNO, CASTELLO DI

Barbaresco Rabajà 1993: Fairly supple tannins, but still quite tight, tart and rather angular. Cherry, tobacco and rusty flavors. Try now. • $NA • (10/31/96) • **82**

Barbaresco Rabajà 1990 • $NA • (10/31/94) • **80**

Barbera d'Alba Bricco del Cuculo 1993 • $NA • (10/31/95) • **79**

Barbera d'Alba Bricco del Cuculo 1992 • $NA • (10/31/94) • **80**

Barolo Vigna Massara 1993: A sweet, ripe, clean and pure Barolo with medium body and firm tannins. Has the stuffing to age past 2000, when it should be silky smooth. • $NA • (10/31/97) • **85**

Barolo Massara 1990 • $NA • (10/31/94) • **81**

VERRAZZANO, CASTELLO DI

Chianti Classico 1995: Good, simple Chianti with berry and cherry aromas and flavors, medium body and a crisp finish. 12,750 cases made. • $11 • (09/30/97) • **82**

Chianti Classico 1994: Plenty of blackberry and wet earth aromas and flavors in this one. Medium-bodied with light tannins and a long, fresh finish. • $13 • (10/31/96) • **84**

Chianti Classico 1993 • $9 • (10/31/95) • **86**

Chianti Classico 1992 • $10 • (02/28/95) • **84**

Chianti Classico 1991 • $9 • (10/31/93) • **84**

Chianti Classico 1990 • $9 • (10/31/93) • **88**

Chianti Classico 1988 • $8 • (09/15/91) • **85**

Chianti Classico Cinquecentenario di Verrazzano Riserva 1985 • $NA • (09/15/91) • **83**

Chianti Classico Riserva 1994: Generous bright cherry character in this medium-bodied wine. It has medium, fine tannins, and is slightly short on the finish. Drink now. • $15 • (09/30/97) • **84**

Chianti Classico Riserva 1993: A light and simple riserva with a cherry character and an herbal finish. Slightly disappointing for this producer. • $18 • (10/31/96) • **79**

Chianti Classico Riserva 1991 • $9 • (10/31/95) • **86**

Chianti Classico Riserva 1988 • $NA • (09/15/92) • **84**

Sassello 1994: Pretty, with berry and dried cherry character throughout. Medium-bodied, with fine tannins. Finishes fresh. Drink now. • $17 • (09/30/97) • **87**

Sassello 1993: A wonderful glass of refined and beautiful wine. Cherry, violet, floral aromas and flavors, fine tannins and a long, silky, succulent finish. Medium body. Drink now. Sangiovese. • $25 • (10/31/96) • **88**

Sassello 1990 • $NA • (10/31/93) • **92**

VESCOVADO DI MURLO

Chianti 1991 • $7 • (09/15/92) • **80**

Chianti 1990 • $6 • (10/31/91) BB • **83**

VESCOVINO, IL

Il Merlotto 1994: Elegant and well-balanced, offering berry and cherry aromas and flavors. Medium in body, with fine tannins and a crisp finish. Drink or hold. • $NA • (09/30/97) • **86**

Il Merlotto 1993: Fresh and simple, offering berry, cherry and mineral aromas and flavors. Medium- to light-bodied, with fine tannins and a crisp finish. Drink now. • $NA • (10/31/96) • **80**

VIALA

Chardonnay delle Venezie 1996: This white from Italy is focused and direct, its apple and pear flavors offset by a slight earthiness. The texture is rich, the finish lingering. At such a bargain price, it's a smart choice when a few bottles are called for. 12,000 cases made. • $6 • (12/15/97) BB • **85**

Sangiovese Ravenna 1996: A basic red, lightly fruity in flavor, crisp enough in texture. Drink now. 8,000 cases made. • $6 • (02/28/98) • **78**

VIBERTI, ERALDO

Barolo 1991: Very fruity, with ample cherry and black currant flavors up front. Firmly textured and tannic, but best to drink now through 2001. • $NA • (10/31/96) • **84**

VIBERTI, GIOVANNI

Barbera d'Alba Bricco Airoli 1994: Lovely, with mature flavors of plum, prune, smoked meat, toasty bread, underbrush and mushroom. Fairly crisp. Drink slightly chilled. • $NA • (10/31/97) • **82**

Barolo 1993: Distinctive, ripe, sweet blackberry flavors, earthy, floral, spicy, tarry accents and well-integrated tannins make this balanced, medium-bodied '93 Barolo a pleasure to drink now through 2002. • $NA • (10/31/97) • **89**

Barolo Bricco delle Viole 1993: Fruity, crisp and intense; the wild raspberry, cherry and dried herbs flavors give it interest, but it's somewhat green and lean, and the drying finish is unfortunate. Drinkable now. • $NA • (10/31/97) • **83**

Barolo Riserva La Volta 1993: Fascinating *terroir* wine, showing a strong mineral, lead-pencil character that plays nicely to the red and blackberry flavors. Medium to full in body, with ripe tannins and a supple, long, balanced finish. Drink from 2000 to 2005. • $NA • (10/31/97) • **90**

Barolo San Pietro 1993: Good winemaking behind this clean, pure, very fruity and floral Barolo. Shows toasty oak, wild raspberry, rose petal, black cherry and cassis notes that bring complexity. Medium-bodied, with well-integrated but crisp, firm tannins that need until 1999 to 2000 to soften. • $NA • (10/31/97) • **88**

Dolcetto di Diano d'Alba Toni 'd Giuspin 1995: Offers spicy, ripe fruit complexity. Medium-bodied, it's still rather crisp and lean, with chewy tannins, but has decent cranberry, black cherry and earth notes. Drink now. • $NA • (10/31/97) • **80**

VICCHIOMAGGIO, CASTELLO DI

Chianti Classico La Prima Riserva 1994: Elegant, with cherry and berry character, and notes of new wood. Medium-bodied, with silky tannins and a medium finish. Drink now or hold. • $29 • (09/30/97) • **86**
Chianti Classico La Prima Riserva 1993: Good fruit in this, with aromas and flavors of plum and chocolate. Medium-bodied with soft tannins, but a slightly dry finish detracts from the total quality. • $23 • (10/31/96) • **83**
Chianti Classico La Prima Riserva 1991 • $NA • (10/31/95) • **86**
Chianti Classico La Prima Riserva 1985 • $20 • (09/15/91) • **86**
Chianti Classico Petri Riserva 1994: Good dried cherry character, with hints of leather. Medium-bodied, with light tannins and finish. • $22 • (09/30/97) • **83**
Chianti Classico Petri Riserva 1993: A light and simple riserva with dried cherry aromas and flavors, a light body, light tannins and a hint of vanilla on the finish. • $17 • (10/31/96) • **80**
Chianti Classico Petri Riserva 1991 • $NA • (10/31/95) • **81**
Chianti Classico Petri Riserva 1990 • $NA • (02/28/95) • **85**
Chianti Classico Petri Riserva 1988 • $NA • (09/15/92) • **87**
Chianti Classico San Jacopo 1995: Simple, with berry and plum flavors and vanilla accents. Light-bodied, with light tannins, and a light finish. Drink now. Tasted twice with consistent notes. • $12 • (09/30/97) • **81**
Chianti Classico San Jacopo 1991 • $9 • (10/31/93) • **80**
Chianti Classico San Jacopo 1990 • $9 • (10/31/93) • **87**
Ripa delle Mandorle 1995: A slightly mean red, with some hard tannins. Velvety and fruity, with a cherry, bark and porcini character. Medium-bodied, with a slightly bitter finish. Drink now. • $19 • (12/31/97) • **81**
Ripa delle More 1994: A very aromatic wine with berry, mushroom and vanilla character. It's of medium body, with velvety tannins and a vanilla finish. Drinkable now. • $31 • (09/30/97) • **87**
Ripa delle More 1991 • $NA • (10/31/95) • **88**
Ripa delle More 1990 • $NA • (10/31/93) • **91**

VICENTINI ORGNANI, FRANCESCO

Chardonnay Grave del Friuli 1996: Simple and straightforward, this shows some nice, crisp appley flavors, but it's a little diluted and on the tart side. Drink now. 2,500 cases made. • $14 • (05/31/98) • **79**
Merlot Grave del Friuli 1996: Muted and round, with moderate cherry and plum flavors, light in weight and finishing with a hint of tannin. Drink through 1999. 2,500 cases made. • $14 • (05/31/98) • **81**
Merlot Grave del Friuli Braide Cjasa 1992: Firm and lean, with plenty of fruit and smoke flavors and some nice herb notes. Good balance. Ripe finish with plenty of tannins. Try now. • $18 • (03/31/97) • **87**
Pinot Grigio Grave del Friuli 1996: Round and juicy, showing moderate concentration of apple and almond flavors. Balanced on the soft side. Drink now. 3,000 cases made. • $14 • (05/15/98) • **84**

VICO, GIACOMO

Barbera d'Alba 1993: Zesty, even a bit spritzy, tasting of freshly crushed grapes, raspberry, black cherry and earth flavors. Lean and quite crisp, but very lively. Ready to drink. • $NA • (10/31/96) • **83**

VIETTI

Barbaresco 1993: Fairly complex and lively flavors of smoky beef and black currant. Full-bodied and ripe, with sweet tannins that need time to come around. Try after 1999. 600 cases made. • $33 • (10/31/96) • **89**
Barbaresco 1985 • $28 • (07/31/89) • **81**
Barbaresco 1982 • $15 • (07/31/87) • **84**
Barbaresco Della Localita Rabajà 1986 • $18 • (10/31/90) • **87**
Barbaresco Masseria 1990 • $26 • (10/31/94) • **82**
Barbaresco Masseria 1989 • $34 • (10/31/93) • **84**
Barbaresco Masseria 1988 • $34 • (10/31/93) • **78**
Barbera d'Alba Pian Romualdo 1991 • $20 • (11/15/93) • **83**
Barbera d'Alba Pian Romualdo 1990 • $20 • (11/15/93) • **85**
Barbera d'Alba Pian Romualdo 1989 • $19 • (11/30/91) • **83**
Barbera d'Alba Pian Romualdo 1988 • $15 • (03/15/91) • **79**
Barbera d'Alba Scarrone 1995: An ambitious Barbera that doesn't quite carry it off. Medium-bodied. Dark in color, it offers hints of sophisticated oak treatment, but the aromas are a bit herbaceous, suggesting unripe fruit, and the finish turns a bit green. • $22 • (10/31/97) • **81**
Barbera d'Alba Scarrone 1992 • $15 • (10/31/94) • **85**
Barbera d'Alba Scarrone 1990 • $11 • (11/15/93) • **84**
Barbera d'Alba Scarrone 1989 • $13 • (03/15/91) • **85**
Barbera d'Alba Scarrone 1987 • $11 • (08/31/89) • **86**
Barolo 1991 • $30 • (10/31/95) • **84**
Barolo 1990 • $NA • (10/31/94) • **82**
Barolo 1978 • $12 • (09/16/84) • **84**
Barolo Brunate 1993: A beautifully balanced, ripe, lush wine that stays elegant, with well-defined flavors of wet earth, truffle, and red and blackberry. Medium-bodied. Nicely integrated, sweet tannins, but needs until around 2000 to 2002 to show it all. • $59 • (10/31/97) • **88**
Barolo Brunate 1990 • $37 • (10/31/94) • **79**
Barolo Brunate 1989 • $30 • (10/31/93) • **91**
Barolo Bussia 1982 • $20 • (09/15/87) • **89**
Barolo Castiglione 1993: Ripe and smooth, this is a sweet-tasting '93 that offers coffee, spice, meaty blackberry, and mineral complexity. Medium-bodied; very flavorful and enticing. Drink now through 2000. • $40 • (10/31/97) • **88**
Barolo Lazzarito 1993: mouthfeel in a traditional style, focusing on wet earth, bark, cherry, and nut flavors. Tannins are firm, but there is enough ripe, sweet fruit in this medium-bodied Barolo to suggest holding it until 2000 when it will be softer and more elegant. • $60 • (10/31/97) • **86**
Barolo Lazzarito 1990 • $37 • (10/31/94) • **85**
Barolo Rocche 1990 • $60 • (10/31/95) • **85**
Barolo Rocche 1989 • $40 • (10/31/94) • **83**
Barolo Rocche 1988 • $50 • (10/31/93) • **78**
Barolo Rocche 1982 • $45 • (07/31/89) • **85**
Barolo Rocche 1980 • $NA • (09/15/88) • **87**
Barolo Rocche 1979 • $NA • (09/15/88) • **79**
Barolo Rocche 1978 • $NA • (09/15/88) • **92**
Barolo Rocche 1971 • $NA • (09/15/88) • **86**
Barolo Rocche 1961 • $NA • (09/15/88) • **93**
Barolo Villero Riserva 1982 • $45 • (09/15/88) • **89**
Dolcetto d'Alba Bussia 1994 • $12 • (10/31/95) • **80**
Dolcetto d'Alba Bussia 1990 • $11 • (11/30/91) • **85**
Dolcetto d'Alba Bussia 1989 • $12 • (02/28/91) • **85**
Dolcetto d'Alba Disa 1988 • $12 • (09/15/90) • **87**
Dolcetto d'Alba Disa 1985 • $7 • (09/15/87) • **74**
Fioretto 1988 • $25 • (06/30/93) • **84**
Fioretto 1987 • $17 • (06/15/90) • **85**

VIGNA DEL CASSERO

Brunello di Montalcino Riserva 1990: Big and powerful, this has everything, but it's slightly overdone. Full-bodied, with full tannins and a dry finish. Needs time. Wait and see. Try after 2000. • $NA • (11/30/96) • **88**

VIGNA PICCOLA

Chianti Classico 1994: A good showing from a new name, this has alluring dried cherry and mineral components. Medium-bodied with light, silky tannins and a fruity finish. From Il Vescovino in Panzano. • $NA • (10/31/96) • **84**

VIGNA SENZA NOME

Moscato d'Asti 1991 • $18 • (05/15/93) • **79**

VIGNAIOLI DA SAN FLORIANO

Pinot Bianco Collio 1994 • $13 • (06/15/96) • **81**
Pinot Grigio Collio 1994 • $13 • (06/15/96) • **84**
Tocai Friulano Collio 1994 • $13 • (06/15/96) • **70**

VIGNALE, FATTORIA

Chianti Classico 1988 • $NA • (09/15/91) • **85**
Chianti Classico Riserva 1988 • $11 • (09/15/92) • **86**
Chianti Classico Riserva 1985 • $NA • (09/15/91) • **88**

Key: SS—Spectator Selection CS—Cellar Selection HR—Highly Recommended BB—Best Buy $NA—Price not available Ⓐ—Auction Price (BT)—Barrel Tasting
Dates in parentheses indicate the issues in which the ratings were published.

VIGNALE, IL

Amarone della Valpolicella Classico 1994: Pleasant and plummy, with firm tannins and pronounced acidity; the structure and alcohol on the finish dominate the modest fruit. Drink now through 2000. 500 cases made. • $20 • (07/31/98) • **83**

Gambellara Vigneti Monte Faldeo 1995: Shows some apple flavors, but contains more earth and straw notes combined with a leaner, racier structure. Slightly bitter on the finish. Drink now. 4,200 cases made. • $10 • (05/15/98) • **79**

Soave Classico 1997: A medium-bodied Soave with subtle almond and mineral aromas, rich texture and a hint of citrus-peel on the finish. Balanced and attractive. Drink now. 3,000 cases made. • $10 • (06/15/98) • **83**

Valpolicella Classico Superiore 1996: Offers light cherry and leather aromas and flavors, yet is basically austere and tannic. Drink through 1999. 900 cases made. • $10 • (07/31/98) • **79**

VIGNALTA

Cabernet Sauvignon Colli Euganei 1990 • $18 • (09/15/92) • **88**
Chardonnay Veneto 1994 • $17 • (06/15/96) • **82**
Colli Euganei Rosso 1994 • $14 • (05/31/96) • **85**
Colli Euganei Rosso 1993 • $14 • (05/31/96) • **87**
Gemola 1993 • $18 • (05/31/96) • **86**
Gemola 1991 • $18 • (05/31/96) • **89**
Gemola 1990 • $18 • (09/15/92) • **85**
Gemola 1988 • $22 • (09/30/91) • **81**
Merlot Veneto 1988 • $18 • (04/15/91) • **80**

Moscato Fior d'Arancio Apianae 1992: The raisin, honey and spice aromas leap out of the glass, but the flavors are more subdued. Good balance and a nutty, butterscotch finish resonates. 300 cases made. • $18/375ml • (01/01/97) • **87**

Moscato Fior d'Arancio Apianae 1991 • $22 • (01/31/95) • **76**
Moscato Fior d'Arancio Apianae 1990 • $24/375ml • (09/15/92) • **85**
Pinot Bianco Colli Euganei 1994 • $12 • (04/30/96) • **81**
Pinot Bianco Colli Euganei 1993 • $11 • (01/31/95) • **81**
Sirio 1994 • $12 • (05/31/96) • **82**
Sirio 1993 • $10 • (01/31/95) • **85**
Zingarello 1993 • $NA • (01/31/95) • **67**

VIGNAMAGGIO, FATTORIA DI

Chianti Classico 1995: Shows plenty of berry and cherry, and a hint of stem. Medium-bodied, with velvety tannins and a fresh finish. Slightly rustic. Drink now. 1,500 cases made. • $16 • (09/30/97) • **84**

Chianti Classico 1992 • $14 • (02/28/95) • **84**
Chianti Classico 1990 • $13 • (09/15/92) • **90**
Chianti Classico 1988 • $17 • (09/15/91) • **85**
Chianti Classico 1986 • $12 • (05/15/90) • **85**
Chianti Classico 1985 • $11 • (08/31/88) • **86**

Chianti Classico Castello di Mona Lisa Riserva 1994: Rather odd and disjointed, it's dark-colored and very young, with stemmy aromas and flavors. Medium body and tannins, with a rough, austere finish. Try now . 2,000 cases made. • $25 • (09/30/97) • **81**

Chianti Classico Castello di Mona Lisa Riserva 1993: Nicely crafted, with loads of spice, black cherry and chocolate flavors. Broad and lush with a ripe finish. Drink now. 2,800 cases made. • $24 • (03/31/97) • **86**

Chianti Classico Mona Lisa Riserva 1990 • $17 • (02/28/95) • **88**
Chianti Classico Mona Lisa Riserva 1988 • $16 • (10/31/94) HR • **91**
Chianti Classico Mona Lisa Riserva 1986 • $20 • (10/31/91) • **88**
Chianti Classico Mona Lisa Riserva 1985 • $17 • (09/15/91) • **89**
Chianti Classico Riserva 1985 • $17 • (09/15/91) • **81**
Chianti Classico Riserva 1983 • $14 • (05/15/90) • **85**

Chianti Classico Terre di Prenzano 1995: Plenty of fruit in this; some herbal, stemmy notes, too. Medium- to light-bodied, with light tannins, and a fresh finish. A bit rustic. Drink now. 900 cases made. • $12 • (09/30/97) • **82**

Gherardino 1993: A rich, autumnal wine with fruit and fresh mushroom aromas. It's medium-bodied, with fine tannins and a sweet, fruity finish. Delicious now or hold. 600 cases made. • $36 • (09/30/97) • **88**

Gherardino 1991 • $NA • (02/28/95) • **79**
Gherardino 1990 • $NA • (02/28/95) • **88**
Gherardino 1987 • $NA • (11/30/89) • **92**
Gherardino 1986 • $NA • (11/30/89) • **91**
Gherardino 1985 • $18 • (01/31/92) • **87**
Tuscany Red 1990 • $NA • (10/31/93) • **94**

Vignamaggio 1993: Inky-colored, with berry, pepper and slightly vegetal aromas. Medium-bodied, with refined tannins and a spicy herbal finish. Herbaceousness detracts overall. Drink now or hold. • $NA • (09/30/97) • **84**

VIGNAVECCHIA

Canvalle 1993: Interesting for its aromas and flavors of dried cherry and mushroom. Medium-bodied and tannic, with a slightly dry finish. A bit too austere. Try now. • $NA • (09/30/97) • **83**

Canvalle 1992 • $NA • (10/31/95) • **78**
Canvalle 1991 • $NA • (10/31/95) • **78**
Canvalle 1990 • $NA • (10/31/93) • **91**

Chianti Classico 1995: Has decent berry and mushroom character, a medium-to-light body, light tannins and a light finish. Drink now. • $NA • (09/30/97) • **80**

Chianti Classico 1993 • $NA • (10/31/95) • **74**
Chianti Classico 1991 • $NA • (10/31/93) • **79**
Chianti Classico 1990 • $12 • (10/31/93) • **74**
Chianti Classico 1988 • $11 • (10/31/91) • **83**
Chianti Classico Riserva 1991 • $NA • (10/31/95) • **76**
Chianti Classico Riserva 1990 • $NA • (02/28/95) • **78**
Raddese 1990 • $NA • (02/28/95) • **87**

Reddege 1993: A pleasant red with vanilla, leather, spice and fruit aromas and flavors. Medium-bodied, with firm tannins and acidity, and a slightly austere finish. Drink now. • $NA • (09/30/97) • **84**

VIGNE DAL LEON

Merlot 1989 • $15 • (05/31/96) • **85**
Pinot Bianco Colli Orientali del Friuli 1993 • $16 • (01/31/95) • **78**
Sauvignon Blanc Colli Orientali del Friuli 1993 • $16 • (01/31/95) • **84**
Tocai Friulano Colli Orientali del Friuli 1993 • $17 • (01/31/95) • **80**

VIGNOLE, TENUTA DI

Chianti Classico 1994: Fruity and simple. Medium- to light-bodied, with light tannins, a crushed berry character and a hint of earth on both the nose and palate. • $NA • (10/31/96) • **81**

Chianti Classico 1993 • $NA • (10/31/95) • **83**
Chianti Classico 1992 • $NA • (02/28/95) • **82**
Chianti Classico 1990 • $NA • (10/31/93) • **85**
Chianti Classico 1988 • $NA • (09/15/91) • **90**

VILLA ABA

Cabernet Sauvignon Grave del Friuli 1995: A robust, medium-bodied red showing black cherry and herbal notes. Balanced, if a bit rustic, with some astringency on the finish. Drink now. • $12 • (04/30/98) • **82**

Chardonnay Grave del Friuli 1996: Floral and citrus, especially grapefruit, are the dominant themes. Soft, straightforward, not much varietal character. • $12 • (12/15/97) • **79**

Merlot Grave del Friuli 1995: Smells like coffee grounds, and there's a hint of coffee on the palate, too. Moderate concentration; cherries fill out the flavor spectrum. • $12 • (12/15/97) • **82**

Pinot Bianco Grave del Friuli 1996: Starts out austere, showing marzipan character that turns dull and plodding on the palate. • $12 • (11/15/97) • **78**

Pinot Grigio Grave del Friuli 1996: Here's a lovely, fresh, floral, apple- and citrus-flavored version, with an herbal note and a mouthwatering finish. Straightforward and quaffable. • $12 • (11/15/97) • **85**

Ribolla Gialla Colli Orientali del Friuli 1996: A soft, medium-bodied white with floral and white peach character. A grapefruit-peel note at the end refreshes the palate and suggests pairing with seafood or light chicken dishes. Drink now. • $15 • (04/30/98) • **83**

Schioppettino Grave del Friuli 1994: A deep-colored red showing loads of spicy berry character and an intriguing, grainy texture. Everything is there in the right proportions. Try this for something different. Drink now. • $26 • (04/30/98) • **87**

VILLA ARCENO

Chianti Classico 1990 • $NA • (10/31/93) • **83**

VILLA BOSCOROTONDO

Chianti Classico 1993: Mature and ready to drink, offering spicy cherry aromas and flavors and a lively texture. 5,000 cases made. • $8 • (10/31/96) • **81**
Chianti Classico 1990 • $NA • (09/15/92) • **81**

VILLA BUONASERA

Chianti Classico 1993 • $NA • (10/31/95) • **78**
Chianti Classico Riserva 1991 • $NA • (10/31/95) • **69**

VILLA CAFAGGIO

Chianti Classico 1995: Good. Offers simple berry and plum aromas and flavors, medium body, light tannins and a fresh finish. 14,000 cases made. • $15 • (09/30/97) • **83**
Chianti Classico 1994: Simple and fresh, with dried cherry and berry aromas and flavors. Medium- to light-bodied with light tannins. Nice served chilled. 7,000 cases made. • $15 • (10/31/96) • **81**
Chianti Classico 1993 • $9 • (10/31/95) • **82**
Chianti Classico 1990 • $14 • (10/31/93) • **82**
Chianti Classico 1989 • $13 • (09/15/92) • **84**
Chianti Classico 1988 • $10 • (11/30/90) • **83**
Chianti Classico 1987 • $9 • (09/15/89) • **86**
Chianti Classico 1986 • $9 • (03/31/90) • **89**
Chianti Classico 1985 • $8 • (05/31/88) • **84**
Chianti Classico 1983 • $11 • (09/15/87) • **91**
Chianti Classico Riserva 1994: Lively. Medium-bodied, showing pretty blackberry and chocolate character, light tannins and a fresh finish. Drink now or hold. 1,800 cases made. • $27 • (09/30/97) • **87**
Chianti Classico Riserva 1993: A riserva with a pretty plum and watermelon character. Medium- to light-bodied, with light tannins and a fresh finish. • $NA • (10/31/96) • **80**
Chianti Classico Riserva 1990 • $17 • (02/28/95) • **87**
Chianti Classico Riserva 1988 • $18 • (09/15/92) • **91**
Chianti Classico Riserva 1986 • $18 • (12/15/90) • **86**
Chianti Classico Riserva 1985 • $13 • (09/15/91) • **91**
Chianti Classico Riserva 1983 • $10 • (05/31/88) • **80**
Cortaccio 1994: Elegant and refined. Medium-bodied, with berry, currant and toasty oak aromas and flavors, fine tannins and a silky finish. Try now. 500 cases made. • $46 • (09/30/97) • **88**
Cortaccio 1993: An absolute beauty. Dark-colored, with complex aromas of mint, berry, cherry and currants that follow through onto the palate. Full-bodied yet wonderfully balanced, with fine, velvety tannins and a long, long aftertaste. Delicious now but will improve into the new century. Made from Cabernet Sauvignon. 300 cases made. • $40 • (03/31/97) • **90**
Cortaccio 1990 • $32 • (10/31/93) • **91**
San Martino 1994: Delicious. Beautiful berry and dark chocolate aromas and flavors flow from this medium-bodied wine. The tannins are fine, and notes of chocolate persist on the finish. Drink now. 800 cases made. • $41 • (09/30/97) • **88**
San Martino 1993: Wonderful aromas of flowers, berries and mint, with a similar character on the palate and fine, silky tannins. Medium-bodied. Try now. Sangiovese. • $30 • (10/31/96) • **88**
San Martino 1990 • $31 • (10/31/93) • **89**
San Martino 1985 • $20 • (09/30/89) • **79**
Solatio Basilica 1990 • $32 • (10/31/93) • **87**
Solatio Basilica 1985 • $20 • (08/31/91) • **83**

VILLA CALCINAIA

Chianti Classico 1992 • $8 • (02/28/95) • **73**
Chianti Classico 1988 • $12 • (09/15/91) • **89**
Chianti Classico Riserva 1993: Light-bodied, with light, yet firm, silky tannins and a fresh finish. Pretty aromas of tea-leaves and berries. Drink now or hold. • $NA • (09/30/97) • **83**
Chianti Classico Riserva 1990 • $NA • (02/28/95) • **84**
Chianti Colli Senesi Geminiano 1994 • $NA • (10/31/95) • **81**
Teodoro 1993 • $NA • (10/31/95) • **80**

Key: SS—Spectator Selection CS—Cellar Selection HR—Highly Recommended BB—Best Buy $NA—Price not available Ⓐ—Auction Price (BT)—Barrel Tasting
Dates in parentheses indicate the issues in which the ratings were published.

VILLA CAPODILISTA

Colli Euganei Rosso 1996: Fresh, with cherry and herb flavors, a lean framework and firm tannins. Well-balanced, but better with food. A blend of 60 percent Merlot and 40 percent Cabernet Sauvignon. Drink through 1999. 20,000 cases made. • $9 • (06/30/98) • **82**
Merlot Colli Euganei 1996: Straightforward, showing good cherry and licorice notes and a chewy texture, it ends up on the rustic side, but has character. Drink through 1999. 5,000 cases made. • $17 • (06/30/98) • **83**

VILLA CARRA

Frascati Superiore 1995: Dull and flat-tasting, with only modest lemony flavors. • $9 • (10/31/97) • **75**

VILLA CERNA

Chianti Classico 1990 • $NA • (09/15/92) • **89**
Chianti Classico 1988 • $9 • (09/15/91) • **89**
Chianti Classico Riserva 1994: Well-crafted, with its balance of berry, cherry character and fine tannins. Medium-bodied and fresh on the finish. Drink now or hold for a few years. • $NA • (09/30/97) • **86**
Chianti Classico Riserva 1991 • $19 • (10/31/95) • **79**
Chianti Classico Riserva 1988 • $NA • (09/15/92) • **88**
Chianti Classico Riserva 1985 • $16 • (09/15/91) • **87**
Chianti Classico Riserva 1983 • $8 • (03/31/89) BB • **84**
Vigneto La Gavina 1988 • $NA • (09/15/91) • **91**

VILLA CERVIA

Montepulciano d'Abruzzo 1995: A big, hearty, full-bodied red that integrates ripe cherry and blackberry flavors with a firmly tannic texture and intriguing spicy accents. Drink now through 2000. 30,000 cases made. • $6 • (01/01/98) • **85**
Montepulciano d'Abruzzo 1993 • $4 • (02/29/96) • **84**
Montepulciano d'Abruzzo 1992 • $4 • (03/31/95) BB • **84**

VILLA CILNIA

Chianti Colli Aretini 1990 • $10 • (01/31/92) • **86**
Chianti Colli Aretini 1989 • $10 • (04/30/91) • **85**
Chianti Colli Aretini 1988 • $10 • (04/15/91) • **89**
Chianti Colli Aretini 1987 • $8 • (10/15/89) • **76**
Chianti Colli Aretini 1986 • $9 • (05/31/89) BB • **87**
Chianti Colli Aretini Riserva 1986 • $18 • (10/31/91) • **76**
Le Vignacce 1988 • $24 • (09/15/91) • **89**
Le Vignacce 1986 • $19 • (11/30/89) • **90**
Le Vignacce 1985 • $20 • (07/15/89) • **88**
Vocato 1986 • $11 • (05/15/89) • **86**

VILLA DAL FERRO

Colli Berici La Rive Rosse 1989 • $NA • (09/15/92) • **73**

VILLA DE MONTE

Chianti Rufina Riserva 1985 • $13 • (04/30/92) • **80**
Chianti Rufina Riserva 1979 • $16 • (04/30/92) • **81**

VILLA DEI LECCHI

Brunello di Montalcino 1991: Good fruit flavor, but a little dry on the cedar- and berry-accented finish. Medium-bodied, with light, dry tannins. Drink now. • $NA • (11/30/96) • **79**
Brunello di Montalcino Riserva 1990: In a traditional style. Shows some pretty, ripe fruit flavors, but slightly austere and drying. Medium-bodied, with high acidity. A cedary, roasted nut note on the finish. Drink now. • $NA • (11/30/96) • **83**
Rosso di Montalcino 1995: A plummy, easy Rosso that caresses and refreshes the palate. Medium in body and soft in texture. • $18 • (09/30/97) • **85**
Rosso di Montalcino 1994: Fresh and fruity, with an attractive berry, dried cherry and dried herb character. Light-bodied, with light tannins and a crisp finish. A little too light. • $NA • (11/30/96) • **79**

Vigna di Bellaria 1993: A good red wine. Pretty, complex aromas and flavors of spice, berry, mint and flowers; similar character on the palate. Drink now. • $NA • (10/31/96) • **84**

VILLA DEL BORGO

Cabernet Sauvignon Grave del Friuli 1996: Assertive aromas of cherry candy, vanilla and earth carry through on the palate to a decent finish. Light and quaffable. Drink now. • $7 • (07/31/98) • **82**
Chardonnay 1993 • $8 • (01/31/95) • **74**
Merlot Grave del Friuli 1997: Light-bodied and straightforward, with a touch of earthiness adding dimension to the plum and spice. Some may find it too earthy. Drink now. • $7 • (07/31/98) • **80**
Pinot Grigio Grave del Friuli 1997: Shy aromas. The flavors are peachlike, and there's body, though this young white is straightforward and a touch earthy. Drink now. • $7 • (07/31/98) • **80**
Pinot Grigio 1993 • $8 • (01/31/95) • **79**
Sauvignon Grave del Friuli 1997: Good Sauvignon character, with the grassy, citrusy elements of the Loire and the richness, though not the assertiveness, of New Zealand. If only it had a little more concentration. Finishes short. Drink now. • $7 • (07/31/98) • **83**

VILLA DI VETRICE

Chianti Classico 1991 • $8 • (10/31/93) • **75**

VILLA FIORE

Pinot Grigio Veneto 1993 • $4 • (04/30/96) • **76**

VILLA FRATTINA

Vigneto Quartarezza Lison-Pramaggiore 1993 • $10 • (10/31/94) • **83**

VILLA IL POGGIOLO

Brunello di Montalcino Sassello 1990: Impressive tobacco, berry and toasty oak character. Full body and round, with fine tannins and slightly dry finish. A bit too much wood. Drinkable now. • $NA • (10/31/95) • **86**
Carmignano Riserva 1985 • $16 • (05/15/90) • **80**

VILLA LA PAGLIAIA

Chianti Classico 1991 • $NA • (10/31/93) • **86**

VILLA LA SELVA

Felciaia 1994: Light, fresh and fruity with plum, berry and delicate earthlike aromas and flavors. 4,000 cases made. • $24 • (09/30/97) • **82**
Felciaia 1993: Smooth and well-rounded. Marked by a silky texture, it's flavorful and elegant, with roasted aromas, good chocolate, plum and cherry flavors and a spicy finish. • $23 • (01/31/97) • **88**
Fiore di Luna 1993: Smells and tastes like a sweet Vin Santo with burnt almond, orange-peel and a hint of honey on nose and palate. Medium-bodied and moderately sweet, with a lively, sweet fruit and almond finish. Drink now. 800 cases made. • $36 • (09/30/97) • **85**
Selvamaggio 1993: Deep, dark ruby in color, with intense berry and violet aromas. Full-bodied and very silky, it has fine tannins and a long finish. Wonderful balance. Drinkable now. 3,300 cases made. • $25 • (09/30/97) • **89**
Selvamaggio 1992: A dark, fruity wine with plenty of berry and cherry flavors, black pepper and spice notes. Reminiscent of Zinfandel. Still lively for its age. Drink now. • $25 • (01/31/97) • **86**
Vin Santo 1993: Cheesy, funky and woody, with a hint of honey, this is medium-bodied, sweet-tasting, and has a barky, woody, honeyed finish. Good traditional VS. 2,000 cases made. • $23 • (09/30/97) • **84**

VILLA MAISANO

Chianti Classico 1995: Clean, fresh fruit flavors, with light body and a crisp, slightly tart finish. Serve chilled. • $14 • (09/30/97) • **80**
Chianti Classico Riserva 1994: Shows spicy berry flavor, but it's rather diluted and sharp on the palate. Not much to it. • $21 • (09/30/97) • **76**

VILLA MONTE RICO

Tuscany Red 1994: Slightly lean, it has a pleasant character of dried cherry and mushroom. Medium-to-light in body, with light tannins and a short finish. Drink now. • $NA • (09/30/97) • **80**
Tuscany White 1995: This slightly unbalanced white emits interesting honey, almond and honeysuckle aromas, is of medium body, and has medium acidity and a toasty oak finish. • $NA • (09/30/97) • **83**

VILLA MONTERSINO

Barolo 1988 • $20 • (12/15/92) • **88**

VILLA NICOLA

Brunello di Montalcino 1985 • $32 • (11/30/90) HR • **91**
Brunello di Montalcino Riserva 1981 • $14 • (09/15/88) • **75**
Rosso di Montalcino 1988 • $15 • (01/31/91) • **89**

VILLA PIGNA

Rozzano 1990 • $13 • (05/31/95) • **87**
Vellutato 1990 • $7 • (05/31/95) • **85**

VILLA PILLO

Chardonnay Toscana 1996: A rather light-bodied Chardonnay, with smoky aromas and milky, appley flavors. Drink now. • $13 • (10/31/97) • **82**
Chardonnay Toscana 1995: A ripe style, reminiscent of California Chardonnay. Nice pear and honey flavors with plenty of spice notes. Smooth finish. 500 cases made. • $10 • (01/31/97) • **84**
Merlot Toscana 1995: An exuberant but polished young Merlot with lots of fresh cherry and raspberry flavors accented by spicy oak, and a wonderfully smooth texture. Best through 1999. 650 cases made. • $15 • (10/31/97) • **88**
Syrah Toscana 1995: A firm-textured, gutsy and appealing Syrah with the typically smoky, peppery, blackberry flavors of many Côtes du Rhônes, with good concentration. Best through 1999. 500 cases made. • $13 • (10/31/97) • **87**
Toscana Borgoforte 1995: A light red with pleasant strawberry and herb flavors and little tannin. Drink now. A blend of Sangiovese, Cabernet and Merlot. 8,000 cases made. • $12 • (10/31/97) • **81**
Toscana Borgoforte 1994: A strong oak flavor pervades this deep-colored, firm-textured wine, dominating its herbal, plummy flavors. A blend of Sangiovese, Cabernet and Merlot. 8,000 cases made. • $10 • (10/31/96) • **82**
Toscana Vivaldaia 1995: Lots of fresh, snappy fruit flavor and modest tannins make this an appealing and well-balanced wine. Medium-bodied. Drink now. 600 cases made. • $17 • (10/31/97) • **85**
Vin Santo 1991: What's not to like about this luscious sweet dessert wine? It has oodles of flavor—butterscotch, toasty almond, honey—plus fine balance and a long, lingering finish. 150 cases made. • $17/375ml • (10/31/97) • **90**

VILLA ROCCA

Amarone della Valpolicella Classico 1989 • $10 • (11/15/94) • **78**

VILLA RUSSIZ

Cabernet Franc Collio 1986 • $15 • (09/15/88) • **83**
Merlot Collio 1989 • $27 • (04/30/92) • **86**
Merlot Collio 1986 • $14 • (09/15/88) • **80**
Pinot Bianco Collio 1996: Loaded with clover honey, apple and almond character that remains vibrant and balanced. The honey note lingers on the finish. Drink through 1999. 250 cases made. • $20 • (06/15/98) • **86**
Pinot Bianco Collio 1993 • $18 • (01/31/95) • **83**
Pinot Grigio Collio 1993 • $18 • (01/31/95) • **80**
Sauvignon Collio 1994 • $19 • (06/15/96) • **85**
Sauvignon Collio 1993 • $18 • (01/31/95) • **86**
Tocai Friulano Collio 1996: Delicious. Smells and tastes like a freshly cut apple, accented by an earthy straw note, all married to a rich yet succulent texture. Drink now. 250 cases made. • $20 • (06/15/98) • **85**
Tocai Friulano Collio 1993 • $18 • (01/31/95) • **83**
Verduzzo 1987 • $NA • (09/15/88) • **76**

VILLA S. ANNA

Vino Nobile di Montepulciano 1994: Exhibits loads of toasty oak which slightly dominates the fruit. Medium-bodied, with strawberry flavors and a vanilla finish. Drink now. 1,250 cases made. • $20 • (09/30/97) • **82**

VILLA SANDI

Cabernet Sauvignon Piave 1996: A softly-textured, berry-flavored red, with bright acidity and a hint of bitter almond on the finish. Drink now. • $NA • (06/30/98) • **82**
Merlot Piave 1996: A solid Merlot, with black cherry and plum notes and a hint of herb, all on a medium-bodied structure. Sinewy tannins emerge on the finish. Drink now through 2000. • $8 • (07/31/98) • **84**
Pinot Grigio Piave 1997: A filigree white, with a translucent texture supporting the peachy, nutty, minerally flavors. Piquant acidity keeps it lively and focused. Drink now. • $8 • (07/31/98) • **84**
Veneto Rosso 1995: An austere, tobacco- and cedar-flavored red, this has a lean, sinewy structure and needs food to tame the stiff tannins. A blend of Cabernet Sauvignon and Cabernet Franc. Drink now through 2000. • $12 • (07/31/98) • **83**

VILLA VITTORIA

Chianti 1994: A refreshingly crisp, straightforward wine that's slightly tannic and nicely fruity. Easy to enjoy. 22,000 cases made. • $6 • (10/31/96) • **83**
Valpolicella 1995: An attempt at a serious style, but not quite there. Tannic, with plum and tealike flavors. 8,300 cases made. • $5 • (01/31/97) • **76**

VILLA ZINGALE

Chianti Riserva 1988 • $8 • (04/30/92) • **77**

VILLADORIA

Barbera d'Alba Superiore 1992 • $NA • (10/31/95) • **82**
Barolo 1993: An interesting wine, with basil, tomato and meat sauce flavors along with the fairly sweet fruit and spice notes. Medium in body, it's quite rough and rustic on the finish. Best from 1999 through 2000. • $21 • (10/31/97) • **79**
Barolo 1991 • $NA • (10/31/95) • **86**
Barolo Riserva 1988 • $NA • (10/31/95) • **85**
Barolo Riserva Spéciale 1978 • $14 • (08/31/86) • **73**

VILLALTA

Amarone della Valpolicella Classico 1988 • $18 • (09/30/95) • **80**
Amarone della Valpolicella Classico I Communali 1991: Deep, concentrated kirsch flavors are buoyed on a firm, tannic texture. Drink now for the fruit character, or wait for the transformation into more tobaccolike, nutty flavors. 500 cases made. • $25 • (06/15/97) • **87**

VINATTIERRI

Rosso 1986 • $18 • (08/31/91) • **83**
Rosso 1985 • $NA • (09/15/87) • **91**
Rosso 1983 • $14 • (09/15/87) • **84**
Rosso II 1986 • $18 • (08/31/91) • **84**

VISTARENNI

Chianti Classico 1995: Light, with leather and berry character, but very diluted on the finish. • $12 • (09/30/97) • **76**
Chianti Classico 1992 • $NA • (02/28/95) • **80**
Chianti Classico 1991 • $11 • (10/31/93) • **75**
Chianti Classico 1990 • $NA • (09/15/92) • **83**
Chianti Classico 1988 • $11 • (09/15/91) • **86**
Chianti Classico 1987 • $10 • (10/15/89) • **89**
Chianti Classico 1986 • $18 • (07/31/89) • **78**

Key: SS—Spectator Selection CS—Cellar Selection HR—Highly Recommended BB—Best Buy $NA—Price not available Ⓐ—Auction Price (BT)—Barrel Tasting
Dates in parentheses indicate the issues in which the ratings were published.

Chianti Classico Riserva 1990 • $NA • (02/28/95) • **87**
Chianti Classico Riserva 1985 • $NA • (09/15/91) • **81**
Chianti Classico Vigneto Assòlo 1990 • $18 • (09/15/92) • **88**
Chianti Classico Vigneto Assòlo 1988 • $16 • (09/15/91) • **78**
Chianti Classico Villa Vistarenni Riserva 1993: A bit simple. Has dried cherry character, medium-to-light body and a light finish. Drink now. • $16 • (09/30/97) • **80**
Codirosso 1993: Medium-bodied, with nice plum, earth and berry character and fine tannins. Delicious, sweet fruit finish. Drink now or hold. • $24 • (09/30/97) • **89**
Codirosso 1990 • $NA • (02/28/95) • **87**
Codirosso 1986 • $22 • (11/30/89) • **90**

VITICCIO

Chianti Classico 1995: A bright, fruity red with black cherry aromas and flavors, medium-to-light body, light tannins and a fresh finish. Drink now. 10,000 cases made. • $11 • (09/30/97) • **84**
Chianti Classico 1993 • $10 • (10/31/95) • **80**
Chianti Classico 1991 • $10 • (10/31/93) • **83**
Chianti Classico 1990 • $11 • (09/15/92) SS • **90**
Chianti Classico 1988 • $10 • (04/30/92) • **81**
Chianti Classico 1987 • $9 • (04/30/90) • **78**
Chianti Classico 1986 • $8 • (03/31/89) BB • **88**
Chianti Classico 1984 • $5 • (11/15/87) • **74**
Chianti Classico Riserva 1993: Pretty black cherry and plum aromas and flavors, with a fresh mushroom accent. Medium-bodied with soft tannins and a delicious, long finish. 2,417 cases made. • $20 • (10/31/96) • **86**
Chianti Classico Riserva 1991 • $16 • (10/31/95) • **85**
Chianti Classico Riserva 1990 • $NA • (02/28/95) • **87**
Chianti Classico Riserva 1988 • $15 • (09/15/92) • **88**
Chianti Classico Riserva 1985 • $11 • (11/30/89) • **85**
Chianti Classico Riserva 1983 • $12 • (11/30/89) • **80**
Chianti Classico Viticcio Riserva 1983 • $8 • (11/15/87) • **77**
Chianti Classico Viticcio Riserva 1982 • $8 • (11/15/87) • **84**
Chianti Classico Viticcio Riserva 1978 • $13 • (11/30/87) • **78**
Chianti Classico Viticcio Riserva 1975 • $14 • (11/15/87) • **71**
Monile 1994: Cassis and berry aromas jump out of the glass. Medium- to full-bodied, with well-integrated tannins and a medium, silky finish. Drinkable now. 500 cases made. • $40 • (09/30/97) • **88**
Monile 1993: A pretty wine with a berry and floral character and a generous accent of cut wood. Medium-bodied, with fine tannins and a short, slightly dry finish. A little too much new wood? Drink now. 1,250 cases made. • $40 • (10/31/96) • **82**
Monile 1991 • $33 • (02/28/95) • **90**
Prunaio 1994: Slightly one-dimensional with its dried cherry character and a hint of earth. Medium- to light-bodied, slightly stemmy on the finish. Drink now. 750 cases made. • $35 • (09/30/97) • **84**
Prunaio 1993: A jammy, rich wine with plummy, smoky aromas and flavors. Medium- to full-bodied, with soft tannins and a sweet fruit finish. Good concentration, but slightly one-dimensional. Try now. 1,833 cases made. • $38 • (10/31/96) • **87**
Prunaio 1990 • $34 • (10/31/93) • **90**
Prunaio 1988 • $28 • (03/31/92) • **88**
Prunaio 1986 • $19 • (03/31/90) SS • **92**
Prunaio 1985 • $18 • (04/30/89) • **88**

VITIGLIANO

Chianti Classico 1995: All on the nose in this one; gorgeous crushed blackberries and strawberries. Medium-bodied, with light tannins and a fresh finish. • $NA • (09/30/97) • **84**
Chianti Classico 1991 • $9 • (10/31/93) • **86**
Chianti Classico La Casina del Diavolo Riserva 1994: Some good fruit, but slightly dry on the palate due to wood maturation. Medium-bodied, with firm tannins and a short finish. Tasted twice, with consistent notes. • $NA • (09/30/97) • **81**

VOERZIO, GIANNI

Barolo La Serra 1991 • $NA • (10/31/95) • **86**
Dolcetto d'Alba Ciabòt della Luna 1995: Medium-bodied, with an abundance of fresh fruit aromas and flavors, black currant accents and ripe tannins. Silky and seductive from start to lingering finish. Try now. • $NA • (10/31/96) • **88**
Dolcetto d'Alba Ciabòt della Luna 1994 • $NA • (10/31/95) • **84**

VOERZIO, ROBERTO

Barolo 1985 • $18 • (01/31/90) • **87**
Barolo 1983 • $15 • (09/15/88) • **88**
Barolo 1982 • $12 • (09/15/88) • **90**
Barolo Brunate 1992: Rich, with ample fruit and spicy oak flavors. More complexity than many 1992s, though still quite tannic. Drinkable now. • $30 • (10/31/96) • **81**
Barolo Cerequio 1991: Soft and supple, with good plum and cherry flavors, and a nice leathery note mixed in. Fully mature and ready to drink. • $48 • (06/30/97) • **84**
Barolo La Serra 1991 • $NA • (10/31/95) • **85**
Barolo La Serra di La Morra 1982 • $12 • (07/31/87) • **91**
Dolcetto d'Alba 1990 • $12 • (01/31/92) • **82**
Dolcetto d'Alba Pria S. Francesco Croera 1994 • $NA • (10/31/95) • **86**
Dolcetto d'Alba Pria S. Francesco Croera 1991 • $12 • (10/31/92) • **81**
Dolcetto d'Alba Priavino 1990 • $14 • (12/15/92) • **86**
Dolcetto d'Alba Priavino 1988 • $11 • (12/31/90) • **87**
Nebbiolo delle Langhe Croera Fossati 1990 • $13 • (10/31/92) • **80**
Vignaserra 1988 • $24 • (03/31/92) • **85**
Vignaserra 1987 • $18 • (08/31/91) • **85**

VOLPAIA, CASTELLO DI

Balifico 1994: Wonderful aromas of flowers, dried cherries and a hint of spice precede a medium-bodied, silky mouthful of berry and cherry flavors. Long finish. Delicious now. 1,650 cases made. • $30 • (09/30/97) • **87**
Balifico 1993: All finesse and class. Interesting aromas of berries, mushrooms and flowers. Medium-bodied, with ultra-fine tannins and a long, sweet fruit finish. Drink now or hold. A blend of Sangioveto and Cabernet Sauvignon. 1,050 cases made. • $30 • (10/31/96) • **90**
Balifico 1991 • $26 • (10/31/95) • **83**
Balifico 1987 • $25 • (12/15/92) • **80**
Balifico 1986 • $19 • (04/30/89) • **83**
Balifico 1985 • $21 • (11/30/89) • **91**
Chianti Borgianni 1992 • $8 • (07/31/95) • **81**
Chianti Classico 1995: Has dried cherry aromas tinged with tobacco and leather, medium body, light tannins and a crisp finish. Rather old-style. 9,150 cases made. • $15 • (09/30/97) • **79**
Chianti Classico 1994: A delicious Chianti with dried cherry and lemon-peel aromas and flavors and a fresh, fruity finish. 3,850 cases made. • $15 • (10/31/96) • **83**
Chianti Classico 1993 • $11 • (10/31/95) • **84**
Chianti Classico 1992 • $10 • (02/28/95) • **76**
Chianti Classico 1991 • $11 • (10/31/93) • **80**
Chianti Classico 1990 • $16 • (09/15/92) • **88**
Chianti Classico 1989 • $12 • (09/15/92) • **79**
Chianti Classico 1988 • $14 • (09/15/91) • **85**
Chianti Classico 1987 • $16 • (11/30/89) • **85**
Chianti Classico 1986 • $10 • (03/31/90) • **75**
Chianti Classico 1985 • $10 • (06/30/89) SS • **90**
Chianti Classico 1983 • $8 • (09/15/87) • **88**
Chianti Classico Riserva 1994: Delicate and fruity, with hints of earth and mushroom. Light- to medium-bodied, with light tannins and a fresh finish. Drink now. Tasted twice, with consistent notes. 5,000 cases made. • $19 • (09/30/97) • **82**
Chianti Classico Riserva 1993: A simple, fresh Riserva with dried cherry and floral aromas and flavors, medium-to-light body and a light finish. 8,225 cases made. • $20 • (10/31/96) • **82**
Chianti Classico Riserva 1991 • $14 • (10/31/95) • **84**
Chianti Classico Riserva 1990 • $14 • (02/28/95) • **86**
Chianti Classico Riserva 1988 • $22 • (09/15/92) • **81**
Chianti Classico Riserva 1987 • $14 • (09/15/92) • **84**
Chianti Classico Riserva 1985 • $13 • (09/15/91) • **84**
Chianti Classico Riserva 1983 • $12 • (05/31/89) • **87**
Chianti Classico Riserva 1982 • $11 • (09/15/87) • **84**
Chianti Classico Riserva 1981 • $NA • (09/15/87) • **86**
Chianti Classico Riserva 1977 • $NA • (09/15/87) • **81**
Chianti Classico Riserva 1970 • $NA • (09/15/87) • **85**
Coltassala 1994: A silky, delicious red with plum and a hint of cedar on the nose and palate. Medium-bodied, with fine tannins and a crisp finish. Drink now. 1,600 cases made. • $30 • (09/30/97) • **87**
Coltassala 1993: A racy Sangiovese with floral, berry and mint aromas and flavors. Medium-bodied, with fine tannins and a silky finish. Try now. A blend of 95 percent Sangiovese and 5 percent Mammolo. 1,125 cases made. • $30 • (10/31/96) • **87**
Coltassala 1991 • $26 • (10/31/95) • **83**
Coltassala 1990 • $26 • (11/30/94) SS • **92**
Coltassala 1988 • $NA • (11/15/93) • **89**
Coltassala 1987 • $NA • (11/15/93) • **86**
Coltassala 1986 • $NA • (11/15/93) • **87**
Coltassala 1985 • $NA • (11/15/93) • **90**
Coltassala 1983 • $22 • (09/15/88) • **86**
Coltassala 1982 • $NA • (11/15/93) • **90**
Coltassala 1981 • $NA • (09/15/87) • **90**
Torniello 1995: Marked by almond and ripe fruit flavors. Medium-bodied, with grassy nuances and a slightly tart finish. 580 cases made. • $16 • (09/30/97) • **81**
Torniello 1994: Yellow-gold in color, with ripe fruit aromas. Medium-bodied and quite thick, with light acidity and an apricot finish. A bit overdone, but delicious. 580 cases made. • $16 • (09/30/97) • **82**
Val d'Arbia 1996: Not much to this white: some citrus character and a bit of ash but light, simple and clean on the finish. 580 cases made. • $10 • (09/30/97) • **80**

VOLPE PASINI

Pinot Bianco Colli Orientali del Friuli Zuc di Volpe 1996: A distinctive earthy character overshadows the modest peach aromas and flavors in this light-bodied, balanced white. Drink now. • $17 • (05/31/98) • **79**
Pinot Grigio Colli Orientali del Friuli Zuc di Volpe 1996: Peach and apple character takes on an almond note at the finish, giving this bright Pinot Grigio some complexity in addition to the rich texture and solid framework. Drink now. • $16 • (05/31/98) • **84**
Ribolla Colli Orientali del Friuli Zuc di Volpe 1996: A delicate white. Floral and citrus flavors play off the balancing acidity nicely. A subtle presentation, easily overwhelmed by food. Drink now. • $16 • (05/31/98) • **82**
Tocai Friulano Colli Orientali del Friuli Zuc di Volpe 1996: A good expression of apple, lemon and mineral notes on a lively framework. It has concentration and a mouthwatering finish, so try as an apéritif. Drink now. • $16 • (05/31/98) • **83**

ZAMÒ & PALAZZOLO

Chardonnay Colli Orientali del Friuli 1994: Seductive and smoky, with a range of spice notes to complement the apple and citrus flavors. Balanced, and the flavors persist on the finish. • $12 • (06/15/97) • **86**
Chardonnay Colli Orientali del Friuli 1993 • $15 • (01/31/95) • **81**
Merlot Colli Orientali del Friuli 1994: Bright cassis and vanilla aromas greet the senses in this medium-weight wine. Lively acidity and modest tannins suggest pairing with light dishes. • $8 • (06/15/97) • **83**
Merlot Colli Orientali del Friuli 1993 • $16 • (02/29/96) • **84**
Pinot Grigio Colli Orientali del Friuli 1994: Exhibits maturity and some red berry character in addition to the marzipan and apple flavors. Ready to drink. • $17 • (06/15/97) • **84**
Pinot Grigio Colli Orientali del Friuli 1993 • $15 • (01/31/95) • **76**
Sauvignon Colli Orientali del Friuli 1994: A full-bodied, textural white exhibiting ripe apple, pear and almost a red fruit character. The firm finish keeps it in balance. Rich enough to pair with food. • $NA • (01/01/97) • **86**
Tocai Friulano Colli Orientali del Friuli 1994 • $17 • (06/15/96) • **82**
Tocai Friulano Colli Orientali del Friuli 1993 • $15 • (01/31/95) • **81**

ZARDETTO

Brut Prosecco di Conegliano NV: Light and bubbly, with modest earth and apple flavors. Drink now. 50,000 cases made. • $12 • (07/31/98) • **78**

ZEMMER, PETER

Chardonnay Alto Adige 1993 • $10 • (01/31/95) • **76**
Gewürztraminer Alto Adige 1997: Rose-petal and litchi aromas are here, as are pronounced mineral and herb elements, lending elegance to the rich texture and lingering flavors. Bitter grapefruit finish, with a lingering note of roses. Drink now. • $13 • (07/31/98) • **85**
Gewürztraminer Alto Adige 1995 • $10 • (06/15/96) • **84**
Gewürztraminer Alto Adige 1993 • $12 • (01/31/95) • **79**
Lagrein Dunkel Alto Adige 1995: Plenty of acidity and tannins in this lean, medium-bodied red, with tobacco, plum and cedar flavors and an intensity that pulses through the finish. Drink through 1999. • $12 • (07/31/98) • **83**

Merlot Alto Adige 1995: Good depth and concentration of cherry, plum and spice in this bright, focused Merlot. The components are in balance and the plum notes resonate on the finish. Drink through 1999. • $12 • (07/31/98) • **85**
Pinot Grigio Alto Adige 1997: Nutty, leesy aromas segue into almond, quince and stone flavors. Good body and intensity. May just need time to soften up. Drink through 1999. • $10 • (07/31/98) • **83**
Pinot Grigio Alto Adige 1995 • $10 • (06/15/96) BB • **87**
Pinot Grigio Alto Adige 1993 • $10 • (01/31/95) • **79**
Sauvignon Alto Adige 1993 • $NA • (01/31/95) • **81**

ZENATO

Amarone della Valpolicella Classico 1990: Already displaying some of the exotic, spicy, nutty characteristics typical of maturing Amarone, yet there's freshness, great balance and depth. Very complex and inviting. Drinkable now, but hold if you like more mature flavors. 45,000 cases made. • $30 • (06/15/97) • **90**
Amarone della Valpolicella Classico 1988 • $25 • (09/30/95) • **86**
Amarone della Valpolicella Classico 1986: Deep color, cassis and new oak flavors dominate this Amarone, which seems very youthful. Should develop some, but doesn't have the depth and complexity of the best in this category. • $25 • (06/15/97) • **87**
Amarone della Valpolicella Classico 1983: Mature in character, showing prune, tobacco and cedar flavors. Dry and austere, with a nutty accent on the finish. Try with cheeses. 45,000 cases made. • $28 • (06/15/97) • **86**
Amarone Recioto della Valpolicella Classico 1981 • $11 • (03/15/89) • **81**
Amarone della Valpolicella Classico Sergio Zenato Riserva 1988: Packed with prune, chocolate, vanilla and spice character, with a slight cheesy note often associated with great, ageable wines. This is young and monolithic, boasting ripe, mouth-coating tannins and vibrant acidity. All the components are here, folks, just be patient. Best from 2000 through 2015. • $48 • (05/31/98) HR • **93**
Amarone Recioto della Valpolicella Classico Signature Label 1983 • $35 • (06/15/96) • **88**
Bardolino Classico Superiore 1990 • $8 • (09/15/92) • **81**
Bardolino Classico Superiore 1989 • $7 • (07/15/91) • **78**
Bardolino Novello 1996: A light, fresh red in a Beaujolais style. Soft, with flavors of strawberry and banana. Ready to drink. • $8 • (06/15/97) • **80**
Bianco di Custoza 1995: Refreshing and full of zesty, citrus character in a straightforward style. Good as an apéritif or with light seafood dishes. • $9 • (06/15/97) • **80**
Bianco di Custoza Sole del Garda 1994 • $10 • (06/15/96) • **84**
Chardonnay Veneto Sergio Zenato 1995: A clove, nutmeg and apple combination holds court in this ambitious Chardonnay, which displays very good concentration and depth. Elegant and seamless, finishing with a fresh citrus note that echoes on the aftertaste. Drink through 1999. • $20 • (05/31/98) • **87**
Lugana S. Benedetto 1996: Serious Trebbiano, offering gentle accents of vanilla along with apple and almond. It's concentrated and rich, finishing with a hint of nutmeg. A fine alternative to Chardonnay. Drink through 1999. • $12 • (05/31/98) • **85**
Lugana S. Benedetto 1995: A generous white wine; full-flavored and full-bodied, but with good balance between its crisp, fruity character and its buttery, spicy undertones. • $10 • (05/31/97) • **87**
Lugana San Benedetto 1994 • $10 • (05/31/96) • **84**
Lugana Sergio Zenato Riserva 1995: This sets a new standard for Trebbiano. Relying more on new oak than fruit, yet there's apple flavor and concentration to back it up, along with a creamy texture and lively acidity. The finish is long, with apple and spice notes intermingling. Drink through 1999. • $21 • (05/31/98) • **86**
Pinot Grigio Veneto 1996: The peach notes of this medium-weight white integrate nicely with a rich mouthfeel and vibrant structure. Moderate finish. Drink now. 25,000 cases made. • $9 • (06/15/98) • **84**
Pinot Grigio Veneto 1995: A fresh, attractive white, with hints of peach accenting the apple flavors. Enjoy now. • $10 • (06/15/97) • **82**
Soave Classico Superiore 1995: Straightforward in its appeal; fresh and clean, redolent of pears and almonds. • $8 • (06/15/97) • **82**
Valpolicella Classico Superiore 1994: Spicy cherry and vanilla accents make this medium-bodied red quite pleasant. Moderately long finish, with tobacco notes. • $9 • (06/15/97) • **83**
Valpolicella Classico Superiore 1990 • $9 • (09/15/92) • **84**
Valpolicella Classico Superiore 1988 • $8 • (04/30/92) BB • **83**
Valpolicella Classico Superiore Ripassa 1994: A modern style of Valpolicella, offering bright plum notes in a restrained, elegant manner. Concentrated and well-balanced, with a lingering finish. Drink now through 2000. 4,500 cases made. • $15 • (05/31/98) • **86**
Valpolicella Classico Superiore Ripassa 1993: This rich, Amarone-like red is full of prune, chocolate and nut flavors. It's full-bodied and concentrated, with a satisfying finish. • $15 • (06/15/97) • **87**
Valpolicella Classico Superiore Ripassa 1992 • $15 • (04/30/96) • **87**

ZERBA, LA

Gavi 1994 • $15 • (07/31/95) • **77**

ZONIN

Amarone Della Valpolicella Il Maso 1991 • $17 • (09/30/95) • **86**
Amarone della Valpolicella Il Maso 1990 • $16 • (09/30/95) • **89**
Amarone Recioto della Valpolicella Il Maso 1988 • $16 • (09/15/92) • **82**
Bardolino Classico 1991 • $7 • (09/15/92) • **82**
Berengario Barrel Aged 1989 • $24 • (03/31/93) • **85**
Berengario Barrel Aged 1988 • $30 • (01/31/92) • **84**
Merlot-Cabernet Aquileia del Friuli 1990 • $7 • (09/15/92) • **74**
Merlot-Cabernet del Friuli 1992 • $6 • (02/28/95) • **82**
Merlot-Cabernet del Friuli 1991 • $6 • (04/30/94) • **75**
Merlot-Cabernet del Friuli 1989 • $6 • (01/31/92) • **78**
Merlot Veneto 1995: Simple cherry and wet earth flavors are allied to a firm, astringent texture in this modest red. • $7 • (09/15/97) • **78**
Merlot Veneto White 1996: Just off-dry, with a hint of berry flavor, this rosé has vinosity but not much fruit. • $7 • (12/15/97) • **75**
Merlot Veneto White 1995: Sweet and cloying, with watermelonlike flavors. • $7 • (10/15/97) • **74**
Montepulciano d'Abruzzo 1995: Light and fruity, showing pretty cherry and red plum flavors that pick up notes of cinnamon and nutmeg on the pleasant finish. • $7 • (07/31/97) • **82**
Montepulciano d'Abruzzo 1993 • $6 • (02/29/96) • **79**
Montepulciano d'Abruzzo 1992 • $6 • (03/31/95) • **77**
Montepulciano d'Abruzzo 1991 • $7 • (07/31/93) • **80**
Montepulciano d'Abruzzo 1990 • $7 • (09/15/92) BB • **83**
Montepulciano d'Abruzzo 1988 • $6 • (06/30/91) BB • **80**
Montepulciano d'Abruzzo 1987 • $5 • (03/31/90) • **78**
Montepulciano d'Abruzzo 1983 • $4 • (05/16/86) BB • **81**
Recioto di Gambellara 1990 • $20 • (09/15/92) • **75**
Valpolicella Classico Il Maso 1990 • $8 • (09/15/92) • **82**

Key: SS—Spectator Selection CS—Cellar Selection HR—Highly Recommended BB—Best Buy $NA—Price not available Ⓐ—Auction Price (BT)—Barrel Tasting
Dates in parentheses indicate the issues in which the ratings were published.

Portugal

Although Portugal produces a wide range of good red, white and rosé table wines, its reputation as a great wine-producing country is based on its production of Port, a sweet wine fortified with brandy. In recent years, however, the quality and value offered by Portugal's dry, unfortified wines has become more appreciated. Both Port and Portugal's other wines now merit the full attention of wine drinkers.

PORT

Although many inferior imitations are produced around the world, true Port comes only from Portugal. The grapes are grown in a designated part of the northern Douro region, while production centers on the city of Oporto. True Port is made in several styles, each with differing characteristics.

Most Ports are wood Ports, which simply means that all of the significant aging takes place in wood barrels before bottling. As a result, wood Ports are ready to drink upon release and do not require aging in the consumer's cellar. The two basic types of wood Ports are ruby Port and tawny Port. Both are usually blends of different vintages (and are thus designated non-vintage or NV). As the names suggest, a chief difference is the color. Ruby Port is red in color, offering vigorous fruit that tastes fresh and shows little evidence of oxidation. It tends to be a younger wine than tawny, and is intended to be enjoyed for its freshness, vivacity, and smoothness.

Tawny Port has a light orange/brown color and a more mature character than does ruby Port. The aromas and flavors typically display notes of caramel, orange-peel and hazelnuts, as opposed to the red-fruit characteristics of ruby Port. Tawnies may be aged for many years, sometimes decades, in wood barrels before being bottled and released. Indeed, some shippers mark their tawnies with designations such as 10, 20 or 30 years, or older to indicate their wines' approximate age. Tawny Port is rarely powerful, but the flavors can have great length and depth. Indeed, a fine aged tawny is often a wine of great subtlety and complexity.

The most revered and collectible Port is vintage Port. Vintage Port is not considered a wood Port, although it does spend its first two years in wood casks. Most of the aging of vintage Port takes place in the bottle, often over a period of decades in the cellars of collectors of this exquisite wine. Vintage Port is not made every year—only in the best years, when the grapes achieve a special ripeness and intensity. Port shippers will then "declare" a vintage, meaning that some of their production will be released with a vintage date, made in the unique style of vintage Port. The decision to declare a vintage is up to the individual Port house, but major houses are usually in agreement.

A recent development has been the increasing availability of so called "single quinta" Ports. These are made exactly like vintage Ports, but are produced from particular estates or vineyards.

DRY PORTUGUESE WINES

Portugal's best known dry wine is Vinho Verde, which literally means "green wine." Vinho Verde can in fact be red or white, as the "greenness" refers to the youth of the wine rather than its color, but most of the

A view of the Quinta do Vesuvio winery—maker of superlative ports—from the Douro River.

James Suckling

exports are white. White Vinho Verde, made primarily from the Loureiro grape and less often the Alvarinho, is a perfect apéritif wine, low in alcohol and nicely crisp. The red can be good, but is often rough around the edges.

Portugal's best known dry wine region is the Dão. Most Dão is red, but about a third is white. Dão reds age well. While vintage dates are not totally reliable, it is not unusual to find Dão reds drinking well after more than a decade in the bottle. Quality is improving markedly here as the influence of the old cooperatives fade. Wineries are now allowed to buy grapes directly from growers and vinify the wines themselves, which has dramatically raised the overall level of the wines. The term "garrafeira" means reserve, and often signifies the best wines of a producer.

The quality potential of the dry red wines of the Douro has long been recognized, even though they are overshadowed by the fame of Port. Red Douro is made from the same grapes as Port; unlike Port, the grapes are allowed to finish their fermentation in the normal way, without the addition of brandy (which arrests the fermentation of wines before all their sugar has turned to alcohol.) Douro reds take wood aging well. The most esteemed is Barca Velha—made by the Ferreira Port house—which is released only in the best vintages.

White wines from the Douro can be pleasant, but they rarely satisfy as fully as the reds.

In recent years, other regions of Portugal have increased in prominence. The Barraida district, located between the Douro River and the Dão, makes fairly highly extracted, Rhône-like reds and lots of rather ordinary white intended for the domestic bulk market. While the principal red grape is the indigenous Baga, some experiments with Cabernet Sauvignon and Merlot have yielded impressive results.

Cabernet Sauvignon is also being planted alongside traditional varieties in the Sebutal district, until now best known for its sweet, Muscat-based wine. The Setubal firm of J.M. da Fonseca (unrelated to the Fonseca of Oporto) also makes an excellent dry red wine from the native Periquita grape.

Until recently the vast Alentejo region in Southern Portugal was known mostly for its light rosés. However, that has changed with the arrival of the Domaines Rothschild (Lafite), which has restored an old estate called Quinta do Carmo and is producing potent, wood-aged reds.

ABRIGADA, QUINTA DE

Alenquer 1992: A luscious wine with good fruit flavors of plum and black cherry with notes of cinnamon and vanilla that build through to the finish. It is well balanced, rich and ready to drink now. 2,666 cases made. • $8 • (09/15/96) • **87**

ALIANÇA, CAVES

Alentejo Alabastro 1996: Simple and a bit lean, with berry and unripe cherry flavors. 40,000 cases made. • $8 • (08/31/97) • **78**
Alentejo Alabastro 1995: Quite a red, and so reasonably priced. This medium-bodied wine is charmingly exuberant, brimming with fresh blueberry flavors and nice, spicy notes that add dimension on the finish. 20,833 cases made. • $9 • (05/31/97) BB • **86**
Alentejo Alabastro 1994 • $8 • (03/31/96) • **78**
Alentejo Alabastro 1993 • $7 • (04/30/95) • **84**
Bairrada 1991 • $8 • (02/28/95) • **78**
Bairrada Aliança Reserva 1994: Peppery aromas and flavors make this red interesting. It's smooth and medium-bodied, with dried cherry flavors and a spicy note which lingers on the finish. 41,667 cases made. • $6 • (05/31/97) • **84**
Bairrada Angelus Reserva 1994: Mature-tasting, with pruny, raisiny flavors and a nice leatherlike note as well. Still a bit tannic, but drink now before it dries out. • $5 • (09/15/97) • **82**
Bairrada Garrafeira 1991: Tannic, with only modest prune- and leatherlike flavors. Turns astringent on the finish. 2,500 cases made. • $10 • (08/31/97) • **74**
Bairrada Garrafeira 1984 • $10 • (04/15/94) • **78**
Bairrada Reserva 1992 • $6 • (04/30/96) • **77**
Bairrada Reserva 1991 • $6 • (04/30/95) • **80**
Bairrada Reserva 1990 • $6 • (03/31/94) BB • **86**
Bairrada Reserva 1989 • $5 • (06/15/93) • **79**
Bairrada Reserva 1987 • $5 • (07/15/91) • **77**
Bairrada Rosé Angelus 1995: A rosé with some character. Offers good cherry and spice flavors that thicken on the finish. A bit heavy-handed, but quite tasty. • $5 • (08/31/97) • **82**
Bairrada White Angelus 1995: Tired and astringent at the same time. Tastes of onion and chalk. Not much fun. Tasted twice, with consistent notes. • $5 • (10/15/97) • **72**
Beiras Garrafeira 1985 • $8 • (06/15/93) • **76**
Beiras Garrafeira 1982 • $9 • (07/15/91) • **84**
Beiras Garrafeira Aliança 1985 • $10 • (04/15/94) • **74**
Bical Bairrada Galeria 1996: Tart, with little fruit flavor. A tough customer. 9,000 cases made. • $8 • (08/31/97) • **75**
Bical Bairrada Galeria 1995: A fairly neutral-tasting white wine dominated by applelike flavors and aromas. 8,333 cases made. • $8 • (05/15/97) • **77**
Brut Bairrada Aliança 1994: An odd mix. Smells fruity and has some nice spice flavors, but turns candied and a little oniony. 8,333 cases made. • $9 • (05/15/97) • **78**
Cabernet Sauvignon Beiras Galeria 1994: A wine of some weight-and tannin. Good plum, spice and currant flavors, with an herbal note. Drink now; hard to say if the fruit will outlive the tannins. 5,000 cases made. • $10 • (08/31/97) • **83**
Cabernet Sauvignon Beiras Galeria 1993 • $10 • (04/30/95) • **79**
Cabernet Sauvignon Beiras Galeria 1991 • $10 • (04/15/94) • **83**
Chardonnay Beiras Galeria 1996: Offers some nice spice and butter flavors. Medium-bodied, with a lingering finish. 3,500 cases made. • $10 • (08/31/97) • **80**
Chardonnay Beiras Galeria 1995: Candied and cloying, with spicy flavors. Simple, and verging on tired. 3,750 cases made. • $9 • (05/15/97) • **76**
Dão Aliança Particular 1992 • $10 • (03/31/96) • **78**
Dão Garrafiera 1989 • $6 • (04/30/95) BB • **85**
Dão Particular 1994: Has a spicy aroma, matched by some nice smoke and ripe plum flavors. A full-bodied red that would serve well at a barbecue. 6,000 cases made. • $10 • (08/31/97) • **84**
Dão Reserva 1992 • $5 • (04/30/95) BB • **85**
Dão Reserva 1990 • $5 • (04/15/94) BB • **82**
Dão Reserva 1989 • $4 • (06/15/93) • **78**
Dão Vinho Tinto 1984 • $8 • (07/15/91) • **74**
Douro Foral 1992 • $8 • (03/31/96) • **82**
Douro Foral 1991 • $5 • (04/30/95) BB • **86**
Douro Foral Garrafeira 1990 • $6 • (04/30/95) BB • **87**
Douro Foral Garrafeira 1989 • $6 • (01/31/95) • **77**
Douro Foral Grande Escolha 1994: Earthy, with musty aromas and harsh tannins. Modest prune and leather flavors. 5,000 cases made. • $12 • (08/31/97) • **73**
Douro Foral Reserva 1995: A green-tasting wine with simple berry flavors, decent body and a spicy finish. 16,000 cases made. • $5 • (08/31/97) • **79**
Douro Foral Reserva 1994: Look at all you get for so few dollars: A rich, round and ripe red, showing delicious blueberry and pepperey flavors with some good, tannic backbone beneath. Drink now. 16,667 cases made. • $5 • (05/31/97) BB • **86**
Douro Foral Reserva 1992 • $5 • (03/31/96) • **78**
Palmela Aliança Particular 1991 • $10 • (03/31/96) • **77**
Palmela Particular 1992: Ripe, and a bit past its prime, it has some prune and leather flavors but little else. 7,000 cases made. • $10 • (08/31/97) • **78**
Vinho de Mesa Cave do Duque NV • $4 • (04/15/94) • **78**

ALTOVISO, CAVES

Dão Fastelo 1991 • $6 • (01/31/95) • **79**

ALVES DE SOUSA, DOMINGOS

Douro Quinta da Gaivosa 1994: A well-rounded and mature red, with good acidity and balance and pleasant dark plum, dried cherry and spice flavors. Pepper and game notes linger on the finish, with smooth tannins. 900 cases made. • $16 • (08/31/97) • **87**
Douro Quinta do Vale da Raposa 1995: Smooth, with modest flavors of dried plum and cherry, but loses charm via a dirty leather taste that turns astringent on the finish. • $7 • (08/31/97) • **80**
Douro White Branco da Gaivosa 1995: Offers some appealing green-peach and almond flavors, but it's a bit unbalanced in the end. 900 cases made. • $16 • (09/15/97) • **78**
Douro White Quinta do Vale da Raposa 1995: A tired and somewhat cloying wine with flavors reminiscent of geraniums and capers. 600 cases made. • $7 • (09/15/97) • **75**

ARRUDA DOS VINHOS

Arruda 1990: Straightforward and mature with ripe plum and black cherry flavors. An herbal note also runs through this wine. • $NA • (09/15/96) • **83**
Estremadura Comenda de Sant'lago 1994: A smooth and supple red with very soft tannins. It features plum and green bean flavors which linger with a hint of leather. • $NA • (09/15/96) • **83**

AVELEDA

Douro Charamba 1995: Simple and grapey-tasting, with pleasant cherry and plum notes. 90,000 cases made. • $5 • (08/31/97) • **81**
Douro Charamba 1992 • $6 • (04/30/95) BB • **86**
Vinho Verde Loureiro da Aveleda 1996: Light and fruity, with green peach flavors. Simple but satisfying. 10,000 cases made. • $7 • (08/31/97) • **80**
Vinho Verde Trajadura da Aveleda 1996: Dull and lifeless, showing only vague apple and citrus flavors. 10,000 cases made. • $7 • (10/15/97) • **75**

BACALHOA, QUINTA DA

Cabernet Sauvignon Terras do Sado 1992 • $14 • (03/31/96) • **85**
Cabernet Sauvignon Terras do Sado 1991 • $15 • (04/30/95) • **83**

BARROCÃO, CAVES DO

Bairrada Garrafeira 1988 • $10 • (04/15/94) • **75**
Bairrada Reserva 1990 • $7 • (04/15/94) • **82**
Dão Garrafeira 1980 • $13 • (04/15/94) • **85**
Dão Reserva 1990 • $7 • (04/15/94) • **77**

BARROS

Douro Vilar da Galeira 1995: A wine of some power, it's thick and supple, with good plum and leather flavors, dried cherry and pepper notes on the finish. • $NA • (08/31/97) • **84**
Late Bottled Port 1992: Refreshing floral, red licorice aromas. Medium-bodied, very sweet with a long, unctuous finish. Delicious. Drink now. • $16 • (02/28/98) • **86**

BLANDYS

Tawny Port 20-year-old NV • $35 • (02/28/90) • **96**
Vintage Port 1995: A ponderous wine, thick and big. Full-bodied, medium sweet, with a big, chewy tannin structure. Slightly one-dimensional but impressively concentrated, with loads of cherry character. Best after 2008. 2,500 cases made. • $22 • (04/30/98) • **87**
Vintage Port 1994: A young, full-bodied Port with plenty of interesting black pepper character, moderate sweetness, well-integrated tannins and a long, silky finish. Very good effort. Try after 2004. • $20 • (04/30/97) • **86**
Vintage Port 1991: Too light to be a good vintage Port. Medium purple to ruby in color, with delicate plum and chocolate aromas. Medium-bodied and medium-sweet, with delicate tannins and a light finish. Tasted twice with consistent notes. Drinkable now. • $NA • (07/31/94) • **79**
Vintage Port 1987: Marks a return to the major leagues for Barros. Good purple color, with a very fresh, grapy, aromatic nose, medium- to full-bodied, with medium tannins and a balance of elegant fruit. No show-stopper, but has some class. • $28 • (01/01/90) • **81**
Vintage Port 1985: This is an early-drinking 1985 but it is nicely crafted all the same. Medium purple with a ruby hue, a very fresh and grapy nose, medium-bodied, with clean, fresh fruit flavors, medium tannins and a long finish. • $29 • (01/01/90) • **80**
Vintage Port 1983 • $30 • (01/01/90) • **76**
Vintage Port 1978 • $30 • (01/01/90) • **75**
Vintage Port 1974 • $40 • (01/01/90) • **74**
Vintage Port 1970 • $60 • (01/01/90) • **82**
White Port Lagrima NV: This unusual white Port is all maple syrup and spice. It's smooth and quite sweet, with a splash of orange-rind flavor as well. Pleasant, if not particularly complex. • $9 • (08/31/97) • **85**

BLANDYS

Bual Madeira 5 Years Old NV: Distinctly sweet, showing plenty of honey and caramel and a touch of rubber at the end. Lacks some complexity and length. • $20 • (11/30/97) • **87**
Malmsey Madeira 15 Years Old NV: This is full-bodied, sweet, complex and long. The burnt caramel and orange-peel notes are balanced by sharp, cutting acidity that provides grip and intensity, followed by a toffee aftertaste. • $45 • (11/30/97) • **89**
Malmsey Madeira 10 Years Old NV: Rich and sweet, yet full of racy acidity that carries the crème brûlée and toffee notes to a graceful, harmonious finish. Tangy and exciting. • $34 • (11/30/97) • **88**
Malmsey Madeira 5 Years Old NV: Sweet, and full of caramel and butterscotch flavors, without the complexity and length. A good introduction to Malmsey. • $20 • (11/30/97) • **86**
Rainwater Madeira NV • $7 • (06/01/85) • **78**
Sercial Madeira 5 Years Old NV: An elegant Sercial that exhibits walnut nuances and a distinct tangy edge leading into a moderate finish. A perfect accompaniment to salted almonds. • $20 • (11/30/97) • **86**
Verdelho Madeira 5 Years Old NV: This rich and honeyed wine, with its apple and floral nuances, is moderately sweet and round until the finish, where it turns dry and nutty. Try as an apéritif or dessert. • $20 • (11/30/97) • **89**

BORBA, ADEGA COOPERATIVA DE

Alentejo 1992 • $5 • (04/30/95) • **83**
Alentejo Borba 1994 • $5 • (04/30/96) • **78**
Alentejo Borba 1991 • $5 • (04/15/94) BB • **82**
Alentejo Convento da Vila 1995: A young and fruity red, with plenty of strawberry and cherry flavors. Lacks complexity, but still satisfying. • $4 • (05/31/97) • **83**
Alentejo Convento da Vila 1994 • $4 • (04/30/96) • **79**
Alentejo Convento da Vila 1992 • $4 • (04/15/94) • **78**
Alentejo Convento da Vila Reserva 1993: Gamy aromas and flavors make this a rather muddled red; has some dried plum flavors as well. • $7 • (05/31/97) • **76**
Alentejo Reserva 1989 • $9 • (04/15/94) • **77**
Alentejo Reserva 1988 • $7 • (04/15/94) • **80**
Alentejo Vila Morena 1994 • $5 • (04/30/96) • **82**
Alentejo White Borba 1994: Dull and tastes slightly sweet, with only modest peach and mineral flavors. Not much of a finish. 80,000 cases made. • $5 • (09/15/96) • **75**
Alentejo White Vila Morena 1994: Distinctive with a mix of apricot and onion flavors. Turns a bit tough on the finish. 40,000 cases made. • $5 • (09/15/96) • **77**
Borba 1995: A fresh and fruity red, with some stuffing. Has a good balance of cherry flavors and moderate tannins. Drinkable now. • $5 • (05/31/97) • **84**
Borba Reserva 1992: Balanced and mature, with good, dried cherry and currant flavors, this full-bodied red is ready to drink. • $8 • (05/31/97) • **85**
Borba White 1995: Tastes spicy and a bit cloying, with only some fading fig and citrus flavors. • $5 • (05/15/97) • **76**

BORGES

Late Bottled Port 1992: Gives much more on the nose than on the palate. Deep, dark color, with very grapey, floral aromas. Medium-bodied, medium sweet, but very short on the finish. Drink now. • $16 • (02/28/98) • **85**
Vintage Port 1994: Slightly premature in style with a red hue and a slightly nutty character, but has pretty aromas of strawberries and raspberries. Medium-bodied, medium-sweet. Slightly peppery finish. Try after 2003. • $25 • (09/15/97) • **81**
Vintage Port 1985: This is so light and ready to drink that it is more like a ruby or a late-bottled vintage. Medium to light red, with simple aromas of cherries and chocolate, light-bodied and clean, with sweet cherry flavors and light tannins on the finish. • $15 • (05/01/90) • **70**
Vintage Port 1983 • $21 • (05/01/90) • **70**
Vintage Port 1982 • $30 • (05/01/90) • **79**
Vintage Port 1980 • $23 • (05/01/90) • **70**

BRIDÃO

Cartaxo 1991 • $7 • (03/31/96) • **74**

BURMESTER

Late Bottled Port 1989: In a state of decline, but some good ripe fruit. Plummy, slightly alcoholic nose. Medium-bodied, a bit dry and spirity on the finish. Drink now or never. • $23 • (02/28/98) • **80**
Late Bottled Port Extra Selected 1992: Lovely LBV with plenty of fresh cherry and berry character. Medium-bodied, medium sweet with a silky, fruity finish. Well made. Drink now or hold. • $21 • (02/28/98) • **87**
Late Bottled Port Extra Selected 1991: Smells like a real vintage Port, with berry, wet earth and fruit. Medium-bodied, with a lovely silky texture and a medium, sweet fruit finish. Delicious. Drink now or hold. • $NA • (02/28/98) • **88**
Late Bottled Port Quinta do Carmo 1992: A bit tough for an LBV, with ripe fruit character and chewy tannins. Medium-bodied, medium sweet, finish is medium. Drink now or hold. • $NA • (02/28/98) • **85**
Tawny Port 20-year-old NV • $40 • (02/28/90) • **95**
Vintage Port 1995: An elegant young Port with lovely, aromatic fruit on the nose and finish. Better than the '94. Good dark-purple color, wet earth and cherry aromas. Medium-bodied, with fine tannins and a sleek, racy, long, sweet fruit finish. Best after 2005. 2,000 cases made. • $22 • (04/30/98) • **88**
Vintage Port 1994: Slightly forward and mature compared to many '94s, with roasted nut and berry character. Medium-bodied and very sweet. Best after 2000. • $NA • (04/30/97) • **82**
Vintage Port 1992: Roasted and ripe; sweet fruit flavors, medium body, round tannins and sweet finish. Drink in 1999. • $NA • (06/15/95) • **85**
Vintage Port 1991: As of 1994, was not showing as well as in a previous tasting. A bit spirited, with grape-skin and brandy aromas. Medium-bodied, with grapey flavors, medium sweetness, tannins and a silky finish. Tasted twice with consistent notes. Try after 1999. 1,500 cases made. • $NA • (07/31/94) • **86**
Vintage Port 1985: This is a great achievement for a 1985, perhaps one of the best wines of the vintage. Inky color, with berry and grape must aromas, full-bodied, with tons of fruit and tannin, very concentrated. Finish is extremely long. Outstanding. • $25 • (01/01/90) • **93**
Vintage Port 1984 • $NA • (01/01/90) • **84**
Vintage Port 1980 • $33 • (01/01/90) • **88**
Vintage Port 1977 • $31 • (01/01/90) • **82**
Vintage Port 1970 • $41 • (01/01/90) • **86**
Vintage Port 1963 • $131 • (01/01/90) • **83**
Vintage Port Quinta do Nova 1992: Not as great as from cask, but very good. Well made Port showing grape-skin, berry and stem aromas, roasted peppery character, full body and plenty of tannins. Try in 1999. • $NA • (06/15/95) • **87**

Key: SS—Spectator Selection CS—Cellar Selection HR—Highly Recommended BB—Best Buy $NA—Price not available Ⓐ—Auction Price (BT)—Barrel Tasting
Dates in parentheses indicate the issues in which the ratings were published.

Vintage Port Quinta Nova de Nossa Senhora do Carmo 1995: Slightly more mature than many '95s at this stage, and considerably lighter. Medium-bodied, medium sweet, with light tannins and a light finish. Best after 2001. 800 cases made. • $43 • (04/30/98) • **80**

CADAVAL, CASA

Cabernet Sauvignon Ribatejo 1994: Stiff and ungenerous, with cedar and tobacco flavors. It has unforgiving tannins as well. • $12 • (10/15/97) • **78**

Pinot Noir Ribatejo 1994: Lots of spicy aromas and flavors in this red, but not much fruit. Sharp-tasting, with a tannic finish. • $12 • (10/15/97) • **79**

Ribatejo 1995: A jammy-tasting red with berry, raspberry and cherry flavors. There's a green note on the finish, but overall it's a decent quaff. • $9 • (10/15/97) • **82**

Trincadeira Preta Ribatejo 1994: A muscular, chewy wine with firm, focused berry and plum flavors and a backbone of tannins. Finishes on a chocolaty note. • $12 • (10/15/97) • **87**

CÁLEM

Late Bottled Port 1992: Doesn't give away much. Seems over-filtered. Medium-bodied, medium sweet, with some fruit character but a short finish. Drink now. • $18 • (02/28/98) • **79**

Tawny Port 20 Años NV • $35 • (04/15/90) • **83**

Vintage Character Port NV • $16 • (03/15/94) • **79**

Vintage Port 1994: Ripe and fruity, but it's slightly musty and lifted in the nose, a bit hard on the finish. Tasted twice, with consistent notes. • $40 • (04/30/97) • **79**

Vintage Port 1991: Early-drinking, harmonious and young, evolving more quickly than anticipated. Attractive floral and berry aromas and flavors. This shows medium-sweet fruit and fine tannins. Tasted three times with consistent notes. Drinkable now. 6,000 cases made. • $NA • (07/31/94) • **80**

Vintage Port 1985: The first vintage that brought Cálem attention. Deep purple, with an intense floral and licorice nose, full-bodied, good grip, a medium concentration of fruit flavors and a long finish. Very good potential. • $42 • (06/01/90) • **88**

Vintage Port 1983 • $40 • (06/01/90) • **84**

Vintage Port 1980 • $38 • (06/01/90) • **78**

Vintage Port 1975 • $37 • (02/01/90) • **86**

Vintage Port 1970 • $14 Ⓐ • (11/01/89) • **80**

Vintage Port 1966 • $85 • (11/01/89) • **82**

Vintage Port 1963 • $85 • (12/01/89) • **82**

Vintage Port Quinta do Foz 1995: Slightly forward, but some interesting character on the nose and palate. Exotic aromas of cumin, tamarind and sweet fruit. Full-bodied and sweet, with more spices on the palate and a sweet fruit finish. Medium, chewy tannins. Best after 2004. • $19 • (04/30/98) • **86**

Vintage Port Quinta do Foz 1992: Better than the '91 Calem blend. Aromatic plum, cherry character; medium in body and sweetness, sporting fine tannins and a medium finish. Try in 1999. • $NA • (06/15/95) • **86**

Vintage Port Quinta do Foz 1987: Made entirely from Calem's Quinta do Foz, this young Port shows lots of fruit, with a rich and velvety mouthfeel. It will be an earlier drinker than the 1985. Purple, with ripe fruit and orange-peel aromas, full-bodied, with lots of fruit flavors. • $28 • (06/01/90) • **84**

Vintage Port Quinta do Foz 1982 • $30 • (06/01/90) • **82**

Vintage Port Quinta do Sagrado 1994: Youthful aromas of fruit and flowers give way to a racy, compacted wine with masses of fruit flavor and tannins, and a long finish. Certainly has grip to it. Try after 2008. • $38 • (04/30/97) • **89**

CALHANDRIZ

Vinho de Mesa White 1995: An easy-to-drink white with a delicious spicy quality and apple, peach and pear flavors of good richness. Lingering finish. • $6 • (08/31/97) • **84**

CAMARATE, QUINTA DE

Azeitão 1986 • $10 • (01/31/93) • **77**

Ribatejo Falcoaria 1989 • $9 • (04/15/94) • **77**

Ribatejo Terra de Lobos 1992 • $4 • (04/15/94) • **81**

CARDO, QUINTA DO

Douro Castelo Rodrigo 1989 • $7 • (12/31/90) BB • **84**

CARMO, QUINTA DO

Alentejo 1994: Thick-tasting, with bitter chocolate and charred flavors, leather and earth notes on the finish. Over the top. Tasted twice, with consistent notes. • $NA • (08/31/97) • **76**

Alentejo 1993: A nicely proportioned wine with good berry and spice flavors that hang together well, and some nice cinnamon flavors on the finish. Juicy and satisfying. 1,000 cases made. • $23 • (07/31/97) • **86**

Alentejo 1988 • $20 • (04/15/94) • **84**

Alentejo 1987 • $20 • (06/15/93) • **80**

CARVALHINHO, QUINTA DO

Bairrada Garrafeira 1990: Smooth and rich, showing good brown sugar and cinnamon flavors. Fully mature, ready to drink. • $14 • (09/15/97) • **84**

Bairrada Reserva 1991 • $10 • (04/30/96) • **78**

CARVALHO, RIBEIRO & FERREIRA

Bairrada Garrafeira 1980 • $8 • (04/15/94) • **77**

Dão Quinta do Serrado 1991 • $7 • (04/15/94) • **84**

Dão Quinta do Serrado 1990 • $7 • (04/15/94) • **82**

Dão Quinta do Serrado 1989 • $7 • (04/15/94) • **76**

Douro Reserva 1990 • $NA • (04/30/95) • **83**

Ribatejo Serradayres 1993 • $6 • (03/31/96) • **83**

Ribatejo Serradayres 1989 • $5 • (04/15/94) • **81**

Tràs-os-Montes Garrafeira 1990 • $14 • (03/31/96) • **74**

Tràs-os-Montes Garrafeira 1985 • $8 • (04/15/94) • **74**

CASAL DE TONDA

Dão 1991 • $9 • (04/30/95) • **77**

Dão 1990 • $8 • (04/15/94) BB • **85**

CASAL FIGUEIRA

Estremadura White 1995: A harsh and ungenerous wine with extremely woody flavors. Not recommended. Tasted twice, with consistent notes. • $10 • (09/30/97) • **65**

CHAMPALIMAUD

Vintage Port 1982 • $20 • (02/01/90) • **86**

CHURCHILL

Late Bottled Port Traditional 1990 • $19 • (01/31/96) • **85**

Late Bottled Port Traditional 1988 • $17 • (11/15/94) • **87**

Ruby Port VC Reserve NV • $11 • (11/15/94) • **86**

Vintage Character Port Finest NV • $19 • (04/15/91) • **83**

Vintage Character Port Finest Reserve NV • $17 • (03/15/94) • **87**

Vintage Port 1994: A gorgeous, voluptuous young Port, best Churchill ever. Intense aromas of dark chocolate and grapes. Full-bodied, with powerful, chewy tannins, yet it's sweet and fruity on the finish. Try after 2010. • $35 • (04/30/97) • **93**

Vintage Port 1991: Impressive. Thick and silky, with an earthy, berry and cherry character. Medium-bodied and medium-sweet with lovely flavors and a long finish. Try after 1999. 3,500 cases made. • $35 • (07/31/94) • **91**

Vintage Port 1985: So much fruit it seems almost drinkable, but give it time. Deep dark color with an attractive raisiny, stemmy nose; very concentrated flavors with a medium grip on the finish. A mid-term wine but will age longer if desired. • $22 • (09/30/87) • **84**

Vintage Port 1982 • $NA • (06/01/90) • **78**

Vintage Port Agua Alta 1995: Muscular style. Closed and not giving much now, but this is a big, burly young Port with loads of violet and berry aromas and flavors and a seriously powerful backbone of tannin. Full-bodied. Long, mouthpuckering finish. Tannic attack. Best after 2008. • $40 • (04/30/98) • **91**

Vintage Port Agua Alta 1992: Rustic monster of a wine; perhaps slightly overdone? Amazing concentration but slightly coarse, like crushed grapes in a lagar. Super raisin extract, almost dry, very tannic. Try in 2005. • $35 • (06/15/95) • **89**

Vintage Port Agua Alta 1987: Dense, fruity and backed by a solid grip of tannin and alcohol. The flavors lean toward berry and cherry, and taper off on the finish. Not a very sweet style. Should be best around 2000 to 2005. • $48 • (04/15/91) • **83**

Vintage Port Fojo 1986: There are some attractive floral fruit flavors, but the nose has a slightly odd component. Medium purple, with a floral, perfumed, slight varnish nose, medium-bodied, with floral, earthy flavors, medium tannins and a good finish. • $NA • (02/01/90) • **78**

Vintage Port Fojo 1984 • $NA • (02/01/90) • **79**

CIMA

Ribatejo 1992 • $6 • (04/30/95) • **82**

COCKBURN

Late Bottled Port Anno 1992: Soft, but slightly aged in style. Ripe, fruity with berry, plum and nutty aromas and flavors. Medium-bodied, medium sweet, with a round texture. Tasted twice, with consistent notes. Drink now. • $20 • (02/28/98) • **81**

Late Bottled Port Anno 1990 • $17 • (01/31/96) • **85**

Late Bottled Port 1987 • $21 • (11/15/94) • **86**

Tawny Port 10 Years Old NV • $24 • (01/31/96) • **88**

Tawny Port 20 Years Old NV • $35 • (02/28/90) • **86**

Tawny Port Directors' Reserve 20 years old NV • $43 • (01/31/96) • **86**

Vintage Character Port Special Reserve NV • $16 • (11/15/94) • **84**

Vintage Port 1994: A big and juicy, young vintage Port. Round, with loads of very ripe roasted and raisiny character. Full-bodied and medium-sweet, with a tannic backbone. Try after 2008. • $45 • (04/30/97) • **92**

Vintage Port 1991: A harmonious wine. Good, deep-purple color and fragrant raspberry and earthy aromas. Full-bodied yet reserved, with fine, full tannins and a long, delicious finish. Tasted twice with consistent notes. Drinkable now. 6,000 cases made. • $36 • (07/31/94) • **88**

Vintage Port 1985: Shows an abundance of thick, rich fruit and plenty of backbone. Very inky, dense color, with a rich, floral nose of berries and cherries. Full-bodied, medium sweet, with massive anise and cherry flavors and extremely well integrated tannins and acidity. • $16 Ⓐ • (06/01/90) • **90**

Vintage Port 1983 • $30 Ⓐ • (06/01/90) • **97**

Vintage Port 1975 • $21 Ⓐ • (01/01/90) • **77**

Vintage Port 1970 • $25 Ⓐ • (12/01/89) • **86**

Vintage Port 1967 • $19 Ⓐ • (12/01/89) • **85**

Vintage Port 1966 • $NA • (10/31/88) • **91**

Vintage Port 1963 • $47 Ⓐ • (12/01/89) • **88**

Vintage Port 1960 • $24 Ⓐ • (10/31/88) • **82**

Vintage Port 1958 • $NA • (11/01/89) • **84**

Vintage Port 1955 • $115 • (11/01/89) • **90**

Vintage Port 1950 • $43 Ⓐ • (11/01/89) • **76**

Vintage Port 1947 • $264 Ⓐ • (11/01/89) • **90**

Vintage Port 1935 • $174 Ⓐ • (02/01/90) • **92**

Vintage Port 1931 • $500 • (01/01/90) • **89**

Vintage Port 1927 • $272 Ⓐ • (12/01/89) • **91**

Vintage Port 1912 • $308 Ⓐ • (10/01/87) • **91**

Vintage Port 1908 • $271 Ⓐ • (10/01/87) • **89**

Vintage Port 1904 • $168 Ⓐ • (10/01/87) • **75**

Vintage Port 1896 • $400 • (02/01/90) • **82**

Vintage Port Quinta da Canias 1992: Better than Cockburn's 1991 blend; a single *quinta* to watch. Ripe, grapey berry and wet earth aromas and flavors, full body, medium sweetness, firm tannins and racy finish. Try in 2000. • $35 • (06/15/95) • **89**

Vintage Port Quinta do Tua 1987 • $28 • (06/15/93) • **89**

Vintage Port Quinta dos Canais 1995: A big and powerful young Port. Grapey, peppery, chewy '95 with lots of grip. Full- to medium-bodied, medium sweet, with a long, tannic, ripe fruit aftertaste. Best after 2006. • $39 • (04/30/98) • **90**

Key: SS—Spectator Selection CS—Cellar Selection HR—Highly Recommended BB—Best Buy $NA—Price not available Ⓐ—Auction Price (BT)—Barrel Tasting

Dates in parentheses indicate the issues in which the ratings were published.

COSSART GORDON

Bual Madeira 5 Years Old NV: This powerful, sweet wine features a burnt caramel nose, and orange, honey and smoke flavors. A racy acidity refreshes the palate, and it finishes with a walnut note. • $21 • (11/30/97) • **88**

Bual Madeira 10 Years Old NV: Medium-bodied for Bual, showing attractive caramel, smoke and earth notes, sharp acidity and a moderately long, clean finish. Just a touch astringent. • $35 • (11/30/97) • **87**

Bual Madeira 15 Years Old NV: A green, eucalyptus note adds dimension to the molasses, smoke and nut flavors in this firmly structured, sleek Bual. Intense and long, with a toffee, clove aftertaste. • $45 • (11/30/97) • **89**

CÔTTO, QUINTA DO

Douro 1995: Rich and juicy, with enticing berry, cherry and dark plum flavors. Also has an appealing leathery flavor which ties it all together. Smooth and supple, with vanilla and nutmeg on the finish. Delicious. Drink now through 2000. 4,000 cases made. • $13 • (04/30/98) • **87**

Douro 1992 • $10 • (04/30/95) • **88**

Douro 1991 • $10 • (04/15/94) • **87**

Douro 1987 • $9 • (04/30/91) • **74**

Douro Grande Escolha 1995: A well-polished wine that's loaded with flavor, made in an international style. Full-bodied, silky and intense, with gorgeous flavors of ripe cherry and spice. Finishes with a burst of blueberry. A wine that glides graciously and sumptuously across the palate. Drink now through 2001. 2,000 cases made. • $50 • (04/30/98) • **90**

Douro Grande Escolha 1994 • $40 • (04/30/96) • **87**

Douro Grande Escolha 1990 • $40 • (04/30/95) • **90**

Douro Grande Escolha 1987 • $18 • (12/31/90) • **81**

Douro White 1996: A wine of some power and finesse. Starts on a peachy note, then develops some intensity, with mineral and spice flavors that linger on the finish. A good alternative to Chardonnay. 1,200 cases made. • $12 • (04/30/98) • **85**

COUTEIRO-MOR

Alentejo 1994: A strange mix of berry and leather flavors with a bit of spritz thrown in. 2,000 cases made. • $5 • (08/31/97) • **73**

Alentejo Colheita Seleccionada 1994: A rough-hewn style, it has some blueberry flavors but also an overwhelming taste of leather. Not much finesse, but plenty of character. 1,000 cases made. • $7 • (08/31/97) • **78**

COVELA, QUINTA DE

Branco Vinho de Mesa 1995: Thick and mature-tasting, with oddly decayed flavors, overripe notes of pear and apple. Comes off unbalanced. • $12 • (10/15/97) • **78**

Rios do Minho White 1996: Crisp and quite citrusy in taste, with good focus, a touch of richness and a clean finish. • $8 • (09/15/97) • **83**

Vinho de Mesa Tinto 1995: A fruity aroma is followed by leather and game-like flavors. Doesn't quite mesh. • $12 • (08/31/97) • **79**

CRASTO, QUINTA DO

Douro 1995: Fairly ripe and concentrated, with lovely berry, cherry and plum flavors and a nice touch of cassis that gives it extra punch. Drink now for its generosity of flavor. 3,400 cases made. • $11 • (07/31/97) • **86**

Douro Reserva 1994: A voluptuous wine, rich and full-bodied, filled with vibrant fruit and spice flavors, notes of plum, cherry and leather. There's a nice juiciness too, and some appealing cinnamon and brown sugar flavors linger on the finish. 900 cases made. • $15 • (07/31/97) • **89**

Late Bottled Port 1992: Dark brick red-colored, with ripe plum and earth aromas and flavors. Medium- to full-bodied with chunky tannins and a sweet, long, fruity finish. Tastes fresher than it looks. Rich and chewy. Drink now or hold. • $19 • (02/28/98) • **87**

Vintage Port 1995: Elegant, well-balanced Port, with floral, berry and mineral aromas and flavors. Medium-bodied, with fine tannins and a long, caressing finish. Best after 2005. • $33 • (04/30/98) • **90**

Vintage Port 1994: Wonderful concentration, with deep color and ripe fruit flavors accented by a hint of green bark. Full-bodied and moderately sweet, with big, chewy tannins, yet the finish is fine and elegant. A single *quinta* to watch in the future. Try after 2008. • $35 • (04/30/97) • **93**

Vintage Port 1987: A balanced yet very simple wine. Shows improvement from earlier vintages. Deep purple, with a black pepper nose, medium-bodied, with medium tannins and very grapy, black pepper flavors. One-dimensional. • $NA • (01/01/90) • **80**

Vintage Port 1985: Short, simple and drinkable. Too light for a 1985. Medium ruby, with a light, grapy, Gamay-like nose, medium-bodied, with light tannins and a light, spicy finish. • $24 • (01/01/90) • **71**

Vintage Port 1978 • $NA • (01/01/90) • **70**

Vintage Port 1958 • $NA • (08/01/90) • **79**

CROFT

Late Bottled Port 1991: Lovely floral aromas with fruity undertones. Medium-bodied, medium sweet, with a soft, silky texture and a plummy chocolate aftertaste. Slightly forward. Drink now. • $20 • (02/28/98) • **83**

Tawny Port 20-year-old NV • $38 • (02/28/90) • **76**

Vintage Port 1994: The essence of grapes. Full-bodied and tannic, yet very classy and refined. It's got grip, but rather than smashing you over the head with structure, it seduces gently with its wonderful, well-toned muscles. Best Croft since 1945. Better after 2010. 3,500 cases made. • $50 • (04/30/97) • **96**

Vintage Port 1991 • $32 • (07/31/94) • **94**

Vintage Port 1985 • $14 Ⓐ • (06/01/90) • **81**

Vintage Port 1977 • $25 Ⓐ • (04/01/90) • **85**

Vintage Port 1975 • $18 Ⓐ • (10/31/88) • **80**

Vintage Port 1970 • $41 Ⓐ • (12/01/89) • **89**

Vintage Port 1966 • $29 Ⓐ • (12/01/89) • **90**

Vintage Port 1963 • $52 Ⓐ • (12/01/89) • **91**

Vintage Port 1960 • $70 • (09/01/89) • **90**

Vintage Port 1955 • $101 Ⓐ • (11/01/89) • **84**

Vintage Port 1950 • $170 • (04/01/90) • **77**

Vintage Port 1945 • $262 Ⓐ • (11/01/89) • **99**

Vintage Port 1935 • $146 Ⓐ • (02/01/90) • **93**

Vintage Port 1927 • $204 Ⓐ • (12/01/89) • **87**

Vintage Port Quinta da Roeda 1995: A '95 with a wonderfully aromatic nose of crushed berries. Full-bodied, with a long, medium-sweet fruit finish and firm, silky tannins. Best after 2006. • $45 • (04/30/98) • **91**

Vintage Port Quinta da Roeda 1987 • $NA • (02/01/90) • **79**

Vintage Port Quinta da Roeda 1983 • $22 • (02/01/90) • **85**

Vintage Port Quinta da Roeda 1980 • $27 • (02/01/90) • **75**

Vintage Port Quinta da Roeda 1978 • $24 • (02/01/90) • **83**

Vintage Port Quinta da Roeda 1967 • $60 • (01/01/90) • **85**

DA SILVA, C.

Vintage Port Presidential 1987: This is a solid 1987 with ample fruit and tannin to give it longevity. Medium purple, with a ripe raisin and tar nose, full-bodied, with full tannins and ripe fruit flavors. A little one-dimensional. • $NA • (02/01/90) • **80**

Vintage Port Presidential 1985: Seems short on grip and flesh for a 1985, but it's nonetheless a pleasant wine. Medium purple, with a perfumed cranberry nose, medium-bodied, with medium fruit flavors, rather delicate tannins and a light finish. • $30 • (02/01/90) • **78**

Vintage Port Presidential 1978 • $37 • (02/01/90) • **77**

Vintage Port Presidential 1977 • $38 • (02/01/90) • **72**

Vintage Port Presidential 1970 • $18 Ⓐ • (02/01/90) • **75**

White Port Presidential NV • $9 • (04/15/92) • **80**

DELAFORCE

Late Bottled Port 1991: Stylish, with cumin, spice and fruit character. Medium-bodied, medium sweet, with a silky texture and a delicious finish. A good glass of Port. • $21 • (02/28/98) • **86**

Tawny Port His Eminence's Choice Reserve NV • $19 • (01/31/96) • **80**

Vintage Character Port NV • $NA • (03/15/94) • **81**

Vintage Port 1994: Wildly plummy, with a meaty, earthy character, and fabulously concentrated. Big, sweet and voluptuous with loads of round tannins and a long, sweet finish. Best Delaforce in decades. Try after 2005. 3,500 cases made. • $40 • (04/30/97) • **92**

Vintage Port 1992: Very grapey, loads of floral character. Full-bodied and medium-sweet, boasting masses of velvety tannins. Tasting this is like getting a good back massage. Try in 2000. • $35 • (06/15/95) • **90**

Vintage Port 1985: A ripe and roasted style of Port. Medium ruby, with a raisiny, slightly burnt nose, medium-bodied, with silky, sweet fruit flavors and medium tannins. • $35 • (06/01/90) • **81**

Vintage Port 1977 • $17 Ⓐ • (02/01/90) • **80**

Vintage Port 1975 • $43 • (02/01/90) • **76**

Vintage Port 1970 • $57 • (02/01/90) • **89**

Vintage Port 1966 • $65 • (02/01/90) • **85**

Vintage Port 1963 • $35 Ⓐ • (02/01/90) • **93**

Vintage Port Quinta da Corte 1995: Fabulous young Port. As good as the '94. Black-colored, with exotic aromas of black currants and spices. Full-bodied, medium-sweet, with classy, silky tannins and a long, long, fruity and caressing finish. Really fine. Best after 2007. 3,500 cases made. • $40 • (04/30/98) • **92**

Vintage Port Quinta da Corte 1991: Not a blockbuster, but well balanced. Pretty and elegant with medium-dark black purple color and plummy, slightly earthy aromas. Medium-to-full body and tannins with a medium aftertaste. Try now. 1,800 cases made. • $29 • (07/31/94) • **87**

Vintage Port Quinta da Corte 1987: Classy and silky in the mouth, showing plenty of elegance and power. Deep purple, with a fresh black olive nose, full-bodied, with medium tannins and balanced tar and blackberry flavors. • $NA • (02/01/90) • **87**

Vintage Port Quinta da Corte 1984 • $NA • (02/01/90) • **84**

Vintage Port Quinta da Corte 1980 • $NA • (02/01/90) • **81**

Vintage Port Quinta da Corte 1978 • $24 • (02/01/90) • **80**

DIEZ HERMANOS

Vintage Port 1977 • $NA • (04/01/90) • **82**

DOM HERMANO

Ribatejo Reserva 1988 • $7 • (04/15/94) • **62**

DOW

Late Bottled Port 1991: Soft and slightly forward. Pretty plum aromas with a hint of berries. Medium-bodied, medium sweet, round and delicious. A touch of nut on the finish. Drink now. • $20 • (02/28/98) • **84**

Tawny Port 10-year-old NV • $23 • (01/31/96) • **89**

Tawny Port 20-year-old NV • $42 • (01/31/96) • **89**

Tawny Port 30-year-old NV • $73 • (01/31/96) • **89**

Tawny Port Boardroom NV • $18 • (01/31/96) • **82**

Tawny Port Fine Tawny NV • $10 • (01/31/96) • **82**

Tawny Port Reserve Single Year 1982 • $25 • (01/31/96) • **84**

Vintage Character Port AJ NV • $19 • (03/15/94) • **79**

Vintage Character Port AJS NV • $17 • (06/15/93) • **83**

Vintage Port 1994: This young Port has superb grip. A mouthpuckering monster with masses of fruit and tannins, it has wonderful ripe, grapey aromas that carry through to the palate. Truly one of the great Dows. Try after 2010. 13,000 cases made. • $80 • (04/30/97) • **97**

Vintage Port 1991: We have underrated this wine in the past; when last tasted it still wasn't showing much at first. However, underneath the pretty fruit is a hard backbone of tannins. It has a full body with loads of fruit concentration and a long and tannic finish. Give it time. Tasted twice; second bottle better. Try after 2000. 6,500 cases made. • $42 • (07/31/94) • **91**

Vintage Port 1985: Fleshy and raw, bursting with fruit on the palate but may have closed up some. Deep dark ruby-purple, with intense tar and berry aromas, full-bodied, with ripe berry flavors, full tannins and a long finish. • $23 Ⓐ • (06/01/90) • **89**

Vintage Port 1983 • $20 Ⓐ • (06/01/90) • **94**

Vintage Port 1980 • $15 • (06/01/90) • **90**

Vintage Port 1977 • $43 Ⓐ • (04/01/90) • **94**

Vintage Port 1975 • $23 Ⓐ • (04/01/89) • **80**

Vintage Port 1972 • $36 • (01/01/90) • **79**

Vintage Port 1970 • $48 Ⓐ • (12/01/89) • **94**

Vintage Port 1966 • $47 Ⓐ • (12/01/89) • **94**

Vintage Port 1963 • $79 Ⓐ • (02/01/90) • **92**

Vintage Port 1960 • $32 Ⓐ • (02/01/90) • **88**

Vintage Port 1955 • $146 Ⓐ • (04/01/90) • **91**

Vintage Port 1950 • $150 • (11/01/89) • **86**

Vintage Port 1947 • $400 • (11/01/89) • **88**

Vintage Port 1945 • $277 Ⓐ • (11/01/89) • **89**

Vintage Port 1935 • $350 • (06/01/90) • **79**

Vintage Port 1934 • $350 • (06/01/90) • **84**

Vintage Port 1927 • $225 Ⓐ • (04/01/90) • **87**

Vintage Port Quinta do Bomfim 1995: Slightly heavy but impressively concentrated, this is a very ripe young Port with plum, raisin and spice aromas and flavors. Full-bodied, very sweet, with sugar-coated, thick tannins. Best after 2004. 6,000 cases made. • $38 • (04/30/98) • **90**

Vintage Port Quinta do Bomfim 1992: Much better than from barrel. Perhaps better than Dow's blended 1991 vintage Port. This is big and concentrated, presenting masses of velvety tannins and intensely ripe violet, raspberry and cherry flavors. It goes on and on. Cellar until 2000. 2,200 cases made. • $30 • (06/30/95) • **92**

Vintage Port Quinta do Bomfim 1990: Firm and fleshy, with ripe black cherry, vanilla and coffee aromas and flavors. Shows a definite grip of tannin and alcohol on the finish, but in balance. A chewy wine that will need until 2000 to 2005 to sort itself out. • $31 • (01/31/93) • **86**

Vintage Port Quinta do Bomfim 1989: Powerful, full of marvelous fruit flavors, yet graceful enough to let them roll across the palate gently. Has the intensity and grip to age well. Expect it to keep developing through at least 2004 to 2010. 2,785 cases made. • $24 • (11/30/91) CS • **90**

Vintage Port Quinta do Bomfim 1987: Extremely impressive, with generous, rich black cherry notes. Deep inky purple, with ripe black cherry aromas, full-bodied, with full tannins and a great concentration of fruit flavors. Very well structured. • $NA • (02/01/90) • **86**

Vintage Port Quinta do Bomfim 1986: Very hard and closed when last tasted, but still showed good fruit flavors and potential. Very dark ruby with a black center, a grape and licorice nose, medium-bodied, with full, hard tannins, blackberry flavors and a closed finish. • $NA • (02/01/90) • **82**

Vintage Port Quinta do Bomfim 1984 • $NA • (02/01/90) • **86**

Vintage Port Quinta do Bomfim 1982 • $NA • (02/01/90) • **82**

Vintage Port Quinta do Bomfim 1979 • $28 • (02/01/90) • **81**

Vintage Port Quinta do Bomfim 1978 • $28 • (11/30/88) • **88**

Vintage Port Quinta do Bomfim 1965 • $NA • (06/01/90) • **87**

DUFF GORDON

Vintage Port 1995: Pretty violet, floral aromas. Medium-bodied, medium sweet, with refined tannins. Slightly simple. Long finish. Best after 2002. From Osborne. 500 cases made. • $40 • (04/30/98) • **87**

EIRA VELHA, QUINTA DA

Vintage Port Martinez 1995: A sweet, mouthfilling young Port. Medium- to full-bodied, with medium tannins and a fruity finish. • $NA • (09/15/97) (BT) • **85-89**

Vintage Port 1987: A good all-around 1987 with excellent fruit and tannins. Dark ruby with a purple center, aromas of grape skins and bitter chocolate, medium- to full-bodied, with grape-skin flavors, medium to full tannins and a long finish. Very good potential. • $NA • (05/01/90) • **86**

Vintage Port 1982 • $NA • (03/01/90) • **81**

Vintage Port 1978 • $22 • (03/01/90) • **85**

ESPORÃO, HERDADE DO

Alentejo Monte Velho 1996: Fruity, simple and light, with good berry and sweet cherry flavors. Could try it slightly chilled. • $8 • (09/15/97) • **80**

Alentejo Monte Velho 1992 • $7 • (03/31/96) • **82**

Alentejo White Monte Velho 1996: A well-rounded white with some nice tropical fruit flavors to it, mango and banana predominating. Flavors linger on the finish. • $7 • (09/15/97) • **83**

Reguengos 1993: Delicious and fruity with its blueberry aroma and flavors of blueberry and raspberry. Well balanced, with shades of nutmeg and cinnamon. Reminiscent of a California Zinfandel. • $12 • (10/15/97) • **85**

Reguengos White 1995: A juicy wine with nice pear, honey and butter flavors. An international style reminiscent of a California Chardonnay. • $12 • (09/15/97) • **84**

FALCOARIA

Almeirim 1990 • $9 • (04/30/95) • **80**

FEIST

Vintage Port 1995: Hard to believe. Best Feist ever made. Dark ink-colored, with wonderful black currant and raspberry aromas. Full-bodied and extremely concentrated, with masses of fruit and ultrafine tannins. Long, long finish. Much better than when tasted from barrel. Tasted twice, with consistent notes. Best after 2006. 1,700 cases made. • $25 • (04/30/98) • **90**

Vintage Port 1991 • $26 • (07/31/94) • **83**

Key: SS—Spectator Selection CS—Cellar Selection HR—Highly Recommended BB—Best Buy $NA—Price not available Ⓐ—Auction Price (BT)—Barrel Tasting
Dates in parentheses indicate the issues in which the ratings were published.

Vintage Port 1985 • $45 • (01/01/90) • **72**

Vintage Port 1982 • $20 • (01/01/90) • **78**

Vintage Port 1978 • $46 • (01/01/90) • **78**

FERREIRA

Douro Barca Velha 1983 • $35 • (04/15/94) • **89**

Late Bottled Port 1991: Very young and slightly rough but there's plenty of berry, grapey character. Medium- to full-bodied, medium sweet, with a licorice, cherry finish. Drink now or hold. • $19 • (02/28/98) • **86**

Tawny Port Duque de Bragança 20 Years Old NV • $49 • (01/31/96) • **73**

Tawny Port Quinta do Porto 10 years old NV • $25 • (01/31/96) • **81**

Vintage Port 1995: Beautifully crafted '95. Better than the '94. Intense aromas of violets. Full-bodied, medium sweet, with super well-integrated tannins. Long and caressing finish. • $37 • (04/30/98) • **90**

Vintage Port 1994: Inky, with intense, ripe fruit flavors, verging on raisin with a hint of citrus. Medium- to full-bodied and lightly sweet, with medium-tough, velvety tannins and a fresh finish. Not quite as impressive as when tasted from barrel, but a well-toned vintage Port nonetheless. Try after 2006. • $42 • (04/30/97) • **89**

Vintage Port 1991: A deceptively fine Port here. Intense grapey, green tea and fruit aromas and flavors. This takes off slowly on the palate and then kicks in at the end. Excellent tannins on the finish; quite dry. Tasted twice; second bottle much better. Try after 1999. 2,000 cases made. • $19 • (07/31/94) • **91**

Vintage Port 1987: Well balanced, with delicious sweet fruit and a firm backbone. Inky color, with a very ripe raisin and grape nose, full-bodied, with sweet fruit flavors, medium tannins and a long finish. • $NA • (11/01/89) • **88**

Vintage Port 1985: A rich, sweet Port that grows in intensity on the palate. Medium to deep purple, with perfumed, earthy raspberry aromas, full-bodied, with very sweet, syrupy fruit flavors and medium tannins. Very round and luscious. • $20 • (11/01/89) • **87**

Vintage Port 1983 • $14 • (11/01/89) • **91**

Vintage Port 1982 • $25 • (11/01/89) • **81**

Vintage Port 1980 • $32 • (11/01/89) • **80**

Vintage Port 1978 • $28 • (11/01/89) • **89**

Vintage Port 1977 • $49 • (11/01/89) • **86**

Vintage Port 1975 • $41 • (11/01/89) • **81**

Vintage Port 1970 • $45 • (04/01/89) • **86**

Vintage Port 1966 • $81 • (11/01/89) • **85**

Vintage Port 1963 • $NA • (08/01/88) • **85**

Vintage Port 1955 • $50 Ⓐ • (11/01/89) • **85**

Vintage Port 1950 • $90 • (11/01/89) • **79**

Vintage Port 1945 • $121 Ⓐ • (11/01/89) • **81**

Vintage Port 1935 • $200 • (02/01/90) • **93**

FERREIRA, ANTONIO ESTEVES

Alvarinho Vinho Verde Soalheiro 1995: Fresh and fairly fruity with tangy apple, citrus and herb flavors. Ends on a sweet, slightly rich note. Try chilled on a summer day. • $15 • (06/30/97) • **84**

Alvarinho Vinho Verde Soalheiro 1994 • $15 • (04/30/96) • **84**

FERREIRINHA, CASA

Douro Vinha Grande 1994: Tightly wound, with plenty of polish and tannin, red plum and spice flavors, a chocolate note on the finish. Smooth, well focused. Try in 1999. 1,000 cases made. • $22 • (07/31/97) • **87**

Douro Vinha Grande 1990 • $10 • (04/15/94) • **83**

FEUERHEERD

Vintage Port 1995: Very good, if slightly one-dimensional. Dark-colored, with an intensely grapey, fruity nose. Full- to medium-bodied, sweet, with firm, velvety tannins and a medium finish. Best after 2004. 850 cases made. • $28 • (04/30/98) • **87**

Vintage Port 1985: There is some fruit here but seemed extremely light on last tasting. Barely passable as a vintage. Medium ruby, with a light grape-skin nose, medium-bodied, with round, light tannins, clean fruit flavors and a very simple finish. • $NA • (01/01/90) • **72**

Vintage Port 1980 • $NA • (01/01/90) • **76**

Vintage Port 1970 • $45 • (01/01/90) • **80**

FONSECA

Late Bottled Port 1991: Slightly disappointing. Fruit, licorice aromas. Medium-bodied, medium sweet, with a fruity yet short finish. Drink now. • $18 • (02/28/98) • **81**
Late Bottled Port 1989 • $18 • (01/31/96) • **85**
Late Bottled Port 1988 • $17 • (11/15/94) • **84**
Tawny Port 10-year-old NV • $23 • (01/31/96) • **86**
Tawny Port 20-year-old NV • $44 • (01/31/96) • **84**
Tawny Port 40-year-old NV • $114 • (01/31/96) • **86**
Vintage Character Port Bin 27 NV • $16 • (03/15/94) • **85**
Vintage Port 1994: Hold on to your hat. This is the best Fonseca since 1977, and it's probably even better than that classic vintage—more like the breathtaking 1948. Mind-blowing, with masses of color, aroma and fruit flavor. Smells like fermenting berries, boasting loads of crushed grape, violet and berry character. Big, full-bodied and very sweet, with tons of tannins and a sweet finish. Tannic and huge, it's a long-term, great Port. Try after 2012. 8,000 cases made. • $120 • (04/30/97) CS • **100**
Vintage Port 1992 • $30 • (06/15/95) CS • **96**
Vintage Port 1991 • $NA • (07/31/94) • **93**
Vintage Port 1985 • $32 • (06/01/90) • **95**
Vintage Port 1983 • $34 • (06/01/90) • **90**
Vintage Port 1980 • $40 • (06/01/90) • **74**
Vintage Port 1977 • $16 • (04/01/90) • **100**
Vintage Port 1975 • $40 • (10/31/88) • **81**
Vintage Port 1970 • $65 • (12/01/89) • **96**
Vintage Port 1966 • $84 • (02/01/90) • **97**
Vintage Port 1963 • $162 • (12/01/89) • **98**
Vintage Port 1960 • $95 • (10/31/88) • **81**
Vintage Port 1955 • $200 • (08/01/88) • **96**
Vintage Port 1948 • $450 • (11/01/89) • **100**
Vintage Port 1945 • $500 • (11/01/89) • **91**
Vintage Port 1934 • $330 • (02/01/90) • **91**
Vintage Port 1927 • $430 • (12/01/89) • **100**
Vintage Port Guimaraens 1995: A gorgeous young thing—even better than I remember from barrel. This is an extremely fresh, floral and fruity young Port, full-to-medium in body and of medium sweetness, with a ripe and plummy aftertaste of good length. Best after 2006. 10,000 cases made. • $39 • (04/30/98) CS • **92**
Vintage Port Guimaraens 1991 • $35 • (07/31/94) • **93**
Vintage Port Guimaraens 1987 • $NA • (02/01/90) • **90**
Vintage Port Guimaraens 1986 • $NA • (02/01/90) • **86**
Vintage Port Guimaraens 1984 • $NA • (02/01/90) • **85**
Vintage Port Guimaraens 1982 • $NA • (02/01/90) • **82**
Vintage Port Guimaraens 1978 • $35 • (02/01/90) • **80**
Vintage Port Guimaraens 1976 • $38 • (02/01/90) • **89**
Vintage Port Guimaraens 1974 • $40 • (01/01/90) • **84**
Vintage Port Guimaraens 1972 • $34 • (02/01/90) • **75**
Vintage Port Guimaraens 1968 • $40 • (02/01/90) • **84**
Vintage Port Guimaraens 1967 • $56 • (02/01/90) • **90**
Vintage Port Guimaraens 1965 • $64 • (02/01/90) • **89**
Vintage Port Guimaraens 1964 • $95 • (02/01/90) • **90**
Vintage Port Guimaraens 1962 • $70 • (02/01/90) • **88**
Vintage Port Guimaraens 1961 • $70 • (02/01/90) • **85**
Vintage Port Guimaraens 1958 • $90 • (02/01/90) • **88**
Vintage Port Quinta do Panascal 1987 • $NA • (02/01/90) • **82**
Vintage Port Quinta do Panascal 1986 • $NA • (02/01/90) • **79**
Vintage Port Quinta do Panascal 1985 • $NA • (02/01/90) • **78**
Vintage Port Quinta do Panascal 1984 • $NA • (02/01/90) • **70**
Vintage Port Quinta do Panascal 1983 • $NA • (02/01/90) • **79**

FONSECA, JOSÉ MARIA DA

Alentejo 1987 • $9 • (04/15/94) • **80**
Alentejo Garrafeira 1988 • $13 • (04/15/94) • **82**
Alentejo Garrafeira AP 1987 • $13 • (04/15/94) • **85**
Alentejo Morgado do Reguengo 1989 • $8 • (04/15/94) • **81**
Alentejo Morgado do Reguengo 1987 • $9 • (11/15/91) • **86**
Arrábida Garrafeira CO 1990: Gamy aromas and flavors dissipate with a few minutes' aeration to make way for some good, dried cherry and tealike flavors. • $20 • (05/31/97) • **82**
Arrábida Garrafeira CO 1982 • $14 • (12/31/90) • **83**
Arrábida Garrafeira TE 1990: A sweet jammy aroma leads into a wine that is past its prime. It has modest dried cherry flavors and an astringent finish. • $19 • (01/01/97) • **78**
Arrábida Garrafeira TE 1988 • $NA • (04/15/94) • **67**
Azeitão Red Periquita 1989 • $5 • (01/31/93) • **80**
Azeitão White Albis 1995: Aromatic, with spicy and herbal flavors. Awkward and overdone. • $9 • (01/01/97) • **76**
Dão Casa da Insua 1988 • $9 • (01/01/95) • **76**
Dão Terras Altas 1991: This red is a bit drying on the palate, with modest, dried cherry flavors and an herbal touch on the finish. Past its prime. • $9 • (05/31/97) • **77**
Dão Terras Altas 1990 • $7 • (04/15/94) • **79**
Dão Terras Altas 1987 • $7 • (11/15/91) • **69**
Moscatel de Setúbal Azeitão 1990: Quite honeyed, with appealing fig and spice flavors, a maplelike flavor on the finish. Has a tealike aroma. • $14 • (05/31/97) • **86**
Moscatel de Setúbal Azeitão 20 Years NV: Hard to beat. Thick and rich, with honey and Sherry-like flavors, this is an enjoyably sweet and fresh dessert wine with great balance and complexity. Nut and chocolate flavors linger on the finish. • $42 • (05/31/97) • **92**
Moscatel de Setúbal Azeitão Roxo 20 Years NV: An elegant and finesseful dessert wine, with peach and apricot flavors, plenty of honey notes and a lingering chocolate flavor on the finish. Complex and full-flavored. Enjoy. • $50/500ml • (05/31/97) • **90**
Moscatel de Setúbal Azeitão Superior 1965: This full-bodied, sweet dessert wine, with its lovely amber color, is rich and voluptuous, with beautiful texture, loads of maple, honey and spice flavors, caramel notes that linger on the finish, and a nice, smoky, oxidized quality overall. It's balanced, and elegant, too. • $57/500ml • (05/31/97) • **94**
Palmela Garrafeira RA 1987: A mature red with leather and dried fruit flavors of good concentration, and spice notes that linger on the finish. Traditional in style. • $20 • (05/31/97) • **85**
Palmela Garrafeira RA 1982 • $14 • (12/31/90) • **88**
Portalegre d'Avillez 1991: A nicely matured red, smooth and rich, with a spicy aroma and plum, cherry and spice flavors that linger on the finish. • $12 • (05/31/97) • **88**
Portalegre d'Avillez 1990: A supple and concentrated red, with some lovely plum and currant flavors. Also has plenty of spice, along with a dollop of tannin. • $12 • (05/31/97) • **87**
Reguengos Garrafeira José de Sousa 1991: A fairly ripe red with some nice concentration, dried cherry and plum flavors. A bit astringent on the finish, though not overly so. • $20 • (05/31/97) • **83**
Reguengos Garrafeira José de Sousa 1990: A smooth and mature red, with leather and dried cherry flavors and some nice peppery notes, all lingering on the finish. Made in a traditional style. • $20 • (05/31/97) • **85**
Reguengos Tinto Velho José de Sousa 1993: A dull, gamy-tasting wine without a lot of finesse or fruit flavor. • $12 • (08/31/97) • **75**
Reguengos Tinto Velho José de Sousa 1992: Reminiscent of a Rioja, with brown sugar, tea, and orange-peel flavors. Medium-bodied, smooth and flavorful. • $12 • (05/31/97) • **85**
Requengos Tinto Velho de Monsarax Colhei 1986 • $10 • (12/31/90) • **82**
Terras do Sado Pasmados 1990: Soft and well proportioned with appealing dried cherry and gamelike flavors. Nice touches of orange-peel and spice mark the finish. It's mature, ready to drink. • $12 • (01/01/97) • **85**
Terras do Sado Pasmados 1989 • $9 • (04/15/94) • **78**
Terras do Sado Pasmados 1984 • $7 • (04/30/91) BB • **83**
Terras do Sado Periquita 1994: A fairly earthy-tasting wine with leather and gamelike flavors. Has a tannic bite on the finish. • $8 • (08/31/97) • **78**
Terras do Sado Periquita 1993: There is a strong menthol taste to this red, and some abrasive tannins. A tough customer. • $9 • (05/31/97) • **76**
Terras do Sado Periquita 1990 • $7 • (04/15/94) BB • **84**
Terras do Sado Periquita 1987 • $6 • (12/31/90) BB • **84**
Terras do Sado Periquita Classico 1992: A mature tasting wine with dark berry and cassis flavors. Still has plenty of tannin, but don't age this red any longer. 3,800 cases made. • $21 • (10/15/97) • **83**
Terras do Sado Periquita Vintage Selection 1987 • $7 • (11/15/91) • **80**
Terras do Sado Quinta de Camarate 1990: A bit dried out, with modest plum and cherry flavors and a tannic finish. • $12 • (01/01/97) • **79**
Terras do Sado Quinta de Camarate 1989 • $10 • (04/15/94) • **68**
Terras do Sado Quinta de Camarate 1984 • $9 • (04/15/94) • **70**

FORUM PRIOR DO CRATO

Dão 1989 • $9 • (04/15/94) • **82**
Planalto Mirandés 1990 • $7 • (04/15/94) • **78**

GILBERT

Vintage Port 1995: Slightly one-dimensional but shows pretty berry aromas and flavors. Medium-bodied, medium sweet, with fine tannins. Medium finish. Best after 2004. 400 cases made. • $45 • (04/30/98) • **85**
Vintage Port 1994: Gorgeously grapey with luscious fruit flavor. Medium- to full-bodied and very sweet, with fine, chewy tannins and a ripe fruit finish. Try after 2004. • $NA • (04/30/97) • **86**
Vintage Port 1992: Pretty plum, meat and berry aromas and flavors. Medium-bodied, sweet and round; a pleasant finish. Drinkable now. • $NA • (06/15/95) • **85**
Vintage Port 1991: Not a big wine, but has some pretty cherry, raspberry and cedar character. Medium body and medium tannins, with a soft finish. Try after 1998. 500 cases made. • $NA • (07/31/94) • **85**

GOULD CAMPBELL

Late Bottled Port 1985 • $15 • (04/15/92) • **86**
Vintage Port 1994: Very perfumed and beautiful, with a generous, ripe berry, cherry and mineral character and masses of fruit. Full-bodied and fat, it's medium-sweet with a long, tannic finish. A big and voluptuous young vintage Port. Better now than when tasted as a barrel sample. Best after 2010. 4,000 cases made. • $55 • (04/30/97) • **92**
Vintage Port 1991: Almost as thick as Graham and a favorite of the vintage. Racy and tannic with super dark color and loads of fruity, peppery aromas. Full-bodied yet reserved; quite dry with sleek tannins and a very long finish. Try after 2000. 500 cases made. • $35 • (07/31/94) • **92**
Vintage Port 1985: A good, standard 1985, quite lean and angular. Deep purple, with very grapy raspberry aromas, full-bodied, with medium tannins, sweet fruit and a slightly short finish. • $23 • (06/01/90) • **85**
Vintage Port 1983 • $31 • (06/01/90) • **90**
Vintage Port 1980 • $35 • (02/01/90) • **86**
Vintage Port 1977 • $29 Ⓐ • (02/01/90) • **93**
Vintage Port 1975 • $33 • (04/15/92) • **82**
Vintage Port 1970 • $54 • (02/01/90) • **88**
Vintage Port 1966 • $80 • (02/01/90) • **84**

GRAHAM

Late Bottled Port 1991: Refined, well-made LBV. Fresh and vibrant, with mineral, cherry and floral aromas and flavors. Medium-bodied, medium sweet, with fine tannins and a silky finish. Delicious. Drink now. 40,000 cases made. • $21 • (02/28/98) • **87**
Ruby Port Fine NV • $7 • (03/31/88) • **74**
Ruby Port Six Grapes NV • $15/375ml • (03/31/88) • **80**
Tawny Port 10 years old NV • $24 • (01/31/96) SS • **91**
Tawny Port 20 years old NV • $45 • (01/31/96) • **88**
Tawny Port 30 years old NV • $75 • (01/31/96) • **87**
Tawny Port 40 years old NV • $122 • (01/31/96) • **87**
Tawny Port Fine Tawny NV • $12 • (01/31/96) • **78**
Vintage Character Port Six Grapes NV • $21 • (03/15/94) • **81**
Vintage Port 1994: A big, tough, young vintage Port that's closed and difficult to taste. Emits lovely aromas of chocolate, berry and plum, and is full-bodied with lots of sweet, fruit flavors and masses of velvety tannins. Long, sweet finish. Try after 2010. 11,000 cases made. • $100 • (04/30/97) • **95**
Vintage Port 1991: Getting better all the time in the bottle. Real blockbuster of a wine that sneaks up on you. Beautiful tar, grape and berry aromas and flavors. It's full-bodied, quite sweet and reserved, but kicks off at the end with loads of fruit and tannins. Tasted twice with consistent notes. Try after 2000. • $45 • (07/31/94) • **93**
Vintage Port 1985: What more could one want in a young vintage Port? It has great elegance and great power. Brilliant deep ruby-purple, with boysenberry and licorice aromas, full-bodied, very fleshy, with a firm backbone of tannins. • $42 • (06/01/90) • **96**
Vintage Port 1983 • $40 • (06/01/90) • **93**
Vintage Port 1980 • $42 • (06/01/90) • **90**
Vintage Port 1977 • $46 Ⓐ • (04/01/90) • **90**
Vintage Port 1975 • $49 • (02/01/89) • **78**
Vintage Port 1970 • $57 Ⓐ • (12/01/89) • **94**
Vintage Port 1966 • $88 • (12/01/89) • **93**
Vintage Port 1963 • $150 • (12/01/89) • **97**
Vintage Port 1960 • $80 • (10/31/88) • **88**
Vintage Port 1955 • $210 • (11/01/89) • **94**
Vintage Port 1954 • $160 • (02/01/90) • **91**
Vintage Port 1948 • $290 • (11/01/89) • **95**
Vintage Port 1945 • $510 • (11/01/89) • **95**
Vintage Port 1942 • $420 • (04/01/90) • **89**
Vintage Port 1935 • $400 • (04/01/90) • **94**
Vintage Port 1927 • $570 • (02/01/90) • **94**
Vintage Port Malvedos 1995: Plenty of plummy, grapey aromas and flavors in this young vintage Port. Medium- to full-bodied, with medium, fine tannins and a sweet fruit aftertaste. Best after 2004. 7,500 cases made. • $43 • (04/30/98) • **89**
Vintage Port Malvedos 1992: Impressively rich and concentrated aromas of currants and fruit, with hints of earth. Big and thick on the palate, showing masses of fruit and tannins. Almost as good as the Graham '91. This one is built for long aging; try in 2000. 3,000 cases made. • $39 • (06/30/95) • **91**
Vintage Port Malvedos Centenary 1990 • $32 • (01/31/93) • **82**
Vintage Port Malvedos 1988: Ripe, opulent and delicious. Beautifully peppery and fruity in flavor, with a silky smooth texture that belies its high alcohol and young age. A very long finish echoes black pepper and chocolate. Tempting to drink now for its fruitiness, but probably best after 2000. 7,000 cases made. • $26 • (01/31/91) HR • **93**
Vintage Port Malvedos 1987: Amazing richness and depth of sweet, chewy fruit flavors. Dark inky color, with intense blackberry and cherry aromas, full-bodied, with sweet grape and cherry flavors and an excellent balance of round, ripe tannins. A great density of ripe fruit. • $NA • (02/01/90) • **91**
Vintage Port Malvedos 1986: A medium-weight vintage Port, with very fine concentration of plum and anise aromas. Not quite so opulent on the palate, where the grip of tannin puts the brakes on any apparent richness, but the spicy finish suggests this is a good candidate for aging. • $20 • (03/31/90) • **84**
Vintage Port Malvedos 1984 • $NA • (02/01/90) • **83**
Vintage Port Malvedos 1982 • $NA • (02/01/90) • **90**
Vintage Port Malvedos 1979 • $NA • (02/01/90) • **74**
Vintage Port Malvedos 1978 • $34 • (02/01/90) • **82**
Vintage Port Malvedos 1976 • $31 • (02/01/90) • **74**
Vintage Port Malvedos 1968 • $50 • (02/01/90) • **70**
Vintage Port Malvedos 1965 • $58 • (02/01/90) • **79**
Vintage Port Malvedos 1964 • $54 • (02/01/90) • **82**
Vintage Port Malvedos 1962 • $62 • (02/01/90) • **89**
Vintage Port Malvedos 1961 • $65 • (02/01/90) • **87**
Vintage Port Malvedos 1958 • $65 • (02/01/90) • **79**
Vintage Port Malvedos 1957 • $70 • (02/01/90) • **84**
Vintage Port Malvedos 1952 • $125 • (11/01/89) • **85**

HENRIQUES & HENRIQUES

Bual Madeira 10 Years Old NV: This notches it up. Sweet, with a thick texture moderated by tangy acidity, the caramel, molasses, walnut and orange flavors accelerate to a long, delineated finish with an aftertaste of the sea. Powerful and complex. • $35 • (11/30/97) • **93**
Madeira Monte Seco NV: Richly textured, dry, with walnut and butterscotch flavors, light caramel, nutty aromas. Good, tangy acidity, yet not so complex. Try as an apéritif. • $15 • (11/30/97) • **84**
Madeira Rainwater NV: Highlights of orange-peel and clove add nuance to the burnt demerara sugar character. Rich and tangy, showing focus and moderate length. • $15 • (11/30/97) • **84**
Malmsey Madeira 5 Years Old NV: Very sweet, with caramel and coffee flavors. The sweet, thick texture doesn't quite mesh with the cutting acidity and alcohol. • $18 • (11/30/97) • **85**
Malmsey Madeira 10 Years Old NV: Full, rich and powerful, yet with a definition that comes from the sharp acidity. The flavors are coffee, caramel, orange peel and vanilla. Long, satisfying finish. • $35 • (11/30/97) • **91**
Sercial Madeira 5 Years Old NV: A richer, fuller style than is typical for a Sercial. The honey and caramel flavors are underscored by a firm backbone and the walnut finish leaves a pleasant sharpness on the gums. • $18 • (11/30/97) • **87**
Sercial Madeira 10 Years Old NV: Offers full, rich, complex aromas and flavors reminiscent of sea air and forest undergrowth, caramel and walnuts. Powerful and long, this has substance and a sharpness at the end that's a little astringent. • $35 • (11/30/97) • **89**
Verdelho Madeira 5 Years Old NV: Displays lovely aromas of caramel that take on depth, with beef bouillon and honey flavors. Rich and round, then

Key: SS—Spectator Selection CS—Cellar Selection HR—Highly Recommended BB—Best Buy $NA—Price not available Ⓐ—Auction Price (BT)—Barrel Tasting
Dates in parentheses indicate the issues in which the ratings were published.

the long finish turns slightly astringent with a smoky aftertaste. • $18 • (11/30/97) • **88**

Verdelho Madeira 10 Years Old NV: Serious stuff. Despite a slightly singed nose, it exhibits complex flavors of honey, smoke, pear and wet pine needles. Rich, with an underlying tang and vibrance that follows through to the long walnut and salt-tang finish. A wine for meditation. • $35 • (11/30/97) • **91**

HOOPER

Tawny Port 20-year-old NV • $35 • (02/28/90) • **78**

Vintage Port 1985: • $20 • (06/01/90) • **80**

HUTCHESON

Vintage Port 1991: An early-maturing Port with pretty fruit, medium-deep ruby color and plummy, earthy aromas. It has a medium body with sweet and velvety fruit, medium tannins and a light finish. From Barros, Almeida. Drink now. 1,000 cases made. • $19 • (07/31/94) • **81**

Vintage Port 1970 • $50 • (01/01/90) • **79**

INFANTADO, QUINTA DO

Tawny Port 10 Years Old NV: Light-colored and quite delicious with its good hazlenut, caramel and toasty almond flavors. Textbook tawny. You could try it slightly chilled. • $32 • (09/15/97) • **87**

Vintage Port 1995: Shows lots of style with its wet earth and berry character, moderate sweetness and good tannic grip on the aftertaste. Almost outstanding. • $NA • (09/15/97) (BT) • **85-89**

Vintage Port 1992: The best ever made at this estate and one to watch in the future. Like a lagar full of grapes fermenting; big and powerful tar and raisin character. Full-bodied, sweet, tannic, in an extracted style. Try in 2000. • $35 • (06/15/95) • **90**

Vintage Port 1991: Deep and dark ruby, with wonderful dark chocolate and berry aromas and flavors. It's medium-bodied and quite sweet, with medium tannins and a fine finish. Try now. • $25 • (07/31/94) • **85**

Vintage Port 1989: This sweet, fruity, agreeable Port offers lots of blackberry and cherry flavors and a smooth finish. Should be at its best now. 1,800 cases made. • $35 • (07/31/93) • **81**

Vintage Port 1985: Pleasant on the palate, this 1985 was quite forward as of 1990. Deep ruby, with a very ripe and roasted nose, medium-bodied with very sweet fruit flavors and a soft mouthfeel. • $33 • (07/01/90) • **76**

Vintage Port 1982 • $35 • (07/01/90) • **70**

Vintage Port 1978 • $NA • (07/01/90) • **75**

J.P. VINHOS

Alentejo Herdade de Santa Marta 1993 • $9 • (03/31/96) • **83**

Alentejo Herdade de Santa Marta 1991 • $10 • (04/15/94) • **85**

Alentejo Tinto da Anfora 1991 • $10 • (03/31/96) • **84**

Alentejo Tinto da Anfora 1990 • $9 • (04/15/94) • **79**

Cabernet Sauvignon Terras do Sado Quinta da Bacalhôa 1995: A delicious wine, ripe, with flavors of red plum and blackberry, and a slightly herbal edge to the finish. Drink now. • $14 • (07/31/97) • **85**

Cabernet Sauvignon Terras do Sado Quinta da Bacalhôa 1990 • $15 • (04/15/94) • **81**

Palmela Garrafeira 1988: Murky and astringent with a lifted aroma and a jammy flavor to it. • $8 • (01/01/97) • **74**

Terras do Sado Má Partilha 1991: Balanced, mature and ready to drink with gamey flavors and aromas. Lively depite its age, it also has some red plum spice flavors that carry through to the finish. • $19 • (01/01/97) • **84**

Terras do Sado Quinta de Santo Amaro 1992 • $8 • (04/15/94) • **78**

Terras do Sado White Catarina 1995: This rich, broad and lush white is notable for its concentration, with loads of butterlike and tropical fruit flavors and some nice spicy notes on the finish. Made in an international style. A real mouthful at a bargain price. 10,000 cases made. • $8 • (06/30/97) BB • **87**

Vinho Espumante Loridos Bruto 1991: A bit austere and rustic-tasting, with modest herbal and canned-fruit flavors. • $12 • (06/30/97) • **76**

Vinho de Mesa J.P. NV • $5 • (03/31/96) • **79**

JOAO PATO

Bairrada 1991 • $9 • (04/15/94) • **86**

KOPKE

Tawny Port 20-year-old NV • $30 • (02/28/90) • **88**

Vintage Port 1995: Pretty young Port. Lovely, balanced, with floral, fruity aromas and flavors, medium body and a medium, firm tannin structure. Best after 2004. 2,500 cases made. • $NA • (04/30/98) • **86**

Vintage Port 1994: Offers plenty of wet earth, toast and blackberry character. Medium-bodied, with well-integrated tannins and a sweet, ripe fruit finish. Very pretty. Best after 2004. • $NA • (04/30/97) • **86**

Vintage Port 1991: Rather forward Port. Round and sweet berry and cherry character, medium to full body, sweet and soft tannins. From Barros, Almeida. Drinkable now. 1,700 cases made. • $NA • (07/31/94) • **82**

Vintage Port 1987: This is an elegant wine with good fruit and structure. Deep purple, with a rich, floral, grapy nose, full-bodied, with a good balance of medium tannins and sweet fruit flavors. • $24 • (01/01/90) • **86**

Vintage Port 1985: A dark horse that should finish among the top 1985s in years to come. Deep purple, with fresh blackberries and raspberries on the nose, full-bodied, with balanced tannins, a firm structure and a lovely finish. • $14 Ⓐ • (01/01/90) • **90**

Vintage Port 1983 • $23 • (01/01/90) • **85**

Vintage Port 1982 • $26 • (01/01/90) • **83**

Vintage Port 1980 • $13 Ⓐ • (01/01/90) • **71**

Vintage Port 1978 • $29 • (01/01/90) • **70**

Vintage Port 1975 • $28 • (01/01/90) • **82**

Vintage Port 1974 • $NA • (01/01/90) • **74**

Vintage Port 1970 • $25 Ⓐ • (01/01/90) • **82**

Vintage Port 1966 • $65 • (01/01/90) • **81**

Vintage Port 1960 • $65 • (01/01/90) • **87**

KROHN

Late Bottled Port 1987: Shows some attractive bottle age. Lovely aromas of berries, flowers and custard. Medium- to light-bodied, with fine tannins and a smooth texture. A little hot on the finish, but still delicate. Drink now. • $19 • (02/28/98) • **84**

Late Bottled Port 1985: A bit tired at this stage, with nut, berry, tobacco and meatlike character. Medium-bodied, medium sweet, with a slightly hot finish. Drink now. • $23 • (02/28/98) • **79**

LAGOALVA, QUINTA DA

Ribatejo 1994: Focused and firm, with decent cherry and dark plum flavors. Drink with food. • $10 • (10/15/97) • **81**

Ribatejo 1992 • $9 • (04/30/96) • **75**

Ribatejo 1991 • $7 • (04/15/94) • **83**

Ribatejo Cima 1992 • $9 • (04/30/96) • **83**

Ribatejo Lagoalva de Cima 1991 • $10 • (04/15/94) • **86**

Ribatejo White 1995: All dressed-up with buttery flavors and aromas, it has some modest fig and pear flavors, too. Enjoyable, but a bit one-dimensional. • $10 • (09/15/97) • **84**

LEACOCK'S

Madeira Rainwater NV: A medium-sweet dessert wine with caramel and smoky notes, it's soft, but comes up short and a little burnt on the finish. • $14 • (11/30/97) • **82**

MADREVINHOS

Cartaxo Três Hastins 1988 • $7 • (04/15/94) • **72**

MANDOS

Bairrada Reserva 1990 • $6 • (04/30/95) • **73**

Dão Reserva 1989 • $7 • (04/30/95) • **76**

MANGUALDE, ADEGA COOPERATIVA DE

Dão Foral D. Henrique Reserva 1990 • $5 • (01/31/95) • **78**

MARTINEZ

Late Bottled Port 1992: Pretty cherry and floral aromas, with a hint of pepper. Of medium body and sweetness, with an earthy, slightly nutty finish. Drink now. • $17 • (02/28/98) • **81**

Tawny Port 20-year-old Directors NV • $25 • (02/28/90) • **93**

Vintage Port 1995: A simple, fruity Port with flavors of plum and earth, a hint of nuts. Slightly forward already. What happened here? Tasted twice, with consistent notes. • $NA • (09/15/97) (BT) • **75-79**

Vintage Port 1994: A classy young Port, full-bodied and brimming with fruit flavor and silky, fine tannins that kick in on the finish. A subtle, young wine that takes you by surprise. Try after 2010. 2,150 cases made. • $30 • (04/30/97) • **95**

Vintage Port 1991: Round and delicious, but slightly forward compared to many. It shows a good balance of fruit, sweetness and tannins. Good aftertaste of minerals and fruit. Drink now. • $NA • (07/31/94) • **85**

Vintage Port 1987: Still very closed when last tasted, but round, ripe and rich, with extremely attractive fruit flavors and plenty of grip on the finish. Deep ruby with a purple center, aromas of flowers, milk chocolate and earth, full-bodied, with round tannins and a long finish. • $NA • (05/01/90) • **84**

Vintage Port 1985: A burly wine with muscles. Deep, dark ruby, with concentrated cherry aromas, full-bodied and tightly structured, with ripe tannins and rich cherry and earth flavors. • $16 Ⓐ • (06/01/90) • **89**

Vintage Port 1982 • $28 • (06/01/90) • **82**
Vintage Port 1975 • $40 • (02/01/90) • **75**
Vintage Port 1970 • $21 Ⓐ • (02/01/90) • **89**
Vintage Port 1967 • $56 • (02/01/90) • **93**
Vintage Port 1963 • $31 Ⓐ • (02/01/90) • **82**
Vintage Port 1955 • $120 • (11/01/89) • **86**

Vintage Port Quinta da Chousa 1995: A light '95 with smoky, berry and tobacco aromas and flavors, medium body and a soft texture. A good glass of Port but not true vintage Port quality. Tasted twice, with consistent notes. Best after 2000. • $39 • (04/30/98) • **79**

Vintage Port Quinta da Eira Velha 1995: Typical top '95. Impressive harmony, with plenty of everything in the right proportion. Full-bodied, medium sweet, with plum, grapey aromas and flavors and a long silky, fruity finish. Best after 2006. • $45 • (04/30/98) • **90**

Vintage Port Quinta da Eira Velha 1994: The sleeper of the vintage. A stunning, huge, amazingly young Port that makes your mouth pucker in delight. Full-bodied and medium-sweet, with masses of fruit and tannins. Try after 2012. 1,000 cases made. • $30 • (04/30/97) • **97**

Vintage Port Quinta da Eira Velha 1992: Better than the declared '91 Martinez. Intense, very ripe fruit character; violet and floral tones. Full-bodied, lightly sweet, quite tough, adding firm tannins and long finish. Try in 2000. • $NA • (06/15/95) • **89**

MATO MIRANDA, QUINTA DE

Ribatejo 1992 • $5 • (03/31/96) • **84**

MESSIA

Vintage Port 1984 • $15 • (02/01/90) • **78**
Vintage Port 1982 • $13 • (02/01/90) • **72**
Vintage Port 1963 • $40 • (02/01/90) • **71**
Vintage Port Quinta do Cachão 1983 • $11 • (02/01/90) • **77**
Vintage Port Quinta do Cachão 1970 • $55 • (02/01/90) • **87**
Vintage Port Quinta do Cachão 1966 • $30 • (02/01/90) • **84**

MINHO, QUINTA DO

Vinha Verde 1994 • $7 • (04/30/96) • **82**

MONÇÃO, ADEGA COOPERATIVA REGIONAL DE

Alvarinho Vinho Verde 1995: Smooth, rich and fairly ripe with appealing grass and citrus flavors and a pleasant finish. In a pleasant, round style, it's delicious and quaffable. • $9 • (05/15/97) • **85**

MORGAN

Vintage Port 1985 • $NA • (02/01/90) • **85**
Vintage Port 1977 • $NA • (01/01/90) • **78**

Key: SS—Spectator Selection CS—Cellar Selection HR—Highly Recommended BB—Best Buy $NA—Price not available Ⓐ—Auction Price (BT)—Barrel Tasting
Dates in parentheses indicate the issues in which the ratings were published.

Vintage Port 1970 • $NA • (02/01/90) • **88**
Vintage Port 1966 • $NA • (02/01/90) • **80**
Vintage Port 1963 • $NA • (02/01/90) • **86**

MURCAS, QUINTA DE

Douro 1992: Mature and somewhat smooth, but the dried plum and cherry flavors are fading. Finish shows a gamy edge. • $10 • (08/31/97) • **80**

MURGAS, QUINTA DAS

Estremadura 1989 • $8 • (04/30/96) • **79**

NAVEGA, ANTONIO AFONSO

Bairrada Quinta do Carvalhinho 1990 • $NA • (04/15/94) • **80**

NIEPOORT

Douro Redoma 1991 • $12 • (03/31/96) • **85**

Late Bottled Port 1992: A fruit-driven, well-blended LBV. Fresh and floral with a pretty, fruity undertone. Medium-bodied, very sweet, with silky tannins and a long, delicious finish. Drink now. • $17 • (02/28/98) • **86**

Tawny Port 10 years old NV • $28 • (01/31/96) • **88**
Tawny Port 20 years old NV • $47 • (01/31/96) • **91**
Tawny Port 30 years old NV • $100 • (01/31/96) • **81**
Tawny Port Colheita 1985 • $29 • (01/31/96) • **87**
Tawny Port Colheita 1983 • $34 • (01/31/96) HR • **95**
Tawny Port Colheita 1978 • $54 • (01/31/96) • **87**
Tawny Port Colheita 1976 • $60 • (01/31/96) • **93**
Tawny Port Colheita 1963 • $160 • (01/31/96) • **91**
Tawny Port Fine Tawny NV • $17 • (01/31/96) • **84**
Vintage Character Port NV • $NA • (03/15/94) • **86**

Vintage Port 1994: A tightly knit young Port with gorgeous plum, berry and earth character on the nose. Full-bodied, full of plummy flavors and velvety tannins, it's beautiful to taste, yet has grip and structure. Try after 2008. • $45 • (04/30/97) • **91**

Vintage Port 1992 • $33 • (06/15/95) • **90**
Vintage Port 1991 • $NA • (07/31/94) • **85**
Vintage Port 1987 • $17 Ⓐ • (11/01/89) • **91**
Vintage Port 1985 • $44 • (06/01/90) • **92**
Vintage Port 1983 • $16 Ⓐ • (06/01/90) • **84**
Vintage Port 1982 • $23 Ⓐ • (06/01/90) • **90**
Vintage Port 1980 • $16 Ⓐ • (06/01/90) • **87**
Vintage Port 1978 • $17 Ⓐ • (11/01/89) • **81**
Vintage Port 1977 • $50 • (04/01/90) • **89**
Vintage Port 1975 • $37 • (11/01/89) • **79**
Vintage Port 1970 • $55 • (01/01/90) • **93**
Vintage Port 1966 • $70 • (11/01/89) • **89**
Vintage Port 1963 • $90 • (11/01/89) • **90**
Vintage Port 1955 • $175 • (08/01/90) • **98**
Vintage Port 1945 • $250 • (02/01/90) • **97**
Vintage Port 1942 • $240 • (04/01/90) • **93**
Vintage Port 1927 • $300 • (04/01/90) • **97**

Vintage Port Petre's 1995: Round, rather soft and fruity, with pretty plum and earth character. • $NA • (09/15/97) (BT) • **80-84**

NOVAL, QUINTA DO

Late Bottled Port 1991: Some decent, clean fruit character, but it's a tad too stripped to be anything more than good. Medium-bodied, medium sweet, short finish. Drink now. • $18 • (02/28/98) • **80**

Late Bottled Port NV • $14 • (11/30/91) • **83**
Tawny Port 20 year old NV • $32 • (02/28/90) • **82**
Vintage Character Port Noval LB NV • $18 • (03/15/94) • **86**

Vintage Port 1995: Outstanding but slightly rustic, with earthy, berry aromas and flavors and chunky, chewy texture. Full in body, medium sweet, with full tannins and a slightly coarse finish. Needs time; best after 2007. • $55 • (04/30/98) • **90**

Vintage Port 1994: Muscular and ripe, showing fabulous potential. The best Noval in decades, it's full-bodied, with a fruity character, well-integrated, chewy tannins and a medium finish. A long-term wine that needs age to mellow; try after 2010. • $50 • (04/30/97) • **95**

Vintage Port 1991 • $25 • (07/31/94) • **87**
Vintage Port 1987 • $30 • (01/01/90) • **89**
Vintage Port 1985 • $NA • (10/31/88) • **91**

Vintage Port 1982 • $36 • (06/01/90) • **78**
Vintage Port 1978 • $17 Ⓐ • (11/01/89) • **72**
Vintage Port 1977 • $50 • (10/31/88) • **78**
Vintage Port 1975 • $52 • (11/01/89) • **81**
Vintage Port 1970 • $60 • (11/01/89) • **89**
Vintage Port 1967 • $60 • (12/01/89) • **88**
Vintage Port 1966 • $75 • (12/01/89) • **91**
Vintage Port 1963 • $90 • (12/01/89) • **84**
Vintage Port 1960 • $84 • (11/01/89) • **82**
Vintage Port 1958 • $100 • (11/01/89) • **82**
Vintage Port 1955 • $100 • (08/01/90) • **88**
Vintage Port 1950 • $180 • (11/01/89) • **85**
Vintage Port 1947 • $200 • (11/01/89) • **93**
Vintage Port 1945 • $310 • (11/01/89) • **92**
Vintage Port 1942 • $200 • (04/01/90) • **86**
Vintage Port 1938 • $110 • (09/01/85) • **71**
Vintage Port 1934 • $310 • (02/01/90) • **98**
Vintage Port 1931 • $850 • (11/01/89) • **99**
Vintage Port 1927 • $360 • (12/01/89) • **93**
Vintage Port Nacional 1994: This is what class is all about in vintage Port. Living up to the greatness of Nacional, this wine shows a stunning nose, with blackberry and cherry perfumes, and is full-bodied and moderately sweet. It has impressively well-integrated, ultrafine tannins and a long, silky finish. Best since the legendary '63. Try after 2012. 250 cases made. • $400 • (04/30/97) CS • **100**
Vintage Port Nacional 1991: There's plenty of grip to this big, racy, young vintage Port, with all the right elements to reward cellaring until after 2004. It's full-bodied, of medium sweetness, with full yet fine tannins and a rich, cherry-charged aftertaste. Delicious. • $180 • (06/15/98) CS • **93**
Vintage Port Nacional 1987 • $145 • (01/01/90) • **94**
Vintage Port Nacional 1985 • $225 • (11/01/89) • **95**
Vintage Port Nacional 1982 • $130 • (11/01/89) • **86**
Vintage Port Nacional 1980 • $150 • (02/01/90) • **80**
Vintage Port Nacional 1978 • $160 • (11/01/89) • **77**
Vintage Port Nacional 1975 • $170 • (11/01/89) • **86**
Vintage Port Nacional 1970 • $300 • (11/01/89) • **98**
Vintage Port Nacional 1967 • $325 • (11/01/89) • **95**
Vintage Port Nacional 1966 • $310 • (11/01/89) • **98**
Vintage Port Nacional 1964 • $250 • (11/01/89) • **84**
Vintage Port Nacional 1963 • $600 • (11/01/89) • **100**
Vintage Port Nacional 1962 • $350 • (11/01/89) • **86**
Vintage Port Nacional 1960 • $300 • (11/01/89) • **84**
Vintage Port Nacional 1950 • $650 • (11/01/89) • **90**
Vintage Port Nacional 1931 • $2500 • (11/01/89) • **100**
Vintage Port Quinta da Silval 1995: Rich and raisiny, if slightly one-dimensional. Not as good as I remember. Full-bodied, sweet and concentrated. Needs time to show what it really has. Best after 2004. • $45 • (04/30/98) • **88**
Vintage Port Quinta do Roriz 1995: An extremely silky, well-made '95 with plum, berry and spice aromas and flavors. Medium- to full-bodied, with well-integrated tannins and a long, silky finish. Best after 2006. • $45 • (04/30/98) • **90**

OFFLEY

Late Bottled Port 1990: A joy to drink. Lovely aromas of violets and berries with a hint of spices. Medium-bodied, medium sweet, with silky, fine tannins and a long, sweet and delicious aftertaste. Drink now. • $19 • (02/28/98) • **88**
Late Bottled Port 1988 • $19 • (11/15/94) • **86**
Tawny Port 20-year-old Baron Forrester NV • $35 • (02/28/90) • **89**
Vintage Character Port Boa Vista Reserve NV • $14 • (03/15/94) • **75**
Vintage Port 1987: Simple, but has very good fruit structure. Dark purple, with grapy, floral aromas, full-bodied, with round, chewy fruit flavors, medium tannins and a long finish. • $NA • (01/01/90) • **84**
Vintage Port Boa Vista 1995: A harmonious young Port. Medium-dark ruby in color, with lovely berry, cherry and black pepper aromas and flavors. Medium-bodied, with medium, firm tannins and a delicious, sweet fruit finish. Best after 2004. 2,100 cases made. • $35 • (04/30/98) • **86**
Vintage Port Boa Vista 1994: One of the sweeter vintage Ports, with fine tannins and fruity character. Medium-bodied, with a silky, elegant finish. Best after 2004. • $30 • (04/30/97) • **84**
Vintage Port Boa Vista 1987: Very classy and well crafted. Deep inky color, very ripe black currant aromas, full-bodied, with plenty of racy fruit flavors, a tough backbone and a long finish. • $NA • (01/01/90) • **88**
Vintage Port Boa Vista 1985: Polished, with good fruit and backbone. Deep inky color, elegant perfumed nose, full-bodied, with silky, elegant fruit flavors, medium tannins and a long finish. • $31 • (06/01/90) • **89**
Vintage Port Boa Vista 1983 • $35 • (01/01/90) • **91**
Vintage Port Boa Vista 1982 • $23 • (06/01/90) • **84**
Vintage Port Boa Vista 1980 • $30 • (06/01/90) • **90**
Vintage Port Boa Vista 1977 • $18 Ⓐ • (01/01/90) • **88**
Vintage Port Boa Vista 1975 • $27 • (02/01/89) • **75**
Vintage Port Boa Vista 1972 • $36 Ⓐ • (02/01/89) • **79**
Vintage Port Boa Vista 1970 • $21 Ⓐ • (02/01/89) • **81**
Vintage Port Boa Vista 1966 • $45 • (02/01/89) • **90**
Vintage Port Boa Vista 1960 • $24 Ⓐ • (02/01/89) • **78**

OSBORNE

Late Bottled Port 1991: Not offering much. Clean and lightly fruity, but it comes across somewhat stripped of character. Drink now. • $15 • (02/28/98) • **77**
Vintage Port 1995: Well structured, if slightly one-dimensional. Loads of crushed blackberries and earth. Full-bodied and very sweet, with plenty of chunky tannins and a long, sweet fruit finish. Best after 2005. 3,000 cases made. • $30 • (04/30/98) • **87**
Vintage Port 1994: An amazing wine for this producer. Osborne means business now. Rich and impressive, with plenty of ripe, fruit character. Full-bodied and very sweet, with a long, tannic, fruity finish. Try after 2010. 2,000 cases made. • $30 • (04/30/97) • **91**
Vintage Port 1992: Loads of grape and berry aromas and flavors, medium body, medium sweetness, fine tannin structure and fresh finish. Try in 1999. • $28 • (06/15/95) • **88**
Vintage Port 1985: Well made, but much too light for such an excellent vintage. Medium ruby with a red hue, peppery aromas, medium-bodied, with elegant medium tannins and a light finish. • $20 • (02/01/89) • **76**
Vintage Port 1982 • $26 • (01/01/90) • **72**
Vintage Port 1970 • $50 • (01/01/90) • **77**
Vintage Port 1960 • $60 • (01/01/90) • **82**

PAÇO, QUINTA DO

Vinho Verde Paço de Teixeiró 1996: Intense and tart, with appealing lemony flavors and herbal notes, and a good crisp finish. Serve well chilled. Try with sushi. 3,500 cases made. • $12 • (04/30/98) • **83**
Vinho Verde Paço de Teixeiró 1995: Fairly rich and mature-tasting with some good ripe apple and spice flavors. Not your typical Vinho Verde, but enjoyable. Finishes with buttery notes. • $11 • (08/31/97) • **83**
Vinho Verde Paço de Teixeiró 1994 • $11 • (04/30/96) • **81**

PALACIO DA BREJOEIRA

Alvarinho Vinho Verde 1995: Past its peak; only some dull, canned fruit flavors remain. Turns harsh on the finish. • $23 • (10/15/97) • **74**

PANCAS, QUINTA DE

Alenquer 1990 • $7 • (04/15/94) BB • **85**
Cabernet Sauvignon Alenquer 1991 • $7 • (04/15/94) BB • **85**
Cabernet Sauvignon Estremadura 1995: Shows some nice concentration, with plum, herb and olive flavors predominant. Drinkable now. • $11 • (08/31/97) • **81**
Cabernet Sauvignon Estremadura 1992 • $NA • (04/30/95) • **83**
Chardonnay Estremadura 1995: A ripe style with plenty of pear and caramel flavors, fairly rich and focused. Nice, spicy finish. • $11 • (06/30/97) • **86**
Chardonnay Estremadura Barrel Fermented 1994: Ripe and almost honeyed apple and cinnamon flavors. Somewhat coarse but firm, adding spicy aftertaste and a nice lemony note as well. 2,000 cases made. • $11 • (10/15/96) • **82**

PARROTES, QUINTA DE

Alenquer 1995: Extreme flavors of leather and game with a harsh finish. Not much fun. • $8 • (08/31/97) • **73**
Alenquer 1992 • $7 • (03/31/96) • **83**
Alenquer 1991 • $NA • (04/30/95) • **84**
Alenquer Periquita 1990 • $6 • (04/15/94) BB • **83**
Vital e Chardonnay Alenquer 1995: Dull tasting, with little fruit flavor and a harsh finish. • $8 • (06/30/97) • **70**

PASSADOURO, QUINTA DO

Vintage Port 1995: A slightly rustic, chunky, sweet young Port. Dark purple, magenta color, with a peppery, berry aroma. Medium-bodied, very sweet, with medium, chunky tannins and a medium finish. Produced and bottled by Niepoort. Best after 2005. • $54 • (04/30/98) • **86**

Vintage Port 1994: Sleek and impressively fruity, with silky tannins and a fresh finish. Medium- to full-bodied, with moderate sweetness and substantial grip on the finish. Produced and bottled by Niepoort. Try after 2004. • $45 • (04/30/97) • **88**

Vintage Port 1992: Not quite as great as when barrel-tasted last year. Ripe and roasted, medium-bodied and sweet, featuring round tannins and ripe fruit finish. Produced and bottled by Niepoort. Try in 1999. • $NA • (06/15/95) • **88**

PATO, LUIS

Bairrada 1988 • $16 • (04/15/94) • **84**

Bairrada Oak Aged 1988 • $17 • (04/15/94) • **85**

Bairrada Quinta do Ribeirinho Primeira Escolha 1995: A well-defined, concentrated wine with lively blackberry and dark plum flavors. Powefully tannic, with vibrant acidity. Coffee and spice flavors linger on the finish. Needs time; try in 1999. 2,750 cases made. • $12 • (09/15/97) • **87**

Bairrada Quinta do Ribeirinho Vinho Tinto 1990 • $7 • (04/15/94) BB • **84**

Bairrada Vinha Barrosa 1995: A ripe style with a wallop of tannins and a beautiful blueberry aroma. Quite fruity and elegant, with lots of blueberry, raspberry and plum flavors. A well-defined and subtle wine. 840 cases made. • $32 • (09/15/97) • **89**

Bairrada Vinha Pan 1995: Smooth and supple. Has blackberry and cherry flavors, some nice peppery and herbal notes and well-integrated tannins. The lingering finish is dominated by a dark chocolate flavor. 575 cases made. • $32 • (09/15/97) • **87**

Bairrada Vinhas Velhas 1995: Good and chewy with leather, plum and dried cherry flavors. This is a full-bodied red with plenty of power and complexity. Finishes on a nice chocolaty note. • $22 • (10/15/97) • **88**

Bairrada Vinhas Velhas 1990 • $12 • (04/15/94) • **86**

PELLADA, QUINTA DA

Dâo 1992 • $10 • (04/30/95) • **80**

PEREIRA, MANUEL SALVADOR

Alvarinho Vinho Verde Dom Salvador 1994 • $10 • (04/30/96) • **85**

PINTOS DOS SANTOS, A.

Vintage Port 1982 • $NA • (01/01/90) • **70**

Vintage Port 1980 • $NA • (01/01/90) • **70**

Vintage Port 1970 • $NA • (01/01/90) • **70**

POCAS, PORTO

Vintage Port 1995: Promises more in color and aroma than is delivered on the palate, showing dark ink-color with wonderful wild berry, currants and raspberry aromas. Full-bodied, very sweet, with soft, velvety tannins and a medium finish. Best after 2004. 2,350 cases made. • $30 • (04/30/98) • **86**

Vintage Port 1994: Unctuous and quite sweet. Medium-bodied, with very fine tannins and a sweet, fruity finish. Try after 2005. • $51 • (04/30/97) • **86**

Vintage Port 1991: A medium-term Port with pretty fruit, medium-deep ruby color and perfumed cherry and blackberry aromas. Medium-bodied and very sweet with soft round texture, focused cherry and chocolate flavors and a medium finish. Drink now. • $NA • (07/31/94) • **84**

POCAS JUNIOR

Tawny Port 20-year-old NV • $35 • (02/28/90) • **89**

Key: SS—Spectator Selection CS—Cellar Selection HR—Highly Recommended BB—Best Buy $NA—Price not available Ⓐ—Auction Price (BT)—Barrel Tasting
Dates in parentheses indicate the issues in which the ratings were published.

Vintage Port 1985: Hard and quite tough for a 1985, with lots of grapy, peppery flavors and a firm backbone, though it was still rather lean when last tasted. Purple with an inky center, black pepper nose, medium-bodied, with black pepper and fruit flavors, medium tannins and a hard finish. • $19 • (02/01/90) • **85**

Vintage Port 1975 • $42 • (02/01/90) • **74**

Vintage Port 1970 • $52 • (02/01/90) • **84**

Vintage Port 1963 • $100 • (02/01/90) • **82**

Vintage Port 1960 • $80 • (02/01/90) • **82**

PORTA DA RAVESSA

Redondo 1995: A fresh, fruity and simple red with strawberry flavors and aromas. Try slightly chilled. • $8 • (08/31/97) • **80**

Redondo 1990 • $4 • (04/15/94) BB • **82**

Redondo White 1995: A muddled white with some canned-fruit flavors and a cloying finish. • $8 • (06/30/97) • **75**

PORTALEGRE, ADEGA COOPERATIVA DE

Alentejo 1990 • $11 • (04/15/94) • **80**

Alentejo Conventual 1995: A ripe style with dark plum and raisinlike flavors, and a good dose of tannins. Somewhat rustic, with some appealing notes. 6,275 cases made. • $13 • (09/15/97) • **84**

Alentejo Conventual 1992 • $12 • (03/31/96) • **76**

Alentejo Conventual 1990 • $9 • (04/15/94) • **78**

Alentejo Terras do Baco 1996: Good cherry and pepper flavors, but it's quite tannic and one-dimensional. • $10 • (10/15/97) • **78**

PRIMAVERA, CAVES

Bairrada Colheita 1990 • $5 • (03/31/96) • **76**

Dão 1989 • $5 • (04/15/94) • **74**

PROVA REGIA

Arinto Bucelas 1995: A fairly simple but satisfying white with some pleasant almond and butter flavors. A one-note wine, but it hits it well. • $7 • (09/15/97) • **82**

QUARLES HARRIS

Port Reserve "Bottled in 1987" 1940 • $70 • (01/31/88) • **96**

Vintage Port 1994: A young Port with lots of roasted fruit and tobacco character, medium body and firm tannins. Lightly sweet. Slightly better than when tasted from barrel. Try after 2003. 3,500 cases made. • $55 • (04/30/97) • **87**

Vintage Port 1985: Firm and well made, with a sufficient structure of fruit and tannin for long-term aging. Medium-to-deep ruby, light tomato and boysenberry nose, medium- to full-bodied, with medium tannins, spicy, peppery fruit flavors and a lingering finish. • $27 • (06/01/90) • **85**

Vintage Port 1983 • $31 • (02/01/90) • **89**

Vintage Port 1980 • $29 • (02/01/90) • **83**

Vintage Port 1977 • $43 • (02/01/90) • **89**

Vintage Port 1975 • $38 • (04/01/90) • **73**

Vintage Port 1970 • $52 • (02/01/90) • **89**

Vintage Port 1966 • $78 • (02/01/90) • **74**

Vintage Port 1963 • $95 • (02/01/90) • **85**

RAMOS-PINTO

Douro 1994: A fruity, concentrated and complex wine with plenty of plum and spice flavors. Well structured and firm, with a nice chocolaty finish. Try now. • $11 • (07/31/97) • **88**

Douro Duas Quintas 1992: Pleasant notes of milk chocolate, plum and a touch of caramel on the finish. Has a bit of richness to boot, and would make a good quaff with grilled foods. • $9 • (09/15/96) • **82**

Douro Duas Quintas 1991 • $7 • (04/15/94) • **82**

Douro Duas Quintas Reserva 1992 • $16 • (03/31/96) • **86**

Douro Duas Quintas Reserva 1991: Rich and full-bodied with plenty of stuffing, it's a concentrated wine in a ripe style with plenty of black cherry, chocolate and plum flavors. Smooth and satisfying. • $18 • (07/31/97) • **87**

Late Bottled Port 1992: Very impressive for a young LBV. As good as many vintage Ports from the same year. Beautiful, bright, ripe fruit, berry and

wet earth character. Medium-bodied, with medium tannins, a silky texture. Long finish. Extremely well made. • $20 • (02/28/98) • **89**
Tawny Port 20 years old Quinta Bom-Retiro NV • $39 • (02/28/90) • **84**
Tawny Port 30 years old NV • $65 • (01/31/96) • **90**
Tawny Port Quinta da Ervamoira 10-year-old NV • $25 • (01/31/96) • **86**
Tawny Port Quinta do Bom-Retiro 20-year-old NV • $48 • (01/31/96) HR • **93**
Tràs-os-Montes Quinta dos Bons Ares 1992 • $NA • (01/01/96) • **84**
Vintage Character Port Quinta da Urtiga NV • $17 • (03/15/94) • **86**
Vintage Port 1995: A softer, early-drinking '95. Enticing plum and black cherry aromas. Full-bodied and very sweet, with light tannins and a sweet finish. Best after 2002. 1,125 cases made. • $35 • (04/30/98) • **83**
Vintage Port 1994: A well balanced, elegant young Port with cherry and roasted fruit character. Medium-bodied and moderately sweet. Spicy finish. Showed slightly better when tasted from barrel. Best after 2004. • $45 • (04/30/97) • **87**
Vintage Port 1991: Big, fat, fruity style. Good, dark purple to ruby color. Grapey plum aromas, full-bodied and sweet, with a wonderfully smooth mouthfeel, loads of fruit and velvety tannins. Try now. 5,500 cases made. • $26 • (07/31/94) • **86**
Vintage Port 1985: Very fine, though perhaps a little too elegant for longevity. Deep ruby, with incredibly fresh violet aromas, medium-bodied, with plenty of lovely, elegant, clean raspberry flavors, medium tannins and a balanced finish. • $21 • (11/01/89) • **85**
Vintage Port 1983 • $35 • (11/01/89) • **89**
Vintage Port 1982 • $15 Ⓐ • (11/01/89) • **79**
Vintage Port 1980 • $25 • (11/01/89) • **74**
Vintage Port 1970 • $85 • (11/01/89) • **81**
Vintage Port 1963 • $80 • (11/01/89) • **83**
Vintage Port Quinta da Ervamoira 1994: A beautifully balanced Port, with ultrafine tannins and lovely, sweet fruit flavors. Medium-bodied, with a fresh, fruity finish. Best after 2004. • $50 • (04/30/97) • **88**

REAL VINÍCOLA

Dão 1990 • $6 • (04/30/95) • **79**
Douro Evel 1994: Has a definite cherry cola flavor, with spicy notes as well. Balanced, with a nice zip. • $7 • (08/31/97) • **83**
Douro Evel 1990 • $6 • (04/30/95) • **84**
Douro White Evel 1995: Interesting flavors of green peaches and herbs, but it turns a bit candied on the finish. • $7 • (06/30/97) • **79**

REBELLO-VALENTE

Vintage Port 1985: Elegant and light for the vintage. Medium ruby, with a light raisin and black pepper nose, medium-bodied, with black pepper and fruit flavors and medium tannins. Lacks punch on the finish. • $33 • (06/01/90) • **81**
Vintage Port 1983 • $24 • (06/01/90) • **78**
Vintage Port 1980 • $41 • (02/01/90) • **80**
Vintage Port 1977 • $40 • (02/01/90) • **89**
Vintage Port 1975 • $53 • (02/01/90) • **75**
Vintage Port 1972 • $53 • (01/01/90) • **83**
Vintage Port 1970 • $50 • (02/01/90) • **92**
Vintage Port 1967 • $77 • (02/01/90) • **91**
Vintage Port 1966 • $60 • (02/01/90) • **82**
Vintage Port 1963 • $92 • (02/01/90) • **85**
Vintage Port 1960 • $55 • (11/01/88) • **85**
Vintage Port 1945 • $195 • (05/01/90) • **92**
Vintage Port 1942 • $140 • (02/01/85) • **75**

REGUENGOS DE MONSARAZ, COOPERATIVA

Alentejo Terras d'el Rei 1994 • $4 • (04/30/96) • **78**
Alentejo Terras d'el Rei NV • $4 • (04/30/95) • **80**
Reguengos 1994 • $5 • (04/30/96) BB • **85**
Reguengos 1992 • $5 • (04/30/95) • **84**
Reguengos 1990 • $5 • (04/15/94) • **71**
Reguengos Garrafeira dos Sócios 1990 • $12 • (04/30/95) • **83**
Reguengos Reserva 1990 • $8 • (04/30/95) • **78**
Reguengos Terras d'el Rei 1992 • $4 • (04/15/94) • **77**
Reguengos Terras d'el Rei Garrafeira 1987 • $10 • (04/15/94) • **77**
Reguengos Terras d'el Rei Reserva 1987 • $7 • (04/15/94) • **77**

ROCHA

Vintage Port 1985: Beautifully focused cherry, nutmeg and exotic spice aromas and flavors carry through to the long, finely balanced finish, offering just the right hint of toast and spirit. A wine with elegance and grip that should age nicely through at least 2000. • $32 • (04/15/91) • **88**
Vintage Port 1977 • $19 • (04/30/91) • **81**

ROMANEIRA, QUINTA DA

Vintage Port 1987: Earthy and well structured, showing aging potential. Medium to deep purple, with earthy grape aromas, full-bodied, with lots of tannins and a good depth of earthy fruit flavors. • $NA • (01/01/90) • **81**
Vintage Port 1985: Very rustic in style. Medium ruby, with an earthy licorice nose, medium-bodied, with round tannins, good fruit flavors and some grip on the finish. • $29 • (01/01/90) • **78**
Vintage Port 1935 • $NA • (02/01/90) • **90**
Vintage Port Quinta das Liceiras 1992: Best ever from here. Very powerful wet earth and ripe fruit character. Medium- to full-bodied, medium-sweet, exhibiting sleek tannins and a medium finish. Try in 1999. • $NA • (06/15/95) • **89**

ROQUEVALE

Alentejo Terras de Xisto 1990 • $5 • (04/15/94) • **77**
Alentejo Tinto da Talha 1992 • $7 • (04/15/94) • **79**
Redondo 1990 • $6 • (04/15/94) • **77**

ROSA, QUINTA DE LA

Douro 1992 • $8 • (04/15/94) • **83**
Douro 1991 • $10 • (04/15/94) • **85**
Late Bottled Port 1992: Solid LBV. Attractive aromas of berries, wet earth. Medium-bodied, medium sweet, with fresh fruit and a velvety texture. Drink now or hold. • $21 • (02/28/98) • **86**
Vintage Character Port Finest Reserve NV • $15 • (03/15/94) • **84**
Vintage Port 1995: Good character, a bit lean. A medium-bodied young Port with spicy, earthy, mushroomy aromas and flavors. Medium sweet, with a rather short finish. Best after 2003. 600 cases made. • $39 • (04/30/98) • **85**
Vintage Port 1994: Aromatic and pretty, with floral, berry and cherry aromas and fruity, citruslike flavors. Medium in body, sweetness and tannin. Best after 2005. • $40 • (04/30/97) • **86**
Vintage Port 1992: Best La Rosa ever made. Very ripe, chocolaty, hot fruit character, medium body, racy tannins and long finish. Well integrated and elegant. Try in 2000. • $NA • (06/15/95) • **88**
Vintage Port 1991: Dark and inky, with green tea, tobacco and raspberry aromas. This is tight and tannic, with a sleek and steely structure. May still need time. Tasted twice; second bottle much better. Try in 1999. 1,600 cases made. • $NA • (07/31/94) • **86**
Vintage Port 1988: Ripe and raisiny, with layers of currant, plum and anise flavors. Is also a bit hot, with chewy tannins and a hint of cedar on the aftertaste. Was rough-edged, but may be better now. • $18 • (04/15/92) • **85**
Vintage Port 1972 • $NA • (10/01/89) • **76**
Vintage Port 1966 • $NA • (10/01/89) • **82**
Vintage Port 1963 • $NA • (10/01/89) • **85**
Vintage Port 1960 • $NA • (10/01/89) • **88**
Vintage Port Feuerheerd Quinta de la Rosa 1927 • $NA • (12/01/89) • **87**

ROYAL OPORTO

Tawny Port 20-year-old NV • $25 • (02/28/90) • **77**
Vintage Port 1987: A hard-edged, brandy-scented style of Port that comes through with enough plum and cherry flavors on the finish to suggest it should age well through 2001 to 2005. • $19 • (11/30/91) • **81**
Vintage Port 1985: This has some fruit but it is too evolved for a 1985. Medium ruby, with a grapey, raisiny nose, medium-bodied, with sweet, berry flavors and round tannins. Maturing quickly. • $16 Ⓐ • (06/01/90) • **71**
Vintage Port 1983 • $14 • (06/01/90) • **76**
Vintage Port 1977 • $30 • (11/01/89) • **74**
Vintage Port 1970 • $36 • (11/01/89) • **75**
Vintage Port 1967 • $30 • (11/01/89) • **72**
Vintage Port 1963 • $55 • (11/01/89) • **73**

Vintage Port 1871 • $NA • (11/01/89) • **98**

ROZES

Late Bottled Port 1992: Good aromas of violets, raspberries and minerals. Medium-bodied, medium sweet, with fine tannins and a short finish. Drink now. • $18 • (02/28/98) • **85**
Late Bottled Port 1985 • $17 • (01/31/96) • **79**
Ruby Port Infanta Isabel 10 years old NV • $20 • (01/31/96) • **85**
Vintage Port 1995: Not a big young Port, but very well balanced. Dark-colored. Loads of raspberry aromas and flavors. Medium-bodied, with medium, fine tannins and a lovely, sweet fruit aftertaste. Best after 2004. 3,000 cases made. • $45 • (04/30/98) • **88**
Vintage Port 1994: Very good wine. Shows violets, plums and chocolate on the nose and palate. Medium- to full-bodied, medium sweet, with medium chewy tannins and a fruity finish. Try after 2003. • $NA • (01/01/97) • **86**
Vintage Port 1991: A relatively new face in Vintage Port and improving. The 1991 Rozes is elegant with solid berry and cherry aromas and flavors, medium body, medium sweetness and tannins and a sweet finish. Try after 1999. 5,000 cases made. • $23 • (07/31/94) • **87**
Vintage Port 1987: Elegant, lovely flavors, but early in maturing. Inky center with a ruby edge, a slight tar and cassis nose, full-bodied, with fresh, sweet, ripe raspberry flavors, firm tannins and a long, elegant, slightly nutty finish. • $NA • (06/01/90) • **86**
Vintage Port 1985: A good, rather chewy 1985 with a solid concentration of flavorful fruit and round tannins. Deep ruby with a red hue, pretty, light cherry aromas, full-bodied, with delicious, round, chewy fruit flavors, medium tannins and a sweet finish. Slightly simple. • $21 • (05/01/90) • **81**
Vintage Port 1982 • $NA • (06/01/90) • **75**

SAES, QUINTA DE

Dão 1995: A fruity wine with good berrylike aromas and flavors. One-dimensional with a slightly astringent finish. • $10 • (10/15/97) • **81**
Dão 1992 • $10 • (04/30/96) • **82**
Dão 1990 • $9 • (04/15/94) • **84**
Dão White 1995: Simple and sappy, with resinous flavors and some astringency on the finish. • $10 • (09/15/97) • **76**

SANDEMAN

Late Bottled Port 1991: Some good berry, chocolate flavors, but slightly mature compared with some LBVs. Medium-bodied, medium sweet, and very soft-textured. Drink now. • $25 • (02/28/98) • **82**
Tawny Port 20 years old NV • $42 • (01/31/96) HR • **91**
Vintage Character Port Founders Reserve NV • $17 • (03/15/94) • **81**
Vintage Port 1994: Big and grapey with loads of sweet fruit flavor, though slightly roasted. Full-bodied, with a short, clumsy finish. Lacks the backbone of tannins and acidity of higher-scoring Ports. Try after 2003. • $40 • (04/30/97) • **85**
Vintage Port 1985: Elegant and balanced, but a little short on concentration. Medium ruby-purple, with a spicy plum nose, medium-bodied, with clean fruit flavors, medium tannins and finish. • $30 • (06/01/90) • **83**
Vintage Port 1982 • $36 • (06/01/90) • **82**
Vintage Port 1980 • $18 Ⓐ • (06/01/90) • **85**
Vintage Port 1977 • $28 Ⓐ • (06/01/90) • **85**
Vintage Port 1975 • $38 • (03/01/90) • **78**
Vintage Port 1970 • $30 Ⓐ • (03/01/90) • **83**
Vintage Port 1967 • $58 • (03/01/90) • **90**
Vintage Port 1966 • $75 • (07/15/90) • **90**
Vintage Port 1963 • $39 Ⓐ • (07/15/90) • **96**
Vintage Port 1960 • $26 Ⓐ • (07/15/90) • **79**
Vintage Port 1958 • $43 Ⓐ • (03/01/90) • **82**
Vintage Port 1957 • $NA • (10/01/88) • **85**
Vintage Port 1955 • $151 Ⓐ • (03/01/90) • **94**
Vintage Port 1950 • $170 • (03/01/90) • **87**
Vintage Port 1947 • $185 Ⓐ • (03/01/90) • **90**
Vintage Port 1945 • $201 Ⓐ • (03/01/90) • **95**
Vintage Port 1942 • $150 • (03/01/90) • **88**

Key: SS—Spectator Selection CS—Cellar Selection HR—Highly Recommended BB—Best Buy $NA—Price not available Ⓐ—Auction Price (BT)—Barrel Tasting
Dates in parentheses indicate the issues in which the ratings were published.

Vintage Port 1935 • $320 • (03/01/90) • **92**
Vintage Port 1934 • $202 Ⓐ • (03/01/90) • **94**
Vintage Port 1927 • $300 • (03/01/90) • **92**
Vintage Port 1920 • $190 • (03/01/90) • **78**
Vintage Port 1917 • $175 • (03/01/90) • **88**
Vintage Port 1911 • $280 • (06/01/90) • **82**
Vintage Port 1908 • $320 • (03/01/90) • **75**
Vintage Port 1904 • $420 • (03/01/90) • **88**
Vintage Port 1896 • $400 • (03/01/90) • **81**
Vintage Port 1887 • $600 • (03/01/90) • **74**
Vintage Port 1870 • $700 • (03/01/90) • **98**

SANTAR, CASA DE

Dão 1992: Shows nice, spicy cinnamon flavors and a dash of brown sugar, but the tannins are overpowering and the finish turns metallic. • $8 • (08/31/97) • **77**
Dão 1990 • $7 • (03/31/96) • **72**
Dão Reserva 1994: A straightforward red with cherry flavors and a leather note. There's a touch of spice on the finish. • $11 • (08/31/97) • **79**
Dão Reserva 1992 • $10 • (03/31/96) • **82**
Dão White 1994: Well crafted and refreshing, with good apple and citrus flavors. Has some richness as well, and a good, crisp finish. • $8 • (06/30/97) • **84**

SÃO JOÃO, CAVES

Bairrada 1985 • $6 • (04/15/94) • **78**
Bairrada Frei João 1989 • $6 • (04/30/95) • **73**
Bairrada Frei João Reserva 1985 • $13 • (04/30/95) • **85**
Bairrada Frei João Reserva 1983 • $13 • (04/15/94) • **81**
Bairrada Reserva 1983 • $14 • (04/15/94) • **79**
Dão Porta dos Cavaleiros 1988 • $6 • (04/30/95) • **79**
Dão Porta dos Cavaleiros 1986 • $6 • (04/15/94) • **80**
Dão Porta dos Cavaleiros 1984 • $12 • (04/30/95) • **78**
Dão Porta dos Cavaleiros Reserva 1985 • $12 • (04/15/94) • **85**
Dão Reserva 1985 • $14 • (04/30/95) • **84**

SAO PEDRO

Tawny Port 10 Years Old NV: A delicate tawny with rich dried-apricot and plum flavors, some walnut notes as well. Balanced and ready to drink. • $40 • (09/15/97) • **88**

SENRA, CASA DA

Vinho Verde Loureiro 1995: Grapefruit flavors to the extreme, with biting acidity and an oxidized note on the finish. • $7 • (06/30/97) • **78**

SEZIM, CASA DE

Vinho Verde 1995: Clean and simple tasting with modest herb and green peach flavors. 1,000 cases made. • $7 • (06/30/97) • **81**

SMITH WOODHOUSE

Late Bottled Port 1984: Like a good single-*quinta* vintage Port with 10 years of bottle age. Medium ruby, with fresh violet, floral aromas. Medium-bodied, medium sweet, with fine tannins. Firm and chewy. Drink now. 1,500 cases made. • $23 • (02/28/98) • **87**
Vintage Character Port Lodge Reserve NV • $15 • (06/15/93) • **82**
Vintage Port Madalena 1995: A serious blackstrap of a wine, and better than the '94. Wild aromas of ripe berries, spices and cedar introduce a full-bodied, medium sweet, very concentrated young Port. It has plenty of tannin, but the fruit is dominating now. Wait and see its true glory, after 2008. 1,700 cases made. • $32 • (04/30/98) CS • **92**
Vintage Port 1994: Emits wonderful aromas of crushed fruits, especially berries. Medium-bodied and very sweet with fine tannins and sweet fruit flavors on the finish. An elegant, young vintage Port for relatively early consumption. Drink after 2000. Tasted twice, with consistent notes. 9,000 cases made. • $45 • (04/30/97) • **86**
Vintage Port 1992: Wet earth, stemmy and ripe fruit character. Fresh; medium in body and sweetness, offering fine tannins and a medium finish. Drink in 1999. • $33 • (06/15/95) • **88**

Vintage Port 1991: Not showing as well as expected when last tasted, but very good nonetheless. Elegant and refined. Lovely and balanced with a silky finish. Medium-bodied, medium-sweet and fruity. Tasted twice with consistent notes. Drinkable now. 2,500 cases made. • $36 • (07/31/94) • **87**
Vintage Port 1985: Medium-deep ruby, with lovely violet aromas, full-bodied, with plenty of grip, full tannins and a powerful finish. • $33 • (06/01/90) • **89**
Vintage Port 1983 • $12 Ⓐ • (06/01/90) • **92**
Vintage Port 1980 • $33 • (06/01/90) • **90**
Vintage Port 1977 • $25 Ⓐ • (02/01/90) • **89**
Vintage Port 1975 • $40 • (02/01/90) • **80**
Vintage Port 1970 • $58 • (02/01/90) • **86**
Vintage Port 1966 • $75 • (02/01/90) • **83**
Vintage Port 1963 • $85 • (02/01/90) • **89**

SOGRAPE

Alentejo Vinha do Monte 1994: Straightforward and fruity with good berry, cherry and plum flavors. A quaffable red with just enough tannin for backbone. 6,227 cases made. • $10 • (08/31/97) • **84**
Alentejo Vinha do Monte 1992 • $9 • (03/31/96) • **85**
Alentejo Vinha do Monte 1991 • $9 • (04/30/95) • **86**
Bairrada Terra Franca 1985 • $7 • (04/15/94) • **72**
Dão Duque de Viseu 1994: A good, hearty red with plum and cherry flavors. Tannins load up on the finish. 13,613 cases made. • $9 • (08/31/97) • **83**
Dão Duque de Viseu 1992 • $9 • (03/31/96) BB • **87**
Dão Duque de Viseu 1990 • $10 • (04/15/94) • **85**
Dão Grão Vasco 1994: Brown sugar and spice flavors dominate this fairly light red. No rough edges; ready now. 100,000 cases made. • $5 • (08/31/97) • **83**
Dão Grão Vasco 1992 • $5 • (03/31/96) • **81**
Dão Grão Vasco 1990 • $7 • (04/15/94) • **77**
Dão Reserva 1985 • $11 • (04/15/94) • **83**
Dão White Duque de Viseu 1996: Pleasant honey and herbal flavors in this fairly rich wine, as well as a slightly spicy edge. 7,187 cases made. • $8 • (07/31/97) • **85**
Douro Mateus Signature 1993: Shows some appealing prune and leather flavors and nice balance. Still a bit tannic, but drink soon with food. 9,500 cases made. • $7 • (08/31/97) • **81**
Douro Mateus Signature 1992 • $6 • (04/30/96) • **80**
Douro Mateus Signature 1989 • $9 • (04/15/94) • **80**
Douro Reserva 1992 • $10 • (03/31/96) • **85**
Douro Reserva 1990 • $10 • (04/30/95) • **89**
Douro Reserva 1987 • $11 • (04/15/94) • **83**
Douro Vila Regia 1990 • $7 • (04/15/94) • **78**
Douro White Mateus Signature 1994: Mature-tasting, with candied, spicy flavors. An extreme style with an astringent finish. 7,915 cases made. • $7 • (10/15/97) • **78**

SOLOURO

Vinho Verde 1995: Simple, with only modest fruit and herb flavors, turning a little earthy on the finish. • $5 • (05/15/97) • **77**

SOPÉ DA ENCOSTA

Ribatejo 1994 • $5 • (03/31/96) • **78**

SOUSELAS, ADEGA COOPERATIVA DE

Bairrada Reserva 1987 • $5 • (04/15/94) • **75**

SYMINGTON

Vintage Port Quinta do Vesùvio 1990 • $45 • (01/31/93) • **83**

TAYLOR FLADGATE

Late Bottled Port 1991: Plummy, slightly earthy character to this LBV. Medium-bodied, sweet, with a velvety texture. On the dull side. Drink now. • $18 • (02/28/98) • **80**
Late Bottled Port 1989 • $16 • (01/31/96) • **87**
Late Bottled Port 1988 • $17 • (11/15/94) • **85**
Late Bottled Port 1986 • $16 • (06/15/93) • **83**
Port First Estate NV • $14 • (04/15/92) • **81**
Tawny Port 10-year-old NV • $22 • (01/31/96) • **84**
Tawny Port 20-year-old NV • $42 • (01/31/96) • **84**
Tawny Port 40-year-old NV • $102 • (01/31/96) • **86**
Vintage Character Port First Estate Lugar das Lages NV • $16 • (03/15/94) • **85**
Vintage Port 1994: In a word, superb. It's full-bodied, moderately sweet and incredibly tannic, but there's amazing finesse and refinement to the texture, not to mention fabulous, concentrated aromas of raspberries, violets and other flowers. Perhaps the greatest Taylor ever, it's better than either the 1992 or the 1970, though it's very like the '70 in structure. Try after 2010. 10,000 cases made. • $120 • (04/30/97) CS • **100**
Vintage Port 1992 • $37 • (06/15/95) • **95**
Vintage Port 1985 • $40 • (06/01/90) • **90**
Vintage Port 1983 • $35 • (06/01/90) • **89**
Vintage Port 1980 • $41 • (06/01/90) • **88**
Vintage Port 1977 • $70 • (04/01/90) • **98**
Vintage Port 1975 • $47 • (12/01/89) • **78**
Vintage Port 1970 • $70 • (12/01/89) • **98**
Vintage Port 1966 • $80 • (12/01/89) • **89**
Vintage Port 1963 • $140 • (12/01/89) • **97**
Vintage Port 1960 • $100 • (10/31/88) • **84**
Vintage Port 1955 • $200 • (11/01/89) • **88**
Vintage Port 1948 • $330 • (11/01/89) • **99**
Vintage Port 1945 • $525 • (11/01/89) • **97**
Vintage Port 1942 • $275 • (04/01/90) • **78**
Vintage Port 1938 • $265 • (04/01/90) • **79**
Vintage Port 1935 • $390 • (02/01/90) • **88**
Vintage Port 1927 • $350 • (12/01/89) • **95**
Vintage Port Quinta de Terra Feita 1995: Outstanding young Port; better than I remember. Best Terra Feita ever. Inky color. Pure aromas of violets and fruit. Full-bodied, medium sweet, with super-racy, silky tannins. Wonderful texture to this wine. Long finish. Try after 2008. • $NA • (04/30/98) • **90**
Vintage Port Quinta de Vargellas 1995: A big, voluptuous wine—decadence in a bottle. Sports a brilliant magenta, purple color and intense aromas of plums and berries with hints of flowers. It's medium- to full-bodied, with a chunky, velvety-tannin mouthfeel and a long aftertaste of chocolate and fruit. Lovely. 9,000 cases made. • $39 • (04/30/98) CS • **92**
Vintage Port Quinta de Vargellas 1991 • $NA • (07/31/94) • **94**
Vintage Port Quinta de Vargellas 1987 • $NA • (02/01/90) • **93**
Vintage Port Quinta de Vargellas 1986 • $45 • (02/01/90) • **88**
Vintage Port Quinta de Vargellas 1984 • $NA • (02/01/90) • **87**
Vintage Port Quinta de Vargellas 1982 • $NA • (02/01/90) • **81**
Vintage Port Quinta de Vargellas 1978 • $34 • (02/01/90) • **85**
Vintage Port Quinta de Vargellas 1976 • $42 • (02/01/90) • **81**
Vintage Port Quinta de Vargellas 1974 • $30 • (02/01/90) • **78**
Vintage Port Quinta de Vargellas 1972 • $48 • (02/01/90) • **84**
Vintage Port Quinta de Vargellas 1969 • $50 • (02/01/90) • **85**
Vintage Port Quinta de Vargellas 1968 • $61 • (02/01/90) • **82**
Vintage Port Quinta de Vargellas 1967 • $50 • (02/01/90) • **82**
Vintage Port Quinta de Vargellas 1965 • $55 • (02/01/90) • **80**
Vintage Port Quinta de Vargellas 1964 • $50 • (07/01/90) • **75**
Vintage Port Quinta de Vargellas 1947: Very mature, with an earthy nose, a bit of sharpness and some nice, smoky, cherry notes on the finish. • $250 • (05/31/97) • **87**
Vintage Port Quinta de Vargellas Vinha Velha 1995: A gloriously crafted young Port. Ancient vines from Vargellas. Inky-colored, with wonderful spice, plum and berry aromas. Full-bodied, medium sweet, with silky tannins and a long, long, sweet fruit finish. Best after 2008. Not available in the U.S. • $NA • (04/30/98) • **95**
Vintage Port Special Quinta 1947: Shows an incredible array of exotic spices, strawberry, raspberry, chocolate and caramel flavors, lovely and floral on the palate with delicate sweetness and tremendous length. • $200 • (07/31/97) • **94**

TEODÓSIO, CAVES DOM

Arinto Tomar Quinta de S. João Batista 1996: A well-defined white, with nice almond, hebal and spice flavors. Crisp, with a good, clean finish. 2,290 cases made. • $7 • (08/31/97) • **82**
Bairrada Teodósio 1994: Extremely peppery-tasting, with some off-putting fruity flavors and an astringent finish. 3,300 cases made. • $7 • (08/31/97) • **71**
Bairrada Teodósio 1990: Smooth and fairly rich with good flavors of dried plum, cherry and leather, and some nice clovelike notes on the finish. Fully mature, ready to drink. • $8 • (08/31/97) • **84**

Cartaxo Falcão de Cima 1996: A bit flat-tasting, with only modest green-apple flavors. Turns slightly bitter on the finish. 2,290 cases made. • $7 • (10/15/97) • **75**

Cartaxo Quinta do Bairro Falcão 1995: Light and fruity, with good currant and cherry flavors. Fresh and well balanced. 3,300 cases made. • $7 • (08/31/97) • **83**

Cartaxo Quinta do Bairro Falcão 1993 • $7 • (03/31/96) • **82**

Cartaxo Quinta do Bairro Falcão 1992 • $NA • (04/30/95) • **75**

Cartaxo Quinta do Bairro Falcão 1991 • $6 • (04/15/94) BB • **84**

Dão Cardeal 1995: This red from Portugal is straightforwardly fruity, with enticing blueberry and currant flavors, turning snazzy on the finish as a spicy note chimes in. Delicious. Drink now. 14,580 cases made. • $7 • (08/31/97) BB • **85**

Dão Cardeal 1991 • $6 • (03/31/96) • **84**

Dão Cardeal 1989 • $5 • (04/30/95) • **85**

Dão Cardeal Reserva 1990: Smooth, with a gush of sweet cherry and spice flavors, a smoke-accented finish. It's mature, drink it now with food. 2,900 cases made. • $9 • (08/31/97) • **86**

Dão Cardeal Reserva 1984: Still quite lively, with well-focused flavors of ripe plum and cherry. Would go well with a cheese course. 2,900 cases made. • $9 • (08/31/97) • **85**

Dão Cardeal Reserva 1983: Shows decent dried-plum and cherry flavors, but turns a bit earthy and tannic on the finish. 2,900 cases made. • $10 • (08/31/97) • **80**

Douro Terra das Fragas 1994: Well balanced, with good plum and currant flavors, a touch of spice. Also has a gamy edge. Smooth and ready to drink. 3,300 cases made. • $8 • (08/31/97) • **84**

Estremoz Casaleiro 1992 • $NA • (04/30/95) • **78**

Estremoz Casaleiro 1990 • $NA • (04/30/95) • **76**

Estremoz Teodósio Garrafiera 1985 • $9 • (04/30/95) • **86**

Estremoz Casaleiro Garrafeira 1982 • $9 • (04/15/94) • **84**

Fernão Pires Tomar Quinta de S. João Batista 1996: Has a peachy flavor to it, good body, and a nice spicy touch on the finish. Not particularly complex, but a good apéritif. 2,290 cases made. • $7 • (08/31/97) • **84**

Garrafeira Particular 1980 • $NA • (04/30/95) • **73**

Palmela Almargem 1992: This has an off-putting, rubbery character. 3,300 cases made. • $8 • (08/31/97) • **73**

Santarém Cabeça de Toiro Reserva 1992: Offers pleasant dried fruit flavors and reveals a lingering, sweet cherry note on the finish. 2,500 cases made. • $8 • (08/31/97) • **81**

Santarém Cabeça de Toiro Reserva 1991 • $10 • (03/31/96) • **79**

Tomar Quinta de S. João Batista 1994: Interesting, with a nicely mature taste to it, some earthy components, some pleasant smoke and dried fruit flavors. Drink now. 11,250 cases made. • $7 • (08/31/97) • **85**

Tomar Quinta de S. João Batista 1992 • $7 • (03/31/96) • **82**

Tomar Quinta de S. João Batista 1991 • $NA • (04/30/95) • **76**

Tomar Quinta de S. João Batista Reserva 1992: A mature wine, with decent brown sugar and spice flavors. Drink now. 2,290 cases made. • $8 • (08/31/97) • **79**

TERRA DE LOBOS

Ribatejo 1992 • $5 • (04/30/95) • **86**

TIA CHICA

Vinho Verde 1995: Provides a nice mouthful of flavors, notably peach, lemon and grapefruit. Balanced, juicy and enjoyable. 1,500 cases made. • $5 • (06/30/97) • **82**

TUKE HOLDSWORTH

Vintage Port 1994: A pretty, young vintage Port with plum, berry and cherry aromas and flavors. Medium- to full-bodied, with racy, fine tannins and a long, fruity finish. Try after 2002. • $33 • (04/30/97) • **88**

Key: SS—Spectator Selection CS—Cellar Selection HR—Highly Recommended BB—Best Buy $NA—Price not available Ⓐ—Auction Price (BT)—Barrel Tasting
Dates in parentheses indicate the issues in which the ratings were published.

VAL DA FIGUEIRA, QUINTA DE

Vintage Port 1987: Extremely well crafted, with a firm structure of medium tannins, fresh strawberry flavors and a floral finish. The fruit and tannins are well integrated and focused on the palate. • $NA • (02/01/90) • **83**

VALDARCOS, CAVES

Bairrada Garrafeira 1987 • $NA • (04/15/94) • **79**

Bairrada Reserva 1989 • $NA • (04/15/94) • **78**

VALE DA MINA, QUINTA

Vintage Port 1995: A pleasant, early drinking '95, with pretty berry, spice and green tobacco aromas and flavors. Medium-ruby, brick red. Medium-bodied, with medium tannins, a sweet finish. Best after 2002. • $NA • (04/30/98) • **84**

VAN ZELLER

Vintage Port 1985: Not as good as the 1983, but it shows some power and robust fruit. It should be ready sooner than the 1983. Deep purple with a red hue, spicy raisin and plum nose, medium-bodied, with sweet raisin flavors that seem slightly burnt. Good tannic backbone. • $NA • (01/01/90) • **80**

Vintage Port 1983 • $22 • (01/01/90) • **84**

Vintage Port Quinta do Roriz 1985: • $NA • (07/01/90) • **87**

Vintage Port Quinta do Roriz 1983 • $22 • (07/01/90) • **84**

Vintage Port Quinta do Roriz 1970 • $NA • (07/01/90) • **86**

Vintage Port Quinta do Roriz 1960 • $NA • (07/01/90) • **83**

VASCONCELLOS

Vintage Port Butler & Nephew 1975 • $30 • (07/01/90) • **74**

Vintage Port Butler & Nephew 1970 • $45 • (07/01/90) • **76**

Vintage Port Gonzalez Byass 1970 • $50 • (06/01/90) • **81**

Vintage Port Gonzalez Byass 1963 • $82 • (07/01/90) • **87**

VELHAS, CAVES

Alentejo 1991 • $6 • (04/15/94) • **76**

Alentejo NV: A wine dominated by fairly strong prune and vegetal flavors. It has balance, but lacks concentration. Quite mature. • $NA • (10/15/96) • **77**

Almeirim Garrafeira 1993: Showing its age with tea, cola and brown sugar flavors. Turns astringent and prunelike on the finish. • $12 • (10/15/97) • **78**

Almeirim Garrafeira 1990 • $12 • (04/30/96) • **82**

Almeirim White 1995: Not much fun with its fruit-cocktail flavors and cloying finish. • $9 • (09/15/97) • **76**

Arinto Bucelas 1995: Has an appealing buttery aroma, but the fruit-cocktail flavors are a bit harsh and unbalanced. • $8 • (09/15/97) • **76**

Bairrada 1992: This is a mature-tasting wine with flavors of spice, tea and a raisiny note as well. Still a bit astringent on the finish, but drink now before its flavors fade. • $9 • (09/15/96) • **82**

Bairrada 1990 • $8 • (04/30/95) • **82**

Bairrada 1989 • $8 • (04/15/94) • **82**

Bairrada Garrafeira 1990: Has a nice beefy aroma to it, as well as pleasant dried cherry and plum flavors. A bit green on the finish. Mature, ready to drink. • $12 • (09/15/97) • **84**

Bairrada Garrafeira 1985 • $12 • (04/30/96) • **83**

Bucelas White 1995: Quite astringent, with neutral fruit flavors and a cloying finish. • $7 • (09/15/97) • **73**

Bucelas White 1994: Pleasant and appealing with peach, tangerine and a nice herbal note on the finish. Tastes a bit sweet. 7,500 cases made. • $8 • (09/15/96) • **84**

Dão 1990 • $8 • (04/30/95) BB • **86**

Dão 1989 • $8 • (04/15/94) • **85**

Dão Reserva 1985 • $10 • (04/30/95) • **85**

Dão White 1994: A rustic style with appealing spice and fig flavors that dominate the finish. A bit thin in the middle. Not for everyone. • $9 • (09/15/96) • **80**

Douro Lagar Velho 1992: Smooth, with a nice smokiness and plummy flavors. Finishes on a pleasant gamy note. Drink now with pasta or red meat. • $8 • (08/31/97) • **84**

PORTUGAL

Douro Lagar Velho Reserva 1990: Mature and smooth, with tea, dried cherry and brown sugar flavors. Also has some good vanilla notes and a lovely, spicy aroma. Drink soon. • $10 • (08/31/97) • **85**
Palmela Romeira 1992: Fairly rich and mature tasting, with flavors of plum, tobacco and a gamy note on the finish. Drink it with a hearty meal. • $8 • (09/15/96) • **83**
Palmela Romeira Garrafeira 1991: Quite dried out, showing only modest tea and prune flavors. • $11 • (10/15/97) • **73**
Palmela Romeira Garrafeira 1990 • $7 • (04/30/95) • **84**
Palmela Romeira Garrafeira 1989: A thick-tasting and mature wine with ripe plum and tealike flavors that linger on the finish. • $11 • (09/15/96) • **81**
Ribatejo Romeira Garrafeira 1988 • $12 • (04/30/96) • **80**
Ribatejo Romeira Garrafeira 1987 • $7 • (04/15/94) • **83**
Ribatejo Romeira Garrafeira 1982 • $11 • (04/15/94) • **79**
Ribatejo Romeira Garrafeira 1980 • $12 • (04/15/94) • **70**

VESÚVIO, QUINTA DO

Vintage Port 1995: A ripe and rich '95 boasting a remarkable essence of crushed berries, this is classic Port. It's full-bodied and quite sweet, with the velvetiest of tannins and a long, long ripe fruit finish. At its best after 2008. 3,000 cases made. • $60 • (04/30/98) CS • **95**
Vintage Port 1994: Terrific aromas of berries and violets, with a hint of mint. Full-bodied and lightly sweet, with fine, silky tannins that build on the palate and caress the tongue. Outstanding concentration and harmony. Greatest Vesúvio this century. Try after 2010. 5,000 cases made. • $70 • (04/30/97) • **96**
Vintage Port 1992: Fabulous Vesuvio; better than remembered and improving all the time. Amazing wet earth and ripe fruit character; full in body and very sleek, offering hard tannins and fresh flavors. Needs time to round off its rough edges; try in 2003. 1,962 cases made. • $49 • (06/15/95) • **94**
Vintage Port 1991: Loads of character in this one. You can almost smell the soil. Very powerful and impressive, with masses of tannins and medium sweetness. It shows opulent aromas and flavors of wet earth, green tea and berry. A tough young wine that needs to age. Tasted twice with consistent notes. Try after 2000. 1,300 cases made. • $48 • (07/31/94) • **91**

VIEIRA DE SOUSA

Vintage Port 1985: Pleasant flavors and aromas, but lacks depth and body. Medium ruby, with a light, earthy beet and berry nose, medium-bodied, with light tannins and advanced flavors. • $NA • (01/01/90) • **70**
Vintage Port 1980 • $NA • (01/01/90) • **70**
Vintage Port 1978 • $NA • (01/01/90) • **74**
Vintage Port 1970 • $NA • (01/01/90) • **71**

VILARINHO DO BAIRRO, ADEGA COOPERATIVA DE

Bairrada Lar de Forno Reserva 1994: This modest but crisp red has a nice menthol flavor to it. 3,000 cases made. • $5 • (08/31/97) • **79**
Bairrada White Reserva 1994: A hard-edged wine with woodlike flavors and a sappy finish.. 2,000 cases made. • $6 • (06/30/97) • **76**

VIMOMPOR

Alvarinho Vinho Verde Quinta da Pedra 1996: An earthy, muddled wine with modest grapefruit flavors. Turns astringent on the finish. • $12 • (10/15/97) • **73**
Vinho Verde Senhoria 1996: A middle-of-the-road white with appealing freshness, but the citrus flavors turn just a tad bitter. • $6 • (10/15/97) • **79**

WARRE

Late Bottled Port 1984: A serious alternative to vintage Port. Good deep color, with complex aromas of cherry, berry and flowers. Medium-bodied, medium sweet, with chewy tannins and a long, fruity finish. Needs decanting. Drink now. • $24 • (02/28/98) • **89**
Tawny Port 20-year-old Nimrod NV • $38 • (02/28/90) • **84**
Tawny Port Reserve 1968 • $65 • (01/31/96) • **88**
Tawny Port Sir William 10 year-old NV • $25 • (01/31/96) • **82**
Tawny Port Very Finest Rare Nimrod NV • $24 • (04/15/91) • **85**
Vintage Character Port Warrior Finest Reserve NV • $14 • (03/15/94) • **80**
Vintage Port 1994: A great surprise for the vintage. Displays fabulous concentration and complex character with it's layers of very sweet fruit, chocolate and cherry aromas and flavors. Full-bodied, with velvety tannins. Long finish with plenty of grip. Beautiful wine. Try after 2008. 13,000 cases made. • $60 • (04/30/97) • **95**
Vintage Port 1991 • $35 • (07/31/94) • **91**
Vintage Port 1985 • $18 Ⓐ • (06/01/90) • **91**
Vintage Port 1983 • $16 Ⓐ • (06/01/90) • **88**
Vintage Port 1980 • $26 Ⓐ • (06/01/90) • **88**
Vintage Port 1977 • $32 Ⓐ • (04/01/90) • **92**
Vintage Port 1975 • $23 Ⓐ • (10/31/88) • **74**
Vintage Port 1970 • $34 Ⓐ • (12/01/89) • **88**
Vintage Port 1966 • $41 Ⓐ • (06/01/89) • **91**
Vintage Port 1963 • $65 Ⓐ • (12/01/89) • **92**
Vintage Port 1960 • $33 • (10/31/88) • **90**
Vintage Port 1958 • $53 Ⓐ • (11/01/89) • **81**
Vintage Port 1955 • $23 • (11/01/89) • **86**
Vintage Port 1947 • $214 Ⓐ • (11/01/89) • **88**
Vintage Port 1945 • $360 • (11/01/89) • **87**
Vintage Port 1934 • $285 • (02/01/90) • **87**
Vintage Port 1927 • $300 • (12/01/89) • **93**
Vintage Port 1900 • $430 • (11/01/89) • **79**
Vintage Port Quinta da Cavadinha 1995: This young Port sneaks up on you and then—bam! Aromas of grapes, flowers and minerals pave the way for a slowly building palate that finishes with a burst of ripe, exotic fruit. Full-bodied, yet very tight and held back. Better than when previously reviewed as a barrel samples. Best after 2008. 7,000 cases made. • $33 • (04/30/98) CS • **92**
Vintage Port Quinta da Cavadinha 1992 • $26 • (06/30/95) • **91**
Vintage Port Quinta da Cavadinha 1987 • $NA • (02/01/90) • **86**
Vintage Port Quinta da Cavadinha 1986 • $NA • (02/01/90) • **85**
Vintage Port Quinta da Cavadinha 1984 • $NA • (02/01/90) • **81**
Vintage Port Quinta da Cavadinha 1982 • $NA • (02/01/90) • **86**
Vintage Port Quinta da Cavadinha 1979 • $25 • (07/31/90) • **82**
Vintage Port Quinta da Cavadinha 1978 • $28 • (02/01/90) • **83**

WIESE & KROHN

Tawny Port 20-year-old NV • $33 • (02/28/90) • **88**
Vintage Port 1985: This has attractive roasted coffee aromas and flavors in a more forward style than many of the top 1985s. Deep ruby with a purple edge, a bitter chocolate and coffee nose, full-bodied, with a velvety mouthfeel, medium tannins and a sweet finish. • $21 • (01/01/90) • **81**
Vintage Port 1984 • $20 • (01/01/90) • **86**
Vintage Port 1982 • $20 • (01/01/90) • **83**
Vintage Port 1978 • $37 • (01/01/90) • **84**
Vintage Port 1975 • $49 • (01/01/90) • **80**
Vintage Port 1970 • $75 • (01/01/90) • **74**
Vintage Port 1967 • $65 • (01/01/90) • **75**
Vintage Port 1965 • $100 • (01/01/90) • **85**
Vintage Port 1963 • $145 • (01/01/90) • **87**
Vintage Port 1961 • $125 • (01/01/90) • **85**
Vintage Port 1960 • $115 • (01/01/90) • **89**
Vintage Port 1958 • $180 • (01/01/90) • **87**

South Africa

Trade embargoes aimed at an apartheid goverment prevented much of world from experiencing South Africa's wines for several decades. But since 1994, the new government's aggressive policy of expanding exports has made South Africa a solid source for quality wines.

1. Swartland
2. Constantia
3. Stellenbosch
4. Paarl
5. Franschhoek
6. Walker Bay
7. Robertson

For the most part, buying South African wine is no different from buying American wine. Wines are usually made from a predominant grape. Chardonnay and Sauvignon Blanc are extremely popular and produce the best white wines. Nonetheless, the variety with the largest plantings is Chenin Blanc, called "Steen" locally, which can produce an array of wines from crisp, clean, dry whites to oaky brandy.

Varietal red wines made from Shiraz (also known as Syrah), Cabernet Sauvignon and Merlot are among the best from South Africa. Their flavors are subtly different from those of their counterparts from other countries. Another favorite red grape is Pinotage, which is grown only here. A cross between the refined Pinot Noir and the rustic Cinsault, it can make light and refreshing rosés as well as powerful, long-lived reds.

SOUTH AFRICAN WINE REGIONS

Images of vineyards growing in arid grasslands amidst zebras and giraffes may come to mind when someone speaks of South Africa. In fact, most of its quality vineyards are located on or near the country's coastal southern tip, and benefit from the cooling influence of the maritime climate.

Constantia—the home of Muscat of Constantia, a sweet wine which graced the tables of 18th-century European aristocracy—is in the southern suburbs of Cape Town, on the thin finger of land that ends in the Cape of Good Hope. Just across the False Bay lies Stellenbosch, a hilly district where yields are low and many of the nation's best red wines are produced. Another 40 miles or so to the southeast is Walker Bay, source of some highly successful recent experiments in the Burgundian varieties Chardonnay and Pinot Noir.

The generally hotter, drier inland wine regions produce large yields under irrigation. Most of the wine destined for domestic consumption is made here, but quality producers are to be found as well. The district of Paarl is home to some of these, and also to KWV, the giant winegrowers' cooperative which for decades bore the blame for keeping South African wine quality low by setting unnecessarily high production quotas. (Its grip on the country's wine industry has since been loosened.) KWV also turns excess grape tonnage into a variety of fortified wines—including some popular and tasty Port and Sherry styles—and brandies.

To the east of Paarl lies Robertson, in the Breede River Valley. The estates and cooperatives here produce almost exclusively white wines, including some notable Chardonnays and dessert wines.

AFRICA COLLECTION, THE

Cabernet Sauvignon Stellenbosch 1991 • $7 • (09/30/95) • **79**
Merlot Stellenbosch 1992 • $7 • (09/30/95) • **77**

ALLESVERLOREN

Cabernet Sauvignon Swartland Region 1989 • $15 • (09/30/95) • **89**

BACKSBERG

Cabernet Sauvignon Paarl 1995: A dark, handsome, brooding style of Cabernet, with well-integrated tannins, concentrated, compelling flavors of black currant, licorice and smoke, and a lingering finish where the flavors persist. The price is a pleasant surprise, too. Drink now through 2001. 4,000 cases made. • $12 • (04/30/98) HR • **88**
Cabernet Sauvignon Paarl 1993: Well made, balanced and complex, with solid Cabernet character. Mingles cherry, cedar and tobacco notes that are starting to evolve, but the fruit is still fresh and the tannins firm. Drink now or hold. 5,000 cases made. • $12 • (07/31/96) • **88**
Cabernet Sauvignon Paarl 1992 • $10 • (03/31/95) • **85**
Cabernet Sauvignon Paarl 1990 • $11 • (06/30/94) • **88**
Chardonnay Paarl 1996: Easy to like. A full-bodied, ripe-tasting Chardonnay with loads of rich flavor, good balance and a lingering, fruity finish. A fine value. Drink now. 4,000 cases made. • $12 • (04/30/98) • **88**
Chardonnay Paarl 1995: A bit bizarre, tasting and smelling of peanuts. There are some oak and nutmeg accents, but not enough to make it appealing. 4,000 cases made. • $12 • (01/31/97) • **75**
Chardonnay Paarl 1993 • $10 • (06/15/95) • **87**
Klein Babylonstoren Paarl 1992 • $13 • (12/31/95) • **84**
Klein Babylonstoren Paarl 1991 • $13 • (09/30/95) • **78**
Merlot Paarl 1995: Smooth and generous, with ample flavors of chocolate, plum and spice on a lush texture. Drink now. 3,000 cases made. • $12 • (04/30/98) • **85**
Merlot Paarl 1994: A hearty, deep-colored, earth-flavored Merlot with a crisp finish. It may not have perfect balance, but it has plenty of presence. 2,000 cases made. • $12 • (01/31/97) • **85**
Merlot Paarl 1993 • $10 • (06/15/95) • **87**
Pinotage Paarl 1994: Like a good Côtes du Rhône, this combines bright fruit flavors and earthy, spicy accents for an interesting flavor spectrum. Medium-bodied, slightly tannic. Ready to drink. 3,500 cases made. • $10 • (05/15/97) • **85**
Pinotage Paarl 1993: Appealing smoke and raspberry aromas give way to ripe fruit on the palate, with firm tannins and good concentration. Drink now. 4,000 cases made. • $10 • (07/31/96) • **87**
Pinotage Paarl 1992 • $8 • (06/15/95) • **86**
Pinotage Paarl 1990 • $10 • (02/15/93) • **86**
Sauvignon Blanc Paarl 1996: A relatively soft-textured, easygoing white, with a hint of sweetness in the simple, applelike flavors. 1,000 cases made. • $10 • (04/30/97) • **78**
Shiraz Paarl 1995: Generous and exuberant. An Aussie-like style, with oodles of blackberry flavor, soft tannins and a lingering, fruity, almost sweet finish. Drink now. 1,500 cases made. • $12 • (04/30/98) • **89**
Shiraz Paarl 1993: This is right-on Shiraz; reminds one of the Northern Rhône, with a deft blend of ripe fruit flavors and peppery, earthy accents. Tannic but well balanced. Drinkable now. 2,000 cases made. • $12 • (05/15/97) • **89**
Shiraz Paarl 1992 • $10 • (04/30/96) • **85**
Shiraz Paarl 1991 • $10 • (09/30/95) • **84**

BECK, GRAHAM

Chardonnay Robertson Lonehill 1997: A fairly fat and broad Chardonnay, with ripe pear, apple and spicy character. What it lacks in power, it makes up for in flavor. 1,500 cases imported. Drink now. • $10 • (06/15/98) • **83**
Shiraz-Cabernet Sauvignon Robertson 1996: An appealing, light, fruity-tasting, almost sweet red, with abundant cherry and raspberry flavors and light tannins. 2,000 cases imported. A blend of 59 percent Shiraz, 41 percent Cabernet Sauvignon. Drink now. • $10 • (07/31/98) • **84**

BELLINGHAM

Merlot Coastal Region 1996: Dominated by dried cherry and smoky flavors, with a rough, gamy edge to the finish. 500 cases imported. Drink now. • $11 • (06/15/98) • **79**
Pinotage Paarl 1990 • $10 • (02/15/93) • **80**
Sauvignon Blanc Coastal Region 1997: Has nice green peach flavors and some good herbal notes as well. Firm and flavorful. 500 cases imported. Drink now. • $10 • (06/15/98) • **84**

BERGSIG

Pinotage South Africa Breede River Valley 1990 • $9 • (10/15/92) • **84**

BERTRAMS

Pinotage South Africa 1988 • $10 • (02/15/93) • **76**

BEYERSKLOOF

Pinotage Stellenbosch 1996: A hearty, jammy-tasting red wine with not much tannin. Simple but satisfying. Drink now. 20,000 cases made. • $11 • (10/15/97) • **84**
Pinotage Stellenbosch 1995: As much like grape juice as wine. Exuberantly fruity, with light herbal flavors. A pricey alternative to Beaujolais. 35,000 cases made. • $10 • (07/31/96) • **82**

BLAAUWKLIPPEN

Cabernet Sauvignon Stellenbosch 1989 • $20 • (09/30/95) • **84**
Cabernet Sauvignon Stellenbosch Reserve Guild Auction Label 1989 • $24 • (09/30/95) • **88**
Zinfandel Reserve Stellenbosch 1990 • $20 • (06/30/95) • **79**
Zinfandel Stellenbosch 1990 • $16 • (06/30/95) • **75**

BOLAND WYNKELDER

Cabernet Sauvignon Paarl 1995: A medium-bodied Cabernet for current drinking, with ample cherry, chocolate and smoke flavors and moderate tannins. Drink now. 5,000 cases made. • $11 • (03/31/98) • **84**
Cabernet Sauvignon Paarl 1992: A well-rounded wine that's fully mature, offering spicy aromas, ripe fruit flavors and modest tannins. Best now. 5,000 cases made. • $10 • (09/15/97) • **84**
Pinotage Paarl 1995: A straightforward, flavorful red, fruity and uncomplicated, featuring ripe cherry and raspberry flavors and a bit of tannin. Drink now. 5,000 cases made. • $NA • (08/31/97) • **83**
Vintage Port Paarl 1992: Fairly rich and smooth, with plenty of chocolaty and plummy flavors. Finishes on a leathery note. Simple and tasty. 2,000 cases made. • $15 • (03/31/98) • **84**

BOPLAAS

South Africa Port 1989 • $NA • (09/30/95) • **82**

BOSCHENDAL

Chardonnay Paarl 1995: This firm-textured Chardonnay has a good base of lively citrus and pear flavors accented by smoky oak. Drink now through 2000. 6,000 cases made. • $13 • (10/15/97) • **84**
Chardonnay Paarl 1994 • $13 • (06/15/95) • **85**
Chardonnay Paarl Reserve 1996: A solid, understated Chardonnay with good pear and citrus flavors accented by subtle creamy, buttery notes. It grows on you. Drink now. 2,000 cases made. • $15 • (03/31/98) • **84**
Chardonnay Paarl Reserve 1995: Appealing character of apple flavors with butter accents. Balanced and fresh, though a little overdone on the finish. 2,000 cases made. • $14 • (01/31/97) • **83**
Le Petit Pavillon Paarl White 1994 • $8 • (06/30/95) • **74**
Le Petit Pavillon Paarl White 1993 • $7 • (01/01/94) • **82**
Premier Cuvée Paarl White 1995: Hot and spicy, with a brownish tint, and pear, ripe apple and nutmeg flavors. Finishes with a note of caramel. 1,000 cases made. • $15 • (01/31/97) • **79**
Sauvignon Blanc Paarl 1994 • $9 • (06/15/95) • **87**
Sauvignon Blanc Paarl Grand Cuvée 1993 • $10 • (03/31/95) • **85**

BOUCHARD FINLAYSON

Blanc de Mer Overberg 1994 • $11 • (09/30/95) • **84**
Chardonnay Overberg 1994 • $NA • (09/30/95) • **82**
Chardonnay Overberg 1993 • $17 • (09/30/95) • **82**
Pinot Noir Walker Bay 1994 • $NA • (06/15/95) • **84**
Pinot Noir Walker Bay 1993 • $NA • (06/15/95) • **85**
Sauvignon Blanc Overberg 1994 • $13 • (06/15/95) • **84**

BOVLEI WINERY

Cabernet Sauvignon Wellington 1992 • $NA • (06/30/95) • **81**
Grand Rouge Wellington 1992 • $NA • (06/30/95) • **85**
Pinotage Wellington 1994 • $NA • (06/30/95) • **81**
Sauvignon Blanc Wellington 1994 • $NA • (06/30/95) • **77**
Shiraz Wellington 1991 • $NA • (06/30/95) • **75**

BREDELL'S

Vintage Reserve Port Stellenbosch Limited Release 1991 • $NA • (09/30/95) • **87**

BUITENVERWACHTING

Buiten Blanc Coastal Region 1994 • $NA • (09/30/95) • **80**
Chardonnay Constantia 1993 • $18 • (09/30/95) • **83**
Christine Constantia 1989 • $20 • (09/30/95) • **88**
Grand Vin Constantia 1990 • $22 • (09/30/95) • **77**
Sauvignon Blanc Constantia 1994 • $16 • (09/30/95) • **82**

CAPE COUNTRY

Cabernet Sauvignon South Africa 1991 • $6 • (06/30/94) • **75**
Pinotage Coastal Region 1990 • $6 • (06/30/94) • **78**
Pinotage Coastal Region 1989 • $5 • (02/15/93) • **77**

CAPE INDABA

Chardonnay Breede River Valley 1996: A smooth, rich Chardonnay but with an odd, underlying earthy, malty sweetness. Drink now. • $8 • (01/01/98) • **82**
Pinotage Coastal Region 1995 • $9 • (04/30/96) • **84**

CAPE SELECTION

Pinotage Stellenbosch 1991 • $8 • (02/15/93) • **83**

CATHEDRAL CELLAR

Cabernet Sauvignon Coastal Region 1995: Smooth and supple with dark plum, sweet cherry and spicy flavors that fill the mouth. Drink now through 2001. 3,000 cases made. • $14 • (06/15/98) • **84**
Cabernet Sauvignon Coastal Region 1994: A smooth, concentrated, well-balanced wine with almost-sweet cherry and currant flavors that linger on the finish. Best now. 2,000 cases made. • $12 • (09/30/97) • **86**
Cabernet Sauvignon Coastal Region 1993: Robust and full-bodied, with ample oak influence in the smoky, cedary aromas and flavors. Tannic and a little tough in texture. Fine but not for everyone. • $12 • (01/31/97) • **84**
Cabernet Sauvignon Coastal Region 1992 • $10 • (06/15/95) • **85**
Cabernet Sauvignon Coastal Region 1990 • $11 • (06/30/94) • **85**
Chardonnay Coastal Region 1995: Ripe and round, with toasty aromas and flavors, and a welcome touch of acidity that gives crispness. • $12 • (01/31/97) • **82**
Chardonnay Coastal Region 1994: Well balanced, with pear, ripe apple and spice flavors. Has some subtlety but not much power or concentration. 1,500 cases made. • $12 • (01/31/97) • **82**
Chardonnay Coastal Region 1993 • $10 • (09/30/95) • **80**
Merlot Coastal Region 1995: Tired tasting, with tobacco and cedarlike flavors and aromas. Ends on a faintly spicy note. Past its prime. 3,000 cases made. • $14 • (06/15/98) • **78**
Merlot Coastal Region 1994: Tannic and oaky, with a good foundation of fruit flavor. Try now. 2,000 cases made. • $12 • (05/15/97) • **82**
Pinotage Coastal Region 1993: A full-bodied, spicy-smelling red with a deep color, smooth tannins and plenty of fruit flavor. Try now. 2,000 cases made. • $12 • (05/31/97) • **88**
Pinotage Coastal Region 1992 • $10 • (09/30/95) • **80**
Triptych Coastal Region 1992 • $10 • (09/30/95) • **82**
Triptych Coastal Region 1990 • $11 • (06/30/94) • **84**

Key: SS—Spectator Selection CS—Cellar Selection HR—Highly Recommended BB—Best Buy $NA—Price not available Ⓐ—Auction Price (BT)—Barrel Tasting
Dates in parentheses indicate the issues in which the ratings were published.

CENTAURUS

Cabernet Sauvignon Durbanville 1991 • $12 • (04/30/96) • **84**
Pinotage Durbanville 1991 • $12 • (04/30/96) • **83**
Zinfandel Stellenbosch 1991: Awkward wine: sweet-and-sour candy notes, some berry flavor, burnt and rubbery finish. Drink up. 6,500 cases made. • $11 • (07/31/96) • **70**

CHATEAU LIBERTAS

Red Coastal Region 1988 • $10 • (06/30/94) • **75**

CHEETAH VALLEY

Cabernet Sauvignon Paarl Reserve 1993: Sleek and well integrated: a generous dollop of oak for chocolaty, toasty flavors, over black cherry and attractive herbal accents. It's for fans of oak. Drinkable now. • $9 • (07/31/96) • **87**
Chardonnay Western Cape 1997: Clean fruit flavors and a polished, silky texture make this quite appealing. Has uncomplicated pear and grapefruit notes with hints of vanilla. Drink now. 10,000 cases made. • $10 • (07/31/98) BB • **86**
Merlot Western Cape 1997: Light and appealing, with fresh strawberry and cherry flavors, an easy-drinking texture and little tannin. Fun for quaffing. Drink now. 10,000 cases made. • $10 • (07/31/98) • **84**
Merlot Western Cape 1993: A full-bodied, full-flavored Merlot with a rather tough texture and smoky, herbal, tomatolike flavors. Not elegant but good. 10,000 cases made. • $9 • (01/31/97) • **83**
Pinotage Paarl Reserve 1993: Mingles plum, smoke and dark chocolate flavors with moderate tannins. Harmonious, aging gracefully, and a fine companion to stews and red meat. • $9 • (07/31/96) • **86**
Pinotage Western Cape 1997: A light, fresh red, with cherry-berry flavors, very little tannin and a sweet finish. Drink now. 10,000 cases made. • $10 • (07/31/98) • **81**
Pinotage Western Cape 1994: A good, medium-bodied, dry red wine with some plummy, herbal character providing substance. 10,000 cases made. • $9 • (05/15/97) • **83**
Vintage Port Western Cape 1994: Pleasant chocolate and plum flavors, with a touch of raisiny spice. More like a tawny than a vintage Port, though. Drink now. 1,000 cases made. • $14 • (06/15/98) • **82**

CLOS MALVERNE

Auret Stellenbosch 1995: Coffee, herb and smoke flavors tend to dominate the fruit here. Big, hearty, full-bodied but very odd. Tasted twice, with consistent notes. A blend of 75 percent Cabernet Sauvignon and 25 percent Pinotage. Drink now. 500 cases made. • $15 • (04/30/98) • **78**
Auret Stellenbosch 1989 • $20 • (10/15/92) • **77**
Cabernet Sauvignon Stellenbosch 1995: Deep, deep color, massively rich fruit flavors and thick but soft tannins make this a Cabernet to watch. Tempting to drink now for its generous cherry-berry flavors and lingering finish but better to wait a bit. Best now through 2005. 500 cases made. • $14 • (03/31/98) • **88**
Cabernet Sauvignon Stellenbosch 1994: Its deep, red-black color, smoky, meaty, gamy flavors and very firm tannins make this full-bodied Cabernet an intriguing specimen. More like Syrah, really, but it lacks charm. 1,500 cases made. • $14 • (01/31/97) • **84**
Cabernet Sauvignon Stellenbosch 1989 • $16 • (10/15/92) • **77**
Pinotage Stellenbosch 1996: Ah, so this is what Pinotage can do. Abundantly fruity, richly textured, densely colored, lightly tannic and easy to enjoy. Drink now. 3,000 cases made. • $12 • (07/31/98) • **87**
Pinotage Stellenbosch 1995: A basic, hearty red wine with earthy aromas, ripe and plummy flavors and rather light tannins. 1,500 cases made. • $12 • (01/01/97) • **81**
Pinotage Stellenbosch 1990 • $10 • (02/15/93) • **87**

DE LEUWEN JAGT

Cabernet Franc Paarl 1993 • $11 • (09/30/95) • **84**

DE WETSHOF

Chardonnay Robertson Bon Vallon 1997: A fresh, straightforward white wine with good balance and appetizing pear and citrus flavors. Drink now. 6,000 cases made. • $10 • (03/31/98) • **83**
Chardonnay Robertson Bon Vallon 1996: Average, with indistinct fruit flavors and a fairly crisp texture. 10,000 cases made. • $10 • (05/15/97) • **78**

Chardonnay Robertson Bon Vallon 1995: Fresh and vibrant, with apple and citrus flavors and hints of spice. Balanced, with a pleasant finish. 12,000 cases made. • $9 • (01/31/97) • **84**
Chardonnay Robertson D' Honneur 1995: This strives for complexity and character in a Burgundian style, showing exuberant toasty, fruity, butterscotchy aromas and flavors, firm acidity and good length on the finish. 1,000 cases made. • $14 • (02/28/97) • **89**
Chardonnay Robertson D'Honneur 1994 • $12 • (09/30/95) • **76**
Chardonnay Robertson D'Honneur 1993 • $12 • (07/31/94) • **84**
Chardonnay Robertson Lesca 1997: Fresh tasting, nicely balanced between crisp and ripe fruit flavors. A good, modestly proportioned Chardonnay. Drink now. 4,000 cases made. • $12 • (04/30/98) • **84**
Chardonnay Robertson Lesca 1995: Fairly rich and flavorful, with good balance and crispness. Offers pear, apple and spice flavors that linger on the finish. 10,000 cases made. • $12 • (01/31/97) • **84**
Chardonnay Robertson Lesca 1994 • $8 • (06/15/95) BB • **86**
Chardonnay Robertson Lesca 1993 • $8 • (07/31/94) BB • **85**

DELHEIM

Chardonnay Stellenbosch 1993 • $12 • (09/30/95) • **72**
Gewürztraminer Stellenbosch 1994 • $10 • (09/30/95) • **83**
Grand Reserve Cabernet Blend Stellenbosch 1991 • $18 • (06/15/95) • **87**
Heerensijn Dry White Stellenbosch 1994 • $7 • (06/30/95) • **78**
Pinotage Stellenbosch 1989 • $10 • (02/15/93) • **81**
Roodenwijn Dry Red Stellenbosch 1994 • $7 • (09/30/95) • **78**
Shiraz Stellenbosch 1991 • $10 • (09/30/95) • **77**

DESTINARE

Cabernet Sauvignon Franschhoek Valley 1995: A medium-bodied Cabernet with sweet cherry flavors and an overpowering gamy component. Comes off awkward and tired in the end. • $8 • (06/15/98) • **76**
Chardonnay Franschhoek Valley 1996: Displays some basic minerally overtones and an earthy finish. 2,000 cases imported. Drink now. • $8 • (06/15/98) • **78**
Chardonnay Franschhoek Valley 1995 • $7 • (05/15/96) • **76**
Grand Rouge Franschhoek Valley 1996: A simple, fruity red that might be best chilled. Light but jammy cherry and strawberry flavors, with a slightly sweet finish. A blend of 86 percent Cinsault and 14 percent Pinotage. Drink now. • $8 • (07/31/98) • **78**
Grand Rouge Franschhoek Valley 1995: Bright cherry flavors laced with herbal notes and hints of black pepper. Light and simple, but fresh, with light tannins. Drinkable now. • $7 • (07/31/96) • **83**
Merlot Worcester 1996: Minty in aroma, with some fading brown sugar and tealike flavors. Flabby and dull. 1,500 cases imported. • $8 • (06/15/98) • **76**
Sauvignon Blanc Franschhoek Valley 1996: Insipid fruit-cocktail aromas and cloying unripe flavors don't add up to much fun. • $8 • (06/15/98) • **71**
Sauvignon Blanc Franschhoek Valley 1995: Without enough fruit flavor to offset the tart, lean texture, it comes up short of balanced. • $7 • (04/30/97) • **74**

DROSTDYHOF

Merlot Coastal Region 1992 • $10 • (09/30/95) • **86**
Pinotage Coastal Region SFW 1989 • $8 • (02/15/93) • **87**

EIKENDAL

Cabernet Sauvignon Stellenbosch 1994: A robust, challenging style that blends smoky, pruny aromas with coffee and tobacco flavors and a tannic, full-bodied texture. Drink now through 2000. 800 cases made. • $16 • (04/30/98) • **85**
Chardonnay Stellenbosch 1997: Oak aged, with plenty of flavor if not finesse. A bit gangly in texture and balance, but has nice pear, pineapple and vanilla notes. Drink now. 2,000 cases made. • $15 • (04/30/98) • **84**
Chardonnay Stellenbosch 1996: A full-bodied style of Chardonnay that's rich in fruit flavor, firm in texture, accented by toasty oak flavors, and long on the finish. Best now. 2,000 cases made. • $15 • (10/15/97) • **89**
Merlot Stellenbosch 1996: Ripe and round, with plum and berry flavors and a leathery note. A nicely focused Merlot, with a chocolaty note on the finish. Drink now. 2,000 cases made. • $15 • (06/15/98) • **84**
Merlot Stellenbosch 1995: For fans of herbaceous Merlots. This wine is green tasting, with some decent plum and spice flavors. 2,000 cases made. • $16 • (08/31/97) • **80**

ELLIS, NEIL

Cabernet Sauvignon Stellenbosch 1995: A focused and intense wine with red cherry and plum flavors and plenty of tannins. A strong minty aroma and flavor smooths out after a few minutes aeration. Powerful; give it some time to let its many components integrate. Best from 2000 through 2004. 2,000 cases made. • $17 • (06/15/98) • **88**
Cabernet Sauvignon Stellenbosch 1994: A really pleasing Cabernet that's saturated with fruit flavor accented by oaky spice notes. It's smooth textured despite firm tannins. Drink now through 2000. 1,000 cases made. • $16 • (09/15/97) • **87**
Cabernet Sauvignon Stellenbosch 1993 • $18 • (12/31/95) • **84**
Cabernet Sauvignon Stellenbosch 1992 • $14 • (03/31/95) • **82**
Cabernet Sauvignon Stellenbosch 1990 • $13 • (06/30/94) • **86**
Chardonnay Elgin 1996: Uncomplicated, ripe and flavorful. A generous Chardonnay, with apple and citrus flavors and a clean, lingering finish. 1,000 cases made. • $15 • (10/15/97) • **86**
Chardonnay Elgin 1995: Not much here, with only modest pear flavors and a bit of spice and butter. Turns astringent on the finish. 1,500 cases made. • $15 • (01/31/97) • **76**
Chardonnay Stellenbosch 1993 • $13 • (06/30/95) • **79**
Sauvignon Blanc Groenkloof 1997: A good expression of Sauvignon Blanc. Crisp and focused, concentrated and full flavored, with citrus, herbal and spice flavors. Herbal flavors linger refreshingly on the finish. Drink now. 1,500 cases made. • $12 • (06/15/98) • **87**
Sauvignon Blanc Groenkloof 1996: Crisply textured and full flavored, capturing the citrus and herb character of the grape. Well balanced. Should prove versatile with food. 1,000 cases made. • $14 • (05/15/97) • **86**

FAIRVIEW ESTATE

Chardonnay Paarl 1996: Thick and juicy, with baked-apple flavors and lots of spice accents. A fairly rich and full-bodied Chardonnay from South Africa. 2,000 cases made. • $17 • (08/31/97) • **86**
Pinot Gris South Africa 1996: Simple, with peach and melon flavors. Turns somewhat astringent on the finish. 2,000 cases made. • $9 • (09/30/97) • **76**
Shiraz Paarl 1996: Eminently likable, fresh, fruity and easy drinking. Slightly tannic. Plenty of grape and blueberry flavor and a lingering finish. Drink now. 2,000 cases made. • $15 • (04/30/98) • **86**
Shiraz Paarl 1992 • $8 • (09/30/95) • **83**
Shiraz-Merlot Paarl 1991 • $8 • (09/30/95) • **85**

FLEUR DU CAP

Cabernet Sauvignon Coastal Region 1989: Showing its age in the interesting, cedary aromas, but it's still tannic and astringent in texture and lean in flavor. A beefy red wine but rather blunt in style. • $12 • (01/31/97) • **80**
Chardonnay Coastal Region 1995: A coarse wine, with earthy flavors and an astringent finish. • $11 • (01/31/97) • **72**
Chardonnay Coastal Region 1994 • $8 • (06/15/95) • **85**
Merlot Coastal Region 1994: Captures the herbal, earthy character of Merlot in a medium-bodied style. On the lean, crisp side in texture, with modest fruit flavors. • $11 • (06/30/97) • **82**
Merlot Coastal Region 1992 • $8 • (06/15/95) • **84**
Merlot Coastal Region 1991 • $8 • (01/01/94) • **78**
Pinotage Coastal Region 1992: A solid red in the Côtes du Rhône style, with peppery, herbal accents to the lean plum flavors. Moderately tannic but ready now. • $11 • (05/31/97) • **83**
Pinotage Coastal Region 1991: An austere style of Pinotage that has firm tannins and less fruit than younger vintages, but emphasizes peppery, smoky flavors instead. Not for everyone. • $9 • (01/01/97) • **80**
Pinotage Coastal Region 1990 • $9 • (09/30/95) • **78**
Pinotage Coastal Region 1989 • $8 • (06/15/95) • **84**
Pinotage Coastal Region 1988 • $10 • (02/15/93) • **88**
Sauvignon Blanc Coastal Region 1996: Light, refreshing and of good quality, this well-balanced white wine has fresh flavors of banana and citrus. • $11 • (06/30/97) • **84**

GLEN CARLOU

Cabernet Sauvignon Paarl 1993 • $20 • (06/15/95) • **88**
Chardonnay Paarl 1997: A spicy, complex, tantalizing Chardonnay with lots to sink your teeth into. Layers of pear, vanilla, nutmeg and pineapple begin in the aroma and last through the lingering finish. 6,000 cases imported. Drink now through 2000. • $15 • (07/31/98) HR • **90**

GOOD HOPE WINES

Chardonnay Paarl 1996: An outstanding Chardonnay in a full-blown style, emphasizing oaky, fruity, buttery flavors and a rich, full texture. Subtle accents of vanilla and a lingering finish give extra appeal. 5,000 cases made. • $15 • (05/15/97) • **90**
Chardonnay Paarl 1994 • $18 • (06/15/95) • **90**
Chardonnay Paarl 1993 • $20 • (02/28/95) • **83**
Chardonnay Paarl Reserve 1996: A gentle, rich Chardonnay with attractive but subtle flavors of pear, nutmeg and vanilla and a pleasantly smooth texture. 400 cases made. • $17 • (12/15/97) • **89**
Chardonnay Paarl Reserve 1995: A richly textured, subtly flavored Chardonnay that grows on you with each sip. It has depth, sophistication and a long finish. Should improve through 2000. • $17 • (05/15/97) • **90**
Chardonnay Paarl Reserve 1994 • $35 • (09/30/95) • **90**
Chardonnay Paarl Reserve Guild Auction Label 1993 • $NA • (09/30/95) • **85**
Grand Classique Reserve Paarl 1993: A rich, densely textured wine with deep color, thick texture and plenty of tannin to support the ample fruit flavors. Try now. A blend of 59 percent Cabernet Sauvignon, 25 percent Merlot, and 16 percent Cabernet Franc. • $16 • (05/15/97) • **85**
Grande Classique Reserve Paarl 1992 • $22 • (09/30/95) • **88**
Les Trois Red Paarl 1993 • $17 • (09/30/95) • **89**
Merlot Paarl 1995: A serious Merlot that is deep in color, packed with fruit flavor accented with oak, and moderately tannic. Has concentration and complexity for extra appeal. Drink now. • $13 • (04/30/97) • **87**
Merlot Paarl 1993 • $18 • (06/15/95) • **89**
Pinot Noir Paarl 1994 • $18 • (06/15/95) • **87**

GOOD HOPE WINES

Chairman's Selection Cabernet Blend Durbanville 1992 • $11 • (04/30/96) • **84**
Merlot Klein Karoo 1992 • $9 • (04/30/96) • **78**
Pinotage Paarl 1994 • $9 • (04/30/96) • **85**

GRANGEHURST

Cabernet Sauvignon Stellenbosch 1992 • $16 • (06/15/95) • **90**
Pinotage Stellenbosch 1992 • $15 • (06/15/95) • **89**

GRANITE CREEK

Sauvignon Blanc Coastal Region 1995: A simple wine, bland and innocuous, with very little taste of the grape. 1,000 cases made. • $9 • (04/30/97) • **74**

GREEN, DOUGLAS

Cabernet Sauvignon Coastal Region Superior 1981 • $21 • (10/15/92) • **83**
Pinotage Coastal Region Superior 1981 • $NA • (02/15/93) • **83**
Pinotage Coastal Region Superior 1980 • $21 • (10/15/92) • **81**
St. Augustine Red Coastal Region 1980 • $21 • (10/15/92) • **82**

GROOT CONSTANTIA

Cabernet Sauvignon Constantia 1992 • $12 • (12/31/95) • **81**
Cabernet Sauvignon Constantia 1990 • $12 • (06/30/94) • **78**
Chardonnay Constantia 1995: Simple, with only modest pear and apple flavors. It has an earthy aroma and turns dull on the finish. 2,000 cases made. • $14 • (01/31/97) • **77**
Constantia Blanc 1994 • $7 • (06/30/95) • **80**
Merlot Constantia 1992 • $12 • (12/31/95) • **79**
Pinotage Constantia 1993: Maturing and shows stewed fruit and raisin flavors with vegetal notes. Lacks balance. 2,000 cases made. • $10 • (07/31/96) • **77**
Pinotage Constantia 1992 • $9 • (09/30/95) • **78**
Pinotage Constantia 1990 • $8 • (06/30/94) • **75**
Pinotage Constantia 1989 • $7 • (02/15/93) • **81**
Rood Constantia Cabernet Blend 1990 • $7 • (06/30/94) • **80**
Sauvignon Blanc Constantia 1994 • $10 • (06/15/95) • **84**
Shiraz Constantia 1991: Extra aging has brought out a nice, spicy bottle bouquet in the aroma, while the texture is still lean and tannic and the fruit flavors are modest. Might have been better two years ago. 1,500 cases made. • $10 • (01/01/97) • **81**

Key: SS—Spectator Selection CS—Cellar Selection HR—Highly Recommended BB—Best Buy $NA—Price not available Ⓐ—Auction Price (BT)—Barrel Tasting
Dates in parentheses indicate the issues in which the ratings were published.

Shiraz Constantia 1989 • $9 • (06/30/94) • **84**
Weisser Riesling Constantia 1994 • $9 • (06/30/95) • **84**

HAMILTON RUSSELL

Chardonnay Walker Bay 1996: Not shy, this is a full-blown, full-bodied white wine that manages to stay harmonious and balanced. It's concentrated and complex, packed with pear, pineapple, fig and vanilla flavors on a rich texture. From South Africa. Drink now through 2000. 7,638 cases made. • $13 • (04/30/98) HR • **89**
Chardonnay Walker Bay 1995: Luscious, superrich and exotic. Packed with ripe fruit flavor, and has a very long, classy finish. From the bright green-gold color to the honeyed, seductive aftertaste, this is something special. Drink now through 2000. • $13 • (01/01/98) • **92**
Chardonnay Walker Bay 1994 • $12 • (06/30/95) • **87**
Pinot Noir Walker Bay 1995: Mature, mellow flavors and a smooth texture make this enjoyable, but it's heavily slanted toward smoky, sweet oak rather than fruit. Interesting, but atypical for Pinot. Drink now. • $15 • (04/30/98) • **80**
Pinot Noir Walker Bay 1992 • $16 • (06/30/95) • **82**

HAUTE PROVENCE VINEYARDS

Angels' Tears White Coastal Region 1997: Easygoing and slightly sweet, with floral, appley flavors. Simple refreshment. A blend of Muscat d'Alexandrie and Chenin Blanc. Drink now. 6,000 cases made. • $9 • (04/30/98) • **80**
Angels' Tears White Coastal Region 1996: An unusually bold style of white wine, with aggressive herbal aromas, somewhat sweet peach flavors and full body. Not for the faint of palate. A blend of Muscat d'Alexandrie and Chenin Blanc. 7,000 cases made. • $10 • (08/31/97) • **78**

IMPALA

Merlot Western Cape 1996: A lively wine with a nice gamy edge to it, along with good herbal and dark cherry flavors. • $10 • (11/15/97) • **83**

JACOBSDAL

Pinotage Stellenbosch 1988 • $10 • (02/15/93) • **86**

KANONKOP

Cabernet Sauvignon Stellenbosch 1991 • $20 • (09/30/95) • **81**
Cabernet Sauvignon Stellenbosch 1990 • $20 • (09/30/95) • **82**
Kadette Stellenbosch 1996: A wild and woolly red, with effusive aromas and flavors that are earthy and smoky but light on fruit. Medium-bodied, not very tannic. Drink now. • $11 • (03/31/98) • **83**
Kadette Stellenbosch 1995: Plush and full-bodied, this succulent red from South Africa offers plenty of yummy plum, cherry and herbal flavors. Rich and fairly distinctive, with a nice leathery note on the finish, it's quite a mouthful for the money. 6,500 cases made. • $10 • (08/31/97) BB • **87**
Paul Sauer Stellenbosch 1993: Smooth and focused, brimming with delicious cherry, red plum, spice and chocolate flavors. It's well crafted, showing abundant character, acidity and reserve. Drinkable now. 1,800 cases made. • $26 • (08/31/97) • **89**
Paul Sauer Stellenbosch 1991 • $25 • (06/15/95) • **90**
Pinotage Stellenbosch 1995: Here's a rich and remarkable South African red, impressively structured, with plenty of jammy flavors in the midpalate framed by chocolate, leather and smoke notes. Has good acidity as well. It's approachable now, but will likely be smoother next year. 14,500 cases made. 14,500 cases made. • $20 • (08/31/97) SS • **91**
Pinotage Stellenbosch 1993 • $14 • (06/15/95) • **88**
Pinotage Stellenbosch 1990 • $10 • (02/15/93) • **84**
Pinotage Stellenbosch Reserve 1993 • $18 • (09/30/95) • **91**
Pinotage Stellenbosch Reserve 1992 • $17 • (09/30/95) • **87**

KLEINBOSCH

Cabernet Sauvignon Paarl 1993: A good, straightforward Cab, with earthy, fruity flavors and moderate tannins. Best now. 5,000 cases made. • $7 • (09/15/97) • **81**
Chardonnay Paarl 1996: A very light, almost watery Chardonnay with simple flavors and a short finish. 5,000 cases made. • $7 • (10/15/97) • **76**
Cinsaut-Cabernet Sauvignon Paarl 1995: A light, rather crisp-textured red wine with little tannin and fresh, jammy fruit flavors. Drink now. 10,000 cases made. • $6 • (10/15/97) • **83**

Pinotage Paarl 1995: A rather light red, almost like Pinot Noir, with fresh cherry flavors and lively texture. Drink now. 5,000 cases made. • $6 • (10/15/97) • **83**
Red Paarl 1996: A very light red, with charming strawberry and cherry flavors. Drink now; best chilled, like a rosé. 20,000 cases made. • $6 • (10/15/97) • **83**
Steen Paarl 1996: A simple white wine with apple and citrus flavors, finishing on a nice grapefruity note. 10,000 cases made. • $6 • (09/30/97) • **79**
White Paarl 1996: A fresh, simple white wine with modest fruit flavors and a soft texture. Drink now. 20,000 cases made. • $6 • (10/15/97) • **80**

KLEINDAL

Pinotage Stellenbosch 1990 • $9 • (10/15/92) • **81**

KRONENDAL

Robertson Port 1991 • $NA • (09/30/95) • **84**
Sauvignon Blanc Breede River 1994 • $7 • (06/30/95) • **72**

KWV

Cabernet Sauvignon Western Cape 1995: A firm and flavorful Cabernet with rich plum, chocolate and cherry flavors, and some spicy notes on the finish. A nice leathery, charred note adds interest. Drink now through 2000. 42,000 cases made. • $14 • (06/15/98) • **84**
Chardonnay Western Cape 1997: A bit rough around the edges, with apple and citrus flavors and some spicy notes on the finish. Drink now. 30,000 cases made. • $8 • (06/15/98) • **79**
Chardonnay Western Cape 1996: A light Chardonnay that comes off as slightly bitter or unripe in character. Drinkable but pretty ordinary. 15,000 cases made. • $8 • (04/30/97) • **75**
Full Cream Sherry NV • $7 • (06/30/95) • **86**
Full Ruby Port NV • $7 • (09/30/95) • **81**
Full Tawny Port NV • $7 • (09/30/95) • **84**
Jerepigo Hanepoot Breede River Valley Dessert Wine 1975 • $10 • (06/30/95) • **85**
Merlot Western Cape 1995: A medium-bodied Merlot with stewed flavors and stemmy, tobaccolike notes on the finish. 20,000 cases made. • $14 • (06/15/98) • **75**
Merlot Western Cape 1994: Nicely mature already, this is spicy, open and intriguing, with cedary aromas, ripe fruit flavors and a broad, moderately tannic texture. Drink soon. 1,500 cases made. • $8 • (01/31/97) • **85**
Noble Late Harvest Coastal Region 1988 • $10 • (06/30/95) • **84**
Pale Medium Dry Sherry Renasans NV • $7 • (06/30/95) BB • **84**
Pinotage Western Cape 1996: Like a good Aussie Shiraz, with abundant fruit flavors, light oak accents, modest tannins and an almost sweet blackberry finish. Drink now. 18,000 cases made. • $9 • (07/31/98) • **84**
Red Muscatel Breede River Valley 1975 • $17 • (06/30/95) • **84**
Roodeberg Red Coastal Region 1991 • $6 • (06/30/95) • **77**
Roodeberg Cabernet Blend Coastal Region 1989 • $7 • (06/30/94) • **78**
Sauvignon Blanc Western Cape 1997: A straightforward white with a pleasant mix of citrus and almond flavors. Drink now. 42,000 cases made. • $7 • (06/15/98) • **81**
Shiraz Western Cape 1996: Straightforward, ripe and appealing. Medium-bodied, with fresh plum and blackberry flavors and light tannins. Easy to enjoy. Drink now. 15,000 cases made. • $8 • (07/31/98) • **84**
Steen Western Cape 1997: Interesting for its mix of ripe apple and cinnamon flavors. Not a blockbuster but an enticing example of this grape variety. Drink now. 65,000 cases made. • $7 • (06/15/98) • **84**
Steen Western Cape 1996: Pleasant, light and fruity in flavor, with a nicely crisp texture and tangy apple and grapefruit accents. 15,000 cases made. • $6 • (04/30/97) • **83**
Vintage Port Stellenbosch 1982 • $17 • (09/30/95) • **74**

LA MOTTE

Cabernet Sauvignon Franschhoek Valley 1992 • $NA • (09/30/95) • **83**
Cabernet Sauvignon Franschhoek Valley 1991: A firm-textured, rather mature and flavorful Cabernet with a ripe, earthy, herbal character. • $18 • (06/30/97) • **84**
Cabernet Sauvignon Franschhoek Valley 1989 • $15 • (06/15/95) • **86**
Cabernet Sauvignon Franschhoek Valley 1987 • $15 • (01/01/94) • **74**
Estate Red Franschhoek Valley 1992: A gutsy, full-bodied red wine that combines powerful fruit flavors with firm tannins and spicy oak accents. • $15 • (06/30/97) • **85**
Estate Red Franschhoek Valley 1990 • $11 • (06/15/95) • **86**
Millenium Franschhoek Valley Red 1992 • $NA • (09/30/95) • **81**
Shiraz Franschhoek Valley 1992 • $NA • (09/30/95) • **87**

LANDSKROON

Cabernet Sauvignon Paarl Estate Wine 1990 • $11 • (01/31/95) • **82**
Pinotage Paarl 1994 • $NA • (09/30/95) • **84**
Pinotage Paarl Estate Wine 1990 • $10 • (02/15/93) • **83**
Steen Dry Chenin Blanc Paarl 1995 • $NA • (09/30/95) • **80**

LANZERAC

Chardonnay Stellenbosch 1994 • $8 • (08/31/95) • **81**

LEBENSRAUM

Chardonnay Breede River Valley 1997: Standard issue, with modest fruit flavors and a certain richness of texture. Not bad, just a bit simple and rough around the edges. Drink now. 1,000 cases made. • $15 • (07/31/98) • **78**
Chenin Blanc Breede River 1997: This hearty but simple white has apricot and apple flavors, a tart texture and a short finish. Drink now. 1,000 cases made. • $10 • (07/31/98) • **78**
Sémillon Breede River 1997: A rich texture and a lingering finish add interest to this subtly flavored, well-balanced white. Not a blockbuster, but intriguing for its fig, melon and apple nuances. Drink now. 800 cases made. • $13 • (07/31/98) • **85**

LIEVLAND

DVB Red Stellenbosch 1992 • $19 • (12/31/95) • **84**
Lievlander Red Stellenbosch 1995: A suave, spicy red that's nicely oaky in aroma, very supple in texture and long on the finish. Firm tannins and solid cherry and plum flavors give it depth. Drink now through 2000. Tasted twice, with consistent notes. 5,000 cases made. • $8 • (11/15/97) • **87**
Lievlander Stellenbosch 1994: Ripe and oozing with blackberry, plum and toasty oak flavors. Generous on the palate but moderate in tannins. Spicy fruit lingers on the finish. Drinkable now. 5,000 cases made. • $9 • (07/31/96) • **87**
Shiraz Stellenbosch 1994: A hearty, enjoyable, full-bodied and rather tannic Shiraz showing spicy oak flavors atop its appealing fruit character. 1,500 cases made. • $19 • (05/15/97) • **85**
Shiraz Stellenbosch 1991 • $18 • (04/30/96) • **81**

LONGRIDGE

Brut Coastal Region Méthode Cap Classique 1992: An appealing, straightforward sparkling wine with enough crisp, dry fruit flavor to give it zing. • $17 • (04/30/97) • **83**
Cabernet Sauvignon Coastal Region 1993: Vanilla and toasty oak flavors dominate the fresh raspberry and cherry flavors. Lean and rather tannic. Needs food to soften and open up. • $16 • (07/31/96) • **83**
Cabernet Sauvignon-Pinotage Western Cape Bay View 1994: The jammy, slightly candied raspberry flavors have some appeal, but lacks finesse and turns dry on the finish. • $10 • (07/31/96) • **77**
Chardonnay Stellenbosch 1995: Oaky tasting and ripe, with loads of butter and spice flavors, though not much fruit. Obvious but tasty. • $16 • (01/31/97) • **82**
Chardonnay Stellenbosch Bay View Reserve 1995: A happy mix of ripe and tropical fruit flavors, and there's some butter and spice notes, too. Balanced, though not complex. • $9 • (01/31/97) • **81**
Merlot Coastal Region Bay View 1995: A soft, fleshy wine with plum and prune flavors and some vegetal and tomato notes. Could stand up to simple grilled meats. • $9 • (07/31/96) • **80**
Pinotage Western Cape Bay View 1994: Bright blackberry flavors, round, fruity and firm on the finish. A bit clumsy and reminiscent of hard candy, but has attractive fruit. Drinkable now. • $9 • (07/31/96) • **83**

L'ORMARINS

Chardonnay Franschhoek Valley 1994: An oddball Chardonnay, with herbal aromas and pine and butter flavors. Awkward, with a floral taste on the finish. • $13 • (01/31/97) • **76**
Chardonnay Franschhoek Valley 1993 • $10 • (09/30/95) • **82**

LOUISVALE

Chardonnay Stellenbosch 1993 • $15 • (07/31/95) • **86**

SOUTH AFRICA

MEERENDAL

Pinotage Durbanville Estate Wine 1988 • $10 • (02/15/93) • **75**

MEERLUST

Cabernet Sauvignon Stellenbosch 1991 • $22 • (06/15/95) • **89**
Cabernet Sauvignon Stellenbosch 1986 • $16 • (11/30/94) • **78**
Merlot Stellenbosch 1993: Like a nice, crisp claret this Merlot emphasizes fresh cranberry and cherry flavors, a light tannic bite and a lingering finish. Should be quite versatile with food. • $22 • (06/30/97) • **86**
Merlot Stellenbosch 1991: A potent blend of black cherry flavors and firm tannins make this enjoyable. Beginning to show maturity in its spicy, cedary aromas. • $22 • (01/31/97) • **84**
Merlot Stellenbosch 1989 • $16 • (06/15/95) • **84**
Rubicon Stellenbosch 1992: A smooth, mellow, enjoyable red with enough ripe fruit flavor for depth, and the right balance of firm tannins and lively acidity. • $22 • (06/30/97) • **85**
Rubicon Stellenbosch 1991: One to sink your teeth into. A vibrant, lively, fruit-packed wine with plenty of flavor and a firm but smooth texture. Well balanced, with a lingering finish. Drink now. • $22 • (01/31/97) • **87**
Rubicon Stellenbosch 1989 • $16 • (06/30/95) • **88**

MIDDELVLEI

Pinotage Stellenbosch 1991: Though somewhat tannic and mature, this nicely balanced red has an elegant mix of firm acidity, subtle fruit flavors and smoky, earthy nuances. Worth a try. • $13 • (05/15/97) • **84**
Pinotage Stellenbosch 1990 • $10 • (09/30/95) • **76**
Pinotage Stellenbosch 1989 • $10 • (02/15/93) • **78**
Shiraz Stellenbosch 1990 • $14 • (04/30/96) • **78**

MORGENHOF

Chardonnay Stellenbosch 1994 • $12 • (06/30/95) • **83**
Merlot Stellenbosch 1993 • $14 • (06/30/95) • **87**
Sauvignon Blanc Stellenbosch 1994 • $12 • (09/30/95) • **80**

MULDERBOSCH

Chardonnay Stellenbosch 1995: Ripe, with a good zing of acidity. Has a bounty of ripe fig, pear and apple flavors, nicely framed by butter and spice notes, all lingering on the long finish. Drink now. • $22 • (08/31/97) SS • **89**
Faithful Hound Stellenbosch 1995: An honest, well-made red, with enough concentration and a firm enough texture to suggest it can age. It combines fresh fruit flavors with intriguing smoky, meaty accents that linger on the finish. Full-bodied and tannic. A blend of 41 percent Merlot, 35 percent Cabernet Sauvignon, 12 percent Malbec, and 12 percent Cabernet Franc. Drink now through 2001. • $19 • (07/31/98) • **87**
Faithful Hound Stellenbosch 1994: Made in a Claret style, with power, it's distinctive and well balanced, with dark plum, currant and herbal flavors, some spice notes, a smooth finish. • $17 • (08/31/97) SS • **88**
Faithful Hound Stellenbosch 1993 • $15 • (09/30/95) • **82**
Sauvignon Blanc Stellenbosch 1997: A crisp, bracing wine with the grapefruit and herb flavors one expects from this varietal. A versatile food wine. Drink now. • $19 • (12/15/97) • **86**
Sauvignon Blanc Stellenbosch 1996: A vividly flavored, classically styled Sauvignon that has crisp acidity, assertive flavors of herbs and grapefruit and a lingering finish. • $18 • (04/30/97) • **88**
Sauvignon Blanc Stellenbosch 1995 • $15 • (09/30/95) • **85**
Sauvignon Blanc Stellenbosch 1994 • $15 • (03/31/95) • **84**

NEDERBURG

Baronne Coastal Region Red 1989 • $10 • (06/30/95) • **77**
Cabernet Sauvignon Paarl 1991 • $10 • (09/30/95) • **76**
Cabernet Sauvignon Paarl 1989 • $10 • (06/30/94) • **84**
Chardonnay Paarl Red 1994 • $10 • (09/30/95) • **84**
Edelrood Paarl Red 1989 • $10 • (06/30/95) • **77**
Pinotage Paarl 1990 • $10 • (09/30/95) • **73**
Pinotage Paarl 1988 • $10 • (06/30/94) • **73**
Prelude Paarl White 1993 • $10 • (06/30/95) • **81**

NEETHLINGSHOF

Cabernet Sauvignon Stellenbosch 1992: Seems tired and past its prime. A smoky, earthy thread runs through this wine from the aroma to the finish. Tasted twice, with consistent notes. 5,000 cases made. • $10 • (09/30/97) • **76**
Cabernet Sauvignon Stellenbosch 1990 • $10 • (09/30/95) • **84**
Chardonnay Stellenbosch 1995: A lean but appealing Chardonnay, with refreshing acidity and bright citrus and mineral flavors that linger on the finish. Drink now. 3,500 cases made. • $10 • (10/15/97) • **85**
Merlot Stellenbosch 1994: Full-bodied, with smoky, plummy flavors, firm tannins and deep color. Hearty, fresh and fruity. Best now through 2000. 3,000 cases made. • $10 • (09/15/97) • **85**
Merlot Stellenbosch 1993 • $10 • (09/30/95) • **72**
Neethlingshoffer Stellenbosch White 1995: A basic, slightly sweet white wine, with apple and herb flavors. 2,500 cases made. • $10 • (10/15/97) • **77**
Neethlingsrood Stellenbosch 1992: An austere red with smoky aromas and flavors, a tart texture and tight tannins. Doesn't give much pleasure. 2,000 cases made. • $10 • (10/15/97) • **76**
Pinotage Stellenbosch 1993: A big, tannic red with smoky, beefy flavors but little fruit character. Austere and tough in style. Drink now. 3,500 cases made. • $10 • (10/15/97) • **78**
Sauvignon Blanc Stellenbosch 1996: The fresh floral character of the aromas turns heavier and more herbal on the palate. A solid, basic Sauvignon. 3,500 cases made. • $10 • (09/15/97) • **82**
Shiraz Stellenbosch 1993: Just about over-the-hill, with unappealing cola and dried cherry flavors. Lacks freshness. Tasted twice, with consistent notes. 2,000 cases made. • $10 • (11/15/97) • **73**
Shiraz Stellenbosch 1992 • $10 • (09/30/95) • **81**
Weisser Riesling Stellenbosch 1996: A well-balanced Riesling with plenty of flavor. Nice and juicy with its good peach, apple and honey notes. Finishes with a touch of spice. 2,000 cases made. • $10 • (09/30/97) • **85**
Weisser Riesling Stellenbosch 1993 • $10 • (08/31/95) • **84**
Weisser Riesling Stellenbosch Noble Late Harvest 1995: A luscious dessert wine overflowing with nectarine, honey and orange-peel aromas and flavors with a hint of clove. Butterscotch and apricot aftertaste. Reminiscent of Sauternes. 400 cases made. • $22/375ml • (09/30/97) • **89**
Weisser Riesling Stellenbosch Off-Dry 1993 • $10 • (08/31/95) • **84**

OVERGAAUW

Cabernet Sauvignon Stellenbosch 1990 • $15 • (09/30/95) • **86**
Cabernet Sauvignon Stellenbosch Landgoedwyn 1987 • $16 • (10/15/92) • **75**
Merlot Stellenbosch Landgoedwyn 1988 • $13 • (10/15/92) • **77**

RED HILL

Cabernet Sauvignon Coastal Region 1996: A simple, hearty, smoky-flavored Cabernet with moderate tannins. Drink now. 3,000 cases made. • $8 • (12/15/97) • **78**
Pinotage Coastal Region 1996: A simple and somewhat dull, smoky-tasting red wine, light in body and tannin. Drink now. 2,500 cases made. • $8 • (03/31/98) • **75**
Shiraz Coastal Region 1996: An agreeable, light style, with smoky, herbal, berrylike flavors and a peppery finish. Like a Côtes du Rhone. 2,000 cases made. • $8 • (12/15/97) • **82**

REDHILL

Pinotage Coastal Region 1993 • $6 • (09/30/95) • **82**

ROOIBERG WYNMAKERY

Cabernet Sauvignon Robertson 1992 • $8 • (09/30/95) • **69**
Chardonnay Robertson 1994 • $8 • (06/30/95) • **80**
Pinotage Robertson 1992 • $8 • (06/15/95) • **84**
Port Eilandia Cape Ruby 1994: An effusively fruity Port that's full-bodied, sweet and well balanced. Its deep, dark color and rich cherry and blackberry flavors make it appealing. Best now through 2002. • $15 • (09/15/97) • **87**

Key: SS—Spectator Selection CS—Cellar Selection HR—Highly Recommended BB—Best Buy $NA—Price not available Ⓐ—Auction Price (BT)—Barrel Tasting
Dates in parentheses indicate the issues in which the ratings were published.

Port Robertson 1993: Enjoyable but rather simple. A full-bodied Port that's agreeably sweet, moderately concentrated and short on the finish. • $NA • (01/01/97) • **78**

Rhine Riesling Vinkrivier 1995: If you want nectarine flavor, this is your wine. Clean, simple and straightforward. 5,000 cases made. • $8 • (09/30/97) • **82**

Sauvignon Blanc Robertson 1994 • $8 • (06/15/95) • **85**

Shiraz Breede River Valley 1993: Ripe and full-bodied, with enticing black-plum and pepper flavors. Robust tannins; drink now with food. 6,000 cases made. • $10 • (08/31/97) • **83**

Shiraz Goree 1989 • $11 • (04/15/92) • **82**

Shiraz Vinkrivier 1991 • $9 • (06/30/94) • **84**

ROOSENVELDT

Cabernet Sauvignon Franschhoek Valley 1993 • $14 • (04/30/96) • **83**

Chardonnay Franschhoek Valley 1995 • $12 • (05/15/96) • **82**

Merlot Franschhoek Valley 1994 • $14 • (04/30/96) • **87**

ROZENDAL FARM

Stellenbosch 1990 • $18 • (06/30/95) • **78**

Stellenbosch 1989 • $18 • (06/15/95) • **86**

RUST EN VREDE

Cabernet Sauvignon Stellenbosch 1989 • $20 • (11/30/94) • **87**

Estate Wine Stellenbosch Cabernet Blend 1992: Firm textured, deep colored, tart cherry flavored. Though enjoyable for its vibrant fruit flavor, it comes off as lean. Seems to be closed in; try now. 1,200 cases made. • $25 • (01/31/97) • **85**

Estate Wine Stellenbosch Cabernet Blend 1991 • $25 • (06/15/95) • **89**

Estate Wine Stellenbosch Cabernet Blend 1990 • $NA • (11/30/94) • **88**

Merlot Stellenbosch 1996: This dry Merlot has smoky aromas, attractive cherry and herb flavors and a clean, fresh texture. It's medium-bodied and not too tannic. Drinkable now. 1,000 cases made. • $12 • (09/15/97) • **84**

Merlot Stellenbosch 1994: Lively, crisp-textured and rather light, this emphasizes herb and smoke flavors backed by enough fruit flavor to balance. 2,000 cases made. • $12 • (01/31/97) • **83**

Merlot Stellenbosch 1993 • $12 • (12/31/95) • **80**

Merlot Stellenbosch 1992 • $11 • (09/30/95) • **73**

Merlot Stellenbosch 1991 • $12 • (11/30/94) • **84**

Shiraz Stellenbosch 1994: Appetizing, well balanced and full flavored, neither too light nor too heavy. Shows pure Shiraz flavors of blackberry and raspberry, good acidity, just enough tannin and light oak accents. 800 cases made. • $16 • (05/15/97) • **88**

Shiraz Stellenbosch 1991: Impressive for its youthful vibrancy at this age, but this moderately tannic, well-balanced Shiraz is turning lean and light on fruit flavor. Drink it soon. 1,500 cases made. • $16 • (01/01/97) • **83**

Shiraz Stellenbosch 1990 • $15 • (04/30/96) • **83**

Shiraz Stellenbosch 1989 • $16 • (11/30/94) • **85**

Tinta Barocca Stellenbosch Red 1994: Lean in flavor and very tannic, this tastes unbalanced. Rough texture. Neither fruity nor fun. 1,500 cases made. • $11 • (01/31/97) • **76**

Tinta Barocca Stellenbosch Red 1993: Polished and accessible, showing lively flavors of cherry and blackberry, with pleasant herbal accents. Balanced and has some elegance. Drinkable now. 1,200 cases made. • $10 • (07/31/96) • **85**

RUSTENBERG

Cabernet Sauvignon Stellenbosch 1990 • $12 • (09/30/95) • **84**

Cabernet Sauvignon Stellenbosch 1988 • $14 • (10/15/92) • **74**

Dry Red Stellenbosch 1991 • $11 • (09/30/95) • **82**

Gold Label Stellenbosch Red 1990 • $17 • (09/30/95) • **84**

Gold Stellenbosch Red 1989 • $19 • (10/15/92) • **82**

Merlot-Cabernet Sauvignon Stellenbosch 1991 • $12 • (09/30/95) • **76**

SABLE VIEW

Cabernet Sauvignon Coastal Region 1990 • $8 • (06/30/94) • **78**

Pinotage Coastal Region 1989 • $8 • (06/30/94) • **76**

SAVANHA

Cabernet Sauvignon Western Cape Agulhas Bank 1996: Offers some basic plum and berry flavors but ends up a bit stewy tasting, with a gamy edge to the finish. 5,000 cases made. • $11 • (06/15/98) • **78**

Chardonnay Western Cape 1996: This Riesling-like Chardonnay has floral aromas, smoky and citrus flavors and plenty of body. Not what you would expect. Drink now. 5,000 cases made. • $10 • (10/15/97) • **78**

Chardonnay Western Cape 1995: A canned-fruit flavor runs through this uninspired wine. Turns bitter on the finish. 15,000 cases made. • $10 • (01/31/97) • **73**

Chardonnay Western Cape Agulhas Bank 1996: Soft and sumptuous, here's a subtle but rich Chardonnay that nicely blends ripe fruit flavors with accents of vanilla and honey. Tasted twice, with consistent notes. Drink now through 2000. 5,000 cases made. • $9 • (10/15/97) • **88**

Chenin Blanc Western Cape Barrel Fermented 1997: A simple, sturdy white, with vague apple flavors and a slightly coarse texture. Drink now. 1,000 cases made. • $7 • (07/31/98) • **75**

Merlot-Cabernet Sauvignon Rosé Western Cape Barrel Fermented 1997: Not a bad rosé. Nicely dry, with light berry flavors and a sense of body and substance that lasts on the finish. Drink now. 1,000 cases made. • $7 • (07/31/98) • **84**

Merlot Western Cape 1995: A smooth, purely fruity Merlot, delivering loads of fresh raspberry flavor with smoky accents, soft tannins and a clean finish. Quite enjoyable in a straightforward way. 15,000 cases made. • $10 • (01/31/97) • **87**

Pinotage Western Cape 1996: Dry, zippy and fresh, this light, spicy and fruity red is reminiscent of Côtes du Rhône. Enjoy. 10,000 cases made. • $11 • (05/31/97) • **85**

Pinotage-Cabernet Sauvignon Western Cape 1996: Generously fruity and medium-bodied, with deep color, subdued tannins and an easy texture. Enjoy now. 5,000 cases made. • $11 • (05/31/97) • **84**

Sauvignon Blanc Western Cape 1997: Nice texture, with citrus and herbal notes mixed in. A quaffable white with an edge to it. Drink now. 1,000 cases made. • $7 • (07/31/98) • **80**

Sauvignon Blanc Western Cape Benguela Current 1997: Simple and fruity, with bright grapefruit and apple flavors, but a bit soft in texture and short on the finish. Drink now. 1,000 cases made. • $7 • (07/31/98) • **77**

Shiraz Western Cape 1996: A light, easygoing Syrah that's not tannic but fresh and ready to drink. 10,000 cases made. • $11 • (05/31/97) • **84**

SAXENBURG

Cabernet Sauvignon Stellenbosch 1995: This melts in your mouth. It has a deep, dark color, ripe and vivid black cherry flavors, smooth tannins and a lingering finish. Best now. 3,000 cases made. • $15 • (09/30/97) • **87**

Merlot Stellenbosch 1996: Flavorful, firm and tannic, with bright cherry flavors and smoky, peppery accents. An ample core of fruit flavor and a lingering finish make it special. Drink now through 2000. 2,000 cases made. • $14 • (06/15/98) • **86**

Merlot Stellenbosch 1995: A generous, fruity, mouthfilling Merlot, with just enough tannin and acidity for balance. The ample cherry and plum flavors linger on the finish. Best now. 1,000 cases made. • $13 • (09/30/97) • **86**

Merlot Stellenbosch 1994: Polished to a glossy sheen. Smooth and shows blackberry, toast, vanilla and light citrus flavors. Pure and clean. Appealing and accessible now. 1,200 cases made. • $14 • (07/31/96) • **86**

Pinotage Stellenbosch 1996: Quite flavorful but extreme in style, with ripe, almost sweet cherry flavors competing with smoky, ashy overtones from the aroma to the finish. Light in tannins, medium in body. Drink now. 2,000 cases made. • $14 • (07/31/98) • **80**

Pinotage Stellenbosch 1995: Concentration and character shine through in this deep-colored, full-bodied red. The flavors are smoky, cherrylike and peppery, reminding us of the Northern Rhône. Firm and tannic but balanced. Drink now through 2000. 1,500 cases made. • $13 • (10/15/97) • **89**

Pinotage Stellenbosch 1994: Balanced and has some depth. Marries ripe black cherry flavor with smoke and licorice. Firm tannins. 2,000 cases made. • $12 • (07/31/96) • **84**

Sauvignon Blanc Stellenbosch 1996: Assertive and distinctive, with powerful aromas of herbs and grapefruit, a vibrant, crisp texture and concentrated fruit flavors that persist on the finish. Mouthwatering. 1,000 cases made. • $10 • (04/30/97) • **88**

Shiraz Stellenbosch 1995: A delicious, juicy red with effusive peppery and leathery flavors, and dark plum and cherry flavors, too. Finishes on a nice, meaty note. Balanced and ready to drink. 800 cases made. • $18 • (11/15/97) • **88**

Shiraz Stellenbosch 1994: Exuberant aromas of black pepper, game and blackberry are true to the variety; the flavors are lively and ripe, with a kick of black pepper. Firm tannins; try now. 1,500 cases made. • $16 • (07/31/96) • **88**

Shiraz Stellenbosch Private Collection 1993 • $16 • (04/30/96) • **90**

SIMONSIG

Cabernet Sauvignon Stellenbosch 1989 • $14 • (10/15/92) • **84**

Pinotage Stellenbosch 1989 • $11 • (10/15/92) • **82**

Pinotage Stellenbosch Private Reserve Estate Wine 1989 • $NA • (02/15/93) • **87**

SIMONSVLEI WYNKELDER

Cabernet Sauvignon-Merlot Coastal Region 1995: A basic style of Cabernet, with smoky, earthy aromas, decent fruit flavors and a tannic texture. 4,000 cases made. • $9 • (09/30/97) • **80**

Pinotage Coastal Region Reserve 1995: Fresh and spicy, with nice black cherry flavors. Chocolate notes linger on the long finish. A delicious and fairly rich wine. 5,000 cases made. • $13 • (08/31/97) • **85**

SORGVLIET

Grand Vin Rouge Stellenbosch 1992 • $7 • (09/30/95) • **87**

SPRINGBOK

Cabernet Sauvignon Coastal Region 1994: Full-bodied, hearty and mature tasting, with jammy, pruny, nutty flavors and moderate tannins. Drink now. 22,000 cases made. • $7 • (01/31/97) • **84**

Cabernet Sauvignon Coastal Region 1992 • $7 • (09/30/95) • **73**

Cabernet Sauvignon Coastal Region 1991 • $7 • (01/01/94) • **79**

Cabernet Sauvignon Coastal Region 1990 • $7 • (06/30/94) • **82**

Cabernet Sauvignon Western Cape 1995: Firm, fruity and focused, here is a well-balanced Cabernet at an impressively low price. Offering satisfying cherry and berry flavors and a smooth, moderately tannic texture, it's best now. 25,000 cases made. • $8 • (09/30/97) BB • **85**

Chardonnay Coastal Region 1995 • $7 • (05/15/96) • **82**

Chardonnay Coastal Region 1994 • $7 • (02/28/95) BB • **86**

Chardonnay Western Cape 1996: An oaky style that has toasty, smoky aromas and flavors, full body and a lingering, oaky finish. Flavorful, if rather one-dimensional. 20,000 cases made. • $8 • (05/15/97) • **84**

Merlot Western Cape 1995: Great balance and serious fruit flavor make this Merlot tempting to drink now, but it should age, too. Has concentrated cherry and currant flavors and a firmly tannic but smooth texture. Best now. 5,000 cases made. • $8 • (09/30/97) • **87**

Merlot Western Cape 1994: A nice, basic Merlot with plummy, herbal flavors. Full-bodied, but not too much tannin. Mature and ready to drink. • $7 • (01/31/97) • **83**

Pinotage Coastal Region 1993 • $7 • (04/30/96) • **87**

Pinotage Coastal Region 1991 • $6 • (09/30/95) • **74**

Pinotage Coastal Region 1990 • $7 • (06/30/94) • **80**

Pinotage Coastal Region 1989 • $7 • (02/15/93) • **82**

Pinotage Western Cape 1995: An appealing and complete South African red, its abundance of fruit flavors nicely accented by sweet oak notes. It's medium-bodied and not too tannic. Ready to drink, and returns change from your $10 bill. 15,000 cases made. • $9 • (10/15/97) BB • **86**

Sauvignon Blanc Coastal Region 1996: A decent white, with just a trace of Sauvignon character. It tastes simple, fruity, on the tart side. 30,000 cases made. • $8 • (04/30/97) • **77**

Sauvignon Blanc Coastal Region 1994 • $6 • (09/30/95) • **79**

Sauvignon Blanc Coastal Region 1993 • $6 • (03/31/95) • **80**

Shiraz Coastal Region 1994: A nicely balanced, flavorful red, with vibrant cherry and raspberry accents and a smooth, elegant texture. Not a powerhouse but a pleasure to drink and a great value, too. 4,500 cases made. • $7 • (05/15/97) • **86**

Shiraz Coastal Region 1989 • $7 • (06/30/94) • **74**

Shiraz Western Cape 1996: Almost sweet, this spicy, oaky red is medium-bodied, fresh, fruity and light in tannin. Best now. 3,000 cases made. • $8 • (09/15/97) • **84**

Key: SS—Spectator Selection CS—Cellar Selection HR—Highly Recommended BB—Best Buy $NA—Price not available (A)—Auction Price (BT)—Barrel Tasting

Dates in parentheses indicate the issues in which the ratings were published.

STELLENRYCK

Cabernet Sauvignon Coastal Region 1991: A big, bold, assertive Cabernet that's tannic, full-bodied and amply fleshed out with fruit flavors. Try now through 2001. • $16 • (05/31/97) • **87**

Cabernet Sauvignon Coastal Region 1989 • $13 • (06/15/95) • **87**

Cabernet Sauvignon Coastal Region 1988 • $13 • (11/30/94) • **82**

Chardonnay Coastal Region 1995: Full in texture and lean in flavor except for a strong buttery note, it's a rather simple Chardonnay. • $11 • (06/30/97) • **79**

Chardonnay Coastal Region 1994: Buttery, simple, pleasant caramel and baked apple flavors. • $9 • (08/31/96) • **78**

STELLENZICHT

Cabernet Sauvignon Stellenbosch 1994: A natural style of Cabernet that bursts at the seams with ripe cherry and plum flavors and shows little oak influence. It's very generous in character, firmly tannic but smooth in texture. Best now through 2000. 5,000 cases made. • $15 • (10/15/97) • **87**

Chardonnay Stellenbosch 1996: A very good Chardonnay in a serious style, with solid, ripe fruit flavors accented by spicy, toasty oak. It's smooth yet crisp in texture and has a lingering finish. Best now. 4,000 cases made. • $15 • (10/15/97) • **87**

Chardonnay Stellenbosch 1993 • $7 • (08/31/95) • **82**

Chenin Blanc Stellenbosch 1996: Rich in flavor and full-bodied, this apple- and honey-scented Chenin Blanc is smooth in texture and lingers on the finish. 350 cases made. • $15 • (09/30/97) • **84**

Merlot Stellenbosch 1994: A reserved, medium-bodied wine with moderate tannins and earthy, tart, cherrylike flavors. Best now. 3,000 cases made. • $15 • (09/15/97) • **81**

Merlot-Cabernet Franc Stellenbosch 1994: A tangy and tannic red with earthy, cherrylike flavors and a smoky finish. Best now. 1,000 cases made. • $15 • (09/30/97) • **83**

Sauvignon Blanc Stellenbosch 1996: Lively, refreshing and full of fruit flavor, this is a well-balanced Sauvignon with a lingering finish. 3,000 cases made. • $15 • (09/15/97) • **85**

Sémillon Stellenbosch Reserve 1996: Stylish and full-bodied, this smooth and complex Sémillon shows the buttery, toasty aromas of new oak backed by good fruit concentration. Best now. 500 cases made. • $20 • (10/15/97) • **88**

Syrah Stellenbosch 1994: A horse of a different color. This inky-black Syrah is closed tight right now, but its underlying black cherry, coffee and chocolate flavors should emerge with time. Quite tannic but well balanced, it should be gorgeous when mature. Best now. 800 cases made. • $35 • (09/15/97) • **92**

SWARTLAND WINERY

Cabernet Sauvignon Swartland Region 1993 • $9 • (09/30/95) • **85**

Dry Red Swartland Region NV • $NA • (09/30/95) • **81**

Merlot Swartland Region 1997: A satisfying Merlot, with a deep color, intriguing tobacco and herb aromas, rich plum and tomato flavors and soft tannins. Drink now. 15,000 cases made. • $10 • (07/31/98) BB • **85**

Merlot Swartland Region 1996: Solid in texture and ample in fruit flavor. Fresh tasting, medium-bodied and not very tannic. Ready to drink. • $11 • (05/15/97) • **84**

Merlot Swartland Region 1995 • $10 • (04/30/96) • **87**

Pinotage Swartland Region 1996: Like a nice, dry Beaujolais, this light-bodied red has abundant fresh fruit flavors, is light in tannins and is ready to drink. • $9 • (05/15/97) • **84**

Pinotage Swartland Region 1995 • $9 • (04/30/96) • **83**

Pinotage Swartland Region 1994 • $6 • (09/30/95) • **83**

Sauvignon Blanc Swartland Region 1996: Fresh, simple and straightforward, it's light on fruit flavor but pleasant. • $8 • (05/15/97) • **78**

Sauvignon Blanc Swartland Region 1994 • $6 • (09/30/95) • **77**

Shiraz Swartland Region 1992 • $9 • (09/30/95) • **80**

THELEMA

Cabernet Sauvignon Stellenbosch 1994: A fine and flavorful Cabernet whose subtle flavors expand on the finish, building layers of complexity. It's deep in color, spicy in aroma, currantlike in flavor, firmly tannic but smooth—a class act all the way around. Best now through 2004. • $30 • (09/15/97) • **90**

Cabernet Sauvignon Stellenbosch 1993: A minty character dominates this delicious, rich, lush Cab, with good plum and chocolate flavors and a

touch of tobacco as well. Inviting and ready to drink. • $20 • (08/31/97) SS • **89**
Cabernet Sauvignon Stellenbosch 1991 • $19 • (06/15/95) • **89**
Cabernet Sauvignon Stellenbosch 1990 • $18 • (01/31/95) • **87**
Cabernet Sauvignon Stellenbosch Reserve 1991 • $22 • (09/30/95) • **91**
Cabernet Sauvignon-Merlot Stellenbosch 1992 • $20 • (06/15/95) • **90**
Chardonnay Stellenbosch 1996: A pumped-up Chardonnay, with strong oaky aromas and a rich texture, but it turns lean on the finish. • $24 • (12/15/97) • **84**
Chardonnay Stellenbosch 1994 • $18 • (06/15/95) • **88**
Chardonnay Stellenbosch Reserve 1993 • $22 • (06/15/95) • **87**
Merlot Stellenbosch 1994: This is a powerful, full-bodied, flavorful and tannic Merlot that needs time to mellow out. Its concentrated cherry, chocolate and tobacco flavors are wrapped tight in tannins, but start to emerge on the finish. Best now. • $24 • (09/15/97) • **89**
Sauvignon Blanc Stellenbosch 1997: Combines tangy citrus flavors with bright herbal accents for a lively, refreshing personality. Drink now. • $19 • (12/15/97) • **85**
Sauvignon Blanc Stellenbosch 1996: A richly flavored, smoothly textured, full-bodied wine that adds buttery accents to its ripe fruit flavors. • $15 • (09/15/97) • **87**
Sauvignon Blanc Stellenbosch 1994 • $14 • (06/15/95) • **87**

UITERWYK

Pinotage Stellenbosch 1992 • $12 • (09/30/95) • **88**

VAN LOVEREN

Chardonnay Robertson 1996: A heavy dose of buttery, oaky flavors puts a spin on this otherwise straightforward Chardonnay. Impressive at first whiff, but turns simple. Drink now. 4,000 cases made. • $12 • (03/31/98) • **78**
Chardonnay Robertson Spes Bona 1997: A pale-colored, simple and fruity-tasting white, with light, fresh, pear and banana flavors and a soft texture. Drink now. 3,000 cases made. • $10 • (03/31/98) • **80**
Gewürztraminer Robertson Special Late Harvest 1997: Candied, tropical fruit flavors dissipate quickly on the palate. 1,000 cases made. • $9 • (04/30/98) • **75**
Muscadel Robertson Blanc de Noir 1997: Nicely fruity and slightly sweet; drinkers of white Zinfandel will find this appealing. It's fresh but simple in flavor. Drink now. 8,000 cases made. • $7 • (03/31/98) • **82**
Pinot Gris Robertson 1997: Very simple. Extremely subdued fruit flavor but a reasonably smooth texture. Drinkable but dull. Ready now. 2,000 cases made. • $9 • (04/30/98) • **77**

VEENWOUDEN

Classic Red Coastal Region 1994: A flavorful, spicy, mature-tasting red, with solid fruit flavors accented by mint. • $30 • (04/30/97) • **83**
Merlot Coastal Region 1994: A powerful style that emphasizes ripe fruit flavors and oak accents on a full-bodied frame. The flavors recall cherry and cranberry; the finish has a tannic bite. • $30 • (04/30/97) • **85**
Merlot Coastal Region 1993 • $NA • (09/30/95) • **87**

VERGELEGEN

Chardonnay Coastal Region 1993 • $NA • (06/15/94) • **80**

VILLIERA ESTATE

Blue Ridge Blanc Paarl 1994 • $8 • (09/30/95) • **82**
Cabernet Sauvignon Paarl 1993 • $NA • (09/30/95) • **77**
Cru Monro Blanc Fumé Oak Matured Paarl 1994 • $NA • (06/15/95) • **88**
Cru Monro Limited Release Oak Matured Paarl Red 1993 • $16 • (09/30/95) • **88**
Cru Monro Limited Release Paarl Red 1992 • $16 • (09/30/95) • **89**
Gewürztraminer Paarl 1993 • $NA • (09/30/95) • **82**
Merlot Paarl 1993 • $15 • (06/15/95) • **89**
Merlot Paarl 1992 • $15 • (06/15/95) • **86**
Sauvignon Blanc Paarl 1994 • $10 • (06/15/95) • **86**

VRIESENHOF

Cabernet Sauvignon Stellenbosch 1990 • $12 • (06/30/94) • **75**
Kallista Stellenbosch Red 1991 • $14 • (06/15/95) • **87**
Kallista Stellenbosch Cabernet Blend 1989 • $13 • (06/30/94) • **75**

WARWICK

Cabernet Franc Stellenbosch 1993 • $15 • (06/30/95) • **85**
Cabernet Sauvignon Stellenbosch 1995: An intense and concentrated Cab, with ripe cherry and currant flavors blanketed in a firm, tannic texture. Worth short-term cellaring; the depth of flavor and lingering aftertaste bode well. Drink now through 2000. 1,000 cases made. • $14 • (03/31/98) • **88**
Cabernet Sauvignon Stellenbosch 1992: For fans of really robust reds. Tannic and full-bodied, with ripe fruit flavors held in check by a stiff texture of acid and tannin. 2,000 cases made. • $15 • (01/31/97) • **82**
Cabernet Sauvignon Stellenbosch 1991 • $15 • (06/30/95) • **85**
Merlot Stellenbosch 1992 • $15 • (06/30/95) • **78**
Trilogy Stellenbosch 1995: An elegant but concentrated Bordeaux-style red, with an intriguing aroma and complex flavors. Enjoyable now, but has the balance, intensity and firm tannins to improve with age. A blend of 60 percent Cabernet Sauvignon, 20 percent Cabernet Franc, 20 percent Merlot. Drink now through 2002. 1,000 cases made. • $18 • (03/31/98) • **87**
Trilogy Stellenbosch 1994: Starts off slowly, then comes on strong with some good herbal, chocolate and plum flavors. Balanced and ready to drink. 1,200 cases made. • $18 • (09/30/97) • **84**
Trilogy Stellenbosch 1992 • $17 • (06/30/95) • **83**

WELMOED WINERY

Sauvignon Blanc Stellenbosch 1994 • $8 • (09/30/95) • **85**

WELTEVREDE

Chardonnay Robertson 1994: Smooth and supple, generous with butter and fig flavors, and shows a bit of zip, as well. Finishes with spice notes. 4,000 cases made. • $12 • (01/31/97) • **83**
Chardonnay Robertson 1993 • $12 • (06/15/94) • **77**
Privé du Bois Robertson 1994: A flavorful but awkward white with thick texture and buttery overtones that don't mesh well with the tart ctirus flavors. 2,000 cases made. • $9 • (05/15/97) • **78**
Privé du Bois Robertson 1993 • $9 • (06/30/95) • **76**

ZANDVLIET

Shiraz Robertson 1989 • $11 • (09/30/95) • **70**

ZONNEBLOEM

Cabernet Sauvignon Stellenbosch 1989 • $11 • (06/30/94) • **82**
Merlot Stellenbosch 1991 • $10 • (09/30/95) • **76**
Pinotage Stellenbosch 1990 • $10 • (06/30/94) • **75**
Pinotage Stellenbosch Vintner's Selection 1988 • $10 • (02/15/93) • **82**
Shiraz Stellenbosch 1989 • $10 • (06/30/94) • **71**

Spain

With 3,500,000 acres, Spain has more vineyards under cultivation than Italy or France. Yet it makes only about half as much wine as Italy and 75 percent as much as France. Moreover, the style of its wine has remained staunchly nationalistic, reflecting the domestic preference for mellow, wood-aged red wines with a strong oak component and light tannins. Many of these wines are made from native grape varieties and vinified in a very traditional style.

However, things are changing. Alongside the traditional styles there is emerging a new breed of modern wines vinified in a fresher, fruitier style. These are becoming more popular, and are helping Spanish wine producers to compete more successfully in the world arena. The Spanish government has actively supported these developments, encouraging investment in new technologies and equipment, and helping its producers to explore world markets. With these efforts and much private initiative, Spain's back-seat position in western European winemaking should soon be a thing of the past.

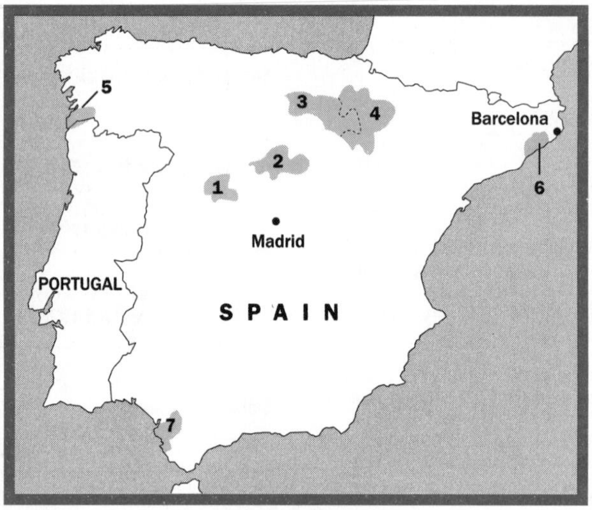

1. Rueda
2. Ribera del Duero
3. Rioja
4. Navarra
5. Rias Baixas
6. Penedès
7. Jerez

SPAIN'S WINE REGIONS

Rioja

Spain has an excellent climate and a vast range of *terroirs* that are suitable for producing quality wines. Rioja is one region that has already made a name for itself. The modern history of Rioja dates back to the last century, when French vignerons from Bordeaux fled the phylloxera epidemic and set up house in this northerly region. As a result of their influence and techniques, the Rioja style offers a good deal of refinement. Basic Rioja, most often designated *crianza* (wood-aged), is marked by the vanilla and smoky tones of American oak overlaying the faintly earthy, spicy notes of the Tempranillo grape. Most *crianza* should be drunk within five years of the vintage. Above the *crianza* level are the reservas and gran reservas. Both are selections from the best vats of the harvest and are usually made only in better years. Gran reservas, which spend the most time in oak, can be profound, provided one has cultivated a taste for the traditional wood-dominated, autumnal flavors and aromas of older Rioja. The best Rioja producers include Marques de Riscal, Marques de Murrieta, Martinez Bujanda and CUNE.

Ribera del Duero

The Ribera del Duero region to the south of Rioja has for decades been producing wines that rival the world's best, including the legendary, fabulously rare and expensive Vega Sicilia, and the less expensive Pesquera. While the average quality in this region is high, styles vary considerably. Vega Sicilia represents the traditional approach, using older wood barrels and extensive aging, and has similarities to Rioja. Recently, the more exuberant style epitomized by Pesquera has taken hold. Pesquera uses new French and American oak, and the flavor has more in common with a vigorous young Bordeaux than with Vega Sicilia. Other producers to watch are Alion and Ismael Arroyo.

Navarra

Next to Rioja is the Navarra district. Once known strictly for its rosés, it is now producing deeply pigmented, often exciting wines from Tempranillo, Grenache (here called Garnacha) and Cabernet.

The sprawling cellars at Marqués de Griñon in Rioja.

Al Goodman

Experimentation with Cabernet and Merlot has added herbal notes to the bouquet and flavors of Tempranillo-dominated wines, as well as a bit more authority on the finish.

Penedès

The Penedès region is home to two of Spain's most forward-thinking wineries, Torres and Jean León. The influence of Cabernet Sauvignon is strongly felt at both wineries, but the indigenous Tempranillo, the Garnacha and the Monastrell are still important here as well.

SPANISH WHITE WINES

The profile of Spanish white wines is changing. In the past these wines tended to be oxidized, tired, and suitable only for domestic consumption. Today, the whites are often fermented in stainless steel at cool temperatures. White Riojas and Ruedas, made from the native Viura grape, now emphasize lemony fruit and freshness, and Spanish Chardonnays are becoming quite good.

On the other hand, the traditional oak-aged style has certainly improved. Many fine Rioja reservas are fermented and aged in American oak. These offer genuine voluptuousness and power, and can be compared to some of the better premium whites of the Graves region of Bordeaux.

Some of the most impressive Spanish white wines come from Galicia, located just north of Portugal. The area's most exciting region now is the Rias Baixas. Its principal grape is the Albariño, which offers an intensity and complexity that calls to mind a French Hermitage blanc or an Alsace Riesling.

CAVA

One couldn't leave a discussion of Spanish wine without mentioning cava, Spain's immensely popular sparkling wine. Cava is made in some of the most technologically advanced, mechanized wineries anywhere in the world. It must spend a minimum of nine months in bottle, and many spend between one and three years. Penedès is the most important region for cava; indigenous grape varieties make up the bulk of the blends, which can be fresh and fruity—and much more affordable than Champagne.

AGAPITO RICO, BODEGAS

Monastrell Jumilla Carchelo 1996: Generous and firm, with bright black cherry, licorice and herbal flavors, mouthfilling tannins. With more muscle than sophistication, it should pair nicely with grilled meats. 10,000 cases made. • $8 • (06/30/97) • **84**
Monastrell Jumilla Carchelo 1995 • $8 • (04/30/96) • **82**
Monastrell Jumilla Carchelo 1994 • $7 • (04/30/95) • **81**
Monastrell Jumilla Carchelo 1993 • $6 • (12/15/94) • **82**

AGE, BODEGAS

La Mancha Vega Serena 1993 • $5 • (02/28/95) • **80**
La Mancha White Vega Serena 1993 • $5 • (12/31/94) • **81**
Rioja Siglo 1988 • $9 • (03/31/93) • **74**
Rioja Siglo Crianza 1991 • $7 • (03/31/96) • **76**
Rioja Siglo Crianza 1990 • $8 • (01/31/95) • **84**
Rioja Siglo Crianza 1989 • $7 • (04/15/94) • **84**
Rioja Siglo Gran Reserva 1984 • $12 • (03/31/93) • **84**
Rioja Siglo Reserva 1988: This silky red offers mature, traditional flavors of dried cherries, caramel, cedar and spices that are balanced and supple and linger on the finish. Nicely crafted. Drink now. • $12 • (11/15/97) • **87**
Rioja Siglo Reserva 1986 • $10 • (04/30/95) • **86**
Rioja Siglo Reserva 1985 • $10 • (03/31/93) • **77**
Rioja White Siglo 1993 • $6 • (02/28/95) • **85**

ALAVESAS, BODEGAS

Rioja Solar de Samaniego 1995: Traditional style, with flavors of dried cherries, brown sugar and tea. Its sweet spiciness is appealing, but masks a lack of structure. Drink now. 20,000 cases made. • $8 • (11/15/97) • **79**
Rioja Solar de Samaniego Crianza 1992: This traditional-style Rioja shows a supple texture, mature flavors of dried cherry, cola and vanilla and a slightly dry finish. Drink now. 20,000 cases made. • $10 • (11/15/97) • **82**
Rioja Solar de Samaniego Reserva 1989: Silky, with mature flavors of raisins, tobacco, dried cherries and spice. Tannins are well integrated but firm; the finish is spicy and clean. Drink now. 10,000 cases made. • $14 • (11/15/97) • **83**

ALBET I NOYA

Cabernet Sauvignon Penedès 1994: Loads of oak-influenced toast and chocolate flavors give an immediate appeal, with enough bitter cherry flavor to keep it mostly balanced. Its firm and chewy berry and floral notes linger on the finish. Accessible now, better in 1999. 3,000 cases made. • $15 • (10/31/97) • **87**
Cabernet Sauvignon Penedès 1993: Big, with more structure than grace. Has aggressive tannins and flavors of smoke, earth and raisins. 2,000 cases made. • $15 • (08/31/96) • **78**
Cabernet Sauvignon Penedès 1991 • $14 • (04/15/94) • **82**
Cabernet Sauvignon Penedès Collecció 1993 • $14 • (04/30/95) • **88**
Cabernet Sauvignon Penedès Collecció 1992 • $14 • (04/30/95) • **83**
Tempranillo Penedès 1995: A compact, well-defined red, with lush, toasty-oak flavors, bright blueberry and black cherry flavors and notes of black pepper, coffee and light herbs. Expressive and firm. Drink now. 3,000 cases made. • $15 • (11/15/97) • **86**
Tempranillo Penedès 1994: Reminiscent of chocolate-covered cherries. You'll love this plush, fruity red with its lavish oak and ripe cherry flavors. It's upfront and pretty, with enough grip for food. Drink now or hold through 1999. 3,000 cases made. • $15 • (11/15/97) • **85**
Tempranillo Penedès 1993: An attractive marriage of sweet vanilla, oak and pretty cherry and blackberry flavors. Still young and fresh, bright and clean. Drink now. 1,000 cases made. • $15 • (08/31/96) • **85**

ALELLA, MARQUÉS DE

Alella White Clasico 1996: This silky white shows straightforward flavors of apples and peaches, soft yet still lively on the palate, turning slightly earthy on the finish. 15,000 cases made. • $10 • (10/31/97) • **83**

Key: SS—Spectator Selection CS—Cellar Selection HR—Highly Recommended BB—Best Buy $NA—Price not available Ⓐ—Auction Price (BT)—Barrel Tasting
Dates in parentheses indicate the issues in which the ratings were published.

ALION, BODEGAS Y VIÑEDOS

Ribera del Duero Reserva 1993: A fleshy, balanced wine with chocolate and coffee aromas as well as pretty blackberry and chocolate flavors. It has firm tannins and a smoky finish. Evolving now, it should peak in 1999. 3,000 cases made. • $25 • (06/15/97) • **87**
Ribera del Duero Reserva 1992: A dark, polished and powerful wine that is loaded with ripe plum, licorice and chocolate flavors of sufficient concentration to match the full tannins. The finish is clean and long. 3,266 cases made. • $22 • (07/31/96) HR • **90**
Ribera del Duero Reserva 1991 • $20 • (04/30/95) • **92**

ALMANSA, CASTILLO DE

Viño de Crianza Almansa 1989 • $9 • (04/30/95) • **77**

AMEZOLA DE LA MORA, BODEGAS

Rioja Señorio Amezola Reserva 1989 • $13 • (04/15/95) • **87**
Rioja Viña Amezola Crianza 1990 • $10 • (04/30/95) • **85**

ARIENZO, MARQUES DE

Rioja 1987 • $7 • (03/31/92) • **84**
Rioja 1986 • $7 • (03/31/92) • **81**
Rioja 1985 • $8 • (07/31/89) BB • **84**
Rioja 1983 • $5 • (06/30/88) BB • **81**
Rioja Gran Reserva 1982 • $23 • (03/31/92) • **83**
Rioja Gran Reserva 1981 • $18 • (03/31/92) • **84**
Rioja Gran Reserva 1978 • $18 • (03/31/90) • **78**
Rioja Gran Reserva 1976 • $18 • (11/15/89) • **88**
Rioja Reserva 1985 • $12 • (03/31/92) • **84**
Rioja Reserva 1983 • $12 • (05/31/91) • **84**
Rioja Reserva 1981 • $12 • (07/31/89) • **83**
Rioja Reserva 1980 • $8 • (06/30/88) • **76**

ARROYO, BODEGAS ISMAEL

Ribera del Duero Mesoñeros de Castilla Crianza 1991 • $14 • (04/30/95) • **89**
Ribera del Duero Mesoñeros de Castilla Crianza 1990 • $14 • (04/15/94) SS • **90**
Ribera del Duero Val Sotillo Crianza 1995: Almost black, this Spanish red is velvety smooth on the palate, but the lush texture cloaks a firm tannic structure and sets off the ripe, beautifully integrated flavors of plums, chocolate and coffee. It's tempting now, but the clamped-down finish suggests it will only improve with time. Best from 2000 through 2010. 8,000 cases made. • $19 • (04/30/98) HR • **92**
Ribera del Duero Val Sotillo Crianza 1994: This big, bold red from Spain delivers toasty, chocolate-scented oak character, and backs it up with ripe plum and blackberry flavors and marked gamy notes that are concentrated yet quite fresh. Big tannins don't get in the way of a long, spicy finish. Try in 1999. 6,000 cases made. • $19 • (10/31/97) HR • **91**
Ribera del Duero Val Sotillo Gran Reserva 1990: Vivid aromas of cassis and blackberry give way to polished berry and tobacco flavors that are beautifully framed by firm yet elegant tannins. Shows a great balance of concentration and finesse. Drink now. Tasted twice, with consistent notes. 300 cases made. • $60 • (10/31/97) • **91**
Ribera del Duero Val Sotillo Gran Reserva 1989: Round and velvety, showing ripe plum, prune and chocolate flavors. The tannins are softening, but still have enough grip for food. Drink now. 1,000 cases made. • $60 • (07/31/96) • **85**
Ribera del Duero Val Sotillo Reserva 1991: This rich, full-bodied red has plenty of tannin, yet the texture is lush. The flavors suggest blackberry, licorice, toast and tar. It's drinkable now with rich food; should improve for years. 3,000 cases made. • $30 • (07/31/96) • **90**
Ribera del Duero Val Sotillo Reserva 1990 • $25 • (04/30/95) • **89**
Ribera del Duero Val Sotillo Reserva 1989 • $27 • (04/15/94) • **87**

ARTADI

Rioja Alavesa 1987 • $6 • (04/30/88) • **80**
Rioja Crianza 1994: Thick and rich. Resembles a ripe California red more than a traditional Rioja in color, body and tannin. Smoky, gamy flavors are

a bit clumsy, but a plummy core keeps it in balance. Try in 2000. • $12 • (02/28/98) • **86**

ARZOBISPO, COOPERATIVA AGRICOLA VILLAR DEL

Valencia Cerro Gordo 1993: This simple red offers straightforward cherry flavors and a soft texture. Quaffable, but marred slightly by hints of plastic. Drink now. Made from Garnacha. 50,000 cases made. • $4 • (12/15/97) • **76**

ARZUAGA, BODEGAS

Ribera del Duero Crianza 1994: Made in a traditional style influenced by Rioja, this smooth red offers coffee, vanilla, brown sugar and raisin flavors, quite concentrated and even a bit sweet. It's ripe and rich, but may be best now while it still shows fruit. Drink now through 2000. • $20 • (04/30/98) • **86**

AS LAXAS, BODEGAS

Albariño Rias Baixas 1996: A ripe, round white with pear and melon flavors and vanilla accents. Has enough acidity for balance, but a musty note detracts. Drink now. 6,000 cases made. • $15 • (05/31/98) • **79**

AYALA LETE E HIJOS, R. DE

Rioja Viña Santurnia Crianza 1994: Assertive, bitter coffee and herbal aromas give way to similar flavors with added layers of cherry and dark chocolate in this round yet firm red. Not powerful, but has enough tannin to go well with food. Drink now through 2000. 4,000 cases made. • $7 • (05/31/98) • **86**

AZPILICUETA, BODEGAS FELIX

Rioja Gran Reserva 1982 • $36 • (03/31/96) • **82**

BAJAMAR, MARQUES DE

Navarra 1995: Though light-colored and light-bodied, this firm red shows a core of berry flavor with smoky and herbal accents. It's still tight, but may open with food. Drinkable now. 160,000 cases made. • $6 • (11/15/97) • **82**

Navarra White 1996: Medium-bodied, basically neutral in flavor, with some light herbal and canned-peach notes. Fairly crisp, but a bit cloying on the finish. 160,000 cases made. • $6 • (11/15/97) • **78**

BALBAS, BODEGAS

Ribera del Duero 1988 • $15 • (09/30/91) • **88**
Ribera del Duero 1987 • $14 • (09/30/90) • **81**
Ribera del Duero 1986 • $15 • (07/31/89) • **87**
Ribera del Duero 1985 • $13 • (09/15/88) • **83**
Ribera del Duero Reserva 1985 • $NA • (03/31/90) • **75**

BALBINO FERNANDEZ

Rioja Don Balbino Reserva 1987 • $NA • (04/15/94) • **82**

BARBADILLO, ANTONIO

Castillo de San Diego Viño de la Tierra de Cadiz Jerez 1994 • $6 • (07/31/95) • **78**

Castillo de San Diego Viño de la Tierra de Cadiz Jerez 1993 • $6 • (03/31/95) • **80**

BARBIER, RENÉ

Cabernet Sauvignon Penedès 1994: Polished and accessible, this round red shows plum, coffee and dark chocolate flavors, with tannins that are just firm enough for food. Not a blockbuster, but harmonious. 5,000 cases made. • $7 • (10/31/97) • **84**

Cabernet Sauvignon Penedès 1987 • $7 • (04/15/94) BB • **84**
Cabernet Sauvignon Penedès 1982 • $3 • (01/31/87) • **77**
Cabernet Sauvignon Penedès 1981 • $5 • (03/31/90) • **74**

Cabernet Sauvignon Penedès Mediterranean Select 1990 • $7 • (03/31/96) • **80**

Merlot Penedès 1993: Toasty, spicy aromas are alluring, but it turns a bit austere on the palate, with smoke, earth and light cherry flavors. The firm structure suggests it will open with food. 4,200 cases made. • $7 • (10/31/97) • **84**

Merlot Penedès Mediterranean Select 1992 • $7 • (03/31/96) • **84**

Penedès Family Reserve NV • $6 • (04/15/94) • **75**

Penedès Mediterranean Red NV: Big-flavored yet light-textured, with hearty plum, smoke and earthy flavors that are balanced and fresh. Modest tannins. • $5 • (08/31/96) • **83**

Penedès Reserva 1978 • $4 • (03/31/90) • **77**

Priorat Clos Mogador 1994: This dark, rich red is packed with ripe, luscious flavors of plums and blackberries, with massive yet perfectly integrated tannins and accents of chocolate and coffee. The fruit is so sweet that you'll be tempted to drink it now, but the wine will be better after 2000. 2,800 cases made. • $35 • (10/31/97) • **91**

Priorat Clos Mogador 1993: This brawny red is almost muscle-bound with tannins, but underneath are a trove of ripe plum flavors and accents of toast and coffee. A tough customer, but should come around in 2000. • $35 • (01/01/97) • **90**

Priorat Clos Mogador 1992: This tough red is tannic and smoky, with slightly charred flavors of game and toast over a core of plum flavors. Despite the moutfilling tannins, the finish is long. Try now. • $35 • (01/01/97) • **87**

Priorat Clos Mogador 1991 • $35 • (04/30/95) • **90**
Priorat Clos Mogador 1990 • $35 • (04/15/94) • **87**

Tempranillo Penedès 1993: Maturing. The raisin and earth flavors dominate the light cherry flavors, and there's a bit of dilution on the palate; further aging isn't advised. 2,500 cases made. • $7 • (11/15/97) • **79**

Viño de Mesa Red Table Wine 1983 • $3 • (03/31/90) BB • **80**

BARCELO, HIJOS DE ANTONIO

Castilla y Leon Peñascal 1994: Light berry, spice and vanilla flavors have a traditional Spanish profile in this light, silky red. Not very concentrated, but it's fresh and somewhat elegant. Drink now. 100,000 cases made. • $6 • (11/15/97) • **84**

Castilla y Leon Peñascal 1987 • $5 • (04/15/94) BB • **83**

Ribera del Duero Viña Mayor 1996: Here's a great buy on a very good wine. Enticing chocolate and ripe cherry aromas lead into rather austere flavors of coffee, tobacco and herbs. Try now. 90,000 cases made. • $6 • (10/31/97) BB • **87**

Ribera del Duero Viña Mayor 1994: Strong but harsh and tannic with smoke and barnyard flavors. Not much fruit or depth. Try now. • $7 • (10/15/96) • **78**

Ribera del Duero Viña Mayor 1992 • $6 • (04/15/94) • **75**
Ribera del Duero Viña Mayor 1991 • $7 • (01/31/93) BB • **86**

Ribera del Duero Viña Mayor Crianza 1994: Borrows its light, polished structure and flavors of strawberries and spices from Rioja, but it shows Ribero's firm tannins and plush texture. Try now. 45,000 cases made. • $8 • (10/31/97) • **85**

Ribera del Duero Viña Mayor Crianza 1992: Plum overlaid with strong toast and vanilla flavors gives this wine depth, but soft tannins make it accessible now. A bit heavy-handed with oak, but still attractive. • $8 • (07/31/96) • **85**

Ribera del Duero Viña Mayor Crianza 1991 • $8 • (04/30/95) BB • **86**
Ribera del Duero Viña Mayor Crianza 1990 • $7 • (02/15/92) BB • **83**
Ribera del Duero Viña Mayor Crianza 1989 • $9 • (12/15/93) • **83**
Ribera del Duero Viña Mayor Crianza 1987 • $9 • (02/15/92) • **82**

Ribera del Duero Viña Mayor Reserva 1991: The vanilla notes are attractive, but the light cherry flavor isn't rich enough to balance it. A light-bodied red that turns a bit dry on the finish. It might soften with food. • $11 • (07/31/96) • **83**

Ribera del Duero Viña Mayor Reserva 1989 • $11 • (04/15/94) • **81**

BARCO, CASA

Viño de Mesa NV • $4 • (06/15/93) • **76**

BARONIA DE TURÍS

Moscatel Valencia NV: Very thick and sweet, this dessert-style white scores points for concentration, but the flavors lean towards the chemical, with notes of orange-peel and rose water. Try it over ice. 10,000 cases made. • $6 • (11/15/97) • **80**

BAZAN, AGRO DE

Albariño Rias Baixas Granbazán 1995: This smooth white offers a pleasant mix of almond, vanilla and melon flavors, kept fresh by crisp, lemony acidity. Clean but short. • $19 • (09/15/97) • **83**

BELONDRADE Y LURTON

Rueda 1994: Toasty oak aromas and flavors dominate this otherwise straightforward white. It's clean and crisp, but doesn't show much fruit now. • $22 • (06/30/97) • **83**

BERBERANA, BODEGAS

Brut Cava Marino NV: Attractive floral and apple aromas turn into harsh and somewhat metallic flavors reminiscent of canned ginger ale in this aggressively fizzy cava. The finish is smoky and bitter. Tasted twice, with consistent notes. Made by Marques de Monistrol for Berberana. 20,000 cases made. • $9 • (10/31/97) • **80**
Rioja Carta de Oro Crianza 1989 • $8 • (08/31/93) • **85**
Rioja Carta de Oro Crianza 1988 • $10 • (03/31/92) • **78**
Rioja Carta de Oro Crianza 1987 • $10 • (03/31/92) • **87**
Rioja Carta de Oro Crianza 1986 • $8 • (03/31/90) • **81**
Rioja Carta de Oro Crianza 1985 • $6 • (07/31/89) • **78**
Rioja Carta de Plata 1989 • $8 • (03/31/92) • **77**
Rioja Carta de Plata 1988 • $7 • (09/30/91) BB • **83**
Rioja Carta de Plata 1987 • $7 • (12/15/90) BB • **84**
Rioja Carta de Plata 1986 • $6 • (05/15/89) BB • **88**
Rioja Carta de Plata 1985 • $6 • (10/31/88) BB • **89**
Rioja Crianza 1991 • $9 • (01/31/96) • **82**
Rioja Dragon Label 1995: Soft and pretty, offering bright raspberry and vanilla flavors, with sufficient tannin to keep it firm enough for food. A fresh, appealing wine. Drink now. 20,000 cases made. • $10 • (10/15/97) • **84**
Rioja Dragon Label 1994 • $10 • (06/30/96) BB • **86**
Rioja Dragon Label 1993 • $10 • (01/31/96) • **83**
Rioja Dragon Label 1992 • $10 • (04/30/95) • **84**
Rioja Gran Reserva 1987: Redolent of flowers, herbs and spices, it's silky yet still has grip on the palate, with raisin, light cherry and cigar-box flavors. Not a powerhouse, but will show well with food. 10,000 cases made. • $18 • (10/15/97) • **87**
Rioja Gran Reserva 1985: Developing well, this elegant wine offers haunting aromas of spice, leather and dried cherry followed up by flavors of cherry, coffee and hints of rose. It's all wrapped in a smooth texture, making this a nicely integrated wine in the traditional style. Tasted twice. 20,000 cases made. • $17 • (09/30/96) HR • **89**
Rioja Gran Reserva 1983 • $15 • (01/31/96) • **85**
Rioja Gran Reserva 1982 • $24 • (11/30/91) • **88**
Rioja Gran Reserva 1980 • $18 • (10/31/88) • **82**
Rioja Gran Reserva 1975 • $13 • (03/31/92) • **88**
Rioja Gran Reserva 1973 • $20 • (03/31/92) • **89**
Rioja Preferido 1992 • $5 • (08/31/93) • **78**
Rioja Reserva 1990: Straightforward, delivering cherry, earth and light spice flavors. It's balanced for drinking now, but lacks the concentration for long aging. 15,000 cases made. • $13 • (12/15/97) • **83**
Rioja Reserva 1988 • $11 • (01/31/96) • **87**
Rioja Reserva 1986 • $11 • (03/31/92) • **81**
Rioja Reserva 1985 • $13 • (03/31/92) • **82**
Rioja Reserva 1983 • $12 • (03/31/92) • **82**
Rioja Reserva 1982 • $20 • (03/31/92) • **85**
Rioja d'Avalos 1994 • $8 • (01/31/96) • **80**
Tempranillo Rioja Crianza 1994: This refreshing red offers well-defined aromas and flavors of cherries, herbs and smoke, with soft tannins and lively acidity. A nice match with lighter foods; drinkable now. 20,000 cases made. • $10 • (11/30/97) • **84**
Tempranillo Rioja Crianza 1992: A vibrant Rioja with good cherry and spice flavors and a tealike note on the finish. Nicely balanced and smooth. Drinkable now. 30,000 cases made. • $10 • (09/15/96) • **84**
Tempranillo Rioja d'Avalos 1995: This firm Spanish red shows personality and grip, with assertive spice, vanilla and earth notes adding dimension to the light berry flavors. An attractive wine that's drinkable now and priced right. 20,000 cases made. • $8 • (07/31/97) BB • **84**
Viño de Mesa Marino NV • $6 • (04/30/96) • **78**

BERONIA, BODEGAS

Rioja Crianza 1994: This light-bodied red is pleasant, if a bit simple. Offers light strawberry, cherry, cinnamon and tea notes, and slips easily across the palate. Drink now. • $9 • (11/15/97) • **81**
Rioja Crianza 1990 • $8 • (04/30/95) • **79**
Rioja Crianza 1989 • $8 • (04/15/94) • **77**
Rioja Gran Reserva 1985: Shows flavors of plums, coffee, vanilla and herbs. It's structure is round but soft, with moderate, well-integrated tannins and a clean finish. Better than previous samples, which were corky. Drink now. • $23 • (05/31/98) • **86**
Rioja Gran Reserva 1981 • $18 • (01/31/96) • **83**
Rioja Gran Reserva 1980 • $18 • (04/15/94) • **85**
Rioja Reserva 1991: Light but appealing flavors of cherry and toast. Round, supple, and traditional in style. A vegetal note detracts, but it's still fresh and lively. Better than previous samples, which were corky. Drink now. • $13 • (05/31/98) • **80**
Rioja Reserva 1985 • $11 • (04/15/94) • **80**
Rioja Reserva 1982 • $12 • (03/31/90) • **82**
Viura Rioja White 1996: Assertive, showing bright lemon and juicy green apple flavors with crisp acidity and notes of herbs and almonds. Very dry, but has distinctive character. Drink now. • $9 • (10/31/97) • **84**
Viura Rioja White Barrel Fermented 1996: Sweet new oak flavors give this assertive white an international character. The vanilla notes are backed by apple and pear flavors and crisp acidity. Fresh and firm. Drink now. • $11 • (10/31/97) • **85**

BILBAINAS, BODEGAS

Rioja Viña Pomal 1983 • $8 • (06/30/90) • **79**
Rioja Viña Pomal Crianza 1990 • $13 • (03/31/96) • **85**
Rioja Viña Pomal Gran Reserva 1980 • $26 • (04/15/94) • **83**
Rioja Viña Pomal Gran Reserva 1978 • $20 • (03/31/90) • **88**
Rioja Viña Pomal Reserva 1988 • $29 • (03/31/96) • **80**
Rioja Viña Pomal Reserva 1985 • $12 • (04/15/94) • **84**

BOADA, BODEGAS

Ribera del Duero Crianza 1991: This maturing red packs a lot of flavor into a lean frame, with notes of cherry, spices, cedar and licorice. Not a blockbuster, but will drink well through 2000. • $15 • (11/30/97) • **84**
Ribera del Duero Reserva 1985: This smooth red is loaded with chocolate and coffee flavors, and there are enough plum and raisin flavors to keep it lively. A solid wine for drinking now through 2000. Made by Los Curros. • $30 • (10/31/97) • **86**

BORJA, AGRICOLA DE

Campo de Borja Borsao 1993 • $4 • (04/30/95) • **81**

BRANAVIEJA, BODEGAS

Navarra Pleno 1988 • $6 • (12/15/90) BB • **85**

BRETÓN, BODEGAS

Rioja Dominio de Conte Reserva 1991: Aromatic with smoke and spices. Bright cherry and spicy flavors with firm tannins on the finish. Well-balanced and should improve. Drink now. 3,000 cases made. • $26 • (08/31/96) • **87**
Rioja Dominio de Conte Reserva 1990 • $24 • (01/31/96) • **84**
Rioja Loriñon Crianza 1994: Vivid and youthful, this fruity and firm light red offers black cherry, chocolate and spice flavors. Balanced and lively, with just enough grip for food. 35,000 cases made. • $10 • (06/30/97) • **86**
Rioja Loriñon Crianza 1991 • $10 • (03/31/96) • **81**
Rioja Loriñon Crianza 1990 • $9 • (04/30/95) • **86**
Rioja Loriñon Crianza 1989 • $9 • (04/15/94) BB • **87**
Rioja Loriñon Crianza 1988 • $10 • (01/31/92) • **83**
Rioja Loriñon Crianza 1985 • $9 • (03/31/90) • **85**
Rioja Loriñon Reserva 1991: Still quite young, this well-structured red shows ripe plum flavors with licorice, spice and cigar-box notes, as well as firm

Key: SS—Spectator Selection CS—Cellar Selection HR—Highly Recommended BB—Best Buy $NA—Price not available Ⓐ—Auction Price (BT)—Barrel Tasting
Dates in parentheses indicate the issues in which the ratings were published.

SPAIN

tannins and bright acidity. Drink now. 6,000 cases made. • $17 • (10/15/97) • **88**
Rioja Loriñon Reserva 1989 • $17 • (04/30/95) • **82**
Rioja Loriñon Reserva 1987 • $15 • (12/15/93) • **77**
Rioja White Loriñon 1993 • $9 • (12/31/94) • **83**
Rioja White Loriñon Barrel Fermented 1996: Balanced, this wine displays a nice mix of bright fruit and herbal flavors that are clean and fresh, and manages to generate character and weight without obvious new oak. 1,250 cases made. • $10 • (10/31/97) • **85**

CÁCERES, MARQUÉS DE

Rioja 1992 • $12 • (03/31/96) • **83**
Rioja 1991 • $10 • (03/31/95) • **84**
Rioja 1989 • $9 • (03/31/93) • **86**
Rioja 1987 • $9 • (03/31/92) • **88**
Rioja 1986 • $9 • (03/31/92) • **82**
Rioja 1985 • $9 • (03/31/90) • **80**
Rioja 1982 • $7 • (11/15/87) • **87**
Rioja 1981 • $5 • (11/01/85) BB • **88**
Rioja Crianza 1994: Gamy, spicy notes give this firm red character, with plenty of black cherry flavor for balance. Has enough tannin to improve through 1999, but it drinks well now. • $12 • (10/15/97) • **86**
Rioja Crianza 1990 • $10 • (04/15/94) • **84**
Rioja Crianza 1989 • $9 • (04/15/94) • **84**
Rioja Gran Reserva 1989 • $NA • (01/01/96) • **85**
Rioja Gran Reserva 1987: This alluring red shows dark, sinuous flavors of coffee, prunes, smoke and spices that are well-concentrated and still quite fresh. Though it seems older than its age, it will provide real pleasure for fans of Rioja's traditional style. • $23 • (11/30/97) • **88**
Rioja Gran Reserva 1986 • $25 • (03/31/96) • **83**
Rioja Gran Reserva 1982 • $25 • (03/31/92) • **89**
Rioja Gran Reserva 1975 • $26 • (03/31/92) • **89**
Rioja Gran Reserva 1973 • $30 • (03/31/92) • **83**
Rioja Reserva 1990: A silky red offering smooth and fresh black cherry, cola and spice flavors that linger on the finish. Drink through 1999. • $17 • (10/15/97) • **86**
Rioja Reserva 1989 • $20 • (03/31/96) • **87**
Rioja Reserva 1986 • $12 • (04/15/94) • **88**
Rioja Reserva 1985 • $19 • (03/31/92) • **87**
Rioja Reserva 1982 • $25 • (03/31/92) • **83**
Rioja Reserva 1981 • $20 • (03/31/90) • **69**
Rioja Rosado 1993 • $7 • (08/31/95) BB • **86**
Rioja White 1996: Light and simple, this tart white shows lemon, light apple and herbal notes, with a clean, neutral finish. A simple summer quaff. • $7 • (10/31/97) • **81**
Rioja White 1993 • $7 • (07/31/95) • **84**
Rioja White Antea 1994: This distinctive white offers vanilla, almond and herbal flavors over firm, cinnamon-spiced apple ones. Lively and crisp, but not quite harmonious; may benefit from another year in the bottle. • $9 • (10/31/97) • **86**
Rioja White Satinela 1996: Peach and floral aromas give way to sweet flavors of peach syrup and candy apples in this soft, rather cloying white. Unusual for the region, but bold and distinctive. • $7 • (10/31/97) • **78**
Rioja White Satinela 1994 • $8 • (02/29/96) • **78**

CACHAZO, BODEGAS ANGEL LORENZO

Rueda Martivillí 1996: A crisp, lean white, with gooseberry and herbal flavors that veer into sharper earthy notes. Tasted twice, with consistent notes. Drink now. • $10 • (04/30/98) • **78**

CACHAZO, BODEGAS FELIX LORENZO

Rueda Gran Cardiel 1996: Very crisp, verging on tart, with gooseberry and herbal flavors that finish dry and clean. Though not complex, it's firm enough for food and brings you back for another sip. 35,000 cases made. • $7 • (10/31/97) • **84**

CALLEJO, BODEGAS FELIX

Ribera del Duero Crianza 1994: Monster tannins get in the way right now, but this very firm red offers bright flavors of cherry, herbs and spices to go with them. May soften by 1999. 10,000 cases made. • $14 • (10/31/97) • **84**
Ribera del Duero Crianza 1991: Supple and straightforward. The lightly herbal, spicy cherry flavors are smooth, but it turns a bit dry on the finish. 10,000 cases made. • $14 • (07/31/96) • **82**
Ribera del Duero Cuatro Meses en Barrica 1996: Round and fairly rich, its ripe plum and smoky tobacco notes show some power, but gamy notes dominate and detract. The tannins are tough, but the wine is concentrated and balanced. May be in an awkward stage. Tasted twice, with consistent notes. 10,000 cases made. • $12 • (11/15/97) • **85**
Ribera del Duero Cuatro Meses en Barrica 1992: In a lighter style that has spice and vanilla notes adding complexity to the strawberry flavors. Attractive and supple. The fruit lingers on the smooth finish. Drink young. 4,500 cases made. • $12 • (07/31/96) • **85**
Ribera del Duero Gran Reserva 1989: Supple and offers aromas of spice and tea, with spicy berry and raisin flavors. Balanced and still has some grip. Drink now. 2,000 cases made. • $30 • (07/31/96) • **85**
Ribera del Duero Joven 1996: Expressive berry and floral aromas are alluring, but turn tough and a bit metallic on the palate. It's not rich, just tannic. Try now. 10,000 cases made. • $8 • (10/31/97) • **79**
Ribera del Duero Reserva 1991: Bold and balanced. The chocolate and walnut notes marry nicely with the plum and blackberry. The round tannins are firm yet harmonious. Attractive now. 3,500 cases made. • $20 • (07/31/96) • **86**
Ribera del Duero Reserva 1989: Supple and silky, offering mature spice, brown sugar, and raisin flavors in a light-bodied red that turns a bit dry on the finish. 2,500 cases made. • $25 • (07/31/96) • **83**
Ribera del Duero Viña Pilar 1994: Made in a soft, Beaujolais style, with grapey, earthy flavors, hints of spice and licorice and slightly chalky texture. 6,000 cases made. • $8 • (07/31/96) • **79**

CAMPANAS, LAS

Cabernet Sauvignon Navarra 1989 • $8 • (04/15/94) • **80**
Navarra 1984 • $6 • (03/31/90) BB • **86**
Navarra Crianza 1994: Fruity, with an international profile of sweet vanilla notes from new oak, ripe flavors of plums and black cherries and a thickish, almost jammy texture. Friendly and easy to drink, it's accessible now. • $8 • (11/15/97) • **84**
Navarra Crianza 1990 • $7 • (04/15/94) BB • **84**
Navarra Rosado 1996: Shows a lovely lilac hue, but it's less expressive on the palate; with light berry flavors and a soft texture. Drink well-chilled. • $7 • (09/15/97) • **80**

CAMPILLO, BODEGAS

Rioja Crianza 1987 • $12 • (06/15/93) • **80**
Rioja Reserva 1985 • $19 • (08/31/93) • **79**

CAMPO, BODEGA COOPERATIVA DEL

Calatayud Viña Alarba 1995: This juicy red makes up in exuberance what it lacks in grace. It offers ripe flavors of plums, chocolate and smoky bacon, with thick tannins and a grapelike finish that's almost sweet. Drink now. • $5 • (10/31/97) • **84**

CAMPO VIEJO, BODEGAS

Rioja 1988 • $NA • (03/31/92) • **83**
Rioja 1987 • $6 • (03/31/92) BB • **83**
Rioja 1986 • $6 • (03/31/92) • **81**
Rioja 1985 • $6 • (03/15/90) BB • **83**
Rioja 1984 • $5 • (01/31/88) BB • **82**
Rioja Albor 1996: Soft in texture, with juicy cherry flavors that pick up a hint of spice on the short, clean finish. An easy quaff for early drinking. • $6 • (12/15/97) • **82**
Rioja Albor 1992 • $6 • (04/30/95) • **81**
Rioja Albor 1991 • $6 • (04/15/94) BB • **85**
Rioja Commemorative Label Crianza 1992 • $7 • (01/31/96) • **73**
Rioja Crianza 1990 • $7 • (01/31/95) • **78**
Rioja Crianza 1989 • $8 • (04/15/94) • **77**
Rioja Gran Reserva 1988: Maturing now, this silky red offers light but balanced cedar, coffee and raisin flavors with a long, spicy finish. A well-made wine in the traditional style. Drink now. • $20 • (10/15/97) • **86**
Rioja Gran Reserva 1981 • $NA • (03/31/92) • **83**
Rioja Gran Reserva 1980 • $15 • (09/30/91) • **88**
Rioja Gran Reserva 1978 • $14 • (09/30/90) • **83**

Rioja Marqués de Villamagna Gran Reserva 1987: Light-bodied and polished, with pretty raisin, tea and vanilla flavors; harmonious and delicate. However, it lacks structure and vibrancy; one wonders what it tasted like five years ago. For fans of traditional Rioja. • $30 • (10/15/97) • **85**
Rioja Marqués de Villamagna Gran Reserva 1982 • $20 • (03/31/92) • **81**
Rioja Marqués de Villamagna Gran Reserva 1978 • $19 • (11/15/91) • **84**
Rioja Marqués de Villamagna Gran Reserva 1975 • $20 • (03/31/92) • **88**
Rioja Marqués de Villamagna Gran Reserva 1973 • $25 • (03/31/92) • **74**
Rioja Marqués de Villamagna Gran Reserva 1970 • $28 • (03/31/92) • **87**
Rioja Reserva 1990: Nicely balanced, still lively, with an appealing mix of young cherry and mature cigar-box flavors. It's supple enough to drink now, firm enough for food, and fresh enough to improve through 2000. • $11 • (11/15/97) • **87**
Rioja Reserva 1989 • $10 • (04/30/95) • **79**
Rioja Reserva 1987 • $NA • (04/15/94) • **77**
Rioja Reserva 1985 • $9 • (03/31/92) • **83**
Rioja Reserva 1983 • $9 • (03/31/92) • **81**
Rioja Reserva 1982 • $9 • (03/31/92) • **84**
Rioja Reserva 1981 • $7 • (11/15/88) • **78**
Rioja Viña Alcorta 1985 • $10 • (09/30/90) • **85**
Rioja Viña Alcorta 1981 • $7 • (10/31/88) • **76**
Rioja Viña Alcorta Crianza 1989 • $7 • (04/30/95) • **83**
Rioja Viña Alcorta Reserva 1987 • $10 • (04/30/95) • **78**
Rioja Viña Alcorta Reserva 1982 • $NA • (11/15/87) • **87**
Rioja White Albor 1996: This crisp white offers lemon and light herbal flavors that turn a bit chalky on the finish. It's clean but simple. • $6 • (10/31/97) • **80**
Rioja White Albor 1993 • $6 • (07/31/95) • **77**

CAN FEIXES

Penedès Blanc Selecció 1993 • $8 • (04/15/94) • **80**
Penedès Negre Selecció 1991 • $12 • (04/15/94) • **82**

CAN RAFOLS DELS CAUS

Penedès Gran Caus 1989 • $14 • (04/15/94) • **80**
Penedès Gran Caus 1988: Still fresh and clean, this balanced red offers black cherry, cedar and light herb flavors, though there is little development evident despite its age. A pleasant match with food, it should hold through 2000. A blend of 43 percent Merlot, 32 percent Cabernet Franc and 25 percent Cabernet Sauvignon. 2,300 cases made. • $20 • (10/31/97) • **85**
Penedès Gran Caus 1986 • $12 • (04/30/89) • **77**
Penedès Gran Caus 1985 • $12 • (10/15/88) • **77**

CARRERAS, BODEGAS JAIME

Valencia 1985 • $4 • (03/31/90) BB • **80**

CASTAÑO, BODEGAS

Yecla Pozuelo Crianza 1987 • $8 • (03/31/93) • **83**
Yecla Pozuelo Reserva 1990: Smooth and simple, this light-bodied red offers spicy black pepper and dried cherry flavors. Drink now. 8,000 cases made. • $10 • (08/31/96) • **82**

CASTELLBLANCH

Brut Cava Brut Zero 1987 • $7 • (05/15/94) BB • **86**
Brut Cava Zero 1987 • $8 • (03/31/93) • **77**
Brut Cava Zero 1985 • $6 • (12/31/88) • **73**
Brut Cava Zero 1982 • $6 • (05/31/88) • **81**

CAVAS HILL

Brut Blanc de Blancs Cava Nature Reserva Oro 1987 • $12 • (03/31/93) • **81**
Seco Blanc de Blancs Cava Reserva Oro 1990 • $9 • (03/31/93) • **80**

Key: SS—Spectator Selection CS—Cellar Selection HR—Highly Recommended BB—Best Buy $NA—Price not available Ⓐ—Auction Price (BT)—Barrel Tasting
Dates in parentheses indicate the issues in which the ratings were published.

CENALSA-MURCHANTE, BODEGAS

Navarra Campo-Nuevo 1991 • $6 • (03/31/93) • **77**

CHENEAU, PAUL

Brut Blanc de Blancs Cava NV: Toasty, smoky aromas and flavors give this sparkler depth on the palate, yet bright acidity keeps it crisp and refreshing. Rather austere, but will match well with food. • $9 • (12/15/97) • **86**

CHIVITE, BODEGAS JULIÁN

Navarra 125 Aniversario 1988 • $19 • (04/15/95) • **85**
Navarra 125 Aniversario 1985 • $31 • (08/31/93) • **82**
Navarra 125 Aniversario Gran Reserva 1988: Attractive aromas and well-integrated flavors of spice, dried cherry and vanilla. This is a well-made example of a traditional Tempranillo. Drinkable now. • $25 • (08/31/96) • **87**
Navarra 125 Aniversario Gran Reserva 1985 • $31 • (08/31/93) • **82**
Navarra Coleccion 125 Reserva 1992: Quite plummy tasting, with some nice spice notes as well. This is rich, full-bodied wine that's ready to drink. • $14 • (05/15/97) • **85**
Navarra Gran Feudo Crianza 1993: Smooth and well balanced, with juicy black cherry and blackberry flavors backed by light, firm tannins. Clean and vibrant. Drink now. • $8 • (08/31/96) • **84**
Navarra Gran Feudo Crianza 1991 • $7 • (04/30/95) BB • **85**
Navarra Gran Feudo Crianza 1990 • $8 • (04/15/94) • **83**
Navarra Gran Feudo Reserva 1992: Clean and well-knit, showing a balance of body and tannin; a clean finish, too, but there's not much flavor, with only hints of cherries, tobacco and herbs. A modest complement to food. • $12 • (11/15/97) • **83**
Navarra Reserva 1991 • $10 • (04/15/94) • **86**
Navarra Reserva 1990 • $9 • (04/15/94) • **85**
Navarra Reserva 1988 • $10 • (12/15/93) • **79**
Navarra Reserva 1987 • $10 • (06/15/93) • **81**
Navarra Rosado Gran Feudo 1996: Light and crisp, this pale rosé offers delicate flavors of strawberries and herbs. Clean and very dry on the palate, it has enough backbone for light foods. • $8 • (10/31/97) • **83**
Navarra Rosado Gran Feudo 1995: Delicate and soft, this wine is a bit low in acidity but has pretty strawberry and raspberry flavors. A nice apéritif, a bit over-matched for food. • $7 • (09/15/97) • **80**
Navarra Rosado Gran Feudo 1993 • $6 • (08/31/95) • **79**
Navarra Viña Marcos 1995: Smoky aromas give way to cherry, smoke, and light earth flavors in this medium-bodied, well-balanced red. An unassuming complement to food, it's approachable now. Made from Tempranillo. • $7 • (10/31/97) • **83**
Navarra Viña Marcos 1992 • $NA • (04/15/94) • **78**
Navarra Viña Marcos 1991 • $6 • (06/15/93) • **77**
Navarra White Coleccion 125 Fermentado En Barrica 1994: Powerful, with cream, spice and almond notes, this is a rich wine with layers of flavor and a mature quality. Try it when in the mood for something different. • $35 • (05/15/97) • **86**
Navarra White Colleccion 125 1993 • $20 • (03/31/95) • **84**

CODORNIU

Blanc de Blancs Cava 1984 • $9 • (05/31/88) • **72**
Brut Blanc de Blancs Cava 1989 • $9 • (06/15/94) • **83**
Brut Blanc de Blancs Cava 1988 • $10 • (03/31/93) • **80**
Brut Blanc de Blancs Cava 1986 • $8 • (07/31/89) • **77**
Brut Cava 1985 • $7 • (05/31/88) • **79**
Brut Cava Anna de Codorniu 1989 • $8 • (05/15/92) • **79**
Brut Cava Anna de Codorniu 1988 • $9 • (03/31/93) • **82**
Brut Cava Anna de Codorniu 1987 • $7 • (08/31/90) • **75**
Brut Cava Anna de Codorniu 1985 • $6 • (07/31/89) • **76**
Brut Cava Anna de Codorniu 1984 • $7 • (05/31/88) • **73**
Brut Cava Chardonnay 1988 • $15 • (05/15/92) • **85**
Brut Cava Chardonnay 1986 • $12 • (07/31/89) • **84**
Brut Cava Clásico 1990 • $7 • (12/15/92) BB • **81**
Brut Cava Clásico 1989 • $9 • (05/15/92) • **75**
Brut Cava Clásico 1986 • $6 • (05/15/89) BB • **82**
Brut Cava Gran Reserve 1983 • $14 • (05/31/88) • **73**
Extra Dry Cava 1985 • $7 • (05/31/88) • **72**

CONCAVINS, BODEGAS

Chardonnay Santara Conca de Barberá 1995: An up-front style with plenty of oaky flavors and ripe overtones that linger on the finish. A bit exaggerated, but still tasty. • $9 • (09/15/96) • **85**

CONDADO DE HAZA

Ribera del Duero Crianza 1995: Very young and quite closed now, this rich Spanish red nonetheless promises a bright future. It shows concentration and balance, offering an intriguing range of coffee, plum, licorice, and tobacco flavors. Oaky notes are dominant, but the wine should improve with time. Try in 2000. Tasted twice, with consistent notes. 30,000 cases made. • $17 • (11/30/97) SS • **90**
Ribera del Duero Crianza 1994: This rich, chewy wine offers vibrant aromas of vanilla, spice and game, with full-bodied flavors of black cherries, spice and toasty oak. Has good concentration and firm tannins. Try now. 8,300 cases made. • $15 • (06/15/97) • **89**

CONTINO

Rioja Reserva 1990: Woody, spicy aromas give way to round flavors of plums, raisins, and earth in this generous but rather soft red. The flavors are just beginning to show maturity, though the structure suggests drinking now. • $22 • (10/15/97) • **85**
Rioja Reserva 1989: A well-integrated marriage of black cherry coffee, and earthy flavors with firm tannins and a spicy finish. Maturing now, it's probably near its best. • $16 • (08/31/96) • **84**
Rioja Reserva 1988 • $16 • (04/30/95) • **84**
Rioja Reserva 1987 • $15 • (04/15/94) • **88**
Rioja Reserva 1985 • $14 • (12/15/90) • **88**
Rioja Reserva 1984 • $12 • (03/31/90) • **84**
Rioja Reserva 1983 • $13 • (03/31/92) • **89**
Rioja Reserva 1982 • $12 • (03/31/92) • **92**
Rioja Reserva 1980 • $11 • (01/31/87) • **83**

CORRAL, BODEGAS

Rioja Don Jacobo 1982 • $7 • (11/15/87) • **79**
Rioja Don Jacobo Crianza 1993: Polished and supple, this traditional red shows strawberry, herbal, cinnamon, and tea flavors, with light tannins that turn a bit dry on the finish. It's harmonious and accessible now. • $9 • (11/15/97) • **83**
Rioja Don Jacobo Crianza 1989 • $7 • (04/30/95) • **86**
Rioja Don Jacobo Crianza 1988 • $7 • (04/15/94) BB • **87**
Rioja Don Jacobo Crianza 1985 • $8 • (03/31/90) • **79**
Rioja Don Jacobo Gran Reserva 1983 • $16 • (04/15/94) • **80**
Rioja Don Jacobo Reserva 1985 • $11 • (04/15/94) • **85**
Rioja Don Jacobo Reserva 1981 • $11 • (03/31/90) • **86**
Rioja Rosado Don Jacobo 1993 • $6 • (08/31/95) • **78**
Rioja White Don Jacobo 1993 • $6 • (07/31/95) • **74**

COSTERS DEL SIURANA

Priorat Clos de L'Obac 1995: Showing off pure fruit and the essence of blackberries, this big red is rich, smooth and irresistible. It has tannin, acidity and alcohol—all in spades—but they are seamlessly integrated and subordinate to ripe, sweet fruit. Hard to resist now; perhaps better in 2002. Much better than when previously reviewed. 1,250 cases made. • $45 • (11/30/97) • **93**
Priorat Clos de L'Obac 1994: Savage and exuberant. Exotic aromas of raspberry, strawberry, heather, iron and game make a potent cocktail and follow through on the lush, tannic palate. A powerful, distinctive wine that will amaze your friends. • $40 • (06/15/97) CS • **92**
Priorat Clos de L'Obac 1993: Lovely raspberry flavor sings in this silky red, and bright acidity keeps it lively and well-defined. Though it lacks the punch of many Priorats, it's fresh and drinking well now. 1,000 cases made. • $60 • (01/01/97) • **86**
Priorat Clos de L'Obac 1992: This meaty red is evolving now, with earthy and smoky accents to the ripe berry and cherry flavors. The tannins are firm but smooth; the finish spicy and a bit hot. Drink now. 950 cases made. • $60 • (01/01/97) • **86**
Priorat Clos de L'Obac 1991: This well-integrated red shows good balance and definition, with firm tannins underlying ripe black cherry, chocolate, and light earthy flavors. Muscular but not clumsy, it should evolve well. Try now. 400 cases made. • $60 • (01/01/97) • **88**
Priorat Clos de L'Obac 1990: Ripe plum and prune flavors, with coffee and chocolate notes that mark maturity. Full-bodied, still tannic. Concentrated, but a bit clumsy; drink now. 1,000 cases made. • $60 • (08/31/96) • **86**
Priorat Clos de L'Obac 1989: Aromas of kirsch and cassis are alluring, but it turns tough, with earth and mineral flavors dominated by firm tannins. Has concentration, but is evolving without much finesse. 550 cases made. • $60 • (01/01/97) • **82**
Priorat Dolç de L'Obac 1995: Where's the vanilla ice cream? This thick, sweet fruit bomb would make a perfect topping. Its amazingly ripe, rich blackberry flavors are syrupy on the palate, but with little tannin or alcohol. Delicious—if you know what to expect. 75 cases made. • $70 • (12/15/97) • **90**
Priorat Dolç de L'Obac 1994: Irresistible! This blue-black-colored dessert wine oozes into the glass, then delivers exotic aromas of raisin, cinnamon and clove, followed by rich, unctuous flavors of plum, raisin and chocolate. It's moderately sweet yet very well balanced, with a long, spicy finish. Have fun stumping your friends with this one. Drinkable now through 2020. 120 cases made. • $75 • (09/15/97) • **94**
Priorat Miserere 1995: Alluring floral and blueberry aromas give way to rich flavors of blueberries, licorice and vanilla in this chewy, tannic red. It gives a starburst of flavors that draws you back for another sip even as the tannins bludgeon your palate. An exciting, distinctive wine. Drink now through 2005. • $35 • (04/30/98) • **91**
Priorat Miserere 1994: Though relatively light in body for the appellation, this punchy red shares the region's bright blueberry, brambly, and vanilla flavors; fresh and well defined. A good match for grilled meats. Drink now through 2005. • $35 • (01/01/98) • **89**
Priorat Miserere 1993: Lush blackberry flavor and punchy notes of licorice, toast, and tar combine in this rich wine. Well integrated, even subtle, despite its size. 1,000 cases made. • $30 • (08/31/96) • **85**
Priorat Miserere 1990 • $30 • (04/30/95) • **91**

COVISA

Elena Talier La Pyramida Somontano 1994: Fresh, firm, and fruity. Exuberant blackberry and cassis flavors with a touch of herb for interest, and just enough tannin for food. Unsophisticated, but pleasant drinking. 20,000 cases made. • $6 • (08/31/96) • **84**

CUEVA DEL GRANERO, BODEGAS

La Mancha Crianza 1988 • $6 • (10/15/92) • **80**

CUNE

Rioja Clarete Crianza 1990 • $8 • (04/15/94) • **81**
Rioja Clarete Crianza 1987 • $7 • (11/15/91) • **78**
Rioja Clarete Crianza 1986 • $7 • (03/31/92) BB • **84**
Rioja Clarete Crianza 1985 • $7 • (03/31/90) • **88**
Rioja Clarete Crianza 1984 • $6 • (10/15/88) BB • **80**
Rioja Clarete Crianza 1982 • $5 • (06/01/85) • **83**
Rioja Clarete Crianza 1978 • $5 • (06/16/85) • **78**
Rioja Imperial Gran Reserva 1989: Mature now, this red shows the alluring smoky, spicy aromas traditional in Rioja, along with light cherry and licorice flavors that linger on the finish; light but firm tannins. A nice accompaniment to lighter dishes. • $33 • (11/30/97) • **87**
Rioja Imperial Gran Reserva 1988: This maturing red offers nice weight and richness on the palate, yet it's smooth and balanced, with plum, prune, coffee, and cedar notes. Good with food. Drink now. • $33 • (11/15/97) • **86**
Rioja Imperial Gran Reserva 1986 • $25 • (04/15/94) • **86**
Rioja Imperial Gran Reserva 1985 • $25 • (04/15/94) • **89**
Rioja Imperial Gran Reserva 1982 • $22 • (03/31/92) • **86**
Rioja Imperial Gran Reserva 1981 • $26 • (03/31/92) • **82**
Rioja Imperial Gran Reserva 1978 • $15 • (03/31/90) • **70**
Rioja Imperial Gran Reserva 1975 • $24 • (03/31/92) • **84**
Rioja Imperial Gran Reserva 1973 • $28 • (03/31/90) • **85**
Rioja Imperial Reserva 1986 • $NA • (03/31/92) • **87**
Rioja Reserva 1991: Tobacco and cedar notes are expressive, but overwhelm the fruit and turn a bit dry on the finish. Medium-bodied. Drink now. Tasted twice, with consistent notes. • $15 • (11/15/97) • **77**
Rioja Reserva 1986 • $10 • (04/15/94) • **76**
Rioja Reserva 1985 • $8 • (03/31/90) • **85**
Rioja Viña Real Crianza 1992: This pleasant red is modest but harmonious, with light black cherry flavors and notes of coffee, brown sugar, and

SPAIN

raisins. Not muscular, but will match easily with food. Drinkable now. • $10 • (11/15/97) • **84**

Rioja Viña Real Crianza 1990 • $9 • (04/30/95) • **84**
Rioja Viña Real Crianza 1989 • $9 • (04/15/94) BB • **87**
Rioja Viña Real Crianza 1988 • $10 • (03/31/92) • **87**
Rioja Viña Real Crianza 1987 • $10 • (03/31/92) • **86**
Rioja Viña Real Crianza 1986 • $8 • (03/31/90) • **81**
Rioja Viña Real Crianza 1985 • $7 • (03/31/90) • **85**
Rioja Viña Real Crianza 1980 • $5 • (06/01/85) • **75**
Rioja Viña Real Gran Reserva 1986 • $19 • (04/30/95) • **77**
Rioja Viña Real Gran Reserva 1985 • $18 • (04/15/94) • **91**
Rioja Viña Real Gran Reserva 1981 • $17 • (03/31/90) • **88**
Rioja Viña Real Gran Reserva 1973 • $24 • (03/31/92) • **84**
Rioja Viña Real Gran Reserva 1970 • $24 • (03/31/92) • **85**
Rioja White Monopole 1994: Spicy vanilla aromas indicate a white in the traditional style, and the flavors follow through, clean and deep, with notes of pear, vanilla and herbs. It's still fresh and firm; a nice match with food. • $12 • (10/31/97) • **87**

CURROS, LOS

Rueda Tierra Buena 1995: The blend of pear, herbal, and light toast flavors in this firm white is reminiscent of a traditional Graves. It's not generous, but can stand up to food. A blend of 50 percent Verdejo and 50 percent Viura. • $5 • (10/31/97) • **84**
Rueda Viña Cantosán 1996: Strong butter and vanilla aromas lighten up on the palate, where flavors of apples and vanilla are backed by firm acidity. An ambitious wine; try now. Made from 100 percent Verdejo. • $9 • (10/31/97) • **82**
Viño de Mesa de Castilla y Leon Yllera Red Label NV: Cherry, cinnamon, and cedar notes mingle in this light-bodied yet quite firm red. Has enough life and grip for simple foods. Drink now. Made from 100 percent Tempranillo from the '89 vintage and aged as a Reserva. • $24 • (11/15/97) • **81**
Viño de Mesa de Castilla y Leon Yllera White Label NV: This off-beat red is a mix of ripe, fresh cherry and more mature, soft, earth and mineral flavors, with round tannins and strong accents of minerals and cedar. It's both accessible and lively. 100 percent Tempranillo from the '94 vintage aged to Crianza level. Drink now. 50,000 cases made. • $9 • (05/15/98) • **84**

DIAZ, J.

Madrid 1985 • $5 • (03/31/90) BB • **85**
Madrid Tinto de Madrid 1985 • $6 • (06/30/88) • **72**

DOMECQ, PEDRO

Amontillado Jerez 51-1a NV: Like a well-oiled knife, this assertive Sherry is smooth and polished, with a keen edge. Tastes of walnuts, raisins, and brown sugar. Though rich, it's dry and refreshing. From a Solera established in 1830. 420 cases made. • $83 • (02/28/98) • **89**
Palo Cortado Jerez Sibarita NV: Mahogany-colored and quite sweet, with maple and walnut flavors. Notes of bitter orange keep it balanced. Full and oily on the palate, and long. From a Solera established in 1792. 370 cases made. • $83 • (02/28/98) • **90**
Pedro Ximenez Jerez Venerable NV: Not your grandmother's Sherry. Black as night, thick as molasses, it coats the palate like motor oil, with flavors of prunes, dark chocolate and sweet Turkish coffee. A fine example of one of the world's most distinctive wines. From a Solera established in 1902. 715 cases made. • $83 • (02/28/98) • **93**

DURON, BODEGAS

Ribera del Duero Gran Reserva 1990: This muscular red shows ripe plum flavor, but it's maturing now and its strongest flavors are earth, coffee, and leather, with dry tannins. A well-built, traditional-style wine. Try in 1999. 2,000 cases made. • $21 • (11/15/97) • **87**
Ribera del Duero Reserva 1991: Kirsch and coffee aromas and flavors make for a vivid character; it's firm and a bit lean on the palate, with slightly drying tannins. May open with time; try in 1999. 4,000 cases made. • $19 • (11/15/97) • **86**

Key: SS—Spectator Selection CS—Cellar Selection HR—Highly Recommended BB—Best Buy $NA—Price not available Ⓐ—Auction Price (BT)—Barrel Tasting
Dates in parentheses indicate the issues in which the ratings were published.

EIRAS, ADEGAS DAS

Albariño Rias Baixas Abadia de San Campio 1996: Pretty peach, citrus, and honey aromas are plump and generous; on the palate, this white is firm and crisp, with bright citrus flavors; a hint of honey on the finish. Lively and refreshing. 2,000 cases made. • $12 • (11/15/97) • **86**
Rias Baixas Terras Gauda 1996: This full-bodied yet very firm white offers muscular flavors of grapefruit, pine-scented herbs, and almonds. Rich yet well defined, with a long, clean finish, it has the weight to stand up to richer foods. • $12 • (11/15/97) • **88**

EL CEP

Brut Cava Marques de Gelida Gran Seleccio NV: Lively, with bright apple flavors, tart acidity, and an aggressive mousse, but a rubbery finish. Drink very cold or in a punch. • $9 • (02/28/98) • **78**

EL COTO

Rioja Coto de Imaz Gran Reserva 1982 • $NA • (11/30/91) • **85**
Rioja Coto de Imaz Reserva 1981 • $9 • (03/31/90) • **81**
Rioja Crianza 1990 • $6 • (04/15/94) • **80**
Rioja Crianza 1987 • $11 • (09/30/91) • **79**
Rioja Crianza 1985 • $5 • (03/31/90) BB • **81**
Rioja Crianza 1984 • $7 • (03/31/90) BB • **81**
Rioja Gran Reserva 1982 • $10 • (04/15/94) • **83**

ELENA TALIER

Chardonnay Somontano Elena Talier La Piedra 1995: A well-focused wine with good ripe apple and spice flavors. Full-bodied with some nice pear notes as well. 50,000 cases made. • $6 • (09/15/96) • **84**

ENVERO

Viño de Mesa Reserva Limousin 1987 • $10 • (08/31/93) • **85**

ERMITA DE PIO

Jumilla 1994 • $8 • (04/30/96) • **79**

ESTOLA

La Mancha Crianza Reserva 1987 • $10 • (12/15/92) • **78**
La Mancha Reserva 1985 • $10 • (02/15/92) • **80**
La Mancha Reserva 1982 • $6 • (11/15/89) BB • **87**

ETXANIZ TXAKOLINA

Getariako Txakolina Txomin Etxaniz 1996: Bracing, sharp and lean, with tart citrus and mineral flavors. A strong dose of carbon dioxide makes it fizzy and even more assertive. Like lemonade on its own, but a great match for shellfish. From the Basque region. • $15 • (02/28/98) • **83**

FARIÑA, BODEGAS

Castilla y Leon Fin del Duero 1990 • $12 • (03/31/95) • **85**
Toro 1994 • $7 • (04/30/95) • **81**
Toro 1993 • $6 • (01/31/95) • **74**
Toro 1992 • $6 • (08/31/93) • **75**
Toro 1990 • $8 • (10/15/92) • **81**
Toro Colegiata 1993 • $9 • (01/31/95) • **77**
Toro Colegiata 1991 • $7 • (04/30/95) • **63**
Toro Colegiata 1986 • $5 • (11/30/89) BB • **82**
Toro Colegiata 1985 • $5 • (11/30/89) BB • **88**
Toro Colegiata Tinto 1990 • $9 • (04/15/94) • **77**
Toro Dama de Toro Reserva 1989 • $10 • (04/15/94) • **83**
Toro Gran Colegiata Crianza 1990 • $10 • (01/31/95) • **81**
Toro Gran Colegiata Crianza 1989 • $11 • (04/15/94) • **83**
Toro Gran Colegiata Crianza 1986 • $7 • (11/30/89) • **77**
Toro Gran Colegiata Crianza 1985 • $5 • (12/31/87) • **85**
Toro Gran Colegiata Crianza 1982 • $6 • (11/30/87) • **78**
Toro Gran Colegiata Riserva 1988 • $12 • (04/30/95) • **79**
Toro Gran Colegiata Riserva 1987 • $12 • (03/31/95) • **80**
Toro Gran Colegiata Riserva 1986 • $20 • (03/31/95) • **76**

Toro Reserva 1987 • $12 • (10/15/92) • **80**
Toro Viño Primero 1995 • $8 • (04/30/96) • **77**
Toro White Colegiata 1994 • $7 • (07/31/95) • **80**
Toro White Colegiata 1993 • $7 • (02/28/95) • **78**
Zamora 1991 • $5 • (04/15/94) • **79**
Zamora Gran Peromato 1990 • $6 • (04/30/96) • **82**
Zamora Gran Peromato Viño de Mesa 1989 • $9 • (02/28/95) • **82**
Zamora Peromato 1990 • $6 • (04/15/94) • **77**
Zamora Peromato Viño de la Tierra 1992 • $6 • (02/28/95) • **79**
Zamora Peromato Viño de la Tierra 1991 • $5 • (02/28/95) • **81**
Zamora Peromato Viño de la Tierra 1986 • $7 • (11/30/89) • **79**

FAUSTINO MARTINEZ, BODEGAS

Rioja 1989 • $10 • (03/31/93) • **83**
Rioja Faustino I Gran Reserva 1988: Spicy dried-fruit aromas are appealing, but flavors are earthy and herbal and the texture is thick. Has concentration, lacks finesse. 30,000 cases made. • $20 • (11/15/97) • **81**
Rioja Faustino I Gran Reserva 1987 • $16 • (04/15/94) • **82**
Rioja Faustino I Gran Reserva 1986 • $21 • (03/31/93) • **86**
Rioja Faustino I Gran Reserva 1982 • $25 • (03/31/92) • **82**
Rioja Faustino I Gran Reserva 1981 • $12 • (10/31/88) • **88**
Rioja Faustino I Gran Reserva 1978 • $NA • (03/31/92) • **76**
Rioja Faustino I Gran Reserva 1973 • $NA • (03/31/92) • **82**
Rioja Faustino I Gran Reserva 1970 • $NA • (03/31/92) • **89**
Rioja Faustino V 1985 • $7 • (10/15/88) • **83**
Rioja Faustino V Reserva 1992: Displays straightforward flavors of black cherry, coffee, and cedar that are harmonious but not intense, over moderate tannins. Still fresh, and will make a modest companion to food. 80,000 cases made. • $11 • (11/15/97) • **83**
Rioja Faustino V Reserva 1991 • $10 • (03/31/96) • **84**
Rioja Faustino V Reserva 1989 • $10 • (04/15/94) • **83**
Rioja Faustino V Reserva 1988 • $14 • (03/31/93) • **81**
Rioja Faustino V Reserva 1987 • $13 • (01/31/92) • **81**
Rioja Faustino V Reserva 1986 • $16 • (03/31/92) • **86**
Rioja Faustino V Reserva 1985 • $18 • (03/31/92) • **82**
Rioja Faustino VII 1995: A chunky red, ripe but clumsy, with generous chocolate, coffee, and prune flavors over thick, chewy tannins. Has good concentration and balance. 100,000 cases made. • $8 • (11/15/97) • **81**
Rioja Faustino VII 1993: Clean and fruity, this wine offers cherry, spice, and light menthol flavors in a supple frame; still fresh, with good balance. A pleasant quaff for lighter foods. 15,000 cases imported. • $8 • (09/30/96) BB • **86**
Rioja Faustino VII 1991 • $6 • (01/31/95) • **81**
Rioja Faustino VII 1990 • $7 • (04/15/94) • **81**
Rioja Faustino VII 1988 • $8 • (01/31/92) BB • **85**
Rioja White Faustino V 1996: This soft, floral-scented white shows modest apple and light vanilla flavors. Makes a light, rather simple apéritif. Drink now. 30,000 cases made. • $9 • (05/31/98) • **81**

FERNANDEZ, BODEGAS ALEJANDRO

Ribera del Duero Pesquera Crianza 1994: The exuberant, ripe fruit flavors of blackberry and cassis are rich and concentrated, the tannins are fine and the wood notes are well integrated in this stylish wine. Quite polished for the appellation. Try now. 35,000 cases made. • $22 • (06/15/97) SS • **90**
Ribera del Duero Pesquera Crianza 1991 • $18 • (04/15/94) • **91**
Ribera del Duero Pesquera Crianza 1990 • $20 • (12/15/93) • **89**
Ribera del Duero Pesquera Crianza 1989 • $20 • (04/15/92) CS • **91**
Ribera del Duero Pesquera Crianza 1988 • $35 • (09/30/91) • **89**
Ribera del Duero Pesquera Crianza 1987 • $25 • (09/30/90) • **84**
Ribera del Duero Pesquera Crianza 1986 • $30 • (04/30/89) • **91**
Ribera del Duero Pesquera Crianza 1985 • $16 • (04/30/88) • **89**
Ribera del Duero Pesquera Crianza 1984 • $14 • (10/15/87) • **89**
Ribera del Duero Pesquera Crianza 1983 • $12 • (11/15/87) • **94**
Ribera del Duero Pesquera Crianza 1982 • $12 • (11/15/87) • **89**
Ribera del Duero Pesquera Crianza 1979 • $11 • (11/15/87) • **90**
Ribera del Duero Pesquera Crianza 1978 • $11 • (11/15/87) • **89**
Ribera del Duero Pesquera Crianza 1975 • $110 • (11/15/87) • **88**
Ribera del Duero Pesquera Gran Reserva 1990 • $80 • (04/30/96) • **91**
Ribera del Duero Pesquera Janus Gran Reserva 1991: This powerhouse red is still young, with loads of vibrant red fruit flavors and notes of violets, spice, and cedar. Massive tannins sneak up on the palate and shut down the finish now, but it should smooth out with time. Try in 2000. 830 cases made. • $120 • (11/30/97) • **91**
Ribera del Duero Pesquera Janus Reserva 1994: Complex and intriguing, this big red shows great concentration, ripeness, and a mix of flavors ranging from plum to smoked meat to chocolate and tobacco. Despite massive tannins, it's balanced, even elegant; though stuffed with fruit, it's incredibly stylish. Distinctive and well crafted. Try in 1999. 2,500 cases made. • $90 • (11/30/97) CS • **95**
Ribera del Duero Pesquera Janus Reserva 1982 • $150 • (09/15/88) • **94**
Ribera del Duero Pesquera Reserva 1991 • $40 • (04/30/95) • **91**
Ribera del Duero Pesquera Reserva 1990 • $25 • (04/15/94) • **89**
Ribera del Duero Pesquera Reserva 1986 • $35 • (09/30/90) • **92**
Ribera del Duero Pesquera Reserva 1985 • $25 • (03/31/90) • **89**

FILLABOA, GRANJA

Albariño Rias Baixas 1996: This firm, clean white has good balance but it's rather neutral in flavor, with notes of apple and hazelnut. Modest but appealing, it's best with food. Drink now. • $14 • (05/31/98) • **82**

FORNELOS, LAGAR DE

Albariño Rias Baixas Lagar de Cervera 1996: This big white offers a round, unctuous texture, bold flavors of pears, toast, and herbs, and a lingering finish. It leans more toward earth than fruit, and tastes quite mature already. • $15 • (10/31/97) • **85**
Albariño Rias Baixas Lagar de Cervera 1995: This firm, rich white, with its toasty almond and vanilla flavors, is smooth and polished on the palate. There's not much fruit, but a core of acidity keeps it lively. Drink now. • $15 • (09/15/97) • **84**
Lagar de Cervera Albariño Rias Baixas 1994 • $15 • (03/31/95) • **87**
Lagar de Cervera Albariño Rias Baixas 1993 • $16 • (12/31/94) • **86**

FREIXENET

Brut Nature Cava 1991: An agreeably fruity, spicy tasting bubbly with a nice soft texture, rich flavors, and a lingering finish. • $13 • (07/31/96) • **85**
Brut Nature Cava 1988 • $10 • (06/15/94) • **86**
Brut Nature Cava 1987 • $10 • (05/15/92) • **80**
Brut Nature Cava 1985 • $10 • (12/31/90) • **81**
Brut Nature Cava 1984 • $8 • (05/31/88) • **75**

FUENTES, J.M.

Priorat Gran Clos 1995: This vivid red shows the ripe, crushed-fruit character typical of Priorat, with notes of blackberry, black pepper, and cola. The texture is lush, with firm, underlying tannins, and a spicy finish. Drink now through 2002. • $NA • (06/30/98) • **87**

GALEGAS, ADEGAS

Albariño Rias Baixas D. Pedro de Soutomaior 1996: This full-bodied white sacrifices harmony for power. Offers ripe melon, honey, and creamy flavors, but is somewhat lacking in focus. Can stand up to boldly spiced dishes. Drink now. • $NA • (05/31/98) • **81**

GANDIA

Cabernet Sauvignon Utiel-Requena 1993 • $6 • (04/30/95) • **78**
Cabernet Sauvignon Utiel-Requena Hoya Valley 1994: Light and rather weedy, this simple red shows light cherry and herbal flavors, with soft tannins that turn a bit dry on the finish. Drink now. • $5 • (10/31/97) • **79**
Chardonnay Utiel-Requena 1993 • $6 • (04/30/95) • **75**
Chardonnay Utiel-Requena Hoya Valley 1995: Round and soft on the palate, offering apple and vanilla flavors, balanced but not very concentrated. It's clean and still fresh. • $6 • (06/30/97) • **83**
Grenache Rosé Utiel-Requena Hoya Valley 1996: This pale rosé shows light fruit and earth aromas, and is lightly sweet, with slightly candied flavors. Simple, a bit cloying. • $5 • (06/30/97) • **79**
Merlot Utiel-Requena 1993 • $6 • (04/30/95) BB • **83**
Merlot Utiel-Requena Hoya Valley 1994: Black cherry, herbal, and light tomato flavors reflect varietal character in this smooth red. Slightly dull on the palate, but firm tannins on the finish promise a satisfying match with food. • $5 • (10/31/97) • **82**
Sauvignon Blanc Utiel-Requena Hoya Valley 1996: Green apple, light peach, and slightly earthy flavors mingle in this tangy white. It has enough acidity

to stand up to food, and the fruit flavors linger on the clean, fresh finish. • $6 • (06/30/97) • **84**

Tempranillo Utiel-Requena Hoya Valley 1992: This light red shows characteristic flavors of tea, spice, and dried cherries, but it's short on structure and turns dry on the finish. Drink now. • $5 • (10/31/97) • **81**

Utiel-Requena Hoya de Cadenas Reserva 1989 • $7 • (04/30/96) • **74**

Utiel-Requena Marques de Chivé 1989 • $6 • (04/15/94) • **81**

Valencia Castillo de Liria NV • $5 • (04/15/94) BB • **80**

GLORIAN, DAPHNE

Priorat Clos Erasmus 1993: Pretty berry aromas give way to berry and licorice flavors that are balanced and lively but get bulldozed by tannin on the finish. May be better in 1999. 250 cases made. • $35 • (09/15/97) • **88**

GONZALEZ BYASS

Dry Oloroso Jerez 1964: Distinctive. Oily and powerful, bone-dry on the palate, this Sherry shows walnut, orange peel, and raisin flavors that linger long on the finish. Ideal served slightly chilled with salted, roasted almonds—or cigars—on a hot afternoon. 240 cases made. • $100 • (10/31/97) • **90**

GRAN CONDAL

Rioja 1987 • $6 • (03/31/90) • **80**

Rioja Gran Reserva 1982 • $10 • (11/15/87) • **79**

Rioja Gran Reserva 1981 • $8 • (11/30/87) • **80**

Rioja Reserva 1980 • $7 • (11/30/87) BB • **82**

GRAN CORPAS

Tarragona 1988 • $6 • (10/15/92) BB • **84**

GRANDES BODEGAS

Ribera del Duero Marques de Velilla 1996: Lush, with vivid ripe cassis and leafy flavor and hints of coffee, all buried under mouthfilling tannins. The elements are strong, but it tastes like a barrel sample. Hard to judge; try now. 20,000 cases made. • $8 • (10/31/97) • **84**

GRIÑON, MARQUÉS DE

Cabernet Sauvignon Viño de Mesa Dominio de Valdepusa 1993: Assertive flavors of smoke and charred meat are bitter and dry in this austere red, with its mouth-gripping tannins and hot finish. Lacks fruit and balance. 4,000 cases made. • $22 • (10/31/97) • **76**

Cabernet Sauvignon Viño de Mesa de Toledo Dominio de Valdepusa 1995: This thick, jammy red shows meat and chocolate flavors, notes of prune and candied black cherry, and firm but well-integrated tannins. A bit clumsy, but shows good concentration and personality. Drink now through 2002. 8,000 cases made. • $22 • (04/30/98) • **84**

Castilla y Leon Durius Red 1993 • $9 • (04/30/96) • **83**

Castilla y Leon Durius Red 1991 • $9 • (03/31/95) • **78**

Chardonnay Viño de Mesa de Toledo Dominio de Valdepusa 1995: Rich, with toasty, smoky flavors; short on fruit with hints of herbs, almonds and dried apples. Concentrated, but lacks freshness. Tasted twice, with consistent notes. 2,000 cases made. • $22 • (02/28/98) • **82**

Rioja 1995: Harmonious, this wine offers black cherry, spice, and cedar notes that are clean and fresh. Firm enough for food yet light enough for drinking now. Marries traditional flavors and contemporary winemaking methods for a very satisfying wine. 20,000 cases made. • $10 • (10/15/97) • **87**

Rioja 1994 • $10 • (06/30/96) BB • **88**

Rioja 1991 • $10 • (04/30/95) • **86**

Rioja Colección Personal Reserva 1990: Powerful for Rioja, this deep wine offers full-bodied flavors of plums, coffee, licorice and spice, with round, firm tannins and a rich finish. Harmonious and drinkable now. 8,000 cases made. • $18 • (10/15/97) • **89**

Rioja Colección Personal Reserva 1988 • $15 • (04/30/95) • **88**

Syrah Viño de Mesa Dominio de Valdepusa 1993: Rich and ripe, this deeply colored red shows plum, black pepper, and cola flavors that are exuberant and fleshy. A bit rustic, but packed with flavor. 3,000 cases made. • $26 • (09/30/96) BB • **85**

Syrah Viño de Mesa de Toledo Dominio de Valdepusa 1995: An exuberant red, with rich tannins and ripe flavors of blackberries and licorice, finishing with notes of bitter herbs and smoke. Has more concentration than elegance, but will stand up to hearty foods. Drink now through 2002. 4,500 cases made. • $22 • (04/30/98) • **84**

Viño de Mesa Dominio de Valdepusa Red 1992 • $19 • (04/30/95) • **87**

Viño de Mesa Durius 1994: Assertive smoke and game aromas follow through on the thick, tannic palate, with plum, meaty, and tarry flavors that turn a bit bitter on the finish. There's concentration here; may soften. 25,000 cases made. • $9 • (07/31/97) • **83**

Viño de Mesa Durius Colección Personal 1994: Assertive aromas and flavors of smoked meats and strong black coffee give this deep red a strong, distinctive character, but there's not much fruit to flesh out the firmly tannic palate. Hard to tell where it's headed; try now. 2,000 cases made. • $15 • (10/31/97) • **83**

Viño de Mesa de Toledo Red 1985 • $12 • (02/28/90) • **86**

Viño de Mesa White Durius 1995: This has quite an earthy aroma at the start, but it opens up with some modest grapefruit and citrus flavors. 25,000 cases made. • $9 • (05/15/97) • **81**

GUELBENZU, BODEGAS

Navarra 1995: This firm red is concentrated but austere now, with black cherry, distinct herbal, and light tobacco flavors backed by very firm tannins. It should bloom around 1999. A blend of Cabernet, Tempranillo, Merlot, and Garnacha. 8,000 cases made. • $10 • (10/31/97) • **86**

Navarra 1994 • $10 • (04/30/96) • **84**

Navarra 1992 • $9 • (04/30/95) • **84**

Navarra 1990 • $9 • (12/15/93) • **82**

Navarra 1989 • $11 • (04/15/92) • **87**

Navarra Evo 1994: Good concentration in this ambitious red, but the flavors are a bit harsh and earthy, and tannins dominate the modest fruit. May soften in 1999. A blend of Cabernet, Tempranillo and Merlot. 3,000 cases made. • $20 • (10/31/97) • **80**

Navarra Evo 1993: Maturing now, this silky red offers coffee, tobacco, and ripe plum flavors, with spicy notes and a slightly dry finish. Balanced, but a bit lean. Drinkable now. 2,500 cases made. • $20 • (06/15/97) • **86**

Navarra Evo 1992 • $17 • (04/30/95) • **87**

Navarra Evo 1989 • $20 • (04/15/92) • **85**

Navarra Jardin 1995: Spicy and fruity, blackberry jamlike flavors dominate this round, fresh wine. Lacks the structure to age, but chill lightly now and take it on a picnic. 5,000 cases made. • $8 • (08/31/96) • **84**

GURPEGUI MUGA, BODEGAS LUIS

Navarra Mendiani 1993 • $NA • (04/15/94) • **82**

Navarra Mendiani 1992 • $4 • (04/15/94) • **78**

Rioja Viña Berceo 1993 • $NA • (04/30/95) • **80**

Rioja Viña Berceo 1992 • $5 • (04/15/94) BB • **84**

GUTIERREZ DE LA VEGA, BODEGAS

Casta Diva Cosecha Miel Alicante 1995: Ripe, round, and very sweet, with nutmeg and cream flavors. Lush and flavorful, it just avoids being overdone via a wild herb note on the finish. 3,000 cases made. • $20/500ml • (05/15/97) • **84**

HERMANOS DEL VILLAR, BODEGA

Rueda Oro de Castilla 1996: Crisp and light. Shows well-defined Sauvignon Blanc character, with citrus, light herb, and grass notes in the style of the Loire Valley. Clean and refreshing. 3,000 cases made. • $9 • (02/28/98) • **83**

HUGUET

Brut Nature Cava Gran Reserva 1989 • $20 • (03/31/93) • **82**

Key: SS—Spectator Selection CS—Cellar Selection HR—Highly Recommended BB—Best Buy $NA—Price not available Ⓐ—Auction Price (BT)—Barrel Tasting

Dates in parentheses indicate the issues in which the ratings were published.

IBERNOBLE

Ribera del Duero 1996: Plum and light vanilla flavors are simple yet appealing in this round, rather soft red. It turns firmer on the short, jammy finish. Accessible now. 25,000 cases made. • $11 • (10/31/97) • **82**
Ribera del Duero Crianza 1994: This balanced red shows well-knit tannins and expressive flavors of black cherry, toast, and vanilla that are intense but not heavy. Not a blockbuster, but will make a consummate partner for food. Try now. 6,667 cases made. • $22 • (10/31/97) • **88**
Ribera del Duero Crianza 1992 • $15 • (04/30/96) • **78**
Ribera del Duero Crianza 1989 • $15 • (04/30/95) • **87**
Ribera del Duero Reserva 1991: This wine is still a baby—a giant baby. Inky-black in color, rich and fruity on the palate, with great concentration and firm, fresh tannins, it's appealing now but promises a long, rich life ahead. The coffee, plum, and cigar-box flavors are reminiscent of a top Bordeaux. 3,000 cases made. • $38 • (10/31/97) • **92**
Ribera del Duero Reserva 1986 • $27 • (04/30/95) • **87**

INVIOSA, BODEGAS

Tierra de Barros Lar de Barros Reserva 1994: Ripe and generous, this full-bodied red offers plum, chocolate, and coffee flavors, round on the palate and buttressed by very firm tannins. Drink now through 2000. 15,000 cases made. • $10 • (06/30/97) • **85**
Tierra de Barros Lar de Barros Reserva 1992: Ripe yet firm, this rustic red shows coffee, earth, and plum flavors over muscular tannins. A good barbecue wine. Drink now. 15,000 cases made. • $10 • (08/31/96) • **83**
Tierra de Barros Lar de Barros Reserva 1991 • $9 • (04/30/95) • **79**
Tierra de Barros Lar de Barros Reserva 1990 • $10 • (12/15/94) • **82**
Tierra de Barros Lar de Barros Reserva 1989 • $9 • (12/15/93) BB • **86**
Tierra de Barros Lar de Barros Reserva 1988 • $10 • (04/15/92) • **79**
Tierra de Barros Lar de Barros Reserva 1986 • $8 • (10/15/90) SS • **91**
Tierra de Barros Lar de Barros Reserva 1983 • $7 • (10/15/87) • **77**
Tierra de Barros Lar de Barros Reserva 1982 • $5 • (05/15/87) BB • **87**

IRACHE, BODEGAS

Navarra Castillo Irache Reserva 1978 • $12 • (03/31/90) • **81**

JUMILLA, CASTILLO

Jumilla 1985 • $5 • (07/31/89) • **75**
Jumilla Bodegas Bleda 1989 • $8 • (12/15/92) • **79**

JUVE Y CAMPS

Brut Cava Extra Reserva de la Familia 1986 • $16 • (03/31/93) • **76**
Brut Cava Natural Reserva de la Familia 1983 • $10 • (05/31/88) • **79**
Brut Cava Natural Reserva de la Familia 1981 • $10 • (07/16/86) • **80**

LAN, BODEGAS

Rioja Crianza 1994: Leans towards the modern style of Rioja with its lush texture and soft, ripe fruit flavors of plum and cherry, and has a pleasant smoky note on the finish. Drink now. 40,000 cases made. • $9 • (05/31/98) • **84**
Rioja Gran Reserva 1987: Round and soft, with light cherry and strawberry flavors accented by tea and vanilla, light, soft tannins and a supple texture. Harmonious, with a clean, lingering finish. Drink now. 15,000 cases made. • $15 • (05/31/98) • **85**
Rioja Lancorta Crianza 1989 • $9 • (01/31/95) • **84**
Rioja Reserva 1988: Pleasant plum and chocolate flavors mark this soft, plush red. The tannins are soft and well integrated, the finish is long and clean. A well-balanced wine for lighter dishes. Drink now through 2000. 20,000 cases made. • $12 • (05/31/98) • **87**
Rioja Viña Lanciano Reserva 1991: This deeply colored red still shows fresh fruit flavors of plums and blackberries, with notes of coffee and licorice. Tannins are firm but not out of balance; the finish is slightly bitter but clean. Drink now through 1999. 12,000 cases made. • $17 • (05/31/98) • **85**

LAR DE LARES

Tierra de Barros Gran Reserva 1989 • $16 • (04/30/96) • **78**
Tierra de Barros Gran Reserva 1982 • $14 • (06/15/91) HR • **90**

LAVERNOYA, CAVAS

Cabernet Sauvignon Penedès 1989 • $9 • (04/15/94) BB • **88**
Cabernet Sauvignon Penedès 1988 • $11 • (03/31/93) • **85**

LEMBEY

Brut Cava 1988 • $6 • (05/15/92) BB • **83**
Brut Cava 1985 • $6 • (05/31/88) • **74**
Brut Cava 1984 • $6 • (05/31/88) • **70**
Brut Cava 1982 • $6 • (12/16/85) BB • **72**
Brut Cava Pedro Domecq 1991 • $6 • (06/15/94) • **79**
Brut Cava Pedro Domecq 1986 • $7 • (07/15/90) • **79**
Brut Cava Première Cuvée 1985 • $14 • (03/31/93) • **87**

LEON, JEAN

Cabernet Sauvignon Penedès 1988 • $26 • (03/31/96) • **85**
Cabernet Sauvignon Penedès 1987 • $15 • (04/15/94) • **84**
Cabernet Sauvignon Penedès 1984 • $12 • (03/31/91) • **77**
Cabernet Sauvignon Penedès 1983 • $8 • (03/31/90) • **85**
Cabernet Sauvignon Penedès Reserva 1990: Thick and ripe, this muscular red shows plum, prune, licorice, and menthol flavors over full, thick tannins. Has more power than elegance, but offers distinctive character. Drinkable now, and could improve by 1999. • $24 • (10/31/97) • **86**
Cabernet Sauvignon Penedès Reserva 1982 • $31 • (03/31/96) • **84**
Cabernet Sauvignon Penedès Reserva 1979 • $34 • (03/31/96) • **85**
Chardonnay Penedès 1995: Appealing toasty oak aromas follow through on the palate, but tend to dominate the apple and spice flavors, leaving the wine a bit heavy on the finish. Has intensity, but lacks grace; may harmonize with food. • $30 • (10/31/97) • **84**
Chardonnay Penedès 1993: Mature, with straightforward fruit flavors and probably some oak influence. Rather tight and tart in texture. • $30 • (02/28/97) • **77**

LEY, BARON DE

Rioja Reserva 1986 • $10 • (04/15/94) • **84**

LLANOS, BODEGAS LOS

Valdepeñas Señorio de Los Llanos Gran Reserva 1984 • $13 • (01/31/93) • **85**
Valdepeñas Señorio de Los Llanos Reserva 1987 • $9 • (01/31/93) • **81**
Valdepeñas Señorio de Los Llanos Reserva 1984 • $6 • (10/15/92) • **79**

LLOPART, P.

Brut Cava Leopardi 1991: Clean, correct, toasty character. Dry and firm, with balance and some depth. • $20 • (02/28/98) • **84**

LÓPEZ DE HEREDIA VIÑA TONDONIA, R.

Rioja Viña Bosconia Crianza 1990: Maturing now, this shows cedar and spice aromas, with tea, spice, and dried fruit flavors over tannins that are just beginning to dry out. This is traditional Rioja, flavorful but a bit meager in structure. 16,000 cases made. • $15 • (12/15/97) • **83**
Rioja Viña Bosconia Gran Reserva 1976 • $14 • (03/31/90) • **72**
Rioja Viña Bosconia Gran Reserva 1973 • $15 • (12/31/87) • **75**
Rioja Viña Bosconia Reserva 1986 • $13 • (03/31/92) • **79**
Rioja Viña Bosconia Reserva 1983 • $13 • (03/31/92) • **78**
Rioja Viña Bosconia Reserva 1982 • $5 • (11/15/87) • **84**
Rioja Viña Bosconia Rioja Full Red 1987 • $NA • (04/30/95) • **83**
Rioja Viña Cubillo 1993: Light and simple, this silky red shows light berry and spice flavors, but it's already drying on the finish. Drink now. 33,000 cases made. • $10 • (11/15/97) • **79**
Rioja Viña Cubillo 1987 • $9 • (03/31/92) • **84**
Rioja Viña Cubillo 1984 • $5 • (03/31/90) • **70**
Rioja Viña Cubillo Crianza 1992: Spicy aromas are appealing, but there's not much stuffing, and the finish is more dry than fruity. It's still fresh though, so drink now. Tasted twice, with consistent notes. 33,300 cases made. • $10 • (12/15/97) • **80**
Rioja Viña Tondonia Gran Reserva 1981 • $NA • (03/31/92) • **79**
Rioja Viña Tondonia Gran Reserva 1978: A classic example of traditional Rioja. If you like subtlety, delicacy, and the mature flavors of dried

cherries, mushrooms and tea, you'll love it. If you want fresh fruit, firm structure, and enough concentration to stand up to food, pass it by. 12,500 cases made. • $35 • (10/15/97) • **85**

Rioja Viña Tondonia Gran Reserva 1976 • $NA • (04/30/95) • **82**

Rioja Viña Tondonia Gran Reserva 1973 • $44 • (03/31/92) • **87**

Rioja Viña Tondonia Gran Reserva 1970 • $44 • (03/31/92) • **75**

Rioja Viña Tondonia Reserva 1990: Firm, with mature flavors of tobacco, cedar, raisin, and spice, but it's still fresh, and a core of cherry flavor keeps it lively. Well made, in the traditional style. Drink now. 40,000 cases made. • $17 • (11/15/97) • **85**

Rioja Viña Tondonia Reserva 1989: Pretty spice and raspberry aromas are still fresh and young in this vibrant, light-bodied red. Soft and spicy on the palate, with dried fruit and cedar flavors. Well integrated and maturing, it's drinkable now. 41,000 cases made. • $17 • (10/15/97) • **86**

Rioja Viña Tondonia Reserva 1987 • $10 • (04/15/94) • **77**

Rioja Viña Tondonia Reserva 1985 • $13 • (03/31/92) • **86**

Rioja Viña Tondonia Reserva 1983 • $5 • (03/31/90) • **79**

LUBERRI, BODEGAS

Rioja Alavesa 1996: This lively, grapey red is a good example of Rioja's Beaujolais style of "vino joven," or young wine. It has light tannins, cherry and slightly bitter flavors, and needs drinking young. Drink now. 10,000 cases made. • $7 • (05/31/98) • **83**

LURTON, J. & F.

Rueda Hermanos Lurton 1995: This round, blowsy white shows ripe apple, bread dough, and vanilla flavors, fat and a bit soft on the palate. Clean, but lacks crispness. 5,000 cases made. • $6 • (10/31/97) • **82**

Tempranillo Viño de Mesa de Castilla y Leon Hermanos Lurton 1995: Lively, with grapey, gamy and smoky flavors, aggressive tannins and a youthful exuberance that probably won't amplify with age. Drink now. • $6 • (11/15/97) • **80**

Tempranillo Viño de Mesa de Castilla y Leon Hermanos Lurton Crianza 1994: A thick veneer of vanilla-scented oak covers a thick layer of jammy black cherry flavor in this solid red. Has a chewy texture and lively fruit flavors. Drink now through 1999. 800 cases made. • $9 • (11/15/97) • **83**

Viño de Mesa de Valladolid Rosado Hermanos Lurton 1996: A deeply colored, blue-tinged rosé, full-bodied and bold, with nearly red-wine flavors of black cherries and herbs. A bit heavy-handed, but it packs a punch. • $6 • (10/31/97) • **82**

LUSCO DO MIÑO

Albariño Rias Baixas Lusco 1996: Ripe peach and fresh vanilla flavors are backed by crisp acidity in this round yet racy white. It has a refreshing combination of mellow flavors and liveliness. 1,100 cases made. • $20 • (09/15/97) • **85**

LUSTAU, EMILIO

Sherry Jerez Dry Oloroso Single Cask NV: Full-bodied and soft, yet quite dry, showing ripe flavors of prunes, coffee, and walnuts. Balanced and generous, with a long, spicy finish. • $37 • (06/30/97) • **88**

Sherry Jerez Dry Solera San Bartolome Gran Reserva NV: Firm and expressive, offering walnut, orange peel, and raisin flavors, dry and lean. Except for the alcohol, it tastes like an aged Spanish brandy. Distinctive; serve slightly cool. • $18 • (06/30/97) • **87**

MAESE JOAN, BODEGAS

Rioja Armorial Crianza 1986 • $8 • (12/15/92) • **82**

Rioja Crianza 1989 • $NA • (04/15/94) • **80**

Rioja El Coro 1990 • $7 • (04/15/94) • **72**

MAGAÑA, BODEGAS

Merlot Navarra Viña Magaña Reserva 1989 • $14 • (04/30/95) • **77**

Merlot Navarra Viña Magaña Reserva 1985 • $35 • (04/15/94) • **78**

Navarra Eventum Finca Paso de la Reina Crianza 1991: A bit tired and over-the-hill with dried-out cherry flavors and an astringent finish. Past its prime. 20,000 cases made. • $10 • (09/15/96) • **78**

Navarra Eventum Finca Paso de la Reina Crianza 1990 • $9 • (04/30/95) • **88**

Navarra Viña Magaña Gran Reserva 1982 • $30 • (04/15/94) • **74**

MAR, SENORIO DEL

Viño Tinto Seco 1987 • $4 • (10/31/91) BB • **81**

MARINO, A. Y B.

Chardonnay Navarra Palacio de Muruzabal Barrel Fermented 1995: A round white, with toast and vanilla flavors dominating the light apple and citrus ones. Has enough acidity to keep it crisp, but a bit clumsy overall. 2,000 cases made. • $20 • (11/15/97) • **78**

Navarra Palacio de Muruzabal Reserva 1992: A jumbled mix of cherry, chocolate, celery, and smoky flavors. It's slightly thin and dry. May come together, but it's a gamble. 1,000 cases made. • $26 • (11/15/97) • **78**

MARTINEZ BUJANDA, BODEGAS

Rioja Conde de Valdemar 1989 • $8 • (12/15/93) • **81**

Rioja Conde de Valdemar Crianza 1994: Ripe and slightly chunky, with jammy flavors of plum and blackberry, notes of chocolate and coffee. Fills the mouth, but the tannins are soft. Drink now through 2000. 50,000 cases made. • $9 • (11/15/97) • **82**

Rioja Conde de Valdemar Crianza 1993: A pleasant spicy note enlivens the cherry and sweet vanilla flavors in this smooth, supple red. It's straightforward, but has enough grip and fruit to match with food. Better than previously reviewed. 40,000 cases made. • $9 • (10/15/96) • **84**

Rioja Conde de Valdemar Crianza 1992 • $10 • (01/31/96) • **82**

Rioja Conde de Valdemar Crianza 1991 • $9 • (04/30/95) • **85**

Rioja Conde de Valdemar Crianza 1990 • $9 • (03/31/94) BB • **87**

Rioja Conde de Valdemar Crianza 1988 • $9 • (03/31/93) • **85**

Rioja Conde de Valdemar Crianza 1987 • $9 • (03/31/92) BB • **90**

Rioja Conde de Valdemar Crianza 1986 • $7 • (03/31/92) • **83**

Rioja Conde de Valdemar Crianza 1985 • $7 • (12/15/88) BB • **89**

Rioja Conde de Valdemar Gran Reserva 1990: Lively and complex, this polished red is maturing now and offers a nice balance of bright cherry and spicy flavors with notes of coffee, cedar, and dried fruits. It's firm, yet turns elegant on the finish. Drink now. 12,000 cases made. • $21 • (11/15/97) • **87**

Rioja Conde de Valdemar Gran Reserva 1989 • $20 • (03/31/96) • **89**

Rioja Conde de Valdemar Gran Reserva 1987 • $20 • (01/31/96) • **83**

Rioja Conde de Valdemar Gran Reserva 1985 • $21 • (04/15/94) HR • **90**

Rioja Conde de Valdemar Gran Reserva 1982 • $22 • (11/30/91) • **89**

Rioja Conde de Valdemar Gran Reserva 1981 • $24 • (03/31/92) • **89**

Rioja Conde de Valdemar Gran Reserva 1975 • $NA • (03/31/92) • **87**

Rioja Conde de Valdemar Gran Reserva 1973 • $30 • (03/31/92) • **86**

Rioja Conde de Valdemar Gran Reserva 1970 • $NA • (03/31/92) • **89**

Rioja Conde de Valdemar Reserva 1992: This supple red offers simple flavors of raisins, coffee, and brown sugar, modest tannins and a clean, almost sweet finish. Drink now. 30,000 cases made. • $14 • (11/15/97) • **80**

Rioja Conde de Valdemar Reserva 1991 • $12 • (03/31/96) • **84**

Rioja Conde de Valdemar Reserva 1990 • $12 • (04/30/95) • **89**

Rioja Conde de Valdemar Reserva 1987 • $12 • (12/15/93) • **84**

Rioja Conde de Valdemar Reserva 1986 • $10 • (03/31/92) • **83**

Rioja Conde de Valdemar Reserva 1985 • $9 • (03/31/92) • **91**

Rioja Conde de Valdemar Reserva 1983 • $14 • (03/31/92) • **88**

Rioja Conde de Valdemar Reserva 1982 • $NA • (03/31/92) • **89**

Rioja Crianza 1990 • $9 • (04/15/94) BB • **87**

Rioja Crianza 1989 • $9 • (04/15/94) BB • **85**

Rioja Garnacha Reserva 1990 • $25 • (03/31/96) • **82**

Rioja Garnacha Reserva 1989 • $22 • (04/30/95) • **86**

Rioja Gran Reserva 1985 • $21 • (04/15/94) • **90**

Rioja Reserva 1990 • $26 • (03/31/96) • **87**

Rioja Reserva 1989: A full-bodied and lively Spanish red that would go well at the dinner table. Ripe and rich, with loads of plum and dried cherry flavors and a spicy finish. Smooth and delicious. • $20 • (05/15/97) • **87**

Rioja Reserva 1987 • $12 • (04/15/94) • **79**

Rioja Reserva Especial 1989 • $25 • (04/30/95) • **87**

Key: SS—Spectator Selection CS—Cellar Selection HR—Highly Recommended BB—Best Buy $NA—Price not available Ⓐ—Auction Price (BT)—Barrel Tasting
Dates in parentheses indicate the issues in which the ratings were published.

Rioja Rosado Conde de Valdemar 1996: Raspberry and watermelon flavors are crisp and well-defined in this generous rosé. Clean and lively, it's a pleasant summer apéritif. 15,000 cases made. • $8 • (09/15/97) • **85**

Rioja Valdemar 1991 • $7 • (03/31/93) BB • **83**

Rioja Valdemar 1989 • $7 • (06/30/90) BB • **83**

Rioja White Conde de Valdemar Fermentado en Barrica 1995: Simply delicious. Tastes like traditional-style Rioja with a strong, spicy aroma and a nice, rich texture. Distinctive, robust and powerful, with flavors of cream, spice, and Sherry and a lingering finish of salt and pepper notes. • $12 • (05/15/97) • **88**

Rioja White Conde de Valdemar Fermentado en Barrica 1994 • $14 • (02/29/96) • **88**

Rioja White Conde de Valdemar Fermentado en Barrica 1993 • $9 • (04/15/94) • **78**

MARTINSANCHO

Verdejo Rueda 1993 • $9 • (12/31/94) • **78**

MAS MARTINET VITICULTORS

Priorat Clos Martinet 1994: This thick, chewy red tastes like sublime blackberry jam, with rich, ripe, concentrated fruit flavors that are almost sweet on the palate. Not truly complex, but there's no denying the allure. Drink now. • $40 • (12/15/97) • **88**

Priorat Martinet Bru 1995: This cheerful, polished red offers bright cherry and licorice flavors, medium-bodied and vibrant, with moderate tannins and a clean finish. Has hints of the crushed-fruit character of Priorat, without the massive structure. Drink now through 2002. • $17 • (06/30/98) • **86**

MASIA BARRIL

Priorat 1996: A hefty dollop of oak gives this velvety red loads of sweet vanilla flavors to back up the ripe cherry ones, but it turns a bit dry on the finish; seems to lack harmony overall. Drink now through 2000. • $17 • (06/30/98) • **84**

Priorat Tipico 1991: A bizarre mix of meaty and sweet flavors give this wine a distinctive but not entirely pleasant character, and big tannins dry out the finish. Tasted twice, with consistent notes. 7,000 cases made. • $16 • (12/15/97) • **73**

MAURO, BODEGAS

Ribera del Duero 1991 • $22 • (04/30/95) • **83**

Ribera del Duero 1990 • $22 • (04/15/94) • **83**

Ribera del Duero 1987 • $17 • (10/15/90) • **82**

Ribera del Duero 1986 • $17 • (03/31/90) • **76**

Ribera del Duero 1985 • $15 • (03/31/90) • **88**

Ribera del Duero 1984 • $16 • (03/31/90) • **78**

Ribera del Duero 1983 • $15 • (10/15/87) • **82**

Viño de Mesa de Castilla y Leon 1995: Chocolate, spice, plum, and herbal flavors mingle in this round, dark red. It shows good balance and a deft use of oak, with moderate concentration. Best from 1999 through 2001. 9,583 cases made. • $25 • (05/15/98) • **85**

Viño de Mesa de Castilla y Leon Selección Especial 1991: Attractive floral, fresh blackberry, and toasty aromas carry through on the palate, which is firm and concentrated, and youthful for its age. Shows a nice balance of sweet fruit and toasty oak, and the tannins are just beginning to soften. Drink now through 2002. 1,247 cases made. • $36 • (05/15/98) • **89**

MENDIANI

Navarra 1990 • $4 • (04/15/92) • **72**

MOLLINA, BODEGAS DE

Ribera del Duero Urbion 1992 • $7 • (04/15/94) • **70**

Ribera del Duero Urbion 1991 • $7 • (04/15/94) • **80**

Ribera del Duero Urbion 1990 • $7 • (04/15/94) • **76**

Ribera del Duero Urbion Crianza 1989 • $11 • (04/15/94) • **89**

Viño de Mesa Tio Vito Red NV • $4 • (04/15/94) • **79**

MONASTERIO, HACIENDA

Ribera del Duero 1992 • $23 • (04/30/96) • **88**

MONISTROL, MARQUÉS DE

Brut Cava Reserva 1992: Nice, rich aromas of cream and butterscotch follow through on the palate. However, it turns a bit candied and rubbery-tasting on the finish. 20,000 cases made. • $10 • (05/15/97) • **78**

Cabernet Sauvignon Penedès 1992: Soft, with pretty berry and cherry flavors that are bright and sweet, light tannins, and enough acidity to keep it lively. Drink now. 7,000 cases made. • $9 • (11/30/97) • **84**

Chardonnay Penedès 1995: Straightforward, with flavors of apples, citrus and bananas, a nice balance of acidity and fruit. The finish is short but clean. Drink it while it's fresh. 7,000 cases made. • $9 • (12/15/97) • **82**

Merlot Penedès 1993: Round and soft, with sweet, jammy flavors of blackberry and boysenberry, soft tannins and a bright, grapey acidity. Quaffable; drink now. 7,000 cases made. • $9 • (12/15/97) • **83**

MONT-MARÇAL

Brut Cava 1994: Earthy, tart aomas are off-putting, but the simple apple cider flavors and aggressive mousse are palatable. Try this sparkler as a base for punch. 50,000 cases made. • $11 • (12/15/97) • **72**

Brut Cava 1993: A nicely perfumed, smooth-textured sparkling wine with subtle fruit, spice and nut flavors. On the soft, light-bodied side and easy to enjoy. 30,000 cases made. • $10 • (07/31/96) • **84**

Brut Cava 1991 • $8 • (06/15/94) • **79**

Brut Cava 1990 • $9 • (03/31/93) • **78**

Cabernet Sauvignon Penedès 1989 • $9 • (12/15/93) • **82**

Penedès 1988 • $8 • (03/31/91) • **83**

Penedès Reserva 1989: This straightforward red is fresh and clean but shows little development for its age, with black cherry, light cola, and herb flavors over moderate tannins. It's balanced and accessible now. A blend of Cabernet, Tempranillo and Merlot. • $10 • (10/31/97) • **84**

MONTE VANNOS

Ribera del Duero 1994 • $11 • (04/30/96) • **77**

Ribera del Duero 1992 • $10 • (04/15/94) • **86**

Ribera del Duero 1991 • $10 • (12/15/92) • **77**

Ribera del Duero Reserva 1989 • $16 • (02/28/95) • **85**

Ribera del Duero Reserva Baños de Valdearados 1985 • $28 • (01/31/93) • **84**

MONTECILLO, BODEGAS

Rioja Gran Reserva 1978 • $30 • (03/31/90) • **85**

Rioja Gran Reserva 1975 • $29 • (12/15/88) • **85**

Rioja Gran Reserva 1973 • $30 • (04/30/95) • **80**

Rioja Gran Reserva 1970 • $45 • (01/31/96) • **87**

Rioja Primera Seleccion 1995: This ripe red shows firm tannins and plush flavors of plums, prunes, and coffee. Turns a bit tough on the finish. Tasted twice, with consistent notes. Drink now. 1,000 cases made. • $14 • (12/15/97) • **78**

Rioja Reserva 1989: Maturing now, this traditional-style Rioja shows classic flavors of tea, spice, dried cherries, and light leather, with a supple texture and a long finish. Has good definition and length. Drink now. 10,000 cases made. • $12 • (10/15/97) • **86**

Rioja Rosado 1995: Round and soft, this offers light watermelon and cherry flavors, and there's a bit of tannin for grip on the finish. It's delicate, but well defined. • $9 • (09/15/97) • **83**

Rioja Viña Cumbrero Crianza 1994: This bright red has soft texture, sweet, toasty oak flavors, and a pretty core of raspberry. It's appealing on its own, but has enough structure to match with lighter dishes. Drink now. • $8 • (10/15/97) • **86**

Rioja Viña Cumbrero Crianza 1993: Light and soft, offering simple cherry and vanilla flavors, balanced for easy drinking now, with just enough tannin for grip. Modest but refreshing. Drink now. • $9 • (12/15/97) • **83**

Rioja Viña Cumbrero Crianza 1991 • $7 • (03/31/96) • **84**

Rioja Viña Cumbrero Crianza 1990 • $7 • (04/30/95) • **87**

Rioja Viña Cumbrero Crianza 1989 • $7 • (04/15/94) BB • **84**

Rioja Viña Cumbrero Crianza 1988 • $NA • (03/31/92) • **89**

Rioja Viña Cumbrero Crianza 1987 • $6 • (08/31/91) BB • **85**

Rioja Viña Cumbrero Crianza 1986 • $5 • (03/31/90) • **66**

Rioja Viña Cumbrero Crianza 1985 • $5 • (11/15/88) BB • **80**
Rioja Viña Cumbrero Crianza 1982 • $4 • (11/15/87) • **79**
Rioja Viña Cumbrero Crianza 1981 • $4 • (06/01/86) BB • **73**
Rioja Viña Monty 1978 • $7 • (09/30/86) • **81**
Rioja Viña Monty 1976 • $6 • (05/16/86) • **70**
Rioja Viña Monty Gran Reserva 1987: Lovely cigar-box and tea aromas, supple, polished texture, flavors of dried fruit, vanilla, and spice. With good body and firm tannins, it's a food wine made in the traditional style. Drink now. 15,000 cases made. • $16 • (10/15/97) • **88**
Rioja Viña Monty Gran Reserva 1986 • $16 • (04/30/95) • **73**
Rioja Viña Monty Gran Reserva 1985 • $15 • (03/31/94) HR • **89**
Rioja Viña Monty Gran Reserva 1982 • $14 • (03/31/92) • **87**
Rioja Viña Monty Gran Reserva 1981 • $13 • (03/31/92) • **88**
Rioja Viña Monty Gran Reserva 1980 • $7 • (11/30/87) • **79**
Rioja Viña Monty Gran Reserva 1978 • $28 • (03/31/92) • **82**
Rioja Viña Monty Gran Reserva 1975 • $28 • (03/31/92) • **86**
Rioja Viña Monty Gran Reserva 1973 • $35 • (03/31/92) • **85**
Rioja Viña Monty Gran Reserva 1970 • $40 • (03/31/92) • **87**
Rioja White Viña Cumbrero 1995: Assertive toasty, smoky flavors dominate and verge on burnt, detracting from the modest apple flavors. Medium-bodied and quite crisp. Drink now. • $9 • (10/31/97) • **80**
Rioja White Viña Cumbrero 1993 • $7 • (07/31/95) • **79**

MONTELEIVA, BODEGAS

Rioja Viña Saseta Gran Reserva 1985 • $31 • (04/30/95) • **83**

MONTEVANNOS, BODEGAS

Ribera del Duero 1996: This lean, dry red offers light berry and herbal flavors and a slight spritz on the palate. It's a bit earthy and quite austere. Try now. 5,000 cases made. • $11 • (10/31/97) • **77**
Ribera del Duero 1995: Balanced and lively, but the fruit flavors are reminiscent of cherry Life-Savers served with an herbal crust, and it lacks concentration on the palate. Accessible now. 4,000 cases made. • $13 • (10/31/97) • **79**
Ribera del Duero Crianza 1994: This well-balanced red is so harmonious, it's almost anonymous; with cherry, licorice and spice flavors tucked inside firm, ripe tannins. A fine match with food. Accessible now. 120,000 cases made. • $13 • (10/31/97) • **86**
Ribera del Duero Reserva 1992: This light red offers pretty flavors of strawberries, tea, and spices, supple yet with some intensity. It's balanced and still fresh, but drink now. 100,000 cases made. • $21 • (10/31/97) • **84**

MONTSARRA

In Fraganti Penedès 1995: This supple, grapey red shows light licorice and herbal accents and soft tannins. It's simple and goes down easily. Drink now. • $8 • (10/15/96) • **81**

MORALES, BODEGAS HERMANOS

La Mancha Gran Creacion Crianza 1992 • $7 • (04/30/95) BB • **84**

MORGADÍO, ADEGAS

Albariño Rias Baixas 1996: This appealing white is both rich and ethereal, delicate on the palate yet assertively flavored with notes of lime, almond, and herbs. It's clean and fresh, yet the harmonious flavors linger on the finish. 8,000 cases made. • $17 • (10/31/97) • **87**
Albariño Rias Baixas 1994 • $18 • (07/31/95) • **80**
Albariño Rias Baixas 1993 • $18 • (12/31/94) • **85**
Albariño Rias Baixas Torre Fornelos 1994 • $13 • (07/31/95) • **82**

MOURE, ADEGAS

Mencía Ribeira Sacra Abadia da Cova 1996: This round, light red offers bright grapey flavors with hints of game and herbs and a soft, Beaujolais-like structure. Drink now. 5,000 cases made. • $6 • (11/15/97) • **81**

Key: SS—Spectator Selection CS—Cellar Selection HR—Highly Recommended BB—Best Buy $NA—Price not available Ⓐ—Auction Price (BT)—Barrel Tasting
Dates in parentheses indicate the issues in which the ratings were published.

MUERZA, BODEGAS

Rioja Vega 1989 • $7 • (03/31/91) • **77**
Rioja Vega Crianza 1994: This exuberant red from Spain shows bright flavors, good balance, and decent concentration. Notes of black cherry, tobacco, and herbs mingle on the lively palate, with vanilla and spice accents and moderate tannins. Makes delicious drinking now, at an attractive price. 12,000 cases made. • $10 • (11/30/97) BB • **88**
Rioja Vega Crianza 1993: Light yet firm, traditional in style, with characteristic flavors of tea, smoke and dried cherries. Not big, but shows some elegance. 13,520 cases made. • $11 • (06/30/97) • **84**
Rioja Vega Crianza 1990 • $9 • (12/15/94) • **84**
Rioja Vega Crianza 1989 • $9 • (04/15/94) • **85**
Rioja Vega Crianza 1986 • $10 • (03/31/91) • **75**

MUGA-VILLFRANCA, BODEGAS

Navarra Mendiani 1989 • $4 • (06/15/91) BB • **82**

MUGA, BODEGAS

Rioja 1990 • $13 • (03/31/95) • **82**
Rioja 1986 • $12 • (05/31/91) • **81**
Rioja 1985 • $12 • (03/31/90) • **83**
Rioja 1984 • $9 • (04/30/89) • **82**
Rioja 1982 • $7 • (11/15/87) • **77**
Rioja Gran Reserva 1976 • $20 • (03/31/90) • **77**
Rioja Prado Enea Gran Reserva 1985 • $35 • (04/30/95) • **87**
Rioja Prado Enea Gran Reserva 1982 • $40 • (11/30/91) • **84**
Rioja Prado Enea Gran Reserva 1981 • $20 • (04/30/89) • **80**
Rioja Prado Enea Gran Reserva 1976 • $60 • (03/31/90) • **84**
Rioja Reserva 1992: Enticing vanilla aromas give way to light but fresh flavors of cherries, vanilla, and licorice. Firm and light-bodied. Drink now. • $14 • (02/28/98) • **84**
Rioja Reserva 1991: A lush texture and a little spice, but not much fruit. Flavors are slightly dull and cooked, though might perk up with food. It's tannic, too; try now. Tasted twice. 6,000 cases made. • $13 • (08/31/96) • **80**
Rioja Reserva 1989 • $13 • (04/15/94) • **85**
Rioja Reserva 1988 • $13 • (04/15/94) • **87**
Rioja Rosado 1995: Dull and flat. Its orange color, candied aromas, and simple fruit flavors suggest it should have been consumed by now. • $9 • (01/01/97) • **74**
Rioja Torre Muga Reserva 1991: This Spanish red is rich and polished, its beautiful aromas of cocoa and coffee testifying to the winemaker's deft use of oak. It's balanced and long and offers ripe, lively flavors of fresh blackberries and plums. Decant one hour before serving. Impressive now, better in 2002. 3,000 cases made. • $50 • (02/28/98) CS • **91**
Rioja White Barrel Fermented 1996: Soft-textured and sunny, in an international style. Combines sweet oaky notes with ripe apple and melon flavors. Drink now. • $10 • (02/28/98) • **84**
Rioja White Barrel Fermented 1995: Heavily toasty, almost charred aromas and flavors may deter all but the most fervent fans of oak. Shows some apple notes, but the finish is almost bitter. 3,000 cases made. • $10 • (12/15/97) • **79**

MURRIETA, BODEGAS MARQUÉS DE

Rioja 1985 • $17 • (02/28/90) • **87**
Rioja Castillo Ygay Gran Reserva 1968 • $85 • (03/31/90) • **92**
Rioja Castillo Ygay Gran Reserva 1952 • $150 • (03/31/90) • **94**
Rioja Crianza 1991 • $11 • (12/15/94) • **86**
Rioja Crianza 1990 • $10 • (04/15/94) BB • **88**
Rioja Gran Reserva 1983 • $20 • (04/15/94) • **88**
Rioja Gran Reserva 1982 • $60 • (04/15/94) • **89**
Rioja Gran Reserva 1978 • $30 • (03/31/92) • **87**
Rioja Gran Reserva 1975 • $35 • (03/31/92) • **93**
Rioja Gran Reserva 1973 • $30 • (03/31/92) • **89**
Rioja Gran Reserva 1970 • $NA • (03/31/92) • **83**
Rioja Reserva 1990 • $15 • (04/30/95) • **81**
Rioja Reserva 1988 • $12 • (04/15/94) • **87**
Rioja Reserva 1986 • $20 • (03/31/92) • **88**
Rioja Reserva 1985 • $20 • (03/31/92) • **90**
Rioja Reserva 1983 • $13 • (03/31/92) • **85**
Rioja Reserva 1982 • $39 • (03/31/92) • **84**

Rioja Reserva 1981 • $39 • (03/31/92) • **88**
Rioja Reserva 1980 • $27 • (03/31/90) • **83**
Rioja White Misela 1993: The price is right for this bold and distinctive white from Spain, delivering a lively mix of vanilla, honey, lemon, and herbal flavors that are more assertive than integrated. It's clean and crisp, and will show best with food. Drink now. 16,000 cases made. • $8 • (10/31/97) BB • **86**
Rioja Ygay Reserva 1992: Shows ripeness and concentration, with plum, toast, and coffee flavors and firm tannins. Drink now. 60,000 cases made. • $15 • (10/15/97) • **85**
Rioja Ygay Reserva Especial 1989: A powerful yet fresh wine, this Spanish red exhibits excellent concentration, with rich, ripe tannins and exuberant fruit flavors of kirsch, blackberry, and licorice. Best now through 2001. Tasted twice, with consistent notes. 30,000 cases made. • $20 • (11/15/97) SS • **89**

NAVARRA, VINICOLA

Navarra Castillo de Tiebas Reserva 1976 • $7 • (01/31/88) • **80**
Navarra Las Campanas Crianza 1991 • $7 • (04/30/96) • **83**
Navarra Las Campanas Tino Tinto 1982 • $5 • (01/31/88) • **77**
Navarra Rosé Las Campanas 1993 • $7 • (08/31/95) • **83**

NEKEAS, BODEGA

Cabernet Sauvignon-Tempranillo Navarra Vega Sindoa 1995: Ripe fruit flavors, well-integrated toasty oak notes, and a polished texture provide a sophisticated appeal to this Cabernet blend from Spain. Harmonious, firm and still quite young, it's a great buy now. Drink now. 5,000 cases available in the U.S. • $7 • (06/15/97) BB • **88**
Cabernet Sauvignon-Tempranillo Navarra Vega Sindoa 1993: Firm and well knit, this lean wine shows spice, tobacco, and cherry flavors with dry tannins in a compact structure. A traditional-style wine. 5,000 cases made. • $6 • (08/31/96) • **81**
Chardonnay Navarra Vega Sindoa Barrel Fermented 1996: Fresh and lively, with round flavors of apples, peaches, and citrus; fruity and crisp. Has enough body to stand up to food. 5,000 cases made. • $9 • (10/31/97) • **84**
Merlot Navarra Vega Sindoa 1995: A polished wine of deep color, toasty oak and ripe plum flavors—hallmarks of the contemporary international style—with spicy undertones and well-balanced acidity that keep it distinctive. Drinkable now, but should improve through 2000. • $9 • (06/15/97) • **89**
Merlot Navarra Vega Sindoa 1993: Bright fruit and sweet oak give immediate appeal. Plump with plum and blackberry flavors and a strong vanilla note on the finish. Balanced and firm. Drink now. 2,000 cases made. • $10 • (08/31/96) • **85**
Navarra Rosado Vega Sindoa 1996: Round and full on the palate. Delivers ripe cherry, herb, and light earth flavors, then finishes with a slightly bitter note. Best with food. • $7 • (02/28/98) • **82**
Viura-Chardonnay Navarra Vega Sindoa 1996: Quite rich, this lush white offers melon, apple, and almond flavors with plenty of acidity to keep them lively. It's full-bodied yet firm, a good match with food. 6,000 cases made. • $6 • (10/31/97) • **85**

OCHOA, BODEGAS

Cabernet Sauvignon Navarra 1987 • $14 • (09/30/91) • **77**
Navarra 1988 • $8 • (09/30/91) BB • **83**
Navarra 1987 • $14 • (09/30/91) • **79**
Navarra 1986 • $6 • (04/15/89) • **73**
Navarra Crianza 1986 • $10 • (11/15/91) • **73**
Navarra Crianza 1984 • $8 • (04/15/89) • **82**
Navarra Reserva 1985 • $10 • (04/15/94) • **83**
Navarra Reserva 1982 • $14 • (09/30/91) • **73**
Navarra Reserva 1980 • $11 • (04/15/89) • **85**
Tempranillo Navarra 1990 • $10 • (04/15/94) • **82**

OLARRA, BODEGAS

Rioja 1983 • $5 • (09/30/86) BB • **87**
Rioja 1982 • $NA • (11/15/87) • **86**
Rioja 1980 • $4 • (03/16/85) BB • **87**
Rioja Añares 1987 • $6 • (03/31/92) • **79**
Rioja Añares 1985 • $6 • (02/28/89) BB • **82**
Rioja Añares 1983 • $6 • (02/28/90) • **76**
Rioja Añares Gran Reserva 1983 • $19 • (03/31/92) • **75**
Rioja Añares Gran Reserva 1982 • $27 • (11/30/91) • **75**
Rioja Añares Gran Reserva 1981 • $25 • (03/31/92) • **76**
Rioja Añares Reserva 1985 • $25 • (03/31/92) • **83**
Rioja Añares Reserva 1983 • $12 • (02/28/90) • **73**
Rioja Añares Reserva 1981 • $8 • (09/30/86) • **88**
Rioja Añares Reserva 1978 • $8 • (03/16/85) • **82**
Rioja Cerro Añon 1984 • $4 • (12/01/85) • **70**
Rioja Cerro Añon 1980 • $4 • (04/01/85) • **75**
Rioja Cerro Añon Gran Reserva 1983 • $19 • (03/31/92) • **83**
Rioja Cerro Añon Gran Reserva 1982 • $27 • (11/30/91) • **71**
Rioja Cerro Añon Gran Reserva 1981 • $25 • (03/31/92) • **87**
Rioja Cerro Añon Gran Reserva 1973 • $NA • (03/31/92) • **81**
Rioja Cerro Añon Gran Reserva 1970 • $NA • (03/31/92) • **75**
Rioja Cerro Añon Reserva 1985 • $NA • (03/31/92) • **73**
Rioja Cerro Añon Reserva 1983 • $11 • (03/31/90) • **61**
Rioja Cerro Añon Reserva 1981 • $8 • (09/30/86) • **78**
Rioja Cerro Añon Reserva 1978 • $8 • (03/01/85) • **83**

OÑA, TORRE DE

Rioja Barón de Oña Reserva 1992: Lean and dry, with flavors of coffee, herbs, and dried fruits, drying tannins and a short finish. A tough wine that lacks fruit character. Drink now. 14,000 cases made. • $14 • (05/31/98) • **78**
Rioja Barón de Oña Reserva 1991: Coffee and tobacco aromas give way to candied-cherry and toast flavors. So ripe and oaky, it's almost sweet, with light tannins and a hot finish. Drink now. Made by La Rioja Alta and aged in barrels used by Château Margaux. • $14 • (02/28/98) • **82**
Rioja Barón de Oña Reserva 1989: Meaty, gamy flavors dominate the light cherry fruit. Thick and rather dull, especially on the finish. • $15 • (08/31/96) • **76**

ONDARRE, BODEGAS

Rioja Ondarre 1984 • $5 • (11/15/88) BB • **80**
Rioja Reserva 1981 • $7 • (12/15/88) BB • **84**
Rioja Tidon 1986 • $4 • (12/15/88) • **78**

ONIX

Priorat 1995: Juicy ripe fruit flavors of blackberries and raspberries marry nicely with spicy cinnamon accents in this lively, well-balanced red. The tannins are firm but well integrated; the wine is accessible now, but should improve through 2000. • $8 • (10/31/97) • **87**
Priorat 1992 • $7 • (04/15/94) BB • **84**
Priorat Collita 1992 • $7 • (04/30/95) • **86**

PADIN, BODEGAS PABLO

Alabariño Rias Baixas Segrel 1996: This vivid white mingles toasty, nutty flavors from oak with mineral and apple notes in a fresh, balanced wine that stays lively through the finish. A good match for grilled fish. Drink now. • $14 • (05/31/98) • **86**
Rias Baixas Segrel Especial 1996: A pleasing mix of vanilla and herbal notes gives this white distinctive character. The melon and apple flavors are ripe yet firm, with good concentration, and linger on the finish. Note: Especial is not designated on the label; only a diagonal orange stripe distinguishes this from the regular bottling. Drink now through 2000. • $18 • (05/31/98) • **88**

PADORNINA

El Bierzo 1987 • $8 • (03/31/90) • **81**
El Bierzo 1985 • $7 • (06/30/90) • **74**

PALACIO DE LA VEGA

Cabernet Sauvignon Navarra Reserva 1993: This herb-scented red is still lively, with crisp cherry flavor and a nice touch of toasty oak. Clean and fresh. Drink now. 36,000 cases made. • $18 • (10/31/97) • **86**
Chardonnay Navarra 1995: Maturing now, this smooth white shows light melon, honey and herbal notes. Lush on the palate, a bit soft on the finish. Harmonious and clean. 24,000 cases made. • $16 • (10/31/97) • **84**
Merlot Navarra Crianza 1994: Lush and generous, this rich red shows ripe cherry, plum, and chocolate flavors in a velvety structure that masks firm tannins. Made in an international style, it shows a good balance of oak and

fruit. Drinkable now and should improve through 1999. 36,000 cases made. • $16 • (10/31/97) • **88**

Navarra Crianza 1994: This rich red shows deep color, good concentration, firm tannins and ripe fruit, with chewy plum, tobacco, licorice, and earth flavors. Try now. Tasted twice, with consistent notes. 600,000 cases made. • $12 • (11/30/97) • **85**

Navarra Crianza 1991 • $NA • (04/15/94) • **83**

Navarra Rosado 1996: This expressive rosé offers vivid strawberry aromas and flavors, yet stays crisp and dry on the palate, with enough body to stand up to food. Not subtle, but it works. Made from 70 percent Grenache and 30 percent Cabernet Sauvignon. 420,000 cases made. • $9 • (09/15/97) • **83**

Tempranillo Navarra 1996: This well-structured wine shows deep color, firm tannins, and crisp acidity. The flavors are rather muted now, but hint at plum, licorice, and cedar. Try now. • $9 • (11/15/97) • **85**

Tempranillo Navarra Reserva 1993: This sturdy red offers thickly textured ripe blackberry flavors backed by notes of herbs and vanilla. Still quite young and firm, but should be enjoyed now for its vigor. 36,000 cases made. • $16 • (11/15/97) • **85**

PALACIO, BODEGAS

Rioja Cosme Palacio y Hermanos 1989 • $13 • (09/30/92) • **84**
Rioja Cosme Palacio y Hermanos 1988 • $13 • (09/30/92) • **84**
Rioja Cosme Palacio y Hermanos 1987 • $13 • (03/31/90) • **83**
Rioja Cosme Palacio y Hermanos 1986 • $9 • (02/28/89) • **88**
Rioja Glorioso 1986 • $8 • (03/31/90) • **80**
Rioja Glorioso 1985 • $7 • (02/28/89) BB • **85**
Rioja Glorioso Gran Reserva 1982 • $19 • (11/30/91) • **84**
Rioja Glorioso Gran Reserva 1981 • $20 • (03/31/93) • **85**
Rioja Glorioso Gran Reserva 1978 • $15 • (02/28/89) • **88**
Rioja Glorioso Reserva 1982 • $18 • (03/31/90) • **79**
Rioja Glorioso Reserva 1981 • $10 • (02/28/89) • **83**

PALACIOS, ALVARO

Priorat Finca Dofí 1995: This intense red hides extraordinary concentration under a smooth, polished surface. The tannins are dominating, but the longer you chew them, the more fruit emerges; ripe and complex, with plum, cassis and blackberry notes. Has the power of vintage Port, with marginally less alcohol. Best from 2000 through 2010. • $40 • (06/30/98) • **93**

Priorat Finca Dofí 1994: A full-bodied Spanish red that attacks the palate with firm tannins and lively acidity, yet there's plenty of raspberry, blackberry, and licorice flavors beneath and the finish is long and clean (and alcoholic). This dry red has the power and profile of a young vintage Port and needs until 2000 to show best. 1,165 cases made. • $35 • (09/15/97) HR • **92**

Priorat Finca Dofí 1990 • $35 • (08/31/93) • **85**
Priorat Finca Dofí 1989 • $40 • (01/31/92) • **89**

Priorat L'Ermita 1995: Such a powerful mouthful of wine that after you swallow, it's almost hard to talk. Explosively aromatic, with jam, tar, licorice, and exotic spices, it leads with concentrated fruit, then follows with a sledgehammer of polished tannins that somehow dissolve on the finish, where the fruit re-emerges like a rainbow. With a huge slab of well-aged, char-grilled beef, paradise. Drink now through 2005. • $135 • (06/30/98) • **97**

Priorat L'Ermita 1994: Rich yet polished, this mouthfilling red adds the chocolate and coffee flavors of new-oak aging to the region's ripe, rich flavors of raspberries and plums. Already harmonious, but should expand and soften starting around 2000. 450 cases made. • $130 • (09/15/97) • **94**

Priorat Les Terrasses 1995: Well crafted, showing a harmonious balance of clean, cherry flavors, firm, ripe tannins and fresh acidity. If it lacks exuberance, it promises smooth, long development. Drink now through 2005. • $20 • (06/30/98) • **88**

PALACIOS REMONDO, BODEGAS

Garnacha Rioja Rosado Herencia Remondo 1996: Hefty, from the weight on the palate to the expressive flavors of strawberries and almonds. Dry and refreshing, with a pretty pink color. • $8 • (02/28/98) • **84**

Rioja Herencia Remondo 1987 • $6 • (03/31/92) • **84**

Key: SS—Spectator Selection CS—Cellar Selection HR—Highly Recommended BB—Best Buy $NA—Price not available Ⓐ—Auction Price (BT)—Barrel Tasting
Dates in parentheses indicate the issues in which the ratings were published.

Rioja Herencia Remondo 1986 • $6 • (03/31/92) • **76**
Rioja Herencia Remondo 1985 • $NA • (03/31/90) • **81**
Rioja Herencia Remondo 1982 • $NA • (11/15/87) • **90**

Rioja Herencia Remondo Crianza 1994: This round and soft red from Spain shows ripe flavors of plums and raisins; a bit sweet, with cinnamon and vanilla notes adding dimension. Its firm tannins kick in on the finish and help it stand up to food. Reasonably priced, and ready to drink. 20,000 cases made. • $10 • (02/28/98) BB • **85**

Rioja Herencia Remondo Gran Reserva 1987: This traditional-style red is fully mature, soft and silky, with light but intense cherry, cedar, vanilla, and herbal flavors. Still has bright acidity, and remains lively, if delicate, on the palate. Tasted twice, with consistent notes. Drink now. • $25 • (05/31/98) • **88**

Rioja Herencia Remondo Gran Reserva 1982 • $13 • (01/31/92) • **78**
Rioja Herencia Remondo Gran Reserva 1975 • $NA • (03/31/92) • **79**
Rioja Herencia Remondo Gran Reserva 1973 • $NA • (03/31/92) • **77**

Rioja Herencia Remondo Reserva 1992: Shows tobacco, coffee, plum, and herb flavors. Round, with balanced acid and tannin, but not much character. Drink now. • $14 • (02/28/98) • **81**

Rioja Herencia Remondo Reserva 1986 • $10 • (03/31/92) • **79**
Rioja Herencia Remondo Reserva 1985 • $NA • (03/31/92) • **71**

Tempranillo Rioja Herencia Remondo 1996: A quasi-Beaujolais style, light but a bit harsh, with grapey and smoky flavors and slightly drying tannins. • $8 • (02/28/98) • **78**

Viura Rioja White Herencia Remondo 1996: Soft, fruity, and light. Floral, apple, and light citrus flavors caress the palate, then disappear. A nice apéritif. • $8 • (02/28/98) • **83**

PATERNINA, BODEGAS FEDERICO

Rioja Banda Azul Crianza 1994: Oodles of oak give strong, sweet vanilla flavors and mouthfilling tannins, but there's sufficient raspberry flavor for balance, at least with food. Drink now. • $8 • (10/15/97) • **84**

Rioja Banda Azul Crianza 1993 • $9 • (03/31/96) • **78**
Rioja Banda Azul Crianza 1985 • $5 • (03/15/90) BB • **80**
Rioja Gran Reserva 1987 • $20 • (03/31/96) • **76**
Rioja Viña Vial Reserva 1991 • $14 • (03/31/96) • **79**

PAZO DE BARRANTES, BODEGAS

Albariño Rias Baixas 1996: This crisp, lean white has the steely acidity and mineral flavors of a Rheingau Riesling. Though the citrus and green apple flavors are a bit muted, the wine has good nerve and intensity; best with food. Drink now through 2000. • $20 • (05/31/98) • **87**

PAZO DE SENORANS

Albariño Rias Baixas 1996: Floral and herbal aromas are alluring, and on the palate this firm white is clean and fresh, with pear, almond, and orange peel flavors. Reminiscent of Viognier, it makes a delightful apéritif. Drink now. • $15 • (05/31/98) • **88**

PAZO DE VILLAREI

Albariño Rias Baixas 1996: Distinctive cinnamon and ginger notes give this white personality. It has softer acidity than many Albariños, but the ripe pear and spicy flavors linger on the finish. • $13 • (09/15/97) • **86**

PENALBA

Ribera del Duero 1983 • $12 • (02/28/90) • **86**
Ribera del Duero Crianza 1985 • $9 • (02/28/90) • **87**
Ribera del Duero Gran Reserva 1980 • $NA • (03/31/90) • **73**
Ribera del Duero Reserva 1982 • $NA • (03/31/90) • **70**

PERELADA, CASTILLO

Cabernet Sauvignon Empordà-Costa Brava 1991 • $10 • (04/30/96) • **80**

Cabernet Sauvignon Empordà-Costa Brava Rosado 1994: Peppery in character, with some pleasant fruit aromas and berry flavors. Simple and satisfying. • $9 • (01/01/97) • **79**

Empordà-Costa Brava Crianza 1993 • $7 • (04/30/96) • **77**
Empordà-Costa Brava Reserva 1990 • $9 • (04/30/96) • **80**

PEREZ PASCUAS, BODEGAS HNOS.

Ribera del Duero Viña Pedrosa 1992 • $23 • (04/30/96) • **87**
Ribera del Duero Viña Pedrosa 1991 • $20 • (04/30/95) • **78**
Ribera del Duero Viña Pedrosa 1990 • $16 • (04/15/94) • **88**
Ribera del Duero Viña Pedrosa 1989 • $18 • (04/15/92) • **86**
Ribera del Duero Viña Pedrosa 1988 • $16 • (05/31/91) • **82**
Ribera del Duero Viña Pedrosa 1987 • $15 • (09/30/90) • **77**
Ribera del Duero Viña Pedrosa 1986 • $14 • (03/31/90) • **88**
Ribera del Duero Viña Pedrosa 1985 • $16 • (09/15/88) • **83**
Ribera del Duero Viña Pedrosa Crianza 1994: This powerful red relies on fruit, not oak, to make its point, with ripe, rich flavors of black cherry, game, and herbs supported by firm, clean tannins and just a hint of toast. It's concentrated but not heavy, with a polished mouthfeel and good acidity for balance. A wonderful example of the traditional style. Best from 2000 through 2010. 25,000 cases made. • $27 • (01/01/98) • **93**
Ribera del Duero Viña Pedrosa Reserva 1990 • $50/1.5 liter • (04/30/96) • **77**

PIEDEMONTE, BODEGAS

Cabernet Sauvignon Navarra Crianza 1994: Plump with fruit yet nicely balanced, this round red offers black cherry, blackberry, and vanilla flavors over moderate tannins, with a clean, refreshing finish. Drinkable now. 2,500 cases made. • $8 • (10/31/97) • **86**
Cabernet Sauvignon Navarra Oligitum 1995: Clean and fresh, this polished red offers well-defined, firm, but accessible black cherry, herb, and toast flavors that linger on the finish. A food-friendly wine for drinking now through 2001. 4,000 cases made. • $6 • (10/31/97) • **87**
Merlot Navarra Oligitum 1995: Ripe, slightly raisiny aromas follow through on the thick palate, with flavors of chocolate and toast. The tannins are firm but well integrated, and black cherry notes emerge on the finish. Try now. 4,000 cases made. • $6 • (10/31/97) • **84**
Navarra Coupage Crianza 1994: Round, lush, and balanced, this red delivers plenty of cherry flavor and accents of toast, vanilla, and spice. It's drinking well now, with just enough grip to match with food. A blend of Cabernet, Tempranillo and Merlot. 12,000 cases made. • $8 • (10/31/97) • **87**
Navarra Oligitum 1995: Plump and fruity, this lively red offers generous dollops of sweet vanilla, Bing cherry, and toast flavors, with just enough tannin for grip. A likable wine that's drinkable now. A blend of Cabernet and Tempranillo. 4,500 cases made. • $6 • (10/31/97) • **85**
Navarra White Agnes de Cleves 1995: Light and very crisp, this clean, neutral white offers hints of mineral and herb. It's refreshing, if simple. 4,500 cases made. • $5 • (06/30/97) • **82**
Tempranillo Navarra Oligitum 1996: This thick, smooth red offers ripe black cherry and smoke flavors, with firm tannins and a fruity finish. Drink now. 10,000 cases made. • $6 • (10/31/97) • **82**

PIQUERAS, BODEGAS

Almansa Castillo de Almansa Crianza 1988 • $NA • (04/15/94) • **82**
Almansa Castillo de Almansa Crianza 1987 • $9 • (01/31/93) • **79**
Almansa Castillo de Almansa Crianza 1986 • $8 • (04/15/92) BB • **83**
Almansa Castillo de Almansa Crianza 1985 • $8 • (09/30/91) BB • **85**
Almansa Castillo de Almansa Crianza 1983 • $6 • (07/31/89) BB • **88**

PIRINEOS, BODEGA

Moristel Somontano Montesierra 1996: This fruity red is soft in texture, with bright flavors of black cherry, smoke, and light herbs. Doesn't show much varietal character, but it's plump and quaffable now. 7,000 cases made. • $7 • (10/31/97) • **83**
Moristel Somontano Montesierra 1995: Light, soft and fruity. Herbal notes perk up the grape flavors. Served chilled, it goes down easily. 4,000 cases made. • $6 • (08/31/96) • **79**
Moristel Somontano Montesierra 1993 • $5 • (01/31/95) • **78**
Moristel Somontano Montesierra 1988 • $6 • (03/31/90) • **81**
Moristel Somontano Montesierra 1987 • $6 • (09/15/88) • **80**
Moristel Somontano Montesierra 1986 • $5 • (11/15/87) • **77**

POBOLEDA

Priorat 1996: This firm red shows flavors of cherries, tobacco, and herbs, with hard tannins and sharp acidity. Unyielding now, it should soften with age. Best from 1999 through 2002. • $10 • (06/30/98) • **84**

POVEDA, SALVADOR

Monastrell Alicante 1987 • $6 • (11/15/91) • **76**
Monastrell Alicante No. 1 Gran Reserva 1985 • $9 • (11/15/91) • **79**
Monastrell Alicante Reserva 1989 • $8 • (04/30/96) • **80**
Monastrell Alicante Reserva 1988 • $9 • (04/15/94) BB • **83**
Monastrell Alicante Reserva 1987 • $9 • (03/31/93) • **82**

PRIMICIA, BODEGAS

Rioja Viña Diezmo Crianza 1994: This dark, brooding red from Spain offers earthy, gamy, and chestnut flavors, concentrated and well-defined, over very firm tannins. Drink now. 26,000 cases made. • $10 • (11/15/97) BB • **86**
Rioja Viña Diezmo Reserva 1989: Ripe and plump, still fresh, with plum and black cherry flavors and accents of vanilla and toast. It has round tannins that will marry well with food. Drinkable now. 20,000 cases made. • $14 • (11/15/97) • **85**

PRINCIPE DE VIANA, BODEGAS

Cabernet Sauvignon Navarra 1989 • $8 • (03/31/91) BB • **83**
Cabernet Sauvignon Navarra Crianza 1990 • $8 • (04/15/94) • **82**

PROTOS, BODEGAS

Ribera del Duero 1996: Exhibits good concentration, with ripe fruit flavors of plum and prune, and firm, full tannins, but a strong gamy note detracts now. Try in 1999. 10,000 cases made. • $9 • (11/15/97) • **84**
Ribera del Duero Crianza 1994: This ripe, well-balanced wine offers vivid flavors of kirsch, blackberry, chocolate, and smoke; the tannins are firm yet ripe, the finish long and subtle. Accessible now, but should be better in 1999. Tasted twice, with consistent notes. 6,000 cases made. • $17 • (11/15/97) • **89**
Ribera del Duero Gran Reserva 1989: Lush, showing mature flavors of dried fruits, tea, and leather, with good concentration and firm tannins, but the finish is still fresh, with pleasant berry notes. A big, slightly clumsy wine with traditional character. Drink now through 2000. 2,000 cases made. • $40 • (11/15/97) • **87**

PUERTO, MARQUÉS DEL

Rioja 1984 • $7 • (02/28/90) • **78**
Rioja 1982 • $6 • (11/15/87) • **78**
Rioja Crianza 1994: A firm red that marries traditional flavors with modern structure. Gamy aromas give way to black cherry, light cola, and cinnamon notes, fresh on the palate and quite long on the finish. Drinkable now. • $9 • (11/15/97) • **85**
Rioja Crianza 1988 • $12 • (03/31/93) • **85**
Rioja Gran Reserva 1985 • $16 • (04/30/95) • **86**
Rioja Gran Reserva 1978 • $20 • (03/31/90) • **85**
Rioja Reserva 1991: Supple and harmonious, still fairly fresh, with cherry, berry, spice, and tea flavors and a pretty berry-scented finish. Well made, in a lighter style. Drink now. • $13 • (11/15/97) • **83**
Rioja Reserva 1987 • $10 • (04/30/95) • **83**
Rioja Roman Paladino Gran Reserva 1975: As delicate as a cobweb, this light, sweet red offers fragile flavors of tea, brown sugar, and spice over light tannins. It's still alive, but barely, so grab it before it blows away. • $35 • (11/15/97) • **78**

PUIG & ROCA, CELLERS

Cabernet Sauvignon Penedès Augustus 1991 • $11 • (03/31/95) • **84**

RAIMAT

Cabernet Sauvignon Costers del Segre 1989 • $8 • (01/31/93) • **81**
Cabernet Sauvignon Costers del Segre 1988 • $8 • (12/15/92) • **80**
Cabernet Sauvignon Costers del Segre 1986 • $10 • (03/31/90) • **81**
Costers del Segre Abadia Red 1989 • $8 • (04/15/94) • **83**
Costers del Segre Abadia Red 1987 • $9 • (03/31/90) • **84**
Merlot Costers del Segre 1990 • $8 • (04/15/94) • **79**
Tempranillo Costers del Segre 1990 • $8 • (04/15/94) BB • **85**

REAL SITIO DE VENTOSILLA, BODEGAS

Ribera del Duero Pradorey 1996: Made in a lighter style for early release. Shows a clumsy mix of bitter cherry and earthy notes, with soft tannins and little focus. Tasted twice, with consistent notes. Drink now. • $7 • (05/15/98) • **78**

REMELLURI, LA GRANJA NUESTRA SEÑORA DE

Rioja 1994: Polished and vivid. Delivers alluring toast and plum aromas that carry through cleanly on the palate. Focused, not overbearing in tannin or alcohol, and accessible now. Decant one hour before serving. Better than previous samples which were corky. 24,000 cases made. • $16 • (02/28/98) • **88**

Rioja 1993: This light-bodied red offers a clean, refreshing character, with cherry, spicy, and herbal flavors, and just enough grip for food. Traditional in style, but clean and fresh. • $16 • (01/01/97) • **84**

Rioja 1989 • $NA • (03/31/92) • **82**
Rioja 1988 • $NA • (03/31/92) • **75**
Rioja 1986 • $11 • (12/15/90) • **87**
Rioja 1985 • $10 • (03/31/90) • **88**
Rioja 1984 • $9 • (03/31/90) • **77**
Rioja 1983 • $12 • (03/31/90) • **77**
Rioja 1982 • $12 • (03/31/90) • **82**
Rioja Alavesa Labastida 1982 • $8 • (09/30/86) • **84**

Rioja Gran Reserva 1990: Balanced and still fresh. Offers ripe plum and dark chocolate flavors with accents of spices and herbs. Well integrated, with firm tannins and a velvety texture. Drink now through at least 2005. Decant one hour before serving. • $40 • (02/28/98) • **88**

Rioja Gran Reserva 1989: Dark and rather heavy, with ripe flavors of raisins and coffee, intense but a bit clumsy, with drying tannins on the finish. Has concentration but lacks grace. Drink now. Tasted twice, with consistent notes. • $40 • (12/15/97) • **82**

Rioja Gran Reserva 1985 • $40 • (03/31/92) • **84**
Rioja Gran Reserva 1982 • $40 • (11/30/91) • **87**
Rioja Reserva 1990 • $14 • (04/30/95) • **88**
Rioja Reserva 1989 • $14 • (04/15/94) • **83**
Rioja Reserva 1987 • $14 • (03/31/92) • **76**
Rioja Reserva 1986 • $14 • (03/31/92) • **78**

Rioja White 1995: Smooth and polished, this deeply-colored white marries the soft, vanilla-flavored character of traditional white Rioja with ripe melon and pear flavors that are fresh and clean, if a bit lacking in acidity. Not entirely harmonious, but distinctive. Tasted three times, with consistent notes. Drink now. • $16 • (05/31/98) • **85**

RETUERTA, ABADIA

Viño de Mesa de Castilla y Leon Rivola 1996: This deeply colored red has intensity and backbone, with gamy, lead pencil, and dark plum flavors overlaid with toasty oak and firm tannins. A bit aggressive now, it should soften and bloom with time. Drink now through 2002. A good value from Pascal Delbeck. A blend of 60 percent Tempranillo and 40 percent Cabernet. 21,000 cases made. • $10 • (05/15/98) BB • **87**

REYES, BODEGAS

Ribera del Duero Teófilo Reyes 1995: This powerful red is chock-full of the chocolate and coffee flavors of new American oak, and ripe fruit notes of plum and cassis. The tannins are firm but not overwhelming, the finish is long and clean. A modern wine in the international style that benefits from decanting before serving. Best from 1999 through 2010. • $25 • (05/15/98) • **91**

Ribera del Duero Teófilo Reyes 1994: Gorgeous. Seriously aromatic, this Spanish red explodes with toast, smoke, coconut, and vanilla aromas and flavors, with plenty of ripe fruit notes beneath. The tannins are big but beautifully framed, the wine is concentrated but completely harmonious and should improve for a decade. 9,000 cases made. • $25 • (06/15/97) CS • **95**

Key: SS—Spectator Selection CS—Cellar Selection HR—Highly Recommended BB—Best Buy $NA—Price not available Ⓐ—Auction Price (BT)—Barrel Tasting
Dates in parentheses indicate the issues in which the ratings were published.

RIBERA, VINICOLA DE LA

Tarragona Mediterráneo NV: Light cherry flavors are undermined by weedy, earthy notes in this light, soft wine. Simple and short. 16,000 cases made. • $4 • (11/15/97) • **76**

RIBERALTA, BODEGAS

Ribera del Duero Vega Izan 1992 • $7 • (04/30/95) • **75**
Ribera del Duero Vega Izan 1991 • $7 • (02/28/95) • **72**
Ribera del Duero Vega Izan Crianza 1991 • $11 • (02/28/95) • **83**

RICAVI

Rioja 1994 • $6 • (04/30/96) • **81**
Rioja 1993 • $6 • (04/30/95) • **82**
Rioja 1992 • $5 • (04/15/94) • **78**
Rioja Crianza 1991 • $8 • (04/30/96) • **83**
Rioja Crianza 1990 • $7 • (04/30/95) • **81**

RIOJA ALTA, LA

Rioja 890 Gran Reserva 1982: This is red Rioja at its most traditional. Mahogany in color, light yet firm in texture, it offers cedar, tea, and raisin flavors and a spicy finish. A mature wine with distinctive character and some elegance. Drink now. • $65 • (11/30/97) • **86**

Rioja 890 Gran Reserva 1981 • $65 • (06/30/96) • **86**
Rioja 890 Gran Reserva 1978 • $50 • (04/30/95) • **89**
Rioja 890 Gran Reserva 1973 • $55 • (03/31/92) • **77**

Rioja 904 Gran Reserva 1987: Still lively, this traditional Rioja shows light but intense flavors of cherries, smoke, brown sugar, and spices over firm tannins that turn a bit dry on the finish. A mature wine with some elegance. Drink now. • $35 • (11/15/97) • **86**

Rioja 904 Gran Reserva 1985 • $35 • (06/30/96) • **82**
Rioja 904 Gran Reserva 1982 • $NA • (03/31/92) • **84**
Rioja 904 Gran Reserva 1981 • $29 • (03/31/92) • **82**
Rioja 904 Gran Reserva 1976 • $17 • (03/31/90) • **90**
Rioja 904 Gran Reserva 1975 • $NA • (03/31/92) • **82**
Rioja 904 Gran Reserva 1973 • $10 • (09/30/86) • **84**
Rioja 904 Gran Reserva 1970 • $NA • (03/31/92) • **75**

Rioja Viña Alberdi Reserva 1994: Firm and lean, showing cherry, berry, vanilla, and herbal flavors, with light yet dry tannins and a slightly dry finish. Should flesh out a bit with food. Drink now through 2000. 9,600 cases made. • $14 • (05/31/98) • **84**

Rioja Viña Alberdi Reserva 1993: Already browning in color, this maturing wine shows dry tannins and flavors of raisins, brown sugar, and leather. Has personality, but doesn't offer much pleasure. • $13 • (11/15/97) • **76**

Rioja Viña Alberdi Reserva 1992: Supple and slightly sweet, the vanilla and raisin flavors slide down easily in combo with the cherry and spice flavors. A medium-weight wine for drinking now. • $14 • (10/15/96) • **84**

Rioja Viña Alberdi Reserva 1991 • $13 • (06/30/96) • **78**
Rioja Viña Alberdi Reserva 1989 • $12 • (04/15/94) • **77**
Rioja Viña Alberdi Reserva 1988 • $11 • (04/15/94) • **86**
Rioja Viña Alberdi Reserva 1987 • $12 • (03/31/92) • **79**
Rioja Viña Alberdi Reserva 1986 • $12 • (03/31/92) • **83**
Rioja Viña Alberdi Reserva 1985 • $8 • (03/15/90) BB • **85**
Rioja Viña Alberdi Reserva Lot 2 1989 • $12 • (04/30/95) • **82**

Rioja Viña Arana Reserva 1991: Traditional in style, showing pale brick color, soft aromas of vanilla and berries and a light, supple texture with cherry, vanilla, and herbal flavors. Harmonious and clean. Drink now. 7,500 cases made. • $18 • (05/31/98) • **85**

Rioja Viña Arana Reserva 1988 • $17 • (06/30/96) • **83**
Rioja Viña Arana Reserva 1986 • $16 • (04/30/95) • **82**
Rioja Viña Arana Reserva 1985 • $15 • (04/15/94) • **76**
Rioja Viña Ardanza Reserva 1989 • $22 • (06/30/96) • **79**
Rioja Viña Ardanza Reserva 1987 • $20 • (04/15/94) • **72**
Rioja Viña Ardanza Reserva 1986 • $20 • (04/15/94) • **85**
Rioja Viña Ardanza Reserva 1985 • $18 • (03/31/92) • **85**
Rioja Viña Ardanza Reserva 1983 • $18 • (03/31/92) • **81**
Rioja Viña Ardanza Reserva 1982 • $17 • (03/31/92) • **84**

RIOJA SANTIAGO, BODEGAS

Rioja 1991 • $6 • (04/15/94) • **82**
Rioja Gran Reserva 1984 • $16 • (04/15/94) • **82**

Rioja Reserva 1986 • $12 • (04/15/94) • **76**

RIOJANAS, BODEGAS

Rioja Canchales 1987 • $4 • (03/15/90) • **75**
Rioja Monte Real Gran Reserva 1985 • $22 • (04/15/94) • **88**
Rioja Monte Real Gran Reserva 1982 • $19 • (03/31/92) • **82**
Rioja Monte Real Gran Reserva 1981 • $19 • (04/15/94) • **89**
Rioja Monte Real Gran Reserva 1975 • $NA • (04/15/94) • **78**
Rioja Monte Real Gran Reserva 1973 • $NA • (04/15/94) • **85**
Rioja Monte Real Gran Reserva 1970 • $NA • (04/15/94) • **72**
Rioja Monte Real Reserva 1986 • $14 • (04/15/94) • **77**
Rioja Monte Real Reserva 1985 • $NA • (03/31/92) • **87**
Rioja Monte Real Reserva 1983 • $7 • (03/31/90) BB • **83**
Rioja Puerta Vieja Crianza 1988 • $9 • (04/15/94) • **80**
Rioja Viña Albina Gran Reserva 1985 • $22 • (04/15/94) • **83**
Rioja Viña Albina Gran Reserva 1982 • $19 • (03/31/92) • **87**
Rioja Viña Albina Gran Reserva 1981 • $19 • (03/31/92) • **86**
Rioja Viña Albina Gran Reserva 1975 • $NA • (03/31/92) • **85**
Rioja Viña Albina Gran Reserva 1973 • $NA • (03/31/92) • **81**
Rioja Viña Albina Gran Reserva 1970 • $NA • (03/31/92) • **70**
Rioja Viña Albina Reserva 1986 • $14 • (04/15/94) • **82**
Rioja Viña Albina Reserva 1985 • $NA • (03/31/92) • **78**
Rioja Viña Albina Reserva 1983 • $8 • (03/31/90) • **68**

RISCAL, MARQUÉS DE

Rioja 1945: Very minty, with cherry, berry and mineral notes. Full-bodied and tannic. A tough and powerful, muscular and strong wine. Like the '45 Latour. Still has ages to go. Will outlive us all. • $NA • (07/31/98) • **99**
Rioja 1938: Slightly simple, but very silky and fine. A caressing old wine, with mint, berry, and chocolate notes and a fine coffee finish. Delicious. • $NA • (07/31/98) • **88**
Rioja 1936: Slightly lifted, with some volatile acidity, but fresh and easy. A bit simple, but ripe and full, with tea-tinged chocolate notes. Medium-bodied, with smooth tannins and a silky finish. • $NA • (07/31/98) • **87**
Rioja 1924: A deep ruby wine, with lovely berry, mineral, and cigar-box aromas. Full-bodied and mouthfilling, with a supervelvety and long finish. A seamless, sexy wine. Wonderful. • $NA • (07/31/98) • **98**
Rioja 1918: Gorgeous aromas of dried berries, with smoke, floral, and milk, chocolate notes. Medium-bodied, with fresh, fine tannins. Lacks a bit of body, but shows a very fine, short finish. • $NA • (07/31/98) • **91**
Rioja 1898: Not a perfect bottle, but very impressive, with loads of dried raisin and ripe fruit character. Full-bodied, with slightly high acidity but a long and silky finish. Outstanding for staying alive for so long. • $NA • (07/31/98) • **90**
Rioja 1897: Fabulous aromas of milk chocolate, with fruit and mint flavors. A full-bodied, silky wine with a long, long finish. Stunning. • $NA • (07/31/98) • **96**
Rioja 1879: A dusty, funky old wine, but rather cuddly and enjoyable, with mushroom, spice, and berry character and mint and meat flavors. Medium- to full-bodied, with medium tannins and a soft texture. Warming finish. • $NA • (07/31/98) • **87**
Rioja Baron de Chirel Reserva 1988 • $36 • (04/30/95) • **90**
Rioja Baron de Chirel Reserva 1986 • $36 • (04/15/94) • **90**
Rioja Gran Reserva 1982 • $NA • (11/30/91) • **84**
Rioja Gran Reserva 1981: Fully mature, starting to fade, this light, drying red shows earthy brown sugar and leather flavors with little depth or length. Drink now. 3,700 cases made. • $18 • (11/15/97) • **78**
Rioja Gran Reserva 1964: A gorgeous wine, with violet and other floral aromas and flavors. Full-bodied and firmly tannic, yet harmonious and long. A truly great wine, like layered silk. Wonderful. • $NA • (07/31/98) • **98**
Rioja Gran Reserva 1958: Very fine Burgundian style. Medium- to light-bodied, with vanilla, cocoa and berry aromas. Fine tannins, with fresh acidity and a long, delicious finish. An elegant, easy wine. • $NA • (07/31/98) • **88**
Rioja Gran Reserva 1952: Lovely notes of raspberry, dried cherry, coffee, and dark chocolate. Full- to medium-bodied, with fine tannins and a chocolaty coconut flavor. Really gorgeous. A very silky, elegant, fine supermodel of a wine. • $NA • (07/31/98) • **93**
Rioja Reserva 1992: Smooth, with pretty, light flavors of cherries, cedar, and smoke, well-integrated if not rich. Tannins are light but will stand up to delicate foods. Drink now. 28,000 cases made. • $12 • (11/15/97) • **81**
Rioja Reserva 1991 • $13 • (03/31/96) • **85**
Rioja Reserva 1990 • $13 • (01/31/96) • **82**
Rioja Reserva 1989 • $11 • (04/30/95) • **90**
Rioja Reserva 1988 • $12 • (04/15/94) • **83**
Rioja Reserva 1985 • $9 • (03/31/90) • **62**
Rioja Reserva 1982 • $7 • (11/15/87) • **84**
Rueda 1996: Fragrant with floral and herbal aromas, this lively white offers juicy peach, citrus and herbal flavors, balanced and food-friendly. Fresh and clean. 12,000 cases made. • $7 • (10/31/97) • **85**
Rueda 1994 • $8 • (02/29/96) • **82**
Sauvignon Blanc Rueda 1994 • $10 • (02/29/96) • **79**
Sauvignon Blanc Rueda 1993 • $7 • (03/31/95) • **85**

ROBLE, ABADIA DEL

La Mancha Fermin Ayuso 1990 • $6 • (12/15/92) BB • **81**

ROMERO, BODEGA

Navarra La Cruceta Crianza 1994 • $7 • (04/30/96) • **81**
Navarra La Cruceta Crianza 1993 • $6 • (04/30/95) • **79**
Navarra La Cruceta Crianza 1990 • $8 • (04/30/95) BB • **84**
Navarra Rosado Malón de Echaide 1993 • $7 • (08/31/95) • **80**
Navarra Señorio de Yaniz 1993 • $4 • (03/31/95) • **75**
Navarra Via Corel 1993 • $6 • (04/30/96) • **82**
Navarra Via Corel 1992 • $5 • (04/30/95) • **83**

ROVIRA, BODEGAS PEDRO

Brut Nature Cava Brut de Belart NV: Fresh apple, light toast, and vanilla flavors mingle in this harmonious sparkler. The mousse is well-integrated and quite delicate, and the finish is clean, with a light herbal note. 2,000 cases made. • $12 • (10/31/97) • **84**
Tarragona Catalonia Reserva 1988: Game and barnyard aromas and earthy flavors combine with drying tannins in this over-the-hill red. Not much pleasure left. 3,500 cases made. • $9 • (11/15/97) • **76**
Tarragona Catalonia Reserva 1987 • $6 • (03/31/93) BB • **82**
Tarragona Gran Corpas 1989 • $6 • (08/31/93) • **79**
Tarragona Gran Reserva 1987: Light strawberry and cherry flavors still spark this mature red, framed by cedar, tobacco, and light earth notes. Tannins are a bit dry. Drink now. 1,700 cases made. • $18 • (11/15/97) • **79**
Tarragona Gran Reserva 1982 • $10 • (03/31/93) • **86**
Tarragona Marqués de Campo Real Crianza 1991: A light-bodied, maturing red, with silky texture, almost neutral flavors, notes of raisins and tea. Drinkable, forgettable. 12,000 cases made. • $6 • (11/15/97) • **77**
Tarragona Rosado Raquel 1995: This dull, nearly brown rosé shows thick caramel and coffee flavors. It's dry but still cloying, with an earthy note on the finish. 3,000 cases made. • $7 • (10/31/97) • **74**
Tarragona Rosado Seco Marqués de Campo Real 1996: A dry, fairly full-bodied rosé, with light but pretty flavors of strawberries and watermelon and firm acidity. Nice as an apéritif. 8,000 cases made. • $6 • (10/31/97) • **84**
Tarragona Señorio del Mar 1989 • $NA • (04/15/94) • **70**
Tarragona Señorio del Mar Crianza 1991: This light-bodied red shows light, mature flavors of coffee, walnuts, and mushrooms. Clean but short. Drink up. 12,000 cases made. • $6 • (11/15/97) • **78**
Tarragona Viña Mater Reserva 1989: Fully mature, with prune, coffee, and brown sugar flavors. It's smooth, and shows some spice on the finish. Drink now. 3,500 cases made. • $9 • (11/15/97) • **79**
Tarragona White Catalonia Select 1995: Apple, butter, and light toast flavors taste more of wood than fruit in this firm white, but it's round on the palate and finishes dry and clean. A modest match for food. 2,500 cases made. • $8 • (10/31/97) • **81**
Tarragona White Marqués de Campo Real Blanc de Blancs 1996: Ripe apple and light spice flavors are soft and simple in this straightforward white. Serve well-chilled as an apéritif. 10,000 cases made. • $6 • (10/31/97) • **79**
Tarragona White Señorio del Mar Blanc de Blancs 1996: Light-bodied and straightforward, this soft white offers mild flavors of cooked apples and herbs. An easy quaff. 10,000 cases made. • $6 • (10/31/97) • **79**
Terra Alta Negre de Belart 1992: Raisin and brown sugar aromas give way to coffee and leather flavors in this light, soft red. It's fully mature; drink up. 1,000 cases made. • $9 • (11/15/97) • **77**
Terra Alta White Alta Mar Blanc de Nectar 1995: Juicy, showing moderate sweetness, with apple and canned-fruit flavors. Round and soft, and might make a pleasant spritzer. 3,000 cases made. • $7 • (10/31/97) • **78**
Terra Alta White Blanc de Belart 1995: This idiosyncratic white marries strong herbal and sweet hard-candy notes in a dry wine that's more perfumed than flavorful. Finishes dry and a bit tannic. 6,500 cases made. • $8 • (10/31/97) • **78**

RUIZ, SANTIAGO

Rias Baixas 1996: This lively white shows ripe pear and honey aromas, then turns crisp and lean on the palate, with lime, green apple and mineral flavors. A bit tart on its own, it should marry nicely with shellfish. Drink now. • $19 • (05/31/98) • **85**

SALNESUR, BODEGAS

Albariño Rias Baixas Condes de Albarei 1996: This lush white shows ripe melon and vanilla aromas and flavors, round on the palate, yet there's enough acidity to keep it firm. The long, honeyed finish brings you back for another sip. Drink now. • $13 • (05/31/98) • **87**

Albariño Rias Baixas Condes de Albarei 1995: This round white shows flavors of vanilla, butter, and coconut. Soft and appealing, with enough lemony acidity for liveliness. Draws you back for another sip. • $15 • (09/15/97) • **87**

SAN JORGE, BODEGA

Ribera del Duero Arroyo 1996: Black cherry and gamelike flavors are vivid, if a bit austere, in this firm red. Has the grip for food, the structure for drinking soon. Try now. 25,000 cases made. • $7 • (10/31/97) • **85**

Ribera del Duero Arroyo 1995: This chunky red offers well-integrated but muted flavors of coffee, leather, and plum, with round, firm tannins that shut down the clean, herb-scented finish. 1,500 cases made. • $7 • (10/31/97) • **84**

Ribera del Duero Arroyo Crianza 1994: You can taste the skilled winemaking here, as layers of sweet, toasty oak, and polished berry flavors fit together like fine carpentry. It's lush and concentrated, but very controlled. Try in 1999. 3,000 cases made. • $12 • (10/31/97) • **89**

SAN VICENTE, SENORIO DE

Tempranillo Rioja 1994: Lush, polished and beautifully textured. Offers plenty of smoky, toasty oak and enough ripe fruit to stay balanced, with flavors of cassis, black cherry and light herbs. Powerful but graceful, made in the international style. Needs until 2002 to show its best. Much better than previously reviewed. Decant one hour before serving. 4,500 cases made. • $25 • (02/28/98) • **92**

Tempranillo Rioja Reserva 1991: Toast, coffee, and chocolate flavors dominate. Heavily oaked, with a core of cherry and enough richness to offset the muscular tannins. Powerful, if a bit clumsy, it should come together this year. • $25 • (02/28/98) • **87**

SANCHO, BODEGAS MANUEL

Mont-Marçal Tinto Reserva Penedès 1989 • $9 • (04/30/95) • **88**

SANTA DARIA

Rioja 1991 • $6 • (04/15/94) BB • **83**
Rioja Crianza 1988 • $10 • (04/15/94) • **74**
Rioja Reserva 1985 • $13 • (04/15/94) • **87**

SARDÀ, BODEGAS J.

Brut Cava NV: A straightforward sparkler offering baked apple, toast, and caramel flavors. Maturing but still dry, with a foamy mouthfeel. Try with salty foods. • $10 • (10/31/97) • **81**

Chardonnay Penedès 1996: A lush white, with bright but rather simple flavors of vanilla, apple, and lime. Clean and soft, with a fresh, modest finish. • $9 • (10/31/97) • **83**

Moscatel Spain NV: A full-bodied, high-octane sweet white, with candied peach and pear flavors. Exaggerated, like a Muscat Life-Saver. • $9 • (11/15/97) • **78**

Tempranillo Penedès Viña Sardà 1993: Bright plum and light meaty flavors mingle in this round, soft red. It's still fresh on the palate, but turns a bit musty on the finish. Drink now. • $6 • (12/15/97) • **78**

Key: SS—Spectator Selection CS—Cellar Selection HR—Highly Recommended BB—Best Buy $NA—Price not available Ⓐ—Auction Price (BT)—Barrel Tasting
Dates in parentheses indicate the issues in which the ratings were published.

SCALA DEI

Priorat El Cipres 1995: The pure, ripe flavors of raspberries and blackberries in this clean, well-balanced red are fresh and likeable. The modest tannins give it backbone, but it's drinkable now. • $8 • (10/31/97) • **85**

Priorat El Cipres 1994: Highly-tannic and alcoholic, it lacks balance but still oozes plenty of ripe blackberry, plum, and licorice flavors. • $10 • (08/31/96) • **84**

Priorat El Cipres 1993 • $8 • (04/30/95) • **82**
Priorat El Cipres 1991 • $9 • (04/30/95) • **85**
Priorat El Cipres 1989 • $10 • (04/15/94) • **85**
Priorat El Cipres 1987 • $18 • (04/15/94) • **83**
Priorat El Cipres 1978 • $25 • (04/15/94) • **86**

SENDA GALIANA, BODEGAS

Rioja Conde Allegre 1993 • $5 • (04/30/95) • **81**
Rioja Crianza 1990 • $7 • (03/31/96) • **72**
Rioja Crianza 1989 • $7 • (01/31/95) • **79**
Rioja Reserva 1989 • $10 • (03/31/96) • **83**
Rioja Reserva 1987 • $10 • (03/31/95) • **81**

SERRA, JAUME

Brut Cava 1991 • $NA • (04/15/94) • **75**
Brut Cava Cristalino 1989 • $10 • (03/31/93) • **76**
Macabeo White Penedès 1993 • $5 • (02/28/95) • **73**
Merlot Penedès 1991 • $13 • (06/15/93) • **72**
Penedès Crianza 1992 • $7 • (03/31/96) • **83**
Penedès Crianza 1991 • $6 • (04/30/95) • **71**
Penedès Crianza 1989 • $7 • (03/31/93) BB • **83**
Penedès Crianza 1985 • $8 • (04/15/92) BB • **80**
Penedès Reserva 1988 • $9 • (04/15/94) • **79**
Penedès Reserva 1986 • $9 • (04/15/94) • **74**

Tempranillo Penedès 1994: Straightforward, delivering fresh cherry and berry flavors with just enough tannin for grip. It's round and balanced. Drinkable now. 100,000 cases made. • $6 • (11/15/97) • **82**

Tempranillo Penedès 1993 • $5 • (03/31/96) • **82**
Tempranillo Penedès 1992 • $5 • (04/30/95) • **75**
Tempranillo Penedès 1991 • $5 • (04/30/95) • **76**
Tempranillo Penedès 1990 • $6 • (03/31/93) • **71**
Tempranillo Penedès 1988 • $6 • (04/15/92) BB • **80**

SIERRA CANTABRIA, BODEGAS

Rioja 1992 • $5 • (04/15/94) • **77**
Rioja 1991 • $8 • (06/30/96) • **81**

Rioja Codice 1995: This simple, grapey wine has earthy notes and a tannic edge that mar its appeal. Resembles a Beaujolais Nouveau grown old. 20,000 cases made. • $7 • (12/15/97) • **77**

Rioja Codice 1993 • $7 • (06/30/96) • **81**
Rioja Codice 1992 • $6 • (04/15/94) • **79**
Rioja Codice 1990 • $6 • (04/15/94) • **84**
Rioja Codice 1989 • $6 • (04/15/92) • **77**
Rioja Codice 1988 • $6 • (06/15/91) • **78**

Rioja Crianza 1994: A bright burst of strawberry and raspberry flavors enlivens this light red, and sweet vanilla notes add to the appeal. It shows good balance for drinking now, and it's affordably priced. 15,000 cases made. • $9 • (10/15/97) BB • **84**

Rioja Crianza 1989 • $7 • (04/30/95) • **85**

Rioja Gran Reserva 1987: Dried flowers and dried fruit character and drying tannins suggest this light-bodied wine is on the way down. Still, offers some spicy notes and it's balanced, so drink up. 500 cases made. • $18 • (12/15/97) • **82**

Rioja Gran Reserva 1982 • $35 • (04/15/94) • **78**

Rioja Reserva 1990: Strawberry and herbal flavors mingle in this soft, ripe red. Still quite fresh, but doesn't have the concentration for long aging. Drink now. • $14 • (10/15/97) • **84**

Rioja Reserva 1987 • $11 • (04/30/95) • **82**

Rioja White Codice 1996: Clean and well balanced, this straightforward white offers fresh apple, citrus, and light herbal flavors. Not distinctive, but easy to drink. • $8 • (10/31/97) • **83**

SOLANA

Cencibel Valdepeñas 1993 • $8 • (02/28/95) • **83**
Torrontés-Treixadura Ribeiro 1993 • $8 • (12/31/94) • **75**

SOLAR, CASA

Viño de Mesa Plata 1994: This light, smooth red offers cinnamon and chocolate notes over cherry flavors. It's not very concentrated, but maintains its balance. Drink now. • $5 • (10/31/97) • **83**

SOLAR DE LIBANO

Rioja Reserva 1992: This ultratraditional wine offers seductive aromas, but the palate is disappointing, with dry tannins, simple earthy flavors. May please fans of the old ways. 6,500 cases made. • $15 • (11/15/97) • **78**

SONSIERRA

Rioja 1993 • $5 • (04/30/95) • **80**
Rioja Crianza 1990 • $7 • (04/30/95) • **79**
Rioja Viña Mindiarte Reserva 1988 • $9 • (04/30/95) • **86**

TAJA

Jumilla Red 1994 • $5 • (04/30/96) • **83**
Jumilla Red 1988 • $6 • (10/15/92) • **73**
Jumilla Red 1987 • $6 • (03/31/90) BB • **80**

TINOS, BODEGA LOS

Casa Barco Red NV • $4 • (04/15/94) BB • **81**
Gran Casa Barco Viño de Mesa Red NV • $5 • (03/31/95) • **78**
Viño de Mesa Casa Barco Red NV • $4 • (04/30/96) • **76**

TORO, EL SENORIO DE

Toro Etiqueta Blanca Red 1989 • $10 • (04/15/92) • **82**

TORRECILLA

Navarra 1993 • $6 • (04/15/94) • **83**
Navarra 1992 • $5 • (08/31/93) BB • **80**
Navarra 1991 • $5 • (04/15/94) • **81**
Navarra Crianza 1990 • $7 • (04/15/94) • **82**

TORRENTE

Jumilla White 1994: A resinous wine with a strongly herbal character. It is a bit rustic-tasting, but still quite flavorful with spice, marzipan, and cream notes. • $6 • (05/15/97) • **84**

TORRES

Chardonnay Penedès Gran Viña Sol 1996: This plump white offers round, ripe apple, vanilla, and butter flavors; a bit simple but well balanced. A pleasant, easy-drinking wine. • $11 • (06/30/97) • **84**
Chardonnay Penedès Gran Viña Sol 1995: Straightforward with good peach and apple flavors. Some nice spice notes chime in on the finish. 33,270 cases made. • $10 • (09/15/96) • **83**
Chardonnay Penedès Gran Viña Sol 1994 • $11 • (02/29/96) • **80**
Chardonnay Penedès Milmanda 1993 • $40 • (02/29/96) • **84**
Merlot Penedès Las Torres 1994: Fruity and fairly rich with some good plum and herbal flavors; soft and straightforward. 12,222 cases made. • $11 • (01/01/97) • **84**
Merlot Penedès Las Torres 1993 • $12 • (04/15/95) • **81**
Merlot Penedès Las Torres 1992 • $12 • (04/15/94) • **82**
Merlot Penedès Las Torres 1990 • $12 • (11/15/91) • **86**
Merlot Penedès Las Torres 1989 • $13 • (10/15/90) • **82**
Merlot Penedès Las Torres 1988 • $10 • (03/31/90) • **83**
Penedès Coronas 1990 • $8 • (02/28/95) • **78**
Penedès Coronas 1989 • $8 • (04/15/92) • **81**
Penedès Coronas 1988 • $7 • (06/15/91) BB • **81**
Penedès Coronas 1987 • $6 • (10/15/90) BB • **80**
Penedès Coronas 1986 • $6 • (11/30/89) • **78**
Penedès Coronas 1985 • $5 • (11/30/88) BB • **86**
Penedès Coronas 1983 • $4 • (06/30/87) BB • **84**
Penedès Coronas 1982 • $4 • (02/16/86) • **76**
Penedès Gran Coronas 1985 • $11 • (11/30/88) • **89**
Penedès Gran Coronas 1979 • $9 • (02/16/86) • **75**
Penedès Gran Coronas Mas La Plana Black Label 1990 • $34 • (04/15/94) • **88**
Penedès Gran Coronas Mas La Plana Black Label 1987 • $33 • (12/15/92) • **85**
Penedès Gran Coronas Mas La Plana Black Label 1985 • $32 • (10/15/90) • **85**
Penedès Gran Coronas Mas La Plana Black Label 1983 • $26 • (03/31/90) • **85**
Penedès Gran Coronas Mas La Plana Black Label 1982 • $29 • (06/15/88) • **85**
Penedès Gran Coronas Mas La Plana Black Label 1981 • $23 • (10/15/87) • **83**
Penedès Gran Coronas Mas La Plana Black Label 1978 • $65 • (02/16/86) • **85**
Penedès Gran Coronas Reserva Cabernet Sauvignon 1993: Maturing flavors of coffee and leather dominate this round red, which also shows raisin and spice flavors and a firm finish. It's ripe, but lacks fruit and freshness; might open up with food. • $15 • (10/31/97) • **80**
Penedès Gran Coronas Reserva Cabernet Sauvignon 1991 • $15 • (04/30/95) • **86**
Penedès Gran Coronas Reserva 1988 • $15 • (04/15/94) • **79**
Penedès Gran Coronas Reserva 1987 • $15 • (04/15/92) • **84**
Penedès Gran Coronas Reserva 1986 • $12 • (11/30/89) • **86**
Penedès Gran Coronas Reserva 1985 • $12 • (03/31/90) • **77**
Penedès Gran Sangre de Toro 1989 • $13 • (12/15/93) • **84**
Penedès Gran Sangre de Toro 1984 • $9 • (09/15/88) • **78**
Penedès Gran Sangre de Toro 1979 • $9 • (02/16/86) • **79**
Penedès Gran Sangre de Toro Reserva 1993: Still lively, this red offers vibrant black cherry, cinnamon, and chocolate flavors, with moderately firm tannins. Drinkable now. A blend of 75 percent Garnacha and 25 percent Cariñena. • $11 • (10/31/97) • **84**
Penedès Gran Sangre de Toro Reserva 1991: Meaty and chock full of ripe berry, smoke, and licorice flavors; what it lacks in refinement, it makes up in exuberance. 87,614 cases made. • $11 • (08/31/96) • **83**
Penedès Gran Sangre de Toro Reserva 1988 • $11 • (12/15/92) • **82**
Penedès Gran Sangre de Toro Reserva 1987 • $10 • (11/15/91) • **83**
Penedès Gran Sangre de Toro Reserva 1986 • $10 • (10/15/90) • **83**
Penedès Gran Sangre de Toro Reserva 1985 • $9 • (11/30/89) • **87**
Penedès Gran Sangre de Toro Reserva 1983 • $9 • (06/15/88) SS • **91**
Penedès Gran Sangre de Toro Reserva 1981 • $5 • (06/15/87) • **80**
Penedès Sangre de Toro 1990 • $8 • (04/15/94) BB • **85**
Penedès Sangre de Toro 1989 • $7 • (04/15/92) BB • **82**
Penedès Sangre de Toro 1988 • $6 • (03/31/91) BB • **82**
Penedès Sangre de Toro 1987 • $5 • (11/30/89) BB • **82**
Penedès Sangre de Toro 1986 • $4 • (12/15/88) BB • **80**
Penedès Sangre de Toro 1985 • $5 • (06/15/88) BB • **81**
Penedès Sangre de Toro 1983 • $4 • (06/15/87) • **79**
Penedès Sangre de Toro 1982 • $NA • (02/16/86) • **83**
Penedès Viña Magdala 1986 • $14 • (11/15/91) • **82**
Penedès Viña Magdala 1984 • $11 • (07/31/89) • **76**
Penedès Viña Magdala 1983 • $9 • (06/15/88) • **74**
Penedès Viña Magdala 1979 • $NA • (02/16/86) • **72**
Penedès White Fransola 1996: Round, ripe apple and peach flavors in this big, rather soft white, with pretty accents of vanilla and cream. Has just enough acidity for balance, and plenty of fruit. Drink now. A blend of 85 percent Sauvignon Blanc and 15 percent Parellada. 7,534 cases made. • $17 • (04/30/98) • **84**
Penedès White Fransola 1993 • $18 • (02/29/96) • **85**
Penedès White Gran Viña Sol 1993 • $11 • (02/28/95) • **83**
Penedès White Milmanda 1995: Lively, with lush oak and tropical fruit flavors of good intensity. The smoky, toasty notes are balanced by vivid acidity. Try now. 3,081 cases made. • $36 • (11/30/97) • **87**
Penedès White Milmanda 1994: Maturing now, this rich white is harmonious and quite deep, with honey and lanolin aromas, flavors of almonds, apples and herbs. Firm acidity gives strength, and the smoky finish is subtle. Drink now. • $36 • (01/01/97) • **87**
Penedès White Viña Esmeralda 1994 • $11 • (02/29/96) • **76**
Penedès White Viña Esmeralda 1993 • $11 • (02/29/96) • **77**
Pinot Noir Penedès Mas Borras 1993: Maturing now, this light red shows alluring tobacco aromas, dried cherry, and herbal flavors, and moderate

tannins that turn a bit dry on the finish. Try with lighter grilled meats. 854 cases made. • $18 • (11/30/97) • **84**
Pinot Noir Penedès Mas Borras 1991 • $20 • (12/15/94) • **76**
Pinot Noir Penedès Mas Borras 1990 • $20 • (04/15/94) • **78**
Pinot Noir Penedès Mas Borras 1989 • $20 • (11/15/91) • **79**
Pinot Noir Penedès Mas Borras 1988 • $18 • (10/15/90) • **79**

TORRES FILOSO, BODEGAS

La Mancha Arboles de Castillejo 1986 • $7 • (04/15/92) • **79**

ULECIA, FAUSTINO RIVERO

Rioja Reserva 1985 • $9 • (03/31/93) • **79**

UNION DE COSECHEROS DE LABASTIDA

Rioja Montebuena 1996: Firm, with black cherry, smoke, and lightly gamy flavors and moderate tannins that turn a bit dry on the finish. Balanced and fresh. Drink now. 35,000 cases made. • $7 • (11/15/97) • **83**
Rioja Solagüen Crianza 1994: Shows good structure, with a nice balance of firm tannins, crisp acidity, and a refreshing texture. The flavors are a bit dull, though, with earthy, gamy notes and not much fruit. Try now. 36,000 cases made. • $10 • (11/15/97) • **83**
Rioja Solagüen Crianza 1990: Generous and deep, this large-production, full-bodied Spanish red still shows dark color and ripe fruit flavors, but also mature notes of spice, tobacco, and cedar. It's balanced and firm, and should drink well through 2000. Hard to beat at this price. 416,000 cases made. • $9 • (06/30/97) BB • **87**
Rioja Solagüen Reserva 1989: Harmonious, elegant, and polished, showing black cherry, spice, and smoke flavors. A bit lean but balanced. Still young, but drinking nicely now. • $10 • (06/30/97) • **86**
Rioja Solagüen Reserva 1985 • $NA • (04/15/94) • **85**
Rioja White Montebuena 1996: Vanilla and lanolin flavors add nuance to this dry, clean, and fresh white, but there isn't much fruit for balance. 30,000 cases made. • $7 • (10/31/97) • **82**

URBION

Ribera del Duero 1991 • $7 • (06/15/93) BB • **82**
Ribera del Duero 1990 • $7 • (12/15/92) • **81**
Ribera del Duero 1989 • $11 • (12/15/92) • **87**

VALDAMOR

Albariño Rias Baixas 1996: Vanilla and toasty aromas and flavors are appealing, but overwhelm the modest fruit character of this slightly soft white. For fans of oak. Drink now. • $15 • (05/31/98) • **82**
Albariño Rias Baixas 1995: Toasty almond and butter flavors dominate this smooth white. There's a jolt of lemony acidity on the finish, but not enough fruit for balance. • $15 • (09/15/97) • **79**
Albariño Rias Baixas 1993 • $14 • (03/31/95) • **79**

VALDEOBISPO

Bierzo 1990 • $7 • (04/15/92) • **80**
Bierzo 1989 • $10 • (04/15/92) • **87**

VALDUMIA

Albariño Rias Baixas 1996: This lush white offers round apple and almond flavors with accents of herbs and lime. It's round and generous on the palate, but firm acidity keeps it well-suited for food. Brings you back for another sip. 40,000 cases made. • $12 • (11/30/97) • **87**

VALLFORMOSA

Brut Cava Metodo Tradicional NV: Very dry, with tart apple and citrus flavors, notes of toast and spice. It's quite austere, but should pair well with food. 15,000 cases made. • $10 • (10/31/97) • **83**
Cabernet Sauvignon Penedès 1990: Light, with flavors of berries, spice and tea, still fresh and firm on the palate. Leans more toward elegance than power, showing good balance and a pretty finish. Accessible now. 5,000 cases made. • $13 • (10/31/97) • **85**
Chardonnay Penedès 1995: This lively white marries melon and apple fruit flavors with crisp acidity and just a touch of oak for a clean, food-friendly wine with balance and grace. 4,000 cases made. • $13 • (10/31/97) • **85**
Penedès Gran Baron Crianza 1988 • $6 • (04/15/94) • **78**
Penedès Gran Baron Reserva 1987 • $8 • (04/15/94) • **74**
Penedès Gran Reserva 1989: Maturing, it's light and soft now, with dried cherry, brown sugar, and spice flavors over soft tannins that are starting to dry out on the finish. Best with food. Drink now. 2,500 cases made. • $16 • (11/15/97) • **83**
Penedès Vall Fort 1986 • $7 • (05/31/91) • **76**
Penedès Vall Fort 1984 • $7 • (03/31/91) BB • **84**
Penedès Vall Fort Crianza 1994: This soft red has a silky texture, very light tannins, and modest flavors of cherries, strawberries, and spice, with a sweet vanilla finish. Easy to drink. 30,000 cases made. • $8 • (11/15/97) • **82**
Penedès Vall Fort Crianza 1990 • $7 • (04/15/94) BB • **81**
Penedès Vall Reserva 1990: Maturing now, this lean red offers harmonious light cinnamon, tea, and dried cherry flavors with some elegance. Drink now. A blend of Tempranillo and Cabernet. • $12 • (10/31/97) • **83**
Penedès Vall Reserva 1987 • $9 • (04/15/94) • **77**
Penedès Viña Blanca 1995: Lively, offering bright citrus, peach, and herbal flavors with crisp acidity. It's sassy enough for an apéritif but has enough grip for food. Balanced and clean. • $8 • (10/31/97) • **84**
Penedès Viña Rosada 1995: More orange than pink, this tastes tired already, with raisin and weed notes. It's dry, but the finish is a bit earthy. Drink up. 10,000 cases made. • $7 • (10/31/97) • **77**

VEGA DE LA REINA, BODEGAS

Viño de Mesa de Castilla y Leon 1985 • $15 • (04/15/94) • **82**

VEGA DE MORIZ

Cencibel Valdepeñas 1989 • $6 • (06/15/91) BB • **81**

VEGA SICILIA, BODEGAS

Ribera del Duero Unico Gran Reserva 1985: Maturing but still fresh. Mingles chocolate, black cherry, raisin, and spice flavors in a harmonious and balanced package. Firm but smooth tannins; aging well. Drink now. 5,062 cases made. • $105 • (07/31/96) • **88**
Ribera del Duero Unico Gran Reserva 1983 • $120 • (04/30/95) • **89**
Ribera del Duero Unico Gran Reserva 1981: This beautiful red would put many a Bordeaux from the same vintage to shame. It's got a deep, youthful color, alluring spice and cherry-pie aromas and a supple yet concentrated palate with cherry, spice, and tobacco flavors. The tannins are softening, yet will still match up with food, and the finish is long and spicy. Drink now through 2005. 4,300 cases made. • $150 • (05/15/98) HR • **93**
Ribera del Duero Unico Gran Reserva 1980 • $130 • (12/15/92) • **86**
Ribera del Duero Unico Gran Reserva 1979 • $150 • (03/31/90) • **95**
Ribera del Duero Unico Gran Reserva 1976 • $NA • (04/30/89) • **91**
Ribera del Duero Unico Gran Reserva 1974 • $160 • (04/15/94) • **87**
Ribera del Duero Unico Gran Reserva 1973 • $NA • (03/31/90) • **90**
Ribera del Duero Unico Gran Reserva 1970 • $180 • (04/30/95) • **92**
Ribera del Duero Unico Gran Reserva 1962 • $295 • (03/31/90) • **89**
Ribera del Duero Unico Reserva Especial NV • $150 • (03/31/90) • **79**
Ribera del Duero Unico Reserva Especial NV • $225 • (04/15/95) • **88**
Ribera del Duero Valbuena 5 Años Reserva 1992: This ripe, lush red offers chocolate, plum, and raspberry flavors, fresh and still lively. Youthful, but drinking nicely, with enough concentration for food. 10,000 cases made. • $75 • (06/15/97) • **88**
Ribera del Duero Valbuena 5 Años Reserva 1991: Sweet vanilla and chocolate from oak are dominant, but enough black cherry peeps through to keep it balanced. The thick, jammy texture needs food. Drink now. 10,262 cases made. • $70 • (07/31/96) • **87**
Ribera del Duero Valbuena 5 Años Reserva 1990 • $60 • (04/30/95) • **86**
Ribera del Duero Valbuena 5 Años Reserva 1988 • $75 • (04/15/94) • **90**
Ribera del Duero Valbuena 5 Años Reserva 1984 • $49 • (03/31/90) • **90**
Ribera del Duero Valbuena 5 Años Reserva 1982 • $35 • (10/15/88) • **91**
Ribera del Duero Valbuena 3 Años Reserva 1986 • $47 • (12/15/90) • **90**
Ribera del Duero Valbuena 3 Años Reserva 1985 • $55 • (03/31/90) CS • **92**

Key: SS—Spectator Selection CS—Cellar Selection HR—Highly Recommended BB—Best Buy $NA—Price not available Ⓐ—Auction Price (BT)—Barrel Tasting
Dates in parentheses indicate the issues in which the ratings were published.

Ribera del Duero Valbuena 3 Años Reserva 1984 • $28 • (04/30/89) • **79**
Ribera del Duero Valbuena 3 Años Reserva 1983 • $22 • (10/15/88) • **88**
Ribera del Duero Valbuena 3 Años Reserva 1982 • $25 • (10/15/88) • **90**

VEGA VIEJA

Rioja Crianza 1987 • $7 • (09/30/92) • **77**
Rioja Gran Reserva 1981 • $16 • (12/15/92) • **67**
Rioja Reserva 1985 • $12 • (12/15/92) • **79**

VEGAVAL PLATA

Valdepeñas Reserva 1987 • $10 • (04/30/96) • **79**

VIDAL, ANGEL RODRIGUEZ

Verdejo Rueda Martinsancho 1996: Clean, fresh, unoaked, and round on the palate, with firm texture and austere flavors of lime, almond, and smoke. A good frame for lighter dishes. 2,000 cases made. • $10 • (02/28/98) • **84**
Verdejo Rueda Martinsancho 1995: Pleasant, with apple, light toast, and spice flavors. It's balanced, but almost anonymous in its straightforward style. 1,500 cases made. • $10 • (10/31/97) • **82**

VILARIÑO-CAMBADOS, BODEGAS

Albariño Rias Baixas Burgáns 1996: There's good intensity in this rich yet nervy white. It offers flavors of white peaches, figs, limes, and almonds. Generous but very crisp, it would be a beautiful complement to grilled shellfish. 2,000 cases imported. 10,000 cases made. • $10 • (09/15/97) BB • **88**
Albariño Rias Baixas Martin Códax 1996: Assertive aromas of lime, grapefruit, and almond are intriguing, but turn lean on the palate. Marrying austere flavors with a rich texture, this white will be better balanced with food. 2,000 cases imported. 20,000 cases made. • $13 • (09/15/97) • **83**
Albariño Rias Baixas Organistrum 1995: Soft and smooth, this delicate yet generous white offers light almond, vanilla, and apple flavors, harmonious and clean. A pleasant apéritif. 200 cases imported. 1,000 cases made. • $17 • (09/15/97) • **84**

VILARNAU, CASTELL DE

Brut Cava NV: This crisp, lively sparkler offers appealing citrus aromas and flavors of apples, spice, and lemon, with a frothy texture. It's grown-up ginger ale. • $12 • (10/31/97) • **83**

VIÑA, CASA DE LA

Cencibel Valdepeñas 1996: Jammy strawberry flavors are soft and pleasant in this round red, with very light tannins and a crisp finish. It's balanced, but light. Drink now. Cencibel is the local Valdepeñas name for Tempranillo. • $5 • (11/15/97) • **83**
Cencibel Valdepeñas 1985 • $6 • (03/31/90) • **82**

VIÑA BERCEO

Rioja Carta de plata 1991 • $5 • (09/30/91) • **70**
Rioja Crianza 1988 • $5 • (11/15/89) • **77**
Rioja Crianza 1987 • $5 • (04/15/89) BB • **86**
Rioja Crianza 1986 • $7 • (09/30/90) BB • **87**
Rioja Crianza 1984 • $5 • (10/15/88) • **76**
Rioja Gran Reserva 1982 • $25 • (11/30/91) • **87**
Rioja Reserva 1985 • $10 • (03/31/90) • **76**
Rioja Reserva 1983 • $10 • (11/15/89) • **69**
Rioja Reserva 1982 • $8 • (10/15/88) • **76**
Rioja Reserva 1980 • $8 • (10/15/88) • **77**

VIÑA IJALBA

Rioja Ijalba Reserva 1990: The ripe plum and pleasant spicy accents add personality, and firm, round tannins give it grip. Tastefully oaked and enjoyable now, this wine still has life ahead of it. 3,550 cases made. • $16 • (10/15/96) • **88**
Rioja Livor 1994: A strong earthy note and dry tannins make this tough to like, though it has concentration and some chocolate and plum flavors underneath. 4,000 cases made. • $10 • (10/15/96) • **77**
Rioja Múrice Crianza 1992: A light-bodied wine whose oak dominates the cherry, chocolate, and vanilla flavors. 20,000 cases made. • $13 • (10/15/96) • **79**
Rioja Rosado Aloque 1994: This rosé has some dried cherry and woodlike flavors to it, as well as some spicy notes. A bit tired. 2,000 cases made. • $9 • (01/01/97) • **77**

VIÑA PEDROSA

Ribera del Duero 1990 • $18 • (12/15/93) • **86**

VIÑA SALCEDA

Rioja 1990 • $11 • (04/30/95) • **83**
Rioja Conde de la Salceda Gran Reserva 1987: Silky and lean, showing coffee and dried cherry flavors before drying tannins shut down the finish. A traditional style, for drinking now. 61,000 cases made. • $23 • (06/30/97) • **78**
Rioja Crianza 1993: Rich and soft, this round red offers chocolate, plum, raisin, and tobacco flavors that linger in a dark, smoky finish. Generous, and still lively. 60,000 cases made. • $13 • (06/30/97) • **84**
Rioja Crianza 1991 • $11 • (03/31/96) • **85**
Rioja Crianza 1989 • $10 • (04/15/94) • **83**
Rioja Cuvée Especial 25 Aniversario Reserva 1987 • $16 • (04/30/95) • **84**
Rioja Gran Reserva 1985 • $20 • (04/15/94) • **89**

VIÑA VALORIA

Rioja 1991 • $8 • (04/30/95) • **78**
Rioja 1989 • $8 • (04/15/94) • **75**
Rioja Crianza 1994: A generous red, with chocolate and tobacco aromas, plum, cedar and tobacco flavors. It has just enough tannin for grip; best now through 2000. 8,000 cases made. • $11 • (11/30/97) • **84**
Rioja Crianza 1987 • $12 • (04/15/94) • **76**
Rioja Reserva 1985 • $15 • (04/15/94) • **85**
Rioja Rosé 1993 • $10 • (08/31/95) • **82**

VIÑAS DE GAIN

Rioja 1988 • $10 • (12/15/92) • **82**

VIÑAS DEL VERO

Cabernet Sauvignon Somontano 1995: Lush and jammy, this fleshy red offers ripe black cherry, licorice, and raisin flavors with firm, chewy tannins. Drink now. 20,000 cases made. • $7 • (10/31/97) • **84**
Cabernet Sauvignon Somontano 1994: This muscular red offers a harmonious blend of vanilla notes, ripe plum flavors, and firm tannins. It has a chewy texture, with licorice and tar notes on the finish. Drinkable now. 5,000 cases made. • $8 • (06/15/97) • **87**
Cabernet Sauvignon Somontano Reserva 1991: Assertive aromas of cherry, vanilla, and cedary minerals give way to fleshy, still-fresh flavors of cherry and toasty oak. A bit rustic, but still kicking. 10,000 cases made. • $8 • (09/30/96) BB • **83**
Chardonnay Somontano Barrel Select 1995: A restrained, elegant style of Chardonnay with buttery aromas, rather lean fruit flavors, and a lingering finish. Not a blockbuster, but it grows on you. • $8 • (02/28/97) • **85**
Chardonnay Somontano La Piedra Barrel Select 1996: This chewy white has firm structure but rather neutral flavors, with light notes of butter, vanilla, and citrus. A crisp finish keeps it refreshing. 15,000 cases made. • $8 • (12/15/97) • **82**
Chardonnay Somontano Saint Marc Estate 1993 • $7 • (03/31/95) • **85**
Chardonnay Somontano Saint Marc Estate Barrel Fermented Reserve 1994 • $9 • (02/29/96) • **80**
Chardonnay Somontano Saint Marc Estate Barrel Select 1994 • $9 • (02/29/96) • **79**
Chardonnay Somontano Saint Marc Reserve 1993 • $11 • (02/29/96) • **83**
Gewürztraminer Somontano 1994 • $10 • (02/29/96) • **79**
Merlot Somontano 1995: Muscular, marrying ripe plum and sweet vanilla flavors in a forceful if not complex wine that has the structure to stand up to food. The finish is short, but fruity and fresh. 8,000 cases made. • $8 • (06/15/97) • **86**

Merlot Somontano 1994: This straightforward, chewy wine offers ripe black cherry flavors with notes of spice and herbs. Round tannins provide grip without astringency. 5,000 cases made. • $8 • (09/30/96) BB • **83**
Merlot Somontano Saint Marc 1993 • $8 • (12/31/95) • **86**
Pinot Noir Somontano Saint Marc Estate 1991 • $10 • (04/30/95) • **78**
Somontano Duque de Azara Crianza 1992: This is a mix of dried cherry and buttery flavors that turns a bit astringent on the finish. 20,000 cases made. • $8 • (01/01/97) • **79**
Somontano La Pyramida 1996: A light red, clean, simple, and refreshing, with cherry and marked herbal flavors, firm tannins, light vanilla notes on the finish. 70,000 cases made. • $5 • (10/15/97) • **84**
Somontano Saint Marc 1990 • $9 • (04/15/94) BB • **86**
Somontano Saint Marc Duque de Azara Crianza 1991 • $9 • (04/30/96) • **83**
Somontano Saint Marc Estate Reserva Especial 1991 • $9 • (04/30/96) • **81**
Somontano Saint Marc Reserva Especial 1990 • $9 • (04/15/94) BB • **86**
Somontano White Saint Marc Estate Duque de Azara 1994 • $8 • (02/29/96) • **81**
Tempranillo Somontano Joven 1994: Flat and dull, as if the heart had been stripped out of it. Simple cherry flavors and light tannins. 3,000 cases made. • $9 • (08/31/96) • **77**

VINEDOS Y BODEGAS, BODEGAS

Ribera del Duero Matarromera 1995: Liked crushed fresh fruit, a mouthful of raspberries and plums, with lots of vanilla notes. Fresher and more exuberant than most Riberas, but has firm tannins on the finish. Drink now. 1,200 cases made. • $31 • (06/15/97) • **87**

VINEGRAS, BODEGAS

Rioja Don Teófilo I Crianza 1994: A lively mix of herbal, bitter cherry, and smoke flavors gives this red a lean but harmonious character. Modest but firm tannins and good balance. Drink now through 2000. 2,500 cases made. • $17 • (05/31/98) • **86**

VINOS DE LA GRANJA, COMPANIA DE

Navarra Alma 1996: This chewy red shows round plum, black cherry, light herb, and game notes, with moderate tannins and a soft mouthfeel. More generous than rich. Drink now though 2000. Made from 100 percent Garnacha. 10,000 cases made. • $7 • (11/15/97) • **83**
Rueda Basa 1996: Full-bodied yet well-knit, this big white offers vanilla, toast, apple, melon, and lightly spicy flavors that linger on the finish. It's clean and fresh, can stand up to food. 15,000 cases made. • $7 • (10/31/97) • **86**

Key: SS—Spectator Selection CS—Cellar Selection HR—Highly Recommended BB—Best Buy $NA—Price not available Ⓐ—Auction Price (BT)—Barrel Tasting
Dates in parentheses indicate the issues in which the ratings were published.

Other International

• Argentina •

ABERDEEN-ANGUS

Sirah Mendoza 1987 • $6 • (09/15/92) BB • **82**

AGRICOLA, LA

Argentinian Red Mendoza Uvas del Sol 1997: Appealing for its fruitiness, with nice berry and cherry flavors. Fairly light but effusive. A nice quaffer. A blend of 50 percent Sangiovese, 30 percent Bonarda and 20 percent Malbec. Drink now. 14,000 cases made. • $7 • (07/31/98) • **83**

Malbec Mendoza Uvas del Sol 1996: A well-focused red, with good coffee, red plum and cassis flavors. Turns just a tad tough on the finish. 12,000 cases made. • $8 • (07/31/98) • **82**

Malbec Mendoza Uvas del Sol 1995: Sturdy, with some good, sweet cherry and berry flavors, but it finishes on a slightly astringent note. Drink now. 15,000 cases made. • $8 • (05/15/98) • **82**

Malbec-Cabernet Sauvignon Mendoza Uvas del Sol 1995: Smooth and supple, with pretty flavors of cherry, berry and plum. Well balanced, with plenty of polish. Finishes on a pleasant leathery note. A blend of 60 percent Malbec and 40 percent Cabernet. 12,000 cases made. • $8 • (05/15/98) • **85**

Torrontes Mendoza Uvas del Sol 1996: Green peach and apricot flavors are matched with some nice spicy notes in this fruity white wine. 10,000 cases made. • $8 • (05/15/98) • **80**

Torrontes-Chenin Blanc Mendoza Uvas del Sol 1997: The floral aroma and attractive peach and spice flavors are reminiscent of Gewürztraminer. An exuberant white that is crisp and enjoyable. Drink well chilled. Drink now. 14,000 cases made. • $7 • (07/31/98) • **84**

Torrontes-Chenin Blanc Mendoza Uvas del Sol 1996: A bit bland, with modest peach and apricot flavors. A blend of 65 percent Torrontes and 35 percent Chenin Blanc. 18,000 cases made. • $7 • (05/15/98) • **76**

ALAMOS RIDGE

Cabernet Sauvignon Mendoza 1994: This firm red shows black cherry, black olive and herbal flavors, with mouthfilling tannins. A bit rustic in style, it may soften with food. Tasted twice, with consistent notes. Drink now. 7,750 cases made. • $9 • (06/15/97) • **83**

Chardonnay Mendoza 1995: Enjoyable, harmonious and well balanced. Brightly fruity, with soft texture, it's a pleasure from the first whiff to the lingering pear and vanilla notes on the finish. 13,800 cases made. • $10 • (02/28/97) • **85**

Chardonnay Mendoza 1993: Well made and flavorful, featuring good apple and lemon notes and a touch of butter on the finish. Crisp and refreshing. • $9 • (07/31/96) • **83**

Malbec Mendoza 1995: Young, exuberant and concentrated, with plenty of plum, blackberry, spice and black pepper flavors. Has some weight to it, with some nice meaty and smoky notes and a thick texture. 2,780 cases made. • $8 • (02/28/97) • **86**

BIANCHI, VALENTIN

Cabernet Sauvignon Mendoza Elsa's Vineyard 1990 • $5 • (06/15/94) • **78**

Cabernet Sauvignon Mendoza Elsa's Vineyard 1987 • $7 • (07/15/91) • **77**

Chenin Blanc Mendoza Elsa's Vineyard 1994 • $5 • (05/15/95) • **84**

Malbec Mendoza Elsa's Vineyard 1994: Straightforward and basic, with a core of cherry and plum flavors and some nice spicy notes on the finish. • $6 • (02/28/97) • **82**

Malbec Mendoza Elsa's Vineyard 1992 • $5 • (07/31/95) • **81**

Malbec Mendoza Elsa's Vineyard 1991 • $6 • (06/15/94) BB • **84**

Malbec Mendoza Elsa's Vineyard 1985 • $6 • (07/15/91) • **76**

BLUE NUN

Merlot Mendoza 1996: Nice plum and coffee flavors, with an herbal note running through. Smooth and ready to drink. Drink now. • $6 • (07/31/98) • **81**

COASTAL CELLARS

Chardonnay Mendoza 1995: Unusual but tasty. Seems sweet and has overt vanilla and nutmeg flavors. Difficult to assess, but might be fine as a dessert. 5,000 cases made. • $7 • (02/28/97) • **81**

COMPASS

Merlot Mendoza 1996: Quite distinctive, with plum and berry flavors and a strong menthol note. Nice concentration, with chocolaty notes on the finish. Drink now. 2,500 cases made. • $9 • (07/31/98) BB • **85**

COMTE DE BELTOUR

Mendoza 1989 • $6 • (09/15/92) • **80**

DOMECQ, BODEGAS

Chardonnay-Sémillon Mendoza Balbi Vineyard 1997: Simple and straightforward, with modest green apple flavors and some earthy notes on the finish. Drink now. • $7 • (07/31/98) • **81**

Malbec-Syrah Mendoza Balbi Vineyard 1997: Fruity and quite jammy tasting, with a nice lushness and pleasant chocolate and spice notes. A rich medium-bodied red from Argentina that would serve well with barbecued food. A blend of 50 percent Malbec and 50 percent Syrah. Drink now. • $7 • (07/31/98) BB • **85**

ESMERALDA, BODEGAS

Cabernet Sauvignon Argentina Trumpeter 1994: Polished and supple, with some concentration, this has cherry and cedar flavors and well-integrated tannins. Drink now. 1,000 cases made. • $8 • (02/28/97) • **86**

Cabernet Sauvignon Maipu Trumpeter 1995: From Argentina comes this firm red, with muscular tannins and ripe, almost roasted flavors of plums, toast and herbs. It has admirable concentration, but needs a little time to gain balance. Should be better next year and, at this price, it's worth setting a few bottles aside. 5,000 cases made. • $9 • (11/30/97) BB • **85**

Cabernet Sauvignon Mendoza Catena Agrelo Vineyard 1994: A nice mix of power and harmony, this marries ripe fruit, plenty of toasty oak and good concentration. Rich yet polished, it needs time to unwind and show its best. Try now. • $16 • (02/28/97) • **89**

Cabernet Sauvignon Mendoza Catena Agrelo Vineyard 1993 • $16 • (06/30/96) • **84**

Cabernet Sauvignon Mendoza Catena Agrelo Vineyard 1992 • $16 • (04/30/95) HR • **91**

Cabernet Sauvignon Mendoza Catena Alta Agrelo Vineyard 1994: This rich red has a core of vivid fruit flavors, but is so lavishly oaked that coffee, toast and vanilla notes dominate, and the tannins are a bit harsh on the finish. An ambitious wine that may harmonize with time in the bottle, but tastes a bit unbalanced now. Try between 1999 and 2003. 194 cases made. • $45 • (02/28/98) • **89**

Cabernet Sauvignon Mendoza Catena Reserve 1990 • $14 • (05/31/94) • **85**

Cabernet Sauvignon Mendoza Trumpeter 1992 • $7 • (04/30/95) • **80**

Cabernet Sauvignon Mendoza Trumpeter 1991 • $10 • (06/15/94) • **77**

Chardonnay Mendoza Catena Agrelo Vineyard 1995: A rich, extroverted California-style Chardonnay that's toasty and buttery in aroma, ripe in flavor, full-bodied and broad in texture. Lingers on the finish. • $16 • (02/28/97) • **88**

Chardonnay Mendoza Catena Alta Tupungato Vineyard 1995: This beautifully focused white offers vibrant, ripe fruit flavors—melon, mango and pineapple—that marry seamlessly with lavish oaky notes of toast, coffee and spice. Though ripe and rich, it remains graceful and lively. Drink now through 2000. 600 cases made. • $45 • (02/28/98) • **91**

Chardonnay Mendoza Trumpeter Tupungato Vineyard 1996: Modest but refreshing, with straightforward apple and vanilla flavors, clean but slightly diluted. An easy quaff. Drink now. 8,000 cases made. • $9 • (03/31/98) • **81**

Chardonnay Mendoza Trumpeter Tupungato Vineyard 1995: Firm textured and oak influenced, this is robust, with crisp fruit flavors, spicy oak nuances and a lingering finish. Clean, fresh and rather strong in character. 3,700 cases made. • $8 • (02/28/97) • **86**

Malbec Vistalba Trumpeter 1996: Fruity and fresh, with berry and cherry flavors and a nice note of pepper. 3,500 cases made. • $10 • (05/15/98) • **82**

Merlot Tupungato Valley Trumpeter 1996: Light yet lush, this gentle red shows round, enticing flavors of ripe plums, milk chocolate and licorice. From a new but promising vineyard region. Drink now. 8,000 cases made. • $10 • (11/30/97) • **84**

Merlot Tupungato Valley Trumpeter 1995: Assertive and full-bodied. Moderately tannic, with plenty of plum, cherry and spice flavors. Something to sink your teeth into. 4,000 cases made. • $9 • (05/15/97) • **86**

ETCHART

Cabernet Sauvignon Mendoza 1995: Black cherry and plum flavors are ripe and clean in this lively red. The tannins are light but have enough grip for food. Drink now. • $NA • (03/31/98) • **83**

Malbec Mendoza 1993 • $6 • (11/15/95) • **84**

Merlot Mendoza 1993 • $6 • (11/15/95) • **78**

FAZIO, NICOLÁS E.

Cabernet Sauvignon Mendoza 1986 • $12 • (04/30/95) • **71**

Cabernet Sauvignon Mendoza 1980 • $11 • (09/15/92) • **70**

Chardonnay Mendoza Fazio & Joyaux 1994 • $12 • (04/30/95) • **77**

Malbec Mendoza 1982 • $12 • (07/31/95) • **83**

Malbec Mendoza 1978 • $12 • (09/15/92) • **79**

Merlot Rio Negro Fabre Montmayou 1988 • $11 • (11/15/95) • **82**

FLICHMAN, FINCA

Argenta Mendoza 1990 • $6 • (09/30/94) • **75**

Argenta Mendoza 1989 • $5 • (09/15/92) BB • **83**

Argenta Mendoza 1988 • $4 • (03/15/91) BB • **84**

Cabernet Sauvignon Mendoza 1991 • $6 • (04/30/95) • **74**

Cabernet Sauvignon Mendoza 1989 • $8 • (06/15/94) • **80**

Cabernet Sauvignon Mendoza Caballero de la Cepa 1991: Has an odd strawberry aroma that seems artificial, plus tired flavors and an astringent finish. No fun. 12,000 cases made. • $11 • (07/31/96) • **72**

Cabernet Sauvignon Mendoza Caballero de la Cepa 1990 • $10 • (04/30/95) • **79**

Cabernet Sauvignon Mendoza Caballero de la Cepa 1989 • $11 • (01/31/95) • **80**

Cabernet Sauvignon Mendoza Caballero de la Cepa 1987 • $11 • (06/15/94) • **74**

Cabernet Sauvignon Mendoza Proprietors Private Reserve 1990 • $8 • (01/31/95) • **84**

Cabernet Sauvignon Mendoza Proprietors Private Reserve 1989 • $7 • (06/15/93) • **81**

Cabernet Sauvignon Mendoza Proprietors Private Reserve 1988 • $7 • (09/15/92) BB • **82**

Cabernet Sauvignon Mendoza Proprietors Private Reserve 1987 • $6 • (03/15/91) BB • **81**

Merlot Mendoza Proprietors Private Reserve 1988 • $6 • (03/15/91) • **66**

Sangiovese Mendoza 1992 • $6 • (11/15/95) • **78**

Syrah Mendoza 1991: Aromas and flavors of ripe plum and raisin, with some floral and light vegetal notes. A bit dry on the finish. Seems to be softening; drink now. 9,000 cases made. • $9 • (07/31/96) • **81**

Syrah Mendoza 1990 • $9 • (04/30/94) • **84**

Key: SS—Spectator Selection CS—Cellar Selection HR—Highly Recommended BB—Best Buy $NA—Price not available Ⓐ—Auction Price (BT)—Barrel Tasting
Dates in parentheses indicate the issues in which the ratings were published.

GROVE STREET

Malbec Mendoza Barrel Reserve 1996: Light, bright and smooth, this is a fruity, easy-going red to drink while it's fresh. 2,300 cases made. • $8 • (06/15/97) • **83**

Merlot Mendoza Barrel Reserve 1996: Surprisingly restrained for such a young wine, with a charred, gamelike flavor to it. Turns tannic and astringent on the finish. 28,600 cases made. • $8 • (06/15/97) • **75**

LAGARDE, HENRY

Cabernet Sauvignon Mendoza Gold Medal 1985: This thick, solid wine has developed appealing nutmeg and cinnamon accents while retaining a core of ripe plum and raisin flavor. Expressive, with impressive backbone, and it still has development ahead. • $12 • (02/28/97) • **87**

Malbec Mendoza 1982: Still lively despite its age. Smooth and supple, with mature flavors of dried cherry and tobacco. Hits some good spicy notes on the finish. • $11 • (02/28/97) • **84**

Merlot Mendoza 1993: Broad-shouldered, with hearty fruit and oak flavors and firm tannins. A bit rough, but should be fine at the dinner table. • $11 • (05/15/97) • **85**

Rosé Mendoza Blanc de Noir 1993: A simple, neutral-tasting rosé dominated by watermelon flavor. • $10 • (05/15/97) • **77**

Sauvignon Blanc Mendoza 1995: Soft in texture, fresh but light in flavor. A simple and delicate white wine. 15,000 cases made. • $10 • (05/15/97) • **82**

Syrah Mendoza 1993: Gamelike and licorice aromas show good varietal character, and pretty cherry flavors emerge on the palate in this lively, well-balanced red. Drink now. 22,000 cases made. • $12 • (06/15/97) • **86**

LEWELLYN ESTATES

Cabernet Sauvignon Mendoza 1994: A bizarre mix of sweet plum and spicy cherry flavors. 20,000 cases made. • $4 • (07/31/98) • **73**

Chardonnay Mendoza 1997: This is dominated by an oniony aroma and flavor that makes it harsh and unappealing. 20,000 cases made. • $4 • (07/31/98) • **72**

Merlot Mendoza 1995: A cloying aroma, with candied flavors and a sweet finish. A bit bizarre in the end. Drink now. 20,000 cases made. • $4 • (07/31/98) • **74**

LURTON, J. & F.

Cabernet Sauvignon Mendoza 1996: Fresh and fruity, with flavors you can sink your teeth into. Raspberry and plum are the primary components, with some nice chocolate and spice notes mixed in as well. • $6 • (09/15/97) • **85**

Cabernet Sauvignon Mendoza Gran Lurton Reserva 1996: An accessible Cabernet, with good concentration. Delicious dark plum, cherry and chocolate flavors, with a spicy, slightly sweet note on the finish. 850 cases made. • $12 • (07/31/98) • **85**

Chardonnay Mendoza 1996: This well-proportioned, quaffable white from Argentina represents real value for all that it offers. It's full-bodied, with good toasty, buttery flavors and an appealing citrus note on the finish. Yummy. 10,000 cases made. • $6 • (09/15/97) BB • **86**

Chenin Blanc Mendoza 1996: Apple and fig flavors dominate this middle-weight wine. Turns a bit vegetal on the finish. • $5 • (09/30/97) • **78**

Malbec Mendoza 1996: A ripe and generous wine with loads of flavor—rich berry, cherry and plum. It's balanced, with a nice crispness to it as well. Finishes on a lovely spice and chocolate note. • $6 • (10/15/97) • **88**

Pinot Gris Mendoza 1996: An awkward wine with some faint peachy flavors and some fairly strong herbal notes as well. Tasted twice, with consistent notes. • $5 • (09/30/97) • **78**

MARIPOSA

Malbec Mendoza 1996: Smooth and well rounded, with appealing berry and cherry flavors. The flavors intensify on the finish, which has a nice spicy quality to it. • $10 • (10/15/97) • **86**

NAVARRO CORREAS

Cabernet Sauvignon Mendoza Colección Privada 1992: A mature-tasting red with herbal and brown sugar flavors. A bit tired, with some prunelike notes on the finish. 30,000 cases made. • $12 • (09/15/97) • **79**

Cabernet Sauvignon Mendoza Colección Privada 1991: Herbal, clove and tobacco flavors give distinction, but it lacks freshness, with drying tannins and little fruit. Drink now. • $12 • (06/15/97) • **77**

Cabernet Sauvignon Mendoza Colección Privada 1990 • $11 • (04/30/95) • **75**

Cabernet Sauvignon Mendoza Colección Privada 1988 • $12 • (05/31/94) • **82**

Cabernet Sauvignon Mendoza Colección Privada 1985 • $10 • (03/31/93) • **79**

Cabernet Sauvignon Mendoza Colección Privada 1981 • $8 • (02/15/89) • **79**

Chardonnay Maipú-Mendoza 1996: Thick and made-up with buttery and toasty flavors, but it's a bit hollow in the middle and turns flat on the finish. 4,000 cases made. • $15 • (09/15/97) • **79**

Chardonnay Maipú-Mendoza 1995: This firm, full-bodied white offers anise, coconut and herbal flavors, with a long vanilla finish. Has just enough acidity for grip. • $15 • (06/15/97) • **84**

Chardonnay Maipú-Mendoza 1994 • $12 • (04/30/95) • **79**

Malbec Mendoza Russell Vineyard 1993: Ends up a bit severe, with gamy, leathery flavors. Mature, and fast going over-the-hill. 25,000 cases made. • $13 • (10/15/97) • **78**

Malbec Mendoza Russell Vineyard 1992: Dry and nicely balanced, this mature red is interesting for its spicy bottle bouquet and elegant, firm texture. Light in flavor. • $12 • (06/15/97) • **84**

Malbec Mendoza Russell Vineyard 1991 • $10 • (07/31/95) • **78**

Malbec Mendoza Russell Vineyard 1988 • $10 • (05/31/94) • **86**

Malbec Mendoza Russell Vineyard 1987 • $10 • (03/31/93) • **80**

Pinot Noir Mendoza 1991: A strange Pinot Noir, too mature for our tastes, with cherry-candy aromas and tired, nutty flavors. • $15 • (09/30/97) • **71**

Pinot Noir Mendoza 1989 • $11 • (07/31/94) • **72**

Syrah Mendoza 1992: More like Rioja than Syrah, this mellow, mature red has intriguing, spicy aromas, a smooth texture and a lingering finish. • $15 • (09/30/97) • **84**

Syrah Mendoza 1991 • $12 • (11/15/95) • **79**

NORTON, BODEGA

Cabernet Sauvignon Mendoza 1995: Ripe, broad and fairly rich, with plum and chocolate flavors and a charred note on the finish. • $9 • (07/31/98) • **83**

Cabernet Sauvignon Mendoza 1994: A plush wine with plenty of ripe plum and chocolate flavors. Has nice concentration as well, and a good dose of tannins. Drinkable now. • $9 • (09/30/97) • **85**

Cabernet Sauvignon Mendoza 1993: Maturing, this shows raisin and spice flavors and a supple texture that turns tough on the finish. Drink now, before it dries out. • $9 • (02/28/97) • **81**

Malbec Mendoza 1996: Nicely sculpted and balanced, with ripe, lush flavors of dark plum, cherry and berry. Chocolaty notes on the lingering finish. • $9 • (07/31/98) BB • **86**

Malbec Mendoza 1995: A rustic wine not for the faint of heart. It's leather- and smoke-flavored, with nice richness and ripeness to it. • $9 • (10/15/97) • **83**

Malbec Mendoza 1994: An earthy style, with stewed flavors and aromas. Very ripe and almost jammy. Finishes on notes of tobacco and spice. • $9 • (02/28/97) • **80**

Merlot Mendoza 1995: Ripe and rich, though a bit rough-hewn, with dark plum and cherry flavors. Finishes with roasted notes. Drink now. • $9 • (07/31/98) • **83**

Merlot Mendoza 1994: Toasty oak aromas are promising, and the wine shows a firm, balanced structure, but right now the full tannins dominate the black cherry flavors. Try with food. • $9 • (10/31/97) • **86**

Merlot Mendoza 1993: An appealing, everyday style, with a soft texture, fresh fruit flavors and moderate tannins. All is in balance. • $9 • (05/15/97) • **85**

Privada Mendoza 1995: Thick and rich, with appealing flavors of ripe plum, cherry and spice, it's a well-balanced, meaty wine that packs plenty of flavor. Nice touch of chocolate on the finish. • $13 • (09/30/97) • **85**

Privada Mendoza 1994: A minty note runs through this concentrated, ripe and full-bodied wine, with red plum, tobacco and dark cherry flavors. Ready to drink. • $12 • (02/28/97) • **85**

Sangiovese Mendoza 1995: Flavorful, but rather light-bodied, with ripe cherry flavors and soft texture. • $9 • (10/15/97) • **81**

Sangiovese Mendoza 1994: Thick and fairly rich, with red plum and berry flavors, and some gamy notes. A bit lumbering but satisfying nonetheless. • $9 • (02/28/97) • **83**

PROVIAR

Clos du Moulin Mendoza 1985 • $10 • (09/30/94) • **76**

RAFAEL

Malbec-Tempranillo Mendoza 1997: A rich and ripe red, with delicious plum, chocolate and cassis. Tightly wound but still enjoyable. A blend of 60 percent Malbec and 40 percent Tempranillo. Drink now through 2001. • $8 • (07/31/98) • **84**

Tempranillo Mendoza 1997: A bit astringent and tired tasting, with modest plum and spice flavors, but there's an overwhelming roasted note that follows through on the finish. • $6 • (07/31/98) • **78**

Trebbiano Mendoza 1997: A fresh white, with a slightly off-dry taste, peachy flavors and herbal notes. Finishes on a slightly earthy note. Drink now. • $6 • (07/31/98) • **81**

SAN TELMO, BODEGAS

Cabernet Sauvignon Mendoza 1985 • $10 • (03/31/93) • **81**

Cabernet Sauvignon Mendoza Cuesta Del Madero 1987 • $4 • (03/31/93) BB • **83**

Malbec Mendoza Malbeck 1986 • $8 • (03/31/93) • **79**

SANTA ANA

Cabernet Sauvignon Mendoza Reserve 1990 • $5 • (08/31/95) • **74**

SANTA JULIA

Cabernet Sauvignon Mendoza 1994: Odd, not very appealing. On the light side for a Cabernet, with chalky, earthy flavors and not much fresh fruit. 11,100 cases made. • $7 • (07/31/96) • **75**

Cabernet Sauvignon Mendoza Oak Reserve 1993: A sturdy but dull Cabernet with mature aromas, vague fruit flavors and a tough texture. 3,350 cases made. • $9 • (07/31/96) • **77**

Chardonnay Mendoza 1997: A full-blown style that verges on the decadent. Has a nutty aroma and some interesting ripe, buttery flavors, but comes off a bit unbalanced in the end. • $7 • (07/31/98) • **79**

Chardonnay Mendoza 1996: A severe style, with woody and buttery flavors and a bitter finish. • $7 • (09/15/97) • **76**

Chardonnay Mendoza 1995: Broad, featuring good acidity and nutty flavors. It also has a just-fermented character that's reminiscent of bread dough. Pleasant apple and lemon notes on the finish. 11,600 cases made. • $7 • (07/31/96) • **83**

Chardonnay Mendoza Oak Reserve 1996: This round white offers ripe melon flavors accented by plenty of sweet vanilla and white chocolate notes. Engaging, but the sweetness cloys a bit. Drink now. • $10 • (03/31/98) • **83**

Malbec Mendoza 1994: Mouthfilling flavors of plum, bacon and black pepper make it rich and chunky. Tannins are firm enough for red meat, but it's round. Drinkable now. 13,300 cases made. • $6 • (07/31/96) • **86**

Malbec Mendoza Oak Reserve 1993: Plum and coffee aromas leap from the glass, followed by smoky, meaty plum flavors. Ripe yet firmly tannic, though it's more exuberance than structure. Drink now. 2,800 cases made. • $8 • (07/31/96) • **82**

Malbec-Cabernet Sauvignon Mendoza 1995: A deliciously spicy wine with loads of cherry and brown sugar flavors. There's a nice coffeelike note to it, too. Balanced and flavorful. A blend of 60 percent Malbec and 40 percent Cabernet. • $7 • (10/15/97) • **86**

Malbec-Cabernet Sauvignon Mendoza 1994: Fruity and accessible, with straightforward black cherry and light herbal flavors, moderate tannins and good balance. Drinkable now. 13,300 cases made. • $6 • (07/31/96) • **83**

Merlot Mendoza 1997: An interesting mix of leather, dark plum and spice flavors. Ripe and round, with a lingering finish dominated by roasted notes. Drink now. • $7 • (07/31/98) • **84**

Pinot Noir Mendoza 1996: Tired and flat, with dried cherry flavors and a tannic finish. • $7 • (10/15/97) • **75**

Sangiovese Mendoza 1997: Light, with berry and spice flavors and a distinctive leathery element. Has a nice grape flavor. Drink now. • $6 • (07/31/98) • **81**

Sangiovese Mendoza Don Alberto 1996: A smooth, simple red with pleasant fruit flavors, light body and soft texture. Drink now. • $7 • (10/15/97) • **79**

Sauvignon Blanc Mendoza 1997: A light floral aroma precedes basically neutral flavors, with some apple and earthy notes, in this round white. Full-bodied but slightly dull. Drink now. • $7 • (06/15/98) • **78**

Syrah Mendoza Don Alberto 1996: Alluring aromas of black pepper and black olives give way to cherry flavors and a gamy note characteristic of the varietal. Chewy and well structured, it could be mistaken for a good Crozes-Hermitage. • $7 • (10/31/97) • **87**

Tempranillo Mendoza 1997: Fruity, with nice berry and plum flavors, though a bit simple in the end. Finishes on an earthy note. Drink now. • $7 • (07/31/98) • **80**

Tempranillo Mendoza Don Alberto 1996: Black cherry and smoke flavors give this soft red an assertive character, turning a bit bitter on the finish. It's nothing like a Rioja, but has an earthy appeal. Drink now. • $7 • (10/31/97) • **82**

Torrontés Mendoza 1997: Light, with a floral aroma and peach and apricot flavors. A bit sweet and simple in the end. • $7 • (05/15/98) • **79**

Torrontés Mendoza 1996: Has a floral aroma and interesting flavors of honey, spice and almond. Finishes on an herbal note. • $6 • (10/15/97) • **82**

SONGMEADOW

Chardonnay Mendoza 1996: Soft and easy going, with slightly sweet pear flavors and a smooth texture. Good in this style. 5,000 cases made. • $7 • (05/15/97) • **83**

Merlot Mendoza 1996: Light, youthful and simple, with appealing cherry and plum flavors and very light tannins. 5,000 cases made. • $7 • (05/15/97) • **81**

TOSO, PASCUAL

Cabernet Sauvignon Mendoza 1992 • $8 • (09/30/95) • **82**
Cabernet Sauvignon Mendoza 1991 • $8 • (06/15/94) • **78**
Cabernet Sauvignon Mendoza 1990 • $7 • (04/30/95) • **72**
Cabernet Sauvignon Mendoza 1988 • $7 • (03/15/91) • **79**
Chardonnay Mendoza 1994 • $8 • (09/30/95) • **76**
Malbec Mendoza 1994 • $6 • (09/30/95) • **83**
Malbec Mendoza 1990 • $6 • (05/31/94) • **74**
Red Mendoza 1994 • $6 • (09/30/95) • **79**
Red Mendoza 1991 • $6 • (05/31/94) • **76**
White Mendoza 1994 • $6 • (11/15/95) • **82**

TRAPICHE

Cabernet Sauvignon Mendoza 1994: A lighter style with decent plum, berry and cherry flavors. There's a hint of olive on the finish. 20,000 cases made. • $6 • (09/15/97) • **83**
Cabernet Sauvignon Mendoza 1990 • $8 • (05/31/94) • **83**
Cabernet Sauvignon Mendoza 1982 • $4 • (02/15/89) BB • **81**
Cabernet Sauvignon Mendoza Fond de Cave 1991 • $12 • (11/15/95) • **83**
Cabernet Sauvignon Mendoza Fond de Cave 1990 • $13 • (06/15/94) • **79**

Cabernet Sauvignon Mendoza Oak Cask 1993: A nicely matured, rich red that's brimming with plum, berry and chocolate flavors and unveils appealing notes of spice on the finsh. It's ripe, generous, well-balanced and affordable, too. 10,000 cases made. • $9 • (09/15/97) BB • **87**
Cabernet Sauvignon Mendoza Oak Cask 1991 • $8 • (04/30/95) • **80**
Cabernet Sauvignon Mendoza Oak Cask 1986 • $10 • (10/15/91) • **82**
Cabernet Sauvignon Mendoza Reserve 1992 • $6 • (11/15/95) • **77**
Cabernet Sauvignon Mendoza Reserve 1988 • $7 • (09/15/92) • **79**
Cabernet Sauvignon Mendoza Reserve 1986 • $6 • (09/15/90) • **77**

Chardonnay Mendoza 1996: Offers some nice mineral flavors, but overall, it's unfocused, and it finishes on a cloying note. • $6 • (09/15/97) • **78**

Chardonnay Mendoza Medalla 1996: Thick and rich, with plenty of butter and caramel flavors. If you like fat, full-bodied Chardonnay, this is your wine. Could use some finesse, but still quite tasty. 800 cases made. • $19 • (09/15/97) • **85**
Chardonnay Mendoza Medalla 1994 • $20 • (04/30/95) • **80**

Chardonnay Mendoza Oak Cask 1996: All dressed up but nowhere to go. Marked by woody flavors and aromas, turns coarse and candied on the finish. Tasted twice, with consistent notes. 10,000 cases made. • $9 • (09/15/97) • **77**

Malbec Mendoza 1995: A nicely matured, well-rounded red from Argentina, offering good smoke, leather and plum flavors. Would be a good partner for well-seasoned foods, especially barbecue, and at this price and score, it's the deal of the month. Ready to drink. 66,000 cases made. • $6 • (10/15/97) BB • **85**

Malbec Mendoza Oak Cask 1993: This chewy red marries sweet, toasty oak flavors with ripe berry and cherry notes. It's harmonious, and though softening now, it still has enough grip for food. 10,000 cases made. • $9 • (10/15/97) • **84**
Malbec Mendoza Oak Cask 1991 • $8 • (08/31/95) BB • **87**
Malbec Mendoza Oak Cask 1990 • $8 • (05/31/94) BB • **86**
Malbec Mendoza Oak Cask 1988 • $8 • (07/15/91) • **74**
Malbec Mendoza Reserve 1991 • $6 • (07/31/95) • **78**
Malbec Mendoza Reserve 1987 • $5 • (09/15/90) BB • **83**

Medalla Mendoza 1994: Smooth and supple, with ripe, prunelike flavors. Has good smoke and leather notes to it, and some tannins on the finish. 4,166 cases made. • $19 • (09/15/97) • **85**
Medalla Mendoza 1991 • $18 • (09/30/94) • **87**
Merlot-Malbec Mendoza Cuvée de Trapiche 1994 • $4 • (11/15/95) • **76**
Pinot Noir Mendoza Reserve 1988 • $7 • (09/15/92) • **80**
Sauvignon Blanc Mendoza Cuvée de Trapiche 1994 • $4 • (11/15/95) • **79**

Sauvignon Blanc-Sémillon Mendoza Falling Star 1996: A lumbering wine with pleasant herbal, onion and spice flavors. Good, though a bit muddled. • $5 • (10/15/97) • **81**

Syrah Maipú-Mendoza 1996: Ripe and round, with plum, berry and cassis flavors. A little thin in the middle. Finishes on a leathery note. Drink now. • $11 • (07/31/98) • **82**

VINTERRA

Cabernet Sauvignon Mendoza 1995: Rustic, with sweet, slightly candied strawberry and spice flavors and firm, drying tannins that take over the finish. Perhaps it will soften with food. Try now. 10,000 cases made. • $6 • (10/31/97) • **79**

Chardonnay Mendoza 1996: Wants to be fresh and fruity, but doesn't quite come together. Has some decent green peach flavors and some buttery notes. 10,000 cases made. • $6 • (09/15/97) • **78**

Malbec Mendoza 1995: A bit stewed tasting, with dried plum and cherry flavors. It has decent richness, though. 10,000 cases made. • $6 • (10/15/97) • **80**

Merlot Mendoza 1996: Quite awkward and unbalanced, with dried leather and plum flavors. 25,000 cases made. • $6 • (09/30/97) • **71**

WEINERT, BODEGA Y CAVAS DE

Cabernet Sauvignon Mendoza Weinert 1992: Quite raisiny tasting, with modest plum flavors. Shows chocolate notes on the finish, but it's still quite tannic. • $17 • (09/15/97) • **80**
Cabernet Sauvignon Mendoza Weinert 1985 • $16 • (04/30/95) • **80**
Cabernet Sauvignon Mendoza Weinert 1983 • $16 • (05/31/94) • **81**

Carrascal Mendoza 1993: Leather and game notes predominate in this muddled red. Turns a bit harsh on the finish. • $13 • (09/15/97) • **78**
Carrascal Mendoza 1989 • $10 • (11/15/95) • **76**
Carrascal Mendoza 1988 • $10 • (05/31/94) • **82**
Carrascal Mendoza 1985 • $10 • (03/31/93) • **75**

Cavas de Weinert Mendoza 1992: Mature and smooth, offering ripe plum and ripe cherry flavors and some peppery notes. Spicy finish. A blend of 60 percent Cabernet, 30 percent Malbec and 10 Merlot. • $21 • (09/15/97) • **84**
Cavas de Weinert Mendoza 1989 • $17 • (11/15/95) • **86**
Cavas de Weinert Mendoza 1985 • $17 • (05/31/94) • **83**
Cavas de Weinert Mendoza 1983 • $16 • (03/31/93) • **77**

Malbec Mendoza Weinert 1992: Ripe, fairly rich and smooth, with good dried cherry and plum flavors, game and leather notes. Mature. Drink now. • $15 • (10/15/97) • **85**

Merlot Mendoza Weinert 1993: An attempt at a serious style, with ripe fruit flavors and herbal notes. Good concentration, but a little tired on the finish. • $15 • (09/30/97) • **82**
Merlot Mendoza Weinert 1990 • $12 • (09/30/94) • **72**
Merlot Mendoza Weinert 1988 • $13 • (03/31/93) • **76**

• Bulgaria •

BULGARE

Chardonnay Varna 1993 • $4 • (06/30/95) • **73**
Merlot & Pinot Noir Sliven 1993 • $4 • (06/30/95) • **84**

COASTAL CELLARS

Merlot Rousse Valley 1995: Light, simple, this offers berry and light cherry flavors with a backbone of lean tannins. Pleasant, but lacking varietal character. 2,500 cases made. • $6 • (02/28/97) • **80**

Key: SS—Spectator Selection CS—Cellar Selection HR—Highly Recommended BB—Best Buy $NA—Price not available Ⓐ—Auction Price (BT)—Barrel Tasting
Dates in parentheses indicate the issues in which the ratings were published.

DALINA, CHATEAU

Cabernet Sauvignon Russe 1996: Nice and juicy, with good cherry, berry and raspberry flavors. Turns a bit coarse on the finish, but still quite tasty. 45,000 cases made. • $4 • (10/31/97) • **82**
Cabernet Sauvignon Russe 1995: Simple and juicy, with berry and currant flavors and an herbal finish. • $5 • (06/30/97) • **78**
Cabernet Sauvignon Russe 1994 • $5 • (12/31/95) • **82**
Cabernet Sauvignon Russe 1993 • $4 • (12/31/94) • **80**
Cabernet Sauvignon Russe 1992 • $4 • (01/01/95) BB • **84**
Chardonnay Russe 1996: There's a strong floral aroma and flavor to this wine. Cloying finish. 45,000 cases made. • $4 • (10/31/97) • **76**
Chardonnay Russe 1995: A solid, full-bodied, oak and herb-flavored Chardonnay with just enough fruit flavor to keep it in balance. • $5 • (02/28/97) • **82**
Chardonnay Russe 1993 • $4 • (03/31/95) • **80**
Merlot Russe 1996: Offers some nice cherry and cedar flavors, but the tannins are a bit coarse, and it has an earthy aroma. Tasted twice, with consistent notes. 60,000 cases made. • $4 • (11/15/97) • **79**
Merlot Russe 1995: Simple and straightforward, with pleasant berry and currant flavors. • $5 • (01/01/97) • **79**
Merlot Russe 1994 • $5 • (12/31/95) • **83**
Merlot Russe 1993 • $4 • (12/31/94) • **84**
Sauvignon Blanc Russe 1995: Simple and fresh, with modest apple and pineapple flavors. Finishes on an earthy note. • $5 • (06/30/97) • **78**

HASKOVO WINERY

Merlot Haskovo 1993: Over the hill, with dried cherry and menthol flavors and a wollop of drying tannins. 25,000 cases made. • $6 • (11/15/97) • **76**
Merlot Sakar 1992: A thick wine, with stewed and prunelike flavors. Coarse on the finish as well. 15,000 cases made. • $8 • (11/15/97) • **78**
Merlot Stambolovo 1991: Dried cherry, tea and stewlike flavors render this a tired wine. 15,000 cases made. • $8 • (11/15/97) • **75**

MARITSA

Merlot Haskovo 1995: A bizarre style of Merlot, more like a Syrah, with smoky, peppery flavors and an overtly woody finish that leaves a bitter, tannic taste. • $7 • (12/31/97) • **74**

MENADA

Cabernet Sauvignon Oriahovitsa Reserve 1992: A bizarre milk and herb flavor runs through this wine. Not recommended. 70,000 cases made. • $6 • (08/31/97) • **70**
Cabernet Sauvignon Oriahovitsa Private Reserve 1991: A thick wine, with spice and cherry flavors. A bit awkward. 12,500 cases made. • $8 • (08/31/97) • **79**
Cabernet Sauvignon-Merlot Oriahovitsa Private Reserve 1990: Quite unappealing, with herbal and rubberlike flavors. 4,000 cases made. • $8 • (08/31/97) • **71**
Merlot Stara Zagora 1995: Fresh and juicy, with straightforward berry and cherry flavors. 20,000 cases made. • $6 • (08/31/97) • **80**

NAZDRAVE

Cabernet Sauvignon Korten 1989 • $5 • (12/31/94) • **81**
Cabernet Sauvignon Sliven Reserve 1988 • $6 • (12/31/94) • **77**
Chardonnay Russe 1993 • $5 • (01/01/96) • **70**
Country Red Russe NV • $4 • (06/30/95) • **82**
Merlot Sliven Reserve 1988 • $6 • (12/31/94) • **80**

NOVA ERA

Mavrud Pulden 1990: Mature, with somewhat appealing gamelike and leather flavors. Lean and tight on the finish. 16,500 cases made. • $7 • (07/31/97) • **79**
Melnik Hursovo Bulgaria 1989: Fruity up front, with dark plum and cherry flavors. Finishes on an herbal note. 8,000 cases made. • $7 • (07/31/97) • **80**
Merlot Trayana 1992: Smooth and fruity, with pleasant plum and berry flavors mixed with notes of smoke. This is a good, quaffable red that will go well with barbecued food. 25,000 cases made. • $7 • (06/30/97) • **84**
Merlot Vinenka Reserve 1991: Interesting for its strong gamelike aroma, this is balanced and full-bodied, with plum, cherry and spice flavors that linger on the finish. 8,300 cases made. • $7 • (06/30/97) • **83**
Merlot/Cabernet Sauvignon Oriahovitsa Reserve 1990: Well made, clean, fruity, with plenty of spice and sweet cherry notes. A bit simple in the end but quite tasty. 2,500 cases made. • $7 • (06/30/97) • **83**
Muscat Ottonel Russe 1994: A slightly sweet white, with simple fruit flavors. Very basic stuff. 1,000 cases made. • $7 • (08/31/97) • **75**

PULDEN

Cabernet Sauvignon Plovdiv 1989 • $5 • (12/31/94) • **84**
Merlot Plovdiv 1990 • $NA • (12/31/94) • **71**

SVISHTOV, VINPROM

Cabernet Sauvignon Svischtov Amphora Series 1988 • $9 • (03/31/95) • **73**

VINI

Cabernet Sauvignon Sliven 1992: A heavy, overwrought style. Smells like sawdust, tastes harsh and woody. Bitter finish, too. Tasted twice, with consistent notes. 15,000 cases made. • $8 • (12/31/97) • **69**
Merlot Sliven 1995: Firm and flavorful, with yummy, sweet cherry, plum and herbal flavors. This Merlot has good varietal character, with chocolaty notes on the lingering finish. 20,000 cases made. • $6 • (11/15/97) • **84**

VINPROM

Bulgare Merlot & Pinot Noir Sliven 1993 • $4 • (06/30/95) BB • **84**
Chardonnay Varna Bulgare 1993 • $4 • (06/30/95) • **73**
Merlot Haskovo 1989 • $5 • (12/31/94) • **74**
Merlot Haskovo Reserve 1987 • $6 • (12/31/94) • **82**

• Canada •

COLIO

Ice Wine Lake Erie North Shore 1992 • $28 • (04/15/95) • **72**

D'ANGELO VINEYARDS

Ice Wine Lake Erie North Shore 1992 • $29 • (04/15/95) • **78**

INNISKILLIN NIAGARA

Cabernet Sauvignon Niagara Peninsula Klose Vineyard 1991 • $15 • (05/15/95) • **82**
Chardonnay Niagara Peninsula Alliánce 1993: A butterball that overwhelms its fruit flavors of pear and apple. Turns earthy on the finish. Not for everyone. 250 cases made. • $20 • (01/31/97) • **80**
Chardonnay Niagara Peninsula Klose Vineyard 1994: Buttery and somewhat rich, with pear and ripe apple flavors. Tastes of clove and vanilla on the finish. A little obvious, but tasty. 889 cases made. • $14 • (01/31/97) • **83**
Chardonnay Niagara Peninsula Reserve 1994: Shows some power in the full-bodied texture, ripe apple flavors and firm acidity, but an herbal edge detracts from the varietal character. 10,000 cases made. • $11 • (01/31/97) • **79**
Ice Wine Niagara Peninsula Brae Burn Vineyard 1990 • $46/375ml • (04/15/95) • **76**
Ice Wine Ontario 1992 • $33/375ml • (04/15/95) • **80**
Ice Wine Ontario Brae Burn Estate 1989 • $71/375ml • (04/15/95) • **76**
Pinot Noir Niagara Peninsula Reserve 1992 • $15 • (05/15/95) • **77**
Pinot Noir Niagara Peninsula Reserve 1991 • $15 • (05/15/95) • **82**

INNISKILLIN OKANAGAN

Chardonnay Okanagan Valley Inkameep Vineyard VQA 1994: Has a strong floral, candied character that trails off into a raw oak note on the finish. Doesn't hang together. • $13 • (08/31/96) • **76**
Ice Wine Okanagan Valley 1994 • $NA • (05/15/96) • **86**

JACKSON-TRIGGS

Chardonnay Okanagan Valley VQA Proprietors' Reserve 1994: Crisp, bright and spicy, with a nice green apple character that lingers on the finish. 1,690 cases made. • $11 • (08/31/96) • **85**

KITTLING RIDGE

Ice Wine Niagara Peninsula Limited Release 1996: Seductive aromas of baked apples, nectarines and vanilla custard are followed by a medium-sweet, viscous texture with just enough acidity to keep it from being cloying. The soft, lush fruit flavors have lingering hints of white pepper and truffle at the edges. 2,000 cases made. • $45/375ml • (12/31/97) • **88**

LEBLANC ESTATE

Ice Wine Lake Erie North Shore 1992 • $31 • (04/15/95) • **76**

MAGNOTTA

Ice Wine Niagara Peninsula Vidal Blanc 1995: A racy dessert wine with vibrant acidity that buoys the orange, spice and tobacco notes and acts as a counterpoint to the sweetness. The finish has a beeswax character. Drinkable now. 4,000 cases made. • $47/375ml • (12/31/97) • **86**

PELLER ESTATES

Ice Wine Ehrenfelser Okanagan Valley 1993 • $25 • (04/15/95) • **83**
Ice Wine Niagara Vidal Blanc Peninsula 1996: Thick, rich and sweet, with well-defined, pretty apricot and peach flavors that linger on the finish. A luscious dessert wine that delivers the goods. • $NA/375ml • (12/31/97) • **88**
Ice Wine Niagara Peninsula Vidal 1991 • $38 • (04/15/95) • **80**
Late Harvest Vidal Blanc Ontario 1996: A light, crisp dessert wine with green apple and honey flavors, and an herbal note on the finish. • $NA/375ml • (12/31/97) • **83**

QUAILS' GATE

Ice Wine Riesling British Columbia 1993 • $33 • (04/15/95) • **86**

REIF ESTATE

Ice Wine Vidal Ontario 1991 • $32 • (04/15/95) • **83**

STONECHURCH

Ice Wine Ontario 1991 • $50 • (04/15/95) • **79**

STONEY RIDGE

Ice Wine Riesling/Traminer Ontario 1992 • $33 • (04/15/95) • **85**

SUMMERHILL

Ice Wine Riesling British Columbia 1992 • $33 • (04/15/95) • **86**
Pinot Noir British Columbia 1993 • $NA • (06/30/95) • **81**

VINELAND ESTATES

Ice Wine Vidal Niagara Peninsula 1992 • $32 • (04/15/95) • **81**
Ice Wine Vidal Niagara Peninsula 1989 • $85 • (04/15/95) • **70**

• Greece •

ANTONOPOULOS VINEYARDS

Antonopoulos Mantinia White 1995: Has fruit-cocktail aromas and flavors that aren't very enticing. • $11 • (04/30/97) • **70**

BOUTARI

Agiorgitiko Nemea 1994: Cherry and leather flavors, with a charred note. Balanced, but not very generous. Finishes on a menthol note. • $24 • (07/31/98) • **76**

Key: SS—Spectator Selection CS—Cellar Selection HR—Highly Recommended BB—Best Buy $NA—Price not available Ⓐ—Auction Price (BT)—Barrel Tasting
Dates in parentheses indicate the issues in which the ratings were published.

Goumenissa Red 1993 • $11 • (05/15/96) • **83**
Kretikos White 1994: Marked by almost medicinal aromas and cloying, sweet flavors. Fruit-cocktail notes on the finish. • $10 • (04/30/97) • **76**
Laoutari White 1995: Smooth and somewhat ripe tasting, with some decent fig and herb flavors, but it turns coarse on the finish. • $19 • (04/30/97) • **78**
Merlot-Xinomavro Vin de Pays d'Imathia 1994: An aromatic wine with coffee, cassis and menthol flavors. Flavorful and tannic but a bit coarse on the finish. Tasted twice, with consistent notes. • $15 • (12/31/97) • **81**
Merlot-Xinomavro Vin de Pays d'Imathia 1993: Thick, broad and juicy, here's a wild bronco of a wine, with plenty of game, plum and herb flavors and a good wollop of tannins. Finishes on a spicy note. Drinkable now. Tasted twice, with consistent notes. • $15 • (05/15/97) • **85**
Naoussa Grande Reserve 1992: Mature, even over-the-hill, with only modest cherry and spice flavors and an astringent finish. • $13 • (05/15/97) • **76**
Naoussa Grande Reserve 1990 • $13 • (05/15/96) • **82**
Naoussa Red 1994: A thin and fairly astringent wine that tastes of cherry and spice. • $7 • (05/15/97) • **75**
Naoussa Red 1993 • $8 • (05/15/96) • **84**
Nemea Red 1993 • $8 • (05/15/96) • **82**
Paros 1995: A tannic Greek red, with dried cherry and juniperlike flavors. Finishes on a spicy note. • $9 • (12/31/97) • **82**
Paros Red 1993 • $13 • (05/15/96) • **78**
Samos NV: A ripe and round dessert wine, sweet and smooth with plenty of body and delicious apricot flavors and aromas, though not a lot of complexity. • $14 • (05/15/97) • **85**
Santorini White 1996: A ride on the wild side, with green peach, herbal and apple flavors. Turns a bit medicinal in the end. • $11 • (12/31/97) • **78**
Santorini White 1995: Quite flat-tasting, with some disjointed herbal flavors. • $10 • (01/01/97) • **70**
Santorini White Kallisti 1994: An interesting and pleasant mix of flavors—plenty of buttery, oaky flavors, some good fig, honey and pear notes. Enjoyable, though turns a bit candied on the finish. • $14 • (04/30/97) • **85**
Vin de Pays d'Arcadia White 1996: Has a somewhat sweet, cloying taste, with fruit-cocktail flavors. A blend of Roditis and Moschofilero. • $NA • (07/31/98) • **74**
Vin de Pays de Pallini Chateau Matsa Vieilles Vignes White 1995: Firm and somewhat structured, with some interesting minerally components, but watch out for those foxy notes. • $NA • (07/31/98) • **78**

CAVA TSANTALIS

Red 1990 • $7 • (05/15/96) • **81**

HATZIMICHALIS, DOMAINE

20th Anniversary 1993 • $NA • (06/30/95) • **77**
Cabernet Sauvignon 1992 • $12 • (04/30/95) • **69**
Chardonnay 1993 • $12 • (06/30/95) • **75**

KOURTAKIS, D.

Kouros Nemea Red 1993: There's some blueberry fruit flavors, but they're fading and turning a wee bit sour. • $8 • (01/31/97) • **78**
Kouros Patras White 1995: Smooth and buttery, with nice fig, honey and lemon flavors, it's a refreshing and somewhat tart white wine with a pleasant finish. • $8 • (04/30/97) • **84**
Kourtaki Vin de Crete Red 1994: Quite herbal tasting, with an earthy aroma. A little thin in the middle, and quite tannic on the finish. Pure, uncomplicated and fresh. • $7 • (01/31/97) • **81**
Kourtaki Vin de Crete White 1994: A good, solid white with a touch of tartness. Offers pleasant honey and pear flavors, with a dash of pepper thrown in as well. • $7 • (04/30/97) • **83**

LAZARIDI, DOMAINE CONSTANTIN

Amethystos 1995: A cherry- and spice-flavored rosé, with a dose of onion and herb. Ends up a bit disjointed. • $13 • (05/15/97) • **76**
Amethystos 1994: Tastes a bit like a Rhône varietal with vibrant berry and cherry flavors. Turns a little green on the finish, but it certainly is lively. • $15 • (01/31/97) • **83**
Amethystos White 1995: A fairly ripe wine, with some earthy notes and a definite oniony streak. Distinctive and tasty, though not for everyone. • $13 • (05/15/97) • **76**
Château Julia White 1995: Coarse and oniony tasting, with a strange mix of herb and honey flavors on the finish. • $14 • (04/30/97) • **75**
Fumé Amethystos 1995: Thick and rustic tasting, with plenty of onionlike and herbal flavors. Try with a salty fish course. • $15 • (04/30/97) • **80**

LIMNOS

Muscat de Lemnos Grand Cru NV: Sweet, with flavors of honey and pine, this is ripe, round and enveloping, with a nice zip to it. An almond note on the finish keeps it in check. • $10 • (05/15/97) • **86**

OINOTHEKIE

Dafnis Red 1994: A well-crafted wine with plenty of punch. Fairly rich and supple, with plum and berry flavors and a prunelike note on the finish. Also has a nice leathery, gamy note running through it. Drink now. 5,000 cases made. • $19 • (04/30/98) • **85**

Dafnis Red NV: A smooth, herbal-tasting wine, with some spicy notes. Not a whole lot of fruit flavor but a distinctive gamy taste on the finish. An ambitious effort. • $19 • (01/31/97) • **85**

RAPSANI

Red 1991 • $11 • (05/15/96) • **83**

SKOURAS

Chardonnay Vin de Pays de Péloponnèse 1996: Thick and buttery tasting, with fig and apple flavors and a coarse finish. 3,000 cases made. • $14 • (04/30/98) • **79**

Matinia Megas Oenos White 1996: A floral aroma and flavor dominates this light white. Simple and a straightforward, with a touch of sweetness. Serve well-chilled. 25,000 cases made. • $12 • (04/30/98) • **81**

Nemea Megas Oenos 1995: Fresh and lively, with appealing berry and plum flavors. Crisp on the finish, with some spicy notes. A blend of 70 percent Saint George and 30 percent Cabernet Sauvignon. Drink now. 5,000 cases made. • $17 • (04/30/98) • **83**

Nemea Megas Oenos 1994: Brimming with blueberry flavors, framed by some nice, spicy notes, this is rich and concentrated. Drink now for its youthfulness. A blend of 70 percent Saint George and 30 percent Cabernet Sauvignon. 4,000 cases made. • $18 • (08/31/97) • **86**

Nemea Megas Oenos 1993: Delivers loads of fruit flavors that echo on the finish, namely, fresh blackberry, black cherry and plum flavors, with some pleasant clove and spice notes. A complex, serious and delicous wine. Drink now. A blend of 70 percent Saint George and 30 percent Cabernet Sauvignon. 5,000 cases made. • $16 • (01/31/97) • **88**

Nemea Saint George 1994: Well structured, with nice herbal and olive flavors. Finishes with drying tannins. 10,000 cases made. • $11 • (08/31/97) • **83**

Nemea Saint George 1993: A good, chunky red, with a nice blast of plum and cherry flavors. Well concentrated, and with plenty of tannins. Enjoy now for its freshness. 10,000 cases made. • $9 • (01/31/97) • **84**

Vin de Pays de Péloponnèse Cambello 1996: Young and juicy, with fresh berry flavors. Made from 100 percent Saint George. 20,000 cases made. • $7 • (08/31/97) • **78**

Vin de Pays de Péloponnèse Cambello 1995: Like a blast of pure fruit, with loads of raspberry and cherry flavors. Fresh and lively, with notes of leather and spice. A solid red. Made from 100 percent Saint George. 20,000 cases made. • $6 • (01/31/97) • **83**

Viognier Vin de Pays de Péloponnèse Cuvée Larsinós 1996: A decent mix of peach and onionlike flavors that turns a little heavy-handed on the finish. 2,000 cases made. • $18 • (04/30/98) • **78**

SPILIOTOPOULOS, CHRISTOS

Dimitra Geromilos Farms 1994: Ripe, and tastes mature, with peppery aromas and stewed flavors. • $14 • (01/31/97) • **78**

• Hungary •

BAKONDI

Eger Egri Bikavér 1993: A bit tired and rustic, with flavors of leather and dried cherry that linger on the finish. 800 cases made. • $12 • (07/31/97) • **78**

BODROG VÁRHEGY

Tokay Aszú 3 Puttonyos 1988 • $16 • (09/15/95) • **83**

Tokay Aszú 3 Puttonyos Citadella 1988: A powerful Tokay, its apricot, orange and spice notes buoyed on a solid framework. Moderately sweet, with firm acidity, this begs for sautéed foie gras. • $14/500ml • (10/31/97) • **87**

Tokay Aszú 5 Puttonyos Citadella 1988: A broad, sweet Tokay that has a hint of rusticity. It has no lack of honey, pistachio and vanilla flavors, but the acidity sticks out. • $20/500ml • (10/31/97) • **86**

Tokay Aszú 5 Puttonyos Messzelátö Dúlö 1988 • $20 • (09/15/95) • **81**

Tokay Szamorodni Citadella Sweet 1988: Touch of oxidation on the nose, showing prominent acidity and apple flavor and finishing on a walnut note. Not as sweet as Tokay can be, and a bit edgy. 3,500 cases made. • $8/500ml • (10/31/97) • **84**

CASTLE HILL CELLARS

Cabernet Sauvignon Villany Barrique 1994: Quite thin, with only modest dried cherry and tobacco flavors. 2,000 cases made. • $8 • (12/31/97) • **75**

Chardonnay Siklós Barrique 1995: A jumbled mix of caramel and floral character; unfinished malolactic perhaps. Tasted twice, with consistent notes. 3,000 cases made. • $8 • (12/31/97) • **69**

Merlot Villany Barrique 1994: Thin and severe, with a green finish. Not much fun. 2,000 cases made. • $8 • (12/31/97) • **70**

DISZNÓKÖ

Tokay Aszú 3 Puttonyos 1990 • $NA • (09/15/95) • **77**

Tokay Aszú 4 Puttonyos 1993: Quite thick and rich, but it remains closed on the nose. Full-bodied, with interesting layers of citrus, honey, cigar-box, smoke and spice flavors, but it finishes angularly. Needs time. Try after 2000. 10,000 cases made. • $25/500ml • (12/31/97) • **85**

Tokay Aszú 4 Puttonyos 1992: Luscious and vibrant at the same time, this rich wine has a thick texture, mouthwatering acidity and lively apricot and honey flavors. A wonderfully long finish completes the package. Drink now through 2005. • $21 • (04/30/97) • **89**

Tokay Aszú 4 Puttonyos 1989 • $NA • (09/15/95) • **80**

Tokay Aszú 5 Puttonyos 1993: Modern-style Tokay. A laser-sharp, pure and clean sweetie, showing great elegance and refinement. Its superb citrusy, crisp structure counterbalances the honey, dried fruit and pineapple character that oozes from start to finish in this full-bodied beauty. Long, spicy and smoky finish makes it tempting to drink now through 2010. 10,000 cases made. • $32/500ml • (12/31/97) • **94**

Tokay Aszú 5 Puttonyos 1992: A truly rich medley of flavors renders this both complex and powerful. Quite sweet, with honey and marzipan flavors, good balance and lingering finish. Drink now through 2005. • $27 • (04/30/97) • **90**

Tokay Aszú 5 Puttonyos 1988 • $18 • (09/15/95) • **86**

Tokay Aszú 6 Puttonyos 1993: Clean and pure, of medium body, with some honey, caramel, maple, honeysuckle and bitter-almond character. The creamy texture turns a bit rough on the finish. Try after 2000. 10,000 cases made. • $40/500ml • (12/31/97) • **87**

Tokay Aszú 6 Puttonyos 1992: Rich in texture but subtle in flavor, this fabulous sweet wine seems to be holding its best in reserve. It has great balance, delicate fruit, honey and butter flavors and a long, long finish. Best after 2000, and should last through 2010. 2,000 cases made. • $32 • (04/30/97) • **94**

Tokay Aszú 6 Puttonyos 1989 • $NA • (09/15/95) • **84**

Tokay Aszú Eszencia 1993: Beautiful sweetie from Tokay. Modern in style, very fresh and stressing fruit over oak and tradition, with an excellent underpinning of acidity. Delivers laser-sharp, fairly crisp honey, citrus, tropical and flowery notes. You wish for a bit more harmony on the finish, so hold until after 2000. To be released in early 1999. • $NA/500ml • (12/31/97) • **95**

Tokay Aszú Eszencia 1988 • $NA • (09/15/95) • **83**

Tokay Eszencia 1992: Very thick and brown-amber in color, this is concentration defined. An oddity as far as wine goes, with spice, chocolate, maple syrup character, but also a slightly rustic chestnut character. Still, it ends on a long, intense, smoky-spicy finish. Drink upon release and into the next century. • $NA/500ml • (12/31/97) • **90**

Tokay Furmint 1994 • $8 • (09/15/95) • **77**

Tokay Furmint 1993 • $7 • (09/15/95) • **78**

Tokay Szamorodni Edes 1993: Like eating a ginger-snap cookie. Lovely and seductive, with honeysuckle, vanilla, cinnamon and apple pie notes. Of medium body, it's just off-dry, with some honey and almond flavors on the clean, spicy finish. Drink now through 2000. • $20/500ml • (12/31/97) • **89**

Tokay Szamorodni Száraz 1990 • $NA • (09/15/95) • **82**

DUNAVÁR

Merlot 1996: Very light, almost a blush wine, with appealing peppery and cherry flavors. 7,800 cases made. • $5 • (10/31/97) • **78**

HETSZOLO

Tokay Aszú 5 Puttonyos 1993 • $NA • (09/15/95) (BT) • **90-94**
Tokay Aszú 5 Puttonyos Dessewffy 1988 • $NA • (09/15/95) • **80**
Tokay Fordítás Dessewffy 1990 • $NA • (09/15/95) • **81**
Tokay Furmint 1994 • $NA • (09/15/95) • **79**
Tokay Hárslevelű 1994 • $NA • (09/15/95) • **79**
Tokay Muscat 1994 • $NA • (09/15/95) • **83**

HICKORY RIDGE

Chardonnay Gyongyos 1996: A lean, straightforward wine that reminds more of Sauvignon. Simple in character, rather green in flavor. Drink now. • $6 • (07/31/98) • **78**

Chardonnay Hincesti 1996: Thin and lean, with celery and lemon flavors that turn watery on the dull finish. Not recommended. Tasted three times, with consistent notes. • $6 • (05/15/98) • **69**

Chardonnay Hincesti 1994 • $5 • (01/01/96) • **78**

IGRISTOJE

Sparkling Dry NV: A simple, slightly sweet (despite the Dry designation) bubbly with fruit-cocktail flavors. • $12 • (12/31/97) • **78**

Sparkling Semi-Dry NV: A sweet, soft, pleasant bottle of bubbly, with fruity, spicy flavors and mouthfilling bubbles. Best as dessert. Drink now. • $12 • (12/31/97) • **81**

MEGYER, CHATEAU

Tokay Aszú 4 Puttonyos 1988 • $NA • (09/15/95) • **78**
Tokay Aszú 5 Puttonyos 1993 • $NA • (09/15/95) (BT) • **90-94**
Tokay Chardonnay 1994 • $NA • (09/15/95) • **75**
Tokay Chardonnay Zempléni 1993 • $NA • (09/15/95) • **75**
Tokay Furmint 1994 • $NA • (09/15/95) • **78**
Tokay Furmint 1993 • $NA • (09/15/95) • **76**
Tokay Muscat 1994 • $NA • (09/15/95) • **80**

OREMUS

Tokay Aszú 5 Puttonyos 1993: Well made, with mineral, stone, honey, lemon and spice character. Medium in body, with a rather subdued finish. Don't expect a showy wine. Try now. • $22/500ml • (12/31/97) • **90**

Tokay Aszú 5 Puttonyos 1989: An exciting dessert wine that exhibits more grace than power. Complex, showing mandarin orange, crème brûlée and spice notes, with an underlying acidity that carries the flavors to a refreshing finish. • $22/500ml • (12/31/97) • **90**

Tokay Aszú 5 Puttonyos 1988 • $NA • (09/15/95) • **82**

Tokay Aszú 6 Puttonyos 1981: Moderately sweet, showing lovely balance and freshness. The apricot, orange, honey and nutlike flavors are sublime, followed by a long, walnut finish. Well made. • $40/500ml • (12/31/97) • **91**

Tokay Aszú 6 Puttonyos 1972 • $NA • (09/15/95) • **89**
Tokay Fordítás 1983 • $NA • (09/15/95) • **74**
Tokay Furmint Mandulás 1993 • $NA • (09/15/95) • **73**

Tokay Szamorodni Száraz 1993: Odd, but fun for the adventurous drinker, this is maderized like a Sherry but fresh and fruity like Pinot Gris. Of medium body, with marzipan, almond, citrus and barklike notes. A good alternative to a Spanish fino to drink as an apéritif. • $8/500ml • (12/31/97) • **83**

Tokay Szamorodni Száraz 1986 • $NA • (09/15/95) • **83**

PAJZOS, CHÂTEAU

Tokay Aszú 4 Puttonyos 1988 • $NA • (09/15/95) • **79**

Tokay Aszú 5 Puttonyos 1993: This honeyed, late-harvest white offers a lush, pillowy texture and rich flavors of dried apricots, toffee and vanilla. It's very sweet, yet quite fresh and still lively. Delicious now, it should age easily until 2020. • $35/500ml • (12/31/97) • **90**

Key: SS—Spectator Selection CS—Cellar Selection HR—Highly Recommended BB—Best Buy $NA—Price not available Ⓐ—Auction Price (BT)—Barrel Tasting
Dates in parentheses indicate the issues in which the ratings were published.

Tokay Aszú 5 Puttonyos 1988 • $21 • (09/15/95) • **82**

Tokay Esszencia 1993: One of the world's finest dessert wines. Sensational, ultrasweet Tokay, yet with a lovely citrus underpinning that keeps it from being heavy. Like melted honey with lime and pineapple, this is one of those marvelous gems that makes you swoon in delight. Tempting now into the 21st century. A collector's item to drink in small portions, by itself, to celebrate life. • $400/500ml • (12/31/97) • **99**

Tokay Furmint 1994 • $9 • (09/15/95) • **72**
Tokay Furmint 1993 • $8 • (09/15/95) • **76**

PETERS' HILL

Chardonnay Möcsényi Bátaapáti Estate 1996: Extreme flavors of onions and herbs. Smells worse. Tasted three times, with consistent notes. 5,000 cases made. • $7 • (10/31/97) • **70**

Möcsényi Red Bátaapáti Estate Special Reserve 1995: Tastes more like a Pinot Noir than a Cabernet blend, with spicy berry flavors and touches of herbs and earth. Lively, moderately concentrated, with light tannins. A blend of Cabernet Franc, Cabernet Sauvignon and Kékfrankos. Drink now. • $7 • (05/15/98) • **83**

ROYAL TOKAJI WINE CO., THE

Tokay Aszú 5 Puttonyos 1990 • $NA • (09/15/95) • **86**

Tokay Aszú 5 Puttonyos Betsek 1991: Smooth and honeyed, this shows the nutty, caramel and spice flavors of the traditional, oxidized style of Tokay. It's medium-sweet, with enough acidity for balance. • $48/500ml • (08/31/96) • **88**

Tokay Aszú 5 Puttonyos Betsek 1990: Light and elegant dessert wine. A vivid orange color, heady aromas of orange and honey, and bright, sweet, tangy fruit flavors make this a vibrant and arresting wine. Its richness and sweetness are well offset by acidity, and the finish is long and appealing. • $50/500ml • (08/31/96) • **89**

Tokay Aszú 5 Puttonyos Birsalmás 1993: Amazingly complex, fat and rich, yet with an undertow of citrus and spice character to keep it on an even keel. Full-bodied and multifaceted, delivering loads of cacao, coffee and orange marmalade flavors. Creamy, intense, harmonious finish. Tempting now through 2015. • $53/500ml • (12/31/97) • **94**

Tokay Aszú 5 Puttonyos Birsalmás 1991: A nice marriage of spice and dried fruit flavors give depth. Shows good concentration, and tastes of raisins, dried apricots and honey. Quite sweet but without much spark. • $48/500ml • (08/31/96) • **87**

Tokay Aszú 5 Puttonyos Birsalmás 1990 • $50 • (09/15/95) • **87**

Tokay Aszú 5 Puttonyos Blue Label 1993: World-class dessert wine. Creamy in texture, full in body, seductive in character, filling your palate with a bouquet of dried figs, vanilla beans, cigar leaves, maple, ginger snaps, cloves and curry. Long, smoky finish with a grip of bitter almond. Tempting now through 2005. • $32/500ml • (12/31/97) • **92**

Tokay Aszú 5 Puttonyos Blue Label 1991: Fresh, complex and lingering. Good balance of sweet and sour with its spicy vanilla, peach and passion fruit flavors. Lively and attractive—would be great with fruit desserts. • $32/500 ml • (08/31/96) • **89**

Tokay Aszú 5 Puttonyos Bojta 1991: Thick but a bit coarse. Offers sweetness but lacks fresh fruit, showing quite a bit of the traditional oxidation. A pleasant accompaniment to dessert; not as intriguing on its own. • $28/500ml • (08/31/96) • **84**

Tokay Aszú 5 Puttonyos Bojta 1990 • $28 • (09/15/95) • **88**

Tokay Aszú 5 Puttonyos Nyulászó 1991: Rich, fresh and juicy, with raisin, orange-peel, nut and spice flavors. Quite sweet, but has plenty of acidity to balance. Intriguing and tempting—take another sip. • $65/500ml • (08/31/96) • **91**

Tokay Aszú 5 Puttonyos Nyulászó 1990 • $65 • (09/15/95) • **89**

Tokay Aszú 5 Puttonyos Red Label 1993: Fabulous harmony in this classy dessert wine. Already, the wood, fruit and acidity have melted together to offer a creamy texture, harmonious finish and loads of complexity, with spice, mocha, curry, pineapple, dried figs and apricot, clove and vanilla beans and plenty of palate-cleansing citrus on the long finish. Tempting now through 2010. • $28/500ml • (12/31/97) HR • **95**

Tokay Aszú 5 Puttonyos Szt. Tamás 1991: Concentrated and quite sweet, this rich white offers apricot, dried pineapple and honey flavors, with enough acidity to maintain freshness. A serious meditation wine. • $65/500ml • (08/31/96) • **90**

Tokay Aszú 6 Puttonyos Nyulászó 1993: Complex and multilayered, sweet and full-bodied. Beautiful flavors, clean and pure, with loads of tropical, dried apricot and dried fig, vanilla bean, ginger snaps and curry. Ends on fresh, palate-cleansing, elegant citrusy notes. Bravo! Tempting now through 2010. • $77/500ml • (12/31/97) • **94**

Tokay Aszú 6 Puttonyos Szt. Tamás 1993: Thick, rich and fat, this full-bodied sweetie is super-round, creamy in texture, voluptuous and showy. Orange marmalade, spice, white chocolate, apple pie and smoky, tobaccolike flavors are terrific. Tempting now through 2010. • $77/500ml • (12/31/97) • **95**

Tokay Aszú Essencia 1993: Amazingly concentrated, this is like liquid gold. Very thick, rich and a bit heavy, with marmalade, honey and pineapple, it almost has the texture of maple syrup. Incredibly intense on the long, smoky, lemony finish. Drink now and well into the next century. • $135/500ml • (12/31/97) • **97**

ST. DONATUS

Chardonnay Balatonlellei 1993 • $6 • (03/31/95) • **78**

White Balatonlellei Muskotály 1994: An interesting character, with cidery aromas and flavors. Lacks concentration. 10,000 cases made. • $NA • (01/01/97) • **77**

VINUM BONUM

Chardonnay Etyeki 1993 • $10 • (03/31/95) • **80**

Sauvignon Blanc Etyeki 1993 • $10 • (03/31/95) • **77**

• Israel •

GAMLA

Cabernet Sauvignon Galil 1990 • $12 • (12/15/94) • **83**

Cabernet Sauvignon Galil 1989 • $12 • (12/15/94) • **78**

Cabernet Sauvignon Galil 1988 • $10 • (07/15/93) • **77**

Cabernet Sauvignon Galil 1987 • $9 • (03/31/91) • **75**

Cabernet Sauvignon Galil Special Reserve 1986 • $12 • (03/31/91) • **83**

Muscat Galil 1995: Orange and spice flavors show varietal character, though with a bit of a canned edge, and there's enough acidity to keep it fresh despite moderate sweetness. • $10 • (04/30/97) • **78**

Sauvignon Blanc Galil 1994: Thick textured but tart, this has little varietal character, only a sharp edge of lemony acidity keeping it from neutrality. • $10 • (04/30/97) • **75**

Sauvignon Blanc Late Harvest Galil 1988 • $14 • (03/31/91) • **75**

GOLAN

Cabernet Sauvignon Galil 1992: Well balanced, offering ripe prune, clove and chocolate flavors with firm but ripe tannins and a rich texture. Maturing, it's ready now. • $13 • (04/30/97) • **85**

Cabernet Sauvignon Galil 1989 • $12 • (12/15/94) • **81**

Cabernet Sauvignon Galil 1987 • $12 • (04/15/92) • **83**

Cabernet Sauvignon Galil 1986 • $11 • (03/31/91) • **85**

Chardonnay Galil 1993: Bright acidity and light vanilla flavors contrast nicely in this medium-weight white. Also has light floral and apple flavors. • $13 • (04/30/97) • **82**

Golan Village Red Galil 1994: A soft red, with cherry, grape and spice flavors that are light and fresh. Round and gentle on the palate, it's a good quaffing wine. • $10 • (04/30/97) • **82**

YARDEN

Cabernet Sauvignon Galil 1993: A luscious red in the international style, with toasty oak, ripe blackberry and chocolate flavors and a velvety texture. Lovely, and ready to drink. • $20 • (04/30/97) • **88**

Cabernet Sauvignon Galil 1990 • $18 • (12/15/94) • **82**

Cabernet Sauvignon Galil 1989 • $18 • (12/15/94) • **79**

Cabernet Sauvignon Galil 1986 • $14 • (06/30/90) • **79**

Cabernet Sauvignon Galil 1985 • $14 • (06/30/90) • **82**

Chardonnay Galil 1995: Heavy oak-induced aromas of vanilla and toast give way to oaky flavors that dominate the ripe melon notes. It's rich and has intensity, but lacks balance. • $15 • (04/30/97) • **84**

Merlot Galil Special Reserve 1988 • $14 • (03/31/91) • **77**

Merlot Galil Special Reserve 1986 • $12 • (06/30/90) • **79**

Mount Hermon Red Galil 1995: This assertive red shows black cherry, coffee and light herb notes in a chewy structure with firm tannins. It's clean, and reveals good concentration. Ready to drink. • $10 • (04/30/97) • **86**

Mount Hermon Red Galil 1989 • $7 • (03/31/91) • **70**

Mount Hermon White Galil 1995: Fruit flavors of pineapple and peach are a bit sweet and sour in this heavy wine. It's rich, but lacks harmony. • $10 • (04/30/97) • **79**

White Riesling Galil 1995: Pine and apricot flavors hint at varietal character, but they're a bit heavy. Moderate sweetness is balanced by crisp acidity. • $12 • (04/30/97) • **80**

• Lebanon •

MUSAR, CHATEAU

Lebanon 1987 • $18 • (09/30/94) • **85**

Lebanon 1983 • $17 • (07/15/91) • **86**

Lebanon 1982 • $17 • (07/15/91) • **87**

Lebanon 1981 • $18 • (07/15/91) • **84**

Lebanon 1980 • $17 • (07/31/88) • **91**

• New Zealand •

ARARIMU

Cabernet Sauvignon Hawke's Bay 1991 • $NA • (05/15/94) • **80**

ATA RANGI

Pinot Noir Martinborough 1995: Smells great, but the texture is a bit tough, with chewy tannins over a core of juicy currant and blackberry flavors. Picks up a smoky note on the finish. Good now, but better in 2000. 400 cases made. • $50 • (06/15/97) • **86**

Pinot Noir Martinborough 1991 • $NA • (05/15/94) • **81**

BABICH

Cabernet Blend Hawke's Bay Irongate 1990 • $NA • (05/15/94) • **79**

Cabernet Sauvignon Hawke's Bay 1989 • $10 • (07/15/91) • **74**

Pinot Noir Henderson Valley 1992 • $NA • (05/15/94) • **77**

Sauvignon Blanc Hawke's Bay 1993 • $10 • (05/15/94) • **80**

Sauvignon Blanc Marlborough 1993 • $11 • (05/15/94) • **82**

BRANCOTT

Chardonnay Gisborne Ormond Estate 1995: Soft, smooth and generous, with spicy pineapple, pear and vanilla flavors, finishing with polish and style. Flavors linger, suggesting that although this is delicious now, it might be best after 1999. • $22 • (05/15/98) • **89**

Chardonnay Marlborough Renwick Estate 1996: A jazzy mouthful of flavor, running from mineral to honey, pear and apricot; balanced with racy acidity, finishing long and vibrant. Feels like a tightly closed bud that should open and flower by 1999 to 2000. • $22 • (05/15/98) • **89**

Sauvignon Blanc Marlborough Brancott Estate 1996: Light and appealing for its modest nectarine and spice flavors, hinting at lemon on the lengthy finish. Delicate and refined, a wine to drink soon. • $24 • (05/15/98) • **87**

Sauvignon Blanc Marlborough Reserve 1997: Bright and fresh; a jazzy, tart mouthful of pear, herb and citrus flavors that meld beautifully on the apricot-scented finish. Lively now. Drink soon. • $16 • (05/15/98) • **88**

CASTLE HILL

Sauvignon Blanc Hawke's Bay 1993 • $NA • (05/15/94) • **82**

CHURCH ROAD

Cabernet Sauvignon Hawke's Bay 1991 • $NA • (05/15/94) • **78**

CLOUDY BAY

Cabernet-Merlot 1991 • $NA • (05/15/94) • **75**

Sauvignon Blanc Marlborough 1996: Superb. Well crafted, it's steely dry but exuberant at the same time, with distinctive, bright passion fruit, nectarine and herb flavors that linger bracingly through the zingy finish. Delicious. 7,000 cases imported. Drink now. • $17 • (06/15/97) SS • **94**

Sauvignon Blanc Marlborough 1993 • $15 • (05/15/94) • **88**

COLLARDS

Sauvignon Blanc Marlborough 1993 • $NA • (05/15/94) • **88**

NEW ZEALAND

COOPERS CREEK

Cabernet-Merlot Huapai 1991 • $NA • (05/15/94) • **77**
Cabernet Sauvignon Huapai 1990 • $12 • (08/31/93) • **83**
Cabernet Sauvignon Huapai 1989 • $10 • (04/15/92) • **79**
Chardonnay Gisborne 1993 • $11 • (05/15/94) • **85**
Merlot Hawke's Bay 1992 • $NA • (05/15/94) • **70**
Sauvignon Blanc Marlborough 1993 • $NA • (05/15/94) • **84**

CORBANS

Cabernet-Merlot Hawke's Bay Private Bin 1995: Firm in texture, with nicely focused currant and blueberry flavors on a modest scale, and velvety tannins on the finish that need until 1999 to 2000. 800 cases made. • $21 • (02/28/98) • **86**

Cabernet Sauvignon Hawke's Bay Private Bin Premium Selection 1994: Light, tart and distinctly herbal, with modest berry flavors to back it up. Drink now. 1,500 cases made. • $18 • (12/15/97) • **81**

Chardonnay Gisborne Private Bin Premium Selection 1995: Toasty, buttery flavors dominate this smooth-textured, polished wine, offering a nice thread of limelike acidity on the balanced finish. Ready now. 2,500 cases made. • $18 • (12/15/97) • **88**

Merlot Marlborough Private Bin 1991 • $15 • (05/15/94) • **88**
Sauvignon Blanc Marlborough Private Bin 1993 • $13 • (05/15/94) • **76**

Sauvignon Blanc Marlborough Private Bin Premium Selection 1996: Crisp and juicy, here's a spiffy mouthful of freshness and citrusy acidity, echoing pear, bay leaf and nectarine flavors on the finish. Ready now. 1,500 cases made. • $18 • (12/15/97) • **87**

CRAWFORD, KIM

Chardonnay Gisborne Tietjen 1997: Ripe, open-textured and engagingly silky, with pear, apricot, vanilla and honey notes fanning out on the finish. Drink now. 200 cases made. • $20 • (06/30/98) • **91**

Chardonnay Marlborough Unoaked 1997: Bright and appealing for its apricot-scented pear and honey flavors, finishing with a touch of spice. The texture could be smoother. Drink now. 200 cases made. • $15 • (06/30/98) • **86**

Sauvignon Blanc Awatere Valley 1996: A bright, herbal style, with a spiky green bean edge to the lemony apple flavors. 75 cases imported. Drink now. • $20 • (06/30/98) • **88**

Sauvignon Blanc Marlborough 1997: Has a sense of ripeness and richness to go along with dead-on herbal and spicy flavors, hinting at apricot on the generous finish. Drink now. 575 cases made. • $15 • (06/30/98) • **89**

DASHWOOD

Sauvignon Blanc Marlborough 1997: Bright and distinctive, with celery and apple flavors lingering on the lively finish. Drink now. • $14 • (06/30/98) • **87**

Sauvignon Blanc Marlborough 1993 • $NA • (05/15/94) • **75**

DE REDCLIFFE

Cabernet-Merlot Hawke's Bay 1990 • $NA • (05/15/94) • **68**
Pinot Noir Hawke's Bay 1991 • $NA • (05/15/94) • **78**
Sauvignon Blanc Marlborough 1993 • $NA • (05/15/94) • **79**

Sauvignon Blanc Marlborough Reserve 1996: Bright, zingy and bubbling over with green apple, passion fruit and herbal aromas and flavors. Light and juicy finish. Drink soon. 3,000 cases made. • $16 • (11/15/97) • **87**

DELEGAT'S

Cabernet-Merlot Hawke's Bay 1992 • $NA • (05/15/94) • **71**
Cabernet Sauvignon Hawke's Bay 1991 • $NA • (05/15/94) • **83**
Merlot Hawke's Bay Proprietor's Reserve 1990 • $NA • (05/15/94) • **70**
Sauvignon Blanc Hawke's Bay 1993 • $NA • (05/15/94) • **84**

Key: SS—Spectator Selection CS—Cellar Selection HR—Highly Recommended BB—Best Buy $NA—Price not available Ⓐ—Auction Price (BT)—Barrel Tasting
Dates in parentheses indicate the issues in which the ratings were published.

DOCTORS CREEK

Chardonnay Marlborough 1996: Packed with bright, ripe fruit character, this pulses with citrusy pear and apple flavors that keep going through the solid finish. Impressive now; should flesh out even more by 1999. 9,000 cases made. • $13 • (02/28/98) • **89**

Sauvignon Blanc Marlborough 1996: Tart, tangy and bright, with lemony pear and green gooseberry flavors, turning almost minty on the finish. Needs food to tame it. 9,000 cases made. • $13 • (01/31/98) • **86**

ESK VALLEY

Cabernet-Merlot Hawke's Bay 1992 • $NA • (05/15/94) • **78**
Cabernet-Merlot Hawke's Bay Reserve 1991 • $NA • (05/15/94) • **86**
Sauvignon Blanc Hawke's Bay 1993 • $NA • (05/15/94) • **83**

FORREST

Chardonnay Marlborough 1993 • $NA • (05/15/94) • **81**

FRAMINGHAM

Riesling Marlborough Classic 1997: Dry style, with exuberant apricot-tinged apple and floral flavors that make it almost seductive. Drink now. 2,000 cases made. • $14 • (05/15/98) • **87**

Sauvignon Blanc Marlborough 1997: Neon-bright in flavor, with colorful fruit tastes ranging from green apple to passion fruit, all nicely balanced. Ready now. 5,000 cases made. • $18 • (12/31/97) • **87**

FRENCH FARM

Sauvignon Blanc Waipara 1993 • $NA • (05/15/94) • **78**

GIBBSTON VALLEY

Sauvignon Blanc Marlborough 1997: Crisp in texture and generous with its spicy citrus and green apple flavors, lingering smoothly on the finish. Has harmony and finesse. Drink now. 1,000 cases made. • $19 • (05/31/98) • **90**

GIESEN

Chardonnay Canterbury 1996: Satiny, spicy and distinctive for its range of citrus, mineral and pineapple flavors. Hangs on nicely on the finish. Drink now through 2000. 8,000 cases made. • $13 • (05/31/98) • **87**

Chardonnay Canterbury Burnham School Road Reserve 1995: Weaves a pleasant blend of mineral, pear, honey and spice flavors through the silky texture, crisply supported by citrusy acidity. Shows maturity and balance. Try now. 1,000 cases made. • $23 • (09/15/97) • **88**

Riesling Canterbury 1996: Bracing acidity keeps this off-dry, peppery wine lively. Has some green apple and mineral notes, too. 2,500 cases made. • $11 • (09/15/97) • **85**

Sauvignon Blanc Marlborough 1997: Very crisp and juicy. A lively wine with flower- and herb-scented apple and pear flavors that linger charmingly on the finish. Delicious now. 8,000 cases made. • $12 • (03/31/98) • **88**

Sauvignon Blanc Marlborough 1996: A racy and zingy white from New Zealand offering high quality at a low price. Refreshing for the dazzling floral, peppery, citrusy flavors that resonate brightly on the long finish, it goes for the high notes. 10,000 cases made. • $9 • (09/15/97) BB • **90**

GOLDWATER

Cabernet-Merlot Waiheke Island 1994: Rich, flavorful and complex, offering a vibrant mouthful of black cherry; gamy, smoky and herbal qualities. Crisp acidity supports the flavors, which persist on the finish. Best from 2000. A blend of 63 percent Cabernet Sauvignon and 37 percent Merlot. 1,000 cases made. • $50 • (10/15/97) • **88**

Cabernet-Merlot Waiheke Island 1990 • $30 • (05/15/94) • **84**
Cabernets-Merlot Waiheke Island 1985 • $27 • (07/15/88) • **73**

Chardonnay Marlborough 1995: Crisp, zingy and refreshing for its citrusy, slightly herbal flavors, shaded nicely with spice. Bracing and pretty. Ready now. 2,500 cases made. • $25 • (10/15/97) • **87**

Chardonnay Waiheke Island Delamore 1995: Crisp and zingy, offering citrus and pear flavors that finish with hints of vanilla and peach. Ready now. 1,000 cases made. • $40 • (10/15/97) • **88**

Sauvignon Blanc Marlborough Dog Point 1996: Tart, citrusy and floral, this is a nice example of New Zealand Sauvignon Blanc that's jazzy, harmonious and appealing early on. 5,000 cases made. • $19 • (10/15/97) • **87**

GROVE MILL

Chardonnay Marlborough 1996: Crisp, bright style of Chardonnay, focusing on citrus, melon and tropical fruit flavors, finishing with zingy acidity. Better in 1999 to 2001. 2,000 cases made. • $20 • (03/31/98) • **90**

Chardonnay Marlborough 1993 • $NA • (05/15/94) • **83**

Chardonnay Marlborough Lansdowne 1996: Bright and appealing for its peach, spice and honey flavors that linger on the beautifully modulated finish. Drink now. 500 cases made. • $30 • (05/31/98) • **90**

Pinot Gris Marlborough 1996: Soft, supple and very tasty, here's a yummy mouthful of floral, melon, pear and pineapple flavors. A stylish wine with intensity and charm. Drink now. 500 cases made. • $20 • (10/15/97) • **89**

Riesling Marlborough 1997: Juicy and bright, rich in flavor, dripping with spicy apple, quince and apricot that reverberate through the pure finish. Delicious now. 1,000 cases made. • $14 • (03/31/98) • **90**

Riesling Marlborough 1996: Soft and generous with its honey-scented apricot and peach flavors that linger long. A pretty wine, perfect for pre-dinner sipping or drinking with crab. 1,100 cases made. • $14 • (10/15/97) • **88**

Sauvignon Blanc Marlborough 1997: Crisp and bright, a zinger of a Sauvignon Blanc with pretty floral and herbal aromas and juicy, citrusy fruit flavors. Ready now. 6,000 cases made. • $17 • (03/31/98) • **90**

Sauvignon Blanc Marlborough 1996: Bright and zingy with its green pepper-tinged pear, apricot and citrus flavors, all resting on a smooth, polished frame that tames the wilder notions of flavor. Drink now. 7,500 cases made. • $17 • (11/15/97) • **88**

Sauvignon Blanc Marlborough 1993 • $NA • (05/15/94) • **83**

HIGHFIELD

Merlot Marlborough 1995: Modest berry flavors with a foxy accent, crisp on the finish. Not your typical Merlot, but a nice red. 800 cases made. • $11 • (06/15/97) • **83**

Riesling Marlborough Dry 1996: Very dry, crisp and bracing; a citrusy wine with modest depth of flavor. 800 cases made. • $9 • (06/15/97) • **81**

Sauvignon Blanc Marlborough 1996: Crisp and lively, with bright, citrusy flavors, especially sweet nectarine, and a dry and steely finish. Ready now. 5,000 cases made. • $10 • (06/15/97) • **86**

HUNTER'S

Cabernet Sauvignon Marlborough 1990 • $NA • (05/15/94) • **77**

Chardonnay Marlborough 1995: Bright and zingy, not crisp but sleek, with a polished texture surrounding the citrus, melon and pear flavors. Hints at spice on the finish. Nicely done. • $24 • (05/15/98) • **88**

Pinot Noir Marlborough 1992 • $NA • (05/15/94) • **76**

Sauvignon Blanc Marlborough 1996: Light enough to aim for elegance, with pretty pear, sweet pea and herb flavors enlivening the finish. Ready now. • $20 • (05/15/98) • **86**

Sauvignon Blanc Marlborough 1993 • $NA • (05/15/94) • **76**

JACKSON

Chardonnay Marlborough 1996: A zingy mouthful of bright and citrusy gooseberry and carambola (star fruit) flavors that just keep coming on the lively finish. A remarkable wine; taut and wiry, full of delicious flavor. Ready now. 4,000 cases made. • $19 • (10/15/97) • **91**

Chardonnay Marlborough Reserve 1994: Smooth and ripe, with a big generous mouthful of buttery, spicy pear, pineapple and honey flavors that linger on the finish. 500 cases made. • $27 • (04/30/97) • **91**

Sauvignon Blanc Marlborough 1996: Dry, bracingly tart and lively, with herb-, celery- and lemon-tinged gooseberry flavor. Distinctive and ready to drink. • $18 • (10/15/97) • **88**

Sauvignon Blanc Marlborough 1993 • $NA • (05/15/94) • **84**

KUMEU RIVER

Chardonnay Kumeu 1996: Ripe flavors are just the beginning in this mouth-filling, buttery beauty. Sleek in style, this New Zealand white wraps its generous peach, pear and honey flavors into a jazzy package that balances everything with delicate acidity. Drinkable now. • $33 • (12/31/97) HR • **92**

Chardonnay Kumeu 1994: Big, rich and powerful. Layered with buttery, spicy pear, honey and hazelnut flavors that fold together luxuriously on a long finish. A most distinctive wine. 3,000 cases made. • $29 • (10/15/96) HR • **93**

Chardonnay Kumeu Maté's Vineyard 1996: A lively mouthful of ripe pear, melon and dusky spices, hinting at honey on the supple finish. Nicely balanced, with hints of citrus on the finish. Ready now. Tasted twice, with consistent notes. • $42 • (12/31/97) • **89**

Chardonnay Kumeu Maté's Vineyard 1995: Polished to a fare-thee-well, this emphasizes spicy, toasty barrel-derived character over fruit, but finishes with a lovely touch of honey. Lacks the zesty backbone of its previous vintages. Best from 1999. • $35 • (12/15/97) • **88**

Chardonnay New Zealand 1995: A serious, distinctive wine, if not as grand as some previous vintages. Earthy, smoky, mineral flavors prevail up front, then picks up plenty of beautiful honey, floral and pear flavors on the long, silky finish. Needs until 2000 to 2002 to fully blossom. • $29 • (11/15/97) • **90**

Merlot-Cabernet Kumeu 1987 • $18 • (12/31/90) • **87**

LAWSONS DRY HILLS

Chardonnay Marlborough 1996: Crisp at first, broadening in texture to become smooth and silky on the finish. Generous with apricot-scented apple and honey flavors that linger nicely. Drink now. 500 cases made. • $17 • (06/30/98) • **89**

Sauvignon Blanc Marlborough 1997: Bright and tangy, exciting for its brilliant pear, pea, passion fruit and thyme flavors that remain vibrant through a long finish. Unmistakable Sauvignon Blanc, but beautifully balanced as well. Drink now through 2000. 500 cases made. • $14 • (06/30/98) • **92**

LONGRIDGE

Cabernet-Merlot Hawke's Bay 1992 • $9 • (05/15/94) • **78**

Chardonnay Hawke's Bay 1994: Bracingly tart, with a raw, racy edge. Try now. 20,000 cases made. • $10 • (08/31/96) • **83**

Chardonnay Hawke's Bay 1993 • $9 • (05/15/94) • **84**

Merlot Hawke's Bay 1991 • $10 • (08/31/93) • **80**

MARTINBOROUGH

Chardonnay Martinborough 1996: Fresh and open-textured, with a slightly bitter edge to the peach and spice flavors that linger gently on the finish. Drink now. 3,000 cases made. • $27 • (05/31/98) • **87**

Chardonnay Martinborough 1995: A tightly focused, medium-weight, zingy wine with citrus and pear flavors that linger on a solid finish. Try now. 3,000 cases made. • $28 • (04/30/97) • **87**

Pinot Noir Martinborough 1996: Shows very pretty currant and blackberry flavors that persist gently on a firm texture, offering a nice balance of fruit and spice on the finish. Best from 2000 through 2003. 4,000 cases made. • $27 • (06/15/98) • **87**

Pinot Noir Martinborough 1995: Bright, focused and generous with its currant and plum aromas and flavors. Some biting tannins on the finish need until 1999 to 2000. 3,000 cases made. • $28 • (04/30/97) • **86**

Pinot Noir Martinborough 1992 • $NA • (05/15/94) • **80**

Pinot Noir Martinborough Reserve 1994: Youthful and bright. A jazzy wine with lots of red cherry, raspberry and cinnamon flavors swirling through the supple finish. Best now. 1,500 cases made. • $36 • (11/15/97) • **88**

Riesling Late Harvest Martinborough 1996: Ripe, deep and vibrant, with explosive apricot, honey and spice flavors that pick up an acetic hint on the long, exotic finish. Lovely now; even better in 2000 to 2002. 1,500 cases made. • $19/375ml • (03/31/98) HR • **94**

Riesling Martinborough 1993 • $NA • (05/15/94) • **76**

Sauvignon Blanc Martinborough 1996: Bright, almost explosive in flavor, yet beautifully lean and lithe in structure, offering pretty citrus, tropical fruit and herb flavors. Drink now through 2000. 1,000 cases made. • $18 • (05/31/98) • **90**

Sauvignon Blanc Martinborough 1993 • $NA • (05/15/94) • **80**

MATUA

Cabernet Blend Hawke's Bay 1995: Soft and supple, with lovely ripe plum and anise flavors that glide smoothly through the velvety finish. Nicely done. A blend of 70 percent Cabernet Sauvignon and 30 percent Merlot. • $NA • (05/15/97) • **85**

Chardonnay Eastern Bays 1996: Bright and refreshing for its zingy fruit character, this offers plenty of passion fruit, citrus and melon flavors that remain lively through the finish. • $NA • (05/15/97) • **89**
Chardonnay Gisborne Judd Estate 1996: Smooth, silky and packed with refreshing layers of spice, orange, pear and mineral flavors that linger nicely on the harmonious finish. Drink soon. 10,000 cases made. • $20 • (09/15/97) • **89**
Chardonnay Gisborne Judd Estate 1995: Broad, ripe and deliciously spicy, dripping with pear flavors, butter, nutmeg and honey overtones and echoing hints of smoke and vanilla. Appealing now, could improve to 2000. 4,000 cases made. • $18 • (05/15/97) • **91**
Muscat Late Harvest Hawke's Bay 1996: Very pretty, with seductive floral and tropical fruit flavors, this is sweet without being cloying. A silky-textured dessert wine with disarming freshness and flavor. • $NA/375ml • (05/15/97) • **89**
Muscat Late Harvest Hawke's Bay 1991 • $NA • (05/15/94) • **86**
Pinot Noir Waimauku 1995: Light in color and flavor, with modest plum and spice flavors. A bit of a green note on the finish. Best now. • $NA • (05/15/97) • **85**
Sauvignon Blanc Hawke's Bay 1995: Light and tart, but silky smooth to show off the mineral-scented citrus and nectarine flavors. • $NA • (05/15/97) • **87**
Sauvignon Blanc Waimauku Reserve 1995: Very crisp and minerally, with spicy floral overtones to the basic green apple flavors. Drink now. • $NA • (05/15/97) • **85**

MILLS REEF

Sauvignon Blanc Hawke's Bay Clifton Road 1993 • $NA • (05/15/94) • **83**

MISSION

Cabernet-Merlot Hawkes Bay 1997: Light in texture, with polished plum and herb flavors. Finishes with chewy tannins. Best from 2000 through 2003. 800 cases made. • $13 • (06/15/98) • **84**
Cabernet Sauvignon Hawkes Bay 1997: Light in texture, with herbal currant flavors that remain sprightly on the crisp finish. Drink now. 700 cases made. • $13 • (06/15/98) • **84**
Chardonnay Hawkes Bay 1997: Fresh and spicy. A racy wine with lean pear and nutmeg flavors that remain balanced through the lively finish. Drink now. 700 cases made. • $15 • (05/31/98) • **86**
Pinot Gris Hawkes Bay 1996: Bright and crisp; refreshing for its straightforward melon and citrus flavors, hinting at almond on the pretty finish. Drink now. 400 cases made. • $11 • (06/15/98) • **87**
Sauvignon Blanc Hawkes Bay 1997: Bright and refreshing for its straightforward citrus and pear flavors, letting the floral notes linger with the fruit on the long finish. Drink now. 500 cases made. • $12 • (05/31/98) • **87**

MONTANA

Cabernet Sauvignon Marlborough 1991 • $NA • (05/15/94) • **75**
Sauvignon Blanc Marlborough 1993 • $NA • (05/15/94) • **80**

MORTON

Cabernet-Merlot Hawke's Bay Black Label 1991 • $NA • (05/15/94) • **76**
Cabernet-Merlot Hawke's Bay White Label 1992 • $NA • (05/15/94) • **74**
Chardonnay Hawke's Bay 1996: A jazzy mouthful of ripe pineapple, lime, lemon and spice, with a smoky edge to the vibrant, fruit-oriented flavors at the core. Delicious now, but it has room to grow through 2000. • $28 • (10/15/97) • **90**
Chardonnay Hawke's Bay 1995: A honey-scented Chardonnay, with ripe, spicy flavors spreading nicely across the tightly wound structure and finishing with real depth. An immensely appealing, polished wine that feels like it has room to grow through 1999 to 2000. Delicious. 3,000 cases made. • $30 • (10/15/97) HR • **94**
Chardonnay Hawke's Bay Black Label 1994: Spicy, woody notes add some class to this full-bodied Chardonnay. Distinctly oaky, it has enough ripe pear flavor to balance. Try now. 2,000 cases made. • $27 • (04/30/97) • **87**

Key: SS—Spectator Selection CS—Cellar Selection HR—Highly Recommended BB—Best Buy $NA—Price not available Ⓐ—Auction Price (BT)—Barrel Tasting
Dates in parentheses indicate the issues in which the ratings were published.

Sauvignon Blanc Hawke's Bay 1996: Bright, bracing and distinctive for its layers of melon, floral, citrus and white peach flavors that keep pulsing through the lively finish. Delicious now. • $14 • (10/15/97) • **88**

NAUTILUS

Chardonnay Marlborough 1996: Crisp, bright and focused, with lovely, zingy green apple, pear and passion fruit flavors tempered with hints of herb and vanilla. Keeps it up on the finish. • $16 • (07/31/97) • **88**
Chardonnay Marlborough 1995: Crisp and focused. Zingy, with passion fruit, spice and vanilla flavors that linger nicely through the long finish. • $14 • (10/15/96) HR • **87**
Sauvignon Blanc Hawke's Bay 1995: Crisp and juicy, offering a lively mouthful of citrus, pineapple and herbal flavors that persist through the finish. • $12 • (11/30/96) • **88**
Sauvignon Blanc Marlborough 1996: Bright and distinctive with its anise- and tropical fruit-scented pear and herb flavors that finish softly and with generosity. 5,000 cases made. • $14 • (05/15/97) • **88**

NEUDORF

Pinot Noir Moutere 1992 • $NA • (05/15/94) • **79**
Sauvignon Blanc Nelson 1993 • $NA • (05/15/94) • **78**

NGATARAWA

Cabernet-Merlot Hawke's Bay Glazebrook 1991 • $NA • (05/15/94) • **79**

NOBILO

Cabernet Sauvignon Hawke's Bay Reserve 1990 • $NA • (05/15/94) • **62**
Pinotage Huapai 1991 • $NA • (05/15/94) • **83**
Pinotage Huapai 1988 • $15 • (07/15/91) • **82**
Sauvignon Blanc Marlborough 1993 • $NA • (05/15/94) • **86**
White Cloud New Zealand 1993 • $NA • (05/15/94) • **83**

OYSTER BAY

Chardonnay Marlborough 1993 • $NA • (05/15/94) • **84**
Sauvignon Blanc Marlborough 1993 • $NA • (05/15/94) • **85**

PALLISER

Chardonnay Martinborough 1995: Bright and spicy, this has a narrow, focused beam of pear, orange and vanilla flavors that remain zingy and crisp through the finish. Drinkable now. • $NA • (05/15/97) • **88**
Pinot Noir Martinborough 1996: Bright and flavorful. A jazzy mouthful of ripe blackberry and mineral flavors that persist on the solid finish. Approachable now, but best to wait until 2000 for it to settle down. 4,000 cases made. • $23 • (05/15/98) • **87**
Pinot Noir Martinborough 1995: Light and sprightly, with pretty currant and earth flavors that fade a mite on the finish. Ready to drink. • $NA • (05/15/97) • **84**
Pinot Noir Martinborough 1992 • $NA • (05/15/94) • **78**
Sauvignon Blanc Martinborough 1997: Bright and jazzy; a mouthful of quince and pepper flavors on a silky texture. Light and vibrant. Ready now. 8,000 cases made. • $17 • (05/15/98) • **88**
Sauvignon Blanc Martinborough 1996: Bold and bright, with very distinctive starfruit, green berry and mineral flavors that cascade across the palate; vibrant and filled with personality. Echoes herb and melon flavors on the finish. • $18 • (05/15/97) • **92**
Sauvignon Blanc Martinborough 1993 • $NA • (05/15/94) • **77**

PASK, C.J.

Cabernet-Merlot Hawke's Bay Gimblett Road 1992 • $NA • (05/15/94) • **73**
Sauvignon Blanc Hawke's Bay Gimblett Road 1993 • $NA • (05/15/94) • **86**

PROVIDENCE

Matakana Red 1994: Earthy, vegetal flavors mingle with sweet spices and ripe currant on a velvety frame. Try after 2000. Tasted twice, with consistent notes. A blend of Merlot, Cabernet Franc and Malbec. 800 cases made. • $75 • (03/31/98) • **81**

REDWOOD VALLEY

Rhine Riesling Late Harvest Nelson 1991 • $NA • (05/15/94) • **91**
Sauvignon Blanc Nelson 1993 • $NA • (05/15/94) • **86**

RIVERSIDE

Sauvignon Blanc Hawkes Bay 1996: Earthy, floral, dusky flavors make this an acquired taste. Not a typical New Zealand Sauvignon Blanc, but it has its charms. Drink now. 1,000 cases made. • $12 • (06/30/98) • **83**

RONGOPAI

Chardonnay Late Harvest Te Kauwhata Botrytised Reserve 1991 • $NA • (05/15/94) • **88**
Riesling Late Harvest Te Kauwhata Botrytised Reserve 1993 • $NA • (05/15/94) • **92**
Sauvignon Blanc Te Kauwhata 1993 • $NA • (05/15/94) • **79**

SACRED HILL

Chardonnay Hawkes Bay Reserve 1996: Silky-smooth and generous in flavor on a lean frame, offering a nice thread of bracing acidity to support the ripe apricot and pear flavors. Hints at honey and lime on the finish. Drink now. • $23 • (05/15/98) • **88**
Chardonnay Hawkes Bay Riflemans 1995: Ripe, rich and layered with flavor; cascading with pear, apricot, honey and spice flavors that linger on the smooth, polished finish. Delicious now, but feels like it could enrich through 2001. • $34 • (05/15/98) • **91**
Sauvignon Blanc Hawkes Bay Reserve 1996: Light, bright and fresh, with citrusy pear flavors that remain zingy on the finish. Drink soon. • $23 • (05/15/98) • **86**
Sauvignon Blanc New Zealand Whitecliff 1997: Light and crisp, with earthy flavors showing more than do the modest citrusy ones, echoing a touch of dusky herbs on the finish. Drink now. • $16 • (05/15/98) • **86**

ST. CLAIR

Riesling Marlborough 1997: Dry, but soft and silky, not crisp, with very pretty green apple, peach and floral flavors that linger with a lovely touch of apricot on the long finish. Drink now. • $12 • (06/30/98) • **90**
Sauvignon Blanc Marlborough 1996: This crisp, lively wine leans strongly toward the herbal side of the spectrum without slipping over the edge. Finishes with citrusy brightness. 8,000 cases made. • $14 • (04/30/97) • **85**

SCOTT, ALLAN

Chardonnay Marlborough 1996: Bright and racy in flavor, with jazzy pineapple and citrus flavors that linger on the crisp finish. Drink now. 12,000 cases made. • $19 • (02/28/98) • **87**
Chardonnay Marlborough 1995: A crisp, steely style of Chardonnay, centering around bright lemon and apple flavors that echo nicely on the finish. 4,500 cases made. • $12 • (06/15/97) • **87**
Chardonnay Marlborough 1993 • $NA • (05/15/94) • **82**
Riesling Marlborough 1997: Dry, crisp and sappy. A lively wine with pretty floral, apple and resiny aromas and flavors that linger. Drink now. 6,000 cases made. • $15 • (02/28/98) • **87**
Riesling Marlborough 1996: Off-dry, but crisp enough to be tangy, with bright apple and floral flavors that are right down the middle. Drink now. 5,000 cases made. • $9 • (06/15/97) • **87**
Riesling Marlborough 1993 • $NA • (05/15/94) • **83**
Sauvignon Blanc Marlborough 1997: Tart and zippy, with lemon, lime and pear flavors, finishing with a bright flash of green-pea and spice. Light on its feet, with flavors that linger. Best with seafood. 10,000 cases made. • $17 • (01/31/98) • **89**
Sauvignon Blanc Marlborough 1996: Tart and zingy, a racy mouthful of grapefruit, passion fruit and green apple flavors that remain lively on the crisp finish. Drink now. 7,000 cases made. • $11 • (06/15/97) • **88**
Sauvignon Blanc Marlborough 1993 • $NA • (05/15/94) • **83**

SELAKS

Ice Wine Marlborough 1995: Smooth and generous with its honey and citrus flavors. A sweet dessert wine with plenty of acidity to balance. Tasty. Drink now. A blend of Riesling and Gewürztraminer. 1,000 cases made. • $13/375ml • (02/28/97) • **83**
Sauvignon Blanc Marlborough 1996: Crisp, almost austere, with its peppery, herbal flavors spreading nicely on the zippy finish. Drink now. 14,000 cases made. • $13 • (04/30/97) • **86**
Sauvignon Blanc Marlborough 1993 • $13 • (05/15/94) • **85**
Sauvignon Blanc-Sémillon Marlborough 1995: A lively wine, with full-blown grass, sweet anise and green olive aromas and flavors coursing through. Finishes with sharp acidity. 4,000 cases made. • $15 • (04/30/97) • **82**

SELWYN RIVER

Chardonnay Marlborough 1996: Bright and refreshing for its apple and spice flavors that linger nicely through the citrusy finish. 10,000 cases made. • $10 • (09/15/97) • **87**
Sauvignon Blanc Marlborough 1996: Bright, crisp and racy. Lemon and floral notes add nice touches to the tart gooseberry flavors. 10,000 cases made. • $9 • (09/15/97) • **86**

SHINGLE PEAK

Chardonnay Marlborough 1996: A crisp, bright style of Chardonnay shaped into a supple package, offering apple, pear and spice flavors that linger on the finish. Drink now. 6,000 cases made. • $15 • (12/31/97) • **88**
Pinot Gris Marlborough 1996: Soft in texture, with pleasant if modest peach and almond flavors gliding gently through the finish. Drink now. 2,000 cases made. • $15 • (12/31/97) • **84**
Riesling Marlborough 1996: Brazenly tart. Racy, with bright lemon and green apple flavors plus some floral notes. Bracing now, may be best after 2000. 5,000 cases made. • $13 • (12/31/97) • **86**
Sauvignon Blanc Marlborough 1996: Juicy, mouthwatering stuff. Lively, with grapefruit and gooseberry flavors that linger bracingly on the tart finish, this vivid wine is jazzy. Try now. 14,000 cases made. • $15 • (12/31/97) • **88**

SPENCER HILL

Chardonnay Marlborough Brentwood Vineyard 1995: Spicy, complex and beautifully balanced, this lets its range of apple, lees and nutmeg-centered flavors unfold over a pinpoint of fine acidity. Has style and elegance, plus plenty of flavor. Drink now. 950 cases made. • $20 • (12/31/96) • **90**
Chardonnay Nelson-Gisborne Moutere Evan's Vineyard 1996: Crisp and zingy, with a spicy anise thread weaving through the pear and toast flavors. Lacks a bit of vibrancy, but offers plenty of soft flavors for current drinking. 375 cases made. • $28 • (03/31/98) • **85**

STONELEIGH

Cabernet Sauvignon Marlborough 1991 • $NA • (05/15/94) • **75**
Chardonnay Marlborough 1994: Silky texture is well balanced with crisp acidity. Has nicely spicy, butterscotch-tinged pear flavors and a jaunty finish. Drinkable now. 20,000 cases made. • $11 • (08/31/96) HR • **88**
Sauvignon Blanc Marlborough 1994: An extreme style, aggressively leafy and green. Surprisingly soft at first, but then the acidity rolls in, finishing with a sweet-and-sour flourish. This will polarize folks. 30,000 cases made. • $10 • (10/31/96) • **83**
Sauvignon Blanc Marlborough 1993 • $9 • (05/15/94) • **83**

STONYRIDGE

Cabernet Larose Waiheke Island 1995: Delicious aromas and flavors centering on fresh currant, plum and spice, with a floral edge to the slightly chewy finish. Flavors linger lightly on aftertaste, but it never shows the depth the nose promises. Drinkable now. 1,200 cases made. • $50 • (04/30/97) • **87**

TASMAN BAY

Chardonnay Marlborough 1996: Ripe and crisp at the same time, this is a distinctive wine with orange and papaya notes riding on a zingy frame, with citrus and apple flavors echoing on the finish. Drink now. 1,975 cases made. • $16 • (09/15/97) • **88**
Chardonnay New Zealand 1995: Smooth and refreshing for its bright citrus-scented apple flavors that linger nicely. 2,600 cases made. • $15 • (12/31/96) • **86**

Sauvignon Blanc Nelson Oak Aged 1997: Ripe and generous; distinct for its spicy overlay of honey-scented oak; very smooth and round, hinting at peach and apple on the rich finish. Atypical for New Zealand, but very well made. Drink now through 2000. 2,800 cases made. • $14 • (05/31/98) • **88**

Sauvignon Blanc-Sémillon Nelson-Gisborne Fumé Reserve 1996: Marked by the spicy, sweet vanilla and caramel flavors of barrel fermentation. Smooth, rich and well proportioned, offering nice citrus and pear notes on the finish. 2,300 cases made. • $16 • (09/15/97) • **87**

TE AWA FARM

Cabernet-Merlot Hawke's Bay Longlands 1996: Bright, silky and generous with its ripe blackberry, spice and vanilla flavors, finishing with a lovely, smooth texture and enough flavor to develop through 2000. 2,000 cases made. • $15 • (02/28/98) • **88**

Merlot Hawke's Bay Longlands 1996: A supple wine; smooth velvety and nicely stuffed with blackberry, currant and gently herbal flavors. Finishes with soft tannins and a stylish touch of oak. Nicely done. 2,000 cases made. • $15 • (02/28/98) • **87**

TE MATA

Cabernet-Merlot Hawke's Bay Coleraine 1991 • $NA • (05/15/94) • **87**

TIMARA

Cabernet Sauvignon Marlborough 1990 • $NA • (05/15/94) • **71**

VAVASOUR

Cabernet Sauvignon Marlborough Reserve 1991 • $NA • (05/15/94) • **84**

Chardonnay Awatere Valley 1996: A bright mouthful of spicy fruit with hints of smoke. A zingy wine with some richness to add flesh to the citrusy pear and passion fruit flavors. Drink now. 2,000 cases made. • $25 • (11/15/97) • **87**

Chardonnay Marlborough Reserve 1993 • $NA • (05/15/94) • **83**

Pinot Noir New Zealand Reserve 1992 • $NA • (05/15/94) • **74**

Sauvignon Blanc Awatere Valley 1996: Crisp, bordering on austere, with citrus and green apple flavors that linger on the juicy finish. 2,000 cases made. • $20 • (11/15/97) • **85**

Sauvignon Blanc Awatere Valley Single Vineyard 1996: Bright, open and impressive for its clarity and balance. A lovely mouthful of green apple and spice flavors that linger on the finish with a spiky herbal note to liven it up further. Ready now. 1,000 cases made. • $23 • (11/15/97) • **89**

VIDAL

Cabernet-Merlot Hawke's Bay Private Bin 1992 • $NA • (05/15/94) • **75**

Sauvignon Blanc Hawke's Bay Private Bin 1993 • $NA • (05/15/94) • **74**

VILLA MARIA

Cabernet-Merlot Hawke's Bay Reserve 1991 • $NA • (05/15/94) • **84**

Cabernet Sauvignon Auckland Reserve 1986 • $30 • (07/15/88) • **74**

Cabernet Sauvignon Hawke's Bay Private Bin 1992 • $NA • (05/15/94) • **74**

Cabernet Sauvignon Hawke's Bay Reserve 1990 • $NA • (05/15/94) • **78**

Cellar Selection Red Hawke's Bay 1995: Bright and jazzy, with distinctly herbal berry notes and a sweet nuance of chocolate on the sharpish finish. Drink now. A blend of Merlot, Cabernet Sauvignon and Malbec. • $20 • (07/31/97) • **83**

Chardonnay Gisborne Private Bin 1996: Bright and friendly, it's a pretty mouthful of pear and spice flavors that stroll nicely through the finish. • $13 • (07/31/97) • **86**

Chardonnay Marlborough Reserve 1996: Bright, with plenty of citrusy pear and melon flavors that remain crisp and lively right through the finish. • $32 • (07/31/97) • **88**

Gewürztraminer Ihumatao Region Private Bin 1993 • $NA • (05/15/94) • **84**

Reserve Hawke's Bay 1995: Lean, almost crisp at the core, but supple and sweet around the edges, offering chocolate-scented berry and mint flavors that linger on the taut finish. Not too tannic, but needs until 2000 to loosen up. • $37 • (07/31/97) • **87**

Riesling Marlborough Private Bin 1993 • $NA • (05/15/94) • **88**

Sauvignon Blanc Marlborough Cellar Selection 1996: Crisp and bright, a racy mouthful of steely fruit, offering passion fruit, green apple and pineapple character that keeps zinging on the finish. Drinkable now. • $19 • (07/31/97) • **89**

Sauvignon Blanc Marlborough-Te Kauwhata-Hawke's Bay Private Bin 1996: Fresh and juicy, a lively medley of peach and pineapple flavors, hinting at rosemary and sage on the long finish. • $10 • (07/31/97) • **88**

Sauvignon Blanc Marlborough Private Bin 1993 • $NA • (05/15/94) • **85**

WAIMARAMA

Cabernet-Merlot Hawke's Bay 1992 • $NA • (05/15/94) • **81**

WAIRAU RIVER

Sauvignon Blanc Marlborough 1997: Bright and citrusy, with tangy passion fruit and some nice herbal overtones. Lovely balance for drinking soon. Drink now. 5,000 cases made. • $20 • (06/30/98) • **89**

Sauvignon Blanc Marlborough 1996: Beautifully balanced, silky and polished, with vibrant flavors of passion fruit, citrus and pear that linger enticingly on the bright finish. Drinkable now. 8,500 cases made. • $14 • (12/31/96) • **90**

Sauvignon Blanc Marlborough 1993 • $NA • (05/15/94) • **85**

• Romania •

CARASU

Cabernet Sauvignon Murfatlar 1992: Camphor, cherry and spice flavors dominate this medium-bodied red wine. A bit bizarre but tasty. 20,000 cases made. • $6 • (01/01/97) • **79**

Merlot Murfatlar 1991: A basic red wine that tastes a little lifted. It has flavors of herbs and currants with a sharp finish. 20,000 cases made. • $6 • (01/01/97) • **77**

LEGACY

Cabernet Sauvignon Murfatlar 1991 • $7 • (01/01/95) • **74**

Muscat Ottonel Murfatlar Special Reserve 1992 • $10 • (06/30/95) • **80**

VAMPIRE

Cabernet Sauvignon Dealul Mare 1991 • $6 • (12/31/95) • **79**

Merlot Dealul Mare 1991 • $6 • (12/31/95) • **76**

• Slovenia •

LJUTOMER WINERY

Chardonnay Slovenia 1994 • $8 • (01/01/96) • **70**

MOVIA ESTATES

Chardonnay Slovenia 1993 • $17 • (01/01/96) • **77**

• Switzerland •

AUVERNIER, CHÂTEAU D'

Chasselas Neuchâtel 1994: Crisp and refreshing, though subtle in its flavors of smoke, mineral and lemon. Clean and light, making for a pleasant apéritif. 10,000 cases made. • $15 • (07/31/96) • **83**

Neuchâtel Rosé Oeil de Perdrix 1996: This coppery rosé is a bit heavy but still crisp, with strawberry and herbal flavors and a nice lemony finish. Drink now. 10,000 cases made. • $17 • (02/28/98) • **79**

Neuchâtel White 1996: Crisp and lively, this very dry white offers peach and mineral flavors and citrusy acidity. It's clean and fresh, a lovely apéritif. 10,000 cases made. • $17 • (02/28/98) • **85**

Key: SS—Spectator Selection CS—Cellar Selection HR—Highly Recommended BB—Best Buy $NA—Price not available Ⓐ—Auction Price (BT)—Barrel Tasting

Dates in parentheses indicate the issues in which the ratings were published.

Pinot Gris Neuchâtel 1996: Verging on late-harvest, with honey, white pepper, smoke and almond notes mingling beautifully in this Pinot Gris-like white. Medium-bodied but quite intense, with a nice, lingering finish. A lovely, balanced surprise from Switzerland. Drink now. 1,500 cases made. • $18 • (02/28/98) • **88**

BADOUX, HENRI

Aigle White Les Murailles 1996: Reserved and delicate on the nose, but nicely structured and minerally on the palate; a nice wine to drink now. We only wish for a bit more fruit complexity. 18,000 cases made. • $28 • (02/28/98) • **84**

Chasselas Aigle les Murailles 1994: Unusually round and soft for Chasselas. Has broad apple and butter flavors with spicy, herbal accents. Appealing on its own but with enough structure for food. 3,334 cases made. • $25 • (07/31/96) • **83**

BONVIN, CHARLES

Amigne Valais Les Cépages 1995: Rich and ripe, yellow in color, with floral, lime, tropical and orange-marmalade character. Quite stony and minerally in the midpalate but supple and fat on the earthy finish. 416 cases made. • $19 • (02/28/98) • **85**

Dôle Valais Matterhorn Mont Cervin 1995: Bright and assertive, this red offers black cherry, herbal and smoky flavors with just enough tannin for grip, and finishes with pleasant notes of spice. Drink now. 1,666 cases made. • $14 • (02/28/98) • **82**

Fendant Valais Matterhorn Mont Cervin 1995: Rich and thick for a Swiss wine, with ripe pear and piecrust flavors. Soft on the palate, it lacks the zesty freshness to keep it interesting. Drink now, chilled. 1,666 cases made. • $14 • (02/28/98) • **83**

Humagne Rouge Valais Les Cépages 1995: Earthy aromas and flavors dominate the simple plum flavor in this rustic, rather tannic red. Will show better with meaty dishes. 666 cases made. • $21 • (02/28/98) • **78**

Marsanne Valais Les Cépages 1995: Interesting. Big, bold and almost tannic, with spinach, mineral, stone and almond flavors. Full-bodied, a bit too chewy and disjointed on the finish. Needs food. Drink now through 2000. 416 cases made. • $17 • (02/28/98) • **84**

Muscat Valais Les Cépages 1995: Lovely fragrant Muscat, true to character of the variety, with rosewater, almond and floral notes, good acidity and medium body. A fresh, fun apéritif. 666 cases made. • $17 • (02/28/98) • **84**

Petite Arvine Valais Les Cépages 1995: Distinctive, pure and fresh, with ripe fruit character. Honey laced, with flavors of lemon, peach, lime and mineral. Medium-bodied and long on the intense, hard finish. Drink now. 666 cases made. • $19 • (02/28/98) • **88**

Pinot Blanc Valais Les Cépages 1995: Quite ripe and off-dry, showing honey, peach and bubble-gum notes. Lacks acidity and length, though. Drink soon, chilled. 583 cases made. • $17 • (02/28/98) • **80**

Valais Cuvée Rouge 1995: Everything about this red screams "prestige cuvée"—the expensive bottle, the lush aromas of new oak, the deep color and polished texture. It shows pretty toasty and black cherry flavors, clean and balanced, and is a sure bet to stump your friends in a blind tasting. Drink now through 2002. 416 cases made. • $24 • (02/28/98) • **86**

Valais Cuvée d'Or 1995: Rich and sweet, this viscous white offers honey, dried apricot and sugar cookie flavors that have enough acidity to keep them lively and lingering on the finish. It's straightforward but luscious. • $NA/375ml • (02/28/98) • **87**

Valais Rosé Oeil de Perdrix Sortilègre 1995: A jammy rosé that offers strawberry flavors almost sweet enough to spread on toast. For fans of white Zinfandel. 666 cases made. • $17 • (02/28/98) • **77**

BOVARD

Dézaley White Medinette 1995: Lovely. Well structured, polished and rich, delicious from start to finish, with melon, prosciutto, lemon, pear and smoke character. Medium to full in body, with a firm backbone carrying it to a long, deep finish. Drink now. 5,000 cases made. • $30 • (02/28/98) • **88**

Epesses White Terre à Boire 1995: Ripe and round. Full-bodied, with blanched-almond, pear and honey flavors, it seems a bit flat despite the chewy texture and good length on the finish. Still good. Drink now. 5,000 cases made. • $20 • (02/28/98) • **81**

St.-Saphorin White L'Archevesque 1995: Soapy and spritzy, lacking in fruit but thick and ripe, with some earthy, mushroom and nutty notes. Drink now. 4,000 cases made. • $24 • (02/28/98) • **76**

GERMANIER-BALAVAUD

Amigne Vétroz 1996: Racy yet ripe, with a lovely, thick, minerally midpalate and loads of fruit. Marvelously complex, with banana, orange, spice and smoke notes. Full-bodied and concentrated. Delicious now. • $24 • (02/28/98) • **88**

Amigne Vétroz Mitis 1994: Distinctive and intriguing, this pillowy soft, richly sweet white offers complex aromas and flavors of herbs, spices, honey, melon and vanilla. Though it lacks acidity for backbone, it's still enticing and long. Drink now. • $32/375ml • (02/28/98) • **89**

Fendant Vétroz Les Terrasses 1995: Flavorful, with a distinctive bouquet of banana, mineral, herbs, flowers and pears. Full-bodied and ripe, it hangs in there on the palate for a fine almond-scented finish. Drink now. • $19 • (02/28/98) • **85**

Syrah Valais 1995: Beautifully defined aromas of licorice, black cherry and black pepper are quintessential Syrah, and though the palate doesn't quite live up to them—a bit tannic and simple—there's still an impressive amount of varietal character. Drinkable now. 833 cases made. • $36 • (02/28/98) • **84**

Vétroz Les Terrasses 1994: Delicate and summery, the subtle but pleasing nuances of flowers, watermelon and apples are light and silky on the palate. Harmonious and reserved. 4,167 cases made. • $17 • (07/31/96) • **86**

GILLIARD, ROBERT

Chasselas Fendant du Valais 1994: Thick, creamy texture with a vivid streak of lemony acidity. Smoky, nutty aromas and flavors are straightforward and harmonious. 25,000 cases made. • $12 • (07/31/96) • **84**

Chasselas Les Murettes Sion 1994: Aggressive and lean; the flavors of smoke, bitter almond and earth don't have much fruit to back them up. 20,000 cases made. • $17 • (07/31/96) • **79**

Dôle Monts 1996: Light-bodied, with straightforward black cherry flavors and soft tannins, but turns slightly bitter on the finish, with herbal and spicy notes. Drink now. 25,000 cases made. • $19 • (02/28/98) • **79**

Petite Arvine Valais Pierre Ollaire 1995: Thick and fat. A ripe style of Petite Arvine, with honey, smoke and hazelnut, but it lacks concentration and fruit. Drink now. 2,000 cases made. • $22 • (02/28/98) • **82**

MATHIER-KUCHLER

Fendant Valais Vins des Chevaliers 1995: Almost yellow in color and quite polished in texture. Tastes neutral and a bit flat, with flavors of cooked apples, herbs and almonds. Drink now. 2,500 cases made. • $17 • (02/28/98) • **79**

MONTMOLLIN, DOMAINE DE

Neuchâtel Rosé Oeil de Perdrix 1996: Shows an unappealing color and aromas of strawberry jam that turn cooked and bitter on the palate. Lacks freshness and verve. 5,555 cases made. • $19 • (02/28/98) • **71**

Neuchâtel White 1996: Delicately structured but a mouthful of flavors: lemon pie, pine, grapefruit and pear, along with a hint of mineral. Very clean and fresh; the spritzy component adds a nice lift. Drink now. 16,666 cases made. • $17 • (02/28/98) • **86**

Pinot Noir Neuchâtel 1995: This crisp, bright red offers lean flavors of berries, herbs and smoke, with light, dry tannins and a clean, short finish. Better with food; drink now. 3,333 cases made. • $21 • (02/28/98) • **80**

PROVINS VALAIS

Cornalin Valais Cuvée du Grand Métral 1995: This inky red shows remarkable concentration, with firm tannins and a chewy texture. The simple flavors range from blueberry to chocolate and earth. A good match for a hearty stew. 1,277 cases made. • $29 • (02/28/98) • **83**

Dôle Valais Chanteauvieux 1995: Round and quite soft on the palate, this pillowy red offers herbal and light earthy flavors, but lacks fruit. It's generous but simple; drink now. 20,833 cases made. • $16 • (02/28/98) • **78**

Fendant Valais Pierrafeu 1996: Ripe and fat. Tropical in style, with pineapple, lemon, apple and pear. Medium-to- full in body, it's a bit short on the finish. Drink chilled. 25,000 cases made. • $16 • (02/28/98) • **80**

Fendant Valais Pierrafeu 1994: Crisp pear and melon flavors with plenty of acidity for balance, and a hint of marzipan on the finish. 25,000 cases made. • $13 • (07/31/96) • **82**

Humagne Rouge Valais Cuvée du Grand Métral 1995: Earthy and plum flavors mingle in this solid, slightly rustic red. Has enough tannin for hearty dishes, but lacks refinement and length. 1,100 cases made. • $26 • (02/28/98) • **78**

Pinot Blanc-Chardonnay Valais Profil 1995: Nice, thick texture, with butter, butterscotch, cream, pear and spice notes, but lacks backbone and acidity. Drink now. 7,100 cases made. • $23 • (02/28/98) • **79**

ROUVINEZ

Dôle Valais de Sierre 1995: The smoky aromas are intriguing and lead to a medium-bodied red with soft tannins and light flavors of black cherries, herbs and dark chocolate that turn slightly bitter on the finish. Drink now. • $19 • (02/28/98) • **81**

Fendant Valais de Sierre 1996: Ripe and fairly rich; a complex mouthful of banana, lime pie, mineral, almond and white pepper flavors. Medium- to full-bodied, it turns chewy and distinctly almondy on the lingering finish. Drink now. • $17 • (02/28/98) • **85**

Fendant Valais de Sierre 1993: Rich and firm, marrying full body and crisp acidity in an assertive package, with smoke, mineral and marzipan flavors. Try with grilled fish. 8,334 cases made. • $13 • (07/31/96) • **85**

Valais Red Le Tourmentin 1995: This international-style red offers sweet berry flavors, bright acidity and firm tannins. It's balanced and polished but rather anonymous. Drink now through 2002. • $34 • (02/28/98) • **84**

Valais White La Trémaille 1994: Honeyed and waxy aromas suggest a sweet, late-harvest-style white, but this rich wine turns dry on the palate, with ripe flavors of figs, almonds and toast. Impressive for its generosity and length but difficult to match with food. • $35 • (02/28/98) • **88**

TAMBORINI, CARLO

Merlot Ticino Collivo Riserva 1995: This inky red shows impressive concentration and plenty of oak, but along the way the fruit gets lost, with flavors of chocolate, toast and licorice that turn slightly bitter on the finish. A strong effort that may come around in 2000. 666 cases made. • $25 • (02/28/98) • **82**

Merlot Ticino Comano 1995: This polished red is focused and harmonious, with bright, ripe cherry flavors and a touch of toasty oak. It's clean and crisp and finishes with a nice burst of fruit. Drink now through 2005. 500 cases made. • $25 • (02/28/98) • **85**

Merlot Ticino San Zeno Riserva 1994: Earthy and a bit hard, this inky red offers flavors of toast, licorice and black cherry, but the tannins dominate the finish. It's fresh and firm; try late this year. 5,000 cases made. • $20 • (02/28/98) • **81**

Merlot Ticino Vigna Vecchia 1995: This ripe red offers plum and chocolate flavors, round and a bit soft on the palate but kept lively by a firm finish. It's generous and clean. Drink now. 833 cases made. • $25 • (02/28/98) • **83**

TESTUZ, JEAN & PIERRE

Dézaley White L'Arbalette 1996: Very attractive, with a distinctive profile of banana pie, bread dough, lemon and mineral flavors. Medium-bodied but rather ripe, with a touch of spritz to keep it lively on the smoky finish. Drink now. 3,000 cases made. • $30 • (02/28/98) • **86**

Dézaley White L'Arbalette 1994: Polished, firm and has good concentration in its light honey, apricot and floral flavors. Though restrained, it's balanced and appealing. 3,000 cases made. • $27 • (07/31/96) • **85**

Epesses Coup de L'Etrier 1994: A simple white wine with light, canned-fruit flavors and short finish. Basically neutral. 1,800 cases made. • $21 • (07/31/96) • **79**

St.-Saphorin White Roche Ronde 1995: This rich white shows generous herbal, almond and toasty flavors; full-bodied and long, with enough acidity to keep it in balance. A distinctive wine with an intriguing marriage of ripeness and austerity, it should age well. 10,000 cases made. • $23 • (01/31/98) HR • **89**

UVAVINS

La Côte Red Les Rocards 1995: This soft red offers a core of ripe berry flavors with notes of chocolate and toast. There's not much structure, but lightly chilled it makes a pleasant apéritif. 2,083 cases made. • $18 • (02/28/98) • **82**

Key: SS—Spectator Selection CS—Cellar Selection HR—Highly Recommended BB—Best Buy $NA—Price not available Ⓐ—Auction Price (BT)—Barrel Tasting

Dates in parentheses indicate the issues in which the ratings were published.

Morges White Vieilles Vignes 1996: Fresh and crisp, with the hallmark blanched-almond, smoke and olive flavors of Swiss whites. Light- to medium-bodied, with some ripe fruit character. Drink now. 2,083 cases made. • $17 • (02/28/98) • **85**

Morges White Vieilles Vignes 1993: This is rich and too heavy-handed. Good honeyed, smoky marzipan flavors but low in acidity and short on fruit. 100 percent Chasselas. 5,834 cases made. • $13 • (07/31/96) • **79**

Nyon White Vieilles Vignes 1995: Very soft but also nutty, buttery, peachy and flowery. Ripe, medium-bodied, and flabby on the finish. Drink now. 2,083 cases made. • $17 • (02/28/98) • **79**

Nyon White Vieilles Vignes 1993: Focused and fresh, with appealing floral, mineral and apple flavors. Not concentrated but still lively. Delicate, and makes a nice apéritif. 100 percent Chasselas. 5,416 cases made. • $12 • (07/31/96) • **84**

VALSANGIACOMO

Merlot Ticino Riserva di Bacco 1994: This tannic red offers vegetal and earthy flavors, with light plum notes. May soften with food, but may not improve with age. 2,500 cases made. • $18 • (02/28/98) • **77**

Merlot Ticino Rubro 1993: This rich red shows concentration and polish. It's stuffed with sweet chocolate and licorice flavors, and the cherry is still fresh and firm. A lively wine in the international style. Drink now through 2002. 2,084 cases made. • $34 • (02/28/98) • **87**

VARONE

Chasselas Uvrier Sion 1994: Rich for Chasselas, offering watermelon, floral and mineral notes and lively acidity. Attractive complexity and good balance. Would work as an apéritif or with food. 1,250 cases made. • $18 • (07/31/96) • **84**

Fendant Sion Soleil du Valais 1996: Has good, lush structure, but the canned-pear, bitter almond and banana aren't too attractive. Medium-bodied. Drink now. 5,000 cases made. • $16 • (02/28/98) • **79**

Valais White Hermitage Grand Glarier 1996: This distinctive white shows rich flavors of almonds, fennel and honey, generous but dry on the palate, and a lingering finish of herbs and litchis. An intriguing wine that's tough to match with food. Made from 100 percent Marsanne. 416 cases made. • $22 • (02/28/98) • **89**

USA

CALIFORNIA

California's first vines were planted by Spanish missionaries only about 200 years ago—not a long time by world wine trade standards. Yet today California produces almost 90 percent of the wine made in the U.S.A. The Mission grape planted by the Spaniards is still cultivated in a few areas, but California's greatest success has been in the cultivation of classic European varietals, such as Cabernet Sauvignon, Chardonnay, Pinot Noir, Merlot and Sauvignon Blanc. These vinifera varietals, which are used almost exclusively for making wine (as opposed to being used as table grapes), now total over 400,000 acres of grapes. Along with France and Italy, California is now regarded as one of the truly great wine-producing regions of the world.

Varietal Labeling

California wines are marketed primarily by varietal categories—by the grape variety (Chardonnay, for instance) that makes up all or most of the wine in the bottle. This method differs from the traditional European approach, which is based primarily on such geographic locations and/or appellations as Bordeaux and the Rhône. The implications of California's system have been enormous. Instead of being limited to a few grape types allowed under an appellation law, California's winemakers have been free to experiment and plant whatever grape variety they wish. This has given them great flexibility in choosing what wines to make and how to make them.

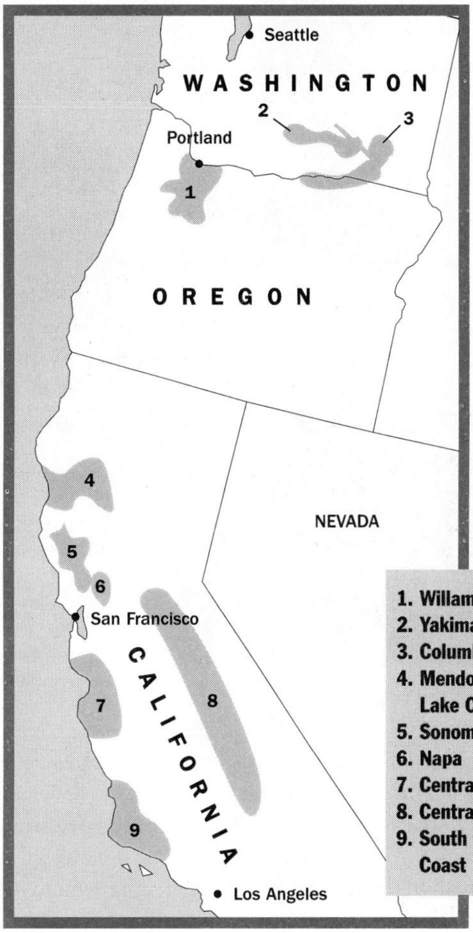

Major California Grape Varieties

Although regional soil differences and variations in microclimate have a significant impact on wine flavors, maintaining and enhancing varietal character remains a key objective of California winemaking. Thus, a knowledge of the leading grape varietals grown in California is central to understanding the state's wines.

Chardonnay. With over 65,000 acres now in production, Chardonnay displaced French Colombard several years ago as the state's most widely planted grape. California Chardonnay displays flavors of fresh-cut yellow fruit, especially apples, melon, pineapple and other tropical fruits. Winemakers build more complexity into these flavors through the use of such techniques as barrel fermentation, *sur lie* aging and malolactic fermentation. California Chardonnay tends to be more full-bodied and plump than French Chardonnay-based wines such as white Burgundy.

With over 13,000 acres planted in the Alexander Valley, Russian River Valley, and parts of Carneros, Sonoma County leads the state in Chardonnay acreage. It is followed by Monterey County, Napa Valley, Santa Barbara, Mendocino and other areas. In recent years, the tendency has been to plant Chardonnay in cooler areas of these regions, leading to wines with less alcohol but with a better balance of fruit and acidity. While many California Chardonnays are quite ordinary, the better ones are undoubtedly among the world's best.

Cabernet Sauvignon. Generally regarded as the king of California red wine, California Cabernet displays the classic varietal characteristics of fresh herbs, cedar, cassis, mint, black currant, and violets. In cooler areas, it can take on a distinct vegetal/bell pepper characteristic, which is increasingly viewed as undesirable.

For many years, it was thought that California Cabernet was sufficiently soft and complex—that it did not benefit from blending with other varietals. While some of the best California Cabernets are still made from 100 percent Cabernet Sauvignon, the trend in recent years has been to add Merlot and other Bordeaux varietals, such as Petit Verdot and Cabernet Franc. Most of the better Cabernet Sauvignons today are aged in small barrels, of both French and American oak, to add appealing vanilla and spice notes. Although many areas of the state now produce top-notch Cabernet, Napa Valley still produces a disproportionate share of the best examples.

Grigich Hills Estate in Napa Valley.

George Olson

Zinfandel. The most widely planted red grape in California. Zinfandel lends itself to an enormous variety of styles, ranging from the rosé style called "white" Zinfandel at one extreme, to inky black late-harvest Zinfandels at the other. Leaving the highly commercial white Zinfandels aside, the true red Zinfandel has a zesty, spicy varietal character, and is loaded with notes of raspberry, plum and red-berry fruit. Winemakers often choose to emphasize one or more of these characteristics. Thus, some Zinfandels are made in a medium-weight, claret style that emphasizes the grape's subtler elements and innate fruitiness. Amador County and a few other regions specialize in blockbusters, characterized by high levels of tannin, extract, and alcohol. Another popular style emphasizes Zinfandel's grapey, Beaujolais character.

Sauvignon Blanc. California Sauvignon Blanc is an often under-appreciated and usually bargain-priced white. Some California Sauvignon Blancs are made in a Loire style, and offer strong grassy, herbal, mineral and citrus (particularly grapefruit) tastes with minimal or no oak flavors. A more recent trend has been to emphasize barrel fermentation, lees stirring, and blending with Sémillon, all of which yields a rich style closer to that of a white Bordeaux.

Merlot. Once thought of as a blending grape, California Merlot has now emerged as a hot new variety on its own. Merlot has been called the "kinder, gentler" alternative to Cabernet Sauvignon. It is sometimes softer than the latter, and can offer more cherry, plum and red fruit flavors. In California, as elsewhere, Merlot is often blended with Cabernet Sauvignon and other Bordeaux grapes to add complexity to the finished wine. Merlot seems to thrive mainly in the regions where Cabernet Sauvignon does best; the finest California examples tend to be from Napa and Sonoma.

Pinot Noir. This grape variety has had a checkered history in California. Many early examples were a bit clumsy and lacked the elegance expected of a good Pinot Noir. But that has very much changed. Today, good California Pinot Noir has layers of pure cherry, raspberry and other red and black fruits that expand across the palate on the finish. Pinot Noir seems to have found a natural home in the cooler regions of California, including the Carneros region, the Russian River Valley and Santa Barbara.

Rhône varieties. The term "Rhône Rangers" has become a catch-all description for a number of California winemakers who are working with grape varieties that originated in France's Rhône Valley; many have already achieved great success with several grape types. Among the red wines, Syrah seems to be achieving the most acclaim at the moment, displaying dense red berry fruit with hints of bacon fat, tar and spice. (Note: Petite Sirah appears to be an unrelated variety; it was long thought to be the Durif of southeastern France, but recent DNA testing has cast doubt on this hypothesis.) Mourvèdre displays characteristics similar to Syrah, but with a bit more earthiness and dustier tannins on the finish. Among whites, Viognier and Roussane show promise. Their primary characteristics are forward fruit, firm acidity and gentle roundness on the finish.

Major California Wine Regions

Napa Valley. Undoubtedly the best known wine region of California, Napa Valley produces a vast array of fine wines; more than 35,000 acres are planted with vines today. Chardonnay and Cabernet Sauvignon account for about 10,000 acres each, and Sauvignon Blanc, Riesling, Pinot Noir, Merlot, and Zinfandel make up most of the rest.

Napa Valley includes a wide range of microclimates and soil types. The northern portion of the Valley, near Calistoga, tends to be the warmest, while the southern end, near Carneros and extending up through Yountville, is cooler due to the moderating influence of San Francisco Bay.

Many of Napa's best known wineries are situated in the central part of the Valley, around Oakville, Rutherford and St. Helena. They include some of the area's oldest wineries—Beaulieu, Robert Mondavi, Beringer, and Louis Martini, for instance. Many of the best vineyards are situated on the so-called Rutherford Bench, a narrow strip of soft loam that is renowned for producing classic, long-lived Cabernet Sauvignon.

A number of sub-regions of Napa have developed individual winemaking identities, and several have been granted appellation status. The Stags Leap District, east of Yountville, is known for its supple, Bordeaux-like Cabernets. It is home to Stag's Leap Wine Cellars, Stags' Leap Winery, Shafer Vineyard Cellars, Pine Ridge, Chimney Rock, S. Anderson, and others.

Los Carneros, which straddles the southern ends of Napa and Sonoma, has developed a reputation for Burgundy-style wines made from Pinot Noir and from Chardonnay. Well-known Carneros wineries include Acacia, Bouchaine, Saintsbury, and Carneros Creek.

In recent years, several regions in the hilly mountainsides of the Valley have achieved special recognition. Howell Mountain, located to the northeast of St. Helena, has volcanic soil that produces especially rich wines. Howell Mountain wineries such as Dunn and La Jota have established well-deserved reputations for producing powerful Cabernets and Zinfandels.

To the west of Yountville is Mount Veeder, a part of the Mayacamas Mountains, which has become known for Cabernet Sauvignon, Chardonnay and Sauvignon Blanc. Leading Mount Veeder wineries include Mayacamas Vineyards, Mount Veeder Winery, Hess Collection, and Château Potelle. The best-known wineries further north in the Mayacamas Mountains include Diamond Creek, Stony Hill and Philip Togni, most of which specialize in Cabernet, Merlot and Chardonnay.

Sonoma County. Sonoma County presents a more varied picture than the Napa Valley. Geographically diverse, with numerous microclimates, it supports many grape varieties and wine styles.

The historic heart of Sonoma County is the Sonoma Valley, where many of its oldest wineries are located. Cabernet Sauvignon has fared well here, as has Zinfandel. Chardonnay and Pinot Noir seem especially well suited to the southern part of the Sonoma Valley. Leading wineries of Sonoma Valley include Kenwood, B.R. Cohn, Kunde, Laurel Glen, Landmark, Chateau St. Jean, Arrowood, Hanzell, and Sebastiani.

Alexander Valley is planted mostly with Cabernet Sauvignon and Chardonnay. The Cabernets produced here have proven to be well balanced and elegant, with many showing a hint of eucalyptus. This region's Chardonnays tend to be full and rich, without the tropical buttery notes found in many other California Chardonnays. Jordan Winery is located here and produces a luxury sparkling wine cuvée called J. The region's other well-known wineries include Chateau Souverain, Geyser Peak, Murphy-Goode, Simi, and Stonestreet.

Dry Creek Valley parallels Alexander Valley, but has a different, often warmer, microclimate. Zinfandel seems to thrive in its benchland soil, but lately Cabernet is making significant inroads. Among whites, Sauvignon Blanc does particularly well here. Leading wineries include Dry Creek Vineyard, Mazzocco, Quivira, A. Rafinelli, Ferrari-Carano, and Preston.

Because of its proximity to the ocean, the Russian River Valley's climate is cooler, which for some years discouraged extensive planting. However, Pinot Noir and Chardonnay have recently been shown to thrive under these conditions, which can be likened to those of Burgundy. The Russian River Valley also encompasses two smaller sub-regions that are attracting increasing attention, Chalk Hill and Green Valley. Both excel in Chardonnay, and Green Valley has been developed by Iron Horse Vineyards as a source of high-quality sparkling wines.

The Hop Kiln Winery in Sonoma's Russian River Valley.

Richard Gillette

Santa Clara, Monterey and San Luis Obispo counties contain a vast number of fine properties. Important viticultural regions in these areas include the Santa Cruz Mountains, Livermore Valley, Carmel, Arroyo Seco, Paso Robles, and Edna Valley. These regions produce a full range of varietal types and make wines that often reach the highest levels of quality.

Other important regions. Santa Barbara County includes two distinct viticultural areas with excellent potential. In northern Santa Barbara County, the Santa Maria Valley is becoming best known for Pinot Noir and Chardonnay; both varieties take on a special intensity and richness of fruit here. Au Bon Climat, Byron and Cambria are among the leading producers. In southern Santa Barbara, the Santa Ynez Valley has also shown an affinity for cool-climate varieties, including Pinot Noir and Chardonnay. The Sanford & Benedict Vineyard in the eastern part of the Valley supplies grapes for some of Sanford Winery's best wines, and supplies other wineries as well. Also in Santa Barbara, experiments with Syrah have produced excellent results; Qupé's and Zaca Mesa's are among the best.

Just north of Napa lies Lake County, which has become an important producer of Chardonnay, Cabernet, Sauvignon Blanc, Merlot, and Pinot Noir. Lake County is the home of the original Kendall-Jackson Winery and Guenoc Winery, among others.

Located just to the west of Lake County, Mendocino is home to a wide array of varietal wines, many of which sell at very modest prices. For many years, Parducci was the only well-known producer here, but Fetzer and several other successful enterprises have now joined its ranks.

OREGON

More than 6,000 acres of vines are planted in Oregon today, and three-quarters of its total wine production comes from the Willamette Valley. The state has shown a particular affinity for the Pinot Noir grape, which constitutes 40 percent of plantings here. The top Oregon Pinot Noirs are competitive with the best of Burgundy and California. Chardonnay, Riesling and other varieties are also widely and successfully cultivated.

Well-known Oregon producers include Eyrie Vineyards, Ponzi, Adelsheim, Erath, Sokol Blosser, Argyle, Beaux Frères, and Willamette Valley Vineyards. Oregon is also the home of Domaine Drouhin, which is owned and operated by the important Burgundian firm of Joseph Drouhin.

WASHINGTON

While Oregon wine has a Burgundian tilt, Washington State's leans toward Bordeaux. Cabernet Sauvignon and Merlot do extremely well here, and now represent nearly a third of Washington's total vine acreage. (Washington Merlot may even have an edge over California's.) Most Washington wineries are located in the Columbia River Valley, which includes the smaller Yakima Valley and Walla Walla districts within its borders. The best-known Washington wineries are Chateau Ste. Michelle and Hogue; other major producers include Columbia Crest, Columbia Winery, Leonetti Cellars, Waterbrook, and Woodward Canyon.

ABBY D'OR | CALIFORNIA

Zinfandel Late Harvest Paso Robles 1991 • $9 • (10/15/94) • **78**

ABREU | CALIFORNIA

Cabernet Sauvignon Napa Valley Madrona Ranch 1987 • $25 • (07/31/91) • **89**

ABUNDANCE | CALIFORNIA

Sangiovese California 1994: Flavors veer off toward green bean and earth. Drinkable now. 1,520 cases made. • $10 • (07/31/97) • **80**

ACACIA | CALIFORNIA

Brut Carneros 1988 • $25 • (12/31/94) • **88**
Brut Carneros 1987 • $25 • (12/31/93) • **81**
Brut Carneros 1986 • $25 • (12/31/92) • **87**
Cabernet Sauvignon Napa Valley 1984 • $15 • (12/15/86) • **75**
Chardonnay California Caviste 1996: A slight metallic edge to the simple pear and pineapple flavors. Turns a little tinny on the finish. The last vintage of this wine. Drink now. 8,000 cases made. • $12 • (07/31/98) • **81**
Chardonnay Carneros 1996: There's a slightly green, leafy edge to this moderately ripe and uncomplicated wine. Picks up some interesting pear and light spicy oak on the finish. Drink now through 2001. 27,200 cases made. • $20 • (05/31/98) • **85**
Chardonnay Carneros 1995: Serves up lots of ripe, pure Chardonnay flavors, with layers of pear, citrus and pineapple. Holds its flavors on the finish, where they fan out. 27,000 cases made. • $19 • (05/31/97) • **90**
Chardonnay Carneros 1994: Serves up a juicy array of tropical fruit flavors, featuring hints of mango, pear, spice and light, toasty oak shadings which add to its finesse and elegance. A nice, complex aftertaste rounds this out. 21,000 cases made. • $18 • (04/30/96) SS • **90**
Chardonnay Carneros 1993 • $17 • (07/31/95) • **84**
Chardonnay Carneros Reserve 1995: A rich, complex style that shows off ripe pear, earth and buttery flavors that are well focused and long on the finish, where the oak is more apparent. Drink now through 2002. 1,168 cases made. • $30 • (07/31/98) • **90**
Chardonnay Carneros Reserve 1994: Ripe and juicy, with a peachlike accent to the pear, spice and pineapple flavors, turning smooth and oaky on the finish, with a creamy edge. Try now. 3,000 cases made. • $28 • (05/31/97) • **91**
Chardonnay Carneros Reserve 1993 • $25 • (04/30/96) • **90**
Merlot Napa Valley 1984 • $15 • (02/28/87) • **83**
Pinot Noir Carneros 1996: Fresh, crisp and snappy, with a grapey edge to the cherry and berry notes. Best now to 2001. 17,350 cases made. • $20 • (01/31/98) • **87**
Pinot Noir Carneros 1995: Smooth and polished, with a supple core of cola and black cherry flavors, finishing with a spicy edge and moderate tannins. 14,500 cases made. • $19 • (07/31/97) • **88**
Pinot Noir Carneros 1994 • $18 • (04/30/96) • **89**
Pinot Noir Carneros 1993 • $15 • (06/30/95) • **83**
Pinot Noir Carneros Reserve 1995: Openly fruity, with complex plum, cherry and spice flavors that are supple and polished, finishing with firm tannins. Drink now. 1,049 cases made. • $30 • (02/28/98) • **90**
Pinot Noir Carneros Reserve 1993 • $25 • (04/30/96) • **86**
Pinot Noir Napa Valley 1991 • $7 • (02/28/93) • **75**
Pinot Noir Napa Valley Carneros 1991 • $15 • (02/28/94) • **83**
Pinot Noir Napa Valley Carneros 1990 • $15 • (02/28/93) • **80**
Pinot Noir Napa Valley Carneros 1989 • $14 • (11/15/91) • **71**
Pinot Noir Napa Valley Carneros 1988 • $14 • (02/28/91) • **89**
Pinot Noir Napa Valley Carneros 1987 • $13 • (02/15/90) • **87**
Pinot Noir Napa Valley Carneros 1986 • $15 • (06/15/88) • **88**
Pinot Noir Napa Valley Carneros 1985 • $12 • (12/15/87) • **84**
Pinot Noir Napa Valley Carneros 1984 • $11 • (12/15/86) SS • **95**
Pinot Noir Napa Valley Carneros lund Vineyard 1991 • $21 • (02/28/94) • **82**
Pinot Noir Napa Valley Carneros lund Vineyard 1984 • $15 • (03/15/87) • **81**
Pinot Noir Napa Valley Carneros lund Vineyard 1983 • $16 • (08/31/86) • **77**
Pinot Noir Napa Valley Carneros lund Vineyard 1982 • $15 • (07/16/84) CS • **91**
Pinot Noir Napa Valley Carneros Lee Vineyard 1983 • $16 • (08/31/86) • **89**
Pinot Noir Napa Valley Carneros Lee Vineyard 1982 • $15 • (07/16/84) • **90**
Pinot Noir Napa Valley Carneros Madonna Vineyard 1986 • $18 • (06/15/88) • **88**
Pinot Noir Napa Valley Carneros Madonna Vineyard 1985 • $16 • (12/15/87) • **88**
Pinot Noir Napa Valley Carneros Madonna Vineyard 1984 • $16 • (03/15/87) • **88**
Pinot Noir Napa Valley Carneros Madonna Vineyard 1983 • $16 • (08/31/86) • **93**
Pinot Noir Napa Valley Carneros St. Clair Vineyard 1991 • $25 • (02/28/94) • **83**
Pinot Noir Napa Valley Carneros St. Clair Vineyard 1990 • $21 • (02/28/93) • **84**
Pinot Noir Napa Valley Carneros St. Clair Vineyard 1989 • $21 • (10/31/91) • **86**
Pinot Noir Napa Valley Carneros St. Clair Vineyard 1988 • $20 • (02/28/91) HR • **91**
Pinot Noir Napa Valley Carneros St. Clair Vineyard 1987 • $18 • (02/15/90) • **89**
Pinot Noir Napa Valley Carneros St. Clair Vineyard 1986 • $18 • (06/15/88) • **91**
Pinot Noir Napa Valley Carneros St. Clair Vineyard 1985 • $16 • (12/15/87) • **91**
Pinot Noir Napa Valley Carneros St. Clair Vineyard 1984 • $16 • (11/30/86) • **93**
Pinot Noir Napa Valley Carneros St. Clair Vineyard 1983 • $15 • (10/01/85) CS • **95**
Pinot Noir Napa Valley Carneros St. Clair Vineyard 1982 • $15 • (07/16/84) • **89**
Pinot Noir Napa Valley Carneros St. Clair Vineyard Reserve 1994: Smooth, ripe and supple. Mature for its age, with earthy plum and berry flavors, herb and tar notes. Best now through 2000. 312 cases made. • $38 • (03/31/98) • **88**
Pinot Noir Napa Valley Carneros St. Clair Vineyard Reserve 1992 • $25 • (06/30/95) • **87**
Pinot Noir Napa Valley Carneros Winery Lake Vineyard 1983 • $15 • (11/16/85) • **78**
Pinot Noir Napa Valley Carneros Winery Lake Vineyard 1982 • $15 • (07/16/84) • **90**
Zinfandel Napa Valley Caviste 1992 • $11 • (10/15/94) • **85**
Zinfandel Napa Valley Caviste 1991 • $12 • (09/30/93) • **87**
Zinfandel Napa Valley Caviste 1990 • $12 • (10/15/92) • **86**
Zinfandel Napa Valley Old Vines 1993 • $10 • (10/15/95) • **85**

ACADEMY, THE | OREGON

Cabernet Sauvignon Rogue Valley 1995: Starts out as a lush mouthful of plum and dusky spice flavors, nicely framed by plush-textured tannins. Hints of leather and game cut in on the finish. Try in 2000. 100 cases made. • $16 • (05/15/98) • **86**
Merlot Rogue Valley 1996: Smooth and supple, with a citrusy note at the center of a lively mouthful of currant and plum flavors. A pretty wine, approachable now or try in 1999 to 2000. 50 cases made. • $16 • (05/15/98) • **86**

ADAMS | OREGON

Pinot Noir Willamette Valley 1990 • $10 • (03/15/94) • **77**
Pinot Noir Willamette Valley 1988 • $12 • (02/28/93) • **79**
Pinot Noir Yamhill County 1985 • $25 • (02/15/90) • **89**
Pinot Noir Yamhill County Peter F. Adams 1983 • $NA • (02/15/90) • **91**
Pinot Noir Yamhill County Reserve 1988 • $18 • (02/28/93) • **86**

ADASTRA | CALIFORNIA

Chardonnay Napa Valley Carneros 1996: Smooth, polished and refined, putting its green apple, spice and honey flavors on a sleek frame. Delicious now. 194 cases made. • $22 • (12/31/97) • **88**

ADELAIDA | CALIFORNIA

Blanc de Blancs California 1984: Hits most of the right notes with its tasty flavors of spicy citrus, toast and pear, traces of ginger and spice on the finish. 1,800 cases made. • $25 • (11/30/96) • **85**
Cabernet Sauvignon Paso Robles 1988 • $15 • (11/15/92) • **87**
Cabernet Sauvignon Paso Robles 1987 • $14 • (02/28/91) • **89**
Cabernet Sauvignon Paso Robles 1983 • $12 • (12/15/89) • **75**
Cabernet Sauvignon Paso Robles 1981 • $7 • (03/01/84) • **88**

Cabernet Sauvignon San Luis Obispo County 1994: Ripe, rich, supple and harmonious, with juicy cherry, plum and berry flavors, finishing with cedar and spice and a touch of earthiness. Best from 1999 through 2004. 1,674 cases made. • $21 • (05/31/98) • **88**
Cabernet Sauvignon San Luis Obispo County 1993: Ripe, supple and harmonious, with an intriguing green olive accent to the spicy currant, plum and blackberry flavors. Has a long, lingering aftertaste that keeps gushing flavors. Ready now through 2004. 1,675 cases made. • $19 • (08/31/97) • **90**
Cabernet Sauvignon San Luis Obispo County 1992: Well proportioned, with ripe, intense flavors of ripe cherry, currant, berry and spice. Finishes with toasty oak notes that add a nice dimension. Ready now through 2000. 995 cases made. • $19 • (11/15/96) • **88**
Cabernet Sauvignon San Luis Obispo County 1991: Ripe and intense; well-oaked, too, with juicy plum and cherry flavors, vanilla-scented oak notes and a dash of herb and spice on the finish. Turns supple and harmonious on the aftertaste, where the tannins are soft and fleshy. Impressive for its balance. Ready now. 1,248 cases made. • $19 • (11/30/96) • **89**
Cabernet Sauvignon San Luis Obispo County 1990 • $22 • (11/15/93) • **81**
Chardonnay San Luis Obispo County 1995: A rich, fat style with lots of flavor—pear, anise, honey, butterscotch, and lees. Hangs nicely on the palate, but shows a little oxidation. Drink now. 282 cases made. • $20 • (07/31/98) • **88**
Chardonnay San Luis Obispo County 1994: Heavy-handed oak flavors dominate, giving a smoky accent, but dashes of pear and vanilla flavors fold in to add interest and dimension. 996 cases made. • $19 • (06/15/97) • **87**
Chardonnay San Luis Obispo County 1993: A full-blown, heavy-handed Chardonnay. Oak and butterscotch flavors outweigh lighter notes of pure fruit. Finishes slightly flat. 703 cases made. • $19 • (07/31/96) • **83**
Chenin Blanc Paso Robles Pavanne 1995: A creamy, firm wine, dry and with finesse. The flavors are subtle, with essence of orange-peel and lime. Finishes fresh and clean. A fine job with this underrated varietal. 614 cases made. • $15 • (10/15/97) • **88**
Pinot Noir Paso Robles HMR Vineyards 1994: An oaky style, with the wood dominating, yet there's enough tart black cherry and plum notes to give a sense of balance. Drink now. 272 cases made. • $24 • (12/15/96) • **84**
Pinot Noir San Luis Obispo County 1993: Quite oaky, giving it a dry, dill-like accent up front that leads into a nice beam of cherry and berry flavors. Tastes complex on the finish. A little more time in the bottle should marry the fruit and oak. 286 cases made. • $24 • (11/30/96) • **87**
Sangiovese San Luis Obispo County 1995: Ripe and chewy, with a solid mouthful of cherry and spice flavors that linger on the finish. Drink through 1999. 159 cases made. • $24 • (07/31/98) • **85**
Sangiovese San Luis Obispo County 1994: A supple, plummy red wine with pretty spice-scented flavor and a soft finish. Ready now. 167 cases made. • $24 • (11/30/97) • **83**
Sangiovese San Luis Obispo County 1993 • $23 • (04/30/96) • **87**
Zinfandel Late Harvest Paso Robles 1992 • $18 • (04/30/96) • **84**
Zinfandel Paso Robles 1994: Ripe, with a jammy wild berry edge to its earthy Brazil nut and meaty notes. Drinks well now, and will through 1999. 380 cases made. • $19 • (08/31/97) • **87**
Zinfandel Paso Robles 1993: Tight and well-focused. This has a tart core of wild berry and cherry flavors, with hints of plum and spice. Finishes with a long, lingering aftertaste. Drink now. 1,020 cases made. • $17 • (12/15/96) • **89**
Zinfandel Paso Robles 1989 • $12 • (10/15/92) • **83**
Zinfandel Paso Robles 1988 • $12 • (04/30/91) • **88**
Zinfandel San Luis Obispo County 1992 • $16 • (04/30/96) • **87**
Zinfandel San Luis Obispo County 1991 • $14 • (10/15/94) • **87**
Zinfandel San Luis Obispo County 1990 • $13 • (09/30/93) • **82**

ADELSHEIM | OREGON

Pinot Gris Oregon 1993 • $11 • (11/30/94) • **80**
Pinot Noir Oregon 1996: Firm in texture, with pretty cherry and raspberry flavors shining through the fine layer of tannins. Has an earthy note on the finish. Best from 1999 or 2000. 3,235 cases made. • $20 • (05/15/98) • **85**
Pinot Noir Oregon 1995: Not much charm. A light, slightly chewy, tobacco-scented wine with some herbal character lurking beneath the tough layer. • $NA • (02/28/97) • **80**
Pinot Noir Oregon 1991 • $15 • (02/28/93) • **84**
Pinot Noir Oregon 1987 • $13 • (02/15/90) • **72**

Key: SS—Spectator Selection CS—Cellar Selection HR—Highly Recommended BB—Best Buy $NA—Price not available Ⓐ—Auction Price (BT)—Barrel Tasting
Dates in parentheses indicate the issues in which the ratings were published.

Pinot Noir Oregon 1985 • $25 • (02/15/90) • **75**
Pinot Noir Polk County 1986 • $15 • (06/15/88) • **87**
Pinot Noir Polk County Seven Springs Vineyard 1992 • $23 • (10/31/94) • **89**
Pinot Noir Polk County Seven Springs Vineyard 1990 • $20 • (02/28/93) • **85**
Pinot Noir Polk County The Eola Hills 1987 • $16 • (02/15/90) • **70**
Pinot Noir Willamette Valley 1988 • $13 • (04/15/91) • **89**
Pinot Noir Willamette Valley Ridgecrest Vineyards 1996: Firm and flavorful, with shots of black cherry and currant flavor piercing the layer of fine-grained tannins that competes on the finish. Needs until 2000 to sort out. 235 cases made. • $40 • (05/15/98) • **88**
Pinot Noir Yamhill County 1985 • $16 • (06/15/87) • **88**
Pinot Noir Yamhill County 1983 • $40 • (02/15/90) • **70**
Pinot Noir Yamhill County Elizabeth's Reserve 1991 • $23 • (11/30/94) • **85**
Pinot Noir Yamhill County Elizabeth's Reserve 1990 • $25 • (02/28/93) • **83**
Pinot Noir Yamhill County Elizabeth's Reserve 1987 • $19 • (02/15/90) • **73**

ADLER FELS | CALIFORNIA

Cabernet Sauvignon Napa Valley 1980 • $10 • (10/01/84) • **74**
Chardonnay Sonoma County 1996: Light and fragrant, with pear and floral flavors. Easy to drink. 2,131 cases made. • $14 • (03/31/98) • **82**
Chardonnay Sonoma County 1995: A straightforward wine with bright citrus flavors and round mouthfeel. • $14 • (07/31/97) • **86**
Chardonnay Sonoma County 1993 • $12 • (03/31/96) HR • **91**
Chardonnay Sonoma County Coleman Reserve 1996: A pretty Chardonnay, offering nicely defined apple, pear, honey and spice flavors. Drink now. 475 cases made. • $16 • (03/31/98) • **86**
Chardonnay Sonoma County Coleman Reserve 1993 • $14 • (03/31/96) • **84**
Fumé Blanc Sonoma County 1996: A bit weedy and grassy up front, it then moves on to touches of almond and guava on the finish, where it could use more zing. 2,150 cases made. • $11 • (05/15/98) • **80**
Fumé Blanc Sonoma County 1995: Different. A pronounced grassiness overwhelms other flavors. Full-bodied with an herbal, butterscotch finish. An older style that might please some. 2,250 cases made. • $11 • (06/30/97) • **86**
Gewürztraminer Sonoma County 1996: Sweet but not cloying; a big mouthful of golden fruit flavors with litchi and honey notes sneaking in on the finish. Nice sipper. 3,018 cases made. • $11 • (07/31/97) • **86**
Gewürztraminer Sonoma County 1995: Silky and spicy, with tangy cinnamon and grapefruit character running through. Finishing gracefully and with a slight sweetness. 3,112 cases made. • $11 • (11/30/96) • **86**
Gewürztraminer Sonoma County 1993 • $9 • (01/31/95) • **80**
Sangiovese Mendocino County 1995: A tart, simple, cherrylike wine with cedary overtones. 741 cases made. • $16 • (09/15/97) • **79**
Sangiovese Mendocino County 1994: Firm and well-focused, with a chewy core of plum- and cherry-accented Sangiovese flavors. Tightly knit, it can stand short-term cellaring. Try now. 460 cases made. • $16 • (12/15/96) • **87**
Sparkling Sonoma County Melange à Deux 1985 • $15 • (10/15/87) • **74**

AETNA SPRINGS | CALIFORNIA

Cabernet Sauvignon Napa Valley 1991 • $18 • (05/15/94) • **81**

AHERN | CALIFORNIA

Zinfandel Amador County 1980 • $6 • (02/15/84) • **78**

AHLGREN | CALIFORNIA

Cabernet Sauvignon Napa Valley 1978 • $20 • (11/15/92) • **80**
Cabernet Sauvignon Santa Cruz Mountains Bates' Ranch 1988 • $20 • (11/15/92) • **76**

AIRLIE | OREGON

Chardonnay Oregon 1994: A medium-weight Chardonnay, with a spicy, somewhat bitter edge that adds an extra dimension. Try now. 400 cases made. • $12 • (02/28/97) • **84**
Chardonnay Oregon Barrel Fermented 1993 • $10 • (03/31/96) • **84**
Gewürztraminer Oregon 1995: Off dry, with pretty floral aromas and metallic flavors. 1,300 cases made. • $7 • (02/28/97) • **78**
Gewürztraminer Oregon 1994 • $6 • (06/15/96) • **84**
Gewürztraminer Oregon 1993 • $6 • (03/31/96) • **84**
Müller-Thurgau Oregon 1995 • $6 • (06/15/96) • **83**
Müller-Thurgau Oregon 1994 • $6 • (01/31/96) • **83**

Müller-Thurgau Oregon 1993 • $7 • (11/30/94) • **83**
Pinot Noir Willamette Valley 1994: Light in texture, with refreshing currant and berry flavors. Try now. 800 cases made. • $11 • (07/31/96) • **82**
Pinot Noir Willamette Valley 1993 • $10 • (01/31/96) • **80**
Pinot Noir Willamette Valley 1992 • $10 • (11/30/94) • **78**
Pinot Noir Willamette Valley 1990 • $10 • (02/28/93) • **60**
Pinot Noir Willamette Valley 1987 • $9 • (02/15/90) • **75**
Riesling Oregon 1995: Earthy, sour and unpleasant. Not recommended. Tasted twice, with consistent notes. 2,200 cases made. • $7 • (11/15/97) • **69**
Riesling Oregon 1994 • $6 • (01/31/96) • **80**
Riesling Oregon 1993 • $7 • (11/30/94) • **83**

ALATERA | CALIFORNIA

Cabernet Sauvignon Napa Valley 1978 • $NA • (11/15/92) • **82**

ALBAN | CALIFORNIA

Grenache Edna Valley 1993 • $28 • (04/30/96) • **86**
Grenache Edna Valley Alban Estate Vineyard 1995: Truly exotic, dark, rich and spicy, with a broad core of plum, blackberry, cherry and raspberry. Holds its flavor on the finish and has the firm tannins to age a few years. Drink now through 2000. 72 cases made. • $28 • (03/31/98) • **88**
Grenache Edna Valley Alban Estate Vineyard 1994: Shows healthy color, with tart cranberry and strawberry notes, and peppery accents. Turns dry and tannic. 112 cases made. • $28 • (08/31/97) • **85**
Roussanne San Luis Obispo County 1994 • $32 • (02/29/96) • **85**
Syrah Edna Valley Alban Estate Reva 1995: Dark, with a rich, smooth texture and lots of flavors built around a core of ripe stewed plum, blackberry, cherry and spice. Finishes with a long, complex aftertaste, with hints of cedar, anise and tar, and supple tannins. Drink now through 2004. 550 cases made. • $21 • (03/31/98) • **89**
Syrah Edna Valley Reva 1994: A racy style, with beef-accented flavors of herb, cola and wild berry Opens slowly, but it's still quite chewy and tannic. Best to cellar into 1999. 950 cases made. • $18 • (08/31/97) • **88**
Syrah Edna Valley Reva 1993 • $18 • (06/15/96) • **87**
Viognier Central Coast 1995: Comes across as simple and ordinary, with its modest band of spice and pear flavor. 650 cases made. • $20 • (11/30/96) • **82**
Viognier Central Coast 1994 • $20 • (02/29/96) • **84**
Viognier Edna Valley Alban Estate Vineyard 1995: A good wine, but awkward; the peach and spicy pine flavors never really take off, as they are hindered by a flat edge. 280 cases made. • $28 • (11/30/96) • **84**
Viognier Edna Valley Alban Estate Vineyard 1994 • $28 • (02/29/96) • **87**

ALBINI | CALIFORNIA

Merlot Sonoma County 1995: A little smoky and spicy, with nice black currant, blackberry and anise notes. Finishes with hints of eucalyptus and herbs. Rustic but rewarding. Best through 2003. 392 cases made. • $21 • (05/31/98) • **86**
Merlot Sonoma County 1994: Decidedly minty, with herbal overtones to the lean core of currant and plum. Finishes with mild tannins. 297 cases made. • $19 • (07/31/97) • **86**

ALDERBROOK | CALIFORNIA

Cabernet Sauvignon Dry Creek Valley 1994: Young and tight, with a supple band of currant, black cherry and wild berry flavors. A good, sound effort at an affordable price. 867 cases made. • $17 • (05/15/97) • **86**
Cabernet Sauvignon Sonoma County 1995: Young and trim, with firm tannins and an earthiness to its currant and plum-tinged Cabernet flavors. Will be even better with short-term cellaring; try now through 2002. 1,961 cases made. • $16 • (08/31/97) • **89**
Chardonnay Dry Creek Valley 1996: A clean and crisp style, with a tightly wound band of citrus, pear and spice-laced Chardonnay flavors. Holds its appealing fruitiness through the finish. Represents significant improvement at this California winery, and it's a great buy at this price. 13,503 cases made. • $13 • (02/28/98) SS • **89**
Chardonnay Dry Creek Valley 1995: Complex in its own way, with citrus, pineapple, spice and pear flavors that are rich and well-focused. At this price, it's more than your money's worth of Chardonnay. 10,153 cases made. • $12 • (05/15/97) • **89**
Chardonnay Dry Creek Valley 1993 • $12 • (07/31/95) • **83**
Chardonnay Dry Creek Valley Dorothy's Vineyard 1995: Rich and complex, with plenty of ripe, concentrated pear, apple, fig and oak shadings, with a slight bitter edge on the finish. Drink now through 2000. 600 cases made. • $20 • (03/31/98) • **89**
Chardonnay Dry Creek Valley Dorothy's Vineyard 1994: Tart and flinty, with citrus flavors, especially grapefruit, at the core. Fans out on the finish, where it picks up a hint of green pear. Those who like non-oaked Chardonnay will find this especially pleasing. Try now. 208 cases made. • $19 • (05/15/97) • **89**
Gewürztraminer Russian River Valley Saralee's Vineyard 1996: Lightly sweet, with modest orange and spice notes that linger on the bitter almond-scented finish. Drinkable now. 2,214 cases made. • $11 • (11/30/97) • **85**
Merlot Sonoma County Kunde Vineyard 1995: Offers some complex oak, currant, herb, sage and tobacco flavors, but lacks the polish and focus of the best. Finishes with firm tannins; cellar into 1999 or 2001. 1,800 cases made. • $20 • (04/30/98) • **86**
Merlot Sonoma County Kunde Vineyard 1994: Well-oaked, young and tight, it slowly opens to reveal more currant, anise, oak and cedar notes. It's a long way from reaching its peak, as it is very compact and firmly tannic. Try around 1999 or 2000. 1,400 cases made. • $22 • (12/31/96) • **86**
Muscat de Frontignan Late Harvest Sonoma County Kunde Vineyard 1995: Very sweet and syrupy, with spicy Muscat flavors layered over the pear and starfruit character. Flavors linger on the finish, picking up a nice tart edge. 362 cases made. • $24/375ml • (12/31/96) • **87**
Muscat de Frontignan Late Harvest Sonoma County Kunde Vineyard 1994: Very ripe and rich honey, spice, pineapple and kumquat flavors are balanced against a zingy thread of racy acidity. This dessert wine is delicious now for its distinctive character, but may improve through 2001 to 2004. 360 cases made. • $20/375ml • (10/31/96) • **92**
Pinot Noir Russian River Valley 1996: Medium weight in body and flavor, with light cherry, spice and vanilla shadings. Given the depth and level of concentration, it's best to drink now through 1999. 2,960 cases made. • $18 • (03/31/98) • **86**
Pinot Noir Russian River Valley 1995: Clean, ripe and spicy. A medium-weight wine, with snappy raspberry and wild cherry flavors, finishing with a slight earthy note. Drink now. 924 cases made. • $18 • (12/31/96) • **87**
Pinot Noir Russian River Valley 1994 • $15 • (01/31/96) • **87**
Sauvignon Blanc Dry Creek Valley 1996: A subdued, fleshy style, showing pleasant mandarin orange and nectarine flavors. Not quite up to the previous vintage. 5,200 cases made. • $11 • (06/30/97) • **86**
Sauvignon Blanc Dry Creek Valley 1995: Crisp and well-focused, offering a generous helping of floral, grapefruit, peach and apricot flavors that linger enticingly on the finish. 5,500 cases made. • $9 • (07/31/96) • **89**
Sauvignon Blanc Dry Creek Valley 1994 • $8 • (08/31/95) • **85**
Sauvignon Blanc Dry Creek Valley 1993 • $8 • (08/31/95) • **82**
Sauvignon Blanc Dry Creek Valley Late Harvest 1989 • $24/375ml • (06/15/92) • **88**
Sémillon Dry Creek Valley 1993 • $8 • (08/31/95) • **83**
Viognier Russian River Valley Timbervine Ranch Alta Vina 1996: Lots of spicy character, with peach and pear flavors filling in the gaps. Drink now. 25 cases made. • $18 • (12/15/97) • **86**
Zinfandel Dry Creek Valley 1993 • $14 • (10/15/95) • **85**
Zinfandel Russian River Valley Gamba Vineyard 1996: Effusively fruity, with bright, ripe flavors of black cherry, wild berry and raspberry, rich and well-focused. Finishes with a rush of fruit and spice, and mild tannins. Drink now through 2002. 340 cases made. • $20 • (03/31/98) • **89**
Zinfandel Russian River Valley Gamba Vineyard 1995: Dark, rich and concentrated, with gobs of complex wild berry, black cherry and plum flavors. This is a fruit-driven wine packed with lively flavors that will please Zin purists who prize unadulterated fruit. Lovely now, with its peppery aftertaste. 197 cases made. • $20 • (12/31/96) • **92**
Zinfandel Sonoma County 1994: Intensely fruity, with lots of spicy ripe cherry and wild berry flavors. It's also crisp and tannic but well-balanced, and the fruit flavors linger on the finish. 1,792 cases made. • $16 • (09/15/96) • **89**
Zinfandel Sonoma County OVOC 1996: Firm and tightly-wound, the hard-edged tannins stand out, yet there's enough ripe berry- and cherry-laced flavors behind them to make it appealing. Short-term cellaring recommended. Best from 1999 through 2003. 8,800 cases made. • $16 • (05/31/98) • **87**
Zinfandel Sonoma County OVOC 1995: Lots of pretty, ripe plum, wild berry and cherry notes mark this supple and forward wine. Drinkable now with its ripe tannins. 5,175 cases made. • $14 • (04/30/97) • **89**

ALEXANDER VALLEY FRUIT & TRADING CO. | CALIFORNIA

Zinfandel Dry Creek Valley 1992 • $9 • (10/15/94) • **81**
Zinfandel Late Harvest Alexander Valley 1991 • $12 • (10/31/95) • **85**
Zinfandel Late Harvest Alexander Valley 1990 • $12 • (10/15/94) • **82**

ALEXANDER VALLEY VINEYARDS | CALIFORNIA

Cabernet Franc Alexander Valley Wetzel Family Estate 1996: Starts up with a green olive facet that fits in nicely with the smooth core of clove, wintergreen, black currant and dried prune flavors. An odd ensemble that nonetheless works. Drink now. 1,000 cases made. • $20 • (03/31/98) • **86**
Cabernet Sauvignon Alexander Valley 1989 • $13 • (08/31/92) • **87**
Cabernet Sauvignon Alexander Valley 1988 • $12 • (09/30/91) • **88**
Cabernet Sauvignon Alexander Valley 1987 • $12 • (05/31/90) • **87**
Cabernet Sauvignon Alexander Valley 1986: Showing balance and grace, this is holding well, with a pleasantly mature band of cedar and cherry flavors and supple tannins. • $NA • (12/15/96) • **86**
Cabernet Sauvignon Alexander Valley 1986 • $12 • (12/31/88) • **89**
Cabernet Sauvignon Alexander Valley 1985 • $11 • (11/15/87) HR • **92**
Cabernet Sauvignon Alexander Valley 1984 • $11 • (05/15/87) SS • **93**
Cabernet Sauvignon Alexander Valley 1983 • $11 • (01/01/86) • **87**
Cabernet Sauvignon Alexander Valley 1982 • $10 • (02/01/85) • **84**
Cabernet Sauvignon Alexander Valley 1981 • $9 • (02/01/86) • **89**
Cabernet Sauvignon Alexander Valley 1980 • $9 • (02/01/86) • **80**
Cabernet Sauvignon Alexander Valley 1978 • $28 • (11/15/92) • **78**
Cabernet Sauvignon Alexander Valley Library Reserve 1986 • $18 • (06/15/93) • **80**
Cabernet Sauvignon Alexander Valley Wetzel Family Estate 1995: Crisp and lean, showing more berry aromas than flavors, with smoky accents on the finish. Could smooth out nicely by 2000. 14,000 cases made. • $16 • (11/15/97) • **82**
Cabernet Sauvignon Alexander Valley Wetzel Family Estate 1994: A bit chewy, with ripe berry overtones-currant, blackberry and a hint of raisin. Smoke and leather on the nose, with a bright, long finish. 13,000 cases made. • $15 • (11/15/97) • **87**
Cabernet Sauvignon Alexander Valley Wetzel Family Estate 1993: A touch earthy, but holds together as hints of plum and cherry fold in on the finish. 8,784 cases made. • $15 • (03/31/97) • **84**
Cabernet Sauvignon Alexander Valley Wetzel Family Estate 1992 • $14 • (05/31/95) • **86**
Cabernet Sauvignon Alexander Valley Wetzel Family Estate 1991 • $13 • (11/15/93) • **84**
Cabernet Sauvignon Alexander Valley Wetzel Family Estate 1990 • $14 • (06/15/93) • **88**
Cabernet Sauvignon Alexander Valley Wetzel Family Estate 1987: Nicely rounded, smooth and elegant, with a pretty array of ripe cherry, plum and spice flavors, turning supple and harmonious on the finish. Drink now through 2000. 10,279 cases made. • $28 • (12/15/97) • **89**
Chardonnay Alexander Valley Wetzel Family Reserve 1996: A delicate coconut aroma precedes the pear and apple flavors inherent in this wine. Acidity seems on the bright side. Finishes with a nice mineral edge. Drink now through 2001. 400 cases made. • $24 • (05/31/98) • **86**
Chenin Blanc Alexander Valley Dry Wetzel Family Estate 1995: With a distinct aroma of hay and green beans, this wine offers up tangy acidity and fresh grapefruit flavors. Dry and refreshing. 1,400 cases made. • $8 • (10/15/97) • **85**
Gewürztraminer North Coast New Gewurz 1997: Fresh, youthful and lightly sweet, with pretty rose-scented pear and apple flavors. Drink now. 7,500 cases made. • $9 • (03/31/98) • **84**
Merlot Alexander Valley 1990 • $13 • (03/31/93) • **87**
Merlot Alexander Valley 1989 • $13 • (11/15/91) • **84**
Merlot Alexander Valley 1985 • $11 • (10/31/87) • **88**
Merlot Alexander Valley Wetzel Family Estate 1995: A racy style, with an herbaceous edge to the cherry and berry flavors, turning crisp and lean on the finish. 12,000 cases made. • $17 • (06/30/97) • **86**
Merlot Alexander Valley Wetzel Family Estate 1993 • $15 • (05/15/96) • **83**
Merlot Alexander Valley Wetzel Family Estate 1992 • $15 • (07/31/95) • **86**
Merlot Alexander Valley Wetzel Family Estate 1991 • $14 • (09/15/94) • **77**
Pinot Noir Alexander Valley 1989 • $10 • (10/31/91) • **65**
Pinot Noir Alexander Valley 1987 • $9 • (05/31/90) • **74**
Pinot Noir Alexander Valley 1985 • $8 • (04/15/88) • **81**
Pinot Noir Alexander Valley 1984 • $7 • (02/15/88) • **87**
Pinot Noir Alexander Valley 1982 • $6 • (11/01/84) • **75**
Pinot Noir Alexander Valley Wetzel Family Estate 1996: Has a distinct herbal edge to the cherry and chocolate aromas and flavors. A soft-textured wine up front, this kicks in with some firm tannins on the finish. Drinkable now. 1,300 cases made. • $13 • (12/15/97) • **84**
Pinot Noir Alexander Valley Wetzel Family Estate 1990 • $11 • (02/28/94) • **83**
Syrah Alexander Valley Vyborny Vineyards 1995: Soft and ripe, with a distinct earthy-tarry edge to the modest blackberry flavors. Drink soon. 400 cases made. • $17 • (12/15/97) • **83**
Zinfandel Alexander Valley 1987 • $9 • (03/31/90) • **82**
Zinfandel Alexander Valley Sin Zin 1993 • $13 • (10/15/95) • **78**
Zinfandel Alexander Valley Sin Zin 1989 • $11 • (10/15/92) • **76**

ALMADEN | CALIFORNIA

Cabernet Sauvignon Monterey County 1981 • $5 • (05/01/84) • **80**
Cabernet Sauvignon Monterey County Vintage Classic Selection 1983 • $5 • (05/01/85) • **74**
Premium California 1982 • $7 • (12/31/86) • **79**

ALPEN | CALIFORNIA

Chardonnay Trinity County 1996: Simple and slightly sweet, with citrus, pear and tart apple. Some light tannins on the finish. 727 cases made. • $7 • (07/31/98) • **81**
Chardonnay Trinity County 1994: Soft in texture, with vanilla aromas and a modest level of pear, spice and toast flavors. Appealing now. 735 cases made. • $7 • (06/15/96) • **82**

ALPINE | OREGON

Pinot Noir Willamette Valley 1989 • $12 • (02/28/93) • **67**
Pinot Noir Willamette Valley Vintage Select 1985 • $17 • (06/15/87) • **80**

ALTAMURA | CALIFORNIA

Cabernet Sauvignon Napa Valley 1994: A big, ripe, well-oaked style that has substantial concentration and complexity, with well-defined currant, black cherry, herb and wild berry flavors, picking up herb and coffee notes. For all its richness and concentration, it's an elegant, delicate wine. Ready now and into the next century. 1,800 cases made. • $33 • (12/15/97) • **91**
Cabernet Sauvignon Napa Valley 1993: Another delicious wine from Altamura, combining ripe, rich, complex fruit with a sense of harmony and finesse. Delivers lots of juicy cherry, currant, anise and light oak shadings. The tannins are smooth and supple, making this one quite enjoyable now and into 2002. • $25 • (02/28/97) • **92**
Cabernet Sauvignon Napa Valley 1992: Dark and complex, with spicy currant, plum and chocolate-cherry flavors that run deep and full into the finish, where it picks up a mineral edge. 1,000 cases made. • $28 • (08/31/96) HR • **92**
Cabernet Sauvignon Napa Valley 1991 • $25 • (05/31/96) • **88**
Cabernet Sauvignon Napa Valley 1990 • $25 • (09/15/95) • **88**
Cabernet Sauvignon Napa Valley 1988 • $18 • (11/15/92) • **85**
Sangiovese Napa Valley 1994: This red serves up lots of flavor and finesse, with spice, anise, cedar, currant and wild berry flavors that fan out and linger on the finish. Impressive for its flavor, richness, elegance and length, it's even better than the outstanding debut '93. Drinks nicely now, but can easily age into 2000. 1,000 cases made. • $22 • (11/30/97) HR • **92**
Sangiovese Napa Valley 1993 • $18 • (04/30/96) • **90**

AMADOR FOOTHILL | CALIFORNIA

Sangiovese Shenandoah Valley 1994: Firm in texture, with modest blackberry and floral flavors that hang on through the finish. Try now. 500 cases made. • $12 • (07/31/97) • **85**
Sangiovese Shenandoah Valley Festa Dell'Uva 1993 • $12 • (11/30/95) • **80**
Sangiovese Shenandoah Valley Festa Dell'Uva 1992 • $12 • (09/15/94) • **79**
Sauvignon Blanc Shenandoah Valley Amador Fumé 1995: The melon and pear flavors have a sour edge with a hint of herb on the soft finish. 1,285 cases made. • $7 • (05/15/97) • **81**

Key: SS—Spectator Selection CS—Cellar Selection HR—Highly Recommended BB—Best Buy $NA—Price not available Ⓐ—Auction Price (BT)—Barrel Tasting
Dates in parentheses indicate the issues in which the ratings were published.

Sémillon Shenandoah Valley 1993 • $9 • (05/31/96) • **76**
Zinfandel Fiddletown Eschen Vineyard 1991 • $10 • (10/15/94) • **78**
Zinfandel Fiddletown Eschen Vineyard 1990 • $10 • (09/30/93) • **82**
Zinfandel Fiddletown Eschen Vineyard 1988 • $10 • (10/15/92) • **73**
Zinfandel Fiddletown Eschen Vineyard 1986 • $9 • (06/15/89) • **82**
Zinfandel Fiddletown Eschen Vineyard 1984 • $9 • (10/15/88) • **86**
Zinfandel Fiddletown Eschen Vineyard Special Selection 1982 • $9 • (04/15/87) • **74**
Zinfandel Shenandoah Valley Ferrero Vineyard 1991 • $10 • (10/15/95) • **83**
Zinfandel Shenandoah Valley Ferrero Vineyard 1990 • $10 • (09/30/93) • **82**
Zinfandel Shenandoah Valley Ferrero Vineyard Special Selection 1989 • $10 • (03/31/92) • **81**
Zinfandel Shenandoah Valley Grand-Père Vineyard 1990 • $10 • (09/30/93) • **83**
Zinfandel Shenandoah Valley Grand-Père Vineyard 1989 • $10 • (10/15/92) • **79**
Zinfandel Shenandoah Valley Grand-Père Vineyard Special Selection 1988 • $10 • (08/31/91) • **75**

AMERICANA | CALIFORNIA

Chardonnay California 1995: A modest ensemble of green apple and herbal flavors. • $11 • (07/31/97) • **84**

AMICI | CALIFORNIA

Cabernet Sauvignon Napa Valley 1994: Smoke, earth and spice tones kick off this wine, which serves up layers of plum, licorice and black currant flavors. An oaky finish. Drink now through 2002. 506 cases made. • $22 • (05/31/98) • **86**
Cabernet Sauvignon Napa Valley 1993: Broad on the palate, this fleshy wine features attractive echoes of plum and tar, tempered by a moderate, herbal finish. 250 cases made. • $18 • (10/15/97) • **86**

AMITY | OREGON

Chardonnay Oregon Winemaker's Reserve 1993: Tastes better than it smells, fading on the nose but showing some spicy walnut and apple flavors on the palate. Seems awkward. 250 cases made. • $18 • (02/28/97) • **81**
Gamay Noir Oregon 1996: Very light, almost airy, with modest strawberry and mint flavors. Drink soon. 761 cases made. • $9 • (05/15/98) • **80**
Gewürztraminer Late Harvest Oregon Juliard Vineyard 1992: Sweet but not cloying, it's fresh and nicely honeyed on the nose but remarkably spicy in the mouth, with its seductive orange, cream and spice flavors lingering on the balanced finish. 266 cases made. • $8 • (04/30/97) • **90**
Gewürztraminer Oregon Dry 1996: Dry, almost austere at first sip, this turns tasty, fresh and ebullient as the bright pineapple, citrus, rose and honey flavors develop. A tad coarse, but the pretty flavors carry the day, and the asking price is quite reasonable for all you get. Drink soon. 2,037 cases made. • $10 • (04/30/98) BB • **87**
Gewürztraminer Oregon Dry 1995: Simple and soft, an off-dry white with modest varietal flavors. 2,676 cases made. • $9 • (02/28/97) • **81**
Pinot Blanc Willamette Valley 1995: Fresh and round, generous with its green plum and spice flavors; finishes a bit crisply. 377 cases made. • $13 • (04/30/97) • **82**
Pinot Blanc Willamette Valley Helmick Vineyards 1996: Flavors reminiscent of unripe melon and apple are pleasant, if unusual. Try now. 1,003 cases made. • $12 • (05/15/98) • **85**
Pinot Noir Oregon 1995: Light and lean, with herbal, minty overtones to the modest currant flavors. Best from 1999. 1,732 cases made. • $16 • (05/15/98) • **82**
Pinot Noir Oregon 1992 • $10 • (11/30/94) • **83**
Pinot Noir Oregon 1988 • $10 • (05/31/91) • **82**
Pinot Noir Oregon 1983 • $15 • (08/31/86) • **85**
Pinot Noir Oregon Eco Wine 1995: Fizzy, stinky flavors reflect a wine gone bad. Tasted twice with consistent notes. 677 cases made. • $12 • (02/28/97) • **72**
Pinot Noir Oregon Gamay Noir 1988 • $9 • (02/15/90) • **84**
Pinot Noir Oregon Winemaker's Reserve 1985 • $NA • (02/15/90) • **80**
Pinot Noir Oregon Winemaker's Reserve 1983 • $30 • (02/15/90) • **75**
Pinot Noir Willamette Valley 1994: Amity's best wine in years. Smooth, polished and elegant, with lovely flavors centering around spicy red berry, plum and exotic spices, gaining richness on the long finish. Tannins bite a bit, but should round off by 1999 or 2001. 1,412 cases made. • $16 • (02/28/97) • **90**
Pinot Noir Willamette Valley 1993: Has more menthol, tea and herb character than fruit. Silky smooth, with decidedly funky notes on the earthy finish. Drink now. 551 cases made. • $16 • (02/28/97) • **81**
Pinot Noir Willamette Valley 1987 • $15 • (02/15/90) • **81**
Pinot Noir Willamette Valley 1986 • $13 • (02/15/90) • **74**
Pinot Noir Willamette Valley 1985 • $25 • (02/15/90) • **85**
Pinot Noir Willamette Valley 1982 • $9 • (03/01/86) • **77**
Pinot Noir Willamette Valley Estate 1987 • $25 • (02/15/90) • **79**
Pinot Noir Willamette Valley Estate 1985 • $25 • (02/15/90) • **79**
Pinot Noir Willamette Valley Estate 1983 • $30 • (02/15/90) • **76**
Pinot Noir Willamette Valley Sunnyside Vineyard 1995: Light and crisp, with pretty strawberry and spice flavors, and a bit of a hard edge on the finish. Drink now. 92 cases made. • $18 • (05/15/98) • **86**
Pinot Noir Willamette Valley Winemaker's Reserve 1994: Firm in texture, with generous black cherry and berry flavors that wind through a layer of firm, but not excessive, tannins on the finish. Has presence and impressive length. Give it until 1999 to 2000 to see how much depth it develops. 308 cases made. • $30 • (05/15/98) • **87**
Pinot Noir Willamette Valley Winemaker's Reserve 1993: Still has a burr of roughness to the tannins, with a streak of black tea running through the black cherry and toast flavors. Best in 1999. 677 cases made. • $35 • (05/15/98) • **85**
Pinot Noir Willamette Valley Winemaker's Reserve 1988 • $25 • (02/28/93) • **80**
Pinot Noir Willamette Valley Winemaker's Reserve 1987 • $30 • (02/15/90) • **83**
Riesling Late Harvest Oregon Juliard Vineyard 1996: Sweet, but not syrupy. A delicate wine with strong floral and haylike aromas and flavors dominating the honey and apple notes, which finally come through on the light finish. 152 cases made. • $10 • (05/15/98) • **86**
Riesling Oregon Dry 1996: Dry and flavorful, but lacking in charm. Offers more earth notes than crisp, green apple ones. Try in 1999. 1,227 cases made. • $9 • (05/15/98) • **80**
Riesling Oregon Dry 1995: Fresh, off-dry, tasting of green apples with vaguely floral overtones. 1,481 cases made. • $9 • (02/28/97) • **81**

AMIZETTA | CALIFORNIA

Cabernet Sauvignon Napa Valley 1985 • $16 • (05/31/88) • **70**

ANAPAMU | CALIFORNIA

Cabernet Sauvignon Monterey County 1994: Marked by weedy, bell pepper and vegetal notes, it struggles to ripen to classic Cabernet flavors. Finishes with soft tannins. 20,000 cases made. • $10 • (02/28/97) • **78**
Chardonnay Central Coast 1996: Elegant and lightly fruity, with hints of pear, apple, citrus and melon, turning simple on the finish, where a dash of oak appears. Drink now through 2000. 50,000 cases made. • $12 • (06/30/98) • **86**
Chardonnay Central Coast 1995: This young Chardonnay shows some nicely mature characteristics, with nutty vanilla flavors backed by citrus and toasty oak notes, and a refreshingly bright finish. A lovely bottle of wine at a more-than-reasonable price. 15,700 cases made. • $10 • (06/15/97) BB • **87**
Pinot Noir Monterey County 1995: Silky-smooth, with pretty cherry, plum, cedar and spice flavors. An herbal thread—thyme and sage—permeates and adds complexity. The finish is bright and long. Drinks well now. 16,000 cases made. • $12 • (01/31/98) • **87**

ANCIEN WINES | CALIFORNIA

Pinot Noir Carneros 1995: Chewy with an earthy note, slowly unveiling its core of plum and black cherry flavors and gaining complexity on the finish, where it's tannic and a shade oaky. 250 cases made. • $23 • (07/31/97) • **88**
Pinot Noir Carneros 1994: Smooth, supple and harmonious, with a velvety texture and a rich, elegant band of ripe cherry, currant and plum flavors. Finishes with a spicy, cedary accent and a mineral note. 215 cases made. • $21 • (09/15/96) • **90**
Pinot Noir Carneros 1993 • $18 • (04/30/96) • **87**

ANDERSON VALLEY VINEYARDS | NEW MEXICO

Cabernet Sauvignon New Mexico 1986 • $11 • (07/31/89) • **80**
Cabernet Sauvignon New Mexico Reserve 1987 • $14 • (02/29/92) • **84**

ANDERSON'S CONN VALLEY | CALIFORNIA

Cabernet Sauvignon Napa Valley 1997: Dense, complex and concentrated, with rich, earthy currant, black cherry, plum and anise. Finishes with gusty tannins, but it's well balanced. • $NA • (07/31/98) (BT) • **90-94**

Cabernet Sauvignon Napa Valley Estate Reserve 1996: Already quite harmonious. Ripe and spicy, with an elegant band of currant, plum and cherry flavors, turning smooth and supple on the finish. 2,500 cases made. • $NA • (06/15/97) (BT) • **90-94**

Cabernet Sauvignon Napa Valley Estate Reserve 1994: Marked by an appetizing gamy edge, the core of cedar and currant is dense and intense, finishing with big, chewy tannins and lots of finesse. Best to hold into 2001. 3,600 cases made. • $40 • (10/15/97) • **91**

Cabernet Sauvignon Napa Valley Estate Reserve 1993: A touch earthy and leathery, but works its way past those flavors into a range of currant and cherry before the tannins kick in and dominate. This young and vibrant wine may move up a notch with time, but for now its rugged and tannic, even as the coffee and currant flavors pour through. 4,700 cases made. • $35 • (11/15/96) • **90**

Cabernet Sauvignon Napa Valley Estate Reserve 1992 • $30 • (11/15/95) HR • **93**

Cabernet Sauvignon Napa Valley Estate Reserve 1991 • $30 • (11/15/94) • **88**

Cabernet Sauvignon Napa Valley Estate Reserve 1990 • $25 • (11/15/93) • **90**

Cabernet Sauvignon Napa Valley Estate Reserve 1989 • $25 • (11/15/92) • **88**

Cabernet Sauvignon Napa Valley Estate Reserve 1988 • $24 • (11/15/91) HR • **92**

Chardonnay Napa Valley Feurnier Vineyard 1995: Sleek and elegant, with a sharply focused core of ripe, rich peach, pear, ginger and spice. Complex and concentrated, this wine packs in the flavor, yet retains its elegance and finesse. 100 cases made. • $40 • (04/30/98) • **91**

Pinot Noir Napa Valley 1992 • $25 • (03/31/95) • **85**

Pinot Noir Napa Valley Valhalla Vineyard 1995: A racy style, intense and lively, with a range of wild berry, beef, leather, earth and cedar. Packs in lots of flavors and finishes with chewy tannins; cellar into 1999 to 2000 in hope it softens. To be released this spring. 250 cases made. • $40 • (01/31/98) • **87**

Pinot Noir Napa Valley Valhalla Vineyards 1993 • $40 • (04/30/96) • **86**

Pinot Noir Napa Valley Valhalla Vineyards 1989 • $25 • (02/28/93) • **84**

ANDERSON, S. | CALIFORNIA

Blanc de Noirs Napa Valley 1993: A delicate style. Floral, black cherry and vanilla flavors turn elegant and spicy on the finish, where the wine picks up a slight earthy quality. 1,880 cases made. • $23 • (11/30/97) • **90**

Blanc de Noirs Napa Valley 1992: Complex, rich and elegant, with a well-focused, delicate core of dried black cherry, pear and anise flavors. A well-crafted wine that captures the essence of Pinot Noir in a sparkling wine. 2,200 cases made. • $22 • (11/30/96) SS • **91**

Blanc de Noirs Napa Valley 1991 • $23 • (12/31/95) • **88**

Blanc de Noirs Napa Valley 1990 • $20 • (11/30/94) SS • **90**

Blanc de Noirs Napa Valley 1989 • $20 • (12/31/93) • **86**

Blanc de Noirs Napa Valley 1988 • $20 • (12/31/92) • **87**

Blanc de Noirs Napa Valley 1987 • $19 • (06/15/91) • **86**

Blanc de Noirs Napa Valley 1986 • $20 • (12/31/90) • **83**

Blanc de Noirs Napa Valley 1985 • $16 • (05/31/89) • **87**

Blanc de Noirs Napa Valley 1984 • $16 • (10/15/88) • **79**

Blanc de Noirs Napa Valley 1983 • $28 • (05/31/89) • **85**

Brut Napa Valley 1993: Toasty, honeyed almond notes draw one into this richly textured California sparkling wine, redolent of lemon, lime, grapefruit and fig. It's powerful yet graceful, and finishes with lingering hints of chocolate and herbs. An outstanding bottle from a winery consistent with this type. 1,950 cases made. • $24 • (04/30/98) SS • **92**

Brut Napa Valley 1992: Honeyed, with hazelnut aromas, this is broad in style and a bit mature, with a smooth, creamy texture. Finishes beautifully, with rich, plum, fig and pear flavors. Complex, soft and tender. Drink now. 1,850 cases made. • $24 • (11/30/97) • **91**

Key: SS—Spectator Selection CS—Cellar Selection HR—Highly Recommended BB—Best Buy $NA—Price not available Ⓐ—Auction Price (BT)—Barrel Tasting
Dates in parentheses indicate the issues in which the ratings were published.

Brut Napa Valley 1991: Ripe and intense, with a pleasant, earthy accent to the pear, vanilla and spice flavors. Turns complex on the finish, where the flavors fold together neatly. 2,400 cases made. • $20 • (09/15/96) • **89**

Brut Napa Valley 1990 • $23 • (11/30/95) • **88**

Brut Napa Valley 1989 • $18 • (11/30/94) • **89**

Brut Napa Valley 1987 • $18 • (12/31/93) • **86**

Brut Napa Valley 1986 • $18 • (12/15/91) • **86**

Brut Napa Valley 1985 • $18 • (06/15/91) • **87**

Brut Napa Valley 1984 • $18 • (10/15/88) • **82**

Brut Napa Valley 1983 • $16 • (05/31/87) • **72**

Brut Napa Valley Reserve 1990: Marked by an earthy edge, the pear and hazelnut flavors are mature and soften on the finish. Drink now. 600 cases made. • $32 • (11/30/97) • **87**

Cabernet Sauvignon Stags Leap District 1994: A bit nervy, with an oddly tangy, oaky edge, which tends to overshadow the currant and herb-tinged Cabernet character. Has a nice texture and the flavors are pleasing. Tasted twice, with consistent notes. 360 cases made. • $24 • (10/31/97) • **89**

Cabernet Sauvignon Stags Leap District 1993: Marked by strong menthol aromas and flavors, with hints of currant and berry and a touch of spice. Turns simple on the finish. It's well-crafted and balanced. 360 cases made. • $22 • (11/15/96) • **87**

Cabernet Sauvignon Stags Leap District Richard Chambers Vineyard 1997: A tremendous effort from barrel. Ripe, complex and aromatic, with layers of rich, plush cherry, currant and coffee. Amazing finesse, polish and length. • $NA • (07/31/98) (BT) • **95-99**

Cabernet Sauvignon Stags Leap District Richard Chambers Vineyard 1996: Young, tight and focused, with a brilliant core of juicy black cherry, currant, anise and spice flavors. Could be stunning. 800 cases made. • $NA • (06/15/97) (BT) • **90-94**

Cabernet Sauvignon Stags Leap District Richard Chambers Vineyard 1994: Tightly wound, with a good dose of oak, the smoky, meaty flavors compete with the currant and plummy ones, but it sorts out on the finish, where the flavors fold together nicely. Best to cellar into 2000. 850 cases made. • $50 • (10/31/97) • **91**

Cabernet Sauvignon Stags Leap District Richard Chambers Vineyard 1993: A well-oaked style, but it manages to balance the woodiness with enough ripe cherry and berry flavors to hold your interest as it gains complexity on the finish. 850 cases made. • $50 • (11/30/96) • **90**

Cabernet Sauvignon Stags Leap District Richard Chambers Vineyard 1992 • $46 • (12/15/95) • **89**

Cabernet Sauvignon Stags Leap District Richard Chambers Vineyard 1991 • $46 • (12/31/94) HR • **91**

Cabernet Sauvignon Stags Leap District Richard Chambers Vineyard 1990 • $42 • (11/15/93) • **90**

Cabernet Sauvignon Stags Leap District Richard Chambers Vineyard 1989 • $36 • (11/15/92) • **90**

Chardonnay Napa Valley Carneros 1996: Clean and crisp, with a trim band of bright citrus, pear and melon flavors. Turns rather simple on the finish, where the flavors taper off. 1,800 cases made. • $22 • (01/31/98) • **87**

Chardonnay Napa Valley Carneros 1995: A racy style, marked by bracing acidity and a strong citrus and grapefruit core, but once the flavors settle in they're bright, complex and distinctive. 1,225 cases made. • $20 • (05/31/97) • **91**

Chardonnay Napa Valley Carneros 1994: Marked by strong citrus and spice character, just enough pear and apple notes coming through to make it interesting. Lacks the extra dimensions hoped for. 1,250 cases made. • $18 • (05/15/96) • **86**

Chardonnay Napa Valley Carneros 1993 • $18 • (04/30/95) • **86**

Chardonnay Napa Valley Proprietor's Reserve 1995: Delivers generous and complex Chardonnay flavors, with layers of ripe pear, citrus, hazelnut and fig. Impressive on the finish, where the flavors fan out to reveal even more depth and concentration. 500 cases made. • $30 • (05/31/97) • **92**

Chardonnay Stags Leap District 1995: A racy style, earthy and leesy, almost Sauvignon Blanc-like, with ripe pear and apple flavors adding interest. 1,550 cases made. • $20 • (06/15/97) • **87**

Chardonnay Stags Leap District 1994: Trim and well balanced, as pleasant spice, vanilla and pear flavors fan out on the finish, delivering a measure of harmony and finesse. This wine has a reputation for improving with age. 1,350 cases made. • $20 • (04/30/96) • **90**

Diva Napa Valley 1987: Ripe, smooth and creamy, with tiers of pear, spice, vanilla and almond flavors. This is a complex and lively wine that hardly tastes like it's 10 years old. 200 cases made. • $86/1.5 liter • (11/30/96) • **90**

Merlot Stags Leap District Reserve 1995: Ripe and fruity, with supple plum, wild berry, cherry and menthol notes, and a smooth, supple texture that lets the flavors run through. Best now to 2002. 210 cases made. • $28 • (03/31/98) • **87**

Merlot Stags Leap District Reserve 1994: Young and vibrant, with a core of cherry, tea, herb and cedary oak flavors, turning crisp and tannic on the finish. An elegantly crafted wine that's well balanced, with a lingering finish. • $28 • (12/31/96) • **88**
Rosé Napa Valley 1992: In a spicy style, its ripe plum and cherry flavors offering a nice dose of Pinot Noir character to the spritz of sparkling wine. 400 cases made. • $25 • (11/30/96) • **86**
Rosé Napa Valley 1991 • $25 • (12/31/95) • **86**

ANDRE | CALIFORNIA

Blush Pink Champagne California NV: A floral quality announces this sweetish, pink bubbly. Simple and cloying. • $4 • (12/15/97) • **79**
Brut California NV: Sweeter than some in this category, with attractive plum and cherry notes. Finishes with enough acidity to keep it from being cloying. • $4 • (12/15/97) • **83**
Extra Dry California NV: Strangely strawlike, with a sweet finish. • $4 • (12/15/97) • **72**

ANDREW WILL | WASHINGTON

Cabernet Sauvignon Washington 1994: Thick, concentrated and chewy, with a solid core of black currant and blackberry flavors shaded with notes of leather and toasty oak. Try now. 700 cases made. • $35 • (02/28/97) • **88**
Cabernet Sauvignon Washington 1992 • $21 • (05/31/95) • **88**
Cabernet Sauvignon Washington 1991 • $20 • (09/30/94) • **85**
Cabernet Sauvignon Washington Reserve 1994: Firm, and nicely packed with spicy, herb-scented black cherry and chocolate flavors. Finishes with a sturdy feel. Needs until 1999 to settle down. • $NA • (02/28/97) • **88**
Cabernet Sauvignon Washington Reserve 1991 • $22 • (09/30/94) • **88**
Chenin Blanc Washington Cuvée Lu Lu 1993 • $10 • (09/30/95) • **73**
Merlot Washington 1994: Light and spicy, with strawberry, raspberry and chocolate flavors balanced nicely. Drinkable now. 600 cases made. • $24 • (09/15/96) • **87**
Merlot Washington 1993 • $21 • (06/15/95) • **89**
Merlot Washington 1992 • $19 • (09/30/94) • **90**
Merlot Washington Ciel du Cheval 1994: A ripe, generous and spicy mouthful that features dark cherry, berry and plum flavors with a toasty oak shadow. 200 cases made. • $27 • (09/15/96) • **89**
Merlot Washington Ciel du Cheval 1993 • $25 • (08/31/95) • **89**
Merlot Washington Pepperbridge 1994: Strikes a lovely balance between generous, jammy berry and plum flavors on the one hand and spicy oak notes on the other. Drinkable now. • $30 • (09/15/96) • **88**
Merlot Washington Pepperbridge 1993 • $25 • (08/31/95) • **86**
Merlot Washington Reserve 1993 • $28 • (09/30/95) • **84**
Merlot Washington Sunshine 1991 • $19 • (09/30/94) • **89**
Merlot Washington Sunshine Reserve 1992 • $21 • (09/30/94) • **82**
Merlot Washington Sunshine Reserve 1991 • $21 • (09/30/94) • **88**

ANGELINE | CALIFORNIA

Zinfandel California Old Vine Cuvée 1992 • $8 • (10/15/95) • **83**

ANGELS CREEK | CALIFORNIA

Merlot California 1989 • $9 • (05/31/92) • **71**

ANTARES | CALIFORNIA

Merlot California 1995: Ripe, rich and generous in flavor, yet it remains airy and lithe. Has plenty of black cherry, chocolate and spice character. Very nicely done. Ready now. • $22 • (12/15/97) • **88**

ANTELOPE VALLEY | CALIFORNIA

Merlot California Bien Nacido Vineyards 1990 • $9 • (09/15/94) • **79**

APEX | WASHINGTON

Cabernet Sauvignon Columbia Valley 1994: Firm in texture and explosive in flavor, it's bursting with blueberry, blackberry, currant and plum, shaded with anise and herbal notes. A smooth package that needs until 2000 to 2001 to settle in. 1,231 cases made. • $35 • (09/15/97) • **90**
Cabernet Sauvignon Columbia Valley 1990 • $18 • (10/15/93) • **88**
Cabernet Sauvignon Yakima Valley 1993: Firm in texture, with generous plum and blackberry flavors that ride effectively through the chewy, fine tannins on the finish. Drinkable now. 401 cases made. • $25 • (09/15/96) • **88**
Chardonnay Columbia Valley 1994: Bright and spicy, with distinctly floral overtones to the pear and honey flavors. Drink now. 1,057 cases made. • $16 • (09/15/96) • **86**
Chardonnay Yakima Valley 1993 • $16 • (09/30/95) • **82**
Gewürztraminer Late Harvest Yakima Valley Ice Wine 1991 • $16 • (09/30/94) • **86**
Gewürztraminer Yakima Valley Barrel Fermented 1993 • $13 • (09/30/95) • **85**
Gewürztraminer Yakima Valley Dry 1994: Broad and flavorful from start to sturdy finish, with distinctive litchi, honey and almond flavors and lingering rose petal aromas. 228 cases made. • $13 • (09/15/96) • **85**
Gewürztraminer Yakima Valley Ice Wine 1991 • $14 • (04/15/95) • **77**
Merlot Columbia Valley 1990 • $15 • (09/30/93) • **84**
Merlot Yakima Valley 1992 • $18 • (09/30/95) • **87**
Merlot Yakima Valley 1989 • $17 • (03/15/93) • **83**
Montage Columbia Valley 1993: Ripe, spicy and polished, with an interesting medley of butterscotch, toast and spice flavors. Hints of honey armwrestle a bitter note on the finish. 269 cases made. • $13 • (09/15/96) • **83**
Pinot Noir Willamette Valley 1995: Light-colored, with pretty berry and black pepper flavors, finishing with a slightly bitter edge. Drink now. 300 cases made. • $18 • (09/15/97) • **85**
Riesling Late Harvest Yakima Valley LHR 1995: The beautiful honey, ripe apricot and spice aromas are betrayed by a very vinegary finish. 401 cases made. • $19 • (09/15/96) • **78**

ARAUJO | CALIFORNIA

Cabernet Sauvignon Napa Valley Eisele Vineyard 1997: Ripe, smooth and polished, this is an elegant, supple, harmonious wine with appealing cherry, berry and currant flavors. Finishes with ripe tannins. • $NA • (07/31/98) (BT) • **90-94**
Cabernet Sauvignon Napa Valley Eisele Vineyard 1994: Massively proportioned, with a dense core of earth-accented cedar and currant-spiked Cabernet flavors that are intense and well-focused and long, with a lively aftertaste and substantial tannins. Finishes with dashes of chocolate and berry. From a vineyard with a distinguished track record. Best to cellar into 2000. A blend of 93 percent Cabernet Sauvignon, 4 percent Cabernet Franc, and 3 percent Petit verdot. 2,400 cases made. • $204 Ⓐ • (10/15/97) HR • **96**
Cabernet Sauvignon Napa Valley Eisele Vineyard 1993: Tight and firm, but quite complex too, with tiers of spice, currant, plum and cherry flavors, picking up traces of herb, mineral and anise. Finishing with a burst of exotic smoky fruit flavor that works its way past the tannins. Cellar 1999 to 2000. 1,285 cases made. • $183 Ⓐ • (11/15/96) CS • **93**
Cabernet Sauvignon Napa Valley Eisele Vineyard 1992 • $40 • (11/15/95) CS • **96**
Cabernet Sauvignon Napa Valley Eisele Vineyard 1991 • $169 Ⓐ • (10/15/94) CS • **90**
Sauvignon Blanc Napa Valley Eisele Vineyard 1996: Fig and melon notes form the core of this firm yet supple wine. The follow-up features herb, vanilla, spice and floral components. 550 cases made. • $22 • (04/30/98) • **87**

ARBIOS | CALIFORNIA

Cabernet Sauvignon Alexander Valley 1995: Austere, with an earthiness that runs through the Cabernet flavors. Tight, with spice, cedar, plum and berry; shows more fruit and finesse with aeration. Best from 1999 through 2008. 500 cases made. • $30 • (06/15/98) • **88**

ARBOR CREST | WASHINGTON

Brut Washington 1990 • $13 • (12/31/94) • **80**
Cabernet Franc Columbia Valley 1993 • $12 • (04/30/95) • **82**
Cabernet Franc Washington 1994: Abundant black cherry, floral and spice flavors are wrapped in a pleasant layer of sweet vanilla and nutmeg that swirls through the finish. Nicely done. 321 cases made. • $12 • (09/15/97) • **88**
Cabernet-Merlot Columbia Valley 1994: A firm, chewy style that shows enough ripe blackberry and toast flavors. Try now. 2,027 cases made. • $12 • (09/15/96) • **84**

Cabernet-Merlot Columbia Valley 1993: Ripe, broad and spicy. A mouthful of plum, cherry and toasty oak keeps singing in harmony through the finish. Try now. • $12 • (07/31/95) • **88**
Cabernet-Merlot Columbia Valley 1992 • $11 • (08/31/94) • **89**
Cabernet-Merlot Washington 1995: Soft, fruity and pleasant to drink now, with floral notes adding a nice touch to the raspberry and spice flavors. 1,547 cases made. • $12 • (08/31/97) • **85**
Cabernet Sauvignon Columbia Valley 1988 • $11 • (09/30/91) • **87**
Cabernet Sauvignon Columbia Valley Bacchus Vineyard 1985 • $11 • (10/15/89) • **80**
Cabernet Sauvignon Columbia Valley Bacchus Vineyard 1983 • $13 • (12/15/87) • **77**
Cabernet Sauvignon Columbia Valley Dionysus Vineyard Block 16 1991 • $11 • (03/15/94) • **83**
Cabernet Sauvignon Washington Dionysus Vineyard Block 16 1994: Supple and generous, nicely modulating its berry and plum flavors with tarry, spicy shadings. Enough tannin to warrant cellaring until 1999 to 2000. 1,231 cases made. • $13 • (09/15/97) • **87**
Cabernet Sauvignon Washington Dionysus Vineyard Block 16 1993: Smooth and generous. A velvety wine with appealing berry, chocolate and spice flavors that linger nicely. 1,065 cases made. • $14 • (09/15/96) • **87**
Chardonnay Columbia Valley Cameo Reserve 1993 • $9 • (04/30/95) • **86**
Chardonnay Washington 1995: Firm, and refreshing for its pear and citrus flavors. Smooth and inviting on the finish. 5,872 cases made. • $8 • (09/15/97) • **85**
Chardonnay Washington 1994: Nicely balanced, simple and pleasant with its juicy pear and toast flavors. 6,750 cases made. • $8 • (09/15/96) • **82**
Chardonnay Washington Cameo Reserve 1995: Polished, ripe and focused, folding some spice and vanilla notes into the pear, orange and melon flavors, all lingering on the finish. 623 cases made. • $12 • (08/31/97) • **88**
Chardonnay Washington Cameo Reserve 1994: Rich and ripe, a silky mouthful of pear, apple, honey and nutmeg notes that swirl nicely through the finish. Try now. 594 cases made. • $11 • (09/15/96) • **88**
Grand Cépage Washington 1995: Straightforward and refreshing for its pure pear and apple flavors, finishing soft and friendly. A blend of 60 percent Sauvignon Blanc, 22 percent Sémillon, and 18 percent Chardonnay. 546 cases made. • $9 • (09/15/97) • **85**
Johannisberg Riesling Late Harvest Columbia Valley Select 1994 • $9/375ml • (09/15/95) • **82**
Johannisberg Riesling Washington 1995: Pretty peach flavors are frankly sweet and gain a leafy note that cuts through the finish. 2,384 cases made. • $5 • (09/15/96) • **82**
Merlot Columbia Valley 1991 • $10 • (06/15/93) • **85**
Merlot Columbia Valley 1990 • $12 • (04/15/92) • **88**
Merlot Columbia Valley 1988 • $9 • (08/31/91) • **81**
Merlot Columbia Valley 1987 • $8 • (10/15/89) • **83**
Merlot Columbia Valley Bacchus Vineyard 1985 • $8 • (07/31/87) • **75**
Merlot Columbia Valley Bacchus Vineyard 1982 • $8 • (11/01/84) • **82**
Merlot Columbia Valley Bacchus Vineyard Cameo Reserve 1985 • $10 • (12/15/87) • **83**
Merlot Columbia Valley Cameo Reserve 1992 • $13 • (08/31/95) • **88**
Merlot Columbia Valley Cameo Reserve 1991 • $13 • (09/30/94) • **86**
Merlot Columbia Valley Cameo Reserve 1989 • $12 • (03/31/92) • **77**
Merlot Columbia Valley Cameo Reserve 1988 • $12 • (08/31/91) • **83**
Merlot Columbia Valley Cameo Reserve 1987 • $11 • (06/15/90) • **85**
Merlot Columbia Valley Rosebud Vineyard Cameo Reserve 1990 • $14 • (01/31/93) • **86**
Merlot Washington Cameo Reserve 1993: Harmonious and tightly knit, weaving its black cherry, plum and spice flavors into a silky whole. Drinkable now. 288 cases made. • $13 • (09/15/96) • **88**
Merlot Washington Dionysus Vineyard Block 16 Cameo Reserve 1994: Tough and austere compared to most Washington Merlots, this packs just enough lithe blackberry and pepper flavors to make it worthy of cellaring until 2000. 1,071 cases made. • $13 • (09/15/97) • **85**
Muscat Canelli Columbia Valley 1994 • $6 • (08/31/95) • **85**
Riesling Columbia Valley Dry Dionysus Vineyard 1993 • $5 • (09/30/94) • **83**
Sauvignon Blanc Columbia Valley Bacchus Vineyard 1994 • $7 • (09/30/95) • **79**
Sauvignon Blanc Columbia Valley Bacchus Vineyard 1993 • $7 • (07/31/94) • **85**

Key: SS—Spectator Selection CS—Cellar Selection HR—Highly Recommended BB—Best Buy $NA—Price not available Ⓐ—Auction Price (BT)—Barrel Tasting
Dates in parentheses indicate the issues in which the ratings were published.

Sauvignon Blanc Columbia Valley Cameo Reserve 1994 • $9 • (09/15/95) • **86**
Sauvignon Blanc Washington 1996: Soft, and generous with its fig, melon and citrus flavors, it emphasizes fruit over herbal notes. Drink soon. 7,200 cases made. • $7 • (09/15/97) • **85**
Sauvignon Blanc Washington Bacchus Vineyard 1995: Fresh flavors, open texture and a pretty nectarine echo on the finish make this an appealing wine to drink now. 10,000 cases made. • $7 • (09/15/96) • **85**
Sémillon Columbia Valley Dionysus Vineyard 1994 • $6 • (07/31/95) • **84**
Sémillon Columbia Valley Dionysus Vineyard 1993 • $6 • (09/30/94) • **85**

ARCACHON | OREGON

Pinot Noir Willamette Valley 1992 • $9 • (03/15/94) • **82**

ARCHERY SUMMIT | OREGON

Pinot Noir Oregon 1993 • $25 • (10/31/95) HR • **90**
Pinot Noir Oregon 100% Whole Cluster 1996: Firm in texture, with ripe plum and anise flavors rounding nicely on the palate. Flavors are a modest presence, but what's there is pretty. Best from 1999. 151 cases made. • $35 • (05/15/98) • **86**
Pinot Noir Oregon Arcus Estate 1995: Silky, polished, generous and heady with berry, anise, pepper and nutmeg notes that mesh harmoniously on the surprisingly delicate finish. Has plenty of intensity and style for the vintage. 250 cases made. • $60 • (08/31/97) • **91**
Pinot Noir Oregon Arcus Estate 1994 • $50 • (06/30/96) • **87**
Pinot Noir Oregon Brick House Vineyard 1996: Ebullient flavors jump out at you from this firm-textured wine, offering a lively mouthful of plum, raspberry and rose petal flavors, along with a nice hint of tobacco on the rich finish. Best from 2000. • $40 • (05/15/98) • **89**
Pinot Noir Oregon Chêne D'Oregon 1996: Soft and generous, appealingly elegant, with pretty plum, berry and spice flavors, marked by sweet oak but not overwhelmed by it. Best by 1999. 151 cases made. • $27 • (03/31/98) • **88**
Pinot Noir Oregon Jeunesse 1996: Light in texture, with distinctive smoky, red berry and red plum flavors that linger on the gentle finish. Best before 1999. 565 cases made. • $23 • (03/31/98) • **85**
Pinot Noir Oregon Premier Cuvée 1995: Light and fragrant. Seductive for its polished texture and sweet, fresh prune, vanilla and berry flavors that linger enticingly on the delicate finish. Ready now. 2,185 cases made. • $35 • (02/28/97) • **87**
Pinot Noir Oregon Premier Cuvée 1994 • $30 • (06/30/96) • **91**
Pinot Noir Oregon Red Hills Estate 1995: A bit tight and chewy, wrapping its nicely focused cherry, smoke and caramel flavors in a layer of fine-grained tannins. Needs until 1999 to settle down. 250 cases made. • $60 • (08/31/97) • **89**
Pinot Noir Oregon Red Hills Estate 1994 • $50 • (06/30/96) • **89**
Vireton White Oregon 1996: Ripe and generous, tightly packed. A serious mouthful of melon and spice flavors that linger on the finish. Made from Pinot Gris. Drink now. 950 cases made. • $21 • (09/15/97) • **85**

ARCIERO | CALIFORNIA

Arpeggio Paso Robles 1995: Light as rosé in color, with a hint of chocolate to make the modest berry flavors a bit more interesting. Made from Nebbiolo. Drink now. 600 cases made. • $12 • (06/30/98) • **80**
Cabernet Franc Paso Robles 1995: Bitter and tannic, with weedy, herbal overtones. 500 cases made. • $11 • (04/30/98) • **75**
Cabernet Sauvignon Paso Robles 1995: Marked by a touch of burnt rubber, the wine redeems itself with cassis, blackberry, licorice and complex herb notes, but then falters with an astringent, short finish. Drink now through 2000. 3,900 cases made. • $11 • (06/30/98) • **81**
Cabernet Sauvignon Paso Robles 1994: Flavors of cedar and spice with herbs mark this wine. A smoky, black cherry finish weaves its way through the smoothly crafted tannins. 1,800 cases made. • $11 • (09/30/97) • **85**
Cabernet Sauvignon Paso Robles 1993: Earthy and a bit diluted, with an herbal, weedy edge to the flavors. 3,000 cases made. • $9 • (12/15/96) • **77**
Cabernet Sauvignon Paso Robles 1992 • $9 • (12/15/95) • **82**
Cabernet Sauvignon Paso Robles 1991 • $9 • (12/15/95) • **72**
Cabernet Sauvignon Paso Robles 1990 • $7 • (11/15/94) • **78**
Cabernet Sauvignon Paso Robles 1989 • $NA • (11/15/93) • **79**
Cabernet Sauvignon Paso Robles 1987 • $8 • (11/15/92) • **81**
Cabernet Sauvignon Paso Robles 1986 • $8 • (11/15/90) • **80**
Cabernet Sauvignon Paso Robles 1985 • $6 • (12/31/87) • **77**
Cabernet Sauvignon Paso Robles Reserve 1990 • $14 • (12/15/95) • **78**

Chardonnay California 1996: A very bright wine that leans toward the lemon end of the spectrum. Kind of one-dimensional. 6,000 cases made. • $9 • (05/15/98) • **78**

Chardonnay Paso Robles 1995: A strange blend of citrus and celery flavors. Bright, and otherwise pleasant. 4,900 cases made. • $9 • (07/31/97) • **84**

Chardonnay Paso Robles 1994: Ripe and generous with its spicy, citrusy pear and apple flavors that are focused and precise. The soft, round structure and reasonable price tag on this California white add to the appeal. 5,500 cases made. • $9 • (06/15/96) BB • **86**

Chardonnay Paso Robles 1993 • $9 • (12/31/95) • **81**

Merlot Paso Robles 1993 • $12 • (03/31/96) • **82**

Muscat Canelli Late Harvest Paso Robles 1995: Sweet and silky. A lovely mouthful of spice, honey and apricot flavors that linger nicely on an almost delicate finish. Delicious now. 600 cases made. • $12/375ml • (01/31/97) • **88**

Muscat Canelli Paso Robles 1994 • $6 • (11/30/95) • **81**

Nebbiolo Paso Robles 1994: Pale, rosélike, lacking in aroma or flavor except for a touch of nuttiness from oxidation. Past its prime. 1,200 cases made. • $10 • (06/30/98) • **72**

Nebbiolo Paso Robles 1993: Firm and flavorful, with blueberry-accented plum and anise flavors that remain generous through the finish. Drinkable now. 2,400 cases made. • $11 • (02/28/97) • **86**

Nebbiolo Paso Robles 1991 • $11 • (09/30/94) • **79**

Petite Sirah Paso Robles 1989 • $8 • (06/15/93) • **81**

Sangiovese Paso Robles 1995: Light enough in color and flavor to qualify as rosé. Smooth in texture, with a pretty layer of oak accompanying modest strawberry notes. Drink now. 1,020 cases made. • $13 • (06/30/98) • **83**

Sangiovese Paso Robles 1994: A very light-colored wine, pleasant and supple for its anise- and caramel-scented berry flavors. 1,260 cases made. • $14 • (02/28/97) • **85**

Sauvignon Blanc California 1997: A peachy wine, with a hint of sweetness that doesn't mask a permeating green core. 550 cases made. • $7 • (04/30/98) • **79**

Sauvignon Blanc Paso Robles 1994 • $6 • (05/31/96) • **87**

Sauvignon Blanc Paso Robles 1993 • $7 • (08/31/95) • **77**

White Riesling Late Harvest Santa Barbara County December Harvest 1985 • $11 • (12/15/89) • **84**

Zinfandel Paso Robles 1995: Ripe and distinctive for its anise-scented black cherry and vanilla flavors. Finishes with a bit of rough tannin, but it's finely balanced and should be fine with hearty food. 2,250 cases made. • $11 • (03/31/98) • **87**

Zinfandel Paso Robles 1994: Young and tight, with a ripe, intense core of spicy, peppery wild berry and cherry flavors that turn slightly earthy on the aftertaste. 750 cases made. • $9 • (04/30/97) • **86**

Zinfandel Paso Robles 1992 • $7 • (10/15/95) • **83**

Zinfandel Paso Robles 1988 • $7 • (10/15/92) • **77**

Zinfandel Paso Robles 1985 • $7 • (12/15/89) • **78**

ARGONAUT | CALIFORNIA

Cabernet Sauvignon Sierra Foothills 1995: Somewhat green and astringent, the wine has an herbal core highlighted by black pepper. 200 cases made. • $12 • (12/15/97) • **79**

Fumé Blanc Sierra Foothills 1996: Firm and tight, in a somewhat restrained style that offers some attractive citrus, celery and herbal notes on the finish. 1,000 cases made. • $10 • (09/15/97) • **83**

ARGYLE | OREGON

Blanc de Blancs Willamette Valley 1987 • $18 • (12/31/93) • **83**

Blanc de Blancs Willamette Valley Cuvée Limited 1987 • $23 • (11/15/91) • **83**

Brut Oregon Cuvée Limited 1988 • $18 • (05/15/92) • **87**

Brut Oregon Cuvée Limited 1987 • $19 • (12/31/90) • **82**

Brut Willamette Valley 1993: Utterly disarming. A complex, polished bubbly with real style and depth, offering a palette of tangy grapefruit and pretty vanilla flavors, with bread dough and spice nuances adding dimension. 5,696 cases made. • $20 • (11/30/97) SS • **91**

Brut Willamette Valley 1988 • $17 • (12/31/93) • **83**

Brut Willamette Valley Cuvée Limited 1991: Pretty floral, butter and pear flavors ride smoothly on its delicate frame. The creamy texture makes it especially appealing. 5,500 cases made. • $19 • (11/30/96) • **87**

Brut Willamette Valley Cuvée Limited 1989 • $17 • (11/30/94) • **85**

Chardonnay Willamette Valley 1994: Dark color, spicy aromas and woody flavors speak more of oak than of fruit, but there's a nice mineral quality that comes through on the finish. Try in 1999. 8,260 cases made. • $13 • (09/15/97) • **87**

Chardonnay Willamette Valley 1993: Strives for elegance and achieves a subtle balance of spicy pear and citrus flavors that linger nicely on the tightly wound finish. Drinkable now. 2,800 cases made. • $12 • (12/31/96) HR • **88**

Chardonnay Willamette Valley Reserve 1994: Ripe with peach, pear and citrus flavors that swirl attractively through the beautifully focused, honey-tinged finish. Delicious now, but should evolve through 1999. 1,900 cases made. • $20 • (11/15/97) • **90**

Pinot Gris Oregon Holstein Vineyards 1993 • $13 • (10/15/94) • **84**

Pinot Noir Oregon Limited Reserve 1993 • $25 • (03/31/96) • **87**

Pinot Noir Oregon Nuthouse Select Barrel 1994: Altogether yummy. This is plush and generous, offering round plum, currant, cola and anise flavors that linger enticingly on the rich finish. Balances its wonderful flavors with polished structure. Tempting now, should be best from 1999. 128 cases made. • $30 • (12/31/96) • **93**

Pinot Noir Willamette Valley 1996: Light and fragrant, a gentle mouthful of plum, rose petal and vanilla flavors that linger delicately on the finish. Nice now, might fill out more by 1999. 3,508 cases made. • $14 • (05/15/98) • **87**

Pinot Noir Willamette Valley 1993 • $9 • (10/31/94) BB • **89**

Pinot Noir Willamette Valley Limited Reserve 1994: There's a strange, herbal-floral edge to the modest berry flavors. Finish is a bit lean. May be better in 1999. 140 cases made. • $30 • (12/31/96) • **81**

Pinot Noir Willamette Valley Nuthouse 1995: Light in texture and modest in flavor, with hints of ripe cherry sneaking in around the earthy spice notes at the core. Firm tannins need until 1999. 147 cases made. • $35 • (05/15/98) • **85**

Pinot Noir Willamette Valley Reserve 1995: Smooth, supple and generous with its plum, vanilla and spice flavors that linger enticingly on the finish. Delicious now, should improve through 1999 or 2000. 809 cases made. • $30 • (10/31/97) • **89**

Pinot Noir Willamette Valley Vintage Select 1995: Light, and refreshing for its nice mix of berry and mint flavors. Ready now. 3,600 cases made. • $14 • (12/31/96) • **83**

Pinot Noir Willamette Valley Vintage Select 1994 • $12 • (03/31/96) • **86**

Riesling Oregon Dry 1995: Light, ever-so-slightly sweet and bright with generous pear, peach and floral flavors that echo on the graceful finish. A totally friendly wine. 2,400 cases made. • $11 • (12/31/96) • **88**

Riesling Oregon Dry Reserve 1993 • $9 • (03/31/96) • **86**

Riesling Willamette Valley Dry Reserve 1996: Light and refreshing for its pretty apple and mineral flavors, finishing dry and delicate. Ready now, but may be best in 1999. 2,205 cases made. • $11 • (05/15/98) • **87**

Rosé Willamette Valley 1987 • $18 • (12/31/93) • **83**

Rosé Willamette Valley Cuvée Limited 1987 • $23 • (11/15/91) • **82**

ARIES | CALIFORNIA

Cabernet Sauvignon Napa Valley 1990 • $11 • (10/31/93) • **87**

Merlot Napa Valley Carneros 1989 • $11 • (11/30/92) • **84**

Pinot Noir California 1995: An understated style, supple and harmonious, with a modest range of plum and cherry flavors. Fans of delicate Pinot Noir will find this appealing, especially at this price. • $10 • (05/15/97) • **85**

Pinot Noir Napa Valley Carneros 1994 • $10 • (01/31/96) BB • **86**

Pinot Noir Napa Valley Carneros 1992 • $10 • (02/28/94) BB • **85**

Pinot Noir Napa Valley Carneros 1991 • $9 • (02/28/93) • **84**

Pinot Noir Napa Valley Carneros Cuvée Vivace 1989 • $8 • (04/30/91) • **70**

ARMIDA | CALIFORNIA

Merlot Russian River Valley 1994: Smooth, ripe and generous with its pure blackberry, currant and vanilla flavors, hints of chocolate on the nicely integrated finish. Best from 1999. 2,072 cases made. • $16 • (07/31/97) • **88**

Merlot Russian River Valley 1993: Medium-weight and a tad spicy. Plum and cherry flavors. 975 cases made. • $14 • (08/31/96) • **81**

Merlot Russian River Valley 1990 • $14 • (05/31/92) • **78**

Pinot Noir Russian River Valley 1992 • $13 • (03/31/95) • **72**

Pinot Noir Russian River Valley 1991 • $12 • (02/28/93) • **84**

ARNS | CALIFORNIA

Cabernet Sauvignon Napa Valley 1994: Tough and tannic, with a chewy leathery flavor that overrides the core of spicy currant and mineral. Takes time to wade through the tannins; there's a lot of substance to this wine, but it doesn't fan out, not yet anyway. Cellaring is a must. Try after 2002. 145 cases made. • $35 • (10/31/97) • **89**

Cabernet Sauvignon Napa Valley 1993: Concentrated, dark, ripe and rich with layers of currant, black cherry, anise and wild berry flavors, all well-focused and tightly wound. Long and lingering aftertaste. Approachable now, or cellar into 2000. 400 cases made. • $30 • (04/30/97) • **93**

ARROWOOD

Cabernet Sauvignon Sonoma County 1997: Hard-edged, firmly tannic, with tight core of currant, dill and berry. Has the depth and concentration for excellence, even in this raw, unevolved form. • $NA • (07/31/98) (BT) • **90-94**

Cabernet Sauvignon Sonoma County 1996: Notable for its pretty fruit, ripe, rich and well-focused layers of currant, black cherry, plum and berry. Should be brilliant. • $NA • (06/15/97) (BT) • **90-94**

Cabernet Sauvignon Sonoma County 1994: Ripe, smooth and polished. A harmonious wine with pretty currant, plum and cherry notes, finishing with supple tannins, good length and a dash of coffee. Drinks well now, but has the depth and balance to age into 2000. 8,421 cases made. • $34 • (10/15/97) • **91**

Cabernet Sauvignon Sonoma County 1993: Complex and well-balanced, showing a fine interplay of ripe plum, currant, cherry, herb and olive flavors. Finishing with a long, lingering aftertaste and a smooth, polished texture. Drinkable now. 8,593 cases made. • $27 • (11/15/96) SS • **92**

Cabernet Sauvignon Sonoma County 1992 • $25 • (11/15/95) HR • **92**

Cabernet Sauvignon Sonoma County 1991 • $25 • (09/30/94) SS • **91**

Cabernet Sauvignon Sonoma County 1990 • $24 • (10/31/93) SS • **91**

Cabernet Sauvignon Sonoma County 1989 • $24 • (11/15/92) • **88**

Cabernet Sauvignon Sonoma County 1988 • $23 • (11/15/91) • **88**

Cabernet Sauvignon Sonoma County 1987: Smooth, supple and harmonious, with a velvety texture, wonderfully integrated flavors and lots of polish and finesse. The core of currant, cherry, chocolate and light toasty oak is sharply focused. Ready to drink. 5,200 cases made. • $26 • (12/15/97) • **93**

Cabernet Sauvignon Sonoma County 1986: Tasted from a magnum. This is a fully mature, even declining, wine, with a modest band of cedar and currant-accented Cabernet flavors. Pleasant enough now, but it was best enjoyed in its youth. • $NA • (12/15/96) • **83**

Cabernet Sauvignon Sonoma County 1985 • $19 • (12/15/88) • **94**

Cabernet Sauvignon Sonoma County Domaine du Grand Archer 1995: A restrained, understated style, with a core of currant, cedar, plum and tar notes that are well-focused and lively through the finish. Drinks well now, but should be best from 1999 to 2004. 1,857 cases made. • $16 • (03/31/98) • **88**

Cabernet Sauvignon Sonoma County Domaine du Grand Archer 1992 • $9 • (11/15/94) • **87**

Cabernet Sauvignon Sonoma County Réserve Spéciale 1994: Beautifully crafted, complex and concentrated, with a tightly-focused core of earthy currant, black cherry, cedary oak and spicy nuances, turning long and full on the finish. Best from 2001 through 2010. 1,208 cases made. • $50 • (07/31/98) • **94**

Cabernet Sauvignon Sonoma County Réserve Spéciale 1993: Firm and tight, with a rich, well-focused core of plum, currant and black cherry flavors, cedary oak and spicy nuances. This compact and concentrated young wine needs cellaring to soften and open. Best now to 2002. 1,000 cases made. • $38 • (12/31/96) • **92**

Cabernet Sauvignon Sonoma County Réserve Spéciale 1992 • $35 • (12/15/95) HR • **92**

Cabernet Sauvignon Sonoma County Réserve Spéciale 1989 • $70/1.5 liter • (11/15/93) • **88**

Chardonnay Sonoma County 1995: Distinctive for its strong citrus, especially grapefuit, accent, with complex and interesting flavors of pear, apple and melon that pick up a buttery note on the finish. 7,409 cases made. • $22 • (05/31/97) • **92**

Chardonnay Sonoma County 1994: Ripe, smooth and supple, with a pretty core of spicy pear, apple and melon notes, finishing with a fruity honey aftertaste. Fans of pure Chardonnay fruit will find this especially pleasing. 7,374 cases made. • $21 • (05/31/96) • **88**

Chardonnay Sonoma County 1993 • $20 • (06/15/95) • **87**

Key: SS—Spectator Selection CS—Cellar Selection HR—Highly Recommended BB—Best Buy $NA—Price not available Ⓐ—Auction Price (BT)—Barrel Tasting
Dates in parentheses indicate the issues in which the ratings were published.

Chardonnay Sonoma County Cuvée Michel Berthoud Réserve Spéciale 1995: An engaging Chardonnay, intense and lively, with a complex, concentrated core of spice, fig, melon and pear flavors. Shows remarkable finesse and polish on the finish, too. From a winery with a good handle on the varietal. 1,192 cases made. • $33 • (09/30/97) HR • **93**

Chardonnay Sonoma County Cuvée Michel Berthoud Réserve Spéciale 1994: Strikes a nice balance between the crisp, well-focused honey, pear, spice and mineral flavors and the lightly toasty oak. It comes together in a nice refrain on the lingering finish. 1,200 cases made. • $27 • (05/31/96) HR • **92**

Chardonnay Sonoma County Cuvée Michel Berthoud Réserve Spéciale 1993 • $24 • (06/15/95) HR • **91**

Chardonnay Sonoma County Domaine du Grand Archer 1996: Smooth, ripe, rich and creamy, with a silky texture and loads of smoky pear, fig, apricot, melon and spice. What a deal at this price. 1,101 cases made. • $14 • (03/31/98) • **89**

Domaine du Grand Archer Sonoma County 1991 • $8 • (04/30/94) SS • **89**

Malbec Sonoma County 1993: Lean and trim, with a stalky, green edge to the plum, tobacco, cedar and spice flavors. The texture is smooth and supple. 250 cases made. • $28 • (04/30/97) • **87**

Merlot Sonoma County 1994: Ripe, round, rich and smoky, with a supple core of ripe plum and black cherry flavors, picking up pleasant spice and vanilla accents. Drinkable now. 3,807 cases made. • $35 • (07/31/97) • **92**

Merlot Sonoma County 1993: Ripe, jammy flavors, with hints of currant and plum and a nice toasty oak accent. Hits all the right notes on the finish, which shows balance and finesse. 2,580 cases made. • $30 • (08/31/96) • **89**

Merlot Sonoma County 1992 • $28 • (12/15/95) • **89**

Merlot Sonoma County 1991 • $28 • (07/31/94) HR • **90**

Merlot Sonoma County 1990 • $25 • (05/31/93) • **89**

Merlot Sonoma County Domaine du Grand Archer 1995: Smooth and polished, with a core of herb, currant, berry, coffee, cedar and spice. Finishes with a complex aftertaste and supple tannins. Drink now into 2001. 500 cases made. • $19 • (03/31/98) • **88**

Merlot Sonoma County Domaine du Grand Archer 1991 • $9 • (09/15/94) • **82**

Pinot Blanc Russian River Valley Saralee's Vineyard 1994 • $28 • (04/30/96) • **91**

Syrah Russian River Valley Saralee's Vineyard 1994: Dark, intense and concentrated, with tiers of black cherry, currant, spice, anise and mineral notes and a dash of leather on the aftertaste. A big, round, rich Syrah that's tempting now for its brilliant fruit flavors, but worthy of cellaring to 2002. 210 cases made. • $33 • (04/30/97) • **92**

Viognier Late Harvest Russian River Valley Saralee's Vineyard Select 1994: Strong, spicy aroma and rich, complex flavors-honey, apricot, vanilla and nectarine-that linger on the finish. 480 cases made. • $28/375ml • (08/31/96) • **88**

Viognier Russian River Valley Saralee's Vineyard 1995: Tastes one-dimensional, with a strong, spicy litchi nut accent and the kind of slight bitterness found in Gewürztraminer. Finishes on a slight sweet note. 948 cases made. • $25 • (11/30/96) • **86**

Viognier Russian River Valley Saralee's Vineyard 1993 • $25 • (01/31/95) • **88**

White Riesling Late Harvest Russian River Valley Oak Meadow Vineyard Select 1991 • $20/375ml • (06/30/93) • **87**

White Riesling Late Harvest Russian River Valley Oak Meadow Vineyard Special Select 1993 • $28/375ml • (04/30/95) HR • **96**

White Riesling Russian River Valley Preston Ranch Select Late Harvest 1995: Weaving its lovely apricot, cream and honey flavors through the light texture, it's a sweet wine that's balanced and elegant. Enticing now, but may develop more complexity with cellaring until 2000 to 2003. 65 cases made. • $28/375ml • (04/30/97) • **92**

White Riesling Sonoma County Domaine du Grand Archer 1996: Soft, bordering on sweet, with pretty honeysuckle-scented apple flavors swirling nicely through the finish. 896 cases made. • $11 • (03/31/98) • **87**

ARROYO, VINCENT | CALIFORNIA

Cabernet Sauvignon Napa Valley 1990 • $15 • (11/15/92) • **88**

Cabernet Sauvignon Napa Valley 1989 • $15 • (11/15/92) • **81**

Cabernet Sauvignon Napa Valley 1988 • $18 • (11/15/92) • **85**

Cabernet Sauvignon Napa Valley 1987 • $12 • (11/15/90) • **91**

ARTERBERRY | OREGON

Pinot Noir Willamette Valley 1990 • $10 • (02/28/93) • **79**

Pinot Noir Willamette Valley Weber Vineyards 1989 • $12 • (11/15/91) • **85**
Pinot Noir Willamette Valley Winemaker's Reserve 1991 • $7 • (03/15/94) • **80**
Pinot Noir Willamette Valley Winemaker's Reserve 1990 • $15 • (02/28/93) • **79**
Pinot Noir Willamette Valley Winemaker's Reserve 1989 • $12 • (11/15/91) • **75**
Pinot Noir Willamette Valley Winemaker's Reserve 1988 • $14 • (01/31/91) • **79**
Pinot Noir Yamhill County Red Hills Vineyard Winemaker's Reserve 1986 • $15 • (06/15/88) • **74**
Pinot Noir Yamhill County Red Hills Vineyard Winemaker's Reserve 1985 • $16 • (06/15/87) • **95**
Pinot Noir Yamhill County Red Hills Vineyard Winemaker's Reserve 1983 • $16 • (02/15/90) • **86**
Pinot Noir Yamhill County Weber Vineyards Winemaker's Reserve 1987 • $14 • (02/15/90) • **90**

ARTHUR, DAVID | CALIFORNIA

Chardonnay Napa Valley Reserve 1996: Light and spicy, with toast and peppery flavors more prominent than the modest green apple ones. Best by 1999. 500 cases made. • $28 • (03/31/98) • **86**
Chardonnay Napa Valley Reserve 1993: Ripe, with a sweet quality to the pear, nectarine and apple notes. Also showing a trace of maturity with its slightly candied aromas and flavors. 1,575 cases made. • $21 • (04/30/97) • **84**
Meritagío Red Napa Valley 1995: Tight and complex, with earthy tannins and cedary currant, spice, cherry and leather notes, this wine needs time. Best to cellar into 2000 in hope it folds together; certainly the elements are there. Best from 2000 to 2004. A blend of Cabernet Sauvignon, Cabernet Franc, Merlot, Petit Verdot, and Sangiovese. 800 cases made. • $32 • (04/30/98) • **88**
Meritagío Red Napa Valley 1992: The ripe, massive style packs plenty of current and plum flavors, but is also overbearingly tannic and bitter. 345 cases made. • $25 • (08/31/96) • **78**

ASHBY, HUNTER | CALIFORNIA

Merlot Napa Valley 1985 • $9 • (07/31/89) • **84**
Zinfandel California 1995: Pretty toast and vanilla notes can't upgrade the lightweight fruit flavors in this wine. Tangy finish doesn't enhance matters. 3,500 cases made. • $12 • (03/31/98) • **81**

ASHLAND PARK | CALIFORNIA

Cabernet Sauvignon Napa Valley 1989 • $5 • (11/15/92) • **75**

ASHLAND VINEYARDS | OREGON

Cabernet Franc Rogue Valley 1995: A nice, sturdy red with chewy plum and berry notes that loll nicely on the finish. Try now. 420 cases made. • $13 • (04/30/97) • **86**
Cabernet-Merlot Rogue Valley 1995: Aggressive flavors of wild berry, tobacco, coffee and chocolate are complemented by slightly aggressive tannins. Give this until 2001 to 2003 to settle down. 620 cases made. • $10 • (04/30/97) • **86**
Cabernet Sauvignon Rogue Valley 1994: Dense and chewy, but crisp acidity keeps it lively and bright. The blueberry, plum and anise flavors linger on the finish. Needs until 2000 to 2002 to shed some tannin. 830 cases made. • $13 • (04/30/97) • **87**
Cabernet Sauvignon Rogue Valley 1993: A bit crisp for a Cabernet, but it has nice, ripe blueberry and currant flavors that are sturdy through the finish. Drink now. 540 cases made. • $13 • (04/30/97) • **85**
Cabernet Sauvignon Rogue Valley 1992 • $11 • (03/31/96) • **85**
Cabernet Sauvignon Rogue Valley 1991 • $14 • (11/30/94) • **87**
Chardonnay Rogue Valley 1995: Ripe and buttery, this is a smooth-textured Chardonnay with lots of spice and caramel, but it remains light in texture and balanced through the supple finish. Drink now. 1,000 cases made. • $10 • (03/31/98) • **87**
Chardonnay Rogue Valley 1994: Leans a bit toward spicy oak, but the bright apple and pear flavors hover in the background. Try now. 600 cases made. • $11 • (04/30/97) • **87**
Chardonnay Rogue Valley Barrel Fermented 1993 • $10 • (03/31/96) • **85**
Merlot Rogue Valley 1995: Soft and lithe, generous with its berry flavors. Has strong coffee undertones and a spicy finish. Ready to drink. 700 cases made. • $12 • (03/31/98) • **86**
Merlot Rogue Valley 1994: Light and simple, with a hint of tar to go with the fresh plum and anise flavors. Ready to drink. 660 cases made. • $14 • (04/30/97) • **82**
Merlot Rogue Valley 1992 • $11 • (03/31/96) • **84**
Merlot Rogue Valley 1991 • $16 • (11/30/94) • **83**
Müller-Thurgau Rogue Valley 1993 • $7 • (11/30/94) • **79**
Pinot Gris Rogue Valley 1994 • $11 • (03/31/96) • **83**
Riesling Oregon Dry 1994 • $5 • (01/31/96) BB • **84**
Sauvignon Blanc Rogue Valley 1994: Light and smooth in texture, with a floral character hovering over the honey and olive flavors. Try now. 370 cases made. • $8 • (04/30/97) • **86**
Sauvignon Blanc Rogue Valley 1993 • $7 • (03/31/96) • **84**

ATLAS PEAK | CALIFORNIA

Cabernet Sauvignon Atlas Peak 1994: Earthy, with a dry, bell-pepper and musty quality that's well off the mark. Disappointing. Tasted three times, with consistent notes. 4,000 cases made. • $18 • (05/15/98) • **75**
Cabernet Sauvignon Atlas Peak 1993: Clean and balanced, with ripe cherry, herb, olive and plummy notes featured before the tannins weigh in. This young wine offers attractive flavors but is somewhat austere; try now. 2,300 cases made. • $18 • (11/15/96) • **87**
Cabernet Sauvignon Atlas Peak 1992 • $18 • (12/15/95) • **89**
Cabernet Sauvignon Atlas Peak 1991 • $18 • (09/15/95) • **86**
Cabernet Sauvignon Atlas Peak Consenso 1993: Smooth and supple, with a core of herb, black olive and currant flavors that are well-focused and balanced. Finish shows a nice interplay of flavors and firm tannins. Drink now. 1,000 cases made. • $22 • (11/15/96) • **87**
Chardonnay Atlas Peak 1996: Clean and correct, with ripe, spicy pear, citrus and melon flavors of modest depth and proportion. Ready to drink. 4,000 cases made. • $16 • (04/30/98) • **86**
Chardonnay Atlas Peak 1995: Marked by a slightly grassy edge, reminiscent of Sauvignon Blanc, and it's a touch herbal, but it turns elegant, with a spicy nuance to the light pear flavors. Oak stays well in the background. 6,000 cases made. • $16 • (03/31/97) • **87**
Chardonnay Atlas Peak 1993 • $16 • (07/31/95) • **85**
Consenso Atlas Peak 1990 • $22 • (12/15/95) • **87**
Consenso Atlas Peak 1989 • $22 • (03/31/95) • **83**
Consenso Napa Valley 1990 • $22 • (11/15/93) • **83**
Consenso Napa Valley 1989 • $22 • (03/31/93) • **82**
Sangiovese Atlas Peak 1995: Earthy, with a slightly sour edge, but it slowly works its way into tartly fruity notes. Tasted twice, with consistent notes. Drink now. 20,000 cases made. • $16 • (05/15/98) • **78**
Sangiovese Atlas Peak 1993 • $16 • (11/30/95) • **84**
Sangiovese Atlas Peak 1992 • $16 • (02/28/95) • **84**
Sangiovese Atlas Peak 1991 • $16 • (05/31/94) • **83**
Sangiovese Atlas Peak Reserve 1992 • $24 • (02/28/95) • **88**
Sangiovese Napa Valley 1990 • $24 • (02/15/93) • **85**
Sangiovese Napa Valley 1989 • $24 • (11/15/91) • **86**
Sangiovese Napa Valley Reserve 1994: Smooth, ripe and harmonious, with a core of pleasant plum and black cherry flavors. Finishes with firm tannins and good length. • $16 • (05/15/97) • **87**

AU BON CLIMAT | CALIFORNIA

Aligoté California Mistral Vineyard 1996: A simple, pretty wine with nice apple flavors. Easy to drink. 200 cases made. • $12 • (03/31/98) • **82**
Chardonnay Arroyo Grande Valley Talley Reserve 1996: Intense, with ripe, rich, creamy Chardonnay character, echoing pear, fig, melon and apple flavors. Long, complex aftertaste. Drink now through 2002. 1,000 cases made. • $25 • (07/31/98) • **92**
Chardonnay Arroyo Grande Valley Talley Reserve 1995: Smooth and polished, young and vibrant, with a pretty band of ripe pear, honey, apple and spice flavors. Impressive for its supple texture and length, with flavors that fan out on the finish. 575 cases made. • $30 • (07/31/97) • **89**
Chardonnay Arroyo Grande Valley Talley Reserve 1994: Simple, with ripe pear and spicy peach flavors. Worthy, though lacking the richness and concentration usually found in ABC's wines. Tasted twice, with consistent notes. 800 cases made. • $25 • (07/31/96) • **84**
Chardonnay Arroyo Grande Valley Talley Reserve 1993 • $25 • (07/31/95) • **90**
Chardonnay Edna Valley Alban Vineyard 1996: A mild vegetal streak runs through this tartly flavored wine, though not to its detriment since the ripe

pear, spice and fig notes fill in the gaps quite nicely. On the finish, it's complex and long on flavor. 640 cases made. • $20 • (11/15/97) • **90**

Chardonnay Edna Valley Alban Vineyard 1995: Marked by a tart, unripe edge as the pear and pineapple flavors lean toward the green side. This lacks the depth of flavor and texture of this producer's other recent releases. 400 cases made. • $20 • (11/30/96) • **87**

Chardonnay Santa Barbara County 1996: Clean, ripe and fruity, with an elegant band of ripe pear, spice, fig and melon flavors. Turns supple on the finish. Very good value from a top-rate producer. 5,500 cases made. • $18 • (11/15/97) • **88**

Chardonnay Santa Barbara County 1995: Complex and full-bodied, with lots of juicy flavors-tiers of ripe pear, spice, hazelnut and honey that pick up hints of mineral and earth on the aftertaste. 5,300 cases made. • $18 • (11/30/96) • **90**

Chardonnay Santa Barbara County 1994: Ripe, juicy pear, peach and spice flavors showcase the Chardonnay grape without letting the oak get in the way. • $15 • (01/31/96) • **88**

Chardonnay Santa Barbara County 1993 • $16 • (07/31/95) • **87**

Chardonnay Santa Barbara County Le Bouge Bien Nacido Vineyard 1995: An intense, well-concentrated white, with tart-edged flavors of ripe pear, citrus, honey and hazelnut that gain complexity on the finish, where they fan out and pick up spicy nuances. 1,400 cases made. • $25 • (07/31/97) • **92**

Chardonnay Santa Barbara County Le Bouge D'à Côté 1996: Intense and a touch coarse, with nothing a little time in the bottle won't solve. The fruit flavors are ripe, complex and appealing, with earthy pear, spice and citrus notes. Drink now through 2001. 1,500 cases made. • $25 • (07/31/98) • **88**

Chardonnay Santa Barbara County Le Bouge D'à Côté 1994: Flavorful, with ripe pear, peach, citrus and hazelnut notes that turn smooth and elegant on the long, complex finish. 1,200 cases made. • $25 • (07/31/96) • **87**

Chardonnay Santa Maria Valley Gold Coast Vineyard 1993 • $20 • (07/31/95) • **89**

Chardonnay Santa Ynez Valley Sanford & Benedict Reserve 1995: Serves up lots of ripe, fresh apple, pear and melon flavors and is intense and concentrated, with a long, full finish. Only needs short-term cellaring to round out the edges. 160 cases made. • $35 • (11/15/97) • **91**

Chardonnay Santa Ynez Valley Sanford & Benedict Reserve 1994: Lithe, smooth and supple, with a pleasant earthy accent to the hazelnut and pineapple notes. Still showing a slight green edge to its flavors, but it's complex and the texture is smooth on the finish. Give it time to open a bit. 275 cases made. • $35 • (11/30/96) • **89**

Chardonnay Santa Ynez Valley Sanford & Benedict Reserve 1993 • $34 • (01/31/96) • **93**

Pinot Blanc Santa Barbara County Bien Nacido Reserve 1996: A big, ripe, full-bodied style, built around a core of fig and melon. Turns elegant and somewhat simple on the finish. Drink now. 140 cases made. • $20 • (02/28/98) • **87**

Pinot Blanc Santa Barbara County Bien Nacido Reserve 1995: A touch earthy and coarse, with unfocused flavors that echo honey and leesy flavors. An attempt to make an interesting wine, but it's rough going most of the wine. 150 cases made. • $20 • (11/30/96) • **86**

Pinot Blanc Santa Barbara County Bien Nacido Vineyard 1994 • $12 • (01/31/96) • **86**

Pinot Noir Arroyo Grande Valley Rincon and Rosemary's 1994: Achieves a nice balance between earthy, leathery notes and ripe cherry and plum flavors. Drinkable now. 300 cases made. • $40 • (11/30/96) • **90**

Pinot Noir Arroyo Grande Valley Rosemary's Talley Vineyard 1993 • $40 • (12/31/95) • **91**

Pinot Noir Arroyo Grande Valley Talley and Paragon Vineyards 1993 • $20 • (09/15/95) • **87**

Pinot Noir California Isabelle 1995: Intense and earthy, built for short-term cellaring, with a spectrum of earthy raspberry, cherry, spice and cola flavors. Finishes with dry, earthy tannins—lay aside to let the tannins subside. 175 cases made. • $50 • (10/31/97) • **88**

Pinot Noir California Isabelle 1994: Smooth and elegant, with a supple core of spicy cherry, plum and berry flavors. The texture is polished and the flavors linger, with fine tannins showing on the finish. Drinks well now, but should only get better; best in 2000. Tasted twice, with consistent notes. 125 cases made. • $50 • (12/31/96) • **89**

Pinot Noir Central Coast 1995-96: Lean, earthy and leathery in character, with drying tannins and just a glimpse of cherry and berry peeking through. Drink now. 2,000 cases made. • $18 • (08/31/97) • **88**

Key: SS—Spectator Selection CS—Cellar Selection HR—Highly Recommended BB—Best Buy $NA—Price not available Ⓐ—Auction Price (BT)—Barrel Tasting

Dates in parentheses indicate the issues in which the ratings were published.

Pinot Noir Central Coast Mistral Vineyard 1995: Attractive for its ripe cherry and raspberry notes, turning elegant and supple in texture. Medium-weight, with a sense of delicacy and finesse. 350 cases made. • $25 • (07/31/97) • **90**

Pinot Noir Santa Barbara County 1989 • $16 • (09/30/92) • **87**

Pinot Noir Santa Barbara County 1988 • $16 • (04/30/91) • **80**

Pinot Noir Santa Barbara County 1987 • $16 • (12/15/89) • **84**

Pinot Noir Santa Barbara County 1985 • $12 • (06/15/88) • **73**

Pinot Noir Santa Barbara County Bien Nacido Vineyard La Bauge 1995: Lean and spicy up front, with herb, tea and leatherlike notes, fanning out on the finish with ripe cherry, cola and berry flavors to reveal its true depth and complexity. 650 cases made. • $30 • (08/31/97) • **92**

Pinot Noir Santa Barbara County La Bauge Au-dessus Bien Nacido Vineyard 1994: Austere with firm tannins, this is tightly wound, with a crisp band of cherry, cola and spice flavors, finishing with a slight leather accent. Drink now. 600 cases made. • $25 • (02/28/97) • **86**

Pinot Noir Santa Barbara County La Bauge Au-dessus Bien Nacido Vineyard 1993 • $25 • (09/15/95) • **85**

Pinot Noir Santa Barbara County La Bauge Au-dessus Bien Nacido Vineyard 1991 • $25 • (02/28/94) HR • **91**

Pinot Noir Santa Barbara County La Bauge Au-dessus Bien Nacido Vineyard 1990 • $30 • (02/28/93) • **87**

Pinot Noir Santa Maria Valley 1996: Light and spicy, with an herb, rhubarb and cola edge to the tea and cherrylike flavors. Finishes with light tannins, making it drinkable now. 3,000 cases made. • $18 • (12/15/97) • **84**

Pinot Noir Santa Maria Valley 1994 • $18 • (02/29/96) • **88**

Pinot Noir Santa Maria Valley 1993 • $14 • (01/31/95) • **86**

Pinot Noir Santa Maria Valley 1990 • $11 • (02/28/93) • **86**

Pinot Noir Santa Maria Valley Rancho Vinedo Vineyard 1992 • $15 • (02/28/94) • **86**

Pinot Noir Santa Maria Valley Rancho Vinedo Vineyard 1988 • $13 • (12/15/89) • **83**

Pinot Noir Santa Ynez Valley 1989 • $30 • (09/30/92) • **81**

Pinot Noir Santa Ynez Valley Sanford & Benedict Reserve 1995: A racy style, with an earth-accented core of cherry and berry flavors, a dash of tea flavor and dry, earthy tannins. Drink now. 125 cases made. • $35 • (10/31/97) • **87**

Pinot Noir Santa Ynez Valley Sanford & Benedict Vineyard 1993: Harmonious, a wine of finesse and subtlety with a spicy, meaty, peppery accent to the ripe plum and cherry flavors that fan out and gain complexity on the finish. Approachable now, but has the intensity and depth to age until 2001 to 2003. 275 cases made. • $35 • (11/30/96) • **89**

Pinot Noir Santa Ynez Valley Sanford & Benedict Vineyard 1991 • $35 • (02/28/94) • **91**

Pinot Noir Santa Ynez Valley Sanford & Benedict Vineyard 1987 • $30 • (12/15/89) • **88**

AUDUBON | CALIFORNIA

Audubon Rouge California NV • $4 • (10/15/88) • **79**

Cabernet Sauvignon Napa Valley 1985 • $11 • (06/15/88) • **77**

Chardonnay Sonoma Valley Carneros Sangiacomo 1995: Earthy and musty, just like an earlier bottle, but has rich toast notes and earthy citrus and crisp green apple flavors that give it limited appeal. Drink now through 2000. 2,000 cases made. • $14 • (07/31/98) • **79**

Chardonnay Sonoma Valley Carneros Sangiacomo Barrel Fermented 1993 • $12 • (07/31/95) • **83**

Sauvignon Blanc Napa Valley Juliana Vineyards 1994 • $9 • (08/31/95) • **84**

Sauvignon Blanc Napa Valley Juliana Vineyards Reserve 1995: Features a more herbal, grassy core backed by hints of fresh pea, hazelnut, citrus and melon. It grows on you, finishing on a clean, refreshing note. Drink now through 2002. 290 cases made. • $13 • (05/31/98) • **87**

Zinfandel Amador County Picnic Hill Vineyard 1995: Brightly acidic, with a doughy, earthy, cheesy core and firm tannins. The John Audubon print on the label is the highlight. Drink now. 1,000 cases made. • $14 • (06/15/98) • **70**

Zinfandel San Luis Obispo County 1983 • $7 • (07/15/88) • **84**

Zinfandel Sonoma County 1990 • $9 • (10/15/92) • **81**

AURORA | OREGON

Chardonnay Willamette Valley 1994: Simple, juicy and refreshing; a mouthful of pear, apple and resiny flavors that linger on the lively finish. 1,345 cases made. • $8 • (03/31/96) BB • **84**

Pinot Noir Willamette Valley 1993 • $9 • (10/31/95) • **85**

Pinot Noir Willamette Valley 1992 • $7 • (03/15/94) • **79**

AUSTIN | CALIFORNIA

A Genoux Santa Barbara County 1986 • $15 • (12/15/89) • **74**
Cabernet Franc Santa Barbara County 1988 • $12 • (11/15/90) • **76**
Cabernet Sauvignon Santa Barbara County Mille Délices 1991 • $20 • (11/15/93) • **84**
Cabernet Sauvignon Santa Barbara County Perry's Reserve 1991 • $15 • (11/15/93) • **80**
Johannisberg Riesling Late Harvest Santa Barbara County Botrytis 1986 • $8/375ml • (12/15/89) • **81**
Pinot Noir Santa Barbara County 1993 • $14 • (02/29/96) • **74**
Pinot Noir Santa Barbara County 1987 • $15 • (12/15/89) • **77**
Pinot Noir Santa Barbara County 1983 • $25 • (12/15/89) • **78**
Pinot Noir Santa Barbara County Artist Series 1988 • $10 • (12/15/89) • **75**
Pinot Noir Santa Barbara County Bien Nacido Vineyard 1982 • $10 • (03/16/85) • **88**
Pinot Noir Santa Barbara County Reserve 1991 • $16 • (02/28/94) • **79**
Pinot Noir Santa Barbara County Sierra Madre Vineyards 1982 • $12 • (05/01/84) • **87**
Sauvignon Blanc Late Harvest Santa Barbara County Botrytis Sierra Madre Vineyards 1985 • $10/375ml • (12/15/89) • **72**

AUTUMN HILL | VIRGINIA

Cabernet Franc Virginia Flarepath Vineyard Monticello 1995: Quite spicy and fruity with good plum and currant flavors liberally dotted with notes of nutmeg and clove. A medium-bodied red that would do well on the dinner table. 104 cases made. • $12 • (04/30/97) • **84**

AUTUMN WIND | OREGON

Chardonnay Oregon 1993 • $10 • (01/31/96) • **87**
Chardonnay Oregon Reserve 1993 • $15 • (03/31/96) • **86**
Pinot Gris Oregon 1994 • $10 • (03/31/96) • **82**
Pinot Gris Oregon 1993 • $10 • (10/31/94) • **83**
Pinot Gris Yamhill County 1996: Has more going on than most Pinot Gris, offering layers of texture and flavors of melon, almond and mineral flavors that swirl through the long finish. 200 cases made. • $15 • (11/30/97) • **88**
Pinot Noir Oregon 1995: Light in color and flavor, showing some pretty raspberry and vanilla flavors that hint at herb on the finish. Drink now. 1,000 cases made. • $10 • (12/15/96) • **84**
Pinot Noir Oregon 1993 • $10 • (01/31/96) • **80**
Pinot Noir Oregon 1992 • $10 • (11/30/94) • **81**
Pinot Noir Oregon Reserve 1994: Spicy and forward, in a fresh style that provides lots of toasty oak notes to keep its black cherry flavors company. Try in 1999. 518 cases made. • $24 • (12/15/96) • **88**
Pinot Noir Oregon Reserve 1993 • $20 • (01/31/96) • **87**
Pinot Noir Oregon Reserve 1992 • $20 • (11/30/94) • **80**
Pinot Noir Oregon Reserve 1990 • $20 • (01/31/94) • **85**
Pinot Noir Oregon Reserve 1989 • $15 • (02/28/93) • **73**
Pinot Noir Willamette Valley 1996: Firm and chewy, sporting enough of a beam of black cherry and currant flavor to push through the tannins easily. Give it until 2000 to 2002. 400 cases made. • $15 • (05/15/98) • **87**
Pinot Noir Willamette Valley 1988 • $12 • (04/15/91) • **80**
Pinot Noir Willamette Valley 1987 • $15 • (02/15/90) • **83**
Pinot Noir Yamhill County Estate Reserve 1996: A seductive, dramatic style of Pinot Noir, offering layers of blackberry, currant, wild plum and smoke flavors that keep swirling through the supple finish. Appealing now, but should settle down a bit by 1999 to 2000. 580 cases made. • $25 • (05/15/98) • **90**
Pinot Noir Yamhill County Estate Reserve 1995: A light, straightforward, citrus peel-scented red with modest berry flavors. Slightly hard on the finish. Give it until 1999. 380 cases made. • $24 • (11/30/97) • **80**
Sauvignon Blanc Oregon 1994: In a smooth, polished style that offers more spicy notes than herb flavors. A nice touch of orange-peel on the finish. Pleasant to drink now. 500 cases made. • $8 • (12/15/96) • **85**
Sauvignon Blanc Oregon 1993 • $8 • (03/31/96) • **80**

AZALEA SPRINGS | CALIFORNIA

Merlot Napa Valley 1995: Good intensity, with complex cedar, spice, currant and berry flavors that are woven together nicely, finishing with supple tannins and good length. Drink now through 2002. 1,327 cases made. • $30 • (03/31/98) • **88**
Merlot Napa Valley 1994: Rich and full-bodied, with lots of plum, currant and cherry notes, a smooth, plush texture and a complex aftertaste where the flavors keep surging. Drinkable now, but short-term cellaring won't hurt. 1,042 cases made. • $24 • (05/15/97) • **91**
Merlot Napa Valley 1992 • $22 • (12/15/95) • **88**
Merlot Napa Valley 1991 • $22 • (09/15/94) • **88**

BABCOCK | CALIFORNIA

Chardonnay San Luis Obispo Talley Vineyard 1993 • $25 • (01/31/95) • **85**
Chardonnay Santa Barbara County 1993 • $16 • (01/31/95) • **85**
Chardonnay Santa Barbara County One Ton Per Acre 1995: Lean, tight and well focused, with a crisp core of tart, lemon-tinged pear and apple flavors which ring true and linger on the finish. Drink through 1999. 983 cases made. • $20 • (06/15/97) • **89**
Chardonnay Santa Maria Valley Bien Nacido Vineyard Block W Gravelly Vein 1996: A solid effort, from the rich, tightly focused tropical fruit, apple and pear notes to the subtle oak shadings. Impressive for its focus, breadth and depth of flavor but also its balance and elegance. Drink now through 2002. 871 cases made. • $30 • (05/31/98) • **91**
Chardonnay Santa Ynez Valley Grand Cuvée 1996: A bright, rich, intensely concentrated wine, packed with ripe spicy pear, pineapple, guava and citrus. The flavors zip across the palate, finishing with a long, zesty aftertaste. Can stand short-term cellaring. Best from 1999 through 2005. 1,886 cases made. • $30 • (06/30/98) • **92**
Chardonnay Santa Ynez Valley Grand Cuvée 1995: Tightly wound now, but rich, intense and lively, with a sharply focused core of pear, citrus and melon flavors. Drink now. 1,090 cases made. • $35 • (05/31/97) • **90**
Chardonnay Santa Ynez Valley Mt. Carmel Vineyard 1996: Lots of ripe, rich, complex fruit flavor and pretty oak nuances, with tiers of spicy pear, apple, melon and hazelnut, finishing with a long, concentrated aftertaste. Best now through 2004. 736 cases made. • $30 • (06/30/98) • **92**
Chardonnay Santa Ynez Valley Mt. Carmel Vineyard 1994: This has ripe pear and peach flavors with light oak and earthy shadings, and an elegant, polished style. • $27 • (01/31/96) • **88**
Chardonnay Santa Ynez Valley Mt. Carmel Vineyard 1993 • $25 • (07/31/95) • **83**
Johannisberg Riesling Late Harvest Santa Ynez Valley Cluster Selected 1987 • $14/375ml • (12/15/89) • **89**
Pinot Gris Santa Barbara County 1996: The focus is a bit muddled, but the core is built around earthy citrus, pear and grapefruit flavors. Gains a little complexity on the finish. Babcock's first Pinot Gris. 359 cases made. • $15 • (05/15/98) • **85**
Pinot Noir Santa Barbara County 1996: The texture is smooth and polished, but the flavors stray into the earthy, spicy, vegetal, peppery side of Pinot Noir. Finishes with a dense, murky aftertaste. Best from 1999. 1,002 cases made. • $20 • (02/28/98) • **86**
Pinot Noir Santa Barbara County 1995: Young, tight and well-focused, with intense black cherry, plum and anise flavors and a wild berry note. The texture is smooth and polished up front, before the tannins weigh in. Best now through 2002. 330 cases made. • $30 • (12/31/96) • **91**
Pinot Noir Santa Barbara County Bien Nacido Vineyard 1994 • $18 • (01/31/96) • **84**
Pinot Noir Santa Ynez Valley 1991 • $22 • (02/28/93) • **79**
Pinot Noir Santa Ynez Valley Benedict Vineyard 1991 • $25/375ml • (02/28/94) • **87**
Pinot Noir Santa Ynez Valley Estate Grown 1996: Smooth, rich and polished, with a well-focused center of black cherry, spice, wild berry, picking up toasty oak, coffee and vanilla notes. Turns expansive on the finish. Drink now. 564 cases made. • $30 • (02/28/98) • **90**
Pinot Noir Santa Ynez Valley Estate Grown 1993 • $30 • (12/31/95) • **84**
Pinot Noir Santa Ynez Valley Estate Grown 1992 • $30 • (03/31/95) • **85**
Pinot Noir Santa Ynez Valley Sanford & Benedict Vineyard 1993 • $25 • (12/31/95) • **83**
Pinot Noir Santa Ynez Valley Sanford & Benedict Vineyard 1992 • $25 • (11/30/94) • **85**
Pinot Noir Santa Ynez Valley Selected Barrels Reserve 1989 • $35 • (02/28/93) • **70**
Sangiovese Santa Ynez Valley Eleven Oaks 1993 • $22 • (11/30/95) • **85**
Sauvignon Blanc Santa Ynez Valley Eleven Oaks 1996: A little earthy on the nose, but on the palate it comes around nicely in the Old World style. It's brightly textured, with a strong herbal, grassy edge backed by plenty of grapefruit, lime and fig flavors. A forceful wine, maybe one for the cellar. 1,228 cases made. • $20 • (03/31/98) • **89**
Sauvignon Blanc Santa Ynez Valley Eleven Oaks 1995: A zingy blend of ripe melon, passion fruit, lemon, orange and a delicate grasslike tone, lightly

framed by sweet oak. Complex and delicious. 1,200 cases made. • $20 • (06/15/97) • **91**

Sauvignon Blanc Santa Ynez Valley Eleven Oaks 1994: Crisp and lively, with sharply focused onion-skin-scented pear, apple and citrus flavors. Long finish has herbal notes. 1,670 cases made. • $20 • (08/31/96) • **89**

Syrah Santa Barbara County Cuvée Lestat 1995: Dark, intense and peppery, with a meaty, vegetal edge to the plum and wild berry flavors. Finishes with a spicy, minty note and earthy tannins. 200 cases made. • $30 • (02/28/97) • **85**

BADGER MOUNTAIN | WASHINGTON

Cabernet Franc Columbia Valley 1994: Ripe and polished, weaving some nice coffee and tobacco notes through the dark berry flavors. Drinkable now. 500 cases made. • $12 • (09/30/96) • **86**

Cabernet Franc Columbia Valley 1993 • $13 • (09/30/95) • **85**

Cabernet Franc Columbia Valley 1992 • $13 • (09/30/95) • **85**

Cabernet Merlot Columbia Valley 1995: Crisp and light, with modest spice and tobacco flavors that pick up some cherry notes on the finish. 1,000 cases made. • $12 • (09/15/96) • **84**

Cabernet Merlot Columbia Valley 1994: Firm and chewy, with a solid core of blackberry and spice flavors that run into a wall of tannin on the finish. Try now. 450 cases made. • $12 • (09/15/96) • **85**

Chardonnay Columbia Valley 1995: Fresh and zingy, with apple, citrus and spice flavors that remain as fresh as a bite of raw fruit right through the finish. A cleanly made white from Washington that's a good value. 2,500 cases made. • $9 • (12/31/96) BB • **86**

Chardonnay Columbia Valley 1994: Light, bright, lively green apple, pear and spice flavors maintain vibrancy through the finish. 1,512 cases made. • $9 • (09/30/95) • **86**

Chardonnay Columbia Valley 1993 • $9 • (09/30/95) • **84**

Gewürztraminer Columbia Valley Mountain Blush 1994 • $6 • (09/30/95) • **76**

Johannisberg Riesling Columbia Valley 1995: Fresh, easy and vaguely fruity with a very light finish. 500 cases made. • $6 • (09/30/96) • **80**

Johannisberg Riesling Columbia Valley 1994 • $6 • (09/30/95) • **79**

Merlot Columbia Valley 1995: Dense and chewy, this spicy wine shows well-rounded berry and smoke flavors that linger engagingly on the finish. Lots of oak, but lots of fruit, too. Appealing now, best from 1999 to 2000. 500 cases made. • $14 • (12/31/96) • **88**

Merlot Columbia Valley 1994: A chewy Merlot that packs lots of spicy black cherry flavor. Drinkable now. 150 cases made. • $12 • (09/15/96) • **85**

Sevé Columbia Valley 1995: Has a simple charm, with nice apple flavors and a hint of mineral. 6,000 cases made. • $6 • (09/15/96) • **81**

Seyval Blanc Columbia Valley Sevé 1994 • $6 • (09/30/95) • **85**

BAILEYANA | CALIFORNIA

Chardonnay Edna Valley 1996: Rich, tropical fruit flavors, with sweet buttery notes. Intense, yet lacking in finesse. Drink now. 3,000 cases made. • $17 • (07/31/98) • **82**

Chardonnay Edna Valley 1994: Tastes ripe and mature, marked by honey, pear and light hazelnut notes that may be a bit heavy-handed for some. 1,500 cases made. • $15 • (06/15/96) • **82**

Chardonnay Edna Valley Paragon Vineyard 1993 • $15 • (07/31/95) • **88**

BAILLY, ALEXIS | MINNESOTA

Country Red Minnesota NV • $7 • (02/29/92) • **78**

Léon Millot Minnesota 1990 • $9 • (02/29/92) • **74**

Maréchal Foch Minnesota 1990 • $9 • (02/29/92) • **77**

BAINBRIDGE ISLAND | WASHINGTON

Dessert Washington Siegerrebe Botrytized 1987 • $15/375ml • (10/15/89) • **71**

Key: SS—Spectator Selection CS—Cellar Selection HR—Highly Recommended BB—Best Buy $NA—Price not available Ⓐ—Auction Price (BT)—Barrel Tasting
Dates in parentheses indicate the issues in which the ratings were published.

BALCOM & MOE | WASHINGTON

Cabernet Sauvignon Washington 1994: Strongly minty, with a rich vein of dill running through the black cherry and spicy oak flavors. Firm enough to hold until 1999. 536 cases made. • $14 • (09/15/96) • **85**

Cabernet Sauvignon Washington 1992 • $14 • (09/30/95) • **87**

Cabernet Sauvignon Washington 1991 • $14 • (09/30/95) • **84**

Chardonnay Washington 1995: Ripe and smooth; generous with its apple, spice and vanilla flavors. It echoes fruit on the round finish. 840 cases made. • $9 • (08/31/96) • **84**

Merlot Washington 1994: Sturdy cherry flavors take an odd turn, picking up a strongly minty pickle-barrel accent. 1,040 cases made. • $14 • (09/15/96) • **77**

Merlot Washington 1992 • $14 • (08/31/95) • **87**

Sauvignon Blanc Washington 1994 • $9 • (09/15/95) • **84**

BALD MOUNTAIN | CALIFORNIA

Zinfandel Napa Valley 1992 • $11 • (10/15/95) • **78**

BALDINELLI | CALIFORNIA

Cabernet Sauvignon Amador County 1989 • $10 • (08/31/92) • **70**

Cabernet Sauvignon Shenandoah Valley 1983 • $7 • (11/30/88) • **86**

Zinfandel Shenandoah Valley 1988 • $7 • (12/31/90) • **82**

Zinfandel Shenandoah Valley 1987 • $8 • (05/15/90) • **85**

Zinfandel Shenandoah Valley Reserve 1986 • $6 • (12/15/88) BB • **83**

BALLATORE | CALIFORNIA

Gran Spumante California NV: Sweet and a bit insipid, with some pleasant apple flavors hiding in the wings. • $7 • (12/15/97) • **77**

BALLENTINE | CALIFORNIA

Cabernet Franc Napa Valley 1992 • $15 • (07/31/95) • **82**

Merlot Napa Valley 1995: Crisp, with firm tannins and just enough plum and wild berry flavors to balance. Finishes with dry tannins, so it's best to cellar into 1999 to 2000. 2,800 cases made. • $18 • (04/30/98) • **86**

Merlot Napa Valley 1994: Focused and flavorful, with raspberry, cassis, blackberry and toasty oak tones all blending harmoniously. Tannins are ripe and firm, and the finish is moderately long. 2,000 cases made. • $18 • (07/31/97) • **89**

Merlot Napa Valley 1992 • $18 • (07/31/95) • **80**

Zinfandel Napa Valley 1995: Ripe and generous, this impressive mouthful of berry, cherry and vanilla flavors takes on a nice layer of earth and spice on the finish. Approachable now, best from 1999. 6,500 cases made. • $16 • (11/30/97) • **88**

Zinfandel Napa Valley 1994: Nicely focused cherry, plum and wild berry flavors; smooth, ripe and complex. Finishes with supple tannins and dashes of smoke and anise. 2,000 cases made. • $14 • (03/31/97) • **88**

Zinfandel Napa Valley 1992 • $14 • (10/15/95) • **85**

BALVERNE | CALIFORNIA

Cabernet Sauvignon Chalk Hill Laurel Vineyard 1983 • $13 • (02/15/89) • **86**

Cabernet Sauvignon Sonoma County 1982 • $12 • (08/31/88) • **88**

BANDIERA | CALIFORNIA

Cabernet Sauvignon California Coastal 1994: Smooth, polished and bright with spicy berry and currant flavors. A layer of spicy oak edges in on the supple finish. Ready to drink. • $8 • (12/31/96) • **82**

Cabernet Sauvignon Napa Valley 1993: Pleasant for its ripe plum, spice and berry flavors and mild tannins. A light dash of oak adds interest in this value red. 26,328 cases made. • $8 • (11/30/95) BB • **85**

Cabernet Sauvignon Napa Valley 1992 • $8 • (09/30/95) • **83**

Cabernet Sauvignon Napa Valley 1991 • $6 • (09/30/94) BB • **85**

Cabernet Sauvignon Napa Valley 1990 • $6 • (04/15/94) BB • **87**

Cabernet Sauvignon Napa Valley 1989 • $6 • (10/31/92) BB • **86**

Cabernet Sauvignon Napa Valley 1988 • $6 • (04/15/92) BB • **80**

Cabernet Sauvignon Napa Valley 1987 • $7 • (11/15/91) BB • **89**

Cabernet Sauvignon Napa Valley 1986 • $6 • (10/31/89) BB • **85**

Cabernet Sauvignon Napa Valley Reserve 5 1993: Spicy, peppery edge to vanilla and toasty oak flavors. Ripe plum, cherry and berry notes underneath emerge on aftertaste to yield a nice sense of balance and proportion. 2,500 cases made. • $12 • (11/30/95) • **87**

Chardonnay California Coastal 1996: Steely, mineral notes in a zesty, tangy white. Finishes with a lemony twist. 18,000 cases made. • $9 • (07/31/97) • **86**

Chardonnay California Coastal 1995: Soft, generous and fresh with spicy, vanilla-scented apple and floral flavors. • $8 • (12/31/96) • **86**

Chardonnay Napa Valley 1994: Bright and flavorful, with lively apple and citrus flavors tempered by a touch of sweet vanilla. Effective subtlety makes this a value. 22,832 cases made. • $8 • (09/30/95) BB • **86**

Chardonnay Napa Valley 1993 • $8 • (07/31/95) • **84**

Merlot Napa Valley Reserve 1993: Dry and tannic. A green, unripe edge pervades the earthy, wild berry flavors. 700 cases made. • $12 • (08/31/96) • **77**

Sauvignon Blanc California Coastal 1995: Seemingly corky. Tasted three times, with consistent notes. 5,000 cases made. • $5 • (08/31/97) • **50**

Sauvignon Blanc Napa Valley 1994 • $5 • (08/31/95) • **83**

Sauvignon Blanc Napa Valley 1993 • $5 • (06/15/94) BB • **86**

White Zinfandel California 1994 • $5 • (09/15/95) • **78**

BANNISTER | CALIFORNIA

Chardonnay Russian River Valley Allen Vineyard 1995: Complex and lively, with a pretty band of ripe pear, apple, light oak and spice flavors that pick up a trace of vanilla. The texture is smooth and polished, and the aftertaste is rich. 432 cases made. • $22 • (06/15/97) • **90**

Chardonnay Russian River Valley Allen Vineyard 1994: Opens with a band of citrus and orange blossom, picking up ripe pear and tart apple notes. A subtle, understated style that finishes with a hint of smoky, toasty oak. 622 cases made. • $20 • (05/31/96) • **88**

Chardonnay Russian River Valley Allen Vineyard 1993 • $18 • (06/15/95) • **89**

Chardonnay Russian River Valley Porter-Bass Vineyard 1995: Smooth, ripe, rich and polished, with juicy pear, fig, melon and apricot flavors, and pretty oak shadings. Turns elegant and silky on the finish, where it picks up a dash of hazelnut. 532 cases made. • $20 • (06/15/97) • **91**

Pinot Noir Anderson Valley Floodgate Vineyard 1995: Exhibits a broad range of flavors, with bright, spicy blueberry, traces of herb, mushroom, tea and earth. Drink now. 102 cases made. • $20 • (08/31/97) • **87**

Pinot Noir Russian River Valley 1995: Young, tight and on the crisp side, it opens to offer ripe cherry- and plum-accented Pinot Noir flavors before shutting down with firm tannins. 192 cases made. • $20 • (08/31/97) • **88**

Pinot Noir Russian River Valley 1994 • $18 • (05/31/96) • **85**

Zinfandel Dry Creek Valley 1994: Strikes a nice balance of ripe cherry, spice and wild berry flavors that pick up a floral note in the aftertaste. 460 cases made. • $15 • (09/15/96) • **85**

Zinfandel Dry Creek Valley 1992 • $12 • (01/31/95) • **84**

Zinfandel Dry Creek Valley 1991 • $12 • (09/30/93) • **83**

Zinfandel Dry Creek Valley Bradford Mountain Vineyard 1995: Moderately rich and well proportioned, this is an elegant, balanced style that captures ripe cherry and plummy flavors. A touch of oak folds in nicely on the finish. Drink now. 370 cases made. • $17 • (06/15/98) • **85**

Zinfandel Dry Creek Valley Bradford Mountain Vineyard 1993 • $15 • (10/15/95) • **86**

Zinfandel Russian River Valley Rochioli Vineyard 1994: Slightly earthy flavors unfold into interesting, tart raspberry, wild berry and blackberry flavors that hit the spot, fanning out on the finish to show more depth and complexity. 169 cases made. • $18 • (04/30/97) • **92**

Zinfandel Russian River Valley Rochioli Vineyard 1993: Marked by a tarry, earthy accent to the spicy wild berry flavors. Finishes with dry tannins. A rustic style that's ready to drink. 150 cases made. • $17 • (09/15/96) • **85**

BARBOURSVILLE | VIRGINIA

Cabernet Franc Monticello 1995: A fruity wine dominated by berry flavors and aromas. Has a green note on the finish, but it's quite enjoyable. 603 cases made. • $15 • (04/30/97) • **82**

Cabernet Franc Monticello 1993 • $12 • (12/31/95) • **81**

Cabernet Sauvignon Monticello Reserve 1991 • $19 • (12/31/95) • **80**

Cabernet Sauvignon Monticello Reserve 1983 • $15 • (02/29/92) • **73**

Chardonnay Monticello Reserve 1994: Vanilla and bread-dough aromas from oak dominate, which makes for a pleasantly smooth texture and sweet flavors, but not much fruit underneath. It's quaffable. 900 cases made. • $15 • (06/30/95) • **80**

Pinot Noir Monticello 1993 • $12 • (05/31/95) • **73**

Riesling Monticello 1994 • $9 • (08/31/95) • **76**

Sauvignon Blanc Monticello 1993 • $10 • (05/31/95) • **79**

BAREFOOT | CALIFORNIA

Chenin Blanc California 1996: A sweet, simple, peachy wine with a solid dose of tangy acidity. • $4 • (09/30/97) • **72**

Zinfandel California NV: Has a medicinal edge to the chewy cherry flavors. • $5 • (11/30/96) • **77**

BARGETTO, LAWRENCE J. | CALIFORNIA

Blanc de Noirs Santa Maria Valley 60th Anniversary 1933-1993 1991 • $11 • (12/31/93) • **79**

Cabernet Sauvignon Central Coast Cyrpress 1991 • $9 • (11/15/94) • **82**

Cabernet Sauvignon Napa Valley Komes Ranch 1988 • $15 • (11/15/93) • **84**

Cabernet Sauvignon Santa Cruz Mountains 1986 • $18 • (08/31/92) • **84**

Cabernet Sauvignon Santa Cruz Mountains Bates Ranch 1991: A touch weedy, with a thin band of cherry-tinged Cabernet flavor that turns earthy and simple on the finish. Not what we've come to expect from Bates Ranch Cabernet. 1,220 cases made. • $18 • (12/15/96) • **79**

Cabernet Sauvignon Santa Cruz Mountains Bates Ranch 1990 • $16 • (12/15/95) • **85**

Cabernet Sauvignon Santa Cruz Mountains Bates Ranch 1989 • $18 • (05/31/95) • **77**

Cabernet Sauvignon Santa Cruz Mountains Bates Ranch 1988 • $15 • (11/15/94) • **78**

Cabernet Sauvignon Santa Cruz Mountains Bates Ranch 1987 • $15 • (11/15/93) • **83**

Cabernet Sauvignon Sonoma County Cypress 1985 • $8 • (11/15/89) • **79**

Chardonnay Central Coast Cypress 1996: A silky white, this is refreshing and distinctive for its focused nectarine and spice flavors, which reverberate through the finish. The asking price is reasonable, and it's ready to drink. 5,000 cases made. • $10 • (12/15/97) BB • **85**

Chardonnay Central Coast Cypress 1995: Delicious mouthful of up front fruit, with juicy pear, melon, fig and spice flavors. Ready to drink. 5,800 cases made. • $9 • (04/30/97) • **87**

Chardonnay Central Coast Cypress 1994: Floral and perfumed, with a pleasant core of pear and citrus flavors. Medium-bodied, soft and ready to drink. 4,400 cases made. • $9 • (05/15/96) • **84**

Chardonnay Central Coast Cypress 1993 • $9 • (07/31/95) • **80**

Chardonnay Santa Clara & Santa Cruz Counties Coastal Reserve 1996: Light, silky and gentle with its spicy pear and quince flavors, gliding smoothly through a persistent finish, echoing a touch of spicy oak. Drink now. 950 cases made. • $15 • (03/31/98) • **86**

Chardonnay Santa Cruz Mountains 1995: Exhibits an earthy nuance up front, unfolding to reveal complex pear, fig and melon flavors, showing more purity on the finish. Appealing, and ready now. 1,650 cases made. • $18 • (04/30/97) • **89**

Chardonnay Santa Cruz Mountains 1993 • $16 • (07/31/95) • **84**

Chardonnay Santa Cruz Mountains Regan Vineyard 1996: A jazzy mouthful of brilliant peach, pear and citrus flavors, delicately shaded with touches of spice and toast. A small package that's packed with flavor. Nicely done. 1,000 cases made. • $18 • (12/15/97) • **87**

Dolcetto Central Coast 1996: Light and simple, this shyly shows some raspberry flavor and finishes smooth and appealing. Ready now. 850 cases made. • $15 • (12/15/97) • **85**

Dolcetto Central Coast 1995: Light and fruity, with an Italianate almond-edge to the modest berry flavors. • $15 • (12/31/96) • **81**

Dolcetto Central Coast 1994: Light and simple, with a spicy, dill-picklelike accent inappropriate to the fruit flavors. 479 cases made. • $15 • (11/30/96) • **79**

Gewürztraminer Monterey County 1996: A crisp texture and a range of bright citrusy flavors make this a refreshing sipper, echoing grapefruit on the finish. 3,800 cases made. • $11 • (07/31/97) • **84**

Gewürztraminer Monterey County 1995: Lightly sweet, with pleasant floral notes gracing mild pineapple flavors. 1,100 cases made. • $9 • (10/31/96) • **83**

Gewürztraminer Monterey County 1993 • $9 • (01/31/95) • **80**

Gewürztraminer Santa Cruz Mountains Barrel Fermented Dry 1994 • $10 • (11/15/95) • **80**

Gewürztraminer Santa Cruz Mountains Dry 1996: Silky and bright, an off-dry style with distinctive rose petal and pear flavors that remain firm on the finish. Label says barrel fermented, but you can't taste it. 1,200 cases made. • $12 • (06/15/97) • **85**

Gewürztraminer Santa Cruz Mountains Dry 1995 • $12 • (06/30/96) • **86**

Gewürztraminer Santa Cruz Mountains Dry 1993 • $9 • (01/31/95) • **77**

Merlot California 1995: Herbal and vegetal, this wine has a green, tarry edge that's hardly offset by the sweetness on the finish. 1,300 cases made. • $18 • (07/31/97) • **79**
Merlot California 1994: Bland and uninteresting; crisp, narrow flavors defy description. 1,700 cases made. • $17 • (08/31/96) • **72**
Merlot California 1993 • $14 • (01/01/96) • **78**
Merlot Central Coast 1989 • $13 • (12/31/93) • **80**
Merlot San Ysidro 1992 • $14 • (06/15/95) • **78**
Pinot Grigio Central Coast 1996: Round on the palate, with melon and citrus flavors backed by an herbal edge. Could use a touch more acidity, but still quite pleasant. 700 cases made. • $15 • (09/15/97) • **84**
Pinot Grigio Central Coast 1995: Light, with a fresh loquat and almond character that lingers. 300 cases made. • $15 • (12/15/96) • **81**
Pinot Noir Carneros Madonna Vineyard 1985 • $13 • (09/15/88) • **83**
Pinot Noir Central Coast Cypress 1989 • $9 • (09/30/92) • **77**
Pinot Noir Santa Cruz Mountains 1994: Lovely, open-textured, with generous currant and black cherry flavors shaded by mineral and spice notes. It all lingers smoothly on the finish. Appealing now. 300 cases made. • $20 • (03/31/98) • **87**
Pinot Noir Santa Cruz Mountains 1993: On the tannic side, so be forewarned, it's a chewy, young wine with tough-edged plum and berry flavors that are struggling to emerge. 366 cases made. • $18 • (11/30/96) • **79**
Pinot Noir Santa Cruz Mountains 1992 • $23 • (12/31/95) • **83**
Pinot Noir Santa Cruz Mountains 1989 • $15 • (02/28/94) • **78**
Pinot Noir Santa Cruz Mountains Sessantesimo 1991 • $18 • (02/28/94) • **87**
Pinot Noir Santa Maria Valley 1987 • $16 • (02/28/91) • **81**

BARNETT | CALIFORNIA

Cabernet Sauvignon Napa Valley 1990 • $25 • (11/15/93) • **83**
Cabernet Sauvignon Napa Valley 1989 • $18 • (11/15/93) • **86**
Cabernet Sauvignon Spring Mountain 1993: Tannic, with an earthy, leathery edge to the ripe cherry, anise and currant flavors. Flavors hang on through the finish. Drink now. 467 cases made. • $32 • (08/31/96) • **85**
Cabernet Sauvignon Spring Mountain 1992 • $32 • (05/31/95) • **87**
Chardonnay Napa Valley 1994: Crisp and bright, with simple, green apple flavors that soften on the finish. 382 cases made. • $18 • (07/31/97) • **85**
Pinot Noir Carneros 1994: A strong minty flavor dominates. Turns a bit funky and peppery on the finish, missing the mark for 1994. 280 cases made. • $23 • (08/31/96) • **80**
Pinot Noir Santa Lucia Highlands 1996: Broad on the palate, with a beefy quality that's balanced nicely by herb notes. Follows up with bright cherry, ginger and cedar tones. Finishes a bit short. 200 cases made. • $20 • (01/31/98) • **86**

BARON HERZOG | CALIFORNIA

Cabernet Sauvignon California 1994: Offers a thin band of cherry and plum flavors. 11,200 cases made. • $13 • (11/30/96) • **76**
Cabernet Sauvignon California 1992 • $9 • (12/31/94) BB • **86**
Cabernet Sauvignon California Selection 1990 • $11 • (06/15/93) • **75**
Cabernet Sauvignon Paso Robles 1987 • $9 • (11/15/92) • **72**
Cabernet Sauvignon Sonoma County 1989 • $11 • (03/31/91) • **73**
Cabernet Sauvignon Sonoma County Special Reserve 1986 • $16 • (03/31/91) • **74**
Chardonnay California 1996: Oak-driven, with lots of butterscotch and toast up front. Flavors of pear, apple and clove take a backseat, but are attractive nonetheless. 17,600 cases made. • $11 • (02/28/98) • **84**
Chardonnay California 1994: Tart, canned pear flavors with a citrus edge. 12,400 cases made. • $11 • (07/31/96) • **79**
Chenin Blanc California 1993 • $6 • (07/31/94) • **74**
Chenin Blanc Clarksburg 1996: Peaches and cream come to mind with this off-dry wine. Simple. 11,800 cases made. • $6 • (09/30/97) • **80**
Johannisberg Riesling Late Harvest California 1989 • $8/375ml • (03/31/91) • **86**
Sauvignon Blanc Shenandoah Valley 1996: Displays an unusual pinelike essence, followed by a strong grapefruit and tangy lemon character. An assertive wine, though not for everyone. 1,800 cases made. • $9 • (10/15/97) • **84**
Zinfandel Sonoma County Special Cuvée 1990 • $10 • (03/31/93) • **86**

Key: SS—Spectator Selection CS—Cellar Selection HR—Highly Recommended BB—Best Buy $NA—Price not available Ⓐ—Auction Price (BT)—Barrel Tasting
Dates in parentheses indicate the issues in which the ratings were published.

BARROW GREEN | CALIFORNIA

Pinot Noir California 1987 • $15 • (10/31/91) • **79**
Pinot Noir California 1986 • $16 • (10/15/89) • **76**

BARTHOLOMEW PARK | CALIFORNIA

Cabernet Sauvignon Sonoma Valley Alta Vista Vineyard 1994: Tea and cedar notes lead into a beefy, gamy brew. Tannins are plush, supporting blackberry, cassis and herb flavors. Moderate finish. Drink now or hold. 480 cases made. • $18 • (10/31/97) • **86**
Cabernet Sauvignon Sonoma Valley Desnudos Vineyard 1994: A focused, seductively smooth wine, with delicately intertwining cassis, blueberry, anise, tar and spice notes. What it lacks in power, it makes up for in finesse. 590 cases made. • $20 • (10/31/97) • **88**
Chardonnay Sonoma Valley Estate Vineyards 1995: Subtle pear and citrus flavors are a bit overloaded with oak. Finishes slightly bitter and on the short side. Drink now. 230 cases made. • $16 • (07/31/98) • **81**
Chardonnay Sonoma Valley Weiler Vineyard 1996: Firm in texture, with modest peach and earthy mineral notes. Drink now. 300 cases made. • $16 • (05/15/98) • **81**
Merlot Sonoma Valley Alta Vista Vineyards 1995: Pretty plum and cherry notes, framed by rich, smoky aromas. Though a bit thin on the palate, it makes a pleasant quaff. 225 cases made. • $18 • (03/31/98) • **84**
Pinot Noir Sonoma Valley Estate Vineyards 1995: Black cherry, cola, cedar and spice mingle well here. It's a little short and tannic on the finish, with a slightly bitter edge. Should smooth out in a year or two. 500 cases made. • $17 • (01/31/98) • **87**

BATTAGLINI | CALIFORNIA

Zinfandel Russian River Valley Twin Pines 1994: Simple, with pleasantly spicy, grapey fruit flavors. Lacks focus on the finish. Drink now. 157 cases made. • $15 • (06/15/98) • **81**

BAY CELLARS | CALIFORNIA

Pinot Noir Los Carneros 1985 • $15 • (06/15/88) • **77**
Pinot Noir Willamette Valley 1985 • $18 • (06/15/88) • **85**

BAYVIEW CELLARS | CALIFORNIA

Cabernet Sauvignon Napa Valley 1992: Tightly wound, with a nice core of currant, plum and black cherry flavors. Picks up a trace of anise and cedar on the finish and has a lively, fruity aftertaste. 670 cases made. • $16 • (09/15/96) • **87**
Cabernet Sauvignon Napa Valley 1991 • $12 • (05/31/95) • **83**
Charbono Napa Valley 1992 • $14 • (11/15/95) • **86**
Chardonnay Napa Valley Carneros 1994: Tart citrus flavors with pear overtones that fan out and pick up light oak flavors on the finish. Simple, but pleasant. 750 cases made. • $16 • (07/31/96) • **84**
Chardonnay Napa Valley Carneros 1993 • $12 • (06/30/96) • **83**
Gewürztraminer Napa Valley 1993 • $7 • (02/28/95) • **77**
Merlot Napa Valley 1992 • $14 • (06/15/96) • **82**

BEARBOAT | CALIFORNIA

Chardonnay Russian River Valley 1995: Distinctive for its ripe apple and pear flavors, this needs but a little time to soften and gain harmony. Drink now. 1,200 cases made. • $18 • (05/15/97) • **89**
Pinot Noir Russian River Valley 1995: Elegant and fruity, with medium-weight tart cherry, wild berry and spice flavors that fan out on the finish before turning dry from the tannins. 1,500 cases made. • $25 • (02/28/98) • **84**
Pinot Noir Russian River Valley 1994: A lighter style, with simple plum and wild berry flavors, and a touch of sage on the finish. Builds intensity on the palate, turning complex. Drink now. • $NA • (01/01/97) • **86**
Pinot Noir Russian River Valley 1992 • $16 • (03/31/95) • **77**

BEAUCANON | CALIFORNIA

Cabernet Sauvignon Napa Valley 1992: Simple style, with earthy, herbal flavors that fail to inspire. 3,000 cases made. • $12 • (11/30/96) • **78**
Cabernet Sauvignon Napa Valley 1991 • $12 • (12/15/95) • **79**
Cabernet Sauvignon Napa Valley 1990 • $11 • (02/28/95) • **86**

Cabernet Sauvignon Napa Valley 1988 • $12 • (12/15/92) • **70**
Cabernet Sauvignon Napa Valley 1986 • $15 • (12/31/88) • **85**
Chardonnay Napa Valley 1994: Very soft, almost flat, with modest fruit character. 3,000 cases made. • $12 • (06/15/96) • **78**
Chardonnay Napa Valley 1993 • $12 • (07/31/95) • **87**
Chardonnay Napa Valley Jacques de Coninck 1996: Earthy and cedary, with a distinct dill note, but slowly reveals fruitier flavors, with spicy pear, citrus, fig and lemony flavors that are intense and focused. Drink now through 2001. 600 cases made. • $28 • (05/15/98) • **89**
Chardonnay Napa Valley Jacques de Coninck 1994: Clean and well-made, but unexciting with its simple pear and citrus notes. Flavors fade on the finish. 110 cases made. • $28 • (07/31/96) • **83**
Chardonnay Napa Valley Reserve 1996: A tangy wine, with subtle pear and mineral notes framed by toasty oak. Finishes on the bright side. Drink now through 2000. 3,000 cases made. • $12 • (05/31/98) • **84**
Merlot Napa Valley 1994: Tough, dry and tannic, with just a hint of mint and currant to the earthy, tarry flavors. 1,000 cases made. • $14 • (08/31/96) • **79**
Merlot Napa Valley 1993: Coffee, currant and berry flavors that quickly fade. Finish is tannic and dry. 2,000 cases made. • $14 • (08/31/96) • **81**
Merlot Napa Valley 1991 • $12 • (02/28/95) • **77**
Merlot Napa Valley 1990 • $12 • (07/15/93) • **81**
Merlot Napa Valley 1989 • $10 • (05/31/92) • **73**
Merlot Napa Valley 1988 • $13 • (03/31/91) • **84**
Merlot Napa Valley 1986 • $13 • (12/31/88) • **78**

BEAULIEU VINEYARD | CALIFORNIA

Brut Napa Valley 1982 • $12 • (05/31/89) • **81**
Brut Napa Valley Champagne de Chardonnay 1982 • $16 • (05/31/89) • **87**
Burgundy Napa Valley 1987 • $5 • (01/31/91) BB • **80**
Burgundy Napa Valley 1984 • $5 • (08/31/89) • **78**
Burgundy Napa Valley 1982 • $5 • (10/15/88) • **79**
Cabernet Sauvignon Napa Valley 1994: Firm and tight, with a tannic edge to the currant, plum and berry flavors. Fans out a little on the finish, where the flavors turn supple. 30,000 cases made. • $15 • (07/31/97) • **85**
Cabernet Sauvignon Napa Valley Beautour 1994: A lighter style, with mint, herb and coffee notes. Tannins are firm yet ripe; delicate enough now to let elegant blueberry and currant flavors sing through on the finish. Drink now or hold. A good value. 120,000 cases made. • $11 • (10/15/97) • **87**
Cabernet Sauvignon Napa Valley Beautour 1991 • $9 • (09/30/94) • **82**
Cabernet Sauvignon Napa Valley Beautour 1990 • $8 • (11/15/93) • **80**
Cabernet Sauvignon Napa Valley Beautour 1988 • $7 • (09/30/90) • **79**
Cabernet Sauvignon Napa Valley Beautour 1987 • $8 • (05/31/89) BB • **81**
Cabernet Sauvignon Napa Valley Beautour 1986 • $7 • (10/31/88) • **83**
Cabernet Sauvignon Napa Valley Beautour 1985 • $7 • (06/15/88) • **83**
Cabernet Sauvignon Napa Valley Claret Special Release 1990 • $7 • (11/15/92) • **79**
Cabernet Sauvignon Napa Valley Georges de Latour Private Reserve 1997: Well focused on the grapey currant core, fanning out into mint and spice. Finishes with richness and length; only a dash of toasty oak. • $NA • (07/31/98) (BT) • **90-94**
Cabernet Sauvignon Napa Valley Georges de Latour Private Reserve 1994: One of the most prestigious wines in California, this shows an impressive core of spicy currant and mineral-laced Cabernet flavors emerging from chewy tannins, picking up cedary oak, coffee and sage notes. Most enjoyable if cellared into 1999 to 2004. 11,000 cases made. • $50 • (10/15/97) CS • **93**
Cabernet Sauvignon Napa Valley Georges de Latour Private Reserve 1993: Complex and harmonious, with a pretty core of ripe plum, cherry and currant flavors and shades of herb and cedary oak. Comes together quite nicely on the finish, where the fruity flavors remain and the tannins weave in. Drinks well now, or can age. 10,000 cases made. • $40 • (11/15/96) CS • **91**
Cabernet Sauvignon Napa Valley Georges de Latour Private Reserve 1992 • $40 • (12/15/95) • **89**
Cabernet Sauvignon Napa Valley Georges de Latour Private Reserve 1991 • $40 • (12/15/95) • **90**
Cabernet Sauvignon Napa Valley Georges de Latour Private Reserve 1990 • $40 • (11/15/94) • **89**
Cabernet Sauvignon Napa Valley Georges de Latour Private Reserve 1989 • $40 • (06/15/94) • **85**
Cabernet Sauvignon Napa Valley Georges de Latour Private Reserve 1988 • $37 • (11/15/92) • **77**
Cabernet Sauvignon Napa Valley Georges de Latour Private Reserve 1987: Elegant and stylish, combining mature and youthful flavors. Shows off cedar, currant and anise. Finishes with a soft, fleshy edge to the tannins. Best now through 2002. 10,000 cases made. • $44 • (12/15/97) • **91**
Cabernet Sauvignon Napa Valley Georges de Latour Private Reserve 1986: For fans of understated, claret-style wines. A bit hollow on the palate initially, this opens gradually to reveal more fruit and anise flavors. Given the dry tannins, it's best to drink soon. • $NA • (12/15/96) • **87**
Cabernet Sauvignon Napa Valley Georges de Latour Private Reserve 1985 • $55 Ⓐ • (03/31/91) • **95**
Cabernet Sauvignon Napa Valley Georges de Latour Private Reserve 1984 • $42 Ⓐ • (03/31/91) • **92**
Cabernet Sauvignon Napa Valley Georges de Latour Private Reserve 1983 • $24 Ⓐ • (03/31/91) • **82**
Cabernet Sauvignon Napa Valley Georges de Latour Private Reserve 1982 • $35 Ⓐ • (03/31/91) • **90**
Cabernet Sauvignon Napa Valley Georges de Latour Private Reserve 1981 • $36 • (03/31/91) • **86**
Cabernet Sauvignon Napa Valley Georges de Latour Private Reserve 1980 • $39 Ⓐ • (03/31/91) • **93**
Cabernet Sauvignon Napa Valley Georges de Latour Private Reserve 1979 • $33 Ⓐ • (03/31/91) • **87**
Cabernet Sauvignon Napa Valley Georges de Latour Private Reserve 1978 • $45 Ⓐ • (03/31/91) • **90**
Cabernet Sauvignon Napa Valley Georges de Latour Private Reserve 1977 • $59 • (03/31/91) • **79**
Cabernet Sauvignon Napa Valley Georges de Latour Private Reserve 1976 • $76 • (03/31/91) • **88**
Cabernet Sauvignon Napa Valley Georges de Latour Private Reserve 1975 • $55 • (03/31/91) • **83**
Cabernet Sauvignon Napa Valley Georges de Latour Private Reserve 1974 • $56 Ⓐ • (11/15/94) • **86**
Cabernet Sauvignon Napa Valley Georges de Latour Private Reserve 1973 • $41 Ⓐ • (03/31/91) • **75**
Cabernet Sauvignon Napa Valley Georges de Latour Private Reserve 1972 • $53 • (03/31/91) • **71**
Cabernet Sauvignon Napa Valley Georges de Latour Private Reserve 1971 • $36 Ⓐ • (03/31/91) • **79**
Cabernet Sauvignon Napa Valley Georges de Latour Private Reserve 1970 • $110 Ⓐ • (03/31/91) • **93**
Cabernet Sauvignon Napa Valley Georges de Latour Private Reserve 1969 • $95 • (03/31/91) • **92**
Cabernet Sauvignon Napa Valley Georges de Latour Private Reserve 1968 • $130 Ⓐ • (03/31/91) • **92**
Cabernet Sauvignon Napa Valley Georges de Latour Private Reserve 1967 • $95 • (03/31/91) • **82**
Cabernet Sauvignon Napa Valley Georges de Latour Private Reserve 1966 • $130 • (03/31/91) • **87**
Cabernet Sauvignon Napa Valley Georges de Latour Private Reserve 1965 • $72 Ⓐ • (03/31/91) • **77**
Cabernet Sauvignon Napa Valley Georges de Latour Private Reserve 1964 • $125 • (03/31/91) • **72**
Cabernet Sauvignon Napa Valley Georges de Latour Private Reserve 1963 • $100 • (03/31/91) • **74**
Cabernet Sauvignon Napa Valley Georges de Latour Private Reserve 1962 • $100 • (03/31/91) • **75**
Cabernet Sauvignon Napa Valley Georges de Latour Private Reserve 1961 • $140 • (03/31/91) • **77**
Cabernet Sauvignon Napa Valley Georges de Latour Private Reserve 1960 • $160 • (03/31/91) • **85**
Cabernet Sauvignon Napa Valley Georges de Latour Private Reserve 1959 • $340 • (03/31/91) • **89**
Cabernet Sauvignon Napa Valley Georges de Latour Private Reserve 1958 • $288 Ⓐ • (03/31/91) • **97**
Cabernet Sauvignon Napa Valley Georges de Latour Private Reserve 1956 • $600 • (03/31/91) • **88**
Cabernet Sauvignon Napa Valley Georges de Latour Private Reserve 1955 • $530 • (03/31/91) • **85**
Cabernet Sauvignon Napa Valley Georges de Latour Private Reserve 1954 • $280 • (03/31/91) • **86**
Cabernet Sauvignon Napa Valley Georges de Latour Private Reserve 1953 • $680 • (03/31/91) • **91**
Cabernet Sauvignon Napa Valley Georges de Latour Private Reserve 1952 • $600 • (03/31/91) • **91**
Cabernet Sauvignon Napa Valley Georges de Latour Private Reserve 1951 • $950 • (03/31/91) • **92**
Cabernet Sauvignon Napa Valley Georges de Latour Private Reserve 1950 • $750 • (03/31/91) • **88**

Cabernet Sauvignon Napa Valley Georges de Latour Private Reserve 1949 • $748 Ⓐ • (03/31/91) • **88**
Cabernet Sauvignon Napa Valley Georges de Latour Private Reserve 1948 • $1500 • (03/31/91) • **79**
Cabernet Sauvignon Napa Valley Georges de Latour Private Reserve 1947 • $1450 • (03/31/91) • **89**
Cabernet Sauvignon Napa Valley Georges de Latour Private Reserve 1945 • $700 • (03/31/91) • **70**
Cabernet Sauvignon Napa Valley Georges de Latour Private Reserve 1944 • $680 • (03/31/91) • **75**
Cabernet Sauvignon Napa Valley Georges de Latour Private Reserve 1943 • $125 • (03/31/91) • **87**
Cabernet Sauvignon Napa Valley Georges de Latour Private Reserve 1942 • $460 Ⓐ • (03/31/91) • **85**
Cabernet Sauvignon Napa Valley Georges de Latour Private Reserve 1941 • $958 Ⓐ • (03/31/91) • **89**
Cabernet Sauvignon Napa Valley Georges de Latour Private Reserve 1940 • $1250 • (03/31/91) • **89**
Cabernet Sauvignon Napa Valley Georges de Latour Private Reserve 1939 • $1550 • (03/31/91) • **91**
Cabernet Sauvignon Napa Valley Georges de Latour Private Reserve 1936 • $1550 • (03/31/91) • **86**
Cabernet Sauvignon Napa Valley Rutherford 1995: Dense, with earthy currant, cedar, sage and plum notes. Given the tannin level, it's best to cellar into 1999 to 2000 in hopes it softens and evolves. Not as good as the '94. 105,000 cases made. • $14 • (04/30/98) • **86**
Cabernet Sauvignon Napa Valley Rutherford 1994: A very impressive BV Rutherford bottling, this California red is deeply concentrated, with a rich core of plum, currant and cherry flavors. It shows remarkable finesse and finishes with a long, full aftertaste. Approachable now, it will soften nicely in a few years. 85,000 cases made. • $15 • (07/31/97) SS • **90**
Cabernet Sauvignon Napa Valley Rutherford 1993: A rustic, tannic style that lacks focus. It's a touch earthy, with a murky core of spicy currant, anise and wild berry flavors. • $15 • (12/15/96) • **83**
Cabernet Sauvignon Napa Valley Rutherford 1992 • $12 • (11/30/95) • **86**
Cabernet Sauvignon Napa Valley Rutherford 1991 • $13 • (10/15/94) • **87**
Cabernet Sauvignon Napa Valley Rutherford 1990 • $11 • (10/31/93) • **85**
Cabernet Sauvignon Napa Valley Rutherford 1989 • $11 • (03/31/92) • **81**
Cabernet Sauvignon Napa Valley Rutherford 1988 • $15 • (07/15/91) • **86**
Cabernet Sauvignon Napa Valley Rutherford 1987 • $11 Ⓐ • (12/15/90) • **85**
Cabernet Sauvignon Napa Valley Rutherford 1986 • $29 Ⓐ • (09/15/89) • **85**
Cabernet Sauvignon Napa Valley Rutherford 1985 • $17 Ⓐ • (06/15/88) • **85**
Cabernet Sauvignon Napa Valley Rutherford 1984 • $9 • (08/31/87) • **78**
Cabernet Sauvignon Napa Valley Rutherford 1983 • $6 • (06/15/87) • **80**
Cabernet Sauvignon Napa Valley Rutherford 1982 • $8 • (04/16/86) • **81**
Cabernet Sauvignon Napa Valley Rutherford 1981 • $9 • (05/16/85) • **81**
Cabernet Sauvignon Napa Valley Rutherford 1980 • $9 • (06/01/85) • **88**
Cabernet Sauvignon Napa Valley Rutherford 1979 • $12 Ⓐ • (06/01/85) • **89**
Cabernet Sauvignon Napa Valley Rutherford 1970 • $NA • (06/01/85) • **90**
Cabernet Sauvignon Rutherford Clone 6 Signet Collection 1994: Ripe, rich, smooth and complex, with deeply concentrated currant, black cherry, herb, spice and vanilla, and a wonderful aftertaste that keeps pumping out the flavors. The tannins, while firm, are physiologically ripe and supple for a wine this young. Tempting now, better in 2000. The first bottling of the Clone 6, which was previously a component of the Private Reserve Cabernet Sauvignon. 250 cases made. • $100 • (11/15/97) • **93**
Chardonnay California Beautour 1996: Toasty, honeyed notes on the nose announce this pretty yet ample white. On the palate, it's rich in pear, apple and citrus flavors, finishing with a touch of butterscotch. A nice wine at a great price. 140,000 cases made. • $10 • (02/28/98) BB • **87**
Chardonnay Carneros 1996: Ripe and earthy, with spicy pear, apple and apricot flavors that are pleasant, if lacking in special attributes. Drink now. 45,000 cases made. • $14 • (05/15/98) • **87**
Chardonnay Carneros 1995: Ripe and spicy, with a Muscat-like accent to the pear, fig and melon flavors. Fans of openly fruity Chardonnay will find this especially appealing. • $13 • (12/31/96) • **86**
Chardonnay Carneros Reserve 1995: An enticing Chardonnay, this is rich and creamy, with an elegant, complex core of fig, melon, pear and citrus flavors tinged with a seductive, smoky oak nuance that adds yet more depth and complexity. Finishes with a dash of hazelnut. 7,200 cases made. • $20 • (05/31/97) SS • **93**

Key: SS—Spectator Selection CS—Cellar Selection HR—Highly Recommended BB—Best Buy $NA—Price not available Ⓐ—Auction Price (BT)—Barrel Tasting
Dates in parentheses indicate the issues in which the ratings were published.

Chardonnay Carneros Reserve 1994: Ripe, rich, smooth and harmonious, offering tiers of pear, honey, vanilla and spice as flavors fan out on the finish, gaining a sense of elegance and finesse. 4,674 cases made. • $18 • (04/30/96) • **91**
Chardonnay Carneros Reserve 1993 • $18 • (12/31/95) • **88**
Chardonnay Napa Valley Beautour 1994: Simple and a little green around the edges of the straightforward apple flavors. • $9 • (07/31/96) • **80**
Chardonnay Napa Valley Beautour 1993 • $10 • (04/30/95) BB • **86**
Chardonnay Napa Valley Carneros 1994: Smooth and elegant, with a pretty band of pear, spice, apple and honey flavors that are well-focused and long on the finish. • $13 • (02/29/96) • **88**
Chardonnay Napa Valley Carneros 1993 • $13 • (09/30/95) • **85**
Ensemble California Signet Collection 1994: Elegant, with ripe cherry and berry flavors that pick up a trace of herb and mineral on the finish. A blend of Mourvèdre, Carignane, Grenache, and Syrah. 1,200 cases made. • $25 • (07/31/96) • **86**
Gamay Beaujolais Napa Valley 1988 • $6 • (08/31/89) • **73**
Gamay Beaujolais Napa Valley 1987 • $6 • (09/30/88) • **76**
Grenache San Benito Solaris Signet Collection 1995: Spicy, cherrylike and enjoyable. This light, fruity blush wine finishes with a strawberry punch. 390 cases made. • $8 • (09/30/97) • **83**
Grenache San Benito South Hart Vineyard Signet Collection 1995: An interesting mix of cherry, bell-pepper and herb flavors captured in a light, fleshy body. Could be enjoyed like a rosé, slightly chilled. 1,300 cases made. • $10 • (09/30/97) • **86**
Meritage Napa Valley 1990 • $20 • (11/15/94) • **85**
Merlot California Coastal 1995: Kind of smoky, with an herbal edge that's backed by currant and blackberry notes. The finish is bright, with a touch of bitterness. Drink now through 2002. 75,576 cases made. • $10 • (07/31/98) • **86**
Merlot Napa Valley 1994: Well-proportioned but nothing special, with an earthy accent to the currant, sage and spice flavors, and a cedary edge on the finish. • $16 • (06/30/97) • **84**
Merlot Napa Valley 1993 • $16 • (06/15/96) • **82**
Merlot Napa Valley Beautour 1994: Fairly herbal, with notes of tea, spice, blackberry and leather. A little more fruit would be nice. Moderate body and finish. 35,000 cases made. • $11 • (07/31/97) • **84**
Merlot Napa Valley Beautour 1993 • $12 • (06/30/96) • **82**
Merlot Napa Valley Beautour 1991 • $10 • (01/31/95) • **82**
Petite Sirah Napa Valley Signet Collection 1995: A dark, rich wine with black cherry, cassis and bell pepper notes. Tannins are coarse, but that's not unusual for this style. • $NA • (09/30/97) • **88**
Pinot Gris Central Coast Signet Collection 1996: A bright wine, with a keen mineral edge, it nonetheless retains a certain fleshiness on the palate. It finishes with hints of lemon-lime. 225 cases made. • $14 • (09/30/97) • **86**
Pinot Noir California Beautour 1996: This sturdy, affable style emphasizes generous berry and woodsy flavors, and has a chewy texture. Drink soon. 28,000 cases made. • $10 • (03/31/98) • **82**
Pinot Noir California Beautour 1995: Straightforward style, with spice, pepper, plum and berry flavors. Turns dry and tannic on the finish. 18,000 cases made. • $11 • (01/31/97) • **81**
Pinot Noir California Beautour 1994 • $10 • (12/31/95) • **82**
Pinot Noir Carneros 1995: Light and simple, but the cherry, strawberry and wild berry flavors are elegant and lively, making it quite appealing to drink now. 17,900 cases made. • $15 • (01/31/98) • **86**
Pinot Noir Carneros Reserve 1995: Wonderfully ripe Pinot Noir fruit comes bursting out of this Beaulieu bottling, with flavors of wild berry, black cherry, plum and spice, framed by light toasty oak that plays well with the fruitiness. Finishes with firm but supple tannins and fine length. Drinkable now, smoother in 1999. 4,000 cases made. • $30 • (01/31/98) SS • **91**
Pinot Noir Carneros Vin Gris Signet Collection 1996: Smoothly-styled but with bite, it combines weight with lightness on the palate, with a mineral-like tint. Refreshing and dry. 390 cases made. • $10 • (09/30/97) • **84**
Pinot Noir Napa Valley 1991 • $8 • (02/28/94) • **81**
Pinot Noir Napa Valley 1990 • $8 • (02/28/93) • **73**
Pinot Noir Napa Valley Beaumont 1986 • $7 • (06/15/88) • **74**
Pinot Noir Napa Valley Beaumont 1985 • $6 • (06/15/88) • **78**
Pinot Noir Napa Valley Beautour 1993 • $10 • (12/31/95) • **81**
Pinot Noir Napa Valley Beautour 1992 • $9 • (03/31/95) • **79**
Pinot Noir Napa Valley Carneros 1995: Marked by a minty, menthol quality up front, then gains dimension as the herb and dried cherry flavors work their way into the flow. Try now. 15,000 cases made. • $15 • (02/28/97) • **84**
Pinot Noir Napa Valley Carneros 1994 • $12 • (03/31/96) • **84**
Pinot Noir Napa Valley Carneros 1993 • $13 • (10/15/95) • **86**
Pinot Noir Napa Valley Carneros 1992 • $13 • (03/31/95) • **78**

Pinot Noir Napa Valley Carneros 1980 • $10 • (08/31/86) • **88**
Pinot Noir Napa Valley Carneros Reserve 1994 • $19 • (03/31/96) HR • **90**
Pinot Noir Napa Valley Carneros Reserve 1993 • $18 • (12/31/95) • **83**
Pinot Noir Napa Valley Carneros Reserve 1992 • $18 • (05/15/95) • **86**
Pinot Noir Napa Valley Carneros Reserve 1991 • $15 • (02/28/94) • **85**
Pinot Noir Napa Valley Carneros Reserve 1990: Good fruit flavors, but they're still straightforward. Crisp finish, with firm, stemmy tannins. Ready now. • $17 • (03/31/97) • **84**
Pinot Noir Napa Valley Carneros Reserve 1989 • $13 • (04/30/91) • **85**
Pinot Noir Napa Valley Carneros Reserve 1988 • $9 • (04/15/90) • **87**
Pinot Noir Napa Valley Carneros Reserve 1987 • $9 • (12/31/88) • **90**
Pinot Noir Napa Valley Carneros Reserve 1986 • $9 • (09/15/88) • **88**
Pinot Noir Napa Valley Carneros Reserve 1985 • $9 • (01/31/88) • **74**
Sangiovese Napa Valley Bianco Signet Collection 1996: Dark for a rosé, it's oaky, plummy character can be overpowering. Lacks the refreshing crispness of good rosé. 130 cases made. • $10 • (09/30/97) • **80**
Sangiovese Napa Valley Signet Collection 1995: A firm, meaty wine with a strong licorice character. Toasty, smoky oak notes add interest as hints of blackberry and cassis unfold on the palate. Shows elegance and finesse. 1,236 cases made. • $16 • (09/15/97) • **90**
Sangiovese Napa Valley Signet Collection 1994: Starts out tight and firm. Softens up nicely, with an anise and cherry edge, and hints of plum and cedar. 600 cases made. • $25 • (07/31/96) • **87**
Sauvignon Blanc California Beautour 1994 • $7 • (06/30/95) • **83**
Sauvignon Blanc Napa Valley 1996: Smooth and silky in texture, with melon-like and tangerine flavors of moderate body. 10,000 cases made. • $11 • (07/31/97) • **87**
Sauvignon Blanc Napa Valley 1995: This won't offend, but won't excite either. Some light citrus flavors pervade the fairly flabby texture and hollow body. • $10 • (08/31/97) • **81**
Sauvignon Blanc Napa Valley 1994: Strongly floral, with rose petal and anise scents. Pear flavors finish with lively intensity. • $8 • (08/31/96) BB • **88**
Sauvignon Blanc Napa Valley 1993 • $10 • (09/15/95) • **80**
Syrah Dry Creek Valley Signet Collection 1995: Ripe, smooth and polished, with a sage and herbal edge to its meaty Syrah flavors. Finishes with a long, spicy aftertaste with lots of plum and berry notes. Drinkable now. 505 cases made. • $25 • (09/30/97) • **91**
Tapestry Napa Valley Reserve 1993: Strikes a good balance of ripe fruit and supple texture, but the flavors lack the extra dimensions of the best, turning dry and tannic on the finish. A blend of 75 percent Cabernet Sauvignon, 17 percent Merlot, 7 percent Cabernet Franc, and 1 percent Malbec. 8,000 cases made. • $20 • (12/15/96) • **85**
Tapestry Napa Valley Reserve 1992 • $20 • (04/30/96) • **88**
Tapestry Napa Valley Signet Collection 1991 • $20 • (12/15/95) • **87**
Tapestry Reserve Napa Valley 1994: A dense and concentrated Bordeaux-style blend, showing promise with its tightly wound core of earthy currant, spice, plum and cherry flavors that fan out nicely on the finish, where the tannins clamp down. Best to cellar into 2001 to 2002. A blend of 79 percent Cabernet Sauvignon, 12 percent Merlot, 5 percent Cabernet Franc, 3 percent Petit Verdot, and 1 percent Malbec. 10,000 cases made. • $20 • (10/31/97) SS • **91**
Viognier Napa Valley Signet Collection 1996: Firmly-textured, with hints of nectarine, orange and spice. It's unusually creamy on the finish, which gives finesse. 1,493 cases made. • $16 • (09/30/97) • **88**
Zinfandel California Beautour 1996: A lighter-styled Zin, appealing for its pretty blueberry, raspberry and vanilla flavors, and the toasty oak nuances that put a nice spin on the finish. 30,000 cases made. • $10 • (03/31/98) BB • **85**
Zinfandel Napa Valley 1996: A lighter style well-suited for near-term consumption, with lively flavors of berry, cherry and spice and surprisingly firm tannins. Drink through 1999. 18,000 cases made. • $14 • (03/31/98) • **85**
Zinfandel Napa Valley 1995: Very impressive, and it's only BV's second vintage with Zinfandel. This is full-bodied and rich, with a jammy, pruny accent to the complex plum, cherry and raspberry flavors. It remains complex and elegant through the finish, and the tannins are supple. 8,000 cases made. • $13 • (04/30/97) SS • **91**
Zinfandel Napa Valley Signet Collection 1995: A delicious Zin from start to finish, with a complex core of spicy oak, ripe cherry, wild berry and currant flavors that are elegant, well-focused, and linger, long and lively, on the finish. Brilliant wine. 283 cases made. • $20 • (04/30/97) • **91**
Zinfandel Napa Valley Signet Collection 1994: A smooth and complex medley of spicy berry, cherry and plum flavors. Impressively fruity and direct finish. BV's first Zinfandel. 800 cases made. • $16 • (08/31/96) • **88**

BEAUX FRÈRES | OREGON

Pinot Noir Willamette Valley 1993 • $35 • (08/31/95) HR • **90**
Pinot Noir Willamette Valley 1992 • $34 • (03/15/94) HR • **91**
Pinot Noir Willamette Valley 1991 • $34 • (03/15/94) • **92**
Pinot Noir Yamhill County 1995: Spicy, peppery flavors make for an unusually zingy Pinot Noir, showing a little more bite than fruit at this point. Has impressive length and generosity as the currant, blackberry and cherry flavors slowly emerge. Try in 1999 to 2000. 2,200 cases made. • $50 • (04/30/97) • **90**
Pinot Noir Yamhill County The Beaux Frères Vineyard 1996: Ripe, supple and velvety; impressive for the purity of its plum, currant and spice flavors that spill out of a generous frame. The flavors are in sharp relief, but the texture remains warm and inviting, folding its tannins into a gentle blanket. Lovely now, best after 2000. 1,700 cases made. • $50 • (05/15/98) HR • **91**
Pinot Noir Yamhill County The Beaux Frères Vineyard 1994 • $40 • (06/30/96) • **93**
Pinot Noir Yamhill County The Beaux Frères Vineyard Belles Soeurs 1996: Light, supple and generous with its raspberry, black cherry and spice flavors, this is a gentle red with appealing character that lingers on the open-textured finish. An initial hint of dissolved gas dissipates with aeration. Drink now. 750 cases made. • $35 • (05/15/98) • **88**

BECKMEN | CALIFORNIA

Cabernet Sauvignon Santa Barbara County 1995: A sturdy red with pretty blackberry and violet flavors that remain fresh and inviting through the firm finish. Good now, but give it until 2000 for the tannins to further soften. 590 cases made. • $20 • (03/31/98) • **87**
Chardonnay Santa Barbara County 1996: A pretty wine, well-balanced and medium-bodied, with hints of vanilla, pear, herbs and spice. Finishes clean. 2,300 cases made. • $16 • (05/15/98) • **87**
Chardonnay Santa Barbara County 1995: Ripe, with grapefruit and pineapple notes that meld nicely with spice and vanilla flavors on the generous finish. Drink now. 1,300 cases made. • $15 • (03/31/98) • **86**
Chardonnay Santa Barbara County Barrel Select 1996: Solid, with ripe, intense, apple- and pear-laced Chardonnay flavors. Shows off some spice and oak on the finish, where it becomes more complex. Drink now through 2001. 670 cases made. • $20 • (06/15/98) • **88**
Chardonnay Santa Ynez Valley 1994: Rich, smoky aromas, but tamer on the palate with a lean, trim band of citrus-accented Chardonnay flavors echoing tart pear notes on the finish. 1,700 cases made. • $14 • (06/15/97) • **88**
Chardonnay Santa Ynez Valley Barrel Select 1994: A curiously flavored wine, with a trace of butterscotch to the mature pear and apple flavors. 190 cases made. • $20 • (07/31/96) • **74**
Sauvignon Blanc Santa Barbara County 1996: Opens with pretty, sweet oak, ripe melon and grapefruit. Follows up with a bright lemony edge. 550 cases made. • $12 • (04/30/98) • **85**
Sauvignon Blanc Santa Barbara County Beckmen Vineyards 1995: Reaches out with a vanilla and nectarine essence, followed by a long finish that showcases tangy lemon-lime and grapefruit flavors. A bit hot. 650 cases made. • $12 • (09/15/97) • **88**
Sauvignon Blanc Santa Ynez Valley 1994: The earthy, gamy, vegetal flavors are not appealing. 850 cases made. • $11 • (08/31/96) • **72**
Sauvignon Blanc Santa Ynez Valley Barrel Select 1994: Ripe, spicy and polished, owing more to the spice and vanilla from oak than anything else. Tasty, though. 125 cases made. • $16 • (08/31/96) • **85**
Syrah Santa Barbara County 1995: A distinctive wine that shows bold blackberry and slightly weedy flavors against a crisp frame of juicy acidity. Not for all tastes, but has a lot of personality. Drink through 1999. 450 cases made. • $18 • (12/15/97) • **87**

BEDELL | NEW YORK

Cabernet Sauvignon North Fork of Long Island 1993: Ripe and supple, with nicely balanced cherry, light chocolate and smoke flavors, and a modest finish. Accessible now. 400 cases made. • $18 • (12/31/96) • **84**
Cabernet Sauvignon North Fork of Long Island 1988 • $15 • (06/30/91) • **86**
Chardonnay North Fork of Long Island 1994: Light floral and apple aromas follow through on the round, soft palate; the wine is tender and fresh, with simple but appealing flavors. 600 cases made. • $12 • (12/31/96) • **83**
Chardonnay North Fork of Long Island Reserve 1993: Piney, nutty and herbal flavors suggest that this has reached full maturity. It's rich in texture, and though lean in flavor, it should perk up with food. Drink now. 700 cases made. • $15 • (12/31/96) • **82**
Dessert North Fork of Long Island 1992 • $24 • (04/15/95) • **84**

Gewürztraminer North Fork of Long Island 1994: Quite sweet and lush on the palate, it has nice texture but it's one-dimensional, with little in the way of Gewürz character or fruit flavor. Pleasant, but not exciting. 400 cases made. • $10 • (12/31/96) • **81**

Merlot North Fork of Long Island 1993: Polished and supple, in an elegant style. The blackberry and toast flavors are focused and balanced, with just enough tannin for grip. Drink now. 1,800 cases made. • $16 • (12/31/96) • **87**

Merlot North Fork of Long Island 1987 • $18 • (03/31/90) • **90**

Merlot North Fork of Long Island 1986 • $11 • (12/15/88) • **88**

Merlot North Fork of Long Island Reserve 1988 • $14 • (06/30/91) • **90**

BEDFORD THOMPSON | CALIFORNIA

Chardonnay Santa Barbara County 1994: Clean and correct, with a simple band of oak and pear flavor. 400 cases made. • $16 • (11/15/96) • **83**

Pinot Blanc Santa Barbara County 1994: Offers modest pear flavors, tinged with notes of pine and resin. Ready to drink. 300 cases made. • $14 • (04/30/97) • **80**

Syrah Santa Barbara County 1995: Smooth, ripe and fleshy, with pretty floral, plum, wild berry and black cherry flavors and supple, tender tannins. Picks up a subtle meaty, smoky note on the aftertaste. Drinks well now into 2000. 1,100 cases made. • $20 • (11/15/97) • **88**

Syrah Santa Barbara County 1994: Dark as night, with a spicy, leathery accent to the plum and wild berry flavors. Finishes with chewy tannins, but enough fruit flavors linger to hold the balance. Try now. 600 cases made. • $18 • (09/30/96) • **88**

BEHRENS & HITCHCOCK | CALIFORNIA

Cabernet Sauvignon Napa Valley Staglin Vineyard 1994: Smooth, rich and enticing, with detailed currant, anise, black cherry, olive and cedar flavors, turning supple and harmonious on the finish where the flavors linger on. Impressive. Enjoyable now through 2004. 100 cases made. • $28 • (11/30/97) • **92**

Merlot Napa Valley Oakville 1995: Soft and fleshy, with a pretty band of cedar, currant and spice nuances, it picks up a trace of black olive on the finish. The texture is smooth and there's plenty of oak. 60 cases made. • $25 • (11/30/97) • **88**

BEL ARBOR | CALIFORNIA

Cabernet Sauvignon America Cask 88 NV • $6 • (11/15/91) • **78**

Cabernet Sauvignon America Founder's Selection NV • $5 • (10/15/89) BB • **82**

Cabernet Sauvignon California 1993: Soft and generous, centered around appealing vanilla-scented raspberry and red currant flavors that linger gently on the finish. A fair price for a Cabernet of good quality. Approachable now. 30,000 cases made. • $7 • (12/15/95) • **84**

Cabernet Sauvignon California 1992 • $7 • (01/31/95) • **78**

Cabernet Sauvignon California 1990 • $6 • (03/15/93) BB • **82**

Cabernet Sauvignon California Founder's Selection 1990 • $6 • (11/15/93) • **80**

Cabernet Sauvignon California Vintner's Selection 1994: On the lean side, with modest flavor notes of herb, cedar and cherry. • $5 • (11/30/96) • **78**

Chardonnay California Vintner's Selection 1995: Soft and fresh, it's generous with its pineapple and floral flavors that linger nicely through the supple finish. • $6 • (11/30/96) • **83**

Chardonnay California Vintner's Selection 1994: Fresh and appealing for its scent of lime and the pineapple and pear flavors, which echo nicely on the finish. Offers some excitement, and is a steal at this price. 150,000 cases made. • $5 • (05/31/96) BB • **85**

Merlot America Cask 89 NV • $6 • (11/15/91) BB • **81**

Merlot America Founder's Selection American Grown NV • $5 • (06/15/90) • **72**

Merlot California 1990 • $7 • (10/31/92) BB • **84**

Merlot California Vintner's Selection 1994 • $6 • (06/30/96) BB • **84**

White Zinfandel California 1994 • $5 • (09/15/95) • **75**

Zinfandel California Founder's Selection 1990 • $6 • (09/30/92) BB • **85**

Key: SS—Spectator Selection CS—Cellar Selection HR—Highly Recommended BB—Best Buy $NA—Price not available Ⓐ—Auction Price (BT)—Barrel Tasting
Dates in parentheses indicate the issues in which the ratings were published.

BELL | CALIFORNIA

Cabernet Sauvignon Rutherford Baritelle Vineyard 1994: Medium-weight, with supple cedar, sage and currant flavors and finishing with a hint of spice, but overall it lacks intensity, focus and concentration. Drink now. 1,270 cases made. • $50 • (04/30/98) • **82**

Cabernet Sauvignon Rutherford Baritelle Vineyard 1992: A bit rustic, with a mineral quality, while currant, cherry and plum flavors emerge to give balance and depth. Picks up a minty note, with supple tannins. Best after 1999. 4,656 cases made. • $50 • (07/31/97) • **89**

Cabernet Sauvignon Rutherford Baritelle Vineyards 1991 • $40 • (12/15/95) • **83**

BELL MOUNTAIN | TEXAS

Cabernet Sauvignon Bell Mountain 1989 • $13 • (02/29/92) • **85**

Pinot Noir Bell Mountain 1989 • $12 • (02/29/92) • **76**

Pinot Noir Bell Mountain Oberhellmann Vineyards 1990 • $12 • (02/28/93) • **64**

BELLEROSE | CALIFORNIA

Cabernet Sauvignon Dry Creek Valley Reserve Cuvée 1987 • $18 • (11/15/91) • **83**

Cuvée Bellerose Sonoma County 1986 • $11 Ⓐ • (01/31/90) • **83**

Cuvée Bellerose Sonoma County 1985 • $19 Ⓐ • (12/15/88) • **82**

Cuvée Bellerose Sonoma County 1984 • $14 • (11/15/87) • **77**

Cuvée Bellerose Sonoma County 1983 • $8 Ⓐ • (01/31/87) • **74**

Cuvée Bellerose Sonoma County 1980 • $11 • (11/01/84) • **79**

Merlot Dry Creek Valley Reserve 1988 • $16 • (05/31/92) • **84**

Merlot Sonoma County 1986 • $16 • (04/15/90) • **69**

Merlot Sonoma County 1985 • $16 • (02/28/89) • **73**

Merlot Sonoma County 1984 • $12 • (12/31/87) • **77**

BELVEDERE | CALIFORNIA

Cabernet Sauvignon Alexander Valley Robert Young Vineyard Gifts of the Land 1985 • $16 • (01/31/91) • **81**

Cabernet Sauvignon Alexander Valley Robert Young Vineyards 1984 • $13 • (07/15/88) • **88**

Cabernet Sauvignon Alexander Valley Robert Young Vineyards 1983 • $12 • (05/15/87) • **88**

Cabernet Sauvignon Alexander Valley Robert Young Vineyards 1982 • $18 • (12/01/85) SS • **95**

Cabernet Sauvignon Dry Creek Valley 1994: Crisp and lively, this jazzy little wine has a slightly volatile, earthy edge to the berry flavors. Ready now. 3,324 cases made. • $14 • (12/15/97) • **82**

Cabernet Sauvignon Lake County Discovery Series 1982 • $4 • (04/01/85) BB • **80**

Cabernet Sauvignon Napa Valley Discovery Series 1982 • $4 • (02/16/86) • **71**

Cabernet Sauvignon Napa Valley York Creek Vineyard 1983 • $12 • (12/31/87) • **79**

Cabernet Sauvignon Napa Valley York Creek Vineyard 1982 • $12 • (09/15/86) • **72**

Cabernet Sauvignon Sonoma County 1992 • $12 • (03/31/96) • **82**

Cabernet Sauvignon Sonoma County 1991 • $10 • (11/15/94) • **82**

Cabernet Sauvignon Sonoma County Discovery Series 1987 • $6 • (06/15/90) • **75**

Cabernet Sauvignon Sonoma County Preferred Stock 1988 • $18 • (11/15/93) • **84**

Chardonnay Alexander Valley 1996: Solid, with pretty fruit shadings, hints of pear, spice and nectarine, and a complex, fruity aftertaste. Drink now. 10,000 cases made. • $14 • (05/15/98) • **87**

Chardonnay Alexander Valley 1995: Delivers a complex and well-balanced array of ripe pear, apple, fig and melon flavors. Ready to drink. 9,400 cases made. • $12 • (06/15/97) • **87**

Chardonnay Alexander Valley 1994: Effusively fruity style sporting a canned fruit cocktail flavor. Shows off ripe fig, pear and apple notes and touches of spice. 6,250 cases made. • $12 • (04/30/96) • **86**

Chardonnay Russian River Valley 1996: Pleasant, with ripe pear, citrus and spice flavors and a dash of toasty oak. Turns simple and fruity on the finish. Drink now through 2000. 7,550 cases made. • $17 • (06/30/98) • **87**

Chardonnay Russian River Valley 1995: Ripe, rich and intense, with complex, concentrated fruit flavors and a pretty dash of smoky, toasty oak. On the finish it all comes together, with layers of fig, melon, pear and apricot. Impressive for its elegance. 7,200 cases made. • $15 • (06/15/97) • **91**

Chardonnay Russian River Valley 1994: Ripe and full-bodied, appealing melon, fig and spice notes picking up a touch of honey and fig on the finish. 5,600 cases made. • $13 • (02/29/96) • **88**

Chardonnay Russian River Valley 1993 • $12 • (10/15/95) • **87**

Chardonnay Sonoma County 1996: Light, straightforward, with citrusy pear and spice flavors that linger on the slightly chewy finish. Could improve by 1999. 34,500 cases made. • $11 • (03/31/98) • **85**

Chardonnay Sonoma County 1995: What a find for so few dollars. This ready-to-drink Chardonnay features a mildly earthy character up front, abdicating to an interesting core of peach, nectarine and pear flavors that linger. 30,000 cases made. • $10 • (04/30/97) BB • **88**

Chardonnay Sonoma County 1994: Ripe, bright, vivid pear, peach and nectarine notes pick up a trace of oak and hazelnut on the lingering finish. A well-crafted white that delivers a load of flavors. 25,000 cases made. • $9 • (02/29/96) BB • **88**

Chardonnay Sonoma County 1993 • $9 • (05/31/95) • **84**

Chardonnay Sonoma County Preferred Stock 1995: Sleek and elegant, rich and polished, with well-focused pear, spice, fig and melon flavors and a long, lingering aftertaste. Drink now through 2000. 480 cases made. • $21 • (05/15/98) • **90**

Chardonnay Sonoma County Preferred Stock 1994: Smooth, ripe, rich and harmonious, with layers of pear, honey, butterscotch and fig flavors. Folds together nicely on the finish, where a spicy edge adds dimension. 779 cases made. • $22 • (04/30/97) • **90**

Discovery Series Red Table Wine Sonoma County 1983 • $3 • (07/31/88) • **78**

Gewürztraminer Anderson Valley Floodgate Vineyard 1996: Supple and generous with its spicy almond and pear flavors. 840 cases made. • $12 • (11/30/97) • **83**

Merlot Alexander Valley Robert Young Vineyards 1986 • $13 • (06/30/89) • **87**

Merlot Alexander Valley Robert Young Vineyards 1984 • $13 • (08/31/88) • **90**

Merlot Alexander Valley Robert Young Vineyards 1983 • $12 • (12/31/87) • **70**

Merlot Alexander Valley Robert Young Vineyards 1982 • $12 • (03/16/86) • **94**

Merlot Dry Creek Valley 1995: Has a bitter thread running through the otherwise attractive berry and spice flavors. Give it until 2000. 4,640 cases made. • $13 • (03/31/98) • **84**

Merlot Dry Creek Valley 1994: Lacking focus and flavor, this tastes bland with but a hint of black cherry. 3,235 cases made. • $14 • (05/15/97) • **80**

Merlot Dry Creek Valley Preferred Stock 1994: Ripe and juicy, with pretty flavors of wild berry and black cherry, hints of plum and currant, all framed with spicy, cedary oak. Long, smooth aftertaste. Drinkable now into 2000. 220 cases made. • $22 • (07/31/97) • **89**

Merlot Sonoma County 1993: Dry and earthy; not showing much in the way of fruit. Dry and bitter on the finish. 1,680 cases made. • $14 • (08/31/96) • **77**

Merlot Sonoma County 1991 • $12 • (09/15/94) • **82**

Muscat Canelli Alexander Valley Late Harvest 1990 • $10/375ml • (06/15/92) • **80**

Pinot Noir Los Carneros Winery Lake 1983 • $12 • (12/15/87) • **73**

Pinot Noir Sonoma County Bacigalupi 1985 • $12 • (06/15/88) • **73**

Zinfandel Dry Creek Valley 1995: A mild-mannered Zin featuring nicely proportioned black cherry and berry flavors on a lithe frame, and echoing hints of vanilla and spice. Ready now. 1,800 cases made. • $18 • (12/15/97) • **87**

Zinfandel Dry Creek Valley 1994: Delivers ripe and chunky plum, pepper, tar and spice flavors in a rustic style. Try now. 1,900 cases made. • $14 • (03/31/97) • **87**

Zinfandel Dry Creek Valley 1993 • $11 • (03/31/96) • **84**

Zinfandel Dry Creek Valley 1991 • $10 • (03/31/94) • **84**

Zinfandel Dry Creek Valley 1990 • $10 • (06/15/93) • **74**

Zinfandel Dry Creek Valley 1989 • $9 • (05/15/92) BB • **85**

BENESSERE | CALIFORNIA

Sangiovese Napa Valley 1995: A somewhat austere style for California, with an appealing smoky quality. Licorice and black currant notes are subtle, positioned behind ripe tannins. Opens up nicely with some exposure to air. 135 cases made. • $25 • (09/15/97) • **89**

BENHAM | CALIFORNIA

Sangiovese California 1992 • $9 • (11/30/95) • **77**

BENICIA | CALIFORNIA

Cabernet Sauvignon Napa Valley Capitol Reserve NV: Ordinary all the way around, with earthy, herbal and spicy flavors. 487 cases made. • $12 • (11/30/96) • **73**

Cabernet Sauvignon Napa Valley Diamond Mountain Capitol Reserve 1993: A sad example of Napa Cabernet, as it tastes dull and stripped of flavor. What's the point? 199 cases made. • $20 • (11/30/96) • **72**

BENTON-LANE | OREGON

Pinot Noir Oregon 1996: Light, crisp structure offers pretty plum and currant flavors that persist on the generous finish. Nice now, seems poised to improve through 2000 to 2001. 13,123 cases made. • $15 • (03/31/98) • **87**

Pinot Noir Oregon 1994 • $14 • (03/31/96) • **87**

Pinot Noir Oregon 1992 • $12 • (11/15/94) • **88**

Pinot Noir Oregon Reserve 1996: Crisp and chewy. A tightly wrapped wine that offers glimpses of blackberry and currant underneath a tough outer layer. Give it until 2000. 300 cases made. • $30 • (03/31/98) • **86**

Pinot Noir Oregon Reserve 1994 • $28 • (06/30/96) • **87**

BENZIGER | CALIFORNIA

A Tribute Red Sonoma Mountain 1990 • $27 • (11/15/94) • **84**

A Tribute Red Sonoma Mountain 1989 • $26 • (11/15/92) • **88**

A Tribute Red Sonoma Mountain 1988 • $26 • (01/31/92) • **88**

A Tribute Red Sonoma Mountain 1987 • $20 • (12/31/90) • **85**

A Tribute Sonoma Mountain 1994: Young, tight and tannic, but once you wade past the tannins the earthy currant, mint and spice flavors are quite appealing. Given the tannic strength, cellar into 2002. A blend of Cabernet Sauvignon, Merlot, Cabernet Franc, and Petit Verdot. 215 cases made. • $25 • (10/31/97) • **87**

Brut Blanc de Blancs Carneros 1988 • $14 • (12/31/92) • **84**

Brut Blanc de Blancs Carneros Late Disgorged 1990: Richly flavored with notes of hazelnut, pear, toast and butterscotch. Shows some age, but it's not over the hill, if you like this style. Lacks zest, but still quite nice. 753 cases made. • $10 • (11/30/97) • **89**

Brut Blanc de Blancs Carneros Late Disgorged 1989 • $14 • (11/30/94) • **86**

Brut Carneros Imagery Series 1990 • $16 • (05/31/95) • **87**

Cabernet Franc Alexander Valley Blue Rock Vineyard Imagery Series 1989 • $16 • (10/15/93) • **85**

Cabernet Franc Alexander Valley Imagery 1995: Well-balanced, with sage, currant, herb and cedary oak flavors folding together nicely. Drink now. 598 cases made. • $20 • (12/15/97) • **85**

Cabernet Franc Alexander Valley Imagery Series 1994: Smooth and supple, with ripe plum, cherry and berry flavors that are rich and complex, firm tannins and a nice dash of oak. Remarkably harmonious on the finish. 800 cases made. • $17 • (04/30/97) • **91**

Cabernet Franc Alexander Valley Imagery Series 1992 • $16 • (02/28/95) • **83**

Cabernet Sauvignon Sonoma County 1995: A well-oaked style, with lots of dill and cedary notes, and enough cherry, herb and currant flavors to broaden the palette. Finishes with supple tannins. 33,607 cases made. • $16 • (11/30/97) • **87**

Cabernet Sauvignon Sonoma County 1992 • $13 • (09/15/95) • **87**

Cabernet Sauvignon Sonoma County 1991 • $12 • (03/15/94) • **88**

Cabernet Sauvignon Sonoma County 1990 • $13 • (09/30/93) • **86**

Cabernet Sauvignon Sonoma County 1989 • $12 • (07/15/92) • **84**

Cabernet Sauvignon Sonoma County 1988 • $12 • (11/15/91) • **84**

Cabernet Sauvignon Sonoma County 1987 • $22 • (09/30/90) SS • **93**

Cabernet Sauvignon Sonoma County 1986 • $10 • (07/31/89) • **82**

Cabernet Sauvignon Sonoma County Five Bordeaux Varietals 1994: A supple, ripe, rich and harmonious Cabernet, with small amounts of Merlot, Cabernet Franc, Malbec, and Petit Verdot adding dimension. With layers of currant, black cherry and spicy oak flavors, and anise and sage notes, this is an exceptionally friendly and complex young wine that's tasty now or can be cellared short-term. An excellent value, too. 34,176 cases made. • $14 • (04/30/97) SS • **90**

Cabernet Sauvignon Sonoma Mountain 1989 • $22 • (11/15/94) • **84**

Cabernet Sauvignon Sonoma Mountain 1988 • $25 • (11/15/91) • **85**

Cabernet Sauvignon Sonoma Mountain Reserve 1994: A touch earthy and marked by gritty, rugged tannins, the core of fruit is solid, showing mineral, currant, leather, anise and sage notes. Has complex flavors on the aftertaste, so it should reward cellaring. Best from 2001 through 2008. 720 cases made. • $32 • (06/30/98) • **88**
Cabernet Sauvignon Sonoma Valley 1986 • $17 • (04/30/90) • **78**
Cabernet Sauvignon Sonoma Valley 1985 • $16 • (12/15/88) • **83**
Cabernet Sauvignon Sonoma Valley Estate Bottled 1987 • $12 • (11/15/90) • **85**
Chardonnay Carneros 1995: Deftly balanced, clean and ripe, with pear, apple, spice and light oak shadings, turning complex on the finish. Ready to drink. 22,117 cases made. • $14 • (04/30/97) • **88**
Chardonnay Carneros 1994: Appealing for its elegance and ripe peach and pear flavors. Smooth and polished in a medium-bodied style. 30,500 cases made. • $13 • (05/15/96) • **84**
Chardonnay Carneros 1993 • $13 • (06/30/95) • **85**
Chardonnay Carneros Reserve 1996: Clean, ripe and refreshing, with spicy peach, pear, fig and melon, picking up a pretty oak flavor on the finish, where the texture is smooth and creamy. Best now through 2002. 1,020 cases made. • $25 • (06/30/98) • **91**
Chardonnay Carneros Reserve 1995: Complex, with its interplay of ripe fruit flavors and spicy, vanilla-tinged oak notes. Hints of pear, apple, melon and apricot are rich and well-focused. Drink now. 550 cases made. • $22 • (05/15/97) • **91**
Chardonnay Carneros Reserve 1994: A supple and complex core of creamy pear, spice, honey and smoky, toasty oak flavors linger well into the aftertaste. An elegant and stylish white that's appealing now. 30,522 cases made. • $13 • (03/31/96) HR • **89**
Chardonnay Carneros Yamakawa Vineyards Reserve 1996: A well-oaked style that has the rich fruit to stand up to it. Serves up complex fig, pear, apricot and ginger notes and holds its focus. Drink now through 2000. 312 cases made. • $25 • (05/31/98) • **91**
Estate Tribute Red Sonoma Mountain 1992: Dark and intense, but with a measure of restraint. A Bordeaux-style blend featuring a range of herb, tea, cherry and currant flavors and finishing with a spicy accent and supple tannins. Ready now and into 2000. 497 cases made. • $20 • (10/15/96) • **87**
Estate Tribute Red Sonoma Mountain 1991 • $20 • (03/31/96) • **84**
Estate Tribute Sonoma Mountain 1993: Tart and spicy, with a trim band of cherry and currant flavors that slowly unfold. Finishes with notes of oak and herb and supple tannins. Drink now. A blend of 55 percent Cabernet Sauvignon, 27 percent Cabernet Franc, 9 percent Merlot, and 9 percent Petit Verdot. 550 cases made. • $22 • (04/30/97) • **87**
Estate Tribute White Sonoma Mountain 1994 • $16 • (06/15/96) • **87**
Fumé Blanc Sonoma County 1996: Marked by lovely melon, citrus and pineapple aromas, this very good California white sits brightly on the palate and finishes with a tangy, lemony edge. A good match for food, and made in a volume that suggests availability. 16,525 cases made. • $10 • (01/31/98) BB • **87**
Fumé Blanc Sonoma County 1995: Buttery, ripe and rich, with spicy oak overtones, generous peach flavors and herb notes. Ready now. 19,284 cases made. • $10 • (12/31/96) BB • **86**
Fumé Blanc Sonoma County 1994 • $10 • (06/30/95) • **84**
Fumé Blanc Sonoma County 1993 • $9 • (02/28/95) • **80**
International Imagery Series (From France, Australia, Chile, California, and Nevada) NV • $28 • (11/15/93) • **82**
Merlot Sonoma County 1995: Pleasant enough, with a smooth, supple texture and attractive herb, currant, sage and cedary oak flavors that fan out, picking up hints of tobacco and coffee. Best to cellar into 1999. 23,105 cases made. • $17 • (11/30/97) • **87**
Merlot Sonoma County 1994: Ripe, smooth and polished, with a pretty array of flavors ranging from currant, cherry and herb to vanilla-tinged oak. Finishes with complexity, finesse and just enough tannins to warrant short-term cellaring. 28,012 cases made. • $15 • (10/15/96) SS • **88**
Merlot Sonoma County 1993 • $14 • (03/31/96) • **82**
Merlot Sonoma County 1992 • $14 • (02/28/95) • **87**
Merlot Sonoma County 1991 • $14 • (09/15/94) • **83**
Merlot Sonoma County 1990 • $14 • (10/15/93) • **85**
Merlot Sonoma County 1989 • $14 • (05/31/92) • **81**
Merlot Sonoma County 1988 • $12 • (11/15/91) • **87**

Key: SS—Spectator Selection CS—Cellar Selection HR—Highly Recommended BB—Best Buy $NA—Price not available Ⓐ—Auction Price (BT)—Barrel Tasting
Dates in parentheses indicate the issues in which the ratings were published.

Merlot Sonoma County Reserve 1995: Solid and balanced, with a well-focused core of tart cherry, currant, anise and cedar flavors. Holds its focus on the finish, where the tannins are well-integrated. Best from 1999 through 2005. 1,018 cases made. • $35 • (06/30/98) • **87**
Merlot Sonoma Mountain A Tribute 1994: Dark, ripe, intense and tannic, with currant, spice, cedar and smoke flavors at its core. Finishes with good length and a wall of tannins. Best to cellar into 1999. 212 cases made. • $25 • (05/31/97) • **88**
Merlot Sonoma Valley 1987 • $12 • (03/31/91) • **86**
Merlot Sonoma Valley 1986 • $16 • (07/31/89) • **84**
Petite Sirah Paso Robles Imagery Series 1994: An oaky style, with stewed plum and pepper notes. The texture is smooth and polished, with a vegetal edge. Drink now through 2000. 1,000 cases made. • $18 • (07/31/97) • **86**
Petite Sirah Paso Robles Shell Creek Vineyard Imagery Series 1993: A well-proportioned Petite Sirah that captures ripe smoke and plum flavors, floral aromas and avoids being overly tannic or dry on the finish. Drinks well now. 500 cases made. • $16 • (11/30/96) • **85**
Petite Sirah Paso Robles Shell Creek Vineyard Imagery Series 1989 • $16 • (10/15/93) • **80**
Pinot Blanc North Coast Imagery Series 1995: Smooth, ripe, round and very pretty with its spicy pear, hazelnut and mineral flavors gliding smoothly through the Chardonnay-like finish. Delicious now. 350 cases made. • $17 • (04/30/97) • **89**
Pinot Blanc Sonoma Mountain Imagery Series 1994: Smooth and spicy, with its tasty pear, apple, honey and vanilla flavors gaining complexity on the finish. Drinks well now. 670 cases made. • $20 • (11/30/96) • **87**
Pinot Blanc Sonoma Mountain Skinner Vineyard Imagery Series 1993 • $16 • (08/31/95) • **84**
Pinot Noir California 1995: Bright and zippy, this is a lively mouthful of raspberry and spice flavors that linger on a slightly chewy finish. Has character and persistence. Drink through 1999. 1,220 cases made. • $17 • (12/15/97) • **87**
Pinot Noir California 1993 • $14 • (06/15/96) • **88**
Pinot Noir California 1992 • $14 • (01/31/95) • **86**
Pinot Noir Sonoma County 1991 • $14 • (08/31/94) • **87**
Pinot Noir Sonoma County 1990 • $14 • (02/28/94) • **87**
Pinot Noir Sonoma County 1989 • $13 • (02/28/93) • **85**
Riesling Late Harvest Santa Maria Valley Imagery Series Bien Nacido Vineyard 1994 • $16/375ml • (06/15/96) • **89**
Sangiovese Dry Creek Valley Imagery Series 1995: Mixes its fruit and spicy, toasty oak flavors well, but ultimately it's simple and uncomplicated. Drink now. 486 cases made. • $18 • (03/31/98) • **83**
Sangiovese Dry Creek Valley Larga Vista Vineyard Imagery Series 1994: Smooth and spicy, with ripe cherry, wild berry and currant flavors. Picks up traces of anise, green olive and cedar on the finish. Drink now. 650 cases made. • $20 • (10/15/96) • **87**
Sangiovese Dry Creek Valley Larga Vista Vineyard Imagery Series 1993 • $16 • (06/15/96) • **88**
Sauvignon Blanc-Sémillon Sonoma Mountain A Tribute 1995: A refreshing blend of light, tangy citrus flavors that linger enjoyably on the palate. A blend of 50 percent Sauvignon Blanc and 50 percent Sémillon. 304 cases made. • $16 • (06/15/97) • **87**
Syrah Central Coast Imagery 1994: Serves up a pretty array of ripe cherry, plum and wild berry flavors, with lots of spice, sage and meat notes. Turns complex on the finish, where the flavors fan out. Try now. 500 cases made. • $19 • (05/15/97) • **88**
Syrah Santa Maria Valley Bien Nacido Vineyard Imagery Series 1990 • $16 • (10/31/93) • **70**
Viognier Sonoma County Imagery Series 1995: Smooth and harmonious for Viognier, with perfumed pear, peach and honeysuckle flavors that linger on the finish. 650 cases made. • $19 • (09/15/96) • **86**
Voignier Sonoma County Moss Oak Vineyard Imagery Series 1993 • $16 • (01/31/95) • **83**
White Burgundy Napa Valley Yountmill Vineyard Imagery Series 1994 • $20 • (06/15/96) • **87**
White Burgundy North Coast Imagery Series 1995: Soft and appealing for its glowing melon, apple and spice flavors, smooth in texture. Drinkable now. 1,300 cases made. • $20 • (04/30/97) • **87**
Zinfandel Port Dry Creek Valley Imagery Series 1994: This is light in flavor and a bit hot, a combination that makes it seem out of balance. 670 cases made. • $20/500 ml • (11/30/96) • **78**
Zinfandel Port Dry Creek Valley Mayo Family & Carreras Vineyard Imagery Series 1990 • $22 • (10/15/94) • **87**
Zinfandel Sonoma County 1993 • $14 • (10/15/95) • **85**
Zinfandel Sonoma County 1992 • $13 • (02/28/95) • **86**
Zinfandel Sonoma County 1991 • $13 • (10/15/94) • **87**

Zinfandel Sonoma County 1990 • $11 • (09/30/93) • **85**
Zinfandel Sonoma County 1989 • $10 • (10/15/92) • **83**
Zinfandel Sonoma County Old Vines 1995: Attractive ripe wild berry, raspberry and cherry flavors are fresh and snappy, gaining a spicy edge on the finish and lingering on. Not too tannic; drink now through 2000. 4,408 cases made. • $17 • (05/15/98) • **87**
Zinfandel Sonoma County Old Vines 1994: Complex, with its array of ripe cherry, wild berry, raspberry and spice flavors. Supple and harmonious on the finish as the flavors linger on. 1,992 cases made. • $15 • (10/15/96) • **89**

BERGFELD | CALIFORNIA

Cabernet Sauvignon Napa Valley 1988 • $14 • (11/15/91) • **83**
Merlot Napa Valley 1989 • $15 • (05/31/92) • **87**

BERINGER | CALIFORNIA

Alluvium Red Knights Valley 1994: Shows off appealing currant, coffee, berry and spicy flavors, the texture is supple and polished, the finish is deceptively complex. A blend of Cabernet Sauvignon, Cabernet Franc, Merlot, Petit Verdot, and Malbec. Best from 2000 through 2006. • $25 • (03/31/98) • **90**
Alluvium Red Knights Valley 1993: Ripe, smooth and spicy, with a pretty core of plum, currant and wild berry flavors that turn elegant and complex on the finish where anise and cedar notes fold in. Finishes with firm tannins. Drink now or age through 2002. A blend of 75 percent Merlot, 14 percent Cabernet Sauvignon, 10 percent Cabernet Franc, and 1 percent Petit Verdot. • $25 • (04/30/97) • **90**
Alluvium White Knights Valley 1996: Touches of butterscotch and cream are followed by hints of lemon and herbs. Tangy acids and a mineral edge firm up the ensemble, which finishes brightly. A blend of Sémillon, Sauvignon Blanc, Chardonnay, and Viognier. • $16 • (03/31/98) • **85**
Alluvium White Knights Valley 1995: Strikes a nice balance between spice and citrusy pineapple flavors, tempering its toasty character with an elegant feel, flavorful without excessive weight. Drinkable now. A blend of 45 percent Sauvignon Blanc, 44 percent Sémillon, 10 percent Chardonnay, and 1 percent Viognier. • $15 • (04/30/97) • **87**
Cabernet Sauvignon Knights Valley 1994: Young, tight and firmly tannic, this well-crafted California Cabernet slowly unwinds its core of ripe and delicious plum, black cherry, currant and spice flavors. Finishes with sufficient tannic strength to maybe merit short-term cellaring. Drink now to 2000. 59,000 cases made. • $20 • (07/31/97) SS • **91**
Cabernet Sauvignon Knights Valley 1993: Well crafted in an elegant style that displays a range of ripe cherry, currant, herb and cedary oak flavors. Not a big, ultra-rich style, but very pleasing to drink now, offering depth and complexity. 38,000 cases made. • $13 • (10/15/96) • **87**
Cabernet Sauvignon Knights Valley 1992 • $15 • (08/31/95) • **87**
Cabernet Sauvignon Knights Valley 1991 • $13 • (05/31/94) • **87**
Cabernet Sauvignon Knights Valley 1990 • $13 • (11/15/93) SS • **90**
Cabernet Sauvignon Knights Valley 1989 • $16 • (11/15/92) • **85**
Cabernet Sauvignon Knights Valley 1988 • $16 • (11/15/91) • **86**
Cabernet Sauvignon Knights Valley 1987 • $20 • (11/15/90) HR • **90**
Cabernet Sauvignon Knights Valley 1985 • $20 • (05/31/88) • **87**
Cabernet Sauvignon Knights Valley 1983 • $17 • (04/15/87) • **83**
Cabernet Sauvignon Knights Valley 1982 • $22 • (04/15/87) • **90**
Cabernet Sauvignon Knights Valley 1981 • $20 • (10/01/85) • **86**
Cabernet Sauvignon Knights Valley 1980 • $20 • (02/15/84) • **88**
Cabernet Sauvignon Knights Valley Appellation Collection 1995: A rich, potent yet elegant, understated style, with ripe, polished currant, blackberry, cherry and spice. Finishes with firm tannins. Best now to 2005. • $NA • (06/15/98) • **91**
Cabernet Sauvignon Napa Valley Bancroft Vineyard 1994: Dark, ripe, rich and plush, with a wonderful core of dense currant, plum, black cherry and wild berry flavors, it fairly gushes with concentrated fruit, all the while maintaining amazing finesse and complexity. 200 cases made. • $85 • (10/31/97) • **97**
Cabernet Sauvignon Napa Valley Chabot Vineyard 1994: A fruit-driven style, ripe and jammy, with rich plum, black cherry and a dash of raspberry. Finishes with a gush of fruit too, backed by firm, dry tannins. 200 cases made. • $85 • (10/31/97) • **92**
Cabernet Sauvignon Napa Valley Chabot Vineyard 1993: Austere, tightly wound, with firm tannins and attractive currant and black cherry flavors. Shows a remarkable purity and depth of flavor, and the finish goes on and on. Given the firmness of the tannins, it's best cellared midterm. Drink now through 2002. • $100 • (06/15/98) • **90**
Cabernet Sauvignon Napa Valley Chabot Vineyard 1992: Dark, ripe, rich and concentrated, brimming with juicy plum, cherry, currant, anise and black cherry flavors. Shows uncommon finesse and polish for a young wine, finishing with ripe, full tannins. Delicious. 200 cases made. • $100 • (12/15/96) • **93**
Cabernet Sauvignon Napa Valley Chabot Vineyard 1988 • $35 • (11/15/93) • **83**
Cabernet Sauvignon Napa Valley Chabot Vineyard 1987: Still young and vibrant, with a firm, intense core of mint-laced currant, cherry and spice flavors. Finishes with a chewy tannic edge. Best from 1999 through 2006. • $80 • (12/15/97) • **93**
Cabernet Sauvignon Napa Valley Chabot Vineyard 1985 • $31 • (11/15/91) • **90**
Cabernet Sauvignon Napa Valley Chabot Vineyard 1984 • $30 • (09/15/90) • **85**
Cabernet Sauvignon Napa Valley Marston Vineyard 1994: Brimming with ripe, rich, concentrated cherry, currant, plum and anise flavors. Tannins are in proportion, finish is long and complex. 200 cases made. • $85 • (10/31/97) • **92**
Cabernet Sauvignon Napa Valley Private Reserve 1993: From Beringer's impressive line of reserve bottlings. Remarkable for its intensity, richness, depth and concentration, this is a big yet elegant wine stuffed with complex currant, leather, spice, sage and cedar flavors that fan out on the palate. Tempting now, but probably best cellared into 1999 to 2001. 11,500 cases made. • $65 • (05/31/97) CS • **93**
Cabernet Sauvignon Napa Valley Private Reserve 1992 • $45 • (11/15/95) CS • **95**
Cabernet Sauvignon Napa Valley Private Reserve 1991 • $40 • (03/31/95) CS • **94**
Cabernet Sauvignon Napa Valley Private Reserve 1990 • $40 • (11/15/94) CS • **92**
Cabernet Sauvignon Napa Valley Private Reserve 1989 • $40 • (07/15/93) CS • **90**
Cabernet Sauvignon Napa Valley Private Reserve 1988 • $40 • (06/15/93) • **88**
Cabernet Sauvignon Napa Valley Private Reserve 1987: Dark, ripe, intense and opulent, this is a remarkably complex and youthful wine. It serves up layers of currant, berry, chocolate, mint, herb and spice, finishing with firm yet supple tannins. Ready to drink, but worthy of cellaring into 2000. May last until 2010. • $86 Ⓐ • (12/15/97) • **97**
Cabernet Sauvignon Napa Valley Private Reserve 1986: *Wine Spectator's* Wine of the Year for 1990, now mature and perhaps a shade past its prime. The flavors are ripe and complex plum and currant, with hints of anise and spice, but it turns dry and tannic on the finish. Quite consistent through several tastings. Drink soon. • $58 Ⓐ • (12/15/96) • **89**
Cabernet Sauvignon Napa Valley Private Reserve 1985 • $94 Ⓐ • (12/15/89) SS • **95**
Cabernet Sauvignon Napa Valley Private Reserve 1984 • $46 Ⓐ • (02/15/89) CS • **94**
Cabernet Sauvignon Napa Valley Private Reserve 1983 • $19 • (04/15/87) • **90**
Cabernet Sauvignon Napa Valley Private Reserve 1982 • $18 • (04/15/87) • **94**
Cabernet Sauvignon Napa Valley Private Reserve 1981 • $18 • (04/15/87) • **93**
Cabernet Sauvignon Napa Valley Private Reserve 1978 • $60 • (11/15/92) • **95**
Cabernet Sauvignon Napa Valley Private Reserve Lemmon Ranch Vineyard 1978 • $15 • (04/30/87) • **92**
Cabernet Sauvignon Napa Valley Private Reserve Lemmon-Chabot Vineyard 1981 • $34 • (04/15/87) • **93**
Cabernet Sauvignon Napa Valley Private Reserve Lemmon-Chabot Vineyard 1980 • $20 • (08/01/84) CS • **93**
Cabernet Sauvignon Napa Valley Private Reserve State Lane Vineyard 1980 • $15 • (08/01/84) • **88**
Chardonnay Napa Valley 1996: Ripe, rich and flavorful, with layers of pear, apple, melon, fig and spice. Shows depth, concentration and complexity on a long, lively finish. • $15 • (01/31/98) • **90**
Chardonnay Napa Valley 1995: Serves up lots of pure, ripe fig, melon and pear flavors in an elegant, understated style. Hints of smoky, toasty oak show through on the finish, where it turns complex. • $15 • (01/31/97) • **89**
Chardonnay Napa Valley 1994: Appealing for its purity of fruit, focusing on ripe pear, nectarine, peach and honey. A complex and well-balanced white with a nicely fruity aftertaste. What a find at this price. 50,000 cases made. • $11 • (03/31/96) SS • **90**

BERNARDUS

Chardonnay Napa Valley 1993 • $11 • (04/30/95) • **84**
Chardonnay Napa Valley Private Reserve 1996: This top-of-the-line Chardonnay lives up to its pedigree, showing ripe pear, smoky oak, fig and vanilla flavors, turning rich and elegant and revealing a fine balance and integration that lets the flavors linger on and on. Another tremendous effort for this wine. Drink now through 2000. 19,800 cases made. • $32 • (03/31/98) HR • **95**
Chardonnay Napa Valley Private Reserve 1995: This reserve is remarkable for its elegance, richness and finesse, not to mention its complex integration of flavors, showing tiers of ripe pear, spicy oak, hints of citrus, pineapple, spice and hazelnut flavors. A dazzling effort from Beringer, it's a worthy successor to the brilliant 1994. 19,500 cases made. • $29 • (04/30/97) HR • **94**
Chardonnay Napa Valley Private Reserve 1994: Ripe, rich, intense and deeply concentrated, packing in tiers of ripe pear, honey, hazelnut and butterscotch. An altogether complex and wonderfully crafted Chardonnay that's long and flavorful on the finish. 19,000 cases made. • $55 Ⓐ • (04/30/96) SS • **95**
Chardonnay Napa Valley Private Reserve 1993 • $20 • (03/31/95) SS • **92**
Chardonnay Napa Valley Sbragia Limited Release 1996: A big, ripe, rich and intense style that's concentrated and full of exotic pear, fig, melon and toasty oak flavors. Remarkably complex, turning elegant and supple on the finish. Another tremendous Chardonnay from Beringer. Drink now through 2002. • $35 • (07/31/98) HR • **94**
Chardonnay Napa Valley Sbragia Limited Release 1995: A well-oaked style, with toasty buttery flavors, but also a core of nectarine, pear, hazelnut and fig flavors that are ripe, rich, focused and concentrated. Finishes with a long, rich aftertaste. Drink now through 2001. • $35 • (06/15/98) • **93**
Chardonnay Napa Valley Sbragia Limited Release 1994: A big, toasty style that supports its fruit with lots of oak flavors. The tiers of pear, fig, honey, melon and spice are rich and concentrated, leading to a tremendous aftertaste. 900 cases made. • $25 • (05/15/96) HR • **94**
Gamay California Beaujolais Nouveau 1997: Here's a light and appealing Gamay in the early-drinking Beaujolais Nouveau style, recommended for its effusion of berry flavors on a supple frame. From a reliable winery, it's of very good quality at an almost unheard-of low price. Drink now. • $7 • (02/28/98) BB • **85**
Gamay California Beaujolais Nouveau 1996: Light, refreshing and not as gaudy as most *nouveau*, this offers appealing flavors of grape and fresh currant. Drink soon. • $6 • (02/28/97) • **84**
Gamay California Beaujolais Nouveau 1995 • $7 • (02/29/96) • **81**
Gamay California Beaujolais Nouveau 1994 • $7 • (01/01/95) • **79**
Meritage Knights Valley 1992 • $13 • (11/15/95) • **87**
Meritage Knights Valley 1991 • $13 • (09/15/94) • **88**
Merlot Howell Mountain Bancroft Ranch 1994: Ruggedly tannic, with a core of strong, earthy currant flavors. Takes some time to work through the tannins, but there's lots to admire in this wine. Still, previous vintages have been suppler and more openly complex at this stage. Tasted three times, with consistent notes. • $45 • (04/30/98) • **89**
Merlot Howell Mountain Bancroft Ranch 1993: Serves up a complex core of earthy cherry, currant and chocolate and frames it with a toasty oak overlay. finishes with a burst of fruit and mineral before the tannins clamp down. Tasted twice with consistent notes. 9,000 cases made. • $29 • (08/31/96) • **89**
Merlot Howell Mountain Bancroft Ranch 1992 • $29 • (12/15/95) SS • **92**
Merlot Howell Mountain Bancroft Ranch 1991 • $29 • (05/31/94) CS • **90**
Merlot Howell Mountain Bancroft Ranch 1990 • $29 • (08/31/93) • **90**
Merlot Howell Mountain Bancroft Ranch 1989 • $29 • (05/31/92) • **91**
Merlot Howell Mountain Bancroft Ranch 1988 • $28 • (05/31/92) • **90**
Merlot Howell Mountain Bancroft Ranch 1987 • $29 • (12/31/90) • **91**
Pinot Noir Napa Valley Stanly Ranch 1994: Rich and flavorful, with ripe and supple black cherry, earth, toast, spice and cedar flavors that stay well focused and lively through the finish, which shows just a trace of tannin. Much better than previously reviewed. Drink now through 2002. 1,700 cases made. • $20 • (12/31/97) • **90**
Sauvignon Blanc-Sémillon Knights Valley Meritage 1994: Broad and buttery, a spicy wine with soft texture and nice hints of honey and pear on the finish. Not much says Sauvignon Blanc, but it's generous. Drink soon. • $9 • (08/31/97) • **87**
Sauvignon Blanc-Sémillon Meritage Knights Valley 1993 • $9 • (08/31/95) BB • **87**

Key: SS—Spectator Selection CS—Cellar Selection HR—Highly Recommended BB—Best Buy $NA—Price not available Ⓐ—Auction Price (BT)—Barrel Tasting
Dates in parentheses indicate the issues in which the ratings were published.

Sauvignon Blanc Napa Valley 1996: A classy, pretty white, with ripe fig, melon, grapefruit and spice flavors, and a hefty shot of oak that marries well with the silky texture. Simply delicious. An excellent value from one of California's most reliable wineries. • $9 • (01/31/98) BB • **90**
Sauvignon Blanc Napa Valley 1995: Bright and appealing for its smoothly textured nectarine and citrus flavors that float gently through the finish. • $10 • (04/30/97) • **87**
Sauvignon Blanc Napa Valley 1994: Soft, fruity and delicious with nectarine and melon flavors that linger in a creamy finish. 18,000 cases made. • $9 • (07/31/96) • **88**
Sauvignon Blanc Napa Valley 1993 • $8 • (08/31/95) • **84**
White Zinfandel California 1994 • $6 • (09/30/95) • **81**
Zinfandel Napa County 1989 • $8 • (10/15/92) • **85**
Zinfandel Napa Valley 1992 • $9 • (09/15/95) BB • **87**
Zinfandel Napa Valley 1991 • $7 • (08/31/94) BB • **86**
Zinfandel Napa Valley 1990 • $8 • (09/30/93) • **86**
Zinfandel North Coast 1994: Ripe, with a jam-accented blackberry, pepper and spicy berry notes. Shows a cedary oak edge and firm tannins. Drink now. • $12 • (08/31/97) • **87**
Zinfandel North Coast 1993: A rustic style with an earthy, metallic edge to the wild berry flavors. Finishes with a slight tarry note and dry tannins. • $10 • (02/28/97) • **82**
Zinfandel North Coast 1992 • $10 • (12/31/95) • **85**
Zinfandel North Coast 1988 • $8 • (02/29/92) BB • **85**
Zinfandel North Coast 1987 • $8 • (09/15/90) • **86**
Zinfandel North Coast 1985 • $6 • (04/30/88) BB • **87**
Zinfandel North Coast Appellation Collection 1995: Solid, with an attractive range of ripe plum, blackberry, cherry and spice, finishing with a light toasty oak flavor that adds dimension and depth. Drink now through 2002. • $12 • (06/15/98) • **88**

BERNARDUS | CALIFORNIA

Chardonnay Monterey County 1996: Distinct for its bright citrus and lemony flavors, it also offers touches of pear, spice, earth and oak, holding its focus while gaining a nuance of oak and hazelnut. Drink now through 2001. 35,500 cases made. • $18 • (06/30/98) SS • **91**
Chardonnay Monterey County 1995: A big, ripe Chardonnay, with an abundance of rich pear, citrus, oak and spice notes. Turns smooth and spicy on the finish, where the flavors fan out. 14,676 cases made. • $17 • (05/31/97) • **90**
Chardonnay Monterey County 1994: A bold, ripe and full-bodied white from California that offers lots of rich pear, spice, honey flavors, all presented with a light shading of hazelnut. This has a sense of elegance and grace that goes on through the finish. 22,000 cases made. • $15 • (05/15/96) SS • **90**
Chardonnay Monterey County 1993 • $15 • (06/30/95) • **87**
Marinus Carmel Valley 1994: Young, tight and well focused, with rich, complex flavors of spicy currant, cedar, leather, anise and berry at the core, it unfolds slowly to reveal some exotic spice and mineral notes. Given the level of intensity, it's best to cellar this one until 2000. 6,585 cases made. • $30 • (04/30/97) • **90**
Marinus Carmel Valley 1993: A new Bordeaux-style blend that's firm and intense, if a bit on the tannic side. Currant, cherry and anise flavors are well focused and well proportioned, and finish with dry tannins. Drink now. 2,200 cases made. • $24 • (08/31/96) • **85**
Pinot Noir Santa Barbara County Bien Nacido Vineyard 1995: Distinctly Santa Barbara Pinot Noir. Complex, elegant and earthy, with spicy cherry, wild berry, tea, herb and sage notes, it turns even more complex on the aftertaste. Beautifully crafted, silky and elegant. 284 cases made. • $35 • (01/31/98) • **91**
Pinot Noir Santa Barbara County Bien Nacido Vineyard 1993 • $25 • (01/31/96) • **86**
Pinot Noir Santa Barbara County Bien Nacido Vineyard 1992 • $18 • (02/28/95) • **86**
Pinot Noir Santa Maria Valley Bien Nacido Vineyard 1994: A ripe, complex style delivering layers of pretty cherry, herb, berry and spice flavors. Impressive for its smooth, fleshy texture and length. 1,216 cases made. • $30 • (11/30/96) • **90**
Sauvignon Blanc Monterey County 1996: A sharp, tangy style, with lots of grapefruit, lemon and herbs. It's a racy wine, but doesn't show the depth of past vintages. 4,339 cases made. • $14 • (11/30/97) • **87**
Sauvignon Blanc Monterey County 1995: Smooth, rich and buttery, a spicy wine with generous layers of pear, honey and exotic tropical fruit character sneaking in on the silky finish. Ready now. 2,100 cases made. • $12 • (02/28/97) • **90**

Sauvignon Blanc Monterey County 1994 • $10 • (12/31/95) BB • **90**
Sauvignon Blanc Monterey County 1993 • $9 • (02/28/95) BB • **87**

BETHEL HEIGHTS | OREGON

Chardonnay Willamette Valley 1994: Lean and a little green in flavor, with apple and delicately bitter spice notes echoing on the finish. Drinkable now. 1,200 cases made. • $12 • (03/31/96) • **82**
Gewürztraminer Willamette Valley 1994 • $7 • (03/31/96) • **79**
Gewürztraminer Willamette Valley 1993 • $7 • (11/30/94) • **82**
Pinot Gris Willamette Valley 1994 • $10 • (01/31/96) • **79**
Pinot Gris Willamette Valley 1993 • $10 • (10/31/94) • **83**
Pinot Noir Willamette Valley 1995: Crisp at first, but pretty blueberry, currant and slightly gamy flavors emerge as the wine warms up on the palate. Echoes of fruit and spice on the finish. Best through 1999. 2,000 cases made. • $17 • (04/30/97) • **87**
Pinot Noir Willamette Valley 1988 • $15 • (04/15/91) • **87**
Pinot Noir Willamette Valley 1987 • $12 • (02/15/90) • **86**
Pinot Noir Willamette Valley 1986 • $15 • (06/15/88) • **86**
Pinot Noir Willamette Valley 1985 • $12 • (02/15/90) • **86**
Pinot Noir Willamette Valley Eola Hills Cuvée 1996: Firm in texture, with edgy tannins. A beam of pretty berry flavor pokes through on the finish. Best from 1999. 650 cases made. • $12 • (05/15/98) • **85**
Pinot Noir Willamette Valley Estate Grown 1996: Light and appealing for its pretty, delicate plum and currant flavors, hinting at gaminess on the long, fragrant finish. Should be at its best after 1999. 2,300 cases made. • $20 • (05/15/98) • **87**
Pinot Noir Willamette Valley Estate Grown 1992 • $16 • (11/30/94) • **81**
Pinot Noir Willamette Valley Estate Grown 1991 • $15 • (06/30/93) • **89**
Pinot Noir Willamette Valley Estate Grown 1990 • $15 • (02/28/93) • **73**
Pinot Noir Willamette Valley Estate Grown First Release 1990 • $10 • (02/28/93) • **85**
Pinot Noir Willamette Valley Estate Grown Flat Block Reserve 1992 • $24 • (11/30/94) • **85**
Pinot Noir Willamette Valley Estate Grown Reserve 1990 • $24 • (02/28/93) • **81**
Pinot Noir Willamette Valley Estate Grown Southeast Block Reserve 1992 • $24 • (11/30/94) • **82**
Pinot Noir Willamette Valley First Release 1994 • $10 • (01/31/96) • **85**
Pinot Noir Willamette Valley Flat Block Reserve 1993 • $24 • (01/31/96) • **83**
Pinot Noir Willamette Valley Flat Rock 1991 • $18 • (09/30/93) • **78**
Pinot Noir Willamette Valley Reserve 1988 • $18 • (04/15/91) • **86**
Pinot Noir Willamette Valley Southeast Block Reserve 1995: Smooth and supple, with pretty plum and spice flavors on a modest scale. Drink now. 400 cases made. • $24 • (12/31/97) • **87**
Pinot Noir Willamette Valley Southeast Block Reserve 1993 • $24 • (01/31/96) • **79**
Pinot Noir Willamette Valley Southeast Block Reserve 1991 • $22 • (09/30/93) • **81**
Pinot Noir Willamette Valley Wädenswil Block Reserve 1995: A crisp Pinot Noir with a raw edge to the berry and earthy flavors, this feels very tight and unyielding. Try in 1999. 396 cases made. • $24 • (12/31/97) • **81**

BETTINELLI | CALIFORNIA

Cabernet Sauvignon Napa Valley 1991 • $14 • (05/31/95) • **82**
Chardonnay Napa Valley 1993 • $12 • (05/15/96) • **82**
Merlot Napa Valley 1993 • $25 • (03/31/96) • **88**

BIALE, ROBERT | CALIFORNIA

Petite Sirah Napa Valley Old Vineyards 1995: Avoids being overly tannic as too many Petite Sirahs are, managing to deliver some tasty plum, cherry, floral and wild berry flavors. Yes, it's tannic, but it's got lots of fruit too. Best after 1999. 225 cases made. • $35 • (04/30/98) • **85**
Zinfandel Napa Valley Aldo's Vineyard Proprietor's Series 1994 • $19 • (05/15/96) HR • **93**
Zinfandel Napa Valley Aldo's Vineyard Proprietor's Series 1993 • $18 • (10/15/95) HR • **91**
Zinfandel Napa Valley Aldo's Vineyard Proprietor's Series 1992 • $14 • (10/15/94) • **84**
Zinfandel Napa Valley Aldo's Vineyard Proprietor's Series 1991 • $15 • (09/30/93) • **86**
Zinfandel Napa Valley Falleri Vineyards 1995: Hints of cedar and smoky oak around a core of herb, sage, cherry and anise flavors. Well-balanced. Drinkable now. 50 cases made. • $26 • (03/31/97) • **88**
Zinfandel Napa Valley Old Crane Ranch 1995: Elegant and delicate, with an appealing core of plum and cherry flavors that turns simple on the finish. Will best please those who like their Zins understated. Ready now. 710 cases made. • $24 • (03/31/97) • **85**
Zinfandel Napa Valley Old Vineyards Late Picked 1995: Brimming with ripe, juicy Zinfandel character, it's definitely sweet, but quite enjoyable for its cherry and berry flavors. Ready now. (Features 1 percent residual sugar and 17.5 percent alcohol.) 388 cases made. • $30 • (03/31/97) • **88**
Zinfandel Napa Valley Two Vineyards 1995: Smooth and elegant. Has a supple core of plum, wild berry and cherry flavors, turning soft and fleshy on the finish where the fruit flavors shine through. Ready now. 719 cases made. • $24 • (03/31/97) • **88**

BIDWELL | NEW YORK

Cabernet Sauvignon North Fork of Long Island 1988 • $12 • (06/30/91) • **82**
Cabernet Sauvignon North Fork of Long Island 1987 • $12 • (06/30/91) • **81**
Merlot North Fork of Long Island 1988 • $11 • (06/30/91) • **85**
Merlot North Fork of Long Island Reserve 1987 • $16 • (03/31/90) • **83**

BILTMORE ESTATE | NORTH CAROLINA

Brut Blanc de Blancs North Carolina NV: A powerful, assertive bottle of bubbly that has a firm, almost coarse texture and strong fruit flavors. Good but unusual. 3,000 cases made. • $17 • (08/31/97) • **80**
Cabernet Sauvignon America 1987 • $16 • (02/29/92) • **84**
Cabernet Sauvignon North Carolina 1993: A straightforward wine with black cherry, currant and pepper flavors. Good, but lacks intensity. Finishes with a touch of spice. 2,100 cases made. • $13 • (12/31/95) • **81**
Cabernet Sauvignon North Carolina 1987 • $16 • (02/29/92) • **76**
Cabernet Sauvignon North Carolina Chateau Biltmore 1993: Austere and tannic, with vegetal flavors and aromas. Very tightly wound, with only modest cherry and plum flavors to back it up. 1,000 cases made. • $20 • (12/31/95) • **79**
Cabernet Sauvignon North Carolina George Washington Vanderbilt Centennial Release 1992 • $25 • (12/31/95) • **83**
Chardonnay North Carolina Cheateau Biltmore 1994: Aggressively oaked, this rich white lacks balance but features toast, coffee and earth aromas and flavors and appley pear accents. 2,000 cases made. • $13 • (10/15/95) • **79**
Chardonnay North Carolina Sur Lies 1993 • $9 • (10/15/95) • **81**
Claret North Carolina 1995: Smoky, herbal notes add dimension to the cherry flavors in this soft, easy-drinking red. The finish is abrupt, slightly astringent. 700 cases made. • $20 • (08/31/97) • **82**
Claret North Carolina George Washington Vanderbilt Centennial Release 1993: Pleasant and flavorful, with good cherry, chocolate and spice components. It is well balanced and has a decent finish. Drinkable now. 584 cases made. • $30 • (12/31/95) • **83**
Johannisberg Riesling North Carolina Cheateau Biltmore 1993 • $10 • (01/31/96) • **73**
Sparkling North Carolina George Washington Vanderbilt Centennial Release 1990 • $35 • (12/15/95) • **81**
White Zinfandel North Carolina American Zinfandel Blanc de Noir 1994 • $6 • (09/15/95) • **83**

BLACK MOUNTAIN | CALIFORNIA

Cabernet Sauvignon Alexander Valley Fat Cat 1990 • $18 • (06/15/93) • **80**
Cabernet Sauvignon Alexander Valley Fat Cat 1988 • $18 • (11/15/92) • **85**
Cabernet Sauvignon Alexander Valley Fat Cat 1986 • $20 • (11/15/91) • **86**
Cabernet Sauvignon Alexander Valley Fat Cat 1985 • $18 • (04/30/90) • **87**
Petite Sirah Alexander Valley Bosun Crest 1990 • $10 • (06/15/93) • **77**
Petite Sirah Alexander Valley Bosun Crest 1987 • $8 • (10/31/91) BB • **87**
Petite Sirah Alexander Valley Bosun Crest 1986 • $8 • (10/31/91) • **67**
Petite Sirah Alexander Valley Bosun Crest 1985 • $9 • (02/15/89) • **81**
Zinfandel Alexander Valley Cramer Ridge 1990 • $10 • (05/31/93) • **78**
Zinfandel Alexander Valley Cramer Ridge 1987 • $10 • (09/30/91) • **77**
Zinfandel Alexander Valley Cramer Ridge 1986 • $9 • (03/31/90) • **82**

BLACK ROCK | CALIFORNIA

Zinfandel Lake County 1996: Rich, charred toast and vanilla flavors last through the tannic finish. Where's the fruit? Drink now. 210 cases made. • $15 • (06/15/98) • **78**

BLACK SHEEP | CALIFORNIA

Zinfandel Sierra Foothills 1995: Firm and chewy, with a raspy edge to the texture and a small bead of ripe berry flavor peeking through. Best in 2000. 1,700 cases made. • $12 • (03/31/98) • **85**

BLACKSTONE | CALIFORNIA

Chardonnay California 1995: Light, but a musty note colors its modest apple and mineral flavors. 12,500 cases made. • $11 • (12/15/96) • **80**
Chardonnay Monterey County Grand Reserve 1994: Soft and generous with its citrus and melon flavors that lose just a bit of focus on the finish. Drinkable now. 15,000 cases made. • $10 • (06/15/96) • **82**
Chardonnay Monterey County Reserve 1993 • $8 • (07/31/95) • **79**
Merlot California 1995: Serves up a modest array of ripe plum and cherry flavors, turning simple on the finish. 30,000 cases made. • $11 • (11/30/96) • **81**
Merlot California Barrel Reserve 1994: Simple, with diluted earthy and berry flavors. Lacks depth and concentration. 18,000 cases made. • $10 • (08/31/96) • **77**
Merlot Napa County Grand Reserve 1994: A nice range of Merlot flavors but is unbalanced by a charred, slightly bitter and vegetal edge. 12,000 cases made. • $14 • (08/31/96) • **77**
Merlot Napa County Reserve 1993 • $10 • (04/30/96) BB • **89**
Merlot Sonoma County Grand Reserve 1994: An unusual melange of raspberry, cherry and green olive flavors, this wine is fairly soft and silky upfront. The oak is a bit aggressive, but the ensemble is sound. 6,000 cases made. • $18 • (07/31/97) • **87**
Pinot Noir Santa Barbara County 1990 • $8 • (02/28/93) • **81**
Zinfandel California Old Vine Cuvée 1994: On solid footing, offering a modest band of spice, berry and cherry flavors. 5,000 cases made. • $12 • (11/30/96) • **81**

BLAKE | CALIFORNIA

Chardonnay Napa Valley 1995: Emphasizes apple and pear character up front, with a thread of spicy oak flavor sneaking in on the soft finish. Ready now. 1,900 cases made. • $20 • (12/15/97) • **84**
Sauvignon Blanc Napa Valley 1995: Lemon-lime and herb notes are up front in this lively, harmonious blend of honey, melon and plums. Finishes with the right touch of grassiness. 2,800 cases made. • $16 • (10/15/97) • **89**

BLOCKHEADIA RINGNOSII | CALIFORNIA

Petite Sirah Napa Valley 1994: Smooth, ripe and juicy, with lots of berry and cherry flavors, balanced tannins. The blend includes Carignane, Alicante, Grenache and Zinfandel, giving it a supple, velvety texture for a wine that's mostly Petite Sirah. Drinkable now to 2002. 140 cases made. • $25 • (05/15/97) • **88**
Zinfandel Napa Valley 1994: Classic Napa Valley Zinfandel mostly from 100-year-old vines, this is ripe and juicy, shows zesty cherry and raspberry flavors and has a firm tannic edge on the anise- and tar-accented finish. 590 cases made. • $20 • (05/15/97) • **90**
Zinfandel Rutherford 1993 • $15 • (10/15/95) • **85**
Zinfandel Rutherford 1992 • $15 • (02/28/95) • **88**

BLOSSOM HILL | CALIFORNIA

Cabernet Sauvignon California 1993: Solid, if unexciting, with a modest range of spicy cherry and berry flavors. • $5 • (12/15/96) • **78**
Chardonnay California 1996: Simple and soft, with light, floral and earthy citrus flavors and a touch of celery. Drink now. 500 cases made. • $5 • (07/31/98) • **78**
Chardonnay California 1995: Light and tart, with flavors reminiscent of canned fruit cocktail. • $5 • (11/30/96) • **79**
Merlot California 1994: Soft, almost sweet, with candied berry flavors and a hint of tannin on the finish. • $6 • (11/30/96) • **77**
Sauvignon Blanc California 1994: Vegetal, peppery flavors overshadow the modest fruit in this soft-finishing white. • $4 • (11/30/96) • **79**

Key: SS—Spectator Selection CS—Cellar Selection HR—Highly Recommended BB—Best Buy $NA—Price not available Ⓐ—Auction Price (BT)—Barrel Tasting
Dates in parentheses indicate the issues in which the ratings were published.

Symphony California 1995: Soft and fragrant, delivering a nice mouthful of fresh peach and pear flavors and finishing gently, with a light floral note. • $5 • (11/30/96) • **84**

BOCAGE | CALIFORNIA

Cabernet Sauvignon Monterey Proprietor's Cuvée 1990 • $10 • (11/15/94) • **70**
Merlot Monterey Proprietor's Cuvée 1990 • $10 • (09/15/94) • **84**
Merlot Monterey Proprietor's Cuvée 1989 • $10 • (10/31/92) • **74**

BOEGER | CALIFORNIA

Barbera El Dorado 1995: Earthy, gamy flavors predominate in this smooth, gentle red, with a touch of plum sneaking in on the finish. Not as rich as previous vintages. Ready now. 1,750 cases made. • $14 • (11/30/97) • **84**
Barbera El Dorado 1993 • $12 • (11/15/95) • **86**
Barbera El Dorado 1992 • $12 • (07/31/95) • **84**
Barbera El Dorado 1991 • $11 • (10/31/93) • **84**
Barbera El Dorado 1990 • $11 • (11/30/92) • **81**
Barbera El Dorado 1989 • $10 • (10/31/91) • **85**
Barbera El Dorado Vineyard Select 1994: A Barbera built for the cellar, or hearty food, this offers anise-scented black cherry flavors and a firm texture. Best from 1999. 500 cases made. • $15 • (07/31/97) • **87**
Cabernet Sauvignon El Dorado 1994: Some earth, herb and cedar notes blend nicely with the plum, black cherry and spice flavors. Full-bodied, with a firm tannic backbone, it's drinking well now. 1,430 cases made. • $12 • (10/15/97) • **85**
Cabernet Sauvignon El Dorado 1993: An earthy, cheesy, rustic quality overshadows the cassis and blackberry flavors timidly hiding in the background. Some merit, however. 1,600 cases made. • $12 • (09/30/97) • **80**
Cabernet Sauvignon El Dorado 1991 • $12 • (12/15/95) • **78**
Cabernet Sauvignon El Dorado 1990 • $12 • (11/15/94) • **83**
Cabernet Sauvignon El Dorado 1989 • $12 • (11/15/92) • **83**
Cabernet Sauvignon El Dorado 1987 • $11 • (03/15/91) • **85**
Cabernet Sauvignon El Dorado 1985 • $11 • (02/15/89) • **77**
Cabernet Sauvignon El Dorado 1984 • $11 • (05/31/88) • **81**
Cabernet Sauvignon El Dorado 1983 • $10 • (08/31/87) • **82**
Cabernet Sauvignon El Dorado 1980 • $8 • (04/16/84) • **76**
Cabernet Sauvignon Napa Valley Joseph A. Nichelini Vineyards 1989 • $12 • (11/15/93) • **77**
Chardonnay El Dorado 1996: A pear and spice core runs through, with a healthy dose of oak on the finish. Drink now. 1,120 cases made. • $12 • (07/31/98) • **83**
Chardonnay El Dorado 1995: Simple and bright, this offers fresh pear and vanilla flavors, youthful and straightforward. Ready to drink. 750 cases made. • $12 • (12/31/96) • **85**
Hangtown Red California 1988 • $5 • (08/31/90) • **78**
Hangtown Red California 1987 • $5 • (02/28/90) BB • **82**
Hangtown Red California 1985 • $5 • (12/31/88) • **73**
Hangtown Red California 1984 • $4 • (01/31/88) • **77**
Hangtown Red California 1983 • $4 • (06/30/87) • **71**
Hangtown Red Lot No. 16 California NV • $5 • (10/31/91) BB • **80**
Majeure Reserve El Dorado 1994: An intriguing bouquet of coffee, tea and herbs. On the palate, this medium-bodied wine offers up bright wild cherry, currant and menthol flavors. A blend of 72 percent Syrah and 28 percent Grenache. 185 cases made. • $15 • (09/30/97) • **87**
Meritage El Dorado 1993: Marked by fresh, fruity blackberry and currant notes, velvety tannins and a zippy, bright finish. Drinking well now but should age nicely, too. A blend of 44 percent Cabernet Sauvignon, 42 percent Cabernet Franc, and 14 percent Merlot. 1,050 cases made. • $15 • (10/15/97) • **87**
Meritage El Dorado 1992 • $15 • (03/31/96) • **77**
Meritage El Dorado 1991 • $15 • (12/15/95) • **86**
Meritage El Dorado 1989 • $14 • (10/15/92) • **83**
Meritage El Dorado Reserve 1994: A little beefy and framed by an herbal component, this also serves up plum, anise and licorice flavors. Brick-color and soft tannins show plenty of bottle evolution. Drink now. 975 cases made. • $15 • (07/31/98) • **84**
Merlot El Dorado 1995: A solid red, with anise-tinged black cherry and toast flavors that prickle just a bit on the finish. Best from 1999. 1,275 cases made. • $15 • (11/30/97) • **83**
Merlot El Dorado 1994: Soft, simple and vaguely cedary to go along with the ripe black cherry flavor, finishing with coarse tannins. Drink sooner rather than later. 1,360 cases made. • $15 • (11/30/96) • **80**

Merlot El Dorado 1993: Solid, though somewhat lacking in finesse and polish on the finish where the currant, tar and cedary oak flavors turn dry, vegatal and a bit rustic. 1,250 cases made. • $13 • (08/31/96) • **82**
Merlot El Dorado 1991 • $13 • (10/15/93) • **86**
Merlot El Dorado 1990 • $13 • (01/31/93) • **78**
Merlot El Dorado 1988 • $13 • (03/31/91) • **78**
Merlot El Dorado 1987 • $13 • (07/15/90) • **81**
Merlot El Dorado 1986 • $13 • (01/31/89) • **73**
Merlot El Dorado 1985 • $13 • (02/15/88) • **82**
Merlot El Dorado 1982 • $10 • (10/01/84) • **74**
Merlot El Dorado Estate Bottled 1992 • $14 • (03/31/95) • **86**
Migliόre Reserve El Dorado 1995: Light in texture, with earthy, spicy flavors that linger. A blend of Barbera, Refosco, Mataro, Grenache, Zinfandel, Nebbiolo, Sangiovese, and Petite Sirah. Drink now. 925 cases made. • $15 • (07/31/98) • **80**
Migliόre Reserve El Dorado 1994: Distinctive for its bay leaf- and spice-accented ripe blackberry and beet flavors, fairly thick and concentrated. Firm and chewy. Try in 1999. 750 cases made. • $14 • (02/28/97) • **87**
Migliόre Reserve El Dorado 1993 • $14 • (11/30/95) • **85**
Sauvignon Blanc El Dorado 1997: Very bright, with a searing core of grapefruit followed by lemon-lime. In spite of its acidity, the texture is fairly broad and creamy on the palate. Good price. 1,500 cases made. • $10 • (04/30/98) • **88**
Sauvignon Blanc El Dorado 1996: A well-balanced style, its ripe melon, honey and fig flavors offset by crisp acidity and notes of mineral and citrus. Lively, fresh and enjoyable, it's a terrific value, too. From California. 1,520 cases made. • $8 • (06/30/97) BB • **89**
Sauvignon Blanc El Dorado 1995: Crisp and flavorful; a zippy wine with focused grapefruit and apple flavors at the core. 1,095 cases made. • $8 • (07/31/96) • **87**
Sauvignon Blanc El Dorado 1993 • $8 • (01/31/95) • **83**
Zinfandel El Dorado 1995: Modest earthy berry, sage, cedar and spice mark this simple, one-dimensional effort. Drink now. 900 cases made. • $12 • (06/15/98) • **81**
Zinfandel El Dorado 1994: A well-focused Zin, supple and harmonious, with earthy plum and black cherry flavors at the center, accented by notes of berry and raspberry. Ready to drink. 925 cases made. • $10 • (04/30/97) • **88**
Zinfandel El Dorado 1993 • $10 • (03/31/96) • **76**
Zinfandel El Dorado 1992 • $10 • (10/15/94) • **84**
Zinfandel El Dorado Walker Vineyard 1995: Offers a complex interplay of earthy raspberry, cherry and spice, picking up a minty note on the finish where the flavors fan out nicely. Drink now through 2002. 1,850 cases made. • $15 • (05/15/98) • **88**
Zinfandel El Dorado Walker Vineyard 1994: Shows off a smoky, meaty edge that's nicely balanced by ripe plum and cherry flavors. Ready now. 1,240 cases made. • $12 • (03/31/97) • **88**
Zinfandel El Dorado Walker Vineyard 1993 • $12 • (10/15/95) • **85**
Zinfandel El Dorado Walker Vineyard 1992 • $12 • (10/15/94) • **87**
Zinfandel El Dorado Walker Vineyard 1991 • $10 • (09/30/93) • **87**
Zinfandel El Dorado Walker Vineyard 1990 • $10 • (10/15/92) HR • **90**
Zinfandel El Dorado Walker Vineyard 1989 • $9 • (09/30/91) • **84**
Zinfandel El Dorado Walker Vineyard 1988 • $8 • (02/15/91) • **85**
Zinfandel El Dorado Walker Vineyard 1987 • $8 • (03/31/90) • **86**
Zinfandel El Dorado Walker Vineyard 1986 • $7 • (07/31/88) • **73**
Zinfandel El Dorado Walker Vineyard 1981 • $6 • (07/16/85) • **76**
Zinfandel Napa Valley Joseph A. Nichelini Vineyards 1993: Ripe and spicy, with smoke and prune tints to the cherry and raspberry flavors. Supple and harmonious, it's drinkable now. 687 cases made. • $12 • (04/30/97) • **87**
Zinfandel Napa Valley Joseph A. Nichelini Vineyards 1990 • $10 • (04/30/93) • **81**
Zinfandel Napa Valley Joseph A. Nichelini Vineyards 1989 • $12 • (10/15/92) • **80**
Zinfandel Napa Valley Joseph A. Nichelini Vineyards 1988 • $12 • (08/31/91) • **85**

BOGLE | CALIFORNIA

Cabernet Sauvignon California 1995: A beefy, oaky medley. Finishes short with touches of tea and tar. 18,000 cases made. • $8 • (12/15/97) • **78**
Cabernet Sauvignon California 1994: Well oaked, bringing a minty, peppery accent. Offers enough ripe berry flavors to give it depth and complexity. 9,000 cases made. • $7 • (11/30/96) • **84**
Cabernet Sauvignon California 1993: Good flavor for the price. Simple and nicely focused currant and blackberry flavors echo nicely on the finish. Drinkable now. 7,000 cases made. • $6 • (11/30/95) BB • **85**
Cabernet Sauvignon California 1992 • $6 • (05/15/94) • **81**
Cabernet Sauvignon California 1990 • $6 • (11/15/92) BB • **83**
Cabernet Sauvignon California 1989 • $7/1.(11/15/92) • **77**
Chardonnay California 1996: Fresh and spicy, with melon and vanilla notes adding interest. Finishes with some solid flavor. 22,000 cases made. • $7 • (11/30/97) • **84**
Chardonnay California 1995: Lacks varietal character, leaving the palate on hold. Tangy yet innocuous. 25,000 cases made. • $7 • (07/31/97) • **79**
Chardonnay California 1993 • $6 • (01/31/95) BB • **82**
Chardonnay California Barrel Fermented Cuvée 1994: A touch earthy, with hints of pineapple and citrus. Also marked by a lightly tinny character. • $6 • (03/31/96) • **81**
Chardonnay California Reserve 1993 • $12 • (05/15/96) • **84**
Chenin Blanc Clarksburg 1996: Peaches-and-cream character starts this off on a good tack, but the finish is somewhat cloying. 300 cases made. • $7 • (09/15/97) • **83**
Chenin Blanc Clarksburg 1993 • $6 • (10/15/95) • **84**
Fumé Blanc California 1996: Fairly mild-mannered. Light citrus and grass flavors are the hallmarks, the finish is clean and bright. 7,000 cases made. • $6 • (07/31/97) • **82**
Fumé Blanc California 1995: A generous portion of pear, apple and honeysuckle flavors that follow through to the finish. Packs a lot of style into a low-cost package. 8,000 cases made. • $6 • (07/31/96) BB • **85**
Fumé Blanc California 1994 • $5 • (05/15/96) BB • **86**
Fumé Blanc Lake County Dry 1993 • $5 • (04/30/95) • **83**
Merlot California 1996: A blend of oak, plum, cherry, smoke and spice flavors. Somewhat cloying on the finish, it tastes a bit manufactured, but is still pleasant. Drink now. 50,000 cases made. • $9 • (07/31/98) • **81**
Merlot California 1995: Herbal, cedary notes come to the fore, with moderate body. Finishes with a licorice accent. 40,000 cases made. • $9 • (07/31/97) • **83**
Merlot California 1994: Earthy and gamy, with strong minty-herbal flavors. Tasted twice with consistent notes. 24,000 cases made. • $9 • (08/31/96) • **72**
Merlot California 1992 • $8 • (09/15/94) BB • **83**
Merlot California 1991 • $8 • (07/15/93) BB • **85**
Merlot California 1990 • $8 • (05/31/92) • **82**
Petite Sirah California 1995: Dense and spicy. A chewy wine with ripe black cherry and black pepper flavors poking through the tannins. Best from 2000 or 2001. 13,000 cases made. • $9 • (03/31/98) BB • **85**
Petite Sirah California 1994: An oaky style, with a odd caramel accent that dominates the fruit flavors beneath. 12,000 cases made. • $8 • (11/30/96) • **78**
Petite Sirah California 1993 • $7 • (11/15/95) BB • **86**
Petite Sirah California 1992 • $7 • (02/28/95) BB • **85**
Petite Sirah California 1991 • $6 • (07/31/93) BB • **88**
Petite Sirah Clarksburg 1988 • $7 • (10/31/89) • **70**
White Zinfandel California 1994 • $5 • (09/15/95) • **76**
Zinfandel California 1993 • $6 • (10/15/95) • **83**
Zinfandel California 1992 • $6 • (05/15/95) • **84**
Zinfandel California Old Vine Cuvée 1995: Bright in flavor but crisp and chewy in texture, with gritty tannins standing in the way of the lean, berryish flavors. Best after 1999 or 2000. 600 cases made. • $11 • (03/31/98) • **82**
Zinfandel California Old Vine Cuvée 1994: Smooth and polished, with a smoky, tarry edge to its cherry and wild berry flavors. Lively aftertaste. Drinks well now. 3,000 cases made. • $9 • (02/28/97) • **87**
Zinfandel California Old Vine Reserve 1994: A big, robust style, blending ripe plum and prune flavors with spicy, tarry notes. Firmly tannic, with a dry aftertaste. Best to drink soon, but let it breathe. 300 cases made. • $18 • (05/15/98) • **84**

BOISSET | CALIFORNIA

Cabernet Sauvignon Napa Valley 1984 • $7 • (12/31/87) • **72**
Cabernet Sauvignon Napa Valley 1981 • $9 • (05/01/85) • **80**
Cabernet Sauvignon Sonoma County 1990 • $15 • (11/15/94) • **70**
Merlot Sonoma County 1991 • $15 • (09/15/94) • **82**

BON MARCHE | CALIFORNIA

Cabernet Sauvignon Alexander Valley 1989 • $8 • (02/28/91) BB • **87**
Cabernet Sauvignon Napa Valley 1992 • $8 • (03/31/94) • **82**
Cabernet Sauvignon Sonoma County 1991 • $7 • (03/31/93) BB • **84**
Pinot Noir Napa Valley 1990 • $7 • (11/15/91) • **79**
Pinot Noir Sonoma County 1991 • $8 • (12/31/92) BB • **86**

BONNY DOON | CALIFORNIA

Ca' Del Solo Il Fiasco California 1995: Distinctive for its tight, tart blueberry and wild berry flavors, this is a compact and narrowly focused wine, young and tannic. Drinkable now. 2,000 cases made. • $15 • (12/31/96) • **86**
Cabernet Franc California Pacific Rim 1994 • $10 • (11/30/95) • **83**
Chenin Blanc California Pacific Rim 1994 • $8 • (10/15/95) • **84**
Chenin Blanc California Pacific Rim 1993 • $8 • (05/31/95) • **78**
Framboise Santa Cruz Mountains NV • $9/375ml • (07/31/95) • **90**
Garnacha California NV: Looks and tastes like a liquified, sour strawberry candy—unusual for a wine but certainly an interesting effort. 395 cases made. • $12 • (12/15/96) • **85**
Gewürztraminer Monterey County Pacific Rim 1996: Soft, and nicely polished to show off its beautifully knit pear, litchi and almond flavors, it hints at citrus and rose petal on the finish. Delicious now. 1,200 cases made. • $12 • (11/30/97) • **88**
Gewürztraminer Monterey County Pacific Rim 1995: Simple and refreshing for its properly spicy, floral flavors, and its dry finish. 900 cases made. • $12 • (07/31/96) • **83**
Gewüztraminer Vin de Glacière Oregon 1990 • $15/375ml • (03/31/92) • **90**
Grahm Crew Vin Rouge California 1989 • $7 • (10/31/90) BB • **82**
Grahm Crew Vin Rouge California 1988 • $7 • (02/15/90) • **83**
Grahm Crew Vin Rouge California 1987 • $8 • (11/30/88) • **85**
Grahm Crew Vin Rouge California 1985 • $6 • (09/30/87) BB • **80**
Grenache America Clos de Gilroy Cuvée St. Marcel NV: Snappy, crushed pepper, cherry and wild berry flavors in a fresh and lively, nouveau style. 3,764 cases made. • $8 • (08/31/96) • **84**
Grenache California Clos de Gilroy 1994 • $8 • (11/15/95) BB • **87**
Grenache California Clos de Gilroy 1993 • $8 • (04/15/94) BB • **87**
Grenache California Clos de Gilroy 1992 • $8 • (02/15/93) • **84**
Grenache California Clos de Gilroy 1991 • $8 • (07/31/92) • **84**
Grenache California Clos de Gilroy 1990 • $8 • (02/15/91) BB • **87**
Grenache California Clos de Gilroy 1989 • $7 • (02/15/90) BB • **88**
Grenache California Clos de Gilroy 1988 • $6 • (02/15/89) BB • **85**
Grenache California Clos de Gilroy 1987 • $6 • (02/29/88) BB • **87**
Grenache California Clos de Gilroy 1986 • $6 • (04/30/87) • **84**
Grenache Late Harvest California Vin de Glacière 1987 • $15/375ml • (12/31/88) • **90**
Le Cigare Volant California 1995: Smooth and spicy, showing cherry and wild berry flavors before working into dry, leathery tannins that emerge on the finish. 3,000 cases made. • $23 • (11/30/97) • **88**
Le Cigare Volant California 1994: Delivers lots of ripe, juicy plum and cherry flavors with zesty spice and leather accents. Turns elegant and complex on the finish, making it appealing to drink now. 5,475 cases made. • $20 • (03/31/97) • **87**
Le Cigare Volant California 1993 • $20 • (10/15/95) • **85**
Le Cigare Volant California 1990 • $18 • (11/30/92) • **87**
Le Cigare Volant California 1989 • $22 Ⓐ • (03/15/92) • **80**
Le Cigare Volant California 1988 • $17 Ⓐ • (12/31/90) • **86**
Le Cigare Volant California 1987 • $28 Ⓐ • (12/15/89) • **85**
Le Cigare Volant California 1986 • $34 Ⓐ • (11/15/88) • **92**
Le Cigare Volant California 1985 • $13 • (01/31/88) • **90**
Le Cigare Volant California 1984 • $11 • (08/31/86) • **87**
Le Gaucher California 1992 • $12 • (03/31/94) • **82**
Le Meunier California Blanc de Meunier 1994 • $15 • (03/31/96) • **88**
Le Sophiste Santa Cruz Mountains 1993 • $25 • (05/15/95) • **87**
Malvasia Bianca Monterey Vin de Glacière 1991 • $15 • (12/15/92) • **85**
Mourvèdre California Old Telegram 1995: Appealing for its core of blackberry, mineral, tar and spice flavors. Finishes with dry, fairly rugged tannins, but this tightly focused red serves up lots of flavor. Drink after 1999. 1,000 cases made. • $30 • (11/30/97) • **89**
Mourvèdre California Old Telegram 1993 • $20 • (12/15/95) • **83**
Mourvèdre California Old Telegram 1991 • $20 • (03/31/94) • **81**
Mourvèdre California Old Telegram 1990 • $20 • (02/15/93) • **84**
Mourvèdre California Old Telegram 1988 • $20 • (12/31/90) • **85**
Mourvèdre California Old Telegram 1986 • $14 • (11/15/88) • **90**
Muscat California Vin de Glacière 1996: Seductive, sweet and silky, remarkable for the purity of its spicy pear, apricot and citrus flavors, hinting at litchi on the slick finish. Utterly delicious now. Why wait? 13,500 cases made. • $15/375ml • (10/31/97) • **93**

Key: SS—Spectator Selection CS—Cellar Selection HR—Highly Recommended BB—Best Buy $NA—Price not available Ⓐ—Auction Price (BT)—Barrel Tasting
Dates in parentheses indicate the issues in which the ratings were published.

Muscat California Vin de Glacière 1995: Sweet and incredibly juicy. The lively mouthful of pineapple, spice and cream flavors dance enthusiastically with juicy acidity. Delicious. Drink now. 5,425 cases made. • $15 • (12/15/96) • **92**
Muscat Canelli Late Harvest California Vin de Glacière 1994 • $15/375ml • (09/30/95) HR • **94**
Muscat Canelli Late Harvest California Vin de Glacière 1990 • $15/375ml • (03/31/92) • **91**
Muscat Canelli Late Harvest California Vin de Glacière 1987 • $15/375ml • (12/31/88) • **91**
Muscat Canelli Late Harvest Monterey Vin de Glacière 1993 • $15 • (04/15/95) • **82**
Muscat Canelli Late Harvest Monterey Vin de Glacière 1992 • $15/375ml • (11/15/93) HR • **92**
Nectarine Eau de Vie Santa Cruz Mountains NV: Plush and velvety on the palate, this displays an almost toasty quality highlighted by a lemony essence. 258 cases made. • $18/375ml • (09/15/97) • **88**
Orange Muscat Late Harvest Monterey Vin de Glacière 1993 • $15 • (04/15/95) • **83**
Paire Eau-de-Vie Santa Cruz Mountains NV: An intriguing black cherry quality precedes a pear and fire-water kick. Despite the heat, it finishes delicately with a lovely floral, especially violet, note. 346 cases made. • $18/375ml • (09/15/97) • **91**
Pear Eau-de-vie Washington Poire NV • $18/375ml • (03/31/92) • **90**
Pinot Meunier California 1991 • $15 • (12/31/93) • **87**
Pinot Noir California 1994: Ripe and spicy, with dried cherry, plum and wild berry flavors. Turns simpler on the finish, but the flavors linger. 910 cases made. • $20 • (08/31/96) • **87**
Pinot Noir Oregon Bethel Heights Vineyard 1985 • $18 • (06/15/88) • **90**
Pinot Noir Oregon Temperance Hill Vineyard 1985 • $18 • (06/15/88) • **88**
Riesling California Pacific Rim 1994 • $8 • (09/15/95) BB • **88**
Riesling California Pacific Rim 1993 • $8 • (02/28/95) • **85**
Sauvignon Blanc Monterey County Pacific Rim 1995: A light, airy style, with modest nectarine flavor and herbal notes. 1,200 cases made. • $9 • (07/31/96) • **83**
Sparkling Pinot Meunier California Le Canard Froid 1993 • $9 • (12/31/94) • **83**
Syrah Santa Cruz Mountains 1994: Dark, ripe and peppery. This offers lots of flavors-exotic wild berry, spice, leather, cedar and anise, and finishes with a smoky accent. Drinkable now. 370 cases made. • $30 • (11/30/96) • **88**
Syrah Santa Cruz Mountains 1988 • $25 • (02/15/91) • **88**
Vin Gris de Cigare California 1995: Intense for a rosé, with snappy cherry, strawberry and watermelon flavors. Altogether pleasing for a hot summer night. 3,300 cases made. • $8 • (09/15/96) • **86**
Vin Gris de Cigare California 1993 • $8 • (12/31/94) BB • **86**
Vin Gris de Cigare California Pink Wine 1994 • $7 • (09/15/95) • **82**
Zinfandel California Cardinal Zin 1996: Well balanced, of medium weight, with ripe blackberry, black cherry and spice. Firm tannins on the finish. Drink now through 2002. 7,500 cases made. • $15 • (06/15/98) • **87**
Zinfandel California Cardinal Zin 1995: Ripe and fleshy, with a solid core of currant, wild berry, cherry and plum notes. Serves up a full range of flavors, while the tannins stay soft and smooth. Ready to drink. 3,800 cases made. • $15 • (03/31/97) • **87**

BONTERRA | CALIFORNIA

Cabernet Sauvignon Mendocino County 1993: A modest wine that strikes a nice balance between its ripe currant and cherry flavors and correct tannins. Drinkable now. 13,000 cases made. • $12 • (03/31/96) • **81**
Cabernet Sauvignon North Coast 1995: An oak-driven wine, with cedar and vanilla dominating. In the background are pleasant, simple cherry and raspberry notes. • $13 • (09/30/97) • **83**
Cabernet Sauvignon North Coast 1994: Simple, with modest currant, earth, tar and cedar notes. 24,000 cases made. • $12 • (05/15/97) • **82**
Chardonnay Mendocino County 1996: Ripe and juicy, with elegant and lively sweet pear, apple, melon and honeysuckle flavors. Holds its fruitiness. Drink now through 2001. • $12 • (06/30/98) • **87**
Chardonnay Mendocino County 1995: Clean and spicy, with a trim band of apple and pear notes. Turns elegant on the finish, where it picks up a hint of pineapple. 60,000 cases made. • $12 • (02/28/97) • **87**
Chardonnay Mendocino County 1994: Floral and spicy flavors dominate an otherwise straightforward style that finishes with a bit of bitterness from the oak. 40,000 cases made. • $12 • (03/31/96) • **83**
Chardonnay Mendocino County Organically Grown Grapes 1993 • $9 • (06/30/95) • **84**

Red Mendocino County Organically Grown Grapes 1991 • $9 • (03/31/94) • **83**
Red Mendocino County Organically Grown Grapes 1990 • $9 • (05/31/93) • **83**
Sangiovese Mendocino County 1995: Light and simple, with hints of green strawberry and berry, but the tannins dominate, leaving a dry, tannic aftertaste and not much fruit. 1,070 cases made. • $22 • (03/31/98) • **79**
Sangiovese Mendocino County 1994: Lacks varietal character, with an earthy, ashlike edge to the modest berry flavors. Hard to tell it's Sangiovese. 460 cases made. • $22 • (02/28/97) • **79**
Sangiovese Mendocino County 1993 • $22 • (04/30/96) • **85**
Syrah Mendocino County 1995: An elegant style, ripe and polished, with spicy plum, blackberry and cherry flavors, complex earth, toasty oak and mushroom notes. Best of both worlds: drinks well now or can age to 2002. 2,500 cases made. • $22 • (03/31/98) • **88**
Syrah Mendocino County 1994: Rich and complex, with an array of smoky, meaty plum, wild berry, currant and anise notes, with a sweet edge. Has firm tannins, but it's well balanced and serves up lots of flavor. 1,200 cases made. • $22 • (02/28/97) • **88**
Syrah Mendocino County 1993 • $22 • (04/30/96) • **86**
Viognier Mendocino County 1995: A spicy, exotic style with lots of pear, litchi nut, fig and Muscat notes. Good, but comes across as a bit one-dimensional. 600 cases made. • $22 • (04/30/97) • **85**
Viognier North Coast 1996: Creamy texture, with toasty, honeyed notes and sprightly acidity. The finish is a tangy blend of lemon, lime and apple. 600 cases made. • $23 • (12/15/97) • **87**

BONVERRE | CALIFORNIA

Cabernet Sauvignon California Lot Number 19 1994: Light and fruity in character, with touches of plum, herb and cedar flavor. 9,812 cases made. • $9 • (11/30/96) • **82**
Cabernet Sauvignon California Lot Number 9 1991 • $7 • (05/15/94) • **83**
Chardonnay California Lot Number 16 1994: Soft, bright and floral—like a Riesling. Spicy apple flavors linger on the finish. 19,278 cases made. • $8 • (07/31/96) • **84**
Merlot California Famille Lot Number 8 NV • $8 • (05/31/93) BB • **84**
Merlot California Lot Number 11 1992 • $8 • (09/15/94) • **76**
Sauvignon Blanc Napa Valley Lot Number 18 1994: Brisk and brightly fruity, with lively citrus, pear and apple flavors. 2,500 cases made. • $7 • (07/31/96) • **85**
Zinfandel Napa Valley 1995: Has a bite to it, with lots of smoke and spice overtones to the modest black cherry flavors. Ready now. • $10 • (04/30/97) • **83**

BOOKWALTER | WASHINGTON

Cabernet Sauvignon Washington 1994: A delicious mouthful of Cabernet flavor, with an earthy mineral quality running through the ripe blackberry, currant, anise and vanilla flavors that persist on the open-textured finish. Drinkable now. 310 cases made. • $20 • (09/30/97) • **91**
Cabernet Sauvignon Washington 1992 • $16 • (08/31/95) • **89**
Cabernet Sauvignon Washington 1990 • $16 • (09/30/94) • **88**
Cabernet Sauvignon Washington Reserve 1989 • $20 • (09/30/94) • **88**
Cabernet Sauvignon Washington Vintner's Select 1994: Jam-packed with flavor, it's a jazzy, berry-intense wine with layers of spice, mint and cedar that keep swirling through the solid finish, hinting at a chocolaty sweetness on the aftertaste. Delicious now. 150 cases made. • $38 • (09/30/97) • **90**
Chardonnay Washington 1994: Ripe and round, spicy around the edges, offering pear and toasty vanilla flavors at the core and a firm texture. Drink now. 1,365 cases made. • $9 • (09/30/95) • **87**
Chardonnay Washington Barrel Fermented Reserve 1993 • $14 • (09/30/95) • **86**
Chardonnay Washington Vintner's Select 1995: Crisp and harmonious. Extremely earthy at first, this improves when it gets some pear flavor going on the finish. 295 cases made. • $18 • (09/30/97) • **86**
Chenin Blanc Washington 1993 • $6 • (09/30/94) • **80**
Merlot Washington 1995: Firm in texture, with earthy blackberry and smoke flavors that remain on the earthy side through the solid finish. Drinkable now. 672 cases made. • $15 • (03/31/98) • **85**
Merlot Washington 1994: Crisp and a bit tight in texture, with a generous range of cherry, earth and smoke flavors lingering behind the fine tannins on the finish. Try in 1999. 308 cases made. • $15 • (03/31/98) • **87**
Merlot Washington 1993 • $14 • (09/30/95) • **87**
Merlot Washington 1992 • $12 • (09/30/94) • **88**
Muscat Washington 1993 • $8 • (09/30/94) • **80**
Red Table Wine Washington NV • $9 • (09/30/95) • **83**
Riesling Washington Vintner's Select 1996: Frankly sweet, silky in texture, but stops short of cloying as the honey and peach flavors swirl through the finish. 907 cases made. • $8 • (10/15/97) • **86**
White Riesling Late Harvest Washington 1994 • $7/375ml • (09/15/95) • **85**
White Riesling Late Harvest Washington 1987 • $5/375ml • (10/15/89) • **78**

BOORDY | MARYLAND

Cabernet Sauvignon Maryland 1989 • $11 • (02/29/92) • **73**
Seyval Blanc Maryland Sur Lie Reserve 1993 • $8 • (01/01/95) • **80**
Vidal Blanc Maryland Semi-Dry 1994 • $6 • (01/01/95) • **77**

BORDONI | CALIFORNIA

Chardonnay Solano County 1994: Marked by lime and citrus flavors, but bordering on unripe, making it seem tart and acidic. 56 cases made. • $16 • (03/31/96) • **78**

BOUCHAINE | CALIFORNIA

Cabernet Franc Sonoma Valley Limited Release 1994: Complex cherry, herb and blueberry flavors blend nicely, backed over-enthusiastically by oak. Moderate finish with a clean, herbal edge. 300 cases made. • $14 • (07/31/97) • **86**
Cabernet Franc Sonoma Valley Limited Release 1993: Starts off with a beefy, herbal profile, then heads into a tangy, raspberry mode. Finishes with an herbaceous note. Drink now. 300 cases made. • $15 • (05/31/98) • **82**
Cabernet Franc Sonoma Valley Limited Release 1991 • $14 • (02/28/95) • **79**
Cabernet Franc Sonoma Valley Limited Release 1990 • $14 • (03/31/93) • **83**
Chardonnay California Q.C. Fly 1994: Simple and appealing for its fresh, floral apple flavors. 5,000 cases made. • $9 • (06/15/96) • **82**
Chardonnay California Q.C. Fly 1993 • $8 • (10/15/95) • **84**
Chardonnay Carneros 1995: Never quite comes into focus; medium-weight, spicy pear and apple notes fold in with light, toasty oak. Perhaps with time the texture will soften. 3,500 cases made. • $18 • (04/30/98) • **84**
Chardonnay Carneros 1994: Has attractive ripe pear, apple and melon flavors, with hints of citrus and spice that fold in on the finish, where the oak folds in, too. 4,100 cases made. • $17 • (11/30/96) • **86**
Chardonnay Carneros 1993 • $15 • (02/29/96) • **85**
Chardonnay Napa Valley Carneros Estate Reserve 1995: Earthy, with chalky, leafy flavors; the pear- and citrus-laced Chardonnay flavors lack focus and purity. Maybe a little time in the bottle will help. Drink through 2000. 400 cases made. • $24 • (06/30/98) • **84**
Chardonnay Napa Valley Carneros Estate Reserve 1994: Solid, with a pleasant core of citrus-accented pear and apple notes, picking up a slight cedary edge on the finish. 400 cases made. • $24 • (07/31/97) • **86**
Chardonnay Napa Valley Carneros Estate Reserve 1993 • $22 • (06/30/96) • **85**
Gewürztraminer Russian River Valley Dry 1996: Light and refreshing. A dry Gewürz with pleasant rose petal and pear flavors. Drink now. 1,300 cases made. • $12 • (03/31/98) • **85**
Gewürztraminer Russian River Valley Dry 1995: On the dry side, this is a firm-textured Gewürz with dead-on spicy grapefruit flavors and a note of apricot on the finish, which balances the wee touch of bitterness. 1,800 cases made. • $10 • (12/15/96) BB • **89**
Gewürztraminer Russian River Valley Dry 1994 • $8 • (05/31/96) • **81**
Gewürztraminer Russian River Valley Dry 1993 • $8 • (02/28/95) • **85**
Pinot Noir California Q.C. Fly 1993 • $8 • (12/31/95) • **82**
Pinot Noir California Q.C. Fly 1992 • $8 • (03/31/95) • **81**
Pinot Noir California Q.C. Fly 1991 • $8 • (02/28/94) • **82**
Pinot Noir California Q.C. Fly 1990 • $8 • (09/30/92) BB • **81**
Pinot Noir Carneros 1992 • $15 • (06/30/95) • **86**
Pinot Noir Los Carneros 1985 • $7 • (06/30/87) • **76**
Pinot Noir Napa Valley 1982 • $20 • (06/30/87) • **81**
Pinot Noir Napa Valley Carneros 1994: Aims for elegance with its body and depth. Flavor hints of tea, cherry and cedar, and spice notes on the finish. 4,000 cases made. • $17 • (01/31/97) • **84**
Pinot Noir Napa Valley Carneros 1991 • $15 • (03/31/95) • **82**
Pinot Noir Napa Valley Carneros 1990 • $15 • (02/28/93) • **86**
Pinot Noir Napa Valley Carneros 1989 • $15 • (09/30/92) • **84**
Pinot Noir Napa Valley Carneros 1988 • $15 • (07/31/91) • **78**
Pinot Noir Napa Valley Carneros 1987 • $13 • (10/31/90) • **82**
Pinot Noir Napa Valley Carneros 1986 • $12 • (05/31/89) • **86**
Pinot Noir Napa Valley Carneros 1985 • $12 • (12/31/88) • **82**
Pinot Noir Napa Valley Carneros Estate Bottled 1989 • $20 • (02/28/93) • **75**

Pinot Noir Napa Valley Carneros Limited Release 1994: Smooth, ripe and elegant, with a supple core of plum, black cherry, wild berry and spice. Turns silky and rich on the aftertaste, where dashes of earth and cola add dimension. Drink now through 2002. 140 cases made. • $33 • (01/31/98) • **87**
Pinot Noir Napa Valley Carneros Reserve 1993: Smooth and spicy, with a mature edge to the dried cherry, spice and subtle leathery notes. Has a polished texture and the flavors are intense. Drink now. 600 cases made. • $25 • (11/30/96) • **87**
Pinot Noir Napa Valley Carneros Reserve 1991 • $20 • (01/31/95) • **88**
Pinot Noir Napa Valley Carneros Reserve 1990 • $20 • (04/30/94) • **82**
Pinot Noir Napa Valley Carneros Reserve 1988 • $25 • (03/31/92) • **83**
Pinot Noir Napa Valley Carneros Reserve 1987 • $20 • (10/31/90) • **85**
Pinot Noir Napa Valley Los Carneros 1982 • $13 • (07/16/85) • **87**
Pinot Noir Napa Valley Los Carneros Winery Lake Vineyard 1982 • $15 • (03/01/86) CS • **91**
Pinot Noir Russian River Valley Limited Release 1991 • $17 • (06/30/95) • **82**

BRANDBORG | CALIFORNIA

Charbono Napa Valley 1989 • $12 • (10/31/91) • **85**
Pinot Noir Anderson Valley 1989 • $11 • (11/15/91) • **86**
Pinot Noir Mendocino 1992 • $13 • (03/31/95) • **82**
Pinot Noir Mendocino County 1991 • $12 • (02/28/94) • **84**
Pinot Noir Mendocino County 1990 • $11 • (02/28/93) • **73**
Pinot Noir Santa Barbara County 1989 • $13 • (11/15/91) • **87**
Pinot Noir Santa Maria Valley Bien Nacido Vineyard 1994: Complex flavors, with earth, spice, cola and wild berry notes that fold together nicely, fanning out on the finish. Ready to drink. 500 cases made. • $15 • (02/28/97) • **86**
Pinot Noir Santa Maria Valley Bien Nacido Vineyard 1992 • $15 • (03/31/95) • **86**
Pinot Noir Santa Maria Valley Bien Nacido Vineyard 1991 • $14 • (02/28/94) • **84**
Pinot Noir Santa Maria Valley Bien Nacido Vineyard 1990 • $13 • (02/28/93) • **78**
Zinfandel Napa Valley 1989 • $10 • (10/15/92) • **84**

BRANDER | CALIFORNIA

Bouchet Tête de Cuvée Santa Ynez Valley 1993: Lean and chewy, but the berry flavors burst through the firm tannins, extending into hints of earth, toast and spice. Try in 2000. 380 cases made. • $22 • (12/15/95) • **86**
Bouchet Tête de Cuvée Santa Ynez Valley 1990 • $18 • (11/15/93) • **79**
Bouchet Tête de Cuvée Santa Ynez Valley 1989 • $20 • (03/31/92) • **84**
Bouchet Tête de Cuvée Santa Ynez Valley 1988 • $20 • (07/15/92) • **83**
Cabernet Franc Santa Ynez Valley High Density Vineyard 1993 • $35 • (04/30/96) • **84**
Chardonnay Santa Ynez Valley Tête de Cuvée 1993 • $15 • (07/31/95) • **84**
Cuvée Natalie Santa Ynez Valley 1996: Full-bodied, and packed with ripe melon and grapefruit flavors, toasty vanilla and peppermint notes. Clean, refreshing finish. A solid wine from a consistent producer of this varietal. A blend of 65 percent Sauvignon Blanc, 26 percent Riesling, and 9 percent Gewürztraminer. 350 cases made. • $14 • (06/30/97) • **89**
Cuvée Natalie Santa Ynez Valley 1995: Rich, ripe, polished and flavorful. The grapefruit, spice, apricot and apple flavors are balanced harmoniously. Drinkable now. 275 cases made. • $14 • (08/31/96) • **89**
Cuvée Natalie Santa Ynez Valley 1994 • $13 • (08/31/95) • **89**
Cuvée Natalie Santa Ynez Valley 1993 • $13 • (12/15/94) • **86**
Merlot Santa Ynez Valley 1995: Weedy, herbaceous, with bell pepper notes and a glimpse of cherry on the finish. True to the appellation, but not mainstream. 2,000 cases made. • $14 • (06/30/97) • **78**
Merlot Santa Ynez Valley 1994: Earthy and pungent, with tarry tobacco flavors. Not much in the way of fruit. 1,200 cases made. • $15 • (08/31/96) • **78**
Merlot Santa Ynez Valley Reserve 1993: Marked by spicy herb, currant and tobacco flavors. This wine delivers more than the 1994 Merlot; as expected from a reserve bottling. 150 cases made. • $18 • (08/31/96) • **83**
Merlot Santa Ynez Valley Three Flags 1989 • $12 • (05/31/92) • **82**
Merlot Santa Ynez Valley Three Flags 1988 • $12 • (05/31/92) • **81**

Key: SS—Spectator Selection CS—Cellar Selection HR—Highly Recommended BB—Best Buy $NA—Price not available Ⓐ—Auction Price (BT)—Barrel Tasting
Dates in parentheses indicate the issues in which the ratings were published.

Sauvignon Blanc Santa Ynez Valley 1997: Kind of lean, with a crisp, grassy edge that's backed by melon and lemon flavors. Light and refreshing. Drink now. 5,000 cases made. • $11 • (06/15/98) • **85**
Sauvignon Blanc Santa Ynez Valley 1996: Citrus, melon and celery flavors make odd bedfellows, but the blend has merit nonetheless. Smooth and supple, with a moderate finish. 10 percent Sémillon. 2,000 cases made. • $11 • (07/31/97) • **87**
Sauvignon Blanc Santa Ynez Valley 1995: Tight and tart, with little charm to balance the hard edge. 2,000 cases made. • $11 • (08/31/96) • **79**
Sauvignon Blanc Santa Ynez Valley 1994 • $10 • (06/30/95) • **84**
Sauvignon Blanc Santa Ynez Valley 1993 • $10 • (04/30/95) • **86**
Sauvignon Blanc Santa Ynez Valley Cuvée Nicolas 1996: A pleasing blend of fresh pea, hazelnut, melon, fig and citrus flavors. A delicate wine with a moderate, light finish. Drink now through 2000. 350 cases made. • $21 • (05/31/98) • **87**
Sauvignon Blanc Santa Ynez Valley Cuvée Nicolas 1995: Crisp and refreshing, with a tartness that's almost overdone. It has style and a raft of vibrant lemon and grapefruit flavors that have plenty of room to grow. Drink now. • $22 • (08/31/96) • **88**
Sauvignon Blanc Santa Ynez Valley Cuvée Nicolas 1994 • $21 • (04/30/96) • **90**
Sauvignon Blanc Santa Ynez Valley Cuvée Nicolas 1993 • $21 • (06/30/95) • **89**
Sauvignon Blanc Santa Ynez Valley au Naturel 1996: A brightly textured wine with hints of peach, nectarine, lemon-lime and grapefruit. A tangy, mineral edge leaves a refreshing impression on the finish. Drink now through 2000. 70 cases made. • $25 • (05/31/98) • **87**
Sémillon Santa Ynez Valley 1994 • $12 • (10/15/95) • **87**

BRAREN PAULI | CALIFORNIA

Cabernet Sauvignon Dry Creek Valley 1990 • $13 • (10/31/93) • **89**
Cabernet Sauvignon Dry Creek Valley Mauritson Vineyard 1989 • $12 • (11/15/93) • **78**
Cabernet Sauvignon Mendocino 1987 • $8 • (03/31/91) BB • **84**
Chardonnay Mendocino Busch Creek Vineyard 1996: Silky in texture. Appealing for its appley and earthy flavors that linger on the solid finish, echoing hints of honey. Drink now. 1,200 cases made. • $13 • (12/15/97) • **86**
Merlot Alexander Valley 1992 • $12 • (03/31/96) • **84**
Merlot Alexander Valley 1991 • $13 • (09/15/94) • **85**
Merlot Alexander Valley Mauritson Vineyard 1989 • $12 • (05/31/92) • **77**
Merlot Alexander Valley Mauritson Vineyard 1987 • $11 • (03/31/91) • **84**
Sauvignon Blanc Mendocino Busch Creek Vineyard 1996: A bit simple and sweet, this is pleasant enough, with hints of pear and lime on the finish. 1,600 cases made. • $9 • (11/15/97) • **82**

BRICK HOUSE | OREGON

Chardonnay Willamette Valley 1996: On the lighter side, this strives for elegance and achieves a lithe balance of fruit, spice and gentle acidity, offering apple, pear and a bitter-almond edge. Flavors grow on the long finish. Drinkable now. 180 cases made. • $24 • (02/28/98) • **88**
Gamay Noir Willamette Valley 1994 • $13 • (03/31/96) • **84**
Pinot Noir Willamette Valley 1995: Crisp and spicy, with floral and tobacco-cinnamon notes adding to the lightish plum flavor. Reflects the lightness of the vintage but maintains its character. Ready to drink. 400 cases made. • $24 • (07/31/97) • **85**
Pinot Noir Willamette Valley 1994 • $22 • (01/31/96) • **91**
Pinot Noir Willamette Valley Cuvée du Tonnelier 1995: Tough and chewy on the surface, smooth and pretty beneath, with solid blackberry and currant flavors that linger nicely on the finish. Ready to drink. 60 cases made. • $34 • (10/15/97) • **87**

BRIDGEHAMPTON | NEW YORK

Cabernet Sauvignon Long Island 1988 • $14 • (06/30/91) • **84**
Cabernet Sauvignon Long Island 1987 • $14 • (06/30/91) • **87**
Cabernet Sauvignon Long Island 1986 • $12 • (12/15/88) • **79**
Merlot Long Island 1988 • $16 • (06/30/91) • **89**
Merlot Long Island 1986 • $11 • (12/15/88) • **78**
Merlot Long Island 1985 • $11 • (12/15/88) • **79**
Pinot Noir Long Island 1984 • $8 • (03/16/86) • **75**
Reserve Red Grand Vineyard North Fork of Long Island 1987 • $17 • (06/30/91) • **80**

BRIDGEVIEW | OREGON

Chardonnay Oregon 1996: This soft-spoken white is appealing for its nicely articulated melon and apple flavors that remain fresh on the gentle finish, and its price tag makes it a smart choice when the occasion calls for multiple bottles. Drink now. 7,250 cases made. • $6 • (06/15/98) BB • **85**

Chardonnay Oregon 1995: Fresh and nicely modulated, neither too exuberant nor too reticent, offering spicy apple and mineral flavors. Drink soon. 4,600 cases made. • $7 • (02/28/97) • **84**

Chardonnay Oregon 1994: Light and brightly fruity, focusing its spicy apple flavors well into its smooth-textured form. A good and inexpensive white that's drinkable now. 10,000 cases made. • $6 • (12/15/95) BB • **85**

Chardonnay Oregon Barrel Select 1995: Round and earthy, generous with its melon and spice flavors, adding some extra nuances on the pretty finish. Drink now through 2000. 318 cases made. • $10 • (06/15/98) • **86**

Chardonnay Oregon Barrel Select 1994: Interesting apricot and mineral overtones accent the solid green apple flavors at the core. Finishes with a smoky edge. Ready to drink. 2,400 cases made. • $10 • (09/15/97) • **85**

Chardonnay Oregon Barrel Select 1993 • $10 • (01/31/96) • **79**

Chardonnay Oregon Blue Moon 1996: Ripe, round and spicy, pretty for its peach, honey and apple flavors that linger enticingly, hinting more strongly at honey on the aftertaste. Drink now through 2000. 3,200 cases made. • $10 • (06/30/98) BB • **87**

Chardonnay Oregon Blue Moon 1995: Fresh, with appealing, spicy apple and citrus flavors. A bit short, but pleasant while it lasts. 3,200 cases made. • $8 • (02/28/97) • **83**

Chardonnay Oregon Blue Moon 1994: Earthy, weedy, stinky flavors up front never quite go away as the fruit comes through on the finish. 500 cases made. • $7 • (01/31/96) • **77**

Early Muscat Oregon 1996: Soft, lightly sweet and pretty for its floral, litchi and pear flavors that linger with a glow on the finish. Drink soon. 350 cases made. • $8 • (11/30/97) • **88**

Early Muscat Oregon 1995: Sweet, light and graceful, with pretty clove-scented melon and vanilla flavors that linger nicely. 250 cases made. • $8 • (11/30/96) • **82**

Gewürztraminer Oregon 1996: Lightly sweet, silky and appealing for its spicy grapefruit and pineapple flavors that linger on the balanced finish. Drink soon. 850 cases made. • $6 • (09/15/97) • **86**

Gewürztraminer Oregon 1993 • $6 • (03/31/96) • **80**

Gewürztraminer Oregon Dry Vintage Select 1994: Aromas are right-on, with a rose petal, citrus and apple character running straight through. A waxy note takes the charm level down a notch. 505 cases made. • $8 • (10/31/96) • **83**

Merlot Oregon Black Beauty 1994: Crisp and focused berry and toast flavors that linger through the smooth finish. 1,590 cases made. • $12 • (07/31/96) • **87**

Merlot Oregon Black Beauty 1993 • $11 • (03/31/96) • **84**

Merlot Paso Robles Black Beauty 1996: Shows strong oak, plum and cherry flavors, but they don't seem very integrated. Woody finish. Drink now. 2,583 cases made. • $17 • (07/31/98) • **80**

Pinot Gris Oregon Cuvée Spéciale 1996: A pleasant mouthful of green plum and melon flavors that linger on the leesy finish. Ready to drink. 2,800 cases made. • $11 • (09/15/97) • **86**

Pinot Gris Oregon Cuvée Spéciale 1995: Light, crisp and lively, this offers citrusy apple and mineral flavors. Finish is a mite astringent, like apple peel. 2,557 cases made. • $10 • (10/31/96) • **83**

Pinot Gris Oregon Cuvée Spéciale 1994 • $10 • (03/31/96) • **84**

Pinot Gris Oregon Cuvée Spéciale 1993 • $9 • (11/30/94) • **80**

Pinot Noir Oregon 1996: Soft, light and fragrant with blackberry and violet-floral aromas and flavors. Finish is simple and refreshing. Drink soon. 6,500 cases made. • $11 • (11/15/97) • **83**

Pinot Noir Oregon 1995: Light in texture, with a layer of firm tannins around a lean core of plum and mineral flavors. Drinkable now. 7,000 cases made. • $7 • (02/28/97) • **85**

Pinot Noir Oregon 1994 • $6 • (03/31/96) • **80**

Pinot Noir Oregon 1988 • $8 • (02/15/90) • **88**

Pinot Noir Oregon 1986 • $8 • (06/15/88) • **87**

Pinot Noir Oregon 1986 • $8 • (02/15/90) • **79**

Pinot Noir Oregon 10th Anniversary 1992 • $30 • (01/31/96) • **81**

Pinot Noir Oregon Reserve 1995: Ripe for the vintage, with pretty plum and currant flavors that linger on the solid finish. Not a powerful wine, but very nicely done. Ready to drink. 1,800 cases made. • $16 • (10/15/97) • **87**

Pinot Noir Oregon Reserve 1993 • $10 • (02/29/96) • **83**

Pinot Noir Oregon Reserve 1992 • $10 • (01/31/96) • **81**

Pinot Noir Oregon Reserve 1990 • $10 • (10/31/94) • **83**

Pinot Noir Oregon Special Reserve 1987 • $12 • (02/15/90) • **80**

Pinot Noir Oregon Winemaker's Reserve 1990 • $13 • (02/28/93) • **70**

Pinot Noir Oregon Winemaker's Reserve 1989 • $13 • (02/28/93) • **83**

Pinot Noir Oregon Winemaker's Reserve 1988 • $12 • (11/15/91) • **87**

Pinot Noir Oregon Winemaker's Reserve 1987 • $15 • (02/15/90) • **89**

Pinot Noir Willamette Valley 1992 • $6 • (03/15/94) • **79**

Pinot Noir Willamette Valley 1991 • $6 • (01/31/93) BB • **83**

Pinot Noir Willamette Valley 1990 • $6 • (02/28/93) • **75**

Riesling Late Harvest Oregon 1992 • $25/375ml • (11/15/94) • **88**

Rosé de Pinot Oregon 1996: Soft and silky, on the dry side, but it feels sweet with its polished berry and spice flavors that linger nicely. Drink now; good by itself or with food. A blend of 65 percent Pinot Noir and 35 percent Pinot Meunier. 70 cases made. • $12 • (11/15/97) • **85**

Sem-Chard Oregon 1995: Crisp, almost bracing, with its green apple and delicate herb flavors hanging nicely on a lean frame. 2,800 cases made. • $5 • (10/31/96) • **84**

BRIDGMAN, W.B. | WASHINGTON

Cabernet Sauvignon Columbia Valley 1993: Harmonious, spicy and elegant, wrapping its spicy, cedary plum and black cherry flavors gently around supple, fine tannins. Appealing to drink now, but could improve through 1999. 543 cases made. • $12 • (09/15/96) • **89**

Cabernet Sauvignon Yakima Valley 1991 • $11 • (07/31/95) • **86**

Chardonnay Columbia Valley 1995: Earthy, stalky flavors sneak into the mix of pear and spice to make this an unusual, if not especially charming, Chardonnay. 2,027 cases made. • $12 • (09/15/97) • **81**

Chardonnay Yakima Valley 1994: Ripe and rich, showing smoothly integrated pineapple and citrus flavors with a buttery accent. Hazelnut and spice flavors haunt the long finish. Drink now. 995 cases made. • $11 • (09/15/96) • **88**

Chardonnay Yakima Valley 1993 • $9 • (09/30/95) • **88**

Lemberger Columbia Valley 1995: Light, crisp and peppery, with a bright streak of blackberry flavor. Finishes with a racy acidity. Drink soon. 254 cases made. • $9 • (09/15/96) • **84**

Merlot Columbia Valley 1995: Light and silky. A wine of lovely texture and delicately etched currant, blueberry and spicy vanilla notes. Best from 1999. 1,333 cases made. • $15 • (09/15/97) • **87**

Merlot Columbia Valley 1994: Ripe and generous, with a zingy streak of acidity running through the sweet black cherry, plum and exotic spice flavors. Finishes with firm tannins. Drink now. 1,332 cases made. • $15 • (09/15/96) • **88**

Merlot Yakima Valley 1992 • $11 • (09/30/95) • **86**

Syrah Yakima Valley 1995: A solid red with rich texture, solid blackberry and mineral flavors and a soft-grained finish. Drink now. 388 cases made. • $15 • (09/15/97) • **86**

BRIGGS, AUGUST | CALIFORNIA

Chardonnay Carneros Leveroni Vineyards 1996: Smooth, ripe and juicy, with lots of spicy pear, fig, melon, apple and citrus notes that are complex and concentrated. For all its size and depth, it's remarkably elegant and refined. Drink now into 2000. 195 cases made. • $25 • (01/31/98) • **92**

Chardonnay Russian River Valley 1996: Shows a remarkable degree of restraint and subtlety, with silky, polished ripe pear, apple, melon and spicy flavors, and a light oaky quality that adds dimension on the finish. Drink now or age into 2000. 145 cases made. • $25 • (01/31/98) • **92**

Pinot Noir Carneros 1995: Ripe, smooth and spicy, with lovely plum and black cherry flavors. Finishes with firm tannins, a dash of oak. Drink now. 197 cases made. • $25 • (07/31/97) • **88**

Pinot Noir Russian River Valley 1995: Marked by an earthy, leathery edge, it's a tightly knit, dry, tannic style, with just a modest core of berry flavor. Atypical Russian River Pinot Noir. Drink now. 194 cases made. • $25 • (07/31/97) • **87**

Zinfandel Napa Valley 1996: Appealing for its spice and pepper notes, with moderately ripe cherry- and berry-laced flavors. Drink now through 2000. 314 cases made. • $20 • (05/31/98) • **83**

Zinfandel Napa Valley 1995: Smooth, ripe, complex and polished, with pretty toasty oak flavors around a juicy core of plum and black cherry. Turns elegant and harmonious on the finish, where the flavors fold together. 397 cases made. • $18 • (08/31/97) • **91**

BRINDIAMO | CALIFORNIA

Cabernet Sauvignon California Limited Bottling 1991 • $8 • (11/15/94) • **76**

Chardonnay California Limited Bottling 1993 • $10 • (07/31/95) • **79**

Gioveto Limited Bottling South Coast 1993 • $14 • (08/31/95) • **86**
Il Bacio Temecula 1990 • $13 • (11/30/92) • **71**
Muscat Alexandria San Diego County Moscato Aromatico Limited Bottling 1994 • $6 • (12/31/95) • **80**
Nebbiolo South Coast Limited Bottling 1993 • $14 • (12/15/95) • **85**
Pinot Noir Edna Valley Limited Bottling 1993 • $10 • (10/15/95) • **84**
Pinot Noir Santa Barbara County Santa Maria Hills Vineyard Limited Bottling 1990 • $9 • (09/30/92) • **77**
Rosso Vecchio South Coast Limited Bottling 1993 • $10 • (06/30/95) • **86**
Rosso Vecchio South Coast Limited Bottling 1992 • $10 • (05/15/95) • **80**

BRITTHILL | CALIFORNIA

Pinot Noir Napa County 1989 • $13 • (02/28/93) • **81**

BROADLEY | OREGON

Pinot Noir Oregon 1990 • $10 • (02/28/93) • **72**
Pinot Noir Oregon 1987 • $8 • (02/15/90) • **76**
Pinot Noir Oregon Claudia's Choice 1994: A profound, graceful Pinot Noir that presents a gamy character on a first whiff, then shows an amazing depth of fruit, expanding into its spicy plum, black cherry and anise flavors that swirl through the long finish. Drink now to 2000. 300 cases made. • $25 • (08/31/96) • **94**
Pinot Noir Oregon Reserve 1995: A gamy edge adds extra, positive character to the spicy blackberry flavors, while the finish is straightforward and sturdy. Needs to soften. 700 cases made. • $15 • (07/31/97) • **87**
Pinot Noir Oregon Reserve 1994: Has a meaty, roasted quality reminiscent of Syrah, but the berry and currant flavors come through and a gamy edge joins in on the fine finish. Drink now. 700 cases made. • $16 • (08/31/96) • **88**
Pinot Noir Oregon Reserve 1992 • $13 • (10/31/94) • **86**
Pinot Noir Oregon Reserve 1987 • $12 • (02/15/90) • **88**
Pinot Noir Oregon Reserve 1986 • $12 • (06/15/88) • **73**
Pinot Noir Willamette Valley Reserve 1996: Feels raw and rough, with berry and anise flavors that veer toward bitterness on the finish. Try in 1999 to 2000. Tasted twice, with consistent notes. 950 cases made. • $18 • (05/15/98) • **80**

BROTHERHOOD | NEW YORK

Johannisberg Riesling New York Late Harvest Eiswein 1991 • $15 • (04/15/95) • **60**

BROWN, STILLMAN | CALIFORNIA

Les Ramones Red California 1995: Smooth and cherrylike, with spice, cedar and herb overtones. Drinks well now, finishing with soft, powdery tannins. A blend of Cabernet Franc, Merlot and Valdigue. 173 cases made. • $20 • (12/15/97) • **86**
Sauvignon Blanc Paso Robles 1994 • $14 • (02/29/96) • **74**
Zinfandel Santa Clara Valley Lion Oaks Ranch 1996: Deeply concentrated with a firm core of black cherry and mineral notes. Velvety, with fine-grained tannins and good length. More reminiscent of Syrah than of Zinfandel. Drink now through 2005. 83 cases made. • $16 • (06/15/98) • **87**

BRUCE, DAVID | CALIFORNIA

Cabernet Sauvignon California Vintner's Select 1983 • $13 • (09/30/86) • **79**
Cabernet Sauvignon Santa Cruz Mountains 1978 • $20 • (11/15/92) • **72**
Mr. Baggins California Red 1990 • $10 • (11/30/92) • **80**
Mrs. Baggins California Red 1990 • $10 • (06/30/92) • **84**
Petite Sirah California Vintner's Select 1991 • $12 • (10/15/93) • **78**
Petite Sirah Central Coast 1996: This California red is complex and well balanced, with ripe dark fruit flavors—lots of plum and wild berry—and pretty dashes of sage and spice adding dimension. Finishes with a complex aftertaste. Needs a little more time to be at its best; drink after 1999. 3,407 cases made. • $15 • (12/31/97) SS • **90**

Key: SS—Spectator Selection CS—Cellar Selection HR—Highly Recommended BB—Best Buy $NA—Price not available Ⓐ—Auction Price (BT)—Barrel Tasting
Dates in parentheses indicate the issues in which the ratings were published.

Petite Sirah Central Coast Vintner's Select 1994: Smooth and harmonious. Ripe, spicy plum and wild berry flavors, and a nice tannin level. Spicy, leathery notes add to the finish. 1,568 cases made. • $12 • (08/31/96) • **86**
Petite Sirah Paso Robles Shell Creek Vineyard 1996: Inky black in color, with rich, intense flavors of meaty plum, black cherry, wild berry and sage. Deliciously fruity, ripe and complex, a real mouthful of Sirah that somehow tames the tannins. 515 cases made. • $18 • (12/31/97) • **93**
Pinot Noir Central Coast 1996: Young and intense, but the flavors hit most of the right notes, with a range of earthy cherry, wild berry, leather, sage and spice. Finishes with firm tannins and a hint of herb. Best now through 2000. 8,820 cases made. • $16 • (01/31/98) • **87**
Pinot Noir Chalone 1995: From a California winery with a focus on Pinot Noir comes this outstanding bottling, well crafted around fruit flavors, with a core of cherry, wild berry, tea, sage, mushroom and spice notes. It has smooth texture and supple tannins, with a complex finish that shows off the flavors. 1,853 cases made. • $30 • (12/15/97) HR • **92**
Pinot Noir Chalone 1994: Complex, with a smoky, meaty edge to the ripe plum and berry flavors. Young and vibrant, the tannins are in check and the flavors linger on the finish. Impressive for its balance and depth. 1,418 cases made. • $30 • (09/30/96) • **89**
Pinot Noir Mendocino Vintner's Select 1990 • $12 • (02/28/94) • **84**
Pinot Noir Russian River Valley Reserve 1995: Lots of ripe, juicy cherry, wild berry and raspberry flavors greet you up front with just a tinge of tartness that adds lively acidity. Finishes with complex fruit flavors and firm tannins. Ready now or into 2000. 2,415 cases made. • $25 • (12/31/97) • **89**
Pinot Noir Russian River Valley Reserve 1994: Young and tight, with a core of spice, black cherry and raspberry flavors, hints of cola. The flavors grow on you as they gain depth and nuance. Not overpowering, it instead succeeds with delicacy. Should age well through 2001 or 2002. 1,540 cases made. • $25 • (12/31/96) • **89**
Pinot Noir Russian River Valley Reserve 1993: Mature, with hints of sage, wild berry, black cherry, spice, and some smoky nuances. Finishing with a dried cherry aftertaste. Drinkable now. 340 cases made. • $25 • (12/31/96) • **88**
Pinot Noir Santa Cruz Mountains 1990: This is an intense and distinctive wine, exotic for its smoky anise, meat and wild berry flavors. Still quite chewy and concentrated, but very well balanced, finishing with complex fruit flavors. Drinkable now. • $12 • (03/31/97) • **91**
Pinot Noir Santa Cruz Mountains 1989 • $18 • (09/30/92) • **75**
Pinot Noir Santa Cruz Mountains 1984 • $15 • (06/30/87) • **81**
Pinot Noir Santa Cruz Mountains 1983 • $15 • (08/31/86) • **78**
Pinot Noir Santa Cruz Mountains Estate Reserve 1993 • $35 • (12/31/95) • **82**
Pinot Noir Santa Cruz Mountains Estate Reserve 1992 • $30 • (03/31/95) • **88**
Pinot Noir Santa Cruz Mountains Estate Reserve 1990: Wonderfully complex and inviting, with tiers of ripe cherry, earth, tar and spice flavors, dash of mushroom. Finishes with a distinctly Burgundian earthiness and complexity. Silky smooth, rich and polished, it proves that David Bruce has made it back. • $20 • (03/31/97) • **93**
Pinot Noir Santa Cruz Mountains Thirtieth Anniversary 1992 • $100 • (03/31/95) • **91**
Pinot Noir Sonoma County 1995: Well balanced, with a pleasant band of dried cherry, wild berry, plum and spice, turning complex on the finish, where the flavors and tannins are well focused, picking up a nice earthy mineral edge. 7,215 cases made. • $18 • (01/31/98) • **88**
Pinot Noir Sonoma County Vintner's Select 1993 • $12 • (12/31/95) • **82**
Pinot Noir Sonoma County Vintner's Select 1992 • $12 • (03/31/95) • **83**
Zinfandel Paso Robles Ranchita Canyon Vineyard 1995: Complex, with a range of beefy, bay leaf flavors along with ripe plum and cherry notes that are still compact and in need of short-term cellaring. 1,741 cases made. • $15 • (03/31/98) • **88**
Zinfandel San Luis Obispo & El Dorado Counties Vintner's Select 1994: Well crafted and fun to drink, in a rustic style. Shows a jammy edge to its plum, cherry and raspberry flavors. Ready now. 1,610 cases made. • $13 • (03/31/97) • **87**
Zinfandel San Luis Obispo County 1990 • $12 • (05/15/92) HR • **90**

BRUCHER | CALIFORNIA

Pinot Noir Santa Barbara County 1992 • $16 • (03/31/95) • **78**

BRUTOCAO | CALIFORNIA

Cabernet Sauvignon Mendocino 1990 • $13 • (05/15/94) • **82**
Cabernet Sauvignon Mendocino 1988 • $13 • (03/31/92) • **83**

Cabernet Sauvignon Mendocino 1986 • $13 • (03/31/92) • **82**
Cabernet Sauvignon Mendocino 1982 • $9 • (11/30/88) • **83**
Cabernet Sauvignon Mendocino Albert Vineyard 1993: Pleasant enough, with wild cherry and berry notes, a touch of tannin and a green edge. Drinkable now. 709 cases made. • $13 • (12/15/95) • **82**
Cabernet Sauvignon Mendocino Albert Vineyard 1992 • $13 • (07/31/95) • **82**
Cabernet Sauvignon Mendocino Proprietor's Special Reserve 1991 • $35 • (07/31/95) • **83**
Chardonnay Mendocino Bliss Vineyard 1995: A snazzy mouthful of bright flavors, offering apple, pear and grapefruit in equal parts, with some almond notes on the lively finish. Drink now. 3,128 cases made. • $12 • (12/15/97) • **88**
Chardonnay Mendocino Bliss Vineyard 1993 • $10 • (07/31/95) • **83**
Merlot Mendocino 1995: A crisp style, offering some pretty raspberry and plum flavors on a lightish frame. Ready to drink. 1,700 cases made. • $18 • (12/15/97) • **86**
Merlot Mendocino 1994: Pleasant enough, with its core of ripe plum and cherry fruit and spicy oak shadings. Emphasizes the fruitiness of Merlot. Ready now. 1,200 cases made. • $15 • (12/15/96) • **82**
Merlot Mendocino 1991 • $15 • (08/31/93) • **87**
Merlot Mendocino 1988 • $13 • (05/31/92) • **84**
Merlot Mendocino Unfiltered Unfined 1993 • $15 • (07/31/95) • **78**
Merlot Mendocino Unfiltered Unfined 1992 • $15 • (09/15/94) • **78**
Pinot Noir Anderson Valley Special Reserve 1993 • $20 • (03/31/95) • **78**
Sauvignon Blanc Mendocino 1994: Soft at first, citrusy-tart on the finish. A stewed onion edge doesn't compliment the pear flavors. 2,500 cases made. • $9 • (08/31/96) • **80**
Sauvignon Blanc Mendocino 1993 • $8 • (08/31/95) • **80**
Zinfandel Mendocino 1992 • $17 • (06/15/94) • **84**
Zinfandel Mendocino Hopland Ranch 1994: Dry, rustic and tannic, the earthy cherry and berry flavors showing a metallic edge. Off the mark compared to the best 1994s. 900 cases made. • $14 • (04/30/97) • **82**
Zinfandel Mendocino Hopland Ranch 1993 • $12 • (06/15/95) • **84**
Zinfandel Mendocino Proprietor's Reserve 1991 • $17 • (09/30/93) • **85**

BRYANT FAMILY | CALIFORNIA

Cabernet Sauvignon Napa Valley 1994: Immense, rich, deep and concentrated, loaded with ripe, sweet currant and black cherry flavors framed by pretty toasty, smoky oak. A wonderful mouthful of wine that finishes with soft, fleshy tannins. Drinkable now, should be softer in 2000. 1,400 cases made. • $370 Ⓐ • (11/30/97) • **94**
Cabernet Sauvignon Napa Valley 1992 • $246 Ⓐ • (05/31/96) • **89**

BUEHLER | CALIFORNIA

Cabernet Sauvignon California 1993: Earthy, simple, a little chewy but flavorful enough to make it appealing now. 4,310 cases made. • $8 • (12/15/95) • **79**
Cabernet Sauvignon Napa Valley 1994: A nice mouthful of lively blueberry, currant and tarry flavors that linger on the solid finish. Firm, chewy and focused. Best from 1999 or 2000. 2,783 cases made. • $20 • (07/31/97) • **87**
Cabernet Sauvignon Napa Valley 1993: Well balanced—the ripe plum and cherry flavors are an equal match for the dry, austere tannins and light oak shadings. 2,600 cases made. • $17 • (11/15/96) • **87**
Cabernet Sauvignon Napa Valley 1992 • $14 • (12/15/95) • **84**
Cabernet Sauvignon Napa Valley 1991 • $13 • (09/15/94) • **86**
Cabernet Sauvignon Napa Valley 1990 • $12 • (11/15/93) • **83**
Cabernet Sauvignon Napa Valley 1989 • $16 • (11/15/92) • **79**
Cabernet Sauvignon Napa Valley 1987 • $21 • (07/31/90) • **85**
Cabernet Sauvignon Napa Valley 1986 • $20 • (04/30/89) • **85**
Cabernet Sauvignon Napa Valley 1985 • $14 • (04/30/88) • **89**
Cabernet Sauvignon Napa Valley 1984 • $13 • (05/31/87) • **92**
Cabernet Sauvignon Napa Valley 1983 • $12 • (07/16/86) SS • **93**
Cabernet Sauvignon Napa Valley Estate 1994: Elegant and focused, with a core of tarry currant, mineral and spice. The texture is supple for a young wine, finishing with firm tannins. The flavors grow on you, making this appealing to drink now. 900 cases made. • $35 • (11/15/97) • **90**
Cabernet Sauvignon Napa Valley Reserve 1991 • $25 • (09/30/95) • **91**
Chardonnay Russian River Valley 1996: Intense and concentrated but lacking focus, its core of pear, spice and cedary oak flavors needs to come together. Try now. 6,600 cases made. • $15 • (04/30/98) • **85**
Chardonnay Russian River Valley 1995: Bright and appealing for its forward apple, pear and spice flavors, finishing with a polished texture and distinctive character. 5,820 cases made. • $15 • (07/31/97) • **86**
Chardonnay Russian River Valley 1994: Appealing for its up-front pear, peach and spicy Chardonnay flavors and light oak shadings on the finish. 5,352 cases made. • $13 • (05/15/96) • **85**
Chardonnay Russian River Valley 1993 • $13 • (01/31/95) • **85**
Chardonnay Russian River Valley Reserve 1996: A gentle, elegant, subtle style, with pretty hints of pear, spice and melon, finishing silky and earthy. Impressive for its delicate texture and rich flavors. 235 cases made. • $30 • (04/30/98) • **90**
Chardonnay Russian River Valley Reserve 1995: Rich and generous with its spicy pear and vanilla flavors; some nice smoky notes on the finish. Tasty now. 200 cases made. • $25 • (06/15/97) • **91**
Pinot Noir Central Coast 1993 • $9 • (03/31/95) • **79**
White Zinfandel Napa Valley 1994 • $6 • (09/15/95) • **79**
Zinfandel Napa Valley 1995: Simple cherry notes combine with what can only be described as fresh Concord grape juice. 4,874 cases made. • $14 • (09/15/97) • **80**
Zinfandel Napa Valley 1994 • $12 • (04/30/96) • **87**
Zinfandel Napa Valley 1993 • $10 • (10/15/95) • **84**
Zinfandel Napa Valley 1992 • $8 • (04/30/94) BB • **88**
Zinfandel Napa Valley 1990 • $9 • (10/15/92) • **77**
Zinfandel Napa Valley 1989 • $9 • (03/31/92) • **83**
Zinfandel Napa Valley 1987 • $9 • (05/15/90) • **89**
Zinfandel Napa Valley 1986 • $8 • (12/15/88) • **83**
Zinfandel Napa Valley 1985 • $8 • (12/31/87) • **89**
Zinfandel Napa Valley 1983 • $6 • (03/15/87) • **71**
Zinfandel Napa Valley 1982 • $6 • (03/01/85) • **91**
Zinfandel Napa Valley 1981 • $6 • (09/16/84) • **80**
Zinfandel Napa Valley Estate 1996: Manages to balance the firm, crisp tannins with a modest core of plum and wild berry. Best by 2000. 1,100 cases made. • $25 • (05/31/98) • **82**
Zinfandel Napa Valley Estate 1995: Delicious, ripe and juicy, with zesty black cherry, wild berry, anise, cedar, pepper and spice flavors. Shows elegance and finesse, with well-integrated tannins and fine length. Drink now through 2002. 1,008 cases made. • $20 • (04/30/98) • **89**
Zinfandel Napa Valley Reserve 1994: Pleasant currant, leather, herb and spicy Zin flavors turn smooth and polished on the finish. Simple, but elegant and easy to drink. 330 cases made. • $25 • (09/15/96) • **85**

BUENA VISTA | CALIFORNIA

Brut Blanc de Blanc Carneros 1991: Fresh toasty aromas and very bright acidity lend a youthful air to this wine, already 7-years-old. It also has a floral component, as well as layers of orange, lemon and pear. Needs a year or two more to calm down. 6,000 cases made. • $17 • (04/30/98) • **88**
Brut Blanc de Blanc Carneros 1990: Ripe, clean and refreshing, with well-integrated layers of spicy pear flavors and hints of cherry. Turns complex on the finish. • $14 • (09/15/96) • **86**
Cabernet Sauvignon Carneros 1994: An elegant style with herb, coffee, currant and cedar notes and fleshy tannins. Smooth and polished, it drinks well now and should hold through 2000. 34,000 cases made. • $16 • (08/31/97) • **88**
Cabernet Sauvignon Carneros 1993: On the tart side. Offers bright black cherry and herb flavors with a crisp finish. Best from 1999. • $NA • (01/01/97) • **82**
Cabernet Sauvignon Carneros 1992 • $12 • (12/15/95) • **80**
Cabernet Sauvignon Carneros 1991 • $12 • (10/15/94) • **87**
Cabernet Sauvignon Carneros 1990 • $11 • (09/15/93) • **82**
Cabernet Sauvignon Carneros 1989 • $9 • (11/15/92) • **74**
Cabernet Sauvignon Carneros 1988 • $8 • (11/15/91) • **79**
Cabernet Sauvignon Carneros 1987 • $11 • (10/15/90) • **83**
Cabernet Sauvignon Carneros 1986 • $11 • (10/15/89) • **91**
Cabernet Sauvignon Carneros 1985 • $10 • (11/15/88) • **84**
Cabernet Sauvignon Carneros 1984 • $10 • (08/31/87) • **94**
Cabernet Sauvignon Carneros 1983 • $9 • (06/15/87) • **77**
Cabernet Sauvignon Carneros 1982 • $11 • (09/16/85) • **85**
Cabernet Sauvignon Carneros 1981 • $11 • (02/16/85) • **89**
Cabernet Sauvignon Carneros Grand Reserve 1993: On the tart side, with dark cherry and plum flavors that are compact and concentrated, finishing with a pretty aftertaste that echoes spicy currant and wild berry. 1,100 cases made. • $26 • (08/31/97) • **90**
Cabernet Sauvignon Carneros Grand Reserve 1992: Marked by an earthy, barnyardy accent and an herb and olive edge, but doesn't show much in the way of ripe fruit flavors. • $24 • (09/15/96) • **80**

Cabernet Sauvignon Carneros Grand Reserve 1990 • $24 • (10/15/94) • **83**
Cabernet Sauvignon Carneros Grand Reserve 1988 • $23 • (03/31/93) • **86**
Cabernet Sauvignon Carneros Private Reserve 1986 • $23 Ⓐ • (03/15/91) • **89**
Cabernet Sauvignon Carneros Private Reserve 1985 • $18 • (10/15/89) SS • **94**
Cabernet Sauvignon Carneros Private Reserve 1983 • $18 • (02/15/88) • **90**
Cabernet Sauvignon Carneros Private Reserve 1982 • $19 • (02/15/87) • **87**
Cabernet Sauvignon Carneros Private Reserve (Special Selection) 1981 • $18 • (07/01/86) • **88**
Cabernet Sauvignon Carneros Special Selection 1978 • $18 • (06/01/86) • **96**
Cabernet Sauvignon Sonoma County 1986 • $11 • (11/15/89) • **90**
Cabernet Sauvignon Sonoma Valley 1978 • $30 • (06/01/86) • **94**
Cabernet Sauvignon Sonoma Valley Special Selection 1978 • $60 • (11/15/92) • **89**
Chardonnay Carneros 1995: Crisp and juicy, offering buttery green pear and nice floral flavors. Ready to drink. 36,000 cases made. • $12 • (07/31/97) • **86**
Chardonnay Carneros 1994: Starts out lean and simple, but the modest pear and apple flavors build to the finish, where they pick up a light oak note. A good, solid wine. 45,565 cases made. • $12 • (12/15/96) • **85**
Chardonnay Carneros Grand Reserve 1995: Ripe, rich, intense and concentrated, with a core of citrus, pear, spice, fig and apricot flavors that fan out, finishing with a spicy quality. 1,176 cases made. • $24 • (12/15/97) • **89**
Chardonnay Carneros Grand Reserve 1994: A big and ripe but somewhat understated style that frames its citrus and pear in a trace of oak. Maintains a sense of elegance and grace. 903 cases made. • $22 • (06/15/96) • **88**
Gamay Beaujolais Carneros 1988 • $7 • (07/15/89) • **84**
Gamay Beaujolais Sonoma Valley Carneros 1987 • $7 • (02/29/88) • **82**
Gamay Beaujolais Sonoma Valley Carneros 1986 • $7 • (05/31/87) • **83**
Gewürztraminer Carneros 1993 • $7 • (02/28/95) • **80**
L'Année Carneros 1986 • $35 • (02/28/91) • **87**
L'Année Carneros 1984 • $32 • (02/15/88) • **88**
Late Harvest Carneros Ingrid's Vineyard 1989 • $18 • (04/30/91) • **87**
Merlot Carneros 1994: An earthy nuance up front fades to reveal currant, tar and cedary oak flavors. The price is appealing and it's ready to drink. 24,086 cases made. • $12 • (05/15/97) • **84**
Merlot Carneros 1993 • $13 • (06/30/96) • **83**
Merlot Carneros 1992 • $13 • (05/15/95) • **82**
Merlot Carneros 1991 • $12 • (12/31/93) • **82**
Merlot Carneros 1990 • $11 • (10/31/92) • **86**
Merlot Carneros 1989 • $11 • (05/31/92) • **71**
Merlot Carneros 1985 • $11 • (06/30/88) • **80**
Merlot Carneros Grand Reserve 1994: A slight green, herbal edge and a whiff of tobacco lead into ripe fruit flavors, a core of plum and wild berry. Has the tannic strength to cellar into 1999 to 2001. 893 cases made. • $26 • (07/31/97) • **88**
Merlot Carneros Grand Reserve 1989 • $20 • (05/31/93) • **82**
Merlot Carneros Private Reserve 1988 • $17 • (05/31/92) • **82**
Merlot Carneros Private Reserve 1987 • $18 • (03/31/91) • **84**
Merlot Carneros Private Reserve 1986 • $17 • (10/31/89) • **86**
Merlot Carneros Private Reserve 1984 • $15 • (02/15/88) • **87**
Merlot Sonoma County 1987 • $11 • (07/31/90) • **86**
Pinot Noir Carneros 1995: Lean and trim, with a modest band of sage-accented Pinot Noir flavors. Drink now. 14,465 cases made. • $16 • (08/31/97) • **86**
Pinot Noir Carneros 1994: In a simple style, with a spicy, peppery accent to the straightforward cherry and strawberry flavors. 17,659 cases made. • $12 • (11/30/96) • **82**
Pinot Noir Carneros 1993 • $10 • (10/15/95) BB • **86**
Pinot Noir Carneros 1992 • $10 • (03/31/95) • **77**
Pinot Noir Carneros 1991 • $10 • (02/28/94) • **80**
Pinot Noir Carneros 1990 • $9 • (09/30/92) • **81**
Pinot Noir Carneros 1989 • $7/5.(07/31/91) • **81**
Pinot Noir Carneros 1988 • $11 • (12/15/90) • **82**
Pinot Noir Carneros 1983 • $14 • (08/31/86) • **75**
Pinot Noir Carneros 1980 • $7 • (04/16/84) • **71**
Pinot Noir Carneros Grand Reserve 1995: A light, uncomplicated style, with more herb, earth, tea and sage notes than fruit. Hard to find much to admire; it simply lacks flavor, depth and concentration. 1,095 cases made. • $26 • (11/15/97) • **79**
Pinot Noir Carneros Grand Reserve 1994 • $20 • (02/29/96) • **84**
Pinot Noir Carneros Grand Reserve 1991 • $20 • (10/31/94) • **86**
Pinot Noir Carneros Grand Reserve 1990 • $16 • (02/28/93) HR • **89**
Pinot Noir Carneros Private Reserve 1987 • $14 • (06/30/91) • **80**
Pinot Noir Carneros Private Reserve 1986 • $14 • (03/31/90) • **85**
Pinot Noir Carneros Private Reserve 1984 • $15 • (02/15/88) • **81**
Pinot Noir Carneros Private Reserve 1981 • $14 • (08/31/86) • **88**
Sauvignon Blanc California 1996: This is a fun, ebullient Sauvignon Blanc, gracefully blending bright melon and grapefruit flavors into an enticing package, lively and with some richness. Quite nice, and check out the price. 70,000 cases made. • $8 • (06/30/97) • **88**
Sauvignon Blanc Lake County 1995: Light-bodied, with a welcome crispness that complements the melon and citrus flavors. 50,000 cases made. • $8 • (08/31/96) BB • **87**
Sauvignon Blanc Lake County 1994 • $7 • (09/15/95) BB • **87**
Sauvignon Blanc Lake County 1993 • $7 • (12/31/94) • **79**
Zinfandel North Coast 1984 • $7 • (04/30/88) • **77**
Zinfandel Sonoma County 1982 • $6 • (04/01/85) • **80**

Key: SS—Spectator Selection CS—Cellar Selection HR—Highly Recommended BB—Best Buy $NA—Price not available Ⓐ—Auction Price (BT)—Barrel Tasting
Dates in parentheses indicate the issues in which the ratings were published.

BULLY HILL | NEW YORK

Brut Seyval Blanc Finger Lakes 1988 • $15 • (12/31/90) • **74**

BURGESS | CALIFORNIA

Cabernet Sauvignon Napa Valley Vintage Selection 1994: An interesting wine with plum, anise, smoke and spice qualities. Finishes with a strong licorice edge and some rustic tannins. 6,600 cases made. • $22 • (11/30/97) • **87**
Cabernet Sauvignon Napa Valley Vintage Selection 1993: Tight and well focused, with cedar, currant, tobacco and spice flavors at the core, finishing with firm tannins. Drinkable now. 6,792 cases made. • $22 • (05/15/97) • **88**
Cabernet Sauvignon Napa Valley Vintage Selection 1992: Elegant and well crafted, with a nice balance between toasty, buttery oak notes and ripe cherry, plum and currant flavors. Finishes with firm tannins, but they're not out of line. Drink now. 8,100 cases made. • $22 • (11/15/96) SS • **90**
Cabernet Sauvignon Napa Valley Vintage Selection 1991 • $20 • (12/15/95) • **83**
Cabernet Sauvignon Napa Valley Vintage Selection 1990 • $18 • (10/15/94) • **88**
Cabernet Sauvignon Napa Valley Vintage Selection 1989 • $18 • (11/15/93) • **86**
Cabernet Sauvignon Napa Valley Vintage Selection 1988 • $17 • (07/31/92) • **85**
Cabernet Sauvignon Napa Valley Vintage Selection 1987 • $20 • (10/15/91) • **85**
Cabernet Sauvignon Napa Valley Vintage Selection 1986 • $20 • (07/15/90) • **88**
Cabernet Sauvignon Napa Valley Vintage Selection 1985 • $24 • (07/15/89) • **92**
Cabernet Sauvignon Napa Valley Vintage Selection 1984 • $17 • (07/31/88) • **92**
Cabernet Sauvignon Napa Valley Vintage Selection 1983 • $17 • (10/15/87) • **85**
Cabernet Sauvignon Napa Valley Vintage Selection 1982 • $16 • (10/15/86) • **81**
Cabernet Sauvignon Napa Valley Vintage Selection 1981 • $16 • (09/16/85) • **87**
Cabernet Sauvignon Napa Valley Vintage Selection 1980 • $16 • (05/01/84) SS • **90**
Cabernet Sauvignon Napa Valley Vintage Selection 1978 • $52 • (11/15/92) • **93**
Cabernet Sauvignon Napa Valley Vintage Selection 1974 • $55 • (11/15/94) • **74**
Chardonnay Napa Valley 1995: Dull, with an earthy edge to the ripe pear and apple. Not very appealing. Tasted twice, with consistent notes. 6,500 cases made. • $15 • (04/30/98) • **78**
Chardonnay Napa Valley Barrel Fermented Debourbage 1993 • $15 • (07/31/95) • **86**
Chardonnay Napa Valley Debourbage 1994: A touch earthy, with murky pear and apple notes. Straightens out nicely on the finish. 11,000 cases made. • $15 • (07/31/96) • **82**
Chardonnay Napa Valley Triere Vineyard Reserve 1994: Good, but the mature, oxidized pear and apple flavors make it taste like it's 6 to 8 years

old. May appeal to those who like Chardonnays with age. 1,950 cases made. • $26 • (04/30/98) • **82**

Chardonnay Napa Valley Triere Vineyard Reserve 1993: Mature, offering flavors of spicy pear, apple, citrus and hazelnut. A solid wine that's ready to drink. 1,636 cases made. • $22 • (11/30/96) • **85**

Merlot Napa Valley 1995: An austere, leathery style, with more sage, herb and cedary notes than pure fruit—but sometimes that's Merlot. Turns meaty and leathery on the finish. Best to cellar into 1999 or 2000. 3,040 cases made. • $22 • (04/30/98) • **84**

Merlot Napa Valley 1994: Complex and well crafted, with a nice interplay between the spicy, toasty oak notes and ripe cherry and berry flavors. A solid effort. 2,980 cases made. • $20 • (11/30/96) • **87**

Merlot Napa Valley 1993 • $20 • (05/31/96) • **84**

Zinfandel Napa Valley 1994: Hard-edged, smoky and meaty, with cedary oak flavors; the fruit struggles to compete. Hints of wild berry and black cherry on the finish suggest cellaring into 1999 might be worthwhile. 4,158 cases made. • $13 • (04/30/97) • **87**

Zinfandel Napa Valley 1993: This is a medium-bodied wine, solid, with a marked herb and currant accent on the palate. 5,185 cases made. • $12 • (11/30/96) • **85**

Zinfandel Napa Valley 1992 • $11 • (10/15/95) • **79**

Zinfandel Napa Valley 1991 • $12 • (10/15/94) • **81**

Zinfandel Napa Valley 1990 • $12 • (09/30/93) • **84**

Zinfandel Napa Valley 1989 • $10 • (10/15/92) • **80**

Zinfandel Napa Valley 1988 • $12 • (07/31/91) • **80**

Zinfandel Napa Valley 1987 • $10 • (05/31/90) • **82**

Zinfandel Napa Valley 1986 • $9 • (07/31/89) • **82**

Zinfandel Napa Valley 1985 • $9 • (06/30/88) • **87**

Zinfandel Napa Valley 1984 • $8 • (11/15/87) • **89**

Zinfandel Napa Valley 1983 • $7 • (10/31/86) • **81**

Zinfandel Napa Valley 1982 • $6 • (07/16/85) • **85**

Zinfandel Napa Valley 1981 • $6 • (04/16/84) • **81**

BURRELL SCHOOL | CALIFORNIA

Cabernet Franc Napa Valley Aviemore Vineyard 1995: A smooth, smoky wine with an interesting floral quality and a bright cherry and raspberry core. Has a lot to offer and should be even better several years from now. 125 cases made. • $18 • (09/15/97) • **87**

BUTTERFLY CREEK | CALIFORNIA

Merlot California 1989 • $15 • (05/31/92) • **77**

Merlot Sierra Foothills Mariposa County 1991 • $10 • (09/15/94) • **82**

BUTTONWOOD | CALIFORNIA

Cabernet Franc Santa Ynez Valley 1994: An interesting blend of herb, tea, chocolate, black cherry and spice flavors in a lean texture. Short finish doesn't quite live up to the opening. Still very nice. Drink now or hold. 301 cases made. • $15 • (03/31/98) • **85**

Cabernet Sauvignon Santa Ynez Valley 1994: Earthy and herbal, having a cedary disposition on the palate. Tannins are firm; perhaps a bit too much so for the beef and currant flavors behind them. 676 cases made. • $16 • (10/31/97) • **83**

Marsanne Santa Ynez Valley 1996: An interesting blend of peach and mineral flavors that lock horns a bit at present, but might come together in three to six months. Dry, with moderate body and finish. 576 cases made. • $12 • (01/31/98) • **86**

Merlot Santa Ynez Valley 1994: Cola, menthol, herbs and spice flavors are followed by black currant, eucalyptus and licorice. Tannins are a bit coarse and bitter, but it should smooth out with time. Better after 2000. 1,467 cases made. • $16 • (02/28/98) • **87**

Merlot Santa Ynez Valley 1993: Smoke and cherries blend nicely, although the oak is a bit forward on the palate. Finishes with a nice, bright, spicy quality. 1,361 cases made. • $16 • (07/31/97) • **87**

Sauvignon Blanc Santa Ynez Valley 1996: Tangy and tight, with a nonetheless silky veneer, the wine shows bright lemon and grapefruit qualities. Finishes squeaky clean. 1,022 cases made. • $10 • (12/15/97) • **86**

Sauvignon Blanc Santa Ynez Valley 1995: Graceful and harmonious, packing lots of lovely pear and quince flavors into a supple frame, balancing the fruit with nice hints of toast and vanilla. An elegant Sauvignon Blanc that's ready to drink. 1,270 cases made. • $10 • (05/15/97) • **88**

Sauvignon Blanc Santa Ynez Valley 1993 • $12 • (08/31/95) • **85**

BYINGTON | CALIFORNIA

Cabernet Sauvignon Alexander Valley Smith Reichel Vineyard 1994: Rich spice, raspberry and vanilla aromas are followed by a somewhat awkward mix of oak, tannin, wintergreen and black currant flavors. Shows potential. 900 cases made. • $18 • (11/30/97) • **83**

Cabernet Sauvignon Alexander Valley Smith Reichel Vineyard 1993: Has an austere tannic edge to the modest range of cherry, tobacco, spice and cedar flavors. Finishes with tart acidity and a clean, though lean, finish. 900 cases made. • $17 • (09/15/96) • **83**

Cabernet Sauvignon Alexander Valley Smith Reichel Vineyard 1992 • $15 • (12/15/95) • **87**

Cabernet Sauvignon Napa Valley 1987 • $16 • (11/15/91) • **86**

Cabernet Sauvignon Santa Cruz Mountains Bates Ranch 1992 • $22 • (12/15/95) • **83**

Cabernet Sauvignon Santa Cruz Mountains Bates Ranch Special Reserve Vineyards 1993: A tightly wound young wine with lively, sour cherry and tart plum flavors that are well focused. 1,200 cases made. • $20 • (09/15/96) • **87**

Cabernet Sauvignon Santa Cruz Mountains Twin Mountains 1994: Cherry and blackberry flavors are backed by a strong charred, herbal, licorice edge. It won't get better; drink now. 500 cases made. • $14 • (11/30/97) • **82**

Chardonnay Mount Veeder 1993 • $14 • (07/31/95) • **83**

Chardonnay Napa Valley Twin Mountains 1996: A bit earthy, with a slight grassy twinge. The ripe pear and melon flavors are supple in texture, finishing with anise and oak on the aftertaste. Drink now through 2001. 1,500 cases made. • $15 • (07/31/98) • **88**

Chardonnay Napa Valley Twin Mountains 1995: A ripe and spicy style, with apple-pie flavors and aromas. Won't shortchange you on flavor, but could use a little more finesse and polish. 2,400 cases made. • $15 • (06/15/97) • **88**

Chardonnay Santa Cruz Mountains 1996: Rich and full-bodied, with complex fig, pear, spice and mineral flavors, turning elegant and earthy on the finish, where the flavors come together. Drink now through 2002. 1,200 cases made. • $20 • (06/30/98) • **90**

Chardonnay Santa Cruz Mountains 1995: Displays wonderful aromas and rich, complex flavors, serving up a mouthful of creamy pear, smoke, fig and melon, adding a dash of hazelnut and spice. Finishes with a long, zesty aftertaste. 600 cases made. • $20 • (06/15/97) • **93**

Chardonnay Santa Cruz Mountains 1993 • $18 • (07/31/95) • **84**

Chardonnay Santa Cruz Mountains Bald Mountain Vineyard Special Reserve Vineyards 1996: Smooth, ripe, rich and creamy, with sharply focused pear, anise, butter, fig and melon. Shows depth and richness, with a dash of hazelnut on the finish. Drink now through 2001. 250 cases made. • $24 • (07/31/98) • **90**

Chardonnay Santa Cruz Mountains Dirk Vineyard Special Reserve Vineyards 1996: Earthy and complex, with a creamy texture, and lots of pear, hazelnut, citrus and spicy, toasty oak and a pretty yeast flavor. Long and full on the finish, it packs in the flavor while remaining elegant and polished. Drink now through 2003. 500 cases made. • $24 • (06/30/98) • **91**

Chardonnay Santa Cruz Mountains Dirk Vineyard Special Reserve Vineyards 1995: Smooth and polished, with a creamy core of ripe pear, apple, spice and hazelnut flavors that stay lively through the finish, where the hazelnut and anise become more pronounced. 300 cases made. • $24 • (06/15/97) • **91**

Chardonnay Santa Cruz Mountains Redwood Hill Vineyard 1993 • $23 • (07/31/95) • **84**

Chardonnay Santa Cruz Mountains Special Reserve Vineyards 1994: Smooth and spicy, with appealing ripe pear, honey and apple notes. Impressive for its purity of fruit and elegance. 800 cases made. • $18 • (06/30/96) • **87**

Chardonnay Santa Cruz Mountains Special Reserve Vineyards Spring Ridge Vineyard 1994: Smooth, rich and creamy, with an alluring, substantial core of pear, spice, honey and vanilla. Altogether impressive for its complexity and finesse. 400 cases made. • $23 • (06/30/96) • **90**

Merlot Sonoma County Bradford Mountain 1994: Smooth and supple, with a spicy edge to the cola, cherry, currant and berry flavors. Picks up traces of oak and chocolate on the finish. 900 cases made. • $18 • (05/15/97) • **87**

Merlot Sonoma County Bradford Mountain 1993: Needs time to open up; has tiers of ripe cherry, plum, currant and spice. Finishes with firm tannins, but good length. Short-term cellaring advised. 1,000 cases made. • $15 • (07/31/96) • **87**

Merlot Sonoma County Bradford Mountain 1991 • $15 • (09/15/94) • **83**

Pinot Noir California 1988 • $15 • (04/30/91) • **83**

Pinot Noir Central Coast 1995: A racy style, with lean, earthy, spicy, herbal qualities and just a dash of cherry to hold your interest. Drink now. 800 cases made. • $18 • (02/28/98) • **84**
Pinot Noir Napa Valley 1987 • $15 • (04/30/91) • **74**
Pinot Noir Santa Barbara County Bien Nacido Vineyard 1991 • $15 • (03/31/95) • **78**
Pinot Noir Santa Cruz Mountains Special Reserve Vineyards 1994 • $25 • (02/29/96) • **88**
Pinot Noir Santa Cruz Mountains St. Charles Vineyard Special Reserve Vineyards 1993 • $30 • (02/29/96) • **85**
Pinot Noir Willamette Valley 1995: Light and pleasant, except for a streak of acrid smoke that overshadows the modest berry notes. Try in 1999. 600 cases made. • $20 • (02/28/98) • **81**
Sauvignon Blanc San Luis Obispo County French Camp Vineyard 1993 • $8 • (08/31/95) • **84**
Zinfandel Howell Mountain 1992 • $10 • (03/31/96) • **86**
Zinfandel Paso Robles Sunny Slope Vineyard 1990 • $12 • (09/30/93) • **85**
Zinfandel Santa Clara County Calle Cielo Vineyard 1992 • $15 • (10/15/94) • **82**

BYNUM, DAVIS | CALIFORNIA

Cabernet Sauvignon Napa Valley Reserve Bottling 1984 • $7 • (12/15/87) • **71**
Cabernet Sauvignon Russian River Valley Hedin Vineyard Limited Edition 1994: Attractive for its ripe cherry and raspberry flavors, this moderately rich wine is complex and concentrated, finishing with mild tannins and good length. Ready now and into 2000. 625 cases made. • $20 • (12/15/97) • **87**
Cabernet Sauvignon Sonoma County 1989 • $11 • (11/15/92) • **81**
Cabernet Sauvignon Sonoma County 1987 • $11 • (11/15/90) • **79**
Cabernet Sauvignon Sonoma County 1986 • $10 • (11/15/89) • **84**
Chardonnay Russian River Valley Allen & McIlroy Vineyards Limited Edition 1994: Bright and lively, with flavors of ripe pear, apple, spice and nutmeg, finishing with fine length and just a dash of oak. Ready to drink. 709 cases made. • $18 • (05/15/97) • **90**
Chardonnay Russian River Valley Limited Edition 1995: Upfront and fruity, with pretty spice, apple and melon notes, finishing with nice length and a light, toasty aftertaste. 640 cases made. • $17 • (11/30/97) • **87**
Eclipse Sonoma County 1994: Tightly wound, with a firm band of currant, black cherry, plum and spice, even a dash of raspberry. Turns complex on the finish, where the flavors remain bright and lively. Best to cellar into 2000 to 2002. 652 cases made. • $28 • (04/30/98) • **87**
Fumé Blanc Russian River Valley Shone Farm Dry 1994 • $8 • (08/31/95) • **82**
Merlot Russian River Valley Laureles Vineyard 1994: An elegant, understated style that delivers some nice currant and black cherry flavors to hold your interest. 1,089 cases made. • $22 • (05/15/97) • **86**
Merlot Russian River Valley Laureles Vineyard 1991 • $20 • (09/15/94) • **81**
Pinot Noir Russian River Valley 1994: Its medium-weight plum and cherry notes taste ripe, but it lacks focus, turning earthy, and the oak flavors bring a dill accent. 2,243 cases made. • $14 • (11/30/96) • **82**
Pinot Noir Russian River Valley 1993 • $12 • (12/31/95) • **82**
Pinot Noir Russian River Valley 1991 • $17 • (02/28/94) • **84**
Pinot Noir Russian River Valley 1990 • $18 • (02/28/94) • **72**
Pinot Noir Russian River Valley Artist Series 1985 • $15 • (06/15/88) • **82**
Pinot Noir Russian River Valley Limited Edition 1995: Ripe and spicy, with a range of herb, dried cherry, stewed plum and anise notes that hold together nicely. 825 cases made. • $28 • (12/15/97) • **86**
Pinot Noir Russian River Valley Limited Edition 1994: Attractive black cherry and raspberry notes are elegant and well focused. Smooth, ripe and spicy, finishing with a nice touch of herb and oak. Drink now. 1,000 cases made. • $24 • (02/28/97) • **88**
Pinot Noir Russian River Valley Limited Edition 1992 • $21 • (09/15/95) • **84**
Pinot Noir Russian River Valley Limited Release 1991 • $18 • (10/31/94) • **88**
Pinot Noir Russian River Valley Limited Release 1990 • $18 • (09/30/92) • **84**
Pinot Noir Russian River Valley Limited Release 1988 • $16 • (04/30/91) • **86**
Pinot Noir Russian River Valley Limited Release 1986 • $14 • (03/31/90) • **83**
Pinot Noir Russian River Valley Limited Release 1984 • $14 • (05/31/88) • **89**
Pinot Noir Russian River Valley Westside Road 1983 • $10 • (07/16/86) • **71**
Pinot Noir Sonoma County Reserve Bottling 1986 • $9 • (09/15/88) • **82**

Key: SS—Spectator Selection CS—Cellar Selection HR—Highly Recommended BB—Best Buy $NA—Price not available Ⓐ—Auction Price (BT)—Barrel Tasting
Dates in parentheses indicate the issues in which the ratings were published.

Sauvignon Blanc Russian River Valley Shone Farm Vineyard Selection 1996: Not shy, it's fresh and lively, with bright green apple, orange and lemon notes, and a tangy, herbal finish that nearly jumps off the palate. 1,830 cases made. • $11 • (06/30/97) • **89**
Zinfandel Russian River Valley 1992 • $12 • (10/15/95) • **88**
Zinfandel Russian River Valley 1991 • $12 • (10/15/94) • **87**
Zinfandel Russian River Valley 1990 • $12 • (10/15/92) • **84**
Zinfandel Sonoma County Old Vines 1995: Smooth and silky, modest in flavor, with some appealing black cherry and tarry flavors. Drink now. 1,946 cases made. • $16 • (12/15/97) • **84**

BYRON | CALIFORNIA

Cabernet Sauvignon Central Coast 1985 • $14 • (12/15/89) • **76**
Cabernet Sauvignon Santa Barbara County 1990 • $16 • (08/31/92) • **85**
Cabernet Sauvignon Santa Barbara County 1989 • $16 • (11/15/93) • **82**
Chardonnay Santa Barbara County 1995: Tight and well focused, with concentrated citrus- and pear-tinged Chardonnay flavors, this is sleek, elegant and complex. Try now. 14,896 cases made. • $17 • (05/31/97) • **90**
Chardonnay Santa Barbara County 1994: Pleasant enough, with ripe pear, honey, apple and spice notes and then a hint of lemon and tangerine on the finish. Well balanced. 20,000 cases made. • $16 • (05/31/96) • **88**
Chardonnay Santa Barbara County 1993 • $15 • (07/31/95) SS • **90**
Chardonnay Santa Barbara County Reserve 1994: An elegant, understated style with flavors that grow on you. It has ripe pear with hints of pineapple and citrus framed in spicy, vanilla-scented oak. Picks up a nice hazelnut taste on the finish. 4,252 cases made. • $23 • (05/31/96) • **90**
Chardonnay Santa Barbara County Reserve 1993 • $23 • (07/31/95) HR • **91**
Chardonnay Santa Maria Valley 1996: Clean and spicy, with plenty of ripe citrus, green pear, apple and melon flavors, finishing with a lingering tropical fruit aftertaste. Drink now through 2000. 24,000 cases made. • $17 • (07/31/98) • **88**
Chardonnay Santa Maria Valley Estate 1995: Ripe, expressive and exotic, with lots of juicy pear, pineapple, citrus, mineral and spice. Elegant, rich, complex and concentrated. Best from 1999 through 2003. 2,860 cases made. • $32 • (07/31/98) • **92**
Chardonnay Santa Maria Valley Estate 1994: Openly fruity, opulent with racy pear and pineapple flavors, but on the finish it turns smooth and silky, revealing more complexity and finesse as the flavors fan out and show more depth and concentration. • $30 • (06/30/97) • **92**
Chardonnay Santa Maria Valley Estate 1993 • $28 • (04/30/96) HR • **93**
Pinot Blanc Santa Maria Valley 1994 • $14 • (04/30/96) • **90**
Pinot Gris Santa Maria Valley 1994: Appealing for its pure peach and nectarine flavors. Finish shows a slight mineral accent. 427 cases made. • $14 • (09/15/96) • **84**
Pinot Noir Santa Barbara County 1995: This California Pinot is intensely flavored, with the rich, earthy cherry, wild berry and spicy features typical of this winery's style with this variety, and its finesse and elegance carry through the substantial finish. 4,181 cases made. • $17 • (11/30/97) SS • **90**
Pinot Noir Santa Barbara County 1994 • $16 • (02/29/96) • **87**
Pinot Noir Santa Barbara County 1992 • $15 • (02/28/94) • **83**
Pinot Noir Santa Barbara County 1986: Mature, with dashes of herb and brown sugar, this is a good example of an aged Santa Barbara Pinot Noir. Finishes with an herbal, vegetal note, little fruit. • $12 • (03/31/97) • **79**
Pinot Noir Santa Barbara County 1985 • $12 • (06/15/88) • **81**
Pinot Noir Santa Barbara County Reserve 1994: Rich, dense and smoky, with firm, dry, leathery tannins. Needs time to open and show its fruit, but for now it's tight and a touch stemmy. Finishes with dashes of black cherry, olive and spice. • $24 • (06/30/97) • **87**
Pinot Noir Santa Barbara County Reserve 1993: Ripe and intense, with exotic herb, spice and black cherry aromas and similar flavors that build on the palate. Smooth texture, right up to the finish, where the tannins become more evident. Drinks well now. 3,043 cases made. • $23 • (01/31/97) • **88**
Pinot Noir Santa Barbara County Reserve 1992 • $23 • (03/31/95) • **86**
Pinot Noir Santa Barbara County Reserve 1991 • $23 • (02/28/94) • **88**
Pinot Noir Santa Barbara County Reserve 1990: Mature, with earthy, spicy flavors that slowly give way to a core of rhubarb, cherry, tar and citrus notes. Elegant and well made. Drink now, before the fruit fades. • $20 • (03/31/97) • **88**
Pinot Noir Santa Barbara County Reserve 1987 • $16 • (12/15/89) • **85**
Pinot Noir Santa Barbara County Reserve 1986 • $12 • (06/15/88) • **84**
Pinot Noir Santa Barbara County Sierra Madre Vineyards 1984 • $13 • (08/31/86) • **85**
Pinot Noir Santa Maria Valley Reserve 1995: Dense and earthy, it unfolds to reveal a core of cherry, berry and beef flavors and dry tannins that make it

chewy and backward. Best to cellar into 1999 to 2000; it may show more fruit complexity. 1,609 cases made. • $25 • (01/31/98) • **87**

Sauvignon Blanc Santa Barbara County 1995: A ripe and generous wine, with buttery, citrusy flavors and a decadent, perfumy edge. 2,195 cases made. • $11 • (07/31/96) • **80**

Sauvignon Blanc Santa Barbara County 1993 • $11 • (08/31/95) • **82**

CA' DEL SOLO | CALIFORNIA

Barbera Monterey 1996: Smooth, supple and seductive, with lovely blackberry, black cherry and spice flavors that spread generously across the palate. Delicious now, but should continue to improve. 2,300 cases made. • $15 • (12/15/97) • **89**

Big House Red California 1992 • $8 • (10/15/93) BB • **84**

Big House Red California 1991 • $7 • (11/30/92) BB • **84**

Big House Red California 1990 • $7 • (06/30/92) BB • **85**

Big House White California 1994 • $7 • (10/15/95) BB • **86**

Big House White California 1993 • $7 • (04/15/95) • **83**

Charbono California La Farfalla 1996: Dark in color and richly concentrated, this shows dense, grapey plum and wild berry flavors and firm tannins. 555 cases made. • $15 • (11/30/97) • **83**

Charbono California La Farfalla 1994: Smells floral and fruity, but is tight and compact on the palate with hints of cherry and berry flavors. 1,500 cases made. • $10 • (08/31/96) • **82**

Grappa di Moscato Santa Cruz Mountains NV: This will knock the socks off (literally). Grappa-esque, with its clean, almost ricelike essence. Caution....flammable. 334 cases made. • $18/375ml • (09/15/97) • **87**

Il Pescatore California 1996: A refreshing, lemony, mineral-tinged wine. A firmness on the tongue adds interest. Not complex, but has some depth and weight. My kind of bistro white—goes with just about anything. 5,360 cases made. • $15 • (03/31/98) • **85**

Il Pescatore California 1993 • $12 • (04/15/95) • **85**

Malvasia Bianca Monterey 1995: Light and refreshing. A zippy mouthful of spicy nectarine and floral flavors that dance nicely through the finish. Drink now. 2,600 cases made. • $9 • (07/31/96) • **86**

Malvasia Bianca Monterey 1994 • $9 • (09/30/95) • **85**

Malvasia Bianca Monterey 1993 • $9 • (04/15/95) • **85**

Muscat Monterey Moscato del Solo 1993 • $9 • (12/31/94) • **85**

Prunus California NV • $15/375ml • (03/31/92) • **92**

Prunus Santa Cruz Mountains NV: Hazelnuts and mirabelles come to mind when sipping this well-proportioned, though somewhat viscous eau-de-vie. It finishes fresh and clean. 681 cases made. • $15/375ml • (09/15/97) • **89**

Sangiovese California Il Fiasco 1996: Packs some jazzy black cherry and anise flavors onto a solid frame with firm, fine-grained tannins, bright acidity and a hint of earth on the long finish. Drink now. 2,400 cases made. • $15 • (12/15/97) • **86**

CAFARO | CALIFORNIA

Cabernet Sauvignon Napa Valley 1994: Starts out lean and trim, with a smoky cedar and tobacco quality, and the core of fruit is tart and firm, but the flavors grow on you and it's well balanced. Short-term cellaring is advised; try in 2001. • $30 • (10/31/97) • **89**

Cabernet Sauvignon Napa Valley 1993: Young and intense, a solid '93 showing nice interplay between the ripe cherry, spice, herb and tar nuances. Well balanced, it finishes with mild tannins, making it approachable now or suitable for into 2000. 960 cases made. • $28 • (10/15/96) • **87**

Cabernet Sauvignon Napa Valley 1992 • $26 • (12/15/95) • **88**

Cabernet Sauvignon Napa Valley 1991 • $28 • (09/15/95) • **88**

Cabernet Sauvignon Napa Valley 1990 • $24 • (11/15/93) • **84**

Cabernet Sauvignon Napa Valley 1989 • $16 Ⓐ • (11/15/92) • **85**

Cabernet Sauvignon Napa Valley 1988 • $25 • (11/15/91) • **81**

Cabernet Sauvignon Napa Valley 1987 • $20 • (11/15/90) • **84**

Cabernet Sauvignon Napa Valley 1986 • $18 • (11/15/89) • **93**

Merlot Napa Valley 1994: A touch herbal, with herb and bell pepper notes, but it also has tart currant and cedary oak flavors to give it added dimension. Finishes with soft, fleshy tannins. Drinkable now. • $30 • (11/15/97) • **88**

Merlot Napa Valley 1988 • $20 • (11/15/91) • **89**

Merlot Napa Valley 1987 • $18 • (12/31/90) • **86**

Merlot Napa Valley 1986 • $18 • (12/31/89) • **84**

CAIN | CALIFORNIA

Cabernet Sauvignon Napa Valley 1986 • $16 • (08/31/90) • **85**

Cabernet Sauvignon Napa Valley 1985 • $16 • (04/15/89) • **81**

Cabernet Sauvignon Napa Valley 1984 • $14 • (05/31/88) • **79**

Cabernet Sauvignon Napa Valley 1983 • $14 • (08/31/87) • **75**

Cabernet Sauvignon Napa Valley 1982 • $11 • (09/30/86) • **78**

Cabernet Sauvignon Napa Valley Estate 1987 • $25 • (10/15/90) • **92**

Cuvée Napa Valley 1994: Dry, earthy, tannic and leathery. Shows enough ripe currant and plum flavors, but the tannin level is troubling—it will take years to soften and by then the fruit may have disappeared. 10,000 cases made. • $19 • (07/31/97) • **85**

Cuvée Napa Valley 1993: Distinguished by earth- and tar-accented herb and cedar flavors that fold together with hints of plum, currant and cherry on the finish. Nicely integrated firm tannins. Try cellaring into 1999 to soften. 7,800 cases made. • $18 • (12/15/96) • **87**

Cuvée Napa Valley 1992 • $16 • (12/15/95) • **83**

Cuvée Napa Valley 1991 • $15 • (12/31/94) • **83**

Cuvée Napa Valley 1989 • $12 • (11/15/93) • **84**

Cuvée Napa Valley 1988 • $12 • (03/31/93) • **87**

Five Napa Valley 1997: A touch stalky with a slight green bean edge, it slowly unfolds into more appealing Cabernet flavors, with currant, herb and cedary flavors. Has fine intensity and concentration. • $NA • (07/31/98) (BT) • **90-94**

Five Napa Valley 1994: Dark, dense and detailed, with pleasant flavors of earthy currant, plum, cedar and spice, and intense, with firm, dry tannins and a complex aftertaste. A blend of 63 percent Cabernet Sauvignon, 25 percent Merlot, 6 percent Cabernet Franc, 4 percent Malbec, and 2 percent Petit Verdot. 5,500 cases made. • $45 • (10/31/97) • **88**

Five Napa Valley 1992: An herbal style with hints of black olive, cedar and currant. Picks up a firm, tannic edge of the finish, suggesting it should age until 2000 or so to soften. Tasted four times, with consistent notes. 6,200 cases made. • $40 • (12/15/96) • **86**

Five Napa Valley 1991 • $40 • (12/15/95) • **89**

Five Napa Valley 1990 • $34 • (09/15/94) CS • **93**

Five Napa Valley 1987: Complex, with a range of flavors stretching from earthy currant to leather, cedar, anise and cherry, finishing with supple tannins. Best now through 2003. • $70 • (12/15/97) • **89**

Five Napa Valley 1986: Cedary currant, spice and earth notes are pleasant enough, but like many '86s, it's losing its fruit flavor. This is fully mature now and not likely to improve or grow out of its drying tannins. Drink soon. 11,000 cases made. • $NA • (12/15/96) • **85**

Five Napa Valley 1985 • $43 Ⓐ • (06/15/89) • **87**

Five Spring Mountain 1996: Elegant and understated in this tasting, marked by subtle herb, earth and currant notes, finishing with mild tannins. Not a showstopper, but shows fine balance and proportion. 7,000 cases made. • $50 • (06/15/97) (BT) • **90-94**

Merlot Napa Valley 1986 • $14 • (02/28/89) • **83**

Merlot Napa Valley 1984 • $12 • (09/30/88) • **89**

Merlot Napa Valley 1982 • $11 • (02/01/85) • **78**

Sauvignon Blanc Monterey Musqué 1994: Light and crisp. Distinct herbal and olive notes complement the citrusy apple flavors. Classic varietal flavors highlight a finish that just doesn't quit. 1,850 cases made. • $15 • (08/31/96) • **89**

Sauvignon Blanc Monterey Musqué 1993 • $14 • (08/31/95) • **80**

Sauvignon Blanc Monterey Musqué Ventana Vineyard 1995: Crisp and lively, this is a juicy mouthful of lime, star fruit and pear flavors that linger on the zippy finish. A refreshing California white. Drinkable now. 1,800 cases made. • $15 • (12/31/96) HR • **89**

Sauvignon Blanc Monterey Ventana Vineyard Musqué 1996: Fragrant and bright, packed with lemon, lime, peach, pear, grapefruit, sweet pea, honey and melon flavors. Not for the faint of heart, it's got an effusive character. The ripe fruit is tempered nicely by subtle grassy notes. Should get even better with a bit more bottle age. 2,300 cases made. • $17 • (01/31/98) • **90**

CAKEBREAD | CALIFORNIA

Cabernet Sauvignon Napa Valley 1994: Beautifully focused while enticingly lush. Ripe and chewy, with complex, concentrated flavors of currant, plum and black cherry with a long, rich aftertaste. Tempting now, better over the next few years. 15,000 cases made. • $25 • (07/31/97) SS • **92**

Cabernet Sauvignon Napa Valley 1993: Forward and supple, with ripe plum and cherry flavors, dashes of spice and herb. Comes across as simple, lacking depth and richness. 12,000 cases made. • $23 • (12/15/96) • **82**

Cabernet Sauvignon Napa Valley 1991 • $22 • (11/15/94) • **88**

Cabernet Sauvignon Napa Valley 1990 • $21 • (09/15/93) • **83**

Cabernet Sauvignon Napa Valley 1989 • $22 • (07/15/92) • **87**

Cabernet Sauvignon Napa Valley 1988 • $24 • (11/15/91) • **86**

Cabernet Sauvignon Napa Valley 1987 • $25 • (10/15/90) • **90**

Cabernet Sauvignon Napa Valley 1986 • $20 • (08/31/89) • 90
Cabernet Sauvignon Napa Valley 1985 • $20 • (04/15/88) • 90
Cabernet Sauvignon Napa Valley 1984 • $16 • (09/30/87) • 87
Cabernet Sauvignon Napa Valley 1983 • $16 • (11/30/86) • 93
Cabernet Sauvignon Napa Valley 1982 • $18 • (07/16/86) • 70
Cabernet Sauvignon Napa Valley Lot 2 1974 • $100 • (11/15/94) • 91

Cabernet Sauvignon Napa Valley Reserve 1993: Crisp and clean, with ripe berry, cherry, currant, cedary oak and spicy nuances built on a lean frame and finishing with firm tannins. Give it a year or two and hope it fills out but, like many 1993s, it's a bit hollow at midpalate. Best from 1999 to 2003. 800 cases made. • $50 • (03/31/98) • **87**

Cabernet Sauvignon Napa Valley Rutherford Reserve 1992: Tight, lean and compact, with a narrow band of spicy currant, plum and berry flavors. Firm tannins clamp down on the aftertaste. Best after 2000 to 2001. 600 cases made. • $44 • (07/31/97) • **87**

Cabernet Sauvignon Napa Valley Rutherford Reserve 1991: Intense and full-bodied, with a core of tarry ripe plum and currant flavors and some herb and dill notes. Young and vibrant, it needs cellaring into 2000 to soften the tannins, but it's well balanced and well proportioned. 600 cases made. • $42 • (11/15/96) • **89**

Cabernet Sauvignon Napa Valley Rutherford Reserve 1990 • $42 • (12/15/95) • **87**

Cabernet Sauvignon Napa Valley Rutherford Reserve 1987 • $23 • (09/15/93) HR • **91**

Cabernet Sauvignon Napa Valley Rutherford Reserve 1986 • $43 • (11/15/91) • **89**

Cabernet Sauvignon Napa Valley Rutherford Reserve 1984 • $35 • (02/15/90) • **85**

Chardonnay Napa Valley 1996: Elegant and refined, with hints of grapefruit, pear, citrus and spice, holding its focus on the aftertaste. Drink now through 2001. 28,000 cases made. • $25 • (05/31/98) • **88**

Chardonnay Napa Valley 1995: A crisp and flinty style, marked by tart green apple, citrus and pear flavors and finishing with a long, clean and lively aftertaste. 25,000 cases made. • $23 • (06/15/97) • **90**

Chardonnay Napa Valley 1994: A pleasantly fruity style with earthy peach and pear notes. Should age a little to soften it and let the flavors develop. Finishes crisp. 36,000 cases made. • $23 • (01/31/96) • **87**

Chardonnay Napa Valley 1993 • $22 • (07/31/95) • **84**

Chardonnay Napa Valley Reserve 1994: Lots of smoky, toasty oak up front, slowly integrating into ripe pear, citrus and spice notes, all coming together with harmony on the finish. Can stand short-term cellaring. 1,100 cases made. • $33 • (06/15/97) • **89**

Merlot Napa Valley 1994: An impressive young wine, firm and tight. A cedary oak quality overshadows the currant, plum and cherry flavors now. Try now. 2,602 cases made. • $27 • (07/31/97) • **89**

Pinot Noir Napa Valley Carneros 1994: Full-bodied, ripe and rich, this serves up lots of complex Pinot Noir flavors, plenty of plum and berry notes and a meaty, leathery nuance. Smooth, it drinks well now. 465 cases made. • $25 • (11/30/96) • **89**

Rosé Napa Valley 1995: A dry rosé, with a snappy wild berry and cherry accent. There's a slight bitter note on the finish. 300 cases made. • $16 • (11/30/96) • **82**

Rubaiyat Napa Valley 1994: A rather anonymous style that features spicy cherry and berry flavors. Simple and easy to drink, but pricey for what's there. 500 cases made. • $18 • (11/30/96) • **82**

Rutherford Reserve Napa Valley 1988 • $39 • (11/15/93) • **81**

Sauvignon Blanc Napa Valley 1996: Bright and tangy, this has pretty grapefruit and melon tones. On the finish, it lingers with a honeyed, lemon-lime accent. 16,000 cases made. • $14 • (01/31/98) • **86**

Sauvignon Blanc Napa Valley 1995: Bright and fruity, with a lively core of nectarine and citrus flavors that are lightly shaded by herbal notes on the finish. 11,000 cases made. • $14 • (08/31/96) • **87**

Sauvignon Blanc Napa Valley 1994 • $13 • (08/31/95) • **87**

Zinfandel Howell Mountain 1994: An elegant Zin from Howell Mountain, this is smooth and spicy, with a peppery accent to the flavors of cherry and currant. Finishes with a dash of earthiness. 1,100 cases made. • $19 • (11/30/96) • **89**

Zinfandel Howell Mountain 1992 • $17 • (09/15/94) HR • **90**

Key: SS—Spectator Selection CS—Cellar Selection HR—Highly Recommended BB—Best Buy $NA—Price not available Ⓐ—Auction Price (BT)—Barrel Tasting

Dates in parentheses indicate the issues in which the ratings were published.

CALE | CALIFORNIA

Chardonnay Carneros Sangiacomo Vineyard 1996: Ripe, with a tart streak to the apple, citrus and pear flavors, and a dash of pineapple. Tightly wound, it can be enjoyed now to 2000. 1,300 cases made. • $20 • (05/15/98) • **88**

Chardonnay Carneros Sangiacomo Vineyard 1995: Clean, ripe and refreshing, with pretty pear, apple, melon and spice notes that fold together nicely on the finish. Has a sense of elegance and finesse. 650 cases made. • $20 • (02/28/97) • **90**

Chardonnay Carneros Sangiacomo Vineyard 1994: Strikes a nice balance between smoky, toasty oak and ripe pear and vanilla notes. An elegant and refined style that's pleasant to drink. 2,300 cases made. • $20 • (05/15/96) • **87**

Chardonnay Carneros Sangiacomo Vineyard 1993 • $18 • (06/15/95) • **88**

Pinot Noir Carneros Sangiacomo Vineyard 1996: Simple, with light, earthy cherry and berry notes; could use more substance. 300 cases made. • $18 • (04/30/98) • **82**

CALERA | CALIFORNIA

Chardonnay Central Coast 1996: The ripe pear, fig, melon and citrus flavors are at first dominated by a toasty, smoky, woody edge, but with a little breathing the fruit opens up and it comes together nicely. 11,442 cases made. • $16 • (03/31/98) • **90**

Chardonnay Central Coast 1995: Classy, smooth and ripe. Creamy in texture, with hints of peach, pear, apple and vanilla flavors that expand and develop, showing more depth and richness on the aftertaste. A great combination of quality and price from this California winery. 9,142 cases made. • $16 • (12/15/96) SS • **91**

Chardonnay Central Coast 1994: A smooth and polished California white with toasty oak, pear, spice and honey notes. It turns elegant and refined on the finish, where the flavors linger. 11,325 cases made. • $15 • (12/31/95) SS • **90**

Chardonnay Central Coast 1993 • $15 • (02/28/95) • **88**

Chardonnay Mount Harlan 1994: Intense and lively, well focused and flavorful. This offers rich pear, hazelnut, mineral and vanilla flavors, well proportioned, with a silky texture and smooth aftertaste. 626 cases made. • $30 • (12/15/96) • **91**

Chardonnay Mount Harlan Twentieth Anniversary Vintage 1995: Smooth, ripe, rich and concentrated, with a focused core of spicy pear, hazelnut, fig, melon and light toasty oak. Complex and inviting, finishing with a spicy flavor and fine length. Drink now to 2001. 1,022 cases made. • $30 • (03/31/98) • **90**

Pinot Noir Central Coast 1996: Austere, with a slight green edge to the black cherry and blackberry flavors, finishing with a dash of spice and firm tannins. Best now to 2000. 9,100 cases made. • $16 • (01/31/98) • **86**

Pinot Noir Central Coast 1995: Shows spicy, peppery qualities, along with more mainstream Pinot Noir flavors of cherry and strawberry. Moderately rich, it's well balanced and long on the finish. Try in 1999. 8,350 cases made. • $16 • (11/30/97) • **88**

Pinot Noir Central Coast 1994 • $16 • (02/29/96) • **85**
Pinot Noir Central Coast 1993 • $15 • (12/31/95) • **83**
Pinot Noir Central Coast 1992 • $15 • (02/28/94) • **73**
Pinot Noir Central Coast 1991 • $14 • (02/28/93) • **84**
Pinot Noir Central Coast 1990 • $14 • (03/31/92) • **87**
Pinot Noir Central Coast 1989 • $14 • (11/15/91) • **85**
Pinot Noir Central Coast 1987 • $14 • (02/15/90) • **82**

Pinot Noir Central Coast Reserve 1993: Elegant, smooth and polished, with a well-focused band of cherry, cola and spice. A complex aftertaste keeps the flavors lively. 1,344 cases made. • $20 • (07/31/96) • **88**

Pinot Noir Mount Harlan 1993 • $35 • (12/31/95) • **85**

Pinot Noir Mount Harlan Jensen 1994: A good, clean, somewhat lean and trim style, especially for Calera, with a pleasant core of earthy currant and black cherry flavors. Drinkable now. 1,289 cases made. • $38 • (07/31/97) • **88**

Pinot Noir Mount Harlan Jensen 1993: Distinct for its exotic, ripe and racy fruit flavors, with layers of juicy cherry, wild berry and plum notes that weave together and echo wonderfully on the finish. A very tasty wine. Drink now. 1,775 cases made. • $38 • (03/31/97) • **91**

Pinot Noir Mount Harlan Jensen 1992: Shows mature Pinot Noir flavors and aromas, with a dry edge to the earthy cherry and mushroom flavors. Drinkable now. 1,481 cases made. • $40 • (01/01/98) • **86**

Pinot Noir Mount Harlan Jensen 1991 • $34 • (03/31/95) • **88**
Pinot Noir Mount Harlan Jensen 1990 • $38 • (02/28/94) • **87**
Pinot Noir Mount Harlan Jensen 1989 • $35 • (02/28/94) • **87**
Pinot Noir Mount Harlan Jensen 1988 • $35 • (11/15/91) • **92**

Pinot Noir Mount Harlan Jensen 1987 • $30 • (04/30/91) • **93**
Pinot Noir Mount Harlan Jensen 1986 • $45 • (05/31/89) • **88**
Pinot Noir Mount Harlan Jensen 1985 • $25 • (06/15/88) • **88**
Pinot Noir Mount Harlan Jensen 1983 • $22 • (08/31/86) • **80**
Pinot Noir Mount Harlan Jensen 1982 • $23 • (01/01/85) • **88**
Pinot Noir Mount Harlan Mills 1994: Smooth, ripe and polished, with a focused core of cherry, sage, earth and spice, holding its flavors through the finish, where it turns supple and elegant. Drink now. 1,176 cases made. • $35 • (02/28/98) • **88**
Pinot Noir Mount Harlan Mills 1993: Young, tight and tannic, with an earthy edge to the cola, cherry, sage and spice flavors. With breathing it shows more cranberry and spice. Drink now. 1,392 cases made. • $35 • (06/30/97) • **86**
Pinot Noir Mount Harlan Mills 1992: Smells terrific, with all kinds of jammy aromas, cherry and raspberry, but on the palate it takes on a racy character, marked by spice and anise notes. Complex and elegant. Ready to drink. 1,552 cases made. • $35 • (03/31/97) • **91**
Pinot Noir Mount Harlan Mills 1990: The complex, exotic wild berry, cherry, anise and spice nuances still show a racy side, but it's well balanced and harmonious. Long, lingering aftertaste. Mature; ready to drink. • $30 • (03/31/97) • **90**
Pinot Noir Mount Harlan Mills 1989 • $32 • (11/15/92) • **91**
Pinot Noir Mount Harlan Mills 1988 • $30 • (11/15/91) • **89**
Pinot Noir Mount Harlan Reed 1994: Distinctively Central Coast, with its earthy flavors. Just enough dried cherry and wild berry emerges to hold your interest, with hints of tea and sage folding in. Drink now. 1,176 cases made. • $35 • (03/31/98) • **88**
Pinot Noir Mount Harlan Reed 1992 • $35 • (03/31/95) • **84**
Pinot Noir Mount Harlan Reed 1988 • $36 • (11/15/91) • **85**
Pinot Noir Mount Harlan Reed 1987 • $35 • (04/30/91) • **80**
Pinot Noir Mount Harlan Reed 1982 • $23 • (08/31/86) • **75**
Pinot Noir Mount Harlan Selleck 1993: On the lighter side, especially for Calera, with herb, rhubarb and cola notes and pretty dashes of cherry and spice. Drink now. 577 cases made. • $38 • (06/30/97) • **85**
Pinot Noir Mount Harlan Selleck 1987 • $30 • (11/15/91) • **92**
Pinot Noir Mount Harlan Selleck 1986 • $30 • (03/31/90) • **85**
Pinot Noir San Benito County Selleck 1986: Offers complex black cherry, spice and cedar flavors that pick up hints of earth, mushroom and smoked meat on the aftertaste. Still has a trace of tannin, but it's best now. • $30 • (03/31/97) • **89**
Pinot Noir Santa Barbara County Bien Nacido Vineyard 1985 • $13 • (06/15/88) • **82**
Rouge de Rouge California NV • $4 • (01/31/87) BB • **80**
Viognier Mount Harlan 1995: Captures the ripe, rich and exotic flavors of the grape, with lots of ripe pear, citrus, spice and hazelnut notes. Finishes with a complex aftertaste. 697 cases made. • $30 • (11/30/96) • **88**
Viognier Mount Harlan 1994 • $30 • (01/31/96) • **89**
Zinfandel California NV • $5 • (07/31/88) • **71**
Zinfandel Cienega Valley 1981 • $7 • (04/16/84) • **81**
Zinfandel Cienega Valley Reserve 1981 • $8 • (01/01/85) • **82**

CALLAGHAN | ARIZONA

Buena Suerte Vineyard Sonoita 1994: An odd wine, with a slightly browning color, ripe, spice and plum aromas and flavors. Shuts down quickly, revealing a tannic finish. A blend of 50 percent Grenache, 25 percent Syrah and 25 percent Cinsault. 25 cases made. • $20 • (08/31/97) • **80**
Buena Suerte Vineyard Cuvée Sonoita 1994: Rich and warm, but quite tannic, this is a full-bodied red with doughy aromas and prunelike, sun-dried flavors. A blend of 70 percent Cabernet Sauvignon and 30 percent Merlot. 640 cases made. • $25 • (06/15/97) • **83**
Caitlin's Selection Sonoita 1995: A spicy tasting, full-bodied red, rough and tannic in texture with insufficient fruit flavor for balance. A blend of 67 percent Cabernet Franc and 33 percent Cabernet Sauvignon. 70 cases made. • $30 • (06/15/97) • **77**
Caitlin's Selection Sonoita 1994: A full-bodied, extremely tannic red with appealing, ripe fruit flavors and spicy oak overtones. Not complex, but good and hearty. A blend of 60 percent Cabernet Franc, 20 percent Merlot and 20 percent Cabernet Sauvignon. 130 cases made. • $25 • (06/15/97) • **83**
Fumé Blanc Cochise County 1996: An unusually heavy style of Sauvignon Blanc with lots of body. The flavors are nutty, oaky and a bit apricotlike. Not for everyone. 140 cases made. • $18 • (06/15/97) • **83**

CALLAHAN RIDGE | OREGON

Pinot Noir Oregon Elkton Vineyards 1987 • $8 • (02/15/90) • **88**
Pinot Noir Umpqua Valley 1991 • $9 • (02/28/93) • **72**

CALLAWAY | CALIFORNIA

Cabernet Sauvignon California 1995: Smooth and silky, with spicy, toasty plum and berry flavors in a light, "drink-me-now" style. • $NA • (12/31/97) • **86**
Cabernet Sauvignon California 1994: Tart and ungenerous, with a sappy, resinous edge to the juicy blackberry flavors. 30,600 cases made. • $10 • (05/15/97) • **78**
Cabernet Sauvignon California 1991 • $10 • (11/15/94) • **79**
Cabernet Sauvignon California 1990 • $8 • (11/15/93) • **79**
Cabernet Sauvignon California 1989 • $9 • (03/31/93) • **80**
Cabernet Sauvignon California America's Cup 1989 • $10 • (11/15/91) • **82**
Chardonnay Temecula Calla-Lees 1996: Marked by a bitter, leesy component, followed by flavors of sweet peas and green apples. Shows balance and harmony, nonetheless. • $10 • (09/15/97) • **81**
Chardonnay Temecula Calla-Lees 1994: Bright, juicy and distinctive for the herbal overtones to its basic green apple flavors. 48,700 cases made. • $10 • (07/31/97) • **83**
Chardonnay Temecula Calla-Lees 1993 • $9 • (07/31/95) • **84**
Chenin Blanc Late Harvest Temecula Sweet Nancy 1991 • $25/375ml • (09/30/95) • **79**
Chenin Blanc Late Harvest Temecula Sweet Nancy NV • $22 • (02/29/96) • **88**
Dolcetto Temecula 1995: Cinnamon and sour cherry flavors clash mightily. • $15 • (09/15/97) • **74**
Dolcetto Temecula 1994: A bit chewy, but offers some well-focused black cherry and spice flavors. Finish is marked by a hint of gaminess. 725 cases made. • $15 • (11/30/96) • **83**
Fumé Blanc Temecula 1995: An odd one. Weedy, asparaguslike flavors are backed by grassy notes. • $8 • (08/31/97) • **77**
Fumé Blanc Temecula 1994: Crisp in texture, with mineral and spice flavors that pick up hints of peach on the finish. 4,000 cases made. • $8 • (11/30/96) • **85**
Fumé Blanc Temecula 1993 • $8 • (08/31/95) • **74**
Pinot Gris Temecula 1996: This mineral-like wine is marked by an odd, smoky quality that never quite blends with the peach and guava finish. • $12 • (09/15/97) • **80**
Pinot Gris Temecula 1995: Sweet, flat and unappealing with a watery, strawberry character. 875 cases made. • $12 • (04/30/97) • **74**
Pinot Gris Temecula 1993 • $14 • (12/15/95) • **84**
Sauvignon Blanc Temecula 1997: Here's a nice bright white from California offering delicate floral, peach, grapefruit, guava and lemon-lime notes. Firmly textured, it blends finesse and richness in a harmonious whole. A real value at this price and score. Tasted three times, with consistent notes. 30,000 cases made. • $8 • (05/15/98) BB • **88**
Sauvignon Blanc Temecula 1996: Tangy acidity meets sweet nectarine in this simple wine. Pleasant quaffer. (0.45 percent residual sugar.) • $8 • (01/31/98) • **82**
Sauvignon Blanc Temecula 1995: Marked by earthy, herbal flavors, with a bitter edge. 16,800 cases made. • $8 • (11/30/96) • **76**
Sauvignon Blanc Temecula 1994 • $7 • (08/31/95) • **78**
Sauvignon Blanc Temecula 1993 • $7 • (04/30/95) • **80**
Viognier Temecula 1996: Interesting, if not for everyone. Smells kind of like a pine forest and on the palate shows melons and apples. Lacks focus. • $15 • (09/30/97) • **83**
Viognier Temecula 1995: Marked by a tinny, canned fruit-cocktail edge to the pear and spice flavors and it's a bit sweaty, but it corrects itself on the finish, where it's more palatable. 2,360 cases made. • $15 • (11/30/96) • **80**
Viognier Temecula 1993 • $16 • (09/15/94) • **81**

CALLE CIELO | CALIFORNIA

Chardonnay Santa Cruz Mountains 1996: An appetizing earthy note upfront is followed by ripe pear, earth, mineral and oak flavors that hold your interest. Lingers on the aftertaste. Drink now through 2001. 300 cases made. • $25 • (06/30/98) • **90**

CAMARADERIE | WASHINGTON

Cabernet Sauvignon Washington 1994: Crisp in texture, with a nice spicy thread running through the tart berry flavors. Best from 1999. 250 cases made. • $19 • (09/30/97) • **84**
Cabernet Sauvignon Washington 1992 • $17 • (09/30/95) • **82**

CAMBRIA | CALIFORNIA

Chardonnay Santa Barbara County 1994: Complex, intriguing array of ripe pear, peach, spice and toasty oak flavors, adding a lingering aftertaste. • $15 • (02/29/96) • **88**
Chardonnay Santa Maria Valley Katherine's Vineyard 1996: Ripe and spicy, with a lively core of tangerine, pear, fig and melon. Spicy vanilla-tinged oak adds dimension, and it holds its flavor on the finish. 70,000 cases made. • $18 • (04/30/98) • **90**
Chardonnay Santa Maria Valley Katherine's Vineyard 1995: Young and tight, with spicy citrus, tangerine, pear and pineapple notes that spead out on the finish, showing elegance and finesse. • $20 • (05/31/97) • **91**
Chardonnay Santa Maria Valley Katherine's Vineyard 1994: Appealing core of ripe peach and pear. Adds a trace of honey and oak on the finish. • $18 • (02/29/96) • **86**
Chardonnay Santa Maria Valley Katherine's Vineyard 1993 • $16 • (02/28/95) • **87**
Chardonnay Santa Maria Valley Reserve 1995: Crisp and flinty up front, the fruit shows more depth and body at midpalate, with complex pear, peach and spicy oak flavors. Drinks well now. 3,500 cases made. • $36 • (04/30/98) • **88**
Chardonnay Santa Maria Valley Reserve 1994: Well balanced, with a nice range of spicy, toasty pear and pineapple flavors, all blending well on the finish. Complex and elegant. • $30 • (06/15/96) • **88**
Chardonnay Santa Maria Valley Reserve 1993 • $25 • (05/31/95) SS • **91**
Pinot Noir Santa Maria Valley Julia's Vineyard 1996: Intense and concentrated, with a range of flavors that stretches from earth to spice, cranberry and cherry. Turns complex on the aftertaste; best now to 2001. 15,000 cases made. • $26 • (01/31/98) • **87**
Pinot Noir Santa Maria Valley Julia's Vineyard 1995: An earthy, beefy style with lots of herb, mushroom, tea and meaty notes. Slowly works in some dried cherry and berry notes, but in the end the meatiness wins out, so be forewarned. Drink now. 3,000 cases made. • $26 • (01/01/97) • **87**
Pinot Noir Santa Maria Valley Julia's Vineyard 1994 • $22 • (02/29/96) • **89**
Pinot Noir Santa Maria Valley Julia's Vineyard 1993 • $18 • (02/28/95) • **86**
Pinot Noir Santa Maria Valley Julia's Vineyard 1992 • $16 • (02/28/94) • **87**
Pinot Noir Santa Maria Valley Julia's Vineyard 1991 • $16 • (02/28/93) • **83**
Pinot Noir Santa Maria Valley Julia's Vineyard 1989 • $15 • (09/30/92) • **80**
Pinot Noir Santa Maria Valley Julia's Vineyard 1988 • $16 • (12/15/90) • **88**
Pinot Noir Santa Maria Valley Reserve 1994: Young, tight and tannic, with a complex array of herb, spice, leather, mineral and cherry flavors. It all adds up to a distinctive style of Pinot Noir, with racy fruit and earthy tannins. Try now to 2000. • $42 • (12/31/96) • **88**
Pinot Noir Santa Maria Valley Reserve 1993 • $35 • (12/31/95) • **85**
Pinot Noir Santa Maria Valley Reserve 1992 • $30 • (03/31/95) • **86**
Sangiovese Santa Maria Valley Tepusquet Vineyard 1994: Serves up lots of ripe, zesty flavors—an array of cranberry, cherry, anise and cedar. Finish shows a nice interplay of fruit and light oak shadings. • $25 • (10/15/96) • **88**
Sangiovese Santa Maria Valley Tepusquet Vineyard 1993 • $18 • (08/31/95) • **86**
Syrah Santa Maria Valley Tepusquet Vineyard 1992 • $30 • (05/15/95) • **88**

CAMELOT | CALIFORNIA

Cabernet Sauvignon Central Coast 1992 • $11 • (11/15/94) • **83**
Cabernet Sauvignon North Coast 1993: Marked by herb, dill and ripe Cabernet flavors, picking up a toasty oak edge on the finish, where the flavors linger. • $12 • (12/15/95) • **87**
Chardonnay Central Coast 1994: Strives for elegance and finesse and succeeds at it. The tiers of honey, pear, nectarine and peach work well together. Impressive for its balance. • $11 • (06/15/96) • **89**
Chardonnay Central Coast 1993 • $12 • (07/31/95) • **88**

Key: SS—Spectator Selection CS—Cellar Selection HR—Highly Recommended BB—Best Buy $NA—Price not available Ⓐ—Auction Price (BT)—Barrel Tasting
Dates in parentheses indicate the issues in which the ratings were published.

Chardonnay Monterey Reserve 1994: A bit musty, with ripe, spicy pear and pineapple flavors. A good, solid white. 978 cases made. • $22 • (06/15/96) • **85**
Chardonnay Santa Barbara County 1995: Smooth and polished, this harmonious wine slides over the palate with pretty orange, pear and toast flavors that have more up front than on the delicate finish. Ready now. 20,000 cases made. • $16 • (11/30/97) • **85**
Chardonnay Santa Barbara County 1994: Smooth and polished, with a delicate balance between the ripe pear, apple and honey notes. Picks up a trace of citrus and spice on the finish. • $18 • (06/15/96) • **87**
Chardonnay Santa Barbara County 1993 • $12 • (01/31/95) HR • **90**
Pinot Noir Central Coast 1994 • $12 • (02/29/96) • **84**
Pinot Noir Central Coast 1993 • $12 • (03/31/95) • **86**

CAMERON | OREGON

Pinot Noir Willamette Valley 1992 • $13 • (11/30/94) • **77**
Pinot Noir Willamette Valley 1987 • $14 • (02/15/90) • **81**
Pinot Noir Willamette Valley 1986 • $15 • (06/15/88) • **86**
Pinot Noir Willamette Valley 1985 • $14 • (02/15/90) • **82**
Pinot Noir Willamette Valley Abbey Ridge Reserve 1990 • $19 • (02/28/93) • **86**
Pinot Noir Willamette Valley Abbey Ridge Reserve 1989 • $19 • (03/31/92) • **86**
Pinot Noir Willamette Valley Reserve 1986 • $18 • (02/15/90) • **80**
Pinot Noir Willamette Valley Vintage Reserve 1987 • $18 • (02/15/90) • **86**

CANARD | CALIFORNIA

Zinfandel Napa Valley 1990 • $12 • (04/30/96) • **85**

CANEPA | CALIFORNIA

Chardonnay Alexander Valley Canepa Vineyard 1993 • $20 • (12/15/95) • **88**
Chardonnay Alexander Valley Gauer Vineyard Adobe III 1996: Pleasantly fruity, with ripe pear, fig and spice notes and spicy, toasty flavors, it's elegant and well focused, with a lingering aftertaste. Drink now through 2000. 614 cases made. • $26 • (05/15/98) • **88**
Chardonnay Alexander Valley Gauer Vineyard Adobe III 1995: Very complex, with an intriguing interplay of ripe pear, apple, toast, fig and butter flavors, turning smooth and smoky on the finish, where it picks up an anise accent. 640 cases made. • $24 • (06/15/97) • **91**
Chardonnay Alexander Valley Gauer Vineyard Adobe III 1994: There's much to like here in the ripe pear and fig notes, but woody tones on the finish come across as heavy-handed and dominating. Lacks grace, despite its attempt to pack in all the flavor. 605 cases made. • $24 • (04/30/96) • **85**

CANOE RIDGE | WASHINGTON

Cabernet Sauvignon Columbia Valley 1994: Firm and chewy in texture, with just enough blackberry and anise flavors behind the layer of fine tannins. Best after 1999. 500 cases made. • $20 • (09/15/97) • **88**
Chardonnay Columbia Valley 1996: Light, lean and earthy, definitely on the mineral side, with modest fruit flavor to balance. Finishes with a mild, citrusy tang. 6,000 cases made. • $12 • (09/15/97) • **86**
Chardonnay Columbia Valley 1995: Lean, crisp and racy, relying on zingy citrus, apple and spice flavors to carry it. Finishes with focus and vibrancy. Drinkable now. 6,200 cases made. • $12 • (09/15/96) • **87**
Chardonnay Columbia Valley 1994: Bright and fruity; effusive peach, apple and vanilla-spice overtones. Ready now. 1,782 cases made. • $12 • (09/30/95) • **86**
Chardonnay Columbia Valley Reserve 1995: Supple and generous, in a lighter style that goes for harmony over drama, focusing on spicy, toasty melon flavor. Drink soon. 500 cases made. • $18 • (09/15/97) • **89**
Columbia Valley 1995: Bright, crisp and focused, with ripe currant, blackberry and tar flavors that finish with more intensity than they start with. Best from 1999. A blend of 70 percent Cabernet Sauvignon and 30 percent Merlot. Available only in Washington. 1,000 cases made. • $14 • (09/15/97) • **86**
Merlot Columbia Valley 1995: On the lighter side, with pretty spice and floral overtones to the core of black cherry flavor. Drink now. 15,200 cases made. • $18 • (09/15/97) • **86**
Merlot Columbia Valley 1994: Firm in texture, with some promising black cherry and spice flavors that never quite open up. Drinkable now. 9,000 cases made. • $18 • (09/15/96) • **84**
Merlot Columbia Valley 1993 • $14 • (09/30/95) • **88**

Red Table Wine Columbia Valley 1992 • $12 • (03/31/95) • **86**

CANTERBURY | CALIFORNIA

Cabernet Sauvignon California 1990 • $7 • (11/15/92) • **81**
Cabernet Sauvignon California 1989 • $6 • (11/15/91) BB • **80**
Merlot California 1991 • $8 • (08/31/93) • **74**
Merlot California 1990 • $7 • (05/31/92) • **79**
Zinfandel California 1990 • $5 • (07/15/92) BB • **84**

CANYON ROAD | CALIFORNIA

Cabernet Sauvignon California 1995: Seeking value in California Cabernet? Here's your wine. It's velvety, spicy and appealing with chocolate-scented berry and currant flavors and a lively yet polished finish. Offers real richness and depth for the price, and as a bonus, it's ready now. 65,000 cases made. • $8 • (05/15/97) BB • **86**

Cabernet Sauvignon California 1994: Unexceptional, with an earthy, herbal accent to the slight Cabernet flavors. 27,000 cases made. • $7 • (11/30/96) • **79**

Cabernet Sauvignon California 1993: Light and fragrant, with a candle wax edge to the raspberry and currant flavors. Ready now. 30,000 cases made. • $6 • (11/15/95) BB • **85**

Cabernet Sauvignon California 1992 • $7 • (11/15/94) • **83**
Cabernet Sauvignon California 1991 • $7 • (06/15/93) • **81**

Cabernet Sauvignon Sonoma County Reserve 1995: A chewy wine, with layers of herb, black currant, anise, cedar and spice. It shows nice length but lacks focus on the midpalate. Drink now or hold. 407 cases made. • $18 • (09/30/97) • **87**

Cabernet Sauvignon Sonoma County Reserve 1994: This mild-mannered red offers pleasant blackberry, herb and anise flavors, packed in moderately firm tannins. 500 cases made. • $18 • (09/30/97) • **84**

Chardonnay California 1997: Pretty citrus and pineapple flavors have refreshing intensity and crispness. Very nicely done, and well priced. Drink now. 75,000 cases made. • $8 • (06/30/98) BB • **85**

Chardonnay California 1996: Candylike, with a bitter edge and woody finish. A highly manipulated wine that's still awkward. 65,000 cases made. • $8 • (07/31/97) • **78**

Chardonnay California 1994: Light, lean and a little grassy behind the narrow beam of spicy apple flavor. Drinkable now. 50,000 cases made. • $7 • (05/15/96) • **81**

Chardonnay California 1993 • $7 • (01/31/95) • **78**

Chardonnay Russian River Valley Reserve 1995: Light and crisp, a steely wine with nice hints of mineral to accent the modest green apple flavor. Drink now. 600 cases made. • $18 • (11/15/97) • **85**

Merlot California 1994 • $7 • (06/15/96) • **80**
Merlot California 1993 • $8 • (12/15/95) • **84**

Sauvignon Blanc California 1997: A racy blend of floral and passion fruit fragrances, evolving on the palate into a silky-textured wine that harbors peach, grapefruit, lemon and anise notes. Tangy finish. 15,000 cases made. • $7 • (05/15/98) • **87**

Sauvignon Blanc California 1996: An easy-drinking white that's fresh and lively, showing its pear and floral flavors in a delicate style, with a simple, lingering finish. Its nice price is the icing on the cake. 17,000 cases made. • $7 • (04/30/97) BB • **85**

Sauvignon Blanc California 1995: Fresh and bright apple and pineapple flavors that narrow a bit on the finish. 15,000 cases made. • $7 • (08/31/96) • **80**

Sauvignon Blanc California 1994 • $6 • (08/31/95) • **83**
Sauvignon Blanc California 1993 • $6 • (09/30/94) BB • **85**

CAP ROCK | TEXAS

Cabernet Sauvignon Texas 1995: A solid Cabernet, with good plum and berry flavors and some herbal notes. Medium-bodied and balanced, with a lingering finish. Drink now. • $8 • (05/15/98) • **84**

Cabernet Sauvignon Texas High Plains Reserve 1995: If you like a slightly herbal style, this is your wine. Those flavors are balanced by appealing raspberry notes and a spicy finish. Drink now. • $13 • (05/15/98) • **83**

Diamond Royale Texas White 1996: A mix of tangerine and canned-fruit flavors that doesn't mesh well. • $7 • (02/28/98) • **75**

Garnet Royale Texas 1996: A simple, light red, with berry and cherry flavors. Could try it slightly chilled. A blend of 53 percent Cabernet Sauvignon, 21 percent Cabernet Franc, 14 percent Barbera, and 12 percent Zinfandel. Drink now. • $7 • (03/31/98) • **78**

Topaz Royale Texas White 1996: Wants to be sweet but ends up awkward, with cloying peach and pineapple flavors. Quite strange. A blend of 63 percent Chenin Blanc, 26 percent Johannisberg Riesling, and 11 percent Muscat Canelli. • $7 • (02/28/98) • **70**

CAPARONE | CALIFORNIA

Cabernet Sauvignon Santa Maria Valley Tepusquet Vineyard 1981 • $10 • (03/16/84) • **80**
Merlot Santa Maria Valley Tepusquet Vineyard 1981 • $10 • (03/16/84) • **88**

CAPIAUX | CALIFORNIA

Pinot Noir Sonoma Coast Hirsch Vineyard 1995: Tightly wound, with earthy sage, dried cherry and wild berry flavors. Finishes with dry, leathery tannins and not much ripe fruit. 50 cases made. • $30 • (02/28/98) • **83**

Pinot Noir Sonoma County Demonstene Vineyard 1995: A touch gamy, with an earthy edge to the dried cherry and leather flavors. May benefit from short-term cellaring. 100 cases made. • $25 • (02/28/98) • **84**

CARDINALE | CALIFORNIA

Meritage California 1992: Dense and chewy, with an earthy, leathery accent to the currant, dried cherry and mineral flavors. More complex on the finish where the flavors fold together nicely. Given the tannin level, cellaring into 2000 is advised. • $60 • (11/15/96) • **89**

Napa Valley-Dry Creek Valley-Knights Valley-Alexander Valley California 1993: Strives for complexity with its aromas and currant, cedar, plum and anise flavors, but the tannins swarm in, and it's dry and not terribly concentrated. Tasted three times, with consistent notes. A blend of Cabernet Sauvignon, Merlot and Cabernet Franc. 2,000 cases made. • $60 • (01/31/98) • **86**

Napa-Alexander Valleys 1995: Massages the intense tannins with supple currant- and plum-laced flavors,while showing off cedar, spice and mineral, too. Holds its focus through the long and complex finish. A blend of Cabernet Sauvignon and Merlot. Best from 2000 through 2008. 2,700 cases made. • $70 • (07/31/98) • **92**

Royale Meritage California 1995: Fairly well balanced, with hints of herbs, citrus and melon. Finishes with bright acidity. • $25 • (06/30/97) • **85**

CAREY CELLARS | CALIFORNIA

Cabernet Sauvignon Santa Ynez Valley 1985 • $10 • (11/15/89) • **83**
Cabernet Sauvignon Santa Ynez Valley 1984 • $9 • (03/31/88) • **72**
Cabernet Sauvignon Santa Ynez Valley Alamo Pintado Vineyard 1981 • $9 • (06/16/84) • **76**
Cabernet Sauvignon Santa Ynez Valley La Cuesta Vineyard 1983 • $9 • (12/15/89) • **83**
Cabernet Sauvignon Santa Ynez Valley La Cuesta Vineyard Reserve 1989 • $16 • (11/15/92) • **77**
Cabernet Sauvignon Santa Ynez Valley La Cuesta Vineyard Reserve 1987 • $16 • (05/31/91) • **81**
Merlot Santa Ynez Valley La Cuesta Vineyard 1988 • $16 • (05/31/92) • **68**
Merlot Santa Ynez Valley La Cuesta Vineyard 1986 • $12 • (12/15/89) • **82**

CARMENET | CALIFORNIA

Cabernet Franc Sonoma Valley Moon Mountain Vineyard 1992 • $20 • (04/30/96) • **82**

Cabernet Sauvignon Sonoma County Moon Mountain Dynamite Cabernet 1992 • $15 • (09/15/95) • **87**

Cabernet Sauvignon Sonoma Valley Dynamite Cabernet 1991 • $15 • (11/15/93) • **85**

Chardonnay Sonoma Valley Carneros Sangiacomo Vineyard 1996: Tight and well focused, with pretty spice, toasty oak, ripe pear and fig flavors that unfold on the finish. Short-term cellaring will soften and smooth the texture; drink through 2002. 2,650 cases made. • $17 • (05/31/98) • **89**

Chardonnay Sonoma Valley Carneros Sangiacomo Vineyard 1995: Rich and complex, with layers of ripe fig, apple, pear and spice flavors, a wonderful sense of harmony and finesse, and a finish that lingers on and on. 3,800 cases made. • $17 • (05/31/97) • **92**

Chardonnay Sonoma Valley Carneros Sangiacomo Vineyard 1993 • $16 • (06/30/96) SS • **91**

Meritage Red Sonoma Valley Moon Mountain Estate Reserve 1994: Smooth, ripe and polished, with a pretty array of currant, toasty oak and vanilla scents, and an elegant aftertaste that keeps flushing out more flavors and nuances, with hints of sage, tobacco and cedar. Best to cellar into 2000. 955 cases made. • $40 • (11/15/97) • **90**

Meritage Red Sonoma Valley Moon Mountain Estate Vineyard 1993: Well focused, with a pretty band of cedar, currant, coffee and light oak, finishing with firm tannins and a pretty aftertaste, where hints of chocolate and mint adds dimension. Best after 1999. 3,735 cases made. • $27 • (11/15/97) • **87**

Meritage Red Sonoma Valley Moon Mountain Estate Vineyard 1992: Elegant and complex, with a pretty band of ripe cherry, currant, plum, anise and spice flavors, framed by light toasty oak notes. The texture is smooth and the tannins are just right, finishing with a fruity aftertaste. Ready now. 3,500 cases made. • $25 • (11/30/96) • **89**

Meritage Red Sonoma Valley Moon Mountain Estate Vineyard 1991: Smooth and supple, showing some mature Cabernet flavors, with hints of herb, currant and black cherry. The finish echoes the fruit and light oak. Drink now. 6,175 cases made. • $25 • (11/15/96) • **88**

Meritage Red Sonoma Valley Moon Mountain Estate Vineyard 1990 • $25 • (11/15/93) • **85**

Meritage Red Sonoma Valley Moon Mountain Estate Vineyard 1989 • $18 • (11/15/92) • **86**

Meritage Red Sonoma Valley Moon Mountain Estate Vineyard Vin de Garde 1989 • $35 • (11/15/93) • **83**

Meritage White Edna Valley Paragon Vineyard 1993 • $12 • (08/31/95) • **83**

Merlot Washington Carmen B 1990 • $10 • (11/30/92) • **86**

Red Sonoma Valley 1988 • $21 • (11/15/91) • **87**

Red Sonoma Valley 1987 • $20 • (11/15/90) • **89**

Red Sonoma Valley 1986: Disappointingly dry, austere and tannic. This wine went south shortly after its release and hasn't really shown much since. • $23 • (12/15/96) • **74**

Red Sonoma Valley 1985 • $19 • (12/31/88) • **91**

Red Sonoma Valley 1984 • $16 • (05/31/87) • **93**

Red Sonoma Valley 1983 • $18 • (09/30/86) • **84**

Red Sonoma Valley 1982 • $16 • (10/16/85) • **93**

Sauvignon Blanc-Sémillon Edna Valley Paragon Vineyard Meritage Reserve 1995: Showing a little age, this blends orange, grapefruit and honeyed notes but finishes with a touch of cheesiness. Rounds off with a pleasant herbal note. A blend of 75 percent Sauvignon Blanc and 25 percent Sémillon. Drink now. 6,150 cases made. • $15 • (05/31/98) • **84**

Zinfandel Contra Costa County Evangelho Vinyard Old Vines Delta Zin 1996: Not entirely ripe-tasting, with a hint of greenness and a tealike edge. Finishes with a hot aftertaste and firm tannins. Drink now through 2002. 2,090 cases made. • $17 • (06/15/98) • **82**

CARMODY MCKNIGHT | CALIFORNIA

Chardonnay Paso Robles 1996: Very pretty for its spice and mineral notes and tangerine and grapefruit rind flavors. Clean and refreshing. Drink now through 2000. 150 cases made. • $15 • (07/31/98) • **84**

CARNEROS BIGHORN RANCH | CALIFORNIA

Chardonnay Napa Valley Carneros Reserve 1995: Ripe and fruity, with zesty pear, apple and citrus notes that are tight and well focused. Picks up a spicy note on the finish. Drink now. 2,041 cases made. • $18 • (05/15/97) • **88**

Chardonnay Napa Valley Reserve 1996: Excellent balance, harmony and finesse, with pretty, ripe pear, hazelnut, light oak and citrus notes. Holds its focus and intensity on a long, rich finish. Drink now through 2002. 9,000 cases made. • $20 • (05/31/98) SS • **91**

CARNEROS CREEK | CALIFORNIA

Cabernet Sauvignon Los Carneros 1985 • $15 • (10/31/89) • **90**

Cabernet Sauvignon Napa Valley 1982 • $11 • (02/16/86) • **71**

Cabernet Sauvignon Napa Valley 1981 • $12 • (12/16/84) • **77**

Cabernet Sauvignon Napa Valley Fay Vineyard 1982 • $14 • (05/15/87) • **70**

Cabernet Sauvignon Napa Valley Reserve 1983 • $14 • (10/15/88) • **83**

Chardonnay California Fleur de Carneros 1993 • $9 • (09/30/95) BB • **87**

Chardonnay Carneros 1996: A dose of toasty oak adds dimension and flavor to this otherwise ripe and fruity wine. Finishes with a clean, refreshing aftertaste. Drink now through 2000. 2,500 cases made. • $16 • (05/15/98) • **87**

Key: SS—Spectator Selection CS—Cellar Selection HR—Highly Recommended BB—Best Buy $NA—Price not available Ⓐ—Auction Price (BT)—Barrel Tasting
Dates in parentheses indicate the issues in which the ratings were published.

Chardonnay Carneros 1995: Starts out simple, with hints of pear and citrus, but the flavors grow on the palate, picking up a nice dash of smoky oak. 2,000 cases made. • $17 • (01/31/97) • **85**

Merlot Napa Valley 1985 • $13 • (02/15/88) • **84**

Merlot Napa Valley 1984 • $11 • (08/31/87) • **87**

Merlot Napa Valley 1982 • $9 • (02/16/86) • **80**

Merlot Napa Valley Truchard Vineyard 1983 • $10 • (10/01/85) • **84**

Pinot Noir Carneros 1995: Supple and elegant, in an understated style. Has an earthy cherry and spicy character, finishing with a slight sour note. 6,000 cases made. • $19 • (12/31/96) • **85**

Pinot Noir Carneros 1994 • $16 • (02/29/96) • **87**

Pinot Noir Carneros 25th Anniversary Signature Reserve 1995: An elegant, understated style, with tea, black cherry, spice and herbal notes, finishing with a beefy, meaty edge. Drink now to 2002. 500 cases made. • $40 • (02/28/98) • **87**

Pinot Noir Carneros Fleur de Carneros 1994 • $10 • (11/30/95) BB • **85**

Pinot Noir Carneros Fleur de Carneros 1993 • $9 • (01/31/95) • **82**

Pinot Noir Carneros Fleur de Carneros 1992 • $9 • (02/28/94) • **79**

Pinot Noir Carneros Fleur de Carneros 1991 • $9 • (02/28/94) • **83**

Pinot Noir Carneros Fleur de Carneros 1990 • $9 • (02/28/93) • **80**

Pinot Noir Carneros Fleur de Carneros 1989 • $9 • (04/30/91) • **82**

Pinot Noir Carneros Fleur de Carneros 1988 • $10 • (02/15/90) • **85**

Pinot Noir Carneros Fleur de Carneros 1987 • $9 • (02/28/89) SS • **92**

Pinot Noir Carneros Las Lomas 1994 • $18 • (02/29/96) • **86**

Pinot Noir Carneros Signature Reserve 1994: Ripe, supple and harmonious, with a complex band of cherry, cedar, earth and spice flavors, and lots of plum and cherry notes chiming in on the finish. Drinks well now, but has the depth and structure to age into 2000. 450 cases made. • $35 • (01/31/97) • **91**

Pinot Noir Carneros Signature Reserve 1993 • $28 • (11/15/95) • **88**

Pinot Noir Carneros Signature Reserve 1991 • $28 • (02/28/93) • **81**

Pinot Noir Carneros Signature Reserve 1989 • $28 • (09/30/92) • **80**

Pinot Noir Carneros Signature Reserve 1988 • $28 • (10/31/90) • **89**

Pinot Noir Carneros Signature Reserve First Release 1987 • $28 • (10/31/90) • **87**

Pinot Noir Los Carneros 1993 • $13 • (09/15/95) • **88**

Pinot Noir Los Carneros 1992 • $15 • (03/31/95) • **86**

Pinot Noir Los Carneros 1991 • $15 • (01/31/94) • **88**

Pinot Noir Los Carneros 1990: Smooth and polished, with mature, complex dried cherry, herb, smoke, anise and jammy berry notes, supple texture. May be a shade past its prime; drink now. • $15 • (03/31/97) • **89**

Pinot Noir Los Carneros 1989 • $15 • (03/31/92) • **85**

Pinot Noir Los Carneros 1988 • $16 • (10/31/90) • **83**

Pinot Noir Los Carneros 1987 • $15 • (02/15/90) • **85**

Pinot Noir Los Carneros 1986: Not a good showing; this wine usually impresses. Has a candied character and turns slightly bitter and metallic on the finish. • $15 • (03/31/97) • **82**

Pinot Noir Los Carneros 1985 • $13 • (04/15/88) • **88**

Pinot Noir Los Carneros 1984 • $15 • (03/15/87) • **92**

Pinot Noir Los Carneros 1983 • $13 • (08/31/86) • **92**

CARNEROS QUALITY ALLIANCE | CALIFORNIA

Pinot Noir Carneros 1986 • $23 • (07/31/89) • **81**

Pinot Noir Carneros 1985 • $25 • (12/31/87) • **90**

CARPE DIEM | CALIFORNIA

Chardonnay San Luis Obispo County 1994: Offers an attractive core of pear, peach and spice notes, picking up a trace of honey and light oak on the finish. Well-focused. 1,000 cases made. • $19 • (02/29/96) • **87**

Pinot Blanc San Luis Obispo 1994 • $19 • (01/31/96) • **88**

Pinot Noir San Luis Obispo County 1994: A Beaujolais-like Pinot Noir. Ripe and fragrant, with a spicy, wild berry accent. 1,000 cases made. • $20 • (09/15/96) • **82**

CARTLIDGE & BROWNE | CALIFORNIA

Chardonnay California 1996: A trim, bright-styled wine, with a tasty touch of pear and apple backed by a judicious use of oak. 20,000 cases made. • $10 • (07/31/98) • **84**

Chardonnay California 1993 • $6 • (04/30/95) • **78**

CASE | CALIFORNIA

Pinot Noir Monterey 1995: Marked by herb, tea and sage notes, with only a glimmer of wild berry and plum flavor. Turns dry and earthy on the finish, where the tannins weigh in. Try now. • $NA • (01/31/98) • **85**

Pinot Noir Monterey 1994: A touch earthy, with a juniper and wild berry accent, finishing with cedar and spice notes. Drinks well now. 475 cases made. • $25 • (02/28/97) • **85**

CASK ONE | CALIFORNIA

Sauvignon Blanc Mendocino County 1994: Crisp and lively. Sharply focused pear, green apple and herbal flavors are balanced and refreshing. 3,000 cases made. • $6 • (08/31/96) BB • **88**

CASTALIA | CALIFORNIA

Pinot Noir Russian River Valley Rochioli Vineyard 1995: Young and tight, with a firm tannic edge, this wine slowly opens to reveal a core of herb- and cherry-accented flavors. Drink now. 245 cases made. • $23 • (05/31/97) BB • **88**

Pinot Noir Russian River Valley Rochioli Vineyard 1994: Dark, ripe and very complex, with a rich core of cherry, currant, tea and spice flavors and just a hint of chocolate and berry on a long, full finish. A new brand that has the good fortune to buy Rochioli Pinot Noir, and preserves the integrity of the fruit. 200 cases made. • $20 • (11/15/96) • **92**

Pinot Noir Russian River Valley Rochioli Vineyard 1993 • $18 • (03/31/96) • **83**

CASTLE CREEK | CALIFORNIA

Chardonnay California 1996: Rich, with lots of voltage to the tropical fruit and toasty oak. Manages to hold everything together with suprising balance. For fans of full-throttle Chardonnay. Drink now. 340 cases made. • $15 • (05/31/98) • **87**

Chardonnay Sonoma County 1995: Simple and light, with pear, lemon, vanilla and spice flavors. Soft and pleasant but unfocused. 2,511 cases made. • $9 • (07/31/98) • **83**

CASTLE ROCK | CALIFORNIA

Cabernet Sauvignon Napa Valley 1993: An earthy, barnyard quality pervades this. Behind it lie some attractive smoke, mint, plum and black cherry flavors, backed by firm tannins. 600 cases made. • $15 • (09/30/97) • **81**

Chardonnay Carneros 1994: Medicinal, vegetal flavors kick this one out of the running. 500 cases made. • $12 • (07/31/97) • **73**

Chardonnay Napa Valley Barrel Fermented 1993 • $10 • (07/31/95) • **84**

Merlot Napa Valley 1993: Flavorful, though a touch funky; earthy currant flavors turn mulchy on the finish. 1,150 cases made. • $13 • (08/31/96) • **82**

CASTLE VINEYARDS | CALIFORNIA

Chardonnay Sonoma Valley 1994: Spicy and refreshing, with a toasty accent and apple flavors. Ready now. 325 cases made. • $15 • (07/31/96) • **85**

Merlot Sonoma Valley 1993 • $17 • (06/30/96) • **82**

Pinot Noir Carneros 1994 • $16 • (01/31/96) • **84**

Zinfandel Sonoma County 1996: Rich plum and raspberry flavors lack focus; turns dilute and tannic on the finish. Drink now. 700 cases made. • $16 • (06/15/98) • **79**

Zinfandel Sonoma Valley 1993 • $15 • (10/15/95) • **83**

CASTLEVIEW | CALIFORNIA

Cabernet Sauvignon Napa Valley Private Reserve 1993: Marked by herb and oaky flavors and modest plum and cherry notes, but the cedary oak flavors stand out. 4,600 cases made. • $9 • (12/15/95) • **84**

Chardonnay Carneros Private Reserve 1993 • $10 • (10/15/95) • **82**

Chardonnay Russian River Valley Private Reserve 1993 • $10 • (12/15/95) • **76**

Chardonnay Sonoma County Private Reserve 1993 • $9 • (10/15/95) • **83**

Merlot Napa Valley Private Reserve 1993: Cherry and currant notes highlight the predominantly earthy, musty flavors. 4,100 cases made. • $12 • (08/31/96) • **74**

CASTORO | CALIFORNIA

Cabernet Sauvignon Paso Robles 1989 • $9 • (07/31/92) • **84**

Cabernet Sauvignon Paso Robles Hope Farms 1986 • $8 • (12/15/89) • **80**

Cabernet Sauvignon Paso Robles Reserve 1991 • $12 • (11/15/94) • **82**

Cabernet Sauvignon Paso Robles Reserve 1990 • $12 • (11/15/93) • **82**

Cabernet Sauvignon Paso Robles The Wine 1991 • $10 • (11/15/94) • **83**

Chardonnay Paso Robles 1996: Well-structured, with a bright citrus and lemon-rind core, hints of butter and toast. Has a trace of bitterness on the finish. 2,518 cases made. • $12 • (07/31/98) • **81**

Chardonnay Paso Robles Reserve 1995: Spice, lemon, orange peel and pear notes weave a brightly textured mosaic in this delicately styled wine. A bit short on the finish, but still quite enjoyable. Drink now. 623 cases made. • $16 • (07/31/98) • **86**

Chardonnay Paso Robles Reserve 1993 • $12 • (07/31/95) • **78**

Chardonnay San Luis Obispo County 1993 • $10 • (07/31/95) • **82**

Dieci Anni Paso Robles 1991 • $16 • (11/15/93) • **79**

Pinot Noir Central Coast 1987 • $4 • (12/15/89) BB • **82**

Pinot Noir Santa Barbara County 1991 • $11 • (02/28/94) • **77**

Pinot Noir Santa Barbara County 1990 • $11 • (02/28/93) • **73**

Zinfandel Paso Robles 1996: Rich and concentrated with black cherry, prune, pepper and tarry notes. Flavors are a bit over-ripe. Finishes short, with an herbal accent and drying tannins. Drink now through 2001. 2,500 cases made. • $13 • (06/15/98) • **82**

Zinfandel Paso Robles 1995: Rich fruit flavors are the redeeming feature of this disjointed wine. Overripe, with spice and lots of heat and tannins on the finish. Drink soon; the alcohol is likely to dominate all else shortly. 2,185 cases made. • $13 • (06/15/98) • **80**

Zinfandel Paso Robles 1992 • $10 • (10/15/95) • **84**

Zinfandel Paso Robles 1990 • $8 • (10/15/92) • **82**

Zinfandel Paso Robles 1987 • $7 • (12/15/89) • **90**

Zinfandel Paso Robles The Wine 1991 • $9 • (10/15/94) • **84**

CATERINA | WASHINGTON

Cabernet Sauvignon Columbia Valley 1995: A snappy wine. Bright with acidity, firm with tannin, generous with its ripe plum and blackberry flavors that glide nicely through the finish. Best now to 2000. 540 cases made. • $18 • (09/15/97) • **87**

Cabernet Sauvignon Columbia Valley 1994: Firmly textured, with pretty currant and blueberry flavors that pick up a hint of sage on the finish. 300 cases made. • $13 • (09/15/96) • **86**

Cabernet Sauvignon Columbia Valley 1993: Gently perfumy at first, exploding on the palate in spicy raspberry and blackberry flavors. Drinkable now. 647 cases made. • $13 • (09/30/95) • **89**

Cabernet Sauvignon Columbia Valley 1992 • $13 • (04/15/95) • **85**

Cabernet Sauvignon Washington Wahluke Slope Vineyard Reserve 1995: Racy acidity makes this a cheek-grabber now, but with time the citrusy berry and herb flavors might meld better. Try into 1999. 150 cases made. • $30 • (10/15/97) • **85**

Chardonnay Columbia Valley 1995: Perfumy aromas and flavors add interest to the bright pineapple and citrus flavors; all linger nicely on the balanced finish. 3,003 cases made. • $10 • (09/15/96) • **87**

Chardonnay Columbia Valley 1994: Smooth and gentle in texture, featuring lively, juicy citrus and pear flavors that linger on the finish. 1,411 cases made. • $10 • (09/30/95) • **87**

Chardonnay Columbia Valley 1993 • $10 • (02/28/95) SS • **89**

Chardonnay Columbia Valley Reserve 1996: Spicy, toasty flavors dominate the fruit in this serious-minded, fully rounded white, finishing with a refreshing touch of citrus. Drinkable now. 350 cases made. • $18 • (10/15/97) • **89**

Chardonnay Columbia Valley Reserve 1995: Bright and appealing, with a parade of showy, hazelnut-scented pear and toast flavors that increase in focus and concentration on the finish. Drink now. 257 cases made. • $14 • (09/15/96) • **90**

Chardonnay Columbia Valley Reserve 1993 • $14 • (04/15/95) • **85**

Johannisberg Riesling Late Harvest Columbia Valley 1994 • $10/375ml • (09/30/95) • **76**

Merlot Columbia Valley 1995: A lithe, supple style offering plenty of raspberry, blackberry and anise flavors that linger gently on the finish. Drink now. 1,700 cases made. • $18 • (09/15/97) • **89**

Merlot Columbia Valley 1994: Firm in texture, with chewy, tarry-but-ripe blackberry and toast flavors that need time to emerge. Drinkable now. 760 cases made. • $16 • (09/15/96) • **87**

Merlot Columbia Valley 1993 • $13 • (09/30/95) • **78**

Merlot Columbia Valley 1992 • $13 • (02/28/95) • **86**

Merlot Columbia Valley 1991 • $13 • (09/30/94) • **81**

Sauvignon Blanc Columbia Valley 1996: Bright in flavor, smooth in texture, this is a well-mannered wine that lets its floral and pear flavors linger on the harmonious finish. 950 cases made. • $9 • (09/15/97) • **87**

Sauvignon Blanc Columbia Valley 1995: Dry and earthy, with mineral and herb flavors that turn a little bitter on the finish. Tasted twice with consistent notes. 838 cases made. • $7 • (09/30/96) • **79**

Sauvignon Blanc Columbia Valley 1994 • $7 • (05/31/96) • **87**

Sauvignon Blanc Columbia Valley 1993 • $8 • (02/28/95) • **77**

Wahluke Slope Reserve Red Columbia Valley 1994: Spicy fruit flavors are marred by a sour accent. Finish shows some pickle-barrel aromas and flavors. 60 cases made. • $25 • (09/15/96) • **79**

CATOCTIN | MARYLAND

Cabernet Sauvignon Maryland 1985 • $8 • (02/29/92) • **82**

CAVATAPPI | WASHINGTON

Nebbiolo Washington Maddalena Red Willow Vineyards 1988 • $19 • (06/15/91) • **83**

CAYMUS | CALIFORNIA

Cabernet Sauvignon Napa Valley 1994: A real mouthful of Cabernet any way you taste it. Bold, ripe, rich and flavorful, with complex layers of currant, black cherry and plum flavors nicely accented with cedary oak. Terrific now. From a producer with a superb track record with Cabernet. 20,000 cases made. • $77 Ⓐ • (05/31/97) CS • **95**

Cabernet Sauvignon Napa Valley 1993: Pleasant for its range of cherry, spice, cedar and currant flavors. Not a big, overbearing style, but rather elegant and refined, with a complex aftertaste. Caymus fans note: A Special Selection was not made in 1993, so the estate grapes went into this wine. 20,000 cases made. • $38 Ⓐ • (11/15/96) SS • **91**

Cabernet Sauvignon Napa Valley 1992 • $58 Ⓐ • (09/30/95) • **89**

Cabernet Sauvignon Napa Valley 1991 • $36 Ⓐ • (11/15/94) SS • **93**

Cabernet Sauvignon Napa Valley 1990 • $115 Ⓐ • (12/15/93) SS • **90**

Cabernet Sauvignon Napa Valley 1989 • $20 • (11/15/92) • **88**

Cabernet Sauvignon Napa Valley 1988 • $20 Ⓐ • (01/31/92) • **87**

Cabernet Sauvignon Napa Valley 1987 • $58 Ⓐ • (09/15/90) • **93**

Cabernet Sauvignon Napa Valley 1986 • $50 Ⓐ • (03/15/90) SS • **94**

Cabernet Sauvignon Napa Valley 1985 • $39 Ⓐ • (11/15/88) • **90**

Cabernet Sauvignon Napa Valley 1984 • $50 Ⓐ • (12/31/87) • **90**

Cabernet Sauvignon Napa Valley 1983 • $26 Ⓐ • (11/30/86) CS • **94**

Cabernet Sauvignon Napa Valley 1982 • $105 Ⓐ • (04/01/86) • **94**

Cabernet Sauvignon Napa Valley 1981 • $14 • (02/01/86) • **93**

Cabernet Sauvignon Napa Valley 1980 • $22 • (02/01/86) • **94**

Cabernet Sauvignon Napa Valley 1979 • $25 • (02/01/86) • **90**

Cabernet Sauvignon Napa Valley 1978 • $67 Ⓐ • (02/01/85) • **91**

Cabernet Sauvignon Napa Valley 1974 • $78 Ⓐ • (02/15/90) • **91**

Cabernet Sauvignon Napa Valley Cuvée 1986 • $37 Ⓐ • (08/31/89) • **90**

Cabernet Sauvignon Napa Valley Cuvée 1985 • $67 Ⓐ • (07/15/88) • **92**

Cabernet Sauvignon Napa Valley Cuvée 1984 • $43 Ⓐ • (08/31/87) • **88**

Cabernet Sauvignon Napa Valley Special Selection 1994: Big, ripe, rich and concentrated, with layers of currant, plum, black cherry, spice, cedary oak and a dash of vanilla. Picks up complex tobacco and coffee notes, and reveals even more flavor nuances on the finish. The texture is smooth and polished, finishing with a thick, plush core of tannins. Drinks well now but can age, too. Best from 1999 to 2005. Tasted twice, with consistent notes. • $153 Ⓐ • (12/31/97) CS • **95**

Cabernet Sauvignon Napa Valley Special Selection 1992 • $120 Ⓐ • (05/15/96) CS • **92**

Cabernet Sauvignon Napa Valley Special Selection 1991 • $155 Ⓐ • (04/15/95) CS • **99**

Cabernet Sauvignon Napa Valley Special Selection 1990 • $192 Ⓐ • (03/31/94) CS • **98**

Cabernet Sauvignon Napa Valley Special Selection 1989 • $60 • (06/30/93) CS • **93**

Cabernet Sauvignon Napa Valley Special Selection 1988 • $60 • (09/30/92) CS • **94**

Key: SS—Spectator Selection CS—Cellar Selection HR—Highly Recommended BB—Best Buy $NA—Price not available Ⓐ—Auction Price (BT)—Barrel Tasting

Dates in parentheses indicate the issues in which the ratings were published.

Cabernet Sauvignon Napa Valley Special Selection 1987: Showing its age with a dry, earthy edge to the cherry, plum and currant flavors, this wine peaked early. Tartness and dry tannins suggest it is fading away. Drink now. • $175 Ⓐ • (12/15/97) • **88**

Cabernet Sauvignon Napa Valley Special Selection 1986: This remains a remarkably complex and flavorful wine, but now it's elegant and refined as well, with polished tannins. Classic Caymus in that it stretches the flavors, with a range that goes from herb and tea to ripe plum and cherry. Finishing with a long, complex aftertaste and still enough tannin to carry it another decade or more. • $189 Ⓐ • (12/15/96) • **95**

Cabernet Sauvignon Napa Valley Special Selection 1985 • $238 Ⓐ • (04/30/90) • **99**

Cabernet Sauvignon Napa Valley Special Selection 1984 • $233 Ⓐ • (07/15/89) CS • **98**

Cabernet Sauvignon Napa Valley Special Selection 1983 • $101 Ⓐ • (05/31/88) • **90**

Cabernet Sauvignon Napa Valley Special Selection 1982 • $119 Ⓐ • (11/30/87) • **90**

Cabernet Sauvignon Napa Valley Special Selection 1981 • $122 Ⓐ • (11/30/86) • **94**

Cabernet Sauvignon Napa Valley Special Selection 1980 • $106 Ⓐ • (03/16/86) SS • **96**

Cabernet Sauvignon Napa Valley Special Selection 1979 • $160 Ⓐ • (06/01/85) SS • **93**

Cabernet Sauvignon Napa Valley Special Selection 1978 • $247 Ⓐ • (04/30/87) • **98**

Conundrum California 1996: This white blend of Chardonnay, Sauvignon Blanc, Sémillon, Viognier and Muscat proves this winery's mastery of more than just Cabernet Sauvignon. It's a complex wine, with an array of ripe, concentrated flavors—pear, honey, fig, vanilla, peach and nectarine, finishing with lots of character and a dash of spice. Delicious. 10,000 cases made. • $20 • (12/15/97) SS • **91**

Conundrum California 1995: Ripe, round and exotic, generous with its melon, citrus and spice flavors, finishing with amazing richness and depth. Delicious now. • $19 • (04/30/97) • **92**

Conundrum California 1994 • $17 • (10/15/95) SS • **91**

Pinot Noir Napa Valley 1981 • $7 • (05/01/84) BB • **85**

Pinot Noir Napa Valley 1980 • $6 • (03/16/84) • **81**

Pinot Noir Napa Valley Special Selection 1990 • $18 • (02/28/94) • **84**

Pinot Noir Napa Valley Special Selection 1989 • $18 • (09/30/92) • **78**

Pinot Noir Napa Valley Special Selection 1988 • $18 • (11/15/91) • **82**

Pinot Noir Napa Valley Special Selection 1987 • $14 • (12/15/90) • **86**

Pinot Noir Napa Valley Special Selection 1986 • $15 • (12/31/89) • **82**

Pinot Noir Napa Valley Special Selection 1985 • $15 • (12/31/88) • **90**

Pinot Noir Napa Valley Special Selection 1984 • $13 • (02/15/88) • **79**

Pinot Noir Napa Valley Special Selection 1982 • $13 • (08/31/86) • **85**

Sauvignon Blanc Napa Valley 1996: This remarkable wine is rich, ripe and packed with fig, melon, lemon and plum flavors. It's got lots of sweet oak too, but stands up to it nicely. The ensemble is tastefully framed by moderate grass and herb tones, making a strong statement for this varietal. Delicious. 18,000 cases made. • $14 • (01/31/98) SS • **91**

Sauvignon Blanc Napa Valley 1995: Spicy oak flavors add an extra dimension to this supple-textured, lively wine, with hints of orange and apricot on the ripe finish. Ready now. • $13 • (04/30/97) • **88**

Sauvignon Blanc Napa Valley 1994: Offers broad, spicy character and a real mouthful of fleshy texture that tends to shoulder past the fruit. A rich wine that has plenty to offer. • $15 • (07/31/96) • **88**

Sauvignon Blanc Napa Valley Barrel Fermented 1993 • $13 • (04/30/95) • **85**

Zinfandel California 1976 • $33 • (06/16/85) • **79**

Zinfandel California 1974 • $29 • (06/16/85) • **83**

Zinfandel California Lot 31-J 1975 • $40 • (06/16/85) • **77**

Zinfandel Napa Valley 1992 • $13 • (09/30/94) SS • **89**

Zinfandel Napa Valley 1991 • $11 • (09/30/93) • **85**

Zinfandel Napa Valley 1990 • $10 • (10/15/92) • **82**

Zinfandel Napa Valley 1989 • $10 • (11/15/91) • **83**

Zinfandel Napa Valley 1988 • $9 • (10/15/90) • **80**

Zinfandel Napa Valley 1987 • $13 • (10/31/89) • **85**

Zinfandel Napa Valley 1986 • $15 • (12/15/88) • **89**

Zinfandel Napa Valley 1985 • $15 • (12/31/87) • **85**

Zinfandel Napa Valley 1984 • $15 • (05/15/87) • **90**

Zinfandel Napa Valley 1983 • $15 • (12/31/86) • **79**

Zinfandel Napa Valley 1982 • $15 • (05/16/86) • **92**

Zinfandel Napa Valley 1981 • $15 • (12/01/84) • **84**

CECCHETTI SEBASTIANI CELLAR | CALIFORNIA

Cabernet Sauvignon Alexander Valley 1989 • $9 • (11/15/92) • **74**
Cabernet Sauvignon Alexander Valley 1988 • $11 • (08/31/92) • **83**
Cabernet Sauvignon Alexander Valley 1986 • $8 • (04/15/89) • **83**
Cabernet Sauvignon Napa Valley 1993: This is a well-focused, well-balanced young wine, ripe with juicy cherry, plum and wild berry flavors and complex oak notes on the finish. Fans of this label will be surprised at the price tag, but the quality is exceptional. Drink now. 326 cases made. • $25 • (11/15/96) • **89**
Cabernet Sauvignon Sonoma County 1983 • $13 • (09/30/86) • **76**
Merlot Napa Valley 1992: An impressive offering from this négociant brand, featuring a well-focused core of spicy currant, herb and berry flavors. Keeps its focus on the finish. Ready now. 500 cases made. • $28 • (12/15/96) • **87**
Merlot Sonoma County 1990 • $10 • (06/15/93) • **78**
Merlot Sonoma County 1989 • $10 • (05/31/92) • **83**

CEDAR BROOK | CALIFORNIA

Cabernet Sauvignon California 1994: A big, coarse, chewy mouthful of oak, plum, cedar and anise. It lacks integration but makes up for it in character. • $9 • (09/15/97) • **84**
Cabernet Sauvignon Napa Valley 1993: Smooth and inviting, a lighter style that unfolds some appealing currant and anise flavors. Drinkable now. 8,500 cases made. • $7 • (12/15/95) • **84**
Cabernet Sauvignon Napa Valley 1992 • $8 • (11/15/94) • **84**
Chardonnay California 1995: Very appealing, with hazelnut, oak and bright lemon flavors rising to the fore. Falters a bit in complexity, finishing a bit short. Still tasty. • $9 • (07/31/97) • **86**
Merlot California 1996: Tough tannins lend an astringency that mutes the core of cassis, blackberry and herb. The oak is toasty yet heavy. • $9 • (07/31/98) • **80**
Merlot California 1995: Somewhat green and herbal, it also shows a few pleasant cherry notes backed by a massive dose of oak. • $9 • (07/31/97) • **80**
Pinot Noir California 1995: Coffee and cola aromas announce an unusually spicy wine, rich in plum, cherry and blackberry flavors, with oak overriding a bit. Diverse components struggle to hold together. Interesting. • $9 • (07/31/97) • **87**
Pinot Noir California 1993 • $7 • (11/15/95) BB • **85**
Zinfandel California 1995: An overriding woodiness detracts from the light cherry and herb flavors. Finish is bitter and astringent. • $9 • (07/31/97) • **79**

CEDAR CREEK | WISCONSIN

American Red 1990 • $6 • (02/29/92) • **78**

CEDAR MOUNTAIN | CALIFORNIA

Cabernet Sauvignon Livermore Valley Blanches Vineyard 1990 • $20 • (11/15/93) • **83**
Chardonnay Livermore Valley Blanches Vineyard 1993 • $15 • (11/15/95) • **80**

CHADDS FORD | PENNSYLVANIA

Cabernet Franc Pennsylvania 1996: Herbal and green pepper flavors dominate this fairly light red. Finishes on a slightly bitter note. Drink now. • $NA • (03/31/98) • **78**
Cabernet Franc Pennsylvania 1995: Very herbal-tasting, with only modest currant flavors. Turns flat on the finish. 580 cases made. • $12 • (04/30/97) • **77**
Cabernet Sauvignon Pennsylvania 1996: A bizarre wine. Has a slight effervescence, with dull berry and earth flavors. • $13 • (05/15/98) • **71**
Chambourcin Pennsylvania Proprietor's Reserve 1989 • $10 • (02/29/92) • **80**
Chambourcin Pennsylvania Seven Valleys Vineyard 1995: Displays nice grapey flavors, with leather and herb notes on the finish. 821 cases made. • $16 • (08/31/97) • **78**
Chambourcin Pennsylvania Seven Valleys Vineyard 1989 • $13 • (02/29/92) • **81**
Chardonnay Pennsylvania 1995: Earthy aromas and flavors, with celery and onion on the finish. Not recommended. Tasted twice with consistent notes. 2,548 cases made. • $12 • (01/31/97) • **65**
Chardonnay Pennsylvania 1994: Lively and crisp, with vibrant lemon and green apple flavors accented by notes of butter and vanilla. Drink now. 1,300 cases made. • $12 • (09/15/96) • **81**
Chardonnay Pennsylvania Philip Roth Vineyard 1995: Spicy oak aromas and a tight, astringent texture make this intriguing, but lean. It has lively acidity and pear and butter that linger on the finish. 196 cases made. • $26 • (06/15/97) • **84**
Chardonnay Pennsylvania Philip Roth Vineyard 1993: Bizarre, sherrylike aromas and flat flavors makes this a tired, over-the-hill wine. • $26 • (01/31/97) • **72**
Chardonnay Pennsylvania Stargazers Vineyard 1994: A full-bodied but subtly flavored Chardonnay with buttery, figgy undertones. 274 cases made. • $24 • (06/15/97) • **83**
Chardonnay Pennsylvania Stargazers Vineyard 1993: Tastes and smells of matchsticks. Flawed. Tasted twice with consistent notes. • $24 • (01/31/97) • **60**
Johannisberg Riesling Pennsylvania 1996: Sweet-tasting, with ripe apple and canned pineapple flavors. 555 cases made. • $13 • (09/30/97) • **75**
Pinot Grigio Pennsylvania 1995: A bit disjointed but still enjoyable with a mature taste to it despite its youth. It has flavors of green apricot, pear and spice. • $12 • (01/01/97) • **82**
Pinot Noir Michigan Lake Erie Region 1988 • $28 • (02/28/93) • **78**
Pinot Noir Pennsylvania 1994: Earthy, tealike flavors and a tannic, astringent texture make this hard to warm up to. Short on fruit and vibrancy. 218 cases made. • $25 • (08/31/97) • **73**
Pinot Noir Pennsylvania Lake Erie Region 1988 • $28 • (02/29/92) • **82**
Proprietor's Reserve Pennsylvania White 1996: A little heavy-handed. Some appealing flavors of fig and spice. Slightly sweet. 2,900 cases made. • $9 • (02/28/98) • **79**
Proprietor's Reserve Pennsylvania White 1995: This wine has an almost sweet taste to it with honey and floral flavors which intensify on the finish. • $9 • (01/01/97) • **78**
Spring Wine Pennsylvania 1994 • $9 • (10/31/95) • **82**

CHALK HILL | CALIFORNIA

Cabernet Sauvignon Chalk Hill 1994: Dense and a touch leathery, with herb, currant, plum and berry notes, finishing with dry, tealike tannins. Best to cellar into 2001 in hopes it softens. 10,600 cases made. • $26 • (10/31/97) • **89**
Cabernet Sauvignon Chalk Hill 1993: Marked by touches of herb and dill, enough currant and berry flavors weave into the blend to give it dimension and complexity. Finishes with firm but supple tannins, notes of herb and cedar. 9,900 cases made. • $23 • (11/15/96) • **88**
Cabernet Sauvignon Chalk Hill 1991 • $21 • (11/15/94) • **85**
Cabernet Sauvignon Chalk Hill 1990 • $17 • (12/15/93) • **86**
Cabernet Sauvignon Chalk Hill 1989 • $13 • (07/15/92) • **75**
Cabernet Sauvignon Chalk Hill 1988 • $12 • (06/15/91) • **87**
Cabernet Sauvignon Chalk Hill 1983 • $10 • (11/15/86) • **78**
Cabernet Sauvignon Chalk Hill 1981 • $8 • (04/01/84) • **83**
Chardonnay Chalk Hill 1996: Bold, ripe, complex and concentrated in style, this California Chardonnay is brimming with flavor—layers of rich fig, pear, pineapple and smoky, toasty oak that linger on the long and complex finish. Drink now through 2002. 38,000 cases made. • $28 • (06/15/98) SS • **93**
Chardonnay Chalk Hill 1995: This Sonoma white offers ripe flavors of pear, grapefruit, guava and nectarine shaded by crisp, flinty, spicy notes, all fanning out into complexity and richness before turning elegant on the finish. It's delicious and, at this case production, it's readily available as well. 45,800 cases made. • $24 • (05/31/97) SS • **93**
Chardonnay Chalk Hill 1994: Rich, intense and full-bodied, the ripe pear, spice, fig and honey flavors framed nicely by toasty oak. An altogether complex and concentrated California white that's brimming with flavor and the finish goes on and on. Drinkable now, but still young. 44,500 cases made. • $20 • (06/15/96) SS • **93**
Chardonnay Chalk Hill 1993 • $19 • (05/15/95) SS • **91**
Chardonnay Chalk Hill Estate Vineyard Selection 1994: Complex for its interplay of ripe pear, peach, fig, vanilla and spicy, toasty oak flavors. Turns elegant, with citrus and spice, on the finish. 600 cases made. • $36 • (10/15/97) • **92**
Pinot Gris Chalk Hill Estate Vineyard Selection 1995: Well made and quite appealing with its rich, spicy fig, pear and anise notes, the palate is smooth

and thick, finishing with a long, complex aftertaste and a twinge of bitterness. Drink now. 600 cases made. • $20 • (02/28/98) • **88**

Sauvignon Blanc Chalk Hill 1995: A rich, full-bodied style that boasts hazelnut, fig, orange and lemon flavors, all framed by a healthy dose of sweet oak. 10,750 cases made. • $16 • (07/31/97) • **90**

Sauvignon Blanc Chalk Hill 1994: Has a welcome subtlety and depth that's missing from many other California Sauvignons. Offers plush pear, tobacco and spice flavors and delicate touches of citrus and parsley on the finish. 12,950 cases made. • $14 • (08/31/96) SS • **90**

Sauvignon Blanc Chalk Hill 1993 • $16 • (08/31/95) • **88**

Sémillon Chalk Hill Botrytized Estate Vineyard Selection 1994: Earthy fig, honey, pear and vanilla flavors swirl generously through the rich, sweet texture in this late-harvest wine of impressive depth and richness, and honey notes linger beautifully on the finish. It's delicious now, could improve through 2003 to 2005. 500 cases made. • $40/375ml • (10/31/97) HR • **97**

Sémillon Late Harvest Chalk Hill 1986 • $10/375ml • (06/15/92) • **91**

CHALONE | CALIFORNIA

Chardonnay Chalone 1996: Elegant and complex. Smooth, ripe, rich and flavorful, with a creamy texture and lots of ripe pear, apple, fig and melon notes. Clean and refreshing, this is an upfront and forward Chalone Chardonnay that should age well. Finishes with light oak and a hint of butterscotch. Drink now through 2002. 19,467 cases made. • $27 • (05/31/98) • **91**

Chardonnay Chalone 1995: Earthy, with a spicy mineral accent to the tightly wound pear and nectarine flavors, as well as that classic, wild and sagelike edge that borders on musty. Drink now. 16,240 cases made. • $27 • (05/31/97) • **91**

Chardonnay Chalone 1994: Strikes a nice balance between its ripe fig, honey, pear, mineral and melon flavors, then expands to show its complexity on the finish. Offers intense flavors and good length. Drinkable now, but will improve through 1999. 13,000 cases made. • $26 Ⓐ • (06/15/96) CS • **91**

Chardonnay Chalone 1993 • $27 • (07/31/95) • **87**

Chardonnay Chalone Gavilan 1994: Bold, rich and complex, with honeyed pear and spicy melon flavors. This is concentrated, yet manages to maintain its elegance and finesse. 6,500 cases made. • $16 • (06/15/96) • **88**

Chardonnay Chalone Gavilan 1993 • $14 • (07/31/95) • **84**

Chardonnay Chalone Reserve 1994: Combines ripe, intense fruit with a sense of elegance and finesse. The ripe pear, honey and butterscotch flavors play into the aftertaste that expands on the theme. 1,400 cases made. • $45 • (05/31/96) • **90**

Pinot Blanc Chalone 1993 • $18 • (05/31/96) • **88**

Pinot Noir Chalone 1994: Greets you with herb, cherry and sage notes and supple tannins. Well balanced, it finishes with touches of smoke, plum and berry. Drinks well now, but can age through 2002. 1,903 cases made. • $27 • (01/31/98) • **88**

Pinot Noir Chalone 1992: Young, firm and tight, with crisp tannins, it slowly unfolds to show more earth, cherry, mushroom and spice nuances. Well balanced, with appealing flavors. Drink now. Better than an earlier sample. 1,875 cases made. • $26 • (03/31/97) • **87**

Pinot Noir Chalone 1991 • $22 • (06/30/95) • **88**

Pinot Noir Chalone 1990: Young and clean, marked by tart cherry and berry flavors that are vibrant and fruity, though understated. Finishing with dashes of tar and anise. Not as dense or as tannic as the reserve. • $30 • (03/31/97) • **87**

Pinot Noir Chalone 1989 • $30 • (02/28/93) • **77**

Pinot Noir Chalone 1986: Dry, earthy and metallic, having lost its fruit. Not much left. • $40 Ⓐ • (03/31/97) • **78**

Pinot Noir Chalone 1985 • $18 • (02/15/90) • **85**

Pinot Noir Chalone 1984 • $19 • (12/15/87) • **88**

Pinot Noir Chalone 1983 • $19 • (08/31/86) • **89**

Pinot Noir Chalone 1981 • $26 Ⓐ • (12/16/84) • **83**

Pinot Noir Chalone Gavilan 1992 • $14 • (10/31/94) • **84**

Pinot Noir Chalone Gavilan 1991 • $13 • (02/28/94) • **78**

Pinot Noir Chalone Gavilan 1990 • $13 • (02/28/93) • **85**

Pinot Noir Chalone Red Table Wine 1983 • $9 • (08/31/86) • **71**

Key: SS—Spectator Selection CS—Cellar Selection HR—Highly Recommended BB—Best Buy $NA—Price not available Ⓐ—Auction Price (BT)—Barrel Tasting

Dates in parentheses indicate the issues in which the ratings were published.

Pinot Noir Chalone Reserve 1990: Elegant, and distinctive for its earth, pepper and spice notes, ripe cherry and berry flavors. Still crisp and tannic, but ready to drink. • $48 • (03/31/97) • **88**

Pinot Noir Chalone Reserve 1989 • $32 • (03/31/95) • **84**

Pinot Noir Chalone Reserve 1988 • $25 • (03/31/95) • **84**

Pinot Noir Chalone Reserve 1987 • $20 • (02/28/93) • **86**

Pinot Noir Chalone Reserve 1986: Still austere, but more generous than in the past with its earthy mushroom and berry notes. Doesn't seem ready to fade away, but remains dry and tannic; the danger being the fruit will dry out. • $50 • (03/31/97) • **85**

Pinot Noir Chalone Reserve 1981 • $28 • (08/31/86) • **92**

CHAMELEON | CALIFORNIA

Barbera Amador County 1996: A firm, straightforward style emphasizing black cherry and citrus flavors that linger nicely on the finish. 119 cases made. • $14 • (12/15/97) • **85**

Sangiovese California 1995: Fairly coarse on the palate, but offers some nice cherry and herb flavors nonetheless. 90 cases made. • $NA • (01/01/97) • **82**

Sangiovese North Coast 1996: Bright and straightforward, here's a jazzy mouthful of black cherry and floral flavors, which remain solid through the not-too-tannic finish. Ready now. 751 cases made. • $16 • (12/15/97) • **85**

CHAMPOEG | OREGON

Chardonnay Willamette Valley 1993: Seems overbalanced toward oak, but there might be enough fresh pear flavor waiting in the wings to bring it around by 1999 or so. 325 cases made. • $8 • (04/30/97) • **83**

Chardonnay Willamette Valley Estate 1994: Earthy, gamy flavors dominate this brassy wine. 288 cases made. • $8 • (05/15/98) • **79**

Chardonnay Willamette Valley Reserve 1993: Smooth, harmonious and pleasing, with its honey-scented pear and pineapple flavors that linger delicately on the finish. Delicious now. 233 cases made. • $12 • (04/30/97) • **88**

Gewürztraminer Willamette Valley 1995: Bright, spicy and citrusy, with more tangerine than grapefruit, both of which linger on the dry finish. Ready now. 133 cases made. • $8 • (05/15/98) • **84**

Gewürztraminer Willamette Valley 1993: An abundant, distinctive floral and spice character in a soft, silky wine that retains its freshness through the finish. 173 cases made. • $8 • (04/30/97) • **85**

Müller-Thurgau Willamette Valley 1993: Spice, floral and almond flavors swirl appealingly through this off-dry, remarkably fresh and complex white. Distinctive and harmonious, it's ready now. 184 cases made. • $6 • (04/30/97) • **87**

Pinot Gris Willamette Valley Estate 1996: Light and crisp, with pretty peach and almond flavors, and a hint of sourness on the finish. Ready now. 132 cases made. • $12 • (05/15/98) • **85**

Pinot Noir Willamette Valley 1991 • $12 • (11/30/94) • **81**

Pinot Noir Willamette Valley Estate 1993: Has mature flavors of cherry, spice and earth that struggle to get past a layer of chewy tannins. Won't be polished, but has style and intensity. 780 cases made. • $10 • (05/15/98) • **84**

White Riesling Willamette Valley 1994: Bright, focused and lively with orange, cream and green apple flavors that linger on the finish. Drink now. • $7 • (04/30/97) • **86**

CHAPPELL FAMILY | CALIFORNIA

Omega Cuvée Sonoma Valley 1990 • $11 • (12/31/93) • **80**

Pinot Noir Carneros Sangiacomo Vineyards 1990 • $14 • (02/28/94) • **80**

Zinfandel Sonoma Valley 75 Year Old Vines Unfiltered 1990 • $12 • (06/15/93) • **84**

CHAPPELLET | CALIFORNIA

Cabernet Sauvignon Napa Valley 1992 • $20 • (03/31/96) • **83**

Cabernet Sauvignon Napa Valley 1991 • $20 • (11/15/94) • **89**

Cabernet Sauvignon Napa Valley 1990 • $25 • (11/15/93) • **81**

Cabernet Sauvignon Napa Valley 1983 • $22 • (02/15/93) • **90**

Cabernet Sauvignon Napa Valley 1982 • $21 • (02/15/93) • **74**

Cabernet Sauvignon Napa Valley 1981 • $23 • (02/15/93) • **85**

Cabernet Sauvignon Napa Valley 1980 • $35 • (02/15/93) • **88**

Cabernet Sauvignon Napa Valley 1979 • $30 • (02/15/93) • **89**

Cabernet Sauvignon Napa Valley 1978 • $41 • (02/15/93) • **75**

Cabernet Sauvignon Napa Valley 1977 • $24 • (02/15/93) • **86**

Cabernet Sauvignon Napa Valley 1976 • $31 • (02/15/93) • **91**

Cabernet Sauvignon Napa Valley 1975 • $16 Ⓐ • (02/15/93) • **81**

Cabernet Sauvignon Napa Valley 1973 • $64 • (02/15/93) • **77**
Cabernet Sauvignon Napa Valley 1972 • $41 • (02/15/93) • **73**
Cabernet Sauvignon Napa Valley 1971 • $40 • (02/15/93) • **78**
Cabernet Sauvignon Napa Valley 1970 • $95 • (02/15/93) • **93**
Cabernet Sauvignon Napa Valley 1969 • $105 • (02/15/93) • **90**
Cabernet Sauvignon Napa Valley Pritchard Hill Estates 1992 • $15 • (09/15/95) • **86**
Cabernet Sauvignon Napa Valley Reserve 1988 • $14 • (02/15/93) • **85**
Cabernet Sauvignon Napa Valley Reserve 1987: Impressive, with a rich core of earthy currant, mineral, cedar and spice, with softening tannins. There's a lot to like in this wine, and it has the intensity and vibrancy to age another decade. Best now through 2002. 4,900 cases made. • $19 Ⓐ • (12/15/97) • **90**
Cabernet Sauvignon Napa Valley Reserve 1986 • $20 • (02/15/93) • **89**
Cabernet Sauvignon Napa Valley Reserve 1985 • $25 • (02/15/93) • **93**
Cabernet Sauvignon Napa Valley Reserve 1984 • $24 • (02/15/93) • **90**
Cabernet Sauvignon Napa Valley Signature 1994: Decidedly herbal and cedary, with lots of tobacco, tar and spice. It slowly works its way into more cherry and plum fruit flavors, but just as it does, the tannins clamp down. Best to cellar into 2002. 5,650 cases made. • $22 • (12/31/97) • **88**
Cabernet Sauvignon Napa Valley Signature 1993: Tight and trim, with a compact band of cedar, leather, green olive, herb and currant notes, finishing with strong, leathery tannins. Best to cellar into 2001, or even longer. 1,685 cases made. • $22 • (05/15/97) • **87**
Cabernet Sauvignon Napa Valley Signature 1989 • $27 • (03/31/93) • **82**
Chardonnay Napa Valley 1995: Fresh, ripe and lively, with a core of rich fig, apple, pear and spice flavors, a hint of honey on the pretty aftertaste. The texture is smooth and creamy. 3,950 cases made. • $14 • (06/15/97) • **89**
Chardonnay Napa Valley 1994: Lean and flinty, with a trim band of spicy pear and fig, but it lacks real finesse and harmony. Finishes a tad on the bitter side. 4,291 cases made. • $15 • (06/15/96) • **80**
Chardonnay Napa Valley 1993 • $15 • (10/31/95) • **86**
Chardonnay Napa Valley Signature Series 1996: Smooth, ripe, rich and creamy, with layers of pear, fig, vanilla, spice and hazelnut. A dramatic departure from previous Chappellet Chardonnays, which have been leaner and more compact. 643 cases made. • $24 • (03/31/98) • **90**
Chardonnay Napa Valley Signature Series 1994: Marked spicy, citrusy accents on its pear and lightly toasty flavors. Its finish is more subtly defined as the flavors trail off. 66 cases made. • $24 • (06/15/96) • **87**
Chenin Blanc Napa Valley Dry 1996: Tart and flinty, with lime, citrus and hints of green apple and pear flavors. 1,560 cases made. • $11 • (05/15/98) • **83**
Chenin Blanc Napa Valley Dry 1994 • $9 • (06/15/96) • **86**
Chenin Blanc Napa Valley Dry 1993 • $7 • (10/15/95) BB • **86**
Chenin Blanc Napa Valley Moelleux 1993: Sweet, dried apricot and earthy tobacco flavors. A bit coarse and short on the finish. A dessert wine that drinks well now. 14 cases made. • $40/375ml • (08/31/96) • **85**
Chenin Blanc Napa Valley Old Vine Cuvée Special Select 1994 • $11 • (06/15/96) • **85**
Chenin Blanc Napa Valley Old Vine Cuvée Special Select 1993 • $11 • (10/15/95) • **88**
Merlot Napa Valley 1993: Elegant, earthy currant and berry flavors, with a slight mineral edge. Turns leathery and a bit peculiar on the finish. 410 cases made. • $18 • (08/31/96) • **85**
Merlot Napa Valley 1992 • $17 • (06/15/95) • **84**
Merlot Napa Valley 1989 • $16 • (05/31/92) • **68**
Merlot Napa Valley 1988 • $15 • (04/15/92) • **85**
Merlot Napa Valley 1987 • $15 • (12/31/90) • **89**
Merlot Napa Valley 1986 • $15 • (01/31/90) • **80**
Merlot Napa Valley 1985 • $12 • (12/31/88) • **78**
Old Vine Cuvée White Napa Valley Special Select 1995: A full-bodied wine with a strong mineral, or flint, edge. It's dry and firm, finishing with hints of vanilla and hazelnuts. Has depth and finesse. 2,850 cases made. • $12 • (10/15/97) • **87**
Sangiovese Napa Valley 1995: Serves up an elegant array of spice, currant and wild berry of moderate depth and richness, finishing with pretty oak shadings and tender tannins. Ready to drink. 385 cases made. • $22 • (12/15/97) • **87**

CHARTRONS | CALIFORNIA

Claret California 1986 • $15 • (11/15/91) • **78**

CHASSEUR | CALIFORNIA

Chardonnay Russian River Valley Dutton 1995: For all its richness and complexity, it's an understated style that relies on finesse and grace rather than sheer power and intensity. Serves up ripe pear, spicy citrus and hazelnut notes, lingering on the finish. 215 cases made. • $28 • (04/30/98) • **88**

CHATEAU BENOIT | OREGON

Müller-Thurgau Willamette Valley 1995: Light, simple and fresh, with a nice apple note highlighting the finish. 8,369 cases made. • $6 • (04/30/97) • **81**
Pinot Noir Oregon 1992 • $9 • (03/15/94) • **77**
Pinot Noir Oregon 1991 • $10 • (02/28/93) • **72**
Pinot Noir Oregon 1989 • $12 • (02/28/93) • **80**
Pinot Noir Oregon Reserve 1992 • $18 • (03/15/94) • **75**
Pinot Noir Oregon Reserve 1989 • $20 • (02/28/93) • **80**
Pinot Noir Oregon Ruby NV • $6 • (03/15/94) • **74**
White Riesling Sweet Oregon Sophia 1995: Richness and sweetness are bracingly balanced by crisp, citrusy acidity, while the lingering finish shows honey and apricot flavors that are just delicious. Ready to drink. 162 cases made. • $14 • (04/30/97) • **88**

CHATEAU BIANCA | OREGON

Chardonnay Oregon Barrel Fermented 1994: Light and fruity, refreshing for its citrusy liveliness. Ready now. 456 cases made. • $8 • (03/31/96) • **85**
Chardonnay Oregon Vintner's Reserve 1994: Grassy, slightly sour flavors make this one forgettable. 140 cases made. • $12 • (01/31/96) • **77**
Chardonnay Oregon Vintner's Reserve 1993 • $12 • (11/30/94) • **85**
Chardonnay Oregon Winemaker's Reserve 1995: Extremely floral, almost decadent flavors, and some medicinal notes, take this one out of contention. Tasted twice, with consistent notes. 123 cases made. • $15 • (04/30/97) • **77**
Gewürztraminer Oregon Dauenhauer Vineyard 1994 • $7 • (03/31/96) • **84**
Pinot Noir Oregon Winemaker's Reserve 1995: Lean and raw, with an herbal streak running through its biting berry and anise flavors. Drinkable now. 212 cases made. • $18 • (02/28/97) • **79**
Pinot Noir Oregon Winemaker's Reserve 1993 • $9 • (01/31/96) • **73**
Pinot Noir Oregon Winemaker's Reserve 1992 • $18 • (11/30/94) • **82**
Riesling Oregon Dauenhauer Vineyard 1994 • $6 • (01/31/96) • **79**

CHATEAU CHEVALIER | CALIFORNIA

Cabernet Sauvignon Napa Valley 1980 • $12 • (01/01/84) • **82**

CHATEAU CHEVRE | CALIFORNIA

Cabernet Franc Napa Valley 1985 • $16 • (07/31/88) • **85**
Chev Reserve Napa Valley 1986 • $25 • (07/31/89) • **88**
Merlot Napa Valley 1985 • $16 • (08/31/88) • **87**
Merlot Napa Valley 1984 • $13 • (10/31/87) • **91**
Merlot Napa Valley 1983 • $13 • (10/15/87) • **85**
Merlot Napa Valley 1982 • $12 • (10/01/85) • **84**
Merlot Napa Valley Reserve 1986 • $25 • (07/31/89) • **80**
Merlot Napa Valley Reserve 1984 • $15 • (12/15/87) • **78**

CHATEAU CHRISTINA | CALIFORNIA

Cabernet Sauvignon Carmel Valley 1994: Firm in texture and nicely packed with earthy blackberry and beet flavors that remain crisp and refined through the juicy finish. Good now, best from 2000. 110 cases made. • $25 • (11/15/97) • **87**
Pinot Noir Monterey County 1996: An earthy, beefy style, with some attractive plum, spice, anise and herb flavors. Texture is a bit chunky. Drink now or hold. 125 cases made. • $25 • (02/28/98) • **84**
Pinot Noir Monterey County 1995: A beefy, earthy style of Pinot Noir, with broad cherry and currant flavors on the finish. Acids are bright, but the ensemble is harmonious. 100 cases made. • $20 • (09/30/97) • **87**

CHATEAU DE BAUN | CALIFORNIA

Brut Rosé Sonoma County Symphony Rhapsody 1988 • $11 • (07/15/91) • **83**
Brut Rosé Sonoma County Symphony Rhapsody 1987 • $12 • (05/31/90) • **78**
Brut Rosé Sonoma County Symphony Rhapsody 1986 • $12 • (09/15/88) • **88**

Brut Sonoma County Symphony Romance 1988 • $11 • (07/15/91) • **84**
Brut Sonoma County Symphony Romance 1987 • $12 • (04/30/90) • **80**
Brut Sonoma County Symphony Romance 1986 • $12 • (07/31/88) • **74**
Chardonnay Russian River Valley 1994: Simple, ordinary pear and spice flavors. Good but nothing more. 12,015 cases made. • $10 • (05/15/96) • **81**
Chardonnay Russian River Valley 1993 • $10 • (04/30/95) • **87**
Chardonnay Russian River Valley Creekside Vineyard Reserve 1993 • $18 • (02/29/96) • **92**
Pinot Noir California Barrel Select Rouge 1991 • $5 • (03/31/95) • **73**
Pinot Noir California Chateau Rouge Barrel Select 1990 • $5 • (02/28/93) • **75**
Pinot Noir Russian River Valley 1994: Light and simple, with an earthy, leathery accent to the modest rhubarb and plum flavors. 4,262 cases made. • $12 • (11/30/96) • **81**
Pinot Noir Russian River Valley 1993 • $10 • (12/31/95) • **82**
Pinot Noir Russian River Valley 1992 • $10 • (12/31/95) • **83**
Pinot Noir Sonoma County 1991 • $10 • (02/28/94) • **82**
Symphony Late Harvest Russian River Valley Finale 1993 • $10/375ml • (07/31/95) • **88**
Symphony Late Harvest Sonoma County Finale 1989 • $6/375ml • (11/15/93) • **87**
Symphony Late Harvest Sonoma County Finale 1988 • $12/375ml • (04/30/91) • **87**
Symphony Late Harvest Sonoma County Finale 1987 • $14/375ml • (04/30/89) • **85**
Symphony Late Harvest Sonoma County Finale 1986 • $14/375ml • (09/15/87) • **81**
Symphony Russian River Valley Stellé 1994 • $12 • (09/30/95) • **84**

CHATEAU DE LEU | CALIFORNIA

Brunolino North Coast 1991 • $6 • (10/15/93) BB • **85**
Brunolino North Coast 1990 • $6 • (07/31/92) • **83**
Pinot Noir Napa Valley 1991 • $9 • (02/28/94) • **83**
Pinot Noir Napa Valley 1990 • $11 • (02/28/93) • **75**
Pinot Noir Solano County Green Valley 1985 • $7 • (02/28/89) • **77**

CHATEAU DIANA | CALIFORNIA

Blanc de Noirs Monterey Special Reserve 1986 • $7 • (06/15/91) • **71**
Cabernet Sauvignon California Limited Edition 1988 • $5 • (10/15/91) • **72**
Cabernet Sauvignon California Limited Edition 1986 • $5 • (10/15/91) BB • **82**
Cabernet Sauvignon Central Coast Limited Edition 1984 • $6 • (11/30/88) BB • **82**

CHATEAU ELAN | CALIFORNIA

Cabernet Sauvignon Napa Valley 1978 • $NA • (11/15/92) • **77**

CHATEAU FRANK | NEW YORK

Brut Finger Lakes 1985 • $18 • (12/31/90) • **80**
Sparkling Finger Lakes Brut 1987 • $15 • (12/15/95) • **82**
Sparkling Finger Lakes Crémant Célèbre NV • $10 • (12/15/95) • **78**

CHATEAU GRAND TRAVERSE | MICHIGAN

Johannisberg Riesling Late Harvest Michigan 1990 • $10 • (02/29/92) • **78**

CHATEAU JULIEN | CALIFORNIA

Cabernet Sauvignon Monterey County Grand Reserve 1992: Lacks body and ripeness. The green bean quality overpowers hints of cherry flavor on the finish. 3,900 cases made. • $7 • (11/30/96) • **71**
Cabernet Sauvignon Monterey County Private Reserve 1992: Firm, intense and tannic, but not out of bounds as there are sufficient currant, herb, oak and cedar flavors providing dimension. Drinkable now. 1,800 cases made. • $18 • (11/30/96) • **86**

Key: SS—Spectator Selection CS—Cellar Selection HR—Highly Recommended BB—Best Buy $NA—Price not available Ⓐ—Auction Price (BT)—Barrel Tasting
Dates in parentheses indicate the issues in which the ratings were published.

Cabernet Sauvignon Monterey County Private Reserve 1989 • $20 • (08/31/92) • **79**
Chardonnay Monterey County Grand Reserve 1995: A spicy, tangy wine, with tropical fruit flavors backed by a lemony finish and a moderate dose of toasty oak. 3,600 cases made. • $8 • (06/15/97) • **87**
Chardonnay Monterey County Grand Reserve 1993 • $7 • (01/01/96) • **79**
Chardonnay Monterey County Private Reserve 1995: A supple, understated style, with a core of smoky oak, creamy pear, citrus and spice flavors. Young and tight, it's rich and well focused, finishing with length. 600 cases made. • $20 • (07/31/97) • **88**
Chardonnay Monterey County Private Reserve 1994: Bright and lively. Citrusy apple and spicy pear flavors with light toasty oak overtones. Flavors carry throughout the finish. 1,200 cases made. • $13 • (07/31/96) • **90**
Chardonnay Monterey County Sur Lie Private Reserve 1993 • $17 • (12/15/95) • **75**
Merlot Monterey County 1991 • $10 • (05/31/93) • **84**
Merlot Monterey County 1989 • $9 • (05/31/92) • **86**
Merlot Monterey County 1988 • $9 • (05/31/92) • **72**
Merlot Monterey County Grand Reserve 1995: Cedar and cinnamon set the tone, followed by pure oak, then, timidly, modest fruit. • $10 • (04/30/98) • **79**
Merlot Monterey County Grand Reserve 1994 • $9 • (06/30/96) • **85**
Merlot Monterey County Private Reserve 1991 • $9 • (09/15/94) BB • **85**
Merlot Santa Barbara County Bien Nacido Vineyard 1984 • $12 • (02/29/88) • **76**

CHATEAU LA GRANDE ROCHE | CALIFORNIA

Pinot Noir Napa Valley 1991 • $16 • (02/28/94) • **85**
Red Napa Valley 1988 • $13 • (10/15/90) • **86**

CHATEAU LAFAYETTE RENEAU | NEW YORK

Johannisberg Riesling Finger Lakes 1995: An odd mix of floral and lanolin aromas and flavors prevent this from being very appetizing. Has sweet and sour components that don't mesh well. • $9 • (10/31/96) • **76**

CHATEAU MARGARITE | CALIFORNIA

Cabernet Sauvignon Napa Valley 1992 • $15 • (12/15/95) • **85**
Cabernet Sauvignon Napa Valley 1991 • $15 • (11/15/93) • **87**
Cabernet Sauvignon Napa Valley 1990 • $12 • (11/15/93) • **86**
Cabernet Sauvignon Napa Valley 1989 • $15 • (11/15/93) • **74**

CHATEAU MONTELENA | CALIFORNIA

Cabernet Napa Valley Calistoga Cuvée 1993: Well balanced, with pleasant cherry, plum and spice notes. Drink now. 10,000 cases made. • $18 • (12/15/95) • **86**
Cabernet Sauvignon Alexander Valley Sonoma 1978 • $68 • (11/15/92) • **86**
Cabernet Sauvignon Alexander Valley Sonoma 1974 • $48 Ⓐ • (11/15/94) • **88**
Cabernet Sauvignon Napa Valley 1997: Tight and unusually backward, even for this wine. So dense and compact it's hard to work through the mineral, currant and sage-laced fruit. Could be a tremendous wine. • $NA • (07/31/98) (BT) • **90-94**
Cabernet Sauvignon Napa Valley 1989 • $30 • (11/15/93) • **85**
Cabernet Sauvignon Napa Valley 1988 • $30 • (11/15/92) • **87**
Cabernet Sauvignon Napa Valley 1987: Dark and still very tightly wound, but the core of earthy currant, mineral, spice and cedar is right on the spot. With aeration, the wine starts to open and the tannins begin to soften a bit. Close to its peak. Ready to drink, but don't be surprised if it's still humming in 2005. 7,200 cases made. • $109 Ⓐ • (12/15/97) • **93**
Cabernet Sauvignon Napa Valley 1986: A candidate for wine of the vintage, this is ripe, rich, complex and deeply concentrated. It has maintained its youthful core of juicy black cherry and plum flavors and, while it remains firmly tannic and potent, the finish is long and complex. Enjoy now or can be cellared—perhaps up to another decade. 11,000 cases made. • $77 Ⓐ • (12/15/96) • **96**
Cabernet Sauvignon Napa Valley 1985 • $85 Ⓐ • (11/15/89) CS • **92**
Cabernet Sauvignon Napa Valley 1984 • $72 Ⓐ • (10/15/88) • **94**
Cabernet Sauvignon Napa Valley 1983 • $53 Ⓐ • (11/15/87) CS • **93**
Cabernet Sauvignon Napa Valley 1982 • $59 Ⓐ • (10/15/86) • **79**
Cabernet Sauvignon Napa Valley 1980 • $16 • (10/01/84) • **83**
Cabernet Sauvignon Napa Valley 1978 • $119 Ⓐ • (11/15/92) • **96**

Cabernet Sauvignon Napa Valley 1974 • $140 • (11/15/94) • **83**

Cabernet Sauvignon Napa Valley Calistoga Cuvée 1995: Openly fruity, with simple but pleasant cherry and berry flavors and just enough tannin to keep your interest. 12,000 cases made. • $18 • (10/31/97) • **82**

Cabernet Sauvignon Napa Valley Calistoga Cuvée 1994: Young and vibrant, it's a bit on the earthy, leathery side, but opens to reveal a rich core of currant, cherry and anise flavors that stay with you even as the tannins weigh in on the finish. Ready now. 13,000 cases made. • $18 • (11/15/96) • **88**

Cabernet Sauvignon Napa Valley Calistoga Cuvée 1992 • $15 • (11/15/94) SS • **90**

Cabernet Sauvignon Napa Valley The Montelena Estate 1993: An assertive young wine, firm, intense and lively, with a complex core of currant, plum and berry flavors, turning smoky and elegant on the finish. Drinkable now, but with its great track record for aging, this estate-grown wine will be best enjoyed from 1999 to 2005, possibly beyond. 10,000 cases made. • $40 • (05/31/97) CS • **92**

Cabernet Sauvignon Napa Valley The Montelena Estate 1991 • $40 • (05/31/95) SS • **92**

Cabernet Sauvignon Napa Valley The Montelena Estate 1990 • $46 Ⓐ • (11/15/94) CS • **90**

Cabernet Sauvignon Napa Valley The Montelena Estate 1972-1992 Anniversary 1992: Serves up a complex, supple band of cherry, plum, coffee and menthol flavors of good depth and concentration. Finishes with a complex aftertaste and enough tannin to warrant cellaring into 1999. 11,000 cases made. • $36 • (11/15/96) CS • **91**

Chardonnay Napa Valley 1995: Good intensity, richness and concentration, with a core of pear, citrus, nectarine, anise and fig, picking up a leafy, earthy flavor on the finish. Has a track record for improving with age, so set a couple bottles aside for 2000 and beyond. Best now through 2004. 9,000 cases made. • $25 • (06/30/98) • **90**

Chardonnay Napa Valley 1994: Crisp and flinty, with a core of citrus flavor that slowly unfolds into pear, apple, spice and cinnamon notes. Drinkable now. 12,000 cases made. • $25 • (06/15/97) SS • **91**

Chardonnay Napa Valley 1993 • $23 • (07/31/95) • **84**

Zinfandel Napa-Alexander Valleys 1974 • $40 • (06/16/85) • **92**

Zinfandel Napa Valley 1991 • $12 • (10/15/94) • **84**

Zinfandel Napa Valley 1989 • $12 • (10/15/92) • **80**

Zinfandel Napa Valley 1987 • $10 • (07/31/90) • **69**

Zinfandel Napa Valley 1986 • $15 • (09/15/89) • **80**

Zinfandel Napa Valley 1985 • $15 • (04/30/88) • **90**

Zinfandel Napa Valley 1983 • $11 • (05/01/86) • **84**

Zinfandel Napa Valley 1982 • $14 • (05/01/84) • **91**

Zinfandel Napa Valley 1981 • $20 • (04/16/84) • **80**

Zinfandel Napa Valley 1973 • $29 • (06/16/85) • **90**

Zinfandel Napa Valley John Rolleri Vineyard 1984 • $18 • (05/15/87) • **91**

Zinfandel Napa Valley The Montelena Estate 1992 • $12 • (07/31/95) • **87**

Zinfandel North Coast 1976 • $25 • (06/16/85) • **78**

CHATEAU MORRISETTE | VIRGINIA

Chardonnay Virginia 1993 • $10 • (06/30/95) • **77**

CHATEAU POTELLE | CALIFORNIA

Cabernet Sauvignon Alexander Valley 1988 • $18 • (11/15/92) • **87**

Cabernet Sauvignon Alexander Valley 1987 • $16 • (08/31/91) • **83**

Cabernet Sauvignon Alexander Valley 1986 • $15 • (10/31/90) • **84**

Cabernet Sauvignon Alexander Valley 1984 • $13 • (12/31/88) • **83**

Cabernet Sauvignon Mount Veeder V.G.S. 1997: Tightly wound, firmly tannic, with tart wild berry, cherry and currant and a long, lingering aftertaste. • $NA • (07/31/98) (BT) • **90-94**

Cabernet Sauvignon Mount Veeder V.G.S. 1996: Young, hard, tart and unevolved, still it's intense, sharply focused and darkly colored. The core of earthy currant, mineral, spice and cedar is most impressive where it should be—on the finish. 1,000 cases made. • $NA • (06/15/97) (BT) • **90-94**

Cabernet Sauvignon Mount Veeder V.G.S. 1993: Dense, tight and chewy, with firm gritty tannins, this is a big, dense, backward-style wine with an uncertain future. If all goes well, the intense core of plum, earth, tar, pepper and cedary flavors will evolve into a complex, deeply-flavored wine. 1,000 cases made. • $39 • (07/31/98) • **88**

Cabernet Sauvignon Mount Veeder V.G.S. 1992: Young, tight and a bit on the green side with its tart plum and berry notes. This is complex and concentrated and will require cellaring to open up, perhaps into 2000 when it may well move up into the outstanding category. Tasted thrice, with consistent notes. 930 cases made. • $39 • (11/30/96) • **88**

Cabernet Sauvignon Napa Valley 1991: Young and tight, still a bit tart, but with pleasant cherry, herb and currant flavors in modest proportions. Turns simple on the finish. Ready now. 4,000 cases made. • $18 • (10/15/96) • **86**

Cabernet Sauvignon Napa Valley Cuvée 95 1990 • $16 • (10/15/94) • **86**

Chardonnay California California Cuvée 1995: A touch earthy with a slight oxidized edge, there's enough ripe pear and apple flavors to make it interesting. 5,000 cases made. • $15 • (07/31/97) • **82**

Chardonnay Central Coast 1995: Ripe, smooth and creamy, with spicy pear, hazelnut, anise and cedary oak flavors that linger on the finish. Drink now through 2001. 3,700 cases made. • $16 • (07/31/98) • **88**

Chardonnay Mount Veeder V.G.S. 1995: Smooth, ripe, rich and buttery, with a creamy texture and lots of complex pear, fig, melon and butterscotch flavors. Turns even more complex and interesting on the finish, where the flavors lift off and linger. Drink now through 2002. 2,000 cases made. • $35 • (06/30/98) • **92**

Chardonnay Mount Veeder V.G.S. 1994: Young, intense and vibrant, with a complex, spicy edge to the ripe pear and apple flavors. Light oak shadings and a flinty citrus note mark the aftertaste. 1,000 cases made. • $35 • (05/31/97) • **92**

Chardonnay Napa Valley-Central Coast 1994: Intense and earthy with pronounced grassy overtones, straying into Sauvignon Blanc territory where it takes a citrus and grapefruit edge. 13,000 cases made. • $9 • (10/15/95) • **85**

Sauvignon Blanc Napa Valley 1996: Fairly complex, with good integration of flavors; thyme, sage, wintergreen, melon and grapefruit interact well. The finish is fresh and clean. 9,000 cases made. • $11 • (04/30/98) • **87**

Sauvignon Blanc Napa Valley 1995: A zippy mouthful of fruit and herb flavors, centering around nectarine and a touch of anise. The finish is bright and lively. A fair price for this quality. 9,000 cases made. • $9 • (10/15/96) BB • **88**

Sauvignon Blanc Napa Valley 1994 • $9 • (08/31/95) • **87**

Sauvignon Blanc Napa Valley 1993 • $9 • (01/31/95) • **85**

Zinfandel Mount Veeder V.G.S 1995: Deftly balances the ripe, intense Zinfandel flavors with pretty toasty oak. The core of zesty, spicy, earth, raspberry and dried cherry is rich, concentrated and focused, finishing with a long, complex aftertaste. Enjoy now. 1,800 cases made. • $35 • (04/30/98) • **91**

Zinfandel Mount Veeder V.G.S. 1994: A classy California Zin from start to finish. Loaded with rich, complex flavors with tiers of cherry, anise, wild berry and plum. Finishes with supple tannins and a pretty, toasty oak accent. Delicious and ready to drink. 1,400 cases made. • $32 • (03/31/97) HR • **92**

Zinfandel Mount Veeder V.G.S. 1993 • $28 • (12/31/95) • **88**

Zinfandel Mount Veeder V.G.S. 1992 • $28 • (10/15/94) • **92**

Zinfandel Mount Veeder V.G.S. 1990 • $27 • (04/30/93) HR • **90**

CHATEAU ST. JEAN | CALIFORNIA

Brut Blanc de Blancs Sonoma County 1987 • $12 • (12/31/89) • **81**

Brut Blanc de Blancs Sonoma County 1984 • $11 • (05/31/89) • **88**

Brut Blanc de Blancs Sonoma County 1983 • $11 • (07/31/87) • **76**

Brut Blanc de Blancs Sonoma County 1982 • $13 • (05/16/86) • **79**

Brut Blanc de Blancs Sonoma County 1981 • $14 • (11/01/84) • **82**

Brut Sonoma County 1987 • $12 • (04/30/90) • **82**

Brut Sonoma County 1986 • $12 • (12/31/89) • **87**

Brut Sonoma County 1985 • $11 • (12/31/88) • **86**

Brut Sonoma County 1984 • $11 • (07/15/88) • **84**

Brut Sonoma County 1983 • $11 • (05/31/87) • **67**

Brut Sonoma County 1981 • $14 • (11/01/84) • **81**

Brut Sonoma County Grande Cuvée 1985 • $19 • (12/31/93) • **88**

Brut Sonoma County Grande Cuvée 1982 • $19 • (06/15/91) • **80**

Cabernet Franc Sonoma Valley Jeanette Vineyards 1989 • $24 • (07/15/93) • **83**

Cabernet Sauvignon Alexander Valley 1987 • $16 • (06/30/91) SS • **92**

Cabernet Sauvignon Alexander Valley 1986 • $19 • (10/15/89) • **90**

Cabernet Sauvignon Alexander Valley 1985 • $19 • (11/15/88) • **86**

Cabernet Sauvignon Alexander Valley Reserve 1987: An impressive array of rich currant, smoke, spice and cedar aromas, softening on the finish. Plenty to admire in this wine. Ready to drink. 500 cases made. • $50 • (12/15/97) • **90**

Cabernet Sauvignon Sonoma County 1997: Graceful, rich and concentrated, with pretty layers of currant, black cherry and toasty oak. Wonderful sense of harmony and finesse. • $NA • (07/31/98) (BT) • **90-94**

Cabernet Sauvignon Sonoma County 1989 • $18 • (06/30/93) • **80**

Cabernet Sauvignon Sonoma County 1988 • $18 • (07/31/92) • **87**

CHATEAU ST. JEAN

Cabernet Sauvignon Sonoma County 1981 • $15 • (11/30/86) • **72**

Cabernet Sauvignon Sonoma County Cinq Cépages 1996: Showing beautiful fruit and oak already, with toasty vanilla and buttery notes and a rich, supple core of currant, berry, cherry and spice flavors. Wonderful. This is only the Cabernet component of the final blend. • $NA • (06/15/97) (BT) • **90-94**

Cabernet Sauvignon Sonoma County Cinq Cépages 1994: A smooth, ripe and fleshy Cabernet blend, with a pretty, concentrated core of plum, cherry, currant and wild berry flavors, and a rich, fruity aftertaste echoing the fruit and light oak. Tempting now, best after 1999. A blend of 76 percent Cabernet Sauvignon, 14 percent Cabernet Franc, 5 percent Merlot, 4 percent Malbec, and 1 percent Petit Verdot. 12,500 cases made. • $24 • (09/30/97) SS • **91**

Cabernet Sauvignon Sonoma County Cinq Cépages 1993: An elegant style that delivers a ripe, intense core of currant, coffee, cedar and cherry flavors while maintaining its balance and finesse. Finishes with a long, fruity aftertaste that lingers on and on. Gives you the flavor, richness and depth of the more expensive Cabernets at about half the price. 9,000 cases made. • $22 • (11/15/96) SS • **91**

Cabernet Sauvignon Sonoma County Cinq Cépages 1992 • $18 • (02/29/96) • **89**

Cabernet Sauvignon Sonoma County Cinq Cépages 1991 • $18 • (11/15/95) HR • **91**

Cabernet Sauvignon Sonoma County Cinq Cépages 1990 • $18 • (09/30/94) • **87**

Cabernet Sauvignon Sonoma County Reserve 1992: Ripe and intense, with firm, chewy tannins, the ripe plum, currant and wild berry flavors pour through, revealing layers of complexity and depth. Finishes with enough tannin to merit cellaring into 2000. 800 cases made. • $45 • (09/30/97) • **92**

Cabernet Sauvignon Sonoma County Reserve 1991: Young and intense, with a significant tannic edge, but the currant, cedar and spice flavors manage to outshine the tannins and it turns complex, adding notes of black cherry and leather to its range of flavors. A big wine that needs cellaring into 2001 or so. • $39 • (11/15/96) • **92**

Cabernet Sauvignon Sonoma County Reserve 1990 • $38 • (04/30/96) CS • **95**

Cabernet Sauvignon Sonoma County Reserve 1989 • $38 • (11/15/95) • **87**

Cabernet Sauvignon Sonoma County Reserve 1988 • $38 • (10/15/93) • **91**

Cabernet Sauvignon Sonoma Valley Wildwood Vineyards 1980 • $17 • (09/01/85) • **82**

Cabernet Sauvignon Sonoma Valley Wildwood Vineyards 1979 • $17 • (07/01/84) • **76**

Chardonnay Alexander Valley Belle Terre Vineyard 1996: An elegant, understated style, with ripe, spicy pear, fig and melon-laced flavors that pick up a smoky, butterscotch edge on the finish. Clean and refreshing, it drinks well now. • $22 • (05/15/98) • **91**

Chardonnay Alexander Valley Belle Terre Vineyard 1995: Notable for its up-front, spicy anise flavors, given depth and complexity as ripe pear and apple flavors fold in and pick up smoky oak and buttery accents on the finish. • $22 • (05/31/97) • **92**

Chardonnay Alexander Valley Belle Terre Vineyards 1994: Rich and full-bodied, showing a complex core of ripe pear, nectarine, honey, spice and toasty oak flavors that are well-focused and long on the finish. A terrific California white from a vineyard that is showing consistently good results. 5,000 cases made. • $18 • (04/30/96) HR • **92**

Chardonnay Alexander Valley Belle Terre Vineyards 1993 • $18 • (07/31/95) • **86**

Chardonnay Alexander Valley Robert Young Vineyard 1995: Smooth, ripe and complex, with nectarine, pear and grapefruit notes that turn elegant and spicy. Finishes with a long, lingering aftertaste. Ready now. • $24 • (11/30/97) • **91**

Chardonnay Alexander Valley Robert Young Vineyard 1994: Complex interplay of ripe pear, apple and spice flavors, with notes of cedary oak which impart a touch of dill, fanning out on the finish to become even more complex. • $24 • (05/31/97) • **92**

Chardonnay Alexander Valley Robert Young Vineyard Reserve 1994: Mature, with subtle, complex pear, citrus, earth and cedary notes, it turns elegant and supple on the finish, with a lingering aftertaste that echoes ripe fruit and light oak shadings. • $57/1.5 liter • (04/30/98) • **90**

Chardonnay Alexander Valley Robert Young Vineyard Reserve 1993: Mature, with a spicy edge to the pear, vanilla, nutmeg and light citrus notes, this turns smooth and polished on the lingering finish. Will be especially appealing for those who like Chardonnays with a little age on them. Available in magnum. • $58/1.5 liter • (05/31/97) • **91**

Chardonnay Sonoma County 1996: Delicious Chardonnay from start to finish. It's smooth, ripe and creamy, with a complex medley of pear, spice, hazelnut flavors, tastily complemented by light oak notes and hints of peach and nectarine. Nice price, too. 117,000 cases made. • $13 • (12/31/97) SS • **89**

Chardonnay Sonoma County 1994: Serves up a ripe and refreshing core of pear, honey, spice and nectarine flavors. A beautifully crafted Chardonnay that delivers the fruit and just a hint of oak. 95,000 cases made. • $11 • (04/30/96) SS • **90**

Chardonnay Sonoma County 1993 • $11 • (05/15/96) • **85**

Chardonnay Sonoma County Private Chateau Select 1994: Simply delicious, and a real value at this price. Pure, ripe and complex, with layers of pear, fig, citrus and melon flavors, and toasty cedar notes on the finish. • $18 • (06/15/97) • **91**

Fumé Blanc Russian River Valley La Petite Etoile Vineyard 1996: A pleasing fruitiness crosses the palate here—melon, mandarin orange and plum—with hints of coconut at the edges. Finishes clean and bright. • $13 • (04/30/98) • **86**

Fumé Blanc Russian River Valley La Petite Etoile Vineyard 1995: A firm, weighty wine that's pleasant on the palate, with light citrus and melonlike flavors. Well made, but lacks varietal distinction. • $13 • (06/15/97) • **88**

Fumé Blanc Russian River Valley La Petite Etoile Vineyard 1994 • $12 • (04/30/96) • **88**

Fumé Blanc Russian River Valley La Petite Etoile Vineyard 1993 • $12 • (08/31/95) • **84**

Fumé Blanc Sonoma County 1996: A mild Fumé, with pretty vanilla notes. The follow-up features grapefruit, clove, lemon and sweet pea. Good price. • $9 • (04/30/98) • **85**

Fumé Blanc Sonoma County 1995: Here's a good-value Sauvignon Blanc from a reputable California producer. It's a nicely balanced mouthful of fruit and acidity, with a blend of mineral, citrus and melon flavors that finish fresh and clean. 30,000 cases made. • $9 • (06/15/97) BB • **87**

Fumé Blanc Sonoma County 1994 • $8 • (04/30/96) • **87**

Fumé Blanc Sonoma County Dry 1993 • $8 • (08/31/95) • **82**

Gewürztraminer Late Harvest Alexander Valley Robert Young Vineyard 1982 • $18/375ml • (07/16/84) • **91**

Gewürztraminer Late Harvest Alexander Valley Robert Young Vineyard Select 1983 • $14/375ml • (11/01/84) • **92**

Johannisberg Riesling Late Harvest Alexander Valley Robert Young Vineyard 1984 • $15/375ml • (03/16/86) • **86**

Johannisberg Riesling Late Harvest Alexander Valley Robert Young Vineyard 1983 • $25/375ml • (08/01/85) SS • **92**

Johannisberg Riesling Late Harvest Alexander Valley Robert Young Vineyard Special Select 1982 • $22/375ml • (09/01/84) • **92**

Johannisberg Riesling Late Harvest Alexander Valley Select 1988 • $20/375ml • (01/31/93) • **88**

Johannisberg Riesling Late Harvest Alexander Valley Select 1987 • $25/375ml • (01/31/93) • **90**

Johannisberg Riesling Late Harvest Alexander Valley Special Select 1989 • $25/375ml • (11/15/93) CS • **95**

Johannisberg Riesling Late Harvest Alexander Valley Special Select 1986 • $25/375ml • (01/31/93) • **94**

Johannisberg Riesling Late Harvest Alexander Valley Special Select Hoot Owl Creek Vineyards 1989 • $22/375ml • (01/31/93) HR • **93**

Johannisberg Riesling Late Harvest Russian River Valley Select 1985 • $12 • (08/31/87) • **84**

Merlot Sonoma County 1995: Serves up ripe cherry, berry, plum and spice flavors and picks up complex cedar and tobacco notes on the finish. Ready to drink. 15,500 cases made. • $18 • (03/31/98) • **87**

Merlot Sonoma County 1994: Serves up lots of sage, cedar and spice notes, with supple plum and black cherry flavors folding in nicely on the finish giving a sense of finesse and polish. 18,000 cases made. • $18 • (06/15/97) • **90**

Merlot Sonoma County 1993: Ripe, smooth and harmonious, with well-focused core flavors of cherry, plum, spice and cedary oak. Finishes with firm but supple tannins. Drink now. 11,000 cases made. • $14 • (07/31/96) SS • **90**

Merlot Sonoma County 1992 • $12 • (04/15/95) • **86**

Merlot Sonoma County 1991 • $12 • (09/15/94) • **84**

Merlot Sonoma County 1990 • $12 • (03/15/94) • **85**

Merlot Sonoma County 1989 • $12 • (12/31/93) • **80**

Merlot Sonoma County Reserve 1993: Elegant and complex, with a pretty array of spicy cedar, currant, black cherry and berry flavors. Turns long and lingering on the finish, where the flavors fan out and reveal their

Key: SS—Spectator Selection CS—Cellar Selection HR—Highly Recommended BB—Best Buy $NA—Price not available Ⓐ—Auction Price (BT)—Barrel Tasting
Dates in parentheses indicate the issues in which the ratings were published.

depth. Tasted three times, with noticeable bottle variation. • $35 • (05/15/98) • **90**

Merlot Sonoma County Reserve 1992: Shows cedar- and ash-accented currant and berry flavors, quite intense and concentrated, finishes with firm tannins and good length. Can stand cellaring into 1999. 500 cases made. • $35 • (06/15/97) • **91**

Merlot Sonoma County Reserve 1991 • $32 • (02/29/96) CS • **92**

Mourvèdre Sonoma Valley 1990 • $17 • (06/15/93) • **83**

Pinot Noir Carneros Durell Vineyard 1995: A beefy, meaty style, with lots of smoky qualities and just enough leathery cherry and berry to sustain it. Tasted twice, with consistent notes. 500 cases made. • $30 • (02/28/98) • **85**

Pinot Noir Sonoma County 1994: Complete and harmonious, it's rich with well-focused currant, black cherry, spice and cedar notes, firm tannins and fine length. Ready now, but holding a bottle or two would also be nice. 700 cases made. • $18 • (01/31/97) • **88**

Pinot Noir Sonoma County 1991 • $16 • (02/28/94) • **86**

Pinot Noir Sonoma County 1990 • $19 • (02/28/93) • **80**

Pinot Noir Sonoma Valley McCrea Vineyards 1983 • $12 • (09/30/87) • **75**

Sauvignon Blanc Late Harvest Sonoma County Sauvignon d'Or 1982 • $15 • (07/01/84) • **85**

Sémillon Late Harvest Sonoma Valley Sémillon D'Or St. Jean Vineyard 1984 • $15 • (11/30/86) • **86**

CHATEAU STE. MICHELLE | WASHINGTON

Cabernet Franc Columbia Valley Cold Creek Vineyard 1995: A very pretty red wine, supple in texture, with pools of blueberry, plum and currant flavor extending into a refined finish. Flavors linger impressively. Delicious now through 2002. 1,500 cases made. • $27 • (06/15/98) • **89**

Cabernet Franc Columbia Valley Cold Creek Vineyard 1992 • $22 • (09/30/95) • **85**

Cabernet Sauvignon Benton County Cold Creek Vineyards Chateau Reserve 1980 • $21 • (10/15/89) • **85**

Cabernet Sauvignon Columbia Valley 1994: A polished Washington Cab that's generous with its spicy blueberry and currant flavors, swirling in some pepper and cola notes for added dimension on the slightly chewy finish. Tannins can use until 1999 to 2000 to soften. 50,000 cases made. • $16 • (08/31/97) SS • **89**

Cabernet Sauvignon Columbia Valley 1993: Richly fruit-flavored and elegant in style, showing impressive depth in black cherry, currant, vanilla and spice notes that echo on the finish. Fine tannins are present but not intrusive. Drinkable now. 66,000 cases made. • $14 • (04/30/96) • **89**

Cabernet Sauvignon Columbia Valley 1992 • $14 • (07/31/95) • **86**

Cabernet Sauvignon Columbia Valley 1991 • $14 • (09/30/94) • **88**

Cabernet Sauvignon Columbia Valley 1990 • $14 • (07/31/94) • **87**

Cabernet Sauvignon Columbia Valley 1989 • $14 • (03/15/93) • **88**

Cabernet Sauvignon Columbia Valley 1988 • $13 • (08/31/91) • **84**

Cabernet Sauvignon Columbia Valley 1986 • $12 • (09/30/90) • **88**

Cabernet Sauvignon Columbia Valley Cold Creek Vineyard 1993: Dense and chewy—a serious wine. Focused berry and chocolate flavors persist on the solid finish. Seems closed at this point, needing more richness on the finish. Allow until 1999-2000 to soften. 2,500 cases made. • $26 • (08/31/96) • **87**

Cabernet Sauvignon Columbia Valley Cold Creek Vineyard 1992 • $26 • (12/15/95) SS • **92**

Cabernet Sauvignon Columbia Valley Cold Creek Vineyard 1991 • $22 • (01/31/95) • **88**

Cabernet Sauvignon Columbia Valley Cold Creek Vineyard Limited Bottling 1987 • $20 • (08/31/91) • **83**

Cabernet Sauvignon Columbia Valley Horse Heaven Vineyard 1994: Firm in texture and generous with its blackberry, blueberry and currant flavors, shaded on the finish with toasty, smoky notes. Chewy, slightly rough tannins need until 2000 to 2002. 550 cases made. • $27 • (08/31/97) • **90**

Cabernet Sauvignon Columbia Valley Horse Heaven Vineyard 1993: Deliciously focused berry and currant flavors over a velvety frame. Echoes of spice and fruit on the lively, complex finish. Try now. • $27 • (08/31/96) • **87**

Cabernet Sauvignon Columbia Valley River Ridge Vineyard Limited Bottling 1987 • $18 • (08/31/91) • **87**

Cabernet Sauvignon Columbia Valley Twentieth Vintage 1987 • $12 • (09/30/90) • **85**

Cabernet Sauvignon Napa Valley Z-91 NV • $NA • (01/31/90) • **90**

Cabernet Sauvignon Washington 1985 • $12 • (10/15/89) • **85**

Cabernet Sauvignon Washington 1984 • $11 • (12/31/88) • **89**

Cabernet Sauvignon Washington 1983 • $10 • (11/15/87) • **81**

Cabernet Sauvignon Washington Cold Creek Vineyard Limited Bottling 1985 • $16 • (10/15/89) • **82**

Cabernet Sauvignon Washington River Ridge Vineyard Limited Bottling 1985 • $17 • (11/30/90) HR • **90**

Chardonnay Columbia Valley 1995: Shows lots of ripe pear and honey flavors on a smooth, well-proportioned frame. Not a huge wine, but the pretty flavors linger on the polished finish. 132,000 cases made. • $14 • (08/31/97) • **89**

Chardonnay Columbia Valley 1994: Bright on a smaller scale, featuring nicely focused peach, apple and spice flavors. Ready now. 150,000 cases made. • $13 • (05/15/96) • **87**

Chardonnay Columbia Valley Barrel Fermented 1993 • $13 • (08/31/95) • **87**

Chardonnay Columbia Valley Canoe Ridge Estate Vineyard 1995: Big, ripe, rich and concentrated, yet balanced for elegance. Shows floral and pepper notes around a core of creamy pineapple and pear flavors and lingers enticingly and harmoniously on the open-textured finish, echoing hazelnut and tropical fruit. Try now. 2,500 cases made. • $28 • (09/15/97) • **92**

Chardonnay Columbia Valley Canoe Ridge Estate Vineyard 1994: Smooth and polished, offering tasty nutmeg-scented pear and honey flavors that linger on a delicate finish. Ready now. 1,200 cases made. • $27 • (09/15/96) • **88**

Chardonnay Columbia Valley Canoe Ridge Estate Vineyard 1993 • $26 • (09/30/95) • **86**

Chardonnay Columbia Valley Chateau Reserve 1994: Rich in texture, bright and expansive in flavor, with lovely walnut, honey, pear and sweet apple flavors that swirl through the smooth, but still tangy, finish. Delicious now, with more maturity than most Chardonnays out there. 1,200 cases made. • $30 • (04/30/97) • **91**

Chardonnay Columbia Valley Chateau Reserve 1993 • $30 • (12/31/95) • **91**

Chardonnay Columbia Valley Cold Creek Vineyard 1995: Silky, harmonious and elegant, it's not especially powerful but displays its pretty pear, honey and pepper notes on a lithe frame. Ready now, but could improve through 1999. 4,500 cases made. • $26 • (09/15/97) • **90**

Chardonnay Columbia Valley Cold Creek Vineyard 1994: Sharply focused pear and citrus flavors hold the spotlight in this crisp, appealing wine with a long, juicy finish. Drink now. 2,500 cases made. • $25 • (09/15/96) SS • **90**

Chardonnay Columbia Valley Cold Creek Vineyard 1993 • $25 • (08/31/95) SS • **90**

Chardonnay Columbia Valley Indian Wells Vineyard 1995: This sturdy Washington white offers crisp, citrusy flavors and a good layer of spice around the edges. Harmonious, elegant and well balanced, it's appealing now, but try to wait until 1999 when it should fill out nicely. 2,500 cases made. • $26 • (09/30/97) SS • **90**

Chardonnay Columbia Valley Indian Wells Vineyard 1994: Finely focused pear, spice, grapefruit and vanilla flavors grace this harmonious, well-balanced wine. Drink now. 1,200 cases made. • $25 • (09/15/96) • **90**

Chardonnay Columbia Valley Indian Wells Vineyard 1993 • $20 • (08/31/95) • **91**

Chardonnay Columbia Valley Reserve 1995: Ripe, broad and generous with its orange-tinged pear and spice flavors; long, silky and harmonious as the flavors linger gently. Drink now. 1,250 cases made. • $31 • (09/30/97) • **92**

Chenin Blanc Columbia Valley 1993 • $7 • (09/30/94) • **84**

Columbia Valley Chateau Reserve Ice Wine 1995: Sweet and silky. A sensational mouthful of pear, honey, apricot and vanilla flavors that swirl and linger through the exceedingly long finish. Seductive now, but could gain yet more depth by 2002 or so. 1,150 cases made. • $30/375ml • (06/15/97) • **95**

Gewürztraminer Columbia Valley 1993 • $7 • (09/30/94) • **79**

Meritage Columbia Valley 1994: Firm in texture, and cascading with pretty berry, anise and vanilla flavors that swirl invitingly through the satiny finish. Mouthfilling but far from heavy, it's a lovely wine that's just starting to show what it has. Best from 2001. A blend of 58 percent Merlot, 37 percent Cabernet Sauvignon, and 5 percent Cabernet Franc. 1,500 cases made. • $50 • (09/15/97) • **91**

Meritage Washington 1993: Crisp and fruity at first, offering nicely articulated berry flavors, although the tannins sneak past these notes by the finish. Try now. 1,250 cases made. • $30 • (09/30/96) • **88**

Merlot Columbia Valley 1994: Crisp and a bit chewy, with a moderate level of spicy, toasty black cherry flavors that linger on the tight finish. Try now. 94,000 cases made. • $18 • (08/31/97) • **85**

Merlot Columbia Valley 1993 • $15 • (05/31/96) • **87**

Merlot Columbia Valley 1992 • $15 • (09/30/95) • **83**

Merlot Columbia Valley 1990 • $14 • (04/15/94) • **87**

Merlot Columbia Valley 1989 • $14 • (06/15/93) • **85**

Merlot Columbia Valley 1988 • $15 • (03/31/92) • **84**

Merlot Columbia Valley 1987 • $12 • (09/30/90) • **84**

Merlot Columbia Valley 1986 • $12 • (09/30/90) • **84**

Merlot Columbia Valley Canoe Ridge Estate Vineyard 1994: Rich, dark and chewy. A generous mouthful of blackberry, chocolate and herbal flavors that wraps tightly around a sinewy texture. Best after 1999. • $31 • (08/31/97) • **90**

Merlot Columbia Valley Canoe Ridge Estate Vineyard 1993 • $28 • (06/15/96) • **88**

Merlot Columbia Valley Cold Creek Vineyard 1994: Bright, smooth and striving for elegance, it's not a big wine, but the pretty raspberry, floral and chocolate notes expand and enrich in the glass. A layer of chewy tannins needs until 1999 to resolve. 2,800 cases made. • $29 • (08/31/97) • **91**

Merlot Columbia Valley Cold Creek Vineyard 1993 • $28 • (06/15/96) HR • **90**

Merlot Columbia Valley Cold Creek Vineyard 1987 • $19 • (06/15/93) • **79**

Merlot Columbia Valley Cold Creek Vineyard Limited Bottling 1987 • $19 • (08/31/91) • **81**

Merlot Columbia Valley Horse Heaven Vineyard 1993 • $27 • (06/15/96) • **88**

Merlot Columbia Valley Indian Wells Vineyard 1994: Refined and elegant in style, showing plenty of tobacco-scented berry and chocolate flavors that glide smoothly through the finish. Ready now. 5,000 cases made. • $31 • (09/15/97) • **87**

Merlot Columbia Valley Indian Wells Vineyard 1992 • $30 • (09/30/95) • **90**

Merlot Columbia Valley Indian Wells Vineyard 1991 • $20 • (09/30/94) • **88**

Merlot Columbia Valley Reserve 1994: A lovely mouthful of ripe, rich blueberry, plum and spice flavors, supple and generous through the fruit-centered finish. Echoes its flavors beautifully, and feels like it can grow through 2000 to 2002. 1,500 cases made. • $42 • (09/15/97) • **92**

Merlot Columbia Valley River Ridge Vineyard 1985 • $18 • (09/30/90) • **89**

Merlot Washington 1983 • $10 • (12/31/88) • **80**

Merlot Washington River Ridge Vineyard 1985 • $14 • (10/15/89) • **87**

Merlot Washington River Ridge Vineyard Château Reserve 1983 • $15 • (12/31/88) • **87**

Pinot Noir Columbia Valley Limited Bottling 1987 • $11 • (08/31/91) • **79**

Riesling Columbia Valley Dry 1993 • $7 • (09/30/94) • **85**

Riesling Washington Ice Wine 1978 • $NA • (04/15/95) • **85**

Sauvignon Blanc Columbia Valley 1993 • $9 • (09/15/95) • **84**

Sauvignon Blanc Columbia Valley Horse Heaven Vineyard 1996: Bright and refreshing for its mineral-scented apple flavors that linger softly. Drink now. 10,000 cases made. • $15 • (06/30/98) • **85**

Sauvignon Blanc Columbia Valley Horse Heaven Vineyard 1995: Bright and mildly citrusy, with spice-accented, soft lemon, pear and lightly herbal flavors that echo with remarkable refinement on the finish. First separate bottling from this vineyard. 3,500 cases made. • $12 • (02/28/97) • **89**

Sémillon Columbia Valley 1995: A pleasant wine, with tobacco-tinged pear and citrus flavors that step lively through the finish. 14,000 cases made. • $7 • (09/15/96) • **86**

Sémillon Columbia Valley 1993 • $7 • (07/31/95) • **82**

Sémillon Columbia Valley Barrel Fermented 1994 • $7 • (07/31/95) BB • **86**

Sémillon Late Harvest Columbia Valley Reserve 1995: Rich, almost syrupy, with enough bright pear, fig and citrus flavors behind the sweetness to keep it in balance. Nice now, best from 1999. 1,190 cases made. • $20/375ml • (03/31/98) • **92**

Sémillon Late Harvest Columbia Valley Reserve 1992 • $20/375ml • (04/30/95) • **90**

White Riesling Late Harvest Columbia Valley Chateau Reserve 1991 • $9/375ml • (09/15/95) HR • **93**

White Riesling Late Harvest Columbia Valley Horse Heaven Vineyard Chateau Reserve 1995: Ripe, sweet, rich and complex. A subtle mouthful of honey, earth, floral and apple pie flavors that linger on the generous finish. 1,000 cases made. • $17/375ml • (02/28/97) SS • **90**

White Riesling Late Harvest Columbia Valley River Ridge Vineyard Hand-Selected Cluster 1989 • $18 • (09/30/91) • **82**

White Riesling Late Harvest Yakima Valley Château Reserve Hand-Selected Cluster 1985 • $22 • (07/31/89) • **91**

CHATEAU SOUVERAIN | CALIFORNIA

Cabernet Sauvignon Alexander Valley 1995: Complex, with smoky, earthy, meaty currant, anise and sage flavors that are tighly focused, finishing with crisp, raw tannins. Best to give this short-term cellaring to soften the rough edges. Best from 2001 through 2009. 40,000 cases made. • $17 • (06/30/98) HR • **89**

Cabernet Sauvignon Alexander Valley 1994: From one of California's more fertile Cabernet-growing regions comes this firm, intense and concentrated red, with layers of currant, plum and black cherry flavors that fan out deliciously. Finishes with a well-focused, fruity aftertaste punctuated with dashes of herb and cedar. 44,000 cases made. • $15 • (06/30/97) SS • **89**

Cabernet Sauvignon Alexander Valley 1992 • $12 • (03/31/95) • **85**

Cabernet Sauvignon Alexander Valley 1991 • $11 • (06/30/94) • **85**

Cabernet Sauvignon Alexander Valley 1990 • $11 • (11/15/93) SS • **90**

Cabernet Sauvignon Alexander Valley 1989 • $10 • (11/15/92) • **85**

Cabernet Sauvignon Alexander Valley 1988 • $10 • (11/15/91) • **85**

Cabernet Sauvignon Alexander Valley 1987 • $9 • (11/15/90) • **87**

Cabernet Sauvignon Alexander Valley 1986 • $8 • (11/15/89) BB • **85**

Cabernet Sauvignon Alexander Valley Barrel Aged 1993: Smooth and elegant, with pretty herb, cherry and currant flavors and a nice touch of cedary oak on the finish. Ready to drink. 48,000 cases made. • $13 • (10/15/96) • **86**

Cabernet Sauvignon Alexander Valley Library Reserve 1993: Complex and richly flavored, with tiers of currant, chocolate, toasty oak and hints of herb and spice. A dense and concentrated style that packs in more flavor than earlier bottlings of Souverain Reserve, and shows a shade more depth and complexity than does even the Winemaker's Reserve. 200 cases made. • $40 • (11/15/96) • **91**

Cabernet Sauvignon Alexander Valley Private Reserve 1987: Drying out, with hints of earth, cedar, plum and currant. Finishes with a pleasing, smoky plum aftertaste. Ready to drink. • $26 • (12/15/97) • **87**

Cabernet Sauvignon Alexander Valley Winemaker's Reserve 1994: Beautifully orchestrated fruit and oak flavors, with tiers of currant, black cherry, herb, sage and spice, a smooth, supple texture and just the right amount of tannin. It's delicious now, but worthy of holding, too. Shoot for drinking the cellared bottles in 2002. 1,000 cases made. • $30 • (10/15/97) • **93**

Cabernet Sauvignon Alexander Valley Winemaker's Reserve 1993: Smooth, rich and harmonious, with a pretty core of anise, currant, herb and spice flavors and well-polished tannins. Not a dazzling style, but one that succeeds due to finesse and harmony. Drinks well now or cellar short-term. 1,000 cases made. • $30 • (11/15/96) • **90**

Cabernet Sauvignon Alexander Valley Winemaker's Reserve 1992 • $16 • (12/15/95) • **89**

Cabernet Sauvignon Alexander Valley Winemaker's Reserve 1991 • $14 • (10/31/94) HR • **91**

Cabernet Sauvignon Alexander Valley Winemaker's Reserve 1990 • $13 • (05/31/94) • **89**

Cabernet Sauvignon Alexander Valley Winemaker's Reserve 1988 • $14 • (11/15/92) • **83**

Cabernet Sauvignon North Coast Vintage Selection 1980 • $13 • (09/16/85) • **83**

Cabernet Sauvignon Sonoma County 1985 • $8 • (11/30/88) • **87**

Cabernet Sauvignon Sonoma County 1984 • $8 • (08/31/87) • **83**

Cabernet Sauvignon Sonoma County 1978 • $50 • (11/15/92) • **82**

Cabernet Sauvignon Sonoma County Vintage Selection 1978 • $28 • (11/15/92) • **83**

Cabernet Sauvignon Sonoma County Vintage Selection 1974 • $50 • (02/15/90) • **84**

Chardonnay Carneros Winemaker's Reserve 1994: Ripe, smooth and elegant, with an alluring spectrum of spicy pear, honey, vanilla and toasty oak flavors that weave into each other nicely. The lingering finish keeps you intrigued. 1,200 cases made. • $16 • (06/15/96) • **91**

Chardonnay Russian River Valley Rochioli Vineyard Reserve 1993 • $16 • (04/30/95) • **89**

Chardonnay Russian River Valley Winemaker's Reserve 1996: Smooth, ripe and creamy, with hints of tropical fruit, ripe pear, fig and melon. Gains a pretty touch of smoky, toasty oak on the aftertaste, where the complex flavors linger on. Impressive texture. Drink now through 2002. 1,000 cases made. • $20 • (07/31/98) HR • **92**

Chardonnay Russian River Valley Winemaker's Reserve 1995: Tightly wound, crisp and flinty, even a touch coarse at this young stage, but it opens to reveal more depth and intensity, with tiers of spicy apple, pear and citrus flavors. 1,000 cases made. • $20 • (05/31/97) • **91**

Chardonnay Sonoma County 1996: Smooth, ripe and creamy in texture, this California Chardonnay features rich pear, fig, melon and spice notes, gaining depth and complexity on the finish, where the flavors flourish. What a buy, from a winemaker with a deft touch with this varietal. 48,000 cases made. • $13 • (01/31/98) SS • **90**

Key: SS—Spectator Selection CS—Cellar Selection HR—Highly Recommended BB—Best Buy $NA—Price not available Ⓐ—Auction Price (BT)—Barrel Tasting
Dates in parentheses indicate the issues in which the ratings were published.

Chardonnay Sonoma County 1995: Pretty pear, apple, hazelnut and vanilla notes are complex and lively. Smooth, supple and harmonious, it's a terrific wine at a value price. 40,000 cases made. • $13 • (04/30/97) • **89**

Chardonnay Sonoma County 1994: Smooth and spicy, ripe with pear and a hint of pineapple, harmonious in the way it folds its sweet oak, vanilla and fruit together. Delicious; amazingly long and drinkable now. An excellent value. 32,000 cases made. • $12 • (04/30/96) SS • **91**

Chardonnay Sonoma County Barrel Fermented 1993 • $12 • (06/15/95) • **85**

Merlot Alexander Valley 1995: Marked by touches of sage and bell pepper, this wine works its way into more complex flavors before turning simpler on the finish. Ready now. 25,000 cases made. • $17 • (11/30/97) • **87**

Merlot Alexander Valley 1994: Pleasant enough; a crisp band of cherry and berry flavors, with a trace of cedary oak. Finishes with soft tannins. 26,000 cases made. • $13 • (07/31/96) • **85**

Merlot Alexander Valley 1993 • $13 • (12/15/95) • **86**

Merlot Alexander Valley 1992 • $12 • (06/30/94) • **85**

Merlot Alexander Valley 1991 • $12 • (06/30/94) • **87**

Merlot Alexander Valley 1990 • $10 • (05/31/93) • **86**

Merlot Alexander Valley 1989 • $10 • (05/31/92) • **89**

Merlot North Coast 1981 • $6 • (10/01/85) • **89**

Merlot Sonoma County 1990 • $10 • (05/31/92) • **86**

Merlot Sonoma County 1986 • $10 • (03/31/89) • **74**

Merlot Sonoma County 1984 • $8 • (07/31/87) • **86**

Pinot Noir Carneros Winemaker's Reserve 1993 • $16 • (03/31/95) • **84**

Pinot Noir Carneros Winemaker's Reserve 1992 • $14 • (04/30/94) • **85**

Pinot Noir Carneros Winemaker's Reserve 1991 • $15 • (02/28/94) • **85**

Sauvignon Blanc Alexander Valley 1996: Lemon-lime and crisp apple flavors in a richly textured wine that finishes with notes of hazelnut, toast and orange essence. 9,000 cases made. • $8 • (06/30/97) • **88**

Sauvignon Blanc Alexander Valley 1995: Soft in the mouth, and light-bodied. Fresh pear and floral flavors. 12,000 cases made. • $7 • (07/31/96) • **82**

Sauvignon Blanc Alexander Valley Barrel Fermented 1994 • $8 • (08/31/95) • **85**

Sauvignon Blanc Alexander Valley Barrel Fermented 1993 • $7 • (12/15/94) BB • **87**

Zinfandel Dry Creek Valley 1995: A jazzy, lively mouthful of Zinfandel flavors, with blackberry, black cherry and vanilla notes that resonate on the intensely generous finish. Best in 1999. 11 percent Syrah, 4 percent Petite Sirah. 15,000 cases made. • $12 • (12/15/97) SS • **89**

Zinfandel Dry Creek Valley 1994: Light and simple, with a grapey cherry and berry accent to the not-quite-ripe flavors. 13,000 cases made. • $9 • (09/15/96) • **82**

Zinfandel Dry Creek Valley 1993 • $9 • (08/31/95) BB • **87**

Zinfandel Dry Creek Valley 1992 • $9 • (08/31/94) BB • **87**

Zinfandel Dry Creek Valley 1991 • $8 • (09/15/93) BB • **87**

Zinfandel Dry Creek Valley 1990 • $7 • (10/15/92) • **84**

Zinfandel Dry Creek Valley 1989 • $7 • (05/15/92) BB • **82**

Zinfandel Dry Creek Valley 1987 • $9 • (05/15/90) • **82**

Zinfandel Dry Creek Valley 1986 • $5 • (03/31/89) BB • **81**

Zinfandel Dry Creek Valley Bradford Mountain Vineyard 1987 • $15 • (05/15/90) • **85**

CHATEAU WOLTNER | CALIFORNIA

Cabernet Sauvignon North Coast 1979 • $3 • (03/16/84) • **76**

Chardonnay Howell Mountain 1996: Has more spice flavor than fruit on its sturdy, straightforward frame. Fresh finish. Try now. 5,000 cases made. • $13 • (11/30/97) • **83**

Chardonnay Howell Mountain 1993 • $10 • (09/30/94) • **86**

Chardonnay Howell Mountain Estate Reserve 1993 • $17 • (07/31/95) • **84**

Chardonnay Howell Mountain Frederique Vineyard 1995: Young and still with a greenness to the pear and apple flavors, it slowly fans out, revealing hints of oak and fig. Try now. 198 cases made. • $40 • (12/31/97) • **88**

Chardonnay Howell Mountain Frederique Vineyard 1994: Tart, lean and crisp, with a flinty core of tangy pear, citrus and melon. Well-crafted and deliberate in style, more like a Chablis than a typical, full-blown California Chardonnay. Try now. 84 cases made. • $40 • (05/15/97) • **88**

Chardonnay Howell Mountain Frederique Vineyard 1993 • $40 • (07/31/95) • **82**

Chardonnay Howell Mountain St. Thomas Vineyard 1995: Tight and crisp, with a flinty lemon and tart pear edge to the core of fruit. Best to cellar into 1999 to let it fan out. 945 cases made. • $23 • (12/31/97) • **87**

Chardonnay Howell Mountain St. Thomas Vineyard 1994: Marked by a strong citrus, particularly grapefruit, edge, this is the most forward of the Woltner Chardonnays, though it's still quite austere by California Chardonnay standards. Try now. 210 cases made. • $23 • (05/15/97) • **89**

Chardonnay Howell Mountain St. Thomas Vineyard 1993 • $23 • (07/31/95) • **83**

Chardonnay Howell Mountain Titus Vineyard 1995: A subtle, understated style that's lean and lemony, with a strong citrus quality to the green pear and apple notes. Drinkable now. 190 cases made. • $40 • (12/31/97) • **88**

Chardonnay Howell Mountain Titus Vineyard 1994: Crisp and tightly wound, showing citrus, especially tart grapefruit, and green pear flavors and finishing with zingy acidity. This is a young, concentrated wine that needs some time to soften and evolve. Try now. 84 cases made. • $40 • (05/15/97) • **89**

Chardonnay Howell Mountain Titus Vineyard 1993 • $40 • (07/31/95) • **82**

CHATOM | CALIFORNIA

Cabernet Sauvignon Calaveras County 1994: Somewhat thin and tannic, its pretty blackberry and cassis flavors don't quite stand up to the oak. 364 cases made. • $18 • (09/15/97) • **81**

Cabernet Sauvignon Calaveras County 1993: Smoky, toasty character blends nicely with plummy, almost prunelike, flavors. Not complex, but enjoyable and ready to drink. 417 cases made. • $16 • (11/30/96) • **85**

Cabernet Sauvignon Calaveras County 1992 • $12 • (06/15/95) • **84**

Cabernet Sauvignon Calaveras County 1991 • $12 • (11/15/94) • **83**

Cabernet Sauvignon Calaveras County 1989 • $14 • (11/15/92) • **84**

Chardonnay Calaveras County 1994: A lighter style of wine with modest green apple flavors and a toasty, cardboardy edge. 339 cases made. • $12 • (07/31/96) • **80**

Chardonnay Calaveras County 1993 • $10 • (07/31/95) • **82**

Merlot Calaveras County 1994: A toasty, dusty wine, with charred, smoky qualities. Fruit takes a backseat, with hints of currant and plum. Finishes oakily. 429 cases made. • $16 • (09/30/97) • **80**

Merlot Calaveras County 1992 • $14 • (07/31/95) • **74**

Merlot Calaveras County 1991 • $14 • (09/15/94) • **85**

Sangiovese Calaveras County 1992 • $14 • (09/30/94) • **70**

Sauvignon Blanc Calaveras County 1993 • $8 • (05/15/95) HR • **90**

Sauvignon Blanc Calaveras County Reserve 1995: Bright and zingy with pineapple and grapefruit flavors that mate nicely with spicy oak notes. Keeps zinging on the finish. 1,002 cases made. • $12 • (04/30/97) • **89**

Sauvignon Blanc Calaveras County Reserve 1994 • $11 • (05/31/96) • **83**

Sémillon Calaveras County 1993 • $8 • (06/30/95) • **87**

Syrah Calaveras County 1995: This firm, yet smoothly crafted wine offers hints of mint, thyme, blackberries and black currants. It finishes with a somewhat herbal edge. 280 cases made. • $20 • (09/30/97) • **86**

Zinfandel Calaveras County 1994: Oak and light cherry flavors struggle to be heard in this lightweight Zin. 455 cases made. • $9 • (09/15/97) • **75**

Zinfandel Calaveras County 1993 • $9 • (04/30/96) • **77**

Zinfandel Calaveras County 1992 • $8 • (07/31/95) • **84**

Zinfandel Calaveras County 1991 • $8 • (10/15/94) • **81**

Zinfandel Calaveras County 1989 • $8 • (09/30/93) • **84**

CHAUFFE-EAU | CALIFORNIA

Cabernet Sauvignon Alexander Valley 1987 • $16 • (08/31/92) • **85**

Cabernet Sauvignon Alexander Valley Smith-Reichel Vineyard 1995: Still tight and young, with powdery, drying tannins, but the flavors are focused and intense, with layers of cassis, black currant, blackberry, black cherry, and an intriguing herbal edge. Could be a real winner in a few years. Drink now through 2002. 240 cases made. • $19 • (06/30/98) • **88**

Chardonnay Carneros Sangiacomo Vineyard 1996: A well-oaked style, but the oak is quite pretty, with spicy, toasty flavors and an elegant, complex aftertaste that lingers. Drink now. 875 cases made. • $20 • (06/15/98) • **88**

Chardonnay Carneros Sans Filtrage Sangiacomo 1993 • $17 • (07/31/95) • **87**

Chardonnay Russian River Valley Sans Filtrage Dutton 1993 • $18 • (07/31/95) • **86**

Merlot Sonoma Valley Kunde Vineyards 1995: Holds back on the nose, but is rich in licorice, cassis, blackberry, cedar and spice on the palate. A leaner style, it may improve in a few years. Drink now through 2003. 190 cases made. • $19 • (05/31/98) • **86**

Merlot Sonoma Valley Kunde Vineyards 1992 • $17 • (09/30/95) • **82**

Pinot Noir Carneros 1996: A nice touch of earth and mushroom starts this out, then it eases into pretty cherry and cola notes. A smooth, easy-drinking Pinot Noir. Drink now. 250 cases made. • $22 • (06/15/98) • **85**

Pinot Noir Carneros 1993 • $19 • (03/31/96) • **71**

CHEHALEM | OREGON

Cerise Willamette Valley Ridgecrest Vineyards NV: Light in color, abbreviated in flavor, with minty overtones to the light berry flavor. Could be more charming. A blend of 80 percent Gamay and 20 percent Pinot Noir. 900 cases made. • $12 • (12/31/97) • **79**

Chardonnay Oregon Ridgecrest Vineyards 1994: Lean, lithe and nicely focused for its pretty pear, spice and vanilla flavors. Ready now. 240 cases made. • $18 • (03/31/96) • **84**

Chardonnay Oregon Ridgecrest Vineyards 1993 • $17 • (01/31/96) • **85**

Chardonnay Willamette Valley 1996: A very pretty Chardonnay, silky in texture and generous with its spicy pear and mineral flavors, finishing with a nice touch of almond. Ready to drink. 690 cases made. • $17 • (05/15/98) • **88**

Chardonnay Willamette Valley Reserve 1996: Ripe, emphasizing fruit character over everything else, with pretty pear, peach and apple flavors swirling generously through the finish. Drink now. 360 cases made. • $27 • (06/30/98) • **88**

Chardonnay Willamette Valley Ridgecrest Vineyard 1995: A tightly structured, lean wine packed with spicy citrus and pear flavors that linger on the lively finish. 400 cases made. • $17 • (02/28/97) • **86**

Pinot Gris Oregon Ridgecrest Vineyards 1994 • $17 • (01/31/96) • **86**

Pinot Gris Oregon Ridgecrest Vineyards 1993 • $11 • (11/30/94) • **81**

Pinot Gris Oregon Ridgecrest Vineyards Reserve 1993 • $15 • (01/31/96) • **86**

Pinot Gris Willamette Valley Ridgecrest Vineyards 1996: Light and airy, modest in intensity, offering some nice apple and melon flavors. Drink soon. 340 cases made. • $14 • (09/15/97) • **82**

Pinot Gris Willamette Valley Ridgecrest Vineyards 1995: Light and oxidized, with unappealing cardboardlike flavors. • $NA • (02/28/97) • **74**

Pinot Gris Willamette Valley Ridgecrest Vineyards Reserve 1996: Ripe and generous with its almond and floral-scented melon flavors. A soft and silky wine with a nice sense of vibrancy. Drink soon. 747 cases made. • $19 • (05/15/98) • **89**

Pinot Gris Willamette Valley Ridgecrest Vineyards Reserve 1995: Soft, ripe and spicy, with chunky pineapple and almond flavors that linger a bit on the finish. 350 cases made. • $17 • (02/28/97) • **81**

Pinot Noir Oregon Ridgecrest Vineyards 1993 • $20 • (01/31/96) • **82**

Pinot Noir Oregon Ridgecrest Vineyards 1992 • $20 • (11/30/94) • **85**

Pinot Noir Oregon Ridgecrest Vineyards 1991 • $16 • (11/30/94) • **88**

Pinot Noir Oregon Ridgecrest Vineyards 1990 • $15 • (11/30/94) • **85**

Pinot Noir Oregon Ridgecrest Vineyards Wadenswil Selection 1993 • $20 • (01/31/96) • **79**

Pinot Noir Willamette Valley 3 Vineyard 1996: Firm and focused, with a lovely mouthful of smoke-tinged black cherry and anise flavors that linger on the chewy finish. Not a huge wine, but articulates its flavors nicely. Best from 2000. 2,200 cases made. • $18 • (05/15/98) • **88**

Pinot Noir Willamette Valley 3 Vineyard 1995: Light, lacking in intensity, but pleasant enough with its sappy black cherry and floral flavors. Try now. 800 cases made. • $15 • (02/28/97) • **80**

Pinot Noir Willamette Valley Ridgecrest Vineyards 1995: Lean and tough in texture, with more earth than fruit in the flavor spectrum. Try now. • $25 • (10/15/97) • **80**

Pinot Noir Willamette Valley Ridgecrest Vineyards 1994: Bright, focused and generous with its black cherry and plum flavors. A welcome note of black pepper on the harmonious finish. Try now. • $23 • (12/31/96) • **88**

Pinot Noir Willamette Valley Ridgecrest Vineyards Rion Reserve 1994: Rich and concentrated, yet remains light enough to provide an elegant, harmonious frame for the dark berry, black cherry and anise flavors. Packed with flavor and a veneer of fine tannins. Try now. • $42 • (01/31/97) • **91**

Pinot Noir Willamette Valley Rion Reserve 1995: A little more tightly packed than most '95s, with ripe blackberry and currant flavors poking through the layer of hard-edged tannin on the surface. Best from 1999 or 2000. 690 cases made. • $34 • (10/15/97) • **86**

Ridgecrest Vineyards Cerise Oregon 1993 • $12 • (01/31/96) • **77**

Ridgecrest Vineyards Oregon 1992 • $12 • (11/30/94) • **82**

Riesling Willamette Valley Corral Creek Vineyard Dry 1995: Ripe and warm, with a delicate frame bordering pretty apple, spice and floral flavors. Ready now. 220 cases made. • $17 • (02/28/97) • **85**

Key: SS—Spectator Selection CS—Cellar Selection HR—Highly Recommended BB—Best Buy $NA—Price not available Ⓐ—Auction Price (BT)—Barrel Tasting
Dates in parentheses indicate the issues in which the ratings were published.

CHERRY HILL | WASHINGTON

Cabernet-Merlot Columbia Valley 1994: Smoky, meaty flavors dominate this olive-accented wine, with a narrow band of cherry flavor at the core. Try now. 400 cases made. • $8 • (09/15/96) • **86**

Chardonnay Columbia Valley 1994: Focused, lively, resiny pear and vanilla flavors remain zingy through the finish, folding in a touch of oak. 2,571 cases made. • $6 • (09/30/95) • **87**

CHESTNUT HILL | CALIFORNIA

Cabernet Sauvignon California 1988 • $7 • (10/15/91) BB • **81**

Cabernet Sauvignon California Coastal Cuvée 1991 • $9 • (05/15/94) • **82**

Cabernet Sauvignon California Coastal Cuvée 1990 • $8 • (05/15/93) • **84**

Cabernet Sauvignon Napa Valley 1983 • $7 • (10/31/86) BB • **91**

Cabernet Sauvignon Sonoma County 1987 • $9 • (03/31/90) • **80**

Cabernet Sauvignon Sonoma County 1985 • $7 • (10/15/88) • **77**

Merlot Napa Valley 1989 • $10 • (11/15/91) • **81**

Merlot North Coast 1985 • $8 • (12/15/87) • **84**

Merlot North Coast Coastal Cuvée 1992 • $10 • (09/15/94) • **78**

Merlot North Coast Coastal Cuvée 1991 • $9 • (03/31/93) • **78**

Zinfandel California Old Vines Cuvée 1990 • $6 • (09/30/93) • **75**

Zinfandel San Luis Obispo 1989 • $6 • (07/31/92) • **83**

Zinfandel San Luis Obispo 1988 • $6 • (08/31/91) BB • **86**

Zinfandel San Luis Obispo County Lot 2 1989 • $6 • (04/30/93) • **77**

CHESTNUT MOUNTAIN | GEORGIA

Cabernet Sauvignon Georgia Mossy Creek Vineyard 1989 • $16 • (02/29/92) • **83**

Merlot Georgia 1990 • $14 • (02/29/92) • **83**

CHIMERE | CALIFORNIA

Chardonnay Santa Barbara County 1995: A ripe, oaky, heavy-handed style that goes over the top with honey and earthy, botrytislike flavors. 1,000 cases made. • $15 • (07/31/97) • **79**

Chardonnay Santa Barbara County 1993 • $13 • (07/31/95) • **82**

Merlot Santa Barbara County 1992 • $16 • (07/31/95) • **83**

Merlot Santa Barbara County Bien Nacido Vineyard 1994: Prematurely aged for a 1994. Has some nice spice, leather and raspberry flavors, but it's not holding together. Past its prime. 500 cases made. • $18 • (05/31/98) • **79**

Nebbiolo Santa Barbara County 1992 • $15 • (12/15/95) • **77**

Pinot Blanc Santa Barbara County 1993 • $10 • (08/31/95) • **76**

Pinot Noir Edna Valley 1995: Turning brown already, it offers up exotic spice and leather but lacks ripe fruit. Sharp on the finish. Past its prime. 1,000 cases made. • $18 • (05/15/98) • **77**

Pinot Noir Edna Valley 1994: Dense and vegetal, with a pickle-barrel and mushroom edge to the sour cherry flavor. Shows the qualities of Edna Valley Pinot Noir, with its marginal ripeness, but the Bien Nacido bottling is better. 1,200 cases made. • $18 • (03/31/97) • **82**

Pinot Noir Santa Barbara County Bien Nacido Vineyard 1994: Ripe and juicy, with a complex array of cherry, creamy vanilla, spice and wild berry notes. Impressive for its supple texture and expression of the Bien Nacido vineyard. Finishes with *terroir*-induced hints of herb and spice. 2,000 cases made. • $24 • (03/31/97) • **88**

CHIMNEY ROCK | CALIFORNIA

Cabernet Sauvignon Napa Valley 1995: This Cabernet is a great bet all around. Not only competitively priced and sufficiently available, it's supple and harmonious, elegant, rich and flavorful, with ripe currant, cherry, berry and spice. Fine tannins on the finish make it appealing to drink now, but it's cellar-worthy, too. Best from 2000 through 2005. 7,481 cases made. • $28 • (05/15/98) SS • **90**

Cabernet Sauvignon Napa Valley 1994: Sharply focused, with a tightly wound core of ripe plum, black cherry and currant flavors. A solid effort, deep and concentrated, turning elegant and supple on the finish. Drinkable now. • $24 • (07/31/97) • **90**

Cabernet Sauvignon Napa Valley Reserve 1997: Complex and well integrated, with layers of black cherry, currant, toasty oak and spice. Impressive balance and texture. • $NA • (07/31/98) (BT) • **90-94**

Cabernet Sauvignon Stags Leap District 1992 • $22 • (05/15/96) • **83**

Cabernet Sauvignon Stags Leap District 1990 • $20 • (04/30/94) • **85**

Cabernet Sauvignon Stags Leap District 1989 • $18 • (03/31/93) • **76**

Cabernet Sauvignon Stags Leap District 1988 • $18 • (08/31/92) • **87**
Cabernet Sauvignon Stags Leap District 1987 • $29 • (07/31/91) SS • **90**
Cabernet Sauvignon Stags Leap District 1986 • $19 • (09/30/89) • **87**
Cabernet Sauvignon Stags Leap District 1985 • $15 • (10/31/88) • **88**
Cabernet Sauvignon Stags Leap District 1984 • $15 • (04/30/88) • **87**
Cabernet Sauvignon Stags Leap District Reserve 1994: Ripe, rich and deeply concentrated, with layers of black cherry, wild berry and currant. More firmly structured that many Stags Leap District Cabernets, but the flavors are complex, pure and long on the finish. 180 cases made. • $50 • (10/15/97) • **91**
Cabernet Sauvignon Stags Leap District Reserve 1993: Tight and firm, with crisp tannins, this serves up a ripe, complex leathery core of currant, spice and cedar flavors that hang with you on the long, full finish. Drinks well now or cellar short-term, into 2000. • $40 • (11/30/96) • **90**
Chardonnay Carneros 1996: A bit disjointed, with chunky, moderately ripe citrus and pear flavors that lose their focus on the finish. Drink now through 2001. 2,960 cases made. • $17 • (05/31/98) • **86**
Chardonnay Carneros 1995: Flavors of fig, melon, apricot and spice unfold slowly from an initial earthiness, picking up a dash of cedar on the finish where all the flavors linger. Ready to drink. 4,800 cases made. • $17 • (05/31/97) • **90**
Chardonnay Carneros 1994: Strikes a good balance between the citrus and pear flavors and the mild oak shadings. 4,300 cases made. • $16 • (06/30/96) • **84**
Chardonnay Carneros 1993 • $16 • (07/31/95) • **82**
Elevage Stags Leap District 1994: Firm and well structured, with a chewy, tannic edge to the earthy currant and leathery notes. Needs time in the bottle to soften a bit and grow into its flavors. A blend of 60 percent Cabernet Sauvignon and 40 percent Merlot. 939 cases made. • $40 • (10/15/97) • **88**
Elevage Stags Leap District 1993: Firm and focused, with a band of ripe cherry, currant, spice and anise flavors, finishing with firm tannins and a good length. Drinks well now or cellar into 2000. • $40 • (11/30/96) • **88**
Elevage Stags Leap District 1992 • $30 • (12/15/95) • **88**
Elevage Stags Leap District 1991 • $30 • (11/15/94) • **90**
Elevage Stags Leap District 1990 • $30 • (11/15/93) • **88**
Fumé Blanc Napa Valley 1996: Pleasant, with mild grapefruit flavors and an air of freshly mowed grass. Clean, flinty finish. 2,340 cases made. • $12 • (05/15/98) • **83**
Fumé Blanc Napa Valley 1995: Straightforward and crisp. The green apple and herb flavors fade a bit on the finish. • $12 • (07/31/96) • **83**
Fumé Blanc Napa Valley 1994 • $11 • (08/31/95) • **80**
Fumé Blanc Napa Valley 1993 • $11 • (08/31/94) • **82**
Reserve Stags Leap District 1992 • $30 • (12/15/95) • **92**

CHINA BEND | WASHINGTON

Gewürztraminer Washington Organic Table Wine 1993 • $12 • (09/30/95) • **82**
Nouveau Organic Red Wine Washington 1994 • $16 • (09/30/95) • **81**
White Riesling Washington Organic Table Wine 1993 • $12 • (09/30/95) • **72**

CHINOOK | WASHINGTON

Merlot Washington 1986 • $13 • (10/15/89) • **83**

CHOUINARD | CALIFORNIA

Chardonnay Monterey Ventana Vineyard 1993 • $12 • (07/31/95) • **80**

CHRISTIAN BROTHERS | CALIFORNIA

Cabernet Sauvignon Napa Valley 1988 • $6 • (11/15/91) • **76**
Cabernet Sauvignon Napa Valley 1987 • $7 • (10/15/91) • **79**
Cabernet Sauvignon Napa Valley 1986 • $9 • (11/15/90) • **88**
Cabernet Sauvignon Napa Valley 1985 • $8 • (06/15/88) HR • **90**
Cabernet Sauvignon Napa Valley 1984 • $7 • (10/15/87) BB • **87**
Merlot Napa Valley 1985 • $8 • (08/31/88) • **80**
Montage Bordeaux & Napa Valley Premier Cuvée NV • $15 • (10/15/88) • **84**
Zinfandel Napa Valley 1986 • $5 • (06/30/88) • **79**

CHRISTINE WOODS | CALIFORNIA

Pinot Noir Alexander Valley 1989 • $10 • (02/28/93) • **69**
Pinot Noir Anderson Valley 1990 • $12 • (02/28/93) • **72**
Pinot Noir Anderson Valley NV • $10 • (12/31/95) • **80**
Pinot Noir Anderson Valley Estate Reserve 1993: In a word, weird, with funky, earthy, murky, metallic flavors that are most unpleasant. Tasted twice with consistent notes. 300 cases made. • $16 • (02/28/97) • **68**
Pinot Noir Anderson Valley Estate Reserve 1992 • $16 • (05/15/95) • **79**

CHRISTOPHE | CALIFORNIA

Cabernet Sauvignon California 1989 • $6 • (08/31/92) • **77**
Cabernet Sauvignon California 1988 • $9 • (03/31/91) • **83**
Cabernet Sauvignon California 1982 • $4 • (12/16/85) BB • **85**
Cabernet Sauvignon Napa County 1994: Has a bitter streak running through its green berry flavors. May settle down by 1999 to 2001. 20,000 cases made. • $9 • (05/15/97) • **79**
Cabernet Sauvignon Napa County 1993: Its ripe plum and cherry flavors and moderate tannins make this wine a decent value. Ready to drink. 3,000 cases made. • $9 • (11/30/96) • **82**
Cabernet Sauvignon Napa County 1992 • $9 • (12/15/95) • **84**
Cabernet Sauvignon Napa County 1991 • $8 • (12/15/95) • **75**
Cabernet Sauvignon Napa Valley 1990 • $9 • (07/15/93) • **78**
Cabernet Sauvignon Napa Valley Reserve 1987 • $8 • (08/31/92) • **80**
Cabernet Sauvignon Napa Valley Reserve 1986 • $12 • (11/15/90) • **78**
Cabernet Sauvignon Napa Valley Reserve 1985 • $13 • (11/15/89) • **74**
Cabernet Sauvignon Napa Valley Reserve 1983 • $9 • (03/31/88) • **82**
Chardonnay Napa County 1994: Light and a tad earthy, but the bright apple flavor wins in the end. 12,000 cases made. • $9 • (06/15/96) • **82**
Chardonnay Napa County 1993 • $8 • (09/30/94) • **79**
Chardonnay North Coast 1993 • $8 • (07/31/95) • **84**
Joliesse California 1987 • $5 • (02/28/90) • **79**
Pinot Noir California 1995: A cherrylike, medicinal quality runs through this wine. An herbal edge frames a short finish. 5,000 cases made. • $9 • (02/28/98) • **79**
Pinot Noir Napa Valley Carneros Reserve 1989 • $9 • (09/30/92) • **84**
Pinot Noir Napa Valley Los Carneros 1992 • $8 • (03/31/95) • **83**
Pinot Noir North Coast 1993: Broad texture. Cheesy, berryish flavors lack harmony. 1,500 cases made. • $9 • (07/31/96) • **79**
Pinot Noir Sonoma County Reserve 1990 • $10 • (02/28/93) • **75**
Sauvignon Blanc Napa County 1995: An interesting blend of cantaloupe and wintergreen flavors emerges, framed by a light, toasty quality. The unusual salt and mineral finish is a bit awkward, however. 20,000 cases made. • $9 • (06/30/97) • **86**
Sauvignon Blanc Napa County 1994: Earthy, candied-leaf flavors predominate, with a sweetish finish. 5,000 cases made. • $10 • (02/28/97) • **74**
Sauvignon Blanc Napa Valley 1993 • $6 • (08/31/94) • **83**

CHRISTOPHER CREEK | CALIFORNIA

Chardonnay Russian River Valley 1993 • $14 • (07/31/95) • **84**
Petite Sirah Russian River Valley 1995: Dense and chewy, striving for elegance beneath the layer of gritty tannins. Give it until 2001 to 2003. 387 cases made. • $18 • (03/31/98) • **85**
Petite Sirah Russian River Valley 1988 • $11 • (10/15/93) • **79**
Syrah Russian River Valley 1993: A tad earthy, but enough plum, leather and berry flavors emerge to hold your interest. Ready to drink. 1,203 cases made. • $14 • (02/28/97) • **84**
Syrah Russian River Valley 1992 • $14 • (05/15/95) • **84**
Syrah Russian River Valley 1990 • $14 • (10/31/93) • **86**

CILURZO | CALIFORNIA

Merlot Temecula Proprietor's Reserve 1991 • $12 • (09/15/94) • **70**
Merlot Temecula Unfiltered Proprietor's Reserve 1990 • $12 • (05/31/92) • **79**

CINNABAR | CALIFORNIA

Cabernet Sauvignon Santa Cruz Mountains 1990 • $20 • (11/15/94) • **84**
Cabernet Sauvignon Santa Cruz Mountains 1989 • $20 • (03/31/93) • **82**
Cabernet Sauvignon Santa Cruz Mountains 1987 • $18 • (03/31/91) • **84**
Cabernet Sauvignon Santa Cruz Mountains 1986 • $15 • (11/15/89) • **93**
Cabernet Sauvignon Santa Cruz Mountains Saratoga Vineyard 1994: A ripe, jammy style, with racy wild berry, black cherry and spicy nuances, finishing with a touch of heat and chewy tannins. Best to cellar short-term to let the tannins soften; try in 1999 to 2000. 1,700 cases made. • $25 • (11/15/97) • **88**
Cabernet Sauvignon Santa Cruz Mountains Saratoga Vineyard 1993: Complex aromas lead to flavors that match, with tiers of spicy currant,

anise, tar and cedary oak nuances. Turns complex on the finish, where the flavors fan out nicely. Supple enough to enjoy now or cellar short-term. 1,450 cases made. • $25 • (10/15/96) • **89**

Cabernet Sauvignon Santa Cruz Mountains Saratoga Vineyard 1992 • $20 • (12/15/95) • **88**

Cabernet Sauvignon Santa Cruz Mountains Saratoga Vineyard 1988 • $20 • (03/15/92) • **82**

Chardonnay Central Coast 1995: Marked by earthy, leesy citrus and pineapple flavors. A tart, crisp young wine that would pair well with seafood. 1,400 cases made. • $17 • (10/15/96) • **84**

Chardonnay Santa Cruz Mountains Saratoga Vineyard 1995: Good intensity, with ripe, spicy pear, citrus and melon notes. Picks up a pleasant earthiness on the finish. Drinkable now, but short-term cellaring should soften it a bit. 1,500 cases made. • $23 • (02/28/97) • **89**

Chardonnay Santa Cruz Mountains Saratoga Vineyard 1994: Rich and enticing, with complex notes of ripe pear, toasty oak, honey and spice. The wood stands out somewhat and the finish is a bit hot, but it should mellow with a little age. 1,500 cases made. • $23 • (06/15/96) • **88**

Merlot Central Coast 1995: Shows off a lot of smoky, toasty oak flavor, with just enough ripe fruit flavor to balance. More for fans of wood-accented Merlots than for those who like fruit up front. 1,375 cases made. • $18 • (03/31/97) • **85**

CIRRI | CALIFORNIA

Cabernet Sauvignon Alexander Valley 1992 • $10 • (12/15/95) • **86**
Cabernet Sauvignon Alexander Valley 1991 • $10 • (11/15/94) • **79**
Chardonnay Sonoma County 1993 • $9 • (07/31/95) • **83**
Merlot Sonoma Valley 1992 • $10 • (03/31/96) • **79**
Merlot Sonoma Valley 1991 • $11 • (09/15/94) • **85**

CLAIBORNE & CHURCHILL | CALIFORNIA

Chardonnay Edna Valley MacGregor Vineyard 1996: Silky-textured, with a slightly earthy component that's followed by lemon, apple and pear flavors. Finishes a bit hot, but still quite interesting. Drink now. 200 cases made. • $18 • (07/31/98) • **87**

Chardonnay Edna Valley MacGregor Vineyard 1994: Clean and correct, with a spicy edge to the ripe pear and pineapple notes. The flavors stay with you on the finish, as the fruit keeps pumping out. 125 cases made. • $18 • (05/31/96) • **88**

Chardonnay Edna Valley MacGregor Vineyard 1993 • $17 • (07/31/95) • **87**

Gewürztraminer Central Coast Alsatian Style Dry 1997: Dry and appealingly floral, with orange-scented pear flavor at the core and a nutty note around the edges. Drink now. 2,000 cases made. • $12 • (07/31/98) • **83**

Gewürztraminer Central Coast Dry 1995: Light, almost crisp in texture, with pleasant grapefruit flavors. Ready now. 1,450 cases made. • $11 • (10/15/96) • **82**

Gewürztraminer Central Coast Dry Alsatian Style 1994 • $10 • (11/15/95) • **87**

Gewürztraminer Central Coast Dry Alsatian Style 1993 • $10 • (05/15/95) BB • **88**

Pinot Noir Edna Valley MacGregor Vineyard 1992 • $15 • (12/31/94) • **88**
Pinot Noir Edna Valley MacGregor Vineyard 1991 • $15 • (02/28/94) • **82**
Pinot Noir Edna Valley MacGregor Vineyard 1990 • $12 • (02/28/93) • **78**
Pinot Noir Edna Valley Runestone 1993 • $16 • (12/31/95) • **78**

Riesling Central Coast Alsatian Style Dry 1997: Dry and refreshing for its green apple and floral flavors, which are light in intensity. A straight-ahead Riesling for easy drinking. Drink now through 2000. 1,000 cases made. • $12 • (07/31/98) • **85**

Riesling Central Coast Dry 1995: Dry, but smooth and generous in flavor, with appealing pear, floral and spice flavors that sail through the finish. 980 cases made. • $10 • (11/15/96) • **87**

Riesling Central Coast Dry Alsatian Style 1994 • $10 • (09/30/95) • **84**
Riesling Central Coast Dry Alsatian Style 1993 • $10 • (06/15/95) • **82**
Riesling Late Harvest Central Coast 1987 • $15/375ml • (12/15/89) • **81**

CLAIRVAUX | CALIFORNIA

Grenache California 1989 • $7 • (03/31/92) BB • **83**

Key: SS—Spectator Selection CS—Cellar Selection HR—Highly Recommended BB—Best Buy $NA—Price not available Ⓐ—Auction Price (BT)—Barrel Tasting
Dates in parentheses indicate the issues in which the ratings were published.

Merlot Napa Valley 1989 • $12 • (05/31/92) • **85**

CLARK-CLAUDON | CALIFORNIA

Cabernet Sauvignon Napa Valley 1995: This wine offers a solid if tannic core of earthy, spicy currant, black cherry and plummy Cabernet flavors. There's a slight bitterness to the tannins and a hint of nail polish. Tasted three times, with noticeable bottle variation. Best from 2001 through 2009. 300 cases made. • $45 • (06/15/98) • **86**

Cabernet Sauvignon Napa Valley 1994: Effusively fruity, with pretty floral aromas and a dense, concentrated core of currant, black cherry and wild berry flavors. Finishes with a solid dose of tannins and a rich aftertaste. Best to cellar this potent wine into 2000. 170 cases made. • $45 • (05/31/97) • **92**

Cabernet Sauvignon Napa Valley 1993: Smooth, supple and harmonious, with lots of complex currant, plum, spice, herb and berry flavors. Finishing with a round, complex aftertaste. Best in 1999. 70 cases made. • $50 • (12/15/96) • **90**

CLAUDIA SPRINGS | CALIFORNIA

Chardonnay Anderson Valley 1996: Delicate and refreshing, with pretty sweet cream, pear and apple flavors. Softly textured, with a lingering finish. Drink now. 250 cases made. • $14 • (07/31/98) • **84**

Chardonnay Anderson Valley 1993 • $10 • (07/31/95) • **83**

Chardonnay Anderson Valley Reserve 1996: Minerally, with a simple range of fruit flavors. Pleasant peach, pear and earth notes linger on the finish. Drink now through 2000. 68 cases made. • $20 • (07/31/98) • **83**

Pinot Noir Anderson Valley 1991 • $13 • (02/28/93) • **86**
Zinfandel Mendocino 1992 • $10 • (10/15/94) • **81**
Zinfandel Mendocino Pacini Vineyard 1993 • $14 • (10/15/95) • **85**

Zinfandel Redwood Valley Vassar Vineyard 1996: Lean and awkward with just a brief window of toast and soft raspberry flavors before the tannins kick in. Flavors re-emerge on the finish. Drink now through 2000. 375 cases made. • $18 • (06/15/98) • **81**

CLINE | CALIFORNIA

California Vin Gris Côtes d'Oakley 1996: Pleasant, round mouthfeel. It finishes with a light cherry and mineral aftertaste. 1,777 cases made. • $8 • (09/30/97) • **82**

Carignane Contra Costa County 1994: Medium weight, with flavors of earth, wild berry and cherry. Finishes with gritty tannins. 825 cases made. • $12 • (11/30/96) • **82**

Carignane Contra Costa County 1990 • $9 • (12/15/92) • **86**

Carignane Contra Costa County Ancient Vines 1995: A touch earthy, with well-proportioned spice and wild berry flavors, finishing with mild tannins and good length. A nice, off-beat wine that's well-made and fun to drink. 1,688 cases made. • $18 • (12/15/97) • **87**

Côtes d'Oakley Contra Costa County 1991 • $7 • (12/31/93) BB • **82**
Côtes d'Oakley Contra Costa County 1990 • $7 • (11/15/92) BB • **85**
Côtes d'Oakley Contra Costa County 1989 • $7 • (05/31/91) • **80**
Côtes d'Oakley Contra Costa County 1988 • $9 • (04/30/90) • **83**
Merlot California 1989 • $17 • (05/31/92) • **75**

Mourvèdre Contra Costa County 1993: A touch meaty and minty in character, turning dry and tannic. Just enough currant flavor comes through to give balance. 1,018 cases made. • $16 • (11/30/96) • **82**

Mourvèdre Contra Costa County 1990 • $20 • (12/15/95) • **81**
Mourvèdre Contra Costa County 1989 • $18 • (11/30/91) • **86**
Mourvèdre Contra Costa County 1988 • $18 • (04/30/90) • **91**
Mourvèdre Contra Costa County 1987 • $18 • (04/15/89) • **82**

Mourvèdre Contra Costa County Ancient Vines 1995: Intensely spicy, with lots of bay leaf and pepper notes. Ripe and concentrated on the palate, with a tight, narrow band of wild berry and black cherry, it finishes where it starts—with lots of spice. 1,933 cases made. • $18 • (12/15/97) • **87**

Mourvèdre Contra Costa County Reserve 1991: A big style of Mourvèdre, with chewy tannins and a core of earth, leather, currant, anise and mineral flavors that fill out nicely on the finish, revealing depth and complexity. Drinks well now or cellar short-term. 193 cases made. • $24 • (11/30/96) • **88**

Mourvèdre Contra Costa County Reserve 1989 • $26 • (03/15/92) • **78**
Oakley Cuvée Contra Costa County 1990 • $12 • (08/31/95) • **85**
Oakley Cuvée Contra Costa County 1989 • $12 • (05/31/91) • **88**
Oakley Cuvée Contra Costa County 1988 • $12 • (02/28/90) • **90**
Oakley Cuvée Contra Costa County NV • $12 • (04/15/89) • **78**

Syrah Carneros 1995: Shows off an herbal, meaty, smoky quality, then reveals its cherry and wild berry flavors. Has the tannic strength to cellar into 1999 to 2000. 1,901 cases made. • $18 • (09/30/97) • **89**
Syrah Carneros 1994: Distinctive, though a bit awkward. Shows a minty accent to ripe berry and cherry flavors and finishes with notes of tea and leather. 853 cases made. • $17 • (01/31/97) • **84**
Syrah Contra Costa County 1991 • $15 • (10/31/93) • **84**
Vin Rouge California Côtes d'Oakley 1996: A blend of Carignane, Mouvèdre, Cinsault, and Alicante Bouschet, this wine is youthfully fresh, while displaying the nicely balanced cherry, spice and plum flavors of a more mature red. Enjoyable now, even better in a year or two. A good buy for all that it offers. 21,140 cases made. • $9 • (03/31/98) BB • **85**
Viognier Contra Costa County 1995: A middle-of-the-road style, with spicy pear and hints of Muscat and honey flavors. Turns simpler on the finish, where the flavors lose their focus. 310 cases made. • $20 • (11/30/96) • **84**
Viognier Los Carneros 1996: A delicate wine that suffers from a bit too much oak. Nonetheless, it displays attractive hazelnut, herb, honey and fig flavors. 613 cases made. • $18 • (12/15/97) • **84**
Zinfandel California 1996: Smooth and silky on the palate, with plum, spice and wild cherry flavors. It's got a bright kick at the end. Would go well with barbecue. 46,000 cases made. • $10 • (11/15/97) • **85**
Zinfandel Contra Costa County 1994 • $12 • (04/30/96) • **87**
Zinfandel Contra Costa County 1993 • $12 • (09/15/95) • **85**
Zinfandel Contra Costa County 1992 • $10 • (10/15/94) • **84**
Zinfandel Contra Costa County 1991 • $10 • (09/30/93) • **84**
Zinfandel Contra Costa County 1990 • $10 • (10/15/92) • **83**
Zinfandel Contra Costa County 1989 • $9 • (05/15/91) • **86**
Zinfandel Contra Costa County 1987 • $9 • (05/15/90) • **89**
Zinfandel Contra Costa County Ancient Vines 1995: With lots of spice and ripe plum and berry flavors, this is a robust, lively, complex wine that's quite pleasing. Shows off earthy bay leaf and minty notes on the finish. Drink now through 2001. 6,692 cases made. • $18 • (03/31/98) • **87**
Zinfandel Contra Costa County Big Break 1995: Starts out tough and chewy, then works its way into more interesting blackberry and raspberry flavors. Finishes with dry tannins. Ready to drink. 1,467 cases made. • $24 • (12/15/97) • **84**
Zinfandel Contra Costa County Big Break 1994: A gutsy style that hits the right notes with its ripe cherry and wild berry flavors and spicy, peppery nuances. The texture is smooth and supple right up to the finish, where the tannins weigh in. 854 cases made. • $22 • (09/30/96) • **90**
Zinfandel Contra Costa County Big Break 1993 • $18 • (09/15/95) • **87**
Zinfandel Contra Costa County Bridgehead 1995: Ripe and racy, with a spicy edge to the black cherry and wild berry flavors, finishing with firm tannins and a hint of tar. 1,467 cases made. • $24 • (12/15/97) • **84**
Zinfandel Contra Costa County Bridgehead 1994: Tight and firm, with a compact core of wildberry, cherry and plum flavors. Needs more time to open and soften, but its solidly packed flavors show promise. 852 cases made. • $22 • (09/30/96) • **87**
Zinfandel Contra Costa County Bridgehead 1993 • $18 • (09/15/95) • **87**
Zinfandel Contra Costa County Live Oak 1995: Complex and concentrated, with a ripe, rich core of mint and cherry, currant and wild berry flavors that are well focused, finishing with firm, chewy tannins. Drink now. 1,288 cases made. • $24 • (11/15/97) • **89**
Zinfandel Contra Costa County Reserve 1994: Despite a few tart notes, this is a rich and complex young wine, brimming with wild berry, cherry and raspberry flavors. It finishes with major-league tannins, but they're not biting. Try now. 862 cases made. • $22 • (09/30/96) • **89**
Zinfandel Contra Costa County Reserve 1993 • $16 • (09/15/95) • **88**
Zinfandel Contra Costa County Reserve 1992 • $12 • (09/15/94) • **89**
Zinfandel Contra Costa County Reserve 1991 • $14 • (09/30/93) • **86**
Zinfandel Contra Costa County Reserve 1990 • $14 • (10/15/92) • **82**
Zinfandel Contra Costa County Reserve 1989 • $12 • (12/31/91) • **84**
Zinfandel Contra Costa County Reserve 1987 • $12 • (05/15/90) • **87**

CLONINGER | CALIFORNIA

Cabernet Sauvignon Carmel Valley 1993: Austere, with firm tannins and just enough light cherry flavors to catch your attention. 756 cases made. • $15 • (11/30/96) • **75**
Cabernet Sauvignon Monterey 1992: A ripe, plummy wine marred by a bit too much barnyard on the palate. 825 cases made. • $11 • (11/30/96) • **78**
Cabernet Sauvignon Monterey 1990 • $15 • (07/15/93) • **82**
Chardonnay Monterey 1995: Smooth, and generous with its citrusy pear flavors that remain lively through the finish. 850 cases made. • $14 • (07/31/97) • **84**
Chardonnay Monterey 1994: A zing of bright acidity cuts through the pineapple and honey flavors, making this difficult to warm up to. May be better in 1999. 1,200 cases made. • $13 • (12/15/96) • **81**
Pinot Noir Monterey 1993: Spicy, with earthy cola and wild berry flavors that are right down the middle. Nothing special. 496 cases made. • $16 • (02/28/97) • **83**

CLOS DANIELLE | CALIFORNIA

Chardonnay Carneros Private Reserve 1993 • $9 • (01/31/95) BB • **87**
Merlot Napa Valley 1993 • $10 • (05/15/95) • **82**

CLOS DU BOIS | CALIFORNIA

Cabernet Franc Sonoma County Winemaker's Reserve 1993: A touch gamy, with a slightly stalky, burnt wood accent to the currant and cherry flavors. Regains its balance on the finish, where the flavors meld. 1,200 cases made. • $20 • (09/15/96) • **85**
Cabernet Sauvignon Alexander Valley 1994: Ripe, smooth and supple, with pleasant currant and berry flavors at the core and mild tannins. Ready to drink. 8,000 cases made. • $17 • (05/15/97) • **85**
Cabernet Sauvignon Alexander Valley 1991 • $12 • (02/28/94) • **86**
Cabernet Sauvignon Alexander Valley 1990 • $13 • (03/31/93) • **87**
Cabernet Sauvignon Alexander Valley 1989 • $11 • (11/15/92) • **80**
Cabernet Sauvignon Alexander Valley 1988 • $14 • (07/15/91) • **77**
Cabernet Sauvignon Alexander Valley 1987 • $11 • (02/15/90) • **86**
Cabernet Sauvignon Alexander Valley 1986 • $12 • (05/31/89) • **86**
Cabernet Sauvignon Alexander Valley 1985 • $19 Ⓐ • (04/15/88) • **87**
Cabernet Sauvignon Alexander Valley 1984 • $10 • (06/15/87) • **87**
Cabernet Sauvignon Alexander Valley 1981 • $9 • (03/01/86) • **91**
Cabernet Sauvignon Alexander Valley Selection 1995: A lot to like in this wine, from its plum, cedar, black cherry and berry flavors to its supple and harmonious texture. While openly fruity and showy up front, it can age short-term. Best from 1999 to 2004. • $18 • (04/30/98) • **88**
Cabernet Sauvignon Alexander Valley Briarcrest Vineyard 1994: Ripe, rich and well-focused, with a tight, complex core of currant, black cherry, berry, coffee and spice. Turns long and lingering on the finish. Best from 2001 through 2010. • $23 • (06/15/98) • **89**
Cabernet Sauvignon Alexander Valley Briarcrest Vineyard 1993: Tight and firm, with a chewy tannic edge to the spicy currant, herb and cedary oak flavors. Can stand cellaring into 1999 or 2000. • $21 • (07/31/97) • **88**
Cabernet Sauvignon Alexander Valley Briarcrest Vineyard 1992 • $20 • (11/30/95) • **89**
Cabernet Sauvignon Alexander Valley Briarcrest Vineyard 1991 • $18 • (11/15/94) • **87**
Cabernet Sauvignon Alexander Valley Briarcrest Vineyard 1990 • $19 • (04/15/94) • **89**
Cabernet Sauvignon Alexander Valley Briarcrest Vineyard 1989 • $19 • (08/31/93) • **80**
Cabernet Sauvignon Alexander Valley Briarcrest Vineyard 1987: Rich and focused, with a wonderful sense of harmony and finesse. Tiers of chocolate, cherry, currant and wildberry turn smooth and supple on the finish, where it picks up tobacco and vanilla accents. Still intense, young and vibrant. Best now through 2004. • $48 • (12/15/97) • **91**
Cabernet Sauvignon Alexander Valley Briarcrest Vineyard 1986 • $17 • (08/31/90) • **87**
Cabernet Sauvignon Alexander Valley Briarcrest Vineyard 1985 • $16 • (06/15/89) • **86**
Cabernet Sauvignon Alexander Valley Briarcrest Vineyard 1984 • $16 • (07/15/88) • **90**
Cabernet Sauvignon Alexander Valley Briarcrest Vineyard 1982 • $14 • (07/31/87) • **91**
Cabernet Sauvignon Alexander Valley Briarcrest Vineyard 1980 • $13 • (04/16/86) • **66**
Cabernet Sauvignon Alexander Valley Briarcrest Vineyard 1978 • $NA • (11/15/92) • **78**
Cabernet Sauvignon Alexander Valley Winemaker's Reserve 1991 • $30 • (10/15/94) CS • **92**
Cabernet Sauvignon Dry Creek Valley Proprietor's Reserve 1982 • $19 • (09/15/87) • **88**
Cabernet Sauvignon Sonoma County 1995: Firm, spicy and chewy, with a thread of blueberry and currant keeping it focused through the delicate finish. Best from 1999. • $15 • (03/31/98) • **84**
Cabernet Sauvignon Sonoma County 1994: Ripe and supple, appealing now for its plum and cherry flavors and soft tannins. Finishes with smoky,

toasty oak notes. Drinks well now. 84,000 cases made. • $13 • (11/15/96) • **86**

Cabernet Sauvignon Sonoma County 1993: Simple but pleasant enough, with supple plum and cherry notes. 79,000 cases made. • $13 • (12/15/95) • **82**

Cabernet Sauvignon Sonoma County 1980 • $9 • (07/01/84) • **81**

Cabernet Sauvignon Sonoma County Dry Creek 1974 • $NA • (02/15/90) • **74**

Chardonnay Alexander Valley Selection 1996: Smooth and spicy. A vibrant mouthful of citrus, pear and pineapple flavors laced with nutmeg and vanilla. Finishes gently. Appealing now, could develop well to 1999 or 2000. • $15 • (03/31/98) • **89**

Chardonnay Alexander Valley Selection 1995: Clean, light and fruity, with a core of spice, apple, melon and grapefruit notes that are refreshing. • $15 • (04/30/97) • **87**

Chardonnay Alexander Valley Barrel Fermented 1994: Tight and compact, showing a narrow band of pear and apple flavor. Decent, but nothing more. 240,000 cases made. • $13 • (04/30/96) • **82**

Chardonnay Alexander Valley Barrel Fermented 1993 • $13 • (01/31/95) • **84**

Chardonnay Alexander Valley Calcaire Vineyard 1996: Clean, crisp and flinty, with an elegant, understated core of citrus and pear. A style well-suited for oysters and other seafood. • $18 • (04/30/98) • **87**

Chardonnay Alexander Valley Calcaire Vineyard 1995: Clean and lively, with a flinty accent to the pear, spice, apple and light oak shadings. Try now. • $18 • (07/31/97) • **89**

Chardonnay Alexander Valley Calcaire Vineyard 1994: Bright and lively, featuring a pretty core of ripe pear, grapefruit, honey and light toasty oak notes that fold together nicely on a tapered finish. Flavors linger on and on, revealing an attractive mineral character. 11,500 cases made. • $18 • (04/30/96) SS • **91**

Chardonnay Alexander Valley Calcaire Vineyard 1993 • $18 • (05/15/95) • **89**

Chardonnay Alexander Valley Winemaker's Reserve 1994: Medium-bodied, with a smattering of pear, citrus, spice and honey notes. Turns delicate and spicy on the finish, but could use a little more depth and complexity. 1,000 cases made. • $24 • (09/15/96) • **86**

Chardonnay Dry Creek Valley Flintwood Vineyard 1996: Elegant, with floral pear, citrus and spice notes, turning flinty with a mineral edge. Delicate finish. • $17 • (05/15/98) • **87**

Chardonnay Dry Creek Valley Flintwood Vineyard 1995: Smooth and polished, with a core of creamy pear, citrus, vanilla, herb and sage flavors, turning elegant and refined on the finish. Drinkable now. • $17 • (07/31/97) • **88**

Chardonnay Dry Creek Valley Flintwood Vineyard 1994: Distinctive for melon and pear flavors in a straightforward style, delivering ripe, full-bodied fruit and light oak shadings. The finish picks up traces of grapefruit. Could profit from a little time in the bottle. 5,650 cases made. • $17 • (04/30/96) • **89**

Chardonnay Dry Creek Valley Flintwood Vineyard 1993 • $17 • (07/31/95) • **86**

Chardonnay Sonoma County 1996: Crisp, spicy and refreshing for its light melon and lemon flavors. Ready now. • $12 • (11/15/97) • **84**

Chardonnay Sonoma County 1995: Ripe and spicy in character, with hints of apple, pear, citrus and spice, turning elegant and delicate on the finish. • $13 • (07/31/97) • **88**

Gewürztraminer Alexander Valley Early Harvest 1993 • $8 • (02/28/95) • **79**

Gewürztraminer Late Harvest Alexander Valley Individual Bunch Selected 1986 • $18/375ml • (08/31/87) • **80**

Johannisberg Riesling Late Harvest Alexander Valley Individual Bunch Selected 1986 • $15/375ml • (08/31/87) • **89**

Malbec Alexander Valley L'Etranger Winemaker's Reserve 1991 • $19 • (03/31/94) • **82**

Malbec Alexander Valley L'Etranger Winemaker's Reserve 1987 • $20 • (01/31/91) • **87**

Marlstone Vineyard Alexander Valley 1994: An elegant style, understated, with ripe plum, currant, spice and herbal notes. Impeccable balance, with fine, detailed tannins and a long, full finish. A blend of 52 percent Cabernet Sauvignon, 34 percent Merlot, 6 percent Malbec, 5 percent Cabernet Franc, and 3 percent Petit Verdot. • $25 • (05/15/98) • **90**

Marlstone Vineyard Alexander Valley 1992 • $21 • (11/30/95) • **89**

Marlstone Vineyard Alexander Valley 1991 • $18 • (01/31/95) • **88**

Marlstone Vineyard Alexander Valley 1990 • $20 • (11/15/93) • **88**

Marlstone Vineyard Alexander Valley 1989 • $20 • (03/31/93) • **85**

Marlstone Vineyard Alexander Valley 1987 • $27 • (07/31/91) HR • **90**

Key: SS—Spectator Selection CS—Cellar Selection HR—Highly Recommended BB—Best Buy $NA—Price not available (A)—Auction Price (BT)—Barrel Tasting

Dates in parentheses indicate the issues in which the ratings were published.

Marlstone Vineyard Alexander Valley 1986 • $24 • (08/31/90) • **85**

Marlstone Vineyard Alexander Valley 1985 • $34 • (06/15/89) • **81**

Marlstone Vineyard Alexander Valley 1984 • $20 • (05/15/88) • **85**

Marlstone Vineyard Alexander Valley 1983 • $20 • (09/15/87) • **88**

Marlstone Vineyard Alexander Valley 1982 • $16 • (09/30/86) • **86**

Marlstone Vineyard Alexander Valley 1981 • $15 • (03/16/86) • **96**

Merlot Alexander Valley Selection 1995: Bright and appealing for its smooth currant and floral flavors, finishing firm and bright. Ready to drink. • $20 • (03/31/98) • **86**

Merlot Alexander Valley Winemaker's Reserve 1993: Smooth, supple and harmonious, with bright, juicy cherry, wild berry and currant flavors. Finish shows a sweet, toasty oak note and a hint of anise. Impressive for its elegance and early-drinking allure. 1,800 cases made. • $28 • (09/15/96) • **89**

Merlot Sonoma County 1995: Generous and supple, here's a nice mouthful of spicy red cherry and plum flavors that linger on the finish. Best from 1999. • $17 • (03/31/98) • **86**

Merlot Sonoma County 1994: Light in color, but shows plenty of flavor, as the spicy, toasty oak notes fold in nicely with the plum and cherry flavors, all turning complex on the aftertaste. Ready to drink. 20,000 cases made. • $17 • (11/30/96) • **87**

Merlot Sonoma County 1993 • $16 • (06/15/96) • **84**

Merlot Sonoma County 1992 • $15 • (01/31/95) • **88**

Merlot Sonoma County 1991 • $15 • (04/15/94) • **86**

Merlot Sonoma County 1990 • $15 • (06/15/93) • **82**

Merlot Sonoma County 1989 • $15 • (05/31/92) • **82**

Merlot Sonoma County 1988 • $15 • (05/31/91) • **81**

Merlot Sonoma County 1987 • $12 • (04/15/90) • **89**

Merlot Sonoma County 1986 • $11 • (10/15/88) • **86**

Merlot Sonoma County 1985 • $10 • (10/31/87) SS • **92**

Merlot Sonoma County 1984 • $9 • (05/16/86) • **87**

Merlot Sonoma County 1983 • $9 • (10/01/85) • **86**

Muscat of Alexandria Late Harvest Alexander Valley Fleur d'Alexandra 1986 • $10 • (05/31/88) • **90**

Pinot Noir Dry Creek Valley Proprietor's Reserve 1980 • $11 • (07/16/84) • **86**

Pinot Noir Sonoma County 1996: Simple, supple and appealing for its currant and red berry flavors, shaded by a touch of creaminess on the finish. Ready to drink. • $14 • (03/31/98) • **85**

Pinot Noir Sonoma County 1990 • $12 • (02/28/93) • **82**

Pinot Noir Sonoma County 1989 • $13 • (10/31/91) • **78**

Pinot Noir Sonoma County 1988 • $12 • (04/30/91) • **80**

Pinot Noir Sonoma County 1987 • $12 • (05/31/90) • **73**

Pinot Noir Sonoma County 1986 • $11 • (10/15/89) • **87**

Pinot Noir Sonoma County 1985 • $11 • (06/15/88) • **70**

Pinot Noir Sonoma County 1984 • $8 • (08/31/86) • **86**

Pinot Noir Sonoma County 1983 • $8 • (08/31/86) • **70**

Sauvignon Blanc Alexander Valley Barrel Fermented 1993 • $8 • (08/31/94) • **80**

Sauvignon Blanc Sonoma County 1997: Bright and lemony. This one's got pucker-power, with grapefruit and herbs bringing up the rear. Drink now. • $9 • (06/30/98) • **84**

Sauvignon Blanc Sonoma County 1996: A more traditional style of Sauvignon Blanc, in which an elegant grassiness dominates a field of flavors that includes grapefruit, melon, figs and cloves. Lively acidity. • $8 • (06/30/97) • **88**

Sauvignon Blanc Sonoma County 1995: A bright and fruity white laced over a silky frame. Offers a simple, fresh punch of peach with a hint of mint. A good value. 67,000 cases made. • $8 • (07/31/96) BB • **85**

Sauvignon Blanc Sonoma County 1994 • $8 • (08/31/95) • **84**

Zinfandel Sonoma County 1995: Pleasant, with ripe cherry and wildberry flavors, turning smooth and supple on the finish. Drink now. • $14 • (06/15/98) • **84**

Zinfandel Sonoma County 1994: Light for the vintage and a bit too reliant on oak for flavor. Just enough cherry and berry notes come through to make it interesting. 20,000 cases made. • $13 • (11/30/96) • **82**

Zinfandel Sonoma County 1993 • $13 • (10/15/95) • **83**

Zinfandel Sonoma County 1992 • $13 • (10/15/94) • **87**

Zinfandel Sonoma County 1991 • $13 • (09/30/93) • **87**

CLOS DU LAC | CALIFORNIA

Muscat Amador County Vin Doux Naturel 1996: Sweet, and stopping just short of syrupy, with floral pear flavors that remain charming through the sweet finish. 711 cases made. • $12/375ml • (11/30/97) • **85**

Sauvignon Blanc Sierra Foothills 1996: Quite fragrant, with floral, peach and grasslike overtones. Flinty, mineral-like quality on the palate. Finishes clean. 396 cases made. • $10 • (07/31/97) • **87**

Zinfandel Shenandoah Valley Twin Rivers Vineyards 1996: Light cherry and charred oak flavors run through. Would be nice to find a tad more intensity in the flavor profile. 227 cases made. • $12 • (03/31/98) • **81**

Zinfandel Sierra Foothills Ghirardelli Vineyard 1996: Bright spice and cherry flavors come to the fore in this rustic-styled wine. Smoke, oak and tar mark a finish that's a bit rough. Drink now. 165 cases made. • $16 • (06/15/98) • **84**

CLOS DU VAL | CALIFORNIA

Cabernet Sauvignon Napa Valley 1994: A supple and restrained style, with spicy currant and berry flavors of modest proportion, finishing with firm, supple, leathery tannins. Those who prefer understated flavors will find this quite appealing. Best from 1999 to 2004. 25,500 cases made. • $24 • (03/31/98) • **86**

Cabernet Sauvignon Napa Valley 1993: Marked by an earthy, leathery edge to the modest currant and spice notes, this is good wine that could use a little more flavor and depth, perhaps with time in the bottle. 16,000 cases made. • $23 • (04/30/97) • **83**

Cabernet Sauvignon Napa Valley 1990 • $12 • (06/30/94) • **84**

Cabernet Sauvignon Napa Valley 1989 • $15 • (11/15/92) • **83**

Cabernet Sauvignon Napa Valley 1974 • $63 Ⓐ • (11/15/94) • **82**

Cabernet Sauvignon Napa Valley Gran Val 1985 • $8 • (05/31/88) • **88**

Cabernet Sauvignon Napa Valley Gran Val 1984 • $8 • (02/15/87) BB • **85**

Cabernet Sauvignon Napa Valley Gran Val 1982 • $7 • (04/16/84) • **88**

Cabernet Sauvignon Napa Valley Joli Val 1988 • $13 • (07/31/91) • **82**

Cabernet Sauvignon Napa Valley Joli Val 1986 • $13 • (12/15/89) • **87**

Cabernet Sauvignon Napa Valley Reserve 1996: Young and rangy, with an herb and earth streak, but the core is built around ripe currant, plum and berry flavors. Turns elegant on the finish. • $NA • (06/15/97) (BT) • **90-94**

Cabernet Sauvignon Napa Valley Reserve 1993: Ripe, smooth and polished, with a rich, complex core of juicy currant, cherry, plum and wild berry flavors. Finishes with depth and concentration. The long, fruity aftertaste picks up oak and anise notes. 1,600 cases made. • $50 • (10/31/97) • **91**

Cabernet Sauvignon Napa Valley Reserve 1992: Young and tight, firm and tannic, but with a well-focused core of earthy currant and cedary flavors. Doesn't yet show the richness and complex range of flavors found in higher scoring '92s, but give it time. Should peak around 1999 or 2000. 1,500 cases made. • $45 • (12/31/96) • **89**

Cabernet Sauvignon Napa Valley Reserve 1990 • $45 • (04/30/95) • **89**

Cabernet Sauvignon Napa Valley Reserve 1987: Smooth and polished. Very complex and compelling, with layers of currant, anise, cedar, tea, sage and spice, finishing with a long, silky aftertaste that spreads out on the palate. Best now through 2005. Tasted from magnum. 1,000 cases made. • $100 • (12/15/97) • **93**

Cabernet Sauvignon Stags Leap District 1991 • $20 • (09/30/95) • **87**

Cabernet Sauvignon Stags Leap District 1990 • $18 • (11/15/94) • **83**

Cabernet Sauvignon Stags Leap District 1988 • $18 • (03/31/92) • **86**

Cabernet Sauvignon Stags Leap District 1987 • $17 • (06/30/91) HR • **92**

Cabernet Sauvignon Stags Leap District 1986: Impressive for its richness, supple texture, ripe tannins and range of flavors, with bright black cherry and subtle earth notes, hints of anise, cedar and coffee. Has reached a nice drinking plateau but, given its balance and youthful flavors, it should age well for another five to ten years. • $NA • (12/15/96) • **89**

Cabernet Sauvignon Stags Leap District 1985 • $32 • (06/15/89) • **90**

Cabernet Sauvignon Stags Leap District 1984 • $16 • (04/15/88) • **86**

Cabernet Sauvignon Stags Leap District 1983 • $15 • (09/15/87) • **77**

Cabernet Sauvignon Stags Leap District 1982 • $13 • (07/01/86) • **91**

Cabernet Sauvignon Stags Leap District 1981 • $NA • (02/01/86) • **89**

Cabernet Sauvignon Stags Leap District 1980 • $14 • (02/01/86) • **83**

Cabernet Sauvignon Stags Leap District 1979 • $16 • (02/01/86) • **93**

Cabernet Sauvignon Stags Leap District 1978 • $45 • (11/15/92) • **91**

Cabernet Sauvignon Stags Leap District Reserve 1979 • $25 • (09/01/84) SS • **91**

Cabernet Sauvignon Stags Leap District Reserve 1978 • $NA • (11/15/92) • **94**

Chardonnay Carneros Special Select 1993 • $20 • (04/30/95) • **86**

Chardonnay Napa Valley Carneros 1996: Clean and spicy, with a dash of light, toasty oak and elegant pear and fig flavors. For those who prefer Chardonnay on the understated side. 15,525 cases made. • $17 • (04/30/98) • **87**

Chardonnay Napa Valley Carneros 1995: This Chardonnay is smooth, ripe, rich and creamy, with a lively medley of spicy pear, apple, hazelnut and cedar flavors at the core, turning supple and complex on the finish. Outstanding. 13,000 cases made. • $16 • (04/30/97) HR • **90**

Chardonnay Napa Valley Carneros 1994: A simple wine, offering a modest band of ripe pear and oak. 8,000 cases made. • $15 • (07/31/96) • **77**

Chardonnay Napa Valley Carneros 1993 • $15 • (12/15/95) • **85**

Chardonnay Napa Valley Carneros Reserve 1995: Impressive. Serves up lots of flavors, spicy pear, smoky oak and hints of anise, apple and citrus, and turns smooth and creamy on the finish. An elegant, stylish yet richly textured wine that's a marked change in style for this winery. 400 cases made. • $24 • (06/15/97) • **91**

Le Clos Napa Valley NV • $5 • (08/31/90) BB • **85**

Merlot Napa Valley 1995: Tightly wound, crisp and closed, with only a glimpse of earthy currant and berry emerging. Shows off a leathery edge on the finish; needs time. Unusually hard-edged for a Clos Du Val Merlot. Best after 2000. 8,992 cases made. • $28 • (04/30/98) • **86**

Merlot Stags Leap District 1994: Young, intense and vibrant, with a rich, lively core of ripe black cherry, currant, anise and cedar notes. Finishes with big, rich, thick tannins, but they're ripe and well rounded. Tempting now, but should be softer if cellared into 1999. 4,400 cases made. • $28 • (12/31/96) • **88**

Merlot Stags Leap District 1993: Crisp and trim, with a narrow band of spicy cherry and plum flavors. Lacks richness and depth. 2,100 cases made. • $21 • (07/31/96) • **81**

Merlot Stags Leap District 1992 • $30 • (07/31/95) • **84**

Merlot Stags Leap District 1991 • $21 • (05/31/94) • **89**

Merlot Stags Leap District 1990 • $22 • (06/15/93) • **86**

Merlot Stags Leap District 1989 • $21 • (05/31/92) • **86**

Merlot Stags Leap District 1988 • $20 • (03/31/91) • **89**

Merlot Stags Leap District 1987 • $17 • (03/31/90) • **85**

Merlot Stags Leap District 1986 • $16 • (08/31/89) • **86**

Merlot Stags Leap District 1985 • $16 • (04/30/88) • **87**

Merlot Stags Leap District 1984 • $15 • (07/31/87) • **88**

Merlot Stags Leap District 1983 • $14 • (06/16/86) • **92**

Merlot Stags Leap District 1982 • $13 • (10/01/85) • **80**

Merlot Stags Leap District 1981 • $14 • (02/15/84) • **88**

Pinot Noir Carneros 1995: The core flavors of ripe cherry, berry and spice are well focused and intense, finishing with firm tannins. Drinkable now. An improvement with this wine for Clos Du Val. 1,565 cases made. • $20 • (12/15/97) • **85**

Pinot Noir Napa Valley 1987 • $14 • (04/30/91) • **84**

Pinot Noir Napa Valley 1986 • $16 • (02/15/90) • **80**

Pinot Noir Napa Valley 1985 • $13 • (06/15/88) • **80**

Pinot Noir Napa Valley 1984 • $12 • (09/30/87) • **78**

Pinot Noir Napa Valley 1982 • $11 • (09/01/84) • **75**

Pinot Noir Napa Valley Carneros 1994 • $15 • (02/29/96) • **83**

Pinot Noir Napa Valley Carneros 1990 • $13 • (03/31/95) • **78**

Pinot Noir Napa Valley Carneros 1989 • $13 • (02/28/94) • **81**

Pinot Noir Napa Valley Carneros 1988 • $14 • (09/30/92) • **80**

Reserve Napa Valley 1988 • $48 • (11/15/93) • **88**

Reserve Stags Leap District 1987 • $45 • (07/15/92) CS • **92**

Reserve Stags Leap District 1985 • $45 • (11/15/90) • **94**

Reserve Stags Leap District 1982 • $28 • (11/15/87) • **88**

Sangiovese Napa Valley Tre Grazie 1994: Young and tight, it's on the austere side with tightly wound but not especially expressive flavors of currant, cedar, spice and strawberry. Tannins are quite strong on the finish. Best to cellar. 750 cases made. • $26 • (12/31/96) • **86**

Zinfandel California 1996: Lean, crisp and tannic, with a thin range of cherry, anise and spice, turning hard and biting on the finish. Drink now through 2001. 3,996 cases made. • $15 • (06/15/98) • **81**

Zinfandel California 1995: Lighter in color and body, with wild berry, plum and dried cherry flavors that are mature and simple on the finish. Drinks well now. 1,977 cases made. • $16 • (03/31/98) • **84**

Zinfandel Stags Leap District 1994: Understated style, with a modest range of cedar, black cherry and wild berry flavors, finishing with crisp, firm tannins. Drink now. 1,450 cases made. • $16 • (06/15/98) • **85**

Zinfandel Stags Leap District 1993: Light and simple, with an earthy, bay leaf shading to the flavors. Lacks concentration, focus and spot-on Zinfandel flavor. The 1992 was much better. 2,100 cases made. • $16 • (03/31/97) • **78**

Zinfandel Stags Leap District 1992: Mature, with spicy cedar, tar and anise flavors, picking up hints of cherry and raspberry flavors. Drinks well now, but will age well, too. 3,500 cases made. • $15 • (02/28/97) • **88**

Zinfandel Stags Leap District 1991 • $15 • (07/31/95) • **84**

Zinfandel Stags Leap District 1990 • $14 • (10/15/94) • **74**

Zinfandel Stags Leap District 1989 • $14 • (09/30/93) • **86**

Zinfandel Stags Leap District 1988 • $15 • (10/15/92) • **85**

Zinfandel Stags Leap District 1987 • $16 • (05/31/90) • **83**
Zinfandel Stags Leap District 1986 • $12 • (05/31/89) • **87**
Zinfandel Stags Leap District 1985 • $12 • (04/30/88) • **90**
Zinfandel Stags Leap District 1984 • $19 • (05/31/87) • **81**
Zinfandel Stags Leap District 1981 • $18 • (05/16/84) CS • **90**
Zinfandel Stags Leap District 1974 • $55 • (06/16/85) • **77**
Zinfandel Stags Leap District 1973 • $50 • (06/16/85) • **86**
Zinfandel Stags Leap District 1972 • $60 • (06/16/85) • **90**

CLOS GARBO | OREGON

Pinot Noir Oregon 1993 • $18 • (05/15/96) • **88**
Pinot Noir Oregon 1992 • $18 • (09/15/94) • **89**

CLOS LACHANCE | CALIFORNIA

Cabernet Sauvignon Santa Cruz Mountains 1993: Smooth, supple cherry and berry flavor, turning earthy and slightly meaty on the finish. Medium- bodied, well proportioned. Drinkable now. 700 cases made. • $23 • (04/30/96) • **86**
Cabernet Sauvignon Santa Cruz Mountains 1992 • $20 • (07/31/95) • **88**
Chardonnay Santa Cruz Mountains 1996: A bit disjointed now, with ripe, concentrated pear, spice, fig and earthy Chardonnay flavors. Finishes with an earthy aftertaste. Drink now through 2001. 1,600 cases made. • $22 • (06/30/98) • **88**
Chardonnay Santa Cruz Mountains 1995: Smooth, ripe and buttery, with a rich core of pear, apple, oak and spice flavors that remain long, full and vibrant on the rich, creamy finish. 1,300 cases made. • $19 • (06/15/97) • **92**
Chardonnay Santa Cruz Mountains 1994: Bold, ripe and generous, with buttery pear, fig and melon notes and finishing with a smoky, toasty oak edge. Shows off its ripe fruit on the finish. 1,125 cases made. • $18 • (05/31/96) • **89**
Chardonnay Santa Cruz Mountains 1993 • $18 • (07/31/95) • **89**
Chardonnay Santa Cruz Mountains Vintner's Reserve 1996: Ripe, rich and concentrated, sharply focused, with pretty mineral, pear, spice and earth, and a complex aftertaste that echoes the fruit, earth, and spice. Drink now through 2002. 300 cases made. • $29 • (06/30/98) • **90**
Pinot Noir Santa Cruz Mountains 1993 • $19 • (12/31/95) • **85**

CLOS PEGASE | CALIFORNIA

Cabernet Sauvignon Napa Valley 1994: Marked by a slight gamelike edge, it also offers enough currant, cherry, sage and spice flavors to hold your interest. Has the tannic strength to age into 2001. 8,963 cases made. • $23 • (10/31/97) • **86**
Cabernet Sauvignon Napa Valley 1993: Smooth and harmonious, with an earthy edge to the plum and currant flavors. Finishes with firm, plush tannins, but its well-balanced and the flavors come through. Drink now. 7,400 cases made. • $20 • (03/31/96) • **87**
Cabernet Sauvignon Napa Valley 1992 • $19 • (10/15/95) • **88**
Cabernet Sauvignon Napa Valley 1991 • $17 • (06/30/94) • **88**
Cabernet Sauvignon Napa Valley 1990 • $17 • (11/15/93) SS • **91**
Cabernet Sauvignon Napa Valley 1987 • $17 • (08/31/92) • **82**
Cabernet Sauvignon Napa Valley 1986 • $17 • (09/30/90) • **88**
Cabernet Sauvignon Napa Valley 1985 • $17 • (05/31/88) • **86**
Cabernet Sauvignon Napa Valley Homage Artist Series Reserve 1994: Distinctive for its cedary oak introduction, the core of plum and cherry flavor fills in the gaps nicely, picking up pretty strawberry and blueberry notes along the way. 1,941 cases made. • $40 • (09/30/97) • **90**
Cabernet Sauvignon Napa Valley Homage Artist Series Reserve 1993: Impressive for its elegance and finesse, this delivers a pleasant core of cherry, currant and wild berry flavors seasoned with spicy, toasty oak notes. 1,000 cases made. • $35 • (11/15/96) • **88**
Chardonnay Napa Valley Carneros 1993 • $15 • (09/30/95) • **86**
Chardonnay Napa Valley Carneros Mitsuko's Vineyard 1996: Elegant and intense, with cedary oak and ripe pear flavors that finish with a touch of spice and citrus. Drink now through 2001. 11,607 cases made. • $19 • (07/31/98) • **87**

Key: SS—Spectator Selection CS—Cellar Selection HR—Highly Recommended BB—Best Buy $NA—Price not available (A)—Auction Price (BT)—Barrel Tasting
Dates in parentheses indicate the issues in which the ratings were published.

Chardonnay Napa Valley Carneros Mitsuko's Vineyard 1995: Appealing for its ripe, smooth core of spice, pear, apple and melon flavors, it turns elegant and sophisticated on the finish, where the flavors resonate. Ready to drink. 14,066 cases made. • $19 • (05/31/97) • **90**
Chardonnay Napa Valley Carneros Mitsuko's Vineyard 1994: Young and tart, adding a distinct lemony flair to the ripe pear and spice flavors. Picks up some toasty oak on the finish, where it turns elegant. 11,300 cases made. • $17 • (05/15/96) • **88**
Chardonnay Napa Valley Carneros Pegase Circle Reserve 1994: An elegant, medium-weight, subtle style, featuring supple texture and bright, lively citrus, pear and nutmeg flavors that finish in a complex and lingering aftertaste. Just misses rating outstanding. 983 cases made. • $23 • (05/15/96) • **89**
Chardonnay Napa Valley Carneros Pegase Circle Reserve 1993 • $20 • (07/31/95) • **87**
Grenache California 1989 • $9 • (08/31/91) • **84**
Hommage California 1989 • $20 • (11/15/93) • **83**
Hommage California 1988 • $25 • (10/15/92) • **84**
Hommage California 1987 • $20 • (08/31/91) HR • **90**
Hommage Napa Valley 1991 • $25 • (11/15/94) • **86**
Hommage Napa Valley 1990 • $20 • (04/15/94) • **87**
Merlot Napa Valley 1993 • $19 • (02/29/96) • **87**
Merlot Napa Valley 1992 • $17 • (09/30/95) HR • **90**
Merlot Napa Valley 1991 • $16 • (09/15/94) • **79**
Merlot Napa Valley 1990 • $16 • (06/15/93) • **83**
Merlot Napa Valley 1989 • $15 • (10/31/92) • **81**
Merlot Napa Valley 1988 • $15 • (11/15/91) • **82**
Merlot Napa Valley 1986 • $16 • (07/15/90) • **84**
Merlot Napa Valley Carneros 1995: Well proportioned, if a bit dry and wanting in fruit. Turns simple on the finish. Drinks well now. 6,000 cases made. • $23 • (11/30/97) • **84**
Pegaso Napa Valley 1988 • $12 • (08/31/92) • **82**
Petite Syrah Napa Valley 1988 • $15 • (10/31/91) • **83**

CLOS ROBERT | CALIFORNIA

Cabernet Sauvignon Napa Valley Proprietor's Reserve 1984 • $7 • (12/31/87) • **71**

CLOS ST. THOMAS | CALIFORNIA

Chardonnay California 1993 • $7 • (03/31/95) • **80**
Pinot Noir California 1993 • $8 • (03/31/95) • **78**
Sauvignon Blanc California 1993 • $6 • (03/31/95) • **79**

CLOVERDALE RANCH | CALIFORNIA

Cabernet Sauvignon Alexander Valley Estate Cuvée 1994: Tar and cedar flavors stand out, followed by cola, strawberry and herbal notes. The blend has some rough edges and finishes short. 1,500 cases made. • $15 • (09/15/97) • **82**
Cabernet Sauvignon Alexander Valley Estate Cuvée 1991 • $12 • (11/15/94) • **83**
Cabernet Sauvignon Alexander Valley Estate Cuvée 1989 • $11 • (03/31/92) • **84**
Cabernet Sauvignon Alexander Valley Pellegrini Family Vineyards 1993: In a forward, ripe and fruity style, with spicy currant, anise and cherry flavors. Not a blockbuster by any means, but the fruit is pure and clean and the wine drinks easily. 1,275 cases made. • $13 • (11/15/96) • **86**
Cabernet Sauvignon Alexander Valley Pellegrini Family Vineyards Estate Cuvée 1995: Fairly thin on the palate, with a light, cherrylike core. 1,100 cases made. • $16 • (05/15/98) • **80**
Merlot Alexander Valley Estate Cuvée 1995: A smoky quality announces a wine rich in licorice, cassis and herbal notes. Tannins are firm but ripe. Should benefit from a few years' cellaring. 1,600 cases made. • $14 • (09/15/97) • **88**

COASTAL CELLARS | WASHINGTON

Chardonnay Yakima Valley 1993 • $6 • (06/30/96) • **87**

COBBLESTONE | CALIFORNIA

Chardonnay Arroyo Seco 1996: A nice blend of toasty oak, pear, apple and spice flavors here, with a brisk, clean finish. 500 cases made. • $23 • (01/31/98) • **87**

Chardonnay Monterey County 1995: Bright, tangy orange and lemon flavors backed by a hint of toasty oak and hazelnut. Well-balanced, good integration. 375 cases made. • $17 • (06/15/97) • **88**
Chardonnay Monterey County 1994: Soft, smoky and spicy, with honeyed pineapple flavors. Finish is as smooth as river pebbles. 200 cases made. • $15 • (07/31/96) • **87**
Chardonnay Monterey County 1993: Smooth and round, with hazelnut and almond notes adding welcome complexity to the pear and apple flavors. Ready now. 200 cases made. • $15 • (07/31/96) • **88**

CODORNIU NAPA | CALIFORNIA

Blanc de Blancs Napa Valley 1991: Has a nutty, slightly sour edge, but it works its way through that to reveal attractive pear and spice flavors. 300 cases made. • $20 • (11/30/97) • **86**
Brut Napa Valley NV: A fresh, lemon-lime theme prevails here, with a bright, long finish. It lacks some depth, but is refreshing and clean. Good value. 15,000 cases made. • $14 • (11/30/97) • **88**
Reserve Napa Valley 1991: Flavorful, with pretty pear, spice and vanilla notes, this picks up an herbal, sagelike edge on the finish, which shows concentration and depth. 300 cases made. • $23 • (11/30/97) • **90**
Rosé Napa Valley NV: A dry, austere, crisp style, with tightly wound notes of black cherry, herb, spice and toast. Finishes with a pleasant dryness, and plenty of flavor. 1,000 cases made. • $18 • (11/30/97) • **89**

COFFARO, DAVID | CALIFORNIA

Cabernet Sauvignon Dry Creek Valley Coffaro Estate Vineyard 1995: Serves up lots of ripe, juicy fruit upfront, with flashes of black cherry, plum and berry, and has mild tannins, making it ideal to drink now through 1999. 130 cases made. • $19 • (10/31/97) • **87**
Cabernet Sauvignon Dry Creek Valley Coffaro Estate Vineyard Old Vines 1994: Ripe, smooth and harmonious, with attractive layers of plum, cherry, currant and cedary oak flavors on the finish. Well-crafted for short-term cellaring. 47 cases made. • $16 • (09/15/96) • **88**
Estate Cuvée Dry Creek Valley Coffaro Estate Vineyard 1995: Smooth, ripe and fruity, with lots of cherry, wild berry, plum and currant notes. Finishes with soft, fleshy tannins, making it ideal to drink now. A blend of Cabernet Sauvignon, Zinfandel, Carignane, Petit Sirah, Merlot, and Cabernet Franc. 300 cases made. • $19 • (11/30/97) • **88**
Estate Cuvée Dry Creek Valley Coffaro Estate Vineyard Old Vines 1994: Combines ripe, complex cherry, plum and raspberry flavors in a supple texture, with an intriguing aftertaste. A blend of Cabernet, Zinfandel, Carignane and Petite Sirah. 190 cases made. • $16 • (09/15/96) • **90**
Zinfandel Dry Creek Valley Coffaro Estate Vineyard 1996: Appealing for its core of ripe plum, blueberry, raspberry and spice. Holds its flavors through the finish, where they linger and gain in complexity and nuance. Drink now through 2002. 434 cases made. • $19 • (05/31/98) • **90**
Zinfandel Dry Creek Valley Coffaro Estate Vineyard 1995: Complex, with elegant cherry, raspberry and spice notes that fold together nicely. Long, lingering aftertaste where pretty pepper notes blend in. Drinkable now, but should hold a few years. 300 cases made. • $17 • (02/28/97) • **90**
Zinfandel Dry Creek Valley Coffaro Estate Vineyard 1994: Ripe and yummy. In a classic style, there's lots of finesse and zesty cherry, plum and wild berry flavors that turn elegant and spicy. Blended with Petite Sirah, Carignane and Cabernet. 200 cases made. • $15 • (08/31/96) • **91**

COHN, B.R. | CALIFORNIA

Cabernet Sauvignon Napa County Silver Label 1989 • $12 • (08/31/92) • **82**
Cabernet Sauvignon Napa Valley Silver Label 1988 • $12 • (09/30/91) • **87**
Cabernet Sauvignon North Coast 1994: A solid core of licorice and tarlike flavors makes this otherwise roughly textured, herbal wine enjoyable. 6,000 cases made. • $14 • (09/15/97) • **82**
Cabernet Sauvignon Sonoma Valley 1991 • $12 • (11/15/94) • **83**
Cabernet Sauvignon Sonoma Valley Olive Hill Estate Vineyards 1995: Austere in style, tight and cedary, with a trim band of currant, tar, sage and berry, this wine will benefit from short-term cellaring. It's dense and concentrated; absolutely needs time to soften and evolve. Best from 2002 through 2010. 3,800 cases made. • $35 • (07/31/98) • **91**
Cabernet Sauvignon Sonoma Valley Olive Hill Estate Vineyards Special Selection 1995: Smooth, ripe, supple and harmonious, with pretty, ripe black cherry, wild berry, currant and plum. Finishes with firm, chewy tannins and a good dose of toasty oak. Still a bit awkward, but give it some time; best from 2002 through 2010. 625 cases made. • $80 • (06/15/98) • **90**
Cabernet Sauvignon Sonoma Valley Olive Hill Vineyard 1994: Dark, immense and firmly tannic, with lots of oak on top of that. Still, there's a lot of rich currant and berry flavor in there to stand up to the wood. Best to cellar into 1999 or 2002. 3,900 cases made. • $35 • (02/28/97) • **89**
Cabernet Sauvignon Sonoma Valley Olive Hill Vineyard 1993: Dark, dense and tannic, with a rich, well-focused core of currant and cherry flavors. Turns substantially tannic on the finish, where the plush texture collides with the firmness. Ripe, fruity finish. 2,000 cases made. • $17 Ⓐ • (04/30/96) • **90**
Cabernet Sauvignon Sonoma Valley Olive Hill Vineyard 1991 • $31 Ⓐ • (04/15/95) HR • **91**
Cabernet Sauvignon Sonoma Valley Olive Hill Vineyard 1990 • $25 • (11/15/93) • **90**
Cabernet Sauvignon Sonoma Valley Olive Hill Vineyard 1989 • $25 • (08/31/92) • **86**
Cabernet Sauvignon Sonoma Valley Olive Hill Vineyard 1988 • $29 Ⓐ • (05/15/91) • **89**
Cabernet Sauvignon Sonoma Valley Olive Hill Vineyard 1987: Marked by a dryness to the fruit and tannins, this is a mature wine with spicy, cedary oak nuances and a modest core of currant and berry flavor. Drink now. • $36 Ⓐ • (12/15/97) • **87**
Cabernet Sauvignon Sonoma Valley Olive Hill Vineyard 1986: This has reached a fine drinking plateau, as the tannins have softened and the sweet plum and black cherry flavors have a nice black olive and herb accent. You'll still encounter firm tannins, but there's lots of richness and flavor, too. • $38 Ⓐ • (12/15/96) • **91**
Cabernet Sauvignon Sonoma Valley Olive Hill Vineyard 1985 • $65 Ⓐ • (11/15/88) • **94**
Cabernet Sauvignon Sonoma Valley Olive Hill Vineyard 1984 • $48 Ⓐ • (06/30/88) • **89**
Chardonnay Carneros 1993 • $28 • (07/31/95) • **84**
Chardonnay Carneros Joseph Herman Vineyard Reserve 1996: Shows off spicy, toasty, vanilla-scented oak and backs it up with ripe pear and appley flavors. A hint of alcohol and bitterness fold in, giving it a coarse texture. Drink now. 914 cases made. • $24 • (05/15/98) • **87**
Chardonnay Carneros Joseph Herman Vineyard Reserve 1995: Complex and elegant, showing a pretty band of ripe pear, apple and citrus flavors with delicate nuances of spice and a light, creamy aftertaste. 486 cases made. • $24 • (03/31/97) • **91**
Chardonnay Carneros Joseph Herman Vineyard Reserve 1993 • $20 • (07/31/95) • **82**
Chardonnay Sonoma Valley 1996: A touch leafy, it works its way into spicy pear and apple flavors, with light oak shadings. Good, but lacks focus, and finishes with an earthy aftertaste. Drink now through 2001. 3,450 cases made. • $14 • (07/31/98) • **87**
Chardonnay Sonoma Valley 1995: Complex, with a rich core of ripe pear, apple and spice flavors and an attractive oak seasoning which keeps the flavors lively through the finish. Ready now. 3,100 cases made. • $14 • (04/30/97) • **89**
Merlot Napa Valley Silver Label 1989 • $14 • (11/15/91) • **82**
Merlot Napa-Sonoma Counties 1992 • $14 • (11/15/94) • **80**
Merlot Napa-Sonoma Counties 1990 • $14 • (10/31/92) • **84**
Merlot Sonoma Valley Olive Hill Vineyard 1994 • $20 • (06/30/96) • **83**
Pinot Noir Sonoma Valley Olive Hill Vineyard 1995: Tart, with sharp-edged earthy mushroom and black cherry flavors. Try now. 145 cases made. • $24 • (03/31/97) • **84**

COLBY | CALIFORNIA

Chardonnay Napa Valley 1996: Somewhat silky on the palate, with hints of butterscotch, toasty oak, pear and spice and a mellow, moderately long finish. Drink now. 622 cases made. • $14 • (07/31/98) • **87**
Chardonnay Napa Valley 1993 • $12 • (05/15/96) • **83**

COLD HEAVEN | CALIFORNIA

Viognier Santa Barbara County Sanford and Benedict Vineyard 1996: The attractively subtle hints of peach, nectarine and hazelnut make you wish it would offer just a bit more. The minerally finish is refreshing. First release from Morgan Toral. 400 cases made. • $25 • (12/15/97) • **86**

COLGIN | CALIFORNIA

Cabernet Sauvignon Napa Valley Herb Lamb Vineyard 1994: This single-vineyard, small-production Cabernet is young and tight, with a complex array of ripe currant, cherry, plum and spice flavors, and a pretty, toasty oak overlay. Given its intensity and depth, it's a remarkably elegant and sophisticated wine. If you're lucky enough to garner a bottle, best to drink it between 2000 and 2010. 500 cases made. • $368 Ⓐ • (07/31/97) HR • **95**

Cabernet Sauvignon Napa Valley Herb Lamb Vineyard 1993: An amazing mouthful of Cabernet—rich, plush and seductive. A complex and concentrated wine that's jam-packed with layers of concentrated plum, currant, cherry and berry flavors. Its texture is smooth and polished, even though the tannins are thick and potent. 400 cases made. • $345 Ⓐ • (11/15/96) • **96**

Cabernet Sauvignon Napa Valley Herb Lamb Vineyard 1992 • $29 • (10/15/95) HR • **92**

COLONY | CALIFORNIA

Cabernet Sauvignon Sonoma County 1982 • $7 • (03/16/86) BB • **89**

COLORADO CELLARS | COLORADO

Grand Gamé Rocky Mountain 1988 • $8 • (02/29/92) • **79**

COLUMBIA | WASHINGTON

Cabernet Franc Yakima Valley Red Willow Vineyard David Lake Signature Series 1995: Has some lovely ripe flavors on a firm, chewy frame, offering berry and spice notes on the generous finish. Best from 1999. 1,000 cases made. • $20 • (03/31/98) • **87**

Cabernet Franc Yakima Valley Red Willow Vineyard David Lake Signature Series 1994: A solid red with a distinctively minty personality centered around a core of vibrant, floral- and pepper-scented blackberry and currant flavors that persist on the supple finish. Tannins would benefit from cellaring until 1999 to 2000. 1,350 cases made. • $22 • (09/15/97) • **89**

Cabernet Franc Yakima Valley Red Willow Vineyard Signature Series 1993 • $16 • (09/30/95) • **87**

Cabernet Franc Yakima Valley Red Willow Vineyard Signature Series 1992 • $16 • (09/30/94) • **87**

Cabernet Franc Yakima Valley Red Willow Vineyard Signature Series 1991 • $15 • (02/28/93) • **86**

Cabernet Sauvignon Columbia Valley 1993: A chewy, snappy wine, firmly tannic, with solid doses of currant and floral flavors. Best after 2000. 10,000 cases made. • $13 • (09/15/97) • **85**

Cabernet Sauvignon Columbia Valley 1992 • $13 • (03/31/96) • **86**

Cabernet Sauvignon Columbia Valley 1991 • $13 • (09/30/94) • **86**

Cabernet Sauvignon Columbia Valley 1990 • $13 • (11/30/93) • **81**

Cabernet Sauvignon Columbia Valley 1989 • $12 • (10/15/92) SS • **90**

Cabernet Sauvignon Columbia Valley 1988 • $10 • (03/31/91) • **86**

Cabernet Sauvignon Columbia Valley 1987 • $9 • (06/15/90) • **87**

Cabernet Sauvignon Columbia Valley 1986 • $10 • (10/15/89) • **85**

Cabernet Sauvignon Columbia Valley 1985 • $9 • (07/15/88) • **79**

Cabernet Sauvignon Columbia Valley Sagemoor Vineyard 1985 • $15 • (10/15/89) • **85**

Cabernet Sauvignon Columbia Valley Sagemoor Vineyard Signature Series 1989 • $18 • (03/31/93) • **83**

Cabernet Sauvignon Columbia Valley Sagemoor Vineyard Signature Series 1988 • $20 • (04/30/92) • **81**

Cabernet Sauvignon Columbia Valley Sagemoor Vineyard Signature Series 25th 1987 • $20 • (06/30/94) • **89**

Cabernet Sauvignon Columbia Valley Sagemoor Vineyard Signature Series 1986 • $16 • (05/15/91) • **85**

Cabernet Sauvignon Washington Bacchus Vineyard 1981 • $12 • (08/01/84) • **86**

Cabernet Sauvignon Yakima Valley 1981 • $8 • (08/01/84) • **76**

Cabernet Sauvignon Yakima Valley Otis Vineyard 1985 • $15 • (10/15/89) • **91**

Cabernet Sauvignon Yakima Valley Otis Vineyard 1981 • $13 • (08/01/84) • **83**

Cabernet Sauvignon Yakima Valley Otis Vineyard Signature Series 1993: Crisp and bright, with layers of blackberry, currant, chocolate and herb flavors that cascade through the finish, echoing juicy berry and spice notes. 1,500 cases made. • $23 • (04/30/97) • **89**

Key: SS—Spectator Selection CS—Cellar Selection HR—Highly Recommended BB—Best Buy $NA—Price not available Ⓐ—Auction Price (BT)—Barrel Tasting

Dates in parentheses indicate the issues in which the ratings were published.

Cabernet Sauvignon Yakima Valley Otis Vineyard Signature Series 1992: Smooth and polished. Harmoniously balances its generous spicy plum, black cherry and vanilla flavors with supple texture, and extends into a long, elegant finish. Tempting now, but give it until 2000 or 2001. 1,250 cases made. • $20 • (12/15/96) • **90**

Cabernet Sauvignon Yakima Valley Otis Vineyard Signature Series 1990 • $19 • (06/30/94) • **85**

Cabernet Sauvignon Yakima Valley Otis Vineyard Signature Series 1989 • $18 • (06/15/93) • **85**

Cabernet Sauvignon Yakima Valley Otis Vineyard Signature Series 1988 • $20 • (04/15/92) • **89**

Cabernet Sauvignon Yakima Valley Red Willow Vineyard 1985 • $15 • (10/15/89) • **82**

Cabernet Sauvignon Yakima Valley Red Willow Vineyard 1981 • $35 • (10/15/89) • **84**

Cabernet Sauvignon Yakima Valley Red Willow Vineyard Signature Series 1993: Made in a sturdy, chewy style, with a pure thread of currant and blueberry flavor at the center that persists through the narrow finish. Best in 1999. 1,400 cases made. • $23 • (04/30/97) • **87**

Cabernet Sauvignon Yakima Valley Red Willow Vineyard Signature Series 1992 • $21 • (05/15/96) • **87**

Cabernet Sauvignon Yakima Valley Red Willow Vineyard Signature Series 1991 • $20 • (08/31/95) • **88**

Cabernet Sauvignon Yakima Valley Red Willow Vineyard Signature Series 1989 • $18 • (05/31/93) • **89**

Cabernet Sauvignon Yakima Valley Red Willow Vineyard Signature Series 1988 • $20 • (04/15/92) • **86**

Cabernet Sauvignon Yakima Valley Red Willow Vineyard Signature Series 25th 1987 • $20 • (06/30/94) • **87**

Chardonnay Columbia Valley Woodburne Cuvée 1995: Strives for delicacy and achieves a sort of crisp elegance, with lively pear and vanilla flavors that linger on a light finish. Drink now. 21,000 cases made. • $12 • (09/15/96) HR • **88**

Chardonnay Columbia Valley Woodburne Cuvée 1994: Refreshingly citrusy and delicately fruity, a mild mannered wine that's clean and immediately drinkable. 14,000 cases made. • $11 • (03/31/96) • **84**

Chardonnay Columbia Valley Woodburne Cuvée 1993 • $12 • (09/30/94) • **88**

Chardonnay Yakima Valley David Lake Signature Series Otis Vineyard 1996: Jazzy and refreshing. A lively Chardonnay, with layers of apple, pear and nutmeg flavors plus a nice earthy touch on the finish. Drink now through 2000. 1,000 cases made. • $24 • (06/30/98) • **90**

Chardonnay Yakima Valley David Lake Signature Series Wyckoff Vineyard 1996: Light and pretty, with gentle pear and floral flavors that pick up a hint of honey on the delicate finish. Drink now. 2,000 cases made. • $24 • (06/15/98) • **86**

Chardonnay Yakima Valley Otis Vineyard David Lake Signature Series 1995: Rich and supple in texture, with spicy tones amid hints of citrus and pear. A graceful wine. Drink now. 500 cases made. • $22 • (09/15/97) • **88**

Chardonnay Yakima Valley Wyckoff Vineyard David Lake Signature Series 1994: Fresh and floral, a silky-textured white that sneaks a delicious, honey edge onto the pear and spice flavors of the finish. Drinkable now. 2,250 cases made. • $15 • (04/30/96) • **88**

Chardonnay Yakima Valley Wyckoff Vineyard Signature Series 1995: Tight and not very generous, with more waxy, mineral flavors than fruit, but it finishes with intensity. Try now. 2,500 cases made. • $18 • (04/30/97) • **84**

Chardonnay Yakima Valley Wyckoff Vineyard Signature Series 1993 • $17 • (04/15/95) • **88**

Chenin Blanc Yakima Valley 1994 • $6 • (09/30/95) • **84**

Gewürztraminer Yakima Valley 1996: A very pretty wine for very few dollars, it's sweet and flowery in character, with distinctly floral-tinged pear and honey flavors and a finish marked by delicacy and grace. 3,500 cases made. • $7 • (09/15/97) BB • **87**

Gewürztraminer Yakima Valley 1995 • $6 • (06/15/96) • **85**

Gewürztraminer Yakima Valley 1994 • $6 • (09/30/95) • **78**

Gewürztraminer Yakima Valley 1993 • $6 • (09/30/94) • **85**

Johannisberg Riesling Columbia Valley 1994 • $6 • (09/30/95) • **83**

Johannisberg Riesling Columbia Valley 1993 • $6 • (09/30/94) • **82**

Johannisberg Riesling Columbia Valley Cellarmaster's Reserve 1995: Frankly sweet, but neither sugary nor thick. Has a light texture, with refreshing pear, ripe peach and floral flavors, and a touch of honey that sneaks in on the finish. 135,000 cases made. • $7 • (09/15/96) BB • **89**

Johannisberg Riesling Columbia Valley Cellarmaster's Reserve 1994 • $6 • (09/30/95) • **82**

Johannisberg Riesling Columbia Valley Cellarmaster's Reserve 1993 • $7 • (09/30/94) • **85**

Johannisberg Riesling Late Harvest Columbia Valley Cellarmaster's Reserve 1988 • $7 • (10/15/89) BB • **85**
Merlot Columbia Valley 1994: Crisp and generous, with extraordinarily supple, spicy black cherry, dark currant and anise flavors that linger smoothly. Delicious now. 14,000 cases made. • $13 • (02/28/97) • **88**
Merlot Columbia Valley 1993 • $13 • (05/15/96) • **85**
Merlot Columbia Valley 1992 • $13 • (05/31/95) • **87**
Merlot Columbia Valley 1991 • $13 • (09/30/94) • **87**
Merlot Columbia Valley 1990 • $13 • (06/15/93) • **80**
Merlot Columbia Valley 1989 • $12 • (03/31/92) • **80**
Merlot Columbia Valley 1988 • $10 • (03/31/91) • **81**
Merlot Columbia Valley 1986 • $10 • (10/15/89) • **84**
Merlot Columbia Valley 1985 • $9 • (05/31/88) • **86**
Merlot Washington 1984 • $9 • (05/15/87) • **75**
Merlot Washington 1981 • $25 • (10/15/89) • **87**
Merlot Yakima Valley Red Willow Vineyard 1989 • $20 • (11/15/91) • **89**
Merlot Yakima Valley Red Willow Vineyard Milestone 1987 • $15 • (10/15/89) • **80**
Merlot Yakima Valley Red Willow Vineyard Milestone Signature Series 1994: Lean and spicy, with flavors that tend strongly toward smoky oak, but there's ju-u-ust enough berry flavor to warrant cellaring until 1999 or 2000 to see what develops. 2,400 cases made. • $23 • (04/30/97) • **85**
Merlot Yakima Valley Red Willow Vineyard Milestone Signature Series 1993 • $20 • (05/15/96) • **87**
Merlot Yakima Valley Red Willow Vineyard Milestone Signature Series 1992 • $20 • (09/30/94) • **85**
Merlot Yakima Valley Red Willow Vineyard Milestone Signature Series 1991 • $20 • (06/15/93) • **84**
Merlot Yakima Valley Red Willow Vineyard Milestone Signature Series 1989 • $18 • (06/15/92) • **88**
Merlot Yakima Valley Red Willow Vineyard Milestone Signature Series 1988 • $16 • (03/31/91) • **82**
Pinot Gris Yakima Valley 1996: Ripe and focused, generous with its pear, almond and peach flavors; long and beautifully balanced. Immensely appealing to drink soon. 1,140 cases made. • $10 • (09/30/97) • **89**
Pinot Gris Yakima Valley Otis Vineyard 1995: Light and mildly fruity, with appealing honeydew and mineral flavors that narrow a bit on the finish. 2,100 cases made. • $12 • (09/15/96) • **82**
Pinot Noir Washington 1996: A light, straightforward red, with pretty black cherry and spice flavors on a firm frame. Best in 1999. 1,500 cases made. • $13 • (03/31/98) • **84**
Pinot Noir Washington Woodburne Cuvée 1994: Plenty of lovely berry, cherry and walnut aromas, but a bit slim on the palate. Drinkable now. 2,400 cases made. • $11 • (09/15/96) • **84**
Pinot Noir Washington Woodburne Cuvée 1993 • $11 • (09/30/95) • **85**
Pinot Noir Washington Woodburne Cuvée 1992 • $12 • (09/30/94) • **82**
Pinot Noir Washington Woodburne Cuvée 1991 • $12 • (02/28/93) • **72**
Pinot Noir Washington Woodburne Cuvée 1990 • $12 • (03/31/92) • **77**
Pinot Noir Washington Woodburne Cuvée 1989 • $12 • (06/15/92) • **84**
Pinot Noir Washington Woodburne Cuvée 1987 • $10 • (03/31/91) • **88**
Pinot Noir Washington Yakima County 1981 • $7 • (09/01/84) • **71**
Riesling Columbia Valley Cellarmaster's Reserve 1996: Bright and refreshing, with citrusy pear and floral flavors that finish smooth and juicy. Drink soon. 22,000 cases made. • $7 • (09/15/97) • **86**
Sauvignon Blanc Columbia Valley 1994 • $8 • (09/30/95) • **82**
Sauvignon Blanc Columbia Valley 1993 • $8 • (07/31/94) BB • **88**
Sémillon-Chardonnay Columbia Valley 1993 • $8 • (09/15/94) BB • **87**
Sémillon-Chardonnay Washington 1994 • $8 • (09/30/95) • **84**
Sémillon Columbia Valley 1995: Light and refreshing. Nicely fruity aromas and a mouthful of citrusy pear and delicately herbal flavors. 12,000 cases made. • $7 • (09/15/96) BB • **87**
Sémillon Columbia Valley 1994 • $6 • (08/31/95) BB • **85**
Sémillon Columbia Valley 1993 • $8 • (08/31/94) BB • **86**
Sémillon Columbia Valley Chevrier 1995: Crisp, light and spicy, with fresh pear and grapefruit notes that linger nicely on the smooth finish. 1,600 cases made. • $12 • (02/28/97) • **86**
Sémillon Columbia Valley Sur Lie Chevrier 1994 • $9 • (05/15/96) • **88**
Sémillon Columbia Valley Sur Lie Chevrier 1993 • $8 • (08/31/95) • **86**
Seyval Blanc Washington 1994 • $8 • (09/30/95) • **84**
Syrah Yakima Valley 1996: Tart, tough and tannic, clearly built for cellaring; nicely packed with berry and coffee flavors. Try in 2002 to 2005. 2,100 cases made. • $14 • (03/31/98) • **85**
Syrah Yakima Valley 1995: Dark and vibrant. A juicy mouthful of red berry, currant and black pepper flavors that linger jazzily on the mildly chewy finish. Drink soon, while it's so exuberant. 1,337 cases made. • $13 • (09/15/97) • **87**
Syrah Yakima Valley Red Willow Vineyard 1994: Focused, flavorful and chewy, this solid red brims with berry and cherry flavors, and finishes with a touch of clove to go along with the fine tannins. Drinkable now. 350 cases made. • $24 • (09/15/97) • **87**
Syrah Yakima Valley Red Willow Vineyard 1993 • $21 • (05/15/96) • **88**
Syrah Yakima Valley Red Willow Vineyard 1992 • $20 • (09/30/95) • **88**
Syrah Yakima Valley Red Willow Vineyard 1991 • $18 • (09/30/94) • **83**
Syrah Yakima Valley Red Willow Vineyard 1990 • $20 • (12/31/93) • **88**
Syrah Yakima Valley Red Willow Vineyard 1989 • $25 • (11/30/92) • **87**
Syrah Yakima Valley Red Willow Vineyard 1988 • $25 • (05/15/91) • **90**
Syrah Yakima Valley Red Willow Vineyard David Lake Signature Series 1995: Dark, dense and peppery, with lots of black cherry and blackberry flavors at the core, chewy tannins and a bite of earthy spice on the finish. Give it until 1999 to 2000 to soften. 2,400 cases made. • $24 • (01/31/98) • **90**

COLUMBIA CREST | WASHINGTON

Cabernet Sauvignon Columbia Valley 1995: A solidly built, harmonious style of Cabernet, offering plenty of pretty black cherry and currant flavor alongside a complement of herb and tobacco notes. Drink now through 2002. 165,000 cases made. • $11 • (07/31/98) • **87**
Cabernet Sauvignon Columbia Valley 1994: This Washington Cab is bursting with character and charm. The ripe currant, blackberry and tarlike flavors emerge brilliantly on the generous, chewy finish, and though it's a little rough up front now, it will reward cellaring with delicious drinking after 2001 or 2002. 65,500 cases made. • $11 • (09/15/97) SS • **90**
Cabernet Sauvignon Columbia Valley 1993: Dense and chewy without being rough, packed with ripe cherry and spice flavors that turn toward elegance on the finish. Delicious now. 130,000 cases made. • $9 • (09/30/96) • **87**
Cabernet Sauvignon Columbia Valley 1992 • $9 • (07/31/95) BB • **85**
Cabernet Sauvignon Columbia Valley 1991 • $9 • (09/30/94) • **84**
Cabernet Sauvignon Columbia Valley 1990 • $10 • (11/30/93) • **82**
Cabernet Sauvignon Columbia Valley 1989 • $8 • (10/15/93) • **82**
Cabernet Sauvignon Columbia Valley 1988 • $9 • (07/31/92) SS • **89**
Cabernet Sauvignon Columbia Valley 1987 • $10 • (08/31/91) • **85**
Cabernet Sauvignon Columbia Valley 1986 • $8 • (01/31/91) BB • **88**
Cabernet Sauvignon Columbia Valley 1985 • $8 • (10/15/89) • **81**
Cabernet Sauvignon Columbia Valley 1984 • $7 • (07/15/88) • **79**
Cabernet Sauvignon Columbia Valley Barrel Select 1991 • $15 • (05/31/96) • **85**
Cabernet Sauvignon Columbia Valley Barrel Select 1990 • $15 • (09/30/94) • **87**
Cabernet Sauvignon Columbia Valley Barrel Select 1989 • $15 • (06/30/94) • **80**
Cabernet Sauvignon Columbia Valley Estate Series 1994: Dense and chewy, with currant and spice flavors coming through on the finish. Drink now. 7,500 cases made. • $20 • (09/15/97) • **85**
Cabernet Sauvignon Columbia Valley Estate Series 1993: Tightly wound, with jammy currant and berry flavors that are graced by all kinds of spicy, chocolaty, toasty overtones. This red from Washington has an austere feel to it right now, mostly from the zippy acidity, but there is also a plushness that can grow with cellaring through 2000 or 2005. 5,500 cases made. • $18 • (02/28/97) SS • **91**
Chardonnay Columbia Valley 1996: Ripe and bright, this Chardonnay is generous with apple, citrus and spice flavors that linger on the soft and supple finish. A good value from one of Washington's largest and most reliable wineries. Drink now. 252,000 cases made. • $9 • (06/15/98) BB • **88**
Chardonnay Columbia Valley 1995: A nice, compact style of Chardonnay, dealing out its lemony pear and mineral flavors slowly, and finishing with a pretty hint of spice. Lovely, at an attractive price. 507,000 cases made. • $9 • (07/31/97) BB • **87**
Chardonnay Columbia Valley 1994: Light, juicy peach and apple flavors, smooth texture. Drinkable now. 330,000 cases made. • $8 • (04/30/96) • **84**
Chardonnay Columbia Valley 1993 • $8 • (01/31/95) BB • **88**
Chardonnay Columbia Valley Barrel Select 1993 • $10 • (09/30/95) • **88**
Chardonnay Columbia Valley Estate Series 1995: An elegant wine, silky smooth and nicely layered with nutmeg, nectarine and apple flavors that linger enticingly on the beautifully balanced finish. Try now. 20,000 cases made. • $14 • (04/30/97) SS • **91**
Chardonnay Columbia Valley Reserve 1995: A serious Chardonnay. Focused, ripe and spicy, dripping with nutmeg, butter and honey overtones to the pear and ripe apple flavors, finishing with some finesse. Drink now. 1,250 cases made. • $14 • (07/31/97) • **90**
Chardonnay Columbia Valley Reserve 1993 • $14 • (03/31/96) • **89**
Gamay Beaujolais Columbia Valley 1993 • $7 • (09/30/94) • **85**

Gewürztraminer Columbia Valley 1997: Soft and off-dry, with lemony pear and honey flavors on a tight frame. Drink now through 1999. • $7 • (07/31/98) • **83**
Gewürztraminer Columbia Valley 1995 • $6 • (06/15/96) • **80**
Gewürztraminer Columbia Valley 1994 • $6 • (09/30/95) • **80**
Gewürztraminer Columbia Valley 1993 • $6 • (02/28/95) BB • **85**
Johannisberg Riesling Columbia Valley 1996: Off-dry, with enough acidity to keep it lively, and modest green apple flavors. Drink now. 45,000 cases made. • $7 • (06/30/98) BB • **85**
Johannisberg Riesling Columbia Valley 1995 • $6 • (06/15/96) BB • **84**
Johannisberg Riesling Columbia Valley 1994 • $6 • (09/30/95) • **86**
Johannisberg Riesling Columbia Valley 1993 • $6 • (09/30/94) BB • **87**
Merlot Columbia Valley 1995: Supple and lithe, a lighter style of Merlot that manages to pack in lots of pretty raspberry and gentle tobacco flavors. Drink now through 2001. 395,000 cases made. • $15 • (06/15/98) • **87**
Merlot Columbia Valley 1994: Great stuff. This Washington red is soft, silky, spicy, and utterly delicious. Remarkable for its elegance and its distinctly nutmeg-tinged plum, berry and chocolate flavors that linger enticingly on the polished finish. 164,000 cases made. • $14 • (06/15/97) SS • **90**
Merlot Columbia Valley 1993 • $10 • (05/31/96) BB • **88**
Merlot Columbia Valley 1992 • $10 • (09/30/94) • **87**
Merlot Columbia Valley 1991 • $10 • (04/15/94) BB • **88**
Merlot Columbia Valley 1990 • $10 • (05/31/93) • **85**
Merlot Columbia Valley 1989 • $10 • (02/29/92) SS • **88**
Merlot Columbia Valley 1987 • $8 • (09/30/90) BB • **86**
Merlot Columbia Valley 1985 • $8 • (10/15/89) • **85**
Merlot Columbia Valley 1984 • $7 • (05/31/88) • **78**
Merlot Columbia Valley Barrel Select 1992 • $15 • (05/15/96) • **88**
Merlot Columbia Valley Barrel Select 1991 • $15 • (09/30/95) • **87**
Merlot Columbia Valley Barrel Select 1990 • $15 • (09/30/94) • **86**
Merlot Columbia Valley Barrel Select 1989 • $15 • (05/31/93) • **88**
Merlot Columbia Valley Barrel Select 1988 • $15 • (07/31/92) • **87**
Merlot Columbia Valley Barrel Select 1987 • $15 • (05/31/91) • **84**
Merlot Columbia Valley Estate Series 1994: Packs a lot of flavor onto a lithe frame, offering black cherry, currant, nutmeg and toast character in a solid package underlined by fine, chewy tannins. Drink now. • $NA • (09/15/97) • **89**
Pinot Noir Willamette Valley Barrel Select 1992 • $15 • (03/31/96) • **81**
Red Reserve Columbia Valley 1993: Strives for subtlety, and comes pretty close, with spicy blackberry and cherry flavors peeking from beneath a layer of fine tannins. Well-balanced. Try in 2000 to 2001. 1,100 cases made. • $17 • (09/15/96) • **87**
Red Reserve Columbia Valley 1992 • $18 • (07/31/95) • **90**
Reserve Columbia Valley 1994: A bit tough and chewy, but packed with solid berry and spice flavors, narrowing a bit on the finish. Best after 2000. A blend of 46 percent Cabernet Sauvignon, 46 percent Merlot, and 8 percent Cabernet Franc. 1,900 cases made. • $22 • (09/30/97) • **85**
Sauvignon Blanc Columbia Valley 1995: An appealing white from Washington, at a price that's hard to beat. Fresh in style, emphasizing light grape and citrus flavors, and finishing with a balanced flourish of fruit and spice notes. 36,000 cases made. • $7 • (06/15/97) BB • **86**
Sauvignon Blanc Columbia Valley 1993 • $7 • (07/31/94) • **82**
Sémillon Chardonnay Columbia Valley 1995: A solid white that doesn't try to be graceful but manages to keep its modest fig, herb and melon flavors in balance. A blend of 70 percent Sémillon and 30 percent Chardonnay. 150,000 cases made. • $8 • (07/31/97) • **84**
Sémillon Chardonnay Columbia Valley 1994 • $7 • (05/15/96) • **84**
Sémillon Chardonnay Columbia Valley 1993 • $7 • (09/30/94) • **84**
Sémillon Columbia Valley 1995: This Washington producer comes through with yet another value-priced wine. It's light and crisp, displaying pretty peach and tobacco flavors that remain fresh through the finish. 10,242 cases made. • $6 • (06/15/97) BB • **85**
Sémillon Columbia Valley 1994 • $6 • (05/15/96) BB • **85**
Sémillon Columbia Valley 1993 • $6 • (09/30/94) • **84**
Sémillon Late Harvest Columbia Valley 1995: Frankly sweet, almost syrupy, with a tobacco note prominent alongside the sugary pear character. Give it until 1999 to settle down. 13.2 percent residual sugar. 1,300 cases made. • $21/375ml • (11/30/97) • **83**
Sémillon Late Harvest Columbia Valley 1992 • $8/375ml • (04/30/95) HR • **93**

Key: SS—Spectator Selection CS—Cellar Selection HR—Highly Recommended BB—Best Buy $NA—Price not available Ⓐ—Auction Price (BT)—Barrel Tasting
Dates in parentheses indicate the issues in which the ratings were published.

Syrah Columbia Valley Reserve 1995: A peppery Syrah, smooth and inviting for its creamy, tarry blackberry and perfumy black cherry flavors. Delicious now, best from 1999. • $24 • (09/15/97) • **89**
Syrah Columbia Valley Reserve 1994: Dark as ink, and dense with plum, berry and sassafrass aromas, but it turns gentle and harmonious on the palate. Drink now to 2000. 325 cases made. • $17 • (09/15/96) • **89**
White Riesling Columbia Valley Ice Wine Reserve 1995: A very pretty wine in a sweet, creamy style, with lovely vanilla-scented pear, pineapple and floral flavors that linger gently. Ready to drink. 16.8 percent residual sugar. • $26/375ml • (05/15/97) • **87**

CONCANNON | CALIFORNIA

Assemblage Livermore Valley Reserve 1996: Shows some nice hazelnut, pear and fresh grass notes. A bit hollow on the midpalate, but still enjoyable. A blend of 59 percent Sémillon and 41 percent Sauvignon Blanc. 394 cases made. • $15 • (05/15/98) • **83**
Assemblage Red Central Coast Reserve 1993: Brimming with ripe, juicy plum and wild berry flavors, this shows a forward and fruity style that is clean and appealing. Not too tannic, it drinks with ease now or can be cellared. 1,642 cases made. • $17 • (11/15/96) • **87**
Assemblage Red Central Coast Reserve 1992 • $15 • (12/15/95) • **86**
Assemblage Red Livermore Valley 1991 • $15 • (11/15/94) • **80**
Assemblage White Livermore Valley 1993 • $15 • (08/31/95) • **80**
Assemblage White Livermore Valley Reserve 1995: The smooth, silky texture is attractive, the subdued flavor profile of mandarin orange and lemon is interesting, if not arresting. The ensemble works well. 79 percent Sauvignon Blanc, 21 percent Sémillon. 581 cases made. • $13 • (06/30/97) • **87**
Assemblage White Livermore Valley Reserve 1994: Floral and citrus-peel aromas and flavors make this one appealing in a zingy sort of way. 1,432 cases made. • $15 • (08/31/96) • **85**
Cabernet Sauvignon Central Coast 1995: A vibrant, grapey wine; it tastes more like Grenache than Cabernet. For quaffing immediately. 9,045 cases made. • $10 • (09/30/97) • **83**
Cabernet Sauvignon Central Coast Selected Vineyard 1994: A fine value at this price for its well-balanced ripe plum, cherry, herb and cedar flavors. Finishes with crisp tannins. Ready now. 16,815 cases made. • $10 • (11/30/96) • **84**
Cabernet Sauvignon Central Coast Selected Vineyard 1993: Spicy aromas are followed by raspberry and cherry flavors that fade into an herbal finish. Drink now. 13,575 cases made. • $10 • (11/30/96) • **83**
Cabernet Sauvignon Central Coast Selected Vineyard 1992 • $10 • (11/15/94) • **84**
Cabernet Sauvignon Livermore Valley 1983 • $12 • (06/15/87) • **77**
Cabernet Sauvignon Livermore Valley 1981 • $12 • (12/16/84) • **82**
Cabernet Sauvignon Livermore Valley Concannon Estate Vineyard 1991 • $9 • (11/15/93) • **79**
Cabernet Sauvignon Livermore Valley Concannon Estate Vineyard 1989 • $10 • (11/15/93) • **78**
Cabernet Sauvignon Livermore Valley Reserve 1987 • $16 • (07/15/91) • **83**
Cabernet Sauvignon Livermore Valley Reserve 1985 • $14 • (02/15/89) • **87**
Chardonnay Central Coast Selected Vineyard 1996: Simple, with appealing apple, pear and hazelnut flavors that are clean and refreshing. Drink now through 2000. 16,400 cases made. • $10 • (07/31/98) BB • **86**
Chardonnay Central Coast Selected Vineyard 1995: A touch vegetal, with a racy edge to the pear, apple, spice and cedar notes, but at this price it offers enough character. 18,000 cases made. • $11 • (04/30/97) • **84**
Chardonnay Central Coast Selected Vineyards 1993 • $10 • (07/31/95) • **84**
Chardonnay Livermore Valley Reserve 1996: Ripe, with appealing pear, spice, fig and melon, picking up traces of citrus and spicy, toasty oak on the finish. A good value at this price. Drink now through 2001. 1,885 cases made. • $16 • (07/31/98) • **87**
Chardonnay Livermore Valley Reserve 1995: Supple and spicy, distinctive for its smoky, nutmeg-tinged pear and citrus flavors that linger on the polished finish. 791 cases made. • $15 • (07/31/97) • **89**
Chardonnay Livermore Valley Reserve 1993 • $15 • (07/31/95) • **87**
Merlot Livermore Valley Beyer's Ranch Limited Bottling 1993: A pleasant wine, with a core of ripe cherry, plum and berry flavors. Shows a slightly waxy edge on the finish. • $NA • (08/31/96) • **84**
Petite Sirah Central Coast Selected Vineyard 1991 • $10 • (02/28/95) • **81**
Petite Sirah Livermore Valley 1987 • $11 • (08/31/91) • **77**
Petite Sirah Livermore Valley Reserve 1985 • $15 • (08/31/91) • **83**
Sangiovese Central Coast Rosé of Sangiovese 1993 • $8 • (09/15/95) • **76**
Sauvignon Blanc Livermore Valley 1996: Tropical aromas of papaya and guava introduce this highly fruity wine. Tangy acidity and a bananalike fla-

vor tend to overwhelm the finish. 17,430 cases made. • $8 • (04/30/98) • **83**

Sauvignon Blanc Livermore Valley James Concannon Vineyard 1994: The pear and lemon flavors have a sour edge that keeps this wine from showing much appeal. 13,215 cases made. • $8 • (08/31/96) • **76**

Sauvignon Blanc Livermore Valley James Concannon Vineyard 1993 • $8 • (08/31/95) • **78**

Sauvignon Blanc Livermore Valley Selected Vineyard 1997: Fairly bright, with zingy lemon-and-lime flavors. A blend of melon and grapefruit flavors come nicely together on the finish. A good buy. Drink now. 24,000 cases made. • $8 • (06/30/98) BB • **86**

Sauvignon Blanc Livermore Valley Selected Vineyard 1995: Fresh and juicy, with a spicy edge to the raw pear and apple flavors that are appealing for their vividness. A reasonable price for this, too. 11,000 cases made. • $8 • (02/28/97) BB • **87**

CONGRESS SPRINGS | CALIFORNIA

Brut Santa Clara County Brut de Pinot 1986 • $8 • (03/31/88) • **77**

Cabernet Franc Santa Cruz Mountains 1986 • $18 • (07/31/89) • **88**

Merlot Santa Clara County 1988 • $14 • (03/31/91) • **74**

Pinot Noir Santa Clara County 1989 • $10 • (04/30/91) • **84**

Pinot Noir Santa Clara County San Ysidro Vineyard 1988 • $9 • (03/31/90) • **87**

Zinfandel Santa Cruz Mountains 1987 • $12 • (03/15/90) • **83**

CONN CREEK | CALIFORNIA

Anthology Napa Valley 1994: Complex, concentrated and well structured, with an intriguing array of ripe currant, plum and cedary oak. A tightly-wound, well-focused style with supple tannins and fine length. Best to cellar into 1999 to 2001, but it should hold into 2005. A blend of 50 percent Merlot, 36 percent Cabernet Sauvignon, and 14 percent Cabernet Franc. 1,420 cases made. • $37 • (03/31/98) • **90**

Anthology Napa Valley 1993: Appealing for its supple texture and bright, forward flavors: layers of juicy cherry, currant, plum and berry. Finishes with a spicy anise aftertaste and notes of tar, herb and cedary oak. Drinkable now if you look past its supple tannins, or age it into 2002; it should only get more harmonious. 1,212 cases made. • $30 • (11/15/96) • **93**

Anthology Napa Valley 1992 • $30 • (12/15/95) • **90**

Anthology Napa Valley 1991 • $30 • (09/30/94) CS • **93**

Cabernet Sauvignon Napa Valley 1981 • $14 • (12/16/84) • **85**

Cabernet Sauvignon Napa Valley 1980 • $29 Ⓐ • (02/15/84) • **86**

Cabernet Sauvignon Napa Valley 1974 • $250 • (11/15/94) • **88**

Cabernet Sauvignon Napa Valley Barrel Select 1991 • $18 • (11/15/94) • **85**

Cabernet Sauvignon Napa Valley Barrel Select 1988 • $15 • (10/31/92) • **84**

Cabernet Sauvignon Napa Valley Barrel Select 1987 • $17 • (07/15/91) • **87**

Cabernet Sauvignon Napa Valley Barrel Select 1986 • $18 • (02/28/91) • **55**

Cabernet Sauvignon Napa Valley Barrel Select 1985 • $29 • (09/15/90) • **90**

Cabernet Sauvignon Napa Valley Barrel Select 1983 • $15 • (12/31/88) • **88**

Cabernet Sauvignon Napa Valley Barrel Select Lot 79 1984 • $13 • (12/31/88) • **86**

Cabernet Sauvignon Napa Valley Barrel Select Private Reserve 1986 • $40 • (12/15/90) HR • **91**

Cabernet Sauvignon Napa Valley Barrel Select Private Reserve 1985 • $45 • (09/15/90) • **91**

Cabernet Sauvignon Napa Valley Collins Vineyard Private Reserve 1984 • $28 • (03/31/89) • **94**

Cabernet Sauvignon Napa Valley Limited Release 1994: On the lighter side, with a modest band of cedar, celery and currant, and glints of leather and oak folding in on the finish. 2,132 cases made. • $20 • (04/30/98) • **84**

Cabernet Sauvignon Napa Valley Limited Release 1993: A middle-of-the-road style. Shows ripe plum, berry and cherry flavors. Turns simple on the finish, where tannins and herbal notes dominate. 1,600 cases made. • $18 • (12/15/96) • **84**

Cabernet Sauvignon Napa Valley Limited Release 1992 • $18 • (12/15/95) • **88**

Cabernet Sauvignon Napa Valley Limited Release 1991 • $18 • (11/15/94) • **88**

Cabernet Sauvignon Napa Valley Lot 1 1978 • $NA • (11/15/92) • **88**

Cabernet Sauvignon Napa Valley Lot 2 1978 • $43 • (11/15/92) • **86**

Cabernet Sauvignon Napa Valley Reserve 1987 • $23 • (08/31/92) • **87**

Merlot Napa Valley Barrel Select 1990 • $14 • (09/15/94) • **84**

Merlot Napa Valley Barrel Select 1989 • $16 • (10/31/92) • **80**

Merlot Napa Valley Barrel Select 1988 • $22 • (11/15/91) • **86**

Merlot Napa Valley Collins Vineyard 1985 • $14 • (03/31/88) • **84**

Merlot Napa Valley Collins Vineyard Barrel Select Limited Bottling 1987 • $22 • (12/31/90) • **87**

Merlot Napa Valley Limited Release 1991 • $15 • (06/30/96) • **83**

Triomphe Napa Valley 1987 • $26 • (07/15/92) • **89**

Zinfandel Napa Valley Barrel Select 1988 • $10 • (10/15/92) • **82**

Zinfandel Napa Valley Barrel Select 1987 • $10 • (11/15/91) • **80**

Zinfandel Napa Valley Barrel Select 1986 • $9 • (10/15/90) • **86**

Zinfandel Napa Valley Collins Vineyard 1983 • $10 • (12/15/88) • **84**

COLIO | MICHIGAN

Ice Wine Lake Erie North Shore 1992 • $28 • (04/15/95 • **72**

COOK'S | CALIFORNIA

Brut America Imperial NV: Simple and semi-sweet, with an attractive hazelnut and plum finish. Sweeter than you'd expect from a label that says "Brut." • $8 • (12/15/97) • **81**

Cabernet Sauvignon California Captain's Reserve 1988 • $5 • (07/15/92) BB • **80**

Extra Dry America Imperial NV: Sweeter than some in the category, this is fairly simple, with citrus and plum essence. Not cloying, however. A quaffer. • $8 • (12/15/97) • **81**

Merlot California Captain's Reserve 1992 • $5 • (09/15/94) BB • **81**

Merlot California Captain's Reserve 1989 • $5 • (05/31/92) • **77**

Spumante America NV: Interesting wintergreen aromas are followed by a sweet, Muscat-like quality. In fact, as the label implies, this resembles Asti Spumante. A fun apéritif. • $8 • (12/15/97) • **84**

COOK, R & J | CALIFORNIA

Delta Clarksburg Red Table Wine NV • $3 • (11/15/87) • **75**

Merlot Clarksburg 1989 • $9 • (05/31/92) • **82**

Petite Sirah Clarksburg 1984 • $6 • (12/31/87) • **73**

Petite Sirah Clarksburg 1981 • $5 • (12/16/84) • **86**

COOPER MOUNTAIN | OREGON

Brut Willamette Valley Cuvée Tradition 1990: Light, crisp, lean and a little spicy. A racy style with a nice toasty edge to the lemony flavors. 230 cases made. • $20 • (02/28/97) • **86**

Chardonnay Willamette Valley 1995: Earthy mineral notes add gentle nuances to the basic pineapple and pear flavors in this lean, tasty Chardonnay that echoes fruit on the smooth finish. 730 cases made. • $12 • (07/31/97) • **89**

Chardonnay Willamette Valley 1994: Fresh and spicy, with a strong toasty note to the core of honey-scented citrus flavors; lean and almost racy. Nicely balanced. Drink now. 650 cases made. • $11 • (02/28/97) • **87**

Chardonnay Willamette Valley 1993 • $13 • (03/31/96) • **85**

Chardonnay Willamette Valley Farmhouse Reserve 1994: Subtle, supple and polished, with lots of caramel, honey and spice notes weaving between the pear and citrus flavors. Ready now. 25 cases made. • $25 • (02/28/97) • **88**

Chardonnay Willamette Valley Meadowlark Reserve 1994: Bright and refreshing, a zingy wine with some refining spice and honey notes to the citrusy pear flavors. Ready now. 25 cases made. • $25 • (02/28/97) • **87**

Chardonnay Willamette Valley Reserve 1994: Crisp and tangy, a zesty wine with citrusy pear flavors and a delicate overlay of spicy oak. Ready now. 90 cases made. • $20 • (02/28/97) • **86**

Pinot Gris Willamette Valley 1997: Fresh and appealing for its pure peach and almond flavors, which charm regardless of the slightly coarse texture. Drink now. 2,250 cases made. • $15 • (07/31/98) • **86**

Pinot Gris Willamette Valley 1996: Fresh and appealing for its melon and spice flavors, hinting at almond on the soft finish. Ready to drink. 3,000 cases made. • $12 • (07/31/97) • **86**

Pinot Gris Willamette Valley 1995: Smooth and ripe. Appealing pear and almond flavors remain fresh through the spicy finish. Ready now. 2,200 cases made. • $12 • (02/28/97) • **87**

Pinot Gris Willamette Valley 1994 • $12 • (01/31/96) • **86**

Pinot Gris Willamette Valley Old Vines Reserve 1994 • $15 • (01/31/96) • **82**

Pinot Noir Willamette Valley 1996: Light in texture and flavor, with pretty cherry notes hovering around a soft core of currant and spice. Drink now through 2000. 3,000 cases made. • $15 • (07/31/98) • **85**

Pinot Noir Willamette Valley 1995: Has a riper flavor than most 1995s, against a crisp background of racy acidity. Polished and almost sweet, with berry flavors on the finish. Lovely. Drink now. 1,000 cases made. • $13 • (07/31/97) • **87**

Pinot Noir Willamette Valley 1994: Earthy tobacco notes add extra interest to this smooth-textured wine, nicely fragrant with notes of berry and anise. Drinkable now. 980 cases made. • $15 • (02/28/97) • **85**
Pinot Noir Willamette Valley 1993 • $13 • (01/31/96) • **83**
Pinot Noir Willamette Valley 1990 • $14 • (02/28/93) • **76**
Pinot Noir Willamette Valley 1988 • $13 • (04/15/91) • **83**
Pinot Noir Willamette Valley 1987 • $13 • (02/15/90) • **87**
Pinot Noir Willamette Valley Reserve 1995: Bright and focused, a crisp wine with a nice bead of ripe black cherry and tobacco flavor that echoes on the polished finish. Ready to drink. 340 cases made. • $25 • (07/31/97) • **88**
Pinot Noir Willamette Valley Reserve 1994: Tightly wound, firm and spicy, packing its narrow frame with prune, blackberry and clove flavors that linger on the hard-edged finish. Try now. 300 cases made. • $30 • (02/28/97) • **86**
Pinot Noir Willamette Valley Reserve 1993 • $19 • (01/31/96) • **85**
Pinot Noir Willamette Valley Reserve 1990 • $20 • (02/28/93) • **76**
Pinot Noir Willamette Valley Reserve 1988 • $20 • (04/15/91) • **83**
White Pinot Noir Willamette Valley 1996: A pretty rosé in color, aroma and flavor, offering delicate strawberry, raspberry and spice notes, finishing dry and fresh. 320 cases made. • $7 • (08/31/97) • **87**

COOPER-GARROD | CALIFORNIA

Cabernet Franc Santa Cruz Mountains 1995: Herbal flavors thread their way through the modest strawberry and rhubarb flavors in this soft-textured, light-ish red. Drinkable now. 850 cases made. • $18 • (11/30/97) • **81**
Cabernet Franc Santa Cruz Mountains 1994 • $18 • (04/30/96) • **77**
Cabernet Franc Santa Cruz Mountains Premier Release 1992 • $16 • (02/28/95) • **80**
Cabernet Sauvignon Santa Cruz Mountains 1994: Marked by charry, black currant, tar and licorice aromas and flavors. The finish features a surprising black cherry core. Despite a few rough edges, it's different and enjoyable. 785 cases made. • $25 • (11/30/97) • **87**
Cabernet Sauvignon Santa Cruz Mountains 1992 • $20 • (03/31/96) • **82**
Cabernet Sauvignon Santa Cruz Mountains Proprietor's Reserve 1993: Distinct for its spicy, peppery accent. The core of currant, cedar, anise and toasty oak flavors are supple and well-focused and the finish turns complex, with just the right dose of tannin. Drinks well now or can be cellared. 208 cases made. • $35 • (11/30/96) • **88**
Chardonnay Santa Cruz Mountains 1996: On solid ground, with traces of mineral and earth working their way into the pear and citrus notes. Finishes with a leafy edge. Drink now through 2000. 860 cases made. • $20 • (07/31/98) • **85**
Chardonnay Santa Cruz Mountains 1995: A bit rustic with its earthy overtones and hints of cedar, it gains in palatability as ripe pear and spicy apple flavors fold in. 825 cases made. • $20 • (07/31/97) • **87**
Chardonnay Santa Cruz Mountains 1994: Strives for complexity with its layers of flavor. Serves up a rich core of pear, apple and oak flavors. Finishes with a long aftertaste. 770 cases made. • $18 • (02/29/96) • **89**

COOPERS' LEGACY | CALIFORNIA

Chardonnay Sonoma County 1993 • $9 • (07/31/95) • **82**
Merlot Sonoma County 1993: Dry and chunky, with hints of currant and berry flavors. Finish is tannic and slightly green. 909 cases made. • $12 • (08/31/96) • **79**

CORBETT CANYON | CALIFORNIA

Cabernet Sauvignon Alexander Valley Reserve 1989 • $8 • (11/15/92) BB • **85**
Cabernet Sauvignon California Coastal Classic 1994: In a simple style, offering a trim band of cherry and currant flavors. 15,000 cases made. • $6 • (11/30/96) • **75**
Cabernet Sauvignon California Coastal Classic 1991 • $6 • (06/15/93) • **80**
Cabernet Sauvignon California Coastal Classic 1989 • $7 • (11/15/91) • **76**
Cabernet Sauvignon Central Coast 1983 • $7 • (05/16/86) BB • **80**
Cabernet Sauvignon Central Coast Coastal Classic 1986 • $6/liter • (12/15/89) • **80**
Cabernet Sauvignon Central Coast Reserve 1987 • $9 • (11/15/91) • **82**
Cabernet Sauvignon Central Coast Select 1984 • $8 • (02/15/87) • **82**
Cabernet Sauvignon Napa County Reserve 1994: Supple and fruity, this has just enough plum and cherry flavor to hold your interest. 4,000 cases made. • $9 • (11/30/96) • **82**
Cabernet Sauvignon Napa Valley Reserve 1991 • $9 • (09/30/94) • **82**
Cabernet Sauvignon Napa Valley Reserve 1990 • $9 • (09/15/93) BB • **84**
Cabernet Sauvignon Santa Barbara-San Luis Obispo Counties Select 1985 • $10 • (05/31/88) • **79**
Cabernet Sauvignon Sonoma-Napa Counties Reserve 1989 • $8 • (11/15/92) • **74**
Chardonnay California Coastal Classic 1995: Light and refreshing for its youthful grapefruit and pineapple flavors. 40,000 cases made. • $6 • (06/15/96) • **82**
Chardonnay California Coastal Classic 1994: Extremely floral, with a sour edge to the grapey flavors. • $5 • (07/31/96) • **77**
Chardonnay Central Coast Coastal Classic 1993 • $5 • (01/31/95) • **80**
Chardonnay Santa Barbara County Reserve 1994: Heavily floral, weedy flavors dominate this wine. 4,000 cases made. • $9 • (07/31/96) • **73**
Chardonnay Santa Barbara County Reserve 1993 • $9 • (01/31/95) • **81**
Merlot California Coastal Classic 1994: Sneaks up on you with a sour, decadent aftertaste that doesn't quit. 15,000 cases made. • $7 • (07/31/96) • **71**
Merlot California Coastal Classic 1992 • $7 • (09/15/94) BB • **82**
Merlot California Coastal Classic 1991 • $6 • (11/30/92) • **79**
Merlot California Coastal Classic 1989 • $7 • (11/15/91) BB • **81**
Merlot California Reserve 1994: Smells muddy and tastes thin and earthy. Not pleasant. 10,000 cases made. • $9 • (07/31/96) • **73**
Pinot Noir Central Coast Reserve 1989 • $9 • (11/15/91) • **81**
Pinot Noir Central Coast Reserve 1986 • $8 • (12/15/89) • **83**
Pinot Noir Santa Barbara County Coastal Classic 1990 • $7/liter • (02/28/93) • **71**
Pinot Noir Santa Barbara County Reserve 1992 • $9 • (03/31/95) • **82**
Pinot Noir Santa Barbara County Reserve 1991 • $9 • (02/28/93) • **72**
Pinot Noir Santa Barbara County Reserve 1990 • $8 • (02/28/93) • **73**
Pinot Noir Santa Maria Valley Sierra Madre Vineyard Reserve 1985 • $12 • (02/15/88) • **81**
Sauvignon Blanc California Coastal Classic 1995: Earthy, cardboardy flavors are unpleasant. • $5 • (09/15/96) • **74**
Sauvignon Blanc Central Coast Costal Classic 1994 • $5 • (08/31/95) • **77**
Zinfandel California Coastal Classic 1996: Simple and diluted with straightforward strawberry and herb flavors. Awkward, slightly sour notes mark the finish. Drink now. 15,000 cases made. • $5 • (06/15/98) • **78**
Zinfandel San Luis Obispo County Select 1984 • $7 • (05/15/88) • **87**

COREY CREEK | NEW YORK

Chardonnay North Fork of Long Island 1994: Assertive yet elegant, this is a dry, clean marriage of crisp lemony acidity, light smoke and mineral flavors. It's understated, but well defined. 1,385 cases made. • $13 • (12/31/96) • **87**
Chardonnay North Fork of Long Island Reserve 1994: Bright and fresh. Vanilla aromas follow through to the palate, with light apple and pear flavors and a hint of spice. It's balanced and has enough body to be matched with food. 296 cases made. • $16 • (12/31/96) • **85**
Merlot North Fork of Long Island 1994: Well made, this shows concentration and intensity yet retains balance. The plum, black chocolate and light herbal flavors are focused and ripe, backed by firm tannins. Drinkable now. 361 cases made. • $17 • (12/31/96) • **88**

CORISON | CALIFORNIA

Cabernet Sauvignon Napa Valley 1994: Young and tight, a bit closed, but enough plum and blackberry flavors peek through to show promise. Lacks the depth and concentration of the best '94s. Drink now or cellar into 1999. 3,000 cases made. • $35 • (09/30/97) • **87**
Cabernet Sauvignon Napa Valley 1993: Elegant, striking a nice balance between smoky, toasty oak shadings and a ripe core of cherry and berry flavors. Finishing with mild tannins, this medium weight wine is appealing to drink now through 2001. 2,700 cases made. • $30 • (10/15/96) • **87**
Cabernet Sauvignon Napa Valley 1992 • $28 • (11/30/95) CS • **92**
Cabernet Sauvignon Napa Valley 1991 • $26 • (10/15/94) • **89**
Cabernet Sauvignon Napa Valley 1990 • $24 • (10/15/93) HR • **91**
Cabernet Sauvignon Napa Valley 1989 • $26 • (11/15/92) • **88**
Cabernet Sauvignon Napa Valley 1988 • $25 • (11/15/91) • **89**
Cabernet Sauvignon Napa Valley 1987 • $41 • (11/15/90) • **92**
Cabernet Sauvignon Napa Valley 1987: Has a ripe, intense and fruity nose, but it's dry and tannic on the palate. The core of cherry- and currant-laced

Key: SS—Spectator Selection CS—Cellar Selection HR—Highly Recommended BB—Best Buy $NA—Price not available Ⓐ—Auction Price (BT)—Barrel Tasting
Dates in parentheses indicate the issues in which the ratings were published.

Cabernet flavor is vibrant and lively, but the dry finish is cause for concern. Best now through 2002. • $41 • (12/15/97) • **89**

CORNERSTONE | CALIFORNIA

Cabernet Sauvignon Howell Mountain Beatty Ranch 1994: Dense and chewy, with firm, earthy tannins and a cedary oak accent to the currant and cherry notes. Picks up a tarry flavor on the finish before the tannins weigh in. There's a lot to like in this wine. Best to cellar into 2001. 750 cases made. • $35 • (10/31/97) • **93**
Cabernet Sauvignon Howell Mountain Beatty Ranch 1993: Smooth and polished, a rich and complex young red boasting tiers of spicy currant, cherry, toasty oak and cedar notes that fan out on the finish. Has major-league tannins, so cellaring into 2000 is advised. 850 cases made. • $33 • (04/30/96) • **93**
Cabernet Sauvignon Howell Mountain Beatty Ranch 1992 • $33 • (12/15/95) • **90**
Cabernet Sauvignon Howell Mountain Beatty Ranch 1991 • $33 • (11/15/94) HR • **93**
Zinfandel Howell Mountain Beatty Ranch 1994: Tight, firm and intense, with a complex core of earth, herb and raspberry flavors that picks up more sage and spice on the finish. Try now, or cellar into 1999. 250 cases made. • $20 • (02/28/97) • **91**
Zinfandel Howell Mountain Cuvée Mysterieuses 1994: Firm, intense and beautifully focused, with tiers of black cherry, herb, spice and light, toasty oak. All the flavors fold together nicely and fan out on a long, lingering finish. Delicious. Has enough tannin to merit short-term cellaring, but don't wait too long—you might miss the fruit. 250 cases made. • $20 • (02/28/97) • **91**

COSENTINO | CALIFORNIA

Cabernet Franc Napa County 1987 • $13 • (09/30/89) • **75**
Cabernet Franc North Coast 1990 • $16 • (11/15/92) • **83**
Cabernet Franc North Coast 1989 • $16 • (11/15/92) • **78**
Cabernet Franc North Coast 1988 • $16 • (11/15/91) • **80**
Cabernet Franc North Coast 1986 • $14 • (07/31/88) • **92**
Cabernet Sauvignon Napa County 1990 • $15 • (11/15/93) • **81**
Cabernet Sauvignon Napa County 1989 • $15 • (03/31/92) • **86**
Cabernet Sauvignon Napa Valley 1993: Of medium weight and well proportioned, with a nice core of currant, cedar, anise and herb flavors. Drinks well now. 2,300 cases made. • $15 • (08/31/96) • **84**
Cabernet Sauvignon Napa Valley 1991 • $16 • (10/31/94) • **86**
Cabernet Sauvignon Napa Valley 1990 • $15 • (11/15/93) • **86**
Cabernet Sauvignon Napa Valley Punched Cap Fermented Unfined 1992 • $16 • (09/15/95) • **88**
Cabernet Sauvignon Napa Valley Reserve 1994: Supple and harmonious, elegant in style, with spicy currant and wild berry flavors that fan out. Builds in intensity and reveals more flavor facets on the finish, with supple tannins. 400 cases made. • $40 • (10/15/97) • **89**
Cabernet Sauvignon Napa Valley Reserve 1993: Packs in lots of ripe, rich, complex flavors, with black cherry, plum and currant the prominent fruit components. Hints of anise, cedar and spice add dimension, and even though the tannins are firm, the texture is supple. Try now. 240 cases made. • $35 • (11/15/96) • **91**
Cabernet Sauvignon Napa Valley Reserve 1991 • $30 • (12/15/95) • **90**
Cabernet Sauvignon Napa Valley Reserve 1990 • $25 • (11/15/94) • **87**
Cabernet Sauvignon Napa Valley The Winemaster 1989 • $20 • (11/15/92) • **80**
Cabernet Sauvignon North Coast 1988 • $15 • (05/31/91) • **88**
Cabernet Sauvignon North Coast 1987 • $16 • (06/30/90) • **80**
Cabernet Sauvignon North Coast 1985 • $11 • (09/15/88) • **84**
Cabernet Sauvignon North Coast Reserve 1988 • $25 • (08/31/92) • **81**
Cabernet Sauvignon North Coast Reserve 1987 • $28 • (02/28/91) • **86**
Cabernet Sauvignon North Coast Reserve 1986 • $18 • (05/15/90) • **90**
Cabernet Sauvignon North Coast Reserve 1985 • $18 • (04/30/89) • **81**
Cabernet Sauvignon North Coast Reserve 1984 • $14 • (03/31/88) • **78**
Chardonnay Napa County 1996: Clean and simple, with modest pear, citrus and hazelnut flavors that gently unfold on the finish. Drink now through 2000. 1,500 cases made. • $18 • (05/15/98) • **87**
Chardonnay Napa County 1995: A heavy-handed style, earthy, with leesy flavors that turn woody on the finish. Hints at Chardonnay flavors, amidst the funkiness. 2,200 cases made. • $16 • (05/15/97) • **84**
Chardonnay Napa Valley 1994: Strikes a nice balance between the ripe pear, citrus and honey notes and the light oak flavors. 2,600 cases made. • $14 • (06/30/96) • **85**
Chardonnay Napa Valley 1993 • $15 • (07/31/95) • **83**
Chardonnay Napa Valley The Sculptor Reserve 1996: Ripe and generous, with pear, spice, floral and fig flavors, turning elegant on the finish where the flavors are earthy and concentrated. Drink now through 2001. 700 cases made. • $30 • (05/15/98) • **90**
Chardonnay Napa Valley The Sculptor Reserve 1995: A subtle style, with understated pear, spice, melon and fig notes. Turns smooth and silky on the finish, where the flavors spread out and linger. Delicious. Drink now. 900 cases made. • $26 • (05/15/97) • **91**
Chardonnay Napa Valley The Sculptor Reserve 1994: Delivers nice oak and ripe fruit flavors that aim for complexity, but comes up just a bit short. 1,050 cases made. • $25 • (06/30/96) • **85**
Chardonnay Napa Valley The Sculptor Reserve 1993 • $24 • (02/28/95) • **86**
Gewürztraminer Napa Valley 1996: Softly sweet, with silky pear and spice flavors that persist on the supple finish. 500 cases made. • $14 • (11/30/97) • **85**
Gewürztraminer Napa Valley 1995: Soft, almost sweet, with honey and spice flavors that make it appealing to drink now. • $12 • (10/15/96) • **84**
Il Chiaretto Classico Napa County 1994: Light in color, but with plenty of zesty ripe cherry, strawberry and plum flavors that turn elegant and spicy on the finish. A distinctive style of Sangiovese that's easy to drink and easy on the pocketbook. 1,200 cases made. • $12 • (11/30/96) • **86**
M. Coz Napa Valley Meritage 1996: Clean, ripe and focused, an understated style with pretty currant and plum notes. Relies on balance and finesse. 400 cases made. • $NA • (06/15/97) (BT) • **90-94**
M. Coz Napa Valley Meritage 1994: Young, tight and tannic, with a rich, dense core of mineral, tar, currant, plum and spice that slowly unfolds and fans out, revealing more dimension and complexity on the finish. Best to cellar into 2000 to 2001. A blend of 48 percent Cabernet Sauvignon, 26 percent Merlot, 21 percent Cabernet Franc, and 5 percent Petit Verdot. 460 cases made. • $60 • (11/15/97) • **91**
M. Coz Napa Valley Meritage 1993: A big, ripe and intense style, with firm, crisp tannins. The ripe currant, coffee and cedary flavors balance it out, giving a sense of proportion. Best to cellar beyond 2000. 400 cases made. • $45 • (11/15/96) • **88**
M. Coz Napa Valley Meritage 1992 • $45 • (12/15/95) • **92**
M. Coz Napa Valley Meritage 1991 • $45 • (11/15/94) • **89**
M. Coz Napa Valley Meritage 1990 • $45 • (11/15/93) • **92**
M. Coz Napa Valley Meritage 1989 • $45 • (11/15/92) • **90**
M. Coz Napa Valley Meritage 1988 • $45 • (11/15/91) • **89**
Merlot Napa County 1988 • $18 • (04/15/91) • **82**
Merlot Napa County 1986 • $14 • (09/30/88) • **85**
Merlot Napa County Reserve 1987 • $18 • (07/31/90) • **80**
Merlot Napa Valley 1994: A wine with a sense of harmony and finesse. Although a touch earthy, it comes together nicely on the palate, offering an array of flavors: ripe cherry, currant and mineral, framed by spicy, toasty oak. 1,800 cases made. • $24 • (07/31/96) • **87**
Merlot Napa Valley 1992 • $19 • (09/15/94) • **88**
Merlot Napa Valley 1991 • $18 • (09/15/94) • **77**
Merlot Napa Valley 1990 • $18 • (06/15/93) • **84**
Merlot Napa Valley Oakville 1995: A well-oaked but richly flavored wine, with layers of ripe cherry and currant framed by vanilla and light, toasty oak flavors. The texture is smooth and polished, making it tempting to drink now. 450 cases made. • $50 • (07/31/97) • **92**
Merlot Napa Valley Oakville 1994 • $38 • (06/30/96) • **87**
Merlot Napa Valley Oakville 1993 • $30 • (12/15/95) • **89**
Merlot Napa Valley Oakville 1992 • $28 • (09/15/94) • **89**
Merlot Napa Valley Reserve 1994: A smooth, complex and seductive style, with lavish oak flavors and a silky texture that let the currant, herb and anise flavors flow. Drinkable now but should age well too, so you win on both counts. 250 cases made. • $34 • (06/30/97) • **91**
Pinot Noir Carneros 1996: Light and fragrant, with modest cherry, spice and floral aromas hidden behind the tea leaf. Simple and uncomplicated, except for its price given the quality. Finishes with crisp tannins. 650 cases made. • $30 • (02/28/98) • **84**
Pinot Noir Carneros 1994 • $25 • (02/29/96) • **84**
Pinot Noir Carneros 1991 • $18 • (02/28/94) • **82**
Pinot Noir Carneros Unfined & Unfiltered 1993 • $25 • (03/31/95) • **84**
Pinot Noir Carneros Unfined & Unfiltered 1992 • $20 • (02/28/94) • **89**
Pinot Noir Napa Valley 1995: Smooth and harmonious. Shows a pleasing array of ripe cherry, plum, anise, smoke and light, toasty oak flavors, turning complex on the finish as the flavors come together. Drink now. 550 cases made. • $25 • (12/31/96) • **89**
Pinot Noir Napa Valley 1990 • $14 • (09/30/92) • **83**
Pinot Noir Napa Valley LZ 1994 • $20 • (02/29/96) • **87**

Pinot Noir Napa Valley Punched Cap Fermented Unfiltered & Unfined 1993 • $25 • (05/15/95) • **86**
Pinot Noir Napa Valley Unfined & Unfiltered 1993 • $18 • (03/31/95) • **83**
Pinot Noir Russian River Valley 1996: Pleasantly balanced, with supple, elegant, dried cherry, spice, plum and smoky oak flavors that glide across the palate, finishing with plush tannins. Drink now to 2000. 200 cases made. • $50 • (02/28/98) • **89**
Pinot Noir Russian River Valley 1994: Smooth-textured range of smoky cherry, herb, cola and mushroom flavors. Finish is complex, with fine tannins. Drink now. 500 cases made. • $38 • (08/31/96) • **88**
Pinot Noir Sonoma County 1990 • $18 • (09/30/92) • **83**
Pinot Noir Sonoma County 1989 • $13 • (06/30/91) • **82**
Rosé California Tenero Rosa 1995: Its lighter style highlights its spicy watermelon and strawberry flavors. 800 cases made. • $8 • (11/30/96) • **83**
The Novelist California Meritage 1996: A nice blend of grapefruit, lemon, melon, celery and grass notes, finishing bright and clean. Refreshing. 85 percent Sauvignon Blanc, 15 percent Sémillon. 1,800 cases made. • $16 • (07/31/97) • **87**
The Novelist Napa Valley Meritage 1995: Classy, rich and distinctive. Nice balance of earthy, citrusy pear and herbal flavors, and a nice note of greengage plum on the finish. 1,300 cases made. • $14 • (08/31/96) • **87**
The Novelist Napa Valley Meritage 1994 • $15 • (12/31/95) • **88**
The Poet California Meritage 1990 • $23 • (05/15/95) • **86**
The Poet California Meritage 1989 • $25 • (11/15/93) • **79**
The Poet California Meritage 1988 • $27 • (05/31/91) • **85**
The Poet California Meritage 1987 • $25 • (09/15/90) • **85**
The Poet California Meritage 1986 • $22 • (07/31/89) • **86**
The Poet California Meritage 1985 • $18 • (08/31/88) • **79**
The Poet Napa Valley Meritage 1994: Dark, ripe and concentrated, with a core of earthy currant, cedar, spice and tar, with hints of vanilla and chocolate folding in on the finish. Needs short-term cellaring to soften and evolve. Best around 2000 to 2001. A blend of 67 percent Cabernet Sauvignon, 20 percent Cabernet Franc, 11 percent Merlot, and 2 percent Petit Verdot. 1,100 cases made. • $30 • (11/15/97) • **89**
The Poet Napa Valley Meritage 1993: Ripe, complex and flavorful, with tiers of ripe cherry, currant, plum and anise flavors and just-right doses of oak and tannin. Shows a sense of harmony and balance, with a long, full aftertaste. 900 cases made. • $26 • (11/15/96) • **91**
The Poet Napa Valley Meritage 1992 • $24 • (12/15/95) • **87**
Zinfandel California Cigarzin 1996: Ripe and pleasing, if on the lighter side, with ripe cherry, strawberry, wild berry and spice. Ready to drink. 1,250 cases made. • $16 • (03/31/98) • **86**
Zinfandel California The Zin 1995: Hits most of the right notes with its zesty plum, cherry, wild berry and spicy nuances, and turns elegant on the finish. Ready now. 1,800 cases made. • $23 • (03/31/97) • **88**
Zinfandel Napa County-Sonoma County The Zin 1994 • $21 • (04/30/96) • **90**
Zinfandel Russian River Valley The Zin 1991 • $15 • (12/31/92) • **89**
Zinfandel Sonoma County The Zin 1992 • $16 • (07/31/94) • **88**
Zinfandel Sonoma County The Zin 1990 • $15 • (10/15/92) • **88**
Zinfandel Sonoma County The Zin Unfined & Unfiltered 1993 • $18 • (09/15/95) • **87**

COTES DE SONOMA | CALIFORNIA

Cabernet Sauvignon Sonoma County 1993: Earthy, with a mature color and flavors, dried fruit and a decadent edge. Spicy currant and cherry flavors hold it together. • $8 • (12/15/95) • **83**
Cabernet Sauvignon Sonoma County 1990 • $6 • (10/31/92) BB • **83**
Cabernet Sauvignon Sonoma County 1989 • $7 • (11/15/91) BB • **83**
Chardonnay Sonoma County 1995: Emphasizes fruit, with green apple and green plum flavors and a lively, almost Muscat-like personality. 9,000 cases made. • $9 • (06/15/96) • **84**
Chardonnay Sonoma County 1994: Lean and crisp, showing plenty of floral, citrus and apple flavors that remain vibrant on the finish. A Chardonnay that still delivers some charm without charging a premium. 10,000 cases made. • $8 • (10/15/95) BB • **86**
Chardonnay Sonoma County 1993 • $8 • (04/15/95) • **84**
Deux Cépages Sonoma County 1990 • $6 • (11/15/91) • **73**
Sauvignon Blanc Sonoma County 1995 • $9 • (06/15/96) • **86**
Sauvignon Blanc Sonoma County 1994 • $7 • (08/31/95) • **83**
Sauvignon Blanc Sonoma County 1993 • $7 • (11/30/94) BB • **85**

Key: SS—Spectator Selection CS—Cellar Selection HR—Highly Recommended BB—Best Buy $NA—Price not available Ⓐ—Auction Price (BT)—Barrel Tasting
Dates in parentheses indicate the issues in which the ratings were published.

COTTONWOOD CANYON | CALIFORNIA

Merlot Central Coast 1995: Medium-weight in concentration and flavor, with hints of plum and strawberry. Tries to compensate with lots of toasty, spicy oak and to some extent succeeds. 286 cases made. • $26 • (05/15/98) • **85**
Merlot Central Coast 1994: Ripe, rich, and smooth, this is a supple wine, packed with blackberry, cassis, plum and smoky oak flavors. Finishes with length and brightness. Elegant. 300 cases made. • $25 • (07/31/97) • **90**
Pinot Noir Santa Barbara County 1991: Tart, with an earthy, vegetal accent to its cherry, rhubarb, celery and spice qualities. An eccentric style that will appeal to some. 364 cases made. • $29 • (02/28/97) • **80**
Pinot Noir Santa Barbara County 1990 • $20 • (02/28/94) • **79**
Pinot Noir Santa Barbara County 1989 • $25 • (02/28/93) • **88**
Pinot Noir Santa Barbara County Barrel Select 1991 • $38 • (12/31/95) • **87**
Pinot Noir Santa Barbara County Barrel Select 1989 • $25 • (02/28/93) • **82**

COTURRI | CALIFORNIA

Merlot Sonoma Mountain 1994: A curious wine that has a vinegary edge to its earthy, nutty and currant flavors. Finishes with chewy tannins. For a walk on the wild side. 200 cases made. • $22 • (07/31/96) • **78**
Zinfandel Sonoma Mountain 1994: Big, ripe and juicy. Packs in lots of spicy berry, cherry, anise and cedary oak flavors with a brambly, gamy accent. Well-balanced, even with its high alcohol level. 350 cases made. • $18 • (09/15/96) • **88**
Zinfandel Sonoma Valley Chauvet Vineyards 1990 • $17 • (10/15/92) • **83**

COULSON | CALIFORNIA

Chardonnay El Dorado Reserve 1996: Starts with delicate, lemony freshness and ripe apple flavors, but finishes with a yeasty note. Drink now. 260 cases made. • $13 • (07/31/98) • **82**

COVEY RUN | WASHINGTON

Cabernet Sauvignon Columbia Valley 1995: Solid, if slightly burnt in flavor, with a smoky cherry and herbal character that echoes on the chewy finish. Best from 1999. 5,300 cases made. • $13 • (09/15/97) • **85**
Cabernet Sauvignon Columbia Valley 1993: A gamy and earthy style, with supple black cherry flavors under a blanket of chewy tannins and a tenacious note of clove. Unusual. Try now. 2,500 cases made. • $12 • (09/15/96) • **85**
Cabernet Sauvignon Yakima Valley 1993: Light and fruity, but dark in flavor, with more black cherry and blackberry than anything. Drinkable now. 2,100 cases made. • $7 • (09/30/94) • **80**
Cabernet Sauvignon Yakima Valley 1992 • $11 • (03/31/95) • **84**
Cabernet Sauvignon Yakima Valley 1990 • $9 • (03/15/94) • **78**
Cabernet Sauvignon Yakima Valley 1989 • $12 • (03/15/93) • **78**
Cabernet Sauvignon Yakima Valley 1988 • $11 • (04/30/92) • **85**
Cabernet Sauvignon Yakima Valley 1986 • $10 • (10/15/89) • **80**
Cabernet Sauvignon Yakima Valley Whiskey Canyon 1993: Has an earthy, gamy streak running through ripe cherry flavors, making for an unusual wine that needs until 2000 to 2003 to settle down. 725 cases made. • $23 • (04/30/97) • **84**
Cabernet Sauvignon Yakima Valley Whiskey Canyon 1992 • $20 • (09/30/95) • **79**
Cabernet Sauvignon Yakima Valley Whiskey Canyon 1991 • $20 • (09/30/95) • **85**
Cabernet-Merlot Washington 1995: Crisp in texture, with pretty blackberry and currant flavors on a modest frame. Drink now through 1999. A blend of 54 percent Cabernet Sauvignon, 24 percent Merlot, and 22 percent Cabernet Franc. 3,000 cases made. • $11 • (04/30/97) • **84**
Chardonnay Columbia Valley 1995: Fresh and simple, with a nice floral and citrus nuance to the flavors. 24,000 cases made. • $11 • (04/30/97) • **81**
Chardonnay Columbia Valley 1994: Light in texture, with resinous, earthy overtones that muscle past the delicate apple and nectarine flavors. Drink now. 7,000 cases made. • $11 • (09/15/96) • **86**
Chardonnay Washington 1996: Has ripeness, but also a layer of earthy flavors that keeps it from being as charming as it could be. Drink now. 10,000 cases made. • $10 • (06/15/98) • **82**
Chardonnay Washington Celilo Vineyard 1995: Spicy, stylish and silky, with very pretty layers of citrus, pear, vanilla and toast flavors plus an exotic patina of Oriental spices and slightly bitter floral notes that linger on the finish. Drinkable now. 350 cases made. • $25 • (09/30/97) • **87**

Chardonnay Washington Celilo Vineyard 1994: Beautifully balanced, harmonious and polished, showing off its elegant, seemingly endless bounty of pear, nectarine, honey and loquat flavors with remarkable grace. Try now. Tasted twice, with consistent notes. 600 cases made. • $20 • (09/30/96) HR • **92**

Chardonnay Yakima Valley 1993 • $10 • (04/15/95) • **74**

Chardonnay Yakima Valley Reserve 1995: Oak character stands out now, putting a rough, woody edge on the basic pear flavors. Feels clumsy. 4,500 cases made. • $17 • (09/15/97) • **80**

Chardonnay Yakima Valley Reserve 1994: Smooth and polished, delivering some pretty pear and nutmeg flavors that linger through the supple finish. 2,400 cases made. • $16 • (09/15/96) • **87**

Chenin Blanc Columbia Valley 1996: Light and fresh, with delicate melon flavors. A bit coarse on the finish. 2,400 cases made. • $8 • (09/15/97) • **82**

Chenin Blanc Columbia Valley 1995: A fresh Washington white that's appealing for its sweet apricot and rhubarb flavors. A bit sugary on the finish, but a great price for what you get. 2,400 cases made. • $6 • (09/30/96) BB • **85**

Fumé Blanc Columbia Valley 1995: Odd, with medicinal smells that wrinkle our noses. 9,500 cases made. • $9 • (04/30/97) • **72**

Fumé Blanc Columbia Valley 1994: Bright and appealing for the vivid peach, pear, floral and vanilla flavors. Gains an herbal accent, particularly a hint of mint, on the polished finish. 4,200 cases made. • $8 • (09/15/96) BB • **88**

Fumé Blanc Washington 1993 • $8 • (03/31/95) BB • **88**

Gewürztraminer Washington 1994 • $7 • (09/30/95) • **78**

Gewürztraminer Washington Celilo Vineyard 1995: Brazenly aromatic. Beautifully floral and citrusy, with a pineapple note adding nice harmony to the dry finish. Has length and distinction. Ready now. 620 cases made. • $13 • (09/15/97) • **89**

Gewürztraminer Washington Celilo Vineyard 1994: A deliciously floral essence surrounds the seductive core of pear and passion fruit flavors; not sweet, but soft and generous. 350 cases made. • $10 • (09/15/96) • **88**

Gewürztraminer Yakima Valley 1993 • $7 • (09/30/94) • **82**

Johannisberg Riesling Columbia Valley 1996: Off-dry, with juicy apple and citrus flavors that are perfumy and persistent on the lively finish. Ready now. 2.6 percent residual sugar. 8,000 cases made. • $6 • (09/15/97) • **86**

Johannisberg Riesling Columbia Valley 1995: Sweet, but nicely balanced to show off the fresh nectarine and floral aromas and flavors. Finishes gently, with a hint of orange. Ready to drink. 10,000 cases made. • $6 • (09/15/96) • **85**

Johannisberg Riesling Yakima Valley 1994 • $7 • (09/30/95) • **83**

Merlot Yakima Valley 1993 • $11 • (05/31/95) • **83**

Merlot Yakima Valley 1992 • $11 • (05/15/94) • **74**

Merlot Yakima Valley 1990 • $12 • (01/31/93) • **82**

Merlot Yakima Valley 1989 • $11 • (06/15/92) • **79**

Merlot Yakima Valley 1988 • $10 • (03/31/91) • **87**

Merlot Yakima Valley 1986 • $9 • (10/15/89) • **82**

Merlot Yakima Valley 1985 • $9 • (04/15/89) • **85**

Merlot Yakima Valley 1984 • $8 • (11/15/87) • **82**

Merlot Yakima Valley Reserve 1994: Lean, austerely styled, with modest berry and earth flavors turning tight and a bit hard on the finish. Hints at chocolate; might be worth trying in 2000. 750 cases made. • $23 • (04/30/97) • **82**

Merlot Yakima Valley Reserve 1993 • $15 • (09/30/95) • **80**

Merlot Yakima Valley Reserve 1989 • $17 • (03/31/92) • **83**

Merlot-Cabernet Columbia Valley 1994: Tangy and bright with tart blackberry and spice flavors, but it has some generosity to soften the zingy acidity. Should complement rich food. A blend of 57 percent Merlot, 33 percent Cabernet Sauvignon and 10 percent Cabernet Franc. 3,600 cases made. • $10 • (09/15/96) • **86**

Muscat Columbia Valley Morio-Muskat 1995: Sweet but a little flat, this shows some nice spice flavors, but finishes simply. 2,000 cases made. • $6 • (09/30/96) • **82**

Muscat Yakima Valley Morio-Muskat 1994 • $7 • (09/30/95) • **81**

Muscat Yakima Valley Morio-Muskat 1993 • $7 • (09/30/94) • **70**

Riesling Columbia Valley Dry 1996: Light, bright and zingy, its citrus and peach flavors picking up hints of green apple on the harmonious finish. Not dry, not sweet either, it's a well-balanced mouthful at an enticing price. 3,000 cases made. • $6 • (09/15/97) BB • **88**

Riesling Columbia Valley Dry 1995: An odd mix of earthy, dusky, floral flavors dominate the fruit in this off-dry wine. 1.9 percent residual sugar. 1,700 cases made. • $7 • (09/15/96) • **79**

Riesling Columbia Valley Dry 1994 • $7 • (09/30/95) • **83**

Riesling Yakima Valley Dry 1993 • $7 • (09/30/94) • **81**

Riesling Yakima Valley Ice Wine 1995: Sweet, smooth and polished, a very pretty wine save for a soapy, perfumy tinge that detracts from the fruit flavor. (18.5 percent residual sugar.) 175 cases made. • $20/375ml • (04/30/97) • **82**

Riesling Yakima Valley Ice Wine 1990 • $20 • (04/15/95) • **83**

Riesling Yakima Valley Ice Wine 1987 • $24 • (04/15/95) • **84**

Sauvignon Blanc Yakima Valley Reserve 1995: Soft and concentrated, with spicy, tobacco-scented pear flavors. Richer and chunkier than most Sauvignons. Drink now. 500 cases made. • $10 • (06/15/98) • **86**

Sémillon Columbia Valley 1994: Pleasantly middle-of-the-road; modest fruit on a modest frame with hints of orange and cream flavors on the finish. 1,100 cases made. • $8 • (09/15/96) • **82**

Sémillon Yakima Valley 1993 • $8 • (09/30/94) • **79**

Sémillon-Chardonnay Columbia Valley 1994: Earthy, mineral flavors dominate this coarse-textured wine. 2,400 cases made. • $9 • (09/15/96) • **77**

White Riesling Columbia Valley Late Harvest 1996: Sweet and silky, with simple flavors of apricot and pear that persist on the long finish. 6 percent residual sugar. 1,300 cases made. • $9 • (09/15/97) • **86**

White Riesling Columbia Valley Late Harvest 1995: Just slightly sweet, with apple and honey flavors that hold their concentration through the soft finish. 1,600 cases made. • $7 • (09/15/96) • **86**

White Riesling Late Harvest Yakima Valley 1994 • $7 • (09/15/95) BB • **91**

White Riesling Late Harvest Yakima Valley 1993 • $7 • (09/30/94) BB • **88**

White Riesling Late Harvest Yakima Valley Mahre Vineyard Botrytis 1986 • $7 • (10/15/89) • **83**

White Riesling Yakima Valley Ice Wine 1990 • $20/375ml • (09/30/94) • **90**

White Riesling Yakima Valley Ice Wine 1987 • $24/375ml • (10/15/89) • **87**

COYNE, THOMAS | CALIFORNIA

Merlot El Dorado Quartz Hill Vineyard 1990 • $12 • (06/30/93) • **84**

Merlot Sonoma County 1990 • $12 • (06/30/93) • **84**

CRAIG, ROBERT | CALIFORNIA

Affinity Napa Valley 1995: A dense and backward style, filled with complex currant and black cherry flavors with cedar, leather and spicy nuances, this red blend opens to reveal rich, seamless fruit flavors, picking up pretty oak shadings and turning complex and elegant on the finish. Contains Cabernet Sauvignon, Merlot and Cabernet Franc. Best from 2000 through 2005. 1,060 cases made. • $34 • (06/15/98) CS • **91**

Affinity Napa Valley 1994: A smooth, rich red, offering a plush mouthful of ripe black cherry, currant, anise and plum flavors, turning silky and polished on the finish, where the flavors linger long. This Cabernet blend drinks well now; can age into 2000. 870 cases made. • $28 • (08/31/97) HR • **94**

Cabernet Sauvignon Howell Mountain 1994: Remarkably elegant and understated for a Howell Mountain Cabernet, this succeeds with harmony and finesse. Displays layers of currant, anise, cedar, sage and spice, and finishes with a mineral edge and dry tannins. Best after 1999 or 2000. 790 cases made. • $28 • (11/30/97) • **90**

Cabernet Sauvignon Howell Mountain 1993: Smooth and harmonious given its youth; the dark cherry, plum, currant and cedary oak flavors turn smoky on the mineral finish. Try now. 300 cases made. • $25 • (10/15/95) • **89**

Cabernet Sauvignon Mount Veeder 1994: A striking example of how elegant and refined Mount Veeder Cabernet can be. Serves up lots of delicious fruit flavors, with elegant, supple black cherry, herb, mineral and spice, showing off a streak of anise, too. Finishes with tender tannins, making it appealing to drink now through 2005. 790 cases made. • $28 • (11/15/97) • **94**

Cabernet Sauvignon Mount Veeder 1993: Plush and harmonious, complex and well crafted, featuring currant, earth, anise and cedary oak flavors. Bold and intense, with a long, full finish. Try now. 370 cases made. • $25 • (10/15/95) • **90**

Cabernet Sauvignon Napa Valley 1992 • $20 • (10/15/95) • **87**

Cabernet Sauvignon Napa Valley Affinity 1993: Smells complex with currant and cherry flavor but turns austere, adding crisp acidity and firm tannins. Softens somewhat on the aftertaste. Drinkable now. 870 cases made. • $25 • (10/15/95) • **87**

CRANE CANYON | CALIFORNIA

Knights Valley Rosé 1994 • $13 • (09/15/95) • **86**

Mourvèdre Sonoma Valley 1993 • $18 • (08/31/95) • **86**

Zinfandel Sonoma Valley 1993 • $18 • (10/15/95) • **83**

CRESTON | CALIFORNIA

Cabernet Sauvignon Central Coast Winemaker's Selection 1985 • $17 • (12/15/89) • **75**
Cabernet Sauvignon Central Coast Winemaker's Selection 1984 • $16 • (12/15/87) • **71**
Cabernet Sauvignon Paso Robles 1993: Fairly austere at first, it ultimately opens to show flavors of cedar, spice, cherry and herbs. Finishes on the tart side. • $13 • (09/15/97) • **84**
Cabernet Sauvignon Paso Robles 1992 • $10 • (12/15/95) • **83**
Cabernet Sauvignon Paso Robles 1989 • $10 • (11/15/93) • **85**
Cabernet Sauvignon Paso Robles 1988 • $10 • (11/15/92) • **81**
Cabernet Sauvignon Paso Robles 1987 • $10 • (11/15/91) • **79**
Cabernet Sauvignon Paso Robles Winemaker's Selection 1991: Floral, cedary aromas introduce this plummy, jammy wine, balanced with mature tannins. Finishes a bit tartly. Drink now. 539 cases made. • $19 • (11/30/96) • **85**
Cabernet Sauvignon Paso Robles Winemaker's Selection 1989 • $17 • (11/15/94) • **83**
Cabernet Sauvignon Paso Robles Winemaker's Selection 1988 • $16 • (11/15/92) • **80**
Cabernet Sauvignon Paso Robles Winemaker's Selection 1987 • $16 • (11/15/91) • **82**
Cabernet Sauvignon San Luis Obispo 1990 • $10 • (11/15/94) • **81**
Chardonnay Paso Robles 1996: Pretty hazelnut and pear flavors, though there is a leesy and slightly cheesy edge that might not please everyone. Drink now. 2,696 cases made. • $13 • (07/31/98) • **83**
Chardonnay Paso Robles 1993 • $10 • (07/31/95) • **80**
Chevrier Blanc Paso Robles 1995: A modest fig and spice character struggles to show through, but is obscured by some earthy flavors. • $10 • (11/15/96) • **80**
Chevrier Blanc Paso Robles 1994 • $9 • (08/31/95) • **86**
Merlot Paso Robles 1991 • $13 • (12/31/93) • **85**
Pinot Noir Paso Robles 1994 • $10 • (01/31/96) • **82**
Pinot Noir Paso Robles 1993 • $10 • (12/31/95) • **80**
Pinot Noir Paso Robles 1992 • $9 • (01/31/94) • **83**
Pinot Noir Paso Robles 1991 • $9 • (02/28/93) • **74**
Pinot Noir Paso Robles 1990 • $8 • (11/15/91) • **70**
Pinot Noir San Luis Obispo County Petit d'Noir 1987 • $8 • (08/31/88) • **80**
Pinot Noir San Luis Obispo County Petit d'Noir Maceration Carbonique 1988 • $8 • (12/15/89) • **74**
Sauvignon Blanc Paso Robles 1995: Ripe and a bit thick in texture, but pleasant for its peach and apple flavors. 664 cases made. • $10 • (08/31/96) • **83**
Sauvignon Blanc Paso Robles 1994 • $9 • (08/31/95) • **79**
Zinfandel Paso Robles 1995: A leaner style with tart cherry notes and herbal, earthy flavors that linger on the drying finish. Drink now through 2000. 660 cases made. • $13 • (06/15/98) • **80**
Zinfandel Paso Robles 1991 • $10 • (09/30/93) • **78**
Zinfandel Paso Robles 1990 • $9 • (10/15/92) • **87**

CRICHTON HALL | CALIFORNIA

Merlot Napa Valley 1993 • $21 • (06/15/96) • **84**
Pinot Noir Napa Valley 1993 • $22 • (01/31/96) • **74**

CRISTOM | WASHINGTON

Chardonnay Columbia Valley 1994: Fresh, focused and zippy, with apricot and apple flavors that linger nicely on the harmonious finish. 249 cases made. • $17 • (06/30/96) • **89**
Chardonnay Columbia Valley 1993 • $16 • (01/31/96) • **87**
Chardonnay Columbia Valley Celilo Vineyard 1996: Quite crisp, with citrusy pear and vanilla flavors that remain fresh through the finish. Best from 1999. 234 cases made. • $20 • (05/15/98) • **86**
Chardonnay Columbia Valley Celilo Vineyard 1995: Ripe, broad and spicy, this is a mouth-filling wine with a delicate thread of spicy oak weaving through the layers of lemon, nectarine and pineapple flavors. Finishes clean and bright. Try now. 242 cases made. • $18 • (10/15/97) • **91**
Chardonnay Willamette Valley 1995: A spicy style of Chardonnay, with some nice smoke and pear flavors that remain juicy through the finish. Stylish now, best through 1999. 548 cases made. • $14 • (10/31/97) • **87**
Chardonnay Willamette Valley 1994: A solid, well-made wine that weaves spicy, slightly toasty flavors into the modest apple and citrus flavors. Drinkable now. 515 cases made. • $13 • (03/31/96) • **85**
Chardonnay Willamette Valley Germaine Vineyard 1996: Light on its feet, but ripe, with a spicy pear and honey character. Finishing light and slightly chalky. Best from 1999. 190 cases made. • $20 • (05/15/98) • **86**
Chardonnay Willamette Valley Louise Vineyard 1995: Smooth, and nicely balanced to show the delicate spice, earth and mineral nuances to the nectarine and citrus flavors. Drink now. 113 cases made. • $17 • (10/31/97) • **87**
Pinot Gris Oregon & Washington 1996: Soft and pleasant, here's a nice mouthful of citrusy green-melon flavor, finishing with a touch of mineral. Ready now. 972 cases made. • $11 • (10/31/97) • **83**
Pinot Gris Oregon & Washington 1994 • $12 • (03/31/96) • **85**
Pinot Gris Willamette Valley 1993 • $10 • (10/15/94) • **86**
Pinot Noir Willamette Valley 1993 • $17 • (01/31/96) • **83**
Pinot Noir Willamette Valley 1992 • $15 • (11/30/94) • **85**
Pinot Noir Willamette Valley Marjorie Vineyard 1995: Crisp in texture, with earthy flavors and a hint of chocolate-scented berry flavor sneaking through on the finish. Shows promise if cellared until 1999 to 2000. 432 cases made. • $27 • (10/31/97) • **85**
Pinot Noir Willamette Valley Marjorie Vineyard 1994: Showing tremendous flavor and finesse in a powerful, elegant package, this plays out its sweet currant, plum and berry flavors on a lush, velvet texture. Tannins are firm and need some time; try in 2001. • $27 • (12/15/96) • **93**
Pinot Noir Willamette Valley Mt. Jefferson Cuvée 1996: Light in color and flavor, very firm in texture, with chewy tannins covering the modest plum and woodsy flavors. Try in 2000. 1,863 cases made. • $20 • (05/15/98) • **84**
Pinot Noir Willamette Valley Mt. Jefferson Cuvée 1995: Very light color, modest flavors; hints of red berry and almond make it quaffable. Drink soon. 2,129 cases made. • $17 • (07/31/97) • **83**
Pinot Noir Willamette Valley Mt. Jefferson Cuvée 1994: Ripe and silky, a medium-weight wine with an herbal tinge to the black cherry flavors. Drinkable now. 1,179 cases made. • $17 • (07/31/96) • **84**
Pinot Noir Willamette Valley Reserve 1995: Light and clearly focused to show its pretty plum and blueberry flavors. A bit chewy, but supple and generous enough to warrant holding until 1999 or 2000 to see how it develops. 687 cases made. • $27 • (10/31/97) • **88**
Pinot Noir Willamette Valley Reserve 1994: Broad, spicy and generous, this delivers plummy, velvety richness without excessive weight, and oak flavors that sneak past the others on the finish. Having finesse and depth, it's ideal for cellaring until 1999 or 2000. • $27 • (12/15/96) • **90**
Pinot Noir Willamette Valley Reserve 1993 • $26 • (01/31/96) • **88**
Pinot Noir Willamette Valley Reserve 1992 • $24 • (11/30/94) • **83**
Viognier Willamette Valley 1996: Ripe, effusive and generous with its floral pear and grapefruit flavors, this is a wonderfully open-textured wine that charms from the first sip to the last echo of the finish. Ready now. 42 cases made. • $20 • (10/31/97) • **90**

CRONIN | CALIFORNIA

Cabernet Sauvignon Santa Cruz Mountains 1994: Marked by cedar, black olive, spice and berry notes, this wine is medium-weight, moderately rich, has pretty oak shadings. Finishes with mild tannins. Drink now through 2006. • $23 • (04/30/98) • **88**
Cabernet Sauvignon Santa Cruz Mountains 1992: Plum and cherry flavors push through an initial, rustic quality to give balance and a sense of elegance. Drinks well now with its supple tannins or can be cellared into 2000. 168 cases made. • $20 • (01/01/97) • **88**
Cabernet Sauvignon Santa Cruz Mountains 1991 • $17 • (04/30/96) • **89**
Cabernet Sauvignon Santa Cruz Mountains 1990 • $17 • (02/28/95) • **85**
Cabernet Sauvignon Santa Cruz Mountains 1989 • $17 • (03/15/94) • **88**
Cabernet Sauvignon-Merlot San Mateo County Shaw & Cronin 1986 • $15 • (02/28/91) • **88**
Cabernet Sauvignon-Merlot Santa Cruz Mountains 1988 • $17 • (03/31/93) • **83**
Cabernet Sauvignon-Merlot Santa Cruz Mountains 1987 • $17 • (03/31/92) • **84**
Cabernet Sauvignon-Merlot Stags Leap District Robinson Vineyard 1989 • $17 • (03/31/93) • **90**
Cabernet Sauvignon-Merlot Stags Leap District Robinson Vineyard 1988 • $17 • (03/31/92) • **88**

Key: SS—Spectator Selection CS—Cellar Selection HR—Highly Recommended BB—Best Buy $NA—Price not available Ⓐ—Auction Price (BT)—Barrel Tasting
Dates in parentheses indicate the issues in which the ratings were published.

Cabernet Sauvignon-Merlot Stags Leap District Robinson Vineyard 1987 • $17 • (02/28/91) • **89**

Cabernet Sauvignon-Merlot Stags Leap District Robinson Vineyard 1986 • $16 • (02/15/90) • **88**

Chardonnay Alexander Valley Stuhlmuller Vineyard 1995: Vibrant, ripe, rich and fleshy, with pretty pear, peach, spice and light oak, turning elegant, creamy and complex on the finish, where a hint of butterscotch folds in. 434 cases made. • $18 • (05/15/98) • **91**

Chardonnay Alexander Valley Stuhlmuller Vineyard 1994: Marked by a distinct peach, pear and nectarine essence, with attractive light oak shadings. Turns elegant on the finish and leaves a pretty fruit aftertaste. 406 cases made. • $18 • (09/15/96) • **87**

Chardonnay Alexander Valley Stuhlmuller Vineyard 1993 • $18 • (07/31/95) • **85**

Chardonnay Monterey County 1995: An earthy, spicy style, with lively pear, citrus and light toasty oak flavors, it shows of attractive floral aromas and lingers on the finish. Drinks well now. 196 cases made. • $16 • (05/15/98) • **88**

Chardonnay Napa Valley 1994: A touch earthy, with a tart leesy and citrus edge to the pear and spice flavors. This is lean and austere in a vintage where opulence is the rule. 182 cases made. • $20 • (09/30/96) • **82**

Chardonnay Napa Valley 1993 • $18 • (07/31/95) • **85**

Chardonnay Santa Cruz Mountains 1995: A touch earthy, it slowly becomes more complex, dominated by anise and pear-laced flavors. Tight and concentrated, it's drinkable now, but stashing a bottle or three in the cellar is a great idea. 448 cases made. • $20 • (05/15/98) • **90**

Chardonnay Santa Cruz Mountains 1994: Simple, with ripe pear and pineapple flavors; lacks the level of complexity and depth often found in Cronin Chardonnays. 658 cases made. • $20 • (09/30/96) • **82**

Chardonnay Santa Cruz Mountains 1993 • $20 • (07/31/95) • **84**

Chardonnay Santa Cruz Mountains Nancy's Cuvée 1994: Complex, with pretty aromas and a rich, silky core of peach, pear, vanilla and smoky, toasty oak flavors. Turns smooth and silky on the finish, with a long, lingering aftertaste that echoes mineral and earth notes. 114 cases made. • $27 • (06/15/97) • **92**

Concerto Robinson Vineyard Stags Leap District 1993: A light, delicate style with supple cherry and berry flavors of modest depth and concentration. Finishes with a pleasant burst of fruit and mild tannins. A blend of 50 percent Cabernet Sauvignon, 25 percent Merlot, and 25 percent Cabernet Franc. 214 cases made. • $18 • (08/31/97) • **88**

Concerto Stags Leap District Robinson Vineyard 1994: Plump, ripe and delicious, with rich, supple plum, cherry, wild berry and currant flavors, and a nice dash of spicy, cedary oak on the finish. Tempting now, best between 2000 and 2008. • $23 • (04/30/98) • **90**

Concerto Stags Leap District Robinson Vineyard 1992 • $17 • (04/30/96) • **93**

Concerto Stags Leap District Robinson Vineyard 1991 • $17 • (02/28/95) • **87**

Concerto Stags Leap District Robinson Vineyard 1990 • $17 • (03/15/94) • **82**

Joe's Cuvée California 1990 • $27 • (03/15/94) • **86**

Pinot Noir Santa Clara County 1989 • $17 • (02/28/94) • **81**

Pinot Noir Santa Cruz Mountains 1993: Mature, at a good drinking stage, with tart cherry, berry, herb and spice notes that pick up nuances of dill and earth on the finish. 140 cases made. • $22 • (04/30/97) • **86**

Pinot Noir Santa Cruz Mountains Peter Martin Ray Vineyard 1992 • $22 • (04/30/96) • **89**

Pinot Noir Santa Cruz Mountains Peter Martin Ray Vineyard 1991 • $20 • (03/31/95) • **82**

Pinot Noir Santa Cruz Mountains Peter Martin Ray Vineyard 1990 • $20 • (04/30/94) • **83**

Pinot Noir Santa Cruz Mountains Peter Martin Ray Vineyard 1988 • $27 • (03/31/92) • **81**

Zinfandel Santa Clara County 1992 • $12 • (10/15/95) • **85**

Zinfandel Sonoma Valley 1992 • $15 • (10/15/95) • **91**

CROSSWOODS | NEW YORK

Merlot North Fork of Long Island Ressler Vineyards 1987 • $10 • (02/29/92) • **84**

CRUVINET | CALIFORNIA

Cabernet Sauvignon Alexander Valley 1985 • $7 • (09/15/88) BB • **85**

CRYSTAL VALLEY | CALIFORNIA

Cabernet Sauvignon Napa Valley Unfined 1989 • $12 • (09/15/93) • **80**

Cabernet Sauvignon North Coast 1983 • $8 • (08/31/86) BB • **89**

Cabernet Sauvignon North Coast Reserve Edition 1984 • $14 • (10/15/87) • **75**

Pinot Noir North Coast Reserve Edition 1986 • $11 • (06/15/88) • **74**

CUISINE CELLARS | CALIFORNIA

California Red NV: A rough-edged wine, with hints of black cherry and cassis. The charry finish ends short. marginal. 1,250 cases made. • $6 • (07/31/98) • **79**

Chardonnay California 1996: Subtle apple and Asian pear flavors weave through the nicely focused, earthy, toasty notes. Finishes with a hint of nuttiness. Drink now through 1999. 1,100 cases made. • $9 • (06/30/98) • **84**

Lighthearted Red California NV: Light and appealing for its gentle berry and vanilla flavors. Simple and soft. • $5 • (12/31/96) • **80**

Merlot California 1996: Hints of blueberry, blackberry and cassis are framed by a smoke and oak edge, but this dries out on the finish. 2,230 cases made. • $9 • (07/31/98) • **83**

Rich Red California NV: Bright and chunky, delivering a generous mouthful of blackberry and anise flavors. Ready to drink. • $5 • (12/31/96) • **84**

CULBERTSON | CALIFORNIA

Blanc de Noir California NV: Toasty, nutty aromas announce this full-bodied bubbly. The flavors lean toward key-lime pie and oranges. A bit heavy, but enjoyable. 8,000 cases made. • $13 • (11/30/97) • **85**

Brut California 1987 • $16 • (12/31/93) • **82**

Brut California 1985 • $14 • (05/31/89) • **83**

Brut California NV: A bit earthy, with essence of orange and lemon. With its rounded, smooth texture and smoky finish, it makes a good quaffer. 10,000 cases made. • $13 • (11/30/97) • **86**

Brut California Reserve 1989: Offers honeyed pear and spice flavors, turning creamy, with an earthy edge. Tastes mature and on the downside, but some may enjoy it for those qualities. 3,000 cases made. • $18 • (11/30/96) • **84**

Brut California Reserve 1988 • $18 • (12/31/93) • **87**

Brut Rosé California 1987 • $16 • (12/31/93) • **85**

Brut Rosé California 1986 • $18 • (05/31/89) • **80**

Natural California 1987 • $16 • (12/31/93) • **74**

Natural California 1986 • $19 • (12/31/90) • **74**

Natural California 1985 • $18 • (05/31/89) • **81**

Natural California 1983 • $17 • (05/16/86) • **72**

CUNEO CELLARS | WASHINGTON

Cana's Feast Columbia Valley 1992 • $25 • (05/15/96) • **85**

CUNEO, RICHARD | CALIFORNIA

Blanc de Blancs Sonoma County Cuvée de Chardonnay 1987 • $14 • (11/15/91) • **84**

Brut Sonoma County Cuvée de Chardonnay 1991 • $15 • (12/15/94) • **88**

Brut Sonoma County Cuvée de Chardonnay 1988 • $15 • (12/15/93) • **88**

CURTIS | CALIFORNIA

Cabernet Franc Santa Ynez Valley Kingsley Vineyard 1994: Delicious mint, blueberry and blackberry flavors progress in a lively manner in this firm, focused wine. Falters on the finish, which is a little short and tart. Should age nicely, though. • $18 • (07/31/97) • **88**

Cabernet Sauvignon Santa Ynez Valley La Cuesta Vineyard 1994: Green and earthy, its vegetal qualities overwhelm. Decent texture. 1,025 cases made. • $18 • (09/30/97) • **77**

Chardonnay Santa Barbara County 1995: Exhibits a complex interplay between ripe pear, peach and citrus notes and pretty, toasty oak shadings, finishing with a pleasant aftertaste. 1,375 cases made. • $17 • (07/31/97) • **88**

Chardonnay Santa Barbara County Reserve 1994: Oxidized. All that remain at this point are an overwhelming butterscotch quality and bright acidity. 169 cases made. • $23 • (07/31/97) • **78**

Merlot Santa Ynez Valley La Cuesta Vineyard 1994: Simple, with modest flavors somewhat atypical of Merlot. Offers a hint of black cherry, dashes of herb and spice. 250 cases made. • $20 • (05/15/97) • **82**

Sauvignon Blanc Santa Ynez Valley 1995: Bright and lively, with an onion-skin grace note to the citrusy pear flavors. Finish is crisp and focused. 1,250 cases made. • $10 • (04/30/97) • **87**

Syrah Santa Ynez Valley Kalina Vineyard 1994: Rich aromas of smoke, spice and cherry pave the way for equally interesting flavors of pepper, anise, cassis and herbs that blend fluidly. 156 cases made. • $18 • (09/15/97) • **88**

CUTLER CELLAR | CALIFORNIA

Cabernet Sauvignon Sonoma Valley 1990 • $19 • (11/15/94) • **88**

Cabernet Sauvignon Sonoma Valley Batto Ranch 1987 • $17 • (03/31/92) HR • **90**

Cabernet Sauvignon Sonoma Valley Batto Ranch 1986 • $17 • (11/15/90) • **86**

Cabernet Sauvignon Sonoma Valley Batto Ranch 1985 • $20 • (07/31/89) • **91**

Satyre Sonoma Valley 1989 • $20 • (12/15/95) • **87**

Satyre Sonoma Valley 1987 • $20 • (07/15/92) • **89**

Satyre Sonoma Valley 1986 • $20 • (02/28/91) • **85**

CUVAISON | CALIFORNIA

Cabernet Sauvignon Napa Valley 1994: Well-balanced, with a supple core of earthy currant, cedar and spice flavors, finishing with firm, but supple tannins. Should drink well after short-term cellaring. Try in 1999. 3,400 cases made. • $25 • (11/15/97) • **89**

Cabernet Sauvignon Napa Valley 1993: Tight, firm and tannic, yet enough earthy currant and cherry flavors emerge to give it balance and proportion. Finishes with a dry edge to the berry and anise notes. 3,218 cases made. • $28 • (11/15/96) • **87**

Cabernet Sauvignon Napa Valley 1992 • $26 • (12/15/95) • **88**

Cabernet Sauvignon Napa Valley 1991 • $22 • (11/15/94) • **88**

Cabernet Sauvignon Napa Valley 1990 • $18 • (03/31/94) • **85**

Cabernet Sauvignon Napa Valley 1989 • $22 • (02/15/93) • **82**

Cabernet Sauvignon Napa Valley 1988 • $19 • (11/15/91) • **82**

Cabernet Sauvignon Napa Valley 1987: Young and lively, with a pleasant balance between ripe cherry and berry notes and hints of cedar and spice. Picks up a trace of chocolate on the finish, where the flavors linger. Ready to drink. • $36 • (12/15/97) • **90**

Cabernet Sauvignon Napa Valley 1986: Still shows enough herb and black cherry flavors to be appealing, but it's starting to decline, losing its intensity and flavor on the finish, where the tannins gain the upper hand. Drink now. • $NA • (12/15/96) • **89**

Cabernet Sauvignon Napa Valley 1985 • $40 • (03/31/89) • **91**

Cabernet Sauvignon Napa Valley 1982 • $15 • (10/15/87) • **90**

Cabernet Sauvignon Napa Valley 1981 • $11 • (11/30/86) • **89**

Cabernet Sauvignon Napa Valley 1980 • $11 • (02/16/85) • **85**

Cabernet Sauvignon Napa Valley 1978 • $14 • (05/16/84) • **65**

Cabernet Sauvignon Napa Valley ATS 1994: Best Cuvaison Cabernet in years, providing the extra richness, depth and dimensions missing in previous vintages. The core of flavors is built around rich currant, spice, herb and mineral and, while it's sturdily built, the tannins are ripe and well integrated. Best to cellar short-term. Try from 2000 to 2006. ATS is in honor of the late and former owner, Alexander "Tai" Schmidheiny. 250 cases made. • $50 • (04/30/98) • **92**

Chardonnay Napa Valley Carneros 1996: Smooth, ripe and polished, with spicy pear flavors, hints of vanilla and nutmeg and a clean, fresh finish. Drink now. • $21 • (06/15/98) • **88**

Chardonnay Napa Valley Carneros 1995: Smooth, ripe, rich and complex, with layers of ripe pear, apple, spice, fig and melon flavors. Elegant and refined on the finish, where a grassy, citrus note makes its entrance. Drinks well now. 40,000 cases made. • $16 • (12/31/96) SS • **89**

Chardonnay Napa Valley Carneros 1993 • $15 • (07/31/95) • **86**

Chardonnay Napa Valley Carneros ATS Selection 1995: Aromatic and spicy, with lots of complex spice, pear, hazelnut, melon and fig flavors that are concentrated and smoothly textured. Long and lingering on the finish, it's another terrific effort from Cuvaison. 350 cases made. • $43 • (04/30/98) • **93**

Chardonnay Napa Valley Carneros ATS Selection 1994: Simply delicious, with a rich, sharply focused core of pear, fig, hazelnut, melon and apricot flavors, turning supple and smooth on the finish, where the flavors show tremendously. 382 cases made. • $40 • (05/31/97) • **93**

Chardonnay Napa Valley Carneros Reserve 1995: A wine of great finesse, texture and balance, with delicate, spicy pear, peach and apple flavors. Holds its elegance and grace on the finish, where the fruit lingers. 1,850 cases made. • $28 • (05/15/98) • **90**

Chardonnay Napa Valley Carneros Reserve 1994: Well-focused, ripe pear, honey, apple and citrus flavors. Holds its fruitiness through the finish because the smoky oak and creamy vanilla flavors aren't overblown. 2,551 cases made. • $30 • (08/31/96) HR • **92**

Chardonnay Napa Valley Carneros Reserve 1993 • $28 • (07/31/95) • **88**

Chardonnay Napa Valley Carneros Twenty-Fifth Anniversary Harvest 1994: Pleasing for its ripe pineapple and apple flavors, it picks up flinty mineral and citrus notes on the finish. 36,959 cases made. • $16 • (06/30/96) • **85**

Meritage Napa Valley Reserve 1991 • $50 • (12/15/95) • **86**

Merlot Napa Valley 1991 • $24 • (09/15/94) • **83**

Merlot Napa Valley 1990 • $23 • (08/31/93) • **87**

Merlot Napa Valley 1988 • $24 • (04/15/91) • **86**

Merlot Napa Valley 1985 • $19 • (06/30/88) • **89**

Merlot Napa Valley Anniversary Release 1984 • $14 • (08/31/87) • **90**

Merlot Napa Valley Twenty-Fifth Anniversary Harvest 1994: Shows off its earthy, herbal flavors but stays well-balanced as its currant and anise flavors provide range and complexity. Finishes with a pleasant aftertaste and good concentration. Best in 2000 or 2001. 4,500 cases made. • $30 • (12/31/96) • **89**

Pinot Noir Napa Valley Carneros 1995: Bold, ripe and flavorful, with layers of black cherry, plum, wild berry and smoky toasty oak, it all works together quite nicely, showing depth, concentration and complexity. Drinks well now with its supple tannins, but can age into 1999 to 2002. • $30 • (01/31/98) • **91**

Pinot Noir Napa Valley Carneros 1993 • $24 • (01/31/96) • **76**

Pinot Noir Napa Valley Carneros 1992 • $22 • (03/31/95) • **84**

Pinot Noir Napa Valley Carneros 1991 • $19 • (02/28/94) • **85**

Pinot Noir Napa Valley Carneros Eris 1995: Offers richness, depth and complexity, with dark, concentrated plum, wildberry, black cherry and earthy, mushroomy nuances. The texture is smooth and plush. 1,988 cases made. • $19 • (12/15/97) • **89**

Pinot Noir Napa Valley Carneros Eris 1994: Supple and elegant, with smoky oak and meaty edges that throw the cherry and berry flavors off a bit. Perhaps a few more months will help integrate the flavors. 969 cases made. • $15 • (02/28/97) • **85**

Zinfandel Napa Valley 1986 • $10 • (03/15/89) • **85**

Zinfandel Napa Valley 1983 • $8 • (09/15/87) • **75**

D-CUBED CELLARS | CALIFORNIA

Zinfandel Howell Mountain 1995: Smooth and supple, even for Howell Mountain, with an earthy, spicy edge to the cherry and wild berry flavors. Drinkable now, but has the balance and depth of flavor to age, too. 520 cases made. • $17 • (04/30/97) • **89**

Zinfandel Howell Mountain 1994 • $15 • (04/30/96) • **90**

Zinfandel Napa Valley 1996: Strikes a nice balance between its modest ripe fruit flavors and firm but supple tannins. Offers enough plum and berry flavors to hold your interest. Drink now through 2000. 498 cases made. • $17 • (05/31/98) • **84**

DA VINCI | CALIFORNIA

Riesling Late Harvest Sierra Foothills 1987: Soft, sweet and gentle, this is layered with spice, pineapple, honey and apricot flavors that swirl through the polished finish. Delicious now. • $8/375ml • (12/31/96) • **90**

Sauvignon Blanc Late Harvest Sierra Foothills 1987: Smooth and tasty, though the flavors are a bit too much like canned fruit cocktail to qualify as elegant. A sweet wine with remarkable freshness for its age. 13 percent residual sugar. Drink soon. • $8/375ml • (12/31/96) • **86**

DALLA VALLE | CALIFORNIA

Cabernet Sauvignon Napa Valley 1996: Effusively fruity, with ripe, rich plum, cherry and wild berry flavors that are bright, smooth and supple. Should be stunning, as it's concentrated and elegant. • $NA • (06/15/97) (BT) • **95-99**

Cabernet Sauvignon Napa Valley 1994: Here's a dense, rich and concentrated young Cabernet, with tiers of currant, black cherry, anise and cedar. It's tightly wound now and will need several years of cellaring to open and soften, but be patient—all the elements are there. Try around 2001. 91 per-

Key: SS—Spectator Selection CS—Cellar Selection HR—Highly Recommended BB—Best Buy $NA—Price not available Ⓐ—Auction Price (BT)—Barrel Tasting

Dates in parentheses indicate the issues in which the ratings were published.

cent Cabernet Sauvignon and 9 percent Cabernet Franc. 2,800 cases made. • $40 • (10/31/97) CS • **93**

Cabernet Sauvignon Napa Valley 1993: Tight and well-focused, showing a firm band of currant and plum flavors, with a spicy, cedary accent. Finishes with firm, gritty tannins. Slightly subdued at midpalate, but has lots of appealing elements. Try in 1999. • $72 Ⓐ • (11/15/96) • **88**

Cabernet Sauvignon Napa Valley 1992 • $83 Ⓐ • (12/15/95) CS • **92**

Cabernet Sauvignon Napa Valley 1991 • $110 Ⓐ • (11/15/94) SS • **92**

Cabernet Sauvignon Napa Valley 1990 • $25 • (09/30/93) HR • **93**

Cabernet Sauvignon Napa Valley 1989 • $25 • (11/15/92) • **85**

Cabernet Sauvignon Napa Valley 1988 • $25 • (11/15/91) • **85**

Cabernet Sauvignon Napa Valley 1986: This was the first Cabernet from this Napa winery, and is on the hard, tannic, thin side—in marked contrast to the bold, rich and complex wines being made now. • $NA • (12/15/96) • **84**

Maya Napa Valley 1994: This is a beautifully crafted wine that will require, and reward, patience. It's tight and intense, with a big, ripe, rich core of spicy currant, plum and berry flavors, finishing with a complex earth and mineral nuance. Turns ruggedly tannic on the finish, so hands off until 2001 or so. A blend of 55 percent Cabernet Sauvignon and 45 percent Cabernet Franc. 480 cases made. • $333 Ⓐ • (10/31/97) HR • **95**

Maya Napa Valley 1993: A magnificent wine, loaded with complex flavors and tiers of currant, anise, mineral and cedar that flow on and on. Rich and concentrated, it shows that truly great wines could be made in 1993 and upholds this vineyard's reputation for producing grand wines. Despite all its intensity and depth, it manages to be elegant. 500 cases made. • $384 Ⓐ • (11/15/96) CS • **96**

Maya Napa Valley 1992 • $377 Ⓐ • (12/15/95) • **94**

Maya Napa Valley 1991 • $354 Ⓐ • (11/15/94) • **90**

Maya Napa Valley 1990 • $50 • (09/30/93) • **89**

Maya Napa Valley 1989 • $50 • (10/15/92) HR • **91**

Maya Napa Valley 1988 • $92 Ⓐ • (11/15/91) • **86**

Pietre Rosse Napa Valley 1995: A bit rustic at first, but quite appealing, with sage, wild berry, cherry and spice flavors, turning complex with cedar and tobacco notes. Made from Sangiovese, and released in California only. 300 cases made. • $25 • (12/15/97) • **86**

Pietre Rosse Napa Valley NV • $35 • (06/15/96) • **82**

Zinfandel Napa Valley 1986 • $25 • (02/15/91) • **84**

D'ANGELO VINEYARDS | MICHIGAN

Ice Wine Lake Erie North Shore 1992 • $29 • (04/15/95) • **78**

DANIEL | CALIFORNIA

Cabernet Sauvignon Napa Valley 1984 • $21 • (07/15/88) • **89**

Cabernet Sauvignon Napa Valley 1983 • $20 • (04/30/89) • **79**

DARK STAR | CALIFORNIA

Merlot Paso Robles Cougar Ridge Vineyards 1995: Cedary oak dominates the fruit in this wine, overriding the modest cherry and berry flavors. 230 cases made. • $18 • (05/15/98) • **80**

DAVIDSON | OREGON

Pinot Noir Umpqua Valley 1989 • $15 • (02/28/93) • **82**

Pinot Noir Umpqua Valley Reserve 1990 • $18 • (02/28/93) • **78**

DAYDREAM | CALIFORNIA

Cabernet Sauvignon Napa Valley 1994: Clean and well-balanced; not flashy, but complex, with cedar, currant and herbal flavors turning smooth and rich on the finish. Drinks well now, should be better around 1999 to 2001. 500 cases made. • $24 • (11/30/97) • **88**

DE LOACH | CALIFORNIA

Cabernet Sauvignon Dry Creek Valley 1984 • $11 • (12/15/87) • **89**

Cabernet Sauvignon Dry Creek Valley 1983 • $11 • (09/30/86) • **85**

Cabernet Sauvignon Dry Creek Valley 1981 • $11 • (04/01/85) • **80**

Cabernet Sauvignon Russian River Valley 1995: Decidedly earthy, with a potent herbal, claylike flavor, but then it reveals more complex currant- and berry-scented flavors. Finishes with firm, earthy tannins. Best from 1999 through 2004. 6,000 cases made. • $18 • (05/31/98) • **87**

Cabernet Sauvignon Russian River Valley 1993: Young and tight, with a trim, tannic band of cherry, currant, herb and chocolate flavors of moderate depth. 5,000 cases made. • $15 • (12/15/96) • **84**

Cabernet Sauvignon Russian River Valley 1992 • $15 • (12/15/95) • **86**

Cabernet Sauvignon Russian River Valley 1991 • $15 • (11/15/94) • **78**

Cabernet Sauvignon Russian River Valley 1990 • $16 • (03/31/93) • **85**

Cabernet Sauvignon Russian River Valley 1989 • $16 • (11/15/91) • **86**

Cabernet Sauvignon Russian River Valley O.F.S. 1994: Dark, ripe and richly flavored, with layers of black cherry, currant, anise and spice, turning supple and harmonious on the finish. 1,000 cases made. • $28 • (09/30/97) • **90**

Cabernet Sauvignon Russian River Valley O.F.S. 1993: Offers a nice core of earthy currant, mineral, tar and cedar flavors and finishes with a dash of oak and firm tannins. Best to cellar into 1999 to let it soften a bit. 600 cases made. • $25 • (01/31/97) • **87**

Cabernet Sauvignon Russian River Valley O.F.S. 1992: Young and tight, with a focused core of currant and cherry flavors that fans out on the finish, where it picks up notes of herb and cedary oak. Drink now through 2002. 1,000 cases made. • $25 • (09/30/96) • **89**

Cabernet Sauvignon Russian River Valley O.F.S. 1991 • $25 • (09/30/95) • **89**

Cabernet Sauvignon Russian River Valley O.F.S. 1987: Mature and a bit dry on the finish, showing nice herb and currant flavors, with hints of anise and sage and a polished texture. Ready to drink. Tasted from magnum. • $50 • (12/15/97) • **87**

Chardonnay Russian River Valley 1996: Has some appealing flavors, with ripe pear, citrus and melon, but the texture is coarse. The finish is more impressive, where the flavors fold together. Drink now to 2002. 28,000 cases made. • $18 • (04/30/98) • **86**

Chardonnay Russian River Valley 1995: From one of California's most respected Chardonnay producers comes this clean and refreshing white, its bright, lively pear, citrus, peach, spice and apricot flavors, uncommonly rich and elegant. A trace of cedary oak chimes in on the finish. 25,000 cases made. • $16 • (06/15/97) SS • **90**

Chardonnay Russian River Valley 1994: Clean and correct, with modest pear and spice notes, and a light, citrusy finish. Solid and well-balanced, but lacking in richness and concentration. 25,000 cases made. • $15 • (06/30/96) • **85**

Chardonnay Russian River Valley 1993 • $15 • (02/29/96) • **85**

Chardonnay Russian River Valley O.F.S. 1995: Brilliant Chardonnay; ripe and complex, with juicy pear, spice, apple and hazelnut notes. Dances on your palate with its fresh, zesty flavors. Drink now. 6,000 cases made. • $25 • (02/28/97) • **92**

Chardonnay Russian River Valley Estate Bottled 1996: Shows off a strong oak presence up front—especially for De Loach—but the fruit pours through too, with the focus on orange-peel, apple, pear and spice. Holds its flavors on the finish. 1,800 cases made. • $20 • (04/30/98) • **89**

Chardonnay Russian River Valley O.F.S. 1996: Tight, ripe and well-focused, with pretty pear, fig, apricot, anise and spice. Rich concentration of flavors and a long, full finish. Impressive. Drink now through 2001. 7,000 cases made. • $28 • (06/30/98) SS • **92**

Chardonnay Russian River Valley O.F.S. 1994: Pleasant fruit, featuring an attractive array of pear, citrus, honey and butterscotch which hangs together nicely, adding a fruity aftertaste. 5,000 cases made. • $25 • (05/15/96) • **89**

Chardonnay Russian River Valley O.F.S. 1993 • $25 • (09/30/95) HR • **90**

Chardonnay Russian River Valley Sonoma Cuvée 1995: Smooth, delicate, all in finesse, this elegant wine has apple and pear flavors that echo through the long, bright finish. 15,000 cases made. • $12 • (06/15/97) • **89**

Chardonnay Sonoma County Sonoma Cuvée 1996: Intense, with a core of pear and pineapple. Holds its fruitiness on the finish, where the pure flavors linger. Drink now through 2000. 8,000 cases made. • $13 • (07/31/98) • **87**

Chardonnay Sonoma County Sonoma Cuvée 1993 • $10 • (05/15/96) • **84**

Fumé Blanc Russian River Valley 1996: Effusive in its lavish menthol, grapefruit, fig and lime flavors. The finish is a bit cloying in spite of its bright acidity, but this wine is tasty nonetheless. 2,500 cases made. • $14 • (06/30/97) • **88**

Fumé Blanc Russian River Valley 1995: A lively mouthful of peachy, floral flavors that carry over into a bright, refreshing finish. 3,900 cases made. • $12 • (07/31/96) • **88**

Fumé Blanc Russian River Valley Dry Sauvignon Blanc 1993 • $10 • (12/31/94) • **84**

Gewürztraminer Late Harvest Russian River Valley 1991 • $14/375ml • (10/15/92) • **86**

Gewürztraminer Late Harvest Russian River Valley 1989 • $10/375ml • (04/30/91) • **88**

Gewürztraminer Late Harvest Russian River Valley 1987 • $10/375ml • (12/31/88) • **93**
Gewürztraminer Late Harvest Russian River Valley 1984 • $10 • (10/01/85) BB • **92**
Gewürztraminer Russian River Valley Early Harvest 1996: Off-dry, bright with spicy fruit, it offers nice nectarine and litchi flavors that linger nicely on the soft finish. 4,500 cases made. • $12 • (07/31/97) • **85**
Gewürztraminer Russian River Valley Early Harvest 1993 • $8 • (01/31/95) • **84**
Merlot Russian River Valley 1995: On the green, herbal side of Merlot, so be advised. Some tart berry and spice notes fold in, but it's on the lean side. 7,000 cases made. • $16 • (06/30/97) • **80**
Merlot Russian River Valley 1994: Medium-weight, with a nice range of cherry, currant, anise and light oak flavors. Comes up short on the finish. 6,500 cases made. • $15 • (08/31/96) • **84**
Merlot Russian River Valley 1993 • $14 • (09/30/95) • **87**
Merlot Russian River Valley 1992 • $14 • (07/31/94) • **86**
Pinot Noir Russian River Valley 1995: Ripe, spicy and elegant, with rich cherry and raspberry flavors that are bright, lively and linger on the finish. Drinks well now. • $15 • (12/31/96) • **88**
Pinot Noir Russian River Valley 1994 • $25 • (02/29/96) • **79**
Pinot Noir Russian River Valley 1992 • $13 • (03/31/95) • **82**
Pinot Noir Russian River Valley 1991 • $13 • (02/28/94) • **74**
Pinot Noir Russian River Valley 1990 • $13 • (09/30/92) • **80**
Pinot Noir Russian River Valley 1986 • $12 • (05/31/90) • **87**
Pinot Noir Russian River Valley 1985 • $12 • (06/15/88) • **72**
Pinot Noir Russian River Valley 1983 • $10 • (03/01/86) • **75**
Pinot Noir Russian River Valley 1982 • $10 • (08/31/86) • **76**
Pinot Noir Russian River Valley O.F.S. 1996: An elegant, understated style, with herb, tea, strawberry, cherry, leather and spice. Tightens up on the finish, where the tannins fold in. Best to cellar now to '99 to let it evolve. 500 cases made. • $28 • (12/31/97) • **89**
Pinot Noir Russian River Valley O.F.S. 1995: Combines ripe, rich, well-focused fruit flavors with a sense of elegance and delicacy, allowing the earthy cherry and wild berry notes to flow across the palate. Long, subtle aftertaste. Impressive. Drinks well now, but should improve through 2000. 720 cases made. • $25 • (12/31/96) • **89**
Pinot Noir Russian River Valley O.F.S. 1994 • $25 • (02/29/96) • **89**
Pinot Noir Russian River Valley O.F.S. 1992 • $25 • (12/31/95) • **88**
Pinot Noir Russian River Valley O.F.S. 1990 • $26 • (02/28/93) • **82**
Pinot Noir Russian River Valley O.F.S. 1987 • $25 • (10/31/90) • **82**
Sauvignon Blanc Russian River Valley 1993 • $10 • (12/31/94) • **81**
White Zinfandel Russian River Valley 1994 • $7 • (09/15/95) • **74**
White Zinfandel Sonoma County 1996: Tutti-frutti, with a cinnamon-cherry hard-candy finish. 22,000 cases made. • $8 • (09/15/97) • **78**
Zinfandel Russian River Valley 1996: Weaves earthy cherry, wild berry and raspberry flavors into a medium-weight, modestly proportioned wine finishing with firm, dry tannins. Drink now through 2000. 3,600 cases made. • $18 • (03/31/98) • **85**
Zinfandel Russian River Valley 1995: A ripe and jammy style with lots of appealing cherry, raspberry and wild berry flavors. Drink now, or hold a few years. 4,200 cases made. • $15 • (02/28/97) • **88**
Zinfandel Russian River Valley 1994 • $14 • (04/30/96) • **86**
Zinfandel Russian River Valley 1993 • $13 • (10/15/95) • **85**
Zinfandel Russian River Valley 1991 • $11 • (05/31/93) • **83**
Zinfandel Russian River Valley 1990 • $12 • (05/15/92) • **89**
Zinfandel Russian River Valley 1989 • $11 • (09/30/91) • **82**
Zinfandel Russian River Valley 1988 • $11 • (09/15/90) • **78**
Zinfandel Russian River Valley 1987 • $10 • (09/15/89) • **90**
Zinfandel Russian River Valley 1986 • $9 • (10/15/88) • **88**
Zinfandel Russian River Valley 1984 • $8 • (07/31/87) • **84**
Zinfandel Russian River Valley 1982 • $8 • (11/01/85) • **77**
Zinfandel Russian River Valley 1981 • $7 • (06/01/85) • **89**
Zinfandel Russian River Valley Barbieri Ranch 1996: Ripe and intense, with firm, gritty tannins, this serves up a modest range of tart wild berry and cherry-laced Zin flavors. Finishes with a simple aftertaste. 400 cases made. • $20 • (05/15/98) • **86**
Zinfandel Russian River Valley Barbieri Ranch 1995: On the tart side, with a sharply focused band of cherry, wild berry and raspberry flavors. Finishes with firm tannins and a peppery accent. • $18 • (02/28/97) • **88**
Zinfandel Russian River Valley Barbieri Ranch 1994 • $15 • (04/30/96) • **85**
Zinfandel Russian River Valley Barbieri Ranch 1993 • $14 • (10/15/95) • **88**
Zinfandel Russian River Valley Barbieri Ranch 1991 • $14 • (01/31/93) • **82**
Zinfandel Russian River Valley Barbieri Ranch 1990 • $14 • (05/15/92) • **82**
Zinfandel Russian River Valley Gambogi Ranch 1996: A lighter style, with pronounced earth and bell pepper flavors and fruit flavors just ripe enough to move into the berry, cherry spectrum. Medium-bodied; should be enjoyed in its youth. 400 cases made. • $20 • (03/31/98) • **84**
Zinfandel Russian River Valley Gambogi Ranch 1995: Fresh and lively; a shade on the tart side, with well-focused berry and cherry flavors that pick up a hint of jamminess on the finish. Drink now or hold. • $18 • (02/28/97) • **88**
Zinfandel Russian River Valley Gambogi Ranch 1994 • $15 • (04/30/96) • **87**
Zinfandel Russian River Valley Gambogi Ranch 1993 • $14 • (10/15/95) • **86**
Zinfandel Russian River Valley O.F.S. 1996: Smooth and polished, in a sophisticated style with a supple texture and elegant, well-focused wild berry, black cherry, earth and spice flavors. Drink now through 2001. 400 cases made. • $28 • (03/31/98) • **90**
Zinfandel Russian River Valley O.F.S. 1995: Gushing with ripe, juicy Zinfandel flavors, with tiers of raspberry, wild berry, spice and cherry. A delicious mouthful of plush, concentrated, complex jammy berry flavors. 500 cases made. • $25 • (02/28/97) • **92**
Zinfandel Russian River Valley O.F.S. 1994 • $25 • (04/30/96) • **88**
Zinfandel Russian River Valley Papera Ranch 1996: Pleasant for its wild berry, anise, sage and raspberry notes, finishing with firm tannins. This moderately rich wine shows more intensity and focus than the Gambogi; still could use more depth and complexity. Drink now. 400 cases made. • $20 • (03/31/98) • **87**
Zinfandel Russian River Valley Papera Ranch 1995: Ripe and full-bodied, with jammy wild berry, cherry and plum flavors and hints of pepper and spice. Packs in lots of flavor and has a long, complex aftertaste that echoes fruit notes, especially berries. Enjoyable now, but can age into 1999. 500 cases made. • $18 • (02/28/97) • **90**
Zinfandel Russian River Valley Papera Ranch 1994 • $15 • (04/30/96) • **87**
Zinfandel Russian River Valley Papera Ranch 1993 • $14 • (10/15/95) • **86**
Zinfandel Russian River Valley Papera Ranch 1991 • $14 • (01/31/93) • **85**
Zinfandel Russian River Valley Papera Ranch 1990 • $14 • (05/15/92) • **81**
Zinfandel Russian River Valley Pelletti Ranch 1996: Modestly proportioned, marked by an earthy touch from start to finish, the barely ripe cherry and wild berry flavors nicely work their way in. Drink now. 400 cases made. • $20 • (03/31/98) • **86**
Zinfandel Russian River Valley Pelletti Ranch 1995: Ripe and complex, with lots of cherry, wild berry and raspberry flavors that are pure and plush. Holds its richness through a long, full finish, with supple tannins. Holds its alcohol well, too, even at 17.5 percent. 300 cases made. • $18 • (02/28/97) • **90**
Zinfandel Russian River Valley Pelletti Ranch 1994 • $15 • (04/30/96) • **86**
Zinfandel Russian River Valley Pelletti Ranch 1993 • $14 • (10/15/95) • **88**
Zinfandel Russian River Valley Pelletti Ranch 1991 • $14 • (01/31/93) • **86**
Zinfandel Russian River Valley Pelletti Ranch 1990 • $14 • (05/15/92) • **87**
Zinfandel Russian River Valley Saitone Ranch 1996: Fresh, crisp and snappy, with crushed pepper, wild berry, raspberry and cherry notes that are supple and lively, finishing with a solid core of ripe fruit and tannin. 400 cases made. • $20 • (03/31/98) • **88**
Zinfandel Russian River Valley Saitone Ranch 1995: Complex and impeccably balanced, with fine interplay of the cherry, wild berry, currant and plum flavors. Finishing with a blast of fruit and firm tannins, it's drinkable now, or cellar into 1999. 200 cases made. • $18 • (02/28/97) • **89**
Zinfandel Russian River Valley Sonoma County 1992 • $12 • (06/15/94) • **88**

DE ROSE | CALIFORNIA

Zinfandel Cienega Valley Cedolini Family Vineyard Hillside Reserve 1993: Ripe and alcoholic, delivering appealing, juicy plum, wild berry and cherry flavors. Finishes with some heat and a tarry edge. 640 cases made. • $19 • (09/15/96) • **85**
Zinfandel Cienega Valley Cedolini Family Vineyard Hillside Reserve 1992: Ripe and spicy, with a raisiny accent to the tarry plum and cherry flavors. Finishes with crisp tannins and a touch of heat. 800 cases made. • $13 • (09/15/96) • **82**

DEAVER | CALIFORNIA

Zinfandel Amador County 1995: A leaner style for Zin, showing subtle blackberry, anise and herb characteristics. The core of ripe flavors may develop nicely with time; drink through 2002. 400 cases made. • $15 • (05/31/98) • **86**

Key: SS—Spectator Selection CS—Cellar Selection HR—Highly Recommended BB—Best Buy $NA—Price not available Ⓐ—Auction Price (BT)—Barrel Tasting
Dates in parentheses indicate the issues in which the ratings were published.

DEBONNE | OHIO

Chambourcin Ohio Lake Erie 1989 • $6 • (02/29/92) • **79**

DECOY | CALIFORNIA

Migration Napa Valley 1995: Light and supple, with pretty floral and leather nuances to the gentle berry and currant flavors. Could finish stronger. Drink now. A blend of Cabernet Franc, Merlot and Cabernet Sauvignon. 3,000 cases made. • $14 • (03/31/98) • **85**

Migration Red Napa Valley 1994: Simple and pleasant, with hints of cherry and berry flavor and light oak shadings. Not as showy as the 1993 was. 1,600 cases made. • $12 • (02/28/97) • **83**

Migration Red Napa Valley 1993: Ripe, well-focused, spicy black cherry, herb and cedar flavors are bright and lively. Well-proportioned and moderately tannic. Deliciously complex and terrific at this price. 4,900 cases made. • $12 • (02/29/96) SS • **90**

Migration White Napa Valley 1996: A pleasant mix of almond, peach, citrus and pineapple, with tangy acidity and firmness on the palate. Finishes clean. A good value at this price. This year it's 100 percent Sémillon. 800 cases made. • $10 • (01/31/98) • **86**

Migration White Napa Valley 1995: Round, fresh and straightforwardly pleasant, offering tobacco-accented light apple flavors. 1,200 cases made. • $7 • (02/28/97) • **81**

Migration White Napa Valley 1994 • $7 • (02/29/96) • **82**

DEER PARK | CALIFORNIA

Cabernet Sauvignon Howell Mountain Beatty Ranch Reserve 1990 • $24 • (10/31/94) • **88**

Cabernet Sauvignon Howell Mountain Beatty Ranch Reserve 1988 • $24 • (11/15/92) • **87**

Petite Sirah Howell Mountain Parks/Muscatine Vineyards 1987 • $14 • (10/31/91) • **82**

Zinfandel Howell Mountain Beatty Ranch 1995: Flavored with bright cherry notes, plum tones and hints of spice, herbs, anise and toasty oak. A charred quality marks the finish. To be released July of this year. Drink now through 2002. 186 cases made. • $17 • (06/15/98) • **85**

Zinfandel Howell Mountain Beatty Ranch 1991 • $14 • (10/15/95) • **83**

Zinfandel Howell Mountain Beatty Ranch 1990 • $14 • (10/15/94) • **81**

Zinfandel Howell Mountain Beatty Ranch 1988 • $13 • (10/15/92) • **83**

Zinfandel Howell Mountain Beatty Ranch 1987 • $14 • (08/31/91) • **79**

Zinfandel Howell Mountain Beatty Ranch Reserve 1987 • $18 • (08/31/91) • **85**

Zinfandel Napa Valley 1991 • $16 • (10/15/95) • **83**

DEER VALLEY | CALIFORNIA

Cabernet Sauvignon Monterey 1985 • $5 • (12/31/87) • **72**

Chardonnay Monterey County 1993 • $7 • (10/31/95) • **81**

Merlot California 1992 • $6 • (09/15/94) • **79**

Merlot California 1990 • $6 • (05/31/92) • **77**

DEERFIELD RANCH | CALIFORNIA

Chardonnay North Coast 1996: Silky, subtle and elegant, with pretty, creamy oak notes and flavors of lemon and vanilla that linger on the palate. Moderate in intensity, but still very nice. Drink now. 115 cases made. • $24 • (07/31/98) • **86**

Sangiovese California 1995: A sturdy red, with straightforward cherry and vaguely floral flavors that balance nicely on the finish. Drink through 1999. 200 cases made. • $18 • (07/31/98) • **84**

Zin'abernet North Coast 1996: Shows tart strawberry flavor, and finishes with firm dry tannins. A blend of Zinfandel and Cabernet. Drink now. 115 cases made. • $20 • (06/15/98) • **79**

DEHLINGER | CALIFORNIA

Cabernet Franc Russian River Valley 1989 • $12 • (03/31/92) • **75**

Cabernet Franc Russian River Valley 1988 • $13 • (04/30/91) • **84**

Cabernet Sauvignon Russian River Valley 1994: Intense and lively, with ripe, juicy, sharply-focused cherry, raspberry and wild berry flavors and a long, full finish that fans out the lovely flavors. 260 cases made. • $25 • (09/30/97) • **91**

Cabernet Sauvignon Russian River Valley 1992: Ripe and spicy layers of plum, cherry and currant flavors. The finish holds the fruit and has firm but balanced tannins. 975 cases made. • $18 • (08/31/96) • **86**

Cabernet Sauvignon Russian River Valley 1991 • $15 • (05/15/95) • **88**

Cabernet Sauvignon Russian River Valley 1990 • $15 • (11/15/94) • **80**

Cabernet Sauvignon Russian River Valley 1989 • $15 • (08/31/93) • **79**

Cabernet Sauvignon Russian River Valley 1988 • $15 • (03/31/92) • **83**

Cabernet Sauvignon Russian River Valley 1987 • $13 • (02/28/91) • **88**

Cabernet Sauvignon Russian River Valley 1986: Impressive for its power and finesse. This remains a big, ripe, intense and tannic wine, still showing hints of bell pepper and herb and plenty of currant, plum and berry flavors. It refuses to show its full hand; hold for another three to five years. • $NA • (12/15/96) • **91**

Cabernet Sauvignon Russian River Valley 1985 • $13 • (05/31/89) • **74**

Cabernet Sauvignon Russian River Valley 1984 • $12 • (02/15/88) • **76**

Cabernet Sauvignon Russian River Valley 1983 • $11 • (06/15/87) • **85**

Cabernet Sauvignon Russian River Valley 1982 • $11 • (08/31/86) • **73**

Cabernet Sauvignon Sonoma County 1981 • $9 • (05/16/85) • **87**

Chardonnay Russian River Valley 1996: Tight, with a crisp, well-focused band of ripe pear, apple, citrus and mineral, the flavors fan out on the aftertaste, where they show more depth and complexity. Drink now through 2002. 2,000 cases made. • $20 • (06/30/98) • **90**

Chardonnay Russian River Valley 1995: Openly fruity, with a pleasing, earthy accent to the ripe pear, fig and melon flavors. Unveils traces of citrus, and hints of mineral and cedar on the finish. What a wine for the price. 2,800 cases made. • $18 • (05/31/97) • **93**

Chardonnay Russian River Valley 1994: Smooth and subtle, with a polished texture and ripe pear, spice and hazelnut notes. Shows off a tart edge on the finish, where the flavors linger. Some age should help. 2,850 cases made. • $16 • (05/31/96) • **88**

Chardonnay Russian River Valley 1993 • $15 • (05/31/95) • **88**

Merlot Sonoma County 1986 • $13 • (07/31/89) • **83**

Merlot Sonoma County 1985 • $11 • (04/30/88) • **89**

Merlot Sonoma County 1984 • $12 • (06/15/87) SS • **94**

Pinot Noir Russian River Valley 1995: This California red has wonderful depth, richness, concentration and purity of flavor. Stuffed with layers of ripe, supple plum, black cherry, currant and berry flavors, it tightens up on the finish where the tannins fold in, but holds its richness and depth. From a winery with a deft hand with Pinot Noir. 1,100 cases made. • $28 • (12/31/97) HR • **94**

Pinot Noir Russian River Valley 1994: Wonderfully rich and complex, with tiers of concentrated black cherry, currant, plum and spice flavors. The texture is smooth and plush, with ripe tannins and impeccable balance. Simply delicious; beautifully crafted and a good bet to get better with another year or two of age. Drinkable now. Tasted twice with consistent notes. 1,200 cases made. • $24 • (12/31/96) • **92**

Pinot Noir Russian River Valley 1993 • $20 • (11/30/95) • **88**

Pinot Noir Russian River Valley 1992 • $18 • (12/31/94) • **88**

Pinot Noir Russian River Valley 1991 • $17 • (02/28/94) • **87**

Pinot Noir Russian River Valley 1990: This wine has really grown up. Tightly structured when youthful, it has evolved into a dark, ripe, rich and effusively fruity wine showing a remarkable amount of ripe cherry, berry and currant flavors and a long, complex aftertaste. • $18 • (03/31/97) • **93**

Pinot Noir Russian River Valley 1989 • $17 • (03/31/92) • **80**

Pinot Noir Russian River Valley 1987 • $14 • (02/15/90) • **91**

Pinot Noir Russian River Valley 1986 • $13 • (05/31/89) • **88**

Pinot Noir Russian River Valley 1985 • $12 • (02/15/88) • **85**

Pinot Noir Russian River Valley 1984 • $11 • (06/30/87) • **89**

Pinot Noir Russian River Valley 1983 • $10 • (08/31/86) • **89**

Pinot Noir Russian River Valley 1982 • $10 • (10/01/85) • **86**

Pinot Noir Russian River Valley Goldridge Vineyard 1995: Smooth, ripe, rich and complex, with a lovely array of ripe cherry, spice, cedar, anise and rhubarb flavors showing remarkable balance, finesse and integration. Best now through 2002. Available in restaurants and by mailing list only. 1,500 cases made. • $23 • (08/31/97) • **91**

Pinot Noir Russian River Valley Goldridge Vineyard 1994: Young and tight, with a firm tannic edge to the currant and wild berry flavors. Turns more interesting on the finish, where the flavors fan out and pick up hints of anise, mineral and oak. Approachable now, but best in 1999. 700 cases made. • $20 • (12/31/96) • **92**

Pinot Noir Russian River Valley Goldridge Vineyard 20-Year-Old Vines 1994: Tight, and a shade more tannic than the other Dehlinger 1994s, this nonetheless exhibits a delicious interplay of flavors: rich currant, black cherry and wild berry, with spicy nuances. Finishes with more tannin and less of the supple flavors found in the producer's other bottlings. Best now through 2002. Tasted twice with consistent notes. 100 cases made. • $32 • (12/31/96) • **93**

Pinot Noir Russian River Valley Octagon Vineyard 1994: Delivers an enormous core of ripe, fleshy, juicy Pinot Noir flavor, with layers of plum, cherry, spice and anise notes that fan out on the finish. The texture is smooth and supple and the aftertaste is long and lingering. Best now through 2007. Tasted twice with consistent notes. 150 cases made. • $32 • (12/31/96) • **92**

Pinot Noir Russian River Valley Reserve 1994: An amazingly complex, rich, plush and concentrated young wine that gushes with tiers of dark, ripe currant, black cherry and wild berry flavors and spicy nuances. Even with its depth and complexity, this wine shows a remarkable sense of elegance and finesse. Finish is long and exciting. Tasted twice with consistent notes. 500 cases made. • $32 • (12/31/96) • **95**

Pinot Noir Russian River Valley Reserve 1992 • $25 • (12/31/94) HR • **91**

Pinot Noir Russian River Valley Reserve 1991 • $23 • (02/28/94) HR • **91**

Pinot Noir Sonoma County Selection 1990 • $10 • (02/28/93) • **81**

Syrah Russian River Valley 1994: Dark, ripe, rich and meaty, with lots of chewy currant, plum and black cherry flavors that are bold and sharply-focused. A young and vibrant wine that features remarkably supple tannins. Lovely now, but worthy of cellaring. Best now through 2004. 700 cases made. • $23 • (08/31/97) • **92**

Syrah Russian River Valley 1993 • $18 • (05/31/96) HR • **90**

Syrah Russian River Valley 1992 • $16 • (05/15/95) HR • **93**

Zinfandel Sonoma County 1983 • $8 • (07/31/87) • **73**

DEL DOTTO | CALIFORNIA

Cabernet Sauvignon Napa Valley 1994: Delicious Cabernet. Displays a sharply-focused core of currant, plum and black cherry, picks up pretty toasty oak and cedar and finishes with a smooth, plush texture. Has the tannic strength to cellar into 2000. 497 cases made. • $42 • (10/31/97) • **92**

Cabernet Sauvignon Napa Valley 1993: Packs a wallop with its rich heart of earthy currant, mineral, spice and cedary oak flavors. Smooth and rich, given its size and concentration of fruit flavors. Drinkable now, but should age into the next century with ease. 497 cases made. • $30 • (04/30/97) • **92**

DELECTUS | CALIFORNIA

Cabernet Sauvignon Napa Valley 1995: Ripe and supple, with an elegant band of currant, chocolate, cherry, cedar, anise and spicy wood flavors. Holds its focus and keeps pumping out the flavors on a long, complex aftertaste. Best from 2000 through 2009. 355 cases made. • $42 • (07/31/98) • **91**

Cabernet Sauvignon Napa Valley 1994: Tightly-wound, with firm tannins and just enough ripe cherry and berry flavors to give interest. More fruit may come through with cellaring through 1999. • $42 • (07/31/97) • **88**

DELILLE | WASHINGTON

Cabernet Sauvignon Yakima Valley Harrison Hill 1994: Breathtakingly pure berry and currant flavors pierce through a layer of a chewy tannins and bright acidity, promising great things by 2000 or 2002. 100 percent Cabernet Sauvignon. 330 cases made. • $32 • (07/31/97) • **92**

Chaleur Estate Yakima Valley 1994: Deep, dark and dense with sweet berry and tobacco flavors, a bit sharp on the finish, but layered with delicious Cabernet flavors. Give it until 1999 to come together. A blend of 66 percent Cabernet Sauvignon, 25 percent Merlot, and 9 percent Cabernet Franc. 1,200 cases made. • $32 • (07/31/97) • **89**

Chaleur Estate Yakima Valley 1993: Ripe, rich, supple and glowing with plum, black cherry, blueberry and gently spicy flavors that last and last on the generous finish. 950 cases made. • $28 • (08/31/96) • **91**

Chaleur Estate Yakima Valley 1992 • $28 • (09/30/95) • **85**

D2 Red Yakima Valley 1994: Bright flavors of blackberry, currant and vanilla shine through a layer of chewy tannins. It's all packed in there, it just needs until 2000 to soften. A blend of 43 percent Cabernet Sauvignon, 40 percent Merlot, and 17 percent Cabernet Franc. 1,050 cases made. • $22 • (07/31/97) • **90**

Key: SS—Spectator Selection CS—Cellar Selection HR—Highly Recommended BB—Best Buy $NA—Price not available Ⓐ—Auction Price (BT)—Barrel Tasting

Dates in parentheses indicate the issues in which the ratings were published.

D2 Red Yakima Valley 1993: Ripe and distinguished for its currant, prune and plum flavors, and its chocolate, coffee and spice overtones, all of which swirl smoothly through the long finish. This Washington red blend has fine tannins now, but try to holding it through 2000 to 2002. 475 cases made. • $18 • (08/31/96) HR • **92**

Sauvignon Blanc-Sémillon Chaleur Estate 1995: Toasty, spicecake flavors shoulder past the raffish green-apple and nectarine notes in this vibrant, if odd-tasting, wine. Not for everyone, but it has style. 250 cases made. • $18 • (04/30/97) • **87**

DELORIMIER | CALIFORNIA

Chardonnay Alexander Valley 1996: Packed with fruit flavor, this has a bright range of citrus and pineapple up front, with hints of caramel and spice on the slightly raisiny finish. Best from 1999. 1,500 cases made. • $16 • (03/31/98) • **87**

Chardonnay Alexander Valley 1995: Shows off a spicy, Muscat-like aroma that makes way for a more complex palate of pear and apple flavors, all the while keeping its spicy edge. 900 cases made. • $16 • (05/15/97) • **88**

Chardonnay Alexander Valley 1994: Distinctly spicy and Muscat-like; fans of this style will like its openly fruity character. 1,000 cases made. • $15 • (07/31/96) • **84**

Chardonnay Alexander Valley 1993 • $14 • (02/29/96) • **85**

Chardonnay Alexander Valley Clonal Select 1994: A medium-weight style of wine, with appealing peach, smoky oak and honey notes, and distinct for its spicy qualities. 208 cases made. • $20 • (06/30/96) • **88**

Mosaic Alexander Valley Meritage 1994: Appealing for its ripe, supple plum and wild berry flavors and modest tannins, this is an approachable wine that's easy to drink now. 900 cases made. • $20 • (11/15/97) • **86**

Mosaic Alexander Valley Meritage 1993: Smells ripe and fruity, with juicy plum and berry flavors on the palate and mild tannins that make it attractive to drink now and through the end of the millennium. Very tasty. 730 cases made. • $20 • (11/15/96) • **89**

Mosaic Alexander Valley Meritage 1992 • $18 • (03/31/96) • **85**

Mosaic Alexander Valley Meritage 1991 • $18 • (08/31/95) • **85**

Mosaic Alexander Valley Meritage 1990 • $18 • (06/15/94) • **77**

Mosaic Alexander Valley Meritage 1988 • $18 • (06/15/93) • **81**

Mosaic Alexander Valley Meritage 1986 • $16 • (10/31/89) • **84**

Mosaic Alexander Valley Mertiage 1987 • $18 • (03/31/92) • **81**

Sauvignon Blanc Alexander Valley 1996: An understated style, with grassy, grapefruit flavors. A little sour on the finish. 2,000 cases made. • $10 • (11/30/97) • **83**

Sauvignon Blanc Alexander Valley 1995: Bright, generous and open-textured, it's centered around fig, melon and grapefruit, all lingering nicely on the finish. A great California Sauvignon, and what a buy for such quality. 1,350 cases made. • $10 • (11/15/96) HR • **90**

Sauvignon Blanc Late Harvest Alexander Valley Lace 1994: Smooth, centered around ripe pear and honey flavors. Not terribly sweet, but balanced and elegant. Ready to drink. 260 cases made. • $16/375ml • (11/30/96) • **86**

Sauvignon Blanc Late Harvest Alexander Valley Lace 1986 • $11/375ml • (02/29/88) • **82**

Spectrum Alexander Valley Meritage 1996: Rich in melon, grapefruit, lemon and sweet-pea flavors, the wine is fairly silky on the palate. A tangy dose of acidity brightens the finish. A blend of 69 percent Sauvignon Blanc and 31 percent Sémillon. 1,200 cases made. • $14 • (03/31/98) • **87**

Spectrum Alexander Valley Meritage 1995: A lively wine with layers of pineapple, herb and citrus flavor bouncing through the finish. Drink soon, while it's fresh. 900 cases made. • $12 • (04/30/97) • **87**

Spectrum Alexander Valley Meritage 1994 • $10 • (06/30/96) • **84**

Spectrum Alexander Valley Meritage 1993: Distinctly herbal, with vanilla and citrus overtones to the creamy, perfumy flavors. Ready now. 935 cases made. • $10 • (09/15/96) • **83**

DEMOOR | CALIFORNIA

Cabernet Sauvignon Napa Valley 1989 • $14 • (05/15/94) • **86**

Cabernet Sauvignon Napa Valley 1987 • $16 • (11/15/91) • **76**

Cabernet Sauvignon Napa Valley 1984 • $14 • (08/31/88) • **89**

Cabernet Sauvignon Napa Valley Napa Cellars 1981 • $13 • (04/16/86) • **95**

Cabernet Sauvignon Napa Valley Owners Select 1986 • $16 • (02/28/91) • **78**

Chardonnay Napa Valley 1993 • $12 • (07/31/95) • **80**

Sauvignon Blanc Late Harvest Napa Valley Fie Doux 1989 • $12/375ml • (03/15/92) • **84**

Zinfandel Napa Valley 1991 • $10 • (09/30/93) • **87**

Zinfandel Napa Valley 1988 • $10 • (04/30/91) • **72**

DENATALE | CALIFORNIA

Pinot Noir Russian River Valley 1990 • $8 • (02/28/93) • **82**

DEUX AMIS | CALIFORNIA

Cabernet Sauvignon Dry Creek Valley 1987 • $14 • (11/15/91) • **83**

Zinfandel Dry Creek Valley Rued Vineyards 1995: Shows off rich raspberry, pepper and spice flavors with surprising finesse. Focused berry and pepper flavors continue to mingle on the long finish. Drink now through 2000. 250 cases made. • $20 • (06/15/98) • **87**

Zinfandel Sonoma County 1995: Hints of plum and cola introduce this wine, which pans out on the palate to feature plums, anise and herbs. A touch of bitterness on the finish. Drink now. 1,450 cases made. • $15 • (05/31/98) • **83**

Zinfandel Sonoma County 1994: Solid, with ripe cherry and berry flavors, hints of cracked pepper and spice. A big, robust style that will please many, and the tannins are in line. 1,400 cases made. • $14 • (04/30/97) • **85**

Zinfandel Sonoma County 1993 • $12 • (10/15/95) • **86**

DEVLIN | CALIFORNIA

Cabernet Sauvignon Santa Cruz Mountains Beauregard Ranch 1991 • $9 • (02/28/95) • **73**

Cabernet Sauvignon Sonoma County 1981 • $6 • (08/01/85) • **83**

Merlot Central Coast 1982 • $8 • (07/16/85) • **80**

DEVON CELLARS | WASHINGTON

Dedication Yakima Valley 1992: Lean and a bit stalky, but bright, berry flavors win in the end. Drinkable now. 85 cases made. • $19 • (07/31/96) • **81**

DI BRUNO | CALIFORNIA

Pinot Grigio Santa Barbara County Sanford & Benedict Vineyard 1996: Firm yet smooth, this displays balanced acidity, with toasty, hazelnut and fresh pea flavors. It has finesse and a lovely lemony finish. A first release from Sanford Winery winemaker Bruno D'Alfonso. 170 cases made. • $14 • (05/15/98) • **87**

DI STEFANO | WASHINGTON

Cabernet Sauvignon Columbia Valley 1994: Ripe, round and powerful in flavor, and nicely sculpted to polish the texture, which lets the earthy, mineral-scented, eucalyptus-shaded blackberry, currant and pepper flavors linger on the concentrated finish. Impressive now, best from 2000 to 2002. 800 cases made. • $26 • (09/30/97) • **92**

Cabernet Sauvignon Columbia Valley 1993: Ripe, smoky and polished, the velvety texture wraps around plush plum, blackberry and spicy oak flavors. A juicy wine with fine tannins and flavor to burn. Drink through 1999. 400 cases made. • $21 • (09/15/96) • **91**

Cabernet Sauvignon Columbia Valley 1991 • $16 • (09/30/94) • **84**

Fumé Blanc Columbia Valley 1995: Bright, crisp and citrusy, with a spicy-herbal character hovering over the lime and green apple flavors. A great value from Washinton that has a distinctive, lively finish. 2,000 cases made. • $8 • (09/30/96) BB • **88**

Fumé Blanc Willamette Valley 1996: Fruity, floral flavors lend plenty of charm to this polished, silky white. Ready to drink. 1,200 cases made. • $9 • (10/31/97) • **85**

DIAMOND CREEK | CALIFORNIA

Cabernet Sauvignon Napa Valley Red Rock Terrace 1979: Austere—in a classy way. Tightly wound, with pretty, mature black cherry- and currant-laced flavors. A fine balance between the fruit and the tannins. Still has time on its side. • $67 • (06/15/98) • **90**

Cabernet Sauvignon Napa Valley Gravelly Meadow 1997: Brimming with ripe, rich, complex fruit, serving up ripe cherry, currant, pepper and spice. Long, sleek, deeply concentrated and firmly tannic. Impressive for its depth and richness. • $NA • (07/31/98) (BT) • **90-94**

Cabernet Sauvignon Napa Valley Gravelly Meadow 1996: The lightest and most supple of the Diamond Creeks, it's a subtle wine with an earthy, clay-like flavor adding dimension to the currant and cherry flavors. • $80 • (06/15/97) (BT) • **90-94**

Cabernet Sauvignon Napa Valley Gravelly Meadow 1995: Simply delicious, with an amazing amount of fruit complexity and tiers of currant, black cherry, plum and spice. Remarkably rich and concentrated on the finish. • $75 • (06/15/98) • **96**

Cabernet Sauvignon Napa Valley Gravelly Meadow 1994: An elegant, sophisticated wine; complex, with ripe cherry, sweet plum and spicy anise and cedary notes. Finishes with a long, full aftertaste and mellow tannins. Best from 2001 through 2010. • $100 • (06/15/98) • **93**

Cabernet Sauvignon Napa Valley Gravelly Meadow 1993: Marked by mint and herbal flavors, it manages to counter with enough coffee and currant notes to keep it in balance. Complex aftertaste. Drinkable now. 650 cases made. • $50 • (12/15/95) • **86**

Cabernet Sauvignon Napa Valley Gravelly Meadow 1992: Supple and showy in this group, with ripe, polished plum, cherry and wild berry flavors. Finishes with elegant tannins. Best from 2001 through 2010. • $50 • (06/15/98) • **92**

Cabernet Sauvignon Napa Valley Gravelly Meadow 1991: Solid, dense and chewy, with a wonderful core of currant, blackberry and spice. Intense and concentrated, it's approachable now but is sure to improve. Best from 2000 through 2010. • $48 Ⓐ • (06/15/98) • **92**

Cabernet Sauvignon Napa Valley Gravelly Meadow 1990: Austere, with a stony, flinty edge to the currant and berry flavors. Muscular tannins on the finish. Best to cellar into 2002. • $41 Ⓐ • (06/15/98) • **88**

Cabernet Sauvignon Napa Valley Gravelly Meadow 1989: Earthy and complex-typical of this vineyard-with layers of clay, spice, berry and cherry; long and lingering on the finish. Needs time. Best from 2002. • $22 Ⓐ • (06/15/98) • **89**

Cabernet Sauvignon Napa Valley Gravelly Meadow 1988: Youthful, medium-weight, with tart berry and cherry-laced flavors. Balanced, with firm tannins. Not from a great vintage, but this wine may well surprise by 2002. • $NA • (06/15/98) • **87**

Cabernet Sauvignon Napa Valley Gravelly Meadow 1987: An earthy wine, crisp and intense, this may well surprise with age. Has plenty of flavor and depth, but remains austere. Best from 1999 through 2005. • $67 Ⓐ • (06/15/98) • **89**

Cabernet Sauvignon Napa Valley Gravelly Meadow 1986: Displays tremendous depth, richness and complexity. Youthful and vibrant, with currant, berry, cherry and spice. Has years to go. Drink now through 2004. • $40 Ⓐ • (06/15/98) • **92**

Cabernet Sauvignon Napa Valley Gravelly Meadow 1985 • $53 Ⓐ • (11/30/87) • **89**

Cabernet Sauvignon Napa Valley Gravelly Meadow 1984: Tight and well-focused, with complex currant and berry-laced flavors that pick up intensity on the finish. Drink now through 2005. • $53 Ⓐ • (06/15/98) • **90**

Cabernet Sauvignon Napa Valley Gravelly Meadow 1983: Shows off plenty of vibrant plum and berry flavor for such a difficult and tannic vintage. A successful 1983, with remarkable length, finesse and texture. • $34 Ⓐ • (06/15/98) • **88**

Cabernet Sauvignon Napa Valley Gravelly Meadow 1982: Elegant and complex, in an understated style, with mature currant, anise, sage, tea and tar flavors that hold on the finish. • $36 Ⓐ • (06/15/98) • **88**

Cabernet Sauvignon Napa Valley Gravelly Meadow 1981: Racy, with an herbaceous streak and not as much fruit as the Red Rock Terrace and Volcanic Hill bottlings. Thins out on the finish. Past its prime. • $34 Ⓐ • (06/15/98) • **84**

Cabernet Sauvignon Napa Valley Gravelly Meadow 1978: Rich and complex, with earthy currant, sage, tar and spice. Has reached a fine drinking plateau, finishing with complex mineral notes. • $104 Ⓐ • (06/15/98) • **91**

Cabernet Sauvignon Napa Valley Gravelly Meadow 1976: Drying, with mature, complex Cabernet flavors that finish with sage and tea notes. • $67 • (06/15/98) • **84**

Cabernet Sauvignon Napa Valley Gravelly Meadow 1975: Dense, with an earthy, slightly medicinal edge. The fruit is very ripe, with hints of Port and raisin. Holds together nicely on the finish, with currant and berry notes. • $NA • (06/15/98) • **90**

Cabernet Sauvignon Napa Valley Gravelly Meadow 1974: Fully mature, still austere, with earthy currant, mineral and spice notes. Complex on the aftertaste, where the flavors linger. Drink now. • $NA • (06/15/98) • **88**

Cabernet Sauvignon Napa Valley Gravelly Meadow Lake 1992: Subtle, with complex earthy currant and berry-laced flavors. Succeeds with its delicacy and finesse. Best to age into 2002. • $NA • (06/15/98) • **90**

Cabernet Sauvignon Napa Valley Gravelly Meadow Lake Blend 1991 • $50 • (11/15/93) • **90**

Cabernet Sauvignon Napa Valley Gravelly Meadow Microclimate 1991: Tighter than the regular bottling, it nonetheless exhibits a firm core of spicy currant and wild berry flavors. With this wonderful dense core of fruit, it just needs time to develop. Best from 2002 through 2012. • $150 • (06/15/98) • **90**

Cabernet Sauvignon Napa Valley Gravelly Meadow Special Select 1982: This lean, earthy wine is devoid of fruit. One of the least interesting and least flavorful of Diamond Creek's wines. • $NA • (06/15/98) • **80**

Cabernet Sauvignon Napa Valley Lake 1994: A tightly wound, deeply concentrated young wine that is years from maturity, with hints of coffee, currant and cedar. Best from 2004 through 2010. • $125 Ⓐ • (06/15/98) • **93**

Cabernet Sauvignon Napa Valley Lake 1992: Wonderful richness, depth and complexity, with tiers of spicy currant, berry and cherry. Delicious fruit and supple texture. • $121 Ⓐ • (06/15/98) • **94**

Cabernet Sauvignon Napa Valley Lake 1990: Graceful and harmonious, with complex spice, currant, cedar and anise flavors. Long and lingering, it has years to go and should start softening by 2000 to 2004; and should then last until 2010. • $191 Ⓐ • (06/15/98) • **92**

Cabernet Sauvignon Napa Valley Lake 1987: Clearly the best of the 1987s. Wonderful aromas and flavors, with ripe plum, black cherry and spice nuances, and a strong anise aftertaste. Fine balance; crisp but ripe tannins. Best from 1999 through 2009. • $242 Ⓐ • (06/15/98) • **93**

Cabernet Sauvignon Napa Valley Lake 1984: Intense and lively, with enormously deep, concentrated flavors. Rich with chocolaty currant, berry and black cherry. Long on the finish. Drink now through 2004. • $201 Ⓐ • (06/15/98) • **94**

Cabernet Sauvignon Napa Valley Lake 1978: Still gets my vote as the finest Diamond Creek ever, though its atypical style isn't as dark in color or as massive as many DC bottlings. Ripe, rich and deeply concentrated, with tiers of plum, currant, berry and spice. Wonderful silky-smooth texture and enticing aromas. Exaggerated fruit flavors and astonishing length on the finish. Best now through 2006. • $528 Ⓐ • (06/15/98) • **97**

Cabernet Sauvignon Napa Valley Red Rock Terrace 1997: Remarkably complex and concentrated, with layers of rich currant, plum, cherry and spicy-peppery notes. Long and complex on the finish. Amazing density and concentration. • $NA • (07/31/98) (BT) • **95-99**

Cabernet Sauvignon Napa Valley Red Rock Terrace 1996: Firm and tight, well-focused, with a juicy core of earthy cherry, currant and berry flavors. Finish is long, with chewy tannins. • $80 • (06/15/97) (BT) • **90-94**

Cabernet Sauvignon Napa Valley Red Rock Terrace 1995: Lovely orchestration of complex cherry, currant and floral flavors. Classic in its balance and grace. Long on the finish. A great young Red Rock Terrace. Best from 2005 through 2012. • $75 • (06/15/98) • **96**

Cabernet Sauvignon Napa Valley Red Rock Terrace 1994: A shade more supple and less flavorful, but nonetheless a complex, tightly-wound, remarkably fruity wine. Best from 2004. • $100 • (06/15/98) • **91**

Cabernet Sauvignon Napa Valley Red Rock Terrace 1993: Medium-bodied, intense and tannic, with a modest core of currant, cedar and berry notes. Comes across as lacking richness and concentration. 750 cases made. • $50 • (12/15/95) • **85**

Cabernet Sauvignon Napa Valley Red Rock Terrace 1992: Elegant but quite complete, with ripe cherry, sage, spice and berry flavors. Youthful, long and vibrant. Best from 2002 through 2010. • $58 • (06/15/98) • **91** • (11/15/93) • **90**

Cabernet Sauvignon Napa Valley Red Rock Terrace 1991: Wonderfully perfumed currant, plum and wild berry, turning rich, intense, focused and concentrated, with a long, lively aftertaste. A great wine with a great future. Best from 2001 through 2011. • $25 Ⓐ • (06/15/98) • **94**

Cabernet Sauvignon Napa Valley Red Rock Terrace 1990: A touch herbaceous if not racy, it combines ripe, intense fruit yet is supple and fleshy. Lacks the depth and concentration of the best Red Rock Terrace bottlings, but is still impressive. • $34 Ⓐ • (06/15/98) • **89**

Cabernet Sauvignon Napa Valley Red Rock Terrace 1989 • $24 Ⓐ • (01/31/92) • **89**

Cabernet Sauvignon Napa Valley Red Rock Terrace 1988: An excellent '88, with ripe cherry and currant, pretty spice shadings, firm but ripe tannins and, most importantly, a long and lingering finish. • $26 Ⓐ • (06/15/98) • **89**

Key: SS—Spectator Selection CS—Cellar Selection HR—Highly Recommended BB—Best Buy $NA—Price not available Ⓐ—Auction Price (BT)—Barrel Tasting
Dates in parentheses indicate the issues in which the ratings were published.

Cabernet Sauvignon Napa Valley Red Rock Terrace 1987: Austere, with a crisp, flinty, citruslike edge to the currant and cherry flavors. Still needs time; may surprise. Drink now through 2004. • $40 Ⓐ • (06/15/98) • **87**

Cabernet Sauvignon Napa Valley Red Rock Terrace 1986: Dark, ripe, rich and concentrated, with vibrant currant, black cherry, tar, sage and spice, it packs in lots of complex flavors. Still has a long way to go. Drink now through 2006. • $40 Ⓐ • (06/15/98) • **92**

Cabernet Sauvignon Napa Valley Red Rock Terrace 1985 • $63 Ⓐ • (11/30/87) • **91**

Cabernet Sauvignon Napa Valley Red Rock Terrace 1984: Ripe and flavorful, this greets you with pretty floral, plum, cherry and spice nuances. Quite complete, with a complex aftertaste. Has the tannin and balance to age through 2006. • $56 Ⓐ • (06/15/98) • **92**

Cabernet Sauvignon Napa Valley Red Rock Terrace 1983: Austere. More typical of the vintage than is the Volcanic Hill, which is more expressive. Serves up crisp cherry and currant flavors. • $32 Ⓐ • (06/15/98) • **84**

Cabernet Sauvignon Napa Valley Red Rock Terrace 1982: A rich, dark-colored wine that's remarkably complex with its earthy currant, herb and tea flavors. Finishes with drying tannins. Drink now through 2000. • $35 Ⓐ • (06/15/98) • **90**

Cabernet Sauvignon Napa Valley Red Rock Terrace 1981: An elegant style; not as dense as most Diamond Creeks, but nonetheless complex and flavorful, with ripe, spicy cherry and berry flavors. Drink now. • $35 Ⓐ • (06/15/98) • **88**

Cabernet Sauvignon Napa Valley Red Rock Terrace 1980: Has the subtle nuances you hope for in a fine, aged Cabernet, with complex, mature cherry, currant, herb and berry. Drink now. • $47 Ⓐ • (06/15/98) • **88**

Cabernet Sauvignon Napa Valley Red Rock Terrace 1978: A grand wine that's still youthful, with ripe, juicy cherry and plummy Cabernet flavors. Elegant, detailed, complex, lively, lingering, spicy and still years from fading. • $104 Ⓐ • (06/15/98) • **96**

Cabernet Sauvignon Napa Valley Red Rock Terrace 1976: Drying, with a slight metallic edge, but the core of flavor is built around earthy, meaty currant, anise and mineral flavors. Hints of cherry and chocolate emerge on the finish. • $63 Ⓐ • (06/15/98) • **88**

Cabernet Sauvignon Napa Valley Red Rock Terrace 1975: Dark, dense, enormously complex and concentrated, with rich currant, mineral, anise, sage and cedar. Long and full-bodied on the aftertaste. Many years to go. • $NA • (06/15/98) • **94**

Cabernet Sauvignon Napa Valley Red Rock Terrace 1974 • $88 Ⓐ • (11/15/94) • **92**

Cabernet Sauvignon Napa Valley Red Rock Terrace 1972: Very complex, with a broad range of earthy currant, plum, berry, sage and spice flavors. Long, intricate, lingering aftertaste. • $NA • (06/15/98) • **90**

Cabernet Sauvignon Napa Valley Red Rock Terrace First Pick 1977: Notably herbaceous, even weedy. It takes time for the earthy, dusty currant flavors to peek through. Still tannic and minty on the finish. • $90 • (06/15/98) • **85**

Cabernet Sauvignon Napa Valley Red Rock Terrace Second Pick 1977: A lean wine, with more cherry tones than the First Pick bottling, but overall not as flavorful. • $30 • (06/15/98) • **84**

Cabernet Sauvignon Napa Valley Red Rock Terrace Microclimate 3 1991 • $50 • (11/15/93) CS • **94**

Cabernet Sauvignon Napa Valley Red Rock Terrace Microclimate 2 1994: Intense, with brilliant fruit concentration. Deep, perfumed and complex currant, cedar, anise and berry. Long and detailed on the finish. • $150 • (06/15/98) • **93**

Cabernet Sauvignon Napa Valley Red Rock Terrace Special Select 1982: Simple for Diamond Creek's lineup, with modest, mature Cabernet flavors. To call this wine special Select is misleading: this was a lighter wine that didn't fit in with the main cuvée, and really isn't special. • $60 • (06/15/98) • **82**

Cabernet Sauvignon Napa Valley Three Vineyard Blend 1990: Ruggedly tannic; backward in many ways, with a decidedly earthy quality. Best to keep until 2002. • $150 • (06/15/98) • **88**

Cabernet Sauvignon Napa Valley Three Vineyard Blend 1989: Solid, crisp and austere, with pleasant currant, berry and cherry flavors and light (for Diamond Creek) tannins. Drink now through 2005. • $150 • (06/15/98) • **87**

Cabernet Sauvignon Napa Valley Three Vineyard Blend 1985: A rare bottling that combines Diamond Creek's three main vineyards (and Lake), this is a complex and flavorful wine, with firm currant, black cherry, anise, herb and spice nuances. Drink now through 2004. • $150 • (06/15/98) • **90**

Cabernet Sauvignon Napa Valley Three Vineyard Blend 1981: Elegant, with pleasant currant, herb and spice; it turns simple on the finish. Drink now. • $150 • (06/15/98) • **84**

UNITED STATES

Cabernet Sauvignon Napa Valley Volcanic Hill 1997: Serves up lots of dense, rich, chewy currant, plum and blackberry. Remarkable finesse and concentration, with a long, complex, fruity aftertaste. • $NA • (07/31/98) (BT) • **95-99**

Cabernet Sauvignon Napa Valley Volcanic Hill 1996: Tight and tannic, with an austere, earthy edge to its currant and cherry flavors. A big, expansive wine that's dense and concentrated. • $80 • (06/15/97) (BT) • **90-94**

Cabernet Sauvignon Napa Valley Volcanic Hill 1995: Intense and deeply concentrated, with an abundance of ripe, rich, lively currant, black cherry and chocolaty Cabernet flavors. Impeccable balance and length. Best from 2004 through 2012. • $75 • (06/15/98) • **94**

Cabernet Sauvignon Napa Valley Volcanic Hill 1994: Tight, complex and backward, with grape, currant- and berry-laced flavors and firm tannins on the finish. Hold off until 2004 to 2006. • $100 • (06/15/98) • **91**

Cabernet Sauvignon Napa Valley Volcanic Hill 1993: Austere, dry and dusty. Tightly-wound and complex, with spicy cherry and currant flavors. • $50 • (06/15/98) • **88**

Cabernet Sauvignon Napa Valley Volcanic Hill 1992: Openly fruity for a young Volcanic Hill. Dense, ripe, rich and concentrated, with tiers of currant, plum and cherry and a long, full, lingering aftertaste. Hands off until 2002; it should age well past 2012. • $50 Ⓐ • (06/15/98) • **92**

Cabernet Sauvignon Napa Valley Volcanic Hill 1991: Wonderfully rich and concentrated, with a complex array of currant, berry, spice, anise and cedar flavors. Long and full on the finish. Still years from peaking. Best from 2001 through 2011. • $37 Ⓐ • (06/15/98) • **93**

Cabernet Sauvignon Napa Valley Volcanic Hill 1990: Intense, lively, complex and concentrated. Rich with vibrant currant, plum, cherry and spice. Long and lingering on the finish. Best from 2003 through 2010. • $38 Ⓐ • (06/15/98) • **93**

Cabernet Sauvignon Napa Valley Volcanic Hill 1989: Surprisingly ripe and complex, it shows off attractive earthy, clay-laced currant notes and finishes with a long, full aftertaste. • $35 Ⓐ • (06/15/98) • **89**

Cabernet Sauvignon Napa Valley Volcanic Hill 1988: Austere, even grapey at age 10. Tight, with a narrow range of cherry and currant flavors, turning dry on the finish. • $29 Ⓐ • (06/15/98) • **87**

Cabernet Sauvignon Napa Valley Volcanic Hill 1987: A touch herbaceous; with racy, leafy, herbal notes, it struggles to show its ripe Cabernet fruit. Drink now through 2004. • $67 Ⓐ • (06/15/98) • **87**

Cabernet Sauvignon Napa Valley Volcanic Hill 1986: Dark, dense, ripe and flavorful, with complex mint, currant, blackberry and earth nuances. Tannins are softening, but this wine can age another decade. Drink now through 2008. • $58 Ⓐ • (06/15/98) • **91**

Cabernet Sauvignon Napa Valley Volcanic Hill 1985: Austere, even at this age. Crisp style, with firm currant, spice, cedar and sage notes. Clearly a restrained, backward wine that needs more time. May surprise by 2002. • $49 Ⓐ • (06/15/98) • **90**

Cabernet Sauvignon Napa Valley Volcanic Hill 1984: A tremendous wine. Ripe, vibrant and fruity, with cherry, currant, anise, sage and cedar. Intensely concentrated, with a long and lingering finish. Drink now through 2006. • $50 Ⓐ • (06/15/98) • **93**

Cabernet Sauvignon Napa Valley Volcanic Hill 1983: Lean and tight, still it slowly fans out to show complex currant, sage and spice nuances. Drink now. • $36 Ⓐ • (06/15/98) • **88**

Cabernet Sauvignon Napa Valley Volcanic Hill 1982: Austere, with a twinge of herbaceousness. Tightly-wound, with spice, mineral, sage and currant. Drink now. • $35 Ⓐ • (06/15/98) • **87**

Cabernet Sauvignon Napa Valley Volcanic Hill 1981: Healthy dark color, with earthy, leathery Cabernet flavors and good length on the finish. Drink now through 2001. • $40 Ⓐ • (06/15/98) • **88**

Cabernet Sauvignon Napa Valley Volcanic Hill 1980: Dark, dense and chewy, with complex earthy, meaty, currant, spice and tar notes. Concentrated and sturdy, with a long, full finish. Can still age. • $50 Ⓐ • (06/15/98) • **91**

Cabernet Sauvignon Napa Valley Volcanic Hill 1979: Youthful, as evidenced by its grapey currant core of fruit. Picks up complex mineral, sage and cedar notes. Still has tannins to shed. • $64 Ⓐ • (06/15/98) • **91**

Cabernet Sauvignon Napa Valley Volcanic Hill 1978: Rich, ripe, complex and concentrated. A racy streak runs through the currant, black cherry and vanilla notes. The finish delivers a wealth of floral and plummy flavors. Delicious. • $105 Ⓐ • (06/15/98) • **93**

Cabernet Sauvignon Napa Valley Volcanic Hill 1976: Mature, with a dry mineral edge to the flinty currant and cedar flavors. Past its prime, but holding up well. Drink now. • $57 Ⓐ • (06/15/98) • **88**

Cabernet Sauvignon Napa Valley Volcanic Hill 1975: A powerful wine with enormous depth, richness and flavor, yet through it all it displays a wonderful measure of finesse. Shows off dense and earthy mineral, currant, herb, sage and tea flavors. May last another 10 years. • $58 Ⓐ • (06/15/98) • **94**

Cabernet Sauvignon Napa Valley Volcanic Hill 1974: Fading now after a long successful run. Turning dry and earthy, with sage and mineral flavors. Drink now. • $70 • (06/15/98) • **86**

Cabernet Sauvignon Napa Valley Volcanic Hill 1973: Austere, with a thin band of mature Cabernet flavors. Less complex, flavorful and interesting than the 1972. • $150 • (06/15/98) • **82**

Cabernet Sauvignon Napa Valley Volcanic Hill 1972: A pleasant surprise. Still youthful, with plum, earth and mushroom flavors. Fine balance and length. Lovely, lingering aftertaste. • $150 • (06/15/98) • **90**

Cabernet Sauvignon Napa Valley Volcanic Hill First Pick 1979: A tremendous vintage for Diamond Creek. Youthful and complex, with appealing earthy currant, mineral and spice and a long, concentrated, vibrant finish. • $90 • (06/15/98) • **93**

Cabernet Sauvignon Napa Valley Volcanic Hill Microclimate 1991: Tightly-wound, much like the other Volcanic Hill bottling, with a trim band of spicy currant, plum and cedar. Firmly tannic; too early to drink. Best from 2002 through 0. • $150 • (06/15/98) • **92**

Cabernet Sauvignon Napa Valley Volcanic Hill Microclimate 4 1991 • $50 • (11/15/93) CS • **93**

Cabernet Sauvignon Napa Valley Volcanic Hill Special Select 1982: Complex, with a pleasant earthiness to the currant and spice flavors. Displays a clay-like aftertaste on the finish. Drink now. • $42 • (06/15/98) • **88**

DICKERSON | CALIFORNIA

Merlot Napa Valley 1994: Young and vibrant, with tart black cherry, spice and cedar flavors. Turns tannic on the finish. 234 cases made. • $16 • (11/30/96) • **84**

Merlot Napa Valley Limited Release 1995: This wine shows bright fruit—blackberry and plums, plus spice notes and a toasty oak component. A little coarse in texture, but still flavorful. Drink now. 200 cases made. • $22 • (06/15/98) • **86**

Merlot Napa Valley Limited Reserve 1993: Young and intense, with a vibrant core of plum, black cherry, herb and toasty oak. Has a big, firm tannic structure. Try now. 229 cases made. • $16 • (08/31/96) • **87**

Merlot Napa Valley Limited Reserve 1992 • $17 • (02/28/95) HR • **90**

Ruby Cabernet Napa Valley 1994: On the tart side, with a green edge to the red cherry and wild berry flavors. Finishes with supple tannins. Ready to drink. 254 cases made. • $10 • (11/15/96) • **84**

Ruby Cabernet Napa Valley 1992 • $10 • (05/15/95) • **85**

Ruby Cabernet Napa Valley 1988 • $9 • (02/28/91) • **79**

Ruby Cabernet Napa Valley Limited Reserve 1993 • $9 • (12/15/95) • **88**

Ruby Cabernet Napa Valley Limited Reserve 1991 • $11 • (11/15/94) • **87**

Zinfandel Napa Valley Limited Reserve 1995: Crisp and tight. Despite its earthy wild berry, sage and cedary oak, it fails to develop extra facets. Available only through the winery. Drink now. 200 cases made. • $22 • (06/15/98) • **84**

Zinfandel Napa Valley Limited Reserve 1994: Lots of ripe, juicy, beefy Zinfandel and raspberry flavors, with a tannic, herbal, minty edge. Lacks the richness and concentration usually found in this wine. Drinks well now. 182 cases made. • $19 • (11/15/96) • **84**

Zinfandel Napa Valley Limited Reserve 1993 • $17 • (12/31/95) • **88**

Zinfandel Napa Valley Limited Reserve 1991 • $19 • (10/15/94) • **92**

DOLAN | CALIFORNIA

Cabernet Sauvignon Mendocino 1984 • $12 • (05/31/88) • **88**

Cabernet Sauvignon Mendocino 1983 • $12 • (02/29/88) • **86**

Merlot California 1986 • $8 • (01/31/89) • **88**

DOLCE | CALIFORNIA

Late Harvest California 1994: Smooth, silky, supple-textured and sweet, this dessert white overflows with lovely honey-scented pear and peach flavors that linger delicately on the finish. It's delicious now, but will deepen further by 2000, so try to hold off until then. 1,000 cases made. • $55/375ml • (03/31/98) • **95**

Late Harvest California 1993: Wonderfully rich and complex, with tiers of honey, pear, apricot, butterscotch, vanilla and spice, all unfolding gracefully onto the palate, where they're smooth and elegant. Finish is long, smooth and refined. Delicious now. 1,500 cases made. • $50/375ml • (02/28/97) • **92**

Late Harvest California 1992 • $50/375ml • (12/31/95) • **90**

Late Harvest California 1991: Smooth and generous. A lush mouthful of fig, honey, pineapple and pear flavors that swirl and linger seductively on the rich texture. Long and delicious, this feels ready now, but could develop more depth with cellaring past 2000. • $NA • (01/01/98) • **94**

Late Harvest California 1990 • $50/375ml • (11/15/93) HR • **92**
Late Harvest California 1989 • $50/375ml • (06/15/92) • **91**
Late Harvest Napa Valley 1995: Sweet but not lush, the nicely layered honey and pear flavors seemingly hold back, giving this an elegant feel. Lovely now, but feels like it can grow through 2002 to 2005. A blend of 90 percent Sémillon and 10 percent Sauvignon Blanc. 2,500 cases made. • $55/375ml • (05/15/98) • **90**

DOMAINE BRETON | CALIFORNIA

Zinfandel Lake County 1989 • $8 • (02/29/92) • **79**
Zinfandel Lake County 1988 • $8 • (02/15/91) • **82**

DOMAINE CARNEROS | CALIFORNIA

Blanc de Blancs Carneros 1989 • $25 • (12/15/94) • **88**
Brut Blanc de Blancs Carneros 1988 • $24 • (12/31/93) • **88**
Brut Carneros 1993: Toasty and bright, this lemony bubbly packs a refreshing mix of citrus and herb flavors. On the finish, it's a touch bitter though quite enjoyable. Drink now through 2001. 31,000 cases made. • $18 • (06/15/98) • **87**
Brut Carneros 1992: Elegant, with a spicy, citrus accent to the modest pear and mineral flavors, which slowly grow on you. Restrained in style. 35,000 cases made. • $21 • (11/30/97) • **87**
Brut Carneros 1991 • $20 • (12/31/95) • **89**
Brut Carneros Blanc de Blancs 1991: Serves up ripe pear and spicy vanilla flavors in a clean, well-balanced, easy-drinking style. Lacks full complexity at this stage, but it's young and may gain nuance with time. 3,000 cases made. • $24 • (11/30/96) • **87**
Brut Carneros Blanc de Blancs 1990: Smooth and complex, with hints of pear, vanilla and spice flavors and aromas. A remarkably elegant and refined finish. • $25 • (09/15/96) • **88**
Brut Carneros Blanc de Blancs 1989 • $25 • (05/15/96) • **90**
Pinot Noir Carneros 1995: Supple and complex, with a range of ripe, spicy cherry, plum and earth notes. It holds together and is well-focused. Ready now. 3,600 cases made. • $20 • (08/31/97) • **88**
Pinot Noir Carneros 1994 • $20 • (02/29/96) • **87**
Pinot Noir Carneros 1993 • $20 • (12/31/95) • **90**
Pinot Noir Carneros The Famous Gate 1995: Smooth and elegant, with a silky texture and pretty plum, wild berry and cherry flavors, framed by light, toasty oak notes. Drinks well now. 1,400 cases made. • $32 • (09/30/97) • **88**
Pinot Noir Carneros The Famous Gate 1994: Marked by herb and cherry flavors, with hints of earth and mushroom. A well-balanced wine with subtle, complex flavors that gently unfold. Give this a year or two to develop and it may well move up a few points. 700 cases made. • $32 • (02/28/97) • **88**
Pinot Noir Carneros The Famous Gate 1993 • $30 • (12/31/95) • **87**
Sparkling Carneros Le Rêve 1992: A bright bubbly, with tangy lemon and mineral notes up front. It's firm and focused, yet made in a delicate style. Flavors fan out on the finish, with hints of gooseberry, mint, citrus, apple and pear. A complex wine with staying power. Drink now through 2002. 3,900 cases made. • $35 • (07/31/98) • **91**

DOMAINE CHANDON | CALIFORNIA

Blanc de Noirs Carneros Cuvée 393 NV: A firm and focused Napa Valley sparkler, with toast, citrus, vanilla and hazelnut accents. The finish is fresh, with an attractive lemon-lime edge. Hard to beat this kind of quality for the price. A blend of 81 percent Pinot Noir and 19 percent Pinot Meunier. 70,000 cases made. • $11 • (11/30/97) BB • **88**
Brut Cuvée Napa-Sonoma Late Disgorged NV: This almost amber-colored wine is full of toasty, nutty, aged qualities, yet maintains racy, bright and youthful character. Flavors are complex, with layers of fig, lemon, wintergreen, almonds, grapefruit and apple. Finishes long. 486 cases made. • $60/1.5 liter • (12/31/97) • **91**
Brut Napa Valley Étoile NV: Smoky, toasty, doughy aromas herald this bright-styled bubbly. On the palate it sings out with green apple, ginger, lemon-lime, grapefruit and vanilla flavors. Fresh and lively on the finish. 10,600 cases made. • $29 • (12/31/97) • **88**

Key: SS—Spectator Selection CS—Cellar Selection HR—Highly Recommended BB—Best Buy $NA—Price not available Ⓐ—Auction Price (BT)—Barrel Tasting
Dates in parentheses indicate the issues in which the ratings were published.

Brut Napa-Sonoma Counties Cuvée 194 NV: Light in style, this California bubbly is a tangy blend of grapefruit, citrus, toast and lemon-lime flavors. It's firm and delicate, with a clean, bright, mineral finish. Tasty and of very good quality, it's also a widely available bargain. 80,000 cases made. • $11 • (12/15/97) BB • **88**
Réserve Cuvée 491 Napa County NV: Has a smooth, earthy quality, perhaps a bit flinty, too. Shows signs of age, but finishes with a fresh, lemon-lime edge. 10,000 cases made. • $19 • (11/30/97) • **86**
Sparkling California Fleur de Vigne NV: Quite fruity, with pronounced peppermint and eucalyptus notes. A bit like Moscato d'Asti. Tangy and refreshing. A fun apéritif. A blend of Chardonnay, Malvasia, Muscat Canelli, Pinot Blanc, and Pinot Noir. Drink now. 3,000 cases made. • $15 • (07/31/98) • **83**
Sparkling Napa County 25th Anniversary Réserve Cuvée NV: Fragrant, with hints of toast and honey, and some nice floral notes. Lemon and lime flavors enhance on the palate, if marred by a slightly bitter note. Drink now. 14,500 cases made. • $24 • (06/15/98) • **85**

DOMAINE CHARBAY | CALIFORNIA

Dessert Chardonnay Sonoma County NV • $5/Q.(03/31/92) • **71**

DOMAINE DE CLARCK | CALIFORNIA

Pinot Noir Monterey County Unfiltered 1991 • $20 • (02/28/94) • **81**
Pinot Noir Monterey County Villages 1992 • $10 • (02/28/94) BB • **85**
Pinot Noir Monterey County Villages 1991 • $11 • (02/28/93) • **77**
Pinot Noir Monterey County Villages 1990 • $10 • (03/31/92) • **82**
Pinot Noir Monterey Première 1989 • $15 • (04/30/91) • **77**
Pinot Noir Sonoma County Villages 1989 • $10 • (03/31/92) • **72**

DOMAINE DE LA TERRE ROUGE | CALIFORNIA

Blanc Sierra Foothills 1996: Light, searching for identity. Flinty and mineral-like on the palate, but lacking fruit. A blend of Sauvignon Blanc, Sémillon and Viognier. 525 cases made. • $14 • (12/15/97) • **80**
Blush Fiddletown Vin Gris d'Amador 1994 • $9 • (03/31/96) • **80**
Noir California 1993: A meaty, beefy, firmly tannic style that loads in plenty of earthy currant and wild berry flavors, though the tannins are rough and rustic. A blend of Grenache, Mourvèdre, Syrah, and Cinsault. 700 cases made. • $16 • (11/15/97) • **86**
Noir Sierra Foothills 1992: Appealing for its ripe, juicy fruit and range of flavors, with hints of plum, cherry and wild berry. Finishes with firm, chewy tannins, but overall it's well balanced, with complex flavors. 700 cases made. • $15 • (02/28/97) • **87**
Reserve Red California 1991 • $15 • (02/29/96) • **86**
Sierra Foothills 1986 • $12 • (04/15/89) • **89**
Syrah Amador County 1995: Quite appealing for its rustic, earthy blackberry, cherry and mineral flavors. Has some gritty tannins to work through—cellaring should help. Best from 1999 to 2001. 600 cases made. • $25 • (03/31/98) • **88**
Syrah Amador County 1994: Dark, ripe and perfumed, with a rich core of plum, wild berry, spice and currant flavors. Fills out on the palate and has good length, finishing with firm but supple tannins. Drinkable now, but another year or two should give it more dimension. 300 cases made. • $20 • (02/28/97) • **88**
Syrah Amador County 1993 • $20 • (06/15/96) • **89**
Tête-à-Tête Sierra Red Foothills 1996: Smooth and appealing for its generous cherry, sweet spice and black pepper flavors that linger gently on the finish. Nice now, better in 1999. A blend of Grenache, Syrah and Mourvèdre. 500 cases made. • $11 • (03/31/98) • **86**
Viognier Shenandoah Valley 1996: An interesting blend of coconut, hazelnut, fig, vanilla and grapefruit flavors. Long finish, with bright mineral and citrus notes. Refreshing. 225 cases made. • $25 • (12/15/97) • **88**

DOMAINE DROUHIN | OREGON

Pinot Noir Oregon 1995: On the light side, but firm enough to pack in some chewy plum, spice and toast flavors. Try now. 8,300 cases made. • $35 • (02/28/97) • **85**
Pinot Noir Oregon 1994: Firm and focused, with a bit of chewiness from the finely grained tannins. A nice thread of peppery blackberry flavor that extends into the finish. May want to cellar until 1999. 6,200 cases made. • $35 • (12/31/96) • **88**
Pinot Noir Oregon 1993 • $30 • (08/31/95) • **87**
Pinot Noir Oregon 1991 • $30 • (03/15/94) • **86**

Pinot Noir Oregon 1990 • $30 • (01/31/93) HR • **90**
Pinot Noir Oregon 1989 • $32 • (01/31/92) • **87**
Pinot Noir Oregon 1988 • $32 • (05/31/91) • **89**
Pinot Noir Oregon Laurène 1995: Pretty black cherry and floral flavors show impressive intensity up front. Gets a bit tough on the finish, but the flavors manage to peek through the firm tannins. Best from 1999. 2,000 cases made. • $45 • (05/15/98) • **88**
Pinot Noir Oregon Laurène 1994: A bright mouthful of sweet currant and blackberry flavors keeps this free and easy, sailing smoothly through the finish. It has terrific length and an amazingly supple texture. Appealing now, best from 1999 to 2000. 1,300 cases made. • $45 • (07/31/97) • **91**
Pinot Noir Oregon Laurène 1993 • $45 • (01/31/96) • **88**
Pinot Noir Oregon Laurène 1992 • $40 • (11/30/94) • **91**
Pinot Noir Oregon Non-Estate 1992 • $30 • (03/15/94) • **85**

DOMAINE MICHEL | CALIFORNIA

Cabernet Sauvignon Dry Creek Valley Michel Vineyard Reserve 1988 • $25 • (11/15/93) • **81**
Cabernet Sauvignon Sonoma County 1990 • $12 • (11/15/94) • **79**
Cabernet Sauvignon Sonoma County 1989 • $15 • (11/15/93) • **81**
Cabernet Sauvignon Sonoma County 1988 • $19 • (03/31/93) • **82**
Cabernet Sauvignon Sonoma County 1987 • $20 • (08/31/92) • **81**
Cabernet Sauvignon Sonoma County 1986 • $19 • (06/30/90) • **75**
Cabernet Sauvignon Sonoma County 1984 • $19 • (09/15/87) • **86**
Merlot Dry Creek Valley 1991 • $15 • (09/15/94) • **80**

DOMAINE NAPA | CALIFORNIA

Cabernet Sauvignon Napa Valley 1987 • $13 • (12/15/92) • **75**
Cabernet Sauvignon Napa Valley 1985 • $12 • (12/15/88) • **81**
Merlot Napa Valley 1990 • $15 • (05/31/92) • **84**

DOMAINE PHILIPPE | CALIFORNIA

Cabernet Sauvignon Napa Valley Select Cuvée 1984 • $6 • (05/15/88) BB • **87**

DOMAINE SAINT GEORGE | CALIFORNIA

Cabernet Sauvignon California Select Reserve 1994: A ripe tasting wine, showing some simple notes of plum and cherry. • $6 • (11/30/96) • **78**
Cabernet Sauvignon California Vintage Reserve 1992 • $6 • (11/15/94) BB • **85**
Cabernet Sauvignon Russian River Valley Premier Cuvée Reserve 1989 • $10 • (11/15/94) • **83**
Cabernet Sauvignon Russian River Valley Select Reserve 1986 • $9 • (05/31/90) • **79**
Cabernet Sauvignon Sonoma County 1988 • $6 • (11/15/90) BB • **83**
Cabernet Sauvignon Sonoma County Premier Cuvée Reserve 1989 • $9 • (11/15/94) • **84**
Cabernet Sauvignon Sonoma County Premier Cuvée Reserve 1988 • $8 • (11/15/93) • **77**
Cabernet Sauvignon Sonoma County Vintage Reserve 1989 • $5 • (11/15/92) • **74**
Chardonnay California Select Reserve 1994: Light and spicy, with more than a touch of bitter almond running through soapy flavors. • $6 • (11/30/96) • **74**
Chardonnay California Vintage Reserve 1993 • $6 • (01/31/95) • **80**
Merlot California Select Reserve 1995: Light, modestly flavorful, with simple black cherry and herb flavors. • $6 • (11/30/96) • **80**
Merlot Chalk Hill Premier Cuvée Reserve 1989 • $11 • (12/31/93) • **69**
Zinfandel California 1989 • $5 • (02/15/91) • **77**

DOMAINE STE. MICHELLE | WASHINGTON

Blanc de Blancs Columbia Valley 1986 • $14 • (01/31/92) • **86**
Blanc de Noirs Columbia Valley 1987 • $20 • (11/15/93) • **80**
Blanc de Noirs Columbia Valley 1986 • $17 • (01/31/92) • **80**
Blanc de Noirs Columbia Valley 1985 • $20 • (12/31/90) • **86**

DOMAINE STE. VINCENT | CALIFORNIA

Cabernet Sauvignon Sonoma County Reserve 1986 • $8 • (11/15/92) • **77**

DOMAINE SAN MARTIN | CALIFORNIA

Cabernet Sauvignon Central Coast 1981 • $7 • (10/01/85) • **76**

DOMAINE SANTA BARBARA | CALIFORNIA

Chardonnay Santa Barbara County 1996: Up front butter flavors stray toward an earthy, cheesy quality. Apple, butter and toast flavors linger on the finish, with finesse. Drink now. 1,200 cases made. • $14 • (05/31/98) • **83**
Chardonnay Santa Barbara County Bien Nacido Vineyard 1996: Bright and almost refreshing, with mango, citrus and toast notes. Has impressive intensity and a long, fruity finish. Drink now. 60 cases made. • $20 • (07/31/98) • **85**
Chardonnay Santa Barbara County Los Olivos Vineyard 1996: Starts off with a bright hazelnut aroma, backed by pretty pear and spice flavors. Smooth finish. Drink now. 200 cases made. • $19 • (07/31/98) • **86**

DOMAINE SERENE | OREGON

Pinot Noir Willamette Valley Evenstad Reserve 1995: Light, lean and crisp; a tight wine with modest berry flavors and a touch of smoky oak on the finish. Try late this year. 975 cases made. • $33 • (02/28/98) • **82**
Pinot Noir Willamette Valley Evenstad Reserve 1991 • $28 • (10/15/94) • **83**
Pinot Noir Willamette Valley Reserve 1992 • $18 • (10/15/94) • **89**
Pinot Noir Willamette Valley Reserve 1991 • $18 • (10/15/94) • **85**

DOMINUS ESTATE | CALIFORNIA

Napa Valley 1990 • $64 Ⓐ • (06/30/94) SS • **91**
Napa Valley 1989 • $45 • (11/15/93) • **89**
Napa Valley 1988 • $45 • (12/15/92) • **87**
Napa Valley 1987: Earthy currant, cherry, anise and mineral flavors work well with the supple texture and fine length. Tannins are softening. Tempting now for its detailed flavors. Best now to 2003. 6,500 cases made. • $72 • (12/15/97) • **92**
Napa Valley 1986: Starts out earthy and leathery, in a rugged style, but works its way into more complex mineral, currant and cedar flavors and finishes with a cedary, earthy note and a good dose of currant flavor. Ready now. • $44 • (12/15/96) • **88**
Napa Valley 1985 • $69 Ⓐ • (02/15/90) • **84**
Napa Valley 1983 • $48 Ⓐ • (04/15/89) • **86**
Napa Valley Napanook Vineyard 1995: A lighter style, with a supple, polished texture and some vegetal notes leading into cherry and plum flavors. Perhaps the lightest Dominus ever, and that's saying a lot. Should drink well early, and does not appear to be a long ager. Tasted twice, with consistent notes. Best from 2000 through 2005. 6,000 cases made. • $90 • (06/30/98) • **87**
Napa Valley Napanook Vineyard 1994: A complex and concentrated red, with a pretty, earthy core of anise- and currant-tinged Cabernet flavors, it slowly unfolds to reveal notes of coffee and spice. Smooth and polished in texture, it's approachable now and over the next few years. The latest in a long line of distinctive Cabernet-blend wines from Dominus. 8,500 cases made. • $75 • (07/31/97) CS • **94**
Napa Valley Napanook Vineyard 1991 • $55 • (11/15/95) CS • **93**

DONNA MARIA | CALIFORNIA

Pinot Noir Chalk Hill 1981 • $6 • (09/16/84) • **79**

DORCICH CELLARS | CALIFORNIA

Cabernet Sauvignon Santa Clara County 1991 • $18 • (07/31/95) • **86**
Cabernet Sauvignon Santa Clara County 1990 • $20 • (07/31/95) • **85**

DORE | CALIFORNIA

Cabernet Sauvignon California Limited Release Lot 102 1987 • $8 • (11/15/91) • **80**

DOS CABEZAS | ARIZONA

Chardonnay Cochise County Arizona 1996: A full-bodied, full-flavored Chardonnay with a deep gold color, lots of spicy oak aromas and enough fruit flavor to keep it interesting. Bold and rather heavy in texture. 160 cases made. • $28 • (06/15/97) • **86**

Pinot Gris Cochise County Arizona Unfiltered 1996: A big, heavy, full-bodied white wine that drips with spice, floral, smoke, butter and fruit flavors—call it a late-harvest, Alsace-style. No finesse but plenty of flavor and impact. 45 cases made. • $20 • (08/31/97) • **85**

Sauvignon Blanc Cochise County Unfiltered 1996: A rich, oaky tasting, thick-textured Sauvignon in an extreme style. Not quite balanced by the acidity and fruit. 300 cases made. • $16 • (06/15/97) • **84**

DOUGLASS HILL | CALIFORNIA

Cabernet Franc Napa Valley 1995: Attractive black cherry and anise take the lead, but a bitter, woody aftertaste brings up the rear. 1,500 cases made. • $16 • (04/30/98) • **80**

Cabernet Sauvignon Napa Valley 1994: An interesting blend of smoky oak and beefy overtones. Firm, supple tannins hold it together. Finishes long, with hints of plum, anise and cassis marred slightly by a bitter edge. 1,500 cases made. • $13 • (10/15/97) • **88**

Cabernet Sauvignon Napa Valley 1992 • $15 • (12/15/95) • **84**

Chardonnay Napa Valley 1993 • $15 • (12/31/95) • **84**

DOVER CANYON | CALIFORNIA

Zinfandel Paso Robles 1995: Pretty crushed raspberry and plum flavors show richness and intensity and the fruit is followed by a layer of pepper, spice and tar notes. A bit overripe, but there's nice depth to the flavors. Drink now. 182 cases made. • $18 • (06/15/98) • **86**

Zinfandel Paso Robles JanKris Vineyard 1996: Rich and Port-like, with concentrated prune and black pepper flavors. Packs in a lot of flavor but lacks finesse. Drink now through 2001. 98 cases made. • $18 • (06/15/98) • **83**

DRAXTON | CALIFORNIA

Sauvignon Blanc Alexander Valley 1995: A sprightly wine, redolent of grapefruit, lemon and lime. It finishes with a clean, mineral edge. Quite attractive. • $NA • (01/31/98) • **88**

DREYER SONOMA | CALIFORNIA

Cabernet Sauvignon Sonoma County 1995: Lean, firm and tight, showing plenty of focused blackberry and currant flavor that keeps singing on the taut finish. Good now, better after 1999 to 2000. 900 cases made. • $11 • (03/31/98) • **87**

Cabernet Sauvignon Sonoma County 1993: Lean and on the cedary side, this is for fans of austere Cabernets rather than folks who favor ripe, up front fruit flavors. 954 cases made. • $10 • (11/30/96) • **82**

Cabernet Sauvignon Sonoma County 1989 • $15 • (08/31/92) • **79**

Chardonnay Sonoma County 1996: Marked by mineral and toast notes, the wine is pleasant, but a little hollow on the midpalate. 4,343 cases made. • $10 • (02/28/98) • **82**

Chardonnay Sonoma County 1995: Solid, with a spicy, cedary accent and hints of pear and vanilla on the finish. An excellent value at this price. 4,000 cases made. • $10 • (04/30/97) • **86**

Chardonnay Sonoma County 1994: Fresh and floral; a Chardonnay of modest scale but charming for its spicy pear flavors. Ready now. 3,000 cases made. • $9 • (04/30/96) • **87**

DRY CREEK | CALIFORNIA

Cabernet Franc Dry Creek Valley 1990 • $18 • (10/15/93) • **83**

Cabernet Sauvignon Dry Creek Valley 1994: A band of cherry, currant, herb and cedary oak flavors that finish with mild tannins. 12,700 cases made. • $17 • (11/30/96) • **86**

Cabernet Sauvignon Dry Creek Valley 1993: Very ripe and somewhat cedary from oak. Plum and cherry notes are bright and jammy, finishing with dry tannins as flavors linger through. Try now. 9,300 cases made. • $16 • (11/30/95) • **88**

Cabernet Sauvignon Dry Creek Valley 1992 • $16 • (10/15/95) • **89**

Cabernet Sauvignon Dry Creek Valley 1974 • $55 • (11/15/94) • **83**

Cabernet Sauvignon Dry Creek Valley 25th Anniversary 1994: Ripe and complex, with concentrated blackberry, currant, plum and spice, showing a nice cedary oak flavor, all adding up to complexity and depth. Drink from 1999 to 2004. 950 cases made. • $30 • (03/31/98) • **89**

Cabernet Sauvignon Dry Creek Valley Reserve 1995: Shows off lots of ripe, spicy flavors and a center of fruit, with wild berry, cherry and plum. Picks up a minty edge on the finish, where it turns tannic. Can stand cellaring into 1999. 2,000 cases made. • $27 • (11/15/97) • **86**

Cabernet Sauvignon Dry Creek Valley Reserve 1994: Medium-weight, with ripe cherry, currant, anise and cedary flavors and soft, fleshy tannins that make it quite enjoyable now. Finishes with a nice, fruity aftertaste. Ready to drink. 2,000 cases made. • $25 • (11/30/96) • **87**

Cabernet Sauvignon Dry Creek Valley Reserve 1993: Offers a decent core of wild berry, blackberry and cherry flavors of some depth and concentration. Finishes with crisp tannins and a touch of dill from the oak. 2,000 cases made. • $22 • (03/31/96) • **83**

Cabernet Sauvignon Dry Creek Valley Reserve 1991 • $20 • (10/31/94) • **89**

Cabernet Sauvignon Sonoma County 1995: Opens with leafy, menthol and earth tones, and clocks in on the finish with plum, cedar and raspberry flavors. A bit chewy. 11,000 cases made. • $19 • (10/31/97) • **84**

Cabernet Sauvignon Sonoma County 1991 • $15 • (11/15/93) • **87**

Cabernet Sauvignon Sonoma County 1989 • $14 • (03/31/92) • **86**

Cabernet Sauvignon Sonoma County 1988 • $14 • (05/31/91) • **81**

Cabernet Sauvignon Sonoma County 1987: Slowly fading, but still in good shape, with light and simple cedar, herb and cherry notes. Better a few years ago. Drink now. 8,300 cases made. • $25 • (12/15/97) • **84**

Cabernet Sauvignon Sonoma County 1986 • $11 • (03/31/89) • **88**

Cabernet Sauvignon Sonoma County 1985 • $11 • (05/31/88) SS • **91**

Cabernet Sauvignon Sonoma County 1984 • $10 • (05/15/87) • **85**

Cabernet Sauvignon Sonoma County 1982 • $9 • (02/01/85) • **81**

Cabernet Sauvignon Sonoma County 1980 • $9 • (04/16/84) • **78**

Cabernet Sauvignon Sonoma County Special Reserve 1980 • $13 • (05/01/86) • **78**

Chardonnay Dry Creek Valley Reserve 1994: A smooth, rich and complex young white, boasting well-integrated pear, fig, melon and toasty oak notes. Turns elegant and flavorful on the finish. 6,000 cases made. • $17 • (05/15/96) • **90**

Chardonnay Dry Creek Valley Wolcott Vineyard Barrel Fermented Reserve 1994: Bold, ripe and full-bodied, offering rich fig, citrus and honey notes. It picks up a good dose of smoky, toasty oak. Packs in lots of flavor. 310 cases made. • $22 • (02/29/96) • **88**

Chardonnay Sonoma County 1996: Offers floral, perfumed Chardonnay character, with ripe pear, apple, mineral and spicy flavors, picking up a hint of toasty oak. Drink now through 2001. 24,000 cases made. • $15 • (06/30/98) • **88**

Chardonnay Sonoma County 1995: Ultra-rich and creamy in style, with layers of ripe fig, pear, hazelnut and apricot flavors accented by a good dose of sweet, toasty oak. An impressive Chardonnay from a producer marking its 25th anniversary in the Dry Creek Valley. 21,000 cases made. • $15 • (05/15/97) SS • **90**

Chardonnay Sonoma County Barrel Fermented 1994: Serves up a pleasing core of ripe, juicy pear, honey and butterscotch notes, turning elegant and complex on the finish. Altogether complex and well balanced. Ready. 25,000 cases made. • $14 • (03/31/96) • **89**

Chardonnay Sonoma County Barrel Fermented 1993 • $14 • (07/31/95) • **84**

Chardonnay Sonoma County Reserve 1996: Serves up attractive spicy pear, citrus and hazelnut flavors in a tightly wound package. Starts to open on the finish, so short-term cellaring might do the trick. 8,500 cases made. • $20 • (04/30/98) • **87**

Chardonnay Sonoma County Reserve 1995: A spicy number, with lots of fresh and lively flavors, ripe pear, apple and melon, and a pretty interplay of cedary oak notes. 6,900 cases made. • $20 • (06/15/97) • **91**

Chenin Blanc California Dry 1993 • $7 • (05/31/95) • **82**

Chenin Blanc Clarksburg Dry 1996: A very good bottling of one of California's rarer varieties, this white is light, lively and bright, offering melon flavors and a hint of passion fruit on the nicely delicate finish. Not totally dry, but artfully balanced. Reasonably priced and ready now. 10,500 cases made. • $8 • (12/15/97) BB • **86**

Chenin Blanc Clarksburg Dry 1994 • $7 • (06/15/96) • **83**

David S. Stare Vintner's Reserve Sonoma County 1984 • $18 • (05/31/88) • **88**

David S. Stare Vintner's Selection Dry Creek Valley 1983 • $15 • (12/31/86) • **74**

Fumé Blanc Dry Creek Valley Barrel Fermented Reserve 1994 • $15 • (02/29/96) • **88**

Fumé Blanc Dry Creek Valley Reserve 1995: An elegant style, full-bodied and focused. Subtle grapefruit and orange flavors are backed by silky smooth viscosity. 4,700 cases made. • $15 • (06/30/97) • **88**

Key: SS—Spectator Selection CS—Cellar Selection HR—Highly Recommended BB—Best Buy $NA—Price not available Ⓐ—Auction Price (BT)—Barrel Tasting
Dates in parentheses indicate the issues in which the ratings were published.

Fumé Blanc Sonoma County 1996: Bright. Filled with lemon and grapefruit flavors, it sings along with a zippy, refreshing edge. Floral and seductive on the finish. 18,600 cases made. • $12 • (11/15/97) • **88**

Fumé Blanc Sonoma County 1995: Open-textured, brightly-flavored and refreshing for its floral, passion fruit and melon flavors on a soft frame. Ready to drink. 24,000 cases made. • $10 • (05/15/97) • **86**

Fumé Blanc Sonoma County 1994: Nicely balanced to show off the herbal and spicy melon-touched-with-vanilla flavors. Smooth and appealing from first to last. 25,600 cases made. • $11 • (07/31/96) HR • **88**

Fumé Blanc Sonoma County 1993 • $9 • (08/31/95) • **84**

Meritage Dry Creek Valley 1995: Showy, with its up front cherry, spice, cedar and wild berry flavors. Quickly turns supple, harmonious and polished, holding and even flaunting its fruitiness on the aftertaste. Grows on you. Drinks well now, should be even better in 1999 to 2003. 5,000 cases made. • $25 • (04/30/98) • **89**

Meritage Dry Creek Valley 1994: Supple and elegant, with cedary oak-accented ripe plum and cherry flavors. Moderate concentration and fleshy tannins. Ready to drink. A blend of 56 percent Cabernet Sauvignon, 23 percent Merlot, 16 percent Cabernet Franc, and 5 percent Petit Verdot. 5,000 cases made. • $25 • (08/31/97) • **88**

Meritage Dry Creek Valley 1993: Effusive cherry, berry and currant flavors. Holds its fruitiness through the finish, avoiding excessive oak or tannins. Try now. 2,000 cases made. • $20 • (11/30/95) • **89**

Meritage Dry Creek Valley 1990 • $18 • (11/15/94) • **89**

Meritage Dry Creek Valley 1988 • $24 • (10/15/93) • **86**

Meritage Dry Creek Valley 1987: Silky-smooth, with an elegant core of dill, currant, plum and cherry flavors. Finishes with soft, fleshy tannins. Ready to drink. 3,021 cases made. • $45 • (12/15/97) • **89**

Meritage Dry Creek Valley 1986 • $22 • (09/15/90) • **80**

Meritage Dry Creek Valley 1985 • $22 • (11/15/89) • **89**

Merlot Dry Creek Valley 1992 • $15 • (06/15/95) • **84**

Merlot Dry Creek Valley 1991 • $15 • (03/15/94) • **84**

Merlot Dry Creek Valley 1990 • $14 • (03/31/93) • **85**

Merlot Dry Creek Valley 1989 • $14 • (04/15/92) • **86**

Merlot Dry Creek Valley 1988 • $15 • (03/31/91) • **83**

Merlot Dry Creek Valley 1985 • $7 • (02/15/88) • **80**

Merlot Dry Creek Valley Bullock House Vineyard 1991 • $20 • (09/15/94) • **85**

Merlot Dry Creek Valley Reserve 1994: Smooth, with an herbal edge to the cherry and currant flavors, finishing with a cedary note and supple tannins. Drinkable now or can age into 2000. 5,000 cases made. • $27 • (06/30/97) • **88**

Merlot Dry Creek Valley Reserve 1993: Ripe and full-bodied, with firm tannins. Delivers lots of ripe cherry and plum flavors with jammy anise and cedary oak shadings. Drink now. 2,000 cases made. • $22 • (08/31/96) • **87**

Merlot Sonoma County 1995: A solid red, packed with blackberry, currant and smoke flavors, finishing tight, with firm tannins that need until 2000 or 2001. 7,500 cases made. • $19 • (03/31/98) • **85**

Merlot Sonoma County 1994: Smooth, ripe and spicy, with a distinct anise accent to the currant and black cherry flavors. Finishes with supple tannins. Ready now. 10,000 cases made. • $17 • (06/30/97) • **86**

Merlot Sonoma County 1986 • $15 • (03/31/89) • **78**

Sauvignon Blanc Dry Creek Valley Reserve 1996: Quite bright, with a strong grassy component. Except for the oak, it resembles a Loire Valley wine. Could use more complexity, but it's intriguing for fans of this style. 8,100 cases made. • $16 • (03/31/98) • **86**

Sauvignon Blanc Late Harvest Dry Creek Valley Soleil Vintner's Reserve David S. Stare 1986 • $15/375ml • (06/15/89) • **90**

Sauvignon Blanc Late Harvest Sonoma County Soleil NV • $18/375ml • (04/30/95) • **85**

Zinfandel Dry Creek Valley 1986 • $9 • (04/15/89) • **85**

Zinfandel Dry Creek Valley Old Vines 1991 • $12 • (08/31/93) • **88**

Zinfandel Dry Creek Valley Old Vines 1990 • $11 • (10/15/92) • **85**

Zinfandel Dry Creek Valley Old Vines 1988 • $11 • (02/15/91) • **86**

Zinfandel Sonoma County Old Vines 1995: A racy, spicy style with wild berry, jam, bay leaf and minty flavors that throw you at first, but gain appeal once you get used to them. Ready to drink. 24 percent Petite Sirah. 8,500 cases made. • $16 • (05/15/98) • **85**

Zinfandel Sonoma County Old Vines 1994: Appealing for its up front fruitiness, this is ripe and juicy, with black cherry, currant and plum notes that turn round and smooth on the finish. 8,500 cases made. • $15 • (04/30/97) • **89**

Zinfandel Sonoma County Old Vines 1993 • $15 • (09/15/95) • **88**

Zinfandel Sonoma County Old Vines 1992 • $14 • (02/28/95) • **83**

Zinfandel Sonoma County Reserve 1995: An elegant style that captures ripe, almost jammy cherry, plum and blueberry flavors, emits pretty floral aromas and finishes with bright fruit and just the right dose of tannin. 23 percent Petite Sirah. Drink now through 2002. 1,400 cases made. • $25 • (06/15/98) • **88**

Zinfandel Sonoma County Reserve 1994: A racy, well-oaked style, with a waxy, dill accent to the wild berry and black cherry flavors that build on the finish to reveal more depth, richness and concentration. Drinkable now, but can be aged, too. Best through 2001. 180 cases made. • $20 • (04/30/97) • **89**

Zinfandel Sonoma County Reserve 1993 • $20 • (05/15/96) • **83**

Zinfandel Sonoma County Reserve 1991 • $20 • (10/15/94) • **84**

DUCK POND | WASHINGTON

Cabernet Sauvignon Columbia Valley Fries Vineyard-Wahluke Slope 1995: Its crisp style offers bright plum and currant flavors and racy acidity. Drinkable now. 900 cases made. • $10 • (10/15/97) • **86**

Chardonnay Columbia Valley 1996: Crisp and bright, centered around pretty nectarine and spice flavors, this zingy wine remains fresh and lively through the finish. Drinkable now. 6,300 cases made. • $8 • (09/30/97) • **87**

Chardonnay Willamette Valley 1996: Light and refreshing Chardonnay, bright with citrusy pear flavors that pick up an enriching hint of honey on the finish. Very nicely done. Ready now. 7,500 cases made. • $8 • (11/15/97) BB • **85**

Chardonnay Willamette Valley 1995: Spicy, earthy flavors mingle with lively citrus and green apple notes in this deftly balanced wine. A fine value. Try now. 10,000 cases made. • $8 • (02/28/97) • **85**

Chardonnay Willamette Valley Barrel Fermented 1994: Youthful, fruity and fresh, like a mouthful of pear. Appealing for its direct fruit flavor. 5,000 cases made. • $8 • (11/15/95) BB • **86**

Gewürztraminer Willamette Valley 1993 • $7 • (11/30/94) BB • **88**

Merlot Columbia Valley 1995: Crisp and bright, it's a fresh mouthful of berry and herb flavors that get smoky and tight on the finish. Approachable now, best in 1999. 12,000 cases made. • $12 • (04/30/97) • **88**

Pinot Gris Willamette Valley 1996: Sleek and appealing for its bright melon and green apple flavor, which lingers gently on the resonant finish. Ready now. 3,300 cases made. • $12 • (12/31/97) • **87**

Pinot Gris Willamette Valley 1995: Round and appealing for its delicate hints of nectarine and almond, finishing on a resinous note. Ready now. 1,000 cases made. • $12 • (02/28/97) • **85**

Pinot Noir Willamette Valley 1996: Light, earthy and unpleasant for its mulchy flavors. Tasted twice, with consistent notes. 13,000 cases made. • $8 • (02/28/98) • **73**

Pinot Noir Willamette Valley 1995: Light-colored and fresh, its almost Beaujolais-like floral and berry flavors make this easy drinking right away. 9,000 cases made. • $8 • (02/28/97) • **82**

Pinot Noir Willamette Valley 1993 • $8 • (03/31/96) • **81**

Pinot Noir Willamette Valley 1992 • $7 • (09/15/94) BB • **87**

Pinot Noir Willamette Valley Reserve 1994: Spicy new oak aromas and flavors make the first impression, but there's plenty of ripe plum, currant and tar character right behind to keep it in balance. Drinkable now. 300 cases made. • $25 • (02/28/97) • **88**

Pinot Noir Yamhill County 1990 • $7 • (03/15/94) • **70**

DUCK WALK | NEW YORK

Chardonnay Long Island 1994: Stewed fruit and dull, vegetal flavors dominate this lifeless wine. • $9 • (12/31/96) • **71**

Chardonnay Long Island Reserve 1994: Solid, with a nice touch of toasty oak, but not much fruit flavor or distinctive character. Would make a nice accompaniment to food. 1,200 cases made. • $13 • (12/31/96) • **82**

Merlot Long Island 1992: A thin wine, drying on the palate, with light berry, brown sugar and vegetal flavors. Reflects a weak vintage and is probably at its best now. • $13 • (12/31/96) • **77**

Pinot Meunier Long Island 1994: Its berry and spice aromas are attractive, but it's light and a bit thin on the palate, with simple strawberry flavors and an herbal accent. 800 cases made. • $13 • (12/31/96) • **78**

DUCKHORN | CALIFORNIA

Cabernet Sauvignon Napa Valley 1997: Ripe, rich and racy, packed with earthy, tannic mint, cherry, currant and wild berry. Finishes with a chewy, tannic aftertaste, but nothing out of bounds for a wine this young. • $NA • (07/31/98) (BT) • **90-94**

Cabernet Sauvignon Napa Valley 1996: Supple and harmonious, rich and polished, impeccably balanced, with a pretty array of floral aromas and juicy cherry, currant and plum flavors. Finishes with supple tannins. • $NA • (06/15/97) (BT) • **90-94**

Cabernet Sauvignon Napa Valley 1994: This is an immense, deeply concentrated, richly flavored wine that's quite tannic at this stage, balancing the currant, plum and berry flavors that persist through the finish. Best to cellar into 2001 or beyond. 7,000 cases made. • $28 • (05/31/97) • **90**

Cabernet Sauvignon Napa Valley 1993: Young and tight, with ripe cherry and cedary oak flavors that are pleasant, but lacking in the extra dimensions you might hope for. Appealing now and through 1999. 1,500 cases made. • $26 • (11/15/96) • **87**

Cabernet Sauvignon Napa Valley 1992 • $24 • (10/31/95) SS • **90**

Cabernet Sauvignon Napa Valley 1990 • $20 • (07/31/93) CS • **93**

Cabernet Sauvignon Napa Valley 1989 • $36 Ⓐ • (12/15/92) • **83**

Cabernet Sauvignon Napa Valley 1988 • $26 Ⓐ • (07/31/91) • **85**

Cabernet Sauvignon Napa Valley 1987: A complex wine. Its smooth, supple texture and an appealing core of currant, black cherry, anise, spice and cedar make up for its lack of sheer power and youthful intensity. • $55 Ⓐ • (12/15/97) • **92**

Cabernet Sauvignon Napa Valley 1986: This remains a big, ripe, intense and concentrated wine, with rich, complex layers of earthy currant, mineral, plum, anise and cedar flavors. Tannins are softening, but it still has a long life ahead. • $54 Ⓐ • (12/15/96) • **94**

Cabernet Sauvignon Napa Valley 1985 • $67 Ⓐ • (06/15/88) CS • **91**

Cabernet Sauvignon Napa Valley 1984 • $17 • (06/15/87) • **87**

Cabernet Sauvignon Napa Valley 1983 • $26 Ⓐ • (07/01/86) • **89**

Cabernet Sauvignon Napa Valley 1982 • $40 Ⓐ • (05/16/85) • **86**

Cabernet Sauvignon Napa Valley 1978 • $64 Ⓐ • (11/15/92) • **92**

Merlot Howell Mountain 1993: Lean and crisp, with a spicy mineral accent to the earthy cherry and berry flavors. Finishes with supple tannins and good length. 2,000 cases made. • $46 Ⓐ • (07/31/97) • **88**

Merlot Napa Valley 1995: Complex in flavor, with currant, cedar, spice and anise notes, and showing deft balance. Finishes with firm but polished tannins; drink now or hold into 2000. 12,000 cases made. • $28 • (03/31/98) • **88**

Merlot Napa Valley 1994: An outstanding Merlot that works its way into complex and interesting flavors, turning up hints of cherry, currant, anise and cedar. Finishes with a firmly tannic edge, but nothing out-of-bounds. Can cellar into 1999. A blend of 82 percent Merlot, 11 percent Cabernet Sauvignon and 7 percent Cabernet Franc. 8,000 cases made. • $29 Ⓐ • (02/28/97) SS • **90**

Merlot Napa Valley 1993 • $24 • (01/31/96) HR • **90**

Merlot Napa Valley 1992 • $36 Ⓐ • (03/31/95) • **88**

Merlot Napa Valley 1990 • $21 • (12/15/92) SS • **89**

Merlot Napa Valley 1989 • $36 Ⓐ • (04/15/92) • **82**

Merlot Napa Valley 1988 • $29 Ⓐ • (12/31/90) • **86**

Merlot Napa Valley 1987 • $38 Ⓐ • (12/31/89) • **91**

Merlot Napa Valley 1986 • $72 Ⓐ • (01/31/89) • **86**

Merlot Napa Valley 1985 • $46 Ⓐ • (12/31/87) CS • **93**

Merlot Napa Valley 1984 • $43 Ⓐ • (12/31/86) SS • **94**

Merlot Napa Valley 1983 • $29 Ⓐ • (11/01/85) CS • **94**

Merlot Napa Valley 1982 • $24 Ⓐ • (10/01/85) • **81**

Merlot Napa Valley Three Palms Vineyard 1991 • $25 • (09/15/94) • **84**

Merlot Napa Valley Three Palms Vineyard 1990 • $45 • (08/31/93) • **83**

Merlot Napa Valley Three Palms Vineyard 1989 • $45 • (05/31/92) • **89**

Merlot Napa Valley Three Palms Vineyard 1988 • $45 • (11/15/91) • **84**

Merlot Napa Valley Three Palms Vineyard 1987 • $60 • (07/31/90) • **92**

Merlot Napa Valley Three Palms Vineyard 1986 • $63 • (07/31/89) • **88**

Merlot Napa Valley Three Palms Vineyard 1985 • $63 • (06/30/88) • **91**

Merlot Napa Valley Three Palms Vineyard 1984 • $75 • (07/31/87) • **89**

Merlot Napa Valley Vine Hill Ranch 1987 • $18 • (07/31/90) • **87**

Merlot Napa Valley Vine Hill Ranch 1986 • $18 • (07/31/89) • **80**

Merlot Napa Valley Vine Hill Ranch 1985 • $16 • (06/30/88) • **91**

Red Howell Mountain 1992: Firm, ripe and intense, with tiers of currant, anise and mineral flavors. Finishes with crisp, chewy tannins. Has the intensity and concentration to age; try now. 4,200 cases made. • $26 • (08/31/96) • **88**

Red Howell Mountain 1991 • $25 • (11/15/94) • **88**

Red Howell Mountain 1990 • $25 • (11/15/93) • **86**

Red Howell Mountain 1989 • $25 • (11/15/92) • **89**

Key: SS—Spectator Selection CS—Cellar Selection HR—Highly Recommended BB—Best Buy $NA—Price not available Ⓐ—Auction Price (BT)—Barrel Tasting

Dates in parentheses indicate the issues in which the ratings were published.

Sauvignon Blanc Napa Valley 1996: Tropical fruit character—mango and papaya come to mind—is the hallmark of this wine. Fig, sweet pea and melon co-star. Though bright and refreshing, it's got a silky-smooth feel on the palate. Rich and lovely. 15,000 cases made. • $15 • (01/31/98) HR • **90**

Sauvignon Blanc Napa Valley 1995: Fresh pear and spice flavors with a welcome wave of herb and cream on the finish, which adds depth. Ready now. 15,000 cases made. • $14 • (02/28/97) • **88**

Sauvignon Blanc Napa Valley 1994 • $12 • (12/31/95) • **89**

Sauvignon Blanc Napa Valley 1993 • $12 • (04/30/95) • **85**

DUNCAN PEAK | CALIFORNIA

Cabernet Sauvignon Mendocino 1994: Marked by an unusual floral quality, this smooth, silky wine, with attractive spice, cinnamon, bright cherry, blueberry and herb flavors, is lovely now. Should improve with time, as well. 572 cases made. • $20 • (11/15/97) • **88**

Cabernet Sauvignon Mendocino County 1993: Lean and trim, offering pleasant cherry, currant and berry flavors of modest depth and proportion. Well-balanced. Try now. 600 cases made. • $18 • (04/30/96) • **86**

Cabernet Sauvignon Mendocino County 1992 • $16 • (11/15/94) • **85**

Cabernet Sauvignon Mendocino County 1991 • $12 • (10/31/93) • **88**

Cabernet Sauvignon Mendocino County 1989 • $10 • (11/15/92) BB • **88**

DUNDEE SPRINGS | OREGON

Pinot Gris Oregon Reserve 1996: Has some ripe flavors, including peach and apple, but remains staunchly crisp, almost chalky on the finish. Best later this year. 80 cases made. • $16 • (05/15/98) • **83**

Pinot Noir Oregon 1995: Light and spicy, with anise and root-beer notes skimming through the light dried cherry and brown sugar flavors. Drink soon. 200 cases made. • $28 • (05/15/98) • **83**

Pinot Noir Oregon Perry Bower Vineyards Reserve 1996: Light and refreshing, a nice mouthful of currant and loganberry flavor that lingers on the pretty finish. Has a good level of intensity for its size. Nice now, better in 1999. 620 cases made. • $35 • (05/15/98) • **87**

Pinot Noir Willamette Valley Reserve 1994: Ripe, open and generous, nicely focused around berry and plum flavors with a hint of chocolate on the harmonious finish. Try now. • $34 • (02/28/97) • **89**

DUNHAM | WASHINGTON

Cabernet Sauvignon Columbia Valley 1995: Herbal and minty notes add a nice touch to the basic berry and anise flavors in this solid, medium-weight Cab. Sweet oak notes blend in on the long finish. Approachable now, best from 1999 or 2000. 200 cases made. • $28 • (09/15/97) • **89**

DUNN | CALIFORNIA

Cabernet Sauvignon Howell Mountain 1997: Earthy, racy, but quite complex and concentrated, with wild berry and floral aromas. An intense, deeply concentrated wine that packs in lots of flavor. • $NA • (07/31/98) (BT) • **90-94**

Cabernet Sauvignon Howell Mountain 1994: Displays the big, ripe, earthy style this location is known for and also manages to stuff plenty of currant, mineral, black cherry and spicy fruit into the bottle. Young and backward, this dense, chewy wine will need a few more years of cellaring to soften. Best from 2000 through 2008. 2,000 cases made. • $45 • (05/15/98) CS • **91**

Cabernet Sauvignon Howell Mountain 1993: Young, tight and marked by cedary flavors, working its way into a core of currant, sage, mineral and spice flavors before the tannins kick in. Typically backward for this wine, so it's best cellared into 2001. 1,670 cases made. • $60 Ⓐ • (04/30/97) • **90**

Cabernet Sauvignon Howell Mountain 1991 • $79 Ⓐ • (12/15/95) CS • **91**

Cabernet Sauvignon Howell Mountain 1990: Openly fruity and quite tannic; wild berry and currant flavors pour through the tightly-wound, tannic structure. Tannins really swarm on the finish. 2,200 cases made. • $92 Ⓐ • (09/15/96) • **88**

Cabernet Sauvignon Howell Mountain 1989 • $39 • (07/31/93) • **88**

Cabernet Sauvignon Howell Mountain 1988 • $50 Ⓐ • (02/29/92) • **86**

Cabernet Sauvignon Howell Mountain 1987: A powerful young wine, even at age 10. Dark, ripe, intense and deeply concentrated, this one is years from peaking. Packed with a rich, earthy core of currant, mineral, anise, sage and cedar. Quite tannic in this tasting, the fruit poured through on the finish. Best from 2000 to 2010, maybe beyond. 2,100 cases made. • $82 Ⓐ • (12/15/97) • **97**

Cabernet Sauvignon Howell Mountain 1986: Still big, ripe, intense and expressive, with tiers of earthy currant, mineral, cedar and spice flavors. Given all its power and richness, it finishes with elegance and finesse. Remarkably well-focused and lively, it has aged very well and shows no signs of fatigue. Try now or cellar longer—it should easily hold until 2001 or 2005. 2,100 cases made. • $86 Ⓐ • (12/15/96) • **94**
Cabernet Sauvignon Howell Mountain 1985 • $69 Ⓐ • (04/15/89) • **88**
Cabernet Sauvignon Howell Mountain 1984 • $122 Ⓐ • (03/31/88) • **93**
Cabernet Sauvignon Howell Mountain 1983 • $40 Ⓐ • (05/15/87) • **95**
Cabernet Sauvignon Howell Mountain 1982 • $112 Ⓐ • (11/30/91) • **94**
Cabernet Sauvignon Howell Mountain 1981 • $47 Ⓐ • (12/16/84) • **93**
Cabernet Sauvignon Howell Mountain 1980 • $117 Ⓐ • (03/16/84) • **87**
Cabernet Sauvignon Howell Mountain 1979 • $128 Ⓐ • (11/30/91) • **94**
Cabernet Sauvignon Napa Valley 1994: Inky dark, intense and tannic, packing in a tightly wound core of currant, mineral, plum and earthy flavors. Dense and chewy; needs cellaring. Drink after 2000. 2,000 cases made. • $39 • (05/15/98) • **88**
Cabernet Sauvignon Napa Valley 1993: A lean and muscular style, with the cedary oak, currant, anise and spice flavors struggling to get past the tannins—which they finally do. This wine will definitely need cellaring into 2000 to 2001. 1,700 cases made. • $50 Ⓐ • (11/15/96) • **89**
Cabernet Sauvignon Napa Valley 1992 • $39 Ⓐ • (12/15/95) • **88**
Cabernet Sauvignon Napa Valley 1991 • $38 Ⓐ • (11/15/94) • **88**
Cabernet Sauvignon Napa Valley 1990 • $41 Ⓐ • (11/15/93) CS • **92**
Cabernet Sauvignon Napa Valley 1989 • $33 Ⓐ • (04/30/93) • **90**
Cabernet Sauvignon Napa Valley 1988 • $48 Ⓐ • (11/15/91) • **87**
Cabernet Sauvignon Napa Valley 1987 • $65 Ⓐ • (11/15/90) • **93**
Cabernet Sauvignon Napa Valley 1986 • $62 Ⓐ • (10/15/89) CS • **95**
Cabernet Sauvignon Napa Valley 1985 • $62 Ⓐ • (09/15/88) CS • **94**
Cabernet Sauvignon Napa Valley 1984 • $48 Ⓐ • (11/30/87) • **90**
Cabernet Sauvignon Napa Valley 1983 • $38 Ⓐ • (10/31/86) SS • **95**
Cabernet Sauvignon Napa Valley 1982 • $99 Ⓐ • (11/01/85) SS • **97**

DUNNEWOOD | CALIFORNIA

Cabernet Sauvignon Alexander Valley Seven Arches Vineyard Gold Label Select 1992 • $10 • (02/29/96) • **82**
Cabernet Sauvignon California 1986 • $7 • (06/15/90) • **73**
Cabernet Sauvignon Napa Valley Napa Reserve 1986 • $11 • (06/15/90) • **82**
Cabernet Sauvignon Napa Valley Reserve 1984 • $11 • (12/31/88) • **85**
Cabernet Sauvignon North Coast Barrel Select 1991 • $7 • (11/15/94) • **84**
Chardonnay Carneros Gold Label Select 1993 • $10 • (07/31/95) • **83**
Chardonnay North Coast Barrel Select 1993 • $8 • (02/28/95) • **80**
Merlot California Barrel Select 1990 • $6 • (04/15/93) BB • **83**
Merlot North Coast Barrel Select 1994: Firm and chewy, with ripe cherry and spice flavors, finishing a bit hot. • $10 • (11/30/96) • **79**
Merlot North Coast Barrel Select 1992 • $7 • (09/15/94) BB • **82**
Sauvignon Blanc North Coast Barrel Select 1995: Sturdy, fresh and appealing for its straightforward pear and earthy flavors. • $7 • (12/31/96) • **82**
Sauvignon Blanc North Coast Barrel Select 1993 • $7 • (08/31/95) • **80**
Zinfandel Mendocino Barrel Select Coastal Series 1995: Lean and a bit on the green side, with spicy cherry flavors of modest depth. Drink now. 3,500 cases made. • $9 • (06/15/98) • **82**
Zinfandel Sonoma Valley Barrel Select 1992 • $10 • (02/28/95) • **80**

DUNNING | CALIFORNIA

Cabernet Sauvignon Paso Robles Westside 1995: A lithe, supple red with distinctive warm black cherry and floral aromas and flavors, nicely balanced to echo on the smooth finish. 300 cases made. • $15 • (03/31/98) • **87**
Cabernet Sauvignon Paso Robles Westside 1994: A solid effort, with lots of ripe, supple plum, currant and wild berry flavors and soft, fleshy tannins, which make it quite appealing to drink now. 250 cases made. • $14 • (11/30/96) • **86**
Chardonnay Paso Robles Westside 1996: Pretty apple and mineral notes are backed by a tad too much oak. It's firm and lean, with a crisp, clean finish. 350 cases made. • $15 • (02/28/98) • **84**
Merlot Paso Robles Westside 1995: Somewhat dense, with a spicy blend of blackberry, currant, smoke and burned sage. It's got some rough edges, but is interesting and exotic nonetheless. 300 cases made. • $15 • (01/31/98) • **87**

DURNEY | CALIFORNIA

Cabernet Sauvignon Carmel Valley 1990 • $17 • (11/15/94) • **89**
Cabernet Sauvignon Carmel Valley 1981 • $13 • (09/01/84) • **82**
Cabernet Sauvignon Carmel Valley Cachagua Dances On Your Palate 1993: Fairly tannic and austere, given the level of fruit concentration. The flavors revolve around cherry and plum. 5,000 cases made. • $13 • (11/30/96) • **78**
Cabernet Sauvignon Carmel Valley Dances On Your Palate 1992: Typically tannic, but this Durney shows a little more Cabernet character, with hints of cherry and berry. 6,000 cases made. • $21 • (11/30/96) • **86**
Cabernet Sauvignon Carmel Valley Dances On Your Palate Private Reserve 1992 • $31 • (03/31/96) • **86**
Cabernet Sauvignon Carmel Valley Private Reserve 1989 • $26 • (11/15/94) • **83**
Cabernet Sauvignon Carmel Valley Private Reserve 1988 • $31 • (11/15/94) • **82**
Cabernet Sauvignon Carmel Valley Private Reserve 1985 • $20/3.(11/15/92) • **86**
Cabernet Sauvignon Carmel Valley Private Reserve 1983 • $20 • (04/30/91) • **86**
Chardonnay Carmel Valley Cachagua Dances On Your Palate 1993 • $11 • (05/15/96) • **76**
Chardonnay Carmel Valley Dances On Your Palate 1994: Earthy, toasty flavors shoulder past the fruit. Tasted twice, with consistent notes. 2,820 cases made. • $18 • (07/31/96) • **76**
Chardonnay Carmel Valley Dances On Your Palate 1993: Rich and complex, with earthy flavors predominating, this fans out its mineral, spice and grapefruit-peel flavors on the finish. Drink now. • $18 • (07/31/96) • **87**
Chenin Blanc Carmel Valley 1994: Off-dry, with pleasant lemon and melon flavors that remain fresh through the finish. Ready to drink. 2,500 cases made. • $10 • (12/15/97) • **83**
Chenin Blanc Carmel Valley 1993 • $9 • (05/31/95) • **85**
Johannisberg Riesling Carmel Valley Late Harvest Dances on Your Palate 1994: Almost amber in color, with earthy, floral flavors and a touch of honey on the relatively unsweet finish. More interesting as an apéritif than a dessert wine. Drink soon. 900 cases made. • $12/375ml • (11/30/97) • **84**
Merlot Carmel Valley 1994: Earth, cola and cherry tones start this off nicely, but it finishes with astringent, bitter tannins and a green edge. 400 cases made. • $25 • (02/28/98) • **80**
Merlot Carmel Valley Dances On Your Palate 1993: Smoky, with licorice, wild cherry, cassis and herb flavors. It's a bit on the lean, astringent side, but enticing nonetheless. Hold for a few years. 400 cases made. • $22 • (07/31/97) • **87**
Pinot Noir Carmel Valley 1993: Fading fast, it's still got some bright cherry notes. The ensemble is bitter, however, astringent and tired. 400 cases made. • $18 • (02/28/98) • **76**
Pinot Noir Carmel Valley 1990 • $18 • (03/31/95) • **80**
Pinot Noir Carmel Valley 1989 • $18 • (02/28/94) • **80**
Pinot Noir Carmel Valley 1988 • $16 • (04/30/91) • **80**
Pinot Noir Carmel Valley Dances On Your Palate 1992 • $24 • (12/31/95) • **81**
Red Carmel Valley NV • $7 • (11/15/92) • **73**

DUXOUP | CALIFORNIA

Charbono Napa Valley 1987 • $9 • (06/15/89) • **88**
Napa Gamay Dry Creek Valley 1990-1991 NV • $9 • (03/31/93) • **85**
Napa Gamay Dry Creek Valley 1988 • $7 • (02/28/90) • **76**
Napa Gamay Dry Creek Valley 1987 • $7 • (02/28/89) BB • **86**
Syrah Dry Creek Valley 1987 • $12 • (04/15/89) • **87**
Syrah Dry Creek Valley 1986 • $9 • (04/15/89) • **85**
Syrah Sonoma County 1982 • $9 • (03/16/84) • **78**

EAGLE RIDGE | CALIFORNIA

Zinfandel Amador County Grandpère Vineyard 1989 • $12 • (10/15/92) • **76**

EASTON | CALIFORNIA

Riesling El Dorado County 1994 • $12 • (06/15/96) • **80**
Zinfandel Fiddletown 1993 • $15 • (03/31/96) • **77**

EATON HILL | WASHINGTON

Cabernet Sauvignon Columbia Valley 1993: Very pretty fruit and spice flavors make this wine appealing, although its soft texture and light intensity level are atypical of Cabernet. Ready now. 222 cases made. • $14 • (09/15/96) • **85**

Chardonnay Yakima Valley 1994: Bright, ripe and appealing for its apricot, pear and spice flavors that linger on the finish. 175 cases made. • $12 • (09/15/96) • **87**

Muscat Canelli Yakima Valley 1994: Light and fruity, delicately spicy and sweet on the finish. 200 cases made. • $8 • (09/30/96) • **84**

EBERLE | CALIFORNIA

Barbera Paso Robles Norman Vineyard 1992 • $18 • (11/15/95) • **83**

Cabernet Sauvignon Paso Robles 1995: Crisp in texture, with a gamy edge to the black cherry and tobacco flavors. Try now. 6,800 cases made. • $18 • (11/15/97) • **83**

Cabernet Sauvignon Paso Robles 1994: Firm, almost chewy, with earthy berry and tobacco flavors that remain crisp on the finish. Best after 1999. 3,749 cases made. • $18 • (11/15/97) • **86**

Cabernet Sauvignon Paso Robles 1991 • $16 • (04/15/95) • **88**

Cabernet Sauvignon Paso Robles 1990 • $15 • (09/15/94) • **84**

Cabernet Sauvignon Paso Robles 1989 • $15 • (11/15/93) • **83**

Cabernet Sauvignon Paso Robles 1988 • $15 • (11/15/92) • **86**

Cabernet Sauvignon Paso Robles 1987 • $22 • (11/15/91) • **76**

Cabernet Sauvignon Paso Robles 1986 • $15 • (11/15/89) • **85**

Cabernet Sauvignon Paso Robles 1985 • $12 • (02/15/89) • **82**

Cabernet Sauvignon Paso Robles 1983 • $12 • (06/15/87) • **79**

Cabernet Sauvignon Paso Robles 1982 • $10 • (09/30/86) • **87**

Cabernet Sauvignon Paso Robles 1981 • $10 • (04/16/85) • **87**

Cabernet Sauvignon Paso Robles Reserve 1991: Ripe, smooth and polished, with a rich core of black cherry, herb, tobacco and cedar notes, finishing with supple tannins and good length. Appealing now, but worthy of cellaring into 1999. 567 cases made. • $35 • (11/15/97) • **91**

Cabernet Sauvignon Paso Robles Reserve 1987 • $26 • (11/15/93) • **86**

Chardonnay Paso Robles 1995: Straightforward, with appealing pear, peach, and grapefruit flavors, finishing with a light dash of oak. 1,171 cases made. • $12 • (07/31/97) • **86**

Chardonnay Paso Robles 1993 • $12 • (07/31/95) • **78**

Muscat Canelli Paso Robles 1997: Lightly sweet, with pretty floral, melon and citrus flavors that linger on the slightly sticky finish. Ready to drink. 1,706 cases made. • $11 • (03/31/98) • **84**

Muscat Canelli Paso Robles 1994 • $9 • (09/30/95) • **82**

Syrah Paso Robles 1991 • $16 • (10/31/93) • **85**

Syrah Paso Robles Fralich Vineyard 1993 • $16 • (08/31/95) • **89**

Syrah Paso Robles Fralich Vineyard 1992 • $16 • (07/31/94) • **86**

Syrah Paso Robles Steinbeck Vineyard 1995: Ripe, rich and concentrated, with tiers of plum, wild berry, cherry and spice flavors. The texture is supple; the tannins are ripe and polished. Drink into 1999. 750 cases made. • $16 • (05/15/97) • **88**

Viognier Paso Robles Fralich Vineyard 1993 • $16 • (09/15/94) • **78**

Zinfandel Paso Robles 1989 • $12 • (10/15/92) • **86**

Zinfandel Paso Robles Sauret Vineyard 1996: Firmly tannic, ripe with black cherry and wild berry flavors, turning even earthier and dry on the finish. Drink now through 2002. 1,223 cases made. • $18 • (06/15/98) • **85**

Zinfandel Paso Robles Sauret Vineyard 1995: Serves up lots of ripe, juicy cherry and wild berry flavors, and a nice pepper and anise edge adds dimension. Not too tannic; drink now or can age. 2,200 cases made. • $16 • (02/28/97) • **90**

Zinfandel Paso Robles Sauret Vineyard 1994 • $16 • (04/30/96) • **87**

Zinfandel Paso Robles Sauret Vineyard 1993 • $13 • (06/15/95) • **86**

Zinfandel Paso Robles Sauret Vineyard 1992 • $13 • (10/15/94) • **82**

Zinfandel Paso Robles Sauret Vineyard 1991 • $12 • (08/31/93) HR • **89**

Zinfandel Paso Robles Sauret Vineyard 1990 • $12 • (12/31/92) • **88**

Zinfandel Paso Robles Steinbeck Vineyard 1996: Light in fruit, with modest cherry and wild berry flavors, turning earthy and leathery, finishing with a short aftertaste. Drink now through 2000. 445 cases made. • $15 • (06/15/98) • **83**

EDDY, TOM | CALIFORNIA

Cabernet Sauvignon Napa Valley 1994: A restrained style, with understated but complex black cherry, tart plum, spice and wild berry flavors that linger on the finish. Tempting now, but better cellared short-term. Best from 2000 through 2005. 450 cases made. • $50 • (05/15/98) • **90**

Cabernet Sauvignon Napa Valley 1993: Lean and trim, with an appealing earthy edge to the ripe currant and berry flavors, picking up leather and cedar flavors on the finish. Has enough tannin to merit cellaring into 1999. 300 cases made. • $40 • (10/31/97) • **90**

Cabernet Sauvignon Napa Valley 1992 • $36 • (05/15/96) • **88**

Cabernet Sauvignon Napa Valley 1991 • $32 • (04/30/95) • **90**

EDEN ROC | CALIFORNIA

Brut California NV: Sits broad on the palate with peach, pear and vanilla flavors. Finishes with a hint of earth and sweetness. • $5 • (12/31/97) • **86**

Extra Dry California NV: Bright and zingy, with apple, peach and vanilla overtones. Finishes clean, with a slightly mineral edge. • $5 • (12/31/97) • **83**

EDGEFIELD | OREGON

Brut Blanc de Noirs Oregon 1992: Crisp and earthy, it strives for elegance but comes off as light and straightforward. 580 cases made. • $20 • (11/30/97) • **82**

Chardonnay Willamette Valley 1996: This shows more alcohol and wood than the modest apple flavors have absorbed. Finishes with a touch of bitterness. 1,500 cases made. • $11 • (05/15/98) • **82**

Chardonnay Willamette Valley Vintage Select 1995: Has beautiful honey-scented apple, nectarine and spice flavors that show richness and subtlety. Ripe and smooth, it has immediate appeal but should develop more depth by 1999 to 2000. 600 cases made. • $15 • (10/31/97) • **89**

Cuvée de L'Abri Rouge Columbia Valley 1995: Crisp and bright, with modest blackberry and beet flavors that cut through the rough layer of tannin. Drink soon with hearty food. A blend of 70 percent Grenache and 30 percent Syrah. 500 cases made. • $18 • (05/15/98) • **83**

Oregon Black Rabbit Red 1996: Pretty berry and spice flavors ride smoothly on a lean, almost racy frame. A lithe wine with a welcome purity of character. Ready now. A blend of 60 percent Cabernet Sauvignon, 20 percent Pinot Noir and 20 percent Zinfandel. 4,500 cases made. • $11 • (05/15/98) • **85**

Pinot Gris Willamette Valley 1996: Soft and broad, generous with its melon and spice flavors, finishing with a touch of apricot. Ready now. 2,185 cases made. • $11 • (10/31/97) • **86**

Pinot Noir Willamette Valley Vintage Select 1995: Lean and crisp, with enough pretty Pinot Noir flavor to keep it charming and harmonious. Ready to drink. 580 cases made. • $18 • (10/15/97) • **86**

Syrah Columbia Valley Chukar Ridge Vineyard 1995: Starts with a burst of plum and berry, narrowing as it glides across the palate, finishing with a bite and echoes of earth and woody flavors. Drink from 1999 or 2000. First Syrah from this Oregon-based winery. 500 cases made. • $18 • (05/15/98) • **86**

White Riesling Yamhill County Hyland Vineyards Vineyard Select 1996: A polished wine, off-dry, with pretty peach, apple and honey flavors swirling through the silky finish. Ready now. 500 cases made. • $12 • (05/15/98) • **87**

EDGEWOOD | CALIFORNIA

Cabernet Franc Napa Valley 1992: Tar and leather, spice and cola flavors blend in an evolved manner. Finishes with a beefy note, a little heavy on the oak. 499 cases made. • $16 • (07/31/97) • **85**

Cabernet Sauvignon Napa Valley 1994: Austere but well focused, with a trim, tightly wound band of currant, plum, spice and cedar. Holds its flavors on the finish, where they turn complex. 1,405 cases made. • $20 • (04/30/98) • **88**

Cabernet Sauvignon Napa Valley 1992: Intense and tightly wound. On the crisp, austere side but there's enough currant and cherry flavors to hold your interest. 2,017 cases made. • $18 • (09/15/96) • **82**

Malbec Napa Valley 1992: Pleasing for its modest band of currant and cherry flavors. Avoids being too tannic; drinkable now. 500 cases made. • $16 • (11/30/96) • **83**

Merlot Napa Valley 1994: Greets you with cedar, plum, sage and spice flavors that are elegant and well-focused, with mild tannins and good length. Lacks the extra dimensions for excellence, but there's a lot to like. Drink now to 2000. 2,040 cases made. • $20 • (03/31/98) • **87**

Petite Sirah Napa Valley 1994: Dense, dark color and lively berry flavors with herbal overtones make this a solid wine for the cellar. Try it in 2001. 966 cases made. • $15 • (03/31/98) • **85**

Petite Sirah Napa Valley 1992: Tastes bitter and overdone, with a sharp green edge to the flavors, and gritty tannins. Misses the mark. 531 cases made. • $14 • (11/30/96) • **76**

Key: SS—Spectator Selection CS—Cellar Selection HR—Highly Recommended BB—Best Buy $NA—Price not available Ⓐ—Auction Price (BT)—Barrel Tasting
Dates in parentheses indicate the issues in which the ratings were published.

Zinfandel Napa Valley 1994: Smoke, spice and a bit of leather introduce this fairly astringent wine; plums and pepper follow. Would benefit from riper fruit. Drink now. 1,337 cases made. • $14 • (06/15/98) • **81**

Zinfandel Napa Valley 1991: Mature, with a nice dash of dried cherry and plum and hints of sage and spice. Drinks well now. 455 cases made. • $14 • (09/15/96) • **84**

EDMEADES | CALIFORNIA

Chardonnay Anderson Valley 1995: Tightly focused, with a core of ripe pear, spice, fig and light oak, showing depth, richness and complexity on the finish, where a dash of pineapple folds in. Drink now through 2001. • $18 • (06/15/98) • **88**

Chardonnay Anderson Valley 1994: Smooth and elegant fig, pear, spice and honey notes. Turns somewhat simple on the finish, where it takes on a candied edge. • $18 • (05/15/96) • **88**

Chardonnay Anderson Valley Anderson Crest Vineyard 1994: Serves up a fruity core of mango, ripe pear and apple flavors complimented by lightly toasty, spicy notes. • $20 • (06/15/96) • **87**

Chardonnay Anderson Valley Dennison Vineyard 1993 • $20 • (07/31/95) • **85**

Chardonnay Mendocino 1993 • $12 • (04/15/95) • **82**

Gewürztraminer Anderson Valley 1994 • $13 • (11/15/95) • **84**

Pinot Noir Anderson Valley 1995: Complex and flavorful, with a range of black cherry, cola, earth and mushroom flavors, it lacks focus and finishes with slightly muddled tannins. Aging it into 1999 may give it more finesse and grace. • $20 • (02/28/98) • **87**

Pinot Noir Anderson Valley 1994: Ripe and fruity, in a lighter style, with delicate fruit notes, hints of cherry and wild berry flavors that linger nicely. • $20 • (02/28/97) • **86**

Pinot Noir Anderson Valley 1982 • $10 • (02/16/85) • **89**

Pinot Noir Anderson Valley Anderson Crest Vineyard 1994 • $23 • (03/31/96) • **85**

Pinot Noir Anderson Valley Dennison Vineyard 1993 • $20 • (09/15/95) • **86**

Zinfandel Mendocino 1996: Elegant, ripe and spicy, with pretty plum-, berry- and cherry-laced flavors. Well-balanced, supple and pleasing. Drink now through 2002. • $18 • (05/31/98) • **87**

Zinfandel Mendocino 1995: Smooth, ripe and spicy, with a pretty core of plum, cherry and wild berry flavors that turn elegant and supple on the finish. • $19 • (04/30/97) • **89**

Zinfandel Mendocino 1994 • $16 • (04/30/96) • **88**

Zinfandel Mendocino Ciapusci Vineyard 1995: Firmly tannic, with a gamy, leathery edge, it slowly reveals complex cherry and berry flavors, showing more complexity on the finish, where the flavors fold together nicely. • $28 • (06/15/98) • **88**

Zinfandel Mendocino Ciapusci Vineyard 1994 • $29 • (04/30/96) • **85**

Zinfandel Mendocino Ciapusci Vineyard 1993 • $20 • (10/15/95) • **86**

Zinfandel Mendocino Ciapusci Vineyard 1990 • $20 • (10/15/92) • **86**

Zinfandel Mendocino Ciapusci Vineyard 1981 • $9 • (03/01/85) • **87**

Zinfandel Mendocino Zeni Vineyard 1994 • $29 • (04/30/96) • **84**

Zinfandel Mendocino Zeni Vineyard 1993 • $20 • (08/31/95) • **88**

Zinfandel North Coast 1992 • $12 • (01/31/95) • **86**

EDMUNDS ST. JOHN | CALIFORNIA

El Niño California 1992 • $11 • (06/30/95) • **84**

Les Côtes Sauvages California 1995: Earthy and meaty, with a smoky accent to the dried plum and cherry flavors. Finishes with austere tannins and a mineral note. Best to cellar into 1999. A blend of Grenache, Syrah, Mourvèdre, and Carignane. 250 cases made. • $20 • (11/30/97) • **87**

Les Côtes Sauvages California 1992 • $16 • (06/30/95) • **88**

Les Côtes Sauvages California 1989 • $19 • (07/15/91) • **79**

Les Côtes Sauvages California 1986 • $14 • (04/15/89) • **88**

Les Côtes Sauvages Cuvée Wahluke 90 American NV • $14 • (01/31/94) • **86**

Les Fleurs du Chaparral Napa Valley 1987 • $15 • (08/31/90) • **91**

Mourvèdre California L'Enfant Terrible 1994: A touch earthy, with a slightly bitter edge. Meager fruit just barely catches your attention. • $12 • (08/31/96) • **76**

Mourvèdre Napa Valley 1986 • $15 • (04/15/89) • **87**

Port O'Call California New World Red 1989 • $9 • (08/31/91) • **84**

Syrah California 1994: Distinct, spicy fruit flavors, and on the tannic side. Finishes with a leathery accent, but plenty of plum and cherry come through. 550 cases made. • $12 • (08/31/96) • **86**

Syrah California 1987 • $18 • (12/15/89) • **81**

Syrah Sonoma County 1986 • $12 • (04/15/89) • **91**

Syrah Sonoma Valley 1988 • $19 • (08/31/91) • **85**

Syrah Sonoma Valley Durell Vineyard 1995: Dark-colored, with rich, complex, meaty currant, plum and wild berry flavors that are tightly wound. Finishes with firm but polished tannins. Best after 1999. 700 cases made. • $30 • (11/30/97) • **88**

Syrah Sonoma Valley Durell Vineyard 1994: Dark, ripe and peppery, with a leathery edge to the plum and wild berry flavors. Finishes with firm tannins. Try now. 800 cases made. • $25 • (02/28/97) • **87**

Syrah Sonoma Valley Durrell Vineyard 1991 • $20 • (12/31/93) • **89**

Zinfandel Amador County 1995: Hits the mark with its well-focused core of wild berry, cherry and spice flavors. Moderately tannic. Drink now. 600 cases made. • $15 • (03/31/97) • **87**

Zinfandel Amador County 1994: A nice medley of cherry, wild berry and spice flavors that maintain elegance and finesse. Well-balanced, with mild tannins on the finish. 700 cases made. • $16 • (09/15/96) • **86**

Zinfandel Amador County 1993 • $16 • (10/15/95) • **86**

Zinfandel Mendocino County Pallini Rosso 1993 • $11 • (10/15/95) • **83**

Zinfandel Napa Valley Amaronese 1988 • $12 • (10/15/92) • **80**

EDNA VALLEY | CALIFORNIA

Brut Edna Valley 1987 • $25 • (12/31/94) • **90**

Chardonnay Edna Valley 1993 • $15 • (06/30/95) • **88**

Chardonnay Edna Valley Paragon 1996: Clean and refreshing, with lively, well-focused pear, apple, peach and spice nuances. Finishes with a crisp, lively aftertaste. Ready now. 69,094 cases made. • $17 • (05/15/98) • **89**

Chardonnay Edna Valley Paragon 1995: A well-focused, complex California white, distinctive for its ripe peach, fig and apricot flavors, complemented by light oak shadings and lingering for a pretty aftertaste. 53,023 cases made. • $17 • (06/30/97) SS • **89**

Chardonnay Edna Valley Paragon 1994: Pear and apple flavors with an earthy, slightly mushroomy edge. A predominantly fruity finish provides interest. 42,093 cases made. • $16 • (07/31/96) • **83**

Pinot Noir Edna Valley 1993 • $15 • (03/31/95) • **73**

Pinot Noir Edna Valley 1992 • $15 • (03/31/95) • **83**

Pinot Noir Edna Valley 1990 • $15 • (02/28/93) • **84**

Pinot Noir Edna Valley 1986 • $15 • (12/15/89) • **76**

Pinot Noir Edna Valley 1985 • $15 • (06/15/88) • **78**

Pinot Noir Edna Valley 1984 • $10 • (12/15/87) • **85**

Pinot Noir Edna Valley 1982 • $12 • (08/31/86) • **80**

Pinot Noir Edna Valley Paragon 1995: Pungent, with an earthy nuance to the black cherry and mushroom flavors. Good dose of oak and firm tannins. 452 cases made. • $17 • (01/31/97) • **81**

Pinot Noir Edna Valley Paragon Vineyard Reserve 1992 • $18 • (03/31/95) • **86**

Pinot Noir Edna Valley Reserve 1988 • $18 • (02/28/93) • **82**

Sémillon-Chardonnay Central Coast Cellar Master's Selection 1995: Rich, round and spicy, this offers toasty vanilla and caramel nuances around a nice core of fig and pineapple flavors. Oak-driven, but not excessively so. Ready now. 422 cases made. • $12 • (11/30/96) • **87**

EHLERS GROVE | CALIFORNIA

Cabernet Sauvignon Napa Valley 1993: Firm and chewy; a lean wine with just about enough berry flavor to sneak through on the finish. Drinkable now. 2,000 cases made. • $11 • (12/15/95) • **83**

Cabernet Sauvignon Napa Valley 1992 • $15 • (12/15/95) • **88**

Cabernet Sauvignon Napa Valley 1983 • $12 • (06/15/87) • **79**

Chardonnay California 1993 • $10 • (07/31/95) • **80**

Chardonnay Sonoma & Napa Counties Winery Reserve 1996: Loaded with peach, pear, apple and lemon flavors, the wine is tempered by plenty of sweet oak, spice and a refreshing mineral edge. Drink now. 225 cases made. • $25 • (06/30/98) • **88**

Sauvignon Blanc Napa Valley 1994 • $9 • (12/15/95) • **81**

Sauvignon Blanc Napa Valley Winery Reserve 1996: Zingy, spicy and refreshing, this squeaky-clean wine is brimming with bright lemon and lime, grapefruit and herb notes. Finishes with finesse. 700 cases made. • $14 • (06/30/97) • **88**

Sauvignon Blanc Napa Valley Winery Reserve 1995: Full-bodied, strongly flavored and citrusy, with blatantly floral aromas. Flavors come bursting out. Grapefruit and spice flavors mark the finish. 500 cases made. • $13 • (07/31/96) • **87**

EISELE, VOLKER | CALIFORNIA

Cabernet Sauvignon Napa Valley 1995: Smooth and spicy, with currant, tobacco, anise, sage and cedary flavors, turning elegant on the finish, where the tannins are polished and supple. Best from 2000 through 2007. 650 cases made. • $35 • (07/31/98) • **88**

Cabernet Sauvignon Napa Valley 1994: Solid, with a pleasing core of currant and cherry flavor, and dashes of cedar and spice on the finish. Contains 10 percent Cabernet Franc. 995 cases made. • $30 • (10/31/97) • **87**

Cabernet Sauvignon Napa Valley 1992: Young and tight, firm and focused, with complex flavors of currant, plum, green olive, cedar and spice. Finishes with firm tannins; cellaring into 1999 to 2002 is advised. 800 cases made. • $26 • (05/15/97) • **88**

EKLUND | CALIFORNIA

Pinot Noir Carneros 1994: Medium-weight, with an earthy streak to the herb, tea and light cherry and strawberry flavors. While elegant and balanced, it lacks the ripe fruit flavors of the top 1994s, and finishes with a stemmy flavor. 253 cases made. • $20 • (11/15/97) • **83**

EL MOLINO | CALIFORNIA

Chardonnay Napa Valley 1996: Crisp and flinty. A subtle, tightly wound, compact style that will need short-term cellaring to blossom. Finishes with a complex array of ripe pear, fig, melon, toast and spice. Best from 1999 through 2004. 710 cases made. • $38 • (06/30/98) • **90**

Chardonnay Napa Valley 1995: Young and sharply focused, with flavors built around ripe pear, nectarine, fig and melon, picking up a complex, spicy quality on the lingering finish. This wine has a knack for improving with age, so set aside a couple of bottles for future enjoyment. 650 cases made. • $38 • (05/31/97) • **91**

Chardonnay Napa Valley 1994: Grows on you, offering ripe pear, spice and honey notes, with light oak shadings folding in on the finish. An elegant, understated wine of great finesse. Will benefit from aging, so look to some future enjoyment from this. 530 cases made. • $35 • (05/31/96) • **91**

Chardonnay Napa Valley 1993 • $30 • (07/31/95) • **88**

Pinot Noir Carneros Abbott's Vineyard 1986: Mature, with an earthy, leafy twist to the supple mushroom and anise notes. Most of the fruit flavor has faded, but it's still enjoyable. Drink it soon, though. • $25 • (03/31/97) • **84**

Pinot Noir Napa County 1990: Fully mature, the earthy mushroom, dried cherry and rhubarb flavors are taking on a pleasant, decadent quality. Best now, before it loses any more fruit. • $30 • (03/31/97) • **89**

Pinot Noir Napa County 1989 • $30 • (09/30/92) • **82**

Pinot Noir Napa County 1988 • $30 • (11/15/91) • **82**

Pinot Noir Napa County 1987 • $29 • (10/31/91) • **85**

Pinot Noir Napa Valley 1995: Lean and trim, with a band of spice, cola, mushroom and berry that's well-focused, if lacking extra dimensions and richness now. Turns complex on the finish; drinkable now through 2000. 750 cases made. • $38 • (01/31/98) • **88**

Pinot Noir Napa Valley 1994: Shows some richness and depth, with layers of black cherry, plum and berry flavors, and nice dashes of smoky oak, herb and mineral on the finish. Drinkable now. 700 cases made. • $35 • (01/31/97) • **89**

Pinot Noir Napa Valley 1993 • $35 • (05/31/96) • **87**

Pinot Noir Napa Valley 1992 • $30 • (02/28/95) HR • **91**

Pinot Noir Napa Valley 1991 • $30 • (02/28/95) • **89**

ELAN | CALIFORNIA

Cabernet Sauvignon Atlas Peak 1992: Smooth and rich, with complex layers of herb, currant and black cherry and picking up a dash of earthiness and anise. Turns even more supple on the finish, where the flavors linger long. Remarkably elegant and approachable, it's an impressive debut from a new wine estate. Drink now through 2004. Tasted twice, with consistent notes. 150 cases made. • $30 • (11/30/97) • **91**

Cabernet Sauvignon Napa Valley 1992: Tight and tannic, in a rustic style with a slightly bitter edge to the coffee and currant flavors. Shows some mature Cabernet flavors too, with cedar and anise on the finish. Try now but be advised, it may always be on the woody, tannic side. 150 cases made. • $29 • (05/15/97) • **86**

Key: SS—Spectator Selection CS—Cellar Selection HR—Highly Recommended BB—Best Buy $NA—Price not available Ⓐ—Auction Price (BT)—Barrel Tasting
Dates in parentheses indicate the issues in which the ratings were published.

ELIZABETH | CALIFORNIA

Zinfandel Mendocino 1992 • $10 • (10/15/94) • **86**

Zinfandel Mendocino 1990 • $10 • (10/15/92) • **85**

Zinfandel Redwood Valley 1996: Lots of vanilla and toast tones and smooth and rich berry flavors. Tarlike, anise and fruit flavors linger on the medium finish. Drink now through 2001. 450 cases made. • $14 • (06/15/98) • **85**

ELK COVE | OREGON

Cabernet Sauvignon Willamette Valley Dundee Hills Vineyard Commander's Cabernet 1987 • $15 • (03/31/91) • **80**

Chardonnay Willamette Valley Clonal Selection Espiguette #352 1996: Fresh and appealing for its bright apple and spice flavors, hinting at earthy mineral notes on the finish. Very good now, better in 1999. 1,043 cases made. • $17 • (03/31/98) • **86**

Chardonnay Willamette Valley Clonal Selection Espiguette #352 1995: Melon, floral and nectarine flavors compete with a resiny edge that detracts a bit from the charm. Ready to drink. 537 cases made. • $17 • (10/31/97) • **84**

Chardonnay Willamette Valley Clonal Selection Espiguette #352 1994: Earthy, almost cardboardlike, adding just a little floral character on the finish to make it interesting. 280 cases made. • $17 • (04/30/96) • **79**

Chardonnay Willamette Valley Reserve Exceptional 1993 • $15 • (11/30/95) • **82**

Gewürztraminer Willamette Valley Ultima 1996: Sweet, with modest spicy overtones to the honey and orange flavors. Finishes with restraint. Drink while it's fresh. 120 cases made. • $25/375ml • (03/31/98) • **88**

Gewürztraminer Willamette Valley Ultima 1994 • $25/375ml • (06/15/96) • **88**

Gewürztraminer Willamette Valley Ultima 1992 • $20 • (05/31/94) • **86**

Pinot Gris Willamette Valley Ultima 1992 • $20 • (05/31/94) • **85**

Pinot Gris Willamette Valley 1996: Very pretty melon, honey and mineral flavors make this a thoroughly attractive wine, its rich texture adding more interest. Drink soon. 5,383 cases made. • $14 • (10/31/97) • **88**

Pinot Gris Willamette Valley 1995: Ripe, bright and plump, with peach and mineral flavors that bounce along nicely, right through the generous finish. Drink soon. 3,932 cases made. • $12 • (10/31/96) • **87**

Pinot Gris Willamette Valley 1994 • $12 • (03/31/96) • **84**

Pinot Gris Willamette Valley 1993 • $10 • (11/30/94) • **74**

Pinot Noir Willamette Valley 1994 • $12 • (03/31/96) • **85**

Pinot Noir Willamette Valley 1992 • $10 • (03/15/94) • **83**

Pinot Noir Willamette Valley 1990 • $10 • (02/28/93) • **83**

Pinot Noir Willamette Valley 1989 • $10 • (03/31/92) • **88**

Pinot Noir Willamette Valley 1988 • $15 • (01/31/91) • **78**

Pinot Noir Willamette Valley 1987 • $15 • (02/15/90) • **78**

Pinot Noir Willamette Valley 1986 • $15 • (06/15/88) • **87**

Pinot Noir Willamette Valley Dundee Hills Vineyard 1990 • $18 • (02/28/93) • **75**

Pinot Noir Willamette Valley Dundee Hills Vineyard 1989 • $18 • (03/31/92) • **84**

Pinot Noir Willamette Valley Dundee Hills Vineyard 1987 • $15 • (02/15/90) • **81**

Pinot Noir Willamette Valley Dundee Hills Vineyard 1986 • $15 • (06/15/88) • **78**

Pinot Noir Willamette Valley Dundee Hills Vineyard 1985 • $15 • (06/15/87) • **85**

Pinot Noir Willamette Valley La Bohème 1993 • $25 • (03/31/96) • **84**

Pinot Noir Willamette Valley Reserve 1994: Very light in color, aroma and flavor. Not characteristic of the vintage, with little to recommend it. 925 cases made. • $25 • (10/15/96) • **77**

Pinot Noir Willamette Valley Reserve 1993 • $20 • (03/31/96) • **79**

Pinot Noir Willamette Valley Reserve 1992 • $18 • (10/31/94) • **88**

Pinot Noir Willamette Valley Reserve 1991 • $18 • (03/15/94) • **82**

Pinot Noir Willamette Valley Reserve 1990 • $22 • (02/28/93) • **83**

Pinot Noir Willamette Valley Reserve 1987 • $15 • (12/15/90) • **85**

Pinot Noir Willamette Valley Reserve 1985 • $15 • (02/15/90) • **79**

Pinot Noir Willamette Valley Reserve 1983 • $15 • (08/31/86) • **81**

Pinot Noir Willamette Valley Wind Hill Vineyards 1990 • $18 • (02/28/93) • **74**

Pinot Noir Willamette Valley Wind Hill Vineyards 1989 • $25 • (03/31/92) • **82**

Pinot Noir Willamette Valley Wind Hills Vineyard 1988 • $18 • (01/31/91) • **80**

Pinot Noir Willamette Valley Wind Hills Vineyard 1987 • $15 • (02/15/90) • **75**

Pinot Noir Willamette Valley Wind Hills Vineyard 1986 • $15 • (06/15/88) • **85**
Pinot Noir Willamette Valley Wind Hills Vineyard 1985 • $15 • (06/15/87) • **91**
Pinot Noir Yamhill County 1995: Light in color and texture, with a chocolaty accent to the mild strawberry flavors. Ready now. 253 cases made. • $18 • (02/28/97) • **84**
Riesling Late Harvest Willamette Valley Ultima 1992 • $20/375ml • (11/30/94) HR • **91**
Riesling Willamette Valley 1993 • $7 • (11/30/94) BB • **85**
Riesling Willamette Valley Ultima 1996: Sweet, balanced with enough gentle, citrusy acidity to keep it from being cloying, with elegant honey and spice overtones on the lithe finish. Delicious now. 220 cases made. • $25/375ml • (03/31/98) • **90**
Riesling Willamette Valley Ultima 1994: Sweet and silky, it's appealing for its polished texture and up-front, honeyed flavors, but the finish is shallow and short. 191 cases made. • $25/375ml • (11/30/96) • **85**
Sauvignon Blanc Willamette Valley Ultima 1992 • $20 • (05/31/94) • **84**

ELKHORN PEAK | CALIFORNIA

Chardonnay Napa Valley Fagan Creek Vineyard 1994: Fairly simple, with light apple and citrus flavors. 820 cases made. • $16 • (07/31/97) • **84**
Chardonnay Napa Valley Fagan Creek Vineyard 1993 • $15 • (07/31/95) • **85**
Pinot Noir Napa Valley Fagan Creek Vineyard 1995: A simple style, with ripe, juicy cherry and herb flavors. Smoothly textured. 525 cases made. • $26 • (12/15/97) • **83**
Pinot Noir Napa Valley Fagan Creek Vineyard 1994: A curious style, with tart, sour cherry flavors, an earthy aftertaste and a touch of ash. 405 cases made. • $24 • (03/31/97) • **78**
Pinot Noir Napa Valley Fagan Creek Vineyard 1993 • $21 • (12/31/95) • **83**
Pinot Noir Napa Valley Fagan Creek Vineyard 1992 • $21 • (03/31/95) • **79**

ELKTON VALLEY | OREGON

Pinot Noir Umpqua Valley 1994 • $9 • (03/31/96) • **83**
Riesling Umpqua Valley Elkton Vineyard 1994 • $7 • (03/31/96) • **82**

ELLENDALE | OREGON

Pinot Noir Willamette Valley 1986 • $12 • (06/15/88) • **71**
Pinot Noir Willamette Valley 1985 • $15 • (06/15/88) • **78**

ELLIOTT | CALIFORNIA

Cabernet Sauvignon Napa Valley 1994: Bold, ripe and juicy, with rich, well-focused currant, anise, black cherry and spicy qualities, turning even more elegant on the aftertaste, where the flavors linger. Best now through 2004. 500 cases made. • $24 • (11/15/97) • **89**
Cabernet Sauvignon Napa Valley 1992: Firm and focused, with a tight core of ripe currant, plum, cherry and berry flavors. Holds its fruitiness through the finish, where the tannins are big and chewy. Best in 1999. 687 cases made. • $14 • (11/15/96) • **86**

ELLISTON | CALIFORNIA

Cabernet Sauvignon Central Coast Sunol Valley Vineyard 1985 • $16 • (11/15/91) • **74**
Cabernet Sauvignon Livermore Valley 1994: Marred by strong vegetal flavors, earthy aromas and rough, green tannins. 408 cases made. • $18 • (11/30/97) • **76**
Captain's Claret California NV • $14 • (11/15/94) • **82**
Captain's Claret Napa Valley 1992 • $14 • (08/31/95) • **84**
Cuvée des Trois Central Coast Sunol Valley Vineyard 1993 • $10 • (12/15/95) • **83**
Pinot Noir Santa Cruz Mountains 1993 • $22 • (12/31/95) • **83**

ELYSE | CALIFORNIA

Cabernet Sauvignon Napa Valley Morisoli Vineyard 1993: A ripe and flavorful style, with a black cherry, cedar, currant and spice character. Picks up hints of anise and tar on the finish, where the tannins weigh in. Needs time to soften; cellar into 1999. 312 cases made. • $30 • (11/15/96) • **87**
Cabernet Sauvignon Napa Valley Morisoli Vineyard 1992 • $30 • (04/30/96) • **89**
Cabernet Sauvignon Napa Valley Tietjen Vineyard 1993: Spicy and aromatic if a bit on the volatile side, giving a zesty, ripe plum and wild berry accent to the flavors, and an almost sweet impression on the finish. 87 cases made. • $24 • (12/15/96) • **85**
Nero Misto Napa Valley 1992 • $14 • (01/31/95) • **84**
Nero Misto Napa Valley 1991 • $14 • (06/15/93) • **86**
Nero Misto Napa Valley 1990 • $15 • (06/30/92) • **86**
Zinfandel Howell Mountain 1994 • $16 • (04/30/96) • **87**
Zinfandel Howell Mountain 1993 • $16 • (10/15/95) • **85**
Zinfandel Howell Mountain 1992 • $14 • (10/15/94) • **87**
Zinfandel Howell Mountain 1991 • $14 • (09/30/93) • **85**
Zinfandel Napa Valley Coeur du Val 1994 • $14 • (04/30/96) • **87**
Zinfandel Napa Valley Coeur du Val 1993 • $14 • (10/15/95) • **83**
Zinfandel Napa Valley Coeur du Val 1992 • $14 • (10/15/94) • **85**
Zinfandel Napa Valley Morisoli Vineyard 1993 • $16 • (10/15/95) • **84**
Zinfandel Napa Valley Morisoli Vineyard 1992 • $14 • (10/15/94) • **88**
Zinfandel Napa Valley Morisoli Vineyard 1991 • $14 • (09/30/93) • **87**
Zinfandel Napa Valley Morisoli Vineyard 1990 • $13 • (10/15/92) • **88**
Zinfandel Napa Valley Morisoli Vineyard 1989 • $13 • (08/31/91) • **85**
Zinfandel Napa Valley Rutherford Bench-Morisoli Vineyard 1994: Well balanced and pleasant to drink, in a claret style that avoids excess. Flavorful, with bright, ripe cherry, strawberry and spice. Only available in California. 1,080 cases made. • $16 • (08/31/96) • **88**

EMMOLO | CALIFORNIA

Sauvignon Blanc Napa Valley 1996: Moderately varietal, with hints of green melon, citrus and spice, finishing with subtle grassy notes. An elegant, understated style. Ready to drink. 525 cases made. • $12 • (09/15/97) • **84**

EOLA HILLS | OREGON

Cabernet Sauvignon Oregon 1995: Sleek and seductive, offering pure, very pretty raspberry, plum and cedar flavors that linger enticingly on the elegantly balanced finish. Texture is smooth and the finish feels like it can grow and grow. Nice now, better after 1999. 316 cases made. • $20 • (05/15/98) • **89**
Cabernet Sauvignon Oregon 1992 • $9 • (11/30/94) • **84**
Cabernet Sauvignon Oregon Visconti Vineyards 1992 • $15 • (03/31/96) • **80**
Chardonnay Oregon 1996: Lithe, supple and generous with its apple, pear and nutmeg flavors. A lively mouthful of fruit and spice. Ready now. 2,500 cases made. • $10 • (05/15/98) • **86**
Chardonnay Oregon 1994: Simple, crisp and lively with apple and spice flavors, finishing with a touch of cream to smooth it out. Ready now. 3,000 cases made. • $9 • (01/31/96) • **84**
Chardonnay Oregon Rivenwood Vineyard 1993 • $12 • (03/31/96) • **85**
Chardonnay Oregon Rivenwood Vineyard Reserve 1994: Light, supple and generous with its spicy, caramel-scented apple and nutmeg flavors, long and appealing on the finish. Ready now. 169 cases made. • $18 • (02/28/97) • **87**
Chardonnay Oregon Temperance Hill Vineyard 1993 • $12 • (01/31/96) • **87**
Gamay Noir Oregon O'Connor Vineyards 1992 • $15 • (11/30/94) • **80**
Gewürztraminer Late Harvest Oregon Vin d'Epice 1996: The dark, almost amber color and thick texture make this apricot- and tangerine-centered wine immensely appealing right now. Flavors linger, but the finish softens, so drink it soon. 830 cases made. • $15/375ml • (05/15/98) • **91**
Gewürztraminer Late Harvest Oregon Vin d'Epice Ultra 1992 • $15/375ml • (11/30/94) • **89**
Gewürztraminer Oregon 1995: Fresh in flavor and soft in texture, with modest melon and pineapple flavors that linger a bit on the finish. 1,000 cases made. • $8 • (02/28/97) • **82**
Merlot Oregon 1995: Smooth, ripe and focused, offering a nice array of spicy, slightly minty black cherry and currant flavors that linger on the deftly balanced finish. Has style and lovely flavors. 1,200 cases made. • $12 • (02/28/97) • **87**
Pinot Gris Oregon 1995: Straightforward and fresh, with some nice citrus and apple-pie flavors that linger appealingly on the soft finish. 1,700 cases made. • $10 • (02/28/97) • **86**
Pinot Gris Oregon 1994 • $10 • (01/31/96) • **85**
Pinot Noir Oregon 1995: Light, simple, soft and silky, a pleasant wine for current drinking, offering some nice strawberry and spice flavors. 2,200 cases made. • $10 • (02/28/97) • **82**
Pinot Noir Oregon 1989 • $10 • (02/28/93) • **73**
Pinot Noir Oregon 1987 • $12 • (02/15/90) • **76**
Pinot Noir Oregon 1986 • $12 • (02/15/90) • **77**
Pinot Noir Oregon Illahe Hills Vineyard 1993 • $12 • (01/31/96) • **80**

Pinot Noir Oregon Temperance Hill Vineyard 1992 • $15 • (11/30/94) • **83**
Sauvignon Blanc Late Harvest Oregon Vin d'Or 1996: Sweet and unctuous. A lush mouthful of apricot, fig and pear flavors, with extra touches of vanilla and smoke around the edges. Aftertaste echoes spices. Appealing to drink now, but could develop further through 2000 or 2001. 810 cases made. • $15/375ml • (05/15/98) • **90**

EOS | CALIFORNIA

Chardonnay Paso Robles Astraeus Vineyard 1996: Opens with pleasant peach and spice aromas, followed by brisk acidity on the palate. An impression of sweetness surprises, later framed by toasty oak. Drink now. 8,000 cases made. • $15 • (07/31/98) • **85**

EPOCH | CALIFORNIA

Chardonnay Central Coast 1993 • $7 • (10/31/95) • **77**

EQUINOX | CALIFORNIA

Blanc de Blanc Santa Cruz Mountains Reserve 1991: Its fruit flavors are tart, and on the green side, with a tinny, canned pineapple accent. 100 cases made. • $40 • (11/30/96) • **78**

ERATH VINEYARDS | OREGON

Chardonnay Willamette Valley 1994: Fresh and lively, its bright peach and melon flavors coming through the polished veneer. Ready now. 3,023 cases made. • $10 • (03/31/96) • **85**
Chardonnay Willamette Valley Reserve 1996: Crisp and lively, a bit raw in texture, but it has pretty pear, peach and mineral flavors. Give it until 1999. 601 cases made. • $19 • (05/15/98) • **87**
Gewürztraminer Late Harvest Willamette Valley 1995: Rich, spicy and elegant. A sweet dessert wine with distinctive apricot, cinnamon, rose petal and honey flavors that keep swirling through the silky finish. Delicious now. 158 cases made. • $18/375ml • (12/31/96) • **92**
Gewürztraminer Willamette Valley 1994 • $18/375ml • (03/31/96) • **91**
Gewürztraminer Willamette Valley Dry 1995: Lightly spicy and floral, with pretty grapefruit and apple flavors on a dry frame. Ready to drink. 448 cases made. • $8 • (12/31/96) • **83**
Pinot Blanc Willamette Valley 1995: Bright and fresh, with a citrusy grace note to the pear and apple flavors. Touches of almond on the finish. 324 cases made. • $12 • (12/31/96) • **85**
Pinot Gris Willamette Valley 1995: Soft, broad and spicy, with a nice almond accent to its peach and pear flavors. Generous, easy to drink. 3,400 cases made. • $12 • (12/31/96) • **87**
Pinot Noir Willamette Valley 1993 • $12 • (01/31/96) • **85**
Pinot Noir Willamette Valley Niederberger Vineyard Reserve 1992 • $25 • (01/31/96) • **80**
Pinot Noir Willamette Valley Reserve 1993 • $20 • (01/31/96) • **87**
Pinot Noir Willamette Valley Reserve 1993: Reveals a crisp core of flavors, with a modest cherry note at the center and smooth, spicy, mushroomy flavors at the edge. Drinkable now. 1,081 cases made. • $21 • (12/31/96) • **85**
Pinot Noir Willamette Valley Twenty-Fifth Anniversary 1994: Crisp in texture, with herbal, earthy notes that cut through the modest berry flavors. Finishing with a harsh edge. May be better in 1999. 2,215 cases made. • $28 • (12/31/96) • **82**
Pinot Noir Willamette Valley Vintage Select 1994: Spicy, buttery flavors add depth to the lovely black cherry and blackberry flavors. Narrows a bit on the finish, where it picks up an anise note. 2,956 cases made. • $17 • (12/31/96) • **88**
Pinot Noir Willamette Valley Vintage Select 1993 • $16 • (01/31/96) • **86**
Pinot Noir Willamette Valley Weber Vineyard Reserve 1994: Dense in flavor, with a green edge to the plum and black cherry flavors. Has a raw feel; may be best from 1999 or 2000. 497 cases made. • $35 • (05/15/98) • **86**
Pinot Noir Willamette Valley Weber Vineyard Reserve 1993 • $28 • (01/31/96) • **88**
Riesling Willamette Valley Dry 1995: Dry and fresh, with a modest level of apple and apricot flavors that finish with a slightly sour edge. Drink soon. 1,542 cases made. • $8 • (12/31/96) • **83**

Key: SS—Spectator Selection CS—Cellar Selection HR—Highly Recommended BB—Best Buy $NA—Price not available Ⓐ—Auction Price (BT)—Barrel Tasting
Dates in parentheses indicate the issues in which the ratings were published.

Sauvignon Blanc Willamette Valley 1994 • $8 • (03/31/96) • **82**

ERIC ROSS | CALIFORNIA

Chardonnay Sonoma County 1995: Medium-bodied, with ripe tropical fruit and green apple flavors and an earthy finish. Drink now. • $15 • (07/31/98) • **82**
Merlot Sonoma County 1995: Lots of ripe, intense cherry, raspberry and wild berry-laced flavors in this, and with a couple more years in the bottle it could be a beauty. Finishes with plenty of fruit and crisp but ripe tannins. Best from 1999 to 2004. 113 cases made. • $22 • (03/31/98) • **88**
Zinfandel Sonoma County Old Vine 1995: Ripe, rich, intense and lively, with tart cherry, pepper, raspberry, bay leaf and tea flavors that are tight and focused. Best to cellar into 1999 to let it soften and evolve. 82 cases made. • $22 • (03/31/98) • **88**

ESTANCIA | CALIFORNIA

Cabernet Sauvignon Alexander Valley 1992 • $10 • (11/15/94) • **82**
Cabernet Sauvignon Alexander Valley 1991 • $9 • (10/31/93) BB • **86**
Cabernet Sauvignon Alexander Valley 1990 • $9 • (06/15/93) BB • **86**
Cabernet Sauvignon Alexander Valley 1989 • $10 • (11/15/92) • **85**
Cabernet Sauvignon Alexander Valley 1988 • $9 • (05/31/91) • **81**
Cabernet Sauvignon Alexander Valley 1987 • $7 • (07/15/90) BB • **80**
Cabernet Sauvignon Alexander Valley 1986 • $8 • (04/15/89) BB • **85**
Cabernet Sauvignon Alexander Valley 1985 • $6 • (06/15/88) BB • **87**
Cabernet Sauvignon Alexander Valley 1984 • $6 • (12/31/87) • **79**
Cabernet Sauvignon Alexander Valley 1982 • $6 • (04/15/87) BB • **87**
Cabernet Sauvignon California 1995: Supple and earthy, with a core of currant, clay and cedar, it holds its fruitiness while turning moderately complex. Drink now through 2002. 45,000 cases made. • $13 • (05/31/98) • **86**
Cabernet Sauvignon Sonoma & Napa Counties 1994: A blend of Cabernet grapes from two of California's finest regions, this wine shows an abundance of ripe, complex flavors, with plum, cherry, currant and anise coming to the fore; ripe, well-balanced tannins; and long, full finish. What a deal! Drink now or age into 2000. 25,000 cases made. • $11 • (03/31/97) BB • **88**
Cabernet Sauvignon Sonoma & Napa Counties 1993: Tight with an earthy, cedary edge to the wild berry and spice notes. Well balanced. • $10 • (12/15/95) • **84**
Chardonnay Monterey County 1994: A remarkably elegant and refined California Chardonnay that strikes a nice balance between the ripe, rich fig, pear and citrus flavors and the deft oak shadings. Very complex on the finish, where the flavors unfold, gaining depth and nuance. What a deal at this price. 140,000 cases made. • $10 • (10/15/96) SS • **89**
Chardonnay Monterey County 1993 • $9 • (04/15/95) BB • **87**
Chardonnay Monterey County Pinnacles 1996: A touch earthy, with a slight grassy edge, pear and spice flavors. Picks up a trace of pineapple, has a spicy oak aftertaste. Drink now through 2001. 100,000 cases made. • $11 • (06/30/98) • **88**
Chardonnay Monterey County Pinnacles 1995: A distinctly spicy style, with a pronounced Muscat-like accent. If you like spice in your Chardonnay, here's a good one: It's easy-drinking and reasonably priced. 130,000 cases made. • $10 • (07/31/97) • **85**
Chardonnay Monterey County Reserve 1993 • $20 • (07/31/95) • **87**
Chardonnay Monterey Reserve 1996: Ripe and full-bodied, with a leesy, toasty oak edge to the ripe pear, anise and hazelnut flavors. Holds together nicely on the finish, where the flavors linger on. Drink now through 2000. 4,000 cases made. • $19 • (06/30/98) • **90**
Chardonnay Monterey Reserve 1995: Exotic fig, pineapple, melon and spice flavors are rich and complex, accented by pretty dashes of smoke and toast. Elegant and well balanced, turning creamy on the aftertaste. Drinkable now. 4,000 cases made. • $20 • (05/15/97) • **91**
Chardonnay Monterey Reserve 1994: Smooth and creamy, with nice, ripe core of pear, apple, melon and spice flavors. It finishes with toasty oak shadings that make an elegant statement. 4,000 cases made. • $20 • (05/31/96) • **90**
Duo Alexander Valley 1995: Smooth, rich and complex, with lots of pretty plum, wild berry, cherry and spicy nuances and soft, fleshy tannins. A blend of 70 percent Cabernet and 30 percent Sangiovese. Drink now or cellar into 2000. 3,000 cases made. • $18 • (11/30/97) • **88**
Meritage Alexander Valley 1994: A Bordeaux-style red blend notable not only for its richness and depth, but for its more-than-reasonable price. Complex and concentrated, this has tiers of ripe plum, currant and sage

flavors with pretty oak shadings, all lingering harmoniously on the supple finish. Tempting now, but softer in 2000. A blend of 66 percent Cabernet Sauvignon, 27 percent Cabernet Franc, and 7 percent Merlot. 18,500 cases made. • $16 • (05/15/97) SS • **92**

Meritage Alexander Valley 1993: A complex and compelling style, with a pretty array of black cherry, currant, anise, cedar and spice notes. Smooth, ripe, rich and polished, finishing with a long, complex aftertaste, full of juicy flavors. Compares quite favorably with wines twice the price. Drink now through 2000. A blend of 65 percent Cabernet Sauvignon, 25 percent Cabernet Franc, and 10 percent Merlot. 12,000 cases made. • $15 • (03/31/97) SS • **90**

Meritage Alexander Valley 1992 • $15 • (09/30/95) • **89**

Meritage Alexander Valley 1991 • $14 • (09/15/94) • **85**

Meritage Alexander Valley 1990 • $14 • (10/15/93) SS • **90**

Meritage Alexander Valley 1989 • $14 • (11/15/92) • **85**

Meritage Alexander Valley 1988 • $14 • (11/15/91) • **83**

Meritage Alexander Valley 1987 • $12 • (01/31/91) • **88**

Meritage White Monterey 1994: Smooth and spicy, with a metallic edge to the pineapple and caramel flavors. 12,000 cases made. • $15 • (11/30/96) • **82**

Meritage White Monterey 1993 • $14 • (05/15/95) • **87**

Merlot Alexander Valley 1995: Soft in texture, with a little gamy edge to the solid blackberry, vanilla and herb flavors. Lingers nicely on the finish. Ready now. 9,000 cases made. • $14 • (12/31/97) • **85**

Merlot Alexander Valley 1994: A simple offering, with a modest band of cedar and cherry flavors that fade on the finish. 6,000 cases made. • $13 • (11/30/96) • **82**

Merlot Alexander Valley 1993: Elegant and supple, with notes of ripe cherries, plums and berries. Finishes with crisp acidity. 11,900 cases made. • $10 • (07/31/96) • **88**

Merlot Alexander Valley 1992 • $10 • (11/15/94) BB • **88**

Pinot Noir Monterey County 1995: A light, simple style, offering plum, cherry and strawberry notes of modest proportion. 4,000 cases made. • $12 • (01/31/97) • **83**

Pinot Noir Monterey County 1994 • $10 • (10/15/95) • **84**

Pinot Noir Monterey County 1993 • $10 • (05/15/95) • **84**

Pinot Noir Monterey Pinnacles 1996: Supple, generous and harmonious, this lovely mouthful of currant, berry, herb and toast flavors has a smooth and promising finish. Best from 1999. 12,000 cases made. • $12 • (11/30/97) • **87**

Pinot Noir Monterey Reserve 1995: Hits the right notes with its ripe cherry and plum and prominent oak flavors. Finishes with firm but polished tannins and good length. 500 cases made. • $18 • (08/31/97) • **88**

Sangiovese Alexander Valley 1994: On the lighter side, with modest plum and cherry flavors. Turns simple on the finish. • $19 • (12/15/96) • **83**

Sangiovese Alexander Valley 1993 • $20 • (11/30/95) • **85**

Sangiovese Alexander Valley 1991 • $12 • (12/15/93) • **83**

Sauvignon Blanc Monterey 1994 • $8 • (08/31/95) • **82**

Sauvignon Blanc Monterey County 1993 • $7 • (08/31/94) • **82**

ESTATE BACCALA | CALIFORNIA

Chardonnay Sonoma County 1995: Shows earthy pear and mineral flavors that finish with a bitter edge. 2,000 cases made. • $12 • (11/15/97) • **77**

Chardonnay Sonoma County 1994: Smooth and creamy, with a pleasant band of flavors: ripe pear, light oak and hints of citrus. 2,511 cases made. • $11 • (07/31/96) • **87**

Chardonnay Sonoma County 1993 • $13 • (02/29/96) • **85**

Merlot Alexander Valley 1984 • $10 • (02/28/87) • **72**

Merlot Napa Valley 1995: Smoke, toast and chocolate aromas lead the way. A little green on the palate, but shows pretty layers of herb, cassis and blackberry. Tannins are a touch astringent. Drink now through 2002. 3,600 cases made. • $16 • (07/31/98) • **84**

Merlot Napa Valley 1994: The wine's smoky, beefy and bacony side is balanced nicely by an herbal, mineral edge. In between lies a core of licorice, plum and cassis. Oak is a bit heavy-handed, but the ensemble remains enjoyable. 2,500 cases made. • $14 • (11/30/97) • **88**

Merlot Napa Valley 1992 • $15 • (06/15/96) • **74**

Merlot Napa Valley 1991 • $14 • (07/31/94) • **86**

Merlot Napa Valley 1990 • $10 • (08/31/93) HR • **90**

Zinfandel Mendocino County Old Vines 1996: Cherries and spice are the hallmarks of this wine, tannins are a bit coarse, however. Pleasant, but shuts down a little quickly in the end. Drink now. 2,200 cases made. • $16 • (06/15/98) • **84**

Zinfandel Mendocino County Old Vines 1995: Juicy, plummy notes are framed by firm yet supple tannins. Spice on the finish adds interest. Better than an earlier sample. Drink now. 1,847 cases made. • $16 • (05/31/98) • **85**

Zinfandel Mendocino County Old Vines 1994: Beautifully crafted, this serves up lots of ripe plum, cherry and wild berry flavors that turn rich, deep and complex on the long, full finish. Delicious, and ready now. 1,200 cases made. • $15 • (12/15/96) • **89**

ESTRELLA RIVER | CALIFORNIA

Blanc de Blancs Paso Robles Star Cuvée 1983 • $13 • (02/29/88) • **81**

Cabernet Sauvignon Paso Robles 1985 • $9 • (11/15/89) • **67**

Cabernet Sauvignon Paso Robles 1983 • $8 • (04/15/88) • **80**

Cabernet Sauvignon Paso Robles 1982 • $10 • (06/15/87) • **85**

Cabernet Sauvignon Paso Robles 1981 • $9 • (05/01/85) • **88**

Cabernet Sauvignon Paso Robles Founders Epic Collection 1983 • $12 • (12/15/89) • **65**

Cabernet Sauvignon San Luis Obispo County 1980 • $10 • (03/16/85) • **77**

Cabernet Sauvignon San Luis Obispo County 1979 • $6 • (03/01/84) BB • **84**

Cabernet Sauvignon San Luis Obispo County 1978 • $20 • (11/15/92) • **74**

Sauvignon Blanc California Proprietor's Reserve 1993 • $5 • (09/30/94) • **80**

Syrah Paso Robles 1986 • $8 • (09/30/89) • **82**

Syrah Paso Robles 1985 • $6 • (03/31/88) • **79**

Syrah Paso Robles 1983 • $6 • (01/31/88) BB • **80**

Zinfandel Paso Robles 1987 • $8 • (12/15/89) • **72**

Zinfandel San Luis Obispo County 1980 • $6 • (12/01/84) • **77**

ETUDE | CALIFORNIA

Cabernet Sauvignon Napa Valley 1996: Young and on the grapey side, with intense, concentrated berry and cherry flavors, a hint of plum. Finishes with a strong, fruity aftertaste; not much sign of oak yet. • $NA • (06/15/97) (BT) • **90-94**

Cabernet Sauvignon Napa Valley 1994: Remarkably complex, with tiers of ripe, juicy currant, plum, cherry and berry, framed by spicy, toasty oak. Altogether harmonious, with well-integrated fruit and wood flavors and a long, supple aftertaste. 1,500 cases made. • $38 • (09/30/97) • **93**

Cabernet Sauvignon Napa Valley 1993: Smooth and harmonious, with layers of spice, currant and plum flavors that fold together nicely, creating a sense of suppleness and finesse. Appealing with its gentle tannins. 1,500 cases made. • $30 • (11/15/96) • **90**

Cabernet Sauvignon Napa Valley 1992 • $30 • (11/30/95) HR • **93**

Cabernet Sauvignon Napa Valley 1989 • $24 Ⓐ • (03/31/93) • **89**

Cabernet Sauvignon Napa Valley 1987: Rich and concentrated, with a dense, complex core of mint, chocolate, currant and berry. A wonderfully complex and enticing wine, impeccably balanced and long on the finish. • $36 • (12/15/97) • **92**

Cabernet Sauvignon Napa Valley 1986: This remains a dark, ripe, rich and flavorful wine, showing lots of currant, mint, plum and spice flavors, finishing with fine length and a tight structure. • $NA • (12/15/96) • **92**

Cabernet Sauvignon Napa Valley 1985 • $16 • (12/15/88) • **92**

Pinot Noir Carneros 1995: Smooth and polished, with dashes of cherry, herb, sage and cedary oak. Needs a little time in the bottle to soften. 5,000 cases made. • $30 • (10/31/97) • **88**

Pinot Noir Carneros 1994: Impressive for its silky texture. It's smooth, supple and polished, with a subtle, elegant core of spice, cherry and wild berry flavors that unfolds slowly. Drinkable now. 5,000 cases made. • $27 • (12/15/96) • **88**

Pinot Noir Carneros 1993 • $27 • (12/31/95) • **84**

Pinot Noir Carneros 1992 • $24 • (01/31/95) • **89**

Pinot Noir Carneros 1990 • $25 • (02/28/93) • **88**

Pinot Noir Carneros 1989 • $20 • (11/15/91) • **85**

Pinot Noir Napa Valley 1988 • $20 • (12/15/90) • **86**

Pinot Noir Napa Valley 1985 • $16 • (06/15/88) • **83**

Pinot Noir Rosé Carneros 1996: A crisp rosé, lightly styled, with mineral and floral notes. 900 cases made. • $12 • (09/30/97) • **83**

EVEREST | CALIFORNIA

Cabernet Sauvignon Dry Creek Valley 1989 • $16 • (11/15/93) • **77**

Cabernet Sauvignon Dry Creek Valley 1987 • $16 • (08/31/92) • **84**

EVESHAM WOOD | OREGON

Pinot Noir Willamette Valley 1995: Tart, tight and slightly bitter, it's a racy wine with little charm. Drinkable now. 700 cases made. • $15 • (11/30/97) • **81**

Pinot Noir Willamette Valley 1992 • $13 • (11/30/94) • **80**
Pinot Noir Willamette Valley 1986 • $11 • (06/15/88) • **84**
Pinot Noir Willamette Valley Cuvée J 1993 • $26 • (02/29/96) • **86**
Pinot Noir Willamette Valley Cuvée J 1992 • $35 • (11/30/94) • **86**

EXPRESSIONS | CALIFORNIA

Cabernet Sauvignon Napa Valley 1993: Ripe and harmonious, offering supple plum and cherry flavors and a dry, tannic finish. Tempting now at this price, but best to wait until 2000. 11,300 cases made. • $10 • (04/30/96) BB • **87**
Cabernet Sauvignon North Coast 1994: Marked by herbal, weedy accents up front, it follows up with pleasant beef, tar and anise flavors on the palate. Finishes like it starts, kind of green. 3,400 cases made. • $10 • (09/30/97) • **82**
Chardonnay Sonoma County 1995: A real find at this price and score, this Chardonnay is clear, bright and appealing for its fresh apple and pear flavors. Finishes with a gentle texture and hints of spice. It's tasty, refreshing and ready to drink. 4,000 cases made. • $10 • (11/15/97) BB • **87**
Chardonnay Sonoma County 1994: Harmonious and focused, letting its peach, pear and vanilla flavors emerge gently on the round finish. A great value that's drinkable now. From Glen Ellen. 35,700 cases made. • $10 • (04/30/96) BB • **88**
Merlot Sonoma County 1995: Modest black currant, anise and herb flavors are backed by smoky oak. Quite enjoyable, though with a bit of a rough edge. Could soften nicely in the next few years. • $13 • (02/28/98) • **85**
Merlot Sonoma County 1994 • $12 • (06/15/96) • **87**
Sangiovese California 1995: Has a bit more density than most California Sangiovese, but the flavors remain muddy, with hints of anise and tar. Try now. Tasted twice, with consistent notes. 1,000 cases made. • $14 • (12/15/97) • **79**
Sangiovese California 1994 • $12 • (04/30/96) • **86**
Viognier San Benito 1995: A core of mineral and spice, notes of coconut as well. The wine is lean but shows a hint of the promise of its French cousins. 1,000 cases made. • $10/375ml • (12/15/97) • **86**
Viognier Santa Clara County 1994: Lots of spice flavors and aromas, with a touch of celery and pear. Thinning out; drink now. 1,100 cases made. • $10/375ml • (07/31/96) • **82**
Zinfandel Sonoma County 1993 • $12 • (04/30/96) • **85**

EYE OF THE SWAN | CALIFORNIA

Cabernet Sauvignon California Limited Edition NV • $7 • (03/31/92) • **77**
Pinot Noir California 1989 • $6 • (04/30/92) • **77**

EYRIE | OREGON

Chardonnay Willamette Valley 1996: Lively and refreshing for its bright lemon, pear and vanilla flavors that pick up a floral note on the well-modulated finish. Enjoy now. • $18 • (01/31/98) • **88**
Chardonnay Willamette Valley Reserve 1994: Disarmingly supple and smooth, generous with its apple, pear and spice flavors, not exuberant but nicely molded for elegance. Drinkable now. • $26 • (01/31/98) • **88**
Chardonnay Yamhill County 1995: Light and tart, a crisp wine with modest pear and citrus notes, appealing for its freshness and racy texture. 260 cases made. • $18 • (02/28/97) • **84**
Chardonnay Yamhill County Reserve 1993: Has more depth and complexity than most, it's still fresh but offering delicate nuances of honey, almond, floral and spice notes on a tight, compact frame. Delicious now. 430 cases made. • $25 • (02/28/97) • **90**
Pinot Gris Willamette Valley 1996: Bright and fruity, a lively mouthful of apple and green melon flavors that remain vivid through the crisp finish. Best now. • $16 • (02/28/98) • **88**
Pinot Gris Yamhill County 1995: Fresh and lively, with attractive pure pear and almond flavors that linger effectively on the finish. Has more intensity than most. 4,780 cases made. • $16 • (02/28/97) • **88**
Pinot Gris Yamhill County 1994 • $15 • (02/29/96) • **87**
Pinot Noir Oregon Reserve 1989 • $25 • (11/30/94) • **86**

Key: SS—Spectator Selection CS—Cellar Selection HR—Highly Recommended BB—Best Buy $NA—Price not available Ⓐ—Auction Price (BT)—Barrel Tasting
Dates in parentheses indicate the issues in which the ratings were published.

Pinot Noir Willamette Valley 1996: Very light in color and flavor, with strong spice notes overshadowing the modest fruit character. • $20 • (02/28/98) • **80**
Pinot Noir Willamette Valley 1991 • $14 • (11/30/94) • **83**
Pinot Noir Willamette Valley 1990 • $18 • (02/28/93) • **77**
Pinot Noir Willamette Valley 1987 • $20 • (02/15/90) • **80**
Pinot Noir Willamette Valley 1986 • $20 • (06/15/88) • **83**
Pinot Noir Willamette Valley 1985 • $19 • (02/15/90) • **91**
Pinot Noir Willamette Valley 1984 • $15 • (08/31/86) • **84**
Pinot Noir Willamette Valley 1983 • $20 • (08/31/86) • **94**
Pinot Noir Willamette Valley Reserve 1994: Light in color and texture, with raspberry, tea and leather flavors on a silky background. Pretty, and ready now. • $40 • (02/28/98) • **85**
Pinot Noir Willamette Valley Reserve 1989 • $24 • (02/28/93) • **80**
Pinot Noir Willamette Valley Reserve 1987 • $25 • (02/15/90) • **86**
Pinot Noir Willamette Valley Special Selection 1992 • $11 • (11/30/94) • **84**
Pinot Noir Yamhill County Reserve 1990: Unusual to find such a mature wine on the market, and it's a nice one, too. Spicy, leathery notes add depth to the graceful black cherry and toasty notes at the core. Fades a bit on the smooth finish. Ready now. • $32 • (02/28/97) • **87**

FACELLI | WASHINGTON

Cabernet Sauvignon Columbia Valley 1993: A solid wine with streaks of mint and pepper running through its soft black cherry and tar flavors. Bright finish. Best from 2001. 240 cases made. • $25 • (09/15/97) • **83**
Cabernet Sauvignon Columbia Valley 1992 • $20 • (09/30/95) • **82**
Cabernet Sauvignon Columbia Valley 1991 • $25 • (07/31/94) • **83**
Chardonnay Columbia Valley 1995: Extremely spicy and rich, dark in color and flavor, with more pepper, clove and nutmeg notes than fruit. Offers touches of pineapple and orange on the solid finish. Drink now. 795 cases made. • $15 • (09/15/97) • **87**
Chardonnay Columbia Valley 1994: A generous, rich mouthful of ripe apple, pear, vanilla and spice flavors that linger enticingly through the finish. Best now. 379 cases made. • $13 • (09/15/96) • **89**
Fumé Blanc Columbia Valley 1995: Bright and citrusy flavors remain lively through the slightly grassy finish, where they pick up nice touches of honey and fig. 1,300 cases made. • $10 • (09/15/96) • **87**
Fumé Blanc Columbia Valley 1993 • $9 • (09/30/95) • **82**
Johannisberg Riesling Columbia Valley Dry 1993 • $8 • (09/30/95) • **74**
Lemberger Yakima Valley 1994: A robust mouthful of cherry and berry flavors, finishing with a chewy edge. 106 cases made. • $12 • (09/15/96) • **86**
Lemberger Yakima Valley Limited Bottling 1993 • $12 • (09/30/95) • **85**
Merlot Columbia Valley 1994: Light and smooth, displaying a nice range of cherry, spice and slightly smoky aromas and flavors that linger on the finish. Ready now. 816 cases made. • $17 • (09/15/97) • **87**
Merlot Columbia Valley 1992 • $15 • (09/30/95) • **81**
Merlot Columbia Valley 1991 • $15 • (09/30/94) • **83**
Pinot Noir Washington 1992 • $20 • (09/30/94) • **85**
Sémillon Columbia Valley 1993 • $9 • (09/30/95) • **73**

FALCONER | CALIFORNIA

Brut Blanc de Blancs Russian River Valley 1984 • $15 • (03/15/91) • **89**

FALL CREEK | TEXAS

Cabernet Sauvignon Texas 1989 • $13 • (02/29/92) • **75**
Cabernet Sauvignon Texas 1988 • $13 • (07/15/91) • **78**
Carnelian Llano County 1988 • $13 • (07/15/91) • **73**
Cascade Texas White 1996: Dominated by dull, floral character, with a blunt finish. Not much fun. A blend of 71 percent Sauvignon Blanc and 29 percent Sémillon. • $NA • (02/28/98) • **73**
Chenin Blanc Texas 1996: Well defined. A tad sweet, dominated by peach and almond flavors. A quaffable wine that should be served well chilled on a warm day. • $NA • (02/28/98) • **82**
Granite Reserve Red Texas 1996: A hearty red with good flavors of leather, spice and berry. Balanced and full-bodied, with a good dose of tannin on the finish. Drink now. • $9 • (05/15/98) • **82**
Merlot Texas 1996: Grapey, with bing-cherry flavor and a touch of spice. Finishes on a slight sweet note. • $NA • (12/31/97) • **80**
Sauvignon Blanc Texas 1996: A raw-tasting wine with a bit of a bite. Has some herbal and oniony flavors, but lacks complexity. • $NA • (12/31/97) • **78**

Sweet Jo Texas Dessert 1996: Redolent of peaches, spice and orange, with plenty of sweetness. Remains fresh and balanced despite its lushness. A delicious dessert wine, light enough to try as an apéritif. • $NA • (12/31/97) • **86**

Vintner's Cuvée Texas White 1996: Some nice apricot and peach flavors, but not much intensity. • $NA • (02/28/98) • **78**

FANUCCHI | CALIFORNIA

Trousseau Gris Russian River Valley Wood Road Vineyard 1996: Bright and lemony, with a flinty edge. It's fairly full-bodied, is pleasant enough, but lacks depth. 335 cases made. • $13 • (03/31/98) • **82**

Trousseau Gris Russian River Valley Wood Road Vineyard 1995: Has a sour, lemon-candy flavor at the core that's not very appealing. 300 cases made. • $11 • (04/30/97) • **76**

Zinfandel Russian River Valley Old Vine 1996: Ripe and full-bodied, with a jammy edge to the earthy plum and wild berry flavors. Finishes with firm but supple tannins and a complex, earthy aftertaste. Drink now to 2002. 498 cases made. • $33 • (03/31/98) • **89**

Zinfandel Russian River Valley Old Vine 1995: A dark, rich and polished wine, with a deep, complex core of black cherry, wild berry, raspberry, tar and spice flavors. Finishes with firm but supple tannins. Delicious now. 200 cases made. • $26 • (04/30/97) • **91**

Zinfandel Russian River Valley Old Vine 1994 • $22 • (10/15/95) • **84**

FAR NIENTE | CALIFORNIA

Cabernet Sauvignon Napa Valley 1997: Complex, with an intriguing interplay of ripe cherry, currant, plum, spice, anise and cedary oak. Wonderful finesse and polish, depth and concentration. • $NA • (07/31/98) (BT) • **95-99**

Cabernet Sauvignon Napa Valley 1996: Impressive for its depth, focus, flavor and balance, as the earthy currant, sage and light, cedary oak flavors fold together nicely, finishing with firm tannins. • $NA • (06/15/97) (BT) • **90-94**

Cabernet Sauvignon Napa Valley 1995: Tight, complex and concentrated, with a pretty core of spicy currant, anise, tar, sage and cedar turning supple and harmonious on the finish, where the flavors fan out and show remarkable depth and finesse. Will reward cellaring; best from 2002 through 2010. 17,000 cases made. • $70 • (06/30/98) HR • **92**

Cabernet Sauvignon Napa Valley 1994: Combines ripe, rich, complex Cabernet flavor with a sense of elegance and harmony, as its spicy currant, cherry, anise and light oak flavors fold together to give depth and fine balance. Drinks well now, but should hold into 2002. 13,000 cases made. • $55 • (02/28/97) • **91**

Cabernet Sauvignon Napa Valley 1993: Big, ripe and intense. Lots of plum and currant flavors that continue to emerge through the finish, where they gain a leathery, slightly bitter edge. 10,700 cases made. • $41 Ⓐ • (08/31/96) • **86**

Cabernet Sauvignon Napa Valley 1992 • $45 • (11/15/95) HR • **93**

Cabernet Sauvignon Napa Valley 1991 • $40 • (09/15/94) • **89**

Cabernet Sauvignon Napa Valley 1990 • $36 • (09/15/93) • **88**

Cabernet Sauvignon Napa Valley 1989 • $36 • (11/15/92) • **86**

Cabernet Sauvignon Napa Valley 1988 • $36 • (11/15/91) • **85**

Cabernet Sauvignon Napa Valley 1987: Smooth and elegant, with plenty of ripe cherry, currant and spicy Cabernet flavors and a smoky edge. Finishes with soft tannins. Best now through 2001. • $46 • (12/15/97) • **91**

Cabernet Sauvignon Napa Valley 1986: This wine was one of Far Niente's early successes, yet, at age 10, it's showing some diluted, earthy flavors. With aeration, however, it exhibits a core of currant, cherry and toasty oak flavors, and it is well balanced. Best to drink soon. 12,000 cases made. • $NA • (12/15/96) • **87**

Cabernet Sauvignon Napa Valley 1985 • $28 • (12/31/88) • **90**

Cabernet Sauvignon Napa Valley 1984 • $25 • (10/15/87) • **92**

Cabernet Sauvignon Napa Valley 1983 • $25 • (06/16/86) • **93**

Cabernet Sauvignon Napa Valley 1982 • $25 • (09/16/85) • **84**

Chardonnay Napa Valley 1996: Tightly wound, with a crisp edge to the core of citrus and grapefruit, finishing with a concentrated lemony aftertaste. Best to cellar short-term, as this wine needs time in the bottle to develop. Best now through 2002. 2,400 cases made. • $40 • (06/30/98) • **90**

Chardonnay Napa Valley 1995: A bright, ripe, brilliantly crafted wine, loaded with juicy pear, apple, spice and citrus notes. Oak is but a subtle background nuance, as it finishes with a burst of fruit and a long aftertaste. 24,000 cases made. • $36 • (02/28/97) • **92**

Chardonnay Napa Valley 1994: A subtle style that shows off its citrus and pear notes, starting out crisp and refreshing and adding more flavor development on the finish. 20,000 cases made. • $32 • (02/29/96) • **86**

Chardonnay Napa Valley 1993 • $32 • (07/31/95) • **85**

FARELLA-PARK | CALIFORNIA

Cabernet Sauvignon Napa Valley 1991 • $25 • (02/28/95) • **85**

Merlot Napa Valley 1990 • $20 • (02/28/95) • **84**

Merlot Napa Valley 1988 • $18 • (08/31/93) • **84**

Sauvignon Blanc Napa Valley 1995: A lighter style of Sauvignon Blanc, with some pleasant melon and citrus tones. A bit hollow on midpalate, but enjoyable. 179 cases made. • $10 • (07/31/97) • **85**

Sauvignon Blanc Napa Valley 1993 • $9 • (08/31/95) • **74**

FARRELL, GARY | CALIFORNIA

Cabernet Sauvignon Sonoma County 1987 • $16 • (10/31/90) • **87**

Cabernet Sauvignon Sonoma County Ladi's Vineyard 1994: Medium-weight, with a modest array of light cherry and berry flavors, crisp tannins, a short aftertaste. Surprisingly uncomplicated for this winery. Best now. Tasted twice, with consistent notes. 500 cases made. • $20 • (11/15/97) • **83**

Cabernet Sauvignon Sonoma County Ladi's Vineyard 1993: A young wine, firm, tight and well focused. A ripe core of plum, black cherry, anise and cedar notes starts to unfold by the third sip, revealing more depth and complexity. With another year in the bottle, it could score higher. 700 cases made. • $20 • (03/31/97) • **88**

Cabernet Sauvignon Sonoma County Ladi's Vineyard 1992 • $20 • (07/31/95) • **89**

Cabernet Sauvignon Sonoma County Ladi's Vineyard 1991 • $18 • (08/31/94) • **87**

Cabernet Sauvignon Sonoma County Ladi's Vineyard 1990 • $18 • (11/15/92) • **90**

Cabernet Sauvignon Sonoma County Ladi's Vineyard 1989 • $18 • (11/15/92) • **81**

Cabernet Sauvignon Sonoma County Ladi's Vineyard 1988 • $18 • (08/31/91) • **86**

Chardonnay Russian River Valley 1994: Openly ripe, sweet-tasting and exotic, distinctive for its range of tangerine, orange and nectarine notes and pouring on more flavors of pear and fig. Delicious now and for the next few years. 325 cases made. • $17 • (05/15/96) • **92**

Chardonnay Russian River Valley Allen Vineyard 1996: Ripe, rich and concentrated, brimming with tiers of pear, fig, apple and apricot. Has a tight focus and a long, lingering finish that keeps pumping out the flavors. Drink now through 2002. 350 cases made. • $28 • (06/30/98) • **93**

Chardonnay Russian River Valley Allen Vineyard 1995: Distinctively flavored, with a flinty, mineral accent to the core of pear and citrus, particularly grapefruit, flavors and light oak notes. Drinkable now. 550 cases made. • $22 • (05/31/97) • **92**

Chardonnay Russian River Valley Allen Vineyard 1994: Bold and intense, boasting rich pear, honey, toast and spice, an altogether mouth-filling white with lots of ripe, bright flavors yet also a measure of finesse. 600 cases made. • $20 • (04/30/96) • **92**

Chardonnay Russian River Valley Allen Vineyard 1993 • $18 • (04/15/95) HR • **92**

Chardonnay Russian River Valley Westside Farms 1993 • $18 • (07/31/95) • **89**

Chardonnay Santa Barbara County Bien Nacido Vineyard 1996: Clean and crisp, with a flinty pear and citrus edge, this is a subdued style with tightly reined fruit flavors. Try in 1999. 550 cases made. • $22 • (04/30/98) • **86**

Chardonnay Santa Barbara County Bien Nacido Vineyard 1995: Wonderful to drink now for its up-front fruitiness, this delivers lots of ripe, bright and juicy tropical fruit flavors, with fig, apricot and apple notes and just a hint of oak lingering in the background. 350 cases made. • $22 • (05/15/97) • **91**

Merlot Russian River Valley 1995: Well proportioned, showing its well-focused core of cedar, plum, anise, coffee and sage flavors before the firm tannins creep in. Intense and concentrated, it's best cellared into 1999 to 2000. 625 cases made. • $23 • (04/30/98) • **88**

Merlot Sonoma County Ladi's Vineyard 1994: The herb, sage and tart black cherry flavors show their appeal, once you get past some chewiness, some firm tannins. Drinkable now. 900 cases made. • $20 • (06/30/97) • **87**

Merlot Sonoma County Ladi's Vineyard 1993 • $20 • (04/30/96) • **87**

Merlot Sonoma County Ladi's Vineyard 1992 • $20 • (07/31/95) • **83**

Merlot Sonoma County Ladi's Vineyard 1991 • $16 • (06/15/94) • **88**

Merlot Sonoma County Ladi's Vineyard 1990 • $16 • (04/15/93) • **88**

Pinot Noir Anderson Valley 1995: On the tart side, with a green edge to the cherry and wild berry flavors, finishing on a slight tealike note. Drinkable now. 300 cases made. • $30 • (05/15/97) • **86**

Pinot Noir Russian River Valley 1996: Attractive for its ripe, bright cherry, blackberry and plum notes, it's tight and trim, turning supple and creamy, gaining richness on the finish, where the flavors are complex. Best now through 2005. 1,500 cases made. • $23 • (06/30/98) • **89**

Pinot Noir Russian River Valley 1995: Lean and trim, with a modest band of black cherry, spice, currant and berry flavors. Finishes with supple tannins and good length. Drinkable now. 1,850 cases made. • $20 • (05/15/97) • **87**

Pinot Noir Russian River Valley 1994: Young, tight and firm, with a tannic edge to the ripe plum and cherry flavors. Also hints of coffee and oak. The texture is smooth and polished and firms up on the finish where the tannins are more evident. Drinkable now. 1,984 cases made. • $19 • (07/31/96) • **90**

Pinot Noir Russian River Valley 1991 • $18 • (02/28/93) • **88**

Pinot Noir Russian River Valley 1990 • $16 • (12/31/92) • **87**

Pinot Noir Russian River Valley 1989 • $16 • (07/31/91) • **88**

Pinot Noir Russian River Valley 1988 • $16 • (10/31/90) • **88**

Pinot Noir Russian River Valley 1986 • $15 • (06/15/88) • **90**

Pinot Noir Russian River Valley 1984 • $12 • (04/15/87) • **79**

Pinot Noir Russian River Valley 1983 • $12 • (08/31/86) • **88**

Pinot Noir Russian River Valley Allen Vineyard 1995: A bottling with an impeccable pedigree, the 1995 version has a well-focused core of plum and wild berry flavors, but is tightly wound, with firm tannins that have a slight tealike edge. Drinkable now. 550 cases made. • $40 • (12/31/97) HR • **90**

Pinot Noir Russian River Valley Allen Vineyard 1994: Young and tight, with a firm, tannic core of ripe currant, plum and wild berry flavors. As it unfolds, more flavors emerge—hints of anise, cedar, nutmeg and spice. Shows greater tannic strength than the Farrell Rochioli bottling. 295 cases made. • $40 • (11/15/96) • **92**

Pinot Noir Russian River Valley Allen Vineyard 1992 • $32 • (11/30/94) • **88**

Pinot Noir Russian River Valley Allen Vineyard 1991 • $32 • (02/28/94) • **87**

Pinot Noir Russian River Valley Allen Vineyard 1990: Rich, dense and earthy, offering complex cherry, mushroom, anise and spice flavors that continue to unfold on the long, full finish. Excellent balance and depth. Ready to drink. • $28 • (03/31/97) • **93**

Pinot Noir Russian River Valley Allen Vineyard 1988 • $25 • (10/31/90) • **87**

Pinot Noir Russian River Valley Olivet Lane Vineyard 1994 • $30 • (06/30/96) • **88**

Pinot Noir Russian River Valley Rochioli Vineyard 1995: Young and tight, with a band of flavors that stretches from tart berry and wild berry to strawberry, herb and spice. Try now to 2002. 300 cases made. • $50 • (12/31/97) • **92**

Pinot Noir Russian River Valley Rochioli Vineyard 1994: Tremendous Pinot Noir, with a wealth of flavors, complexity and finesse. The ripe cherry, currant and plum flavors are amazingly well focused, bright and lively, finishing with a wonderful interplay of fruit and light oak notes. Picks up traces of herb and cedar, too. Has the tannic strength for cellaring, but the vibrance of the young fruit is alluring. 113 cases made. • $50 • (11/15/96) • **94**

Pinot Noir Santa Barbara County Bien Nacido Vineyard 1996: A lighter style, with fresh berry and strawberry fruit, finishing with a dash of pepper and oak. While not especially rich or concentrated, short-term cellaring should give it more breadth and texture; drink through 2004. 450 cases made. • $28 • (06/30/98) • **87**

Pinot Noir Santa Barbara County Bien Nacido Vineyard 1992 • $28 • (11/30/94) • **85**

Pinot Noir Santa Barbara County Bien Nacido Vineyard 1990 • $24 • (09/30/92) • **88**

Pinot Noir Sonoma County Howard Allen Vineyard 1986: Shows mature plum, cherry and wild berry notes that are soft and fleshy, with hints of earth and mushroom. The tannins have softened, the flavors are elegant and complex; drink now. (Price upon release). • $15 • (03/31/97) • **91**

Zinfandel Dry Creek Valley Grist Ranch 1995: Tart, with an ever-so-slight green edge to the wild berry and blackberry flavors. Opens to show more juicy fruit, so cellar short-term to let it come together. The texture is smooth and polished, the tannins are round and fine. 300 cases made. • $20 • (06/15/98) • **88**

Key: SS—Spectator Selection CS—Cellar Selection HR—Highly Recommended BB—Best Buy $NA—Price not available Ⓐ—Auction Price (BT)—Barrel Tasting

Dates in parentheses indicate the issues in which the ratings were published.

Zinfandel Russian River Valley 1995: Serves up a bonanza of ripe, juicy flavors, with spice, anise, tar, raspberry, cherry and plum, holding its fruit and turning smooth and polished. Ready to drink. 841 cases made. • $20 • (08/31/97) • **90**

Zinfandel Russian River Valley 1992 • $15 • (08/31/94) HR • **92**

Zinfandel Russian River Valley 1991 • $15 • (04/30/93) • **88**

Zinfandel Russian River Valley Collins Vineyard 1994 • $16 • (04/30/96) • **88**

Zinfandel Russian River Valley Collins Vineyard 1993 • $15 • (07/31/95) • **89**

Zinfandel Russian River Valley Collins Vineyard 1990 • $14 • (10/15/92) • **88**

Zinfandel Sonoma County 1985 • $10 • (04/30/88) • **91**

Zinfandel Sonoma County Old Vine Selection 1996: Firm, crisp, dry and tannic, with hard-edged cherry and wild berry flavors. Slowly opens to show more depth and fruitiness. Drink now through 2002. • $22 • (06/15/98) • **86**

FATHOM | CALIFORNIA

Cabernet Franc Santa Ynez Valley 1992 • $17 • (02/28/95) • **70**

Cabernet Sauvignon Santa Ynez Valley 1992 • $24 • (11/15/94) • **86**

Merlot Santa Ynez Valley 1992 • $18 • (02/28/95) • **84**

FENESTRA | CALIFORNIA

Cabernet Sauvignon Livermore Valley 1991 • $11 • (06/15/95) • **79**

Cabernet Sauvignon Livermore Valley 1990 • $12 • (11/15/93) • **82**

Cabernet Sauvignon Livermore Valley 1989 • $13 • (11/15/92) • **79**

Cabernet Sauvignon Livermore Valley 1988 • $12 • (11/15/91) • **85**

Cabernet Sauvignon Monterey Smith & Hook Vineyard 1989 • $14 • (11/15/93) • **79**

Cabernet Sauvignon Monterey Smith & Hook Vineyard 1988 • $15 • (11/15/92) • **86**

Cabernet Sauvignon Monterey Smith & Hook Vineyard 1987 • $14 • (11/15/91) • **75**

Cabernet Sauvignon Monterey Smith & Hook Vineyard 1986 • $14 • (11/15/93) • **83**

Cabernet-Merlot Livermore Valley 1990 • $35 • (12/15/95) • **78**

Chardonnay Livermore Valley 1996: Sweet, but well-focused flavors of fresh pineapple. Well balanced, with hints of vanilla and toast. The emphasis is on the refreshing, zingy fruit. Drink now. 199 cases made. • $15 • (07/31/98) • **84**

Chardonnay Livermore Valley Toy Vineyard 1993 • $12 • (07/31/95) • **82**

Merlot Livermore Valley 1991 • $11 • (09/15/94) • **83**

Merlot Livermore Valley 1990 • $13 • (09/15/94) • **78**

Merlot Livermore Valley 1989 • $13 • (05/31/92) • **87**

Merlot Livermore Valley Special Reserve 1989 • $40/1.5 liter • (05/31/92) • **89**

Merlot Sonoma County 1986 • $11 • (10/15/89) • **83**

Zinfandel Livermore Valley 1990 • $8 • (09/30/93) • **80**

Zinfandel Livermore Valley 1989 • $8 • (10/15/92) • **87**

Zinfandel Livermore Valley Special Reserve 1991 • $11 • (10/15/95) • **78**

FENN VALLEY | MICHIGAN

Chancellor Lake Michigan Shore 1989 • $9 • (02/29/92) • **81**

FENSALIR | CALIFORNIA

Cabernet Sauvignon Napa Valley 1989 • $10 • (11/15/92) • **83**

Cabernet Sauvignon Napa Valley 1988 • $14 • (11/15/91) • **85**

FERMENTATIONS & MORE | CALIFORNIA

Cabernet Sauvignon San Luis Obispo Silver Canyon Vineyard 1993: Tastes odd, with a weird vinegary edge to the prune and plum flavors. Best to avoid. 120 cases made. • $16 • (11/30/96) • **70**

Chardonnay Edna Valley MacGregor Vineyard 1994: Crisp and refreshing for its lively pineapple and spice flavors, although there is a candied edge that lowers the charm quotient somewhat. • $13 • (04/30/96) • **86**

Zinfandel Paso Robles Benito Dusi Vineyard 1993 • $14 • (04/30/96) • **88**

FERRARI-CARANO | CALIFORNIA

Cabernet Sauvignon Alexander Valley 1997: Dark, grapey and concentrated, on the tart side with wild berry, cherry and raspberry; reduced now, with firm tannins. • $NA • (07/31/98) (BT) • **90-94**

Cabernet Sauvignon Alexander Valley 1988 • $14 • (08/31/92) • **84**

Cabernet Sauvignon Alexander Valley 1987 • $18 • (07/15/91) • **84**
Cabernet Sauvignon Alexander Valley 1986 • $18 • (09/15/90) • **80**
Cabernet Sauvignon Alexander Valley Reserve 1988 • $40 • (11/15/93) • **86**
Cabernet Sauvignon Alexander Valley Special Selection 1987 • $24 • (03/31/93) • **83**
Cabernet Sauvignon Sonoma County 1996: Wonderful aromas with ripe, bright, rich fruit. Deeply concentrated, with layers of currant, cherry, anise and spice. Finishes with supple tannins. • $NA • (06/15/97) (BT) • **90-94**
Cabernet Sauvignon Sonoma County 1993: Austere, with crisp, dry tannins and a modest range of cedar, currant, tea and sagelike notes. Turns even drier on the finish, so be forewarned. May be more appealing by 1999, if the tannins soften. 13,500 cases made. • $23 • (11/15/97) • **87**
Cabernet Sauvignon Sonoma County 1992: Ripe and well balanced, with a nice core of black cherry, plum, spice and berry flavors. Turns supple on the finish, where the tannins weigh in. Drink now. • $22 • (11/15/96) • **89**
Cabernet Sauvignon Sonoma County 1991 • $16 • (09/15/95) • **86**
Cabernet Sauvignon Sonoma County 1990 • $15 • (09/30/94) • **89**
Chardonnay Alexander Valley 1996: Elegant, even delicate, with spicy pear, apple, melon and light oak shadings. Finishes with a complex interplay of fruit and oak. Drink now through 2000. 35,000 cases made. • $21 • (07/31/98) SS • **90**
Chardonnay Alexander Valley 1995: Yet another example of this producer's mastery of Chardonnay. This wine shows off tropical fruit flavors, with loads of ripe pear, melon, fig and butterscotch notes, holding its fruit and keeping its focus through a long, lingering finish. 30,000 cases made. • $21 • (05/31/97) SS • **92**
Chardonnay Alexander Valley 1994: Serves up a pretty array of fig, pear, spice and smoky, toasty oak flavors. This California Chardonnay turns on the elegance and complexity on the finish, where the flavors take on a sense of delicacy. 30,000 cases made. • $22 • (05/15/96) SS • **90**
Chardonnay Alexander Valley 1993 • $20 • (04/30/95) SS • **91**
Chardonnay Alexander Valley Tre Terre 1995: Fresh and lively, with a complex array of smoky, toasty oak and a core of pear, melon, fig and spice flavors. Long, lingering aftertaste keeps pumping out the flavor. 825 cases made. • $26 • (09/30/97) • **92**
Chardonnay Alexander Valley Tre Terre 1994: Openly fruity, remarkably complex and subtle, sporting ripe pear, peach, nectarine and pretty toasty, smoky oak shadings and a long, elegant aftertaste. 467 cases made. • $24 • (05/15/96) • **91**
Chardonnay Alexander Valley Tre Terre 1993 • $22 • (02/29/96) • **93**
Chardonnay Napa & Sonoma Counties Reserve 1995: Shows impressive depth and concentration of fruit, brimming with ripe, rich, complex and concentrated fruit flavors, tiers of pear, tropical fruit, fig, melon and citrus shadings, yet manages to remain elegant and refined, too. Delicious. Drink now through 2002. 4,000 cases made. • $34 • (05/15/98) HR • **93**
Chardonnay Napa & Sonoma Counties Reserve 1994: Remarkably complex and well balanced, with brilliant pear, honey, spice and butter flavors that glide along, smooth and creamy on the palate. A winner, from a winery that seemingly never fails with this varietal. 3,500 cases made. • $32 • (05/31/97) • **93**
Chardonnay Napa & Sonoma Counties Reserve 1993 • $30 • (05/15/96) • **91**
Eldorado Gold Late Harvest Alexander Valley 1989 • $17/375ml • (09/15/91) • **88**
Eldorado Gold Late Harvest Dry Creek Valley 1994 • $18/375ml • (12/31/95) • **91**
Eldorado Gold Late Harvest Sonoma County 1991 • $17/375ml • (04/15/93) • **83**
Fumé Blanc Sonoma County 1996: Ripe melon, grapefruit and fig notes are prominent, but still have the awkwardness of youth. Should pull together nicely over the next year. 30,000 cases made. • $11 • (06/30/97) • **87**
Fumé Blanc Sonoma County 1995: Crisp and citrusy; the lemon and melon flavors are touched with a floral note, and bounce through the finish nicely. 30,000 cases made. • $11 • (07/31/96) • **87**
Fumé Blanc Sonoma County 1994 • $11 • (12/15/95) • **88**
Fumé Blanc Sonoma County 1993 • $11 • (08/31/94) • **88**
Fumé Blanc Sonoma County Reserve 1996: A tangy mix of grapefruit, lemon and lime. Almost sears the palate with freshness, and finishes with just a touch of toasty oak. 5,800 cases made. • $18 • (01/31/98) • **87**
Fumé Blanc Sonoma County Reserve 1995: Swirls spicy vanilla notes into lively apple, pear and citrus flavors. A barrel-fermented white of great finesse and character. 4,100 cases made. • $17 • (07/31/96) HR • **91**
Fumé Blanc Sonoma County Reserve 1994 • $15 • (12/15/95) • **90**
Fumé Blanc Sonoma County Reserve 1993 • $14 • (11/30/94) • **87**
Merlot Alexander Valley 1987 • $17 • (07/31/90) • **84**
Merlot Alexander Valley 1986 • $15 • (06/30/89) • **87**
Merlot Sonoma County 1994: Smooth, ripe and polished, with gentle tannins and a pretty core of juicy plum and blackberry flavors. Drinks well now and through 1999. 19,800 cases made. • $23 • (09/30/97) • **87**
Merlot Sonoma County 1993 • $23 • (06/30/96) • **83**
Merlot Sonoma County 1992 • $20 • (09/30/95) • **89**
Merlot Sonoma County 1991 • $17 • (05/31/94) • **89**
Merlot Sonoma County 1990 • $15 • (07/15/93) • **81**
Merlot Sonoma County 1989 • $15 • (05/31/92) • **86**
Merlot Sonoma County 1988 • $18 • (08/31/91) • **85**
Pinot Noir Napa & Sonoma Counties Rhonda's Reserve 1990 • $30 • (02/28/93) • **82**
Reserve Red Sonoma County 1992: Remarkably complex, with tiers of currant, spice, cedar and dill, turning elegant and supple on the finish, where the flavors linger. Drink now or cellar into 2000. 2,651 cases made. • $47 • (09/30/97) • **91**
Reserve Red Sonoma County 1991: Big, ripe and ruggedly tannic, this is a blockbuster style that some may find overpowering at this stage. Once past the tannins, the core of spicy cherry, wild berry and currant flavors runs deep and is complex, with a touch of anise and a chewy aftertaste. 1,694 cases made. • $47 • (11/15/96) • **90**
Reserve Red Sonoma County 1990 • $47 • (11/30/95) • **91**
Reserve Red Sonoma County 1989 • $40 • (11/15/94) • **85**
Siena Sonoma County 1995: A remarkably harmonious and well integrated red, smooth, ripe, rich and concentrated, with complex black cherry, raspberry, anise, sage and spice flavors. Finishes with a long, fruity aftertaste. Enjoyable now through 2002. A blend of Sangiovese, Cabernet Sauvignon and Malbec. 9,100 cases made. • $28 • (12/31/97) SS • **91**
Siena Sonoma County 1994: Harmonious and smooth, with a core of black cherry, plum, anise and berry notes that fan out on the palate. Finishes with a complex interplay of flavors and supple tannins. A blend of Sangiovese, Cabernet Sauvignon and Merlot. 2,800 cases made. • $28 • (04/30/97) • **89**
Siena Sonoma County 1993 • $24 • (11/30/95) HR • **90**
Siena Sonoma County 1992 • $20 • (09/30/95) • **89**
Siena Sonoma County 1991 • $20 • (11/15/93) • **90**
Sémillon-Sauvignon Blanc Dry Creek Valley Late Harvest Eldorado Gold 1996: Strongly tobacco-scented, its pear and caramel flavors mingle pleasantly on the vanilla-laced finish. Best from 2000. 500 cases made. • $23/375ml • (03/31/98) • **89**
Zinfandel Dry Creek Valley 1992 • $15 • (09/30/94) • **89**
Zinfandel Dry Creek Valley 1991 • $14 • (09/30/93) • **85**
Zinfandel Dry Creek Valley 1990 • $15 • (01/31/93) • **90**
Zinfandel Sonoma County 1995: Dense and chewy, with a firm wall of tannins and earthy wild berry and black cherry flavors that are slow to emerge. Strong oak and slight bitterness on the finish. Needs food. 6,800 cases made. • $18 • (05/15/98) • **84**
Zinfandel Sonoma County 1994: Firm, tight and tannic—not as supple and harmonious as Ferrari-Carano usually is. The core is built around racy wild berry and raspberry notes, but there's a good dose of tar and earth, too. Drinkable now. 4,000 cases made. • $18 • (03/31/97) • **85**
Zinfandel Sonoma County 1993 • $14 • (08/31/95) • **88**

FETZER | CALIFORNIA

Cabernet Sauvignon California 1988 • $8 • (01/31/91) BB • **81**
Cabernet Sauvignon California Barrel Select 1990 • $12 • (11/15/93) • **87**
Cabernet Sauvignon California Barrel Select 1989 • $11 • (03/15/93) • **87**
Cabernet Sauvignon California Barrel Select 1988 • $11 • (08/31/92) • **86**
Cabernet Sauvignon California Barrel Select 1983 • $8 • (06/15/87) • **70**
Cabernet Sauvignon California Bel Arbors 1993: Soft and generous, centered around appealing vanilla-scented raspberry and red currant flavors that linger gently on the finish. Approachable now. • $7 • (12/15/95) BB • **84**
Cabernet Sauvignon California Reserve 1985 • $17 • (11/15/89) • **87**
Cabernet Sauvignon California Valley Oaks 1994: A solid effort, with spicy currant and berry flavors, light oak shadings. Drinks well now. 300,000 cases made. • $8 • (11/30/96) BB • **84**
Cabernet Sauvignon California Valley Oaks 1994: Fairly simple yet enjoyable, it's a woody, plummy blend finishing with a quick, dry edge. • $9 • (09/30/97) • **81**
Cabernet Sauvignon California Valley Oaks 1993: Light, straightforward, showing nice plum and berry flavors that fade a bit on the finish. Ready now. • $8 • (12/15/95) • **82**
Cabernet Sauvignon California Valley Oaks 1990 • $8 • (03/15/93) • **83**
Cabernet Sauvignon California Valley Oaks 1989 • $8 • (08/31/92) BB • **85**
Cabernet Sauvignon California Valley Oaks 1988 • $8 • (11/15/91) • **82**
Cabernet Sauvignon Lake County 1985 • $6 • (08/31/87) BB • **82**

FETZER

Cabernet Sauvignon Lake County 1984 • $8 • (05/15/87) • **74**
Cabernet Sauvignon Lake County 1983 • $5 • (05/01/86) • **83**
Cabernet Sauvignon Lake County 1982 • $5 • (05/16/84) • **78**
Cabernet Sauvignon Mendocino Barrel Select 1985 • $10 • (12/15/88) • **85**
Cabernet Sauvignon Mendocino Barrel Select 1984 • $9 • (11/30/87) • **82**
Cabernet Sauvignon Mendocino Barrel Select 1982 • $7 • (02/01/85) • **73**
Cabernet Sauvignon Mendocino County 1981 • $7 • (12/16/84) • **86**
Cabernet Sauvignon Mendocino Special Reserve 1984 • $14 • (12/31/88) • **85**
Cabernet Sauvignon Napa Valley Toga Red 1994: Grapey and peppery, with a spicy edge that reminds you of Zinfandel; finishes with hard tannins, so be forewarned. • $24 • (11/15/97) • **82**
Cabernet Sauvignon Napa Valley Usibelli Vineyard Reserve 1994: Strikes a nice balance between its ripe currant, black cherry and plummy notes, light cedary oak shadings and fine tannins. Most impressive on the finish, where the flavors fold together well. • $24 • (11/15/97) • **89**
Cabernet Sauvignon North Coast Barrel Select 1994: A rich blend of licorice, cassis and coffee notes, framed by firm but ripe tannins and a minty finish. It's well balanced and drinking nicely now but should improve within five years. • $14 • (09/30/97) • **88**
Cabernet Sauvignon North Coast Barrel Select 1993: Complex with its interplay of ripe currant, plum and berry flavors and light toasty oak notes. Finishes with modest tannins and good length. Drinks well now. 40,000 cases made. • $13 • (11/30/96) • **87**
Cabernet Sauvignon North Coast Barrel Select 1992 • $12 • (12/15/95) • **85**
Cabernet Sauvignon North Coast Barrel Select 1991 • $12 • (11/15/94) • **83**
Cabernet Sauvignon Sonoma County Reserve 1992: Lean and trim, with a narrow band of appealing flavors—cedar, currant and berry. Dries out on the finish, where the tannins dominate. 700 cases made. • $24 • (04/30/97) • **86**
Cabernet Sauvignon Sonoma County Reserve 1989 • $24 • (12/15/95) • **85**
Cabernet Sauvignon Sonoma County Reserve 1988 • $24 • (11/15/94) • **83**
Cabernet Sauvignon Sonoma County Reserve 1987: Drying out, but still plenty to admire. Shows ripe currant, plum and cherry notes before the dry tannins kick in. Drink soon. 3,250 cases made. • $75 • (12/15/97) • **87**
Cabernet Sauvignon Sonoma County Reserve 1986: Still showing a slight gaminess, but there are enough currant, plum and black cherry flavors to provide balance and interest to the palate. Finishes with firm, dry tannins. • $NA • (12/15/96) • **86**
Cabernet Sauvignon Sonoma County Reserve 1985 • $24 • (08/31/90) • **86**
Chardonnay California Sundial 1997: Simple, clean and spicy, with bright pear, nectarine and citrus flavors that linger. Drink now. 1,000,000 cases made. • $8 • (07/31/98) BB • **85**
Chardonnay California Sundial 1996: Crisp, simple and pleasant for its nectarine and sweet, grapey flavors. Ready to drink. 850,000 cases made. • $7 • (07/31/97) • **80**
Chardonnay California Sundial 1993 • $8 • (07/31/95) • **81**
Chardonnay Mendocino Barrel Select 1996: Ripe and spicy, with a nice core of pear and caramel flavor that extends into a delicate finish. Feels a little chunky up front but finishes well. Drinkable now. • $12 • (03/31/98) • **86**
Chardonnay Mendocino County Barrel Select 1995: Fresh and lively, with a ripe core of pear, peach, honey and butterscotch flavors. Smooth and harmonious, it's ready now. • $11 • (04/30/97) • **88**
Chardonnay Mendocino Reserve 1993 • $24 • (07/31/95) • **88**
Chardonnay North Coast Barrel Select 1994: Smooth in texture, with spicy apple and pear flavors in balance and echoing nicely on the finish. • $10 • (06/15/96) • **86**
Chardonnay North Coast Barrel Select 1993 • $11 • (06/30/95) • **87**
Chardonnay North Coast Sundial 1995: Ripe, bright and attractive for its citrusy melon and pear flavors that remain fresh through the finish. • $7 • (07/31/96) • **84**
Chardonnay Sonoma County Carneros Sangiacomo Vineyard 1995: Marked by spicy pear, vanilla, fig and apricot flavors, it's solid with a sense of elegance and finesse. Smooth and polished texture. Ready to drink. 1,000 cases made. • $17 • (04/30/97) • **88**
Chardonnay Sonoma County Carneros Sangiacomo Vineyard Special Reserve 1994: A touch earthy, with mature pear, citrus and light oak shadings. • $15 • (07/31/96) • **81**
Fumé Blanc California Echo Ridge 1996: Peachy and cloying, this is a simple quaff. • $8 • (11/15/97) • **77**

Key: SS—Spectator Selection CS—Cellar Selection HR—Highly Recommended BB—Best Buy $NA—Price not available Ⓐ—Auction Price (BT)—Barrel Tasting
Dates in parentheses indicate the issues in which the ratings were published.

Fumé Blanc California Echo Ridge 1995: Light and crisp, with peach and floral flavors that linger nicely through the finish. • $7 • (10/31/96) • **84**
Fumé Blanc Mendocino County 1995: A mouthful of vivid, fruit flavors—crisp apple, citrus and peach—that have just a hint of herb. 50,000 cases made. • $6 • (08/31/96) • **86**
Fumé Blanc Mendocino County 1993 • $7 • (07/31/95) BB • **87**
Gamay Beaujolais Mendocino County 1988 • $5 • (07/15/89) • **74**
Gamay Beaujolais Mendocino County 1987 • $6 • (07/15/88) • **83**
Gamay Beaujolais Mendocino County 1986 • $4 • (01/31/88) • **80**
Gewürztraminer California 1997: Soft, off dry and layered with pretty apple, spice and floral flavors that linger gently on the sweet finish. Drink now. 300,000 cases made. • $7 • (07/31/98) BB • **85**
Gewürztraminer California 1996: Sweet, soft and pleasant, with modest pear and floral flavors. • $7 • (11/30/97) • **81**
Gewürztraminer Mendocino County Dry Beckstoffer Vinifera Vineyards Dry Reserve 1996: Vibrantly fruity and pretty, a bright mouthful of citrus, pineapple and rose petal aromas and flavors. Finishes dry. Drink soon. • $18 • (04/30/98) • **88**
Gewürztraminer Mendocino County Beckstoffer Vinifera Vineyards Reserve 1995: A gorgeous Gewürztraminer, this shows dry, spicy, floral, litchi and grapefruit aromas and flavors and picks up a delicious vanilla and rose-petal note that lingers on the finish. Tasty now. 220 cases made. • $18 • (04/30/97) • **90**
Johannisberg Riesling Late Harvest Sonoma County Reserve 1988 • $10/375ml • (03/31/91) • **91**
Merlot California Eagle Peak 1995: Offers toasty oak, cherry and herb flavors that finish simply with a dusty nuance. 365,000 cases made. • $8 • (07/31/97) • **81**
Merlot California Eagle Peak 1994 • $8 • (06/15/96) BB • **85**
Merlot California Eagle Peak 1992 • $8 • (09/15/94) • **81**
Merlot North Coast Barrel Select 1994 • $12 • (06/30/96) • **85**
Merlot Sonoma County Barrel Select 1995: Enters with smoke and charred notes, then follows up with licorice and black currant, but the ensemble remains a little disjointed and bitter. • $14 • (02/28/98) • **83**
Petite Sirah California Petite Syrah Reserve 1986 • $14 • (08/31/90) • **74**
Petite Sirah Mendocino County Eagle Point Ranch Reserve 1994: A touch earthy, with a minty juniper-berry accent and drying tannins. It certainly is intense and firmly tannic. Try now. 200 cases made. • $24 • (08/31/97) • **86**
Petite Sirah Mendocino Petite Syrah 1982 • $5 • (04/16/85) • **78**
Pinot Blanc Santa Barbara County Bien Nacido Vineyard Reserve 1995: Soft and pretty, with effusive mineral and pineapple flavors that remain refreshing through the finish. 240 cases made. • $20 • (04/30/97) • **88**
Pinot Noir California Barrel Select 1996: Light, smooth and pretty, offering lovely raspberry, currant and vanilla flavors. Ready now. • $13 • (12/31/97) • **83**
Pinot Noir California Barrel Select 1991 • $13 • (02/28/94) • **88**
Pinot Noir California Reserve 1990 • $13 • (02/28/93) • **85**
Pinot Noir Mendocino 1981 • $5 • (04/01/84) • **80**
Pinot Noir Mendocino County Reserve 1986 • $18 • (10/31/90) • **87**
Pinot Noir Mendocino County Special Reserve 1985 • $13 • (06/15/88) • **78**
Pinot Noir North Coast Barrel Select 1994 • $13 • (02/29/96) • **81**
Pinot Noir North Coast Barrel Select 1992 • $13 • (01/31/95) • **82**
Pinot Noir Santa Barbara County Bien Nacido Vineyard Reserve 1995: Cherry, plum and wild berry flavors emerge to give added dimension to this racily styled Pinot with its streaks of herb and cola. The texture is smooth and polished. 350 cases made. • $24 • (05/15/97) • **90**
Pinot Noir Santa Barbara County Bien Nacido Vineyards 1994 • $17 • (02/29/96) • **82**
Pinot Noir Santa Barbara County Bien Nacido Vineyards 1992 • $24 • (01/31/95) • **86**
Pinot Noir Sonoma County Barrel Select 1994: A medium weight wine, with modest cherry and wild berry flavors of good length. 4,000 cases made. • $13 • (01/31/97) • **84**
Pinot Noir Sonoma County Carneros Sangiacomo Vineyard Reserve 1994: Young, tight and tannic, with a slightly stemmy, astringent edge to the muted black cherry and earth notes. Drinkable now. 1,000 cases made. • $24 • (12/31/96) • **82**
Pinot Noir Sonoma County Olivet Lane Vineyard 1992 • $24 • (01/31/95) • **87**
Port Mendocino County Eagle Point 1993 • $19 • (05/15/96) • **85**
Premium Red California 1985 • $4 • (03/15/88) • **78**
Sauvignon Blanc Mendocino County Barrel Select 1995: Soft, silky and definitely earthy, with a peppery edge to the grapefruit and pineapple flavors. Drink soon. • $10 • (02/28/97) • **83**

Sauvignon Blanc Mendocino County Barrel Select 1993 • $10 • (08/31/95) • **79**

Sauvignon Blanc North Coast Barrel Select 1994: Light-bodied and crisp. Has citrusy apple flavors with a distinctly herbal tang. 18,000 cases made. • $10 • (08/31/96) • **85**

White Zinfandel California 1994 • $7 • (09/15/95) • **80**

Zinfandel California 1995: A bright and chewy red, its spicy berry flavors emerging nicely from the base of fine-grained tannins. Drinkable now. 30,000 cases made. • $9 • (03/31/98) BB • **86**

Zinfandel California 1989 • $6 • (11/30/90) • **76**

Zinfandel California 1986 • $6 • (09/15/88) • **78**

Zinfandel California Barrel Select 1989 • $9 • (07/31/92) • **84**

Zinfandel El Dorado County Reserve 1993: Showing some maturity, this is a rustic style with an earthy, chunky quality to the plum and berry flavors. 665 cases made. • $13 • (03/31/97) • **84**

Zinfandel Lake County 1986 • $6 • (02/15/88) BB • **83**

Zinfandel Lake County 1984 • $5 • (04/15/87) • **81**

Zinfandel Lake County 1983 • $4 • (07/16/86) BB • **83**

Zinfandel Mendocino 1982 • $5 • (04/01/85) • **81**

Zinfandel Mendocino 1980 • $5 • (04/01/84) • **78**

Zinfandel Mendocino County Barrel Select 1994: Smells better than it tastes; the flavors are thin with hints of cherry and spice. 24,000 cases made. • $9 • (03/31/97) • **82**

Zinfandel Mendocino County Barrel Select 1992 • $9 • (09/30/94) BB • **86**

Zinfandel Mendocino County Barrel Select 1991 • $9 • (12/31/93) BB • **86**

Zinfandel Mendocino County Reserve 1991 • $13 • (03/31/94) • **87**

Zinfandel Mendocino County Reserve 1986 • $14 • (07/31/90) • **83**

Zinfandel Mendocino Home Vineyard 1982 • $8 • (11/01/84) • **77**

Zinfandel Mendocino Lolonis Vineyards 1982 • $8 • (11/01/84) • **79**

Zinfandel Mendocino Ricetti Vineyard 1985 • $14 • (10/15/88) • **79**

Zinfandel Mendocino Ricetti Vineyard 1983 • $8 • (02/16/86) • **82**

Zinfandel Mendocino Ricetti Vineyard 1982 • $8 • (10/16/84) • **79**

Zinfandel Mendocino Ricetti Vineyard Reserve 1986 • $14 • (07/31/90) • **74**

Zinfandel Mendocino Scharffenberger Vineyard 1982 • $8 • (10/16/84) • **85**

Zinfandel Mendocino Special Reserve 1985 • $14 • (12/15/88) • **81**

FICKLIN | CALIFORNIA

Port California Special Bottling No. 6 1983 • $25 • (11/30/91) • **87**

Port California Special Bottling No. 5 1980 • $19 • (04/30/91) • **84**

Port California Tinta NV • $10 • (04/30/91) • **78**

Port Madera County 1988: Mature, spicy flavors layer nicely with hints of tobacco and leather around a core of sweet plum and black cherry flavor. A soft, mature style of Port, delicious to drink now. 1,000 cases made. • $25 • (12/31/97) • **88**

Tawny Port Madera County Aged 10 Years NV • $20 • (05/15/96) • **87**

FIDDLEHEAD | CALIFORNIA

Pinot Noir Santa Maria Valley 1993 • $25 • (05/31/96) • **88**

Pinot Noir Santa Maria Valley 1992 • $25 • (02/28/95) • **88**

Pinot Noir Santa Maria Valley 1990 • $25 • (02/28/94) • **82**

Pinot Noir Willamette Valley 1995: Spicy, toasty flavors and supple texture make this appealing. Try now. 900 cases made. • $36 • (11/30/97) • **84**

Pinot Noir Willamette Valley 1994 • $34 • (05/31/96) • **91**

Pinot Noir Willamette Valley 1992 • $29 • (02/28/95) • **88**

Sauvignon Blanc Santa Ynez Valley 1995: Crisp yet well balanced, this wine offers a complex blend of herb, grapefruit, lime and light grass flavors. Finishes elegantly and with length. 800 cases made. • $18 • (06/30/97) • **89**

Sauvignon Blanc Santa Ynez Valley 1994 • $17 • (05/31/96) • **84**

FIELD STONE | CALIFORNIA

Cabernet Sauvignon Alexander Valley 1994: An herbal core wends its way through this wine, which fans out to include smoke, tar, currant and blackberry notes. Pulls up a bit short at the end, but still attractive. Drink now through 2002. 3,400 cases made. • $18 • (07/31/98) • **85**

Cabernet Sauvignon Alexander Valley 1993: A supple-textured Cabernet with bright cherry and cassis flavors framed nicely by a smoky, herbal edge. Moderate finish. 2,000 cases made. • $17 • (09/30/97) • **87**

Cabernet Sauvignon Alexander Valley 1992: A touch earthy, with a slight tart accent to the cherry and berry flavors. Holds together on the finish even though the tannins are firm and crisp. 3,700 cases made. • $16 • (11/30/96) • **85**

Cabernet Sauvignon Alexander Valley 1991 • $14 • (11/15/94) • **84**

Cabernet Sauvignon Alexander Valley 1989 • $14 • (11/15/92) • **85**

Cabernet Sauvignon Alexander Valley 1987 • $14 • (02/28/91) • **85**

Cabernet Sauvignon Alexander Valley 1983 • $11 • (10/15/88) • **74**

Cabernet Sauvignon Alexander Valley Home Ranch Vineyard 1985 • $14 • (04/15/89) • **70**

Cabernet Sauvignon Alexander Valley Hoot Owl Barrel Select 1990 • $16 • (05/15/94) • **80**

Cabernet Sauvignon Alexander Valley Hoot Owl Creek Vineyards 1985 • $20 • (03/31/89) • **87**

Cabernet Sauvignon Alexander Valley Hoot Owl Creek Vineyards 1984 • $14 • (10/15/88) • **82**

Cabernet Sauvignon Alexander Valley Hoot Owl Reserve 1986 • $20 • (12/15/90) • **85**

Cabernet Sauvignon Alexander Valley Staten Family Reserve 1994: A smoky blend of cassis, blackberry, licorice, pepper and herbs couched in a medium-bodied, even lean-textured wine. Finishes fairly long. Drink now through 2003. 600 cases made. • $28 • (07/31/98) • **88**

Cabernet Sauvignon Alexander Valley Staten Family Reserve 1993: A spicy blend of licorice, cherry, blackberry, cassis and herbs. The tannins, however, are quite rough. Perhaps time will soften it a bit. 250 cases made. • $25 • (11/30/97) • **86**

Cabernet Sauvignon Alexander Valley Staten Family Reserve 1991: Hits enough of the right notes to make it interesting, as it features ripe plum and cherry flavors before turning gritty and tannic. Try now. 600 cases made. • $23 • (11/30/96) • **86**

Cabernet Sauvignon Alexander Valley Staten Family Reserve 1990 • $20 • (11/15/94) • **84**

Cabernet Sauvignon Alexander Valley Staten Family Reserve 1989 • $20 • (11/15/92) • **82**

Cabernet Sauvignon Alexander Valley Staten Family Reserve 1987 • $25 • (11/15/91) • **72**

Cabernet Sauvignon Alexander Valley Turkey Hill Vineyard 1985 • $18 • (02/28/91) • **84**

Cabernet Sauvignon Alexander Valley Turkey Hill Vineyard 1984 • $16 • (12/31/88) • **88**

Cabernet Sauvignon Alexander Valley Turkey Hill Vineyard 1982 • $12 • (03/16/86) • **78**

Cabernet Sauvignon Alexander Valley Vineyard Blend 1990 • $14 • (11/15/93) • **84**

Chardonnay Sonoma County 1996: A tropical blend, with mango and papaya in the lead. Fairly full-bodied, with a fruity, toasty oak finish. Drink now. 1,500 cases made. • $15 • (06/30/98) • **87**

Chardonnay Sonoma County 1994: Smooth and refined, with a core of fresh pear and honey flavors that keep the palate lively, finishing with polish and style. Ready to drink. 1,500 cases made. • $14 • (12/15/96) • **87**

Chardonnay Sonoma County 1993 • $14 • (07/31/95) • **82**

Gewürztraminer Sonoma County 1996: Simple, fruity and soft, a generous mouthful of pear and grapefruit character. Ready to drink. 1,500 cases made. • $10 • (12/15/97) • **84**

Gewürztraminer Sonoma County 1995: Appropriately spicy, and appealing for its harmonious litchi and rose petal flavors that finish softly and with generosity. 800 cases made. • $9 • (11/15/96) • **85**

Petite Sirah Alexander Valley 1988 • $15 • (12/31/90) • **85**

Petite Sirah Alexander Valley 1987 • $15 • (12/31/90) • **84**

Petite Sirah Alexander Valley 1986 • $15 • (09/30/89) • **79**

Petite Sirah Alexander Valley 1985 • $11 • (02/15/89) • **83**

Petite Sirah Alexander Valley 1984 • $11 • (10/15/88) • **88**

Petite Sirah Alexander Valley Old Vines 1990 • $16 • (06/15/93) • **83**

Sauvignon Blanc Sonoma County 1996: A medium-bodied wine with hints of melon, grapefruit and herbs. Finishes fresh and clean. 1,500 cases made. • $15 • (10/15/97) • **85**

Sauvignon Blanc Sonoma County 1995: Very pretty cantaloupe and spice flavors dance nicely through this harmonious, elegantly balanced white. Delicious now. 1,200 cases made. • $10 • (08/31/97) • **86**

Sauvignon Blanc Sonoma County 1994 • $9 • (08/31/95) • **83**

FIELDBROOK | CALIFORNIA

Chardonnay Trinity County 1995: Smooth, ripe and generous, its flavor profile different from most California Chardonnays, offering more tobacco and leafy flavors along with some ripe apple notes. 420 cases made. • $13 • (07/31/97) • **83**

Chardonnay Trinity County Meredith Vineyard 1994: Ripe, full-bodied and rich, with spicy pineapple and apple flavors. 160 cases made. • $14 • (07/31/96) • **87**

Merlot Napa Valley Frediani Vineyard 1991 • $15 • (09/15/94) • **84**

Pinot Noir Napa Valley Beard Vineyard 1992 • $18 • (10/31/94) • **87**

Pinot Noir Napa Valley Beard Vineyard 1988 • $12 • (02/28/93) • **77**

Sauvignon Blanc Mendocino Webb Vineyard 1995: Light in texture, but nicely mouthfilling with distinctive mineral and melon flavors that linger on the polished finish. 275 cases made. • $11 • (04/30/97) • **86**

Sauvignon Blanc Mendocino County Webb Vineyard 1994 • $10 • (08/31/95) • **83**

Sauvignon Blanc Mendocino County Webb Vineyard 1993 • $9 • (09/30/94) • **87**

Sauvignon Blanc Redwood Valley Elizabeth Vineyard 1997: Pretty melon and citrus flavors lead the way with this somewhat understated yet pleasant wine. Drink now. 220 cases made. • $13 • (06/15/98) • **83**

Sauvignon Blanc Redwood Valley Elizabeth Vineyard 1996: Fairly firm—almost austere for this usually effusive grape. This wine is driven more by its texture and mineral components than by its fruit flavors. Inquisitive palates will find refreshing grapefruit and anise on the finish. 207 cases made. • $11 • (03/31/98) • **86**

Zinfandel Mendocino County Pacini Vineyard 50-year-old vines 1996: Effusively fruity, with jammy strawberry and raspberry. The finish detracts, with a bitter note and firm tannins. Drink now. 225 cases made. • $18 • (06/15/98) • **82**

Zinfandel Mendocino County Pacini Vineyard 1995: Smooth and ripe, with tar-accented black berry and cherry flavors. Finishes with fleshy tannins and pretty fruit and chocolate aftertaste. 219 cases made. • $13 • (04/30/97) • **91**

Zinfandel Mendocino County Pacini Vineyard 1994: Smooth, ripe and spicy, this offers hints of blackberry, wild berry, spice and pepper flavors with a long, clean aftertaste. 200 cases made. • $13 • (04/30/97) • **87**

Zinfandel Mendocino County Pacini Vineyard 1993 • $12 • (10/15/94) • **87**

Zinfandel Mendocino County Pacini Vineyard 1991 • $11 • (03/15/93) • **84**

Zinfandel Mendocino County Pacini Vineyard Reserve 1992 • $12 • (10/15/94) • **86**

FIELDS OF FAIR | KANSAS

Concord Kansas 1991 • $5 • (02/29/92) • **70**

Flint Hills Red Proprietor's Reserve Kansas 1990 • $6 • (02/29/92) • **70**

FIFE | CALIFORNIA

Cabernet Sauvignon Napa Valley Estate Vineyard 1995: Young and vibrant, with a tightly focused core of currant, cedar, plum and vanilla. Finishes with gentle tannins and a complex aftertaste. Best now through 2005. 231 cases made. • $24 • (05/15/98) • **90**

Cabernet Sauvignon Spring Mountain Reserve 1993: Big, ripe and intense, but stays in balance as the ripe smoky currant, black cherry, mineral, anise and oaky flavors fall into place with a sense of depth, proportion and complexity. Finishes with earthy tannins, but nothing to be afraid of. Drinkable now. 765 cases made. • $28 • (11/15/96) • **90**

Max Cuvée Napa Valley 1995: Serves up complex smoky, meaty Petite Sirah-like flavors yet manages to put enough ripe cherry and berry flavor to give it more depth and suppleness. Drinks well now, but given the tannin level, it won't hurt to cellar into 1999 to 2000. A blend of Petite Sirah, Zinfandel, Barbera, and Syrah. 437 cases made. • $24 • (12/31/97) • **89**

Max Cuvée Napa Valley 1994: Delicious, with juicy plum and cherry flavors, dashes of spice and pretty oak and most notably, exotic fruit flavors that go on and on. Drinkable now. A blend of Petite Sirah, Syrah, Zinfandel, and Charbono. 380 cases made. • $19 • (07/31/97) HR • **93**

Merlot Napa Valley 1995: Strives for complexity but comes up short, as the core of herb, currant, tobacco and toasty oak seem a bit muted. 1,900 cases made. • $20 • (12/31/97) • **84**

Merlot Napa Valley Old Vines 1993: Intense and tannic, this backward, tightly wound young wine isn't showing much-the currant and peppery flavors wrapped in firm, chewy tannins. Try now. 300 cases made. • $20 • (10/15/96) • **86**

Petite Sirah Napa Valley 1994: Spicy in character, with a core of earthy currant and cherry flavors, although it turns simpler on the finish. Drinkable now. 677 cases made. • $16 • (07/31/97) • **87**

Petite Sirah Napa Valley Les Vieilles Vignes 1991 • $16 • (06/15/93) • **87**

Key: SS—Spectator Selection CS—Cellar Selection HR—Highly Recommended BB—Best Buy $NA—Price not available Ⓐ—Auction Price (BT)—Barrel Tasting

Dates in parentheses indicate the issues in which the ratings were published.

Petite Sirah Napa Valley Old Vines 1993: Dennis Fife continues to show a deft touch with old-vine Petite Sirah. This wine captures the essence of the varietal with its grapey, spicy, peppery flavors, yet manages to tame the tannins so they don't overwhelm. Finishes with an anise and smoke accent. 545 cases made. • $16 • (11/30/96) • **88**

Petite Sirah Redwood Valley Redhead Vineyard 1995: Distinct for its spicy, peppery aromas and chewy, gritty tannins. Fans of Petite Sirah will be able to look past its enormous tannic strength to taste the delicious core of wild berry and black cherry flavor buried beneath. Drinkable now. 500 cases made. • $19 • (12/31/97) • **89**

Zinfandel Mendocino 1996: Well balanced, if on the trim side, with attractive plum, cherry and wild berry flavors, finishing with austere tannins. Cellar short-term; drink through 2002. 2,000 cases made. • $17 • (06/15/98) • **87**

Zinfandel Napa Valley Les Vieilles Vignes 1992 • $16 • (09/15/95) • **89**

Zinfandel Napa Valley Les Vieilles Vignes 1991 • $16 • (06/15/93) • **85**

Zinfandel Napa Valley Old Vines 1996: A touch on the green side, this is a lighter style, with moderately ripe plum and berry flavors and firm, dry tannins. Drink now through 2001. 1,700 cases made. • $20 • (05/31/98) • **84**

Zinfandel Napa Valley Old Vines 1995: Ripe and roasted, with a smoky, meaty edge to the raspberry and wild berry flavors. Tannins clamp down on the finish. Drinks well now. Contains 6 percent Petite Sirah. 1,200 cases made. • $19 • (09/30/97) • **89**

Zinfandel Napa Valley Old Vines 1994: An oaky style of Zin, with a slight earthy accent to the ripe plum and wild berry flavors. It opens up, though, and turns more interesting, picking up anise and mineral notes. Finishes with a tannic edge. Ready to drink. 1,029 cases made. • $16 • (11/30/96) • **88**

Zinfandel Redwood Valley Redhead Vineyard 1996: Firm and tight, with intense cherry and berry flavors that finish with crisp, lean tannins. Doesn't quite fill out at midpalate. Drink now through 2001. 1,600 cases made. • $20 • (06/15/98) • **86**

Zinfandel Redwood Valley Redhead Vineyard 1995: A medium-weight style, with a grapey side to its plum and wild berry flavors. Finishes with firm tannins and a dry, oaky, smoky edge. Best to drink now. 11 percent Petite Sirah. 1,500 cases made. • $19 • (09/30/97) • **88**

Zinfandel Redwood Valley Redhead Vineyard 1994: Smells ripe and juicy, with a racy streak to its cherry, raspberry and spice notes. A real mouthful of Zinfandel, with classic peppery nuances. Finishing with a dry edge to the tannins. 420 cases made. • $19 • (03/31/97) • **91**

Zinfandel Spring Mountain 1994: Dense and concentrated, with lots of rich berry, currant and cherry flavors at the forefront. Remarkably supple and harmonious but also deeply concentrated, it's drinkable now. 420 cases made. • $19 • (03/31/97) • **91**

FILIPPI, JOSEPH | CALIFORNIA

Angelica Elena Cucamonga Valley Limited Release Winemaker's Reserve NV • $10/375ml • (06/15/96) • **82**

Ruby Port California Limited Release Winemaker's Reserve NV • $8 • (06/15/96) • **81**

Sauvignon Blanc Monterey Biane Guasti Vineyard Limited Release Winemaker's Reserve 1994 • $8 • (08/31/95) • **80**

White Grenache Cucamonga Valley Limited Release Winemaker's Reserve 1996: Resembles cough medicine, but not as good. 580 cases made. • $9 • (09/15/97) • **59**

Zinfandel Cucamonga Valley Limited Release Winemaker's Reserve 1994 • $9 • (04/30/96) • **76**

Zinfandel Cucamonga Valley Nouveau Winemaker's Reserve Limited Release 1996: Awkward, with leathery, menthol flavors that override hints of dried fruit. Rough, drying tannins. Drink now. 454 cases made. • $11 • (06/15/98) • **72**

FIRELANDS | OHIO

Cabernet Sauvignon Ohio Lake Erie 1988 • $10 • (02/29/92) • **82**

FIRESTEED | OREGON

Pinot Noir Oregon 1996: Very light, almost a rosé, with strawberry and spice notes lingering on the delicate finish. Drink soon. 25,000 cases made. • $10 • (11/30/97) • **83**

Pinot Noir Oregon 1995: Light, soft and simple, with fragrant berry and spice flavors that do linger a bit on the finish. Drinkable now. 28,000 cases made. • $10 • (02/28/97) • **81**

Pinot Noir Oregon 1994 • $10 • (01/31/96) BB • **86**

Pinot Noir Oregon 1993 • $7 • (11/30/94) BB • **83**
Pinot Noir Oregon 1992 • $9 • (09/30/93) • **82**

FIRESTONE | CALIFORNIA

Blanc de Noirs Santa Ynez Valley 1985 • $15 • (12/31/88) • **79**
Cabernet Sauvignon Santa Barbara County 1978 • $20 • (11/15/92) • **65**
Cabernet Sauvignon Santa Ynez Valley 1994: A smooth-textured wine with bright cherry, licorice and spicy cedar notes. The finish is moderate, with a pleasant herbal edge. Drink now. 9,000 cases made. • $12 • (10/31/97) • **85**
Cabernet Sauvignon Santa Ynez Valley 1993: Complex, with layers of cherry, currant, herb and cedar flavors. Anise flavors fold in on the supple and harmonious finish. 6,500 cases made. • $12 • (09/15/96) • **85**
Cabernet Sauvignon Santa Ynez Valley 1992 • $12 • (12/15/95) • **83**
Cabernet Sauvignon Santa Ynez Valley 1991 • $12 • (11/15/94) • **84**
Cabernet Sauvignon Santa Ynez Valley 1990 • $12 • (11/15/93) • **81**
Cabernet Sauvignon Santa Ynez Valley 1989 • $12 • (11/15/92) • **78**
Cabernet Sauvignon Santa Ynez Valley 1988 • $12 • (11/15/91) • **75**
Cabernet Sauvignon Santa Ynez Valley 1987 • $11 • (05/31/90) • **82**
Cabernet Sauvignon Santa Ynez Valley 1986 • $10 • (12/15/89) • **81**
Cabernet Sauvignon Santa Ynez Valley 1985 • $9 • (08/31/88) • **72**
Cabernet Sauvignon Santa Ynez Valley 1984 • $9 • (03/31/88) • **72**
Cabernet Sauvignon Santa Ynez Valley 1983 • $9 • (06/15/87) • **77**
Cabernet Sauvignon Santa Ynez Valley 1981 • $8 • (03/01/85) • **89**
Cabernet Sauvignon Santa Ynez Valley Reserve 1990 • $20 • (11/15/94) • **85**
Cabernet Sauvignon Santa Ynez Valley Reserve 1988 • $18 • (02/28/91) • **84**
Cabernet Sauvignon Santa Ynez Valley Special Release 1977 • $9 • (04/16/85) • **77**
Cabernet Sauvignon Santa Ynez Valley Vintage Reserve 1990 • $20 • (02/15/93) • **84**
Cabernet Sauvignon Santa Ynez Valley Vintage Reserve 1985 • $25 • (12/15/89) • **67**
Cabernet Sauvignon Santa Ynez Valley Vintage Reserve 1979 • $12 • (03/16/86) • **73**
Chardonnay Santa Ynez Valley 1996: This one strikes a fairly complex pose, with spice, pear, apple, toast and hazelnut. The finish is bright and lemony. A refreshing wine. Drink now. 26,111 cases made. • $13 • (07/31/98) • **87**
Chardonnay Santa Ynez Valley 1995: Complex and bright. Extremely lemony, showing the tangy acidity common to this region, it also displays just the right amount of earth tones—all harmoniously blended into a well-balanced whole. A terrific value. 20,000 cases made. • $13 • (06/15/97) • **90**
Chardonnay Santa Ynez Valley 1994: Light toasty oak frames a core of ripe pear and spicy apple flavors. Well crafted and complex on the finish. 28,000 cases made. • $13 • (07/31/96) HR • **87**
Chardonnay Santa Ynez Valley Barrel Fermented 1994: Clean, ripe, appealing apple, pear and spice flavors. The finish is somewhat coarse, but time may soften it a bit. • $13 • (05/15/96) • **84**
Chardonnay Santa Ynez Valley Barrel Fermented 1993 • $12 • (11/30/94) • **87**
Gewürztraminer Santa Barbara County 1994 • $9 • (05/31/96) • **77**
Johannisberg Riesling Santa Barbara County Selected Harvest 1991 • $12/375ml • (12/15/92) • **84**
Johannisberg Riesling Santa Barbara County Selected Harvest 1989 • $12/375ml • (04/30/91) • **84**
Johannisberg Riesling Santa Ynez Valley Ambassador's Vineyard Selected Harvest 1988 • $9/375ml • (12/15/89) • **79**
Johannisberg Riesling Santa Ynez Valley Ambassador's Vineyard Selected Harvest 1986 • $9/375ml • (02/28/89) • **89**
Johannisberg Riesling Santa Ynez Valley Selected Harvest 1995: Very sweet and spicy, with a peppery accent to the honey, apricot and floral flavors, which swirl through the unctuous finish. Delicious to drink now. 800 cases made. • $15/375ml • (11/30/96) • **89**
Johannisberg Riesling Santa Ynez Valley Selected Harvest 1993 • $15/375ml • (06/15/96) • **85**
Merlot Santa Ynez Valley 1993 • $13 • (03/31/96) • **84**
Merlot Santa Ynez Valley 1992 • $12 • (11/15/94) • **81**
Merlot Santa Ynez Valley 1991 • $12 • (12/31/93) • **83**
Merlot Santa Ynez Valley 1990 • $13 • (11/30/92) • **79**
Merlot Santa Ynez Valley 1989 • $12 • (08/31/91) • **86**
Merlot Santa Ynez Valley 1988 • $11 • (03/31/91) • **82**
Merlot Santa Ynez Valley 1987 • $9 • (12/15/89) • **83**
Merlot Santa Ynez Valley 1986 • $9 • (09/30/88) • **83**
Merlot Santa Ynez Valley 1985 • $9 • (04/30/88) • **78**
Pinot Noir Santa Ynez Valley 1986 • $10 • (12/15/89) • **77**
Pinot Noir Santa Ynez Valley 1983 • $9 • (11/15/87) • **71**
Pinot Noir Santa Ynez Valley 1981 • $8 • (05/16/86) • **73**
Prosperity Red Santa Ynez Valley NV • $5 • (03/31/93) • **75**
Red Table Wine Santa Ynez Valley 1990 • $6 • (04/30/92) • **74**
Reserve Santa Ynez Valley 1993: A distinctly herbaceous style that will deter some, with its racy bell pepper, onion and herb-laced cherry flavors. Finishes with chewy tannins, too. Drink now. 900 cases made. • $30 • (12/31/96) • **84**
Sauvignon Blanc Santa Barbara County 1996: An elegant and flavorful Sauvignon Blanc, fleshy in texture, with a core of orange and other citrus notes framed by a just-right toasty edge. Finishes with an appetizing spicy clove and ginger quality. Nice wine, nice price. 10,100 cases made. • $9 • (04/30/98) BB • **86**
Sauvignon Blanc Santa Ynez Valley 1995: A smooth, ripe and generous mouthful of slightly spiced, silky pear, toast and butterscotch flavors that linger nicely. A touch of herb on the finish. 6,000 cases made. • $7 • (07/31/96) BB • **89**
Sauvignon Blanc Santa Ynez Valley 1994 • $8 • (02/29/96) • **87**
Sauvignon Blanc Santa Ynez Valley 1993 • $7 • (08/31/95) • **81**
Vintage Reserve Santa Ynez Valley 1991 • $22 • (12/15/95) • **89**

FISHER | CALIFORNIA

Cabernet Sauvignon Napa & Sonoma Counties Coach Insignia 1990 • $20 • (06/15/93) • **86**
Cabernet Sauvignon Napa & Sonoma Counties Coach Insignia 1989 • $18 • (03/31/92) • **82**
Cabernet Sauvignon Napa & Sonoma Counties Coach Insignia 1987: Smells and tastes mature, with an earthy, cheesy edge to the dried-out Cabernet flavors. Hard to warm up to. • $NA • (11/15/97) • **78**
Cabernet Sauvignon Napa Valley Coach Insignia 1994: Solid, with a good core of earthy currant, cedar and tar, and it's nicely balanced, if a bit on the tannic side at this stage. Approachable now through 2002. 1,750 cases made. • $24 • (10/31/97) • **87**
Cabernet Sauvignon Napa Valley Coach Insignia 1993: Ripe and chunky, with currant, plum and berry flavors, but it lacks focus and harmony at this stage, finishing with a tannic, waxy accent. 1,706 cases made. • $22 • (12/15/96) • **85**
Cabernet Sauvignon Napa Valley Coach Insignia 1991 • $20 • (11/15/94) • **84**
Cabernet Sauvignon Napa Valley Coach Insignia 1986: Mature, with drying tannins, this delivers just enough cherry, herb and cedar-tinged flavors to hold your interest. Ready to drink. • $NA • (12/15/96) • **86**
Cabernet Sauvignon Napa Valley Lamb Vineyard 1994: Big, ripe, intense and concentrated, with a firmly tannic core of earthy currant, spice, plum and cherry flavors. Given the tannin level, it's best to cellar this into 2001. 570 cases made. • $50 • (10/31/97) • **92**
Cabernet Sauvignon Napa Valley Lamb Vineyard 1993: Tight and tannic, firmly structured, but the ripe cherry and currant flavors turn supple and slowly open to reveal more depth, richness and complexity, reaching a nice climax on the finish where the fruit really pours through. Best now to 2000. 488 cases made. • $45 • (11/15/96) • **90**
Cabernet Sauvignon Sonoma County 1983 • $13 • (06/15/87) • **73**
Cabernet Sauvignon Sonoma County 1982 • $13 • (11/01/85) • **88**
Cabernet Sauvignon Sonoma County 1981 • $12 • (12/01/84) • **85**
Cabernet Sauvignon Sonoma County Coach Insignia 1986 • $20 • (01/31/90) • **87**
Cabernet Sauvignon Sonoma County Coach Insignia 1985 • $18 • (09/15/88) • **91**
Cabernet Sauvignon Sonoma County Coach Insignia 1984 • $18 • (11/15/87) • **90**
Cabernet Sauvignon Sonoma County Wedding Vineyard 1994: Tough and leathery, with chewy, gritty tannins and just a modest amount of Cabernet flavor. May come around and grow more supple with time in the bottle, but for now it's rough-and-tumble. Cellar into 2001. 492 cases made. • $50 • (10/31/97) • **88**
Cabernet Sauvignon Sonoma County Wedding Vineyard 1993: Firm, ripe and intense, this is a bit gritty in texture but the flavors are right on, with tiers of currant, mint, cherry and berry that fold together nicely on the finish. 584 cases made. • $33 • (11/15/96) • **90**
Cabernet Sauvignon Sonoma County Wedding Vineyard 1991 • $28 • (11/15/94) • **88**
Chardonnay Sonoma County Coach Insignia 1995: Lots of flavor, complexity and finesse, with layers of ripe fig, apple, pear and spice, finishing with a citrus, especially grapefruit, edge. Ready now. 3,377 cases made. • $18 • (05/31/97) • **90**

Chardonnay Sonoma County Coach Insignia 1994: The spicy, earthy pear, toast, honey and apple flavors weave together intricately on the finish. 3,300 cases made. • $18 • (06/15/96) • **86**

Chardonnay Sonoma County Whitney's Vineyard 1995: Appealing for its ripe fruit flavors, ranging from pear to citrus, and a dash of vanilla on the finish. Also has a slightly bitter note from oak that detracts slightly. 297 cases made. • $26 • (06/15/97) • **89**

Chardonnay Sonoma County Whitney's Vineyard 1994: Ripe and flavorful, but a touch on the mature side, which gives a leesy quality to the pear, pineapple and butterscotch flavors. 430 cases made. • $26 • (06/15/96) • **87**

Chardonnay Sonoma County Whitney's Vineyard 1993 • $26 • (07/31/95) • **85**

Merlot Napa Valley RCF Vineyard 1994: A well-oaked style, with a leathery, herbal, dry oak flavor. Finishes with anise and dried-plum notes, but also dry tannins. 787 cases made. • $26 • (06/30/97) • **84**

Merlot Napa Valley RCF Vineyard 1993 • $26 • (06/30/96) • **84**

Merlot Napa Valley RCF Vineyard 1991 • $22 • (10/31/93) • **84**

FITCH MOUNTAIN | CALIFORNIA

Cabernet Sauvignon Napa Valley 1985 • $9 • (04/15/89) • **74**

Merlot Napa Valley 1986 • $9 • (09/30/88) • **84**

Merlot Napa Valley 1985 • $9 • (12/15/87) • **89**

Zinfandel Dry Creek Valley 1989 • $10 • (03/31/92) • **86**

FLEUR DE CARNEROS CELLARS | CALIFORNIA

Chardonnay California 1995: Elegant and complex, with layers of ripe, spicy pear and creamy vanilla flavors and hints of anise and cedar that echo on the finish. Very appealing, especially at this price. 1,500 cases made. • $12 • (12/31/96) • **87**

Pinot Noir Carneros 1995: Simple, with an earthy accent to herb and cedar notes. Comes up short on fruit, with just a hint of cherry. Tasted twice, with consistent notes. 16,000 cases made. • $12 • (03/31/97) • **79**

FLORA SPRINGS | CALIFORNIA

Cabernet Sauvignon Napa Valley 1986: Thin and uninspiring when released, much the same now. • $NA • (12/15/96) • **76**

Cabernet Sauvignon Napa Valley 1985 • $15 • (07/31/89) • **90**

Cabernet Sauvignon Napa Valley 1984 • $25 • (07/31/88) • **71**

Cabernet Sauvignon Napa Valley 1983 • $20 • (12/15/86) • **79**

Cabernet Sauvignon Napa Valley 1982 • $9 • (10/15/86) • **78**

Cabernet Sauvignon Napa Valley 1981 • $25 • (12/16/84) • **82**

Cabernet Sauvignon Napa Valley Cellar Select 1988 • $24 • (02/29/92) • **85**

Cabernet Sauvignon Napa Valley Cellar Select 1987 • $25 • (11/15/90) • **91**

Cabernet Sauvignon Napa Valley Reserve 1996: Impressive for its finesse and elegance, this wine is smooth, ripe and polished, with pretty floral aromas and a generous core of rich currant, wild berry, plum and black cherry flavors. • $NA • (06/30/97) (BT) • **90-94**

Cabernet Sauvignon Napa Valley Reserve 1991 • $33 • (09/30/94) CS • **97**

Cabernet Sauvignon Napa Valley Reserve 1990 • $33 • (02/28/94) • **85**

Cabernet Sauvignon Napa Valley Reserve 1989 • $25 • (11/15/92) • **88**

Cabernet Sauvignon Napa Valley Rutherford Hillside Reserve 1994: Displays all the ingredients for excellence, offering impressive mëaty, smoky, oaky flavors before the leathery currant and dried cherry fold in. Young, dense and tightly wound, it needs time in the cellar, but the flavors build to a wonderful aftertaste. 800 cases made. • $65 • (10/15/97) HR • **96**

Cabernet Sauvignon Napa Valley Rutherford Reserve 1993: Shows off lots of ripe cherry, strawberry jam and berry flavors, with hints of blackberry, currant, and black cherry. Holds its flavors while maintaining balance and finesse, and the finish turns complex and lingers. Another winner from Flora Springs. Drinks well already. 800 cases made. • $45 • (11/15/96) • **90**

Cabernet Sauvignon Napa Valley Rutherford Reserve 1992 • $40 • (11/15/95) HR • **96**

Cabernet Sauvignon Rutherford Hillside Reserve 1997: Still tasting sweet, as if the fermentation isn't complete, this is an enormously complex and concentrated wine, brimming with currant and black cherry. • $NA • (07/31/98) (BT) • **90-94**

Chardonnay Carneros 1995: Ripe and complex, with a well-focused core of apple, pear, spice and light oak shadings. Turns smooth and creamy on the finish and the flavors linger. All silk and polish. 800 cases made. • $24 • (04/30/97) • **92**

Chardonnay Carneros 1994: Strikes a nice balance between the ripe pear, apple and nectarine flavors and the toasty oak. An elegant, well-crafted Chardonnay that's new from Flora Springs. 200 cases made. • $20 • (06/30/96) • **89**

Chardonnay Napa Valley 1996: Begins with a slight leafy, earthy edge, and right now the smoky, toasty oak stands out. The core flavors are built around ripe, rich, intense pear, smoky oak, hazelnut and spice. Finishes with a long, full aftertaste. Best from 1999 through 2004. 8,500 cases made. • $20 • (06/30/98) • **91**

Chardonnay Napa Valley 1995: An exotic style with a strong, spicy aroma, followed by complex and interesting flavors including grapefruit, pear, citrus and melon. Try now. 1,700 cases made. • $13 • (04/30/97) • **88**

Chardonnay Napa Valley Barrel Fermented 1993 • $20 • (07/31/95) • **84**

Chardonnay Napa Valley Lavender Hill Vineyard 1996: Ripe and complex, with a tight focus on the rich pear, anise, fig and spice notes, finishing with light oak shadings and fine length. Drink now through 2002. 800 cases made. • $23 • (06/30/98) • **91**

Chardonnay Napa Valley Reserve 1995: A young, intense and lively Chardonnay that's deep and concentrated, its creamy pear, citrus, melon and light, spicy oak flavors accented by an earthy mineral nuance. Shows a remarkable amount of finesse. 7,500 cases made. • $20 • (04/30/97) • **93**

Chardonnay Napa Valley Reserve 1994: Pleasant enough, with ripe pear, spice and honey notes that turn creamy on the finish. 3,900 cases made. • $18 • (07/31/96) • **87**

Merlot Napa Valley 1994 • $14 • (06/30/96) • **87**

Merlot Napa Valley 1993 • $12 • (09/30/95) • **87**

Merlot Napa Valley 1988 • $15 • (08/31/91) • **83**

Merlot Napa Valley 1987 • $17 • (07/31/90) • **87**

Merlot Napa Valley 1985 • $15 • (06/30/88) • **82**

Merlot Napa Valley Floréal 1991 • $12 • (10/31/93) • **86**

Merlot Napa Valley Floréal 1990 • $14 • (11/30/92) • **79**

Merlot Napa Valley Windfall Vineyard 1995: Supple and harmonious, with a complex core of plum, black cherry, currant and berry. Finishes with firm but polished tannins and good length. Best now to 2002. 600 cases made. • $40 • (03/31/98) • **89**

Pinot Noir Carneros Lavender Hill Vineyard 1996: Graceful, with supple plum, black cherry, spice and berry notes and light oak shadings. Complex and flavorful, with pretty flavors. Best now to 2002. 500 cases made. • $30 • (04/30/98) • **88**

Pinot Noir Napa Valley Floréal 1989 • $12 • (09/30/92) • **78**

Sangiovese Napa Valley 1996: Decent fruit, with hints of earthy plum and strawberry, but it lacks focus and depth. Tasted twice, with consistent notes. Drink now. 3,300 cases made. • $15 • (05/15/98) • **82**

Sangiovese Napa Valley 1995: Openly fruity, with lots of ripe blackberry and black cherry flavors that pick up dashes of anise and cedar; long, complex aftertaste. Delicious from start to finish. 3,000 cases made. • $15 • (04/30/97) • **92**

Sangiovese Napa Valley 1993 • $15 • (02/28/95) • **86**

Sauvignon Blanc California 1995: Brightly focused and fruity, with green apple, parsley and vanilla flavors. 3,700 cases made. • $8 • (08/31/96) • **85**

Sauvignon Blanc Napa Valley 1996: Fairly full on the palate, velvety, in a firm yet supple style, offering up classy and complex toast, melon, citrus and anise flavors. Not effusive, but very well integrated and balanced. 4,000 cases made. • $15 • (03/31/98) • **89**

Sauvignon Blanc Napa Valley 1993 • $8 • (08/31/95) • **85**

Sauvignon Blanc Napa Valley Soliloquy 1995: Fairly full-bodied, it offers hints of melon, grapefruit, passion fruit and kiwi and a long, mineral-like finish. The creamy texture blends well with the bright acidity. 900 cases made. • $17 • (06/30/97) • **89**

Sauvignon Blanc Napa Valley Soliloquy 1994: Pleasant and distinctive mineral, floral and grassy qualities give a gratifying sense of weightiness. 2,000 cases made. • $15 • (08/31/96) • **87**

Sauvignon Blanc Napa Valley Soliloquy 1993 • $15 • (08/31/95) • **77**

Trilogy Napa Valley 1994: A hearty, rustic style with chewy tannins and a spicy mineral edge to the currant and wild berry flavors. Finishes with dashes of herb and cedar; given the chewy tannins, it's best to lay it away until 2000. A blend of 41 percent Cabernet Sauvignon, 37 percent Merlot and 22 percent Cabernet Franc. 2,000 cases made. • $33 • (10/15/97) • **90**

Trilogy Napa Valley 1993: Ripe and juicy, with an alluring core of black cherry, currant, plum and berry flavors. Hints of sage, spice and herb add

Key: SS—Spectator Selection CS—Cellar Selection HR—Highly Recommended BB—Best Buy $NA—Price not available Ⓐ—Auction Price (BT)—Barrel Tasting
Dates in parentheses indicate the issues in which the ratings were published.

dimension and though the tannins stand up on the finish, it can be enjoyed now. A blend of 40 percent Cabernet Sauvignon, 40 percent Merlot and 20 percent Cabernet Franc. 1,900 cases made. • $30 • (11/15/96) • **89**

Trilogy Napa Valley 1992 • $27 • (11/30/95) CS • **92**

Trilogy Napa Valley 1991 • $25 • (11/15/94) • **86**

Trilogy Napa Valley 1990 • $33 • (02/28/94) • **85**

Trilogy Napa Valley 1989 • $33 • (11/15/92) • **87**

Trilogy Napa Valley 1988 • $33 • (02/29/92) • **86**

Trilogy Napa Valley 1987 • $33 • (05/15/91) • **90**

Trilogy Napa Valley 1986: Even in its youth, this didn't show well and, now, it's rather simple and diluted, in sharp contrast to the richer, full-bodied efforts of '90s vintages. • $37 • (12/15/96) • **82**

Trilogy Napa Valley 1985 • $33 • (02/15/89) • **87**

Trilogy Napa Valley 1984 • $30 • (02/29/88) • **73**

FLOWERS | CALIFORNIA

Chardonnay Sonoma Coast Camp Meeting Ridge Vineyard 1995: Wonderfully rich and complex, with layers of sharply focused spicy pear, apple, citrus and melon flavors that are long and intense on the finish, where the texture turns silky. 500 cases made. • $36 • (04/30/98) • **91**

FLYNN | OREGON

Blanc de Blancs Willamette Valley Brut Cuvée 1988 • $16 • (11/30/94) • **72**

Blush Willamette Valley 1993 • $8 • (11/30/94) • **79**

Brut Willamette Valley Premier Cuvée 1988 • $16 • (11/30/94) • **83**

Brut Willamette Valley Premier Cuvée 1987 • $14 • (05/15/92) • **81**

Pinot Noir Oregon Clos d'Or Lot Twenty Seven NV • $7 • (02/28/93) • **75**

Pinot Noir Willamette Valley 1992 • $12 • (10/31/94) • **85**

Pinot Noir Willamette Valley 1991 • $10 • (02/28/93) • **74**

FOGARTY, THOMAS | CALIFORNIA

Blanc de Blancs Santa Cruz Mountains 1989 • $22 • (12/31/93) • **80**

Brut Blanc de Blancs Santa Cruz Mountains 1989 • $22 • (12/31/92) • **74**

Brut Santa Cruz Mountains 1990 • $22 • (12/31/95) • **87**

Cabernet Sauvignon Napa Valley 1985 • $15 • (07/15/91) • **70**

Cabernet Sauvignon Napa Valley Vallerga Vineyards 1992 • $25 • (04/30/96) • **90**

Chardonnay Santa Cruz Mountains 1994: Ripe and intense, with an elegant core of earthy pear, honey and hazelnut flavors that are well focused and lively right through to the long, lingering finish. Has a lot of finesse and grace. 1,394 cases made. • $17 • (02/29/96) HR • **90**

Chardonnay Santa Cruz Mountains Estate Reserve 1995: Serves up lots of ripe, bright, juicy Chardonnay fruit, with plenty of pear, apple and spice flavors that turn elegant on the finish, where the spiciness kicks in. 450 cases made. • $28 • (12/31/97) • **89**

Chardonnay Santa Cruz Mountains Estate Reserve 1994: Complex, with a pretty array of smoky, toasty oak and ripe pear, citrus and melon notes. The flavors expand and linger on the long, elegant finish. 550 cases made. • $23 • (06/30/96) • **91**

Gewürztraminer Monterey Ventana Vineyards 1994 • $12 • (11/15/95) • **88**

Pinot Noir Napa Valley 1988 • $15 • (02/28/91) • **86**

Pinot Noir Napa Valley Carneros 1985 • $15 • (06/15/88) • **73**

Pinot Noir Santa Cruz Mountains 1994: Lean and a bit tannic, with a tight core of sour cherry and berry flavors. Finishes with a wall of firm tannins. 1,100 cases made. • $25 • (01/31/97) • **80**

Pinot Noir Santa Cruz Mountains 1992 • $21 • (12/31/95) • **84**

Pinot Noir Santa Cruz Mountains Estate 1993: Strives for elegance and delicacy with its spicy cherry, berry and mushroom flavors but loses a bit of its charm on the finish where it turns more rustic and tart. 800 cases made. • $22 • (09/15/96) • **85**

Pinot Noir Santa Cruz Mountains Estate 1989 • $16 • (02/28/93) • **74**

Pinot Noir Santa Cruz Mountains Estate 1988 • $15 • (02/28/91) • **83**

Pinot Noir Santa Cruz Mountains Estate Reserve 1995: Well focused and flavorful, with flashes of wild berry, mushroom, cedar, sage and spice. Finishes with firm tannins and a dash of color. Ready now through 2000. 998 cases made. • $28 • (01/31/98) • **87**

Pinot Noir Santa Cruz Mountains Reserve 1994: Smooth, ripe and fruity, with layers of cherry, berry, earth and tar, all young and vibrant, finishing with a tannic edge that comes up short. Ready now. 400 cases made. • $32 • (02/28/97) • **87**

FOLIE A DEUX | CALIFORNIA

Brut Napa Valley Fantasie 1989 • $18 • (06/15/91) • **81**

Cabernet Sauvignon Napa Valley 1995: Shows off its sage and dill notes up front, picks up a peppery flavor, too. Elegant and supple, easy to drink with its currant and sage notes. Ready now. 715 cases made. • $18 • (10/31/97) • **84**

Cabernet Sauvignon Napa Valley 1993: Marked by a spicy anise edge, this is a ripe and fruity style. The plum and currant flavors pick up leathery notes on the finish. 1,200 cases made. • $14 • (12/15/95) • **85**

Cabernet Sauvignon Napa Valley 1988 • $18 • (08/31/92) • **83**

Cabernet Sauvignon Napa Valley 1987 • $18 • (11/15/90) • **92**

Cabernet Sauvignon Napa Valley 1986 • $17 • (04/15/90) • **85**

Cabernet Sauvignon Napa Valley 1984 • $15 • (05/31/88) • **88**

Cabernet Sauvignon Napa Valley Reserve 1995: Supple, elegant and complex, with herb, cherry, toasty oak, chocolate and currant flavors and a long, full finish where the flavors stay lively. Approachable now. 2,200 cases made. • $22 • (11/30/97) • **88**

Chardonnay Napa Valley Reserve 1996: Clean and refreshing, with flinty citrus, pear, spice and smoky oak flavors, but it turns simple on the finish. Drink now through 2001. 580 cases made. • $25 • (05/15/98) • **84**

Merlot Napa Valley 1988 • $18 • (03/31/91) • **82**

Merlot Napa Valley Reserve 1995: An exotic, smoky, well-oaked style of Merlot that manages to provide enough ripe plum and cherry flavors to give it balance and finesse. Still, the oak is quite prevalent. Drink now through 2002. 530 cases made. • $22 • (11/30/97) • **88**

Merlot Napa Valley Reserve 1993: Marked by minty, cedary flavors that override the ripe plum and berry flavors. It comes across disjointed and out of balance, certainly lacking in harmony and finesse. 1,000 cases made. • $25 • (08/31/96) • **81**

Zinfandel Amador County Old Vine 1996: Dry, earthy and tannic, with just enough berry-laced Zinfandel flavor emerging to hold your interest. Chewy and compact on the finish. Drink now through 2001. 1,544 cases made. • $18 • (06/15/98) • **82**

Zinfandel Amador County Old Vine 1995: Shows off the appellation's rustic properties yet tames the tannins, focusing on wild berry, black cherry and plum notes, picking up a spicy anise accent. The tannins, while firm, have a gentle edge; drink now. 1,330 cases made. • $16 • (09/15/97) • **88**

Zinfandel Fiddletown Eschen Vineyard Old Vine 1996: Modest cherry and blackberry flavors briefly hold their own before giving way to firm, dry, earthy tannins. Finishes with dashes of spice and mint and a burst of fruit. Drink now through 2002. 472 cases made. • $22 • (06/15/98) • **84**

FOOTE, E.B. | WASHINGTON

Cabernet Sauvignon Columbia Valley 1993: Has a strong streak of pickle-barrel flavor that cuts through the modest fruit. Try it in 1999. 390 cases made. • $10 • (08/31/96) • **79**

Cabernet Sauvignon Columbia Valley 1992 • $13 • (09/30/94) • **85**

Cabernet-Merlot Columbia Valley 1994: Firm in texture, with sharply focused berry, currant and smoke flavors plus a hint of green pepper. Flavors unfold nicely on the solid frame. Best from 1999. 125 cases made. • $15 • (09/30/97) • **89**

Chardonnay Columbia Valley 1995: Ripe and juicy, brimming with pear, citrus and spice flavors that linger on the bright finish. Appealing now, but its layers of flavor should keep evolving through 1999 to 2000. 141 cases made. • $12 • (09/30/97) • **89**

Chardonnay Columbia Valley 1993 • $9 • (09/30/95) • **88**

Merlot Columbia Valley 1994: Brilliant blackberry, currant and delicate toast flavors swirl appetizingly. Notes of fruit and spice on the long finish. 183 cases made. • $10 • (08/31/96) • **88**

Merlot Columbia Valley 1993 • $8 • (09/30/95) • **85**

Pinot Noir Washington NV • $7 • (09/30/94) • **73**

Pinot Noir Washington La Center Vineyard 1993 • $7 • (09/30/95) • **80**

FOPPIANO | CALIFORNIA

Cabernet Sauvignon Russian River Valley 1994: Somewhat thin and restrained, it nonetheless shows some delicate coffee and blackberry notes. Finishes tartly. 4,200 cases made. • $14 • (10/31/97) • **82**

Cabernet Sauvignon Russian River Valley 1990 • $9 • (11/15/94) • **80**

Cabernet Sauvignon Russian River Valley 1985 • $9 • (06/30/89) • **71**

Cabernet Sauvignon Russian River Valley 1984 • $8 • (04/30/88) • **77**

Cabernet Sauvignon Russian River Valley 1981 • $7 • (04/16/85) • **81**

Cabernet Sauvignon Sonoma County 1989 • $9 • (03/15/92) • **82**

Cabernet Sauvignon Sonoma County 1986 • $9 • (11/15/90) • **79**

Merlot Russian River Valley 1994: Tough and tannic, with a dry, austere edge. Plum and currant flavors make it interesting—but just barely. 4,600 cases made. • $12 • (08/31/96) • **82**
Merlot Russian River Valley 1992 • $10 • (09/15/94) • **83**
Petite Sirah Napa Valley Reserve La Grande Petite 1991 • $20 • (04/30/95) • **80**
Petite Sirah Russian River Valley 1994: Big, ripe and expressive, with enough cherry and berry flavor lurking to merit attention. Try now. 6,000 cases made. • $11 • (08/31/97) • **86**
Petite Sirah Russian River Valley 1988 • $8 • (08/31/90) • **86**
Petite Sirah Russian River Valley 1986 • $8 • (06/15/89) • **83**
Petite Sirah Russian River Valley 1984 • $7 • (05/31/88) • **84**
Petite Sirah Russian River Valley Centennial Selection La Grande Anniversaire 1993: Long part of the Foppiano lineup, this is a solid effort, with alluring ripe cherry, plum, spice and floral notes and firm if a bit chewy tannins. Also good length, the flavors hang with you. 1,047 cases made. • $25 • (11/30/96) • **88**
Petite Sirah Russian River Valley Reserve Le Grande Petite 1987 • $20 • (08/31/90) • **79**
Petite Sirah Sonoma County 1992 • $9 • (11/15/95) • **82**
Petite Sirah Sonoma County 1991 • $11 • (02/28/95) • **82**
Petite Sirah Sonoma County 1990 • $10 • (06/30/92) • **87**
Pinot Noir Russian River Valley 1996: An earthy component sets the tone, with cola, herbs and licorice following closely. It doesn't taste like Pinot Noir, but it can be enjoyed with a meal. Drink now. 800 cases made. • $16 • (06/15/98) • **82**
Sauvignon Blanc Dry Creek Valley 1993 • $8 • (08/31/95) • **85**
Zinfandel Dry Creek Valley 1994: Medium-weight, with an herbal, especially sagelike, edge to the spicy, supple cherry and wild berry flavors. Appealing for its elegance and early-drinking allure. 4,000 cases made. • $11 • (08/31/97) • **86**
Zinfandel Dry Creek Valley 1993 • $11 • (06/15/95) • **81**
Zinfandel Dry Creek Valley 1991 • $10 • (09/30/93) • **87**
Zinfandel Dry Creek Valley Proprietor's Reserve 1987 • $12 • (12/31/90) • **86**

FOREST GLEN | CALIFORNIA

Cabernet Sauvignon California Barrel Select 1995: Strikes a balance between green beans, tar and a touch of burnt rubber. Look hard and you'll also find some blackberry and spice. Drink now. • $10 • (06/30/98) • **78**
Cabernet Sauvignon California Barrel Select 1994: Light cedar, plum and spice flavors blend nicely in this simple, pleasurable wine. 48,000 cases made. • $10 • (10/31/97) • **82**
Cabernet Sauvignon Sonoma County 1991 • $10 • (04/30/94) • **85**
Cabernet Sauvignon Sonoma County 1990 • $12 • (09/15/93) • **83**
Cabernet Sauvignon Sonoma County Barrel Select 1992 • $10 • (11/15/94) • **83**
Chardonnay California 1996: Flavors of dark spices and raisins make this an unusual style at this price. Finishes with a smoky character. Drink soon. 240,000 cases made. • $10 • (03/31/98) • **83**
Chardonnay California 1995: Tries too hard to match the fruit and oak, and the result is a curiously oaky style, with hints of honey, pear and butterscotch. • $10 • (01/31/97) • **82**
Chardonnay California Barrel Fermented 1994: Distinctive for its core of butterscotch flavors, it also has a nice band of pear and spice, at a very attractive price. 30,000 cases made. • $10 • (05/15/96) • **85**
Chardonnay Sonoma County Barrel Fermented 1993 • $10 • (12/31/94) • **83**
Merlot California 1992 • $10 • (09/15/94) • **82**
Merlot California Barrel Select 1996: Tight, almost crisp in texture, with pretty raspberry and vanilla flavors that linger gently on the finish. Ready now. • $NA • (12/31/97) • **86**
Merlot California Barrel Select 1995: Complex with its notes of vanilla, beef and currant, all framed by smoky, toasty oak. While far from classic, it serves up plenty of flavor. 125,000 cases made. • $10 • (02/28/97) • **84**
Merlot Sonoma County Barrel Select 1994 • $10 • (05/31/96) • **77**
Shiraz California Barrel Select 1996: Starts off with a gamy, woody character, followed by nice plum, spice and herb qualities. The finish is a little bitter and oaky. Drink now. • $10 • (06/15/98) • **82**
Shiraz California Barrel Select 1995: A silky-textured red wine that greets the nose with an interesting mix of cedar, leather and meatlike aromas, greets the palate with jammy blueberry and plum flavors, and deliciously stretches your wine budget. 10,000 cases made. • $10 • (09/15/97) BB • **88**

FOREST HILL | CALIFORNIA

Chardonnay Napa Valley Private Reserve 1995: Intense and spicy, with a tight core of pear, grapefruit and tart apple flavors that are crisp and lively. Drink now and into 2000. 551 cases made. • $30 • (04/30/98) • **88**
Chardonnay Napa Valley Private Reserve 1994: Simple, with a modest band of citrus and pear, and crisp acidity, which a little age should soften. 750 cases made. • $32 • (06/30/96) • **83**
Chardonnay Napa Valley Private Reserve 1993 • $28 • (07/31/95) • **85**

FOREST LAKE | CALIFORNIA

Cabernet Sauvignon California 1991 • $6 • (05/31/94) BB • **83**
Cabernet Sauvignon California 1989 • $6 • (11/15/92) BB • **82**
Cabernet Sauvignon California 1988 • $6 • (11/15/91) • **81**

FOREST VILLE | CALIFORNIA

Cabernet Sauvignon California 1993: Coffee and herb flavors frame a somewhat lean fruit core. Finishes with a strong licorice flavor. 5,000 cases made. • $6 • (11/30/96) • **81**
Cabernet Sauvignon California 1992 • $6 • (11/15/94) • **78**
Chardonnay California 1994: Light, simple and appealing for its almond-scented apple flavors that persist on the smooth finish. 12,000 cases made. • $6 • (06/30/96) BB • **84**
Chardonnay California 1993 • $6 • (01/31/95) • **77**
Merlot California 1992 • $6 • (09/15/94) • **79**
Sauvignon Blanc California 1994 • $5 • (10/31/95) • **81**
Zinfandel California 1993 • $5 • (10/15/95) • **83**

FORGERON | OREGON

Pinot Noir Oregon 1985 • $19 • (02/15/90) • **89**
Pinot Noir Oregon Vinters Reserve 1987 • $12 • (02/15/90) • **76**

FORIS | OREGON

Cabernet Sauvignon Rogue Valley 1991 • $9 • (11/30/94) • **82**
Cabernet Sauvignon Rogue Valley Reserve 1992 • $16 • (03/31/96) • **87**
Cabernet Sauvignon Rogue Valley Reserve 1991 • $15 • (11/30/94) • **83**
Cabernet Sauvignon Washington Klipsun Vineyard 1993: Tough, chewy texture barely lets the black cherry, currant and perfumy flavors through, but they do surface, and linger on the tannic finish. Best now. • $13 • (01/31/98) • **84**
Cabernet Sauvignon Washington Klipsun Vineyard 1992: Firm and a little chewy, packing some solid blackberry and leafy flavors into its lean frame. Drinkable now. 342 cases made. • $15 • (09/30/96) • **82**
Cabernet Sauvignon-Merlot-Cabernet Franc Oregon 1994: Tart, tough and excessively herbal. 953 cases made. • $9 • (02/28/97) • **76**
Chardonnay Rogue Valley 1994: A medium-weight wine that goes for elegance. Has a spicy, caramel-scented nuance to the modest pear flavors. 1,677 cases made. • $9 • (02/28/97) • **85**
Chardonnay Rogue Valley Barrel Fermented 1993 • $10 • (03/31/96) • **86**
Chardonnay Rogue Valley Reserve 1994: Simple and straightforward, with cider and brown sugar overtones to the basic pear flavors. Ready now. 1,342 cases made. • $15 • (02/28/97) • **82**
Chardonnay Rogue Valley Reserve 1993 • $16 • (03/31/96) • **82**
Gewürztraminer Rogue Valley 1995: Smooth, off-dry and appealing for its pineapple and floral flavors. Touching on litchi and other exotic fruit flavors on the finish. 1,166 cases made. • $8 • (10/31/96) • **87**
Gewürztraminer Rogue Valley 1994 • $8 • (06/15/96) • **84**
Gewürztraminer Rogue Valley 1993 • $7 • (03/31/96) BB • **87**
Merlot Rogue Valley 1993 • $15 • (03/31/96) • **86**
Merlot Rogue Valley 1992 • $14 • (11/30/94) • **86**
Merlot Rogue Valley Reserve 1994: Smooth, lithe and fragrant, with mint and black cherry flavors that narrow a bit on the polished finish. Drinkable now. 953 cases made. • $20 • (11/30/96) • **85**
Merlot Rogue Valley Reserve 1992 • $25 • (03/31/96) • **79**
Merlot Washington Klipsun Vineyard 1994: The blackberry and cedar flavors have a hard edge, finishing tautly and without generosity. Drinkable now. 1,029 cases made. • $17 • (11/30/96) • **83**
Pinot Blanc Rogue Valley 1995: Bright and fresh, with a resiny tinge to the apple flavors. 237 cases made. • $11 • (10/31/96) • **80**

Key: SS—Spectator Selection CS—Cellar Selection HR—Highly Recommended BB—Best Buy $NA—Price not available Ⓐ—Auction Price (BT)—Barrel Tasting
Dates in parentheses indicate the issues in which the ratings were published.

Pinot Gris Rogue Valley 1995: Refreshing and tasty, this wine is brimming with bright pineapple and citrus flavors and shows a hint of almond on the polished finish. 1,650 cases made. • $11 • (12/15/96) • **87**

Pinot Gris Rogue Valley 1994 • $11 • (03/31/96) • **83**

Pinot Noir Rogue Valley 1995: Light and simple, with grape and spice flavors echoing softly on the finish. 3,223 cases made. • $11 • (02/28/97) • **83**

Pinot Noir Rogue Valley 1994 • $11 • (04/30/96) • **87**

Pinot Noir Rogue Valley 1993 • $11 • (03/31/96) • **87**

Pinot Noir Rogue Valley 1992 • $10 • (11/30/94) • **82**

Pinot Noir Rogue Valley Maple Ranch 1994: Light in texture, with a distinctive range of flavors, from blackberry to smoke, and a touch of sage on the finish. Drinkable now. 221 cases made. • $25 • (10/31/96) • **85**

Ruby Oregon 1995: Sweet, but not quite syrupy, this is something like a light Port that lacks grip, with pretty plum flavors. Should be nice with a plate of cheese and walnuts. Made from Pinot Noir. 350 cases made. • $10/375ml • (12/31/97) • **85**

Ruby Oregon 1993 • $10/375ml • (03/31/96) • **87**

FORMAN | CALIFORNIA

Cabernet Sauvignon Napa Valley 1997: Intense, lively, well focused, rich and brimming with racy wild berry, cherry, anise, cedar and spice. Finishes with a long, lingering aftertaste. • $NA • (07/31/98) (BT) • **95-99**

Cabernet Sauvignon Napa Valley 1996: Brilliant fruit, ripe and lively, supple and polished, with pretty plum, wild berry, cherry and spice notes. Picks up an elegant oak flavor on the finish. Very complete and harmonious. 1,800 cases made. • $37 • (06/15/97) (BT) • **90-94**

Cabernet Sauvignon Napa Valley 1995: Ripe, rich, smooth and concentrated, still rangy and a bit raw around the edges, but the core of fruit is sharply focused on currant, black cherry, sage, cedar and spice. Finishes with a long, complex aftertaste. Best from 2001 through 2010. 1,900 cases made. • $38 • (06/30/98) • **91**

Cabernet Sauvignon Napa Valley 1994: Elegant, smooth and smoky, with a leather and herb edge which, with aeration, gives way to a rich, concentrated core of currant, mineral, and berry flavors. Unusually firm and concentrated for a Forman, it needs time; best after 2002. 1,900 cases made. • $35 • (05/31/97) • **92**

Cabernet Sauvignon Napa Valley 1993: Crisp cedar, cherry and currant flavor and firmly tannic finish. This is a well-crafted young Cabernet which lacks the richness of the 1991 or '92 vintages but is impressive nonetheless. 1,800 cases made. • $32 • (04/30/96) • **88**

Cabernet Sauvignon Napa Valley 1992 • $36 Ⓐ • (06/15/95) CS • **93**

Cabernet Sauvignon Napa Valley 1991 • $30 • (03/15/94) CS • **89**

Cabernet Sauvignon Napa Valley 1990 • $30 • (07/15/93) • **89**

Cabernet Sauvignon Napa Valley 1989 • $22 Ⓐ • (07/15/92) • **87**

Cabernet Sauvignon Napa Valley 1988 • $25 Ⓐ • (08/31/91) • **88**

Cabernet Sauvignon Napa Valley 1987: Starts out with a meaty, earthy, slightly cheesy quality, along with hints of currant, in the aroma, then unveils complex fruit flavors, with hints of cherry, plum and currant and a dash of cedar, and finishes with a tarry edge. Well balanced, quite firm and tannic. In need of further cellaring. 1,567 cases made. • $41 Ⓐ • (12/15/97) • **90**

Cabernet Sauvignon Napa Valley 1986: Strikes a fine balance of ripe, rich, highly extracted currant, plum and mineral flavors, cedary oak nuances and chewy tannins. The tannins are strong, but they aren't dry, so what emerges on the finish is a nice core of fruit flavor. Ready for drinking. • $31 Ⓐ • (12/15/96) • **92**

Cabernet Sauvignon Napa Valley 1985 • $51 Ⓐ • (06/15/88) • **92**

Cabernet Sauvignon Napa Valley 1984 • $17 • (04/30/87) • **92**

Chardonnay Napa Valley 1996: A zingy style, with zesty grapefruit, lemon, pear and fig flavors that are rich and concentrated. Finishes with a long, lingering aftertaste and a nice earthy quality. Drinkable now. 2,000 cases made. • $27 • (11/30/97) • **90**

Chardonnay Napa Valley 1995: Young and a bit awkward, but there's also a lot to like. The ripe pear, smoky oak, toast, hazelnut and buttery flavors develop complexity on the finish and fold together nicely. Drinkable now. 2,059 cases made. • $28 • (02/28/97) • **91**

Chardonnay Napa Valley 1994: A delicious young wine that balances intensity with elegance in a ripe, fruity, moderately rich style. Features ripe pear, spice, melon and fig notes, finishing with toasty oak and smoky nuances. 1,800 cases made. • $23 • (07/31/96) HR • **91**

Merlot Napa Valley 1995: A dry, ruggedly earthy style, with leathery flavors and hard-edged tannins. It's high in extract, but the flavors are a bit murky; may focus better with time. Tasted twice, with consistent notes. 380 cases made. • $35 • (11/30/97) • **85**

Merlot Napa Valley 1994: Young, tight and tannic, with a smoky, leathery edge to the currant, cedar and plum notes. Needing short-term cellaring to soften the rough edges, it will be best after 1999. First Merlot from Forman. 200 cases made. • $40 • (09/15/97) • **89**

FOSS CREEK | CALIFORNIA

Cabernet Sauvignon Sonoma County 1991 • $7 • (11/15/94) • **82**

FOUNTAIN GROVE | CALIFORNIA

Cabernet Sauvignon California 1994: A pleasant blend of spice, herb and cherry flavors mark this medium-bodied wine. 1,518 cases made. • $10 • (09/15/97) • **82**

Chardonnay California 1996: Rich, toasty, buttery flavors, with hints of citrus and green apple on the finish and a interesting floral note. Drink now. 3,000 cases made. • $10 • (07/31/98) • **84**

Chardonnay California 1995: Broad, ripe and generous with its fresh nectarine and vanilla flavors that linger gently on the finish. 4,363 cases made. • $10 • (07/31/97) • **85**

Petit Noir Russian River Valley 1995: Light in texture and in color, with bright cherry and mint flavors. A refreshing, versatile wine made from a clone of Pinot Noir. 1,200 cases made. • $8 • (07/31/97) • **87**

Sauvignon Blanc California 1996: Zingy acidity, fresh herbs, melon, hazelnut and grass notes shape the face of this wine. It's a fairly pure and pretty expression of the grape with a price tag that can't be beat. 1,500 cases made. • $9 • (03/31/98) • **88**

Sauvignon Blanc Lake County 1995: Creamy and melonlike in character, with hints of fig, herb, citrus and toast. Finishes with a refreshing dose of lemon-lime and green apple flavors. 551 cases made. • $9 • (06/30/97) • **87**

FOUR CORNERS | CALIFORNIA

Chardonnay California 1995: Earthy aromas are off-putting, but on the palate it's got some nice peach and honey tones. Finishes a bit sourly, though. 200 cases made. • $15 • (09/30/97) • **79**

FOWLER | CALIFORNIA

Pinot Noir Central Coast 1995: Starts out slowly, but expands into rich cherry, herb, earth, cola and spice flavors, finishes with tight tannins. Best to cellar into 1998. New from the winemaker at Mumm Cuvée Napa and Sterling Vineyards. Available at the Mumm tasting room only. 150 cases made. • $32 • (08/31/97) • **88**

FOX MOUNTAIN | CALIFORNIA

Cabernet Sauvignon Russian River Valley Reserve 1986 • $20 • (11/15/92) • **87**

Cabernet Sauvignon Russian River Valley Reserve 1985 • $19 • (09/15/89) • **75**

Cabernet Sauvignon Russian River Valley Reserve 1982 • $18 • (12/31/87) • **77**

Cabernet Sauvignon Russian River Valley Reserve 1981 • $16 • (12/15/86) • **79**

Cabernet Sauvignon Sonoma County Reserve 1987 • $15 • (11/15/94) • **79**

Chardonnay California Limited Release 1996: Simple and sweet, with canned-fruit flavors. Flavors straighten out, become more palatable on the finish. Drink now. 5,926 cases made. • $12 • (07/31/98) • **78**

Chardonnay Russian River Valley 1994: This shows tart, thin, metallic flavors, with just a hint of honey revealed on the finish. 3,000 cases made. • $12 • (11/30/96) • **77**

Sauvignon Blanc Dry Creek Valley Limited Release 1995: An oak-centered wine, dominated by floral and spice flavors. 1,600 cases made. • $10 • (07/31/96) • **80**

Sauvignon Blanc Sonoma County Limited Release 1996: Effusively fruity, with melon, grapefruit and even some grapey notes. Brisk acidity softens the almost sweet quality. A quaffer. 1,200 cases made. • $10 • (04/30/98) • **85**

FOX RUN | NEW YORK

Blanc de Blancs Finger Lakes Méthode Champenoise NV: Really appetizing. A bright, lively bubbly with great balance and a crisp texture backed by light citrus flavors that linger on the finish. Drink now. • $NA • (05/15/98) • **86**

Brut Finger Lakes 1993 • $NA • (06/30/95) • **78**

Brut Finger Lakes 1991 • $NA • (06/30/95) • **78**

Chardonnay Finger Lakes 1996: Like a good Mâcon, this is a lean, nervy Chardonnay with lemon and mineral flavors accented by butter on the finish. Its crisp texture is appetizing. Drink now. • $8 • (03/31/98) • **84**

Chardonnay Finger Lakes 1995: Pear and butter flavors dominate this medium-bodied wine. Has good concentration and a slight sweetness on the finish. 1,000 cases made. • $8 • (01/31/97) • **83**

Chardonnay Finger Lakes Reserve 1996: Not flashy, but very good. This pale-colored, lean-textured, dry Chardonnay with crisp citrus and mineral flavors is lightly accented by the spicy, vanilla notes of new oak barrels. Drink now. • $12 • (03/31/98) • **87**

Chardonnay Finger Lakes Reserve 1995: Good and juicy, with plenty of apple and toast flavors. Vibrant acidity and a spicy finish. Nicely crisp, as well. 500 cases made. • $11 • (01/31/97) • **85**

Meritage Finger Lakes 1995: A noble attempt at a Bordeaux-style red that comes off as awkward. The fresh cherry and raspberry flavors are appealing, but tart acidity, tight tannins and a strong, smoky oak flavor throw it out of balance. • $20 • (05/31/97) • **80**

Pinot Noir Finger Lakes 1995: A lively and fairly lush wine with pretty cherry and berry flavors. Clean, straightforward, with a spicy finish. • $15 • (12/31/97) • **83**

Riesling Finger Lakes 1996: Peachy tasting and slightly sweet, with some decent mineral and spice notes as well. Drink now. • $9 • (03/31/98) • **82**

Riesling Finger Lakes 1995: An effusive wine that tastes enticingly of peaches and cream. It is ripe, quite concentrated, and its unique flavors linger on the finish. • $9 • (01/31/97) • **85**

Riesling Finger Lakes 1994 • $9 • (01/31/96) • **85**

Riesling Finger Lakes Dry 1996: Offers some nice mineral and green peach flavors, but it turns a bit earthy and candied on the finish. Drink now. • $10 • (03/31/98) • **81**

Vintage Port Finger Lakes 1996: A medium-bodied dessert wine with sweet cherry and spice flavors, some chocolaty notes on the finish. Drink now. • $20/375ml • (06/15/98) • **80**

Vintage Port Finger Lakes 1995: An interesting mix. Quite jammy-tasting, with maple syrup and anise flavors, a chocolaty finish. Well-crafted; a solid effort. • $20/375ml • (10/31/97) • **84**

FOXEN | CALIFORNIA

Cabernet Franc Santa Maria Valley Tinaquaic Vineyard 1994: Marked by cedar and dill notes and a dash of green pepper, it's tilted toward the herbal side, but a thorough search turns up some attractive dark fruit flavors, too. 300 cases made. • $24 • (05/31/97) • **84**

Cabernet Franc Santa Maria Valley Tinaquaic Vineyard 1993 • $24 • (04/30/96) • **90**

Cabernet Sauvignon Santa Barbara County 1994: Ripe and fruity. Has a juicy core of plum and wild berry flavors that are bright and lively, and finishes with a burst of fruit flavor and mild tannins. 800 cases made. • $24 • (11/15/96) • **88**

Cabernet Sauvignon Santa Barbara County 1993: Smooth and generous, with some vegetal aromas, but the flavors center around currant and raspberry. Delicious now. 1,000 cases made. • $22 • (12/15/95) • **86**

Cabernet Sauvignon Santa Barbara County 1992 • $20 • (10/31/94) • **87**

Cabernet Sauvignon Santa Barbara County 1991 • $20 • (02/28/94) HR • **90**

Cabernet Sauvignon Santa Barbara County 1990 • $20 • (11/15/92) • **84**

Cabernet Sauvignon Santa Barbara County 1989 • $20 • (11/15/91) • **91**

Cabernet Sauvignon Santa Barbara County 1988 • $18 • (11/15/91) • **89**

Chardonnay Santa Maria Valley 1996: Intense and lively, with a distinct earthiness that adds an attractive element to the core of fig, tropical fruit and spice. Turns complex and creamy on the aftertaste. 2,500 cases made. • $20 • (07/31/98) • **88**

Chardonnay Santa Maria Valley 1995: Pungently earthy and leesy with strong sulfurous flavors that are quite unappealing. Tasted twice, with consistent notes. • $NA • (07/31/97) • **68**

Chardonnay Santa Maria Valley 1994: A truly funky style, with sour, earthy, off-beat flavors and aromas that override the fruit. Tasted twice with consistent notes. 1,000 cases made. • $20 • (07/31/96) • **72**

Chardonnay Santa Maria Valley 1993 • $20 • (04/15/95) HR • **90**

Key: SS—Spectator Selection CS—Cellar Selection HR—Highly Recommended BB—Best Buy $NA—Price not available Ⓐ—Auction Price (BT)—Barrel Tasting

Dates in parentheses indicate the issues in which the ratings were published.

Chardonnay Santa Maria Valley Tinaquaic Vineyard 1995: A tight, dense, richly flavored wine that's earthy, leesy and a bit sour; be forewarned. 250 cases made. • $30 • (07/31/97) • **74**

Chardonnay Santa Maria Valley Tinaquaic Vineyard 1994: Well oaked and offers an abundance of spicy flavors, though the pear and apple notes lack focus. Seems one dimensional. Tasted twice, with consistent notes. 600 cases made. • $30 • (07/31/96) • **82**

Chardonnay Santa Maria Valley Tinaquaic Vineyard 1993 • $28 • (07/31/95) • **85**

Chenin Blanc Santa Barbara County 1993 • $12 • (05/31/95) • **83**

Merlot Santa Barbara County 1995: Smooth and supple, a harmonious wine with a core of ripe cherry, sage, cedar and spice, and a slight vegetal edge. Firms up on the finish, where its shows its tannic strength. Best now to 2003. 700 cases made. • $24 • (04/30/98) • **88**

Merlot Santa Barbara County 1994: Tightly wound, firm and marked by strong cedar and spice notes, with just a hint of cherry flavor in the background. Difficult to warm up to, especially at this price. 600 cases made. • $24 • (03/31/97) • **84**

Merlot Santa Barbara County 1992 • $22 • (12/15/95) • **84**

Merlot Santa Barbara County 1991 • $22 • (03/15/94) • **88**

Merlot Santa Maria Valley Tinaquaic Vineyard 1993 • $24 • (04/30/96) • **90**

Pinot Noir Santa Barbara County 1995: Marked by spicy herb, earth, cola and cherry flavors, this style is true to the Santa Barbara area. Finishes with complex flavors and a good dose of tannin. Drink now. 650 cases made. • $24 • (12/31/96) • **86**

Pinot Noir Santa Maria Valley 1996: Rich and exotic, with ripe and spicy stewed-plum, wild berry and cranberry nuances, finishing with an earthy edge. 1,700 cases made. • $24 • (01/31/98) • **87**

Pinot Noir Santa Maria Valley 1994 • $20 • (01/31/96) • **87**

Pinot Noir Santa Maria Valley 1993 • $20 • (11/15/95) • **88**

Pinot Noir Santa Maria Valley 1992 • $30 • (11/30/94) • **87**

Pinot Noir Santa Maria Valley 1991 • $20 • (01/31/94) HR • **89**

Pinot Noir Santa Maria Valley 1990 • $20 • (09/30/92) • **89**

Pinot Noir Santa Maria Valley 1987 • $16 • (12/15/89) • **78**

Pinot Noir Santa Maria Valley Bien Nacido Vineyard 1995: A touch racy, with a slightly herbaceous edge. Ripe cherry and sage-laced berry flavors fold in to give it balance and breadth. 144 cases made. • $30 • (07/31/97) • **88**

Pinot Noir Santa Maria Valley Bien Nacido Vineyard 1993 • $26 • (11/15/95) • **90**

Pinot Noir Santa Ynez Valley Sanford & Benedict Vineyard 1995: A touch earthy, with a spicy cola edge to the cherry and wild berry flavors. Turns elegant and spicy on the finish, where the flavors linger on. 140 cases made. • $30 • (09/30/97) • **88**

Pinot Noir Santa Ynez Valley Sanford & Benedict Vineyard 1993 • $30 • (11/15/95) • **90**

Pinot Noir Santa Ynez Valley Sanford & Benedict Vineyard 1992 • $30 • (01/31/95) • **87**

Pinot Noir Santa Ynez Valley Sanford & Benedict Vineyard 1991 • $30 • (02/28/94) • **89**

Syrah Santa Ynez Valley Morehouse Vineyard 1995: Smooth, ripe and polished, with a pretty core of juicy black cherry, plum, wild berry and spice flavors, picking up a zesty mint and herb nuance and finishing with a long, plush aftertaste. 240 cases made. • $25 • (08/31/97) • **92**

Syrah Santa Ynez Valley Morehouse Vineyard 1994: Dark, ripe and complex, with a pretty array of juicy, wild berry and peppery plum flavors. Drinkable now. 100 cases made. • $25 • (07/31/96) • **88**

FOXHOLLOW | CALIFORNIA

Cabernet Sauvignon California Barrel Select 1994: Toasty oak and licorice flavors lead the way, followed by black cherry and plum. This medium-bodied, straightforward wine is ready to drink. 5,000 cases made. • $9 • (10/31/97) • **84**

Cabernet Sauvignon Paso Robles 1991 • $10 • (06/30/94) • **82**

Chardonnay California Barrel Select 1996: Smooth, open and generous with its pear and spice flavors, this is a well-mannered wine with a distinct flavor. Ready now. • $9 • (12/15/97) • **84**

Chardonnay California Barrel Select 1995: Lemony, tangy, toasty-but without much depth. 2,500 cases made. • $10 • (07/31/97) • **83**

Chardonnay California Barrel Select 1994: There's a toasty edge to the bright pear and citrus flavors, and a fresh finish. 2,500 cases made. • $10 • (07/31/96) • **80**

Merlot California 1992 • $10 • (09/15/94) • **81**

Merlot California Barrel Select 1996: Light, with distinctly herbal overtones to the basic raspberry flavors. Finishes with a crisp zing of citrusy acidity. Best now. • $9 • (12/15/97) • **82**

FRANCAL | CALIFORNIA

Mourvèdre California 1988 • $7 • (02/15/93) • **78**

FRANCISCAN OAKVILLE ESTATE CALIFORNIA

Cabernet Sauvignon Alexander Valley 1980 • $7 • (10/16/84) • **86**
Cabernet Sauvignon Napa Valley 1994: An elegant style, well focused, with pretty currant, cedar, sage and spice notes. Finishes with supple tannins and a sense of harmony. Ready to drink. 25,000 cases made. • $16 • (05/15/97) • **88**
Cabernet Sauvignon Napa Valley 1993: Smooth and creamy, with pretty oak and ripe cherry flavors that pick up hints of cedar and spice. Appealing to drink now as the flavors are ripe and juicy. 15,000 cases made. • $15 • (12/15/96) • **87**
Cabernet Sauvignon Napa Valley 1992 • $15 • (12/15/95) • **87**
Cabernet Sauvignon Napa Valley 1991 • $13 • (11/15/94) • **82**
Cabernet Sauvignon Napa Valley 1990 • $13 • (10/31/93) • **88**
Cabernet Sauvignon Napa Valley 1989 • $13 • (05/15/93) • **87**
Cabernet Sauvignon Napa Valley 1988 • $12 • (08/31/92) • **81**
Cabernet Sauvignon Napa Valley 1987 • $12 • (02/15/91) • **89**
Cabernet Sauvignon Napa Valley Library Selection 1987: Mature, with soft tannins and dashes of tea and bell pepper over the currant and plum flavors. Drink now. 7,000 cases made. • $20 • (12/15/97) • **86**
Cabernet Sauvignon Napa Valley 1986: This is lean and thin. It showed little upon release, and not much now. • $NA • (12/15/96) • **80**
Cabernet Sauvignon Napa Valley 1985 • $11 • (05/15/89) • **86**
Cabernet Sauvignon Napa Valley 1984 • $9 • (09/15/88) • **84**
Cabernet Sauvignon Napa Valley 1983 • $9 • (04/30/87) • **75**
Cabernet Sauvignon Napa Valley Reserve 1988 • $18 • (03/15/93) • **81**
Cabernet Sauvignon Napa Valley Reserve 1985 • $15 • (05/31/90) • **88**
Chardonnay Napa Valley 1996: Clean and fruity, with ripe pear, fig and spicy flavors, a creamy texture and a long, lingering finish, where a touch of earthiness adds dimension. A bit coarse in texture now, but give it a few months in the bottle. Drink now through 2002. 15,000 cases made. • $15 • (06/30/98) SS • **90**
Chardonnay Napa Valley 1995: Deftly balanced, with a pretty band of ripe pear, spice, citrus and light oak shadings, gaining depth and complexity on the finish. 19,000 cases made. • $16 • (07/31/97) • **89**
Chardonnay Napa Valley Barrel Fermented 1994: Complex and well focused, boasting a solid core of ripe, spicy pear and apple flavors and pretty dashes of toasty oak. Finishes with intensity and concentration and a long aftertaste. Terrific value. 20,000 cases made. • $13 • (04/30/96) • **90**
Chardonnay Napa Valley Barrel Fermented 1993 • $12 • (04/15/95) SS • **90**
Chardonnay Napa Valley Cuvée Sauvage 1995: Well focused, with a tightly wound core of ripe pear, apple, spice and hazelnut flavors that turn rich and concentrated on the finish. Well-integrated toasty oak flavors add dimension. 3,500 cases made. • $30 • (01/31/98) • **91**
Chardonnay Napa Valley Cuvée Sauvage 1994: Tart and a bit leesy, not the rich, polished wine it usually is. This vintage seems to reflect a stylistic change, with grapefruit and citrus flavors in place of the creamy pear and vanilla flavors of years past. Perhaps it will grow more complex and compelling with time. • $30 • (10/15/96) • **86**
Chardonnay Napa Valley Cuvée Sauvage 1993 • $30 • (05/31/95) • **89**
Johannisberg Riesling Napa Valley Late Harvest Select 1983 • $10/375ml • (01/31/88) • **88**
Magnificat Meritage Napa Valley 1994: Complex, with ripe cherry, cedar and currant flavors, dashes of anise and spice and firm but polished tannins on the finish, which turns elegant and supple. A blend of Cabernet Sauvignon, Merlot and Cabernet Franc. 5,000 cases made. • $25 • (11/30/97) • **89**
Magnificat Meritage Napa Valley 1993: Elegant and sophisticated, a complex blend of flavor and texture-bright, lively cherry, plum and currant flavors and a smooth, supple texture. The tannnins are there, for sure, but the fruit flavor works its way past them for a fine finish. Best now through 2002. 800 cases made. • $20 • (11/15/96) • **91**
Meritage Magnificat Napa Valley 1991 • $20 • (12/15/95) • **89**
Meritage Magnificat Napa Valley 1990 • $20 • (11/15/94) • **85**
Meritage Magnificat Napa Valley 1989 • $18 • (11/15/93) • **86**
Meritage Napa Valley 1988 • $18 • (07/15/92) • **89**
Meritage Napa Valley 1987 • $17 • (04/30/91) • **87**
Meritage Napa Valley 1986 • $15 • (07/31/90) • **79**
Meritage Napa Valley 1985 • $16 • (03/31/90) • **90**
Merlot Napa Valley 1994: Tough and tannic, with just enough cherry, plum and berry flavors emerging to hold your interest. Not as generous and forthcoming as Franciscan Merlot usually is. • $17 • (10/15/96) • **84**
Merlot Napa Valley 1993 • $16 • (12/15/95) • **89**
Merlot Napa Valley 1990 • $12 • (07/15/93) • **87**
Merlot Napa Valley 1989 • $12 • (05/31/92) • **79**
Merlot Napa Valley 1987 • $13 • (06/15/90) • **88**
Merlot Napa Valley 1986 • $12 • (07/31/89) • **80**
Merlot Napa Valley 1985 • $9 • (05/31/88) • **89**
Merlot Napa Valley 1984 • $8 • (06/30/87) SS • **90**
Merlot Napa Valley 1983 • $8 • (02/28/87) • **88**
Merlot Napa Valley 1981 • $8 • (10/01/85) • **91**
Merlot Napa Valley Reserve 1991 • $25 • (01/31/95) • **89**
Zinfandel Napa Valley 1994: Elegant and refined. Marked by light spice and pepper notes, with ripe cherry and raspberry flavors coming through on the finish. Not too tannic; drink it now. • $15 • (10/15/96) • **88**
Zinfandel Napa Valley 1993 • $11 • (06/15/95) • **86**
Zinfandel Napa Valley 1992 • $12 • (10/15/94) • **80**
Zinfandel Napa Valley 1991 • $10 • (09/30/93) • **85**
Zinfandel Napa Valley 1990 • $10 • (07/31/92) • **87**
Zinfandel Napa Valley 1989 • $10 • (07/31/91) • **88**
Zinfandel Napa Valley 1988 • $9 • (05/31/90) • **87**

FRANK-ROMBAUER LARKMEAD | CALIFORNIA

Cabernet Sauvignon Napa Valley 1993: Ripe and rustic, with decent cherry and berry flavors, but it turns earthy, tannic and oaky on the aftertaste, slightly bitter. Will always be on the tannic side. 450 cases made. • $50 • (05/15/97) • **84**
Sangiovese Napa Valley 1992: Smooth and supple, in an elegant, understated style highlighted by ripe plum, black cherry and berry notes. Turns fruity on the finish. 600 cases made. • $23 • (05/15/97) • **87**

FRANK, DR. KONSTANTIN | NEW YORK

Cabernet Finger Lakes NV: A good, meaty-tasting red with plenty of dark plum, cherry and spice flavors. Finishes with nice leather and chocolate notes. A blend of 65 percent Cabernet Franc and 35 percent Cabernet Sauvignon. 650 cases made. • $15 • (10/31/97) • **85**
Cabernet Sauvignon Finger Lakes 1995: Interesting combination of spice and herb flavors, with a tealike note mixed in. Balanced and delicious, with a chocolate note on the finish. Drink now. 450 cases made. • $22 • (06/15/97) • **85**
Cabernet Sauvignon Finger Lakes 1993: The deep color and spicy aromas are promising, but it turns lean, tart and green on the palate. Has some cranberry and tart cherry flavor, along with sweet oak, but we would like more ripe fruit. 150 cases made. • $22 • (06/30/95) • **79**
Cabernet Sauvignon Finger Lakes 1991 • $22 • (06/30/95) • **84**
Chardonnay Finger Lakes 1995: A forward style of Chardonnay that emphasizes smoky, oaky aromas, ripe, almost sweet, fruit flavors and a soft texture. Easy to enjoy. 1,500 cases made. • $11 • (05/31/97) • **84**
Chardonnay Finger Lakes Barrel Fermented 1996: Clean and crisp, with lively acidity buoying the apple and citrus flavors. Has vanilla accents from light oak treatment. Finishes a bit short. Drink now. 2,200 cases made. • $11 • (05/15/98) • **84**
Chardonnay Finger Lakes Reserve 1993 • $15 • (10/15/95) • **79**
Gewürztraminer Finger Lakes 1996: This wine wants to go somewhere, with some buttery and apricot flavors, but it ends up hollow in the middle and cidery on the finish. 450 cases made. • $13 • (07/31/98) • **76**
Gewürztraminer Finger Lakes 1995: Sweet and simple in flavor, with a thick texture and herbal, earthy overtones. 300 cases made. • $13 • (06/15/97) • **75**
Gewürztraminer New York 1994 • $12 • (01/31/96) • **76**
Johannisberg Riesling Finger Lakes Dry 1996: Offers some good apple and peach flavors, but its turns a bit earthy on the finish. 2,200 cases made. • $10 • (10/31/97) • **81**
Johannisberg Riesling Finger Lakes Dry 1995: A simple, straightforward white wine with modest fruit flavors. 1,600 cases made. • $9 • (10/31/96) • **77**
Johannisberg Riesling Finger Lakes Dry 1994 • $9 • (08/31/95) • **79**
Johannisberg Riesling Finger Lakes Dry 1993 • $8 • (09/15/94) • **85**
Johannisberg Riesling Finger Lakes Ice Wine 1995: Sweet and rich, straightforward and delicious. This is a balanced and lush wine that's generous on the palate, with loads of honey, pear and ripe apple flavors. 200 cases made. • $30/375ml • (05/31/97) • **88**
Johannisberg Riesling Finger Lakes Salmon Run 1996: Clean and crisp, with good peach and apple flavors and a nice richness as well. Tastes slightly sweet. Drink well-chilled. 1,100 cases made. • $9 • (10/31/97) • **84**

Johannisberg Riesling Finger Lakes Semi-Dry 1996: Frankly sweet, with peach and apple flavors. One-dimensional, but good for what it is and has a nice, rich texture. 1,900 cases made. • $10 • (10/31/97) • **83**
Johannisberg Riesling Finger Lakes Semi-Dry 1995: Great, fresh fruit flavors accented by honey and framed by lively acidity and moderate sweetness make this a harmonious, well-balanced, Spätlese style of Riesling. 960 cases made. • $9 • (10/31/96) • **86**
Johannisberg Riesling Finger Lakes Semi-Dry 1994 • $9 • (08/31/95) • **84**
Johannisberg Riesling New York Semi-Dry 1993 • $8 • (09/15/94) BB • **86**
Pinot Noir Finger Lakes 1995: Bright, fruity, spicy, it's lively in texture and accented strongly with spicy oak, especially on the finish. A bit heavy with oak, but fun anyway. 830 cases made. • $19 • (08/31/97) • **84**
Pinot Noir Finger Lakes 1992 • $18 • (05/15/95) • **79**
Pinot Noir Finger Lakes 1990 • $18 • (05/15/95) • **83**
Pinot Noir Finger Lakes 1985 • $15 • (06/15/88) • **75**
Pinot Noir Finger Lakes Fleur de Pinot Noir NV: Mature-tasting, with stewy, leathery flavors, touches of spice and brown sugar on the finish. 950 cases made. • $12 • (07/31/98) • **79**
Rkatsiteli Finger Lakes 1995: A nicely crafted wine with good flavors of apple, almond and honey and a slightly spicy finish. 395 cases made. • $13 • (08/31/97) • **82**
Rkatsiteli Finger Lakes 1993 • $12 • (06/30/95) • **77**

FRANUS | CALIFORNIA

Zinfandel Contra Costa County Planchon Vineyard 1996: Ripe, rich and spicy, with complex plum, wild berry, black cherry, tar, spice and cedar notes. Turns elegant on the finish, where the flavors are well balanced and lively. Well made. Drink now through 2002. 700 cases made. • $17 • (06/15/98) • **89**
Zinfandel Mount Veeder Brandlin Ranch 1992 • $16 • (01/31/95) • **88**
Zinfandel Mount Veeder Brandlin Ranch 1991 • $13 • (09/30/93) • **86**
Zinfandel Napa Valley Hendry Vineyard 1993 • $14 • (10/15/95) • **85**
Zinfandel Napa Valley Hendry Vineyard 1992 • $13 • (07/31/94) • **88**
Zinfandel Napa Valley Hendry Vineyard 1991 • $13 • (09/30/93) • **88**
Zinfandel Napa Valley Hendry Vineyard 1989 • $13 • (10/15/92) • **83**

FRAZIER | CALIFORNIA

Merlot Napa Valley Lupine Hill Vineyard 1995: A touch gamy and leathery, this slowly works its way into more mainstream flavors of cherry, currant, anise and sage. Finishes with a complex aftertaste. Best now through 2005. 330 cases made. • $28 • (06/30/98) • **85**

FREEMARK ABBEY | CALIFORNIA

Cabernet Bosché Napa Valley Bosché Estate 1993: Rich and complex, with a tight, well-focused core of currant, black cherry, anise, sage and spice. Turns supple and generous on the palate, with well-integrated tannins and a long, full aftertaste. Best from 2000 through 2010. 2,000 cases made. • $35 • (06/30/98) CS • **92**
Cabernet Sauvignon Napa Valley 1994: Young, tight and firmly tannic, but the core of Cabernet flavor is ripe and juicy, with hints of currant, black cherry, leather, sage and tar. Finishes with a complex aftertaste that echoes the flavors. Best after 2000. 10,000 cases made. • $18 • (10/31/97) • **89**
Cabernet Sauvignon Napa Valley 1993: A medium-bodied style that hits the right notes, with ripe cherry, berry and cedary oak flavors, mild tannins. Complex enough to cellar, or drink now. 10,922 cases made. • $18 • (11/15/96) • **87**
Cabernet Sauvignon Napa Valley 1991 • $17 • (11/15/94) • **85**
Cabernet Sauvignon Napa Valley 1990 • $16 • (11/15/94) • **83**
Cabernet Sauvignon Napa Valley 1989 • $16 • (11/15/93) • **81**
Cabernet Sauvignon Napa Valley 1988 • $16 • (08/31/92) • **81**
Cabernet Sauvignon Napa Valley 1987: Solid, with a supple, well-integrated core of ripe plum, herb and cherry flavors. • $22 Ⓐ • (12/15/97) • **88**
Cabernet Sauvignon Napa Valley 1986 • $15 • (11/15/90) • **83**
Cabernet Sauvignon Napa Valley 1985 • $21 Ⓐ • (10/31/89) • **79**
Cabernet Sauvignon Napa Valley 1984 • $14 • (02/15/89) • **84**
Cabernet Sauvignon Napa Valley 1983 • $12 • (02/15/88) • **68**
Cabernet Sauvignon Napa Valley 1982 • $12 • (02/15/87) • **84**

Key: SS—Spectator Selection CS—Cellar Selection HR—Highly Recommended BB—Best Buy $NA—Price not available Ⓐ—Auction Price (BT)—Barrel Tasting
Dates in parentheses indicate the issues in which the ratings were published.

Cabernet Sauvignon Napa Valley 1981 • $20 Ⓐ • (10/01/85) • **79**
Cabernet Sauvignon Napa Valley 1980 • $22 • (05/16/84) • **84**
Cabernet Sauvignon Napa Valley 1979 • $29 Ⓐ • (01/01/84) • **89**
Cabernet Sauvignon Napa Valley 1974 • $50 • (11/15/94) • **83**
Cabernet Sauvignon Napa Valley Bosché 1992: Ripe, smooth and harmonious, impeccably balanced, long and tasty, boasting a delicious core of plum and wild berry flavors that gracefully unfold into a lengthy, complex aftertaste. Ageworthy, it has just the right amount of tannin for cellaring into 2003. 2,015 cases made. • $32 • (09/30/97) CS • **93**
Cabernet Sauvignon Napa Valley Bosché 1991: Young and tight, well focused and lively, with ripe flavors of rich cherry, currant, anise and a nice touch of earth. Finishes with smooth, well-integrated tannins and fine length. Can be enjoyed now, but cellaring should only soften the tannins; this vineyard has a reputation for wines that age well for six to 10 years after the vintage. 2,032 cases made. • $24 • (11/30/96) • **90**
Cabernet Sauvignon Napa Valley Bosché 1989 • $22 Ⓐ • (11/15/94) • **85**
Cabernet Sauvignon Napa Valley Bosché 1987: Still lean and trim, with an earthy edge to the herb, green olive and currant notes. Finishes with crisp tannins and a dash of sage. Very well proportioned and quite elegant. Best now through 2003. • $22 Ⓐ • (12/15/97) • **88**
Cabernet Sauvignon Napa Valley Bosché 1986: A curious wine with a tart, cedary accent to the anise and cherry flavors. Turns thin and uninteresting on the finish, as most of its fruit flavor has dried out. • $26 Ⓐ • (12/15/96) • **78**
Cabernet Sauvignon Napa Valley Bosché 1985 • $25 Ⓐ • (07/31/89) • **90**
Cabernet Sauvignon Napa Valley Bosché 1984 • $29 Ⓐ • (04/30/88) • **80**
Cabernet Sauvignon Napa Valley Bosché 1983 • $18 • (06/15/87) • **80**
Cabernet Sauvignon Napa Valley Bosché 1982 • $20 Ⓐ • (05/16/86) CS • **93**
Cabernet Sauvignon Napa Valley Bosché 1981 • $20 Ⓐ • (07/01/85) • **89**
Cabernet Sauvignon Napa Valley Bosché 1980 • $24 • (02/01/86) • **84**
Cabernet Sauvignon Napa Valley Bosché 1979 • $29 Ⓐ • (02/01/86) • **86**
Cabernet Sauvignon Napa Valley Bosché 1978 • $56 • (11/15/92) • **86**
Cabernet Sauvignon Napa Valley Bosché 1978 • $13 • (04/30/87) • **92**
Cabernet Sauvignon Napa Valley Bosché 1974 • $75 • (11/15/94) • **85**
Cabernet Sauvignon Napa Valley Sycamore Vineyards 1992: Mature and supple, with a complex interplay of currant, plum, cedar and coffee notes. Finishes with a smooth, polished texture and good length. Drinks well now, but can age into 2002. 2,159 cases made. • $30 • (09/30/97) • **89**
Cabernet Sauvignon Napa Valley Sycamore Vineyards 1991: Smooth and harmonious, with a supple texture, ripe tannins and pleasing core of cherry and wild berry flavors. Shows more complexity and finesse on the finish, and also more tannic strength. Drinkable now. 1,551 cases made. • $22 • (11/30/96) • **88**
Cabernet Sauvignon Napa Valley Sycamore Vineyards 1990 • $23 • (12/15/95) • **88**
Cabernet Sauvignon Napa Valley Sycamore Vineyards 1989 • $20 • (12/15/95) • **80**
Cabernet Sauvignon Napa Valley Sycamore Vineyards 1988 • $25 • (11/15/94) • **84**
Cabernet Sauvignon Napa Valley Sycamore Vineyards 1987: Firm, with chewy tannins and a meaty, herbal edge to its Cabernet flavors. Lacks harmony and focus. • $35 • (12/15/97) • **84**
Cabernet Sauvignon Napa Valley Sycamore Vineyards 1986 • $25 • (11/15/91) • **91**
Cabernet Sauvignon Napa Valley Sycamore Vineyards 1985 • $25 • (10/31/89) • **88**
Cabernet Sauvignon Napa Valley Sycamore Vineyards 1984 • $20 • (12/15/88) • **91**
Chardonnay Napa Valley 1996: An elegant, understated style, with attractive citrus, pear, lemon and earthy nuances that hang together nicely through the finish. Ready to drink. 8,129 cases made. • $17 • (04/30/98) • **88**
Chardonnay Napa Valley 1995: Earthy, with a twinge of bitterness that disrupts the flow of apple and pear-scented flavors. Smoky, toasty oak shows up on the finish. 8,200 cases made. • $18 • (03/31/98) • **85**
Chardonnay Napa Valley 1994: On the tart side, with a green apple accent to the flavors. Fans of a crisp, flinty style will find this appealing. 7,800 cases made. • $14 • (02/28/97) • **84**
Chardonnay Napa Valley 1993 • $16 • (06/30/96) • **84**
Chardonnay Napa Valley Carpy Ranch 1996: Clean and well focused, with spice, pear, light oak and cedar notes. Finishes with a spicy, fruity aftertaste. 1,400 cases made. • $24 • (05/15/98) • **88**
Chardonnay Napa Valley Carpy Ranch 1994: Young, tight and concentrated, with a pretty band of ripe pear, spice, nutmeg and vanilla flavors, turning smooth and creamy on the finish. Ready to drink. 893 cases made. • $24 • (05/31/97) • **90**

Johannisberg Riesling Late Harvest Napa Valley Edelwein Gold 1991 • $25/375ml • (10/15/92) CS • **92**
Johannisberg Riesling Late Harvest Napa Valley Edelwein Gold 1989 • $22/375ml • (07/15/90) • **92**
Johannisberg Riesling Late Harvest Napa Valley Edelwein Gold 1988 • $18/375ml • (06/15/89) • **87**
Johannisberg Riesling Late Harvest Napa Valley Edelwein Gold 1986 • $19/375ml • (06/15/87) • **87**
Johannisberg Riesling Late Harvest Napa Valley Edelwein Gold 1973 • $NA/375ml • (02/28/87) • **91**
Merlot Napa Valley 1995: Ripe, rich and complex, with tiers of spicy currant, black cherry, herb, cedar and tobacco. Shows depth and concentration, with a long, full aftertaste. Impressive. Best now to 2003. 9,000 cases made. • $21 • (04/30/98) • **88**
Merlot Napa Valley 1994: Distinctive for its spicy wild berry and black cherry flavors. Not your classic Merlot, but it's a solid red wine with lots of spice and currant flavors. Drinkable now. 8,500 cases made. • $18 • (12/31/96) • **87**
Merlot Napa Valley 1993: Smooth and harmonious, with a pretty core of plum and cherry framed by light toasty oak. Finishes with a pretty, fruity aftertaste. Drinkable now. 4,800 cases made. • $16 • (08/31/96) • **87**
Merlot Napa Valley 1992 • $15 • (03/31/95) • **83**
Merlot Napa Valley 1991 • $15 • (04/15/94) • **86**
Merlot Napa Valley 1989 • $15 • (07/15/93) • **80**
Merlot Napa Valley 1985 • $10 • (12/31/88) • **90**
Petite Sirah Napa Valley 1980 • $NA • (02/01/88) • **78**
Petite Sirah Napa Valley 1979 • $NA • (02/01/88) • **87**
Petite Sirah Napa Valley 1978 • $NA • (02/01/88) • **80**
Petite Sirah Napa Valley 1977 • $NA • (02/01/88) • **82**
Petite Sirah Napa Valley 1976 • $NA • (02/01/88) • **77**
Petite Sirah Napa Valley 1975 • $NA • (02/01/88) • **73**
Petite Sirah Napa Valley 1974 • $NA • (02/01/88) • **80**
Petite Sirah Napa Valley 1973 • $NA • (02/01/88) • **86**
Petite Sirah Napa Valley 1972 • $NA • (02/01/88) • **76**
Petite Sirah Napa Valley 1971 • $NA • (02/01/88) • **90**
Petite Sirah Napa Valley 1969 • $NA • (02/01/88) • **81**

FREESTONE | CALIFORNIA

Cabernet Sauvignon Napa Valley 1994: Roundly textured, with cedar, spice and plum overtones. Fairly simple, firm, and finishes with a tangy, herbal edge. 3,864 cases made. • $15 • (10/15/97) • **85**
Cabernet Sauvignon Napa Valley 1993: Trim and compact, with some mature cedary oak flavors and traces of cherry and berry. Second label for von Strasser. 2,700 cases made. • $14 • (09/15/96) • **82**
Sauvignon Blanc Napa Valley 1996: Very bright. This has pucker-power, backed by intense citrus and herb flavors. The grassiness is under control, however. Refreshing and light. 1,950 cases made. • $11 • (11/15/97) • **86**

FREMONT CREEK | CALIFORNIA

Cabernet Sauvignon Mendocino & Napa Counties 1988 • $10 • (11/15/92) • **77**
Cabernet Sauvignon Mendocino & Napa Counties 1986 • $8 • (04/30/91) BB • **85**
Cabernet Sauvignon Mendocino & Napa Counties 1985 • $9 • (03/31/88) • **78**
Cabernet Sauvignon Mendocino & Napa Counties Beckstoffer Vineyards 1990 • $9 • (11/15/94) • **77**
Cabernet Sauvignon Mendocino & Napa Counties Beckstoffer Vineyards 1989 • $9 • (11/15/93) • **71**

FRENCH CREEK | WASHINGTON

Cabernet Sauvignon Washington 1988 • $9 • (04/15/92) • **73**
Cabernet Sauvignon Washington 1985 • $8 • (10/15/88) • **82**
Merlot Washington 1985 • $12 • (12/31/88) • **83**

FREY | CALIFORNIA

Pinot Noir Mendocino 1991 • $11 • (02/28/93) • **62**
Sauvignon Blanc Late Harvest Mendocino NV • $8 • (12/31/95) • **72**
Sauvignon Blanc Mendocino Organically Grown Grapes No Sulfites Added 1993 • $7 • (08/31/95) • **73**
Syrah Mendocino Bulow Vineyard 1986 • $10 • (04/15/89) • **82**
Zinfandel Mendocino 1993 • $8 • (10/15/95) • **83**
Zinfandel Mendocino 1992 • $8 • (10/15/94) BB • **84**
Zinfandel Mendocino 1990 • $8 • (10/15/92) • **84**

FRICK | CALIFORNIA

Cabernet Sauvignon Dry Creek Valley 1994: Tea, herbs and mint come to mind with this somewhat meaty wine. It finishes long and loudly with attractive layers of plum, cassis, and toasty oak. 340 cases made. • $20 • (09/15/97) • **89**
Cabernet Sauvignon Dry Creek Valley 1993: Simple, with an earthy anise accent to the plum and currant flavors. Gains more flavor on the finish and the tannins are mild, so it's drinkable now. 250 cases made. • $16 • (11/30/96) • **85**
Cinsaut Dry Creek Valley 1995: Southern Rhône grape, usually part of a Châteauneuf blend in France, plays a very pretty solo in this light wine prettily packed with blackberry flavor. Ready to drink. 335 cases made. • $15 • (03/31/98) • **85**
Grenache Napa County 1985 • $7 • (04/15/89) • **86**
Merlot Dry Creek Valley 1995: Bright and tangy, with a spicy black currant and cherry core. It sits cleanly on the palate, and finishes with a refreshing minty edge. 600 cases made. • $20 • (03/31/98) • **85**
Petite Sirah Monterey County 1985 • $8 • (02/15/89) • **87**
Pinot Noir California 1981 • $12 • (08/31/86) • **89**
Pinot Noir Santa Maria Valley 1984 • $12 • (02/28/89) • **75**
Syrah Dry Creek Valley 1995: Firm in texture, ripe in flavor, with pretty blackberry and spice notes echoing on the chewy finish. Best after 1999. 350 cases made. • $21 • (03/31/98) • **86**
Viognier Dry Creek Valley 1996: A little earthy, with peach and banana flavors and a touch of spice. Drink now. 120 cases made. • $21 • (05/15/98) • **83**
Zinfandel Dry Creek Valley 1993: A bit on the weird side. Has ripe, bordering on prunelike, flavors with a cedary oak accent that turns vinegary on the aftertaste. 420 cases made. • $14 • (04/30/97) • **82**
Zinfandel Dry Creek Valley 1991 • $13 • (10/15/94) • **79**
Zinfandel Russian River Valley 1990 • $13 • (09/30/93) • **70**

FRITZ, J. | CALIFORNIA

Cabernet Sauvignon Dry Creek Valley 1989 • $12 • (08/31/92) • **86**
Chardonnay Russian River Valley Dutton Ranch 1996: Shows off some pretty, toasty oak, but has the rich, concentrated fruit to stand up to it, with layers of ripe fig, pear, apricot and hazelnut. Holds its focus on a long, lingering aftertaste. Drink now through 2002. 2,000 cases made. • $20 • (06/30/98) • **91**
Chardonnay Russian River Valley Dutton Ranch Cuvée de Terre 1994: A ripe and full-flavored wine that shows off firm oak shadings and a core of ripe pear, melon and apple flavors. Finishes on the dry side. 300 cases made. • $20 • (11/30/96) • **89**
Chardonnay Russian River Valley Dutton Vineyard Ruxton Ranch 1996: Pure fruit. Ripe with honeysuckle, melon and pear flavors, with good intensity and concentration. Finishes with a pretty, spicy aftertaste. Drink now through 2000. 400 cases made. • $26 • (06/30/98) • **87**
Chardonnay Russian River Valley Dutton Vineyard Shop Block 1996: Well oaked, with lots of toast and smoke, the rich, concentrated core of pear, fig, spice and anise works its way into the mainstream. Long and full-bodied on the aftertaste. Drink now through 2002. 200 cases made. • $30 • (06/30/98) • **91**
Chardonnay Russian River Valley Poplar Vineyard 1996: Pleasantly fruity, ripe with spicy pear, apple and light oak shadings, turning simpler on the finish. Drink now through 2000. 500 cases made. • $22 • (06/30/98) • **87**
Chardonnay Sonoma County 1993 • $10 • (07/31/95) • **82**
Melon Russian River Valley 1994 • $12 • (05/31/96) • **83**
Sauvignon Blanc Dry Creek Valley 1994 • $9 • (08/31/95) • **83**
Sauvignon Blanc Dry Creek Valley 1993 • $8 • (06/30/94) BB • **86**
Sauvignon Blanc Dry Creek Valley Jenner Vineyard 1996: Marked by a buttery quality, this also offers almond, fig and sugar snap flavors. Finishes with nice touches of sweetness and toast. • $12 • (03/31/98) • **87**
Sauvignon Blanc Russian River Valley Poplar Vineyard 1996: An effusive style, redolent of wildflowers and hazelnuts. On the palate, it serves up bright citrus, especially grapefruit, flavors. Finishes a bit short, but quite attractive overall. • $12 • (03/31/98) • **89**
Zinfandel Dry Creek Valley 1986 • $9 • (03/15/89) • **86**
Zinfandel Dry Creek Valley 1984 • $7 • (02/15/88) • **84**
Zinfandel Dry Creek Valley Eighty-Year-Old Vines 1993 • $12 • (10/15/95) • **84**

Zinfandel Dry Creek Valley Eighty-Year-Old Vines 1992 • $10 • (10/15/94) • **83**

Zinfandel Dry Creek Valley Eighty-Year-Old Vines 1991 • $10 • (09/30/93) • **82**

Zinfandel Dry Creek Valley Eighty-Year-Old Vines 1990 • $10 • (10/15/92) • **82**

Zinfandel Dry Creek Valley Eighty-Year-Old Vines 1989 • $10 • (03/31/92) • **84**

Zinfandel Dry Creek Valley Eighty-Year-Old Vines 1988 • $10 • (07/31/91) • **79**

Zinfandel Dry Creek Valley Old Vine 1996: Medium-bodied, with a focused core of wild berry, black cherry, strawberry and tealike flavors. Well balanced, with firm, grainy tannins and good length. Drink now through 2002. 800 cases made. • $20 • (06/15/98) • **88**

Zinfandel Dry Creek Valley Rogers' Reserve Eighty-Year-Old-Vines 1996: Crisp, with firm tannins and a modest core of plum and black cherry flavors. Fills out a bit at midpalate. Drink now through 2002. 100 cases made. • $28 • (06/15/98) • **86**

Zinfandel Dry Creek Valley Rogers' Reserve Eighty-Year-Old Vines 1994: A ripe and flavorful style, brimming with zesty cherry, raspberry, plum and wild berry flavors. Finishes with firm tannins, but they're gentle enough to let the fruit shine through. 200 cases made. • $18 • (10/15/96) • **88**

FROG'S LEAP | CALIFORNIA

Cabernet Sauvignon Napa Valley 1994: Well focused, with ripe, complex plum, raspberry, cherry and currant flavors of good intensity. Keeps its fruit and focus through the finish, where the tannins are lively but ripe. Impressive now. A blend of 88 percent Cabernet Sauvignon and 12 percent Cabernet Franc. 3,800 cases made. • $20 • (11/15/96) • **88**

Cabernet Sauvignon Napa Valley 1990 • $17 • (09/30/93) • **88**

Cabernet Sauvignon Napa Valley 1989 • $17 • (07/15/92) • **79**

Cabernet Sauvignon Napa Valley 1988 • $16 Ⓐ • (12/15/90) • **88**

Cabernet Sauvignon Napa Valley 1987: Starting to fade, as the drying tannins dominate the leathery currant and black cherry flavors. Still enjoyable, but the fruit is dropping out. 5,000 cases made. • $39 • (12/15/97) • **84**

Cabernet Sauvignon Napa Valley 1986: Big and ripe still, a bit dry and tannic, but shows more depth and concentration than many subsequent releases from this producer. The currant, cedar, herb and spice flavors are mature. 2,600 cases made. • $NA • (12/15/96) • **88**

Cabernet Sauvignon Napa Valley 1985 • $12 • (12/31/87) • **82**

Cabernet Sauvignon Napa Valley 1984 • $12 • (03/31/87) SS • **95**

Cabernet Sauvignon Napa Valley 1983 • $10 • (05/16/86) • **85**

Chardonnay Carneros 1996: Simple, with tart, earthy pear and citrus flavors of modest depth and proportion. Drink now. 6,900 cases made. • $19 • (05/15/98) • **85**

Chardonnay Carneros 1995: Delivers some earth tones and attractive apple and lemon flavors offset by judicious use of oak and backed by bright, but not overwhelming, acidity. 6,000 cases made. • $19 • (06/15/97) • **88**

Leapfrögmilch Napa Valley 1997: Bright and lemony, refreshing and light. On the finish, it has a mineral edge that adds a bit of complexity. Drink now. 2,000 cases made. • $16 • (06/30/98) • **83**

Merlot Napa Valley 1994: Lean and trim, with a supple band of cedar, currant, herb and tobacco flavors. Finishes with a firm tannic edge. Drinkable now. 10,000 cases made. • $20 • (06/30/97) • **87**

Merlot Napa Valley 1993 • $NA • (04/30/96) • **87**

Merlot Napa Valley 1991 • $17 • (05/31/94) • **88**

Merlot Napa Valley 1990 • $17 • (01/31/93) • **84**

Sauvignon Blanc Late Harvest Napa Valley Late Leap 1989 • $14/375ml • (10/31/91) • **84**

Sauvignon Blanc Late Harvest Napa Valley Late Leap 1986 • $9/375ml • (09/30/88) • **85**

Sauvignon Blanc Napa Valley 1996: A bit green, its grassiness dominating the sweet pea and lime flavors behind it. Finishes a bit short. 16,000 cases made. • $13 • (06/30/97) BB • **83**

Sauvignon Blanc Napa Valley 1995: Unripe grapefruit flavors are too tart, unwelcoming. Tasted twice with consistent notes. 20,000 cases made. • $13 • (09/15/96) • **76**

Sauvignon Blanc Napa Valley 1994 • $11 • (09/15/95) • **80**

Key: SS—Spectator Selection CS—Cellar Selection HR—Highly Recommended BB—Best Buy $NA—Price not available Ⓐ—Auction Price (BT)—Barrel Tasting
Dates in parentheses indicate the issues in which the ratings were published.

Zinfandel Napa Valley 1995: An elegant style that doesn't try to overpower, succeeding with its ripe plum and cherry flavors and fine, polished tannins. Drink now through 2000. 7,100 cases made. • $16 • (06/15/98) • **87**

Zinfandel Napa Valley 1994: This bold Zin unfolds to reveal interesting flavors of wild berry, cherry, raspberry and spice. Finishes with a distinctive dash of sage and a sense of elegance. Ready to drink. 5,500 cases made. • $15 • (03/31/97) SS • **89**

Zinfandel Napa Valley 1992 • $13 • (10/15/94) • **68**

Zinfandel Napa Valley 1991 • $12 • (09/30/93) • **85**

Zinfandel Napa Valley 1990 • $12 • (10/15/92) • **80**

Zinfandel Napa Valley 1989 • $12 • (11/15/91) • **83**

Zinfandel Napa Valley 1988 • $12 • (12/15/90) • **88**

Zinfandel Napa Valley 1987 • $11 • (03/15/90) • **86**

Zinfandel Napa Valley 1986 • $10 • (12/15/88) • **85**

Zinfandel Napa Valley 1985 • $9 • (11/15/87) • **79**

G'SELL | CALIFORNIA

Chardonnay Alexander Valley Limited Reserve 1996: Toasty oak and pretty pear flavors blend well, but it finishes with a hint of bitterness. 600 cases made. • $15 • (07/31/98) • **83**

Chardonnay Sonoma County Limited Reserve 1995: Sweet, with a tutti-frutti, canned fruit-cocktail edge. Lacks focus and depth on the finish. Drink now. 600 cases made. • $15 • (05/15/98) • **83**

Zinfandel Sonoma County 1996: Licorice and herb flavors set the tone in this rustic wine. It's a little weedy, but is enhanced by blackberry and mint character. Drink now. 380 cases made. • $15 • (06/15/98) • **82**

GABRIELLI | CALIFORNIA

Pinot Noir Anderson Valley Floodgate Vineyard 1995: A decidedly herbal edge leads the way in this lighter-styled wine. Crisp and tangy, it also shows layers of clove, spice, anise and black currant. Tannins are a bit coarse. 500 cases made. • $18 • (09/30/97) • **87**

Pinot Noir Mendocino County 1995: A smooth-textured wine, with pretty cherry, cola and herb flavors. Firm, powdery tannins give it a fresh, clean finish. 600 cases made. • $14 • (01/31/98) • **87**

Pinot Noir Mendocino County Weir Vineyard 1995: A bit rough-edged, but with nice blackberry, licorice and herb notes. Chunky texture might be do to overextraction from skins. Needs a year or two to soften. 500 cases made. • $18 • (02/28/98) • **84**

Pinot Noir Mendocino Reserve 1995: A focused wine, with plush, round tannins that frame bright black cherry, cola, clove and other spice flavors. Good integration, with sweet oak on the finish. 60 cases made. • $25 • (09/30/97) • **88**

Sangiovese Mendocino 1995: Ripe and generous with its blackberry and anise flavors, a polished mouthful of fruit and spice that lingers nicely. Ready now. 985 cases made. • $14 • (11/30/96) • **87**

Syrah Redwood Valley 1995: Firm, chewy red with solid blackberry flavors hiding beneath a layer of tannin. Needs until 1999 to 2000 to open up. 1,007 cases made. • $18 • (03/31/98) • **86**

Zinfandel Mendocino 1993 • $12 • (07/31/95) • **86**

Zinfandel Mendocino 1992 • $12 • (10/15/94) • **85**

Zinfandel Mendocino 1991 • $10 • (12/31/93) • **85**

Zinfandel Mendocino 1990 • $10 • (10/15/92) • **85**

Zinfandel Mendocino County 1995: Woody and astringent up front. On the finish, some pleasant pepper, green olive and black currant flavors arise. 2,500 cases made. • $14 • (03/31/98) • **82**

Zinfandel Mendocino Reserve 1994: This rustic wine shows hefty tannins that still can't hide its robust leather, blackberry and licorice flavors. 500 cases made. • $18 • (09/15/97) • **84**

Zinfandel Mendocino Reserve 1992 • $18 • (10/15/94) • **84**

Zinfandel Mendocino Reserve 1991 • $16 • (03/31/94) • **84**

Zinfandel Mendocino Reserve 1990 • $16 • (10/15/92) • **82**

Zinfandel Redwood Valley Goforth Vineyard 1995: Black pepper, spice, juicy black cherry, plum and toasty oak conspire to create an enjoyable red. A bit on the bright side though. 500 cases made. • $18 • (06/15/98) • **85**

GAINEY | CALIFORNIA

Cabernet Franc Santa Ynez Valley Limited Selection 1990 • $16 • (10/15/93) • **88**

Cabernet Sauvignon Santa Barbara County 1987 • $13 • (11/15/90) • **82**

Cabernet Sauvignon Santa Barbara County Limited Selection 1989 • $20 • (11/15/92) • **83**

Cabernet Sauvignon Santa Barbara County Limited Selection 1986 • $15 • (12/15/89) • **89**
Cabernet Sauvignon Santa Maria Valley 1988 • $13 • (03/15/92) • **77**
Cabernet Sauvignon Santa Ynez Valley 1989 • $13 • (11/15/92) • **77**
Cabernet Sauvignon Santa Ynez Valley Limited Selection 1988 • $20 • (03/10/92) • **75**
Chardonnay Santa Barbara County 1993 • $14 • (07/31/95) • **86**
Chardonnay Santa Barbara County Limited Selection 1996: An exotic yet elegant style, with an earthy streak running through the stream of ripe pear, fig, apricot and melon. Holds its flavor and gains finesse on the finish. Drink now through 2002. 1,500 cases made. • $25 • (07/31/98) • **91**
Chardonnay Santa Ynez Valley Limited Selection 1995: Ripe and full-bodied, with an exotic mix of complex and concentrated flavors—creamy pear, pineapple, citrus, honey and hazelnut—finishing with a beautiful anise and butter aftertaste. 886 cases made. • $25 • (06/15/97) • **93**
Chardonnay Santa Ynez Valley Limited Selection 1994: Pleasantly balanced, ripe and elegant, with layers of rich pear, honey, vanilla and spice. The flavors become delicate and elegant on the finish. 701 cases made. • $25 • (06/30/96) • **88**
Chardonnay Santa Ynez Valley Limited Selection 1993 • $25 • (07/31/95) • **91**
Johannisberg Riesling Santa Barbara County 1995 • $9 • (06/15/96) • **83**
Johannisberg Riesling Santa Ynez Valley 1996: Frankly sweet, but soft and appealing for its delicate pear flavors that linger on the finish. Ready now. 3,125 cases made. • $10 • (11/30/97) • **83**
Johannisberg Riesling Santa Ynez Valley 1994 • $8 • (09/15/95) • **87**
Merlot Santa Barbara County 1989 • $14 • (05/31/92) • **70**
Merlot Santa Barbara County 1988 • $13 • (04/15/91) • **82**
Merlot Santa Ynez Valley 1990 • $14 • (07/15/93) • **83**
Merlot Santa Ynez Valley Limited Selection 1990 • $20 • (10/15/93) • **76**
Merlot Santa Ynez Valley Limited Selection 1988 • $20 • (02/29/92) • **89**
Pinot Noir Santa Barbara County 1990 • $15 • (02/28/94) • **87**
Pinot Noir Santa Barbara County 1986 • $15 • (12/15/89) • **88**
Pinot Noir Santa Maria Valley 1989 • $18 • (09/30/92) • **74**
Pinot Noir Santa Ynez Valley Limited Reserve 1991 • $30 • (02/28/94) • **88**
Pinot Noir Santa Ynez Valley Limited Selection 1990 • $25 • (02/28/94) • **85**
Pinot Noir Santa Ynez Valley Limited Selection 1989 • $25 • (02/28/93) • **83**
Pinot Noir Santa Ynez Valley Limited Selection 1988 • $25 • (11/15/91) • **86**
Pinot Noir Santa Ynez Valley Sanford and Benedict Vineyard 1993 • $30 • (04/30/96) • **84**
Sauvignon Blanc Santa Ynez Valley Limited Selection 1993 • $16 • (08/31/95) • **83**

GALANTE | CALIFORNIA

Cabernet Sauvignon Carmel Valley Blackjack Pasture 1994: Young and tight, with a note of green olive to the cherry and currant flavors. Finishes with mild tannins. Drinkable now. 570 cases made. • $30 • (10/15/96) • **86**
Cabernet Sauvignon Carmel Valley Red Rose Hill 1994: Intense and tannic, but not out of bounds for a wine this young. Shows off cedar, herb and currant flavors but they're tightly wound, as Carmel Valley Cabernets often are. Drinkable now. 1,400 cases made. • $25 • (10/15/96) • **85**

GALLERON | CALIFORNIA

Cabernet Sauvignon Napa Valley 1994: Smooth, ripe and juicy, with lots of ripe, rich, complex currant, plum and wild berry flavors. Turns complex on the finish, where it shows its depth and concentration, with flavors fanning out. 150 cases made. • $50 • (09/30/97) • **91**
Cabernet Sauvignon Napa Valley 1993: Smooth and supple, with a nice interplay of ripe cherry, plum and currant flavors that turn elegant and spicy on the finish. Light oak notes and mild tannins make it pleasing now. From Gary Galleron, winemaker at Whitehall Lane.• $40 • (11/15/96) • **88**

GALLO, E. & J. | CALIFORNIA

Cabernet Sauvignon California NV • $5 • (08/31/92) BB • **80**
Cabernet Sauvignon California Limited Release Reserve 1980 • $8 • (11/15/86) • **78**
Cabernet Sauvignon California Reserve NV • $6 • (11/15/91) • **84**
Cabernet Sauvignon Northern Sonoma 1985 • $8 • (08/31/92) • **80**
Cabernet Sauvignon Northern Sonoma Estate Bottled 1993: Well focused, if a bit dry and earthy around the edges, its core of ripe plum and cherry flavor is ripe, dense and complex. Turns dry on the finish; cellar into 1999 to 2000. 1,792 cases made. • $45 • (10/31/97) • **90**
Cabernet Sauvignon Northern Sonoma Estate Bottled 1992: A remarkably ripe, rich and complex wine, tight and firm. Well structured and well endowed with currant, mineral, anise and berry flavors. Finishes with a long, complex aftertaste that echoes fruit and oak flavors. Drink now. 3,671 cases made. • $45 • (11/15/96) • **92**
Cabernet Sauvignon Northern Sonoma Estate Bottled 1991 • $50 • (11/15/94) HR • **91**
Cabernet Sauvignon Northern Sonoma Estate Bottled 1990 • $60 • (10/31/93) CS • **93**
Cabernet Sauvignon Northern Sonoma Limited Release 1981 • $5 • (12/31/88) • **75**
Cabernet Sauvignon Northern Sonoma Reserve 1984 • $7 • (10/15/91) • **80**
Cabernet Sauvignon Northern Sonoma Reserve 1982 • $6 • (05/31/91) BB • **82**
Chardonnay Northern Sonoma Estate Bottled 1995: A well-oaked style, with toast, vanilla and smoky flavors up front, it's core of rich, concentrated Chardonnay fruit easily rises to the occasion, adding loads of fig, pear, spice and melon flavors to the mix and finishing with a satisfying, long and lively aftertaste. • $35 • (02/28/98) HR • **94**
Chardonnay Northern Sonoma Estate Bottled 1994: Elegant and complex, with layers of ripe, rich pear, fig, melon and citrus accented by a slightly smoky, toasty note. Gains depth on the finish, where the flavors fan out. Delicious now. 700 cases made. • $30 • (09/30/96) • **92**
Chardonnay Northern Sonoma Estate Bottled 1993 • $30 • (07/31/95) • **88**
Classic Burgundy California NV: Earthy barnyard notes add some welcome complexity to the spicy cherry flavors. Has a touch of bitterness on the finish, but drinks well now. • $11/1.5 liter • (05/15/98) • **81**
White Zinfandel California 1994 • $3 • (09/15/95) • **79**
Zinfandel North Coast 1992 • $6 • (08/31/95) • **82**
Zinfandel Northern Sonoma 1990 • $5 • (08/31/94) BB • **88**
Zinfandel Northern Sonoma 1987 • $5 • (09/30/93) BB • **84**

GALLO OF SONOMA | CALIFORNIA

Cabernet Sauvignon Dry Creek Valley Frei Ranch Vineyard 1993: Dense and chewy, with a wall of firm tannins and a core of tarry plum and dried cherry flavors. Quite dry on the finish. Drinkable now, but stay mindful of the tannins' status. 3,100 cases made. • $18 • (11/15/97) • **87**
Cabernet Sauvignon Dry Creek Valley Frei Ranch Vineyard 1992 • $16 • (11/15/95) • **89**
Cabernet Sauvignon Sonoma County 1994: Beef, black cherry, cedar and spice flavors rise to the fore in this medium-bodied, somewhat effusive yet tannic wine. Drink now or hold. 35,000 cases made. • $10 • (10/31/97) • **84**
Cabernet Sauvignon Sonoma County 1992 • $12 • (11/15/95) • **87**
Cabernet Sauvignon Sonoma County 1991 • $12 • (03/31/95) SS • **90**
Cabernet Sauvignon Sonoma County 1990 • $10 • (11/15/94) BB • **86**
Chardonnay Dry Creek Valley Stefani Vineyard 1996: A crisp, flinty style, with fresh pear, quince and tart apple. Not as rich and opulent as the Laguna Ranch bottling, but still well-balanced, with attractive, complex flavors. Drink now through 2000. 17,000 cases made. • $16 • (05/31/98) • **88**
Chardonnay Dry Creek Valley Stefani Vineyard 1995: An estate-bottled Chardonnay from Gallo's quality-oriented holdings in northern Sonoma, this is fresh and lively, with complex pear, apple, spice and nutmeg notes, turning smooth and silky on the finish where it unveils a smoky accent. Delicious, and a value at this price and score. 5,500 cases made. • $14 • (05/15/97) SS • **91**
Chardonnay Dry Creek Valley Stefani Vineyard 1994: Clean, vibrant, appealing pear and spice notes finish in light, toasty oak shadings. Solid, if unspectacular. 4,108 cases made. • $16 • (05/15/96) • **87**
Chardonnay Russian River Valley 1996: Crisp, with a flinty edge to the core of citrus, pear and earthy Chardonnay flavors. A good value. Drink now. • $11 • (06/30/98) • **84**
Chardonnay Russian River Valley Laguna Ranch Vineyard 1996: Delicious, rich and flavorful, loaded with spice, pear, apple, fig and melon. Turns elegant and refined on the finish, where the flavors linger. Drink now through 2001. 17,000 cases made. • $18 • (05/31/98) SS • **91**
Chardonnay Russian River Valley Laguna Ranch Vineyard 1995: From Gallo's quality-oriented holdings comes this bright and lively Chardonnay, with a juicy core of citrus, pear and spice flavors underscored by firm acidity that keeps the flavors lively. Finishes with a clean, elegant aftertaste. 11,000 cases made. • $16 • (09/30/97) SS • **90**

Chardonnay Russian River Valley Laguna Ranch Vineyard 1994: The seductive, complex smoky oak and exotic fruit flavors turn more elegant and refined on the palate as the tiers of earthy pear, grapefruit and spice show through. Finishes with a delicate touch. The first Gallo Chardonnay from Laguna Ranch Vineyard. 6,195 cases made. • $16 • (04/30/96) HR • **92**
Chardonnay Sonoma County 1995: A bright and polished white, with a strong layer of spicy oak complementing its generous portion of citrusy peach and honey flavors. It's tasty, ready to drink and reasonably priced. 35,000 cases made. • $10 • (11/30/97) BB • **87**
Chardonnay Sonoma County 1993 • $12 • (06/30/95) • **87**
Merlot Dry Creek Valley Frei Ranch Vineyard 1992 • $15 • (05/15/95) • **82**
Merlot Dry Creek Valley Frei Ranch Vineyard 1991 • $15 • (09/15/94) • **84**
Merlot Northern Sonoma 1993 • $15 • (04/30/96) • **87**
Valdiguié Alexander Valley Barrelli Creek Vineyard 1994: A rustic style with chunky berry and earth notes, even a slight metallic edge on the finish. Worth a try for a trip down memory lane. 4,000 cases made. • $12 • (05/15/97) • **82**
Zinfandel Alexander Valley Barrelli Creek Vineyard 1995: Ripe, with lovely jam, wild berry, cherry and plum-laced Zinfandel flavors that are complex, concentrated and well proportioned. It's long and fruity on the aftertaste, where the tannins feel smooth and rich. Ready to drink, and a value, too. 2,200 cases made. • $14 • (06/15/98) SS • **90**
Zinfandel Dry Creek Valley Chiotti Vineyard 1995: Well crafted and complex, with interesting, earth-accented wildberry, raspberry, tar and sage flavors. Best now. What a find at this price. 2,038 cases made. • $12 • (06/15/97) • **90**
Zinfandel Dry Creek Valley Frei Ranch Vineyard 1995: Elegant and refined. Firm and tightly wound, well focused, too, with ripe, complex raspberry, cherry, earth and cedary notes. Drink now through 2001. 9,900 cases made. • $14 • (06/15/98) • **87**
Zinfandel Dry Creek Valley Frei Ranch Vineyard 1994: Austere, with a dry edge to the modest plum and wild berry flavors; dryness on the finish is difficult to overlook. 5,300 cases made. • $14 • (08/31/97) • **84**
Zinfandel Dry Creek Valley Frei Ranch Vineyard 1993 • $14 • (04/30/96) • **87**
Zinfandel Dry Creek Valley Frei Ranch Vineyard 1992 • $15 • (09/15/95) • **85**
Zinfandel Dry Creek Valley Frei Ranch Vineyard 1991 • $14 • (02/28/95) SS • **90**
Zinfandel Dry Creek Valley Frei Ranch Vineyard 1990 • $14 • (07/31/94) SS • **90**
Zinfandel Sonoma County 1995: Displays appetizing earthy and meaty aromas followed by a mouthful of focused plum, currant and blackberry jam flavors that glide to a long and silky finish. A best buy. 10,000 cases made. • $10 • (11/15/97) BB • **87**

GAN EDEN | CALIFORNIA

Black Muscat San Joaquin County 1995: Smells pleasant, with berry and spice notes, but it wimps out on the palate, fading fast. Has 3.75 percent residual sugar. 3,000 cases made. • $10 • (05/15/97) • **78**
Black Muscat San Joaquin County 1993 • $7 • (05/15/95) • **80**
Cabernet Sauvignon Alexander Valley 1989 • $14 • (07/31/95) • **83**
Cabernet Sauvignon Alexander Valley 1988 • $18 • (03/31/93) • **77**
Cabernet Sauvignon Alexander Valley 1987 • $18 • (03/31/91) • **90**
Cabernet Sauvignon Alexander Valley 1986 • $15 • (02/15/89) • **86**
Chardonnay Sonoma County 1994: Like canned pears with a tangy finish. Strange. 4,000 cases made. • $12 • (07/31/97) • **77**
Chardonnay Sonoma County 1993 • $12 • (07/31/95) • **88**
Chardonnay Sonoma County Reserve 1993 • $14 • (07/31/95) • **78**
Chenin Blanc Lake County 1995: Unusually crisp and mineral-like for Chenin Blanc. Its bright edge and lemony finish make it a fine candidate for the catch of the day. 1,500 cases made. • $9 • (09/15/97) • **87**
Gewürztraminer Late Harvest Monterey County 1993 • $8 • (09/30/95) • **81**
Moscato Nero San Joaquin County 1995: Flavors of sweet peas and cherries are highlighted by a peppery quality. Finishes with a clean, herbal edge. Has 2 percent residual sugar. 1,200 cases made. • $10 • (09/15/97) • **82**
Sauvignon Blanc Sonoma County 1993 • $8 • (08/31/94) • **83**
Sémillon Sonoma County 1993 • $14 • (06/30/95) • **83**

Key: SS—Spectator Selection CS—Cellar Selection HR—Highly Recommended BB—Best Buy $NA—Price not available Ⓐ—Auction Price (BT)—Barrel Tasting
Dates in parentheses indicate the issues in which the ratings were published.

GARLAND RANCH | CALIFORNIA

Cabernet Sauvignon Central Coast 1986 • $6 • (10/31/89) • **70**
Cabernet Sauvignon Monterey County 1984 • $6 • (08/31/88) BB • **84**
Merlot California 1986 • $6 • (05/31/92) • **76**

GAUER ESTATE | CALIFORNIA

Cabernet Sauvignon Alexander Valley 1988 • $18 • (08/31/92) • **84**
Merlot Alexander Valley 1990 • $16 • (06/15/93) • **84**

GEHRS, DANIEL | CALIFORNIA

Chenin Blanc Monterey County Carmel Vineyard Le Cheniere 1996: Minerals and herbs mesh cleanly in this crisp, almost bracing style of Chenin Blanc. A certain weightiness on the midpalate brings it back to earth with a moderate finish. 1,344 cases made. • $9 • (09/15/97) • **86**
Chenin Blanc Monterey County Carmel Vineyard Le Cheniere 1994 • $8 • (06/15/96) • **82**
Chenin Blanc Monterey County Le Chenay 1993 • $8 • (12/31/94) • **84**
Chenin Blanc Santa Barbara County Le Cheniere 1993 • $8 • (12/31/94) • **83**
Fleetwood Cucamonga Valley 1996: Simple, straightforward and cherrylike. Finishes with a waxy, herbal edge. A blend of Grenache, Mourvèdre and Syrah. 543 cases made. • $9 • (09/30/97) • **80**
Muscadet Monterey County Carmel Vineyard 1995: Crisp and tight, with a bright, narrow beam of Jonathan apple flavor that echoes lightly on the finish. 350 cases made. • $9 • (12/15/96) • **82**
Muscadet Monterey County Carmel Vineyard 1994 • $8 • (05/31/96) • **82**
Muscadet Monterey County Carmel Vineyard 1993 • $8 • (12/15/94) • **84**
Pinot Blanc Monterey County Carmel Vineyard 1996: Fairly sweet. A simple quaffer with peach and melon overtones. Drink well chilled. 1,222 cases made. • $11 • (09/15/97) • **82**
Pinot Blanc Monterey County Carmel Vineyard 1995: A fresh and open texture shows off the melon and citrus flavors, hitting a resiny note on the finish. 560 cases made. • $10 • (04/30/97) • **83**
Pinot Blanc Monterey County Carmel Vineyard 1994 • $10 • (04/30/96) • **84**
Pinot Blanc Monterey County Carmel Vineyard 1993 • $10 • (12/15/94) • **81**
Pinot Noir Monterey County El Segundo Vineyard 1996: Marked by pretty cherry, cola and spice flavors, with a bright, tangy finish. Light on the palate. 545 cases made. • $14 • (01/31/98) • **85**
Rosé Monterey County El Segundo Vineyard Fleetwood 1995: Pale pink in color, with a fragrant strawberry and black cherry accent. Finishes with a delicate aftertaste. 100 percent Pinot Noir. 332 cases made. • $9 • (09/15/96) • **84**
Sauvignon Blanc Monterey County Carmel Vineyard Fumé En Vogue 1996: Ripe fig and melon qualities are attractive, but clash rather than blend with what should be classic herbaceousness. The sweetness on the finish is the culprit. 1,398 cases made. • $10 • (09/15/97) • **81**
Sauvignon Blanc Monterey County Carmel Vineyard Fumé En Vogue 1995: Crisp and flavorful. Shows a nice core of peach flavor, with pleasant grass and spice notes floating on top. Finish is zingy and polished. 840 cases made. • $9 • (10/31/96) • **89**
Sauvignon Blanc Monterey County Carmel Vineyard Fumé En Vogue 1993 • $9 • (12/15/94) • **83**

GEMELLO | CALIFORNIA

Zinfandel Mendocino 1993 • $16 • (10/15/95) • **80**
Zinfandel Mendocino 60th Anniversary 1934-1994 1992 • $16 • (10/15/95) • **82**
Zinfandel Mendocino County 1990 • $16 • (09/30/93) • **84**

GEORIS | CALIFORNIA

Merlot Carmel Valley 1994: Difficult to warm up to with its tart, green, earthy flavors and dry, leathery tannins. Best to cellar in hopes it will improve. 1,200 cases made. • $35 • (06/30/97) • **80**
Merlot Carmel Valley 1992: Smooth, polished and tannic, offering cherry and wild berry notes and hints of sage and spice. Firm tannins on the finish; good depth of flavor. 800 cases made. • $28 • (08/31/96) • **89**
Merlot Carmel Valley 1989 • $25 • (05/15/93) • **87**
Merlot Carmel Valley 1987 • $27 • (03/31/91) • **89**
Merlot Carmel Valley 1986 • $25 • (12/31/90) • **77**
Merlot Carmel Valley 1985 • $20 • (04/15/89) • **83**

GEYSER PEAK | CALIFORNIA

Cabernet Sauvignon Alexander Valley 1993: Clean and well balanced, with spicy berry and cherry flavors. Drink now. 38,000 cases made. • $10 • (12/15/95) • **83**
Cabernet Sauvignon Alexander Valley 1989 • $9 • (11/15/92) • **82**
Cabernet Sauvignon Alexander Valley 1984 • $7 • (03/15/88) • **77**
Cabernet Sauvignon Alexander Valley 1983 • $7 • (03/15/87) BB • **87**
Cabernet Sauvignon Alexander Valley 1982 • $7 • (09/15/86) • **68**
Cabernet Sauvignon Alexander Valley 1980 • $6 • (01/01/85) • **57**
Cabernet Sauvignon Alexander Valley Reserve 1996: Complex, lean and trim now, but the herb, cherry and currant flavors are attractive, with hints of plum, green olive, herb and tea. Chewy tannins. 6,000 cases made. • $25 • (06/15/97) (BT) • **85-89**
Cabernet Sauvignon Alexander Valley Reserve 1994: A well-oaked style that's marked by herb and cedar notes, it opens to show more currant and black cherry flavors. Given its youthful vibrancy and strong oak influence, best to cellar into 2000. May move up a point or two with time. 5,700 cases made. • $28 • (05/31/97) • **89**
Cabernet Sauvignon Alexander Valley Reserve 1993: Smooth and polished, with a marked herbal edge to the ripe berry and cherry flavors. Appealing now and into 1997. 2,733 cases made. • $20 • (12/15/95) • **88**
Cabernet Sauvignon Alexander Valley Reserve 1991 • $20 • (03/15/94) SS • **90**
Cabernet Sauvignon Alexander Valley Reserve 1990 • $15 • (06/15/93) HR • **90**
Cabernet Sauvignon Alexander Valley Reserve 1989 • $14 • (11/15/92) • **87**
Cabernet Sauvignon Alexander Valley Reserve 1987: Plenty of ripe, juicy cherry, currant and plummy Cabernet flavors, and a shade of dill-laced oak flavors. Turns dry and tannic on the finish, where hints of sage and black olive add a nice dimension. Best now through 2000. • $28 • (12/15/97) • **89**
Cabernet Sauvignon Alexander Valley Reserve 1986 • $15 • (09/30/90) • **85**
Cabernet Sauvignon Alexander Valley Reserve 1985 • $15 • (05/15/89) • **77**
Cabernet Sauvignon Sonoma County 1995: Showing focus and finesse, this packs a core of bright cherry, blackberry and anise flavors. Has a meaty texture supported by velvety tannins, and a long, smoky finish. A fine value and widely available. 46,000 cases made. • $15 • (10/31/97) • **88**
Cabernet Sauvignon Sonoma County 1994: Supple and well balanced, with a smooth texture and a band of ripe plum, cherry and currant flavors. Turns supple on the finish, where the tannins are ripe and elegant. 40,000 cases made. • $10 • (11/15/96) BB • **86**
Cabernet Sauvignon Sonoma County 1991 • $10 • (03/15/94) • **84**
Cabernet Sauvignon Sonoma County 1990 • $10 • (06/15/93) • **81**
Cabernet Sauvignon Sonoma County 1987 • $8 • (11/30/90) BB • **88**
Cabernet Sauvignon Sonoma County 1981 • $7 • (06/16/85) • **83**
Chardonnay Alexander Valley Reserve 1996: Serves up lots of ripe, creamy pear, spice, fig and melon flavors, which linger on the elegant, polished finish. Drink now through 2001. 4,000 cases made. • $20 • (07/31/98) • **89**
Chardonnay Alexander Valley Reserve 1995: Generous with its ripe, rich pear, fig, melon and anise flavors that are intense and lively. Clamps down a bit on the finish and it's a touch coarse, but a few more months in the bottle should do the trick. 3,740 cases made. • $23 • (05/31/97) • **90**
Chardonnay Alexander Valley Reserve 1994: Strikes a nice balance between ripe pear, fig and honey notes and traces of citrus and spice. Turns elegant on the finish, but loses some of its intensity. 3,500 cases made. • $20 • (05/15/96) • **89**
Chardonnay Alexander Valley Reserve 1993 • $20 • (04/15/95) HR • **90**
Chardonnay Sonoma County 1996: A crisp, refreshing, fruit-up-front style, with ripe pear, grapefruit and pear flavors unobstructed by toasty oak. Drink now. 50,000 cases made. • $14 • (06/15/98) • **87**
Chardonnay Sonoma County 1995: Shows off its ripe pear and citrus flavors, especially tangerine, in a crisp, elegant style. 50,000 cases made. • $12 • (01/31/97) • **85**
Chardonnay Sonoma County 1993 • $10 • (12/15/94) BB • **85**
Gewürztraminer California 1997: Peachy aromas and a canned, syrupy sweet edge make this wine a little hard to swallow. Marginal. 15,000 cases made. • $8 • (06/30/98) • **74**
Gewürztraminer California 1996: Simple and sweet, with an odd, peppery floral character. Awkward finish. Tasted twice, with consistent notes. 15,700 cases made. • $7 • (11/30/97) • **79**
Gewürztraminer California 1995 • $7 • (06/15/96) BB • **86**
Gewürztraminer North Coast 1993 • $6 • (01/31/95) • **84**
Johannisberg Riesling California 1997: An off-dry style, with tangy peach and apple notes. Fairly simple and easy to quaff. Drink now. 39,000 cases made. • $8 • (06/30/98) • **82**
Johannisberg Riesling California 1996: Simple and refreshing, lightly sweet, with hints of resin and flower amidst the modest apple flavors. 36,000 cases made. • $8 • (05/15/97) • **84**
Johannisberg Riesling California Soft 1995 • $7 • (06/15/96) BB • **84**
Johannisberg Riesling Late Harvest Mendocino County Selected Dried Berry 1990 • $13/375ml • (08/31/91) • **93**
Johannisberg Riesling Late Harvest Russian River Valley Selected Dried Berry 1991 • $16/375ml • (10/15/92) HR • **90**
Johannisberg Riesling North Coast Soft 1994 • $6 • (09/30/95) BB • **85**
Malbec Alexander Valley 1991 • $10 • (03/31/94) • **85**
Malbec Alexander Valley Trione Vineyards Winemaker's Selection 1993 • $18 • (03/31/96) • **83**
Merlot Alexander Valley 1992 • $12 • (01/31/95) • **85**
Merlot Alexander Valley 1991 • $13 • (06/15/93) • **87**
Merlot Alexander Valley 1989 • $9 • (05/31/92) • **79**
Merlot Alexander Valley 1987 • $8 • (07/15/90) • **82**
Merlot Alexander Valley 1985 • $7 • (10/15/88) • **77**
Merlot Alexander Valley 1983 • $7 • (12/31/86) • **80**
Merlot Alexander Valley Reserve 1995: Offers ripe, complex, chewy plum, mineral, sage, tea and herbal flavors, turning deep and rich on the finish, where the flavors are focused and lively. Has the tannic strength to age. Best from 2000 through 2006. 470 cases made. • $32 • (07/31/98) • **88**
Merlot Alexander Valley Reserve 1994: Strikes a nice balance between ripe fruit and spicy oak, picking up a cedary edge on the finish, where the flavors linger. Drinkable now. 500 cases made. • $30 • (07/31/97) • **86**
Merlot Sonoma County 1995: Crisp, with ripe, plummy fruit and hints of cherry, spice and berry, and drying, earthy tannins that are edgy on the finish. Drink now through 2002. 34,000 cases made. • $16 • (05/31/98) • **86**
Merlot Sonoma County 1994: Supple and well balanced, with just enough plum and berry flavors to fill out the frame. A graceful style that doesn't overwhelm, as the currant, cedar and spice flavors are in balance. 30,000 cases made. • $16 • (02/28/97) • **87**
Opulence California NV • $7 • (01/31/87) • **80**
Petite Sirah Alexander Valley 1989 • $15 • (06/30/92) • **79**
Pinot Noir Sonoma County Carneros 1985 • $6 • (06/15/88) • **82**
Pinot Noir Sonoma County Carneros 1981 • $5 • (08/31/86) • **82**
Réserve Alexandre Alexander Valley 1994: Well focused, with a ripe, complex core of cherry, currant and berry flavors. Smooth and supple right up to the finish, where the tannins weigh in. Deft oak shadings add flavor dimensions. Try now. 3,850 cases made. • $28 • (10/31/97) • **91**
Réserve Alexandre Alexander Valley 1993: Complex, with its array of spicy currant, plum and berry flavors, and the texture is smooth despite firm tannins. Finishes with hints of leather, herb, tea and cherry. Drinks well now. 2,397 cases made. • $27 • (11/15/96) • **88**
Réserve Alexandre Alexander Valley 1991 • $30 • (07/31/94) CS • **91**
Réserve Alexandre Alexander Valley 1990 • $30 • (11/15/93) • **90**
Réserve Alexandre Alexander Valley 1987: Rich, intense and concentrated, showing well-focused flavors of ripe plum, currant, black cherry and anise, with a dash of spicy oak. Finishes with firm but polished tannins. Best now through 2000. • $18 • (12/15/97) • **92**
Réserve Alexandre Alexander Valley 1986 • $20 • (09/30/90) • **89**
Réserve Alexandre Alexander Valley 1985 • $19 • (09/30/89) • **88**
Réserve Alexandre Alexander Valley 1984 • $19 • (08/31/88) • **89**
Réserve Alexandre Alexander Valley 1983 • $15 • (04/30/87) • **80**
Riesling Late Harvest Sonoma County Trione Vineyards Reserve 1993 • $16/375ml • (07/31/95) • **87**
Sauvignon Blanc Sonoma County 1997: Check out the price on this vivid and refreshing white, filled with bright grapefruit and lemon-lime flavors. It's firm and focused, with the kind of up-front character many California vintners seem to shy away from. 39,000 cases made. • $7 • (05/15/98) BB • **88**
Sauvignon Blanc Sonoma County 1996: A well-crafted, bright and fruity style delivering more nectarine and spice notes than are typical for Sauvignon Blanc, this white is soft up front, then finishes with a nice burst of citrusy freshness. A solid value from a winery on the upswing. 18,000 cases made. • $9 • (05/15/97) BB • **87**
Sauvignon Blanc Sonoma County 1995 • $8 • (05/15/96) BB • **89**
Sauvignon Blanc Sonoma County 1994 • $7 • (08/31/95) • **85**
Semchard California 1993 • $7 • (12/15/94) • **81**
Shiraz Port Sonoma County Trione Vineyards Henry's Reserve 1993 • $15 • (12/31/95) • **73**
Shiraz Sonoma County 1994: Tastes like Shiraz with its meaty, earthy, wild berry and cherry flavors. It's well-balanced, fanning out on the finish. Drinks well now. 4,600 cases made. • $14 • (02/28/97) • **87**
Shiraz Sonoma County Reserve 1994: Flavors are dense and somewhat muddled, but with breathing the core of meaty currant and berry flavor comes to the fore. 995 cases made. • $32 • (09/30/97) • **87**

Syrah Alexander Valley Reserve 1991 • $18 • (12/31/93) HR • **91**
Syrah Alexander Valley Shiraz 1993 • $12 • (06/15/96) • **89**
Zinfandel Alexander Valley 1984 • $7 • (07/31/88) • **79**
Zinfandel Sonoma County 1995: Crisp and tight, with a modest band of spicy berry and sage notes, finishing with a slightly green, tealike flavor. Drink now through 2001. 5,000 cases made. • $16 • (06/15/98) • **85**

GICOMA | CALIFORNIA

Cabernet Sauvignon Napa Valley Pointer Run Vineyards 1992 • $14 • (03/31/96) • **78**

GIRARD | CALIFORNIA

Cabernet Sauvignon Napa Valley 1996: Young, tight, dense and well focused, with a pretty core of earthy currant, cedar and toasty oak flavors. Quite complete and harmonious. • $NA • (06/15/97) (BT) • **90-94**
Cabernet Sauvignon Napa Valley 1994: Deftly balanced, with a fine core of earthy currant, cedar, herb and spice flavors. Finishing with dry tannins, it's best cellared into 1999 to 2000. 2,464 cases made. • $25 • (10/31/97) • **88**
Cabernet Sauvignon Napa Valley 1993: Tight and spicy, with a trim band of currant, cedar and berry flavors that fan out on the finish and give it some finesse. Drinkable now. 2,400 cases made. • $22 • (11/15/96) • **89**
Cabernet Sauvignon Napa Valley 1991 • $18 • (05/31/94) • **86**
Cabernet Sauvignon Napa Valley 1990 • $16 • (11/15/93) • **87**
Cabernet Sauvignon Napa Valley 1989 • $20 Ⓐ • (11/15/92) • **82**
Cabernet Sauvignon Napa Valley 1988 • $16 • (11/15/91) • **85**
Cabernet Sauvignon Napa Valley 1987 • $16 • (11/15/90) • **86**
Cabernet Sauvignon Napa Valley 1986 • $16 • (11/15/89) • **89**
Cabernet Sauvignon Napa Valley 1985 • $22 Ⓐ • (09/15/88) • **88**
Cabernet Sauvignon Napa Valley 1984 • $35 Ⓐ • (11/30/87) • **88**
Cabernet Sauvignon Napa Valley 1983 • $15 • (12/15/86) • **71**
Cabernet Sauvignon Napa Valley 1982 • $13 • (02/16/86) • **89**
Cabernet Sauvignon Napa Valley 1981 • $14 • (08/01/85) • **89**
Cabernet Sauvignon Napa Valley Reserve 1994: A wonderfully elegant, understated style that grows on you; offers lovely currant, spice, vanilla, cedar and herb notes. Opts for charm, finesse and delicacy rather than extract and power. Approachable now, best by 2001. 887 cases made. • $40 • (11/15/97) • **93**
Cabernet Sauvignon Napa Valley Reserve 1993: Young, tight, firm, crisp and tannic. It finally reveals ripe cherry, plum, anise and berry flavors. Try now. 800 cases made. • $45 • (11/15/96) • **88**
Cabernet Sauvignon Napa Valley Reserve 1992 • $40 • (12/15/95) • **88**
Cabernet Sauvignon Napa Valley Reserve 1991 • $35 • (11/15/94) • **87**
Cabernet Sauvignon Napa Valley Reserve 1990 • $25 • (04/15/94) • **86**
Cabernet Sauvignon Napa Valley Reserve 1989 • $25 • (11/15/93) • **84**
Cabernet Sauvignon Napa Valley Reserve 1988 • $25 • (11/15/92) • **84**
Cabernet Sauvignon Napa Valley Reserve 1987 • $25 • (11/15/91) • **88**
Cabernet Sauvignon Napa Valley Reserve 1986 • $34 • (11/15/90) • **87**
Cabernet Sauvignon Napa Valley Reserve 1985 • $35 • (02/15/90) • **86**
Cabernet Sauvignon Napa Valley Reserve 1984 • $25 • (12/15/88) • **93**
Cabernet Sauvignon Napa Valley Reserve 1983 • $20 • (12/15/87) • **86**
Chardonnay Napa Valley 1995: Rich and flavorful, with lots of ripe pear, fig and melon flavors, picking up pretty oak flavors and finishing with a citrus edge. Ready to drink. 3,981 cases made. • $25 • (05/31/97) • **91**
Chardonnay Napa Valley 1994: Combines ripe, rich fruit with a sound measure of finesse and harmony. Lots of juicy pear, honey and butterscotch flavors dovetail on the finish and linger. 7,700 cases made. • $18 • (06/15/96) SS • **91**
Chardonnay Napa Valley Old Vines 1993 • $19 • (12/15/95) • **88**
Chardonnay Napa Valley Reserve 1995: Bold, ripe and generous, with a complex interplay of ripe, rich fig, vanilla, pear and spice flavors and toast notes. Drinkable now. 1,086 cases made. • $40 • (05/31/97) • **91**
Chardonnay Napa Valley Reserve 1994: A bold, ripe, rich and dramatic style that's loaded with concentrated pear, spice, honey, toast and pineapple flavors. It shows the extra depth and dimensions of a great wine in the making. 800 cases made. • $32 • (05/31/96) • **93**
Chardonnay Napa Valley Viridian Vineyard 1993 • $38 • (12/15/95) • **87**

Key: SS—Spectator Selection CS—Cellar Selection HR—Highly Recommended BB—Best Buy $NA—Price not available Ⓐ—Auction Price (BT)—Barrel Tasting
Dates in parentheses indicate the issues in which the ratings were published.

GIRARDET | OREGON

Cabernet Sauvignon Umpqua Valley 1995: On the light side, but has pretty raspberry and currant flavors—and a hint of volatility—that shine through the layer of modest tannins. Best now through 2003. 215 cases made. • $14 • (07/31/98) • **85**
Pinot Noir Oregon 1989 • $11 • (11/30/92) • **79**
Pinot Noir Oregon 1987 • $12 • (02/15/90) • **67**
Pinot Noir Umpqua Valley 1987 • $12 • (02/15/90) • **75**
Pinot Noir Umpqua Valley Barrel Select 1995: Light and soft, with pretty chocolate overtones to the modest berry and orange peel flavors. Feels mature and ready. Drink now. 487 cases made. • $22 • (07/31/98) • **83**

GLASS MOUNTAIN QUARRY | CALIFORNIA

Cabernet Sauvignon California 1992 • $10 • (12/15/95) • **84**
Cabernet Sauvignon California 1990 • $9 • (06/15/93) • **84**
Cabernet Sauvignon Napa Valley 1988 • $8 • (10/15/91) BB • **85**
Chardonnay California 1993 • $9 • (06/30/95) • **84**
Petite Sirah Napa Valley 1988 • $8 • (10/31/91) BB • **81**
Rubis du Val Napa Valley 1988 • $8 • (10/31/91) BB • **82**

GLEN ELLEN | CALIFORNIA

Cabernet Franc Alexander Valley Imagery Series 1988 • $16 • (03/31/92) • **86**
Cabernet Sauvignon California Proprietor's Reserve 1995: A bit chewy, with some anise and herbs on the palate. A pleasant, if simple, cherry note finishes it off. 530,000 cases made. • $6 • (10/31/97) • **80**
Cabernet Sauvignon California Proprietor's Reserve 1994: An average-quality Cabernet, showing a touch of herb and currant flavor, but not much more. • $6 • (11/30/96) • **77**
Cabernet Sauvignon California Proprietor's Reserve 1993: Light, focused around raspberry and a touch of mint; smooth and drinkable now. • $6 • (12/15/95) • **82**
Cabernet Sauvignon California Proprietor's Reserve 1991 • $6 • (11/15/93) • **78**
Cabernet Sauvignon California Proprietor's Reserve 1989 • $6 • (11/15/92) BB • **84**
Cabernet Sauvignon California Proprietor's Reserve 1988 • $6 • (11/15/91) BB • **79**
Cabernet Sauvignon California Proprietor's Reserve 1987 • $6 • (01/31/91) • **79**
Cabernet Sauvignon California Proprietor's Reserve 1986 • $4 • (07/15/88) BB • **82**
Cabernet Sauvignon Sonoma Valley Benziger Family Selection 1984 • $14 • (10/15/87) • **82**
Cabernet Sauvignon Sonoma Valley Benziger Family Selection 1983 • $9 • (05/15/87) • **91**
Cabernet Sauvignon Sonoma Valley Glen Ellen Estate 1982 • $9 • (02/01/85) • **85**
Cabernet Sauvignon Sonoma Valley Imagery Series 1985 • $13 • (02/15/89) • **86**
Chardonnay California Proprietor's Reserve 1997: Simple and easy-drinking, with earthy citrus and apple flavors. Drink now. 1,000,000 cases made. • $6 • (06/30/98) • **81**
Chardonnay California Proprietor's Reserve 1996: Simple, with tart apple and mineral flavors. Slightly herbal on the short finish. Drink now. • $6 • (07/31/98) • **78**
Chardonnay California Proprietor's Reserve 1995: Light and inoffensive, with pleasant pear and honey flavors. • $5 • (11/30/96) • **80**
Chardonnay California Proprietor's Reserve 1993 • $5 • (07/31/95) BB • **85**
Fumé Blanc California Proprietor's Reserve 1994 • $6 • (05/31/96) • **82**
Merlot California Proprietor's Reserve 1994: Light, simple and low-key; a bit peppery but otherwise undistinguished. 360,000 cases made. • $6 • (07/31/96) • **78**
Merlot California Proprietor's Reserve 1992 • $5 • (09/15/94) • **82**
Merlot California Proprietor's Reserve 1991 • $6 • (04/15/93) BB • **82**
Merlot California Proprietor's Reserve 1990 • $6 • (05/31/92) • **79**
Merlot California Proprietor's Reserve 1986 • $6 • (01/31/89) BB • **84**
Petit Verdot Alexander Valley Imagery Series 1988 • $16 • (03/31/92) • **88**
Riesling Late Harvest Santa Maria Valley Imagery Series 1989 • $10/375ml • (03/31/92) • **79**
Sauvignon Blanc California Proprietor's Reserve 1996: An unusual style, with a slightly waxy texture. Flavors and aromas lean to the green side, with green pea, wintergreen and fresh-mowed grass. • $5 • (04/30/98) • **84**

Sauvignon Blanc California Proprietor's Reserve 1995: Light and citrusy in character, with bright fruit flavors at its core. • $5 • (11/30/96) • **82**
Sauvignon Blanc California Proprietor's Reserve 1993 • $5 • (06/30/95) • **80**
White Zinfandel California Proprietor's Reserve 1994 • $5 • (09/15/95) • **79**
Zinfandel California Proprietor's Reserve 1996: Dilute and innocuous, with artificial strawberry flavors and a bitter, jasmine tea-flavored finish. Drink now. • $6 • (06/15/98) • **70**

GLEN FIONA | WASHINGTON

Grenache Columbia Valley Noir 1995: Gives a solid blast of blackberry and tobacco flavor. It's a bit chewy but packed with character and style. Approachable now, with hearty food. 167 cases made. • $16 • (09/30/97) • **87**
Sauvignon Blanc-Sémillon Walla Walla County 1995: A sweet wine with a nice range of honey, pear and tobacco flavors that remain harmonious through the gentle finish. Ready now. 125 cases made. • $16/375ml • (10/15/97) • **85**
Syrah Walla Walla County 1995: A bright, open-textured Syrah, untannic, and appealing for its bright berry flavors shaded with spicy oak. Ready now. 279 cases made. • $25 • (09/30/97) • **88**

GLENORA | NEW YORK

Blanc de Blancs Finger Lakes 1987 • $12 • (12/31/90) • **85**
Blancs de Blancs New York 1991 • $15 • (02/28/95) • **84**
Brut New York 1989 • $13 • (06/30/95) • **84**
Brut New York 1987 • $12 • (12/31/90) • **81**
Brut Rosé New York 1991 • $20 • (02/28/95) • **84**
Chardonnay Finger Lakes 1993: Nicely balanced, crisp and fruity, with lemon, apple and grapefruit flavors accented by a bit of butter. • $9 • (09/15/96) • **83**
Chardonnay Finger Lakes Barrel Fermented 1993: A very simple, acceptable wine, with unusual aromas and fruit-cocktail flavors. • $12 • (09/15/96) • **75**
Johannisberg Riesling Finger Lakes 1995: Nice and peachy, this is a slightly sweet but well-balanced Riesling to drink now, while it's fresh. • $8 • (10/31/96) • **84**
Johannisberg Riesling Finger Lakes 1994 • $8 • (01/31/96) • **78**
Johannisberg Riesling Finger Lakes 1993 • $8 • (12/15/94) • **79**
Riesling Finger Lakes Dry 1995: Very bland and slightly sweet, with a soft texture. Boring. • $8 • (10/31/96) • **70**
Riesling Finger Lakes Dry 1994 • $8 • (01/31/96) • **85**

GLORIA FERRER | CALIFORNIA

Blanc de Noirs Sonoma County Carneros NV: Exhibiting pretty berry and wild cherry flavors with a dash of mango, this fruit-driven style has richness and depth. Drinks well now. 15,000 cases made. • $15 • (11/30/97) • **89**
Brut Carneros Carneros Cuvée Late Disgorged 1989: Rich, toasty aromas announce this wine, followed by orange, lemon, spice and honey notes. With brisk acidity yet ample body, it's showing a rewarding touch of age. Drink now. 1,500 cases made. • $28 • (06/30/98) • **91**
Brut Carneros Carneros Cuvée Late Disgorged 1988: Youthful for its age, it retains some austerity with its flavors of citrus and lemon, touches of pear and mushroom. Aging exceptionally well. 1,500 cases made. • $25 • (11/30/97) • **89**
Brut Carneros Carneros Cuvée Late Disgorged 1987 • $25 • (12/31/94) • **87**
Brut Carneros Cuvée 1985 • $20 • (05/15/92) • **81**
Brut Carneros Royal Cuveé 1989: Complex and inviting, with a trim, well-focused core of ripe pear, citrus and spice qualities that hang with you. Good value. 10,000 cases made. • $19 • (11/30/97) • **88**
Brut Carneros Royal Cuvée 1988 • $18 • (12/15/95) SS • **91**
Brut Carneros Royal Cuvée 1987 • $17 • (12/31/94) • **85**
Brut Carneros Royal Cuvée 1986 • $17 • (12/31/91) • **84**
Brut Rosé Sonoma County NV: Serves up a complex array of dried black cherry, herb, spice and vanilla flavors, before turning even more complex on the finish, where the texture is smooth and creamy. 2,000 cases made. • $20 • (11/30/97) • **90**
Brut Sonoma County NV: Smoky, and creamy in texture, with hints of plum and citrus. Delicate, with finesse, this is a lovely wine at a good price. 30,000 cases made. • $15 • (11/30/97) • **90**
Brut Sonoma County Royal Cuvée 1986 • $16 • (04/30/91) • **84**
Brut Sonoma County Royal Cuvée 1985 • $16 • (03/15/91) • **83**
Brut Sonoma County Royal Cuvée 1984 • $15 • (04/15/88) • **89**
Chardonnay Carneros 1996: A ripe, rich and full-bodied style of California Chardonnay, with a track record for quality since its first vintage. Brimming with complex, concentrated fig, pear, melon and honeyed flavors that are long and tasty through the finish. Drink now through 2000. 9,500 cases made. • $19 • (05/15/98) SS • **90**
Chardonnay Carneros 1995: Smooth and creamy, with a polished texture and pretty pear, nectarine, anise and light buttery oak flavors finishing with complexity. 9,500 cases made. • $17 • (06/15/97) • **90**
Chardonnay Carneros 1994: Impressive flavor and finesse. Layers of ripe pear, apple and toasty oak that fold out on the finish. 9,000 cases made. • $16 • (07/31/96) • **89**
Chardonnay Carneros 1993 • $15 • (03/31/95) SS • **91**
Pinot Noir Carneros 1995: Appealing for its simple cherry, wild berry, earth and herbal notes, this is a clean, well-made wine that lacks extra dimensions. Best now through 2000. 2,900 cases made. • $19 • (02/28/98) • **85**
Pinot Noir Carneros 1994 • $16 • (02/29/96) • **79**
Pinot Noir Carneros 1993 • $16 • (12/31/95) • **81**
Pinot Noir Carneros 1992 • $16 • (12/31/95) • **86**
Pinot Noir Carneros 1991 • $15 • (02/28/94) • **85**

GODSPEED | CALIFORNIA

Cabernet Sauvignon Mount Veeder 1991 • $15 • (12/15/95) • **82**
Chardonnay Mount Veeder 1996: A bit of an oddball. Minerally seashell and sour notes detract from the otherwise crisp citrus flavors. Drink now through 2000. 300 cases made. • $17 • (07/31/98) • **75**
Chardonnay Mount Veeder 1993 • $15 • (07/31/95) • **85**

GODWIN | CALIFORNIA

Chardonnay Alexander Valley 1995: Crisp and citrusy, with a nice thread of pear and vanilla flavor shining through the finish. Best from late this year. 1,300 cases made. • $20 • (07/31/97) • **86**
Chardonnay Alexander Valley 1994: Toasty, smoky notes add class to the aromas, and it does seem rich, although loses some charm as wood covers the fruit on the medium-weight palate. 600 cases made. • $20 • (04/30/96) • **82**
Merlot Alexander Valley 1995: Shows an earthy side, followed by hints of licorice, cassis and blackberry. Fairly lean and a little rustic, though it may smooth out with time. Drink now through 2005. 1,960 cases made. • $20 • (05/31/98) • **84**

GOLD HILL | CALIFORNIA

Merlot El Dorado 1991 • $11 • (09/15/94) • **79**

GOLDEN CREEK | CALIFORNIA

Caberlot Reserve Sonoma County 1991 • $15 • (11/15/94) • **83**
Cabernet Sauvignon Sonoma County 1990 • $12 • (11/15/94) • **80**
Merlot Sonoma County 1989 • $13 • (05/31/92) • **81**
Merlot Sonoma County Reserve 1991 • $15 • (09/15/94) • **84**
Merlot Sonoma County Reserve 1990 • $15 • (09/15/94) • **82**
Merlot Sonoma County Reserve 1989 • $16 • (05/31/92) • **87**

GORDON BROTHERS | WASHINGTON

Cabernet Sauvignon Columbia Valley 1993: Light, showing more spice and tobacco flavors than fruit, finishing soft and appealing. Approachable now. 1,236 cases made. • $17 • (09/15/97) • **82**
Cabernet Sauvignon Washington 1991 • $15 • (09/30/95) • **85**
Cabernet Sauvignon Washington 1990 • $14 • (03/15/94) • **77**
Cabernet Sauvignon Washington 1989 • $16 • (07/31/92) • **83**
Cabernet Sauvignon Washington 1988 • $19 • (11/15/91) • **89**
Chardonnay Columbia Valley 1995: Ripe and focused, with a slightly bitter edge that soon disappears under a blanket of rich, artfully balanced pear, cream and grapefruit flavors. Finishes smooth and elegant. Drink now. 1,609 cases made. • $17 • (09/15/97) • **89**
Chardonnay Washington Reserve 1994: A sturdy white with flavors akin to apple cider at first, but it develops some honey, spice and earth flavors through the long finish. 3,000 cases made. • $14 • (09/15/96) • **86**
Merlot Columbia Valley 1994: Light and smooth, inviting for its delicately herbal prune, tar and mineral flavors, all doing a decrescendo on the finish. 2,029 cases made. • $19 • (09/15/97) • **85**

Merlot Washington 1993: Pretty berry and cherry flavors are well balanced on a light frame. Slow-fading finish shows hints of spice and vanilla. 3,000 cases made. • $16 • (09/15/96) • **82**
Merlot Washington 1992 • $15 • (09/30/95) • **87**
Merlot Washington 1990 • $14 • (06/15/93) • **78**
Tradition Washington 1991 • $20 • (01/31/95) • **88**

GOSSAMER BAY | CALIFORNIA

Cabernet Sauvignon California 1995: An easy-to-drink, supple wine with silky texture and pretty plum flavors that echo on the finish. Syrupy flavors are not for everyone, but it has its charms. Drink now. • $9 • (03/31/98) • **85**
Chardonnay California 1995: A fruit-driven style, with a core of pear, peach and grapefruit flavors and a finish marked by good, zingy acidity. • $9 • (01/31/97) • **84**
Zinfandel California 1995: Tastes mid-way between rosé and Zinfandel, but it's pleasant enough with its cracked pepper and wild berry notes. • $9 • (02/28/97) • **80**

GRACE FAMILY | CALIFORNIA

Cabernet Sauvignon Napa Valley 1995: Tightly wound, with dense, rich, well-focused cherry and currant flavor that's bright and vivid. This is a compact wine with lovely focus on the fruit, and smooth, polished tannins. 426 magnums produced. Best from 2002 through 2010. • $475/1.5 liter • (06/15/98) • **92**
Cabernet Sauvignon Napa Valley 1994: A well-crafted red from a small-production winery, this Cabernet is young, tight and well concentrated, with a brilliant core of currant, black cherry, cedar and spice nuances. Big, ripe, complex and firmly tannic, it should age well for up to a decade and, given the tannin level (and price), it's best cellared until 2002. 175 cases made. • $307 Ⓐ • (05/31/97) CS • **94**
Cabernet Sauvignon Napa Valley 1993: A lean, trim, leathery style, offering more oak and cedary flavors than obvious fruit, which is usually the most evident feature of this wine. Tasted twice, with consistent notes. 187 cases made. • $259 Ⓐ • (05/15/96) • **85**
Cabernet Sauvignon Napa Valley 1991 • $238 Ⓐ • (11/15/94) • **88**
Cabernet Sauvignon Napa Valley 1990 • $225 Ⓐ • (08/31/93) • **90**
Cabernet Sauvignon Napa Valley 1988 • $216 Ⓐ • (06/30/91) • **92**
Cabernet Sauvignon Napa Valley 1987: Probably the best Grace of the 1980s. A supple, showy wine with a bounty of silky currant, plum and spicy Cabernet flavors. Shows a wonderful sense of harmony and finesse, finishing with a long, complex aftertaste. Best now through 2004. • $242 Ⓐ • (12/15/97) • **94**
Cabernet Sauvignon Napa Valley 1986: Impressive for its range of flavors, touching on cedar, spice, currant and cherry. The texture is smooth and polished, the finish is complex. This is fully mature, ready to drink. 175 cases made. • $245 Ⓐ • (12/15/96) • **91**
Cabernet Sauvignon Napa Valley 1985 • $288 Ⓐ • (12/15/88) • **93**
Cabernet Sauvignon Napa Valley 1984 • $211 Ⓐ • (04/15/88) • **90**
Cabernet Sauvignon Napa Valley 1983 • $173 Ⓐ • (06/15/87) • **85**

GRACELAND | CALIFORNIA

Cabernet Sauvignon Napa Valley Going Home 1994: Big, intense and tannic, marked by a stalky, green bean flavor and finishing with charred, stiff tannins. Shame what they've done to The King. 2,500 cases made. • $23 • (10/31/97) • **77**

GRAESER | CALIFORNIA

Cabernet Sauvignon Napa Valley 1991 • $14 • (12/15/95) • **79**

GRAFF, RICHARD | CALIFORNIA

Mourvèdre Chalone 1992 • $16 • (01/31/96) • **86**
Pinot Noir Central Coast 1994: Bold, ripe and lush, with pleasant, earthy mushroom, plum, wild berry and cherry flavors shaded with hints of anise and cedar. Drinks well now, but should hold until 2002, at least. Alas, only 125 cases made. 125 cases made. • $18 • (01/31/97) • **90**

Key: SS—Spectator Selection CS—Cellar Selection HR—Highly Recommended BB—Best Buy $NA—Price not available Ⓐ—Auction Price (BT)—Barrel Tasting
Dates in parentheses indicate the issues in which the ratings were published.

GRAHAM, GREGORY | CALIFORNIA

Pinot Noir Carneros 1994: Marked by strong earthy flavors, though with aeration it shows hints of cherry and plum. Dries out, with a tannic finish. Tasted twice, with consistent notes. 315 cases made. • $22 • (03/31/97) • **83**
Pinot Noir Carneros 1992 • $18 • (03/31/95) • **86**
Viognier Knights Valley 1996: Rich and flavorful, with lots of ripe pear, honey, fig, nectarine and spicy flavors, holding its focus and turning complex on the finish. Very well made in a bold, ripe style. 226 cases made. • $24 • (04/30/98) • **88**
Viognier Knights Valley 1995: Starts out ripe and spicy with hints of pear and honeysuckle, and holds those flavors through the finish where it picks up traces of melon and nutmeg. 347 cases made. • $22 • (11/30/96) • **88**
Viognier Knights Valley 1994: Elegant and refined, smooth and polished, with a ripe, complex core of pear, peach, honey and melon, with a touch of spice on the finish. From Greg Graham, winemaker at Rombauer. 207 cases made. • $23 • (07/31/96) • **90**
Viognier Napa Valley 1996: Elegant and spicy, with a core of ripe pear, honey, fig and melon. Picks up a trace of bitterness on the finish, but still it's tasty and well made. 260 cases made. • $22 • (04/30/98) • **87**

GRAND CRU | CALIFORNIA

Cabernet Sauvignon Alexander Valley Collector's Reserve 1986 • $22 • (05/15/90) • **85**
Cabernet Sauvignon Alexander Valley Collector's Reserve 1985 • $18 • (07/15/89) • **81**
Cabernet Sauvignon Alexander Valley Collector's Reserve 1982 • $15 • (09/30/87) • **70**
Cabernet Sauvignon Alexander Valley Collector's Reserve 1980 • $15 • (11/01/84) • **85**
Cabernet Sauvignon Sonoma County 1984 • $8 • (12/31/87) • **75**
Cabernet Sauvignon Sonoma County 1983 • $8 • (11/16/85) • **68**
Cabernet Sauvignon Sonoma County Premium Selection 1988 • $12 • (03/15/92) • **84**
Cabernet Sauvignon Sonoma County Premium Selection 1987 • $12 • (11/15/91) • **85**
Cabernet Sauvignon Sonoma County Premium Selection 1986 • $12 • (04/30/90) • **79**
Cabernet Sauvignon Sonoma County Premium Selection 1985 • $9 • (06/15/89) • **79**
Chardonnay California Premium Selection 1996: Coconut and toast flavors dominate, but there are also some nice, tart apple and pear notes. No attempt to integrate the oak with the fruit, but it has a silky texture and a long finish. Drink now. 15,000 cases made. • $8 • (07/31/98) • **82**
Chardonnay California Premium Selection 1994: Simple and refreshing, with nectarine and citrus flavors lingering briefly on the finish. 7,000 cases made. • $8 • (06/30/96) • **83**
Gewürztraminer California Premium Selection 1993 • $7 • (02/28/95) • **80**
Gewürztraminer Late Harvest Sonoma County Select 1987 • $10/375ml • (03/31/90) • **72**
Johannisberg Riesling California Premium Selection 1993 • $7 • (06/15/95) • **83**
Merlot California Premium Selection 1996: A bright cherry core is the focus, with pretty almond and smoke tones. The finish is a bit tart and short. 25,000 cases made. • $8 • (04/30/98) • **83**
Merlot California Premium Selection 1992 • $8 • (09/15/94) • **81**
Sauvignon Blanc California 1994 • $7 • (05/31/96) • **83**
Zinfandel California Premium Selection 1992 • $7 • (10/15/95) • **78**

GRANITE SPRINGS | CALIFORNIA

Zinfandel El Dorado 1990 • $8 • (09/30/93) • **82**
Zinfandel El Dorado 1989 • $8 • (10/15/92) • **75**

GREEN & RED | CALIFORNIA

Chardonnay Napa Valley Catacula Vineyard 1995: Ripe and flavorful, with a spicy core of apple and pear that holds true through the finish. Ready to drink. 594 cases made. • $18 • (06/15/97) • **87**

Chardonnay Napa Valley Catacula Vineyard 1994: A medium-bodied white serving up a nice core of ripe, spicy pear and citrus flavors, and finishing with a light dash of oak. 690 cases made. • $18 • (06/30/96) • **84**
Chardonnay Napa Valley Catacula Vineyard 1993 • $16 • (07/31/95) • **84**
Gamay Napa Valley 1996: A friendly wine, generous with its juicy berry and spice flavors. Ready to drink. 322 cases made. • $14 • (03/31/98) • **84**
Zinfandel Napa Valley 1989 • $11 • (10/15/92) • **81**
Zinfandel Napa Valley 1987 • $9 • (02/15/91) • **77**
Zinfandel Napa Valley 1986 • $9 • (03/15/90) • **76**
Zinfandel Napa Valley 1985 • $8 • (06/15/89) • **73**
Zinfandel Napa Valley 1984 • $7 • (11/15/87) • **82**
Zinfandel Napa Valley 1982 • $7 • (12/16/85) • **82**
Zinfandel Napa Valley Chiles Mill Vineyard 1996: The ripe berry- and cherry-laced flavors are ripe and pleasant, with a light peppery note. Lacking in depth and extra facets. Give it short-term cellaring in the hope it will fill out a bit; drink through 2001. 1,279 cases made. • $18 • (05/31/98) • **85**
Zinfandel Napa Valley Chiles Mill Vineyard 1995: Young, vibrant and fruity, with a boysenberry, raspberry, anise and pepper character. A complex and well-focused wine, driven by fruit. Another excellent Zin from Green & Red. 660 cases made. • $17 • (04/30/97) • **90**
Zinfandel Napa Valley Chiles Mill Vineyard 1994 • $16 • (04/30/96) • **88**
Zinfandel Napa Valley Chiles Mill Vineyard 1992 • $14 • (07/31/94) • **88**
Zinfandel Napa Valley Chiles Mill Vineyard 1991 • $12 • (09/30/93) • **85**
Zinfandel Napa Valley Chiles Mill Vineyard 1990 • $12 • (03/15/93) HR • **90**
Zinfandel Napa Valley Chiles Mill Vineyard Unfiltered 1993 • $15 • (09/30/95) HR • **90**

GREENSTONE | CALIFORNIA

Zinfandel Amador County 1990 • $9 • (09/30/93) • **84**
Zinfandel Amador County Special Release 1987 • $10 • (09/30/93) • **84**

GREENVALE | NEW ENGLAND

Chardonnay Southeastern New England 1995: A fairly tart wine with lemony and buttery flavors. A bit awkward in the end, but still flavorful. 550 cases made. • $13 • (10/31/97) • **80**

GREENWOOD RIDGE | CALIFORNIA

Cabernet Sauvignon Anderson Valley 1994: Shows sage and bell pepper notes before developing into truer Cabernet flavors of currant and plum, with light, toasty oak. Finishes with firm tannins. Drinkable now. 130 cases made. • $36 • (11/15/97) • **89**
Cabernet Sauvignon Anderson Valley 1992 • $18 • (09/15/95) • **89**
Cabernet Sauvignon Anderson Valley 1991 • $14 • (11/15/94) • **82**
Cabernet Sauvignon Anderson Valley 1989 • $12 • (08/31/92) • **74**
Cabernet Sauvignon Anderson Valley Reserve 1990 • $16 • (06/15/93) • **75**
Cabernet Sauvignon Anderson Valley Reserve 1989 • $16 • (11/15/92) • **87**
Cabernet Sauvignon Mendocino 1988 • $15 • (02/29/92) • **83**
Chardonnay Anderson Valley Du Pratt Vineyard 1996: An openly fruity style, floral and spicy, with ripe apple, melon, fig and citrus flavors that are well focused. Drink now. 833 cases made. • $22 • (03/31/98) • **88**
Chardonnay Anderson Valley Du Pratt Vineyard 1995: Marked by a spicy, grassy edge, with ripe pear, apple and hazelnut notes that are fresh and lively, finishing with a trace of grapefruit. 876 cases made. • $20 • (02/28/97) • **88**
Chardonnay Anderson Valley Du Pratt Vineyard 1994: Ripe and refreshing, featuring complex pear, tangerine, honey and spice flavors and a delicate finish. Impressive for its finesse and grace. 500 cases made. • $19 • (04/30/96) • **90**
Chardonnay Late Harvest Anderson Valley 1993 • $18 • (06/15/94) • **85**
Merlot Anderson Valley 1995: Serves up lots of ripe, bright fruit, with ripe plum, cherry and berry notes. Finishes with soft, fleshy tannins. Ready to drink. 600 cases made. • $22 • (11/30/97) • **89**
Merlot Anderson Valley 1994: A bit stalky, showing notes of cedar and currant with dashes of bell pepper and oregano. It's a good red, though it won't remind you much of Merlot. Drink through 1999. 2,145 cases made. • $20 • (02/28/97) • **84**
Merlot Anderson Valley 1993: Rich and well focused, with chewy currant, black cherry, plum and berry notes. Picks up a spicy anise edge with light toasty oak. Finishes with firm tannins. Drinkable now. 950 cases made. • $20 • (08/31/96) • **89**
Merlot Anderson Valley 1992 • $20 • (04/15/95) • **86**
Merlot Anderson Valley 1991 • $16 • (03/15/94) • **78**
Merlot Anderson Valley 1989 • $16 • (11/15/91) • **85**
Pinot Noir Anderson Valley 1996: Smooth, ripe and juicy, with pretty plum, black cherry and light oak shadings. Turns elegant and supple on the finish, with a delicate, fruity aftertaste. Drink now. 1,075 cases made. • $22 • (02/28/98) • **88**
Pinot Noir Anderson Valley 1995: Captures lots of pretty fruit flavors, with plum, cherry, strawberry and watermelon notes. Flavors hold on the long finish, where it picks up a trace of earthiness, smoky notes. Drinks well now. • $19 • (12/31/96) • **88**
Pinot Noir Anderson Valley 1994 • $16 • (01/31/96) HR • **90**
Pinot Noir Anderson Valley 1990: Complex, with refreshing wild berry, raspberry and cherry notes that linger long on the finish. Appealing for its upfront, pure fruitiness. Ready now. • $15 • (03/31/97) • **89**
Pinot Noir Anderson Valley 1989 • $14 • (06/30/91) • **87**
Pinot Noir Anderson Valley Roederer Estate Vineyards 1993 • $15 • (03/31/95) • **89**
Pinot Noir Anderson Valley Roederer Estate Vineyards 1992 • $15 • (10/31/94) SS • **90**
Pinot Noir Mendocino County 1991 • $15 • (02/28/93) • **87**
Sauvignon Blanc Anderson Valley 1994 • $9 • (02/29/96) • **87**
Sauvignon Blanc Anderson Valley 1993 • $9 • (08/31/95) • **80**
Sauvignon Blanc Mendocino 1996: Kind of sweet and syrupy, lacking acidity and firmness. Melony flavors are rather simple, yet finish with a pleasant spiciness. 1,116 cases made. • $10 • (07/31/97) • **82**
White Riesling Anderson Valley 1994 • $8 • (06/15/96) • **84**
White Riesling Anderson Valley 1993 • $8 • (02/28/95) • **85**
White Riesling Late Harvest Mendocino 1989 • $18/375ml • (08/31/91) • **89**
Zinfandel Sonoma County 1991 • $12 • (05/31/93) • **85**
Zinfandel Sonoma County 1990 • $13 • (07/31/92) • **86**
Zinfandel Sonoma County 1989 • $12 • (10/15/92) • **81**
Zinfandel Sonoma County 1988 • $11 • (05/15/91) • **86**
Zinfandel Sonoma County Scherrer Vineyards 1996: Medium-weight, with a pleasant core of earthy cherry, wild berry, light vanilla, oak and spice. Ready to drink. 1,021 cases made. • $18 • (03/31/98) • **86**
Zinfandel Sonoma County Scherrer Vineyards 1995: A well-oaked style that offers toasty, buttery nuances and lots of wild berry, black cherry and spicy flavors. Has a nice sense of balance and proportion, with a long, lingering finish. Drinks well now. 1,036 cases made. • $16 • (02/28/97) • **89**
Zinfandel Sonoma County Scherrer Vineyards 1994 • $15 • (04/30/96) • **90**
Zinfandel Sonoma County Scherrer Vineyards 1993 • $14 • (01/31/95) • **87**
Zinfandel Sonoma County Scherrer Vineyards 1992 • $14 • (09/15/94) • **88**
Zinfandel Sonoma County Scherrer Vineyards 1991 • $12 • (08/31/93) HR • **91**

GRGICH HILLS | CALIFORNIA

Cabernet Sauvignon Napa Valley 1994: Starts out on the green side, with herb and spice notes, then reveals more compelling flavors, with hints of tea, currant and wild berry. Finishes with firm but smooth tannins, so cellaring into 2001 is advised. Tasted twice, with consistent notes. 16,800 cases made. • $30 • (10/31/97) • **88**
Cabernet Sauvignon Napa Valley 1993: Well made, if shy of outstanding, with an array of ripe plum, cherry and toasty oak flavors that make it appealing to drink now, as the flavors linger on the finish and it's not too tannic. 6,000 cases made. • $28 • (11/15/96) • **88**
Cabernet Sauvignon Napa Valley 1992: Lean, tart and tannic, with just a glimpse of cherry and cedar flavors peeking through. Lacks the charm and harmony usual to Grgich. Try now. 9,000 cases made. • $26 Ⓐ • (08/31/96) • **79**
Cabernet Sauvignon Napa Valley 1991 • $26 Ⓐ • (12/15/95) • **83**
Cabernet Sauvignon Napa Valley 1990 • $22 • (04/30/95) • **87**
Cabernet Sauvignon Napa Valley 1989 • $22 • (11/15/94) • **81**
Cabernet Sauvignon Napa Valley 1988 • $22 • (11/15/93) • **84**
Cabernet Sauvignon Napa Valley 1987: Harmonious, with ripe plum, cherry and berry notes and dashes of cedar and dill, finishing with soft tannins. Very well balanced and quite appealing. Best now through 2001. • $NA • (12/15/97) • **88**
Cabernet Sauvignon Napa Valley 1986: Well balanced, as the ripe cherry and plum flavors show through quite well and the tannins and oak flavors are in check. The fruit flavor is still strong on the finish, too. Ready to drink. 13,000 cases made. • $29 Ⓐ • (12/15/96) • **89**
Cabernet Sauvignon Napa Valley 1985 • $40 Ⓐ • (10/31/90) • **90**
Cabernet Sauvignon Napa Valley 1984 • $35 Ⓐ • (04/30/89) • **87**
Cabernet Sauvignon Napa Valley 1983 • $17 • (04/30/88) • **90**
Cabernet Sauvignon Napa Valley 1982 • $17 • (04/15/87) • **92**
Cabernet Sauvignon Napa Valley Yountville Selection 1991 • $35 • (12/15/95) • **89**

Chardonnay Napa Valley 1996: A pure, crisp expression of Chardonnay, with a citrus edge. Fans out on the aftertaste, with hints of pear and toasty oak. Has a track record for improving with age, so stash a couple of bottles. Best now through 2002. 34,000 cases made. • $30 • (07/31/98) • **89**
Chardonnay Napa Valley 1995: Brilliantly made. Ripe and elegant, with a spicy core of ripe pear, apple, citrus and melon flavors, this white reveals even more depth and concentration on the finish as the flavors linger. A feather in the cap of this California winemaker. 36,000 cases made. • $28 • (05/31/97) HR • **92**
Chardonnay Napa Valley 1994: Crisp and flinty, with a well-focused core of pear, citrus, lemon and spice, graced by a pretty overlay of smoky, toasty oak. Impressive for its balance and length. Will age well. 35,000 cases made. • $26 • (05/31/96) • **90**
Chardonnay Napa Valley 1993 • $24 • (12/15/95) • **86**
Fumé Blanc Napa Valley 1996: Here's a wonderfully flavorful white for drinking now, rich with melon, grapefruit and spice flavors backed by bracing acidity. This wine pulls no punches, framed with distinctive grassiness and herbal complexity. Reminiscent of Sancerre. 10,864 cases made. • $15 • (03/31/98) SS • **90**
Fumé Blanc Napa Valley 1995: Lively, complex flavors of melon, passion fruit, grapefruit and a touch of grassiness. Tangy, long finish. 15,000 cases made. • $14 • (06/30/97) • **89**
Fumé Blanc Napa Valley 1994 • $14 • (02/29/96) • **82**
Fumé Blanc Napa Valley 1993 • $13 • (03/31/95) • **85**
Johannisberg Riesling Late Harvest Napa Valley 1993 • $50/375ml • (04/30/95) • **88**
Violetta Napa Valley Late Harvest 1994: Rich, honeyed and elegant, its concentrated orange and apricot flavors wrapped in layers of vanilla, nutmeg and cream. Deliciously sweet and balanced, it's a wine to drink by itself for dessert. Terrific now, might improve through 2005. A blend of Riesling and Chardonnay. 4,000 cases made. • $26/375ml • (04/30/97) • **95**
Zinfandel Alexander Valley 1986 • $19 • (05/15/90) • **85**
Zinfandel Alexander Valley 1985 • $19 • (07/31/89) • **84**
Zinfandel Alexander Valley 1984 • $19 • (03/15/87) • **90**
Zinfandel Alexander Valley 1983 • $191 • (05/01/86) • **85**
Zinfandel Alexander Valley 1982 • $18 • (05/16/85) SS • **91**
Zinfandel Sonoma County 1995: An understated style that's supple and complex, with ripe cherry, raspberry, earth, mushroom and cedar flavors. Finishes with soft, fleshy tannins and a hint of anise. Drink now through 2001. 15,000 cases made. • $18 • (03/31/98) • **88**
Zinfandel Sonoma County 1993: Intense. Marked by strong flavors of pepper and peppermint that override the cherry and raspberry flavors, making for a rather one-dimensional taste. Tannic, too. Approachable now, but cellaring will soften and, hopefully, subdue the mintiness a bit. 4,500 cases made. • $16 • (10/15/96) • **85**
Zinfandel Sonoma County 1992 • $14 • (07/31/95) • **84**
Zinfandel Sonoma County 1991 • $13 • (10/15/94) • **84**
Zinfandel Sonoma County 1990 • $13 • (04/30/94) • **85**
Zinfandel Sonoma County 1989 • $13 • (04/30/93) • **85**
Zinfandel Sonoma County 1988 • $12 • (03/31/92) • **85**
Zinfandel Sonoma County 1987 • $22 • (10/15/90) • **84**
Zinfandel Sonoma County 1984 • $11 • (10/31/88) • **86**
Zinfandel Sonoma County 1981 • $10 • (04/01/84) • **80**

GRIFFIN, BARNARD | WASHINGTON

Cabernet-Merlot Columbia Valley 1992 • $10 • (08/31/94) • **86**
Cabernet-Merlot Columbia Valley 1990 • $10 • (03/15/94) BB • **88**
Cabernet Sauvignon Columbia Valley 1993: Rich, supple and generous, loaded with spicy plum, black cherry and lightly smoky flavors that linger and swirl on the finish. Modest tannins. Try now. 490 cases made. • $15 • (03/31/96) • **88**
Cabernet Sauvignon Columbia Valley 1991 • $15 • (09/30/95) • **86**
Cabernet Sauvignon Columbia Valley 1990 • $15 • (09/30/94) • **78**
Chardonnay Columbia Valley 1994: Nicely focused pear and vanilla flavors remain clear and bright in this easy-to-drink Chardonnay. • $13 • (04/30/96) • **86**
Chardonnay Columbia Valley Barrel Fermented 1993 • $13 • (09/30/95) • **84**
Fumé Blanc Columbia Valley 1994 • $9 • (09/30/95) • **87**
Fumé Blanc Columbia Valley 1993 • $9 • (09/15/94) • **83**
Merlot Washington 1993 • $15 • (09/30/95) • **85**

Key: SS—Spectator Selection CS—Cellar Selection HR—Highly Recommended BB—Best Buy $NA—Price not available Ⓐ—Auction Price (BT)—Barrel Tasting
Dates in parentheses indicate the issues in which the ratings were published.

Merlot Washington 1992 • $15 • (12/31/94) • **82**
Merlot Washington 1991 • $15 • (09/30/94) • **78**

GRISTINA | NEW YORK

Cabernet Sauvignon North Fork of Long Island 1993: Harsh and tannic in texture and way out of balance, with too much charred oak for the relatively weak, tart, tomato and plum flavors. Tasted twice, with consistent notes. 335 cases made. • $16 • (05/31/97) • **69**
Cabernet Sauvignon North Fork of Long Island 1988 • $14 • (06/30/91) • **90**
Chardonnay North Fork of Long Island 1994: Crisp and lemony, this well-balanced white has an attractive austerity that will complement food. It's straightforward and lively. 1,800 cases made. • $14 • (12/31/96) • **84**
Chardonnay North Fork of Long Island Andy's Field 1993 • $19 • (10/15/95) • **83**
Merlot North Fork of Long Island 1993: Tannic and has power, but the smoky, earthy flavors outweigh the modest fruit flavors. Try now. 1,010 cases made. • $15 • (12/31/96) • **82**
Merlot North Fork of Long Island Andy's Field 1993: Ripe and well structured, it's deeply-colored, tannic and offers concentrated plum and blackberry flavors with chocolate and burnt coffee accents. Drinkable now. 200 cases made. • $27 • (12/31/96) • **87**
Pinot Noir North Fork of Long Island 1993: Deep color and smoky oak aromas make a good first impression, and are followed up by ripe cherry, smoke and light earth flavors, and firm tannins. Drinkable now. 112 cases made. • $25 • (12/31/96) • **84**

GROTH | CALIFORNIA

Cabernet Sauvignon Napa Valley 1994: Medium-weight, with attractive cedar, herb, and currant notes, it's an elegant style with a supple texture. Mildly tannic. Drink now through 2000. 15,000 cases made. • $27 • (08/31/97) • **88**
Cabernet Sauvignon Napa Valley 1993: Ripe, with chunky cherry and currant flavors, a touch of earthiness and some coffee and weedy herbal notes. The texture is smooth and polished and it turns elegant and supple on the finish. 15,500 cases made. • $20 • (11/15/96) • **88**
Cabernet Sauvignon Napa Valley 1992 • $20 • (09/30/95) CS • **91**
Cabernet Sauvignon Napa Valley 1991 • $55 Ⓐ • (10/15/94) SS • **90**
Cabernet Sauvignon Napa Valley 1990 • $17 • (09/30/93) SS • **90**
Cabernet Sauvignon Napa Valley 1989 • $17 • (11/15/92) • **81**
Cabernet Sauvignon Napa Valley 1988 • $15 Ⓐ • (11/15/91) • **75**
Cabernet Sauvignon Napa Valley 1987 • $43 Ⓐ • (10/31/90) • **81**
Cabernet Sauvignon Napa Valley 1986: Somewhat weedy with an earthy coffee accent at the start, but then plenty of currant and berry flavors burst through and, after a couple of sips, the combination grows on you. Aging well, its tannins are well integrated and the finish lingers. 6,400 cases made. • $55 Ⓐ • (12/15/96) • **90**
Cabernet Sauvignon Napa Valley 1985 • $58 Ⓐ • (11/15/88) • **93**
Cabernet Sauvignon Napa Valley 1984 • $48 Ⓐ • (02/15/88) • **86**
Cabernet Sauvignon Napa Valley 1983 • $13 • (08/31/86) • **85**
Cabernet Sauvignon Napa Valley 1982 • $13 • (11/01/84) • **84**
Cabernet Sauvignon Napa Valley Reserve 1994: Enormously complex, firm and tightly wound, with ripe, firm tannins and a wide range of rich, concentrated flavors, cherry, wild berry, plum, cedar, coffee and spice. Shows remarkable finesse and polish for a young wine. Tempting now for its suppleness, but sure to age for another decade. Michael Weiss was winemaker. Best from 2001 through 2009. 1,650 cases made. • $100 • (05/15/98) CS • **96**
Cabernet Sauvignon Napa Valley Reserve 1992 • $125 Ⓐ • (04/30/96) CS • **98**
Cabernet Sauvignon Napa Valley Reserve 1991 • $58 Ⓐ • (04/15/95) CS • **95**
Cabernet Sauvignon Napa Valley Reserve 1990 • $73 Ⓐ • (11/15/94) CS • **94**
Cabernet Sauvignon Napa Valley Reserve 1989 • $40 • (11/15/93) • **88**
Cabernet Sauvignon Napa Valley Reserve 1988 • $40 • (06/15/93) • **85**
Cabernet Sauvignon Napa Valley Reserve 1987: Smooth and supple, marked by nuances of herb, sage, tea, ash and bell pepper. Underneath is a tasty, flavorful core of ripe black cherry, stewed plum and currant. Tannins are mild and polished. Best now through 2005. • $77 Ⓐ • (12/15/97) • **90**
Cabernet Sauvignon Napa Valley Reserve 1986: Rich, complex, deep and concentrated, with a broad array of spicy currant, coffee, herb, tea and black cherry flavors. The texture is broad and supple and the tannins, while firm, are well integrated, leading to a long, satisfying aftertaste. Drink now through 2005. 475 cases made. • $81 Ⓐ • (12/15/96) • **92**
Cabernet Sauvignon Napa Valley Reserve 1985 • $400 Ⓐ • (04/15/90) • **95**
Cabernet Sauvignon Napa Valley Reserve 1984 • $77 Ⓐ • (04/15/89) • **84**

Cabernet Sauvignon Napa Valley Reserve 1983 • $25 • (12/15/88) • **92**

Chardonnay Napa Valley 1996: A fresh, crisp, flinty style, with tart apple, pear and citrus notes and a pleasant dash of smoky, toasty oak showing through on the finish. Well crafted. A fine value at this price. Drink now through 2000. 5,000 cases made. • $18 • (03/31/98) • **88**

Chardonnay Napa Valley 1995: Tiers of ripe pear, melon and apple flavors emerge from an up-front oaky note, build on the palate and pick up spice and fig accents on the finish. 8,770 cases made. • $15 • (05/15/97) • **88**

Chardonnay Napa Valley 1994: Ripe pear, nut, light oak and spice flavors add up to an enjoyable wine. Finishes with a fruity aftertaste. 9,000 cases made. • $15 • (06/30/96) • **84**

Chardonnay Napa Valley 1993 • $14 • (04/15/95) • **84**

Merlot Napa Valley 1994: Marked by an herbal accent and cedar and spice notes, with currant and berry flavors adding interest. Give it another year or two in the bottle. 1,300 cases made. • $27 • (06/30/97) • **87**

Merlot Napa Valley 1992 • $20 • (09/30/95) • **89**

Merlot Napa Valley 1991 • $17 • (09/15/94) • **82**

Merlot Napa Valley 1990 • $15 • (08/31/93) • **83**

Sauvignon Blanc California 1995: Light, lean and simple, showing modest fruit flavors and an abundance of earthy, mineral notes that build up on the finish. 17,049 cases made. • $10 • (10/31/96) • **80**

Sauvignon Blanc Napa Valley 1994 • $9 • (08/31/95) • **83**

GROVE STREET | CALIFORNIA

Cabernet Sauvignon California Barrel Reserve 1993: Serves up clean, ripe cherry and berry flavors. 13,000 cases made. • $7 • (11/30/96) • **79**

Cabernet Sauvignon California Vineyard Select 1992 • $7 • (11/15/94) • **75**

Chardonnay California Barrel Reserve 1995: Displays some pretty pear and spice flavors that feel solid and straightforward. Ready now. 13,500 cases made. • $8 • (11/30/97) • **82**

Chardonnay California Barrel Reserve 1994: A light and simple Chardonnay, with a mineral scent that adds character to the nectarine flavors. For drinking now. 20,000 cases made. • $7 • (11/30/96) • **81**

Chardonnay Sonoma County Healdsburg Vineyard Select 1993 • $7 • (07/31/95) • **77**

GRUET | NEW MEXICO

Blanc de Blancs New Mexico 1992: Something unexpected from New Mexico. Citrus and herb flavors and bracing acidity give this well-made bubbly a forceful personality. Has a full, persistent mousse. Drink now. • $20 • (12/31/97) • **85**

Blanc de Noirs New Mexico NV: Very dry and lean in style, this green-apple flavored bubbly shows ample acidity, very tight flavors and a green finish. Drink now. • $14 • (12/31/97) • **79**

Brut New Mexico NV: Full-bodied, flavorful, mouthfilling bubbly with layers of bold, fresh fruit flavors accented by butter and vanilla and vivid acidity. Not subtle, but quite enjoyable. Drink now. • $14 • (12/31/97) • **87**

Grand Rosé New Mexico NV: Full-bodied and mouthfilling, but not very flavorful, this is dry and slightly toasty in character. Drink now. • $28 • (12/31/97) • **81**

GUENOC | CALIFORNIA

Cabernet Franc Lake County 1985 • $12 • (02/15/89) • **70**

Cabernet Franc Napa Valley 1990 • $14 • (11/15/93) • **83**

Cabernet Sauvignon Guenoc Valley Premier Cuvée 1985 • $17 • (10/15/90) • **84**

Cabernet Sauvignon Guenoc Valley Tephra Ridge Reserve 1997: Tight, a bit tart, and a bit awkward at this very early stage. The core of cherry and currant is firmly tannic. • $NA • (07/31/98) (BT) • **85-89**

Cabernet Sauvignon Guenoc Valley Tephra Ridge Reserve 1996: Elegant in style. Ripe and spicy, with plum, cherry and berry flavors and a light oak note, finishing with a plummy aftertaste. 300 cases made. • $NA • (06/15/97) (BT) • **85-89**

Cabernet Sauvignon Guenoc Valley Tephra Ridge Reserve 1993: Appealing for its ripe, bright fruit flavors of cherry, plum and wild berry, turning tart and simple on the finish. 310 cases made. • $30 • (12/15/95) • **86**

Cabernet Sauvignon Lake County 1994: A chewy wine that has bright cherry and herb overtones and tannins that are slightly coarse. Drink now or hold. 14,530 cases made. • $15 • (11/15/97) • **84**

Cabernet Sauvignon Lake County 1993: Young and vibrant, offering ripe, fresh cherry, currant, herb and tea flavors. Finish has a tart, slightly green edge. Ready now. 12,029 cases made. • $15 • (10/15/96) • **85**

Cabernet Sauvignon Lake County 1992 • $15 • (12/15/95) • **85**

Cabernet Sauvignon Lake County 1991 • $15 • (11/15/94) • **85**

Cabernet Sauvignon Lake County 1990 • $11 • (04/15/94) • **84**

Cabernet Sauvignon Lake County 1989 • $12 • (11/15/92) • **77**

Cabernet Sauvignon Lake County 1987 • $12 • (07/15/91) • **89**

Cabernet Sauvignon Lake County 1986 • $13 • (04/30/91) • **78**

Cabernet Sauvignon Lake County 1983 • $9 • (09/30/86) • **89**

Cabernet Sauvignon Lake County 1981 • $8 • (12/16/84) • **78**

Cabernet Sauvignon Napa Valley Beckstoffer IV Vineyard Reserve 1994: Sharply focused, with a pretty core of ripe cherry, currant, plum and berry, showing remarkable polish and finesse, and even though the flavors are young and the tannins are crisp, the finish is long and lively. Tempting now, but worthy of cellaring into 2000. 1,708 cases made. • $40 • (10/31/97) • **93**

Cabernet Sauvignon Napa Valley Beckstoffer IV Vineyard Reserve 1993: Young and vibrant, with a tart cherry and wild berry accent to the flavors. A good Beckstoffer Vineyard bottling, but not as rich or dramatic as in past vintages. Drinks well now. 1,965 cases made. • $40 • (11/15/96) • **88**

Cabernet Sauvignon Napa Valley Beckstoffer IV Vineyard Reserve 1992 • $40 • (12/15/95) • **90**

Cabernet Sauvignon Napa Valley Beckstoffer Vineyard Reserve 1991 • $35 • (09/30/94) CS • **94**

Cabernet Sauvignon Napa Valley Beckstoffer Vineyard Reserve 1990 • $35 • (11/15/93) HR • **92**

Cabernet Sauvignon Napa Valley Beckstoffer Vineyard Reserve 1989 • $30 • (03/31/93) • **85**

Cabernet Sauvignon Napa Valley Beckstoffer Vineyard Reserve 1987: Still quite youthful and vibrant, with rich currant, cedar, black cherry and anise flavors and a firm but supple wall of tannin. Turns supple and fleshy as it unfolds, with dashes of herb and spice on the finish. Best now through 2002. 1,304 cases made. • $65 • (12/15/97) • **91**

Cabernet Sauvignon Napa Valley Bella Vista Vineyard Reserve 1994: Smooth, ripe and juicy, with a pretty array of plum, cherry and berry flavors. Finishing with firm, but supple tannins and fine length. Best to cellar into 1999 to 2000. 764 cases made. • $26 • (09/30/97) • **90**

Cabernet Sauvignon Napa Valley Bella Vista Vineyard Reserve 1993: Distinctive for its spicy cherry and wild berry flavors, gaining complexity and finesse on the finish. In an elegant, understated style, it's well balanced and has a lingering finish. 787 cases made. • $25 • (11/15/96) • **88**

Cabernet Sauvignon Napa Valley Bella Vista Vineyard Reserve 1992 • $25 • (12/15/95) • **90**

Cabernet Sauvignon North Coast 1991 • $12 • (11/15/94) • **82**

Cabernet Sauvignon North Coast 1988 • $12 • (08/31/92) • **79**

Chardonnay Guenoc Valley 1995: Clean and elegant, with pretty citrus, pear and light pineapple shadings, a touch of grapefruit on the finish. Tastes much better than an earlier bottle. 15,194 cases made. • $15 • (06/15/97) • **89**

Chardonnay Guenoc Valley 1994: Sleek and elegant, a trim and focused style showing nectarine, pear and citrus flavors that turn flinty on the finish. 11,913 cases made. • $15 • (04/30/96) • **87**

Chardonnay Guenoc Valley 1993 • $15 • (02/28/95) • **86**

Chardonnay Guenoc Valley Genevieve Magoon Vineyard Reserve 1996: Intense and lively, with a core of citrus, grassy pear and spice, finishing with subtle oak shadings and fine length. Packs in lots of flavor and nuance, built on an elegant frame. Best now through 2003. 3,143 cases made. • $25 • (06/30/98) • **90**

Chardonnay Guenoc Valley Genevieve Magoon Vineyard Reserve 1995: Smooth, ripe and harmonious, with a complex core of ripe pear, spice, apple and hazelnut flavors that are deep, concentrated and linger on the aftertaste. 3,567 cases made. • $23 • (05/31/97) • **92**

Chardonnay Guenoc Valley Genevieve Magoon Vineyard Reserve 1994: Marked by grassy nuances to the pear and tangerine flavors, and holds together nicely on the palate, finishing in a slight citrus edge. 3,200 cases made. • $23 • (04/30/96) • **88**

Chardonnay Guenoc Valley Genevieve Magoon Vineyard Reserve 1993 • $25 • (05/31/95) HR • **90**

Chardonnay Guenoc Valley Genevieve Magoon Vineyard Unfiltered Reserve 1996: Starts out lean and trim, but slowly builds in flavor. The citrus, pear and pippin apple flavors are tight and flinty, with an earthy, mineral flavor on the finish. Toasty oak lingers in the background. Best now through 2004. 446 cases made. • $30 • (06/30/98) • **92**

Chardonnay Guenoc Valley Genevieve Magoon Vineyard Unfiltered Reserve 1995: Delicious, with layers of flavors, ranging from ripe pear, fig and apple to spice, anise, vanilla and cedar, that really take off on the long, lively finish, revealing extra complexity and concentration. 459 cases made. • $30 • (05/31/97) • **93**

Chardonnay Guenoc Valley Genevieve Magoon Vineyard Unfiltered Reserve 1994: Intense, elegant, attractive pear, spice, fig and melon notes. This is a solid Chardonnay that holds together well. 396 cases made. • $30 • (05/15/96) • **88**
Chardonnay North Coast 1996: Distinctively spicy, with a Muscat-like edge. Ripe pear and apple fold in to give a broader range of flavors. 6,000 cases made. • $16 • (05/15/98) • **87**
Langtry California Meritage Red 1993: Ripe, smooth and elegant. Spicy black cherry and wild berry flavors, with hints of currant, finishing with a firm, dry tannic edge. Try now. 1,960 cases made. • $41 • (11/15/96) • **88**
Langtry California Meritage Red 1992 • $35 • (12/15/95) • **89**
Langtry California Meritage Red 1991 • $35 • (09/30/94) HR • **91**
Langtry Guenoc Valley Meritage White 1993 • $17 • (04/30/95) • **88**
Langtry Lake County Meritage Red 1990 • $35 • (11/15/93) HR • **91**
Langtry Lake County Meritage Red 1989 • $35 • (11/15/92) • **88**
Langtry Lake-Napa Counties Meritage Red 1988 • $35 • (11/15/91) • **86**
Langtry Lake-Napa Counties Meritage Red 1987 • $35 • (04/15/91) • **88**
Langtry Napa Valley Meritage Red 1994: Young and fruity, with a supple texture and appealing plum and cherry flavors. Builds intensity on the finish as the flavors linger. Drinkable now. A blend of 46 percent Cabernet Sauvignon, 31 percent Petit Verdot, 16 percent Merlot, 6 percent Cabernet Franc, and 1 percent Malbec. 2,549 cases made. • $41 • (09/30/97) • **90**
Meritage Red Lake County 1994: The firm core of mint, herbs, cassis, and blackberry flavors is tightly wound and the tannins are big, but ripe and smooth. Will benefit from a few more years in the cellar. A blend of Cabernet Franc, Merlot, Cabernet Sauvignon, Malbec, and Petit Verdot. 4,459 cases made. • $15 • (11/15/97) • **86**
Meritage Red Lake County 1992 • $15 • (12/15/95) • **88**
Meritage Red Lake County 1991 • $15 • (10/31/94) SS • **89**
Meritage Red Lake County 1990 • $18 Ⓐ • (11/15/93) SS • **91**
Meritage Red Lake County 1989 • $17 • (11/15/92) • **83**
Merlot Guenoc Valley 1985 • $15 • (03/31/89) • **85**
Merlot Lake-Napa Counties 1987 • $14 • (11/15/91) • **86**
Merlot Lake-Napa Counties 1986 • $12 • (06/15/90) • **80**
Petit Verdot Napa Valley 1993: Tart and a bit tannic, with a narrow band of spicy cherry and wild berry flavors. 614 cases made. • $18 • (11/30/96) • **83**
Petite Sirah California 1995: Tames some of the rugged tannins in Petite Sirah, allowing the fruit to shine through—ripe cherry, plum and wild berry flavors. Drink now with hearty fare or cellar into 2000. • $16 • (04/30/98) • **87**
Petite Sirah Guenoc Valley 1988 • $10 • (08/31/91) • **86**
Petite Sirah Guenoc Valley 1985 • $7 • (02/15/89) • **83**
Petite Sirah Guenoc Valley 1984 • $7 • (11/15/87) • **77**
Petite Sirah North Coast 1992: Supple and aromatic, with pretty floral and fruity aromas. Lots of pure cherry and berry flavors with minerally nuances. Manages to tame the tannins throughout. 6,180 cases made. • $14 • (08/31/96) • **89**
Petite Sirah North Coast 1990 • $13 • (09/30/94) • **84**
Petite Sirah North Coast 1989 • $14 • (06/30/92) • **82**
Port California 1994: Rich and spicy, with lots of stewed prune, chocolate, cinnamon and vanilla aromas and flavors competing for attention. Has plenty of style a sense of elegance, and a nice grip on the finish. Best from 2003 or so. 850 cases made. • $25 • (02/28/97) • **88**
Port California 1992 • $15 • (05/31/95) • **89**
Sauvignon Blanc Guenoc Valley 1995: Spicy and fruity, like applesauce. Has a smooth texture and an odd floral overtone on the finish. Ready now. 2,322 cases made. • $11 • (07/31/96) • **83**
Sauvignon Blanc Guenoc Valley 1994 • $11 • (07/31/95) • **87**
Sauvignon Blanc Guenoc Valley 1993 • $11 • (01/31/95) • **82**
Sauvignon Blanc North Coast 1996: A lighter-styled wine, with lemon, green pea, melon and herb flavors. Refreshing and simple. 927 cases made. • $14 • (04/30/98) • **84**
Sauvignon Blanc-Sémillon Guenoc Valley Langtry Meritage 1996: A blend of nut and herb essence, followed by notes of grapefruit, melon and grass. The wine is well balanced, with good integration, firm, yet smooth in texture. 82 percent Sauvignon Blanc, 18 percent Sémillon. 2,675 cases made. • $21 • (04/30/98) • **87**
Zinfandel California 1991 • $9 • (09/30/93) • **86**
Zinfandel California 1990 • $10 • (09/30/92) • **84**
Zinfandel California 1989 • $9 • (05/15/92) • **85**

Key: SS—Spectator Selection CS—Cellar Selection HR—Highly Recommended BB—Best Buy $NA—Price not available Ⓐ—Auction Price (BT)—Barrel Tasting
Dates in parentheses indicate the issues in which the ratings were published.

Zinfandel California 1988 • $7 • (09/15/90) • **76**
Zinfandel Guenoc Valley 1987 • $8 • (05/15/90) • **84**
Zinfandel Lake County 1985 • $5 • (03/31/89) • **79**
Zinfandel Lake County 1981 • $5 • (05/16/84) • **78**

GUGLIELMO | CALIFORNIA

Cabernet Sauvignon Monterey County 1989 • $8 • (11/15/94) • **74**
Cabernet Sauvignon Santa Clara County Private Reserve 1986 • $12 • (11/15/93) • **75**
Merlot Monterey County Private Reserve 1995: A brightly textured red, with layers of cherry, spice, licorice, blackberry and herbs. Hints of cedar linger on the finish. Shows complexity, lacks integration. 834 cases made. • $15 • (04/30/98) • **86**
Merlot Napa Valley 1990 • $8 • (09/15/94) • **78**
Petite Sirah Santa Clara Valley 1993: A dense, intense color and flavors of blueberry, black cherry and black pepper make this a good match for meaty, gamy food. Not terribly tannic, so have at it right away. 1,000 cases made. • $11 • (11/30/96) • **86**
Pinot Noir Santa Clara Valley Private Reserve 1990 • $10 • (02/28/93) • **75**
Sangiovese California 1994: Crisp, bordering on tart, with definite tar and anise overtones, finishing a bit thin. Ready now. 500 cases made. • $10 • (11/30/96) • **82**
Sangiovese California Private Reserve 1995: Has a sweet-and-sour feel to it, with earthy, almost medicinal overtones to the black cherry flavor, and finishing very soft. 500 cases made. • $12 • (11/30/97) • **77**
Zinfandel Santa Clara Valley Private Reserve 1991 • $9 • (10/15/95) • **78**
Zinfandel Santa Clara Valley Private Reserve 1989 • $NA • (10/15/94) • **79**
Zinfandel Santa Clara Valley Private Reserve 1988 • $8 • (09/30/93) • **84**

GUILLIAMS | CALIFORNIA

Cabernet Sauvignon Napa Valley Spring Mountain District 1990 • $15 • (11/15/94) • **86**
Cabernet Sauvignon Spring Mountain 1993: There's a lot going on in this wine's flavor profile—not all of it charming. A strong herbal streak runs through the earthy berry and mineral flavors. Drink now. 1,200 cases made. • $20 • (12/15/97) • **81**
Cabernet Sauvignon Spring Mountain 1991 • $17 • (12/15/95) • **88**

GUNDLACH BUNDSCHU | CALIFORNIA

Bearitage Sonoma Valley 1990 • $10 • (05/15/93) • **81**
Cabernet Franc Sonoma Valley Rhinefarm Vineyards 1994: Smooth, with lots of spice, plum, currant and cedary oak flavors that fold together harmoniously on the finish. Drinkable now. 2,155 cases made. • $14 • (12/15/96) • **86**
Cabernet Franc Sonoma Valley Rhinefarm Vineyards 1989 • $12 • (02/29/92) • **87**
Cabernet Franc Sonoma Valley Rhinefarm Vineyards 1987 • $12 • (09/15/90) • **89**
Cabernet Sauvignon Sonoma Valley 1986 • $9 • (11/15/89) • **87**
Cabernet Sauvignon Sonoma Valley 1981 • $10 • (05/16/85) • **85**
Cabernet Sauvignon Sonoma Valley Batto Ranch 1983 • $14 • (02/15/88) • **74**
Cabernet Sauvignon Sonoma Valley Batto Ranch 1982 • $12 • (06/16/85) • **89**
Cabernet Sauvignon Sonoma Valley Rhinefarm Vineyards 1994: Dense, chewy and earthy. The currant and berry flavors have a cheesy, leathery edge to them which time may help straighten out. Try in 1999 to 2000. 8,500 cases made. • $20 • (01/01/97) • **82**
Cabernet Sauvignon Sonoma Valley Rhinefarm Vineyards 1992 • $15 • (10/31/95) • **87**
Cabernet Sauvignon Sonoma Valley Rhinefarm Vineyards 1991 • $15 • (10/31/94) • **88**
Cabernet Sauvignon Sonoma Valley Rhinefarm Vineyards 1990 • $14 • (11/15/93) • **83**
Cabernet Sauvignon Sonoma Valley Rhinefarm Vineyards 1989 • $15 • (11/15/92) • **80**
Cabernet Sauvignon Sonoma Valley Rhinefarm Vineyards 1987 • $15 • (05/15/91) • **85**
Cabernet Sauvignon Sonoma Valley Rhinefarm Vineyards 1985 • $12 • (03/31/89) • **78**
Cabernet Sauvignon Sonoma Valley Rhinefarm Vineyards 1984 • $10 • (09/30/88) • **84**

Cabernet Sauvignon Sonoma Valley Rhinefarm Vineyards 1974 • $40 • (11/15/94) • **74**
Cabernet Sauvignon Sonoma Valley Rhinefarm Vineyards Reserve 1989 • $24 • (11/15/93) • **84**
Cabernet Sauvignon Sonoma Valley Rhinefarm Vineyards Reserve 1986 • $25 • (08/31/91) • **83**
Cabernet Sauvignon Sonoma Valley Rhinefarm Vineyards Reserve 1982 • $20 • (09/15/87) • **71**
Cabernet Sauvignon Sonoma Valley Rhinefarm Vineyards Reserve 1981 • $20 • (11/30/86) • **88**
Cabernet Sauvignon Sonoma Valley Rhinefarm Vineyards Vintage Reserve 1993: Lean and trim, with an earthy, herbal, slightly weedy edge to the currant and berry flavors. Fills out a bit on the finish, where the vanilla and chocolate notes emerge. 1,250 cases made. • $34 • (09/30/97) • **85**
Cabernet Sauvignon Sonoma Valley Rhinefarm Vineyards Vintage Reserve 1992: In a complex and harmonious style, with a pretty array of currant, wild berry and cherry flavors, notes of herb, cedar and spice. The texture is smooth and supple, showing its tannic strength on the finish. Given its intensity and tannin level, best to cellar this one 1999 to 2003. 1,260 cases made. • $30 • (11/15/96) • **90**
Cabernet Sauvignon Sonoma Valley Rhinefarm Vineyards Vintage Reserve 1987 • $22 • (07/31/92) • **89**
Chardonnay Sonoma Valley Rhinefarm Vineyards 1996: A grassy, herbaceous style that's a bit like Sauvignon Blanc, with a tangy, racy streak of citrus and grapefruit. Drink now through 2000. 4,900 cases made. • $14 • (07/31/98) • **83**
Chardonnay Sonoma Valley Sangiacomo Ranch 1996: Bright and lively, with intense citrus, pear and pineapple flavors that are crisp and refreshing. Finishes with herb and leaf notes. Drink now through 2001. 1,200 cases made. • $16 • (07/31/98) • **87**
Chardonnay Sonoma Valley Sangiacomo Ranch 1995: Tight and firm, with a crisp, juicy band of citrus, pear, pineapple and spice flavors. 1,260 cases made. • $17 • (02/28/97) • **86**
Chardonnay Sonoma Valley Sangiacomo Ranch 1994: Nice blend of pear and apple flavors, accented with a hint of gragefruit. Clean and correct, though somwhat one dimensional. 1,245 cases made. • $15 • (07/31/96) • **85**
Chardonnay Sonoma Valley Sangiacomo Ranch Special Selection 1993 • $15 • (11/15/95) • **89**
Gewürztraminer Sonoma Valley 1994 • $9 • (11/15/95) • **84**
Gewürztraminer Sonoma Valley Rhinefarm Vineyards 1997: Somewhat one-dimensional for this multifaceted varietal. Bright, lemony flavors start this off nicely, but the follow-up is weak. Drink now. 5,500 cases made. • $12 • (06/30/98) • **81**
Gewürztraminer Sonoma Valley Rhinefarm Vineyards 1996: Starts off bright and fruity, offering orange-scented nectarine and spice flavors. 3,900 cases made. • $10 • (07/31/97) • **85**
Merlot Sonoma Valley Rhinefarm Vineyards 1994: Solid, if still tight and unevolved, but the core of plum and currant flavor is well focused and the tannins are in check. Pleasant aftertaste. Try now to 2000. • $21 • (03/31/97) • **88**
Merlot Sonoma Valley Rhinefarm Vineyards 1993: Marked by a cedary edge, this medium-weight wine offers a modest core of currant and herb flavors. Should soften and may flesh out a bit more. 9,900 cases made. • $18 • (08/31/96) • **84**
Merlot Sonoma Valley Rhinefarm Vineyards 1992 • $16 • (01/31/95) • **88**
Merlot Sonoma Valley Rhinefarm Vineyards 1990 • $16 • (10/15/93) • **85**
Merlot Sonoma Valley Rhinefarm Vineyards 1989 • $16 • (05/31/92) • **80**
Merlot Sonoma Valley Rhinefarm Vineyards 1988 • $20 • (05/31/91) • **81**
Merlot Sonoma Valley Rhinefarm Vineyards 1987 • $18 • (10/31/89) SS • **93**
Merlot Sonoma Valley Rhinefarm Vineyards 1986 • $19 • (12/31/88) • **91**
Merlot Sonoma Valley Rhinefarm Vineyards 1985 • $20 • (02/29/88) SS • **92**
Merlot Sonoma Valley Rhinefarm Vineyards 1984 • $20 • (02/28/87) • **88**
Merlot Sonoma Valley Rhinefarm Vineyards 1983 • $15 Ⓐ • (05/01/86) HR • **92**
Merlot Sonoma Valley Rhinefarm Vineyards 1982 • $19 • (10/01/85) • **88**
Pinot Noir Sonoma Valley Rhinefarm Vineyards 1995: Earthy up front, with a dry, leathery quality that dominates both flavor and texture, and finishing with a sage, tea, dried cherry and earth edge. Best to cellar short-term. 1,100 cases made. • $14 • (08/31/97) • **86**
Pinot Noir Sonoma Valley Rhinefarm Vineyards 1994: Made in an elegant, understated style that succeeds with its ripe, spicy cherry and berry flavors and light tannins. Drinks well now. 2,100 cases made. • $14 • (11/30/96) • **84**
Pinot Noir Sonoma Valley Rhinefarm Vineyards 1993 • $14 • (12/31/95) • **85**
Pinot Noir Sonoma Valley Rhinefarm Vineyards 1992 • $14 • (03/31/95) • **82**
Pinot Noir Sonoma Valley Rhinefarm Vineyards 1991 • $14 • (02/28/94) • **78**
Pinot Noir Sonoma Valley Rhinefarm Vineyards 1989 • $14 • (10/31/91) • **83**
Pinot Noir Sonoma Valley Rhinefarm Vineyards 1988 • $12 • (02/28/91) • **88**
Pinot Noir Sonoma Valley Rhinefarm Vineyards 1986 • $14 • (06/15/88) • **89**
Pinot Noir Sonoma Valley Rhinefarm Vineyards 1985 • $10 • (02/29/88) • **81**
Pinot Noir Sonoma Valley Rhinefarm Vineyards 1982 • $9 • (05/01/84) • **75**
Red #2 Sonoma Valley NV • $5 • (11/15/89) • **77**
Riesling Sonoma Valley Dresel's Sonoma Riesling 1993 • $9 • (06/15/95) • **83**
Zinfandel Sonoma Valley 1994: A wonderful Zin at a great price. Ripe cherry and berry flavors, with a classic, spicy, peppery edge, finishing with a hint of tar. A supple, easy-drinking wine that hits the spot. Ready now. • $12 • (12/15/96) • **88**
Zinfandel Sonoma Valley 1992 • $10 • (09/15/94) SS • **92**
Zinfandel Sonoma Valley 1991 • $10 • (09/30/93) • **85**
Zinfandel Sonoma Valley 1989 • $7 • (07/31/91) • **84**
Zinfandel Sonoma Valley 1988 • $7 • (05/31/90) BB • **88**
Zinfandel Sonoma Valley 1987 • $7 • (03/31/89) • **87**
Zinfandel Sonoma Valley Morse Vineyard 1996: Quite fruity, with strawberry, cherry candy and herbs coming to the fore. A bit odd in style; more like Beaujolais. 1,495 cases made. • $14 • (06/15/98) • **80**
Zinfandel Sonoma Valley Rhinefarm Vineyards 1996: An openly fruity style, with lots of ripe black cherry, plum and blueberry flavors and mild, supple tannins. Fruit lingers on the complex aftertaste. Drink now through 2002. 1,934 cases made. • $16 • (06/15/98) • **88**
Zinfandel Sonoma Valley Rhinefarm Vineyards 1994: Well crafted, this strikes a nice balance between spicy sage and minty notes and wild berry flavors. Turns elegant on the finish. 2,050 cases made. • $16 • (03/31/97) • **88**
Zinfandel Sonoma Valley Rhinefarm Vineyards 1993 • $14 • (10/15/95) • **88**
Zinfandel Sonoma Valley Rhinefarm Vineyards 1990 • $9 • (09/30/92) • **87**
Zinfandel Sonoma Valley Rhinefarm Vineyards 1989 • $12 • (07/31/91) • **87**
Zinfandel Sonoma Valley Rhinefarm Vineyards 1988 • $10 • (12/15/90) • **88**
Zinfandel Sonoma Valley Rhinefarm Vineyards 1987 • $8 • (09/15/89) • **71**
Zinfandel Sonoma Valley Rhinefarm Vineyards 1986 • $8 • (09/15/88) • **90**
Zinfandel Sonoma Valley Rhinefarm Vineyards 1985 • $8 • (02/29/88) • **84**
Zinfandel Sonoma Valley Rhinefarm Vineyards 1984 • $7 • (04/30/87) BB • **87**
Zinfandel Sonoma Valley Rhinefarm Vineyards 1982 • $7 • (02/16/86) • **87**

HACIENDA | CALIFORNIA

Antares Sonoma County 1987 • $28 • (11/15/90) • **91**
Antares Sonoma County 1986 • $28 • (07/31/89) • **91**
Cabernet Sauvignon California Clair de Lune 1992 • $7 • (11/15/94) • **72**
Cabernet Sauvignon Sonoma County 1987 • $15 • (11/15/92) • **81**
Cabernet Sauvignon Sonoma County 1986 • $15 • (11/15/91) • **87**
Cabernet Sauvignon Sonoma County 1985 • $15 • (09/30/90) • **83**
Cabernet Sauvignon Sonoma Valley 1983 • $11 • (05/31/88) • **86**
Cabernet Sauvignon Sonoma Valley 1982 • $11 • (09/01/85) • **63**
Cabernet Sauvignon Sonoma Valley Reserve 1985 • $18 • (11/15/92) • **78**
Cabernet Sauvignon Sonoma Valley Reserve 1984 • $18 • (05/31/91) • **87**
Cabernet Sauvignon Sonoma Valley Selected Reserve 1982 • $18 • (03/31/87) • **86**
Chardonnay California Clair de Lune 1994: Soft, fragrant floral and honey notes, but a little funky, too, its modest fruit hanging on the finish. Ready now. 6,000 cases made. • $7 • (05/15/96) • **81**
Chardonnay California Clair de Lune 1993 • $6 • (02/28/95) • **83**
Merlot California Clair de Lune 1996: Sports a kind of candied-cherry flavor backed by rough-hewn oak. 30,000 cases made. • $7 • (03/31/98) • **79**
Merlot California Clair de Lune 1992 • $8 • (09/15/94) • **81**
Pinot Noir Sonoma Valley 1982 • $12 • (12/16/84) • **85**
Pinot Noir Sonoma Valley Estate Reserve 1989 • $17 • (11/30/92) • **81**
Pinot Noir Sonoma Valley Estate Reserve 1987 • $15 • (10/31/90) • **78**
Pinot Noir Sonoma Valley Estate Reserve 1986 • $15 • (06/15/88) • **80**
Pinot Noir Sonoma Valley Estate Reserve 1985 • $15 • (06/15/88) • **86**

HAGAFEN | CALIFORNIA

Cabernet Sauvignon Napa Valley 1995: Firm in texture, modest in flavor, with some pretty berry notes sneaking through the layer of chewiness. Best after 2000. 1,000 cases made. • $20 • (12/15/97) • **85**
Cabernet Sauvignon Napa Valley 1993: Smooth and graceful, a veil of tough tannins covering the bright currant and blackberry flavors. Drink now. 900 cases made. • $20 • (12/15/95) • **83**
Cabernet Sauvignon Napa Valley 1990 • $20 • (05/15/94) • **77**
Cabernet Sauvignon Napa Valley 1989 • $20 • (12/15/92) • **68**
Cabernet Sauvignon Napa Valley 1988 • $20 • (03/31/91) HR • **88**
Cabernet Sauvignon Napa Valley 1987 • $20 • (04/30/90) • **88**
Cabernet Sauvignon Napa Valley Reserve 1989 • $28 • (12/15/95) • **84**

Cabernet Sauvignon Napa Valley Reserve 1988 • $28 • (03/31/93) • **85**
Chardonnay Napa Valley 1996: Shows nice tropical fruit and a pretty oak edge, though it's lacking in depth and complexity. Clean on the finish. 700 cases made. • $14 • (02/28/98) • **83**
Chardonnay Napa Valley 1995: Delightful for its delicious sweet apple, quince and vanilla flavors on a crisp, tangy background. Bright, light and ready now for its freshness. 900 cases made. • $14 • (06/15/97) • **87**
Chardonnay Napa Valley Reserve 1995: Lea and mineral-tinged, but with a soft texture, nonetheless. On the palate, the flavors run mildly tropical—mangoes, perhaps. The finish is moderate, with hints of apple and pear. 400 cases made. • $18 • (01/31/98) • **87**
Chardonnay Napa Valley Reserve 1993: Tropical fruit and spicy, toasty flavors. A modest wine with some extra dimensions. 600 cases made. • $17 • (07/31/96) • **83**
Harmonia Napa Valley 1994 • $8 • (11/30/95) • **77**
Johannisberg Riesling Napa Valley 1996: On the dry side, with very pretty nectarine, peach and spice flavors swirling through the generous finish. Very tasty now as an apéritif. 900 cases made. • $10 • (05/15/97) • **87**
Johannisberg Riesling Napa Valley 1994 • $8 • (06/15/95) • **86**
Pinot Noir Napa Valley 1996: A lighter style, with hints of cherry, cola and spice. The texture is smooth, almost waxy. The short finish has a slightly bitter, smoky edge. 1,300 cases made. • $13 • (02/28/98) • **84**
Pinot Noir Napa Valley 1994: Has a harsh, chemical edge to the coarse berry flavors. Not charming. • $12 • (07/31/96) • **77**
Pinot Noir Napa Valley 1991 • $11 • (02/28/94) • **77**
Red Table Wine Napa Valley NV • $7 • (06/30/92) • **75**

HAHN | CALIFORNIA

Cabernet Franc Santa Lucia Highlands 1995: Marked by strongly vegetal flavors, it has some interesting herbal elements as well, but it's just not made from ripe grapes. 29,637 cases made. • $12 • (09/15/97) • **77**
Cabernet Franc Santa Lucia Highlands 1994: Emits distinctly herbal aromas, but the flavors center around berry and mint. Finishing with some richness. Ready to drink. 2,792 cases made. • $10 • (11/30/96) BB • **85**
Cabernet Sauvignon Monterey 1989 • $10 • (06/15/93) • **73**
Cabernet Sauvignon Monterey 1988 • $10 • (11/15/92) • **80**
Cabernet Sauvignon Santa Lucia Highlands 1994: A bit disjointed, with strong cola and herb flavors coming to the fore. Finishes with a green edge. 7,206 cases made. • $10 • (09/30/97) • **79**
Cabernet Sauvignon Santa Lucia Highlands 1993: This offers a modest band of cedar-accented Cabernet flavors, picking up hints of toasty oak and spice on the finish. A good value. 9,025 cases made. • $10 • (12/15/96) • **83**
Cabernet Sauvignon Santa Lucia Highlands 1992 • $10 • (08/31/95) • **83**
Cabernet Sauvignon Santa Lucia Highlands 1991 • $10 • (11/15/94) • **80**
Cabernet Sauvignon Santa Lucia Highlands 1990 • $10 • (05/15/94) • **80**
Chardonnay Monterey 1996: A strange character—more kerosene and smoke than fruit—derails this wine. 26,500 cases made. • $10 • (11/30/97) • **78**
Chardonnay Monterey 1995: Smooth, with a spicy nuance to the toast and honey flavors, which overshadow the fruit. 22,500 cases made. • $10 • (12/15/96) • **82**
Chardonnay Monterey 1994: Crisp, simple and appealing, a little short on fruit but adding citrus notes on the finish. 12,391 cases made. • $10 • (10/31/95) • **81**
Chardonnay Monterey 1993 • $10 • (03/31/95) • **85**
Merlot Monterey 1992 • $10 • (09/15/94) • **81**
Merlot Monterey 1991 • $10 • (06/15/93) • **84**
Merlot Monterey 1990 • $10 • (05/31/92) • **83**
Merlot Monterey 1989 • $10 • (05/31/92) • **86**
Merlot Santa Lucia Highlands 1995: Musty, beefy aromas permeate. A wild cherry note struggles to emerge, but falters on the slightly vinegarlike finish. • $NA • (03/31/98) • **76**
Merlot Santa Lucia Highlands 1994: Cedary oak flavors, punctuated by strong herb, particularly dill, and green bean accents. 18,000 cases made. • $11 • (08/31/96) • **78**
Merlot Santa Lucia Highlands 1993 • $10 • (12/15/95) • **82**

HALLCREST | CALIFORNIA

Barbera El Dorado Ritchie Vineyard 1990 • $12 • (11/30/92) • **80**

Key: SS—Spectator Selection CS—Cellar Selection HR—Highly Recommended BB—Best Buy $NA—Price not available Ⓐ—Auction Price (BT)—Barrel Tasting
Dates in parentheses indicate the issues in which the ratings were published.

Cabernet Sauvignon El Dorado County Covington Vineyard 1990 • $19 • (11/15/94) • **86**
Cabernet Sauvignon El Dorado County Covington Vineyard 1989 • $12 • (11/15/92) • **76**
Cabernet Sauvignon El Dorado County De Cascabel Vineyard 1989 • $14 • (06/15/93) • **70**
Cabernet Sauvignon El Dorado County De Cascabel Vineyard 1988 • $15 • (11/15/92) • **81**
Cabernet Sauvignon El Dorado County De Cascabel Vineyard 1987 • $13 • (11/15/91) • **83**
Cabernet Sauvignon El Dorado County De Cascabel Vineyard Proprietors Reserve 1990 • $13 • (11/15/94) • **85**
Cabernet Sauvignon Santa Cruz Mountains Beauregard Ranch Proprietors Reserve 1990 • $23 • (11/15/94) • **84**
Clos de Jeannine California 1990 • $7 • (05/31/93) • **84**
Clos de Jeannine California 1989 • $8 • (10/31/91) • **82**
Merlot El Dorado County De Cascabel Vineyard 1991 • $14 • (07/15/93) • **83**
Merlot El Dorado County De Cascabel Vineyard 1989 • $15 • (05/31/92) • **74**
Merlot El Dorado County De Cascabel Vineyard 1988 • $15 • (05/31/92) • **78**
Merlot El Dorado County De Cascabel Vineyard Proprietors Reserve 1991 • $19 • (11/15/94) • **87**
Syrah California Doe Mill Cuvée 1989 • $7 • (04/30/91) • **86**
Veilig (Sanctuary) California NV • $11 • (11/15/94) • **79**
Zinfandel California Doe Mill Vineyard 1990 • $8 • (10/15/92) • **83**
Zinfandel Santa Cruz Mountains Beauregard Ranch Proprietors Reserve 1988 • $13 • (10/15/92) • **76**

HAMACHER | OREGON

Chardonnay Oregon Cuvée Forêts Diverses 1995: A serious-minded wine with polish, displaying deft orange-tinged pear, honey and nutmeg flavors and finishing with a peppery note. Shows lots of oak. Ready now. 250 cases made. • $20 • (11/30/97) • **87**

HAMBRECHT | CALIFORNIA

Cabernet Sauvignon Dry Creek Valley Bradford Mountain 1991 • $14 • (11/15/94) • **83**
Cabernet Sauvignon Dry Creek Valley Bradford Mountain Vineyard 1990 • $13 • (11/15/93) • **86**
Zinfandel Dry Creek Valley 1992 • $14 • (10/15/94) • **86**

HAMEL | CALIFORNIA

Syrah Russian River Valley Alegría Vineyard 1995: Inky dark in color, dense and concentrated, with a potent core of rich currant, plum, mineral and spice flavors stacked up, finishing with a classic smoky, meaty edge and thick but plush tannins. Finish goes on and on. Best now to 2004. 416 cases made. • $24 • (12/31/97) • **92**
Syrah Sonoma County 1994: Dark, ripe, rich and spicy, with a tannic, leathery edge to the black cherry and wild berry flavors. Drinkable now. 528 cases made. • $22 • (07/31/97) • **88**

HANDLEY | CALIFORNIA

Blanc de Blancs Anderson Valley 1990 • $18 • (12/15/95) • **88**
Blanc de Blancs Anderson Valley 1989 • $18 • (12/31/94) • **84**
Blanc de Blancs Anderson Valley 1988 • $18 • (12/31/93) • **84**
Brut Anderson Valley 1992: A fresh, floral, applelike quality pervades this firm and focused wine, which shows hints of pear, hazelnut and grapefruit. A tangy finish makes it most refreshing. 350 cases made. • $20 • (11/30/97) • **89**
Brut Anderson Valley 1991: The citrus and green apple flavors are tart, somewhat green in character. Turns earthy, with a slight metallic edge, on the finish. 925 cases made. • $18 • (11/30/96) • **80**
Brut Anderson Valley 1990 • $15 • (12/31/95) • **87**
Brut Anderson Valley 1989 • $15 • (12/31/94) • **86**
Brut Anderson Valley 1988 • $15 • (05/31/93) • **86**
Brut Anderson Valley 1984 • $15 • (10/15/88) • **81**
Brut Rosé Anderson Valley 1994: A peaches-'n-cream quality is balanced by toast, herb and mineral notes. The finish is dry and refreshing, with a slight vanilla accent. 175 cases made. • $19 • (11/30/97) • **86**
Brut Rosé Anderson Valley 1993: A subtle style of rosé, with its emphasis on fruitiness. Serves up attractive Pinot Noir flavors echoing cherry, plum and berry notes. 200 cases made. • $19 • (12/15/96) • **87**
Brut Rosé Anderson Valley 1990 • $17 • (12/31/94) • **85**

Brut Rosé Anderson Valley 1989 • $17 • (12/31/93) • **83**
Brut Rosé Anderson Valley 1988 • $17 • (05/31/93) • **86**
Brut Rosé Anderson Valley 1984 • $17 • (12/31/88) • **75**
Chardonnay Anderson Valley 1996: Crisp and earthy, with nicely focused pear, mineral and green apple notes. Finishes with a touch of spice. Drink now through 2000. 2,800 cases made. • $17 • (07/31/98) • **84**
Chardonnay Anderson Valley 1995: Light and fresh, showing pleasant melon and pear flavors that linger on the gentle finish. 2,196 cases made. • $18 • (07/31/97) • **84**
Chardonnay Anderson Valley 1994: Ripe and smooth, with an elegant core of pear, spice, honey and apple notes. 1,267 cases made. • $13 • (07/31/96) • **87**
Chardonnay Anderson Valley 1993 • $11 • (06/15/96) • **81**
Chardonnay Dry Creek Valley 1995: Bright and crisp, a straightforward style with the appealing snap of green apple, and a hint of nutmeg. Ready to drink. 3,070 cases made. • $18 • (07/31/97) • **85**
Chardonnay Dry Creek Valley 1994: Has an elegant style. Smooth, creamy and ripe with hints of pear, light oak, spice and citrus. Complex and well proportioned. 1,804 cases made. • $17 • (07/31/96) • **88**
Chardonnay Dry Creek Valley 1993 • $15 • (06/30/96) • **87**
Chardonnay Dry Creek Valley Cellar Select 1993: Ripe, smooth and polished, with a silky texture and lots of pretty fig, melon, pear and apricot notes, and a trace of honey on the finish. Ready to drink. 245 cases made. • $20 • (06/15/97) • **89**
Chardonnay Dry Creek Valley Handley Vineyard 1996: A smoothly textured wine, with hints of peach, apricot, apple, spice and vanilla. Clean, moderate finish. Drink now through 2000. 2,900 cases made. • $17 • (05/31/98) • **88**
Gewürztraminer Anderson Valley 1996: Bright and refreshing. A lively mouthful of litchi, grapefruit, spice and rose petal. The finish is dry and remarkably long. 1,075 cases made. • $11 • (12/15/97) • **89**
Gewürztraminer Anderson Valley 1995: Bright, fragrant and fresh. Marked by dryness through the finish, which shows off the pretty grapefruit, pineapple and floral flavors nicely. 982 cases made. • $12 • (10/15/96) • **87**
Gewürztraminer Anderson Valley 1994 • $9 • (11/15/95) • **79**
Gewürztraminer Anderson Valley 1993 • $8 • (02/28/95) • **85**
Pinot Meunier Anderson Valley Pinot Mystère 1996: A versatile wine in a pleasantly delicate style, with hints of cherry, toast and spice. The finish is moderate. 844 cases made. • $19 • (01/31/98) • **85**
Pinot Noir Anderson Valley 1995: Floral and toast aromas lead the way, backed by pretty cherry, herb and anise notes. Tannins are a touch rough, though, and it finishes short. Better in a year or two. 1,218 cases made. • $20 • (01/31/98) • **87**
Pinot Noir Anderson Valley 1994 • $15 • (02/29/96) • **84**
Pinot Noir Anderson Valley 1993 • $15 • (12/31/95) • **84**
Pinot Noir Anderson Valley 1992 • $14 • (10/31/94) • **84**
Pinot Noir Anderson Valley 1991 • $13 • (06/15/93) • **84**
Pinot Noir Anderson Valley Reserve 1995: An intense style, with a tart edge to the black cherry and wild berry flavors. Finishes with firm, crisp tannins. Drinkable now. 160 cases made. • $28 • (02/28/98) • **87**
Pinot Noir Anderson Valley Reserve 1994: Appealing, snappy grape accent to the nice core of ripe cherry and plum flavors. Drinks well now. 487 cases made. • $24 • (09/15/96) • **84**
Sauvignon Blanc Dry Creek Valley 1996: Made in an older style, with some attractive herb, citrus and melon flavors. Crisp finish. 2,240 cases made. • $12 • (06/30/97) • **86**
Sauvignon Blanc Dry Creek Valley 1995: A bright and refreshing, zingy mouthful of citrus and pear flavors that keep dancing on the finish. 2,000 cases made. • $11 • (08/31/96) • **87**
Sauvignon Blanc Dry Creek Valley 1993 • $9 • (08/31/95) • **87**

HANNA | CALIFORNIA

Cabernet Sauvignon Alexander Valley 1995: This offers light black cherry and berry flavors that are smooth and easy to drink. Good intensity, although lacking in concentration. 2,000 cases made. • $20 • (11/15/97) • **86**
Cabernet Sauvignon Alexander Valley 1994: A good, solid if simple effort, with ripe cherry and berry notes of modest proportion. 2,500 cases made. • $20 • (05/15/97) • **82**
Cabernet Sauvignon Alexander Valley 1993: Delivers a tasty core of ripe Cabernet flavor, with notes of currant, cherry, plum and berry in the mix. Finishes with supple tannins and a complex, fruity aftertaste. Drinks well now. 2,500 cases made. • $18 • (11/15/96) • **88**
Cabernet Sauvignon Alexander Valley 1992 • $16 • (12/15/95) • **84**
Cabernet Sauvignon Alexander Valley 1991 • $14 • (02/28/95) • **85**
Cabernet Sauvignon Alexander Valley 1990 • $18 • (11/15/93) • **87**
Cabernet Sauvignon Sonoma County 1988 • $16 • (11/15/91) • **86**
Cabernet Sauvignon Sonoma County 1987 • $16 • (08/31/90) • **80**
Cabernet Sauvignon Sonoma County 1986 • $16 • (07/31/89) • **87**
Cabernet Sauvignon Sonoma Valley 1985 • $14 • (06/30/88) • **86**
Chardonnay Russian River Valley 1996: Weaves a wide range of jazzy flavors into a nice, tight package of juicy fruit and spice character. Green apple, nectarine, greengage plum and nutmeg flavors finish brightly. Ready to drink. 6,000 cases made. • $16 • (12/15/97) • **88**
Chardonnay Russian River Valley 1995: A heavy-handed style, with a slightly sour, underripe twinge to the flavors. 3,000 cases made. • $15 • (04/30/97) • **82**
Chardonnay Russian River Valley Reserve 1993 • $18 • (06/30/96) • **85**
Chardonnay Sonoma County 1994: Smooth, adding a peppermint note to the modest apple and spice flavors. Ready now. 1,820 cases made. • $14 • (04/30/96) • **84**
Merlot Alexander Valley 1995: Firm and a little chewy, with modest blackberry and plum flavors picking up some steam on the finish. Drinkable now. • $NA • (12/31/97) • **85**
Merlot Alexander Valley 1994: Well crafted. Young, tight and complex, with concentrated flavors of currant, smoke, herb and black cherry and a cedar-accented finish. Drinkable now. 1,509 cases made. • $20 • (05/15/97) • **88**
Merlot Alexander Valley 1993 • $16 • (06/15/96) • **87**
Merlot Alexander Valley 1991 • $14 • (12/31/93) • **82**
Merlot Alexander Valley 1990 • $14 • (12/15/92) • **87**
Pinot Noir Russian River Valley 1992 • $14 • (01/31/94) • **86**
Sauvignon Blanc Russian River Valley 1996: Sports some nice, silky citrus, herb and mineral qualities, but doesn't quite achieve the potential inherent in Russian River grapes. 6,000 cases made. • $11 • (09/15/97) • **86**
Sauvignon Blanc Russian River Valley Reserve 1996: This lively wine displays lovely ripe peach, mango, melon and grapefruit flavors. It's got a racy, refreshing, orange-peel finish. 900 cases made. • $21 • (01/31/98) • **88**
Sauvignon Blanc Sonoma County 1995: Fresh and appealing for its aromas and flavors of green apple and sweet pea, which linger with clarity. The price makes it even nicer. 10,000 cases made. • $10 • (12/15/96) BB • **87**
Sauvignon Blanc Sonoma County 1994 • $10 • (08/31/95) • **87**
Sauvignon Blanc Sonoma County 1993 • $10 • (08/31/94) • **85**
Zinfandel Alexander Valley Pourroy Vineyard 1995: Marked by ripe, racy cherry, wild berry and raspberry flavors, this is a young and vibrant wine with lots of zest and personality. Drink it now for its youthful vibrancy, or hold and see what happens. 200 cases made. • $20 • (04/30/97) • **90**
Zinfandel Alexander Valley Pourroy Vineyard Reserve 1996: Straddles a fine line between spicy, vanilla-laced oak and wild berry and spicy Zinfandel flavors. Shows modest complexity, finishes with soft, supple tannins. Drink now through 2000. 350 cases made. • $35 • (05/31/98) • **83**

HANZELL | CALIFORNIA

Cabernet Sauvignon Sonoma Valley 1990 • $20 • (11/15/94) • **83**
Cabernet Sauvignon Sonoma Valley 1989 • $19 • (11/15/93) • **82**
Cabernet Sauvignon Sonoma Valley 1988 • $22 • (11/15/92) • **82**
Cabernet Sauvignon Sonoma Valley 1987 • $22 • (11/15/91) • **84**
Cabernet Sauvignon Sonoma Valley 1986 • $22 • (10/31/90) • **90**
Cabernet Sauvignon Sonoma Valley 1982 • $20 • (03/31/87) • **76**
Chardonnay Sonoma Valley 1995: Beautifully crafted, rich and harmonious, with tiers of ripe pear, fig and citrus and light oak shadings. Really zooms on the finish, where the flavors are complex and concentrated. Delicious now, but has a great track record for aging, so don't worry about cellaring it another 5 to 7 years, drinking through 2004. 1,750 cases made. • $30 • (01/31/98) CS • **92**
Chardonnay Sonoma Valley 1994: Spicy, perfumed aromas lead to an elegant, complex array of ripe pear, tart pineapple, citrus and light oak flavors. If you're inclined to cellar Chardonnay, this tightly wound young wine is one of your best candidates. It has a superb track record for improving in the bottle; try in 2006. 1,850 cases made. • $28 • (11/30/96) • **90**
Chardonnay Sonoma Valley 1993: Fresh and lively if a bit on the crisp, tart side. This shows a nice range of ripe apple, pear and melonlike flavors with hints of spice and light oak. Finishes with a zesty aftertaste. Given the wine's track record of improving with age, cellaring a few years should add more dimension. 1,700 cases made. • $26 • (10/15/96) CS • **90**
Pinot Noir Sonoma County 1989 • $19 • (02/28/94) • **87**
Pinot Noir Sonoma County 1987 • $19 • (02/15/92) • **84**
Pinot Noir Sonoma Valley 1993: Shows off some mature aromas and flavors, with earthy sage, tar, spice and plum notes, and turns complex on the fin-

ish as rose petal and cherry notes fold in. Approachable now, best before 2001. 730 cases made. • $25 • (01/31/98) • **87**

Pinot Noir Sonoma Valley 1992: A true-to-style Hanzell Pinot Noir, this shows its earthier side. Mature in color, with attractive earth and mushroom flavors, notes of dried cherry, tar and spice. Finishes with firm tannins and a slightly bitter edge. Try now. 980 cases made. • $23 • (01/31/97) • **86**

Pinot Noir Sonoma Valley 1991 • $19 • (06/30/95) • **86**

Pinot Noir Sonoma Valley 1990: Age has benefited Hanzell, again: This once-austere and crisp wine has flowered, displaying more plum, cherry and spice flavors now than it did on release. It's still young and vibrant enough for further cellaring, but approachable now. • $21 • (03/31/97) • **90**

Pinot Noir Sonoma Valley 1988 • $19 • (02/28/93) • **88**

Pinot Noir Sonoma Valley 1986: Once again, time plays in Hanzell's favor: This shows healthier color and younger flavors than most '86s. A ripe, intense, well-structured wine with lively cherry and berry flavors. Greatly improved since an earlier tasting, but may still need another year or two to be at its best. • $32 Ⓐ • (03/31/97) • **88**

Pinot Noir Sonoma Valley 1985 • $19 • (03/31/90) • **82**

Pinot Noir Sonoma Valley 1984 • $17 • (05/31/89) • **78**

Pinot Noir Sonoma Valley 1983 • $17 • (04/15/88) • **70**

Pinot Noir Sonoma Valley 1981 • $17 • (08/31/86) • **93**

HARBOR | CALIFORNIA

Merlot Napa Valley Narsai David Vineyard 1991 • $9 • (09/15/94) • **78**

HARGRAVE | NEW YORK

Blanc Fumé North Fork of Long Island 1995: A very drinkable marriage of melon and pear aromas, balanced flavors of ripe fruit and clean acidity. A slight herbaceousness adds interest to the palate. 500 cases made. • $11 • (12/31/96) • **86**

Cabernet Franc North Fork of Long Island 1988 • $14 • (06/30/91) • **81**

Cabernet Sauvignon North Fork of Long Island 1986 • $22 • (12/15/88) • **87**

Cabernet Sauvignon North Fork of Long Island 1985 • $22 • (12/15/88) • **82**

Cabernet Sauvignon North Fork of Long Island 1983 • $22 • (12/15/88) • **86**

Cabernet Sauvignon North Fork of Long Island Reserve 1982 • $22 • (12/15/88) • **70**

Cabernet Sauvignon North Fork of Long Island Vintner's Signature 1981 • $29 • (12/15/88) • **78**

Cabernet Sauvignon North Fork of Long Island Vintner's Signature 1980 • $NA • (12/15/88) • **79**

Chardonnay North Fork of Long Island 1993: The light herb and apple flavors are straightforward and rather neutral; the wine is balanced but lacks distinction. 2,000 cases made. • $15 • (12/31/96) • **77**

Merlot North Fork of Long Island 1988 • $18 • (06/30/91) • **81**

Merlot North Fork of Long Island 1985 • $19 • (12/15/88) • **85**

Merlot North Fork of Long Island 1980 • $NA • (12/15/88) • **78**

HARLAN ESTATE | CALIFORNIA

Napa Valley 1997: Serves up lots of complexity, with dark, ripe, rich currant, anise, cedar and spice, and frames it with spicy, toasty, cedary oak. This sample was 100 percent Cabernet Sauvignon. The finished wine will contain a small amount of Merlot and possibly Cabernet Franc. • $NA • (07/31/98) (BT) • **95-99**

Napa Valley 1994: Another terrific wine from Harlan. This Bordeaux-style red blend is muscular yet beautifully focused, rich and complex, with concentrated and lively layers of deep currant, spice and black cherry. Finishes with a long, fruity aftertaste. Best from 2001 through 2008. A blend of 70 percent Cabernet Sauvignon, 18 percent Merlot and 12 percent Cabernet Franc. 1,700 cases made. • $100 • (05/15/98) CS • **95**

Napa Valley 1993: Beautifully crafted, this is a seamless, deeply concentrated wine with lots of ripe, juicy currant, wild berry and plum flavors, along with a smoky, cedary edge from new oak. Impressive for its balance and finesse, finishing with a spicy anise quality and a long aftertaste. Has the tannic strength to age into 2002 and beyond. A blend of 75 percent Cabernet Sauvignon, 18 percent Merlot and 7 Cabernet Franc. 844 cases made. • $85 • (10/15/97) • **93**

Napa Valley 1992: Young, firm and tannic, with a cedary oak accent. Once it opens up, it shows more currant and plum flavors, but it takes a while to work through the tannic veneer. On the finish the flavors rush through, but cellaring into 2001 or longer is recommended. 909 cases made. • $75 • (11/15/96) • **91**

Napa Valley 1991 • $65 • (11/30/95) • **90**

HARMONY CELLARS | CALIFORNIA

Cabernet Sauvignon Paso Robles 1994: Opens with a rich, heady aroma of thyme and other Provençal herbs. On the palate, it calls forth focused mint, cassis, black currant. Loses its way a bit on the finish, but a nice wine. 405 cases made. • $14 • (10/15/97) • **87**

Cabernet Sauvignon Paso Robles 1993: More like Zinfandel than Cabernet, this has spicy, jammy plum aromas and bright cherry flavors that finish with a smoky, slightly bitter quality. 420 cases made. • $13 • (11/15/97) • **83**

Cabernet Sauvignon Paso Robles 1990 • $12 • (11/15/93) • **77**

Cabernet Sauvignon Paso Robles 1989 • $12 • (11/15/92) • **85**

Chardonnay San Luis Obispo 1996: Lots of smoky, toasty oak, with pretty honeysuckle, peach and coconut. Well focused, with concentrated flavors and a long finish. Drink now. 730 cases made. • $14 • (07/31/98) • **86**

Chardonnay San Luis Obispo County 1995: A bright wine, with hints of lemon, orange and spice. The whole is framed in subtle oak and tapers to an elegant finish. 730 cases made. • $13 • (01/31/98) • **88**

Pinot Noir Paso Robles 1994: Fresh mint and raspberries come to mind, followed by saddle-leather and currants. This is a firm, crisp Pinot, with a bright, herbal finish. 350 cases made. • $13 • (09/30/97) • **88**

Pinot Noir Paso Robles 1990 • $11 • (02/28/93) • **88**

HARRIS, RANDALL | WASHINGTON

Merlot-Cabernet Washington 1995: Bright and flavorful, smoothly polished and brimming with floral, berry and currant flavors. Hints of chocolate mark the open-textured finish. Best now to 2001. • $10 • (04/30/97) • **87**

HARRISON | CALIFORNIA

Cabernet Sauvignon Napa Valley 1994: Supple, elegant and understated in style, showcasing a complex array of currant, earth, cedar and spice flavors. Finishes with dashes of anise and coffee, and a long, full aftertaste. This California red is enticing now, can be held to 2000. 790 cases made. • $33 • (07/31/97) HR • **93**

Cabernet Sauvignon Napa Valley 1993: Pleasant, moderately rich currant and cherry flavors lose intensity and fade on the finish. Good now but may have more depth after 1999. 945 cases made. • $33 • (09/15/96) • **87**

Cabernet Sauvignon Napa Valley 1992 • $33 • (11/15/95) • **90**

Cabernet Sauvignon Napa Valley 1991 • $30 • (11/15/94) • **82**

Cabernet Sauvignon Napa Valley 1990 • $30 • (07/15/93) • **87**

Cabernet Sauvignon Napa Valley 1989 • $30 • (04/15/92) • **91**

Cabernet Sauvignon Napa Valley Reserve 1990 • $40 • (10/15/94) • **91**

Chardonnay Napa Valley 1996: An ultrarich style that's visibly unfined and unfiltered, with exotic, buttery pear, fig, apricot and spicy, toasty oak flavors. Zooms along on the finish. Drink now through 2002. 594 cases made. • $32 • (07/31/98) • **92**

Chardonnay Napa Valley 1995: Interesting flavors, tiers of pear, spice and melon, unfold from an initial earthiness, and a hint of spicy oak peeks in on the finish. 620 cases made. • $30 • (05/15/97) • **90**

Chardonnay Napa Valley 1994: Smooth, ripe and creamy, the pretty honey, pear, spice and vanilla flavors picking up a trace of tangerine and nutmeg on the finish. Wonderful sense of harmony and finesse. 870 cases made. • $26 • (04/30/96) • **90**

Chardonnay Napa Valley 1993 • $26 • (07/31/95) • **86**

Merlot Napa Valley 1994: Simple and direct. On the austere side with spice, cedar, herb and tobacco notes, and just a hint of currant and cherry flavor emerging from behind the tannins. Gains interest when aired, as more currant and oak flavors emerge. 125 cases made. • $33 • (10/15/96) • **87**

HART | CALIFORNIA

Cabernet Sauvignon Temecula Hansen Vineyard 1989 • $15 • (11/15/92) • **82**

Merlot Temecula 1989 • $15 • (05/31/92) • **80**

HART'S DESIRE | CALIFORNIA

Cabernet Sauvignon Alexander Valley Hidden Spring Vineyard 1995: Starts off with a charry note, followed by herbs, plum, anise and cassis. Finishes with vegetal edge. Drink now. 200 cases made. • $20 • (06/30/98) • **80**

Cabernet Sauvignon Napa Valley 1993: Medium-bodied, with an herbal weediness to the flavors and a flat edge to the tannins on the finish. What's lacking is a core of ripe fruit flavor. 100 cases made. • $15 • (11/30/96) • **79**

Cabernet Sauvignon Napa Valley Draper Vineyard 1995: Light, straightforward, with ripe currant and blackberry flavors and crisp tannins that sneak in on the finish. Best to drink soon with hearty food. 110 cases made. • $17 • (11/15/97) • **84**

Chardonnay Edna Valley MacGregor Vineyard 1995: Bright and crisp, this has toasty overtones yet is packed with juicy ripe fruit: mango, peach and pear. It finishes with a long, refreshing lemon-lime flavor. 308 cases made. • $15 • (09/30/97) • **89**

Zinfandel Russian River Valley Ponzo Vineyard 1995: Serves up plenty of raspberry and cherry on the nose and sails forth on the palate with more of the same, plus licorice, blackberry, cassis and spice. A bit astringent on the edges. Drink now or hold. 130 cases made. • $18 • (03/31/98) • **87**

Zinfandel Russian River Valley Ponzo Vineyard 1994 • $14 • (05/15/96) • **85**

HARTFORD COURT | CALIFORNIA

Pinot Noir Russian River Valley Arrendell Vineyard 1995: Tough, earthy and leathery, with just enough ripe plum and black cherry. Cellar into 1999 in hopes the fruit pushes to the fore. Tasted twice, with consistent notes. 400 cases made. • $45 • (02/28/98) • **85**

Pinot Noir Russian River Valley Arrendell Vineyard 1994 • $42 • (02/29/96) • **89**

Pinot Noir Russian River Valley Dutton Ranch-Sanchietti Vineyard 1995: Lightly flavored, elegant and delicate, with earthy cherry and raspberry flavors that are clean and simple. Drinks well now. 400 cases made. • $40 • (10/31/97) • **87**

Pinot Noir Russian River Valley Dutton Ranch-Sanchietti Vineyard 1994 • $35 • (02/29/96) • **86**

Pinot Noir Sonoma Coast 1995: Smooth and elegant, with subtle herb, cherry, tea, earth and spice notes. Firms up on the finish, where the tannins show some strength. Try now. 400 cases made. • $32 • (12/15/97) • **87**

Zinfandel Russian River Valley Hartford Vineyard 1995: Has a nice sense of harmony and finesse, striking a fine balance between its core of cherry and raspberry flavors and its light oak shadings. Drinkable now. 300 cases made. • $32 • (10/31/97) • **90**

Zinfandel Russian River Valley Hartford Vineyard 1994 • $30 • (04/30/96) • **92**

HARTWELL | CALIFORNIA

Cabernet Sauvignon Stags Leap District 1992 • $50 • (11/15/95) • **90**

Cabernet Sauvignon Stags Leap District 1991 • $55 • (11/15/94) • **92**

Cabernet Sauvignon Stags Leap District Grace Vineyard 1994: Young and tight, this shows a rich, concentrated core of ripe plum, currant and black cherry, with a nice accent of toasty, cedary oak adding dimension and backbone. Has a wonderful sense of harmony, balance, extract and finesse. Should be a beauty by 2001. 207 cases made. • $63 • (11/30/97) • **94**

Cabernet Sauvignon Stags Leap District Sunshine Vineyard 1995: Well balanced, supple and harmonious, with spicy currant, black cherry and anise, gaining a complex earthy quality on the finish. Intense and concentrated, it's tempting now, best from 2000 to 2005. 700 cases made. • $50 • (05/15/98) • **92**

Cabernet Sauvignon Stags Leap District Sunshine Vineyard 1994: More elegant and less concentrated than this winery's Grace Vineyard bottling, it is nonetheless richly flavored, with pretty plum, wild berry and cherry flavors and soft tannins. Approachable now. 433 cases made. • $40 • (11/30/97) • **89**

HAVENS | CALIFORNIA

Merlot Napa Valley 1994: Smooth and supple, with light, toasty oak adding interest to the ripe cherry and plum flavors. Well balanced and easy to drink now. 4,000 cases made. • $18 • (07/31/96) • **85**

Merlot Napa Valley 1993: Marked by a nice, earthy sage and herb edge, it picks up enough minty cherry and berry flavors to achieve balance. 4,394 cases made. • $16 • (07/31/96) • **86**

Merlot Napa Valley 1991 • $15 • (07/15/93) HR • **90**

Merlot Napa Valley 1990 • $15 • (06/15/93) • **87**

Merlot Napa Valley 1989 • $14 • (05/31/92) • **84**

Merlot Napa Valley 1988 • $14 • (03/31/91) • **82**

Merlot Napa Valley 1987 • $14 • (07/15/90) • **89**

Merlot Napa Valley 1986 • $14 • (03/31/90) • **72**

Merlot Napa Valley 1985 • $13 • (05/31/88) • **84**

Merlot Napa Valley Carneros Reserve 1993: A pleasant core of plum and cherry, though a touch tannic and a bit hollow at midpalate. Tannins quite noticeable in the finish. 1,048 cases made. • $24 • (07/31/96) • **85**

Merlot Napa Valley Carneros Truchard Vineyard 1988 • $20 • (08/31/91) • **76**

Merlot Napa Valley Carneros Truchard Vineyard Reserve 1990 • $20 • (06/15/93) • **88**

Merlot Napa Valley Carneros Truchard Vineyard Reserve 1989 • $20 • (05/31/92) • **82**

Sauvignon Blanc Napa Valley Clock Vineyard 1995: Straightforward fruit and herb flavors, with a touch of spice to liven up the finish. 1,000 cases made. • $11 • (07/31/96) • **83**

Sauvignon Blanc Napa Valley Clock Vineyard 1994 • $10 • (08/31/95) • **84**

Syrah Carneros 1995: Dense, earthy, leathery, gamy flavors override the core of meaty currant and wild berry. May improve if the gaminess and tannins subside. 950 cases made. • $20 • (11/30/97) • **83**

HAWK CREST | CALIFORNIA

Cabernet Sauvignon California 1995: A bit rough-and-tumble, the chewy tannins still don't obscure a firm core of currant, cherry, blackberry, clove and charry smoke. A country wine for full-bodied eating. 40,000 cases made. • $12 • (03/31/98) • **85**

Cabernet Sauvignon California 1994: A lighter style showing modest tannins and supple flavors of currant and cherry. Drinks well now. 30,000 cases made. • $10 • (12/15/96) • **83**

Cabernet Sauvignon California 1991 • $9 • (03/31/94) • **78**

Cabernet Sauvignon California 1990 • $9 • (04/30/93) • **82**

Cabernet Sauvignon California 1989 • $9 • (03/15/92) • **77**

Cabernet Sauvignon Mendocino 1981 • $5 • (03/16/85) BB • **84**

Cabernet Sauvignon North Coast 1987 • $8 • (03/31/90) • **79**

Cabernet Sauvignon North Coast 1986 • $7 • (10/15/88) BB • **82**

Cabernet Sauvignon North Coast 1985 • $6 • (07/31/88) • **75**

Cabernet Sauvignon North Coast 1984 • $7 • (10/15/87) • **76**

Cabernet Sauvignon North Coast 1981 • $5 • (02/01/86) • **65**

Chardonnay California 1996: Spice, toast and pear notes announce this pretty, delicate wine. It's a bit lean on the palate, but works well, and the price is right, too. The second label of renowned Stag's Leap Wine Cellars. 32,000 cases made. • $10 • (01/31/98) BB • **86**

Chardonnay California 1994: Nice enough, with simple pear, spice and apple notes. Good but nothing exceptional. • $9 • (05/15/96) • **82**

Merlot California 1995: Redolent of cherries and stewed prunes, framed in toasty oak. Fairly straightforward, but enjoyable. Finishes with a licorice tinge. 9,497 cases made. • $12 • (01/31/98) • **83**

Sauvignon Blanc California 1994 • $8 • (02/29/96) • **85**

Sauvignon Blanc California 1993 • $6 • (08/31/95) • **79**

HAWLEY | CALIFORNIA

Merlot Dry Creek Valley 1995: Lean, tart, with hard, sharp tannins and an earthy side to the barely ripe currant and plum flavors. Lacks harmony and finesse; perhaps short-term cellaring will help. From John Hawley, formerly winemaker at Clos du Bois and Kendall-Jackson. 403 cases made. • $30 • (11/15/97) • **83**

Viognier Dry Creek Valley 1996: Lots of spicy flavors, but needs a little more of the pear and apple notes to add dimension. 368 cases made. • $22 • (12/15/97) • **83**

HAYWOOD | CALIFORNIA

Cabernet Sauvignon California 1991 • $8 • (11/15/94) • **83**

Cabernet Sauvignon California Vintner's Select 1995: Light, smooth and appealing. The black cherry, currant and spice flavors linger on the solid finish. Drink soon. 47,000 cases made. • $8 • (11/15/97) • **84**

Cabernet Sauvignon California Vintner's Select 1994: Pretty oaky, with some bright cherry notes on the finish. Drink now. 20,200 cases made. • $8 • (10/31/97) • **82**

Cabernet Sauvignon California Vintner's Select 1993: Smells funky, but the flavors pick up lovely raspberry accents, polished by spicy, toasty notes. Drinkable now. 25,000 cases made. • $8 • (12/15/95) • **84**
Cabernet Sauvignon California Vintner's Select 1990 • $8 • (03/15/93) • **82**
Cabernet Sauvignon California Vintner's Select 1989 • $8 • (03/15/92) • **80**
Cabernet Sauvignon Sonoma Valley 1988 • $16 • (02/28/91) • **82**
Cabernet Sauvignon Sonoma Valley 1986 • $19 • (11/15/89) • **92**
Cabernet Sauvignon Sonoma Valley 1985 • $15 • (03/15/88) • **91**
Cabernet Sauvignon Sonoma Valley 1984 • $13 • (10/31/87) • **93**
Cabernet Sauvignon Sonoma Valley 1983 • $13 • (05/15/87) • **77**
Cabernet Sauvignon Sonoma Valley 1981 • $11 • (09/01/84) • **84**
Cabernet Sauvignon Sonoma Valley 1980 • $9 • (02/15/84) • **78**
Cabernet Sauvignon Sonoma Valley Los Chamizal Vineyards 1989 • $12 • (11/15/94) • **84**
Cabernet Sauvignon Sonoma Valley Los Chamizal Vineyards 1988 • $16 • (11/15/91) • **85**
Chardonnay California Vintner's Select 1996: Tastes tart and a bit raw, but the grapefruit and pineapple notes are harmonious and a nice touch of vanilla helps smooth it out. 74,000 cases made. • $8 • (11/15/97) • **82**
Chardonnay California Vintner's Select 1994: Soft and broad in texture, centered around citrusy pear and toasty earthy flavors that spread on the finish. Ready now. 60,000 cases made. • $8 • (11/15/95) BB • **85**
Chardonnay California Vintner's Select 1993 • $8 • (02/28/95) • **82**
Merlot California Vintner's Select 1995: Here's a good-drinking Merlot at a very reasonable price. Smooth in texture, it does a nice job of balancing its pretty plum and berry flavor against overtones of gaminess. Ready to drink. 4,942 cases made. • $10 • (12/31/97) BB • **84**
Spaghetti Red California NV • $6 • (02/15/90) • **74**
Spaghetti Red Sonoma County NV • $4 • (04/30/87) • **74**
Zinfandel Sonoma Valley 1986 • $11 • (09/15/88) • **89**
Zinfandel Sonoma Valley 1985 • $9 • (11/15/87) • **85**
Zinfandel Sonoma Valley 1984 • $9 • (05/31/87) • **92**
Zinfandel Sonoma Valley 1983 • $8 • (01/01/86) • **85**
Zinfandel Sonoma Valley 1982 • $8 • (11/01/84) • **89**
Zinfandel Sonoma Valley Los Chamizal Vineyard 1995: An elegant wine, less flavorful and distinctive than Haywood's Rocky Terrrace bottling, this offers medium-weight cherry, wild berry and spice flavors and mild tannins. Drink now through 2000. 3,350 cases made. • $18 • (06/15/98) • **87**
Zinfandel Sonoma Valley Los Chamizal Vineyard 1994: Smooth, ripe and polished, with a supple range of cherry, anise, raisin, raspberry, sage, smoke and tea flavors, finishing with a complex aftertaste and a touch of heat. Drink now to 2001. 2,696 cases made. • $16 • (01/01/98) • **88**
Zinfandel Sonoma Valley Los Chamizal Vineyard 1993: A touch earthy, with herb, sage and cedar notes, though enough cherry and currant flavors emerge to give this the depth and proportion it needs. Drinks well now but can hold into 1999. 1,714 cases made. • $15 • (02/28/97) • **88**
Zinfandel Sonoma Valley Los Chamizal Vineyard Rocky Terrace 1995: Beautifully crafted, intense, ripe, rich and distinctive with its spice, mineral, sage, earth and wild berry flavors. Finishes with firm, crisp but well-integrated tannins. Drink now through 2004. 982 cases made. • $25 • (06/15/98) • **90**
Zinfandel Sonoma Valley Los Chamizal Vineyard 1994: Smooth, ripe and polished, with a supple range of cherry, anise, raisin, raspberry, sage, smoke and tea flavors, finishing with a complex aftertaste and a touch of heat. Drink now to 2001. 2,696 cases made. • $16 • (01/01/98) • **88**
Zinfandel Sonoma Valley Los Chamizal Vineyards 1992 • $14 • (10/15/95) • **84**
Zinfandel Sonoma Valley Los Chamizal Vineyards 1991 • $14 • (10/15/94) • **84**
Zinfandel Sonoma Valley Los Chamizal Vineyards 1990 • $14 • (10/15/92) • **83**
Zinfandel Sonoma Valley Los Chamizal Vineyards 1989 • $14 • (11/15/91) • **85**
Zinfandel Sonoma Valley Los Chamizal Vineyards 1988 • $13 • (11/30/90) • **89**
Zinfandel Sonoma Valley Rocky Terrace 1992 • $18 • (10/15/94) • **88**
Zinfandel Sonoma Valley Rocky Terrace Los Chamizal Vineyard 1994: Combines ripe, mature fruit flavors with firm tannins and a sense of elegance. The core of earthy cherry, raspberry and anise flavors slowly unfolds to reveal more complexity. Tannins are mild enough to drink this now through 2001. 910 cases made. • $25 • (01/01/98) • **89**

Key: SS—Spectator Selection CS—Cellar Selection HR—Highly Recommended BB—Best Buy $NA—Price not available Ⓐ—Auction Price (BT)—Barrel Tasting
Dates in parentheses indicate the issues in which the ratings were published.

HAZLITT 1852 | NEW YORK

Johannisberg Riesling Finger Lakes 1995: A very simple, quite sweet, white wine without much fruit flavor or distinction. • $9 • (10/31/96) • **72**

HECKER PASS | CALIFORNIA

Zinfandel Santa Clara Valley 1988 • $7 • (10/15/92) • **75**

HEDGES | WASHINGTON

Cabernet-Merlot Columbia Valley 1995: Very pretty berry and spice flavors dance along the velvety texture and remain bright and lively through the generous finish. Drinkable now. 46,000 cases made. • $11 • (09/15/96) HR • **87**
Cabernet-Merlot Columbia Valley 1994: Light and velvety, as modest red berry and cedary flavors linger tentatively on the finish. Ready now. 39,500 cases made. • $9 • (05/15/96) • **83**
Cabernet-Merlot Columbia Valley 1990 • $9 • (06/15/92) BB • **88**
Cabernet-Merlot Columbia Valley 1989 • $7 • (09/30/91) BB • **89**
Cabernet-Merlot Washington 1996: Bright and jazzy, a lively mouthful of raspberry, spice and chocolate flavors that linger delicately on the light finish. Ready to drink. 26,000 cases made. • $11 • (12/15/97) • **85**
Cabernet-Merlot Washington 1993: Ripe and generous, showing nicely articulated berry and black cherry flavors that extend into a delicious finish, shading with herb flavors at the end. 55,000 cases made. • $9 • (08/31/94) BB • **87**
Cabernet-Merlot Washington 1992 • $9 • (12/31/93) BB • **86**
Cabernet-Merlot Washington 1991 • $9 • (03/31/93) BB • **88**
Cabernet Sauvignon Columbia Valley Three Vineyards at Red Mountain 1994: Rich, generous and spicy, filling the mouth with ripe blackberry, currant, tar and tobacco flavors that don't let go even when met by the chewy tannins on the finish. Give until 2000 to 2002 for best drinking. 1,000 cases made. • $18 • (09/15/96) • **90**
Fumé-Chardonnay Columbia Valley 1995: Bright and fruity, offering up a generous mouthful of fresh apple and peach flavors that remain lively through the herb-accented finish. • $8 • (08/31/96) BB • **86**
Fumé-Chardonnay Columbia Valley 1994 • $6 • (05/15/96) • **85**
Fumé-Chardonnay Washington 1993 • $8 • (09/30/94) • **80**
Fumé-Chardonnay Washington-Oregon 1996: Soft and smooth, showing distinctive nectarine and spice flavors that linger on the finish. Interesting, a bargain, too. A blend from Oregon and Washington vineyards: 52 percent Sauvignon Blanc, 48 percent Chardonnay. 11,500 cases made. • $8 • (06/15/97) BB • **86**
Red Mountain Reserve Columbia Valley 1994: Gnashingly tannic. A thresher of a wine that works ju-u-st enough ripe berry and spice flavor into the mix to make it worth cellaring until 2001 to 2002. A blend of 55 percent Merlot and 45 percent Cabernet Sauvignon. 1,000 cases made. • $30 • (09/15/97) • **87**
Red Mountain Reserve Columbia Valley 1993: Deep, dark, dense and dazzling, with spicy, herb-scented berry, currant and plum flavors that are layered beautifully on the complex finish and hint at chocolate on the aftertaste. Has great style without excess weight. Polished tannins can use until 2000. A blend of 68 percent Cabernet Sauvignon and 32 percent Merlot. 995 cases made. • $30 • (04/30/97) • **92**
Red Mountain Reserve Columbia Valley 1991 • $23 • (09/30/95) • **85**
Red Mountain Reserve Columbia Valley 1990 • $25 • (03/15/94) • **84**
Red Mountain Reserve Columbia Valley 1989 • $25 • (03/31/93) • **87**

HEITZ | CALIFORNIA

Cabernet Sauvignon Napa Valley 1993: Starts out tight and compact, slowly opening to more rich and supple flavors, with currant, berry and plum notes. Finishes with drying tannins. • $21 • (05/15/98) • **88**
Cabernet Sauvignon Napa Valley 1992: Solid Cabernet, with a core of rich, earthy currant and berry flavors and hints of cedar and spice on the finish. Drinkable now, though the tannins are a bit chewy, but best now to 2004. 11,850 cases made. • $20 • (05/31/97) • **89**
Cabernet Sauvignon Napa Valley 1991 • $29 Ⓐ • (04/30/96) • **85**
Cabernet Sauvignon Napa Valley 1990 • $18 • (04/30/95) HR • **90**
Cabernet Sauvignon Napa Valley 1989 • $20 Ⓐ • (07/31/94) • **88**
Cabernet Sauvignon Napa Valley 1988 • $18 • (03/31/93) • **88**
Cabernet Sauvignon Napa Valley 1987 • $60 Ⓐ • (04/15/92) SS • **90**
Cabernet Sauvignon Napa Valley 1986 • $24 Ⓐ • (04/15/91) • **88**
Cabernet Sauvignon Napa Valley 1985 • $29 Ⓐ • (05/15/90) • **80**

Cabernet Sauvignon Napa Valley 1984 • $30 • (01/31/90) • **89**
Cabernet Sauvignon Napa Valley 1983 • $20 • (01/31/90) • **85**
Cabernet Sauvignon Napa Valley 1982 • $14 • (06/15/87) • **74**
Cabernet Sauvignon Napa Valley 1982 • $30 • (01/31/90) • **80**
Cabernet Sauvignon Napa Valley 1981 • $30 • (01/31/90) • **86**
Cabernet Sauvignon Napa Valley 1980 • $28 • (01/31/90) • **88**
Cabernet Sauvignon Napa Valley 1979 • $18 Ⓐ • (01/31/90) • **86**
Cabernet Sauvignon Napa Valley 1978 • $24 Ⓐ • (01/31/90) • **90**
Cabernet Sauvignon Napa Valley 1977 • $48 • (01/31/90) • **83**
Cabernet Sauvignon Napa Valley 1973 • $41 Ⓐ • (01/31/90) • **78**
Cabernet Sauvignon Napa Valley 1970 • $100 • (01/31/90) • **74**
Cabernet Sauvignon Napa Valley Bella Oaks Vineyard 1993: Best version of this Rutherford-grown wine in nearly a decade. Aromatically complex, with pretty floral and plummy aromas, the lean, austere style slowly unfolds to reveal a broad range of complex flavors, with currant, spice, sage and cedar notes. Impeccably balanced, this late-release Cabernet will be best from 1999 to 2005. 1,521 cases made. • $28 • (05/15/98) CS • **91**
Cabernet Sauvignon Napa Valley Bella Oaks Vineyard 1990 • $44 Ⓐ • (04/30/95) • **85**
Cabernet Sauvignon Napa Valley Bella Oaks Vineyard 1989 • $24 Ⓐ • (07/31/94) • **85**
Cabernet Sauvignon Napa Valley Bella Oaks Vineyard 1988 • $32 • (03/31/93) • **81**
Cabernet Sauvignon Napa Valley Bella Oaks Vineyard 1987 • $33 • (06/30/92) • **85**
Cabernet Sauvignon Napa Valley Bella Oaks Vineyard 1986: Shows an odd cedary component that's perilously close to mossy and, though time has integrated the woodiness somewhat, it still causes a sour edge. Too bad, because the ripe cherry and currant flavors are right on the mark. Passable, with food. 4,974 cases made. • $43 Ⓐ • (12/15/96) • **82**
Cabernet Sauvignon Napa Valley Bella Oaks Vineyard 1985 • $59 Ⓐ • (05/15/90) CS • **92**
Cabernet Sauvignon Napa Valley Bella Oaks Vineyard 1984 • $35 Ⓐ • (05/15/89) • **86**
Cabernet Sauvignon Napa Valley Bella Oaks Vineyard 1983 • $31 Ⓐ • (04/30/88) • **90**
Cabernet Sauvignon Napa Valley Bella Oaks Vineyard 1982 • $21 • (04/30/87) • **91**
Cabernet Sauvignon Napa Valley Bella Oaks Vineyard 1978 • $20 • (01/01/84) • **90**
Cabernet Sauvignon Napa Valley Bella Oaks Vineyard 1977 • $51 Ⓐ • (01/01/84) • **89**
Cabernet Sauvignon Napa Valley Bella Oaks Vineyard 1976 • $29 Ⓐ • (01/01/84) • **92**
Cabernet Sauvignon Napa Valley Fay Vineyard 1978 • $52 • (01/01/84) • **80**
Cabernet Sauvignon Napa Valley Fay Vineyard 1977 • $35 • (01/01/84) • **78**
Cabernet Sauvignon Napa Valley MZ-1 NV • $NA • (01/31/90) • **75**
Cabernet Sauvignon Napa Valley Martha's Vineyard 1992: A smooth, rich and harmonious Cabernet from what is perhaps Heitz's best-known vineyard, this shows the signature minty-accented currant and black cherry flavors. It turns supple and silky on the way to a long, complex aftertaste, where it picks up cedar and chocolate notes. Drinkable now, but concentrated enough to cellar. 2,518 cases made. • $67 Ⓐ • (05/31/97) CS • **93**
Cabernet Sauvignon Napa Valley Martha's Vineyard 1991 • $62 Ⓐ • (04/30/96) CS • **91**
Cabernet Sauvignon Napa Valley Martha's Vineyard 1990 • $63 Ⓐ • (04/30/95) CS • **90**
Cabernet Sauvignon Napa Valley Martha's Vineyard 1989 • $64 Ⓐ • (06/30/94) CS • **90**
Cabernet Sauvignon Napa Valley Martha's Vineyard 1988 • $71 • (03/31/93) • **87**
Cabernet Sauvignon Napa Valley Martha's Vineyard 1987: Despite serious bottle variation, with some wines marked by sour aromas and flavors, the best bottles were elegant, with spicy, minty currant and chocolate character and smooth, fleshy tannins. Tasted four samples: Two were flawed, one was slightly off, but the last was in fine shape. Best now through 2003. • $96 Ⓐ • (12/15/97) • **92**
Cabernet Sauvignon Napa Valley Martha's Vineyard 1986: Smooth and spicy, with characteristic mintiness. Rich currant, chocolate and mineral flavors add dimension and depth and the finish is complex and well focused. Drinks well now, but should hold until 2006 with ease, as the tannins are fine and well integrated. 6,938 cases made. • $125 Ⓐ • (12/15/96) • **91**
Cabernet Sauvignon Napa Valley Martha's Vineyard 1985 • $212 Ⓐ • (04/30/90) • **98**
Cabernet Sauvignon Napa Valley Martha's Vineyard 1984 • $124 Ⓐ • (03/15/89) SS • **97**
Cabernet Sauvignon Napa Valley Martha's Vineyard 1983 • $50 Ⓐ • (04/30/88) • **90**
Cabernet Sauvignon Napa Valley Martha's Vineyard 1982 • $62 Ⓐ • (04/15/87) CS • **94**
Cabernet Sauvignon Napa Valley Martha's Vineyard 1979 • $115 Ⓐ • (02/15/84) SS • **94**
Cabernet Sauvignon Napa Valley Martha's Vineyard 1978 • $100 • (11/15/92) • **92**
Cabernet Sauvignon Napa Valley Martha's Vineyard 1977 • $68 Ⓐ • (01/31/90) • **90**
Cabernet Sauvignon Napa Valley Martha's Vineyard 1976 • $65 Ⓐ • (01/01/84) • **94**
Cabernet Sauvignon Napa Valley Martha's Vineyard 1975 • $91 Ⓐ • (01/01/84) • **90**
Cabernet Sauvignon Napa Valley Martha's Vineyard 1974 • $310 Ⓐ • (11/15/94) • **97**
Cabernet Sauvignon Napa Valley Trailside Vineyard 1992: Smooth, ripe and harmonious, with a supple core of currant, herb, dill and sage notes, the flavors fanning out on the finish to reveal a coffee note. The texture is silky and the finish lingers. Drinks well now, but can age into 2000. 3,220 cases made. • $48 • (09/30/97) • **90**
Cabernet Sauvignon Napa Valley Trailside Vineyard 1991: Well oaked, with a leathery edge to the mature currant and plum flavors. Picks up a cedary accent on the finish, where the tannins are supple and fleshy. Drink now through 2000. 2,688 cases made. • $45 • (11/15/96) • **88**
Cabernet Sauvignon Napa Valley Trailside Vineyard 1990 • $45 • (10/15/95) CS • **91**
Cabernet Sauvignon Napa Valley Trailside Vineyard 1989 • $35 • (09/30/94) • **89**
Chardonnay Napa Valley Estate Selection 1993 • $18 • (07/31/95) • **78**
Grignolino Rosé Napa Valley 1994 • $5 • (09/30/95) • **82**
Port Napa Valley Grignolino Port 1992 • $13 • (09/30/95) • **85**
Ryan's Red Napa Valley NV • $6 • (02/28/89) • **74**
Zinfandel Napa Valley Heitz Vineyard 1989 • $8 • (09/30/93) • **67**
Zinfandel Napa Valley Heitz Vineyard 1988 • $7 • (10/15/92) • **78**

HELENA VIEW | CALIFORNIA

Cabernet Franc Napa Valley Johnston Vineyards 1992: Firm in texture, with a nice bead of blueberry and plum flavor weaving through the fine tannins. Drinkable now. 280 cases made. • $21 • (11/30/96) • **85**
Cabernet Sauvignon Napa Valley 1992: Serves up a pretty core of ripe berry, plum and cherry flavors framed by a spicy, toasty oak accent. Finishes with mild tannins and a rich, fruity aftertaste. Appealing now. Appealing price, too. 260 cases made. • $12 • (11/30/96) • **87**
Cabernet Sauvignon Napa Valley 1991: Simple with a modest band of cedar, spice and berry flavors. Tastes oxidized on the finish. 60 cases made. • $12 • (11/30/96) • **79**
Cabernet Sauvignon Napa Valley Moon Mountain 1992: A touch earthy, with mature cherry and plum flavors, but for the price you get a rustic Cabernet with some character. 200 cases made. • $7 • (11/30/96) • **83**

HELMS, H.W. | CALIFORNIA

Chardonnay Carneros 1994: Smooth, polished and straightforward with ripe pear, spice and light honey notes. From Trent Moffit. 642 cases made. • $11 • (07/31/96) • **86**

HENDRY RANCH | CALIFORNIA

Cabernet Sauvignon Napa Valley Block 8 1995: Distinctively minty, with a whiff of bay leaf, it offers ripe currant, berry, spice and cedar. The texture is smooth and supple, with a long, lingering finish. Best after 2000. 500 cases made. • $24 • (05/15/98) • **90**
Chardonnay Napa Valley Block 9 1996: Hits most of the right notes with its ripe pear, apple, melon and spicy fruit flavors, supple texture and lingering aftertaste, where the toasty oak folds in nicely. Drink now through 2000. 350 cases made. • $22 • (05/31/98) • **88**
Zinfandel Mount Veeder Brandlin Vineyard 1994: Distinct for its mintiness and its spice and cedar notes. Ripe berry and cherry flavors unfold gracefully, picking up a nice dash of oak. 850 cases made. • $17 • (01/31/97) • **88**
Zinfandel Mount Veeder Brandlin Vineyard 1992 • $15 • (10/15/95) • **86**
Zinfandel Napa Valley Hendry Block 7 1994: Smooth, ripe and polished, with a jammy cherry and wild berry accent to the Zinfandel grape flavors. Appealing to drink now. 860 cases made. • $17 • (01/31/97) • **90**

Zinfandel Napa Valley Hendry Block 7 1992 • $14 • (10/15/95) • **88**

HENRY ESTATE | OREGON

Cabernet Sauvignon Umpqua Valley 1992 •$12 •(03/31/96) • **78**
Chardonnay Oregon Umpqua Cuvée 1993 • $9 •(11/30/95) • **85**
Chardonnay Umpqua Valley 1994: Earth and mineral flavors weave through the modest apple and spice notes in this complex, serious wine. Could use more charm. 573 cases made. • $15 • (09/15/97) • **87**
Chardonnay Umpqua Valley Umpqua Cuvée 1995: Has a sour, lemon-candy flavor that permeates the otherwise creamy, fresh-tasting core of pear and spice. 900 cases made. • $10 • (02/28/97) • **81**
Gewürztraminer Umpqua Valley Dry 1996: On the dry side, with simple pear flavor and slightly bitter overtones. 954 cases made. • $9 • (02/28/98) • **81**
Gewürztraminer Umpqua Valley Dry 1995: Light, refreshingly spicy, off dry, with pretty rose petal nuances to the citrusy flavors. A generous wine, but not too strong in character, either. • $NA • (02/28/97) • **86**
Gewürztraminer Umpqua Valley Dry 1994 • $8 • (03/31/96) • **83**
Gewürztraminer Umpqua Valley Dry 1993 • $8 • (11/30/94) • **83**
Gewürztraminer Umpqua Valley Select Harvest 1995: Very soft, sweet and spicy, with an earthy edge to the floral character. Sweet finish. 125 cases made. • $10 • (02/28/97) • **79**
Müller-Thurgau Umpqua Valley 1996: Lightly sweet, with modest green apple and spice flavors. 635 cases made. • $8 • (09/15/97) • **83**
Müller-Thurgau Umpqua Valley 1995: On the sweet side, with lemon and cream flavors running through its supple structure, finishing with some length. Drink soon. 322 cases made. • $8 • (02/28/97) • **85**
Pinot Noir Oregon Umpqua Cuvée 1996: Light and fragrant, with spicy black cherry, blackberry and lime flavors that linger on the taut finish. Drinkable now. 2,650 cases made. • $10 • (02/28/98) • **84**
Pinot Noir Oregon Umpqua Cuvée 1995: Fresh and youthful, rather more like Gamay than Pinot Noir, but it has charm. Drink soon. 2,159 cases made. • $10 • (12/31/96) • **82**
Pinot Noir Oregon Umpqua Cuvée 1994 • $9 • (12/31/95) • **84**
Pinot Noir Oregon Umpqua Cuvée 1993 • $9 • (11/30/94) • **79**
Pinot Noir Oregon Umpqua Cuvée 1992 • $9 • (11/30/94) BB • **86**
Pinot Noir Umpqua Valley 1995: Shows pretty plum and berry flavors on a light frame, finishes with a touch of smoke. Best to drink soon. 1,707 cases made. • $13 • (09/15/97) • **85**
Pinot Noir Umpqua Valley 1993: Light, and a bit chewy with tannins that obscure the nice layer of anise-scented berry flavor. Drinkable now. 1,048 cases made. • $10 • (09/30/96) • **83**
Pinot Noir Umpqua Valley 1990 • $11 • (11/30/94) • **83**
Pinot Noir Umpqua Valley 1986 • $10 • (04/15/91) • **81**
Pinot Noir Umpqua Valley 1985 • $15 • (02/15/90) • **85**
Pinot Noir Umpqua Valley Barrel Select 1994: Lithe and fragrant. A lively mouthful of plum and berry flavor on a supple frame. Shows some elegance and persistence on the finish. Drink by 2000. 804 cases made. • $24 • (02/28/98) • **87**
Pinot Noir Umpqua Valley Barrel Select 1992 • $18 • (12/31/95) • **88**
Pinot Noir Umpqua Valley Barrel Select 1991 • $18 • (11/30/94) • **85**
Pinot Noir Umpqua Valley Barrel Select 1990 • $18 • (11/30/94) • **88**
Pinot Noir Umpqua Valley Barrel Select 1988 • $15 • (02/28/93) • **84**
Pinot Noir Umpqua Valley Winemakers Reserve 1990 • $25 • (10/31/95) • **84**
White Riesling Umpqua Valley Select Harvest 1995: Has a strong bitter edge to very sweet, creamy flavors; not everyone will like the mix. 680 cases made. • $9 • (02/28/97) • **82**

HERON HILL | NEW YORK

Chardonnay Finger Lakes Ingle Vineyard 1995: There are attractive minerally flavors to this wine, which also has a good, tart, lemony edge. Light and refreshing. 946 cases made. • $10 • (10/31/97) • **83**
Riesling Finger Lakes Dry 1995: This is a severe wine with overwhelming green apple and lime flavors. 738 cases made. • $9 • (09/30/97) • **76**

HERON LAKE | CALIFORNIA

Pinot Noir Wild Horse Valley 1994 • $24 • (02/29/96) • **87**
Pinot Noir Wild Horse Valley 1990 • $12 • (12/31/95) • **82**

Key: SS—Spectator Selection CS—Cellar Selection HR—Highly Recommended BB—Best Buy $NA—Price not available Ⓐ—Auction Price (BT)—Barrel Tasting
Dates in parentheses indicate the issues in which the ratings were published.

Pinot Noir Wild Horse Valley Reserve 1994: Pleasant enough, with hints of plum, cherry and berry, set off with a dash of oak. Well balanced, with appealing flavors and supple tannins. 325 cases made. • $26 • (02/28/97) • **86**

HESS COLLECTION, THE | CALIFORNIA

Cabernet Sauvignon Mount Veeder 1997: Shows off a racy, spicy, minty flavor, with a core of cherry and currant, finishing with firm, gritty tannins and a hint of bay leaf. • $NA • (07/31/98) (BT) • **90-94**
Cabernet Sauvignon Napa Valley 1996: Has all the raw ingredients for excellence. Unfolds slowly, showing earth-accented currant and plum flavors, picking up a minty edge on the finish. • $20 • (06/15/97) (BT) • **90-94**
Cabernet Sauvignon Napa Valley 1994: Solid, with ripe, intense, earthy currant, black cherry and berry flavors, dashes of mint and cedar. Turns complex on the finish, where the flavors fold together nicely. Best now to 2005. • $20 • (05/15/98) • **88**
Cabernet Sauvignon Napa Valley 1993: Clean and crisp, it then opens to reveal riper flavors, with currant, chocolate, berry and cedar notes. The finish comes up a bit short and shows an earthy note. Best to cellar into 2000. 16,000 cases made. • $20 • (05/15/97) • **88**
Cabernet Sauvignon Napa Valley 1992 • $18 • (11/15/95) SS • **94**
Cabernet Sauvignon Napa Valley 1991 • $34 Ⓐ • (11/15/94) SS • **92**
Cabernet Sauvignon Napa Valley 1990 • $18 • (04/15/94) CS • **90**
Cabernet Sauvignon Napa Valley 1989 • $17 • (02/15/93) • **82**
Cabernet Sauvignon Napa Valley 1988 • $18 • (01/31/92) CS • **90**
Cabernet Sauvignon Napa Valley 1987: Smooth and supple (especially compared with the Hess Reserve, which is quite tannic), this is a complex and harmonious wine, with layers of currant, cedar, spice, sage, tar, chocolate and berry. Intense finish, with a firm tannic edge marked by earthiness. Best now. • $30 Ⓐ • (12/15/97) • **94**
Cabernet Sauvignon Napa Valley 1986: Shows the same ripe, vibrant cherry, wild berry and spice flavors that have made it likable ever since its release. What it may lack in tannin and extraction, compared to the réserve, it makes up in youthful vitality. Ready now into 2000. • $36 Ⓐ • (12/15/96) • **90**
Cabernet Sauvignon Napa Valley 1985 • $37 Ⓐ • (11/15/88) • **91**
Cabernet Sauvignon Napa Valley 1983 • $14 • (11/15/87) • **82**
Cabernet Sauvignon Napa Valley Reserve 1993: Dark in color but lean on the palate, with tart cherry and wild berry flavors that slowly unfold. A wine that will need time—perhaps until 2002 to open and show its best. Finishes with rich fruit and firm tannins, so be advised. Sold only at the winery. • $40 • (05/15/98) • **90**
Cabernet Sauvignon Napa Valley Reserve 1992: Complex, with an elegant band of currant, anise, cedar and spice flavors, showing a hint of mineral on the aftertaste. For all its intensity and concentration, it's texture is smooth and polished. Best after 2000. 400 cases made. • $39 • (11/15/96) • **90**
Cabernet Sauvignon Napa Valley Reserve 1991 • $39 • (04/30/96) • **91**
Cabernet Sauvignon Napa Valley Reserve 1990 • $38 • (11/15/94) • **90**
Cabernet Sauvignon Napa Valley Reserve 1989 • $35 • (11/15/93) • **84**
Cabernet Sauvignon Napa Valley Reserve 1987: Firm, dark, ripe and intense. A young, vibrant wine with lots of earthy currant, spice, cedar and sage notes, finishing with a tight band of tannin and good length. Best now. • $41 Ⓐ • (12/15/97) • **94**
Cabernet Sauvignon Napa Valley Reserve 1986: Dense and concentrated, packed with ripe, rich flavors of earthy currant, mineral, anise, tar and spice. Finishes with firm, chewy tannins, but plenty of fruit flavor works its way through, providing depth and complexity. Can stand aging into 2000. 350 cases made. • $NA • (12/15/96) • **91**
Cabernet Sauvignon Napa Valley Reserve 1984 • $23 • (11/15/88) • **92**
Cabernet Sauvignon Napa Valley Reserve 1983 • $36 Ⓐ • (09/15/88) • **89**
Chardonnay Napa Valley 1996: Tightly wound, with a crisp, complex core of ripe pear, apple, spice and light oak. Sharply focused, well balanced and intense, with clean, refreshing flavors and a floral note on the aftertaste. Best now through 2003. • $18 • (06/30/98) • **90**
Chardonnay Napa Valley 1995: Complex aromatics lead to a core of juicy apple, pear and citrus flavors, turning elegant and refined, persisting on a long, complex aftertaste. Wonderful, and a good price. 25,000 cases made. • $16 • (06/30/97) • **91**
Chardonnay Napa Valley 1994: Appealing ripe pear, spice and apple flavors. An elegant and understated wine that succeeds through subtlety. 20,000 cases made. • $12 • (07/31/96) • **87**
Chardonnay Napa Valley 1993 • $15 • (07/31/95) • **84**
Merlot Napa Valley 1994: Smooth, ripe and polished, with a pretty interplay between the plum, black cherry, wild berry and spicy, toasty oak. Complex

and concentrated, it drinks well now but can age into 2002. Sold only at the winery. • $20 • (05/15/98) • **88**

Merlot Napa Valley 1993: Firm and tight, a compact style with currant, herb, earth and cedar notes, finishing with a short, tannic aftertaste. Available at the winery only. • $NA • (08/31/97) • **86**

Merlot Napa Valley 1992 • $18 • (06/30/96) • **88**

Merlot Napa Valley 1991 • $18 • (01/01/96) • **83**

Merlot Napa Valley 1989 • $25 • (05/31/92) • **86**

Zinfandel Napa Valley 1992 • $15 • (10/15/95) • **87**

HESS SELECT | CALIFORNIA

Cabernet Sauvignon California 1995: Pleasing, if a bit tannic. The core of plum and cherry is upfront and tasty. Drink now through 2001. 60,000 cases made. • $10 • (04/30/98) • **86**

Cabernet Sauvignon California 1994: A rustic style, with a chewy, tannic edge to its currant, earth and tar flavors. Drink now through 2000. • $10 • (01/31/97) • **83**

Cabernet Sauvignon California 1993: Ripe and compact, with attractive cherry and berry flavors that are well focused. This delivers a good bang for the buck, finishing with spicy, earthy notes. 50,000 cases made. • $9 • (11/30/95) BB • **85**

Cabernet Sauvignon California 1992 • $9 • (11/15/94) BB • **87**

Cabernet Sauvignon California 1991 • $9 • (02/28/94) • **82**

Cabernet Sauvignon California 1990 • $9 • (11/15/92) • **80**

Cabernet Sauvignon California 1988 • $9 • (03/31/91) • **86**

Chardonnay California 1996: Intense and concentrated, with a core of citrus, especially grapefruit, and subtle notes of spice and green apple. Finishes with a pleasant, fruity aftertaste. A well-made version of a popular varietal at a reasonable price. • $10 • (01/31/98) BB • **87**

Chardonnay California 1995: Smooth and polished, with creamy pear, apple, spice and hazelnut flavors. Drinks well now, and priced right. 80,000 cases made. • $10 • (01/31/97) BB • **86**

Chardonnay California 1994: Fresh and flavorful, with apricot and pear flavors swirling refreshingly through it. Drinkable now. 80,000 cases made. • $9 • (06/30/96) BB • **87**

Chardonnay California 1993 • $9 • (12/15/94) BB • **86**

Pinot Noir Santa Barbara County Bien Nacido Vineyard 1994: Earthy in character, with a leathery nuance to the herb, cherry, cola and rhubarb notes. Try now. 3,500 cases made. • $13 • (05/15/97) • **86**

Pinot Noir Santa Barbara County Bien Nacido Vineyard Q Block 1994: Dry, with an earthy, tannic edge that leaves the hints of herb, tar and dried cherry struggling for equal billing. 300 cases made. • $15 • (01/31/97) • **78**

Pinot Noir Santa Barbara County Bien Nacido Vineyard Unfiltered 1993 • $14 • (12/31/95) • **84**

HEWN, HANS | CALIFORNIA

Red California NV: Round in texture, with smoky, toasty accents over a bright cherry and spice facade. Somewhat simple and finishes with a rough edge, however. 4,600 cases made. • $5 • (09/15/97) • **84**

HICKOK | CALIFORNIA

Claret Napa Valley 1992: Toast and coffee notes lead the way in this meaty wine. Tannins are still rough despite its age, but the ensemble is enjoyable. Finishes with hints of cassis and mint. Would benefit from additional age. 3,500 cases made. • $25 • (11/15/97) • **86**

HIDDEN CELLARS | CALIFORNIA

Alchemy White Mendocino 1995: Toasty oak and vanilla aromas rise to the fore, and the mineral-like flavors are backed by honey tones, but it's a bit short on the effusive qualities of this varietal. A blend of 67 percent Sauvignon Blanc and 33 percent Sémillon. 1,400 cases made. • $18 • (06/30/97) • **86**

Alchemy White Mendocino Mendocino Heritage 1995: Marked by sweet oak, vanilla and hazelnuts, this has weight on the palate but lacks complexity and finesse. The finish is moderate, with fig and grapefruit overtones. A blend of 67 percent Sauvignon Blanc and 33 percent Sémillon. 1,380 cases made. • $20 • (12/15/97) • **87**

Alchemy White Mendocino County 1993 • $18 • (06/30/96) • **87**

Cabernet Sauvignon Mendocino County Mountanos Vineyard 1984 • $12 • (08/31/88) • **88**

Chanson d'Or Mendocino County Bailey J. Lovin Vineyard 1989 • $15/375ml • (09/15/91) • **84**

Chardonnay Mendocino County 1994: An understated, medium-weight wine, with balanced measures of pear, spice and light oak flavors. 4,600 cases made. • $13 • (07/31/96) • **85**

Chardonnay Mendocino County 1993 • $10 • (07/31/95) • **83**

Chardonnay Mendocino County Organically Grown Grapes 1993 • $10 • (09/30/95) • **86**

Chardonnay Mendocino Mendocino Heritage 1995: Earthy, spicy flavors predominate in this smooth-textured Chardonnay, some modest apple flavors slipping in as well. Ready now. 435 cases made. • $25 • (12/31/97) • **85**

Chauché Gris Mendocino County Organically Grown Grapes 1994 • $8 • (09/30/95) • **81**

Chaucé Gris Mendocino 1996: A slightly sweet, peachy blend. Fortunately, it's balanced by a mineral and lemon edge. Might want to drink as an apéritif. 1,850 cases made. • $9 • (03/31/98) • **81**

Cote du Nord California 1986 • $7 • (11/15/88) • **83**

Hillside Red Mendocino Old Vines 1995: A solid red with pretty berry and spice flavors. Drink with dinner. Ready now. A blend of Carignane, Zinfandel and Petite Sirah. 950 cases made. • $11 • (03/31/98) • **84**

Johannisberg Riesling Mendocino 1995: Bright, light and effusively fruity, offering citrus, apple and floral flavors that remain zingy through the finish. 1,150 cases made. • $8 • (07/31/96) • **85**

Johannisberg Riesling Mendocino County 1993 • $8 • (02/28/95) • **86**

Petite Sirah Mendocino 1995: Deep and chewy, with a layer of black pepper seasoning the ripe berry flavor beneath. Tannic enough to want until 2002 to 2004. 650 cases made. • $16 • (03/31/98) • **86**

Petite Sirah Mendocino Eaglepoint Ranch Mendocino Heritage 1995: Dense and peppery, in a chewy, tannic style loaded with spicy wild berry and plummy flavors that coat the palate. Not for everyone, but fans of this full-throttle style will find it especially distinctive. Best now to 2004. 165 cases made. • $25 • (04/30/98) • **88**

Riesling Late Harvest Mendocino Bailey J. Lovin Vineyard 1984 • $10 • (10/16/85) • **94**

Sauvignon Blanc Mendocino 1996: Subtle melon and lemon notes sit nicely on the silky texture. A hint of vanilla rounds things out, though on the finish it's a bit tart. 2,100 cases made. • $11 • (04/30/98) • **85**

Sauvignon Blanc Mendocino 1994 • $9 • (12/15/95) • **85**

Sauvignon Blanc Mendocino 1993 • $8 • (04/30/95) • **85**

Sauvignon Blanc Mendocino Organically Grown Grapes 1995: Dry, crisp, almost austere, with modest floral and apple flavors. 2,200 cases made. • $9 • (10/31/96) • **82**

Sauvignon Blanc Mendocino County Organically Grown Grapes 1993 • $8 • (01/01/95) • **76**

Sorcery Mendocino Mendocino Heritage 1995: A solid red, likable for its raspberry and tobacco notes, which linger on the slightly chewy finish. Best now. A blend of 75 percent Zinfandel, 10 percent Syrah, 10 percent Petite Sirah, and 5 percent Carignane. 410 cases made. • $25 • (12/15/97) • **85**

Syrah Mendocino 1995: A splashy mouthful of berry, spice and earth flavors lingers effectively on the solid, smoothly sculpted finish. Ready now, could be best around 2000. 800 cases made. • $16 • (03/31/98) • **87**

Zinfandel Mendocino County 1992 • $10 • (10/15/94) • **85**

Zinfandel Mendocino County 1991 • $11 • (09/15/93) • **88**

Zinfandel Mendocino County 1990 • $10 • (10/15/92) • **85**

Zinfandel Mendocino County Pacini Vineyard 1989 • $10 • (02/29/92) • **81**

Zinfandel Mendocino County Pacini Vineyard 1988 • $10 • (12/31/90) • **85**

Zinfandel Mendocino County Pacini Vineyard 1986 • $7 • (10/31/88) • **86**

Zinfandel Mendocino County Pacini Vineyard 1984 • $7 • (04/15/87) • **88**

Zinfandel Mendocino Ford & Hitzman Vineyards Mendocino Heritage 1995: Tough, tart, tannic and chewy, but packed with flavors, this wine will require some patience. The core of leathery raspberry and cherry is tightly wound and compact, so cellaring into 2000 is advised. 163 cases made. • $30 • (03/31/98) • **90**

Zinfandel Mendocino Hildreth Ranch Mendocino Heritage 1995: Clean and refreshing, with lively wild berry, plum and cherry flavors. Finishes with firm tannins, dashes of earth and leather and, most importantly, plenty of fruit. Ready to drink. 165 cases made. • $25 • (03/31/98) • **88**

Zinfandel Mendocino McAdams Vineyard 1994: Smooth, ripe and supple, with a pleasing core of black cherry, wild berry, spice and plum notes. Finishes with finesse and mild tannins. Ready to drink. 1,200 cases made. • $14 • (04/30/97) • **89**

Zinfandel Mendocino McAdams Vineyard 1993 • $10 • (10/15/95) • **83**

Zinfandel Mendocino Old Vines 1995: Not fully ripe, the green flavors are interwoven with tart berry and cherry notes. 9 percent Petite Sirah, 5 percent Carignane. Drink now. 3,200 cases made. • $16 • (06/15/98) • **80**

Zinfandel Mendocino Old Vines 1994: Chunky and chewy, with firm tannins and a leathery accent to its currant, anise and spice flavors. Turns more leathery, and dry, on the finish. 1,800 cases made. • $15 • (11/30/96) • **84**

HIDDEN SPRINGS | OREGON

Pinot Noir Oregon 1989 • $12 • (02/28/93) • **62**
Pinot Noir Oregon 1985 • $12 • (06/15/88) • **78**

HIGH PASS | OREGON

Pinot Noir Willamette Valley 1995: Crisp in texture but generous in flavor, with sweet plum, prune and spice notes collecting nicely on the lengthy finish. Lovely to drink now; a superb value, too. 220 cases made. • $11 • (07/31/97) • **88**
Pinot Noir Willamette Valley Reserve 1995: Tightly packed with ripe cherry, plum and spice flavors, this is a narrow-gauge wine with firm texture and length. Best from 2000. 110 cases made. • $15 • (07/31/97) • **87**
Sauvignon Blanc Willamette Valley 1995: Strongly herbal, with peppery, floral qualities as well. Finishes soft. 90 cases made. • $9 • (09/15/97) • **83**

HILL & THOMA WINEGROWERS | CALIFORNIA

Cabernet Sauvignon Napa Valley Clos Fontaine du Mont Reserve 1992 • $32 • (12/15/95) • **87**
Cabernet Sauvignon Napa Valley Clos Fontaine du Mont Reserve 1991 • $32 • (12/31/94) • **85**
Chardonnay Napa Valley Carneros Bighorn Ranch Reserve 1994: Elegant, understated pear and citrus flavors are supported by light oak shadings. Delicate and nicely done. 600 cases made. • $19 • (09/15/96) • **86**
Chardonnay Napa Valley Clos Fontaine du Mont Reserve 1993 • $20 • (05/31/96) • **88**

HILL, WILLIAM | CALIFORNIA

Cabernet Sauvignon Napa Valley 1995: Decidedly herbal, with sage, bell pepper and weedy currant aromas. More impressive on the palate, where the flavors straighten out and the texture is smooth. Already approachable. 16,000 cases made. • $16 • (11/30/97) • **86**
Cabernet Sauvignon Napa Valley 1994: Leads off with a strong earth, mushroom and barnyard edge. If you can handle that, what follows is good: anise, mint, coffee, tar, cedar and currant flavors. Long finish. Drink now, though. It's not going to improve. • $14 • (09/30/97) • **86**
Cabernet Sauvignon Napa Valley 1993: Goes for elegance, and packs a lot of sweet berry, currant and cedar flavors into a lean and lively package. Approachable now. • $14 • (07/31/97) • **87**
Cabernet Sauvignon Napa Valley 1992 • $14 • (12/15/95) • **84**
Cabernet Sauvignon Napa Valley 1986: Tight, austere and tannic, this is less concentrated than when tasted just two or three years ago. Now it shows more structure than fruit flavor, with hints of tart, dried cherry and berry that pick up an earthy accent. • $NA • (12/15/96) • **84**
Cabernet Sauvignon Napa Valley Gold Label 1983 • $18 Ⓐ • (08/31/87) • **89**
Cabernet Sauvignon Napa Valley Gold Label 1982 • $24 Ⓐ • (06/16/86) SS • **94**
Cabernet Sauvignon Napa Valley Gold Label 1981 • $17 • (12/15/84) • **88**
Cabernet Sauvignon Napa Valley Gold Label 1978 • $46 Ⓐ • (11/15/92) • **94**
Cabernet Sauvignon Napa Valley Reserve 1994: Smooth, ripe and complex, with lots of currant, cedar, plum and spice flavors that are rich and well focused. Just the right amount of tannins. Drinkable now to 2001. 6,000 cases made. • $27 • (12/15/97) • **88**
Cabernet Sauvignon Napa Valley Reserve 1992 • $24 • (12/15/95) • **85**
Cabernet Sauvignon Napa Valley Reserve 1991 • $14 • (10/15/94) • **84**
Cabernet Sauvignon Napa Valley Reserve 1990 • $24 • (11/15/93) • **88**
Cabernet Sauvignon Napa Valley Reserve 1989 • $29 • (03/31/93) • **87**
Cabernet Sauvignon Napa Valley Reserve 1988 • $26 • (11/15/91) • **84**
Cabernet Sauvignon Napa Valley Reserve 1987 • $39 • (11/15/90) SS • **95**
Cabernet Sauvignon Napa Valley Reserve 1986 • $29 • (11/15/89) • **91**
Cabernet Sauvignon Napa Valley Reserve 1985 • $22 • (11/15/88) • **92**
Cabernet Sauvignon Napa Valley Reserve 1984 • $18 • (04/15/88) CS • **91**
Cabernet Sauvignon Napa Valley Silver Label 1989 • $14 • (03/31/93) • **82**

Key: SS—Spectator Selection CS—Cellar Selection HR—Highly Recommended BB—Best Buy $NA—Price not available Ⓐ—Auction Price (BT)—Barrel Tasting
Dates in parentheses indicate the issues in which the ratings were published.

Cabernet Sauvignon Napa Valley Silver Label 1987 • $14 • (11/15/90) • **85**
Cabernet Sauvignon Napa Valley Silver Label 1985 • $12 • (04/30/88) • **90**
Cabernet Sauvignon Sonoma County Silver Label 1988 • $14 • (11/15/91) • **82**
Chardonnay Napa Valley 1996: A wine of polish and finesse. A touch earthy up front, before the core of pear and vanilla-scented Chardonnay flavor works in. Turns supple and silky on the finish. 34,000 cases made. • $15 • (04/30/98) • **87**
Chardonnay Napa Valley 1995: Fruity, with a flinty citrus accent to the ripe pear and apple flavors. Finishes with a clean aftertaste. • $12 • (07/31/97) • **87**
Chardonnay Napa Valley 1994: Simple, light and fruity. Pleasant apple flavors with earthy notes. 32,000 cases made. • $13 • (07/31/96) • **83**
Chardonnay Napa Valley Reserve 1996: A subtle, understated style, with earthy pear, fig and melon flavors that linger on the finish, with a touch of cedary oak. Drink now through 2001. 12,000 cases made. • $20 • (06/30/98) • **87**
Chardonnay Napa Valley Reserve 1995: One of the better William Hill wines of late, this is smooth, ripe and harmonious, with complex pear, fig, melon and citrus notes. • $18 • (06/15/97) • **89**
Chardonnay Napa Valley Reserve 1994: Comes across as elegant and subtle, with light pear, citrus and oak shadings, but comes up short on distinction and length. Ready to drink. 4,000 cases made. • $18 • (12/31/96) • **85**
Chardonnay Napa Valley Reserve 1993: Mature, showing a complex array of ripe pear, melon, honey and fig flavors that turn elegant and spicy on the finish, where a light oak flavor surfaces. • $18 • (12/15/96) • **87**
Merlot Napa Valley 1995: Well proportioned, with appealing coffee, currant, herb and spice flavors of modest depth and complexity. Drink now through 2000. 15,000 cases made. • $19 • (03/31/98) • **86**
Merlot Napa Valley 1994: A touch of green, cedary herb to the cherry and currant flavors. Finishes with crisp tannins. 9,000 cases made. • $16 • (08/31/96) • **82**
Merlot Napa Valley 1992 • $18 • (01/31/95) • **82**
Merlot Napa Valley Premier Release 1991 • $15 • (09/15/94) • **84**
Sauvignon Blanc Napa Valley 1994: Earthy flavors predominate in this medium-weight, nicely balanced, spicy wine. 4,200 cases made. • $9 • (07/31/96) • **85**
Sauvignon Blanc Napa Valley 1993 • $9 • (08/31/95) • **81**

HINMAN | OREGON

Chardonnay Oregon 1995: Earthy, metallic flavors intrude on the modest fruit in this raucous white wine. 3,868 cases made. • $11 • (05/15/98) • **78**
Chardonnay Oregon 1994: Fresh, fruity and appealing, brimming with pear and citrus flavors that remain juicy through the finish. Ready now. 2,136 cases made. • $10 • (01/31/96) • **83**
Pinot Gris Oregon 1996: Bright and jazzy, offering lots of raw-edged peach and citrus flavors, finishing with a slightly acrid edge. Lacks charm. 1,244 cases made. • $11 • (05/15/98) • **78**
Pinot Gris Oregon 1993 • $14 • (08/31/95) • **83**
Pinot Noir Oregon 1996: Lean and crisp, a layer of chewy, earthy tannin covering the modest berry flavors at this point. Try in 2000. 2,675 cases made. • $11 • (05/15/98) • **83**
Pinot Noir Oregon 1994 • $10 • (01/31/96) • **83**

HITCHING POST | CALIFORNIA

Pinot Noir Central Coast 1996: Flavors are built around herb, sage and tea, with hints of cherry and spice working their way to the forefront. 950 cases made. • $18 • (02/28/98) • **84**
Pinot Noir Santa Barbara County 1994 • $14 • (12/31/95) • **84**
Pinot Noir Santa Barbara County Sierra Madre and Gold Coast Vineyards 1993 • $14 • (12/31/95) • **86**
Pinot Noir Santa Maria Valley 1994: A touch earthy, with a slightly tart accent to its cherry, pepper and spice flavors. Turns elegant on the finish. 400 cases made. • $18 • (09/15/96) • **83**
Pinot Noir Santa Maria Valley 1993 • $16 • (10/15/95) • **87**
Pinot Noir Santa Maria Valley Bien Nacido Vineyard 1995: A racy style, smooth and spicy, with cola, cherry, berry and cedar notes. Turns complex on the finish where the flavors fan out and intermingle. Drink now. 250 cases made. • $25 • (05/15/97) • **88**
Pinot Noir Santa Maria Valley Bien Nacido Vineyard 1994: Smooth and polished, with a supple array of spicy cherry, currant, herb and cedary oak flavors. Turns complex and elegant on the finish, where the flavors linger. Approachable now. 100 cases made. • $25 • (09/15/96) • **89**

Pinot Noir Santa Maria Valley Bien Nacido Vineyard 1993 • $25 • (10/15/95) • **88**

Pinot Noir Santa Maria Valley Sierra Madre & Riverbench Vineyards 1995: Distinctive for its smoky, gamy, meaty edge, the core of currant and cherry flavors fills the gaps to provide depth and dimension. Enjoyable now. 350 cases made. • $20 • (05/15/97) • **87**

Pinot Noir Santa Ynez Valley Sanford & Benedict Vineyard 1995: Greets you with rather firm tannins, but the core of fruit is complex and appealing, with intense spice and meaty-beefy notes, mushroom and dried cherry flavors. Drinks well now. 75 cases made. • $30 • (01/31/98) • **90**

Pinot Noir Santa Ynez Valley Sanford & Benedict Vineyard 1994: Austere, with a meaty, barnyardy accent to the cherry and berry flavors and a funky aftertaste. Try now to 2000. 100 cases made. • $30 • (01/31/97) • **86**

Pinot Noir Santa Ynez Valley Sanford & Benedict Vineyard 1993 • $25 • (10/15/95) • **88**

Zinfandel California 1995: Marked by exotic spicy nuances around a core of meaty plum and wild berry flavors. Long, spicy aftertaste. 270 cases made. • $14 • (04/30/97) • **87**

HOBBS, PAUL | CALIFORNIA

Cabernet Sauvignon Howell Mountain Liparita Vineyard 1994: Young, lean, firm and tight, with a well-focused core of earthy currant, mineral and tar flavors. Finishes with a long, lively aftertaste and fine length. Best after 2001. 778 cases made. • $45 • (10/31/97) • **91**

Cabernet Sauvignon Howell Mountain Liparita Vineyard 1993: Plum and cherry flavors give body and flesh to this wine that's a touch on the green side otherwise, with herb and sage notes. Best to give it a year or two in the bottle. Tasted twice, with consistent notes. 469 cases made. • $35 • (06/15/97) • **88**

Cabernet Sauvignon Howell Mountain Liparita Vineyard 1992 • $35 • (05/15/96) • **84**

Cabernet Sauvignon Napa Valley Carneros Hyde Vineyard 1994: Smooth and polished in texture, with a flavor profile built around dill, sage, tea and currant that slowly unfold to gain complexity and interest. Best now. 1,044 cases made. • $40 • (10/31/97) • **89**

Cabernet Sauvignon Napa Valley Carneros Hyde Vineyard 1993: Marked by herb and black olive flavors, with hints of currant and strawberry. Turns elegant and refined on the finish, where the flavors linger and the tannins are smooth and polished. 490 cases made. • $30 • (11/30/96) • **89**

Cabernet Sauvignon Napa Valley Carneros Hyde Vineyard 1992 • $30 • (12/15/95) HR • **93**

Cabernet Sauvignon Napa Valley Carneros Hyde Vineyard 1991 • $30 • (10/31/94) HR • **91**

Chardonnay Sonoma Mountain Kunde Vineyard 1995: Bold, ripe, rich and exotic, with tiers of juicy pear, apple, fig and melon flavors and light oak shadings, this is a remarkably complex and beautifully integrated young wine that promises several more years of fine drinking. 825 cases made. • $28 • (05/31/97) • **93**

Chardonnay Sonoma Mountain Richard Dinner Vineyard 1996: An appealing, fruit-driven style, with ripe apple, pear, nectarine, melon and spice, turning complex and lively on the finish. Drink now through 2001. 1,000 cases made. • $39 • (06/30/98) • **91**

Chardonnay Sonoma Mountain Richard Dinner Vineyard 1995: Amazingly elegant and flavorful, with a complex core of ripe pear, apple, spice and melon flavors that gently and deliciously unfold. Concentrated too, the long, lingering finish keeps pumping out flavors. A very impressive wine in only its fourth vintage. 700 cases made. • $30 • (05/31/97) HR • **94**

Chardonnay Sonoma Mountain Richard Dinner Vineyard 1994: An openly oaky style, with mature, medium-bodied honey, citrus and earthy pear notes, and an elegant finish. Well balanced and drinkable now. Tasted twice with consistent notes. 1,800 cases made. • $28 • (06/30/96) • **89**

Chardonnay Sonoma Mountain Richard Dinner Vineyard 1993 • $28 • (07/31/95) • **86**

Chardonnay Sonoma Valley Kunde Vineyard 1996: Ripe, fruity and complex, with elegant pear, spice, fig and melon notes that are polished and sophisticated, and a lingering finish. Drink now through 2002. 435 cases made. • $35 • (06/30/98) • **91**

Pinot Noir Napa Valley Carneros Hyde Vineyard 1994: An elegant, delicate style, with subtle cherry, earth, mineral, spice and cedar flavors, a trace of tar on the finish. Well crafted and drinking well now, but capable of aging into 2000. 796 cases made. • $24 • (01/31/97) • **89**

Pinot Noir Napa Valley Carneros Hyde Vineyard 1993 • $23 • (05/15/96) • **84**

Pinot Noir Napa Valley Carneros Hyde Vineyard 1992 • $24 • (03/31/95) • **81**

Pinot Noir Napa Valley Carneros Hyde Vineyard 1991 • $25 • (02/28/94) • **86**

HOGUE | WASHINGTON

Cabernet Franc Yakima Valley Genesis 1994: Dense and chewy, with gritty tannins and a modest level of berryish flavor, layered with hints of iris and spice. Drinkable now. 200 cases made. • $14 • (01/31/98) • **82**

Cabernet Sauvignon Columbia Valley 1993: Firm in texture, with solid Cabernet flavor and smoky anise shadings. Drinkable now. 2,814 cases made. • $15 • (11/15/96) SS • **88**

Cabernet Sauvignon Columbia Valley 1992: An open-textured red, with tightly packed blackberry and bright currant flavors and a nice hint of cedar on the finish. 11,776 cases made. • $15 • (09/15/96) • **87**

Cabernet Sauvignon Columbia Valley 1991 • $14 • (06/15/95) • **85**

Cabernet Sauvignon Columbia Valley Barrel Select 1994: A crisp mouthful of Cabernet fruit, with currant and raspberry notes swirling through the supple finish. Very good now, better from 1999 or 2000. 9,496 cases made. • $15 • (03/31/98) • **86**

Cabernet Sauvignon Columbia Valley Barrel Select 1993: Light, and surprisingly delicate, with pretty currant and plum flavors weaving through the fine-grained tannins. 2,814 cases made. • $14 • (09/15/97) • **84**

Cabernet Sauvignon Columbia Valley Genesis 1994: Has a sharp edge to its spicy currant flavors, and finishes with a bite of tannin and acidity that will need until 2000 to soften. 800 cases made. • $21 • (01/31/98) • **81**

Cabernet Sauvignon Washington 1990 • $14 • (09/30/94) • **85**

Cabernet Sauvignon Washington 1989 • $12 • (11/15/91) • **84**

Cabernet Sauvignon Washington 1988 • $12 • (03/31/92) • **88**

Cabernet Sauvignon Washington Reserve 1992: This wine is nicely balanced, harmonious with its tobacco-scented blackberry and cedar flavors, finishes smooth as glass. Best now. 1,068 cases made. • $18 • (09/15/97) • **87**

Cabernet Sauvignon Washington Reserve 1991: Light in texture, with chewy, currant flavors. Finishes with restraint. 950 cases made. • $20 • (09/15/96) • **82**

Cabernet Sauvignon Washington Reserve 1990 • $18 • (09/30/95) • **90**

Cabernet Sauvignon Washington Reserve 1989 • $18 • (09/30/94) • **86**

Cabernet Sauvignon Washington Reserve 1988 • $18 • (11/15/91) • **89**

Cabernet Sauvignon Washington Reserve 1987 • $19 • (03/31/91) • **88**

Cabernet Sauvignon Washington Reserve 1985 • $18 • (10/15/89) • **81**

Cabernet-Merlot Columbia Valley 1995: Light, bright and refreshing. A lithe wine with pleasant strawberry and raspberry flavors plus a touch of tobacco on the finish. Drink soon. A blend of 68 percent Cabernet Sauvignon and 32 percent Merlot. 18,075 cases made. • $10 • (09/15/97) • **85**

Cabernet-Merlot Columbia Valley 1994: Lean and chewy, a tight wine with restrained berry and herb flavors. Drinkable now. 4,000 cases made. • $9 • (09/15/96) • **81**

Chardonnay Columbia Valley 1995: Soft and simple, with appealing nectarine and mineral flavors that linger harmoniously. • $10 • (09/15/97) • **86**

Chardonnay Columbia Valley 1994: A smooth and spicy white that's nicely balanced to show off its pineapple, pear and nutmeg flavors. The finish lingers pleasantly, and this looks good for its value, too. Drinkable now. 59,200 cases made. • $9 • (08/31/95) BB • **88**

Chardonnay Columbia Valley 1993 • $10 • (04/15/95) SS • **89**

Chardonnay Columbia Valley Barrel Select 1996: Bright and appealing for its peppery apple and pear flavors, with mineral notes hinting on the finish. Best now. 5,000 cases made. • $14 • (03/31/98) • **88**

Chardonnay Washington 1996: Here's a crisp and juicy style, with a jazzy range of citrus, pear and apple flavors that pick up hints of spice on the finish. Makes tasty drinking now through 2000, and is all the more enticing for its reasonable price. 46,000 cases made. • $9 • (06/15/98) BB • **88**

Chardonnay Washington Reserve 1995: A straightforward wine, refreshing for its melon, spice and apple flavors that linger appealingly. 4,631 cases made. • $14 • (09/15/97) • **87**

Chardonnay Washington Reserve 1994: A smooth and spicy, medium-weight Chardonnay with tasty hazelnut notes on the finish. Drinkable now. 4,000 cases made. • $15 • (09/15/96) • **88**

Chardonnay Washington Reserve 1993 • $13 • (08/31/95) • **89**

Chardonnay Yakima Valley Genesis Crawford Vineyard 1996: A solid white wine with pretty pear and tobacco flavors that linger on the slightly rough finish. Drinkable now. 500 cases made. • $19 • (01/31/98) • **84**

Chenin Blanc Columbia Valley 1997: Off-dry, with simple apple and slightly herbal flavors on a soft frame. Drink now. 12,000 cases made. • $7 • (06/30/98) • **80**

Chenin Blanc Columbia Valley 1996: Off-dry, ripe, harmonious, balanced and utterly charming, with plenty of sweet melon and apple flavors. A simple wine for casual sipping. 3,780 cases made. • $7 • (09/15/97) • **85**

Chenin Blanc Columbia Valley 1995: Light and fruity, like biting into a fresh nectarine. Finish is off-dry. 11,180 cases made. • $6 • (09/30/96) • **84**

Chenin Blanc Columbia Valley 1994 • $6 • (09/30/95) • **84**

Chenin Blanc Columbia Valley 1993 • $6 • (09/30/94) • **84**

Chenin Blanc Columbia Valley Dry 1997: On the dry side, with simple pear and leaf aromas and flavors, finishing with a touch of honey. Drink now. 2,400 cases made. • $7 • (06/30/98) • **81**

Chenin Blanc Columbia Valley Dry 1996: Crisp and light, refreshing for its fragile melon and green berry flavors. Finishes dry. 1,266 cases made. • $7 • (09/15/97) • **84**

Chenin Blanc Columbia Valley Dry 1995: Fresh and light, with simple, citrusy apple flavors. Not sweet. 2,420 cases made. • $6 • (09/15/96) • **82**

Chenin Blanc Columbia Valley Dry 1994 • $6 • (09/30/95) • **84**

Chenin Blanc Columbia Valley Dry 1993 • $6 • (09/30/94) • **82**

Fumé Blanc Columbia Valley 1996: Soft and smooth, generous with its nectarine and spice flavors, finishing freshly. 24,949 cases made. • $9 • (09/15/97) • **87**

Fumé Blanc Columbia Valley 1995: Decidedly floral and light in texture, with a white pepper accent to the modest peach flavors. 48,355 cases made. • $7 • (09/15/96) • **83**

Fumé Blanc Columbia Valley 1994 • $7 • (09/15/95) BB • **86**

Fumé Blanc Columbia Valley Dry 1993 • $7 • (12/31/94) BB • **88**

Gewürztraminer Columbia Valley 1997: Soft and somewhat sweet, with pretty orange, cream and delicate rose petal flavors folding into a gentle finish. Drink now. 9,500 cases made. • $7 • (06/30/98) • **84**

Gewürztraminer Columbia Valley 1996: Lightly sweet, with simple, modest pear flavors that linger on the finish. 4,554 cases made. • $7 • (09/15/97) • **84**

Gewürztraminer Columbia Valley 1995: Light and toasty, but gains your interest on the finish where black pepper and spice flavors make an unexpected arrival. 8,360 cases made. • $6 • (09/15/96) • **85**

Gewürztraminer Columbia Valley 1994 • $6 • (09/30/95) • **83**

Gewürztraminer Columbia Valley 1993 • $6 • (09/30/94) • **84**

Johannisberg Riesling Columbia Valley 1996: Has a strong mineral streak running through the pleasant peach and pear flavors. Off-dry, and easy to drink. 13,276 cases made. • $7 • (09/15/97) • **84**

Johannisberg Riesling Columbia Valley 1995: A wonderful sipping wine, inviting you to indulge, especially at this price. Pretty peach and green apple flavors bounce through this lively, refreshing Riesling from Washington. 38,830 cases made. • $6 • (09/15/96) BB • **87**

Johannisberg Riesling Columbia Valley Dry 1996: Dry, almost delicate, with a pleasant raw-fruit character including peach and green apple notes. Finish is a bit rough, but it's a nice summertime quaffer. 5,470 cases made. • $7 • (09/15/97) • **82**

Johannisberg Riesling Columbia Valley Dry 1995: Charmingly fruity, but dry enough to discipline the impetuous lemon, apple and floral aromas and flavors. 11,520 cases made. • $6 • (09/15/96) • **85**

Johannisberg Riesling Columbia Valley Dry 1994 • $6 • (09/30/95) • **85**

Johannisberg Riesling Washington 1997: Soft, slightly sweet, with plenty of pretty pear, orange and floral flavors that linger gently on the generous finish. Drink now. 48,000 cases made. • $7 • (06/30/98) BB • **86**

Johannisberg Riesling Yakima Valley 1993 • $6 • (09/30/94) • **83**

Johannisberg Riesling Yakima Valley Dry 1993 • $6 • (09/30/94) • **81**

Lemberger Columbia Valley 1994: A light, dry wine with a sweet-feeling texture and appealing cherry flavors. 1,580 cases made. • $9 • (09/15/96) • **82**

Lemberger Columbia Valley 1992 • $9 • (09/30/95) • **82**

Lemberger Columbia Valley Genesis Blue Franc 1995: Bright and jazzy, with a bit of a prickle to the texture, showing pretty black cherry and cream flavors that do a gradual diminuendo on the finish. Ready now. 500 cases made. • $12 • (01/31/98) • **85**

Lemberger Yakima Valley 1993 • $9 • (09/30/95) • **82**

Lemberger Yakima Valley 1991 • $10 • (12/31/93) • **85**

Merlot Columbia Valley 1994: A lovely mouthful of black cherry, blueberry, spice and cedar flavors that's soft and mellow. This Washington red is supple and tasty now. A blend of 84 percent Merlot and 16 percent Cabernet Sauvignon. 18,284 cases made. • $15 • (11/15/96) SS • **89**

Merlot Columbia Valley 1993: A light, pleasant red with berry and vanilla flavors that linger delicately on the herbal finish. • $15 • (09/15/96) • **85**

Merlot Columbia Valley 1992 • $14 • (06/15/95) • **86**

Merlot Columbia Valley 1991 • $14 • (09/30/94) • **84**

Merlot Columbia Valley Barrel Select 1995: Light, fragrant Merlot with pretty strawberry, blackberry and spice notes lingering on the modestly chewy finish. Drink now. 35,214 cases made. • $15 • (03/31/98) • **85**

Merlot Columbia Valley Genesis 1994: Light in style, with chewy texture and modest anise and blackberry flavors that echo solidly on the finish. Best now. 900 cases made. • $21 • (01/31/98) • **85**

Merlot Washington 1990 • $12 • (01/31/93) • **86**

Merlot Washington 1989 • $12 • (10/15/91) SS • **92**

Merlot Washington 1986 • $12 • (04/15/89) • **85**

Merlot Washington 1985 • $12 • (11/15/87) • **80**

Merlot Washington Reserve 1993: Lean in texture, but solidly packed with berry, earth and spice flavors that echo nicely on the on the open-textured finish. Drink soon. Tasted twice, with consistent results. 972 cases made. • $18 • (10/15/97) • **85**

Merlot Washington Reserve 1992: Currant and berry flavors with delicate spice, chocolate and earth nuances in a crisp and refreshing texture. A harmonious wine, with subtlety. Ready now. 982 cases made. • $20 • (09/15/96) • **88**

Merlot Washington Reserve 1991 • $18 • (09/30/95) • **89**

Merlot Washington Reserve 1990 • $18 • (09/30/94) • **87**

Merlot Washington Reserve 1989 • $18 • (06/15/93) • **88**

Merlot Washington Reserve 1988 • $18 • (11/15/91) • **90**

Merlot Washington Reserve 1987 • $19 • (03/31/91) • **89**

Riesling Columbia Valley Dry Schwartzman Vineyard Reserve 1994: Intensely pinelike aromas and flavors surround ripe fruit flavors that simplify into a nice apple note on the finish. 220 cases made. • $7 • (09/15/96) • **86**

Riesling Washington Dry Schwartzman Vineyard Reserve 1995: Bright, floral and fresh, with mineral accents and a disturbing touch of soapiness among the floral notes. • $NA • (09/15/97) • **80**

Sémillon Columbia Valley 1996: This Washington white offers a nice change of pace at an affordable price. It's soft in texture, with bright apple, fig and coffee flavors that linger on the gentle finish. Inviting now. 24,000 cases made. • $8 • (06/15/98) BB • **86**

Sémillon Columbia Valley 1995: Shows a distinctive, oddly floral character and watermelon and lime flavors that never quite achieve balance. 5,140 cases made. • $7 • (09/15/96) • **82**

Sémillon Columbia Valley 1994 • $7 • (09/30/95) • **85**

Sémillon Columbia Valley 1993 • $8 • (03/31/95) BB • **85**

Sémillon Yakima Valley Genesis 1996: Light and smooth in texture, this subtle wine yields its anise and fig flavors on the finish. Drinkable now. 750 cases made. • $12 • (03/31/98) • **85**

Sémillon-Chardonnay Columbia Valley 1996: Herb and tobacco flavors are more prominent than the fruit, which sneaks in with a bite of green apple on the finish. Ready now. 7,260 cases made. • $9 • (03/31/98) • **82**

Sémillon-Chardonnay Columbia Valley 1995: A snappy mouthful of citrusy pear and tobacco flavors that remain solid and rich through the finish. Ready now. A blend of 73 percent Sémillon and 27 percent Chardonnay. 5,650 cases made. • $9 • (09/15/97) • **86**

Sémillon-Chardonnay Columbia Valley 1994: Light and floral, but with a medicinal edge that detracts. 7,860 cases made. • $7 • (09/15/96) • **80**

Sémillon-Chardonnay Columbia Valley 1993 • $7 • (04/30/95) • **85**

Seyval Blanc Columbia Valley 1994 • $7 • (09/30/95) • **86**

Syrah Columbia Valley Genesis 1995: Richly flavorful on a supple frame, offering plenty of black cherry and berry flavors shaded with litchi and spice nuances, and finishing smooth, with immediate appeal. Delicious now. 1,000 cases made. • $14 • (01/31/98) • **87**

White Riesling Late Harvest Columbia Valley 1996: Sweet, but balanced by crisp acidity and an explosion of honey-tinged pear, pineapple and floral flavors that persist through the rich finish. Not a "sticky", but a lovely mouthful of Riesling intensity from Washington. Delicious now, may be at its best after 2000. 17,400 cases made. • $7 • (09/15/97) SS • **90**

White Riesling Late Harvest Columbia Valley 1994 • $6 • (08/31/95) BB • **88**

White Riesling Late Harvest Columbia Valley 1993 • $6 • (09/30/94) • **85**

White Riesling Late Harvest Yakima Valley Markin Vineyard 1987 • $7 • (10/15/89) • **79**

HOMEWOOD | CALIFORNIA

Cabernet Sauvignon Alexander Valley 1990: A touch on the rustic side, showing off herb and green olive flavors, but enough cherry and plum flavors fold in to provide added dimension. • $14 • (11/30/96) • **88**

Cabernet Sauvignon Alexander Valley 1989 • $14 • (11/15/92) • **80**

Cabernet Sauvignon Alexander Valley 1988 • $13 • (11/15/92) • **83**

Zinfandel Dry Creek Valley Quinn Vineyard 1993 • $12 • (04/30/96) • **80**

Zinfandel Dry Creek Valley Quinn Vineyard 1992 • $9 • (03/31/94) • **79**

Zinfandel Sonoma Valley 110 Year Old Vines 1992 • $12 • (03/31/94) • **83**

Key: SS—Spectator Selection CS—Cellar Selection HR—Highly Recommended BB—Best Buy $NA—Price not available Ⓐ—Auction Price (BT)—Barrel Tasting

Dates in parentheses indicate the issues in which the ratings were published.

HONIG | CALIFORNIA

Cabernet Sauvignon Napa Valley 1995: Crisp and tight, with pretty plum and cherry-laced flavors. Solid, well balanced and flavorful, with a complex aftertaste. Best after 2000. 4,000 cases made. • $22 • (05/15/98) • **89**
Cabernet Sauvignon Napa Valley 1988 • $14 • (08/31/92) • **83**
Sauvignon Blanc Napa Valley Barrel Fermented 1993 • $10 • (08/31/95) • **80**
Sauvignon Blanc Napa Valley Reserve 1996: Pretty peach, citrus and honey flavors, but framed in a little too much toasty oak for the delicate fruit. Still enjoyable. 2,800 cases made. • $17 • (05/15/98) • **84**

HOODSPORT | WASHINGTON

Cabernet Sauvignon Washington Limited Artist Edition 1994: A lively and generous swallow of red berry, currant and sweetly leathery flavors that remain fiesty through the finish. 260 cases made. • $21 • (09/15/96) • **85**
Cabernet Sauvignon Yakima Valley Reserve 1996: Light, more like a Merlot than a Cabernet, with pretty currant and tobacco flavors that remain gentle on the finish. Drink now. 92 cases made. • $17 • (03/31/98) • **83**
Chardonnay Yakima Valley Skagit Valley Tulip Festival 1995: Crisp and citrusy, this wine is bright with grapefruit and melon flavors that linger on the smart finish. Best to drink sooner rather than later. 1,434 cases made. • $11 • (09/15/97) • **86**
Gewürztraminer Washington 1994 • $8 • (09/30/95) • **83**
Gewürztraminer Washington 1993 • $8 • (09/30/94) • **78**
Johannisberg Riesling Washington 1995: Light but vibrant, with juicy citrus and green apple flavors. Soft finish shows a hint of honey. Yummy to drink now. 1,388 cases made. • $8 • (09/15/96) • **87**
Johannisberg Riesling Washington 1994 • $8 • (09/15/95) • **85**
Johannisberg Riesling Washington 1993 • $8 • (09/30/94) • **80**
Lemberger Washington 1992 • $8 • (09/30/94) • **73**
Lemberger-Cab Washington 1994: Light and appealing with its cola-scented berry flavors. Best when served slightly chilled. The unique blend of grapes makes for a fresh red that delivers good value. 1,536 cases made. • $9 • (09/30/96) BB • **85**
Lemberger-Cab Washington 1993 • $10 • (09/30/95) • **77**
Lemberger-Cab Yakima Valley 1996: Light, simple and distinctive for its fruit profile, offering blackberry, blueberry and cherry flavors. Drink now. A blend of 81 percent Lemberger and 19 percent Cabernet. 590 cases made. • $11 • (03/31/98) • **83**
Lemberger-Cab Yakima Valley 1995: Light, pretty and smooth, offering a hint of chocolate to go along with the fragile raspberry and floral flavors. Ready to drink. 1,787 cases made. • $11 • (08/31/97) • **86**
Merlot Washington 1994: Notes of floral and mint trickle through the core of cherry flavors. Finish is a tad bitter considering the modest level of flavor and tannin. 627 cases made. • $11 • (09/15/96) • **82**
Merlot Washington 1992 • $11 • (09/30/94) • **80**
Sauvignon Blanc Washington 1995: A pretty, polished wine offering plenty of melon and grapefruit flavors that unfold gracefully on the palate. 462 cases made. • $8 • (09/15/96) • **89**
Sauvignon Blanc Yakima Valley 1996: Appealing for its silky texture and refreshing peach and delicately herbal flavors. Ready now. 585 cases made. • $9 • (11/30/97) • **85**
Sémillon Washington 1995: Lean and lively. Citrusy pear and tobacco flavors nip the palate with a touch of astringency, then linger on the finish. 462 cases made. • $8 • (09/15/96) • **84**
Sémillon Washington 1993 • $8 • (09/30/95) • **76**
Sémillon Washington Limited Aritist Edition 1994 • $8 • (05/15/96) • **79**

HOP KILN | CALIFORNIA

Cabernet Sauvignon Alexander Valley 1984 • $10 • (03/31/88) • **77**
Cabernet Sauvignon Dry Creek Valley 1986 • $12 • (06/15/89) • **69**
Cabernet Sauvignon Dry Creek Valley 1985 • $10 • (10/15/88) • **75**
Cabernet Sauvignon Russian River Valley 1991 • $14 • (11/15/94) • **83**
Cabernet Sauvignon Russian River Valley 1990 • $14 • (09/15/93) • **84**
Cabernet Sauvignon Sonoma County 1989 • $14 • (11/15/92) • **73**
Chardonnay Russian River Valley M. Griffin Vineyards 1993 • $15 • (02/28/95) • **89**
Gewürztraminer Russian River Valley M. Griffin Vineyards 1993 • $7 • (11/15/94) • **82**
Johannisberg Riesling Russian River Valley M. Griffin Vineyards 1993 • $8 • (02/28/95) • **83**
Marty Griffin's Big Red Russian River Valley 1988 • $7 • (11/30/90) BB • **85**
Marty Griffin's Big Red Russian River Valley 1987 • $7 • (12/15/89) BB • **89**
Marty Griffin's Big Red Russian River Valley 1986 • $6 • (06/15/89) BB • **85**
Marty Griffin's Big Red Sonoma County 1994: Intense and a touch woody, but there's enough plum and cherry flavors to keep it in balance. Not the blockbuster Big Red it has been in the past. 6,264 cases made. • $9 • (09/15/96) • **83**
Marty Griffin's Big Red Sonoma County 1991 • $8 • (09/15/93) BB • **88**
Petite Sirah Russian River Valley M. Griffin Vineyards 1987 • $11 • (02/28/90) • **82**
Petite Sirah Russian River Valley M. Griffin Vineyards 1985 • $11 • (03/31/88) • **77**
Petite Sirah Russian River Valley M. Griffin Vineyards 1984 • $10 • (02/15/87) • **90**
Petite Sirah Sonoma County 1991 • $15 • (10/15/93) • **84**
Valdiguié M. Griffin Vineyards Russian River Valley 1991 • $15 • (10/15/93) • **82**
Valdiguié M. Griffin Vineyards Russian River Valley 1990 • $15 • (06/30/92) • **77**
Zinfandel Russian River Valley 1992 • $14 • (06/15/95) • **86**
Zinfandel Russian River Valley 1988 • $12 • (12/15/90) • **88**
Zinfandel Russian River Valley 1986 • $10 • (06/15/89) • **85**
Zinfandel Russian River Valley 1982 • $8 • (11/01/85) • **85**
Zinfandel Russian River Valley M. Griffin Vineyards 1994: Shows a ripe core of cherry and raspberry flavors, is of medium weight and intensity and turns complex on the lingering finish. Ready now. 650 cases made. • $15 • (10/15/96) • **85**
Zinfandel Russian River Valley Marty Griffin's Big Red 1990 • $8 • (04/30/93) • **81**
Zinfandel Russian River Valley Primitivo 1995: Young and tart, with grape-tinged cherry and wild berry flavors. A vibrant wine to be enjoyed now. 832 cases made. • $22 • (03/31/97) • **87**
Zinfandel Russian River Valley Primitivo 1992 • $18 • (02/28/95) • **85**
Zinfandel Russian River Valley Primitivo 1985 • $12 • (03/15/88) • **80**
Zinfandel Russian River Valley Primitivo Reserve 1985 • $12 • (06/15/89) • **90**
Zinfandel Sonoma County 1996: Serves up a broad range of Zinfandel flavors, from tart, slightly green berry notes to riper flavors, which stay focused on the finish. Firmly tannic. Drink now through 2000. 2,180 cases made. • $16 • (06/15/98) • **85**
Zinfandel Sonoma County 1995: A complex wine with an inviting array of supple, concentrated black cherry, wild berry and raspberry notes that linger on the finish. Not too tannic, it's drinkable now. 1,075 cases made. • $16 • (03/31/97) • **90**
Zinfandel Sonoma County 1991 • $12 • (10/15/94) • **84**
Zinfandel Sonoma County 1990 • $12 • (10/15/92) • **85**
Zinfandel Sonoma County Marty Griffin's Big Red 1992 • $8 • (02/28/95) • **81**
Zinfandel Sonoma County Marty Griffin's Big Red Reserve NV • $8 • (09/15/94) BB • **87**
Zinfandel Sonoma County Primitivo 1996: Tart, with a green streak running through the wild berry and cherry-laced flavors. Finishes with firm, crisp tannins and dashes of pepper and spice. Drink now through 2000. 500 cases made. • $22 • (06/15/98) • **84**
Zinfandel Sonoma County Primitivo 1994: Marked by tar and wild berry flavors, but it also has a slightly green, stemmy edge which gives a somewhat bitter flavor. Typically more ripe. 650 cases made. • $18 • (10/15/96) • **81**
Zinfandel Sonoma County Primitivo 1993 • $18 • (10/15/95) • **86**
Zinfandel Sonoma County Primitivo 1991 • $15 • (09/15/93) • **87**
Zinfandel Sonoma County Primitivo 1990 • $15 • (10/15/92) • **85**
Zinfandel Sonoma County Primitivo 1988 • $14 • (12/31/90) • **89**

HOPE FARMS | CALIFORNIA

Cabernet Sauvignon Paso Robles 1992: Ruby-red color yields to cinnamon, spice and leather aromas. Powdery tannins frame a nice blend of herbal, anise and chocolate flavors. Finish is somewhat tart. Drink now. 640 cases made. • $13 • (11/30/96) • **85**
Cabernet Sauvignon Paso Robles 1990 • $9 • (11/15/94) • **84**
Cabernet Sauvignon Paso Robles 1989 • $16 • (11/15/93) • **84**
Claret Paso Robles 1991 • $10 • (11/15/94) • **81**
Sauvignon Blanc Paso Robles 1994: Bright and simple, showing some nice pear flavor. 167 cases made. • $NA • (09/15/96) • **81**
Zinfandel Paso Robles NV • $7 • (09/30/93) BB • **84**

HORIZON'S EDGE | WASHINGTON

Muscat Canelli Yakima Valley Nouveaux Riche 1993 • $10/375ml • (09/30/95) • **81**

HORTON | VIRGINIA

Cabernet Franc Orange County 1996: Meaty and leathery flavors and aromas are the hallmarks of this average wine. Also contains 17 percent Cabernet, 5 percent Touriga Nacional and 3 percent Tannat. 2,000 cases made. • $12 • (07/31/98) • **77**

Cabernet Franc Orange County 1995: Stewy-tasting, with some plum and berry flavors, but ends up a bit dried out. Also contains Cabernet Sauvignon, Tannat and Tinta Cão. 2,000 cases made. • $12 • (07/31/98) • **78**

Cabernet Franc Orange County 1994: Smooth, ripe and well concentrated, with plenty of plum, cherry and chocolate flavors. This is a delicious wine that is ready to drink. 1,918 cases made. • $12 • (04/30/97) • **86**

Chardonnay Monticello Montdomaine Reserve 1993 • $13 • (10/15/95) • **82**

Chardonnay Virginia 1994: Pleasant, sweet vanilla-oaky aromas and flavors dominate this light-bodied white, adding some melon and fig notes underneath. It's clean and rather simple, best for fans of oak. • $15 • (10/15/95) • **83**

Côtes d'Orange Orange County Red 1995: A mature, unusual red, with pronounced cherry, cola and spice flavors and earthy-foxy overtones. Not bad, but not our cup of tea. A blend of Grenache, Mourvèdre, Tinta Cão, Syrah, Touriga Nacional, and Viognier. Drink now. 450 cases made. • $15 • (07/31/98) • **78**

Dionysus Orange County 1995: Distinguished by coffeelike aromas and flavors, with some plum and berry notes. A thick, full-bodied red that finishes on a spicy note. A blend of Touriga Nacional, Tinta Cão and Cabernet Sauvignon. 500 cases made. • $25 • (07/31/98) • **83**

Norton Orange County 1996: Fruity and lively, if overdone, with a distinctive charred note. Just doesn't hang together in the end. A blend of Norton, Cabernet Sauvignon and Mourvèdre. 2,500 cases made. • $11 • (07/31/98) • **73**

Norton Orange County 1995: Leathery aromas and flavors dominate this red wine. Tired and overblown. A blend of Norton, Touriga Nacional, Mourvèdre, and Cabernet Franc. 2,500 cases made. • $11 • (07/31/98) • **74**

Viognier Orange County 1997: Cloying flavors and aromas make this awkward. Candied banana and insipid fruit-cocktail flavors dominate. 1,600 cases made. • $20 • (07/31/98) • **74**

Viognier Orange County Reserve 1997: There's nothing resembling Viognier in this awkward, overblown wine. Has an astringent finish and almost no fruit. 85 cases made. • $30 • (07/31/98) • **73**

Viognier Virginia 1993 • $23 • (12/31/94) • **86**

HOWELL MOUNTAIN VINEYARD | CALIFORNIA

Zinfandel Howell Mountain 1995: A ripe, high-octane style, with juicy plum and wild berry flavors, turning slightly hot on the finish where a peppery note comes through. Grapes come from the Black Sears Vineyard. 900 cases made. • $16 • (08/31/97) • **89**

Zinfandel Howell Mountain 1994: Typical spice and pepper aromas of Zinfandel lead to a ripe, lean, elegant young wine, with hints of cherry, sage and wild berry. Finishes with firm tannins, but you can still drink it now. • $15 • (02/28/97) • **88**

Zinfandel Howell Mountain 1988 • $11 • (10/15/92) • **74**

HUNT COUNTRY VINEYARDS | NEW YORK

Johannisberg Riesling Finger Lakes 1995: This has a nice, thick texture and plenty of body, but the fruit flavors are subdued. An atypical Riesling; more like a Pinot Blanc. • $9 • (10/31/96) • **80**

HUNTER, ROBERT | CALIFORNIA

Brut de Noirs Sonoma Valley 1992: Toasty, earthy, nutty aromas are followed by honeyed, melon and citrus flavors, but the final effect is a bit cloying. Bright acidity on the finish saves the day. 1,000 cases made. • $25 • (11/30/97) • **87**

Brut de Noirs Sonoma Valley 1991 • $25 • (09/15/95) • **85**

Brut de Noirs Sonoma Valley 1984 • $15 • (10/15/88) • **84**

Brut de Noirs Sonoma Valley 1983 • $15 • (01/31/88) • **84**

Brut de Noirs Sonoma Valley 1982 • $14 • (12/31/86) • **90**

Brut de Noirs Sonoma Valley 1981 • $14 • (12/16/84) • **87**

Key: SS—Spectator Selection CS—Cellar Selection HR—Highly Recommended BB—Best Buy $NA—Price not available (A)—Auction Price (BT)—Barrel Tasting
Dates in parentheses indicate the issues in which the ratings were published.

Brut de Noirs Sonoma Valley Extended Tirage 1992: Refreshing citrus aromas—mandarin orange comes to mind—lend an appealing air. A blend of minerals, herbs and toast, pear and floral notes shows nicely on the palate. Drink now. 1,000 cases made. • $25 • (06/15/98) • **88**

HUNTINGTON | CALIFORNIA

Cabernet Sauvignon Alexander Valley 1989 • $8 • (08/31/92) • **68**

HUSCH | CALIFORNIA

Cabernet Sauvignon Mendocino La Ribera Vineyards 1994: Rich aromas of chocolate and coffee announce this silky-textured wine. On the palate lie layers of black currant and herbs. Finishes with a slightly bitter aftertaste. Good now or hold. 1,915 cases made. • $15 • (10/15/97) • **88**

Cabernet Sauvignon Mendocino La Ribera Vineyards 1993: An herbal quality dominates the field here, backed by hints of anise and cassis. Finishes with a tart edge. 1,939 cases made. • $15 • (09/30/97) • **83**

Cabernet Sauvignon Mendocino La Ribera Vineyards 1992 • $8 • (11/15/94) • **83**

Cabernet Sauvignon Mendocino La Ribera Vineyards 1991 • $14 • (03/31/95) • **84**

Cabernet Sauvignon Mendocino La Ribera Vineyards 1990 • $14 • (08/31/93) • **88**

Cabernet Sauvignon Mendocino La Ribera Vineyards 1989 • $8 • (11/15/93) • **79**

Cabernet Sauvignon Mendocino La Ribera Vineyards 1988 • $12 • (06/30/91) • **86**

Cabernet Sauvignon Mendocino La Ribera Vineyards 1987: Well proportioned, with a pretty core of ripe and juicy plum, cherry and berry flavors. Intense and lively. Finishes with firm tannins and good length. Best now through 2002. • $25 • (12/15/97) • **89**

Cabernet Sauvignon Mendocino La Ribera Vineyards 1986 • $12 • (02/15/90) • **84**

Cabernet Sauvignon Mendocino La Ribera Vineyards 1985 • $5 • (11/30/87) BB • **84**

Cabernet Sauvignon Mendocino La Ribera Vineyards 1984 • $10 • (12/31/87) • **73**

Cabernet Sauvignon Mendocino North Field Select 1991 • $18 • (03/31/95) • **81**

Cabernet Sauvignon Mendocino North Field Select 1990 • $18 • (11/15/93) • **87**

Cabernet Sauvignon Mendocino North Field Select 1989 • $18 • (08/31/93) • **87**

Cabernet Sauvignon Mendocino North Field Select 1988 • $18 • (08/31/92) • **84**

Cabernet Sauvignon Mendocino North Field Select 1987 • $16 • (11/15/90) • **87**

Chardonnay Mendocino 1995: Clean and a bit grassy, with a band of citrus, pear and lemon flavors. For fans of pure Chardonnay, not for fans of oak. 17,000 cases made. • $12 • (11/30/96) • **84**

Chardonnay Mendocino 1993 • $12 • (11/30/94) • **85**

Chenin Blanc Mendocino La Ribera Vineyard 1994 • $8 • (06/15/95) • **85**

Chenin Blanc Mendocino La Ribera Vineyards 1993 • $7 • (07/31/94) • **82**

Gewürztraminer Anderson Valley 1993 • $9 • (01/31/95) • **81**

Gewürztraminer Late Harvest Anderson Valley 1993 • $14/375ml • (07/31/95) • **87**

Pinot Noir Anderson Valley 1994: With it's modest band of dried cherry and light toast flavors, it's good, but nothing to write home about. 2,800 cases made. • $16 • (11/30/96) • **81**

Pinot Noir Anderson Valley 1993 • $15 • (12/31/95) • **72**

Pinot Noir Anderson Valley 1992 • $14 • (11/30/94) • **88**

Pinot Noir Anderson Valley 1991 • $14 • (04/30/94) • **84**

Pinot Noir Anderson Valley 1990 • $14 • (02/28/93) • **81**

Pinot Noir Anderson Valley 1989 • $14 • (11/15/91) • **87**

Pinot Noir Anderson Valley 1988 • $13 • (12/15/90) • **84**

Pinot Noir Anderson Valley 1987 • $13 • (02/15/90) • **80**

Pinot Noir Anderson Valley 1986 • $13 • (10/15/89) • **81**

Pinot Noir Anderson Valley 1985 • $10 • (06/15/88) • **84**

Pinot Noir Anderson Valley 1983 • $9 • (05/31/88) • **74**

Pinot Noir Anderson Valley 1982 • $9 • (08/31/86) • **88**

Pinot Noir Anderson Valley Reserve 1992: Earthy, with a mature edge to the currant and berry notes. It slowly grows more interesting though, bringing out hints of mushroom. 482 cases made. • $24 • (02/28/97) • **82**

Sauvignon Blanc Mendocino La Ribera Vineyards 1996: Spice, vanilla, toast and fresh peach lead the way in this full-bodied wine. Oak influence is a bit strong, though, and steamrolls much of the fruit. 7,600 cases made. • $11 • (04/30/98) • **83**

Sauvignon Blanc Mendocino La Ribera Vineyards 1995: Crisp and refreshing for the grapefruit and honey notes that linger on the delicate finish. 7,918 cases made. • $9 • (04/30/97) • **87**

Sauvignon Blanc Mendocino La Ribera Vineyards 1994 • $9 • (08/31/95) • **87**

HYATT | WASHINGTON

Black Muscat Yakima Valley 1994 • $7 • (03/31/96) • **85**

Black Muscat Yakima Valley Ice Wine 1996: Deep, brilliant amber color is striking, with sweet, intense flavors of plum and spice to match. Has plenty of zingy acidity for balance, keeping it lively through the sweet finish. Nice now. 265 cases made. • $30/375ml • (10/15/97) • **88**

Black Muscat Yakima Valley Royale 1993 • $7 • (09/30/94) • **82**

Cabernet-Merlot Yakima Valley 1992 • $9 • (08/31/94) • **84**

Cabernet Sauvignon Yakima Valley 1993: Light, chewy and distinctive, with mint, mineral and berry flavors cutting through the firm tannins. Best from 1999 or 2000. 1,003 cases made. • $12 • (09/15/97) • **86**

Cabernet Sauvignon Yakima Valley 1991 • $13 • (03/31/96) • **83**

Cabernet Sauvignon Yakima Valley Reserve 1994: Firmly tannic, with a strong core of ripe currant and cedar flavors showing through the layers of chewy tannins. Needs until 2000 to 2001. 270 cases made. • $32 • (09/15/97) • **88**

Cabernet Sauvignon Yakima Valley Reserve 1992 • $25 • (03/31/96) • **84**

Cabernet Sauvignon Yakima Valley River's Bend Vineyard 1990 • $13 • (10/15/93) • **82**

Chardonnay Yakima Valley 1995: Distinctive, with earthy, gamy notes adding depth and richness, and notes of ripe pear integrating smoothly on the finish. Drink now. 1,760 cases made. • $10 • (09/15/97) • **87**

Chardonnay Yakima Valley 1993 • $8 • (04/30/96) • **84**

Chardonnay Yakima Valley Reserve 1995: Fresh, focused and finely balanced to show pretty spice and honey notes along with the pear character at the core. 230 cases made. • $18 • (09/15/97) • **87**

Johannisberg Riesling Yakima Valley 1995: Lightly sweet, and generous with its pear and floral flavors. 717 cases made. • $6 • (09/15/97) • **85**

Merlot Columbia Valley 1991 • $11 • (05/15/94) • **75**

Merlot Columbia Valley 1989 • $11 • (11/30/92) • **87**

Merlot Yakima Valley 1993 • $11 • (03/31/96) • **85**

Merlot Yakima Valley 1992 • $11 • (08/31/95) • **88**

Merlot Yakima Valley 1990 • $13 • (06/15/93) • **85**

Merlot Yakima Valley Reserve 1993 • $25 • (03/31/96) • **84**

Riesling Late Harvest Yakima Valley 1994 • $9 • (03/31/96) • **87**

Riesling Late Harvest Yakima Valley 1987 • $8 • (10/15/89) • **87**

ICI/LA-BAS | OREGON

Pinot Noir Oregon Les Révélés 1995: Has a softness and a spiciness absent from many 1995s, along with pretty chocolate and herbal overtones to its supple berry flavors. Ready to drink. 600 cases made. • $25 • (10/31/97) • **87**

IL CUORE | CALIFORNIA

Cabernet Sauvignon North Coast 1995: Fairly smooth, with tar, licorice, and black currant notes. A clean, spare wine with a moderate finish. 4,300 cases made. • $9 • (09/15/97) • **84**

Chardonnay Sonoma County 1995: Simple, fruity and appealing for its bright pear flavors and smooth finish. 5,300 cases made. • $10 • (07/31/97) • **82**

Rosso Classico California 1994: A crisp red with a spicy, leathery accent to the lightish-cherry aromas and flavors. A blend of Sangiovese, Syrah and Zinfandel. 7,200 cases made. • $10 • (04/30/97) • **85**

IL PODERE DELL'OLIVOS | CALIFORNIA

Arneis Central Coast 1995: Offers a spicy anise accent to the core of peach and apple flavors, but ultimately, it's simple. 50 cases made. • $10 • (09/15/96) • **83**

Barbera California 1995: A light wine that's a bit chewy, with modest flavors of berry and citrus. • $12 • (12/15/96) • **81**

Barbera California Ragazzo Legnoso Riserva 1993 • $18 • (10/15/95) • **90**

Barbera Santa Barbara County Ragazzo Legnoso Riserva 1995: Generous and supple, distinctive for its earthy undertones to the ripe cherry and plum flavors. Finishes softly, with a light layer of fine tannin. Ready to drink. 800 cases made. • $12 • (03/31/98) • **86**

Fiano Central Coast 1996: Peach and melon aromas give way to a lemon-lime flavored wine. Zippy acids leave a fresh, lively imprint on the tongue. An old Italian grape with a California twist. 100 cases made. • $18 • (03/31/98) • **86**

Ragazzo Legnoso California Riserva 1994: A blend of Barbera and Nebbiolo that doesn't optimize the qualities of either. Shows tart plum and berry flavors. 300 cases made. • $18 • (08/31/96) • **81**

Tocai Friulano Central Coast 1996: Rich and creamy, with distinct hazelnut and pear flavors. Judicious use of oak lightly frames the whole. Finishes with a delicate lemon zest. Better than many of its Italian brethren. 500 cases made. • $15 • (03/31/98) • **88**

Tocai Friulano Central Coast 1995: A juicy core of ripe and spicy peach and nectarine flavors. Turns simple on the finish. 300 cases made. • $12 • (09/15/96) • **83**

INDIAN SPRINGS | CALIFORNIA

Cabernet Sauvignon Nevada County 1993: This is somewhat green on the palate but shows a nice, supple texture. 902 cases made. • $10 • (11/30/96) • **82**

Cabernet Sauvignon Nevada County 1991 • $9 • (11/15/94) • **82**

Cabernet Sauvignon Nevada County 1990 • $8 • (11/15/93) • **80**

Merlot Nevada County 1992 • $12 • (09/15/94) • **84**

Merlot Nevada County 1991 • $12 • (08/31/93) • **84**

Merlot Nevada County Sierra Foothills 1990 • $12 • (06/15/93) • **84**

Merlot Sierra Foothills 1989 • $10 • (11/30/92) • **85**

Sémillon Nevada County 1993 • $8 • (10/15/95) • **74**

Syrah Nevada County 1995: Smooth and generous with its gentle prune, blackberry and spice flavors, nicely modulated for a harmonious wine that's pretty to drink now. 521 cases made. • $15 • (03/31/98) • **86**

INDIGO HILLS | CALIFORNIA

Brut Chardonnay North Coast NV: Firmly textured, with citrus, starfruit, apple and melon flavors at the fore. Bright and refreshing, with a tangy, mineral finish. • $9 • (12/15/97) • **88**

Chardonnay Mendocino County 1996: Light and bright, with straightforward green apple and vanilla flavors. Ready to drink. 42,000 cases made. • $10 • (03/31/98) BB • **85**

Chardonnay Mendocino County 1995: Smooth and polished, this light-style Chardonnay shows generous apple, honey and butter flavors that linger on the toasty finish. Ready now. • $9 • (12/15/97) • **86**

Pinot Noir North Coast 1995: A pretty wine with bright raspberry and vanilla flavors and a hint of candy sneaking in on the silky finish. Ready now. • $NA • (12/31/97) • **86**

Sauvignon Blanc Mendocino County 1996: Bright grapefruit and melon flavors are the hallmarks of this California white. Light in style and body, it finishes with a flinty, mineral-like edge. Refreshing for both palate and pocketbook. 33,000 cases made. • $10 • (03/31/98) BB • **85**

Zinfandel North Coast 1995: Black cherry and smoke lead the way. It gains some complexity on the palate, but remains a little light, with a somewhat sharp finish. • $10 • (03/31/98) • **83**

INGLENOOK | CALIFORNIA

Classic Burgundy Premium Select California NV: Soft and straightforward, with pleasant peppery rhubarb and strawberry flavors. Ultimately simple, finishing short, but makes a nice sipper. Drink now. • $8/1.5 liter • (05/15/98) • **81**

INGLENOOK-NAPA VALLEY | CALIFORNIA

Cabernet Sauvignon Napa Valley 1989 • $10 • (11/15/92) • **80**

Cabernet Sauvignon Napa Valley 1988 • $10 • (11/15/92) • **80**

Cabernet Sauvignon Napa Valley 1987 • $10 • (11/15/91) • **86**

Cabernet Sauvignon Napa Valley 1986 • $10 • (02/28/91) BB • **85**

Cabernet Sauvignon Napa Valley 1985 • $10 • (03/31/89) • **83**

Cabernet Sauvignon Napa Valley 1983 • $10 • (03/15/88) • **80**

Cabernet Sauvignon Napa Valley 1980 • $22 • (09/16/84) • **89**

Cabernet Sauvignon Napa Valley 1978 • $9 • (04/30/87) • **90**

Cabernet Sauvignon Napa Valley 1977 • $8 • (06/01/85) • **92**

Cabernet Sauvignon Napa Valley 1974 • $9 • (06/01/85) • **94**

Cabernet Sauvignon Napa Valley 1970 • $6 • (06/01/85) • **90**

Cabernet Sauvignon Napa Valley 1966 • $NA • (06/01/85) • **84**

Cabernet Sauvignon Napa Valley 1960 • $125 • (06/01/85) • **89**

Cabernet Sauvignon Napa Valley 1958 • $125 • (06/01/85) • **88**

Cabernet Sauvignon Napa Valley 1955 • $NA • (06/01/85) • **93**

Cabernet Sauvignon Napa Valley 1941 • $ • (06/01/85) • **95**
Cabernet Sauvignon Napa Valley Cask A-4 1974 • $59 • (11/15/94) • **67**
Cabernet Sauvignon Napa Valley Cask F-11 1958 • $NA • (02/28/87) • **79**
Cabernet Sauvignon Napa Valley Reserve Cask 1988 • $19 • (03/15/94) • **84**
Cabernet Sauvignon Napa Valley Reserve Cask 1987 • $21 • (11/15/92) • **89**
Cabernet Sauvignon Napa Valley Reserve Cask 1986 • $25 • (10/31/91) HR • **91**
Cabernet Sauvignon Napa Valley Reserve Cask 1985 • $19 • (02/15/91) CS • **90**
Cabernet Sauvignon Napa Valley Reserve Cask 1984 • $22 • (07/31/90) • **90**
Cabernet Sauvignon Napa Valley Reserve Cask 1983 • $20 • (09/15/87) • **88**
Cabernet Sauvignon Napa Valley Reserve Cask 1982 • $19 • (02/15/87) • **93**
Cabernet Sauvignon Napa Valley Reserve Cask 1981 • $16 • (10/15/86) • **92**
Charbono Napa Valley 1984 • $8 • (04/15/88) • **82**
Charbono Napa Valley 1980 • $8 • (03/01/85) • **79**
Gewürztraminer Late Harvest Napa Valley 1986 • $9/375ml • (05/15/88) • **78**
Merlot Napa Valley 1981 • $12 • (10/01/85) • **77**
Merlot Napa Valley Reserve 1988 • $12 • (05/31/92) • **83**
Merlot Napa Valley Reserve 1986 • $12 • (10/31/89) • **81**
Merlot Napa Valley Reserve 1985 • $14 • (10/15/88) SS • **91**
Merlot Napa Valley Reserve 1983 • $9 • (10/15/87) • **85**
Merlot Napa Valley Reserve 1981 • $12 • (02/16/85) • **80**
Niebaum Claret Napa Valley 1986 • $13 • (06/30/91) • **74**
Niebaum Claret Napa Valley 1985 • $12 • (03/15/89) • **82**
Niebaum Claret Napa Valley 1983 • $12 • (11/30/87) • **88**
Petite Sirah Napa Valley 1982 • $5 • (12/31/86) BB • **87**
Petite Sirah Napa Valley 1981 • $6 • (02/01/85) BB • **86**
Pinot Noir Napa Valley 1985 • $9 • (06/15/88) • **82**
Pinot Noir Napa Valley 1980 • $6 • (03/01/84) • **71**
Reunion Napa Valley 1985 • $35 • (07/15/89) • **91**
Reunion Napa Valley 1984 • $35 • (10/15/88) • **87**
Reunion Napa Valley 1983 • $33 • (11/30/87) CS • **95**
Zinfandel Napa Valley 1986 • $8 • (04/30/91) • **73**
Zinfandel Napa Valley 1983 • $7 • (03/15/88) • **81**
Zinfandel Napa Valley 1981 • $7 • (02/01/85) • **79**

INGLESIDE PLANTATION | VIRGINIA

Cabernet Franc Virginia 1993: Quite light and spicy-tasting, almost like a medium-weight Pinot Noir. Tasting a bit mature now, but still decent. 500 cases made. • $12 • (04/30/97) • **80**

INNISFREE | CALIFORNIA

Cabernet Sauvignon Napa Valley 1990 • $11 • (04/30/93) • **88**
Cabernet Sauvignon Napa Valley 1988 • $11 • (04/30/91) • **84**
Cabernet Sauvignon Napa Valley 1986 • $11 • (06/30/90) • **73**
Cabernet Sauvignon Napa Valley 1985 • $9 • (03/15/89) • **86**
Cabernet Sauvignon Napa Valley 1984 • $9 • (12/15/87) • **68**
Cabernet Sauvignon Napa Valley 1983 • $9 • (11/15/86) • **82**
Cabernet Sauvignon Napa Valley 1982 • $9 • (12/16/85) • **80**
Pinot Noir California 1990 • $11 • (09/30/92) • **84**
Pinot Noir California 1989 • $11 • (04/30/91) • **84**

INTAGLIO | CALIFORNIA

Pinot Noir Russian River Valley Saralee's Vineyard 1992 • $14 • (03/31/95) • **70**

IRON HORSE | CALIFORNIA

Blanc de Blancs Sonoma County Green Valley 1989 • $24 • (12/31/94) • **88**
Blanc de Blancs Sonoma County Green Valley 1988 • $25 • (07/31/93) HR • **90**
Blanc de Blancs Sonoma County Green Valley 1987 • $25 • (12/31/91) • **89**
Blanc de Blancs Sonoma County Green Valley 1986 • $22 • (12/31/90) • **87**
Blanc de Blancs Sonoma County Green Valley 1985 • $21 • (12/31/89) • **85**
Blanc de Blancs Sonoma County Green Valley 1984 • $19 • (12/31/88) • **79**
Blanc de Blancs Sonoma County Green Valley 1982 • $17 • (05/16/86) • **78**
Blanc de Blancs Sonoma County Green Valley 1981 • $18 • (11/01/84) • **86**

Key: SS—Spectator Selection CS—Cellar Selection HR—Highly Recommended BB—Best Buy $NA—Price not available Ⓐ—Auction Price (BT)—Barrel Tasting
Dates in parentheses indicate the issues in which the ratings were published.

Blanc de Blancs Sonoma County Green Valley Late Disgorged 1990: Toasty, with mature honey, pear and spice notes, and shows its wide array of flavors while maintaining its youthful vitality. Rich and full-bodied, with a complex finish. 2,000 cases made. • $45 • (11/15/96) • **90**
Blanc de Blancs Sonoma County Green Valley Late Disgorged 1982 • $24 • (12/31/87) • **85**
Blanc de Noirs Sonoma County Green Valley Wedding Cuvée 1989 • $23 • (08/31/92) • **82**
Blanc de Noirs Sonoma County Green Valley Wedding Cuvée 1988 • $24 • (10/31/91) • **84**
Blanc de Noirs Sonoma County Green Valley Wedding Cuvée 1986 • $19 • (05/31/89) • **90**
Blanc de Noirs Sonoma County Green Valley Wedding Cuvée 1985 • $17 • (12/31/88) • **86**
Blanc de Noirs Sonoma County Green Valley Wedding Cuvée 1984 • $17 • (12/31/87) • **85**
Blanc de Noirs Sonoma County Green Valley Wedding Cuvée 1983 • $17 • (12/31/86) • **82**
Brut Rosé Sonoma County Green Valley 1992: Smoke, toast and mountain herbs make an interesting blend here, backed by melon and citrus flavors. The ensemble is elegant, with a lengthy finish. 2,155 cases made. • $25 • (11/30/97) • **88**
Brut Rosé Sonoma County Green Valley 1991: Marked by dried cherry and berry flavors and a coarse texture. Shows some Pinot Noir character on the finish. 1,200 cases made. • $28 • (09/15/96) • **86**
Brut Rosé Sonoma County Green Valley 1990 • $28 • (12/31/94) • **84**
Brut Rosé Sonoma County Green Valley 1989 • $28 • (12/31/93) • **81**
Brut Rosé Sonoma County Green Valley 1988 • $28 • (12/15/91) • **87**
Brut Rosé Sonoma County Green Valley 1987 • $28 • (12/31/90) • **84**
Brut Rosé Sonoma County Green Valley 1986 • $23 • (12/31/89) • **80**
Brut Rosé Sonoma County Green Valley 1985 • $20 • (12/31/88) • **88**
Brut Sonoma County Green Valley 1991 • $24 • (12/31/95) • **88**
Brut Sonoma County Green Valley 1990 • $24 • (12/31/94) • **87**
Brut Sonoma County Green Valley 1989 • $20 • (12/31/93) • **85**
Brut Sonoma County Green Valley 1988 • $23 • (08/31/92) • **84**
Brut Sonoma County Green Valley 1987 • $21 • (11/15/90) • **89**
Brut Sonoma County Green Valley 1986 • $20 • (12/31/89) • **82**
Brut Sonoma County Green Valley 1985 • $18 • (12/31/88) • **83**
Brut Sonoma County Green Valley 1984 • $17 • (12/31/87) • **79**
Brut Sonoma County Green Valley 1983 • $17 • (12/31/86) • **87**
Brut Sonoma County Green Valley 1982 • $17 • (05/16/86) • **80**
Brut Sonoma County Green Valley Classic Vintage 1992: Light in style, with citrusy lemon-lime qualities. Pleasant, but doesn't really take off with any great complexity. 14,181 cases made. • $20 • (11/30/97) • **86**
Brut Sonoma County Green Valley Late Disgorged 1989 • $45 • (12/31/95) • **88**
Brut Sonoma County Green Valley Late Disgorged 1988 • $25 • (12/31/93) • **82**
Brut Sonoma County Green Valley Late Disgorged 1987 • $25 • (12/31/92) • **87**
Brut Sonoma County Green Valley Late Disgorged 1984 • $23 • (12/31/89) • **80**
Brut Sonoma County Green Valley Late Disgorged Vrais Amis 1986 • $25 • (12/15/91) HR • **90**
Cabernet Sauvignon Alexander Valley 1994: Smoke, spice and cherries are followed by a distinctive, herbal core that adds depth to the ensemble. Bright on the finish. 2,570 cases made. • $19 • (11/30/97) • **86**
Cabernet Sauvignon Alexander Valley 1981 • $14 • (12/16/84) • **92**
Cabernet Sauvignon Alexander Valley Barrel Fermented 1994: A fairly bright, cherrylike wine. Shows depth and focus, though, with follow-up hints of anise, blueberry, sage, and thyme. Silky-smooth. Drink now. 159 cases made. • $19 • (11/30/97) • **88**
Cabernet Sauvignon Alexander Valley Cuveé Joy 1994: Firm and complex, with a solid core of currant, spice, cedar and tobacco flavors, crisp tannins and good length. Drink now. 156 cases made. • $25 • (11/15/97) • **87**
Cabernet Sauvignon Alexander Valley T-T Vineyards 1993: Raw and rustic, with harsh tannins and a biting aftertaste that are hard to overlook, even though the fruit flavors are ripe and plummy. 2,100 cases made. • $20 • (12/15/96) • **78**
Cabernet Sauvignon Alexander Valley T-T Vineyards Reserve 1992 • $20 • (04/30/96) • **82**
Cabernets Alexander Valley 1990 • $19 • (11/15/93) • **88**
Cabernets Alexander Valley 1988 • $22 • (03/31/92) • **85**
Cabernets Alexander Valley 1987 • $20 • (03/15/91) • **86**
Cabernets Alexander Valley 1986 • $22 • (04/15/90) • **90**
Cabernets Alexander Valley 1985 • $16 • (12/31/88) • **88**

Cabernets Alexander Valley T-T Vineyards 1992: Firm, dark and intense, with strong oak, austere cherry and plum flavors. Finishes with crisp acidity and biting tannins. 1,970 cases made. • $16 • (09/15/96) • **83**
Cabernets Alexander Valley T-T Vineyards 1991 • $19 • (12/15/95) • **87**
Cabernets Alexander Valley T-T Vineyards 1990 • $15 • (10/31/94) • **86**
Cabernets Alexander Valley T-T Vineyards 1989 • $15 • (05/15/94) • **86**
Chardonnay Sonoma County Green Valley 1996: Tight and a touch flinty, with fresh pear, fig, apricot and spice. Finishes with a touch of oak. Best to cellar short-term. Drink now to 2001. 9,183 cases made. • $22 • (07/31/98) • **88**
Chardonnay Sonoma County Green Valley 1995: Clean and simple, with a cedary accent to the pear and citrus flavors. Ready to drink. 9,000 cases made. • $18 • (07/31/97) • **85**
Chardonnay Sonoma County Green Valley 1994: Lean and tart, a trim band of pippin apple flavors giving it tangy character. 11,702 cases made. • $18 • (05/15/96) • **87**
Chardonnay Sonoma County Green Valley 1993 • $18 • (05/15/95) • **87**
Chardonnay Sonoma County Green Valley Cuvée Joy 1995: Enormously complex with its ripe fig, melon, apple pear and spice flavors and distinctive lime and mineral accents. Turns smooth and silky on the finish while the flavors linger. Best Iron Horse Chardonnay in some time. 99 cases made. • $50/1.5 liter • (05/31/97) • **92**
Chardonnay Sonoma County Green Valley Cuvée Joy 1993 • $19 • (05/15/95) • **90**
Demi-Sec Sonoma County Green Valley 1990: A touch of sweetness adds a nice dimension to the spice, vanilla and subtle pear flavors. Finishes with a hint of earthiness. 169 cases made. • $20 • (11/30/96) • **86**
Demi-Sec Sonoma County Green Valley 1989 • $20 • (12/31/93) • **82**
Fumé Blanc Alexander Valley T-T Vineyards 1996: Bright melon, citrus and herbal notes rise to the fore in this tangy, medium-bodied wine. Finishes with length. 1,970 cases made. • $18 • (06/30/97) • **87**
Fumé Blanc Alexander Valley T-T Vineyards 1995 • $13 • (06/30/96) • **88**
Fumé Blanc Alexander Valley T-T Vineyards 1994 • $12 • (08/31/95) • **87**
Fumé Blanc Alexander Valley T-T Vineyards 1993 • $12 • (11/30/94) • **87**
Merlot Alexander Valley T-T 1994: Tight and on the austere side, with a narrow band of cherry, currant, herb and tar notes. The flavors fan out a bit more on the finish, but still don't fully uncoil. Try now. 256 cases made. • $18 • (12/15/96) • **84**
Pinot Noir Sonoma County Green Valley 1996: Pretty and smooth, with lovely cherry, sage, toast and anise notes. Displays good integration of its elements and sits cleanly on the palate, though it finishes with a hint of bitterness. 1,076 cases made. • $23 • (01/31/98) • **88**
Pinot Noir Sonoma County Green Valley 1995: The aroma smacks of cherry candy, but the wine is mercifully dry on the palate. A bit hollow, nonetheless. Hints of black cherry, herbs and peppermint. 1,293 cases made. • $19 • (12/15/97) • **81**
Pinot Noir Sonoma County Green Valley 1994: Just ripe, with cola, tea and herb flavors and a trace of black cherry. Finishes with a slightly green accent. 1,900 cases made. • $18 • (08/31/96) • **82**
Pinot Noir Sonoma County Green Valley 1993 • $18 • (12/31/95) • **84**
Pinot Noir Sonoma County Green Valley 1992 • $19 • (10/31/94) • **87**
Pinot Noir Sonoma County Green Valley 1987 • $19 • (10/31/90) • **72**
Pinot Noir Sonoma County Green Valley 1986 • $18 • (06/15/88) • **92**
Pinot Noir Sonoma County Green Valley 1985 • $18 • (06/15/88) • **77**
Pinot Noir Sonoma County Green Valley 1982 • $10 • (10/01/85) • **76**
Russian Cuvée Sonoma County Green Valley 1992: A fruity style, with hints of mango, papaya, pear and nutmeg. Interesting, though atypical in style. 1,000 cases made. • $24 • (11/30/97) • **87**
Sangiovese Alexander Valley T-T Vineyards 1995: Serves up lively ripe plum, cherry and strawberry flavors on an elegant frame. Could use a little more depth and complexity, but it's well made and ready to drink. 480 cases made. • $18 • (03/31/98) • **82**
Sangiovese Alexander Valley T-T Vineyards 1994: Elegant and well focused, with a bright, tight core of spicy cherry and raspberry flavors. Gains complexity and nuance on the finish, where the flavors fan out nicely. Mildly tannic, drinks well now. Includes Merlot and Cabernet Sauvignon. 662 cases made. • $15 • (11/30/96) • **88**
Sangiovese Alexander Valley T-T Vineyards 1993 • $18 • (04/30/96) • **87**
Viognier Alexander Valley T-T Vineyards 1995: Elegant and spicy, with a supple mouthfeel and pear flavor touched by spicy, earthy notes. 350 cases made. • $16 • (07/31/96) • **86**
Vrais Amis Sonoma County Green Valley 1992: Shows a clean, floral quality, backed by a trace of smoke and accents of citrus, hazelnut and mineral. Has upfront appeal, finishes just short of outstanding. 1,000 cases made. • $24 • (11/30/97) • **89**
Vrais Amis Sonoma County Green Valley 1991: Lean and trim, with a band of spicy citrus flavors. An austere style that would work well paired with oysters. • $21 • (11/15/96) • **87**
Vrais Amis Sonoma County Green Valley 1990 • $25 • (12/31/95) • **88**
Vrais Amis Sonoma County Green Valley 1989 • $25 • (12/31/93) • **87**
Vrais Amis Sonoma County Green Valley 1987 • $25 • (12/31/92) • **85**
Wedding Cuvée Sonoma County Green Valley 1994: Fresh, yet rich in aromas of raspberry, plum and nectarine. Smooth, almost velvety, although a bit hollow on the midpalate. 2,862 cases made. • $20 • (11/30/97) • **87**
Wedding Cuvée Sonoma County Green Valley 1993 • $19 • (04/30/96) • **87**
Wedding Cuvée Sonoma County Green Valley 1992 • $25 • (12/31/95) • **84**
Wedding Cuvée Sonoma County Green Valley 1991 • $20 • (11/15/94) • **87**
Wedding Cuvée Sonoma County Green Valley 1990 • $20 • (12/31/93) • **86**
Zinfandel Alexander Valley 1982 • $7 • (10/16/84) • **81**

IRONSTONE | CALIFORNIA

Cabernet Franc California 1995: The mix of cherry, green bean and olive is a bit odd here. On the finish, however, the fruit wins out, leaving a pleasant lasting impression. A light style for drinking now. 11,500 cases made. • $10 • (03/31/98) • **83**
Merlot California Highlands 1990 • $10 • (03/31/93) • **76**
Shiraz California 1995: Nicely balanced to show off its pretty plum and anise flavors, with hints of blackberry and spice sneaking in on the silky finish. Drink now. 3,850 cases made. • $11 • (03/31/98) • **87**

J | CALIFORNIA

Pinot Noir Russian River Valley Nicole's Vineyard 1995: A lighter-styled wine, slightly waxy in texture, with light cherry and spice notes. A touch of anise on the finish adds interest. The first still-Pinot Noir from this sparkling producer. Drink now. • $33 • (06/15/98) • **83**
Sonoma County 1993: An interesting wine, with a dash of ginger and grapefruit. Finishes long, with hints of lemon and lime. 25,000 cases made. • $25 • (11/30/97) • **89**
Sonoma County 1991: Smooth and spicy, with hints of vanilla, almond, pear and anise flavors. Turns creamy on the palate, where the flavors fold together nicely. 25,000 cases made. • $26 • (11/30/96) • **89**
Sonoma County 1990 • $23 • (11/30/95) SS • **91**
Sonoma County 1989 • $24 • (07/31/93) • **89**
Sonoma County 1987 • $22 • (05/15/91) • **88**
Sonoma County Late Disgorged 1988: Tart on the palate, with spicy green apple and pear notes that are lean and tight. Remarkably youthful and well focused, it holds its flavors through the finish, turning crisp on the aftertaste. Not showing the open complexity expected of a wine this age but, with more time, it may. 34 cases made. • $33 • (11/30/96) • **88**

JACKSON VALLEY | CALIFORNIA

Chardonnay Amador County 1994: Spicy, toasty flavors characterize this wine, which finishes a bit short on fruit. 200 cases made. • $7 • (06/15/96) • **80**
Zinfandel Amador County 1990 • $9 • (10/15/92) • **83**

JACUZZI | CALIFORNIA

Zinfandel Contra Costa County Reserve 1994: Ruggedly tannic and earthy, but as the tightly wound core of cedar, mint, currant and tar peeks through, the flavors start to grow on you. Will benefit from short-term cellaring. 284 cases made. • $40 • (11/15/97) • **88**

JADE MOUNTAIN | CALIFORNIA

Cabernet Sauvignon Alexander Valley Icaria Creek Vineyard deCarteret 1984 • $8 • (06/30/88) • **75**
Côtes du Soleil California 1994: Has dusty, meaty flavors and ripe cherry too, but it's coarse and tannic on the finish. • $8 • (08/31/96) • **81**
Grenache American NV • $8 • (03/31/92) • **82**
La Provençale California 1994: Rustic and tannic. Wild berry and cherry flavors have a strong, meaty, peppery edge. Finishes with firm tannins and a touch of heat. • $15 • (08/31/96) • **84**
La Provençale California 1992 • $14 • (06/30/95) • **88**
La Provençale California 1990 • $12 • (03/15/92) • **80**
Les Jumeaux California 1994: Distinct, smoky, meaty and peppery flavors. Nice touches of berry and cherry come through on the finish, giving balance to the hard, green tannins. • $18 • (08/31/96) • **85**

Merlot Napa Valley 1993 • $25 • (03/31/96) • **87**

Merlot Napa Valley Caldwell Vineyard 1995: An oaky, hard-edged style with charred wood flavors dominating the currant, herb, leather and sage notes. Finishes with a bitter edge. Best to cellar into 2000. 730 cases made. • $30 • (03/31/98) • **83**

Mourvèdre California 1991 • $15 • (12/15/95) • **74**

Mourvèdre California 1990 • $15 • (03/15/92) • **81**

Mourvèdre California Unfiltered 1990 • $15 • (03/15/92) • **83**

Syrah Mount Veeder 1995: Dry and earthy, with leathery tannins that override the currant, oak and cedary flavors, finishing with big, ripe, chewy tannins. Best to cellar into 2000, hoping the tannins subside. 370 cases made. • $40 • (03/31/98) • **87**

Syrah Napa Valley 1993: Firm and intense, with ripe currant, cherry and anise flavors. The fruit is pure and focused, but it struggles to stand up to the tannins, which are dry and coarse. Anyone's guess as to whether the tannins will soften. • $18 • (08/31/96) • **85**

Syrah Napa Valley 1992 • $18 • (06/30/95) • **87**

Zinfandel California 1991 • $13 • (10/15/95) • **85**

JAEGER | CALIFORNIA

Merlot Napa Valley Inglewood Vineyard 1989 • $19 • (09/15/94) • **77**

Merlot Napa Valley Inglewood Vineyard 1988 • $17 • (08/31/93) • **81**

Merlot Napa Valley Inglewood Vineyard 1987 • $15 • (05/31/92) • **81**

Merlot Napa Valley Inglewood Vineyard 1986 • $15 • (05/31/92) • **88**

Merlot Napa Valley Inglewood Vineyard 1985 • $16 • (02/15/90) • **89**

Merlot Napa Valley Inglewood Vineyard 1983 • $14 • (02/29/88) • **87**

JAFFURS | CALIFORNIA

Chardonnay Santa Barbara County Bien Nacido Vineyard 1994: Smooth and elegant, with a pleasant band of typical Chardonnay flavors that center on pear and citrus. Finishes simple, with a tart edge. 150 cases made. • $15 • (03/31/96) • **84**

Grenache Santa Barbara County 1995: Complex, with a jammy accent to the ripe black cherry, plum and blackberry-scented flavors. Fans out on the finish, with a fruity aftertaste. 69 cases made. • $18 • (01/01/97) • **88**

Syrah Santa Barbara County 1996: A racy style, with firm tannins and earthy, herbal, meaty Syrah flavors; turns tannic and dry on the aftertaste. Best to cellar into 1999. 587 cases made. • $22 • (04/30/98) • **86**

Syrah Santa Barbara County 1995: Exhibits lots of ripe plum, cherry and spicy flavors, with a supple texture. 339 cases made. • $20 • (01/01/97) • **88**

Syrah Santa Barbara County Thompson Vineyard 1996: Lots of ripe, juicy, complex Syrah flavors, with plum, black cherry, wild berry and spice. Finishes with a fruity aftertaste that offers depth and richness. Best now to 2002. 50 cases made. • $25 • (04/30/98) • **89**

Syrah Santa Barbara County Thompson Vineyard 1994 • $14 • (02/29/96) • **91**

Viognier Santa Barbara County Bien Nacido Vineyard 1996: A spicy mix of bright lemon, mandarin orange and papaya, smoothly blended. Coats the palate with an almost thick texture, yet finishes with a bright, tangy edge. A fun wine. 138 cases made. • $19 • (02/28/98) • **88**

JAMES SCOTT | OREGON

Pinot Noir Willamette Valley 1992 • $15 • (05/31/95) • **85**

Pinot Noir Willamette Valley Signature Reserve 1992 • $29 • (12/31/95) • **84**

Pinot Noir Willamette Valley Signature Reserve 1991 • $28 • (01/31/95) • **89**

JAMESPORT | NEW YORK

Brut North Fork of Long Island Grand Cuvée 1991: Austere, with hard acidity and an agressive mousse. Shows light baked-apple flavors, then finishes short. May soften if served with food. 450 cases made. • $16 • (12/31/96) • **78**

Cabernet Franc North Fork of Long Island 1995: Lean and almost astringent, with only modest berry and cherry flavors. 500 cases made. • $15 • (07/31/98) • **77**

Key: SS—Spectator Selection CS—Cellar Selection HR—Highly Recommended BB—Best Buy $NA—Price not available Ⓐ—Auction Price (BT)—Barrel Tasting
Dates in parentheses indicate the issues in which the ratings were published.

Cabernet Sauvignon North Fork of Long Island North House 1987 • $10 • (06/30/91) • **78**

Chardonnay North Fork of Long Island Cox Lane Vineyard 1995: This is straightforward, full-bodied yet neutral, showing modest butter and apple flavors, but little distinctive character. 800 cases made. • $13 • (12/31/96) • **77**

Chardonnay North Fork of Long Island Three Barrel Select 1993: Pleasant aromas of vanilla and butter give way to a round mouthful of simple fruit flavors, canned peaches and pears, soft and almost sweet. Drink now. 215 cases made. • $18 • (12/31/96) • **80**

Mélange de Trois Red North Fork of Long Island 1993: It's sturdy, with some spicy, minty notes, but the cherry and tomato flavors are slightly candied. Maturing already; drink soon. 215 cases made. • $16 • (12/31/96) • **78**

Merlot North Fork of Long Island 1994: This is simple with its light berry and herbal flavors, light, dry tannins and short finish. It's supple and ready to drink. 220 cases made. • $20 • (12/31/96) • **79**

Merlot North Fork of Long Island 1986 • $9 • (06/30/91) • **72**

Merlot North Fork of Long Island Reserve 1993: Light-bodied and simple, with a supple texture. Flavors of berry, brown sugar and spice, with little tannin or concentration. Ready now. 250 cases made. • $27 • (12/31/96) • **77**

Riesling North Fork of Long Island 1995: Sweet, simple and rather flat, this supple wine offers light pineapple and cooked apple flavors, somewhat lifeless, without much acidity. Drink well chilled. 200 cases made. • $14 • (12/31/96) • **79**

Sauvignon Blanc North Fork of Long Island 1995: Very dry and austere, this sharp wine has smoke and mineral flavors, without much fruit flavor to soften the palate. It has character, but needs food to bring it into balance. 600 cases made. • $11 • (12/31/96) • **80**

JANKRIS | CALIFORNIA

Merlot Paso Robles 1992 • $12 • (09/15/94) • **85**

Merlot Paso Robles 1991 • $11 • (08/31/93) • **84**

Zinfandel Paso Robles 1993 • $9 • (10/15/95) • **87**

Zinfandel Paso Robles 1992 • $10 • (10/15/94) • **78**

Zinfandel Paso Robles 1991 • $8 • (09/30/93) • **81**

JARVIS | CALIFORNIA

Cabernet Franc Napa Valley 1994: Lean and trim, with a narrow band of currant and cedar flavors that picks up a buttery note on the finish. Given the tannin level, it's best to cellar this into 1999. 375 cases made. • $45 • (05/31/97) • **87**

Cabernet Franc Napa Valley 1992 • $40 • (08/31/95) • **86**

Cabernet Sauvignon Napa Valley 1993: Smooth, ripe and fleshy, with currant, black cherry, cedar and spice flavors at the core. Long finish, pleasant aftertaste. Best given a year or so in the cellar; try after 1999. 2,440 cases made. • $55 • (05/31/97) • **88**

Cabernet Sauvignon Napa Valley 1992 • $48 • (08/31/95) • **90**

Chardonnay Napa Valley 1994: A subtle style, clean and spicy, with citrus, pear and grapefruit accents and just a dash of cedary oak. Drinkable now, but put a bottle aside to see what develops. 1,000 cases made. • $36 • (05/15/97) • **87**

Chardonnay Napa Valley 1993: Elegant and understated, with pure ripe apple, spice and hints of hazelnut. Finishes with a fruity aftertaste; not reliant on oak. 800 cases made. • $34 • (07/31/96) • **88**

Lake William Napa Valley 1993: Young and tight, with a band of flavors ranging from cherry to herb, tobacco and currant. Turns smooth and supple on the finish, picking up flavor nuances and a green olive note. Try cellaring into 1999. 500 cases made. • $45 • (11/30/96) • **90**

Merlot Napa Valley 1994: Complex, with a pretty interplay of ripe cherry, currant, anise and cedar flavors that turn spicy and linger for a long aftertaste. Drinkable now to 2004. 220 cases made. • $45 • (05/31/97) • **88**

JASON | CALIFORNIA

Chardonnay California 1995: Tangerine and mineral flavors produce a lean, clean effect. Bright, refreshing finish. 2,000 cases made. • $6 • (06/15/97) • **86**

JC CELLARS | CALIFORNIA

Zinfandel Redwood Valley Rhodes 1996: Complex and rich in flavor, with lots of wild berry, cherry and spice, turning smooth and supple and holding its fruit on the finish. Drink now through 2002. 75 cases made. • $27 • (06/15/98) • **91**

JEFFERSON VINEYARDS | VIRGINIA

Cabernet Franc Virginia 1995: A bit tough and herbal tasting with only modest fruit flavors and an astringent finish. Tasted twice, with consistent notes. 500 cases made. • $12 • (06/15/97) • **72**
Cabernet Sauvignon Monticello 1995: Awkward and pruny, with brewed-tea flavors that linger unappealingly on the finish. 500 cases made. • $17 • (06/15/98) • **72**
Meritage Monticello 1995: Candied in aroma, with a jumbled mix of pruny, bacony flavors and harsh, uneven tannins. A blend of 66 percent Merlot, 26 percent Cabernet Franc, and 8 percent Cabernet Sauvignon. 500 cases made. • $28 • (06/15/98) • **73**

JEKEL | CALIFORNIA

Cabernet Franc Monterey 1990 • $13 • (07/31/95) • **82**
Cabernet Sauvignon Arroyo Seco 1990 • $13 • (11/15/94) • **84**
Cabernet Sauvignon Arroyo Seco 1989 • $13 • (04/30/93) • **81**
Cabernet Sauvignon Arroyo Seco 1988 • $12 • (03/15/93) • **80**
Cabernet Sauvignon Arroyo Seco 1986 • $13 • (11/15/90) • **83**
Cabernet Sauvignon Arroyo Seco Sanctuary Estate 1992 • $13 • (12/15/95) • **87**
Cabernet Sauvignon Monterey 1984 • $12 • (07/31/89) • **63**
Cabernet Sauvignon Monterey 1983 • $8 • (02/15/89) • **67**
Cabernet Sauvignon Monterey 1982 • $11 • (01/31/87) • **71**
Cabernet Sauvignon Monterey Home Vineyard Private Reserve 1982 • $20 • (02/01/86) • **69**
Cabernet Sauvignon Monterey Home Vineyard Private Reserve 1981 • $18 • (02/01/86) • **76**
Cabernet Sauvignon Monterey Home Vineyard Private Reserve 1980 • $25 • (02/01/86) • **63**
Cabernet Sauvignon Monterey Home Vineyard Private Reserve 1979 • $18 • (02/01/86) • **77**
Cabernet Sauvignon Monterey Home Vineyard Private Reserve 1978 • $22 • (11/15/92) • **68**
Chardonnay Arroyo Seco Gravelstone 1995: Mature for its age, with earthy honey and apricot flavors; a troubling sign for a wine this young. 52,000 cases made. • $12 • (05/15/97) • **77**
Chardonnay Arroyo Seco Gravelstone 1994: Light in style, and appealing for its spicy, caramel-tinged melon flavors. Ready now. • $11 • (11/30/96) • **81**
Chardonnay Arroyo Seco Gravelstone 1993 • $10 • (07/31/95) • **82**
Chardonnay Monterey County Gravelstone 1996: Intense, sweet pineapple and rich, spicy toast flavors are well focused but could use more finesse. Impressive for its rich, mouthfilling flavors. Drink now. 53,025 cases made. • $15 • (05/31/98) • **86**
Johannisberg Riesling Arroyo Seco Gravelstone 1995: Dry, tangy and citrusy, with a touch of peach flavor that never breaks out of its narrow, acidic bounds. Drinkable now. 7,860 cases made. • $9 • (11/30/96) • **82**
Meritage Arroyo Seco Sanctuary Estate 1992 • $13 • (12/15/95) • **83**
Meritage Symmetry Arroyo Seco Sanctuary Estate 1989 • $20 • (11/15/93) • **85**
Meritage Symmetry Arroyo Seco Sanctuary Estate 1987 • $25 • (03/31/93) • **77**
Merlot Arroyo Seco Sanctuary Estate 1994: A bit green and tannic. Underneath, however, there's a nice layer of flavors—clove, anise, cassis and herbs. 17,000 cases made. • $15 • (07/31/97) • **84**
Merlot Arroyo Seco Sanctuary Estate 1993: Clean and correct, with cedar, herb and some very nice dried cherry notes. 10,000 cases made. • $13 • (08/31/96) • **82**
Merlot Arroyo Seco Sanctuary Estate 1992 • $15 • (09/15/94) • **83**
Merlot California 1995: Simple, with light cherry, anise and herb notes offset by toasty oak flavors. Drink now. 12,000 cases made. • $15 • (06/15/98) • **80**
Pinot Noir Arroyo Seco 1992 • $14 • (02/28/94) • **84**
Pinot Noir Arroyo Seco Gravelstone 1994: An austere style with trim cedar, earth and spice notes, but not much fruit flavor and it finishes with a slight sour edge. 4,000 cases made. • $15 • (03/31/97) • **78**
Pinot Noir Arroyo Seco Gravelstone 1993 • $15 • (01/31/96) • **82**
Riesling Late Harvest Arroyo Seco Gravelstone 1987 • $14/375ml • (02/28/89) • **77**

JENNER | CALIFORNIA

Cabernet Sauvignon Dry Creek Valley 1992 • $6 • (03/31/96) • **75**

JEPSON | CALIFORNIA

Blanc de Blanc Mendocino 1989 • $16 • (12/31/94) • **85**
Blanc de Blanc Mendocino 1988 • $16 • (12/15/93) • **88**
Blanc de Blanc Mendocino 1986 • $16 • (04/30/91) • **86**
Blanc de Blanc Mendocino County 10th Anniversary 1985: Youthful for its age. Shows off spicy ginger, pear and citrus flavors in a moderately complex style. Finish offers hints of vanilla and apple. 395 cases made. • $24 • (11/30/96) • **87**
Blanc de Blanc Mendocino County Burnee Hill Vineyard 1992: Crisp, lively and delicate, the wine shows the appealing essence of pear, citrus, toast, honey and herbs. Finishes clean and fresh. 2,100 cases made. • $17 • (11/30/97) • **87**
Blanc de Blanc Mendocino County Burnee Hill Vineyard 1991: Clean and spicy, with a palate of ripe pear, citrus and ginger notes that turn elegant on the finish. 1,300 cases made. • $16 • (11/30/96) • **86**
Brut Mendocino 1985 • $16 • (12/31/88) • **82**
Chardonnay Mendocino County Estate Select 1996: Somewhat chunky, with bold butterscotch, spice, citrus and apple notes. The oak stands out, though, along with a hint of bitterness on the finish. Drink now. 7,990 cases made. • $15 • (07/31/98) • **83**
Chardonnay Mendocino County Estate Select 1995: A full-bodied, creamy, buttery, toasty mouthful, with notes of orange, melon and starfruit followed by a lingering, somewhat complex finish. 7,000 cases made. • $14 • (09/15/97) • **87**
Chardonnay Mendocino County Estate Select 1994: Lean and spicy, with prominent oak flavors that stand out more than fruit. • $14 • (06/15/96) • **82**
Pinot Noir Sonoma County 1994: A curious style, with just a trace of berry flavor and a slight vinegar note. With food, you might look past its peculiarities. 965 cases made. • $16 • (01/31/97) • **78**
Sauvignon Blanc Mendocino 1993 • $8 • (08/31/95) • **82**
Sauvignon Blanc Mendocino County Estate Select 1996: Peaches and ripe melons come to mind in this soft, velvety yet somewhat sweet wine. A bit hollow on the midpalate, finishing with a distinctly herbal edge. 5,600 cases made. • $9 • (06/30/97) • **86**
Sauvignon Blanc Mendocino County Estate Select 1994 • $8 • (05/31/96) • **87**

JESSANDRA VITTORIA | CALIFORNIA

Santa Vittoria Sonoma Valley 1994: A touch leathery, but enough cherry and currant flavors emerge to give it polish and a measure of finesse. A blend of 70 percent Cabernet Sauvignon and 30 percent Sangiovese. 396 cases made. • $25 • (08/31/96) • **83**

JOHNS | WASHINGTON

Vintage Port Yakima Valley 1993: Looks, smells and feels light for a Port, with pleasantly mild, tawny aromas and flavors. Ready for sipping. 350 cases made. • $16 • (09/15/96) • **80**

JOHNSON TURNBULL | CALIFORNIA

Cabernet Sauvignon Napa Valley 1991 • $18 • (10/31/94) • **89**
Cabernet Sauvignon Napa Valley 1990 • $16 • (03/31/94) • **81**
Cabernet Sauvignon Napa Valley 1989 • $16 • (08/31/93) • **85**
Cabernet Sauvignon Napa Valley 1988 • $16 • (11/15/91) • **84**
Cabernet Sauvignon Napa Valley 1987 • $16 • (11/15/90) • **80**
Cabernet Sauvignon Napa Valley 1985 • $15 • (07/15/88) • **88**
Cabernet Sauvignon Napa Valley 1984 • $15 • (07/31/87) • **73**
Cabernet Sauvignon Napa Valley 1983 • $13 • (09/15/86) • **86**
Cabernet Sauvignon Napa Valley 1982 • $13 • (10/16/85) • **86**
Cabernet Sauvignon Napa Valley 1981 • $12 • (04/16/84) • **76**
Cabernet Sauvignon Napa Valley Oakville 1994: Young, tight and tannic, with leather and earthlike nuances to the currant, plum and berry notes. Shows a lot of wood tannin at this stage; best to cellar into 1999 to 2000 and hope it evolves. 4,600 cases made. • $22 • (04/30/97) • **87**
Cabernet Sauvignon Napa Valley Vineyard Selection 67 1990 • $34 • (04/30/94) • **87**

Cabernet Sauvignon Napa Valley Vineyard Selection 67 1989 • $16 • (11/15/93) • **87**
Cabernet Sauvignon Napa Valley Vineyard Selection 67 1988 • $22 • (08/31/93) • **86**
Cabernet Sauvignon Napa Valley Vineyard Selection 67 1987 • $22 • (06/30/91) • **89**
Cabernet Sauvignon Napa Valley Vineyard Selection 67 1986 • $25 • (04/15/90) • **86**
Cabernet Sauvignon Napa Valley Vineyard Selection 82 1986 • $25 • (08/31/89) • **95**

JOLIESSE | CALIFORNIA

Cabernet Sauvignon California Reserve 1994: Don't let the reserve designation fool you, this is a tart, nearly sour wine with cherry flavors. 15,000 cases made. • $7 • (11/30/96) • **73**
Chardonnay California Reserve 1995: A fruity blend of lemon, lime and passion fruit flavors, backed by tangy acidity. 40,000 cases made. • $7 • (07/31/97) • **85**
Chardonnay California Reserve 1994: Zingy, fruity and a bargain too. This offers a real mouthful of complex peach, pear and spice flavors. 15,000 cases made. • $7 • (05/31/96) BB • **86**
Sauvignon Blanc California Reserve 1995: Extremely earthy and metallic. Not a friendly wine. 15,000 cases made. • $7 • (02/28/97) • **70**
Sauvignon Blanc California Reserve 1994 • $7 • (05/31/96) • **82**

JORDAN | CALIFORNIA

Cabernet Sauvignon Alexander Valley 1994: Tight, firmly tannic and well focused, with complex cherry, currant, menthol and cedar flavors. Turns dry and tannic on the finish, but it's not out of line for its age. Needs cellaring. Best from 2000 through 2008. 52,000 cases made. • $34 • (06/30/98) • **88**
Cabernet Sauvignon Alexander Valley 1993: Lean and tannic at first, with just enough ripe cherry and plum flavors to hold your interest. Slowly opens to reveal more fruit flavors, with hints of currant and spice. A little more tannic than Jordan's usual; cellar into 1999. 43,000 cases made. • $29 • (12/15/97) • **87**
Cabernet Sauvignon Alexander Valley 1992: Dry and tannic, with a musty, earthy note to the wild berry and cherry flavors. Finishes with yet more dry tannins. • $27 Ⓐ • (08/31/96) • **83**
Cabernet Sauvignon Alexander Valley 1991 • $32 Ⓐ • (06/15/95) • **84**
Cabernet Sauvignon Alexander Valley 1990 • $25 • (06/30/94) • **87**
Cabernet Sauvignon Alexander Valley 1989 • $24 • (11/15/93) • **80**
Cabernet Sauvignon Alexander Valley 1988 • $27 • (11/15/92) • **85**
Cabernet Sauvignon Alexander Valley 1987 • $26 Ⓐ • (11/15/91) HR • **90**
Cabernet Sauvignon Alexander Valley 1986: This wine has been mature for years. What's left is a modest range of cedary cherry and currant flavors with notes of herb, especially dill. • $38 Ⓐ • (12/15/96) • **82**
Cabernet Sauvignon Alexander Valley 1985 • $44 Ⓐ • (09/15/89) • **88**
Cabernet Sauvignon Alexander Valley 1984 • $42 Ⓐ • (07/15/88) • **86**
Cabernet Sauvignon Alexander Valley 1983 • $31 Ⓐ • (07/15/87) • **81**
Cabernet Sauvignon Alexander Valley 1978 • $59 • (11/15/92) • **80**
Chardonnay Sonoma County 1995: Ripe and elegant, with spicy pear, citrus and melon notes. Well balanced, with a clean, fruity aftertaste. Drink now through 2000. 25,000 cases made. • $24 • (05/15/98) • **88**
Chardonnay Sonoma County 1994: An elegant and spicy style, with complex ripe fruit flavors that grow on you. The core of apple, spice and pear is vibrant. Drinkable now. 25,000 cases made. • $20 • (06/15/97) • **89**
Chardonnay Sonoma County 1993 • $20 • (06/30/96) • **84**

JORY | CALIFORNIA

Black Hand Mano Nera California 1995: Dark and ripe, generous with its currant and blueberry notes, this is a solid wine packed with delicious fruit flavor that keeps pumping through the rich finish. Appealing now, but should improve through 1999. A blend of Petite Sirah, Carignane, Zinfandel, Mourvèdre, Syrah, and Sangiovese. 714 cases made. • $15 • (04/30/97) • **88**
Black Hand Mano Nera California 1993 • $13 • (04/30/95) • **85**

Key: SS—Spectator Selection CS—Cellar Selection HR—Highly Recommended BB—Best Buy $NA—Price not available Ⓐ—Auction Price (BT)—Barrel Tasting
Dates in parentheses indicate the issues in which the ratings were published.

Claret California Old Barrister 1990 • $13 • (10/15/92) • **84**
Fumé Blanc Sierra County New Mexico 1996: Pretty, peachy, passion fruit flavors are framed by a refreshing mineral-like edge. Bright on the finish, with a hint of grapefruit. 560 cases made. • $15 • (05/15/98) • **86**
Pinot Noir California Santa Clara County San Ysidro 1989 • $20 • (02/28/93) • **81**
Pinot Noir Santa Clara County 1986 • $19 • (06/15/88) • **76**
Pinot Noir Santa Clara Valley San Ysidro Bon Jory 1989 • $9 • (02/28/93) • **76**
Red Zeppelin Bon Jory Red California 1991 • $10 • (09/30/94) • **80**
Red Zeppelin Bon Jory Red California 1989 • $10 • (11/30/92) • **88**
Red Zeppelin II The Emperor's Reserve Red California 1990 • $15 • (10/15/93) • **86**
Zinfandel California Old Barrister Cuvée 91 1991 • $13 • (10/15/94) • **81**

JOULLIAN | CALIFORNIA

Cabernet Sauvignon Carmel Valley 1994: Texture is smooth and plush, but the cherry and herb flavors are a bit muddy and the beef and menthol aromas are kind of weird. Not for everyone. 3,056 cases made. • $20 • (10/31/97) • **80**
Cabernet Sauvignon Carmel Valley 1990 • $14 • (12/15/95) • **83**
Cabernet Sauvignon Carmel Valley 1989 • $14 • (11/15/94) • **81**
Cabernet Sauvignon Carmel Valley 1987 • $14 • (07/31/91) • **81**
Chardonnay Monterey 1995: A shade on the tart side, with a green edge to the apple and pear flavors. 4,565 cases made. • $14 • (07/31/97) • **84**
Chardonnay Monterey 1994: Smooth and spicy, showing some nice pear and subtle, raisinlike flavors that linger. 4,410 cases made. • $12 • (06/15/96) • **87**
Chardonnay Monterey 1993 • $11 • (07/31/95) • **82**
Chardonnay Monterey Family Reserve 1993 • $20 • (06/15/96) • **86**
Merlot Carmel Valley Family Reserve 1994: Bursts with tea, cinnamon, coffee and spice notes on the nose, and has some nice currant and blackberry qualities, but it's burnt and smoky on the palate, with plenty of earth. Not for everyone. 223 cases made. • $25 • (04/30/98) • **84**
Sauvignon Blanc Carmel Valley 1994: Lots of mineral aromas and flavors come to the fore in this lean, spicy wine. A hint of oak on the finish. 2,057 cases made. • $9 • (08/31/96) • **81**
Sauvignon Blanc Carmel Valley 1993 • $8 • (08/31/95) • **81**
Sauvignon Blanc Carmel Valley Family Reserve 1995: Generous with its spicy flavors and herbal, slightly oniony overtones, but the texture is velvety. 616 cases made. • $15 • (04/30/97) • **85**
Sauvignon Blanc Carmel Valley Family Reserve 1994: Crisp and lively in the mouth. Spicy, citrus flavors include an attractive essence of orange peel. 200 cases made. • $14 • (08/31/96) • **85**
Sauvignon Blanc Carmel Valley Family Reserve 1993 • $13 • (08/31/95) • **83**

JOYA | CALIFORNIA

Zinfandel Napa Valley 1992 • $9 • (08/31/94) • **86**

JUDD'S HILL | CALIFORNIA

Cabernet Sauvignon Napa Valley 1994: Elegant and refined, with complex currant, iodine, mint, spice and cedary flavors. Finishes with chewy tannins but nothing out of bounds; short-term cellaring is advised. Best from 2001 through 2006. 1,293 cases made. • $30 • (05/15/98) • **87**
Cabernet Sauvignon Napa Valley 1993: Offers a smooth and polished texture, ripe cherry and currant flavors. Finishing with soft, supple tannin and a hint of dill. Appealing to drink now and through the coming decade. 1,500 cases made. • $28 • (11/15/96) • **88**
Cabernet Sauvignon Napa Valley 1992 • $26 • (12/15/95) • **91**
Cabernet Sauvignon Napa Valley 1991 • $24 • (09/30/94) SS • **93**
Cabernet Sauvignon Napa Valley 1989 • $20 • (04/15/92) • **89**

JUSTIN | CALIFORNIA

Blanc de Noir Paso Robles 1985 • $23 • (12/31/91) • **84**
Cabernet Franc Paso Robles 1989 • $20 • (11/15/92) • **86**
Cabernet Franc San Luis Obispo County 1993: Dark, ripe and plush, marked by rich currant, wild berry, cherry, sage and leather notes. Holds its focus through the finish, where the flavors work their way past chewy tannins. Drink now. 1,500 cases made. • $20 • (05/31/97) • **90**
Cabernet Franc San Luis Obispo County 1991 • $20 • (12/31/94) • **87**
Cabernet Sauvignon Paso Robles 1989 • $19 • (11/15/92) • **81**
Cabernet Sauvignon Paso Robles 1988 • $19 • (11/15/91) • **72**

Cabernet Sauvignon San Luis Obispo County 1993: Notable for its complexity, this offers an intriguing interplay of ripe, spicy cherry, berry, currant and sage notes. Intense and concentrated, with impressive depth and polish, it can be enjoyed now or held into 2000 to 2001. 4,000 cases made. • $20 • (04/30/97) HR • **92**

Cabernet Sauvignon San Luis Obispo County 1992 • $18 • (12/15/95) • **88**

Cabernet Sauvignon San Luis Obispo County 1990 • $19 • (11/15/93) • **80**

Cabernet Sauvignon San Luis Obispo County Reserve 1994: Harmonious, with a complex core of currant and cherry flavors, light, toasty oak and spice nuances. Smooth and supple. Drinkable now. 2,800 cases made. • $20 • (03/31/97) • **89**

Cabernet Sauvignon San Luis Obispo County Society Reserve 1991 • $19 • (11/15/94) • **88**

Chardonnay San Luis Obispo County 1994: Marked by complex oak and butterscotch flavors, with fig, pear and honey notes that add dimension. Finishes with touches of citrus and spice. 3,500 cases made. • $17 • (04/30/97) • **89**

Dessert San Luis Obispo County Cabernet Sauvignon Obtuse 1992 • $23 • (09/30/95) • **84**

Isosceles Paso Robles 1994: Quite pleasing. Smooth and flavorful, with a pretty array of cherry, berry and chocolate flavors. Finishes with deep, plush tannins, and the kind of concentration and focus that bodes well for future drinking. Try in 2001 to 2003 and beyond. 2,050 cases made. • $33 • (10/31/97) • **92**

Isosceles Paso Robles Reserve 1989 • $23 • (11/15/92) • **86**

Isosceles San Luis Obispo County Reserve 1993: Firm, ripe and intense, with tiers of currant, cedar, anise and spice, but it still has some rough edges from tannin, and a curious, earthy, leathery quality. Best to cellar into 2000. 3,800 cases made. • $28 • (01/31/97) • **87**

Isosceles San Luis Obispo County Reserve 1992 • $25 • (12/15/95) HR • **92**

Isosceles San Luis Obispo County Reserve 1991 • $23 • (11/15/94) • **84**

Isosceles San Luis Obispo County Reserve 1990 • $23 • (11/15/93) • **88**

Justification San Luis Obispo County 1992 • $20 • (05/15/95) • **87**

Merlot Paso Robles 1994: Ripe, with a smoky accent to the cherry and berry flavors, and it shows a good dose of oak—almost to the point of overdoing it. Best to cellar short-term. 602 cases made. • $20 • (06/30/97) • **86**

Merlot San Luis Obispo County 1993: Impressive. Firm and tight, with a core of cherry, sage, herb and cedary oak notes, this is a wonderfully crafted, well-focused wine that's intense and concentrated. Try now. 1,500 cases made. • $20 • (05/15/97) • **89**

Merlot San Luis Obispo County 1992 • $20 • (12/31/95) HR • **91**

Reserve Paso Robles 1988 • $23 • (11/15/91) • **75**

Reserve Paso Robles 1987: Still firmly tannic, though softening, with an earthy, cedary edge to the ripe Cabernet flavors. Impressive for its long, elegant, flavorful finish. Best now through 2002. • $NA • (12/15/97) • **90**

KALIN | CALIFORNIA

Cabernet Sauvignon Sonoma County Reserve 1988 • $26 • (08/31/92) • **81**

Cabernet Sauvignon Sonoma County Reserve 1985 • $23 • (04/15/91) • **83**

Pinot Noir Sonoma County Cuvée DD 1986 • $20 • (04/30/91) • **80**

KALINDA | CALIFORNIA

Zinfandel Paso Robles 1991 • $9 • (10/15/95) • **84**

KARL LAWRENCE | CALIFORNIA

Cabernet Sauvignon Napa Valley 1994: A bit on the rustic side, with a claylike flavor to the earthy currant and cherry notes. Finishes with a nice touch of fruit, which works its way through the tannins. 650 cases made. • $28 • (09/30/97) • **88**

Cabernet Sauvignon Napa Valley 1993: Strives for complexity with its spicy oak accent, but comes up a little short on richness and concentration. The currant, cherry and berry flavors are pleasant, picking up a fruity note on the finish. Ready now. 350 cases made. • $25 • (09/15/96) • **88**

KARLY | CALIFORNIA

Cabernet Sauvignon El Dorado Stromberg Carpenter Vineyard 1991 • $15 • (11/15/94) • **82**

Marsanne Amador County 1995: A smooth, classy wine, with a silky texture. The subtle flavors—hazelnuts, minerals, sweet pea and citrus come to mind—blend nicely on a long finish. 224 cases made. • $17 • (0/31/98) • **89**

Orange Muscat Amador County 1995: Sweet, syrupy and smooth, with a nice floral note riding above the modest apricot flavors. Ready to drink. 415 cases made. • $14/375ml • (11/30/96) • **85**

Petite Sirah Amador County 1989 • $12 • (03/15/92) • **65**

Petite Sirah Amador County Not So Petite Sirah 1991 • $12 • (09/30/94) • **83**

Petite Sirah Amador County Not So Petite Sirah 1988 • $14 • (12/31/90) • **81**

Sangiovese Amador County 1994: Ripe and complex, with a pleasant, earthy edge to the ripe cherry and plumlike flavors. Finishes with a zesty aftertaste. 830 cases made. • $13 • (10/15/96) • **87**

Sauvignon Blanc Amador County 1997: Still quite young and spritzy; needs to settle down. Light in texture, with grapefruit, almond and mineral touches. Clean finish. 1,867 cases made. • $10 • (05/15/98) • **84**

Sauvignon Blanc Amador County 1996: Somewhat delicate, with a nice blend of grapefruit and lime flavors backed by this varietal's signature grassy tones. Finishes clean and fresh. 1,804 cases made. • $9 • (06/30/97) • **87**

Sauvignon Blanc Amador County 1995: Rich; spicy nectarine and floral flavors glide smoothly through and finishing on a grassy note. 2,340 cases made. • $9 • (07/31/96) • **87**

Sauvignon Blanc Amador County 1993 • $8 • (01/31/95) • **83**

Syrah Amador County 1995: Focused, with hints of blackberry and plum framed in pretty, toasty oak. Plush on the palate, with supple tannins and a moderate finish. Drink now through 2002. 775 cases made. • $18 • (06/15/98) • **87**

Syrah Amador County 1992 • $13 • (01/31/95) • **85**

Zinfandel Amador County 1994 • $12 • (04/30/96) • **79**

Zinfandel Amador County 1993 • $10 • (10/15/95) • **82**

Zinfandel Amador County 1992 • $9 • (10/15/94) • **82**

Zinfandel Amador County 1990 • $9 • (09/15/93) • **86**

Zinfandel Amador County 1989 • $9 • (10/15/92) • **74**

Zinfandel Amador County 1988 • $9 • (12/31/90) • **83**

Zinfandel Amador County 1987 • $9 • (03/31/90) • **83**

Zinfandel Amador County 1986 • $9 • (03/31/89) • **79**

Zinfandel Amador County 1985 • $8 • (12/31/87) • **72**

Zinfandel Amador County Pokerville 1995: A touch sweet, with lots of earthlike, sage and wild berry flavors, but a glimpse of its varietal soul holds it together. 4,500 cases made. • $8 • (03/31/97) • **82**

Zinfandel Amador County Pokerville 1993 • $8 • (10/15/95) BB • **87**

Zinfandel Amador County Pokerville 1990 • $6 • (09/15/93) BB • **88**

Zinfandel Amador County Sadie Upton Vineyard 1992 • $14 • (01/31/95) • **88**

Zinfandel Amador County Sadie Upton Vineyard 1991 • $15 • (10/15/94) • **77**

Zinfandel Amador County Sadie Upton Vineyard 1989 • $15 • (03/31/92) • **81**

Zinfandel Amador County Warrior Fires 1995: Very ripe, expressive and intense, with a rich core of earthy wild berry, cherry and plum. Deeply concentrated, with an attractive earthiness, it is well focused, firmly tannic and worthy of short-term cellaring. Best now through 2004. 1,105 cases made. • $20 • (06/15/98) • **89**

Zinfandel Amador County Warrior Fires 1994: Layers of complex currant, cherry, plum and berry flavors render this dark, rich and plush. It's big, concentrated and well crafted, finishing with firm tannins and a nice touch of chocolate. Drinkable now. 804 cases made. • $20 • (03/31/97) • **90**

KAZ | CALIFORNIA

Pinot Noir Sonoma County Ashton Vineyard 1995: Young, tight and tannic, with a distinct, mintlike edge to the cherry and berry flavors. Best to give it a year or so of cellaring to soften. 175 cases made. • $19 • (04/30/97) • **85**

KEEBLE, ROBERT | CALIFORNIA

Cabernet Franc Sonoma County 1988 • $12 • (11/15/91) • **79**

Cabernet Sauvignon Napa Valley 1989 • $14 • (11/15/92) • **80**

Cabernet Sauvignon Napa Valley 1987 • $14 • (10/15/91) • **89**

KEEGAN | CALIFORNIA

Chardonnay Knights Valley 1995: A modestly proportioned, ripe and complex wine with layers of pear, spice and light toasty oak. An elegant, understated style that drinks well now. 207 cases made. • $20 • (11/30/97) • **87**

Pinot Noir Russian River Valley 1994: Well oaked, with an elegant band of spicy cherry and plum flavors. Well balanced. Finishes with soft tannins and good length. 244 cases made. • $18 • (07/31/96) • **87**

KEENAN | CALIFORNIA

Cabernet Sauvignon Napa Valley 1992: Hard-edged and leathery with a young, green streak to the currant and cedar flavors. Aggressive tannins are unpleasant. 2,349 cases made. • $20 • (12/15/96) • **74**
Cabernet Sauvignon Napa Valley 1991 • $21 • (12/15/95) • **85**
Cabernet Sauvignon Napa Valley 1989 • $18 • (11/15/93) • **83**
Cabernet Sauvignon Napa Valley 1988 • $18 • (03/31/92) • **85**
Cabernet Sauvignon Napa Valley 1987 • $19 • (05/31/90) • **86**
Cabernet Sauvignon Napa Valley 1986 • $20 • (08/31/89) • **93**
Cabernet Sauvignon Napa Valley 1985 • $15 • (03/31/89) • **79**
Cabernet Sauvignon Napa Valley 1984 • $14 • (10/15/87) SS • **94**
Cabernet Sauvignon Napa Valley 1983 • $11 • (02/15/87) • **87**
Cabernet Sauvignon Napa Valley 1982 • $13 • (01/01/86) • **91**
Cabernet Sauvignon Napa Valley 1980 • $14 • (01/01/84) • **85**
Cabernet Sauvignon Napa Valley 1978 • $28 • (11/15/92) • **78**
Chardonnay Napa Valley 1996: Crisp and clean, with attractive earthy pear, citrus and spice flavors and a lingering finish. Can stand short-term cellaring. Drinkable now through 2001. 2,300 cases made. • $20 • (07/31/98) • **86**
Chardonnay Napa Valley 1995: Marked by a ripe pear and pineapple edge, it hits a few sour notes along the way but holds its balance before finishing with a earthy note. 2,160 cases made. • $17 • (07/31/97) • **85**
Chardonnay Napa Valley 1993 • $15 • (10/15/95) • **88**
Chardonnay Napa Valley Hillside 1995: A bit brackish, with a strong earthy, leesy edge, finishing with a metallic note and little fruit. 150 cases made. • $20 • (07/31/97) • **78**
Chardonnay Napa Valley Hillside 1994: A juicy wine with spicy citrus, grapefruit and tart pear notes that finish crisply. 1,750 cases made. • $15 • (06/15/96) • **83**
Merlot Napa Valley 1995: Young and tight, with a firm band of earthy currant, sage, mineral, cedar and spice. Finishes with chewy tannins and a twinge of bitterness; best to cellar short-term. 2,500 cases made. • $30 • (04/30/98) • **87**
Merlot Napa Valley 1994: Chewy but flavorful, showing plenty of smoke and berry flavors that linger on the tight finish. Needs until 2000 to soften. • $NA • (03/31/98) • **86**
Merlot Napa Valley 1993 • $25 • (06/30/96) • **86**
Merlot Napa Valley 1992 • $17 • (09/30/95) • **83**
Merlot Napa Valley 1990 • $18 • (07/15/93) • **83**
Merlot Napa Valley 1989 • $18 • (05/31/92) • **82**
Merlot Napa Valley 1988 • $18 • (05/31/92) • **84**
Merlot Napa Valley 1987 • $20 • (03/31/90) • **88**
Merlot Napa Valley 1986 • $18 • (06/30/89) • **90**
Merlot Napa Valley 1985 • $19 • (05/31/88) • **83**
Merlot Napa Valley 1984 • $30 • (07/31/87) CS • **94**
Merlot Napa Valley Vintners Selection 1990 • $25 • (07/15/93) • **88**

KELTIE BROOK | CALIFORNIA

Pinot Noir Carneros Unfiltered 1991 • $10 • (02/28/93) • **84**

KENDALL-JACKSON | CALIFORNIA

Cabernet Franc California Vintner's Reserve 1992 • $15 • (01/31/95) • **82**
Cabernet Sauvignon Alexander Valley Buckeye Vineyard Single Vineyard Series 1994: Smooth, ripe and lush, with a pretty core of herb-accented plum and cherry flavors. Turns supple and fleshy on the finish. Ready to drink. • $24 • (08/31/97) • **88**
Cabernet Sauvignon California Cardinale 1986: Despite its early promise, this wine's tart acidity, shallow flavors and hard-edged tannins make it one of the bigger disappointments. It's now thin, austere and tannic, having lost the sumptuous fruit flavors it showed in youth. • $NA • (12/15/96) • **78**
Cabernet Sauvignon California Cardinale 1985 • $45 • (11/15/89) • **97**
Cabernet Sauvignon California Cardinale 1984 • $45 • (07/31/87) • **84**
Cabernet Sauvignon California Cardinale 1983 • $50 • (10/16/85) • **82**
Cabernet Sauvignon California Grand Reserve 1997: Dark, grapey, with spicy plum, currant and wild berry. Finishes with firm tannins and fine balance. Notably elegant at this early stage. • $NA • (07/31/98) (BT) • **90-94**

Key: SS—Spectator Selection CS—Cellar Selection HR—Highly Recommended BB—Best Buy $NA—Price not available Ⓐ—Auction Price (BT)—Barrel Tasting
Dates in parentheses indicate the issues in which the ratings were published.

Cabernet Sauvignon California Grand Reserve 1996: Vibrant and tannic, with a rich, concentrated core of currant, anise and earthy Cabernet flavors. • $NA • (06/15/97) (BT) • **90-94**
Cabernet Sauvignon California Grand Reserve 1994: Crisp, with firm tannins and just enough spicy currant and berry flavor to give it the depth and complexity you might hope for at this price. • $39 • (07/31/97) • **87**
Cabernet Sauvignon California Grand Reserve 1992 • $35 • (11/30/95) • **91**
Cabernet Sauvignon California Grand Reserve 1991 • $30 • (11/15/94) • **89**
Cabernet Sauvignon California Grand Reserve 1990 • $30 • (11/15/93) • **90**
Cabernet Sauvignon California Proprietor's Grand Reserve 1988 • $23 • (03/15/93) • **83**
Cabernet Sauvignon California Proprietor's Grand Reserve 1987 • $16 • (03/31/92) • **87**
Cabernet Sauvignon California Proprietor's Reserve 1986 • $24 • (03/15/90) • **85**
Cabernet Sauvignon California Proprietor's Reserve 1985 • $20 • (12/15/88) • **95**
Cabernet Sauvignon California Vintner's Reserve 1994: Firm and intense, with a narrow band of earthy currant and cedar flavors, but it lacks focus and it's coarse. • $16 • (02/28/97) • **81**
Cabernet Sauvignon California Vintner's Reserve 1993: Supple and harmonious, with a range of cherry, herb and olive flavors that linger. Drinks well now. • $15 • (03/31/96) • **85**
Cabernet Sauvignon California Vintner's Reserve 1992 • $14 • (04/30/95) • **82**
Cabernet Sauvignon California Vintner's Reserve 1991 • $15 • (07/31/94) • **83**
Cabernet Sauvignon California Vintner's Reserve 1990 • $13 • (11/15/92) • **83**
Cabernet Sauvignon California Vintner's Reserve 1989 • $13 • (07/31/92) • **84**
Cabernet Sauvignon California Vintner's Reserve 1987 • $14 • (11/15/91) • **82**
Cabernet Sauvignon California Vintner's Reserve 1986 • $11 • (12/31/88) • **85**
Cabernet Sauvignon Lake County 1986 • $7 • (07/31/88) • **74**
Cabernet Sauvignon Lake County 1984 • $7 • (11/15/87) BB • **81**
Cardinale California Meritage 1991 • $60 • (12/15/95) • **91**
Cardinale California Meritage 1990 • $50 • (10/15/94) HR • **91**
Cardinale California Meritage 1989 • $50 • (05/15/94) • **88**
Cardinale California Meritage 1988 • $50 • (11/15/93) • **85**
Cardinale California Meritage 1987 • $44 Ⓐ • (03/31/92) HR • **95**
Chardonnay Arroyo Seco Paradise Vineyard 1995: Clean and attractive, with a core of ripe peach and citrus flavors. Fans out on the finish, picking up toasty oak and spice notes. • $19 • (07/31/97) • **87**
Chardonnay Arroyo Seco Paradise Vineyard Single Vineyard Series 1996: A touch earthy, it works its way into more mainstream fruit flavors, with ripe pear, apricot and toasty oak. Finishes with complex oak and more fruit. Drink now through 2001. • $20 • (06/15/98) • **88**
Chardonnay California Grand Reserve 1996: Clean, with ripe, moderately rich and complex pear, fig, apple and smoky oak nuances. Finishes with a sense of elegance and polish and hints of pear and lime. Drink now through 2000. • $26 • (05/31/98) • **89**
Chardonnay California Grand Reserve 1995: Elegant and flavorful, ripe and creamy, with juicy pear, apple, melon and fig notes that fan out on the finish where nice touch of spicy oak adds dimension. • $26 • (05/15/97) • **91**
Chardonnay California Grand Reserve 1994: Intense yet with a sense of elegance and finesse, with ripe pear, melon, nutmeg and apple flavors. Finishes with a light touch of oak and a fruity aftertaste. • $26 • (03/31/96) • **90**
Chardonnay California Grand Reserve 1993 • $24 • (06/30/95) HR • **90**
Chardonnay California Vintner's Reserve 1996: Simple, straightforward, soft and pleasant for its spice and melon flavors. • $15 • (11/30/97) • **81**
Chardonnay California Vintner's Reserve 1995: Features ripe, intense, concentrated flavors of pear, spice, apple and hazelnut that are pure and refreshing, if a tad on the sweet side. • $15 • (01/31/97) • **87**
Chardonnay California Vintner's Reserve 1994: Openly fruity, with ripe pear, melon, apple and spice notes, a straightforward and appealing wine that's drinkable now. • $14 • (12/15/95) • **86**
Chardonnay California Vintner's Reserve 1993 • $14 • (09/15/94) • **85**
Chardonnay Santa Maria Valley Camelot Vineyard 1995: Ripe, rich and complex, with tiers of spice, toast, honey and nectarine accented by hints of peach and pineapple. A up-front and openly fruity style that is appealing now. • $18 • (02/28/97) • **91**
Chardonnay Santa Maria Valley Camelot Vineyard 1994: Smooth, ripe and creamy, striking a nice balance between its rich pear, fig, melon and spice

character and the toasty, buttery oak. Finishes with a creamy flavor and texture. Keeps up the track record for this leading California winery. 10,000 cases made. • $18 • (03/31/96) SS • **90**

Chardonnay Santa Maria Valley Camelot Vineyard 1993 • $16 • (07/31/95) • **88**

Chardonnay Santa Maria Valley Camelot Vineyard Single Vineyard Series 1995: Ripe, rich and complex, with tiers of spice, toast, honey and nectarine accented by hints of peach and pineapple. A up-front and openly fruity style that is appealing now. • $18 • (02/28/97) • **91**

Gewürztraminer California Vintner's Reserve 1996: Soft, and generous with its spicy pear and pepper flavors, harmonious and frankly sweet on the finish. Drink soon. • $10 • (11/30/97) • **84**

Gewürztraminer California Vintner's Reserve 1993 • $10 • (02/28/95) • **82**

Johannisberg Riesling California Vintner's Reserve 1996: Sweet but juicy and flavorful, offering plenty of floral, grape and honeyed apple flavors that linger on the soft, balanced finish. • $11 • (07/31/97) • **85**

Johannisberg Riesling California Vintner's Reserve 1993 • $9 • (06/15/95) • **80**

Merlot Alexander Valley 1986 • $16 • (12/31/88) • **93**

Merlot California Grand Reserve 1994: Pleasant enough, with ripe cherry, smoky oak and cedar notes, but it tastes tightly wound and finishes with crisp, firm tannins. • $39 • (06/30/97) • **85**

Merlot California Grand Reserve 1993 • $42 • (06/30/96) • **86**

Merlot California Grand Reserve 1992 • $30 • (09/30/95) • **90**

Merlot California Grand Reserve 1991 • $30 • (09/15/94) • **86**

Merlot California Vintner's Reserve 1994: Pleasant enough, with hints of cherry, herb, cedar and spice. Drinks well now. • $18 • (02/28/97) • **84**

Merlot California Vintner's Reserve 1993: Pleasant enough, with its uncomplicated ripe cherry and light oak flavors. • $NA • (08/31/96) • **84**

Merlot California Vintner's Reserve 1992 • $15 • (09/15/94) • **82**

Merlot California Vintner's Reserve 1991 • $14 • (10/15/93) • **87**

Merlot California Vintner's Reserve 1990 • $14 • (01/31/93) • **83**

Merlot California Vintner's Reserve 1989 • $14 • (05/31/92) • **75**

Merlot California Vintner's Reserve 1988 • $14 • (11/15/91) • **84**

Merlot Sonoma County The Proprietor's 1987 • $20 • (12/31/90) • **87**

Pinot Noir California Grand Reserve 1994: Shows off earthy cola and wild berry notes with a leathery edge that carries over to the finish, where a funky note chimes in. Tastes like an old-style California Pinot Noir. • $30 • (02/28/97) • **84**

Pinot Noir California Grand Reserve 1993 • $30 • (03/31/95) • **88**

Pinot Noir California Proprietor's Grand Reserve 1992 • $30 • (10/31/94) • **86**

Pinot Noir California Proprietor's Grand Reserve 1991 • $30 • (02/28/94) • **82**

Pinot Noir California Vintner's Reserve 1996: Light and refreshing for its soft berry and spice flavors. Ready now. • $15 • (12/31/97) • **83**

Pinot Noir California Vintner's Reserve 1994 • $14 • (11/15/95) • **88**

Pinot Noir California Vintner's Reserve 1993 • $14 • (03/31/95) • **83**

Pinot Noir California Vintner's Reserve 1992 • $13 • (02/28/94) • **82**

Pinot Noir California Vintner's Reserve 1991 • $13 • (09/15/93) • **80**

Pinot Noir California Vintner's Reserve 1990 • $13 • (02/28/93) • **82**

Pinot Noir Santa Maria Valley Julia's Vineyard 1988 • $14 • (11/15/91) • **82**

Riesling Late Harvest California Select 1993 • $15 • (07/31/95) • **86**

Royale California Meritage 1994 • $15 • (07/31/95) • **89**

Sauvignon Blanc California Grand Reserve 1994 • $20 • (06/30/96) • **87**

Sauvignon Blanc California Grand Reserve 1993 • $14 • (12/31/94) • **86**

Sauvignon Blanc California Vintner's Reserve 1996: Pleasant enough, with mild acidity and a grassy edge, finishing with hints of lemon and grapefruit. A bit hot on the palate, though. • $11 • (12/15/97) • **82**

Sauvignon Blanc California Vintner's Reserve 1995: Fresh and fruity, with lively pear and pineapple flavors that finish bright and clean. Ready now. • $10 • (08/31/97) • **84**

Sauvignon Blanc California Vintner's Reserve 1994 • $9 • (08/31/95) • **82**

Sauvignon Blanc California Vintner's Reserve 1993 • $9 • (01/31/95) • **82**

Sémillon California Vintner's Reserve 1994 • $12 • (06/30/96) • **87**

Syrah California Grand Reserve 1992: Pleasantly fruity, with spicy cherry and wild berry flavors. Turns a bit hollow at midpalate and ends with firm tannins. • $20 • (07/31/96) • **86**

Syrah California Grand Reserve 1991 • $20 • (09/30/94) • **88**

Syrah California Proprietor's Grand Reserve 1990 • $16 • (02/15/93) • **88**

Syrah California Vintner's Reserve 1990 • $14 • (10/31/93) • **83**

Syrah Sonoma Valley Durell Vineyard 1990 • $16 • (05/15/95) • **85**

Syrah Sonoma Valley Durell Vineyard 1988 • $24 • (08/31/91) • **89**

Syrah Sonoma Valley Durell Vineyard 1987 • $17 • (12/15/89) • **90**

Syrah Sonoma Valley Durell Vineyard 1986 • $14 • (11/30/88) • **92**

Viognier California Grand Reserve 1995: Tightly wound, with a snappy edge to the ripe pear and apple flavors, but it never really takes off. 2,000 cases made. • $25 • (12/15/97) • **82**

Viognier California Grand Reserve 1994: Has hints of spice and pear, but it's straightforward. A good, quenching quaff. • $25 • (07/31/96) • **84**

Zinfandel Anderson Valley DuPratt Vineyard 1990 • $20 • (09/30/93) • **88**

Zinfandel Anderson Valley DuPratt Vineyard 1987 • $20 • (07/31/91) HR • **90**

Zinfandel Anderson Valley DuPratt-DePatie Vineyard 1986 • $16 • (12/15/89) • **85**

Zinfandel Anderson Valley DuPratt-DePatie Vineyard 1983 • $10 • (11/01/85) • **76**

Zinfandel California Grand Reserve 1994: Delivers a ripe, complex, supple core of blackberry and cherry flavors, dashes of spice and sage and adds subtle earth notes. Turns elegant and complex on the finish, where the tannins are soft and fleshy. Ready now through 2000. 1,500 cases made. • $25 • (04/30/97) • **90**

Zinfandel California Grand Reserve 1993: Lean and spicy, with more herb and dried cherry than ripe fruit flavors. Unexpectedly modest, given the price and reserve status. • $25 • (08/31/96) • **82**

Zinfandel California Grand Reserve 1992 • $20 • (01/31/95) • **84**

Zinfandel California Grand Reserve 1991 • $20 • (10/15/94) • **86**

Zinfandel California Proprietor's Grand Reserve 1990 • $16 • (01/31/93) • **89**

Zinfandel California Vintner's Reserve 1995: Toasty cola and black cherry notes surface despite a hollow core. Backed by somewhat rough-edged tannins. A blend of 11 percent Carignane, 3 percent Petite Sirah and 1 percent Mataro. • $18 • (07/31/97) • **82**

Zinfandel California Vintner's Reserve 1994 • $14 • (04/30/96) • **83**

Zinfandel California Vintner's Reserve 1993 • $14 • (10/15/95) • **83**

Zinfandel California Vintner's Reserve 1992 • $12 • (10/15/94) • **83**

Zinfandel California Vintner's Reserve 1991 • $10 • (09/30/93) • **84**

Zinfandel California Vintner's Reserve 1990 • $9 • (12/15/92) • **78**

Zinfandel California Vintner's Reserve 1989 • $11 • (09/30/91) • **84**

Zinfandel Clear Lake Vina Las Lomas Vineyard 1983 • $7 • (06/01/85) • **80**

Zinfandel Mendocino 1987 • $9 • (03/15/90) • **88**

Zinfandel Mendocino 1986 • $9 • (09/15/88) • **86**

Zinfandel Mendocino Ciapusci Vineyard 1989 • $20 • (10/15/92) • **82**

Zinfandel Mendocino Ciapusci Vineyard 1988 • $20 • (10/15/92) • **77**

Zinfandel Mendocino Ciapusci Vineyard 1984 • $16 • (12/15/89) • **86**

Zinfandel Mendocino County DuPratt Vineyard Proprietor's Grand Reserve 1990 • $23 • (10/15/92) • **84**

Zinfandel Mendocino Zeni Vineyard 1990 • $20 • (10/15/92) • **83**

KENNEDY, KATHRYN | CALIFORNIA

Cabernet Sauvignon Santa Cruz Mountains 1993: A tight, tart, richly flavored wine with tightly packed currant and berry flavors and firm, rustic tannins but, on the finish, the flavors are long and true. There's a lot to like in this wine, but it needs cellaring into 2001 to 2002. 700 cases made. • $70 • (10/31/97) • **91**

Cabernet Sauvignon Santa Cruz Mountains 1992: An attractive blend of ripe plum, cherry and currant flavors. Finishes with a slightly nutty edge to the tannins. Drink now. 600 cases made. • $35 Ⓐ • (07/31/96) • **87**

Cabernet Sauvignon Santa Cruz Mountains 1991 • $54 • (11/15/94) • **87**

Cabernet Sauvignon Santa Cruz Mountains 1990 • $54 • (06/15/94) • **89**

Cabernet Sauvignon Santa Cruz Mountains 1989 • $54 • (03/31/93) • **87**

Cabernet Sauvignon Santa Cruz Mountains 1988 • $60 • (11/15/91) • **88**

Cabernet Sauvignon Santa Cruz Mountains 1987: Aging beautifully, with a healthy dark color, lots of rich currant, black cherry, chocolate and spice flavors, and a smooth, polished texture right up to the finish, where it dries ever so slightly with tannin. Best now through 2002. • $100 • (12/15/97) • **92**

Cabernet Sauvignon Santa Cruz Mountains 1986 • $37 • (03/15/90) • **81**

Cabernet Sauvignon Santa Cruz Mountains 1985 • $33 • (12/15/88) • **93**

Lateral California 1995: Serves up a modest band of spicy currant and cherry before losing its intensity. Best now to 2000. 700 cases made. • $26 • (04/30/98) • **83**

Lateral California 1993: Openly fruity, with jammy cherry and berry notes of medium depth and richness. Mild tannins and pleasant aftertaste. Drink now. 700 cases made. • $25 • (12/15/95) • **86**

Lateral California 1991 • $18 • (11/15/93) • **86**

Lateral California 1990 • $17 • (10/15/92) • **88**

Lateral California 1989 • $17 • (11/15/91) • **86**

Lateral California 1988 • $15 • (10/15/90) • **87**

KENWOOD | CALIFORNIA

Cabernet Sauvignon Sonoma Valley 1997: Smooth, ripe and already plush in texture. Sharply focused, rich with currant, black cherry, herb and olive. Elegant and supple, long on the finish. • $NA • (07/31/98) (BT) • **90-94**

Cabernet Sauvignon Sonoma Valley 1996: A touch earthy and reduced, but not out of bounds for a barrel sample. Young and unevolved, lacking focus and not showing much fruit. Hard to judge. • $NA • (06/15/97) (BT) • **85-89**

Cabernet Sauvignon Sonoma Valley 1994: Dark, rich, focused—this has muscle, with a core of black cherry, licorice, toasty oak and spice. Drinks well now, but should improve in two to five years. 23,000 cases made. • $18 • (10/31/97) • **88**

Cabernet Sauvignon Sonoma Valley 1991 • $16 • (11/15/94) • **82**

Cabernet Sauvignon Sonoma Valley 1990 • $17 • (11/15/93) • **84**

Cabernet Sauvignon Sonoma Valley 1989 • $15 • (11/15/92) SS • **91**

Cabernet Sauvignon Sonoma Valley 1987: Ripe and complex, somewhat lacking in extra dimensions and finesse, but solid and complete on its own terms. Shows a smoky, roasted edge to the currant and berry flavors, turning supple on the finish. Ready to drink. 14,180 cases made. • $25 • (12/15/97) • **88**

Cabernet Sauvignon Sonoma Valley 1986: Simple as the vintage goes, this is a mature wine with a cedar, currant and earth edge and drying tannins. Enjoyable, though not as complex as many '86s. 15,400 cases made. • $NA • (12/15/96) • **84**

Cabernet Sauvignon Sonoma Valley 1985 • $15 • (02/15/89) • **91**

Cabernet Sauvignon Sonoma Valley 1984 • $12 • (05/31/88) • **83**

Cabernet Sauvignon Sonoma Valley 1983 • $10 • (02/15/88) • **85**

Cabernet Sauvignon Sonoma Valley 25th Anniversary Vintage 1993: Tough and chewy now, but it has some currant and cherry flavors underneath the tannins. Try now. 36,000 cases made. • $16 • (12/15/96) • **85**

Cabernet Sauvignon Sonoma Valley 25th Anniversary Vintage 1992 • $16 • (10/31/95) • **86**

Cabernet Sauvignon Sonoma Valley Artist Series 1993: A bottling from this winery's flagship lineup, characteristically tight and firm, with chewy tannins. The core of spicy currant, earthy anise and cedary oak flavors folds together nicely on the finish. Best cellared into 2000 to 2001, when it should be smoother and softer. Tasted twice, with consistent notes. 3,100 cases made. • $50 • (10/31/97) CS • **90**

Cabernet Sauvignon Sonoma Valley Artist Series 1992: Marked by herb and cedar flavors, its currant and plum flavors are a bit muted and struggle to work their way through, but they do. The tannins are thick and chocolaty, with hints of currant and berry peeking in on the finish. Try in 2000. 3,000 cases made. • $50 • (12/15/96) • **91**

Cabernet Sauvignon Sonoma Valley Artist Series 1991 • $34 Ⓐ • (11/15/94) • **89**

Cabernet Sauvignon Sonoma Valley Artist Series 1990 • $30 • (12/15/93) • **86**

Cabernet Sauvignon Sonoma Valley Artist Series 1989 • $36 • (10/31/92) CS • **93**

Cabernet Sauvignon Sonoma Valley Artist Series 1988 • $19 Ⓐ • (03/15/92) • **83**

Cabernet Sauvignon Sonoma Valley Artist Series 1987: Smooth, ripe and complex, with a pretty array of spicy currant, black cherry, anise, sage and cedary oak flavors. Rich and concentrated. Most of the tannin has softened quite enjoyably. Best now through 2002. 4,200 cases made. • $32 Ⓐ • (12/15/97) • **91**

Cabernet Sauvignon Sonoma Valley Artist Series 1986: Young, tight and tannic. A ripe, complex and concentrated young wine, with earthy currant, mineral, cedar and spice flavors that linger on. Approachable now to 2000, though it can easily be held into 2006. 3,800 cases made. • $40 Ⓐ • (12/15/96) • **90**

Cabernet Sauvignon Sonoma Valley Artist Series 1985 • $26 Ⓐ • (02/15/89) • **91**

Cabernet Sauvignon Sonoma Valley Artist Series 1984 • $27 Ⓐ • (11/30/87) • **93**

Cabernet Sauvignon Sonoma Valley Artist Series 1983 • $34 Ⓐ • (11/15/86) CS • **92**

Cabernet Sauvignon Sonoma Valley Artist Series 1982 • $25 • (11/01/85) • **89**

Key: SS—Spectator Selection CS—Cellar Selection HR—Highly Recommended BB—Best Buy $NA—Price not available Ⓐ—Auction Price (BT)—Barrel Tasting

Dates in parentheses indicate the issues in which the ratings were published.

Cabernet Sauvignon Sonoma Valley Artist Series 1981 • $25 • (09/16/84) SS • **89**

Cabernet Sauvignon Sonoma Valley Artist Series 1978 • $NA • (11/15/92) • **90**

Cabernet Sauvignon Sonoma Valley Jack London Vineyard 1994: Needs some time to work through the earthy, claylike tannins, but you get a hint of the currant, sage and leather flavors. Cellar into 2000 to 2001 to let it soften. 12,000 cases made. • $25 • (10/31/97) • **88**

Cabernet Sauvignon Sonoma Valley Jack London Vineyard 1993: An herbal style with hints of sage and anise, but currant, cherry and berry flavors fold in to provide added dimension and depth. Intense but not overly tannic, it's well crafted and well balanced. 7,000 cases made. • $25 • (11/15/96) • **88**

Cabernet Sauvignon Sonoma Valley Jack London Vineyard 1992 • $20 • (10/31/95) • **87**

Cabernet Sauvignon Sonoma Valley Jack London Vineyard 1991 • $20 • (11/15/94) • **83**

Cabernet Sauvignon Sonoma Valley Jack London Vineyard 1989 • $20 • (11/15/92) • **89**

Cabernet Sauvignon Sonoma Valley Jack London Vineyard 1987: Smooth and supple, with a rich, smoky accent to the ripe currant and plum flavors. Could stand to shed more tannin. Best now through 2002. 10,000 cases made. • $45 • (12/15/97) • **89**

Cabernet Sauvignon Sonoma Valley Jack London Vineyard 1986: This is a remarkably tame Jack London bottling, without the usual heavy dose of tannin. It offers a supple core of earthy currant, spicy oak, herb and mineral flavors and tannins that are firm, but not out of line. Can age a bit. 4,994 cases made. • $NA • (12/15/96) • **89**

Cabernet Sauvignon Sonoma Valley Jack London Vineyard 1985 • $24 Ⓐ • (10/15/88) • **89**

Cabernet Sauvignon Sonoma Valley Jack London Vineyard 1984 • $21 • (11/30/87) • **91**

Cabernet Sauvignon Sonoma Valley Jack London Vineyard 1983 • $21 • (02/15/87) • **86**

Cabernet Sauvignon Sonoma Valley Jack London Vineyard 1980 • $25 • (05/16/84) • **80**

Chardonnay Sonoma County-Santa Maria Valley Reserve 1996: A racy style, with a grassy, Sauvignon Blanc-like edge and hints of oak, pear, cedar and spice. The texture is a bit rough, unlike the rich, polished wine that emerged in a previous tasting. Drink now through 2001. 2,396 cases made. • $22 • (07/31/98) • **88**

Chardonnay Sonoma County-Santa Maria Valley Reserve 1995: Shows a spicy, Muscat-like edge and complex, interesting flavors of tropical fruits, pear, guava, citrus and spice. A delicious blend of Sonoma Valley and Santa Maria Valley grapes. 2,092 cases made. • $20 • (05/31/97) • **92**

Chardonnay Sonoma County 1996: A spicy style, with a hint of litchi nut, and ripe pear and apple flavors that are ripe and refreshing if lacking in extra complexities. Drink now. 28,000 cases made. • $15 • (06/15/98) • **87**

Chardonnay Sonoma County 25th Anniversary Vintage 1995: Ripe and spicy, in an early-drinking style that features pear, spice and apple flavors and a clean, fruity aftertaste that picks up a hint of citrus, but not much oak. 22,900 cases made. • $15 • (11/15/96) • **85**

Chardonnay Sonoma County 25th Anniversary Vintage 1994: Light, lean, fresh and fruity, zingy apple and melon flavors lingering spicily on the finish. Ready now. 17,700 cases made. • $14 • (12/15/95) • **87**

Chardonnay Sonoma Valley 1993 • $14 • (07/31/95) • **84**

Chardonnay Sonoma Valley Beltane Ranch 1993 • $18 • (07/31/95) • **84**

Chardonnay Sonoma Valley Reserve 1994: A bit heavy-handed and a touch bitter, and the pear and apple notes struggle to keep pace with the oaky flavors. It becomes more interesting on the finish. 185 cases made. • $18 • (07/31/96) • **81**

Chardonnay Sonoma Valley Reserve 1993 • $18 • (07/31/95) • **84**

Chardonnay Sonoma Valley Yulupa 1993 • $14 • (07/31/95) • **83**

Johannisberg Riesling Late Harvest Sonoma Valley 1985 • $10/375ml • (02/28/87) BB • **89**

Johannisberg Riesling Late Harvest Sonoma Valley 1984 • $8/375ml • (09/16/85) • **79**

Merlot Sonoma County 1992 • $16 • (07/31/95) • **83**

Merlot Sonoma County 1991 • $16 • (09/15/94) • **80**

Merlot Sonoma County 1990 • $16 • (06/15/93) • **86**

Merlot Sonoma County 1989 • $15 • (01/31/93) • **83**

Merlot Sonoma County Jack London Vineyard 1992 • $18 • (09/30/95) • **88**

Merlot Sonoma Mountain Jack London Vineyard 1991 • $18 • (06/30/94) • **87**

Merlot Sonoma Mountain Jack London Vineyard 1990 • $18 • (06/15/93) • **82**

Merlot Sonoma Valley Jack London Vineyard 1993: Earthy and tannic, with a dense, leathery edge and not much fruit. Hints of pepper and spice poke through. 4,000 cases made. • $18 • (07/31/96) • **81**
Merlot Sonoma Valley Massara Vineyards 1994: Well balanced, with attractive herb, currant and cedary oak flavors that are intense and concentrated; best to cellar into 1999. 1,600 cases made. • $25 • (11/30/97) • **85**
Merlot Sonoma Valley Massara Vineyards 1992 • $18 • (02/28/95) • **84**
Pinot Noir Russian River Valley 1995: Very light in color, with more spicy, toasty and pickle-barrel notes than berry flavors. A harsh edge mars the finish. Try in 1999 to see how it develops. 8,700 cases made. • $16 • (11/30/97) • **82**
Pinot Noir Russian River Valley 1993 • $14 • (10/15/95) • **84**
Pinot Noir Russian River Valley Olivet Lane 1993 • $22 • (10/15/95) • **87**
Pinot Noir Sonoma Valley Jack London Vineyard 1992 • $18 • (03/31/95) • **80**
Pinot Noir Sonoma Valley Jack London Vineyard 1990 • $18 • (09/30/92) • **85**
Pinot Noir Sonoma Valley Jack London Vineyard 1989 • $15 • (10/31/91) • **80**
Pinot Noir Sonoma Valley Jack London Vineyard 1984 • $15 • (05/31/89) • **77**
Sauvignon Blanc Sonoma County 1996: A crisply sweet medley of melon, sweet pea, grapefruit, fig and herb notes, all coming together harmoniously into an elegant, multitiered white that's drinkable now. The price is right, and there's plenty to go around. 40,000 cases made. • $11 • (07/31/97) BB • **88**
Sauvignon Blanc Sonoma County 1995: Simple and direct, with appealing citrus and spicy nectarine flavors. 50,000 cases made. • $9 • (08/31/96) • **83**
Sauvignon Blanc Sonoma County 1993 • $9 • (05/31/95) • **84**
Sauvignon Blanc Sonoma County 25th Anniversary Vintage 1994 • $9 • (12/15/95) BB • **87**
Sauvignon Blanc Sonoma Valley Reserve 1996: Fairly complex, with a blend of melon, grapefruit, lemon and herbal aspects. A light touch on the palate makes it refreshing and quite enjoyable. 3,000 cases made. • $15 • (03/31/98) • **88**
Sauvignon Blanc Sonoma Valley Reserve 1995: Bright grapefruit, melon and kiwi flavors pack a tangy, refreshing punch here. Finishes with a hint of hazelnut and just the right touch of grassiness. 3,800 cases made. • $15 • (06/30/97) • **89**
Sauvignon Blanc Sonoma Valley Reserve 1994 • $15 • (12/15/95) • **85**
Vintage Red California 1988 • $5 • (12/31/90) • **77**
Vintage Red California 1986 • $5 • (11/30/88) • **74**
Vintage Red Sonoma County 1983 • $4 • (05/31/88) • **77**
Zinfandel Geyserville Mazzoni 1995: Complex, with lots of ripe, spicy cherry and wild berry flavors, turning smooth and supple on the finish. Drink now through 2002. 1,000 cases made. • $20 • (06/15/98) • **87**
Zinfandel Geyserville Mazzoni 1994: Ripe, smooth and spicy, with lively blackberry, cherry and raspberry notes. Finish is of good length. Fine balance, with a sense of harmony and finesse. 1,300 cases made. • $20 • (04/30/97) • **88**
Zinfandel Sonoma County Geyserville Mazzoni 1993 • $15 • (09/30/95) • **89**
Zinfandel Sonoma Mountain Jack London Vineyard 1991 • $14 • (09/30/93) • **86**
Zinfandel Sonoma Valley 1995: Captures just enough ripe plum and black cherry to sustain itself. The texture turns supple, before the tannins kick in. Drink now through 2001. 11,944 cases made. • $15 • (06/15/98) • **85**
Zinfandel Sonoma Valley 1994: Complex, if a bit rustic with its band of earthy cherry, zesty raspberry, pepper and spice flavors. Finishing with earthy tannins, it's drinkable now. 8,500 cases made. • $14 • (04/30/97) • **87**
Zinfandel Sonoma Valley 1992 • $12 • (07/31/95) • **84**
Zinfandel Sonoma Valley 1991 • $12 • (10/15/94) • **82**
Zinfandel Sonoma Valley 1990 • $12 • (09/30/93) • **86**
Zinfandel Sonoma Valley 1988 • $14 • (12/31/90) • **82**
Zinfandel Sonoma Valley 1987 • $15 • (10/31/89) • **90**
Zinfandel Sonoma Valley 1985 • $15 • (05/15/88) • **89**
Zinfandel Sonoma Valley 1984 • $16 • (09/15/87) • **90**
Zinfandel Sonoma Valley 1983 • $16 • (11/15/86) • **88**
Zinfandel Sonoma Valley 1982 • $16 • (07/16/86) • **90**
Zinfandel Sonoma Valley Barricia Vineyard 1994: Claret-style, with supple plum, cherry and wild berry notes, finishing with mild tannins and good length. Ready to drink. 1,000 cases made. • $20 • (04/30/97) • **88**
Zinfandel Sonoma Valley Barricia Vineyard 1993 • $16 • (01/01/95) • **85**
Zinfandel Sonoma Valley Barricia Vineyard 1991 • $16 • (10/15/94) • **84**
Zinfandel Sonoma Valley Barricia Vineyard 1990 • $12 • (10/15/92) • **89**
Zinfandel Sonoma Valley Jack London Vineyard 1995: Lean and earthy, with hints of cherry and wild berry followed by cedar, tar and sage. On solid footing even if it fails to excite. Well balanced. Drink now. 5,988 cases made. • $20 • (03/31/98) • **87**
Zinfandel Sonoma Valley Jack London Vineyard 1994: Shows spicy qualities along with a little gaminess, but the ripe cherry and berry flavors overcome, gaining complexity and interest along the way. 5,500 cases made. • $20 • (09/30/96) • **85**
Zinfandel Sonoma Valley Jack London Vineyard 1993 • $14 • (10/15/95) • **84**
Zinfandel Sonoma Valley Jack London Vineyard 1992 • $14 • (10/15/94) • **82**
Zinfandel Sonoma Valley Jack London Vineyard 1990 • $14 • (10/15/92) • **84**
Zinfandel Sonoma Valley Jack London Vineyard 1989 • $14 • (09/30/91) • **83**
Zinfandel Sonoma Valley Jack London Vineyard 1987 • $12 • (12/15/89) • **88**
Zinfandel Sonoma Valley Nuns Canyon 1995: There's a green, slightly unripe streak that runs through this wine, interrupting the core of sage and wild berry. Drink now through 2000. 679 cases made. • $20 • (06/15/98) • **84**
Zinfandel Sonoma Valley Nuns Canyon 1994: Tart and earthy, but hits the right notes with its black cherry, raspberry, spice and anise flavors at the center, finishing with a good dose of tannins. 1,200 cases made. • $20 • (04/30/97) • **89**
Zinfandel Sonoma Valley Nuns Canyon 1993 • $16 • (04/30/96) • **90**
Zinfandel Sonoma Valley Upper Weise Ranch 1995: Pleasant enough, with crushed black pepper and earth, sage and wild berry flavors, turning tart on the finish. Drink now through 2000. 1,933 cases made. • $20 • (06/15/98) • **84**
Zinfandel Sonoma Valley Upper Weise Ranch Old Vine 1994: Smooth and spicy, with a nice overlay of toasty oak, but also a tasty core of wild berry, cherry, anise and spice flavors. Finishes with tar-accented fruit and spice notes. 1,200 cases made. • $20 • (04/30/97) • **89**

KERR, J. | CALIFORNIA

Pinot Noir Santa Barbara County 1991 • $19 • (08/31/94) • **85**
Pinot Noir Santa Barbara County 1990 • $19 • (03/31/95) • **80**

KESTREL | CALIFORNIA

Merlot Sierra Foothills Limited Release 1996: Shows pretty plum flavors with hints of earth and mushrooms. Tannins and acids are a bit pronounced, however. Short finish. Drink now through 2002. 214 cases made. • $17 • (05/31/98) • **81**
Trinity Amador County Limited Release 1994: Rich, smoky, tarry licorice notes lead the way to a charry palate backed by nice currant and blackberry flavors. Roughish finish. Should age well. A blend of 62 percent Merlot and 38 percent Cabernet Sauvignon. 35 cases made. • $27 • (11/30/97) • **85**

KINDERWOOD | CALIFORNIA

Merlot California 1992 • $6 • (09/15/94) BB • **83**

KING ESTATE | OREGON

Cabernet Sauvignon Oregon 1994: On the light side for Cabernet, but the spicy thwack of oak tends to obscure the modest berry and herb flavors. Best from 2000 through 2003. 1,218 cases made. • $30 • (07/31/98) • **81**
Cabernet Sauvignon Oregon 1992: Lean in style, tight and tart, with blackberry flavors at the core and an earthy streak running through the narrow finish. Try in 1999. 900 cases made. • $30 • (04/30/97) • **84**
Chardonnay Oregon 1995: A generous mouthful of harmoniously balanced pear, honey and spice flavors, polished and supple. Approachable now. 11,500 cases made. • $14 • (03/31/98) • **87**
Chardonnay Oregon 1994: Generous with its almond-scented peach, pear and mineral flavors that linger enticingly on the finish. Ripe, supple and spicy. Drink now. 8,500 cases made. • $13 • (04/30/97) • **89**
Pinot Gris Oregon 1996: Very crisp and bright, with strong mineral and almond flavors. Needs food to show its best. 31,000 cases made. • $13 • (03/31/98) • **80**
Pinot Gris Oregon 1995: Fresh and appealing for its peach and apple flavors. Generous and immediately likable. 24,000 cases made. • $12 • (12/31/96) • **86**
Pinot Gris Oregon 1994 • $11 • (01/31/96) • **87**
Pinot Gris Oregon 1993 • $11 • (11/30/94) • **85**
Pinot Gris Oregon Reserve 1996: Supple and appealing for its up front, bright melon and pear flavors, finishing with a slight bite of acidity and

touch of spice. Best for summer drinking. 4,000 cases made. • $18 • (03/31/98) • **87**

Pinot Gris Oregon Reserve 1995: A bit more aromatic and focused than most Pinot Gris, adding a layer of definition to the basic pear, floral and almond flavors, and finishing with style. 350 cases made. • $15 • (12/31/96) • **88**

Pinot Gris Oregon Reserve 1994 • $14 • (01/31/96) • **88**

Pinot Gris Oregon Reserve 1993 • $14 • (11/30/94) • **85**

Pinot Noir Oregon 1995: Soft, gentle style has a slight bite of tannin on the finish, but otherwise feels supple and offers a nice layer of light cherry and cinnamon flavors. Drinkable now. 25,500 cases made. • $18 • (03/31/98) • **86**

Pinot Noir Oregon 1994: Light and artfully balanced to show off its red plum, chocolate and spice flavors that linger on the delicate finish. Doesn't overpower, but seduces quite effectively. Drink now. 24,000 cases made. • $18 • (02/28/97) • **88**

Pinot Noir Oregon 1993 • $18 • (03/31/96) • **87**

Pinot Noir Oregon 1992 • $18 • (11/30/94) • **85**

Pinot Noir Oregon Reserve 1994: A beautiful Pinot Noir with plenty of currant, blackberry and sweet cream flavors that deploy themselves elegantly and hang on through a long finish. Drinkable now. 1,890 cases made. • $35 • (06/15/97) • **91**

Zinfandel Oregon 1994: A supple, harmonious red with pretty plum and spice flavors that linger on the moderately chewy finish. Best now through 2001. 265 cases made. • $20 • (07/31/98) • **85**

KINGS RIDGE | OREGON

Pinot Noir Oregon 1990 • $9 • (02/28/93) • **78**

KIONA | WASHINGTON

Cabernet Sauvignon Washington 1996: Light, smooth and silky, with a pretty plum and grape character that lingers gently on the finish. Ready now. 1,000 cases made. • $15 • (01/31/98) • **85**

Cabernet Sauvignon Washington 1995: Smooth, ripe and generous with its sweet berry, currant, beet and tealeaf flavors, but biting tannins grab at the back, and need until 2000 to 2003. Don't worry; it has the intensity and richness to get there. 600 cases made. • $15 • (08/31/97) • **90**

Cabernet Sauvignon Washington 1993: Firmly textured, with smoky, floral accents to the sturdy base of currant flavors. Finishes smoothly; try now. 850 cases made. • $15 • (09/15/96) • **86**

Cabernet Sauvignon Washington 1991 • $12 • (09/30/94) • **86**

Cabernet Sauvignon Washington 1990 • $12 • (07/31/94) • **84**

Cabernet Sauvignon Yakima Valley 1992: Packs a lot of flavor onto a lean frame, offering a minty berry and floral character and a firmly tannic finish. Best after 1999. 800 cases made. • $20 • (01/01/97) • **85**

Cabernet Sauvignon Yakima Valley 1991 • $18 • (09/30/95) • **86**

Cabernet Sauvignon Yakima Valley 1990 • $18 • (08/31/95) • **89**

Cabernet Sauvignon Yakima Valley 1989 • $15 • (07/31/94) • **87**

Cabernet Sauvignon Yakima Valley 1986 • $14 • (10/15/89) • **89**

Cabernet Sauvignon Yakima Valley Reserve 1993: Dark and peppery, firm in texture, with a gamy edge to the ripe cherry and currant flavors. Has a hint of leather at the end. Chewy at this stage. Best from 2000 through 2005. 400 cases made. • $28 • (06/15/98) • **87**

Cabernet Sauvignon Yakima Valley Tapteil Vineyard 1989 • $12 • (03/15/93) • **89**

Cabernet Sauvignon Yakima Valley Tapteil Vineyard 1988 • $12 • (03/31/92) • **85**

Chardonnay Washington 1995: Bright and flavorful, with enticing nectarine and spice flavors that hold on through the finish. Drinkable now. 1,100 cases made. • $12 • (09/15/96) • **86**

Chardonnay Yakima Valley 1995: Bright, peppery and lively, it's a crisp mouthful of citrusy apple flavors with layers of spice and vanilla folding in on the finish. 900 cases made. • $15 • (08/31/97) • **86**

Chardonnay Yakima Valley Barrel Fermented 1993: A supple wine with an earthy, almost gamy accent to the flavors. Finishes with style. Ready now. 1,200 cases made. • $15 • (09/15/96) • **85**

Chardonnay Yakima Valley Reserve 1996: Ripe, and bright with flavor, all reined nicely into a supple, polished framework. Feels fresh and lively. Drink now through 2000. 600 cases made. • $18 • (06/15/98) • **87**

Key: SS—Spectator Selection CS—Cellar Selection HR—Highly Recommended BB—Best Buy $NA—Price not available Ⓐ—Auction Price (BT)—Barrel Tasting
Dates in parentheses indicate the issues in which the ratings were published.

Chenin Blanc Columbia Valley 1996: Soft and appealing for its melon and floral aromas and flavors. Charming to the end. Drink now. 1,800 cases made. • $6 • (09/15/97) • **83**

Chenin Blanc Late Harvest Yakima Valley Ice Wine 1993 • $19/375ml • (09/30/94) • **80**

Chenin Blanc Yakima Valley 1995: Soft, sweet and simple, offering a pleasant mouthful of melon and peach flavors. Finish is a bit subdued. 1,800 cases made. • $7 • (09/30/96) • **83**

Chenin Blanc Yakima Valley 1994 • $6 • (09/30/95) • **85**

Chenin Blanc Yakima Valley 1993 • $6 • (09/30/94) • **87**

Chenin Blanc Yakima Valley Ice Wine 1993 • $19 • (04/15/95) • **78**

Chenin Blanc Yakima Valley Ice Wine 1989 • $20 • (04/15/95) • **68**

Gewürztraminer Late Harvest Yakima Valley 1994 • $7/375ml • (09/30/95) • **87**

Gewürztraminer Late Harvest Yakima Valley 1993 • $6 • (09/30/94) • **89**

Lemberger Washington 1995: Soft texture, dark color and bright berry flavors add up to a pleasant, quaffable wine to wash down a casual dinner. 1,400 cases made. • $10 • (09/15/97) • **84**

Lemberger Yakima Valley 1994: Ripe and rich. A polished wine with generous black cherry and berry flavors wrapped in a light cloak of oak. Drinkable now 1,100 cases made. • $10 • (09/15/96) • **88**

Lemberger Yakima Valley 1993 • $10 • (09/30/95) • **85**

Lemberger Yakima Valley 1992 • $10 • (09/30/94) • **84**

Lemberger Yakima Valley 1990 • $10 • (09/30/94) • **79**

Lemberger Yakima Valley 1989 • $9 • (05/15/92) • **76**

Merlot-Cabernet Washington 1995: Smooth and spicy around a core of bright, citrusy flavors. Some black cherry and tarry notes develop on the finish. Drink now. 630 cases made. • $12 • (09/15/96) • **85**

Merlot Columbia Valley 1994: Firm in texture, deep in color. A chewy wine with a nice core of blackberry flavor overlapped with some toasty and earthy notes. Tannins need at least until 2000. 1,400 cases made. • $18 • (09/15/96) • **85**

Merlot Columbia Valley 1993: Firm, a bit tannic for the weight, but has some nice blackberry, tar and mineral flavors. Drink now. 1,400 cases made. • $15 • (07/31/96) • **85**

Merlot Columbia Valley 1992 • $12 • (09/30/95) • **91**

Merlot Columbia Valley 1991 • $12 • (09/30/94) • **87**

Merlot Columbia Valley 1990 • $12 • (06/15/93) • **81**

Merlot Columbia Valley 1989 • $12 • (03/31/92) • **86**

Merlot Columbia Valley 1988 • $12 • (05/31/91) • **84**

Muscat Late Harvest Yakima Valley 1994 • $7/375ml • (09/30/95) • **82**

Muscat Late Harvest Yakima Valley 1993 • $7/375ml • (09/30/94) • **89**

Rosé Washington Vintage 1995: Off-dry and modestly fruity, offering watermelon and raspberry flavors. A rosé made from Lemberger. 400 cases made. • $6 • (09/30/96) • **82**

Rosé Washington Vintage 1993 • $6 • (09/30/95) • **85**

White Riesling Columbia Valley 1997: Off-dry, with pretty, resiny apple flavors that linger lightly on the finish. Drink now. 5,000 cases made. • $7 • (06/30/98) • **84**

White Riesling Columbia Valley 1996: A sweet, complex wine, generous with its ripe red apple, pineapple and citrus flavors. Better focused in the middle than on the finish. Drink soon. 5,000 cases made. • $6 • (09/15/97) • **87**

White Riesling Columbia Valley 1995: Freshly sweet, like biting into a bright, green apple after a bite of ripe peach. Shows some restraint on the light finish. 1,800 cases made. • $7 • (09/15/96) • **87**

White Riesling Columbia Valley 1994 • $6 • (06/30/96) • **86**

White Riesling Late Harvest Yakima Valley 1994 • $6/375ml • (09/15/95) • **85**

White Riesling Late Harvest Yakima Valley 1991 • $6/375ml • (09/30/94) • **86**

White Riesling Yakima Valley 1993 • $6 • (09/30/94) • **87**

White Riesling Yakima Valley Dry 1995: Light and brightly fruity, with appealing floral, peach and green apple flavors that linger nicely on the crisp, dry finish. 1,800 cases made. • $7 • (09/15/96) • **85**

White Riesling Yakima Valley Dry 1994 • $6 • (09/30/95) • **81**

White Riesling Yakima Valley Dry 1993 • $6 • (09/30/94) • **86**

KISTLER | CALIFORNIA

Cabernet Sauvignon Sonoma Valley Kistler Estate Vineyard 1991 • $30 • (06/15/95) HR • **90**

Cabernet Sauvignon Sonoma Valley Kistler Estate Vineyard 1990 • $30 • (02/28/94) • **86**

Cabernet Sauvignon Sonoma Valley Kistler Estate Vineyard 1988 • $25 • (08/31/92) • **86**

Cabernet Sauvignon Sonoma Valley Kistler Estate Vineyard 1987 • $33 • (02/28/91) • **83**

Cabernet Sauvignon Sonoma Valley Kistler Estate Vineyard 1986 • $26 Ⓐ • (09/30/89) • **84**

Cabernet Sauvignon Sonoma Valley Kistler Estate Vineyard 1985 • $17 • (05/31/88) • **92**

Chardonnay Carneros Hudson Vineyard 1995: Young and crisp, with a flint, grapefruit, citrus and pear core. It's tightly wound and sharply focused. Best from 1999 through 2002. 288 cases made. • $48 • (06/30/98) • **92**

Chardonnay Russian River Valley Dutton Ranch 1995: A smoky, earthy style that's a bit heavy-handed, but the core of fruit is intense and concentrated, with rich fig, pear, anise, hazelnut and cedary oak. Best to cellar short-term. Best from 1999 through 2004. 1,876 cases made. • $42 • (07/31/98) • **91**

Chardonnay Russian River Valley Dutton Ranch 1994: A pure, simple, delicious Chardonnay that's brimming with ripe, juicy pear, apple, apricot and exotic spicy notes. Fills out the palate with a load of complexity that gives long, lingering flavors. Has a good dose of toasty oak, but the wine wears it well. Ready now. 1,844 cases made. • $36 • (02/28/97) • **94**

Chardonnay Russian River Valley Dutton Ranch 1993 • $35 • (06/30/96) • **89**

Chardonnay Russian River Valley Vine Hill Vineyard 1995: Crisp and lively, with a rich, concentrated, tightly wound band of nectarine, pear, citrus and spice. Gains momentum and finishes with a wonderful display of fruit and oak complexity. Best from 1999 through 2006. 2,782 cases made. • $42 • (06/30/98) HR • **94**

Chardonnay Russian River Valley Vine Hill Vineyard 1994: Displays remarkable depth and integration, slowly unfolding to show flavors of pear, vanilla, fig, anise, smoke, butter and spice that loll, smooth, rich and creamy, on the palate. An altogether complex and concentrated young wine that packs in flavor while maintaining harmony and finesse. 2,748 cases made. • $38 • (06/30/97) HR • **95**

Chardonnay Russian River Valley Vine Hill Vineyard 1993 • $35 • (06/30/96) • **92**

Chardonnay Sonoma Coast 1995: Bold, ripe, rich and complex, with exotic fig, pear, melon and spicy Chardonnay flavors that pick up a trace of toasty oak on the finish. Beautifully balanced. Drink now. 7,017 cases made. • $31 • (05/15/97) • **92**

Chardonnay Sonoma Coast 1993 • $26 • (06/15/95) • **89**

Chardonnay Sonoma Coast Camp Meeting Ridge 1995: Kistler strikes again with this rich and unctuous Chardonnay. Bold, flavorful and fleshy, its layers of ripe pear, fig, citrus and honeysuckle flavors gain depth and complexity thanks to judicious oak seasoning, which adds toast and anise nuances. Delicious. 282 cases made. • $42 • (04/30/98) HR • **95**

Chardonnay Sonoma County Cuvée Cathleen 1994: Ripe, rich and opulent, with tiers of spicy pear, apple, melon and citrus flavors. Finishes with a complex, concentrated aftertaste that keeps pumping out the flavors. Drinkable now, or cellar into 2000. 540 cases made. • $50 • (06/30/97) • **93**

Chardonnay Sonoma County Cuvée Cathleen 1993 • $50 • (06/30/96) • **90**

Chardonnay Sonoma Mountain McCrea Vineyard 1995: From Kistler's impressive Chardonnay lineup comes this smooth, ripe, rich and polished wine, with a succulent core of ripe pear, spice, hazelnut, fig and honey flavors. Notable for its depth, concentration, complexity and finesse, with a long, full aftertaste. Best now through 2001. 2,791 cases made. • $42 • (03/31/98) CS • **93**

Chardonnay Sonoma Mountain McCrea Vineyard 1994: Manages to deliver a rich core of flinty, spicy pear and anise notes while showing its young, tight, complex and concentrated nature. A remarkably well-focused Chardonnay with a long, full finish that keeps pumping out the flavors. 2,765 cases made. • $38 • (02/28/97) HR • **95**

Chardonnay Sonoma Mountain McCrea Vineyard 1993 • $35 • (06/30/96) HR • **91**

Chardonnay Sonoma Valley Durell Vineyard 1995: Yet another winner from this winery. Remarkably complex and concentrated, serving up a lot of intense fruit flavors, with ripe pear, citrus, fig and toasty oak and hazelnut notes. This is a young and tightly wound Chardonnay that should only get better with age. Drink now through 2002. 2,735 cases made. • $40 • (03/31/98) CS • **93**

Chardonnay Sonoma Valley Durell Vineyard 1993 • $34 • (06/15/95) HR • **91**

Chardonnay Sonoma Valley Kistler Vineyard 1994: Ripe and full-bodied, with a core of smoky pear, spice and citrus flavors, turning buttery on the finish and picking up a pretty anise note. Still young and vibrant, it's worthy of another couple of years in the cellar. 522 cases made. • $45 • (06/30/97) • **92**

Chardonnay Sonoma Valley Kistler Vineyard 1993 • $40 • (06/30/96) CS • **94**

Pinot Noir Russian River Valley Dutton Ranch 1987 • $15 • (03/31/90) • **85**

Pinot Noir Russian River Valley Dutton Ranch 1986 • $14 • (06/15/88) • **89**

Pinot Noir Russian River Valley Kistler Vineyard Cuvée Catherine 1994: Kistler's best Pinot Noir to date. Showing healthy, dark plumlike color and lots of ripe, rich flavor, with tiers of black cherry, plum, spice and lightly toasted oak. Impeccably balanced. Attests to the California producer's mastery of this grape, in a great vintage. Delicious now to 2001. 192 cases made. • $45 • (03/31/97) HR • **95**

Pinot Noir Russian River Valley Kistler Vineyard Cuvée Catherine 1992 • $40 • (12/31/95) • **90**

Pinot Noir Sonoma Coast Camp Meeting Ridge 1994: Impressive with its dense, concentrated core of black cherry, plum and berry flavors, picking up a pretty oak shading and a slight meaty accent, both of which add dimension. Firmly tannic on the finish, so if you're lucky enough to have a bottle or two, cellar into 1999 for best results. 190 cases made. • $38 • (06/30/97) • **94**

Pinot Noir Sonoma Coast Hirsch Vineyard 1995: Dense, dark and concentrated, with a tightly wound core of wild blackberry, cherry, anise, sage and spice. A unique expression of Sonoma Coast Pinot Noir. Finishes with a slight tannic bitterness and a dash of new oak. 164 cases made. • $50 • (06/30/98) • **90**

Pinot Noir Sonoma Mountain McCrea Vineyard 1992 • $22 • (03/31/95) • **88**

KLEIN | CALIFORNIA

Cabernet Sauvignon Santa Cruz Mountains 1990 • $25 • (11/15/93) • **81**
Cabernet Sauvignon Santa Cruz Mountains 1989 • $25 • (08/31/92) • **85**
Cabernet Sauvignon Santa Cruz Mountains 1988 • $25 • (01/31/92) • **83**
Cabernet Sauvignon Santa Cruz Mountains 1987 • $19 • (10/15/90) • **87**
Cabernet Sauvignon Santa Cruz Mountains 1986 • $22 • (09/30/89) • **89**

KNAPP | NEW YORK

Pinot Noir Finger Lakes 1992 • $13 • (11/15/94) • **78**
Prism Finger Lakes 1993 • $NA • (06/30/95) • **76**
Riesling Finger Lakes 1995: A mix of herb and peach flavors that ends up a bit awkward, earthy and dull. • $9 • (01/31/97) • **76**
Vignoles Finger Lakes Late Harvest 1991 • $17 • (06/30/95) • **86**

KNIPPRATH | WASHINGTON

Cabernet Sauvignon Columbia Valley 1994: A crisp Cabernet, but it has distinctive blackberry and currant flavors that persist on the vibrant finish. Good now, but it has room to grow through 2000 to 2002 and beyond. 250 cases made. • $12 • (09/30/97) • **88**

Chardonnay Columbia Valley 1995: Earthy, slightly bitter flavors make this seem charmless. 500 cases made. • $10 • (09/30/97) • **79**

Fumé Blanc Washington 1995: Smooth, soft and generous with its spicy, buttery pineapple flavors. Ready now. 250 cases made. • $10 • (11/30/97) • **83**

Lemberger Yakima Valley Pleasant Vineyards 1992 • $8 • (09/30/94) • **81**

Merlot Washington 1995: This is a smooth, silky Merlot, on the lighter side, with floral overtones to its modest berry flavors. A pretty wine to drink soon. 500 cases made. • $13 • (10/15/97) • **86**

Pinot Noir Columbia Valley 1994: Light, simple and pleasant for its smooth texture and black cherry flavors shaded by hints of tobacco and spice. Ready now. 400 cases made. • $10 • (11/30/97) • **85**

Port Washington NV: On the dry side for Port, but offers some ripe berry and plum flavors, a spirity edge and some grip on the finish. Drink soon. 220 cases made. • $17 • (11/30/97) • **84**

White Riesling Columbia Valley 1995: Strongly floral, almost bitter, this soft, generous wine shows hints of peach and cream around the edge. Ready now. 500 cases made. • $7 • (11/30/97) • **82**

KNUDSEN ERATH | OREGON

Cabernet Sauvignon Oregon NV • $7 • (04/30/88) • **79**
Chardonnay Willamette Valley 1993 • $10 • (10/31/94) BB • **86**
Pinot Gris Willamette Valley 1994 • $12/375ml • (03/31/96) • **84**
Pinot Gris Willamette Valley 1993 • $12 • (10/15/94) • **85**
Pinot Noir Oregon Dundee Villages NV • $7 • (02/28/93) • **70**
Pinot Noir Willamette Valley 1993 • $12 • (03/31/96) • **81**
Pinot Noir Willamette Valley 1992 • $10 • (03/15/94) • **80**
Pinot Noir Willamette Valley 1991 • $10 • (03/15/94) • **79**
Pinot Noir Willamette Valley 1990 • $12 • (02/28/93) • **72**
Pinot Noir Willamette Valley 1988 • $11 • (05/31/91) • **82**
Pinot Noir Willamette Valley 1987 • $11 • (02/15/90) • **65**
Pinot Noir Willamette Valley 1986 • $10 • (06/15/88) • **72**

Pinot Noir Willamette Valley NV • $6 • (06/16/86) BB • **81**
Pinot Noir Willamette Valley Leland Vineyards Reserve 1987 • $24 • (02/15/90) • **89**
Pinot Noir Willamette Valley Reserve 1991 • $22 • (11/30/94) • **84**
Pinot Noir Willamette Valley Vintage Select 1992 • $16 • (02/28/95) • **85**
Pinot Noir Willamette Valley Vintage Select 1991 • $16 • (01/31/94) • **86**
Pinot Noir Willamette Valley Vintage Select 1987 • $16 • (03/15/94) • **72**
Pinot Noir Willamette Valley Vintage Select 1986 • $15 • (06/15/88) • **87**
Pinot Noir Willamette Valley Vintage Select 1985 • $NA • (09/30/87) • **90**
Pinot Noir Yamhill County Vintage Select 1985 • $21 Ⓐ • (02/15/90) • **75**
Pinot Noir Yamhill County Vintage Select 1983 • $12 • (07/01/86) SS • **94**
Riesling Willamette Valley 1994 • $7 • (01/31/96) BB • **85**
Riesling Willamette Valley Dry 1993 • $8 • (01/31/96) • **82**
White Riesling Late Harvest Willamette Valley 1994 • $8 • (03/31/96) • **86**

KONOCTI | CALIFORNIA

Cabernet Franc Lake County 1988 • $9 • (02/28/91) • **83**
Cabernet Sauvignon Lake County 1990 • $10 • (11/15/93) • **82**
Cabernet Sauvignon Lake County 1989 • $9 • (11/15/92) • **81**
Cabernet Sauvignon Lake County 1986 • $9 • (04/30/90) • **80**
Cabernet Sauvignon Lake County 1985 • $7 • (11/15/89) BB • **89**
Cabernet Sauvignon Lake County 1984 • $7 • (02/15/89) • **76**
Cabernet Sauvignon Lake County 1983 • $6 • (06/15/87) BB • **84**
Cabernet Sauvignon Lake County 1982 • $7 • (11/15/86) • **78**
Meritage Clear Lake 1987 • $17 • (11/15/92) • **84**
Merlot Lake County 1989 • $10 • (02/29/92) • **85**
Merlot Lake County 1988 • $9 • (03/31/91) BB • **83**
Merlot Lake County 1987 • $9 • (12/31/90) • **73**
Merlot Lake County 1985 • $8 • (12/31/88) • **83**
Merlot Lake County Mount Konocti Kelsey 1992 • $10 • (06/30/94) BB • **86**
Red Table Wine Lake County NV • $5 • (11/15/92) BB • **80**

KONRAD | CALIFORNIA

Barbera Amador County 1992 • $12 • (07/31/95) • **85**
Charbono Mendocino 1992 • $11 • (11/15/95) • **81**
Chardonnay Mendocino 1993 • $11 • (06/15/96) • **83**
Mélange à Trois Mendocino 1992 • $13 • (12/15/95) • **85**
Mélange à Trois Mendocino 1991 • $12 • (03/15/94) • **86**
Mélange à Trois Mendocino County 1989 • $16 • (07/15/92) • **87**
Petite Sirah Mendocino 1991 • $11 • (09/30/94) • **84**
Port Mendocino Petite Sirah Port Admiral's Quinta 1990 • $18 • (11/15/93) • **74**
Zinfandel Mendocino 1992 • $10 • (10/15/95) • **79**
Zinfandel Mendocino 1991 • $9 • (10/15/94) • **80**
Zinfandel Mendocino County 1990 • $9 • (09/30/93) BB • **88**
Zinfandel Mendocino County 1989 • $10 • (03/31/92) • **84**

KORBEL | CALIFORNIA

Blanc de Noirs California Cuvée Master's Reserve 1990 • $15 • (05/31/95) • **78**
Blanc de Noirs California Cuvée Pinot Noir Champagne Master's Reserve 1991: Tart, earthy and a bit tinny. Shows hints of spice, citrus and black cherry flavors, but it's coarse and biting on the finish. 3,500 cases made. • $15 • (11/30/96) • **82**
Brut California NV: Shows attractive citrus and hazelnut flavors but the finish is a bit short, with a trace of sweetness. A fine quaffer. 619,000 cases made. • $11 • (11/30/97) • **84**
Brut Rosé California Jane Seymour NV: Sweet and simple, with a strong raspberry edge. Bottle design by actress Jane Seymour adds little. • $13 • (05/15/98) • **80**
Brut Rosé California Sinatra NV: Fairly simple, with raspberry and cherry flavors, it's not quite as sparkling as its namesake, but should please some. • $13 • (11/30/97) • **80**
Cabernet Sauvignon Alexander Valley 1991 • $13 • (11/15/94) • **73**
Chardonnay Champagne California NV: A strange, mildly candylike quality pervades. Mint, wintergreen, toast and citrus are also in evidence. Somewhat awkward, but enjoyable. 100,000 cases made. • $13 • (11/30/97) • **82**
Chardonnay Russian River Valley 1993 • $15 • (06/30/95) • **85**
Chardonnay Russian River Valley Heck Family Cellar Selection 1996: A jazzy wine, ripe and juicy, with pineapple, pear, resin and vanilla flavors tumbling over each other. Finishes fresh and lively. May be best in 1999 or 2000. 750 cases made. • $15 • (03/31/98) • **88**
Kosher California NV: Light in style, showing citrus and pear on the finish. A fairly simple wine. 26,000 cases made. • $12 • (11/30/97) • **83**
Le Premier Reserve California 1991: Marked by depth, finesse and elegance, this is toasty and smooth, yet still bright, with a nutty quality that's tempered by notes of citrus, herbs, spice and dried cherry. Complex and delicious. Top-of-the-line bubbly from this often-underrated producer. 1,400 cases made. • $20 • (12/15/97) HR • **91**
Natural California NV: Lovely floral aromas lead the way in this sparkler, followed by a medley of tangy grapefruit, lemon, pear and mineral flavors that waltz to a long and graceful finish. A fine wine at a great price. 37,000 cases made. • $12 • (11/30/97) SS • **89**
Rouge California NV: Somewhat earthy, with distinct Cabernet-like flavors of tar, plums and cassis. Reminiscent of a bubbly "kir" apéritif, it might shock some, but this sparkler from Cabernet and Pinot Noir is interesting and flavorful. 2,840 cases made. • $12 • (11/30/97) • **84**

KORNELL, HANNS | CALIFORNIA

Blanc de Blancs California 1982 • $15 • (11/30/86) • **77**
Blanc de Noirs California 1987 • $15 • (06/15/91) • **87**
Sparkling California Sehr Trocken 1984 • $15 • (06/15/91) • **74**

KRAMER | OREGON

Chardonnay Willamette Valley 1993: A nice, crisp frame surrounds some lovely honey-scented pear and floral flavors that linger enticingly on the finish. Drinkable now. 160 cases made. • $10 • (12/31/96) • **88**
Chardonnay Willamette Valley Estate Bottled 1993: Ripe, spicy and soft, this offers a nice touch of lime to enliven its generous caramel and pear flavors. Ready to drink. 160 cases made. • $15 • (12/31/96) • **87**
Müller-Thurgau Willamette Valley 1995: A gentle mouthful of peach and apple flavors, fresh and simple. Finish is clean and refreshing. 399 cases made. • $6 • (04/30/97) • **85**
Pinot Gris Willamette Valley 1995: Fresh and simple, with pear flavors and earth notes. Ready now. 479 cases made. • $12 • (12/31/96) • **80**
Pinot Gris Willamette Valley 1993 • $10 • (10/31/94) • **83**
Pinot Gris Willamette Valley Reserve 1995: Ripe, flavorful and exquisitely balanced to show-off sappy pear, almond and honey flavors on a silky frame. Delicious now. 72 cases made. • $15 • (12/31/96) • **88**
Pinot Noir Willamette Valley 1994: Gentle and fresh, with modest plum and vanilla flavors. Drink now. 330 cases made. • $15 • (12/31/96) • **81**
Pinot Noir Willamette Valley 1993 • $18 • (01/31/96) • **87**
Pinot Noir Willamette Valley 1992 • $18 • (03/15/94) • **84**
Pinot Noir Willamette Valley 1991 • $18 • (02/28/93) • **86**
Pinot Noir Yamhill County 1993: Harsh, bitter and earthy in character. Tasted twice with consistent notes. • $NA • (02/28/97) • **73**
Pinot Noir Yamhill County 1991 • $14 • (02/28/93) • **83**
Pinot Noir Yamhill County Reserve 1992 • $22 • (01/31/96) • **86**
Pinot Noir Yamhill County Reserve 1991 • $22 • (03/15/94) • **82**
Riesling Willamette Valley 1993 • $6 • (10/31/94) • **84**
Riesling Willamette Valley Select Cluster 1992 • $12/375ml • (11/30/94) • **77**

KRISTONE | CALIFORNIA

Blanc de Blancs California 1992: Complex in its own way, and a bit curious at first for its range of flavors. Showing pear, vanilla and a dash of oak, it turns creamy and smooth, with a distinctive, yeasty bread-dough quality that adds dimension. Complex aftertaste. 2,500 cases made. • $40 • (11/30/97) • **90**
Blanc de Blancs California 1991 • $60 • (11/30/95) • **87**
Blanc de Noirs California 1992: Prematurely aged, with strong hazelnut, earth and slightly cheesy flavors. The finish is a bit dull. Fans of old bubbly might enjoy it. 2,300 cases made. • $40 • (12/15/97) • **82**
Blanc de Noirs California 1991 • $60 • (11/30/95) • **91**
Brut Rosé California 1991 • $60 • (11/30/95) • **90**

Key: SS—Spectator Selection CS—Cellar Selection HR—Highly Recommended BB—Best Buy $NA—Price not available Ⓐ—Auction Price (BT)—Barrel Tasting
Dates in parentheses indicate the issues in which the ratings were published.

KRUG, CHARLES | CALIFORNIA

Cabernet Sauvignon Napa Valley 1993: Dry, with a tease of currant and cherry flavors. Turns simple on the finish. 29,000 cases made. • $12 • (09/15/96) • **83**
Cabernet Sauvignon Napa Valley 1992 • $12 • (12/15/95) • **84**
Cabernet Sauvignon Napa Valley 1991 • $12 • (11/15/94) • **81**
Cabernet Sauvignon Napa Valley 1990 • $12 • (10/31/93) • **88**
Cabernet Sauvignon Napa Valley 1989 • $12 • (11/15/92) • **77**
Cabernet Sauvignon Napa Valley 1988 • $12 • (03/15/92) • **73**
Cabernet Sauvignon Napa Valley 1987 • $11 • (11/15/91) • **79**
Cabernet Sauvignon Napa Valley 1986 • $11 • (02/28/91) • **87**
Cabernet Sauvignon Napa Valley 1985 • $23 Ⓐ • (01/31/90) • **77**
Cabernet Sauvignon Napa Valley 1982 • $7 • (10/31/87) • **79**
Cabernet Sauvignon Napa Valley 1965 • $35 • (07/16/85) • **74**
Cabernet Sauvignon Napa Valley 1962 • $65 • (07/16/85) • **84**
Cabernet Sauvignon Napa Valley 1961 • $125 • (07/16/85) • **84**
Cabernet Sauvignon Napa Valley 1952 • $250 • (07/16/85) • **86**
Cabernet Sauvignon Napa Valley 1951 • $250 • (07/16/85) • **80**
Cabernet Sauvignon Napa Valley 1947 • $300 • (07/16/85) • **89**
Cabernet Sauvignon Napa Valley 1944 • $NA • (07/16/85) • **95**
Cabernet Sauvignon Napa Valley Peter Mondavi Family 1994: Young and tight, with a rich core of currant, berry and spice flavors, finishing with a pretty dash of cedary oak. Impressive for its balance, finesse and finish. 14,600 cases made. • $14 • (08/31/97) • **89**
Cabernet Sauvignon Napa Valley Vintage Selection 1994: A well-oaked style with vanilla and butter notes, currant and cherry flavors that are smooth and supple, and a pretty aftertaste that turns elegant. Best after 1999. 1,600 cases made. • $35 • (10/31/97) • **88**
Cabernet Sauvignon Napa Valley Vintage Selection 1993: Dark in color, with a strong, smoked wood quality that dominates the ripe plum and berry notes. Finishes with a stalky, cedarlike edge, drying tannins. 1,545 cases made. • $35 • (06/30/97) • **79**
Cabernet Sauvignon Napa Valley Vintage Selection 1991 • $28 • (12/15/95) • **89**
Cabernet Sauvignon Napa Valley Vintage Selection 1988 • $28 • (07/31/93) • **87**
Cabernet Sauvignon Napa Valley Vintage Selection 1986 • $28 • (10/31/92) HR • **92**
Cabernet Sauvignon Napa Valley Vintage Selection 1985 • $29 • (03/15/92) • **89**
Cabernet Sauvignon Napa Valley Vintage Selection 1984 • $16 Ⓐ • (06/30/90) • **87**
Cabernet Sauvignon Napa Valley Vintage Selection 1983 • $24 • (06/30/90) • **81**
Cabernet Sauvignon Napa Valley Vintage Selection 1981 • $25 • (09/30/90) • **90**
Cabernet Sauvignon Napa Valley Vintage Selection 1978 • $31 • (11/15/92) • **78**
Cabernet Sauvignon Napa Valley Vintage Selection 1974 • $29 Ⓐ • (11/15/94) • **81**
Cabernet Sauvignon Napa Valley Vintage Selection 1966 • $53 • (06/01/85) • **87**
Cabernet Sauvignon Napa Valley Vintage Selection 1957 • $135 • (07/16/85) • **81**
Chardonnay Carneros Peter Mondavi Family Reserve 1996: Simple, with modest apple, pear and spicy flavors that are pleasant, if without extra dimension. Drink now. 2,150 cases made. • $20 • (05/15/98) • **86**
Chardonnay Carneros Peter Mondavi Family Reserve 1995: Appealing flavors of ripe pear, spice, citrus and a hint of herb are a bit clumsy at first, gaining complexity on the finish, with pretty oak shadings. 1,200 cases made. • $20 • (06/15/97) • **87**
Chardonnay Carneros Peter Mondavi Family Reserve 1994: Dull, earthy and a bit waxy, with a slightly sour, leesy pineapple accent to the flavors. Doesn't quite earn the reserve status. 985 cases made. • $20 • (09/15/96) • **78**
Chardonnay Napa Valley 1994: A simple Chardonnay of modest intensity and flavor. A hint of spice on the finish. 14,000 cases made. • $12 • (07/31/96) • **82**
Chardonnay Napa Valley 1993 • $11 • (05/15/95) • **81**
Chardonnay Napa Valley Peter Mondavi Family 1996: Light and simple, with a modest band of citrus- and pear-laced flavors that thin out on the finish. Drink now. 9,700 cases made. • $15 • (05/31/98) • **83**
Chardonnay Napa Valley Peter Mondavi Family 1995: Flavors of ripe apple, pear and spice are appealing, if lacking in focus. Turns smooth and polished on the finish, where toasty oak folds in. 10,255 cases made. • $13 • (07/31/97) • **85**
Chenin Blanc Napa Valley Pineau 1996: A crisp wine with a lemon and mineral edge backed by hazelnut and subtle honeyed tones. It's dry yet rich, and finishes with a toasty oak accent. 625 cases made. • $13 • (10/15/97) • **88**
Generations Napa Valley Peter Mondavi Family 1994: Ruggedly tannic, with a range of tea, sage, spice and wild berry flavors that are intense and compact. Needs some time to flesh out its texture. Best after 1999. A blend of 49 percent Cabernet Sauvignon, 29 percent Merlot, and 22 percent Cabernet Franc. 2,085 cases made. • $30 • (10/31/97) • **87**
Generations Napa Valley Peter Mondavi Family 1993: Well oaked, with a smoky, leathery edge and a dry, tannic core of spicy Cabernet flavors. Finishes with a dry, tannic aftertaste. A blend of 50 percent Cabernet Sauvignon, 26 percent Cabernet Franc and 24 percent Merlot. 990 cases made. • $30 • (06/30/97) • **84**
Generations Napa Valley Peter Mondavi Family 1992: An austere style that's tannic and lean, with a band of cedar, currant, herb and spice that stretches the range of flavors. Finishes with a firm tannic grip, so cellaring into 1999 is advised. 428 cases made. • $30 • (02/28/97) • **84**
Generations Napa Valley Peter Mondavi Family 1991: Appealing for its ripe currant, black cherry and plum flavors, and hints of cedar and spice. Finishes with mild tannins and a moderately complex aftertaste. 664 cases made. • $30 • (09/15/96) • **85**
Merlot Napa Valley 1993: A touch earthy and leathery, with just enough plum and berry flavors to create a balance. Let it breath.... 6,800 cases made. • $14 • (08/31/96) • **79**
Merlot Napa Valley 1992 • $14 • (03/31/95) • **83**
Merlot Napa Valley 1991 • $13 • (09/15/94) • **81**
Merlot Napa Valley 1990 • $14 • (06/15/93) • **85**
Merlot Napa Valley 1989 • $13 • (05/31/92) • **84**
Merlot Napa Valley Peter Mondavi Family 1995: Delivers plenty of detailed flavors, with pretty currant, plum and cherry notes complemented by lovely toasted oak shadings, all coming together quite nicely on the finish where the texture is polished. An impressive offering, it's this winery's best Merlot yet. 8,700 cases made. • $15 • (07/31/97) SS • **92**
Merlot Napa Valley Peter Mondavi Family 1994: Marked by herb and wild berry flavors, this turns thin and lean on the finish where it picks up a smoky, mineral accent. 12,500 cases made. • $14 • (11/30/96) • **86**
Merlot Napa Valley Peter Mondavi Family Reserve 1994: Earthy, with leathery, currant and cherry flavors. Slowly comes into focus. Best to cellar into 1999 to 2001 in hopes it's more forthcoming. 2,075 cases made. • $23 • (04/30/98) • **86**
Merlot Napa Valley Peter Mondavi Family Reserve 1993: A touch on the green side, with herb, tea and spice notes, it turns lean and leathery, missing the rich core of Merlot fruit you'd expect from a Reserve style wine. 1,520 cases made. • $22 • (02/28/97) • **84**
Merlot Napa Valley Peter Mondavi Family Reserve 1992: Intense and spicy, but the nice cherry and currant aromas are overcome by murky, earthy flavors. 615 cases made. • $22 • (08/31/96) • **82**
Pinot Noir Napa Valley Carneros 1994: Light, with floral aromas and spicy nuances of flavor. Fades a bit on the finish. 17,700 cases made. • $9 • (07/31/96) • **83**
Pinot Noir Napa Valley Carneros 1993 • $9 • (12/31/95) • **81**
Pinot Noir Napa Valley Carneros 1992 • $9 • (01/31/95) • **82**
Pinot Noir Napa Valley Carneros 1991 • $9 • (02/28/94) • **78**
Pinot Noir Napa Valley Carneros 1990 • $9 • (02/28/93) • **78**
Pinot Noir Napa Valley Carneros 1989 • $10 • (02/15/92) • **82**
Pinot Noir Napa Valley Carneros 1987 • $8 • (02/28/91) BB • **87**
Pinot Noir Napa Valley Carneros 1985 • $8 • (02/15/90) • **81**
Sangiovese Napa Valley Family Reserve 1993: Tired and earthy, with a slightly dirty edge to the cherry and berry flavors. Rather uninspiring, despite attractive new packaging. 925 cases made. • $16 • (09/15/96) • **80**
Sangiovese Napa Valley Peter Mondavi Family Reserve 1995: Earthy and diluted, with murky flavors that lack focus and depth. 2,625 cases made. • $16 • (05/15/98) • **80**
Sangiovese Napa Valley Peter Mondavi Family Reserve 1993: A middleweight with ripe plum, berry, anise and cedar notes. Somewhat simple on the finish, but good. 1,175 cases made. • $22 • (02/28/97) • **83**
Sauvignon Blanc Napa Valley 1993 • $9 • (10/31/95) • **81**
Zinfandel Napa Valley 1993: A safe style with moderate plum and cherry flavors. A good wine at a fair price, but we'd like to see a little more pizzazz. 2,700 cases made. • $7 • (11/30/96) • **81**
Zinfandel Napa Valley 1992 • $7 • (10/15/94) • **81**
Zinfandel Napa Valley 1990 • $6 • (09/30/93) • **74**
Zinfandel Napa Valley 1989 • $6 • (12/15/90) BB • **83**

KUNDE | CALIFORNIA

Cabernet Sauvignon Sonoma Valley 1994: Marked by a cheesy note, the currant and plum flavors are tart and compact, finishing with a slightly yeasty edge. May settle down with time. 4,980 cases made. • $17 • (08/31/97) • **82**

Cabernet Sauvignon Sonoma Valley 1993: Medium weight, with tart, simple cherry and berry flavors that gain interest on the finish as they fan out. Drinks well now. 5,000 cases made. • $15 • (10/15/96) • **85**

Cabernet Sauvignon Sonoma Valley 1990 • $15 • (03/15/93) • **88**

Cabernet Sauvignon Sonoma Valley Reserve 1993: Hard tannins and a lot of earthy, cedary flavors dominate the currant, dried berry, dusty flavors. Not likely to improve. Ready now through 2000. 744 cases made. • $24 • (11/15/97) • **81**

Cabernet Sauvignon Sonoma Valley Reserve 1991 • $23 • (05/31/96) • **85**

Cabernet Sauvignon Sonoma Valley Reserve 1990 • $23 • (11/15/93) • **82**

Chardonnay Sonoma Valley 1996: Complex, with pretty, ripe pear, spice, apple and melon flavors and a nice dash of spicy, toasty oak. Finishes with a complex aftertaste and more pretty interplay of fruit and oak. 28,500 cases made. • $15 • (04/30/98) • **87**

Chardonnay Sonoma Valley 1995: A fruit-driven style, with ripe pear and apple flavors and dashes of spice, toast and honey on the finish. 27,000 cases made. • $14 • (11/30/96) • **85**

Chardonnay Sonoma Valley 1994: A pleasant wine that offers spicy pear and apple notes, with a smooth and creamy mouthfeel. 23,000 cases made. • $14 • (01/31/96) • **86**

Chardonnay Sonoma Valley Kinneybrook 1995: Ripe and spicy, with a solid core of pear, vanilla, hazelnut and nutmeg. Shows a trace of alcohol on the finish, where the flavors turn complex. 945 cases made. • $20 • (03/31/98) • **88**

Chardonnay Sonoma Valley Kinneybrook 1994: An elegant and detailed young wine with bright, vivid pear, spice and citrus flavors that keep their focus on a long, complex finish. 500 cases made. • $20 • (05/31/96) • **89**

Chardonnay Sonoma Valley Kinneybrook 1993 • $17 • (01/31/96) • **90**

Chardonnay Sonoma Valley Reserve 1995: Elegant and understated, with a core of spice and hazelnut-tinged pear and apple flavors. Doesn't try to overpower, yet could use a little more richness and depth. 3,100 cases made. • $22 • (12/15/97) • **87**

Chardonnay Sonoma Valley Reserve 1994: A subtle, elegant style that opens up an attractive core of ripe pear, apple and honey notes, then adds a trace of hazelnut on the finish. 3,000 cases made. • $22 • (06/15/96) • **87**

Chardonnay Sonoma Valley Reserve 1993: Smooth, ripe and buttery, sporting tiers of honey, pear, fig and toast notes that fold together nicely on the finish. Impressive for its flavor and balance. 3,000 cases made. • $20 • (07/31/96) • **89**

Chardonnay Sonoma Valley Wildwood Vineyard 1995: Ripe and a bit alcoholic, with a core of earthy pear, fig and vanilla flavors that are raw and in need of short-term cellaring to be more harmonious. 662 cases made. • $20 • (03/31/98) • **87**

Chardonnay Sonoma Valley Wildwood Vineyard 1994: Smooth, rich and creamy, with tiers of honey, pear, vanilla and spice. A complex and well-crafted wine that finishes with a pleasant aftertaste. 500 cases made. • $20 • (05/31/96) • **89**

Chardonnay Sonoma Valley Wildwood Vineyard 1993 • $17 • (01/31/96) • **89**

Claret Sonoma Valley Louis Kunde Founder's Reserve 1990 • $17 • (11/15/93) • **88**

Claret Sonoma Valley Louis Kunde Founder's Reserve 1989 • $15 • (11/15/92) • **90**

Gewürztraminer Sonoma Valley Louis Kunde Founder's Reserve 1995: Bright and floral, with a nice core of pear and clove flavors to balance the rose-petal notes that linger a bit on the finish. 500 cases made. • $10 • (04/30/97) • **82**

Merlot Sonoma Valley 1995: A touch earthy and leathery, with just enough ripe currant and berry flavor to maintain a delicate balance. 14,200 cases made. • $17 • (11/30/97) • **82**

Merlot Sonoma Valley 1993 • $17 • (12/31/95) • **88**

Merlot Sonoma Valley 1991 • $15 • (09/15/94) • **77**

Muscat Canelli Late Harvest Sonoma Valley Louis Kunde Founder's Reserve 1995: Sweet, fruity and fresh, with a lively core of pear and litchi flavors that last through the smooth finish. Ready to drink. 1,100 cases made. • $11/375ml • (11/30/96) • **88**

Sauvignon Blanc Sonoma Valley Magnolia Lane 1996: Richly textured, with toasty oak and hazelnut flavors up front. Finishes moderately, with hints of grapefruit, herb and vanilla. 10,500 cases made. • $11 • (10/15/97) • **85**

Sauvignon Blanc Sonoma Valley Magnolia Lane 1995: Crisp and straightforward, with a pleasant range of pear flavors, notes of floral and vanilla. 9,000 cases made. • $11 • (07/31/96) • **83**

Sauvignon Blanc Sonoma Valley Magnolia Lane 1994 • $10 • (10/31/95) • **82**

Sauvignon Blanc Sonoma Valley Magnolia Lane 1993 • $10 • (02/28/95) • **80**

Syrah Sonoma Valley 1995: Dark, ripe, intense and concentrated. The meaty, beefy, plum, currant and wild berry flavors stay with you on the aftertaste. Drink now. 1,200 cases made. • $18 • (11/15/97) • **88**

Viognier Sonoma Valley 1996: Offers some interesting facets, with pretty spice, apple, pear and citrus notes, but finishes with a trace of bitterness. 1,880 cases made. • $18 • (12/15/97) • **84**

Viognier Sonoma Valley 1995: Rich and flavorful, showing more depth and range of flavor than most Viogniers, with tiers of peach, pear, honey and spice. An altogether complex and alluring wine. 2,200 cases made. • $18 • (10/15/96) SS • **90**

Viognier Sonoma Valley 1994 • $17 • (09/30/95) • **85**

Viognier Sonoma Valley 1993 • $15 • (09/15/94) • **88**

Zinfandel Sonoma Valley 1996: Supple and fruity, with simple cherry, berry and raspberry flavors and nice touches of anise and spice. Finishes with firm tannins, but it's a ready-to-drink style, pleasant but not overly concentrated. 5,650 cases made. • $15 • (03/31/98) • **85**

Zinfandel Sonoma Valley Century Vines 1994: Earthy and a bit cheesy, with a tannic accent to the wild berry and raspberry flavors. Turns dry and tannic on the finish. 6,050 cases made. • $14 • (11/15/96) • **82**

Zinfandel Sonoma Valley Century Vines The Shaw Vineyard 1995: A light style of Zin, with earthy, gamy notes adding interest to the straightforward black cherry flavor. Ready now. 5,400 cases made. • $15 • (12/15/97) • **85**

Zinfandel Sonoma Valley Robusto 1995: Smooth, ripe, rich and supple, with layers of coffee, currant, spice and anise, it flows across the palate with a silky-smooth texture and a pleasing, earthy aftertaste. 497 cases made. • $24 • (07/31/97) • **94**

Zinfandel Sonoma Valley The Shaw Vineyard 1990 • $14 • (12/31/92) • **84**

Zinfandel Sonoma Valley The Shaw Vineyard Century Vines 1993 • $14 • (03/31/96) • **85**

Zinfandel Sonoma Valley The Shaw Vineyard Century Vines 1992 • $14 • (10/15/94) • **74**

Zinfandel Sonoma Valley The Shaw Vineyard Century Vines 1991 • $14 • (06/15/94) • **82**

KYNSI | CALIFORNIA

Chardonnay Santa Ynez Valley Sanford & Benedict Vineyard 1995: Smooth, polished and inviting for its citrusy pear and spice flavors, hinting at honey on the delicate, long finish. Drink now. 140 cases made. • $25 • (03/31/98) • **88**

Pinot Noir Edna Valley 1995: Elegant and spicy, with pretty plum-, wild berry- and cherry-laced flavors that turn supple and polished on the finish. Mild tannins on the finish make it appealing now through 2000. 400 cases made. • $18 • (03/31/98) • **88**

Syrah San Luis Obispo County 1995: Of medium weight and intensity, with attractive plum, wild berry, sage and light oak shadings. Loses its focus and turns simpler on the finish. Best now. 295 cases made. • $20 • (03/31/98) • **86**

L'ECOLE NO. 41 | WASHINGTON

Apogee Pepper Bridge Vineyard Walla Walla Valley 1995: Ripe in flavor, lean in structure, with lovely floral overtones to the blackberry, currant and vanilla flavors, hinting at peach on the long, supple finish. Best from 1999 through 2005. A blend of 67 percent Cabernet Sauvignon, 33 percent Merlot. 405 cases made. • $30 • (06/15/98) • **89**

Apogee Pepper Bridge Vineyard Walla Walla Valley 1994: Ripe, with distinctive deep-dish blueberry, currant and spicy oak flavors that keep skittering around through the long, mouthfilling finish. Has lots of character packed into an elegant frame. Tannins need until 1999 to 2000 to resolve. A blend of 67 percent Merlot and 33 percent Cabernet Sauvignon. 288 cases made. • $28 • (04/30/97) • **90**

Cabernet Sauvignon Columbia Valley 1995: Ripe and generous, with rich, spicy black cherry and currant flavors on a sleek frame, echoing fruit and spice on the surprisingly delicate finish. Best from 1999 through 2005. 1,344 cases made. • $25 • (05/15/98) • **90**

Key: SS—Spectator Selection CS—Cellar Selection HR—Highly Recommended BB—Best Buy $NA—Price not available Ⓐ—Auction Price (BT)—Barrel Tasting

Dates in parentheses indicate the issues in which the ratings were published.

Cabernet Sauvignon Columbia Valley 1994: Distinctive for its rich flavors and explosive finish, this wine is loaded with personality. Understated up front, it finishes with elegance and lots of currant, spice and chocolate flavors. Delicious now, should improve through 2000. 672 cases made. • $24 • (04/30/97) • **90**
Cabernet Sauvignon Columbia Valley 1993: Has a smooth, supple texture and plenty of berry, tobacco and spice flavors that narrow out on the finish. Drink now. 657 cases made. • $22 • (09/15/96) • **87**
Cabernet Sauvignon Columbia Valley 1992 • $22 • (07/31/95) • **88**
Cabernet Sauvignon Walla Walla Valley Windrow Vineyard 1995: Distinctly floral, with violet and iris overtones to the smooth-textured berry and red currant flavors. Firm in texture. Best from 2001 through 2005. 354 cases made. • $30 • (05/15/98) • **88**
Cabernet Sauvignon Washington 1991 • $19 • (09/30/94) • **87**
Cabernet Sauvignon Washington 1989 • $18 • (05/31/93) • **88**
Chardonnay Washington 1996: Very pretty flavors of peach, vanilla and mineral swirl smoothly through the polished texture. Delicious now. 1,558 cases made. • $20 • (05/15/98) • **87**
Chardonnay Washington 1995: Ripe and supple, offering a lovely mouthful of spicy pear and toast flavors that take their time opening up, getting richer and spicier on the finish. 1,087 cases made. • $20 • (04/30/97) • **88**
Chardonnay Washington 1993 • $16 • (09/30/95) • **88**
Merlot Columbia Valley 1995: This tight package sports all manner of flavors: pretty currant, blackberry, floral, earthy and tobacco notes are packed on a slim frame. Spicy oak nuances weave through it all. Tannins want until 2000. 3,434 cases made. • $24 • (07/31/97) • **88**
Merlot Columbia Valley 1994: Supple and generous, with vanilla-scented plum and blackberry flavors coasting on a sleek framework of fine tannins. Drink now. 2,484 cases made. • $22 • (09/15/96) • **89**
Merlot Columbia Valley 1993 • $19 • (08/31/95) SS • **90**
Merlot Columbia Valley 1992 • $17 • (09/30/94) • **87**
Merlot Walla Walla Valley Seven Hills Vineyard 1995: Dense with delicious berry, plum and spice flavors, it's a lithe wine that delivers plenty of flavor on a lean frame, remaining elegant and generous through the long finish. Best from 2000. 395 cases made. • $30 • (07/31/97) • **91**
Merlot Walla Walla Valley Seven Hills Vineyard 1994: Rich, polished and seductive, folding sweet, spicy notes into the generous layers of currant and chocolate flavors. Marked by oak, but the mouthfull of fruit prevails. Drink now. 288 cases made. • $28 • (09/15/96) • **90**
Merlot Walla Walla Valley Seven Hills Vineyard 1993 • $22 • (09/30/95) • **91**
Merlot Washington 1990 • $17 • (04/15/94) • **83**
Merlot Washington 1989 • $16 • (05/31/93) • **82**
Merlot Washington 1987 • $13 • (11/30/91) • **90**
Sémillon Washington 1996: Crisp in texture, with nice touches of honey and pineapple around the chalky center. Finishes smooth and inviting. Not as fat as previous vintages. Ready now. 1,503 cases made. • $14 • (05/15/98) • **87**
Sémillon Washington 1995: Polished in texture and distinctive in character, with earthy, woodsy notes surrounding a crisp core of citrus and fig flavors. Ready to drink. 1,274 cases made. • $13 • (06/15/97) • **87**
Sémillon Washington 1994: Nice pear, honey and tobacco aromas and flavors have substance, but aren't quite rich enough to match the dense texture. Drinkable now. 1,254 cases made. • $12 • (09/15/96) • **86**
Sémillon Washington Barrel Fermented 1993 • $12 • (08/31/95) • **88**
Sémillon Washington Fries Vineyard Wahluke Slope 1996: Round and polished. A ripe, smooth-textured wine with spicy pineapple flavors that turn a bit woody on the finish. Ready now. 244 cases made. • $22 • (05/15/98) • **85**

L'ECOSSE | CALIFORNIA

Cabernet Franc Napa Valley Cuvée Hommage de Jeanne d'Arc 1995: A touch of earthiness up front paves the way for complex flavors with notes of celery, cherry, leather, anise and cedar. The smooth and polished texture makes it quite drinkable now. 230 cases made. • $22 • (04/30/97) • **87**

LA BOHEME | OREGON

Pinot Noir Willamette Valley 1991 • $25 • (10/31/94) • **86**
Pinot Noir Willamette Valley 1990 • $25 • (02/28/93) • **86**

LA CASA SENA | CALIFORNIA

Chardonnay Santa Clara Valley 1994: Mature and a bit herbal in flavor, hitting some pineapple and pine notes as it reaches the finish. Drink now. 1,194 cases made. • $12 • (04/30/96) • **81**

LA CREMA | CALIFORNIA

Chardonnay California Grand Cuvée 1993 • $20 • (05/31/95) • **85**
Chardonnay California Reserve 1993 • $12 • (05/31/95) • **85**
Chardonnay Sonoma Coast 1995: Remarkable for its creamy peach and pear flavors, it picks up a nice smoke and toast nuance and then keeps the flavors lively through its long, complex finish. • $20 • (06/15/97) • **90**
Chardonnay Sonoma Coast Reserve 1995: Serves up a moderate range of ripe pear- and apple-laced Chardonnay flavors and picks up dashes of spice and mineral on the finish. Shows only a small oak influence; drinks well now. 1,500 cases made. • $26 • (12/15/97) • **88**
Chardonnay Sonoma County 1994: Marked by spicy oak and spicy fruit, with hints of pear and nutmeg coming through. It's solid and finishes with a creamy mouthfeel. • $15 • (03/31/96) • **88**
Chardonnay Sonoma County Sonoma Reserve 1994: Very good. Ripe and fruity, with an elegant core of pear, honey, spice and apple flavors that linger on the finish. • $23 • (09/15/96) • **87**
Pinot Noir California 1992 • $12 • (02/28/94) • **78**
Pinot Noir California 1991 • $12 • (02/28/94) • **78**
Pinot Noir California 1986 • $12 • (12/31/88) • **89**
Pinot Noir California 1985 • $11 • (09/30/87) • **90**
Pinot Noir California 1984 • $11 • (03/15/87) • **89**
Pinot Noir California Grand Cuvée 1993 • $19 • (03/31/95) • **86**
Pinot Noir California Reserve 1993 • $11 • (03/31/95) • **84**
Pinot Noir California Reserve 1992 • $20 • (02/28/94) • **83**
Pinot Noir California Reserve 1991 • $20 • (02/28/94) • **79**
Pinot Noir California Reserve 1990 • $17 • (02/28/93) • **85**
Pinot Noir California Reserve 1986 • $22 • (05/31/89) • **85**
Pinot Noir California Reserve 1985 • $18 • (12/31/87) • **82**
Pinot Noir Sonoma Coast 1995: Elegant, with an earthy, chewy edge to the wild berry and cherry flavors. Try in 1999. • $21 • (10/15/97) • **87**
Pinot Noir Sonoma Coast Reserve 1995: Offers a nice balance between its ripe blackberry, cola and spicy flavors and ripe but firm tannins. Picks up traces of tea, spice and earthiness on the finish. Try now. 1,500 cases made. • $26 • (12/15/97) • **88**
Pinot Noir Sonoma County 1994 • $17 • (03/31/96) • **88**
Pinot Noir Sonoma County Reserve 1994 • $14 • (02/29/96) • **87**
Zinfandel Sonoma Coast Reserve 1995: Ripe, bright and lively, with grapey cherry, snappy raspberry and wild berry flavors. Finishes with lots of fruit, firm tannins and good length. Drink now. 1,200 cases made. • $24 • (12/15/97) • **87**

LA CROSSE | CALIFORNIA

Cabernet Sauvignon Napa Valley 1993: Simple, with modest cherry and currant flavors, cedary notes. Ready to drink. 2,000 cases made. • $8 • (12/15/96) • **82**
Cabernet Sauvignon Napa Valley 1991 • $7 • (02/28/95) • **77**
Cabernet Sauvignon Napa Valley 1989 • $6 • (12/15/92) • **77**
Chardonnay Napa Valley 1993 • $7 • (04/30/95) • **83**
Merlot Napa Valley 1994: A sturdy red with modest flavors and rough tannins that will need until 1999 to settle down. 5,000 cases made. • $9 • (07/31/96) • **81**
Merlot Napa Valley 1993 • $8 • (05/15/95) • **85**

LA FERRONNIERE | CALIFORNIA

Cabernet Sauvignon Napa Valley 1985 • $14 • (01/31/90) • **80**

LA GARZA | OREGON

Cabernet Sauvignon Umpqua Valley 1995: Has earthy, smoky flavors up front, but the bright raspberry and red currant flavors come through on the finish of this crisp-style red. Fine-grained tannins want until 2000 or so. 400 cases made. • $15 • (05/15/98) • **85**
Cabernet Sauvignon Umpqua Valley Reserve 1993: A chunky red with a gamy edge to the black cherry flavors, and chewy tannins that want until 2000 to settle down. 244 cases made. • $25 • (05/15/98) • **84**
Chardonnay Oregon 1995: Earthy, smoky flavors dominate this lean, crisp wine. 285 cases made. • $10 • (05/15/98) • **80**
Riesling Umpqua Valley Bradley Vineyards Dry 1996: A simple, pretty, dry white with floral and green apple flavors. Drink now. 204 cases made. • $8 • (05/15/98) • **82**

LA JOTA | CALIFORNIA

Cabernet Franc Howell Mountain 1995: Ruggedly tannic and earthy, with a coarse texture, a hint of prune and a stalky tobacco, oak and currant flavor spectrum. 225 cases made. • $36 • (03/31/98) • **84**
Cabernet Franc Howell Mountain 1994: Has an intriguing spicy edge to the currant, cedar, anise and leathery tree bark flavors, that gives way to hints of sassafras and mineral. Drink now for all its exotic flavors. 240 cases made. • $32 • (04/30/97) • **88**
Cabernet Franc Howell Mountain 1993 • $28 • (04/30/96) • **88**
Cabernet Franc Howell Mountain 1992 • $28 • (07/31/95) • **89**
Cabernet Franc Howell Mountain 1991 • $28 • (12/31/94) • **84**
Cabernet Franc Howell Mountain 1990 • $28 • (11/15/93) • **80**
Cabernet Franc Howell Mountain 1988 • $28 • (08/31/91) • **89**
Cabernet Franc Howell Mountain 1986 • $25 • (10/15/89) • **81**
Cabernet Sauvignon Howell Mountain 1997: Tightly wound, quite tannic and earthy, but the core of fruit is dense and chewy. Will need a long, long time to come around, but has the raw ingredients. 1,800 cases made. • $48 • (07/31/98) (BT) • **90-94**
Cabernet Sauvignon Howell Mountain 1990 • $28 • (11/15/93) • **85**
Cabernet Sauvignon Howell Mountain 1989 • $29 • (11/15/92) • **78**
Cabernet Sauvignon Howell Mountain 1988 • $17 Ⓐ • (08/31/91) • **85**
Cabernet Sauvignon Howell Mountain 1987 • $31 Ⓐ • (07/31/90) SS • **95**
Cabernet Sauvignon Howell Mountain 1986 • $38 Ⓐ • (10/15/89) • **85**
Cabernet Sauvignon Howell Mountain 1985 • $18 • (11/15/88) • **91**
Cabernet Sauvignon Howell Mountain 1984 • $15 • (11/15/87) • **84**
Cabernet Sauvignon Howell Mountain 1983 • $15 • (03/31/87) • **90**
Cabernet Sauvignon Howell Mountain Selection 1995: Tight, tannic and leathery, with a tobacco and cedar edge to the core of earthy currant. Well balanced and in need of short-term cellaring. Best from 2000 through 2008. Tasted twice, with consistent notes. 1,270 cases made. • $28 • (06/30/98) • **86**
Cabernet Sauvignon Howell Mountain Selection 1994: Rich and exotic, with layers of ripe currant, plum, anise, cedar and mineral flavors that pick up traces of tobacco and toast on the finish. The texture is smooth and supple for a young Howell Mountain. Drinkable now or cellar it into 2000. 1,050 cases made. • $28 • (05/15/97) • **90**
Cabernet Sauvignon Howell Mountain Selection 1993: Tight and a touch earthy, sporting cedar, currant, cherry and pepper notes. Drink now. 1,240 cases made. • $24 • (04/30/96) • **87**
Cabernet Sauvignon Howell Mountain Selection 1992 • $18 • (06/15/95) • **88**
Cabernet Sauvignon Howell Mountain Selection 1991 • $NA • (06/15/94) • **79**
Cabernet Sauvignon Howell Mountain 15th Anniversary Release 1996: Tame for a Howell Mountain barrel-sample, with beautiful plum, currant, earth, mineral and anise notes. Tannins are supple. 1,200 cases made. • $48 • (06/15/97) (BT) • **90-94**
Cabernet Sauvignon Howell Mountain 14th Anniversary Release 1995: A dark, intense wine with a solid core of currant-, black cherry-, and anise-laced Cabernet flavors, but also a strong dose of cedary oak. Give it some time to come together. Best from 2002 through 2010. 930 cases made. • $48 • (06/30/98) • **89**
Cabernet Sauvignon Howell Mountain 13th Anniversary Release 1994: Bold, rich and concentrated, this wine packs in lots of thick, complex, concentrated currant, black cherry, anise and cedar flavors that fan out on the finish. This is a big, ripe style with well-proportioned fruit, oak and tannins. Best to cellar into 2002. 1,430 cases made. • $46 • (04/30/97) • **93**
Cabernet Sauvignon Howell Mountain 12th Anniversary Release 1993: A well-oaked style, featuring lots of vanilla and toasty, smoky oak. Underneath, the currant, cherry and mineral flavors are full-blown, finishing in strong wood and plush tannins. Can stand aging into 1999—maybe longer. 1,450 cases made. • $42 • (04/30/96) • **91**
Cabernet Sauvignon Howell Mountain 11th Anniversary Release 1992: Ripe and intense, rich and complex, with layers of currant, anise, mineral and cedary oak flavors. Finishes with a firm, dry tannic aftertaste that shows some polish. Needs cellaring into 2000 or so. 1,000 cases made. • $42 • (01/01/97) • **89**
Cabernet Sauvignon Howell Mountain 10th Anniversary Release 1991 • $38 • (06/15/94) CS • **90**
Cabernet Sauvignon Napa Valley Little J NV • $9 • (10/15/92) • **81**

Key: SS—Spectator Selection CS—Cellar Selection HR—Highly Recommended BB—Best Buy $NA—Price not available Ⓐ—Auction Price (BT)—Barrel Tasting
Dates in parentheses indicate the issues in which the ratings were published.

Petite Sirah Howell Mountain 1995: A ruggedly tannic style with floral plum and berry notes, but at this stage they're fairly buried beneath the tannins. Try after 1999 or 2000. 300 cases made. • $28 • (04/30/98) • **85**
Petite Sirah Howell Mountain 1994: Dense, earthy, and ruggedly tannic, but once you push past the tannins there's a core of spicy currant and peppery fruit that's quite appealing. Drink from 1999 to 2005. 360 cases made. • $24 • (01/01/97) • **88**
Petite Sirah Howell Mountain 1992 • $18 • (02/28/95) • **87**
Viognier Howell Mountain Barrel Fermented 1996: Distinctively spicy with litchi nut, hazelnut, melon, spice, fig and pear. A complex and sophisticated wine that's supple and balanced. 250 cases made. • $24 • (04/30/98) • **88**
Viognier Howell Mountain Barrel Fermented 1995: Pretty, with ripe, spicy peach, pear and nectarine flavors that turn elegant and linger; has lively fruit and vanilla notes on the aftertaste. 300 cases made. • $25 • (01/01/97) • **90**
Viognier Howell Mountain Cold Fermented 1995: Shows lots of spice, with pretty pear, nectarine and melon notes, picking up a trace of bitterness on the finish. Still, quite complete. 300 cases made. • $24 • (01/01/97) • **88**
Viognier Howell Mountain Cold Fermented 1993 • $24 • (01/31/95) • **87**
Viognier Howell Mountain Sweet 1993 • $36 • (04/30/95) • **85**
Viornier Howell Mountain Barrel Fermented 1993 • $24 • (01/31/95) • **80**
Zinfandel Howell Mountain 1987 • $12 • (10/31/89) • **83**
Zinfandel Howell Mountain 1986 • $10 • (10/31/88) • **89**
Zinfandel Howell Mountain 1985 • $10 • (04/30/88) • **85**
Zinfandel Howell Mountain 1984 • $10 • (11/15/87) • **88**

LA PETITE VIGNE | CALIFORNIA

Chenin Blanc Napa Valley 1993 • $14 • (07/31/94) • **88**

LA ROUGETTE | CALIFORNIA

Pinot Noir Carneros Truchard Vineyard 1992 • $11 • (03/31/95) • **86**

LA SIRENA | CALIFORNIA

Sangiovese Napa Valley 1994: Young and vibrant, with a dry edge to the cherry and plum flavors. The texture is round and smooth right up to the finish when the tannins become more evident. 250 cases made. • $24 • (07/31/96) • **88**

LA VIEILLE MONTAGNE | CALIFORNIA

Cabernet Sauvignon Napa Valley 1988 • $15 • (11/15/92) • **81**
Cabernet Sauvignon Napa Valley 1987 • $14 • (06/15/91) • **81**
Cabernet Sauvignon Napa Valley 1986 • $14 • (06/30/90) • **84**

LAETITIA | CALIFORNIA

Brut San Luis Obispo County Sélect NV: Toasty hazelnut flavors lead the way here, with a slightly sweet, earth and herb finish. Lacks complexity, but remains enjoyable. 1,000 cases made. • $15 • (11/30/97) • **84**
Chardonnay San Luis Obispo County Laetitia Vineyard 1996: A juicy mouthful of Chardonnay, with ripe pear, citrus, light toasty oak and melon flavors that are smooth and creamy, finishing with a light hazelnut aftertaste. Best now through 2002. 215 cases made. • $25 • (06/30/98) • **91**
Chardonnay San Luis Obispo County Laetitia Vineyard 1995: A shade coarse, with a oaky edge, the core of Chardonnay flavor is built around pear, spice, apricot and fig notes that are rich and long on the finish. 400 cases made. • $25 • (10/15/97) • **90**
Chardonnay San Luis Obispo County Reserve 1996: Starts out with a slight herbal edge before working into more mainstream Chardonnay flavors, showing ripe pear, melon and cedary oak. Well balanced. Drink now through 2001. 440 cases made. • $17 • (06/30/98) • **88**
Chardonnay San Luis Obispo County Reserve 1995: Ripe, with lots of complex flavors built around the core of creamy pear, toast and spicy qualities. Comes up a bit short on the finish. 1,500 cases made. • $17 • (12/15/97) • **86**
Crémant de Noirs San Luis Obispo County NV: Orange peel and lemon notes lead the way through a toasty, clean finish. Though not terribly complex, the blend is refreshing. 300 cases made. • $15 • (11/30/97) • **86**
Pinot Blanc San Luis Obispo County La Colline Vineyard 1995: Marked by tart, flinty, citrus, green pear and apple notes. A touch of spicy, toasty oak works its way into the finish, adding dimension. 115 cases made. • $25 • (04/30/98) • **85**

Pinot Blanc San Luis Obispo County Reserve 1995: A well-oaked Pinot Blanc, starting to show some age. Bright in acidity, yet creamy. Somewhat lacking in varietal distinction, however. 400 cases made. • $17 • (05/15/98) • **84**
Pinot Noir San Luis Obispo County Laetitia Vineyard 1995: Dense and chewy, this young, tannic wine will need cellaring into 1999 to show its best, but the core of mineral and black cherry is impressive. 250 cases made. • $25 • (10/15/97) • **88**
Pinot Noir San Luis Obispo County Reserve 1995: Shows off strong, earthy tannins but there's enough fruit concentration behind to merit attention, as the plum and cherry flavors are ripe and tasty. Drink now. 650 cases made. • $19 • (10/15/97) • **87**
Rosé San Luis Obispo County Rosé Elégance 1993: Straight down the middle, with pleasant spice, black cherry and light toast qualities. Good length on the finish. Ready now. 300 cases made. • $25 • (11/30/97) • **87**
Sparkling San Luis Obispo County Elégance 1992: Displaying a mature, dark-straw color and a yeasty nose, this is rather heavy in style, ripe and buttery, but with a vaguely bitter edge. Still, enjoyable. 400 cases made. • $23 • (11/30/97) • **86**

LAKE SONOMA | CALIFORNIA

Chardonnay Russian River Valley 1996: Rich and juicy, with ripe, buttery flavors and notes of toast, fig and Asian pear. Focused and refreshing, with a long, full finish. 1,200 cases made. • $15 • (07/31/98) • **86**
Cinsault Dry Creek Valley Vintner's Reserve 1991 • $16 • (02/15/93) • **73**
Merlot Dry Creek Valley Yoakim Bridge Ranch 1991 • $14 • (03/31/93) • **83**
Merlot Dry Creek Valley Yoakim Bridge Ranch 1990 • $14 • (05/31/92) • **86**
Zinfandel Dry Creek Valley 1995: Crisp acidity and a bright cherry flavor are the hallmarks of this wine. Smoke, licorice and herb notes linger on the finish. Showing a hint of age, however. Drink now. 870 cases made. • $17 • (07/31/98) • **85**
Zinfandel Dry Creek Valley 1990 • $10 • (09/30/93) • **72**
Zinfandel Dry Creek Valley 1989 • $9 • (10/15/92) • **84**

LAKESPRING | CALIFORNIA

Cabernet Sauvignon Napa Valley 1993: Medium-bodied, with a modest band of currant, cedar and spicy flavors. • $12 • (03/31/96) • **80**
Cabernet Sauvignon Napa Valley 1990 • $10 • (05/15/94) • **87**
Cabernet Sauvignon Napa Valley 1987 • $17 • (10/15/91) • **84**
Cabernet Sauvignon Napa Valley 1985 • $12 • (07/15/88) • **92**
Cabernet Sauvignon Napa Valley 1983 • $11 • (12/15/86) • **77**
Cabernet Sauvignon Napa Valley 1981 • $11 • (09/16/84) • **87**
Cabernet Sauvignon Napa Valley Reserve Selection 1988 • $18 • (11/15/92) • **74**
Cabernet Sauvignon Napa Valley Reserve Selection 1984 • $15 • (10/31/88) SS • **92**
Cabernet Sauvignon Napa Valley Vintage Selection 1982 • $14 • (12/15/86) • **94**
Chardonnay California 1995: Bright and flavorful, offering a juicy mouthful of pear, quince and spice flavors that linger nicely. Ready now. 9,000 cases made. • $11 • (12/31/96) • **87**
Chardonnay Napa Valley 1994: Complex, appealing array of fig, toast, spice and pear flavors. Strikes a nice balance between its ripe fruit and toasty oak. Ready now. • $12 • (02/29/96) • **88**
Elixia Late Harvest Napa Valley 1989 • $12/375ml • (03/01/92) • **75**
Merlot Napa Valley 1994 • $14 • (03/31/96) • **78**
Merlot Napa Valley 1987 • $14 • (06/15/90) • **85**
Merlot Napa Valley 1986 • $14 • (03/31/89) • **79**
Merlot Napa Valley 1985 • $15 • (03/31/88) SS • **91**
Merlot Napa Valley 1984 • $12 • (05/15/87) • **88**
Merlot Napa Valley 1983 • $11 • (05/16/86) • **87**
Merlot Napa Valley 1982 • $10 • (10/01/85) • **78**
Merlot Napa Valley Yount Mill Vineyard 1990 • $14 • (07/15/93) • **88**
Merlot Napa Valley Yount Mill Vineyard 1988 • $15 • (02/29/92) • **85**
Sauvignon Blanc California 1995: Crisp, light and pleasant at first, but an acidic finish robs it of its charm. • $10 • (12/15/96) • **79**
Sauvignon Blanc Napa Valley Yount Mill Vineyard 1993 • $8 • (08/31/94) • **83**

LAKEWOOD | CALIFORNIA

Chevriot Clear Lake 1993 • $12 • (08/31/95) • **86**
Finger Lakes Glaciovinum Delaware Ice Wine 1993 • $9 • (04/15/95) • **81**
Riesling Finger Lakes 1995: Ripe, with plenty of apple, peach and mineral flavors, framed by notes of spice. Clean and well made. • $9 • (01/31/97) • **85**
Sauvignon Blanc Clear Lake 1994 • $10 • (12/31/95) • **87**
Sauvignon Blanc Clear Lake 1993 • $9 • (12/15/94) • **84**
Sémillon Clear Lake 1993 • $12 • (12/15/94) • **85**

LAMBERT BRIDGE | CALIFORNIA

Cabernet Sauvignon Dry Creek Valley 1994: Complex and concentrated, featuring a core of supple plum, currant and wild berry flavors that finish with spicy, toasty oak accents. 675 cases made. • $20 • (11/15/97) • **89**
Cabernet Sauvignon Dry Creek Valley Crane Creek 1989 • $28 • (11/15/92) • **80**
Cabernet Sauvignon Sonoma County 1993: Clean and correct, with ripe plum, spice and berry notes, finishing with mild oak and tannins. Well proportioned. 420 cases made. • $15 • (12/15/95) • **86**
Cabernet Sauvignon Sonoma County 1992 • $15 • (12/15/95) • **87**
Cabernet Sauvignon Sonoma County 1991 • $14 • (10/15/94) • **84**
Cabernet Sauvignon Sonoma County 1984 • $10 • (04/15/87) • **80**
Cabernet Sauvignon Sonoma County 1981 • $12 • (01/01/85) • **75**
Chardonnay Sonoma County 1996: Complete and harmonious, with ripe pear, hazelnut, light oak and spicy apple flavors that are supple and focused, long and lingering. Drink now through 2000. 3,270 cases made. • $17 • (07/31/98) • **88**
Chardonnay Sonoma County 1995: Ripe, smooth and elegant, with a complex core of spicy pear, apple, melon and smoky oak flavors, especially pleasing on the finish, where the flavors gain depth and length. 3,000 cases made. • $16 • (06/15/97) • **90**
Chardonnay Sonoma County 1994: Nicely ripe pear, spicy apple and oak flavors blend elegantly. A complex aftertaste defines the finish. 3,000 cases made. • $15 • (07/31/96) • **87**
Chardonnay Sonoma County Barrel Fermented 1993 • $13 • (04/15/95) • **86**
Crane Creek Cuvée Dry Creek Valley 1994: Firm, dark and intense. Features ripe, spicy, juicy plum, black cherry and currant flavors framed by lightly toasty oak. Altogether complex and supple, elegant and inviting, with a long, lively finish. Ready now through 2004. 450 cases made. • $28 • (11/15/97) • **91**
Fumé Blanc Dry Creek Valley 1995: A bright, fresh mouthful, blending pear and spice flavors. Very nice. 1,000 cases made. • $9 • (07/31/96) • **85**
Fumé Blanc Sonoma County 1993 • $8 • (02/28/95) • **81**
Merlot Dry Creek Valley 1994: Young and tight, with a spicy, minty accent to its firm currant and herb flavors. Finishes with dry tannins. Drinkable now. 3,734 cases made. • $18 • (12/15/96) • **86**
Merlot Dry Creek Valley Tzabaco Vineyard 1994: Complex with its mint and chocolate notes, the currant and cherry flavors come through on the finish. Drinkable now through 2002. 307 cases made. • $24 • (06/30/97) • **88**
Merlot Sonoma County 1995: Lean and trim, with spicy cherry, berry and dusty, cedary oak. Turns supple at midpalate, but then shortens up on the finish. Best now to 2002. 6,560 cases made. • $20 • (05/15/98) • **85**
Merlot Sonoma County 1993 • $15 • (12/15/95) • **86**
Merlot Sonoma County 1992 • $14 • (09/15/94) • **87**
Merlot Sonoma County 1991 • $14 • (09/15/94) • **79**
Merlot Sonoma County 1982 • $12 • (12/16/84) • **79**
Merlot Sonoma County Library Reserve 1989 • $24 • (11/30/92) • **85**
Pinot Noir Oregon Muirfield Vineyards 1993 • $16 • (02/28/95) • **82**
Sauvignon Blanc Dry Creek Valley 1996: Green apple, cloves and lemon-lime come to mind with this refreshing, medium-bodied wine. A bit dry on the finish, but a good effort. 885 cases made. • $12 • (06/30/97) • **87**
Zinfandel Dry Creek Valley 1996: Hits most of the right notes, with an attractive, supple core of plum- and berry-laced flavors that is smooth and polished. Drink now through 2002. A blend of 12 percent Syrah, 4 percent Petite Sirah, 2 percent Carignane. 418 cases made. • $20 • (05/31/98) • **87**
Zinfandel Dry Creek Valley 1995: Supple and elegant, with a nice core of ripe cherry, plum and raspberry flavors that remain focused and intense through the finish. 563 cases made. • $15 • (03/31/97) • **90**
Zinfandel Dry Creek Valley 1994: Supple and fruity, with plum and cherry notes of moderate depth and complexity. Finishes with crisp tannins, on the simple side. • $13 • (11/15/96) • **85**
Zinfandel Dry Creek Valley 1992 • $11 • (10/15/94) • **84**

LAMBORN FAMILY | CALIFORNIA

Zinfandel Howell Mountain 1990 • $12 • (10/15/92) • **80**
Zinfandel Howell Mountain 1988 • $11 • (02/15/91) • **89**
Zinfandel Howell Mountain 1987 • $10 • (03/15/90) • **84**

Zinfandel Howell Mountain The French Connection 1995: Zesty, with spicy, peppery flavors and a supple, complex texture that lets the ripe raspberry, wild berry and cherry notes flow smoothly and evenly. 1,500 cases made. • $19 • (09/15/97) • **90**

Zinfandel Howell Mountain The French Connection Unfiltered 1995: Openly spicy and peppery, with a tight, crisp band of wild berry, finishing with firm, earthy tannins. Drink now through 2002. 200 cases made. • $22 • (06/15/98) • **85**

Zinfandel Howell Mountain The Hang Time Vintage 1993: Captures the essence of Howell Mountain Zin with its spicy, earthy, wild berry flavors. Manages to tame the tannins too, making it elegant and tasty to drink now. 2,150 cases made. • $15 • (11/30/96) • **89**

Zinfandel Howell Mountain The Phoenix Vintage 1991 • $12 • (09/30/93) • **82**

Zinfandel Howell Mountain The Queen's Vintage 1994: Firm, intense and tannic, with classic Zin flavors. The wild berry, raspberry and fresh cracked pepper notes fold together nicely, though the tannins stick out a bit on the finish. 1,900 cases made. • $17 • (02/28/97) • **88**

LAMOREAUX LANDING | NEW YORK

Blanc de Noirs Finger Lakes 1990 • $15 • (12/31/94) • **83**

Brut Finger Lakes 1990 • $15 • (12/31/94) • **80**

Chardonnay Finger Lakes 1993 • $12 • (10/15/95) • **85**

Pinot Noir Finger Lakes 1993 • $12 • (09/30/95) • **82**

Riesling Finger Lakes Dry 1995: An average-quality Riesling with modest, grapey flavors and a rather simple structure. Could be more lively. 619 cases made. • $10 • (10/31/96) • **77**

Riesling Finger Lakes Dry 1994 • $8 • (01/31/96) • **83**

Riesling Finger Lakes Semi-Dry 1995: An off-dry wine, with good body and peach flavors. A bit one-dimensional, but appealing. 758 cases made. • $10 • (01/31/97) • **83**

Riesling Finger Lakes Semi-Dry 1994 • $8 • (01/31/96) • **83**

Riesling Finger Lakes Semi-Dry 1993 • $8 • (12/15/94) • **82**

LANDMARK | CALIFORNIA

Chardonnay Alexander Valley Damaris Reserve 1993 • $19 • (12/31/94) HR • **90**

Chardonnay Russian River Valley Lorenzo 1996: A tremendous Chardonnay from Landmark. Delicious, ripe, rich, full-bodied and loaded with complex pear, fig, citrus and honey notes, finishing with a broad, rich aftertaste. Drink now through 2002. 400 cases made. • $35 • (06/30/98) • **93**

Chardonnay Sonoma County Damaris Reserve 1996: Tasty Chardonnay. Ripe, rich and complex, with layers of pear, vanilla, honey and citrus, and a creamy, smooth texture. Long and sophisticated on the finish. Drink now through 2002. 2,500 cases made. • $32 • (06/30/98) • **92**

Chardonnay Sonoma County Damaris Reserve 1994: Rich and creamy, with a good dose of toasty, buttery oak and just the right amount of spicy pear and honey-laced Chardonnay. Finishes with a complex encore of fruit and smoky oak. 1,400 cases made. • $23 • (03/31/96) • **89**

Chardonnay Sonoma County Overlook 1996: A very spicy, rich, flavorful and complex Chardonnay, with concentrated pear, fig, apple, melon and spice flavors that unfold in tiers. Finishes with a long, full, complex aftertaste that keeps pumping out the intense fruit flavors and toasty oak notes. 12,000 cases made. • $21 • (03/31/98) SS • **92**

Chardonnay Sonoma County Overlook 1995: A remarkably elegant California Chardonnay that's overflowing with ripe fruit flavors, notes of pear and apple, spice and cedar nuances. Good length on the finish, which echoes the complex flavors. 15,000 cases made. • $18 • (03/31/97) SS • **91**

Chardonnay Sonoma County Overlook 1994: A fabulous California Chardonnay. Well oaked, rich and creamy, with a pretty core of melon, fig, honey and pear flavors that hold on through the finish. This builds on the palate, offering more complexity as it goes. 17,000 cases made. • $16 • (03/31/96) SS • **91**

Chardonnay Sonoma County Overlook 1993 • $14 • (02/28/95) • **88**

Chardonnay Sonoma Valley Damaris Reserve 1995: This California Chardonnay is highlighted by a smooth, polished texture that lets the complex array of buttery pear, honey, butterscotch and spice flavors flow on and on. Delicious now. 1,400 cases made. • $28 • (03/31/97) HR • **92**

Key: SS—Spectator Selection CS—Cellar Selection HR—Highly Recommended BB—Best Buy $NA—Price not available Ⓐ—Auction Price (BT)—Barrel Tasting
Dates in parentheses indicate the issues in which the ratings were published.

Pinot Noir Sonoma County 1994: Ripe, intense and complex. The rich plum, cherry and currant flavors have peppery and floral overtones. Succeeds with its supple texture, firm tannins and mushroom-edged finish. 500 cases made. • $22 • (07/31/96) • **90**

Pinot Noir Sonoma County Grand Detour 1995: Smooth and silky, with a lovely texture and a pretty array of black cherry, anise, wild berry, plum and cedar notes. Finishes with a long, full, complex aftertaste and elegant tannins. Tasted twice, with consistent notes. 900 cases made. • $30 • (09/15/97) • **90**

LANG | CALIFORNIA

Zinfandel El Dorado Twin Rivers Vineyards 1992 • $6 • (09/15/95) • **87**

LANG & REED | CALIFORNIA

Cabernet Franc Napa Valley 1996: Ripe, rich and lush, with generous, currant, herb, sage, cedar and spice flavors. Impressive for its supple texture and mild, tender tannins. Best now to 2002. 400 cases made. • $18 • (03/31/98) • **89**

Cabernet Franc Napa Valley 1993: Smooth, rich and supple, with pleasant currant, mineral, cedar, herb, tar and spice flavors, finishing with round, fleshy tannins and good length. Drink now through 2000 to 2002. 125 cases made. • $20 • (03/31/98) • **88**

LANGE | OREGON

Chardonnay Willamette Valley Reserve 1996: A bit on the tart side, with flavors centering on green apple. Still very youthful, lively and crisp. Drink now. 400 cases made. • $20 • (05/15/98) • **85**

Chardonnay Willamette Valley Reserve 1995: Light in texture, with fresh, citrusy flavors that linger nicely on the finish, echoing lime and vanilla. 350 cases made. • $16 • (02/28/97) • **86**

Chardonnay Willamette Valley Reserve 1994: Light, bright, fruity and racy enough to show its lemony apple flavors to advantage on the solid finish. Ready now. 350 cases made. • $20 • (01/31/96) • **85**

Pinot Gris Willamette Valley 1996: Peach and melon flavors are exuberant enough to make up for the slightly raw texture. Almond notes add interest to the finish. Ready now. 1,700 cases made. • $12 • (05/15/98) • **84**

Pinot Gris Willamette Valley 1995: Fresh and generous with its cantaloupe, honey and spicy walnut flavors that fold together appealingly on the vibrant finish. 600 cases made. • $16 • (02/28/97) • **87**

Pinot Gris Willamette Valley Reserve 1994 • $14 • (01/31/96) • **83**

Pinot Gris Willamette Valley Yamhill Vineyards Reserve 1996: Soft, light and supple, pretty for its melon and apple flavors, finishing with delicacy. Ready now. 500 cases made. • $16 • (05/15/98) • **86**

Pinot Noir Willamette Valley 1994: On the light side, with modest currant and plum flavors shaded by a touch of tobacco. Drinkable now. 350 cases made. • $18 • (02/28/97) • **85**

Pinot Noir Willamette Valley 1993 • $35 • (01/31/96) • **89**

Pinot Noir Willamette Valley 1992 • $14 • (11/30/94) • **83**

Pinot Noir Willamette Valley Eola Hills 1990 • $20 • (02/28/93) • **84**

Pinot Noir Willamette Valley Estate 1995: Light in color and flavor, with nice cherry and vanilla flavors hiding behind a layer of chewy tannins and raw acidity. Drink now. 350 cases made. • $40 • (05/15/98) • **83**

Pinot Noir Willamette Valley Reserve 1995: Very light color, not much to the nose, but the flavors are soft and pretty, offering delicate plum and vanilla notes. Ready now. 300 cases made. • $40 • (05/15/98) • **82**

Pinot Noir Willamette Valley Reserve 1994: A firm, chewy, austere wine with earthy, spicy flavors that pick up nice hints of plum and chocolate on the long finish. Give it until 2000. 300 cases made. • $40 • (02/28/97) • **88**

Pinot Noir Willamette Valley Reserve 1992 • $30 • (11/30/94) • **86**

Pinot Noir Willamette Valley Reserve 1991 • $30 • (03/15/94) • **79**

Pinot Noir Willamette Valley Reserve 1990 • $25 • (02/28/93) • **88**

LAS VINAS | CALIFORNIA

Cabernet Sauvignon California Private Reserve 1988 • $6 • (10/31/92) • **78**

LATAH CREEK | WASHINGTON

Cabernet Sauvignon Washington 1993: Firm in texture, with soft plum and currant flavors that linger on the finish. Drinkable now. 800 cases made. • $12 • (07/31/95) • **85**

Cabernet Sauvignon Washington 1986 • $13 • (10/15/88) • **80**

Cabernet Sauvignon Washington Limited Bottling 1992 • $12 • (09/30/94) • **77**

Cabernet Sauvignon Washington Limited Bottling 1990 • $12 • (06/15/93) • **85**

Cabernet Sauvignon Washington Limited Bottling 1988 • $13 • (10/15/91) • **91**

Cabernet Sauvignon Washington Limited Bottling 1987 • $13 • (10/15/89) • **83**

Cabernet Sauvignon Washington Reserve 1991: Very firm and chewy, but there's a rich vein of ripe blackberry and plum flavors in the tannins. Give until 2000 to 2002 for the flavors to blossom. 200 cases made. • $20 • (09/15/96) • **88**

Cabernet Sauvignon Washington Wahluke Slope Vineyards 1995: Gamy, earthy, slightly sour flavors rob this wine of its charm. 600 cases made. • $13 • (09/30/97) • **73**

Chardonnay Washington 1996: Crisp and bright, brimming with citrus, green apple and pear flavors, layered with nutmeg and vanilla grace notes that keep peeking through the long finish. Refreshing for its seductive fruit character. 1,700 cases made. • $11 • (09/30/97) • **89**

Chardonnay Washington 1995: Polished, smooth and generous with vanilla and pear flavors and lots of oaky, spicy notes on the finish. 2,000 cases made. • $10 • (09/15/96) • **85**

Chardonnay Washington 1993 • $10 • (04/30/95) BB • **88**

Chardonnay Washington Feather 1993 • $7 • (09/30/94) • **82**

Chardonnay Washington Reserve 1996: Bright and refreshing with its jazzy nectarine and spice flavors that linger on the generous finish. Not a typically woody Reserve. Ready now. 600 cases made. • $16 • (09/15/97) • **88**

Chenin Blanc Washington 1994 • $6 • (09/30/95) • **83**

Gewürztraminer Washington 1993 • $6 • (09/30/94) • **73**

Johannisberg Riesling Washington 1996: Sweet and soft, with a peppery, slightly bitter edge to the floral and citrus flavors. Drink now. 1,200 cases made. • $7 • (10/15/97) • **85**

Johannisberg Riesling Washington 1994 • $6 • (09/30/95) • **80**

Lemberger Washington 1995: A bright, peppery, zingy wine with generous blackberry and spice flavors. Ready now. 600 cases made. • $9 • (09/15/97) • **86**

Lemberger Washington 1994: Ripe and peppery, like Syrah, a chewy wine with concentrated berry and spice flavors. Drink now. 600 cases made. • $8 • (09/15/96) • **87**

Lemberger Washington 1992 • $8 • (12/31/93) • **80**

Lemberger Washington 1991 • $8 • (04/30/93) • **82**

Lemberger Washington 1990 • $8 • (01/31/92) • **85**

Merlot Washington 1993 • $12 • (09/30/95) • **85**

Merlot Washington 1986 • $10 • (05/31/88) • **89**

Merlot Washington Limited Bottling 1992 • $12 • (12/31/93) • **82**

Merlot Washington Limited Bottling 1991 • $12 • (05/31/93) • **87**

Merlot Washington Limited Bottling 1989 • $11 • (09/30/91) HR • **91**

Merlot Washington Limited Bottling 1987 • $10 • (10/15/89) • **90**

Merlot Washington Wahluke Slope Vineyards 1995: Firm, focused and flavorful, showing a sharp beam of raspberry and currant flavor overlaid with a spicy, pickle-barrel, oak character. Try now. 1,500 cases made. • $14 • (09/15/97) • **85**

Muscat Canelli Washington 1996: Lightly sweet, spicy and refreshing for its melon and litchi flavors that linger on the gentle finish. 700 cases made. • $8 • (10/15/97) • **85**

Muscat Canelli Washington 1995: Simple, and balanced on the sweet-side with a floral character and modest fruit flavors. 600 cases made. • $7 • (09/30/96) • **81**

Muscat Canelli Washington 1994 • $6 • (09/30/95) • **80**

Muscat Canelli Washington 1993 • $6 • (09/30/94) • **79**

Riesling Washington 1995: A lovely touch of honey adds depth to the sweet apricot and apple flavors, but the fruit medley narrows a bit on the finish. 800 cases made. • $6 • (09/15/96) • **84**

Sauvignon Blanc Washington 1995: Lacks liveliness and charm, finishing with more mineral and earthy notes than fruit flavors. 500 cases made. • $8 • (09/15/96) • **78**

Sauvignon Blanc Washington 1994 • $8 • (09/15/95) • **87**

LAUREL ESTATE | CALIFORNIA

Cabernet Sauvignon North Coast 1989 • $8 • (11/15/92) • **77**

LAUREL GLEN | CALIFORNIA

Cabernet Sauvignon Sonoma Mountain 1997: Tight, lean, even a bit tart, but the concentration is there, focused on currant and blackberry. • $NA • (07/31/98) (BT) • **90-94**

Cabernet Sauvignon Sonoma Mountain 1996: Marked by inky color and dense, rich, sharply focused fruit, with loads of juicy currant and black cherry flavors. Could be a stunner. • $NA • (06/15/97) (BT) • **90-94**

Cabernet Sauvignon Sonoma Mountain 1994: Tight, lean, firm and tannic. Shows a green, stalky edge to the moderately ripe cherry and currant flavors, and is ruggedly tannic with crisp acidity; best cellared into 2000. Tasted twice with consistent notes. 1,829 cases made. • $35 • (08/31/97) • **86**

Cabernet Sauvignon Sonoma Mountain 1993: Firm and intense, with chewy tannins and a slight, green, tealike accent to the cherry and currant flavors. Finishes with a hard edge. Best to cellar a few years to soften. Tasted twice, with consistent notes. 2,827 cases made. • $39 Ⓐ • (02/28/97) • **85**

Cabernet Sauvignon Sonoma Mountain 1992 • $33 • (12/15/95) • **85**

Cabernet Sauvignon Sonoma Mountain 1991 • $42 Ⓐ • (11/15/94) • **89**

Cabernet Sauvignon Sonoma Mountain 1990 • $22 Ⓐ • (11/15/93) • **89**

Cabernet Sauvignon Sonoma Mountain 1989 • $34 • (08/31/92) • **88**

Cabernet Sauvignon Sonoma Mountain 1988 • $29 Ⓐ • (05/15/91) CS • **90**

Cabernet Sauvignon Sonoma Mountain 1987: Dark, ripe, intense and concentrated, packed with rich currant, mineral, spice, cedar and berry flavors. While mellowing, it's still quite vibrant and dense. Can go another decade. Tasted from magnum. 50 cases made. • $38 Ⓐ • (12/15/97) • **93**

Cabernet Sauvignon Sonoma Mountain 1986: This still seems on the way up. It's firm and tannic and may dry out, but the currant, cherry and mineral flavors are young and vibrant, turning more complex on the finish where herb and tobacco flavors fold in. Well balanced for drinking now. Tasted from magnum. 3,941 cases made. • $24 Ⓐ • (12/15/96) • **91**

Cabernet Sauvignon Sonoma Mountain 1985 • $46 Ⓐ • (04/30/88) • **91**

Cabernet Sauvignon Sonoma Mountain 1984 • $53 Ⓐ • (04/30/87) • **87**

Cabernet Sauvignon Sonoma Mountain 1982 • $13 • (06/01/86) • **83**

Cabernet Sauvignon Sonoma Mountain 1981 • $13 • (02/16/85) SS • **93**

Cabernet Sauvignon Sonoma Mountain 1978 • $NA • (11/15/92) • **92**

Cabernet Sauvignon Sonoma Mountain Counterpoint 1993: Tightly wound and quite tannic; the cherry and currant flavors struggle to work their way to the forefront and hold on through the finish. This wine needs time to soften. Best after 2000. 1,987 cases made. • $17 • (09/15/96) • **87**

Cabernet Sauvignon Sonoma Mountain Counterpoint 1992 • $16 • (12/15/95) • **88**

Cabernet Sauvignon Sonoma Mountain Counterpoint 1991 • $15 • (11/30/93) SS • **90**

Cabernet Sauvignon Sonoma Mountain Counterpoint 1990 • $15 • (03/15/93) • **87**

Cabernet Sauvignon Sonoma Mountain Counterpoint 1989 • $15 • (01/31/92) • **85**

Cabernet Sauvignon Sonoma Mountain Counterpoint 1988 • $13 • (07/15/91) • **83**

Cabernet Sauvignon Sonoma Mountain Counterpoint 1987 • $13 • (10/31/89) • **94**

Cabernet Sauvignon Sonoma Mountain Counterpoint Cuvée 85-86 NV • $11 • (05/31/88) • **89**

Cabernet Sauvignon Sonoma Mountain Reserve 1990 • $75 • (11/15/93) • **88**

Reds California 1996: A smoky, charry blend of plum and cassis flavors. Somewhat rustic and chunky. Finishes a bit short. Drink now. 25,000 cases made. • $7 • (07/31/98) • **82**

Reds California 1994: A blend of Grenache, Zinfandel, Syrah, Carignane and Malbec. A sturdy, complex red table wine that's quite tasty, and very appealing at this price. 24,000 cases made. • $6 • (10/15/96) BB • **86**

Reds California 1993 • $7 • (11/30/95) BB • **87**

LAUREL RIDGE | OREGON

Brut Oregon 1991: A bright mouthful of lively pear, apple and vanilla flavor that echoes prettily on the soft finish. Flavorful and generous in style. 450 cases made. • $15 • (03/31/98) • **87**

Pinot Noir Willamette Valley 1995: Light in texture, with a creamy note adding a little something to the basic berry flavors. Finish is supple and balanced. Try in 1999. 328 cases made. • $12 • (02/28/98) • **85**

Pinot Noir Willamette Valley Vintner's Reserve 1995: Tart and more than a little bitey in texture, but there's a smooth, supple wine beneath with pretty plum and spice flavors that linger. Try now. 198 cases made. • $16 • (02/28/98) • **86**

Riesling Willamette Valley Select Harvest 1995: Moderately sweet, with spicy, peppery honey and pineapple flavors balanced with enough jazzy acidity to keep it feeling fresh. Tasty now, so why wait? 168 cases made. • $8/375ml • (05/15/98) • **88**

Sauvignon Blanc Willamette Valley Vintner's Reserve 1995: Bright, fresh and lightly herbal, with pretty floral and spice notes to go along with its citrusy fruit flavors. Ready now. 1,200 cases made. • $10 • (01/31/98) • **88**

Sauvignon Blanc Willamette Valley Vintner's Reserve 1994: Smooth, rich and spicy, showing more honey and nutmeg than herbs. Nicely balanced and ready now. 450 cases made. • $10 • (05/15/97) • **86**

LAURENT CELLARS | CALIFORNIA

Red Napa Valley 1988 • $30 • (06/30/93) • **87**

LAURIER | CALIFORNIA

Cabernet Sauvignon Sonoma County Green Valley 1982 • $12 • (02/16/85) • **82**

Chardonnay Sonoma County 1996: Intense and ripe spicy pear, apple, citrus and light oak flavors. Focused, it turns a bit leafy and earthy on the finish; short-term cellaring should help. Best now through 2002. 6,000 cases made. • $15 • (07/31/98) • **88**

Chardonnay Sonoma County 1995: Gentle and generous. A pretty mouthful of apple, spice and cream flavors that echo on the finish, picking up a nice hint of honey as well. Delicious now. 11,000 cases made. • $15 • (03/31/98) • **88**

Chardonnay Sonoma County 1994: Distinct for its flinty edge and tart nectarine and peach notes, this wine builds slowly on the palate, revealing more depth and breadth of flavor right up to the finish, where it picks up hints of spice and hazelnut. Ready now. 9,800 cases made. • $15 • (05/31/97) • **90**

Chardonnay Sonoma County 1993 • $15 • (03/31/96) • **88**

Pinot Noir Sonoma County 1995: A touch earthy, showing a mushroomy accent to the cola and cherry flavors. Well balanced, but lacks focus and extra dimensions. 3,900 cases made. • $20 • (01/31/97) • **84**

Pinot Noir Sonoma County 1994 • $15 • (03/31/96) • **88**

Pinot Noir Sonoma County Green Valley 1986 • $10 • (06/15/88) • **90**

Pinot Noir Sonoma County Green Valley 1981 • $10 • (02/16/85) • **78**

LAVA CAP | CALIFORNIA

Cabernet Sauvignon El Dorado 1989 • $10 • (11/15/93) • **85**

Merlot El Dorado 1990 • $13 • (07/15/93) • **84**

Zinfandel El Dorado 1991 • $10 • (10/15/94) • **73**

Zinfandel El Dorado 1990 • $8 • (09/30/93) • **77**

Zinfandel El Dorado 1989 • $8 • (10/15/92) • **77**

LAWRENCE, DANIEL | CALIFORNIA

Chardonnay California Vineyard Select 1996: Simple, floral and earthy, with hints of citrus and herb. Drink now. 1,150 cases made. • $12 • (07/31/98) • **80**

Chardonnay Santa Cruz Mountains Vineyard Reserve 1996: Sweet citrus and ripe pineapple flavors turn awkward, finishing soft with a note of bitterness. 350 cases made. • $15 • (07/31/98) • **79**

Syrah Alexander Valley Vineyard Reserve 1996: A solid red, with earthy beet and mineral overtones to the basic blackberry flavors. Finishes smooth and long, with bead-on fruit character. Best from 1999 to 2000. 2,100 cases made. • $13 • (03/31/98) • **86**

Zinfandel California Vineyard Select 1996: Sour candy and spicy herbal notes predominate. Decadent rotting fruit flavors on the finish. Drink now. 2,000 cases made. • $12 • (06/15/98) • **75**

LAZY CREEK | CALIFORNIA

Chardonnay Anderson Valley 1996: Has a lean, citrusy edge to the basic green apple flavor, finishing with a hint of spice. Drink now. 750 cases made. • $10 • (05/15/98) • **82**

Key: SS—Spectator Selection CS—Cellar Selection HR—Highly Recommended BB—Best Buy $NA—Price not available Ⓐ—Auction Price (BT)—Barrel Tasting

Dates in parentheses indicate the issues in which the ratings were published.

Chardonnay Anderson Valley 1995: Bright and fruity, a smooth-textured white with pretty apricot and pear flavors. Ready to drink. 1,000 cases made. • $10 • (07/31/97) • **85**

Chardonnay Anderson Valley 1993 • $10 • (06/15/96) • **84**

Pinot Noir Anderson Valley 1991 • $12 • (02/28/93) • **83**

LE DUCQ | CALIFORNIA

Red Napa Valley 1994: An elegant, understated style with a modest range of currant, cedar, spice and berry flavors. Finishes with mild tannins and good length but, as a 1994, it fails to excite. Drink from 2000 to 2004. A blend of Cabernet Sauvignon, Merlot, Cabernet Franc and Petit Verdot. 300 cases made. • $99 • (03/31/98) • **85**

Red Napa Valley 1993: This is a dry, intense and concentrated wine with cedar, herb, currant and spice flavors that are quite tannic. Anyone's guess how (or if) it will come around. Try after 1999. A blend of Cabernet Sauvignon, Merlot, Cabernet Franc and Petit Verdot. 415 cases made. • $91 • (03/31/98) • **86**

LEBLANC ESTATE | MICHIGAN

Ice Wine Lake Erie North Shore 1992 • $31 • (04/15/95) • **76**

LEEWARD | CALIFORNIA

Cabernet Sauvignon Alexander Valley 1991 • $15 • (11/30/93) • **81**

Cabernet Sauvignon Alexander Valley 1988 • $13 • (11/15/92) • **78**

Cabernet Sauvignon Alexander Valley 1987 • $13 • (11/15/90) • **84**

Cabernet Sauvignon Alexander Valley 1986 • $12 • (10/15/89) • **79**

Cabernet Sauvignon Alexander Valley 1985 • $12 • (10/31/87) • **83**

Chardonnay Central Coast 1996: Light, lean and crisp in texture, with lively nectarine and green-leaf aromas and flavors, a fresh finish. Drink now. 8,199 cases made. • $11 • (12/15/97) • **85**

Chardonnay Central Coast 1995: Crisp, bright and refreshing. Shows appealing flavors of citrusy pear and vanilla, fresh and inviting on the finish. 2,065 cases made. • $11 • (12/15/96) • **85**

Chardonnay Central Coast 1993 • $11 • (10/15/95) • **83**

Chardonnay Edna Valley Reserve 1995: Heavy-handed, with rich, overripe pineapple flavors and nutty notes. Still, it packs a lot of flavor, which lingers on the finish. Drink now. 1,438 cases made. • $15 • (07/31/98) • **83**

Chardonnay Edna Valley Reserve 1993 • $15 • (05/31/95) • **86**

Chardonnay Monterey County Reserve 1994: Bright and crisp. Refreshing for its citrus and hazelnut flavors that bounce merrily into a nicely defined finish. 920 cases made. • $15 • (12/15/96) • **86**

Merlot Napa Valley 1995: Hard in texture, with slightly sour flavors that never let the berry notes come through. Not for all tastes. Try in 2000. 933 cases made. • $18 • (12/15/97) • **78**

Merlot Napa Valley 1993 • $15 • (02/29/96) • **84**

Merlot Napa Valley 1992 • $15 • (09/15/94) • **74**

Merlot Napa Valley 1991 • $15 • (09/15/94) • **81**

Merlot Napa Valley 1989 • $14 • (11/15/91) • **83**

Merlot Napa Valley 1985 • $10 • (05/15/87) • **88**

Merlot San Ysidro 1996: Stewed cherries and lemons pave the way. Coarse tannins rip up the palate. 1,100 cases made. • $15 • (05/15/98) • **74**

Pinot Noir Santa Barbara County 1993 • $14 • (09/15/95) • **86**

Pinot Noir Santa Barbara County 1990 • $14 • (02/28/93) • **76**

Pinot Noir Santa Barbara County 1989 • $16 • (02/28/93) • **82**

LEFRANC, CHARLES | CALIFORNIA

Cabernet Sauvignon Monterey County 1981 • $8 • (09/16/85) • **76**

Cabernet Sauvignon Napa County 1984 • $12 • (10/15/87) • **80**

Gewürztraminer Late Harvest San Benito County Selected 1984 • $11 • (03/16/86) • **75**

Merlot Monterey County San Lucas Ranch 1984 • $8 • (12/15/87) • **70**

LENZ | NEW YORK

Cabernet Sauvignon North Fork of Long Island 1993: Quite ripe, resembling young Port in its sweet, grapey flavors and thick texture. Rustic but appealing, although an earthy aroma detracts. • $20 • (12/31/96) • **79**

Chardonnay North Fork of Long Island Barrel Fermented 1993: Oak is the dominant element, joined by assertive smoke, toast and caramel flavors that overwhelm the modest apple flavors and linger on the finish. It's unbalanced, but distinctively styled. • $20 • (12/31/96) • **82**

Chardonnay North Fork of Long Island Vineyard Selection 1994: Very firm and fresh, this well-balanced white marries pear, citrus and apple flavors with notes of vanilla and cream that add texture and complexity. A good match with food. • $11 • (12/31/96) • **87**

Cuvée North Fork of Long Island 1991: Toasted almond and spice aromas and flavors show sophistication and maturity. It's crisp, well structured and clean on the finish. • $20 • (12/31/96) • **85**

Gewürztraminer North Fork of Long Island 1993: Distinctive, but not Gewürz-like, this is dry, rather austere and offers vanilla aromas, tobacco and earth flavors and hard acidity. Try with food. • $20 • (12/31/96) • **78**

Merlot North Fork of Long Island 1993: Rich, delivering concentrated plum flavors and firm tannins, but there's a burnt, earthy note that detracts from the pleasure. Try now. • $25 • (12/31/96) • **78**

Merlot North Fork of Long Island 1987 • $12 • (06/30/91) • **80**

Merlot North Fork of Long Island 1986 • $12 • (12/15/88) • **83**

Merlot North Fork of Long Island 1985 • $11 • (12/15/88) • **84**

Merlot North Fork of Long Island 1984 • $12 • (12/15/88) • **74**

Pinot Blanc North Fork of Long Island Lieb Vineyards 1994: Opulent aromas of peaches, figs and honey give way to vivid, crisp flavors of peaches, limes and green apples. With its clarity and expressiveness, it's a nice example of the varietal. • $13 • (12/31/96) • **86**

LEONETTI | WASHINGTON

Cabernet Sauvignon Columbia Valley 1995: Ripe and supple, this spicy mouthful of black cherry, plum and tar flavors remains smooth and elegant through the harmonious finish, which is wrapped in a layer of spiciness. Drink now through 2005. 1,961 cases made. • $50 • (06/15/98) • **91**

Cabernet Sauvignon Columbia Valley 1994: A deep-pile, plush carpet of a Cabernet, from Washington, this is smooth and velvety, with layer upon layer of juicy blackberry, prune, plum, spice and vanilla flavors that linger beautifully and get richer with each sip. Tempting now, but likely best from 2002 or so. 2,500 cases made. • $45 • (06/15/97) HR • **94**

Cabernet Sauvignon Columbia Valley 1992 • $33 • (06/15/95) HR • **91**

Cabernet Sauvignon Columbia Valley 1986 • $20 • (10/15/89) • **81**

Cabernet Sauvignon Walla Walla Valley Seven Hills Vineyard 1988 • $25 • (08/31/91) • **91**

Cabernet Sauvignon Walla Walla Valley Seven Hills Vineyard 1985 • $22 • (10/15/89) • **85**

Cabernet Sauvignon Walla Walla Valley Seven Hills Vineyard Reserve 1990 • $50 • (08/31/95) • **90**

Cabernet Sauvignon Washington 1991 • $29 • (06/30/94) CS • **95**

Cabernet Sauvignon Washington 1990 • $26 • (06/15/93) CS • **96**

Cabernet Sauvignon Washington 1989 • $25 • (07/31/92) HR • **96**

Cabernet Sauvignon Washington 1988 • $22 • (08/31/91) • **87**

Cabernet Sauvignon Washington 1987 • $22 • (06/15/90) • **91**

Cabernet Sauvignon Washington Reserve 1985 • $40 • (06/15/91) • **84**

Merlot America 1996: Lithe and polished, a gorgeous example of fruit-centered Merlot, layering its berry, black cherry and vanilla flavors with hints of pepper and olive notes that swirl through the elegant finish. A blend of 50 percent Washington fruit, 50 percent Dry Creek Valley. Drink now through 2003. 1,963 cases made. • $50 • (06/15/98) • **91**

Merlot Columbia Valley 1995: A distinctive beauty, if not the blockbuster of previous vintages. Light in texture but ripe in flavor, with black cherry, spice and vanilla notes ringing on the long finish, which grows richer with each sip. Oak notes add depth. Best from 1999. 2,400 cases made. • $40 • (11/30/97) • **91**

Merlot Columbia Valley 1987 • $16 • (10/15/89) • **88**

Merlot Washington 1994: Smooth and broad. Disarmingly pure berry and cherry flavors with lovely, complex notes of spice, leather and vanilla on the finish. Drink now. 1,300 cases made. • $40 • (07/31/96) CS • **94**

Merlot Washington 1993 • $29 • (06/15/95) SS • **91**

Merlot Washington 1992 • $25 • (05/15/94) CS • **96**

Merlot Washington 1991 • $22 • (05/31/93) HR • **92**

Merlot Washington 1990 • $22 • (06/15/92) • **92**

Merlot Washington 1989 • $18 • (05/31/91) HR • **93**

Merlot Washington 1988 • $17 • (04/15/90) • **90**

Sangiovese Walla Walla Valley 1995: Distinctive berry and spice flavors shine through a polished overlay of toasted oak in this soft, smooth-textured red. Has some real character. Try in 1999. 297 cases made. • $45 • (06/15/97) • **90**

Select Walla Walla Valley 1990 • $28 • (06/15/93) • **90**

LEWELLING | CALIFORNIA

Cabernet Sauvignon Napa Valley 1993: Openly fruity, offering ripe black cherry, wild berry and cassislike flavors before finishing with crisp, firm tannins. A new wine that's well focused and laden with fruit. Worth watching. Best from 2000 through 2005. 265 cases made. • $30 • (05/31/98) • **88**

LEWIS CELLARS | CALIFORNIA

Cabernet Sauvignon Napa Valley Oakville Ranch 1993: Young, tight, vibrant cedar, currant and spice pick up bright cherry flavors on the finish, where the tannins fold in. Best to cellar into 1999 to 2001 to let it soften a bit. 1,200 cases made. • $32 • (04/30/96) • **88**

Cabernet Sauvignon Napa Valley Oakville Ranch 1992 • $30 • (11/30/95) HR • **94**

Cabernet Sauvignon Napa Valley Reserve 1995: An outstanding '95. Intense and concentrated, with supple currant, sage, spice, cedar and coffee notes. Sharply focused and deeply concentrated, with a long, full finish that keeps pumping out the flavors. Best from 2001 through 2008. 1,800 cases made. • $40 • (05/15/98) HR • **93**

Cabernet Sauvignon Napa Valley Reserve 1994: This is a dramatic California Cabernet, rich and explosive, with layers of bold, ripe currant, black cherry, anise, plum and spice flavors framed by nuances of toasty, buttery oak and finishing long and full. We tasted this reserve wine twice, with consistently delicious notes. 1,900 cases made. • $36 • (06/15/97) HR • **94**

Chardonnay Napa Valley Oakville Ranch Reserve 1994: Big, ripe, complex pear, apple, fig and melon notes accompany lots of pretty, smoky, toasty oak. Shortens up somewhat on the finish, but give this a few more months for the flavors to round out. 1,400 cases made. • $28 • (05/15/96) • **90**

Chardonnay Napa Valley Oakville Ranch Reserve 1993 • $26 • (07/31/95) • **90**

Chardonnay Napa Valley Reserve 1996: A rich, earthy style, with pronounced ripe fruit, spicy aromatics and lots of complex Chardonnay flavors, echoing ripe pear, fig, melon and buttery nuances. There's a pretty dash of toasty oak on the lengthy finish. Drink now through 2002. 2,100 cases made. • $32 • (05/15/98) • **93**

Chardonnay Napa Valley Reserve 1995: Ripe and juicy, with spicy pear, apple, fig and melon notes, turning supple and elegant on the finish, where the flavors fan out and hints of butter and butterscotch fold in. 1,600 cases made. • $30 • (06/15/97) • **93**

Merlot Napa Valley Oakville Ranch 1993: Firm and compact, with a tight core of black cherry and currant flavors, and hints of herb and spice. Well balanced. 300 cases made. • $32 • (01/31/97) • **88**

Merlot Napa Valley Reserve 1995: Complex and inviting, with supple, well-integrated plum, currant, anise, cedar and tobacco flavors, finishing with a long, concentrated aftertaste. Has tannin to shed, so can cellar short-term; drink through 2004. 150 cases made. • $45 • (05/31/98) • **91**

Merlot Napa Valley Reserve 1994: Young, intense and vibrant, with a rich, complex core of plum, black cherry, anise and cedar flavors that really take off on the finish, picking up notes of chocolate and coffee, soaring through firm, polished tannins. 300 cases made. • $40 • (06/15/97) • **93**

LIBERTY SCHOOL | CALIFORNIA

Cabernet Sauvignon Alexander Valley Lot 13 NV • $6 • (01/01/86) • **64**

Cabernet Sauvignon California Lot 17 NV • $6 • (02/29/88) • **73**

Cabernet Sauvignon California Lot 18 NV • $7 • (04/30/89) BB • **81**

Cabernet Sauvignon California Lot 19 NV • $7 • (11/15/89) • **77**

Cabernet Sauvignon California Vintner Select Series 2 NV • $7 • (11/15/91) BB • **82**

Cabernet Sauvignon California Vintner Select Series 3 1990 • $7 • (06/15/93) • **83**

LIMERICK LANE | CALIFORNIA

Zinfandel Russian River Valley 1991 • $12 • (06/15/93) • **88**

Zinfandel Russian River Valley 1990 • $13 • (10/15/92) • **88**

Zinfandel Russian River Valley Collins Vineyard 1996: Crisp and firm, with earthy raspberry, cherry, cedar and spice. The tannins turn especially firm on the finish. Drink now through 2002. 3,360 cases made. • $19 • (05/31/98) • **87**

Zinfandel Russian River Valley Collins Vineyard 1995: An effusively fruity style, with a range of exotic flavors—including bright blueberry, black cherry and wild berry—that dance with exuberance across the palate before turning smooth and polished on the finish. 2,870 cases made. • $18 • (06/30/97) SS • **91**

Zinfandel Russian River Valley Collins Vineyard 1994: An elegant and lively Zin from California that showcases lots of rich, complex cherry, berry and raspberry flavors, which persist through the long, fruity finish, with just the right dose of tannin. 2,360 cases made. • $16 • (12/15/96) HR • **90**

Zinfandel Russian River Valley Collins Vineyard 1993 • $14 • (10/15/95) • **85**

LINDEN | VIRGINIA

Cabernet Franc Virginia 1995: A sappy flavor runs throughout this somewhat cloying red wine. 480 cases made. • $15 • (03/31/98) • **75**

Cabernet Franc Virginia 1994: Herbal aromas and flavors dominate, and there's a roasted note. Somewhat coarse on the finish. 520 cases made. • $15 • (04/30/97) • **79**

Cabernet Sauvignon Virginia 1994: Smooth and polished, with berry, cherry and spice flavors. A fairly rich wine, with nice chocolaty notes on the finish. Drink now. 820 cases made. • $16 • (05/15/98) • **84**

Cabernet Sauvignon Virginia 1990 • $16 • (09/30/93) • **86**

Cabernet Virginia 1991 • $16 • (12/31/95) • **88**

Cabernet Virginia 1988 • $15 • (02/29/92) • **84**

Chardonnay Virginia 1994: An oaky style with some good pear and melon flavors. A straightforward, clean Chardonnay. 1,600 cases made. • $15 • (12/31/97) • **81**

Chardonnay Virginia 1993: On the lean side, but interesting for its toasty aromas, light but bright fruit flavors and crisp finish. Quite narrow in focus. 1,200 cases made. • $15 • (09/15/96) • **85**

Vidal Blanc Late Harvest Virginia 1996: Quite thick and peachy-sweet, with enough acidity to keep it lively. Finishes smooth and spicy. 400 cases made. • $16/375ml • (12/31/97) • **84**

LIPARITA | CALIFORNIA

Cabernet Sauvignon Howell Mountain 1994: From a great vintage, this is still tightly wound, with an austere, earthy band of currant, spice, cedar, coffee, sage and wild berry flavors that persist on the finish, turning rich and complex, with a long, full aftertaste. Best from 2001 through 2009. 1,900 cases made. • $32 • (05/15/98) HR • **93**

Cabernet Sauvignon Howell Mountain 1993: Young and vibrant, with rich, earthy currant, tar and cedary oak flavors. A touch of green olive weaves its way into the finish, where the tannins are firm but polished. 1,000 cases made. • $32 • (10/15/96) • **88**

Cabernet Sauvignon Howell Mountain 1992 • $28 • (12/15/95) • **84**

Cabernet Sauvignon Howell Mountain 1991 • $28 • (11/15/94) • **86**

Cabernet Sauvignon Howell Mountain 1990 • $28 • (11/15/93) • **89**

Chardonnay Howell Mountain 1996: Perfumed and floral, with flinty mint and mineral notes, hints of pear, and lingering citrus flavors. Drink now through 2001. 1,400 cases made. • $24 • (05/15/98) • **88**

Chardonnay Howell Mountain 1995: A touch earthy in character, with flinty, mineral and anise nuances to the pear and apple notes. Try now. 750 cases made. • $22 • (05/15/97) • **89**

Chardonnay Howell Mountain 1994: Tight and firm, a crisp, well-focused style that gently unfolds, revealing complex mineral, pear, spice, honey and vanilla notes. Deceptively subtle and understated, but the flavors are wonderful and they grow on you. 800 cases made. • $18 • (04/30/96) • **92**

Chardonnay Howell Mountain 1993 • $16 • (10/31/95) HR • **90**

Merlot Howell Mountain 1994: Young, tight and well focused, this throws a lot of flavors at you while maintaining a sense of harmony and finesse. Complex flavors of black cherry, currant, anise, cedar and spice are at the core, and the finish shows dashes of currant and coffee. 1,400 cases made. • $28 • (05/15/97) • **90**

Merlot Howell Mountain 1993 • $26 • (04/30/96) • **88**

Merlot Howell Mountain 1991 • $24 • (09/15/94) • **83**

Sauvignon Blanc Howell Mountain 1996: Crisp and clean, showcasing subtle flavors of hazelnut, melon, grapefruit and lemon backed by a judicious dose of oak. Tangy acidity. 400 cases made. • $18 • (06/30/97) • **88**

Sauvignon Blanc Howell Mountain 1994 • $14 • (10/31/95) • **85**

Key: SS—Spectator Selection CS—Cellar Selection HR—Highly Recommended BB—Best Buy $NA—Price not available Ⓐ—Auction Price (BT)—Barrel Tasting
Dates in parentheses indicate the issues in which the ratings were published.

LITTORAI | CALIFORNIA

Chardonnay Russian River Valley Mays Canyon 1993 • $25 • (12/31/95) • **91**

Chardonnay Sonoma Coast Occidental 1995: Shows off a complex range of ripe pear, citrus, fig and melon, with pretty spicy, toasty oak. All folds together nicely on the finish, where the flavors are rich and concentrated. 463 cases made. • $30 • (12/31/97) • **90**

Chardonnay Sonoma Coast Occidental 1994: Serves up lots of ripe, juicy Chardonnay flavors with tiers of honey, pear, spice and citrus, and frames them with just the right dash of smoky, toasty oak. A rich and full-bodied style. 294 cases made. • $28 • (11/30/96) • **92**

Pinot Noir Sonoma Coast Hirsch Vineyard 1994: Lean and earthy, with a tightly wound, trim band of dried cherry, wild berry, spice and sage. Finishes with crisp, firm tannins. Shows more depth and concentration with aeration; best to cellar into 1999. • $NA • (01/01/97) • **88**

LIVINGSTON

Cabernet Sauvignon Napa Valley Gemstone Vineyard 1997: Intense and concentrated, loaded with wild berry, currant, anise and sage. Rough and a bit raw in texture, it has the right stuff. • $NA • (07/31/98) (BT) • **90-94**

Cabernet Sauvignon Napa Valley Gonser Vineyard 1993: An earthy, leathery style with drying tannins and a meaty edge. Good, if not exciting. 120 cases made. • $25 • (06/15/97) • **83**

Cabernet Sauvignon Napa Valley Moffett Vineyard 1996: Rich and sharply focused, with a pretty core of ripe currant, plum, black cherry and anise flavors framed by toasty, smoky oak. 1,000 cases made. • $36 • (06/15/97) (BT) • **90-94**

Cabernet Sauvignon Napa Valley Moffett Vineyard 1994: A bottling with a track record for quality and ageability, and this year's version is no exception, delivering a wonderful core of deep, concentrated, earthy currant, plum and cherry flavors that turn smooth and silky on the lingering finish. Best after 2000. 1,400 cases made. • $36 • (10/31/97) HR • **94**

Cabernet Sauvignon Napa Valley Moffett Vineyard 1993: Firm, compact and tightly wound. Marked by a cedar-anise-tar accent, but cherry and currant flavors give it depth and dimension. Drinkable now. 1,500 cases made. • $33 • (11/15/96) • **89**

Cabernet Sauvignon Napa Valley Moffett Vineyard 1992 • $30 • (12/15/95) • **89**

Cabernet Sauvignon Napa Valley Moffett Vineyard 1991 • $30 • (11/15/94) • **89**

Cabernet Sauvignon Napa Valley Moffett Vineyard 1990 • $30 • (11/15/93) HR • **91**

Cabernet Sauvignon Napa Valley Moffett Vineyard 1989 • $30 • (11/15/92) • **81**

Cabernet Sauvignon Napa Valley Moffett Vineyard 1988 • $30 • (11/15/91) • **85**

Cabernet Sauvignon Napa Valley Moffett Vineyard 1987: The best Livingston of the 1980s and a candidate for best Livingston ever. Dark, ripe, complex and concentrated, with a solid core of minty currant, anise, cedar and spice flavors. Still firm and finishing with chewy tannins, this remains a formidable wine. Best now to 2006. • $63 • (12/15/97) • **94**

Cabernet Sauvignon Napa Valley Moffett Vineyard 1986 • $19 Ⓐ • (11/30/89) • **88**

Cabernet Sauvignon Napa Valley Moffett Vineyard 1985 • $18 • (10/15/88) • **85**

Cabernet Sauvignon Napa Valley Moffett Vineyard 1984 • $18 • (11/15/87) • **86**

Cabernet Sauvignon Napa Valley Rockpile 1993: Tightly wound, with ripe plum, cherry and berry flavors, finishing with firm, dry tannins. Can stand cellaring into 1999. 120 cases made. • $25 • (06/15/97) • **87**

Cabernet Sauvignon Napa Valley Stanley's Selection 1995: Well crafted, with an appealing core of ripe plum, currant and spice and a pretty dash of cedary, buttery oak. Could use just a touch more depth and richness, but most will find this quite appealing. 2,120 cases made. • $22 • (03/31/98) • **88**

Cabernet Sauvignon Napa Valley Stanley's Selection 1994: Young and unevolved, with only a modest band of spicy currant and berry flavors emerging on the finish, with just a hint of oak. 1,800 cases made. • $20 • (05/15/97) • **84**

Cabernet Sauvignon Napa Valley Stanley's Selection 1993: Earthy and a touch herbal, with chewy tannins and a smoky accent to the currant and chocolate flavors. Still a bit rustic, murky and tannic; cellaring into 1999 to 2002 is your best bet. 1,500 cases made. • $20 • (12/15/96) • **84**

Cabernet Sauvignon Napa Valley Stanley's Selection 1992 • $18 • (08/31/95) • **87**

Cabernet Sauvignon Napa Valley Stanley's Selection 1991 • $20 • (11/15/94) • **83**
Cabernet Sauvignon Napa Valley Stanley's Selection 1990 • $20 • (03/15/93) • **88**
Cabernet Sauvignon Napa Valley Stanley's Selection 1989 • $26 • (07/15/92) • **85**
Chardonnay Napa Valley 1996: Lots of flavor and finesse, with complex, rich flavors—hints of pear, fig, melon, anise and citrus—that fold together nicely on the finish. Drink now through 2002. 250 cases made. • $40 • (05/31/98) • **92**
Sangiovese Sonoma County 1996: Openly fruity, with a tight core of spicy berry, strawberry and cherry, picking up earthy, herbal notes on the finish. Shows more depth and complexity than most Sangioveses. Drink now through 2000. 198 cases made. • $20 • (05/15/98) • **87**

LIVINGSTONE, STEVEN THOMAS | WASHINGTON

Merlot Columbia Valley 1990 • $13 • (11/30/92) • **89**
Merlot Columbia Valley 1989 • $11 • (08/31/91) • **84**

LLANO ESTACADO | TEXAS

Cabernet Sauvignon Texas 1988 • $12 • (02/29/92) • **81**
Cabernet Sauvignon Texas High Plains 1992 • $12 • (01/31/95) • **85**
Cabernet Sauvignon Texas High Plains Cellar Select 1994: Dense, chewy, overripe and harsh. • $19 • (11/30/96) • **79**
Chardonnay Texas Cellar Select 1995: Soft, fresh and distinctive for its salty mineral and citrus flavors. • $19 • (11/30/96) • **81**
Merlot Texas 1991 • $12 • (06/30/93) • **81**
Merlot Texas Cellar Select 1995: Light, crisp and spicy, with a cedary tone over the modest berry flavors. Drink now. • $19 • (11/30/96) • **83**
Port Texas High Plains Cellar Select NV: Quite sweet-tasting, with chocolate, orange, and plum flavors. Could have more structure, but still satisfying. Reminiscent of a tawny. 1,100 cases made. • $20 • (12/31/97) • **83**
Signature Edition Texas 1992 • $8 • (01/31/95) BB • **83**
Viviano Noble Cepagé Texas 1994: A sinewy wine with some power. A nice spicy aroma leads into concentrated ripe plum, cherry and spice flavors. Still a bit tannic, try in 1999. 200 cases made. • $40 • (09/30/97) • **84**
Zinfandel Texas 1996: A meaty red with charred bacon flavors and aromas. Flavors linger on the finish. Drink now. • $15 • (05/15/98) • **81**

LOCKWOOD | CALIFORNIA

Cabernet Sauvignon Monterey 1994: Distinct oak-fostered nuances of vanilla and butter fold nicely into the core of cherry, berry and currant, giving this wine a broad range of flavors. Finishes with smooth, supple texture. 14,800 cases made. • $15 • (05/31/97) • **88**
Cabernet Sauvignon Monterey 1993: Smooth and harmonious, with lots of plum, currant and cherry flavors. Finishes with a supple aftertaste. Ready now. 5,969 cases made. • $14 • (09/15/96) • **85**
Cabernet Sauvignon Monterey 1992 • $14 • (09/30/95) • **86**
Cabernet Sauvignon Monterey 1991 • $12 • (10/31/93) • **88**
Cabernet Sauvignon Monterey Partners' Reserve 1994: Smooth, ripe, rich and concentrated. Has layers of currant, black cherry and wild berry flavors, spicy accents, supple tannins and lots of finesse. Drinkable now. 1,024 cases made. • $21 • (11/15/97) • **88**
Cabernet Sauvignon Monterey Partners' Reserve 1993: A touch on the green side, with cedar, anise and spice flavors that show a stalky edge. Never quite gets into gear, as the oak and fruit don't appear happily married. 1,000 cases made. • $18 • (11/30/96) • **83**
Cabernet Sauvignon Monterey Partners' Reserve 1991 • $16 • (11/15/94) • **84**
Cabernet Sauvignon Monterey Partners' Reserve 1990 • $18 • (10/31/93) • **88**
Chardonnay Monterey 1996: Silky, spicy style offers a nice core of pear and a touch of mint on the smooth finish. Drink now. 18,293 cases made. • $16 • (03/31/98) • **85**
Chardonnay Monterey 1995: A yummy California Chardonnay with a complex interplay of ripe, juicy pear, smoky oak, vanilla and butterscotch flavors. It folds together nicely to leave a long, lingering impression on the palate. Delicious now, but put a bottle or two away for future enjoyment. 14,800 cases made. • $15 • (02/28/97) SS • **91**
Chardonnay Monterey 1994: Spicy and generous with its oak-wrapped pineapple and honey flavors, smooth and rich through the finish. 8,004 cases made. • $15 • (04/30/96) • **87**
Chardonnay Monterey 1993 • $15 • (12/15/95) • **86**
Chardonnay Monterey Partners' Reserve 1995: An oaky style, distinct for its smoky overtones and butterscotch flavors, but there are sufficient fig and pear flavors to stand up to it. Drink now. 2,005 cases made. • $21 • (05/31/97) • **90**
Chardonnay Monterey Partners' Reserve 1994: Rich and exotic, if bordering on overblown with its bold apricot, honey and fig flavors. Turns spicy on the finish, where the flavors linger long. Enjoy it for its hedonistic flavors, paired with ultrarich fare. 1,993 cases made. • $21 • (05/31/97) • **90**
Chardonnay Monterey Partners' Reserve 1993 • $17 • (06/30/96) • **86**
Merlot Monterey 1995: Ripe and generous, this stylish wine has beautifully articulated blackberry, currant, anise and spice flavors that swirl harmoniously through the supple finish. Delicious now. 15,000 cases made. • $17 • (11/30/97) • **88**
Merlot Monterey 1994: Strives for complexity with its blend of ripe cherry, currant and cedary oak flavors, and is pleasant enough right through the finish, where the flavors persist. Ready to drink. 7,741 cases made. • $17 • (02/28/97) • **87**
Merlot Monterey 1993: Well-balanced currant and cherry flavors play off notes of light cedary oak. Appealing, but pricey. 8,050 cases made. • $16 • (08/31/96) • **85**
Merlot Monterey 1992 • $15 • (09/15/94) • **86**
Merlot Monterey 1991 • $12 • (05/31/94) • **89**
Merlot Monterey Partners' Reserve 1995: Dark and complex, oozing with ripe, juicy plum and wild berry flavors, finishing with crisp tannins and good length. Drink now to 2002. 330 cases made. • $25 • (03/31/98) • **89**
Merlot Monterey Partners' Reserve 1994: Ripe and opulent in style if a bit on the pruny side. Walks a tightrope and just hangs on, as the oak is strong on the finish. Drink now. 234 cases made. • $25 • (06/30/97) • **87**
Pinot Blanc Monterey 1996: A moderately ripe and flinty style, with a twinge of greenness. Marked by green pear and apple notes, finishing with a spicy, lemony edge. 2,500 cases made. • $12 • (04/30/98) • **86**
Pinot Blanc Monterey 1995: Tasty, with tangy flavors ranging from ripe pear to apple, citrus and spice. A slight smoky accent marks the finish. 2,162 cases made. • $12 • (11/30/96) • **84**
Pinot Blanc Monterey 1994 • $11 • (05/31/96) • **86**
Pinot Blanc Monterey 1993 • $9 • (11/15/95) • **82**
Sangiovese Monterey 1995: Silky, polished and spicy with the influence of new oak barrels, the character of which dominates the palate. Has some solid black cherry flavor, too, and finishes with promise. Drink now. 1,400 cases made. • $16 • (12/15/97) • **87**
Sauvignon Blanc Monterey 1996: Bright acidity is the hallmark of this tasty California white, along with hazelnut, vanilla, melon and citrus flavors packed tightly together, finishing with moderate length and intensity. A satisfying wine at a pleasing price. 7,202 cases made. • $10 • (11/30/97) BB • **85**
Sauvignon Blanc Monterey 1995: Mouth-filling butterscotch, citrus and herb flavors seem a little raucous at this point, but the crisp finish brings it together nicely. 6,450 cases made. • $10 • (08/31/96) • **87**
Sauvignon Blanc Monterey 1994 • $9 • (05/31/96) BB • **88**
Sauvignon Blanc Monterey 1993 • $9 • (08/31/95) • **86**
Syrah Monterey 1995: Serves up pretty black cherry, plum and toasty oak flavors and holds its focus while turning smooth and supple on the finish. Best to cellar short-term to soften. 1,650 cases made. • $16 • (04/30/98) • **87**

LOGAN | CALIFORNIA

Chardonnay Monterey 1996: Shows off an earthy, gamy side before the ripe pear, citrus and spicy oak flavors work their way to the mainstream. Solid. Drink now through 2000. 7,000 cases made. • $17 • (07/31/98) • **86**
Chardonnay Monterey 1994: A touch earthy with a slight tinny edge to the pear and pineapple notes, but it folds together nicely, keeping the fruit up front. 7,500 cases made. • $14 • (05/15/96) • **87**
Chardonnay Monterey 1993 • $14 • (07/31/95) • **84**
Pinot Noir Monterey 1995: Light and fruity, with an herbal edge to the cherry and berry notes. Modest tannins on the finish, with a touch of earthiness. • $18 • (02/28/98) • **84**
Pinot Noir Monterey 1994: Holds together nicely, showing dried cherry and tea flavors, finishing with an earthy, tarry accent. 750 cases made. • $18 • (01/31/97) • **84**

LOHR, J. | CALIFORNIA

Cabernet Sauvignon California 1987 • $7 • (02/15/90) BB • **84**
Cabernet Sauvignon California 1986 • $6 • (04/15/89) BB • **84**

LOLONIS

Cabernet Sauvignon California 1984 • $5 • (11/30/86) BB • **82**
Cabernet Sauvignon California Cypress 1993: Bright, fruity and simple, generous with its berry flavors, finishing soft. 45,000 cases made. • $8 • (12/15/95) • **82**
Cabernet Sauvignon California Cypress 1992 • $9 • (11/30/95) BB • **86**
Cabernet Sauvignon California Cypress 1991 • $8 • (11/15/94) • **82**
Cabernet Sauvignon California Cypress 1990 • $7 • (11/15/93) BB • **86**
Cabernet Sauvignon California Cypress 1989 • $7 • (05/15/93) BB • **83**
Cabernet Sauvignon California Cypress 1988 • $7 • (11/15/91) • **80**
Cabernet Sauvignon Napa Valley Carol's Vineyard Reserve 1985 • $15 • (12/15/88) • **89**
Cabernet Sauvignon Napa Valley Carol's Vineyard Reserve Lot 2 1985 • $18 • (09/30/90) • **88**
Cabernet Sauvignon Paso Robles Seven Oaks 1995: Complex for its interplay of toasty, cedary oak and supple plum and berry flavors, this wine impresses with its balance and grace. Drink now through 2002. 50,000 cases made. • $14 • (04/30/98) • **85**
Cabernet Sauvignon Paso Robles Seven Oaks 1994: Ripe and smooth, with a spicy floral-and-oak streak running through that's reminiscent of certain Washington reds, backed up with ripe black cherry and tarlike flavors. Drink now. 50,000 cases made. • $14 • (07/31/97) • **87**
Cabernet Sauvignon Paso Robles Seven Oaks 1993: Marked by strong toasty, buttery oak flavor, it matches this with ripe, complex plum, currant and cherry notes. 65,000 cases made. • $12 • (11/30/95) • **87**
Cabernet Sauvignon Paso Robles Seven Oaks 1991 • $11 • (07/31/94) • **84**
Cabernet Sauvignon Paso Robles Seven Oaks 1990 • $11 • (11/15/93) • **88**
Cabernet Sauvignon Paso Robles Seven Oaks 1989 • $12 • (11/15/92) • **89**
Cabernet Sauvignon Paso Robles Seven Oaks 1988 • $13 • (03/15/92) • **83**
Cabernet Sauvignon Paso Robles Seven Oaks 1987 • $12 • (04/30/91) • **86**
Cabernet Sauvignon Paso Robles VS 1991 • $22 • (11/30/95) • **87**
Cabernet Sauvignon Paso Robles VS 1990 • $22 • (03/31/95) • **88**
Chardonnay Arroyo Seco VS 1994: A complex white with an enticing array of ripe pear, fig and celery flavors, picking up some nicely smoky, toasty oak character to help carry it all through the long finish. 1,200 cases made. • $23 • (06/15/96) • **89**
Chardonnay California Cypress 1993 • $9 • (12/15/95) • **85**
Chardonnay Monterey Riverstone 1996: Shows off toasty, smoky aromas and flavors, with fresh, ripe pear, peach, nectarine and tangerine flavors. Elegant and flavorful. Drink now. 55,000 cases made. • $14 • (06/15/98) • **88**
Chardonnay Monterey Riverstone 1995: This California Chardonnay performs a wonderful balancing act—between its core of juicy pear, apple, pineapple and citrus flavors and the toasty, vanilla, oak shadings that keep the flavors fresh and lively. Delicious now. 55,000 cases made. • $14 • (04/30/97) SS • **90**
Chardonnay Monterey Riverstone 1994: A complex array of elegant pear, spice, honey and hazelnut notes, leading up to a nicely, smoky, toasted oak finish. Combines richness with depth, concentration and finesse. Has the flavor and complexity of wines two to three times its price. 86,000 cases made. • $12 • (02/29/96) SS • **90**
Chardonnay Monterey Riverstone 1993 • $12 • (12/15/95) • **87**
Fumé Blanc California Cypress 1993 • $7 • (03/31/95) BB • **86**
Gamay Monterey County Monterey Gamay 1987 • $5 • (07/15/88) • **78**
Gamay Monterey Wildflower 1995: A light and fruity wine, charming for its lively, fresh flavors of raspberry and blueberry. Polished and vibrant on the finish. Drinkable now. 8,500 cases made. • $7 • (11/30/96) BB • **86**
Gamay Monterey Wildflower 1993 • $8 • (09/15/95) • **78**
Johannisberg Riesling Late Harvest Monterey Bay Mist 1993 • $10/375ml • (10/31/95) HR • **93**
Merlot California Cypress 1995: Has some nice cola, cedar and tar notes framed by coarse tannins. Finishes short. 50,000 cases made. • $11 • (07/31/97) • **82**
Merlot California Cypress 1993 • $10 • (12/31/95) • **86**
Merlot California Cypress 1992 • $9 • (06/15/94) BB • **86**
Merlot California Cypress 1991 • $9 • (05/31/93) • **82**
Merlot California Cypress 1989 • $8 • (02/29/92) BB • **85**
Pinot Blanc Monterey October Night 1995: Fragrant citrus and peach aromas lead the way, lightly accented by toasty oak and mango. It finishes with a clean, mineral edge. 2,500 cases made. • $14 • (09/30/97) • **87**
Pinot Blanc Monterey October Night 1994 • $14 • (06/30/96) • **88**

Key: SS—Spectator Selection CS—Cellar Selection HR—Highly Recommended BB—Best Buy $NA—Price not available Ⓐ—Auction Price (BT)—Barrel Tasting
Dates in parentheses indicate the issues in which the ratings were published.

Syrah Paso Robles South Ridge 1994: Intense and lively, with smoky, beefy, currant and wild berry flavors that linger nicely. Finishes with modest tannins and good length. Ready now. 2,800 cases made. • $14 • (11/15/97) • **86**
Syrah Paso Robles South Ridge 1993: Dark color and hard, chewy tannins are promising, but insufficient flavor and a hollowness in the middle detract. 2,500 cases made. • $14 • (08/31/96) • **80**
Valdiguié Monterey Wildflower 1996: Fresh and young, this quaffer has plenty of bright plum and grape flavors. Drink now, preferably at picnics and barbecues. 10,000 cases made. • $7 • (07/31/97) • **86**

LOLONIS | CALIFORNIA

Cabernet Sauvignon Mendocino County 1994: While it has fairly supple texture, the flavors are restrained, with hints of cherry, cola and coffee. Finish is short and herbal. 1,800 cases made. • $15 • (10/31/97) • **83**
Cabernet Sauvignon Mendocino County Lolonis Vineyards Private Reserve 1989 • $15 • (11/15/91) • **86**
Cabernet Sauvignon Mendocino County Private Reserve 1993: A perfumed, sandalwood note announces this unusual wine. On the palate, it's beefy and smoky, with cassis and herb notes. Tannins are a bit coarse. • $20 • (12/15/97) • **85**
Cabernet Sauvignon Mendocino County Private Reserve 1989 • $16 • (08/31/92) • **84**
Cabernet Sauvignon Mendocino County Private Reserve 1986 • $15 • (05/15/90) • **83**
Eugenia Mendocino County Late Harvest Private Reserve 1993: Sweet and honey-scented, but the focused apricot flavors are balanced nicely by tangy, citrus acidity. Ready to drink. 500 cases made. • $28 • (06/15/97) • **88**
Merlot Mendocino County Private Reserve 1995: Combines ripe cherry and berry with sage and herbal notes, turning elegant and spicy, with a dusty oak edge on the finish and just a twinge of bitterness. 900 cases made. • $22 • (05/15/98) • **84**
Merlot Mendocino County Private Reserve 1994: Shows menthol and anise qualities backed by firm tannins, and finishes moderately with cassis and blackberry overtones. 1,200 cases made. • $23 • (07/31/97) • **87**
Merlot Mendocino County Private Reserve 1993: Ultra fruity, ripe and jammy, with a racy edge to the wild berry, raspberry and spicy flavors. Not your typical Merlot, but a distinctive wine nonetheless. Drinkable now. 900 cases made. • $18 • (08/31/96) • **88**
Petite Sirah Mendocino Orpheus Private Reserve 1994: Underneath the chewy tannins beats a heart lively with bright blackberry and coffee flavors. Give it until 2000 or 2002 to chip off some of the tannins. 700 cases made. • $16 • (03/31/98) • **85**
Zinfandel Mendocino County 1995: Ripe, with earthy, leathery flavors woven into the core of plum and blackberry. Turns even more complex on the finish, where the flavors fan out with pretty floral notes. Best now through 2004. 2,500 cases made. • $16 • (06/15/98) • **89**
Zinfandel Mendocino County 1994: A bold and juicy California red, with black cherry, plum, wild berry and raspberry flavors that are ripe, plush and concentrated and finish in a complex aftertaste. A great find at this price and score. 2,000 cases made. • $12 • (04/30/97) HR • **92**
Zinfandel Mendocino County 1992 • $10 • (10/15/95) • **84**
Zinfandel Mendocino County 1991 • $10 • (10/15/94) • **83**
Zinfandel Mendocino County 1990 • $10 • (09/30/93) • **85**
Zinfandel Mendocino County Lolonis Vineyards Private Reserve Lot 1 1989 • $12 • (08/31/91) • **83**
Zinfandel Mendocino County Lolonis Vineyards Private Reserve Lot 2 1989 • $8 • (10/15/92) • **76**
Zinfandel Mendocino County Private Reserve 1994: Dark, ripe, rich and spicy, this is a high-octane-style Zinfandel with layers of juicy plum, black cherry and raspberry flavors, a hint of Port and lots of sage and spice flavors. Finishes off with a burst of fruit and just the right amount of tannin. It's drinking well now, and will into 2000. 1,300 cases made. • $19 • (12/31/97) SS • **92**
Zinfandel Mendocino County Private Reserve 1993: Funky. Its earthy flavors have a spicy, cedary edge and it picks up some odd notes on the finish. 600 cases made. • $17 • (04/30/97) • **79**
Zinfandel Mendocino County Private Reserve 1992 • $16 • (10/15/95) • **88**
Zinfandel Mendocino County Private Reserve 1991 • $16 • (10/15/94) • **85**
Zinfandel Mendocino County Private Reserve 1990 • $13 • (10/15/92) • **89**
Zinfandel Redwood Valley Private Reserve 1995: Shows off a range of ripe Zinfandel flavors, with tar, earth and sage built around the core of ripe plum and wild berry. Finishes with complex flavors and good length. Drink now to 2001. 800 cases made. • $22 • (03/31/98) • **87**

LONE OAK | CALIFORNIA

Cabernet Sauvignon Monterey 1992 • $6 • (11/15/94) • **79**

LONETREE | CALIFORNIA

Sangiovese Mendocino 1995: Smoke and cherry notes are fine, but harsh tannins make them hard to distinguish. Perhaps a few years in the cellar would help. 600 cases made. • $14 • (03/31/98) • **82**

Syrah Mendocino 1995: Supple and generous, its plum and currant flavors shaded nicely with hints of pepper and vanilla. Appealing now, should develop through 1999 to 2000. 600 cases made. • $14 • (03/31/98) • **87**

Zinfandel Mendocino 1996: Herbs, spice, black currant, blackberry and anise conspire here in a dark, intricate blend. The wine has both depth and finesse, though the tannins remain quite firm. Drink now through 2002. 602 cases made. • $14 • (06/15/98) • **88**

LONG | CALIFORNIA

Cabernet Sauvignon Napa Valley 1995: Complex interplay of toasty, cedary oak and ripe cherry, currant and plum, with an especially supple and silky texture and smooth, polished tannins. Turns even more complex on the finish, where the coffee, anise and spicy flavors fan out. Best from 1999 to 2006. 300 cases made. • $40 • (03/31/98) • **90**

Cabernet Sauvignon Napa Valley 1994: Smooth and supple, with a sense of harmony and finesse, this serves up an appealing array of ripe cherry, earth, coffee, chocolate and wild berry notes. Drink now. 175 cases made. • $35 • (01/31/97) • **90**

Cabernet Sauvignon Napa Valley 1993: Young and tannic, with strong wood flavors. Offers hints of ripe raisin and plum, but a hot, tannic aftertaste presides on the finish. 200 cases made. • $32 • (08/31/96) • **84**

Cabernet Sauvignon Napa Valley 1990 • $30 • (08/31/93) • **89**

Cabernet Sauvignon Napa Valley 1986: Mature, and losing its once delicious core of cherry and currant flavors. Not too tannic, it's enjoyable now, but best consumed before it loses any more flavor. • $NA • (12/15/96) • **86**

Cabernet Sauvignon Napa Valley 1984 • $38 • (12/15/88) • **88**

Cabernet Sauvignon Napa Valley 1983 • $36 • (08/31/87) • **72**

Chardonnay Napa Valley 1996: Crisp and flinty, with fresh, lively pear, melon and apple and a hint of citrus. Well focused, with a long, fruity aftertaste that lingers. Drink now through 2002. 1,400 cases made. • $31 • (05/31/98) • **91**

Chardonnay Napa Valley 1995: Bright, fresh and lively, with a hazelnut accent to the ripe, complex pear, fig and apricot flavors. Turns elegant and refined on the finish, where it shows a flinty edge. Drinkable now, but ageable, too. 1,690 cases made. • $31 • (05/31/97) • **91**

Chardonnay Napa Valley 1994: Clean, ripe and refreshing, with a lively core of ripe apple, pear, spice and honey notes that are well focused. Has a long, lingering aftertaste and is elegant for its touch of smoky oak. 1,800 cases made. • $30 • (02/28/97) • **91**

Chardonnay Napa Valley 1993 • $30 • (01/31/96) • **90**

Johannisberg Riesling Late Harvest Napa Valley Botrytis 1996: Sweet and wide-open in flavor, showing a purity of pear and honey character that glides and lingers on the nicely balanced finish. Drink now through 2001. 500 cases made. • $25 • 500ml • (05/15/98) • **92**

Johannisberg Riesling Late Harvest Napa Valley Botrytis 1990 • $18 • (09/15/91) • **86**

Pinot Grigio Napa Valley 1996: Firm and flinty, this refreshing wine offers hints of orange peel, lemon and grapefruit. It's begging for shellfish. 640 cases made. • $18 • (10/15/97) • **86**

Sangiovese Sonoma County Seghesio Vineyards 1995: Strives for complexity, with a broad range of rich, earthy, meaty currant, plum and berry flavors, shows off a supple texture and finishes with length and grace. 200 cases made. • $20 • (07/31/97) • **90**

Sauvignon Blanc Napa Valley 1995: Starts with earthy, mineral aromas, and the bright, delicately fashioned nectarine and apple flavors linger on the elegant, polished finish. 700 cases made. • $15 • (02/28/97) • **90**

Sauvignon Blanc Napa Valley 1994 • $14 • (05/15/96) • **87**

Sauvignon Blanc Sonoma County 1996: Marked by melon and citrus flavors, framed by subtle herb- and grass-tones. Bright and firm, it's a serious palate-cleanser. 600 cases made. • $15 • (01/31/98) • **85**

LONGORIA | CALIFORNIA

Cabernet Franc Santa Ynez Valley Blues Cuvée 1995: Lots of smoke and wood to this, with cherries and herbs taking a backseat. Tannins are manageable. Drink now. 435 cases made. • $21 • (03/31/98) • **81**

Cabernet Franc Santa Ynez Valley Blues Cuvée 1993 • $20 • (11/30/95) • **84**

Cabernet Sauvignon Santa Ynez Valley 1990 • $15 • (06/15/93) • **83**

Chardonnay Santa Ynez Valley Huber Vineyard 1994: Smooth and elegant, with a ripe, spicy core of pear, cream and vanilla notes; finishes with a trace of earthiness. 555 cases made. • $21 • (06/30/96) • **88**

Chardonnay Santa Ynez Valley Huber Vineyard 1993 • $16 • (07/31/95) • **86**

Chardonnay Santa Ynez Valley Santa Rita Cuvée 1996: Tight, firm and concentrated, with a rich, complex core of green apple, pear, melon and fig, turning subtle and polished on the finish, where the flavors linger on. This wine tames the sometimes exotic fruit from this appellation with harmony and grace. Drink now through 2002. 650 cases made. • $25 • (06/30/98) • **91**

Chardonnay Santa Ynez Valley Santa Rita Cuvée 1995: Ripe pear, fig and anise flavors are interesting, with added dimension from a gamy note. 455 cases made. • $23 • (06/15/97) • **87**

Merlot Santa Ynez Valley 1995: Well balanced, its spicy sage, herb, dried cherry and leather flavors working in sync with the supple texture and mild tannins. Finishes with a complex interplay of leather and fruit. Best now through 2002. 646 cases made. • $23 • (04/30/98) • **87**

Merlot Santa Ynez Valley 1994: Firm, tight and tannic, with a slight leathery accent to the plum and cherry notes. Finishes with a dry, tannic aftertaste; cellar into 1999. 468 cases made. • $21 • (07/31/97) • **88**

Merlot Santa Ynez Valley 1990 • $16 • (07/15/93) • **85**

Pinot Noir Santa Maria Valley Bien Nacido Vineyard 1995: Shows off flashes of pepper, herb and spice, with a core built around beefy herb, plum and earthy Pinot Noir flavors that turn elegant and delicate on the aftertaste. Drink now. 105 cases made. • $32 • (01/31/98) • **88**

Pinot Noir Santa Maria Valley Bien Nacido Vineyard 1994 • $23 • (04/30/96) • **86**

Pinot Noir Santa Maria Valley Bien Nacido Vineyard 1993 • $20 • (09/15/95) • **86**

Pinot Noir Santa Ynez Valley Benedict Vineyard 1989 • $28 • (02/28/93) • **86**

LORANE VALLEY | OREGON

Chardonnay Oregon 1996: On the crisp side, with simple melon and green apple flavors. Drink now. 9,000 cases made. • $10 • (06/15/98) • **83**

Pinot Noir Oregon 1995: Light and charming, with pretty strawberry and chocolate notes gliding delicately through the polished finish. Drink now. 20,000 cases made. • $10 • (06/15/98) • **84**

LORENZA-LAKE | CALIFORNIA

Petite Sirah Napa Valley Blockheadia Ringnosii 1996: Dark, dense and chewy, with glimpses of plum and wild berry. The aromas offer floral and raspberry notes. This is a lovely wine to drink now and for the next two to three years; but don't bet on it gaining. • $25 • (05/15/98) • **88**

Zinfandel Napa Valley Blockheadia Ringnosii 1996: Ripe, with complex wild berry, blackberry and raspberry flavors that are tightly wound. Finishes with mild tannins and fine length. 590 cases made. • $20 • (05/15/98) • **88**

LOS ENCANTOS | CALIFORNIA

Cabernet Sauvignon Napa Valley Covenant Reserve 1992 • $14 • (02/29/96) • **85**

Chardonnay Edna Valley Covenant Reserve 1996: Has a raw edge to its modest nutmeg and pear flavors. Drinkable now. 2,000 cases made. • $16 • (11/30/97) • **85**

Chardonnay Santa Maria Covenant Reserve 1994: Firm and tight, sporting a pretty focus to the spice, pear and apple notes, turning complex on the finish. Young and vibrant, it's well crafted. 5,000 cases made. • $14 • (02/29/96) • **88**

Pinot Noir Arroyo Grande Valley Covenant Reserve 1996: A blend of bell pepper, cherry and spice. The wine is soft, yet firm on the palate. The finish is a bit short. 1,000 cases made. • $16 • (11/30/97) • **84**

Pinot Noir Edna Valley Covenant Reserve 1994 • $14 • (01/31/96) • **84**

LOS OLIVOS | CALIFORNIA

Chardonnay Santa Barbara County 1993 • $18 • (09/30/95) • **90**

Pinot Noir Santa Barbara County 1993 • $20 • (02/29/96) • **75**

LUNA | CALIFORNIA

Sangiovese Napa Valley 1996: Captures the essence of Sangiovese with its ripe, bright cherry, berry and strawberry flavors, supple tannins and elegant aftertaste. Drink now. 1,600 cases made. • $18 • (05/15/98) • **87**

LYETH | CALIFORNIA

A Red Blend Alexander Valley 1992 • $18 • (08/31/95) • **87**
A Red Blend Alexander Valley 1991 • $14 • (10/15/94) SS • **89**
A Red Blend Alexander Valley 1990 • $13 • (06/30/93) • **87**
Chardonnay Sonoma County 1994: Elegant with a pretty band of pear, apple and spice, finishing with a trace of oak and a lingering finish. 8,000 cases made. • $11 • (02/29/96) • **87**
Chardonnay Sonoma County 1993 • $12 • (12/15/94) • **82**
Meritage Red California 1993: Soft around the edges, but the bright berry and herb flavors shine through brightly. Drinkable now. 25,000 cases made. • $13 • (11/15/95) • **86**
Meritage Red Napa-Sonoma Counties Reserve 1993: Complex and inviting, with well-integrated cedary oak, anise, currant and plum flavors. Finishes with supple tannins and hints of fruit and spice. Best in 1999. 2,000 cases made. • $29 • (02/28/97) • **87**
Meritage White North Coast 1995: A classy wine, a terrific value. It's well integrated, with melon, fig and lemon flavors that finish with elegance. A blend of 66 percent Sauvignon Blanc, 34 percent Sémillon. 16,000 cases made. • $9 • (06/30/97) • **88**
Meritage White Sonoma County 1994 • $7 • (06/15/96) • **86**
Red Alexander Valley 1988 • $12 • (11/15/92) • **84**
Red Alexander Valley 1987 • $15 • (10/15/92) • **83**
Red Alexander Valley 1986 • $23 • (11/15/90) • **88**
Red Alexander Valley 1985 • $19 Ⓐ • (05/31/89) • **86**
Red Alexander Valley 1984 • $18 • (03/15/88) • **91**
Red Alexander Valley 1983 • $17 • (06/30/87) • **91**
Red Alexander Valley 1982 • $16 • (06/16/86) • **86**

LYNMAR | CALIFORNIA

Chardonnay Russian River Valley Quail Hill Vineyard 1995: Intensely spicy, with an exotic Muscat-like flavor, the spiciness overrides the core of Chardonnay fruit, with just a hint of pear and melon creeping through. Finishes with a twinge of bitterness. Tastes more like Gewürztraminer than Chardonnay. 400 cases made. • $20 • (03/31/98) • **84**
Chardonnay Russian River Valley Quail Hill Vineyard 1994: Ripe and full-bodied, with a rich core of fig, pear, apple and melon flavors that turn a bit cloying on the slightly alcoholic finish. 313 cases made. • $20 • (06/15/97) • **88**
Pinot Noir Russian River Valley 1993 • $17 • (03/31/96) • **83**
Pinot Noir Russian River Valley 1992 • $16 • (05/15/95) • **88**
Pinot Noir Russian River Valley Quail Hill Vineyard 1995: Well proportioned, with elegant, spicy plum and cherry flavors and hints of mushroom and sage. Best now to 2000. 600 cases made. • $26 • (03/31/98) • **87**
Pinot Noir Russian River Valley Quail Hill Vineyard 1994: Young and still a bit woody, with a core of berry, rhubarb and mushroom flavors that are still a bit chunky. Drinkable now. 451 cases made. • $26 • (03/31/97) • **86**
Pinot Noir Russian River Valley Quail Hill Vineyard 1992 • $24 • (05/15/95) • **90**
Pinot Noir Russian River Valley Quail Hill Vineyard Reserve 1994: Polished and smooth, with a complex core of ripe cherry, raspberry and smoky, toasty oak flavors. Well balanced, with a slightly earthy, meaty edge that adds a nice dimension. 114 cases made. • $45 • (03/31/97) • **91**

LYTTON SPRINGS | CALIFORNIA

Cabernet Sauvignon Mendocino County Private Reserve 1988 • $18 • (11/15/91) • **80**
Cabernet Sauvignon Mendocino County Private Reserve 1987 • $18 • (09/15/90) • **88**
Palette Sonoma-Mendocino Counties NV • $10 • (11/15/91) • **83**
Zinfandel Sonoma County 1994 • $18 • (04/30/96) • **88**
Zinfandel Sonoma County 1992 • $16 • (08/31/94) • **89**
Zinfandel Sonoma County 1989 • $15 • (08/31/91) • **84**
Zinfandel Sonoma County 1988 • $12 • (07/31/90) • **90**
Zinfandel Sonoma County 1987 • $12 • (05/31/89) • **88**
Zinfandel Sonoma County 1986 • $10 • (10/15/88) • **87**
Zinfandel Sonoma County 1985 • $8 • (08/31/87) • **90**
Zinfandel Sonoma County 1984 • $36 Ⓐ • (10/31/86) • **70**
Zinfandel Sonoma County Valley Vista Vineyard Private Reserve 1981 • $12 • (01/01/85) • **85**

MAACAMA CREEK | CALIFORNIA

Cabernet Sauvignon Alexander Valley Melim Vineyard Reserve 1991 • $9 • (11/15/93) • **75**
Cabernet Sauvignon Alexander Valley Reserve 1992 • $12 • (11/15/94) • **77**
Cabernet Sauvignon Alexander Valley Reserve 1990 • $14 • (11/15/92) • **81**
Cabernet Sauvignon Sonoma County Melim Vineyard 1989 • $8 • (11/15/91) BB • **86**

MACGREGOR, CATHY | CALIFORNIA

Chardonnay Edna Valley MacGregor Vineyard 1994: An oak-driven wine, with a surprisingly dark, apricot color. Smoky, nutty, apricot flavors blend together in a rich texture, but in a somewhat awkward manner. An unusual style. 210 cases made. • $22 • (07/31/97) • **86**

MACKINAW | CALIFORNIA

Chardonnay California 1993: Has a sour, metallic edge that robs it of its charm. 2,611 cases made. • $11 • (07/31/96) • **74**

MACMILLAN | CALIFORNIA

Sauvignon Blanc San Luis Obispo French Camp Vineyard 1995: Sulfurous aromas tend to override the ripe pear and nectarine flavors hiding behind. Finish is bitter. 400 cases made. • $10 • (01/01/97) • **78**

MACROSTIE | CALIFORNIA

Chardonnay Carneros 1996: Intense, with spicy, cedary oak and a solid core of ripe pear-, melon- and peach-laced flavors. Finishes with toasty, smoky oak and a bit of coarseness, so short-term cellaring is advised. Best from 1999 through 2002. 8,000 cases made. • $18 • (07/31/98) • **87**
Chardonnay Carneros 1995: A ripe and generous style, sporting a complex array of pear, spice, apple, citrus and anise flavors that linger through a smooth and elegant finish. 6,800 cases made. • $18 • (06/15/97) SS • **91**
Chardonnay Carneros 1994: Bold, ripe and delicious, brimming with ripe pear, honey, hazelnut and light oak shadings. Gets extra marks for its silky texture and long aftertaste. Has a wonderful sense of harmony and finesse. 6,500 cases made. • $17 • (04/30/96) • **91**
Chardonnay Carneros 1993 • $16 • (02/28/95) • **85**
Chardonnay Carneros Reserve 1995: Showing some mature Chardonnay flavors, the core of earthy pineapple, citrus and butterscotch is quite rich, finishing with cedary oak and anise. Drink now through 2001. 604 cases made. • $25 • (07/31/98) • **90**
Chardonnay Carneros Reserve 1994: Rich and flavorful, loaded with spicy pear, peach, honey and citrus notes. Showing fine depth and concentration and finishing with a tightness that bodes well for short-term cellaring. 483 cases made. • $25 • (11/15/96) • **88**
Chardonnay Carneros Reserve 1993 • $23 • (01/31/96) • **92**
Merlot Carneros 1995: Greets you with ripe cherry, tobacco, cedar and spice flavors, turning crisp and firmly tannic on the finish. Drink now through 2002. 1,500 cases made. • $21 • (05/31/98) • **87**
Merlot Carneros 1994: Austere, with an earthy, metallic edge to the rustic berry and cherry flavors. Short-term cellaring might help soften the rough edges. 1,600 cases made. • $22 • (05/31/97) • **84**
Merlot Carneros 1993 • $19 • (02/29/96) • **86**
Merlot Carneros 1992 • $18 • (02/28/95) • **87**
Merlot Carneros 1991 • $18 • (09/15/94) • **82**
Pinot Noir Carneros 1995: Smooth, ripe and spicy, with pretty black cherry, plum and berry notes, finishing with a dash of anise and firm tannins. Ready now. 2,200 cases made. • $18 • (12/15/97) • **88**
Pinot Noir Carneros 1994: Subtle, with understated spicy cola, cherry and earthy mushroom flavors. Drinkable now. 700 cases made. • $17 • (08/31/96) • **85**

Key: SS—Spectator Selection CS—Cellar Selection HR—Highly Recommended BB—Best Buy $NA—Price not available Ⓐ—Auction Price (BT)—Barrel Tasting
Dates in parentheses indicate the issues in which the ratings were published.

Pinot Noir Carneros 1993 • $17 • (01/31/96) • **87**
Pinot Noir Carneros 1992 • $16 • (02/28/94) • **84**
Pinot Noir Carneros Reserve 1995: Supple and elegant, with silky tannins and pretty dried cherry, herb, sage, tar and spice flavors that glide along on the finish. Ready to drink. 400 cases made. • $26 • (12/15/97) • **88**
Pinot Noir Carneros Reserve 1994: Young, tight and intense, with a cedary oak accent that overrides the ripe cherry and plum flavors. Finishes with hints of tea and mint. Drinkable now. 150 cases made. • $25 • (11/15/96) • **87**

MADDALENA | CALIFORNIA

Cabernet Sauvignon Alexander Valley Reserve 1986 • $10 • (03/31/90) • **77**
Cabernet Sauvignon Alexander Valley Reserve 1985 • $11 • (06/30/89) • **78**
Cabernet Sauvignon Sonoma County 1990 • $8 • (11/15/94) • **76**
Cabernet Sauvignon Sonoma County 1988 • $7 • (03/31/92) • **79**
Cabernet Sauvignon Sonoma County 1985 • $6 • (05/31/88) • **74**
Cabernet Sauvignon Sonoma County Vintner's Reserve 1984 • $9 • (03/31/87) • **82**
Chardonnay Central Coast San Simeon Reserve 1996: Minerally, with a nice core of citrus, pear and toast. Delicate flavors linger on the crisp finish. Drink now. 6,000 cases made. • $14 • (07/31/98) • **84**
Chardonnay Monterey 1996: Starts with an awkward floral note, but straightens out with simple citrus and apple flavors. Drink now. 25,000 cases made. • $10 • (07/31/98) • **79**
Johannisberg Riesling Central Coast 1993 • $6 • (02/28/95) • **78**
Johannisberg Riesling Monterey County 1996: Shows earthy, peppery, floral aromas and flavors that turn very soft on the gentle finish. 5,000 cases made. • $8 • (03/31/98) • **81**
Merlot Central Coast San Simeon Collection 1990 • $9 • (09/15/94) • **77**
Merlot Central Coast San Simeon Collection 1989 • $12 • (05/31/92) • **73**
Merlot Central Coast San Simeon Reserve 1996: Marked by black cherry, licorice, spice and vanilla, the wine is made in a rustic style, with chunky tannins and bright acidity. Pretty oaky. Drink now. 10,000 cases made. • $15 • (07/31/98) • **83**
Muscat Canelli Central Coast 1996: Nicely fruity and sweet, not especially characteristic of Muscat in flavor, but very pretty in a peachy-apple way. Ready now. 3,000 cases made. • $8 • (03/31/98) BB • **85**
Muscat Canelli Central Coast 1993 • $6 • (12/31/94) • **82**

MADIGAN | CALIFORNIA

Cabernet Sauvignon Napa Valley 1991 • $10 • (11/15/93) • **79**
Cabernet Sauvignon Napa Valley 1989 • $10 • (11/15/93) • **78**

MADRON LAKE HILLS | MICHIGAN

White Riesling Late Harvest Lake Erie Heartland Vineyards Semi-Dry 1990 • $10 • (02/29/92) • **74**

MADRONA | CALIFORNIA

Cabernet Franc El Dorado 1986 • $11 • (03/31/92) • **73**
Cabernet Sauvignon El Dorado 1992: This restrained and oaky wine packs a tannic punch but never delivers on flavor. 785 cases made. • $12 • (11/30/96) • **73**
Cabernet Sauvignon El Dorado 1991 • $11 • (05/31/95) • **81**
Cabernet Sauvignon El Dorado 1985 • $12 • (04/15/92) • **82**
Chardonnay El Dorado 1996: Smoothly textured and well focused, with green apple, apricot and earthy orange peel notes. The intensity picks up on the long, concentrated finish. Drink now through 2000. 1,100 cases made. • $12 • (07/31/98) • **86**
Chardonnay El Dorado 1994: Light and crisp, with modest pear and citrus flavors that turn a bit earthy on the finish. 629 cases made. • $12 • (07/31/96) • **81**
Chardonnay El Dorado 1993 • $12 • (07/31/95) • **85**
Johannisberg Riesling El Dorado 1996: Light, slightly resiny in flavor, with nice apple notes to keep it balanced. Drink soon. 624 cases made. • $8 • (03/31/98) • **80**
Johannisberg Riesling El Dorado 1993: Light and crisp, but with a surprisingly bitter edge to the modest apple flavors. 488 cases made. • $7 • (07/31/96) • **80**
Zinfandel El Dorado 1995: A solid red, packed with ripe blackberry flavor. Slightly toasty. A firm wine with a racy acidity balance. Drink now. 959 cases made. • $10 • (12/15/97) • **85**
Zinfandel El Dorado 1993 • $9 • (04/30/96) • **83**
Zinfandel El Dorado 1992 • $8 • (10/15/95) • **84**
Zinfandel El Dorado 1989 • $8 • (10/15/92) • **64**

MAISON DEUTZ | CALIFORNIA

Brut San Luis Obispo County Reserve 1992: Marked by ripe, spicy pear and apple flavors, with hints of lemon and vanilla. Turns elegant and supple, finishing with notes of toast and earth. 1,000 cases made. • $18 • (11/30/96) • **88**
Brut San Luis Obispo County Reserve 1990 • $23 • (12/31/94) • **85**
Brut San Luis Obispo County Reserve 1987 • $22 • (10/31/91) • **88**
Brut San Luis Obispo County Reserve 1986 • $22 • (04/30/91) • **77**

MAKOR | CALIFORNIA

Pinot Blanc Santa Barbara County Bien Nacido Vineyard 1995: Good, with appealing pear and subtle peach flavors. 329 cases made. • $11 • (08/31/96) • **83**
Zinfandel California 1995: Very complete and harmonious, with layers of rich plum, blackberry, cherry and spice flavors framed by spicy oak notes. Smooth, ripe and complex, with a long aftertaste. 365 cases made. • $12 • (04/30/97) • **90**

MANISCHEWITZ | CALIFORNIA

Pinot Noir Russian River Valley 1989 • $9 • (03/31/91) • **74**

MANZANITA RIDGE | CALIFORNIA

Zinfandel Alexander Valley 1988 • $8 • (07/15/92) BB • **89**

MARBLE CREST | WASHINGTON

Cabernet Sauvignon Columbia Valley 1993: Soft and generous, centered around gentle plum and berry flavors. Ready now. 4,200 cases made. • $8 • (09/30/95) • **82**
Chardonnay Columbia Valley 1993 • $8 • (09/30/95) • **84**
Merlot Columbia Valley 1993 • $10 • (09/30/95) • **80**

MARCASSIN | CALIFORNIA

Chardonnay Alexander Valley Gauer Vineyard Upper Barn 1995: Truly exotic, ripe, rich and flavorful, with complex, concentrated pear, fig, citrus, anise and spicy oak flavors, long and lingering on the aftertaste. Ready now. 144 cases made. • $45 • (06/15/97) • **94**
Chardonnay Alexander Valley Gauer Vineyard Upper Barn 1994: Bold, ripe, ultrarich and creamy, loaded with tiers of pear, fig and melon flavors, adding some complexity on the finish with its echoes of anise and spice. A real mouthful of Chardonnay that will do well in the cellar. 275 cases made. • $39 • (05/15/96) CS • **94**
Chardonnay Alexander Valley Gauer Vineyard Upper Barn 1993 • $36 • (06/30/95) HR • **92**
Chardonnay Carneros Hudson Vineyard 1994: Serves up a mouthful of ripe pear, grapefruit and lemon flavors framed by toasty, smoky oak. The texture is smooth and polished, leading to its long, rich, complex aftertaste. 200 cases made. • $39 • (05/15/96) • **93**
Chardonnay Carneros Hudson Vineyard 1993 • $36 • (06/30/95) • **90**
Chardonnay Carneros Hudson Vineyards E Block 1995: This California Chard is impeccably balanced, with a smooth, rich with a buttery texture and a generous core of ripe pear, citrus, tart pineapple and spice flavors that linger for a long, tapered aftertaste. Delicious. 240 cases made. • $45 • (06/30/97) HR • **95**
Chardonnay Sonoma Coast Lorenzo Vineyard 1995: A bold, ripe and flavorful style, loaded with spicy anise and vanilla-tinged Chardonnay flavors. Picks up creamy pear and vanilla notes on the lingering finish. 168 cases made. • $45 • (06/15/97) • **92**
Chardonnay Sonoma Coast Lorenzo Vineyard 1993 • $36 • (06/30/95) • **91**

MARCELINA | CALIFORNIA

Cabernet Sauvignon Napa County 1993: Well focused, with spicy currant, sage, mineral and tar notes and firm tannins on the finish. Drink now. From Gallo. 19,000 cases made. • $20 • (12/15/97) • **87**
Chardonnay Napa Valley 1995: Complex. Shows a range of cedary oak and fruit flavors, with its layers of ripe pear, fig, peach and apple, and picks up

a spicy edge on the finish. From Gallo. 10,000 cases made. • $18 • (12/15/97) • **88**

MARIETTA | CALIFORNIA

Cabernet Sauvignon Sonoma County 1987 • $10 • (02/28/91) • **87**
Cabernet Sauvignon Sonoma County 1985 • $10 • (06/30/90) • **83**
Cabernet Sauvignon Sonoma County 1984 • $10 • (12/31/87) • **78**
Cabernet Sauvignon Sonoma County 1981 • $9 • (06/16/84) • **78**
Old Vine Red Sonoma County Lot No. Three NV • $4 • (04/16/86) BB • **85**
Old Vine Red Sonoma County Lot No. Five NV • $5 • (12/31/87) • **77**
Old Vine Red Sonoma County Lot No. Seven NV • $6 • (11/15/89) BB • **82**
Old Vine Red Sonoma County Lot No. Eight NV • $5 • (05/31/90) BB • **81**
Old Vine Red Sonoma County Lot No. Ten NV • $6 • (04/30/92) • **79**
Old Vine Red Sonoma County Lot No. Eleven NV • $6 • (03/31/93) • **79**
Old Vine Red Sonoma County Lot No. Fourteen NV • $8 • (04/30/95) • **83**
Old Vine Red Sonoma County Lot No. Seventeen NV: With lots of ripe flavors on a chewy texture, this is a red wine with some grip. Drink with hearty food. 13,000 cases made. • $9 • (12/31/96) • **83**
Petite Sirah Sonoma County 1988 • $10 • (03/15/92) • **84**
Port Alexander Valley 1989 • $16 • (05/31/95) • **86**
Zinfandel Geyserville 1995: Good intensity and plenty of plum, cherry and berry. Turns simple on the finish, but holds its flavors and is well balanced. Drink now. 5,000 cases made. • $14 • (06/15/98) • **84**
Zinfandel Sonoma County 1992 • $11 • (09/15/95) • **85**
Zinfandel Sonoma County 1988 • $8 • (12/31/91) BB • **87**
Zinfandel Sonoma County 1987 • $8 • (11/30/90) • **79**
Zinfandel Sonoma County 1985 • $7 • (12/31/87) • **87**
Zinfandel Sonoma County 1984 • $7 • (01/31/87) • **90**
Zinfandel Sonoma County 1982 • $6 • (06/16/84) • **73**
Zinfandel Sonoma County Reserve 1985 • $10 • (12/31/87) • **88**

MARILYN MERLOT | CALIFORNIA

Merlot Napa Valley 1990 • $14 • (06/15/93) • **85**
Merlot Napa Valley 1989 • $14 • (05/31/92) • **87**
Merlot Napa Valley 1988 • $13 • (05/31/91) • **85**
Merlot Napa Valley 1986 • $13 • (12/31/88) • **85**

MARION | CALIFORNIA

Cabernet Sauvignon California 1989 • $9 • (11/15/91) • **83**
Cabernet Sauvignon California 1985 • $5 • (12/31/87) • **62**
Merlot Napa Valley 1991 • $9 • (04/15/93) • **84**
Pinot Noir Sonoma County 1991 • $8 • (02/28/94) • **75**

MARK RIDGE | CALIFORNIA

Cabernet Sauvignon California 1994: An essence of green beans fades into a wooden finish. • $NA • (11/30/96) • **70**
Chardonnay California 1995: Soft and inviting, this has pretty honey and green apple flavors that linger gently on the finish. • $NA • (07/31/97) • **84**

MARK WEST | CALIFORNIA

Blanc de Noirs Russian River Valley 1984 • $17 • (12/31/88) • **71**
Chardonnay Russian River Valley 1996: A medium-weight, fruit-driven style, with ripe pear, peach and spicy Chardonnay flavors. Holds its fruitiness through the finish. Drink now. 9,876 cases made. • $15 • (05/15/98) • **86**
Chardonnay Russian River Valley 1995: Delivers ripe, complex fruit flavors, notes of apple, pear, melon and fig, in a straightforward style. 4,300 cases made. • $14 • (06/15/97) • **87**
Chardonnay Russian River Valley 1994: A good Chardonnay, straightforward in style, with ripe pear, citrus and apple notes. 6,000 cases made. • $13 • (01/01/97) • **85**
Chardonnay Russian River Valley 1993 • $13 • (05/31/96) SS • **89**
Chardonnay Russian River Valley Reserve 1995: Delicious Chardonnay, with a broad array of ripe pear, spice, apple and hazelnut flavors, a rich, silky texture, and a long, full aftertaste. 556 cases made. • $20 • (06/15/97) • **90**

Key: SS—Spectator Selection CS—Cellar Selection HR—Highly Recommended BB—Best Buy $NA—Price not available Ⓐ—Auction Price (BT)—Barrel Tasting
Dates in parentheses indicate the issues in which the ratings were published.

Gewürztraminer Russian River Valley 1996: Fresh and zingy, with citrusy flavors but not much to distinguish it as Gewürz. Pleasant sipper. 2,700 cases made. • $10 • (07/31/97) • **82**
Gewürztraminer Russian River Valley 1994 • $9 • (06/30/96) • **86**
Johannisberg Riesling Late Harvest Russian River Valley 1983 • $10/375ml • (03/16/86) • **79**
Pinot Noir Russian River Valley 1995: Young and vibrant, with a slightly meaty accent to the ripe plum and berry flavors. Turns more complex on the finish, where the flavors fold together nicely. Drinkable now. 750 cases made. • $14 • (07/31/97) • **87**
Pinot Noir Russian River Valley 1993: Light-bodied and supple, with pleasant berry and earth flavors. 2,012 cases made. • $13 • (07/31/96) • **82**
Pinot Noir Russian River Valley 1991 • $10 • (02/28/94) • **84**
Pinot Noir Russian River Valley 1990 • $14 • (02/28/93) • **82**
Pinot Noir Russian River Valley Ellis Vineyard 1986 • $14 • (03/31/90) • **81**
Pinot Noir Russian River Valley Ellis Vineyard 1984 • $10 • (03/15/87) • **84**
Pinot Noir Sonoma County 1986 • $8 • (02/28/89) • **80**
Sauvignon Blanc Russian River Valley 1996: A bright blend of herb and grapefruit flavors, with tangy acidity and a racy finish. 446 cases made. • $9 • (06/30/97) • **87**
Sauvignon Blanc Russian River Valley 1994 • $9 • (05/31/96) • **83**
Zinfandel Sonoma County Robert Rue Vineyard 1987 • $17 • (05/15/92) • **86**
Zinfandel Sonoma County Robert Rue Vineyard 1986 • $14 • (03/15/90) • **83**
Zinfandel Sonoma County Robert Rue Vineyard 1985 • $14 • (07/31/88) • **85**

MARKHAM | CALIFORNIA

Cabernet Sauvignon Napa Valley 1994: This seductive wine not only grows on you with each sip, it's a tremendous value, too. Its core of ripe, rich currant and black cherry flavors unfolds into a supple, polished texture, and the flavors are pure, focused and linger long on the finish—a most encouraging sign. Best after 2000. 13,350 cases made. • $15 • (10/31/97) SS • **92**
Cabernet Sauvignon Napa Valley 1993: Clean and well balanced, a touch on the simple side. Offers modest cherry and berry flavors that linger on the finish. 10,710 cases made. • $15 • (11/15/96) • **86**
Cabernet Sauvignon Napa Valley 1992 • $17 • (11/30/95) • **88**
Cabernet Sauvignon Napa Valley 1991 • $17 • (11/15/94) • **88**
Cabernet Sauvignon Napa Valley 1990 • $17 • (11/15/93) SS • **90**
Cabernet Sauvignon Napa Valley 1989 • $17 • (11/15/92) • **88**
Cabernet Sauvignon Napa Valley 1988 • $16 • (11/15/92) • **80**
Cabernet Sauvignon Napa Valley 1987: A lighter style, with clean, simple cherry, cedar and berry notes. Pleasant and ready to drink. • $15 • (12/15/97) • **86**
Cabernet Sauvignon Napa Valley 1986: A solid, if unspectacular, effort. This is a mature wine with enough ripe, juicy plum and cherry flavors to hold your interest. Drinkable now. • $NA • (12/15/96) • **87**
Cabernet Sauvignon Napa Valley 1985 • $17 • (04/15/90) • **91**
Cabernet Sauvignon Napa Valley 1984 • $12 • (10/31/88) • **87**
Cabernet Sauvignon Napa Valley 1983 • $26 • (07/31/89) • **90**
Cabernet Sauvignon Napa Valley 1982 • $13 • (11/15/87) • **92**
Cabernet Sauvignon Napa Valley 1978 • $30 • (11/15/92) • **86**
Chardonnay Napa Valley 1996: Smooth, ripe and spicy, with appealing pear, apple, spice and vanilla notes. Of medium weight, it's not especially concentrated, so drink soon. 26,500 cases made. • $16 • (05/15/98) • **87**
Chardonnay Napa Valley 1995: Distinguished by its spice, ripe apple and peach accents, and hints of tangerine. It's a medium-weight style that turns elegant and has an impressive aftertaste. Ready now. 25,000 cases made. • $15 • (12/31/96) • **88**
Chardonnay Napa Valley 1994: Bold, ripe, complex and showing a broad spectrum of pear, honey, spice and mineral notes. It picks up a toasty oak character, then keeps echoing fruit in its long, complex aftertaste. 26,700 cases made. • $15 • (06/15/96) SS • **90**
Chardonnay Napa Valley Barrel Fermented 1993 • $17 • (06/15/95) SS • **91**
Chardonnay Napa Valley Reserve 1995: Smooth, ripe, rich and creamy, with tiers of ripe pear, vanilla, fig and melon flavors, a long, rich, concentrated aftertaste. 500 cases made. • $28 • (08/31/97) • **92**
Laurent Napa Valley Reserve 1990 • $25 • (12/31/94) • **85**
Merlot Napa Valley 1995: Lively ripe fruit up front, with cherry, plum and blackberry notes, but it lacks the complexity, depth and polish usually found in this wine. Drink now to 2004. 49,000 cases made. • $18 • (05/15/98) • **87**
Merlot Napa Valley 1994: Supple and well balanced, with a zesty core of currant, anise and cedary oak flavors. Medium- to full-bodied, it's an attractive wine that's tightly wound now and needs cellaring into 2000, or even 2001. 42,000 cases made. • $18 • (12/31/96) • **88**
Merlot Napa Valley 1993 • $16 • (12/15/95) • **89**

Merlot Napa Valley 1992 • $17 • (04/15/95) • **88**
Merlot Napa Valley 1991 • $16 • (05/31/94) • **87**
Merlot Napa Valley 1990 • $15 • (05/31/93) HR • **91**
Merlot Napa Valley 1989 • $15 • (05/31/92) • **85**
Merlot Napa Valley 1988 • $14 • (04/15/91) HR • **90**
Merlot Napa Valley 1987 • $14 • (10/15/89) • **91**
Merlot Napa Valley 1985 • $11 • (04/30/88) • **88**
Merlot Napa Valley 1981 • $8 • (08/01/84) • **86**
Merlot Napa Valley Reserve 1994: Rich and flavorful, with tiers of ripe, spicy black cherry, currant, plum and mineral flavors, turning elegant and complex on the finish. Shows great depth and concentration. 1,000 cases made. • $35 • (08/31/97) • **91**
Muscat Napa Valley Blanc 1996: Rich, sweet and appealing for its uncomplicated pear and litchi flavors, finishing sweet but not cloying. Ready now. 1,700 cases made. • $9/375ml • (05/15/98) • **87**
Petite Sirah Napa Valley 1993: A big, hearty, chewy style that packs in lots of flavor, this California red exhibits good varietal character. It's dark, firm, rich and tannic, with a spicy mineral accent to the plum and currant flavors. Drink now. 3,000 cases made. • $17 • (08/31/97) SS • **90**
Sauvignon Blanc Napa Valley 1996: Bright and zippy, this white sings harmoniously with lemon-lime high notes and an herbal, minerally bass. It's not afraid of making a strong varietal statement and does so with elegance and enthusiasm. A delicious example of California's strides with Sauvignon Blanc, and so reasonably priced. 19,000 cases made. • $12 • (09/15/97) SS • **90**
Sauvignon Blanc Napa Valley 1995: Light and remarkably fruity, with subtle, resiny, floral and apricot flavors that linger on the finish. 28,500 cases made. • $10 • (09/15/96) BB • **88**
Sauvignon Blanc Napa Valley 1994 • $8 • (08/31/95) BB • **87**
Sauvignon Blanc Napa Valley 1993 • $8 • (06/30/95) SS • **89**
Zinfandel Napa Valley 1995: Tight and firm, with earthy wild berry, plum and cedar notes, finishing with firm tannins and a hint of raisin and tar. Drink now through 2002. 2,250 cases made. • $16 • (05/31/98) • **86**
Zinfandel Napa Valley 1994: Tightly focused around a core of black cherry and wild berry flavors, it's a classic old-vine style of Zin that avoids excessive alcohol or heat. Turns tannic on the finish, but it's comfortably drinkable now, and into 2000. 204 cases made. • $17 • (08/31/97) • **89**

MARKKO | OHIO

Cabernet Sauvignon Conneaut 1988 • $10 • (02/29/92) • **76**
Pinot Noir Conneaut 1989 • $15 • (02/29/92) • **76**

MARQUAM HILL | OREGON

Chardonnay Willamette Valley 1993: A medium-weight wine with appealing pear, honey and spice flavors, plus a touch of acacia on the round finish. Smooth and ripe. Ready to drink. 675 cases made. • $12 • (04/30/97) • **87**
Gewürztraminer Willamette Valley 1993: Has a character of decaying flowers, in an off-dry frame. 200 cases made. • $8 • (04/30/97) • **76**
Gewürztraminer Willamette Valley Semi-Sweet 1996: Extremely earthy, sour and unpleasant. Past its prime. • $8 • (06/30/98) • **74**
Müller-Thurgau Willamette Valley Dry 1995: Fresh and soft, with pretty Golden Delicious apple and citruslike flavors. 365 cases made. • $8 • (02/28/97) • **83**
Pinot Gris Willamette Valley 1995: Crisp and bright, with citrusy apple and melon flavors that swirl around enticingly on the racy finish. Drink now. 400 cases made. • $12 • (02/28/97) • **88**
Pinot Gris Willamette Valley 1993 • $12 • (11/30/94) • **81**
Pinot Noir Willamette Valley 1993: Minty, fresh and zingy, a tart wine with splashes of berry and oak flavors bubbling on the finish. Drink now. 675 cases made. • $12 • (02/28/97) • **83**
Pinot Noir Willamette Valley 1991 • $14 • (02/28/93) • **71**
Pinot Noir Willamette Valley Barrel Aged 1992 • $12 • (11/30/94) • **80**
Riesling Willamette Valley Off-Dry 1993: Remarkably fresh and appealing for a 4-year-old Riesling, nicely balanced and charming. Ready to drink. 350 cases made. • $8 • (04/30/97) • **85**
Riesling Willamette Valley Semi-Sweet 1997: Light and gentle, off-dry, with simple apple and floral flavors. Drink now. 1,300 cases made. • $8 • (06/30/98) • **81**
Riesling Willamette Valley Semi-Sweet 1995: Soft, fresh and inviting for its spicy, green apple flavors and gentle texture. Ready now. 700 cases made. • $8 • (04/30/97) • **86**

MARTIN BROTHERS | CALIFORNIA

Aleatico California 1990 • $10/375ml • (03/15/92) • **78**
Cabernet Sauvignon Paso Robles 1989 • $12 • (11/15/91) • **77**
Cabernet Sauvignon Paso Robles Etrusco 1995: Smooth, ripe and flavorful, with harmonious currant, sage, tea and cedar flavors and mild, supple tannins. Finishes with an odd flavor from oak, which may dissipate with time. 2,150 cases made. • $18 • (10/31/97) • **85**
Chardonnay Paso Robles in Botti 1996: Sweet, sour and bitter, with metallic flavors. Not a nice combination. Tasted twice, with consistent notes. Drink now. 2,606 cases made. • $10 • (07/31/98) • **69**
Chardonnay Paso Robles in Botti 1995: Excessively earthy for the modest citruslike flavors. 2,668 cases made. • $12 • (07/31/97) • **77**
Chardonnay Paso Robles in Botti 1994: Light and silky, showing the effects of barrel fermentation with spicy, leesy flavors and smooth texture; some length on aftertaste. Drinkable now. 2,328 cases made. • $12 • (09/30/95) • **84**
Chardonnay Paso Robles in Botti 1993 • $12 • (07/31/95) • **81**
Etrusco Paso Robles 1993: Bright and lively, with a pretty, toasty oak overlay to the ripe plum and cherry flavors, finishing with a smoky edge to the fruit. 1,500 cases made. • $16 • (12/15/95) • **90**
Etrusco Paso Robles 1992 • $18 • (02/28/95) • **79**
Etrusco Paso Robles 1991 • $18 • (06/30/93) • **89**
Etrusco Paso Robles 1990 • $18 • (11/15/92) • **85**
Gemelli Paso Robles NV • $25 • (10/15/95) • **86**
Malvasia Bianca California Vin Santo 1990 • $15/5.(03/15/92) • **81**
Moscato Allegro California 1992 • $10 • (05/15/93) • **77**
Moscato Frizzante California 1991 • $9 • (03/31/92) • **88**
Muscat Canelli Paso Robles Allegro Moscato 1994 • $10 • (11/30/95) • **85**
Nebbiolo California 1989 • $9 • (11/15/91) • **76**
Nebbiolo California 1987 • $12 • (12/15/89) • **75**
Nebbiolo California 1986 • $12 • (12/15/89) • **75**
Nebbiolo California 1982 • $7 • (04/01/84) • **78**
Nebbiolo California Vecchio 1992 • $20 • (12/15/95) • **84**
Nebbiolo California Vecchio 1990 • $18 • (05/31/93) • **83**
Nebbiolo Central Coast 1995: Canned cherries and thyme flavors recline on a thinly layered, somewhat tannic bed. 1,780 cases made. • $11 • (09/15/97) • **81**
Nebbiolo Central Coast 1993 • $10 • (12/15/95) • **84**
Nebbiolo Central Coast Vecchio 1994: Toasty oak and plum flavors dominate this lighter-style Nebbiolo. Finishes with an herbal edge. 493 cases made. • $20 • (09/15/97) • **83**
Nebbiolo Paso Robles 1987 • $12 • (12/15/89) • **85**
Pinot Grigio Central Coast 1994 • $12 • (11/30/95) • **84**
Pinot Grigio Central Coast 1993 • $12 • (01/01/95) • **85**
Sangiovese Central Coast Il Palio 1996: Rich, juicy and fragrant with plum and floral character, this is unusual in style but nicely balanced. Ready now. 1,550 cases made. • $12 • (11/30/97) • **83**
Sangiovese Paso Robles Il Palio 1994 • $12 • (06/15/96) • **84**
Sangiovese Paso Robles Il Palio 1992 • $12 • (05/31/94) • **82**
Zinfandel Paso Robles 1986 • $8 • (12/15/89) • **78**
Zinfandel Paso Robles 1985 • $6 • (02/15/88) • **83**
Zinfandel Paso Robles La Primitiva 1995: Ripe and spicy, with lots of cherry and berry notes that are quite pleasing. Drinkable now. 630 cases made. • $12 • (04/30/97) • **84**
Zinfandel Paso Robles La Primitiva 1994: A medium-weight wine, tart and a bit earthy, with hints of wild berry, raspberry and spice. Ready to drink. 619 cases made. • $11 • (04/30/97) • **82**
Zinfandel Paso Robles La Primitiva 1993 • $10 • (10/15/95) • **84**
Zinfandel Paso Robles La Primitiva 1992 • $10 • (06/15/95) • **83**
Zinfandel Paso Robles La Primitiva 1991 • $10 • (10/15/94) • **84**
Zinfandel Paso Robles La Primitiva 1990 • $9 • (03/31/93) • **82**
Zinfandel Port Paso Robles La Primitiva Appassito 1990 • $12 • (03/15/92) • **83**

MARTINELLI | CALIFORNIA

Chardonnay Russian River Valley Gold Ridge 1995: Smooth, ripe, complex and harmonious, with layers of fig, melon, apricot and pear flavors, turning spicy and showing off its oaky attributes. Finishes with touches of hazelnut and spice. Ready now. 500 cases made. • $20 • (05/31/97) • **93**
Chardonnay Russian River Valley Gold Ridge 1994: Ripe, rich and full-bodied, with tiers of ripe pear, fig, honey and melon flavors. Well oaked too, but the flavors marry well together, rendering an altogether rich and complex wine. 325 cases made. • $18 • (11/15/96) • **92**

Chardonnay Sonoma Coast Charles Ranch 1995: Complex, with ripe, intense, concentrated pear, spice, melon and fig flavors, turning elegant and seamless on the finish, where a hint of tangerine adds dimension. 500 cases made. • $25 • (02/28/98) • **91**
Gewürztraminer Russian River Valley 1995: Beautifully structured to highlight its pretty floral and grapefruit flavors and luscious undertone of apricot and mineral notes—all of which persist through the off-dry finish. Ready now. 585 cases made. • $9 • (10/15/96) • **90**
Gewürztraminer Russian River Valley Dry Select 1995: Soft, round and fresh. A generous mouthful of pineapple, citrus and rose petal flavors. Ready now. 86 cases made. • $12 • (10/15/96) • **86**
Gewürztraminer Russian River Valley Martinelli Vineyard 1996: Soft, not very sweet, with simple pear and citrus flavors and a hint of rose petal on the finish. Drink now. 750 cases made. • $12 • (03/31/98) • **83**
Gewürztraminer Russian River Valley Martinelli Vineyard Dry Select 1996: Bright, pull-out-the-stops Gewürz flavors fill this lively, smooth-textured wine. On the dry side, it has litchi, grapefruit and dusky spice flavors that linger on the smooth finish. No bitterness. Drink now. 145 cases made. • $18 • (03/31/98) • **88**
Pinot Noir Russian River Valley 1994: A delicate style, ripe, smooth and elegant, with a creamy texture and complex cherry, berry and spice flavors that linger long on the finish. 250 cases made. • $25 • (09/30/96) • **88**
Pinot Noir Russian River Valley Martinelli Vineyard 1995: Showing some mature earth and cola flavors, with hints of cherry and berry folding in on the finish. Has a pretty, spicy oak aftertaste. 500 cases made. • $25 • (05/31/97) • **87**
Pinot Noir Russian River Valley Martinelli Vineyard Reserve 1995: Marked by a smoky, meaty edge, it slowly unveils some cola and wild berry flavors before the wood and tannins weigh in. Best to cellar short-term. 250 cases made. • $36 • (01/31/98) • **87**
Sauvignon Blanc Russian River Valley 1993 • $9 • (08/31/94) • **71**
Sauvignon Blanc Russian River Valley Martinelli Vineyard 1996: Rich on the palate, with almost a hint of sweetness, displaying attractive melon, pineapple, lemon and lime notes. The finish is bright and refreshing. 700 cases made. • $12 • (01/31/98) • **87**
Zinfandel Russian River Valley Jackass Vineyard 1996: A big, potent, high-extract wine that takes time to open up. Once it does, it's packed with chewy, earthy black cherry, mineral, sage and spice, finishing with a strong cedary oak flavor. High in alcohol, it has a hot aftertaste. Drink now through 2004. • $25 • (06/15/98) • **89**
Zinfandel Russian River Valley Jackass Vineyard 1995: Smooth, ripe and smoky, with lots of black cherry, wild berry, cola and plum flavors that pick up a complex earthy, spicy edge. 550 cases made. • $25 • (06/15/97) • **91**
Zinfandel Russian River Valley Jackass Vineyard 1994: Dark, ripe and intense. Delivers an elegant core of complex, rich, plush plum, cherry, currant and berry flavors, with a tarry, spicy aftertaste. Delicious now. 275 cases made. • $25 • (09/30/96) • **92**
Zinfandel Russian River Valley Jackass Vineyard 1992 • $14 • (10/15/94) • **88**
Zinfandel Russian River Valley Jackass Vineyard 1991 • $12 • (05/31/93) • **81**
Zinfandel Russian River Valley Jackass Vineyard 1990 • $13 • (12/15/92) • **91**
Zinfandel Russian River Valley Martinelli Vineyard 1989 • $13 • (12/15/92) • **81**
Zinfandel Russian River Valley Martinelli Vineyard 1988 • $11 • (04/30/91) • **85**

MARTINI & PRATI | CALIFORNIA

Barbera California 1994: Light and earthy, having lost whatever fruit-flavored charm it once had. Fading. 1,481 cases made. • $10 • (11/30/96) • **78**
Fuoco di Sant' Elmo California 1993: A bright and flavorful red on a soft frame, offering a nice burst of blackberry and cherry flavors, finishing with polish. Ready now. 600 cases made. • $20 • (02/28/97) • **85**
Muscat California Gato Selvaggio Moscato Bianco 1995: Offers pretty fruit and floral flavors that are simple and a wee bit syrupy. 1,313 cases made. • $10 • (04/30/97) • **80**

Key: SS—Spectator Selection CS—Cellar Selection HR—Highly Recommended BB—Best Buy $NA—Price not available Ⓐ—Auction Price (BT)—Barrel Tasting
Dates in parentheses indicate the issues in which the ratings were published.

Pinot Bianco Monterey 1996: Pretty mandarin orange, spice and vanilla notes highlight this bright but fleshy wine. A slight mineral edge leads to an attractive finish. 786 cases made. • $10 • (05/15/98) • **87**
Sangiovese California 1994: A lighter style, in color and in body, with an herb and olive accent to the flavors. Lacks varietal distinction. • $10 • (12/15/96) • **78**
Vino Grigio California 1996: Bright and fresh, offering a burst of apple and melon flavor on a open-textured frame. A blend of 60 percent Pinot Blanc and 40 percent Trousseau Gris. Drink now. 1,560 cases made. • $10 • (05/15/98) • **85**
Zinfandel California 1995: Straightforward Zin, serving up bright strawberry, cherry and spice flavors. Drink now. 786 cases made. • $10 • (06/30/98) • **83**
Zinfandel California 1993: A touch earthy and rustic in style, with a slight metallic accent to the cherry and wild berry flavors. Finishes with a dry, tannic edge. 1,280 cases made. • $13 • (04/30/97) • **82**
Zinfandel Sonoma County 1991 • $7 • (10/15/94) • **72**

MARTINI, LOUIS M. | CALIFORNIA

Barbera California 1992: On the lighter side, with modest hints of cherry and berry flavor. Drinks well now. 2,410 cases made. • $12 • (10/15/96) • **82**
Barbera California 1991 • $12 • (10/15/95) • **85**
Barbera California 1987 • $6 • (12/31/90) BB • **83**
Barbera California 1984 • $7 • (11/15/89) • **80**
Barbera Napa Valley 1981 • $6 • (12/31/87) BB • **80**
Cabernet Sauvignon California Private Reserve 1952 • $2 • (02/28/87) • **93**
Cabernet Sauvignon California Private Reserve Villa del Rey 1943 • $1 • (06/01/85) • **77**
Cabernet Sauvignon California Special Reserve 1939 • $1 • (06/01/85) • **90**
Cabernet Sauvignon California Special Selection 1974 • $45 • (11/15/94) • **68**
Cabernet Sauvignon California Special Selection 1968 • $6 • (06/01/85) • **90**
Cabernet Sauvignon California Special Selection 1964 • $6 • (06/01/85) • **86**
Cabernet Sauvignon California Special Selection 1957 • $3 • (06/01/85) • **92**
Cabernet Sauvignon California Special Selection 1955 • $2 • (06/01/85) • **89**
Cabernet Sauvignon California Special Selection 1951 • $2 • (02/28/87) • **90**
Cabernet Sauvignon California Special Selection 1945 • $1 • (06/01/85) • **75**
Cabernet Sauvignon Napa Valley Reserve 1993: There are attractive currant flavors and minty, smoky, spicy notes here, but heavy oak and astringent tannins hinder the enjoyment. 1,900 cases made. • $18 • (11/15/97) • **84**
Cabernet Sauvignon Napa Valley Reserve 1992: Wraps ripe black cherry and spice flavors in a smooth, polished package, hinting at chocolate and spice on the finish. Drinkable now, capable of growing through 2000. 2,000 cases made. • $15 • (07/31/97) • **86**
Cabernet Sauvignon Napa Valley Reserve 1991: A tight and austere wine of modest proportions, with a narrow band of cedar, currant and cherry flavors. 986 cases made. • $15 • (09/15/96) • **83**
Cabernet Sauvignon Napa Valley Reserve 1989 • $14 • (11/15/94) • **81**
Cabernet Sauvignon Napa Valley Reserve 1988 • $14 • (11/15/92) • **78**
Cabernet Sauvignon Napa Valley Reserve 1987 • $14 • (10/15/90) • **87**
Cabernet Sauvignon North Coast 1993: Pleasant enough, with ripe plum and cherry flavors and a touch of cedary oak on the finish. 34,042 cases made. • $11 • (09/15/96) • **82**
Cabernet Sauvignon North Coast 1992 • $9 • (12/15/95) • **82**
Cabernet Sauvignon North Coast 1990 • $8 • (11/15/94) • **79**
Cabernet Sauvignon North Coast 1986 • $9 • (09/15/89) • **80**
Cabernet Sauvignon North Coast 1985 • $8 • (10/31/88) • **76**
Cabernet Sauvignon North Coast 1983 • $7 • (03/31/87) • **69**
Cabernet Sauvignon North Coast 1981 • $6 • (03/01/85) • **83**
Cabernet Sauvignon North Coast Special Selection 1980 • $12 • (12/15/86) • **78**
Cabernet Sauvignon Sonoma County 1988 • $9 • (04/30/91) BB • **81**
Cabernet Sauvignon Sonoma Valley Monte Rosso 1990 • $23 • (09/30/94) • **85**
Cabernet Sauvignon Sonoma Valley Monte Rosso 1988 • $25 • (11/15/91) • **81**
Cabernet Sauvignon Sonoma Valley Monte Rosso 1987 • $20 • (11/15/90) HR • **93**
Cabernet Sauvignon Sonoma Valley Monte Rosso 1981 • $15 • (12/15/86) • **90**
Cabernet Sauvignon Sonoma Valley Monte Rosso Vineyard 1993: A straightforward style—ripe, spicy, with clean cherry and currant flavors and a crisply tannic finish. Drink now. 800 cases made. • $22 • (11/15/96) • **86**

Cabernet Sauvignon Sonoma Valley Monte Rosso Vineyard 1991 • $22 • (12/15/95) • **78**

Cabernet Sauvignon Sonoma Valley Monte Rosso Vineyard 1989 • $23 • (12/15/95) • **71**

Cabernet Sauvignon Sonoma Valley Monte Rosso Vineyard Selection Heritage Collection 1994: Bright, with wild cherry, mint and anise overtones. Oak is a little heavy-handed, though, with rough tannins. Still, a very enjoyable wine. Drink now or hold. 750 cases made. • $30 • (11/30/97) • **87**

Chardonnay California 1995: Like a fruit cocktail blend, backed by notes of spice, particularly cinnamon. 16,363 cases made. • $11 • (07/31/97) • **82**

Chardonnay Napa Valley 1994: Has more going for it than most Chardonnays at this price. Spice and tobacco nuances support the pear and apple flavors and it finishes with pizzazz. Drinkable now. 21,385 cases made. • $11 • (06/15/96) • **87**

Chardonnay Russian River Valley Reserve 1995: Smooth and immensely appealing for its peach, spice and vanilla flavors that emerge gently and linger smoothly on the finish. Ready to drink. 3,000 cases made. • $18 • (06/15/97) • **88**

Chardonnay Russian River Valley Reserve 1994: An oaky style where the woody flavors dominate and the ripe pear and apple notes linger in the background. 3,000 cases made. • $15 • (07/31/96) • **82**

Folle Blanche Sonoma Valley Heritage Collection 1996: Steely, almost austere, with just enough jazzy fruit and mineral flavor to make it appealing. Drink soon. 225 cases made. • $12 • (12/15/97) • **83**

Gewürztraminer Russian River Valley 1996: Spicy and refreshing, with lively orange and rose petal flavors that linger on the round, dry finish. Delicious now. 700 cases made. • $12 • (03/31/98) • **88**

Heritage Collection Sonoma Valley White 1995: Offers a ripe and generous helping of nectarine, apple and gentle herb flavors, finishing brightly. Drink now, while it's fresh. 250 cases made. • $12 • (04/30/97) • **86**

Merlot North Coast 1995: Light, simple and refreshing for its bright currant flavors, which fade slightly on the finish. 51,000 cases made. • $10 • (12/15/97) • **80**

Merlot North Coast 1994 • $9 • (06/30/96) • **83**

Merlot North Coast 1993 • $9 • (06/15/96) • **81**

Merlot North Coast 1992 • $9 • (07/31/95) • **81**

Merlot North Coast 1991 • $8 • (09/15/94) • **82**

Merlot North Coast 1990 • $10 • (08/31/93) • **79**

Merlot North Coast 1989 • $9 • (05/31/92) • **74**

Merlot North Coast 1988 • $10 • (08/31/91) • **85**

Merlot North Coast 1986 • $12 • (10/31/89) • **79**

Merlot North Coast 1984 • $6 • (02/15/88) • **79**

Merlot North Coast 1982 • $5 • (02/16/86) • **71**

Merlot Russian River Valley Los Vinedos del Rio 1990 • $20 • (09/15/94) • **87**

Merlot Russian River Valley Los Vinedos del Rio 1988 • $22 • (05/31/92) • **74**

Merlot Russian River Valley Los Vinedos del Rio 1986 • $20 • (03/31/90) • **79**

Merlot Russian River Valley Los Vinedos del Rio 1984 • $12 • (02/15/88) • **82**

Merlot Russian River Valley Los Vinedos del Rio 1981 • $10 • (10/01/85) • **81**

Merlot Russian River Valley Los Vinedos del Rio Vineyard Selection 1991: Simple, with earthy and light berry flavors that turn dry and almost sour on the finish. Disappointing, given this vineyard's track record. 400 cases made. • $20 • (08/31/96) • **78**

Merlot Russian River Valley Reserve 1992: Nice array of smoky herb, plum and cherry flavors. Texture is a bit coarse and the finish turns rustic. 928 cases made. • $15 • (08/31/96) • **84**

Petite Sirah Napa Valley 1985 • $7 • (10/31/89) BB • **85**

Petite Sirah Napa Valley 1983 • $6 • (12/31/87) • **76**

Petite Sirah Napa Valley 1982 • $5 • (09/15/86) BB • **80**

Petite Sirah Napa Valley Reserve 1987 • $11 • (11/30/91) • **85**

Petite Sirah Napa Valley Reserve 1986 • $12 • (10/31/90) • **81**

Pinot Noir Los Carneros 1993 • $8 • (01/31/96) BB • **85**

Pinot Noir Los Carneros 1990 • $8 • (02/28/94) • **79**

Pinot Noir Los Carneros 1988 • $8 • (07/15/91) BB • **85**

Pinot Noir Los Carneros La Loma Vineyard 1990 • $16 • (02/28/94) • **82**

Pinot Noir Napa Valley 1986 • $8 • (12/31/89) BB • **85**

Pinot Noir Napa Valley Carneros 1992 • $7 • (05/15/95) BB • **86**

Pinot Noir Napa Valley Carneros 1987 • $7 • (02/28/91) BB • **82**

Pinot Noir Napa Valley Carneros La Loma Vineyard 1988 • $18 • (03/31/92) • **75**

Pinot Noir Napa Valley Carneros Las Amigas Vineyard Selection 1982 • $12 • (03/31/90) • **85**

Sauvignon Blanc Napa Valley 1994 • $8 • (02/29/96) • **81**

Zinfandel California 1974 • $NA • (06/16/85) • **78**

Zinfandel California 1973 • $NA • (06/16/85) • **87**

Zinfandel North Coast 1985 • $6 • (03/31/89) • **80**

Zinfandel North Coast 1984 • $6 • (02/15/88) BB • **84**

Zinfandel North Coast 1983 • $7 • (10/15/86) • **87**

Zinfandel Paso Robles 1989 • $8 • (08/31/91) • **83**

Zinfandel Sonoma & Napa Counties 1989 • $7 • (06/15/93) • **73**

Zinfandel Sonoma & Napa Counties 1988 • $7 • (10/15/92) • **79**

Zinfandel Sonoma County 1995: A medium-weight style that hits the right pepper, cherry and wild berry flavors while maintaining a sense of elegance. • $NA • (04/30/98) • **84**

Zinfandel Sonoma County 1986 • $7 • (10/31/89) • **79**

Zinfandel Sonoma County Heritage Collection 1994: Starts off with pretty hints of smoke, anise and plum on the nose, but falls short on the palate. A slight bitterness marks the finish. Drink now. 1,500 cases made. • $12 • (06/15/98) • **81**

Zinfandel Sonoma Valley 1992 • $8 • (08/31/95) • **84**

Zinfandel Sonoma Valley Gnarly Vine Monte Rosso Vineyard 1994: Tart, with a green, peppery edge, picking up cedar and wild berry flavors before finishing with earthy tannins. Drink now through 2002. 233 cases made. • $30 • (06/15/98) • **84**

Zinfandel Sonoma Valley Heritage Collection 1993: Simple, but pleasant enough with its modest core of spice, pepper and berry flavors. Easy-drinking for fans of a lighter, more elegant style. 4,440 cases made. • $12 • (03/31/97) • **84**

Zinfandel Sonoma Valley Monte Rosso Vineyard Gnarly Vine 1993: Hits the right notes for Zin, with its crushed berry, pepper and spice flavors. Turns elegant and refined on the finish. Ready now. 250 cases made. • $20 • (09/15/96) • **86**

MASO | CALIFORNIA

Red Table Wine Napa Valley 1991 • $8 • (03/31/95) • **80**

Rosé California Rosatta 1993 • $5 • (09/15/95) • **73**

MASON | CALIFORNIA

Chardonnay Napa Valley 1994: Clean and well balanced, though turning simple on the finish. Flavors are attractive; ripe pear, apple and citrus. 550 cases made. • $12 • (07/31/96) • **83**

Merlot Napa Valley 1995: Clean and well balanced, with cedary oak showing the way for ripe cherry and currant notes. Needs some time to soften and come together. Best now through 2004. 1,545 cases made. • $20 • (06/15/98) • **87**

Merlot Napa Valley 1994: Tight and firm, with crisp tannins, the core of cherry and plum flavors is juicy and lively. Ready now. 640 cases made. • $20 • (07/31/97) • **87**

Merlot Napa Valley 1993 • $20 • (04/30/96) • **89**

Sauvignon Blanc Napa Valley 1997: Richly textured, with a complex blend of melon, fig and grapefruit as well as assertive grassy, herbal notes. The wine doesn't shy away from the multifaceted character of this grape. Drink now through 2000. 3,900 cases made. • $14 • (05/31/98) • **90**

Sauvignon Blanc Napa Valley 1996: Honey, fig, melon, citrus and herb flavors blend beautifully, with great finesse. Fragrant and refreshing, right through the lengthy finish. An elegant example of what can be done with Sauvignon Blanc. 1,745 cases made. • $12 • (07/31/97) • **91**

MASSON | CALIFORNIA

Blanc de Noirs Monterey Centennial Cuvée 1984 • $9 • (12/31/87) • **83**

Cabernet Sauvignon California Vintners Selection 1986 • $6 • (06/30/89) • **84**

Cabernet Sauvignon Monterey County Vintage Selection 1986 • $9 • (11/15/89) • **79**

Cabernet Sauvignon Monterey County Vintage Selection 1985 • $8 • (09/15/88) • **78**

Chardonnay Monterey County 1993: Soft and spicy, smooth in texture and modest with its vanilla-scented pear flavors. Ready now. • $10 • (07/31/96) • **78**

Merlot California Vintners Selection 1989 • $4 • (04/15/92) BB • **80**

Merlot Monterey County 1988 • $8 • (05/31/92) • **79**

Merlot Monterey County Vintage Selection 1987 • $8 • (07/15/90) • **83**

MASTANTUONO | CALIFORNIA

Carminello California 1988 • $7 • (07/15/91) • **79**
Zinfandel San Luis Obispo County Dante Dusi Vineyards 1989 • $9 • (09/30/93) • **77**
Zinfandel San Luis Obispo County Dante Dusi Vineyards 1986 • $9 • (08/31/91) • **84**
Zinfandel San Luis Obispo County Dante Dusi Vineyards 1984 • $18 • (07/31/91) • **73**

MATANZAS CREEK | CALIFORNIA

Cabernet Sauvignon Sonoma Valley 1983 • $14 • (07/16/86) • **75**
Cabernet Sauvignon Sonoma Valley 1982 • $14 • (08/01/85) • **88**
Cabernet Sauvignon Sonoma Valley 1981 • $16 • (04/16/84) • **84**
Chardonnay Sonoma Valley 1995: Remarkably elegant and sophisticated, this Chardonnay displays a pretty core of spicy citrus, pear, fig and melon flavors, with amazing detail and a polished texture. Finishes with a long, smooth aftertaste. From a winery with a real handle on this varietal. 12,417 cases made. • $30 • (10/15/97) CS • **94**
Chardonnay Sonoma Valley 1994: An openly fruity style with appealing floral aromas to match the hints of apple, pear and spice, with flavors to match. Finishes rich and fruity, with just a kiss of smoky oak tones. 16,195 cases made. • $18 Ⓐ • (05/31/96) • **90**
Chardonnay Sonoma Valley 1993 • $23 • (09/30/95) SS • **91**
Chardonnay Sonoma Valley Journey 1993: A fresh, lively, enormously complex and concentrated white with ripe, intense layers of honey, pear, peach and nectarine flavors that fan out on the finish to reveal even more complexities. Delicious now, but still youthful in flavor, with the intensity to age well. 428 cases made. • $75 • (02/28/97) HR • **95**
Merlot Sonoma County 1987 • $25 • (06/15/90) SS • **92**
Merlot Sonoma County 1986 • $20 • (06/30/89) • **92**
Merlot Sonoma Valley 1994: Young, tight and focused, with a brilliant core of cedar-tinged currant and black cherry flavors and, on the finish, a pretty floral and spice edge. Best cellared into 1999 to 2001. 5,500 cases made. • $43 • (06/15/97) • **92**
Merlot Sonoma Valley 1993 • $48 Ⓐ • (06/30/96) • **88**
Merlot Sonoma Valley 1992 • $54 Ⓐ • (04/15/95) SS • **91**
Merlot Sonoma Valley 1991 • $29 • (09/15/94) • **89**
Merlot Sonoma Valley 1990 • $28 • (05/15/93) HR • **89**
Merlot Sonoma Valley 1989 • $28 • (04/15/92) HR • **90**
Merlot Sonoma Valley 1988 • $28 • (08/31/91) • **88**
Merlot Sonoma Valley 1985 • $29 Ⓐ • (05/31/88) • **88**
Merlot Sonoma Valley 1984 • $23 Ⓐ • (06/30/87) • **91**
Merlot Sonoma Valley 1982 • $14 • (10/01/85) • **88**
Merlot Sonoma Valley 1981 • $13 • (04/16/84) • **80**
Merlot Sonoma Valley Journey 1992: Dark, dense, ripe and intense, with tiers of rich berry, black cherry, anise and spice flavors that fan out and reveal an amazing concentration of tannin. Best to cellar this one at least to 1999, or even 2004, to let it soften. 144 cases made. • $125 • (02/28/97) • **94**
Pinot Noir Sonoma County Quail Hill Ranch 1980 • $9 • (07/01/84) • **82**
Sauvignon Blanc Sonoma County 1996: A fine blend of tangy citrus flavors and pretty, ripe melon notes framed in sweet oak. This is a bright, refreshing, lighter-styled wine with a squeaky-clean finish. Tasted three times, with consistent notes. 9,000 cases made. • $18 • (04/30/98) • **86**
Sauvignon Blanc Sonoma County 1995: Crisp, floral and generous with its silky pear and melon flavors that linger on the bright finish, with a burnt tinge. Tasted twice, with consistent notes. 13,300 cases made. • $17 • (02/28/97) • **85**
Sauvignon Blanc Sonoma County 1994 • $15 • (02/29/96) • **87**
Sauvignon Blanc Sonoma County 1993 • $14 • (12/31/94) • **87**

MATTHEWS | WASHINGTON

Cabernet Sauvignon Washington Reserve 1994: Has a burnt, ashy edge and astringent texture that detract from a narrow core of berry flavors. 98 cases made. • $30 • (08/31/96) • **78**
Merlot Washington Reserve 1993: Very smoky, almost like ash. Lean berry flavors turn tart on the finish. Not much charm. • $NA • (09/30/96) • **77**

Key: SS—Spectator Selection CS—Cellar Selection HR—Highly Recommended BB—Best Buy $NA—Price not available Ⓐ—Auction Price (BT)—Barrel Tasting
Dates in parentheses indicate the issues in which the ratings were published.

Washington 1995: Light and crisp, with a smooth surface that shows off the pretty plum, smoke and spice flavors. Drinkable now. A blend of 50 percent Cabernet Sauvignon, 40 percent Merlot, and 10 percent Cabernet Franc. 500 cases made. • $30 • (09/30/97) • **85**
Washington 1994: Supple and generous at first, takes a dip after the first sip, then redeems itself with a chewy licorice-tobacco streak and plum flavors. Drink now. 191 cases made. • $21 • (08/31/96) • **85**

MATTITUCK HILLS | NEW YORK

Cabernet Sauvignon North Fork of Long Island 1987 • $9 • (06/30/91) • **82**

MAURICE CAR'RIE | CALIFORNIA

Pinot Noir Santa Barbara County 1990 • $8 • (02/28/93) • **67**

MAYACAMAS | CALIFORNIA

Cabernet Sauvignon Napa Valley 1990 • $26 Ⓐ • (12/15/95) • **85**
Cabernet Sauvignon Napa Valley 1989 • $20 • (12/15/95) • **82**
Cabernet Sauvignon Napa Valley 1987: Tight, tart and lean, showing a core of earthy cherry and currant with anise and cedar accents. Will likely remain on the tart side. Best now to 2005. • $45 • (12/15/97) • **87**
Cabernet Sauvignon Napa Valley 1986: Better now than on release. Not the rich, potent Mayacamas style of the 1970s, but the cedar, herb, dill and currant flavors have come together and the texture is smooth and polished. Tannins are quite evident on the finish, but altogether it's a complex wine that reveals new facets with each sip. 2,210 cases made. • $NA • (12/15/96) • **88**
Cabernet Sauvignon Napa Valley 1985 • $46 Ⓐ • (01/31/90) • **92**
Cabernet Sauvignon Napa Valley 1984 • $45 • (04/15/89) • **80**
Cabernet Sauvignon Napa Valley 1983 • $40 Ⓐ • (09/15/88) • **80**
Cabernet Sauvignon Napa Valley 1982 • $25 Ⓐ • (03/31/87) • **77**
Cabernet Sauvignon Napa Valley 1978 • $82 • (11/15/92) • **88**
Cabernet Sauvignon Napa Valley 1974 • $89 Ⓐ • (11/15/94) • **88**
Cabernet Sauvignon Napa Valley 1971 • $8 • (04/01/86) • **87**
Chardonnay Napa Valley 1993 • $18 • (05/15/96) • **88**
Pinot Noir California 1981 • $12 • (08/31/86) • **74**
Pinot Noir Napa Valley 1988 • $14 • (02/28/93) • **68**
Pinot Noir Napa Valley 1987 • $14 • (04/30/91) • **80**
Pinot Noir Napa Valley 1986 • $14 • (03/31/90) • **67**
Pinot Noir Napa Valley 1985 • $12 • (06/15/88) • **72**
Pinot Noir Napa Valley 1984 • $12 • (12/31/88) • **71**
Sauvignon Blanc Napa Valley 1994 • $12 • (05/15/96) BB • **86**
Sauvignon Blanc Napa Valley 1993 • $10 • (08/31/95) • **88**
Zinfandel Late Harvest Napa Valley 1984 • $18 • (11/15/89) • **84**

MAYO | CALIFORNIA

Cabernet Sauvignon Dry Creek Valley 1995: Bright cherry flavors lead the way in this unusually tangy Cabernet. It's pleasant and fairly simple, finishing moderately. 135 cases made. • $18 • (09/30/97) • **84**
Cabernet Sauvignon Sonoma Valley Los Chamizal Vineyard 1995: Smooth and spicy, supple in texture and spiky in flavor, with woodsy, tealeaf notes wafting through the modest level of berry flavors. Ready now; best by 2000. 110 cases made. • $24 • (03/31/98) • **85**
Chardonnay Sonoma Valley 1996: Bright and fruity, with a resinous edge to the peach and pear flavors. Finishes with some intensity. Best now through 2000. 509 cases made. • $17 • (05/15/98) • **85**
Chardonnay Sonoma Valley 1995: Ripe and spicy, with hints of pear, spice and citrus flavors, finishing with a dash of cedary oak. Drinkable now. 813 cases made. • $15 • (06/15/97) • **88**
Chardonnay Sonoma Valley 1994: Showing signs of oxidation, this wine displays nutty flavors backed by a citruslike finish. 950 cases made. • $15 • (01/01/97) • **81**
Chardonnay Sonoma Valley Barrel Select 1996: Smooth and silky, appealing more for its texture than its modest apple and earthy flavors. Drink now. 458 cases made. • $22 • (05/15/98) • **82**
Chardonnay Sonoma Valley Barrel Select 1995: Smooth, ripe, rich and polished, brimming with layers of smoky pear, hazelnut, vanilla and apple flavors, turning complex on the aftertaste. 297 cases made. • $20 • (06/15/97) • **88**
Merlot Sonoma Valley 1995: Tastes green and unripe, with tart cherry, cedar and spice, turning woody on the finish. 261 cases made. • $20 • (06/15/98) • **78**

Pinot Noir Carneros 1996: A bright-tasting blend of cherry and anise flavors, backed by seductive cola and clove notes. It's a little bitter on the finish, but quite pleasant nonetheless. 147 cases made. • $20 • (02/28/98) • **86**

Zinfandel Sonoma County Three Valley 1996: Lightly fruity, with earthy wild berry and plummy notes of modest depth and proportion. Loses its focus, turning minty. 203 cases made. • $18 • (06/15/98) • **80**

MAZZOCCO | CALIFORNIA

Cabernet Sauvignon Alexander Valley Claret Style 1988 • $18 • (03/15/92) • **85**

Cabernet Sauvignon Alexander Valley Claret Style 1987: Attractive, with a fruity profile, the cherry, plum and wild berry flavors are ripe and juicy. Quite appealing medium body. Finishes with mild tannins. Ready now. 1,200 cases made. • $20 • (12/15/97) • **88**

Cabernet Sauvignon Alexander Valley Claret Style 1986 • $20 • (07/31/89) • **78**

Cabernet Sauvignon Sonoma County 1993: Light in style and fairly simple, with cherry and herb notes. Finishes short. 3,200 cases made. • $18 • (11/30/97) • **81**

Cabernet Sauvignon Sonoma County 1992 • $18 • (04/30/96) • **88**

Cabernet Sauvignon Sonoma County 1991 • $18 • (11/15/94) • **88**

Cabernet Sauvignon Sonoma County 1989 • $15 • (06/15/93) • **81**

Chardonnay Sonoma County River Lane 1996: Smooth and spicy, with pretty apple, melon, pear and fig notes, finishing with a dash of grapefruit. Drinks well now. 6,600 cases made. • $15 • (12/15/97) • **87**

Chardonnay Sonoma County River Lane 1995: Smooth, ripe and creamy, with pretty pear, apple, melon and spice flavors, this is a delicate, lively young wine that's appealing to drink now. 4,500 cases made. • $15 • (05/15/97) • **89**

Chardonnay Sonoma County River Lane 1994: An elegant style that's fresh and vibrant. Has an attractive core of ripe pear, citrus and melon flavors and finishes with traces of light oak. 7,000 cases made. • $14 • (06/30/96) • **87**

Chardonnay Sonoma County River Lane 1993 • $15 • (07/31/95) • **83**

Chardonnay Sonoma County Winemaker's Select 1994: Lean and trim, crisp and well focused, with a core of citrus, particularly tart lime, and green pear flavors. A flinty style that doesn't overpower with oak. Ready to drink. 286 cases made. • $18 • (05/15/97) • **88**

Chardonnay Sonoma County Winemaker's Select 1993 • $18 • (06/30/96) • **84**

Matrix Dry Creek Valley 1993: Medium-weight, with a modest range of currant, cedar and spice flavors. Finishes with supple tannins, dashes of olive and sage. A blend of Cabernet Sauvignon, Cabernet Franc, Malbec and Petit Verdot. Ready now. 500 cases made. • $28 • (11/30/97) • **84**

Matrix Dry Creek Valley 1992: Firm and tight, with focused currant, cherry and cedary oak flavors and a hint of anise. Finishes with a nice burst of fruit, and the tannins are soft and round. 350 cases made. • $28 • (08/31/96) • **87**

Matrix Dry Creek Valley 1991 • $28 • (12/15/95) • **87**

Matrix Sonoma County 1990 • $28 • (11/15/94) • **82**

Matrix Sonoma County 1989 • $28 • (11/15/93) • **86**

Matrix Sonoma County 1987: Quite ripe, nearly pruny, with juicy plum and cherry flavors. For all its ripeness, it's somewhat one-dimensional, lacking the extra flavor facets of the Cabernet. Ready now. 215 cases made. • $28 • (12/15/97) • **87**

Merlot Dry Creek Valley 1994: Light, velvety and a wee bit gamy, with black cherry flavor behind. Has a nice sense of harmony and balance. Drinkable now. 837 cases made. • $18 • (11/30/97) • **84**

Merlot Dry Creek Valley 1993: Smooth and supple, with an elegant band of ripe cherry, plum and currant flavors, as well as hints of herb and cedar. Finishes with fine length and plenty of fruit complexity. Ready now. 840 cases made. • $18 • (07/31/96) • **88**

Merlot Dry Creek Valley 1992 • $15 • (05/31/96) • **84**

Merlot Dry Creek Valley 1991 • $15 • (11/15/94) • **78**

Merlot Dry Creek Valley 1989 • $14 • (06/15/93) • **78**

Merlot Dry Creek Valley Estate Unfiltered 1989 • $14 • (05/31/92) • **89**

Petite Sirah Dry Creek Valley 1993: Effusively fruity, with pretty floral and jam notes to the ripe, juicy plum, wild berry and black cherry flavors. Fans of fruity Petite Sirah will love this one. Avoids being overly tannic, too, which is a big plus. 175 cases made. • $21 • (08/31/97) • **90**

Viognier Dry Creek Valley 1996: Peachy. On the palate, it's a little thin and one-dimensional. Drink now. 115 cases made. • $25 • (05/15/98) • **82**

Zinfandel Alexander Valley 1994: Light and uncomplicated, with simple cherry and berry notes. Not what you'd expect from a 1994 Zin. 400 cases made. • $20 • (04/30/97) • **80**

Zinfandel Dry Creek Valley Cuneo & Saini 1994: Smooth, ripe and concentrated, with a pretty core of black cherry, raspberry, anise and buttery oak flavors that keep pumping through the long, lively aftertaste. 400 cases made. • $20 • (04/30/97) • **89**

Zinfandel Dry Creek Valley Cuneo & Saini 1993 • $20 • (10/15/95) • **83**

Zinfandel Dry Creek Valley Quinn Vineyard 1995: A bit thin and mature. Pretty cherry notes try to emerge, but are eclipsed by the coarse texture. Tasted twice, with consistent notes. 400 cases made. • $22 • (06/15/98) • **79**

Zinfandel Sonoma County 1995: Light in color and flavor, it's a modest red with simple red cherry and spice flavors. Finishes a bit tart. Ready now. 4,100 cases made. • $16 • (12/15/97) • **81**

Zinfandel Sonoma County 1994: Ripe and flavorful, with plum and berry notes of medium weight and intensity. 3,500 cases made. • $15 • (03/31/97) • **82**

Zinfandel Sonoma County 1993 • $14 • (08/31/95) • **86**

Zinfandel Sonoma County 1992 • $14 • (10/15/94) • **86**

Zinfandel Sonoma County 1991 • $14 • (09/30/93) • **88**

Zinfandel Sonoma County 1990 • $13 • (10/15/92) • **87**

Zinfandel Sonoma County Traditional Style 1988 • $13 • (10/15/90) • **89**

Zinfandel Sonoma County Traditional Style 1986 • $10 • (12/15/88) • **90**

MCCOY, PETER | CALIFORNIA

Chardonnay Knights Valley Clos des Pierres 1994: Oxidized, with nutty pear, dried apricot and honey flavors. Drink now. Tasted twice, with consistent notes. 1,600 cases made. • $24 • (06/15/98) • **75**

Chardonnay Knights Valley Clos des Pierres 1993 • $20 • (06/15/96) • **85**

MCDOWELL | CALIFORNIA

Bistro Red LVC Mendocino NV • $7 • (06/30/92) • **79**

Cabernet Sauvignon California 1988 • $10 • (11/15/91) • **78**

Cabernet Sauvignon California 1987 • $9 • (11/15/90) • **78**

Cabernet Sauvignon McDowell Valley 1986 • $8 • (04/30/90) • **70**

Cabernet Sauvignon McDowell Valley 1983 • $11 • (04/15/88) • **76**

Cabernet Sauvignon McDowell Valley 1982 • $11 • (12/15/86) • **89**

Cabernet Sauvignon McDowell Valley 1981 • $11 • (12/16/84) • **78**

Cabernet Sauvignon Mendocino 1992 • $10 • (12/15/95) • **85**

Cabernet Sauvignon Mendocino 1990 • $9 • (07/15/93) • **82**

Cabernet Sauvignon Mendocino 1989 • $9 • (11/15/92) • **75**

Chardonnay Mendocino 1994: Simple and pleasant enough, delivering a modest range of pear, spice, apple and melon flavors. • $10 • (05/15/96) • **84**

Grenache Rosé Mendocino 1995: A cherrylike blend that would be much more refreshing with higher acidity and less sweetness. 5,000 cases made. • $10 • (09/15/97) • **80**

Grenache Rosé Mendocino 1994: A welcome spiciness weaves through the watermelon and strawberry flavors in this soft, sippable California rosé. Interesting flavors and affordable, too. 4,500 cases made. • $8 • (07/31/96) BB • **85**

Grenache Rosé Mendocino 1993 • $7 • (09/15/95) • **83**

Les Vieux Cépages Les Trésor McDowell Valley Red 1990 • $13 • (10/15/93) • **86**

Les Vieux Cépages Les Trésor McDowell Valley Red 1988 • $12 • (06/30/92) • **75**

Les Vieux Cépages Les Trésor McDowell Valley Red 1987 • $14 • (08/31/90) • **82**

Les Vieux Cépages Les Trésor McDowell Valley Red 1986 • $13 • (09/30/89) • **86**

Marsanne Mendocino 1994: Tight, firm and focused, with a complex band of pear, apricot and hazelnut flavors that linger on the long, lively finish. 150 cases made. • $14 • (09/15/96) • **87**

Syrah McDowell Valley 1985 • $12 • (09/30/89) • **90**

Syrah McDowell Valley 1984 • $9 • (02/15/89) • **86**

Syrah McDowell Valley 1982 • $10 • (01/31/87) • **75**

Syrah McDowell Valley 1981 • $10 • (12/16/84) • **90**

Syrah McDowell Valley Bistro Syrah LVC 1991 • $9 • (03/31/93) • **79**

Syrah McDowell Valley Bistro Syrah LVC 1990 • $9 • (06/30/92) • **76**

Syrah McDowell Valley Les Vieux Cépages 1987 • $16 • (03/31/91) • **74**

Syrah McDowell Valley Les Vieux Cépages 1986 • $14 • (08/31/90) • **80**

Syrah Mendocino 1996: Here's a young California red that's upfront and fruity, featuring snappy cherry and wild berry flavors, floral aromas and supple tannins. Very appealing, especially at this price and score. 9,000 cases made. • $10 • (12/15/97) BB • **87**

Syrah Mendocino 1995: This Rhône-style California red, from a producer with a track record for the same, offers early drinking appeal at a bargain price, serving up mineral-accented ripe plum and wild berry flavors and a fruit-driven finish. 6,500 cases made. • $10 • (05/15/97) BB • **87**

Syrah Mendocino 1993 • $10 • (10/15/95) BB • **87**

Syrah Mendocino 1990 • $17 • (07/31/94) • **82**

Syrah Mendocino Bistro Syrah 1992 • $10 • (07/31/94) • **85**

Syrah Mendocino McDowell Valley Estate 1995: Complex aromatics lead to a ripe, supple core of plum, wild berry, cherry and spice. Moderately rich and elegant, it's a tasty wine with lots of flavor and finesse. Best now to 2002. 650 cases made. • $16 • (04/30/98) • **90**

Syrah Mendocino McDowell Valley Estate 1992 • $15 • (05/31/96) • **84**

Viognier Mendocino 1996: Honey, hazelnuts, minerals and spice intertwine in a refreshing, light blend. 750 cases made. • $15 • (12/15/97) • **83**

Viognier Mendocino 1994: Smooth and polished, with nice melon, honey, pear and spice flavors. Finishes almost Muscat-like. Very attractive. 1,000 cases made. • $14 • (07/31/96) • **88**

Zinfandel McDowell Valley 1990 • $9 • (04/30/93) • **79**

Zinfandel McDowell Valley 1989 • $9 • (10/15/92) • **80**

Zinfandel McDowell Valley 1988 • $9 • (12/31/90) • **80**

Zinfandel McDowell Valley 1987 • $8 • (12/15/89) BB • **87**

MCGREGOR | NEW YORK

Blanc de Blancs Finger Lakes 1985 • $15 • (12/31/90) • **64**

Pinot Noir Finger Lakes 1986 • $13 • (06/15/88) • **70**

MCILROY | CALIFORNIA

Chardonnay Russian River Valley Aquarius Ranch 1996: Smooth and velvety on the palate, with subtle hints of hazelnut, peach, pear, spice and toasty oak. Complex yet quite easy to drink. The finish is long and mellow. Drink now. 560 cases made. • $18 • (06/30/98) • **90**

Chardonnay Russian River Valley Aquarius Ranch 1995: Has some character and style despite a slightly bitter edge, offering spicy nectarine and passion fruit flavors that soften on the finish. Drink now. 729 cases made. • $18 • (06/15/97) • **87**

Red Russian River Valley 1993: Has bright acidity for a red wine. The bright cherry, wild berry and licorice flavors are attractive, however, framed by smoky oak. A blend: 60 percent Cabernet Sauvignon, 40 percent Merlot. • $15 • (12/15/97) • **83**

Zinfandel Russian River Valley Porter-Bass Vineyard 1996: Bright cherry and raspberry flavors are the hallmark of this juicy wine, redolent of fresh fruit. Tannins are a little powdery. Finishes with touches of pepper and anise. Drink through 2002. 457 cases made. • $18 • (06/15/98) • **86**

Zinfandel Russian River Valley Porter-Bass Vineyard 1995: A multifaceted wine, with layers of blackberry, black cherry, sage, thyme and perhaps a touch of eucalyptus. Lean in texture, it is nonetheless complex, though a bit short on the finish. Drink now through 2002. 322 cases made. • $18 • (01/01/98) • **88**

Zinfandel Russian River Valley Porter-Bass Vineyard 1994: Tart, lean and a bit on the green side, right through the finish. An austere young wine that doesn't show the ripeness of the vintage. • $15 • (02/28/97) • **82**

MCKINLAY | OREGON

Pinot Noir Willamette Valley 1990 • $15 • (02/28/93) • **84**

Pinot Noir Willamette Valley 1988 • $13 • (04/15/91) • **90**

Pinot Noir Willamette Valley Special Selection 1994: Tart and tangy, it's a bit hot but packed with juicy berry and tar flavors that linger on the finish. See what develops by 1999 or 2000. 300 cases made. • $31 • (02/28/97) • **86**

Pinot Noir Willamette Valley Special Selection 1993 • $23 • (01/31/96) • **83**

Pinot Noir Willamette Valley Special Selection 1991 • $23 • (11/30/94) • **86**

MEADOW GLEN | CALIFORNIA

Merlot Napa Valley 1989 • $8 • (05/31/92) • **81**

Key: SS—Spectator Selection CS—Cellar Selection HR—Highly Recommended BB—Best Buy $NA—Price not available Ⓐ—Auction Price (BT)—Barrel Tasting
Dates in parentheses indicate the issues in which the ratings were published.

MEDICI | OREGON

Pinot Noir Willamette Valley 1995: Light in color and texture but surprisingly bright in flavor. A silky-smooth red with Pommard-like raspberry, strawberry, coffee and spice flavors that linger attractively on the finish. Has little of the harshness associated with this vintage. Drink now. 300 cases made. • $20 • (05/15/98) • **85**

MEEKER | CALIFORNIA

Cabernet Sauvignon Dry Creek Valley 1988 • $14 • (08/31/92) • **85**

Cabernet Sauvignon Dry Creek Valley 1987 • $14 • (10/15/91) • **87**

Cabernet Sauvignon Dry Creek Valley 1986 • $19 • (02/15/90) • **72**

Cabernet Sauvignon Dry Creek Valley 1985 • $18 • (04/30/89) • **76**

Cabernet Sauvignon Dry Creek Valley 1984 • $18 • (06/15/88) • **78**

Cabernet Sauvignon Dry Creek Valley Gold Leaf Cuvée 1994: Shows depth, with rich currant and blueberry notes. Silky texture is followed by powdery tannins and a moderate finish. Drink now or hold. • $18 • (11/15/97) • **88**

Cabernet Sauvignon Dry Creek Valley Gold Leaf Cuvée 1991 • $14 • (11/15/94) • **78**

Cabernet Sauvignon Dry Creek Valley Gold Leaf Cuvée 1990 • $14 • (09/15/93) • **82**

Cabernet Sauvignon Dry Creek Valley Red Table Wine Fourth Rack 1992: A lighter style that's smooth and fruity, with supple cherry, plum and raspberry notes. Drinks well now and is fairly priced. The label is cute, too. 520 cases made. • $9 • (11/30/96) • **83**

Cabernet Sauvignon Dry Creek Valley Red Table Wine Second Rack NV • $8 • (11/15/94) • **79**

Cabernet Sauvignon Dry Creek Valley Scharf Family Vineyard 1990 • $14 • (11/15/94) • **84**

Chardonnay Sonoma County Incognito 1995: Smooth and refreshing for its bright apple and polished, sweet nectarine notes that linger on the smooth, creamy finish. Its texture is its strong point. 557 cases made. • $18 • (07/31/97) • **87**

Chardonnay Sonoma County Incognito 1994: Refreshing; apple and lightly spicy flavors with a smoky edge. 190 cases made. • $18 • (07/31/96) • **83**

Four Kings Scharf Family Vineyard Sonoma County 1994: Smoky, tarry flavors are followed by licorice, leather, cassis and black currant. Well balanced, though a bit austere in style. Ready to drink, should also age nicely. A blend of Cabernet Sauvignon, Merlot, Cabernet Franc, and Petit Verdot. 400 cases made. • $20 • (11/15/97) • **87**

Fumé Blanc Dry Creek Valley Gold Label Cuveé 1993 • $9 • (10/15/94) • **85**

Merlot Sonoma County Winemakers' Handprint Collection 1992: A big, ripe style with lots of oak seasoning, with bold black berry and cherry flavors and firm dry tannins. This tense and tannic wine definitely needs cellaring, but may always be on the tannic side. 200 cases made. • $18 • (08/31/96) • **87**

Petite Sirah Napa County Gold Leaf Cuvée 1994: Offers a wide range of flavors—from floral to ripe plum to cherry and a whiff of black pepper—but it has the requisite, firm core of drying tannins, so it's best consumed with hearty fare. 220 cases made. • $18 • (01/01/97) • **88**

Sauvignon Blanc Late Harvest Dry Creek Valley Gold Leaf Cuveé 1992 • $16 • (09/30/95) • **88**

Zinfandel Dry Creek Valley 1991 • $8 • (09/30/93) • **82**

Zinfandel Dry Creek Valley 1989 • $10 • (10/15/92) • **80**

Zinfandel Dry Creek Valley 1988 • $10 • (08/31/91) • **82**

Zinfandel Dry Creek Valley 1987 • $10 • (03/31/90) • **85**

Zinfandel Dry Creek Valley 1986 • $9 • (03/15/89) • **83**

Zinfandel Dry Creek Valley 1985 • $8 • (05/15/88) • **90**

Zinfandel Dry Creek Valley Gold Leaf Cuvée 1994: Serves up zesty ripe plum and wild berry flavors, picking up a dash of oak and spice on the finish. Drinks well now. 1,344 cases made. • $14 • (02/28/97) • **84**

Zinfandel Dry Creek Valley Gold Leaf Cuvée 1992 • $12 • (10/15/94) • **80**

Zinfandel Dry Creek Valley Gold Leaf Cuvée 1991 • $11 • (09/30/93) • **84**

Zinfandel Dry Creek Valley Gold Leaf Cuvée 1990 • $10 • (01/31/93) SS • **90**

Zinfandel Dry Creek Valley Gold Leaf Reserve 1989 • $14 • (10/15/92) • **81**

Zinfandel Dry Creek Valley Red Table Wine Fifth Rack 1994: Simple, with light cherry and berry flavors, turning earthy on the aftertaste. 504 cases made. • $9 • (04/30/97) • **80**

Zinfandel Dry Creek Valley Red Table Wine First Rack 1991 • $8 • (09/30/93) BB • **86**

Zinfandel Sonoma County Sonoma Cuvée 1992 • $10 • (10/15/94) • **84**

MEITZ | CALIFORNIA

Merlot Sonoma County 1991 • $15 • (04/15/94) • **85**

MENDOCINO ESTATE | CALIFORNIA

Cabernet Sauvignon Mendocino 1985 • $5 • (02/15/88) • **61**
Cabernet Sauvignon Mendocino 1984 • $4 • (06/15/87) • **78**
Cabernet Sauvignon Mendocino 1982 • $4 • (10/15/86) BB • **87**
Zinfandel Mendocino 1985 • $4 • (02/15/88) • **79**

MENDOCINO HILL | CALIFORNIA

Cabernet Sauvignon Mendocino County 1989 • $15 • (03/31/93) • **88**
Cabernet Sauvignon Mendocino County Private Reserve 1992: Bright cherry, spice and smoke aromatics get this off to a good start, but the tannins remain drying and the finish is rough. 900 cases made. • $14 • (09/15/97) • **86**

MER SOLEIL | CALIFORNIA

Chardonnay Central Coast 1995: Compact, with toasty, cedary oak and a rich core of pear, fig and citrus. Turns complex and sophisticated, with a long, lingering aftertaste. Drinkable now through 2001. 5,000 cases made. • $36 • (01/31/98) • **91**
Chardonnay Central Coast 1994: A bold, ripe, rich and full-bodied style of California Chardonnay that laces the honey, pear and pineapple flavors with nice spicy, toasty shadings. A concentrated white with a long, lingering aftertaste. Delicious. 2,400 cases made. • $32 • (05/31/96) HR • **93**

MEREDYTH | VIRGINIA

Cabernet Sauvignon Virginia 1989 • $11 • (02/29/92) • **79**
Merlot Virginia 1989 • $25 • (02/29/92) • **81**

MERIDIAN | CALIFORNIA

Cabernet Sauvignon California 1994: Heavy on the smoke and vanilla, but with enough plush plum, anise and tar flavors to balance things out. With supple tannins and a moderate finish, it's ready for quaffing now. • $11 • (09/30/97) • **86**
Cabernet Sauvignon Paso Robles 1990 • $14 • (09/30/93) • **87**
Cabernet Sauvignon Paso Robles 1989 • $14 • (07/31/92) • **85**
Cabernet Sauvignon Paso Robles 1988 • $12 • (09/30/91) SS • **92**
Chardonnay Edna Valley 1993 • $14 • (04/30/95) • **85**
Chardonnay Edna Valley Coastal Reserve 1996: Beautifully crafted, this California white is rich, complex, concentrated and sharply focused, with layers of ripe pear, fig, peach and honeydew melon. Turns elegant and spicy on a long, lingering finish that echoes fruit and vanilla. Hard to go wrong at this price and score. 15,000 cases made. • $14 • (03/31/98) SS • **92**
Chardonnay Edna Valley Reserve 1995: Delivers complex and interesting flavors, with hints of peach, fig and melon, that crowd out an initial earthy note to turn rich and elegant on the finish. Impressive for its depth and concentration. • $15 • (05/15/97) • **90**
Chardonnay Edna Valley Reserve 1994: Serves up a modest band of citrus and pineapple notes; becomes simple on the finish while maintaining the fruit. • $14 • (06/30/96) • **85**
Chardonnay Santa Barbara County 1996: Smooth, silky and distinctive, especially for the price, with nectarine, grapefruit and mineral flavors, plus a touch of earthiness on the finish. Ready now. • $11 • (11/15/97) • **87**
Chardonnay Santa Barbara County 1995: Highlighted by a nice core of ripe tangerine and tropical fruit flavors, which will wow fans of pure, unadulterated California Chardonnay. 100,000 cases made. • $11 • (01/31/97) HR • **88**
Chardonnay Santa Barbara County 1994: Brimming with fresh, ripe pear, apricot, peach and spicy fruit flavors, a rich and forward style that leads into a pretty, creamy, fruity aftertaste. Hard to beat at this—or even twice—this price. 100,000 cases made. • $10 • (02/29/96) BB • **89**
Chardonnay Santa Barbara County 1993 • $10 • (06/15/95) • **85**
Chardonnay Santa Barbara County Limited Release 1995: Marked by a spicy, Muscat-like quality, the ripe, juicy Chardonnay flavors fold in, with ripe pear, fig and citrus notes adding dimension to the light, toasted oak shadings. Complex and long on the finish. • $25 • (05/31/97) • **91**
Chardonnay Santa Barbara County Limited Release 1994: Soft and pillowy, a gentle wine with a nice core of apple and peach flavors. Drinkable now. • $17 • (06/30/96) • **86**
Merlot California 1994: Starts out smooth and spicy, with a toasty edge to the modest plum and berry flavors. Finishes with a dash of sage. • $15 • (11/30/97) • **84**
Merlot California 1993: Lovely currant and chocolate flavors. Finish is a bit coarse, as the tannins kick in. • $16 • (08/31/96) • **82**
Pinot Blanc Santa Barbara County 1993 • $14 • (04/15/95) • **86**
Pinot Noir Edna Valley Reserve 1991 • $16 • (04/30/94) • **86**
Pinot Noir Santa Barbara & San Luis Obispo Counties 1993 • $14 • (09/15/95) • **82**
Pinot Noir Santa Barbara & San Luis Obispo Counties Reserve 1995: Delicious fruit that's ripe, rich and focused, with juicy, supple and elegant black cherry, sage, plum and spice flavors that unfold and fan out on the finish. A classy style that packs in lots of fruit and finesse. Drink now to 2000. Tasted twice, with consistent notes. 520 cases made. • $20 • (03/31/98) • **91**
Pinot Noir Santa Barbara & San Luis Obispo Counties Reserve 1994: Marked by a strongly earthy, barnyardy accent at first, it then reveals more pleasing flavors—cola, leather and wild berry. • $17 • (01/31/97) • **84**
Pinot Noir Santa Barbara & San Luis Obispo Counties Reserve 1993 • $16 • (11/30/95) • **87**
Pinot Noir Santa Barbara County 1996: Light, herbal, spicy and laced with black cherry flavor on the widening finish. Drink now. • $14 • (12/15/97) • **83**
Pinot Noir Santa Barbara County 1995: Best yet from Meridian, with more bright, ripe fruit flavor than usual from Santa Barbara. Dark, ripe and concentrated, with complex black cherry, currant, plum and berry flavors, mild tannins. Bold, fruity finish, with a dash of pepper. 8,000 cases made. • $14 • (01/31/97) • **88**
Pinot Noir Santa Barbara County 1994 • $14 • (03/31/96) • **86**
Pinot Noir Santa Barbara County 1992 • $14 • (11/30/94) • **83**
Pinot Noir Santa Barbara County 1991 • $14 • (02/28/94) • **80**
Pinot Noir Santa Barbara County 1990 • $14 • (02/28/93) • **80**
Pinot Noir Santa Barbara County Riverbench Vineyard 1988 • $14 • (02/28/91) • **86**
Sauvignon Blanc California 1997: A touch of oak, a honeyed note, a bit of grass, fresh pea and citrus all lead to a pleasant quaff. • $9 • (06/30/98) • **83**
Sauvignon Blanc California 1996: Refreshing, and fairly light, with a solid core of citrus flavors backed by a pleasing touch of traditional herbaceousness. • $9 • (09/15/97) • **85**
Sauvignon Blanc California 1995: Smooth, aiming for elegance over exuberance, with pleasant orange and cream flavors and a hint of herb. Ready now. • $8 • (02/28/97) • **87**
Sauvignon Blanc California 1994 • $8 • (06/15/96) • **79**
Sauvignon Blanc California 1993 • $8 • (05/15/95) • **86**
Syrah Paso Robles 1991 • $14 • (07/31/94) • **83**
Syrah Paso Robles 1990 • $15 • (03/31/93) • **85**
Syrah Paso Robles 1988 • $14 • (03/31/91) HR • **91**
Zinfandel Paso Robles 1990 • $14 • (09/30/93) • **86**
Zinfandel Paso Robles 1989 • $9 • (10/15/92) • **85**

MERLION | CALIFORNIA

Cabernet Sauvignon Napa Valley 1986 • $17 • (11/15/90) • **84**
Cabernet Sauvignon Napa Valley 1985 • $14 • (08/31/88) • **85**

MERRYVALE | CALIFORNIA

Cabernet Sauvignon Napa Valley 1994: Compact, with earthy currant, cherry, cedar and spice flavors that are pleasantly focused, although it becomes a bit disjointed and hard on the finish. Best after 2001. 3,040 cases made. • $27 • (10/31/97) • **87**
Cabernet Sauvignon Napa Valley 1993: Solid if unexciting, this wine delivers a tannic core of currant, cherry and herb flavors. Turns rustic and austere on the finish. 3,450 cases made. • $25 • (12/15/96) • **83**
Cabernet Sauvignon Napa Valley 1992 • $24 • (12/15/95) • **88**
Cabernet Sauvignon Napa Valley 1991 • $23 • (11/15/94) • **87**
Cabernet Sauvignon Napa Valley 1990 • $20 • (06/30/93) • **88**
Cabernet Sauvignon Napa Valley 1989 • $16 • (10/31/92) SS • **92**
Cabernet Sauvignon Napa Valley 1988 • $18 • (07/15/91) • **86**
Chardonnay Napa Valley Reserve 1996: Serves up lots of tasty, sharply focused Chardonnay flavors, with ripe, creamy pear, hazelnut, fig and toasty oak. Turns intricate and delicate on the finish, where the flavors are bright and lively. Best now through 2002. 2,150 cases made. • $30 • (07/31/98) • **92**

MESSINA HOF

Chardonnay Napa Valley Reserve 1995: Bold, ripe and flavorful, with tiers of ripe pear, apple, spice and light oak flavors, turning elegant on the finish with a smoky nectarine aftertaste that lingers long. 3,600 cases made. • $25 • (06/15/97) • **93**

Chardonnay Napa Valley Reserve 1993 • $25 • (07/31/95) • **88**

Chardonnay Napa Valley Silhouette 1993 • $36 • (05/31/96) • **89**

Chardonnay Napa Valley Starmont 1996: Smooth, ripe, rich and creamy, with layers of complex pear, fig and hazelnut flavors, finishing with a long, lingering, intricate aftertaste. Drink now through 2002. 12,000 cases made. • $18 • (07/31/98) SS • **91**

Chardonnay Napa Valley Starmont 1995: A remarkably complex California white, with tiers of ripe pear, fig, apple and vanilla flavors that linger for a long aftertaste. The texture is smooth and polished finishing with a creamy quality. 10,000 cases made. • $18 • (06/15/97) SS • **93**

Chardonnay Napa Valley Starmont 1994: Starts out with subtle notes that gradually build into a more interesting wine, with ripe pear, apple, citrus and honey notes. Doesn't rely on heavy oak for its flavors. 10,000 cases made. • $16 • (05/31/96) • **88**

Chardonnay Napa Valley Starmont 1993 • $16 • (07/31/95) • **84**

Late Harvest Alexander Valley Solstice 1989 • $24/375ml • (06/30/93) • **85**

Meritage White Napa Valley 1993 • $14 • (08/31/95) • **78**

Merlot Napa Valley 1994: Firm and focused, with a tightly knit core of cedar, spice and currant flavors, picking up dashes of tobacco and herb. Finishes with firm tannins, so cellar short-term. 3,500 cases made. • $28 • (06/30/97) • **87**

Merlot Napa Valley 1993: A dose of mint cannot help the modest cherry flavors overcome the high tannin level. 3,000 cases made. • $25 • (07/31/96) • **78**

Merlot Napa Valley 1992 • $24 • (09/30/95) • **85**

Merlot Napa Valley 1991 • $28 • (09/15/94) • **84**

Merlot Napa Valley 1990 • $18 • (12/15/92) • **85**

Merlot Napa Valley 1989 • $16 • (05/31/92) • **84**

Muscat de Frontignan Napa Valley Antigua NV • $12 • (11/30/91) • **86**

Profile Napa Valley 1992: Smooth and supple, with a rich core of currant, anise, mint and cherry flavors that fan out nicely on the palate. Not a wine that dazzles, but wins you over with subtlety and finesse. Has enough tannin to merit cellaring into 2000. 1,375 cases made. • $36 • (11/15/96) • **88**

Profile Napa Valley 1991 • $36 • (12/15/95) • **90**

Profile Napa Valley 1990 • $36 • (12/15/95) • **78**

Profile Napa Valley 1989 • $30 • (06/30/93) • **86**

Profile Napa Valley 1988 • $25 • (11/15/92) • **85**

Profile Napa Valley 1987 • $25 • (11/15/91) • **83**

Red Napa Valley 1986 • $24 • (10/15/90) • **86**

Red Napa Valley 1985 • $25 • (11/15/88) • **87**

Red Napa Valley 1984 • $24 • (10/31/87) • **90**

Red Napa Valley 1983 • $20 • (02/15/87) • **94**

Sauvignon Blanc Napa Valley 1996: A very bright wine that leans toward lemon and grapefruit. Firm yet round, it tapers off with a sharp mineral edge. Not for wimps. 2,800 cases made. • $17 • (04/30/98) • **85**

Sauvignon Blanc Napa Valley 1995: Crisp, with floral and lightly spicy flavors surrounding a center of green apple. Finishes with some finesse. 2,650 cases made. • $12 • (07/31/96) • **86**

Sauvignon Blanc Napa Valley 1993 • $10 • (06/30/95) • **83**

Sauvignon Blanc-Sémillon Napa Valley Vignette 1996: Toasty, flinty notes frame pretty mango and peach flavors. The finish is bright and clean, with subtle grass tones. A blend of 69 percent Sauvignon Blanc and 31 percent Sémillon. 750 cases made. • $22 • (04/30/98) • **86**

MESSINA HOF | TEXAS

Cabernet Sauvignon Texas Barrel Reserve 1989 • $10 • (03/15/93) • **84**

Cabernet Sauvignon Texas Private Reserve 1990 • $15 • (01/31/95) • **81**

Chardonnay Texas Barrel Reserve 1994: A broad and pungent wine that's ultimately simple and sweet. Tastes more like Muscat or Niagara than Chardonnay. 2,000 cases made. • $11 • (09/15/96) • **71**

Muscat Canelli Late Harvest Texas 1995: Sweet, and a bit cloying, with peach and herbal flavors. An odd mix. • $17 • (01/01/97) • **78**

Pinot Noir Texas Reflections 1991 • $10 • (02/28/93) • **80**

Port Texas Papa Paulo 1993: An unusual style of Port that's full-bodied, spicy-oaky in flavor and not too sweet. Like a turbo-charged Cabernet. 1,000 cases made. • $20 • (01/01/97) • **82**

Key: SS—Spectator Selection CS—Cellar Selection HR—Highly Recommended BB—Best Buy $NA—Price not available Ⓐ—Auction Price (BT)—Barrel Tasting
Dates in parentheses indicate the issues in which the ratings were published.

Reflections Texas 1988 • $15 • (02/29/92) • **77**

Sémillon Late Harvest Texas 1995: A sweet and fairly rich wine with oniony flavors that are not off-putting. Distinctive and quite tasty. • $17 • (01/01/97) • **83**

MICHAEL, PETER | CALIFORNIA

Cabernet Sauvignon Knights Valley Les Pavots 1992 • $29 • (12/15/95) • **90**

Cabernet Sauvignon Knights Valley Les Pavots 1991 • $46 Ⓐ • (05/15/95) • **87**

Cabernet Sauvignon Knights Valley Les Pavots 1989 • $24 • (12/15/92) • **79**

Cabernet Sauvignon Knights Valley Les Pavots 1988 • $25 • (11/15/91) • **90**

Chardonnay Knights Valley Belle Côte 1996: Elegant and understated at first, with delicate pear, tangerine and vanilla flavors that build into a more complex and concentrated wine, with hazelnut, citrus, and fig. Drink now through 2002. 2,423 cases made. • $42 • (07/31/98) • **93**

Chardonnay Napa County Clos du Ciel 1996: Distinct for its rich, creamy tangerine flavors. The core of pear, fig and citrus is intense and lively, finishing with a long, complex, lingering aftertaste. Shows a remarkable amount of elegance and finesse for a wine that packs in so much flavor. Drink now through 2004. 1,700 cases made. • $38 • (07/31/98) HR • **93**

Chardonnay Napa County Clos du Ciel 1995: Opens with spicy, toasty oak and fruit aromas and then shows off its ripe, rich, concentrated core of pear, fig and citrus flavors. Try now. 1,500 cases made. • $35 • (05/31/97) • **94**

Chardonnay Napa County Clos du Ciel 1994: Pleasant, spicy notes accent the ripe pear and honey flavors that glide into an elegant finish. 2,800 cases made. • $32 • (06/15/96) • **87**

Chardonnay Sonoma County Cuvée Indigène 1994: Serves up tiers of rich, complex, concentrated flavors—ripe pear, fig, butterscotch and honey that combine intensity and flavor with elegance and finesse. Amazingly complex on the finish, with a smoky, toasty aftertaste. 750 cases made. • $60 • (12/31/96) • **95**

Chardonnay Sonoma County Cuvée Indigène 1993 • $40 • (01/31/96) • **93**

Chardonnay Sonoma County Mon Plaisir 1994: Combines a rich, complex core of ripe pear, honey, peach and hazelnut flavors with a dash of toasty oak. Shows both depth and richness, along with a sense of elegance and finesse. The finish is long and complex. 2,200 cases made. • $40 • (12/31/96) HR • **94**

Chardonnay Sonoma County Mon Plaisir 1993 • $35 • (01/31/96) HR • **93**

Les Pavots Knights Valley 1995: A wine of enormous intensity, concentration and complexity, it's packed with crisp, firm, currant, spice, cedar, tar and wild berry flavors, and the finish just goes on and on. Best on the aftertaste, where the flavors fold together ever so nicely. Best from 2001 through 2010. • $50 • (07/31/98) • **93**

Les Pavots Knights Valley 1994: Wonderful complexity, depth and concentration, with layers of ripe, juicy plum, currant and black cherry flavors tinged with spice, smoke, toast and buttery oak notes. Delicious aftertaste keeps pumping out flavors. A blend of 68 percent Cabernet Sauvignon, 16 percent Merlot and 16 percent Cabernet Franc. Best from 1999 to 2005. 3,000 cases made. • $35 • (08/31/97) CS • **94**

Les Pavots Knights Valley 1993: A young and tight Cabernet blend that adds a cedary grace note to the ripe cherry, currant, anise and spice flavors. A complex and complete California wine that shows finesse and careful attention to detail. Finishes with firm tannins. Keep it cellared into 1999 or 2000. 2,016 cases made. • $35 • (09/30/96) CS • **90**

Sauvignon Blanc Napa County L' Après-Midi 1996: Quite lemony, with a silky texture, this wine also boasts a medley of melon, fig and grapefruit flavors. A polished effort, with plenty of oak yet lots of finesse too. Drink now. • $30 • (07/31/98) • **90**

Sauvignon Blanc Napa County L' Après-Midi 1995: A tangy, citruslike wine that packs a punch, and finishes with bright lemon-orange flavors. 575 cases made. • $24 • (06/15/97) • **88**

Sauvignon Blanc Napa County L' Après-Midi 1994: Flavors are spicy and toasty, with highlights of lemon and apple. Some rich textures on the finish. 857 cases made. • $21 • (07/31/96) • **88**

MICHAEL-SCOTT | CALIFORNIA

Zinfandel Napa Valley 1996: Delicious old-vine Zinfandel from a new producer. Serves up lively, fresh and rich cherry, raspberry, wild berry, plum and spice and finishes with a gush of fruit and firm but supple tannins. Drink now through 2001. 140 cases made. • $22 • (04/30/98) • **90**

Zinfandel Napa Valley Old Vine 1996: Beaujolais-like in its weight and fruitiness, with lots of ripe plum and wild berry flavor that's soft and fleshy, and finishing with easygoing tannins. A joy to drink already. 17 percent Petite Sirah. 140 cases made. • $22 • (11/30/97) • **87**

MICHEL-SCHLUMBERGER | CALIFORNIA

Cabernet Sauvignon Dry Creek Valley 1993: A fairly rich wine, somewhat hot though. Its cedar, currant and blackberry notes are framed by an herbal core and it finishes with a licorice twist. 2,547 cases made. • $20 • (10/31/97) • **86**

Cabernet Sauvignon Dry Creek Valley 1991 • $18 • (11/15/94) • **81**

Cabernet Sauvignon Dry Creek Valley Reserve 1990 • $35 • (11/15/94) • **82**

Chardonnay Dry Creek Valley 1995: Earthy, mineral flavors come forward in this off-beat Chardonnay. Firm finish, with hints of honey. Drink now. 1,900 cases made. • $20 • (12/15/97) • **85**

MIDNIGHT CELLARS | CALIFORNIA

Cabernet Franc Paso Robles Crescent 1995: Fairly soft and supple, with ripe plum and blackberry flavors. Smoky oak lends an attractive dimension. On the finish, it's bright and firm but still balanced. Drink now through 2003. 265 cases made. • $15 • (05/31/98) • **88**

Cabernet Sauvignon Paso Robles 1994: Nicely textured, firm, with cedar, smoke and wild cherry flavors. A slightly vegetal quality kicks in disappointingly on the finish, however. 681 cases made. • $16 • (09/15/97) • **85**

Cabernet Sauvignon Paso Robles Limited Reserve 1993: Marked by rich aromas of plum, fig and black cherry. It's quite ripe, almost too much so, with a big, Port-like kick. Racy and powerful, but perhaps lacking in elegance. Drink now. 232 cases made. • $17 • (02/28/98) • **87**

Cabernet Sauvignon Paso Robles Nocturne 1995: Smoke, blackberry and plum flavors announce this wine. A cherrylike core shines through. Finishes a little short, however. Drink now through 2000. 100 cases made. • $16 • (06/30/98) • **84**

Chardonnay Central Coast 1996: A neat blend of hazelnut, pear, anise, spice and ginger flavors in a silky structure. Long finish. Drink now. 313 cases made. • $16 • (07/31/98) • **88**

Chardonnay Central Coast 1995: A creamy, smooth wine, with full, tropical flavors of mango and papaya. It's somewhat bitter on the finish though, and marked by an almost smoky edge. 1,736 cases made. • $15 • (01/31/98) • **86**

Merlot Paso Robles Eclipse 1995: This is a pretty, delicately styled Merlot, with cherry, blueberry, anise and cedar notes. It's silky and smooth, drinking well now, but should last for the cellar, too. 231 cases made. • $19 • (04/30/98) • **88**

Sauvignon Blanc Paso Robles 1995: Ripe and straightforward in style, it's big and lengthy, but marked by spicy oak that overwhelms. 720 cases made. • $9 • (04/30/97) • **84**

Zinfandel Paso Robles 1995: A little too much toasty oak in here for the modest cherry and plum flavors behind it. Pleasant enough, with a tangy finish. 832 cases made. • $18 • (07/31/97) • **82**

MIETZ | CALIFORNIA

Merlot Sonoma County 1995: Tough and leathery, showing lots of cedar, herb and sage notes before working into some currant, tobacco and berry. Try now to 2002. 1,800 cases made. • $21 • (03/31/98) • **87**

Merlot Sonoma County 1994 • $18 • (06/30/96) • **82**

Merlot Sonoma County 1993: Tannic with a green herbal edge to the modest core of plum and berry flavors, but overall the impression is of barely ripe fruit. 1,855 cases made. • $17 • (08/31/96) • **81**

Merlot Sonoma County 1990 • $14 • (11/30/92) • **81**

Merlot Sonoma County 1989 • $14 • (04/15/92) • **91**

Zinfandel Sonoma County 1996: The fruit is just ripe enough to sustain this wine, with tart berry, wild berry and spice. Turns bitingly tannic on the finish. Drink now through 2000. 728 cases made. • $18 • (05/31/98) • **84**

Zinfandel Sonoma County 1995: Smooth, supple and harmonious, with attractive black cherry, spice, wild berry and anise notes. Finishes with a long, lingering aftertaste and a trace of bitterness. Drink now or cellar into 1999. • $15 • (04/30/97) • **88**

MILANO | CALIFORNIA

Cabernet Sauvignon Mendocino County Sanel Valley Vineyard 1993: Bright, spicy and cherrylike. Not much like Cabernet, it resembles a Zin/Pinot Noir blend. Pleasant enough, though out of character. 120 cases made. • $13 • (11/30/97) • **80**

Cabernet Sauvignon Mendocino County Sanel Valley Vineyard 1985 • $18 • (09/30/89) • **80**

Cabernet Sauvignon Mendocino County Sanel Valley Vineyard 1982 • $13 • (12/15/87) • **83**

Cabernet Sauvignon Mendocino County Sanel Valley Vineyards Vino di Famiglia NV: The bright cherry and spice character heralds a well-balanced effort that integrates flavors of herbs, oak, coffee and leather. A slightly bitter finish disappoints, but the big picture is harmonious. 250 cases made. • $25 • (11/30/96) • **86**

Chardonnay Late Harvest Anderson Valley Marguerite Vineyards 1993: Rich and spicy, this is marked more by oak nuances than by fruit flavors. Firm and spicy finish. Drink now. 120 cases made. • $15/375ml • (11/30/96) • **80**

Echo Red Mendocino County Bells Echo Vineyard 1994: Cola, tar and coffee flavors are followed by plum, oak and spice notes. The velvety texture dries out a bit on the finish. Drink now. A blend of Merlot, Petit Verdot and Cabernet Sauvignon. 143 cases made. • $30 • (11/30/97) • **83**

Zinfandel Mendocino County 1981 • $6 • (10/01/84) • **80**

Zinfandel Mendocino County Sanel Valley Vineyard 1994: Plump, ripe and juicy, with lots of tasty plum, berry, cherry and spice flavors, finishing with a chalky edge to the tannins. Drinkable now. 506 cases made. • $12 • (04/30/97) • **89**

Zinfandel Mendocino County Sanel Valley Vineyard 1993 • $10 • (10/15/95) • **85**

Zinfandel Mendocino County Sanel Valley Vineyard 1990 • $8 • (09/15/94) • **85**

Zinfandel Mendocino County Sanel Valley Vineyard 1988 • $8 • (04/30/91) • **85**

MILAT | CALIFORNIA

Cabernet Sauvignon Napa Valley 1990 • $14 • (11/15/94) • **83**

MILL CREEK | CALIFORNIA

Cabernet Sauvignon Dry Creek Valley 1993: A touch earthy in character, with a cedary oak edge, but there's enough ripe Cabernet flavor there to offset the earth and wood elements. 863 cases made. • $12 • (11/30/96) • **83**

Cabernet Sauvignon Dry Creek Valley 1992 • $12 • (12/15/95) • **85**

Cabernet Sauvignon Dry Creek Valley 1991 • $12 • (11/15/94) • **83**

Cabernet Sauvignon Dry Creek Valley 1990 • $12 • (11/15/93) • **74**

Cabernet Sauvignon Dry Creek Valley 1988 • $12 • (11/15/91) • **78**

Cabernet Sauvignon Dry Creek Valley 1982 • $9 • (06/15/88) • **68**

Cabernet Sauvignon Dry Creek Valley Estate Bottled 1982 • $8 • (12/31/87) • **81**

Cabernet Sauvignon Sonoma County 1995: Subdued, still quite young, though cassis, blackberry, anise and herbs are nonetheless in evidence. Tannins are silky, but another year of aging would be beneficial. 978 cases made. • $17 • (03/31/98) • **83**

Cabernet Sauvignon Sonoma County 1994: Bright acidity and vivid, wild cherry and spice flavors are surprisingly lively, but it's one-dimensional and the finish is bitter. 499 cases made. • $15 • (11/15/97) • **81**

Chardonnay Dry Creek Valley 1996: An unusual style that offers more minty, leafy notes than fruit at first, but it all comes together smoothly on the finish, hinting at peach and honey. Ready now. 2,100 cases made. • $13 • (11/30/97) • **85**

Chardonnay Dry Creek Valley 1995: Crisp and bright with lemony pear flavors, hints of spices on the juicy finish. Ready to drink. 1,582 cases made. • $12 • (07/31/97) • **83**

Chardonnay Dry Creek Valley 1994: Light and bright, with nectarine and spice flavors that linger nicely on the finish. Drinkable now. 1,559 cases made. • $12 • (06/30/96) • **86**

Chardonnay Dry Creek Valley 1993 • $12 • (05/15/95) • **87**

Gewürztraminer Dry Creek Valley 1993 • $7 • (02/28/95) • **84**

Gewürztraminer North Coast 1994 • $8 • (06/15/96) • **83**

Merlot Dry Creek Valley 1995: Light and silky, with modest raspberry and currant flavors and a hint of dill on the finish. Nice now. 6,061 cases made. • $18 • (11/30/97) • **85**

Merlot Dry Creek Valley 1994: Achieves a nice balance between its ripe cherry and currant flavors and light oak shadings. Impressive finish. 5,896 cases made. • $14 • (08/31/96) • **86**

Merlot Dry Creek Valley 1993: Smoky, toasty oak notes add dimension to the ripe cherry and plum flavors. 2,848 cases made. • $14 • (08/31/96) • **84**

Merlot Dry Creek Valley 1991 • $12 • (09/15/94) • **83**

Merlot Dry Creek Valley 1990 • $14 • (10/15/93) • **84**

Merlot Dry Creek Valley 1989 • $12 • (03/31/93) • **82**

Merlot Dry Creek Valley 1988 • $12 • (05/31/92) • **77**

Merlot Dry Creek Valley 1987 • $12 • (11/15/91) • **84**
Merlot Dry Creek Valley 1983 • $9 • (10/01/85) • **80**
Merlot Dry Creek Valley 1982 • $8 • (04/01/85) • **85**
Pinot Noir Dry Creek Valley 1982 • $6 • (08/31/86) • **71**
Sauvignon Blanc Dry Creek Valley 1994 • $8 • (10/31/95) • **86**
Sauvignon Blanc Dry Creek Valley 1993 • $8 • (10/15/94) • **86**
Sauvignon Blanc North Coast 1995: In a smooth and polished style, with pretty melon and earth flavors that linger. 2,370 cases made. • $10 • (11/30/96) • **83**

MILLBROOK | CALIFORNIA

Arneis Central Coast Mistral Vineyard 1996: Fresh, fruity and lively, with good citrus and pear flavors and hints of almond. Has a bit of a bite on the finish. 187 cases made. • $12 • (12/31/97) • **82**
Cabernet Franc Hudson River Region Proprietor's Special Reserve 1995: A medium-bodied red, with a touch of richness and good cherry, herb and plum flavors. Has a nice gamy edge on the finish. Drink now. 227 cases made. • $19 • (03/31/98) • **82**
Cabernet Sauvignon Hudson River Region Proprietor's Special Reserve 1993: Fairly rich with a nice mix of herbal and plum flavors. Tannic with a lingering finish that has some nice spice nuances. A ripe and well-rounded wine. 260 cases made. • $17 • (12/31/95) • **85**
Cabernet Sauvignon New York 1995: A vibrant, fruity red, exhibiting cherry and bell-pepper flavors, accents of vanilla. Medium-bodied, with fine tannins and moderate length. Drinkable now. • $NA • (08/31/97) • **85**
Chardonnay Central Coast Mistral Vineyard 1996: Buttery and smoky aromas give way to smoky and toasty flavors in this oak-dominated white. Also has crisp acidity, some light apple and citrus notes. Tasted twice, with consistent notes. 2,160 cases made. • $13 • (11/15/97) • **83**
Chardonnay Central Coast Mistral Vineyard 1993 • $8 • (02/28/95) • **89**
Chardonnay Hudson River Region Proprietor's Special Reserve 1996: A rich, complex Chardonnay, with a nice blend of creamy, citrusy, spicy flavors, that turns slightly astringent on the finish. Drink now. 2,400 cases made. • $19 • (03/31/98) • **85**
Chardonnay Hudson River Region Proprietor's Special Reserve 1995: Lacks finesse, but has plenty of apple and butter flavors, with an earthy note for good measure. A bit astringent on the finish. 1,250 cases made. • $19 • (05/15/97) • **81**
Chardonnay Hudson River Region Proprietor's Special Reserve 1994: Melts in your mouth. Enticing spicy aromas, ripe but subtle pear and peach flavors and a lingering finish make this silky-textured Chardonnay something special. Easily mistaken for a Puligny-Montrachet. 500 cases made. • $17 • (09/15/96) • **90**
Chardonnay Hudson River Region Proprietor's Special Reserve 1993 • $16 • (02/28/95) • **88**
Chardonnay New York 1996: Almost like an Australian Chardonnay with its deep gold color, honeyed flavors and thick texture. A fat, ripe style that's easy to like. Drink now. 5,400 cases made. • $13 • (03/31/98) • **85**
Chardonnay New York 1995: Full-bodied, with flavors of butter and apples. It finishes with notes of cream and butterscotch. 4,000 cases made. • $12 • (05/15/97) • **82**
Chardonnay New York 1994: A full-blown, fairly oaky style of Chardonnay—from the toasty, spicy aromas to the buttery vanilla flavors. Could only use more fruit. 3,600 cases made. • $12 • (09/15/96) • **84**
Fernão Pires Central Coast Mistral Vineyard 1996: An awkward wine that smells and tastes like pineapple juice. 75 cases made. • $12 • (08/31/97) • **72**
Fiano Central Coast Mistral Vineyard 1996: Dominated by a buttery flavor, and lacks enough fruit to balance. Turns cloying on the finish. 58 cases made. • $12 • (07/31/97) • **77**
Gamay Noir Hudson River Region 1996: Grapey and almost sweet, with maraschino cherry flavors. 210 cases made. • $11 • (08/31/97) • **77**
Merlot Central Coast Mistral Vineyard 1996: Intensely herbal in aroma and flavor, with some decent gamy notes wrapped in. An assertive style that's not for everyone. Finishes on a chocolaty note. Drink now. 690 cases made. • $14 • (03/31/98) • **81**
Moscato Bianco Central Coast Mistral Vineyard 1996: This lively white offers well-defined melon, orange peel and spice flavors, with an engaging balance of acidity and slight sweetness. A good example of the varietal. 193 cases made. • $16 • (11/15/97) • **85**

Key: SS—Spectator Selection CS—Cellar Selection HR—Highly Recommended BB—Best Buy $NA—Price not available Ⓐ—Auction Price (BT)—Barrel Tasting
Dates in parentheses indicate the issues in which the ratings were published.

Pinot Grigio Central Coast Mistral Vineyard 1996: A bit of a muddle. Shows melon and herbal flavors, a slight saltiness on the finish. 117 cases made. • $13 • (12/31/97) • **79**
Pinot Noir Central Coast Mistral Vineyard 1996: A stewy-tasting Pinot Noir with dried cherry flavors. Flavorful, but lacks finesse. 640 cases made. • $14 • (12/31/97) • **79**
Pinot Noir Central Coast Mistral Vineyard 1993 • $9 • (11/15/94) • **80**
Pinot Noir Hudson River Region Proprietor's Special Reserve 1995: Firm and flavorful, with dried cherry flavors and some good spicy notes. Turns a bit astringent and stewy-tasting on the finish, though. Drink now. 375 cases made. • $19 • (03/31/98) • **81**
Pinot Noir Hudson River Region Proprietor's Special Reserve 1993: A solid but basic Pinot Noir, with toasty aromas, a fairly full body and tea and berry flavors. 402 cases made. • $17 • (09/15/96) • **80**
Pinot Noir New York 1995: A reasonable Pinot Noir with the characteristic cherry, spice and cola flavors, medium body and an oaky aftertaste. 330 cases made. • $14 • (08/31/97) • **79**
Pinot Noir New York 1994: A grayish tint and a smoky flavor make this atypical. Has some varietal characteristics, but not much appeal. 900 cases made. • $12 • (09/15/96) • **77**
Roussanne Central Coast Mistral Vineyard 1996: Fruity, with apricot and herbal flavors. A soft wine that should be served chilled. 150 cases made. • $12 • (07/31/97) • **78**
Tocai Friulano Hudson River Region 1996: Full-bodied and firm, this no-nonsense white offers light pear, almond and smoke flavors. A bit hard, but balanced. Try with richer fish dishes. 540 cases made. • $12 • (11/15/97) • **83**
Tocai Friulano Hudson River Region 1995: A lively, fruity white, full of melon and butter flavors wrapped up in a fat, rich texture. Soft, and easy to drink. 400 cases made. • $11 • (05/31/97) • **82**
Verdelho Central Coast Mistral Vineyard 1996: A nice, peachy-tasting wine with good body and a touch of richness. Flavors linger on the finish. 71 cases made. • $12 • (07/31/97) • **83**
Vernaccia Central Coast Mistral Vineyard 1996: A medium-bodied white that shows the almond and spicy notes typical of this Italian varietal, with firm backbone and a fruity finish. A refreshing apéritif. • $NA • (11/15/97) • **84**

MILLSTREAM | CALIFORNIA

Cabernet Sauvignon California 1993: Smooth and exuberantly fruity, wheeling its raspberry, tobacco and spice flavors through the polished finish. Ready now. 3,000 cases made. • $5 • (12/15/95) • **84**

MIRABELLE | CALIFORNIA

Brut North Coast NV: Clean and smooth, with bright apple and mineral tones. The finish is fresh but not terribly complex. 10,000 cases made. • $12 • (12/31/97) • **86**

MIRASSOU | CALIFORNIA

Blanc de Noirs Monterey Cuvée 1989 • $13 • (05/15/92) • **82**
Blanc de Noirs Monterey Cuvée 1987 • $12 • (11/15/91) • **77**
Blanc de Noirs Monterey Fifth Generation Cuvée 1991 • $14 • (12/31/93) • **80**
Brut Monterey 1987 • $13 • (12/31/91) • **76**
Brut Monterey 1982 • $12 • (09/16/85) • **78**
Brut Monterey Cuvée 1989 • $13 • (12/31/92) • **87**
Brut Monterey Cuvée 1988 • $13 • (05/15/92) • **78**
Brut Monterey Cuvée 1984 • $12 • (06/15/91) • **84**
Brut Monterey Cuvée Au Naturel 1989 • $15 • (12/31/92) • **72**
Brut Monterey Cuvée Au Naturel 1988 • $15 • (05/15/92) • **85**
Brut Monterey Cuvée Au Naturel 1987 • $15 • (11/15/91) • **85**
Brut Monterey Cuvée Au Naturel 1984 • $15 • (06/15/91) • **83**
Brut Monterey Cuvée Reserve 1985 • $15 • (12/31/92) • **82**
Brut Monterey Cuvée Reserve 1984 • $15 • (12/31/91) • **85**
Brut Monterey Fifth Generation Cuvée 1991 • $12 • (12/31/95) • **84**
Brut Monterey Fifth Generation Cuvée 1990 • $12 • (07/31/93) • **83**
Brut Monterey Fifth Generation Cuvée Reserve 1988 • $14 • (12/31/93) • **73**
Brut Monterey Fifth Generation Cuvée Reserve Au Naturel 1989 • $14 • (12/31/93) • **82**
Brut Monterey Reserve 1983 • $15 • (12/31/89) • **76**
Cabernet Sauvignon California Family Selection 1986 • $9 • (05/31/91) • **83**

Cabernet Sauvignon Monterey County 1993: Distinctly herbal, with a strong, mintlike component to the soft berry and tobacco flavors. Ready to drink. 8,700 cases made. • $12 • (07/31/97) • **83**
Cabernet Sauvignon Monterey County 1992: You get a whiff of bell pepper and herb, but it delivers enough currant and plum character to hold your interest. Drinks well now. 15,450 cases made. • $11 • (12/15/96) • **85**
Cabernet Sauvignon Monterey County Fifth Generation Family Selection 1991 • $9 • (12/15/95) • **74**
Cabernet Sauvignon Monterey County Fifth Generation Family Selection 1990 • $9 • (09/15/93) • **81**
Cabernet Sauvignon Monterey County Fifth Generation Harvest Reserve 1991 • $12 • (12/15/95) • **87**
Cabernet Sauvignon Monterey County Fifth Generation Harvest Reserve Limited Bottling 1990 • $12 • (11/15/93) • **79**
Cabernet Sauvignon Monterey County Harvest Reserve 1992: Serves up ripe, pure plum and cherry flavors that are well focused, tight and structured. It picks up anise, cedar, tar and spice notes on the finish. Drinkable now. 6,311 cases made. • $15 • (11/15/96) • **88**
Cabernet Sauvignon Monterey County Harvest Reserve 1988 • $13 • (11/15/92) • **76**
Cabernet Sauvignon Monterey County Harvest Reserve 1987 • $13 • (11/15/91) • **86**
Cabernet Sauvignon Monterey County Harvest Reserve 1986 • $13 • (07/31/91) • **60**
Cabernet Sauvignon Napa Valley Harvest Reserve 1985 • $12 • (11/15/89) • **81**
Cabernet Sauvignon Napa Valley Harvest Reserve 1983 • $12 • (12/15/86) • **67**
Cabernet Sauvignon Napa Valley Harvest Reserve 1982 • $12 • (04/16/86) • **82**
Cabernet Sauvignon Napa Valley Harvest Reserve Limited Bottling 1994: An austere style with an earthy, cedary edge to its currant and cherry flavors. Finishes with a cheeselike accent; definitely needs food. 2,332 cases made. • $18 • (05/15/97) • **85**
Cabernet Sauvignon North Coast 1982 • $7 • (10/16/85) BB • **82**
Cabernet Sauvignon Stags Leap District Showcase Selection Harvest Reserve 1994: Smells of earthy, dill-scented oak, with light cherry and plummy Cabernet flavor that doesn't quite fill in the gaps. Best from 2000 through 2007. Tasted twice, with consistent notes. 370 cases made. • $30 • (06/15/98) • **80**
Chardonnay Monterey County 1995: Clean and refreshing, with lively citrus, pear, apple and melon notes that pick up a nice, spicy oak accent. A tremendous value in first-class Chardonnay. 8,500 cases made. • $12 • (05/15/97) • **90**
Chardonnay Monterey County Family Selection 1996: Fruit, fruit and more fruit in this exuberant, fresh-tasting Chardonnay. Apple, pear and tangerine notes mingle nicely, with a light touch of oak on the finish. Drink now. 15,616 cases made. • $12 • (12/31/97) • **88**
Chardonnay Monterey County Fifth Generation Family Selection 1994: Light, fragrant and supple, showing off lovely pear, spice and toast flavors that swirl deliciously and elegantly through the finish. 16,500 cases made. • $11 • (06/15/96) • **88**
Chardonnay Monterey County Fifth Generation Harvest Reserve 1993 • $12 • (07/31/95) • **87**
Chardonnay Monterey County Fifth Generation Harvest Reserve Limited Bottling 1994: Smooth and spicy, with tiers of ripe pear and apple flavors. A touch of jalapeño pepper adds interest. Finishes with a silky texture. 4,500 cases made. • $15 • (07/31/96) • **87**
Chardonnay Monterey County Harvest Reserve 1996: Clean, ripe and richly flavored, with tiers of spicy melon, pear, apple and citrus, fanning out and turning complex on the finish. Drinks well now. 9,395 cases made. • $16 • (05/15/98) • **89**
Chardonnay Monterey County Harvest Reserve Limited Bottling 1995: Features an intriguing range of pretty Chardonnay flavors, with layers of pear, apple, melon and butterscotch and a dash of spicy oak that folds in on the finish. Quality is definitely on the upswing at this winery. 5,500 cases made. • $16 • (05/15/97) • **90**
Chardonnay Monterey County Showcase Selection Harvest Reserve 1996: Smooth, ripe, rich and creamy, with tiers of pear, vanilla, citrus, spice and earthy nuances, finishing with a long, rich aftertaste that keeps pumping out the flavors. Drink now through 2002. 1,085 cases made. • $28 • (06/30/98) • **91**
Chardonnay Monterey Showcase 1995: Young and vibrant, with a rich, complex core of pear, spice, citrus (especially nectarine) flavors. Turns elegant and complex on the finish, where it unveils a smoky oak note. 80 cases made. • $25 • (06/30/97) • **91**
Chenin Blanc Monterey County Fifth Generation Family Selection Dry 1993 • $6 • (06/30/95) • **85**
Johannisberg Riesling Late Harvest Monterey Fifth Generation Select Harvest Reserve 1992 • $13 • (04/15/94) • **85**
Johannisberg Riesling Late Harvest Monterey Select Harvest Reserve 1987 • $13/375ml • (08/31/91) • **87**
Merlot Central Coast Family Selection 1991 • $9 • (06/15/93) • **80**
Merlot Central Coast Fifth Generation Family Selection 1992 • $9 • (04/15/95) • **84**
Merlot Central Coast Fifth Generation Family Selection 1991 • $9 • (09/15/94) • **84**
Merlot Monterey County Family Selection 1990 • $9 • (03/31/93) • **80**
Merlot Monterey County Harvest Reserve Limited Bottling 1994: Racy, with bell pepper and herbaceous notes, while cherry and currant flavors fold in for balance. Ready to drink. 1,985 cases made. • $18 • (07/31/97) • **85**
Petite Sirah Monterey County Family Selection 1989 • $7 • (03/15/92) • **79**
Petite Sirah Monterey County Family Selection Commemorative Bottling 1990 • $9 • (03/31/93) • **75**
Petite Sirah Monterey County Fifth Generation Family Selection 1993: A nice find a this price. This dark, ripe, richly flavored Sirah exhibits classic plum, earth, mineral and pepper flavors and the tannins, while firm, are not overbearing. Ready to drink. 4,067 cases made. • $11 • (11/30/96) • **86**
Petite Sirah Monterey County Fifth Generation Family Selection 1991 • $9 • (02/28/95) • **81**
Pinot Blanc Monterey County Fifth Generation Family Selection 1993 • $7 • (04/15/95) • **81**
Pinot Blanc Monterey County Fifth Generation Harvest Reserve 1993 • $12 • (08/31/95) • **82**
Pinot Blanc Monterey County Harvest Reserve 1995: Smooth, ripe, rich and creamy, with spicy pear, vanilla, toast and anise flavors that are complex and concentrated. Long finish. 2,000 cases made. • $16 • (04/30/98) • **87**
Pinot Blanc Monterey County White Burgundy 1996: Showing bright acidity and a touch of sweetness on the palate, the wine displays light citrus and mineral flavors. 21,894 cases made. • $11 • (05/15/98) • **82**
Pinot Blanc Monterey County White Burgundy Fifth Generation Family Selection 1995: A spicy character tints its ripe pear, apple and melon flavors, which turn simple on the finish. • $8 • (11/30/96) • **82**
Pinot Noir Central Coast Family Selection 1995: Bright cherry and menthol flavors rise to the fore; the ensemble yields a light, refreshing blend. 6,900 cases made. • $11 • (12/15/97) • **85**
Pinot Noir Monterey County 1994: Light in color, body and flavor, with hints of dried cherry, herb and spice. 4,233 cases made. • $11 • (01/31/97) • **77**
Pinot Noir Monterey County 1990 • $7 • (09/30/92) • **72**
Pinot Noir Monterey County Family Selection 1990 • $7 • (02/28/93) • **75**
Pinot Noir Monterey County Family Selection 1988 • $7 • (04/30/91) BB • **81**
Pinot Noir Monterey County Fifth Generation Family Selection 1993: Ripe and spicy on the palate, this medium-weight Pinot offers ripe cherry, plum and wild berry flavors. Easy to drink, especially at this price. 4,173 cases made. • $8 • (11/30/96) • **84**
Pinot Noir Monterey County Fifth Generation Family Selection 1992 • $7 • (12/31/95) • **80**
Pinot Noir Monterey County Fifth Generation Harvest Reserve 1993: Marked by a strong, spicy herb and cedar accent to cherry and berry flavors. Finish reveals some slightly bitter tannins. • $15 • (09/15/96) • **82**
Pinot Noir Monterey County Fifth Generation Harvest Reserve 1992 • $12 • (10/15/95) • **86**
Pinot Noir Monterey County Fifth Generation Harvest Reserve Limited 1991 • $12 • (03/31/95) • **83**
Pinot Noir Monterey County Harvest Reserve 1995: Serves up lots of ripe cherry and berry flavor, and the vanilla-flavored oak is complex, yet it comes across as a bit disjointed. Ready now. 1,600 cases made. • $16 • (02/28/98) • **85**
Pinot Noir Monterey County Harvest Reserve 1989 • $13 • (09/30/92) • **80**
Pinot Noir Monterey County Harvest Reserve 1988 • $13 • (04/30/92) • **84**
Pinot Noir Monterey County Harvest Reserve 1986 • $12 • (04/30/91) • **78**
Pinot Noir Monterey County Harvest Reserve Limited Bottling 1994: In a lighter style, with ripe, bright cherry and raspberry flavors. Appealing to drink now. 1,250 cases made. • $16 • (01/31/97) • **84**
Riesling Monterey County 1995: Sweet but tangy, with little fruit to overcome the acidity. • $7 • (11/30/96) • **78**
Sauvignon Blanc California 1995: Celery, green bean and herb notes mark this stalky, grassy wine that somehow comes out of a nosedive with a fairly clean finish. 5,900 cases made. • $7 • (08/31/97) • **79**
Sauvignon Blanc California 1993 • $6 • (08/31/95) • **85**
White Zinfandel California 1994 • $10 • (09/15/95) • **82**

Zinfandel California 1989 • $5 • (04/30/93) • **72**
Zinfandel California Dry Red Lot No. 3 NV • $5 • (07/31/91) • **73**
Zinfandel California Lot No. 4 NV • $5 • (07/31/91) BB • **81**
Zinfandel California Lot No. 6 NV • $5 • (09/15/92) • **73**
Zinfandel Central Coast Fifth Generation Family Selection 1992 • $7 • (08/31/95) • **83**
Zinfandel Santa Clara Valley Fifth Generation Harvest Reserve 1992 • $12 • (10/15/95) • **83**
Zinfandel Santa Clara Valley Fifth Generation Harvest Reserve Limited Bottling 1991 • $12 • (10/15/94) • **79**
Zinfandel Santa Clara Valley Harvest Reserve 1995: Lightly fruity, with plum, prune and black cherry flavors of modest depth and proportion. Drink now. 873 cases made. • $16 • (06/15/98) • **82**
Zinfandel Santa Clara Valley Harvest Reserve 1990 • $13 • (03/15/93) • **82**
Zinfandel Santa Clara Valley Harvest Reserve 1988 • $13 • (10/15/92) • **85**

MISSION CANYON | CALIFORNIA

Chardonnay Santa Barbara County 1994: Round and herbal, with pinelike nuances adding to the apple and spice flavors. 400 cases made. • $9 • (06/15/96) • **84**
Chardonnay Santa Barbara County 1993 • $9 • (07/31/95) • **79**

MISSION MOUNTAIN | WASHINGTON

Cabernet Sauvignon Columbia Valley 1990 • $15 • (03/31/95) • **79**
Merlot Columbia Valley Reserve 1995: Light and simple, with nice touches of grape, raspberry and floral. Notes of spicy oak fold in on the finish. Best from 1999. 700 cases made. • $25 • (01/31/98) • **85**

MISSION VIEW | CALIFORNIA

Cabernet Sauvignon Paso Robles 1994: Marked by a slight cedary accent, enough plum and cherry flavors surface to give it balance and proportion. Drinks well now. 566 cases made. • $13 • (11/30/96) • **84**
Cabernet Sauvignon Paso Robles 1993: Thin and vegetal in character, with a touch of anise flavor on the finish that acts as a saving grace. 224 cases made. • $13 • (11/30/96) • **79**
Cabernet Sauvignon Paso Robles 1990 • $12 • (11/15/94) • **82**
Cabernet Sauvignon Paso Robles 1989 • $12 • (11/15/92) • **85**
Cabernet Sauvignon Paso Robles 1988 • $12 • (11/15/92) • **86**
Cabernet Sauvignon Paso Robles 1986 • $12 • (12/15/89) • **72**
Chardonnay Paso Robles 1995: A strong resiny streak cuts through the spicy fruit flavors in this oaky white. 1,074 cases made. • $10 • (06/15/96) • **79**
Chardonnay Paso Robles 1994: Soft and fragrant, a chunky white which adds a spicy, perfumy edge to the pear and orange flavors. Ready now. 294 cases made. • $10 • (10/31/95) • **85**
Chardonnay San Luis Obispo 1993 • $10 • (07/31/95) • **77**
Classic Cuvée Paso Robles 1993: A lean wine that shows some cassis, licorice and tarlike flavors. Tannins are firm but supple. Drink now. 261 cases made. • $18 • (11/30/96) • **84**
Fumé Blanc Paso Robles Barrel Fermented & Aged 1995 • $10 • (06/15/96) • **79**
Fumé Blanc Paso Robles Barrel Fermented & Aged 1994 • $9 • (09/15/95) • **84**
Merlot Paso Robles Limited Release 1992 • $14 • (06/15/95) • **76**
Pinot Noir Monterey County Limited Release 1990 • $14 • (02/28/93) • **77**
Sauvignon Blanc San Luis Obispo 1993 • $9 • (08/31/95) • **78**
Zinfandel Paso Robles 1993 • $12 • (01/01/95) • **85**
Zinfandel Paso Robles 1990 • $11 • (09/30/93) • **81**

MISTY MOUNTAIN | VIRGINIA

Cabernet Sauvignon Virginia 1988 • $18 • (02/29/92) • **82**
Merlot Virginia 1988 • $18 • (02/29/92) • **77**

Key: SS—Spectator Selection CS—Cellar Selection HR—Highly Recommended BB—Best Buy $NA—Price not available Ⓐ—Auction Price (BT)—Barrel Tasting
Dates in parentheses indicate the issues in which the ratings were published.

MITCHELL, CHARLES B. | CALIFORNIA

Cabernet Sauvignon El Dorado 1994: Firm, chunky and tannic. Serves up an austere band of earthy currant flavors. 700 cases made. • $12 • (11/30/96) • **79**
Cabernet Sauvignon El Dorado 1993: Pleasant enough, with ripe, spicy cherry and wild berry flavors that pick up an earthy accent. 227 cases made. • $10 • (11/30/96) • **82**
Cabernet Sauvignon El Dorado Grand Reserve 1995: Black cherry, licorice and herbs are followed by a distinctly charred note; the ensemble is attractive, however. Tannins are a little harsh. Drink now or hold. 500 cases made. • $28 • (11/30/97) • **86**
Cabernet Sauvignon El Dorado Reserve 1995: A restrained wine, showing tea, beef and herb qualities framed by smoky oak notes and chunky tannins. Drink now, or wait to see what happens. 200 cases made. • $16 • (10/31/97) • **82**
Cabernet Sauvignon El Dorado Reserve 1993: Light and straightforward, with an earthy edge to the modest strawberry flavors. 157 cases made. • $14 • (12/15/95) • **80**
Cabernet Sauvignon El Dorado Vintner's Cuvée 1995: Somewhat chewy, with smoky, toasty overtones that precede layers of plum, mint, cassis and anise. Tannins shut down the finish early. Better in a few years. 600 cases made. • $11 • (10/31/97) • **85**
Chardonnay El Dorado 1995: Bright and spicy, a different flavor profile than most Chardonnays, with grapefruit and raisin character sneaking in on the finish. 700 cases made. • $12 • (07/31/97) • **84**
Chenin Blanc El Dorado Dry 1994 • $6 • (06/15/96) • **77**
Fumé Blanc El Dorado 1995: Has a nice almond edge to the light pear flavor, giving it an Italianate feel. 215 cases made. • $8 • (07/31/96) • **82**
Fumé Blanc El Dorado 1994 • $7 • (08/31/95) • **82**
Johannisberg Riesling El Dorado 1995: Frankly sweet, almost syrupy, with honey and caramel nuances that overshadow any fruit flavor. 300 cases made. • $7 • (11/30/96) • **80**
Port California NV • $15/500 ml • (06/15/96) • **83**
Sauvignon Blanc El Dorado 1995: Oddly floral and vegetal in character, with a peppery accent to the coarse flavors. 700 cases made. • $7 • (11/30/96) • **77**
Sauvignon Blanc El Dorado 1993 • $6 • (08/31/95) • **83**
Sauvignon Blanc Sierra Foothills 1996: Honeyed melon and nectarine tones announce this refreshing, enjoyable wine. 1,000 cases made. • $8 • (07/31/97) • **87**
Sauvignon Blanc-Sémillon El Dorado 1995: Solidly fruity, with lemony-accented fig and melon flavors that persist on the finish. 350 cases made. • $11 • (08/31/97) • **87**
Sauvignon Blanc-Sémillon El Dorado Euphoria 1996: An austere wine, with sharp acidity and a bright, lemony flavor. Needs food. A blend of 70 percent Sauvignon Blanc and 30 percent Sémillon. Drink now. 500 cases made. • $11 • (05/31/98) • **80**
Zinfandel El Dorado Special Selection 1996: Firm, with strawberry, anise and tar notes resting on a supple frame. Finishes long, with lingering flavors of pepper and berries. Drink now through 2001. 500 cases made. • $15 • (06/15/98) • **85**
Zinfandel El Dorado Vintners' Cuvée 1996: Simple and dilute, with strawberry and spice notes. Finishes with drying, bitter tannins. Drink now. 600 cases made. • $10 • (06/15/98) • **76**
Zinfandel Sierra Foothills Special Selection 1995: Plum- and cherrylike qualities in a waxy base. Shows promise at first but finishes with a short, herbal burst. 500 cases made. • $14 • (07/31/97) • **82**

MONDAVI, CK | CALIFORNIA

Cabernet Sauvignon California 1996: Tart and tannic, with a canned-cherry quality. • $7 • (05/15/98) • **75**
Cabernet Sauvignon California 1995: Smooth, polished and a bit sweet, with pretty plum, strawberry and spice flavors that linger on the solid finish. Ready to drink. • $7 • (05/15/97) • **84**
Cabernet Sauvignon California 1994: In a light style, with simple herb, dill and mild berry flavors. 80,000 cases made. • $6 • (11/30/96) • **79**
Cabernet Sauvignon California 1993: Light and gently fruity, hinting at plum and currant on the modest finish. • $6 • (12/15/95) • **80**
Chardonnay California 1997: Simple, earthy and disjointed. Has a supple texture and some pear flavors but finishes with an odd menthol note. Drink now. • $7 • (06/30/98) • **78**
Chardonnay California 1995: Light-bodied and soft. Fruity flavors—pineapple and pear—remain lively through the finish. 100,000 cases made. • $6 • (07/31/96) • **83**

Chardonnay California 1994: Soft, fruity and appealing for its snappy tropical fruit and floral flavors. Ready now. 36,000 cases made. • $6 • (05/15/96) • **80**

Merlot California 1995: Light and supple, with earthy dried cherry and candied nuances to the flavors. • $7 • (05/15/97) • **80**

Sauvignon Blanc California 1997: Light melon and lemon-lime flavors are couched in a bright but somewhat simple structure. Drink now. • $6 • (05/31/98) • **81**

Zinfandel California 1996: Disjointed, with sour cherry flavors and an earthy, floral aftertaste. Tastes manufactured. Drink now. • $7 • (06/15/98) • **72**

Zinfandel California 1992 • $5 • (10/15/94) • **81**

Zinfandel California 1991 • $5 • (10/15/94) • **79**

MONDAVI, ROBERT | CALIFORNIA

Brut Napa Valley Chardonnay Reserve 1987 • $28 • (12/31/93) • **86**

Brut Napa Valley Chardonnay Reserve 1985 • $35 • (12/31/91) • **85**

Brut Napa Valley Reserve 1987 • $28 • (12/31/93) • **90**

Brut Napa Valley Reserve 1985 • $35 • (12/31/91) • **90**

Cabernet Sauvignon California Cabernet 1986 • $5 • (12/15/88) BB • **80**

Cabernet Sauvignon California Cabernet 1985 • $4 • (10/31/87) BB • **78**

Cabernet Sauvignon California Woodbridge 1992 • $6 • (11/15/94) BB • **82**

Cabernet Sauvignon California Woodbridge 1991 • $7 • (11/15/93) • **80**

Cabernet Sauvignon California Woodbridge 1990 • $8 • (10/31/92) • **81**

Cabernet Sauvignon California Woodbridge 1988 • $6 • (02/28/91) BB • **81**

Cabernet Sauvignon California Woodbridge 1987 • $6 • (09/15/89) • **74**

Cabernet Sauvignon Napa Valley 1994: Slightly earthy and leathery at first, the herb, currant and black cherry flavors slowly become more complex and interesting. Finish is firmly tannic, but the fruit pours through on the aftertaste. Best after 1999. • $22 • (11/15/97) • **90**

Cabernet Sauvignon Napa Valley 1993: Ripe and a touch earthy, with hints of herb and anise and a slight leathery edge, but it folds together nicely on the finish and the tannins are well proportioned. 80,000 cases made. • $20 • (11/15/96) • **88**

Cabernet Sauvignon Napa Valley 1990 • $15 • (10/31/93) SS • **90**

Cabernet Sauvignon Napa Valley 1989 • $18 • (03/31/93) • **84**

Cabernet Sauvignon Napa Valley 1988 • $18 • (11/15/92) • **84**

Cabernet Sauvignon Napa Valley 1987: Still quite young and vibrant, with a firm tannic edge, its earthy currant, sage, spice and cedar flavors unfold gently on the palate. • $72 Ⓐ • (12/15/97) • **90**

Cabernet Sauvignon Napa Valley 1986 • $38 Ⓐ • (07/31/89) • **93**

Cabernet Sauvignon Napa Valley 1985 • $30 Ⓐ • (12/15/88) SS • **94**

Cabernet Sauvignon Napa Valley 1984 • $31 • (12/31/87) • **80**

Cabernet Sauvignon Napa Valley 1983 • $25 Ⓐ • (04/15/87) • **94**

Cabernet Sauvignon Napa Valley 1982 • $20 Ⓐ • (07/01/85) • **90**

Cabernet Sauvignon Napa Valley 1981 • $29 Ⓐ • (12/16/84) • **90**

Cabernet Sauvignon Napa Valley 1979 • $19 Ⓐ • (07/16/85) • **85**

Cabernet Sauvignon Napa Valley 1978 • $26 Ⓐ • (11/15/92) • **86**

Cabernet Sauvignon Napa Valley 1977 • $24 Ⓐ • (07/16/85) • **89**

Cabernet Sauvignon Napa Valley 1976 • $40 • (07/16/85) • **84**

Cabernet Sauvignon Napa Valley 1975 • $14 Ⓐ • (11/30/91) • **85**

Cabernet Sauvignon Napa Valley 1974 • $26 Ⓐ • (02/15/90) • **79**

Cabernet Sauvignon Napa Valley 1973 • $19 Ⓐ • (07/16/85) • **86**

Cabernet Sauvignon Napa Valley 1972 • $16 Ⓐ • (07/16/85) • **80**

Cabernet Sauvignon Napa Valley 1971 • $23 Ⓐ • (07/16/85) • **87**

Cabernet Sauvignon Napa Valley 1970 • $44 Ⓐ • (11/30/91) • **92**

Cabernet Sauvignon Napa Valley 1969 • $38 Ⓐ • (11/30/91) • **91**

Cabernet Sauvignon Napa Valley 1968 • $79 Ⓐ • (11/30/91) • **88**

Cabernet Sauvignon Napa Valley 1967 • $70 • (11/30/91) • **79**

Cabernet Sauvignon Napa Valley 1966 • $110 • (11/30/91) • **88**

Cabernet Sauvignon Napa Valley Oakville District 1994: Smooth and supple, with a spicy accent to the medium-weight currant, plum and cherry notes. Flavors hold and fan out on the finish. Drinkable now or can be cellared into 2000. • $28 • (06/30/97) • **88**

Cabernet Sauvignon Napa Valley Oakville District 1993: Complex, with intense plum, cherry and wild berry flavors and nice dashes of spice, cedar and leather on the finish, where the flavors fan out. Overall it's very pleasing and well balanced. 3,000 cases made. • $28 • (11/15/96) • **88**

Cabernet Sauvignon Napa Valley Oakville District 1992 • $28 • (12/15/95) • **91**

Cabernet Sauvignon Napa Valley Reserve 1997: A touch earthy and leathery, it quickly works its way into more complex and sophisticated flavors. Well integrated, supple in texture, actually quite elegant. • $NA • (07/31/98) (BT) • **90-94**

Cabernet Sauvignon Napa Valley Reserve 1996: Ripe, rich and well focused, with a solid core of currant, plum and cherry flavors. Finishes with firm tannins, fine structure. • $NA • (06/15/97) (BT) • **90-94**

Cabernet Sauvignon Napa Valley Reserve 1995: Ripe, dark, dense and earthy, with a rich core of currant, mineral and spice. Shows off pretty, toasty, spicy oak too, all the while maintaining a tremendous sense of elegance and finesse. Best from 2002 through 2010. • $80 • (07/31/98) • **94**

Cabernet Sauvignon Napa Valley Reserve 1994: A supple, complex and harmonious reserve, sporting a broad range of currant, anise, coffee, cedar and spice flavors, picking up light toasty oak notes and finishing with a smooth texture. Delicious now, but worthy of cellaring, too. • $64 Ⓐ • (07/31/97) CS • **94**

Cabernet Sauvignon Napa Valley Reserve 1993: Dark, ripe and intense, with a tight core of currant, mineral, earth and spice flavors. Turns dry and austere on the finish, where the flavors show more earthy qualities. Best to cellar into 1999. 17,000 cases made. • $41 Ⓐ • (11/30/96) CS • **90**

Cabernet Sauvignon Napa Valley Reserve 1992 • $55 • (07/31/95) CS • **91**

Cabernet Sauvignon Napa Valley Reserve 1991 • $68 Ⓐ • (11/15/94) • **90**

Cabernet Sauvignon Napa Valley Reserve 1990 • $55 • (10/31/93) HR • **91**

Cabernet Sauvignon Napa Valley Reserve 1989 • $19 Ⓐ • (11/15/92) • **85**

Cabernet Sauvignon Napa Valley Reserve 1988 • $36 Ⓐ • (05/31/91) CS • **91**

Cabernet Sauvignon Napa Valley Reserve 1987: Dark, ripe and intense, with a rich core of cedar, currant, anise and spice flavors, finishing with a firm tannic edge. Impressive for its detailed, integrated flavors and fine balance. Best now through 2003. • $81 Ⓐ • (12/15/97) • **93**

Cabernet Sauvignon Napa Valley Reserve 1986: Ripe, smooth, elegant and polished, with its rich core of currant and plum flavors holding very well, if drying out just a tad on the finish. Time to enjoy this one. • $57 Ⓐ • (12/15/96) • **89**

Cabernet Sauvignon Napa Valley Reserve 1985 • $63 Ⓐ • (11/15/89) SS • **95**

Cabernet Sauvignon Napa Valley Reserve 1984 • $53 Ⓐ • (12/31/88) • **90**

Cabernet Sauvignon Napa Valley Reserve 1983 • $31 Ⓐ • (11/30/87) • **91**

Cabernet Sauvignon Napa Valley Reserve 1982 • $43 Ⓐ • (02/15/87) • **95**

Cabernet Sauvignon Napa Valley Reserve 1981 • $26 Ⓐ • (02/16/86) CS • **94**

Cabernet Sauvignon Napa Valley Reserve 1980 • $29 Ⓐ • (11/30/91) • **86**

Cabernet Sauvignon Napa Valley Reserve 1979 • $37 Ⓐ • (11/30/91) • **91**

Cabernet Sauvignon Napa Valley Reserve 1978 • $57 Ⓐ • (11/15/92) • **91**

Cabernet Sauvignon Napa Valley Reserve 1977 • $52 Ⓐ • (11/30/91) • **89**

Cabernet Sauvignon Napa Valley Reserve 1976 • $26 Ⓐ • (11/30/91) • **84**

Cabernet Sauvignon Napa Valley Reserve 1975 • $34 Ⓐ • (07/16/85) • **89**

Cabernet Sauvignon Napa Valley Reserve 1974 • $85 Ⓐ • (11/15/94) • **87**

Cabernet Sauvignon Napa Valley Reserve 1973 • $55 Ⓐ • (11/30/91) • **92**

Cabernet Sauvignon Napa Valley Reserve 1972 • $NA • (11/30/91) • **78**

Cabernet Sauvignon Napa Valley Reserve 1971 • $125 • (11/30/91) • **91**

Cabernet Sauvignon Napa Valley Unfiltered 1991 • $18 • (11/15/94) SS • **90**

Cabernet Sauvignon Napa Valley Unfiltered 1970 • $90 • (07/16/85) • **93**

Cabernet Sauvignon North Coast Coastal 1995: Light and refreshing, showing bright currant and berry flavors and smooth, polished tannins. Drink soon. • $11 • (11/15/97) • **85**

Cabernet Sauvignon North Coast Coastal 1994: A touch herbal, with a modest range of cherry, plum, earth and anise flavors. Finishes with a cedary note and dry tannins. May show more finesse and depth in 1999. • $11 • (12/31/96) • **85**

Cabernet Sauvignon North Coast Coastal 1993: Ripe, smooth and harmonious, laced with plum, herb and currant flavors, picking up a trace of mineral and spice on the finish, where the tannins become more prominent. • $11 • (02/29/96) • **85**

Cabernet Sauvignon North Coast Coastal 1991 • $11 • (09/30/94) • **83**

Chardonnay Carneros 1995: Easily the best Mondavi Carneros to date. Firm and compact, with a rich core of spicy citrus, pear and light oak shadings. On the finish, this wine really shows its stuff as the flavors are deep and complex. • $23 • (05/31/97) • **92**

Chardonnay Carneros 1994: Smells fresh and ripe, with a tart, citrus accent to the pear and apple flavors. Picks up a nice spicy note on the finish, where the texture is smooth and polished. Drinks well now. 10,260 cases made. • $23 • (12/31/96) HR • **89**

Chardonnay Carneros 1993 • $23 • (05/15/96) • **88**

Chardonnay Central Coast Coastal 1996: Smooth and clean, with ripe pear and apple flavors that are focused and pleasing. Finishes with a glimmer of oak. Drink now. • $10 • (06/15/98) • **84**

Chardonnay Central Coast Coastal 1995: Fresh, ripe and lively, with plenty of zesty pear, citrus and vanilla notes. Doesn't try to wow you with toasty oak, but gives you lots of flavor at a very decent price. 285,000 cases made. • $11 • (01/31/97) • **87**

MONDAVI, ROBERT

Chardonnay Central Coast Coastal 1994: Ripe and spicy, showing a juicy—almost sweet—core of citrus and grapefruit flavors. 200,000 cases made. • $10 • (05/15/96) • **82**

Chardonnay Central Coast Coastal 1993 • $11 • (12/15/94) • **84**

Chardonnay Napa Valley 1996: Ripe, rich and complex, with concentrated fruit flavors, lots of pretty spicy, toasty nuances and a core of rich pear, fig and melon. Finishes with a long, lingering aftertaste. Drink now through 2002. • $19 • (07/31/98) • **90**

Chardonnay Napa Valley 1995: Clean and snappy, with citrus, pear and grapefruit flavors at the core and just a hint of oak on the finish. Ready to drink. • $17 • (04/30/97) • **88**

Chardonnay Napa Valley 1994: Young and vibrant, with a focused core of spicy pear, citrus and lemon flavors, picking up a trace of toasty oak on the finish. Impressive for its length. 100,000 cases made. • $17 • (05/31/96) • **89**

Chardonnay Napa Valley Reserve 1995: Smooth, ripe and creamy, with hints of pear, lemon, light oak and spice, it turns elegant on the finish. A delicate style. Drink now. Tasted twice, with consistent notes. • $31 • (11/30/97) • **90**

Chardonnay Napa Valley Reserve 1994: The best Mondavi reserve Chardonnay ever, this is trim and compact at first, with tartly accented, ripe pear, apple and citrus notes. The flavors fan out on the finish, showing a good measure of elegance and finesse. Has a wonderful aftertaste where the notes linger long. Put a couple of bottles away for 1999 to 2000. 7,000 cases made. • $30 • (04/30/97) HR • **95**

Chardonnay Napa Valley Reserve 1993 • $29 • (07/31/95) HR • **91**

Chardonnay Napa Valley Unfiltered 1993 • $15 • (07/31/95) • **85**

Fumé Blanc Napa Valley 1995: Ripe and refreshing, with a lively herbal streak and a hint of anise to shade the green apple and light, citrusy flavors. Drink now. • $12 • (04/30/97) • **88**

Fumé Blanc Napa Valley 1994 • $11 • (05/15/96) • **85**

Fumé Blanc Napa Valley 1993 • $10 • (05/31/95) BB • **88**

Fumé Blanc Napa Valley To-Kalon Vineyard I Block 1995: Rich and exotic, with butterscotch, pear, melon and citrus flavors at the fore. Bracing acidity refreshes the palate, with a finish that echoes sage and fresh-cut hay. From some of California's oldest Sauvignon Blanc vines. 300 cases made. • $50 • (04/30/98) • **89**

Fumé Blanc Napa Valley To-Kalon Vineyard Reserve 1995: A richly textured wine with ripe pear and melon flavors. It's seen a bit too much oak, though, so it's overly rich in coconut and vanilla. • $22 • (11/30/97) • **88**

Fumé Blanc Napa Valley To-Kalon Vineyard Reserve 1994: Dry, almost austere, with grapefruit flavor at the core and pretty vanilla and floral notes that linger on the finish. Significantly better than in an earlier tasting. 3,900 cases made. • $20 • (10/31/96) • **86**

Fumé Blanc Napa Valley To-Kalon Vineyard Reserve 1993 • $19 • (05/31/95) • **86**

Fumé Blanc Napa Valley Unfiltered 1994: A fresh and lively mouthful of nice green apple and floral flavors that linger on the finish. 5,000 cases made. • $11 • (08/31/96) • **86**

Fumé Blanc Stags Leap District 1994: Tangy and refreshing aromas and flavors—herb, sweet pea and melon—that linger nicely on the finish. 5,000 cases made. • $18 • (09/15/96) • **88**

Johannisberg Riesling Central Coast Coastal 1996: Bright and appealing for its straight-ahead apple and sweet grapefruit flavors, which fade gently on the finish. Ready now. • $9 • (03/31/98) • **83**

Merlot Central Coast Coastal 1996: Light and pretty, with plum and vanilla flavors riding on a layer of fine tannins. Very nice now, best in 1999. • $11 • (03/31/98) • **84**

Merlot Napa Valley 1994: Emerging from some distinct, slightly bitter, herb and tar notes is an interesting core of smoky, toasty oak, plush currant, tea, sage and mineral flavors. Drinkable now. 14,000 cases made. • $22 • (04/30/97) • **90**

Merlot Napa Valley 1993 • $19 • (05/31/96) • **84**

Merlot Napa Valley 1992: Dense and cedary, with a tightly wound core of earthy currant, tobacco, mineral and spice. Drink now. 9,500 cases made. • $19 • (08/31/96) • **87**

Merlot Napa Valley 1991 • $21 • (06/15/94) • **89**

Merlot Napa Valley 1990 • $21 • (03/31/93) • **86**

Merlot Napa Valley 1989 • $21 • (05/31/92) • **87**

Key: SS—Spectator Selection CS—Cellar Selection HR—Highly Recommended BB—Best Buy $NA—Price not available Ⓐ—Auction Price (BT)—Barrel Tasting
Dates in parentheses indicate the issues in which the ratings were published.

Pinot Noir Carneros 1995: Earthy and quite tannic, with a stemmy, tealike edge, it takes some time to unfold its core of cherry and wild berry flavors. Drink now. • $26 • (01/31/98) • **87**

Pinot Noir Carneros 1994: Elegant, with supple earth and black cherry flavors and a pretty dash of smoky oak. Drink now. Tasted twice, with consistent notes. 6,500 cases made. • $26 • (12/31/96) • **87**

Pinot Noir Carneros 1991 • $20 • (02/28/94) • **83**

Pinot Noir Carneros Unfiltered 1992 • $24 • (03/31/95) • **86**

Pinot Noir Central Coast Coastal 1996: Crisp and appealing for its mineral-scented currant flavors, finishing a bit tight. Try in 1999. • $11 • (03/31/98) • **84**

Pinot Noir Central Coast Coastal 1995: Pleasant enough, with a core of spice, herb, cola and cherry flavors that hang together for a full-flavored finish. Ready to drink. 35,000 cases made. • $12 • (01/31/97) • **84**

Pinot Noir Central Coast Coastal 1994 • $11 • (05/31/96) • **82**

Pinot Noir Napa Valley 1995: Attractive for its range of wild berry, black cherry, sage, tea and spice. It's moderately rich and concentrated, but turns simpler and loses its focus on the aftertaste. • $19 • (02/28/98) • **85**

Pinot Noir Napa Valley 1994: An austere style, with a crisp, somewhat green edge to its cherry and berry flavors. Fans of delicate, understated Pinot Noir will find this attractive. 35,000 cases made. • $17 • (01/31/97) • **86**

Pinot Noir Napa Valley 1991 • $14 • (02/28/94) • **85**

Pinot Noir Napa Valley 1990 • $18 • (03/31/92) • **86**

Pinot Noir Napa Valley 1989 • $15 • (04/30/91) • **86**

Pinot Noir Napa Valley 1988 • $13 • (02/15/90) • **89**

Pinot Noir Napa Valley 1987 • $12 • (07/31/89) • **88**

Pinot Noir Napa Valley 1985 • $11 • (06/15/88) • **79**

Pinot Noir Napa Valley 1984 • $8 • (11/15/87) • **75**

Pinot Noir Napa Valley 1982 • $9 • (08/31/86) • **79**

Pinot Noir Napa Valley 1981 • $7 • (11/01/84) • **80**

Pinot Noir Napa Valley Carneros Unfiltered 1993 • $26 • (11/30/95) • **89**

Pinot Noir Napa Valley Reserve 1995: Marked by mint and sage notes, the core of cherry and plum flavors is intense and concentrated, slowly weaving through the firm tannins. Finishes with dashes of blackberry and spice. Drink now. • $31 • (08/31/97) • **91**

Pinot Noir Napa Valley Reserve 1994: Lean and trim, with a smoky, meaty accent to cherry and berry flavors that slowly build and fan out on the finish, where they show more character. Drink now. 5,000 cases made. • $31 • (01/31/97) • **89**

Pinot Noir Napa Valley Reserve 1993 • $30 • (05/31/96) • **89**

Pinot Noir Napa Valley Reserve 1991 • $28 • (02/28/94) • **89**

Pinot Noir Napa Valley Reserve 1990: Smooth and elegant, marked by dried cherry, herb, sage, tea, anise and spice notes, this is a fully mature wine of finesse and understatement, not power and rich fruit. Approachable now, but should hold into 2000. (Price upon release). • $30 • (03/31/97) • **89**

Pinot Noir Napa Valley Reserve 1988 • $26 • (10/31/90) • **82**

Pinot Noir Napa Valley Reserve 1986: Decadent and drying, but holding. Earthy mushroom and dried cherry flavors dominate up front, with more appealing tea and herb-accented flavors on the finish. Best to drink soon. • $22 • (03/31/97) • **87**

Pinot Noir Napa Valley Reserve 1985 • $31 • (04/15/89) SS • **92**

Pinot Noir Napa Valley Reserve 1983 • $25 • (11/15/87) • **80**

Pinot Noir Napa Valley Reserve 1982 • $25 • (08/31/86) • **78**

Pinot Noir Napa Valley Reserve 1981 • $17 • (08/31/86) • **86**

Pinot Noir Napa Valley Reserve 1980 • $13 • (08/01/84) • **81**

Pinot Noir Napa Valley Unfiltered 1993 • $16 • (09/15/95) • **86**

Pinot Noir Napa Valley Unfiltered 1992 • $14 • (11/30/94) • **84**

Pinot Noir Napa Valley Unfiltered Reserve 1992 • $29 • (03/31/95) • **87**

Red California 1984 • $5 • (01/31/87) • **75**

Sauvignon Blanc North Coast Coastal 1996: Pretty flavors of plum, honey, lemon and spice form the core element here, with a tangy, slightly bitter finish. • $9 • (04/30/98) • **86**

Sauvignon Blanc North Coast Coastal 1995: Frank and enjoyable for its racy, mineral-scented pear and herb flavors. Drink soon. • $9 • (12/31/96) • **85**

Sauvignon Blanc North Coast Coastal 1994 • $9 • (02/29/96) • **83**

Sauvignon Blanc Stags Leap District 1995: Subtle, toasty aromas are backed by bright acidity and tangerine, lemon-lime flavors. It's tightly wound, somewhat bracing, with a slightly bitter finish. • $18 • (06/30/97) • **87**

Sauvignon Blanc Stags Leap District 1994: Tangy and refreshing aromas and flavors—herb, sweet pea and melon—that linger nicely on the finish. 5,000 cases made. • $18 • (09/15/96) • **88**

Sauvignon Blanc Stags Leap District 1993 • $18 • (09/15/95) • **88**

Zinfandel California Woodbridge 1992 • $6 • (10/15/94) • **77**

Zinfandel California Woodbridge 1991 • $5 • (06/15/93) • **79**

Zinfandel California Woodbridge 1990 • $7 • (07/15/92) BB • **84**

Zinfandel Napa Valley 1996: Smooth, ripe and supple, with pretty plum, cherry and wild berry flavors and hints of jam and floral. Finishes with polished tannins. Drink now through 2001. • $18 • (06/15/98) • **87**
Zinfandel Napa Valley 1995: The best Zin yet from Robert Mondavi. Bright, ripe and juicy on the palate, with a pretty core of ripe cherry, wild berry, plum and currant notes. Turns supple and elegant on the finish, where the flavors are smooth and spicy. Approachable now, but should age well into 2000. 8,100 cases made. • $18 • (04/30/97) SS • **92**
Zinfandel Napa Valley 1994 • $16 • (04/30/96) • **91**
Zinfandel Napa Valley 1993 • $16 • (07/31/95) • **86**
Zinfandel Napa Valley 1992 • $14 • (10/15/94) SS • **92**
Zinfandel North Coast Coastal 1995: With its earthy, candied aromas, this gets off to a rough start, but improves noticeably on the palate with spice, black cherry, blackberry and blueberry flavors. Drink now. • $10 • (03/31/98) • **85**
Zinfandel North Coast Coastal 1994: Not terribly distinctive, this offers a modest core of ripe Zinfandel flavors, with notes of berry and spice. 14,000 cases made. • $11 • (11/30/96) • **82**

MONDAVI, LA FAMIGLIA DI ROBERT | CALIFORNIA

Barbera California 1995: Crisp, with tart wild berry and cherry flavors and light, earthy tannins. Drink now. 1,500 cases made. • $18 • (05/15/98) • **84**
Barbera California 1994: Tart and well focused, with an earth accent to the cherry and berry flavors. Ready to drink. • $18 • (04/30/97) • **85**
Barbera California 1993 • $15 • (08/31/95) • **85**
Malvasia Bianca California 1995: Fresh and appealing for its spicy pear and vaguely citrusy flavors that linger on the gently sweet finish. • $11 • (04/30/97) • **87**
Muscat California Moscato Bianco 1995: Lightly fizzy and sweet, and though it's a bit watery, the fresh litchi and pear flavors have charm. • $12 • (04/30/97) • **84**
Pinot Grigio California 1996: Light and silky, generous with its pear and almond flavors, finishing with an open texture. Drink now. 4,500 cases made. • $16 • (05/15/98) • **85**
Rosato California 1995: A light, refreshing style with hints of cherries and herbs on the finish. • $12 • (09/15/97) • **84**
Sangiovese California 1995: Pleasant, lightly fruity, with a dry, earthy quality and modest plum and strawberry notes. Drink now. 1,500 cases made. • $22 • (05/15/98) • **83**
Sangiovese California 1994: Marked by cedary oak, the core of cherry and berry flavors struggles to rise about the wood and barely does. Perhaps cellaring into 1999 will soften it a bit. • $22 • (04/30/97) • **85**
Sangiovese California 1993 • $22 • (08/31/95) • **83**
Tocai Friulano California 1995: Simple, short and odd-tasting, sort of lemony, but not charming. • $18 • (04/30/97) • **79**

MONT ST. JOHN | CALIFORNIA

Cabernet Sauvignon Napa Valley 1987 • $14 • (11/15/92) • **70**
Cabernet Sauvignon Napa Valley 1986 • $14 • (04/30/91) • **87**
Cabernet Sauvignon Napa Valley 1983 • $15 • (07/31/89) • **78**
Cabernet Sauvignon Napa Valley 1982 • $15 • (03/15/89) • **82**
Cabernet Sauvignon Napa Valley Private Reserve 1980 • $12 • (05/16/84) • **75**
Chardonnay Carneros 1996: Toasty oak and hazelnut lead the way, with a blend of citrus, tangerine and pear. Moderate finish. Drink now. 2,341 cases made. • $15 • (07/31/98) • **87**
Chardonnay Carneros 1994: Soft and spicy, with a moderate level of citrus to balance the toasty flavors. 2,800 cases made. • $13 • (06/15/96) • **80**
Chardonnay Carneros Organically Grown Grapes 1993 • $13 • (07/31/95) • **85**
Chardonnay Napa Valley Carneros Madonna Vineyards 1993 • $18 • (07/31/95) • **82**
Pinot Noir Carneros 1995: The bright, tangy texture is balanced by a slight waxiness on the palate. Finishes with fresh cherry and herb notes. • $16 • (07/31/97) • **86**
Pinot Noir Carneros 1993 • $15 • (12/31/95) • **81**
Pinot Noir Napa Valley Carneros 1989 • $11 • (09/30/92) • **85**
Pinot Noir Napa Valley Carneros 1988 • $14 • (04/30/91) • **81**
Pinot Noir Napa Valley Carneros 1987 • $15 • (03/31/90) • **76**
Pinot Noir Napa Valley Carneros 1985 • $15 • (10/15/89) • **82**
Pinot Noir Napa Valley Carneros 1981 • $9 • (05/16/84) • **73**
Pinot Noir Napa Valley Carneros Madonna Vineyard 1985 • $11 • (06/15/88) • **78**

MONTDOMAINE | VIRGINIA

Cabernet Franc Virginia 1993: A solid, chewy red, well-balanced and fairly rich, with pleasant cherry, smoke and spice flavors and an herbal nuance on the finish. 802 cases made. • $12 • (04/30/97) • **83**
Meritage Monticello 1988 • $14 • (02/29/92) • **82**
Merlot Monticello Reserve 1987 • $15 • (02/29/92) • **86**

MONTE CARASSO | CALIFORNIA

Sangiovese Napa Valley 1994 • $17 • (02/29/96) • **84**

MONTE VERDE | CALIFORNIA

Cabernet Sauvignon California Proprietor's Reserve 1988 • $5 • (12/15/92) • **79**
Cabernet Sauvignon California Proprietor's Reserve 1987 • $6/liter • (12/15/89) • **80**

MONTE VOLPE | CALIFORNIA

Barbera California 1995: Tart and spicy, with pretty cherry, berry and strawberry notes. Finishes with a pretty burst of fruit and supple tannins. Drink now through 2000. 1,968 cases made. • $14 • (05/15/98) • **87**
Barbera California 1994: Tart and refreshing for its bright black cherry, vanilla and slightly floral flavors. Has style and polish. 2,050 cases made. • $14 • (02/28/97) • **85**
Barbera California 1992 • $9 • (11/15/95) • **82**
Barbera Mendocino 1991 • $8 • (03/31/93) BB • **87**
Dolcetto Mendocino 1996: Ripe and supple, open-textured, with a slight bite of tannin to the woodsy black cherry and anise flavors. Drink now. 800 cases made. • $20 • (06/30/98) • **84**
Dolcetto Mendocino 1995: Lots of wild berry and almond aromas and flavors make this an aggressive young wine, fresh and zingy. 192 cases made. • $16 • (05/15/97) • **85**
Moscato Mendocino 1995: Soft and floral, with a white pepper accent to the grapefruit and sweet pear flavors, plus a refreshing lemony zing on the finish. 709 cases made. • $9 • (04/30/97) • **85**
Nebbiolo Mendocino 1994: A solid red wine, a bit rough at the edges, with mature floral and earthlike flavors around a light core of raspberry and spice. Ready to drink. 563 cases made. • $16 • (05/15/97) • **85**
Nebbiolo Mendocino 1993: Firm in texture, this delivers rich black cherry and earth flavors that linger on the chewy finish. Drinkable now. 315 cases made. • $14 • (11/30/96) • **84**
Peppolino Mendocino 1992 • $14 • (10/15/95) • **85**
Pinot Bianco Mendocino 1996: A little sweetness doesn't help the ripe pear and peach flavors in this wine. Bright acidity gives it balance, however. 824 cases made. • $13 • (05/15/98) • **81**
Pinot Bianco Mendocino 1995: A smooth-textured white with spicy melon and apple flavors that are fresh and lively. 1,400 cases made. • $12 • (04/30/97) • **85**
Pinot Bianco Mendocino 1993 • $9 • (04/15/95) • **84**
Sangiovese Mendocino 1995: Fresh and generous with its berry and black cherry aromas and flavors. A bit short on the palate, but has refinement and character. Drink now. 1,218 cases made. • $16 • (04/30/97) • **85**
Sangiovese Mendocino 1994: Tingles on the tongue but it brings some nice raspberry, leather and cola flavors to the party. 991 cases made. • $16 • (02/28/97) • **84**
Sangiovese Mendocino 1992 • $14 • (09/30/94) • **86**
Sesso Mendocino 1994: Rich, ripe and spicy, broad-textured and deep, with vanilla notes and flavors from the lees that linger on the firm finish. Drink now. 188 cases made. • $25 • (02/28/97) • **86**
Tocai Friulano Mendocino 1995: Fresh and simple, with pleasant flavors of apple and pear, plus a hint of almond on the finish. • $12 • (12/31/96) • **84**

MONTEREY PENINSULA | CALIFORNIA

Barbera California Vineyard View Pleasant Hill 1989 • $12 • (10/31/93) • **78**
Black Burgundy California NV • $6 • (10/15/93) • **75**
Cabernet Sauvignon Monterey County 1991 • $12 • (12/15/95) • **80**
Cabernet Sauvignon Monterey County 1986 • $10 • (11/15/94) • **84**
Cabernet Sauvignon Monterey County 1985 • $12 • (11/15/92) • **82**
Cabernet Sauvignon Monterey County 1982 • $11 • (03/31/87) • **74**
Cabernet Sauvignon Monterey County Doctors' Reserve 1986 • $18 • (11/15/94) • **86**

MONTEREY VINEYARD

Cabernet Sauvignon Monterey County Doctors' Reserve 1985 • $25 • (11/15/92) • **76**
Cabernet Sauvignon Monterey County Monterey Cellars 1986 • $8 • (11/15/92) • **77**
Cabernet Sauvignon Monterey Doctors' Reserve 1984 • $18 • (11/15/92) • **78**
Cabernet Sauvignon Monterey Doctors' Reserve Lot II 1982 • $14 • (06/15/87) • **83**
Chardonnay Central Coast 1996: A peaches-and-cream medley that finishes with a crisp lemon-orange edge. The contrast is pleasing, if unusual. 4,240 cases made. • $13 • (01/31/98) • **86**
Chardonnay Central Coast 1995: Simple, with spice and citrus accents to the ripe pear and apple notes and a hint of butterscotch on the finish. 1,400 cases made. • $14 • (05/15/97) • **82**
Chardonnay Monterey County Sleepy Hollow Vineyard Reserve 1995: Heavily oaked, even to a fault, as the woody flavors give a bitter edge that overrides the citrus and pear flavors beneath. 900 cases made. • $20 • (05/15/97) • **79**
Merlot Monterey County Doctors' Reserve 1987 • $18 • (07/15/93) • **81**
Merlot Monterey Doctors' Reserve 1986 • $16 • (05/31/92) • **83**
Merlot Monterey Doctors' Reserve 1985 • $14 • (01/31/89) • **83**
Merlot Monterey Doctors' Reserve 1984 • $12 • (12/15/87) • **74**
Pinot Blanc Monterey County Cobblestone Vineyard 1995: Appealing, fresh and vibrant, with apple, peach and nutmeg flavors that remain generous through the finish. 967 cases made. • $15 • (04/30/97) • **86**
Pinot Noir Monterey County Sleepy Hollow Vineyard 1995: Marked by herb and spice notes, the core of leather, cola and berry flavors is well focused and the flavors linger on the finish. 900 cases made. • $17 • (02/28/97) • **86**
Pinot Noir Monterey County Sleepy Hollow Vineyard 1992 • $12 • (01/31/95) • **85**
Pinot Noir Monterey County Sleepy Hollow Vineyard 1989 • $12 • (02/28/93) • **76**
Pinot Noir Monterey County Sleepy Hollow Vineyard 1987 • $18 • (02/28/91) • **86**
White Riesling Late Harvest Monterey County Sleepy Hollow 1989 • $15 • (06/30/93) • **89**
Zinfandel Amador County Ferrero Ranch 1990 • $10 • (09/30/93) • **80**
Zinfandel Amador County Ferrero Ranch Doctors' Reserve 1987 • $15 • (05/15/91) • **83**
Zinfandel Amador County Ferrero Ranch Doctors' Reserve 1982 • $10 • (02/29/88) • **83**
Zinfandel Amador County Ferrero Vineyard 1991 • $9 • (10/15/94) • **80**
Zinfandel Mendocino M & M Vineyard 1994: Ripe and flavorful, with juicy wild berry and cherry flavors and touches of anise and spice. Borders on being slightly sour on the finish, but should work well with food. 291 cases made. • $15 • (04/30/97) • **83**

MONTEREY VINEYARD | CALIFORNIA

Cabernet Sauvignon Monterey County 1995: Smoothly textured, with cedar and cherry notes coming to the fore. Simple and pleasant. 83 cases made. • $7 • (09/15/97) • **82**
Cabernet Sauvignon Monterey County 1994: Light for a Cabernet, this offers some berry flavors then finishes a bit tartly. • $7 • (12/15/96) • **79**
Cabernet Sauvignon Monterey County Classic 1994: A simple wine, with a trim band of cedar and berry flavors. Usually better from this producer. 89,000 cases made. • $7 • (11/30/96) • **76**
Cabernet Sauvignon Monterey County Classic 1990 • $6 • (03/31/93) BB • **80**
Cabernet Sauvignon Monterey County Classic 1989 • $6 • (03/15/92) BB • **83**
Cabernet Sauvignon Monterey County Classic 1987 • $6 • (01/31/91) BB • **83**
Cabernet Sauvignon Monterey County Classic 1986 • $5 • (10/31/89) • **76**
Cabernet Sauvignon Monterey County Limited Release 1990 • $11 • (11/15/94) • **84**
Cabernet Sauvignon Monterey County Limited Release 1986 • $8 • (08/31/92) • **79**
Cabernet Sauvignon Monterey County Limited Release 1985 • $10 • (08/31/88) • **75**
Cabernet Sauvignon Monterey-Sonoma-San Luis Obispo Counties Classic 1985 • $5 • (02/15/89) • **73**
Chardonnay Central Coast 1995: Ripe, and generous with its apple and pear flavors, which echo nicely on the soft, harmonious finish. Ready to drink. 151,000 cases made. • $7 • (12/31/96) BB • **84**
Chardonnay Monterey County Classic 1993 • $6 • (02/28/95) • **79**
Chardonnay Monterey County Limited Release 1993 • $13 • (07/31/95) • **85**
Chardonnay Monterey-San Joaquin-Napa Counties 1996: Simple, with flavors of spice, pear and apple. Has a nice focus on the finish. Drink now. 278,000 cases made. • $7 • (07/31/98) • **82**
Chardonnay Monterey-San Joaquin-Stanislaus Counties 1996: Toasty oak blends with mild citrus and apple flavors in this pleasant, simple wine. 120,000 cases made. • $7 • (09/15/97) • **84**
Classic Red California 1982 • $4 • (06/16/86) • **74**
Classic Red Monterey 1984 • $4 • (11/15/87) • **74**
Classic Red Monterey County 1990 • $5 • (03/31/93) • **76**
Merlot Monterey County 1992 • $6 • (09/15/94) • **80**
Merlot Monterey County Classic 1989 • $6 • (02/29/92) BB • **84**
Merlot Monterey County Classic 1988 • $6 • (12/31/90) • **76**
Merlot Monterey County Limited Release 1994: A smoky aroma soon takes a backseat to layers of cassis, blackberry and menthol, but a piney, bitter edge mars the finish. 500 cases made. • $15 • (04/30/98) • **83**
Pinot Noir Monterey County 1995: A rounder, lighter style that offers pleasing cherry flavors and finishes with a surprising hint of chocolate. 15,000 cases made. • $7 • (09/15/97) • **84**
Pinot Noir Monterey County 1987 • $8 • (03/31/90) • **84**
Pinot Noir Monterey County 1986 • $7 • (06/15/88) • **83**
Pinot Noir Monterey County Classic 1992 • $6 • (03/31/95) • **77**
Pinot Noir Monterey County Classic 1991 • $6 • (02/28/94) • **79**
Pinot Noir Monterey County Limited Release 1994: Lean and trim, with a slim range of cedar, plum and berry flavors that quickly fades. 500 cases made. • $14 • (02/28/97) • **81**
Pinot Noir Monterey County Limited Release 1990 • $8 • (02/28/93) • **78**
Pinot Noir Monterey County Limited Release 1989 • $8 • (09/30/92) • **71**
Pinot Noir Monterey County Limited Release 1988 • $9 • (02/28/91) • **80**
Sauvignon Blanc Central Coast Classic 1994 • $5 • (08/31/95) • **82**
Sauvignon Blanc Monterey County 1996: Offers subtle hints of hazelnut, herb and sugar snap, but lacks a ripe fruit core. It strives for depth through oak. • $6 • (04/30/98) • **81**
Sauvignon Blanc Monterey County 1995: Earthy and mushroomy flavors dominate. • $5 • (12/15/96) • **77**
White Zinfandel Central Coast Classic 1994 • $5 • (09/30/95) • **78**

MONTERRA | CALIFORNIA

Cabernet Sauvignon Monterey 1991 • $7 • (11/15/94) • **81**
Merlot Monterey 1991 • $7 • (05/31/94) BB • **86**
Merlot Monterey Sand Hill 1992 • $10 • (02/29/96) • **86**

MONTEVINA | CALIFORNIA

Aleatico Amador County 1993 • $7/375ml • (01/01/95) • **78**
Barbera Amador County 1995: Ripe and juicy, this is a lively, fresh mouthful of berry and anise flavors that linger on the smooth finish. A nice streak of bright acidity balances it. 10,000 cases made. • $12 • (11/30/97) • **86**
Barbera Amador County 1994: An intriguing aroma of smoke and blueberry, with flavors to match. Texture is a bit chunky and tannic. 7,500 cases made. • $10 • (10/15/96) • **84**
Barbera Amador County 1993 • $9 • (05/15/96) • **84**
Barbera Amador County Reserve 1990 • $15 • (12/15/92) • **82**
Barbera Amador County Terra d'Oro 1995: Lean and spicy, with distinct clove overtones to the berry and earthy flavors. Drink now. 2,680 cases made. • $18 • (12/15/97) • **81**
Barbera Amador County Terra d'Oro 1993 • $16 • (05/15/96) • **86**
Barbera Shenandoah Valley 1984 • $6 • (10/15/88) • **78**
Cabernet Sauvignon California 1992 • $9 • (12/15/95) • **83**
Cabernet Sauvignon California 1990 • $9 • (05/15/93) • **80**
Cabernet Sauvignon California 1989 • $9 • (08/31/92) • **78**
Cabernet Sauvignon California 1988 • $8 • (02/15/90) • **77**
Cabernet Sauvignon Shenandoah Valley Limited Release 1984 • $7 • (08/31/88) BB • **86**
Chardonnay California 1993 • $8 • (07/31/95) • **78**
Fumé Blanc California 1993 • $7 • (08/31/95) • **78**
Matrimonio Amador County 1992 • $8 • (08/31/95) • **84**
Montanaro Amador County 1992 • $7 • (08/31/95) • **85**
Montanaro Amador County 1989 • $10 • (11/30/92) • **80**

Key: SS—Spectator Selection CS—Cellar Selection HR—Highly Recommended BB—Best Buy $NA—Price not available Ⓐ—Auction Price (BT)—Barrel Tasting
Dates in parentheses indicate the issues in which the ratings were published.

Nebbiolo Rosato Amador County 1996: A vaguely sweet, cherrylike theme dominates this wine, which is much improved by a somewhat drying astringency on the finish. 1,600 cases made. • $7 • (09/15/97) • **81**

Refosco Amador County 1995: Firm and focused, with layers of wintergreen, thyme, cassis, anise and black cherry flavors. Tannins are a bit dry and acidity is bright, creating a lean-textured finish. 1,000 cases made. • $8 • (09/15/97) • **87**

Sangiovese Amador County 1995: A jazzy wine with berry and floral flavors plus overtones reminiscent of root beer. Has more up front than on the finish. Ready through 1999. 3,500 cases made. • $12 • (11/30/97) • **84**

Sangiovese Amador County 1992 • $12 • (08/31/95) • **86**

Sangiovese Amador County Terra d'Oro 1995: Light in texture and flavor, with modest plum and earthy notes scattered through the slightly volatile and chewy finish. Drink now. 1,203 cases made. • $16 • (12/15/97) • **81**

Sangiovese Amador County Terra d'Oro 1993 • $15 • (04/30/96) • **80**

Zinfandel Amador County 1996: Tightly wound, with firm tannins built around a core of wild berry and cherry flavors. Turns dry on the finish. Drink now through 2002. 25,000 cases made. • $10 • (06/15/98) • **82**

Zinfandel Amador County 1995: Laced with pickle-barrel and orange-peel notes that make it distinctive, if odd, this has enough berry flavor lurking in the background. Best from 1999. 20,000 cases made. • $10 • (12/15/97) • **81**

Zinfandel Amador County 1994: A simple palate of modest cherry and berry flavors gives way to a dry, tannic finish. • $NA • (09/15/96) • **79**

Zinfandel Amador County 1993 • $7 • (10/15/95) • **83**

Zinfandel Amador County 1992 • $7 • (10/15/95) • **84**

Zinfandel Amador County 1990 • $6 • (06/15/94) BB • **83**

Zinfandel Amador County 1989 • $8 • (10/15/92) • **72**

Zinfandel Amador County 1987 • $7 • (03/31/90) • **75**

Zinfandel Amador County Brioso 1996: One shade darker than rosé, it's a lightish wine appealing for its restraint. Shows modest strawberry and leafy flavors. Ready now. 10,000 cases made. • $7 • (12/15/97) • **82**

Zinfandel Amador County Brioso 1995: Light in color, smooth and spicy in flavor, with some nice hints of raspberry and strawberry jam on the finish. Ready now. 7,000 cases made. • $7 • (04/30/97) • **84**

Zinfandel Amador County Brioso 1994 • $6 • (04/30/96) • **83**

Zinfandel Amador County Brioso 1993 • $7 • (10/15/95) • **83**

Zinfandel Amador County Brioso 1992 • $7 • (09/30/93) • **83**

Zinfandel Amador County Brioso 1991 • $7 • (06/15/93) • **77**

Zinfandel Amador County Brioso 1990 • $7 • (07/15/92) BB • **86**

Zinfandel Amador County Reserve 1991 • $12 • (10/15/94) • **82**

Zinfandel Amador County Reserve 1989 • $12 • (10/15/92) • **87**

Zinfandel Amador County Terra d'Oro 1995: Not your classic Zin, as the aroma is meaty and not especially varietal. To the taste, though, it's ripe and fruity, with a slight gamy edge. Best now through 2000. 4,449 cases made. • $16 • (06/15/98) • **86**

Zinfandel Amador County Terra d'Oro 1993 • $15 • (04/30/96) • **89**

Zinfandel Shenandoah Valley Montino 1985 • $5 • (10/15/88) • **75**

Zinfandel Shenandoah Valley Winemaker's Choice 1984 • $9 • (08/31/87) • **75**

Zinfandel Shenandoah Valley Winemaker's Choice 1980 • $9 • (04/16/84) • **78**

MONTHAVEN | CALIFORNIA

Cabernet Sauvignon Napa Valley 1995: Tarry and licoricelike, with smoky overtones. A bit chewy and tough, but should tackle a thick steak well enough. Drink now or hold. 10,000 cases made. • $10 • (03/31/98) • **84**

Cabernet Sauvignon Napa Valley 1994: A decent value, offering cedary currant and cherry flavors, but it dries out and turns tannic on the finish. 5,000 cases made. • $9 • (12/15/96) • **81**

Cabernet Sauvignon Napa Valley 1993: Pleasant enough, with ripe cherry, currant and berry flavors of modest proportion. 3,000 cases made. • $8 • (03/31/96) • **81**

Chardonnay Monterey 1996: Starts coarsely, with rich butter, toast and citrus flavors. Straightens out on the finish, where the citrus, pear and toast notes linger. Drink now. 5,000 cases made. • $10 • (06/30/98) • **82**

Chardonnay Napa Valley 1996: A light-bodied wine, with hints of mineral and pear at the fore. Smooth and refreshing. 5,275 cases made. • $10 • (03/31/98) • **84**

Chardonnay Napa Valley 1995: Light and refreshing, but a spicy, woody character overshadows the modest fruit flavors. 10,000 cases made. • $9 • (11/30/96) • **79**

Chardonnay Napa Valley 1994: Clean and spicy, with a modest core of citrus, pear and spice flavors. A decent wine for the price. 3,000 cases made. • $8 • (03/31/96) • **82**

Malbec Napa Valley 1993 • $8 • (03/31/96) • **81**

Sauvignon Blanc Napa Valley 1996: This kicks off with some bright, flinty, mineral tones. It carries through with firm texture and a blend of sweet pea, lemon-lime and grapefruit. Tangy finish. 801 cases made. • $9 • (03/31/98) • **86**

Sauvignon Blanc Napa Valley 1995: An earthy, spicy style, with grassy pear and mineral flavors that are less than charming. 2,500 cases made. • $9 • (10/31/96) • **78**

Sauvignon Blanc Napa Valley 1994 • $6 • (03/31/96) • **83**

Syrah California 1995: Smoky, with rich plum flavors orbited by herbs and spices. Finishes with a touch of bitterness, but still quite nice. A good value. 1,771 cases made. • $10 • (07/31/97) • **87**

Viognier California 1995: Simple, with a citrus, especially grapefruit, and pear edge that turns tart on the finish. 1,800 cases made. • $9 • (04/30/97) • **80**

Zinfandel California 1996: Earth and oak take the upper hand here, with a nod to blackberries, spice and herbs. Rough on the finish. Drink now. 3,000 cases made. • $10 • (06/15/98) • **79**

Zinfandel Napa Valley 1995: Cola and black cherry notes are attractive, framed by smoky, toasty aromas. Texture is a bit rough, though, with an earthy finish. 1,986 cases made. • $10 • (03/31/98) • **83**

MONTICELLO | CALIFORNIA

Cabernet Sauvignon Napa Valley 1981 • $14 • (07/16/84) • **74**

Cabernet Sauvignon Napa Valley Corley Reserve 1990 • $25 • (11/15/93) • **88**

Cabernet Sauvignon Napa Valley Corley Reserve 1989 • $25 • (11/15/92) • **85**

Cabernet Sauvignon Napa Valley Corley Reserve 1987 • $26 • (11/15/90) • **90**

Cabernet Sauvignon Napa Valley Corley Reserve 1986 • $33 • (03/15/90) • **92**

Cabernet Sauvignon Napa Valley Corley Reserve 1985 • $35 • (07/31/89) • **92**

Cabernet Sauvignon Napa Valley Corley Reserve 1984 • $29 • (11/30/87) • **90**

Cabernet Sauvignon Napa Valley Corley Reserve 1982 • $15 • (12/16/85) • **92**

Cabernet Sauvignon Napa Valley Corley Select Reserve 1993: Fresh and vibrant, if a bit lean, with ripe currant and black cherry flavors and spicy, cedar notes to fill in the gaps. Tannins may have subsided by now. 495 cases made. • $35 • (06/30/97) • **89**

Cabernet Sauvignon Napa Valley Corley Select Reserve 1992 • $28 • (12/15/95) • **83**

Cabernet Sauvignon Napa Valley Corley Select Reserve 1991 • $25 • (12/15/95) • **85**

Cabernet Sauvignon Napa Valley Jefferson Cuvée 1993: Strikes a nice balance between spicy, black cherry-tinged Cabernet flavors and firm tannins. The tannins are dry and dominant on the finish. Best to drink over the next couple of years, before it dries out. 2,400 cases made. • $18 • (07/31/97) • **87**

Cabernet Sauvignon Napa Valley Jefferson Cuvée 1992 • $18 • (12/15/95) • **89**

Cabernet Sauvignon Napa Valley Jefferson Cuvée 1989 • $15 • (11/15/93) • **86**

Cabernet Sauvignon Napa Valley Jefferson Cuvée 1988 • $16 • (11/15/91) • **85**

Cabernet Sauvignon Napa Valley Jefferson Cuvée 1987 • $14 • (09/30/90) • **90**

Cabernet Sauvignon Napa Valley Jefferson Cuvée 1986 • $14 • (04/15/89) • **89**

Cabernet Sauvignon Napa Valley Jefferson Cuvée 1985 • $12 • (02/29/88) • **87**

Cabernet Sauvignon Napa Valley Jefferson Cuvée 1984 • $11 • (11/30/87) • **90**

Cabernet Sauvignon Napa Valley Jefferson Cuvée 1983 • $10 • (11/30/86) • **77**

Cabernet Sauvignon Napa Valley Jefferson Cuvée 1982 • $10 • (02/01/86) • **91**

Chardonnay Napa Valley Corley Estate Reserve 1995: Clean and vibrant, with a complex range of ripe pear, spice, lemon and apricot. Finishes with a cedary oak aftertaste. Drink now through 2002. 1,855 cases made. • $26 • (07/31/98) • **88**

Chardonnay Napa Valley Corley Estate Reserve 1994: Ripe and complex, with a rich, full-bodied core of fig, pear, apricot and pineapple flavors, finishing with a good splash of oak and cedar. Mature, it's ready now. 1,350 cases made. • $26 • (06/15/97) • **89**

Chardonnay Napa Valley Corley Estate Reserve 1993 • $26 • (05/15/96) • **82**

Chardonnay Napa Valley Corley Family Vineyards 1994: Ripe and flavorful, with a pretty array of pear, tropical fruit, apple and spice nuances, and finishing with a dash of buttery oak. 1,300 cases made. • $18 • (07/31/97) • **90**

Chardonnay Napa Valley Corley Wild Yeast Estate Reserve 1994: Has a cedary edge to the the pear and citrus notes, and a tart, leesy quality emerges on the finish. A touch too oaky now, but should pull together by 1997. 230 cases made. • $33 • (06/15/96) • **85**

Merlot Napa Valley 1990 • $17 • (07/15/93) • **86**

Merlot Napa Valley Corley Family Vineyards 1993: Firm and tight, though a bit dry and tannic. Ripe plum and currant flavors are intense enough to hold your interest. Ready to drink. 1,100 cases made. • $20 • (08/31/96) • **85**

Merlot Napa Valley Corley Family Vineyards 1992 • $18 • (09/30/95) • **88**

Pinot Noir Napa Valley 1994: Mature, with dried fruit, sage, earth, tea and spicy flavors that are complex, but drying on the aftertaste. Drinkable now. 1,500 cases made. • $18 • (01/31/98) • **87**

Pinot Noir Napa Valley 1991 • $18 • (02/28/94) • **81**

Pinot Noir Napa Valley 1990 • $18 • (09/30/92) • **86**

Pinot Noir Napa Valley 1987 • $15 • (10/15/89) • **85**

Pinot Noir Napa Valley 1986 • $12 • (06/15/88) • **89**

Pinot Noir Napa Valley 1985 • $12 • (12/15/87) • **89**

Pinot Noir Napa Valley Corley Estate Reserve 1995: Well oaked, with supple flavors of butter and vanilla, the core of cherry and wild berry slowly unfolds to reveal more depth and complexity. Drinks well now. 224 cases made. • $32 • (01/31/98) • **88**

Pinot Noir Napa Valley Corley Estate Reserve 1994: Mature in color and flavor, with cedar, herb and berry flavors that turn supple and complex. Finishes with firm, dry tannins and good length. Drinkable now. 1,000 cases made. • $30 • (01/31/98) • **87**

Pinot Noir Napa Valley Corley Family Vineyards 1993: Attractive for its plum and cherry flavors, and hints of cola and wild berry that fold in on the finish. Well crafted, it's drinkable now or can be cellared a bit. 2,400 cases made. • $18 • (01/31/97) • **87**

Pinot Noir Napa Valley Corley Family Vineyards 1992 • $18 • (09/15/95) • **88**

Pinot Noir Napa Valley Monticello Vineyards Estate Reserve 1993 • $30 • (11/30/95) • **89**

MONTINORE | OREGON

Chardonnay Willamette Valley 1995: Fresh and zingy, with lots of citrusy overtones to the apple and pear flavors, finishing with a touch of honey. This Oregon Chardonnay is on the lighter side, but not lacking in character. Ready now. 3,880 cases made. • $10 • (02/28/97) BB • **88**

Chardonnay Willamette Valley 1993 • $9 • (03/31/96) • **84**

Chardonnay Willamette Valley Vintner's Cuvée 1996: Crisp and appealing for its bright apple flavors and honeyed floral notes, prettily accenting the fruit. Ready to drink. 4,000 cases made. • $5 • (07/31/97) • **85**

Chardonnay Willamette Valley Winemaker's Reserve 1995: Light and delicately spicy, nicely polished in texture, with modest apple and vanilla flavors echoing on the finish. 2,036 cases made. • $14 • (02/28/97) • **84**

Gewürztraminer Late Harvest Willamette Valley 1993 • $6/375ml • (11/30/94) • **85**

Gewürztraminer Willamette Valley 1996: Here's a light, supple and refreshing white, enticing for its pure litchi and grapefruit flavors that linger nicely on the long finish. It's ready for sipping, at a price that invites you to imbibe freely. 3,000 cases made. • $5 • (07/31/97) BB • **87**

Gewürztraminer Willamette Valley 1995: Has a sweet character, with some nice honey notes to round off the spicy floral flavors at the center. Appealing now. 966 cases made. • $6 • (02/28/97) • **86**

Gewürztraminer Willamette Valley 1993 • $6 • (03/31/96) • **87**

Müller-Thurgau Willamette Valley 1996: Fresh and simple, appealing for its spicy apple flavors, finishing soft and pleasant. 3,000 cases made. • $5 • (07/31/97) • **83**

Key: SS—Spectator Selection CS—Cellar Selection HR—Highly Recommended BB—Best Buy $NA—Price not available Ⓐ—Auction Price (BT)—Barrel Tasting

Dates in parentheses indicate the issues in which the ratings were published.

Müller-Thurgau Willamette Valley 1995: Fresh and spicy, with modest, simple flavors that hold together on the slightly sweet finish. 2,993 cases made. • $6 • (02/28/97) • **81**

Müller-Thurgau Willamette Valley 1993 • $6 • (11/30/94) BB • **83**

Pinot Gris Willamette Valley 1996: A light, refreshing style of white wine with modest peach and almond flavors. 6,000 cases made. • $8 • (07/31/97) • **83**

Pinot Gris Willamette Valley 1995: On the tart side, but shows some pleasant almond and tar-scented pear flavors. Ready now. 3,604 cases made. • $10 • (02/28/97) • **83**

Pinot Gris Willamette Valley 1994 • $10 • (11/30/95) • **83**

Pinot Gris Willamette Valley 1993 • $10 • (10/31/94) SS • **88**

Pinot Noir Oregon Vintner's Cuvée NV • $5 • (11/30/94) • **73**

Pinot Noir Washington County 1989 • $12 • (02/28/93) • **73**

Pinot Noir Washington County 1988 • $14 • (04/15/91) • **88**

Pinot Noir Washington County 1987 • $13 • (02/15/90) • **81**

Pinot Noir Willamette Valley 1995: Very light color and herbal flavors make this a question mark. 4,000 cases made. • $9 • (07/31/97) • **79**

Pinot Noir Willamette Valley 1994: Has ripe flavors, but it's a bit chewy on the finish; needs time for the texture to smooth out and reveal flavors beneath. Improved since an earlier tasting. Try now. 5,000 cases made. • $8 • (04/30/97) • **83**

Pinot Noir Willamette Valley 1993 • $10 • (01/31/96) • **82**

Pinot Noir Willamette Valley 1992 • $12 • (11/30/94) • **79**

Pinot Noir Willamette Valley 1990 • $12 • (02/28/93) • **83**

Pinot Noir Willamette Valley NV • $7 • (02/28/93) • **79**

Pinot Noir Willamette Valley Vintner's Cuvée 1996: Looks like a rosé, it's so light—smells and tastes like it, too, with cherry-candy flavors that linger appealingly. Drink slightly chilled. 6,000 cases made. • $5 • (07/31/97) • **84**

Pinot Noir Willamette Valley Winemaker's Reserve 1995: Light and appealing for its spicy strawberry flavors, finishing harmoniously. Ready now. 4,065 cases made. • $14 • (02/28/97) • **85**

Pinot Noir Willamette Valley Winemaker's Reserve 1994: Has ripe flavors against a tart background; a firm, almost austere wine that offers fresh blackberry and anise flavors. Best from 1999. Better than a sample reviewed earlier. • $NA • (02/28/97) • **87**

Pinot Noir Willamette Valley Winemaker's Reserve 1992 • $18 • (11/30/94) • **82**

Pinot Noir Willamette Valley Winemaker's Reserve 1990 • $18 • (11/15/94) • **87**

Pinot Noir Willamette Valley Winemaker's Reserve 1989 • $20 • (02/28/93) • **85**

White Riesling Late Harvest Oregon Ultra 1987 • $22/375ml • (03/31/91) • **83**

White Riesling Late Harvest Washington County Ultra 1987: Sweet and rich, with a spice and tobacco character interwoven with caramel and other mature flavors. 1,441 cases made. • $11 • (02/28/97) • **80**

White Riesling Late Harvest Willamette Valley 1996: Sweet-and-sour character goes over the top, turning oxidized and tired on the finish. 3,000 cases made. • $5 • (07/31/97) • **79**

White Riesling Late Harvest Willamette Valley 1993 • $6/375ml • (11/30/94) • **84**

White Riesling Late Harvest Yamhill County 1989 • $7 • (03/31/91) • **84**

White Riesling Late Harvest Yamhill County Ultra 1987: Dark in color, bordering on amber, with mature flavors of honey, caramel and a touch of mushroom. A sweet, silky wine, very tasty to drink now. 737 cases made. • $11 • (02/28/97) • **88**

White Riesling Willamette Valley 1996: Tastes harsh, oxidized and slightly fishy. 3,000 cases made. • $5 • (07/31/97) • **72**

White Riesling Willamette Valley 1995: Offers freshness, but it's soft, almost flabby, on the sweet finish. 1,999 cases made. • $6 • (02/28/97) • **79**

White Riesling Willamette Valley 1993 • $6 • (03/31/96) • **83**

MONTPELLIER | CALIFORNIA

Cabernet Sauvignon California 1993: Earthy aromas and toasty anise and coffee flavors give this wine character though it may lack finesse. Drink now. 8,000 cases made. • $8 • (11/30/96) • **83**

Cabernet Sauvignon California 1990 • $8 • (11/15/94) • **83**

Cabernet Sauvignon California 1988 • $7 • (07/31/91) BB • **83**

Chardonnay California 1994: A light, simple wine, with pleasant floral and apple flavors. Drinkable now. 12,000 cases made. • $8 • (06/30/96) • **83**

Merlot California 1996: A mild-mannered wine with violet and cherry notes. The texture is waxy, the ensemble shows a hint of earthiness. 15,000 cases made. • $8 • (03/31/98) • **80**

Merlot California 1993 • $8 • (11/15/95) • **83**
Merlot California 1992 • $8 • (09/15/94) • **80**
Pinot Noir California 1993 • $8 • (12/31/95) • **78**
Zinfandel California 1993 • $7 • (10/15/95) • **83**

MONTREAUX | CALIFORNIA

Brut Napa Valley 1987 • $26 • (12/31/94) • **86**
Brut Napa Valley 1986 • $26 • (12/31/93) • **76**
Brut Napa Valley 1985 • $32 • (12/31/90) • **79**

MOONDANCE | CALIFORNIA

Cabernet Sauvignon Napa Valley 1992 • $10 • (07/31/95) • **82**
Merlot Napa Valley 1994: Light, supple and generous with its plum and vanilla flavors. Some nice blackberry flavors pop up at the fresh finish. 900 cases made. • $18 • (12/31/96) • **85**
Merlot Napa Valley 1993: Ripe and openly fruity, with wild berry, cherry and currant notes. Finishes with firm tannins and a slightly coarse texture. Short-term cellaring advised. 1,000 cases made. • $15 • (08/31/96) • **83**
Merlot Napa Valley 1992 • $12 • (11/15/94) • **87**
Merlot Napa Valley 1990 • $10 • (03/31/93) • **86**
Moontage California NV: Light and ebulliently fruity, this is pleasant for its blackberry flavors, hints of chocolate. 3,000 cases made. • $7 • (12/31/96) • **84**
Petite Sirah Napa Valley 1992 • $16 • (09/30/95) • **88**
Sangiovese Alexander Valley 1993 • $13 • (11/30/95) • **80**
Zinfandel Sonoma Valley 1992 • $12 • (10/15/94) • **88**

MOONSHINE VINEYARD | CALIFORNIA

Chardonnay California 1995: Smoky, bitter overtones steal the charm from this light, apple-scented Chardonnay. 18,600 cases made. • $12 • (07/31/97) • **78**
Fumé Blanc California 1995: Tutti-frutti, canned aromas leave much to be desired. On the palate, it's clean, bright, simple and short. 4,334 cases made. • $10 • (08/31/97) • **80**

MOORE, Z | CALIFORNIA

Danato Sonoma-Mendocino Counties 1990 • $22 • (09/30/93) • **87**

MORAGA | CALIFORNIA

Bel Air 1993: Smooth, rich and supple, with delicious spicy currant, plum and wild berry flavors. The texture is silky right up to the finish. Try in 1999 to 2002. 80 percent Cabernet Sauvignon, the remainder being Cabernet Franc and Merlot. 423 cases made. • $50 • (07/31/97) • **91**
Cabernet Sauvignon Bel Air 1990 • $50 • (11/15/94) • **80**
Cabernet Sauvignon Bel Air 1989 • $50 • (06/30/93) • **87**
Red Bel Air 1994: Wonderfully complex, with ripe, rich, vibrant flavors and a smooth, supple texture that lets the core of currant, tobacco, cedar and spice flavors glide across the palate. But it's also a strongly oaked style, with lots of up-front smoke and cedar. Forward enough to enjoy now, but should age well until 2005. A blend of Cabernet Sauvignon, Merlot and Cabernet Franc. 600 cases made. • $55 • (05/15/98) • **90**

MORGAN | CALIFORNIA

Cabernet Sauvignon Carmel Valley 1991 • $15 • (11/15/94) • **88**
Cabernet Sauvignon Carmel Valley 1990 • $14 • (11/15/93) • **77**
Cabernet Sauvignon Carmel Valley 1989 • $15 • (08/31/92) • **83**
Cabernet Sauvignon Carmel Valley 1988 • $19 • (11/15/91) • **81**
Cabernet Sauvignon Carmel Valley 1987 • $16 • (09/30/90) • **92**
Cabernet Sauvignon Carmel Valley 1986 • $16 • (09/15/89) • **90**
Chardonnay Monterey 1996: Impressively smooth, ripe, rich and creamy, this California white offers well-focused pear, vanilla, nutmeg and spice, holding its focus and flavors through the finish, where it turns even more complex. Delicious. Drink now through 2002. 16,013 cases made. • $18 • (04/30/98) SS • **90**
Chardonnay Monterey 1995: Opens on an earthy note, then unveils some exotic citrus and tart pineapple flavors. Finishes crisply and with more earthiness. Drink now. 13,000 cases made. • $18 • (05/31/97) • **90**
Chardonnay Monterey 1994: Marked by citrus notes, especially grapefruit. Made more interesting by hints of pear and honey flavors. 12,000 cases made. • $18 • (07/31/96) • **85**
Chardonnay Monterey Reserve 1995: Complex, with deep, earthy pear, pineapple and citrus flavors, dashes of hazelnut and nectarine. Young and vibrant; by 1999 it may have softened and come together. 1,690 cases made. • $26 • (03/31/98) • **89**
Chardonnay Monterey Reserve 1994: Rich and full-bodied, with a juicy core of ripe pear and pineapple flavors. Finishes with a lively aftertaste and a kiss of spicy oak. Ready to drink. 1,521 cases made. • $24 • (04/30/97) • **89**
Chardonnay Monterey Reserve 1993 • $23 • (06/15/96) • **88**
Malvasia Bianca Monterey 1996: Fresh, delicate and very pretty for its floral pear, citrus and litchi flavors. Dry, and appealing for drinking soon, while it's fresh. 765 cases made. • $12 • (03/31/98) • **86**
Malvasia Bianca Monterey 1995: An unusual blend of lush tropical flavors and steely mineral notes. Fresh mango, peach, citrus and anise flavors taper off with a steely, dry edge. Interesting, if not for everyone. 300 cases made. • $14 • (09/30/97) • **86**
Pinot Noir California 1995: A touch earthy and smoky, with a charred edge to the cherry and berry flavors, it's best to let this soften and integrate a while. Try now. 6,285 cases made. • $18 • (05/31/97) • **87**
Pinot Noir California 1994: Misses the mark, with only a modest cherry note and lots of tannic, leathery flavors. 5,500 cases made. • $17 • (03/31/97) • **78**
Pinot Noir California 1993 • $15 • (06/30/95) • **83**
Pinot Noir California 1992 • $15 • (03/31/95) • **85**
Pinot Noir California 1991 • $15 • (02/28/93) • **81**
Pinot Noir California 1990: Supple and harmonious, with mature cherry, plum and berry notes. Finishing with a slight tarry edge. Ready now. • $15 • (03/31/97) • **85**
Pinot Noir California 1989 • $14 • (03/31/92) • **85**
Pinot Noir California 1988 • $14 • (04/30/91) • **75**
Pinot Noir California 1987 • $15 • (07/31/89) • **81**
Pinot Noir California 1986: This has taken a curious turn for the worse, with earthy, mulchy, bitter dried-fruit flavors. Marginal at best. • $14 • (03/31/97) • **70**
Pinot Noir Carneros Reserve 1993: Tastes and looks mature, with dried leaf and dried cherry flavors. Finishes with a slight edge to the tannins. Best for drinking now. 400 cases made. • $27 • (02/28/97) • **85**
Pinot Noir Carneros Reserve 1992 • $27 • (03/31/95) • **87**
Pinot Noir Carneros Reserve 1991 • $23 • (02/28/94) • **84**
Pinot Noir Carneros Reserve 1990: Tight, lean and still a bit tannic, with a chewy side to the ripe berry flavors. Perhaps holding will have softened the tannins a bit more. Try now. • $23 • (03/31/97) • **86**
Pinot Noir Monterey 1991 • $25 • (02/28/94) • **81**
Pinot Noir Monterey Reserve 1995: Begins with a complex smoky, meaty, fruity character and shows fine concentration of cherry, berry, mushroom and spice. Builds to a rich, well-focused aftertaste, with mild tannins. Tempting now, also worthy of short-term cellaring. 600 cases made. • $28 • (01/31/98) • **90**
Pinot Noir Monterey Reserve 1994: Tastes mature, with pleasant, earthy mushroom flavors and hints of currant and berry. Shows lots of polish and delicate notes on the finish. Impressive for its balance and finesse. 800 cases made. • $27 • (02/28/97) • **89**
Pinot Noir Monterey Reserve 1993 • $25 • (12/31/95) • **86**
Pinot Noir Monterey Reserve 1992 • $27 • (03/31/95) • **87**
Pinot Noir Monterey Reserve 1990: Nice interplay between complex flavors, with ripe cherry, berry, earth, tar and spice nuances that weave together well on the finish. The best of the three Morgan '90s, outscoring both the Carneros Reserve and California bottlings. • $30 • (03/31/97) • **89**
Sauvignon Blanc Sonoma & Monterey 1996: Toasty oak aromas are seductive, but they dominate the melon and citrus flavors. It remains, nonetheless, a pretty wine. 10,500 cases made. • $11 • (09/15/97) • **86**
Sauvignon Blanc Sonoma County 1995: Ripe, bright and focused. Weaves spicy, herbal notes with citrus and pear flavors. Finishes with a delicate touch of oak. 10,000 cases made. • $12 • (07/31/96) • **88**
Sauvignon Blanc Sonoma County 1994 • $11 • (06/30/95) • **86**
Viognier Sonoma County VNA 1994 • $18 • (11/30/95) • **82**
Zinfandel Dry Creek Valley 1995: Austere, with earthy cherry and raspberry flavors, turning dry and cedary on the finish. Drink now through 2000. 2,980 cases made. • $15 • (06/15/98) • **84**
Zinfandel Dry Creek Valley 1994: A rustic style, with some tartness to its cherry and berry flavors. Doesn't offend, but lacks harmony. 3,000 cases made. • $14 • (03/31/97) • **83**

Zinfandel Dry Creek Valley Grist Vineyard 1996: A blend of anise, cherry and spice and a touch of toasty oak create a brightly styled wine, a little short on the finish yet tasty. Drink now. 147 cases made. • $19 • (06/15/98) • **85**
Zinfandel Sonoma County 1993 • $14 • (10/15/95) • **82**

MOROVINO | CALIFORNIA

Chardonnay Santa Barbara County 1996: Intense and lively, well focused on the core of ripe pear and spicy, toasty oak. Fine balance, with pretty flavors on the finish. Drink now. • $16 • (06/15/98) • **88**
Merlot Santa Barbara County 1995: Displays bright flavors on a crisp frame, offering blackberry and plum notes with an overlay of mineral on the finish. Try now. • $18 • (12/15/97) • **82**
Sauvignon Blanc Santa Barbara County 1995: Tart, crisp and tangy, with citrusy herbal flavors that hold on through a zingy finish. 350 cases made. • $10 • (08/31/96) • **85**
Zinfandel Central Coast French Camp Vineyards 1994: Ripe and complex, with an appealing core of plum and cherry flavors. Finishes with supple tannins and a sense of elegance. Too bad there aren't more cases to go around. 70 cases made. • $14 • (10/15/96) • **88**

MORRIS, J.W. | CALIFORNIA

Cabernet Sauvignon Alexander Valley 1985 • $8 • (02/15/89) • **74**
Cabernet Sauvignon California Private Reserve 1989 • $6 • (11/15/92) • **79**
Cabernet Sauvignon California Private Reserve 1988 • $7 • (11/15/91) • **74**
Cabernet Sauvignon California Private Reserve 1987 • $8 • (03/31/90) • **83**
Private Reserve California 1987 • $3 • (06/30/90) • **70**
Private Reserve California 1986 • $3 • (12/31/88) • **78**
Private Reserve California 1984 • $3 • (11/15/87) BB • **79**

MORRO BAY | CALIFORNIA

Chardonnay Central Coast Special Edition 1995: Marked by strong spice and Muscat-like flavors, this hardly reminds one of Chardonnay—it's more like a Muscat-Chardonnay blend. 36,000 cases made. • $10 • (05/15/97) • **80**
Chardonnay Central Coast Special Edition 1994: Has a distinct earthy edge with hints of celery on top of a sweet apple flavor. It definitely has personality. Drink soon. 35,000 cases made. • $10 • (12/31/95) • **83**
Chardonnay Central Coast Special Edition 1993 • $10 • (05/15/95) • **84**

MOSBY | CALIFORNIA

Nebbiolo Santa Barbara County Rosso di Nebbiolo 1991 • $12 • (09/30/94) • **83**
Pinot Grigio Santa Barbara County 1994 • $11 • (12/15/95) • **86**
Sangiovese Santa Barbara County Vigna Della Casa Vecchia 1993 • $16 • (08/31/95) • **79**

MOSHIN | CALIFORNIA

Blanc de Noir Russian River Valley Dry 1993 • $9 • (09/15/95) • **86**
Pinot Noir Russian River Valley 1995: Spicy and almost jammy, but with enough edge to keep it firm and refreshing. This wine is filled with pretty wild cherry, thyme, sage and cedar notes. 483 cases made. • $16 • (01/31/98) • **87**
Pinot Noir Russian River Valley 1994: Moderate strawberry and mushroom flavors turn simple, with hints of tea and herb, grainy tannins. • $16 • (01/01/97) • **84**
Pinot Noir Russian River Valley 1992 • $13 • (03/31/95) • **83**
Pinot Noir Russian River Valley 1989 • $9 • (02/28/93) • **75**
Pinot Noir Russian River Valley Proprietor's Select 1995: This wine has weight, yet feels light on the palate, with a smooth, velvety texture. Marked by cherry, tea, spice and herbs, all harmoniously folded together. Drink now or hold. 515 cases made. • $24 • (01/31/98) • **88**
Pinot Noir Russian River Valley Proprietor's Select 1994: Well-focused, with strawberry, tea, mushroom and spice notes, turning lightly tannic on the finish. Drink now. • $30 • (08/31/97) • **85**
Pinot Noir Russian River Valley Reserve 1991 • $25 • (03/31/95) • **81**

Key: SS—Spectator Selection CS—Cellar Selection HR—Highly Recommended BB—Best Buy $NA—Price not available Ⓐ—Auction Price (BT)—Barrel Tasting
Dates in parentheses indicate the issues in which the ratings were published.

MOUNT BAKER | WASHINGTON

Cabernet Sauvignon Washington 1989 • $19 • (09/30/94) • **83**
Cabernet Sauvignon Washington 1988 • $16 • (03/31/92) • **84**

MOUNT EDEN | CALIFORNIA

Cabernet Sauvignon Santa Cruz Mountains 1994: Interesting flavors, hints of currant, anise and chocolate, steal the show after a tart, earthy note at the outset. Finishing with firm tannins, it is drinkable now but can be cellared into 2002. 1,522 cases made. • $20 • (05/15/97) • **88**
Cabernet Sauvignon Santa Cruz Mountains 1993: Marked by strong oak and chewy tannins, dense and backward, tasting more like a raw barrel sample than a finished wine. Will require patience and may always be tannic. Best to wait until 2002. 1,261 cases made. • $18 • (04/30/96) • **84**
Cabernet Sauvignon Santa Cruz Mountains 1992 • $16 • (05/31/95) • **83**
Cabernet Sauvignon Santa Cruz Mountains 1989 • $25 • (11/15/92) • **86**
Cabernet Sauvignon Santa Cruz Mountains 1988 • $26 • (11/15/92) • **86**
Cabernet Sauvignon Santa Cruz Mountains 1987 • $28 • (04/30/91) • **65**
Cabernet Sauvignon Santa Cruz Mountains 1986 • $16 Ⓐ • (08/31/90) • **83**
Cabernet Sauvignon Santa Cruz Mountains 1985 • $26 Ⓐ • (11/15/89) • **81**
Cabernet Sauvignon Santa Cruz Mountains 1984 • $22 Ⓐ • (10/31/88) • **90**
Cabernet Sauvignon Santa Cruz Mountains 1981 • $18 • (11/01/84) • **81**
Cabernet Sauvignon Santa Cruz Mountains 1978 • $24 Ⓐ • (11/15/92) • **84**
Cabernet Sauvignon Santa Cruz Mountains 1974 • $75 • (11/15/94) • **88**
Cabernet Sauvignon Santa Cruz Mountains Kennedy Vineyard 1978 • $NA • (11/15/92) • **85**
Cabernet Sauvignon Santa Cruz Mountains Lathweisen Ridge 1990 • $15 • (06/15/93) • **88**
Cabernet Sauvignon Santa Cruz Mountains Lathweisen Ridge 1989 • $14 • (08/31/92) • **85**
Cabernet Sauvignon Santa Cruz Mountains Lathweisen Ridge 1988 • $12 • (04/30/91) • **87**
Cabernet Sauvignon Santa Cruz Mountains Old Vine Reserve 1994: Earthy and well-oaked, but problematic, with a strong raw-cedar character and a dense, unyielding core of currant, blackberry and anise. Given the tannin level, cellar into 2002. Tasted twice, with consistent notes. 532 cases made. • $36 • (03/31/98) • **84**
Cabernet Sauvignon Santa Cruz Mountains Old Vine Reserve 1993: A big, rustic, mountain-grown style, with notes of mineral, currant, oak and cedar, finishing with chewy tannins. Unevolved and deeply concentrated, it will appeal most to those who favor old-style California Cabernet. Best in 2004. 425 cases made. • $36 • (01/31/97) • **88**
Cabernet Sauvignon Santa Cruz Mountains Old Vine Reserve 1992 • $35 • (06/15/96) • **90**
Cabernet Sauvignon Santa Cruz Mountains Old Vine Reserve 1991 • $35 • (04/15/95) • **88**
Cabernet Sauvignon Santa Cruz Mountains Old Vine Reserve 1990 • $30 • (11/15/93) • **85**
Cabernet Sauvignon Santa Cruz Mountains Young Vine Cuvée 1987 • $12 • (04/15/90) • **85**
Chardonnay Edna Valley MacGregor Vineyard 1996: Rich, elegant and complex for California's Edna Valley, this wine shows off well-defined Chardonnay flavors, with ripe pear, spice, melon and fig, and the finish goes on and on, turning creamy and complex. Good price, too. 10,500 cases made. • $16 • (03/31/98) SS • **91**
Chardonnay Edna Valley MacGregor Vineyard 1995: Offers interesting, earth-accented flavors of pear and pineapple, turning smooth and silky on the finish. Drink now. 3,825 cases made. • $16 • (06/30/97) • **89**
Chardonnay Edna Valley MacGregor Vineyard 1994: Moderate pear and citrus notes float through this. Doesn't have the richness of some earlier vintages, but good nonetheless. 5,000 cases made. • $16 • (06/15/96) • **84**
Chardonnay Edna Valley MacGregor Vineyard 1993 • $15 • (03/31/95) SS • **90**
Chardonnay Santa Cruz Mountains 1995: Marked by snappy acidity, the earthy mineral and light oak shadings add dimension to the pear and melon notes. Finishes with complexity and fine length. 1,175 cases made. • $38 • (09/30/97) • **91**
Chardonnay Santa Cruz Mountains 1994: Bold, ripe and intense, loaded with rich pear and hazelnut flavors, and well-oaked, with smoky, toasty flavors. Delicious now, but still big and unevolved at this stage. Sure to age well. 1,386 cases made. • $36 • (02/28/97) • **92**
Pinot Noir Edna Valley 1991 • $15 • (02/28/94) • **83**
Pinot Noir Santa Cruz Mountains 1995: Starts out with an earthy, gamy edge before working into more interesting dried fruit flavors. Finishes with a

touch of earthiness and drying tannins. Can stand cellaring into 1999. 386 cases made. • $35 • (01/31/98) • **87**

Pinot Noir Santa Cruz Mountains 1994: Remarkably complex, with a ripe core of currant, coffee, wild berry and cedar flavors. Young and tight, with a pleasant earthy edge and hints of fruit. Grows on you. Drinks well now, but put a bottle or two aside for future drinking. 400 cases made. • $34 • (02/28/97) • **90**

Pinot Noir Santa Cruz Mountains 1990 • $30 • (02/28/94) • **86**

Pinot Noir Santa Cruz Mountains 1989 • $30 • (02/28/94) • **85**

Pinot Noir Santa Cruz Mountains 1987 • $25 • (04/15/90) • **79**

Pinot Noir Santa Cruz Mountains 1985 • $35 • (06/15/88) • **90**

Pinot Noir Santa Cruz Mountains 1984 • $35 • (04/15/88) • **86**

Pinot Noir Santa Cruz Mountains 1983 • $35 • (08/31/86) • **77**

MOUNT KONOCTI | CALIFORNIA

Cabernet Franc Lake County Kelsey 1992 • $7 • (02/28/95) • **84**

Cabernet Sauvignon Lake County 1993: A bit rustic, with chewy tannins and earthy wild berry flavors. 4,500 cases made. • $10 • (12/15/95) • **82**

Cabernet Sauvignon Lake County Kelsey 1992 • $10 • (11/15/94) • **84**

Fumé Blanc Lake County 1994 • $8 • (08/31/95) • **85**

Fumé Blanc Lake County 1993 • $7 • (12/31/94) BB • **85**

Fumé Blanc Lake County Grand Fumé Barrel Fermented Reserve 1993 • $12 • (08/31/95) • **84**

Sémillon-Chardonnay Lake County 1993 • $7 • (04/15/95) • **82**

MOUNT MAROMA | CALIFORNIA

Cabernet Sauvignon Napa Valley 1993: Decent, but lacks focus. Serves up some off-beat, earthy, cedary flavors that some may find interesting. 5,583 cases made. • $14 • (11/30/96) • **80**

Chardonnay Napa Valley 1993: Sturdy and simple. Spicy, citrusy flavors lurk in the background. 4,024 cases made. • $14 • (07/31/96) • **82**

MT. MADONNA | CALIFORNIA

Merlot San Luis Obispo County 1987 • $8 • (05/31/92) • **69**

MOUNT PALOMAR | CALIFORNIA

Cabernet Sauvignon Temecula 1991 • $10 • (11/15/94) • **74**

Cabernet Sauvignon Temecula 1990 • $12 • (07/15/93) • **83**

Chardonnay Temecula 1993 • $10 • (02/28/95) • **79**

Chardonnay Temecula Reserve 1993 • $16 • (07/31/95) • **83**

Cortese Temecula Castelletto 1994: Soft and appealing, with sweetly spicy pear flavors. Made from Cortese, used to make Gavi in Piedmont, this wine has unusual character. Ready now. 360 cases made. • $16 • (07/31/96) • **83**

Cortese Temecula Castelletto 1993 • $16 • (12/31/94) • **87**

Johannisberg Riesling Temecula 1993 • $6 • (09/15/95) • **73**

Sangiovese Temecula Castelletto 1993: Smooth and spicy, this has a slight, peppery edge to the flavors of herb, olive and plum. 950 cases made. • $18 • (12/15/96) • **82**

Sangiovese Temecula Castelletto 1992 • $18 • (08/31/95) • **73**

Sangiovese Temecula Castelletto 1991 • $20 • (09/30/94) • **82**

Sauvignon Blanc Temecula 1993 • $7 • (08/31/94) • **79**

Sauvignon Blanc Temecula Reserve 1993 • $10 • (08/31/94) • **74**

MOUNT VEEDER | CALIFORNIA

Cabernet Sauvignon Napa Valley 1994: Clean, ripe and flavorful, with pretty black cherry, herb, plum and berry notes, holding its flavors through the lingering finish. 8,000 cases made. • $25 • (08/31/97) • **88**

Cabernet Sauvignon Napa Valley 1993: Firm and compact, with a nice core of ripe cherry, plum and cedary oak flavors that linger on the finish. The tannins are mild enough to make it drinkable now. 7,000 cases made. • $25 • (11/15/96) • **87**

Cabernet Sauvignon Napa Valley 1992 • $25 • (12/15/95) • **87**

Cabernet Sauvignon Napa Valley 1991 • $18 • (01/31/95) • **85**

Cabernet Sauvignon Napa Valley 1990 • $15 • (10/31/93) SS • **94**

Cabernet Sauvignon Napa Valley 1989 • $15 • (06/15/93) • **82**

Cabernet Sauvignon Napa Valley 1987 • $22 • (04/30/91) • **85**

Cabernet Sauvignon Napa Valley 1986 • $20 • (11/15/90) • **83**

Cabernet Sauvignon Napa Valley 1984 • $14 • (11/15/88) • **83**

Cabernet Sauvignon Napa Valley 1983 • $14 • (10/31/87) • **75**

Cabernet Sauvignon Napa Valley 1982 • $13 • (06/15/87) • **64**

Cabernet Sauvignon Napa Valley 1981 • $13 • (07/16/86) • **81**

Cabernet Sauvignon Napa Valley 1974 • $53 • (11/15/94) • **85**

Cabernet Sauvignon Napa Valley Bernstein Vineyards 1980 • $12 • (05/16/84) • **85**

Cabernet Sauvignon Napa Valley Bernstein Vineyards 1978 • $31 • (11/15/92) • **78**

Cabernet Sauvignon Napa Valley Mount Veeder Vineyards 1987: Tart, with a firm tannic backbone and some earthy notes, this remains young and intensely flavored. True to its appellation, with hard-edged, slightly green, wild berry flavors. 2,500 cases made. • $50 • (12/15/97) • **87**

Meritage Napa Valley 1989 • $24 • (06/15/93) • **88**

Meritage Napa Valley 1988 • $24 • (07/15/92) • **83**

Merlot Napa Valley 1994: Built around a core of ripe plum and currant flavors, with a good dose of spicy, toasted oak adding dimension. Smooth, supple tannins. 450 cases made. • $22 • (06/30/97) • **87**

Reserve Napa Valley 1993: Tight, firm and tannic, with a core of currant, plum and wild berry flavors. Finishes with an austere edge and drying tannins; best to cellar into 1999. A blend of Cabernet Sauvignon, Merlot, Cabernet Franc, Petit Verdot and Malbec. 2,500 cases made. • $40 • (08/31/97) • **90**

Reserve Napa Valley 1992: Tightly-wound currant, cherry and berry flavors and lively tannins on the finish. Vibrant and young; needs cellaring into 1999. 3,000 cases made. • $40 • (08/31/96) • **88**

Reserve Napa Valley 1991 • $40 • (09/15/95) • **84**

Reserve Napa Valley 1990 • $25 • (09/15/94) CS • **92**

Zinfandel Napa County 1982 • $8 • (03/16/85) • **86**

Zinfandel Napa Valley 1994: In a lighter style, yet it captures lots of ripe cherry, strawberry and pepper notes and the flavors linger without getting too tannic. Ready to drink. 1,000 cases made. • $22 • (03/31/97) • **86**

Zinfandel Napa Valley 1993 • $20 • (03/31/96) • **83**

MOUNTAIN DOME | WASHINGTON

Brut Rosé Washington NV: Dry, slightly bitter, but balanced with watermelon and strawberry notes that add life to the base of spicy flavors. 450 cases made. • $17 • (09/30/97) • **87**

Brut Washington 1991: Spicy, almost peppery, in flavor, this is a firm-textured wine that's supple around the edges, flavorful and sprightly. 530 cases made. • $16 • (09/30/97) • **88**

Brut Washington 1990 • $16 • (09/30/94) • **85**

Brut Washington 1988: Rich and complex, its flavors center around toast, honey and pepper, all very gentle, richly grapey and harmonious. 350 cases made. • $20 • (09/30/97) • **89**

Brut Washington NV: Round and generous in flavor, broad in texture, it's a tasty mouthful of spicy, slightly earthy flavors. Balanced and appealing. 1,600 cases made. • $10 • (09/30/97) • **87**

MOUNTAIN VALLEY | TENNESSEE

Dessert Tennessee Blackberry Table Wine 1991 • $8 • (02/29/92) • **75**

MOUNTAIN VIEW | CALIFORNIA

Cabernet Sauvignon Mendocino County 1986 • $6 • (03/31/90) • **79**

Cabernet Sauvignon Mendocino County 1985 • $6 • (02/15/89) • **77**

Cabernet Sauvignon North Coast 1992 • $6 • (11/15/94) • **79**

Cabernet Sauvignon North Coast 1990 • $6 • (06/15/93) • **76**

Cabernet Sauvignon North Coast 1989 • $6 • (11/15/92) • **71**

Cabernet Sauvignon North Coast 1988 • $6 • (04/30/91) BB • **80**

Chardonnay Monterey 1993: Light and citrusy, with a strong oaky streak running through the narrow flavors. Ready now. 50,000 cases made. • $6 • (07/31/96) • **80**

Merlot Napa County 1989 • $6 • (05/31/91) • **72**

Pinot Noir Carneros 1986 • $6 • (02/28/89) BB • **80**

Pinot Noir Monterey-Napa Counties 1992 • $6 • (02/28/94) • **81**

Pinot Noir Monterey-Napa Counties 1991 • $6 • (02/28/93) • **74**

Pinot Noir Monterey-Napa Counties 1990 • $6 • (04/30/92) BB • **82**

Pinot Noir Monterey-Napa Counties 1989 • $6 • (02/28/91) BB • **82**

Pinot Noir Monterey-Napa Counties 1988 • $6 • (03/31/90) • **72**

Zinfandel Amador County Lot #91 NV • $5 • (10/15/94) • **79**

Zinfandel Amador County Lot #93 NV • $6 • (10/15/95) • **82**

MUELLER | CALIFORNIA

Chardonnay Alexander Valley Gauer Ranch 1995: Ripe, rich and full-bodied, with pretty pear, peach, spice and nectarine notes, finishing with a spicy, fruity aftertaste that lingers. 667 cases made. • $18 • (08/31/97) • **90**

Chardonnay Alexander Valley Gauer Ranch 1994: Begins with spicy, toasty oak and turns toward lean citrus and pear flavors. 508 cases made. • $15 • (05/15/96) • **89**

Chardonnay Russian River Valley 1995: An ultrarich mouthful, in a big, bold, ripe and buttery style. This California Chardonnay is impressively complex-loaded with fresh pear, anise, fig and spice flavors that linger on the finish, along with pretty smoke and toast notes. 1,460 cases made. • $15 • (06/30/97) HR • **92**

Chardonnay Russian River Valley 1994: Clean and lively, as an attractive band of citrus, apple, pear and spice finishes in a subtle nutmeg and honey aftertaste. Complex and refined style that offers lots of finesse and grace. 592 cases made. • $13 • (05/15/96) • **90**

Chardonnay Russian River Valley LB 1996: Complex, with ripe fruit, creamy nuances and lots of pear, earth and spice. Finishes with hints of citrus and light oak shadings. Drink now through 2001. 1,163 cases made. • $18 • (06/30/98) • **90**

Chardonnay Russian River Valley Oak Meadow Vineyard 1996: A subtle style that packs in lots of ripe, intense flavors, with a pretty array of rich pear, toasty oak, spice, mineral and citrus, turning complex with a hint of anise on the finish. Drink now through 2001. 510 cases made. • $18 • (07/31/98) • **90**

Chardonnay Sonoma County Gauer Ranch 1993 • $15 • (03/31/96) • **88**

Pinot Noir Russian River Valley Emily's Cuvée 1995: Smooth, ripe, supple and polished, with a creamy texture and lots of ripe plum and black cherry flavors. Turns silky on the finish, where the flavors linger long. Drink now or cellar until 1999. 429 cases made. • $22 • (07/31/97) • **91**

Pinot Noir Russian River Valley Emily's Cuvée 1994 • $20 • (04/30/96) • **91**

Pinot Noir Russian River Valley Ranch 23 1996: Medium-weight, with earthy cherry and wild berry fruit. Finishes with firm, dry tannins, so a short spell in the cellar should help; drink through 2004. 288 cases made. • $25 • (06/30/98) • **87**

MUMM CUVÉE NAPA | CALIFORNIA

Blanc de Blancs Napa Valley NV: Fragrant, with toasty, floral overtones. Shows complex pear, hazelnut and vanilla flavors with an interesting lemon-lime core. Long finish. Nice price. • $18 • (11/30/97) • **91**

Blanc de Noirs Napa Valley NV: Lots of Pinot Noir character to this, with pretty black cherry, spice and creamy vanilla flavors, a smooth texture and a long, rich aftertaste. A wonderful buy, too. Ready. • $15 • (11/30/97) • **90**

Brut Napa Valley Carneros Winery Lake 1990 • $18 • (11/30/95) • **89**

Brut Napa Valley Carneros Winery Lake 1989 • $20 • (12/31/94) • **86**

Brut Napa Valley Carneros Winery Lake 1988 • $22 • (11/15/91) • **89**

Brut Napa Valley Carneros Winery Lake 1986 • $23 • (12/10/90) • **87**

Brut Napa Valley Vintage Reserve 1989 • $18 • (12/31/94) • **87**

Brut Napa Valley Vintage Reserve 1987 • $22 • (12/31/90) • **87**

Brut Napa Valley Vintage Reserve 1985 • $21 • (05/31/89) • **86**

Brut Prestige Napa Valley NV: Has a real lemony edge, almost too tart. It's a bit disjointed but remains refreshing and bright. Clean finish. 15,000 cases made. • $15 • (11/30/97) • **86**

DVX Napa Valley 1993: A toasty, creamy wine, with hints of pear, nutmeg, and citrus. An elegant, complex blend. 1,900 cases made. • $40 • (11/30/97) • **91**

DVX Napa Valley 1992: Deliciously complex, with layers of ripe pear, fig, anise, toast and vanilla flavors. The texture is smooth and supple, with lots of zesty flavors coming through on the finish. 2,000 cases made. • $30 • (11/30/96) HR • **92**

DVX Napa Valley 1991 • $30 • (12/31/95) • **89**

DVX Napa Valley 1990 • $25 • (12/15/94) SS • **91**

Key: SS—Spectator Selection CS—Cellar Selection HR—Highly Recommended BB—Best Buy $NA—Price not available Ⓐ—Auction Price (BT)—Barrel Tasting
Dates in parentheses indicate the issues in which the ratings were published.

MURPHY-GOODE | CALIFORNIA

Cabernet Sauvignon Alexander Valley 1995: Light and simple, with a pleasing band of currant, berry, herb and cedar, finishing with mild tannins. Ready to drink. 3,700 cases made. • $19 • (03/31/98) • **84**

Cabernet Sauvignon Alexander Valley 1988 • $16 • (11/15/91) • **87**

Cabernet Sauvignon Alexander Valley Brenda Block Reserve 1994: Firm, tight and tannic, with a rich, concentrated core of currant, plum, anise and tobacco flavors. Finishes with a smooth aftertaste, light toast notes. Try now and into 2002. 1,800 cases made. • $30 • (07/31/97) • **89**

Cabernet Sauvignon Alexander Valley Goode-Ready 1989 • $10 • (06/15/91) • **80**

Cabernet Sauvignon Alexander Valley Murphy Ranch 1994: Appealing for its up-front ripe currant, plum and cherry flavors and supple tannins. It grows on you, especially on the finish, where a nice dash of oak adds dimension. 5,100 cases made. • $18 • (11/15/96) • **88**

Cabernet Sauvignon Alexander Valley Murphy Ranch 1993: Dense and compact, with chewy tannins and rich plum and cherry-laced Cabernet flavors. Was a bit rustic, but a little aging should have done the trick. 2,900 cases made. • $16 • (11/15/95) • **88**

Cabernet Sauvignon Alexander Valley Murphy Ranch 1992 • $15 • (05/15/95) • **87**

Cabernet Sauvignon Alexander Valley Murphy Ranch 1991 • $15 • (11/15/94) • **83**

Cabernet Sauvignon Alexander Valley Murphy Ranch 1990 • $15 • (10/15/93) • **87**

Cabernet Sauvignon Alexander Valley Murphy Ranch 1989 • $16 • (11/15/92) • **84**

Cabernet Sauvignon Alexander Valley Premier Vineyard 1987 • $17 • (05/31/90) • **89**

Cabernet Sauvignon Alexander Valley Premier Vineyard 1986 • $16 • (11/15/89) • **90**

Chardonnay Alexander Valley 1995: Smooth and polished, with ripe pear, vanilla and honey flavors that finish on a spicy oak note. Appealing now. 19,500 cases made. • $14 • (01/31/97) • **87**

Chardonnay Alexander Valley 1994: Soft and fruity, offering tasty, bright melon and green grape flavors and a nice addition of resiny oak. Ready now. • $14 • (12/31/95) • **86**

Chardonnay Alexander Valley 1993 • $13 • (07/31/95) • **86**

Chardonnay Alexander Valley Island Block Reserve 1996: Smooth, ripe, rich and creamy, with pretty pear and hazelnut flavors, smoky, toasty oak notes and a long, complex, concentrated aftertaste. Drink now through 2000. 3,500 cases made. • $24 • (05/15/98) • **90**

Chardonnay Alexander Valley Island Block Reserve 1995: Smells ripe and spicy, with lots of apple and pear flavors, turning elegant and subtle on the finish, where light oak shadings fold in. 1,400 cases made. • $24 • (06/15/97) • **88**

Chardonnay Alexander Valley Island Block Reserve 1994: Serves the ripe pear and pineapple flavors up front, with a spicy oak dimension that's complex and compelling. An openly fruity white that finishes with a rich, smoky aftertaste. 1,400 cases made. • $24 • (01/31/96) • **89**

Chardonnay Russian River Valley J & K Murphy Vineyard Reserve 1996: Generous for its up-front fruitiness, with ripe pear, spice, peach and light oak shadings, it remains supple and fruity on the finish. Drink now. 2,900 cases made. • $24 • (05/15/98) • **89**

Chardonnay Russian River Valley J & K Murphy Vineyard Reserve 1995: Creamy and ripe, with a pretty core of ripe pear, apple and spice flavors. Shows depth, richness and concentration while maintaining its elegance and finesse. 2,400 cases made. • $24 • (06/15/97) • **91**

Chardonnay Russian River Valley J & K Murphy Vineyard Reserve 1994: Marked by an openly spicy edge, it's an elegant and refined style with flavors that build on the finish, picking up a smoky, toasty edge. Very appealing now. 1,350 cases made. • $24 • (05/31/96) • **89**

Chardonnay Russian River Valley J & K Murphy Vineyard Reserve 1993 • $24 • (07/31/95) • **90**

Chardonnay Sonoma County 1996: A bit disjointed, as the smoky wood flavors stand apart from the core of ripe pear, peach and apple, finishing with a bitter twinge. 27,000 cases made. • $15 • (02/28/98) • **87**

Fumé Blanc Alexander Valley 1994 • $10 • (07/31/95) • **87**

Fumé Blanc Alexander Valley 1993 • $10 • (09/30/94) • **86**

Fumé Blanc Alexander Valley Reserve 1996: Lots of toasty oak here, plus hazelnut, sweet pea and an attractive grassiness that lends a complexity to the blend. Brisk acidity on the finish makes it refreshing. 14,000 cases made. • $17 • (03/31/98) • **88**

Fumé Blanc Alexander Valley Reserve 1995: Smooth, rich and elegant, offering a deliciously honeyed finish after displaying lovely pineapple, pear and

herb flavors along the way. Ready now, why wait? 13,000 cases made. • $16 • (12/31/96) • **90**
Fumé Blanc Alexander Valley Reserve 1994 • $16 • (02/29/96) • **85**
Fumé Blanc Alexander Valley Reserve 1993 • $15 • (02/28/95) • **89**
Fumé Blanc Sonoma County 1996: Quite bright and perky. Firm and tightly wound around a core of vivid grapefruit, anise and lemon flavors. Squeaky clean, and more fruit-driven than the reserve version. 26,000 cases made. • $12 • (06/30/97) • **88**
Fumé Blanc Sonoma County 1995: Good balancing act; spicy, distinctly herbal, nectarine and apple flavors hang on a lighter-than-air framework. What it lacks in finish it makes up for in finesse. 31,000 cases made. • $11 • (09/15/96) • **87**
Merlot Alexander Valley Murphy Ranch 1990 • $15 • (03/31/93) • **83**
Merlot Alexander Valley Murphy Ranch 1989 • $15 • (05/31/92) • **82**
Merlot Alexander Valley Murphy Ranches 1995: Supple and well-balanced, with a rich, complex core of currant, berry, anise and buttery oak flavors. Finishes with smooth, polished tannins and a lively aftertaste. 5,350 cases made. • $18 • (06/30/97) • **89**
Merlot Alexander Valley Murphy Ranches 1994: Medium-bodied, with ripe cherry and berry flavors and modest tannins. It's Murphy good, but nothing more. Drink now. 4,000 cases made. • $16 • (11/30/96) • **84**
Merlot Alexander Valley Murphy Ranches 1993 • $16 • (12/15/95) • **85**
Merlot Alexander Valley Murphy Ranches 1992 • $15 • (01/31/95) • **83**
Merlot Alexander Valley Murphy Ranches 1991 • $15 • (03/15/94) • **83**
Merlot Alexander Valley Premier Vineyard 1986 • $14 • (01/31/89) • **90**
Pinot Blanc Alexander Valley 1994 • $13 • (11/15/95) • **83**
Pinot Blanc Alexander Valley 1993 • $13 • (04/15/95) • **88**
Pinot Blanc Russian River & Alexander Valleys 1995: Young and on the tart side, with a lean band of apple, pear and spice flavors that are clean, turning simple on the finish. 3,300 cases made. • $13 • (02/28/97) • **86**
Pinot Blanc Sonoma County 1996: Marked by pear and apple flavors, on the tart side, turning crisp and flinty on the aftertaste. 3,300 cases made. • $14 • (04/30/98) • **84**
Sauvignon Blanc Alexander Valley Fumé II The Deuce 1996: A rich wine, packed with layers of butterscotch, herbs, lemon-lime, grapefruit and hazelnuts. Firm and focused on the palate with a bright, zingy finish. 2,100 cases made. • $24 • (03/31/98) • **90**
Sauvignon Blanc Alexander Valley Fumé II The Deuce 1995: Toasty vanilla aromas are followed by a wine of creamy texture, full body and an interesting blend of orange and mineral flavors. 1,000 cases made. • $24 • (06/15/97) • **88**
Zinfandel Dry Creek-Alexander Valleys 1995: Silky and spicy, this is a lovely mouthful of distinctive wild berry and toasty vanilla flavors that swirl nicely through the lithe, intense finish. Best in 1999. 2,000 cases made. • $16 • (12/15/97) • **88**
Zinfandel Sonoma County 1996: Offers appealing pepper and wild berry flavors up front, then shows off some tar and sage notes before finishing with a burst of spicy fruit. Firmly tannic, it can benefit from short-term cellaring; drink through 2001. 5,050 cases made. • $16 • (05/31/98) • **88**
Zinfandel Sonoma County 86% Cuneo & Saini Vineyard 14% Capener Vineyard 1994: A well-oaked style, with spicy, buttery, smoky wood flavors that add a nice dimension to the ripe cherry and wild berry notes. Ready to drink. 600 cases made. • $16 • (03/31/97) • **88**

MURRAY, ANDREW | CALIFORNIA

Syrah Santa Barbara County 1994: An austere style with a modest range of flavors and hints of sage, spice and berry, but it could use a little more stuffing. • $20 • (05/15/97) • **84**
Syrah Santa Barbara County 1993: Spicy currant flavors touched with green notes; herb, tea and bell pepper. Finish is slightly lean, with a tannic edge. 80 cases made. • $25 • (07/31/96) • **85**

MURRIETA'S WELL | CALIFORNIA

Vendimia Livermore Valley 1993: Smooth, ripe and harmonious, with supple currant, plum and berry notes, finishing with a spicy aftertaste and a dash of cedary oak. Delicious now, also worthy of cellaring into 1999 to 2001. 60 percent Cabernet Sauvignon, 16 percent Cabernet Franc, 12 percent Merlot and 12 percent Zinfandel. 3,900 cases made. • $28 • (04/30/97) • **90**
Vendimia Livermore Valley 1991 • $28 • (05/31/95) • **84**
Vendimia Livermore Valley 1990 • $28 • (11/15/94) • **89**
Vendimia White Livermore Valley 1993: Somewhat viscous, with a cinnamon nuance preceding essence of star fruit, melon and citrus flavors. Lacks the bright acidity of many other Sauvignon Blancs due to its relative age. 55 percent Sauvignon Blanc, 43 percent Sémillon and 2 percent Muscat de Frontignan. 2,000 cases made. • $20 • (06/30/97) • **88**
Zinfandel Livermore Valley 1994: Ripe and spicy, with a wild berry and sage accent. Picks up more plum and cherry notes and an intriguing, complex earthy quality on the finish, where the tannins are mild and well integrated. Drinkable now. 1,150 cases made. • $18 • (03/31/97) • **90**
Zinfandel Livermore Valley 1991 • $16 • (10/15/94) • **89**
Zinfandel Livermore Valley 1989 • $16 • (10/15/94) • **83**

NALLE | CALIFORNIA

Cabernet Sauvignon Dry Creek Valley 1990 • $18 • (11/15/93) • **85**
Cabernet Sauvignon Dry Creek Valley 1987 • $18 • (01/31/91) • **89**
Zinfandel Dry Creek Valley 1993 • $16 • (08/31/95) • **87**
Zinfandel Dry Creek Valley 1992 • $15 • (10/15/94) • **85**
Zinfandel Dry Creek Valley 1991 • $14 • (09/30/93) • **86**
Zinfandel Dry Creek Valley 1990 • $14 • (10/15/92) • **89**
Zinfandel Dry Creek Valley 1989 • $14 • (07/31/91) • **85**
Zinfandel Dry Creek Valley 1988 • $25 • (07/31/90) • **89**
Zinfandel Dry Creek Valley 1987 • $22 • (05/31/89) SS • **92**
Zinfandel Dry Creek Valley 1986 • $9 • (06/30/88) • **90**
Zinfandel Dry Creek Valley 1985 • $8 • (09/15/87) • **91**
Zinfandel Dry Creek Valley 1984 • $7 • (10/15/86) • **91**

NAPA CELLARS | CALIFORNIA

Cabernet Sauvignon California 1990 • $8 • (11/15/94) • **78**
Chardonnay Napa Valley 1993 • $7 • (07/31/95) • **72**
Merlot California 1990 • $7 • (05/31/92) • **79**
Merlot California 1989 • $7 • (05/31/91) • **70**

NAPA CREEK | CALIFORNIA

Cabernet Sauvignon Napa Valley 1991 • $12 • (11/15/94) • **82**
Chardonnay California Barrel Select 1995: Hazelnuts, citrus and mineral flavors mesh somewhat disjointedly here. Still pleasant, however. 4,000 cases made. • $9 • (07/31/97) • **84**
Merlot Napa Valley 1988 • $13 • (03/31/91) • **75**
Merlot Napa Valley 1987 • $14 • (06/15/90) • **83**
Pinot Noir California Barrel Select 1995: Heavily oaked, to the wine's detriment, with more cedar and vanilla flavors than fruit. • $NA • (03/31/97) • **77**

NAPA RIDGE | CALIFORNIA

Cabernet Sauvignon Central Coast 1992 • $8 • (10/15/95) BB • **87**
Cabernet Sauvignon Central Coast Oak Barrel 1995: A focused wine, yet not heavy, bringing to mind flavors of cassis, mint, wintergreen, blackberry and clove that mingle with a-tad-coarse tannins in a harmonious ensemble. This very good California Cabernet is a bargain, and readily available. 95,000 cases made. • $9 • (10/15/97) BB • **87**
Cabernet Sauvignon Central Coast Oak Barrel 1994: A well-oaked style, with spicy vanilla and cedar notes that add flavor and dimension to the cherry and wild berry flavors. With its supple tannins, it drinks well now. 65,900 cases made. • $8 • (02/28/97) BB • **87**
Cabernet Sauvignon Central Coast Oak Barrel 1991 • $8 • (11/15/94) • **84**
Cabernet Sauvignon Napa Valley 1980 • $5 • (03/16/84) • **75**
Cabernet Sauvignon Napa Valley Reserve 1994: Somewhat spicy, with a bright cherrylike center enhanced by smoky oak and anise notes. Tannins are supple yet firm, and the finish is moderate. • $15 • (10/15/97) • **87**
Cabernet Sauvignon Napa Valley Reserve 1992: Medium-bodied, with a pleasant band of cherry, currant, spice and cedar flavors, but not really a reserve-style wine. • $15 • (10/15/96) • **84**
Cabernet Sauvignon Napa Valley Reserve 1989 • $12 • (07/15/93) • **85**
Cabernet Sauvignon North Coast 1989 • $6 • (11/15/91) • **79**
Cabernet Sauvignon North Coast 1982 • $5 • (03/31/87) • **72**
Cabernet Sauvignon North Coast Oak Barrel 1994: Openly fruity, with ripe cherry, plum and berry flavors and light, toasty oak shadings. An excellent value at this price, as the flavors are pure and pleasing. • $7 • (11/15/96) BB • **87**
Cabernet Sauvignon North Coast Oak Barrel 1993: Has appealing spicy berry and toasty oak flavors that are pleasantly well-proportioned. Another terrific value from this California winery. 38,000 cases made. • $7 • (11/30/95) BB • **87**
Cabernet Sauvignon North Coast Oak Barrel 1992 • $8 • (11/15/94) • **79**
Cabernet Sauvignon North Coast Oak Barrel 1991 • $8 • (11/15/93) • **77**

Cabernet Sauvignon North Coast Reserve 1991 • $13 • (10/15/95) • **87**
Cabernet Sauvignon North Coast Reserve 1990 • $13 • (11/15/94) • **82**
Cabernet Sauvignon North Coast Reserve 1989 • $13 • (11/15/93) • **87**
Chardonnay Central Coast 1993 • $7 • (06/15/94) BB • **87**
Chardonnay Central Coast Coastal Vines 1996: Smooth and appealing for its soft pear and nutmeg flavors. Harmonious, even delicate, straightforward and ready to drink. • $9 • (12/15/97) • **85**
Chardonnay Central Coast Coastal Vines 1995: Ripe and racy, with a zesty citrus accent to the pear and melon notes. Finishes with a clean, complex aftertaste. • $7 • (11/30/96) • **85**
Chardonnay Central Coast Coastal Vines 1994: Soft, creamy and disarmingly tasty, showing spicy orange and pear flavors that glide smoothly through the supple finish. • $7 • (10/15/95) • **85**
Chardonnay Central Coast Coastal Vines 1993 • $8 • (11/30/94) BB • **85**
Chardonnay Napa Valley Frisinger Vineyard 1994: Toasty, spicy, earthy notes add some extra dimension to the pear flavors. Ready now. 224 cases made. • $11 • (06/30/96) • **85**
Chardonnay Napa Valley Frisinger Vineyard 1993 • $11 • (04/15/95) • **88**
Chardonnay Napa Valley Reserve 1995: Delicious Chardonnay, smooth, rich and concentrated, with complex pear, honey, hazelnut, citrus and melon flavors that fan out nicely on the finish, revealing more depth and nuance. • $15 • (01/31/98) • **91**
Chardonnay Napa Valley Reserve 1994: Broad and ripe, with floral, earthy notes that add complexity, and just a hint of honey on the aftertaste. Ready now. 850 cases made. • $12 • (06/30/96) • **86**
Chardonnay Napa Valley Reserve 1993 • $13 • (07/31/95) • **86**
Chardonnay North Coast Coastal Vines 1996: Attractive, with ripe, tart peach, pear and apple flavors and firm structure. It's clean and refreshing, if missing the extra depth of some Napa Ridge Chardonnays. Drink now. 90,000 cases made. • $9 • (05/31/98) BB • **86**
Chardonnay North Coast Coastal Vines 1995: Light and fruity, with appealing apple, pear, apricot and light spice notes. Finishes with a dash of oaky flavor. • $8 • (02/28/97) • **87**
Gewürztraminer Central Coast 1995: Soft, simple and pleasant for its honeyed peach flavors, twist of grapefruit. • $5 • (10/31/96) • **83**
Merlot North Coast 1993 • $10 • (06/30/96) BB • **85**
Merlot North Coast 1992 • $9 • (03/31/95) BB • **87**
Merlot North Coast 1991 • $9 • (09/15/94) • **84**
Merlot North Coast 1990 • $7 • (06/15/93) • **81**
Pinot Noir Carneros Reserve 1995: Lean, beefy and well-oaked, with chewy tannins and decent dried cherry and plum flavors. 490 cases made. • $15 • (03/31/98) • **84**
Pinot Noir North Coast 1994 • $7 • (01/31/96) BB • **86**
Pinot Noir North Coast 1993 • $8 • (12/15/94) BB • **84**
Pinot Noir North Coast 1991 • $6 • (02/28/94) BB • **83**
Pinot Noir North Coast 1989 • $7 • (07/31/91) BB • **82**
Pinot Noir North Coast Coastal 1996: Medium-weight, with earthy cherry and berry-laced flavors and more Gamay-like flavors than classic Pinot Noir ones. Still, it's a solid effort at a good price. Drink now. • $11 • (06/30/98) • **84**
Pinot Noir North Coast Coastal 1995: What a deal in California Pinot Noir. Full-flavored yet elegant, with classic, complex flavors, touches of ripe cherry, wild berry and light oak, accented by touches of mushroom- and cola-accented earthiness, and a silky texture. Retasted, and upgraded appropriately from an earlier note. 54,000 cases made. • $10 • (05/15/97) BB • **89**
Sauvignon Blanc North Coast 1996: Rich hazelnut and sweet pea aromas announce this tasty, balanced white with its flavors of almonds, grapefruit and herbs. A bit oily on the finish, but still quite nice and, at this price, you can afford to keep a few bottles on hand. 18,000 cases made. • $6 • (03/31/98) BB • **86**
Sauvignon Blanc North Coast 1995: Light and simple, with some pear flavors and toasty notes. • $5 • (11/30/96) • **80**
Sauvignon Blanc North Coast 1994 • $5 • (12/15/95) BB • **86**
Sauvignon Blanc North Coast 1993 • $4 • (03/31/95) • **81**
Zinfandel Central Coast 1995: Silky and generous, soft and supple, and shows pretty blackberry and vanilla flavors that linger gently on the finish. Ready to drink. 22,500 cases made. • $9 • (12/15/97) BB • **86**
Zinfandel Central Coast 1990 • $7 • (09/30/93) • **76**

Key: SS—Spectator Selection CS—Cellar Selection HR—Highly Recommended BB—Best Buy $NA—Price not available Ⓐ—Auction Price (BT)—Barrel Tasting
Dates in parentheses indicate the issues in which the ratings were published.

NATHANSON CREEK | CALIFORNIA

Cabernet Sauvignon California NV: Light, fruity, spicy cherry flavors are nice, if not very Cabernet-like. Ready now. 136,000 cases made. • $6 • (11/15/97) • **78**
Pinot Noir California NV: Interesting flavors of black cherry, tobacco and cola weave through a layer of coarse tannins. Finishes with balance, so it may be best from 1999 or 2000. • $14/1.5 liter • (05/15/98) • **80**

NAVARRO | CALIFORNIA

Brut Gewürztraminer Anderson Valley 1989 • $9 • (05/15/92) • **82**
Brut Mendocino 1988 • $16 • (12/31/93) • **81**
Cabernet Sauvignon Mendocino 1992: Young, chunky and firmly tannic. The core of herb- and currant-laced Cabernet flavor is a little rough around the edges, but will soften with short-term cellaring. 657 cases made. • $19 • (11/15/97) • **89**
Cabernet Sauvignon Mendocino 1991: Shows soft, mature flavors and it's deftly balanced, well-focused and drinks well. Shows a nice core of ripe currant, cherry and plum flavors with hints of herb and cedar. Drink now. 719 cases made. • $18 • (11/15/96) • **88**
Cabernet Sauvignon Mendocino 1990 • $17 • (10/15/95) • **88**
Cabernet Sauvignon Mendocino 1989 • $16 • (11/15/94) • **82**
Cabernet Sauvignon Mendocino 1988 • $16 • (10/15/93) • **86**
Cabernet Sauvignon Mendocino 1987 • $16 • (11/15/92) • **88**
Cabernet Sauvignon Mendocino 1986 • $16 • (10/15/91) • **87**
Cabernet Sauvignon Mendocino 1985 • $14 • (11/15/90) • **87**
Chardonnay Anderson Valley 1993 • $8 • (07/31/95) • **83**
Chardonnay Anderson Valley Première Reserve 1995: Opens up to reveal a core of ripe apple, pear and melon notes—even dashes of fig and spice. Earthy accent up front. Ready to drink. 3,275 cases made. • $16 • (06/15/97) • **88**
Chardonnay Anderson Valley Première Reserve 1994: Bright and lively, with a tight core of pear, peach, honey and nectarine flavors, yet maintains its delicacy and finesse. Young and vibrant; it can age too. 3,272 cases made. • $15 • (06/15/96) • **89**
Chardonnay Anderson Valley Première Reserve 1993 • $NA • (02/29/96) • **88**
Chardonnay Mendocino 1995: A solid wine, ripe and generous, with pretty pear, peach, melon and spice flavors that intensify and fan out on the finish. 2,230 cases made. • $12 • (06/15/97) • **89**
Chardonnay Mendocino 1994: Ripe and spicy, with a juicy core of citrus, pear and spice. Drinks well now. 1,258 cases made. • $8 • (02/29/96) • **85**
Chardonnay Mendocino Special 1994: Distinctive for its spicy grapefruit accent, this is a solid, fruit-driven Chardonnay, with lots of ripe pear and spice flavors. Drinks well now. 1,702 cases made. • $16 • (11/30/96) • **88**
Edelzwicker California 1995: Charming. This is off-dry and fruity, with spicy apricot and apple flavors that linger on the finish. 1,471 cases made. • $7 • (10/31/96) • **85**
Edelzwicker Mendocino 1993 • $6 • (12/31/94) • **86**
Gewürztraminer Anderson Valley Dry 1996: Firmly textured, with a classy blend of spice, litchi, citrus, grapefruit and apple flavors. Bright acidity keeps the finish long and refreshing. Drink now. 5,418 cases made. • $14 • (06/30/98) • **89**
Gewürztraminer Anderson Valley Dry 1995: Soft and polished, shining some pretty litchi and citrus flavors through the hints of rose petal on the off-dry finish. 1,354 cases made. • $14 • (04/30/97) • **87**
Gewürztraminer Anderson Valley Dry 1994 • $11 • (05/31/96) • **88**
Gewürztraminer Anderson Valley Dry 1993 • $9 • (02/28/95) • **84**
Gewürztraminer California Dry Cuvée Traditional 1995: Extraordinary balance and flavor, with finesse and charm. Bright and floral, with lots of pineapple, citrus and spice flavors competing for attention. Finish is dry and inviting. 3,323 cases made. • $11 • (04/30/97) • **90**
Gewürztraminer Late Harvest Anderson Valley Sweet 1989 • $12 • (04/30/91) • **86**
Gewürztraminer Late Harvest Anderson Valley Sweet Cluster Selected 1989 • $15/375ml • (03/15/92) • **86**
Gewürztraminer Late Harvest Anderson Valley Vineyard Selection 1986 • $19 • (02/28/89) • **93**
Gewürztraminer Late Harvest North Coast Sweet 1991 • $14 • (12/31/93) • **90**
Muscat Blanc Anderson Valley Dry 1996: A dry Muscat, still redolent of litchi, lemons, peaches and spice. It's got a lot of character, perhaps too much for dinner, but do try it as an apéritif. Drink now. 301 cases made. • $14 • (06/30/98) • **85**

Muscat Blanc Anderson Valley Dry 1995: Dry, spicy and steely. Not a frou-frou Muscat, but one with a little backbone and mineral character, like a Muscat from Alsace. 160 cases made. • $14 • (04/30/97) • **85**
Petits Villages Mendocino 1993 • $8 • (04/30/95) • **83**
Pinot Gris Anderson Valley 1995: Soft and ever-so-slightly syrupy, with honey, walnut and melon flavors that hover on the finish. 567 cases made. • $14 • (04/30/97) • **83**
Pinot Gris Anderson Valley 1994 • $12 • (11/30/95) • **85**
Pinot Gris Anderson Valley 1993 • $8/375ml • (12/31/94) • **87**
Pinot Noir Anderson Valley 1984 • $12 • (01/31/88) • **91**
Pinot Noir Anderson Valley 1982 • $9 • (04/15/87) • **82**
Pinot Noir Anderson Valley Clone 54 1992 • $12 • (11/30/94) • **87**
Pinot Noir Anderson Valley Cuvée 90/91 NV • $9 • (02/28/94) BB • **83**
Pinot Noir Anderson Valley Deep End Blend 1989 • $18 • (02/28/93) • **88**
Pinot Noir Anderson Valley Méthode à l'Ancienne 1994: An openly fruity style, ripe and intense, brimming with juicy black cherry, wild berry, currant and spice flavors that linger on the finish. Mildly tannic; drink now to 2002. 2,575 cases made. • $18 • (02/28/98) • **88**
Pinot Noir Anderson Valley Méthode à l'Ancienne 1993: From one of the most respected and most consistent names in Anderson Valley wines comes this mature, well-focused red. With its complex array of black cherry, tea, sage, earth and mushroom notes and a dash of tannin, it's at a great drinking stage through 1999. 3,068 cases made. • $17 • (05/15/97) SS • **90**
Pinot Noir Anderson Valley Méthode à l'Ancienne 1992 • $15 • (03/31/96) • **85**
Pinot Noir Anderson Valley Méthode à l'Ancienne 1991 • $15 • (12/31/94) • **86**
Pinot Noir Anderson Valley Méthode à l'Ancienne 1990: An understated style that serves up rich cherry, mushroom, earth and spice flavors with a soft, fleshy aftertaste. Tasted from magnum. Drink now. • $15/1.5 liter • (03/31/97) • **88**
Pinot Noir Anderson Valley Méthode à l'Ancienne 1989 • $15 • (02/28/93) • **87**
Pinot Noir Anderson Valley Méthode à l'Ancienne 1988 • $14 • (03/31/92) • **89**
Pinot Noir Anderson Valley Méthode à l'Ancienne 1987 • $14 • (04/30/91) • **85**
Pinot Noir Anderson Valley Méthode à l'Ancienne 1986: A delicate style that's aged well, with hints of dried cherry, earth, spice, smoke and mushroom flavors. Most of the tannins having faded, it's ready to drink. • $14/1.5 liter • (03/31/97) • **88**
Pinot Noir Anderson Valley Méthode à l'Ancienne 1985 • $14 • (02/28/89) • **85**
Pinot Noir Anderson Valley Méthode à l'Ancienne Unfiltered 1994: Still young, tight and tannic, with a slightly green, tealike accent to the plum and black cherry flavors. Needs time to soften; perhaps the greenness will settle into the wine's mainstream flavors. Best from 1999 to 2004. 1,104 cases made. • $19 • (03/31/98) • **87**
Pinot Noir Anderson Valley Table Wine 1993 • $10 • (12/31/95) • **81**
Pinot Noir Anderson Valley Whole Berry Fermentation 1987 • $9 • (02/28/89) • **81**
Pinot Noir Mendocino 1995: Elegant, showing a spicy, earthy edge to the cherry and wild berry flavors, finishing with supple tannins and good length. A terrific buy in first-class Pinot Noir. 2,057 cases made. • $13 • (10/15/97) • **88**
Pinot Noir Mendocino 1994: Elegant, with pretty black cherry, ripe plum and spice flavors. Finishes with supple tannins, good length and a smoky, toasty note from oak. An excellent value. 1,166 cases made. • $12 • (12/15/96) • **87**
Sauvignon Blanc Mendocino Cuvée 128 1996: A heady blend of lemon-lime and grapefruit essences with a powerful, fruit-driven follow-up. It's not shy, packed with pear, hazelnut, orange and peach flavors, and is lots of fun to drink. 1,583 cases made. • $13 • (03/31/98) • **90**
Sauvignon Blanc Mendocino Cuvée 128 1995: Bright and zingy, with well-articulated passion fruit and green berry flavors that remain lively through the floral, peppery finish. 1,334 cases made. • $12 • (04/30/97) • **89**
Sauvignon Blanc Mendocino Cuvée 128 1994 • $11 • (02/29/96) • **90**
Sauvignon Blanc Mendocino Cuvée 128 1993 • $10 • (04/30/95) • **88**
White Riesling Anderson Valley 1994: Crisp, bright peach and floral flavors, with a distinct stalky character to the finish. 1,000 cases made. • $9 • (07/31/96) • **81**
White Riesling Anderson Valley Late Harvest Very Sweet Cluster Select 1994: Ripe orange and apricot flavors have a strong, spicy bite. The finish is sweet, but not cloying thanks to the spiciness. 297 cases made. • $20/375ml • (04/30/97) • **87**
White Riesling Anderson Valley Late Harvest Cluster Selected 1985 • $10/375ml • (05/15/87) • **81**
White Riesling Anderson Valley Late Harvest Sweet 1994: Frankly sweet but balanced, with enough racy acidity to showcase the pineapple, honey and apricot flavors with great style. Finish is long and luxuriant. Delicious now, it should keep improving through 2000 to 2004. 369 cases made. • $14 • (10/31/96) • **93**
White Riesling Anderson Valley Late Harvest Sweet Cluster Selected 1989 • $15 • (03/31/92) • **83**
White Riesling Anderson Valley Late Harvest Sweet Cluster Selected 1986 • $25 • (03/31/90) • **85**
Zinfandel Mendocino 1993 • $15 • (03/31/96) • **83**
Zinfandel Mendocino 1992 • $15 • (02/28/95) • **85**
Zinfandel Mendocino 1991 • $14 • (03/31/94) • **86**

NAYLOR | PENNSYLVANIA

Chambourcin York County 1986 • $10 • (02/29/92) • **70**
Dessert York County Ekem 1990 • $9 • (02/29/92) • **77**

NEGOCIANTS, THE | CALIFORNIA

Cabernet Sauvignon Napa Valley 1990 • $10 • (03/31/94) • **85**
Chardonnay Central Coast 1993 • $7 • (02/28/95) • **74**
Merlot Napa Valley Reserve 1992 • $8 • (03/31/95) • **84**

NELSON ESTATE | CALIFORNIA

Cabernet Franc Sonoma County 1990 • $15 • (02/28/95) • **78**
Cabernet Franc Sonoma County 1987 • $16 • (04/30/91) • **82**

NEUHARTH | WASHINGTON

Merlot Washington 1991 • $14 • (09/30/94) • **71**

NEVADA CITY | CALIFORNIA

Cabernet Sauvignon Sierra Foothills Nevada County 1989 • $11/3.(11/15/92) • **81**
Chardonnay Nevada County Barrel Fermented 1993 • $11 • (07/31/95) • **86**
Claret Nevada County The Director's Reserve 1989 • $15 • (05/31/92) • **83**
Claret Sierra Foothills The Directors' Reserve 1990 • $14 • (11/15/93) • **79**
Merlot Nevada County 1994: Starting off with cola, herb and celery notes, this one strikes an unusual pose at first. Anise, cedar and smoke flavors follow nicely, though, with a finish that's a bit short. 310 cases made. • $14 • (09/30/97) • **84**
Merlot Nevada County 1989 • $14 • (05/31/92) • **80**
Merlot Sierra Foothills 1991 • $14 • (09/15/94) • **74**
Zinfandel Sierra Foothills 1991 • $9 • (09/30/93) • **85**
Zinfandel Sierra Foothills 1990 • $8 • (10/15/92) • **84**

NEVADA COUNTY WINE GUILD | CALIFORNIA

Pinot Noir Nevada County 1991 • $11 • (02/28/93) • **70**

NEW LAND | NEW YORK

Pinot Noir Finger Lakes Reserve 1993 • $15 • (06/30/95) • **82**

NEWLAN | CALIFORNIA

Cabernet Sauvignon Napa Valley 1994: A pleasant blend of cedar, herb, anise, spice and plum flavors. The tannins are smooth and the finish is moderate. Drink now. 512 cases made. • $19 • (10/15/97) • **87**
Cabernet Sauvignon Napa Valley 1993: A dusty, fragrant and focused wine, rich in cedar, spice, currant and plum flavors. Finish is a bit short, but it's still a pretty package. 716 cases made. • $19 • (09/15/97) • **87**
Cabernet Sauvignon Napa Valley 1991 • $16 • (11/30/95) • **89**
Cabernet Sauvignon Napa Valley 1990 • $26 • (02/28/95) • **86**
Cabernet Sauvignon Napa Valley 1988 • $16 • (02/28/95) • **84**
Cabernet Sauvignon Napa Valley 1987 • $15 • (11/15/92) • **88**
Cabernet Sauvignon Napa Valley 1986 • $15 • (04/30/91) • **89**
Cabernet Sauvignon Napa Valley 1985 • $15 • (03/31/90) • **87**
Century Selection Napa Valley 1989 • $11 • (11/30/92) • **78**

Chardonnay Napa Valley 1995: Has a strong grasslike edge to its apple flavors. Not as charming as it could be. 1,021 cases made. • $15 • (07/31/97) • **81**
Johannisberg Riesling Late Harvest Napa Valley 1993 • $22 • (12/31/95) • **94**
Johannisberg Riesling Late Harvest Napa Valley 1992 • $22/375ml • (04/30/95) • **88**
Johannisberg Riesling Late Harvest Napa Valley 1991 • $20/375ml • (12/31/93) • **89**
Pinot Noir Central Coast 1995: Hints of leather, plum, cedar and spice start this off nicely but lose focus, ceding to a rough texture and a slightly bitter finish. 1,500 cases made. • $14 • (09/15/97) • **83**
Pinot Noir Napa County School House Vieilles Vignes 1991 • $25 • (03/31/95) • **79**
Pinot Noir Napa Valley 1995: Plummy cola flavors are the profile here. It's pretty bright for Pinot, but finishes with a delicate anise edge. 1,375 cases made. • $19 • (02/28/98) • **85**
Pinot Noir Napa Valley 1994: Simple in style, with a modest range of dried cherry, floral and cedar flavors. Not as inspiring as many '94s scoring higher. 1,222 cases made. • $19 • (12/15/96) • **81**
Pinot Noir Napa Valley 1993 • $18 • (02/29/96) • **87**
Pinot Noir Napa Valley 1992 • $18 • (03/31/95) • **83**
Pinot Noir Napa Valley 1991 • $18 • (02/28/94) • **80**
Pinot Noir Napa Valley 1989 • $18 • (02/28/93) • **87**
Pinot Noir Napa Valley 1988 • $18 • (11/15/91) • **81**
Pinot Noir Napa Valley 1987 • $16 • (03/31/90) • **81**
Pinot Noir Napa Valley 1985 • $12 • (06/15/88) • **88**
Pinot Noir Napa Valley Napa-Villages 1991 • $10 • (03/31/95) • **81**
Pinot Noir Napa Valley Reserve 1994: Straightforward style, with hints of cedar, cherry and berry, but it remains austere. May benefit from short-term cellaring. 255 cases made. • $28 • (02/28/97) • **83**
Pinot Noir Napa Valley Reserve 1993 • $28 • (05/15/96) • **82**
Pinot Noir Napa Valley Reserve 1991 • $28 • (02/28/94) • **84**
Pinot Noir Napa Valley Vieilles Vignes 1986 • $19 • (03/31/90) • **76**
Pinot Noir Napa Valley Vieilles Vignes 1985 • $16 • (06/15/88) • **80**
Zinfandel Napa Valley 1995: A jazzy, earthy style of Zin, with a distinct gamy streak running through the black cherry and vanilla notes. A touch of herb on the finish. Best in 1999. 916 cases made. • $16 • (12/15/97) • **84**
Zinfandel Napa Valley 1994: Young, rich and complex, with a pretty array of earthy currant, plum and wild berry flavors. Finish reveals the thick, chewy tannins and a mineral-and-leather edge. 1,550 cases made. • $16 • (04/30/97) • **89**
Zinfandel Napa Valley 1992 • $14 • (10/15/94) • **86**
Zinfandel Napa Valley 1991 • $15 • (03/31/94) • **86**
Zinfandel Napa Valley 1990 • $12 • (09/30/93) • **88**

NEWTON | CALIFORNIA

Cabernet Sauvignon Napa County 1991: A mouthful of Cabernet that's smooth, ripe, rich and harmonious, with tiers of currant, black cherry, chocolate, berry, spice and cedar. Finishes with a firm tannic wall, but the tannins are plush and ripe. Tempting now, but worthy of cellaring into 1999. • $NA • (01/01/97) • **93**
Cabernet Sauvignon Napa Valley 1994: Tightly wound, with a firm tannic wall built around the core of currant, anise, cherry and berry-laced flavors. Finishes with complex coffee and leather flavors and a dash of fruit. • $30 • (01/31/98) • **89**
Cabernet Sauvignon Napa Valley 1993: A dense, rich and chewy style with a pronounced leatherlike edge to the core of currant and earth flavors. Some may find the tannins overbearing. 1,000 cases made. • $25 • (05/31/97) • **87**
Cabernet Sauvignon Napa Valley 1989 • $19 • (11/15/93) • **84**
Cabernet Sauvignon Napa Valley 1988 • $17 • (11/15/92) • **87**
Cabernet Sauvignon Napa Valley 1987 • $17 • (11/15/91) • **87**
Cabernet Sauvignon Napa Valley 1986 • $16 • (05/31/90) • **91**
Cabernet Sauvignon Napa Valley 1985 • $31 Ⓐ • (01/31/89) • **89**
Cabernet Sauvignon Napa Valley 1984 • $14 • (09/30/87) • **91**
Cabernet Sauvignon Napa Valley 1983 • $19 Ⓐ • (04/15/87) SS • **96**
Cabernet Sauvignon Napa Valley 1981 • $13 • (12/16/84) • **91**
Chardonnay Napa Valley 1994: Combines ripe fig and pear flavors with light smoky notes from oak. Develops more nuances on the creamy finish. Elegant and well-crafted. • $19 • (03/31/96) • **90**

Key: SS—Spectator Selection CS—Cellar Selection HR—Highly Recommended BB—Best Buy $NA—Price not available Ⓐ—Auction Price (BT)—Barrel Tasting
Dates in parentheses indicate the issues in which the ratings were published.

Chardonnay Napa Valley Unfiltered 1995: Smooth, rich and spicy. A delicious, fragrant, effusively fruity style that packs in lots of apple, pear, fig and melon flavors while maintaining a sense of elegance and finesse. • $NA • (01/31/98) • **91**
Chardonnay Napa Valley Unfiltered 1994: A wonderful 1994. Complex, with rich, spicy accents to the ripe pear, melon and apple flavors. Picks up a nice oak-induced dimension on the finish, where the flavors fold together nicely. 4,000 cases made. • $30 • (02/28/97) • **92**
Chardonnay Napa-Sonoma Counties 1996: Delicious, rich and elegant describes this Napa-Sonoma blend. It's a smooth, ripe and creamy Chardonnay, brimming with lots of ripe fig and pear flavors accented by a tasty dash of hazelnut. Finishes with a long, full aftertaste. 6,000 cases made. • $22 • (11/15/97) SS • **91**
Chardonnay Napa-Sonoma Counties 1995: A wonderful Chardonnay blended from two of California's more impressive regions, this silky textured wine is elegant, concentrated and sophisticated, with smooth, ripe, rich and creamy layers of fig, pear and apricot flavors and a dash of toasty oak. A delight to drink. 6,000 cases made. • $20 • (05/15/97) SS • **93**
Claret Napa Valley 1995: Solid, with appealing cherry, spice, cedar and light toasty oak shadings, turning supple and complex on the aftertaste. Drinks well now. • $NA • (11/30/97) • **87**
Claret Napa Valley 1994: An understated, middle-of-the-road style, with modest currant, cherry and plum flavors that lack focus. Finishes with firm tannins and an odd, woody quality. 9,000 cases made. • $16 • (02/28/97) • **85**
Claret Napa Valley 1992 • $13 • (11/15/94) • **88**
Claret Napa Valley 1991 • $12 • (06/15/93) • **87**
Claret Napa Valley 1990 • $12 • (08/31/92) • **83**
Claret Napa Valley 1988 • $11 • (03/15/91) • **89**
Merlot Napa Valley 1995: Tight and firm, with a narrow band of currant, cedar, oak and spicy nuances. Never really unfolds to reveal extra dimensions of depth, richness or concentration. Drink now through 2000. • $NA • (01/31/98) • **86**
Merlot Napa Valley 1994: Ripe, smooth and supple, with a rich core of currant, berry, cherry and cedary oak flavors that fan out on the finish, where the tannins are tight and spicy. 6,000 cases made. • $25 • (05/15/97) • **87**
Merlot Napa Valley 1989 • $20 • (05/31/92) • **88**
Merlot Napa Valley 1987 • $17 • (07/31/90) • **81**
Merlot Napa Valley 1986 • $15 • (12/31/88) • **83**
Merlot Napa Valley 1985 • $14 • (03/31/88) • **93**
Merlot Napa Valley 1983 • $12 • (02/28/87) • **90**
Merlot Napa Valley 1982 • $12 • (10/01/85) • **83**
Merlot Napa Valley 1981 • $13 • (12/16/84) • **91**
Merlot Napa Valley Special Cuvée 1994: Lean and trim, with a narrow band of cedar, currant and berry flavors. Well-balanced, with firm tannins and good length. Drink now through 2001. 3,200 cases made. • $22 • (05/15/97) • **87**
Pinot Noir Napa Valley Special Cuvée 1995: Clean and simple, it offers a pleasant core of black cherry, herb and sage, finishing with a spicy edge and clean tannins. New from Newton. • $NA • (01/31/98) • **86**

NEYERS | CALIFORNIA

Cabernet Franc Napa Valley 1987 • $16 • (11/15/90) • **79**
Cabernet Sauvignon Napa Valley 1995: Tightly wound, with firm plum, currant, cedar and spice, but the supple texture and rich flavors will need time to soften. Best from 2002 through 2009. 775 cases made. • $40 • (05/31/98) • **88**
Cabernet Sauvignon Napa Valley 1988 • $15 • (11/15/91) • **82**
Cabernet Sauvignon Napa Valley 1985 • $14 • (07/15/89) • **83**
Cabernet Sauvignon Napa Valley 1984 • $13 • (04/30/88) • **75**
Cabernet Sauvignon Napa Valley 1983 • $12 • (08/31/87) • **79**
Chardonnay Carneros 1996: Tight and flinty up front, with dashes of lemon and spice, it slowly unfolds to reveal more facets, with pretty ripe pear, fig and smoky oak flavors that linger on the aftertaste. 1,991 cases made. • $25 • (11/15/97) • **92**
Chardonnay Carneros 1995: Ripe, rich and creamy, with tiers of spicy pear, honey, apricot and light oak flavors. A complex and appealing effort from Neyers, which has made a real turnaround in quality over the past few vintages. Ready to drink. 1,500 cases made. • $22 • (11/30/96) • **90**
Chardonnay Carneros 1993 • $16 • (02/28/95) • **86**
Chardonnay Napa Valley 1996: Elegant and complex, with ripe pear, spice, apple and citrus flavors, and a pretty overlay of smoky, toasty oak, which adds a nice dimension. 1,011 cases made. • $25 • (11/15/97) • **91**
Chardonnay Sonoma Coast Thieriot Vineyard 1996: Wonderful Chardonnay. Intense and lively, with a complex, concentrated core of ripe fig, peach,

pear and melon. Finishes with a long, lively aftertaste and loads of flavor. 227 cases made. • $35 • (11/15/97) • **93**

Chardonnay Sonoma Coast Thieriot Vineyard 1995: An impressive offering, this is a bold, ripe and complex style that packs in lots of flavor, with hints of ripe pear, apple, pineapple and spice, and a dash of oak on the finish. 140 cases made. • $30 • (12/15/96) • **90**

Merlot Napa Valley 1995: Dark, intense and concentrated, with a complex core of currant and berry flavors, turning supple and harmonious on the finish. This is a big, ripe, full-bodied wine that's best cellared into 1999. 1,124 cases made. • $25 • (11/15/97) • **91**

Merlot Napa Valley 1994: Young, tight and firmly tannic, but the earthy currant, mineral and cedary oak flavors are rich and concentrated. Drink now. 1,100 cases made. • $24 • (10/15/96) • **86**

Merlot Napa Valley 1992 • $18 • (05/15/95) • **84**

Merlot Napa Valley Neyers Ranch-Conn Valley 1995: Well-oaked, with pretty spice and toasty notes, and a supple, rich and complex center of ripe plum and currant. Finishes with a long, concentrated aftertaste that echos plum and wild berry. 275 cases made. • $35 • (11/15/97) • **91**

Zinfandel Contra Costa County Pato Vineyard 1996: A big, ripe, intense and juicy style, with a slight vinegary edge to the jammy cherry and wild berry. Finishes with a hot note and a hint of prune. Drink now through 2002. • $25 • (06/15/98) • **87**

Zinfandel Contra Costa County Pato Vineyard 1995: An exotic style, rich and flavorful, well-oaked and offering lots of juicy plum, wild berry, cherry and vanilla flavors that pick up meaty, smoky, anise notes on the finish. Impressive. 650 cases made. • $20 • (06/30/97) • **92**

NICHELINI | CALIFORNIA

Cabernet Sauvignon Napa Valley 1991: Clean and correct, with a modest band of cedar and berry flavors finishing with crisp tannins. Can stand short-term cellaring. 300 cases made. • $17 • (11/30/96) • **82**

Cabernet Sauvignon Napa Valley 1988 • $15 • (11/15/93) • **81**

Cabernet Sauvignon Napa Valley Joseph A. Nichelini Vineyards 1989 • $12 • (06/15/95) • **77**

Merlot Napa Valley 1992 • $20 • (03/31/96) • **81**

Merlot Napa Valley Joseph A. Nichelini Vineyard 1994: Leathery, bitter flavors mar this chewy red. May be better after 2000. 310 cases made. • $18 • (03/31/98) • **79**

Sauvignon Blanc Napa Valley Joseph A. Nichelini Vineyards 1993 • $9 • (05/15/95) • **82**

Sauvignon Vert Napa Valley 1996: This bright wine is marked by an unusually fruity, grapey quality. Pleasant as a simple quaffer. 700 cases made. • $12 • (09/15/97) • **82**

Sauvignon Vert Napa Valley 1995: Has a bit of nectarine flavor in its favor, but otherwise like a canned grapefruit juice, complete with the racy acidity and tinny quality. 212 cases made. • $10 • (08/31/96) • **80**

Sauvignon Vert Napa Valley Joseph A. Nichelini Vineyard 1994 • $9 • (05/31/96) • **83**

Zinfandel Napa Valley 1993: Leather, tar and spice notes introduce this brightly styled red, marked by cedar, licorice and black cherry flavors. 800 cases made. • $15 • (09/15/97) • **87**

Zinfandel Napa Valley 1992: Supple, ripe and harmonious, with lots of spice, cedar and pepper notes adding dimension to the currant and wild berry flavors. Delicious aftertaste. 1,000 cases made. • $14 • (04/30/97) • **88**

Zinfandel Napa Valley 1991 • $12 • (03/31/96) • **87**

Zinfandel Napa Valley Centennial Vintage 1990 • $10 • (06/15/95) • **79**

Zinfandel Napa Valley Joseph A. Nichelini Vineyard 1994: Brimming with spices like clove and cinnamon, it also serves up a vanilla-tinged core of black cherry and licorice. Cedary aromas conjure visions of fresh wine in barrels. 400 cases made. • $15 • (03/31/98) • **87**

NICHOL'S, DAVE | CALIFORNIA

Cabernet Sauvignon Napa Valley Stags Leap Hillside Personal Selection Reserve 1991: Big, ripe and a touch leathery, with an earthy accent to the currant and cherry flavors. Finish shows prune, anise and cedary flavors. Best after 1999. 400 cases made. • $18 • (09/15/96) • **83**

Cabernet Sauvignon Napa Valley Stags Leap Hillside Reserve 1993: Dark, ripe and intense. The rich core of currant, anise, cedar and herb flavors is well focused, and the finish shows a nice burst of fruit and toasty oak. Best after 1999. 600 cases made. • $18 • (09/15/96) • **89**

NICHOLS | CALIFORNIA

Chardonnay Arroyo Grande Valley Talley Vineyard 1996: On the tart side, with a crisp lemon-lime streak. A lean and flinty style that's well made and well focused. Short-term cellaring is advised. Drink now through 2002. 639 cases made. • $28 • (07/31/98) • **88**

Chardonnay Arroyo Grande Valley Talley Vineyards 1995: A ripe, spicy, complex and beautifully crafted wine that deftly balances its ripe pear, melon, apple and light oak shadings. On the finish, the flavors linger, with a pleasant earthiness. 420 cases made. • $28 • (05/15/97) • **92**

Chardonnay Arroyo Grande Valley Talley Vineyards 1994: Bold, ripe and juicy notes of rich pear, honey, peach and nectarine pick up toasty, smoky oak on the finish, where the flavors linger on and on. 1,100 cases made. • $23 • (04/30/96) • **92**

Chardonnay Arroyo Grande Valley Talley Vineyards 1993 • $20 • (12/31/95) • **87**

Chardonnay Central Coast Blend 1996: Clean and well-focused, with crisp citrus, pear, light oak and hazelnut shadings. Offers excellent depth, richness and concentration. May be better with time in the bottle; try now through 2000. • $NA • (03/31/98) • **89**

Chardonnay Central Coast Reserve 1996: Starts out lean and tight, with a crisp band of citrus, pear and lemon that slowly unfolds to reveal more depth, intensity and complexity. Finishes with a long, mineral and toasty oak aftertaste. 265 cases made. • $33 • (02/28/98) • **88**

Chardonnay Edna Valley Paragon Vineyard 1996: Tightly wound, with a narrow band of citrus, especially grapefruit, flavors dominating the pear and melon notes. Needs some time in the bottle to open up. 290 cases made. • $28 • (03/31/98) • **87**

Chardonnay Santa Barbara County Bien Nacido Vineyards 1996: Lean and crisp, with a trim range of citrus, pear, lemon and earthy flavors that are well focused and lively, with good intensity and depth. Tightly wound, it may show more breadth and complexity with age. Drink now to 2000. 340 cases made. • $26 • (03/31/98) • **87**

Chardonnay Santa Barbara County Cottonwood Canyon Vineyard 1996: Tightly wound and well focused, with a core of citrus and pear flavors that's intense and concentrated. Best to cellar short-term to let the acidity subside, but there's lot to like in this wine. 260 cases made. • $30 • (11/30/97) • **91**

Pinot Blanc Arroyo Grande Valley La Colline Vineyard 1996: Smooth and spicy, with flavors of ripe pear, fig and melon, picking up dashes of citrus and oak on the finish. 195 cases made. • $21 • (04/30/98) • **86**

Pinot Noir Arroyo Grande Valley La Colline Vineyards 1996: Young, tight, complex and tannic, with layers of cherry, plum, tomato and berry. Finishes with a zesty, spicy quality, but then the tannins fold in, giving it an earthy aftertaste. Drinks well now through 1999. 105 cases made. • $33 • (02/28/98) • **87**

Pinot Noir Central Coast Blend 1996: Smooth and polished, with a pretty core of earthy cherry, spice, wild berry and leather notes, turning complex on the aftertaste, where the flavors fan out. Drink now to 2001. 190 cases made. • $36 • (02/28/98) • **88**

Pinot Noir Central Coast Reserve 1996: Shows off a smoky, meaty edge before the dried cherry and berry flavors emerge, filling in the gaps and expanding on the palate, turning complex and rich on the finish, sailing on and on. Drink now to 2001. 265 cases made. • $45 • (02/28/98) • **89**

Pinot Noir Edna Valley Paragon Vineyard 1996: Smooth, ripe and supple, with an array of plum, cherry, wild berry and spice. Shows a lot of rich fruit and plenty of elegance and finesse. Drink now through 2002. 150 cases made. • $28 • (02/28/98) • **89**

Pinot Noir Monterey County Pisoni Vineyards 1996: Dark in color and rich in flavor, with complex earthy currant, plum and mushroomlike flavors, picking up a spicy edge. Finishes with fine length and finely integrated tannins. 420 cases made. • $42 • (02/28/98) • **89**

Pinot Noir Santa Barbara County Cottonwood Canyon Vineyard 1996: Leans toward the vegetal side of Pinot Noir, with spicy cherry, earth and leather notes that turn elegant and supple on the finish. 645 cases made. • $33 • (02/28/98) • **87**

Pinot Noir Santa Barbara County Sierra Madre Vineyard 1995: Dark, ripe, rich and exotic, with a tightly focused core of tart berry and cherry flavors, finishing with a spice and cedar aftertaste. Distinct, with a bold personality. Drink now or cellar into 1999. Tasted twice with consistent notes. 240 cases made. • $32 • (02/28/97) • **87**

Pinot Noir Santa Barbara County Sierra Madre Vineyard 1994 • $24 • (04/30/96) • **89**

Pinot Noir Santa Barbara County Sierra Madre Vineyard 1993 • $24 • (12/31/95) • **91**

NIEBAUM-COPPOLA | CALIFORNIA

Cabernet Franc Napa Valley Francis Coppola Family Wines 1995: Ripe, smooth and supple, with lots of pretty flavors of spice, currant, wild berry and cherry, and just the right touch of tannins. 901 cases made. • $20 • (12/15/97) • **88**
Cabernet Franc Napa Valley Francis Coppola Family Wines 1991 • $14 • (01/31/95) • **81**
Cabernet Franc Napa Valley Francis Coppola Family Wines 1990 • $12 • (03/31/93) • **84**
Chardonnay Napa Valley Francis Coppola Family Wines 1995: Smooth and creamy, with a dash of Viognier that adds a spicy dimension. It doesn't rely on heavy oak for flavor, emphasizing instead the ripe pear and citrus notes. 95 percent Chardonnay and 5 percent Viognier. 2,376 cases made. • $18 • (11/15/96) • **87**
Merlot Napa Valley Francis Coppola Family Wines 1995: Firm, rich and concentrated, with crisp black cherry and blackberry flavors, touches of mineral and spice. Finishes with firm tannins, herb and cedary oak flavors. Needs short-term cellaring; best 1999 to 2003. 1,850 cases made. • $32 • (05/15/98) • **88**
Merlot Napa Valley Francis Coppola Family Wines 1994: Remarkably supple and elegant, with a juicy core of ripe black cherry, plum and currant flavors that pick up nuances of spice and herb. The tannins are soft and fleshy and the finish lingers on and on. 1,045 cases made. • $24 • (04/30/97) • **92**
Merlot Napa Valley Francis Coppola Family Wines 1993 • $18 • (05/15/96) • **89**
Merlot Napa Valley Francis Coppola Family Wines 1991 • $16 • (10/15/93) • **86**
Rubicon Napa Valley 1990 • $35 • (12/15/95) • **90**
Rubicon Napa Valley 1989 • $30 • (11/15/94) • **83**
Rubicon Napa Valley 1988 • $30 • (11/15/94) • **83**
Rubicon Napa Valley 1987: Dry, austere and leathery, this is losing its fruit, offering only a modest hint of ripe Cabernet flavor. Not going anywhere. • $30 • (12/15/97) • **84**
Rubicon Napa Valley 1986: A curiously tight, austere and crisply tannic wine—it hasn't evolved into the complex wine it appeared it might. It still tastes ruggedly tannic and oaky, the currant and earthy flavors still struggle to emerge. 3,500 cases made. • $NA • (12/15/96) • **85**
Rubicon Napa Valley 1985 • $29 Ⓐ • (11/15/90) • **87**
Rubicon Napa Valley 1982 • $44 Ⓐ • (10/15/89) • **88**
Rubicon Napa Valley 1981 • $35 • (11/15/88) • **89**
Rubicon Napa Valley 1980 • $34 Ⓐ • (10/15/87) • **92**
Rubicon Napa Valley 1979 • $38 Ⓐ • (02/28/87) • **81**
Rubicon Napa Valley 1978 • $53 • (11/15/92) • **88**
Rubicon Napa Valley 1977 • $NA • (02/28/87) • **93**
Rubicon Rutherford 1996: Dense and well focused, with a core of earthy currant, chocolate and black cherry flavors. Finishes with firm, chewy tannins. • $NA • (06/15/97) (BT) • **90-94**
Rubicon Rutherford 1994: A well-regarded blend of Cabernet Sauvignon, Merlot and Cabernet Franc, this year's version shows impressive balance and finesse. Firm and tightly wound, with a sharply focused, deeply concentrated core of currant, black cherry, cedar, toast and spice flavors, this is a muscular yet polished wine that should be best from 2002 through 2010. 3,481 cases made. • $65 • (06/15/98) CS • **92**
Rubicon Rutherford 1993: Distinct for its minty, herbal and earthy flavors, it slowly unveils more interesting currant and cedary oak notes. But it's intense and tannic from start to finish, turning dry on the aftertaste. Best from 1999 through 2004. 2,800 cases made. • $55 • (05/15/98) • **90**
Rubicon Rutherford 1992: Distinctly minty, firm and austere, slowly evolving into a more supple and flavorful wine, with a core of currant and berry. A ruggedly tannic young wine, it will need cellaring until 2002. 2,956 cases made. • $50 • (05/31/97) • **92**
Rubicon Rutherford 1991: Firm and focused, with a dense core of smoky currant, plum, black cherry, anise and tar flavors. Finishes with a wall of tannins, but they're soft and they let the fruit come through. Best to cellar into 2000. 1,165 cases made. • $40 • (09/15/96) CS • **91**
Zinfandel Napa Valley Edizione Pennino 1995: Elegant and refined, ripe, smooth and polished, with just the right proportion of black cherry, plum and blackberry flavors and spicy, minty nuances. Finishes with a burst of fruit and supple tannins. Drink now through 2002. 2,800 cases made. • $24 • (03/31/98) SS • **91**
Zinfandel Napa Valley Edizione Pennino 1994: Big, ripe and intense, with a wild, minty streak to its earthy cherry and berry flavors. Folds together nicely on the finish, where the tannins turn supple. Drink now. 1,720 cases made. • $20 • (03/31/97) • **88**
Zinfandel Napa Valley Edizione Pennino 1993 • $16 • (10/15/95) • **87**
Zinfandel Napa Valley Edizione Pennino 1992 • $15 • (10/15/94) • **88**
Zinfandel Napa Valley Edizione Pennino 1991 • $14 • (10/15/94) • **88**
Zinfandel Napa Valley Edizione Pennino 1990 • $14 • (09/30/93) • **88**
Zinfandel Napa Valley Edizione Pennino 1989 • $14 • (09/30/93) • **87**

NIEBAUM, GUSTAVE | CALIFORNIA

Cabernet Sauvignon Napa Valley Mast Vineyard 1987 • $14 • (08/31/92) • **89**
Cabernet Sauvignon Napa Valley Reference 1989 • $11 • (07/31/92) • **85**
Cabernet Sauvignon Napa Valley Reference 1985 • $14 • (10/31/89) • **89**
Cabernet Sauvignon Napa Valley Tench Vineyard 1988 • $15 • (07/31/92) • **80**
Cabernet Sauvignon Napa Valley Tench Vineyard 1986 • $16 • (10/15/89) • **93**
Merlot Napa Valley Reference 1989 • $11 • (10/31/92) • **72**

NOCETO | CALIFORNIA

Sangiovese Shenandoah Valley 1995: Marked by unusual coffee, tea and earth notes, it packs a punch, but not as expected from this grape. Fairly rich, but somewhat heavy. Try now or hold. 1,633 cases made. • $12 • (10/15/97) • **85**
Sangiovese Shenandoah Valley 1994: Ripe and attractive layers of currant and black cherry flavors, with spice and anise notes. Well balanced, nicely focused and flavorful on the finish. 1,338 cases made. • $10 • (08/31/96) • **87**
Sangiovese Shenandoah Valley 1993 • $10 • (08/31/95) • **82**
Sangiovese Shenandoah Valley 1992 • $8 • (09/30/94) • **77**
Sangiovese Shenandoah Valley 1991 • $8 • (07/31/93) • **81**

NOMINEE | CALIFORNIA

Cabernet Sauvignon Napa Valley 1992 • $7 • (11/15/94) • **75**
Cabernet Sauvignon Napa Valley 1991 • $7 • (07/15/93) • **83**
Cabernet Sauvignon Paso Robles 1995: Ripe cherry flavors add some interest to this solid, early-drinking style of Cabernet. 4,000 cases made. • $8 • (12/31/97) • **82**
Cabernet Sauvignon Paso Robles 1994: Simple, with modest cherry flavors and spice notes. 4,000 cases made. • $8 • (11/30/96) • **78**
Cabernet Sauvignon Paso Robles 1993: Firm and tight, with a well-balanced band of currant, cedar and spice. 10,000 cases made. • $7 • (12/15/95) • **83**
Chardonnay Paso Robles 1996: Simple, crisp, flinty lemon flavors are straightforward. Not a lot of personality, but a good wine in a lighter style. 15,000 cases made. • $8 • (07/31/98) • **82**
Chardonnay Paso Robles 1994: Harmoniously plays its light, smooth spice and fruit flavors off a touch of toasty oak. Ready now. 32,000 cases made. • $7 • (12/15/95) • **83**
Chardonnay Paso Robles 1993 • $6 • (06/30/94) • **79**
Merlot Napa Valley 1992 • $8 • (09/15/94) • **83**

NORMAN | CALIFORNIA

Cabernet Sauvignon Paso Robles 1994: Bright and appealing for its grapey flavors, offering herb-scented currant and smoky notes on the crisp finish. Give it until 2000. 540 cases made. • $16 • (11/15/97) • **86**
Cabernet Sauvignon Paso Robles 1993: Young, tight and with earthy, leathery tannins, but just enough cherry and berry flavors come through for it to achieve balance. Drink now. 560 cases made. • $16 • (12/15/96) • **85**
Cabernet Sauvignon Paso Robles 1992 • $13 • (11/15/94) • **87**
Cabernet Sauvignon Paso Robles No Nonsense Red 1992 • $9 • (11/15/94) • **82**
Chardonnay Paso Robles 1995: Simple, straightforward stuff with a gamelike edge that doesn't fade. 940 cases made. • $15 • (07/31/97) • **80**
Chardonnay San Luis Obispo County 1994: Vibrant and fruity, sporting pretty pear, nectarine and tangerine flavors that turn elegant and refined on the finish. Especially attractive price. 600 cases made. • $12 • (05/15/96) • **88**
Claret Paso Robles No Nonsense Red 1995: A bit coarse, with tea and herb flavors most prominent. The fruit takes a backseat in this wine, squeaking

Key: SS—Spectator Selection CS—Cellar Selection HR—Highly Recommended BB—Best Buy $NA—Price not available Ⓐ—Auction Price (BT)—Barrel Tasting
Dates in parentheses indicate the issues in which the ratings were published.

blackberry and anise into the moderate finish. A blend of Cabernet Sauvignon, Merlot and Cabernet Franc. 670 cases made. • $14 • (10/31/97) • **81**

Claret Paso Robles No Nonsense Red 1994: On solid footing, with a nice core of ripe currant, berry, cedar and spice flavors that are well focused and linger on the finish. Medium-weight, and not too tannic. Drink now. 285 cases made. • $12 • (11/15/96) • **86**

Pinot Noir Paso Robles William Cain Vineyard 1995: Marked by strong core of cola and herb that branches out on the palate to reveal pretty plum, cherry, anise and spice flavors. Drink now or hold. 740 cases made. • $16 • (01/31/98) • **86**

Sauvignon Blanc Paso Robles Morrow Vineyard 1996: Zippy acidity and an intriguing core of flint, orange peel, grapefruit and clove mark this as a wine of interest. Firm and focused, it holds together nicely. 540 cases made. • $12 • (03/31/98) • **87**

Sauvignon Blanc Paso Robles Morrow Vineyard 1995: Smooth and a little spicy, with pleasant, mild flavors of apple and herb. 320 cases made. • $10 • (10/15/96) • **82**

Zinfandel Late Harvest Paso Robles 1994 • $15/375ml • (10/31/95) • **79**

Zinfandel Paso Robles 1993 • $13 • (10/15/95) • **90**

Zinfandel Paso Robles 1992 • $11 • (07/31/94) • **88**

Zinfandel Paso Robles The Classic 1995: Lean and crisp, with a narrow band of green, cedary Zinfandel flavors. Offers glimpses of tart wild berry and spice. Drink now. 906 cases made. • $16 • (06/15/98) • **83**

Zinfandel Paso Robles The Classic 1994 • $13 • (04/30/96) • **88**

Zinfandel Paso Robles The Monster 1994: A monster with a smile. Smooth and supple, with ripe cherry, plum and berry flavors that are rich, concentrated and well focused. Finishes with a lively aftertaste and a sense of harmony and finesse. 720 cases made. • $18 • (04/30/97) • **90**

NORTHSTAR | WASHINGTON

Merlot Columbia Valley 1994: Rich, ripe and welcoming up front, but then the tannins clamp down. Has some impressive plum and black cherry flavors, shaded with an earthy tobacco edge. Best from 1999. 1,029 cases made. • $50 • (12/15/97) • **88**

OAK FALLS | CALIFORNIA

Chardonnay Central Coast 1995: Soft and generous, with spice-accented nectarine and pear flavors. 3,000 cases made. • $9 • (07/31/97) • **83**

Merlot Napa Valley 1992 • $9 • (06/15/95) • **80**

Merlot Napa Valley Private Reserve 1990 • $8 • (03/31/93) • **82**

Sauvignon Blanc California 1993 • $4 • (02/28/95) • **76**

Zinfandel Amador County 1991 • $6 • (10/15/95) • **82**

OAK KNOLL | OREGON

Chardonnay Willamette Valley 1993 • $12 • (01/31/96) • **80**

Gewürztraminer Willamette Valley 1995: Has some ugly aspects, including a decadent, dead-flower taste. 428 cases made. • $8 • (02/28/97) • **73**

Pinot Gris Willamette Valley 1996: Broad in texture, almost resiny, with a slightly bitter edge to the generous melon and apple flavors. Needs food to soften it. 5,700 cases made. • $13 • (03/31/98) • **82**

Pinot Gris Willamette Valley 1995: A pleasantly soft white wine with some richness and pretty melon and almond notes on the delicate finish. 3,856 cases made. • $13 • (02/28/97) • **85**

Pinot Gris Willamette Valley 1994 • $10 • (01/31/96) • **86**

Pinot Noir Oregon Vintage Select 1983 • $20 • (02/15/90) • **78**

Pinot Noir Oregon Vintage Select 1982 • $25 • (02/15/90) • **77**

Pinot Noir Willamette Valley 1992 • $12 • (11/30/94) • **83**

Pinot Noir Willamette Valley 1991 • $12 • (03/15/94) • **83**

Pinot Noir Willamette Valley 1990 • $12 • (02/28/93) • **80**

Pinot Noir Willamette Valley 1989 • $12 • (02/28/93) • **70**

Pinot Noir Willamette Valley 1988 • $11 • (04/15/91) • **81**

Pinot Noir Willamette Valley Silver Anniversary Reserve 1994: Chocolate, leather and ripe berry flavors compete for attention in this artfully balanced wine. Its focused character lingers on the spicy finish. Best from 1999. 1,880 cases made. • $20 • (02/28/97) • **87**

Pinot Noir Willamette Valley Vintage Reserve 1994: Ripe and jazzy, with black cherry and berry flavors shaded with hints of smoke and bitter almond. A solid wine that needs cellar time; best from 1999 or 2000. 540 cases made. • $34 • (02/28/98) • **86**

Pinot Noir Willamette Valley Vintage Reserve 1992 • $24 • (01/31/96) • **85**

Pinot Noir Willamette Valley Vintage Reserve 1990 • $20 • (03/15/94) • **86**

Pinot Noir Willamette Valley Vintage Select 1989 • $18 • (02/28/93) • **79**

Pinot Noir Willamette Valley Vintage Select 1988 • $18 • (05/31/91) • **81**

Pinot Noir Willamette Valley Vintage Select 1987 • $18 • (02/15/90) • **77**

Pinot Noir Willamette Valley Vintage Select 1985 • $15 • (06/15/87) • **70**

Riesling Willamette Valley 1993 • $7 • (01/31/96) • **76**

OAK LANE | CALIFORNIA

Cabernet Sauvignon Napa Valley 1990: This is earthy—with a dirty, metallic accent and just a trace of fruit flavor. Unappealing. 670 cases made. • $10 • (11/30/96) • **71**

OAK RIDGE | CALIFORNIA

Chardonnay California Bighorn 1993 • $7 • (06/30/94) • **74**

Fumé Blanc California Swan Lake 1993 • $4 • (08/31/94) • **73**

OAKFORD | CALIFORNIA

Cabernet Sauvignon Napa Valley 1993: Already showing signs of drying out, with a slightly bitter edge to the plum and cherry flavors. The finish shows depth and length. Best over the next few years. 921 cases made. • $32 • (11/30/97) • **86**

Cabernet Sauvignon Napa Valley 1992: Complex aromas, an array of cherry, currant, anise and earthy notes, that follow through onto the palate. Finishes with firm, crisp tannins. Drink now or cellar into 1999. 1,000 cases made. • $30 • (11/15/96) • **89**

Cabernet Sauvignon Napa Valley 1991 • $30 • (12/15/95) • **88**

Cabernet Sauvignon Napa Valley 1990 • $25 • (11/15/94) • **88**

Cabernet Sauvignon Napa Valley 1989 • $25 • (11/15/94) • **88**

Cabernet Sauvignon Napa Valley 1988 • $25 • (11/15/94) • **87**

Cabernet Sauvignon Napa Valley 1987 • $25 • (11/15/90) • **91**

OAKVILLE BENCH | CALIFORNIA

Cabernet Sauvignon Napa County 1990 • $12 • (05/15/94) • **82**

Cabernet Sauvignon Napa Valley 1989 • $12 • (03/15/92) • **87**

OAKVILLE RANCH | CALIFORNIA

Cabernet Sauvignon Napa Valley 1994: Quite attractive, with juicy currant and plum flavors, pretty oak shadings. Turns complex on the finish, but could use a little more pizzazz. Drinkable now or cellar into 1999. 1,800 cases made. • $30 • (07/31/97) • **88**

Cabernet Sauvignon Napa Valley 1993: Young and spicy, with a pleasing core of cherry, currant, herb and anise flavors that are tight and compact; can stand to open it up a bit. 1,200 cases made. • $28 • (11/15/96) • **88**

Cabernet Sauvignon Napa Valley 1992 • $24 • (12/15/95) • **90**

Cabernet Sauvignon Napa Valley 1991 • $24 • (09/30/94) • **89**

Cabernet Sauvignon Napa Valley 1990 • $23 • (10/15/93) HR • **93**

Cabernet Sauvignon Napa Valley 1989 • $20 • (11/15/92) • **90**

Cabernet Sauvignon Napa Valley Lewis Select 1991 • $28 • (09/30/94) • **91**

Cabernet Sauvignon Napa Valley Reserve 1991 • $32 • (05/15/95) HR • **92**

Chardonnay Napa Valley ORV 1996: Distinct for its butterscotch flavors, this wine is ripe, rich and focused, with well-defined fruit flavors, hints of pear, apricot and butter, and finishing with smoky, toasty oak. Drink now through 2001. 700 cases made. • $32 • (05/15/98) • **92**

Chardonnay Napa Valley ORV 1995: Young, tight and concentrated, with a pretty core of spice, apple, pear and peach flavors, turning complex on the finish where the flavors fully unfold. Drink now. 700 cases made. • $30 • (05/31/97) • **91**

Chardonnay Napa Valley ORV 1994: Young and tight, showing citrus, pear and toasty vanilla flavors and a long, complex aftertaste. Picks up a trace of herb on the finish and it's slightly tannic; some aging should help. 400 cases made. • $28 • (05/15/96) • **89**

Chardonnay Napa Valley Vista Vineyard 1996: A rich and spicy style, backed up with ripe pear and fig notes, gaining a smoky nuance and turning long and lingering on the finish. Drink now through 2001. 433 cases made. • $26 • (05/31/98) • **90**

Chardonnay Napa Valley Vista Vineyard 1995: Beautifully crafted, rich and complex, with a wonderful core of ripe pear, fig, melon and peach flavors. Finishes with impressive depth, complexity and a smoky oak aftertaste that turns elegant and refined. 600 cases made. • $22 • (05/31/97) • **93**

Chardonnay Napa Valley Vista Vineyard 1994: Not quite together when tasted, it certainly has enough ripe and complex pear, pineapple and spice flavors that are a bit tannic and woody on the finish. Some aging should help. 1,400 cases made. • $20 • (05/15/96) • **88**

■ ■ ■ ■

OAKWOOD

Chardonnay Napa Valley Vista Vineyards 1993 • $18 • (06/15/95) HR • **90**

Merlot Napa Valley 1994: Young, firm, tight and focused. A rich and flavorful wine that's brimming with cherry, currant and spice nuances and finishes with a long, complex aftertaste. 400 cases made. • $28 • (07/31/97) • **92**

Merlot Napa Valley 1993: Dark, with a tart accent to the ripe cherry and currant flavors. Well-focused and turning somewhat simpler at midpalate, although the flavors hang together through the finish. Drink now. 300 cases made. • $26 • (11/30/96) • **87**

Merlot Napa Valley 1992 • $24 • (05/15/96) • **83**

Old Vine Field Blend Napa Valley 1993 • $18 • (11/30/95) • **87**

Robert's Blend Napa Valley 1994: Lean and trim, with a narrow band of cedar, currant and spice. Perhaps will fill out with cellaring, but for now it's hollow in the middle and tannic on the finish. Drink now to 2002. A blend of 70 percent Cabernet Franc and 30 percent Cabernet Sauvignon. 160 cases made. • $45 • (03/31/98) • **85**

Robert's Blend Napa Valley 1993: A touch herbal, with dashes of cedar, tobacco and currant, unfolding to reveal elegant fruit flavors, finishing with firm tannins. Best after 1999. A blend of 70 percent Cabernet Franc and 30 percent Cabernet Sauvignon. 140 cases made. • $42 • (07/31/97) • **88**

OAKWOOD | WASHINGTON

Cabernet Sauvignon Yakima Valley 1989 • $14 • (09/30/95) • **87**

Cabernet Sauvignon Yakima Valley Reserve 1987 • $20 • (11/30/93) HR • **92**

Lemberger Yakima Valley 1991 • $10 • (09/30/95) • **78**

Muscat Canelli Yakima Valley 1993 • $6 • (09/30/95) • **85**

Riesling Late Harvest Yakima Valley 1995: Frankly sweet, but its nectarine, spice and honey flavors are nicely balanced and linger on the generous finish. 229 cases made. • $10/375ml • (09/30/96) BB • **88**

OASIS | VIRGINIA

Brut Virginia NV: Not bad, but not everyone's cup of tea. Rich-textured, but unusual-tasting, blending buttery, waxy, earthy flavors up front with a lean, slightly green-tinged finish. Drink now. • $NA • (03/31/98) • **78**

Brut Virginia Cuvée D'Or 1990 • $25 • (12/31/94) • **81**

Cabernet Sauvignon Virginia 1995: Shows some elegance, but it's quite herbal and stemmy-tasting. There are some spicy notes on the finish. Drink now. • $20 • (05/15/98) • **78**

Chardonnay Virginia 1995: Modestly appealing, with pine and apple flavors, but it turns a bit bitter on the finish. 2,400 cases made. • $12 • (01/31/97) • **77**

Chardonnay Virginia 1994: Clumsy, mingling celery and canned peach aromas. Sweet and syrupy on the palate. Flavorful, but doesn't hold together. 2,400 cases made. • $10 • (06/30/95) • **77**

Chardonnay Virginia 1993 • $10 • (02/28/95) • **82**

Meritage Virginia 1993: On the lean and green side of the flavor spectrum, with herbal aromas and flavors, and a strong streak of wood throughout. Drinkable, but awkward. 101 cases made. • $15 • (06/30/95) • **77**

Merlot Virginia 1995: A medium-weight Merlot with flavors of rhubarb and red plum. Finishes on a charry note. Drink now. • $NA • (03/31/98) • **78**

Merlot Virginia 1992 • $12 • (12/31/95) • **74**

Vidal Blanc Virginia Great Falls Vineyard 1994 • $15 • (10/31/95) • **77**

OBESTER | CALIFORNIA

Pinot Noir Anderson Valley 1995: A curious style—a combination of wild berry, rhubarb and celery flavors that turn earthy and dry. 440 cases made. • $17 • (03/31/97) • **72**

Pinot Noir Anderson Valley 1992 • $15 • (04/30/94) • **78**

Sangiovese Mendocino County 1993 • $10 • (08/31/95) • **83**

Sangiovese Mendocino County 1992 • $14 • (03/31/94) • **79**

Sauvignon Blanc Mendocino County 1993 • $8 • (08/31/95) • **80**

Zinfandel Mendocino 1995: The bright strawberry flavor has a sour, herbal streak running through it. Finishes short, with astringency. Drink now. 248 cases made. • $15 • (06/15/98) • **74**

Zinfandel Mendocino County 1991 • $11 • (06/15/94) • **84**

Key: SS—Spectator Selection CS—Cellar Selection HR—Highly Recommended BB—Best Buy $NA—Price not available Ⓐ—Auction Price (BT)—Barrel Tasting
Dates in parentheses indicate the issues in which the ratings were published.

OCTOPUS MOUNTAIN | CALIFORNIA

Cabernet Sauvignon Anderson Valley Dennison Vineyard 1991 • $13 • (11/15/94) • **82**

Cabernet Sauvignon Anderson Valley Dennison Vineyards 1989 • $13 • (07/31/91) • **83**

Pinot Noir Anderson Valley 1989 • $13 • (10/31/91) • **86**

Pinot Noir Anderson Valley Dennison Vineyard 1991 • $14 • (12/15/93) • **85**

OJAI | CALIFORNIA

Cabernet Sauvignon-Syrah California 1986 • $7 • (04/15/89) • **74**

Chardonnay Arroyo Grande Valley 1995: Combines bold, ripe, grapey flavors with layers of pear, spice and citrus subtly and with finesse. Finishes with nice touches of oak and spice. 460 cases made. • $16 • (06/30/97) • **89**

Chardonnay Arroyo Grande Valley 1993 • $18 • (07/31/95) • **86**

Chardonnay Arroyo Grande Valley Reserve 1995: A restrained style, with a trim band of citrus-tinged pear and apple notes, turning flinty and austere on the finish. Try now. 192 cases made. • $28 • (12/15/97) • **85**

Chardonnay Santa Barbara County Bien Nacido Vineyard 1996: Intense and spicy, with an earthy side to the core of ripe pear and melon flavors. Turns complex on the finish, so short-term cellaring is advised. 600 cases made. • $20 • (12/15/97) • **87**

Chardonnay Santa Barbara County Reserve 1993 • $21 • (07/31/95) • **87**

Pinot Noir Santa Barbara County 1993 • $25 • (06/30/95) • **86**

Pinot Noir Santa Barbara County Bien Nacido Vineyard Benjamin Lorenzo 1995: Dark, ripe, intense and flavorful, with lots of rich, racy Pinot Noir flavors. The black cherry, cola, spice and wild berry flavors dance on the palate. Finishes with complex anise and wild berry notes. Drinks well now through 2001. 110 cases made. • $36 • (01/31/98) • **91**

Syrah California 1996: Dark, ripe and spicy, with juicy plum, wild berry, cherry and spice, firming up on the finish, where the tannins make their presence known. Give it a year or two; best from 1999 to 2004. 1,050 cases made. • $18 • (04/30/98) • **88**

Syrah California 1995: Smooth, rich and supple, with a generous core of ripe plum, blackberry, spice and anise flavors, finishing with firm tannins and good length. • $13 • (07/31/97) • **89**

Syrah California 1994: Dark and intense, tannic too, but it delivers a nice, rich core of plum, currant, mineral and spice flavors and a slightly smoky note on the finish. Tasty through 1999. • $15 • (09/30/96) • **88**

Syrah California 1992 • $15 • (01/31/95) • **84**

Syrah California 1991 • $15 • (12/31/93) • **87**

Syrah California 1986 • $7 • (04/15/89) • **77**

Syrah Santa Barbara County Bien Nacido Vineyard 1995: Dark, ripe, rich and concentrated, with intense meat, smoke, currant, mineral, spice and leather notes that are sharply focused and long on the finish. Has the tannic strength to cellar into 2000 with ease. 480 cases made. • $32 • (11/15/97) • **91**

Viognier California Roll Ranch Vineyard 1996: Good, but rather one-dimensional in flavor, with hints of pear and spice. 180 cases made. • $20 • (12/15/97) • **83**

OL' BLUE JAY | CALIFORNIA

Zinfandel California Blue Blood NV • $11 • (12/31/92) • **81**

OLD BROOKVILLE | NEW YORK

Chardonnay Nassau County 1995: Clean, well-made and quite buttery, with some nice fig and apple flavors. Spicy on the finish, with a citrus note. Well done. 1,200 cases made. • $12 • (05/15/97) • **86**

OLIVER | INDIANA

Merlot Indiana 1988 • $15 • (02/29/92) • **82**

OLIVET LANE | CALIFORNIA

Chardonnay Russian River Valley 1995: Ripe, smooth and creamy, with a distinct, smoky oak accent to the pear and fig flavors. A little heavy-handed on the finish, but it's young. Cellaring into 1999 is advised. 3,412 cases made. • $14 • (03/31/97) • **88**

Chardonnay Russian River Valley Pellegrini Family Vineyards 1996: Ripe and spicy, with pretty pear, nectarine and cedary oak flavors. Nonetheless, there's a slight mustiness that's troubling. Tasted twice, with consistent notes. Drink now. 4,200 cases made. • $14 • (05/15/98) • **82**

Chardonnay Russian River Valley Pellegrini Family Vineyards 1994: Strives for complexity in its honey and butterscotch notes. An elegant, subtle style where flavors build on the palate, fanning out on aftertaste. 2,595 cases made. • $12 • (02/29/96) • **87**

Pinot Noir Russian River Valley 1993 • $13 • (12/31/95) • **84**

Pinot Noir Russian River Valley 1992 • $12 • (02/28/94) • **84**

Pinot Noir Russian River Valley 1991 • $10 • (02/28/93) • **84**

Pinot Noir Russian River Valley 1988 • $9 • (06/30/91) BB • **85**

Pinot Noir Russian River Valley Pellegrini Family Vineyards 1996: Light in texture, with more spice and earth overtones than fruit, but the leather and raspberry notes echo nicely on the finish. Ready now. 4,200 cases made. • $16 • (12/31/97) • **84**

Pinot Noir Russian River Valley Pellegrini Family Vineyards 1995: Clean and fruity, with simple cherry and berry notes that develop a slight jammy accent. 3,250 cases made. • $15 • (01/31/97) • **84**

Pinot Noir Russian River Valley Pellegrini Family Vineyards 1994 • $15 • (01/31/96) • **86**

OLSON | CALIFORNIA

Merlot California 1989 • $11 • (05/31/92) • **76**

ONE VINEYARD | CALIFORNIA

Cabernet Sauvignon Napa Valley 1993: Cedar, spice, plums and black currant make for a juicy blend here. Turns somewhat astringent and angular on the finish, though. • $NA • (12/15/97) • **86**

Cabernet Sauvignon Napa Valley 1989 • $18 • (03/31/93) • **72**

Cabernet Sauvignon Napa Valley 1988 • $15 • (11/15/92) • **77**

Sauvignon Blanc Napa Valley 1995: Fairly smooth, with pleasing melon and citrus notes. A restrained herbal finish adds interest. 870 cases made. • $11 • (04/30/98) • **86**

ONE WORLD WINERY | CALIFORNIA

Cabernet Sauvignon Russian River Valley 1991 • $15 • (05/15/94) • **82**

Sauvignon Blanc Russian River Valley 1993 • $9 • (08/31/94) • **70**

Zinfandel Russian River Valley 1993 • $14 • (04/30/96) • **70**

Zinfandel Russian River Valley 1992 • $11 • (04/30/94) • **85**

OPTIMA | CALIFORNIA

Cabernet Sauvignon Alexander Valley 1994: Smooth, ripe, rich and harmonious, with supple texture and lots of ripe plum, cherry and berry notes. Delicious now and over the next four or five years. 2,400 cases made. • $28 • (08/31/97) • **89**

Cabernet Sauvignon Alexander Valley 1992 • $25 • (12/15/95) • **89**

Cabernet Sauvignon Alexander Valley 1991 • $25 • (02/28/95) • **88**

Cabernet Sauvignon Alexander Valley 1990 • $27 • (06/15/94) • **82**

Cabernet Sauvignon Sonoma County 1989 • $25 • (11/15/92) • **88**

Cabernet Sauvignon Sonoma County 1987 • $22 • (12/15/90) HR • **92**

Cabernet Sauvignon Sonoma County 1986 • $22 • (02/15/90) • **91**

Cabernet Sauvignon Sonoma County 1985 • $19 • (12/15/88) • **93**

Cabernet Sauvignon Sonoma County 1984 • $17 • (02/29/88) • **90**

Chardonnay Carneros 1995: For fans of well-oaked Chardonnay. Shows a lot of wood, but there's plenty of pear and butterscotch flavors too, with a smoky oak aftertaste. 400 cases made. • $28 • (06/15/97) • **89**

Chardonnay Carneros 1994: An elegant style, with a medium-bodied core of pear, spice, hazelnut and anise, turning complex on the finish. 300 cases made. • $28 • (02/29/96) • **87**

Chardonnay Carneros 1993 • $25 • (10/15/95) • **89**

Pinot Noir Russian River Valley 1995: Not your classic Pinot Noir, but a solid red nonetheless; smooth and spicy, with lots of cola, wild berry and cherry notes. The price, however, is high for what's there. 225 cases made. • $45 • (01/31/97) • **84**

Pinot Noir Russian River Valley 1994 • $40 • (04/30/96) • **87**

OPUS ONE | CALIFORNIA

Napa Valley 1994: The fruit emerges gloriously from beneath a subtle earthiness in this wine, the flavors gushing forward, with layers of currant, dried cherry, sage and cedar. Impressive for its depth, concentration and finesse, with a long, lively aftertaste. A blend of 93 percent Cabernet Sauvignon, 4 percent Cabernet Franc, 4 percent Merlot and 1 percent Malbec. 30,000 cases made. • $90 • (10/15/97) CS • **94**

Napa Valley 1993: Big, ripe and intense. Offers a rich band of currant, anise, mineral and spice flavors, with nice touches of anise, cedar and blackberry coming through on the long, rich finish. Has the tannic strength to cellar into 2000, but you can enjoy it now for its finesse and polish. 28,000 cases made. • $80 • (11/30/96) CS • **91**

Napa Valley 1992 • $75 • (12/15/95) CS • **91**

Napa Valley 1991 • $65 • (11/15/94) CS • **93**

Napa Valley 1990 • $65 • (11/30/93) CS • **92**

Napa Valley 1989 • $63 • (12/15/92) • **89**

Napa Valley 1988 • $91 Ⓐ • (10/31/91) HR • **92**

Napa Valley 1987: This has evolved into a supple, complex and harmonious wine, with a range of herb, tea, sage, anise, currant and berry flavors. Finishes with silky texture and excellent length. Best now through 2002. • $164 • (12/15/97) • **94**

Napa Valley 1986: This tastes like a highly extracted, concentrated wine, but there isn't as much flavor as you would hope. The earthy currant, leather and spice notes seem wrapped in a veil of tannin, rendering the finish short and tight. Can still age, but will it evolve into something more interesting, or turn simpler as it seems to have done since last tasted, just two years ago. • $NA • (12/15/96) • **88**

Napa Valley 1985 • $95 • (06/15/89) • **95**

Napa Valley 1984 • $50 • (05/31/88) • **94**

Napa Valley 1983 • $53 • (06/15/87) • **89**

Napa Valley 1982 • $50 • (05/01/86) CS • **93**

Napa Valley 1981 • $50 • (05/16/85) CS • **94**

Napa Valley 1980 • $50 • (04/01/84) CS • **91**

OREGON VINEYARDS | OREGON

Pinot Gris Oregon 1993 • $9 • (11/30/94) • **79**

Pinot Noir Oregon 1992 • $9 • (09/15/94) • **83**

ORFILA | CALIFORNIA

California Tawny Port NV • $13 • (05/31/95) • **78**

Chardonnay San Diego-Monterey Counties Coastal California 1996: Soft and pleasant, with apple, pear, sweet vanilla and butter notes. Drink now. 1,300 cases made. • $11 • (07/31/98) • **83**

Chardonnay San Diego-Monterey-Santa Barbara Counties 1994: Marked by a candied quality, there are enough ripe pear and spicy apple flavors to hold your interest, especially at this price. 1,500 cases made. • $10 • (07/31/97) • **83**

Chardonnay San Diego-San Luis Obispo Counties Ambassador's Reserve 1995: Heavily oxidized, with well-oaked tropical fruit flavors that turn nutty. Tasted twice, with consistent notes and scores. Drink now. 1,300 cases made. • $15 • (07/31/98) • **70**

Merlot California 1992 • $15 • (05/15/95) • **79**

Merlot California 1991 • $16 • (03/31/95) • **79**

Merlot San Diego County 1991 • $25 • (03/31/95) • **78**

Merlot San Diego County Ambassador's Reserve 1993: Not especially varietal, but pleasant enough as a table wine with its plum, cherry and berry notes. Finishes with a simple aftertaste and modest tannins. • $NA • (02/28/97) • **85**

Merlot San Diego County Ambassador's Reserve 1992 • $25 • (03/31/95) • **85**

Sangiovese San Diego County Di Collina 1995: Clean, ripe and refreshing, with bright, complex cherry, raspberry and plum notes and a distinctive floral twist. Very well made; shows promise for an area that's still untested. • $NA • (02/28/97) • **87**

Syrah San Diego County Val De La Mer 1994: Impressive, showing the meaty, smoky plum and wild berry flavors of Syrah and smooth, fleshy texture. Another excellent effort from this San Diego County winery. Drinkable now, but can age into 2000. • $NA • (02/28/97) • **87**

ORGANIC WINE WORKS | CALIFORNIA

Barbera El Dorado 1991 • $9 • (06/15/93) • **76**

Merlot Butte County 1992 • $12 • (08/31/93) • **80**

Merlot Napa Valley Thompson Ranch 1991 • $13 • (05/31/92) • **84**

Pinot Noir Mendocino County 1992 • $12 • (06/15/93) • **73**

Red Table Wine California à Notre Terre 1992 • $8 • (07/31/93) • **79**

Red Table Wine California à Notre Terre 1991 • $7 • (05/31/93) • **83**

Zinfandel California 1991 • $8 • (10/15/92) • **86**

Zinfandel Napa County 1992 • $10 • (05/31/93) • **80**

OSPREY'S DOMINION | NEW YORK

Cabernet Sauvignon North Fork of Long Island 1993: Cherry, chocolate and cola flavors give this sweet appeal and, though it's concentrated, the tannins are kept in check. A ripe, jammy red that's accessible now. 1,800 cases made. • $14 • (12/31/96) • **86**

Chardonnay North Fork of Long Island 1995: Distinctive. This fat white offers marked vanilla, honey, nutmeg and allspice flavors that linger like mulled wine on the palate. Not your typical Chardonnay, but not unattractive. 2,500 cases made. • $13 • (12/31/96) • **84**

Merlot North Fork of Long Island 1993: Generous and ripe, this thick-textured wine offers cassis and blackberry flavors with pleasant toasty, spicy accents that linger on the finish. Drink now. 450 cases made. • $14 • (12/31/96) • **88**

Riesling North Fork of Long Island 1995: Off-dry, showing canned-fruit flavors of pineapple and citrus, with a slightly soapy texture. It has some Riesling character, but lacks clarity. 485 cases made. • $10 • (12/31/96) • **76**

PACHECO RANCH | CALIFORNIA

Cabernet Sauvignon Marin County 1985 • $10 • (11/15/91) • **76**

PACIFIC ECHO | CALIFORNIA

Brut Mendocino County NV: This sparkling wine starts off with toasty, citrusy aromas, a touch of honey on the nose. On the palate, a pleasing blend of herb, lemon, pear and nut flavors hold on for a lengthy finish. It's new from California bubbly-maker Scharffenberger. Drink now. 40,000 cases made. • $19 • (06/15/98) SS • **89**

Brut Mendocino County Private Reserve 1992: Starts off a bit doughy, then kicks in with fresh floral notes and complex citrus, pear and apple flavors. The acidity is bright and refreshing, and the finish is long and clean. A new name, made by Scharffenberger. Drink now. • $30 • (06/30/98) • **90**

Brut Rosé Mendocino County NV: A pretty salmon color and a light, refreshing style mark this wine. Floral, citrus and apple notes lead the way. A bit short on the finish. Drink now. • $24 • (06/30/98) • **86**

PAGE MILL | CALIFORNIA

Cabernet Sauvignon Napa Valley V. & L. Eisele Vineyard 1990 • $18 • (03/31/96) • **80**

Cabernet Sauvignon Napa Valley V. & L. Eisele Vineyard 1989 • $22 • (11/15/93) • **74**

Cabernet Sauvignon Napa Valley V. & L. Eisele Vineyard 1988 • $18 • (11/15/93) • **84**

Merlot Santa Maria Valley Bien Nacido Vineyard 1993 • $12 • (03/31/96) • **80**

Pinot Noir Santa Barbara County Bien Nacido Vineyard 1990 • $18 • (02/28/93) • **68**

Pinot Noir Santa Barbara County Bien Nacido Vineyard 1985 • $13 • (06/15/88) • **87**

Pinot Noir Santa Maria Valley Bien Nacido Vineyard 1991 • $18 • (02/28/94) • **86**

Port California Lewis 1995: Ripe and exotic, sweet, harmonious and rich, with prune, plum, blueberry and smoke flavors that linger on the finish. Has a firm grip, too. Best from 2002. A blend of Cabernet Sauvignon and Cabernet Franc. 117 cases made. • $20 • (10/15/97) • **89**

PAGOR | CALIFORNIA

Cabernet Sauvignon California 1992 • $12 • (03/31/96) • **73**
Merlot Santa Maria Valley 1984 • $11 • (04/30/88) • **70**
Pinot Noir Santa Barbara County 1990 • $14 • (02/28/93) • **65**
Pinot Noir Santa Barbara County 1987 • $11 • (12/15/89) • **85**

PAHLMEYER | CALIFORNIA

Caldwell Vineyard Napa Valley 1990 • $32 • (10/15/93) • **90**

Caldwell Vineyard Napa Valley 1989 • $24 Ⓐ • (10/15/92) • **83**
Caldwell Vineyard Napa Valley 1988 • $24 Ⓐ • (11/15/91) • **89**

Caldwell Vineyard Napa Valley 1987: Smells more complex than it tastes. Austere, dry and tannic. The hints of mint, cedar and currant are lean and trim, and the finish is still quite hard. Best after 1999. • $41 • (12/15/97) • **86**

Caldwell Vineyard Napa Valley 1986 • $39 Ⓐ • (11/15/89) • **89**
Caldwell Vineyard Napa Valley Minty Cuvée 1990 • $NA • (12/15/95) • **82**

Chardonnay Napa Valley 1996: Rich and smoky, with complex fig, melon, toast and anise flavors that are still a bit disjointed, but all the ingredients are there and a little more time in the bottle should smooth things out. Drink now through 2002. 1,000 cases made. • $50 • (05/31/98) • **90**

Chardonnay Napa Valley 1995: A touch earthy and a bit leesy, this is an elegant, richly flavored, deeply complex wine with a core of grapefruit, citrus and green pear flavors. Impressive for its length and its smoky anise aftertaste. 2,200 cases made. • $40 • (05/31/97) • **92**

Chardonnay Napa Valley 1994: Starts out with a smoky, toasty oak aroma and follows up with elegant, spicy pear, honey and butterscotch flavors that blend together. Finishes with complex and concentrated flavors. 2,100 cases made. • $41 Ⓐ • (05/31/96) • **92**

Chardonnay Napa Valley 1993 • $26 Ⓐ • (04/30/95) • **89**
Jayson Napa Valley 1992 • $20 • (12/31/94) • **88**

Merlot Napa Valley 1995: Well focused, with ripe black cherry, plum and wild berry flavors, a hint of cedar and spice and mild but firm tannins on the finish. Best to give this a year or two in the cellar; drink through 2004. 2,000 cases made. • $50 • (05/31/98) • **90**

Merlot Napa Valley 1994: Young and fleshy in texture, with a mere hint of herb accenting the currant, spice and cedar flavors, the fruit flavors fanning out on the finish. Try now. 2,000 cases made. • $40 • (11/30/96) • **89**

Merlot Napa Valley 1991 • $24 • (09/15/94) • **85**
Merlot Napa Valley Caldwell Vineyard 1990 • $24 • (10/15/93) • **85**

Napa Valley Red 1997: Dense and grapey, with rich, concentrated cherry, plum and currant, spice notes, a supple texture and a remarkably long and sophisticated finish. • $NA • (07/31/98) (BT) • **95-99**

Napa Valley Red 1994: Ripe, complex and full-bodied, with pretty currant, black cherry, spice and cedary oak flavors that continue to develop far into the finish. The tannins are a little rough around the edges, but they're not out of line for a wine this young. Best after 2000. Tasted twice, with consistent notes. To be released in April 1997. 2,000 cases made. • $40 • (11/30/96) HR • **92**

Napa Valley Red 1993: A ripe, rich, full-bodied Bordeaux-style red that shows its plush and complex side already, though still young. The tiers of cherry, currant, anise and spice finish with thick but polished tannins and a rich aftertaste. Impressive for its depth and concentration. 3,000 cases made. • $36 • (05/31/96) CS • **91**

Napa Valley Red 1992 • $34 • (12/15/95) • **89**
Napa Valley Red 1991 • $32 • (11/15/94) • **82**

Napa Valley Red 1986: Elegant and refined, with a distinctly minty edge to the sweet, ripe cherry and currant flavors. Finishes with a complex array of flavors and ripe, sweet tannins. Ready now into 2000. Tasted from a half (375ml) bottle. • $39 • (12/15/96) • **89**

PALMER | NEW YORK

Blanc de Blanc North Fork of Long Island Special Reserve 1989: Muscular and full-bodied, with an exuberant mousse and firm acidity, but the fruit flavors are simple and slightly candied. It's serious, but not sophisticated. 264 cases made. • $20 • (12/31/96) • **81**

Cabernet Franc North Fork of Long Island Proprietor's Reserve 1994: This is supple and polished, showing good varietal character with its leafy, berry flavors and light smoke accent. For pleasant drinking now. 761 cases made. • $14 • (12/31/96) • **86**

Cabernet Franc North Fork of Long Island Proprietor's Reserve 1991 • $15 • (12/31/95) • **79**

Cabernet Franc North Fork of Long Island's Proprietor's Reserve 1989 • $13 • (11/15/91) • **76**

Cabernet Sauvignon North Fork of Long Island 1993: Dark aromas of tar and coffee give way to a polished palate with plenty of cherry flavor to balance the tar and earth notes. It's well structured, yet smooth. Drink now. 833 cases made. • $13 • (12/31/96) • **87**

Cabernet Sauvignon North Fork of Long Island 1988 • $14 • (06/30/91) • **83**
Cabernet Sauvignon North Fork of Long Island 1986 • $10 • (12/15/88) • **82**

Chardonnay North Fork of Long Island Barrel Fermented 1994: Buttery-tasting, with a soft structure, and some good pear and ripe apple flavors. Drink now. 2,485 cases made. • $15 • (06/15/98) • **81**

Key: SS—Spectator Selection CS—Cellar Selection HR—Highly Recommended BB—Best Buy $NA—Price not available Ⓐ—Auction Price (BT)—Barrel Tasting
Dates in parentheses indicate the issues in which the ratings were published.

Chardonnay North Fork of Long Island Barrel Fermented 1993: Its aromas of butter, butterscoch and nuts, and its thick texture, show maturity, but fresh flavors of pears and melons keep the palate lively and linger on the finish. Ready to drink. Slightly better than in an earlier tasting. 2,500 cases made. • $15 • (12/31/96) • **88**

Chardonnay North Fork of Long Island Estate 1995: Ripe and exuberant, this offers truckloads of tropical fruit flavors—pineapple, melon and mango—in a firm, toasty frame. It's vivid yet deep, a rich wine with distinctive character. 1,519 cases made. • $10 • (12/31/96) • **90**

Chardonnay North Fork of Long Island Free Range 1994: Rich, offering toasty, smoky flavors, adequate acidity and modest fruit flavors of melons and apples. A little clumsy, but will appeal to fans of oak. 230 cases made. • $15 • (12/31/96) • **84**

Gewürztraminer North Fork of Long Island 1995: Full-bodied, with ripe Gewürz flavors of orange peel, spice and toast and just enough acidity to balance its moderate sweetness. Well made, a fine apéritif. 620 cases made. • $10 • (12/31/96) • **85**

Gewürztraminer North Fork of Long Island Select Harvest 1994: This has loads of lovely honey and sweet peach flavors. Lush and full-flavored, with maple sugar notes on the finish. A focused dessert wine that would finish any meal well. Drink now. 434 cases made. • $16/375ml • (06/15/98) • **87**

Merlot North Fork of Long Island 1994: Ripe, round and supple. Flavors of plum, sweet tomato and chocolate, with just enough tannin for grip. Enjoy it now. 1,925 cases made. • $15 • (12/31/96) • **84**

Merlot North Fork of Long Island 1989 • $13 • (07/31/92) • **82**

Merlot North Fork of Long Island 1988 • $13 • (06/30/91) • **86**

Merlot North Fork of Long Island 1986 • $10 • (12/15/88) • **80**

Merlot North Fork of Long Island Reserve 1995: A serious effort, with appealing spice, cherry and plum flavors. Ripe and fairly rich, it just lacks a little punch in the middle. Perhaps some time in the cellar; drink through 2001. 295 cases made. • $29 • (05/31/98) • **85**

Pinot Blanc North Fork of Long Island Lieb Vineyards 1996: Dominated by green peach and green apple flavors, with a buttery note. A little muddled in the end. 266 cases made. • $12 • (07/31/98) • **77**

Riesling North Fork of Long Island 1993 • $8 • (08/31/95) • **80**

Sauvignon Blanc North Fork of Long Island 1995: This Loire-style Sauvignon shows herbaceous aromas and flavors, with mineral accents and sharp acidity. The finish is a bit bitter; try with food. 1,464 cases made. • $9 • (12/31/96) • **80**

Sauvignon Blanc North Fork of Long Island 1993 • $9 • (01/01/95) • **86**

Select Reserve White North Fork of Long Island 10th Anniversary 1995: Attractive, making up in flavor what it lacks in harmony. Mineral, smoky aromas give way to soft-textured tropical flavors of figs and vanilla that linger on the finish. 378 cases made. • $20 • (12/31/96) • **84**

White Riesling North Fork of Long Island 1995: Appealing in an understated way, this is just off-dry, with applelike acidity and light flavors of nectarine, orange and honey. Try as a nice afternoon quaff. 337 cases made. • $8 • (12/31/96) • **82**

PALOMA | CALIFORNIA

Merlot Napa Valley 1995: Emitting attractive aromas, this slowly unveils appealing currant, cedar, spice and tobacco flavors that fill out on the palate, showing nice focus and a rich aftertaste. Approachable now, but worthy of cellaring into 1999. 674 cases made. • $26 • (12/15/97) • **90**

PANTHER CREEK | OREGON

Pinot Noir Willamette Valley 1994: Solidly built to showcase the ripe currant and toast flavors. Closed-up tightly at this stage, but it should unfold by 1999. 500 cases made. • $15 • (10/15/96) • **87**

Pinot Noir Willamette Valley 1988 • $15 • (04/15/91) • **75**

Pinot Noir Willamette Valley 1987 • $17 • (04/15/90) • **74**

Pinot Noir Willamette Valley Bednarik Vineyard 1995: Flavors are nice, with spicy herb and earthy notes adding depth to the modest berry and cherry flavors, but scratchy tannins make the finish a bit rough. Best after 2000. 240 cases made. • $33 • (11/30/97) • **86**

Pinot Noir Willamette Valley Bednarik Vineyard 1994: Dark and dense, this shows chewy tannins and intense anise and mineral flavors that shoulder past the berrylike flavors. Drink now. 250 cases made. • $36 • (10/15/96) • **85**

Pinot Noir Willamette Valley Canary Hill Barn Block 1993 • $30 • (03/31/96) • **85**

Pinot Noir Willamette Valley Canary Hill Vineyard 1992 • $35 • (11/30/94) • **87**

Pinot Noir Willamette Valley Carter Vineyard 1993 • $30 • (03/31/96) • **88**

Pinot Noir Willamette Valley Carter Vineyard 1992 • $30 • (11/30/94) • **86**

Pinot Noir Willamette Valley Carter Vineyard 1990 • $30 • (02/28/93) • **89**

Pinot Noir Willamette Valley Freedom Hill Vineyard 1995: Shows plenty of ripe fruit on a raw frame, centering on pure plum and currant flavors, shaded nicely with hints of smoke and toast. Needs until 1999 or so to soften and fill in the missing pieces. 650 cases made. • $33 • (12/31/97) • **85**

Pinot Noir Willamette Valley Freedom Hill Vineyard 1994: Smooth and nicely focused with its flavors of currant and berry and hints of vanilla. Finishes with fine tannins that need until 1998. 540 cases made. • $36 • (10/15/96) • **87**

Pinot Noir Willamette Valley Freedom Hill Vineyard 1993 • $30 • (03/31/96) • **85**

Pinot Noir Willamette Valley Freedom Hill Vineyard Winemaker's Cuvée 1995: Has some lovely ripe berry and root-beer notes that focus nicely on the firm-textured finish. Balanced with crisp acidity, it should be best from 1999. 120 cases made. • $38 • (11/30/97) • **88**

Pinot Noir Willamette Valley Reserve 1995: Practically weightless on the palate, this light wine exhibits very pretty berry and spice notes that linger on the finish. May have filled out by 1999. 1,250 cases made. • $25 • (11/30/97) • **86**

Pinot Noir Willamette Valley Reserve 1994: Ripe and generous with its focused currant, black cherry and toasty vanilla flavors. Tries to finish with delicacy; the finely integrated tannins may need into 1999 to soften. 925 cases made. • $25 • (10/15/96) • **89**

Pinot Noir Willamette Valley Reserve 1993 • $21 • (01/31/96) • **90**

Pinot Noir Willamette Valley Reserve 1992 • $20 • (11/30/94) • **80**

Pinot Noir Willamette Valley Reserve 1990 • $18 • (02/28/93) • **86**

Pinot Noir Willamette Valley Shea Vineyard 1995: Lean and tight, with very interesting flavors of black cherry, tea, herb and cola lurking beneath a layer of chewy tannins. Try now. 400 cases made. • $33 • (11/30/97) • **86**

Pinot Noir Willamette Valley Shea Vineyard 1994: Rich and complex, this layers spicy berry and cherry flavors with meaty, smoky, slightly herbal notes. Drink now. 130 cases made. • $36 • (10/15/96) • **91**

Pinot Noir Willamette Valley Winemaker's Cuvée 1993 • $28 • (01/31/96) • **89**

PAOLETTI | CALIFORNIA

Cabernet Sauvignon Napa Valley 1994: Big, ripe, intense and concentrated, with firm, chewy tannins and an earthy streak that runs through the currant and berry flavors. This is a rough-and-tumble style that needs cellaring, with hope the tannins soften. 650 cases made. • $30 • (12/15/97) • **87**

La Forza Red Napa Valley 1995: Delivers lots of ripe plum, black cherry, wild berry and spice flavors, with good depth, richness and concentration. Finishes with firm, chewy tannins. Approachable now, best from 2000 to 2005. A blend of 85 percent Sangiovese and 15 percent Cabernet Sauvignon. 58 cases made. • $30 • (03/31/98) • **88**

PARADIGM | CALIFORNIA

Cabernet Sauvignon Napa Valley 1992 • $28 • (12/15/95) • **87**

Cabernet Sauvignon Napa Valley 1991 • $26 • (11/15/94) • **90**

Cabernet Sauvignon Napa Valley Oakville 1994: Young and intense, with a lively core of wild berry, plum and blackberry flavors that fan out and pick up a nice spicy edge. Has the tannic strength to age for a decade, yet the texture is smooth enough to enjoy now. 2,230 cases made. • $30 • (09/30/97) • **92**

Cabernet Sauvignon Napa Valley Oakville 1993: Smooth and harmonious, with plenty of rich plum, currant and anise flavors that turn supple on the finish, where the tannins are plush and concentrated. 1,300 cases made. • $28 • (11/15/96) • **89**

Merlot Napa Valley Oakville 1994: Ripe and flavorful, with a rich, complex core of currant, black cherry, plum and anise flavors. Finishes with plush, supple tannins and a long, full aftertaste. Impressive all around. Drinkable now through 2002. 400 cases made. • $30 • (06/30/97) • **92**

Merlot Oakville 1995: Touches of earth and leather, with a charred oak edge, introduce this tightly focused, firm and tannic, even a bit chunky, wine. The flavors are rich and supple, with tar, spice, currant and meaty flavors on the finish. Needs short-term cellaring. Best from 1999 through 2005. 650 cases made. • $32 • (07/31/98) • **91**

Zinfandel Oakville 1995: Ripe, intense, well focused and rich in wild berry, cherry, anise, sage and mineral flavors. Manages to pack in lots of flavor and still be polished and elegant. Finishes with firm, ripe tannins. Drink now through 2002. 80 cases made. • $22 • (06/15/98) • **89**

PARADISE RIDGE | CALIFORNIA

Blanc de Blanc Sonoma County Private Reserve 1995: Light toast and lemon flavors are offered in this somewhat simple sparkler. Bright and zingy. 450 cases made. • $19 • (05/15/98) • **83**

Chardonnay Sonoma County Nagasawa Vineyard 1995: Pleasant enough, with simple pear and toast flavors that turn slightly bitter on the finish. Ready to drink. 482 cases made. • $15 • (07/31/97) • **81**

Sauvignon Blanc Sonoma County 1995: Tastes sweet and bitter, with heavy anise-licorice character on the palate. 574 cases made. • $13 • (05/15/97) • **77**

Sauvignon Blanc Sonoma County Grandview Vineyard 1996: A light style, showing subtle snap-pea and lemon characteristics. Clean on the finish. 550 cases made. • $13 • (04/30/98) • **82**

PARADISE VALLEY | ARIZONA

Cabernet Sauvignon Arizona 1994: There's a cooked edge to its soft black cherry and beet flavors. 1,703 cases made. • $8 • (12/15/96) • **79**

PARADUXX | CALIFORNIA

Napa Valley 1994: A good, solid, red table wine, with a modest core of ripe plum and berry. A blend of 36 percent Zinfandel, 32 percent Merlot, 19 percent Cabernet Sauvignon and 13 percent Petite Sirah. Made by Duckhorn. 596 cases made. • $22 • (08/31/97) • **84**

PARAISO SPRINGS | CALIFORNIA

Chardonnay Santa Lucia Highlands 1996: Really bright and lemony—too much so, in fact, with peach, apple and earth flavors that blend with difficulty. Tasted twice, with consistent notes. 2,000 cases made. • $16 • (01/31/98) • **78**

Chardonnay Santa Lucia Highlands 1995: Offering bright, mandarin-orange flavors blended with toasty oak and earth tones, this wine is fairly complex and elegant, if somewhat leesy. 900 cases made. • $13 • (07/31/97) • **88**

Chardonnay Santa Lucia Highlands 1994: Soft and pillowy, with honey, spice and earthy notes that linger on the finish. Unusually mature at this stage, so drink soon. 1,200 cases made. • $12 • (06/30/96) • **83**

Chardonnay Santa Lucia Highlands 1993 • $12 • (07/31/95) • **86**

Gewürztraminer Santa Lucia Highlands 1993 • $7 • (02/28/95) • **84**

Johannisberg Riesling Late Harvest Santa Lucia Highlands 1993 • $20 • (07/31/95) • **85**

Johannisberg Riesling Santa Lucia Highlands 1996: Light and delicately sweet, this charming California white offers floral, nectarine and apple flavors that linger gently on the soft finish. Enjoyable now, it's a good value, too. 2,300 cases made. • $9 • (07/31/97) BB • **87**

Pinot Blanc Santa Lucia Highlands 1996: This well-oaked, buttery bombshell bears little resemblance to Pinot Blanc. If, however, you like full-bodied Chardonnay with butterscotch, toast, melon and tangy citrus notes on the finish, you'll like this. 1,985 cases made. • $13 • (09/15/97) • **88**

Pinot Blanc Santa Lucia Highlands 1994 • $9 • (05/31/96) • **80**

Pinot Blanc Santa Lucia Highlands 1993 • $9 • (11/15/95) • **87**

Pinot Blanc Santa Lucia Highlands Reserve 1996: Starts off with floral and apricot and a fresh, forestlike aroma. On the palate, it's a fine blend of bright citrus flavors—mandarin orange and lemon—followed by a subtle oak edge. 1,000 cases made. • $23 • (05/15/98) • **88**

Pinot Blanc Santa Lucia Highlands Reserve 1995: Lean and trim. Delicate peach and nectarine flavors have a spicy accent and pick up a note of citrus on the finish. 220 cases made. • $15 • (08/31/96) • **85**

Pinot Noir Carneros 1991 • $8 • (02/28/94) • **77**

Pinot Noir Santa Lucia Highlands 1995: Coffee and cinnamon aromas yield to plum, cola, spice and raspberry flavors on the palate. Finishes with a pleasant, almost juicy texture. 1,000 cases made. • $23 • (02/28/98) • **85**

PARDUCCI | CALIFORNIA

Bono-Sirah Mendocino 1990 • $7 • (11/15/92) BB • **82**

Cabernet Franc Mendocino County 1989 • $10 • (11/15/91) • **85**

Cabernet Sauvignon Mendocino 1995: A fairly lean blend of herb, plum and menthol flavors. Finishes moderately, with a dash of toasty oak. 28,000 cases made. • $11 • (09/30/97) • **81**

Cabernet Sauvignon Mendocino County 1992 • $8 • (11/15/95) BB • **88**

Cabernet Sauvignon Mendocino County 1991 • $8 • (02/28/95) BB • **84**

Cabernet Sauvignon Mendocino County 1989 • $7 • (04/15/94) • **84**

Cabernet Sauvignon Mendocino County 1984 • $8 • (07/31/88) • **74**

Cabernet Sauvignon Mendocino County 1981 • $6 • (02/01/86) • **73**

Cabernet Sauvignon Mendocino County 1980 • $6 • (02/01/86) • **79**

Cabernet Sauvignon Mendocino County 1979 • $8 • (02/01/86) • **69**

Cabernet Sauvignon Mendocino County 1978 • $5 • (02/01/86) • **75**

Cabernet Sauvignon North Coast 1990 • $7 • (11/15/94) • **79**

Cabernet Sauvignon North Coast 1988 • $8 • (11/15/92) • **80**

Cabernet Sauvignon North Coast 1987 • $9 • (04/30/91) • **80**

Cabernet-Merlot Mendocino County Cellarmaster Selection 1993: Smooth and generous, round-textured, with focused berry, vanilla and spice flavors that linger on the finish. • $15 • (11/15/95) • **88**

Cabernet-Merlot Mendocino County Cellarmaster Selection 1986 • $15 • (11/15/92) • **80**

Cabernet-Merlot Mendocino County Cellarmaster Selection 1978 • $12 • (02/01/86) • **75**

Charbono Mendocino Old Vines 1994: Rich with currant and blackberry, and sweet with spicy oak, this is a solid red, velvety in texture, that finishes spicily. Drink now with roast chicken. 2,250 cases made. • $10 • (03/31/98) BB • **87**

Chardonnay Mendocino County 1994: Smooth, fruity and distinctly spicy, weaving a nutmeg-cinnamon character through its pear and smoke flavors. It's a good value to boot. 25,000 cases made. • $8 • (09/30/95) BB • **87**

Chardonnay Mendocino County 1993 • $8 • (02/28/95) • **81**

Chardonnay Mendocino Old Vines 1996: Has some pretty citrus and peach notes around a basic flavor of toasty spice, all of it on a modest scale. Drink now. 42,799 cases made. • $10 • (11/30/97) • **83**

Chardonnay North Coast 1995: A clean, ripe and fruity wine, with a core of spice, apple, pear and melon flavors that are pure and direct. 40,000 cases made. • $10 • (11/30/96) • **86**

Merlot California 1994 • $8 • (12/31/95) BB • **88**

Merlot Mendocino County 1983 • $8 • (12/15/87) • **75**

Merlot North Coast 1992 • $9 • (06/15/94) • **85**

Merlot North Coast 1990 • $8 • (10/31/92) BB • **82**

Merlot North Coast 1989 • $10 • (11/15/91) • **85**

Merlot North Coast 1988 • $9 • (04/30/91) • **78**

Petite Sirah California 1994: Starts out earthy, but evolves to show some fun flavors in layers of ripe cherry, plum and wild berry. Finishes with a vanilla-scented accent and the requisite tannins. 29,443 cases made. • $10 • (10/15/96) BB • **87**

Petite Sirah California Old Vines 1995: Here's a red wine bargain that's enjoyable now. More supple and ready to drink sooner than most Petite Sirahs, this one offers pretty raspberry and blackberry flavors that linger on the lithe finish. Drink now through 1999 or 2001. 40,000 cases made. • $10 • (03/31/98) BB • **86**

Petite Sirah Mendocino County 1992 • $6 • (09/30/95) BB • **86**

Petite Sirah Mendocino County 1991 • $7 • (02/28/95) BB • **84**

Petite Sirah Mendocino County 1989 • $7 • (11/30/92) • **80**

Pinot Noir Mendocino County 1995: Marked by strong oak flavors that overpower whatever fruit flavor it may have started with. 15,000 cases made. • $10 • (03/31/97) • **74**

Pinot Noir Mendocino County 1994 • $8 • (01/31/96) BB • **87**

Pinot Noir Mendocino County 1993 • $7 • (12/31/95) • **79**

Pinot Noir Mendocino County 1992 • $7 • (01/31/94) BB • **83**

Pinot Noir Mendocino County 1990 • $7 • (09/30/92) BB • **85**

Pinot Noir Mendocino County 1988 • $7 • (04/15/90) BB • **85**

Pinot Noir Mendocino County 1986 • $7 • (06/15/88) • **70**

Pinot Noir Mendocino County 1985 • $5 • (11/15/87) • **76**

Pinot Noir Mendocino County Cellarmaster Selection 1987 • $15 • (04/30/91) • **84**

Pinot Noir Mendocino County Old Vines 1996: A bit one-dimensional, with a solid cherry core. Lacks the complexity and finesse of great Pinot, but still an enjoyable quaff. Drink now. 15,000 cases made. • $10 • (06/15/98) • **83**

Sauvignon Blanc Mendocino 1996: Restrained and herbal in character, with bright acidity, it's a racy style that would flesh out well with shellfish or the like. • $8 • (06/30/97) BB • **83**

Sauvignon Blanc Mendocino County 1995: Bright and fruity. Central flavors are nectarine and spice. Ready now. 670 cases made. • $7 • (07/31/96) • **84**

Sauvignon Blanc North Coast 1993 • $6 • (02/28/95) • **79**

Key: SS—Spectator Selection CS—Cellar Selection HR—Highly Recommended BB—Best Buy $NA—Price not available Ⓐ—Auction Price (BT)—Barrel Tasting
Dates in parentheses indicate the issues in which the ratings were published.

Syrah Mendocino Old Vines 1995: A smooth-textured red, emphasizing spice and toast over fruit, with a thread of plum flavor keeping it honest. Drink now. 1,200 cases made. • $10 • (03/31/98) • **86**

Zinfandel Mendocino County 1994: Simple, delivering ripe plum and cherry flavors of modest proportions. 4,206 cases made. • $8 • (11/30/96) • **82**

Zinfandel Mendocino County 1993 • $7 • (10/15/95) • **77**

Zinfandel Mendocino County 1992 • $6 • (10/15/94) BB • **82**

Zinfandel Mendocino County 1991 • $6 • (09/15/93) BB • **82**

Zinfandel Mendocino County 1990 • $6 • (09/30/93) • **78**

Zinfandel Mendocino County 1986 • $5 • (07/15/88) • **80**

Zinfandel Mendocino County Cellarmaster Selection 1990 • $12 • (10/15/94) • **83**

Zinfandel Mendocino Old Vines 1996: Light and simple, with modest plum and berry flavors that turn diffuse. Drink now. 22,000 cases made. • $10 • (05/31/98) • **82**

Zinfandel North Coast 1995: Cherry-candy flavors dominate here. The wine is fairly one-dimensional, and bright enough to be called unbalanced. 21,000 cases made. • $10 • (11/15/97) • **78**

Zinfandel North Coast 1988 • $6 • (10/15/92) • **74**

PARKER, FESS | CALIFORNIA

Chardonnay Santa Barbara County 1995: Elegant and well balanced, with a cedary oak edge giving way to a core of pear and peach flavors. 6,356 cases made. • $16 • (07/31/97) • **87**

Chardonnay Santa Barbara County 1994: Shows off its ripe pear, peach and nectarine flavors in a clean, correct, well-balanced style. The flavors linger on the finish. 7,683 cases made. • $16 • (06/30/96) • **87**

Chardonnay Santa Barbara County 1993 • $13 • (01/31/95) • **87**

Chardonnay Santa Barbara County American Tradition Reserve 1995: Lean and trim, but well focused, with hints of citrus, pear, apple and spice, turning elegant and refined on the finish. 2,125 cases made. • $22 • (07/31/97) • **88**

Chardonnay Santa Barbara County American Tradition Reserve 1994: Elegant and complex, with a ripe, rich core of pear, apple, citrus flavors and dashes of honey and oak. Finishes with a long, complex aftertaste that shows a hint of earthiness. 2,300 cases made. • $22 • (11/30/96) • **88**

Chardonnay Santa Barbara County American Tradition Reserve 1993 • $18 • (06/15/95) • **88**

Chardonnay Santa Barbara County Marcella's Vineyard American Tradition Reserve 1996: Smooth, ripe and creamy, with a range of spicy pear, vanilla, honey, fig and anise notes, turning complex on the finish, where the flavors linger on. Drink now through 2002. 1,039 cases made. • $24 • (06/30/98) • **90**

Chardonnay Santa Barbara County Marcella's Vineyard American Tradition Reserve 1995: A touch sour, with an earthy, leesy accent to the pear and pineapple flavors. Straightens out on the finish, where the flavors are more pleasing. 298 cases made. • $28 • (07/31/97) • **86**

Johannisberg Riesling Santa Barbara County 1993 • $9 • (02/28/95) • **84**

Merlot Santa Barbara County 1995: Smooth and velvety, with modest berry and dill flavors that linger gently on the finish. Ready now. 3,750 cases made. • $18 • (11/30/97) • **87**

Pinot Noir Santa Barbara County 1994 • $16 • (02/29/96) • **86**

Pinot Noir Santa Barbara County 1993 • $15 • (12/31/94) • **86**

Pinot Noir Santa Barbara County American Tradition Reserve 1995: Distinct for its herb and spice aromatics, this is a firmly tannic wine with a slightly stemmy edge that overshadows the tart cherry and berry flavors. 1,229 cases made. • $28 • (12/31/96) • **84**

Pinot Noir Santa Barbara County American Tradition Reserve 1994 • $25 • (02/29/96) • **88**

Pinot Noir Santa Barbara County American Tradition Reserve 1993 • $NA • (02/29/96) • **86**

Syrah Santa Barbara County 1995: The cedary oak stands out a bit in this, but with time it should reveal its plum and smoky berry flavors. Finishes with crisp tannins, making it drinkable now and into 2000. 3,500 cases made. • $18 • (11/15/97) • **86**

Syrah Santa Barbara County 1994: Rich and exotic aromas and a complex core of meaty currant, plum, mineral, leather and smoke flavors. Finishes with lots of flavor, moderate, well-integrated tannins and fine length. 2,450 cases made. • $18 • (11/30/96) • **90**

Syrah Santa Barbara County 1992 • $15 • (09/30/94) • **85**

Syrah Santa Barbara County American Tradition Reserve 1993 • $34 • (05/31/96) • **87**

PASO ROBLES | CALIFORNIA

Zinfandel Paso Robles 1993: Shows a wild accent of licorice and cola that wraps around the chewy frame of dark berry flavors. Drink now. 300 cases made. • $14 • (11/30/96) • **85**

PATZ & HALL | CALIFORNIA

Chardonnay Carneros Hyde Vineyard 1996: Distinct for its rich, spicy flavors and subtle oak shadings, the core of ripe pear, apple and melon is complex and concentrated, showing a measure of elegance and restraint on the finish. Drinkable now. 550 cases made. • $35 • (01/31/98) • **93**

Chardonnay Mount Veeder Carr Vineyard 1996: An elegant, refined style, with pretty floral and spicy aromas and a silky texture that lets the pear, melon and fig flavors glide across the palate. Beautifully crafted, with lots of subtle nuances and finesse. Best now through 2003. 723 cases made. • $42 • (06/30/98) HR • **93**

Chardonnay Mount Veeder Carr Vineyard 1995: A single-vineyard California Chardonnay in a Burgundian style, this wine is generous with its complex fruit flavors, and though it's well oaked, it's not overdone, allowing the core of ripe pear, apple, hazelnut and toast flavors to fold together nicely. Shows a trace of tannin, but should be in fine shape by later this year. 500 cases made. • $40 • (05/15/97) HR • **94**

Chardonnay Mount Veeder Carr Vineyard 1994: Bold, ultrarich and complex, with tiers of concentrated pear, spice, honey and hazelnut flavors that fan out on the finish. Shows uncommon richness and depth of flavor, with a long, full aftertaste. A new vineyard-designated wine from Patz & Hall. 350 cases made. • $38 • (02/29/96) • **94**

Chardonnay Napa Valley 1996: A wonderfully ripe and complex Chardonnay, with a pretty core of rich pear, fig and apple flavors, and a silky smooth texture that keeps them pumping. Picks up lots of subtle flavor nuances, hazelnut notes. 2,100 cases made. • $29 • (01/31/98) HR • **94**

Chardonnay Napa Valley 1995: Bold, ripe, rich and fruity. This has an amazing core of fresh, ripe pear, apple, fig and melon flavors. The pretty oak shadings give it some hazelnut and woody nuances that are remarkably complex and flavorful. Delicious now. 1,400 cases made. • $27 • (12/31/96) HR • **93**

Chardonnay Napa Valley 1994: Another winner from this exceptional California winery. A rich yet elegant white, that's brimming with complex flavors of pear, spice, vanilla and hazelnut, with lovely length. 2,000 cases made. • $28 • (02/29/96) HR • **91**

Chardonnay Napa Valley 1993 • $25 • (06/15/95) HR • **91**

Chardonnay Russian River Valley 1996: Intense and lively, with a smoky oak edge to the core of ripe apple, pear, fig and melon notes, and picking up a dash of nutmeg. Well focused, rich and lively, with lots of subtle flavors emerging on the finish. Drink now through 2000. 150 cases made. • $29 • (01/31/98) • **93**

Chardonnay Russian River Valley 1995: Smooth and creamy. Shows subtle pear, fig, melon and spice flavors with light smoky oak shadings. Turns complex on the finish, where the flavors fold together nicely. Drinks well now. 250 cases made. • $27 • (12/31/96) • **91**

Pinot Noir Carneros Hyde Vineyard 1996: Tight and compact, with pretty dark berry and black cherry fruit, firm tannins and light oak. Finishes with a burst of fruit and firm tannins, so give it some time in the cellar; drink through 2004. 121 cases made. • $35 • (06/30/98) • **88**

Pinot Noir Russian River Valley 1996: Lean and earthy, slowly revealing hints of tea, sage, berry and cherry flavors of moderate ripeness. Finishes with firm, dry tannins; best to cellar short-term; drink through 2004. 783 cases made. • $29 • (06/30/98) • **86**

Pinot Noir Russian River Valley 1995: Smooth and supple, intense and lively, with a spicy core of zesty cherry and wild berry. Was a young, unbridled wine. Should be showing more harmony by now. First Pinot Noir from Patz & Hall. 500 cases made. • $27 • (12/31/96) • **89**

PAUL, PATRICK M. | WASHINGTON

Cabernet Franc Walla Walla Valley 1988 • $12 • (02/29/92) • **84**

Cabernet Franc Walla Walla Valley Reserve 1994: Very firm and chewy, but not heavy, offering wonderful plum and berry flavors under the veil of fine tannins. At its best now. 200 cases made. • $12 • (09/30/96) • **87**

Cabernet Franc Walla Walla Valley Reserve 1992 • $14 • (09/30/94) • **78**

Cabernet Franc Washington 1993 • $9 • (09/30/95) • **89**

Cabernet Sauvignon Columbia Valley 1994: Burnt, foxy flavors, reminiscent of Concord grapes, make this unpalatable. 120 cases made. • $12 • (09/15/96) • **78**

Merlot Columbia Valley 1994: Has a foxy, Concord grape quality that makes it seem coarse. 120 cases made. • $12 • (09/15/96) • **77**

PAULSEN, PAT | CALIFORNIA

American Gothic California 1984 • $6 • (12/31/86) BB • **80**
Cabernet Sauvignon Alexander Valley 1984 • $11 • (04/30/87) • **70**
Cabernet Sauvignon Alexander Valley 1983 • $11 • (07/01/86) • **84**
Cabernet Sauvignon Alexander Valley 1982 • $10 • (03/01/85) BB • **85**
Cabernet Sauvignon Sonoma County 1985 • $11 • (12/31/87) • **78**
Cabernet Sauvignon Sonoma County 1981 • $8 • (01/01/84) • **78**

PAUMANOK | NEW YORK

Assemblage North Fork of Long Island 1995: Impressive for its deep color and opulent aromas, but turns overly oaky and dry on the finish. Fans of tannins will find it attractive, but we'd like more fruit concentration and a better finish. A blend of 55 percent Cabernet Sauvignon, 35 percent Merlot and 10 percent Cabernet Franc. Drink now through 2000. 400 cases made. • $24 • (03/31/98) • **85**
Assemblage North Fork of Long Island 1993: This rich, dark wine is stuffed with ripe fruit and tannin; the plum, coffee and smoke flavors are intense, but need time to come into harmony. 400 cases made. • $22 • (12/31/96) • **88**
Cabernet Sauvignon North Fork of Long Island 1991 • $12 • (12/31/95) • **75**
Cabernet Sauvignon North Fork of Long Island Grand Vintage 1995: Wow. An impressive Cabernet from Long Island that combines a deep color, powerful and enticing aromas, rich fruit and oak flavors and a velvety texture. It has firm but smooth tannins and a lingering finish. Drink now through 2001. 650 cases made. • $19 • (03/31/98) • **88**
Cabernet Sauvignon North Fork of Long Island Grand Vintage 1993: A rich wine whose power is restrained by good balance. Delivers ripe plum and blackberry flavors with firm tannins and plenty of smoky oak nuances. Should live long. 325 cases made. • $22 • (12/31/96) • **88**
Cabernet Sauvignon North Fork of Long Island Tuthills Lane Vineyard 1995: This full-bodied Cabernet has the firm tannins and restrained but intriguing flavors of a St.-Estèphe. It's concentrated, powerful but somehow subtle. A promising wine for the cellar, if it opens as it should. Best from 1999 through 2005. • $29 • (03/31/98) • **89**
Chardonnay North Fork of Long Island Barrel Fermented 1995: An inviting Chardonnay with lots of ripe, juicy fruit flavors and a slightly sweet balance. Smooth and easy to swallow. Drink now. 1,560 cases made. • $15 • (03/31/98) • **84**
Chardonnay North Fork of Long Island Barrel Fermented 1994: This muscular wine shows ripe melon and butterscotch flavors, but has enough firm acidity to keep it lively and in balance. Try now. 750 cases made. • $15 • (12/31/96) • **87**
Chardonnay North Fork of Long Island Barrel Fermented 1993 • $15 • (06/30/95) • **82**
Chardonnay North Fork of Long Island Grand Vintage 1995: An attractive, seemingly sweet Chardonnay with piney aromas, ripe fruit and butter flavors and a soft texture. Tasted twice, with consistent notes. Drink now. 420 cases made. • $22 • (05/15/98) • **82**
Chenin Blanc North Fork of Long Island 1995: An awkward mix of canned fruit and herbal flavors with a strong, oniony aroma. 250 cases made. • $10 • (01/01/97) • **72**
Late Harvest North Fork of Long Island 1994: Firm, with a good honeyed flavor and texture. However, there' s an off-putting earthy note that runs through it and grows stronger on the finish. 90 cases made. • $26 • (01/01/97) • **77**
Merlot North Fork of Long Island 1992 • $13 • (12/31/95) • **81**
Merlot North Fork of Long Island 1991 • $13 • (12/31/95) • **82**
Merlot North Fork of Long Island Grand Vintage 1995: Don't be put off by the earthy aroma—this wine has good concentration to it, with lovely red cherry, plum and berry flavors and, on the finish, some beautiful notes of nutmeg, cinammon and cedar. Best from 1999 through 2001. 620 cases made. • $19 • (05/31/98) • **88**
Merlot North Fork of Long Island Grand Vintage 1993: A harmonious, ripe wine that marries intensity and balance. Appealing blackberry and tar aromas give way to bright berry, plum and chocolate flavors, and ripe tannins. This has improved in the bottle. Drink now. 560 cases made. • $19 • (12/31/96) • **89**
Riesling North Fork of Long Island Semi-Sweet 1995: Quite sweet, it shows Muscat-like flavors of orange, spice and nectarine. There's enough acidity for crispness, but a soapy note detracts. Finish is short and a bit cloying. 600 cases made. • $11 • (12/31/96) • **78**

PAVONA | CALIFORNIA

Pinot Blanc Monterey County Paraiso Springs Vineyard 1996: Peach and floral aromas lead the way. On the palate, mineral flavors dominate to make a refreshing statement. Clean on the finish. 500 cases made. • $15 • (05/15/98) • **84**
Pinot Blanc Monterey County Paraiso Springs Vineyard 1995: Shows character and finesse. Fresh melon and citrus coat the palate and finish with a clean, toast and mineral edge. 600 cases made. • $14 • (09/15/97) • **87**
Pinot Blanc Monterey County Paraiso Springs Vineyard 1994 • $12 • (05/31/96) • **87**
Pinot Noir Monterey County Paraiso Springs Vineyard 1995: Old-style Monterey Pinot Noir, with its earthy, herbal and weedy edges. Picks up a soft, sour cherry accent that some may find interesting. 600 cases made. • $16 • (08/31/97) • **82**
Pinot Noir Monterey County Paraiso Springs Vineyard 1994 • $15 • (04/30/96) • **86**
Twin Hills Vineyard Peacock Port Paso Robles NV: Toast and medicinal black cherry flavors seem out of synch with each other, making this Port seem surprisingly unrich. 75 cases made. • $23 • (06/15/97) • **80**
Zinfandel Paso Robles Twin Hills Vineyard 1994: A rich, spicy, high-alcohol style. Has lots of overripe flavors laced with pepper. Finishes hot, but wins points for its rich plum and prune flavors. Drink now. 400 cases made. • $18 • (06/15/98) • **83**
Zinfandel Paso Robles Twin Hills Vineyard 1993: Big, broad and chewy. A mouthful of ripe plum and spice that shows more up front than on the finish. Drink with hearty food. 400 cases made. • $16 • (12/15/97) • **86**

PEACHY CANYON | CALIFORNIA

Cabernet Sauvignon Central Coast 1994: A touch earthy, this medium-bodied wine is marked by herb, cedar and light currant flavors, finishing on the crisp, simple side, with a hint of mint. Ready now. 568 cases made. • $20 • (12/15/96) • **84**
Cabernet Sauvignon Central Coast 1993: Smooth and supple, with pretty black cherry, plum and currant notes of modest depth and richness. Pleasant, relying more on finesse and balance than sheer power. 400 cases made. • $20 • (12/15/95) • **88**
Cabernet Sauvignon Central Coast 1992 • $18 • (11/15/94) • **87**
Cabernet Sauvignon Paso Robles 1995: Strikes a good balance between the core of herb and cherry-laced Cabernet flavors and light, spicy, toasty oak. Drink now through 2002. 933 cases made. • $20 • (04/30/98) • **86**
Cabernet Sauvignon Paso Robles 1991 • $18 • (11/15/93) • **90**
Cabernet Sauvignon Paso Robles 1990 • $15 • (03/31/93) • **85**
Merlot Paso Robles 1995: Distinctively herbal and earthy, but well within Merlot's boundaries, showing off ripe plum and berry flavors on the finish. Turns tannic there too, so cellar into 1999 to 2000. 765 cases made. • $23 • (04/30/98) • **87**
Merlot Paso Robles 1993 • $22 • (03/31/96) • **88**
Merlot Paso Robles 1992 • $22 • (07/31/95) • **91**
Para Siempre Central Coast 1994: Crisp, lean and tannic, with an herbal streak running through the plum and wild berry flavors. Best to cellar short-term. 60 percent Cabernet Sauvignon, 30 percent Merlot and 10 percent Cabernet Franc. 200 cases made. • $28 • (08/31/97) BB • **86**
Para Siempre Central Coast 1993: Starts out with dusty oak and currant notes with flavors to match, it picks up a trace of black cherry and anise on the finish, where the tannins are smooth and integrated. 140 cases made. • $28 • (03/31/96) • **87**
Para Siempre Paso Robles 1995: A ripe and fruity style, with plum and berry notes and a vegetal hint. Best to enjoy it now while the fruit is ripe. A blend of 60 percent Cabernet Sauvignon, 30 percent Merlot and 10 percent Cabernet Franc. 245 cases made. • $28 • (05/15/98) • **86**
Zinfandel Late Harvest Paso Robles Leona's Vineyard 1995: Big, bold and dripping with plum and jazzy berry flavors. Modestly sweet, this is wine to drink with cheese, not dessert. Finishes with balance, neither hot nor soft. Drink it young, while the fruit is fresh. 3.8 percent residual sugar. 110 cases made. • $15/375ml • (12/31/97) • **88**
Zinfandel Paso Robles 1995: Good, with modest cherry and wild berry flavors that come across as simple and uncomplicated, but attractive. Finishes

Key: SS—Spectator Selection CS—Cellar Selection HR—Highly Recommended BB—Best Buy $NA—Price not available Ⓐ—Auction Price (BT)—Barrel Tasting
Dates in parentheses indicate the issues in which the ratings were published.

UNITED STATES

with a spicy, peppery edge, but not the depth or concentration you might expect at this price. 75 cases made. • $30 • (11/15/97) • **85**

Zinfandel Paso Robles 1989 • $10 • (12/31/91) • **82**

Zinfandel Paso Robles Dusi Ranch 1995: Ripe, with a core of jammy cherry and wild berry flavor that's supple and complex, finishing with tar and vanilla accents and a dash of coffee. Ready now. 1,075 cases made. • $23 • (11/15/97) • **87**

Zinfandel Paso Robles Dusi Ranch 1994: A touch on the austere side, with a slight, green cedar edge to its flavors of wild berry and cherry. Try now. 750 cases made. • $22 • (12/15/96) • **87**

Zinfandel Paso Robles Dusi Ranch 1993 • $20 • (10/15/95) • **88**

Zinfandel Paso Robles Dusi Ranch 1992 • $18 • (10/15/94) • **85**

Zinfandel Paso Robles Eastside 1995: Smooth, ripe and fruity, with hints of cherry, wild berry and plum that make it tasty now. Of moderate concentration and depth; drink up. 302 cases made. • $15 • (11/15/97) • **84**

Zinfandel Paso Robles Eastside 1994: Lean and tight, with a tart, sour cherry edge to the wild berry and pepper flavors. Good, and ready now. 668 cases made. • $15 • (03/31/97) • **84**

Zinfandel Paso Robles Eastside 1993 • $12 • (10/15/95) • **87**

Zinfandel Paso Robles Especial 1995: Medium in color and weight, but with appealing cherry and berry flavors of modest proportion. Supple and easy to drink. 205 cases made. • $25 • (11/15/97) • **84**

Zinfandel Paso Robles Especial 1991 • $18 • (06/15/94) • **85**

Zinfandel Paso Robles Especial 1990 • $13 • (08/31/93) • **90**

Zinfandel Paso Robles Especial Reserve 1989 • $12 • (12/31/91) • **89**

Zinfandel Paso Robles Incredible Red Bin 102 NV • $9 • (03/31/96) • **83**

Zinfandel Paso Robles Incredible Red Bin 103 NV: An elegant style, smooth and spicy, with a pretty core of plum and black cherry flavors spiced with a minty edge. 3,000 cases made. • $9 • (06/30/97) • **88**

Zinfandel Paso Robles Incredible Red Bin 104 NV: Marked by a vinegary flavor, with a modest range of cherry and strawberry. Avoid. 2,874 cases made. • $11 • (06/15/98) • **72**

Zinfandel Paso Robles Leona's Vineyard Second Crop 1995: Dry, tannic and earthy, with spicy, mature-tasting cherry and wild berry flavors. Ready now, even with the tannins, for the fruit is fading. 150 cases made. • $23 • (11/15/97) • **81**

Zinfandel Paso Robles Leona's Vineyard Second Crop 1994: This shows a jammy blackberry and black cherry accent that's quite rich and distinctive, ripe and juicy. Proffers lots of spice and pepper notes, too. Finishes with a tarry, smoky edge and some firm tannins. Cellaring should have softened it a bit. 200 cases made. • $22 • (12/15/96) • **90**

Zinfandel Paso Robles Old Bailey Ranch 1995: Elegant and spicy, with pretty cherry and strawberry flavors that make for pleasing drinking now. Finishes with a dry herb note and a tannic edge. 411 cases made. • $23 • (11/15/97) • **86**

Zinfandel Paso Robles Westside 1995: Ripe and juicy, with a jammy quality to the ripe plum and raspberry flavors. Picks up earthy mushroom flavor on the finish. Ready to drink. 2,015 cases made. • $19 • (11/15/97) • **86**

Zinfandel Paso Robles Westside 1994: Zesty, with lots of pepper and spice notes joined by ripe cherry, wild berry and plum flavors. Finishes with a tart, tannic edge that should be helped by short-term cellaring. 1,603 cases made. • $18 • (12/15/96) • **88**

Zinfandel Paso Robles Westside 1993 • $15 • (10/15/95) • **86**

Zinfandel Paso Robles Westside 1992 • $12 • (10/15/94) • **88**

Zinfandel Paso Robles Westside 1991 • $12 • (08/31/93) • **84**

Zinfandel Paso Robles Westside 1990 • $12 • (10/15/92) HR • **91**

PEBBLEWOOD | CALIFORNIA

Merlot Alexander Valley Limited Release 1987 • $9 • (05/31/92) • **76**

PECONIC BAY | NEW YORK

Cabernet Sauvignon North Fork of Long Island 1994: A deep and harmonious package of blackberry, floral and spice flavors bolstered by ripe, unobtrusive tannins. Ripe, yet polished. Drink now. 550 cases made. • $19 • (12/31/96) • **87**

Cabernet Sauvignon North Fork of Long Island 1988 • $13 • (06/30/91) • **81**

Cabernet Sauvignon North Fork of Long Island 1987 • $13 • (06/30/91) • **78**

Cabernet Sauvignon North Fork of Long Island 1986 • $11 • (12/15/88) • **84**

Cabernet Sauvignon North Fork of Long Island 1985 • $11 • (12/15/88) • **78**

Chardonnay North Fork of Long Island 1995: Herbaceous, citrusy flavors dominate this lean wine, with only modest green apple flavors for balance. A tart style that needs food to soften it. 1,350 cases made. • $12 • (12/31/96) • **79**

Chardonnay North Fork of Long Island Rolling Ridge 1995: Straighforward but pleasant, this round white offers modest flavors of apple, melon and vanilla that finish short but clean. Drink soon. 250 cases made. • $18 • (12/31/96) • **82**

Chardonnay North Fork of Long Island Sandy Hill 1995: Made in a light, elegant style, this gentle wine offers modest toasty and spicy oak notes and nicely balanced melon and citrus flavors. It's restrained, but harmonious. 100 cases made. • $18 • (12/31/96) • **85**

Merlot North Fork of Long Island 1989 • $13 • (06/30/91) • **78**

Merlot North Fork of Long Island Wesley Hall Vineyard 1994: Very ripe, this offers raisin and milk chocolate aromas, raisin and stewed fruit flavors and hard tannins. It has muscle, but lacks finesse. 450 cases made. • $19 • (12/31/96) • **76**

White Riesling North Fork of Long Island 1995: The earthy, smoky aromas are off-putting, and the sweet-and-sour flavors don't overcome them. 600 cases made. • $10 • (12/31/96) • **72**

PECOTA, ROBERT | CALIFORNIA

Cabernet Sauvignon Napa Valley Kara's Vineyard 1995: Combines elegance with lively Cabernet flavors. Bright and refreshing, even sleek, with juicy wild berry, black cherry, plum and spice, finishing with crisp tannins and fine length. Best from 1999 through 2005. 2,500 cases made. • $25 • (05/31/98) • **90**

Cabernet Sauvignon Napa Valley Kara's Vineyard 1994: Young and compact, with a green olive accent to the currant and berry flavors. This tightly wound wine will need time to sort out its flavors and tannins; it lacks focus and length now. Try in 1999. 2,100 cases made. • $23 • (11/15/96) • **88**

Cabernet Sauvignon Napa Valley Kara's Vineyard 1993: Offers a decent core of ripe plum and currant flavors with a spicy edge, finishing with mild tannins and medium weight. Well balanced. Ready now. 1,300 cases made. • $20 • (12/15/95) • **86**

Cabernet Sauvignon Napa Valley Kara's Vineyard 1991 • $20 • (09/15/94) HR • **91**

Cabernet Sauvignon Napa Valley Kara's Vineyard 1990 • $16 • (09/15/93) • **86**

Cabernet Sauvignon Napa Valley Kara's Vineyard 1989 • $17 • (11/15/92) • **78**

Cabernet Sauvignon Napa Valley Kara's Vineyard 1988 • $16 • (11/15/91) • **89**

Cabernet Sauvignon Napa Valley Kara's Vineyard 1987 • $16 • (10/15/90) • **90**

Cabernet Sauvignon Napa Valley Kara's Vineyard 1986 • $16 • (09/15/89) • **86**

Cabernet Sauvignon Napa Valley Kara's Vineyard 1985 • $16 • (12/15/88) • **89**

Cabernet Sauvignon Napa Valley Kara's Vineyard 1984 • $14 • (10/15/87) • **91**

Merlot Napa Valley Steven André Vineyard 1995: Intense and tannic, with a core of earthy currant, coffee, cedar and spice, finishing with a hard, unyielding edge. Best to cellar into 2000 and hope it softens. 3,000 cases made. • $25 • (03/31/98) • **87**

Merlot Napa Valley Steven André Vineyard 1994: Tight and intense, a compact young wine with rich cherry, currant, anise and cedary flavors. Needs to soften a bit, but it's well focused, lively and flavorful. 3,200 cases made. • $23 • (09/15/96) • **88**

Merlot Napa Valley Steven André Vineyard 1993 • $20 • (12/15/95) • **85**

Merlot Napa Valley Steven André Vineyard 1992 • $18 • (11/15/94) • **87**

Merlot Napa Valley Steven André Vineyard 1991 • $18 • (10/31/93) • **89**

Merlot Napa Valley Steven André Vineyard 1990 • $17 • (06/15/93) • **86**

Merlot Napa Valley Steven André Vineyard 1989 • $17 • (11/15/91) • **86**

Muscat Canelli Napa Valley Moscato d'Andrea 1996: Sweet but not syrupy, with lots of pretty pear, litchi and spice flavors that linger on the balanced finish. 2,600 cases made. • $9/375ml • (11/30/97) • **87**

Muscat Napa Valley Moscato d'Andrea 1994 • $11 • (09/30/95) • **84**

Muscat Napa Valley Muscato d'Andrea Late Harvest 1990 • $16/375ml • (12/15/92) • **81**

Sauvignon Blanc California 1997: Bright acidity carries the grapefruit and melon flavors along, framed in a subtle grassiness. 1,400 cases made. • $11 • (03/31/98) • **86**

Sauvignon Blanc Napa Valley 1995: Round and flavorful. Pear flavors have a strong herbal-weedy edge that persists through the finish. 4,200 cases made. • $7 • (08/31/96) • **84**

Sauvignon Blanc Napa Valley 1994 • $7 • (08/31/95) • **85**

Sauvignon Blanc Napa Valley 1993 • $7 • (08/31/94) BB • **83**

PEDRONCELLI | CALIFORNIA

Brut Rosé Sonoma County 1986 • $10 • (07/31/89) • **84**
Cabernet Sauvignon Alexander Valley Fay Vineyard 1992 • $13 • (12/15/95) • **84**
Cabernet Sauvignon Alexander Valley Morris Fay Vineyards Single Vineyard Selection 1992 • $13 • (03/31/96) • **84**
Cabernet Sauvignon Dry Creek Valley 1991 • $9 • (11/15/94) • **75**
Cabernet Sauvignon Dry Creek Valley 1990 • $9 • (11/15/93) • **73**
Cabernet Sauvignon Dry Creek Valley 1989 • $9 • (08/31/92) • **75**
Cabernet Sauvignon Dry Creek Valley 1987 • $8 • (11/15/90) BB • **85**
Cabernet Sauvignon Dry Creek Valley 1986 • $7 • (09/15/89) BB • **83**
Cabernet Sauvignon Dry Creek Valley 1985 • $7 • (10/15/88) • **79**
Cabernet Sauvignon Dry Creek Valley 1983 • $6 • (08/31/87) • **75**
Cabernet Sauvignon Dry Creek Valley 1981 • $6 • (12/01/84) BB • **80**
Cabernet Sauvignon Dry Creek Valley Raymond Burr Vineyards 1993: Coffee, tea, green beans and earth make strange bedfellows here. Has blackberry and herb flavors too, but a coarse texture shuts it down fast. 1,800 cases made. • $20 • (11/30/97) • **80**
Cabernet Sauvignon Dry Creek Valley Raymond Burr Vineyards 1991: On the lean, trim side for a 1991, striking simple notes of cherry and currant. Rather ordinary. 2,000 cases made. • $20 • (11/30/96) • **80**
Cabernet Sauvignon Dry Creek Valley Reserve 1988 • $14 • (11/15/92) • **78**
Cabernet Sauvignon Dry Creek Valley Reserve 1986 • $14 • (11/15/92) • **78**
Cabernet Sauvignon Dry Creek Valley Reserve 1985 • $14 • (03/31/90) • **85**
Cabernet Sauvignon Dry Creek Valley Reserve 1982 • $13 • (10/15/89) • **73**
Cabernet Sauvignon Dry Creek Valley Three Vineyards 1994: A medium-weight wine, with a modest band of cedar-edged cherry and currant flavors. Turns earthy on the finish. 6,000 cases made. • $12 • (04/30/97) • **82**
Cabernet Sauvignon Sonoma County 1988 • $9 • (10/15/91) • **83**
Cabernet Sauvignon Sonoma County 1974 • $40 • (11/15/94) • **78**
Chardonnay Dry Creek Valley 1993 • $9 • (07/31/95) • **80**
Chardonnay Dry Creek Valley F. Johnson Vineyard Single Vineyard Selection 1995: Somewhat medicinal, this herbal, bitter wine seems barely related to Chardonnay. Tastes stripped. 5,000 cases made. • $12 • (07/31/97) • **72**
Chardonnay Dry Creek Valley Vintage Selection 1996: Bright and straightforward, with pretty pear and grape flavors. Drink now. 4,500 cases made. • $10 • (05/15/98) • **83**
Chardonnay Dry Creek Valley Vintage Selection 1995: Crisp and simple, with fresh apple and floral flavors. 9,000 cases made. • $10 • (07/31/97) • **80**
Fumé Blanc Dry Creek Valley 1996: A fresh, peachy wine that stumbles with some hollowness on the palate. Some herbal, minty qualities fill things out a bit. 2,500 cases made. • $9 • (04/30/98) • **82**
Fumé Blanc Dry Creek Valley 1994: Fruity and floral, with citrus and pear flavors. Some zingy herb and, surprise, even chocolate overtones. 4,800 cases made. • $8 • (08/31/96) • **86**
Fumé Blanc Dry Creek Valley Vintage Selection 1995: Earth and pinelike flavors overtake the sweet, spicy oak notes. Has a juicy finish, but its flavors aren't crowd-pleasers. 5,800 cases made. • $9 • (04/30/97) • **80**
Gamay Beaujolais Sonoma County 1987 • $4 • (01/31/88) • **77**
Gamay Beaujolais Sonoma County 1984 • $4 • (08/31/87) BB • **87**
Merlot Dry Creek Valley 1991 • $10 • (09/15/94) • **82**
Merlot Dry Creek Valley 1990 • $10 • (08/31/93) • **83**
Merlot Dry Creek Valley Benchlands 1994: Oaky for Pedroncelli, but plenty of light cherry and berry flavors pull it into balance. 6,300 cases made. • $12 • (08/31/96) • **83**
Merlot Sonoma County 1989 • $13 • (02/29/92) • **76**
Pinot Noir Dry Creek Valley 1993 • $9 • (12/31/95) • **78**
Pinot Noir Dry Creek Valley 1992 • $9 • (03/31/95) • **79**
Pinot Noir Dry Creek Valley 1991 • $8 • (01/31/94) • **82**
Pinot Noir Dry Creek Valley 1990 • $8 • (02/28/93) • **79**
Pinot Noir Dry Creek Valley 1989 • $8 • (03/31/92) • **75**
Pinot Noir Dry Creek Valley 1988 • $8 • (02/28/91) BB • **84**
Pinot Noir Dry Creek Valley 1986 • $7 • (05/31/90) • **70**
Pinot Noir Dry Creek Valley 1985 • $7 • (06/15/88) • **76**
Pinot Noir Dry Creek Valley F. Johnson Vineyard Single Vineyard Selection 1994: A lighter style, with modest cherry and berry notes, but it drinks easily and has soft tannins. Ready now. 3,700 cases made. • $13 • (01/31/97) • **83**
Primitivo Misto Sonoma County 1991 • $6 • (01/31/95) • **75**

Key: SS—Spectator Selection CS—Cellar Selection HR—Highly Recommended BB—Best Buy $NA—Price not available Ⓐ—Auction Price (BT)—Barrel Tasting
Dates in parentheses indicate the issues in which the ratings were published.

Zinfandel Dry Creek Valley 1991 • $7 • (10/15/94) • **83**
Zinfandel Dry Creek Valley 1990 • $7 • (04/30/93) • **80**
Zinfandel Dry Creek Valley 1989 • $7 • (10/15/92) • **77**
Zinfandel Dry Creek Valley 1988 • $7 • (11/30/90) BB • **84**
Zinfandel Dry Creek Valley 1987 • $7 • (07/31/90) • **65**
Zinfandel Dry Creek Valley 1986 • $6 • (03/31/89) BB • **86**
Zinfandel Dry Creek Valley 1984 • $5 • (07/15/88) BB • **88**
Zinfandel Dry Creek Valley Mother Clone Special Vineyard Selection 1996: Brightly textured, with wild blackberry and licorice flavors that at first struggle for integration but come together nicely on the finish. Drink now. 6,000 cases made. • $12 • (06/15/98) • **84**
Zinfandel Dry Creek Valley Mother Clone Special Vineyard Selection 1993 • $11 • (10/15/95) • **85**
Zinfandel Dry Creek Valley Pedroni-Bushnell Vineyard Single Vineyard Selection 1994: A rustic style that delivers chewy cherry, pepper, wild berry and spice flavors, with more depth and richness than the past few vintages from this winery; a positive sign. 1,750 cases made. • $12 • (03/31/97) • **87**
Zinfandel Dry Creek Valley Pedroni-Bushnell Vineyard Single Vineyard Selection 1993 • $12 • (10/15/95) • **84**
Zinfandel Rosé Sonoma County 1994 • $5 • (09/15/95) • **76**
Zinfandel Sonoma County 1983 • $4 • (09/15/87) • **77**
Zinfandel Sonoma County 1982 • $4 • (10/31/86) BB • **79**
Zinfandel Sonoma County 1981 • $4 • (01/01/85) • **78**
Zinfandel Sonoma County Reserve 1981 • $8 • (11/15/87) • **82**

PEIRANO ESTATE | CALIFORNIA

Chardonnay Lodi 1995: Reminiscent of peaches and cream, with toast. Though not complex, this modest wine is balanced and well made. 281 cases made. • $9 • (09/30/97) • **85**
Zinfandel Lodi 1994: Simple, with modest varietal character but it's sturdy overall, with spicy wild berry and earthy notes. 1,241 cases made. • $9 • (12/15/96) • **79**
Zinfandel Lodi 1993 • $10 • (08/31/95) • **87**
Zinfandel Lodi 1992 • $10 • (06/15/95) • **86**

PEJU | CALIFORNIA

Cabernet Franc Napa Valley 1994: Smoke, earth, anise and tar aromas stand out, while cassis, blackberry, herb and spice flavors linger. On the finish, it's sagelike, though a bit astringent. Drink now through 2003. 724 cases made. • $25 • (05/31/98) • **87**
Cabernet Sauvignon Napa Valley 1993: Mature tasting, with a supple core of ripe cherry, plum and berry flavors, notes of anise and spice. Finishing with mild tannins and a cedary edge. Drinks well now. 2,800 cases made. • $18 • (11/30/96) • **88**
Cabernet Sauvignon Napa Valley 1992 • $18 • (12/15/95) • **84**
Cabernet Sauvignon Napa Valley 1991 • $18 • (09/15/95) • **85**
Cabernet Sauvignon Napa Valley 1989 • $15 • (08/31/92) • **85**
Cabernet Sauvignon Napa Valley HB Vineyard 1994: Displays a lot of complex elements, showing an array of cedar, spice, currant, black cherry and plum flavors, picking up sage and tarry notes on the finish. Rich and concentrated, it's best to cellar this into 2001. 1,088 cases made. • $55 • (10/31/97) • **92**
Cabernet Sauvignon Napa Valley HB Vineyard 1993: Ripe and complex, with tiers of black cherry, berry, plum and spice flavors. Holds its fruitiness on the finish, even when the tannins weigh in. Best to cellar into 1999 to 2000. 1,200 cases made. • $35 • (11/30/96) • **89**
Cabernet Sauvignon Napa Valley HB Vineyard 1992 • $35 • (12/15/95) • **91**
Cabernet Sauvignon Napa Valley HB Vineyard 1991 • $35 • (09/15/95) • **86**
Cabernet Sauvignon Napa Valley HB Vineyard 1990 • $35 • (11/15/94) • **88**
Cabernet Sauvignon Napa Valley HB Vineyard 1989 • $30 • (08/31/92) • **84**
Cabernet Sauvignon Napa Valley HB Vineyard 1988 • $30 • (08/31/91) • **82**
Cabernet Sauvignon Napa Valley HB Vineyard 1987 • $20 • (11/15/90) • **87**
Cabernet Sauvignon Napa Valley HB Vineyard 1986 • $20 • (11/15/89) • **92**
Cabernet Sauvignon Napa Valley HB Vineyard Special Selection 1988 • $24 • (08/31/92) • **87**
Chardonnay Late Harvest Napa Valley Select 1989 • $13/375ml • (03/15/92) • **88**
Chardonnay Napa Valley 1995: Openly fruity, showing complex pear, apple, peach and nectarine flavors framed by spicy, toasty oak notes. Has a sense of elegance and finesse. 1,098 cases made. • $16 • (05/15/97) • **90**
Chardonnay Napa Valley 1994: An attractive core of ripe pear, spice, honey and nectarine flavors. Picks up a butterscotch note on the finish. 1,050 cases made. • $15 • (06/30/96) • **86**

Chardonnay Napa Valley 1993 • $16 • (07/31/95) • **86**

Chardonnay Napa Valley HB Vineyard 1996: Strays into the earthy side of Chardonnay and stays there, although hints of ripe pear and anise work their way to the forefront. Drink now through 2000. 800 cases made. • $26 • (07/31/98) • **83**

Chardonnay Napa Valley HB Vineyard 1995: Ripe pear and apple flavors successfully outmaneuver the oak notes to make this interesting. Finishes with a smoked wood edge. Ready to drink. 405 cases made. • $24 • (05/15/97) • **88**

Chardonnay Napa Valley HB Vineyard 1994: An unusual wine, with ripe, sweet-tasting tangerine and floral flavors; not quite a classic Chardonnay, but enjoyable nonetheless. 950 cases made. • $22 • (06/30/96) • **83**

Chardonnay Napa Valley HB Vineyard 1993 • $22 • (12/31/94) • **88**

Meritage Napa Valley 1992 • $24 • (11/15/94) • **87**

Merlot Napa Valley 1994: Lean and trim, with pretty cherry and berry flavors. Stays compact on the finish; cellaring may have softened it a bit. 350 cases made. • $30 • (07/31/97) • **85**

Sauvignon Blanc Late Harvest Napa Valley Special Select 1992 • $14 • (06/15/94) • **87**

Sauvignon Blanc Late Harvest Napa Valley Special Select 1991 • $15 • (01/31/93) • **81**

PELLEGRINI | CALIFORNIA

Barbera Sonoma Valley Old Vines 1995: Crisp in texture, with an unripe edge to the berry and earth flavors. Drink now. 554 cases made. • $14 • (12/15/96) • **80**

Barbera Sonoma Valley Old Vines 1994: Smooth and harmonious, this is generous with its blackberry, vanilla and spice flavors that hold on impressively for a long finish. 328 cases made. • $11 • (11/30/96) • **88**

Barbera Sonoma Valley Old Vines 1993 • $10 • (07/31/95) • **81**

Cabernet Sauvignon Alexander Valley Cloverdale Ranch Estate Cuvée 1988 • $12 • (06/15/91) • **82**

Carignane Alexander Valley Old Vines 1995: Lacks the effusive fruit qualities that small production Carignane can display. While quite astringent, it shows some enjoyable herb, cherry and anise notes on the finish. 1,500 cases made. • $10 • (09/15/97) • **84**

Carignane Alexander Valley Old Vines 1994: A light wine that's a bit chewy. Bright on the palate, with purple plum and spice flavors that linger nicely on the finish. Ready to drink. 1,700 cases made. • $9 • (11/30/96) • **85**

Côtes de Sonoma Sonoma County Deux Cépages 1991 • $6 • (03/31/93) BB • **83**

Zinfandel Sonoma County Old Vines 1993 • $9 • (02/28/95) • **81**

PELLEGRINI VINEYARDS | NEW YORK

Cabernet Franc North Fork of Long Island 1995: Full of leather and spice flavors, with a gamy note on the finish. It's fairly lively, though a bit muddled. Drink now. 120 cases made. • $24 • (06/15/98) • **82**

Cabernet Sauvignon North Fork of Long Island 1994: Ripe and smooth, with dark plum, cherry and spice flavors. An accessible wine that finishes on an appealing cinnamon note. Drink now. 1,139 cases made. • $15 • (06/15/98) • **84**

Cabernet Sauvignon North Fork of Long Island 1993: Layers of ripe, seductive flavors, redolent of blackberry and cassis, are framed by lovely toasty oak notes and tannins that are firm but ripe; this wine is harmonious and should improve through 1999. • $15 • (12/31/96) • **89**

Cabernet Sauvignon North Fork of Long Island 1991 • $15 • (11/15/94) • **86**

Chardonnay North Fork of Long Island 1994: A rich, buttery wine, with intensely smoky and toasty aromas and flavors that will please fans of oak, and ripe pear and melon flavors that emerge on the finish. Distinctive, if a bit unbalanced. 1,900 cases made. • $13 • (12/31/96) • **84**

Chardonnay North Fork of Long Island 1993: The honeyed aromas are promising, but it's lean and a bit short on the palate, with simple apple and smoke flavors and lively acidity. 2,764 cases made. • $13 • (12/31/96) • **82**

Chardonnay North Fork of Long Island Eastend Select 1996: This brisk white offers delicate floral aromas and flavors of crisp grapefruit and light smoke. Tight and fresh, with a nervy intensity that compensates for its leanness. • $9 • (11/15/97) • **85**

Chardonnay North Fork of Long Island Eastend Select 1994: An oaky tasting wine; the peach flavors are outweighed by the spicy vanilla and maple syrup influence of the barrels. • $9 • (09/15/96) • **79**

Chardonnay North Fork of Long Island Vintner's Pride 1995: A full-bodied Chardonnay with plenty of pear, cream, spice and ripe apple flavors. Though a little rough around the edges, it's still balanced, with vanilla flavors that linger on the finish. Drink now. 290 cases made. • $23 • (05/31/98) • **86**

Chardonnay North Fork of Long Island Vintner's Pride 1994: Rich butter and wax aromas persist on the palate in this smooth, rich white. Displays intriguing minty and white chocolate flavors. Try now. • $20 • (11/15/97) • **83**

Chardonnay North Fork of Long Island Vintner's Pride 1993: Big-boned and deep-colored, this offers plenty of toasty nutmeg and buttery oak flavors, and enough melon and spice character to keep the balance. A winner for fans of oak. 325 cases made. • $20 • (12/31/96) • **86**

Dessert North Fork of Long Island Finale 1993 • $25 • (04/15/95) • **78**

Dessert North Fork of Long Island Finale 1992 • $25 • (04/15/95) • **79**

Encore North Fork of Long Island Vintner's Pride 1993: A frame of toasty oak engenders appealing toast, chocolate and vanilla flavors, and there's just enough black cherry and cranberry flavors to fill in the gaps. The finish is a bit tannic, though. • $20 • (12/31/96) • **85**

Encore North Fork of Long Island Vintner's Pride 1992 • $20 • (12/31/95) • **81**

Merlot North Fork of Long Island 1995: An exuberantly spicy Merlot, with plenty of luscious plum, ripe cherry, cinnamon and chocolate flavors. Easy to like. Drink now. 1,790 cases made. • $17 • (05/31/98) • **87**

Merlot North Fork of Long Island 1994: Pretty blackberry and black cherry aromas carry through on the round, soft palate of this appealing red. It offers its ripe fruit and light vanilla flavors without harsh tannins; perfect for drinking now. 1,380 cases made. • $17 • (12/31/96) • **86**

Merlot North Fork of Long Island 1992 • $16 • (11/15/94) • **84**

PEPI, ROBERT | CALIFORNIA

Cabernet Sauvignon Napa Valley Vine Hill Ranch 1991 • $18 • (12/15/95) • **86**

Cabernet Sauvignon Napa Valley Vine Hill Ranch 1989 • $18 • (11/15/94) • **85**

Cabernet Sauvignon Napa Valley Vine Hill Ranch 1988 • $18 • (11/15/92) • **89**

Cabernet Sauvignon Napa Valley Vine Hill Ranch 1987 • $24 • (04/30/91) HR • **90**

Cabernet Sauvignon Napa Valley Vine Hill Ranch 1986 • $18 • (10/31/90) • **88**

Cabernet Sauvignon Napa Valley Vine Hill Ranch 1985 • $16 • (07/31/90) • **85**

Cabernet Sauvignon Napa Valley Vine Hill Ranch 1984 • $21 • (08/31/89) • **80**

Cabernet Sauvignon Napa Valley Vine Hill Ranch 1983 • $16 • (05/31/88) • **89**

Cabernet Sauvignon Napa Valley Vine Hill Ranch 1982 • $14 • (03/31/87) • **84**

Cabernet Sauvignon Napa Valley Vine Hill Ranch 1981 • $14 • (01/01/86) CS • **93**

Sangiovese California Two-Heart Canopy 1995: Takes a while to warm up to; it has an odd iodine edge from which the core of cherry and berry struggles to free itself. Turns herbal on the finish. 5,500 cases made. • $18 • (12/31/97) • **84**

Sangiovese California Two-Heart Canopy 1994: Ripe and spicy, with juicy red cherry, currant and plum flavors that are elegant and lively. Impressive for its purity of fruit. • $18 • (09/15/96) • **86**

Sangiovese Grosso Napa Valley Colline di Sassi 1991 • $20 • (11/30/95) • **87**

Sangiovese Grosso Napa Valley Colline di Sassi 1990 • $25 • (02/15/93) • **75**

Sangiovese Grosso Napa Valley Colline di Sassi 1989 • $25 • (10/31/91) • **83**

Sangiovese Grosso Napa Valley Colline di Sassi 1988 • $25 • (11/10/90) • **87**

Sangiovese Napa Valley Colline di Sassi 1994: Young and tight, with spice, black cherry and a hint of strawberry flavor emerging on the finish where the tannins are smooth and polished. Approachable now, but should age well through 1999. • $25 • (04/30/97) • **88**

Sauvignon Blanc Napa Valley Reserve 1995: Light, refreshing, with hints of lemon and mandarin orange. Simple, yet pleasant. The regular bottling is more interesting. • $20 • (06/30/97) • **83**

Sauvignon Blanc Napa Valley Reserve Selection 1994 • $20 • (03/31/96) • **89**

Sauvignon Blanc Napa Valley Reserve Selection 1993 • $20 • (06/30/95) • **88**

Sauvignon Blanc Napa Valley Two-Heart Canopy 1996: Spice, cloves, mandarin orange and overly bright grapefruit flavors are effusive but not quite integrated in this bouncy white. Finishes on the tart side. 11,500 cases made. • $15 • (12/15/97) • **84**

Sauvignon Blanc Napa Valley Two-Heart Canopy 1995: Very direct peach and spicy apple flavors are appealing, though atypical of Sauvignon Blanc. • $12 • (08/31/96) • **84**

Sauvignon Blanc Napa Valley Two-Heart Canopy 1994 • $11 • (08/31/95) • **84**
Sauvignon Blanc Napa Valley Two-Heart Canopy 1993 • $9 • (01/31/95) BB • **86**

PEPPERWOOD GROVE | CALIFORNIA

Cabernet Franc California 1995: Woody, herbal and somewhat vegetal. Flavors of cherries and raspberries tentatively show themselves, but not enough. 16,000 cases made. • $7 • (07/31/97) • **78**
Cabernet Franc California 1994: Firm, chewy and modestly endowed with cherry and meaty flavors. Drinkable now. • $7 • (11/30/96) • **81**
Cabernet Sauvignon California 1995: Light in texture and flavor, offering currant and raspberry flavors in modest proportion. Drink soon. 15,045 cases made. • $7 • (05/15/97) • **82**
Cabernet Sauvignon California 1993: Strongly herbal, almost medicinal and not as charming as some others. 8,400 cases made. • $6 • (12/15/95) • **78**
Cabernet Sauvignon California 1991 • $6 • (06/15/93) • **77**
Cabernet Sauvignon California 1990 • $5 • (11/15/92) • **74**
Chardonnay California 1996: Fresh and flavorful, with nectarine and apricot notes echoing through the round finish. 26,000 cases made. • $7 • (07/31/97) • **84**
Merlot California 1996: This red is light, bright and fruity, reminiscent of Beaujolais. It's silky in texture and nicely focused to show off the raspberry and strawberry flavors. A real value in one of California's hottest varieties. Drink soon. 8,500 cases made. • $7 • (12/15/97) BB • **85**
Pinot Noir California 1993 • $6 • (02/28/95) BB • **83**
Pinot Noir California Cask Lot 1 1993 • $6 • (12/31/95) BB • **83**
Pinot Noir California Cask Lot 1 1992 • $5 • (02/28/94) • **78**
Pinot Noir California Cask Lot 2 1992 • $5 • (01/31/94) BB • **86**
Pinot Noir California Cask Lot 3 1992 • $5 • (11/30/94) BB • **84**
Pinot Noir Sonoma County 1994: Light-bodied, and mildly spicy. Strawberry and leather flavors work nicely on the finish. • $8 • (07/31/96) • **84**
Sauvignon Blanc California 1996: Lacking in substance, the wine is thin and one-dimensional, finishing with a resinous edge. 3,300 cases made. • $7 • (12/15/97) • **78**
Sauvignon Blanc California 1995: Simple and straightforward in style, with vegetal notes against the grapey flavors. 857 cases made. • $7 • (11/30/96) • **81**
Zinfandel California 1996: Rich and sappy, with concentrated mineral, mocha and lingering blackberry flavors. Rustic, with nothing indicating Zinfandel, but it's interesting. Drink now. 3,000 cases made. • $7 • (06/15/98) • **83**
Zinfandel California 1994: Light-bodied, thin and a bit tart on the palate, this lacks suppleness and grace. • $7 • (11/30/96) • **78**
Zinfandel California 1993 • $6 • (10/15/95) • **83**

PEPPERWOOD SPRINGS | CALIFORNIA

Pinot Noir Anderson Valley 1991 • $15 • (02/28/93) • **79**
Pinot Noir Mendocino County Vidmar Vineyard 1991 • $10 • (02/28/93) • **74**

PER SEMPRE | CALIFORNIA

Cabernet Sauvignon Napa Valley 1994: Difficult to judge because of its tannic strength. Dense, earthy and leathery, with a core of currant, anise and black cherry, it takes a while to work through the tannins. Improves with aeration, showing more depth to the earthy currant flavor. Better than in an earlier tasting. 860 cases made. • $35 • (01/31/98) • **87**
Cabernet Sauvignon Napa Valley 1993: Strives for complexity with its range of flavors, but lacks depth. The currant, leather, cedar and spice flavors are pleasant. • $31 • (09/15/96) • **84**
Cabernet Sauvignon Napa Valley Select Reserve 1994: Dense, tannic and leathery. Backward, it takes time to reveal its core of earthy currant and tar flavors. Finishes with a strong, woody, oaky flavor. Lacks the depth of fruit of the regular bottling, though it showed better here than in an earlier tasting. Needs aeration so decanting is a must. 220 cases made. • $43 • (01/31/98) • **86**
Sangiovese Napa Valley Davide 1994: A well-made wine, with ripe and complex flavors of plum, cherry and currant. Finish shows a firm, tannic edge. 260 cases made. • $27 • (12/15/96) • **87**

Key: SS—Spectator Selection CS—Cellar Selection HR—Highly Recommended BB—Best Buy $NA—Price not available Ⓐ—Auction Price (BT)—Barrel Tasting
Dates in parentheses indicate the issues in which the ratings were published.

PERELLI-MINETTI, MARIO | CALIFORNIA

Cabernet Sauvignon Napa Valley 1994: Thick in texture, packed with mint-scented berry flavors that finish strong, with a hint of earthiness. Best from 1999. • $NA • (03/31/98) • **85**
Cabernet Sauvignon Napa Valley 1991 • $13 • (05/31/96) • **86**
Cabernet Sauvignon Napa Valley 1990 • $15 • (11/15/94) • **88**
Cabernet Sauvignon Napa Valley 1988 • $13 • (11/15/92) • **86**
Cabernet Sauvignon Napa Valley 1987 • $12 • (04/30/91) • **83**

PERRY CREEK | CALIFORNIA

Zinfandel Sierra Foothills Zin Man 1996: Rich strawberry tones and peppery flavors, with a strong dose of charred oak. Finishes with firm tannins. Lacks finesse. Drinkable now. Includes 10 percent Carignane and 6 percent Syrah. 1,964 cases made. • $12 • (06/15/98) • **82**

PESENTI | CALIFORNIA

Cabernet Sauvignon Paso Robles Family Reserve 1990 • $12 • (11/15/92) • **82**
Cabernet Sauvignon Paso Robles Family Reserve 1989 • $13 • (11/15/92) • **82**
Cabernet Sauvignon San Luis Obispo County Family Reserve 1987 • $8 • (12/15/89) • **84**
Cabernet Sauvignon San Luis Obispo County Family Reserve 1985 • $13 • (12/15/89) • **77**
Zinfandel Paso Robles 1994: Firm and flavorful. A jazzy mouthful of wild berry, cherry and anise flavors that linger on the solid finish. Drinkable now. 710 cases made. • $12 • (11/30/96) • **86**
Zinfandel Paso Robles 1993 • $12 • (09/30/95) • **88**
Zinfandel Paso Robles 1992 • $12 • (10/15/94) • **78**
Zinfandel Paso Robles Dry Late Harvest Family Reserve 1993: Firm and chewy in texture, this is a tight wine with a spicy palate and cedary nuances on the finish. 1,428 cases made. • $7 • (11/30/96) • **82**
Zinfandel Paso Robles Dry Late Harvest Family Reserve 1990 • $7 • (10/15/94) • **72**
Zinfandel San Luis Obispo County Family Reserve 1984 • $6 • (12/15/89) • **79**

PETERSON | CALIFORNIA

Cabernet Sauvignon Dry Creek Valley 1992 • $16 • (09/15/95) • **83**
Chardonnay Anderson Valley 1993 • $13 • (07/31/95) • **84**
Zinfandel Dry Creek Valley 1995: Slightly earthy in character, with hints of cherry, berry and spice. A dash of cedar at the finish. Ready to drink. 1,500 cases made. • $15 • (03/31/97) • **87**
Zinfandel Dry Creek Valley 1994: Underscored by a complex core of flavors—wild berry, raspberry, earth and game. Drinkable now, but it's on the tannic side, with a leathery aftertaste. 1,500 cases made. • $15 • (03/31/97) • **86**
Zinfandel Dry Creek Valley 1993 • $15 • (10/15/95) • **84**
Zinfandel Dry Creek Valley Bradford Mountain Vineyard 1995: Austere, crisp and firmly tannic, with a streak of green that detracts. Needs food to soften the hard edge. Drink through 2003. 450 cases made. • $18 • (06/15/98) • **79**
Zinfandel Dry Creek Valley Bradford Mountain Vineyard 1994: Earthy cherry and raspberry flavors mark the complex core, and it picks up dashes of anise and pepper on the finish. Ready to drink. 350 cases made. • $18 • (04/30/97) • **87**

PEZZI KING | CALIFORNIA

Cabernet Sauvignon Dry Creek Valley 1995: Blackberry, cherry and currant-tinged flavors hold your interest, overcoming a dry, earthy and tannic quality up front. Best to cellar into 1999 to 2001. 3,500 cases made. • $20 • (04/30/98) • **88**
Cabernet Sauvignon Dry Creek Valley 1994: Smooth, ripe, supple and well proportioned, with hints of plum and cherry, turning complex on the aftertaste. Finishes with firm tannins. 3,500 cases made. • $18 • (04/30/97) • **89**
Chardonnay Sonoma County 1996: Elegant and spicy, with ripe, smooth pear, grapefruit, melon and light oak flavors. Impressive for its texture and balance. 1,500 cases made. • $17 • (04/30/98) • **89**

Chardonnay Sonoma County 1995: Unfolds beautifully, opening with crisp apple and spice flavors and sliding in some lovely butter and honey notes as the finish rolls on and on. Not a big wine, but it has plenty of class. Enjoy now. 750 cases made. • $20 • (12/31/97) • **90**

Chardonnay Sonoma County 1994: Serves up an odd combination of perfumed fruit flavors and smoky oak notes—and it doesn't quite pull together. Tastes like a highly manipulated wine that's stripped. 780 cases made. • $18 • (11/30/96) • **83**

Fumé Blanc Sonoma County 1996: Steely, mineral notes blend nicely with light citrus tones. What it lacks in intensity, it makes up for in harmony. 2,200 cases made. • $15 • (09/15/97) • **84**

Zinfandel Dry Creek Valley 1996: Lightly fruity, with modest cherry and strawberry flavors that expand on the finish. Drink now through 2000. 1,100 cases made. • $25 • (06/15/98) • **86**

Zinfandel Dry Creek Valley 1995: Remarkably rich and well focused, with a ripe, plush core of raspberry, cherry, currant and plum flavors, and lots of spice and pepper notes. Finishes with supple tannins and excellent length. Delicious now through 2002. 1,500 cases made. • $20 • (04/30/97) • **92**

Zinfandel Dry Creek Valley 1994: Ripe, juicy cherry, currant, plum and berry flavors, finishing with touches of herb and spice and a complex aftertaste. Supple in texture. Ready now, but should age well through 2000. 1,500 cases made. • $18 • (09/15/96) • **89**

PHANTOM HILL | OREGON

Pinot Noir Oregon Corral Creek Vineyard 1996: Pretty flavors of plum and spice do a delicate dance around a thin layer of firm tannins. Promises more depth as it develops through 2000 or 2001. 170 cases made. • $38 • (05/15/98) • **86**

Pinot Noir Willamette Valley 1996: Light in texture, with very pretty raspberry, cola and tobacco flavors. Has hints of peach and vanilla on the elegant finish. Ready now, could improve through 2000. 350 cases made. • $24 • (05/15/98) • **87**

PHEASANT RIDGE | TEXAS

Cabernet Franc Lubbock County Cox Family Vineyards 1988 • $12 • (02/29/92) • **79**

Cabernet Sauvignon Lubbock County 1988 • $13 • (02/29/92) • **83**

Pinot Noir Texas 1989 • $14 • (02/28/93) • **67**

PHELPS, JOSEPH | CALIFORNIA

Cabernet Sauvignon Napa Valley 1995: Tightly wound, a touch earthy and leathery, but the core of currant, berry, cherry and spice flavors is rich and focused, finishing with a long, lively aftertaste. Definitely needs cellaring. Best from 2001 through 2010. 5,000 cases made. • $27 • (06/30/98) SS • **91**

Cabernet Sauvignon Napa Valley 1994: Big, ripe, bold and intense, with concentrated currant, plum, cedar and spice flavors. Picks up an intriguing raspberry flavor on the finish, where it turns complex. Given its size, best to cellar into 2000. 15,000 cases made. • $24 • (02/28/97) • **89**

Cabernet Sauvignon Napa Valley 1993: Dry and a bit rustic; cedary, currant flavors have an earthy accent. Struggles a bit to open up. Try now. 12,167 cases made. • $22 • (08/31/96) • **86**

Cabernet Sauvignon Napa Valley 1992 • $46 Ⓐ • (09/30/95) • **87**

Cabernet Sauvignon Napa Valley 1991 • $23 Ⓐ • (10/15/94) • **89**

Cabernet Sauvignon Napa Valley 1990 • $24 Ⓐ • (06/15/93) • **85**

Cabernet Sauvignon Napa Valley 1989 • $20 • (04/15/92) • **78**

Cabernet Sauvignon Napa Valley 1988 • $23 • (11/15/91) • **86**

Cabernet Sauvignon Napa Valley 1987 • $50 Ⓐ • (07/15/91) • **75**

Cabernet Sauvignon Napa Valley 1985 • $23 Ⓐ • (05/15/89) • **84**

Cabernet Sauvignon Napa Valley 1984 • $24 Ⓐ • (10/31/88) • **91**

Cabernet Sauvignon Napa Valley 1983 • $17 Ⓐ • (08/31/87) • **84**

Cabernet Sauvignon Napa Valley 1982 • $24 Ⓐ • (12/15/86) • **82**

Cabernet Sauvignon Napa Valley 1981 • $13 Ⓐ • (09/01/85) • **86**

Cabernet Sauvignon Napa Valley 1980 • $20 Ⓐ • (07/01/84) • **89**

Cabernet Sauvignon Napa Valley Backus Vineyard 1994: Marked by dense, earthy, chewy tannins and a strong minty edge, the latter so strong it overshadows the currant and berry flavors. Definitely needs time in the bottle to round out and soften, so hands off until 2000. 600 cases made. • $70 • (10/15/97) • **89**

Cabernet Sauvignon Napa Valley Backus Vineyard 1992 • $51 Ⓐ • (12/15/95) • **89**

Cabernet Sauvignon Napa Valley Backus Vineyard 1991 • $33 Ⓐ • (10/15/94) CS • **90**

Cabernet Sauvignon Napa Valley Backus Vineyard 1990 • $30 • (11/15/93) • **88**

Cabernet Sauvignon Napa Valley Backus Vineyard 1989 • $30 • (11/15/92) • **88**

Cabernet Sauvignon Napa Valley Backus Vineyard 1987 • $48 Ⓐ • (07/15/91) • **88**

Cabernet Sauvignon Napa Valley Backus Vineyard 1986: Starting to dry out, with coarse tannins, yet a ripe band of currant, cedar and spicy oak flavors emerges. The tannins dominate the finish, though, and even turn a tad bitter. • $26 • (12/15/96) • **84**

Cabernet Sauvignon Napa Valley Backus Vineyard 1985 • $34 Ⓐ • (12/31/88) • **91**

Cabernet Sauvignon Napa Valley Backus Vineyard 1984 • $41 Ⓐ • (12/31/87) • **88**

Cabernet Sauvignon Napa Valley Backus Vineyard 1983 • $64 Ⓐ • (06/15/87) • **85**

Cabernet Sauvignon Napa Valley Backus Vineyard 1981 • $24 Ⓐ • (04/16/85) • **90**

Cabernet Sauvignon Napa Valley Eisele Vineyard 1991 • $48 Ⓐ • (10/15/94) • **89**

Cabernet Sauvignon Napa Valley Eisele Vineyard 1989 • $40 • (06/15/93) • **83**

Cabernet Sauvignon Napa Valley Eisele Vineyard 1986 • $40 Ⓐ • (08/31/90) • **77**

Cabernet Sauvignon Napa Valley Eisele Vineyard 1985 • $64 Ⓐ • (05/31/89) • **81**

Cabernet Sauvignon Napa Valley Eisele Vineyard 1984 • $62 Ⓐ • (03/15/88) • **88**

Cabernet Sauvignon Napa Valley Eisele Vineyard 1983 • $40 Ⓐ • (08/31/87) • **76**

Cabernet Sauvignon Napa Valley Eisele Vineyard 1982 • $46 Ⓐ • (12/15/86) • **84**

Cabernet Sauvignon Napa Valley Eisele Vineyard 1981 • $25 Ⓐ • (11/16/85) • **78**

Cabernet Sauvignon Napa Valley Eisele Vineyard 1979 • $62 Ⓐ • (01/01/84) • **86**

Cabernet Sauvignon Napa Valley Eisele Vineyard 1978 • $89 • (11/15/92) • **97**

Chardonnay Los Carneros 1996: Distinct for its rich, spicy flavors, it opens to reveal perfumed grapelike pear and citrus notes, and even a hint of bitterness. On the finish it fans out, turning complex and fruity but slightly coarse. 9,500 cases made. • $20 • (05/31/98) • **88**

Chardonnay Los Carneros 1995: Marked by its spicy flavors, this is a ripe, full-bodied style, with hints of apple, pear and melon and a long, full, fruity aftertaste. 13,000 cases made. • $19 • (05/15/97) • **90**

Chardonnay Los Carneros 1994: Well oaked, but the pear, peach and nectarine flavors stand up to it. Elegant and refined, with a finish that lingers and gains a spicy edge. 17,426 cases made. • $17 • (07/31/96) SS • **90**

Chardonnay Los Carneros 1993 • $17 • (08/31/95) HR • **89**

Chardonnay Napa Valley Ovation 1994: Ripe and intense, with a rich core of pear, pineapple and spice flavors. Well oaked, but the wood and fruit fold together nicely on the finish and gain complexity. 800 cases made. • $30 • (09/15/96) • **92**

Gewürztraminer Anderson Valley 1996: Soft and appealing for its generous apple and vanilla flavors, shaded with Gewürztraminer spiciness on the finish. Ready now. 900 cases made. • $15 • (12/15/97) • **85**

Gewürztraminer California 1994 • $14 • (11/15/95) • **82**

Grenache Rosé California Vin du Mistral 1996: A touch of tannin provides a nice edge to balance the raspberry and herb flavors. Finish is dry and peppery. 8,000 cases made. • $13 • (09/15/97) • **86**

Grenache Rosé California Vin du Mistral 1995: Appealing for the strawberry and cherry notes that emphasize its red wine qualities just enough to please those who might otherwise avoid rosé. 2,938 cases made. • $12 • (09/30/96) • **87**

Grenache Rosé California Vin du Mistral 1994 • $NA • (01/01/95) • **80**

Grenache Rosé California Vin du Mistral 1993 • $10 • (06/30/95) • **87**

Insignia Napa Valley 1997: Wonderful fruit complexity and concentration, with smoky tar, black currant, cherry, anise, earth and cedar. Finishes with a wall of tannins, but they're friendly. • $NA • (07/31/98) (BT) • **95-99**

Insignia Napa Valley 1996: What a mouthful. Big, ripe, rich and concentrated, jammed with juicy plum, currant, anise and black cherry flavors, turning smooth and polished on the finish. A real beauty. • $NA • (06/15/97) (BT) • **95-99**

Insignia Napa Valley 1994: This Bordeaux-inspired red blend is remarkably elegant and supple, with a silky smooth texture and a wonderful array of ripe currant, plum, cedar, coffee and vanilla flavors that keep pumping through the long, full, lingering aftertaste. Delicious. A blend of 88 percent Cabernet Sauvignon, 10 percent Merlot, and 2 percent Cabernet Franc. 8,000 cases made. • $70 • (09/30/97) CS • **96**

Insignia Napa Valley 1993: Shows a nice balance of ripe, spicy currant, cedar, anise and tobacco flavors and supple texture. Finishes with a long, complex aftertaste, retaining elegance and focus. Not too tannic; enjoy now. 5,486 cases made. • $62 Ⓐ • (10/15/96) HR • **90**

Insignia Napa Valley 1992 • $100 Ⓐ • (09/30/95) CS • **90**

Insignia Napa Valley 1991 • $62 Ⓐ • (05/31/95) CS • **90**

Insignia Napa Valley 1990 • $53 Ⓐ • (11/15/94) • **86**

Insignia Napa Valley 1989 • $35 • (11/15/93) • **87**

Insignia Napa Valley 1988 • $35 Ⓐ • (11/15/91) • **86**

Insignia Napa Valley 1987: Magnificent. Dark, ripe, dense, chewy and enormously concentrated, it's clearly one of the stars of the vintage. Packed with rich currant, mineral, earth, cedar, spice, anise and coffee notes, it turns plush and thick on the finish, where the flavors are young and vibrant. A wonderful aftertaste keeps pumping out the flavors. Drink now through 2004. 2,500 cases made. • $71 Ⓐ • (12/15/97) • **96**

Insignia Napa Valley 1986: Distinctive for its ripe wild berry, cherry, earth and mint flavors. It's complex, elegant and well-focused, still firm, intense and a shade on the tannic side. Given the youthful vitality of the fruit and tannins, this can easily age until 2006. • $91 • (12/15/96) • **92**

Insignia Napa Valley 1985 • $90 Ⓐ • (07/31/89) CS • **93**

Insignia Napa Valley 1984 • $74 Ⓐ • (11/15/88) • **91**

Insignia Napa Valley 1983 • $46 Ⓐ • (11/30/87) • **90**

Insignia Napa Valley 1980 • $67 Ⓐ • (07/01/84) CS • **90**

Insignia Napa Valley 1978 • $85 • (11/15/92) • **92**

Insignia Napa Valley 1974 • $173 Ⓐ • (11/15/94) • **88**

Johannisberg Riesling Late Harvest Napa Valley 1985 • $12 • (12/15/86) • **93**

Johannisberg Riesling Late Harvest Napa Valley 1983 • $25 • (03/16/86) • **75**

Johannisberg Riesling Late Harvest Napa Valley 1982 • $23/375ml • (04/16/84) • **92**

Marsanne Napa Valley Vin du Mistral 1995: Marked by dashes of citrus and just a tinge of bitterness, enough pear and citrus flavors pour through to hold one's interest. Best with food. 250 cases made. • $20 • (12/15/97) • **83**

Merlot Napa Valley 1994: A complex weave of ripe currant, plum and berry flavors with spicy, toasty oak notes. It's firmly structured and has ample tannins. Drink now. • $24 • (02/28/97) • **89**

Merlot Napa Valley 1993 • $22 • (06/15/96) • **83**

Merlot Napa Valley 1991 • $18 • (09/15/94) • **83**

Merlot Napa Valley 1990 • $16 • (06/15/93) • **83**

Merlot Napa Valley 1989 • $15 • (05/31/92) • **88**

Merlot Napa Valley 1987 • $18 • (07/31/90) • **80**

Merlot Napa Valley 1986 • $15 • (06/30/88) • **84**

Sauvignon Blanc Napa Valley 1996: A bit earthy, with a grassy strain as the main theme. The wine is firm and well balanced, with melon and citrus notes as well. Clean on the finish. 4,500 cases made. • $14 • (03/31/98) • **86**

Sauvignon Blanc Napa Valley 1995: Balanced for smoothness, and offers well-integrated melon, grapefruit and grapefruit-rind flavors that finish with richness and zing. Ready to drink. 8,000 cases made. • $15 • (02/28/97) • **88**

Sauvignon Blanc Napa Valley 1994: Soft in texture, with a slightly bitter edge to the vaguely floral flavors. Never quite comes into focus. 9,545 cases made. • $13 • (09/15/96) • **78**

Sauvignon Blanc Napa Valley 1993 • $12 • (08/31/95) • **77**

Scheurebe Late Harvest Napa Valley 1990 • $13/375ml • (06/15/92) • **81**

Scheurebe Late Harvest Napa Valley 1985 • $15 • (08/31/86) SS • **94**

Scheurebe Late Harvest Napa Valley 1983 • $15 • (09/16/84) • **87**

Scheurebe Late Harvest Napa Valley 1982 • $15 • (04/16/84) CS • **90**

Scheurebe Late Harvest Napa Valley Special Select 1989 • $18/375ml • (04/30/91) • **88**

Scheurebe Late Harvest Napa Valley Special Select 1982 • $25/375ml • (05/16/85) • **88**

Syrah Napa Valley 1984 • $8 • (11/15/88) • **89**

Syrah Napa Valley 1983 • $8 • (11/15/87) • **71**

Syrah Napa Valley 1979 • $7 • (09/16/84) • **78**

Syrah Napa Valley Vin du Mistral 1994: Big, ripe, dark and meaty, delivering a rich, concentrated core of plum, meat, mineral, herb and cedar note and finishing with ripe, plush tannins. Tempting now, best after 1999. 500 cases made. • $26 • (09/30/97) • **92**

Syrah Napa Valley Vin du Mistral 1993: Dark, ripe and intense, a full-throttle style that shows ripe currant, mineral, smoke and anise flavors while keeping its tannic strength in check. Finishes with a complex aftertaste and enough depth and richness to age into 1999 and beyond. 942 cases made. • $24 • (09/30/96) • **89**

Syrah Napa Valley Vin du Mistral 1992 • $22 • (12/15/95) HR • **92**

Syrah Napa Valley Vin du Mistral 1991 • $22 • (01/31/95) • **88**

Syrah Napa Valley Vin du Mistral 1990 • $18 • (10/31/93) • **81**

Syrah Napa Valley Vin du Mistral 1989 • $18 • (12/31/92) • **81**

Syrah Napa Valley Vin du Mistral 1988 • $16 • (06/30/92) • **87**

Syrah Napa Valley Vin du Mistral 1987 • $14 • (08/31/91) • **81**

Syrah Napa Valley Vin du Mistral 1986 • $14 • (10/31/90) • **88**

Sémillon Late Harvest Napa Valley Délice du Sémillon 1989 • $13/375ml • (04/30/91) • **89**

Sémillon Late Harvest Napa Valley Délice du Sémillon 1985 • $8/375ml • (08/31/87) • **91**

Vin du Mistral California Rouge 1993 • $15 • (12/15/95) • **88**

Vin du Mistral California Le Mistral 1991 • $14 • (07/31/93) • **84**

Vin du Mistral California Le Mistral 1990 • $14 • (11/30/92) • **85**

Vin du Mistral California Rouge 1989 • $14 • (07/15/91) • **85**

Viognier Napa Valley Vin du Mistral 1995: Elegant, with a spicy accent to the peach and nectarine flavors, tapering off on the finish. 2,400 cases made. • $26 • (01/01/97) • **87**

Viognier Napa Valley Vin du Mistral 1994 • $27 • (02/29/96) • **89**

Viognier Napa Valley Vin du Mistral 1993 • $27 • (01/31/95) • **89**

Zinfandel Alexander Valley 1990 • $12 • (10/15/92) • **88**

Zinfandel Alexander Valley 1989 • $12 • (10/15/92) • **82**

Zinfandel Alexander Valley 1985 • $10 • (07/31/87) • **74**

Zinfandel Alexander Valley 1981 • $6 • (04/16/85) • **80**

Zinfandel Alexander Valley 1980 • $6 • (07/16/84) • **85**

Zinfandel Napa Valley 1985 • $6 • (12/31/86) • **82**

PHILIPPE-LORRAINE | CALIFORNIA

Cabernet Sauvignon Napa Valley 1990 • $10 • (09/15/93) • **82**

Cabernet Sauvignon Napa Valley 1989 • $10 • (07/15/92) • **84**

Merlot Napa Valley 1989 • $15 • (05/31/92) • **89**

PHILLIPS, R.H. | CALIFORNIA

Alliance California 1992 • $9 • (04/30/96) • **80**

Alliance California 1990 • $10 • (05/31/93) • **80**

Alliance California 1989 • $10 • (11/30/91) • **88**

Cabernet Sauvignon California 1992 • $7 • (05/15/96) • **82**

Cabernet Sauvignon California 1991 • $8 • (05/15/94) • **82**

Cabernet Sauvignon California 1990 • $8 • (11/15/92) • **80**

Cabernet Sauvignon California 1989 • $8 • (07/31/91) BB • **82**

Cabernet Sauvignon California 1985 • $6 • (11/30/88) • **80**

Cabernet Sauvignon California Night Harvest NV • $4 • (11/30/88) BB • **83**

Cabernet Sauvignon Dunnigan Hills Barrel Cuvée 1994: Light and simple, with a thin band of spicy cherry and berry flavors. 26,600 cases made. • $8 • (11/30/96) • **80**

Cabernet-Syrah California Toasted Head 1995: Fairly oaky, but there's depth to the blackberry and cassis notes. The finish shows anise and herb; it's somewhat rustic, yet enjoyable. Drink now through 2002. 2,000 cases made. • $15 • (06/15/98) • **86**

Chardonnay California Barrel Cuvée 1993 • $7 • (06/30/95) BB • **85**

Chardonnay Dunnigan Hills Barrel Cuvée 1996: A brisk and sprightly California white, showing hints of almonds and toast, minerals and green apples. Refreshing, and a real find at this price and score. 140,000 cases made. • $8 • (09/15/97) BB • **86**

Chardonnay Dunnigan Hills Barrel Cuvée 1994: Light, elegant and surprisingly deep in flavor, which makes this low-priced California white quite notable. Nuances of spice and hazelnut add nicely to the pear and apricot flavors. 160,000 cases made. • $8 • (05/31/96) BB • **87**

Chardonnay Dunnigan Hills Toasted Head 1996: An elegant, polished, supple style, with a creamy texture and pretty pear, citrus, melon and toasty oak flavors, all deftly balanced. Best now through 2001. 12,000 cases made. • $12 • (06/30/98) HR • **89**

Chardonnay Dunnigan Hills Toasted Head 1995: Bright, smooth and refreshing for its apple, spice and citrus flavors, polished and generous through the finish. 5,000 cases made. • $12 • (06/15/97) • **88**

Cuvée Rouge California Night Harvest NV • $3/5.(11/15/92) BB • **80**

Key: SS—Spectator Selection CS—Cellar Selection HR—Highly Recommended BB—Best Buy $NA—Price not available Ⓐ—Auction Price (BT)—Barrel Tasting

Dates in parentheses indicate the issues in which the ratings were published.

Mistura Dunnigan Hills Night Harvest 1994: Simple, modest fruit flavors that develop a dry, claylike edge when mixed with the tannins. 32,500 cases made. • $6 • (08/31/96) • **80**
Mourvèdre California EXP 1990 • $15 • (10/15/93) • **83**
Mourvèdre California EXP 1988 • $13/375ml • (04/30/91) • **74**
Sauvignon Blanc Dunnigan Hills Night Harvest 1997: Light in style, with fresh grapefruit, lemon and herb flavors. Finishes crisp and bright. 60,000 cases made. • $6 • (04/30/98) • **84**
Sauvignon Blanc Dunnigan Hills Night Harvest 1996: This California white is understated in style, avoiding the varietal's excesses to achieve even balance and finishing with some nice citrus and honey notes. An appealing wine offering good value. 66,000 cases made. • $6 • (06/30/97) BB • **85**
Sauvignon Blanc Dunnigan Hills Night Harvest 1995: Open-textured and bright. Pear and vanilla flavors gain a hint of herb on the finish. 70,600 cases made. • $5 • (08/31/96) • **84**
Sauvignon Blanc Dunnigan Hills Night Harvest 1994 • $5 • (12/15/95) • **83**
Syrah California EXP 1993 • $10 • (12/31/95) BB • **88**
Syrah California EXP 1989 • $15 • (12/31/92) • **86**
Syrah California EXP 1988 • $15 • (11/15/91) HR • **91**
Syrah California Reserve 1987 • $13 • (12/31/90) • **80**
Syrah Dunnigan Hills EXP 1995: Tea and cherry notes rise to the fore, backed by a touch of toasty oak. 8,000 cases made. • $12 • (09/30/97) • **84**
Syrah Dunnigan Hills EXP 1994: Chunky, with a meaty, leathery edge to the plum and berry flavors, this is firm and tannic but has a lot of substance. Try now. 5,500 cases made. • $12 • (04/30/97) • **88**
Viognier Dunnigan Hills EXP 1996: Smoothly textured, with nectarine, peach, honey and herb notes. The finish has a somewhat bitter, mineral edge. 1,200 cases made. • $12 • (12/15/97) • **84**
Viognier Dunnigan Hills EXP 1995: Shows off an attractive array of citrus and floral aromas, spice, pear and fig flavors. Turns a bit simpler on the finish. 2,200 cases made. • $12 • (10/15/96) • **86**
Viognier Dunnigan Hills EXP 1994 • $NA • (02/29/96) • **82**
Viognier Dunnigan Hills EXP 1993 • $10 • (07/31/95) • **86**

PHOENIX | CALIFORNIA

Cabernet Sauvignon Napa Valley 1992: Spicy aromas blend well with the blackberry flavors and slightly chocolaty finish. Tannins are smooth and firm. Drink now. 200 cases made. • $16 • (11/30/96) • **85**
Hillside Princess Napa Valley 1994: Spicy, slightly bitter notes intrude upon the pear and honey flavors; finishes with a strong floral note. 112 cases made. • $13 • (07/31/96) • **81**
Hillside Rogue Napa Valley 1992 • $16 • (04/30/96) • **77**
Zinfandel Napa Valley 1996: Complex, with earthy wild berry, black cherry, spice and sage, still a bit rough around the edges, but overall, well made and appealing. Drink now through 2002. 150 cases made. • $15 • (06/30/98) • **87**

PIEDMONT | VIRGINIA

Chardonnay Virginia Native Yeast 1995: Beautifully balanced, elegant in texture and rich with bright fruit flavors accented by hints of vanilla and honey. Great tasting and long on the finish. 460 cases made. • $24 • (09/15/96) • **89**
Chardonnay Virginia Special Reserve 1993 • $15 • (02/28/95) HR • **91**

PIETRA SANTA | CALIFORNIA

Dolcetto San Benito County 1996: Earthy, gamy notes are a bit more prominent than the berrylike flavor in this sturdy, simple red. Drink now. 500 cases made. • $10 • (07/31/98) • **81**
Dolcetto San Benito County 1995: Firm and flavorful with spicy berry flavors that rise above the fine tannins. Ready now. 450 cases made. • $14 • (12/31/96) • **85**
Sangiovese California Sassolino 1993 • $13 • (04/30/96) • **83**
Sangiovese San Benito County 1993 • $19 • (02/29/96) • **74**
Sangiovese San Benito County 1992 • $12/500 ml • (02/28/95) • **84**
Sassolino California 1995: Supple, open-textured and generous with its pure blackberry flavors shaded with hints of dried peach and earth. Pretty now, so why wait? A blend of Sangiovese and Cabernet Sauvignon. 1,200 cases made. • $15 • (06/30/98) • **83**

PINDAR | NEW YORK

Brut North Fork Premier Cuvée North Fork of Long Island 1986 • $13 • (12/31/90) • **80**
Cabernet Sauvignon North Fork of Long Island 1986 • $13 • (12/15/88) • **86**
Cabernet Sauvignon North Fork of Long Island 1984 • $9 • (03/16/86) • **71**
Cabernet Sauvignon North Fork of Long Island Reserve 1993: Rustic and well concentrated. The bright strawberry and cherry flavors, over very firm tannins, are jammy on the palate but dry on the finish. Try now. 900 cases made. • $17 • (12/31/96) • **82**
Cabernet Sauvignon North Fork of Long Island Reserve 1988 • $14 • (06/30/91) • **85**
Chardonnay North Fork of Long Island 1995: Rich, with good concentration and stucture, firm acidity and dark, toasty oak accents. It's not showing much fruit flavor now, but may come around. 6,000 cases made. • $10 • (12/31/96) • **85**
Chardonnay North Fork of Long Island Reserve 1995: Pretty vanilla and butter aromas give way to bright flavors of apple, melon and lime in this lively, balanced wine. It's vivid and fresh; enjoy its youth. 1,750 cases made. • $15 • (12/31/96) • **86**
Chardonnay North Fork of Long Island Sunflower Special Reserve 1995: A big wine with plenty of flavor, this leans heavily on oak for its toasty, buttery flavors, but comes through with ripe melon and pineapple flavors, too. There's just enough acidity to keep it in balance and earn it a place with food. 500 cases made. • $17 • (12/31/96) • **88**
Merlot North Fork of Long Island 1987 • $13 • (12/15/90) • **80**
Merlot North Fork of Long Island 1986 • $13 • (12/15/88) • **84**
Merlot North Fork of Long Island Reserve 1993: Makes an impact with its very ripe flavors of plums, prunes and earth, backed by firm tannins and a pleasant, spicy finish. But despite its concentration, it was somewhat coarse. May have improved; try now. 1,500 cases made. • $15 • (12/31/96) • **85**
Merlot North Fork of Long Island Reserve 1988 • $14 • (06/30/91) • **83**
Mythology North Fork of Long Island 1993: Rich and chewy, packing plenty of cassis and plum flavors, with accents of coffee and herb, into a velvety texture. It's ripe and clean and should drink well through 1999. 1,000 cases made. • $23 • (12/31/96) • **86**
Mythology North Fork of Long Island 1988 • $20 • (06/30/91) • **83**
Mythology North Fork of Long Island 1987 • $20 • (06/30/91) • **81**
Natural North Fork of Long Island Cuvée Rare 1992: Crisp and refreshing, this very dry sparkler offers light pear and toast flavors, a rather aggressive mousse and a clean finish. A good match for food. 2,000 cases made. • $28 • (12/31/96) • **84**

PINE RIDGE | CALIFORNIA

Andrus Reserve Howell Mountain 1988 • $15 • (11/15/91) • **82**
Andrus Reserve Napa Valley 1995: Offers a lot of intense, complex flavors, with tiers of cherry, currant, berry and spice, finishing with firm but polished tannins and a dash of cedary oak. Fans out on the finish. Needs time in the cellar. A blend of Cabernet Sauvignon, Merlot, Cabernet Franc, Petit Verdot, and Malbec. Best from 2001 through 2010. 496 cases made. • $85 • (06/30/98) • **92**
Andrus Reserve Napa Valley 1994: A big, ripe, rich and flavorful wine, with tiers of currant, anise, black cherry and spice, picking up pretty, toasted oak flavors and finishing with a silky-smooth texture. Very impressive, although the price is way up there. 990 cases made. • $85 • (07/31/97) • **93**
Andrus Reserve Napa Valley Diamond Mountain 1988 • $32 • (11/15/91) • **82**
Andrus Reserve Napa Valley Rutherford Cuvée 1988 • $19 • (11/15/91) • **65**
Andrus Reserve Stags Leap District 1988 • $15 • (11/15/91) • **82**
Cabernet Sauvignon Howell Mountain 1995: Remarkably supple and refined for Howell Mountain, with spicy currant, herb, sage and mineral, finishing with dashes of tar and cedar. The tannins slowly work their way to the forefront, so it's best cellared into 2000. 1,640 cases made. • $38 • (04/30/98) • **88**
Cabernet Sauvignon Howell Mountain 1994: Broad-shouldered, dense and tannic, but loaded with concentrated anise, cherry, currant and earthy nuances. Finishes with chewy tannins and a good dose of cedary oak. Best cellared into 2001. 1,515 cases made. • $35 • (10/31/97) • **90**
Cabernet Sauvignon Howell Mountain 1993: Well oaked, with a smoky edge to the currant and berry edge. Tight and a bit lean, though it fans out on the finish. Drink now. 1,526 cases made. • $31 • (12/15/95) • **88**
Cabernet Sauvignon Napa Valley Andrus Reserve 1991 • $60 • (11/15/93) • **85**
Cabernet Sauvignon Napa Valley Andrus Reserve 1986: Earthy, with a tart, sour cherry note and not a whole lot more in the way of fruit flavor. Turns mildly tannic on the finish. • $48 • (12/15/96) • **80**

Cabernet Sauvignon Napa Valley Andrus Reserve 1984 • $38 • (06/30/88) • **90**
Cabernet Sauvignon Napa Valley Andrus Reserve 1980 • $35 • (12/01/84) CS • **93**
Cabernet Sauvignon Napa Valley Andrus Reserve Cuvée Duet 1985 • $40 • (10/15/88) • **83**
Cabernet Sauvignon Napa Valley Diamond Mountain 1987 • $35 • (11/15/90) • **84**
Cabernet Sauvignon Napa Valley Diamond Mountain 1986: Enjoyable, though its earthy currant flavors are simple and not especially concentrated. • $NA • (12/15/96) • **82**
Cabernet Sauvignon Napa Valley Rutherford Cuvée 1992 • $16 • (11/15/95) SS • **91**
Cabernet Sauvignon Napa Valley Rutherford Cuvée 1991 • $17 • (11/15/94) • **84**
Cabernet Sauvignon Napa Valley Rutherford Cuvée 1990 • $16 • (11/15/93) • **84**
Cabernet Sauvignon Napa Valley Rutherford Cuvée 1987 • $16 • (03/15/92) • **77**
Cabernet Sauvignon Napa Valley Rutherford Cuvée 1986: A modest band of cedar and currant flavors. Has already lost a lot of its zip and vitality. Finishes with an odd, mossy edge to the mostly oak flavors. • $NA • (12/15/96) • **78**
Cabernet Sauvignon Napa Valley Rutherford Cuvée 1985 • $16 • (02/15/89) • **88**
Cabernet Sauvignon Napa Valley Rutherford Cuvée 1984 • $14 • (08/31/87) • **87**
Cabernet Sauvignon Napa Valley Rutherford Cuvée 1983 • $14 • (04/30/87) • **81**
Cabernet Sauvignon Napa Valley Rutherford Cuvée 1982 • $13 • (10/01/85) • **86**
Cabernet Sauvignon Napa Valley Rutherford Cuvée 1981 • $13 • (12/16/84) • **93**
Cabernet Sauvignon Napa Valley Rutherford Cuvée 1978 • $7 • (04/30/87) • **90**
Cabernet Sauvignon Rutherford 1995: Medium-weight but quite appealing, with a supple band of cherry, currant, cedar and spice, finishing with fleshy tannins and good length. Grows on you. Best from 1999 to 2004. 9,200 cases made. • $24 • (03/31/98) • **89**
Cabernet Sauvignon Rutherford 1994: Smooth and polished, with a pretty interplay of ripe cherry, currant and spicy, toasty oak. This is an especially appealing wine to drink now, as the tannins are smooth and fleshy. 8,300 cases made. • $22 • (10/31/97) • **89**
Cabernet Sauvignon Stags Leap District 1995: Tight, rich and concentrated, with a complex array of currant, anise, cedar and spice. Turns plush and dense on the finish, where the flavors slowly fan out and gain nuance. Needs cellaring. Best from 2001 through 2010. 2,230 cases made. • $38 • (06/15/98) • **90**
Cabernet Sauvignon Stags Leap District 1994: Dense and concentrated, with a ripe, rich core of currant, anise, plum and spice flavors, it fills out the palate with gobs of fruit and ripe, smooth tannins. Supple enough to drink now, or cellar into 2000. 2,100 cases made. • $35 • (10/31/97) • **92**
Cabernet Sauvignon Stags Leap District 1992 • $31 • (12/15/95) • **90**
Cabernet Sauvignon Stags Leap District 1991 • $30 • (11/15/94) • **88**
Cabernet Sauvignon Stags Leap District 1990 • $30 • (11/15/93) • **83**
Cabernet Sauvignon Stags Leap District 1987 • $28 • (01/31/92) • **85**
Cabernet Sauvignon Stags Leap District 1981 • $20 • (02/01/85) • **88**
Cabernet Sauvignon Stags Leap District Pine Ridge Stags Leap Vineyard 1986: Tart and thin, with just a whiff of earthiness and simple cherry and green plum flavors. Tastes like a highly acidic wine that will age for a long time, but never offer much pleasure. • $NA • (12/15/96) • **78**
Cabernet Sauvignon Stags Leap District Pine Ridge Stags Leap Vineyard 1985 • $30 • (04/10/89) • **80**
Cabernet Sauvignon Stags Leap District Pine Ridge Stags Leap Vineyard 1984 • $25 • (02/15/88) • **91**
Cabernet Sauvignon Stags Leap District Pine Ridge Stags Leap Vineyard 1983 • $20 • (07/15/87) • **79**
Cabernet Sauvignon Stags Leap District Pine Ridge Stags Leap Vineyard 1982 • $20 • (10/31/86) CS • **91**
Chardonnay Napa Valley Carneros Dijon Clones 1996: Tightly wound but with attractive flavors emerging, the core of citrus, pear, apple and melon are rich and concentrated. Try now or can stand cellaring into 1999. 700 cases made. • $20 • (01/31/98) • **90**
Chardonnay Napa Valley Knollside Cuvée 1996: Solid but lacking a tight focus, as the smoky, toasty oak isn't quite in sync with the ripe apple and pear flavors. A little more time should help. Drink through 2000. 7,550 cases made. • $18 • (02/28/98) • **87**
Chardonnay Napa Valley Knollside Cuvée 1995: Clean and ripe, emphasizing fruit, with pear, apple, honeysuckle and cedary oak notes. 9,300 cases made. • $17 • (06/15/97) • **89**
Chardonnay Napa Valley Knollside Cuvée 1994: Strikes a nice balance between ripe, juicy pear, apple and honey notes and smoky, toasty oak shadings. Flavors linger on the finish. 3,300 cases made. • $16 • (05/31/96) • **88**
Chardonnay Stags Leap District 1995: A remarkably understated and elegant wine that's rich in flavor and deceptively concentrated. The core of ripe pear, citrus, apple and melon flavors is complex and concentrated, the finish is long and lively. 1,498 cases made. • $30 • (03/31/98) • **92**
Chardonnay Stags Leap District 1994: Ripe, rich and complex, with lots of juicy pear, apricot, fig and spicy flavors, and finishing with a dash of toasty oak. Delicious wine from start to finish. 800 cases made. • $25 • (11/30/97) • **92**
Chardonnay Stags Leap District 1993 • $25 • (06/30/95) • **89**
Chardonnay Stags Leap District Dijon Clones 1996: Remarkably complex, deep, rich and flavorful, with tiers of peach, pear, spice and toasty oak. Very concentrated, well balanced and long on the finish. 1,650 cases made. • $34 • (05/15/98) • **91**
Chenin Blanc California 1996: Fruity though dry, this enticing white reaches out with distinctive peach and mandarin orange flavors, balanced nicely by a flinty edge. A lovely sipper at a reasonable price. 18,000 cases made. • $8 • (10/15/97) BB • **85**
La Petite Vigne TSIFG White Napa Valley 1996: Crisp, with a lean, spicy, lemony edge and hints of tart melon and pear. Distinctive in style, if a bit on the austere side. A blend of 85 percent Chenin Blanc, 15 percent Viognier. 3,500 cases made. • $12 • (05/15/98) • **85**
Merlot Napa Valley Carneros 1995: Rich and complex, with deep currant, spice, coffee and cherry, showing an element of finesse and harmony and finishing with a lively aftertaste that echoes ripe fruit and toasty oak. 1,000 cases made. • $33 • (03/31/98) • **90**
Merlot Napa Valley Carneros 1994 • $29 • (06/30/96) • **87**
Merlot Napa Valley Carneros 1993 • $28 • (05/15/96) • **85**
Merlot Napa Valley Crimson Creek 1995: Medium-weight, with pleasant cedar, currant and spicy berry flavors that turn simple on the aftertaste. Drink now. 12,800 cases made. • $35 • (03/31/98) • **85**
Merlot Napa Valley Selected Cuvée 1994: On solid ground with its ripe plum and cherry flavors. Lacks richness and depth on the finish. 12,000 cases made. • $19 • (07/31/96) • **84**
Merlot Napa Valley Selected Cuvée 1993 • $18 • (05/15/96) • **84**
Merlot Napa Valley Selected Cuvée 1991 • $17 • (09/15/94) • **85**
Merlot Napa Valley Selected Cuvée 1989 • $17 • (05/31/92) • **73**
Merlot Napa Valley Selected Cuvée 1988 • $17 • (08/31/91) • **80**
Merlot Napa Valley Selected Cuvée 1987 • $15 • (04/15/90) • **88**
Merlot Napa Valley Selected Cuvée 1986 • $15 • (06/30/89) • **80**
Merlot Napa Valley Selected Cuvée 1985 • $13 • (02/15/88) SS • **91**
Merlot Napa Valley Selected Cuvée 1984 • $18 • (05/15/87) • **80**
Merlot Napa Valley Selected Cuvée 1983 • $13 • (12/16/85) • **83**
Merlot Napa Valley Selected Cuvée 1982 • $13 • (10/01/85) • **90**
Merlot Napa Valley Selected Cuvée 1981 • $13 • (03/16/84) • **82**

PINNACLES | CALIFORNIA

Pinot Noir Monterey Pinnacles Vineyard 1991 • $16 • (02/28/93) • **84**
Pinot Noir Monterey Pinnacles Vineyard 1990 • $16 • (02/28/93) • **79**
Pinot Noir Monterey Pinnacles Vineyard 1988 • $16 • (10/31/91) • **74**

PINTLER | IDAHO

Cabernet Sauvignon Idaho 1988 • $16 • (02/29/92) • **81**

PIPER SONOMA | CALIFORNIA

Blanc de Noirs Sonoma County 1988 • $14 • (12/31/92) • **86**
Blanc de Noirs Sonoma County 1987 • $16 • (06/15/91) • **83**
Blanc de Noirs Sonoma County 1986 • $15 • (05/31/89) • **87**
Blanc de Noirs Sonoma County 1983 • $15 • (12/31/86) • **88**
Blanc de Noirs Sonoma County 1982 • $15 • (04/01/86) • **86**

Key: SS—Spectator Selection CS—Cellar Selection HR—Highly Recommended BB—Best Buy $NA—Price not available Ⓐ—Auction Price (BT)—Barrel Tasting
Dates in parentheses indicate the issues in which the ratings were published.

Blanc de Noirs Sonoma County NV: Floral overtones are followed by a doughy, appley, citrusy character. Broad on the palate, with a moderate finish. • $16 • (12/15/97) • **87**
Brut Rosé Sonoma County 1990 • $19 • (12/31/95) • **84**
Brut Rosé Sonoma County 1989 • $19 • (11/15/94) • **88**
Brut Sonoma County 1988 • $14 • (01/31/92) • **88**
Brut Sonoma County 1987 • $16 • (06/15/91) • **87**
Brut Sonoma County 1986 • $14 • (05/31/89) • **82**
Brut Sonoma County 1985 • $14 • (07/15/88) • **79**
Brut Sonoma County 1983 • $22 • (01/31/88) • **74**
Brut Sonoma County NV: Upfront and fruity, with lemon, lime, spice, ginger and even a touch of mint to its character. Tangy acidity carries the wine nicely. • $15 • (12/15/97) • **85**
Brut Sonoma County Reserve 1982 • $20 • (12/31/89) • **93**
Brut Sonoma County Tête de Cuvée 1985 • $28 • (12/31/94) • **86**
Brut Sonoma County Tête de Cuvée 1981 • $29 • (05/31/89) • **88**

PLAM | CALIFORNIA

Cabernet Sauvignon California 1992 • $6 • (12/15/95) • **82**
Cabernet Sauvignon Napa Valley 1992 • $30 • (11/15/94) • **88**
Cabernet Sauvignon Napa Valley 1988 • $28 • (09/30/91) • **79**
Cabernet Sauvignon Napa Valley 1986 • $24 • (09/15/89) • **92**
Cabernet Sauvignon Napa Valley 1985 • $24 • (06/30/88) • **91**
Merlot Napa Valley 1993 • $25 • (03/31/96) • **78**

PLUM CREEK | COLORADO

Chardonnay Colorado 1995: A blowsy style for fans of oak, with decent pear and apple flavors. A one-note wine that does the job. 2,549 cases made. • $10 • (12/31/97) • **80**
Chardonnay Colorado Redstone Reserve 1995: An overblown and blowsy style with buttery flavors verging on rancidity. Has a tannic finish as well. 464 cases made. • $13 • (08/31/97) • **76**
Merlot Colorado 1995: Tannic, dominated by fairly rich and concentrated chocolate and ripe cherry flavors, turning a little bitter on the finish. 856 cases made. • $11 • (12/31/97) • **80**
Merlot Colorado Redstone Reserve 1994: Loads of spicy, sawdust aromas and flavors mingle with the plum notes in this assertive red. The finish has some dry tannins, but overall it's tasty. For fans of oak. 1,008 cases made. • $13 • (08/31/97) • **84**
Riesling Colorado 1996: A bizarre mix of onion and apple flavors. Finishes on a funky note. 439 cases made. • $8 • (08/31/97) • **73**
Sauvignon Blanc Colorado Whitecliff 1996: Herbal, almost salty-tasting, with an astringent finish. A tough customer. 436 cases made. • $8 • (12/31/97) • **76**

PLUMPJACK | CALIFORNIA

Cabernet Sauvignon Napa Valley McWilliam's Mt. Eden Vineyard 1995: A supple and forward style, openly fruity, also well-oaked with toasty, spicy flavors and an elegant band of spice and currant-laced Cabernet flavors. Complex and intense; drinkable now, but worthy of cellaring into 2002. 1,000 cases made. • $30 • (11/15/97) • **92**
Cabernet Sauvignon Napa Valley McWilliam's Mt. Eden Vineyard Reserve 1995: Intense and concentrated, with a firm band of cedar, spice, earth, mineral and currant flavors. Tightens up on the finish, where the tannins fold in and the wine displays lots of finesse and complexity. Best to cellar into 2001 to 2002. 500 cases made. • $65 • (11/15/97) • **92**

PONTIN DEL ROZA | WASHINGTON

Cabernet Sauvignon Columbia Valley 1993: Has a distinct pickle-barrel note that runs through the modest blackberry flavors. Drinkable now. 375 cases made. • $22 • (08/31/96) • **84**
Chenin Blanc Columbia Valley 1995: Soft and pleasant. Slightly sweet pear and almond flavors. Drink it soon. 500 cases made. • $6 • (08/31/96) • **82**
Merlot Columbia Valley 1993: Fresh, lively and focused, playing out its berry, spice and vanilla flavors with style and flair. Tasty now. 540 cases made. • $11 • (08/31/96) • **87**
White Riesling Columbia Valley 1995: Sweet, floral aromas and flavors are insufficient to balance some off-notes. 575 cases made. • $6 • (09/15/96) • **73**

PONZI | OREGON

Arneis Willamette Valley 1996: Exhibits a distinctive range of flavors, hitting pear, almond, hazelnut and orange-peel notes along the way. A full-bodied wine that emphasizes rich fruit. Drink soon. 311 cases made. • $18/500ml • (10/31/97) • **86**
Chardonnay Willamette Valley 1996: A fresh, pretty white wine, with modest pear and apple flavors that pick up a touch of rose petal and a hint of spice and grow on the finish. Ready now. 1,132 cases made. • $16 • (05/15/98) • **88**
Chardonnay Willamette Valley Clonal Selection 1996: Bright and focused, crisply balanced, with a fine layer of acidity to enhance the ripe pear, caramel and spice flavors that weave through the finish. Nice now, best from 1999. 122 cases made. • $24 • (05/15/98) • **89**
Pinot Gris Willamette Valley 1996: Has a smoky edge to its pretty melon and floral flavors, and finishes with freshness and balance. 2,400 cases made. • $13 • (09/15/97) • **87**
Pinot Gris Willamette Valley 1994 • $13 • (11/30/95) • **85**
Pinot Noir Oregon Reserve 1992 • $30 • (10/15/94) HR • **92**
Pinot Noir Willamette Valley 1995: Very light in color and flavor, a delicate wine with a hint of orange peel to the soft currant flavor. Ready now. 2,100 cases made. • $20 • (10/31/97) • **86**
Pinot Noir Willamette Valley 1994: Smooth and sophisticated, with a nice core of ripe cherry and plum flavors wrapped in a currently obtrusive layer of sophisticated new oak. Should be at its best now. 1,400 cases made. • $20 • (12/15/96) • **88**
Pinot Noir Willamette Valley 1988 • $16 • (05/31/91) • **76**
Pinot Noir Willamette Valley 1987 • $15 • (02/15/90) • **88**
Pinot Noir Willamette Valley 1985 • $20 • (02/15/90) • **84**
Pinot Noir Willamette Valley 20th Anniversary Edition 1990 • $35 • (02/28/93) • **91**
Pinot Noir Willamette Valley Reserve 1995: Light, crisp and juicy at first, with an anise accent to the black cherry and smoke flavors that rev up nicely on the finish, gaining depth and sweet, earthy complexity. Grows with each sip. Best from 2000. 1,600 cases made. • $48 • (10/31/97) • **89**
Pinot Noir Willamette Valley Reserve 1994: Ripe and rich, elegant and complex. A profound wine that balances its black cherry, currant and anise flavors with fine touches of spicy oak and silky texture. Tannins barely show, but they're there, making this a great bet for cellaring well past 2000 or 2001. 1,059 cases made. • $35 • (12/15/96) CS • **94**
Pinot Noir Willamette Valley Reserve 1991 • $25 • (01/31/94) • **86**
Pinot Noir Willamette Valley Reserve 1990 • $25 • (02/28/93) • **73**
Pinot Noir Willamette Valley Reserve 1988 • $25 • (04/15/91) • **86**
Pinot Noir Willamette Valley Reserve 1987 • $20 • (02/15/90) • **91**
Pinot Noir Willamette Valley Reserve 1986 • $15 • (06/15/88) • **81**

POPE VALLEY | CALIFORNIA

Cabernet Sauvignon Napa Valley 1990 • $14 • (11/15/94) • **84**
Cabernet Sauvignon Napa Valley La Dolce DeVita Vineyard 1992 • $15 • (12/15/95) • **87**
Port Napa Valley 1994 • $18 • (10/31/95) • **88**
Port Napa Valley 1993 • $18 • (05/31/95) • **83**

POPPY HILL | CALIFORNIA

Cabernet Sauvignon California 1987 • $7 • (05/31/91) • **78**
Merlot Napa Valley Founder's Selection 1991 • $10 • (09/15/94) • **84**

PORTER CREEK | CALIFORNIA

Chardonnay Russian River Valley 1993 • $14 • (07/31/95) • **82**
Chardonnay Russian River Valley Unfiltered Reserve 1993 • $23 • (07/31/95) • **83**

PORTTEUS | WASHINGTON

Cabernet Sauvignon Yakima Valley 1991 • $19 • (09/30/94) • **71**
Cabernet Sauvignon Yakima Valley 1990 • $19 • (09/30/95) • **72**
Cabernet Sauvignon Yakima Valley 1988 • $19 • (02/28/93) • **85**
Cabernet Sauvignon Yakima Valley 1987 • $18 • (03/31/92) • **86**
Cabernet Sauvignon Yakima Valley Estate Bottled 1991 • $23 • (09/30/94) • **85**
Lemberger Yakima Valley 1992 • $12 • (09/30/94) • **85**

POWERS | WASHINGTON

Cabernet Sauvignon Columbia Valley 1993: Silky smooth and beautifully polished, a mouthful of sweet plum, blackberry and vanilla flavor that glides smoothly through the finish. Drink now. 300 cases made. • $12 • (09/30/95) • **91**

Cabernet Sauvignon Columbia Valley Mercer Ranch Vineyard 1994: Packs a lot of delicious currant, boysenberry and plum flavors into a tight package, making the spicy, toasty notes seem almost racy. Should develop into an elegant, deep wine by 1999 to 2000. 1,500 cases made. • $18 • (09/15/96) • **88**

Cabernet-Merlot Columbia Valley 1995: A solid wine, offering ripe Cabernet flavors on a firm frame, finishing with a velvety cast to the tannins. A blend of 88 percent Cabernet Sauvignon and 12 percent Merlot. 2,100 cases made. • $12 • (09/15/97) • **86**

Cabernet-Merlot Columbia Valley 1994: Bright, plummy flavors make this a lively blend, balancing its zesty fruit against a firm frame of fine tannin and some spiciness. Drink now. 1,000 cases made. • $10 • (05/15/96) • **87**

Cabernet-Merlot Columbia Valley 1993: Packs a rich vein of spicy plum, currant and berry flavor on an airy, elegant frame. Disarming in its purity of sweet fruit combined with polished texture and nice touches of minty oak. Drink now. 550 cases made. • $10 • (05/15/96) • **91**

Cabernet-Merlot Columbia Valley 1992 • $8 • (10/15/93) • **79**

Chardonnay Columbia Valley 1995: A fresh and fragrant white with apple, pine and spice flavors that linger gently on the finish. A good value. 2,500 cases made. • $10 • (12/31/96) BB • **87**

Chardonnay Columbia Valley 1994: Light and spicy, sneaking some toasty oak into the mix on the finish. 1,500 cases made. • $8 • (09/30/95) • **82**

Chardonnay Columbia Valley 1993 • $8 • (09/30/95) • **87**

Fumé Blanc Columbia Valley 1996: Crisp and zingy, this is a sharp-edged Sauvignon with vaguely citrusy flavors. 2,600 cases made. • $8 • (09/15/97) • **81**

Fumé Blanc Columbia Valley 1995: Soft and floral on the nose and palate, with a distinct, rose petal accent setting off the pear and toast flavors. 2,000 cases made. • $7 • (09/15/96) • **85**

Fumé Blanc Columbia Valley 1994 • $8 • (09/30/95) • **83**

Lemberger Columbia Valley Mercer Ranch Vineyard 1995: Dense color, chewy texture and strong blackberry and anise flavors that actually remain light enough on their feet to be charming. Ready now. 1,000 cases made. • $10 • (12/31/96) • **85**

Merlot Columbia Valley 1995: Lean and lithe, with nicely focused black cherry and spice flavors that linger on the gentle finish. Drink now. 2,000 cases made. • $18 • (09/15/97) • **88**

Merlot Columbia Valley 1993 • $13 • (05/31/96) • **85**

Merlot Columbia Valley 1992 • $12 • (09/30/94) • **80**

Muscat Canelli Columbia Valley 1996: Frankly sweet, open and generous with its fresh pear and litchi flavors. 500 cases made. • $7 • (09/15/97) • **85**

Pinot Noir Columbia Valley 1996: Youthful and bright, with a solid core of currant and mineral flavors that linger on the soft finish. Best to drink soon. 2,850 cases made. • $9 • (09/15/97) • **83**

PRADEL, BERNARD | CALIFORNIA

Cabernet Sauvignon Howell Mountain Ranch 1991 • $21 • (09/15/95) • **87**

Cabernet Sauvignon Napa Valley 1987 • $20 • (10/15/90) • **86**

Cabernet Sauvignon Napa Valley 1986 • $12 • (01/31/90) • **82**

Cabernet Sauvignon Napa Valley 1985 • $12 • (04/30/89) • **91**

Cabernet Sauvignon Napa Valley 1984 • $11 • (02/29/88) • **88**

Cabernet Sauvignon Napa Valley Limited Barrel Selection 1990 • $14 • (09/15/95) • **85**

Cabernet Sauvignon Napa Valley Limited Barrel Selection 1989 • $18 • (08/31/92) • **81**

Cabernet Sauvignon Napa Valley Limited Barrel Selection 1988 • $20 • (11/15/91) • **80**

Sauvignon Blanc Late Harvest Napa Valley Allais Vineyard Botrytis 1985 • $9/375ml • (05/31/88) • **75**

Key: SS—Spectator Selection CS—Cellar Selection HR—Highly Recommended BB—Best Buy $NA—Price not available Ⓐ—Auction Price (BT)—Barrel Tasting
Dates in parentheses indicate the issues in which the ratings were published.

PREJEAN | NEW YORK

Johannisberg Riesling Finger Lakes Dry 1995: Flavorful enough, with its peach, honey and grapefruit notes. Rather soft and slightly sweet. • $10 • (10/31/96) • **82**

Johannisberg Riesling Finger Lakes Semi-Dry 1995: A well-rounded and lively tasting Riesling that blends honey, peach and herb flavors with a smooth mouthfeel. • $NA • (10/31/96) • **84**

PRESTON | CALIFORNIA

Barbera Dry Creek Valley 1992 • $13 • (11/15/95) • **89**

Barbera Dry Creek Valley 1990 • $13 • (11/30/92) • **82**

Barbera Dry Creek Valley 1989 • $13 • (03/15/92) • **86**

Barbera Dry Creek Valley 1985 • $8 • (01/31/88) • **85**

Cabernet Sauvignon Dry Creek Valley 1990 • $12 • (11/15/94) • **88**

Cabernet Sauvignon Dry Creek Valley 1989 • $12 • (11/15/93) • **81**

Cabernet Sauvignon Dry Creek Valley 1988 • $14 • (03/15/92) • **80**

Cabernet Sauvignon Dry Creek Valley 1987 • $14 • (10/31/90) • **88**

Cabernet Sauvignon Dry Creek Valley 1986 • $12 • (03/15/90) • **87**

Cabernet Sauvignon Dry Creek Valley 1985 • $11 • (09/30/88) • **86**

Cabernet Sauvignon Dry Creek Valley 1984 • $11 • (10/15/87) • **91**

Cabernet Sauvignon Dry Creek Valley 1983 • $11 • (07/16/86) • **86**

Cabernet Sauvignon Dry Creek Valley 1982 • $11 • (07/01/85) • **84**

Estate Red Dry Creek Valley 1989 • $5 • (06/30/90) • **77**

Estate Red Dry Creek Valley 1988 • $5 • (08/31/89) BB • **82**

Faux Dry Creek Valley 1995: This Rhône blend is racy, with an earthy, herbal edge to the cherry and plum flavors. Drinkable now. 4,866 cases made. • $10 • (07/31/97) • **85**

Faux Dry Creek Valley 1993 • $9 • (04/30/95) • **85**

Faux Dry Creek Valley 1992 • $9 • (12/31/93) BB • **83**

Faux-Castel Dry Creek Valley 1991 • $9 • (11/30/92) • **85**

Faux-Castel Dry Creek Valley 1990 • $9 • (06/30/92) • **82**

Gamay Beaujolais Dry Creek Valley 1996: Deep purple in color and brimming with licorice, herb, blackberry and cassis flavors. A tart finish and pronounced acidity detract from this otherwise interesting wine. 800 cases made. • $11 • (09/15/97) • **87**

Gamay Beaujolais Dry Creek Valley 1995 • $9 • (02/29/96) • **86**

Gamay Beaujolais Dry Creek Valley 1994 • $8 • (04/30/95) • **87**

Gamay Beaujolais Dry Creek Valley 1988 • $7 • (02/15/89) • **85**

Gamay Beaujolais Dry Creek Valley 1987 • $6 • (01/31/88) • **78**

Gamay Beaujolais Dry Creek Valley 1986 • $6 • (02/15/87) • **88**

Gamay Beaujolais Dry Creek Valley 1985 • $5 • (02/01/86) • **88**

Gamay Dry Creek Valley 1997: Light, bright and appropriately fruity. Not too exuberant so it shows a little more balance and suppleness than most Gamays. Ready now. 2,400 cases made. • $12 • (03/31/98) • **86**

Le Petit Faux Dry Creek Valley Rosé 1996: This somewhat floral-scented wine has body but lacks flavor. Finishes hot. 510 cases made. • $10 • (09/15/97) • **80**

Marsanne Dry Creek Valley 1995: A smooth, subtle wine, revealing layers of toasty hazelnut, vanilla, fig and herbs. The finish is crisp and clean, with a bright mineral edge. 545 cases made. • $18 • (12/15/97) • **87**

Marsanne Dry Creek Valley 1994 • $18 • (07/31/95) • **87**

Muscat Canelli Late Harvest Dry Creek Valley 1989 • $12/375ml • (03/15/92) • **82**

Muscat Canelli Late Harvest Dry Creek Valley 1987 • $12/375ml • (08/31/89) • **91**

Sauvignon Blanc Dry Creek Valley 1994 • $12 • (02/29/96) • **82**

Sauvignon Blanc Dry Creek Valley 1993 • $12 • (08/31/95) • **83**

Sauvignon Blanc Dry Creek Valley Cuvée de Fumé 1996: Fairly viscous in texture, yet balanced by good acidity. Flavors include wintergreen, grapefruit, herbs and a touch of vanilla. 3,900 cases made. • $12 • (12/15/97) • **87**

Sauvignon Blanc Dry Creek Valley Cuvée de Fumé 1995: Round and spicy, with a floral, herbal accent to the toasty pear flavors. Has more character than most California Sauvignon Blancs. 5,800 cases made. • $10 • (02/28/97) • **87**

Sauvignon Blanc Dry Creek Valley Cuvée de Fumé 1994: Soft and weedy, with a sweet vanilla overtone to the floral flavors. Lacks fruit; not the norm for Preston. 1,594 cases made. • $9 • (09/15/96) • **78**

Sauvignon Blanc Dry Creek Valley Cuvée de Fumé 1993 • $9 • (05/31/95) BB • **86**

Syrah Dry Creek Valley 1994: A medium-weight Syrah, with a spicy, meaty edge to the plum and berry notes. Try now. 973 cases made. • $20 • (05/15/97) • **87**

Syrah Dry Creek Valley 1993 • $18 • (02/29/96) • **88**

Syrah Dry Creek Valley 1992 • $18 • (05/15/95) • **88**
Syrah Dry Creek Valley 1990 • $18 • (12/31/92) • **85**
Syrah-Sirah Dry Creek Valley 1989 • $18 • (03/15/92) • **78**
Syrah-Sirah Dry Creek Valley 1986 • $11 • (02/15/89) • **90**
Syrah-Sirah Dry Creek Valley 1985 • $9 • (01/31/88) • **91**
Sémillon Dry Creek Valley 1994 • $13 • (05/31/96) • **83**
Viognier Dry Creek Valley 1996: Tart, and with an ever-so-slightly bitter edge, enough spicy pear and green fig flavors fold in to hold your interest. Try now. 810 cases made. • $20 • (08/31/97) • **85**
Viognier Dry Creek Valley 1995: Spicy and floral, with a core of citrus, pear and peach-scented flavors. Turns soft and elegant on the finish. 890 cases made. • $20 • (10/15/96) • **86**
Viognier Dry Creek Valley 1994 • $17 • (07/31/95) • **85**
Viognier Dry Creek Valley 1993 • $18 • (01/31/95) • **87**
White Zinfandel Dry Creek Valley Le Petit Faux 1994 • $10 • (09/15/95) • **78**
Zinfandel Dry Creek Valley 1992 • $12 • (09/15/94) SS • **89**
Zinfandel Dry Creek Valley 1991 • $11 • (09/30/93) • **88**
Zinfandel Dry Creek Valley 1990 • $12 • (12/15/92) • **87**
Zinfandel Dry Creek Valley 1989 • $11 • (10/15/92) • **86**
Zinfandel Dry Creek Valley 1988 • $10 • (10/15/90) • **86**
Zinfandel Dry Creek Valley 1987 • $10 • (03/15/90) • **83**
Zinfandel Dry Creek Valley 1986 • $8 • (12/15/88) • **84**
Zinfandel Dry Creek Valley 1985 • $8 • (11/15/87) • **91**
Zinfandel Dry Creek Valley 1984 • $8 • (12/31/86) • **80**
Zinfandel Dry Creek Valley Old Vines-Old Clones 1996: Shows off a ripe, perfumed plum aroma, turning elegant and supple in texture. The black cherry and raspberry flavors are ripe and rich, persist for a long, full finish. Drink now through 2001. 2,655 cases made. • $18 • (05/15/98) • **88**
Zinfandel Dry Creek Valley Old Vines-Old Clones 1995: Appealing for its upfront juicy cherry and wild berry flavors. Picks up spice, sage and raspberry notes along the way, and retains its fruitiness on the finish. Ready to drink. 2,987 cases made. • $15 • (02/28/97) • **87**
Zinfandel Dry Creek Valley Old Vines-Old Clones 1993 • $13 • (06/15/95) • **88**

PRESTON PREMIUM WINES | WASHINGTON

Cabernet Franc Columbia Valley 1995: Crisp and chewy, it's a tough little wine with modest berry and tar notes poking through the tannins. Try in 2000. 1,100 cases made. • $17 • (01/31/98) • **80**
Cabernet Sauvignon Columbia Valley 1995: Light for a Cabernet, with slightly cooked cherry and tobacco flavors that remain sturdy on the finish. 6,000 cases made. • $14 • (09/15/97) • **85**
Cabernet Sauvignon Columbia Valley 1994: Was firm and chewy, with more herb than fruit flavors. Try in 1999. • $10 • (09/15/96) • **79**
Cabernet Sauvignon Columbia Valley Reserve 1994: Smooth, ripe and brightly focused to show off jazzy black cherry, raspberry and currant flavors that are wrapped in a layer of spice and vanilla. Delicious now, best from 1999. 1,150 cases made. • $19 • (09/15/97) • **89**
Cabernet Sauvignon Columbia Valley Reserve 1993: Smooth, supple and polished to show off its brilliant plum, black currant, vanilla and floral flavors. Finishes with welcome richness and fine texture. Approachable now, best from 2000. • $22 • (09/15/96) • **91**
Cabernet Sauvignon Columbia Valley Western White Oak Aged 1993: Firm and focused, with spicy, grapey blueberry and gentle herb flavors that remain velvety-textured and polished through the finish. 527 cases made. • $18 • (09/15/96) • **88**
Cabernet Sauvignon Washington 1992 • $12 • (03/15/94) • **82**
Cabernet Sauvignon Washington 1982 • $8 • (05/31/88) • **84**
Cabernet Sauvignon Washington Oak Aged 1993: Smooth, ripe and generous, opening up to a cascade of berry, plum, spice and vanilla flavors that swirl around elegantly on the finish. Drinkable now. 1,600 cases made. • $10 • (09/30/95) • **89**
Cabernet Sauvignon Washington Oak Aged 1989 • $10 • (05/15/91) • **85**
Cabernet Sauvignon Washington Preston Vineyard Oak Aged 1990 • $12 • (04/30/92) • **76**
Cabernet Sauvignon Washington Preston Vineyard Reserve 1990 • $21 • (03/31/92) • **91**
Cabernet Sauvignon Washington Preston Vineyard Selected Reserve 1987 • $14 • (10/15/89) • **62**
Cabernet Sauvignon Washington Reserve 1992 • $27 • (09/30/95) • **90**
Cabernet Sauvignon Washington Reserve 1991 • $28 • (10/15/93) • **84**
Cabernet Sauvignon Washington Reserve 1989 • $24 • (08/31/91) • **90**
Cabernet Sauvignon Washington Western White Oak Aged 1992 • $24 • (04/30/96) • **81**
Cabernet Sauvignon Washington Western White Oak Aged 1991 • $18 • (10/15/93) • **81**
Chardonnay Columbia Valley 1995: Generous without being weighty, this is a smooth-textured wine that emphasizes spice and hazelnut flavors over ripe fruit. Feels substantial enough to improve through 1999. 1,700 cases made. • $11 • (09/15/97) • **88**
Chardonnay Columbia Valley Reserve 1994: Silky, supple, subtle and substantial, it's a lovely mouthful of pear, nutmeg and cream flavors that linger seductively on the harmonious finish. Delicious now, likely better in 1999. 1,150 cases made. • $13 • (09/15/97) • **90**
Chardonnay Washington 1993 • $9 • (12/31/94) • **73**
Chardonnay Washington All Around Cowboy Limited Edition 1993 • $14 • (04/30/95) • **84**
Fumé Blanc Columbia Valley 1995: A barrel-fermented style delivering plenty of buttery spice flavors and a touch of honey on a supple frame, hinting at fig and melon on the finish. Ready now. 1,200 cases made. • $8 • (09/15/97) • **86**
Fumé Blanc Washington Bareback Riding Limited Edition 1993 • $9 • (09/30/95) • **77**
Gamay Beaujolais Rosé Blush Washington 1994 • $5 • (09/30/95) • **82**
Gewürztraminer Columbia Valley 1995: Soft and pleasant, with a slight mineral accent to the light peach flavors. 550 cases made. • $6 • (09/15/96) • **80**
Gewürztraminer Washington 1993 • $5 • (09/30/95) • **85**
Merlot Columbia Valley 1995: A light, simple red with basic berry and herbal flavors. Drinkable now. 6,000 cases made. • $14 • (09/15/97) • **80**
Merlot Columbia Valley 1994: An earthy, foxy character permeates the modest fruit flavors in this sturdy red. Drink right away. 2,700 cases made. • $10 • (09/15/96) • **76**
Merlot Columbia Valley Reserve 1994: Long, rich and flavorful, leaning strongly toward spicy oak flavors, but it has enough ripe blackberry and tarlike flavors to promise fine things by 1999 or so, when the firm tannins start to loosen their grip. 1,150 cases made. • $19 • (09/15/97) • **88**
Merlot Columbia Valley Reserve 1993: Soft and supple, with a gamy edge to the harmonious boysenberry and tobacco flavors. Ready now. 560 cases made. • $20 • (09/15/96) • **88**
Merlot Columbia Valley Western White Oak Aged 1995: Ripe, dark and spicy, with focused blackberry and anise flavors that linger, wrapped in a cloud of spicy oak, on the velvety finish. Impressive now, but hold until 1999 to 2000 to see what develops. 1,100 cases made. • $16 • (01/31/98) • **88**
Merlot Washington Bareback Riding Limited Edition 1992 • $18 • (06/15/95) • **84**
Merlot Washington Oak Aged 1993 • $10 • (09/30/95) • **83**
Merlot Washington Oak Aged 1988 • $7 • (08/31/91) • **77**
Merlot Washington Reserve 1990 • $26 • (09/30/93) • **80**
Platinum Red Columbia Valley NV: More generous with its aromas than with its flavors, but the blackberry, vanilla and toasty oak notes come into their own on the finish. Drink now. 190 cases made. • $22 • (09/15/96) • **85**
Port Columbia Valley Tenrebac 1993: A solid Port with style and substance, offering cinnamon-scented plum and coffee flavors that linger on the firm finish. Best from 2000. Made from Cabernet Sauvignon. 100 cases made. • $22 • (10/15/97) • **87**
Riesling Washington Ice Wine 1986 • $32 • (04/15/95) • **79**
Riesling Washington Ice Wine 1978 • $42 • (04/15/95) • **72**
White Riesling Late Harvest Washington Ice Wine 1986 • $38 • (10/15/89) • **80**

PRIDE | CALIFORNIA

Cabernet Franc Napa Valley 1992 • $18 • (12/31/94) • **83**
Cabernet Franc Sonoma County 1995: Shows some backbone and substance, along with a wall of rich tannins and oak. The currant and berry flavors do come slowly to the fore, but at this stage the tannins rule. Best to cellar into 1999. 400 cases made. • $24 • (12/15/97) • **85**
Cabernet Franc Sonoma County 1993 • $20 • (04/30/96) • **88**
Cabernet Sauvignon Napa Valley 1995: Dark, ripe and high in extract, this wine is overflowing with young currant, anise, plum and spicy Cabernet flavors from the first sip to the last. Turns complex on the finish, where it picks up a dusty, cedary, chocolaty accent. Will be best after 1999, peaking into 2004. 2,252 cases made. • $24 • (11/30/97) HR • **91**
Cabernet Sauvignon Napa Valley 1994: Dense and chewy, with lots of earthy leather, currant and berry flavors. A big, ripe and concentrated wine, it needs cellaring into 2001 to soften. 1,965 cases made. • $24 • (10/31/97) • **90**
Cabernet Sauvignon Napa Valley 1993: Complex interplay of ripe cherry, currant and spicy, toasty oak flavors. Shows fine depth and structure and

the flavors hold on through the finish. Best now to 2001. 1,715 cases made. • $22 • (09/15/96) • **90**

Cabernet Sauvignon Napa Valley 1992 • $18 • (12/15/95) • **87**

Cabernet Sauvignon Napa Valley 1991 • $18 • (05/15/94) HR • **92**

Cabernet Sauvignon Napa Valley Reserve 1994: Dark in color, sharply focused on the core of currant, wild berry and black cherry. Young and intense, it will need another 3 to 4 years cellaring to reach its peak. Try in 2001. 200 cases made. • $65 • (03/31/98) • **91**

Chardonnay Napa Valley 1996: Spicy and elegant, with understated ripe pear, green fig, melon and spicy nuances, turning especially complex on the finish where the oak and citrus flavors marry. Drink now through 2002. 592 cases made. • $20 • (05/15/98) • **91**

Chardonnay Napa Valley 1995: Distinct for its floral, pear and nectarine flavors, it's a spicy style that's ripe and flavorful, turning complex on the finish. 700 cases made. • $18 • (07/31/97) • **89**

Chardonnay Napa Valley 1994: Strikes a nice balance between its ripe pear and spicy oak flavors. Finesse and grace characterize this Chardonnay. 700 cases made. • $18 • (05/15/96) • **87**

Chardonnay Napa Valley 1993 • $18 • (07/31/95) • **87**

Merlot Napa Valley 1995: Lean and trim, with a narrow band of spicy blackberry and currant flavor that fans out on the finish, where the flavors show more depth and complexity. Best to cellar into 1999. 3,900 cases made. • $24 • (09/30/97) • **89**

Merlot Napa Valley 1994: Impressive. Smooth, rich and flavorful, with lots of currant, wild berry and cherry flavors shaded nicely with oaky nuances. Finishes with a broad, intense flourish of fruit and spice, with a sweet edge to the fruitiness. Best now into 1999. 3,200 cases made. • $20 • (06/30/97) HR • **91**

Merlot Napa Valley 1993 • $20 • (12/15/95) • **89**

Merlot Napa Valley 1992 • $18 • (01/31/95) • **85**

Merlot Napa Valley 1991 • $18 • (03/15/94) • **89**

Reserve Claret Napa Valley 1994: This is a dark, rich, complex wine, loaded with plush currant, black cherry, plum, mineral, spice and cedary oak flavors. Deeply concentrated, the tannins are ripe and polished. Approachable now, but worthy of cellaring into 2002. Another impressive offering from this Spring Mountain winery. 100 cases made. • $50 • (03/31/98) • **92**

Reserve Claret Napa Valley 1993: Impressive for its focus and core of ripe, spicy currant, plum and wild berry flavors, subtle oak nuances and lingering aftertaste. Best to cellar short-term into 1999 to let the tannins subside a bit. A blend of 48 percent Merlot, 47 percent Cabernet Sauvignon and 5 percent Cabernet Franc. 100 cases made. • $50 • (09/30/97) • **90**

Viognier Napa Valley 1994 • $24 • (05/31/96) • **89**

Viognier Sonoma County 1995: Ripe and understated in style, this offers a modest core of ripe, spicy pear, melon and a dash of honey and citrus flavors. 70 cases made. • $24 • (11/30/96) • **86**

PRINCE MICHEL | VIRGINIA

Cabernet Franc Virginia De Virginia Reserve 1994: Like smoky, gamy flavors? This is your wine. It's smooth and appealing in texture, with ripe plum and spice notes wrapped in. 108 cases made. • $20 • (04/30/97) • **85**

Cabernet-Merlot Virginia Reserve 1990 • $15 • (01/31/93) • **87**

Cabernet Sauvignon America De Rapidan Cask 92 NV • $12 • (01/31/95) • **83**

Chardonnay Virginia 1996: Bright and lively, with delicious pear, lemon and minerally flavors. A medium-bodied Chardonnay that's nicely nuanced, and appealing for its freshness. Drink now. 1,100 cases made. • $13 • (05/31/98) • **85**

Chardonnay Virginia 1994: Subtle pear and spice flavors are inviting and it has a smooth, agreeable texture. 4,500 cases made. • $12 • (09/15/96) • **83**

Chardonnay Virginia Barrel Select 1995: A fairly ripe-tasting wine with nice pear, apple and spice flavors, though it's a bit hollow in the middle. Drink now. 2,200 cases made. • $18 • (05/31/98) • **82**

Chardonnay Virginia Barrel Select 1994: A solid wine with ripe fruit flavors and spicy accents in a rich texture. Lingering finish. Drink right away. 1,200 cases made. • $16 • (09/15/96) • **87**

Le Ducq Lot 87 California-Virginia NV • $50 • (02/29/92) • **79**

Le Ducq Lot 88 America NV • $65 • (01/31/95) • **84**

Virginia De Virginia Reserve 1991 • $16 • (01/31/95) • **76**

Key: SS—Spectator Selection CS—Cellar Selection HR—Highly Recommended BB—Best Buy $NA—Price not available Ⓐ—Auction Price (BT)—Barrel Tasting

Dates in parentheses indicate the issues in which the ratings were published.

PUGLIESE | NEW YORK

Blanc de Blanc Brut North Fork of Long Island 1992: An exuberantly bubbly bubbly, fruity and frothy, offering simple apple and brown sugar flavors, with tart acidity and a dry finish. 1,400 cases made. • $15 • (12/31/96) • **80**

Cabernet Sauvignon North Fork of Long Island Reserve 1993: Straightforward but well defined, showing typical cassis, cedar and green bean flavors of moderate finish. Drink immediately. 600 cases made. • $14 • (12/31/96) • **84**

Chardonnay North Fork of Long Island Reserve 1994: Light and lively, this is refreshing and well balanced. Offering bright floral, pine and butter flavors, it's best as an apéritif. 800 cases made. • $13 • (12/31/96) • **84**

Merlot North Fork of Long Island Reserve 1993: This velvety red offers light, sweet berry flavors with milk chocolate accents, and light but firm tannins. Appealing to drink now. 700 cases made. • $14 • (12/31/96) • **83**

PYRAMIDS | CALIFORNIA

Chardonnay Sonoma County 1996: Notes of green apple and pear run through this tight, silky-textured young wine. Finishes with notes of toast and nuts. Drink now. 1,500 cases made. • $16 • (06/15/98) • **86**

Chardonnay Sonoma County Ranch Vineyards 1995: Ripe and generous, a breezy blend of peach and apple flavors, with pleasant touches of vanilla on the soft finish. Drink now through 2000. 1,500 cases made. • $16 • (05/15/98) • **87**

QUADY | CALIFORNIA

Black Muscat California Elysium 1996: Disarmingly ripe and fruity, this sweet wine shows plenty of plum with hints of cinnamon and vanilla, and a touch of mint on the open-textured finish. Ready now. 5,042 cases made. • $14 • (11/30/97) • **88**

Black Muscat California Elysium 1995: Syrupy, with a jazzy raspberry flavor at the core and a sweet finish that shows a hint of plum. Should be served cold. 2,910 cases made. • $15 • (11/30/96) • **86**

Black Muscat California Elysium 1993 • $13 • (05/15/95) • **87**

Black Muscat California Elysium 1992 • $12 • (11/15/93) • **82**

Black Muscat California Elysium 1990 • $12 • (11/30/91) • **86**

Black Muscat California Elysium 1989 • $12 • (10/15/90) • **85**

Black Muscat California Elysium 1988 • $11 • (08/31/89) • **90**

Black Muscat California Elysium 1987 • $11 • (09/30/88) • **82**

Black Muscat California Elysium 1985 • $11 • (09/15/86) • **85**

Black Muscat California Elysium 1984 • $11 • (08/01/85) • **87**

Orange Muscat California Electra 1996: Light, fizzy and refreshing for its unassuming pear, peach and litchi-fruit flavors. Finish is sweet and balanced. Drink while it's fresh. 4,191 cases made. • $7 • (04/30/97) • **88**

Orange Muscat California Electra 1993 • $9 • (04/30/95) • **83**

Orange Muscat California Electra 1992 • $9 • (06/30/93) BB • **86**

Orange Muscat California Electra 1991 • $9 • (06/15/92) • **84**

Orange Muscat California Essensia 1995: A jazzy mouthful of spicy honey and dried apricot flavors, this is sweet, not at all delicate, open-textured-appealing for its range of pretty characteristics. Drink soon. 883 cases made. • $14 • (10/31/97) • **88**

Orange Muscat California Essensia 1994: Fragrant, with orange blossom and spice aromas, but it turns a tad bitter on the palate in an attempt to balance the sweetness, and loses charm. 3,194 cases made. • $15 • (11/30/96) • **80**

Orange Muscat California Essensia 1993 • $13 • (05/15/95) • **84**

Orange Muscat California Essensia 1990 • $12 • (11/30/91) • **83**

Orange Muscat California Essensia 1989 • $12 • (10/15/90) • **89**

Orange Muscat California Essensia 1987 • $11 • (08/31/89) • **78**

Orange Muscat California Essensia 1985 • $11 • (09/30/86) • **79**

Orange Muscat California Essensia 1984 • $11 • (07/01/85) • **88**

Port Amador County 1984 • $9 • (10/01/85) • **82**

Port Amador County Frank's Vineyard 1986 • $12 • (10/15/90) • **75**

Port Amador County LBV 1993: Has a spicy, almost Muscat-like edge to the rich plum and black cherry flavors, which remain balanced and not too sweet through the dusty finish. Approachable now, should keep improving through 2005. 668 cases made. • $12 • (12/15/97) • **87**

Port Amador County Starboard 1987 • $25 • (03/31/91) • **81**

Port Amador County Starboard Batch 88 Rich Ruby 1988 • $15 • (11/30/91) • **87**

Port Amador County Starboard Frank's Vineyard 1990: Spicy, heady aromas and flavors center around cooked plum, chocolate and exotic spices, finishing smooth and rich. A powerful wine that needs until 2002 or 2005 to settle down. • $22 • (02/28/97) • **88**

Port Amador County Starboard Frank's Vineyard 1989: Port-like, with fine-grained tannins and a lovely core of pure blueberry and plum that extends into a long, firm, elegant finish. Tempting now, but better in 1999. 590 cases made. • $19 • (11/30/96) • **90**

Port California 1985 • $9 • (08/31/89) • **73**

Port California LBV 1991 • $9 • (05/31/95) • **81**

Port California Starboard Batch 88 NV: Properly Port-like, with some prominent, ripe black cherry and spice flavors, a gentle grip and a nice touch of spice on the finish. 1,169 cases made. • $16 • (11/30/96) • **85**

QUAFF | CALIFORNIA

White Riesling Monterey County 1993 • $7 • (10/15/95) • **85**

QUAIL RIDGE | CALIFORNIA

Cabernet Sauvignon Napa Valley 1995: Ripe and interesting for its strongly herbal flavors backed by round berry and currant. Needs until 1999 to 2000 to soften the finish. 5,651 cases made. • $16 • (03/31/98) • **85**

Cabernet Sauvignon Napa Valley 1992: Dry and tannic, with herb, sage and dill notes and a narrow band of currant and spice flavors, turning leathery and even drier on the finish. 2,068 cases made. • $15 • (04/30/97) • **84**

Cabernet Sauvignon Napa Valley 1990 • $13 • (11/15/94) • **85**

Cabernet Sauvignon Napa Valley 1989 • $16 • (06/15/93) • **82**

Cabernet Sauvignon Napa Valley 1988 • $16 • (08/31/92) • **80**

Cabernet Sauvignon Napa Valley 1987 • $16 • (09/30/91) HR • **93**

Cabernet Sauvignon Napa Valley 1986 • $15 • (11/15/90) • **89**

Cabernet Sauvignon Napa Valley 1985 • $15 • (07/31/89) • **82**

Cabernet Sauvignon Napa Valley 1984 • $15 • (03/31/89) • **88**

Cabernet Sauvignon Napa Valley 1982 • $13 • (09/16/85) • **86**

Cabernet Sauvignon Napa Valley Reserve 1987 • $25 • (11/15/92) • **87**

Cabernet Sauvignon Napa Valley V. & L. Eisele Vineyard Reserve 1989 • $30 • (12/15/95) • **82**

Cabernet Sauvignon Napa Valley Volker Eisele Vineyard Reserve 1992: Tannic and marked by a green streak, this is a hard-edged and unyielding wine that lacks focus and harmony, and comes up short on fruit, too. 474 cases made. • $40 • (05/15/97) • **82**

Merlot California 1994: Tart and crisp, offering pleasant, straightforward berry and tangy citruslike flavors. Ready to drink. 2,532 cases made. • $19 • (07/31/97) • **85**

Merlot Napa Valley 1991 • $14 • (12/15/95) • **82**

Merlot Napa Valley 1990 • $15 • (09/15/94) • **82**

Merlot Napa Valley 1989 • $15 • (07/15/93) • **79**

Merlot Napa Valley 1988 • $15 • (05/31/92) • **84**

Merlot Napa Valley 1987 • $15 • (06/15/90) • **86**

Merlot Napa Valley 1985 • $14 • (03/31/89) • **90**

Sauvignon Blanc Napa Valley 1996: Here's a nicely crafted Sauvignon Blanc at a reasonable price. It's firm and well balanced, bright and grassy, with hints of sweet pea and melon, and a touch of toast on the finish. 2,025 cases made. • $10 • (03/31/98) BB • **85**

Sauvignon Blanc Napa Valley 1995: Fresh, simple and appealing, with peachy apple flavors. 2,846 cases made. • $12 • (04/30/97) • **84**

Sauvignon Blanc Napa Valley 1993 • $11 • (05/15/96) BB • **75**

Sauvignon Blanc Napa Valley Reserve 1996: Fairly light and clean, it's bright and refreshing, with a lemony finish. Lacks complexity, however. 928 cases made. • $15 • (01/31/98) • **82**

QUATRO | CALIFORNIA

Cabernet Sauvignon Sonoma County 1994: Barely ripe, with a mild green streak to the plum and berry flavors. Lean and trim, it could use a little more stuffing; finishes with firm tannins. Available in restaurants only. 850 cases made. • $18 • (08/31/97) • **85**

Pinot Noir Sonoma County 1994: Somewhat tight and a bit smoky, this won't offend—or inspire, either. Lean, with hints of anise and black currant, some bitterness on the finish. 1,200 cases made. • $13 • (02/28/98) • **81**

QUILCEDA CREEK | WASHINGTON

Cabernet Sauvignon Washington 1993: Smoky, toasty flavors and firm tannins almost mask the pretty berry tones that emerge gradually in the glass, growing polished and almost plush. Needs until 2000 or so to see if the fruit can make itself heard. 1,300 cases made. • $40 • (08/31/97) • **91**

Cabernet Sauvignon Washington 1992: Dense, rich and dynamic, packed with mouth-filling blackberry, currant and blueberry flavors with hints of anise and sweet spices. A glorious mélange of flavors that shows both substance and subtlety. Needs until 2002 to 2005. 950 cases made. • $31 • (09/15/96) CS • **92**

Cabernet Sauvignon Washington 1990 • $24 • (05/15/94) • **89**

Cabernet Sauvignon Washington 1989 • $24 • (10/15/93) • **87**

Cabernet Sauvignon Washington 1988 • $22 • (02/28/93) HR • **89**

Cabernet Sauvignon Washington 1985 • $17 • (10/15/89) • **74**

Cabernet Sauvignon Washington Reserve 1992 • $49 • (09/30/95) • **95**

Merlot Washington 1993: Ripe, round and complex, layering its spice, toast, berry, plum and tobacco flavors with depth and harmony. A bit chunky now, but should develop well through 1999 or 2001. 50 cases made. • $45 • (12/31/96) • **91**

QUINTESSA | CALIFORNIA

Rutherford Napa Valley 1994: Rich, supple and forward, this drinks well now but is worthy of cellaring into 2000. The core of currant, anise, cedar, vanilla and spice flavors are smooth and polished, as are the tannins. A blend of Cabernet Sauvignon, Cabernet Franc and Merlot. 500 cases made. • $70 • (11/30/97) • **91**

QUIVIRA | CALIFORNIA

Cabernet Cuvée Dry Creek Valley 1991 • $15 • (07/31/95) • **82**

Cabernet Cuvée Dry Creek Valley 1990 • $15 • (11/15/94) • **85**

Cabernet Cuvée Dry Creek Valley 1989 • $15 • (11/15/92) • **84**

Cabernet Sauvignon Dry Creek Valley 1988 • $18 • (11/15/91) • **84**

Cabernet Sauvignon Dry Creek Valley 1987 • $15 • (11/15/90) • **87**

Dry Creek Cuvée Dry Creek Valley 1995: Tight and tart, with pretty black cherry, wild berry and spice flavors, turning elegant and supple on the finish. 1,400 cases made. • $13 • (07/31/97) • **87**

Dry Creek Cuvée Dry Creek Valley 1994: Simple and drinkable, with nicely spicy plum and berry notes. 1,000 cases made. • $13 • (08/31/96) • **82**

Dry Creek Cuvée Dry Creek Valley 1993 • $12 • (06/30/95) • **84**

Dry Creek Cuvée Dry Creek Valley 1992 • $12 • (09/30/94) • **83**

Sauvignon Blanc Dry Creek Valley 1996: A bright, lean wine with a subtle core of hazelnut and grapefruit flavors. Firm and refreshing. 3,837 cases made. • $10 • (04/30/98) • **84**

Sauvignon Blanc Dry Creek Valley 1995: Crisp and light, with honey and toast notes and a melon and tangy lemon finish. 5,300 cases made. • $10 • (07/31/97) • **87**

Sauvignon Blanc Dry Creek Valley 1993 • $10 • (08/31/95) • **85**

Sauvignon Blanc Dry Creek Valley Reserve 1995: A steely wine, with hints of orange, lemon and lime. Bright acidity carries the flavors forward to a moderate finish. 1,500 cases made. • $16 • (06/30/97) • **86**

Sauvignon Blanc Dry Creek Valley Reserve 1993 • $14 • (08/31/95) • **84**

Zinfandel Dry Creek Valley 1996: A medium-weight style, with moderately ripe plum and wild berry flavors that, while good, fail to excite. Drink now through 2000. 4,875 cases made. • $17 • (05/31/98) • **85**

Zinfandel Dry Creek Valley 1995: Ripe and appealing in a rustic style, with a jammy edge to the red cherry, raspberry and plum flavors. 4,500 cases made. • $16 • (08/31/97) • **87**

Zinfandel Dry Creek Valley 1994 • $15 • (04/30/96) • **88**

Zinfandel Dry Creek Valley 1993 • $14 • (04/30/96) • **87**

Zinfandel Dry Creek Valley 1992 • $14 • (09/30/94) • **89**

Zinfandel Dry Creek Valley 1991 • $13 • (09/30/93) • **88**

Zinfandel Dry Creek Valley 1990 • $13 • (10/15/92) HR • **90**

Zinfandel Dry Creek Valley 1989 • $13 • (07/31/91) • **84**

Zinfandel Dry Creek Valley 1988 • $12 • (05/31/90) • **88**

Zinfandel Dry Creek Valley 1987 • $11 • (07/31/89) • **88**

Zinfandel Dry Creek Valley 1986 • $9 • (12/15/88) • **88**

Zinfandel Dry Creek Valley 1984 • $7 • (04/15/87) • **88**

Zinfandel Dry Creek Valley 1983 • $7 • (01/01/86) • **75**

QUPÉ | CALIFORNIA

Bien Nacido Cuvée Santa Barbara County 1996: A blend of 67 percent Chardonnay and 33 percent Viognier, this exhibits the body and pear flavors of the former and the spicy qualities of the latter. 1,008 cases made. • $16 • (08/31/97) • **87**

Bien Nacido Cuvée Santa Barbara County 1995: Simple and uncomplicated, with flavors of pear, spice, honey and oak. A blend of Chardonnay and Viognier that does little to benefit either wine. • $16 • (09/15/96) • **82**

Bien Nacido Cuvée Santa Barbara County 1994 • $15 • (01/31/96) • **88**

Chardonnay Santa Barbara County Bien Nacido Vineyard 1996: Intense and concentrated, with a nice core of pear, fig and melon flavors, picking up traces of citrus and honey on the aftertaste. 3,300 cases made. • $18 • (11/15/97) • **89**

Chardonnay Santa Barbara County Sierra Madre Reserve 1994: Shows off a hint of honeyed botrytis on the nose and palate, but the apple and pear notes fold in nicely on the finish and it's well balanced. 680 cases made. • $25 • (05/31/96) • **88**

Chardonnay Santa Barbara County Sierra Madre Reserve 1993 • $25 • (07/31/95) • **88**

Chardonnay Santa Barbara County Sierra Madre Vineyards 1993 • $11 • (04/30/95) SS • **90**

Los Olivos Cuvée Santa Barbara County 1995: Elegant and spicy, with supple herb, berry and cherry flavors that pick up a complex, earthy component on the finish. A blend of 50 percent Syrah and 50 percent Mourvèdre. 500 cases made. • $18 • (08/31/97) • **88**

Los Olivos Cuvée Santa Barbara County 1994: Simple and not quite ripe, with a tart, green edge to the meaty berry and leathery flavors. Tasted twice with consistent notes. A blend of Syrah and Mourvèdre. • $18 • (09/15/96) • **79**

Los Olivos Cuvée Santa Barbara County 1993 • $15 • (08/31/95) • **88**

Los Olivos Cuvée Santa Barbara County 1989 • $15 • (08/31/91) • **85**

Marsanne Santa Barbara County Los Olivos Vineyard 1994 • $12 • (11/30/95) • **81**

Syrah Central Coast 1996: The core of meaty cherry and plum flavors shows off a slight candied edge, finishing with firm tannins. Drink through 1999. 6,100 cases made. • $13 • (12/15/97) • **84**

Syrah Central Coast 1995: Young and tight, with a firm core of plum and berry flavors. Picks up some spicy cherry notes on the finish, as well as a nice pepper and leather accent. Drinks well now. 5,600 cases made. • $13 • (11/30/96) • **88**

Syrah Central Coast 1993 • $11 • (08/31/95) • **88**

Syrah Central Coast 1988 • $11 • (12/15/89) • **90**

Syrah Central Coast 1987 • $9 • (04/15/89) • **88**

Syrah Central Coast 1986 • $9 • (04/15/89) • **79**

Syrah Central Coast 1985 • $5 • (04/15/88) • **78**

Syrah Santa Barbara County Bien Nacido Hillside Estate 1995: Complex and well made. Lots of pepper and spice up front, a vegetal note, too, it slowly unfolds into more interesting flavors of beefy, stewed plums and berries. The texture is smooth and supple. 380 cases made. • $35 • (12/31/97) • **90**

Syrah Santa Barbara County Bien Nacido Hillside Select 1994: Spicy and meaty in character, with a strong vegetal accent, but it straightens out, showing toast, plum, currant and anise notes along with the meaty flavors. Rich and concentrated, it makes quite a statement about Syrah in Santa Barbara county. Try now. 110 cases made. • $35 • (11/30/96) • **90**

Syrah Santa Barbara County Bien Nacido Reserve 1995: Dense and chewy, with a pretty array of meaty plum, cherry and herb notes. Fans out to reveal greater depth and concentration, and finishes with a meaty aftertaste. 1,354 cases made. • $23/375ml • (08/31/97) • **91**

Syrah Santa Barbara County Bien Nacido Reserve 1994: Dark, ripe, and concentrated, with a tannic core of cherry and leather Syrah flavors. Shows a lot of substance and depth, finishing with a mineral accent. 1,320 cases made. • $22 • (09/15/96) • **88**

Syrah Santa Barbara County Bien Nacido Reserve 1993 • $17 • (08/31/95) SS • **91**

Syrah Santa Barbara County Bien Nacido Vineyard 1989 • $20 • (08/31/91) • **89**

Syrah Santa Barbara County Bien Nacido Vineyard 1987 • $20 • (02/28/90) • **81**

Syrah Santa Barbara County Los Olivos Reserve 1993 • $20 • (08/31/95) • **88**

Viognier Santa Barbara County Ibarra-Young Vineyard 1995: Ripe, with a slightly bitter edge to the spicy pear and hazelnut flavors. Tasted twice with consistent notes. • $18/500ml (09/15/96) • **80**

Viognier Santa Barbara County Los Olivos Vineyard 1994 • $22 • (09/30/95) • **89**

RABBIT RIDGE | CALIFORNIA

Allure Red California 1995: What a deal. Bright and appealing for its harmony and balance, this blend of blend of Syrah, Mourvèdre, Carignane, Grenache and Cinsault isn't a blockbuster, but a nicely restrained mouthful of tasty juice. Ready to drink. 20,000 cases made. • $7 • (03/31/98) BB • **85**

Allure Red California 1991 • $7 • (06/30/95) • **82**

Allure Red California 1990 • $8 • (10/15/93) • **83**

Allure Red California 1989 • $7 • (05/31/93) • **81**

Avventura Sonoma County Migliore di Vigneto Reserve 1994: Elegant and well proportioned, this wine shows off appealing ripe plum and wild berry flavors and picks up a pretty, spicy aftertaste. Mild tannins make it appealing now through 2001. A blend of Sangiovese, Cabernet Sauvignon and Merlot. 750 cases made. • $30 • (05/15/98) • **88**

Cabernet Sauvignon Russian River Valley Rabbit Ridge Ranch Winemaker's Grand Reserve 1994: Appealing for its purity of flavor and focus, with ripe plum, cherry and berry, hints of anise and cedar and a rich aftertaste of pretty, ripe fruit. Finishes with firm tannins. Best to cellar into 2000. 450 cases made. • $40 • (03/31/98) • **87**

Cabernet Sauvignon Sonoma County 1989 • $12 • (11/15/94) • **77**

Cabernet Sauvignon Sonoma County 1988 • $12 • (08/31/91) • **89**

Cabernet Sauvignon Sonoma County Rabbit Ridge Ranch Estate Reserve 1990 • $20 • (11/15/94) • **86**

Chardonnay Carneros Sangiacomo Vineyard Reserve 1995: Young and fruity, with flavors of ripe apple, pear, fig and melon that slowly build. Turns elegant and harmonious on the finish, where the flavors fan out. 465 cases made. • $18 • (12/15/96) • **89**

Chardonnay Russian River Valley Rabbit Ridge Ranch Estate Reserve 1996: Smooth, rich and flavorful. In a well-oaked style with plenty of fruit complexity and concentration, its pretty fig, apricot, melon and pear flavors linger on. Drink now. 1,730 cases made. • $18 • (04/30/98) • **89**

Chardonnay Russian River Valley Rabbit Ridge Ranch Estate Reserve 1994: Pleasant enough, as its ripe, spicy pear and melon notes persist to the finish, where toasty oak folds in nicely. 1,400 cases made. • $16 • (05/15/96) • **87**

Chardonnay Russian River Valley Rabbit Ridge Ranch Estate Reserve 1993 • $16 • (07/31/95) • **88**

Chardonnay Sonoma County 1996: Ripe and full-bodied, with an earthy, grassy edge to the pear- and apple-laced flavors, finishing with a dash of vanilla-tinged oak. Drinks well now. 1,400 cases made. • $12 • (05/15/98) • **87**

Chardonnay Sonoma County Winemaker's Grand Reserve 1995: Rich, elegant and creamy, with complex pear, vanilla, spice and anise flavors, picking up an earthy quality on the aftertaste. Another winner from Rabbit Ridge. 300 cases made. • $30 • (03/31/98) • **91**

Dolcetto Paso Robles 1995: Supple and appealing, with pretty plum and cherry flavors in a soft frame, finishing with some intensity. Gets the feel of Dolcetto nicely. Drink now. 900 cases made. • $12 • (06/30/98) • **85**

Merlot California Barrel Cuvée 1996: A bit tanky at first, but the oak, blackberry and herb flavors ultimately kick in for a nice, simple quaff. Finishes short. Drink now through 2002. 34,500 cases made. • $9 • (07/31/98) • **84**

Merlot Carneros Sangiacomo Vineyard 1994: Supple and spicy, with a soft, fleshy texture. The pretty Merlot flavors echo plum and berry accents. Smells and tastes complex, with a nice integration of fruit and oak. Shows a lot of finesse on the finish, where the flavors fan out nicely. Best in 1999. 850 cases made. • $20 • (12/31/96) HR • **91**

Merlot Carneros Sangiacomo Vineyard 1992 • $15 • (06/15/95) • **86**

Merlot Carneros Sangiacomo Vineyard Reserve 1995: Intense and complex, with a nice interplay of herb and currant-laced Merlot flavors and spicy, cedary oak. Drinks well now but has the tannic strength to age into 2000. 2,700 cases made. • $23 • (04/30/98) • **89**

Merlot Sonoma County 1994: Supple and elegant, with traces of currant and spice. Finishes with lightly toasted oak flavors. 2,500 cases made. • $16 • (07/31/96) • **84**

Merlot Sonoma County Winemaker's Grand Reserve 1994: Smooth, supple and elegant, with pretty dashes of spicy, toasty oak and just the right amount of ripe plum and cherry flavors that gently unfold and ease into a long, complex aftertaste. 235 cases made. • $28 • (04/30/97) • **90**

Montepiano Red California 1995: Flavorful and sturdy, not tannic, generous with its blackberry and floral flavors. Finishes softly. Ready to drink. A blend of Sangiovese, Barbera, Lambrusco and Cabernet Franc. 7,500 cases made. • $10 • (03/31/98) BB • **85**

Mystique North Coast 1993 • $7 • (06/30/95) • **85**

Nebbiolo California Barrique Riserva 1994: Smooth and supple, with flavors of tar, plum and wild berry. Finishes with a smoky aftertaste, a slight burnt quality. Tasted twice, with consistent notes. 475 cases made. • $18 • (12/31/97) • **83**

Oddux Red California Reserve 1990 • $15 • (03/31/93) • **78**

Petite Sirah Sonoma County 1990 • $10 • (03/31/93) • **80**

Sangiovese California Coniglio Selezione 1992 • $12 • (08/31/95) • **84**

Key: SS—Spectator Selection CS—Cellar Selection HR—Highly Recommended BB—Best Buy $NA—Price not available Ⓐ—Auction Price (BT)—Barrel Tasting
Dates in parentheses indicate the issues in which the ratings were published.

Sangiovese Sonoma County Coniglio Selezione 1994: Might be the best California Sangiovese going. Harmonious, smooth and supple, with plum, cherry and berry flavors that fold together nicely on the finish, with a nice streak of spicy, toasty oak. Wow, what a wonderful wine. Drinkable now. 2,500 cases made. • $13 • (04/30/97) HR • **92**

Sangiovese Sonoma County Coniglio Selezione 1993 • $13 • (11/30/95) • **85**

Sangiovese Sonoma County Coniglio Selezione Reserve 1995: Lightly fruity, with ripe cherry and strawberry flavors, turning earthy on the finish, where it loses its velocity. Drink now. 4,500 cases made. • $13 • (05/15/98) • **85**

Sauvignon Blanc Russian River Valley 1997: Fig and melon notes lead the way here, with grassy overtones. The wine shows moderate body and finishes with a distinct grapefruit edge. Drink now. 3,100 cases made. • $10 • (06/30/98) BB • **86**

Sauvignon Blanc Russian River Valley 1996: An intriguing blend of melon, grapefruit, herbs, lemon and spice flavors, it's well-balanced and focused, delivering lots of flavor and character with finesse. Drink now. 1,300 cases made. • $9 • (06/30/97) • **89**

Sauvignon Blanc Russian River Valley Rabbit Ridge Ranch 1995: Simple and straightforward. Favoring nectarine and herb flavors that lose definition on the finish. 900 cases made. • $8 • (07/31/96) • **83**

Viognier Sonoma County Heartbreak Hill 1995: Shows off its spicy, exotic Viognier character, but finishes with a slightly bitter edge. With food, more of the pear and apple flavors might shine through. 1,400 cases made. • $15 • (09/15/96) • **81**

Zinfandel California Barrel Cuvée 1995: Bright and zingy, marked by wild cherry and spice tones. Simple and pleasant. 45,000 cases made. • $9 • (11/15/97) • **83**

Zinfandel Dry Creek Valley 1993 • $11 • (06/15/95) • **85**

Zinfandel Dry Creek Valley 1992 • $11 • (10/15/94) • **80**

Zinfandel Dry Creek Valley 1991 • $10 • (05/31/93) • **87**

Zinfandel Dry Creek Valley 1990 • $9 • (10/15/92) • **73**

Zinfandel Dry Creek Valley Olsen Vineyard 1995: A yummy wine, ripe and complex, with a minty, spicy edge to the rich plum and wild berry flavors. Enjoy now and through 2000. 600 cases made. • $22 • (12/15/96) • **88**

Zinfandel Dry Creek Valley Olsen Vineyard 1994 • $16 • (04/30/96) • **92**

Zinfandel Dry Creek Valley Olson Vineyard Reserve 1996: Complex and fruity, with ripe plum, berry, cherry and spicy nuances that hang with you. Turns smooth and supple on the finish. Drink now through 2001. 750 cases made. • $23 • (05/31/98) • **88**

Zinfandel Paso Robles Westside Vines 1996: Of medium weight, smooth, ripe and polished, with a core of currant, plum and wild berry. Finishes with supple tannins and good length. Drink now through 2001. 6,300 cases made. • $16 • (06/15/98) • **85**

Zinfandel Russian River Valley Hedin Vineyard Reserve 1996: Good intensity and focus for the vintage, with ripe, racy cherry, wild berry, strawberry and spice. Finishes with firm tannins. Drink now through 2001. 350 cases made. • $23 • (06/15/98) • **86**

Zinfandel Russian River Valley Rabbit Ridge Ranch 1988 • $8 • (04/30/91) • **86**

Zinfandel Russian River Valley Rabbit Ridge Ranch Estate Reserve 1996: An elegant, tasty Zin that's ideal for drinking now. Smooth and supple, with ripe plum, cherry, raspberry and spice. Turns complex on the finish. 740 cases made. • $30 • (05/15/98) • **87**

Zinfandel Russian River Valley Rabbit Ridge Ranch Estate Reserve 1995: Ripe and racy, with a dense, jammy quality to the plum and wild berry flavors. Fills out the palate, picking up a cedar accent on the tannic finish. Drink now. 261 cases made. • $25 • (06/15/97) • **90**

Zinfandel Sonoma County 1996: Well proportioned, with spicy, peppery wild berry and cherry flavors that linger on the finish. Drink now through 2000. 32,000 cases made. • $14 • (06/15/98) • **86**

Zinfandel Sonoma County 1995: This California Zin offers an impressive combination of flavor, finesse, depth and polish, especially at this price. The tiers of ripe cherry and wild berry flavors and toasty oak and anise notes fold together nicely and linger on the finish. Ready to drink. 9,000 cases made. • $13 • (03/31/97) SS • **90**

Zinfandel Sonoma County 1994 • $10 • (03/31/96) • **84**

Zinfandel Sonoma County 1989 • $9 • (08/31/91) • **86**

Zinfandel Sonoma County OVZ Reserve 1995: Lovely Zinfandel, ripe, smooth and fleshy, with a creamy quality to its black cherry, plum and wild berry flavors. Finishes with a long, fruity aftertaste. 1,700 cases made. • $26 • (09/30/97) • **92**

Zinfandel Sonoma County San Lorenzo Reserve 1994: A touch earthy and waxy, but still serving up lots of flavor and finesse, with hints of wild berry, cherry and hazelnut. Finishes with a cedary edge and crisp tannins. 600 cases made. • $23 • (08/31/96) • **91**

Zinfandel Sonoma County San Lorenzo Reserve 1993 • $18 • (09/15/95) HR • **93**

Zinfandel Sonoma County San Lorenzo Reserve 1991 • $14 • (09/30/93) • **90**

Zinfandel Sonoma County Winemaker's Grand Reserve 1996: Strikes a nice balance between spicy, creamy, vanilla-laced oak and a solid core of blackberry, wild berry and cherry-scented Zinfandel flavors. The texture is smooth and polished, finishing with supple tannins and fine length. Drink now through 2004. 840 cases made. • $32 • (06/15/98) • **90**

Zinfandel Sonoma County Winemaker's Grand Reserve 1995: Rich, smooth, ripe and polished, with a supple core of wild berry, black cherry, raspberry and spicy flavors framed by creamy vanilla oak. Turns complex on the finish, where the flavors fan out. 650 cases made. • $30 • (03/31/98) • **91**

RADANOVICH | CALIFORNIA

Cabernet Sauvignon Sierra Foothills 1993: Hard, with a green edge that engenders herbal, cedary flavors, with touches of dill and unripe berry. 200 cases made. • $15 • (12/15/96) • **77**

Cabernet Sauvignon Sierra Foothills Mariposa County 1989 • $18 • (12/15/92) • **77**

Merlot Sierra Foothills Mariposa County 1991 • $15 • (09/15/94) • **82**

Sauvignon Blanc Sierra Foothills 1994 • $8 • (05/31/96) • **80**

Zinfandel Sierra Foothills 1993 • $9 • (04/30/96) • **80**

Zinfandel Sierra Foothills Mariposa County 1989 • $11 • (12/15/92) • **72**

RAFANELLI, A. | CALIFORNIA

Cabernet Sauvignon Dry Creek Valley 1997: Brilliant fruit. Distinct for its earthy, racy wild berry and blackberry, and tight focus. Fine balance, firm tannins. • $NA • (07/31/98) (BT) • **90-94**

Cabernet Sauvignon Dry Creek Valley 1994: Well proportioned, with a complex array of black cherry, plum, anise and cedary notes. Finishes with mild tannins and good length. Drink now or cellar into 1999 to 2001. 2,750 cases made. • $20 • (09/30/97) • **88**

Cabernet Sauvignon Dry Creek Valley 1993: A bit rustic and rugged, but well balanced overall. Has chunky currant, black cherry, cedar and spice flavors and a chewy, dry tannic finish. 2,600 cases made. • $18 • (09/15/96) • **85**

Cabernet Sauvignon Dry Creek Valley 1992 • $17 • (09/30/95) SS • **92**

Cabernet Sauvignon Dry Creek Valley 1991 • $15 • (09/15/94) SS • **90**

Cabernet Sauvignon Dry Creek Valley 1990 • $15 • (09/15/93) HR • **90**

Cabernet Sauvignon Dry Creek Valley 1989 • $14 • (09/30/92) • **84**

Cabernet Sauvignon Dry Creek Valley 1988 • $13 • (08/31/91) HR • **90**

Cabernet Sauvignon Dry Creek Valley 1987: Starts out lean and earthy and remains a trim, tannic wine, but as it breathes, more currant, leather, anise and cedar flavors emerge, giving breadth, depth and complexity. Best now through 2002, but it may always be on the tannic side. • $NA • (12/15/97) • **91**

Cabernet Sauvignon Dry Creek Valley 1986: Starts out earthy and chewy, but the core of rich mineral, currant, wild berry and cherry flavors builds, showing uncommon depth and intensity. Quite tannic, but the fruit holds its own. One of the more complex and concentrated Dry Creek Cabernets, the flavors turn sweet on the finish. • $NA • (12/15/96) • **92**

Cabernet Sauvignon Dry Creek Valley 1985 • $8 • (09/15/88) • **78**

Zinfandel Dry Creek Valley 1995: Classy. This formidable red delivers a complex palette, with wild berry, raspberry and cherry notes and spicy nuances, and exhibits great concentration, finishing with depth and firm, dry tannins. Drink through 1999. 6,150 cases made. • $18 • (12/15/97) SS • **90**

Zinfandel Dry Creek Valley 1994: With a core of spicy anise, raspberry and cherry flavors, turning supple and harmonious on the finish, it's not quite up to the barrel sample, but better now than when first reviewed. 5,900 cases made. • $16 • (06/30/97) • **90**

Zinfandel Dry Creek Valley 1993 • $14 • (12/31/95) • **88**

Zinfandel Dry Creek Valley 1992 • $13 • (10/15/94) SS • **88**

Zinfandel Dry Creek Valley 1991 • $13 • (12/15/93) SS • **89**

Zinfandel Dry Creek Valley 1990 • $12 • (09/30/92) • **88**

Zinfandel Dry Creek Valley 1989 • $11 • (09/30/91) • **85**

Zinfandel Dry Creek Valley 1988 • $9 • (09/15/90) • **90**

Zinfandel Dry Creek Valley 1987 • $9 • (12/15/89) • **84**

Zinfandel Dry Creek Valley 1986 • $7 • (09/15/88) • **91**

Zinfandel Dry Creek Valley 1985 • $6 • (12/31/87) • **77**

Zinfandel Dry Creek Valley 1983 • $6 • (03/01/86) BB • **91**

RAINSONG | OREGON

Pinot Noir Oregon 1995: Has a definite bite, bordering on bitterness, but there's enough ripe berry flavor behind to suggest it should balance out by 1999. 425 cases made. • $14 • (10/31/97) • **82**

RAMSAY | CALIFORNIA

Merlot Napa Valley 1992 • $14 • (09/15/94) • **87**
Merlot Napa Valley 1991 • $13 • (06/15/93) • **88**
Merlot Napa Valley 1989 • $12 • (04/15/92) • **86**
Pinot Noir California 1994: Earthy and dirty-tasting. A soulless wine with herb and vegetal notes and not much in the way of fruit. Tasted twice, with consistent notes. 2,078 cases made. • $15 • (03/31/97) • **70**
Pinot Noir California Lot #7 1995: Solid, with ripe, spicy, earthy cherry flavors of modest depth and proportion. 1,500 cases made. • $12 • (02/28/97) • **84**
Pinot Noir California Lot #8 1996: An herbal style, with hints of anise, cola and thyme backed by black cherry and spice. Tannins are a little rough , but might soften with time. 6,585 cases made. • $16 • (02/28/98) • **83**
Pinot Noir Carneros 1993 • $12 • (12/31/95) • **86**
Pinot Noir Carneros 1992 • $12 • (03/31/95) • **82**
Pinot Noir Carneros 1991 • $12 • (02/28/94) • **81**
Sangiovese California 1993 • $14 • (02/29/96) • **74**
Sangiovese California 1992 • $14 • (02/28/95) • **82**
Trebbiano California 1993 • $8 • (12/15/95) • **76**

RAMSPECK | CALIFORNIA

Pinot Noir Napa Valley 1994 • $16 • (01/31/96) • **88**

RANCHO SISQUOC | CALIFORNIA

Cabernet Sauvignon Santa Maria Valley 1994: A country wine with some quirky barnyard aromas. Aside from that, the texture is plush and the finish is redolent of ripe plums and black currants. 800 cases made. • $18 • (09/15/97) • **83**
Cabernet Sauvignon Santa Maria Valley 1993: The plum and cherry flavors make a brief appearance on the palate then fade on the finish, where the tannins fold in. 600 cases made. • $18 • (11/30/96) • **84**
Cabernet Sauvignon Santa Maria Valley 1992 • $15 • (12/15/95) • **82**
Cabernet Sauvignon Santa Maria Valley 1991 • $15 • (11/15/94) • **84**
Cabernet Sauvignon Santa Maria Valley 1990 • $14 • (11/15/93) • **76**
Cabernet Sauvignon Santa Maria Valley 1989 • $14 • (11/15/92) • **85**
Cabernet Sauvignon Santa Maria Valley 1986 • $10 • (12/15/89) • **73**
Cabernet Sauvignon Santa Maria Valley 1974 • $NA • (11/15/94) • **74**
Cellar Select Red Santa Maria Valley 1990 • $25 • (11/15/93) • **88**
Cellar Select Red Santa Maria Valley 1989 • $25 • (11/15/92) • **87**
Chardonnay Santa Maria Valley 1995: Pretty earth tones announce this spicy, zippy wine. Firm and lean, yet polished, it's nuanced with layers of lemon and beach plum. 1,200 cases made. • $15 • (09/30/97) • **88**
Chardonnay Santa Maria Valley 1994: Ripe and round, with an interesting complexity of earthy, minerally flavors that lift it out of the ordinary. 2,200 cases made. • $15 • (07/31/96) • **85**
Chardonnay Santa Maria Valley 1993 • $15 • (07/31/95) • **82**
Johannisberg Riesling Santa Maria Valley 1995: Unpleasantly metallic, with a bitter edge to the modest pear flavors. 500 cases made. • $8 • (04/30/97) • **79**
Merlot Santa Maria Valley 1994: A lean but focused wine, its spicy, minty overture followed by dark wild berry, cassis and anise flavors. Tannins are firm but ripe. Better in a few years. 2,300 cases made. • $16 • (07/31/97) • **88**
Merlot Santa Maria Valley 1991 • $13 • (09/15/94) • **80**
Merlot Santa Maria Valley 1989 • $12 • (05/31/92) • **81**
Merlot Santa Maria Valley 1986 • $9 • (12/15/89) • **77**
Sauvignon Blanc Santa Maria Valley 1996: With its hazelnut, melon, lemon-lime and grapefruit qualities, this wine strikes a fine profile for the varietal. Brisk acidity and a subtle herbal touch on the finish make it a fine choice for dinner. 700 cases made. • $12 • (04/30/98) • **88**
Sauvignon Blanc Santa Maria Valley 1995: Ripe and creamy, generous with its grapefruit and floral flavors, finishing with a spicy note. 1,600 cases made. • $12 • (04/30/97) • **85**
Sauvignon Blanc Santa Maria Valley 1994: Some nice orange, cream and earthy flavors that fade a bit on the finish. 1,800 cases made. • $12 • (09/15/96) • **79**
Sauvignon Blanc Santa Maria Valley 1993 • $10 • (08/31/95) • **87**
Sylvaner Santa Maria Valley 1995: This tastes strange, with earth and game notes that lack charm. 750 cases made. • $8 • (04/30/97) • **78**

RANDOM RIDGE | CALIFORNIA

Red Table Wine Mount Veeder 1993: Lean and trim, with a narrow band of cedar, cherry, plum and spice flavors. Has elegance and balance, and the tannins, while crisp, aren't overbearing. Drink now. 240 cases made. • $20 • (11/15/96) • **86**
Sangiovese Mount Veeder 1993 • $27 • (02/29/96) • **83**
Zinfandel Sonoma Valley Old Wave 1994: Lots of berry flavor, pure and simple. Tart and spicy, with bright blackberry, cherry and wild berry notes. 200 cases made. • $16 • (04/30/97) • **88**
Zinfandel Sonoma Valley Old Wave 1993 • $14 • (10/15/95) • **85**

RAPIDAN RIVER | VIRGINIA

Merlot Virginia 1991 • $9 • (01/31/93) • **86**

RASMUSSEN, KENT | CALIFORNIA

Cabernet Sauvignon Napa Valley 1988 • $20 • (11/15/91) • **83**
Chardonnay Napa Valley 1996: Ripe fruit and toasty oak fold together nicely, with complex pear, apple, citrus and woody flavors that add depth and dimension. Drink now through 2001. 2,000 cases made. • $23 • (05/31/98) • **89**
Chardonnay Napa Valley 1995: Strikes a nice balance between ripe, spicy Chardonnay flavors and pale oak shadings, creating a clean wine, delicate and understated but building to a complex aftertaste, with pear, apple and hazelnut notes. Impressive. 1,727 cases made. • $21 • (06/15/97) • **92**
Chardonnay Napa Valley 1994: Serves up a nice core of ripe pear and apple, but the flavors lack the extra dimensions and finesse you might hope for at this price. 1,100 cases made. • $21 • (02/29/96) • **86**
Dolcetto Napa Valley 1990 • $20 • (03/15/92) • **85**
Pinot Noir Carneros 1995: A bit disjointed now, the ripe plum and black cherry flavors aren't quite in sync with the spicy oak, and the tannins merit another year or two in the bottle. 2,042 cases made. • $26 • (01/31/98) • **86**
Pinot Noir Carneros 1994: Marked by spicy, peppery flavors, it's an elegant, understated style with hints of herb and cherry, on the lighter side. 2,000 cases made. • $22 • (01/31/97) • **84**
Pinot Noir Carneros 1993 • $20 • (12/31/95) • **87**
Pinot Noir Carneros 1992 • $19 • (01/31/95) • **87**
Pinot Noir Carneros 1991 • $18 • (02/28/94) • **88**
Pinot Noir Carneros 1990 • $19 • (02/28/93) • **86**
Pinot Noir Carneros 1988 • $22 • (10/31/90) • **84**

RATTLESNAKE RIDGE | WASHINGTON

Lemberger Yakima Valley 1992 • $6 • (09/30/94) • **74**

RAVENSWOOD | CALIFORNIA

Cabernet Sauvignon Sonoma County 1993: Dry and austere with a touch of wild berry and spice. Hangs together with chunky fruit flavors, but the tannins tend to dominate. Try now. 3,600 cases made. • $15 • (12/15/95) • **87**
Cabernet Sauvignon Sonoma County 1992 • $15 • (11/15/94) • **86**
Cabernet Sauvignon Sonoma County 1991 • $14 • (11/15/94) • **84**
Cabernet Sauvignon Sonoma County 1989 • $14 • (11/15/92) • **84**
Cabernet Sauvignon Sonoma County 1988 • $14 • (03/15/91) • **89**
Cabernet Sauvignon Sonoma County 1987 • $11 • (05/31/90) • **84**
Cabernet Sauvignon Sonoma County 1986 • $12 • (12/31/88) • **88**
Cabernet Sauvignon Sonoma County 1985 • $12 • (05/31/88) • **83**
Cabernet Sauvignon Sonoma County 1984 • $12 • (09/15/87) • **68**
Cabernet Sauvignon Sonoma County 1982 • $11 • (04/01/86) SS • **95**
Cabernet Sauvignon Sonoma Valley Gregory 1994: Firm and tight, with a slight camphor edge to the cherry and currant flavors. Finishes with firm tannins, but the fruit keeps pumping through. Drinkable now. 1,070 cases made. • $20 • (02/28/97) • **88**

Key: SS—Spectator Selection CS—Cellar Selection HR—Highly Recommended BB—Best Buy $NA—Price not available Ⓐ—Auction Price (BT)—Barrel Tasting
Dates in parentheses indicate the issues in which the ratings were published.

Cabernet Sauvignon Sonoma Valley Gregory 1993: Marked by minty notes and hints of sage and herb, but enough currant and cherry come through. Supple and harmonious on the finish, even with substantial tannins. Try now. 960 cases made. • $20 • (12/15/95) • **89**
Cabernet Sauvignon Sonoma Valley Gregory 1990 • $18 • (04/30/93) • **84**
Cabernet Sauvignon Sonoma Valley Gregory 1989 • $18 • (11/15/92) • **85**
Cabernet Sauvignon Sonoma Valley Gregory 1988 • $18 • (11/15/91) • **80**
Cabernet Sauvignon Sonoma Valley Olive Hill 1978 • $31 • (11/15/92) • **80**
Chardonnay California Vintners Blend 1996: Simple and straightforward, with delicate notes of citrus, green apple and sweet pea. Drink now. 16,000 cases made. • $10 • (07/31/98) • **82**
Chardonnay North Coast Vintners Blend 1993 • $9 • (07/31/95) • **84**
Chardonnay Sonoma Valley Sangiacomo 1996: A bit disjointed, with leafy pear and cedary oak, it slowly works its way into more appealing flavors, with smoky, toasty oak and hints of pear and melon. Best from 1999 through 2002. 4,127 cases made. • $20 • (07/31/98) • **87**
Merlot Carneros Sangiacomo 1990 • $20 • (12/15/92) • **88**
Merlot Carneros Sangiacomo 1989 • $18 • (11/15/91) • **90**
Merlot Napa & Sonoma Counties Vintners Blend 1989 • $18 • (03/31/91) BB • **84**
Merlot North Coast Vintners Blend 1992 • $10 • (09/15/94) • **84**
Merlot North Coast Vintners Blend 1991 • $10 • (05/31/93) • **83**
Merlot North Coast Vintners Blend 1990 • $9 • (05/31/92) BB • **84**
Merlot Sonoma County 1994: A racy style, with a spicy oregano nuance to the plum and cherry notes. The flavors start to grow on you by the second or third sip. Try now or cellar into 1999. 7,000 cases made. • $18 • (06/30/97) • **87**
Merlot Sonoma County 1993: Young, firm and tight, with compact currant, chocolate, mint and herbal notes. Drink now. • $18 • (07/31/96) • **87**
Merlot Sonoma County 1992 • $15 • (02/28/95) • **85**
Merlot Sonoma County 1990 • $15 • (06/15/93) • **85**
Merlot Sonoma County 1989 • $15 • (05/31/92) • **86**
Merlot Sonoma County 1987 • $18 • (01/31/90) • **87**
Merlot Sonoma County 1986 • $18 • (12/31/88) • **80**
Merlot Sonoma County 1984 • $11 • (02/28/87) • **85**
Merlot Sonoma Valley Gregory Vineyard 1994: Marked by a strongly spicy, minty, bay leaf accent, the core of cherry and wild berry flavors struggles to compete. If you like mintiness in your wine, okay, but some will find it overpowering. 90 cases made. • $30 • (02/28/97) • **85**
Merlot Sonoma Valley Sangiacomo 1994: Smooth and supple, slowly building to show more tannic strength on the finish. The flavors range from earthy currant to cedar, tar, coffee and herb. Drinkable now or can cellar short-term. 1,965 cases made. • $20 • (10/15/96) • **88**
Merlot Sonoma Valley Sangiacomo 1992 • $20 • (06/15/95) • **86**
Mountain Claret Sonoma County 1992 • $12 • (09/15/95) • **84**
Pickberry Sonoma Mountain 1994: Tight and restrained, slowly unwinding to reveal its complexity and completeness with a band of earth, tar, currant and berry flavors that fill out on the palate. Best from 1999. A blend of 63 percent Merlot, 21 percent Cabernet Sauvignon, and 16 percent Cabernet Franc. 1,150 cases made. • $30 • (03/31/97) • **90**
Pickberry Sonoma Mountain 1990 • $26 • (11/15/93) • **86**
Pickberry Sonoma Mountain 1989 • $37 • (11/15/92) • **89**
Pickberry Sonoma Mountain 1988 • $27 • (04/30/91) • **82**
Pickberry Sonoma Mountain 1987: Has good intensity, but the flavors lack focus. The core is built around cedar, plum and berry. Supple tannins. Drink now. A blend of 50 percent Cabernet Sauvignon, 35 percent Cabernet Franc, and 15 percent Merlot. • $48 • (12/15/97) • **87**
Pickberry Sonoma Mountain 1986: Fully mature, but holding well, with spicy cherry, herb, anise and currant flavors. Ready for consumption. • $30 • (12/15/96) • **87**
Rancho Salina Vineyards Sonoma Valley 1994: Firm, tight and tannic, this compact young wine is marked by minty, leathery flavors, but its range is broadened, its depth increased, by currant and cherry notes folding in. A blend of 67 percent Cabernet Sauvignon, 22 percent Merlot, and 11 Cabernet Franc. 700 cases made. • $25 • (02/28/97) • **87**
Zinfandel Alexander Valley 1994: A solid effort, with its spice, modest berry and cherry flavors and hints of tea and sage. Ready now. A new bottling from Ravenswood. 1,615 cases made. • $14 • (03/31/97) • **86**
Zinfandel Napa & Sonoma Counties Vintners Blend 1986 • $5 • (06/30/88) BB • **85**
Zinfandel Napa Valley Canard 1988 • $12 • (08/31/91) • **75**
Zinfandel Napa Valley Canard 1986 • $11 • (03/15/90) • **81**
Zinfandel Napa Valley Canard 1985 • $10 • (03/15/89) • **85**
Zinfandel Napa Valley Dickerson 1995: Tinges its ripe cherry, raspberry and wild berry flavors with an appealing jammy quality. Finishes with firm, chewy tannins and lots of mint and sage; best to cellar into 1999. 1,912 cases made. • $22 • (09/30/97) • **89**
Zinfandel Napa Valley Dickerson 1994: Marked by a minty sage accent, with ripe plum and wild berry flavors at the core. Flavors fold together quite nicely on the finish, where the tannins stand out. Drink now. 874 cases made. • $20 • (03/31/97) • **89**
Zinfandel Napa Valley Dickerson 1993 • $20 • (09/15/95) • **89**
Zinfandel Napa Valley Dickerson 1992 • $18 • (09/15/94) SS • **91**
Zinfandel Napa Valley Dickerson 1991 • $18 • (09/30/93) • **87**
Zinfandel Napa Valley Dickerson 1990 • $16 • (09/30/92) SS • **92**
Zinfandel Napa Valley Dickerson 1989 • $13 • (11/15/91) • **87**
Zinfandel Napa Valley Dickerson 1988 • $13 • (08/31/91) • **84**
Zinfandel Napa Valley Dickerson 1987 • $13 • (03/15/90) • **86**
Zinfandel Napa Valley Dickerson 1986 • $12 • (12/15/88) • **88**
Zinfandel Napa Valley Dickerson 1985 • $11 • (12/31/87) • **80**
Zinfandel Napa Valley Vintners Blend 1985 • $6 • (05/31/87) • **80**
Zinfandel North Coast Vintners Blend 1992 • $8 • (10/15/94) • **83**
Zinfandel North Coast Vintners Blend 1991 • $7 • (05/31/93) • **84**
Zinfandel North Coast Vintners Blend 1990 • $7 • (10/15/92) • **81**
Zinfandel North Coast Vintners Blend 1989 • $7 • (07/31/91) BB • **83**
Zinfandel North Coast Vintners Blend 1988 • $7 • (10/15/90) BB • **81**
Zinfandel Russian River Valley Wood Road Belloni 1995: Shows off lots of pretty fruit flavors, with a core of dark cherry and plum. Has lively acidity and floral notes that linger on the finish. Try now. 3,015 cases made. • $22 • (09/30/97) • **88**
Zinfandel Russian River Valley Wood Road Belloni 1994: Ripe and spicy, with pretty cherry and wild berry flavors that pick up a spicy, minty accent on the finish, where the flavors fan out and linger. 2,680 cases made. • $20 • (09/30/96) • **88**
Zinfandel Russian River Valley Wood Road Belloni 1993 • $20 • (09/15/95) • **87**
Zinfandel Sonoma County 1994: Comes together well. Though there are a few green notes, the core of berry and cherry flavor is appealing, as is the peppery note on the finish. Ready now. 8,060 cases made. • $15 • (03/31/97) • **88**
Zinfandel Sonoma County 1993 • $15 • (09/15/95) • **89**
Zinfandel Sonoma County 1992 • $12 • (08/31/94) SS • **91**
Zinfandel Sonoma County 1987 • $11 • (03/15/90) • **88**
Zinfandel Sonoma County 1986 • $9 • (12/15/88) HR • **90**
Zinfandel Sonoma County 1985 • $8 • (12/31/87) • **80**
Zinfandel Sonoma County Belloni 1992 • $18 • (09/15/94) • **89**
Zinfandel Sonoma County Dry Creek Benchland 1981 • $6 • (04/01/84) • **81**
Zinfandel Sonoma County Old Vine 1990 • $11 • (10/15/92) • **89**
Zinfandel Sonoma County Old Vine 1989 • $11 • (12/31/91) • **82**
Zinfandel Sonoma County Old Vine 1988 • $11 • (11/30/90) • **87**
Zinfandel Sonoma County Vintners Blend 1987 • $6 • (06/15/89) BB • **88**
Zinfandel Sonoma Valley Belloni 1991 • $18 • (09/30/93) • **89**
Zinfandel Sonoma Valley Cooke 1995: Ripe, rich and complex, with spice and pepper-accented ripe cherry and wild berry flavors. Finishes with firm tannins, but also loads of fruit. Drink now through 2002. 838 cases made. • $22 • (09/30/97) • **91**
Zinfandel Sonoma Valley Cooke 1994: A rustic style, marked by spicy, peppery wild berry and cherry flavors. Turns quite tannic on the finish, but the fruit flavors hold on and push through. 495 cases made. • $20 • (09/30/96) • **88**
Zinfandel Sonoma Valley Cooke 1993 • $20 • (09/15/95) • **89**
Zinfandel Sonoma Valley Cooke 1992 • $18 • (10/15/94) HR • **91**
Zinfandel Sonoma Valley Cooke 1991 • $18 • (09/30/93) • **88**
Zinfandel Sonoma Valley Cooke 1990 • $16 • (10/15/92) • **90**
Zinfandel Sonoma Valley Cooke 1987 • $13 • (03/15/90) • **84**
Zinfandel Sonoma Valley Monte Rosso 1995: A heady wine, with lots of fruit and tannin from start to finish. The core of chewy plum and wild berry flavors finishes with dashes of sage and spice. Best to cellar into 1999 to 2000 to let the tannins subside. 1,664 cases made. • $22 • (09/30/97) • **89**
Zinfandel Sonoma Valley Monte Rosso 1994: Well focused, with bright, ripe and lively currant, cherry and wild berry flavors that show touches of cedar and spice on the finish. Drinks well now. From the Louis Martini-owned Monte Rosso Vineyard. 2,660 cases made. • $20 • (09/30/96) • **90**
Zinfandel Sonoma Valley Monte Rosso 1993 • $20 • (09/15/95) • **88**
Zinfandel Sonoma Valley Old Hill Vineyard 1992 • $20 • (10/15/94) • **92**
Zinfandel Sonoma Valley Old Hill Vineyard 1991 • $20 • (09/30/93) • **87**
Zinfandel Sonoma Valley Old Hill Vineyard 1990 • $18 • (10/15/92) • **89**
Zinfandel Sonoma Valley Old Hill Vineyard 1987 • $15 • (03/15/90) • **87**
Zinfandel Sonoma Valley Old Hill Vineyard 1986 • $13 • (12/15/88) • **92**
Zinfandel Sonoma Valley Old Hill Vineyard 1985 • $12 • (12/31/87) • **87**

Zinfandel Sonoma Valley Old Hill Vineyard Limited Edition 1995: Open-throttle Zinfandel from its ripe, juicy black cherry, raspberry and wild berry flavors, to its firm, structured tannins. Boasts lots of flavor while keeping its balance. Drinkable now, but worthy of cellaring, too. 1,722 cases made. • $24 • (09/30/97) • **92**

Zinfandel Sonoma Valley Old Hill Vineyard Limited Edition 1994: Tightly wound and firmly tannic, the leathery currant and cherry flavors just now beginning to emerge, revealing more depth. Still, needs more time for tannins to soften. 700 cases made. • $22 • (09/30/96) • **87**

Zinfandel Sonoma Valley Old Hill Vineyard Limited Edition 1993 • $22 • (09/15/95) • **90**

RAY, MARTIN | CALIFORNIA

Cabernet Sauvignon California Saratoga Cuvée 1994: Young, tight and intense, with a range of herb, currant, black cherry and spice, finishing with cedary oak and chewy tannins. Needs time; try after 2001. 2,700 cases made. • $30 • (12/15/97) • **88**

Cabernet Sauvignon California Saratoga Cuvée 1993: Ripe cherry and currant flavors are generous—avoiding the hollow middle found in so many 1993 Cabernets. Finishes with a fruity aftertaste and crisp tannins. Ready now. 650 cases made. • $32 • (08/31/96) • **86**

Cabernet Sauvignon California Saratoga Cuvée 1992 • $28 • (10/31/95) • **89**

Cabernet Sauvignon Napa Valley 1993: Well balanced, given the vintage, and there's plenty of cherry, coffee and currant flavors to offset the crisp tannins. Try now. 875 cases made. • $32 • (08/31/96) • **86**

Cabernet Sauvignon Napa Valley 1992 • $28 • (10/31/95) • **86**

Cabernet Sauvignon Napa Valley 1991 • $28 • (11/15/94) HR • **94**

Cabernet Sauvignon Napa Valley Diamond Mountain 1995: Dark, ripe, rich and plush, with dense, chewy, complex currant, anise, mineral, cedar and spice. Tightly focused, deep and concentrated, with lots more anise, currant, tar and berry flavors on the amazingly long finish. Tasted twice, with consistent notes. Best from 2001 through 2010. 400 cases made. • $45 • (07/31/98) • **95**

Chardonnay California Mariage 1996: Solid, with fresh, ripe pear, tangerine, nectarine and peach notes. Complex and elegant, with a clean, fruity aftertaste. Drink now through 2001. 2,000 cases made. • $25 • (07/31/98) • **89**

Chardonnay California Mariage 1995: Complete and well balanced, with a combination of ripe pear, apple, melon and spice flavors that pick up a hint of cedar on the finish. 3,000 cases made. • $28 • (07/31/97) • **88**

Chardonnay California Mariage 1994: Ripe, complex and elegant, with tiers of bright, spicy pear, apple, honey and light citrus shadings. Impressive for its purity of flavor and long, lingering finish. A wonderful Chardonnay from this upstart winery. 700 cases made. • $25 • (05/31/96) • **93**

Chardonnay California Mariage 1993 • $24 • (08/31/95) • **89**

Pinot Noir California 1995: A racy, spicy style, with earthy cherry, pepper, spice and leathery notes, complex in its own way. Finishes with firm tannins and good length. Best now to 2001. 1,300 cases made. • $28 • (02/28/98) • **84**

Pinot Noir California 1994: An elegant style, with ripe cherry, plum and strawberry flavors and supple tannins. Drinks well now. 500 cases made. • $28 • (11/15/96) • **88**

RAYMOND | CALIFORNIA

Cabernet Sauvignon California Amberhill 1995: Simple cherry notes mark this lightweight Cabernet. Finishes fairly short with a parting shot of oak. 24,000 cases made. • $13 • (06/30/98) • **77**

Cabernet Sauvignon California Amberhill 1994: Light, fresh and crisp, with modest berry flavors and fine tannins. Try now. 11,000 cases made. • $10 • (11/15/97) • **80**

Cabernet Sauvignon California Amberhill 1993: Marked by gritty tannins (more than you'd expect from a wine at this price) but the flavors are good, with hints of herb and currant. 20,000 cases made. • $10 • (12/15/96) • **81**

Cabernet Sauvignon California Amberhill 1991 • $8 • (11/15/94) • **84**

Cabernet Sauvignon California Amberhill 1990 • $8 • (11/15/94) • **78**

Cabernet Sauvignon Napa Valley 1992 • $17 • (11/30/95) • **88**

Cabernet Sauvignon Napa Valley 1991 • $17 • (11/15/94) • **88**

Cabernet Sauvignon Napa Valley 1990 • $17 • (11/15/93) • **88**

Cabernet Sauvignon Napa Valley 1989 • $17 • (02/15/93) • **88**

Key: SS—Spectator Selection CS—Cellar Selection HR—Highly Recommended BB—Best Buy $NA—Price not available Ⓐ—Auction Price (BT)—Barrel Tasting

Dates in parentheses indicate the issues in which the ratings were published.

Cabernet Sauvignon Napa Valley 1988 • $18 • (08/31/92) • **85**

Cabernet Sauvignon Napa Valley 1987: Smooth and supple, with a silky band of herb, chocolate and cherry. Youthful and lively, finishing with fleshy tannins. Best now through 2001. 12,000 cases made. • $26 • (12/15/97) • **88**

Cabernet Sauvignon Napa Valley 1986 • $16 • (05/31/90) • **90**

Cabernet Sauvignon Napa Valley 1985 • $16 • (12/15/89) • **84**

Cabernet Sauvignon Napa Valley 1984 • $28 • (02/15/89) • **90**

Cabernet Sauvignon Napa Valley 1983 • $30 • (02/15/88) • **89**

Cabernet Sauvignon Napa Valley 1982 • $22 • (11/15/86) • **91**

Cabernet Sauvignon Napa Valley 1981 • $12 • (05/01/85) • **77**

Cabernet Sauvignon Napa Valley 1980 • $12 • (01/01/84) • **81**

Cabernet Sauvignon Napa Valley 1978 • $31 • (11/15/92) • **86**

Cabernet Sauvignon Napa Valley 1974 • $40 • (11/15/94) • **78**

Cabernet Sauvignon Napa Valley Estates 1995: Decidedly earthy, with a slight murky edge that slowly works into sage and herb-laced Cabernet flavors. Best with food, which will soften the earthy edge. Drink now through 2002. 8,700 cases made. • $15 • (05/31/98) • **85**

Cabernet Sauvignon Napa Valley Estates 1994: Lean and trim, with a tobacco and herb edge to the currant and cherry flavors. Can stand cellaring into 1999 to 2000, when it should be softer. 23,000 cases made. • $14 • (05/31/97) • **87**

Cabernet Sauvignon Napa Valley Estates 1993: Supple and harmonious, with a pleasant core of plum and cherry flavors. Appealing now. 9,000 cases made. • $12 • (03/31/96) • **84**

Cabernet Sauvignon Napa Valley Generations 1994: Dense, chewy and concentrated, with an appetizing, earthy side to the substantial currant, black cherry, cedar and spice flavors, this California Cabernet is built for aging, with all the right ingredients to reward cellaring until 2000. 3,000 cases made. • $35 • (10/31/97) SS • **93**

Cabernet Sauvignon Napa Valley Private Reserve 1992: Complex, with a nice interplay of ripe cherry, currant and anise flavors and buttery, toasty oak notes. The texture is smooth and polished and the flavors linger on the finish, with a well-focused, fruity aftertaste. Drinks well now, should improve through 2000. • $26 • (11/15/96) • **90**

Cabernet Sauvignon Napa Valley Private Reserve 1991 • $25 • (12/15/95) • **84**

Cabernet Sauvignon Napa Valley Private Reserve 1990 • $25 • (10/31/94) • **88**

Cabernet Sauvignon Napa Valley Private Reserve 1988 • $26 • (07/31/93) • **88**

Cabernet Sauvignon Napa Valley Private Reserve 1987: This reserve shows a shade more depth, complexity and finesse than the Raymond Napa Valley, with a pretty core of ripe black cherry, herb, anise, sage and berry that picks up nice vanilla and coffee accents on the finish. Ready now. 4,000 cases made. • $20 • (12/15/97) • **90**

Cabernet Sauvignon Napa Valley Private Reserve 1986: Still showing a lot of woody character and engendering a waxy aroma and dryness in the mouth; most of the fruit flavors are fading—just a hint of currant and berry remain. Drink now. 3,500 cases made. • $NA • (12/15/96) • **82**

Cabernet Sauvignon Napa Valley Private Reserve 1985 • $30 • (07/15/90) CS • **91**

Cabernet Sauvignon Napa Valley Private Reserve 1984 • $25 • (07/15/89) • **87**

Cabernet Sauvignon Napa Valley Private Reserve 1983 • $18 • (06/30/88) • **91**

Cabernet Sauvignon Napa Valley Private Reserve 1982 • $16 • (06/15/87) • **88**

Cabernet Sauvignon Napa Valley Private Reserve 1981 • $16 • (08/31/86) • **92**

Cabernet Sauvignon Napa Valley Reserve 1994: Cherry and currant flavors give dimension and breadth and, with aeration, its green olive and dill notes become more appealing. Finishes with supple tannins. Best from 1999 to 2005. 30,000 cases made. • $20 • (05/31/97) • **89**

Cabernet Sauvignon Napa Valley Reserve 1993: Smooth and harmonious, featuring a supple core of cherry, currant and berry notes. Turns complex and fleshy on aftertaste where the flavors unfold, revealing anise and spice. 20,500 cases made. • $17 • (04/30/96) • **90**

Chardonnay California Amberhill 1996: Strays a bit from the main core of Chardonnay fruit, with racy, grassy, leesy flavors. 10 percent Chenin Blanc. Drink now. 65,000 cases made. • $9 • (07/31/98) • **78**

Chardonnay California Amberhill 1995: Canned peaches and toasty oak are the leading elements in this vaguely sweet sipper. 70,000 cases made. • $10 • (07/31/97) • **80**

Chardonnay California Amberhill 1994: Oddly spicy and medicinal around the edge of the tangy apple flavor. 100,000 cases made. • $10 • (06/15/96) • **76**
Chardonnay California Amberhill 1993 • $11 • (02/28/95) • **83**
Chardonnay Monterey Estates 1996: Ripe and creamy, with pear, spice and a hint of tangerine on the finish. Clean and easy-drinking. Drink now. 35,000 cases made. • $13 • (06/15/98) • **84**
Chardonnay Monterey Estates 1995: Creamy and ripe, with a core of silky pear, peach and nectarine flavors that unfold and linger. A lot of wine, flavor and texture at this price. 27,000 cases made. • $12 • (06/15/97) • **89**
Chardonnay Monterey Estates 1994: A racy style, with a distinctive grassy edge to the grapefruit and citrus flavors, graced by pear and spice notes. Comes together on the finish, where the flavors evolve. 30,000 cases made. • $12 • (03/31/96) • **87**
Chardonnay Napa Valley 1993 • $14 • (12/15/95) • **87**
Chardonnay Napa Valley Generations 1996: Slowly unfolds to reveal complex pear, spice, honey and vanilla, adding dashes of hazelnut and smoke. Succeeds with its elegance, richness, depth and complexity. 3,000 cases made. • $27 • (05/15/98) • **91**
Chardonnay Napa Valley Generations 1995: Packs in lots of flavors, with hints of pear, hazelnut, fig and spice, finishing with a toasty oak flourish and a sense of elegance and finesse. Ready to drink. 3,400 cases made. • $25 • (05/31/97) • **91**
Chardonnay Napa Valley Private Reserve 1994: An oaky style, with lots of buttery, smoky wood flavors, but enough ripe pear, apple and honey notes arrive to keep it in balance. 3,500 cases made. • $18 • (05/31/96) • **89**
Chardonnay Napa Valley Reserve 1996: Appealing for its ripe, spicy pear and apple flavors, but for a reserve, it comes across as simple. 40,000 cases made. • $15 • (05/15/98) • **86**
Chardonnay Napa Valley Reserve 1995: Distinct for its effusive fruitiness, this overflows with ripe citrus, peach, pear and vanilla notes, turning smooth and elegant on the aftertaste. 32,000 cases made. • $14 • (06/15/97) • **90**
Chardonnay Napa Valley Reserve 1994: Grows into a complex and attractive wine, marked by cedar, toast and spicy wood shadings that add dimensions and richness to the ripe pear, grapefruit and melon notes. 35,000 cases made. • $14 • (05/31/96) • **89**
Johannisberg Riesling Late Harvest Napa Valley 1985 • $8 • (09/15/86) • **91**
Meritage Napa Valley 1989 • $35 • (11/15/93) • **89**
Meritage Napa Valley Private Reserve 1991 • $40 • (12/15/95) • **87**
Meritage Napa Valley Private Reserve 1990 • $40 • (10/31/94) HR • **90**
Merlot California Amberhill 1996: Tastes of raspberry and candied cherry with an herbal, oaky edge. Cinnamon on the finish adds some interest. Drink now. 24,000 cases made. • $13 • (07/31/98) • **83**
Merlot Napa Valley 1992 • $17 • (11/15/95) • **89**
Merlot Napa Valley Reserve 1993 • $17 • (06/30/96) • **83**
Pinot Noir Napa Valley 1992 • $17 • (09/15/95) • **83**
Pinot Noir Napa Valley Reserve 1995: Lean and trim, with a slightly earthy metallic flavor that overrides the muddled cherry and mushroomlike notes. Tasted twice, with consistent notes. 1,200 cases made. • $17 • (02/28/98) • **81**
Sauvignon Blanc Napa Valley 1994 • $9 • (12/31/95) • **77**
Sauvignon Blanc Napa Valley 1993 • $9 • (08/31/95) • **81**
Sauvignon Blanc Napa Valley Reserve 1996: Lemon-lime, grapefruit, melon and herbs blend well in this medium-bodied wine. Refreshing acidity carries the flavors nicely on the finish. 13,000 cases made. • $11 • (04/30/98) • **86**
Sauvignon Blanc Napa Valley Reserve 1995: Bright and fruity pear and floral flavors with a smoky accent. 9,800 cases made. • $10 • (08/31/96) • **85**
Vintage Select Red California 1984 • $4 • (02/15/88) • **75**
Vintage Select Red North Coast 1982 • $4 • (04/01/86) BB • **82**

RED HILL | CALIFORNIA

Chardonnay California 1993 • $4 • (07/31/95) • **79**
Sauvignon Blanc California 1993 • $3 • (05/15/95) • **81**

REDHAWK | OREGON

Cabernet Sauvignon Umpqua Valley Safari Vineyard Reserve 1992 • $15 • (11/30/94) • **86**
Evan's Creek Reserve Rogue Valley 1990 • $25 • (11/30/94) • **83**
Pinot Noir Grateful Red 1992 • $8 • (03/15/94) • **79**
Pinot Noir Grateful Red 1990 • $10 • (06/15/92) • **84**
Pinot Noir Willamette Valley 1992 • $10 • (03/15/94) • **80**
Pinot Noir Willamette Valley 1991 • $13 • (03/15/94) • **77**
Pinot Noir Willamette Valley Vintage Select 1992 • $15 • (11/30/94) • **78**

REDWOOD CANYON | CALIFORNIA

Cabernet Sauvignon Napa Valley 1993: Ripe and fruity, with a spicy edge to the plum and berry flavors. Simple but pleasant. 7,000 cases made. • $13 • (12/15/95) • **84**

REMICK RIDGE | CALIFORNIA

Cabernet Sauvignon Sonoma Valley 1992 • $19 • (05/31/96) • **88**
Chardonnay Sonoma Valley 1994: Distinctive for its fresh, ripe peach, pear and melon notes, and it finishes with complex toasty oak accents. The texture turns a bit coarse, but only a bit. A little age should bring it into line. 300 cases made. • $16 • (06/15/96) • **88**
Merlot Sonoma Valley Marcy's Vineyard 1992 • $30 • (05/31/96) • **88**

RENAISSANCE | CALIFORNIA

Cabernet Sauvignon North Yuba 1994: Pretty lean, but with good texture, nonetheless. The core is marked by smoke, anise, cassis and herbal flavors. It's a tight package, but well done. Drink now or hold. 12,000 cases made. • $13 • (10/31/97) • **86**
Cabernet Sauvignon North Yuba 1993: In a simple style, with a modest range of cedar and currant flavors that turn earthy on the finish. 11,916 cases made. • $15 • (11/30/96) • **79**
Cabernet Sauvignon North Yuba 1991 • $12 • (12/15/95) • **78**
Cabernet Sauvignon North Yuba 1990 • $14 • (11/15/94) • **81**
Cabernet Sauvignon North Yuba 1988 • $12 • (11/15/93) • **76**
Cabernet Sauvignon North Yuba 1987 • $15 • (08/31/92) • **76**
Cabernet Sauvignon North Yuba 1986 • $21 • (11/15/94) • **78**
Cabernet Sauvignon North Yuba Reserve 1994: A rustic wine, with chewy tannins, tar and licorice up front. Finishes with a hefty dose of black cherry, blackberry and cassis. Drink now through 2003. 1,500 cases made. • $20 • (07/31/98) • **86**
Cabernet Sauvignon North Yuba Reserve 1987 • $35 • (12/15/95) • **88**
Cabernet Sauvignon North Yuba Reserve 1985 • $45 • (11/15/92) • **82**
Chardonnay North Yuba 1996: Fairly mineral-like in character, with an herbal note framed in toasty oak. Drink now. 1,842 cases made. • $18 • (07/31/98) • **82**
Chardonnay North Yuba 1995: Crisp at the center, but smooth and generous around the edges, it develops on the finish into a rich, comfortable Chardonnay with green apple and spice flavors that linger. 1,100 cases made. • $18 • (07/31/97) • **87**
Chardonnay North Yuba 1994: Simple, with spicy pear flavors that turn a bit earthy on the finish. 1,534 cases made. • $15 • (07/31/96) • **81**
Chardonnay North Yuba Barrel Select 1993 • $20 • (07/31/95) • **76**
Chardonnay North Yuba Reserve 1994: Clean and refined, with a modest band of Chardonnay flavors that fan out on the finish into hints of ripe pear and hazelnut. 240 cases made. • $35 • (07/31/97) • **85**
Chardonnay North Yuba Reserve 1993: Strong woody notes dominate, and the pear flavors have an odd edge to them. It's a weak wine that's been overoaked. 50 cases made. • $20 • (07/31/96) • **78**
Merlot North Yuba 1994: Solid, with an earthy, tarry nuance to the Merlot flavors. Finishes with a dry, tannic edge. 400 cases made. • $18 • (12/15/96) • **79**
Merlot North Yuba 1993 • $16 • (03/31/96) • **74**
Riesling Late Harvest North Yuba Special Select 1986 • $15/375ml (09/30/95) • **89**
Sauvignon Blanc Late Harvest North Yuba 1990 • $12/375ml • (12/31/93) • **78**
Sauvignon Blanc Late Harvest North Yuba Select 1991 • $13 • (05/15/95) • **85**
Sauvignon Blanc Late Harvest North Yuba Select 1985 • $13/375ml (09/30/95) • **89**
Sauvignon Blanc North Yuba 1996: A bit lean, with grassy, melonlike notes up front. The finish is crisp and clean, with a mineral edge. 2,634 cases made. • $10 • (11/30/97) • **83**
Sauvignon Blanc North Yuba 1995: A pleasant, straightforward wine with light flavors of grapefruit and lemon. Finishes with a refreshing mineral edge. 3,900 cases made. • $10 • (06/30/97) BB • **85**
Sauvignon Blanc North Yuba 1994: Pear and grassy flavors that are typical of this varietal. Earthy, spicy and floral notes add flair and complexity. 2,033 cases made. • $9 • (08/31/96) • **87**
Sauvignon Blanc North Yuba 1993 • $9 • (08/31/95) • **77**

Sauvignon Blanc North Yuba Barrel Select 1996: Rich melon, peach and citrus flavors mark this tangy white. Sharp on the finish but mellowed by a velvety texture, framed by hints of herbs, honey and hazelnuts. Much better than the regular bottling. 334 cases made. • $12 • (04/30/98) • **88**

Sauvignon Blanc North Yuba Barrel Select 1995: Butterscotch and toast aromas in a medium-bodied mix of lemon-lime and grapefruit flavors. Bright, clean finish. 200 cases made. • $15 • (06/30/97) • **86**

Sauvignon Blanc North Yuba Barrel Select 1994: Rich and mouth-filling, with butterscotch accents to the bright pear and caramel flavors. Finish is soft and plush. 190 cases made. • $12 • (08/31/96) • **89**

RENWOOD | CALIFORNIA

Barbera Amador County 1995: Tart and trim, with pleasing wild berry and cherry flavors and crisp tannins. Shows more complexity and finesse on the finish, where the flavors fan out. 550 cases made. • $16 • (11/30/97) • **88**

Barbera Amador County 1992 • $16 • (07/31/95) • **82**

Barbera Amador County Linsteadt Vineyard 1995: A touch earthy and leathery, with ripe berry, cherry and raspberry flavors that finish with a slightly gamy edge. Should work well with food. 550 cases made. • $18 • (11/30/97) • **87**

Port Shenandoah Valley Late Bottled Vintage 1989 • $18 • (05/31/95) • **85**

Syrah Amador County 1995: Austere with a spicy, cedary edge to its notes of ripe plum and cherry. Tannins should be softer now, so drink soon. 1,444 cases made. • $22 • (09/30/97) • **86**

Viognier Amador County 1996: This one suffers from a slight petrol quality. Finishes with a tangy grapefruit, mineral edge. 643 cases made. • $22 • (12/15/97) • **81**

Zinfandel Amador County 1991 • $12 • (03/31/94) • **83**

Zinfandel Amador County Amador Ice 1994: Very sweet, almost syrupy, with delicious, concentrated strawberry and distinctive, exotic spice and melon flavors that hint of chocolate on the long finish. Tempting now, but could improve through 2005. 252 cases made. • $20 • (04/30/97) • **92**

Zinfandel Amador County Grandmère 1994: Ripe and intense, with a core of chunky cherry, chocolate and cedary oak flavors. A rustic style that manages to shave off the rough edges. Ready to drink. 1,261 cases made. • $23 • (10/15/96) • **86**

Zinfandel Amador County Grandpère 1995: Ripe to the point of jamminess, with lots of cherry and wild berry aromas and flavors that persist for a long, fruity aftertaste. Drinks well now. 1,225 cases made. • $23 • (11/15/97) • **88**

Zinfandel Amador County Grandpère 1994: Supple, complex and elegant, with pretty ripe cherry, blackberry, spice and cedar notes. Only mildly tannic, it's approachable now. 1,008 cases made. • $25 • (04/30/97) • **88**

Zinfandel Amador County Jack Rabbit Flat Fox Creek Vineyard 1995: Displays pretty, complex fruit flavors, with dashes of ripe cherry, plum and wild berry, before turning smooth and supple on the finish. Impressive for its balance and purity of flavor. 1,175 cases made. • $25 • (11/15/97) • **89**

Zinfandel Amador County Old Vine 1994: Smooth, ripe, rich and exotic, with layers of ripe plum, cherry and berry, showing fine depth and richness before a wave of tannins moves in. Best to cellar into 1999. 8,023 cases made. • $17 • (04/30/97) • **90**

Zinfandel Amador County Old Vine 1993 • $15 • (09/15/95) • **89**

Zinfandel Fiddeltown Eschen Vineyard 1994: Austere and still quite tannic, but shows more finesse than most Zins from this area. The sharply focused cherry, currant and wild berry flavors slowly unfold, gaining depth and complexity. 850 cases made. • $25 • (02/28/97) • **89**

Zinfandel Fiddletown Eschen Vineyard 1995: Dense, earthy and quite tannic, yet the core of wild berry, cherry and raspberry flavors shows through nicely, picking up a tarry edge and hints of cedar and spice. Packs a wallop that many Zin fans will love. Try now (for the hearty) or cellar into 1999. 1,525 cases made. • $23 • (11/15/97) • **89**

Zinfandel Fiddletown Old Vine 1993 • $22 • (04/30/96) • **87**

Zinfandel Shenandoah Valley Grandpère 1993 • $21 • (10/15/95) • **87**

Zinfandel Shenandoah Valley Grandpère 1992 • $18 • (08/31/94) • **88**

Zinfandel Shenandoah Valley Grandpère 1991 • $16 • (03/31/94) • **86**

Key: SS—Spectator Selection CS—Cellar Selection HR—Highly Recommended BB—Best Buy $NA—Price not available Ⓐ—Auction Price (BT)—Barrel Tasting
Dates in parentheses indicate the issues in which the ratings were published.

RETZLAFF | CALIFORNIA

Cabernet Sauvignon Livermore Valley 1991 • $16 • (11/15/93) • **68**

Meritage Livermore Valley 1990 • $18 • (11/15/93) • **81**

Merlot Livermore Valley 1991 • $14 • (09/15/94) • **79**

REX HILL | OREGON

Cabernet Sauvignon Oregon Reserve 1994: Ripe, gentle and nicely proportioned to show off its black cherry and currant flavors, shaded with hints of pepper and earth. Best from 1999 or 2000. 300 cases made. • $30 • (05/15/98) • **88**

Cabernet Sauvignon Oregon Reserve 1992 • $30 • (11/30/94) • **85**

Chardonnay Willamette Valley 1996: Crisp, bright and appealing for its spicy pear and apricot flavors that linger pleasantly on the finish. Remains delicate without sacrificing intensity. Best from 1999. 1,300 cases made. • $14 • (05/15/98) • **87**

Pinot Gris Oregon Kings Ridge 1993 • $9 • (10/15/94) BB • **86**

Pinot Gris Oregon Reserve 1993 • $15 • (10/15/94) • **84**

Pinot Gris Willamette Valley 1996: Simple and straightforward, with modest melon and floral flavors. Ready now. 3,000 cases made. • $14 • (10/31/97) • **82**

Pinot Noir Oregon 1985 • $15 • (02/15/90) • **81**

Pinot Noir Oregon Archibald Vineyards 1990 • $22 • (03/15/94) • **85**

Pinot Noir Oregon Archibald Vineyards 1985 • $30 • (02/15/90) • **84**

Pinot Noir Oregon Dundee Hills Vineyards 1989 • $22 • (02/28/93) • **86**

Pinot Noir Oregon Dundee Hills Vineyards 1985 • $19 Ⓐ • (02/15/90) • **74**

Pinot Noir Oregon Dundee Hills Vineyards 1983 • $18 • (08/31/86) • **86**

Pinot Noir Oregon Kings Ridge 1996: Light in texture, with green, leafy flavors dominating the very modest fruit, finishing with a bite of tannin. Try in 1999. 9,650 cases made. • $13 • (10/31/97) • **80**

Pinot Noir Oregon Kings Ridge 1995: Light, soft and simple, with a low level of pretty plum and toast flavors that fade quickly. 7,800 cases made. • $12 • (02/28/97) • **79**

Pinot Noir Oregon Kings Ridge 1992 • $10 • (03/15/94) • **81**

Pinot Noir Oregon Maresh Vineyard 1989 • $22 • (02/28/93) • **84**

Pinot Noir Oregon Maresh Vineyard 1985 • $18 • (06/15/88) • **79**

Pinot Noir Oregon Medici Vineyard 1985 • $28 • (02/15/90) • **77**

Pinot Noir Oregon Reserve 1994: Soft and generous with its cola-scented black cherry and tar flavors. An open-textured wine with a wild berry edge that keeps it interesting right through the slightly biting finish. Best from 1999. 2,000 cases made. • $40 • (02/28/97) • **86**

Pinot Noir Oregon Reserve 1992 • $30 • (11/30/94) • **82**

Pinot Noir Oregon Wirtz Vineyards 1985 • $18 • (06/15/88) • **82**

Pinot Noir Willamette Valley 1995: Light and spicy, it's distinctive for its cigar box and red cherry flavors that extend into a narrow finish. Has length and possibilities for growth through 1999 or 2000. 5,200 cases made. • $17 • (02/28/97) • **85**

Pinot Noir Willamette Valley 1990 • $15 • (03/15/94) • **79**

Pinot Noir Willamette Valley 1989 • $15 • (02/28/93) • **77**

Pinot Noir Willamette Valley 1988 • $18 • (04/15/91) • **88**

Pinot Noir Willamette Valley 1985 • $15 • (06/15/88) • **79**

Sauvignon Blanc Oregon 1995: Bright and fruity up front, with a spicy, violet-floral accent to the orange and vaguely medicinal flavors. 370 cases made. • $9 • (04/30/97) • **80**

White Riesling Oregon 1996: Light, with modest citrus and apple flavors. Drink soon. 1,500 cases made. • $8 • (05/15/98) • **83**

REY SOL | CALIFORNIA

Syrah Temecula 1995: Cassis and spice notes herald this silky-textured wine. A smoky quality borders on charcoal, and the finish is touched with herbs. Drink now through 2001. 351 cases made. • $16 • (06/15/98) • **86**

Syrah Temecula 1994: Earthy, musty notes divert the focus of the modest pepper and berry flavors. 300 cases made. • $10 • (08/31/96) • **81**

RICH PASSAGE | OREGON

Chardonnay Oregon 1993: A flavorful white with burnt flavors that might be from the oak. Was awkward, but it may have melded together by now. 85 cases made. • $12 • (01/31/97) • **78**

Fumé Blanc Washington 1995: Bright and citrusy, with a metallic flavor edging past the herbal character. Finishes with some nice fruit and smoke flavors. 450 cases made. • $8 • (11/30/97) • **83**

Fumé Blanc Washington 1994: The floral, spicy flavors are reminiscent of Muscat. This has charm and the lively fruit flavors persist on the finish. 225 cases made. • $8 • (08/31/96) • **85**
Fumé Blanc Washington 1993 • $9 • (09/30/95) • **83**
Merlot Washington 1994: Pale in color, and stingy with its orange-peel and berry flavors. A touch of vinegar sneaks in on the finish. 110 cases made. • $13 • (09/15/96) • **78**
Pinot Noir Oregon 1993: Light, smooth and velvety, with a smoky edge to the spicy cherry flavors. Drinkable now. 115 cases made. • $13 • (08/31/96) • **83**
Pinot Noir Oregon Winemaker's Reserve 1991 • $13 • (11/30/94) • **81**
Pinot Noir Oregon Winemaker's Reserve 1990 • $15 • (02/28/93) • **79**
Pinot Noir Washington Morgan Vineyard 1990 • $12 • (02/28/93) • **68**

RICH, ANDREW | WASHINGTON

Cabernet Sauvignon Yakima Valley Les Vigneaux 1996: Generous and supple, smooth-textured, with raspberry and spice flavors that remain smooth and spicy through the soft finish. Good now, best from 1999 through 2002. 140 cases made. • $16 • (05/15/98) • **87**
Gewürztraminer Willamette Valley Les Vigneaux 1996: This ice wine, while sweet, is remarkably light and elegant. A lovely mouthful of pear, honey, floral and nectarine flavors that linger enticingly on the long finish. Delicious now, may be best from 1999. 250 cases made. • $15/375ml • (11/30/97) • **92**
Pinot Noir Rosé Willamette Valley Tabula Rasa 1996: Dry, with slightly peppery watermelon and light berry flavors, finishing simple and austere. Not a casual sipper; best with food. 150 cases made. • $10 • (11/15/97) • **81**
Pinot Noir Yamhill County Les Vigneaux 1996: Firm in texture, with a thin layer of coarse tannins covering the light plum and berry flavors for now. Best from 1999. 350 cases made. • $16 • (05/15/98) • **80**

RICHARDSON | CALIFORNIA

Cabernet Franc Sonoma Valley Giles Vineyard 1993 • $15 • (05/15/96) • **83**
Cabernet Sauvignon Sonoma Valley 1985 • $12 • (11/30/88) • **78**
Cabernet Sauvignon Sonoma Valley Horne Vineyard 1995: Surprisingly herbal for this region, it also shows some nice anise, cherry and blackberry notes. Tannins are coarse, but nothing a good steak couldn't fix. 400 cases made. • $18 • (11/30/97) • **83**
Cabernet Sauvignon Sonoma Valley Horne Vineyard 1992 • $12 • (11/15/94) • **81**
Cabernet Sauvignon Sonoma Valley Horne Vineyard 1991 • $14 • (11/15/93) • **89**
Cabernet Sauvignon Sonoma Valley Horne Vineyard 1990 • $12 • (11/15/93) • **73**
Cabernet Sauvignon Sonoma Valley Horne Vineyard 1989 • $14 • (11/15/91) • **78**
Merlot Carneros Sangiacomo Vineyard 1995: Firm and focused, with a complex band of earthy currant, cedar, cherry and plum flavors that fan out nicely on the finish, revealing depth and richness. 950 cases made. • $17 • (07/31/97) • **88**
Merlot Carneros Sangiacomo Vineyard 1994: Clean and correct, with a narrow band of cedar, plum and cherry flavors. Lacks depth and concentration. 500 cases made. • $18 • (07/31/96) • **82**
Merlot Carneros Sangiacomo Vineyard 1993: Tart and trim, with a narrow band of cedar, tart black cherry, plum and wild berry. Tastes better on the finish, where the oak flavors fold in together nicely with the fruit. Drink now. 750 cases made. • $18 • (08/31/96) • **87**
Merlot Sonoma Valley Los Carneros Vineyard 1992 • $15 • (09/15/94) • **87**
Merlot Sonoma Valley Los Carneros Gregory Vineyard 1991 • $18 • (06/15/93) • **86**
Merlot Sonoma Valley Los Carneros Gregory Vineyard 1990 • $15 • (05/31/92) • **89**
Merlot Sonoma Valley Los Carneros Gregory Vineyard 1989 • $14 • (03/31/91) • **83**
Merlot Sonoma Valley Los Carneros Sangiacomo Vineyard 1990 • $15 • (05/31/92) • **87**
Merlot Sonoma Valley Los Carneros Sangiacomo & Gregory Vineyards 1991 • $15 • (06/15/93) • **85**
Pinot Noir Carneros Sangiacomo Vineyard 1996: Bright cherry, spice and mint flavors are the hallmarks of this wine, though it's a bit unbalanced on the palate. It lacks integration and smoothness. Try in 1999. 800 cases made. • $19 • (02/28/98) • **84**
Pinot Noir Carneros Sangiacomo Vineyard 1995: Clean and vibrant, with fresh cherry, plum and berry notes and a trace of spice on the finish. Not too tannic, it can be enjoyed now. 950 cases made. • $18 • (02/28/97) • **86**
Pinot Noir Carneros Sangiacomo Vineyard 1993 • $15 • (03/31/95) • **84**
Pinot Noir Sonoma Valley Los Carneros Sangiacomo Vineyard 1992 • $14 • (12/31/95) • **74**
Pinot Noir Sonoma Valley Los Carneros Sangiacomo Vineyard 1991 • $15 • (02/28/93) • **80**
Pinot Noir Sonoma Valley Los Carneros Sangiacomo Vineyard 1990 • $14 • (09/30/92) • **81**
Pinot Noir Sonoma Valley Los Carneros Sangiacomo Vineyard 1989 • $14 • (04/30/91) • **86**
Pinot Noir Sonoma Valley Los Carneros Sangiacomo Vineyard 1987 • $12 • (10/15/89) • **88**
Pinot Noir Sonoma Valley Los Carneros Sangiacomo Vineyard 1986 • $12 • (06/15/88) • **87**
Synergy Sonoma & Napa Valleys 1989 • $15 • (05/31/92) • **84**
Synergy Sonoma Valley 1994: A touch earthy and leathery, though it still serves up well-proportioned currant and cherry flavors. Hold off until 1999 for smoother tannins. 1,000 cases made. • $15 • (12/15/95) • **86**
Zinfandel Sonoma Valley 1995: Starts out on a minty note, followed by some black cherry and plum flavors. Young and tight, it needed aging; hopefully the tannins have softened. 400 cases made. • $16 • (04/30/97) • **87**
Zinfandel Sonoma Valley NV • $9 • (07/31/89) • **76**
Zinfandel Sonoma Valley Nora's Vineyard 1993 • $15 • (10/15/95) • **84**
Zinfandel Sonoma Valley Nora's Vineyard 1992 • $12 • (08/31/94) • **89**

RIDGE | CALIFORNIA

Cabernet Sauvignon Howell Mountain 1983 • $14 Ⓐ • (03/16/86) • **83**
Cabernet Sauvignon Howell Mountain 1982 • $12 • (06/01/85) • **88**
Cabernet Sauvignon Napa County York Creek 1991 • $16 • (11/15/94) • **85**
Cabernet Sauvignon Napa County York Creek 1990 • $16 • (11/15/93) • **88**
Cabernet Sauvignon Napa County York Creek 1987 • $21 • (11/15/92) • **85**
Cabernet Sauvignon Napa County York Creek 1985 • $21 • (06/15/89) • **78**
Cabernet Sauvignon Napa County York Creek 1984 • $14 • (02/15/87) • **78**
Cabernet Sauvignon Napa County York Creek 1981 • $12 Ⓐ • (12/16/84) • **89**
Cabernet Sauvignon Napa County York Creek 1978 • $33 • (11/15/92) • **87**
Cabernet Sauvignon Napa County York Creek Spring House Vineyard 1981 • $12 • (01/01/84) • **63**
Cabernet Sauvignon Santa Barbara County Tepusquet Vineyard 1981 • $9 • (04/16/84) • **83**
Cabernet Sauvignon Santa Cruz Mountains 1993: Pleasant, with a touch of herb and currant, this medium-weight wine reflects the character of the 1993 vintage with its trim band of flavors. 7,193 cases made. • $NA • (12/15/95) • **83**
Cabernet Sauvignon Santa Cruz Mountains 1992 • $16 • (11/15/94) • **89**
Cabernet Sauvignon Santa Cruz Mountains 1991 • $16 • (10/15/93) • **89**
Cabernet Sauvignon Santa Cruz Mountains 1990 • $14 • (02/15/93) • **85**
Cabernet Sauvignon Santa Cruz Mountains 1989 • $12 • (03/31/92) • **82**
Cabernet Sauvignon Santa Cruz Mountains 1986 • $15 • (10/31/89) • **68**
Cabernet Sauvignon Santa Cruz Mountains 1985 • $12 • (06/15/89) • **64**
Cabernet Sauvignon Santa Cruz Mountains 1984 • $12 • (06/15/87) • **64**
Cabernet Sauvignon Santa Cruz Mountains Jimsomare 1985 • $16 • (02/15/89) • **87**
Cabernet Sauvignon Santa Cruz Mountains Jimsomare 1984 • $16 • (10/31/87) • **69**
Cabernet Sauvignon Santa Cruz Mountains Jimsomare 1983 • $10 • (11/30/86) • **78**
Cabernet Sauvignon Santa Cruz Mountains Jimsomare & Monte Bello Vineyards 1981 • $12 • (01/01/85) • **87**
Cabernet Sauvignon Santa Cruz Mountains Monte Bello 1988 • $43 Ⓐ • (01/31/92) • **84**
Cabernet Sauvignon Santa Cruz Mountains Monte Bello 1987 • $44 Ⓐ • (11/15/90) • **88**
Cabernet Sauvignon Santa Cruz Mountains Monte Bello 1986 • $53 Ⓐ • (09/15/89) • **82**
Cabernet Sauvignon Santa Cruz Mountains Monte Bello 1985 • $74 Ⓐ • (07/15/88) CS • **95**
Cabernet Sauvignon Santa Cruz Mountains Monte Bello 1984 • $88 Ⓐ • (09/15/87) CS • **95**
Cabernet Sauvignon Santa Cruz Mountains Monte Bello 1982 • $21 Ⓐ • (11/30/86) • **75**
Cabernet Sauvignon Santa Cruz Mountains Monte Bello 1981 • $62 Ⓐ • (08/01/85) • **89**

UNITED STATES

Cabernet Sauvignon Santa Cruz Mountains Monte Bello 1980 • $26 Ⓐ • (04/01/85) • **70**
Cabernet Sauvignon Santa Cruz Mountains Monte Bello 1978 • $81 Ⓐ • (11/15/92) • **92**
Cabernet Sauvignon Santa Cruz Mountains Monte Bello 1974 • $123 Ⓐ • (11/15/94) • **94**
Cabernet Sauvignon Santa Cruz Mountains Monte Bello 1971 • $10 • (04/01/86) • **85**
Chardonnay California 1995: Intense and earthy, with a hard, cedary edge to the ripe pear and melon flavors, finishing with smoky oak notes. Not the norm for Ridge Chardonnay of late-but it's the California appellation, not the Santa Cruz Mountains bottling, which has been excellent. Tasted twice, with consistent notes. 1,200 cases made. • $16 • (07/31/97) • **83**
Chardonnay Santa Cruz Mountains 1996: Elegant and complex, with pretty peach, pear, spice and mineral flavors, picking up hints of anise and toasty oak. Lingering finish. Drink now through 2002. 2,000 cases made. • $25 • (06/30/98) • **92**
Chardonnay Santa Cruz Mountains 1994: The ripe pear and smoky oak flavors finish a bit astringent at this point, but it should smooth out; needs time for the fruit and oak to blend. 761 cases made. • $16 • (06/15/96) • **82**
Chardonnay Santa Cruz Mountains Monte Bello Ridge Vineyards 1995: Starts out with a wonderful, earthy aroma, then moves into more complex and intricate flavors showing layers of pear, spice, hazelnut and light oak. Smooth and harmonious, with a silky texture. 1,800 cases made. • $23 • (05/31/97) • **93**
Chardonnay Santa Cruz Mountains Monte Bello Ridge Vineyards 1994: Smells complex, featuring creamy pear, fig and vanilla notes, and it's elegant and refined, as young, vibrant, concentrated flavors finish with a trace of tannin and a hint of mineral. 809 cases made. • $20 • (05/15/96) • **90**
Geyserville Sonoma County 1996: Brimming with ripe, zesty Zinfandel-laced flavors: spicy wild berry, blackberry, cherry and plum. Finishes with a hot aftertaste and firm tannins, but delivers a lot of impressive flavor. A blend of Zinfandel, Carignane, Petite Sirah, and Mourvèdre. • $NA • (05/31/98) • **90**
Geyserville Sonoma County 1995: Smooth and polished, with a perfumed edge to the ripe plum and black cherry flavors. Turns supple and fleshy on the finish, with lots of pretty, dark fruit flavors. A blend of 62 percent Zinfandel, 18 percent Petite Sirah, 15 percent Carignane, and 5 percent Mataro. Drink now. 11,000 cases made. • $25 • (11/15/97) • **89**
Geyserville Sonoma County 1994: The complex cedar, coffee and currant aromas lead to flavors that match in this Zinfandel-based red. Impressive for its long-lasting flavor, elegance and smooth, polished texture. A winner from this quality leader in Zinfandel. 11,167 cases made. • $20 • (09/30/96) SS • **91**
Geyserville Sonoma County 1993 • $20 • (09/15/95) SS • **91**
Geyserville Sonoma County 1992 • $18 • (08/31/94) • **86**
Geyserville Sonoma County 1991 • $18 • (09/15/93) HR • **90**
Geyserville Sonoma County 1990 • $16 • (10/15/92) • **87**
Geyserville Sonoma County 1989 • $14 • (11/15/91) • **84**
Lytton Springs Dry Creek Valley 1996: Without the stamp of one particular varietal, this wine manages to provide complex, well-integrated, spicy plum and wild berry and toasty, cedary oak flavors. A touch hot on the finish, but it's rich and intense, with lots of power and flavor. A blend of 78 percent Zinfandel, 19 percent Petite Sirah, 2 percent Carignane, and 1 percent Grenache. Drink now through 2003. 10,800 cases made. • $25 • (05/31/98) • **88**
Lytton Springs Dry Creek Valley 1995: This single-vineyard bottling is altogether pleasing for its earthy wild berry, plum and anise flavors that fan out on the lingering finish. Not your run-of-the-mill Zin. A blend of 84 percent Zinfandel, 14 percent Petite Sirah, and 2 percent Carignane. Drink now. 11,900 cases made. • $23 • (07/31/97) SS • **92**
Lytton Springs Dry Creek Valley 1994: Tarry and a bit leathery, with dry berry and cherry flavors. It opens up to show more spice and cedar, but it's still tightly wound. Drinkable now. 7,389 cases made. • $14 • (09/30/96) • **87**
Lytton Springs Dry Creek Valley 1993 • $19 • (07/31/95) SS • **91**
Mataro California Bridgehead Century-Old Vines 1995: Complex, with a meaty edge to plum, currant and cedar notes. Finishes with good length and supple tannins. Although the label shows a California appellation, the grapes come from 100-year-old vines in Contra Costa County. Mataro is another name for Mourvèdre. Drink now. 2,126 cases made. • $18 • (08/31/97) • **87**
Merlot Napa County York Creek 1991 • $18 • (11/15/94) • **80**
Merlot Santa Cruz Mountains Monte Bello Ridge 1994: Young, firm, tight and peppery, with an earthy, cedary nuance to the spicy currant and cherry notes. This compact wine is quite tannic; try now. 500 cases made. • $40 • (06/30/97) • **89**
Merlot Santa Cruz Mountains Monte Bello Ridge 1993 • $24 • (06/15/96) • **88**
Merlot Santa Cruz Mountains Monte Bello Ridge 1992 • $16 • (01/31/96) • **91**
Merlot Santa Cruz Mountains Monte Bello Ridge 1974 • $175 • (11/15/94) • **84**
Merlot Sonoma County Bradford Mountain 1990 • $18 • (03/15/94) HR • **89**
Merlot Sonoma County Bradford Mountain 1989 • $18 • (10/31/92) • **82**
Merlot Sonoma County Bradford Mountain 1987 • $17 • (07/15/90) • **75**
Merlot Sonoma County Bradford Mountain 1986 • $16 • (07/31/89) • **64**
Monte Bello Santa Cruz Mountains 1997: Fine intensity, focused, rich and concentrated, with currant, wild berry, anise and spice. Finishes with firm tannins and a sense of elegance. • $NA • (07/31/98) (BT) • **90-94**
Monte Bello Santa Cruz Mountains 1994: Young and tight, a touch earthy with tart currant and wild berry flavors. Takes time to unfold, but the depth and concentration become evident on the finish, where the flavors linger. Give this time; best after 2001. A blend of 73 percent Cabernet Sauvignon, 15 percent Merlot, 9 percent Petit Verdot, and 3 percent Cabernet Franc. 4,000 cases made. • $100 • (09/30/97) • **93**
Monte Bello Santa Cruz Mountains 1993: Elegant and understated, its core of fruit is built around ripe cherry and plummy flavors, finishing with supple tannins and a dash of cedar. A claret style that grows on you. Appealing now and into 2004. A blend of 86 percent Cabernet Sauvignon, 7 percent Merlot and 7 percent Petit Verdot. 2,754 cases made. • $80 • (10/15/97) • **89**
Monte Bello Santa Cruz Mountains 1992: Dark, young and tight, it's firmly tannic, but with enough black cherry, currant and smoky oak flavors. The woodiness dominates the finish at this young stage. Best to cellar into 2000 in hopes it softens. Finishes with intensity and concentration. 3,985 cases made. • $80 • (11/15/96) CS • **91**
Monte Bello Santa Cruz Mountains 1991 • $75 • (11/15/95) CS • **91**
Monte Bello Santa Cruz Mountains 1990 • $60 • (11/15/93) • **89**
Monte Bello Santa Cruz Mountains 1989 • $40 • (11/15/92) HR • **91**
Mourvèdre California Evangelo Vineyards Mataro 1990 • $14 • (03/15/92) • **73**
Mourvèdre Contra Costa County Bridgehead Mataro 1993 • $16 • (12/15/95) • **84**
Petite Sirah Napa County York Creek 1991 • $18 • (09/30/95) • **85**
Petite Sirah Napa County York Creek 1990 • $18 • (05/31/94) • **83**
Petite Sirah Napa County York Creek 1988 • $16 • (03/15/92) • **80**
Petite Sirah Napa County York Creek 1987 • $12 • (08/31/91) • **76**
Petite Sirah Napa County York Creek 1985 • $9 • (10/31/89) • **87**
Petite Sirah Napa County York Creek 1984 • $10 • (01/31/88) • **70**
Petite Sirah Napa County York Creek 1983 • $9 • (03/15/87) • **86**
Petite Sirah Napa County York Creek 1981 • $8 • (10/01/84) • **90**
Petite Sirah Spring Mountain York Creek 1994: Dark and dense, with exotic, spicy aromas and a chewy core of earthy currant, mineral and tarlike nuances. Approachable now, or cellar short-term. 1,325 cases made. • $18 • (07/31/97) • **88**
Zinfandel Dry Creek Valley Lytton Springs 1992 • $18 • (08/31/94) SS • **90**
Zinfandel Dry Creek Valley Lytton Springs 1991 • $18 • (08/31/93) CS • **91**
Zinfandel Dry Creek Valley Lytton Springs 1990 • $15 • (10/15/92) • **89**
Zinfandel Howell Mountain 1990 • $12 • (10/15/92) • **80**
Zinfandel Howell Mountain 1989 • $12 • (03/31/92) • **87**
Zinfandel Howell Mountain 1988 • $12 • (07/31/91) • **82**
Zinfandel Howell Mountain 1987 • $10 • (05/31/90) • **83**
Zinfandel Howell Mountain 1985 • $9 • (05/15/88) • **73**
Zinfandel Howell Mountain 1984 • $9 • (06/30/87) • **81**
Zinfandel Howell Mountain 1983 • $9 • (05/01/86) • **89**
Zinfandel Howell Mountain 1982 • $9 • (06/01/85) • **85**
Zinfandel Napa County York Creek 1985 • $11 • (12/31/87) • **82**
Zinfandel Napa County York Creek 1984 • $23 Ⓐ • (03/15/87) • **86**
Zinfandel Napa County York Creek 1982 • $22 • (07/16/85) SS • **91**
Zinfandel Napa County York Creek 1981 • $9 • (01/01/84) • **89**
Zinfandel Paso Robles 1990 • $10 • (10/15/92) • **84**
Zinfandel Paso Robles 1989 • $10 • (11/15/91) • **84**
Zinfandel Paso Robles 1987 • $10 • (03/15/90) • **85**
Zinfandel Paso Robles Dusi Ranch 1996: Supple and elegant, with a fleshy texture and ripe plum, cherry and wild berry flavors that are complex and

Key: SS—Spectator Selection CS—Cellar Selection HR—Highly Recommended BB—Best Buy $NA—Price not available Ⓐ—Auction Price (BT)—Barrel Tasting
Dates in parentheses indicate the issues in which the ratings were published.

well focused. Drinks well now, but can age short-term; try through 2002. 5 percent Petite Sirah. 1,800 cases made. • $20 • (05/31/98) • **89**

Zinfandel Paso Robles Dusi Ranch 1995: Lavish with its ripe, complex cherry, plum and wild berry flavors, and it gains a nice meaty, nutty edge that enhances complexity on the finish. Another wonderful Zin from Ridge. 3,129 cases made. • $20 • (04/30/97) • **91**

Zinfandel Paso Robles Dusi Ranch 1994: Impressive for its polish and finesse, this smooth and complex California wine serves up tasty cherry, berry and spice flavors, yet manages to avoid excessive tannins. Finishes with a zesty, peppery note. 2,934 cases made. • $16 • (09/30/96) HR • **90**

Zinfandel Paso Robles Dusi Ranch 1993 • $14 • (09/30/95) • **86**

Zinfandel Paso Robles Dusi Ranch 1992 • $14 • (08/31/94) • **90**

Zinfandel Paso Robles Dusi Ranch 1991 • $12 • (09/15/93) HR • **90**

Zinfandel Paso Robles Dusi Ranch 1986 • $7 • (10/31/88) • **81**

Zinfandel Paso Robles Dusi Ranch 1982 • $8 • (01/01/85) • **90**

Zinfandel Sonoma County 1994: On solid ground with its core of ripe cherry and wild berry flavors, light toasty oak accent and hints of herb and spice. Ready to drink. 7,389 cases made. • $14 • (09/30/96) • **87**

Zinfandel Sonoma County 1993 • $12 • (09/15/95) • **88**

Zinfandel Sonoma County 1991 • $10 • (08/31/93) SS • **90**

Zinfandel Sonoma County 1990 • $8 • (12/31/92) BB • **86**

Zinfandel Sonoma County 1989 • $8 • (03/31/92) • **80**

Zinfandel Sonoma County 1988 • $8 • (02/15/91) BB • **88**

Zinfandel Sonoma County Geyserville 1988 • $19 • (11/30/90) SS • **90**

Zinfandel Sonoma County Geyserville 1987 • $15 • (10/31/89) • **90**

Zinfandel Sonoma County Geyserville 1986 • $30 • (10/31/88) • **79**

Zinfandel Sonoma County Geyserville 1985 • $25 • (09/15/87) • **83**

Zinfandel Sonoma County Geyserville 1984 • $18 • (12/31/86) • **79**

Zinfandel Sonoma County Geyserville 1982 • $32 • (09/16/84) • **90**

Zinfandel Sonoma County Geyserville 1975 • $35 • (06/16/85) • **67**

Zinfandel Sonoma County Geyserville 1974 • $44 • (06/16/85) • **79**

Zinfandel Sonoma County Geyserville 1973 • $55 • (06/16/85) • **80**

Zinfandel Sonoma County Lytton Springs 1989 • $13 • (11/15/91) • **82**

Zinfandel Sonoma County Lytton Springs 1988 • $12 • (11/30/90) • **82**

Zinfandel Sonoma County Lytton Springs 1987 • $18 • (10/31/89) • **91**

Zinfandel Sonoma County Lytton Springs 1986 • $25 • (10/15/88) • **88**

Zinfandel Sonoma County Lytton Springs 1985 • $22 • (09/15/87) • **81**

Zinfandel Sonoma County Lytton Springs 1984 • $17 • (11/15/86) • **79**

Zinfandel Sonoma County Sonoma Station 1996: Well balanced and proportioned, with appealing ripe berry, cherry, plum and anise, finishing with complex flavors and a long, lingering aftertaste. A blend of 8 percent Petite Sirah, 8 percent Alicante Bouschet and 4 percent Carignane. Drink now through 2002. 9,500 cases made. • $16 • (05/31/98) • **88**

Zinfandel Sonoma County Sonoma Station 1995: Good, ripe berry, cherry and plum notes fill out the frame, luckily diverting attention from an odd earthy flavor up front. Ready to drink. 10,080 cases made. • $18 • (04/30/97) • **88**

Zinfandel Sonoma Valley Pagani Ranch 1995: A Zinfandel of harmony and finesse, it offers smooth, ripe and fruity flavors of cherry, jam, wild berry and strawberry that gently unfold. The texture is silky and supple, with fine length. A blend of 13 percent Mataro, 3 percent Alicante Bouschet and 2 percent Petite Sirah. 4,000 cases made. • $25 • (10/31/97) SS • **92**

Zinfandel Sonoma Valley Pagani Ranch 1994: Firm and intense, with a tight core of leathery currant, herb and cedary oak flavors that open up to reveal more depth and richness just before the tannins kick in. Drink now. 3,804 cases made. • $20 • (09/30/96) • **90**

Zinfandel Sonoma Valley Pagani Ranch 1993 • $20 • (09/15/95) CS • **90**

Zinfandel Sonoma Valley Pagani Ranch 1992 • $16 • (10/15/94) SS • **93**

Zinfandel Sonoma Valley Pagani Ranch 1991 • $14 • (09/30/93) • **86**

Zinfandel Spring Mountain York Creek 1995: Intense and lively, with a ripe, complex core of cherry, raspberry, pepper and spice flavors. Finishes with crisp tannins that are well proportioned. Appealing now. 6 percent Petite Sirah, 4 percent Alicante Bouschet. 2,900 cases made. • $23 • (11/15/97) • **88**

RITCHIE CREEK | CALIFORNIA

Cabernet Sauvignon Napa Valley 1991 • $18 • (04/15/95) • **85**

Cabernet Sauvignon Napa Valley 1978 • $22 • (11/15/92) • **78**

RIVER ROAD | CALIFORNIA

Cabernet Sauvignon Napa County 1993: Light, smooth and appealing, its berry and currant flavors nicely integrated. 2,400 cases made. • $9 • (12/15/95) • **83**

Chardonnay Sonoma County Proprietor's Reserve 1996: Simple and earthy, with notes of citrus, apple and toast. A bit leesy on the finish, where the earthy notes compete with the fruit. Drink now. 1,000 cases made. • $10 • (07/31/98) • **81**

RIVER RUN | CALIFORNIA

Syrah Monterey County Ventana Vineyard 1994: Intensely varietal, with strong pepper, bell pepper and wild berry flavors. Dark in color, it's a potent wine that some will find overbearing. Drink now. 670 cases made. • $18 • (02/28/97) • **86**

Zinfandel Paso Robles Beckwith Ranch Vineyard 1996: Tightly structured, with concentrated, gamy leather flavors. Lingering notes of bright strawberry, spice and herbs add dimensions. Finishes with firm tannins. Drink now through 2001. 200 cases made. • $15 • (06/15/98) • **84**

RIVERSIDE FARM | CALIFORNIA

Cabernet Sauvignon California 1991 • $7 • (11/15/94) • **78**

Cabernet Sauvignon California 1990 • $7 • (11/15/92) • **79**

Cabernet Sauvignon California 1985 • $4 • (05/31/88) • **72**

Cabernet Sauvignon North Coast 1983 • $3 • (09/15/86) • **77**

Zinfandel California 1992 • $7 • (10/15/94) • **74**

Zinfandel California 1990 • $5 • (04/30/93) • **79**

RIVERVIEW | NEW YORK

Blanc de Blancs New York 1989: Appetizingly dry, with tight texture and subtle fruit, yeast and smoke flavors. A restrained bubbly in the Champagne style, still lively and fresh after eight years. 2,000 cases made. • $17 • (05/15/97) • **88**

Merlot North Fork of Long Island Barrel Reserve 1993: A quirky, deep-colored Merlot with doughy aromas, dull fruit flavors and a stiff, tannic texture. Not our cup of tea. 700 cases made. • $16 • (06/15/97) • **73**

RIZZA | OREGON

Pinot Noir Oregon Limited Release 1989 • $10 • (02/28/93) • **74**

ROBERT ALISON | CALIFORNIA

Cabernet Sauvignon California 1993: A strong tobacco flavor runs through the light currant flavors in this soft-textured red. • $6 • (12/15/95) • **81**

Cabernet Sauvignon California 1989 • $5 • (11/15/92) • **78**

Chardonnay California 1994: Soft, almost sweet, with a pleasant note of peach flavor ringing through. Ready now. • $6 • (12/31/95) • **82**

ROCHE | CALIFORNIA

Pinot Noir Carneros 1990 • $15 • (09/30/92) • **83**

Pinot Noir Carneros 1989 • $15 • (04/30/91) • **81**

Pinot Noir Carneros 1988 • $14 • (12/31/89) • **89**

Pinot Noir Carneros Reserve 1990 • $19 • (02/28/93) • **83**

Pinot Noir Carneros Unfiltered 1991 • $16 • (12/31/93) • **84**

Pinot Noir Carneros Unfiltered 1989 • $19 • (04/30/91) • **78**

ROCHIOLI | CALIFORNIA

Cabernet Sauvignon Russian River Valley Neoma's Vineyard Reserve 1993: Attractive for its bright, tart cherry, currant and raspberry flavor. It's intense and well balanced and shows good depth and concentration. Drink now. 146 cases made. • $28 • (04/30/96) • **86**

Cabernet Sauvignon Russian River Valley Neoma's Vineyard Reserve 1991 • $26 • (12/15/95) • **87**

Cabernet Sauvignon Russian River Valley Neoma's Vineyard Reserve 1990 • $24 • (06/15/93) • **86**

Chardonnay Russian River Valley 1996: Tightly focused, rich with complex pear, citrus, tangerine and smoky, toasty oak flavors, it turns smooth and polished on the finish, where the flavors fan out and linger. Elegant. Drink now through 2002. 2,100 cases made. • $24 • (05/31/98) • **91**

Chardonnay Russian River Valley 1995: Young and tight, with a spicy, flinty accent to the pear and vanilla flavors. Clean and refreshing. Drinks well now, but should only get better. 1,721 cases made. • $18 • (12/31/96) • **88**

Chardonnay Russian River Valley 1994: A wine of delicate style that laces its spicy ripe pear flavors with hints of honey, then floats them nicely through the finish. 1,800 cases made. • $17 • (06/15/96) • **89**

Chardonnay Russian River Valley 1993 • $16 • (07/31/95) • **85**

Chardonnay Russian River Valley Allen Vineyard 1996: A wonderful orchestration of fruit and oak, with a ripe, rich, tightly focused core of spicy pear, apple and hazelnut. Pretty smoke and toasted oak flavors fold in on the finish. Drink now through 2003. 75 cases made. • $38 • (07/31/98) • **94**

Chardonnay Russian River Valley Allen Vineyard Reserve 1995: Elegant and refined, with a supple, complex core of ripe pear, anise, apricot and fig flavors, it gains momentum and length on the finish, where the flavors fan out and linger. First bottling from Allen Vineyard—alas, only 75 cases made. 75 cases made. • $35 • (05/31/97) • **94**

Chardonnay Russian River Valley Estate Cuvée Reserve 1995: Elegant and complex, with subtle ripe pear, apricot, melon and fig notes that slowly unfold on the palate, work their way into some pretty toasty, smoky oak nuances and turn delicate and intricate on the finish. 223 cases made. • $30 • (05/31/97) • **93**

Chardonnay Russian River Valley Reserve 1994: Amazingly ripe, rich and complex, with tiers of concentrated pear, hazelnut, honey and toasty oak flavors all folding together into a remarkably sophisticated Chardonnay. A tremendous effort that matches intensity of fruit, elegance and grace. 210 cases made. • $28 • (04/30/96) • **95**

Chardonnay Russian River Valley Reserve 1993 • $28 • (06/15/95) • **90**

Chardonnay Russian River Valley River Block 1996: Elegant and understated, with complex pear, hazelnut, honey and anise flavors that slowly build on the finish, revealing more depth and richness. Impressive for its fruit complexity. Best now through 2004. 153 cases made. • $32 • (07/31/98) • **93**

Chardonnay Russian River Valley South River Vineyard Reserve 1995: Big, ripe, rich and concentrated, this is a real mouthful of Chardonnay, with layers of ripe fig, pear and melon, hints of cedar and vanilla. Finishes with a long, intense aftertaste that keeps pumping out the flavors. 78 cases made. • $40 • (11/15/97) • **94**

Gewürztraminer Russian River Valley McIlroy Vineyard 1995: In a subtle, off-dry style that wraps the generous flavors and fragrances in a smooth package, showing the rose petal, citrus and spice flavors to good effect. 274 cases made. • $9 • (10/31/96) • **87**

Pinot Noir Russian River Valley 1995: Has a wonderful sense of harmony and finesse, with a pretty, fleshy core of plum, cherry, wild berry and spice. Finishes with light, toasty oak notes. Drinks well now, through 2002. 2,162 cases made. • $24 • (07/31/97) • **92**

Pinot Noir Russian River Valley 1994: Smooth, rich and complex, with a nice integration of cherry, berry and currant flavors and light toasty oak shadings. Delicious, from start to finish. Ready to drink. 1,800 cases made. • $22 • (02/28/97) • **91**

Pinot Noir Russian River Valley 1992 • $18 • (12/15/94) • **88**

Pinot Noir Russian River Valley 1991 • $19 • (02/28/94) SS • **90**

Pinot Noir Russian River Valley 1990 • $16 • (02/28/93) • **80**

Pinot Noir Russian River Valley 1989 • $16 • (11/15/91) • **84**

Pinot Noir Russian River Valley 1988 • $15 • (10/31/90) • **85**

Pinot Noir Russian River Valley 1987 • $15 • (05/31/90) • **89**

Pinot Noir Russian River Valley 1986 • $15 • (10/15/89) • **87**

Pinot Noir Russian River Valley 1985 • $13 • (06/15/88) • **92**

Pinot Noir Russian River Valley 1984 • $12 • (11/15/87) • **84**

Pinot Noir Russian River Valley 1982 • $13 • (08/31/86) • **89**

Pinot Noir Russian River Valley East Block Reserve 1994: Tightly wound, with a rich, complex core of anise, black cherry, oak and mineral flavors. The fruit flavors expand on the finish to reveal notes of plum and berry, and a firm core of tannins. Drink now, as this concentrated young wine has all the right ingredients. 70 cases made. • $60 • (11/15/96) • **95**

Pinot Noir Russian River Valley Little Hill Block Reserve 1995: Earthy mushroom and tarry aromas lead to a tightly wound core of cherry and berry Pinot Noir flavors. Try in 1999. Tasted twice, with consistent notes. 171 cases made. • $38 • (11/15/97) • **89**

Pinot Noir Russian River Valley Reserve 1991 • $35 • (02/28/94) SS • **92**

Pinot Noir Russian River Valley Reserve 1990 • $30 • (11/15/92) • **92**

Pinot Noir Russian River Valley Reserve 1990: A curiously complex and tasty wine. Some earthy mushroom flavors up front make way for a wonderful array of mature cherry, anise, cedar and spice flavors that fold together with style. All you would hope for from a wine this age. Delicious now and into 2000. 154 cases made. • $30 • (03/31/97) • **92**

Key: SS—Spectator Selection CS—Cellar Selection HR—Highly Recommended BB—Best Buy $NA—Price not available Ⓐ—Auction Price (BT)—Barrel Tasting

Dates in parentheses indicate the issues in which the ratings were published.

Pinot Noir Russian River Valley Three Corner Vineyard Reserve 1995: Smooth, ripe and elegant, with a pretty array of earthy cherry and currant flavors, picking up flashes of tar and tea on the finish. Drink now. Tasted twice, with consistent notes. 121 cases made. • $40 • (11/15/97) • **89**

Pinot Noir Russian River Valley Three Corner Vineyard Reserve 1994: Delicious Pinot Noir from the first sip. Serves up lots of complex flavors, with layers of ripe cherry, plum and raspberry and finishes with notes of tea, anise and spice. Tannins are smooth and polished and the finish goes on and on, revealing more nuances and subtelties. 83 cases made. • $40 • (11/15/96) • **94**

Pinot Noir Russian River Valley West Block Reserve 1995: Shows more fruit and depth than the other Rochioli Reserve Pinot Noirs, as the plum and cherry flavors have touches of earthy mushroom and spice that add dimension. Drink now. 325 cases made. • $50 • (11/15/97) • **89**

Pinot Noir Russian River Valley West Block Reserve 1994: Stunning, with an amazing core of ripe, rich, complex and concentrated fruit; tiers of brilliant black cherry, plum, currant and raspberry flavors-and just the right amount of oak shading, giving it a light, toasty vanilla accent that adds dimension. A sensational wine from a winery that is right on target. 243 cases made. • $48 • (11/15/96) • **96**

Pinot Noir Russian River Valley West Block Reserve 1993 • $38 • (10/15/95) • **89**

Pinot Noir Russian River Valley West Block Reserve 1992 • $36 • (12/15/94) HR • **92**

Sauvignon Blanc Russian River Valley 1997: Highly aromatic, redolent of fig, fresh pea, passion fruit, grapefruit and herbs. On the palate, it's rich and weighty, well-oaked, yet still brimming with ripe fruit. The finish is tangy and long. Drink now. 3,072 cases made. • $14 • (06/30/98) SS • **91**

Sauvignon Blanc Russian River Valley 1996: Delicious. Rich, ripe melon, fig and passion fruit flavors coat the palate and linger, thanks to bright acidity. Finishes with just the right touch of grassiness. 1,850 cases made. • $15 • (06/15/97) • **90**

Sauvignon Blanc Russian River Valley 1995: Smooth and bright. Brimming with citrus, pear and herb flavors, with an echo of anise. Flavors linger nicely. 2,850 cases made. • $11 • (07/31/96) • **89**

Sauvignon Blanc Russian River Valley 1994 • $11 • (08/31/95) • **84**

Sauvignon Blanc Russian River Valley 1993 • $10 • (06/30/94) BB • **87**

Sauvignon Blanc Russian River Valley Old Vines Reserve 1996: This wine strikes a fine balance between ripe pear, tangy grapefruit and fresh melon flavors. It's crisp and refreshing, with a spicy, though slightly bitter, finish. 143 cases made. • $20 • (11/30/97) • **90**

Sauvignon Blanc Russian River Valley Old Vines Reserve 1995: Bright and brilliant; generous grapefruit, pear, herb and spice flavors held tightly in focus by crisp, lively acidity. 145 cases made. • $19 • (07/31/96) • **91**

Sauvignon Blanc Russian River Valley Old Vines Reserve 1994: Elegant, lively and balanced, weaving its spice, herb and rich pear flavors around a smooth, focused beam of cream. Flavors last and last on the finish. 102 cases made. • $19 • (09/15/96) • **91**

Sauvignon Blanc Russian River Valley Reserve 1993 • $19 • (02/28/95) • **88**

Zinfandel Russian River Valley 1996: Pleasantly complex and fruity, with appealing cherry, raspberry, plum and spice. Finishes with a burst of fruit and pretty oak shadings. Drink now through 2002. 452 cases made. • $20 • (06/15/98) • **89**

Zinfandel Russian River Valley Sodini Vineyard 1994: Impressive for its ripe, bright cherry, berry, currant and spice flavors. Keeps its focus on the finish, where it gains complexity and elegance. 200 cases made. • $15 • (09/30/96) • **89**

Zinfandel Russian River Valley Sodini Vineyard 1993 • $15 • (08/31/95) • **88**

Zinfandel Russian River Valley Sodini Vineyard 1992 • $14 • (09/30/94) • **91**

ROCKING HORSE | CALIFORNIA

Cabernet Sauvignon Napa Valley Garvey Family Vineyard 1994: While it's firmly tannic around the edges and in need of short-term cellaring to soften, its core of plum, currant and black cherry flavors is rich and supple, deep and concentrated. Hold until 1999 to 2001. 850 cases made. • $24 • (11/30/97) • **90**

Cabernet Sauvignon Napa Valley Garvey Family Vineyard 1993: Somewhat earthy and leathery but the Cabernet fruit rises, giving it a sense of balance and finesse. Should drink well early, as the tannins are modest. 1,000 cases made. • $20 • (04/30/96) • **87**

Cabernet Sauvignon Napa Valley Hillside Cuvée 1991 • $18 • (03/15/94) • **84**

Cabernet Sauvignon Napa Valley Hillside Cuvée 1989 • $17 • (03/31/92) • **85**

Cabernet Sauvignon Stags Leap District Robinson Vineyard 1993: Appealing, fruity flavors that turn spicy and simple at midpalate. Drinks well now with its soft tannins. 200 cases made. • $28 • (08/31/96) • **83**

Cabernet Sauvignon Stags Leap District Robinson Vineyard 1992 • $24 • (04/15/95) • **86**
Cabernet Sauvignon Stags Leap District Robinson Vineyard 1991 • $24 • (03/31/94) HR • **90**
Cabernet Sauvignon Stags Leap District Robinson Vineyard 1990 • $22 • (02/15/93) • **91**
Zinfandel Howell Mountain 1994: Pure Zinfandel from the first whiff, with zesty pepper, spice and wild berry flavors that turn smooth and supple on the finish, picking up a juniper note. Drink now through 2001. 1,500 cases made. • $16 • (05/15/97) • **88**
Zinfandel Howell Mountain Lamborn Vineyard 1995: Attractive spicy, peppery, wild berry and plummy notes hold your interest, but it loses focus on the finish, turning earthy. Best now to 2000. 2,000 cases made. • $16 • (05/15/98) • **85**
Zinfandel Howell Mountain Lamborn Vineyard 1993 • $15 • (04/30/96) • **89**
Zinfandel Howell Mountain Lamborn Vineyard 1991 • $14 • (03/31/94) • **88**
Zinfandel Howell Mountain Lamborn Vineyard 1989 • $13 • (10/15/92) • **81**
Zinfandel Napa Valley Old Paint 1993: Lean and a bit green, with a slightly stemmy, tannic edge to the ripe cherry and wild berry flavors. Finishes on the rustic side with crisp tannins. Try now. 300 cases made. • $18 • (09/15/96) • **84**

ROCKLAND | CALIFORNIA

Cabernet Sauvignon Napa Valley 1994: Truly exotic, rich and complex. Lots of currant, anise, smoke, mineral and berry flavors that fold together quite nicely and turn even more complex on the finish where they show more depth and nuance. Tempting now for its vibrant fruitiness, but worthy of cellaring. Its one shortcoming: only 125 cases made. • $30 • (11/15/96) • **93**
Cabernet Sauvignon Napa Valley 1993: Smooth, ripe and polished, marked by spicy plum, currant and cherry notes and finishing with soft, fleshy tannins and a touch of cedar. Well balanced and enjoyable now; should age well into 2000. 80 cases made. • $30 • (05/15/96) • **89**
Petite Sirah Napa Valley 1995: Ripe, sturdy, rustic style. Hints of plum and berry peek through, but at this stage the tannins have the upper hand. Needs some time, but may always be on the tannic side. Best from 2000 to 2004. 268 cases made. • $22 • (04/30/98) • **85**
Petite Sirah Napa Valley 1993 • $17 • (05/15/96) • **89**

ROEDERER ESTATE | CALIFORNIA

Brut Anderson Valley NV: An outstanding California Brut from a French Champagne producer, it offers lots of richness, depth and flavor with its well-focused pear, hazelnut, honey, fig and spice character. Displays wonderful finesse and has a long, lingering finish, where it picks up a trace of almond. A great value, too. 30,000 cases made. • $17 • (11/30/97) SS • **92**
Brut Anderson Valley L'Ermitage 1992: Creamy and complex, with rose petal notes, it sits delicately on the palate, with toasty, hazelnut flavors and a fresh citrus-and-herb finish. 5,400 cases made. • $33 • (11/30/97) • **90**
Brut Anderson Valley L'Ermitage 1991: Supple and complex, showing zesty citrus and grapefruit flavors, picking up hints of pear and vanilla. Turns elegant and refined on the finish. Altogether, a sophisticated wine. 2,600 cases made. • $35 • (11/30/96) • **91**
Brut Anderson Valley L'Ermitage 1990 • $35 • (12/31/95) • **90**
Brut Anderson Valley L'Ermitage 1989 • $35 • (11/30/93) SS • **92**
Brut Rosé Anderson Valley NV: Full of wonderful, complex aromas and flavors. Shows smooth, creamy vanilla notes, lots of delicate black cherry, herb, spice and pear flavors and much finesse. Long and complex on the finish. 3,000 cases made. • $21 • (11/30/97) • **92**

ROLIN, NICOLAS | OREGON

Pinot Noir Willamette Valley 1994: Warm and ripe, it's generous with its fresh and supple plum and chocolate flavors. An oak character sticks out a bit now, but there's enough depth and flavor to suggest an improved future; best after 1999. • $27 • (02/28/97) • **89**

ROMBAUER | CALIFORNIA

Cabernet Franc Napa Valley 1994: Lean, with hints of bell pepper, cedar and black cherry. Turns stalky and woody on the finish. 500 cases made. • $20 • (12/15/97) • **79**
Cabernet Franc Napa Valley 1990 • $16 • (07/15/93) • **87**
Cabernet Sauvignon Napa Valley 1994: An earthy, rustic style with a core of tart cherry, wild berry and spice. Slowly straightens out on the finish, where the flavors come into better focus. For now, it's a little rough-and-tumble; drink after 1999. 1,500 cases made. • $27 • (11/15/97) • **87**
Cabernet Sauvignon Napa Valley 1993: A bit rustic, with a modest minty-menthol edge to the plum and currant flavors, but it turns dry and tannic on the finish. • $27 • (12/15/96) • **85**
Cabernet Sauvignon Napa Valley 1991 • $20 • (12/15/95) • **84**
Cabernet Sauvignon Napa Valley 1990 • $18 • (11/15/94) • **86**
Cabernet Sauvignon Napa Valley 1989 • $15 • (11/15/93) • **78**
Cabernet Sauvignon Napa Valley 1987: Crisp, showing firm, dry tannins. Somewhat unevolved, with a coarse texture. Plum and berry notes fade on the finish, indicating it's in danger of drying out. • $50 • (12/15/97) • **85**
Cabernet Sauvignon Napa Valley 1986 • $18 • (04/15/90) • **88**
Cabernet Sauvignon Napa Valley 1985 • $20 • (04/30/89) • **85**
Cabernet Sauvignon Napa Valley 1984 • $14 • (02/15/88) • **80**
Cabernet Sauvignon Napa Valley 1983 • $14 • (09/15/87) • **73**
Cabernet Sauvignon Napa Valley 1982 • $13 • (02/16/86) • **91**
Cabernet Sauvignon Napa Valley 1981 • $13 • (12/16/84) • **88**
Cabernet Sauvignon Napa Valley Diamond Mountain Selection 1994: Young, dense and chewy, with a complex core of cedar, spice, currant and wild berry flavors, finishing with cedar and vanilla-tinged oak flavors. Has a lot going for it and once it smooths out it should be delicious. Try after 1999 or 2000. 1,200 cases made. • $50 • (11/15/97) • **90**
Chardonnay Carneros 1995: This elegant California white serves up lots of ripe, juicy, complex flavors with hints of pear, apple, pineapple and guava. Finishes with a sense of finesse. The flavors persist, picking up a hint of butterscotch. 9,000 cases made. • $24 • (02/28/97) SS • **91**
Chardonnay Carneros 1994: An oaky California style, with ripe fig, pear, spice and hazelnut flavors that are smooth and opulent, finishing with a long, rich aftertaste. The smoky oak finish adds a nice dimension. 9,000 cases made. • $21 • (12/31/95) SS • **93**
Chardonnay Carneros 1993 • $18 • (03/31/95) SS • **92**
Le Meilleur du Chai Napa Valley 1990: Ripe and harmonious, with fresh, lively red cherry, plum and spice nuances, finishing with supple tannins and a stream of anise and tobacco. Drink now through 2002. A blend of 70 percent Cabernet Sauvignon, 20 percent Cabernet Franc, and 10 percent Merlot. 600 cases made. • $40 • (08/31/97) • **90**
Le Meilleur du Chai Napa Valley 1989 • $35 • (12/15/95) • **84**
Le Meilleur du Chai Napa Valley 1987 • $35 • (11/15/93) • **83**
Le Meilleur du Chai Napa Valley 1986: A wine that has dried up and turned overly tannic. Most of the bright, rich cherry and currant flavors that made it so appealing years ago have now faded. • $NA • (12/15/96) • **83**
Le Meilleur du Chai Napa Valley 1985 • $48 • (10/31/89) • **90**
Le Meilleur du Chai Napa Valley 1984 • $33 • (03/31/89) • **94**
Merlot Napa Valley 1994: Complex for its array of currant, olive, dill and cedar notes. Turns smooth and supple on the finish, where the flavors linger. 5,000 cases made. • $25 • (06/30/97) • **88**
Merlot Napa Valley 1993: Ripe and complex, with lots of heady plum, cherry and berry flavors. Offers depth and richness, finishing with firm tannins. Drink now. 4,500 cases made. • $20 • (07/31/96) • **88**
Merlot Napa Valley 1991 • $20 • (03/15/94) • **82**
Merlot Napa Valley 1990 • $16 • (07/15/93) • **84**
Merlot Napa Valley 1989 • $16 • (11/15/91) • **84**
Merlot Napa Valley 1987 • $14 • (02/15/90) • **87**
Merlot Napa Valley 1986 • $14 • (07/31/89) • **78**
Zinfandel Napa Valley 1996: Ripe, with rich, jammy wild berry, black cherry and plummy, minty notes, turning rustic and tannic on the finish, with a tarry, anise flavor. Drink now through 2002. 1,500 cases made. • $20 • (05/31/98) • **86**
Zinfandel Napa Valley 1995: Ripe and complex, concentrated with rich, juicy, bright plum, wild berry, black cherry and spicy, peppery notes. Impressive for its core of fruit, balance, supple tannins and fruity aftertaste. Drink now through 2004. 1,500 cases made. • $20 • (06/15/98) • **90**
Zinfandel Napa Valley 1994: Well crafted in a big, robust style. Features a rich core of pepper, wild berry, raspberry and cedar flavors framed by pretty oak notes. Drink now. 900 cases made. • $20 • (03/31/97) • **89**
Zinfandel Napa Valley 1993 • $18 • (07/31/95) • **88**

ROSENBLUM | CALIFORNIA

Black Muscat California 1995: Fresh, with a plummy and spicy character, it's charming for its straightforward fruit flavors and zing. Drink soon. 1,200 cases made. • $9/375ml • (11/30/96) • **85**
Cabernet Sauvignon Napa Valley 1989 • $17 • (08/31/92) • **80**
Cabernet Sauvignon Napa Valley George Hendry Vineyard 1990 • $14 • (11/15/93) • **84**

Cabernet Sauvignon Napa Valley George Hendry Vineyard Reserve 1995: Firmly tannic, but the core of plum, currant and wild berry is fresh and lively, with good intensity and cedar notes. Best from 2000 through 2006. 450 cases made. • $40 • (05/31/98) • **88**

Cabernet Sauvignon Napa Valley George Hendry Vineyard Reserve 1991 • $30 • (11/15/94) • **88**

Cabernet Sauvignon Napa Valley Holbrook Mitchell Vineyard 1995: An elegant, flavorful, well-proportioned Cabernet, with dashes of herb, currant, spice, berry and cherry, finishing with a long, complex fruit aftertaste and fine, firm tannins. Drink now through 2004. 600 cases made. • $30 • (04/30/98) • **89**

Cabernet Sauvignon Napa Valley Holbrook Mitchell Vineyard 1991 • $14 • (10/31/94) HR • **90**

Cabernet Sauvignon Napa Valley Yountville Vineyards 1994: Young and spicy, with hints of plum and black cherry flavors. Finish shows a trace of green olive. Drinks well now, even though it's a shade tannic. 850 cases made. • $20 • (11/30/96) • **85**

Carignane Napa Valley Kenefick Ranch 1995: Medium-weight, with spice, stewed-plum and wild berry notes of modest depth and richness, finishing with a flash of black cherry. Drinks well now. 300 cases made. • $15 • (12/15/97) • **87**

Carignane Napa Valley TLK Ranch 1994: Austere, with its firm tannins, but it also offers a zesty core of plum and anise flavors. Ready to drink. 200 cases made. • $11 • (11/30/96) • **83**

Chardonnay Edna Valley 1996: Bright, lean and spicy. A distinctive Chardonnay with spicy tobacco and honey notes sweeping in on the finish, all wrapped in a smooth, silky frame. 600 cases made. • $24 • (12/15/97) • **87**

Chardonnay Edna Valley 1995: Impressive new bottling for Rosenblum. Ripe and juicy, with lots of rich pear, vanilla, peach and pineapple flavors finishing in a complex, spicy aftertaste. 250 cases made. • $16 • (06/30/97) • **90**

Gewürztraminer California 1996: Definitely on the dry side, with distinctive orange, flower-scented pear and spice flavors that linger on the taut finish. Ready now. 200 cases made. • $10 • (11/30/97) • **86**

Gewürztraminer Sonoma County 1996: On the nose, it resembles a sparkling sweet Moscato from Italy, but on the palate, the bubbles accentuate the natural spiciness and bitter qualities of the grape. The net result is awkward, almost medicinal. 250 cases made. • $15 • (05/15/98) • **79**

Holbrook Mitchell Trio Napa Valley 1995: Firm and tight, with currant, plum, black cherry and cedary oak flavors that are compact and in need of cellaring to soften and unfold. Best from 2000 to 2004. 650 cases made. • $35 • (04/30/98) • **88**

Holbrook Mitchell Trio Napa Valley 1994: Well balanced, with a complex band of currant, cedar, leather and spice flavors that fan out on the finish, where they gain harmony and finesse. Ready to drink. 750 cases made. • $24 • (11/30/96) • **88**

Holbrook Mitchell Trio Napa Valley 1993: Simple with light spice and berry notes of modest proportion. Picks up a trace of herb on the finish. Ready now. 600 cases made. • $23 • (12/15/95) • **80**

Holbrook Mitchell Trio Napa Valley 1992 • $23 • (11/15/94) • **85**

Holbrook Mitchell Trio Napa Valley 1991 • $22 • (11/15/93) • **86**

Holbrook Mitchell Trio Napa Valley 1990 • $22 • (11/15/92) • **87**

Merlot Napa Valley Holbrook Mitchell Vineyard 1989 • $20 • (05/31/92) • **80**

Merlot Russian River Valley Lone Oak Vineyard 1995: Supple and elegant, with ripe currant, cherry, sage, cedar and spice flavors, polished tannins and good length. A complete and well-proportioned wine that drinks well now. 1,200 cases made. • $20 • (03/31/98) • **88**

Merlot Russian River Valley Lone Oak Vineyard 1990 • $15 • (07/15/93) • **81**

Merlot Russian River Valley Lone Oak Vineyard 1989 • $14 • (05/31/92) • **85**

Mourvèdre Contra Costa County Chateau La Paws Côte Du Bone 1996: Medium-weight, with spicy plum, wild berry and strawberry flavors that are supple and easy-going. 3,000 cases made. • $13 • (11/30/97) • **85**

Mourvèdre Contra Costa County Chateau La Paws Côte du Bone 1995: A delicious Mourvèdre, with juicy plum, blackberry, spice and anise flavors that are complex and lively. Terrific price, too. 2,750 cases made. • $10 • (11/30/96) BB • **87**

Palomino White Contra Costa County Fleur de Hoof 1996: Peaches-and-cream quality makes this an enjoyable quaff. Full and fat on the palate, but lacking in finesse and complexity. Cute label. 1,800 cases made. • $8 • (03/31/98) • **83**

Key: SS—Spectator Selection CS—Cellar Selection HR—Highly Recommended BB—Best Buy $NA—Price not available (A)—Auction Price (BT)—Barrel Tasting

Dates in parentheses indicate the issues in which the ratings were published.

Petite Sirah Napa Valley 1992 • $13 • (09/30/95) • **86**

Petite Sirah Napa Valley Kenefick Ranch 1995: Dense and dark, with a firm, earthy, tannic edge to the ripe plum and wild berry flavors. Finishes with chewy tannins. 320 cases made. • $17 • (07/31/97) • **88**

Petite Sirah Napa Valley Palisades Vineyard 1994: Dark, ripe, plummy and firmly tannic, this is a solid, old-style Petite Sirah, the kind of intense, compact wine that stands up well to hearty fare. Finishes with hints of cherry flavor and a whiff of floral aroma. Approachable now. 225 cases made. • $15 • (11/30/96) • **87**

Pinot Noir Napa Valley George Hendry Vineyard 1990 • $12 • (02/28/93) • **73**

Pinot Noir Russian River Valley Ellis Ranch 1991 • $9 • (02/28/94) • **80**

Port California 1994: Delicious already, bursting with berry, black cherry, spice and vanilla flavors that remain juicy through the racy finish. With a bit more grip it would be a real ager, too. Made from Zinfandel and Petite Sirah. Contains 9.3 percent residual sugar. 300 cases made. • $15 • (04/30/97) • **88**

Sauvignon Blanc Late Harvest Napa Valley Concento d'Oro 1991: Smoky, earthy, oniony notes sneak in amongst the honey and caramel flavors in this odd dessert wine. 850 cases made. • $15/375ml (11/30/96) • **79**

Sémillon Sonoma Valley 1996: Citrus and honey are the hallmarks of this tangy, refreshing wine. It finishes with zippy lemon, grapefruit and herbal notes. 200 cases made. • $14 • (09/15/97) • **87**

Sémillon-Chardonnay Livermore Valley 1996: Pleasant mandarin orange, lemon and nut flavors course over the palate. Finishes with tangy acidity. 3,600 cases made. • $11 • (09/15/97) • **84**

Sémillon-Chardonnay Sonoma County 1995: Firm in texture, with a tart, citrusy edge to the lean pineapple flavors. Try now. 1,700 cases made. • $9 • (11/15/96) • **82**

Zinfandel Alexander Valley Harris Kratka Vineyard 1996: Ripe and spicy, with jammy plum and black cherry flavors and hints of spice and sage. Finishes with firm, chewy tannins and pretty floral notes. Drink now through 2004. 750 cases made. • $22 • (06/15/98) • **88**

Zinfandel Alexander Valley Harris Kratka Vineyard 1995: Beautifully focused, with a pretty array of ripe plum, black cherry, wild berry and strawberry flavors, turning elegant and supple on the finish where the flavors linger long. 600 cases made. • $20 • (08/31/97) • **92**

Zinfandel Alexander Valley Harris Kratka Vineyard 1994: Fresh and lively, with compact cherry, wild berry, spice and anise flavors. Its 22 percent Carignane lends elegance. 750 cases made. • $16 • (09/30/96) • **87**

Zinfandel Alexander Valley Harris Kratka Vineyard 1993 • $15 • (10/15/95) • **83**

Zinfandel California Vintner's Cuvée IV NV • $7 • (10/15/92) • **84**

Zinfandel California Vintner's Cuvée V NV • $7 • (10/15/92) BB • **82**

Zinfandel California Vintner's Cuvée VI NV • $7 • (09/30/93) BB • **85**

Zinfandel California Vintner's Cuvée IX NV • $8 • (10/15/94) • **81**

Zinfandel California Vintner's Cuvée X NV • $8 • (10/15/95) • **83**

Zinfandel California Vintner's Cuvée XIV NV: Reasonably priced, this delicious blend of Zinfandel from throughout the state is ripe and juicy with up-front flavors of wild berry, cherry, plum and raspberry that are supple and appealing. Ready to drink. 8,000 cases made. • $9 • (03/31/97) BB • **88**

Zinfandel California Vintner's Cuvée XVI NV: Pleasantly fruity, with ripe cherry, berry and raspberry flavors and mild, integrated tannins. Drink now through 2002. 6,000 cases made. • $10 • (06/15/98) • **86**

Zinfandel Contra Costa County 1996: A ripe, full-bodied but not especially varietal wine, more reminiscent of a generic red table wine with plummy and tarry notes. 3,000 cases made. • $15 • (05/15/98) • **83**

Zinfandel Contra Costa County 1995: Ripe and brimming with spice, sage and wild berry flavors, unfolding to reveal more cherry, plum and raspberry flavors. Continues to show its fruit on a long, full finish. Drinkable now. 7,000 cases made. • $14 • (06/30/97) • **89**

Zinfandel Contra Costa County 1994 • $11 • (04/30/96) • **89**

Zinfandel Contra Costa County 1993 • $11 • (09/30/95) • **86**

Zinfandel Contra Costa County 1992 • $10 • (10/15/94) • **83**

Zinfandel Contra Costa County 1991 • $9 • (09/30/93) • **90**

Zinfandel Contra Costa County 1990 • $9 • (10/15/92) • **87**

Zinfandel Contra Costa County Continente Vineyard Old Vine 1996: Dry and earthy, with ripe plum and tar flavors that are awkward and show a high level of alcohol. Turns bitter and coarse on the finish. Drink now through 2000. 250 cases made. • $20 • (06/15/98) • **83**

Zinfandel Contra Costa County Continente Vineyard Old Vine 1995: Delivers a pretty array of ripe plum, raspberry and cherry-tinged Zin flavors, with moderate depth and mild tannins. Appealing now. 150 cases made. • $18 • (06/30/97) • **88**

Zinfandel Contra Costa County Pato Vineyard Reserve 1996: Serves up ripe, supple cherry, plum and spicy Zinfandel flavors. Holds its focus on the finish, where anise and spice fold in. Drink now through 2000. 250 cases made. • $19 • (06/15/98) • **85**

Zinfandel Contra Costa County Pato Vineyard Reserve 1995: Ripe and balanced, with a slight tarlike edge to the ripe plum and wild berry flavors. Turns smooth and supple on the finish. Ready to drink. 250 cases made. • $18 • (06/30/97) • **88**

Zinfandel Dry Creek Valley Rockpile Vineyard 1996: Clean and fruity, with firm cherry and wild berry flavors. Strikes a nice balance between fruit and tannins. Drink now through 2000. 1,182 cases made. • $18 • (06/15/98) • **86**

Zinfandel Howell Mountain White Cottage Vineyard 1996: Earthy, with a supple texture and racy wild berry flavor, this is a lighter style for Rosenblum but quite appealing on its own terms. Drink now through 2002. 200 cases made. • $21 • (06/15/98) • **86**

Zinfandel Mount Veeder Brandlin Ranch 1996: Complex, with ripe, rich, plush layers of blackberry, cherry, wild berry and spice. Bold and supple in texture, it packs in lots of flavor while maintaining a sense of elegance and grace. Drink now through 2004. 350 cases made. • $23 • (06/15/98) • **91**

Zinfandel Mount Veeder Brandlin Ranch 1995: Complex, with a spicy, peppery edge to the wild berry and black cherry flavors. Flirts with elegance before the leathery tannins fold in on the finish. 560 cases made. • $23 • (09/30/97) • **89**

Zinfandel Mount Veeder Brandlin Ranch 1994: This wine has a great sense of harmony and finesse. The texture is fleshy and polished, the flavors ripe with complex tiers of plum, wild berry, cherry and currant that continue to unfold through the finish. 625 cases made. • $20 • (09/30/96) • **92**

Zinfandel Mount Veeder Brandlin Ranch 1993 • $19 • (10/15/95) • **87**

Zinfandel Mount Veeder Brandlin Ranch 1992 • $19 • (10/15/94) • **86**

Zinfandel Mount Veeder Brandlin Ranch 1991 • $15 • (09/30/93) • **88**

Zinfandel Napa Valley 1995: Lovely integration of plum, wild berry, cherry and spice flavors, with a supple texture, firm tannins and a pretty dash of toasty oak. Drinks well now, should hold through 2002. 3,000 cases made. • $18 • (04/30/98) • **89**

Zinfandel Napa Valley 1994: A bit rustic, with a core of tart, chewy, earthy cherry and wild berry flavors. Turns dry on the finish, but should work well with food. 4,000 cases made. • $14 • (02/28/97) • **84**

Zinfandel Napa Valley 1993 • $14 • (04/30/96) • **87**

Zinfandel Napa Valley 1987 • $9 • (10/31/89) • **77**

Zinfandel Napa Valley Ballentine Vineyard 1996: Ultraripe and jammy, with a slight Port-like flavor and high alcohol that sticks out, giving it a coarse texture and heat on the finish. Drink now through 2002. 3,000 cases made. • $19 • (06/15/98) • **84**

Zinfandel Napa Valley George Hendry Vineyard 1989 • $13 • (10/15/92) • **84**

Zinfandel Napa Valley George Hendry Vineyard Reserve 1996: Smooth, ripe and elegant, with a pretty core of plum and blackberry-laced flavor. Finishes with a nice floral touch and firm tannins. Short-term cellaring is advised; try through 2002. 740 cases made. • $26 • (06/15/98) • **88**

Zinfandel Napa Valley George Hendry Vineyard Reserve 1995: Big, ripe, robust and tannic, with a good dose of toasty oak and a solid core of rich plum, black cherry, wild berry and spicy, peppery flavors that are intense, complex and concentrated. Drinks well now, even with its crisp tannins. Best to 2002. 700 cases made. • $25 • (04/30/98) • **90**

Zinfandel Napa Valley George Hendry Vineyard Reserve 1994: Smooth, ripe and polished, with pretty notes of plum, wild berry, cherry and anise. Finishes with a flourish of fruit and a chunky aftertaste. Ready now. 952 cases made. • $24 • (03/31/97) • **89**

Zinfandel Napa Valley George Hendry Vineyard Reserve 1993 • $22 • (04/30/96) • **90**

Zinfandel Napa Valley George Hendry Vineyard Reserve 1992 • $20 • (10/15/94) • **86**

Zinfandel Napa Valley George Hendry Vineyard Reserve 1988 • $14 • (04/30/91) • **84**

Zinfandel Napa Valley Michael Marston Vineyard 1990 • $14 • (10/15/92) • **84**

Zinfandel Paso Robles Richard Sauret Vineyard 1996: Ripe and fruity, with jammy plum, blackberry, cherry and wild berry flavors that linger on the supple, elegant finish. 2,200 cases made. • $17 • (05/15/98) • **88**

Zinfandel Paso Robles Richard Sauret Vineyard 1995: A racy style with ripe cherry, plum and berry notes, picking up pretty pepper and spice flavors and finishing with firm, dry tannins. Drink now. 3,500 cases made. • $16 • (06/30/97) • **88**

Zinfandel Paso Robles Richard Sauret Vineyard 1994 • $12 • (04/30/96) • **87**

Zinfandel Paso Robles Richard Sauret Vineyard 1993 • $12 • (09/30/95) • **88**

Zinfandel Paso Robles Richard Sauret Vineyard 1992 • $11 • (10/15/94) • **87**

Zinfandel Paso Robles Richard Sauret Vineyard 1991 • $10 • (09/30/93) • **88**

Zinfandel Paso Robles Richard Sauret Vineyard 1990 • $10 • (10/15/92) • **87**

Zinfandel Redwood Valley Rhodes Vineyard Annette's Reserve 1996: Clean, ripe and spicy, with attractive cherry, wild berry, raspberry and plum notes. Holds its fruit on the long, lingering finish. Nice now with its well-integrated tannins. Drink through 2002. 1,450 cases made. • $22 • (06/15/98) • **89**

Zinfandel Redwood Valley Rhodes Vineyard Annette's Reserve 1995: Lean, ripe and spicy, with crushed berry and cherry flavors that finish with a trace of astringency. Drink now. 650 cases made. • $19 • (12/15/97) • **84**

Zinfandel Sonoma County 1991 • $11 • (09/30/93) • **86**

Zinfandel Sonoma County 1990 • $12 • (09/30/92) HR • **90**

Zinfandel Sonoma County Old Vines 1995: Distinctly peppery, with lots of berry and cherry flavors that fold in nicely. Finishes with mild tannins and good length. 1,200 cases made. • $18 • (06/30/97) • **89**

Zinfandel Sonoma County Old Vines 1994: Smooth and polished. Reveals a ripe core of cherry and wild berry flavors that pick up leather and spice notes on the finish. 4,400 cases made. • $13 • (09/30/96) • **88**

Zinfandel Sonoma County Old Vines 1993 • $13 • (09/30/95) • **88**

Zinfandel Sonoma County Old Vines 1992 • $12 • (10/15/94) • **85**

Zinfandel Sonoma County St. Peters Church Vineyard 1996: A ripe, potent style, with jammy berry, cherry, currant and plum flavors that are rich and well focused. Holds its flavors on a long, full finish. Drink now through 2002. 100 cases made. • $20 • (06/15/98) • **89**

Zinfandel Sonoma Valley Cullinane Vineyard 1996: Some curious fruit flavors up front, then a core of black cherry and plum Zinfandel flavor emerges. Finishes with a hint of mint and supple tannins. Drink now through 2002. 250 cases made. • $23 • (06/15/98) • **87**

Zinfandel Sonoma Valley Samsel Vineyard Maggie's Reserve 1996: Floral, with ripe, spicy berry and cherry flavors, turning supple and elegant on the finish. Avoids the over-ripeness of the vintage. Drink now through 2002. 600 cases made. • $28 • (06/15/98) • **88**

Zinfandel Sonoma Valley Samsel Vineyard Maggie's Reserve 1995: Smooth and supple, with lots of ripe, juicy cherry, raspberry and wild berry flavors and pretty dashes of spice and oak. Impressive from start to finish. 625 cases made. • $25 • (09/30/97) • **92**

Zinfandel Sonoma Valley Samsel Vineyard Maggie's Reserve 1994: Features ripe, bright, juicy cherry and wild berry flavors that hold their focus through a long, lively finish. 700 cases made. • $24 • (09/30/96) • **89**

Zinfandel Sonoma Valley Samsel Vineyard Maggie's Reserve 1993 • $22 • (09/30/95) • **89**

Zinfandel Sonoma Valley Samsel Vineyard Maggie's Reserve 1992 • $22 • (10/15/94) • **87**

Zinfandel Sonoma Valley Samsel Vineyard Maggie's Reserve 1991 • $16 • (09/30/93) • **91**

Zinfandel Sonoma Valley Samsel Vineyard Maggie's Reserve 1990 • $15 • (10/15/92) • **90**

ROSENTHAL-THE MALIBU ESTATE
CALIFORNIA

Cabernet Sauvignon California 1992 • $22 • (12/15/95) • **89**

Cabernet Sauvignon California 1991 • $20 • (11/15/94) • **91**

Cabernet Sauvignon Malibu & Newton Canyon 1994: Rich, ripe, intense and focused, with loads of currant, dill, cedar and spice. Shows excellent depth and concentration and a long, complex aftertaste. A bit hot on the finish, where the tannins are ripe. Best from 2001 through 2008. 720 cases made. • $25 • (05/15/98) • **90**

Cabernet Sauvignon Malibu & Newton Canyon 1993: A heavy-handed style in which strong, pungent menthol flavors dominate the tart cherry and wild berry flavors. Best to cellar into 1999, hoping for integration. 1,623 cases made. • $22 • (01/31/97) • **84**

ROSEWOOD | CALIFORNIA

Chardonnay Monterey 1994: Ripe, spicy and sturdy, with slightly bitter but solid pineapple and caramel flavors. Second wine of Talbott. 1,000 cases made. • $10 • (06/15/96) • **80**

ROSS VALLEY | CALIFORNIA

Merlot Sonoma Valley 1992: Tart and a bit sour; concentrated cherry and berry flavors have a distinctly grapy accent. Finish is dry, and has a tannic edge it may or may not outgrow. • $13 • (08/31/96) • **82**

Zinfandel Russian River Valley Tom and Kelly Parsons' Vineyard 1993 • $12 • (05/15/96) • **83**

Zinfandel Sonoma County Tom and Kelley Parsons' Vineyard 1988 • $11 • (08/31/91) • **83**

ROUDON-SMITH | CALIFORNIA

Cabernet Sauvignon California 1991 • $10 • (11/15/93) • **77**
Cabernet Sauvignon Santa Cruz Mountains 1986 • $12 • (03/15/91) • **81**
Cabernet Sauvignon Santa Cruz Mountains 1984 • $12 • (06/30/88) • **78**
Cabernet Sauvignon Santa Cruz Mountains 1978 • $20 • (11/15/92) • **65**
Claret California Cuvée Five NV • $4 • (03/31/89) • **78**
Petite Sirah San Luis Obispo County 1984 • $8 • (09/30/88) • **84**
Pinot Noir Santa Cruz Mountains 1989 • $15 • (02/28/93) • **70**
Pinot Noir Santa Cruz Mountains 1985 • $15 • (06/15/88) • **86**
Pinot Noir Santa Cruz Mountains Cox Vineyard 1989 • $15 • (06/15/93) • **82**
Pinot Noir Santa Cruz Mountains Cox Vineyard 1987 • $15 • (02/28/91) • **84**
Zinfandel San Luis Obispo County 1989 • $8 • (10/15/92) • **80**
Zinfandel San Luis Obispo County Beckwith Vineyard 1990 • $10 • (05/31/93) • **81**
Zinfandel Sonoma County 1988 • $12 • (02/15/91) • **87**
Zinfandel Sonoma Valley Chauvet Vineyard 1985 • $8 • (03/31/89) • **80**

ROUND HILL | CALIFORNIA

Cabernet Sauvignon California 1995: Pleasant, with a range of currant, berry, cedar and earth flavors. Hard to beat at this price. Drink now through 2000. 54,000 cases made. • $8 • (05/31/98) BB • **85**
Cabernet Sauvignon California 1993: Marked by notes of herb, dill and bell pepper, it provides just enough currant and berry flavors to achieve balance. 25,000 cases made. • $8 • (04/30/97) • **83**
Cabernet Sauvignon California 1992 • $7 • (12/15/95) • **83**
Cabernet Sauvignon California 1991 • $7 • (11/15/94) • **80**
Cabernet Sauvignon California 1990 • $7 • (05/31/94) BB • **84**
Cabernet Sauvignon California 1989 • $6 • (12/15/92) BB • **82**
Cabernet Sauvignon California House Lot 5 NV • $5 • (09/30/86) BB • **76**
Cabernet Sauvignon California House Lot 6 NV • $5 • (10/15/87) • **72**
Cabernet Sauvignon California House Lot 7 NV • $6 • (10/31/90) • **79**
Cabernet Sauvignon California House Lot 8 NV • $6 • (07/31/91) • **79**
Cabernet Sauvignon California House Lot 89 NV • $6 • (11/15/92) BB • **80**
Cabernet Sauvignon Napa Valley 1993: Austere with a narrow band of cedar, anise and currant flavors. A good value in a clean, flavorful, well-balanced wine. 5,050 cases made. • $12 • (02/28/97) • **84**
Cabernet Sauvignon Napa Valley 1992 • $12 • (12/15/95) • **85**
Cabernet Sauvignon Napa Valley 1988 • $9 • (11/15/91) • **81**
Cabernet Sauvignon Napa Valley 1986 • $8 • (10/15/88) • **82**
Cabernet Sauvignon Napa Valley 1984 • $8 • (05/31/88) • **84**
Cabernet Sauvignon Napa Valley 1982 • $9 • (05/16/86) • **88**
Cabernet Sauvignon Napa Valley 1981 • $9 • (03/16/85) • **86**
Cabernet Sauvignon Napa Valley 1980 • $7 • (04/16/84) • **81**
Cabernet Sauvignon Napa Valley Reserve 1990 • $11 • (11/15/94) • **84**
Cabernet Sauvignon Napa Valley Reserve 1989 • $11 • (11/15/94) • **83**
Cabernet Sauvignon Napa Valley Reserve 1988 • $10 • (02/15/93) • **75**
Cabernet Sauvignon Napa Valley Reserve 1987 • $11 • (11/15/91) • **77**
Cabernet Sauvignon Napa Valley Reserve 1986 • $9 • (06/30/90) • **80**
Cabernet Sauvignon Napa Valley Reserve 1985 • $11 • (05/31/88) • **86**
Cabernet Sauvignon Napa Valley Reserve 1984 • $10 • (10/31/87) • **88**
Cabernet Sauvignon Napa Valley Reserve 1983 • $9 • (12/15/86) • **92**
Cabernet Sauvignon Napa Valley Signature Reserve 1990: Soft and fleshy, with herb, tobacco and tar accents added to the dried cherry and currant flavors. Finishes with a sense of elegance and a meaty edge. 250 cases made. • $20 • (09/15/96) • **85**
Chardonnay California 1995: On the crisp, zingy side of the flavor spectrum, with notes of peach, apple and citrus, even a dash of lime. Ready now, and a bargain for this popular white variety. 100,000 cases made. • $7 • (02/28/97) BB • **86**
Chardonnay California 1993 • $7 • (04/30/95) BB • **86**
Chardonnay Napa Valley 1995: Nicely balanced to show off the pear and apple flavors, which linger nicely on the delicate finish. Best now. 6,000 cases made. • $12 • (11/30/97) • **86**
Chardonnay Napa Valley 1994: In a light style, with an oaky accent to the pear and apple flavors. Finish features a touch of honey. 4,198 cases made. • $12 • (09/15/96) • **83**
Chardonnay Napa Valley Reserve 1993 • $11 • (07/31/95) • **82**

Key: SS—Spectator Selection CS—Cellar Selection HR—Highly Recommended BB—Best Buy $NA—Price not available (A)—Auction Price (BT)—Barrel Tasting
Dates in parentheses indicate the issues in which the ratings were published.

Chardonnay Napa Valley Van Asperen Selection Reserve 1993 • $12 • (07/31/95) • **83**
Fumé Blanc Napa Valley 1993 • $7 • (08/31/95) • **85**
Merlot California 1995: A charming red wine offering spicy raspberry flavors on a light frame, this bottling is ooh-what-a-deal in one of California's hottest varieties. There's plenty to go around and it's ready to drink. 46,000 cases made. • $9 • (12/31/97) BB • **83**
Merlot California 1994: Light and simple. The cherry and berry flavors are unassuming, but the fruit is pure. 31,000 cases made. • $8 • (08/31/96) • **82**
Merlot California 1993: Simple and rustic, with cedary, cherry flavors that are dry at the start and become even dryer on the finish. 24,000 cases made. • $8 • (08/31/96) • **80**
Merlot California 1992 • $7 • (09/15/94) • **77**
Merlot California 1990 • $7 • (01/31/93) BB • **84**
Merlot Napa Valley 1994: Marked by stalky cedar, tar and anise notes and just a glimpse of currant and berry flavors. Turns dry and tannic on the finish. 7,860 cases made. • $12 • (04/30/97) • **85**
Merlot Napa Valley 1993: Pleasant, if unassuming, with plum and currant flavors. Turns thin and tannic on the finish, where the flavors taper off. 5,700 cases made. • $14 • (08/31/96) • **80**
Merlot Napa Valley 1984 • $9 • (05/15/87) • **87**
Merlot Napa Valley 1983 • $7 • (01/31/87) SS • **92**
Merlot Napa Valley Reserve 1991 • $11 • (09/15/94) • **78**
Merlot Napa Valley Reserve 1990 • $11 • (06/15/93) • **78**
Merlot Napa Valley Reserve 1989 • $11 • (05/31/92) • **78**
Merlot Napa Valley Reserve 1988 • $11 • (11/15/91) • **80**
Merlot Napa Valley Reserve 1986 • $11 • (12/31/88) • **82**
Merlot Napa Valley Reserve 1985 • $10 • (05/31/88) • **84**
Sauvignon Blanc Napa Valley 1995: Bright and citrusy, with a smoky accent to the lemon and mineral flavors. 1,000 cases made. • $9 • (10/31/96) • **83**
Zinfandel Napa Valley 1993 • $10 • (03/31/96) • **83**
Zinfandel Napa Valley 1992 • $8 • (10/15/95) • **85**
Zinfandel Napa Valley 1990 • $6 • (10/15/92) BB • **85**
Zinfandel Napa Valley 1989 • $6 • (03/31/92) BB • **81**
Zinfandel Napa Valley 1988 • $6 • (02/15/91) BB • **89**
Zinfandel Napa Valley 1985 • $5 • (05/15/88) BB • **82**
Zinfandel Napa Valley 1981 • $5 • (04/16/84) • **84**
Zinfandel Napa Valley Select 1987 • $6 • (03/31/90) BB • **84**

ROYCE | CALIFORNIA

Cabernet Sauvignon Napa Valley 1989 • $10 • (12/15/92) • **77**
Cabernet Sauvignon Sonoma County 1987 • $12 • (11/15/92) • **80**
Merlot Napa Valley Reserve 1990 • $16 • (01/31/93) • **81**
Merlot Sonoma County 1991 • $12 • (06/30/93) • **85**

RUBISSOW-SARGENT | CALIFORNIA

Cabernet Sauvignon Mount Veeder 1992: A touch herbal, with a weedy side to the flavors and just a modest band of mineral, currant and tobacco. Finishes with firm, dry tannins; try in 1999 to 2000. 785 cases made. • $19 • (11/15/97) • **88**
Cabernet Sauvignon Mount Veeder 1991 • $16 • (12/15/95) • **84**
Cabernet Sauvignon Mount Veeder 1990 • $16 • (11/15/94) • **84**
Cabernet Sauvignon Mount Veeder 1988 • $16 • (04/15/92) • **87**
Les Trompettes Mount Veeder 1992: Austere, with dry, crisp tannins and a tightly wound band of cedar, spice and currant. Best to let the tannins soften a bit. Try in 1999 to 2000. 465 cases made. • $22 • (11/15/97) • **88**
Les Trompettes Mount Veeder 1990 • $18 • (11/15/94) • **85**
Les Trompettes Mount Veeder 1989 • $18 • (11/15/94) • **79**
Merlot Mount Veeder 1994: Lean and tannic, with an earthy band of currant, tar and spice flavors. Best to cellar into 2000. 432 cases made. • $21 • (07/31/97) • **86**
Merlot Mount Veeder 1992 • $16 • (05/15/96) • **85**
Merlot Mount Veeder 1990 • $15 • (09/15/94) • **86**
Merlot Mount Veeder 1989 • $15 • (08/31/93) • **76**
Merlot Mount Veeder 1988 • $15 • (05/31/92) • **84**

RUNQUIST, J. | CALIFORNIA

Zinfandel Amador County Z Massoni Ranch 1996: A pleasing blend of plum and cherry starts this off. Rough tannins cut the flavors a bit short, but it's enjoyable nonetheless, with a bright finish. Drink now through 2001. 691 cases made. • $18 • (06/15/98) • **84**

RUSTRIDGE | CALIFORNIA

Cabernet Sauvignon Napa Valley 1991 • $20 • (12/15/95) • **87**
Cabernet Sauvignon Napa Valley 1990 • $30 • (12/15/95) • **82**
Chardonnay Napa Valley 1994: Flavors reminiscent of burnt buttered popcorn dominate this wine. Unpleasant. Tasted twice, with consistent notes. 386 cases made. • $17 • (06/15/98) • **70**
Zinfandel Napa Valley 1996: Dominated by rich, smoky oak flavors, but the ripe cherry and berry flavors almost measure up to the wood. Nicely textured. Drink now through 2000. 530 cases made. • $18 • (06/15/98) • **84**
Zinfandel-Cabernet Napa Valley 1991 • $18 • (09/30/93) • **82**

RUTHERFORD ESTATE | CALIFORNIA

Cabernet Sauvignon Napa Valley 1992: Fairly austere and tart. The fruit flavor seems to be hiding behind pronounced acidity and a low-grade tannic wall. 50,000 cases made. • $7 • (11/30/96) • **77**
Cabernet Sauvignon Napa Valley 1991 • $7 • (11/15/94) • **81**
Cabernet Sauvignon Napa Valley 1987 • $6 • (08/31/92) BB • **84**
Cabernet Sauvignon Napa Valley 1986 • $7 • (11/15/91) • **80**
Cabernet Sauvignon Napa Valley 1984 • $5 • (11/15/87) • **72**
Chardonnay California Barrel Select 1994: Bright and citrusy, a lively mouthful of peach and citrus flavor, softening on the finish. Drinkable now. • $7 • (05/15/96) • **84**
Merlot Napa Valley 1991 • $7 • (06/30/94) BB • **84**
Pinot Noir Napa Valley 1992 • $7 • (01/31/95) • **81**
White Zinfandel California 1994 • $7 • (09/15/95) • **83**

RUTHERFORD GROVE | CALIFORNIA

Cabernet Sauvignon Napa Valley 1993: Well balanced, with just enough ripe cherry and plummy Cabernet flavor to give it depth and proportion. Finishes with crisp acidity and the right amount of tannins for its weight. Ready to drink. 1,783 cases made. • $20 • (11/30/96) • **87**
Chardonnay Napa Valley 1994: Tries to be subtle and complex, but ends up emphasizing honey and almond flavors, with little fruit character to complete the picture. Try now. 1,282 cases made. • $16 • (12/15/96) • **83**
Merlot Napa Valley 1995: Appealing for its supple texture and understated flavors, but it lacks richness and depth. The earthy black cherry, herb, coffee and leather flavors start out OK, but they lose focus on the finish. Drink now through 2002. 517 cases made. • $22 • (04/30/98) • **85**

RUTHERFORD HILL | CALIFORNIA

Cabernet Sauvignon Napa Valley 1991 • $14 • (11/15/94) • **81**
Cabernet Sauvignon Napa Valley 1987 • $16 • (11/15/92) • **85**
Cabernet Sauvignon Napa Valley 1986 • $14 • (02/28/91) • **68**
Cabernet Sauvignon Napa Valley 1985 • $17 • (04/30/90) • **82**
Cabernet Sauvignon Napa Valley 1984 • $13 • (08/31/88) • **88**
Cabernet Sauvignon Napa Valley 1983 • $13 • (09/15/87) • **83**
Cabernet Sauvignon Napa Valley 1982 • $13 • (11/15/86) • **88**
Cabernet Sauvignon Napa Valley 1981 • $12 • (06/01/86) • **90**
Cabernet Sauvignon Napa Valley 1980 • $12 • (10/16/84) • **82**
Cabernet Sauvignon Napa Valley 1978 • $25 • (11/15/92) • **78**
Cabernet Sauvignon Napa Valley Cask Lot 2 Limited Edition 1980 • $15 • (07/31/87) • **92**
Cabernet Sauvignon Napa Valley XVS 1987 • $26 • (11/15/92) • **86**
Cabernet Sauvignon Napa Valley XVS 1986: Dry and tannic, not showing much flavor. • $NA • (12/15/96) • **75**
Cabernet Sauvignon Napa Valley XVS 1985 • $29 • (04/30/89) • **88**
Chardonnay Napa Valley Exceptional Vineyard Selection Reserve 1993: Has a greenish edge to the basic pear and spice flavors. Drinkable now. 1,600 cases made. • $18 • (07/31/96) • **81**
Chardonnay Napa Valley Jaeger Vineyards American Canyon Ranch 1993: Spicy, peachy, toasty flavors turn slightly bitter on the finish. Try now. 9,200 cases made. • $12 • (07/31/96) • **80**
Merlot Napa Valley 1991 • $16 • (09/15/94) • **82**
Merlot Napa Valley 1989 • $14 • (05/31/92) • **70**
Merlot Napa Valley 1988 • $15 • (05/31/92) • **82**
Merlot Napa Valley 1987 • $14 • (03/31/91) • **74**
Merlot Napa Valley 1986 • $13 • (06/15/90) • **68**
Merlot Napa Valley 1985 • $12 • (01/31/89) • **92**
Merlot Napa Valley 1984 • $11 • (04/30/88) • **84**
Merlot Napa Valley 1983 • $10 • (08/31/87) • **87**
Merlot Napa Valley 1982 • $11 • (05/16/86) • **79**
Merlot Napa Valley 1981 • $10 • (10/01/85) • **78**
Merlot Napa Valley Exceptional Vineyard Selections Reserve 1993: Thin and earthy, with a narrow stripe of leathery flavors. Lacks focus and depth. 50,000 cases made. • $15 • (08/31/96) • **77**
Merlot Napa Valley Reserve 1995: Complex, with a pretty integration of ripe plum and berry and light, spicy vanilla-oak flavors. Shows the balance, depth and richness that's been missing for so long from this winery's Merlot. 475 cases made. • $40 • (05/15/98) • **89**
Merlot Napa Valley Twentieth Anniversary 1994: A good balance of ripe cherry and currant flavors, light oak accents and firm tannins. On the finish, the fruit comes through. 58,000 cases made. • $15 • (08/31/96) • **85**
Merlot Napa Valley XVS Reserve 1992 • $21 • (06/15/95) • **85**

RUTHERFORD RANCH | CALIFORNIA

Cabernet Sauvignon Napa Valley 1993: Lean and tight, with cedary flavors overtaking the modest blackberry character. Likely best from 1999. 7,000 cases made. • $11 • (07/31/97) • **82**
Cabernet Sauvignon Napa Valley 1992: An understated style, smooth and complex, with pleasant currant, cedar, spice and light oak flavors. Not too tannic and beginning to show some mature Cabernet flavors. A good value to drink now. 11,200 cases made. • $11 • (11/15/96) • **87**
Cabernet Sauvignon Napa Valley 1991 • $10 • (11/15/94) • **86**
Cabernet Sauvignon Napa Valley 1987 • $13 • (04/30/91) • **83**
Cabernet Sauvignon Napa Valley 1985 • $11 • (05/15/90) SS • **92**
Cabernet Sauvignon Napa Valley 1984 • $13 • (05/31/89) • **85**
Cabernet Sauvignon Napa Valley 1983 • $11 • (12/31/87) • **83**
Cabernet Sauvignon Napa Valley 1982 • $11 • (06/15/87) • **84**
Chardonnay Napa Valley 1995: Light, lean and tight, not showing much fruit or charm, just hints of lemon and lime on the finish. 9,000 cases made. • $9 • (07/31/97) • **80**
Chardonnay Napa Valley 1994: Ripe, and though it's labeled "dry style", it has a sweet edge. It's effusively fruity, with hints of ripe pear, apple, melon and spice. Appealing now. 1,500 cases made. • $9 • (12/15/96) • **86**
Chardonnay Napa Valley 1993 • $9 • (07/31/95) • **82**
Merlot Napa Valley 1995: Somewhat herbal and thin on the palate, but a hard look finds black cherry, leather and toast, too. Finishes with yet more herbal flavor. 7,450 cases made. • $13 • (01/31/98) • **80**
Merlot Napa Valley 1994: Tight and austere, its plum and cherry flavors unfolding slowly. Finishes with firm tannins, but enough fruit and buttery oak notes sneak through to hold your interest. Try now. 4,460 cases made. • $12 • (12/15/96) • **85**
Merlot Napa Valley 1992 • $10 • (04/15/95) • **82**
Merlot Napa Valley 1990 • $9 • (03/31/93) • **82**
Merlot Napa Valley 1988 • $12 • (08/31/91) • **80**
Merlot Napa Valley 1986 • $12 • (12/31/88) • **87**
Merlot Napa Valley 1985 • $11 • (04/30/88) • **92**
Merlot Napa Valley 1984 • $9 • (10/15/87) • **83**
Quintessence Napa Valley Meritage 1991 • $20 • (12/15/95) • **86**
Quintessence Napa Valley Meritage 1989 • $NA • (11/15/94) • **83**
Sauvignon Blanc Napa Valley 1994: Light and straighforward, with appealing, juicy nectarine and spice flavors that keep singing through the finish. 1,480 cases made. • $7 • (08/31/97) BB • **87**
Sauvignon Blanc Napa Valley 1993 • $7 • (05/15/94) • **85**
Zinfandel Napa Valley 1992 • $8 • (08/31/95) • **85**
Zinfandel Napa Valley 1985 • $7 • (03/15/88) • **89**
Zinfandel Napa Valley 1982 • $6 • (09/16/85) • **80**

RUTHERFORD VINTNERS | CALIFORNIA

Cabernet Sauvignon California Barrel Select 1993: Tastes sweet beyond ripeness, with a slight Port and raisiny accent to the Cabernet flavors. • $8 • (12/15/96) • **78**
Cabernet Sauvignon Napa Valley Rutherford Bench 1992 • $8 • (12/15/95) • **87**
Cabernet Sauvignon Sonoma County Barrel Select 1995: Pronounced barnyard aromas may not be for everyone. Behind them lie some nice licorice, cassis, herb, plum and blackberry notes. Drink now. Winery formerly Rutherford Vineyards. • $9 • (10/15/97) • **86**
Chardonnay Lodi Barrel Select 1996: Soft and pleasant, with pretty pear and vanilla flavors that dance lightly through the finish. Ready now. • $9 • (11/30/97) • **85**
Chardonnay Napa Valley 1993 • $8 • (06/15/95) BB • **86**
Fumé Blanc Napa Valley 1993 • $8 • (08/31/95) • **87**

Zinfandel Lodi Barrel Select 1995: Attractive smoke and earth aromas are followed by bright plummy flavors. Not terribly complex, but quite enjoyable. • $9 • (11/15/97) • **85**

RUTZ | CALIFORNIA

Cabernet Sauvignon Napa Valley 1994: Bright in style, with hints of chocolate, herbs and black currant. Finishes moderately, with some astringency. 1,120 cases made. • $26 • (11/30/97) • **86**

Chardonnay Russian River Valley 1996: A crisp, elegant style, with floral and earthy notes orbiting a core of spice, anise, pear and apricot. Drink now through 2001. • $22 • (06/30/98) • **88**

Chardonnay Russian River Valley 1994: Ripe, with citrus, pear and spice flavors that run toward the tart side, but it's well balanced and well made. 300 cases made. • $20 • (10/15/96) • **86**

Chardonnay Russian River Valley 1993: Ripe and fruity, with a smoky edge to the pear, honey, melon and spice notes. Picks up a slightly bitter edge from the oak on the finish. • $18 • (07/31/96) • **83**

Chardonnay Russian River Valley Dutton Ranch 1996: Clean, elegant and refined, with ripe, spicy pear, fig, vanilla and hazelnut flavors. Not overpowering, it succeeds with its elegance and finesse. Drink now through 2002. 900 cases made. • $30 • (05/15/98) • **89**

Chardonnay Russian River Valley Dutton Ranch 1995: Spicy and smoky, with a strong core of anise and pear that's rich and full-bodied. Shows depth and concentration, with a complex mineral flavor on the aftertaste. 700 cases made. • $30 • (01/01/98) • **89**

Chardonnay Russian River Valley Dutton Ranch 1994: Starts out with a touch of earthiness, but layers of citrus, pear and butterscotch flavors fold in nicely, adding depth. Turns a bit coarse on the finish, short-term cellaring may help. 200 cases made. • $25 • (10/15/96) • **88**

Chardonnay Russian River Valley Maison Grand Cru 1996: Smells earthy yet serves up plenty of ripe, fruity flavors. Lacks focus and maintains a slightly coarse texture from start to finish. Best to cellar short-term; drink from 2000 through 2004. 700 cases made. • $25 • (05/15/98) • **86**

Chardonnay Russian River Valley Quail Hill Vineyard 1994: Shows an array of citrus and pineapple flavors in a lean, crisp style. Finishes with a slightly cheesy accent to the oak flavors. 400 cases made. • $25 • (10/15/96) • **85**

Pinot Noir Mendocino County Weir Vineyard 1995: Rich in plum, earth and anise aromas. On the palate, it's a bit less opulent, marked by herbal, wild berry, smoke and licorice flavors. Moderate tannins. Ready now. 300 cases made. • $35 • (12/15/97) • **86**

Pinot Noir Russian River Valley 1995: Somewhat austere, displaying a drying, tannic edge. Flavors are pleasant enough, however, with anise, black cherry, cedar and herbs. 1,300 cases made. • $20 • (12/15/97) • **84**

Pinot Noir Russian River Valley 1994: Marked by earthy cola, rhubarb and leathery notes. The tannins on the finish are bitter and biting. • $NA • (11/15/96) • **76**

Pinot Noir Russian River Valley Dutton Ranch 1994: A soft, pretty nose of mushroom and tea leads to fruit, spice, cherry-rhubarb and more mushroom flavors on the palate. Turns silky and spicy on the finish. 400 cases made. • $25 • (08/31/97) • **86**

Pinot Noir Russian River Valley Dutton Ranch 1993 • $24 • (01/31/96) • **85**

Pinot Noir Russian River Valley Quail Hill Vineyard 1994: This has ripe strawberry flavors laced with herb and tea notes, picks up a woody mushroom nuance, and finishes with dashes of caramel and cola. Drink now. 400 cases made. • $25 • (08/31/97) • **85**

Pinot Noir Russian River Valley Quail Hill Vineyard 1993 • $24 • (01/31/96) • **87**

RYAN, SETH | WASHINGTON

Cabernet Franc Yakima Valley 1994: Soft, light and round, with nice plum, berry and vanilla aromas and flavors that are artfully balanced, emphasizing the fruit. Finish has a pickle-barrel note. Ready to drink. 91 cases made. • $16 • (09/30/96) • **86**

Cabernet Sauvignon Yakima Valley 1993: Very firm, but bright with raspberry, plum and olive flavors that sit lightly on the chewy layer of tannins. Drink now. 184 cases made. • $21 • (09/15/96) • **86**

Cabernet Sauvignon Yakima Valley 1992: A strong smell of nail polish remover takes this wine out of contention. 217 cases made. • $24 • (09/15/96) • **74**

Merlot Columbia Valley 1994: Firm, chewy and a bit wild in character, showing plenty of ripe berry flavors up front and a pickle-barrel note on the finish. Try now. 84 cases made. • $22 • (09/15/96) • **81**

SADDLEBACK | CALIFORNIA

Cabernet Sauvignon Napa Valley 1994: Young and rangy now, but it has the right stuff, with a rich core of plum, currant and red cherry flavors that are deep and concentrated. Best to cellar into 2002. 1,092 cases made. • $23 • (09/30/97) • **91**

Cabernet Sauvignon Napa Valley 1993: Dark, ripe, plush and concentrated, with layers of currant, plum, black cherry and mineral. Finishes with a hint of anise and cedar, all adding to its complexity. Ready now, but should age well into 2000 and beyond. 963 cases made. • $19 • (05/31/96) • **92**

Cabernet Sauvignon Napa Valley 1992 • $17 • (12/15/95) • **87**

Cabernet Sauvignon Napa Valley 1991 • $17 • (10/31/94) HR • **90**

Cabernet Sauvignon Napa Valley 1990 • $15 • (11/15/93) • **84**

Cabernet Sauvignon Napa Valley 1988 • $14 • (08/31/92) • **73**

Cabernet Sauvignon Napa Valley Family Reserve 1989 • $25 • (11/15/94) • **85**

Cabernet Sauvignon Napa Valley Family Reserve 1988 • $24 • (11/15/93) • **81**

Chardonnay Napa Valley 1996: Young and still a bit tannic, with ripe pear, spice and melon flavors that blend in nicely with the spicy oak shadings. A good value at this price. 710 cases made. • $18 • (12/31/97) • **87**

Chardonnay Napa Valley 1995: Marked by a crisp citrus, especially grapefruit, edge, with tart pear and pineapple flavors folding in to provide added depth and dimension. 1,012 cases made. • $16 • (06/15/97) • **87**

Chardonnay Napa Valley 1994: A simple, easy-to-drink wine, with modest pear, spice and vanilla shadings. 1,012 cases made. • $15 • (07/31/96) • **82**

Chardonnay Napa Valley 1993 • $13 • (07/31/95) • **81**

Pinot Blanc Napa Valley 1994: Clean and refresing, with a simple core of ripe pear, vanilla and spice. 11,000 cases made. • $10 • (07/31/96) • **84**

SAGPOND | NEW YORK

Chardonnay Long Island Domaine Wolffer Reserve 1994: Generous in fruit and spice flavors, well rounded in texture, and fairly complex, too. A very good, all-around Chardonnay. 1,541 cases made. • $15 • (09/15/96) • **85**

Chardonnay Long Island La Ferme Martin 1994: This crisp, lemony wine bears a passing resemblance to a Mâcon-Villages. However, it has been inconsistent in multiple tastings, with other bottles coarse and dull. 2,272 cases made. • $12 • (12/31/96) • **79**

Merlot Long Island 1994: Straightforward in flavor, with meager fruit and toasty, spicy oak accents. Medium-bodied, with light tannins and a licorice note on the finish. 1,100 cases made. • $14 • (12/31/96) • **78**

Pinot Noir Long Island 1994: Soft and straightforward, this offers light spice, black pepper and black cherry flavors with a whisper of tannin and a slightly bitter, herbal finish. 210 cases made. • $22 • (12/31/96) • **79**

Pinot Noir Long Island 1993: Buttery, candied aromas and tomatolike flavors make this a bit of an oddball. 150 cases made. • $18 • (09/15/96) • **75**

Rosé Long Island 1995: Quite herbal and stemmy tasting, with little fruit flavor. 1,000 cases made. • $9 • (01/01/97) • **73**

Sparkling Long Island Christian Wolffer Cuvée 1993: Mellow. A soft texture and mature flavors make this modestly proportioned bubbly easy to enjoy. Drink now. 130 cases made. • $23 • (05/15/98) • **84**

ST. AMANT | CALIFORNIA

Port Amador County Late Bottled 1991 • $12 • (05/15/96) • **86**

Port Amador County Reserve 1992 • $18 • (05/15/96) • **88**

ST. ANDREW'S VINEYARD | CALIFORNIA

Chardonnay Napa Valley 1994: Offers a modest band of tart citrus, pear and grapefruit flavors and turns even simpler on the finish. • $10 • (11/15/96) • **82**

Chardonnay Napa Valley 1993 • $12 • (07/31/95) • **82**

ST. ANDREW'S WINERY | CALIFORNIA

Cabernet Sauvignon Napa Valley 1986 • $15 • (04/30/90) • **87**

Cabernet Sauvignon Napa Valley 1985 • $11 • (05/15/88) • **89**

Key: SS—Spectator Selection CS—Cellar Selection HR—Highly Recommended BB—Best Buy $NA—Price not available Ⓐ—Auction Price (BT)—Barrel Tasting

Dates in parentheses indicate the issues in which the ratings were published.

ST. CLEMENT | CALIFORNIA

Cabernet Sauvignon Howell Mountain White Cottage Ranch 1994: A bit rustic, with an earthy, tarry edge, but opens to reveal more complex and supple flavors, with layers of plum, cherry and wild berry. Finishes with firm tannins; cellaring into 2002 is advised. 250 cases made. • $45 • (09/30/97) • **92**

Cabernet Sauvignon Howell Mountain White Cottage Ranch 1993: Remarkably supple and harmonious for a Howell Mountain red at this youthful stage. Shows off lots of ripe red cherry, currant, anise and cedary oak flavors, gaining complexity on the finish. Tempting now, but worthy of cellaring into 2000. 250 cases made. • $45 • (11/15/96) • **90**

Cabernet Sauvignon Napa Valley 1997: Beautifully crafted; impressive from the barrel. Dark, dense and concentrated, with a plush texture and rich, smooth currant, berry, chocolate and vanilla. • $NA • (07/31/98) (BT) • **90-94**

Cabernet Sauvignon Napa Valley 1996: Quite grapey, with plum and berry notes, turning smooth and polished on the finish. Has a pretty floral aroma and soft tannins. 4,000 cases made. • $28 • (06/15/97) (BT) • **90-94**

Cabernet Sauvignon Napa Valley 1994: A well-oaked style with lots of cherry, currant, berry and spice flavors, it turns supple and elegant on the finish where the anise and berry flavors re-emerge. Drinks well now but can age into 2000 with ease. 3,600 cases made. • $27 • (07/31/97) • **91**

Cabernet Sauvignon Napa Valley 1993: Smooth and polished for a young wine. Offers ripe cherry, currant and berry flavors that linger on the finish. Well balanced, in a moderately rich, complex style. 3,500 cases made. • $24 • (10/15/96) • **88**

Cabernet Sauvignon Napa Valley 1992 • $24 • (10/31/95) • **90**

Cabernet Sauvignon Napa Valley 1991 • $23 • (09/30/94) SS • **90**

Cabernet Sauvignon Napa Valley 1990 • $22 • (10/31/93) • **90**

Cabernet Sauvignon Napa Valley 1989 • $23 • (11/15/92) • **84**

Cabernet Sauvignon Napa Valley 1988 • $22 • (03/31/92) • **86**

Cabernet Sauvignon Napa Valley 1987: Has evolved into a supple, harmonious, complex wine, with ripe, well-focused plum, currant, black cherry and spice notes. Smooth tannins. Elegant aftertaste, where the flavors linger. 2,248 cases made. • $18 • (12/15/97) • **90**

Cabernet Sauvignon Napa Valley 1986: Elegant and refined, offering a core of ripe cherry, currant and plum flavors, tinged with a nice earthiness. Finishes with good fruit flavor and firm, drying tannins. At a good stage; drink now through 2002. 1,872 cases made. • $18 • (12/15/96) • **87**

Cabernet Sauvignon Napa Valley 1984 • $15 • (10/15/88) • **90**

Cabernet Sauvignon Napa Valley 1983 • $15 • (06/01/86) • **89**

Cabernet Sauvignon Napa Valley 1982 • $14 • (03/16/85) CS • **92**

Cabernet Sauvignon Napa Valley 1981 • $13 • (06/01/84) SS • **89**

Chardonnay Napa Valley Carneros Abbott's Vineyard 1996: Ripe and creamy, with well-focused pear, hazelnut, spice and toasty oak. Turns complex on the finish, where the flavors fan out, pick up a pretty anise note. Drink now through 2002. 2,500 cases made. • $20 • (05/31/98) • **89**

Chardonnay Napa Valley Carneros Abbott's Vineyard 1995: Ripe and creamy smooth, in an elegant style, with hints of pear, citrus, melon and spice and a richly fruity aftertaste. 2,600 cases made. • $20 • (06/15/97) • **90**

Chardonnay Napa Valley Carneros Abbott's Vineyard 1994: Light and simple, with a modest band of pear, spice and vanilla flavors that fan out on the finish. A pleasant, easy-drinking wine. 3,000 cases made. • $21 • (06/30/96) • **84**

Chardonnay Napa Valley Carneros Abbott's Vineyard 1993 • $18 • (07/31/95) • **84**

Merlot Columbia Valley 1995: Fresh, bright and appealing for its generous cherry and currant flavors, overlaid with a light blanket of spicy oak, finishing sweet and silky. Nice now, better in 2000. 1,000 cases made. • $22 • (09/30/97) • **88**

Merlot Napa Valley 1995: A touch austere with its crisp tannins, but it has enough herb, currant and plum-laced flavors to broaden the palette and give some depth and personality. Young and tight, it's best cellared short-term into 2000. 3,930 cases made. • $24 • (04/30/98) • **88**

Merlot Napa Valley 1994: The core of herb and currant flavors and hints of bell-pepper and sage are harmonious and supple. Finishes with a slight leathery edge to the tannins, which cellaring into 1999 might help soften. 4,100 cases made. • $24 • (04/30/97) • **89**

Merlot Napa Valley 1993 • $18 • (04/30/96) • **87**

Merlot Napa Valley 1992 • $21 • (03/31/95) • **88**

Merlot Napa Valley 1991 • $20 • (09/15/94) • **83**

Merlot Napa Valley 1990 • $20 • (05/31/93) • **88**

Merlot Napa Valley 1989 • $18 • (05/31/92) • **87**

Merlot Napa Valley 1987 • $16 • (12/31/90) • **85**

Merlot Napa Valley 1986 • $15 • (10/31/89) • **74**

Merlot Napa Valley 1985 • $15 • (03/31/89) • **91**

Merlot Napa Valley 1983 • $15 • (05/31/88) • **81**

Oroppas Napa Valley 1995: A wonderfully rich, supple, complex and harmonious young wine, elegant and flavorful, with layers of ripe cherry, plum, currant, coffee and spicy oak. Silky tannins on the finish make it appealing now. A blend of 62 percent Cabernet Sauvignon, 25 percent Cabernet Franc, and 13 percent Merlot. 960 cases made. • $35 • (08/31/97) • **93**

Oroppas Napa Valley 1994: Smooth, supple and harmonious, with tiers of anise, black cherry and spicy, cedary oak flavors. Manages to pack in lots of flavor while maintaining a sense of elegance and finesse, and the finish lingers. Drinks well now but is worthy of cellaring. A blend of 60 percent Cabernet Sauvignon, 27 percent Cabernet Franc, and 13 percent Merlot. 650 cases made. • $30 • (11/15/96) • **91**

Oroppas Napa Valley 1993: Strikes a fine balance between toasty, buttery oak and ripe, juicy plum and currant flavors-a wine of elegance and finesse. Doesn't have quite the depth and richness of the past two vintages, but still impressive. 650 cases made. • $30 • (10/31/95) HR • **92**

Oroppas Napa Valley 1992 • $25 • (09/30/94) CS • **95**

Oroppas Napa Valley 1991 • $22 • (10/31/93) HR • **94**

Sauvignon Blanc Napa Valley 1996: A tangy blend, rich with grapefruit, lemon, clove, a hint of honey and toasty oak. The finish is long and steady. A solid effort. 3,200 cases made. • $15 • (06/30/97) • **88**

Sauvignon Blanc Napa Valley 1995: Smooth in texture, with focused Sauvignon flavors-herb, gooseberry and green apple-that persist nicely through the vanilla-scented finish. 3,300 cases made. • $12 • (07/31/96) • **88**

Sauvignon Blanc Napa Valley 1994 • $12 • (08/31/95) • **87**

Sauvignon Blanc Napa Valley 1993 • $11 • (02/28/95) • **84**

ST. FRANCIS | CALIFORNIA

Brut Sonoma Valley 1984 • $9 • (12/16/85) • **82**

Cabernet Franc Sonoma Valley 1989 • $14 • (11/15/93) • **83**

Cabernet Sauvignon California 1985 • $9 • (11/30/87) • **88**

Cabernet Sauvignon Sonoma County 1995: Supple and fruity, with smoke, currant, plum and berry flavors. Easy to drink for its fleshy tannins and light oak shadings. 30,000 cases made. • $14 • (11/15/97) • **85**

Cabernet Sauvignon Sonoma County 1994: An herbal style, with tea and tobacco notes complementing currant and cedar flavors. With its supple texture, it's appealing to drink now. 25,000 cases made. • $10 • (10/15/96) BB • **86**

Cabernet Sauvignon Sonoma County 1993: Ripe and intense, with earthy plum, cherry, anise and leather, finishing with firm tannins and crisp acidity. Hangs together but not as much complexity as previous vintages. 25,000 cases made. • $12 • (11/30/95) • **85**

Cabernet Sauvignon Sonoma County 1992 • $10 • (11/15/94) • **85**

Cabernet Sauvignon Sonoma County 1991 • $10 • (09/15/93) • **84**

Cabernet Sauvignon Sonoma County 1990 • $10 • (09/30/93) • **89**

Cabernet Sauvignon Sonoma County 1989 • $10 • (09/30/93) • **84**

Cabernet Sauvignon Sonoma County 1988 • $14 • (08/31/91) HR • **90**

Cabernet Sauvignon Sonoma County 1986 • $12 • (01/31/90) • **89**

Cabernet Sauvignon Sonoma County Reserve 1992 • $24 • (11/30/95) HR • **92**

Cabernet Sauvignon Sonoma County Reserve 1991 • $24 • (11/15/94) • **88**

Cabernet Sauvignon Sonoma County Reserve 1990 • $24 • (09/30/93) HR • **91**

Cabernet Sauvignon Sonoma Valley Reserve 1994: An outstanding California Cabernet. Tightly wound, with firm tannins and good spicy currant, plum and cherry flavors that slowly come shining through the tannic veil. This deeply concentrated wine has lots of pretty oak to show off, too. Best to cellar into 2000. 4,200 cases made. • $30 • (10/15/97) SS • **93**

Cabernet Sauvignon Sonoma Valley Reserve 1993: Distinctive for its minty, wild berry flavors, this is tamed with aeration to show more plum and cherry flavors. Finishes with a complex array of fruit and well-toned smoky oak notes. Impressive texture and balance. 3,500 cases made. • $29 • (12/15/96) • **90**

Cabernet Sauvignon Sonoma Valley Reserve 1989 • $24 • (11/15/92) • **89**

Cabernet Sauvignon Sonoma Valley Reserve 1988 • $24 • (08/31/91) • **87**

Cabernet Sauvignon Sonoma Valley Reserve 1986 • $20 • (11/30/89) • **94**

Chardonnay Sonoma County 1996: Earthy, minty character adds interest to the crisp, green apple flavors. Unusual profile, but it finishes with a good balance of flavors and textures. Ready to drink. 50,000 cases made. • $12 • (03/31/98) • **85**

Chardonnay Sonoma County 1995: A spicy style of Chardonnay, with a Muscat-like accent to the pear and apple flavors. Finishes with a smoky oak note. 50,000 cases made. • $12 • (11/30/96) • **82**

Chardonnay Sonoma County 1994: A sweet and fruity white that's light and straightforward; a good value at this price. 50,000 cases made. • $10 • (05/15/96) • **84**

Chardonnay Sonoma County 1993 • $12 • (11/30/94) • **82**

Chardonnay Sonoma Valley Reserve 1996: Outstanding, offering a core of smoky, toasty oak and intense pear and citrus-laced Chardonnay flavors, and finishing with a complex aftertaste. Drink now to 2000. 5,000 cases made. • $22 • (03/31/98) • **90**

Chardonnay Sonoma Valley Reserve 1995: Spicy and well oaked, with toasty vanilla flavors, but it has a nice core of pear and apple flavors, too. Strikes a nice balance between the two now, but short-term cellaring will add extra dimensions. 5,000 cases made. • $20 • (01/31/97) • **88**

Chardonnay Sonoma Valley Reserve 1994: Strives for complexity in toast and butterscotch flavors. Ripe pear and smoky oak notes fold in nicely on the finish, as its depth becomes more evident. 4,500 cases made. • $20 • (05/15/96) • **90**

Chardonnay Sonoma Valley Reserve 1993 • $19 • (04/15/95) HR • **90**

Merlot Sonoma County 1995: Decidedly herbal, opening with sage and tobacco flavors, it works its way into cedary currant, coffee and spice flavors and finishes with supple tannins. Drink now to 2002. 25,000 cases made. • $23 • (03/31/98) • **87**

Merlot Sonoma County 1994: Not a great St. Francis Merlot, but on solid ground. Delivers ripe plum, spice, mint and currant flavors, with mild tannins, and cedary oak nuances on the finish. 30,500 cases made. • $18 • (11/30/96) • **87**

Merlot Sonoma County 1993: Young and tight, with trim, crisp, cherry and spice flavors. Lacks the depth and character of the winery's Reserve, as expected of the vintage. 16,000 cases made. • $18 • (07/31/96) • **83**

Merlot Sonoma Valley 1992 • $17 • (02/29/96) • **86**

Merlot Sonoma Valley 1991 • $18 • (07/31/94) • **86**

Merlot Sonoma Valley 1990 • $18 • (05/31/93) • **88**

Merlot Sonoma Valley 1989 • $14 • (05/31/92) • **79**

Merlot Sonoma Valley 1988 • $16 • (11/15/91) • **82**

Merlot Sonoma Valley 1987 • $14 • (06/15/90) • **80**

Merlot Sonoma Valley 1986 • $14 • (06/30/89) • **85**

Merlot Sonoma Valley 1985 • $12 • (10/15/88) • **66**

Merlot Sonoma Valley 1984 • $12 • (10/31/87) • **88**

Merlot Sonoma Valley 1983 • $11 • (07/31/87) • **80**

Merlot Sonoma Valley 1982 • $11 • (10/01/85) • **78**

Merlot Sonoma Valley Reserve 1994: Harmonious and rich, with layers of well-oaked plum, wild berry, cherry and spice flavors that finish with length and complexity. A delicious Merlot from a California producer with a track record for same. Drinkable now, but worthy of cellaring, too. 5,000 cases made. • $29 • (06/15/97) HR • **92**

Merlot Sonoma Valley Reserve 1993: Smooth and supple, with ripe cherry, currant and berry notes. Holds its fruity flavors through the finish, when the sweet toasty oak folds in. Drinkable now. 5,000 cases made. • $26 • (08/31/96) • **88**

Merlot Sonoma Valley Reserve 1992: Smooth, rich and complex. A plethora of cherry, currant, spice, light herb and a trace of coffee flavors with an elegant and supple texture. Finishes with soft tannins and fine length. 3,500 cases made. • $24 • (07/31/96) SS • **92**

Merlot Sonoma Valley Reserve 1991 • $24 • (09/15/94) • **89**

Merlot Sonoma Valley Reserve 1990 • $24 • (05/31/93) HR • **91**

Merlot Sonoma Valley Reserve 1989 • $24 • (05/31/92) HR • **90**

Merlot Sonoma Valley Reserve 1988 • $24 • (11/15/91) • **82**

Merlot Sonoma Valley Reserve 1986 • $28 • (01/31/90) • **94**

Merlot Sonoma Valley Reserve 1985 • $15 • (12/31/88) • **81**

Merlot Sonoma Valley Reserve 1984 • $16 • (02/15/88) • **74**

Pinot Noir Sonoma Valley 1986 • $14 • (06/15/88) • **74**

Zinfandel Sonoma County Old Vines 1996: Tight and backward, with plum and wild berry lurking in the background, it slowly opens up to reveal some earthy, meaty, leathery flavors and hints of blackberry and spice. Best from 2000 through 2004. 7,500 cases made. • $20 • (05/31/98) • **88**

Zinfandel Sonoma County Old Vines 1995: A bit rustic with forest-floor and mushroomlike tones up front, its complexity emerges slowly, finishing with a wild berry and cherry flourish. Ready to drink. 3,500 cases made. • $22 • (08/31/97) • **88**

Zinfandel Sonoma County Old Vines 1994: An elegant style of Zin that strives for harmony and finesse rather than sheer power. Shows an especially pretty core of cherry and wild berry notes on the finish. 2,400 cases made. • $18 • (09/15/96) HR • **89**

Zinfandel Sonoma Valley Old Vines 1993 • $18 • (10/15/95) • **91**

Zinfandel Sonoma Valley Old Vines 1992 • $14 • (10/15/94) • **87**

Zinfandel Sonoma Valley Old Vines 1990 • $12 • (10/15/92) • **88**

Zinfandel Sonoma Valley Old Vines 1989 • $12 • (03/31/92) • **76**

Zinfandel Sonoma Valley Pagani Vineyard Reserve 1996: A big, ripe, oaky style that lumbers along. The fruit is rich, concentrated and quite tannic, and the oak stands out on the finish. Best to cellar short-term; drink from 1999 through 2003. 10 percent Alicante Bouschet, 5 percent Petite Sirah. Best now through 2003. 960 cases made. • $28 • (06/15/98) • **90**

Zinfandel Sonoma Valley Pagani Vineyard Reserve 1995: Ripe and juicy, with an array of plum, strawberry, currant and raspberry flavors, enriching and fanning out on the finish, where it shows uncommon depth and concentration. Drink now through 2000. 900 cases made. • $28 • (08/31/97) • **92**

Zinfandel Sonoma Valley Pagani Vineyard Reserve 1994: A seductive, ripe and juicy young wine, brimming with rich, complex currant, black cherry, plum and raspberry flavors. Lots of flavor, yet smoothly textured with a long, full finish. 800 cases made. • $24 • (09/15/96) • **92**

SAINT GREGORY | CALIFORNIA

Chardonnay Mendocino 1994: Decadent, earthy flavors take this one below the median. 609 cases made. • $15 • (07/31/97) • **77**

Chardonnay Mendocino 1993: Ripe, juicy pear and apple flavors hold the spotlight in this appealing fruit-centered wine. 1,000 cases made. • $16 • (07/31/96) • **85**

Pinot Blanc Mendocino 1994: Extra spicy flavors make this a bit more interesting than most, creating a soy-sauce accent to the pear notes. 577 cases made. • $14 • (04/30/97) • **83**

Pinot Noir Mendocino 1994: Earthy tasting up front, but straightens out as more berry and cherry flavor comes to the rescue. With its spicy edge, it tastes like it could have a splash of Zin. • $14 • (03/31/97) • **84**

Pinot Noir Mendocino 1993 • $14 • (12/31/95) • **81**

Pinot Noir Mendocino 1992 • $14 • (03/31/95) • **81**

Pinot Noir Mendocino 1991 • $14 • (02/28/94) • **84**

Pinot Noir Mendocino 1990 • $14 • (09/30/92) • **86**

ST. INNOCENT | OREGON

Pinot Noir Willamette Valley Freedom Hill Vineyard 1995: Packed with pretty flavors of bright currant, blueberry and earth, which linger nicely on the finish. Give it until 1999 to see if it fills out its frame. 508 cases made. • $27 • (12/31/97) • **89**

Pinot Noir Willamette Valley Freedom Hill Vineyard 1994: Ripe and supple, with a strong overlay of spicy oak to the berry and anise flavors. Not a big wine, but it has a harsh bite that needs until 1999 or 2000 to smooth out. 419 cases made. • $NA • (02/28/97) • **85**

Pinot Noir Willamette Valley O'Connor Vineyard 1995: Has pretty Pinot Noir aromas and toasty notes on the palate, finishing a bit rough. Best from 1999. 918 cases made. • $22 • (10/15/97) • **85**

Pinot Noir Willamette Valley Seven Springs Vineyard 1995: Very light, but has pleasant plum and currant flavors nicely set off on a sturdy but lightweight frame. A sleek wine with modest flavors. Drink soon. 946 cases made. • $27 • (12/31/97) • **87**

Pinot Noir Willamette Valley Seven Springs Vineyard 1994: Packs delicious plum and berry flavors into a firm frame with chewy tannins and a harmonious zing of citrusy acidity. It's youthful now, but should be harmonious in '99. • $NA • (02/28/97) • **88**

Pinot Noir Willamette Valley Seven Springs Vineyard 1992 • $16 • (11/30/94) • **85**

ST. JOSEF'S | OREGON

Cabernet Sauvignon Oregon 1989 • $14 • (03/31/96) • **83**

Cabernet Sauvignon Oregon 1988 • $12 • (03/31/96) • **84**

Cabernet Sauvignon Oregon 1986 • $12 • (08/31/91) • **68**

Cabernet Sauvignon Oregon 1985 • $15 • (03/31/91) • **87**

Pinot Noir Oregon 1993 • $9 • (04/30/96) • **72**

Pinot Noir Oregon 1987 • $8 • (04/15/91) • **76**

Pinot Noir Oregon 1985 • $16 • (02/15/90) • **89**

Zinfandel Oregon 1990 • $10 • (03/31/96) • **78**

Key: SS—Spectator Selection CS—Cellar Selection HR—Highly Recommended BB—Best Buy $NA—Price not available Ⓐ—Auction Price (BT)—Barrel Tasting

Dates in parentheses indicate the issues in which the ratings were published.

ST. JULIAN | MICHIGAN

Cabernet Franc Michigan 1996: Firm, and nicely concentrated with plum flavors that are definitely on the herbal side. Not particularly complex, but a lot of upfront flavor and finishes on an appealing spicy note. Best from 1999 through 2001. 150 cases made. • $20 • (07/31/98) • **83**
Chambourcin Lake Michigan Shore 1989 • $8 • (02/29/92) • **76**
Chardonnay Michigan 1996: A serviceable Chardonnay with lemony, buttery flavors that could harmonize better. Has an attractive spiciness on the finish. Drink now. 1,200 cases made. • $12 • (07/31/98) • **82**
Merlot Michigan 1996: A jumbled mix of herbal, menthol and plummy flavors that finish on a somewhat sweet, spicy note. 400 cases made. • $20 • (07/31/98) • **74**
Pinot Gris Michigan 1997: On the sweet side, with simple peach and apple flavors and a clean finish. 600 cases made. • $10 • (07/31/98) • **79**
Riesling Michigan 1997: Sweet and peachy, with some green apricot notes but not much complexity. 2,200 cases made. • $10 • (07/31/98) • **78**
Solera Light Cream Sherry Michigan NV • $12 • (02/29/92) • **88**

ST. SUPÉRY | CALIFORNIA

Cabernet Sauvignon Napa Valley Dollarhide Ranch 1993: Lean and trim, with a medium-weight band of cedar, currant, anise and spice notes. Doesn't quite fill out on the palate, but it's ready now. 24,000 cases made. • $15 • (03/31/97) • **83**
Cabernet Sauvignon Napa Valley Dollarhide Ranch 1991: Serves up lots of ripe, juicy Cabernet flavors, with tiers of plum, cherry, berry and currant. Finishes with a nice dash of spicy oak and tame tannins. Well proportioned. Drink now. 13,652 cases made. • $15 • (11/15/96) • **88**
Cabernet Sauvignon Napa Valley Dollarhide Ranch 1990 • $14 • (05/15/94) • **86**
Cabernet Sauvignon Napa Valley Dollarhide Ranch 1989 • $19 • (07/31/94) • **86**
Cabernet Sauvignon Napa Valley Dollarhide Ranch 1988 • $14 • (09/30/91) • **85**
Cabernet Sauvignon Napa Valley Dollarhide Ranch 1987 • $13 • (07/15/90) • **85**
Cabernet Sauvignon Napa Valley Dollarhide Ranch Limited Edition 1991: Smooth and complex, with an elegant swirl of cedar, cherry, currant and spice flavors. Holds together nicely through the finish, where the flavors fan out and gain nuance. • $25 • (11/15/96) • **88**
Chardonnay Napa Valley Dollarhide Ranch 1993 • $13 • (07/31/95) • **81**
Merlot Napa Valley Dollarhide Ranch 1993: Complex and appealing with currant, black cherry, herb and tobacco flavors. A well-crafted wine with substance and depth. 17,215 cases made. • $17 • (08/31/96) • **86**
Merlot Napa Valley Dollarhide Ranch 1992 • $15 • (05/15/95) • **80**
Merlot Napa Valley Dollarhide Ranch 1991 • $14 • (12/31/93) • **85**
Merlot Napa Valley Dollarhide Ranch 1990 • $14 • (11/30/92) • **86**
Merlot Napa Valley Dollarhide Ranch 1989 • $14 • (05/31/92) • **89**
Moscato California 1992 • $11 • (05/15/93) • **76**
Sauvignon Blanc Napa Valley Dollarhide Ranch 1996: Straightforward, with citrusy lime and orange peel notes followed by a touch of grassiness. Finishes cleanly and quickly. • $10 • (06/30/97) • **86**
Sauvignon Blanc Napa Valley Dollarhide Ranch 1995: Light, unfocused and vaguely fruity. Little in the way of distinctive characteristics. • $9 • (09/15/96) • **79**
Sauvignon Blanc Napa Valley Dollarhide Ranch 1994: Soft texture and smooth finish. Spice and milky herb flavors. 11,830 cases made. • $9 • (07/31/96) • **80**
Sauvignon Blanc Napa Valley Dollarhide Ranch 1993 • $8 • (08/31/95) • **80**

STE. CHAPELLE | IDAHO

Cabernet Sauvignon Idaho 73% Arena Valley Vineyard/27% Symms Old 1990 • $12 • (03/31/94) • **74**
Cabernet Sauvignon Idaho Reserve 1988 • $20 • (02/29/92) • **74**
Cabernet Sauvignon Washington 1993: Firm in texture, with brightly focused grapey berry flavors that remain lively on the finish. Drinkable now. 2,773 cases made. • $10 • (11/15/95) BB • **87**
Cabernet Sauvignon Washington 1992 • $10 • (01/31/95) • **83**
Cabernet Sauvignon Washington 1989 • $10 • (03/15/93) • **79**
Cabernet Sauvignon Washington 1988 • $10 • (02/29/92) • **84**
Cabernet Sauvignon Washington 1986 • $10 • (08/31/91) • **83**
Cabernet Sauvignon Washington 1983 • $9 • (04/30/88) • **77**
Cabernet Sauvignon Washington 1981 • $9 • (05/15/87) • **80**
Cabernet Sauvignon Washington Canyon 1992 • $7 • (01/31/95) BB • **86**
Cabernet Sauvignon Washington Collectors Series 1988 • $16 • (10/15/93) • **73**
Cabernet Sauvignon Washington Collectors Series 1981 • $18 • (10/15/89) • **81**
Cabernet Sauvignon Washington Mercer Ranch Vineyard 1989 • $16 • (01/31/94) • **80**
Chardonnay Idaho 1994: Softly rounded texture and pleasant, mature flavors; subdued pear and pineapple. 5,400 cases made. • $10 • (08/31/96) • **84**
Chardonnay Idaho Reserve 1994: Spicy, butterscotch flavors come to the fore in this broad-structured wine that finishes with an herbal note. 601 cases made. • $15 • (06/15/96) • **85**
Fumé Blanc Idaho 1994: Simple and earthy, with a slight vegetative edge to the pear flavors. 1,146 cases made. • $7 • (08/31/96) • **79**
Fumé Blanc Idaho 1993 • $7 • (05/31/95) • **82**
Fumé Blanc Idaho Dry 1996: Fragrant, with hints of anise, wildflowers, melon, lemon and herbs. Bright, delicate and clean. Drink now through 2000. 3,000 cases made. • $8 • (05/31/98) • **84**
Johannisberg Riesling Late Harvest Idaho Botrytis 1986 • $15 • (02/15/88) • **79**
Merlot Idaho 1992 • $10 • (09/15/94) • **85**
Merlot Washington 1987 • $10 • (09/30/90) • **73**
Merlot Washington Dionysus Vineyard 1986 • $12 • (05/31/88) • **81**
Pinot Noir Idaho 1988 • $8 • (02/29/92) • **74**
Syrah Idaho Reserve 1994 • $20 • (06/30/96) • **84**

STE. CLAIRE | CALIFORNIA

Cabernet Sauvignon California 1992 • $11 • (11/15/94) • **82**

STE. GENEVIEVE | TEXAS

Cabernet Sauvignon Escondido Valley NV: Dominated by leathery and meaty aromas and flavors, with some plummy notes. Finishes with tealike and brown sugar flavors. Drink now. • $5 • (05/15/98) • **81**
Gamay Nouveau Texas 1997: Fresh and fruity, with an interesting mix of strawberry and red plum flavors. Finishes on a sweet note. Serve well chilled. Drink now. • $5 • (03/31/98) • **80**
Pinot Noir Escondido Valley NV: Hearty and earthy-tasting, with berry and cherry flavors, and a hint of brown sugar. A light-styled Pinot Noir with a dull finish. • $9/1.5 liter • (12/31/97) • **81**

SAINTSBURY | CALIFORNIA

Chardonnay Carneros 1996: Well focused, with a snappy edge to the peach, pear and apple flavors. Clean and refreshing, it drinks well now through 2000. 13,664 cases made. • $17 • (05/15/98) • **88**
Chardonnay Carneros 1995: Nicely styled to emphasize its supple texture and ripe fruit flavors, this wine is silky smooth and creamy, with an elegant band of fig, apple and pear flavors brightened by spicy notes that echo on the aftertaste. From one of California's best Chardonnay-growing regions. 13,905 cases made. • $17 • (05/31/97) SS • **92**
Chardonnay Carneros 1994: A heavy-handed, cedary style, but enough pear and spice-laced Chardonnay fruit rises to the occasion to keep it in balance. Has richness and concentration. 12,900 cases made. • $15 • (07/31/96) • **88**
Chardonnay Carneros 1993 • $15 • (07/31/95) • **85**
Chardonnay Carneros Reserve 1995: Crisp and lively, with a core of citrus flavors, especially grapefruit, that slowly unfolds, revealing more depth and elegance and a green pear and tropical fruit accent. Best now. 2,041 cases made. • $30 • (05/31/97) • **93**
Chardonnay Carneros Reserve 1994: Bold, ripe, smooth and creamy, a real mouthful of Chardonnay. Its tiers of ripe pear, fig and honey flavors are framed by smoky, toasty oak. An altogether complex and beautifully crafted young wine, with a rich butterscotch aftertaste that still has all those delicious flavors chiming in. Kudos to this California winery. 1,130 cases made. • $25 • (05/31/96) HR • **95**
Chardonnay Carneros Reserve 1993 • $25 • (05/31/95) • **89**
Pinot Noir Carneros 1996: Crisp and spicy, with a band of cola, black cherry, spice and cedar. Shows lots of richness and depth on the finish. Best now to 2002. 20,347 cases made. • $20 • (01/31/98) • **88**
Pinot Noir Carneros 1995: Elegant, with spicy cherry and earthy nuances, hints of plum and strawberry and a complex aftertaste of lingering flavors. Drinks well now, but has the intensity and concentration for short-term cellaring. 17,400 cases made. • $18 • (12/31/96) • **88**
Pinot Noir Carneros 1992 • $16 • (02/28/95) • **85**
Pinot Noir Carneros 1991 • $17 • (02/28/94) • **87**

Pinot Noir Carneros 1990: At a nice drinking stage, this wine shows a ripe, fruity core of spicy black cherry along with hints of mushroom, sage, earth, tea and anise. The tannins having softened, it's ready now through 2000. • $15 • (03/31/97) • **89**

Pinot Noir Carneros 1989 • $17 • (02/15/92) • **85**

Pinot Noir Carneros 1988 • $20 • (12/15/90) SS • **91**

Pinot Noir Carneros 1987 • $15 • (07/31/89) • **86**

Pinot Noir Carneros 1986 • $14 • (06/15/88) • **92**

Pinot Noir Carneros 1985 • $13 • (11/30/87) • **92**

Pinot Noir Carneros 1984 • $12 • (12/15/86) • **93**

Pinot Noir Carneros 1983 • $12 • (12/01/85) • **93**

Pinot Noir Carneros 1982 • $8 • (11/30/87) • **86**

Pinot Noir Carneros Garnet 1996: Starts out simple, with modest berry and cherry flavors, but the flavors unfold to reveal more complexity and depth, and for this price, you get a lot of Pinot Noir for your dollar. Pick up six bottles or a case. Ready now through 2000. 10,500 cases made. • $13 • (01/31/98) • **87**

Pinot Noir Carneros Garnet 1995: Light and fragrant. An easy drinking, young Pinot Noir with spicy cherry and strawberry flavors and a trace of stemminess on the finish. Drinks well now. 10,500 cases made. • $13 • (12/31/96) • **84**

Pinot Noir Carneros Garnet 1994 • $11 • (11/15/95) • **85**

Pinot Noir Carneros Garnet 1993 • $11 • (12/15/94) • **86**

Pinot Noir Carneros Garnet 1992 • $10 • (02/28/94) • **84**

Pinot Noir Carneros Garnet 1991 • $10 • (12/31/92) • **88**

Pinot Noir Carneros Garnet 1990 • $10 • (02/15/92) • **86**

Pinot Noir Carneros Garnet 1989 • $9 • (12/15/90) • **88**

Pinot Noir Carneros Garnet 1988 • $9 • (03/31/90) • **84**

Pinot Noir Carneros Garnet 1987 • $9 • (12/31/88) • **91**

Pinot Noir Carneros Garnet 1986 • $8 • (12/15/87) • **87**

Pinot Noir Carneros Garnet 1985 • $9 • (03/15/87) • **86**

Pinot Noir Carneros Garnet 1984 • $8 • (08/31/86) • **76**

Pinot Noir Carneros Garnet 1983 • $8 • (11/30/87) • **73**

Pinot Noir Carneros Rancho 1981 • $NA • (11/30/87) • **80**

Pinot Noir Carneros Reserve 1995: Smooth and silky. An elegant style, with dense, rich black cherry, plum, leather, earth and beef flavors, picking up a nice touch of toasty oak on the finish, where the tannins kick in. Delicious now. 2,700 cases made. • $35 • (01/31/98) HR • **93**

Pinot Noir Carneros Reserve 1994: Amazingly harmonious, smooth and supple, with ripe, rich, complex black cherry, berry, strawberry and anise flavors, picking up a hint of currant on the finish. The best Saintsbury Reserve since 1990—and quite probably the best this winery has made. Tasted twice with consistent notes. 2,575 cases made. • $35 • (12/31/96) • **92**

Pinot Noir Carneros Reserve 1993 • $30 • (12/31/95) • **88**

Pinot Noir Carneros Reserve 1992 • $30 • (12/15/94) • **89**

Pinot Noir Carneros Reserve 1991 • $30 • (02/28/94) • **88**

Pinot Noir Carneros Reserve 1990: Mature now, this is quite complete and compelling. It's dark, smooth, rich and polished, with a supple core of black cherry, anise, mushroom and spice flavors and, on the finish, soft, fleshy tannins. Ready to drink. • $30 • (03/31/97) • **92**

SAKONNET | NEW ENGLAND

Cabernet Franc Rosé Southeastern New England 1996: A blend of herbal, watermelon and strawberry flavors that don't quite come together. 572 cases made. • $10 • (12/31/97) • **78**

Cabernet Franc Southeastern New England 1994: A modest, elegant Cab Franc, with bell-pepper and green olive flavors framed by toasty oak. Good length and intensity on the palate. 435 cases made. • $20 • (08/31/97) • **82**

Chardonnay Southeastern New England 1995: A fruity, lively, slightly sweet style, with oodles of floral and apple flavors and a nice, crisp texture. Great for picnics. 840 cases made. • $13 • (06/15/97) • **85**

Chardonnay Southeastern New England 1994: Searing, lemony acidity renders this too tart to enjoy. May be good to cook with. • $14 • (09/15/96) • **72**

Fumé-Vidal Southeastern New England 1995: Full-bodied, somewhat pleasant, with spicy aromas and flavors. 954 cases made. • $10 • (08/31/97) • **77**

Fumé-Vidal Southeastern New England 1994: This wine has buttery aromas, but turns tart and almost cidery in the mouth. • $10 • (01/01/97) • **74**

Gewürztraminer Southeastern New England 1995: Aromatic, spicy and crisp, this is an appealing, well-balanced, dry white that tastes fresh and lively. 480 cases made. • $12 • (06/15/97) • **85**

Mariner Red France-America NV: A bizarre mix of cherry and herbal flavors with an off-putting spritz. Not recommended. A blend of 85 percent Merlot and 15 percent American Chancellor. 2,790 cases made. • $9 • (01/01/97) • **65**

Vidal Blanc Southeastern New England 1995: Canned-fruit flavors and a stale aroma don't add up to much fun. 3,716 cases made. • $9 • (01/01/97) • **68**

Vidal Blanc Southeastern New England 1994: Appley flavors dominate this wine. It has a mature aroma, but lacks depth or finesse. • $8 • (01/01/97) • **78**

SALAMANDRE | CALIFORNIA

Chardonnay Arroyo Seco 1994: Tart, with a strong edge of citrus. Fans of flinty Chardonnays will find it appealing. Doesn't rely heavily on oak for its flavor. 180 cases made. • $15 • (07/31/96) • **84**

Chardonnay Arroyo Seco 1993 • $16 • (07/31/95) • **77**

Chardonnay Arroyo Seco Hunter Moon Reserve 1994: Simple, tart citrus and pear flavors fan out on the finish. Lacks the expected richness and extra dimensions of Reserve style wines. 84 cases made. • $22 • (07/31/96) • **84**

Chardonnay Santa Cruz Mountains Matteson Vineyard 1994: Smooth and creamy, with an appealing honey note to the spicy pear, citrus and light oak flavors. Turns complex on the finish. 84 cases made. • $24 • (07/31/96) • **88**

Chardonnay Santa Cruz Mountains Matteson Vineyard 1993 • $16 • (07/31/95) • **86**

SALISHAN | WASHINGTON

Cabernet Sauvignon Washington 1992 • $12 • (09/30/95) • **78**

Pinot Noir Washington 1991 • $9 • (09/30/95) • **83**

Pinot Noir Washington Lot 1 1992: A light red that still has some spicy character. The cherrylike flavor is pleasant though simple. 502 cases made. • $6 • (08/31/96) • **80**

Pinot Noir Washington Lot 1 1989 • $9 • (02/28/93) • **77**

Pinot Noir Washington Silver Anniversary NV: Toasty and chewy, with a hint of anise adding a welcome touch to the finish. 263 cases made. • $8 • (08/31/96) • **81**

SALMON CREEK | CALIFORNIA

Chardonnay Carneros 1993 • $12 • (07/31/95) • **85**

Chardonnay Sonoma County Carneros Bad Dog Ranch West 1995: The lightish apple flavors have unusual, minty herbal overtones to them and finish with a chemical-like accent. 5,500 cases made. • $15 • (07/31/97) • **79**

Syrah California 1996: Plums, berries and spices lead the way in a pleasant blend, but the wine could use a bit more ripeness. Finishes a little short. Drink now. 300 cases made. • $12 • (06/15/98) • **83**

SALVESTRIN | CALIFORNIA

Cabernet Sauvignon Napa Valley 1994: Opens with ripe, supple currant, plum and black cherry, but then turns a bit earthy and oaky and finishes with a slight bitterness. 160 cases made. • $26 • (03/31/98) • **83**

SAN SABA | CALIFORNIA

Cabernet Sauvignon Monterey 1994: Weedy aromas remind one of the old-style Monterey reds. On the palate it's dominated by vegetal flavors-green beans and asparagus, backed by hints of cherry and herbs. Marginal. 1,100 cases made. • $17 • (06/30/98) • **75**

Cabernet Sauvignon Monterey 1990 • $15 • (11/15/94) • **88**

Chardonnay Monterey 1996: Hazelnut and fig aromas introduce this full-bodied wine, with melon, lemon and applelike notes on the palate. Fairly silky texture, with a clean finish. Drink now. 972 cases made. • $20 • (05/31/98) • **87**

Chardonnay Monterey 1995: Ripe and creamy, with a mildly bitter streak that robs the wine of some charm. Try now. 500 cases made. • $20 • (07/31/97) • **80**

Key: SS—Spectator Selection CS—Cellar Selection HR—Highly Recommended BB—Best Buy $NA—Price not available Ⓐ—Auction Price (BT)—Barrel Tasting
Dates in parentheses indicate the issues in which the ratings were published.

SANFORD | CALIFORNIA

Chardonnay Santa Barbara County 1996: Tight and flinty, with crisp citrus, pear and earthy Chardonnay flavors, it's not quite as flashy as in most vintages, but it has lots of flavor and richness. 19,895 cases made. • $18 • (01/31/98) • **88**

Chardonnay Santa Barbara County 1995: Delivers ripe, clean, zingy Chardonnay fruit and hints of peach, fig, pear and melon, all fanning out on the finish. Another winner from Sanford. 20,000 cases made. • $18 • (05/31/97) • **91**

Chardonnay Santa Barbara County 1994: Hits all the right notes with its ripe pear, light oak shadings and hints of vanilla, pineapple and citrus. An elegant and complex Chardonnay from this California Winery. 19,000 cases made. • $17 • (05/31/96) SS • **90**

Chardonnay Santa Barbara County 1993 • $18 • (06/30/95) SS • **90**

Chardonnay Santa Barbara County Barrel Select 1996: Ripe, smooth and creamy, with well-integrated fruit flavors and hints of pear, melon, apple and spice, finishing with a pretty aftertaste of silky oak. Best now through 2004. 2,005 cases made. • $30 • (06/30/98) • **92**

Chardonnay Santa Barbara County Barrel Select 1995: Intense and compact, with a tightly wound core of pear, peach and tropical fruit flavors that carry through on the finish. This enormously concentrated wine drinks well now, should be even better in 1999. 1,332 cases made. • $30 • (01/31/98) • **91**

Chardonnay Santa Barbara County Barrel Select 1994: Ripe and flavorful, with bold pear, honey, fig and butterscotch flavors that are complex and concentrated. Finishes with a pretty array of tropical fruit flavors—guava included. 2,250 cases made. • $30 • (05/31/97) • **92**

Chardonnay Santa Barbara County Barrel Select 1993: Ripe and fruity, offering an elegant core of earthy pear and apple tones. Picks up light oak, hazelnut and spice notes on the finish, where the flavors turn complex and tropical. 1,500 cases made. • $30 • (07/31/96) • **90**

Chardonnay Santa Ynez Valley 1994: A brilliant Chardonnay, with an amazing core of ripe pear, vanilla, hazelnut, anise and citrus flavors that pick up pretty oak shadings and finish with a rich, complex aftertaste. Simply delicious. 750 cases made. • $24 • (05/31/97) • **94**

Chardonnay Santa Ynez Valley 1993 • $24 • (07/31/95) • **86**

Chardonnay Santa Ynez Valley Estate Bottled 1996: Elegant and sophisticated, with hints of green apple, pear, citrus and spice, tightly focused, crisp and lively. Best now through 2004. 685 cases made. • $26 • (06/30/98) • **91**

Pinot Noir Carneros Vin Gris 1996: Somewhat angular in scope, with good body, bright texture and fairly complex flint, citrus and raspberry flavors. Long, refreshing finish. 1,297 cases made. • $12 • (09/30/97) • **87**

Pinot Noir Central Coast 1994: Austere, with a marked herbal edge and gritty, chewy tannins up front. Picks up more interesting flavors, especially hints of sour black cherry, but never quite sheds its vegetal edge. 9,000 cases made. • $19 • (01/31/97) • **86**

Pinot Noir Central Coast 1984 • $12 • (05/15/87) • **85**

Pinot Noir Santa Barbara County 1996: Gamy, with a range of earthy herb, dried cherry and stewed plum flavors. Finishes with dry tannins. Best to give it some time; drink through 2003. 12,200 cases made. • $22 • (06/30/98) • **87**

Pinot Noir Santa Barbara County 1995: Well focused, unveiling a supple core of spicy cherry and wild berry flavors shaded lightly with a toasted oak quality, this is an elegant and understated California red that delivers lots of flavor and finesse, and is ready to drink. 4,100 cases made. • $20 • (10/31/97) SS • **90**

Pinot Noir Santa Barbara County 1994 • $18 • (12/31/95) • **88**

Pinot Noir Santa Barbara County 1992 • $18 • (01/31/95) • **88**

Pinot Noir Santa Barbara County 1991 • $17 • (09/15/93) • **87**

Pinot Noir Santa Barbara County 1990: Brick-brown color announces a mature wine and, sure enough, the first sniff is of brown sugar and leafy, mushroomlike aromas. Actually, it tastes better than it smells—sweet, fairly balanced and delicate, with soft, ripe tannins. Some fresh acidity remains, but tannins are a bit drying. • $50 • (05/15/98) • **84**

Pinot Noir Santa Barbara County 1989 • $15 • (03/31/92) • **85**

Pinot Noir Santa Barbara County 1988 • $15 • (06/30/91) • **78**

Pinot Noir Santa Barbara County 1987 • $14 • (02/28/91) • **76**

Pinot Noir Santa Barbara County 1986 • $14 • (12/15/89) • **75**

Pinot Noir Santa Barbara County 1985 • $14 • (06/15/88) • **74**

Pinot Noir Santa Barbara County Barrel Select 1986 • $20 • (12/15/89) • **78**

Pinot Noir Santa Barbara County Barrel Select 1985 • $20 • (06/15/88) • **75**

Pinot Noir Santa Barbara County Sanford & Benedict Vineyard Barrel Select 1995: Smooth, rich and complex, with appealing wild berry, cherry, tea and spice flavors. Tightly wound, but the texture is smooth and polished, finishing with a lively aftertaste. Drinkable now, but should be cellared into 1999 to 2001. 1,600 cases made. • $34 • (01/31/98) • **91**

Pinot Noir Santa Barbara County Sanford & Benedict Vineyard Barrel Select 1992 • $30 • (01/31/95) • **88**

Pinot Noir Santa Barbara County Sanford & Benedict Vineyard Barrel Select 1991 • $30 • (02/28/94) • **88**

Pinot Noir Santa Barbara County Sanford & Benedict Vineyard Barrel Select 1990: Highlighted by beautifully proportioned, rich and concentrated flavors of complex cherry, earth, tar and anise. Mature, it's drinkable now, but should hold, and might even gain, through 1999. 700 cases made. • $30 • (03/31/97) • **92**

Pinot Noir Santa Barbara County Vin Gris 1994 • $10 • (09/15/95) • **74**

Pinot Noir Santa Ynez Valley Barrel Select 1994: Smooth and polished, with rich flavors-cherry, herb, spice and dried berry. Complex, well-crafted and long on the finish, where the supple tannins fold in. 1,300 cases made. • $30 • (08/31/96) HR • **91**

Pinot Noir Santa Ynez Valley Barrel Select 1993 • $30 • (12/31/95) • **88**

Sauvignon Blanc Central Coast 1996: A spicy mix of honeydew melon, figs, lemons and limes make this an enticing wine. Racy acidity and a squeaky-clean finish are particularly attractive. 7,000 cases made. • $12 • (06/30/97) • **89**

Sauvignon Blanc Santa Barbara County 1995: A smooth and artfully balanced mouthful of pear, honey, fig and sage flavors. Slightly tart on the finish, but ready to drink. 7,000 cases made. • $10 • (09/15/96) • **88**

Sauvignon Blanc Santa Barbara County 1993 • $9 • (08/31/95) • **82**

SANTA BARBARA WINERY | CALIFORNIA

Cabernet Sauvignon Santa Ynez Valley 1991 • $11 • (11/15/94) • **75**

Cabernet Sauvignon Santa Ynez Valley 1990 • $11 • (11/15/93) • **83**

Cabernet Sauvignon Santa Ynez Valley 1989 • $11 • (11/15/92) • **79**

Cabernet Sauvignon Santa Ynez Valley 1988 • $12 • (11/15/91) • **83**

Cabernet Sauvignon Santa Ynez Valley Reserve 1992 • $16 • (12/15/95) • **86**

Cabernet Sauvignon Santa Ynez Valley Reserve 1991 • $16 • (11/15/94) • **84**

Cabernet Sauvignon Santa Ynez Valley Reserve 1990 • $16 • (11/15/93) • **83**

Cabernet Sauvignon Santa Ynez Valley Reserve 1989 • $16 • (11/15/92) • **82**

Cabernet Sauvignon Santa Ynez Valley Reserve 1988 • $18 • (11/15/91) • **83**

Cabernet Sauvignon Santa Ynez Valley Reserve 1987 • $18 • (11/15/90) • **77**

Cabernet Sauvignon Santa Ynez Valley Reserve 1984 • $14 • (10/31/87) • **81**

Cabernet Sauvignon Santa Ynez Valley Reserve 1974 • $16 • (12/15/89) • **81**

Chardonnay Santa Barbara County 1996: Full-bodied, with a rich core of melon, peach, mineral and citrus qualities. Tangy finish. Drink now. 5,600 cases made. • $15 • (07/31/98) • **86**

Chardonnay Santa Barbara County 1995: Ripe, rich and smoky, with a spicy core of pear, fig and melon flavors that linger for a long aftertaste, with a dash of spicy oak. 2,153 cases made. • $14 • (06/30/97) • **89**

Chardonnay Santa Barbara County Reserve 1995: Lean and trim, with a hint of celery to the citrus, particularly lemon, and pear flavors. Snappy aftertaste. 1,232 cases made. • $23 • (07/31/97) • **88**

Chardonnay Santa Ynez Valley 1994: Solidly built to show off its spicy pear and anise flavors. Drinkable now. 2,661 cases made. • $13 • (07/31/96) • **82**

Chardonnay Santa Ynez Valley Lafond Vineyard 1994: A firm but subtle wine, with hints of hazelnut, citrus and pear flavors. Finishes with elegance. 204 cases made. • $30 • (06/15/97) • **87**

Chardonnay Santa Ynez Valley Lafond Vineyard 1993 • $30 • (05/15/96) • **90**

Chardonnay Santa Ynez Valley Reserve 1994: Ripe and spicy, with a pleasant band of pear, melon and apricot flavors that become complex on the finish and linger. 1,859 cases made. • $22 • (06/30/96) • **87**

Chardonnay Santa Ynez Valley Reserve 1993 • $20 • (07/31/95) • **89**

Johannisberg Riesling Late Harvest Santa Ynez Valley Botrytised Grapes 1986 • $15/375ml • (10/15/87) • **88**

Johannisberg Riesling Santa Ynez Valley 1994: A light wine, citrusy in character, with an orange-peel accent to the apple and pine flavors. 1,026 cases made. • $6 • (11/30/96) • **82**

Pinot Noir Santa Barbara County 1995: Uncommonly dark for Pinot Noir, this is dense and chewy, with a meaty, weedy, earthy quality that sidetracks you from the core of cherry and berry flavors. Finishes with chewy tannins; cellar into 1999. 293 cases made. • $20 • (11/15/97) • **88**

Pinot Noir Santa Barbara County 1994 • $15 • (02/29/96) • **84**

Pinot Noir Santa Barbara County 1993 • $12 • (03/31/95) • **83**

Pinot Noir Santa Barbara County 1991 • $11 • (02/28/94) • **82**

Pinot Noir Santa Barbara County 1990 • $11 • (02/28/93) • **87**

Pinot Noir Santa Barbara County 1989 • $11 • (07/31/91) • **84**

Pinot Noir Santa Barbara County 1986 • $11 • (06/15/88) • **80**

Pinot Noir Santa Barbara County Reserve 1995: Dense, dark and tannic, so patience is required. If you're willing to wait out the tannins, the core of beefy Pinot Noir flavor might reward. For now, the tannins dominate. 359 cases made. • $40 • (11/15/97) • **84**
Pinot Noir Santa Barbara County Reserve 1994 • $24 • (02/29/96) • **82**
Pinot Noir Santa Barbara County Reserve 1993 • $20 • (12/31/95) • **84**
Pinot Noir Santa Barbara County Reserve 1992 • $20 • (03/31/95) • **86**
Pinot Noir Santa Barbara County Reserve 1991 • $20 • (02/28/94) • **79**
Pinot Noir Santa Barbara County Reserve 1990 • $20 • (09/30/92) • **89**
Pinot Noir Santa Barbara County Reserve 1989 • $20 • (11/15/91) • **87**
Pinot Noir Santa Ynez Valley Reserve 1987 • $20 • (12/15/89) • **89**
Sauvignon Blanc Late Harvest Santa Ynez Valley 1995: Very sweet and rich, with unctuous fig, honey and vanilla flavors that linger on the spicy finish. Disarming for its seductive flavors and smooth texture. Lovely now, it may be better after 2000. 184 cases made. • $35/375ml • (05/15/98) • **93**
Sauvignon Blanc Late Harvest Santa Ynez Valley 1994: Juicy, ripe peach and nectarine flavors, finishing with an earthy, sweaty accent. 563 cases made. • $18/375ml (08/31/96) • **83**
Sauvignon Blanc Late Harvest Santa Ynez Valley 1993 • $14/375ml • (05/15/95) • **90**
Sauvignon Blanc Late Harvest Santa Ynez Valley Lafond Vineyard 1990 • $12 • (03/10/92) • **72**
Sauvignon Blanc Santa Ynez Valley 1996: This melony, lemon-lime white has a slight candylike twist to it. 1,384 cases made. • $11 • (11/30/97) • **81**
Sauvignon Blanc Santa Ynez Valley 1994: Soft, broad and spicy, with a strong, toasted onion character. 665 cases made. • $9 • (07/31/96) • **78**
Sauvignon Blanc Santa Ynez Valley 1993 • $8 • (08/31/95) • **83**
Sauvignon Blanc Santa Ynez Valley Reserve 1993 • $12 • (08/31/95) • **80**
Syrah Santa Ynez Valley 1994 • $16 • (05/15/96) • **85**
White Riesling Santa Ynez Valley Paradis 1993 • $8 • (06/15/96) • **78**
Zinfandel Central Coast Beaujour 1991 • $7 • (07/31/92) BB • **84**
Zinfandel Late Harvest Santa Ynez Valley Essence 1993 • $20/375ml • (05/31/95) • **87**
Zinfandel Late Harvest Santa Ynez Valley Essence 1987 • $15/375ml • (12/15/89) • **74**
Zinfandel San Luis Obispo County Saucelito Canyon Vineyard 1990 • $11 • (10/15/92) • **84**
Zinfandel San Luis Obispo County Saucelito Canyon Vineyard 1989 • $11 • (10/15/92) • **82**
Zinfandel Santa Ynez Valley 1987 • $8 • (12/15/89) • **82**
Zinfandel Santa Ynez Valley Beaujour 1994 • $9 • (02/28/95) • **82**
Zinfandel Santa Ynez Valley Beaujour 1993 • $9 • (10/15/94) • **84**
Zinfandel Santa Ynez Valley Beaujour 1992 • $8 • (03/15/93) • **80**
Zinfandel Santa Ynez Valley Beaujour 1988 • $7 • (12/15/89) • **80**
Zinfandel Santa Ynez Valley Lafond Vineyard 1993: Ripe and racy, with a core of plum, prune, chocolate and berry flavors. A completely different style, akin to that of a Napa or Sonoma Zin. Best with hearty fare. 938 cases made. • $14 • (04/30/97) • **87**
Zinfandel Santa Ynez Valley Lafond Vineyard 1992 • $10 • (10/15/94) • **85**
Zinfandel Santa Ynez Valley Lafond Vineyard 1991 • $10 • (09/30/93) • **83**

SANTA CRUZ MOUNTAIN | CALIFORNIA

Cabernet Sauvignon Santa Cruz Mountains Bates Ranch 1991: Serves up lots of currant and berry flavors. Remarkably supple in texture, but the finish turns dry and a bit bitter. Not for everyone, but an exotic and daring style. • $18 • (11/15/96) • **86**
Cabernet Sauvignon Santa Cruz Mountains Bates Ranch 1990 • $15 • (12/15/95) • **85**
Cabernet Sauvignon Santa Cruz Mountains Bates Ranch 1989 • $15 • (11/15/93) • **71**
Cabernet Sauvignon Santa Cruz Mountains Bates Ranch 1988 • $14 • (11/15/93) • **87**
Cabernet Sauvignon Santa Cruz Mountains Bates Ranch 1987: Big, ripe, dense and chewy, loaded with thick, earthy currant, sage, cherry and spice flavors, but also the kinds of tannins that plead for another few years of cellaring. Best after 2000. • $NA • (12/15/97) • **89**
Cabernet Sauvignon Santa Cruz Mountains Bates Ranch 1986: Big, ripe and, as in the past, on the tannic side, but it's also aging well as it's quite rich in earth, spice, anise-accented cherry, plum and currant flavors. Drink now or can hold short-term. • $75 • (12/15/96) • **89**

Key: SS—Spectator Selection CS—Cellar Selection HR—Highly Recommended BB—Best Buy $NA—Price not available Ⓐ—Auction Price (BT)—Barrel Tasting
Dates in parentheses indicate the issues in which the ratings were published.

Cabernet Sauvignon Santa Cruz Mountains Bates Ranch 1983 • $27 • (06/15/89) • **80**
Cabernet Sauvignon Santa Cruz Mountains Bates Ranch 1981 • $13 • (03/01/85) • **88**
Cabernet Sauvignon Santa Cruz Mountains Bates Ranch 1978 • $35 • (11/15/92) • **88**
Chardonnay Santa Cruz Mountains S. Miller Vineyard 1996: Takes some getting used to, with earthy, leafy pear and spice notes, yet focused, with enough Chardonnay fruit to hold your interest. Drink now through 2001. 221 cases made. • $19 • (07/31/98) • **87**
Chardonnay Santa Cruz Mountains S. Miller Vineyard 1995: Offers ripe, creamy pear, vanilla and fig flavors that come into focus and linger on the finish. 78 cases made. • $18 • (07/31/97) • **88**
Duriff Santa Cruz Mountains 1992: Ripe and generous. Offering blackberry, plum and anise flavors that become richer and broader, finishing with both power and grace. A real find, distinctive and approachable now despite its tannins. 312 cases made. • $14 • (11/30/96) • **88**
Merlot California 1993 • $15 • (04/30/96) • **86**
Merlot California 1991 • $14 • (07/31/94) • **89**
Merlot California 1989 • $12 • (11/30/92) • **83**
Merlot California 1983 • $10 • (10/01/85) • **82**
Pinot Noir Santa Cruz Mountains 1992: Smells exotic, with spicy cherry, plum and floral aromas. More austere, tannic and leathery on the palate, but well balanced overall. Try now. 108 cases made. • $25 • (09/15/96) • **88**
Pinot Noir Santa Cruz Mountains 1990 • $18 • (02/28/94) • **81**
Pinot Noir Santa Cruz Mountains 1989 • $15 • (02/28/93) • **90**
Pinot Noir Santa Cruz Mountains 1985 • $15 • (06/15/88) • **89**
Pinot Noir Santa Cruz Mountains Estate Vineyard 1990: Smells exotic, with floral and wild berry aromas, but on the palate as the tannins clamp down, the flavors show a dry, metallic edge. Tannins may have softened by now, but then again, maybe not. 297 cases made. • $18 • (03/31/97) • **84**
Pinot Noir Santa Cruz Mountains Estate Vineyard 1987 • $18 • (02/28/94) • **84**
Pinot Noir Santa Cruz Mountains Estate Vineyard 1986: Rustic, dry and tannic, with earth and mushroom flavors that slowly give way to hints of black cherry and wild berry. Needs time to breathe, and may always be on the tannic side. 331 cases made. • $18 • (03/31/97) • **84**
Pinot Noir Santa Cruz Mountains Jarvis Vineyard 1981 • $15 • (08/31/86) • **89**
Pinot Noir Santa Cruz Mountains Matteson Vineyard 1995: Bold, ripe and racy, with hints of plum, wild berry, cherry and spice. Turns complex and earthy on the aftertaste. Drinks well now but has the intensity and stuffing for aging into 2002. 145 cases made. • $18 • (01/31/98) • **89**
Pinot Noir Santa Cruz Mountains Matteson Vineyard 1993: A touch earthy and leathery, with hints of herb and wild berry, it slowly grows on you, with a range of complex flavors that echo coffee, tar and cedar. Drinks well now, but can age into 1999. 285 cases made. • $18 • (02/28/97) • **88**
Pinot Noir Santa Cruz Mountains Matteson Vineyard 1992 • $16 • (04/30/96) • **89**
Pinot Noir Santa Cruz Mountains Matteson Vineyard 1991 • $15 • (04/30/96) • **88**
Pinot Noir Santa Cruz Mountains Matteson Vineyard 1990 • $15 • (02/28/93) • **87**
Pinot Noir Santa Cruz Mountains Matteson Vineyard 1989 • $18 • (02/28/93) • **87**

SANTA YNEZ VALLEY | CALIFORNIA

Cabernet-Merlot Santa Barbara County 1987 • $13 • (03/31/90) • **72**
Pinot Noir Santa Maria Valley 1987 • $13 • (03/31/90) • **62**
Zinfandel Paso Robles 1987 • $8 • (03/31/90) • **84**

SANTINO | CALIFORNIA

Alfresco Amador County NV • $6 • (08/31/91) BB • **83**
Barbera Amador County Aged Release 1988 • $12 • (10/31/91) • **85**
Fumé Blanc Amador County 1995: Ripe fig, honey, pear and melon notes precede a layer of lemon, herb and tangy acidity. The wine is viscous, yet finishes with a refreshing lemon-lime edge. Lots of flavor for your dollar here. 773 cases made. • $9 • (10/15/97) • **89**
Johannisberg Riesling Late Harvest Sonoma County Dry Berry Select 1989 • $18/375ml • (11/30/91) • **92**
Muscat Canelli Amador County Moscato del Diavolo 1994: Sweet, syrupy and simple, with modest nectarine notes but not much charm. 2,280 cases made. • $10/375ml • (11/30/97) • **78**

Satyricon California 1988 • $14 • (10/31/91) • **83**
Zinfandel Amador County Aged Release 1990 • $9 • (09/30/93) • **84**
Zinfandel Amador County Aged Release 1989 • $7 • (10/15/92) • **81**
Zinfandel Amador County Aged Release 1988 • $7 • (02/29/92) • **75**
Zinfandel California 1995: Nicely structured and richly textured, with a touch of tannin on the finish. Intriguing earthy, leathery flavors dominate the Zinfandel characteristics. Drink now through 2000. 550 cases made. • $10 • (06/15/98) • **84**
Zinfandel Fiddletown Eschen Vineyards 1983 • $7 • (04/15/87) • **84**
Zinfandel Shenandoah Valley Grandpère Vineyards 1989 • $12 • (10/15/92) • **83**
Zinfandel Shenandoah Valley Grandpère Vineyards 1988 • $12 • (08/31/91) • **79**

SARAFORNIA | CALIFORNIA

Zinfandel Napa Valley 1988 • $8 • (02/15/91) • **81**
Zinfandel Napa Valley 1987 • $7 • (03/15/90) • **78**

SARAH'S VINEYARD | CALIFORNIA

Chardonnay Santa Clara County 1993 • $42 • (07/31/95) • **89**
Chardonnay Santa Clara County Gold Label 1994: A wonderfully rich, ripe and seductive style, loaded with fig, apricot, pear and spice, turning elegant on the finish, where hints of hazelnut and butter add complexity and dimension. 200 cases made. • $45 • (03/31/98) • **92**
Grenache California Cadenza 1988 • $NA • (04/15/89) • **80**
L'Audace Santa Clara County 1988 • $30 • (11/15/92) • **82**
Merlot San Luis Obispo County John Radike Vineyard 1991: Lean and trim, with a modest band of fruit flavors and tart-tasting notes of herb, cherry and anise. Doesn't offer much fruit or complexity for its age. 191 cases made. • $30 • (03/31/97) • **83**
Merlot San Luis Obispo County John Radike Vineyard 1987 • $30 • (05/31/92) • **65**
Pinot Noir Santa Clara County 1993 • $50 • (10/15/95) • **92**

SATTUI, V. | CALIFORNIA

Cabernet Sauvignon Napa Valley 1991 • $14 • (11/15/94) • **85**
Cabernet Sauvignon Napa Valley Julian Schwinger Reserve Stock 1992 • $50 • (04/30/96) • **87**
Cabernet Sauvignon Napa Valley Mario's Reserve Stock 1991 • $35 • (11/15/94) • **90**
Cabernet Sauvignon Napa Valley Morisoli Vineyard 1994: Dark, ripe and intense, with a tannic core of cherry, plum and wild berry flavors that are deep and concentrated. A bit rustic, it can stand short-term cellaring; try in 2000 and beyond. 1,000 cases made. • $27 • (05/15/97) • **88**
Cabernet Sauvignon Napa Valley Preston Vineyard 1993: Smooth and supple, with a understated band of currant and cherry flavors and modest amount of tannin. 1,200 cases made. • $24 • (10/15/96) • **83**
Cabernet Sauvignon Napa Valley Preston Vineyard 1991 • $22 • (11/15/94) • **87**
Cabernet Sauvignon Napa Valley Preston Vineyard 1988 • $20 • (11/15/91) • **86**
Cabernet Sauvignon Napa Valley Preston Vineyard Reserve Stock 1988 • $35 • (11/15/92) • **87**
Cabernet Sauvignon Napa Valley Preston Vineyard Reserve Stock 1987 • $35 • (11/15/92) • **88**
Cabernet Sauvignon Napa Valley Suzanne's Vineyard 1993: Supple and elegant, with a range of herb, cherry, berry and spice flavors. Well balanced and drinking well now. 1,500 cases made. • $18 • (10/15/96) • **85**
Cabernet Sauvignon Napa Valley Suzanne's Vineyard 1991 • $16 • (11/15/94) • **86**
Cabernet Sauvignon Napa Valley Suzanne's Vineyard 1989 • $15 • (11/15/92) • **82**
Chardonnay Napa Valley Carsi Vineyard 1995: Good, but the citrus, pear and spicy oak flavors lack focus and never quite come together. Spicy oak aftertaste. Sold only at the winery. 1,200 cases made. • $20 • (05/15/97) • **84**
Chardonnay Napa Valley Carsi Vineyard 1994: Marked by an abundance of spicy flavors. Significant notes of ripe pear and honey trickle in on the finish. 2,100 cases made. • $19 • (07/31/96) • **87**
Chardonnay Napa Valley Carsi Vineyard 1993 • $18 • (02/28/95) • **89**
Merlot Napa Valley 1994: This offers a simple band of herb, tea and light plum flavors, turning more simple on the finish. Good, but lacks the extra dimensions to score higher. 800 cases made. • $20 • (11/30/96) • **83**
Merlot Napa Valley 1989 • $16 • (09/15/94) • **80**
Sauvignon Blanc Napa Valley 1994 • $11 • (08/31/95) • **83**
Sauvignon Blanc Napa Valley 1993 • $10 • (01/31/95) • **82**
Zinfandel Howell Mountain 1994: Classic Howell Mountain in its earth and pepper flavors and tannic structure, this is a distinctive wine with appealing Zinfandel flavors. Best to cellar into 1999 to let it soften just a bit. Sold only at the winery. 800 cases made. • $20 • (04/30/97) • **89**
Zinfandel Howell Mountain 1993 • $18 • (04/30/96) • **84**
Zinfandel Howell Mountain 1991 • $14 • (02/28/95) • **86**
Zinfandel Napa Valley Suzanne's Vineyard 1994: Complex and supple, with appealing ripe cherry, plum and wild berry flavors, finishes with a dash of spice and pepper. Mild tannins make it drinkable now. Sold only at the winery. 2,000 cases made. • $14 • (04/30/97) • **88**

SAUCELITO CANYON | CALIFORNIA

Zinfandel Arroyo Grande Valley 1996: Lots of spice, earth, mineral and leather before the raspberry, rhubarb and berry flavors kick in. Clean and refreshing on the finish, where the fruit keeps pumping. Drink now through 2001. 2,424 cases made. • $19 • (06/15/98) • **87**
Zinfandel Arroyo Grande Valley 1995: Multidimensional, with lots of ripe, complex plum, wild berry, black cherry and spice qualities adding interest. Finishes with a broad aftertaste that echoes the fruit flavors. Ready to drink. 2,222 cases made. • $17 • (04/30/97) • **92**
Zinfandel Arroyo Grande Valley 1993 • $14 • (10/15/95) SS • **91**
Zinfandel Arroyo Grande Valley 1992 • $12 • (08/31/94) • **87**
Zinfandel Arroyo Grande Valley 1991 • $12 • (09/30/93) • **88**
Zinfandel Arroyo Grande Valley 1990 • $13 • (10/15/92) • **85**
Zinfandel Arroyo Grande Valley 1989 • $13 • (10/15/92) • **89**
Zinfandel San Luis Obispo County 1986 • $9 • (12/15/89) • **87**

SAUSAL | CALIFORNIA

Cabernet Sauvignon Alexander Valley 1992 • $14 • (10/31/95) • **88**
Cabernet Sauvignon Alexander Valley 1988 • $14 • (07/15/93) • **80**
Cabernet Sauvignon Alexander Valley 1987 • $14 • (11/15/92) • **79**
Cabernet Sauvignon Alexander Valley 1985 • $12 • (07/31/89) • **74**
Zinfandel Alexander Valley 1995: Ripe, if a bit tarry, its plum and cherry flavors are supple until the finish, where the tannins are chewy and coarse. Drink now. 8,500 cases made. • $10 • (06/15/98) • **84**
Zinfandel Alexander Valley 1994 • $10 • (04/30/96) • **84**
Zinfandel Alexander Valley 1993 • $9 • (07/31/95) BB • **88**
Zinfandel Alexander Valley 1992 • $9 • (01/31/95) SS • **89**
Zinfandel Alexander Valley 1990 • $9 • (12/15/92) • **82**
Zinfandel Alexander Valley 1989 • $8 • (03/31/92) • **79**
Zinfandel Alexander Valley 1988 • $8 • (04/30/91) • **82**
Zinfandel Alexander Valley 1987 • $7 • (09/15/89) • **83**
Zinfandel Alexander Valley 1986 • $6 • (03/31/89) SS • **90**
Zinfandel Alexander Valley 1985 • $6 • (10/15/88) • **72**
Zinfandel Alexander Valley 1984 • $6 • (05/31/88) • **78**
Zinfandel Alexander Valley 1983 • $5 • (09/15/87) BB • **82**
Zinfandel Alexander Valley Century Vines 1995: Supple and harmonious, a claret style that features ripe plum, cherry and blackberry flavors. Soft and fleshy. Drink now through 2002. 500 cases made. • $18 • (06/15/98) • **88**
Zinfandel Alexander Valley Century Vines 1993 • $15 • (03/31/96) • **84**
Zinfandel Alexander Valley Private Reserve 1995: Offers a well-focused core of fruit. Though tight, with an unyielding edge to the wild berry and blackberry-laced Zinfandel flavors, a little time in the bottle should work to its advantage. Firmly tannic. Best from 1999 through 2002. 2,000 cases made. • $16 • (06/15/98) • **88**
Zinfandel Alexander Valley Private Reserve 1994: Appealing for its fruity core, with hints of sage, plum, berry and pepper and a touch of earth. A claret style that features understated flavors and smooth texture. 1,500 cases made. • $14 • (03/31/97) • **89**
Zinfandel Alexander Valley Private Reserve 1992 • $14 • (01/31/95) • **87**
Zinfandel Alexander Valley Private Reserve 1991 • $14 • (10/15/94) • **87**
Zinfandel Alexander Valley Private Reserve 1988 • $14 • (04/30/91) • **88**
Zinfandel Alexander Valley Private Reserve 1984 • $10 • (02/15/88) • **86**

SCHARFFENBERGER | CALIFORNIA

Blanc de Blancs Mendocino County 1991: Smooth, ripe and flavorful, with complex pear, spice, apple and hazelnut flavors, finishing with a toasty, yeasty note. 10,000 cases made. • $23 • (11/30/97) • **87**
Blanc de Blancs Mendocino County 1988 • $22 • (08/31/92) HR • **90**
Blanc de Blancs Mendocino County 1987 • $20 • (12/31/91) • **83**

Blanc de Blancs Mendocino County 1986 • $20 • (03/15/91) HR • **91**
Blanc de Blancs Mendocino County 1985 • $18 • (12/31/88) • **85**
Blanc de Blancs Mendocino County 1984 • $18 • (12/31/87) • **78**
Brut Blanc de Blancs Mendocino County 1989 • $20 • (12/31/93) • **89**
Brut Blanc de Blancs Mendocino County Prestige Cuvée 1991 • $23 • (12/31/95) • **90**
Brut Blanc de Blancs Mendocino County Prestige Cuvée 1989 • $20 • (12/15/94) • **89**
Brut Mendocino County 1983 • $13 • (09/30/87) • **84**
Brut Mendocino County 1982 • $13 • (02/01/86) • **85**
Brut Mendocino County NV: Emits toast and yeast on the nose, but the fruit has a bit of a green edge. Still, it has pleasant nut, fig and citrus qualities. 30,000 cases made. • $18 • (11/30/97) • **87**
Brut Rosé Mendocino County 1992: Impressive for its ripe, juicy plum and black cherry flavors and the smoky vanilla accent that emerges on the finish. 2,160 cases made. • $23 • (11/30/96) • **87**
Brut Rosé Mendocino County 1989 • $18 • (12/31/94) • **87**
Brut Rosé Mendocino County NV: Features ripe and pretty notes of black cherry and berry, and picks up a dash of herb on the aftertaste. Well made; drinks well now. 10,000 cases made. • $23 • (11/30/97) • **87**

SCHEID | CALIFORNIA

Cabernet Sauvignon Monterey 1994: Lighter style of Cabernet, offering a modest level of berry and smoke flavor, and a touch of green bean on the finish. Drink now. 426 cases made. • $18 • (03/31/98) • **83**
Chardonnay Monterey 1995: Marked by hazelnut, mandarin orange and toast components, this wine has a good foundation, but lacks elegance. Still, enjoyable. 269 cases made. • $16 • (01/31/98) • **85**
Chardonnay Monterey 1994: Very spicy. A dusky wine with distinctive cinnamon, peppermint and honey flavors overshadowing the core of bright fruit. Try now. 413 cases made. • $18 • (03/31/98) • **82**

SCHERRER, F. | CALIFORNIA

Zinfandel Alexander Valley Old & Mature Vines 1996: Smooth, ripe and polished, with black cherry, wild berry, strawberry and spice. Elegant and supple on the finish, with a soft, fleshy texture. Drink now through 2002. 600 cases made. • $23 • (07/31/98) • **89**
Zinfandel Alexander Valley Old & Mature Vines 1995: Inviting ripe, fruity aromas, and a core of juicy plum and cherry flavors that linger on the finish, picking up a hint of sage. 1,000 cases made. • $18 • (06/30/97) • **89**
Zinfandel Alexander Valley Old & Mature Vines 1994: Smooth and polished, striking a nice balance between ripe cherry, plum and berry flavors and spicy vanilla and oak notes. Drinks well now. • $16 • (09/30/96) • **86**
Zinfandel Alexander Valley Old & Mature Vines 1993 • $15 • (10/15/95) • **87**
Zinfandel Alexander Valley Old Vines 1992 • $14 • (09/15/94) HR • **90**
Zinfandel Alexander Valley Old Vines 1991 • $14 • (08/31/93) • **87**
Zinfandel Alexander Valley The Shale Terrace 1996: Serves up lots of ripe, juicy plum, cherry and blackberry flavors, picking up mint, sage and spice notes while keeping a tight focus. Long on the finish. A new bottling from a section within Scherrer Vineyard. Drink now through 2004. 200 cases made. • $20 • (07/31/98) • **89**

SCHNEIDER | NEW YORK

Cabernet Franc North Fork of Long Island 1994: Bright in flavor, serious and lush in texture, this Cabernet Franc is quite like a good Bordeaux. Best now. 255 cases made. • $19 • (09/30/97) • **86**
Merlot North Fork of Long Island 1994: A serious, tannic, deep-colored Merlot with enough ripe fruit flavor to match the stiff structure. Has flavors of black cherry, menthol and spice that linger on the finish. Best now through 2000. 85 cases made. • $19 • (09/30/97) • **89**

SCHOOL HOUSE | CALIFORNIA

Pinot Noir Spring Mountain 1993 • $35 • (12/31/95) • **77**

Key: SS—Spectator Selection CS—Cellar Selection HR—Highly Recommended BB—Best Buy $NA—Price not available Ⓐ—Auction Price (BT)—Barrel Tasting
Dates in parentheses indicate the issues in which the ratings were published.

SCHRAMSBERG | CALIFORNIA

Blanc de Blancs Napa Valley 1993: A bit oxidized, with some earth tones, too. Rich in caramel, honey and cream. A heavy style, perhaps not for everyone. 12,000 cases made. • $25 • (11/30/97) • **86**
Blanc de Blancs Napa Valley 1992: Simple and spicy, with hints of pear, melon and light toast flavors, but it loses focus and concentration on the finish. 12,000 cases made. • $23 • (11/30/96) • **86**
Blanc de Blancs Napa Valley 1989 • $22 • (12/31/94) • **87**
Blanc de Blancs Napa Valley 1988 • $22 • (12/31/93) • **87**
Blanc de Blancs Napa Valley 1987 • $21 • (12/15/91) • **87**
Blanc de Blancs Napa Valley 1986 • $20 • (12/31/90) • **89**
Blanc de Blancs Napa Valley 1985 • $20 • (05/31/89) • **84**
Blanc de Blancs Napa Valley 1983 • $18 • (05/16/86) • **82**
Blanc de Blancs Napa Valley Late Disgorged 1988: Ripe and full-bodied, with complex pear, vanilla and spicy hazelnut flavors. Still young and vibrant, it finishes with lots of intensity and flavor. 400 cases made. • $28 • (11/30/96) • **89**
Blanc de Blancs Napa Valley Late Disgorged 12/90 1985 • $27 • (06/15/91) • **87**
Blanc de Noirs Napa Valley 1990: Delivers lots of ripe, complex black cherry, vanilla and citrus flavors, but shows a trace of bitterness, as well as maturity, on the finish. 5,000 cases made. • $26 • (11/30/97) • **88**
Blanc de Noirs Napa Valley 1989: A touch earthy and yeasty, with hints of citrus, especially grapefruit, adding dimension to the light cherry flavor. Finishes with a complex aftertaste of lingering flavors. 7,000 cases made. • $25 • (11/30/96) • **89**
Blanc de Noirs Napa Valley 1988: Mature, with an earthy, drying edge to the pear and spice flavors. Turns a bit cloying on the finish, but unveils a nice rose petal note on the long aftertaste. • $30 • (11/30/97) • **87**
Blanc de Noirs Napa Valley 1987 • $24 • (12/31/94) • **87**
Blanc de Noirs Napa Valley 1986 • $24 • (12/31/93) • **87**
Blanc de Noirs Napa Valley 1985 • $22 • (12/31/91) • **83**
Blanc de Noirs Napa Valley 1984 • $22 • (12/31/90) • **82**
Blanc de Noirs Napa Valley 1983 • $21 • (05/31/89) • **90**
Blanc de Noirs Napa Valley 1981 • $20 • (05/16/86) • **91**
Blanc de Noirs Napa Valley 30th Anniversary 1965-1995 1984 • $32 • (12/31/95) • **88**
Blanc de Noirs Napa Valley Late Disgorged 12/90 1983 • $28 • (06/15/91) • **87**
Brut Napa Valley Reserve 1983 • $29 • (12/31/90) • **82**
Brut Napa Valley Reserve 1982 • $28 • (05/31/89) • **85**
Brut Napa Valley Reserve 1981 • $27 • (07/31/87) • **78**
Brut Rosé Napa Valley Cuvée de Pinot 1994: A spicy style, with understated black cherry and strawberry notes of modest proportion, finishing with a toasty edge. Ready to drink. 2,000 cases made. • $25 • (11/30/97) • **88**
Brut Rosé Napa Valley Cuvée de Pinot 1992: Shows off the delicate side of rosé, with smooth, creamy strawberry and cherry flavors that are elegant and refined. There's a sweetish edge to the finish. 2,200 cases made. • $23 • (11/30/96) • **89**
Brut Rosé Napa Valley Cuvée de Pinot 1990 • $23 • (12/31/94) • **87**
Brut Rosé Napa Valley Cuvée de Pinot 1989 • $22 • (12/31/93) • **84**
Brut Rosé Napa Valley Cuvée de Pinot 1987 • $20 • (12/31/90) • **81**
Brut Rosé Napa Valley Cuvée de Pinot 1986 • $19 • (05/31/89) • **76**
Brut Rosé Napa Valley Cuvée de Pinot 1985 • $17 • (04/30/88) • **80**
Brut Rosé Napa Valley Cuvée de Pinot 1984 • $17 • (05/31/87) • **83**
Demi-Sec Napa Valley Crémant 1992: Ripe and sweet without being cloying, with nice spice, honey, pear and earth flavors. Pleasant before or after a meal. A rare wine made from the Flora grape. 2,000 cases made. • $23 • (11/30/96) • **86**
Demi-Sec Napa Valley Crémant 1989 • $22 • (12/31/94) • **87**
Demi-Sec Napa Valley Crémant 1987 • $20 • (12/31/91) • **80**
Demi-Sec Napa Valley Crémant 1986 • $20 • (12/31/90) • **77**
Demi-Sec Napa Valley Crémant 1985 • $19 • (05/31/89) • **85**
J. Schram Napa Valley 1990: Complex and concentrated, with a pretty array of black cherry, toast and spice flavors, and a smooth, delicate aftertaste where the vanilla and cherry flavors flow through. Shows a measure of finesse and harmony. Has improved with a year in bottle. • $50 • (11/30/97) • **92**
J. Schram Napa Valley 1989 • $50 • (06/30/95) HR • **90**
J. Schram Napa Valley 1988 • $50 • (12/31/93) • **90**
J. Schram Napa Valley 1987 • $50 • (12/31/92) • **85**
Reserve Napa Valley 1987: Complex and spicy, with layers of pear, honey, vanilla and lightly toasty flavors. The texture is smooth and creamy and the finish is rich, lively and lingering. Tasty now, but can age a few more years. 2,500 cases made. • $33 • (12/31/96) • **91**

Reserve Napa Valley 1986 • $32 • (12/31/93) • **85**

SCHUETZ OLES | CALIFORNIA

Chardonnay Napa Valley Chappell Vineyard 1993 • $14 • (07/31/95) • **82**
Zinfandel Napa Valley Korte Ranch 1993 • $14 • (10/15/95) • **88**
Zinfandel Napa Valley Korte Ranch 1992 • $14 • (06/15/95) • **89**

SCHUG | CALIFORNIA

Brut Carneros Rouge de Noir 1995: Darker than rosé, this has a bitter quality that overrides the hints of cherry and spice. 300 cases made. • $25 • (12/15/97) • **78**
Cabernet Sauvignon Napa Valley 1994: Well proportioned, with a core of currant, herb, tobacco and spice flavors, and firm but supple tannins. Finishes with a complex array of flavors and good length. 1,053 cases made. • $18 • (12/15/97) • **88**
Cabernet Sauvignon Sonoma Valley Heritage Reserve 1994: Intense and concentrated, with firm, raw tannins and a band of spice, currant, cherry and wild berry flavor that's dense and chewy, so cellaring into 1999 to 2001 is advised. 524 cases made. • $30 • (12/15/97) • **89**
Cabernet Sauvignon Sonoma Valley Heritage Reserve 1992 • $25 • (11/15/94) • **86**
Chardonnay Carneros 1996: Shows a measure of restraint and finesse, with complex citrus, pear and green apple hints, picking up a spicy, earthy note on the finish where the flavors linger. 1,850 cases made. • $18 • (05/15/98) • **90**
Chardonnay Carneros 1995: Marked by intense, earthy citrus and pear flavors, along with a dash of minty spice, this can use short-term cellaring to soften and round out its rough edges. Try now to 2000. 1,450 cases made. • $18 • (04/30/98) • **88**
Chardonnay Carneros 1994: A medium-bodied white, with a trim, somewhat tart band of light oak, spice and pear. Appealing for its fruit. 1,800 cases made. • $18 • (06/30/96) • **85**
Chardonnay Carneros 1993 • $16 • (07/31/95) • **78**
Chardonnay Carneros Heritage Reserve 1996: A bit tart, with ripe pear and appley flavors that while elegant are also earthy, with citrus notes. Drink now through 2000. 320 cases made. • $25 • (05/15/98) • **87**
Chardonnay Carneros Heritage Reserve 1995: Smooth and silky, with a rich, complex, earthy core of fruit built around ripe pear, citrus, melon and hazelnut. Drinks well now, but has the depth and concentration to hold into 2000. 290 cases made. • $25 • (04/30/98) • **90**
Chardonnay Carneros Heritage Reserve 1994: Marked by earthy citrus and tart pineapple notes, it becomes elegant and spicy on the finish. Well crafted. The wines from this winery just keep getting more complex and interesting. 300 cases made. • $25 • (06/30/96) • **88**
Chardonnay Carneros Heritage Reserve 1993 • $25 • (07/31/95) • **88**
Chardonnay North Coast 1996: A creamy-textured wine, with tropical fruit flavors of orange, mango and lemon. A hint of earth and spice adds interest. Drink now. 2,150 cases made. • $14 • (06/30/98) • **87**
Chardonnay Sonoma Valley 1995: A lean, crisp style with citrus, especially lemon, notes. A twinge of earthiness on the finish adds dimension, but more flavor and depth would be nice. 1,800 cases made. • $14 • (04/30/98) • **83**
Chardonnay Sonoma Valley 1994: A pleasant white with a good band of citrus, pear and apple flavors. 1,950 cases made. • $14 • (06/30/96) • **85**
Chardonnay Sonoma Valley 1993 • $12 • (11/30/94) • **85**
Merlot North Coast 1995: Gamy, barnyardy flavors shoulder past the modest plum flavors, making this an acquired taste. Solid otherwise. Ready now. 533 cases made. • $20 • (12/31/97) • **81**
Pinot Noir Carneros 1996: Crisp and tart, with simple blackberry and cherry flavors. Finishes with spice and earth nuances. Best now to 2000. 5,000 cases made. • $18 • (02/28/98) • **83**
Pinot Noir Carneros 1995: Serves up an attractive core of earthy cherry and wild berry flavors, even throws in a dash of strawberry on the finish. Finishes with firm tannins. Cellar into 1999. 3,500 cases made. • $18 • (02/28/98) • **84**
Pinot Noir Carneros 1994 • $16 • (02/29/96) • **87**
Pinot Noir Carneros 1993 • $16 • (12/31/95) • **86**
Pinot Noir Carneros 1992 • $15 • (03/31/95) • **78**
Pinot Noir Carneros 1991 • $15 • (03/31/95) • **78**
Pinot Noir Carneros 1990 • $14 • (02/28/94) • **78**
Pinot Noir Carneros Beckstoffer Vineyard 1990: Impressive for its ripe cherry and plum flavors and hints of tar and anise. Shows more fruit complexity now than on release. Ready to drink. • $16 • (03/31/97) • **87**
Pinot Noir Carneros Beckstoffer Vineyard 1989 • $14 • (02/28/93) • **74**
Pinot Noir Carneros Beckstoffer Vineyard 1988 • $13 • (09/30/92) • **79**
Pinot Noir Carneros Beckstoffer Vineyard 1987 • $13 • (02/28/91) • **81**
Pinot Noir Carneros Beckstoffer Vineyard 1986: Despite faint hints of spice and mushroom on the nose, there isn't much flavor on the palate. • $13 • (03/31/97) • **77**
Pinot Noir Carneros Heritage Reserve 1995: A touch earthy, it slowly unfolds to reveal a broader range of berry and spice notes, all the while showing off its mushroomy flavors. Ready to drink. 481 cases made. • $30 • (12/15/97) • **87**
Pinot Noir Carneros Heritage Reserve 1994: Smooth and polished. A delicate, understated style that's quite attractive with its spice, cherry, and strawberry flavors and subtle herb notes. Another fine effort from Schug. 300 cases made. • $25 • (10/15/96) • **88**
Pinot Noir Carneros Heritage Reserve 1992 • $25 • (12/31/95) • **86**
Pinot Noir Carneros Heritage Reserve 1991 • $25 • (12/15/94) • **87**
Pinot Noir Napa Valley Heinemann Vineyard Reserve 1990: Still rustic, with firm, dry tannins and muddled focus. With its earth, mushroom and dried cherry flavors, it would be best served with creamy or strongly flavored cheese. • $20 • (03/31/97) • **84**
Pinot Noir Napa Valley Heinemann Vineyard Reserve 1989 • $18 • (02/28/94) • **80**
Pinot Noir Napa Valley Heinemann Vineyard Reserve 1986: Hasn't outgrown its stemmy austerity in all these years, rendering it crisp and blandly flavored. • $18 • (03/31/97) • **74**
Pinot Noir Napa Valley Heinemann Vineyard Reserve 1985 • $15 • (11/15/91) • **83**
Pinot Noir North Coast 1994: Simple, showing tart herb, tea and rhubarb flavors before the plum notes fold in. Ready to drink. 2,900 cases made. • $14 • (10/15/96) • **83**
Rouge de Noirs Carneros 1992 • $20 • (12/31/94) • **85**
Rouge de Noirs Carneros 1987 • $18 • (12/15/91) • **85**
Sauvignon Blanc North Coast 1996: Ripe fig and melon flavors turn to more subtle star fruit and honey notes on the finish. Well balanced and enjoyable. 1,282 cases made. • $12 • (09/15/97) • **87**
Sauvignon Blanc Sonoma Valley 1993 • $8 • (01/31/95) • **73**

SCHWARZENBERG | OREGON

Blush Willamette Valley Blanc de Pinot Noir Dry 1993 • $7 • (08/31/95) • **74**
Pinot Noir Oregon 1987 • $14 • (02/15/90) • **70**
Pinot Noir Willamette Valley 1992 • $10 • (10/31/94) BB • **86**
Pinot Noir Willamette Valley 1991 • $7 • (03/15/94) • **82**
Pinot Noir Willamette Valley Dry Blanc de Pinot Noir 1992 • $9 • (11/30/94) • **81**

SCOTLAND CRAIG | CALIFORNIA

Pinot Noir Atlas Peak 1995: Austere in style, with firm, earthy tannins and a murky core of wild berry and black cherry, finishing with dry, earthy tannins. Drinkable now. • $22 • (01/31/98) • **87**
Pinot Noir Russian River Valley Rochioli Vineyard 1993 • $35 • (12/31/95) • **85**

SCREAMING EAGLE | CALIFORNIA

Cabernet Sauvignon Napa Valley 1994: Broad, smooth, ripe and harmonious, with supple texture and tannins and a wonderful core of plush currant, black cherry, anise and light cedary oak flavors. 175 cases made. • $604 Ⓐ • (10/31/97) • **95**
Cabernet Sauvignon Napa Valley 1993: Dark, ripe, intense and concentrated, with lots of currant, earth, leather and anise flavors. Comes across as a rustic, concentrated style with a chewy core of flavors. Finishes with a dry tannic edge and gritty tannins. Not as plush as the 1992, but still packs a wallop. • $579 Ⓐ • (12/31/96) • **91**
Cabernet Sauvignon Napa Valley 1992 • $678 Ⓐ • (02/29/96) • **94**

SEA RIDGE | CALIFORNIA

Chardonnay California 1996: Simple, tastes more like a Chenin Blanc than Chardonnay, with coarse, earthy grapefruit flavors. Drink now. 5,000 cases made. • $10 • (06/30/98) • **78**
Merlot California 1996: Fairly complex, with ripe cherry, blackberry and herbal notes. Oak is a bit heavy, but the ensemble is attractive. Finishes moderately. Drink now through 2002. 5,000 cases made. • $10 • (07/31/98) • **86**
Merlot Sonoma Coast Occidental Vineyard 1989 • $15 • (05/31/92) • **86**

Pinot Noir Sonoma Coast Hirsch Vineyard 1990 • $20 • (03/31/92) • **82**
Pinot Noir Sonoma Coast Hirsch Vineyard 1989 • $18 • (03/31/92) • **81**
Pinot Noir Sonoma County 1982 • $11 • (08/31/86) • **72**
Zinfandel California 1996: A bit herbal and tanky, the wine shows pleasant cherry notes, but fails to deliver the ripe, juicy promise inherent in this grape. Drink now. 5,000 cases made. • $10 • (07/31/98) • **78**
Zinfandel Late Harvest Sonoma Coast Morelli Vineyards 1991 • $12 • (10/15/94) • **83**
Zinfandel Sonoma Coast Occidental Vineyard 1991 • $12 • (10/15/94) • **82**
Zinfandel Sonoma Coast Occidental Vineyard 1990 • $12 • (09/30/93) • **80**

SEAVEY | CALIFORNIA

Cabernet Sauvignon Napa Valley 1994: Tough and chewy, with an earthy edge to the currant, herb, and tobacco flavors. With aeration, it opens up to reveal more complexity and depth, finishing with a nice interplay of flavors. Best to cellar into 1999 to 2001. 950 cases made. • $30 • (12/31/97) • **89**
Cabernet Sauvignon Napa Valley 1993: Strikes a nice balance between ripe, complex cherry and plum Cabernet flavors and smooth, supple texture. Finishes with nice length and soft tannins. Can be enjoyed now or cellared into 2000. 1,200 cases made. • $28 • (11/15/96) • **88**
Cabernet Sauvignon Napa Valley 1992: Tightly wound and less concentrated than the 1991. Still, delivers pleasant herb, olive, cedar, currant and spice flavors and a pretty aftertaste. Drink now. 750 cases made. • $28 • (07/31/96) • **88**
Cabernet Sauvignon Napa Valley 1991 • $26 • (07/31/95) • **89**
Cabernet Sauvignon Napa Valley 1990 • $24 • (08/31/94) • **89**
Chardonnay Napa Valley 1995: An elegant and sophisticated style, smooth, ripe and creamy, that relies on subtle pear, apple, melon and oak shadings. Drinkable now. 275 cases made. • $18 • (06/15/97) • **91**
Chardonnay Napa Valley 1994: Fragrant, delicate honey, pear, peach and nectarine notes of moderate concentration and richness. A subtle, understated style. Tasted twice, with consistent notes. 395 cases made. • $16 • (05/15/96) • **88**
Merlot Napa Valley 1994: Ripe, smooth and complex, with pretty currant, light cedary oak and spicy qualities. Has a lot going for it, with balance, tender tannins and a long, rich aftertaste. Drink now into 2001 or 2002. 350 cases made. • $24 • (11/30/97) • **91**

SEBASTIANI | CALIFORNIA

Barbera Sonoma County 1994: Very pretty strawberry and anise flavors swirl through this supple wine and even linger a bit on the finish. 2,800 cases made. • $14 • (07/31/97) • **86**
Barbera Sonoma County 1989 • $10 • (03/31/93) • **81**
Barbera Sonoma Valley 1992 • $14 • (07/31/95) • **86**
Barbera Sonoma Valley 1987 • $11 • (04/30/91) • **86**
Cabernet Franc California 1988 • $8 • (07/15/91) • **77**
Cabernet Franc Sonoma County 1989 • $10 • (03/31/93) • **88**
Cabernet Sauvignon California Proprietor's Reserve 1974 • $40 • (11/15/94) • **68**
Cabernet Sauvignon North Coast 1986 • $13 • (03/31/92) • **71**
Cabernet Sauvignon Sonoma County 1994: California Cabernets of this quality at this price are few and far between. This wine is smooth, ripe and spicy, with an elegant band of currant, herb, sage and spice nuances that hang on and tannins that are soft and fleshy. An exceptional value. 55,000 cases made. • $10 • (04/30/97) BB • **87**
Cabernet Sauvignon Sonoma County 1992 • $10 • (11/15/95) BB • **87**
Cabernet Sauvignon Sonoma County 1991 • $10 • (11/15/94) • **85**
Cabernet Sauvignon Sonoma County 1990 • $10 • (11/15/94) • **80**
Cabernet Sauvignon Sonoma County 1989 • $9 • (04/30/93) • **82**
Cabernet Sauvignon Sonoma County 1988 • $8 • (11/15/92) • **77**
Cabernet Sauvignon Sonoma County 1985 • $8 • (10/15/88) • **80**
Cabernet Sauvignon Sonoma County Reserve 1988 • $12 • (10/31/92) • **83**
Cabernet Sauvignon Sonoma County Reserve 1986 • $13 • (01/31/91) • **86**
Cabernet Sauvignon Sonoma County Reserve 1985 • $13 • (11/15/90) • **86**
Cabernet Sauvignon Sonoma County Reserve 1978 • $25 • (11/15/92) • **83**
Cabernet Sauvignon Sonoma Valley 1982 • $27 • (09/15/86) • **75**
Cabernet Sauvignon Sonoma Valley 1981 • $25 • (08/01/85) • **91**

Key: SS—Spectator Selection CS—Cellar Selection HR—Highly Recommended BB—Best Buy $NA—Price not available Ⓐ—Auction Price (BT)—Barrel Tasting
Dates in parentheses indicate the issues in which the ratings were published.

Cabernet Sauvignon Sonoma Valley Cherryblock 1992: A balancing act between currant and cherry flavors and some mature Cabernet flavors, with sage and bell-pepper notes. Picks up a cedary edge on the finish, with firm tannins. Try this with a classified Bordeaux. 2,300 cases made. • $35 • (04/30/97) • **89**
Cabernet Sauvignon Sonoma Valley Cherryblock 1987 • $14 • (07/15/92) • **84**
Cabernet Sauvignon Sonoma Valley Cherryblock 1985 • $17 • (03/31/90) • **89**
Cabernet Sauvignon Sonoma Valley Cherryblock Old Vines 1991 • $24 • (11/15/94) • **88**
Cabernet Sauvignon Sonoma Valley Cherryblock Old Vines 1989 • $15 • (06/15/93) • **82**
Cabernet Sauvignon Sonoma Valley Reserve 1982 • $11 • (12/31/87) • **74**
Chardonnay California 1996: Complex, with plenty of ripe, rich pear, fig, apple and melon flavors and a pretty dash of toasty oak. Drink now. 58,000 cases made. • $12 • (06/15/98) • **88**
Chardonnay California Heritage 1995: Pleasantly soft, and nicely fruity. 800,000 cases made. • $12/1.5 liter • (07/31/96) • **81**
Chardonnay Russian River Valley Dutton Ranch 1996: A delicate, understated style, with lovely floral, light oak, ripe pear, fig, apple and melon flavors, which are supple and fleshy on the elegant finish. Drink now through 2001. 1,000 cases made. • $30 • (07/31/98) • **91**
Chardonnay Russian River Valley Dutton Ranch 1995: Ripe and complex, with tiers of ripe pear, fig, toasty oak and citrus, all well proportioned and finishing in a lingering aftertaste. In a word, impressive. Drinkable now, but should age well, too. 2,000 cases made. • $25 • (05/31/97) • **90**
Chardonnay Russian River Valley Dutton Ranch 1994: Delivers a nice core of ripe pear, peach and nectarine flavors with a light dash of oak. Well balanced, with a lingering aftertaste. 2,000 cases made. • $18 • (06/30/96) • **86**
Chardonnay Russian River Valley Dutton Ranch 1993 • $18 • (05/31/95) • **89**
Chardonnay Sonoma County 1995: Impressive for its elegance, finesse and core of complex fruit and oak flavors, with tiers of ripe pear, melon, cedar and spice. Delicious, and a wonderful bargain at this price-comparable to wines two to three times as expensive. 80,000 cases made. • $10 • (04/30/97) BB • **88**
Chardonnay Sonoma County 1994: Fresh, spicy and simple, a nice mouthful of green apple and nutmeg flavors. 65,000 cases made. • $11 • (06/15/96) • **82**
Chardonnay Sonoma County 1993 • $10 • (06/15/95) BB • **87**
Merlot California Country NV • $4 • (05/31/92) • **72**
Merlot Sonoma County 1995: A soft, lush mouthful of blackberry, anise and tar flavors. Tannins are gentle and nicely integrated, flavors linger prettily. Nice now, better in 1999 to 2000. 15,000 cases made. • $16 • (03/31/98) • **87**
Merlot Sonoma County 1994 • $14 • (06/30/96) • **82**
Merlot Sonoma County 1993 • $12 • (11/15/95) • **87**
Merlot Sonoma County 1992 • $12 • (09/15/94) • **79**
Merlot Sonoma County 1991 • $8 • (05/15/93) BB • **84**
Merlot Sonoma County 1990 • $9 • (03/31/93) • **82**
Merlot Sonoma County 1989 • $9 • (05/31/92) • **85**
Merlot Sonoma County 1985 • $7 • (09/30/88) • **85**
Merlot Sonoma Valley Town 1994: Rich and supple, tight, firm and well focused, with a complex core of earthy currant, plum, black cherry, spicy oak and anise notes. A beautifully-crafted young Merlot that's wonderfully balanced and worthy of a few more years of cellaring. 900 cases made. • $25 • (06/30/97) • **89**
Mourvèdre California Old Vines 1993: Smooth and supple core of mineral, currant and wild berry flavors that hold together nicely on the finish. • $14 • (08/31/96) • **85**
Red Hill Vineyard Sonoma Valley 1989 • $14 • (11/15/93) • **79**
Sauvignon Blanc California Propreietor's 1993 • $6 • (08/31/94) • **75**
Sémillon-Chardonnay California Heritage 1995: Slight, simple flavors that are pretty, but lack oomph. • $9/1.5 liter • (07/31/96) • **80**
Syrah Dry Creek Valley 1995: A spicy style, emphasizing nutmeg and cinnamon notes. Ripe blackberry and earth flavors, finishing smooth and polished, with hints of vanilla and mineral. Tempting now, best from 1999 to 2001. 1,100 cases made. • $15 • (03/31/98) • **89**
Syrah Sonoma County 1992 • $14 • (01/31/95) • **86**
White Zinfandel California Proprietor's 1994 • $7/1.5 liter • (09/15/95) • **75**
Wildwood Sonoma Valley 1987 • $15 • (08/31/91) • **86**
Zinfandel Dry Creek Valley Cuneo-Saini Farms Old Vines 1994 • $12 • (10/15/95) • **88**
Zinfandel Sonoma County 1991 • $8 • (10/15/94) • **83**
Zinfandel Sonoma County 1989 • $7 • (03/31/93) BB • **85**

Zinfandel Sonoma County 1988 • $6 • (09/15/92) • **78**
Zinfandel Sonoma County 1985 • $5 • (09/15/88) BB • **88**
Zinfandel Sonoma County Old Vines Cuvée 1995: Tight and tart, with a core of blackberry, black cherry and wild berry. Finishes with crisp acidity and a twinge of green astringency. Drink now. 2,450 cases made. • $20 • (06/15/98) • **82**
Zinfandel Sonoma Valley Domenici Vineyard Old Vines 1995: Well focused on spicy, peppery, wild berry and cherry flavors, with a seamless texture and an elegant aftertaste. Ripe, but not overly rich or powerful, it finishes with dashes of herb and sage. Drink now. 1,000 cases made. • $17 • (05/15/98) • **87**
Zinfandel Sonoma Valley Proprietor's Reserve 1980 • $9 • (12/16/85) • **76**

SEBASTOPOL | CALIFORNIA

Chardonnay Russian River Valley Dutton Ranch 1996: Smooth, ripe and spicy, with a pleasant core of ripe pear, fig and apple. Holds its flavors on the finish, where it picks up a trace of citrus. Drink now. 700 cases made. • $24 • (05/15/98) • **87**
Chardonnay Russian River Valley Dutton Ranch 1995: A crisp, clean wine that nonetheless sports plenty of character-with ripe apple, fig and citrus flavors and a judicious use of oak that blends well with the delicacy of the wine. A fine first release from this renowned grape-growing family. 700 cases made. • $18 • (01/31/98) • **90**
Pinot Noir Russian River Valley Dutton Ranch 1995: Clean, ripe and spicy, with attractive cherry, wild berry, plum and sage notes, finishing with mild tannins and a touch of earthiness. Drink through 2001. 300 cases made. • $24 • (01/31/98) • **86**

SECRET HOUSE | OREGON

Pinot Noir Willamette Valley 1994: Firm, focused and elegant, this delivers a rich mouthful of spicy plum and currant flavor that extends into a long, harmonious, nicely proportioned finish. Delicious now, but has the stuffing to improve through 2000. 980 cases made. • $17 • (11/30/96) • **89**

SEGHESIO | CALIFORNIA

Arneis California Vitigno Piemonte 1995: Earthy, slightly grassy and with a mildly sweaty accent, it manages to keep its balance with tart citrus and pineapple flavors. 500 cases made. • $14 • (09/15/96) • **84**
Barbera California Noble Vines 1996: Bright, smooth and fruity, with pretty plum and berry flavors on a light frame. Drink now. 900 cases made. • $17 • (06/30/98) • **84**
Barbera California Vitigno Piemontese 1995: Bright and juicy, brimming with zingy berry and plum flavors, and finishing with a stylish hint of spice. Drink now. • $15 • (11/30/97) • **87**
Cabernet Sauvignon Northern Sonoma 1986 • $8 • (06/30/90) • **76**
Cabernet Sauvignon Northern Sonoma 1985 • $5 • (04/15/89) BB • **84**
Cabernet Sauvignon Northern Sonoma 1983 • $6 • (07/15/88) • **69**
Cabernet Sauvignon Northern Sonoma 1982 • $5 • (04/30/87) • **77**
Cabernet Sauvignon Sonoma County 1993: Good intensity, with lively mint, cherry and plum-laced flavors before the tannins kick in. A solid value at this price. 13,000 cases made. • $9 • (02/29/96) • **84**
Cabernet Sauvignon Sonoma County 1992 • $9 • (11/15/94) • **84**
Cabernet Sauvignon Sonoma County 1991 • $9 • (03/31/94) • **83**
Cabernet Sauvignon Sonoma County 1990 • $9 • (06/15/93) • **79**
Cabernet Sauvignon Sonoma County 1989 • $9 • (11/15/92) • **82**
Cabernet Sauvignon Sonoma County 1987 • $9 • (04/30/91) • **85**
Carignane Alexander Valley Old Vine 1992 • $12 • (12/31/93) • **84**
Chardonnay Russian River Valley 1994: Somewhat coarse, featuring spicy pear and vanilla notes. Straightfoward style that's a decent value. 10,000 cases made. • $10 • (05/15/96) • **84**
Chardonnay Sonoma County 1993 • $9 • (07/31/95) • **82**
Omaggio Four Generations Red Sonoma County 1995: Tightly wound, with cedary oak almost overshadowing the core of spicy plum, black cherry, raspberry and spice flavors. Turns complex on the finish, where the flavors fold together. Drink now or age short-term. A blend of Cabernet Sauvignon, Merlot, Sangiovese, and Barbera. 600 cases made. • $30 • (12/31/97) • **88**
Pinot Noir Northern Sonoma 1983 • $5 • (04/15/87) • **72**
Pinot Noir Russian River Valley 1995: Pretty light. If you're looking for subtlety, try this. Pretty cherry and spice flavors are hiding behind a mildly tannic edge. Not likely to improve. 1,600 cases made. • $14 • (02/28/98) • **82**
Pinot Noir Russian River Valley 1994: Young, firm and tight, with a narrow band of black cherry, spice and cedary oak flavors. Try now. An improvement over earlier efforts. 4,000 cases made. • $12 • (02/28/97) • **86**
Pinot Noir Russian River Valley 1991 • $9 • (02/28/94) • **81**
Pinot Noir Russian River Valley 1990 • $9 • (02/28/93) • **78**
Pinot Noir Russian River Valley 1988 • $9 • (10/31/91) • **83**
Pinot Noir Russian River Valley 1987 • $8 • (04/15/90) • **84**
Pinot Noir Russian River Valley Reserve 1987 • $13 • (04/15/90) • **83**
Pinot Noir Sonoma & Mendocino Counties 1984 • $6 • (05/31/88) • **84**
Pinot Noir Sonoma County 1993 • $12 • (11/15/95) • **86**
Pinot Noir Sonoma County 1989 • $9 • (04/30/92) • **79**
Sangiovese Alexander Valley Chianti Station Old Vine 1990 • $30 • (12/15/92) • **86**
Sangiovese Alexander Valley Nonno's Clones 1996: This modest red offers some chewy black cherry and floral flavors, remaining rustic and simple through the solid finish. Drink now through 2000. 3,000 cases made. • $15 • (06/30/98) • **86**
Sangiovese Alexander Valley Vitigno Toscano 1995: Somewhat mild-mannered, with a strawberry backdrop and powdery tannins. 1,800 cases made. • $15 • (10/15/97) • **80**
Sangiovese Alexander Valley Vitigno Toscano 1992 • $14 • (05/31/94) • **87**
Sangiovese Alexander Valley Vitigno Toscano 1991 • $14 • (12/15/92) • **80**
Sauvignon Blanc Sonoma County 1994 • $9 • (08/31/95) • **85**
Sauvignon Blanc Sonoma County 1993 • $7 • (09/30/94) BB • **88**
Sonoma Red Lot 3 Sonoma County NV • $4 • (05/31/88) • **78**
Sonoma Red Lot 4 Sonoma County NV • $5 • (06/30/90) • **75**
Zinfandel Alexander Valley 1996: Shows more depth, richness and complexity than the other Seghesio bottlings, with ripe, spicy plum, blackberry, raspberry and cedary oak notes. Turns elegant on the finish, where the tannins are soft and fleshy. 350 cases made. • $18 • (05/15/98) • **87**
Zinfandel Alexander Valley Old Vine Reserve 1990 • $14 • (12/15/92) • **83**
Zinfandel Alexander Valley Reserve 1988 • $12 • (08/31/91) • **88**
Zinfandel Alexander Valley Reserve 1986 • $9 • (10/31/89) • **80**
Zinfandel Alexander Valley San Lorenzo 1996: Ripe and flavorful, with supple plum, black cherry, raspberry and spicy Zinfandel flavors. Not too tannic; drink now through 2000. 300 cases made. • $20 • (05/15/98) • **86**
Zinfandel Alexander Valley San Lorenzo 1995: Ripe, smooth and spicy before the tannins weigh in and wrap themselves around the core of mint, berry, sage and spice for a dry, tannic finish. Best from now to 2002. 260 cases made. • $20 • (05/15/98) • **88**
Zinfandel Dry Creek Valley 1993 • $12 • (10/15/95) • **85**
Zinfandel Northern Sonoma 1987 • $6 • (07/31/90) BB • **85**
Zinfandel Northern Sonoma 1986 • $6 • (05/15/90) BB • **80**
Zinfandel Northern Sonoma 1985 • $5 • (03/15/89) BB • **80**
Zinfandel Northern Sonoma 1984 • $5 • (06/30/88) • **76**
Zinfandel Sonoma County 1995: A fresh and lively Zin, with ripe cherry and wild berry flavors at the core. Develops a spicy, peppery edge on the finish that's tasty and adds interest. The price is right, and it's ready to drink. 16,000 cases made. • $10 • (04/30/97) BB • **87**
Zinfandel Sonoma County 1994: A nice core of cherry and berry flavors, but they're somewhat overwhelmed by the dry, cedary oak. 18,000 cases made. • $10 • (09/15/96) • **83**
Zinfandel Sonoma County 1993 • $9 • (10/15/95) • **85**
Zinfandel Sonoma County 1992 • $9 • (09/15/94) BB • **88**
Zinfandel Sonoma County 1991 • $7 • (09/30/93) • **84**
Zinfandel Sonoma County 1990 • $7 • (10/15/92) BB • **85**
Zinfandel Sonoma County 1989 • $7 • (07/31/92) BB • **84**
Zinfandel Sonoma County 1988 • $6 • (09/30/91) BB • **86**
Zinfandel Sonoma County Old Vine 1996: Impressive. Smooth, ripe, rich and concentrated, with broad black cherry, plum and wild berry flavors, touches of cedar and spice. Finishes with complex fruit flavors and fleshy tannins. Drink now through 2004. 2,200 cases made. • $21 • (06/15/98) • **90**
Zinfandel Sonoma County Old Vine 1995: Intense and focused, with a core of ripe plum, raspberry and toasty oak. The finish is impressive for its bright, juicy fruit. Tight and compact now, it can stand short-term cellaring to soften a bit. Try late this year to 2002. 1,700 cases made. • $20 • (04/30/98) • **90**
Zinfandel Sonoma County Old Vine 1994: Firm, dry and tannic, but enough wild berry, cracked pepper, spice and cherry flavors come through to hold your interest. Turns complex on the finish. Try now. 2,000 cases made. • $14 • (10/15/96) • **88**
Zinfandel Sonoma County Sonoma 1996: Medium-bodied, with ripe and supple plum and blackberry flavors and modest tannins. A ready-to-drink style that's simple but complete; drink to 2000. 20,000 cases made. • $13 • (05/15/98) • **85**

SELBY | CALIFORNIA

Chardonnay Sonoma County 1996: Smooth and silky, with rich, polished pear, spice, fig and melon flavors that are complex and concentrated, well focused and elegant. Finish goes on and on. 1,050 cases made. • $23 • (04/30/98) • **90**

Chardonnay Sonoma County 1995: Solid, with lots of ripe fruit, layers of pear, fig, apple and melon, showing more complexity and finesse on the finish, where the flavors fan out and gain depth. 840 cases made. • $20 • (06/15/97) • **90**

Chardonnay Sonoma County 1994: Big, ripe and intense, loaded with bold tropical fruit notes and layers of ripe pear, guava, honeysuckle and spice, an altogether rich and fruity style that doesn't shortchange you on flavor. 198 cases made. • $18 • (04/30/96) • **90**

Merlot Sonoma County 1994: Heavily reliant on oak, as the toasty vanilla flavors and woody texture dominate. Too bad, because underneath is a core of currant and cherry flavor that's quite appealing. Try now. 483 cases made. • $23 • (05/15/97) • **88**

Pinot Noir Russian River Valley 1994 • $16 • (05/15/96) • **85**

Syrah Sonoma County 1994: Smooth and polished, with supple tannins and a rich core of smoky, meaty currant, black cherry, herb and anise. Well balanced, with a spicy aftertaste that lingers. Best now to 2002. 800 cases made. • $20 • (04/30/98) • **88**

Syrah Sonoma County 1993: Trim with a narrow band of spice, plum and earth notes, picking up a trace of spice and leather. Drink now. 430 cases made. • $20 • (02/28/97) • **87**

Zinfandel Sonoma County Old Vines 1995: Clean, and well focused on its wild berry, plum and cherry flavors. Of medium weight and intensity, it's a wine that's best enjoyed now and for the next year. 1,000 cases made. • $20 • (05/15/98) • **85**

SELENE | CALIFORNIA

Merlot Napa Valley 1995: Intense and spicy, but lacking focus and purity of flavor. The spice tends to dominate the modest currant and berry flavor underneath. 700 cases made. • $28 • (12/31/97) • **85**

Merlot Napa Valley 1994: Tight and firm, with a narrow focus of cedar, coffee and herbed currant flavors. Not as much fruit flavor as in many Merlots, but fans of this style will appreciate this wine for its varietal character. It's well balanced, with fine texture. Tasted twice, with consistent notes. 600 cases made. • $26 • (11/30/96) • **88**

Merlot Napa Valley 1993 • $25 • (06/15/96) • **84**

Merlot Napa Valley 1992: Ripe, with layers of herb, currant, cherry and cedar flavors. Complex through the finish, where the flavors fold together. Delicious now, but worth aging. • $25 • (08/31/96) • **89**

Merlot Napa Valley 1991 • $22 • (07/31/94) • **88**

Sauvignon Blanc Carneros Hyde Vineyards 1996: A blend of fig, melon, anise and grapefruit flavors, this is soft in texture, full and round. 400 cases made. • $20 • (11/30/97) • **87**

Sauvignon Blanc Carneros Hyde Vineyards 1995: This wine displays light grapefruit and lemon character and a crisp, clean, mineral finish. 650 cases made. • $18 • (06/30/97) • **87**

Sauvignon Blanc Carneros Hyde Vineyards 1994 • $18 • (02/29/96) • **88**

Sauvignon Blanc Carneros Hyde Vineyards 1993 • $18 • (08/31/95) • **86**

SEQUOIA GROVE | CALIFORNIA

Cabernet Sauvignon Alexander Valley 1981 • $12 • (12/16/84) • **87**

Cabernet Sauvignon Napa & Alexander Valleys 1983 • $13 • (02/15/87) • **88**

Cabernet Sauvignon Napa & Alexander Valleys 1982 • $12 • (12/16/85) • **83**

Cabernet Sauvignon Napa County 1986 • $16 • (09/30/89) • **78**

Cabernet Sauvignon Napa County 1985 • $16 • (12/15/88) • **86**

Cabernet Sauvignon Napa Valley 1995: Opens with earthy, leathery flavors that make way for ripe plum, cherry, blackberry and spice, and finishes with cedary oak nuances. Best from 2001 through 2008. • $22 • (06/15/98) • **88**

Cabernet Sauvignon Napa Valley 1992 • $18 • (07/31/95) SS • **90**

Cabernet Sauvignon Napa Valley 1991 • $18 • (11/15/94) • **88**

Cabernet Sauvignon Napa Valley 1990 • $16 • (03/31/94) SS • **90**

Cabernet Sauvignon Napa Valley 1989 • $16 • (11/15/92) • **80**

Key: SS—Spectator Selection CS—Cellar Selection HR—Highly Recommended BB—Best Buy $NA—Price not available Ⓐ—Auction Price (BT)—Barrel Tasting
Dates in parentheses indicate the issues in which the ratings were published.

Cabernet Sauvignon Napa Valley 1988 • $20 • (11/15/92) • **87**

Cabernet Sauvignon Napa Valley 1987 • $19 • (11/15/91) • **70**

Cabernet Sauvignon Napa Valley 1984 • $13 • (11/15/87) • **82**

Cabernet Sauvignon Napa Valley 1981 • $12 • (03/01/84) • **87**

Cabernet Sauvignon Napa Valley Estate 1988 • $25 • (11/15/92) • **87**

Cabernet Sauvignon Napa Valley Estate 1987 • $31 • (11/15/91) • **87**

Cabernet Sauvignon Napa Valley Estate 1986 • $28 • (09/30/89) • **84**

Cabernet Sauvignon Napa Valley Estate 1985 • $30 • (08/31/88) • **92**

Cabernet Sauvignon Napa Valley Estate Reserve 1991 • $26 • (07/31/94) • **91**

Cabernet Sauvignon Napa Valley Estate Reserve 1990 • $25 • (12/15/93) • **90**

Cabernet Sauvignon Napa Valley Estate Reserve 1989 • $25 • (10/31/92) HR • **93**

Cabernet Sauvignon Napa Valley Rutherford Estate Reserve 1993: Combines ripe, complex fruit flavors with a sense of balance and finesse. Shows off currant, cedar, tobacco and spice flavors and finishes with a pleasantly fruity aftertaste. Drink now. • $30 • (11/15/96) • **88**

Cabernet Sauvignon Rutherford Estate Reserve 1994: Shows better than in an earlier tasting, but it's still hard to look past the up-front oak and cedary flavors. Does unveil some pleasant currant and berry flavors, making this a good but unexceptional 1994. 3,233 cases made. • $37 • (03/31/98) • **83**

Cabernet Sauvignon Rutherford Estate Reserve 1992 • $30 • (07/31/95) • **89**

Chardonnay Napa Valley Carneros 1996: Clean, crisp and simple, with pleasantly ripe and spicy citrus, pear and apple flavors that linger. Drink now. 7,677 cases made. • $18 • (05/15/98) • **87**

Chardonnay Napa Valley Carneros 1995: Young and tightly wound, this is austere in style with hints of pear, grapefruit and melon. Finishing with crisp, lively acidity, it can stand short-term cellaring. 8,506 cases made. • $14 • (05/15/97) • **88**

Chardonnay Napa Valley Carneros 1994: Marked by bracing acidity, it slowly unfolds to reveal more depth and flavors of pear and citrus with an earthy, leesy accent. Short-term cellaring may soften it a bit. Drink now. Much better than an earlier sample. 6,999 cases made. • $16 • (10/15/96) • **87**

Chardonnay Napa Valley Carneros 1993 • $14 • (07/31/95) • **83**

Chardonnay Napa Valley Estate Reserve 1993 • $18 • (07/31/95) • **82**

Chardonnay Rutherford Estate Reserve 1995: Clean and tart, with a nice core of citrusy pear and apple notes. This tight young wine can stand short-term cellaring, and it has a reputation for aging well. 1,551 cases made. • $18 • (06/15/97) • **88**

Chardonnay Rutherford Estate Reserve 1994: Bright and lively, with hints of pear and citrus, particularly lime. Finish has a nicely fruity aftertaste, with a pleasing touch of oak. 2,050 cases made. • $21 • (07/31/96) • **88**

SEVEN HILLS | OREGON

Cabernet Sauvignon Columbia Valley Klipsun Vineyard 1994: A firm, chunky, chewy style that packs a lot of berry, herb and chocolate flavors between the layers of gritty tannins, making this a wine to cellar until at least 2001 to 2004. 400 cases made. • $22 • (07/31/97) • **88**

Cabernet Sauvignon Columbia Valley Klipsun Vineyard 1993: Bright and lively. Jammy blackberry, raspberry and currant flavors are accented by slightly sweet, spicy notes from oak, but the fruit is front and center. Finish could be richer. Drink now. 180 cases made. • $20 • (09/15/96) • **88**

Cabernet Sauvignon Columbia Valley Klipsun Vineyard 1992: Ripe, round and generous, a silky mouthful of black cherry and plum fruit with minty-vanilla grace notes, wrapping smoothly around the fine tannins on the finish. Drink now. 440 cases made. • $20 • (07/31/96) • **90**

Cabernet Sauvignon Columbia Valley Klipsun Vineyard 1991 • $20 • (10/15/94) • **81**

Cabernet Sauvignon Oregon 1993: Pleasantly fruity and light, with a spicy, minty character that adds some interest to the flavors. Soft and drinkable now. 600 cases made. • $12 • (03/31/96) • **82**

Cabernet Sauvignon Oregon 1991 • $10 • (10/15/94) • **85**

Cabernet Sauvignon Walla Walla Valley 1990 • $20 • (09/30/93) • **90**

Cabernet Sauvignon Walla Walla Valley 1989 • $20 • (03/31/92) • **85**

Cabernet Sauvignon Walla Walla Valley Seven Hills Vineyard 1995: Has a tough shell around a lithe core of blackberry and currant flavors that echo on the coffee-scented finish. Best from 2000. 550 cases made. • $23 • (03/31/98) • **87**

Cabernet Sauvignon Walla Walla Valley Seven Hills Vineyard 1991 • $22 • (10/15/94) • **87**

Merlot Columbia Valley 1995: Goes for intensity of flavor, with a solid, driving core of blueberry, plum and spicy chocolate overtones and hints of pepper. Picks up a layer of spicy oak on the vibrant finish. Drink now. 400 cases made. • $20 • (08/31/97) • **90**

Merlot Columbia Valley 1994: An open texture allows the plum, berry and anise flavors to take the spotlight. Drink now. 200 cases made. • $18 • (09/15/96) • **87**
Merlot Columbia Valley Klipsun Vineyard 1995: Crisp, bright and generous with its blueberry and currant flavors that persist in a lively bead of jazzy fruitiness on the long finish. Needs to develop a little more richness; try now. 200 cases made. • $24 • (08/31/97) • **89**
Merlot Walla Walla Valley 1990 • $18 • (03/15/93) • **88**
Merlot Walla Walla Valley Seven Hills Vineyard 1995: Tight, chewy and smoky, with pretty berry flavor sneaking through on the finish, where a significantly smoky, ashy layer makes itself felt. Drink now. 600 cases made. • $24 • (08/31/97) • **85**
Merlot Walla Walla Valley Seven Hills Vineyard 1994: Marked by a silky texture and straightforward flavors of toasty plum and berry. Lighter than most Washington Merlots. Drinkable now. 350 cases made. • $24 • (09/15/96) • **86**
Merlot Walla Walla Valley Seven Hills Vineyard 1993 • $22 • (09/30/95) • **88**
Merlot Walla Walla Valley Seven Hills Vineyard 1992 • $20 • (11/30/94) • **84**
Pinot Gris Willamette Valley 1996: A solid white wine with pretty melon and almond flavors that turn slightly rough on the finish. Ready to drink. 750 cases made. • $13 • (08/31/97) • **83**
White Riesling Columbia Valley 1995: Off-dry, bright and lively, with disarmingly fresh peach and floral flavors. 900 cases made. • $7 • (08/31/96) • **85**
White Riesling Columbia Valley 1994 • $7 • (09/30/95) • **85**
White Riesling Oregon 1993 • $6 • (10/31/94) • **85**

SEVEN PEAKS | CALIFORNIA

Chardonnay California 1996: Smoothly textured, with a strong melony flavor. Finishes with pleasant lemon-lime notes. 25,000 cases made. • $12 • (09/30/97) • **87**
Chardonnay Edna Valley Reserve 1996: Smooth, ripe and creamy, with complex and sharply focused vanilla, pear, citrus and spice flavors. Drink now through 2001. • $18 • (06/30/98) • **88**

SHADOW BROOK | CALIFORNIA

Cabernet Sauvignon Napa Valley 1985 • $9 • (07/15/91) • **84**
Pinot Noir Napa Valley 1990 • $9 • (09/30/92) • **79**

SHAFER | CALIFORNIA

Cabernet Sauvignon Stags Leap District 1994: Clean, ripe and supple, marked by cherry, currant and anise notes before the earthy, leathery tannins clamp down. Try now. 5,000 cases made. • $28 • (06/30/97) • **88**
Cabernet Sauvignon Stags Leap District 1993: Smooth and supple, particularly for a '93, with a pleasant band of ripe cherry, plum and currant flavors. Drinks well now. 5,000 cases made. • $24 • (09/15/96) • **86**
Cabernet Sauvignon Stags Leap District 1992 • $22 • (09/30/95) CS • **91**
Cabernet Sauvignon Stags Leap District 1991 • $21 • (08/31/94) HR • **90**
Cabernet Sauvignon Stags Leap District 1990 • $20 • (11/15/93) • **90**
Cabernet Sauvignon Stags Leap District 1989 • $19 • (08/31/92) • **86**
Cabernet Sauvignon Stags Leap District 1988 • $20 • (08/31/91) • **88**
Cabernet Sauvignon Stags Leap District 1987 • $19 • (07/31/90) • **92**
Cabernet Sauvignon Stags Leap District 1986 • $20 • (09/30/89) SS • **93**
Cabernet Sauvignon Stags Leap District 1985 • $16 • (11/15/88) • **88**
Cabernet Sauvignon Stags Leap District 1984 • $14 • (12/15/87) SS • **93**
Cabernet Sauvignon Stags Leap District 1982 • $13 • (06/16/85) • **90**
Cabernet Sauvignon Stags Leap District 1980 • $11 • (02/15/84) • **73**
Cabernet Sauvignon Stags Leap District 1978 • $50 • (11/15/92) • **91**
Cabernet Sauvignon Stags Leap District Hillside Select 1997: A bit reduced, with floral and currant notes, this is a dense, chewy, complex young wine, overflowing with earthy currant, plum, black cherry and spice. Finishes with chewy but ripe and complex tannins. • $NA • (07/31/98) (BT) • **95-99**
Cabernet Sauvignon Stags Leap District Hillside Select 1996: Smooth, rich and polished, loaded with complex currant, black cherry, anise, sage and mineral flavors, this is a deeply concentrated and beautifully crafted young wine. 2,000 cases made. • $NA • (06/15/97) (BT) • **95-99**
Cabernet Sauvignon Stags Leap District Hillside Select 1994: Deliciously complex, with a wide array of flavors—earthy currant, black cherry, dusty sage and cedary oak. Serves up lots of goodies, revealing depth and concentration, and the long, full finish picks up cedar and coffee notes. Best after 1999 or 2001. 2,000 cases made. • $75 • (10/15/97) • **95**
Cabernet Sauvignon Stags Leap District Hillside Select 1993: A big, broad wine, generous and lush in flavor, packed with rich currant, leather, earth, tar, cedar, anise, mint and smoke nuances. There's plenty of depth and concentration to the flavors, and the tannins are big-league. Has a long, rich aftertaste. Best now to 2001. 2,000 cases made. • $60 • (10/31/97) CS • **94**
Cabernet Sauvignon Stags Leap District Hillside Select 1992: Offers a world of flavor, complex and well focused; a rich, concentrated band of cherry, currant, mineral and spice. Holds its flavor, focus and intensity through a long aftertaste. Can easily age into 2000 and beyond. 2,000 cases made. • $50 • (11/15/96) HR • **93**
Cabernet Sauvignon Stags Leap District Hillside Select 1991 • $45 • (11/15/95) CS • **93**
Cabernet Sauvignon Stags Leap District Hillside Select 1990 • $38 • (12/15/95) • **90**
Cabernet Sauvignon Stags Leap District Hillside Select 1989 • $35 • (05/15/94) • **90**
Cabernet Sauvignon Stags Leap District Hillside Select 1988 • $35 • (03/31/93) • **88**
Cabernet Sauvignon Stags Leap District Hillside Select 1987 • $56 • (07/31/92) • **88**
Cabernet Sauvignon Stags Leap District Hillside Select 1987: An amazing wine, perhaps the most youthful in this tasting. Serves up layers of ripe, rich currant, cherry, chocolate, spice, anise and vanilla flavors that are plush, supple and deeply concentrated, all the while maintaining its supple tannins. Delicious now, it appears to have the depth and concentration to age another decade with ease. 2,000 cases made. • $56 • (12/15/97) • **96**
Cabernet Sauvignon Stags Leap District Hillside Select 1986 • $45 • (03/15/91) HR • **91**
Cabernet Sauvignon Stags Leap District Hillside Select 1986: Dark, ripe, rich and intense, it's one of the more complex and concentrated '86s, with a long life still ahead. The core of currant, mineral, cherry, coffee and herb flavors is young and lively, and the tannins are ripe and vibrant. 2,000 cases made. • $32 • (12/15/96) • **90**
Cabernet Sauvignon Stags Leap District Hillside Select 1985 • $48 Ⓐ • (05/31/90) CS • **91**
Cabernet Sauvignon Stags Leap District Hillside Select 1984 • $35 • (04/30/89) • **89**
Cabernet Sauvignon Stags Leap District Hillside Select 1983 • $22 • (07/31/88) • **84**
Chardonnay Napa Valley Barrel Select 1993 • $16 • (04/30/95) • **87**
Chardonnay Napa Valley Carneros Red Shoulder Ranch 1996: Elegant and refined, with subtle notes of creamy pear, vanilla, citrus and apple that are well focused and long, lively on the finish. Drink now through 2001. 5,000 cases made. • $30 • (05/31/98) HR • **92**
Chardonnay Napa Valley Carneros Red Shoulder Ranch 1995: Spicy and perfumed, with a floral Muscat-like edge, but there's plenty of fruit to like, as hints of pear, melon and apple come through. Fans of spicy Chardonnays will find this especially pleasing. 3,500 cases made. • $30 • (05/31/97) • **91**
Chardonnay Napa Valley Carneros Red Shoulder Ranch 1994: Big, ripe, intense and juicy, loaded with rich, complex flavors. The echoes of ripe pear, anise, fig and spice are cast nicely in a full-bodied style. Yet for all its size and depth, it maintains a sense of elegance and finesse right through the long finish. 3,500 cases made. • $23 • (06/15/96) HR • **93**
Firebreak Napa Valley 1994: Young, tight and tannic, offering lots of flavor, with currant, anise, mineral and spicy nuances, and a long, full finish. Ready to drink. A blend of Sangiovese and Cabernet Sauvignon. 500 cases made. • $25 • (07/31/97) • **88**
Firebreak Stags Leap District 1993 • $24 • (02/29/96) • **84**
Firebreak Stags Leap District 1992 • $22 • (11/30/94) • **89**
Firebreak Stags Leap District 1991 • $20 • (12/15/93) • **85**
Merlot Napa Valley 1995: Smooth, ripe and supple, with a pleasant band of currant, herb and sage notes, finishing with tender tannins and good length. Drinks well now. 6,000 cases made. • $28 • (12/15/97) • **86**
Merlot Napa Valley 1994: Lean and leathery, with a narrow band of cherry and plum-tinged Merlot flavors. Slowly opens up to reveal more complexity, but it's not up to par for this winery. 6,000 cases made. • $26 • (06/30/97) • **85**
Merlot Napa Valley 1993 • $24 • (12/15/95) • **88**
Merlot Napa Valley 1992 • $21 • (06/15/95) • **88**
Merlot Napa Valley 1991 • $20 • (09/15/94) • **83**
Merlot Napa Valley 1990 • $18 • (05/31/92) HR • **91**
Merlot Napa Valley 1989 • $18 • (08/31/91) • **87**
Merlot Napa Valley 1988 • $17 • (12/31/90) • **83**
Merlot Napa Valley 1987 • $15 • (10/15/89) • **92**
Merlot Napa Valley 1986 • $13 • (12/31/88) • **91**
Merlot Napa Valley 1985 • $NA • (12/15/87) HR • **90**
Merlot Napa Valley 1984 • $13 • (02/28/87) • **87**
Merlot Napa Valley 1983 • $10 • (02/16/86) • **93**

Zinfandel Napa Valley Last Chance 1983 • $7 • (02/16/86) • **73**

SHAFER VINEYARD CELLARS | OREGON

Gewürztraminer Willamette Valley 1993 • $6 • (11/30/94) • **78**
Pinot Noir Willamette Valley 1988 • $14 • (02/28/93) • **74**
Riesling Willamette Valley Miki's Sweet Delight 1991 • $11/375ml • (11/30/94) • **80**

SHALE RIDGE | CALIFORNIA

Chardonnay Monterey 1996: Bright and refreshing, with a minty-herbal accent to the pretty lemon flavors. A new wine from Lockwood. 20,000 cases made. • $10 • (11/15/97) • **83**
Merlot Monterey 1996: Smoke, licorice and small berries lead the way in this lean, somewhat tight wine. The finish is short, due to coarse tannins. May flesh out in a few years. 5,000 cases made. • $12 • (02/28/98) • **84**

SHENANDOAH | CALIFORNIA

Barbera Amador County Sobon Family Vineyards 1996: Light, spicy, distinctly woodsy, with a supple core of anise-scented plum flavor. Ready to drink. 620 cases made. • $15 • (03/31/98) BB • **84**
Black Muscat Amador County 1992 • $10 • (11/15/93) • **84**
Cab-Shiraz Amador County 1993: Broad and chewy, providing a nice mouthful of berry and spice flavors wrapped in a layer of tannin. Try now. 450 cases made. • $10 • (12/15/95) • **85**
Cabernet Franc Amador County Varietal Adventure Series 1989 • $10 • (08/31/91) • **87**
Cabernet Sauvignon Amador County 1994: Ripe and plummy, with supple cherry, berry and spice notes and smooth, fleshy tannins. Finishes with a pleasant, fruity aftertaste. 583 cases made. • $10 • (11/30/96) • **86**
Cabernet Sauvignon Amador County 1992 • $10 • (11/15/94) BB • **88**
Cabernet Sauvignon Amador County 1991 • $10 • (11/15/94) • **79**
Cabernet Sauvignon Amador County 1990 • $10 • (11/15/92) • **74**
Cabernet Sauvignon Amador County Artist Series 1987 • $10 • (02/28/91) • **80**
Cabernet Sauvignon Amador County Artist Series 1986 • $12 • (10/31/88) • **86**
Cabernet Sauvignon Amador County Artist Series 1984 • $9 • (08/31/87) • **89**
Orange Muscat Amador County 1992 • $10 • (11/15/93) • **84**
Orange Muscat Amador County 1990 • $10 • (06/15/92) • **84**
Port Amador County 1989 • $7/375ml • (09/30/95) • **81**
Sangiovese Amador County 1995: Earthy, gamy flavors overtake the modest fruit in this distinctive but overly chewy red. Best from 1999. 379 cases made. • $12 • (07/31/97) • **81**
Sangiovese Amador County 1994 • $12 • (04/30/96) • **84**
Sauvignon Blanc Amador County 1997: Starts off with an earthy aroma but follows up with pleasant sweet-pea, fig, lemon and grapefruit flavors. Firm and bright on the palate, it finishes with a touch of anise. 4,600 cases made. • $8 • (05/15/98) • **86**
Sauvignon Blanc Amador County 1996: Crisp and floral, with lovely citrus, green apple and passion fruit flavors, finishing brightly and with appealing zinginess. 2,958 cases made. • $8 • (04/30/97) • **88**
Sauvignon Blanc Amador County 1995 • $8 • (05/31/96) • **89**
Sauvignon Blanc Amador County 1994 • $7 • (08/31/95) • **84**
Sauvignon Blanc Amador County 1993 • $8 • (02/28/95) • **82**
Serene Varietal Adventure Series Amador County 1989 • $8 • (03/31/91) • **74**
Zinfandel Amador County Classico Varietal Adventure Series 1990 • $6 • (09/15/92) BB • **82**
Zinfandel Amador County Classico Varietal Adventure Series 1989 • $6 • (04/30/91) BB • **82**
Zinfandel Amador County Sobon Family Vineyards Vintner's Selection 1995: A soft, supple wine that balances pretty raspberry and tar flavors with the spice of new oak barrels, maintaining a welcome sense of harmony. Ready to drink. 600 cases made. • $15 • (12/15/97) • **86**
Zinfandel Amador County Special Reserve 1996: Ripe and broad, with a generous layer of blueberry and smoke flavor coursing through the medium-weight finish. Delivers the goods at a reasonable price. Nice now, best from 1999. 4,643 cases made. • $9 • (03/31/98) BB • **85**
Zinfandel Amador County Special Reserve 1995: Marked by a racy, earthy edge, this shows off lots of pepper and raspberry flavors. Ready to drink. 3,572 cases made. • $9 • (04/30/97) • **84**
Zinfandel Amador County Special Reserve 1994 • $8 • (04/30/96) • **87**
Zinfandel Amador County Special Reserve 1993 • $8 • (10/15/95) • **87**
Zinfandel Amador County Special Reserve 1992 • $8 • (02/28/95) • **83**
Zinfandel Amador County Special Reserve 1991 • $6 • (06/15/93) • **76**
Zinfandel Amador County Special Reserve 1990 • $8 • (06/15/93) • **78**
Zinfandel Amador County Special Reserve 1989 • $8 • (02/29/92) • **84**
Zinfandel Amador County Special Reserve 1987 • $8 • (07/31/89) • **81**
Zinfandel Amador County Special Reserve 1986 • $7 • (07/15/88) • **86**
Zinfandel Amador County Special Reserve 1985 • $7 • (02/15/88) • **85**
Zinfandel Fiddletown Special Reserve 1983 • $7 • (10/15/86) • **74**
Zinfandel-Sirah Late Harvest Sierra Foothills 1991 • $8 • (10/15/94) • **81**
Zingiovese Amador County 1993 • $9 • (05/15/95) • **77**

SHOOTING STAR | CALIFORNIA

Cabernet Franc Clear Lake 1995: Silky, supple and generous with its spicy blackberry and smoke flavors. Tannins maintain a grip, but it shows signs of softening nicely by 1999. 500 cases made. • $10 • (11/30/97) • **87**
Cabernet Franc Clear Lake 1994: Well oaked, with lots of smoky, toasty, vanilla-scented flavors, but the ripe currant and cherry flavors stand up to it. Finishes with firm but supple tannins. Ready to drink. 400 cases made. • $8 • (09/15/96) BB • **87**
Cabernet Franc Clear Lake 1992 • $9 • (12/31/94) • **84**
Cabernet Franc Clear Lake 1991 • $9 • (10/15/93) BB • **85**
Chardonnay California 1996: Solid if unexciting. The core of spicy pear and light oak is tasty, though somewhat one-dimensional and simple. Drink now through 2000. 1,000 cases made. • $14 • (07/31/98) • **83**
Chardonnay Mendocino 1993 • $9 • (11/15/94) • **82**
Chardonnay Sonoma County 1994: Distinctive for its nectarine and tangerine accents, featuring complex flavors of modest proportions. 800 cases made. • $10 • (05/15/96) • **84**
Grenache Washington Côte de Columbia 1995: Balances ripe, bright fruit flavors against an undertone of earthy, gamy notes for a smooth, easy-to-drink wine with real personality. Ready now. 600 cases made. • $9 • (04/30/97) • **87**
Grenache Washington Côte de Columbia 1994 • $8 • (09/30/95) • **85**
Lemberger Washington Blue Franc 1995: A sturdy wine with bright plum and currant flavors that dance lightly across the finish. Ready to drink. 1,200 cases made. • $8 • (04/30/97) • **84**
Merlot Clear Lake 1996: A ripe, juicy style, with a core of herb and mint to balance the plum and raspberry flavors. Toasty, smoky oak aromas round things off nicely, with a plush finish hinting at licorice. Drink now. 1,200 cases made. • $14 • (07/31/98) • **89**
Merlot Clear Lake 1994: Serves up a rich, chewy core of currant, cherry, plum and toasty oak, with a lot more substance and richness than expected from Clear Lake. Tasty now; can age short term. 500 cases made. • $12 • (07/31/96) • **89**
Merlot Clear Lake 1992 • $9 • (06/30/94) • **87**
Pinot Noir Mendocino 1994: Marked by ripe cherry, berry and spicy leather aromas and flavors. On solid footing, if somewhat one-dimensional. A good value at this price. 500 cases made. • $9 • (01/31/97) • **82**
Pinot Noir Mendocino 1993 • $9 • (02/28/95) BB • **86**
Rosé Mendocino Pacini Vineyard Zin Gris 1995: Pleasant ripe cherry and strawberry flavors that pick up a hint of watermelon on the finish. • $8 • (09/15/96) • **87**
Sauvignon Blanc Lake County 1996: An odd one, with peach and lemon-lime flavors at the fore. The blend is fairly simple and a bit cloying on the finish. 1,000 cases made. • $9 • (11/30/97) • **81**
Sauvignon Blanc Lake County 1995: Broad and smooth, with a racy, steely note at the center that makes the orange and pear flavors vibrant. Ready now. 400 cases made. • $9 • (02/28/97) • **87**
Syrah Lake County 1996: Firmly tannic, with chewy currant, plum, black cherry, tobacco and spicy notes all adding up to a complex flavor profile. Can use a little time to shed some of its tannins; best from now to 2004. 1,500 cases made. • $12 • (04/30/98) • **88**
Zinfandel Lake County 1996: Well focused and balanced, with appealing ripe cherry, wild berry and briary notes. Becomes diffused on the finish, but altogether a nice wine—especially at this price. Drink now through 2000. 900 cases made. • $11 • (05/31/98) • **86**
Zinfandel Lake County 1995: A touch earthy and murky, with a strong oak presence that adds a tarry dill character, but in the end the flavors come

Key: SS—Spectator Selection CS—Cellar Selection HR—Highly Recommended BB—Best Buy $NA—Price not available Ⓐ—Auction Price (BT)—Barrel Tasting
Dates in parentheses indicate the issues in which the ratings were published.

together, showing enough complexity to hold your interest. 1,000 cases made. • $11 • (02/28/97) • **83**

Zinfandel Lake County 1994 • $8 • (04/30/96) • **89**

Zinfandel Lake County 1993 • $8 • (02/28/95) BB • **87**

Zinfandel Mendocino 1995: Ripe and earthy, with a spicy core of ripe plum and cherry flavors and a minty edge. Complex and well balanced, with supple tannins that are just a touch coarse. Ready to drink. 400 cases made. • $10 • (04/30/97) • **88**

Zinfandel Mendocino Zin Gris Pacini Vineyard 1994 • $8 • (10/15/95) • **78**

SIDURI | CALIFORNIA

Pinot Noir Anderson Valley Rose Vineyard 1995: Smooth, ripe and generous, with pretty plum, cherry, berry and vanilla shadings, it turns even more complex on the finish. Very pretty, supple and harmonious, with a wonderful aftertaste. 75 cases made. • $40 • (05/31/97) • **92**

Pinot Noir Anderson Valley Rose Vineyard 1994 • $30 • (01/31/96) • **89**

Pinot Noir Oregon 1996: Light and smooth, aiming for delicacy over power, with pretty plum and vanilla flavors that linger gently on the finish. Very nice now, could be best in 2000. 200 cases made. • $28 • (05/15/98) • **88**

Pinot Noir Oregon 1995: Just delicious; a mouthful of concentrated blackberry, chocolate, black cherry and spice flavors that swirl, swivel, glide and soar through the elegant finish. Lovely and supple now, it's hard to imagine it getting much better, but should be fine through 2000. 147 cases made. • $20 • (11/30/96) • **91**

Pinot Noir Sonoma Coast Hirsch Vineyard 1996: Strives for complexity, with appealing toasty oak, berry and cherry flavors up front, but could use a bit more concentration, richness and depth. Drink now. 40 cases made. • $40 • (04/30/98) • **86**

Pinot Noir Sonoma Coast Hirsch Vineyard 1995: Marked by spicy cola and earth flavors up front, this wine evolves slowly, ending with a complex interplay of flavors. Ready to drink. 50 cases made. • $40 • (05/31/97) • **88**

Pinot Noir Sonoma Mountain Van Der Kamp Vineyard 1996: Up-front plum and cherry flavors are appealing in a light, elegant manner, but it loses intensity and turns simpler on the finish. Still, it's better than the 1996 Siduri Carneros bottlings. 275 cases made. • $40 • (04/30/98) • **86**

SIERRA VISTA | CALIFORNIA

Cabernet Sauvignon El Dorado 1989 • $11 • (11/15/92) • **76**

Cabernet Sauvignon El Dorado 1988 • $11 • (04/15/92) • **84**

Cabernet Sauvignon El Dorado 1984 • $9 • (03/31/88) • **86**

Cabernet Sauvignon El Dorado Five Star Reserve 1991 • $22 • (11/15/94) • **86**

Chardonnay El Dorado 1996: Somewhat meaty in texture, this wine offers pleasant orange and honeyed tones, but is lacking in complexity. Finishes with some nice, toasty oak. 800 cases made. • $16 • (01/31/98) • **84**

Fleur de Montage Red El Dorado 1996: Ripe, generous and beautifully balanced to show off black cherry, blackberry, spice and tar flavors. Flavorful, but stops just this side of effusive or hearty. Very nicely done all around. Best through 1999. A blend of Syrah, Grenache, Mourvèdre, and Cinsault. 500 cases made. • $14 • (12/15/97) • **89**

Syrah El Dorado 1995: Distinctly earthy. A chewy wine with solid blackberry and anise flavors. Needs until 1999 or 2000 to fill itself out. 1,200 cases made. • $10 • (12/15/97) • **86**

Syrah El Dorado Sierra Syrah 1985 • $9 • (04/15/89) • **82**

Syrah El Dorado Sierra Syrah 1983 • $9 • (04/15/89) • **89**

Viognier El Dorado 1996: Nice body, with a smooth, silky quality. The flavors hint at hazelnut, pear and peach, with attractively moderate acidity. Clean and bright on the finish. 400 cases made. • $20 • (02/28/98) • **86**

Zinfandel El Dorado 1996: A silky-smooth texture lends an attractive mouthfeel, with mild flavors redolent of plum and blackberry. A licorice touch on the finish adds interest. Drink now. 1,000 cases made. • $13 • (06/15/98) • **85**

Zinfandel El Dorado 1990 • $9 • (10/15/92) • **73**

Zinfandel El Dorado 1989 • $9 • (03/31/92) • **78**

Zinfandel El Dorado Five Star Reserve 1995: Firm, with a layer of toasty oak running through lush black cherry and clove flavors. Unfortunately, it dries out on the mouth-puckering finish. Best from 2000 through 2003. 500 cases made. • $22 • (06/15/98) • **82**

Zinfandel El Dorado Herbert Vineyards 1986 • $8 • (03/31/89) • **84**

Zinfandel El Dorado Reeves Vineyard Special Reserve 1985 • $12 • (04/30/88) • **73**

SIGNORELLO | CALIFORNIA

Cabernet Sauvignon Napa Valley 1995: Dark, ripe and intense, with spicy currant, plum and blackberry flavors, picking up pretty, spicy oak, anise and tobacco notes. Remains remarkably elegant and spicy for all its dark fruit flavors. Has the tannic strength to age. Best from 2000 through 2008. 1,600 cases made. • $30 • (07/31/98) • **93**

Cabernet Sauvignon Napa Valley 1994: A well-proportioned, medium-bodied style with attractive green olive, currant and cherry flavors, and just the right dash of oak and tannin. Best after 1999 or 2000. 1,325 cases made. • $30 • (11/15/97) • **88**

Cabernet Sauvignon Napa Valley Founder's Reserve 1995: Ripe and plummy, with a firm tannic backbone and plenty of black cherry, smoky, toasty oak, anise, earth and tarry nuances that are rich and focused. Finishes with a long, complex, intricate aftertaste echoing currant, coffee and spice. Best from 2001 through 2010. • $55 • (07/31/98) • **93**

Cabernet Sauvignon Napa Valley Founder's Reserve 1994: Distinctive for its earthy mineral notes, this is an intense, deeply concentrated, firmly tannic wine laced with currant and wild berry flavors. Will need several years cellaring to soften and reveal all its nuances. 431 cases made. • $55 • (09/30/97) • **90**

Cabernet Sauvignon Napa Valley Founder's Reserve 1993: Ripe and fruity, as complex flavors echo black cherry, currant, anise and light oak shadings. Try now. 575 cases made. • $32 • (05/15/96) • **88**

Cabernet Sauvignon Napa Valley Founder's Reserve 1992 • $32 • (09/15/95) CS • **90**

Cabernet Sauvignon Napa Valley Founder's Reserve 1991 • $30 • (09/30/94) • **90**

Cabernet Sauvignon Napa Valley Founder's Reserve 1990 • $30 • (10/15/93) • **92**

Cabernet Sauvignon Napa Valley Founder's Reserve 1989 • $25 • (07/15/92) • **85**

Cabernet Sauvignon Napa Valley Founder's Reserve 1988 • $25 • (05/15/91) • **92**

Chardonnay Napa Valley 1996: Sharply focused, ripe, rich and lively, with complex, concentrated pear, apple, spice and peach flavors. A bright and lively style that finishes with vanilla and hazelnut. Drink now through 2002. 1,000 cases made. • $30 • (07/31/98) • **92**

Chardonnay Napa Valley 1995: Rich and complex, in a bold style, with layers of ripe fig, pear, apple and pretty toasty oak shadings that add dimension and depth on the finish. 992 cases made. • $28 • (06/15/97) • **92**

Chardonnay Napa Valley 1994: An elegant style where the ripe fig, pear and melon flavors are shaded by toasty oak. Turns complex and spicy on the finish, where the smoky flavors are a touch astringent. 1,200 cases made. • $20 • (03/31/96) • **89**

Chardonnay Napa Valley 1993 • $20 • (04/15/95) • **88**

Chardonnay Napa Valley Founder's Reserve 1996: Intense, supple and complex, with a creamy texture and ripe, rich pear, fig, melon and apricot flavors that are sharply focused. Long and full-bodied on the finish, with vanilla and hazelnut notes. Drink now through 2002. 434 cases made. • $48 • (07/31/98) HR • **93**

Chardonnay Napa Valley Founder's Reserve 1995: Ripe, elegant and complex, with a wonderful array of fruit flavors, notes of pear, apple, citrus and hazelnut, and a lingering aftertaste. 470 cases made. • $44 • (06/15/97) • **92**

Chardonnay Napa Valley Founder's Reserve 1994: Bold, ripe, rich and complex, offering tiers of ripe fig, pear, apple and honeysuckle notes before picking up pleasant, toasty oak and hazelnut. Still a bit tannic, but very concentrated and deep in flavor. 475 cases made. • $30 • (05/15/96) • **92**

Chardonnay Napa Valley Founder's Reserve 1993 • $30 • (07/31/95) • **90**

Chardonnay Napa Valley Hope's Cuvée 1995: Bold and concentrated, brimming with layers of ripe, rich fig, pear, citrus and buttery hazelnut flavors, this is an impressive wine all-around, with a wonderful aftertaste. 42 cases made. • $60 • (06/15/97) • **93**

Il Taglio Napa Valley 1991 • $9 • (03/31/94) • **86**

Merlot Napa Valley 1990 • $25 • (03/15/94) • **82**

Petite Sirah Napa Valley 1990 • $15 • (10/15/93) • **84**

Pinot Noir Carneros Las Amigas Vineyard 1995: Serves up ripe cherry, strawberry, earth, tea and spice, along with some firm, chewy tannins, finishing with dill and sweet oak flavors. Drink now to 2001. 400 cases made. • $48 • (03/31/98) • **88**

Pinot Noir Carneros Las Amigas Vineyard 1994: Ripe, bright and lively, with attractive plum, cherry and wild berry flavors that come across as simple and uncomplicated. 200 cases made. • $35 • (01/31/97) • **85**

Pinot Noir Napa Valley 1988 • $25 • (02/28/91) • **85**

Pinot Noir Napa Valley Founder's Reserve 1992 • $28 • (03/31/95) • **87**

Pinot Noir Napa Valley Founder's Reserve 1991 • $28 • (02/28/94) • **87**
Pinot Noir Napa Valley Founder's Reserve 1990 • $25 • (02/28/93) • **82**
Pinot Noir Napa Valley Founder's Reserve 1989 • $25 • (11/15/91) • **78**
Pinot Noir North Coast 1994: Young, tight and a bit on the tart side, this is well focused, with crisp cherry and wild berry notes that persist on the finish. Drinks well now. 650 cases made. • $22 • (01/31/97) • **85**
Pinot Noir North Coast Founder's Reserve 1993 • $28 • (12/31/95) • **86**
Sauvignon Blanc Napa Valley 1993 • $15 • (02/28/95) • **89**
Sémillon Napa Valley 1995: Dark straw-colored, with hazelnut and charred aromas. On the palate, it shows honeyed, buttery notes and finishes with bright acidity. 556 cases made. • $20 • (11/30/97) • **87**
Sémillon Napa Valley 1994 • $18 • (05/15/96) • **87**
Sémillon Napa Valley 1993 • $18 • (08/31/95) • **86**
Zinfandel Napa Valley 1993 • $18 • (09/15/95) • **86**
Zinfandel Napa Valley 1990 • $15 • (06/15/93) • **75**

SILVAN RIDGE | OREGON

Chardonnay Oregon 1994: Crisp in texture, offering a nice layer of spicy apple and caramel flavors that remain taut and fresh on the finish. Ready now. 1,232 cases made. • $15 • (05/15/98) • **87**
Chardonnay Oregon 1993 • $19 • (01/31/96) • **88**
Chardonnay Willamette Valley Brunker Hall Vineyard 1995: Soft, open-textured Chardonnay, offering pretty pear and nutmeg flavors that whittle down to a thin stream on the finish. Ready now. 144 cases made. • $18 • (05/15/98) • **84**
Merlot Oregon 1994: A firm, chewy texture doesn't get in the way of the tangy berry, chocolate and spice flavors. Try now. 162 cases made. • $25 • (11/30/96) • **86**
Merlot Rogue Valley 1995: Soft and fruity, with pretty raspberry and strawberry notes that linger on the finish. A streak of woodsy flavor peeks through. Drink now. 782 cases made. • $22 • (05/15/98) • **84**
Merlot Walla Walla Valley Seven Hills Vineyard 1994: The brilliant color and powerful berry and spice aromas make this a wine worth cellaring. Flavors are densely layered under chewy, fine tannins and crisp acidity. Best from now to 2000. 114 cases made. • $28 • (01/31/97) • **88**
Muscat Oregon Early Semi-Sparkling 1995: Lightly sparkling, and charming for its floral, spicy pear and vanilla flavors that linger nicely on the sweet but balanced finish. 895 cases made. • $12 • (02/28/97) • **86**
Muscat Oregon Early Semi-Sparkling 1994 • $12 • (03/31/96) • **90**
Muscat-Huxelrebe Oregon Early Late Harvest 1995: Sweet, almost syrupy, with a citrusy streak that nearly keeps it in balance, finishing with pear-nectar flavors. Ready now. 223 cases made. • $16 • (02/28/97) • **85**
Muscat-Huxelrebe Oregon Early Late Harvest Ultra 1994 • $16/375ml • (03/31/96) • **90**
Pinot Gris Oregon 1995: Light, soft and delicate, with a nice array of orange, pear and hazelnut flavors that linger with freshness on the finish. 3,133 cases made. • $15 • (02/28/97) • **86**
Pinot Gris Oregon 1994 • $15 • (01/31/96) • **86**
Pinot Gris Oregon 1993 • $12 • (08/31/95) • **85**
Pinot Noir Willamette Valley 1995: Has pretty berry and spice aromas and flavors, turning thin and hard on the finish. Try in 1999. 2,257 cases made. • $19 • (05/15/98) • **82**
Pinot Noir Willamette Valley 1994: Ripe and generous with its aromas and flavors of black currant and spice that pick up a smoky note on the finish. Has firm tannins, but an open texture. Try now. 1,252 cases made. • $22 • (10/31/96) • **88**
Pinot Noir Willamette Valley 1993 • $19 • (01/31/96) • **84**
Pinot Noir Willamette Valley 1992 • $19 • (11/30/94) • **82**
Pinot Noir Willamette Valley Bockelman Vineyard 1994: Smooth and appealing for its generous plum, prune, vanilla and spice flavors that linger on the polished finish. Delicious now. 33 cases made. • $30 • (10/15/96) • **89**
Pinot Noir Willamette Valley Hoodview Vineyard 1995: Shows some ripe black cherry flavor, shaded with earthy spice notes. Despite some rough tannins, this has charm. Try now. 250 cases made. • $22 • (05/15/98) • **85**
Pinot Noir Willamette Valley Visconti Vineyard 1994: Light in color and texture, with plum and spice flavors that pick up a toasty accent on the finish. Drinkable now. 250 cases made. • $26 • (10/15/96) • **86**
Riesling Late Harvest Oregon Botrytised Cluster Select 1994 • $30/375ml • (03/31/96) • **88**

Key: SS—Spectator Selection CS—Cellar Selection HR—Highly Recommended BB—Best Buy $NA—Price not available Ⓐ—Auction Price (BT)—Barrel Tasting
Dates in parentheses indicate the issues in which the ratings were published.

Riesling Willamette Valley Forgeron Vineyard Dry 1993 • $8 • (01/31/96) • **81**

SILVER FALLS | OREGON

Pinot Noir Willamette Valley 1987 • $10 • (02/15/90) • **75**

SILVER HORSE | CALIFORNIA

Cabernet Sauvignon Paso Robles 1993: Medium-weight, with a simple band of cherry and berry fruit and a vegetal edge. 1,000 cases made. • $13 • (03/31/96) • **79**
Cabernet Sauvignon Paso Robles 1990 • $10 • (11/15/94) • **82**
Chardonnay Paso Robles 1994: Clean and well crafted, with lots of smoky, toasty oak and a nice core of pear and apple fruit. 1,200 cases made. • $11 • (02/29/96) • **87**
Pinot Noir Paso Robles 1994 • $13 • (02/29/96) • **81**
Zinfandel Paso Robles 1992 • $12 • (02/28/95) • **84**

SILVER LAKE | WASHINGTON

Cabernet Sauvignon Columbia Valley 1994: A tart, jazzy style, offering more bracing acidity than focused flavor, but what's there is nice—berry, cedar and vanilla. Try now. 650 cases made. • $13 • (09/30/97) • **83**
Cabernet Sauvignon Columbia Valley 1993: Lean and crisp. A zingy mouthful of tart berry and toast flavors. Drink now. 1,613 cases made. • $11 • (09/15/96) • **83**
Cabernet Sauvignon Columbia Valley 1991 • $13 • (09/30/94) • **80**
Cabernet Sauvignon Columbia Valley Reserve 1993: Tart and lively. A juicy mouthful of currant and plum flavor with a hint of citrus on the finish. Try now. 375 cases made. • $16 • (09/30/97) • **88**
Cabernet Sauvignon Columbia Valley Reserve 1992: Firm and fresh, offering spicy, caramel-scented blackberry and plum flavors that glide effortlessly through the finish. Try now. 214 cases made. • $25 • (09/30/96) • **85**
Cabernet Sauvignon Columbia Valley Reserve 1989 • $16 • (09/30/94) • **86**
Cabernet-Merlot Columbia Valley 1995: Lean, crisp and juicy, with berry and tobacco flavors that remain tart and bracing on the finish. Drinkable now. A blend of 60 percent Cabernet Sauvignon and 40 percent Merlot. 1,100 cases made. • $9 • (09/30/97) • **85**
Chardonnay Columbia Valley 1995: Ripe, and generous with its perfumy melon and pear flavors. Drink soon. 2,700 cases made. • $10 • (09/15/97) • **85**
Chardonnay Columbia Valley 1994: Open-textured, with generous pear, orange and mineral flavors that provide plenty of muscle and character. Drinkable now. 1,960 cases made. • $10 • (09/15/96) • **87**
Chardonnay Columbia Valley 1993 • $8 • (09/30/95) • **83**
Chardonnay Columbia Valley Reserve 1995: Very ripe and generous with its spicy pear flavors, it's a crisp wine with solid character. Ready now. 800 cases made. • $16 • (09/30/97) • **86**
Chardonnay Columbia Valley Reserve 1994: Firm and chewy, its modest pear and toast flavors still lurk below the surface. Drinkable now. 556 cases made. • $13 • (09/15/96) • **80**
Chardonnay Columbia Valley Reserve 1993 • $13 • (09/30/95) • **82**
Chardonnay Columbia Valley Sentinel Peak 1994: Lacks the polish and charm to support the overly earthy and leesy flavors. 1,424 cases made. • $7 • (09/15/96) • **74**
Chardonnay Columbia Valley Sentinel Peak 1993 • $7 • (09/30/95) • **84**
Fumé Blanc Columbia Valley 1995: Soft, silky and floral, offering enough pear and herb flavors to make for solid drinking sooner rather than later. 1,300 cases made. • $8 • (09/30/97) • **84**
Fumé Blanc Columbia Valley 1994: Polished and refreshing, with its lime-scented nectarine and sage flavors. Ready to drink. 751 cases made. • $6 • (09/30/96) • **84**
Fumé Blanc Columbia Valley 1993 • $6 • (09/30/95) • **80**
Fumé-Chardonnay Columbia Valley Sentinel Peak 1994: Light, smooth and appealing for its creamy apple and spice flavors. Just a hint of tangy, green citrus flavor suggests Sauvignon Blanc. 280 cases made. • $6 • (09/30/96) • **86**
Fumé-Chardonnay Columbia Valley Sentinel Peak 1993 • $6 • (09/30/95) • **78**
Ice Wine Columbia Valley 1989 • $25 • (06/15/91) • **85**
Johannisberg Riesling Columbia Valley 1994: Soft and frankly sweet, with caramel and pine flavors that rob it of liveliness. 1,921 cases made. • $5 • (09/15/96) • **79**

Merlot Columbia Valley 1994: Firm in texture, vibrant in flavor, emphasizing blackberry and smoke flavors that remain lively through the solid finish. Try now. 1,550 cases made. • $13 • (09/30/97) • **88**

Merlot Columbia Valley 1993: Rich and focused, showing smoothly concentrated toasty plum flavors that narrow on the finish. Drinkable now. 1,185 cases made. • $13 • (09/15/96) • **87**

Merlot Columbia Valley 1990 • $16 • (09/30/94) • **86**

Merlot Columbia Valley Reserve 1993: A firm, chewy style of Merlot, tannic on the surface with juicy plum and tobacco flavors lurking beneath. Try now. 375 cases made. • $16 • (09/30/97) • **86**

Merlot Columbia Valley Reserve 1992: Has an earthy, gamy edge to the solid prune and black cherry flavors. Finishes with firm tannins that need from now to 2000 to settle down. 214 cases made. • $25 • (09/30/96) • **85**

Merlot Columbia Valley Sentinel Peak 1993 • $8 • (09/30/95) • **78**

Pinot Noir Willamette Valley Reserve 1993: Smells riper than it tastes, but the currant and smoke aromas and flavors hang in there against a cedary, chewy texture. 575 cases made. • $13 • (10/15/96) • **87**

Pinot Noir Willamette Valley Reserve 1992 • $13 • (03/31/96) • **84**

Reserve Columbia Valley 1993: Tart but juicy. A zingy wine with bright raspberry, mint and vanilla flavors that swirl through the nicely polished finish. Needs until 2000 to settle down. A blend of 58 percent Cabernet Sauvignon, 20 percent Merlot, 11 percent Cabernet Franc, and 11 percent Malbec. 250 cases made. • $16 • (09/30/97) • **87**

Reserve Columbia Valley 1992: Firm and chewy, its currant and blueberry flavors are buried under a layer of fine tannins that will soften by 2000 to 2002. 201 cases made. • $25 • (09/15/96) • **85**

Reserve Columbia Valley 1990 • $16 • (09/30/95) • **84**

Riesling Columbia Valley Dry 1994: Focused, resiny notes puncuate the modest green apple flavors in this off-dry sipper. 795 cases made. • $5 • (09/15/96) • **81**

Riesling Columbia Valley Ice Wine 1989 • $25 • (04/15/95) • **85**

Riesling Late Harvest Columbia Valley 1994: Sweet, in a dessert style, but neither gooey nor syrupy, showing spicy pear and apricot flavors and a touch of honey on the finish. 488 cases made. • $8 • (09/30/96) • **86**

Sémillon Chardonnay Columbia Valley 1995: Crisp and bright, it's a juicy wine with pretty melon and herbal flavors. 500 cases made. • $7 • (09/30/97) • **85**

Sémillon Columbia Valley 1995: Crisp in texture, with flavors on the earthy side. A solid wine with more tobacco and spice than fruit. Try now. 700 cases made. • $6 • (09/30/97) • **81**

Sentinel Peak Columbia Valley 1993: Lean and tangy, offering an unusual zing of acidity. The flavors are reminiscent of unripe berry. 1,800 cases made. • $7 • (09/30/95) • **79**

SILVER OAK | CALIFORNIA

Cabernet Sauvignon Alexander Valley 1993: One of this appellation's most consistent Cabernet bottlings, it's a bit awkward at this young stage, but most of the pieces are in place. The currant, plum and cedary oak flavors are outstanding. Should be softer in a year or two, likely best in 2001. 40,000 cases made. • $40 • (09/30/97) CS • **90**

Cabernet Sauvignon Alexander Valley 1992: Smooth and polished, with well-focused cherry, plum and currant flavors wrapped in a firm dose of dill-scented oak. Still a bit awkward, but has all the right ingredients of an outstanding bottle of wine. Drinkable now and into 2000. • $58 Ⓐ • (11/15/96) • **90**

Cabernet Sauvignon Alexander Valley 1991 • $32 • (11/15/95) HR • **91**

Cabernet Sauvignon Alexander Valley 1990 • $64 Ⓐ • (11/15/94) • **89**

Cabernet Sauvignon Alexander Valley 1989 • $29 • (11/15/93) • **82**

Cabernet Sauvignon Alexander Valley 1988 • $38 • (10/31/92) HR • **91**

Cabernet Sauvignon Alexander Valley 1987: Intense and concentrated, with plenty of exotic, spicy cedar and sage notes and a rich core of currant, vanilla, berry, anise and tar flavors. The finish lingers long. Ready to drink. 20,000 cases made. • $72 Ⓐ • (12/15/97) • **93**

Cabernet Sauvignon Alexander Valley 1986: Smooth, supple and harmonious. Shows flavors of spicy mineral, currant, anise and cedar, and a long plummy aftertaste. Wonderful balance and finesse on the finish. Drinkable now. This is the most elegant and refined of the 1986s from Silver Oak, all of which are outstanding. • $96 Ⓐ • (12/15/96) • **92**

Cabernet Sauvignon Alexander Valley 1985 • $87 Ⓐ • (10/31/89) • **86**

Cabernet Sauvignon Alexander Valley 1984 • $75 Ⓐ • (12/15/88) • **85**

Cabernet Sauvignon Alexander Valley 1983 • $48 Ⓐ • (11/30/87) • **82**

Cabernet Sauvignon Alexander Valley 1982 • $36 Ⓐ • (02/15/87) • **90**

Cabernet Sauvignon Alexander Valley 1981 • $38 Ⓐ • (09/30/86) • **92**

Cabernet Sauvignon Alexander Valley 1980 • $62 Ⓐ • (03/01/85) • **90**

Cabernet Sauvignon Alexander Valley 1979 • $55 Ⓐ • (02/15/84) • **81**

Cabernet Sauvignon Alexander Valley 1978 • $86 Ⓐ • (11/15/92) • **91**

Cabernet Sauvignon Napa Valley 1993: Starts with a cedary aroma and keeps a woody edge, but delivers enough chewy currant and plummy flavors to merit attention. Still a bit rough around the edges, and the tannins still stick out with a drying sensation. Try now, but be wary of it drying out. Tasted twice, with consistent notes. • $50 • (10/15/97) • **88**

Cabernet Sauvignon Napa Valley 1992: Big, ripe and oaky in style, but has the flavors to match. This is loaded with currant, plum and wild berry flavors framed by smoky, toasty oak nuances, and finishes with a long, complex, concentrated aftertaste. Tempting now, but worthy of cellaring too; buy one for tonight and a couple to cellar. 8,000 cases made. • $75 Ⓐ • (11/15/96) CS • **93**

Cabernet Sauvignon Napa Valley 1991 • $36 • (11/15/95) • **90**

Cabernet Sauvignon Napa Valley 1990: A complex marriage of cedar and dill flavors, tart cherry, berry and tarry accents. Flavors remain intense and concentrated on the finish, with chewy tannins. Try now. • $78 Ⓐ • (09/15/96) • **89**

Cabernet Sauvignon Napa Valley 1989 • $29 • (11/15/93) • **86**

Cabernet Sauvignon Napa Valley 1988 • $40 • (10/31/92) • **88**

Cabernet Sauvignon Napa Valley 1987: Starts out earthy, with a slight cheesy edge, then more fruit emerges, with hints of currant and berry. A metallic quality stays with the wine, and while it doesn't ruin the flavor, it's a mild distraction. Quite tannic on the aftertaste. 3,000 cases made. • $89 Ⓐ • (12/15/97) • **87**

Cabernet Sauvignon Napa Valley 1986: Shows the same exotic oak and spice character of the Bonny's Vineyard bottling, but is a shade less concentrated and perhaps more elegant. Features lots of complex flavors, ranging from plum and black cherry to dill and spice. Finishes with smooth tannins. • $104 Ⓐ • (12/15/96) • **92**

Cabernet Sauvignon Napa Valley 1985 • $75 Ⓐ • (10/31/89) • **88**

Cabernet Sauvignon Napa Valley 1984 • $55 Ⓐ • (12/15/88) • **88**

Cabernet Sauvignon Napa Valley 1983 • $40 Ⓐ • (11/30/87) • **87**

Cabernet Sauvignon Napa Valley 1982 • $56 Ⓐ • (02/15/87) CS • **96**

Cabernet Sauvignon Napa Valley 1981 • $62 Ⓐ • (09/15/86) • **75**

Cabernet Sauvignon Napa Valley 1980 • $64 Ⓐ • (03/01/85) • **80**

Cabernet Sauvignon Napa Valley 1979 • $41 Ⓐ • (03/01/84) • **83**

Cabernet Sauvignon Napa Valley Bonny's Vineyard 1991: Dark, rich and complex, with tiers of polished currant, cherry, herb, dill and tea flavors. A delicious mouthful of Cabernet that packs in lots of flavor yet manages to remain elegant and not overly tannic. Picks up a complex tarry note on the aftertaste. • $125 Ⓐ • (09/15/96) CS • **93**

Cabernet Sauvignon Napa Valley Bonny's Vineyard 1987: Shows wonderful complexity and density of flavor, with layers of smoky currant, coffee, plum, cherry, cedar, dill and oak. A beautifully orchestrated wine, young and oozing with fruit flavors. The tannins are smooth and supple, and the flavors go on and on. Best now through 2004. 460 cases made. • $85 • (12/15/97) • **95**

Cabernet Sauvignon Napa Valley Bonny's Vineyard 1986: A delicious treat. Ripe, rich and complex, it's a remarkably well-balanced and flavorful wine, still tasting young, with tiers of smoke, toasty oak, ripe plum, cherry and berry flavors, and lots of exotic spicy notes on the finish. Drinks well now, but can surely age until 2004 or 2006. • $77 Ⓐ • (12/15/96) • **94**

Cabernet Sauvignon Napa Valley Bonny's Vineyard 1985 • $134 Ⓐ • (11/15/90) • **83**

Cabernet Sauvignon Napa Valley Bonny's Vineyard 1984 • $85 • (10/15/89) • **84**

Cabernet Sauvignon Napa Valley Bonny's Vineyard 1982 • $44 Ⓐ • (09/15/87) • **66**

Cabernet Sauvignon Napa Valley Bonny's Vineyard 1979 • $67 Ⓐ • (06/16/84) • **81**

Cabernet Sauvignon North Coast 1974 • $77 Ⓐ • (11/15/94) • **83**

SILVER RIDGE | CALIFORNIA

Cabernet Sauvignon California Barrel Select 1994: A light-textured Cabernet, with strawberry and cherry flavors leading the way. Simple and supple. 5,000 cases made. • $10 • (10/31/97) • **82**

Cabernet Sauvignon Napa Valley 1989 • $10 • (11/15/94) • **84**

Cabernet Sauvignon Napa Valley Barrel Select 1992: A fairly simple, straightforward wine with toasty aromas. Blackberry and herb flavors mark the finish. 3,000 cases made. • $10 • (11/30/96) • **83**

Chardonnay California 1996: Although dominated by rich toasty oak flavors, this wine finds balance with pear, apple and spice emerging on the finish. Drink now. 10,000 cases made. • $10 • (06/30/98) • **83**

Chardonnay California 1995: Toasty, smoky notes precede a core of hazelnut and lemon flavors. Finishes brightly, but lacks depth. • $10 • (07/31/97) • **85**

Chardonnay California Barrel Fermented 1994: Ripe and spicy, with generous nutmeg, toast and pear flavors that narrow to a sharp focus on the finish. 5,000 cases made. • $10 • (06/30/96) • **86**

Merlot California 1992 • $12 • (09/15/94) • **80**

Merlot California Barrel Select 1996: A lightweight blend of plum, cherry, cedar and smoke flavors. Straightforward and simple, yet tasty. 10,000 cases made. • $15 • (03/31/98) • **82**

Merlot California Barrel Select 1992: Medium-bodied, with simple cherry and berry fruit flavors and light oak shadings with mild tannins. Good but nothing more. 2,000 cases made. • $10 • (08/31/96) • **81**

Pinot Noir California Barrel Select 1996: Light, floral and fragrant, a simple wine with modest herb and berry flavors. Ready now. 2,500 cases made. • $10 • (12/31/97) • **83**

SILVERADO HILL CELLARS | CALIFORNIA

Cabernet Sauvignon Napa Valley 1995: Simple and sweet, with juicy sour cherry and butterscotch flavors. A bit too candied to be recommended. Drink now. 1,200 cases made. • $13 • (07/31/98) • **78**

Cabernet Sauvignon Napa Valley 1992: This wine has a nice sense of proportion as its currant, herb and berry flavors are offset by light oak flavors and firm tannins. Drinks well now. 1,100 cases made. • $15 • (11/15/96) • **87**

Chardonnay Napa Valley 1994: A light style that's harmonious and delicately spicy, accenting the green apple flavor. 3,500 cases made. • $10 • (06/15/96) • **85**

Chardonnay Napa Valley Art Cuvée 1996: Slightly sour, with a hint of oxidation. Finishes with metallic flavors. 5,000 cases made. • $10 • (06/15/98) • **70**

Chardonnay Napa Valley Art Cuvée 1995: A straightforward, hard-edged Chardonnay, lean in structure, with modest pear and orange flavors. 7,000 cases made. • $10 • (12/15/96) • **80**

Chardonnay Napa Valley Founder's Reserve 1994: Tart lime and earthy pineapple flavors. A touch on the lean side. 450 cases made. • $15 • (07/31/96) • **82**

Chardonnay Napa Valley Le Mélange Supérieur 1996: Earthy, sour and bitter, with rancid butter and toast notes. Avoid. Tasted twice, with consistent notes and scores. Past its prime. 1,600 cases made. • $13 • (07/31/98) • **65**

Chardonnay Napa Valley Le Mélange Supérieur Select Reserve 1995: Earthy, minty, soapy flavors make this unappealing. 1,508 cases made. • $14 • (07/31/97) • **75**

Chardonnay Napa Valley Traditional Cuvée 1996: Softly textured, with subtle, pleasant flavors of citrus, butter and toast. Doesn't have intensity, but the flavors are focused and linger on the finish. Drink now. 300 cases made. • $10 • (07/31/98) • **84**

Chardonnay Napa Valley Traditional Cuvée 1995: Soft and simple, with a cardboardy nuance to the simple pear flavors. 6,236 cases made. • $11 • (07/31/97) • **81**

Chardonnay Napa Valley Winemaker's Traditional Méthode 1994: Distinctive, with a character reminiscent of apple cider that persists on the supple finish. 4,500 cases made. • $10 • (06/15/96) • **83**

Chardonnay Napa Valley Winemaker's Traditional Méthode 1993 • $10 • (07/31/95) • **83**

SILVERADO VINEYARDS | CALIFORNIA

Cabernet Sauvignon Napa Valley 1993: Well crafted, with attractive herb, cherry and currant flavors. Finishes with the requisite tannins, but they're not excessive for a wine this young. 9,500 cases made. • $20 • (08/31/96) • **87**

Cabernet Sauvignon Napa Valley 1992 • $19 • (03/31/95) SS • **90**

Cabernet Sauvignon Napa Valley 1987: Smooth, ripe and harmonious, with layers of black cherry, plum, currant and anise, finishing with a smooth texture and a long, lingering aftertaste. Best now through 2000. 11,025 cases made. • $41 Ⓐ • (12/15/97) • **92**

Cabernet Sauvignon Napa Valley 1986: This shows that you don't need high extraction or massive amounts of fruit. You need balance, and this wine's got it. The currant, anise and cherry flavors are youthful, with supple tannins and fine length. Shows more rich, complex, fruit flavor than many of the higher-priced heavy hitters. 9,800 cases made. • $13 • (12/15/96) • **91**

Cabernet Sauvignon Napa Valley Limited Reserve 1994: A dramatic effort. This Cabernet is bold, ripe, rich and concentrated, gushing with minty currant, black cherry, plum and wild berry flavors. It's highly extracted and delivers a long, rich aftertaste. Drinks well now, will be even better from 2000 to 2002. 3,369 cases made. • $72 Ⓐ • (11/30/97) HR • **93**

Cabernet Sauvignon Napa Valley Limited Reserve 1993: A solid effort, with a tight band of herb, currant and cherry. Well balanced, with a pleasing dash of toasty oak, it holds together nicely on the finish. With its tannic strength, best to try it in 2000. 2,447 cases made. • $60 Ⓐ • (02/28/97) • **90**

Cabernet Sauvignon Napa Valley Limited Reserve 1990 • $40 • (10/31/93) CS • **97**

Cabernet Sauvignon Napa Valley Limited Reserve 1987: An exotic style, rich in flavor, texture and body, with layers of ripe currant, black cherry, anise, mint, sage and tea, finishing with supple tannins and a long, lingering aftertaste. Has a way to go yet. 763 cases made. • $69 Ⓐ • (12/15/97) • **96**

Cabernet Sauvignon Napa Valley Limited Reserve 1986: This lived up to its billing, and may well be the wine of the vintage. It's ultra rich, deep and complex, loaded with cassis, currant, plum and black cherry flavors. Finishes with ripe, sweet tannins, not the dryness and austerity found in so many '86s. Drinkable now. 1,400 cases made. • $35 • (12/15/96) • **97**

Cabernet Sauvignon Stags Leap District 1991 • $17 • (04/30/94) SS • **93**

Cabernet Sauvignon Stags Leap District 1990 • $16 • (06/30/93) HR • **90**

Cabernet Sauvignon Stags Leap District 1989 • $19 • (08/31/92) • **81**

Cabernet Sauvignon Stags Leap District 1988 • $18 • (03/31/91) • **86**

Cabernet Sauvignon Stags Leap District 1987 • $25 • (04/15/90) SS • **92**

Cabernet Sauvignon Stags Leap District 1986 • $25 • (08/31/89) SS • **94**

Cabernet Sauvignon Stags Leap District 1985 • $13 • (11/15/88) SS • **91**

Cabernet Sauvignon Stags Leap District 1984 • $12 • (11/30/87) • **89**

Cabernet Sauvignon Stags Leap District 1983 • $12 • (12/31/86) • **92**

Cabernet Sauvignon Stags Leap District 1982 • $12 • (09/30/86) • **82**

Cabernet Sauvignon Stags Leap District 1981 • $10 • (12/16/84) • **91**

Cabernet Sauvignon Stags Leap District Limited Reserve 1991 • $40 • (11/15/94) CS • **93**

Cabernet Sauvignon Stags Leap District Limited Reserve 1987 • $45 • (10/31/91) HR • **93**

Chardonnay Napa Valley 1995: Smooth, rich and creamy, with a lovely array of citrus, especially grapefruit, pear and melon notes that are clean, attractive and well focused. Lots of fruit with just the slightest trace of oak in the background. 29,696 cases made. • $18 • (04/30/97) • **89**

Chardonnay Napa Valley 1994: Well made. Though a touch tart and flinty, pear and citrus flavors, particularly grapefruit, preside. An elegant, understated wine for those who don't want to be blown away by oak. 32,213 cases made. • $11 • (07/31/96) • **87**

Chardonnay Napa Valley 1993 • $15 • (05/31/95) • **87**

Chardonnay Napa Valley Limited Reserve 1995: Elegant and complex, with a band of smoky oak, ripe pear, fig and melon flavors, and lots of spicy nuances. Finishes with good length, depth and concentration. 1,151 cases made. • $36 • (03/31/98) • **88**

Chardonnay Napa Valley Limited Reserve 1994: Smooth, rich and harmonious, with layers of ripe fig, melon, pear and toasted oak. Given its concentration and flavor, it's remarkably elegant and supple, with a long, complex aftertaste. Ready now through 2001. 2,244 cases made. • $36 • (05/31/97) • **93**

Merlot Napa Valley 1994: Decidedly herbal, with a strong mint and pickle-barrel quality that's unsettling. A curious, eccentric style that somehow pleases, even if it doesn't remind you of pure Merlot. 11,108 cases made. • $20 • (02/28/97) • **85**

Merlot Napa Valley 1992 • $18 • (01/31/95) • **85**

Merlot Napa Valley 1991 • $17 • (09/15/94) • **85**

Merlot Napa Valley Limited Reserve 1992: Supple and fruity, with bright, lively, juicy cherry and currant, picking up a trace of herb and chocolate. Finishes with crisp acidity and firm tannins, but they're not overbearing. 1,279 cases made. • $45 • (08/31/96) • **89**

Merlot Stags Leap District 1990 • $17 • (06/15/93) • **87**

Merlot Stags Leap District 1989 • $16 • (04/15/92) • **87**

Merlot Stags Leap District 1988 • $16 • (05/31/91) • **86**

Merlot Stags Leap District 1987 • $14 • (04/15/90) • **92**

Merlot Stags Leap District 1986 • $12 • (08/31/89) • **91**

Merlot Stags Leap District 1984 • $13 • (12/15/87) • **78**

Sangiovese Napa Valley 1995: Pushes the style envelope, perhaps too far, with some unusually high-toned flavors. Shows strong candied berry and cherry flavors with plenty of oak. Drinkable now. 2,038 cases made. • $20 • (12/15/97) • **84**

Key: SS—Spectator Selection CS—Cellar Selection HR—Highly Recommended BB—Best Buy $NA—Price not available Ⓐ—Auction Price (BT)—Barrel Tasting
Dates in parentheses indicate the issues in which the ratings were published.

Sangiovese Napa Valley 1994: A well-oaked style, with a stalky, green edge to the plum and berry notes, but it lacks focus and harmony. 1,873 cases made. • $20 • (02/28/97) • **82**

Sauvignon Blanc Napa County 1996: A bit clumsy at first, with piney, grassy notes, it calms down to show vanilla, melon and grapefruit and modest acidity. 18,754 cases made. • $11 • (11/30/97) • **84**

Sauvignon Blanc Napa Valley 1995: Ripe, mouth-filling and flavorful; a core of pear, citrus and smoky flavors and a smooth, round finish. 21,411 cases made. • $10 • (08/31/96) • **86**

Sauvignon Blanc Napa Valley 1994 • $9 • (02/29/96) • **86**

Sauvignon Blanc Napa Valley 1993 • $9 • (08/31/94) • **84**

Sauvignon Blanc-Chardonnay-Sémillon Late Harvest Napa Valley Limited Reserve NV • $25/375ml • (04/30/95) • **90**

SILVERWOOD | CALIFORNIA

Claret Napa Valley 1988 • $9 • (10/15/92) • **70**

SIMI | CALIFORNIA

Altaire North Coast 1992 • $8 • (07/31/93) • **78**

Cabernet Sauvignon Alexander Valley 1997: Grapey, with a smooth texture and bright cherry, plum and wild berry flavors. Finishes with smoky, toasty oak and firm tannins. • $NA • (07/31/98) (BT) • **90-94**

Cabernet Sauvignon Alexander Valley 1996: Ripe, rich and grapey with lots of pretty flavors and aromas, it's gushing with currant, black cherry and spicy, toasty oak. Tannins are intense but supple. • $NA • (06/15/97) (BT) • **95-99**

Cabernet Sauvignon Alexander Valley 1994: Young, tight and tannic, but the core of currant, herb, tea and leather slowly comes to the fore, and it's nicely balanced. Cellar this for a couple years for optimum drinking. Best after 2000. 20,000 cases made. • $18 • (10/31/97) • **88**

Cabernet Sauvignon Alexander Valley 1993: Smooth and polished, this is appealing for its ripe plum and cherry flavors and supple, balanced tannins. Well crafted for drinking now. 20,000 cases made. • $17 • (11/15/96) • **88**

Cabernet Sauvignon Alexander Valley 1992 • $15 • (10/15/95) • **89**

Cabernet Sauvignon Alexander Valley 1989 • $14 • (06/15/93) • **77**

Cabernet Sauvignon Alexander Valley 1988 • $15 • (07/31/92) • **84**

Cabernet Sauvignon Alexander Valley 1981 • $20 • (11/01/85) • **79**

Cabernet Sauvignon Alexander Valley 1980 • $28 • (07/01/84) • **81**

Cabernet Sauvignon Alexander Valley 1979 • $28 • (04/01/84) SS • **91**

Cabernet Sauvignon Alexander Valley Reserve 1992: Best Simi Reserve in years. Fresh and vibrant, this is a remarkably complex and concentrated young wine that serves up lots of fresh cherry, currant, plum and berry flavors. Shows a notable amount of finesse and harmony, as the tannins are supple and well-integrated, with a long aftertaste. Drinkable now. 4,000 cases made. • $31 Ⓐ • (11/15/96) CS • **93**

Cabernet Sauvignon Alexander Valley Reserve 1991 • $35 • (10/15/95) HR • **92**

Cabernet Sauvignon Alexander Valley Reserve 1988 • $33 • (03/31/93) • **87**

Cabernet Sauvignon Alexander Valley Reserve 1987: Dark, ripe, rich and intense, with a solid core of currant, anise, berry and spice, picking up a trace of cedary oak. With breathing, it shows more finesse and polish. Still a long way to go. 1,700 cases made. • $29 Ⓐ • (12/15/97) • **92**

Cabernet Sauvignon Alexander Valley Reserve 1986: Supple and harmonious, this wine is drinking well now—the tannins are softening and the core of herb, currant and berry flavor is developing complexity and finesse. Avoids the drying tannins of many from this vintage. Ready now, but worthy of cellaring into 2000. 1,800 cases made. • $29 Ⓐ • (12/15/96) • **91**

Cabernet Sauvignon Alexander Valley Reserve 1985 • $34 Ⓐ • (08/31/90) SS • **94**

Cabernet Sauvignon Alexander Valley Reserve 1981 • $30 • (12/15/88) • **86**

Cabernet Sauvignon Alexander Valley Reserve 1980 • $NA • (06/01/86) • **87**

Cabernet Sauvignon Alexander Valley Reserve 1979 • $NA • (02/01/86) • **77**

Cabernet Sauvignon Alexander Valley Reserve 1978 • $17 • (02/01/86) • **69**

Cabernet Sauvignon Alexander Valley Reserve 1974 • $46 Ⓐ • (02/15/90) • **85**

Cabernet Sauvignon Alexander Valley Special Reserve 1974 • $54 • (11/15/94) • **82**

Cabernet Sauvignon Mendocino-Sonoma-Napa Counties Reserve 1982 • $50 • (04/15/89) • **90**

Cabernet Sauvignon Sonoma County 1987 • $17 • (05/15/91) • **89**

Cabernet Sauvignon Sonoma County 1985 • $21 • (09/30/89) • **91**

Cabernet Sauvignon Sonoma County 1984 • $20 • (10/31/88) • **86**

Cabernet Sauvignon Sonoma County 1982 • $15 • (11/15/86) • **90**

Cabernet Sauvignon Sonoma County Centennial Edition 1990 • $14 • (11/15/94) • **84**

Chardonnay Carneros 1996: A sleek, elegant style that delivers a lot of complex flavors ranging from ripe pear to spicy, toasty oak, to fig, melon and nutmeg. Wonderful balance, polish and finesse. Drink now through 2001. 6,000 cases made. • $21 • (07/31/98) • **91**

Chardonnay Sonoma County 1996: Appealing green apple, pear, honeysuckle and spicy apricot flavors emerge from behind a green note up front for a long, rich aftertaste. Drink now through 2001. 80,000 cases made. • $17 • (07/31/98) • **90**

Chardonnay Sonoma County 1995: Tight and firm, well focused, with a compact band of ripe pear, citrus and apple flavors, and even a hint of lime. Finishes with a crisp, lively aftertaste. 45,000 cases made. • $18 • (05/31/97) • **90**

Chardonnay Sonoma County Reserve 1995: Smooth, ripe, rich and creamy, with pretty pear, vanilla, tangerine and spicy flavors. Turns silky-smooth on the palate and finishes with a long, rich, complex aftertaste, where hints of anise and butterscotch emerge. Drink now through 2002. 3,500 cases made. • $29 • (07/31/98) • **93**

Chardonnay Sonoma County Reserve 1994: Truly exotic for its range of fig, tropical fruit, melon, grapefruit and spice flavors, and it shows a sense of elegance and finesse on the finish. Try now. 3,000 cases made. • $28 • (05/31/97) • **91**

Chardonnay Sonoma County Reserve 1993 • $28 • (06/15/96) HR • **92**

Pinot Noir Carneros 1994: The debut Pinot Noir from Simi. A cautious, understated style, with hints of herb, dried cherry, sage and spice. Fails to excite, but it's a pleasant enough bottle of wine. • $18 • (03/31/97) • **84**

Sauvignon Blanc Sonoma County 1996: A lighter-styled wine, with hints of grass, melon, lemon and spice. Bright and refreshing. 20,000 cases made. • $12 • (04/30/98) • **84**

Sauvignon Blanc Sonoma County 1995: Refined and focused, with subtle grapefruit, melon and starfruit tones. Finishes clean but quickly. 24,000 cases made. • $11 • (06/30/97) • **87**

Sauvignon Blanc Sonoma County 1993 • $9 • (08/31/95) • **84**

Sauvignon Blanc-Sémillon Sonoma County Sendal 1995: Starts off with hints of toffee, caramel, sage, pear and clove. Sits broadly on the palate, with brisk acidity and a moderate, vanillalike finish. A blend of 68 percent Sauvignon Blanc and 32 percent Sémillon. 1,500 cases made. • $18 • (04/30/98) • **87**

Sendal Sonoma County 1994: Lemon and spice flavors jump smartly to the fore in this polished, oak-accented Sauvignon Blanc-Sémillon blend. 1,100 cases made. • $16 • (08/31/96) • **85**

Shiraz Sonoma County 1995: Ripe and spicy, with lots of plum, cherry and berry flavors that fill out on the palate, before the firm tannins kick in. Drinks well now, can age, too. 300 cases made. • $17 • (09/30/97) • **87**

SINE QUA NON | CALIFORNIA

Queen of Spades Santa Barbara County 1994: Dark enough to remind you of a barrel sample, and while you might expect it to be tannic, it's not. It is delicious, though, with tiers of ripe black cherry, currant, anise and spice. Finishes with a complex smoky edge. Drinkable now, but worthy of short-term cellaring. 100 cases made. • $31 • (11/30/96) • **92**

Red Handed California 1995: Dark, ripe and complex, with a pretty array of plum, cherry and wild berry flavor that's rich and concentrated. Finishes with pretty spice and mineral notes. Delicious now, but worthy of short-term cellaring. A blend of Grenache, Syrah, and Mourvèdre. 80 cases made. • $31 • (12/15/97) • **92**

Syrah California The Other Hand 1995: Marked by a beefy, meaty, earthy quality, and the wood sticks out; try cellaring it in the hopes that it comes together. Try now. Tasted twice, with consistent notes. 400 cases made. • $31 • (12/31/97) • **84**

The Bride Arroyo Grande Valley 1995: Luscious. This intriguing blend is packed with passion fruit, citrus, fig and melon flavors, backed by bright acidity and a serious dose of sweet oak. Exotic and yummy. A blend of 50 percent Chardonnay and 50 percent Roussane. 180 cases made. • $31 • (06/15/97) • **92**

SINEANN | WASHINGTON

Cabernet Sauvignon Columbia Valley Block One Vineyard 1995: Crisp, focused and chewy. Not an elegant style, but likeable for its generous ripe currant, prune and anise flavors. Best from 2000 or 2002. 45 cases made. • $30 • (09/15/97) • **86**

Zinfandel Columbia Valley Old Vine 1994: Ripe and generous with its blackberry, wild strawberry and black pepper flavors that show plenty of richness on a supple frame. Drinkable now. 128 cases made. • $15 • (09/30/96) • **88**

SINSKEY, ROBERT | CALIFORNIA

Cabernet Sauvignon Stags Leap District 1989 • $22 • (11/15/92) • **89**
Chardonnay Napa Valley Los Carneros 1993 • $20 • (07/31/95) • **87**
Claret Carneros 1990 • $28 • (05/15/94) • **87**
Claret Carneros 1989 • $28 • (02/15/93) • **85**
Claret Carneros 1988 • $28 • (11/15/91) • **89**
Claret Stags Leap District 1993: A tight, crisp, firm young wine, with a solid core of spicy currant, anise, sage and herb. Finishes with firm tannins. Best to cellar short term. 1,059 cases made. • $30 • (05/15/98) • **89**
Claret Stags Leap District 1991 • $28 • (11/15/94) • **88**
Merlot Los Carneros 1995: Crisp tannins lead to ripe cherry and berry flavors of moderate depth and richness. Turns complex on the aftertaste, with a hint of cherry, but the tannins are firm. Best after 2000. 2,800 cases made. • $30 • (05/15/98) • **87**
Merlot Napa Valley 1987 • $18 • (03/31/91) • **88**
Merlot Napa Valley 1986 • $17 • (10/15/89) • **83**
Merlot Napa Valley Los Carneros 1992 • $18 • (04/30/96) • **85**
Merlot Napa Valley Los Carneros 1990 • $18 • (12/31/93) • **86**
Merlot Napa Valley Los Carneros 1989 • $18 • (05/31/92) • **83**
Pinot Noir Carneros 1995: Shows a nice core of concentrated plum, cherry and berry flavors, with fine oaky shadings. Drinks well now, but can stand a year in the cellar. 5,850 cases made. • $22 • (09/30/97) • **87**
Pinot Noir Napa Valley Carneros 1987 • $14 • (03/31/90) • **86**
Pinot Noir Napa Valley Carneros 1986 • $12 • (06/15/88) • **79**
Pinot Noir Napa Valley Los Carneros 1992 • $19 • (03/31/95) • **83**
Pinot Noir Napa Valley Los Carneros 1991 • $19 • (02/28/94) • **82**
Pinot Noir Napa Valley Los Carneros 1990 • $18 • (09/30/92) • **85**
Pinot Noir Napa Valley Los Carneros 1988 • $18 • (02/28/91) • **81**
Pinot Noir Napa Valley Los Carneros Reserve 1990 • $32 • (11/30/92) • **80**

SISKIYOU | OREGON

Pinot Noir Oregon Estate 1987 • $13 • (02/15/90) • **80**

SKY | CALIFORNIA

Zinfandel Mount Veeder 1990 • $16 • (09/30/93) • **88**
Zinfandel Mount Veeder 1989 • $13 • (10/15/92) • **87**
Zinfandel Napa Valley 1988 • $12 • (08/31/91) • **78**
Zinfandel Napa Valley 1987 • $17 • (10/15/90) • **90**
Zinfandel Napa Valley 1985 • $9 • (10/31/88) • **88**

SLAUGHTER LEFTWICH | TEXAS

Cabernet Sauvignon Texas 1989 • $9 • (02/29/92) • **76**

SMITH & HOOK | CALIFORNIA

Cabernet Sauvignon Monterey 1983 • $14 • (11/15/87) • **78**
Cabernet Sauvignon Monterey 1981 • $14 • (12/16/84) • **90**
Cabernet Sauvignon Napa County 1985 • $12 • (09/30/89) • **88**
Cabernet Sauvignon Napa County 1982 • $17 • (06/15/87) • **79**
Cabernet Sauvignon Santa Lucia Highlands 1994: Smoke, mint, bacon and herbs conspire happily, though unusually. Anise and black currant flavors are tempered, however, by a somewhat bitter, weedy edge. 4,239 cases made. • $18 • (09/30/97) • **85**
Cabernet Sauvignon Santa Lucia Highlands 1993: Firm and tight, but the cedar, herb and currant flavors work their way to the forefront. 2,753 cases made. • $18 • (11/15/96) • **87**
Cabernet Sauvignon Santa Lucia Highlands 1992 • $18 • (12/15/95) • **83**
Cabernet Sauvignon Santa Lucia Highlands 1991 • $18 • (11/15/94) • **86**
Cabernet Sauvignon Santa Lucia Highlands 1990 • $18 • (03/31/94) • **87**
Cabernet Sauvignon Santa Lucia Highlands 1988 • $15 • (11/15/91) • **80**
Cabernet Sauvignon Santa Lucia Highlands Masterpiece Edition 1994: Fairly smooth in texture, this displays strong smoke, beef and leather qualities, also anise, black currant and herbal flavors. A bit on the bright side. 419 cases made. • $35 • (11/30/97) • **86**
Cabernet Sauvignon Santa Lucia Highlands Masterpiece Edition 1992 • $30 • (12/15/95) • **88**
Merlot Napa County 1987 • $15 • (12/31/90) • **83**
Merlot Napa County 1986 • $20 • (08/31/89) • **86**
Merlot Santa Lucia Highlands 1995: Light, tart and distinctive for its racy cranberry and raspberry flavors, which linger on the finish as it becomes silkier. Ready to drink. 8,511 cases made. • $19 • (12/15/97) • **83**
Merlot Santa Lucia Highlands 1994: A hard-edged, stylized wine with pungent herbal and vegetal flavors that made this area's reds so controversial in the late 1970s and 1980s. 4,238 cases made. • $18 • (12/15/96) • **80**
Merlot Santa Lucia Highlands 1993: Lean and tough, with a band of cedar, herb, light cherry and currant flavors. 2,783 cases made. • $18 • (08/31/96) • **83**
Merlot Santa Lucia Highlands 1992 • $18 • (07/31/95) • **85**
Merlot Santa Lucia Highlands 1991 • $18 • (09/15/94) • **78**
Merlot Santa Lucia Highlands 1990 • $18 • (09/15/94) • **81**
Merlot Santa Lucia Highlands 1989 • $15 • (05/31/92) • **70**
Merlot Santa Lucia Highlands 1988 • $15 • (05/31/92) • **80**
Viognier Arroyo Seco 1996: Attractive nut, starfruit and peach flavors are followed by tangy acidity and a bright finish. A slight candied edge is somewhat distracting, however. 835 cases made. • $18 • (02/28/98) • **84**
Viognier Arroyo Seco 1995: A weird attempt at Viognier, with a thin band of innocuous flavors that are without any real substance. 288 cases made. • $18 • (04/30/97) • **70**

SMITH WINES, W.H. | CALIFORNIA

Pinot Noir Sonoma Coast 1996: Light and uncomplicated, with modest tea and wild berry flavors. Tasted twice, with consistent notes. 450 cases made. • $26 • (02/28/98) • **79**
Pinot Noir Sonoma Coast Hellenthal Vineyard 1996: Light in color, with plum and berry notes of modest concentration and complexity. Turns simple on the finish. 550 cases made. • $36 • (12/15/97) • **84**
Pinot Noir Sonoma Coast Hellenthal Vineyard 1995: A tremendous effort. Smooth, ripe, rich and flavorful, with a supple, elegant core of ripe cherry, plum, wild berry and nutmeg flavors, finishing with a cola and chocolate aftertaste. • $32 • (07/31/97) • **93**
Pinot Noir Sonoma Coast Hellenthal Vineyard 1994: Mature in color, but the flavors are ripe and fresh, with zesty cherry and plum notes. Picks up traces of earth and anise on the finish, where the tannins are smooth. 176 cases made. • $28 • (11/15/96) • **87**
Pinot Noir Sonoma Coast Hellenthal Vineyard Young Vines 1994 • $22 • (04/30/96) • **91**

SMITH-MADRONE | CALIFORNIA

Cabernet Sauvignon Napa Valley 1993: Solid if unexciting, with a modest band of Cabernet flavor, offering up hints of pepper and plum. 185 cases made. • $20 • (12/15/96) • **83**
Cabernet Sauvignon Napa Valley 1992: A big, ripe and powerful wine that needs time to settle out. The flavors are ripe, but the tannins are still rough and the alcohol stands out. Best after 2000. 600 cases made. • $17 • (12/15/96) • **82**
Cabernet Sauvignon Napa Valley 1985 • $19 • (04/15/90) • **74**
Cabernet Sauvignon Napa Valley 1984 • $14 • (12/31/88) • **92**
Cabernet Sauvignon Napa Valley 1980 • $13 • (01/01/84) • **83**

SMOTHERS BROTHERS | CALIFORNIA

Cabernet Sauvignon Sonoma Valley 1988 • $17 • (11/15/94) • **82**
Cabernet Sauvignon Sonoma Valley Remick Ridge Ranch 1990 • $18 • (11/15/94) • **87**
Cabernet Sauvignon Sonoma Valley Remick Ridge Ranch 1989 • $16 • (11/15/94) • **82**

SNOQUALMIE | WASHINGTON

Cabernet Sauvignon Columbia Valley 1989 • $11 • (03/15/94) • **87**
Cabernet Sauvignon Columbia Valley 1987 • $10 • (09/30/90) • **90**
Cabernet-Merlot Columbia Valley 1992 • $8 • (02/28/95) BB • **85**
Gewürztraminer Columbia Valley 1994 • $6 • (09/30/95) • **83**
Gewürztraminer Columbia Valley 1993 • $7 • (09/30/94) • **78**
Johannisberg Riesling Columbia Valley 1994 • $6 • (09/30/95) • **84**
Johannisberg Riesling Columbia Valley 1993 • $6 • (09/15/95) BB • **87**

Key: SS—Spectator Selection CS—Cellar Selection HR—Highly Recommended BB—Best Buy $NA—Price not available Ⓐ—Auction Price (BT)—Barrel Tasting
Dates in parentheses indicate the issues in which the ratings were published.

Johannisberg Riesling Columbia Valley Dry 1994 • $6 • (09/30/95) • **86**
Merlot Columbia Valley Reserve 1987 • $12 • (09/30/90) • **91**
Muscat Canelli Columbia Valley 1994 • $8 • (09/30/95) • **82**
Muscat Canelli Columbia Valley 1993 • $7 • (09/30/94) • **78**
Sémillon Columbia Valley 1994 • $6 • (07/31/95) • **81**
Sémillon Columbia Valley 1993 • $7 • (09/30/94) • **84**
White Riesling Late Harvest Columbia Valley 1988 • $7 • (10/15/89) • **84**

SNOWDEN

Cabernet Sauvignon Napa Valley 1997: Dark, ripe, rich and racy. Still malolactic but brimming with juicy, grapey Cabernet fruit, with lots of fresh, complex berry, cherry, currant and floral notes. Elegant finish. • $NA • (07/31/98) (BT) • **90-94**
Cabernet Sauvignon Napa Valley 1993: Deep, rich and concentrated, with layers of earthy currant, spice, cedar and berry flavors that pick up a nice, light, toasted oak edge and finish with length and complexity. Drink now. 385 cases made. • $35 • (07/31/97) • **92**

SOBON ESTATE | CALIFORNIA

Blush Shenandoah Valley Rosé 1994 • $6 • (09/15/95) • **82**
Cabernet Franc Shenandoah Valley 1990 • $12 • (08/31/92) • **81**
Cabernet Sauvignon Shenandoah Valley 1988 • $14 • (08/31/92) • **78**
Cabernet Sauvignon Shenandoah Valley 1987 • $15 • (11/30/90) • **83**
Rhône Rouge Shenandoah Valley 1992 • $8 • (05/15/95) • **86**
Syrah Shenandoah Valley 1996: Fairly dense, with blackberry, black cherry, anise, sage and thyme flavors, all backed by plenty of oak. The finish is a bit smoky. Well balanced, it should age nicely. Drink through 2002. 990 cases made. • $13 • (06/15/98) • **87**
Syrah Shenandoah Valley 1995: Some funky "off" odors make it difficult to appreciate the otherwise attractive black currant and black pepper flavors struggling to surface. 607 cases made. • $12 • (09/15/97) • **80**
Syrah Shenandoah Valley 1993 • $10 • (09/30/95) • **82**
Syrah Shenandoah Valley 1991 • $12 • (01/31/95) • **82**
Syrah Shenandoah Valley 1990 • $12 • (12/31/92) • **86**
Viognier Shenandoah Valley 1996: Juicy and fruity, chock full of spicy lemon, grapefruit, anise and herb flavors. Though somewhat bitter on the finish, this lusty wine is quite enjoyable. 892 cases made. • $15 • (02/28/98) • **87**
Viognier Shenandoah Valley 1994 • $17 • (09/30/95) • **80**
Viognier Shenandoah Valley 1993 • $17 • (09/15/94) • **86**
Zinfandel Amador County Vintners Selection 1996: Charry and smoky on the nose, with herbal underpinnings to the toast, licorice and blackberry qualities. Moderate finish. Drink now. 1,080 cases made. • $15 • (06/15/98) • **83**
Zinfandel Fiddletown 1996: Austere, with a green streak running through. Unusually tannic. Needs more fruit. Marginal quality. 890 cases made. • $15 • (06/15/98) • **77**
Zinfandel Fiddletown 1995: Shows lots of deep, concentrated raspberry, earth, mineral and spicy meat flavors before chewy, rustic tannins kick in. Finishes with a tarry edge. 950 cases made. • $15 • (08/31/97) • **88**
Zinfandel Fiddletown Lubenko 1994: Dry and leathery, in an unendearing, rustic, tannic style. Offers some chunky Zinfandel flavors, though. 570 cases made. • $14 • (09/15/96) • **78**
Zinfandel Fiddletown Lubenko 1993 • $14 • (03/31/96) • **83**
Zinfandel Fiddletown Lubenko 1992 • $14 • (06/15/95) • **82**
Zinfandel Shenandoah Valley 1992 • $10 • (10/15/95) • **81**
Zinfandel Shenandoah Valley 1988 • $10 • (11/30/90) • **88**
Zinfandel Shenandoah Valley Cougar Hill 1996: Dry, tannic and leathery, with a modest core of earthy currant and plummy Zinfandel flavors. Drink now through 2000. 1,139 cases made. • $15 • (06/15/98) • **78**
Zinfandel Shenandoah Valley Cougar Hill 1995: Tough and chewy, with a tannic, leathery edge to the spicy wild berry and plum flavors. Drinkable now. 680 cases made. • $15 • (04/30/97) • **86**
Zinfandel Shenandoah Valley Cougar Hill 1994: Marked by a dry leather and tar edge, the cherry and berry flavors struggle to keep pace with the tannins. 390 cases made. • $14 • (09/15/96) • **81**
Zinfandel Shenandoah Valley Cougar Hill 1993 • $13 • (03/31/96) • **83**
Zinfandel Shenandoah Valley Old Vines Sobon Estate 1990 • $16 • (09/30/93) • **78**
Zinfandel Shenandoah Valley Rocky Top 1996: An earthy, rustic, tarry style, with hints of wild berry, sage and mineral, and smoky flavors on the finish. Compact and concentrated, this hearty wine is well balanced and very tasty. Drink now through 2002. 1,500 cases made. • $15 • (05/31/98) • **88**
Zinfandel Shenandoah Valley Rocky Top 1995: Marked by great density and length, with delicious, smoky mineral notes and blueberry and plum flavors peeking through the rustic meat, mineral and herb core. Pair with a rare steak. 970 cases made. • $15 • (08/31/97) • **88**
Zinfandel Shenandoah Valley Rocky Top 1993 • $13 • (03/31/96) • **85**
Zinfandel Shenandoah Valley Rocky Top 1992 • $14 • (02/28/95) • **82**
Zinfandel Sierra Foothills 1990 • $10 • (09/30/93) • **81**
Zinfandel Sierra Foothills 1989 • $10 • (07/31/92) • **86**

SOKOL BLOSSER | OREGON

Cabernet Sauvignon Yamhill County 1994: Smooth, silky and spicy, with prominent new oak flavors, it's almost sweet with the vanilla nuances to the modest currant and blackberry. Very smooth, it's drinkable now. 91 cases made. • $30 • (01/31/98) • **86**
Cabernet Sauvignon Yamhill County 1992: A lighter style of Cabernet, its pretty cherry and currant flavors, shaded with vanilla and nutmeg, rest on a modest frame. Drinkable now. 100 cases made. • $30 • (01/31/98) • **83**
Chardonnay Yamhill County 1994: Round and generous, its nose and palate center around earthy, mineral aromas and flavors that never broaden or pick up much fruit character. 4,100 cases made. • $15 • (10/31/96) • **81**
Chardonnay Yamhill County 1993 • $12 • (03/31/96) • **74**
Chardonnay Yamhill County Redland 1993: Butterscotch aromas and flavors dominate, but it's not too broad for the crisp apple and spice flavors at the core. Finishes with a flinty edge. 1,450 cases made. • $19 • (10/31/96) • **84**
Chardonnay Yamhill County Redland Winemaker's Reserve 1994: A ripe, generous wine with layers of nutmeg, citrus and pear that echo, with touches of pineapple and toast, on the finish. Has elegance and intensity without excess weight. 850 cases made. • $20 • (01/31/98) • **90**
Müller-Thurgau Yamhill County 1995: Fresh and simple. A nice mouthful of orange and cream flavors that soften on the finish. 2,000 cases made. • $NA • (02/28/97) • **83**
Pinot Noir Oregon 1993 • $7 • (11/30/94) • **78**
Pinot Noir Willamette Valley 1994: Has a cooked quality that detracts from the freshness and focus. Finishing with smooth texture, but not much intensity. 4,100 cases made. • $15 • (10/15/96) • **82**
Pinot Noir Willamette Valley Red Hills Vineyard 1985 • $NA • (09/30/87) • **92**
Pinot Noir Yamhill County 1993 • $14 • (01/31/96) • **81**
Pinot Noir Yamhill County 1992 • $13 • (10/31/95) • **85**
Pinot Noir Yamhill County 1991 • $10 • (11/30/94) • **80**
Pinot Noir Yamhill County 1990 • $13 • (02/28/93) • **81**
Pinot Noir Yamhill County 1989 • $13 • (02/28/93) • **83**
Pinot Noir Yamhill County Hyland Vineyards 1986 • $15 • (06/15/88) • **79**
Pinot Noir Yamhill County Hyland Vineyards 1985 • $15 • (06/15/87) • **86**
Pinot Noir Yamhill County Hyland Vineyards 1983 • $14 • (08/31/86) • **82**
Pinot Noir Yamhill County Hyland Vineyards Reserve 1985 • $18 • (06/15/88) • **86**
Pinot Noir Yamhill County Hyland Vineyards Reserve 1983 • $30 • (02/15/90) • **67**
Pinot Noir Yamhill County Red Hills 1986 • $15 • (06/15/88) • **77**
Pinot Noir Yamhill County Red Hills 1985 • $15 • (06/15/87) • **80**
Pinot Noir Yamhill County Red Hills Reserve 1985 • $30 • (02/15/90) • **74**
Pinot Noir Yamhill County Redland 1994: Fresh and lightly spicy around the supple core of currant and black cherry flavors. A wine of moderate intensity that keeps its flavors on the finish. Ready now. 1,250 cases made. • $NA • (02/28/97) • **87**
Pinot Noir Yamhill County Redland 1993: Has some pretty blackberry and cherry aromas and flavors and a firm, almost bitter, green accent on the finish. 1,100 cases made. • $25 • (10/15/96) • **84**
Pinot Noir Yamhill County Redland 1992 • $25 • (02/29/96) • **86**
Pinot Noir Yamhill County Redland 1991 • $23 • (11/15/94) • **88**
Pinot Noir Yamhill County Redland 1989 • $24 • (02/28/93) • **83**
Pinot Noir Yamhill County Redland 1988 • $13 • (04/15/91) • **82**
Pinot Noir Yamhill County Redland 1987 • $13 • (02/15/90) • **66**
Sémillon-Chardonnay Oregon NV • $9 • (11/30/95) • **81**
Sémillon-Chardonnay Washington & Oregon 1995: Its pretty melon and apple flavors make this a pleasant white for sipping. 73 percent Sémillon from Washington, 27 percent Chardonnay from Oregon. • $8 • (11/15/96) • **84**
White Riesling Columbia Valley Sweet Reserve 1995: Unpleasantly strange, with flavors that taste a lot less sweet than the 12.2 percent residual sugar listed on the back label would imply . 800 cases made. • $12 • (10/31/96) • **76**

SOLARI | CALIFORNIA

Cabernet Sauvignon Napa Valley Larkmead Vineyards 1985 • $10 • (03/15/90) • **80**

Cabernet Sauvignon Napa Valley Larkmead Vineyards 1984 • $12 • (04/15/88) • **80**

SOLEO | CALIFORNIA

California White 1996: An intriguing aroma of freshly ground black pepper does little to prepare the palate for this sweet yet balanced apéritif wine. The flavors suggest kiwi, peach, melon and honey. Made by Sutter Home, it's a bargain at twice the price. 220,000 cases made. • $NA • (09/15/97) BB • **87**

Rosé California 1995: A fairly dry rosé sporting light cherry and herb flavors and a short finish. • $NA • (09/15/97) • **80**

SOLIS | CALIFORNIA

Merlot Monterey County 1988 • $11 • (05/31/92) • **73**

Merlot Santa Clara County 1991 • $11 • (11/30/92) • **81**

Pinot Noir Santa Clara County 1988 • $9 • (04/30/91) • **78**

SOLITUDE | CALIFORNIA

Chardonnay Carneros Sangiacomo Vineyard 1995: An excellent California Chardonnay—bright, ripe, rich and lively. Delivers lots of juicy pear, apple, honey, spice and fig flavors that turn complex, with light oak shadings on the finish. 2,700 cases made. • $20 • (12/15/96) SS • **90**

Chardonnay Carneros Sangiacomo Vineyard 1994: Serves up pretty peach and nectarine flavors, a fruit-driven wine that's smooth and refreshing. The finish brings out more pretty fruit couched in light oak shadings. • $19 • (01/31/96) • **91**

Chardonnay Carneros Sangiacomo Vineyard 1993 • $18 • (05/31/95) HR • **90**

Pinot Noir Carneros Sangiacomo Vineyard 1994: Austerely styled with a strong earth-and-game edge that's hard to overlook. Tasted thrice, with consistent notes. 611 cases made. • $18 • (03/31/97) • **79**

Pinot Noir Carneros Sangiacomo Vineyard 1993 • $18 • (01/31/96) • **84**

Pinot Noir Carneros Sangiacomo Vineyard 1991 • $18 • (02/28/94) • **75**

Pinot Noir Russian River Valley Rochioli Vineyard 1994: Young and on the tart side with fresh black cherry and wild berry notes. Drinks well now, but lacks the depth and richness of the best '94s. Considering the source vineyard, it's disappointing. Tasted twice, with consistent notes. 94 cases made. • $25 • (02/28/97) • **84**

Pinot Noir Sonoma County 1992 • $17 • (03/31/95) • **84**

SONOITA | ARIZONA

Cabernet Sauvignon Soñoita Private Reserve 1987 • $15 • (02/29/92) • **79**

Cabernet Sauvignon Soñoita Private Reserve 1985 • $22 • (02/29/92) • **71**

Pinot Noir Soñoita 1989 • $30 • (02/29/92) • **75**

SONOMA CREEK | CALIFORNIA

Cabernet Sauvignon California 1994: Shows more substance and tannin than most wines at this price, but it's still on the austere side, with its cherry and currant flavors working against the tannins. 5,000 cases made. • $11 • (11/30/96) • **80**

Cabernet Sauvignon Napa Valley Reserve 1991 • $15 • (11/15/94) • **84**

Cabernet Sauvignon Sonoma County 1991 • $15 • (11/15/93) • **78**

Cabernet Sauvignon Sonoma Valley 1991 • $15 • (11/15/94) • **82**

Cabernet Sauvignon Sonoma Valley 1988 • $12 • (11/15/91) • **74**

Cabernet Sauvignon Sonoma Valley Rancho Salina Vineyard 1994: Coffee and tea, mint, spice and herbs blend in an intriguing manner, backed by earth, berry, black cherry, leather and tar. It's a wild cocktail, currently somewhat disjointed, but outstanding nonetheless. 800 cases made. • $28 • (10/31/97) • **90**

Key: SS—Spectator Selection CS—Cellar Selection HR—Highly Recommended BB—Best Buy $NA—Price not available Ⓐ—Auction Price (BT)—Barrel Tasting

Dates in parentheses indicate the issues in which the ratings were published.

Chardonnay Carneros Reserve 1994: Simple, with a pleasant band of spicy pear flavors that become even more interesting on the finish. 2,000 cases made. • $15 • (07/31/96) • **85**

Chardonnay Carneros Reserve 1993: Pleasant enough; the ripe pear and apple flavors are touched with cedary oak. Finish is mature and flavorful. 3,000 cases made. • $15 • (07/31/96) • **83**

Chardonnay Sonoma County 1995: Has a pleasant, spicy nuance to its modest pear and toast flavors, all lingering nicely on the finish. 12,000 cases made. • $12 • (07/31/97) • **83**

Chardonnay Sonoma County 1994: A straightforward quaff. Offers pear, melon and spice flavors, with hints of apple and herb. 10,000 cases made. • $12 • (07/31/96) • **83**

Gewürztraminer Mendocino County 1995: Fresh and fruity, frankly sweet but not cloying, offering pleasant peach and mild, citruslike flavors. 1,200 cases made. • $10 • (07/31/97) • **82**

Meritage Sonoma County 1994: Strong coffee and herb notes are featured in the aromatics. On the palate, it's bright, actually tart, with cherry, cedar and herbs. 1,200 cases made. • $18 • (10/31/97) • **82**

Merlot Sonoma Valley Sangiacomo Vineyard 1994: An interesting blend of coffee, tar, blackberries and herbs that sits smoothly on the palate and ends in a silky finish. 1,000 cases made. • $28 • (07/31/97) • **88**

Merlot Sonoma Valley Sangiacomo Vineyard 1992 • $25 • (11/15/94) • **85**

Pinot Noir Carneros 1992 • $10 • (03/31/95) • **77**

Pinot Noir Sonoma County 1995: Coffee and earth qualities make this seem a bit older than it is. Lots of cedar and vanilla on the palate; finishes brightly. 5,000 cases made. • $12 • (07/31/97) • **85**

Pinot Noir Sonoma County 1993 • $10 • (12/31/95) • **83**

Zinfandel California 1994: On the simple side, with a sprinkling of cherry and spice notes. 6,800 cases made. • $11 • (12/15/96) • **79**

Zinfandel Contra Costa County 1994: Lean and trim, with ripe blueberry notes that are tasty, if simple. Ready to drink. 2,800 cases made. • $11 • (12/15/96) • **81**

Zinfandel Sonoma County 1994: Crisp, lean and tannic, with a shallow band of spicy cherry flavors. Finishes with an earthy aftertaste. Try now. 1,200 cases made. • $14 • (12/15/96) • **81**

Zinfandel Sonoma County 1992 • $10 • (10/15/94) • **78**

Zinfandel Sonoma Valley 1990 • $9 • (10/15/92) • **78**

SONOMA-CUTRER | CALIFORNIA

Chardonnay Russian River Valley Russian River Ranches 1995: Bright, fresh and lively, with a pleasing interplay of ripe pear, citrus, melon and spice notes. A light toasty-oak aftertaste and a hint of mineral mark the finish. • $16 • (04/30/97) • **90**

Chardonnay Sonoma Coast Cutrer Vineyard 1995: Intense and lively, rich and concentrated, with anise, pear, hazelnut and light vanilla shadings. Well focused, with a long, rich aftertaste. Drink now to 2000. • $28 • (03/31/98) • **90**

Chardonnay Sonoma Coast Cutrer Vineyard 1994: Overflowing with complex fig, pear, melon and butterscotch notes; smooth, ripe, rich and creamy. Reveals yet more depth and richness on the finish, while the flavors linger. Looks like Sonoma-Cutrer is back on track. 10,000 cases made. • $25 • (05/31/97) • **92**

Chardonnay Sonoma Coast Les Pierres 1995: Crisp and intense, with a flinty band of pear, hazelnut, light oak and spice, gaining complexity on the finish. Drinkable now but tightly wound; it can stand cellaring to 2000. • $28 • (03/31/98) • **89**

Chardonnay Sonoma Coast Les Pierres 1994: Elegant and refined, with a flinty, citrus accent to the tart pear and light spice notes. A very delicate and understated style that relies more on finesse than power. • $28 • (07/31/97) • **88**

Chardonnay Sonoma Coast Russian River Ranches 1996: Intense and spicy, with a fruit core built around racy citrus and pineapple flavors. Well focused and lively through the finish, it is crisp enough to cellar to 2000. • $17 • (03/31/98) • **89**

Chardonnay Sonoma Coast Russian River Ranches 1995: Bright, fresh and lively, with a pleasing interplay of ripe pear, citrus, melon and spice notes. A light toasty-oak aftertaste and a hint of mineral mark the finish. • $16 • (04/30/97) • **90**

Chardonnay Sonoma Coast Russian River Ranches 1994: Smooth and ripe, with an array of pear, apple, spice and cedary oak flavors. Fine balance from start to lingering finish. • $15 • (07/31/96) • **89**

Chardonnay Sonoma Coast Russian River Ranches 1993 • $14 • (04/30/95) • **84**

SONOMA-LOEB | CALIFORNIA

Cabernet Sauvignon Alexander Valley 1988 • $10 • (02/29/92) • **82**
Chardonnay Sonoma County 1996: Brimming with ripe, juicy pear, apple, apricot and melon notes, this elegant and spicy style drinks well now. 805 cases made. • $20 • (11/30/97) • **89**
Chardonnay Sonoma County 1995: Holds your interest with its complexity and finesse, exhibiting a nice interplay of ripe pear, apple, fig and melon flavors. Finishes with a hint of toasty oak. 2,039 cases made. • $20 • (12/15/96) • **89**
Chardonnay Sonoma County 1994: Smooth and polished, with ripe pear and buttery oak flavors that show a moderate level of richness and complexity, followed by a spicy, smoky aftertaste. 1,257 cases made. • $18 • (03/31/96) • **88**
Chardonnay Sonoma County 1993 • $16 • (07/31/95) • **86**
Chardonnay Sonoma County Private Reserve 1995: Smooth and spicy, with a silky texture and lots of pretty pear, spice, apricot and honey flavors that turn elegant and smoky on the finish. Impressive for its texture and length. 581 cases made. • $30 • (05/31/97) • **92**
Chardonnay Sonoma County Private Reserve 1994: Ripe, complex pear, spice and apple notes pick up a pretty, toasty oak edge on the finish. Try now. 372 cases made. • $25 • (02/29/96) • **88**
Chardonnay Sonoma County Private Reserve 1993 • $26 • (07/31/95) • **89**

SONOMA MISSION | CALIFORNIA

Chardonnay Sonoma County 1993 • $8 • (07/31/95) • **82**

SOOS CREEK | WASHINGTON

Cabernet Sauvignon Columbia Valley 1995: An earthy, gamy edge to the ripe black cherry flavors makes this a distinctive red but not one to appeal to everyone. Finishes with some intensity. Best from 2000 or 2002. 173 cases made. • $21 • (05/15/98) • **87**
Cabernet Sauvignon Columbia Valley 1994: Crisp and bright, with a streak of black pepper and sage running through its moderate blackberry and tar flavors. Best from now or 2000. 123 cases made. • $19 • (08/31/97) • **86**
Cabernet Sauvignon Columbia Valley 1993: Stylish, with lots of ripe plum, currant and spicy oak character swirling through the velvety frame. Holds its character and is firm on the finish. Drinkable now or hold until 2001. 142 cases made. • $17 • (02/28/97) • **88**
Cabernet Sauvignon Columbia Valley 1992: Very firm and focused. A harmonious wine with layers of spicy black currant and tar flavors that persist through the finish. Drinkable now. 75 cases made. • $16 • (09/15/96) • **88**
Cabernet Sauvignon Columbia Valley 1991 • $15 • (04/30/96) • **84**
Cabernet Sauvignon Columbia Valley 1989 • $15 • (10/15/93) • **86**

SOQUEL | CALIFORNIA

Cabernet Sauvignon Santa Cruz Mountains 1994: Beef, coffee, leather, cedar and spice mingle in an arresting manner here. The finish is plush and long, though a touch too bright and tangy. Drinks well now. 450 cases made. • $22 • (10/31/97) • **87**
Cabernet Sauvignon Santa Cruz Mountains 1991 • $20 • (04/15/94) • **86**
Cabernet Sauvignon Santa Cruz Mountains 1990 • $16 • (03/31/93) • **88**
Cabernet Sauvignon Santa Cruz Mountains Partners' Reserve 1994: Generous in flavor, with a strong earthy edge to the jammy strawberry and spice character. Ready now. Tasted twice, with consistent notes. 190 cases made. • $40 • (12/15/97) • **80**
Cabernet Sauvignon Santa Cruz Mountains Special Reserve 1992: Even with its bottle age, the bright acidity of this wine remains a little top-heavy. Bright cherry and plum flavors are nonetheless attractive in this zingy red. Drink now. 275 cases made. • $22 • (05/31/98) • **83**
Cabernet Sauvignon Santa Cruz Mountains Special Reserve 1989 • $25 • (08/31/92) • **85**
Cabernet Sauvignon Stags Leap District 1992: Tannins and acids are a bit harsh here. It's a combination that doesn't help the otherwise pretty cassis, blackberry, anise and herb flavors. Moderate finish. Drink now through 2002. 750 cases made. • $20 • (05/31/98) • **83**
Cabernet Sauvignon Stags Leap District 1991 • $18 • (05/15/94) • **83**
Cabernet Sauvignon Stags Leap District 1990 • $20 • (02/29/96) • **80**
Cabernet Sauvignon Stags Leap District 1989 • $16 • (02/15/93) • **85**
Chardonnay California Coastal Cellars 1993: Smooth and fruity, with a spicy edge to the grapefruit flavors that keep resonating on the finish. • $6 • (07/31/96) • **86**
Chardonnay Monterey County 1996: A blend of pear, apple and mineral components, this wine shows tangy acidity and a bright though moderate finish. Drink now. 320 cases made. • $16 • (06/30/98) • **87**
Chardonnay Monterey County 1995: Bright and supple, with a nice core of pear and spice flavors that persist through the finish. Ready to drink. 501 cases made. • $15 • (07/31/97) • **84**
Chardonnay Santa Cruz Mountains 1996: Butterscotch and spice notes sing loudly here, followed by creamy peach, pear and honey flavors. Firm, almost meaty on the palate, with a refreshing lemon lift at the end. Drink now. 240 cases made. • $20 • (06/30/98) • **89**
Pinot Noir Santa Cruz Mountains 1991 • $16 • (02/28/94) • **80**
Pinot Noir Santa Cruz Mountains 1990 • $18 • (09/30/92) • **86**
Pinot Noir Santa Cruz Mountains Longridge Vineyard 1994 • $25 • (02/29/96) • **85**
Pinot Noir Santa Cruz Mountains Special Reserve 1994 • $25 • (03/31/96) • **83**
Pinot Noir Santa Cruz Mountains Special Reserve 1993 • $25 • (12/31/95) • **81**
Zinfandel Alexander Valley 1991 • $8 • (06/15/93) • **79**

SPARROW LANE | CALIFORNIA

Zinfandel Howell Mountain Beatty Ranch 1996: Tight, tannic and earthy, with hard edges to the dense pepper and wild berry flavors. Not for the faint of heart, it finishes with a chewy core of tannins; the dryness on the finish is a big question mark. Best from 2000 through 2005. 700 cases made. • $22 • (06/15/98) • **86**
Zinfandel North Coast 1994: Lighter than most Zins, with a slightly herbal accent to its polished berry and chocolate flavors. Ready to drink. 700 cases made. • $15 • (04/30/97) • **84**
Zinfandel North Coast 1993 • $12 • (10/15/95) • **88**

SPENKER | CALIFORNIA

Zinfandel Lodi 1996: Earthy and vinegary, with paintlike flavors. Downright ugly. A second bottle was equally flawed. Avoid. 1,150 cases made. • $15 • (06/15/98) • **60**
Zinfandel Lodi 1995: This robust wine is packed with fat, ripe fruit—cherries, cassis, blackberries—yet has enough acidity to give it lift. Smoky, cola flavors are almost overpowering but not quite. A terrific wine from an underrated region. 570 cases made. • $14 • (07/31/97) • **90**

SPOTTSWOODE | CALIFORNIA

Cabernet Sauvignon Napa Valley 1997: Openly fruity, supple, with plum and cherry-laced flavors, this is a notably harmonious and well-balanced young wine. • $NA • (07/31/98) (BT) • **90-94**
Cabernet Sauvignon Napa Valley 1996: Young and grapey, focused on bright cherry and plummy Cabernet flavors. Solid and concentrated, nothing flashy yet. • $NA • (06/15/97) (BT) • **90-94**
Cabernet Sauvignon Napa Valley 1994: From a classic vintage, this California Cabernet is supple and harmonious at but three years of age, with a ripe, complex core of cherry, plum and wild berry flavors that fan out nicely, finishing with firm tannins and good length. Best now through 2004. Contains 8 percent Cabernet Franc. 5,000 cases made. • $45 • (10/15/97) CS • **92**
Cabernet Sauvignon Napa Valley 1993: Supple and elegant, with tiers of currant, cherry and spice flavors. Finishes with round, smooth tannins and a lingering aftertaste. A solid effort that shows off its complexity and finesse on the finish. 5,150 cases made. • $42 • (11/15/96) • **90**
Cabernet Sauvignon Napa Valley 1992 • $39 • (11/30/95) CS • **90**
Cabernet Sauvignon Napa Valley 1991 • $40 • (11/15/94) CS • **93**
Cabernet Sauvignon Napa Valley 1990: Well structured, with a nice balance of focused ripe plum and currant flavors and firm tannins. Young and compact, it needs more time to open. Drinkable now. • $69 • (09/15/96) • **93**
Cabernet Sauvignon Napa Valley 1988 • $52 • (11/15/91) • **90**
Cabernet Sauvignon Napa Valley 1987: Despite bottle variation, the best was ripe, smooth, rich and plush—much as it was in its youth—with plenty of currant, black cherry, wild berry and spicy anise flavors. Tannins have softened, but the depth and concentration remain impressive. Best now through 2005. 2,700 cases made. • $77 • (12/15/97) • **95**
Cabernet Sauvignon Napa Valley 1986: Youthful and vibrant, with well-preserved black cherry and currant flavors, still remarkably well focused, long and full on the aftertaste, where it picks up an earthy note. Drinks well now or may be cellared into 2001, with the chance that by then the fruit may not shine as brightly. 2,400 cases made. • $75 • (12/15/96) • **92**

Cabernet Sauvignon Napa Valley 1985: A tight and somewhat tart wine, with crisp black cherry, currant and spice flavors that turn elegant and supple on the finish. Not the massively concentrated wine it was in its youth but still very complex and age-worthy. Best now and into 2000. • $91 • (09/15/96) • **89**
Cabernet Sauvignon Napa Valley 1984 • $25 • (11/30/87) • **92**
Cabernet Sauvignon Napa Valley 1983 • $25 • (11/15/86) • **81**
Cabernet Sauvignon Napa Valley 1982 • $18 • (11/01/85) • **86**
Sauvignon Blanc Napa Valley 1996: Bright lemon and tart plum flavors come to the fore, backed by a light, toasty quality. 3,500 cases made. • $18 • (06/15/97) • **87**
Sauvignon Blanc Napa Valley 1995: Smooth, silky and almost sweet, with ripe apricot, pear and lightly minty-herbal overtones. A distinctive wine that finishes with a polished feel. 4,150 cases made. • $15 • (08/31/96) • **89**
Sauvignon Blanc Napa Valley 1994 • $14 • (06/30/95) • **87**
Sauvignon Blanc Napa Valley 1993 • $12 • (08/31/94) • **85**

SPRING MOUNTAIN | CALIFORNIA

Cabernet Sauvignon Napa Valley 1985 • $20 • (10/15/89) • **85**
Cabernet Sauvignon Napa Valley 1984 • $15 • (03/15/89) • **89**
Cabernet Sauvignon Napa Valley 1983 • $15 • (09/30/87) • **80**
Cabernet Sauvignon Napa Valley 1982 • $15 • (12/15/86) • **87**
Cabernet Sauvignon Napa Valley Miravalle-Alba-Chevalier 1993: Crisp and tight, with a coffee and cedary accent to the ripe cherry and currant flavors. Finishes with firm tannins and an earthy edge, so prepare to cellar this one into 2000. 7,000 cases made. • $30 • (11/15/96) • **87**
Red Napa Valley 1994: Shows restraint while delivering the goods, with tightly reined currant, black cherry, cedar, anise and plum, fanning out on the finish where it holds its focus and flavors. Best between now and 2004. A blend of Cabernet Sauvignon, Merlot, and Cabernet Franc. 5,000 cases made. • $36 • (04/30/98) • **90**

SPRINGHILL | OREGON

Pinot Noir Oregon Barrel Select 1992 • $15 • (11/30/94) • **85**
Pinot Noir Willamette Valley 1996: Nicely focused to show off its pretty black cherry and mineral flavors, with fine tannins that need until 2000 to settle down. 280 cases made. • $20 • (05/15/98) • **87**
Pinot Noir Willamette Valley 1990 • $8 • (11/30/94) • **78**
Pinot Noir Willamette Valley Reserve 1996: Firm, chewy and distinctive for an earthy-minty streak running through the solid black cherry flavors. Give it until 2000 to come together. 270 cases made. • $35 • (05/15/98) • **87**
Pinot Noir Willamette Valley Reserve 1995: Has plenty of ripeness and richness, focused flavors of black cherry, blackberry, currant and smoke, and is nicely fashioned to show off its pretty side. Finish turns chewy with tannin. Best from 2000. 240 cases made. • $25 • (07/31/97) • **90**
Pinot Noir Willamette Valley Reserve 1993 • $20 • (01/31/96) • **85**
Riesling Late Harvest Willamette Valley Select Cluster Botrytized 1994 • $12 • (01/31/96) • **83**
Riesling Willamette Valley 1996: On the dry side, with crisp green apple and honeydew flavors, picking up a touch of honeysuckle on the slick finish. Drink soon. 360 cases made. • $9 • (05/15/98) • **84**
Riesling Willamette Valley 1993 • $8 • (11/30/94) • **81**
Riesling Willamette Valley TBA 1994: This sweet, golden wine layers its honey, pineapple, orange blossom, pear and ever-so-slightly vinegary flavors on a silky frame. Delicious now. 53 cases made. • $20/375ml • (05/15/98) • **88**

STAG HOLLOW | OREGON

Pinot Noir Oregon Celebré 1995: Crisp in texture, with meaty and berry flavors that linger on the still-rough finish. Give it until 1999. 74 cases made. • $21 • (02/28/98) • **85**
Pinot Noir Oregon Celebré 1994: Displays its ripe, Zinfandel-like berry and spice flavors on a lean, chewy frame, then expands them on a spicy finish. Try now. 72 cases made. • $32 • (04/30/97) • **88**
Pinot Noir Oregon Vendange Sélection 1995: A solid wine, with firm texture and a modest level of ripe blackberry and spice flavors, finishing with a touch of earth and mineral. Has more going for it than the sample reviewed earlier. Best from now through 2002. 126 cases made. • $28 • (06/15/98) • **86**

STAG'S LEAP WINE CELLARS | CALIFORNIA

Cabernet Sauvignon Napa Valley 1995: Appealing for its ripe, supple plum and wild berry flavors. Well focused, moderately rich and tannic, it's well suited for near-term drinking. 24,167 cases made. • $26 • (04/30/98) • **87**
Cabernet Sauvignon Napa Valley 1994: Shows off earthy, spicy Cabernet flavors, with hints of wild berry, cherry, sage and cedar, and finishes with firm tannins and good length. 15,000 cases made. • $19 Ⓐ • (05/15/97) • **88**
Cabernet Sauvignon Napa Valley 1993: Medium weight, with spicy currant, light oak, cherry and cedar nuances. Gains complexity and finesse on the finish, where the texture is smooth and shows fine interplay with the flavors. Drink now and through 2000. 10,000 cases made. • $22 • (10/15/96) • **88**
Cabernet Sauvignon Napa Valley 1991 • $18 • (03/31/94) • **87**
Cabernet Sauvignon Napa Valley 1990 • $18 • (05/15/93) SS • **91**
Cabernet Sauvignon Napa Valley 1989 • $18 • (09/30/92) • **83**
Cabernet Sauvignon Napa Valley 1988 • $18 • (06/15/91) • **90**
Cabernet Sauvignon Napa Valley 1987 • $18 • (08/31/90) • **75**
Cabernet Sauvignon Napa Valley 1986 • $18 • (06/15/89) • **82**
Cabernet Sauvignon Napa Valley 1985 • $16 • (09/15/88) • **90**
Cabernet Sauvignon Napa Valley 1984 • $15 • (07/15/87) • **83**
Cabernet Sauvignon Napa Valley 1981 • $15 • (12/16/84) • **82**
Cabernet Sauvignon Napa Valley Fay 1994: There's lots to admire in this Cab, with its core of currant, anise, cedar, sage and black olive flavors, and tannins that are firm but supple. It's marked by more substance, depth and tannin than is the SLV bottling, if not as concentrated as the Cask 23. Drinkable now, and worthy of cellaring to 2003. 5,000 cases made. • $50 • (03/31/98) CS • **92**
Cabernet Sauvignon Napa Valley Fay 1993: A seductive style, with ripe, rich, sweet fruit that unfolds to offer a core of cherry, currant, plum and wild berry flavors. Picks up herb, cedar and coffee notes on its long, complex finish. At this stage, the showiest of the Stag's Leap Wine Cellars' Cabernets. 1,500 cases made. • $40 • (11/15/96) • **91**
Cabernet Sauvignon Napa Valley Fay 1992 • $35 • (12/15/95) CS • **91**
Cabernet Sauvignon Napa Valley Fay 1991 • $30 • (12/31/94) • **88**
Cabernet Sauvignon Napa Valley Fay 1990 • $30 • (03/31/94) • **88**
Cabernet Sauvignon Napa Valley S.L.V. 1994: Shows lovely fruit, with tiers of spicy currant, black cherry, olive, sage and tar flavors, and a remarkably supple and fleshy texture that makes it quite appealing now. Medium in color and medium-weight in texture, it's an elegant and understated but quite fruity Cabernet Sauvignon from a great year. Drink now through 2004. 3,819 cases made. • $50 • (11/30/97) CS • **91**
Cabernet Sauvignon Napa Valley S.L.V. 1993: Ripe and flavorful, with a nice band of earthy cherry, currant and plum flavors that pick up hints of coffee, herb and anise before turning more complex on the finish, where the flavors fan out. 3,000 cases made. • $40 • (11/15/96) • **90**
Cabernet Sauvignon Napa Valley S.L.V. 1992 • $35 • (12/15/95) • **88**
Cabernet Sauvignon Napa Valley S.L.V. 1990 • $30 • (03/31/94) HR • **89**
Cabernet Sauvignon Napa Valley S.L.V. 1988 • $38 • (11/15/91) • **85**
Cabernet Sauvignon Napa Valley S.L.V. 1987 • $33 • (11/15/90) • **77**
Cabernet Sauvignon Napa Valley S.L.V. 1986: A ripe, supple, rich and complex wine, with layers of currant, cherry, coffee, cedar and spice flavors, and a texture that is classic Stag's Leap in its softness. Drinks exceptionally well now through 2004. • $36 • (12/15/96) • **91**
Cabernet Sauvignon Napa Valley S.L.V. 1985 • $26 • (10/31/88) • **90**
Cabernet Sauvignon Napa Valley S.L.V. Fay 1989 • $25 • (11/15/92) • **80**
Cabernet Sauvignon Napa Valley Stag's Leap Vineyards 1984 • $21 • (11/30/87) • **81**
Cabernet Sauvignon Napa Valley Stag's Leap Vineyards 1983 • $18 • (11/15/86) • **77**
Cabernet Sauvignon Napa Valley Stag's Leap Vineyards 1982 • $17 • (10/01/85) • **69**
Cabernet Sauvignon Napa Valley Stag's Leap Vineyards 1981 • $15 • (09/16/84) CS • **90**
Cabernet Sauvignon Napa Valley Stag's Leap Vineyards 1974 • $95 • (02/15/90) • **83**
Cabernet Sauvignon Napa Valley Stag's Leap Vineyards 1973 • $NA • (04/01/86) • **82**
Cabernet Sauvignon Napa Valley Stag's Leap Vineyards Cask 23 1984 • $40 • (12/31/88) • **90**

Key: SS—Spectator Selection CS—Cellar Selection HR—Highly Recommended BB—Best Buy $NA—Price not available Ⓐ—Auction Price (BT)—Barrel Tasting
Dates in parentheses indicate the issues in which the ratings were published.

Cabernet Sauvignon Napa Valley Stag's Leap Vineyards Cask 23 1983 • $32 • (10/15/88) • **82**
Cabernet Sauvignon Napa Valley Stag's Leap Vineyards Cask 23 1978 • $200 • (11/15/92) • **92**
Cabernet Sauvignon Napa Valley Stag's Leap Vineyards Cask 23 1977 • $30 • (01/01/83) CS • **91**
Cabernet Sauvignon Napa Valley Stag's Leap Vineyards Cask 23 1974 • $150 • (11/15/94) • **94**
Cabernet Sauvignon Napa Valley Stag's Leap Vineyards Lot 2 1978 • $56 • (11/15/92) • **88**
Cabernet Sauvignon Stag's Leap District Fay 1997: A subtle style, supple, with currant, herb, sage and anise. Turns complex on the finish, where the flavors linger. • $NA • (07/31/98) (BT) • **90-94**
Cask 23 Napa Valley 1994: This red blend is intense and concentrated, with a rich, supple texture and loads of currant, anise, black cherry, plum and berry notes. On the finish, the flavors weave together in a complex tapestry, and though firmly tannic, it's perfectly balanced. Tempting now; at its best from 2000 to 2006, maybe beyond. 2,093 cases made. • $100 • (03/31/98) CS • **93**
Cask 23 Napa Valley 1993: A touch earthy, but the flavors turn complex with hints of cedar, coffee, currant and anise. Impressive for its depth and finesse, it finishes with fine texture and lingering flavors. Drinkable now. 3,000 cases made. • $80 • (03/31/97) • **88**
Cask 23 Napa Valley 1992 • $80 • (12/15/95) CS • **94**
Cask 23 Napa Valley 1991 • $70 • (12/31/94) CS • **92**
Cask 23 Napa Valley 1990 • $80 • (10/31/93) CS • **92**
Cask 23 Napa Valley 1987: A lighter style, with a modest band of herb, currant and cedar. The tannins are soft and the texture is fleshy; what's missing is the depth, richness and concentration found in the top Cask 23s. Best now through 2000. 593 cases made. • $78 • (12/15/97) • **87**
Cask 23 Napa Valley 1986: Despite the mature garnet color, this wine offers a complex array of herb, cedar, anise, leaf, mineral, currant and slightly pruny flavors, with smooth, supple tannins. Dries out on the finish. It showed better in this tasting than in three previous encounters, when it tasted earthy and mulchy. Best to drink it soon. • $67 • (12/15/96) • **88**
Cask 23 Napa Valley 1985 • $180 • (11/30/89) • **96**
Chardonnay Napa Valley 1996: An elegant, understated style, with lots of spicy pear, apple and hazelnut notes. Finishes with a smooth, silky texture and a lingering aftertaste. 21,428 cases made. • $24 • (04/30/98) • **89**
Chardonnay Napa Valley 1995: Ripe and fruity, with a complex core of apple, melon, fig and hazelnut flavors that are elegant and refreshing. 15,000 cases made. • $24 • (05/15/97) • **90**
Chardonnay Napa Valley 1994: Clean and sound, with ripe pear, apple and spice flavors than grow on the finish. A subtle style that draws you in. 15,000 cases made. • $22 • (06/15/96) • **89**
Chardonnay Napa Valley 1993 • $19 • (07/31/95) • **88**
Chardonnay Napa Valley Beckstoffer Ranch 1996: Sleek and elegant, with pretty pear, spice, nutmeg and hazelnut flavors. Finishes with a long, subtle aftertaste that echoes citrus and apple flavors. Drink now through 2001. 569 cases made. • $28 • (05/15/98) • **91**
Chardonnay Napa Valley Beckstoffer Ranch 1995: A deliciously fruity and complex young wine, brimming with bright, ripe pear, apple, citrus, spice and melon flavors. The long, lingering aftertaste keeps pumping out the flavors. 700 cases made. • $28 • (10/15/97) • **92**
Chardonnay Napa Valley Beckstoffer Ranch 1994: Openly fruity, with an elegant core of ripe pear, apple, fig and melon notes framed by toasty, creamy oak. Finishes with echoes of the fruit and smoky oak. Only available at the winery. 400 cases made. • $24 • (05/31/96) • **91**
Chardonnay Napa Valley Reserve 1996: Elegant and complex, with well-focused pear, apple, spice and pretty toasty, smoky oak flavors, finishing with a long, intriguing aftertaste. Delicious. Drink now through 2001. 1,086 cases made. • $37 • (05/15/98) • **91**
Chardonnay Napa Valley Reserve 1995: Lots of complexity to this wine, with its ripe pear, fig, apple, citrus and light oak shadings, and it turns even richer and more complex on the finish, where the flavors pick up a smoky edge, fan out and linger. 875 cases made. • $35 • (05/31/97) • **93**
Chardonnay Napa Valley Reserve 1994: Pretty pear, apple, melon and spice flavors dance through this smooth, ripe and creamy wine, picking up a dash of nutmeg and turning elegant and complex on the lingering finish. Ready to drink. 1,931 cases made. • $32 • (05/15/97) • **91**
Chardonnay Napa Valley Reserve 1993 • $28 • (05/31/95) • **89**
Merlot Napa Valley 1994: Firm, well focused and richly flavored, with pretty black cherry, currant, anise, sage and spice notes, finishing with nice dashes of cedar and buttery oak. 3,000 cases made. • $26 • (06/30/97) • **88**
Merlot Napa Valley 1992 • $24 • (12/15/95) • **88**
Merlot Napa Valley 1991 • $22 • (05/31/94) • **86**
Merlot Napa Valley 1990 • $22 • (03/31/93) • **87**
Merlot Napa Valley 1985 • $16 • (05/31/88) • **86**
Merlot Napa Valley 1984 • $15 • (05/15/87) • **78**
Merlot Napa Valley 1982 • $14 • (10/01/85) • **78**
Merlot Napa Valley 1981 • $14 • (04/16/84) • **82**
Petite Sirah Napa Valley 1993: Dark and chewy, with intense pepper and plum flavors and a hint of cherry that emerges on the finish. Drinkable now, if you can wade through the tannins. 600 cases made. • $18 • (10/15/96) • **85**
Petite Sirah Napa Valley 1992 • $18 • (09/30/95) • **83**
Petite Sirah Napa Valley 1991 • $19 • (02/28/95) • **85**
Petite Sirah Napa Valley 1987 • $12 • (08/31/90) • **87**
Petite Sirah Napa Valley 1985 • $9 • (10/15/88) • **85**
Petite Sirah Napa Valley 1982 • $7 • (12/01/85) • **73**
Sauvignon Blanc Napa Valley 1996: Honey and hazelnut tones set the stage for a well-balanced wine redolent of grapefruit, fig, melon and herbs. Shows depth, along with a velvety texture. Finishes bright and clean. 2,197 cases made. • $15 • (04/30/98) • **88**
Sauvignon Blanc Napa Valley 1995: Tries to be delicate, but comes off as fresh and simple, with lively pear and light floral flavors. 5,000 cases made. • $12 • (05/15/97) • **84**
Sauvignon Blanc Napa Valley 1994: Soft and simple. Displays some varietal qualities, but stops short of achieving harmony. 5,000 cases made. • $12 • (07/31/96) • **81**
Sauvignon Blanc Napa Valley Rancho Chimiles 1993 • $11 • (08/31/95) • **77**
White Riesling Late Harvest Napa Valley Birkmyer Vineyards 1983 • $14/375ml • (10/01/84) • **85**
White Riesling Napa Valley 1996: Soft, simple and pleasant for its pear and honey flavors, finishing light and sweet. Ready now. 1,039 cases made. • $13 • (11/30/97) • **83**

STAGLIN FAMILY | CALIFORNIA

Cabernet Sauvignon Napa Valley 1993: Appealing for its spicy, zesty cherry and plum notes, this medium-weight red offers a nice core of flavors, inserting hints of smoky oak on the firmly tannic finish. 3,000 cases made. • $30 • (04/30/96) • **89**
Cabernet Sauvignon Napa Valley 1992 • $28 • (12/15/95) • **91**
Cabernet Sauvignon Napa Valley 1991 • $26 • (11/15/94) • **89**
Cabernet Sauvignon Napa Valley 1989 • $22 • (11/15/92) • **87**
Cabernet Sauvignon Rutherford 1994: Firm, tight and tannic, with a chewy edge to the earthy currant and black cherry flavors. Picks up pretty coffee and cedar notes on the aftertaste. Best to hold this dense, compact wine until 2001 or after. 4,000 cases made. • $40 • (06/15/97) • **90**
Sangiovese Napa Valley Stagliano 1994 • $34 • (04/30/96) • **87**
Sangiovese Napa Valley Stagliano 1993 • $34 • (02/28/95) • **88**

STAGS' LEAP WINERY | CALIFORNIA

Burgundy Napa Valley 1983 • $5 • (09/15/87) • **71**
Cabernet Sauvignon Napa Valley 1991 • $20 • (11/15/94) • **85**
Cabernet Sauvignon Napa Valley 1989 • $19 • (03/15/93) • **86**
Cabernet Sauvignon Napa Valley 1987 • $18 • (06/30/91) • **89**
Cabernet Sauvignon Napa Valley 1984 • $14 • (07/15/88) • **90**
Cabernet Sauvignon Napa Valley 1981 • $14 • (03/01/85) • **86**
Merlot Napa Valley 1994: Lean and herbal, with an earthy, tannic edge to the flavors, picking up a bitter, leathery note on the finish. Lacks charm. 17,516 cases made. • $25 • (06/30/97) • **82**
Merlot Napa Valley 1990 • $20 • (06/15/93) • **78**
Merlot Napa Valley 1989 • $17 • (05/31/92) • **88**
Merlot Napa Valley 1987 • $17 • (11/15/91) • **85**
Merlot Napa Valley 1986 • $17 • (12/31/90) • **84**
Merlot Napa Valley 1981 • $12 • (02/16/85) • **83**
Petite Sirah Napa Valley 1990 • $17 • (09/30/94) • **81**
Petite Sirah Napa Valley 1988 • $15 • (11/30/92) • **88**
Petite Sirah Napa Valley 1987 • $14 • (10/31/91) • **82**
Petite Sirah Napa Valley 1980 • $10 • (03/01/85) • **84**
Petite Sirah Napa Valley Stags' Leap Reserve 1993: Dense and chewy, packed with rugged tannins that only allow a glimpse of the ripe plum and spicy berry flavors, which are pretty. Finishes with a dash of spice. Best from now to 2005. 448 cases made. • $45 • (04/30/98) • **88**

STAIGER, P. & M. | CALIFORNIA

Chardonnay Santa Cruz Mountains 1994: A flinty style that serves up an attractive range of ripe pear, spice and fig flavors. Drink now. 230 cases made. • $12 • (06/15/96) • **86**

Pinot Noir Monterey 1987 • $12 • (02/28/93) • **67**

STALEY, PHILIP | CALIFORNIA

Grenache Russian River Valley Staley Vineyard 1995: Chewy, country-style red, on the rustic side but nicely laden with berry and jam flavors. Drinkable now with something hearty. 225 cases made. • $13 • (03/31/98) • **83**

Mourvèdre Russian River Valley Staley Vineyard 1995: Firm and tight, with chewy tannins, but there's some nice berry flavor popping through on the generous finish. Drinkable now. 375 cases made. • $15 • (03/31/98) • **85**

Rue Rivage Red Russian River Valley 1994: Supple and juicy, a lighter style with cherry, anise and tar flavors plus a hint of bitterness on the finish. Drink now. A blend of Grenache, Mourvèdre and Syrah. 600 cases made. • $10 • (03/31/98) • **84**

Sangiovese Dry Creek Valley Somers Vineyard 1995: The opening notes feature a modest band of dried cherry, coffee, herb and spice before turning dry and tannic. Cellar short term. 575 cases made. • $20 • (03/31/98) • **83**

Syrah Russian River Valley Staley Vineyard 1995: Tart and tight. Packed with pretty blackberry and earth flavors, but wound up like a rubber band on a toy airplane. Give it until 2001 to see how it will fly. 375 cases made. • $18 • (03/31/98) • **85**

STANDING STONE | NEW YORK

Gewürztraminer Finger Lakes 1996: A good, firm Gewürz with appealing grapefruit and spice flavors. Well structured, with a nice raciness and a long, clean finish. Well done. Drink now. 680 cases made. • $11 • (03/31/98) • **87**

Gewürztraminer Finger Lakes 1995: Not a bad substitute for an Alsatian Gewürz, this has the classic floral, spicy aromas and rich fruit flavors. Good balance, too. • $11 • (06/15/97) • **85**

Riesling Finger Lakes 1996: A good, quaffable Riesling with appealing peach, apple and spice flavors. Fairly ripe and round with a smooth texture. 2.3 percent residual sugar. Drink now. 611 cases made. • $9 • (03/31/98) • **84**

Riesling Finger Lakes 1995: Well balanced with peach, citrus and mineral flavors. Crisp and fairly ripe, with a hint of spice on the finish. A very good Finger Lakes Riesling. • $9 • (01/31/97) • **86**

Riesling Finger Lakes Dry 1996: A focused Riesling that will go well with food. Clean, crisp and lively with green peach and mineral flavors and some nice spicy notes on the finish. Drink now. 375 cases made. • $11 • (03/31/98) • **86**

STANGELAND | OREGON

Chardonnay Willamette Valley Estate Reserve 1994: Some slightly bitter, earthlike flavors detract from the delicate fruity charm of this toasty, medium-weight wine. Try now. 145 cases made. • $18 • (04/30/97) • **81**

Gewürztraminer Oregon 1995: Silky smooth, and pretty for its floral aromas and flavors but a bit washed-out in the fruit flavor department. Drink now. 115 cases made. • $7 • (04/30/97) • **82**

Pinot Gris Willamette Valley 1995: Earthy, sweaty, decadent flavors are ruinous. 250 cases made. • $12 • (02/28/97) • **70**

Pinot Gris Willamette Valley 1994 • $12 • (03/31/96) • **85**

Pinot Noir Willamette Valley 1995: Light, crisp and appealing for its pretty berry flavors. 289 cases made. • $12 • (02/28/97) • **82**

Pinot Noir Willamette Valley Estate Reserve 1994: Light in color and intensity, with more oak character than fruit flavor. 184 cases made. • $18 • (02/28/97) • **77**

Pinot Noir Willamette Valley Rob Roy Red NV • $8 • (01/31/96) • **82**

Key: SS—Spectator Selection CS—Cellar Selection HR—Highly Recommended BB—Best Buy $NA—Price not available Ⓐ—Auction Price (BT)—Barrel Tasting

Dates in parentheses indicate the issues in which the ratings were published.

STAR HILL | CALIFORNIA

Cabernet Sauvignon Napa Valley Bartolucci Vineyard Doc's Reserve 1990 • $24 • (02/15/93) • **82**

Cabernet Sauvignon Napa Valley Doc's Reserve 1987 • $24 • (11/15/91) • **88**

Pinot Noir Napa Valley Doc's Reserve 1988 • $19 • (02/15/92) • **82**

Pinot Noir Napa Valley Doc's Reserve 1987 • $19 • (05/31/90) • **87**

STARR | OREGON

Chardonnay Willamette Valley Reserve 1995: Offers plenty of complex, beautifully developed flavors on a crisp, elegant frame. Spicy, toasty pear and lime flavors swirl through the gentle finish. Try now. 72 cases made. • $20 • (05/15/98) • **88**

Pinot Noir Willamette Valley 1996: Light and bright, here's a refreshing red with pretty strawberry and spice flavors. Try now. 525 cases made. • $14 • (05/15/98) • **83**

Pinot Noir Willamette Valley Bert's Blend Reserve 1996: Light in texture, with a lovely ruby color and pretty berry and currant flavors that remain lithe and smooth through the long, elegant finish. Best from now through 2002. 110 cases made. • $28 • (06/15/98) • **89**

STATON HILLS | WASHINGTON

Cabernet Sauvignon Columbia Valley Unfiltered 1993: A bit tough around the edges, but it has a nice bead of currant and blackberry flavor that extends into the finish. Try in 2000 to 2002. 3,600 cases made. • $18 • (09/15/97) • **86**

Cabernet Sauvignon Washington 1992 • $12 • (06/15/96) • **87**

Cabernet Sauvignon Washington 1989 • $14 • (01/31/95) • **87**

Cabernet Sauvignon Washington 1988 • $15 • (03/31/92) • **81**

Cabernet Sauvignon Washington 1987 • $13 • (03/31/91) • **86**

Cabernet Sauvignon Washington 1986 • $12 • (10/15/89) • **80**

Cabernet Sauvignon Washington Estate 1987 • $20 • (02/29/92) • **79**

Cabernet Sauvignon Washington Estate 1986 • $20 • (03/31/91) • **83**

Cabernet Sauvignon Washington Reserve 1987 • $22 • (03/31/92) • **85**

Cabernet Sauvignon Washington Reserve 1986 • $22 • (08/31/91) • **83**

Cabernet Sauvignon Yakima Valley 1992: Crisp in structure, with a polished texture that shows off its nice mouthful of minty black cherry flavors. Drinkable now. 12,000 cases made. • $14 • (11/30/96) • **86**

Chardonnay Columbia Valley 1994: Pretty pear, vanilla and nutmeg flavors glide smoothly, almost unobtrusively, through this mild-mannered wine. Ready to drink. 3,600 cases made. • $12 • (11/30/96) • **85**

Fumé Blanc Washington 1994 • $9 • (05/31/96) • **84**

Fumé Blanc Washington 1993 • $7 • (07/31/94) • **83**

Merlot Washington 1992 • $13 • (06/15/96) • **85**

Merlot Washington 1988 • $15 • (03/31/92) • **82**

Merlot Washington 1987 • $14 • (08/31/91) • **79**

Merlot Washington Reserve 1987 • $22 • (10/15/92) • **87**

Phoenix Yakima Valley 1992 • $18 • (06/15/96) • **82**

Phoenix Yakima Valley Lot #2 1992: Crisp, earthy and chewy, it's a tight little wine that never shows much flavor or richness. Tasted twice, with consistent notes. A blend of 56 percent Cabernet Sauvignon, 33 percent Merlot, and 11 percent Cabernet Franc. 350 cases made. • $30 • (09/30/97) • **78**

Pinot Noir Oregon 1990 • $10 • (11/30/94) • **79**

Pinot Noir Oregon 1988 • $15 • (02/28/93) • **78**

Pinot Noir Oregon 1987 • $13 • (04/15/91) • **84**

Riesling Late Harvest Washington 1987 • $10/375ml • (03/31/92) • **82**

STAUB, RUSTY | CALIFORNIA

Cabernet Sauvignon California 1992 • $10 • (12/15/95) • **83**

STEELE | CALIFORNIA

Cabernet Franc Clear Lake 1994: Interesting flavors of rich currant and berry, and a dash of mineral, happily override an earthy, barnyardy edge. Ruggedly tannic, but try now. 300 cases made. • $15 • (04/30/97) • **86**

Cabernet Sauvignon Anderson Valley 1994: Starts off with leafy sage and bell-pepper flavors, but notes of ripe currant and plum fold in for added dimension. Has a rich, intense finish with a long, complex aftertaste showing pretty oak shadings. 500 cases made. • $24 • (12/15/97) • **91**

Cabernet Sauvignon Anderson Valley 1993: Shows off pretty toast, vanilla and smoky oak before the currant and cherry flavors come through, adding hints of anise and spice. Has a nice sense of balance and proportion, despite firm tannins. 250 cases made. • $22 • (04/30/96) • **90**

Chardonnay California 1994: Bold, ripe and exotic, boasting complex fig, apricot, honey, pear and vanilla notes, an altogether opulent and mouth-filling bottle of Chardonnay. Packs in lots of flavor, yet manages to maintain its finesse. 5,000 cases made. • $18 • (05/15/96) SS • **92**

Chardonnay California 1993 • $18 • (07/31/95) • **86**

Chardonnay California Steele Cuvée 1996: A smooth, rich and creamy style, with complex anise, buttery pear and fig flavors, and spicy, toasty oak nuances. Manages to balance its richness with a sense of elegance and finesse. Drink now through 2002. 9,200 cases made. • $19 • (05/31/98) SS • **90**

Chardonnay California Steele Cuvée 1995: Complex, with a creamy core of pear, spice, apple and melon flavors. Turns elegant and supple on the finish, where the flavors linger. Wonderful. Ready to drink. 5,000 cases made. • $18 • (05/15/97) • **91**

Chardonnay Carneros Durell Vineyard 1996: Thick and concentrated, with an earthy streak through the core of pear, spice and vanilla, but make no mistake, this is a wonderful wine, with lots of extra facets. Drink now through 2002. 800 cases made. • $24 • (06/30/98) • **93**

Chardonnay Carneros Sangiacomo Vineyard 1996: An ultrarich, almost cloying style, with ripe, sweet-tasting fruit, lots of fig, pear and honey flavors, but it manages to keep focused, hold its rich flavors and finish with a complex aftertaste. Drink now through 2001. 700 cases made. • $24 • (05/15/98) • **90**

Chardonnay Carneros Sangiacomo Vineyard 1995: Smooth, rich and creamy layers of ripe fig, pear, melon and apricot that fan out and linger on the finish, turning elegant and silky. Delicious now. 500 cases made. • $22 • (05/15/97) • **93**

Chardonnay Carneros Sangiacomo Vineyard 1994: Well oaked, with ripe, rich, complex fruit to match. The layers of pear, spice, honey, fig and melon all meld together quite nicely on the finish and linger on. 500 cases made. • $22 • (05/31/96) • **93**

Chardonnay Mendocino Dennison Vineyard 1995: Smooth and creamy, with a pretty core of pear- and peach-laced Chardonnay flavors, finishing on a spicy note and with good length. 250 cases made. • $22 • (08/31/97) • **90**

Chardonnay Mendocino Dennison Vineyard 1994: A subtle white that grows on you, with an elegant band of spicy, toasty oak, ripe pear and apple notes. A graceful style with flavors that expand on the finish. 250 cases made. • $22 • (05/31/96) • **90**

Chardonnay Mendocino DuPratt Vineyard 1996: Rich and focused, with a complex core of pear, fig, apple, spice and mineral. Showing off some pretty, spicy oak flavors, too, with hints of nutmeg and honeysuckle. Drink now through 2002. 800 cases made. • $26 • (06/30/98) • **92**

Chardonnay Mendocino DuPratt Vineyard 1995: Rich and concentrated, this is a bold and complex young wine oozing with juicy pear, melon, apricot and hazelnut flavors that keep pumping through a long, lingering aftertaste. 600 cases made. • $25 • (05/15/97) • **92**

Chardonnay Mendocino DuPratt Vineyard 1994: Smooth and complex, with a pretty array of ripe pear, honey and apple flavors set in a creamy texture. Shows fine depth and integration of the fruit and oak flavors that continue to expand on the finish. 400 cases made. • $24 • (05/31/96) • **92**

Chardonnay Mendocino DuPratt Vineyard 1993 • $24 • (07/31/95) • **91**

Chardonnay Mendocino Lolonis Vineyard 1996: Starts out earthy, then unveils more appealing flavors, with pear, apple, butterscotch and citrus, and even adds touches of mineral and oak on the finish. Drink now through 2002. 1,000 cases made. • $26 • (06/30/98) • **93**

Chardonnay Mendocino Lolonis Vineyard 1995: Brings ripe, creamy pear, fig, apricot and peach flavors to the party, and turns smooth and elegant on the finish, where the flavors dance along. 950 cases made. • $26 • (08/31/97) • **91**

Chardonnay Mendocino Lolonis Vineyard 1994: Serves up an attractive array of ripe pear and tangerine flavors in a smooth and elegant style. Lacks the extra dimensions and complexity of the best from this vintage. 600 cases made. • $26 • (05/31/96) • **88**

Chardonnay Mendocino Lolonis Vineyard 1993 • $20 • (07/31/95) • **90**

Chardonnay Santa Barbara County Bien Nacido Vineyard 1996: A wine with rich flavors and lots of finesse, this offers a smooth, creamy texture and lots of pear, tropical fruit, guava and fig. Turns ever more elegant on the aftertaste, with delicate fruit notes that linger. Drink now through 2002. 800 cases made. • $26 • (05/31/98) • **92**

Chardonnay Santa Barbara County Bien Nacido Vineyard 1995: Bold, ripe and complex, with a rich core of tropical fruit, hints of pear, pineapple and guava. Turns smooth and supple on the finish. Wonderful finesse. 500 cases made. • $25 • (05/31/97) • **92**

Chardonnay Santa Barbara County Bien Nacido Vineyard 1994: An elegant, refined style with smooth, polished pear and honey flavors laced with hints of toasty oak. Has a creamy texture, and the flavors sail on and on. A beautifully crafted white. 400 cases made. • $24 • (05/31/96) • **91**

Chardonnay Santa Barbara County Bien Nacido Vineyard 1993 • $22 • (07/31/95) • **88**

Chardonnay Santa Barbara County Goodchild Vineyard 1996: Smooth, rich and creamy, with sharply focused tropical fruit flavors, hints of pear, guava, spice and nectarine. Turns elegant on the finish, where its depth and concentration become ever more apparent. Drink now through 2002. 800 cases made. • $26 • (05/31/98) • **92**

Chardonnay Santa Barbara County Goodchild Vineyard 1995: Ripe and full-bodied, with an earthy side to the pear, fig and spicy flavors, but the finish is most impressive, where the flavors fan out and show added dimension. 700 cases made. • $24 • (09/30/97) • **92**

Chardonnay Santa Barbara County Goodchild Vineyard 1994: A wonderfully crafted, ripe, rich and complex white that takes you through tiers of honey, spice, fig and melon flavors, then gives you a lovely hazelnut finish. A complex and racy yet elegant and refined style. 350 cases made. • $24 • (05/31/96) • **92**

Chardonnay Sonoma Valley Durell Vineyard 1995: Ripe, rich and full-bodied, with complex flavors of spice, pear, apple and honey, turning silky and polished on the finish, where the fruit flavors really fan out. 750 cases made. • $24 • (08/31/97) • **92**

Chardonnay Sonoma Valley Durell Vineyard 1994: A complex array of ripe tropical fruit, with tiers of honey, pear and butterscotch flavors. Picks up a toasty oak edge on the finish. 400 cases made. • $24 • (05/31/96) • **88**

Chardonnay Sonoma Valley Parmelee-Hill Vineyard 1996: Bright and lively, with well-focused anise, pear and spicy nuances, turning tight and even more focused on the finish. Good intensity and subtle oak flavors, which, combined with the fruit, grow on you. Drink now through 2001. 175 cases made. • $26 • (06/30/98) • **90**

Pinot Blanc Santa Barbara County Bien Nacido Vineyard 1996: Remarkable both for its complexity and finesse, this California Pinot Blanc offers rich pear, fig, melon and vanilla that pick up an attractive spice and hazelnut edge on the finish. Simply delicious—not a bit surprising from winemaker Jed Steele and this vineyard. 1,800 cases made. • $15 • (02/28/98) SS • **92**

Pinot Blanc Santa Barbara County Bien Nacido Vineyard 1995: Young, tight and a bit backward, showing hints of peach, pear and spice flavors that fold together nicely. 700 cases made. • $15 • (02/28/97) • **88**

Pinot Blanc Santa Barbara County Bien Nacido Vineyard 1994 • $14 • (11/15/95) • **85**

Pinot Blanc Santa Barbara County Bien Nacido Vineyard 1993 • $14 • (12/31/94) • **89**

Pinot Gris Anderson Valley Romani Family Vineyard 1996: Rich, smooth and creamy, with ripe, well-defined pear, vanilla, citrus and earth flavors and a long, complex aftertaste. 150 cases made. • $18 • (04/30/98) • **87**

Pinot Noir Anderson Valley 1995: Distinct for its smoky cola and raspberry notes, finishing with coffee and cedary notes. It's tight and firmly tannic: Try now. 500 cases made. • $22 • (10/15/97) • **88**

Pinot Noir Anderson Valley 1994: Young and tight, barely showing its plum and berry flavors, but as it opens up, it shows more spice and oak. Try now. 500 cases made. • $22 • (04/30/97) • **88**

Pinot Noir Carneros 1995: A reliable performer vintage after vintage, this year's bottling is ripe, smooth and polished, with a rich array of smoky, tarry plum and cherry flavors that fold together nicely, finishing with an array of sage, tea and anise notes. Drink now. 3,000 cases made. • $18 • (10/15/97) SS • **90**

Pinot Noir Carneros 1993 • $18 • (09/15/95) HR • **90**

Pinot Noir Carneros 1992 • $16 • (02/28/94) • **87**

Pinot Noir Carneros 1991 • $18 • (02/15/93) HR • **90**

Pinot Noir Carneros Durell Vineyard 1995: An elegant style that shows off tea, herb, sage and dried cherry flavors, turning dry on the finish. Drinkable now. 350 cases made. • $24 • (10/31/97) • **88**

Pinot Noir Carneros Durell Vineyard 1993 • $19 • (09/15/95) • **88**

Pinot Noir Carneros Durell Vineyard 1992 • $20 • (02/28/94) • **87**

Pinot Noir Carneros Sangiacomo Vineyard 1995: Smooth, ripe and juicy, with a pretty medley of ripe plum, cherry, sage, tea and spice flavors. Turns elegant on the finish, where it shows a measure of finesse. 500 cases made. • $24 • (10/15/97) • **90**

Pinot Noir Carneros Sangiacomo Vineyard 1994: Features a wonderful conglomeration of well-integrated flavors—layers of black cherry, cola, earth and light, spicy oak. Gains complexity on the finish, where the flavors fold together nicely. 400 cases made. • $22 • (04/30/97) • **91**

Pinot Noir Carneros Sangiacomo Vineyard 1993 • $22 • (09/15/95) • **88**

Pinot Noir Carneros Sangiacomo Vineyard 1991 • $22 • (02/28/93) • **88**
Pinot Noir Mendocino DuPratt Vineyard 1995: Young, tightly wound and firmly tannic, with a wonderful core of plum, wild berry and blueberry flavors, picking up tasty cedar, anise and tarry notes on the finish, where the flavors linger. 70 cases made. • $28 • (10/15/97) • **92**
Pinot Noir Mendocino DuPratt Vineyard 1994: Complex with its ripe plum, cherry, berry and cedary oak flavors, it shows a measure of elegance and finesse, turning delicate on the aftertaste. Drinkable now. 70 cases made. • $26 • (04/30/97) • **91**
Pinot Noir Mendocino DuPratt Vineyard 1992 • $26 • (02/28/94) • **86**
Pinot Noir Santa Barbara County Bien Nacido Vineyard 1995: Displays wonderful fruit intensity and is sharply focused, with bright, lively wild berry, cherry, spice and earthy raspberry flavors and a long, complex aftertaste. Can stand short-term cellaring. 210 cases made. • $38 • (10/31/97) • **93**
Pinot Noir Santa Barbara County Bien Nacido Vineyard 1994 • $20 • (04/30/96) • **90**
Pinot Noir Santa Barbara County Bien Nacido Vineyard 1993 • $22 • (09/15/95) • **86**
Viognier Clear Lake Dorn Vineyard 1996: Clean and spicy, with a modest serving of ripe pear and apple notes. The aftertaste shows a slight peachy note. 70 cases made. • $16 • (12/15/97) • **86**
Zinfandel Clear Lake Catfish Vineyard 1996: Intense, concentrated and marked by spice, mint and wild berry flavors. It lacks the rich fruitiness of previous vintages, but is restrained and well balanced. Drink now through 2002. 800 cases made. • $18 • (05/31/98) • **87**
Zinfandel Clear Lake Catfish Vineyard 1994: Delivers lots of complex flavors, with tiers of spice, raspberry, earth, cherry and wild berry; finishes with good depth and a long, lingering finish. Has elegance and finesse. Drinks well now. 700 cases made. • $18 • (10/31/97) • **91**
Zinfandel Clear Lake Catfish Vineyard 1993 • $13 • (09/30/95) • **89**
Zinfandel Clear Lake Catfish Vineyard 1992 • $13 • (09/15/94) HR • **90**
Zinfandel Clear Lake Catfish Vineyard 1991 • $13 • (09/30/93) • **90**
Zinfandel Mendocino DuPratt Vineyard 1995: Big, ripe, rich and tannic, it's a blockbuster style that packs in lots of exotic mineral and wild berry flavors but offers little in the way of polish or finesse. Needs hearty fare. Try now. 1,400 cases made. • $20 • (10/31/97) • **89**
Zinfandel Mendocino DuPratt Vineyard 1994: A big, ripe and intense California Zin, with juicy wild berry, cherry, anise and raspberry flavors. Showing off a rich and plush, long, lingering aftertaste that throws in dashes of pepper and spice. Drinks well now. 1,400 cases made. • $18 • (02/28/97) HR • **93**
Zinfandel Mendocino DuPratt Vineyard 1993 • $18 • (04/30/96) • **91**
Zinfandel Mendocino Pacini Vineyard 1996: Features bright, ripe, juicy Zinfandel fruit, with spicy cherry, wild berry, plum and cedar notes, finishing with ripe, firm tannins and a rich anise aftertaste. Drink now through 2002. 1,200 cases made. • $20 • (05/31/98) • **90**
Zinfandel Mendocino Pacini Vineyard 1995: Bold and ripe, with Port-like aromas and flavors, it's a big, assertive, chewy wine that stretches into the extremes for Zinfandel. Given its weight, intensity and tannin level, it will be best with food. 1,500 cases made. • $16 • (10/31/97) • **88**
Zinfandel Mendocino Pacini Vineyard 1994 • $15 • (04/30/96) • **88**
Zinfandel Mendocino Pacini Vineyard 1993 • $14 • (09/30/95) • **87**
Zinfandel Mendocino Pacini Vineyard 1992 • $13 • (10/15/94) • **82**
Zinfandel Mendocino Pacini Vineyard 1991 • $13 • (09/30/93) • **84**

STELTZNER | CALIFORNIA

Cabernet Sauvignon Napa Valley Stags Leap District 1988 • $19 • (11/15/92) • **82**
Cabernet Sauvignon Napa Valley Stags Leap District 1987 • $25 • (11/15/91) • **86**
Cabernet Sauvignon Napa Valley Stags Leap District 1986: Mature, with strikingly firm tannins and sharp acidity that distract your attention somewhat from the nice herb, black cherry and spice nuances. • $NA • (12/15/96) • **87**
Cabernet Sauvignon Napa Valley Stags Leap District 1985 • $16 • (11/15/88) • **92**
Cabernet Sauvignon Napa Valley Stags Leap District 1984 • $33 • (03/31/88) • **91**
Cabernet Sauvignon Napa Valley Stags Leap District 1983 • $NA • (06/30/87) • **88**
Cabernet Sauvignon Napa Valley Stags Leap District 1982 • $14 • (09/01/85) CS • **91**
Cabernet Sauvignon Napa Valley Stags Leap District 1981 • $NA • (06/30/87) • **91**
Cabernet Sauvignon Napa Valley Stags Leap District 1980 • $NA • (06/30/87) • **88**
Cabernet Sauvignon Napa Valley Stags Leap District 1979 • $NA • (06/30/87) • **89**
Cabernet Sauvignon Napa Valley Stags Leap District 1978 • $45 • (11/15/92) • **88**
Cabernet Sauvignon Napa Valley Stags Leap District 1977 • $NA • (06/30/87) • **88**
Cabernet Sauvignon Stags Leap District 1994: The dusty, cedary oak flavors override the modest core of plum and berry. Needs some time to work out the rough spots. Try after 1999. Much better than previously reviewed. 2,565 cases made. • $21 • (03/31/98) • **83**
Cabernet Sauvignon Stags Leap District 1991 • $18 • (03/31/95) • **85**
Cabernet Sauvignon Stags Leap District Barrel Select Reserve 1994: Good, with appealing cherry and currant flavors, but there's also a strongly earthy, somewhat cheesy edge. Best to cellar in hope it comes together. Try from 2000 to 2004. Better than an earlier tasting. 220 cases made. • $35 • (03/31/98) • **84**
Cabernet Sauvignon Stags Leap District Commemorative 1991 • $45 • (03/31/95) • **85**
Claret Stags Leap District 1993: Light and simple, coming across a bit watery, lacking focus and depth. 3,200 cases made. • $11 • (12/15/95) • **77**
Claret Stags Leap District 1992 • $11 • (03/31/95) • **84**
Claret Stags Leap District 1991 • $10 • (02/28/94) • **84**
Claret Stags Leap District 1990 • $11 • (11/15/92) • **88**
Merlot Stags Leap District 1994: Marked by a slight candied edge, the ripe cherry and berry flavors turn elegant and spicy, finishing with mild tannins. Ready now. 2,500 cases made. • $20 • (07/31/97) • **87**
Merlot Stags Leap District 1993: Marked by ripe fruity flavors, with hints of spice, cherry and plum, but the texture is a bit coarse and the tannins stand out on the finish. Drinkable now. 2,120 cases made. • $19 • (08/31/96) • **83**
Merlot Stags Leap District 1992 • $19 • (03/31/95) • **82**
Merlot Stags Leap District 1991 • $17 • (09/15/94) • **83**
Merlot Stags Leap District 1990 • $20 • (08/31/93) • **85**
Merlot Stags Leap District 1989 • $15 • (11/15/91) • **85**
Sauvignon Blanc Napa Valley 1996: Earthy, cloying and heavy. Lacks finesse, but offers some nice hazelnut, melon and grapefruit flavors nonetheless. 2,665 cases made. • $9 • (07/31/97) • **81**
Sauvignon Blanc Napa Valley 1995: Bright, focused and almost hot, with peppery pear and leafy, slightly vegetal flavors. 3,050 cases made. • $9 • (07/31/96) • **81**

STEMMLER, ROBERT | CALIFORNIA

Cabernet Sauvignon Sonoma County 1982 • $15 • (04/01/85) • **66**
Pinot Noir Sonoma County 1995: An interesting blend of wild cherry and spicy herbal notes. The texture is smooth and supple. Ready to drink. 2,823 cases made. • $26 • (11/30/97) • **86**
Pinot Noir Sonoma County 1994: Young, with a green, tannic edge to the barely ripe cherry and plum flavors. Try now. 4,725 cases made. • $22 • (02/28/97) • **80**
Pinot Noir Sonoma County 1993: A touch leathery and earthy in character. The plum and cherry flavors that do emerge are modest. 4,760 cases made. • $20 • (11/30/96) • **79**
Pinot Noir Sonoma County 1992 • $20 • (12/31/95) • **84**
Pinot Noir Sonoma County 1991 • $20 • (03/31/95) • **78**
Pinot Noir Sonoma County 1990 • $20 • (02/28/94) • **80**
Pinot Noir Sonoma County 1989 • $20 • (02/28/93) • **71**
Pinot Noir Sonoma County 1988 • $20 • (02/28/93) • **71**
Pinot Noir Sonoma County 1987 • $19 • (10/31/90) • **82**
Pinot Noir Sonoma County 1986 • $18 • (06/15/88) • **84**
Pinot Noir Sonoma County 1985 • $18 • (09/30/87) • **79**
Pinot Noir Sonoma County 1984 • $15 Ⓐ • (08/31/86) • **90**
Pinot Noir Sonoma County 1983 • $15 • (03/16/85) SS • **93**

STEPHEN ROSS | CALIFORNIA

Chardonnay Edna Valley Edna Ranch 1996: Tightly wound and sharply focused, with an intense core of citrus, pear, apple and guava, showing a touch of elegance and finesse. 161 cases made. • $18 • (07/31/98) • **89**

Key: SS—Spectator Selection CS—Cellar Selection HR—Highly Recommended BB—Best Buy $NA—Price not available Ⓐ—Auction Price (BT)—Barrel Tasting
Dates in parentheses indicate the issues in which the ratings were published.

Chardonnay Edna Valley Edna Ranch 1995: Solid, with ripe pear and pineapple flavors, and a grapefruit note on the finish. Complex and well balanced, it drinks well now. 269 cases made. • $18 • (06/15/97) • **87**

Chardonnay Edna Valley Linda's Vineyard 1996: Ripe and clean, with a pleasant range of spicy melon and pear flavors. Picks up a little more depth and complexity on the finish, while maintaining its elegance. Drinks well now. 201 cases made. • $18 • (07/31/98) • **87**

Chardonnay Santa Maria Valley Bien Nacido Vineyard 1995: Well focused, in a clean, ripe style, with zingy pear, citrus and apple flavors. 118 cases made. • $18 • (07/31/97) • **86**

Pinot Noir Arroyo Grande Valley La Colline Vineyard 1996: Pleasant enough, but never really gets going. The modest cherry, spice and berry flavors are smooth and simple, and the finish lacks the extra dimensions you hope for. Ready now. 143 cases made. • $20 • (02/28/98) • **85**

Pinot Noir Edna Valley Edna Ranch 1996: Tight and crisp, with a well-focused core of black cherry, wild berry, plum and spice. Flavors fan out on the finish. Drinkable now or cellar into 2000. 409 cases made. • $22 • (01/31/98) • **87**

Pinot Noir Edna Valley Edna Ranch 1995: Dark, ripe, rich and concentrated, offering well-integrated black cherry, spice, cedar and anise flavors, pretty on the aftertaste. Finishes with smooth, polished tannins. Drinkable now. 189 cases made. • $18 • (02/28/97) • **91**

Pinot Noir Santa Maria Valley Bien Nacido Vineyard 1996: Smooth and polished, with a supple texture, ripe cherry, plum and berry notes and a pretty, spicy oak aftertaste. Appealing now. 195 cases made. • $24 • (01/31/98) • **88**

STERLING | CALIFORNIA

Cabernet Sauvignon Napa Valley 1995: Fans of understated, Bordeaux-style Cabernet will find this California red quite appealing, especially at this price. It's lean and trim, with a tight, narrow band of currant, cedar, earth and claylike flavors, finishing with firm tannins. Needs short-term cellaring; will be best from now to 2004. 76,000 cases made. • $14 • (04/30/98) HR • **88**

Cabernet Sauvignon Napa Valley 1994: Solid, with a band of leathery currant, cherry and cedary oak flavors and a finish marked by firm tannins. Try now. 66,000 cases made. • $14 • (12/15/96) • **84**

Cabernet Sauvignon Napa Valley 1993: Shows herb and cedary notes laced with just enough cherry and berry flavors to keep it interesting. Turns simple on the finish. 32,000 cases made. • $14 • (09/15/96) • **84**

Cabernet Sauvignon Napa Valley 1992 • $14 • (11/30/95) • **85**

Cabernet Sauvignon Napa Valley 1991 • $14 • (11/15/94) • **82**

Cabernet Sauvignon Napa Valley 1990 • $14 • (11/15/93) • **83**

Cabernet Sauvignon Napa Valley 1989 • $18 • (11/15/92) • **83**

Cabernet Sauvignon Napa Valley 1988 • $15 • (11/15/91) • **80**

Cabernet Sauvignon Napa Valley 1987 • $14 • (05/15/90) • **91**

Cabernet Sauvignon Napa Valley 1986 • $29 Ⓐ • (03/31/89) • **91**

Cabernet Sauvignon Napa Valley 1985 • $29 Ⓐ • (05/15/88) • **89**

Cabernet Sauvignon Napa Valley 1983 • $18 • (02/15/87) • **81**

Cabernet Sauvignon Napa Valley 1982 • $16 • (05/16/86) • **66**

Cabernet Sauvignon Napa Valley 1981 • $20 • (08/01/85) • **88**

Cabernet Sauvignon Napa Valley 1980 • $28 • (02/15/84) • **84**

Cabernet Sauvignon Napa Valley 1978 • $22 • (06/01/86) • **95**

Cabernet Sauvignon Napa Valley 1974 • $26 Ⓐ • (11/15/94) • **82**

Cabernet Sauvignon Napa Valley Diamond Mountain Ranch 1990 • $18 • (11/15/93) • **81**

Cabernet Sauvignon Napa Valley Diamond Mountain Ranch 1989 • $18 • (11/15/92) • **79**

Cabernet Sauvignon Napa Valley Diamond Mountain Ranch 1987 • $16 • (11/15/90) • **91**

Cabernet Sauvignon Napa Valley Diamond Mountain Ranch 1986: Ruggedly earthy and tannic, still. Hints of currant and spice flavor emerge but, in the end, the tannins win out. • $NA • (12/15/96) • **80**

Cabernet Sauvignon Napa Valley Diamond Mountain Ranch 1985 • $21 • (05/31/89) • **88**

Cabernet Sauvignon Napa Valley Diamond Mountain Ranch 1984 • $16 • (02/15/88) • **84**

Cabernet Sauvignon Napa Valley Diamond Mountain Ranch 1983 • $15 • (11/30/86) • **74**

Cabernet Sauvignon Napa Valley Diamond Mountain Ranch 1982 • $15 • (11/16/85) CS • **94**

Cabernet Sauvignon Napa Valley Diamond Mountain Ranch Vineyard 1994: Ruggedly tannic, with a strong leathery edge; the fruit is deeply submerged. On the finish, hints of currant, sage and spice peek through. Fans of this style might be rewarded if it's cellared, or they might be disappointed by its austerity. 7,000 cases made. • $18 • (10/31/97) • **85**

Cabernet Sauvignon Napa Valley Diamond Mountain Ranch Vineyard 1993: Young, tight and tannic, this well-structured wine offers a pleasant array of earthy currant, mineral, smoky oak and herbal flavors. Folds together nicely on the finish, though the tannins are substantial and will require cellaring into 2000. 5,000 cases made. • $18 • (11/15/96) • **88**

Cabernet Sauvignon Napa Valley Diamond Mountain Ranch Vineyard 1992 • $17 • (10/31/95) • **88**

Cabernet Sauvignon Napa Valley Diamond Mountain Ranch Vineyard 1991 • $18 • (11/15/94) • **86**

Cabernet Sauvignon Napa Valley Reserve 1997: Still quite grapey, with fermentation aromas, it's tart and focused, with black cherry, blackberry, cedar and spice. • $NA • (07/31/98) (BT) • **90-94**

Cabernet Sauvignon Napa Valley Reserve 1996: Young, tight and well stuctured. A touch of earthiness, but it adds dimension to the rich currant and mineral flavors. • $NA • (06/15/97) (BT) • **90-94**

Cabernet Sauvignon Napa Valley Reserve 1984 • $24 Ⓐ • (03/31/89) CS • **92**

Cabernet Sauvignon Napa Valley Reserve 1983 • $26 Ⓐ • (06/15/87) • **86**

Cabernet Sauvignon Napa Valley Reserve 1980 • $17 Ⓐ • (11/01/84) CS • **90**

Cabernet Sauvignon Napa Valley Reserve 1979 • $29 Ⓐ • (02/15/84) • **91**

Cabernet Sauvignon Napa Valley Reserve 1978 • $41 • (11/15/92) • **90**

Cabernet Sauvignon Napa Valley Reserve 1974 • $61 Ⓐ • (11/15/94) • **83**

Chardonnay Napa Valley 1996: Ripe and intense, with a core of apple, fig and melon, turning to citrus and cedar on the finish. Drinks well now. 65,000 cases made. • $14 • (01/31/98) • **87**

Chardonnay Napa Valley 1995: An elegant wine featuring pretty pear, apple and melon notes and picking up a trace of cedary oak on the finish. Smooth, ripe and creamy, it's a good value. 49,000 cases made. • $14 • (05/15/97) • **87**

Chardonnay Napa Valley 1993 • $14 • (04/30/95) • **82**

Chardonnay Napa Valley Carneros Winery Lake Vineyard 1996: Simple, clean and pleasant, offering ripe pear, vanilla and spicy notes, but a bit short on the extra dimensions you might hope for from this vineyard and vintage. Drink now through 2000. 4,000 cases made. • $18 • (05/31/98) • **86**

Chardonnay Napa Valley Carneros Winery Lake Vineyard 1995: Strives for complexity, with its focused citrus and pear flavors and spicy, toasty oak nuances. Shows hints of honey and apricot on the finish. A marked improvement over the previous few vintages. 6,500 cases made. • $18 • (01/31/97) • **88**

Chardonnay Napa Valley Carneros Winery Lake Vineyard 1994: A rustic style, with a waxy, earthy accent to the pear and fig notes. Lacks focus and has some off-beat flavors. Tasted twice, with consistent notes. • $18 • (12/31/96) • **78**

Chardonnay Napa Valley Carneros Winery Lake Vineyard 1993 • $18 • (07/31/95) • **78**

Chardonnay Napa Valley Diamond Mountain Ranch Vineyard 1996: Pleasant, with ripe pear and apple notes and a hint of spicy, toasty oak on the finish. Drink now through 2002. 3,000 cases made. • $18 • (05/31/98) • **87**

Chardonnay Napa Valley Diamond Mountain Ranch Vineyard 1993: Lean and a touch bitter, with a simple band of pear and spice notes. Tasted twice, with consistent notes. 3,300 cases made. • $19 • (07/31/96) • **79**

Chardonnay Napa Valley Z Lot 1993 • $20 • (07/31/95) • **85**

Dolcetto Napa Valley 1994 • $10 • (01/01/95) • **80**

Malvasia Bianca California 1995: Fresh and lively, with lots of apricot, passion fruit and spice flavors that linger nicely on the soft finish. 213 cases made. • $15 • (12/31/96) • **85**

Merlot Napa Valley 1995: Marked by a modest core of cedar, currant, tar and oak, this wine is nonetheless well-balanced, and the tannins are in proportion. Picks up a tobacco note on the aftertaste. Try now through 2002. 80,000 cases made. • $14 • (04/30/98) • **86**

Merlot Napa Valley 1994: Lean and trim, with a narrow band of earthy currant, spice and cedar notes. Finishes with a smoky, tobacco edge and good length, but it's shy on depth and complexity. Drinkable now. 95,000 cases made. • $14 • (03/31/97) • **87**

Merlot Napa Valley 1993 • $14 • (03/31/96) • **82**

Merlot Napa Valley 1991 • $14 • (09/15/94) • **74**

Merlot Napa Valley 1990 • $14 • (06/15/93) • **82**

Merlot Napa Valley 1989 • $15 • (05/31/92) • **82**

Merlot Napa Valley 1988 • $15 • (04/15/91) • **83**

Merlot Napa Valley 1987 • $13 • (06/15/90) • **83**

Merlot Napa Valley 1986 • $14 • (03/31/89) • **85**

Merlot Napa Valley 1985 • $14 • (03/31/88) • **87**

Merlot Napa Valley 1984 • $12 • (04/30/87) • **93**

Merlot Napa Valley 1983 • $11 • (06/01/86) • **91**

Merlot Napa Valley 1982 • $12 • (10/01/85) • **83**

Merlot Napa Valley 1981 • $11 • (03/01/84) • **83**
Merlot Napa Valley Carneros Winery Lake 1987 • $25 • (12/31/90) • **90**
Merlot Napa Valley Diamond Mountain Ranch Vineyard 1994: Supple and harmonious, with a dense core of earthy currant, spice and herbal notes, and a pretty overlay of buttery oak. Try now, or cellar to 2001. • $NA • (06/30/97) • **88**
Merlot Napa Valley Three Palms Vineyard 1994: Dense and chewy, with firm, earthy tannins and a slight leathery edge to the currant and plum flavors. Try now. • $NA • (06/30/97) • **85**
Merlot Napa Valley Three Palms Vineyard 1992 • $22 • (03/31/96) • **83**
Merlot Napa Valley Three Palms Vineyard 1990 • $18 • (04/15/94) • **85**
Pinot Grigio Napa Valley 1995: A simple wine, tasting vaguely of honey and almond. 943 cases made. • $15 • (12/15/96) • **80**
Pinot Grigio Napa Valley 1994 • $12 • (12/15/95) • **80**
Pinot Noir Napa Valley Carneros Winery Lake 1991 • $18 • (02/28/93) • **78**
Pinot Noir Napa Valley Carneros Winery Lake 1990 • $14 • (11/30/92) • **73**
Pinot Noir Napa Valley Carneros Winery Lake 1990: Tastes simple—the modest band of tart cherry and berry notes fail to evolve into something more interesting. Finishes with crisp acidity. • $14 • (03/31/97) • **82**
Pinot Noir Napa Valley Carneros Winery Lake 1989 • $14 • (03/31/92) • **87**
Pinot Noir Napa Valley Carneros Winery Lake 1988 • $14 • (04/30/91) • **87**
Pinot Noir Napa Valley Carneros Winery Lake 1987 • $18 • (12/31/89) • **86**
Pinot Noir Napa Valley Carneros Winery Lake 1986: Aging well. Still holding its fruit, with fresh, ripe plum, cherry and wild berry notes, and the finish is complex and lingering. This was winemaker Bill Dyer's first Winery Lake Pinot, and may have been his best. Drink now to 2000. • $18 • (03/31/97) • **90**
Pinot Noir Napa Valley Carneros Winery Lake Vineyard 1995: A touch earthy, but it works its way into more interesting flavors, all the while retaining its austerity and firm, crisp tannins. Cellar short term. 7,750 cases made. • $16 • (12/15/97) • **84**
Pinot Noir Napa Valley Carneros Winery Lake Vineyard 1994 • $18 • (02/29/96) • **82**
Pinot Noir Napa Valley Carneros Winery Lake Vineyard 1993 • $18 • (12/31/95) • **82**
Pinot Noir Napa Valley Carneros Winery Lake Vineyard 1992 • $15 • (03/31/95) • **73**
Reserve Napa Valley 1994: Firm and well oaked, with a hard edge to its cedar, currant and tobacco flavors, it's solid but lacks the extra dimensions you might expect from this wine. Tasted three times, with consistent notes. A blend of 70 percent Cabernet Sauvignon, 11 percent Cabernet Franc, 10 percent Merlot, 8 percent Petit Verdot, and 1 percent Malbec. 6,400 cases made. • $40 • (12/15/97) • **88**
Reserve Napa Valley 1993: Pleasant enough, with its spicy currant and plum flavors, and finishes with a sense of elegance and finesse, but it loses its intensity and lacks the extra richness and dimensions found in great wines. 1,820 cases made. • $40 • (11/15/96) • **88**
Reserve Napa Valley 1992 • $40 • (12/15/95) • **87**
Reserve Napa Valley 1991 • $30 • (11/15/94) • **88**
Reserve Napa Valley 1990 • $30 • (11/15/94) • **87**
Reserve Napa Valley 1989 • $35 • (06/30/93) • **88**
Reserve Napa Valley 1988 • $40 • (03/31/92) • **85**
Reserve Napa Valley 1987 • $43 • (11/15/90) • **93**
Reserve Napa Valley 1987: Round, smooth and supple, with an elegant core of earthy currant, tar, black cherry, sage and herbs, it holds its flavors through the complex finish. Best now and through 2002. • $43 • (12/15/97) • **90**
Reserve Napa Valley 1986 • $43 • (03/15/90) CS • **95**
Reserve Napa Valley 1986: This has turned into an elegant, complex wine, offering ripe cherry, currant, anise, smoke and meatlike flavors and fine tannins. Finishes with good fruit flavors and avoids being overly dry or tannic. Wows you subtly and with finesse. • $41 • (12/15/96) • **90**
Reserve Napa Valley 1985 • $42 • (07/15/89) SS • **96**
Sangiovese Atlas Peak 1993 • $14 • (11/30/95) • **82**
Sauvignon Blanc Napa Valley 1995: Crisp and appealing for its bright apple, vanilla and grapefruit flavors that linger nicely on the finish. 80,000 cases made. • $8 • (08/31/96) • **85**
Sauvignon Blanc Napa Valley 1994 • $9 • (03/31/96) • **85**
Sauvignon Blanc Napa Valley 1993 • $9 • (05/31/95) • **80**
Sauvignon Blanc North Coast 1996: Here's a mouthful of Sauvignon Blanc, its blend of melon, grapefruit and hazelnut qualities sitting broadly on the palate, supported by a steely counterpoint. Finishes a bit short but still delicious and a good value. 68,000 cases made. • $8 • (10/15/97) BB • **85**
Three Palms Vineyard Napa Valley 1988 • $19 • (11/15/92) • **85**
Three Palms Vineyard Napa Valley 1987 • $23 • (11/15/90) • **87**
Three Palms Vineyard Napa Valley 1986 • $22 • (12/31/89) • **86**
Three Palms Vineyard Napa Valley 1985 • $22 • (12/31/88) • **93**

STEVENOT | CALIFORNIA

Cabernet Franc Sierra Foothills 1995: Earthy, stalky flavors prevail over the modest fruit. Not fun to drink. 400 cases made. • $15 • (11/30/97) • **78**
Cabernet Sauvignon Amador County Grand Reserve 1988 • $10 • (11/15/92) • **83**
Cabernet Sauvignon Calaveras County 1985 • $7 • (06/30/89) • **76**
Cabernet Sauvignon Calaveras County Grand Reserve 1987 • $9 • (03/31/92) • **82**
Cabernet Sauvignon Calaveras County Grand Reserve 1984 • $15 • (12/31/87) • **75**
Cabernet Sauvignon Calaveras County Reserve 1993: A solid, young wine, well focused, with an earthy accent to its plum and currant flavors. Well balanced and flavorful, it's a fine value at this price, and it's ready now. 4,000 cases made. • $12 • (11/15/96) • **87**
Cabernet Sauvignon Calaveras County Reserve 1992 • $10 • (07/31/95) • **82**
Cabernet Sauvignon Calaveras County Reserve 1991 • $11 • (11/15/94) • **84**
Cabernet Sauvignon Calaveras County Reserve 1990 • $10 • (07/31/93) • **86**
Cabernet Sauvignon Calaveras County Reserve 1989 • $10 • (03/15/93) • **82**
Cabernet Sauvignon California 1991 • $8 • (04/30/93) BB • **83**
Cabernet Sauvignon California 1990 • $8 • (11/15/92) • **79**
Cabernet Sauvignon California 1989 • $7 • (11/15/92) • **79**
Cabernet Sauvignon Sierra Foothills 1993: Strikes a nice balance between smoky, toasty oak and ripe, spicy berry flavor. 7,000 cases made. • $7 • (12/15/95) • **83**
Chardonnay Calaveras County Reserve 1994: Good intensity, showing pear and peach notes of modest proportions and a strong citrus finish. 1,500 cases made. • $10 • (05/15/96) • **84**
Chardonnay Calaveras County Reserve 1993 • $11 • (02/28/95) • **82**
Chardonnay Calaveras County Shaw Ranch 1996: Toasty oak frames pretty pear, citrus and mineral flavors. The wine is smooth yet lean, with a moderate finish. Drink now. 1,000 cases made. • $20 • (05/31/98) • **85**
Chardonnay Calaveras County Shaw Ranch 1995: Smooth, creamy and generous with its apple, pear, spice and vanilla flavors, finishing gracefully. Ready to drink. 500 cases made. • $18 • (06/15/97) • **87**
Chardonnay Sierra Foothills 1996: Here's a very good value in California Chardonnay. It's redolent of butter and smoke, but it's graceful, not heavy, on the palate, and finishes with a smattering of honey and papaya notes that give plenty of style. 6,000 cases made. • $10 • (11/30/97) BB • **88**
Chardonnay Sierra Foothills 1995: Fresh, fruity and inviting for its simple, straightforward character and soft texture. • $10 • (07/31/97) • **82**
Chardonnay Sierra Foothills 1993 • $8 • (02/28/95) • **82**
Chardonnay Sierra Foothills Reserve 1995: Crisp and simple, a tart mouthful of lemon and chalky spice flavors. 4,000 cases made. • $10 • (07/31/97) • **81**
Merlot California Reserve 1995: Light, crisp and refined, a smooth-textured wine with pretty blackberry and cranberry flavors. Ready to drink. 10,000 cases made. • $12 • (07/31/97) • **86**
Merlot North Coast Reserve 1991 • $10 • (03/31/93) • **75**
Merlot North Coast Reserve 1990 • $10 • (11/30/92) • **80**
Merlot North Coast Reserve 1989 • $10 • (05/31/92) • **83**
Merlot Sierra Foothills Reserve 1992 • $11 • (09/15/94) • **77**
Sangiovese Calaveras County Reserve 1994: Pale in color, but quite tannic, with an earthy accent to the modest plum and berry flavors. Ready to drink. 500 cases made. • $12 • (12/15/96) • **80**
Sauvignon Blanc Calaveras County 1996: Bright and tangy, with a strong thread of lemon-lime and grapefruit. Minerals and a hint of coconut round out the edges in this refreshingly assertive wine. Great price—too bad there's not much to go around. 270 cases made. • $10 • (03/31/98) • **88**
Sauvignon Blanc Calaveras County 1995: Bright and refreshing for its lively grapefruit and rose-petal flavors that remain crisp and vibrant through the focused finish. 500 cases made. • $9 • (10/31/96) • **89**
Sauvignon Blanc Calaveras County Reserve 1993 • $7 • (08/31/95) • **79**
Zinfandel Amador County Grand Reserve 1985 • $7 • (12/31/87) • **72**
Zinfandel Calaveras County 1986 • $7 • (07/31/89) BB • **84**
Zinfandel Calaveras County 1984 • $6 • (06/30/87) • **73**
Zinfandel Calaveras County Reserve 1991 • $10 • (06/15/94) • **73**
Zinfandel Calaveras County Reserve 1990 • $10 • (06/15/93) • **77**
Zinfandel California 1989 • $6 • (04/30/93) • **79**

Key: SS—Spectator Selection CS—Cellar Selection HR—Highly Recommended BB—Best Buy $NA—Price not available Ⓐ—Auction Price (BT)—Barrel Tasting
Dates in parentheses indicate the issues in which the ratings were published.

Zinfandel Sierra Foothills Reserve 1993 • $8 • (10/15/95) • **80**

STEWART | WASHINGTON

Cabernet Sauvignon Columbia Valley 1993: Charming, light and fragrant, with pleasant berry and spice flavors that linger delicately on the finish. 350 cases made. • $10 • (09/15/96) • **85**
Cabernet Sauvignon Columbia Valley 1988 • $11 • (08/31/91) • **79**
Chardonnay Columbia Valley 1994: On the earthy side, with an uplifting wisp of apple and oak aromas and flavors on the finish. 220 cases made. • $10 • (09/15/96) • **80**
Chardonnay Columbia Valley 1993 • $9 • (09/30/95) • **85**
Chardonnay Columbia Valley Barrel Fermented Reserve 1993 • $14 • (09/30/95) • **85**
Gewüztraminer Late Harvest Yakima Valley 1994 • $8/375ml • (09/30/95) • **88**
Gewürztraminer Yakima Valley 1993 • $5 • (09/30/95) • **79**
Johannisberg Riesling Columbia Valley 1994 • $5 • (09/30/95) • **84**
White Riesling Late Harvest Columbia Valley 1987 • $8 • (07/31/89) • **83**
White Riesling Late Harvest Columbia Valley Select 1986 • $6 • (10/15/89) • **80**

STONE CELLARS | WASHINGTON

Cabernet Sauvignon Columbia Valley 1993: Youthful, with plenty of fruit and some tannin. Try now. 20,000 cases made. • $5 • (05/31/95) • **83**
Chardonnay Central Coast 1995: Fresh and appealing for its smooth-textured pear and citrus flavors. Ready to drink. 4,000 cases made. • $9 • (07/31/97) • **83**
Chardonnay Columbia Valley 1993 • $5 • (01/31/95) • **81**
Merlot Columbia Valley 1993 • $6 • (05/31/95) BB • **83**

STONE CREEK | CALIFORNIA

Cabernet Sauvignon California Special Selection 1995: Smooth and appealing for its bright berry and vanilla flavors, this is nice to drink now, while it's fresh. 38,000 cases made. • $7 • (11/15/97) • **83**
Cabernet Sauvignon California Special Selection 1994: Sturdy, simple and generous with its black cherry and herb flavors. Nice to drink now, if a bit coarse. 20,000 cases made. • $7 • (12/31/96) • **82**
Cabernet Sauvignon California Special Selection 1989 • $6 • (11/15/93) • **72**
Cabernet Sauvignon Napa Valley Chairman's Reserve 1990 • $10 • (11/15/93) • **68**
Cabernet Sauvignon Napa Valley Limited Bottling 1986 • $10 • (06/15/90) • **85**
Cabernet Sauvignon Napa Valley Special Selection 1986 • $10 • (11/15/91) • **80**
Cabernet Sauvignon Napa Valley Special Selection 1983 • $8 • (05/31/87) BB • **91**
Cabernet Sauvignon Sonoma County Chairman's Reserve 1995: A juicy, bright wine with cherry, licorice, herb and cassis flavors. Hangs on the finish with moderate tannins and a spicy edge. Drink now or hold. 2,100 cases made. • $16 • (10/15/97) • **87**
Chardonnay California Special Selection 1996: Refreshing, with nicely focused mineral and juicy lemon flavors. Hints of toast and cream linger on the finish. Drink now. 36,000 cases made. • $7 • (05/31/98) • **84**
Chardonnay California Special Selection 1995: Ripe and spicy, with more than a hint of mineral and earth character sneaking in with the decadent pear flavors. Ready to drink. 40,000 cases made. • $7 • (12/31/96) • **83**
Chardonnay California Special Selection 1994: Light and a little spicy, centered around simple peach fruit that lingers on the finish. Ready now. 40,000 cases made. • $7 • (07/31/96) BB • **83**
Chardonnay Napa Valley Chairman's Reserve 1994: Has an earthiness that lends some character to the simple, spicy pear flavors. Ready to drink. 2,500 cases made. • $15 • (06/15/97) • **82**
Merlot California Special Selection 1995: Shows herbal, tarry, blackberry flavors backed by coarse tannins. Finishes short. 70,000 cases made. • $8 • (07/31/97) • **80**
Merlot California Special Selection 1990 • $7 • (11/30/92) • **80**
Merlot California Special Selection 1989 • $6 • (05/31/92) • **79**
Merlot Columbia Valley 1989 • $7 • (05/31/91) BB • **86**
Merlot Columbia Valley 1988 • $6 • (09/30/90) • **78**
Merlot Sonoma County Chairman's Reserve 1994: Light in texture and color, with modest earth and berry flavors fading fast. 2,655 cases made. • $17 • (07/31/97) • **77**
Merlot Washington Special Selection 1993 • $8 • (05/15/96) BB • **84**
Pinot Noir Sonoma County Chairman's Reserve 1996: A pleasant, cherrylike wine with a smooth, almost waxy texture. A simple quaff to drink young. 1,300 cases made. • $14 • (11/30/97) • **83**
Zinfandel California 1991 • $6 • (09/30/94) BB • **85**
Zinfandel California Special Selection 1995: A straightforward style, with ripe berry, spice, tar and cedar notes. Solid, if unexciting. 7,000 cases made. • $7 • (04/30/97) • **84**
Zinfandel California Special Selection 1991 • $7 • (10/15/95) • **83**

STONE HILL | MISSOURI

Norton Missouri 1992 • $NA • (10/31/95) • **85**
Port Missouri 1992 • $NA • (10/31/95) • **83**

STONEGATE | CALIFORNIA

Cabernet Franc Napa Valley 1990 • $NA • (11/15/93) • **81**
Cabernet Sauvignon Napa Valley 1991 • $18 • (12/15/95) • **82**
Cabernet Sauvignon Napa Valley 1990 • $14 • (11/15/94) • **81**
Cabernet Sauvignon Napa Valley 1989 • $15 • (11/15/93) • **80**
Cabernet Sauvignon Napa Valley 1988 • $14 • (11/15/92) • **84**
Cabernet Sauvignon Napa Valley 1987 • $14 • (03/31/92) • **82**
Cabernet Sauvignon Napa Valley 1986: This is mature, with coffee and currant notes that dry out the palate, but it's a good effort from a winery that has suffered from inconsistency. • $NA • (12/15/96) • **84**
Cabernet Sauvignon Napa Valley 1985 • $17 • (08/31/90) • **86**
Cabernet Sauvignon Napa Valley 1984 • $13 • (02/15/89) • **86**
Cabernet Sauvignon Napa Valley 1981 • $12 • (11/15/86) • **78**
Cabernet Sauvignon Napa Valley 1978 • $27 • (11/15/92) • **87**
Chardonnay Sonoma County Bella Vista Vineyard 1995: Quite good. Broad, smooth and appealing for its spice and earth overtones to the basic, ripe apple flavors. Ready to drink. 2,500 cases made. • $14 • (07/31/97) • **85**
Meritage Reserve Napa Valley 1988 • $17 • (11/15/93) • **85**
Meritage Reserve Napa Valley 1987 • $17 • (11/15/93) • **86**
Merlot Napa Valley 1989 • $17 • (10/31/92) • **86**
Merlot Napa Valley 1988 • $17 • (05/31/92) • **81**
Merlot Napa Valley 1986 • $15 • (04/15/90) • **84**
Merlot Napa Valley Pershing Vineyard 1987 • $17 • (03/31/91) • **83**
Merlot Napa Valley Spaulding Vineyard 1987 • $17 • (03/31/91) • **86**
Merlot Napa Valley Spaulding Vineyard 1984 • $15 • (12/31/88) • **85**
Merlot Napa Valley Spaulding Vineyard 1982 • $14 • (02/28/87) • **84**
Merlot Napa Valley Spaulding Vineyard 1980 • $12 • (10/01/85) • **68**
Reserve Napa Valley 1989 • $24 • (12/15/95) • **88**
Sauvignon Blanc Napa Valley 1993 • $9 • (08/31/95) • **76**
Sauvignon Blanc-Sémillon Late Harvest Napa Valley 1989 • $13 • (04/30/91) • **87**
Sémillon-Sauvignon Blanc Late Harvest Napa Valley 1990 • $9 • (03/31/92) • **83**

STONEHEDGE | CALIFORNIA

Cabernet Sauvignon Napa Valley 1995: A rustic style, marked by chewy tannins and leathery, tealike notes, followed by cassis and blackberry flavors. Better in a couple of years. 9,500 cases made. • $15 • (10/31/97) • **86**
Cabernet Sauvignon Napa Valley Winemaker's Reserve 1994: This is a thin, narrow wine with just a trace of cedar and currant flavor. 5,000 cases made. • $10 • (11/30/96) • **77**
Cabernet Sauvignon Napa Valley Winemaker's Reserve 1993: Earthy and tannic, with just enough currant and berry showing through to make it palatable, but it won't lose its tannins. 1,500 cases made. • $10 • (03/31/96) • **79**
Cabernet Sauvignon Napa Valley Winemaker's Reserve 1992 • $10 • (11/30/95) BB • **89**
Chardonnay California 1996: Bright and appealing for its simple nutmeg-scented pear flavors. 12,000 cases made. • $10 • (11/30/97) • **82**
Chardonnay California Barrel Fermented 1995: Smooth and creamy. A richly textured wine with very pretty pear, spice, vanilla and floral flavors that float through the finish. It comes at a fair price, and it's ready now. 18,500 cases made. • $10 • (12/31/96) BB • **87**
Chardonnay Napa Valley 1995: Ripe in flavor and beautifully focused, with smoky pear and nutmeg flavors that fold gently into the long finish. Ready to drink. 6,000 cases made. • $13 • (12/31/96) • **88**
Malbec Napa Valley 1994: Leans to the earthy, leathery side, though enough ripe cherry and wild berry flavors emerge to give it a sense of balance and proportion. Finishes with firm tannins. 1,000 cases made. • $15 • (11/30/96) • **84**
Malbec Napa Valley 1993 • $15 • (03/31/96) • **79**

STONESTREET

Marsanne Mendocino County 1995: Intriguing, tropical and guava aromas turn into an almost sweet peach flavor on the palate. Fans of Marsanne may not recognize the varietal, however. Those who like viscous, fruity whites will love this. 500 cases made. • $15 • (01/31/98) • **87**

Sauvignon Blanc California 1996: Here's a substantial Sauvignon Blanc at an inviting price, offering fleshy layers of melon, grapefruit, fresh pea, herbs and lemon flavors. It's bright and firm, if just a bit short on the finish. Drink now. 15,000 cases made. • $8 • (05/31/98) BB • **86**

Viognier Mendocino County 1995: Almonds and hazelnuts blend nicely in this mineral-like wine. Crisp and light. 500 cases made. • $15 • (12/15/97) • **83**

Zinfandel Napa Valley 1995: A little green, though it shows some spice and plum flavors. Very tannic. Short on the finish. Drink now. 2,500 cases made. • $15 • (06/15/98) • **78**

Zinfandel Napa Valley 1994: A plush-textured Zin, but with enough edge to give it good structure. Peppery and plummy, with hints of raspberry, leather and spice. Finishes cleanly, with class. 2,500 cases made. • $13 • (11/15/97) • **89**

STONESTREET

Cabernet Sauvignon Alexander Valley 1997: Dark, rich, intense and tannic, with roasted coffee, currant and toasty oak flavors. Hard and unyielding now, but has a solid core of fruit and oak. • $NA • (07/31/98) (BT) • **90-94**

Cabernet Sauvignon Alexander Valley 1996: Dark, ripe and intense. A potent barrel sample showing lots of smoky, toasty oak and a dense core of earthy currant flavors. Given its weight, it's rather elegant on the finish. 11,000 cases made. • $NA • (06/15/97) (BT) • **90-94**

Cabernet Sauvignon Alexander Valley 1994: Well balanced, with supple coffee, herb, currant and cedary oak flavors, it turns smooth and polished on the finish, where the flavors fan out. Drinks well now. 4,947 cases made. • $35 • (10/31/97) • **91**

Cabernet Sauvignon Alexander Valley 1993: Pleasant band of cedar, spice and currant flavors, but they lack richness and lose concentration on the finish. 4,879 cases made. • $30 • (09/15/96) • **84**

Cabernet Sauvignon Alexander Valley 1992 • $25 • (10/31/95) HR • **91**

Cabernet Sauvignon Alexander Valley 1991 • $22 • (05/15/95) • **88**

Cabernet Sauvignon Alexander Valley 1990 • $20 • (11/15/94) • **87**

Cabernet Sauvignon Alexander Valley 1989 • $24 • (11/15/92) • **84**

Cabernet Sauvignon Alexander Valley 1988 • $24 • (08/31/92) • **82**

Chardonnay Alexander Valley Upper Barn Block Alexander Mountain Estate 1995: Smooth, ripe and creamy, with rich apple, pear, citrus and spice notes, and even a touch of greeness around the edges. Flavors linger on the aftertaste. 450 cases made. • $30 • (12/15/97) • **88**

Chardonnay Sonoma County 1995: A big, ripe and intense style, with flavors of rich fig, melon, apple, pear and apricot, finishing long and full, with a smoky oak accent. Delicious now. • $25 • (05/31/97) • **91**

Chardonnay Sonoma County 1994: A smooth, rich and complex white that has an attractive array of honey, pear and butterscotch flavors kissed by spicy toasty oak. Deep and concentrated, finishing with a satisfying complexity. 13,018 cases made. • $25 • (05/31/96) SS • **91**

Chardonnay Sonoma County 1993 • $21 • (04/30/95) SS • **92**

Gewürztraminer Anderson Valley 1993 • $13 • (02/28/95) • **85**

Legacy Alexander Valley 1994: A smooth and supple Meritage, deeply concentrated, with a rich, detailed core of mineral, coffee, currant, cherry and sage flavors and a long, complex aftertaste where the flavors keep pumping. Drinks well now, but should be a beauty in another year or two. Best after 1999. A blend of 51 percent Cabernet Sauvignon, 39 percent Merlot, 9 percent Cabernet Franc, and 1 percent Petit Verdot. 2,451 cases made. • $50 • (10/15/97) HR • **93**

Legacy Alexander Valley 1993: Dark, intense and tannic, but the tannins are smooth and polished, allowing the ample currant, chocolate, anise, cedar and spice flavors to pour through. Drink now. A blend of Merlot, Cabernet Sauvignon, and Cabernet Franc. 942 cases made. • $40 • (09/30/96) • **90**

Legacy Alexander Valley 1992 • $35 • (09/30/95) CS • **92**

Legacy Alexander Valley 1991 • $35 • (11/15/94) • **91**

Legacy Alexander Valley 1990 • $35 • (11/15/93) • **85**

Merlot Alexander Valley 1994: Young and firm. Has pretty core of currant, chocolate, berry and spice flavors, picking up a slight leather note on the aftertaste and finishing with firm tannins and good length. Drink now. • $30 • (06/30/97) • **88**

Key: SS—Spectator Selection CS—Cellar Selection HR—Highly Recommended BB—Best Buy $NA—Price not available Ⓐ—Auction Price (BT)—Barrel Tasting

Dates in parentheses indicate the issues in which the ratings were published.

Merlot Alexander Valley 1993 • $30 • (06/30/96) • **86**

Merlot Alexander Valley 1992 • $22 • (05/15/95) SS • **90**

Merlot Alexander Valley 1991 • $24 • (09/15/94) • **85**

Merlot Alexander Valley 1990 • $20 • (09/15/94) • **82**

Merlot Alexander Valley 1989 • $24 • (05/31/92) • **88**

Pinot Noir Russian River Valley 1995: An elegant style. Ripe and spicy, with pretty plum, wild berry, tea, herb and cherry flavors and a long, fruity aftertaste with mild, polished tannins. Drinks well now. 1,613 cases made. • $30 • (12/15/97) • **89**

Pinot Noir Russian River Valley 1994 • $30 • (02/29/96) • **87**

Pinot Noir Russian River Valley 1990 • $30 • (09/30/92) • **84**

Pinot Noir Sonoma County 1993 • $25 • (12/31/95) • **87**

Pinot Noir Sonoma County 1992 • $20 • (03/31/95) • **86**

Pinot Noir Sonoma County 1991 • $30 • (02/28/94) • **89**

Pinot Noir Sonoma County Reserve 1992 • $34 • (12/15/94) • **89**

Sauvignon Blanc Alexander Valley Pinnacle Block Alexander Mountain Estate 1996: A full-textured, somewhat oily wine, with hints of gooseberry, herb, lemon and grapefruit. Toasty butterscotch notes add to the complexity. Distinctive. Drink now. 325 cases made. • $24 • (07/31/98) • **88**

Sauvignon Blanc Alexander Valley Pinnacle Vineyard 1995: A delicately textured wine that is nonetheless packed with complex flavors of green apple, citrus, pear and melon, and just the right touch of grassy herbality. • $20 • (06/15/97) • **89**

STONINGTON | NEW ENGLAND

Chardonnay Southeastern New England 1994: This rustic white mingles apple, smoke and herbaceous flavors and very tart acidity. May show better balance with food. 2,400 cases made. • $13 • (11/15/97) • **79**

STONY HILL | CALIFORNIA

Chardonnay Napa Valley 1993 • $21 Ⓐ • (06/15/96) • **85**

Chardonnay Napa Valley SHV 1993 • $23 • (07/31/95) • **86**

STONY RIDGE | CALIFORNIA

Cabernet Sauvignon California 1989 • $6 • (08/31/92) • **78**

Cabernet Sauvignon Napa Valley Limited Release 1989 • $9 • (11/15/92) • **78**

Merlot North Coast Limited Release 1991 • $10 • (06/30/93) • **85**

Merlot North Coast Limited Release 1990 • $9 • (11/30/92) • **82**

Zinfandel Livermore Valley 1980 • $7 • (06/16/84) • **75**

STORRS | CALIFORNIA

Chardonnay Santa Cruz Mountains Christie Vineyard Mountain Vineyard Collection 1993 • $17 • (07/31/95) • **85**

Chardonnay Santa Cruz Mountains Meyley Vineyard 1995: Ripe flavors at the core, with slightly vegetal, buttery oak and spice flavors picking up a touch of honey on the long finish. Feels able to develop nicely into 2001. 180 cases made. • $20 • (03/31/98) • **88**

Chardonnay Santa Cruz Mountains Vanumanutagi Vineyards 1993 • $19 • (05/31/95) • **86**

Zinfandel California Ben Lomond Mountain Beauregard Ranch 1992 • $15 • (10/15/95) • **82**

Zinfandel California Ben Lomond Mountain Beauregard Ranch 1990 • $15 • (10/15/92) • **82**

Zinfandel California Ben Lomond Mountain Beauregard Ranch 1989 • $13 • (10/15/92) • **81**

STORY | CALIFORNIA

Zinfandel Amador County 1980 • $6 • (04/01/84) • **73**

Zinfandel Shenandoah Valley 1992 • $10 • (10/15/95) • **83**

Zinfandel Shenandoah Valley 1991 • $10 • (09/30/93) • **86**

Zinfandel Shenandoah Valley 1990 • $8 • (09/30/93) • **83**

Zinfandel Shenandoah Valley 1989 • $9 • (09/30/93) • **82**

Zinfandel Shenandoah Valley 1987 • $8 • (04/30/91) • **84**

Zinfandel Shenandoah Valley 1986 • $8 • (08/31/91) • **80**

Zinfandel Shenandoah Valley Picnic Hill Vineyard Old Vines 1993 • $16 • (10/15/95) • **84**

Zinfandel Shenandoah Valley Private Reserve 1992 • $16 • (10/15/95) • **82**

Zinfandel Shenandoah Valley Private Reserve 1984 • $14 • (04/30/91) • **79**

STORYBOOK MOUNTAIN | CALIFORNIA

Zinfandel Howell Mountain 1992 • $14 • (10/15/95) • **83**
Zinfandel Howell Mountain 1991 • $15 • (10/15/94) • **87**
Zinfandel Napa Valley 1992 • $14 • (10/15/95) • **86**
Zinfandel Napa Valley 1991 • $14 • (09/30/93) • **87**
Zinfandel Napa Valley 1990 • $14 • (03/15/93) • **83**
Zinfandel Napa Valley 1989 • $15 • (03/31/92) • **80**
Zinfandel Napa Valley 1988 • $13 • (12/31/90) • **75**
Zinfandel Napa Valley 1987 • $12 • (12/15/89) • **88**
Zinfandel Napa Valley 1986 • $11 • (12/15/88) • **88**
Zinfandel Napa Valley 1985 • $10 • (12/31/87) • **90**
Zinfandel Napa Valley 1984 • $9 • (03/15/87) • **80**
Zinfandel Napa Valley 1983 • $19 Ⓐ • (04/16/86) • **90**
Zinfandel Napa Valley 1982 • $8 • (12/01/84) • **86**
Zinfandel Napa Valley Eastern Exposures 1995: Austere, even tart, with a mix of ripe and not-quite-ripe fruit flavors; the sage, tart berry, mineral and spice flavors are firm and structured, finishing with tight tannins. Drink now through 2002. 803 cases made. • $19 • (05/31/98) • **87**
Zinfandel Napa Valley Eastern Exposures 1994: Tight and tart, with a pretty core of black cherry, wild berry, earth, anise and spice flavors. Only mildly tannic, it's drinkable now. 850 cases made. • $19 • (04/30/97) • **88**
Zinfandel Napa Valley Eastern Exposures 1992 • $17 • (10/15/95) • **89**
Zinfandel Napa Valley Estate Reserve 1992: Vibrant, with a complex, zesty core of spice, pepper, wild berry and cherry notes. This is a supple, harmonious, well-integrated Zinfandel that finishes with firm but supple tannins and a pleasant earthiness. 759 cases made. • $25 • (03/31/97) • **90**
Zinfandel Napa Valley Estate Reserve 1991 • $25 • (10/15/95) • **86**
Zinfandel Napa Valley Estate Reserve 1989 • $19 • (06/15/93) • **71**
Zinfandel Napa Valley Estate Reserve 1988 • $20 • (03/31/92) • **84**
Zinfandel Napa Valley Estate Reserve 1987 • $25 • (12/31/90) • **89**
Zinfandel Napa Valley Estate Reserve 1986 • $27 • (05/15/90) • **82**
Zinfandel Napa Valley Estate Reserve 1985 • $29 • (05/31/89) • **88**
Zinfandel Napa Valley Estate Reserve 1984 • $22 • (04/30/88) • **92**
Zinfandel Napa Valley Estate Reserve 1983 • $22 • (07/31/87) • **81**
Zinfandel Napa Valley Estate Reserve 1981 • $9 • (04/16/84) • **86**
Zinfandel Napa Valley Mayacamas Range 1996: Appealing for its ripe, up-front fruitiness, with plum, floral and wild berry flavors. Turns firmly tannic on the finish, but the fruit manages to push through. Drink now through 2001. 4,300 cases made. • $17 • (05/31/98) • **88**
Zinfandel Napa Valley Mayacamas Range 1994: Ripe and juicy, with layers of plum, black cherry, spice and cedar, this is young and vibrant, in a zesty style that's lively and compelling. Drinkable now, but could use a year or two in the cellar. Significantly better than an earlier sample. 4,900 cases made. • $15 • (04/30/97) • **90**
Zinfandel Napa Valley Reserve 1992: Vibrant, with a complex, zesty core of spice, pepper, wild berry and cherry notes. This is a supple, harmonious, well-integrated Zinfandel that finishes with firm but supple tannins and a pleasant earthiness. 759 cases made. • $25 • (03/31/97) • **90**
Zinfandel Sonoma County 1986 • $8 • (10/15/88) • **87**
Zinfandel Sonoma County 1982 • $7 • (09/16/85) • **81**

STRATFORD | CALIFORNIA

Cabernet Sauvignon California 1990 • $12 • (11/15/92) • **81**
Cabernet Sauvignon California 1985 • $10 • (11/30/88) • **83**
Cabernet Sauvignon California 1983 • $8 • (02/15/87) • **86**
Cabernet Sauvignon Napa Valley 1993: A lean wine with flavors that run toward pickle barrel and toast, modest on the fruit. Drinkable now. 3,000 cases made. • $10 • (12/15/95) • **81**
Cabernet Sauvignon Napa Valley 1987 • $12 • (04/30/90) • **85**
Cabernet Sauvignon Napa Valley Partners' Reserve 1988 • $16 • (03/15/92) • **68**
Cabernet Sauvignon Napa Valley Partners' Reserve 1987 • $16 • (04/30/91) • **90**
Chardonnay California 1996: Smooth, almost silky on the palate, with subtle hints of apricot, nectarine, herbs, minerals and citrus. A touch of bitterness on the finish. 500 cases made. • $12 • (05/15/98) • **85**
Dolcetto Napa Valley 1994 • $8 • (11/15/95) • **83**
Merlot California 1991 • $11 • (07/15/93) • **84**
Merlot California 1990 • $9 • (05/31/92) BB • **85**
Merlot California 1987 • $13 • (10/31/89) • **83**
Merlot California 1986 • $10 • (01/31/89) • **78**
Merlot California 1983 • $8 • (09/30/86) • **79**
Merlot Sierra Foothills 1996: Plum and cherry flavors form the core of this pleasant though not complex wine. Round and accessible, with a touch of herbs on the finish. Drink now. 3,000 cases made. • $14 • (06/15/98) • **84**
Zinfandel California 1991 • $7 • (06/15/93) BB • **83**

STRAUS | CALIFORNIA

Merlot Napa Valley 1991 • $17 • (05/15/95) • **85**
Merlot Napa Valley 1990 • $16 • (08/31/93) • **85**
Merlot Napa Valley 1989 • $15 • (11/15/91) • **81**
Merlot Napa Valley 1988 • $14 • (12/31/90) • **82**
Merlot Napa Valley 1987 • $12 • (02/15/90) • **90**
Merlot Napa Valley 1986 • $11 • (02/28/89) • **93**
Merlot Napa Valley 1985 • $10 • (02/15/88) • **81**

STREBLOW | CALIFORNIA

Cabernet Sauvignon Napa Valley 1987 • $16 • (10/15/90) • **79**
Cabernet Sauvignon Napa Valley 1986 • $16 • (07/31/89) • **87**
Cabernet Sauvignon Napa Valley 1985 • $15 • (06/15/88) • **89**
Merlot Napa Valley 1989 • $20 • (05/31/92) • **89**

STRONG, RODNEY | CALIFORNIA

Cabernet Sauvignon Alexander Valley Alexander's Crown Vineyard 1987 • $17 • (07/15/91) • **89**
Cabernet Sauvignon Alexander Valley Alexander's Crown Vineyard 1985 • $17 • (05/31/91) • **87**
Cabernet Sauvignon Alexander Valley Alexander's Crown Vineyard 1984 • $12 • (04/30/89) • **80**
Cabernet Sauvignon Alexander Valley Alexander's Crown Vineyard 1982 • $12 • (10/31/88) • **80**
Cabernet Sauvignon Alexander Valley Alexander's Crown Vineyard 1981 • $12 • (11/30/87) • **77**
Cabernet Sauvignon Alexander Valley Alexander's Crown Vineyard 1980 • $11 • (04/16/85) • **86**
Cabernet Sauvignon Alexander Valley Alexander's Crown Vineyard 1979 • $12 • (04/16/84) • **79**
Cabernet Sauvignon Alexander Valley Alexander's Crown Vineyard 1978 • $12 • (01/01/84) • **80**
Cabernet Sauvignon Alexander Valley Alexander's Crown Vineyard 1974 • $50 • (11/15/94) • **74**
Cabernet Sauvignon Alexander Valley Reserve 1988 • $30 • (11/15/92) • **84**
Cabernet Sauvignon Alexander Valley Reserve 1987 • $28 • (09/30/91) HR • **92**
Cabernet Sauvignon Northern Sonoma Alexander's Crown Vineyard 1994: Clean and ripe, with appealing black cherry, currant, herb, earth and spice, firming up on the finish, where the tannins kick in. Drink now or cellar into 2002. • $23 • (03/31/98) • **86**
Cabernet Sauvignon Northern Sonoma Alexander's Crown Vineyard 1993: Elegant, with a supple, well-balanced core of currant, plum and wild berry flavors. Finishes with firm tannins and good length. Moderately rich and concentrated, it can be enjoyed now through 2002. • $22 • (08/31/97) • **88**
Cabernet Sauvignon Northern Sonoma Alexander's Crown Vineyard 1992: Smooth and polished, with a focused, deftly balanced core of currant, plum and cherry flavors. Finishes with mild, smooth tannins and good length. Drinkable now. • $20 • (09/15/96) • **87**
Cabernet Sauvignon Northern Sonoma Alexander's Crown Vineyard 1991 • $20 • (12/15/95) • **86**
Cabernet Sauvignon Northern Sonoma Alexander's Crown Vineyard 1990 • $20 • (11/15/93) • **86**
Cabernet Sauvignon Northern Sonoma Alexander's Crown Vineyard 1988 • $18 • (09/30/92) HR • **91**
Cabernet Sauvignon Northern Sonoma Reserve 1993: Lean and trim, with a spicy band of black cherry, plum and berry notes. Drinks well now; can age into 2000. • $30 • (09/30/97) • **87**
Cabernet Sauvignon Northern Sonoma Reserve 1992: Ripe, smooth and harmonious. Shows a supple core of ripe plum, cherry, currant and mineral flavors, finishing with a touch of spice, herb and cedar. Plenty of tannins show up on the finish, but they're smooth and round. Drinks well now. • $30 • (11/15/96) • **89**
Cabernet Sauvignon Northern Sonoma Reserve 1991 • $30 • (12/15/95) • **86**
Cabernet Sauvignon Northern Sonoma Reserve 1990 • $30 • (06/15/94) • **88**
Cabernet Sauvignon Sonoma County 1994: Modestly proportioned, with an earthy, cedary accent to the moderate currant and berry notes. • $12 • (04/30/97) • **82**

Cabernet Sauvignon Sonoma County 1993: Well balanced, with pretty oak, currant and plum flavors; a well-executed style that turns complex on the finish. Drinkable now. • $11 • (12/15/95) • **86**
Cabernet Sauvignon Sonoma County 1992 • $10 • (06/15/95) • **83**
Cabernet Sauvignon Sonoma County 1991 • $10 • (11/15/94) • **82**
Cabernet Sauvignon Sonoma County 1990 • $11 • (11/15/93) • **81**
Cabernet Sauvignon Sonoma County 1989 • $10 • (09/30/92) • **84**
Cabernet Sauvignon Sonoma County 1988 • $10 • (11/15/91) • **80**
Cabernet Sauvignon Sonoma County 1987 • $10 • (06/30/91) • **85**
Cabernet Sauvignon Sonoma County 1982 • $7 • (12/15/86) • **69**
Cabernet Sauvignon Sonoma County 1981 • $7 • (12/16/84) • **86**
Chardonnay Chalk Hill Chalk Hill Vineyard 1996: Intense, with spicy pear, apple and melon flavors framed by light toast and cedary oak. Drink now. • $16 • (02/28/98) • **87**
Chardonnay Chalk Hill Chalk Hill Vineyard 1995: Complex with ripe pear, citrus, honey and hazelnut notes, the flavors fanning out on the finish. Ready to drink. • $15 • (04/30/97) • **88**
Chardonnay Chalk Hill Chalk Hill Vineyard 1994: Fruit-centered white packs some concentration on a medium frame, offering apple, spice and vanilla notes and a touch of green flavor on the finish. • $14 • (04/30/96) • **85**
Chardonnay Chalk Hill Chalk Hill Vineyard 1993 • $14 • (07/31/95) • **85**
Chardonnay Sonoma County 1996: Light, smooth and silky, with pretty nectarine and vanilla flavors that show more up front than they do on the finish. • $12 • (11/15/97) • **83**
Chardonnay Sonoma County 1995: Smooth, ripe and spicy, with lots of pear, melon and apricot flavors that are pure and pleasing. Ready now. • $12 • (04/30/97) • **87**
Chardonnay Sonoma County 1994: A fruity style that adds a touch of hazelnut to its pear, honey and melon flavors. The understated toastiness lets the ripe fruit shine. • $11 • (06/15/96) • **87**
Chardonnay Sonoma County 1993 • $11 • (04/30/95) • **83**
Merlot Russian River Valley River West Vineyard 1985 • $12 • (02/28/89) • **79**
Merlot Sonoma County 1995: Supple, with a modest range of currant, clay, herb and cedar notes that are simple, finishing with mild tannins. A good but unexceptional offering. Best now to 2000. • $16 • (04/30/98) • **83**
Merlot Sonoma County 1994: A touch woody in character, with its cedary edge, it nonetheless delivers enough fruit flavor to fill out the frame, with hints of cherry and berry. Ready to drink. 28,108 cases made. • $12 • (03/31/97) • **84**
Merlot Sonoma County 1993: Supple and well oaked, with a toasty, buttery edge to the plum and cherry-laced fruit. Well made, with a complex aftertaste. Drink now. • $16 • (08/31/96) • **87**
Merlot Sonoma County 1992 • $14 • (02/28/95) • **84**
Pinot Noir Russian River Valley River East Vineyard 1994: Ripe, clean and correct, with a well-proportioned and balanced core of cherry, plum and rhubarb flavors. • $16 • (11/15/96) • **85**
Pinot Noir Russian River Valley River East Vineyard 1993 • $16 • (12/31/95) • **87**
Pinot Noir Russian River Valley River East Vineyard 1992 • $14 • (03/31/95) • **83**
Pinot Noir Russian River Valley River East Vineyard 1991 • $14 • (02/28/94) • **87**
Pinot Noir Russian River Valley River East Vineyard 1990 • $14 • (09/30/92) • **82**
Pinot Noir Russian River Valley River East Vineyard 1985 • $10 • (02/28/91) • **83**
Pinot Noir Russian River Valley River East Vineyard 1984 • $8 • (11/15/87) • **78**
Pinot Noir Russian River Valley River East Vineyard 1981 • $8 • (08/31/86) • **63**
Pinot Noir Russian River Valley River East Vineyard 1980 • $10 • (07/01/84) • **78**
Sauvignon Blanc Northern Sonoma Charlotte's Home 1997: A richly textured wine, with passion fruit, fig and lemon-lime flavors. The acidity is refreshing, with a bright mineral and spice component. A reliable producer—a great price. Drink now. 20,000 cases made. • $10 • (06/30/98) BB • **88**
Sauvignon Blanc Northern Sonoma Charlotte's Home 1996: Bright, fresh green apple and grapefruit notes blend elegantly with an interesting herbal, grassy edge. Perfumed and refreshing. • $10 • (06/30/97) • **88**

Key: SS—Spectator Selection CS—Cellar Selection HR—Highly Recommended BB—Best Buy $NA—Price not available Ⓐ—Auction Price (BT)—Barrel Tasting
Dates in parentheses indicate the issues in which the ratings were published.

Sauvignon Blanc Northern Sonoma Charlotte's Home 1995 • $10 • (06/15/96) • **86**
Sauvignon Blanc Northern Sonoma Charlotte's Home 1994 • $9 • (08/31/95) • **84**
Sauvignon Blanc Northern Sonoma Charlotte's Home 1993 • $10 • (08/31/94) • **85**
Zinfandel Northern Sonoma Old Vines 1995: A restrained nose leads to a modest offering of ripe plum and berry flavors. Ready now. • $16 • (05/15/98) • **86**
Zinfandel Northern Sonoma Old Vines 1994: Marked by spicy, cedary oak notes, around a modest core of spicy berry flavor. Good, but doesn't offer the expected richness, depth or concentration. • $14 • (04/30/97) • **82**
Zinfandel Northern Sonoma Old Vines 1993 • $14 • (03/31/96) • **84**
Zinfandel Russian River Valley River West Vineyard Old Vines 1992 • $14 • (07/31/95) • **86**
Zinfandel Russian River Valley River West Vineyard Old Vines 1991 • $14 • (04/30/94) • **82**
Zinfandel Russian River Valley River West Vineyard Old Vines 1990 • $14 • (12/15/92) • **86**
Zinfandel Russian River Valley River West Vineyard Old Vines 1988 • $15 • (10/15/92) • **89**
Zinfandel Russian River Valley River West Vineyard Old Vines 1987 • $14 • (08/31/91) • **82**
Zinfandel Russian River Valley River West Vineyard Old Vines 1980 • $12 • (11/15/87) • **68**
Zinfandel Russian River Valley River West Vineyard Old Vines 1979 • $10 • (03/15/87) • **71**
Zinfandel Sonoma County 1986 • $5 • (03/31/89) • **79**
Zinfandel Sonoma County 1982 • $5 • (12/31/87) • **70**

STUHLMULLER | CALIFORNIA

Chardonnay Alexander Valley 1996: Fresh, with complex, concentrated spicy apple, pear, citrus and melon notes. Firm and tightly wound. Cellar short term. New from a vineyard that's been selling grapes to Cronin, which has made a vineyard-designated wine from this property. Best from now through 2001. 657 cases made. • $21 • (07/31/98) • **90**

SUGARLOAF RIDGE | CALIFORNIA

Cabernet Sauvignon Sonoma Valley 1986 • $13 • (03/31/90) • **82**

SULLBERG, MICHAEL | CALIFORNIA

Cabernet Sauvignon California Lot 66 Reserve 1994: Cherry, herb and tarlike notes rise to the top of this otherwise herbal, somewhat hot, wine. 5,000 cases made. • $7 • (09/15/97) • **80**
Cabernet Sauvignon Central Coast 1992 • $6 • (12/15/95) • **84**
Cabernet Sauvignon Napa Valley 1991 • $7 • (11/15/94) • **79**
Chardonnay California Lot 65 Barrel Select 1995: Fairly insipid, with citrus and cardboard qualities. 5,000 cases made. • $7 • (07/31/97) • **79**
Chardonnay Knights Valley Lot 54 Barrel Fermented 1994: Light in texture but bright, featuring pear and vanilla flavors that finish with some restraint. Ready now. 2,200 cases made. • $8 • (02/29/96) • **86**
Merlot California Barrel Reserve 1991 • $7 • (09/15/94) • **81**
Merlot-Cab Cuvée Mount Veeder Reserve NV • $6 • (12/15/95) • **80**
Pinot Noir Anderson Valley 1992 • $6 • (03/31/95) • **81**
Zinfandel California Old Vine Reserve 1990 • $5 • (10/15/94) • **79**

SULLIVAN | CALIFORNIA

Cabernet Sauvignon Napa Valley 1993: Smoothly textured up front, with licorice, raspberry and herb flavors. The finish is good, though the tannins are a bit drying. Drink now or hold. 3,000 cases made. • $26 • (11/30/97) • **86**
Cabernet Sauvignon Napa Valley 1991 • $23 • (11/15/94) • **85**
Cabernet Sauvignon Napa Valley 1989 • $23 • (11/15/92) • **85**
Coeur de Vigne Napa Valley Private Reserve 1993: Ripe, seductive plum and earth aromas rise gracefully from this silky-smooth wine, followed by cassis, blackberry and black currant flavors. A fairly astringent finish detracts slightly. A blend of 80 percent Cabernet Sauvignon and 20 percent Merlot. 280 cases made. • $40 • (11/30/97) • **88**
Coeur de Vigne Napa Valley Private Reserve 1991 • $30 • (11/15/94) • **82**
Coeur de Vigne Napa Valley Private Reserve 1989 • $25 • (08/31/92) • **82**
Meritage Coeur de Vigne Napa Valley 1988 • $25 • (07/15/92) • **83**

Merlot Napa Valley 1994: A rustic style, rough and chewy, showing lots of cedary oak and a curious range of flavors that don't quite say Merlot. As a red table wine, it's gutsy and tannic, with a vinegary edge. 800 cases made. • $35 • (02/28/97) • **77**
Merlot Napa Valley 1991 • $22 • (09/15/94) • **83**
Merlot Napa Valley 1990 • $20 • (06/15/93) • **87**
Merlot Napa Valley 1989 • $20 • (04/15/92) HR • **92**

SUMMERFIELD | CALIFORNIA

Chardonnay California Vintner's Reserve 1996: Simple, with pleasant notes of peach and almond and a soft finish. Drink now. 10,000 cases made. • $9 • (07/31/98) • **83**
Chardonnay California Vintner's Reserve 1995: Very spicy aromas and flavors and some nice pear notes on the smoky finish make this a pleasant wine for immediate drinking. • $8 • (12/31/96) • **85**
Chardonnay California Vintner's Reserve 1994: Balances its spicy oak and fresh pear flavors nicely on a medium-bodied frame. 15,000 cases made. • $8 • (06/15/96) • **82**
Chardonnay California Vintner's Reserve 1993 • $6 • (07/31/95) • **82**
Merlot California Vintner's Reserve 1995: Soft and generous, with ripe black cherry, plum and blueberry flavors, each vying for attention. Finishes with moderate richness. Tasty now. 4,243 cases made. • $8 • (11/30/96) • **85**
Sauvignon Blanc California 1993 • $4 • (06/30/95) • **81**

SUMMERS RANCH | CALIFORNIA

Chardonnay Napa Valley 1996: A pleasant wine, with lemon and pear notes and perhaps just a touch too much toasty oak. Drink now. 500 cases made. • $20 • (05/15/98) • **83**
Merlot Knights Valley 1995: Smooth and polished, with ripe currant, plum and cherry notes, picking up sage and herb before finishing with mild, supple tannins. Drink now through 2002. 900 cases made. • $24 • (04/30/98) • **88**
Merlot Knights Valley 1992 • $21 • (02/29/96) • **87**

SUMMIT LAKE | CALIFORNIA

Cabernet Sauvignon Howell Mountain Emily Kestrel 1992: Strong peppery flavors give way to hints of ripe, earthy Cabernet flavors; it shows off the austerity of the appellation, along with its gritty tannins. Drink now or cellar into 2000 in hopes the tannins fade. 210 cases made. • $25 • (11/30/96) • **87**
Zinfandel Howell Mountain 1995: Firmly structured, with an unyielding core of tart strawberry, mineral and spice flavors. Firm tannins need time to resolve. Should develop nicely. Best from now through 2003. 1,200 cases made. • $16 • (06/15/98) • **84**
Zinfandel Howell Mountain 1994: Quite peppery, with tart cherry and bay leaf notes, the peppery, earthy flavors linger on the moderate finish. Howell Mountain intensity is there, but it lacks extra dimension. Drink now. 630 cases made. • $16 • (06/15/98) • **82**
Zinfandel Howell Mountain 1992 • $13 • (03/31/96) • **83**
Zinfandel Howell Mountain 1991 • $12 • (10/15/95) • **87**
Zinfandel Howell Mountain 1989 • $9 • (08/31/93) • **84**
Zinfandel Howell Mountain 1988 • $11 • (10/15/92) • **82**
Zinfandel Howell Mountain 1987 • $11 • (02/15/91) • **87**
Zinfandel Howell Mountain 1986 • $11 • (03/15/90) • **84**
Zinfandel Howell Mountain 1985 • $9 • (12/15/88) • **88**
Zinfandel Howell Mountain 1984 • $8 • (04/30/88) • **90**

SUNCREST | WASHINGTON

Gewürztraminer Washington Organically Grown Grapes 1993 • $7 • (09/30/95) • **72**

SUNNY ST. HELENA | CALIFORNIA

Cabernet Sauvignon California 1989 • $10 • (11/15/91) • **86**
Cabernet Sauvignon Napa Valley 1985 • $9 • (10/31/87) • **81**
Cabernet Sauvignon North Coast 1988 • $13 • (04/30/91) • **85**

SUNRIDGE | CALIFORNIA

Cabernet Sauvignon Napa Valley 1989 • $6 • (08/31/92) • **78**

SUNSTONE | CALIFORNIA

Cabernet Sauvignon Santa Barbara County 1994: Marked by earthy, vegetal flavors, and the silky texture doesn't help it break out of the doldrums, either. Finishes on a brighter note, with anise and herb overtones. 729 cases made. • $18 • (10/31/97) • **79**
Cabernet Sauvignon Santa Ynez Valley 1993: A touch leathery in character, with trim cherry and currant flavors at the core. 215 cases made. • $18 • (11/30/96) • **77**
Chardonnay Santa Barbara County 1996: Starts off with earth and mineral aromas. Firm and lemony on the palate, with a solid core of nectarine, fresh pea, mineral and herb flavors. Crisp, complex finish. Drink now through 2001. 880 cases made. • $18 • (07/31/98) • **87**
Chardonnay Santa Barbara County 1994: Elegant and understated, with pure pear, melon, grapefruit, and honey flavors. The aftertaste lingers with hints of citrus. 785 cases made. • $18 • (07/31/96) • **86**
Chardonnay Santa Barbara County 1993 • $14 • (07/31/95) • **78**
Equinox Santa Barbara County 1994: A good wine that lacks concentration and depth, this is forward and fruity, with an earthy, herbal, green olive accent to the Cabernet flavors. A blend of Cabernet Sauvignon, Merlot, and Cabernet Franc. 470 cases made. • $21 • (12/15/96) • **84**
Merlot Santa Barbara County 1994: Marked by olive, red pepper and herb flavors, with a slightly bitter edge. Has the texture of Merlot, but not quite the flavor. 3,175 cases made. • $18 • (08/31/96) • **80**
Syrah Santa Barbara County 1995: Starts off with a meaty note. A fairly complex wine that leans toward herbs and stewed tomatoes, with plum and anise influences. Soft, supple texture. Has character. Drink now. 330 cases made. • $24 • (06/15/98) • **87**

SUTTER HOME | CALIFORNIA

Cabernet Sauvignon California 1991 • $6 • (11/15/94) • **81**
Cabernet Sauvignon California 1990 • $6 • (09/15/93) BB • **81**
Cabernet Sauvignon California 1989 • $5 • (10/15/91) BB • **83**
Cabernet Sauvignon California 1988 • $5 • (11/15/90) BB • **81**
Cabernet Sauvignon California 1987 • $5 • (06/30/89) • **77**
Cabernet Sauvignon California 1986 • $5 • (11/30/88) • **79**
Cabernet Sauvignon Napa Valley Centennial Selection Reserve 1990 • $12 • (10/31/93) • **87**
Cabernet Sauvignon Napa Valley Reserve 1992: This is a ripe and full-bodied wine, with a core of anise, cherry and currant flavors flanked by firm, tight tannins. Firmer and more tannic than you might expect from Sutter Home. A solid effort and good value at this price. 2,040 cases made. • $12 • (11/15/96) • **87**
Cabernet Sauvignon Napa Valley Reserve 1991 • $12 • (11/15/94) • **82**
Chardonnay California 1995: Light and tangy, with a spicy mineral character to the citrus and apple flavors. 900,000 cases made. • $6 • (11/30/96) • **82**
Chardonnay California 1993 • $6 • (04/30/95) • **74**
Chenin Blanc California 1993 • $4 • (06/15/95) • **79**
Gewürztraminer California 1996: Sweet and simple, a nice mouthful of orange and pear flavors. 70,000 cases made. • $6 • (11/30/97) • **80**
Gewürztraminer California 1994 • $5 • (01/01/95) • **79**
Merlot California 1996: Beefy and herbal, marked by a strong vegetal quality on the finish. 400,000 cases made. • $6 • (07/31/97) • **77**
Merlot California 1992 • $6 • (09/15/94) • **79**
Merlot California 1991 • $6 • (08/31/93) • **78**
Merlot California Merlot Rosé 1997: Lightly fruity, a touch sweet, with earthy herb, cherry and strawberry flavors, it's clean and refreshing and captures enough Merlot flavor to make it interesting. Drink now. 125,000 cases made. • $6 • (06/30/98) • **82**
Moscato California 1996: A peppery nose leads the way in this sweet, pleasant, simple quaffer. 23,000 cases made. • $6 • (09/15/97) • **80**
Muscat Alexandria California 1994 • $5 • (09/30/95) BB • **84**
Sauvignon Blanc California 1996: Bright grapefruit flavors, backed by light grass and earth tones and a clean finish, make this a refreshing quaff. Can't beat it at this price. 120,000 cases made. • $5 • (07/31/97) • **85**
Sauvignon Blanc California 1994: Light and fragrant, this is charming for its nectarine, citrus and floral flavors that hold on through the generous finish. Delicious to drink now. 70,000 cases made. • $5 • (11/30/96) • **86**
Sauvignon Blanc California 1993 • $5 • (02/28/95) • **82**
Sauvignon Blanc Monterey County Signature Series 1997: A rich blend of ripe fig, fresh pea, herb, citrus and earth tones, this wine shows flair, leaning toward a traditional, grassy style. Texturally smooth and silky. First in the Signature Series from Sutter Home. Drink now through 2000. 1,156 cases made. • $14 • (05/31/98) • **88**
White Zinfandel California 1994 • $4 • (09/15/95) • **73**

Zinfandel Amador County 1981 • $6 • (05/16/84) • **80**
Zinfandel Amador County 1973 • $NA • (06/16/85) • **86**
Zinfandel Amador County 1972 • $NA • (06/16/85) • **85**
Zinfandel Amador County 1970 • $NA • (06/16/85) • **80**
Zinfandel Amador County Centennial Selection Reserve 1990 • $10 • (10/15/94) • **83**
Zinfandel Amador County Reserve 1989 • $10 • (10/15/92) • **79**
Zinfandel Amador County Reserve 1988 • $10 • (03/31/92) • **84**
Zinfandel Amador County Reserve 1987 • $9 • (05/15/91) • **79**
Zinfandel Amador County Reserve 1984 • $9 • (07/31/89) • **82**
Zinfandel California 1994: Modestly varietal in character, with mature berry and anise flavors and hints of pepper and cedar. 204,000 cases made. • $10 • (04/30/97) • **81**
Zinfandel California 1993 • $5 • (04/30/96) • **77**
Zinfandel California 1992 • $5 • (10/15/94) • **75**
Zinfandel California 1991 • $5 • (04/30/93) BB • **82**
Zinfandel California 1990 • $5 • (09/15/92) • **77**
Zinfandel California 1989 • $5 • (05/15/91) BB • **85**
Zinfandel California 1988 • $5 • (03/31/91) • **72**
Zinfandel California 1987 • $5 • (07/31/89) • **78**
Zinfandel California 1986 • $7 • (10/15/88) • **76**
Zinfandel California 1984 • $6 • (12/31/86) • **77**

SUTTER RIDGE | CALIFORNIA

Chardonnay Amador County 1994: A round wine with modest pear and spice flavors. 300 cases made. • $8 • (06/15/96) • **81**

SWAN, JOSEPH | CALIFORNIA

Cabernet Sauvignon Sonoma Mountain Steiner Vineyard 1990 • $18 • (11/15/93) • **84**
Chardonnay Russian River Valley 1994: An odd, curious style, with earthy, funky flavors that miss the mark and turn slightly sour on the finish. 240 cases made. • $18 • (07/31/96) • **78**
Chardonnay Russian River Valley Estate 1996: A twinge of earthiness interrupts the flow of ripe pear and apple, but it fills out at midpalate, where the texture is creamy. Finishes with spice and vanilla notes. Drink now through 2002. 50 cases made. • $25 • (07/31/98) • **88**
Côtes du Rosa Russian River Valley 1991 • $10 • (11/30/92) • **88**
Pinot Noir Russian River Valley 1994: The ripe cherry, plum and berry flavors are appealing, but the texture is tough and coarse now. Best to give this another year or two in the bottle. • $30 • (06/30/97) • **88**
Pinot Noir Russian River Valley 1993 • $14 • (12/31/95) • **82**
Pinot Noir Russian River Valley 1992 • $22 • (12/31/95) • **87**
Pinot Noir Russian River Valley 1991 • $20 • (03/31/95) • **83**
Pinot Noir Russian River Valley 1990: A delicious Pinot Noir, pure and simple. Has a juicy core of ripe, rich raspberry, black cherry, anise and plum flavors that are deep, complex and concentrated, and a long, fruity, full-flavored aftertaste. Softened tannins make it drinkable now through 2001. • $20 • (03/31/97) • **94**
Pinot Noir Russian River Valley 1988 • $20 • (06/30/91) • **79**
Pinot Noir Russian River Valley 1986: Aging well, in a rustic style, this retains lots of racy raspberry, wild cherry and anise notes and plenty of tannin, too. Impresses with its spicy aftertaste. Ready. • $20 • (03/31/97) • **87**
Pinot Noir Russian River Valley 1985 • $18 • (06/15/88) • **89**
Pinot Noir Russian River Valley 1982 • $13 Ⓐ • (08/31/86) • **82**
Pinot Noir Sonoma Coast 1986: Aging well, in a rustic style, this retains lots of racy raspberry, wild cherry and anise notes and plenty of tannin, too. Impresses with its spicy aftertaste. Ready. • $20 • (03/31/97) • **87**
Pinot Noir Sonoma Mountain Steiner Vineyard 1995: A touch earthy and herbal, with cedar, tar and spicy berry flavors, finishing with chewy tannins. Try now. 275 cases made. • $18 • (07/31/97) • **87**
Pinot Noir Sonoma Mountain Steiner Vineyard 1994 • $17 • (04/30/96) • **86**
Pinot Noir Sonoma Mountain Steiner Vineyard 1993 • $15 • (03/31/95) • **84**
Pinot Noir Sonoma Mountain Steiner Vineyard 1992 • $16 • (02/28/95) • **88**
Pinot Noir Sonoma Mountain Wolfspierre Vineyard 1995: Decidedly minty, with a bay leaf and sage edge to its dried cherry flavors. Turns crisp and tannic on the finish. Try now. 70 cases made. • $16 • (01/01/97) • **88**

Key: SS—Spectator Selection CS—Cellar Selection HR—Highly Recommended BB—Best Buy $NA—Price not available Ⓐ—Auction Price (BT)—Barrel Tasting
Dates in parentheses indicate the issues in which the ratings were published.

Pinot Noir Sonoma Mountain Wolfspierre Vineyard 1992 • $14 • (03/31/95) • **86**
Zinfandel California 1973 • $NA • (06/16/85) • **84**
Zinfandel California 1969 • $NA • (06/16/85) • **83**
Zinfandel Russian River Valley Frati Ranch 1995: Ripe, juicy, rich and flavorful, brimming with black cherry, wild berry, plum and raspberry. Shows a remarkable depth and richness on the finish, where the flavors are complex and the tannins detailed. Best from now through 2004. 242 cases made. • $24 • (06/15/98) • **91**
Zinfandel Russian River Valley Frati Ranch 1993 • $18 • (10/15/95) • **90**
Zinfandel Russian River Valley Frati Ranch 1992 • $16 • (10/15/94) • **92**
Zinfandel Russian River Valley V.H.S.R. Vineyard 1993 • $15 • (10/15/95) • **85**
Zinfandel Russian River Valley V.H.S.R. Vineyard 1992 • $15 • (10/15/94) HR • **92**
Zinfandel Russian River Valley Zeigler Vineyard 1995: Still crisp and tight, with a focused core of peppery cherry and raspberry-scented flavor that's elegant and refined, finishing with a long, complex, lingering aftertaste. Can stand short-term cellaring. 268 cases made. • $20 • (06/15/98) • **90**
Zinfandel Sonoma County 1989 • $13 • (10/15/92) • **80**
Zinfandel Sonoma County 1988 • $16 • (08/31/91) • **82**
Zinfandel Sonoma County 1987 • $16 • (07/31/90) • **86**
Zinfandel Sonoma County 1986 • $16 • (03/15/90) • **89**
Zinfandel Sonoma County 1985 • $17 • (03/15/89) • **82**
Zinfandel Sonoma County Ziegler Vineyard 1993 • $15 • (10/15/95) • **81**
Zinfandel Sonoma County Ziegler Vineyard 1987 • $16 • (09/15/90) • **86**
Zinfandel Sonoma Valley Stellwagen Vineyard 1995: Lots of ripe spice, cherry, wild berry, raspberry and anise notes. An elegant, polished, rich and complex wine that's well focused and long on the finish. Drink now through 2004. 338 cases made. • $20 • (06/15/98) • **90**
Zinfandel Sonoma Valley Stellwagen Vineyard 1993 • $16 • (10/15/95) • **88**
Zinfandel Sonoma Valley Stellwagen Vineyard 1992 • $14 • (10/15/94) • **77**
Zinfandel Sonoma Valley Stellwagen Vineyard 1989 • $14 • (10/15/92) • **80**
Zinfandel Sonoma Valley Stellwagen Vineyard 1987 • $13 • (09/15/90) • **86**

SWANSON | CALIFORNIA

Alexis Napa Valley 1995: Impressive. Smooth, ripe, rich and harmonious, with plenty of soaring, complex spice, cherry, currant and chocolate flavors that really take off on the finish, complemented by a pretty dash of oak and supple tannins. A blend of 65 percent Cabernet Sauvignon and 35 percent Syrah. 1,035 cases made. • $40 • (12/15/97) HR • **92**
Alexis Napa Valley 1994: Combines ripe, rich, complex fruit flavors with elegance and finesse. Loaded with tiers of plum, black cherry, currant and wild berry flavors that pick up traces of cedar and spice on the finish, where the tannins are mild and polished. Ready now. A blend of 55 percent Cabernet, 40 percent Syrah and 5 percent Merlot. 500 cases made. • $33 • (03/31/97) • **91**
Cabernet Sauvignon Napa Valley 1995: Complex, with a pretty interplay of ripe cherry and plummy Cabernet flavor and mineral notes. Turns a bit minty and earthy on the finish, where leather and tobacco notes add dimension. Supple texture. Best from 2001 through 2010. 804 cases made. • $26 • (07/31/98) • **91**
Cabernet Sauvignon Napa Valley 1994: Smooth, ripe and supple, with a pretty core of chocolate, vanilla, black cherry and currant flavors. Gains complexity on the finish, revealing more concentration and depth. Has the tannic strength to cellar into 2000 with ease. 1,116 cases made. • $24 • (07/31/97) • **91**
Cabernet Sauvignon Napa Valley 1993: Marked by spicy currant, tobacco and cedary oak flavors. Balanced enough for early drinking, despite the tannin level. Finishes on the dry side. Try now. 1,093 cases made. • $22 • (08/31/96) • **83**
Cabernet Sauvignon Napa Valley 1992 • $22 • (12/15/95) • **90**
Cabernet Sauvignon Napa Valley 1991 • $20 • (11/15/94) • **89**
Cabernet Sauvignon Napa Valley 1990 • $23 • (11/15/93) • **89**
Cabernet Sauvignon Napa Valley 1988 • $23 • (11/15/92) • **82**
Cabernet Sauvignon Napa Valley 1987: Quite tannic, with a hollowness to the core of earthy currant, anise, sage, cedar and spice. Don't rule this out; its flavors are still young and vibrant, but it is somewhat awkward and lacking in focus. Drink now. • $25 • (12/15/97) • **88**
Chardonnay Napa Valley Carneros 1996: Good intensity, with ripe pear, spice, vanilla, anise and smoky notes. Can stand short-term cellaring to soften and evolve. Drink now through 2001. 1,991 cases made. • $26 • (05/31/98) • **88**

Chardonnay Napa Valley Carneros 1995: Complex, its band of earthy citrus, pear and pineapple flavors fan out on the finish, where it picks up a dash of creamy oak. Try now. 2,785 cases made. • $24 • (04/30/97) • **89**

Chardonnay Napa Valley Carneros 1994: Young and tight, offering trim citrus, pear and grapefruit flavors. It fans out a bit on the finish, where toasty oak folds in. 1,489 cases made. • $22 • (05/15/96) • **87**

Chardonnay Napa Valley Carneros 1993 • $20 • (07/31/95) • **88**

Merlot Napa Valley 1995: Marked by a racy, oaky edge, the core of fruit flavor is deep and intense, with blackberry, spice, herb and spicy oak notes. Rounding out nicely on the finish; drinkable now. 7,559 cases made. • $24 • (09/30/97) • **89**

Merlot Napa Valley 1994: Has interesting flavors, notes of currant, chocolate and cedar, and there's a nice dash of spice on the finish. Has the tannic weight to cellar into 2002. 5,539 cases made. • $22 • (05/15/97) • **89**

Merlot Napa Valley 1993: Young and intense, with firm tannins and crisp acidity, it's a bit raw and in need of cellaring to soften the tannins and rough edges. Still, the earthy currant and berry flavors are appealing if unevolved. 4,272 cases made. • $18 • (08/31/96) • **85**

Merlot Napa Valley 1992 • $16 • (07/31/95) • **86**

Merlot Napa Valley 1991 • $15 • (05/31/94) • **84**

Merlot Napa Valley 1990 • $16 • (05/31/92) • **82**

Sangiovese Napa Valley 1995: Smooth and supple, with a pleasant range of cherry, vanilla, spice and cedary oak flavors that gain amplitude on the finish. 2,060 cases made. • $24 • (12/15/97) • **87**

Sangiovese Napa Valley 1994: Young; the cherry and wild berry flavors have a slight green edge, but they build on the finish, gaining a nuance of spicy anise. Try now. 1,477 cases made. • $22 • (04/30/97) • **88**

Sangiovese Napa Valley 1993 • $18 • (06/15/96) • **88**

Sangiovese Napa Valley 1992 • $18 • (11/30/94) SS • **90**

Sangiovese Napa Valley 1991 • $16 • (05/31/94) • **84**

Sangiovese Rosato Napa Valley 1996: Somewhat waxy and herbal, but has an attractive brightness backed by light cherry qualities and a clean finish. 620 cases made. • $12 • (09/15/97) • **83**

Sangiovese Rosato Napa Valley 1995: Light and fruity with attractive cherry and strawberry flavors. 533 cases made. • $11 • (09/15/96) • **86**

Sangiovese Rosato Napa Valley 1994 • $9 • (09/15/95) • **84**

Sémillon Late Harvest Napa Valley 1992 • $25/375ml • (12/31/95) • **97**

Sémillon Late Harvest Napa Valley 1991 • $25/375ml • (05/15/95) • **88**

Sémillon Late Harvest Napa Valley 1988 • $25/375ml • (06/30/93) • **80**

Syrah Napa Valley 1995: Greets you with lots of exotic spicy flavors and nuances, and then a core of dark wild berry and blackberry. Finishes with firm tannins and a burst of spice. Given the tannin level and this vineyard's reputation for wines that age well, drink it from now to 2003. 360 cases made. • $40 • (03/31/98) • **88**

Syrah Napa Valley 1994: Big, ripe, rich and concentrated, this delivers a bounty of chewy currant, anise, leather, plum and spice flavors and, on the finish, a meaty note. Delicious; jam-packed with flavor. Drink now through 2004. 1,091 cases made. • $33 • (04/30/97) • **93**

Syrah Napa Valley 1993 • $30 • (02/29/96) • **89**

Syrah Napa Valley 1992 • $25 • (01/31/95) • **87**

Zinfandel Napa Valley 1988 • $12 • (03/31/93) • **86**

SWEDISH HILL | NEW YORK

Brut Finger Lakes 1990 • $15 • (12/31/94) • **71**

Johannisberg Riesling Finger Lakes 1995: Leafy, herbal aromas and lively, citrus flavors make this a zingy, satisfying, interesting and slightly sweet Riesling. • $9 • (10/31/96) • **86**

Optimus Finger Lakes 1991 • $15 • (11/15/94) • **75**

Riesling Finger Lakes Dry 1995: Fruity, but fairly simple in scope, with mild peach and floral flavors. Soft and smooth in texture. • $8 • (10/31/96) • **80**

Vignoles Finger Lakes Late Harvest 1992 • $11 • (06/30/95) • **83**

SYCAMORE CREEK | CALIFORNIA

Cabernet Sauvignon Central Coast 1978 • $NA • (11/15/92) • **70**

Zinfandel California 1982 • $9 • (06/16/84) • **87**

Zinfandel Santa Clara Valley 1988 • $8 • (10/15/92) • **84**

SYLVESTER | CALIFORNIA

Cabernet Sauvignon Paso Robles Kiara Reserve 1988 • $9 • (07/15/93) • **82**

SYLVIANE | CALIFORNIA

Cabernet Sauvignon Napa Valley Le Ducq Vineyards 1995: Complex, in an understated way, with pleasant currant, cedar, earth and tarry notes. Finishes with firm tannins and good length. Best from now to 2004. 300 cases made. • $30 • (04/30/98) • **87**

Merlot Napa Valley 1994: Soft and herbal, with a modest core of tar, tobacco and currant, finishing with an earth and leather edge and supple tannins. Very good, but fails to excite. Drink now through 2000. From Le Ducq. 350 cases made. • $30 • (03/31/98) • **86**

T VINE | CALIFORNIA

Zinfandel Napa Valley 1992 • $10 • (10/15/95) • **83**

TABLAS HILLS | CALIFORNIA

Cuvée Rouge Paso Robles 1995: Offers a medium-weight range of modestly ripe fruit, with hints of plum and cherry; finishes with crisp, austere tannins. A blend of Grenache, Syrah, and Mourvèdre. Drink now through 2001. • $NA • (05/31/98) • **82**

TABULA RASA | WASHINGTON

Red Columbia Valley 1995: Its light color is deceptive, because the palate is rich and spicy. A nice core of berrylike flavors. Ready to drink. 450 cases made. • $10 • (11/30/96) • **86**

Rosé Columbia Valley 1995: Bright and refreshing on the palate, it's on the dry side, with appealing watermelon and berry flavors that linger. 100 cases made. • $10 • (11/30/96) • **84**

TAFT STREET | CALIFORNIA

Cabernet Sauvignon California 1995: Cedar and spice, anise, blackberry and cassis flavors blend well. Finishes moderately, with pretty herb notes. 4,796 cases made. • $12 • (04/30/98) • **84**

Cabernet Sauvignon California 1994: Licorice, blackberry and herb flavors are framed nicely by cedar notes in this fairly smooth, easy-drinking Cabernet. 4,000 cases made. • $11 • (09/15/97) • **84**

Cabernet Sauvignon California 1992 • $9 • (12/15/95) • **85**

Cabernet Sauvignon California 1985 • $7 • (10/15/88) • **78**

Cabernet Sauvignon Napa Valley 1983 • $9 • (01/31/87) • **84**

Cabernet Sauvignon Sonoma County 1991 • $11 • (03/15/94) • **81**

Chardonnay Sonoma County 1996: Focused, with a pear and mineral core. Moderate body and medium balance lend elegance, while the finish is clean and refreshing. Drink now. 20,162 cases made. • $10 • (07/31/98) BB • **86**

Chardonnay Sonoma County 1995: Misses the mark with its earthy, canned pineapple-juice flavors. 16,500 cases made. • $10 • (05/15/97) • **77**

Chardonnay Sonoma County 1994: Soft and charming, offering up a nice mouthful of lightly spicy melon and pear flavors. This is a value white for drinking now. 14,400 cases made. • $10 • (06/15/96) BB • **86**

Chardonnay Sonoma County 1993 • $9 • (01/31/95) BB • **86**

Merlot Sonoma County 1995: Has a weedy, green edge framed by too much oak. 5,663 cases made. • $14 • (04/30/98) • **77**

Merlot Sonoma County 1994: Somewhat herbal, with hints of cherry and toast. Finishes with a dill and licorice edge. 6,200 cases made. • $14 • (07/31/97) • **83**

Merlot Sonoma County 1993: Ripe, with spicy cherry, plum and berry flavors and light oak shadings. 4,100 cases made. • $13 • (08/31/96) • **83**

Merlot Sonoma County 1992 • $11 • (01/31/95) • **81**

Merlot Sonoma County 1991 • $11 • (07/15/93) • **83**

Merlot Sonoma County 1990 • $12 • (05/31/92) • **89**

Merlot Sonoma County 1989 • $12 • (05/31/92) • **85**

Merlot Sonoma County 1985 • $10 • (05/31/88) • **83**

Pinot Noir Monterey County 1982 • $7 • (05/01/84) • **76**

Pinot Noir Santa Maria Valley 1983 • $9 • (04/15/87) • **76**

Sauvignon Blanc Russian River Valley 1996: Some pretty herb, wintergreen and floral qualities are evident but overshadowed slightly by oak. 2,798 cases made. • $9 • (03/31/98) • **84**

Sauvignon Blanc Sonoma County 1995: Fresh and appealing for its lively apple, pear and grapefruit flavors that keep step nicely through the finish. 3,200 cases made. • $8 • (04/30/97) • **85**

Sauvignon Blanc Sonoma County 1994 • $8 • (05/31/96) • **80**

Sauvignon Blanc Sonoma County 1993 • $6 • (08/31/94) • **77**

Zinfandel Sonoma County 1996: A big, ripe and chewy mouthful of dark plum, blueberry and anise flavors that remain strong through the finish. Needs until 2000 to shed some of its grainy tannins. 4,203 cases made. • $13 • (03/31/98) • **87**

TAGARIS | WASHINGTON

Blanc de Noirs Washington 1988 • $12 • (01/31/94) • **79**

Cabernet Sauvignon Columbia Valley 1995: Crisp and fairly generous with its cedary blackberry and gently herbal flavors, which continue through the softening finish. Approachable now. 700 cases made. • $15 • (09/30/97) • **86**

Cabernet Sauvignon Columbia Valley 1994: Very firm and chewy, with extremely fine tannins. Not as dense as the deep ruby color would suggest, but has enough berry and leathery spice flavors to make it worth cellaring until 2000 to 2002. 165 cases made. • $13 • (09/15/96) • **87**

Chardonnay Columbia Valley 1995: Crisp and intense, with well-focused pear, vanilla and citrus flavors that linger nicely on the finish. 1,500 cases made. • $10 • (09/15/96) • **88**

Chardonnay Columbia Valley 1994: Wood flavors dominate in this tight, youthful wine. Feels a bit hollow but drinkable now. 185 cases made. • $9 • (09/15/96) • **80**

Chardonnay Columbia Valley 1993 • $6 • (04/15/95) • **81**

Fumé Blanc Columbia Valley 1996: Bright and flavorful, offering refreshing nectarine, nutmeg and vanilla flavors that linger on the appealing finish. Ready now. 400 cases made. • $8 • (09/30/97) • **87**

Fumé Blanc Columbia Valley 1995: Has pleasant melon and spice aromas and flavors. Not tangy, but there's a celery note that clearly says Sauvignon Blanc. 300 cases made. • $8 • (09/15/96) • **85**

Johannisberg Riesling Columbia Valley 1994: Crisp in texture and only slightly sweet, with vibrant apple, green peach and resinous flavors that persist through the finish. Ready now. 450 cases made. • $7 • (09/15/96) • **86**

Johannisberg Riesling Columbia Valley 1993 • $6 • (09/30/95) • **77**

Johannisberg Riesling Columbia Valley Reserve 1994 • $6 • (09/30/95) • **87**

Merlot Columbia Valley 1995: Crisp in texture, with juicy prune, berry and spice flavors that remain bright and juicy through the finish. Drinkable now. 950 cases made. • $15 • (09/30/97) • **87**

Merlot Columbia Valley 1994: Disarmingly ripe, bright and generous with blackberry, vanilla and currant flavors that keep swirling right through to the finish. Delicious now. 165 cases made. • $13 • (09/15/96) • **89**

TALBOTT | CALIFORNIA

Chardonnay Monterey Cuvée Cynthia 1995: Ripe, rich and buttery, with a creamy texture and intense pear, spice, pineapple and citrus notes. Long and lingering on the finish. Best now through 2002. 500 cases made. • $45 • (06/30/98) • **92**

Chardonnay Monterey Cuvée Cynthia 1994: Marked by exotic tropical fruit flavors, with tiers of pineapple, pear, guava and spice. Well oaked, too, but the fruit more than stands up to it. Finishes with a lively aftertaste that brings out hints of citrus, especially grapefruit. Ready now and into 2000. 329 cases made. • $45 • (02/28/97) • **91**

Chardonnay Monterey Diamond T Estate 1995: Ripe, complex and exotic, with pineapple, citrus and grapefruit notes. Intense and lively, with a long, lingering finish. Drink now through 2002. 1,500 cases made. • $45 • (07/31/98) • **91**

Chardonnay Monterey Diamond T Estate 1994: Smells complex, with its spice, nectarine and light oak shadings; turns elegant and reveals tropical fruit flavors. Drinks well now. 1,100 cases made. • $40 • (07/31/97) • **90**

Chardonnay Monterey Diamond T Estate 1993 • $34 • (05/31/96) • **90**

Chardonnay Monterey Sleepy Hollow Vineyard 1995: Ripe, rich and creamy, with layers of pear, pineapple, fig and spice and a pretty dose of smoky, toasty oak folding in on the long, luxurious finish. Drink now through 2002. 7,000 cases made. • $30 • (06/30/98) SS • **93**

Chardonnay Monterey Sleepy Hollow Vineyard 1994: A subtle, well-integrated, flavorful wine that manages to maintain its sense of elegance even with its rich core of honey, pear, pineapple, vanilla and butterscotch flavors. Finishes with a long, complex aftertaste. 7,750 cases made. • $28 • (02/28/97) • **90**

Chardonnay Monterey Sleepy Hollow Vineyard 1993 • $26 • (12/31/95) CS • **91**

Key: SS—Spectator Selection CS—Cellar Selection HR—Highly Recommended BB—Best Buy $NA—Price not available Ⓐ—Auction Price (BT)—Barrel Tasting
Dates in parentheses indicate the issues in which the ratings were published.

TALLEY | CALIFORNIA

Chardonnay Arroyo Grande Valley 1996: Supple and creamy, with rich, attractive pear, vanilla, spice and citrus flavors that linger on the elegant, delicate finish. Drink now through 2001. 6,294 cases made. • $20 • (07/31/98) SS • **90**

Chardonnay Arroyo Grande Valley 1995: Crisp, lean and flinty, with a tart core of pear, nectarine and spice flavors that fan out and linger on the palate, finishing with a clean aftertaste and hints of fruit and spice. 2,689 cases made. • $20 • (05/31/97) • **91**

Chardonnay Arroyo Grande Valley 1994: Ripe with spicy pear, melon and hazelnut flavors, showing a sense of elegance and finesse on the finish, where the flavors linger on, gaining complexity and nuance. Better than an earlier sample. 4,399 cases made. • $18 • (11/30/96) • **89**

Chardonnay Arroyo Grande Valley 1993 • $18 • (07/31/95) • **88**

Chardonnay Arroyo Grande Valley Rincon Vineyard 1996: Aromatically complex, with yeast, oak and earth aromas. A supple, elegant, concentrated center of ripe pear, fig and melon flavors come together on the finish. Best now through 2002. 277 cases made. • $30 • (07/31/98) • **93**

Chardonnay Arroyo Grande Valley Rincon Vineyard 1994: A stylish wine that serves up lots of ripe pear, spice and subtle honey flavors, with some nice oak seasoning on the finish. Loses a bit of intensity on the finish, but it's still a pleasant bottle. 60 cases made. • $28 • (11/30/96) • **90**

Chardonnay Arroyo Grande Valley Rosemary's Vineyard 1996: Smooth, ripe, rich and creamy, with pretty pear, nectarine, peach, fig and melon flavors, all sharply focused and deeply concentrated. Wonderful texture, balance and finesse. Best now through 2002. 133 cases made. • $30 • (07/31/98) • **93**

Chardonnay Arroyo Grande Valley Rosemary's Vineyard 1995: Intense and tightly wound, with rich, complex flavors of pear, citrusy nectarine and light oak, this is a remarkably deep and concentrated young wine that should improve during the next 6 to 12 months. The finish is long and sophisticated; very flavorful. 68 cases made. • $30 • (05/31/97) • **93**

Chardonnay Edna Valley Oliver's Vineyard 1996: Delicious. Intense and spicy, rich and concentrated, this California Chardonnay is a well-focused, complex wine with tiers of buttery pear, honey, hazelnut and spice notes that cascade into a pretty, fruity flourish on the finish. 1,348 cases made. • $18 • (12/31/97) SS • **92**

Chardonnay Edna Valley Oliver's Vineyard 1994: Attractive for its ripe pear and citrus flavors and light shades of pineapple. Finishes clean and fruity, with just a dash of oak. 680 cases made. • $15 • (06/15/96) • **87**

Pinot Noir Arroyo Grande Valley 1994: An elegant, delicate style that captures ripe black cherry, spice and plum flavors. Well focused, with supple tannins and fine length, it can be enjoyed now. 840 cases made. • $22 • (12/31/96) • **88**

Pinot Noir Arroyo Grande Valley 1993: Ripe and fruity, with a smooth, polished texture. Shows hints of black cherry, herb and spice, and finishes with a complex array of Pinot Noir flavors. Better than when reviewed in December '95. 1,258 cases made. • $22 • (09/15/96) • **87**

Pinot Noir Arroyo Grande Valley 1992 • $20 • (03/31/95) • **82**

Pinot Noir Arroyo Grande Valley 1990 • $17 • (09/30/92) • **87**

Pinot Noir Arroyo Grande Valley 1989 • $17 • (10/31/91) • **75**

Pinot Noir Arroyo Grande Valley Rincon Vineyard 1995: Deeply flavored, rich and complex, showing concentrated cherry, currant and wild berry flavors, and a dash of raspberry. The flavors are beautifully integrated, and they hold their focus through a long, lively, flavorful aftertaste. Best now through 2000. 331 cases made. • $30 • (12/15/97) • **92**

Pinot Noir Arroyo Grande Valley Rincon Vineyard 1994: Deliciously complex, with layers of ripe plum, cherry, wild berry and spicy, toasty oak flavors. This is an elegant, classy style of Pinot Noir, delivering lots of flavors with no one of them dominant. Impressive texture, too. 94 cases made. • $32 • (12/31/96) • **91**

Pinot Noir Arroyo Grande Valley Rincon Vineyard 1993 • $30 • (12/31/95) • **85**

Pinot Noir Arroyo Grande Valley Rosemary's Vineyard 1995: Dark, rich and complex, with deep currant, wild berry, black cherry, plum and spice flavors all folding together in a harmonious style, finishing with hints of smoke, toasty oak and spice. Has just the right dose of tannin. Best now. 42 cases made. • $32 • (12/15/97) • **93**

Pinot Noir Arroyo Grande Valley Rosemary's Vineyard 1994: A delicious mouthful of Pinot Noir. Captures perfectly ripe, complex fruit flavors, with layers of black cherry, plum, anise, smoke and light oak. This is a wonderfully balanced wine that should age well through 2001 or 2003. 94 cases made. • $32 • (12/31/96) • **93**

Pinot Noir Arroyo Grande Valley Rosemary's Vineyard 1993 • $30 • (12/31/95) • **90**

TALUS | CALIFORNIA

Cabernet Sauvignon California 1994: A strong licorice flavor dominates, leaving little room for much else. Simple, and coarse in texture. 70,000 cases made. • $9 • (09/15/97) • **78**
Cabernet Sauvignon California 1993: Ripe and fruity, with supple plum and currant notes of modest proportion. Picks up a spicy edge on the finish. • $8 • (12/15/95) • **84**
Chardonnay California 1996: Supple and fruity, with ripe, clean pear, apple, citrus and melon flavors that are easygoing. Drink now. 120,000 cases made. • $9 • (07/31/98) • **83**
Chardonnay California 1995: Lightly fruity, with an appealing core of ripe pear, apple, melon and cedary oak flavors. 44,000 cases made. • $8 • (07/31/97) • **85**
Chardonnay California 1994: A solid Chardonnay, with ripe, juicy pear, apple and spice notes. Appealing for its fruitiness. 68,000 cases made. • $8 • (03/31/96) • **83**
Merlot California 1995: Some nice black cherry, cedar and leather notes give this fairly straightforward wine some depth. Coarse tannins cut off the finish early. 55,000 cases made. • $9 • (07/31/97) • **82**
Merlot California 1994 • $8 • (06/30/96) • **82**
Pinot Noir California 1995: Fairly refined and understated, with cherry and herb notes and firm yet smooth tannins. 20,000 cases made. • $10 • (07/31/97) • **85**
White Zinfandel California 1996: Pretty floral and raspberry aromas are marred by a tinny, artificial fruit quality. 165,000 cases made. • $7 • (09/15/97) • **77**
Zinfandel California 1995: Cedar and toast notes blend nicely, with a floral twist. Hints of plum and cherry are cut short by rough tannins, though. 8,000 cases made. • $7 • (07/31/97) • **82**
Zinfandel California 1994: Soft and earthy, with a mineral quality to the modest berry flavors. Ready now. • $8 • (11/30/96) • **82**
Zinfandel California 1993 • $7 • (03/31/96) • **82**

TAMAS, IVAN | CALIFORNIA

Cabernet Sauvignon Livermore Valley 1992 • $7 • (12/15/95) • **80**
Cabernet Sauvignon Livermore Valley Le Clan des Quatre Vineyards 1991 • $8 • (11/15/93) • **77**
Cabernet Sauvignon Livermore Valley Reserve 1992: This wine has had some time to settle down and exhibits smoothness on the palate. Herbs, plums, anise, cedar and spice flavors blend nicely, finish moderately. 1,166 cases made. • $14 • (09/15/97) • **86**
Cabernet Sauvignon Mendocino McNab Ranch 1984 • $6 • (02/15/87) BB • **84**
Cabernet Sauvignon North Coast 1985 • $7 • (12/31/87) • **79**
Chardonnay Central Coast 1996: Bright and simple, with pleasant, earthy citrus notes. Drink now. 10,000 cases made. • $9 • (07/31/98) • **82**
Chardonnay Central Coast 1995: Nice texture, but the flavors don't quite blossom. Remains light, spicy and modestly fruity. 10,000 cases made. • $9 • (07/31/97) • **80**
Chardonnay Central Coast 1994: Light and bright, offering a nice core of floral and apple flavors. Drinkable now. 8,000 cases made. • $9 • (06/15/96) • **82**
Chardonnay Central Coast Reserve 1995: Tropical fruit, vanilla and butterscotch blend nicely in this creamy-textured wine. Finishes with toasty oak and hints of pear, pineapple and refreshing mineral notes. Drink now. 800 cases made. • $14 • (07/31/98) • **88**
Chardonnay Central Coast Reserve 1994: Smooth and generous with its spicy pear and honey flavors, finishing a bit soft. 1,000 cases made. • $18 • (07/31/97) • **82**
Chardonnay Livermore Valley Hayes Ranch 1993 • $8 • (07/31/95) • **84**
Pinot Grigio Monterey County 1995: In a light, airy style, with soft pear and almond flavors that linger gently on the finish. 929 cases made. • $9 • (04/30/97) • **83**
Pinot Grigio Monterey County 1993 • $9 • (12/15/95) • **82**
Sauvignon Blanc Livermore Valley Figoni Ranch 1994: Frankly varietal, with anise and celery flavors weaving through the bright, citrusy fruit. Drink it soon. 2,813 cases made. • $9 • (08/31/96) • **84**
Trebbiano Livermore Valley 1994: Fresh, simple and appealing for its peach and almond flavors. 6,362 cases made. • $8 • (04/30/97) • **82**
Zinfandel Livermore Valley 1993: Earthy and a bit rustic, with a leathery twist to the sage and wild berry flavors, but with food some of the crispness will fade. 1,500 cases made. • $9 • (04/30/97) • **82**
Zinfandel Livermore Valley Beyer Ranch 1994: Pleasant, with fresh berry flavors, spice and lots of smoky oak. Flavors persist on the drying finish. Drink now. 1,200 cases made. • $9 • (06/15/98) • **83**

TANNER, LANE | CALIFORNIA

Pinot Noir Santa Barbara County 1992 • $20 • (03/31/95) • **84**
Pinot Noir Santa Barbara County 1991 • $20 • (02/28/93) • **75**
Pinot Noir Santa Barbara County Benedict Vineyard 1989 • $25 • (11/15/91) • **85**
Pinot Noir Santa Barbara County Sanford & Benedict Vineyard 1993: Tart, bordering on sour, with some supple cherry and plum flavors that pick up notes of leather and earth on the finish. Drink now. 200 cases made. • $30 • (01/31/97) • **85**
Pinot Noir Santa Barbara County Sanford & Benedict Vineyard 1992 • $30 • (03/31/95) • **82**
Pinot Noir Santa Barbara County Sanford & Benedict Vineyard 1991 • $25 • (02/28/94) • **88**
Pinot Noir Santa Barbara County Sierra Madre Vineyard 1990 • $22 • (09/30/92) • **84**
Pinot Noir Santa Barbara County Sierra Madre Vineyard Hitching Post 1987 • $25 • (02/28/93) • **81**
Pinot Noir Santa Maria Valley Bien Nacido Vineyards 1995: A touch earthy, with a slightly stemmy edge to the tart cherry and wild berry flavors. Leaner and sculpted, as is usual for this winery. Finishes with dashes of cola, earth and spice. 300 cases made. • $30 • (12/31/96) • **85**
Pinot Noir Santa Maria Valley Bien Nacido Vineyards 1994 • $20 • (02/29/96) • **86**
Pinot Noir Santa Maria Valley Bien Nacido Vineyards Picked Under A Blue Moon 1993 • $22 • (12/31/95) • **84**
Pinot Noir Santa Maria Valley Sierra Madre Plateau 1995: Tart, with a sour cherry edge to the plum and wild berry flavors. Turns racy on the finish, where it picks up oak and raisin notes. 125 cases made. • $25 • (01/31/97) • **82**
Pinot Noir Santa Maria Valley Sierra Madre Plateau 1994 • $20 • (02/29/96) • **88**

TANTALUS | CALIFORNIA

Meritage Sonoma County 1991 • $16 • (07/31/95) • **83**
Meritage Sonoma County 1989 • $15 • (07/15/92) • **86**

TARARA | VIRGINIA

Cabernet Frederick County 1989 • $12 • (02/29/92) • **82**

TAY | CALIFORNIA

Cabernet Sauvignon Napa Valley 1993: Aromatically complex, as pretty currant, black cherry and toasty oak flavors gain nuance and finesse on the finish, where accents of anise and cedar fold in neatly. Rich and concentrated, adding a long, full aftertaste. Drinkable now. 150 cases made. • $35 • (04/30/96) • **92**

TEAL LAKE | CALIFORNIA

Pinot Noir Monterey 1991 • $12 • (02/28/93) • **82**

TEDESCHI VINEYARDS | HAWAII

Brut Blanc de Noirs Maui 1984 • $19 • (02/29/92) • **79**

TEFFT | WASHINGTON

Cabernet Sauvignon Yakima Valley 1995: Dense and chewy. Front-loaded with plenty of black cherry and anise flavor, adding a mouthful of chewy tannins to the finish. Needs time. Best from 2001 through 2010. 665 cases made. • $22 • (07/31/98) • **86**
Cabernet Sauvignon Yakima Valley 1994: A solid Cabernet, offering firm texture and some pretty berry flavors that are more expressive up front than on the finish. Drinkable now. 350 cases made. • $25 • (11/30/97) • **85**
Cabernet Sauvignon Yakima Valley 1993: Lean and firm in texture, with currant and anise flavors that don't quite have the horsepower to get past the tannins. Try now. 230 cases made. • $23 • (09/15/96) • **84**
Cabernet Sauvignon Yakima Valley 1992 • $20 • (09/30/95) • **91**

Cabernet Sauvignon Yakima Valley 1991 • $13 • (09/30/94) • **79**
Cabernet Sauvignon Yakima Valley Winemakers Reserve 1994: Despite a sour edge to the berry and mint flavors, this is a smooth-textured red with a distinctive, if oddball, character. Try now. 135 cases made. • $30 • (11/30/97) • **83**
Chardonnay Columbia Valley Winemakers Reserve 1995: Fresh and lively, but well modulated to keep the bright citrus and honey flavors gliding smoothly through the finish. 216 cases made. • $15 • (09/15/97) • **88**
Chardonnay Yakima Valley 1995: Awkward, harsh and off-putting for its perfumy excess. 250 cases made. • $10 • (08/31/96) • **74**
Merlot Columbia Valley 1991 • $13 • (06/15/93) • **88**
Merlot Columbia Valley NV: A bit coarse and rustic, but the black cherry and slightly herbal flavors have enough pizzazz to carry it. Drink now. 630 cases made. • $15 • (07/31/98) • **83**
Merlot Yakima Valley 1995: Ripe, and nicely focused to show its black cherry and herb flavors, with a lively, chunky finish. Drink now. 1,000 cases made. • $16 • (11/30/97) • **87**
Merlot Yakima Valley 1994: A little chewy, but the currant and blackberry flavors push gently to the fore on the finish. 520 cases made. • $16 • (09/15/96) • **85**
Merlot Yakima Valley 1993 • $14 • (09/30/95) • **83**
Pinot Grigio Columbia Valley Crystal Pheasant Vineyard 1997: Bright, crisp and light textured, with floral, citrusy pear flavors on a sleek frame. Drink for its freshness. Drink now. 200 cases made. • $8 • (07/31/98) • **85**
Proprietor's Red Columbia Valley NV • $10 • (09/30/95) • **85**
Red Table Wine Yakima Valley NV • $10 • (09/30/94) • **83**
Sauvignon Blanc Late Harvest Yakima Valley River Mist 1992 • $10 • (09/30/94) • **87**

TELDESCHI | CALIFORNIA

Moscato Dry Creek Valley Frontignan NV • $11 • (12/31/95) • **87**
Zinfandel Dry Creek Valley 1991: Supple and well balanced, mature with ripe berry, pepper, tar and spicy notes. Appealing now. 2,000 cases made. • $15 • (07/31/96) • **85**
Zinfandel Sonoma County 1990 • $10 • (10/15/95) • **84**

TENNESSEE VALLEY | TENNESSEE

Cabernet Sauvignon Tennessee 1988 • $14 • (02/29/92) • **72**

TENREBAC | WASHINGTON

Port Washington 1989 • $24 • (11/30/91) • **74**

TERRA | CALIFORNIA

Cabernet Franc Napa Valley 1990 • $15 • (02/28/95) • **82**
Cabernet Sauvignon Napa Valley 1990 • $13 • (01/01/94) • **79**
Chardonnay Carneros Sangiacomo Vineyard 1993 • $19 • (06/30/96) • **88**
Merlot Napa Valley 1988 • $14 • (05/31/92) • **84**

TERRA ROSA | CALIFORNIA

Cabernet Sauvignon Napa Valley 1990 • $9 • (09/30/93) BB • **89**
Cabernet Sauvignon North Coast 1995: What a deal in California Cabernet! Young and still quite tannic, with an earthy anise edge to its currant and tobacco notes. This well-crafted red evolves into a supple, elegant wine as you sip—even with the tannins. Best cellared short term. Made by Laurel Glen, which also offers a Terra Rosa bottling from Chilean grapes. 10,000 cases made. • $11 • (08/31/97) BB • **87**
Cabernet Sauvignon North Coast 1994: A ready-to-drink style, with green olive, herb and cherry flavors. A blend of 87 percent Cabernet Sauvignon, 8 percent Cabernet Franc and 5 percent Merlot. Made by Laurel Glen. 28,596 cases made. • $11 • (10/15/96) • **82**
Cabernet Sauvignon North Coast 1992 • $10 • (04/30/95) SS • **88**
Cabernet Sauvignon Sonoma County 1989 • $9 • (07/15/92) • **86**
Red Napa Valley 1988 • $12 • (11/15/90) • **85**
Red Napa Valley 1987 • $14 • (07/31/90) • **86**

Key: SS—Spectator Selection CS—Cellar Selection HR—Highly Recommended BB—Best Buy $NA—Price not available Ⓐ—Auction Price (BT)—Barrel Tasting
Dates in parentheses indicate the issues in which the ratings were published.

TERRA VIN | CALIFORNIA

Red Napa Valley Vigil Vineyard NV • $11 • (02/29/96) • **88**

TERRACES | CALIFORNIA

Cabernet Sauvignon Napa Valley 1993: Complex, with a nice interplay of spicy, toasty oak and rich currant. Turns smooth and polished on the finish, where it picks up coffee and herb notes. Ready now through 2002. 300 cases made. • $40 • (11/30/97) • **91**
Cabernet Sauvignon Napa Valley 1992: Complex and well balanced, striking a nice balance between ripe cherry, plum and wild berry flavors and dashes of anise and oak. Drinks well now, with its supple tannins, but can surely age until 2002. Tasted twice, with consistent notes. 256 cases made. • $40 • (02/28/97) • **88**
Cabernet Sauvignon Napa Valley 1991 • $40 • (10/31/95) • **88**
Cabernet Sauvignon Napa Valley 1990 • $40 • (11/15/94) • **86**
Cabernet Sauvignon Napa Valley 1989 • $40 • (11/15/93) • **89**
Cabernet Sauvignon Napa Valley 1988 • $40 • (03/31/93) • **88**
Cabernet Sauvignon Napa Valley 1987: Mature, and in fine shape as the currant, black cherry, anise and earth flavors are round and supple, turning smooth and polished on the finish. Best now through 2002. • $38 • (12/15/97) • **90**
Cabernet Sauvignon Napa Valley 1986: Complex plum, herb and cherry flavors still hold the fort, with a pruny accent, but it's starting to dry out. Mature. Drinks well now. • $NA • (12/15/96) • **89**
Zinfandel Napa Valley 1995: Well oaked, but there's plenty of fruit to match it. Generous spice, tart raspberry, black cherry and wild berry flavors fan out on the finish, picking up an array of nuances. Best now through 2000. 400 cases made. • $20 • (12/15/97) • **92**
Zinfandel Napa Valley 1994: Well crafted, striking a nice balance between its spicy currant, wild berry and cherry notes and light, toasty oak shadings. Finishes with a zingy, fruity aftertaste. Has the structure for short-term aging. 452 cases made. • $20 • (02/28/97) • **90**
Zinfandel Napa Valley 1993: Smooth and spicy, with a nice dash of smoky, toasty oak to complement the spicy cherry and berry flavors as they fan out. Has a pleasant aftertaste. 375 cases made. • $20 • (09/15/96) • **87**
Zinfandel Napa Valley 1992 • $16 • (10/15/95) • **88**
Zinfandel Napa Valley 1991 • $13 • (10/15/94) • **87**
Zinfandel Napa Valley 1990 • $15 • (06/15/94) • **84**
Zinfandel Napa Valley 1989 • $13 • (03/31/93) • **87**
Zinfandel Napa Valley 1988 • $13 • (02/29/92) • **86**
Zinfandel Napa Valley 1987 • $13 • (02/15/91) • **89**
Zinfandel Napa Valley Hogue Vineyard 1985 • $13 • (10/31/88) • **87**

TESSERA | CALIFORNIA

Cabernet Sauvignon California 1995: Cola, blackberry, vanilla and spice blend nicely in this soft-styled wine that finishes with touches of smoke and licorice. Drink now. 91,000 cases made. • $10 • (06/30/98) • **84**
Cabernet Sauvignon California 1994: Clean and simple, showing some currant and cedar flavors. 31,000 cases made. • $9 • (11/30/96) • **80**
Chardonnay California 1996: Clean and lively, with pleasant citrus-laced pear and apple flavors. Drink now. • $10 • (07/31/98) • **81**
Chardonnay California 1995: Offers toasty oak and lemony flavors. Lacks depth. 63,000 cases made. • $10 • (07/31/97) • **80**
Chardonnay California 1994: Serves up a modest portion of ripe, spicy pear and hints of oak. Straightforward on the finish. 18,800 cases made. • $9 • (06/15/96) • **84**
Merlot California 1996: Smoothly textured, with tangy cherry flavors up front, but not much behind it. Ends on a woody note. Drink now. • $10 • (07/31/98) • **80**
Merlot California 1995: Starts out with a spicy, cedary oak note, then proceeds into pleasing cherry and berry flavors. All-in-all, it's a pleasant and well-balanced red wine that's affordable. 67,000 cases made. • $10 • (02/28/97) BB • **86**
Merlot California 1994 • $9 • (06/30/96) BB • **86**
Zinfandel California Old Vine 1996: Austere, with a compact range of modest spice and berry flavors. Drink now. 11,000 cases made. • $10 • (06/15/98) • **78**
Zinfandel California Old Vine 1995: Ripe and chewy, a solid wine packed with black cherry and anise flavors. Finish is smooth and gutsy at the same time. Ready now. 38,000 cases made. • $10 • (12/31/96) • **85**

TESTAROSSA | CALIFORNIA

Chardonnay California George Troquato Signature Reserve 1995: Intense and smoky, with a good dose of toasty oak. Underneath, the core of citrus, pear, fig and melon flavors is complex and lively, finishing in a long, rich aftertaste. Alas, only 85 cases made. • $38 • (03/31/98) • **92**

Chardonnay Chalone 1995: Complex and richly flavored, with elegant, sharply focused, creamy pear, vanilla, spice, nutmeg and anise notes that fold together nicely. 460 cases made. • $28 • (03/31/98) • **91**

Chardonnay Chalone 1994: Ripe and complex. Its juicy pear, apple, melon and fig flavors turn rich and concentrated, revealing their depth on the finish, where they pick up a smoky, toasty oak accent. 150 cases made. • $22 • (12/15/96) • **91**

Chardonnay Chalone Michaud Vineyard Reserve 1995: Young, tight and concentrated, this is a rich, complex and vibrant wine with a band of pear, apple, citrus and mineral. Drink now or lay a few bottles away in your cellar. 110 cases made. • $38 • (03/31/98) • **88**

Chardonnay Santa Barbara County Bien Nacido Vineyard 1995: Ultrarich and concentrated, with ripe pear, fig, melon and spice and lots of pretty smoky, toasty oak flavors. Finishes with subtle notes of complexity. Drink now through 2001. 79 cases made. • $27 • (03/31/98) • **92**

Pinot Blanc Chalone 1995: Ripe pear, mineral and spice flavors work their way past a touch of earthiness to capture your interest. Drinks well now. 47 cases made. • $21 • (04/30/98) • **86**

TEWKSBURY | NEW JERSEY

Cherry Wine New Jersey NV • $6 • (02/29/92) • **78**

TEYSHA | TEXAS

Cabernet Sauvignon Texas Late Harvest 1990 • $10 • (02/29/92) • **78**

THACKREY, SEAN H. | CALIFORNIA

Mourvèdre California Taurus 1989 • $24 • (08/31/91) • **86**

Mourvèdre California Taurus 1988 • $24 • (09/30/90) • **86**

Petite Sirah Napa Valley Marston Vineyard Sirius Old Vines 1989 • $24 • (08/31/91) • **87**

Petite Sirah Napa Valley Sirius Doomed Vines 1992: Dark, ripe, intense and spicy, with a core of minty currant, wild berry and cherry flavors that turn meaty and tannic on the finish. Try now. 110 cases made. • $24 • (11/30/96) • **91**

Pleiades California NV • $15 • (06/30/92) • **83**

Pleiades California Old Vines 1991 • $20 • (10/31/93) • **84**

Pleiades California Old Vines NV • $15 • (12/15/95) • **88**

Pleiades California Old Vines V NV: This is the wine to drink while Thackrey's heavyweights are aging. Supple and polished, with ripe plum and mineral flavors, and subtle, earthy nuances. 1,500 cases made. • $15 • (11/30/96) • **88**

Syrah California Orion 1994: Dark, ripe, intense and spicy, with a minty edge to the smoky, meaty currant, berry and cedary flavors. Turns complex and leathery on the finish. Not too tannic, it can be enjoyed now or cellared into 2000. 600 cases made. • $38 • (11/30/96) • **91**

Syrah California Orion 1992 • $30 • (12/15/95) • **91**

Syrah California Rossi Vineyard Orion Old Vines 1995: Pronounced minty, bay leaf flavors distinguish this wine, rendering a potent flavor that makes it seem one-dimensional. With time, it reveals wild berry, cherry and currant flavors, with a finish that is rich, complex, and full of firm tannins. Try from now to 2001. 490 cases made. • $45 • (03/31/98) • **88**

Syrah Napa Valley Orion 1990 • $NA • (10/31/93) • **83**

Syrah Napa Valley Orion 1989 • $45 • (12/31/91) • **90**

Syrah Napa Valley Orion 1988 • $30 • (09/30/90) • **89**

Syrah Napa Valley Orion 1987 • $30 • (09/30/89) • **92**

Syrah Napa Valley Orion 1986 • $26 • (04/15/89) • **83**

Syrah Napa Valley Rossi Vineyard Orion 1993 • $30 • (04/30/96) • **91**

THOMAS | OREGON

Pinot Noir Willamette Valley 1994: Packed with delicious berry, coffee and spice flavors that swirl nicely through the velvety finish. Tannins can use until 2000 to soften. 450 cases made. • $27 • (07/31/97) • **90**

THOMAS, JOHN | OREGON

Pinot Noir Willamette Valley 1991 • $17 • (11/15/94) HR • **91**

THOMAS, PAUL | WASHINGTON

Cabernet Sauvignon Columbia Valley 1993: A ripe and nicely focused Washington Cab, showing well-defined plum, currant and spice flavors that linger on the smooth, elegant finish. Drinkable now. 3,600 cases made. • $9 • (03/31/95) BB • **87**

Cabernet Sauvignon Columbia Valley 1992 • $10 • (09/30/94) • **78**

Cabernet Sauvignon Washington 1995: Light and fragrant, with currant and boysenberry flavors that linger with freshness on the open-textured finish. 20,000 cases made. • $8 • (06/15/97) • **85**

Cabernet Sauvignon Washington 1994: A little light and lean but showing enough freshness on the finish to make it approachable. Drinkable now. 7,500 cases made. • $9 • (03/31/96) • **84**

Cabernet Sauvignon Washington 1989 • $12 • (03/31/92) • **80**

Cabernet Sauvignon Washington 1986 • $14 • (09/30/90) • **84**

Cabernet Sauvignon Washington 1985 • $20 • (10/15/89) • **88**

Cabernet Sauvignon Washington Reserve 1995: Not a huge wine, but nicely focused to show off its currant and blackberry flavors. Shadings of spice and vanilla add interest, and it remains smooth through the finish. Drinkable now. 300 cases made. • $15 • (09/15/97) • **88**

Cabernet Sauvignon Washington Reserve 1988 • $15 • (03/15/94) • **80**

Cabernet Sauvignon Washington Reserve 1987 • $16 • (03/31/92) • **86**

Cabernet-Merlot Columbia Valley 1993: Delicious blend from Washington that offers ripe, elegant plum, berry and spicy vanilla flavors that remain focused and bright on the finish. Drinkable now. 7,200 cases made. • $9 • (03/31/95) BB • **87**

Cabernet-Merlot Columbia Valley 1992 • $10 • (08/31/94) • **87**

Cabernet-Merlot Columbia Valley 1991 • $10 • (12/31/93) • **80**

Cabernet-Merlot Washington 1995: Characterized by generous, bright fruit and smooth texture, this has plenty of charm. An early drinking style, best now. A blend of 57 percent Cabernet Sauvignon and 43 percent Merlot. 20,000 cases made. • $10 • (06/15/97) • **84**

Cabernet-Merlot Washington 1994: Open-textured and plummy, a bit light on intensity but very pretty. Approachable now. 8,500 cases made. • $9 • (06/15/96) • **84**

Chardonnay Columbia Valley 1993 • $10 • (08/31/94) BB • **90**

Chardonnay Washington 1995: Crisp and bright but not especially deep. A simple white with spice overtones. Ready to drink. 50,000 cases made. • $8 • (06/15/97) • **81**

Chardonnay Washington 1994: Bright and resiny, with a mouthful of green apple and pine flavors that are distinctive and fresh. Drinkable now. 18,500 cases made. • $9 • (05/15/96) • **85**

Chenin Blanc Washington 1993 • $6 • (09/30/94) • **86**

Gewürztraminer Columbia Valley 1994 • $6 • (09/30/95) • **82**

Gewürztraminer Columbia Valley 1993 • $NA • (05/31/94) • **78**

Johannisberg Riesling Columbia Valley 1995: Definitely sweet, with pretty apple and honey flavors that open up and fan out nicely on the finish. 4,000 cases made. • $6 • (09/15/97) • **85**

Johannisberg Riesling Columbia Valley 1994 • $6 • (09/30/95) • **80**

Johannisberg Riesling Columbia Valley Dry 1994 • $6 • (09/15/95) • **84**

Johannisberg Riesling Columbia Valley Select Harvest 1994 • $6 • (09/30/95) • **85**

Johannisberg Riesling Washington 1993 • $6 • (09/30/94) • **87**

Lemberger Columbia Valley 1993 • $8 • (09/30/95) • **83**

Merlot Columbia Valley 1993 • $9 • (06/15/95) • **78**

Merlot Columbia Valley 1992 • $9 • (04/30/95) • **87**

Merlot Washington 1995: Soft and appealing for its ripe berry and herbal flavors. Shows hints of tobacco on the firm finish. Drink soon. 20,000 cases made. • $13 • (09/15/97) • **84**

Merlot Washington 1987 • $16 • (09/30/90) • **89**

Merlot Washington Reserve 1990 • $15 • (05/15/94) • **79**

Merlot Washington Reserve 1989 • $15 • (03/31/92) • **79**

Rattlesnake Red Washington 1995: Light, smooth and appealing with its delicate raspberry and plum flavors that linger, with a touch of vanilla, on the finish. Drink soon. A blend of 77 percent Merlot, 17 percent Cabernet Sauvignon, 3 percent Pinot Noir, and 3 percent Cabernet Franc. 3,000 cases made. • $10 • (09/15/97) • **85**

Riesling Columbia Valley Dry 1995: Off-dry, with flavors that seem less than fresh. 1,800 cases made. • $7 • (09/15/97) • **78**

Riesling Columbia Valley Select Harvest 1994: Piles a little too much earthy flavor on top of the sweet fruit. 550 cases made. • $8 • (09/15/97) • **78**

Riesling Washington Dry 1993 • $6 • (09/30/94) • **86**

THORNHILL

Sauvignon Blanc Columbia Valley 1994 • $8 • (09/30/95) • **82**
Sauvignon Blanc Columbia Valley 1993 • $9 • (09/30/94) • **77**
Sémillon Columbia Valley 1993 • $6 • (03/31/95) • **80**
Sémillon-Chardonnay Washington 1995: Light, fruity and simple, with a pleasant touch of fig to the pear and tobacco flavors. 2,000 cases made. • $7 • (09/15/97) • **82**
Seyval Blanc Columbia Valley 1993 • $7 • (09/30/95) • **77**
Seyval Blanc Washington 1994 • $8 • (09/30/95) • **83**

THORNHILL | CALIFORNIA

Cabernet Sauvignon Napa Valley 1991 • $10 • (11/15/94) • **83**

THORNTON | CALIFORNIA

Blanc de Blancs California 1985: Mature and slightly oxidized, with a dry nutlike accent to the pear, ginger and spice flavors. Fans of mature, austere sparkling wines may find this attractive. 750 cases made. • $30 • (11/30/96) • **86**
Chardonnay California Coastal Reserve 1994: Smooth, with inviting aromas. A strong earthy element overrides the fruit on the finish. 3,000 cases made. • $14 • (07/31/96) • **81**
Gioveto South Coast Limited Bottling 1994: A stylish wine, this has a polished texture and appealing spicy red cherry and chocolate flavors that linger on the finish. Drink now. A blend of Sangiovese, Merlot, and Cabernet Sauvignon. 900 cases made. • $16 • (11/30/96) • **88**
Moscato South Coast Limited Bottling 1995: A fresh and spicy offering, with a snappy pepper, clove and apple character. Finish is ever so slightly sweet. Ready now. 800 cases made. • $7 • (11/30/96) • **85**
Pinot Noir San Luis Obispo County Coastal Reserve 1994 • $18 • (02/29/96) • **72**
Zinfandel South Coast Limited Bottling 1994 • $12 • (03/31/96) • **85**

THUNDER MOUNTAIN | CALIFORNIA

Cabernet Sauvignon Santa Cruz Mountains Bates Ranch 1995: Shows off a distinct herb, olive and tomatolike edge before moving into more mainstream Cabernet flavors of cherry and berry. Pleasant enough and drinkable now. 411 cases made. • $35 • (11/15/97) • **85**
Chardonnay Santa Cruz Mountains Bald Mountain Vineyard 1996: Well oaked and unctuous, this wine is redolent of butterscotch, melon, menthol, peach and pear. It's complex and elegant, full-bodied and powerful. The finish is long and smooth. Drink now. 144 cases made. • $29 • (06/30/98) • **91**
Chardonnay Santa Cruz Mountains Matteson Vineyard 1996: A brilliant yellow color, this wine is brimming with ripe, rich, complex flavors of pear, honey, butter and toasty vanilla, with spicy anise and yeasty notes on the finish. Best now through 2001. 72 cases made. • $29 • (06/30/98) • **92**

TIJSSELING | CALIFORNIA

Blanc de Blancs Mendocino 1986 • $13 • (12/31/91) • **72**
Blanc de Blancs Mendocino Cuvée de Chardonnay 1985 • $13 • (12/31/89) • **80**
Brut Mendocino 1987 • $12 • (12/31/91) • **81**
Brut Mendocino 1986 • $12 • (12/31/89) • **89**
Cabernet Sauvignon Mendocino 1990 • $8 • (11/15/92) • **77**
Cabernet Sauvignon Mendocino 1986 • $8 • (01/31/90) BB • **85**

TITUS | CALIFORNIA

Cabernet Sauvignon Napa Valley 1994: Very good if you like tannin. Has a tightly knit core of currant, blackberry, cedar, sage and spice. Finishes with a dry edge and cedary oak extract; drink now or cellar into 2000 in hopes it softens. 885 cases made. • $22 • (04/30/98) • **87**
Cabernet Sauvignon Napa Valley 1992 • $19 • (12/15/95) • **85**
Zinfandel Napa Valley 1996: Manages to pull out enough plum and berry flavors to make it interesting, but clearly it's medium-weight, modestly complex and best to drink by 2000. 1,800 cases made. • $17 • (05/31/98) • **83**

Key: SS—Spectator Selection CS—Cellar Selection HR—Highly Recommended BB—Best Buy $NA—Price not available Ⓐ—Auction Price (BT)—Barrel Tasting
Dates in parentheses indicate the issues in which the ratings were published.

TOAD HALL | CALIFORNIA

Bodacious Napa Valley 1988 • $20 • (11/15/92) • **81**
Bodacious Napa Valley 1987 • $20 • (11/15/92) • **83**

TOBIN JAMES | CALIFORNIA

Cabernet Franc San Luis Obispo County Constellation 1994: Ripe and tangy in character, with a tart edge to its ripe blackberry and herb flavors. Notes of coffee echo on the finish. Try now. 225 cases made. • $14 • (11/30/96) • **86**
Cabernet Franc San Luis Obispo County Quasar 1995: Bright cherry flavors are headed over the top, finishing with a sharp edge. Fairly one-dimensional. 225 cases made. • $18 • (03/31/98) • **78**
Cabernet Sauvignon Paso Robles Private Stash 1990 • $12 • (11/15/92) • **84**
Cabernet Sauvignon Paso Robles Private Stash 1989 • $12 • (08/31/92) • **88**
Cabernet Sauvignon San Luis Obispo County Morning Star 1995: Shows some attractive fruit beneath a layer of earthy-woodsy character, echoing berry on the lightish finish. Ready now. 1,078 cases made. • $14 • (03/31/98) • **83**
Cabernet Sauvignon San Luis Obispo County Star Light 1993: Ripe and fruity, with a simple core of plum- and cherry-laced fruit that's bright and lively. Finishes with modest tannins. Ready now. 919 cases made. • $14 • (03/31/96) • **84**
Cabernet Sauvignon San Luis Obispo County Super Star 1994: An austere style, with tart, sour cherry and berry flavors and very firm tannins. 500 cases made. • $14 • (11/30/96) • **79**
Cabernet Sauvignon San Luis Obispo County Twilight 1991 • $12 • (11/15/93) • **86**
Chardonnay Paso Robles Solid Gold 1995: Has an unusually floral, stalky overtone to the butterscotch and pear flavors. Distinctive, if not for everyone. 800 cases made. • $13 • (07/31/97) • **81**
Chardonnay Paso Robles Summer Sunshine 1996: Smells enticing, but the flavors veer off toward perfumy, floral notes that do not meld well with the pineapple and citrus flavors. Ready now. 870 cases made. • $13 • (12/31/97) • **80**
Chateau Le Cacheflo Central Coast NV: Light and modestly fruity, with a bit of a bite on the finish. 750 cases made. • $8 • (11/30/96) • **80**
Chateau Le Cacheflo Paso Robles NV • $6 • (07/31/93) BB • **82**
Merlot Paso Robles Full Moon 1991 • $14 • (06/15/93) • **86**
Merlot Paso Robles Lucky Star 1994: Firm in texture and ripe in flavor, with a cooked edge to the black cherry flavors. 400 cases made. • $15 • (12/31/96) • **84**
Merlot Paso Robles Midnight Star 1995: Has a distinctive range of red cherry and floral flavors that doesn't taste like other Merlots. Pleasant for its fleetness and lightness. Ready to drink. 508 cases made. • $16 • (03/31/98) • **83**
Merlot San Luis Obispo County Made in the Shade 1992 • $14 • (03/31/95) • **84**
Pinot Noir Monterey County Elegance 1995: Firm yet smooth, this wine shows pretty cherry and cassis flavors. It's got focus and finesse, with just a touch of bitterness on the finish. 415 cases made. • $16 • (01/31/98) • **87**
Pinot Noir Monterey County High Noon 1994: A chunky style, with an earthy, herbal edge to the modest plum and cherry notes. Hard to warm up to. 375 cases made. • $14 • (02/28/97) • **82**
Pinot Noir Santa Barbara County Black Tie 1992 • $13 • (03/31/95) • **84**
Pinot Noir Santa Barbara County Sunshine 1990 • $14 • (11/30/92) • **86**
Syrah Paso Robles Bodacious 1995: Fresh and youthful, with a floral accent to the peppery berry flavors. A sturdy wine to drink now through 2000. 695 cases made. • $14 • (03/31/98) • **82**
Syrah Paso Robles High Five 1992 • $13 • (08/31/95) • **87**
Syrah Paso Robles Smokey 1994: Smooth and focused, showing plenty of black cherry, licorice and spice flavors that swirl through the long finish. Try now. 275 cases made. • $13 • (11/30/96) • **88**
Zinfandel Late Harvest Paso Robles James Gang Reserve 1994: Very ripe and smoky, with a core of concentrated blueberry flavor that extends into a chewy, but not terribly tannic, finish. Best now to 2000. 5 percent residual sugar. 330 cases made. • $1/375ml • (11/30/96) • **85**
Zinfandel Late Harvest Paso Robles Solar Flair 1991 • $11 • (10/15/94) • **85**
Zinfandel Paso Robles Big Time 1991 • $12 • (06/15/93) • **82**
Zinfandel Paso Robles Blue Moon Reserve 1991 • $14 • (06/15/93) • **84**
Zinfandel Paso Robles Blue Moon Reserve 1990 • $12 • (12/15/92) • **84**
Zinfandel Paso Robles Flag Ship 1993 • $14 • (04/30/96) • **84**
Zinfandel Paso Robles James Gang Reserve 1996: A late-harvest-style Zin. Dark, dense and sweet, with an herbal streak running through the sweet

plum and spice flavors. Delicious. Drink now. 6 percent residual sugar. 800 cases made. • $16/375ml • (12/31/97) • **89**

Zinfandel Paso Robles James Gang Reserve 1995: Ripe, with a slight jam and raisin edge, but it hangs together with plenty of plum, wild berry, sage, tar and anise. Finishes with firm tannins and an earthy accent. Drink now. 300 cases made. • $20 • (03/31/98) • **87**

Zinfandel Paso Robles James Gang Reserve 1994: Ripe and approaching jammy, it delivers a full-bodied thrust of wild berry, cherry, plum and raspberry flavors. Finishing with firm, dry, chewy tannins, it should be especially appealing to fans of big, robust Zinfandels. 150 cases made. • $20 • (10/15/96) • **87**

Zinfandel Paso Robles James Gang Reserve 1993 • $20 • (04/30/96) • **81**

Zinfandel Paso Robles Solar Flair 1992 • $10 • (10/15/94) • **84**

Zinfandel Paso Robles Solar Flair 1991 • $12/375ml • (01/31/93) • **87**

Zinfandel Paso Robles Sure Fire 1991 • $18 • (05/31/95) • **86**

Zinfandel Paso Robles Wild Child 1994: With some breathing it opens to reveal cherry, plum and raspberry flavors, and it finishes with a lively aftertaste and lots of fruit notes. Ready to drink. 850 cases made. • $18 • (04/30/97) • **88**

TOGNI, PHILIP | CALIFORNIA

Ca' Togni Napa Valley 1992: Ultraripe and spicy dessert wine with zesty pepper, anise, mint and wild berry flavors. Finishes with an appealing hot-and-sweet tobacco accent. 175 cases made. • $20/375ml • (08/31/96) • **88**

Cabernet Sauvignon Napa Valley 1994: Strikes a nice balance between toasty, buttery oak and ripe cherry and plum flavors. It's not as big or as intense as this wine can be, but it still packs in enough racy Cabernet flavor to hold your interest. Tannic, but balanced. Try in 2001. 1,752 cases made. • $39 • (11/15/96) • **90**

Cabernet Sauvignon Napa Valley 1993: Starts with an herbal accent—like dill weed—then works its way into a core of currant and cherry before finishing with dry tannins and a hint of olive. 2,000 cases made. • $35 • (05/31/96) • **87**

Cabernet Sauvignon Napa Valley 1992 • $32 • (11/15/94) CS • **91**

Cabernet Sauvignon Napa Valley 1991 • $30 • (11/15/93) • **90**

Cabernet Sauvignon Napa Valley 1990 • $30 • (11/15/92) • **92**

Cabernet Sauvignon Napa Valley 1989 • $30 • (08/31/92) • **84**

Cabernet Sauvignon Napa Valley 1988 • $26 • (07/15/91) • **92**

Cabernet Sauvignon Napa Valley 1987: This remains a dazzling wine—big, ripe and bountiful, with loads of exotic plum and wild berry flavors and enough chewy, supple tannins to support another decade in the bottle. Best now through 2005. • $72 • (12/15/97) • **93**

Cabernet Sauvignon Napa Valley 1986: Dark and intense, with a ripe, exotic core of anise, plum and mineral flavors, showing signs of dryness on the finish. Ready now into 2000. • $NA • (12/15/96) • **89**

Cabernet Sauvignon Napa Valley Tanbark Hill Vineyard 1988 • $24 • (06/30/91) • **87**

TOPAZ | CALIFORNIA

Rouge de Trois Napa Valley 1991 • $17 • (12/15/95) • **84**

Rouge de Trois Napa Valley 1990 • $16 • (06/30/93) • **82**

Rouge de Trois Napa Valley 1988 • $15 • (11/15/91) • **87**

Sauvignon Blanc-Sémillon Late Harvest Napa Valley Special Select 1994: Rich and spicy. Not terribly sweet, this is centered more around honey-caramel flavors, with fig, pineapple and spicy oak notes swirling through. Has harmony and length. Delicious; ready now. 550 cases made. • $25/375ml • (11/30/96) • **91**

Sauvignon Blanc-Sémillon Late Harvest Napa Valley Special Select 1991 • $19 • (06/15/94) • **87**

Sauvignon Blanc-Sémillon Late Harvest Napa Valley Special Select 1989 • $19/375ml • (08/31/91) • **90**

TOPEL | CALIFORNIA

Cabernet Sauvignon Mendocino Proprietor's Reserve 1993: Classic 1993 in its rugged tannic framework and drying fruit flavors. The center of earthy currant, sage and berry is appealing. Dubious future; best from now to 2004. 400 cases made. • $40 • (04/30/98) • **84**

TOPOLOS | CALIFORNIA

Cabernet Sauvignon Sonoma County 1992 • $18 • (11/15/94) • **83**

Pinot Noir Sonoma Mountain Dry Farmed 1992 • $12 • (02/28/94) • **79**

Riserva Sonoma County 1991 • $18 • (11/15/93) • **79**

Sauvignon Blanc Sonoma County 1994 • $8 • (08/31/95) • **76**

Sauvignon Blanc Sonoma County 1993 • $8 • (08/31/95) • **76**

Zinfandel California 1996: Pretty bright—too bright, in fact. The cherry notes are nice, but the wine suffers from an awkward, bitter finish. Marginal. 3,000 cases made. • $9 • (06/15/98) • **78**

Zinfandel Napa County 1993 • $8 • (10/15/95) • **83**

Zinfandel Russian River Valley Bella Lisa 1996: Lightly fruity, with an elegant floral, plummy flavor that makes for easy drinking. Ready now. 575 cases made. • $16 • (06/15/98) • **83**

Zinfandel Russian River Valley Pagani Ranch Old Vines Reserve 1995: Dark, ripe and racy, with spicy raspberry, black cherry and plum, it's rich and concentrated, finishing with firm tannins and rich Zinfandel character. Drink now through 2002. 202 cases made. • $30 • (06/15/98) • **86**

Zinfandel Russian River Valley Piner Heights Old Vines 1995: Cherry, spice and smoke notes lead the way. Moderate body and finesse. The color is brick red, so go for it now. 2,954 cases made. • $17 • (06/15/98) • **83**

Zinfandel Russian River Valley Rossi Ranch 86-Year-Old Vines 1996: Pleasantly fruity, with ripe cherry and berry flavors and hints of spice and sage, but lacking in extra dimensions. Drink now through 2000. 1,060 cases made. • $27 • (06/15/98) • **83**

Zinfandel Sonoma County 1992 • $8 • (10/15/94) • **84**

Zinfandel Sonoma County 1991 • $8 • (09/30/93) • **81**

Zinfandel Sonoma County Piner Heights Old Vines 1994 • $13 • (10/15/95) • **83**

Zinfandel Sonoma County Piner Heights Old Vines 1993 • $13 • (10/15/95) • **84**

Zinfandel Sonoma County Rossi Ranch 1991 • $14 • (09/30/93) • **85**

Zinfandel Sonoma County Rossi Ranch 1990 • $24 Ⓐ • (10/15/92) • **84**

Zinfandel Sonoma County Rossi Ranch 1989 • $10 • (10/15/92) • **84**

Zinfandel Sonoma County Rossi Ranch 80 Year Old Vines 1992 • $15 • (10/15/94) • **78**

Zinfandel Sonoma County Rossi Ranch 80 Year Old Vines Late Picked 1993 • $18 • (10/15/95) • **83**

Zinfandel Sonoma County Ultimo 1991 • $18 • (09/30/93) • **84**

Zinfandel Sonoma County Ultimo 1988 • $12 • (05/15/92) • **77**

Zinfandel Sonoma County Ultimo Old Vines 1993 • $20 • (10/15/95) • **86**

Zinfandel Sonoma County Ultimo Old Vines 1992 • $18 • (10/15/94) • **83**

TORII MOR | OREGON

Pinot Noir Yamhill County 1995: Silky, polished, finishing with crispness and offering some nice tea-scented plum and spice flavors. Ready to drink. 1,825 cases made. • $18 • (06/15/97) • **86**

Pinot Noir Yamhill County 1994: Smooth in texture, with a firm backbone supporting lively blackberry, spice and delicate citruslike flavors that get a bit chewy on the solid finish. Best from now to 2000. 1,850 cases made. • $19 • (02/28/97) • **88**

Pinot Noir Yamhill County Reserve 1995: A distinctive wine, showing a level of soft ripeness unusual for the vintage, along with hints of mint and dill that sneak in on the silky finish. Has more up front than on the finish. Best from now or 2000. 115 cases made. • $37 • (11/30/97) • **88**

Pinot Noir Yamhill County Reserve 1994: Ripe, generous and complex, this is a mouthfilling wine with a broad range of black currant, plum and berry flavors shaded with spice and toast. Rich, it may need until 2000 for its boisterous edges to soften. 100 cases made. • $36 • (02/28/97) • **91**

TORRES, MARIMAR | CALIFORNIA

Chardonnay Sonoma County Green Valley Don Miguel Vineyard 1995: A lovely white, ripe and fruity, with lots of rich tangerine, pear, melon and spice flavors and a long, lingering aftertaste where the flavors resonate with intensity. From the California branch of the well-known Torres wine family of Spain. 9,192 cases made. • $22 • (10/15/97) SS • **90**

Chardonnay Sonoma County Green Valley Don Miguel Vineyard 1994: Distinct for its spicy flavors, with layers of ripe pear, peach and smoky oak, all tightly wound. Finishes with a flinty, green apple edge. • $20 • (11/15/96) • **90**

Chardonnay Sonoma County Green Valley Don Miguel Vineyard 1993 • $20 • (05/15/96) • **88**

Pinot Noir Sonoma County Green Valley Don Miguel Vineyard 1995: A delicious young Pinot Noir from a distinguished California vineyard, delivering ripe, rich and supple black cherry, wild berry, plum and spice flavors that are well focused, deep and lively. The wine finishes with just the right amount of tannin, and the aftertaste is rich and complex. Best now to 2002. 3,656 cases made. • $25 • (02/28/98) SS • **91**

Pinot Noir Sonoma County Green Valley Don Miguel Vineyard 1994: Young, firm and tannic. With a slight green edge, and its cherry, tea, leather and spice flavors wrapped up in tannins. Drink now. • $25 • (11/15/96) • **87**
Pinot Noir Sonoma County Green Valley Don Miguel Vineyard 1993 • $25 • (12/31/95) • **84**
Pinot Noir Sonoma County Green Valley Don Miguel Vineyard 1992 • $25 • (03/31/95) • **86**
Pinot Noir Sonoma County Green Valley Don Miguel Vineyard Vineyard Selection 1992 • $35 • (04/30/96) • **87**

TOTIER CREEK | VIRGINIA

Cabernet Franc Monticello 1995: Fruity in character, with some peppery notes. Tastes of red plum, with a tobaccolike nuance on the finish. 310 cases made. • $13 • (04/30/97) • **79**

TOTT'S | CALIFORNIA

Blanc de Noir California Reserve Cuvée NV: Simple and sweet, with a cloying candylike finish. • $7 • (12/31/97) • **71**
Brut California Reserve Cuvée NV: This one sports some doughy, floral aromas and a tight, firm core of lemon-lime and grapefruit flavors. It finishes long with zingy acidity. • $7 • (12/31/97) • **87**
Extra Dry California Reserve Cuvée NV: Fairly simple, with good acidity to balance its touch of sweetness. Finishes with hints of peach and pear. • $7 • (12/31/97) • **81**

TRAIL RIDGE | COLORADO

Cabernet Franc Colorado 1994: Fairly rich and concentrated, with appealing ripe plum and spice flavors. An up front, blousy style. Drink now. 125 cases made. • $15 • (03/31/98) • **83**
Chardonnay Colorado 1996: Overdone. Not much fruit flavor and has a green finish. 400 cases made. • $12 • (12/31/97) • **73**
Merlot Colorado Reserve 1994: A heavy-handed Merlot with chocolate, bacon- and Port-like flavors. Turns thin on the finish. 140 cases made. • $16 • (12/31/97) • **79**

TRAULSEN | CALIFORNIA

Zinfandel Napa Valley 1989 • $18 • (09/30/93) • **82**

TREFETHEN | CALIFORNIA

Cabernet Sauvignon California Eshcol 1994: A bit rustic, but the chunky cherry and wild berry flavors are ripe and lively and finish with a pure fruit aftertaste. 25,000 cases made. • $10 • (11/30/96) BB • **85**
Cabernet Sauvignon California Eshcol 1993: Green, unripe aromas are the hallmark here, followed by a beefy, herbal character on the palate. The finish is woody and resinous. 10,000 cases made. • $10 • (11/30/96) • **78**
Cabernet Sauvignon Napa Valley 1994: Dark, dense and intense, with a tightly wound core of black cherry, currant, cedar and spice, picking up traces of oak and cedar on the finish. 16,000 cases made. • $24 • (11/15/97) • **87**
Cabernet Sauvignon Napa Valley 1993: Marked by herb and tea notes, with a tart edge, and cherry, tobacco and herbal flavors. The tannins are supple on the finish. 11,000 cases made. • $23 • (12/15/96) • **83**
Cabernet Sauvignon Napa Valley 1992 • $21 • (02/29/96) • **87**
Cabernet Sauvignon Napa Valley 1991 • $19 • (12/15/95) • **84**
Cabernet Sauvignon Napa Valley 1990 • $19 • (11/15/95) • **87**
Cabernet Sauvignon Napa Valley 1989 • $18 • (07/31/94) • **84**
Cabernet Sauvignon Napa Valley 1988 • $16 • (04/30/93) • **82**
Cabernet Sauvignon Napa Valley 1987: Mature, with complex currant, cedar and cherry notes and a sense of elegance and balance. Finishes with a dryness to the tannins. Ready to drink. • $50 • (12/15/97) • **88**
Cabernet Sauvignon Napa Valley 1986 • $16 • (10/31/89) • **84**
Cabernet Sauvignon Napa Valley 1984 • $14 • (05/31/88) • **88**
Cabernet Sauvignon Napa Valley 1983 • $12 • (07/15/87) • **90**
Cabernet Sauvignon Napa Valley 1982 • $11 • (03/16/86) • **63**
Cabernet Sauvignon Napa Valley 1981 • $11 • (12/16/84) SS • **88**
Cabernet Sauvignon Napa Valley 1974 • $37 • (11/15/94) • **78**

Key: SS—Spectator Selection CS—Cellar Selection HR—Highly Recommended BB—Best Buy $NA—Price not available Ⓐ—Auction Price (BT)—Barrel Tasting
Dates in parentheses indicate the issues in which the ratings were published.

Cabernet Sauvignon Napa Valley Hillside Selection 1985 • $30 • (11/15/90) • **80**
Cabernet Sauvignon Napa Valley Library Selection 1983 • $30 • (10/15/90) • **80**
Cabernet Sauvignon Napa Valley Reserve 1991: A bit on the tart side with its cherry and currant flavors. It's a young wine and it's balanced, so cellaring into 2000 to 2002 should soften the rough edges. 1,100 cases made. • $40 • (11/15/96) • **86**
Cabernet Sauvignon Napa Valley Reserve 1989 • $30 • (07/31/94) • **86**
Cabernet Sauvignon Napa Valley Reserve 1986: There wasn't much to work with in the first place; now it's dry and thin, without much fruit flavor. • $NA • (12/15/96) • **80**
Chardonnay Napa Valley 1995: Veers toward the earthy side, with lots of mineral and spice shading the modest pear flavors. Best now. 23,000 cases made. • $20 • (11/30/97) • **83**
Chardonnay Napa Valley 1994: A touch earthy, with hints of grapefruit and citrus in the pear and pineapple notes. Finishes with a spicy citrus edge. 25,000 cases made. • $19 • (06/30/96) • **83**
Chardonnay Napa Valley 1993 • $19 • (07/31/95) • **85**
Chardonnay Napa Valley Eshcol 1995: Light and fragrant with spicy pear flavors that remain fresh on the finish. • $10 • (12/15/96) • **82**
Chardonnay Napa Valley Eshcol 1994: Simple, smooth and generous with its juicy apple and spice flavors. Drinkable now. 15,000 cases made. • $10 • (04/30/96) • **84**
Eshcol Red Napa Valley NV • $8 • (11/15/94) • **80**
Merlot Napa Valley 1994: A touch on the tart side, showing tight, bright black cherry, currant, anise and sage notes before the dry, firm tannins fold in on the finish. Try now. 3,500 cases made. • $24 • (11/30/97) • **87**
Pinot Noir Napa Valley 1986 • $13 • (07/31/89) • **68**
Pinot Noir Napa Valley 1985 • $12 • (06/15/88) • **74**
Pinot Noir Napa Valley 1984 • $9 • (05/31/88) • **80**
Riesling Napa Valley Dry 1996: Soft, floral and spicy, this smooth-textured wine has modest peach flavors to balance. Ready now. 3,100 cases made. • $12 • (11/30/97) • **84**
Riesling Napa Valley Dry 1994 • $9 • (09/15/95) • **85**

TRELEAVEN | NEW YORK

Riesling Cayuga Lake Semi-Dry 1995: Straightforward appeal, offering mineral, apple and peach flavors that finish off-dry. 489 cases made. • $9 • (01/31/97) • **84**

TRENTADUE | CALIFORNIA

Cabernet Sauvignon Dry Creek Valley 1989 • $10 • (11/15/93) • **77**
Old Patch Red Sonoma County 1994: Pleasant black cherry and chocolate flavors quickly turn tart and tannic. Lacks depth and finesse. A blend of Zinfandel, Petite Sirah and Carignane. Drink now. 623 cases made. • $12 • (06/15/98) • **79**
Sangiovese Alexander Valley 1994: Has a crispness and freshness that's balanced with some mature red-wine flavors, offering hints of blackberry and tar on the finish. Drink now through 2000. 568 cases made. • $18 • (07/31/98) • **86**
Zinfandel Sonoma County 1993 • $11 • (10/15/95) • **83**
Zinfandel Sonoma County 1992 • $10 • (10/15/94) BB • **88**

TRIA | CALIFORNIA

Cabernet Franc Dry Creek Valley 1993 • $24 • (05/15/96) • **83**
Claret Dry Creek Valley 1993: Drinks well now, highlighting its appealing black cherry flavor with spicy, cedary, earthy tones and finishing with the right amount of tannins. 130 cases made. • $24 • (05/31/96) • **87**
Labyrinth Red California 1995: A racy style, with a leathery, gamy streak that runs through the wild berry, cherry, cedar and spice, but even on the finish it fails to shake its earthiness. A blend of Merlot, Cabernet Sauvignon, Petit Verdot and Cabernet Franc. Drink now through 2002. 600 cases made. • $18 • (05/31/98) • **86**
Labyrinth Red California 1994: Complex, with ripe, juicy flavors and a meaty accent. Good, but lacking the depth and richness of the best '94s. Drinks well now. A blend of Merlot, Malbec, Cabernet Sauvignon and Cabernet Franc. 300 cases made. • $18 • (11/15/97) • **86**
Pinot Noir Late Harvest Carneros 1994 • $20/500 ml • (06/30/96) • **83**
Port Monterey County Souzao 1994: Dark, sweet and brimming with raspberry and blackberry flavors, finishing with just enough bite and smoky crispness to qualify as grip. Best from 2004 to 2005. 175 cases made. • $15 • (04/30/97) • **86**

Syrah Dry Creek Valley 1994: Young, tight and tannic, with a leathery accent to the ripe plum, berry and mineral flavors. Try now. 180 cases made. • $20 • (04/30/97) • **88**
Syrah Dry Creek Valley 1993 • $20 • (05/15/96) • **89**
Syrah Sonoma County 1995: Crisp and lively, with a trim band of spicy currant and wild berry flavors, finishing with a leathery edge and dry tannins. 670 cases made. • $20 • (11/15/97) • **84**
Zinfandel Dry Creek Valley 1996: Supple and complex, with a pretty array of ripe plum, berry, cherry and spice. Finishes with gentle, polished tannins and good length. Drink now through 2002. 650 cases made. • $18 • (05/31/98) • **88**
Zinfandel Dry Creek Valley 1995: Opens with an earthy accent, then works its way into more appealing flavors of sage, raspberry, cherry and spice. Turns dry and tannic on the finish; try now. 675 cases made. • $16 • (03/31/97) • **86**
Zinfandel Dry Creek Valley 1994 • $16 • (05/15/96) • **83**
Zinfandel Napa Valley 1996: Tight and austere, with a narrow band of spicy berry, cherry and cedar flavors. Best to cellar short term to let it soften; drink through 2001. 1,000 cases made. • $16 • (05/31/98) • **84**
Zinfandel Napa Valley 1995: Smooth, ripe and juicy, with spicy cherry, wild berry, raspberry and earthlike nuances that fold together nicely on the finish. 420 cases made. • $16 • (03/31/97) • **87**
Zinfandel Napa Valley 1994 • $16 • (05/15/96) • **89**

TRIBAUT | CALIFORNIA

Brut Monterey County 1985 • $13 • (05/31/89) • **91**
Brut Monterey County 1984 • $14 • (12/31/87) • **85**
Brut Monterey County 1983 • $14 • (02/15/87) • **81**
Rosé Monterey County 1984 • $14 • (12/31/87) • **80**

TRINCHERO, M. | CALIFORNIA

Chardonnay Napa Valley 1996: Elegant, with pretty toasty oak nuances and a core of lemon, pear and spice. Gains points for its delicacy, but could use a shade more depth and richness. Clean and refreshing on the finish. Overall, an impressive new wine from Sutter's Home new ultrapremium brand. 1,200 cases made. • $35 • (07/31/98) • **88**

TROQUATO | CALIFORNIA

Zinfandel Santa Clara County 1991 • $8 • (10/15/94) • **85**

TROUT GULCH | CALIFORNIA

Pinot Noir Santa Cruz Mountains 1995: A strange brew. Tea, cola, earth, beef, tomato and leather flavors conspire to produce a wine uncharacteristic of the varietal. Tastes prematurely aged. 300 cases made. • $16 • (02/28/98) • **83**
Pinot Noir Santa Cruz Mountains 1994: Opens with some interesting earth, stem, smoke, cedar and plum aromas that lead to complex layers of anise, currant, tea, ginger and other spice flavors. Finishes a bit sharply, but still intriguing. 325 cases made. • $16 • (01/31/98) • **87**

TRUCHARD | CALIFORNIA

Cabernet Sauvignon Napa Valley Carneros 1994: Marked by earthy, leathery shadings up front, the currant, herb and spice flavors come slowly to the forefront. Picks up a peppery, dill-like and coffee edge on the finish. Needs time to soften a bit; try now. 1,894 cases made. • $24 • (09/30/97) • **91**
Cabernet Sauvignon Napa Valley Carneros 1993: Supple and harmonious, with a nice toasty, buttery oak accent to the ripe currant and plummy flavors. Avoids being overly tannic or hard and finishes with hints of sweet fruit. Drink now. Tasted twice, with consistent notes. 1,470 cases made. • $22 • (11/15/96) • **90**
Cabernet Sauvignon Napa Valley Carneros 1992 • $20 • (03/31/96) • **88**
Cabernet Sauvignon Napa Valley Carneros 1991 • $18 • (11/15/94) • **87**
Cabernet Sauvignon Napa Valley Carneros 1990 • $18 • (11/15/93) • **87**
Cabernet Sauvignon Napa Valley Carneros 1989 • $18 • (12/15/92) • **87**
Chardonnay Napa Valley Carneros 1996: Smooth, ripe, rich and creamy, with lots of complex pear, anise, fig, hazelnut and earthy nuances. The texture is silky-smooth and the finish echoes fruit, spice and light oak. Delicious now through 2002. 1,323 cases made. • $24 • (04/30/98) • **92**
Chardonnay Napa Valley Carneros 1995: Well focused and well made, this is young and a touch on the austere side, with flavors built around a core of citrus and green pear. Will be especially appealing to those who like their Chardonnays on the flinty side. 1,150 cases made. • $22 • (05/15/97) • **91**
Chardonnay Napa Valley Carneros 1994: Bold, ripe, rich and exotic, with layers of pear, honey, toast and smoky oak flavors. An altogether complex and enticing style that is deep and concentrated, with a smooth, supple texture. Finishes with a wonderful display of flavors. 1,120 cases made. • $19 • (03/31/96) HR • **94**
Chardonnay Napa Valley Carneros 1993 • $17 • (07/31/95) • **87**
Merlot Napa Valley Carneros 1995: Complex, with rich, spicy, exotic currant, berry and plum flavors. Turns elegant and supple on the finish, with delicate tannins and fine length. Drink now through 2004. 2,786 cases made. • $24 • (05/15/98) • **91**
Merlot Napa Valley Carneros 1994: A well-oaked and concentrated style, this has a rich core of currant, spice, pepper and cedar flavors and finishes with firm, earthy tannins. Try now to 2000. 2,814 cases made. • $22 • (06/30/97) • **89**
Merlot Napa Valley Carneros 1993 • $20 • (04/30/96) • **89**
Merlot Napa Valley Carneros 1992 • $18 • (09/30/95) • **87**
Merlot Napa Valley Carneros 1991 • $18 • (06/30/94) • **87**
Merlot Napa Valley Carneros 1990 • $18 • (07/15/93) • **85**
Merlot Napa Valley Carneros 1989 • $18 • (05/31/92) • **81**
Pinot Noir Napa Valley Carneros 1995: Brimming with juicy plum, strawberry and black cherry flavors, with decidedly earthy and herbal notes, and finishing with firm, tealike tannins. Try now. 1,416 cases made. • $23 • (08/31/97) • **91**
Pinot Noir Napa Valley Carneros 1994: Takes a while to unfold, but as it does the cherry, spice, herb and berry notes are ripe, rich and well focused. Finishing with a long, full aftertaste. Try now. 1,350 cases made. • $21 • (02/28/97) • **91**
Pinot Noir Napa Valley Carneros 1993 • $18 • (11/30/95) • **88**
Pinot Noir Napa Valley Carneros 1992 • $18 • (02/28/94) • **84**
Pinot Noir Napa Valley Carneros 1991 • $18 • (02/28/93) • **82**
Pinot Noir Napa Valley Carneros 1990 • $18 • (09/30/92) • **86**
Pinot Noir Napa Valley Carneros 1989 • $18 • (10/31/91) • **90**
Syrah Napa Valley Carneros 1995: Dense and earthy, with a smoky, meaty, leathery edge to the ripe currant and berry flavors. Finishing with a chewy, tannic aftertaste, drink now. 1,212 cases made. • $24 • (07/31/97) • **90**
Syrah Napa Valley Carneros 1994: Remarkably concentrated and distinctive. Ripe and complex tiers of currant flavor with smoky, meaty nuances and just enough oak. Finishes with a long, full aftertaste. Drink now. 888 cases made. • $21 • (08/31/96) • **91**
Syrah Napa Valley Carneros 1993 • $18 • (05/15/95) HR • **92**
Syrah Napa Valley Carneros 1992 • $16 • (07/31/94) • **84**
Zinfandel Napa Valley Carneros 1996: Dark, rich and structured, with thick, opulent black cherry, berry, pepper, sage and spice notes, turning minty on the aftertaste. Amazing depth, richness and concentration for Carneros Zinfandel—a tribute to the diversity and excellence of this vineyard. Best from now through 2004. 637 cases made. • $18 • (05/31/98) • **91**
Zinfandel Napa Valley Carneros 1994 • $15 • (03/31/96) • **88**

TRUMPETVINE | CALIFORNIA

Syrah California Berkeley Red NV • $5 • (04/15/89) • **79**

TUALATIN | OREGON

Blush Willamette Valley 1993 • $5 • (11/30/94) • **70**
Chardonnay Willamette Valley 1994: Earthy, peppery flavors run through this wine, making it distinctive if outside the mainstream. Has some nice grapefruit and apple notes to balance. Ready to drink. 1,300 cases made. • $10 • (11/15/97) • **83**
Chardonnay Willamette Valley Barrel Fermented 1993 • $10 • (03/31/96) • **84**
Chardonnay Willamette Valley Barrel Selected Private Reserve 1993 • $15 • (03/31/96) • **88**
Gewürztraminer Willamette Valley 1993 • $6 • (03/31/96) • **83**
Müller-Thurgau Willamette Valley 1996: Soft, lightly sweet and fragrant, offering lots of appealing peach, pear and light floral aromas and flavors. Ready now. 270 cases made. • $7 • (11/15/97) • **85**
Müller-Thurgau Willamette Valley 1995: Bordering on sweet, with grapey, floral flavors. 200 cases made. • $6 • (02/28/97) • **80**
Müller-Thurgau Willamette Valley 1993 • $6 • (11/30/94) BB • **87**
Pinot Noir Oregon 1990 • $8 • (02/28/93) • **80**
Pinot Noir Willamette Valley 1995: Light in color, with straightforward plum and toast flavors that linger, with a bit of a bite, on the finish. Ready now. 2,200 cases made. • $13 • (10/31/97) • **84**
Pinot Noir Willamette Valley 1992 • $10 • (10/15/94) • **87**
Pinot Noir Willamette Valley Barrel Aged 1994 • $10 • (01/31/96) BB • **87**

Pinot Noir Willamette Valley Barrel Aged 1993 • $10 • (12/31/95) • **83**
Pinot Noir Willamette Valley Barrel Selected Private Reserve 1994: Light in texture, with earthy black cherry and metallic flavors that get in the way. 300 cases made. • $20 • (12/31/96) • **75**
Pinot Noir Willamette Valley Barrel Selected Private Reserve 1993 • $25 • (03/31/96) • **84**
Pinot Noir Willamette Valley Barrel Selected Private Reserve 1992 • $20 • (10/15/94) • **90**
Pinot Noir Willamette Valley Estate Bottled 1987 • $14 • (02/15/90) • **79**
Pinot Noir Willamette Valley Estate Bottled 1986 • $14 • (06/15/88) • **85**
Pinot Noir Willamette Valley Private Reserve 1985 • $14 • (02/15/90) • **84**
Riesling Late Harvest Willamette Valley 1994: Sweet, ripe and remarkably fresh, this is bright with grapey pear flavors and peppery, floral overtones, finishing with fruit over all else. Ready now. 80 cases made. • $9/375ml • (12/31/96) • **87**
Riesling Willamette Valley 1996: Light, sweet and lemony, with modest melon overtones and peppery, floral notes that make it seem slightly bitter. Ready to drink. 5,200 cases made. • $7 • (11/15/97) • **81**
Riesling Willamette Valley 1994 • $5 • (01/31/96) • **82**
Riesling Willamette Valley 1993 • $6 • (10/31/94) BB • **87**

TUCKER | WASHINGTON

Gewürztraminer Yakima Valley 1994 • $6 • (09/30/95) • **86**
Muscat Canelli Yakima Valley 1993 • $7 • (09/30/95) • **83**
Pinot Noir Yakima Valley 1989 • $8 • (02/28/93) • **72**

TUDAL | CALIFORNIA

Cabernet Sauvignon Napa Valley 1992 • $18 • (12/15/95) • **83**
Cabernet Sauvignon Napa Valley 1990 • $17 • (02/28/94) • **88**
Cabernet Sauvignon Napa Valley 1989 • $17 • (11/15/92) • **74**
Cabernet Sauvignon Napa Valley 1988 • $17 • (11/15/92) • **80**
Cabernet Sauvignon Napa Valley 1986 • $15 • (12/15/89) • **91**

TULOCAY | CALIFORNIA

Cabernet Sauvignon Napa Valley 1986 • $12 • (06/30/90) • **70**
Cabernet Sauvignon Napa Valley 1978 • $NA • (11/15/92) • **78**
Cabernet Sauvignon Napa Valley Cliff Vineyard 1994: A dense wine, with rough, powdery tannins. Behind the astringency, however, are layers of chocolate, coffee, herb, plum, cassis, prune and spice. With time, may soften. 506 cases made. • $22 • (11/30/97) • **87**
Cabernet Sauvignon Napa Valley Cliff Vineyard 1993: Crisp, trim and firmly tannic, but with enough ripe plum and cherry flavors to keep it interesting. Best enjoyed soon. 403 cases made. • $18 • (11/15/96) • **86**
Cabernet Sauvignon Napa Valley Cliff Vineyard 1991 • $12 • (11/15/94) • **86**
Cabernet Sauvignon Napa Valley Cliff Vineyard 1990 • $12 • (11/15/94) • **74**
Cabernet Sauvignon Napa Valley De Celles Vineyard 1991 • $12 • (11/15/94) • **87**
Cabernet Sauvignon Napa Valley De Celles Vineyard 1993: Appealing for its band of cherry, currant, plum and spice flavors, but it lacks depth and richness and turns simple on the finish. 118 cases made. • $18 • (12/15/96) • **84**
Cabernet Sauvignon Napa Valley Egan Vineyard 1988 • $15 • (11/15/91) • **86**
Cabernet Sauvignon Napa Valley Egan Vineyard 1987 • $17 • (02/15/91) • **74**
Chardonnay Napa Valley De Celles Vineyard 1993 • $14 • (07/31/95) • **83**
Pinot Noir Napa Valley Haynes Vineyard 1992 • $15 • (11/30/95) • **87**
Pinot Noir Napa Valley Haynes Vineyard 1989 • $16 • (03/31/92) • **76**
Pinot Noir Napa Valley Haynes Vineyard 1988 • $15 • (03/31/92) • **75**
Pinot Noir Napa Valley Haynes Vineyard 1985 • $18 • (02/28/91) • **83**

TURLEY | CALIFORNIA

Petite Sirah Napa Valley Aïda Vineyard 1995: Inky dark, dense and chewy, this is a potent Petite Sirah with a peppery edge to the plum and currant flavors, and a dash of black cherry. Needs time; try after 2000. 325 cases made. • $25 • (07/31/97) • **88**
Petite Sirah Napa Valley Aïda Vineyard 1993 • $21 • (09/30/95) • **90**

Key: SS—Spectator Selection CS—Cellar Selection HR—Highly Recommended BB—Best Buy $NA—Price not available Ⓐ—Auction Price (BT)—Barrel Tasting
Dates in parentheses indicate the issues in which the ratings were published.

Petite Sirah Napa Valley Hayne Vineyard 1995: Big, ripe, dark and richly flavored, this has a tight core of juicy plum, currant and black cherry, and finishes with a mouthful of chewy tannins and a spicy aftertaste. 300 cases made. • $30 • (07/31/97) • **91**
Sauvignon Blanc Napa Valley Turley Vineyard 1994 • $16 • (10/31/95) • **87**
Zinfandel Alexander Valley Vineyard 101 1996: Ripe and complex, with pretty, spicy, toasty oak and a pretty core of juicy plum, blackberry, cherry and spice. Deliciously fruity and complex on the finish. Tasty now for its fruit, yet mildly tannic, so you can age it short term. A new wine from Turley's estate vineyard near Geyserville. Drink now through 2004. 150 cases made. • $35 • (07/31/98) • **91**
Zinfandel California Old Vines 1996: A ripe, jammy style, with lots of fresh strawberry, black cherry and raspberry flavors that are rich, supple and focused. Finishes with a long, fruity aftertaste and hints of anise and sage. Drink now through 2004. 1,000 cases made. • $20 • (07/31/98) • **90**
Zinfandel Contra Costa County Duarte Vineyard 1996: Ripe, almost sweet, with a range of plum, sage and blackberry. Turns earthy and dry on the aftertaste, with a slight candied flavor on the finish. Drink now through 2002. 600 cases made. • $22 • (07/31/98) • **86**
Zinfandel Dry Creek Valley Grist Vineyard 1996: Ripe, almost raisiny, with dry, earthy sage, wild berry and black cherry flavors. A mouthful of Zin. Finishes with firm tannins, so drink now or cellar short term, through 2002. 300 cases made. • $32 • (07/31/98) • **89**
Zinfandel Dry Creek Valley Grist Vineyard 1995: Smooth, ripe and juicy, a late-harvest style that serves up lots of juicy black cherry, blackberry, currant and plum flavors. Impressive as it stays in balance, even with its high (17.3 percent) alcohol level and 1 percent residual sugar. • $30 • (07/31/97) • **93**
Zinfandel Howell Mountain Black-Sears Vineyard 1996: Marked by distinctive spice, mint and pepper flavors built around a core of plum and blackberry. Finishes with a long, lingering aftertaste and remarkably plush, polished tannins. Drink now through 2004. 600 cases made. • $26 • (07/31/98) • **91**
Zinfandel Howell Mountain Black-Sears Vineyard 1995: This Turley Zin is characteristically intense and deeply concentrated, showing off complex cherry, berry and plum flavors, with distinct pepperlike and herbaceous accents, and a long, lingering aftertaste. Bravo. 700 cases made. • $26 • (07/31/97) HR • **95**
Zinfandel Howell Mountain Black-Sears Vineyard 1994 • $24 • (04/30/96) • **93**
Zinfandel Napa Valley Aïda Vineyard 1996: A big, ripe, massive style that packs in lots of flavor, with tiers of mineral, spice, blackberry, black cherry and currant. Finishes with firm but supple tannins and a long, full, lingering aftertaste that keeps pumping out the flavor. A highly individual style. Best from now through 2005. 500 cases made. • $25 • (07/31/98) • **94**
Zinfandel Napa Valley Aïda Vineyard 1995: Smooth, dark, rich and polished, with a supple core of coffee, spicy oak, currant and wild berry flavors. Finishes with an unusual dried fruit accent, a prunelike edge. • $25 • (07/31/97) • **90**
Zinfandel Napa Valley Aïda Vineyard 1994 • $20 • (04/30/96) • **90**
Zinfandel Napa Valley Aïda Vineyard 1993 • $20 • (09/30/95) • **93**
Zinfandel Napa Valley Hayne Vineyard 1996: Dense, chewy and jam-packed with rich, concentrated plum, black cherry, blackberry and spice. A big, ripe mouthful of Zinfandel. You can feel the energy in this seductive wine. Best from now through 2004. 600 cases made. • $40 • (07/31/98) CS • **95**
Zinfandel Napa Valley Hayne Vineyard 1995: Dark, ripe, rich and expansive, loaded with smoky currant, plum, blackberry and black cherry flavors, it fairly oozes with Zinfandel character. Finishes with dry tannins. • $105 Ⓐ • (07/31/97) • **94**
Zinfandel Napa Valley Hayne Vineyard 1994 • $115 Ⓐ • (04/30/96) HR • **96**
Zinfandel Napa Valley Hayne Vineyard 1993 • $22 • (09/30/95) HR • **95**
Zinfandel Napa Valley Moore "Earthquake" Vineyard 1996: Spot-on Napa Zinfandel, with lots of cherry, blackberry, spice, pepper and oak. Tightly focused, finely balanced and quite pleasurable. Drink now through 2002. 600 cases made. • $30 • (07/31/98) • **91**
Zinfandel Napa Valley Moore "Earthquake" Vineyard 1995: A sweet, late-harvest style, it's ripe and juicy, brimming with cherry, wild berry, plum and coffee notes and picking up a hint of caramel. The alcohol is way up there, 16.8 percent, and it has 1 percent residual sugar. • $30 • (07/31/97) • **93**
Zinfandel Napa Valley Moore "Earthquake" Vineyard 1994 • $25 • (04/30/96) HR • **94**
Zinfandel Napa Valley Moore "Earthquake" Vineyard 1993 • $20 • (09/30/95) • **90**
Zinfandel Napa Valley Tofanelli Vineyard 1996: A potent, powerful wine with rough edges, it nonetheless delivers a ripe, juicy, tannic core of black cher-

ry, wild berry, plum and cedar. Finishes with firm, chewy tannins, so short-term cellaring is advised. Another new vineyard for Turley. Best from now through 2004. 350 cases made. • $28 • (07/31/98) • **92**

Zinfandel Napa Valley Whitney Tennessee Vineyard 1996: Hits the right notes, with pretty blackberry, black cherry, pepper and spice. The flavors zoom along the palate, revealing depth, richness and concentration. Has the tannic strength to cellar short term. The last Whitney Tennessee bottling for Turley. Drink now through 2004. 250 cases made. • $28 • (07/31/98) • **92**

Zinfandel Napa Valley Whitney Tennessee Vineyard 1995: Young and tight, with a rich, complex core of blueberry, blackberry and cherry flavors, turning smooth and polished on the finish. • $25 • (07/31/97) • **90**

Zinfandel Napa Valley Whitney Vineyard 1994 • $115 Ⓐ • (04/30/96) • **91**

Zinfandel Oakley Duarte Vineyard 1995: Smooth, rich and harmonious, exhibiting wonderfully integrated ripe, spicy cherry, currant and wild berry flavors shaded with just-right notes of toasty oak. Has an amazingly long, full-bodied finish. A delectable wine from a winery specializing in Zinfandel. 400 cases made. • $22 • (07/31/97) HR • **95**

TURNBULL | CALIFORNIA

Cabernet Sauvignon Napa Valley Oakville 1994: Young, tight and tannic, with leather and earthlike nuances to the currant, plum and berry notes. Shows a lot of wood tannin; try now or cellar to 2000 and hope it evolves. 4,600 cases made. • $22 • (04/30/97) • **87**

Syrah Napa Valley Oakville 1995: Greets you with smoky wild berry, plum and raspberry-laced flavors, showing depth, richness and concentration before turning tannic. But the fruit shines through on the finish, gaining a spicy edge. Best now to 2002. 250 cases made. • $25 • (04/30/98) • **88**

TURNING LEAF | CALIFORNIA

Cabernet Sauvignon California 1995: A solid red, firm in texture but not too tannic, with appealing blackberry and gently herbal flavors. Ready now. • $8 • (12/15/97) • **85**

Cabernet Sauvignon Sonoma County Sonoma Reserve 1993: Smooth, ripe and well focused, with a core of plum, currant and cherry flavor that gains touches of anise and spice. The complex aftertaste echoes fruit and oak. Ready to drink. 50,000 cases made. • $10 • (02/28/97) BB • **87**

Chardonnay California 1996: Marked by a leesy, slightly sour edge to the modest pear and melon flavors. Average; not as good as last year's model. Drink now. • $7 • (07/31/98) • **77**

Chardonnay California 1995: A good, straightforward Chardonnay with modest herb and citrus aromas, a soft texture and simple fruit flavors. • $7 • (07/31/97) • **81**

Chardonnay Sonoma County Sonoma Reserve 1995: Creamy and complex, with an elegant band of pear, vanilla, citrus and spice. Holds its focus, with a long, lingering aftertaste. Impressive. Drink now through 2000. • $10 • (07/31/98) • **87**

Chardonnay Sonoma County Sonoma Reserve 1994: Smooth and fragrant, with a well-focused core of ripe pear, fig, melon and vanilla flavors. Perfectly drinkable, with a lively, spicy aftertaste. • $10 • (12/31/96) • **85**

Fumé Blanc California 1995: An herbal style, backed by subtle pear, fig and spice notes. Finishes with a bitter edge. • $8 • (12/15/97) • **84**

Merlot California 1995: Light and crisp, offering some nice, pretty raspberry and floral flavors. Ready now. • $8 • (12/15/97) • **84**

Merlot Sonoma County Sonoma Reserve 1994: Tasty for its spicy licorice overtones, underscored toasty oak, herb and wild berry flavors that mingle on the palate with some rough-and-ready tannins. A very nice bottle of red wine, at a very nice price. 25,000 cases made. • $10 • (07/31/97) BB • **86**

Pinot Noir Sonoma County Sonoma Reserve 1995: Soft and appealing for its delicate currant, plum and spice flavors. Finishes with a sweet sensation. Ready now. • $8 • (12/15/97) • **84**

Pinot Noir Sonoma County Sonoma Reserve 1994: Shows off attractive ripe plum and cherry flavors, simple and pleasant. 40,000 cases made. • $10 • (01/31/97) • **83**

Zinfandel California 1996: Smooth and generous with blackberry, mint and spice flavors that linger enticingly on the polished finish. Tasty now through 2000. • $8 • (12/15/97) • **87**

Zinfandel Sonoma County Sonoma Reserve 1994: Smooth and supple, with complex fruit flavors that echo notes of cherry, raspberry and plum. Finishes with firm tannins. It's tasty and very affordable. 40,000 cases made. • $10 • (12/31/96) BB • **87**

TWIN HILLS | CALIFORNIA

Cabernet Sauvignon Paso Robles 1991 • $7 • (11/15/94) • **72**

Cabernet Sauvignon Paso Robles 1989 • $13 • (11/15/93) • **69**

Cabernet Sauvignon Paso Robles 1988 • $8 • (11/15/92) • **76**

Chardonnay Paso Robles 1993 • $9 • (07/31/95) • **79**

Chardonnay Paso Robles Reserve 1993: Acrid, sour flavors dominate the modest fruit in this otherwise smooth wine. 500 cases made. • $13 • (07/31/96) • **74**

Zinfandel Paso Robles 1991 • $9 • (09/30/93) • **80**

TYEE | OREGON

Pinot Noir Willamette Valley 1994: Packed with jazzy black cherry, spice and earthy mineral flavors, adding a limelike nuance that persists on the finish. Drink now or cellar until 2000. 600 cases made. • $20 • (07/31/97) • **87**

Pinot Noir Willamette Valley 1989 • $12 • (02/28/93) • **68**

Pinot Noir Willamette Valley 1988 • $13 • (02/28/93) • **63**

UNALII | CALIFORNIA

Chardonnay Sonoma County Hillside Estates 1996: Smooth and creamy on the palate, with attractive pear, spice, apple and mineral flavors. On the finish however, it's a little bitter. 1,057 cases made. • $14 • (01/31/98) • **87**

UNIONVILLE VINEYARDS | NEW JERSEY

Hunter's White Reserve New Jersey 1994 • $6 • (01/01/95) • **80**

Seyval Blanc New Jersey Windfall 1994 • $9 • (01/01/95) • **82**

Seyval Blanc New Jersey Windfall 1993 • $9 • (01/01/96) • **83**

UNISSENT | CALIFORNIA

Cabernet Sauvignon California 1988 • $15 • (11/15/91) • **83**

UVE CELLARS | CALIFORNIA

Vin Santo Napa Valley 1992: Amber in color, with woody aromas, but the flavors run toward caramel, almond and nutmeg, hitting a peppery note on the finish. Ready now. 400 cases made. • $20 • (11/30/96) • **85**

Vin Santo Napa Valley 1991 • $19/375ml • (12/31/95) • **89**

VALLEJO, M.G. | CALIFORNIA

Cabernet Sauvignon California 1994: Light cedar and plum notes make this simple wine enjoyable now. 170,000 cases made. • $7 • (10/31/97) • **81**

Cabernet Sauvignon California 1992 • $6 • (11/30/95) BB • **85**

Cabernet Sauvignon California 1990 • $6 • (11/15/92) BB • **80**

Cabernet Sauvignon California 1986 • $5 • (06/15/90) BB • **82**

Cabernet Sauvignon California 1985 • $4 • (02/15/89) • **78**

Cabernet Sauvignon California 1983 • $4 • (08/31/87) • **67**

Cabernet Sauvignon California Harvest Select 1991 • $6 • (11/15/94) • **79**

Cabernet Sauvignon California Harvest Select 1990 • $7 • (06/15/93) • **78**

Chardonnay California 1995: Fresh, simple and appealing for its pineapple and mineral flavors. • $7 • (11/30/96) • **81**

Chardonnay California 1994: Smooth and flavorful, showing plenty of vanilla-scented pear and citrus character. Ready now. • $6 • (11/15/95) • **84**

Chardonnay California 1993 • $6 • (07/31/95) • **82**

M.G.V. Red California NV • $3 • (05/31/90) • **74**

Merlot California 1994: Very light flavors, with minty, herbal notes that keep playing on the finish. 123,000 cases made. • $8 • (07/31/96) • **80**

Merlot California 1991 • $6 • (11/30/92) BB • **84**

Merlot California 1990 • $6 • (05/31/92) BB • **80**

Merlot California 1987 • $5 • (06/15/90) • **77**

Merlot California Harvest Select 1992 • $6 • (09/15/94) JL • **82**

Merlot California Harvest Select 1991 • $7 • (06/15/93) • **79**

Pinot Noir California 1995: Blessed with some pretty plum, cherry and herb flavors, this is a simple wine but pleasant nonetheless. 16,000 cases made. • $7 • (02/28/98) • **82**

Pinot Noir California 1994: Simple, light and fruity, this has more Gamay flavor than Pinot. • $7 • (12/15/96) • **76**

Pinot Noir California Harvest Select 1994 • $8 • (01/31/96) • **80**

Sauvignon Blanc California 1994: Light, showing an earthy and vaguely spicy character around modest citrus flavors. • $6 • (11/30/96) • **81**

Sauvignon Blanc California 1993 • $5 • (08/31/95) • **82**

White Zinfandel California 1994 • $6 • (09/15/95) • **80**

VALLEY OF THE MOON | CALIFORNIA

Zinfandel Sonoma Valley 1984 • $9 • (03/15/90) • **76**
Zinfandel Sonoma Valley Reserve 1990 • $10 • (10/15/94) • **80**

VALLEY RIDGE | CALIFORNIA

Cabernet Sauvignon Sonoma County 1989 • $9 • (11/15/91) • **83**
Zinfandel Sonoma County 1988 • $9 • (11/15/91) • **86**

VALLEY VIEW | OREGON

Anna Maria Red Rogue Valley Reserve 1995: Firm in texture, with a nice beam of earth-scented cherry flavor cutting through the fine tannins. Approachable now; best from 2000. A blend of Cabernet Sauvignon, Cabernet Franc and Merlot. 1,000 cases made. • $18 • (05/15/98) • **86**
Anna Maria Red Rogue Valley Reserve 1994: Crisp tannins and earthy flavors tend to cover the bright streaks of red cherry and berry, and it finishes with a chewy texture that needs to soften. Try now. A blend of Merlot, Cabernet Sauvignon and Cabernet Franc. 1,200 cases made. • $20 • (10/31/97) • **85**
Anna Maria Red Rogue Valley Reserve 1992 • $20 • (11/30/94) • **77**
Anna Maria Red Rogue Valley Reserve 1990 • $27 • (05/15/94) • **87**
Anna Maria Red Rogue Valley Vintners Reserve 1994: Offers a lush mouthful of spicy berry flavors; very much a Zinfandel-style red with some extra nuances of currant and herb. Has substance in the middle and grace on the finish. Good now to 2000. A blend of 52 percent Zinfandel, 19 percent Cabernet Franc,18 percent Cabernet Sauvignon and 11 percent Merlot. 300 cases made. • $20 • (05/15/98) • **90**
Cabernet Franc Rogue Valley Anna Maria 1994: A solid red wine packing delicious berry, cherry and cedar into a trim package dripping with flavor. Drinkable now. 25 percent Cabernet Sauvignon. 200 cases made. • $20 • (10/31/97) • **87**
Cabernet Sauvignon Rogue Valley 1995: A solid Cabernet, firm in texture, with nicely proportioned flavors. Offers ripe berry and smoke notes that linger on the finish. Drink now. 1,800 cases made. • $12 • (10/31/97) • **86**
Cabernet Sauvignon Rogue Valley 1992: Modest berry and brick flavors, with an earthy, ashy edge. 550 cases made. • $10 • (07/31/96) • **78**
Cabernet Sauvignon Rogue Valley 1991 • $6 • (05/15/94) • **75**
Cabernet Sauvignon Rogue Valley Anna Maria 1990 • $18 • (05/15/94) • **86**
Cabernet Sauvignon Rogue Valley Barrel Select 1991 • $13 • (11/30/94) • **84**
Cabernet Sauvignon Rogue Valley Barrel Select 1989 • $13 • (06/15/92) • **83**
Chardonnay Rogue Valley 1993: Bright and fresh. Bursting with delicious peach, pineapple and honey flavors that swirl solidly through the finish. 900 cases made. • $10 • (07/31/96) • **87**
Chardonnay Rogue Valley Anna Maria 1996: Ripe, fat style of Chardonnay emphasizing pear and honey flavors that expand and linger on the round finish. Not subtle, but a nice mouthful of flavor. Drink now. 502 cases made. • $15 • (05/15/98) • **87**
Chardonnay Rogue Valley Anna Maria 1994: Spicy, toasty flavors, with modestly fruity foundation. 752 cases made. • $16 • (07/31/96) • **82**
Chardonnay Rogue Valley Anna Maria 1993 • $14 • (03/31/96) • **85**
Fumé Blanc Rogue Valley 1995: Light and fruity, with a spicy peach zing that shines through on the soft finish. 826 cases made. • $10 • (07/31/96) • **83**
Fumé Blanc Rogue Valley Anna Maria 1993 • $10 • (11/30/94) • **87**
Merlot Oregon 1983 • $10 • (05/31/88) • **78**
Merlot Rogue Valley 1995: Ripe and supple, appealing for its currant, herb and plum flavors that linger gently on the velvety finish. Ready to drink. 2,100 cases made. • $12 • (10/31/97) • **86**
Merlot Rogue Valley 1991 • $10 • (11/30/94) • **78**
Merlot Rogue Valley Anna Maria 1992 • $18 • (03/31/96) • **85**
Merlot Rogue Valley Anna Maria Old Stage 1994: Very firm in texture, almost tough, with pretty berry and herbal flavors lurking behind the tannins. Try now. 150 cases made. • $30 • (10/31/97) • **85**
Merlot Rogue Valley Jazz Label 1992 • $10 • (11/30/94) • **85**
Pinot Noir Oregon 1982 • $8 • (03/01/86) • **73**
Pinot Noir Oregon 1980 • $7 • (09/16/84) • **76**
Red Rogue Oregon NV • $3 • (02/15/88) • **74**

Key: SS—Spectator Selection CS—Cellar Selection HR—Highly Recommended BB—Best Buy $NA—Price not available Ⓐ—Auction Price (BT)—Barrel Tasting
Dates in parentheses indicate the issues in which the ratings were published.

VAN ASPEREN | CALIFORNIA

Zinfandel Napa Valley 1995: Distinct for its up-front spice and pepper flavors, it turns lean and trim on the palate. Well balanced, but missing extra flavor dimensions. Drink now. 1,600 cases made. • $10 • (06/15/98) • **84**

VAN DER HEYDEN | CALIFORNIA

Cabernet Sauvignon Alexander Valley 1987 • $18 • (08/31/92) • **80**

VAN DER KAMP | CALIFORNIA

Brut Rosé Sonoma Valley Midnight Cuvée 1989 • $15 • (12/31/94) • **83**
Brut Rosé Sonoma Valley Midnight Cuvée 1988 • $12 • (05/15/92) • **75**
Brut Rosé Sonoma Valley Midnight Cuvée 1987 • $15 • (11/15/90) • **81**
Brut Rosé Sonoma Valley Midnight Cuvée 1986 • $15 • (05/31/89) • **83**
Brut Rosé Sonoma Valley Midnight Cuvée 1985 • $18 • (12/31/87) • **84**
Brut Sonoma Valley 1988 • $15 • (12/15/93) • **86**
Brut Sonoma Valley 1985 • $15 • (12/15/91) • **84**
Brut Sonoma Valley 1984 • $15 • (05/31/89) • **86**
Brut Sonoma Valley 1983 • $18 • (12/31/87) • **86**
Brut Sonoma Valley English Cuvée 1986 • $15 • (12/31/92) • **89**
Brut Sonoma Valley Reserve 1986 • $16 • (12/31/94) • **84**

VAN DUZER | OREGON

Chardonnay Oregon Eola Selection 1995: Crisp in texture, with citrusy pear and honey flavors that linger on the tight finish. Has some nice stuff packed into a narrow frame. Try now. 900 cases made. • $12 • (10/31/97) • **87**
Chardonnay Oregon Eola Selection 1994: Ripe, focused and more than a little spicy, which adds character to the mineral-scented apple, orange peel and honey flavors. Not a big wine, but it has style and finishes gracefully. Ready now. 830 cases made. • $12 • (02/28/97) • **89**
Chardonnay Oregon Eola Selection 1993 • $12 • (03/31/96) • **82**
Chardonnay Oregon Reserve 1994: Creamy, elegant and crisp all at the same time, with juicy acidity supporting the apple, honey, spice and pear flavors as they echo deliciously on the spicy finish. A harmonious wine, ready now. 1,325 cases made. • $17 • (02/28/97) • **90**
Chardonnay Oregon Reserve 1993 • $17 • (06/15/96) • **87**
Pinot Noir Oregon Appellation Selection 1992 • $10 • (03/31/96) • **87**
Pinot Noir Oregon Domain Hill & Mayes Reserve 1991 • $15 • (11/30/94) • **83**
Pinot Noir Oregon Eola Selection 1996: On the light side, with pretty, pure currant, plum and vanilla flavors that glide smoothly through the velvety finish. Ends with a crisp underpinning and a nice echo of the flavors. Try now. 1,200 cases made. • $13 • (05/15/98) • **87**
Pinot Noir Oregon Eola Selection 1994: Oak tends to to dominate the fruit in this spicy, almost resiny wine. Reveals just enough ripe berry flavor on the finish to keep it in balance. Try now. 1,400 cases made. • $13 • (02/28/97) • **84**
Pinot Noir Oregon Eola Selection 1993: Light in style, with hints of leather to the modest blackberry and smoke flavors. 1,000 cases made. • $14 • (09/30/96) • **81**
Pinot Noir Oregon Reserve 1994: Ripe flavors leap forward from the first sip of this spicy, berry-scented Pinot, firm in texture and long on the finish. Tasty now, but it can use until 2000 to soften the crisp tannins. 1,400 cases made. • $18 • (10/31/97) • **88**
Pinot Noir Oregon Reserve 1989 • $16 • (06/15/92) • **87**
Pinot Noir Willamette Valley Reserve 1990 • $16 • (03/15/94) • **74**
Riesling Oregon Domain Hill & Mayes Dry Reserve 1993 • $8 • (11/30/94) • **79**
Riesling Oregon Dry Reserve 1994 • $8 • (01/31/96) BB • **87**
Riesling Oregon Dry Reserve 1994: Smells like rotting flowers, and the flavors displease as well. Tasted twice, with consistent notes. 3,400 cases made. • $9 • (11/15/97) • **71**
Riesling Oregon Reserve 1996: Dry, lean and sappy, with a strong resinous streak running through the light, green apple flavors. Ready now. 2,100 cases made. • $8 • (05/15/98) • **82**

VEEDERCREST | CALIFORNIA

Cabernet Sauvignon Napa Valley 1978 • $NA • (11/15/92) • **74**

VENDANGE | CALIFORNIA

Cabernet Sauvignon California 1991 • $6 • (11/15/94) • **76**

Cabernet Sauvignon California 1990 • $6 • (08/31/92) • **73**

Cabernet Sauvignon California Autumn Harvest NV: Dried cherry and berry flavors and light oak notes have some focus. Simple, yet there is structure and depth to the varietally correct flavors. Finishes with light tannins. Tasted twice, with consistent notes. • $12/1.5 liter • (05/15/98) • **80**

Chardonnay California Autumn Harvest 1995: A tangy blend of green apple and citrus flavors. Weak in aromatics but enjoyable nevertheless. 600,000 cases made. • $NA • (07/31/97) • **84**

Chardonnay California Autumn Harvest 1993 • $7 • (06/30/94) • **79**

Merlot California 1990 • $6 • (05/31/92) BB • **80**

Merlot California Autumn Harvest 1992 • $7 • (09/15/94) • **78**

Pinot Noir California 1990 • $6 • (02/28/94) • **78**

Pinot Noir California Autumn Harvest 1993 • $6 • (03/31/95) • **76**

Sauvignon Blanc California Autumn Harvest 1996: A soft style, marked by snap-pea and herbal notes. Good length and concentration, but turns a touch bitter on the finish. • $6/1.5 liter • (05/15/98) • **80**

Sauvignon Blanc California Autumn Harvest 1995: Has a flavor like canned fruit juice that has turned. 90,000 cases made. • $5 • (08/31/96) • **72**

Sauvignon Blanc California Autumn Harvest 1993 • $7 • (08/31/94) • **77**

White Zinfandel California Autumn Harvest 1994 • $6 • (09/15/95) • **81**

Zinfandel California 1991 • $7 • (12/31/93) • **78**

Zinfandel California 1989 • $6 • (07/31/92) BB • **84**

Zinfandel California 1987 • $5 • (09/15/90) • **78**

Zinfandel California Autumn Harvest 1993 • $6 • (10/15/94) • **79**

VENEZIA | CALIFORNIA

Bianco Nuovo Mondo Alexander Valley Meritage 1994 • $18 • (03/31/96) • **89**

Bianco Nuovo Mondo Northern Sonoma Meritage 1995: Shows real complexity and style as spicy, barrel-fermented flavors add a layer of sophistication to this zingy wine, which offers a lovely mouthful of fig, melon, star fruit and pineapple flavors to go along with the spice and vanilla notes. A blend of 56 percent Sauvignon Blanc and 44 percent Sémillon. 1,365 cases made. • $22 • (05/15/97) • **91**

Cabernet Sauvignon Alexander Valley 1993: Lots of toasty vanilla notes and tasty black cherry, plum and wild berry flavors, turning tight and firmly tannic on the finish. Drinkable now. New from Geyser Peak. 400 cases made. • $20 • (04/30/96) • **88**

Cabernet Sauvignon Alexander Valley Meola Vineyards 1994: Bold, ripe and concentrated, with tiers of flavors—cherry, spice, currant and plum—that linger on and on. A distinctive and well-crafted wine that's drinkable now but can age, too. 1,220 cases made. • $25 • (05/15/97) • **91**

Chardonnay Alexander Valley Beaterra Vineyard 1995: Clean and refreshing, with a spicy, lively tangerine edge to the pear and melon notes. Finishes with a long, lingering aftertaste that echos the fruitiness. 1,780 cases made. • $20 • (09/30/97) • **91**

Chardonnay Napa Valley Regusci Vineyard 1995: Remarkably complex, with ripe, rich, concentrated pear, spice, apple and hazelnut shadings, turning elegant and harmonious on the finish, where the flavors linger. 1,630 cases made. • $20 • (04/30/97) • **91**

Sangiovese Alexander Valley Trione Vineyards Hoffman Ranch 1995: Strives for complexity, with a range of berry and cherry flavors, but there's a hollowness at midpalate, and it turns simple on the finish. Ready to drink. 400 cases made. • $24 • (12/15/97) • **85**

Sangiovese California Nuovo Mondo 1995: A strange style, with a strong menthol accent and not much in the way of ripe fruit flavor. Way too much oak for the fruit. 2,500 cases made. • $24 • (02/28/97) • **78**

Sangiovese Mendocino County Eagle Point Ranch 1995: Firm and tight, with a pretty band of cherry and raspberry flavors, picking up wild berry and floral notes on the finish. 350 cases made. • $24 • (07/31/97) • **88**

Sangiovese Russian River Valley Alegría Vineyard 1995: Ripe, with a smoky edge to the cherry and berry flavors, finishing with a tannic aftertaste. Could use short-term cellaring. 620 cases made. • $24 • (07/31/97) • **87**

Stella Bianco California 1995: Sweet oak, vanilla and hazelnuts provide a nice opening note, though the flavors aren't quite as forthcoming as the aromas—dominated by mineral, herb, fig and citrus notes. Iconoclastic and interesting. A blend of 50 percent Sémillon, 49 percent Chardonnay and 1 percent Sauvignon Blanc. 1,950 cases made. • $20 • (07/31/97) • **89**

VENGE | CALIFORNIA

Cabernet Sauvignon Napa Valley Family Reserve 1992: Dark, tight and intense, with a rich core of currant and cherry, finishing with firm tannins and a touch of heat. Drinkable now. 90 cases made. • $35 • (08/31/96) • **88**

Merlot Napa Valley 1995: Tough and chewy, with leathery tannins that dominate the plum, currant and wild berry flavors beneath. Finishes with a strong, oaky aftertaste; cellar into 2001 in hope it comes around. 120 cases made. • $28 • (03/31/98) • **88**

VENTANA | CALIFORNIA

Chardonnay Monterey Gold Stripe 1996: A solid white, youthful and exuberant, with orange and pear flavors weaving through the slightly raw texture. Drink now. 7,000 cases made. • $12 • (12/15/97) • **86**

Chardonnay Monterey J. Douglas Meador Winegrower's Grand Reserve 1996: Showing off ripe peach, nectarine and honeyed notes on the nose, this tangy, fruity wine packs a bright, lemony finish. Drink now through 2000. 400 cases made. • $25 • (05/15/98) • **85**

Chardonnay Monterey Reserve 1996: Earthy, spicy flavors mingle with smoke and a touch of apple to make this a sophisticated if low-powered wine. Ready now. 400 cases made. • $18 • (12/31/97) • **84**

Chenin Blanc Monterey 1993 • $6 • (06/30/95) • **81**

Chenin Blanc Monterey Dry 1996: A pretty wine, with some weight on the palate. Nicely balanced with hints of star fruit, peach and vanilla. 700 cases made. • $8 • (09/30/97) • **84**

Johannisberg Riesling Monterey 1994 • $6 • (06/15/96) • **84**

Johannisberg Riesling Monterey 1993 • $6 • (06/15/95) • **84**

Magnus Monterey Meritage 1986 • $20 • (10/31/89) • **79**

Merlot Monterey 1996: Fairly herbal, weedy and vegetal, it reminds one of the old Monterey reds—unripe and unyielding. • $13 • (05/15/98) • **77**

Riesling Monterey Dry 1996: Balances its ripe apricot flavors with a zippy grapefruit and slate character that adds depth to this medium-weight wine. Not sweet; ready now. 1,000 cases made. • $8 • (07/31/97) • **87**

Riesling Monterey Dry 1994 • $6 • (06/15/96) • **85**

Sauvignon Blanc Monterey 1996: Toasty, nutty qualities herald a firmly textured, tangy, mineral-laced wine. Finishes with a subtle blend of melon, tangerine and lemon-lime flavors. A terrific value. 700 cases made. • $10 • (07/31/97) • **88**

Sauvignon Blanc Monterey 1994 • $9 • (05/31/96) • **85**

Sauvignon Blanc Monterey 1993 • $8 • (04/30/95) BB • **89**

White Riesling Late Harvest Monterey Hand-Selected Clusters 1987 • $14/375ml • (08/31/89) • **70**

VERITAS | OREGON

Pinot Gris Yamhill County 1993 • $8 • (11/30/94) • **82**

Pinot Noir Oregon 1985 • $15 • (06/15/87) • **88**

Pinot Noir Willamette Valley 1989 • $9 • (11/30/94) • **80**

Pinot Noir Willamette Valley 1988 • $15 • (05/31/91) • **87**

Pinot Noir Willamette Valley 1987 • $15 • (02/15/90) • **77**

Pinot Noir Willamette Valley Reserve 1989 • $15 • (03/15/94) • **80**

Pinot Noir Yamhill County 1990 • $11 • (11/30/94) • **78**

VIADER | CALIFORNIA

Napa Valley 1997: Ripe, round, rich and complex, with well-focused plum, cherry, currant and spice. A deceptively elegant and understated style. Finishes with a long, fruity aftertaste. This sample was 100 percent Cabernet Sauvignon. The finished wine will contain Cabernet Franc as well. • $NA • (07/31/98) (BT) • **90-94**

Napa Valley 1996: Young and grapey, with beautiful fruit. Lots of plum, cherry, berry and floral notes, with a wonderful aftertaste. Mostly Cabernet (86 percent) this time. • $NA • (06/15/97) (BT) • **95-99**

Napa Valley 1995: A ripe and complex Cabernet blend, with pretty plum, black cherry and wild berry flavors. The texture is smooth and polished, right up until the finish, where the supple tannins kick in. Finishes with a dash of toasty oak, which adds a nice dimension. Tempting now; best after 2000. A blend of 53 percent Cabernet Sauvignon and 47 percent Cabernet Franc. 4,400 cases made. • $33 • (01/31/98) HR • **92**

Napa Valley 1994: Smooth, ripe and smoky, with an elegant core of currant, plum, cherry, sage and mineral flavors that are thick and plush. Flavors fan out and unfold on the finish. A blend of 55 percent Cabernet Sauvignon and 45 percent Cabernet Franc. 3,400 cases made. • $30 • (05/31/97) • **93**

Napa Valley 1993: Dark and intense currant, anise, chocolate and berry, adding a nice array of flavors on the aftertaste, where the tannins fold in. 2,613 cases made. • $29 • (05/15/96) • **89**
Napa Valley 1992 • $28 • (07/31/95) • **88**
Napa Valley 1991 • $28 • (11/15/94) HR • **91**
Napa Valley 1990 • $25 • (07/15/93) HR • **91**
Napa Valley 1989 • $25 • (11/15/92) • **90**

VIANO | CALIFORNIA

Cabernet Sauvignon California Reserve Selection 1988 • $9 • (11/15/94) • **81**
Zinfandel Contra Costa County Reserve Selection 1993: A real mouthful of berry, cherry, plum and smoke flavors; dark, ripe, rich and plush, picking up a meaty note on the finish. A bit dry on the aftertaste, but quite flavorful. 550 cases made. • $9 • (04/30/97) • **90**
Zinfandel Contra Costa County Sand Rock Hill Reserve Selection 1994: What a find! Yummy plum, blueberry and currant flavors swirl through a rich, almost plush texture. A seductive wine that will win you over with sheer tastiness. Best around 2000. 850 cases made. • $10 • (12/15/97) • **90**
Zinfandel Contra Costa County Sand Rock Hill Reserve Selection 1992 • $9 • (10/15/95) • **89**
Zinfandel Contra Costa County Sand Rock Hill Reserve Selection 1991 • $8 • (10/15/94) • **80**
Zinfandel Contra Costa County Sand Rock Hill Reserve Selection 1989 • $7 • (06/15/93) • **81**
Zinfandel Late Harvest Contra Costa County Reserve Selection 1989 • $9 • (12/31/95) • **76**
Zinfandel Late Harvest Contra Costa County Reserve Selection 1988 • $8 • (10/15/94) • **86**
Zinfandel Port Contra Costa County Vintage Old Vines Reserve Selection NV: Has rich, full Zinfandel character in the aroma but feels a bit rough and youthful in the mouth, with a hint of earthiness on the finish. 400 cases made. • $10 • (02/28/97) • **86**

VIANSA | CALIFORNIA

Cabernet Sauvignon Napa & Sonoma Counties 1988 • $17 • (11/15/92) • **76**
Cabernet Sauvignon Napa & Sonoma Counties 1986 • $15 • (07/31/90) • **77**
Cabernet Sauvignon Napa & Sonoma Counties 1985 • $13 • (09/15/89) • **72**
Cabernet Sauvignon Napa & Sonoma Counties 1984 • $13 • (07/31/88) • **85**
Cabernet Sauvignon Napa & Sonoma Counties 1983 • $15 • (11/30/86) • **88**
Cabernet Sauvignon Napa & Sonoma Counties Reserve 1988 • $23 • (11/15/93) • **78**
Cabernet Sauvignon Napa Valley Reserve 1994: Serves up lots of ripe, juicy plum, currant and black cherry flavor, all the while maintaining a sense of elegance and grace. Gains complexity on the finish, where coffee and herb notes fold in. Drinks well now, but can age, too. • $30 • (11/30/97) • **89**
Cabernet Sauvignon Sonoma Valley Grand Reserve 1983 • $35 • (10/15/88) • **88**
Cabernet Sauvignon Sonoma Valley Reserve 1983 • $18 • (10/15/88) • **88**
Nebbiolo California Northern California 1990 • $15 • (11/30/92) • **81**
Obsidian Napa & Sonoma Counties 1987 • $65 • (07/15/91) • **85**
Ossidiana Napa Valley 1994: Young and tight, with intense leather and currant flavors and a dash of spice. Finishes with a slight bitter edge and drying tannins. Try now. A blend of 55 percent Cabernet Franc and 45 percent Cabernet Sauvignon. • $70 • (11/30/97) • **87**
Prindelo California 1996: Rich, complex and flavorful, with loads of ripe plum, black cherry, pepper and spice flavors, finishing with ripe, plush tannins and good length. A blend of Primitivo, Zinfandel, Charbono and Teroldigo. Try now to 2000. • $28 • (11/30/97) • **89**
Prindelo Sonoma Valley 1993 • $20 • (10/15/95) • **92**
Prindelo Sonoma Valley 1991 • $16 • (12/31/93) • **82**
Riserva Anatra Rosso Napa & Sonoma Counties 1989 • $18 • (11/15/93) • **80**
Sangiovese California Piccolo Toscano 1995: Spicy, it has the strength of aftershave and an overbearing personality. Hold a year or two in hopes the spiciness subsides. • $18 • (12/31/97) • **80**
Thalia Napa County 1990 • $22/5.(11/30/92) • **83**

Key: SS—Spectator Selection CS—Cellar Selection HR—Highly Recommended BB—Best Buy $NA—Price not available Ⓐ—Auction Price (BT)—Barrel Tasting
Dates in parentheses indicate the issues in which the ratings were published.

VICHON | CALIFORNIA

Cabernet Sauvignon California Coastal Selection 1994: Simple with modest fruit flavors shaded by notes of dill, herb and light currant. • $11 • (11/30/96) • **79**
Cabernet Sauvignon California Coastal Selection 1992 • $9 • (01/31/95) BB • **87**
Cabernet Sauvignon California Coastal Selection 1991 • $11 • (09/30/94) • **82**
Cabernet Sauvignon California Coastal Selection 1990 • $9 • (11/15/93) • **82**
Cabernet Sauvignon California Coastal Selection 1989 • $10 • (11/15/92) • **84**
Cabernet Sauvignon Napa Valley 1993: Very complete and appealing for the vintage. Rich, firm, ripe and intense, with complex layers of currant, anise, cedar, tar and spice flavors. • $20 • (08/31/96) • **87**
Cabernet Sauvignon Napa Valley 1992 • $16 • (12/15/95) • **87**
Cabernet Sauvignon Napa Valley 1991 • $16 • (04/30/94) • **81**
Cabernet Sauvignon Napa Valley 1990 • $16 • (08/31/93) HR • **89**
Cabernet Sauvignon Napa Valley 1989 • $16 • (11/15/92) • **89**
Cabernet Sauvignon Napa Valley 1988 • $16 • (05/15/91) • **84**
Cabernet Sauvignon Napa Valley 1985 • $14 • (11/15/88) • **91**
Cabernet Sauvignon Napa Valley 1983 • $12 • (11/30/86) • **91**
Cabernet Sauvignon Napa Valley 1982 • $13 • (07/16/86) • **89**
Cabernet Sauvignon Napa Valley 1981 • $14 • (12/16/84) • **89**
Cabernet Sauvignon Stags Leap District 1992 • $31 • (03/31/96) • **84**
Cabernet Sauvignon Stags Leap District 1991 • $28 • (12/15/95) • **88**
Cabernet Sauvignon Stags Leap District 1990 • $24 • (11/15/93) HR • **91**
Cabernet Sauvignon Stags Leap District 1989 • $24 • (08/31/93) • **83**
Cabernet Sauvignon Stags Leap District 1988 • $24 • (11/15/91) • **90**
Cabernet Sauvignon Stags Leap District 1987 • $17 • (07/31/90) • **87**
Cabernet Sauvignon Stags Leap District 1986 • $21 • (10/31/89) • **91**
Cabernet Sauvignon Stags Leap District 1985 • $20 • (01/31/89) • **93**
Chardonnay California Coastal Selection 1994: Bright, generous and round, with a spicy character to the pear flavor. 50,000 cases made. • $10 • (06/15/96) • **83**
Chardonnay California Coastal Selection 1993 • $10 • (01/31/95) • **82**
Chardonnay Napa Valley 1994: Ripe and fruity, moderately rich, as tiers of apple, fig and melon gain depth and complexity on the finish, where the flavors fold together nicely. • $NA • (02/29/96) • **89**
Chardonnay Napa Valley 1993 • $14 • (07/31/95) • **83**
Chevrignon Napa Valley 1994 • $NA • (02/29/96) • **87**
Chevrignon Napa Valley 1993 • $8 • (05/15/95) • **85**
Merlot California Coastal Selection 1994: Soft texture, and the plum flavors are edged with spice. 18,000 cases made. • $11 • (08/31/96) • **84**
Merlot California Coastal Selection 1993: Lean and herbal, with some nice cherry and berry flavors providing balance. Ready. 19,500 cases made. • $10 • (07/31/96) • **84**
Merlot California Coastal Selection 1992 • $10 • (01/31/95) • **83**
Merlot Napa Valley 1993: Serves up earthy, leathery, coffee and currant flavors. Turns dry and tannic on the finish, where the flavor thins out. • $21 • (07/31/96) • **83**
Merlot Napa Valley 1992 • $18 • (01/31/96) • **90**
Merlot Napa Valley 1991 • $19 • (09/15/94) • **84**
Merlot Napa Valley 1990 • $18 • (06/30/93) • **89**
Merlot Napa Valley 1989 • $17 • (04/15/92) • **88**
Merlot Napa Valley 1988 • $16 • (12/31/90) • **81**
Merlot Napa Valley 1987 • $16 • (02/15/90) • **91**
Merlot Napa Valley 1986 • $16 • (08/31/89) • **86**
Merlot Napa Valley 1985 • $14 • (12/15/87) • **88**
Sémillon Late Harvest Napa Valley Botrytis 1986 • $15/375ml • (12/31/88) • **86**
Sémillon Late Harvest Napa Valley Botrytis 1985 • $15/375ml • (07/15/88) • **88**
Syrah California 1993: Mature plum and berry notes fold together nicely, while spicy, peppery, gamy notes lend distinction. • $13 • (08/31/96) • **85**

VIENTO | OREGON

Riesling Hood River County Columbia Gorge Vineyard 1993 • $7 • (10/31/94) • **84**

VIGIL | CALIFORNIA

Cabernet Franc Napa Valley 1995: Very pretty wine, with lovely raspberry, spice and chocolate flavors that linger elegantly on the finish. Has style and grace. Delicious now. 423 cases made. • $20 • (11/30/97) • **89**

Cabernet Sauvignon Napa Valley 1994: Tannic and unyielding, with only hints of wild cherry and spice peeking through. One expects more from the region and the vintage. 744 cases made. • $18 • (10/31/97) • **81**
Cabernet Sauvignon Napa Valley NV • $12 • (12/15/95) • **84**
Terra Vin California 1995: Looking a little old for a '95, this wine sports cedar, spice, raspberry and vanilla flavors. Soft textured, with a touch of herbs on the finish. A blend of Zinfandel and Carignane. Drink now. 1,472 cases made. • $12 • (01/01/98) • **82**
Terra Vin Napa Valley Reserve 1996: A smoky, ripe blend of beach plum, anise, prune and spice flavors weaves across the palate. Finishes a bit short, but it's still quite nice. Drink now. 207 cases made. • $20 • (06/15/98) • **87**
Valiente Claret Napa Valley 1995: A wine of some distinction. Offers a lovely, almost delicate array of raspberry, currant and herbal, violetlike overtones, poised on a smooth frame. Drinkable now. A blend of Cabernet Sauvignon, Cabernet Franc, Merlot, Malbec and Petite Verdot. 1,050 cases made. • $20 • (12/31/97) • **87**
Zinfandel California Tres Condados 1996: A tangy blend of cherry, anise and charred toast flavors. Tannins are a little rustic, however, and the finish is short. Drink now. 2,200 cases made. • $13 • (06/15/98) • **82**
Zinfandel California Tres Condados 1995: Not an effusive wine, but it holds its own with pretty raspberry, spice and tar flavors that linger on the silky finish. 933 cases made. • $14 • (12/15/97) • **85**
Zinfandel Howell Mountain 1995: Surprisingly light for a mountain-grown Zin, showing an earthy edge to the plum and spice flavors. Try now. 546 cases made. • $16 • (11/30/97) • **79**
Zinfandel Lodi Mohr-Fry Ranch Old Vines 1996: Openly fruity, with ripe, complex plum, blackberry, cherry and spice, finishing with supple tannins while holding its fruitiness. Drink now. 610 cases made. • $16 • (06/15/98) • **86**

VILLA ANDRIANA | CALIFORNIA

Bianco di Palisades Napa Valley 1996: Sweet, silky and a little short in the flavor department, offering modest honeydew flavors that linger gently. A blend of Muscat Canelli and Chardonnay. Contains between 5 and 7 percent residual sugar. Drink now. 300 cases made. • $9 • 500 ml (03/31/98) • **83**
Charbono Napa Valley 1996: Velvety, ripe and generous with its black cherry, blackberry and mineral flavors, which linger nicely on the firm finish. Approachable now, should age well through 2002 to 2004. 500 cases made. • $16 • (03/31/98) • **87**

VILLA HELENA | CALIFORNIA

Cabernet Sauvignon Napa Valley Atlas Peak Baron von Kees Vineyard 1990 • $22 • (11/15/93) • **71**

VILLA MT. EDEN | CALIFORNIA

Cabernet Sauvignon California 1995: Simple, earthy, somewhat diluted Cabernet flavors are appealing only when you factor in the price. Hints of mature-tasting cherry and currant emerge on the finish. 31,200 cases made. • $12 • (04/30/98) • **82**
Cabernet Sauvignon California 1994: Well balanced, with a core of cedar, spice, plum and herb flavors. Smooth on the palate, with a moderate finish. Drink now or hold. 36,800 cases made. • $12 • (10/15/97) • **86**
Cabernet Sauvignon California Cellar Select 1993: Simple, with dashes of herb and cedar to flesh out the modest plum and currant flavors. 10,000 cases made. • $9 • (09/15/96) • **82**
Cabernet Sauvignon California Cellar Select 1991 • $10 • (05/15/94) • **82**
Cabernet Sauvignon California Cellar Select 1990 • $10 • (03/31/93) • **83**
Cabernet Sauvignon California Cellar Select 1989 • $10 • (03/31/93) • **85**
Cabernet Sauvignon California Cellar Select 1988 • $8 • (07/15/92) BB • **85**
Cabernet Sauvignon Mendocino Signature Series 1994: A big, ripe and plush wine that shows its earthy, leathery tannins right away, only slowly revealing its ripe currant and cherry flavors. Given the tannin level, cellar it into 2002. 750 cases made. • $50 • (10/31/97) • **92**
Cabernet Sauvignon Mendocino Signature Series 1993: Trim and well focused, with supple cherry, plum and currant flavors of moderate depth and richness. Finishes with supple tannins and dashes of coffee and cedar. Drinkable now. 500 cases made. • $45 • (04/30/97) • **88**
Cabernet Sauvignon Mendocino Signature Series 1992 • $45 • (03/31/95) HR • **92**
Cabernet Sauvignon Napa Valley 1987 • $13 • (02/15/91) • **88**
Cabernet Sauvignon Napa Valley 1986 • $13 • (02/15/91) • **84**
Cabernet Sauvignon Napa Valley 1982 • $10 • (04/15/88) • **71**
Cabernet Sauvignon Napa Valley 1980 • $12 • (01/01/84) • **86**
Cabernet Sauvignon Napa Valley 1978 • $45 • (11/15/92) • **85**
Cabernet Sauvignon Napa Valley 1974 • $95 • (11/15/94) • **90**
Cabernet Sauvignon Napa Valley Grand Reserve 1993: Dry, tannic and austere, with a leathery quality that overshadows the ripe plum and cherry flavors. More interesting on the finish. 2,400 cases made. • $16 • (09/15/96) • **82**
Cabernet Sauvignon Napa Valley Grand Reserve 1992 • $16 • (04/30/96) • **88**
Cabernet Sauvignon Napa Valley Grand Reserve 1991 • $14 • (03/31/95) • **83**
Cabernet Sauvignon Napa Valley Grand Reserve 1990 • $16 • (11/15/93) • **86**
Cabernet Sauvignon Napa Valley Grand Reserve 1989 • $14 • (10/31/92) • **84**
Cabernet Sauvignon Napa Valley Grand Reserve 1988 • $12 • (07/15/92) • **87**
Cabernet Sauvignon Napa Valley Reserve 1983 • $13 • (10/15/90) • **90**
Cabernet Sauvignon Napa Valley Reserve 1981 • $17 • (02/01/86) • **81**
Cabernet Sauvignon Napa Valley Reserve 1980 • $25 • (10/01/84) • **89**
Chardonnay California 1996: Solid, with a modest core of ripe pear and melon flavors. A bit cloying on the finish, which has a hint of oak. Drink now. 78,000 cases made. • $12 • (07/31/98) • **84**
Chardonnay California 1995: A well-oaked style that delivers more than enough varietal flavor in its ripe pear, peach and pineapple notes. And it's a great value to boot. 75,000 cases made. • $9 • (02/28/97) BB • **88**
Chardonnay California Cellar Select 1994: Crisp and flavorful, with pleasant pear and spice flavors that soften on the finish. 60,000 cases made. • $9 • (06/30/96) • **84**
Chardonnay California Cellar Select 1993 • $8 • (04/30/95) • **85**
Chardonnay California Grand Reserve 1995: This reserve bottling is ripe, rich and full-bodied, with layers of creamy pear, fig, melon and honeysuckle flavors that slowly unfold, revealing ever-greater depth and concentration right through to the long, delicious aftertaste. The price is reasonable, too. 10,000 cases made. • $18 • (08/31/97) • **92**
Chardonnay Carneros Grand Reserve 1993 • $14 • (04/30/95) HR • **91**
Chardonnay Napa Valley Grand Reserve 1994: Rich, smooth and creamy, a complex and exotic style that offers lots of bold pear, spice, vanilla and hazelnut notes, picking up a citrus edge on the finish. Impressive flavor and texture. 3,000 cases made. • $16 • (04/30/96) • **92**
Chardonnay Santa Barbara County Signature Series 1993 • $30 • (07/31/95) HR • **93**
Chardonnay Santa Maria Valley Bien Nacido Vineyards Signature Series 1996: This wine has a wonderful sense of harmony and finesse, balancing its ripe, complex tiers of peach, pear and nectarine with a silky-smooth texture and long, rich, smoky aftertaste. Drink now through 2002. 744 cases made. • $35 • (05/31/98) HR • **95**
Chardonnay Santa Maria Valley Bien Nacido Vineyard Signature Series 1995: Bold, ripe and intense, with rich, spicy fruit, hints of pear, fig, melon and apple, and just a trace of alcohol on an otherwise creamy finish. A delicous wine that should age well for another few years. Drink now through 2002. 750 cases made. • $35 • (01/01/98) • **92**
Chardonnay Santa Maria Valley Bien Nacido Vineyard Signature Series 1994: A bold, ripe, rich and seductive style that places its pear, peach, honey and smoke flavors into a smooth, creamy texture. A trace of green plum adds to its complexity. Finishes amazingly plush and elegant. 500 cases made. • $30 • (05/31/96) • **94**
Merlot Napa Valley Grand Reserve 1994 • $16 • (06/30/96) • **85**
Merlot Napa Valley Grand Reserve 1993 • $16 • (12/31/95) • **86**
Merlot Napa Valley Grand Reserve 1991 • $15 • (05/31/94) • **88**
Merlot Napa Valley Grand Reserve 1990 • $15 • (03/31/93) • **88**
Pinot Blanc Santa Maria Valley Bien Nacido Vineyard Grand Reserve 1996: Tight and compact, with earthy peach, pear and melon flavors, turning simple and fruity on the finish. 1,400 cases made. • $20 • (02/28/98) • **86**
Pinot Blanc Santa Maria Valley Bien Nacido Vineyard Grand Reserve 1995: Fresh and lively, with ripe peach, pear and honey flavors that pick up a spicy note on the finish, where it turns elegant. 700 cases made. • $16 • (02/28/97) • **89**
Pinot Blanc Santa Maria Valley Bien Nacido Vineyard Grand Reserve 1994 • $16 • (01/31/96) • **88**
Pinot Blanc Santa Maria Valley Bien Nacido Vineyard Grand Reserve 1993 • $14 • (04/15/95) • **88**
Pinot Noir California 1996: Shows some nice cinnamon overtones to the modest raspberry flavors, broadening nicely on the finish. Ready now. 10,500 cases made. • $12 • (12/31/97) • **85**
Pinot Noir California Cellar Select 1994 • $8 • (01/31/96) • **82**

Pinot Noir California Cellar Select 1993 • $8 • (03/31/95) • **83**
Pinot Noir Carneros Grand Reserve 1991 • $14 • (02/28/94) • **86**
Pinot Noir Napa Valley 1988 • $12 • (02/28/91) • **82**
Pinot Noir Napa Valley Tres Ninos Vineyard 1981 • $5 • (04/16/85) BB • **86**
Pinot Noir Santa Maria Valley Bien Nacido Vineyard 1995: Ripe cherry and berry flavors come to the forefront, working past a strong earth and mushroom edge. Turns elegant and supple on the finish. 1,100 cases made. • $20 • (10/31/97) • **89**
Pinot Noir Santa Maria Valley Bien Nacido Vineyard Grand Reserve 1996: Serves up an appealing range of ripe plum, wild berry, cherry and earth flavors, and turns smooth and polished on the aftertaste. Drink now. 4,000 cases made. • $20 • (01/31/98) • **88**
Pinot Noir Santa Maria Valley Bien Nacido Vineyard Grand Reserve 1994 • $12 • (01/31/96) • **86**
Pinot Noir Santa Maria Valley Bien Nacido Vineyard Grand Reserve 1993 • $14 • (03/31/95) • **84**
Sauvignon Blanc Late Harvest Napa Valley 1989 • $13 • (04/30/91) • **83**
Sauvignon Blanc Late Harvest Napa Valley 1986 • $10 • (05/15/88) • **89**
Syrah California Grand Reserve 1995: Ripe, smooth and harmonious, with spicy stewed plum, black cherry and wild berry flavors, a supple texture and good length. Shows intensity, richness and concentration. Best from now to 2003. 1,300 cases made. • $20 • (04/30/98) • **89**
Zinfandel California 1995: Earthy, spicy notes add an extra dimension to the supple plum and light cherry flavors. Ready now. A blend of 7 percent Petite Sirah and 4 percent Cabernet Franc. 5,800 cases made. • $12 • (11/30/97) • **85**
Zinfandel California Cellar Select 1994: Nothing fancy; middle-of-the-road style balancing modest raspberry and cherry flavors with cedary oak notes. 24,000 cases made. • $9 • (11/30/96) • **82**
Zinfandel California Cellar Select 1993 • $8 • (09/15/95) BB • **88**
Zinfandel California Cellar Select 1992 • $8 • (10/15/94) BB • **84**
Zinfandel California Cellar Select 1991 • $8 • (08/31/93) BB • **86**
Zinfandel California Cellar Select 1990 • $8 • (09/15/92) • **84**
Zinfandel California Cellar Select 1989 • $8 • (09/15/92) BB • **86**
Zinfandel Napa Valley 1986 • $8 • (12/15/88) • **90**
Zinfandel Sonoma Valley Monte Rosso Vineyard Grand Reserve 1995: Dry and earthy, with modest fruit flavors peeking through dry tannins. Finishes with lots of pepper and berry and an astringent texture. 1,250 cases made. • $20 • (12/15/97) • **84**
Zinfandel Sonoma Valley Monte Rosso Vineyard Grand Reserve 1994: Ripe and zesty, with rich pepper and wild berry flavors and lots of spicy nuances. A well-mannered, big style of Zin with ample tannins and a hot finish. Drinkable now. 1,200 cases made. • $16 • (01/31/97) • **88**
Zinfandel Sonoma Valley Monte Rosso Vineyard Grand Reserve 1993 • $16 • (09/15/95) • **88**

VILLA ZAPU | CALIFORNIA

Cabernet Sauvignon Napa Valley 1988 • $20 • (11/15/91) • **86**
Cabernet Sauvignon Napa Valley 1986 • $16 • (10/31/89) • **79**

VINA VISTA | CALIFORNIA

Merlot Alexander Valley 1988 • $12 • (05/31/92) • **86**
Merlot Alexander Valley 1985 • $8 • (10/31/87) • **90**

VINE CLIFF | CALIFORNIA

Cabernet Sauvignon Napa Valley 1992 • $30 • (05/15/96) • **83**
Cabernet Sauvignon Napa Valley 1991 • $25 • (04/30/95) • **88**
Cabernet Sauvignon Napa Valley 1990 • $35 • (11/15/93) • **85**
Cabernet Sauvignon Napa Valley Oakville Estate 1994: Dense and chewy, with a ripe, tight, well-focused core of earthy currant, black cherry and wild berry flavors. Finishes with firm, earthy tannins and fine length. Drinkable now. 1,700 cases made. • $36 • (10/15/97) • **90**
Cabernet Sauvignon Napa Valley Oakville Estate 1993: Firm, ripe and intense, with a complex band of currant, plum, cherry and anise flavors that fan out and linger long on the finish. Drinking between now and 2000 is your best bet. 850 cases made. • $30 • (11/15/96) • **90**

Key: SS—Spectator Selection CS—Cellar Selection HR—Highly Recommended BB—Best Buy $NA—Price not available Ⓐ—Auction Price (BT)—Barrel Tasting
Dates in parentheses indicate the issues in which the ratings were published.

Chardonnay Napa Valley 1996: Impressive for its impeccable balance, with generous, supple, up-front fruitiness, this outstanding Chardonnay delivers seamless pear, apple, apricot and melon flavors that glide into a gentle, rich, lingering aftertaste. Drink now into 2000. 1,460 cases made. • $25 • (04/30/98) HR • **93**
Chardonnay Napa Valley 1995: Very complete and harmonious, with a complex array of ripe pear, melon, hazelnut and spice flavors. Turns elegant and refined on the finish, where it shows great depth and flavor. A terrific wine at a reasonable price. 1,200 cases made. • $23 • (04/30/97) • **93**
Chardonnay Napa Valley 1994: Remarkably complex and well focused, with a pretty core of ripe pear and citrus flavors couched in light, spicy oak shadings. Try now. 1,000 cases made. • $23 • (05/31/96) • **90**
Chardonnay Napa Valley Proprietress Reserve 1995: An elegant, understated style, with attractive lemon, citrus, pear and honey flavors that fan out, picking up smoky, toasty oak nuances. Most impressive on finish, where the flavors linger long. 300 cases made. • $34 • (11/15/97) • **92**
Chardonnay Napa Valley Proprietress Reserve 1994: A tight, complex, well-focused, flinty style with lots of depth, richness and flavor. Fans out to offer clean pear, apple and mineral notes with a slightly chalky edge. Long aftertaste. 310 cases made. • $30 • (11/15/96) • **91**
Chardonnay Napa Valley Proprietress Reserve 1993 • $35 • (05/31/95) • **89**
Merlot Napa Valley 1995: Tough and chewy, but the core of flavors is appealing, built around ripe cherry and currant, sage and mineral. Turns complex on the finish, but given the level of tannin, try now or cellar into 2001. 820 cases made. • $27 • (04/30/98) • **88**

VINEYARD 29 | CALIFORNIA

Cabernet Sauvignon Napa Valley 1994: Marked by spice, cedar and dill notes, with just enough ripe cherry and currant flavors to fill in the gaps. Fans out with more flavor and depth with aeration. Best to cellar short term into 2000. 490 cases made. • $55 • (09/30/97) • **90**
Cabernet Sauvignon Napa Valley 1993: Firm and trim, with an attractive band of currant, coffee, anise and cedar. A well-proportioned, moderately rich and complex young red that finishes with mild tannins. Drinkable now. 200 cases made. • $33 • (03/31/96) • **88**
Cabernet Sauvignon Napa Valley 1992: Smooth and supple, with a band of cedar, spice, dried cherry and plum flavors. Finishes with fleshy tannins and modest length. New from Tom Paine's and Teresa Norton's vineyard in St. Helena, produced at Grace Family Vineyards. Ready now. • $50 • (09/15/96) • **86**

VISTA DEL REY | CALIFORNIA

Zinfandel Paso Robles 1996: Gamy, with stewed-tomato flavors and sour fruit. Dries out on the finish. Drink now. 216 cases made. • $16 • (06/15/98) • **79**
Zinfandel Paso Robles 1995: Shows broad raspberry jam flavors with touches of spice, tar and earth. Considering the ripeness of the flavors, the texture is a bit thin. Drink now. 225 cases made. • $15 • (06/15/98) • **85**

VITA NOVA | CALIFORNIA

Cabernet Franc Santa Barbara County 1994: Lean, chewy and tart. Try now. 400 cases made. • $8 • (11/30/96) • **81**
Chardonnay Santa Barbara County Rancho Vinedo Vineyards 1994: Mature pear and pineapple flavors are a touch earthy, but hang together. Somewhat one-dimensional. 750 cases made. • $15 • (07/31/96) • **85**
Red Central Coast 1994 • $16 • (06/15/96) • **83**
Reservatum Santa Barbara County 1986 • $20 • (12/15/89) • **87**

VOILA! | CALIFORNIA

Melange Napa Valley 1994: A bit weedy on the nose, but chock full of plummy, tarry, anise, prune and herb flavors on the palate. An unusual wine, it finishes long, with a nod to the herbal spectrum. Drink now through 2002. 190 cases made. • $18 • (07/31/98) • **86**

VON STRASSER | CALIFORNIA

Cabernet Sauvignon Napa Valley Diamond Mountain 1995: Delicious Cabernet. Ripe, plummy, with complex cedar, black cherry, spice and herbal menthol notes, it zooms along the palate and shows remarkable texture and suppleness on the finish. Has firm, polished tannins. Best from 2002 through 2011. 1,500 cases made. • $36 • (07/31/98) • **93**

Cabernet Sauvignon Napa Valley Diamond Mountain 1994: Lots of complex coffee, currant, cherry and tealike notes, with a smooth texture and lots of finesse. Finishes with firm, chewy tannins, but the flavors are well focused and offer lots of depth and complexity. Try after 2000. 1,300 cases made. • $32 • (10/31/97) • **92**

Cabernet Sauvignon Napa Valley Diamond Mountain 1993: Attractive floral and blackberry flavors follow through on the palate, picking up a nice, toasty, smoky oak feel. Firmly tannic but balanced. Try now. 1,173 cases made. • $28 • (04/30/96) • **89**

Cabernet Sauvignon Napa Valley Diamond Mountain 1992 • $28 • (02/28/95) • **88**

Cabernet Sauvignon Napa Valley Diamond Mountain 1991 • $25 • (03/31/94) • **88**

Cabernet Sauvignon Napa Valley Diamond Mountain 1990 • $25 • (11/15/93) • **87**

Chardonnay Napa Valley 1996: Lots of ripe, fresh, up-front fruitiness, with gentle peach, apricot, fig and pear flavors that linger. Impressive for its elegance and balance. Drink now through 2002. 490 cases made. • $30 • (05/31/98) • **90**

Chardonnay Napa Valley 1995: A spicy style with a tinge of bitterness on the finish. The core of pear and apple-scented fruit flavor is a bit out of focus; try short-term cellaring. May get more complex, too. 450 cases made. • $30 • (11/30/97) • **87**

Chardonnay Napa Valley 1994: Spicy, mature pear and citrus flavors dominate in this classy Chardonnay. 406 cases made. • $30 • (06/15/96) • **86**

VOSE | CALIFORNIA

Cabernet Sauvignon Napa Valley 1978 • $NA • (11/15/92) • **76**

VOSS | CALIFORNIA

Chardonnay Napa Valley 1993 • $NA • (02/29/96) • **89**

Merlot Napa Valley 1995: An elegant, understated style with a pretty interplay of ripe plum and cherry flavors and notes of spicy, cedary, toasty oak. Turns complex on the finish, where the flavors fold together quite well. 1,124 cases made. • $18 • (04/30/98) • **88**

Merlot Napa Valley 1994: Wonderful aromas, young, tight and tannic, but the core of fruit flavor is well focused and concentrated, with a band of currant, earth, herb and cedar. Drink now or cellar to 2000. 1,281 cases made. • $18 • (07/31/97) • **88**

Merlot Napa Valley 1993 • $16 • (05/31/96) • **75**

Merlot Napa Valley 1992 • $15 • (04/15/95) • **83**

Merlot Napa Valley 1991 • $18 • (09/15/94) • **75**

Sauvignon Blanc Napa Valley 1996: Somewhat outspoken, with melon, grass, herbs, celery, honey and citrus flavors circulating freely. An interesting mélange. 4,195 cases made. • $12 • (06/30/97) • **87**

Sauvignon Blanc Napa Valley 1995: Smooth, polished and vibrant, with sweet-pea, pear and ever-so-slightly gamy flavors. Has real complexity and depth. Delicious now. 2,200 cases made. • $10 • (08/31/96) BB • **90**

Sauvignon Blanc Napa Valley 1994 • $9 • (07/31/95) • **87**

Sauvignon Blanc Napa Valley 1993 • $10 • (08/31/94) • **88**

Sauvignon Blanc Napa Valley Botrytis 1996: Golden color and ripe, honeyed aromas set up surprisingly unsweet flavors; definitely a dessert wine but not unctuous. Mild flavors center around apricot and honey. Contains 8.9 percent residual sugar. Drink now. 328 cases made. • $19/375ml • (05/15/98) • **85**

Zinfandel Alexander Valley 1994: Solid if unexciting, with a chunky core of anise, wild berry and smoky oak. Finishes with chewy tannins. 1,397 cases made. • $14 • (03/31/97) • **84**

Zinfandel Alexander Valley 1992 • $13 • (01/31/95) • **77**

Zinfandel Alexander Valley 1991 • $13 • (05/31/93) • **88**

WAGNER | NEW YORK

Chardonnay Finger Lakes Grace House 1993 • $10 • (01/31/96) • **83**

Gewürztraminer Finger Lakes 1993 • $8 • (01/31/96) • **78**

Johannisberg Riesling Finger Lakes 1994 • $8 • (01/31/96) • **80**

Johannisberg Riesling Finger Lakes Fermented Dry 1994 • $8 • (01/31/96) • **78**

Johannisberg Riesling Finger Lakes Ice Wine 1990 • $15 • (04/15/95) • **76**

Johannisberg Riesling Finger Lakes Ice Wine 1989 • $14/375ml • (01/31/92) • **85**

Ravat Blanc Finger Lakes Ice Wine 1990 • $14 • (04/15/95) • **79**

WALLA WALLA VINTNERS | WASHINGTON

Cabernet Franc Yakima Valley 1995: Light, silky and appealing for its gentle blackberry and currant flavors, hinting at spice and tobacco on the finish. Ready now. 170 cases made. • $14 • (12/15/97) • **88**

Cabernet Sauvignon Columbia Valley 1995: Unfolding impressively, this silky-smooth wine emphasizes berry, black cherry and currant flavors up front, then folds in harmonious touches of pretty oak and sweet spices. Appealing now, but give it until 2000 to settle down. 165 cases made. • $20 • (12/15/97) • **91**

Cabernet Sauvignon Washington 1995: Ripe and rich, with a solid core of bright raspberry and cherry notes surrounded by blankets of spicy oak and tobacco flavors. Finishes with silky, pretty fruit. Drinkable now. 165 cases made. • $22 • (12/15/97) • **88**

Merlot Washington 1995: Rich in flavor, noble in stature, with spicy, tobacco-scented black cherry and dark plum flavors that linger on the generous finish, which picks up a distinct floral note. Delicious now, but promises to keep developing from now to 2000 at least. 168 cases made. • $18 • (12/15/97) • **90**

WASHINGTON HILLS | WASHINGTON

Cabernet Sauvignon Columbia Valley Varietal Select 1994: Lean, almost crisp in texture, with appealing berry, spice and smoke flavors that narrow a bit on the finish. Best from now to 2000. 4,402 cases made. • $10 • (09/15/96) • **85**

Cabernet Sauvignon Columbia Valley Varietal Select 1993: Lean and chewy, flirting with oak up front, but ripe fruit comes bouncing back on the tannic finish, echoing currant and plum. 3,500 cases made. • $9 • (09/30/95) • **86**

Cabernet-Merlot Columbia Valley 1992 • $8 • (08/31/94) • **83**

Cabernet-Merlot Columbia Valley Varietal Select 1994: A bit chewy, but it tries to be light and elegant underneath, offering some pretty blackberry and tar flavors. Drink now. 4,079 cases made. • $10 • (09/15/96) • **85**

Cabernet-Merlot Columbia Valley Varietal Select 1993: Lean and a little chewy, appealing cherry and tarry flavors showing on the finish. Best now. 3,500 cases made. • $9 • (09/30/95) • **83**

Chardonnay Columbia Valley Varietal Select 1994: Bright and appealing, with spicy pineapple and citrus flavors that keep step through the lively finish. 4,924 cases made. • $10 • (09/15/96) • **86**

Chenin Blanc Columbia Valley Varietal Select Dry 1996: Crisp and bright, almost racy, with lemony green-apple flavors and enough melony sweetness to make it feel balanced—and dry. Ready now. 1,291 cases made. • $6 • (09/15/97) • **85**

Gewürztraminer Columbia Valley 1993 • $6 • (09/30/94) • **81**

Gewürztraminer Columbia Valley Varietal Select 1995: Soft and floral, with appealing rose petal and gentle peach flavors. 1,270 cases made. • $6 • (09/15/96) • **84**

Gewürztraminer Columbia Valley Varietal Select 1994 • $7 • (09/30/95) • **85**

Johannisberg Riesling Columbia Valley 1993 • $6 • (09/30/94) BB • **86**

Johannisberg Riesling Columbia Valley Varietal Select 1996: Bright, lightly sweet and refreshingly crisp, showing off melon and nectarine flavors with floral hints on the silky finish. Ready now. 5,284 cases made. • $6 • (10/15/97) • **87**

Johannisberg Riesling Columbia Valley Varietal Select 1995: Soft, round and off-dry. Shows polished, Golden Delicious apple and floral flavors. 5,042 cases made. • $6 • (09/15/96) • **85**

Johannisberg Riesling Columbia Valley Varietal Select 1994 • $7 • (09/15/95) • **86**

Merlot Columbia Valley 1992 • $9 • (09/30/94) • **81**

Merlot Columbia Valley Varietal Select 1995: Light, with tough tannins for its size and just enough pretty berry flavors to bring it into balance. Try now. 9,950 cases made. • $13 • (09/15/97) • **81**

Merlot Columbia Valley Varietal Select 1994: A nice, small-scale Merlot with pretty black cherry and spice flavors that soften on the modest finish. 4,310 cases made. • $10 • (09/15/96) • **84**

Merlot Columbia Valley Varietal Select 1993 • $9 • (09/30/95) • **85**

Riesling Columbia Valley Varietal Select Dry 1993 • $6 • (09/15/95) • **84**

Sauvignon Blanc Columbia Valley Varietal Select 1995: Pretty apple, fig and olive flavors wrap nicely around a fresh, wiry frame. Has a mineral note on the finish. 1,995 cases made. • $7 • (09/15/96) • **86**

Sauvignon Blanc Columbia Valley Varietal Select 1993 • $7 • (09/30/95) • **80**

Sémillon Columbia Valley Varietal Select 1995: Aggressively floral, with an acidic edge that keeps the flavors from blossoming. 1,822 cases made. • $6 • (09/15/96) • **78**

Sémillon-Chardonnay Columbia Valley Varietal Select 1995: Soft, silky and smooth. A lovely mouthful of pear, peach and melon, with a touch of tobacco swirling through the lively finish. Ready now. A blend of 67 percent Sémillon and 33 percent Chardonnay. 2,225 cases made. • $8 • (09/15/97) • **88**

Sémillon-Sauvignon Blanc Columbia Valley Varietal Select 1995: Tobacco and herb flavors dominate in this austere but distinctive wine; it finishes a bit flat. A blend of 65 percent Sémillon, 35 percent Sauvignon Blanc. 1,814 cases made. • $8 • (09/15/97) • **82**

Sémillon-Sauvignon Blanc Columbia Valley Varietal Select 1994: A sturdy wine showing tobacco and mineral flavors, hinting at vegetal notes on the finish. 1,178 cases made. • $7 • (09/15/96) • **80**

Seyval Blanc Columbia Valley Varietal Select 1993 • $7 • (09/30/95) • **82**

Varietal Select Red Columbia Valley 1995: A crisp, firm style that emphasizes ripe blackberry and herbal flavors. Finishes with chewy tannins that need until 2000. A blend of 67 percent Cabernet Sauvignon and 33 percent Merlot. 7,160 cases made. • $12 • (09/15/97) • **84**

White Riesling Columbia Valley Special Harvest 1993 • $6 • (09/30/94) BB • **86**

White Riesling Columbia Valley Varietal Select Special Harvest 1993 • $7 • (09/30/95) • **81**

White Riesling Late Harvest Columbia Valley Varietal Select 1996: Sweet, but lively enough to keep the nectarine and melon flavors in balance. Ready now. 2,126 cases made. • $7 • (10/15/97) • **85**

White Riesling Late Harvest Columbia Valley Varietal Select 1995: Sweet and lightly honeyed apricot and spice flavors are elevated by a distinctive remnant note of noble rot. Nicely balanced, too. 2,183 cases made. • $7 • (09/15/96) • **88**

WATERBROOK | WASHINGTON

Cabernet Franc Columbia Valley 1994: Bold, ripe and generous with its spice-scented blackberry, black cherry and cola flavors that expand on the palate. Delicious now, but the fine tannins can help it develop through 2000 to 2001. 267 cases made. • $20 • (12/31/96) • **89**

Cabernet Sauvignon Columbia Valley 1995: Firm in texture, with fine-grained tannins around a nice core of bright currant and cherry flavors that meld with spicy oak notes and linger on the harmonious finish. Good now, but might develop more depth by 2000. 1,500 cases made. • $24 • (05/15/98) • **88**

Cabernet Sauvignon Columbia Valley 1994: Filled with gorgeous blackberry and currant flavors that swirl through the finish with anise and toast accents. Supple, elegant, superbly balanced, it has the polish to drink now and the fine-grained tannins to hold well past 2000. 1,216 cases made. • $20 • (12/15/96) • **92**

Cabernet Sauvignon Columbia Valley 1993: Ripe and generous, a mouthful of spicy black cherry and berry flavors, feeling almost thick on the palate. Try now. 1,100 cases made. • $18 • (12/15/95) • **88**

Cabernet Sauvignon Columbia Valley 1992 • $16 • (04/15/95) SS • **91**

Cabernet Sauvignon Columbia Valley 1991 • $15 • (09/30/94) • **88**

Cabernet Sauvignon Columbia Valley 1989 • $13 • (10/15/93) • **86**

Cabernet Sauvignon Columbia Valley 1988 • $14 • (04/15/92) • **85**

Chardonnay Columbia Valley 1996: Smooth and fragrant with its pear, vanilla and cream aromas and flavors that linger gently on the supple finish. Nice now, better later this year. 11,036 cases made. • $11 • (01/31/98) • **87**

Chardonnay Columbia Valley 1995: Bright, lively and flavorful, with apple, pear and spice notes that linger on the nicely modulated finish. 24,000 cases made. • $10 • (08/31/96) BB • **86**

Chardonnay Columbia Valley 1994: A bright, ripe and fruity Washington white that offers good flavors for the dollars. A nice thread of spicy oak runs through this to balance it out. Drinkable now. 11,500 cases made. • $10 • (12/15/95) BB • **87**

Chardonnay Columbia Valley 1993 • $9 • (12/31/94) BB • **88**

Chardonnay Walla Walla Valley Cottonwood Creek Estate 1993 • $14 • (12/31/94) • **89**

Merlot Columbia Valley 1995: Smooth and supple, a pretty mouthful of black cherry, currant and spice that lingers gently on the finish. Not quite the depth of previous vintages. Ready now. 5,414 cases made. • $22 • (05/15/98) • **86**

Merlot Columbia Valley 1994: Brilliantly aromatic and bursting with juicy berry and plum flavors from start to finish. A stylish, beautifully crafted wine that floats its yummy flavors over a silky frame. Drink now. 1,640 cases made. • $20 • (12/15/96) HR • **91**

Key: SS—Spectator Selection CS—Cellar Selection HR—Highly Recommended BB—Best Buy $NA—Price not available Ⓐ—Auction Price (BT)—Barrel Tasting
Dates in parentheses indicate the issues in which the ratings were published.

Merlot Columbia Valley 1993 • $18 • (05/15/96) • **90**

Merlot Columbia Valley 1992 • $15 • (09/30/95) • **90**

Merlot Columbia Valley 1991 • $14 • (12/31/93) • **86**

Merlot Columbia Valley 1990 • $15 • (06/15/93) • **84**

Merlot Columbia Valley 1989 • $14 • (04/30/92) HR • **94**

Merlot Columbia Valley Reserve 1995: Firm in texture, with a nice range of plum, berry and spice flavors showing more up front than on the finish. Drink through 2000. 1,500 cases made. • $32 • (05/15/98) • **86**

Merlot Columbia Valley Reserve 1992 • $22 • (05/31/95) • **89**

Sauvignon Blanc Columbia Valley 1996: A spicy, toasty style that retains a steely core to support the pear and mineral flavors. Juicy finish. Drink soon. 725 cases made. • $11 • (09/15/97) • **86**

Sauvignon Blanc Columbia Valley 1995: Crisp and bright, with melon, green apple and spice flavors. This is appealingly zingy and develops complexity with each sip. The long finish gives it a nice follow-through. 2,280 cases made. • $10 • (08/31/96) • **88**

Sauvignon Blanc Columbia Valley 1993 • $9 • (03/31/95) • **86**

WATTLE CREEK | CALIFORNIA

Sauvignon Blanc Alexander Valley 1996: A toasty, tangy mélange of grapefruit, apple and herbs, finishing crisply with a strong hint of Meyer lemon. Brisk and refreshing. 500 cases made. • $16 • (09/15/97) • **89**

WEIBEL | CALIFORNIA

Cabernet Sauvignon Mendocino County 1988 • $8 • (03/15/92) BB • **81**

Cabernet Sauvignon Mendocino County 1987 • $8 • (02/28/91) BB • **84**

Cabernet Sauvignon Mendocino Limited Reserve 1989 • $10 • (11/15/93) • **77**

Pinot Noir Mendocino County 1988 • $6 • (02/28/91) • **74**

WEINSTOCK | CALIFORNIA

Cabernet Sauvignon Sonoma County 1994: Thin and bland, with barely any fruit flavors showing. 1,500 cases made. • $10 • (11/30/96) • **72**

Cabernet Sauvignon Sonoma County 1992 • $9 • (05/31/95) • **85**

Gamay Sonoma County 1989 • $8 • (03/31/91) • **75**

Pinot Noir Sonoma County Winemaker Selection Reserve 1989 • $13 • (11/15/91) • **79**

WEISINGER'S | OREGON

Cabernet Sauvignon Rogue Valley Layne Vineyard Vintage Select 1990 • $23 • (11/30/94) • **79**

Mescolare Red Oregon NV: This sturdy, flavorful red blend features berry, plum and smoke flavors. A blend of Cabernet Sauvignon, Pinot Noir, Zinfandel and Nebbiolo. Drink now. 300 cases made. • $11 • (05/15/98) • **84**

Petite Pompadour Rogue Valley Pompadour Vineyard 1995: A supple red, with solid structure and an appealing core of currant and herb flavors that linger on the nicely defined finish. Best from 2000. A blend of Cabernet Franc, Cabernet Sauvignon, Merlot and Malbec. 450 cases made. • $17 • (05/15/98) • **87**

Petite Pompadour Rogue Valley Pompadour Vineyard 1993: Lean, crisp and a bit austere, with a tart quality to the berry and smoke flavors. Drink soon. 290 cases made. • $15 • (12/31/96) • **81**

Petite Pompadour Rogue Valley Pompadour Vineyard 1992 • $15 • (03/31/96) • **86**

Pinot Noir Rogue Valley 1992 • $15 • (01/31/96) • **86**

Sémillon Rogue Valley 1993 • $9 • (11/30/94) • **85**

Sémillon-Chardonnay Rogue Valley 1995: Fresh, open textured and generous with its apricot-scented pear and almond flavors. Tasty to drink now. 200 cases made. • $10 • (12/31/96) • **85**

Sémillon-Chardonnay Rogue Valley 1994 • $10 • (01/31/96) • **88**

WELLINGTON | CALIFORNIA

Cabernet Franc Mount Veeder 1990 • $13 • (11/15/92) • **80**

Cabernet Sauvignon Mount Veeder Random Ridge 1993: Firm and trim, this shows compact cedar, currant and cherry flavors. Turns crisp and tannic on the finish, where it picks up a nice earthy edge. Drink now. 600 cases made. • $16 • (11/15/96) • **87**

Cabernet Sauvignon Mount Veeder Random Ridge 1992 • $16 • (12/15/95) • **83**

Cabernet Sauvignon Mount Veeder Random Ridge 1991 • $16 • (11/15/94) • **84**

Cabernet Sauvignon Mount Veeder Random Ridge 1990 • $16 • (10/15/93) • **86**

Cabernet Sauvignon Sonoma County Mohrhardt Ridge Vineyard 1994: Somewhat earthy on the nose, with layers of black currant, licorice, smoke, cassis and tar. Firmly textured, it should mature well in the cellar; drinks well now, too. 548 cases made. • $15 • (11/15/97) • **87**

Cabernet Sauvignon Sonoma County Mohrhardt Ridge Vineyard 1993: A racy style, marked by exotic oak flavors and dashes of herb and dill. Still, the smoky flavors are balanced by currant and cherry notes that enhance the depth and proportion. 600 cases made. • $14 • (11/15/96) • **87**

Cabernet Sauvignon Sonoma County Mohrhardt Ridge Vineyard 1992 • $14 • (12/15/95) • **84**

Cabernet Sauvignon Sonoma County Mohrhardt Ridge Vineyard 1991 • $14 • (11/15/94) • **85**

Cabernet Sauvignon Sonoma County Mohrhardt Ridge Vineyard 1990 • $14 • (09/15/93) • **83**

Cabernet Sauvignon Sonoma County Mohrhardt Ridge Vineyard 1989 • $14 • (08/31/92) • **85**

Cabernet Sauvignon Sonoma Valley Glen Lyon Vineyard 1993: Light and brightly focused, a mouthful of minty, earthy berry flavors that finish solidly, if not with great depth. 215 cases made. • $14 • (12/15/95) • **84**

Chardonnay Sonoma County 1996: A smoothly textured wine, with hints of vanilla, pear, peach and toasty oak. Finishes with a mild, mineral edge. Drink now. 1,003 cases made. • $13 • (06/30/98) • **86**

Chardonnay Sonoma County Barrel Fermented Lot 2 1993 • $8 • (07/31/95) • **81**

Chardonnay Sonoma Valley 1995: Pretty nectarine flavors are punctuated by unfortunate metallic and bitter notes. It's drinkable, but a bit off. 600 cases made. • $12 • (07/31/97) • **81**

Chardonnay Sonoma Valley 1994: Simple, with a modest band of spicy pear, citrus and light oak notes, but nothing more. 520 cases made. • $11 • (06/30/96) • **84**

Chardonnay Sonoma Valley Barrel Fermented 1993 • $12 • (07/31/95) • **84**

Chardonnay Sonoma Valley Reserve 1995: Bright and spicy, a tad bitter, but the fresh green apple and citrus notes harmonize nicely on the finish. Ready to drink. 225 cases made. • $16 • (07/31/97) • **86**

Criolla Sonoma Valley Old Vines 1991 • $7 • (06/15/93) • **85**

Criolla Sonoma Valley Old Vines 1990 • $7 • (03/31/92) • **85**

Merlot Sonoma County 1992 • $15 • (11/15/95) • **86**

Merlot Sonoma County 1991 • $11 • (09/15/94) • **85**

Merlot Sonoma Valley 1995: Earthy, gamy flavors prevail in this somewhat austere red. Drinkable now. 1,300 cases made. • $16 • (12/15/97) • **80**

Merlot Sonoma Valley 1994: Young and chewy, with firm tannins and an earthy nuance to its currant and berry flavors. Needs time to shed its tannins, though it may always be on the tannic side. 840 cases made. • $15 • (12/15/96) • **84**

Merlot Sonoma Valley 1993: Crisp and trim, with medium-depth herb, tobacco and cherry flavors. 600 cases made. • $15 • (08/31/96) • **83**

Red Mount Veeder Random Ridge 1989 • $16 • (11/15/92) • **86**

Syrah Russian River Valley Alegría Vineyard 1995: Nicely packed with currant and blackberry flavors, with reined-in tannins and a generous mouthful of fruit flavor on the finish. Ready now to 2001. 420 cases made. • $16 • (03/31/98) • **88**

Syrah Russian River Valley Alegría Vineyard 1994: Dark, ripe and spicy, with a plum and currant edge, but it it would benefit from greater richness, depth and concentration. 394 cases made. • $15 • (09/15/96) • **84**

Syrah Russian River Valley Alegría Vineyard 1993 • $12 • (09/30/95) • **89**

Victory Reserve Sonoma County 1991: Offers an elegant and appealing array of ripe, mature cherry, currant and plum flavors. Finishes with a dry edge and hints of spice and cedar. 220 cases made. • $20 • (09/15/96) • **86**

Zinfandel Russian River Valley 1996: Bright and fruity, with spice and herbs to add complexity. Black cherry, raspberry, anise and a touch of vanilla make this an enjoyable quaff. Drink now. 1,142 cases made. • $14 • (05/31/98) • **85**

Zinfandel Sonoma County 1994: Ripe and supple, with cherry, berry, spice and cedary oak flavors. Has a complex, earthy, peppery accent on the finish. 840 cases made. • $10 • (08/31/96) • **88**

Zinfandel Sonoma County Old Vines 1993 • $9 • (10/15/95) • **72**

Zinfandel Sonoma Valley 100-Year-Old Vines 1995: Charged with plum, anise and blackberry flavors, it's got bite on the finish with a pleasing herbal edge. Doesn't sail at the end, but it carries enough weight to make it worth exploring. Drink now through 2002. 110 cases made. • $20 • (06/15/98) • **87**

Zinfandel Sonoma Valley 100-Year-Old Vines 1994: Shows off a tart, wild berry edge, so fans of that style will find it quite pleasing, but it doesn't quite fill out at midpalate. Finishes with a crisp, simple edge. 143 cases made. • $18 • (02/28/97) • **83**

Zinfandel Sonoma Valley 100-Year-Old Vines 1993 • $15 • (10/15/95) • **87**

Zinfandel Sonoma Valley 100-Year-Old Vines 1992 • $13 • (10/15/94) • **87**

Zinfandel Sonoma Valley Casa Santinamaria 1996: Fairly focused, with jammy blackberry flavors, balanced spice and licorice highlights and a smooth-textured finish. To be released July of this year; drink through 2000. 553 cases made. • $16 • (05/31/98) • **86**

Zinfandel Sonoma Valley Casa Santinamaria 1995: Ripe and earthy in character, showing juicy plum and wild berry notes and a touch of earthiness on the finish. 625 cases made. • $16 • (03/31/97) • **86**

Zinfandel Sonoma Valley Casa Santinamaria 1994: Ripe and juicy, with pretty plum and cherry flavors. It loses a bit of its zest on the finish, where it picks up a minty flavor. 500 cases made. • $15 • (08/31/96) • **87**

Zinfandel Sonoma Valley Casa Santinamaria 1993 • $12 • (10/15/95) • **86**

Zinfandel Sonoma Valley Casa Santinamaria 1992 • $10 • (10/15/94) • **84**

WENTE | CALIFORNIA

Blanc de Noir Arroyo Seco 1983 • $15 • (03/31/89) • **78**

Brut Arroyo Seco 1983 • $10 • (08/31/88) • **79**

Brut Arroyo Seco 1982 • $8 • (12/31/86) • **84**

Brut Arroyo Seco 1981 • $8 • (04/01/86) • **78**

Cabernet Sauvignon California 1981 • $7 • (12/16/85) • **65**

Cabernet Sauvignon Central Coast 1985 • $8 • (11/15/89) • **78**

Cabernet Sauvignon Livermore Valley 1995: Smoke, spice, coffee and toast blend nicely in this lighter-styled Cabernet. The finish is herbal, fresh and clean. Drinks well now. 7,000 cases made. • $11 • (10/15/97) • **85**

Cabernet Sauvignon Livermore Valley 1993: A sturdy California wine that offers a lot for a fair price. The solid, beet-scented berry and herb flavors pick up interesting notes of spice and pickle barrel on the finish. Drinkable now. 28,000 cases made. • $8 • (11/15/95) BB • **85**

Cabernet Sauvignon Livermore Valley 1991 • $10 • (11/15/94) • **82**

Cabernet Sauvignon Livermore Valley 1990 • $8 • (11/15/93) • **81**

Cabernet Sauvignon Livermore Valley Charles Wetmore Vineyard Reserve 1990 • $16 • (08/31/94) • **86**

Cabernet Sauvignon Livermore Valley Charles Wetmore Vineyard Reserve 1989 • $18 • (11/15/93) • **85**

Cabernet Sauvignon Livermore Valley Charles Wetmore Vineyard Reserve 1987 • $18 • (04/30/91) • **86**

Cabernet Sauvignon Livermore Valley Charles Wetmore Vineyard Reserve 1986 • $12 • (10/15/90) • **82**

Chardonnay Arroyo Seco Riva Ranch 1993 • $8 • (05/15/96) • **85**

Chardonnay Arroyo Seco Riva Ranch Reserve 1994: Clean, crisp and well focused, with ripe, lively flavors, hints of melon, pear and citrus and a spicy, elegant aftertaste. 5,000 cases made. • $15 • (04/30/98) • **88**

Chardonnay Central Coast 1994: Light and straightforward, with modest apple and vaguely toasty flavors. Drinkable now. 40,000 cases made. • $9 • (06/15/96) • **81**

Chardonnay Central Coast 1993 • $9 • (04/30/95) • **85**

Chardonnay Livermore Valley Herman Wente Reserve 1995: Big, ripe and complex, with loads of vanilla and smoky oak flavors, but also a pretty core of well-focused Chardonnay flavors, with citrus, pear, spice and melon. Complex aftertaste. 2,500 cases made. • $23 • (04/30/98) • **89**

Chardonnay Livermore Valley Herman Wente Reserve 1994: Elegant and refreshing, with spicy pear, tangerine, citrus and smoky oak flavors that add dimension and complexity to the finish. 2,000 cases made. • $22 • (06/30/96) • **88**

Chardonnay Livermore Valley Herman Wente Reserve 1993 • $14 • (09/30/95) • **88**

Merlot Livermore Valley Crane Ridge 1993: Rings true for the varietal, with herb, currant, cherry and berry flavors that finish with light, toasty oak shadings. 9,000 cases made. • $13 • (08/31/96) • **84**

Merlot Livermore Valley Crane Ridge 1991 • $12 • (09/15/94) • **84**

Merlot Livermore Valley Crane Ridge 1990 • $12 • (12/31/93) • **84**

Pinot Noir Arroyo Seco Reliz Creek Reserve 1994: Mature in color, with a thin band of peppery flavors. More like red table wine than Pinot Noir. 2,500 cases made. • $15 • (03/31/97) • **78**

Riesling Late Harvest Arroyo Seco Auslese 1973 • $NA • (02/28/87) • **95**

Riesling Late Harvest Arroyo Seco November Harvest Reserve 1987 • $12 • (07/15/90) • **76**

Sauvignon Blanc Livermore Valley 1996: Bright melon aromas and flavors lead the charge in this crisp-yet-ripe-style white from a long-established California winery. Woven into the blend are lemon, lime, grapefruit and fig elements, all finishing cleanly with a mineral accent. It doesn't get much better at this price. 5,661 cases made. • $8 • (03/31/98) BB • **88**

Sauvignon Blanc Livermore Valley 1995: Straightforward, with melon, spice and citrus flavors that unfold nicely, finish clean. A good value. • $9 • (06/30/97) • **87**

Sauvignon Blanc Livermore Valley 1994: Crisp, and somewhat elegant, with sharply focused melon, sage and citrusy flavors. Drinkable now. 5,000 cases made. • $9 • (08/31/96) • **88**

Sauvignon Blanc Livermore Valley 1993 • $7 • (06/30/95) BB • **85**

Zinfandel Livermore Valley Raboli Vineyards 1985 • $10 • (12/15/89) • **77**

WESTBEND | NORTH CAROLINA

Cabernet Sauvignon North Carolina 1994: Awkward and almost medicinal-tasting, with dark cherry and menthol flavors. 245 cases made. • $14 • (06/15/98) • **72**

Cabernet Sauvignon North Carolina 1993: A bit astringent but still very juicy and fruity with some good dark cherry and plum flavors and a touch of spice. 561 cases made. • $14 • (04/30/97) • **82**

Cabernet Sauvignon North Carolina 1992: Fairly light and a bit tannic, with roasted flavors and aromas, this also has dark cherry flavors and good spiciness on the finish. 406 cases made. • $14 • (04/30/97) • **82**

Chardonnay North Carolina 1995: Almost amber in color with a slight diesel-like aroma. Overdone with buttery, oaky flavors that aren't backed up by fruit. 1,100 cases made. • $11 • (01/31/97) • **72**

Chardonnay North Carolina Barrel Fermented 1995: Has a strong aroma and flavor of pineapple, which remains fresh and gives the wine a nice focus. Drink now. 615 cases made. • $17 • (05/31/98) • **82**

Chardonnay North Carolina Barrel Fermented 1994: Surprisingly lively despite its ripeness and butter notes. Flavors of pear, lemon and ripe apple, with spice accents. Won't win any contests for finesse, but still delicious. 615 cases made. • $17 • (01/31/97) • **85**

Chardonnay North Carolina Silver Creek Vineyards 1996: A ripe-tasting wine with buttery and creamy flavors that are appealing if a bit overpowering. Smooth and satisfying. Drink now. 74 cases made. • $13 • (05/31/98) • **84**

Muscat Canelli North Carolina 1995: A pleasant, fruity wine with peach and apple flavors, tobacco notes on the finish. Fairly light-bodied. 110 cases made. • $10 • (05/31/97) • **81**

Sauvignon Blanc North Carolina 1995: A good, basic white with appealing grapefruit and herbal flavors and some nice spicy notes on the finish. 485 cases made. • $10 • (05/15/97) • **83**

Seyval Blanc North Carolina 1995: A nice, rich white if you can get past the pronounced earthy-grapey character of this French-American grape variety. Barrel-fermented style, with buttery aromas, full body and a lingering finish. Drink now. 855 cases made. • $8 • (07/31/98) • **84**

Vidal Blanc North Carolina 1994: Well-crafted dessert wine for this hybrid grape variety. Smooth and full-flavored, with honey, caramel and ripe pear flavors blending fairly elegantly. Still, way overpriced. Drink now. 120 cases made. • $35 • (06/15/98) • **86**

Vidal Blanc North Carolina Late Harvest Botrytis 1993: Crisp and appley with some tobacco notes in it as well. Well-structured and semi-dry this wine leaves a nice, clean taste on the palate. 1,252 cases made. • $24/375ml • (01/01/97) • **82**

White Gamay North Carolina 1996: An innocuous rosé, with only modest strawberry and watermelon flavors. 409 cases made. • $8 • (07/31/98) • **75**

White Gamay North Carolina 1994: This semi-sweet rosé, though drinkable, is rendered unappealing by an odd flavor, like pickled beets. 1,200 cases made. • $8 • (05/31/97) • **73**

WESTPORT RIVERS | NEW ENGLAND

Blanc de Blancs Southeastern New England 1991: Good in a mature style, showing nutty, smoky flavors and a firm, dry texture. Austere at first, but improves as you sip. 103 cases made. • $35 • (05/15/97) • **84**

Brut Southeastern New England Cuvée RJR 1993: Elegant, crisp-textured and restrained in flavor, this is appealing and refreshing. It has subtle cherry and citrus flavors and great balance. Drink now. 604 cases made. • $25 • (03/31/98) • **86**

Key: SS—Spectator Selection CS—Cellar Selection HR—Highly Recommended BB—Best Buy $NA—Price not available Ⓐ—Auction Price (BT)—Barrel Tasting
Dates in parentheses indicate the issues in which the ratings were published.

Brut Southeastern New England Cuvée RJR 1992: An average sparkling wine with simple apple flavors, slightly coarse texture. 1,040 cases made. • $21 • (05/15/97) • **78**

Chardonnay Southeastern New England Gold Label 1995: Pleasant and fruity, with good peach and green apple flavors, and a clean finish dominated by appealing herbal notes. Drink now. 800 cases made. • $22 • (05/31/98) • **84**

Chardonnay Southeastern New England Gold Label 1994: A bit heavy-handed with butter and spice flavors, and only modest fruit flavors. 236 cases made. • $19 • (01/31/97) • **79**

Chardonnay Southeastern New England Gold Label 1993: A reduced aroma is followed by appealing toasty, tobaccolike flavors with a hazelnut accent. Drink now, before it fades. 236 cases made. • $19 • (01/31/97) • **84**

Chardonnay Southeastern New England Noble 1994: Semi-sweet, dominated by apricot and pear flavors. Not deep or intense but still pleasant, with plenty of acidity. Try with a light dessert. 600 cases made. • $15/375ml • (01/31/97) • **84**

Chardonnay Southeastern New England Silver Label 1995: Thin and tart, with lemon and herbal flavors and aromas. Drink now. 780 cases made. • $14 • (05/31/98) • **76**

Chardonnay Southeastern New England Silver Label 1994: A ripe style, though a bit coarse and astringent on the finish. Where's the fruit? 2,072 cases made. • $13 • (01/31/97) • **76**

Chardonnay Southeastern New England Silver Label 1993: Crisp, with plenty of apple flavors and a zippy finish. Clean, well made and balanced, with a complementary touch of spice. 2,072 cases made. • $13 • (01/31/97) • **85**

Johannisberg Riesling Southeastern New England 1994: Flat and uninspiring; like biting into an overripe apple. 846 cases made. • $15 • (01/01/97) • **70**

Johannisberg Riesling Southeastern New England 1993: Tart, with green apple and tealike flavors. 547 cases made. • $11 • (01/01/97) • **71**

Pinot Noir Blanc Southeastern New England 1995: An admirably dry rosé that's clean, crisp and lightly fruity—a step up from the average white Zinfandel. 345 cases made. • $12 • (05/31/97) • **84**

Signature Reserve North Fork of Long Island Red 1994: A cloying red wine, with an overt green bell-pepper flavor to it. 600 cases made. • $22 • (07/31/98) • **71**

Sparkling Johannisberg Riesling Southeastern New England Imperial Sec 1994: Serviceable, but a bit off-kilter. Has a cheesy-doughy aroma, sweet-and-sour flavors. Drink now. 141 cases made. • $25 • (03/31/98) • **75**

WESTREY | OREGON

Pinot Noir Willamette Valley Reserve 1995: Tight, tough, tart and tannic, it's not charming but has some solid flavor to it. Try now. 198 cases made. • $26 • (10/31/97) • **83**

WESTWOOD | CALIFORNIA

Barbera El Dorado Ritchie Vineyard 1991 • $7 • (12/15/92) • **81**
Pinot Noir California 1991 • $10 • (02/28/93) • **73**
Pinot Noir California 1990 • $9 • (09/30/92) • **82**
Pinot Noir California 1989 • $9 • (04/30/91) • **75**
Pinot Noir Napa Valley Haynes Vineyard Reserve 1989 • $18 • (02/28/93) • **82**

WHALER | CALIFORNIA

Zinfandel Mendocino 1992 • $10 • (10/15/94) • **84**
Zinfandel Mendocino 1991 • $10 • (09/30/93) • **84**
Zinfandel Mendocino 1990 • $10 • (10/15/92) • **81**
Zinfandel Mendocino 1989 • $10 • (10/15/92) • **83**
Zinfandel Mendocino Flagship 1992 • $14 • (10/15/94) • **87**
Zinfandel Mendocino Flagship 1991 • $14 • (09/30/93) • **87**
Zinfandel Mendocino Flagship 1990 • $14 • (10/15/92) • **85**

WHEELER | CALIFORNIA

Cabernet Franc California 1994: Herbal, oaky and banal. Finishes with a cloying quality. This producer's Malbec is much better. 475 cases made. • $19 • (07/31/97) • **76**

Cabernet Sauvignon California 1995: Crisp in style, with zingy acidity and decent currant and black cherry flavors that linger on the finish. 375 cases made. • $15 • (05/15/97) • **85**

Cabernet Sauvignon Dry Creek Valley 1989 • $12 • (06/15/93) • **81**
Cabernet Sauvignon Dry Creek Valley 1988 • $15 • (08/31/92) • **83**
Cabernet Sauvignon Dry Creek Valley 1987 • $14 • (11/15/91) • **84**

Cabernet Sauvignon Dry Creek Valley 1986 • $12 • (08/31/90) • **83**
Cabernet Sauvignon Dry Creek Valley 1985 • $12 • (07/15/89) • **76**
Cabernet Sauvignon Dry Creek Valley 1984 • $11 • (04/15/88) • **75**
Cabernet Sauvignon Dry Creek Valley Norse Vineyard Private Reserve 1985 • $18 • (11/15/90) • **83**
Cabernet Sauvignon Dry Creek Valley Norse Vineyard Private Reserve 1984 • $15 • (07/31/89) • **60**
Cabernet Sauvignon Dry Creek Valley Norse Vineyard Reserve 1991 • $12 • (11/15/94) • **84**
Chardonnay Sonoma County 1993 • $11 • (07/31/95) • **84**
Malbec California 1994: A tightly wound wine, with charred, herbal, plum and spice flavors. A bit on the lean side, yet with punch. It's screaming for a rare steak. 450 cases made. • $19 • (07/31/97) • **86**
Merlot Dry Creek Valley 1992 • $12 • (04/15/95) • **79**
Quintet California 1990 • $7 • (05/31/93) • **76**
RS Reserve California Red 1989 • $11 • (10/31/91) • **77**
RS Reserve California Red 1988 • $10 • (08/31/90) • **83**
Sangiovese California 1994: Pale in color, pallid in flavor, vaguely cherryish. 450 cases made. • $19 • (04/30/97) • **80**
Viognier California 1995: Marked by spicy notes, this serves up a modest band of pear and peach flavors but turns simple on the finish. 500 cases made. • $19 • (04/30/97) • **82**
Zinfandel California 1994: Rather ordinary, with light notes of meat and cherry that are thin and watery. 4,000 cases made. • $15 • (04/30/97) • **78**
Zinfandel Dry Creek Valley 1992 • $11 • (08/31/95) • **87**
Zinfandel Dry Creek Valley 1991 • $12 • (09/30/93) • **80**

WHIDBEY ISLAND | WASHINGTON

Cabernet Sauvignon Yakima Valley 1995: Offers a range of pretty raspberry, cinnamon and vanilla flavors that glide smoothly across the firmly textured frame. Try now. 75 cases made. • $14 • (09/15/97) • **86**
Lemberger Yakima Valley 1995: Light and tart, with modest vinous flavors. Ready now. 270 cases made. • $10 • (09/15/97) • **79**
Madeleine Angevine Puget Sound 1995: A sturdy wine with soft edges and appealing pear flavors. Has a touch of violet to its character. 250 cases made. • $8 • (09/15/97) • **80**

WHITCRAFT | CALIFORNIA

Chardonnay Santa Maria Valley 1995: Smooth, ripe and creamy, with a bright, ripe core of pear, apple, citrus and melon flavors, it turns even more complex on the finish, where the flavors fan out and linger. Drinkable now. 875 cases made. • $22 • (05/31/97) • **91**
Chardonnay Santa Maria Valley Bien Nacido Vineyard 1996: A lean, crisp style, with a band of lemon and grapefruit-scented flavors that zip across your palate. Best to cellar a year or two to let it fill out. 950 cases made. • $22 • (11/30/97) • **89**
Chardonnay Santa Maria Valley Bien Nacido Vineyard 1994: Filled with flavors of pear, spice, honey and nectarine. Perhaps in time a little more polish and finesse will develop as well. 950 cases made. • $17 • (06/15/96) • **88**
Chardonnay Santa Maria Valley Bien Nacido Vineyard 1993 • $22 • (05/31/95) • **89**
Chardonnay Santa Ynez Valley Sanford & Benedict Vineyard 1995: Tart, with a green edge to the pineapple, citrus and guava notes, but once past the bracing acidity the flavors show remarkable depth and concentration. Can stand short-term cellaring. 150 cases made. • $35 • (05/31/97) • **91**
Chardonnay Santa Ynez Valley Sanford & Benedict Vineyard 1994: Clean and correct, showing a trim band of leesy pear and light, toasty oak shadings. Comes across as an elegant, understated white. 120 cases made. • $35 • (05/15/96) • **88**
Petite Sirah Santa Barbara County 1995: Marked by complex spice, plum and pepper notes, it shortens up on the finish and turns tannic. Try now. 165 cases made. • $22 • (07/31/97) • **86**
Pinot Noir Russian River Valley Olivet Lane Vineyard 1992 • $30 • (02/28/94) • **90**
Pinot Noir Russian River Valley Olivet Lane Vineyard 1991 • $25 • (02/28/93) • **81**
Pinot Noir Santa Maria Valley Bien Nacido Vineyard 1996: A racy style. Shows peppery, wild berry and black cherry flavors that are supple and elegant, finishing with a spicy aftertaste. Ready now. 285 cases made. • $35 • (01/31/98) • **88**
Pinot Noir Santa Maria Valley Bien Nacido Vineyard 1995: Ripe and zesty, this is exotic in style, with tart, meaty, sour cherry and wild berry flavors that push the limits for Pinot Noir. It's dark, concentrated, young, peppery and intense; drinkable now. 72 cases made. • $35 • (12/31/96) • **88**
Pinot Noir Santa Maria Valley Bien Nacido Vineyard 1994 • $30 • (12/31/95) • **93**
Pinot Noir Santa Maria Valley Bien Nacido Vineyard 1993 • $30 • (12/31/94) • **88**
Pinot Noir Santa Maria Valley Bien Nacido Vineyard 1992 • $30 • (02/28/94) • **88**
Pinot Noir Santa Maria Valley Bien Nacido Vineyard 1991 • $25 • (02/28/93) • **83**
Pinot Noir Santa Maria Valley Bien Nacido Vineyard 1990 • $25 • (02/28/93) • **88**
Pinot Noir Santa Maria Valley Bien Nacido Vineyard N Block 1996: Strays out-of-bounds for Pinot Noir, with intense spicy, racy vegetal flavors, wild berry, tomato and minty notes—take your pick. 300 cases made. • $40 • (02/28/98) • **79**
Pinot Noir Santa Maria Valley Bien Nacido Vineyard N Block 1994 • $40 • (05/15/96) • **89**
Pinot Noir Santa Maria Valley Bien Nacido Vineyard N Block 1993 • $35 • (12/31/95) • **87**
Pinot Noir Santa Maria Valley Bien Nacido Vineyard Q Block 1996: Dark, ripe, rich and complex, with black cherry, herb, tea and spicy flavors that turn smooth and supple. Finishes with a tinge of herb and a vegetal note. Drinks well now. 295 cases made. • $40 • (01/31/98) • **88**
Pinot Noir Santa Maria Valley Bien Nacido Vineyard Q Block 1995: Young, tart, tight and exotic, with lots of spice, wild berry, black cherry and spicy oak flavors that are well focused and show lots of meaty, leathery nuances. Drink now or cellar or 2000. 72 cases made. • $40 • (12/31/96) • **88**
Pinot Noir Santa Maria Valley Bien Nacido Vineyard Q Block 1994 • $35 • (12/31/95) • **88**
Pinot Noir Santa Maria Valley Bien Nacido Vineyard Q Block 1993 • $35 • (12/31/94) • **89**
Pinot Noir Santa Maria Valley Bien Nacido Vineyard Q Block 1992 • $40 • (02/28/94) • **88**
Pinot Noir Sonoma Coast Hirsch Vineyard 1996: Intense and tannic, with racy blackberry, wild berry and cherry flavors that are young and vibrant but in need of short-term cellaring. Tasted twice, this is a somewhat worrisome wine whose future is in doubt. 120 cases made. • $40 • (02/28/98) • **82**
Pinot Noir Sonoma Coast Hirsch Vineyard 1995: Unusual. Truly exotic in its spicy character, this has a tart, tightly wound core of wild blackberry flavor with hints of clove. Not a typical Pinot Noir, but shows good concentration. 98 cases made. • $40 • (12/31/96) • **87**
Pinot Noir Sonoma Coast Hirsch Vineyard 1994 • $40 • (05/15/96) • **92**

WHITE COTTAGE | CALIFORNIA

Cabernet Sauvignon Howell Mountain 1994: Tight and sharply focused, with a wonderful core of currant, wild berry, mineral and spice flavors. Delivers the goods with richness, concentration, length and complexity. Best to cellar into 2000. 120 cases made. • $35 • (10/15/97) • **93**

WHITE HALL | VIRGINIA

Cabernet Franc Virginia 1995: An herbal style with green pepper and berry flavors. It's a bit spritzy, too. 100 cases made. • $18 • (04/30/97) • **79**

WHITE HERON | WASHINGTON

Chantepierre Washington 1992 • $10 • (09/30/95) • **80**
Chantepierre Washington 1990 • $10 • (09/30/94) • **83**
Chantepierre Washington 1989 • $10 • (03/15/93) • **70**
Chantepierre Washington 1988 • $11 • (04/15/92) • **80**
Pinot Noir Washington 1990 • $7 • (09/30/94) • **81**

WHITE OAK | CALIFORNIA

Cabernet Franc Alexander Valley 1992 • $17 • (12/31/94) • **85**
Cabernet Franc Alexander Valley 1989 • $12 • (11/15/92) • **84**
Cabernet Sauvignon Alexander Valley 1992 • $14 • (12/15/95) • **85**
Cabernet Sauvignon Alexander Valley 1991 • $14 • (11/15/94) • **84**
Cabernet Sauvignon Alexander Valley 1990 • $14 • (11/15/93) • **87**
Cabernet Sauvignon Alexander Valley 1988 • $14 • (11/15/92) • **85**
Cabernet Sauvignon Alexander Valley Myers Limited Reserve 1985 • $18 • (07/31/89) • **85**
Cabernet Sauvignon Sonoma County 1987 • $14 • (02/29/92) • **85**

Chardonnay Russian River Valley Poplar Ranch Private Reserve 1995: Has a bitter edge to its bright apple flavor, making it feel a bit raw. Try now. 458 cases made. • $18 • (07/31/97) • **80**
Chardonnay Russian River Valley Poplar Ranch Private Reserve 1994: A pleasant, well-oaked wine with intense ripe pear, spice and nutmeg flavors. Could ultimately be more complex. 250 cases made. • $18 • (06/30/96) • **84**
Chardonnay Russian River Valley Poplar Ranch Private Reserve 1993 • $18 • (07/31/95) • **82**
Chardonnay Sonoma County 1995: Solid, with a complex core of ripe pear, apple and melon flavors and finishing with a dash of oak. 3,000 cases made. • $13 • (06/15/97) • **87**
Chardonnay Sonoma County 1994: A clumsy wine whose wood and fruit flavors don't marry: The pear is marred in bitter oak. 3,100 cases made. • $13 • (07/31/96) • **79**
Chardonnay Sonoma County 1993 • $11 • (07/31/95) • **83**
Chardonnay Sonoma County Myers Limited Reserve 1996: Bright in flavor, open-textured, with appealing apple, pear and spice flavors that echo on the soft finish. Drink now. 410 cases made. • $20 • (05/15/98) • **87**
Chardonnay Sonoma County Myers Limited Reserve 1995: A resinous note to the bright apple fruit gives this supple Chardonnay a jazzy feel. Easy to drink and pleasing. 411 cases made. • $17 • (07/31/97) • **86**
Chardonnay Sonoma County Myers Limited Reserve 1993 • $16 • (10/15/95) • **87**
Chenin Blanc California 1993 • $7 • (06/15/95) • **87**
Sauvignon Blanc Napa Valley 1995: Floral and citrus notes announce this zingy wine, rich in bright grapefruit, lemon-lime and melon flavors, with a tasteful touch of grassiness on the finish. The ensemble is complex, spritely and inspiring. 2,040 cases made. • $11 • (06/30/97) • **89**
Sauvignon Blanc Sonoma County 1993 • $9 • (09/30/94) • **83**
Zinfandel Alexander Valley 1994: Shows off ripe fruit flavors aplenty, with smoke-accented plum and cherry notes, and has finesse and grace that make it quite appealing. Drink now. 2,200 cases made. • $15 • (04/30/97) • **89**
Zinfandel Alexander Valley 1993 • $15 • (10/15/95) • **88**
Zinfandel Alexander Valley 1990 • $10 • (12/15/92) • **75**
Zinfandel Alexander Valley Church Vineyard 1992 • $14 • (10/15/94) • **82**
Zinfandel Dry Creek Valley Saunders Vineyard 1992 • $16 • (10/15/94) • **85**
Zinfandel Dry Creek Valley Saunders Vineyard 1991 • $16 • (09/15/93) • **89**
Zinfandel Dry Creek Valley Saunders Vineyard 1990 • $13 • (10/15/92) • **91**
Zinfandel Sonoma County 1994: A touch brambly, with a core of spice and cherry flavors and a berry note on the finish. Drinkable now. 600 cases made. • $13 • (04/30/97) • **86**
Zinfandel Sonoma County 1992 • $9 • (10/15/94) BB • **85**
Zinfandel Sonoma County 1991 • $10 • (09/15/93) • **87**
Zinfandel Sonoma County 1989 • $10 • (02/29/92) • **87**
Zinfandel Sonoma County Limited Reserve 1993 • $13 • (10/15/95) • **85**
Zinfandel Sonoma County Limited Reserve 1992 • $13 • (10/15/94) • **86**
Zinfandel Sonoma County Limited Reserve 1991 • $13 • (09/15/93) • **88**
Zinfandel Sonoma Valley 1993 • $9 • (10/15/95) • **87**

WHITE ROCK | CALIFORNIA

Chardonnay Napa Valley 1996: Light and simple, with cedary oak and ripe, spicy pear and apple flavors. Turns elegant on the finish, where the fruit comes through. 770 cases made. • $20 • (05/15/98) • **87**
Chardonnay Napa Valley 1995: Marked by ripe fruit flavors and a spicy, Muscat-like edge, its pear, hazelnut and nutmeg flavors are elegant and well focused. Very appealing and ready now. 1,370 cases made. • $19 • (05/15/97) • **89**
Claret Napa Valley 1992: Firm and tannic, with mint and anise accents to the currant and berry flavors, a strong eucalyptus edge on the finish and leathery tannins. Try now. A blend of 55 percent Cabernet Sauvignon, 37 percent Cabernet Franc, 6 percent Petite Verdot and 2 percent Merlot. 1,100 cases made. • $24 • (05/15/97) • **87**
Claret Napa Valley 1991 • $22 • (12/15/95) • **85**
Claret Napa Valley 1990 • $19 • (04/15/94) • **88**
Claret Napa Valley 1989 • $18 • (11/15/93) • **83**
Claret Napa Valley 1988 • $18 • (11/15/93) • **84**
Claret Napa Valley 1986 • $18 • (10/31/89) • **80**

Key: SS—Spectator Selection CS—Cellar Selection HR—Highly Recommended BB—Best Buy $NA—Price not available Ⓐ—Auction Price (BT)—Barrel Tasting
Dates in parentheses indicate the issues in which the ratings were published.

WHITEHALL LANE | CALIFORNIA

Cabernet Franc Napa Valley 1990 • $15 • (07/15/93) • **86**
Cabernet Franc Napa Valley 1989 • $18 • (08/31/92) • **79**
Cabernet Franc Napa Valley 1988 • $19 • (11/15/90) • **88**
Cabernet Sauvignon California NV • $7 • (10/15/88) • **70**
Cabernet Sauvignon California Le Petit NV • $8 • (03/31/90) • **81**
Cabernet Sauvignon Napa Valley 1995: Rich, complex and flavorful, with a concentrated core of earthy currant, plum and berry-scented flavors, and firm, dry tannins. Finishes with dense sage and herbal overtones and enough tannin to merit cellaring. Best from 2000 to 2004. 5,800 cases made. • $20 • (04/30/98) • **88**
Cabernet Sauvignon Napa Valley 1994: Ripe and grapey, with lots of currant, black cherry, anise and plummy notes and a smooth, supple texture. Appealing for its generous fruitiness. 5,000 cases made. • $18 • (11/15/96) • **89**
Cabernet Sauvignon Napa Valley 1992 • $15 • (10/15/95) • **87**
Cabernet Sauvignon Napa Valley 1991 • $14 • (11/15/94) • **88**
Cabernet Sauvignon Napa Valley 1990 • $13 • (12/15/93) • **88**
Cabernet Sauvignon Napa Valley 1988 • $18 • (11/15/91) • **87**
Cabernet Sauvignon Napa Valley 1987 • $18 • (09/15/90) • **84**
Cabernet Sauvignon Napa Valley 1986 • $16 • (08/31/89) • **89**
Cabernet Sauvignon Napa Valley 1985 • $16 • (11/15/88) • **93**
Cabernet Sauvignon Napa Valley 1984 • $14 • (12/31/87) • **84**
Cabernet Sauvignon Napa Valley 1983 • $14 • (11/30/86) • **77**
Cabernet Sauvignon Napa Valley 1982 • $12 • (02/16/85) • **86**
Cabernet Sauvignon Napa Valley NV • $6 • (12/31/87) • **77**
Cabernet Sauvignon Napa Valley Morisoli Vineyard 1992 • $28 • (10/15/95) HR • **93**
Cabernet Sauvignon Napa Valley Morisoli Vineyard 1991 • $36 • (05/31/95) • **89**
Cabernet Sauvignon Napa Valley Morisoli Vineyard Reserve 1993: Intense and well focused, with a spicy, minty band of cherry and currant flavors. Gains complexity on the finish, where it picks up herb, cedar and wild berry flavors. Drinkable now. 1,200 cases made. • $30 • (11/15/96) • **91**
Cabernet Sauvignon Napa Valley Reserve 1992 • $23 • (10/15/95) HR • **92**
Cabernet Sauvignon Napa Valley Reserve 1991 • $26 • (05/31/95) • **89**
Cabernet Sauvignon Napa Valley Reserve 1990 • $23 • (02/28/95) • **88**
Cabernet Sauvignon Napa Valley Reserve 1989 • $19 • (11/15/93) • **89**
Cabernet Sauvignon Napa Valley Reserve 1988 • $27 • (11/15/92) • **86**
Cabernet Sauvignon Napa Valley Reserve 1987 • $28 • (11/15/91) • **90**
Cabernet Sauvignon Napa Valley Reserve 1986 • $30 • (11/15/90) • **77**
Cabernet Sauvignon Napa Valley Reserve 1985 • $30 • (11/30/89) • **88**
Cabernet Sauvignon Rutherford Morisoli Vineyard Reserve 1994: Young, dark and concentrated, with sharply focused currant, black cherry, plum and spicy flavors, smooth, supple tannins and a long, rich aftertaste. Tempting now, but worthy of cellaring, too. Best after 2002. 2,000 cases made. • $36 • (09/30/97) • **92**
Chardonnay Napa Valley 1995: Lightly oaked, with nutmeg and hazelnut accents, the flavors are built around moderately ripe green apple and tart pear notes. 3,100 cases made. • $15 • (08/31/97) • **88**
Chardonnay Napa Valley 1994: A touch earthy, with muted pear, apple and spice flavors in modest proportions. Loses focus on the finish, as flavors become muddled. 2,800 cases made. • $13 • (07/31/96) • **80**
Chardonnay Napa Valley 1993 • $11 • (05/15/95) • **82**
Chardonnay Napa Valley Barrel Fermented 1993 • $13 • (05/15/95) • **84**
Johannisberg Riesling Late Harvest Napa Valley 1994 • $12/375ml • (12/31/95) • **88**
Meritage Napa Valley 1991 • $15 • (11/15/94) • **85**
Merlot Knights Valley 1992 • $17 • (05/15/95) • **88**
Merlot Knights Valley 1991 • $15 • (09/15/94) • **86**
Merlot Knights Valley 1987 • $16 • (07/15/90) • **77**
Merlot Knights Valley 1984 • $14 • (12/31/87) • **87**
Merlot Knights Valley 1983 • $12 • (10/01/85) • **85**
Merlot Knights Valley 1982 • $10 • (06/01/85) CS • **92**
Merlot Knights Valley Reserve 1986 • $15 • (07/31/89) • **72**
Merlot Knights Valley Summers Ranch 1990 • $16 • (06/15/93) • **86**
Merlot Knights Valley Summers Ranch 1989 • $18 • (04/15/92) • **84**
Merlot Knights Valley Summers Ranch 1988 • $18 • (03/31/91) • **82**
Merlot Napa Valley 1995: A young, bright and well-focused Merlot, unveiling a rich, complex core of currant, black cherry, cedar and toasty oak flavors. Notable for its length and concentration, it finishes with a long, lively aftertaste. This California red is drinkable now. From a winery worth watching. 4,500 cases made. • $20 • (11/15/97) SS • **92**

Merlot Napa Valley 1994: Simple, with juicy ripe cherry and plum flavors, hints of anise and cedar on the finish. Avoids being too tannic, and the texture is smooth. 3,800 cases made. • $18 • (11/30/96) • **86**
Merlot Napa Valley 1993 • $18 • (12/15/95) • **86**
Merlot Napa Valley Leonardini Vineyard Reserve 1995: Dark, ripe, intense and concentrated. Well oaked but with the fruit depth and concentration to match. Finishes with a rich core of black cherry, chocolate and wild berry flavors, even a dash of charred oak. Try now. 600 cases made. • $36 • (09/30/97) • **90**
Merlot Napa Valley Leonardini Vineyard Reserve 1994: Bold, ripe and delicious, with tiers of rich plum, currant and black cherry flavor, smooth, polished tannins and a rich, deep aftertaste, where the flavors linger on and on. Drinks well now but worthy of cellaring, too. 560 cases made. • $30 • (11/30/96) • **92**
Merlot Napa Valley Leonardini Vineyard Reserve 1993 • $28 • (12/15/95) • **88**
Pinot Noir Alexander Valley 1990 • $12 • (02/28/94) • **82**
Pinot Noir Alexander Valley 1988 • $14 • (10/31/90) • **82**
Pinot Noir Napa Valley 1987 • $12 • (10/15/89) • **88**
Pinot Noir Napa Valley 1985 • $7 • (06/15/88) • **82**
Pinot Noir Napa Valley 1984 • $7 • (03/01/86) • **86**
Primavera Late Harvest California NV • $8 • (10/15/92) • **74**
Sauvignon Blanc Napa Valley Barrel Fermented 1993 • $10 • (05/31/95) • **81**
Sauvignon Blanc Rutherford 1995: Unpleasant—tastes burnt and acrid. Tasted twice with consistent notes. 1,190 cases made. • $11 • (09/15/96) • **72**
Sauvignon Blanc Rutherford Bommarito Vineyard 1996: A chewy wine, well integrated, with ripe melon, fig, lime and grapefruit flavors all blending harmoniously. Lengthy, lemony finish. 2,000 cases made. • $12 • (06/30/97) • **88**
Zinfandel Napa Valley 1995: Young and trim, in an austere style, with crisp tannins and firm acidity. The core of cherry and wild berry flavors is well focused, finishing with dry tannins. Try now. 18 percent Petite Sirah. 260 cases made. • $20 • (09/30/97) • **89**
Zinfandel Napa Valley 1994: The wild berry, cherry and raspbery flavors hold reign, even as the tannins and a slightly waxy green olive accent kick in on the finish. 250 cases made. • $16 • (08/31/96) • **89**

WHITTLESEY MARK | OREGON

Brut Oregon 1987 • $17 • (05/15/92) • **78**
Brut Oregon Grand Cuvée 1987 • $17 • (12/15/92) • **78**

WIEDERKEHR | ARKANSAS

Cabernet Sauvignon Arkansas Mountain 1978 • $35 • (02/29/92) • **70**
Muscat di Tanta Maria Altus Arkansas 1990 • $9 • (02/29/92) • **71**

WIEMER, HERMANN J. | NEW YORK

Blanc de Noirs Finger Lakes 1989 • $14 • (12/31/94) • **74**
Chardonnay Finger Lakes 1995: Nicely crafted, with apple and butterlike flavors and a fairly rich texture. An earthy note on the finish gives it a pleasant zip. 1,500 cases made. • $12 • (05/15/97) • **83**
Chardonnay Finger Lakes Reserve 1995: Buttery and toasty, with some nice pear and ripe apple flavors. Ripe and rich, with a spicy finish. It would stand up well to a cream sauce. 1,300 cases made. • $16 • (01/31/97) • **84**
Chardonnay Finger Lakes Reserve 1994: Fig, banana and brown sugar flavors give this round white personality, if not typical Chardonnay character. It finishes dry and short. 500 cases made. • $16 • (01/31/96) • **80**
Johannisberg Riesling Finger Lakes Dry 1995: Balanced and refreshing, with good peach and apple flavors in a dry style. 2,600 cases made. • $9 • (01/31/97) • **81**
Johannisberg Riesling Finger Lakes Dry 1994 • $8 • (01/31/96) • **84**
Johannisberg Riesling Finger Lakes Semi-Dry 1994 • $10 • (01/31/96) BB • **88**
Johannisberg Riesling Late Harvest Finger Lakes 1995: Quite applelike in character and slightly sweet, with balance. Nice acidity on the finish. Good, though not complex. 1,500 cases made. • $16 • (01/31/97) • **83**
Johannisberg Riesling Late Harvest Finger Lakes 1994 • $16 • (01/31/96) • **88**
Johannisberg Riesling Late Harvest Finger Lakes 1990 • $13 • (09/15/94) • **87**
Johannisberg Riesling Late Harvest Finger Lakes 1984 • $9 • (03/16/86) • **82**
Johannisberg Riesling Late Harvest Finger Lakes Bunch Select 1987 • $16 • (09/15/94) • **87**
Naturel Finger Lakes 1988 • $12 • (02/28/95) • **79**

WILD HOG HILL | CALIFORNIA

Pinot Noir Sonoma County 1990 • $14 • (02/28/93) • **82**

WILD HORSE | CALIFORNIA

Arneis Central Coast 1995: A soft, low-key sort of wine with dusky pear flavors, finishing with a touch of mineral character. Drink soon. 274 cases made. • $16 • (04/30/97) • **82**
Cabernet Sauvignon Paso Robles 1987 • $13 • (04/30/91) • **88**
Cabernet Sauvignon Paso Robles 1985 • $11 • (06/30/88) • **70**
Cabernet Sauvignon San Luis Obispo County 1994: Complex and well balanced, serving up a pleasant core of cedar, cherry and currant flavors before the tannins kick in. Drink now. • $16 • (12/15/96) • **86**
Chardonnay Central Coast 1996: Ripe, creamy pear and melon-scented Chardonnay flavors combine with toasty oak. Turns complex and elegant on the finish, where the fruit shines through. Drink now through 2000. 10,500 cases made. • $16 • (07/31/98) • **88**
Chardonnay Central Coast 1995: Offers an appealing core of pear, apple and hazelnut flavors that fold together on the finish. Young, tight and a bit on the tart side. Drinkable now. • $14 • (12/15/96) • **87**
Chardonnay Central Coast 1994: Smooth and creamy, with a spicy edge to the ripe pear, peach and vanilla notes. Develops elegance and complexity on the finish. 12,943 cases made. • $14 • (06/30/96) SS • **89**
Chardonnay Central Coast 1993 • $13 • (01/31/95) • **88**
Dolcetto Central Coast 1994: Young, tight and a bit on the tart side, with an earthy streak to the wild berry flavors. Can stand short-term cellaring to soften a bit. 275 cases made. • $14 • (12/31/96) • **86**
Malvasia Bianca Monterey 1996: Spicy and somewhat exotic, with peach and tangy citrus, ginger and clove notes. Displays bracing acidity, nicely tempered with a touch of sweetness. A fine match for Asian flavors. 3,117 cases made. • $13 • (03/31/98) • **87**
Malvasia Bianca Monterey 1995: Fresh and appealing for its buoyant pear, spice and honey flavors. 1,339 cases made. • $14 • (12/31/96) • **85**
Malvasia Bianca Monterey 1994: Spicy aromas and sappy flavors characterize this fresh, simple white. • $13 • (12/31/96) • **81**
Malvasia Bianca Monterey 1993 • $13 • (04/15/95) • **84**
Merlot Central Coast 1989 • $15 • (05/31/92) • **76**
Merlot Central Coast 1986 • $11 • (07/31/89) • **77**
Merlot Paso Robles 1995: A nice red wine with some pretty currant flavors and a slightly vinegary streak running through the otherwise solid finish. Drink now. 20,206 cases made. • $16 • (12/31/97) • **85**
Merlot Paso Robles Cheval Sauvage 1990 • $28 • (03/31/93) • **87**
Merlot San Luis Obispo 1991 • $14 • (02/28/95) • **85**
Negrette Cienega Valley 1992 • $16 • (01/31/95) • **85**
Pinot Blanc Monterey 1995: Ripe and generous with its mineral flavors, which weave between the orange and pear notes to make a delicious wine. 3,650 cases made. • $13 • (04/30/97) • **86**
Pinot Blanc Monterey 1993 • $12 • (04/15/95) • **83**
Pinot Blanc Monterey County 1996: Spicy and full-bodied, with an array of anise, pear, fig and melon notes, turning rich and complex on the finish. Good price. 3,376 cases made. • $13 • (04/30/98) • **87**
Pinot Blanc Santa Barbara County Bien Nacido Vineyard 1993 • $13 • (12/31/94) • **90**
Pinot Noir Central Coast 1996: Lean and racy, with spicy cherry, herb and wild berry flavors that are true to the area. Cellar short term to soften its wild, rangy flavors. 16,200 cases made. • $18 • (02/28/98) • **85**
Pinot Noir Central Coast 1995: Boasts a nice, ripe core of plum and cherry flavors with a slight tangy accent. Drinkable now, but can age a few years, too. 9,053 cases made. • $18 • (01/31/97) • **87**
Pinot Noir Central Coast 1993 • $12 • (02/28/95) • **85**
Pinot Noir Central Coast 1992 • $14 • (01/31/95) • **84**
Pinot Noir Central Coast 1991 • $16 • (02/28/94) • **87**
Pinot Noir Central Coast 1990: Smooth and mellow, perked up by a racy accent to the herb, cherry, anise, smoke and earth flavors. Finishes with a fleshy aftertaste. Ready now. • $13 • (03/31/97) • **88**
Pinot Noir Central Coast Cheval Sauvage 1994: Elegant and lively, with a pretty, spicy edge to the tea leaf, plum and cherry flavors. Finishes with dashes of strawberry and spice. Try now. 189 cases made. • $35 • (09/30/97) • **88**
Pinot Noir Paso Robles 1987 • $14 • (10/15/89) • **90**
Pinot Noir Paso Robles Cheval Sauvage 1993: Mature, with a complex array of ripe plum, black cherry, wild berry and spice flavors. Toasty oak notes

come through on the finish, where the flavors turn even more complex. 193 cases made. • $35 • (12/31/96) • **92**

Pinot Noir Paso Robles Cheval Sauvage 1990 • $28 • (02/28/93) • **90**

Pinot Noir Santa Barbara County 1990 • $14 • (02/28/93) • **86**

Pinot Noir Santa Barbara County 1988 • $14 • (04/30/91) • **79**

Pinot Noir Santa Barbara County 1987 • $14 • (03/31/90) • **82**

Pinot Noir Santa Barbara County 1986: Its dry, earthy, tannic edge and fading fruit flavors spell maturity. Picks up a hint of orange-peel on the finish, but it's best to drink it soon. • $12 • (03/31/97) • **84**

Pinot Noir Santa Barbara County 1985 • $13 • (06/15/88) • **86**

Pinot Noir Santa Barbara County Cheval Sauvage 1990 • $25 • (02/28/94) • **88**

Pinot Noir Santa Barbara County Cheval Sauvage 1989 • $28 • (02/28/93) • **85**

Sauvignon Blanc Late Harvest Edna Valley 1994: Sweet and rich, this offers a ripe, succulent mouthful of spicy apricot, pineapple and fig flavors that keep swirling through the rich, silky finish. Beautifully made, it's approachable now, but may further develop through 2000 to 2010. 418 cases made. • $14/375ml • (12/31/96) • **91**

Syrah Central Coast 1994: Complex and well crafted, with a spicy, wild berry and earth accent. Finishes with soft tannins and a sense of elegance. Delicious now. 863 cases made. • $16 • (03/31/97) • **89**

Zinfandel Paso Robles 1989 • $11 • (09/30/93) • **85**

Zinfandel Paso Robles Unbridled 1990 • $16 • (09/15/94) • **88**

WILDCAT | CALIFORNIA

Merlot Sonoma Valley 1989 • $20 • (05/31/92) • **74**

Merlot Sonoma Valley 1988 • $18 • (05/31/92) • **78**

WILDHURST | CALIFORNIA

Cabernet Sauvignon Clear Lake 1991 • $9 • (11/15/93) • **76**

Cabernet Sauvignon Clear Lake 1990 • $10 • (07/31/92) • **83**

Cabernet Sauvignon Clear Lake Private Reserve 1993: A coarse one. Mouth-puckering tannins reveal only modestly ripe fruit and cedar. Pleasant enough. 499 cases made. • $16 • (10/31/97) • **84**

Chardonnay California 1995: Simple peach and citrus flavors blend nicely, with a vaguely sweet finish. 1,360 cases made. • $11 • (09/30/97) • **81**

Chardonnay California 1994: A sturdy, fresh, fragrant white with spicy apple flavors. 1,500 cases made. • $11 • (06/15/96) • **81**

Chardonnay California 1993 • $10 • (07/31/95) • **85**

Chardonnay Sonoma County Reserve 1993: Earthy, metallic flavors pick up enough nice apricot notes on the finish to save it. 840 cases made. • $12 • (07/31/96) • **80**

Fumé Blanc Clear Lake Reserve 1993 • $11 • (08/31/95) • **84**

Merlot Clear Lake 1994: Pleasant and light textured, with modest herbal, strawberry and cherry flavors. Drinkable now. 5,119 cases made. • $12 • (07/31/96) • **80**

Merlot Clear Lake 1991 • $8 • (03/31/93) BB • **84**

Merlot Lake County Reserve 1992 • $15 • (09/15/94) • **84**

Merlot Lake County Reserve 1991 • $15 • (10/15/93) • **87**

Pinot Noir Mendocino County 1992 • $9 • (02/28/94) • **74**

Sauvignon Blanc Clear Lake 1994 • $9 • (06/15/96) • **83**

Sauvignon Blanc Clear Lake 1993 • $9 • (08/31/95) • **81**

Zinfandel Clear Lake 1996: Simple, with toast, strawberry and spice flavors. A pleasant, straightforward wine, but the chunky, oaky finish is a bit awkward. Drink now through 2000. 575 cases made. • $14 • (06/15/98) • **80**

Zinfandel Clear Lake 1992 • $9 • (10/15/94) • **80**

Zinfandel Clear Lake 1991 • $7 • (09/30/93) BB • **86**

Zinfandel Clear Lake 1990 • $7 • (07/15/92) BB • **85**

WILE & SONS, J. | CALIFORNIA

Cabernet Sauvignon Napa Valley 1991 • $7 • (11/15/93) • **74**

Cabernet Sauvignon Napa Valley 1987 • $10 • (05/31/91) • **78**

Cabernet Sauvignon Napa Valley 1986 • $7 • (09/15/88) • **75**

Cabernet Sauvignon Napa Valley 1985 • $7 • (11/15/87) • **78**

Merlot Napa Valley 1989 • $10 • (05/31/92) • **77**

Key: SS—Spectator Selection CS—Cellar Selection HR—Highly Recommended BB—Best Buy $NA—Price not available Ⓐ—Auction Price (BT)—Barrel Tasting

Dates in parentheses indicate the issues in which the ratings were published.

WILLAKENZIE | OREGON

Gamay Noir Willamette Valley 1996: Bright and effusive in flavor, but feels less frivolous than most Gamay. Has intensity and a slight bite of tannin to add a serious edge to the strawberry and cherry flavors. Drink soon. 1,160 cases made. • $16 • (05/15/98) • **87**

Gamay Noir Yamhill County 1995: Has more stuffing and brighter fruit flavors than most 1995 Pinot Noir. A lively and generous drink with some actual richness and charm. Ready now. 750 cases made. • $15 • (02/28/97) • **87**

Pinot Blanc Oregon 1996: Soft and appealing for its gentle green-melon and almond flavors. Harmonious, fresh and ready now. 633 cases made. • $14 • (11/30/97) • **86**

Pinot Blanc Willamette Valley 1995: Soft and fragrant. Offers orange-peel and floral scents against a pleasant background of gentle pear flavors. Drink soon. 940 cases made. • $15 • (10/31/96) • **83**

Pinot Gris Oregon 1996: A smooth, silky Pinot Gris offering pretty melon and pineapple flavors that linger gently on the finish. Ready now. 2,912 cases made. • $14 • (11/30/97) • **89**

Pinot Gris Willamette Valley 1995: Ripe, generous and disarmingly appealing for its melon, almond, rose petal and spice flavors that linger on the generous finish. 2,700 cases made. • $15 • (11/15/96) • **88**

Pinot Meunier Willamette Valley 1996: Fresh and jazzy. A lively mouthful of blackberry and black cherry flavors that remain crisp and vivid through the finish. Drink soon. 420 cases made. • $16 • (05/15/98) • **87**

Pinot Noir Willamette Valley 1996: Light in texture, with pretty plum and spice flavors that remain delicate and pure through the slightly chewy finish. Drink soon. 1,960 cases made. • $18 • (05/15/98) • **86**

Pinot Noir Willamette Valley 1995: Has more ripeness and richness than most '95s, more layers than most, too, showing toasty black cherry and anise flavors that persist on the solid finish. Try now. 1,300 cases made. • $18 • (10/31/97) • **88**

Pinot Noir Willamette Valley Aliette 1996: Packs a lot of flavor into a racy, high-energy package, offering wild berry, cherry, anise and sassafras flavors that linger on the jazzy finish. Impressive now, but feels like it needs until 2000 to 2002 to settle down. 300 cases made. • $25 • (05/15/98) • **90**

Pinot Noir Willamette Valley Aliette 1995: Riper than most '95s, with a solid range of black cherry, floral and spice flavors that linger nicely on the firm finish. Ready to drink. 200 cases made. • $25 • (10/31/97) • **87**

Pinot Noir Willamette Valley Pierre Léon 1996: Strikes a lovely balance between ripe, pure black cherry and plum flavors and fine, chewy tannins, making for an approachable wine that could pick up more depth with cellaring. Best from 2000. 891 cases made. • $22 • (05/15/98) • **88**

Pinot Noir Willamette Valley Pierre Léon 1995: Has some interesting coffee and cola flavors threading through its supple berry flavors. Ready to drink. 1,400 cases made. • $21 • (10/31/97) • **86**

WILLAMETTE VALLEY VINEYARDS | OREGON

Blush Oregon Blossom 1996: Light and delicate, but it can't decide whether it wants to be fruity or austere and falls short either way. Drink now. 4,509 cases made. • $7 • (11/30/97) • **79**

Cabernet Sauvignon Oregon Founders' Reserve 1992 • $17 • (03/31/96) • **82**

Cabernet Sauvignon Oregon Karina's Vineyard OVB 1992: Soft and distinctly minty, with a spicy berry note that persists on the silky finish. Best from now or 2000. 210 cases made. • $27 • (12/31/96) • **85**

Cabernet Sauvignon Oregon OVB 1992 • $25 • (03/31/96) • **84**

Chardonnay Oregon 1996: A supple, spicy Chardonnay offering a nice range of melon, green apple and honey flavors, with a tinge of caramel on the smooth finish. A very nice price for all you get, from an Oregon winery to watch. Ready now. 9,788 cases made. • $10 • (05/15/98) BB • **87**

Chardonnay Oregon 1995: Crisp and light, it's a wine of delicacy, grace and pretty apple and caramel flavors that linger on the finish. 5,979 cases made. • $13 • (02/28/97) • **88**

Chardonnay Oregon 1994: Ripe, round, lightly spicy with oak surrounding the honeyed pineapple and pear flavors. Smooth and generous on the lengthy finish. Drinkable now. 2,839 cases made. • $12 • (12/15/95) • **87**

Chardonnay Oregon Estate Founders' Reserve 1996: Open textured, fresh and pure, with pretty pear and spice flavors lingering on the lively finish. Ready now. To be released September of this year. 378 cases made. • $22 • (05/15/98) • **86**

Chardonnay Oregon Founders' Reserve 1996: Soft, supple, harmonious and spicy, offering hazelnut-tinged pear and honey flavors that linger gently on the finish. To be released September of this year. 2,157 cases made. • $18 • (05/15/98) • **89**

Chardonnay Oregon Founders' Reserve 1995: Packs quite a bit of fresh pear, spice and citrus flavors into a tight package, wrapping its sweet character in a cloak of firm, toasty oak. Never tastes woody, but feels firm and a bit austere. Try now or give until 2001 to flesh out. 2,072 cases made. • $18 • (02/28/97) • **88**

Chardonnay Oregon Founders' Reserve 1994: Ripe and vivid in flavor, letting its peach, pear and nutty spice flavors swirl effectively on the lively finish. Nice now. 608 cases made. • $15 • (03/31/96) • **87**

Chardonnay Oregon Shea Vineyard OVB 1995: Fresh and carefully crafted, with citrus and spice flavors lingering on the nicely focused finish. Has style and grace, and it should fill out from now to 2000. 1,095 cases made. • $21 • (02/28/97) • **89**

Chardonnay Oregon Shea Vineyard OVB 1994: Smooth and spicy, striving for an elegant style that results in polished, subtle flavors that extend into a long, delicate finish. Drinkable now. 608 cases made. • $21 • (01/31/96) • **86**

Gewürztraminer Oregon 1996: Has spot-on rose petal and grapefruit aromas and flavors, plus a touch of berry and a roundness that smooths it all out on the bracing finish. Ready now. 1,344 cases made. • $8 • (11/15/97) • **87**

Gewürztraminer Oregon 1995: Soft, light and refreshing. This offers a nice touch of citrus flavor and finishes with a tart kick. 1,000 cases made. • $8 • (10/31/96) • **80**

Gewürztraminer Oregon 1993 • $8 • (11/30/94) • **79**

Merlot Oregon Whittaker Vineyards 1992 • $25 • (11/30/94) • **85**

Müller-Thurgau Oregon 1995: Soft and vaguely fruity, dishing up some melon and nectarine flavors. 1,990 cases made. • $7 • (11/30/96) • **83**

Pinot Gris Oregon 1996: Soft, generous and fragrant with melon, almond and apple flavors that linger gently on the finish. Appealing now. Drink soon. 7,200 cases made. • $13 • (11/15/97) • **87**

Pinot Gris Oregon 1994 • $13 • (03/31/96) • **83**

Pinot Noir Oregon 1995: Light and undistinguished, with modest wild berry and anise flavors. 10,100 cases made. • $13 • (02/28/97) • **79**

Pinot Noir Oregon 1994 • $12 • (01/31/96) • **84**

Pinot Noir Oregon 1993 • $12 • (03/31/96) • **86**

Pinot Noir Oregon 1992 • $12 • (11/30/94) • **79**

Pinot Noir Oregon 1991 • $15 • (01/31/94) • **83**

Pinot Noir Oregon Burger Vineyard Reserve 1991 • $25 • (10/15/94) • **88**

Pinot Noir Oregon Commemorative Release 1992 • $9 • (01/31/94) • **82**

Pinot Noir Oregon Founders' Reserve 1995: Light and charming, distinctive for the herbal notes weaving through the red berry and tobacco flavors. Finishes with a spicy edge. Drink now. 3,373 cases made. • $18 • (02/28/97) • **85**

Pinot Noir Oregon Founders' Reserve 1994 • $18 • (04/30/96) • **87**

Pinot Noir Oregon Founders' Reserve 1993 • $18 • (01/31/96) • **86**

Pinot Noir Oregon Founders' Reserve 1991 • $15 • (01/31/94) • **83**

Pinot Noir Oregon Founders' Reserve Nectar 1993 • $14 • (11/30/94) • **83**

Pinot Noir Oregon OVB 1994 • $30 • (04/30/96) • **90**

Pinot Noir Oregon OVB 1993 • $25 • (01/31/96) • **86**

Pinot Noir Oregon Whole Berry Fermented 1996: Light and fruity like a Beaujolais, this is a supple wine with nicely nuanced strawberry and watermelon notes on a modest scale. Drink soon. 8,800 cases made. • $13 • (10/31/97) • **84**

Pinot Noir Oregon Whole Berry Fermented 1994 • $12 • (03/31/96) • **85**

Pinot Noir Oregon Whole Berry Fermented 1993 • $12 • (11/30/94) • **83**

Pinot Noir Willamette Valley Founders' Reserve 1992 • $16 • (10/15/94) • **84**

Port Oregon Quinta Reserva Pinot Noir 1993 • $18 • (03/31/96) • **83**

Riesling Oregon 1996: Sweet tasting, but not a late-harvest style, it's nicely balanced with lemony acidity. Green apple and lightly floral aromas and flavors. Ready now. 18,000 cases made. • $8 • (11/15/97) • **84**

Riesling Oregon Dry 1996: Dry, crisp and vibrant for its tart grapefruit, apple and floral aromas and flavors that keep singing on the finish. Delicious now. 2,000 cases made. • $8 • (11/15/97) • **89**

Riesling Oregon Dry 1995: Soft and generous, this isn't really sweet but bright, with apple, peach and floral flavors that linger nicely on the off-dry finish. 2,400 cases made. • $8 • (10/31/96) • **85**

Riesling Oregon Dry 1994 • $8 • (03/31/96) • **85**

White Riesling Oregon 1994: Sweet but not rich in flavor; canned fruit flavors hold the reigns. 7,000 cases made. • $7 • (10/31/96) • **75**

WILLIAMS SELYEM | CALIFORNIA

Chardonnay Russian River Valley Allen Vineyard 1995: Pure and simple, a delicious Chardonnay. Rich in flavor and body, with a silky smooth texture and a bounty of spicy pear, apple, peach and hazelnut. Wood stays out of the way in this opulent young wine. Drink now to 2002. • $42 • (03/31/98) • **95**

Chardonnay Russian River Valley Allen Vineyard 1993 • $35 • (06/30/95) • **91**

Pinot Noir Anderson Valley Ferrington Vineyard 1995: Tight, young and tannic, with hints of floral, berry and dried cherry. Try now. • $40 • (10/31/97) • **90**

Pinot Noir Anderson Valley Ferrington Vineyard 1994: Ripe and juicy, brimming with black cherry, earth, mushroom and berry flavors. Tightly focused, dense and concentrated. Drink now through 2002. • $50 • (10/31/97) • **91**

Pinot Noir Anderson Valley Ferrington Vineyard 1993: Well focused, plush and concentrated, it's an impressive '93 for its color and depth of plum and cherry flavors. • $60 • (10/31/97) • **91**

Pinot Noir Anderson Valley Ferrington Vineyard 1992 • $65 • (12/15/94) • **92**

Pinot Noir Russian River Valley 1995: Ripe and flavorful, with layers of plum, cherry and wild berry; still tight, with enough tannin to merit cellaring. • $35 • (10/31/97) • **90**

Pinot Noir Russian River Valley 1994: Delivers plenty of ripe cherry, plum and berry flavors, turns smooth and elegant on the finish. Drinks well now. • $65 • (10/31/97) • **89**

Pinot Noir Russian River Valley 1993: Light and elegant, with a slight tea and herbal edge to the modest cherry flavors. • $60 • (10/31/97) • **85**

Pinot Noir Russian River Valley 1992: A touch coarse and tannic, but the core of plum and cherry is solid and complex. Worth holding. • $75 • (10/31/97) • **89**

Pinot Noir Russian River Valley 1991: Ripe, rich, smooth and supple; very complete, with lots of berry flavors and a silky texture, long on the finish. • $80 • (10/31/97) • **93**

Pinot Noir Russian River Valley 1990: Serves up lots of ripe, rich, concentrated black cherry, wild berry, plum and spice flavors. Deeply complex and concentrated, finishing with a minty note. • $85 • (10/31/97) • **91**

Pinot Noir Russian River Valley 1989: Ripe and complex, with a smoky, meaty flavor that adds to the cherry and wild berry character. Youthful, with plenty of flavor and depth. • $70 • (10/31/97) • **89**

Pinot Noir Russian River Valley 1988: Dark, ripe and intense, with a citrus accent to the racy blackberry flavors. Would benefit from additional aging. Tasted from magnum. • $75 • (10/31/97) • **90**

Pinot Noir Russian River Valley Allen Vineyard 1995: Quite seductive, with supple oak, cherry, wild berry and spicy nuances. Impressive for its delicacy and finesse. • $50 • (10/31/97) • **93**

Pinot Noir Russian River Valley Allen Vineyard 1994: Smooth and polished, supple and harmonious, nicely perfumed, with cherry and wild berry flavors that are young and vibrant. • $70 • (10/31/97) • **92**

Pinot Noir Russian River Valley Allen Vineyard 1993: Young and crisp but complete, with pretty cherry and strawberry notes. • $80 • (10/31/97) • **88**

Pinot Noir Russian River Valley Allen Vineyard 1992: Smooth, ripe, rich and polished, loaded with ripe plum and cherry-laced flavors. Still young and tight, impressive for its length. • $64 Ⓐ • (10/31/97) • **93**

Pinot Noir Russian River Valley Allen Vineyard 1991: A delicious wine. Minty, deep, rich and concentrated, with layers of plum and raspberry, a long, long finish. • $100 • (10/31/97) • **95**

Pinot Noir Russian River Valley Allen Vineyard 1990: Complex, with an herb and olive edge to its spicy cherry flavors, picking up a smoky orange and dried cherry nuance. • $115 • (10/31/97) • **90**

Pinot Noir Russian River Valley Allen Vineyard 1989: Complex with its mature, ripe, dried cherry and strawberry flavors. Turns elegant on the finish. • $100 • (10/31/97) • **89**

Pinot Noir Russian River Valley Allen Vineyard 1988: Ripe and forward, with juicy plum and cherry-laced Pinot Noir flavors. Long and lingering. • $125 • (10/31/97) • **91**

Pinot Noir Russian River Valley Allen Vineyard 1987: Smoky and tarry, with a strong anise and herbal edge to the ripe cherry flavors. Best now through 2000. • $130 • (10/31/97) • **90**

Pinot Noir Russian River Valley Cohn Vineyard 1993: Tight and focused, young and unevolved, with a core of spice and raspberry flavors. Best from now to 2000. • $50 • (10/31/97) • **88**

Pinot Noir Russian River Valley Olivet Lane 1995: Full-bodied, rich and complex, with lovely aromas and plum, cherry and oak flavors. An impressive Olivet Lane bottling. • $50 • (10/31/97) • **93**

Pinot Noir Russian River Valley Olivet Lane 1994: Lean for this vintage, with herb and tea accents to the lightly scented cherry and berry flavors. Ready. • $65 • (10/31/97) • **88**

Pinot Noir Russian River Valley Olivet Lane 1993: Austere, with firm tannins, crisp acidity and spicy cherry notes. Try now. • $75 • (10/31/97) • **88**

Pinot Noir Russian River Valley Olivet Lane 1992: Well focused, with a core of spicy cherry and berry flavors, finishing with crisp acidity. • $85 • (10/31/97) • **88**

Pinot Noir Russian River Valley Olivet Lane 1991: Juicy, with pretty, supple plum and black cherry flavors and a cola accent on the finish. Impressive for its texture and finesse. • $100 • (10/31/97) • **92**

Pinot Noir Russian River Valley Olivet Lane 1990: A higher-acidity style, lean and trim, with a tart band of spicy cherry flavor. • $110 • (10/31/97) • **87**

Pinot Noir Russian River Valley Olivet Lane 1989: Light in aromatics, but builds depth and complexity on the palate, where the ripe plum and cherry flavors fill in the gaps. • $100 • (10/31/97) • **89**

Pinot Noir Russian River Valley Olivet Lane Vineyard 1994: Appealing, with its ripe plum, cherry and wild berry flavors. Tannins kick in on the finish, with nice tea and herb notes. 1,100 cases made. • $88 Ⓐ • (07/31/96) • **90**

Pinot Noir Russian River Valley Olivet Lane Vineyard 1993 • $75 • (09/15/95) • **85**

Pinot Noir Russian River Valley Olivet Lane Vineyard 1992 • $85 • (12/15/94) • **89**

Pinot Noir Russian River Valley Olivet Lane Vineyard 1991 • $100 • (02/28/94) HR • **92**

Pinot Noir Russian River Valley Olivet Lane Vineyard 1990 • $110 • (09/30/92) • **84**

Pinot Noir Russian River Valley Olivet Lane Vineyard 1989 • $100 • (11/15/91) • **90**

Pinot Noir Russian River Valley Riverblock Vineyard 1995: Takes a while to develop, but once the core of cherry, berry and spice unfolds, it reveals more complexity and nuance, with hints of tea, cedar, anise and oak on the finish. Try now. • $36 • (12/31/97) • **90**

Pinot Noir Russian River Valley Riverblock Vineyard 1994: Dense and chewy, with a well-focused core of plum, cherry and wild berry. Drink now or cellar to 2001. • $50 • (10/31/97) • **91**

Pinot Noir Russian River Valley Rochioli Vineyard 1995: A wine of great subtlety and finesse, with slowly unfolding black cherry, berry, vanilla and spice. The texture is smooth and polished; the finish long and lingering. Most impressive is the finish, where the flavors fold together nicely. Drinks well now, but should only get better until 2003. • $65 • (12/31/97) • **94**

Pinot Noir Russian River Valley Rochioli Vineyard 1994: Deliciously complex, ripe, rich and vibrant, with a youthful core of plum, cherry and wild berry flavors. Drink now or cellar to 2002. • $60 • (10/31/97) • **93**

Pinot Noir Russian River Valley Rochioli Vineyard 1993 • $70 • (02/29/96) • **88**

Pinot Noir Russian River Valley Rochioli Vineyard 1993: Ripe and very complete, with plum, cherry and wild berry flavors. Like many '93s, it's somewhat unevolved. • $70 • (10/31/97) • **88**

Pinot Noir Russian River Valley Rochioli Vineyard 1992: Has it all. Combines richness with power, finesse, depth and concentration. Packs in lots of ripe, juicy plum, black cherry, spicy, toasty oak and finishes with a long, rich aftertaste. Drink now through 2004. • $80 • (10/31/97) • **97**

Pinot Noir Russian River Valley Rochioli Vineyard 1991: Shows tremendous complexity, with a pretty interplay of vanilla-tinged oak notes and lots of currant and black cherry flavors. Long finish. • $90 • (10/31/97) • **95**

Pinot Noir Russian River Valley Rochioli Vineyard 1990: Young, intense and firmly tannic, with a racy edge to the black cherry and wild berry flavors. Finishes with zingy acidity and fine length, but not a great 1990. • $100 • (10/31/97) • **89**

Pinot Noir Russian River Valley Rochioli Vineyard 1989: Rich, supple and polished, with lots of ripe plum and wild berry flavors and gentle, supple texture. • $100 • (10/31/97) • **92**

Pinot Noir Russian River Valley Rochioli Vineyard 1988: Delicious wine, ripe, smooth and juicy, with tiers of plum, black cherry, anise and spice. Amazingly elegant, complex and delicate. • $120 • (10/31/97) • **95**

Pinot Noir Russian River Valley Rochioli Vineyard 1987: Distinct for its spicy raspberry flavors and firm tannins, it's aging well with no signs of fatigue. • $135 • (10/31/97) • **88**

Pinot Noir Russian River Valley Rochioli Vineyard 1986: Deep in color and rich in flavor, this exhibits a bounty of cherry, currant and plum flavors that are complex and lively. Aging gracefully. • $140 • (03/31/97) • **92**

Pinot Noir Russian River Valley Rochioli Vineyard 1986: Corked this time, but in true form it's a classic, with a deep, rich, complex core of cherry, currant and plum flavors, turning silky. • $140 • (10/31/97) • **92**

Pinot Noir Russian River Valley Rochioli Vineyard 1985: Mature but holding, with a tarry, herb and earthy edge to the currant and plum flavors. Best now. • $145 • (10/31/97) • **90**

Key: SS—Spectator Selection CS—Cellar Selection HR—Highly Recommended BB—Best Buy $NA—Price not available Ⓐ—Auction Price (BT)—Barrel Tasting
Dates in parentheses indicate the issues in which the ratings were published.

Pinot Noir Sonoma Coast 1995: Tight and detailed, with a tart quality to the ripe plum and berry flavors. Shows off spicy, toasty oak; try now. • $40 • (10/31/97) • **88**

Pinot Noir Sonoma Coast 1994: Smooth and polished, with herb, smoky oak, cherry and berry flavors. Comes together nicely on the finish. • $66 Ⓐ • (10/31/97) • **89**

Pinot Noir Sonoma Coast 1993: Finely knit, supple in texture, with elegant, understated flavors that gently unfold. A most elegant and sophisticated wine. • $50 • (10/31/97) • **91**

Pinot Noir Sonoma Coast 1991: Smooth and harmonious, with pretty tea and sage accents to the spice and cherry flavors. • $60 • (10/31/97) • **90**

Pinot Noir Sonoma Coast 1990: Lean and trim, with herb, tart cherry, spice and anise notes. Best now through 2000. • $65 • (10/31/97) • **87**

Pinot Noir Sonoma Coast 1989: Marked by smoky, tarry notes, with ripe and tart cherry flavors that fill in nicely. • $70 • (10/31/97) • **87**

Pinot Noir Sonoma Coast 1988 • $75 • (05/31/90) • **92**

Pinot Noir Sonoma Coast Coastlands Vineyard 1995: Ripe, smooth and polished, with a silky texture and lots of pretty plum, black cherry, spice and berry flavors that glide across the palate. Finishes with a long, complex aftertaste that reveals tremendous concentration. Drinks well now, but can age into 2000. • $40 • (12/31/97) • **92**

Pinot Noir Sonoma Coast Coastlands Vineyard 1994: Smooth, rich and smoky, with a pretty toasty oak accent to the plum and cherry flavors. Turns elegant and spicy on the finish. • $45 • (10/31/97) • **92**

Pinot Noir Sonoma Coast Hirsch Vineyard 1995: Remarkably complex and flavorful. Rich, supple, concentrated, loaded with plum, cherry and wild berry flavors. Long, satisfying aftertaste. • $40 • (10/31/97) • **94**

Pinot Noir Sonoma Coast Hirsch Vineyard 1994: Offers lots of wild berry and cherry flavors, picks up an exotic toasty oak edge and finishes with a long, full aftertaste. Can stand cellaring. Best from now to 2002. • $45 • (10/31/97) • **92**

Pinot Noir Sonoma Coast Summa Vineyard 1993: Smells more attractive than it tastes, as the plum, cherry and berry notes are austere, adding a touch of tea and herb on the finish. An elegant style that's appealing already. • $50 • (10/31/97) • **85**

Pinot Noir Sonoma Coast Summa Vineyard 1991: Dark, ripe, rich and potent, with a distinctly spicy edge to the blackberry and black cherry flavors. Amazing depth and finesse. • $75 • (10/31/97) • **96**

Pinot Noir Sonoma Coast Summa Vineyard 1988: Lean, with a smoky orange-rind and tea-leaf edge to the barely ripe fruit flavors. • $100 • (10/31/97) • **86**

Pinot Noir Sonoma County 1994: Complete on its own terms, if lacking the depth and complexity of the best from this vintage. • $30 • (10/31/97) • **87**

Pinot Noir Sonoma County 1987 • $65 • (05/31/89) • **88**

Pinot Noir Sonoma County 1986: The mature Pinot Noir flavors exhibit an earthy dryness. Fading. • $70 • (10/31/97) • **82**

Pinot Noir Sonoma County 1985: A lighter style that has matured, with a spicy rhubarb accent that's elegant. • $75 • (10/31/97) • **87**

Pinot Noir Sonoma County 1984: Muddled and murky, with mature ripe fruit flavors of modest proportions. • $80 • (10/31/97) • **82**

Pinot Noir Sonoma County 1983: Stalky, with a green-bean edge to the barely ripe cherry and berry flavors. Lacks concentration; holds together but turning spicy. • $85 • (10/31/97) • **85**

Pinot Noir Sonoma County 1982: A touch waxy, with dried cherry, spice and earth notes, but finishes with a long aftertaste. A blend of Rochioli and Iron Horse vineyards. • $90 • (10/31/97) • **90**

Pinot Noir Sonoma County 1981: Fading, with a floral, wilted rose, strawberry character; finishing with a subtle, elegant aftertaste. Worth the taste of history. • $95 • (10/31/97) • **88**

Zinfandel Mendocino County 1994: Supple and elegant, not the big, ripe style of Zin that used to come from Dry Creek. Marked by cherry and berry flavors, it picks up a trace of tar and spice on the finish. Ready now. • $17 • (02/28/97) • **88**

Zinfandel Russian River Valley 1992 • $30 • (04/30/96) • **89**

Zinfandel Russian River Valley 1991 • $20 • (09/30/94) • **92**

Zinfandel Russian River Valley Leno Martinelli Vineyard 1985 • $10 • (07/31/88) • **79**

WILLIAMSBURG | VIRGINIA

Chardonnay Virginia Acte 12 of Sixteen Nineteen 1993: A flavorful but extreme Chardonnay that emphasizes nutty, oaky, earthy flavors over fruit. Heavy. 5,200 cases made. • $13 • (09/15/96) • **78**

Chardonnay Virginia John Adlum 1993: Rich and extroverted, but odd flavors. Has strong nut and butterscotch aromas and a thick texture, but only earthy, funky flavors. 4,900 cases made. • $10 • (09/15/96) • **76**

Chardonnay Virginia Reserve 1993: Thick, mature and overblown. Has buttery, oaky aromas and flavors but not much fruit. Drinkable, but simple. 650 cases made. • $16 • (09/15/96) • **79**

WILLOW CREEK | CALIFORNIA

Cabernet Sauvignon Napa & Alexander Valleys 1986 • $9 • (07/31/89) • **82**
Cabernet Sauvignon Napa Valley 1984 • $8 • (03/31/88) • **73**

WILRIDGE | WASHINGTON

Cabernet Sauvignon Columbia Valley Crawford Vineyard 1994: This odd combination of grapey and floral flavors is unusual for Cabernet. It's strange, but certainly drinkable. 200 cases made. • $19 • (09/15/96) • **80**
Cabernet Sauvignon Columbia Valley Crawford Vineyard 1991 • $19 • (09/30/94) • **86**
Cabernet Sauvignon Columbia Valley Klipsun Vineyard 1994: Youthful, exuberant fruit flavors in a raw texture. Showing as many floral and stalky notes as fruit flavors at this stage. Try now. 200 cases made. • $19 • (09/15/96) • **84**
Cabernet Sauvignon Columbia Valley Klipsun Vineyard 1993: Bright and flavorful, featuring zingy blackberry and herb notes; tannins closing down on the finish. Try now. 200 cases made. • $19 • (09/30/95) • **88**
Cabernet Sauvignon Columbia Valley Klipsun Vineyard 1992 • $19 • (09/30/95) • **87**
Cabernet Sauvignon Yakima Valley Crawford Vineyard 1995: Grapey, minty flavors dominate up front, turning earthy and chewy on the finish. Best from 2000. 200 cases made. • $19 • (09/30/97) • **83**
Cabernet Sauvignon Yakima Valley Klipsun Vineyard 1995: Intensely grapey, but also intensely gravel-like in flavor, with a strong minty edge to the ripe currant and black cherry flavors. Has lots of personality, not all of it immediately likeable. Try in 2000. 200 cases made. • $19 • (09/30/97) • **87**
Merlot Columbia Valley Crawford Vineyard 1994: Good texture and balance, but some wild, fruity flavors, reminiscent of Concord grapes, make this an odd duck. 200 cases made. • $19 • (09/15/96) • **81**
Merlot Columbia Valley Klipsun Vineyards 1994: Has a wild, floral, almost soapy flavor that obscures the otherwise pretty Merlot flavors. Seems off-kilter now, although it may improve by 2001 to 2003. 200 cases made. • $19 • (09/15/96) • **79**
Merlot Columbia Valley Klipsun Vineyards 1993 • $19 • (09/30/95) • **86**
Merlot Yakima Valley Crawford Vineyard 1995: Grapey, herbal flavors dominate this open-textured, appealingly generous wine. Ready now. 200 cases made. • $19 • (09/30/97) • **85**
Merlot Yakima Valley Klipsun Vineyards 1995: Crisp in texture but exotic in flavor, with an array of spice notes to season the focused blackberry flavors. It's all packed in there, waiting for time to smooth it out. Try soon. 200 cases made. • $19 • (09/30/97) • **87**

WILSON DANIELS | CALIFORNIA

Chardonnay Napa Valley 1993 • $10 • (05/15/96) • **87**
Pinot Noir Carneros 1995: Solid if unexciting, with a modest core of cherry, wild berry, earth and spice, turning simple on the finish. • $18 • (02/28/98) • **84**

WINDEMERE | CALIFORNIA

Cabernet Sauvignon Napa Valley 1991 • $16 • (03/31/96) • **82**
Cabernet Sauvignon Napa Valley 1989 • $16 • (08/31/92) • **83**
Cabernet Sauvignon Napa Valley Diamond Mountain 1990 • $14 • (08/31/93) • **88**
Chardonnay Edna Valley Mac Gregor Vineyard 1996: Zingy acidity and bright lemon flavors give this wine pucker-power. A bit meaty and earthy, it finishes with a touch of honey. Struggles for balance. Drink now. 1,200 cases made. • $18 • (07/31/98) • **81**
Zinfandel Paso Robles Benito Dusi Vineyard 1993 • $15 • (03/31/96) • **86**

WINDSOR | CALIFORNIA

Cabernet Sauvignon Russian River Valley River West Vineyard 1987 • $20 • (11/15/92) • **87**
Cabernet Sauvignon Sonoma County Signature Series 1988 • $26 • (11/15/92) • **83**
Chardonnay Russian River Valley Signature Series 1996: A toasty introduction leads to layers of hazelnut, pear, apple and spice, with a clean, moderate finish. Drink now. • $16 • (06/30/98) • **87**
Merlot Russian River Valley Signature Series 1987 • $25 • (05/31/92) • **84**
Pinot Noir California Signature Series 1993 • $15 • (12/31/95) • **82**
Pinot Noir Russian River Valley Winemaster's Private Reserve 1985 • $8 • (06/15/88) • **83**
Pinot Noir Sonoma County Private Reserve 1993 • $14 • (12/31/95) • **84**
Zinfandel Alexander Valley Signature Series 1995: Supported by an oaky frame, the cherry notes can't keep up with the vanilla and charry wood flavors. Finishes with grainy tannins. Drink now through 2000. • $15 • (06/15/98) • **81**

WINDWALKER | CALIFORNIA

Cabernet Sauvignon El Dorado 1994: Some cassis and blackberry flavors struggle to surface from behind a wall of green astringency. 410 cases made. • $11 • (04/30/98) • **79**
Chardonnay El Dorado 1996: Offers citrus and heavy-handed butterscotch flavors of pleasant focus, but finishes abruptly. The finish shows some spice. 910 cases made. • $11 • (07/31/98) • **80**
Sauvignon Blanc El Dorado 1997: An unusual licorice-and-lemon streak courses through this tangy wine. It's firm and bright. 1,000 cases made. • $8 • (05/15/98) • **83**
Sauvignon Blanc El Dorado 1996: A pleasant lemon, lime and mineral core runs through. Definitely a lightweight, however. 820 cases made. • $8 • (03/31/98) • **82**

WINDWARD | CALIFORNIA

Pinot Noir Paso Robles 1994: Pleasant enough, with bright strawberry and cherry flavors, streaks of mint and herb. Well balanced, and ready to drink. 1,500 cases made. • $19 • (08/31/97) • **85**
Pinot Noir Paso Robles Monopole 1995: Pleasantly fruity and rather uncomplicated, with ripe plum and berry flavors of moderate depth and concentration. Ready now. 1,150 cases made. • $25 • (02/28/98) • **83**

WINEGLASS CELLARS | WASHINGTON

Cabernet Sauvignon Yakima Valley Elerding Vineyard 1994: Beneath its fine texture and chewy tannins lurks a taut layer of blackberry and spice flavors struggling to get free. Give it until 2000. 105 cases made. • $28 • (11/30/97) • **85**
Merlot Yakima Valley 1995: Focused and bright, this crisp wine sports jazzy berry and herb flavors that finish with wisps of tea and earth. Drinkable now. 230 cases made. • $16 • (11/30/97) • **86**
Merlot Yakima Valley 1994: Deep color and dense flavors, not all of them pretty, with burnt, earthy notes intruding upon the berry flavors. Try soon to see how it's resolving. 116 cases made. • $16 • (09/15/96) • **83**
Merlot Yakima Valley Reserve 1994: Crisp in texture, offering pretty berry and tobacco flavors that remain zingy on the sturdy finish. Try now. 50 cases made. • $25 • (09/15/97) • **84**
Pinot Noir Oregon 1994 • $21 • (05/15/96) • **91**

WINTERBROOK | CALIFORNIA

Cabernet Sauvignon Napa County 1991 • $8 • (05/15/94) • **81**
Cabernet Sauvignon Napa County 1990 • $9 • (08/31/92) • **81**
Cabernet Sauvignon Napa Valley Grand Reserve 1991 • $18 • (01/31/95) • **84**
Cabernet Sauvignon Napa Valley Grand Reserve 1990 • $19 • (09/15/93) • **85**
Merlot Sonoma County Reserve 1991: Earthy, funky, cedary flavors that need more fruit. Finishes with a strange, meaty taste that's not very pleasant. 900 cases made. • $12 • (08/31/96) • **70**

WITNESS TREE | OREGON

Chardonnay Willamette Valley 1994: Deep, rich and smoky, spreading its spicy pear flavor nicely while keeping a crisp, juicy underpinning. Delicious now. 1,028 cases made. • $13 • (06/30/96) • **88**
Chardonnay Willamette Valley 1993 • $14 • (11/15/95) • **85**
Chardonnay Willamette Valley Vintage Select 1994: Rich, supple and complex, a lovely mouthful of apple, pear, hazelnut and spice flavors that keep swirling throughout the finish. Delicious now. 144 cases made. • $20 • (06/30/96) • **92**
Chardonnay Willamette Valley Vintage Select 1993 • $22 • (03/31/96) • **71**
Pinot Noir Oregon 1989 • $14 • (02/28/93) • **82**

Pinot Noir Willamette Valley 1995: Light in texture, with a rough edge of tannin to the modest berry and tobacco flavors. Try now or 2000. 2,000 cases made. • $17 • (05/15/98) • **83**
Pinot Noir Willamette Valley 1994: Light-textured, with bright blackberry, vanilla and cherry flavors to balance the fine tannins. Tasty now. 1,277 cases made. • $16 • (07/31/96) • **85**
Pinot Noir Willamette Valley 1992 • $13 • (03/15/94) • **83**
Pinot Noir Willamette Valley Vintage Select 1994 • $30 • (06/30/96) • **87**
Pinot Noir Willamette Valley Vintage Select 1993 • $25 • (10/31/95) • **88**

WOLFE, THURSTON | WASHINGTON

Black Muscat Washington 1992 • $9 • (09/30/94) • **85**
Black Muscat Washington 1987 • $9 • (10/15/89) • **85**
Grenache Columbia Valley 1994: Light, smooth and fruity. Like a chewy Beaujolais with its appealing berry, spice and coffee flavors. Ready to drink. 280 cases made. • $10 • (09/30/96) • **84**
Lemberger Columbia Valley 1992 • $10 • (09/30/94) • **77**
Lemberger Columbia Valley RW Reserve 1994: Firm, focused and chewy with black cherry and anise flavors at the fore. Drink now. 168 cases made. • $10 • (09/30/96) • **85**
Port Columbia Valley JTW's 1992 • $17 • (09/30/95) • **85**
Port Columbia Valley Late Bottled 1988 • $9 • 500 ml (09/30/95) • **89**
Port Washington JTW's Port 1991 • $10 • (06/15/95) • **87**
Sauvignon Blanc Late Harvest Washington Sweet Rebecca 1987 • $9 • (10/15/89) • **83**
Sweet Rebecca Late Harvest Yakima Valley 1992 • $10 • (09/30/94) • **85**
Zinfandel Columbia Valley 1992 • $12 • (09/30/94) • **85**
Zinfandel Port Columbia Valley Burgess Vineyard 1992 • $20 • (09/30/95) • **87**

WOLLERSHEIM | WISCONSIN

Domaine du Sac Dry Red Wine Wisconsin 1990 • $8 • (02/29/92) • **81**
Domaine Reserve Wisconsin 1989 • $12 • (02/29/92) • **73**
Pinot Noir Wisconsin Sugarloaf Hill 1989 • $NA • (02/29/92) • **75**

WOODBRIDGE | CALIFORNIA

Cabernet Sauvignon California 1994: Marked by vegetal notes, with hints of turnip and asparagus, you finally find enough dark cherry and berry flavors to hold your interest. • $8 • (05/31/97) • **83**
Cabernet Sauvignon California Barrel Aged 1992 • $6 • (12/15/95) • **83**
Cabernet Sauvignon California Lot No. 295 1995: On the tart side, with a chewy layer of tannin over the modest strawberry and currant flavors. Best now. • $8 • (11/15/97) • **79**
Cabernet Sauvignon California Twin Oaks 1995: Smooth, silky texture frames a wine that doesn't quite meet the same flavor standard. Some blackberry and mint, but the ensemble leans more toward coffee and stems. Drink now. 15,000 cases made. • $9 • (06/30/98) • **80**
Chardonnay California 1995: A blend of lemon-lime and mineral flavors. Finishes on a bitter note. • $8 • (07/31/97) • **83**
Chardonnay California Barrel Aged 1993 • $6 • (07/31/95) • **81**
Chardonnay Monterey County Lot No. 196 1996: Tropical notes; melon and citrus lead the way. The texture remains thin, however, and the finish is a bit short. • $8 • (03/31/98) • **81**
Port Lodi Portocinco Limited Edition 1992: Ripe, sweet and complex, with layers of prune, black cherry and plum flavors that stand up straight with a backbone of firm tannins and acidity. Tempting now, but should improve for decades. Only available in restaurants. 1,000 cases made. • $15 • (04/30/97) • **91**
Sauvignon Blanc California 1995: A pleasant-enough wine, with a floral edge and some nice, melonlike flavors. A bit hollow on the midpalate. • $6 • (07/31/97) • **83**
Sauvignon Blanc California Barrel Aged 1993 • $5 • (06/30/95) BB • **85**
Sauvignon Blanc California Lot No. 396 1996: A mildly herbal, grassy style, finishing with hints of lime and grapefruit. A lighter-bodied wine; quite refreshing. • $7 • (03/31/98) • **84**
White Zinfandel California 1996: If you like drinking cherry candy, this wine is for you. • $5 • (09/15/97) • **76**

Key: SS—Spectator Selection CS—Cellar Selection HR—Highly Recommended BB—Best Buy $NA—Price not available Ⓐ—Auction Price (BT)—Barrel Tasting
Dates in parentheses indicate the issues in which the ratings were published.

Zinfandel California 1996: Ordinary, with tart strawberry flavors and a tannic edge. Tasted twice, with consistent notes. Drink now. • $NA • (06/16/98) • **74**
Zinfandel California 1995: A pleasant blend of plum, cherry and herb notes couched in a somewhat silky texture. Won't knock your socks off, but won't disappoint, either, and you can't beat the price. • $6 • (07/31/97) • **85**
Zinfandel California Barrel Aged 1993 • $5 • (08/31/95) • **82**
Zinfandel California Lot No. 496 1996: Fairly vegetal, with a slightly sour quality. • $7 • (03/31/98) • **79**

WOODBURY | NEW YORK

Brut Blanc de Blancs New York 1987 • $12 • (12/31/90) • **82**
Port Alexander Valley Old Vines 1981 • $10 • (01/01/86) • **91**

WOODSIDE | CALIFORNIA

Cabernet Sauvignon Santa Cruz Mountains 1990 • $24 • (11/15/93) • **75**
Chardonnay Santa Cruz Mountains 1996: Awkward, with a bitterness to the simple apple and butter flavors. Drink now. 374 cases made. • $17 • (07/31/98) • **78**
Chardonnay Santa Cruz Mountains Estate Reserve 1996: Simple and pleasant, with hints of apple, citrus and toasty oak. Drink now. 120 cases made. • $21 • (07/31/98) • **81**
Zinfandel Santa Cruz Mountains Vineyard Hill Vineyards 1991 • $14 • (10/15/94) • **77**

WOODWARD CANYON | WASHINGTON

Cabernet Sauvignon Columbia Valley 1994: Dense, dark, chewy and delicious, overflowing with ripe berry, vanilla, floral and herbal flavors that meander for a long finish. A serious wine with distinctive character, it needs cellaring until 2001 to 2003 to settle down. 2,691 cases made. • $34 • (07/31/97) • **92**
Cabernet Sauvignon Columbia Valley 1991 • $29 • (07/31/94) HR • **93**
Cabernet Sauvignon Columbia Valley 1989 • $27 • (05/15/92) HR • **92**
Cabernet Sauvignon Columbia Valley 1988 • $24 • (04/15/92) • **93**
Cabernet Sauvignon Columbia Valley 1987 • $35 • (04/15/92) • **95**
Cabernet Sauvignon Columbia Valley 1986 • $35 • (04/15/92) • **87**
Cabernet Sauvignon Columbia Valley 1985 • $30 • (04/15/92) • **86**
Cabernet Sauvignon Columbia Valley 1984 • $27 • (04/15/92) • **81**
Cabernet Sauvignon Columbia Valley 1983 • $30 • (04/15/92) • **88**
Cabernet Sauvignon Columbia Valley 1982 • $28 • (04/15/92) • **83**
Cabernet Sauvignon Columbia Valley 1981 • $30 • (04/15/92) • **85**
Cabernet Sauvignon Columbia Valley Dedication Series #10 1990 • $27 • (07/31/93) HR • **91**
Cabernet Sauvignon Columbia Valley Dedication Series #12 1992 • $27 • (08/31/95) CS • **90**
Cabernet Sauvignon Columbia Valley Dedication Series #13 1993: On the crisp side, but nicely packed with spicy plum and coffee flavors. Remains lean and balanced toward spicy oak on the finish. Should be best now. 2,447 cases made. • $30 • (06/15/96) • **88**
Cabernet Sauvignon Washington Canoe Ridge Vineyard 1992 • $20 • (05/31/95) • **90**
Cabernet Sauvignon Washington Canoe Ridge Vineyard Artist Series #2 1993: Smooth and inviting for its spicy currant and black cherry flavors that jump right up and show from the first sip, then remain lively through the supple finish. 297 cases made. • $25 • (06/15/96) • **90**
Charbonneau Walla Walla County 1994: Lithe, with generous ripe blackberry, plum and tobacco flavors, and a swirl of exotic orange blossom and spice notes on the lingering finish. Ripe, sweet and focused. Drinkable now. A blend of 68 percent Cabernet Sauvignon and 32 percent Merlot. 291 cases made. • $38 • (07/31/97) • **90**
Charbonneau Walla Walla County 1989 • $30 • (05/15/92) • **88**
Charbonneau Walla Walla County 1988 • $NA • (04/15/92) • **95**
Charbonneau Walla Walla County 1987 • $30 • (12/31/90) • **89**
Charbonneau Walla Walla County 1985 • $30 • (04/15/92) • **86**
Chardonnay Columbia Valley 1994: Bright and flavorful, a little astringent around the edges but shining, with pear, apple and vanilla flavors. Drink now. 2,000 cases made. • $23 • (03/31/96) • **88**
Chardonnay Columbia Valley 1993 • $23 • (01/31/95) SS • **90**
Chardonnay Walla Walla Valley 1995: A ripe, rich and silky-smooth Washington Chard, layered with distinctively spicy, honey-scented pear, apricot and citrus flavors that linger enticingly on the harmonious finish. Tempting now, even better through 2000. 2,200 cases made. • $25 • (09/15/97) HR • **92**

Chardonnay Washington Celilo Vineyard 1995: Juicy nectarine and fresh prune flavors slide across a lean, lively frame. Packs a lot of character into its compact structure, and finishes with notes of spice and toast. Ready to drink. 415 cases made. • $30 • (07/31/97) • **90**

Chardonnay Washington Celilo Vineyard 1994: Bright, flavorful and elegant, weaving some lovely nutmeg and pepper flavors through the silky pear and vanilla core. Echoes the flavors on the long finish, too. 240 cases made. • $30 • (06/15/96) • **91**

Chardonnay Washington Reserve 1994: Ripe, focused and elegant, swirling its pear, spice and honey flavors in a finish that fans out appealingly. Drinkable now. 642 cases made. • $28 • (03/31/96) • **91**

Chardonnay Washington Reserve 1993 • $28 • (01/31/95) HR • **91**

Merlot Columbia Valley 1995: A crisp style, but with enough juicy prune, tobacco and exotic spice flavors swirling through it to make it appealing. Ready now. 1,467 cases made. • $30 • (09/30/97) • **88**

Merlot Columbia Valley 1994 • $27 • (06/15/96) HR • **91**

Merlot Columbia Valley 1993 • $23 • (09/30/95) • **89**

Merlot Columbia Valley 1992 • $21 • (09/30/94) • **86**

Merlot Columbia Valley 1991 • $22 • (11/15/93) • **84**

Red Columbia Valley NV: Aims for elegance and achieves a lithe balance of spicy tobacco notes and sweet berry flavor that holds through the fine-grained tannins on the finish. Best from now to 2000. A blend of 80 percent Merlot and 20 percent Cabernet Sauvignon. 1,236 cases made. • $14 • (07/31/97) • **88**

White Riesling Walla Walla County 1995: Sweet, with flavors that seem more decadent and sour than fresh. Simple finish. Tasted twice, with consistent notes. • $8 • (09/15/97) • **80**

WORDEN | WASHINGTON

Cabernet-Merlot Washington 1993: Harmony and elegance on a lean frame, with its spicy berry flavors swirling around on the finish. Best now. 827 cases made. • $15 • (09/15/96) • **85**

Cabernet-Merlot Washington 1992 • $12 • (09/30/95) • **84**

Cabernet-Merlot Washington 1991 • $12 • (08/31/94) • **83**

Cabernet-Merlot Washington 1990 • $10 • (07/31/92) • **73**

Cabernet-Merlot Washington 1989 • $10 • (02/29/92) • **86**

Cabernet-Merlot Washington Cascade Collection 1994: A satiny, expansive wine, generous with its nutmeg-scented, ripe blackberry, currant, anise and cedar flavors, and beautifully focused to show them off. Long and harmonious, it should be best from now. A blend of 63 percent Cabernet Sauvignon and 37 percent Merlot. 808 cases made. • $15 • (09/15/97) • **90**

Chenin Blanc Washington 1993 • $7 • (09/30/94) • **86**

Chenin Blanc Washington Cascade Collection 1995: On the sweet side, with leafy apple and honey flavors that fade on the light finish. 378 cases made. • $7 • (09/30/96) • **81**

Claret Washington 1994: Has the light, fruity aromas and flavors of Lemberger up front, fading a bit on the finish. 804 cases made. • $10 • (09/15/96) • **81**

Claret Washington 1993 • $8 • (09/30/95) • **79**

Claret Washington 1992 • $9 • (09/30/94) • **87**

Gewüztraminer Late Harvest Washington 1992 • $7 • (09/30/94) • **83**

Gewürztraminer Washington 1995: A lovely mouthful of effusive fruit, offering litchi, pear and a touch of rose petal through the dry, full-bodied finish. Drink soon. 248 cases made. • $7 • (09/15/97) • **86**

Johannisberg Riesling Washington 1993 • $6 • (09/30/95) • **73**

Johannisberg Riesling Washington Cascade Collection 1995: Bright and vibrant, offering a generous mouthful of peach, apple and spicy floral flavors that linger on the off-dry finish. 201 cases made. • $7 • (09/30/96) • **87**

Merlot Washington 1993 • $8 • (09/30/95) • **81**

Merlot Washington 1992 • $12 • (05/15/94) • **76**

WRIGHT, KEN | OREGON

Chardonnay Washington Celilo Vineyard 1994: A smooth, polished, spicy wine with earthy, toasty, nutty flavors dominating moderate fruit. Try now. 550 cases made. • $18 • (08/31/96) • **81**

Pinot Noir Willamette Valley 1995: Lean and a bit rough, but pleasantly aromatic, with plum and spice flavors that linger gently on the finish. Pretty, but one might wish for more intensity. Best now. 1,500 cases made. • $21 • (11/30/97) • **86**

Pinot Noir Willamette Valley 1994: Satiny smooth, ripe and supple, packed with black cherry, blackberry and earthy notes that take on hints of thyme and floral flavors. The finish lingers enticingly. Try now. 2,100 cases made. • $21 • (08/31/96) SS • **90**

Pinot Noir Willamette Valley Abbey Heights 1994: One for the cellar. It's firm and chewy, with a strong current of berry and spice flavors fighting through the fine tannins. Try now. 125 cases made. • $28 • (08/31/96) • **90**

Pinot Noir Willamette Valley Abbey Heights Whistling Ridge 1994: Disarming for its delicious fruit, centering around plum and anise, with a touch of tar on the chewy finish. Should develop into an opulent wine from now to 2000. 50 cases made. • $28 • (08/31/96) • **92**

Pinot Noir Willamette Valley Canary Hill Vineyard 1995: Crisp and appealing for its bright plum and cherry flavors, it's jazzy and harmonious but not especially deep. Drink now. 250 cases made. • $28 • (11/30/97) • **86**

Pinot Noir Willamette Valley Canary Hill Vineyard 1994: Firm in texture, with just enough berry and plum flavor to show promise. Drinkable now. 200 cases made. • $28 • (08/31/96) • **84**

Pinot Noir Willamette Valley Carter Vineyard 1995: Light and unimposing, it's a gentle wine with modest plum and spice flavors and an evanescent finish. Drink now. 250 cases made. • $28 • (11/30/97) • **85**

Pinot Noir Willamette Valley Carter Vineyard 1994: Silky smooth, polished and elegant, balancing its blackberry, blueberry and currant flavors against a spicy note. Delicious now. 200 cases made. • $28 • (08/31/96) • **91**

Pinot Noir Willamette Valley Freedom Hill Vineyard 1995: Has more silkiness and richness of flavor than most '95s, with pretty blackberry and raspberry flavors lingering on the sharp finish. Drinkable now. 50 cases made. • $28 • (11/30/97) • **88**

Pinot Noir Willamette Valley Guadalupe Vineyard 1995: Firm in texture, with a jazzy core of blackberry and cherry flavors plus some nice hints of tobacco and spice. Try it now. 180 cases made. • $28 • (11/30/97) • **87**

Pinot Noir Willamette Valley Shea Vineyard 1995: Light and fragrant, this is a gentle wine with a bit more intensity than most '95s, focusing its berry and plum flavors that linger with hints of spice and tobacco on the harmonious finish. Drinkable now. 200 cases made. • $28 • (11/30/97) • **88**

Pinot Noir Willamette Valley Shea Vineyard 1994: A solidly built, chunky red. Try it now. 125 cases made. • $28 • (08/31/96) • **90**

YAKIMA RIVER | WASHINGTON

Cabernet Sauvignon Columbia Valley 1992: Ripe, round and earthy, with decadent mineral, black cherry and leather flavors that linger on a long finish. Not for all palates; a serious wine. Drinkable now. 1,200 cases made. • $14 • (07/31/96) • **87**

Cabernet Sauvignon Columbia Valley 1988 • $15 • (03/31/92) • **74**

Cabernet Sauvignon Yakima Valley 1993: Leans a bit heavily on exotic, spicy elements from aging in oak, coupled with a slightly sour streak, and finishes smooth. 1,308 cases made. • $15 • (07/31/97) • **81**

Cabernet Sauvignon Yakima Valley 1991 • $13 • (03/31/96) • **79**

Cabernet Sauvignon Yakima Valley 1990 • $15 • (04/15/95) • **84**

Cabernet Sauvignon Yakima Valley Winemaker's Reserve 1989 • $25 • (09/30/94) • **83**

Chenin Blanc Yakima Valley 1995: Light, soft, and semisweet. Flavors are simple and nondistinctive. 360 cases made. • $6 • (08/31/96) • **79**

Fumé Blanc Yakima Valley Dry 1993 • $9 • (09/30/94) • **71**

Johannisberg Riesling Yakima Valley 1995: Fresh apple and peach flavors are soft and appealing. 1,200 cases made. • $6 • (08/31/96) • **84**

Lemberger Sof/Lem Yakima Valley 1995: A simple and dryish rosé. Appealing raspberry and rhubarb flavors linger on the finish. 1,000 cases made. • $8 • (08/31/96) • **82**

Lemberger Yakima Valley Rendezvous 1996: Peppery berry flavors pump their way through this supple, high-energy red, finishing with a nice sense of balance. 812 cases made. • $10 • (07/31/97) • **84**

Lemberger Yakima Valley Rendezvous 1995: Earthy, stalky flavors crash detrimentally through an otherwise exuberantly fruity wine. 650 cases made. • $10 • (07/31/96) • **73**

Lemberger Yakima Valley Rendezvous 1989 • $7 • (03/31/92) • **81**

Merlot Columbia Valley 1988 • $15 • (04/15/92) • **83**

Merlot Yakima Valley 1993: Strongly herbal, with flavors more from a pickle barrel than a fruit basket. Not for all tastes, but it holds together within its style. 2,315 cases made. • $15 • (07/31/97) • **81**

Merlot Yakima Valley 1992 • $12 • (05/15/96) • **86**

Merlot Yakima Valley 1991 • $15 • (06/15/95) • **88**

Merlot Yakima Valley 1990 • $15 • (09/30/94) • **85**

Port Yakima Valley Johns Vintage Port 1994: Harmonious, nicely balanced to show off its tobacco-scented plum and black cherry flavors, yet there's enough tannin and alcohol for grip. Approachable now, best from 2001 to 2004. Made from Merlot. 645 cases made. • $17 • (09/15/97) • **87**

Port Yakima Valley Johns Vintage Port 1992 • $16 • (06/15/95) • **82**

White Riesling Late Harvest Yakima Valley Late Harvest 1996: Sweet but blowsy, with a metallic edge to the flavors. 565 cases made. • $10 • (09/15/97) • **78**

YAMHILL VALLEY | OREGON

Pinot Blanc Oregon 1996: A solid, refreshing wine, brimming with citrusy peach and apple flavors that linger gently on the smooth, open-textured finish. Ready now. 45 cases made. • $17 • (11/15/97) • **87**
Pinot Gris Willamette Valley 1993 • $10 • (11/30/94) • **80**
Pinot Noir Oregon 1985 • $16 • (06/15/87) • **86**
Pinot Noir Oregon 1983 • $17 • (08/31/86) • **92**
Pinot Noir Willamette Valley 1995: Light in texture, with exuberant berry, cinnamon and vanilla flavors. Try now. 1,000 cases made. • $17 • (02/28/97) • **85**
Pinot Noir Willamette Valley 1992 • $11 • (11/30/94) • **83**
Pinot Noir Willamette Valley 1988 • $12 • (01/31/91) • **76**
Pinot Noir Willamette Valley 1983 • $35 • (02/15/90) • **87**
Pinot Noir Willamette Valley Reserve 1994: Offers rich, ripe berry and spice flavors, but it also has a hard, tannic veneer that needs until 2000 to soften. Pretty chocolate and prune notes mark the finish. 1,000 cases made. • $35 • (11/15/97) • **86**
Pinot Noir Willamette Valley Reserve 1991 • $22 • (11/30/94) • **82**
Pinot Noir Willamette Valley Reserve 1988 • $18 • (11/15/91) • **78**

YORK MOUNTAIN | CALIFORNIA

Cabernet Sauvignon San Luis Obispo County 1990 • $14 • (12/15/95) • **85**
Cabernet Sauvignon San Luis Obispo County 1989 • $14 • (11/15/94) • **71**
Cabernet Sauvignon San Luis Obispo County 1988 • $12 • (11/15/92) • **83**
Cabernet Sauvignon San Luis Obispo County 1987 • $12 • (11/15/92) • **84**
Cabernet Sauvignon San Luis Obispo County 1986 • $14 • (11/15/92) • **84**
Cabernet Sauvignon San Luis Obispo County 1985 • $15 • (12/15/89) • **83**
Cabernet Sauvignon San Luis Obispo County Carver Vineyard 1993: Leads off with smoky, charry notes followed by tar, leather and blackberry flavors. Tannic, bitter finish. 550 cases made. • $18 • (05/15/98) • **77**
Cabernet Sauvignon San Luis Obispo County Reserve 1990 • $16 • (12/15/95) • **82**
Chardonnay San Luis Obispo County 1996: Odd, with heavy mineral notes and traces of citrus and herb. Drink now. 555 cases made. • $14 • (07/31/98) • **78**
Chardonnay San Luis Obispo County 1995: Has a green edge, with a bitter, resinous note intruding on the modest apple flavors. 1,050 cases made. • $12 • (07/31/97) • **79**
Chardonnay San Luis Obispo County 1994: Crisp and brightly fruity, with a zippy mouthful of apple and spice flavors. 900 cases made. • $12 • (06/30/96) • **85**
Chardonnay San Luis Obispo County 1993 • $12 • (07/31/95) • **84**
Merlot San Luis Obispo County 1993: Bizarre, with an unattractive prune and vinegary flavor. Hard to warm up to. 350 cases made. • $12 • (08/31/96) • **70**
Merlot San Luis Obispo County 1991 • $12 • (09/15/94) • **79**
Merlot San Luis Obispo County 1990 • $12 • (09/15/94) • **77**
Merlot San Luis Obispo County 1989 • $13 • (05/31/92) • **84**
Merlot San Luis Obispo County 1986 • $10 • (12/15/89) • **80**
Pinot Noir Central Coast 1986 • $6 • (06/15/88) • **81**
Pinot Noir San Luis Obispo County 1993: Earthy, with dry tannins and a slight green herb edge to the modest cherry flavors. 950 cases made. • $14 • (02/28/97) • **81**
Pinot Noir San Luis Obispo County 1992 • $10 • (12/31/95) • **78**
Pinot Noir San Luis Obispo County 1991 • $10 • (12/31/95) • **73**
Pinot Noir San Luis Obispo County 1990 • $10 • (03/31/95) • **82**
Pinot Noir San Luis Obispo County 1989 • $9 • (02/28/93) • **76**
Pinot Noir San Luis Obispo County 1985 • $9 • (06/15/88) • **80**
Pinot Noir San Luis Obispo County William Cain Vineyard 1994: A bit on the light side, with a tart cherry core. The follow-up features smoke, leather and herbs. 595 cases made. • $14 • (05/15/98) • **82**
Zinfandel San Luis Obispo County 1991 • $9 • (10/15/95) • **83**
Zinfandel San Luis Obispo County 1990 • $9 • (06/15/94) • **82**
Zinfandel San Luis Obispo County 1989 • $7 • (09/30/93) • **78**

Key: SS—Spectator Selection CS—Cellar Selection HR—Highly Recommended BB—Best Buy $NA—Price not available Ⓐ—Auction Price (BT)—Barrel Tasting
Dates in parentheses indicate the issues in which the ratings were published.

Zinfandel San Luis Obispo County 1988 • $9 • (10/15/92) • **74**
Zinfandel San Luis Obispo County 1986 • $8 • (12/15/89) • **85**

YORKVILLE | CALIFORNIA

Cabernet Franc Mendocino 1994: Smoke, cedar and chocolate notes blend harmoniously, followed by nuances of cherry and herbs. The finish is somewhat bitter, though—shut down by coarse tannins. 800 cases made. • $13 • (09/15/97) • **84**
Chardonnay Anderson Valley 1993 • $10 • (07/31/95) • **81**
Sauvignon Blanc Mendocino Randle Hill Vineyard 1995: Fresh, crisp and lively, with an elegant band of citrus, particularly grapefruit, and fig flavors. Finishes with a complex earthiness and good length. Brand new winery. • $10 • (02/28/97) • **87**
Sauvignon Blanc Mendocino Randle Hill Vineyard 1994 • $8 • (05/31/96) • **77**
Sauvignon Blanc Mendocino Randle Hill Vineyard 1993 • $8 • (08/31/95) • **80**
Sémillon Mendocino 1993 • $9 • (08/31/95) • **83**
Sémillon Mendocino Randle Hill Vineyard 1995: Earthy, with dashes of fig and citrus. This is a compact, tightly wound young wine that will benefit from short-term cellaring, but try now. • $11 • (02/28/97) • **87**
Sémillon-Sauvignon Blanc Mendocino 1995: Shows a stronger oak profile than the other Yorkville Winery whites and is more ponderous, as the fig and citrus flavors are dominated by this oaky presence. • $16 • (02/28/97) • **84**
Sémillon-Sauvignon Blanc Mendocino Eleanor of Aquitaine 1995: Finely focused spicy pear and nectarine flavors, ripe and rich, remain exuberant and generous through the nutmeg-tinged finish. Ready to drink. 200 cases made. • $16 • (04/30/97) • **90**

YOUNGBERG HILL | OREGON

Pinot Noir Willamette Valley 1996: Earthy, gamy flavors take over the fruit in this firm, hard-edged red. 400 cases made. • $24 • (06/15/98) • **78**

ZABACO | CALIFORNIA

Pinot Noir Russian River Valley 1995: Here's a deal in quality California Pinot. Enters with earth and cola notes, and stretches out with plum and wintergreen flavors. Not a blockbuster, but a pleasing, delicate wine at an equally appealing price. 14,000 cases made. • $10 • (01/31/98) BB • **84**
Sauvignon Blanc Sonoma County 1996: Extremely bright acidity is the hallmark of this lemony wine. Firm-textured and full-bodied, it finishes with a spicy air. 22,000 cases made. • $9 • (04/30/98) • **84**
Zinfandel Sonoma County 1994: A new brand from Gallo that features soft, ripe, slightly jammy, smoky, wild berry flavors and supple tannins. It's a style that's quite drinkable now. 45,000 cases made. • $10 • (02/28/97) • **86**

ZACA MESA | CALIFORNIA

Cabernet Sauvignon Central Coast 1988 • $12 • (11/15/91) • **58**
Cabernet Sauvignon Central Coast Reserve 1987 • $25 • (11/15/91) • **83**
Cabernet Sauvignon Santa Barbara County 1986 • $9 • (12/15/89) • **78**
Cabernet Sauvignon Santa Barbara County 1984 • $8 • (10/31/88) • **79**
Cabernet Sauvignon Santa Barbara County 1981 • $8 • (04/01/84) • **76**
Cabernet Sauvignon Santa Barbara County American Reserve 1983 • $13 • (03/31/87) • **87**
Cabernet Sauvignon Santa Barbara County Reserve 1986 • $15 • (12/15/88) • **80**
Cabernet Sauvignon Santa Barbara County Reserve 1985 • $15 • (10/15/88) • **79**
Chardonnay Santa Barbara County Alumni Winemaker Series James A. Clendenen 1993 • $18 • (02/29/96) • **88**
Chardonnay Santa Barbara County Chapel Vineyard 1995: A touch earthy, but enough pear and pineapple flavors peek through to keep it interesting. 1,762 cases made. • $18 • (07/31/97) • **84**
Chardonnay Santa Barbara County Chapel Vineyard 1994: Smooth and nicely spicy, with pleasant pear, peach and nectarine flavors that linger through a long finish. 1,500 cases made. • $18 • (07/31/96) • **86**
Chardonnay Santa Barbara County Zaca Vineyards 1996: Bright and lively, with distinctly spicy tangerine, nectarine and peach flavors that are smooth and concentrated, finishing with a long, spicy aftertaste. 20,000 cases made. • $14 • (05/15/98) • **89**

Chardonnay Santa Barbara County Zaca Vineyards 1995: Clean and refreshing, with a slight celerylike accent to the ripe pear and spicy citrus flavors; bright aftertaste. 11,600 cases made. • $15 • (07/31/97) • **87**
Chardonnay Santa Barbara County Zaca Vineyards 1994: Ripe and spicy, a generous wine that pours out its distinctive herb-tinged pear and caramel flavors on the supple finish. Drinkable now. 20,000 cases made. • $13 • (05/15/96) • **87**
Chardonnay Santa Barbara County Zaca Vineyards 1993 • $12 • (01/31/95) • **87**
Cuvée Z Santa Barbara County 1996: Young and grapey, with snappy wild berry and raspberry flavors that are clean and refreshing. Ready now. A blend of Grenache, Mourvèdre, Syrah, Cinsault and Counoise. 5,400 cases made. • $15 • (12/15/97) • **86**
Cuvée Z Santa Barbara County 1995: Ripe, rich and exotic. Layers of ripe plum, cherry, anise and spice flavors finish with a slight meaty edge. Drink now or age short term. A blend of Mourvèdre, Grenache, Syrah and Cinsault. 2,600 cases made. • $15 • (04/30/97) • **88**
Cuvée Z Santa Barbara County 1994 • $14 • (04/30/96) • **85**
Cuvée Z Santa Barbara County 1993 • $14 • (04/30/95) • **85**
Cuvée Z Santa Barbara County 1992 • $14 • (09/30/94) • **78**
Pinot Noir Santa Barbara County Alumni Winemaker Series Lane Tanner 1993 • $18 • (03/31/95) • **84**
Pinot Noir Santa Barbara County American Reserve 1984 • $13 • (02/15/87) • **93**
Pinot Noir Santa Barbara County Reserve 1990 • $16 • (02/28/93) • **74**
Pinot Noir Santa Barbara County Reserve 1989 • $16 • (09/30/92) • **73**
Pinot Noir Santa Barbara County Reserve 1988 • $16 • (10/31/90) • **86**
Pinot Noir Santa Barbara County Reserve 1987 • $15 • (12/15/89) • **82**
Pinot Noir Santa Barbara County Reserve 1986 • $15 • (06/15/88) • **91**
Pinot Noir Santa Barbara County Sierra Madre Vineyard 1990 • $16 • (08/31/94) • **82**
Roussanne Santa Barbara County Zaca Vineyards 1995: An openly fruity, floral style, with attractive pear, peach, fig and honeysuckle flavors. Shortens up on the finish, but overall it's quite distinctive and appealing. 2,039 cases made. • $15 • (04/30/98) • **87**
Syrah Santa Barbara County 1990 • $12 • (12/31/92) • **83**
Syrah Santa Barbara County 1989 • $12 • (08/31/91) • **83**
Syrah Santa Barbara County Alumni Winemaker Series Bob Lindquist 1993 • $18 • (02/29/96) • **88**
Syrah Santa Barbara County Alumni Winemaker Series Bob Lindquist 1992 • $18 • (01/31/95) • **90**
Syrah Santa Barbara County Chapel Vineyard 1992 • $19 • (01/31/95) • **85**
Syrah Santa Barbara County Zaca Vineyards 1995: Clean, ripe and juicy, with a core of beefy, meaty currant and blackberry flavors, turning elegant and supple on the finish. Drinks well now, but can age a year or two. 4,300 cases made. • $20 • (11/15/97) • **88**
Syrah Santa Barbara County Zaca Vineyards 1994: Dark and spicy, with an earthy accent to its wild berry and cherry flavors. Picks up a leathery edge on the finish. Try now. 2,700 cases made. • $20 • (02/28/97) • **89**
Syrah Santa Barbara County Zaca Vineyards 1993 • $13 • (11/30/95) SS • **94**
Z Gris Santa Barbara County Rosé 1996: Somewhat austere, this wine is a pleasing blend of mildly smoky thyme and sage flavors backed by hints of peppermint. It finishes cleanly, with just a touch of bitterness. 3,600 cases made. • $8 • (09/15/97) • **85**

ZAYANTE | CALIFORNIA

Chardonnay Santa Cruz Mountains 1993 • $14 • (07/31/95) • **83**

ZD WINES | CALIFORNIA

Cabernet Sauvignon California 1982 • $12 • (07/16/86) • **66**
Cabernet Sauvignon Napa Valley 1995: Dark, ripe, rich and chocolaty, with a slight leather accent to the dense currant, plum and spicy herbal flavors. Finishes with a complex aftertaste. Best from 2001 through 2008. 2,836 cases made. • $32 • (05/15/98) • **91**
Cabernet Sauvignon Napa Valley 1994: Firm, with crisp tannins, and tightly wound flavors of currant and cherry that pick up an earthy, leathery edge. Drink now or cellar into 2002. 2,300 cases made. • $30 • (07/31/97) • **88**
Cabernet Sauvignon Napa Valley 1990 • $20 • (11/15/92) • **86**
Cabernet Sauvignon Napa Valley 1989 • $20 • (11/15/92) • **78**
Cabernet Sauvignon Napa Valley 1988 • $20 • (04/30/91) • **86**
Cabernet Sauvignon Napa Valley 1987 • $16 • (02/15/91) • **78**
Cabernet Sauvignon Napa Valley 1985 • $14 • (05/15/89) • **81**
Cabernet Sauvignon Napa Valley Estate Bottled 1987 • $40 • (01/31/91) • **90**
Cabernet Sauvignon Napa Valley Reserve 1994: Tightly wound, firm and compact, with ripe, rich floral, plum and berry flavors; turns rich with mineral and spicy flavors. Muscular but ripe; rustic tannins finish it off. Best into 2000. 620 cases made. • $55 • (05/15/98) • **90**
Cabernet Sauvignon Napa Valley Reserve 1993: Just shy of outstanding. This wine has a lot going for it—elegance, a range of spicy currant, cherry, berry and light oak shadings. Needs only a little more richness and concentration. • $40 • (03/31/97) • **88**
Cabernet Sauvignon Napa Valley Reserve 1992 • $34 • (04/30/96) • **88**
Chardonnay California 1996: Crisp, with a core of citrus, pear, nectarine, herb and spice. The texture is a bit raw, but the wine is concentrated. Drink now through 2000. 20,000 cases made. • $25 • (07/31/98) • **88**
Chardonnay California 1995: Intensely flavored, with a slight leesy, earthy accent to the ripe pear, pineapple and spicy Chardonnay flavors. Try now. 19,362 cases made. • $24 • (07/31/97) • **87**
Chardonnay California 1994: Ordinary, with simple pear, citrus and light pineapple flavors. Finishes with an odd, woolly aftertaste. 19,000 cases made. • $18 • (07/31/96) • **81**
Chardonnay California 1993 • $23 • (02/28/95) • **85**
Pinot Noir Carneros 1995: A well-oaked style, but the fruit stands up to it, with moderately rich cherry, herb and tobacco flavors. Finishes with firm, dry tannins. 3,300 cases made. • $25 • (11/15/97) • **84**
Pinot Noir Napa Valley 1982 • $13 • (08/31/86) • **75**
Pinot Noir Napa Valley Carneros 1991 • $20 • (02/28/94) • **78**
Pinot Noir Napa Valley Carneros 1990 • $20 • (09/30/92) • **83**
Pinot Noir Napa Valley Carneros 1989 • $16 • (11/15/91) • **82**
Pinot Noir Napa Valley Carneros 1988 • $17 • (06/30/91) • **82**
Pinot Noir Napa Valley Carneros 1985 • $14 • (07/31/89) • **79**

ZELLERBACH ESTATES | CALIFORNIA

Cabernet Sauvignon Alexander Valley 1988 • $10 • (10/31/90) • **82**
Cabernet Sauvignon Alexander Valley 1984 • $8 • (11/30/88) • **86**
Cabernet Sauvignon Alexander Valley 1982 • $6 • (11/30/86) • **80**
Cabernet Sauvignon Alexander Valley 1980 • $8 • (04/01/85) • **77**
Cabernet Sauvignon California 1991 • $9 • (03/31/94) • **78**
Cabernet Sauvignon Sonoma County 1978 • $NA • (11/15/92) • **84**
Chardonnay California 1994: A fresh and spicy mouthful of nectarine, resin and vanilla flavors that soften on the finish. Drinkable now. • $8 • (10/31/95) • **83**
Chardonnay California 1993 • $8 • (01/31/95) • **83**
Chardonnay Sonoma County 1995: Earthy, mineral flavors dominate the fruit in this odd Chardonnay. Has a tobacco edge on the finish. Drink now. 6,000 cases made. • $10 • (11/15/97) • **80**
Chardonnay Sonoma County 1994: Bright and fruity, offering a bitter woody streak that takes away some of the charm. Try now. • $12 • (05/15/96) • **80**
Merlot Alexander Valley 1982 • $8 • (10/01/85) • **84**
Merlot Alexander Valley 1980 • $8 • (05/01/84) • **68**
Merlot Napa Valley 1993 • $14 • (06/15/96) • **75**
Sauvignon Blanc Sonoma County 1993 • $7 • (08/31/95) BB • **88**

ZIA | CALIFORNIA

Cabernet Sauvignon Napa Valley 1992 • $24 • (04/30/96) • **90**

ZILLAH OAKES | WASHINGTON

Aligoté Yakima Valley 1993 • $10 • (09/30/95) • **84**
Cabernet Franc Yakima Valley 1993 • $10 • (09/30/95) • **79**
Muscat Canelli Yakima Valley 1994 • $7 • (08/31/95) • **87**
Riesling Late Harvest Yakima Valley 1993 • $9 • (09/15/95) • **84**
Sémillon Yakima Valley 1994 • $7 • (09/30/95) • **85**

ZOOM | CALIFORNIA

Zinfandel Contra Costa County 102-Year-Old Vines 1996: Captures more ripeness, richness and depth than most '96s, showing plum, cherry, wild berry and spicy raspberry flavors and round, supple tannins. Drink now through 2002. From John Eppler of Rosenblum. 289 cases made. • $20 • (05/31/98) • **88**

Winery Index

Abarbanel, France, 282
Abbaye De Tholomies, France, 282
Abbaye De Valmagne, France, 282
Abbey Vale, Australia, 212
Abbona, Marziano & Enrico, Italy, 644
Abby D'Or, USA, California, 819
Abeille De Fieuzal, France, 282
Abelé, Henri, France, 282
Aberdeen-Angus, Argentina, 799
Abreu, USA, California, 819
Abrigada, Quinta De, Portugal, 747
Abundance, USA, California, 819
Acacia, USA, California, 819
Acacias, Domaine Des, France, 282
Academy, The, USA, Oregon, 819
Accomasso & Figlio, Giovanni, Italy, 644
Acinum, Italy, 644
Adam, J.-B., France, 282
Adams, USA, Oregon, 819
Adams, Tim, Australia, 212
Adastra, USA, California, 819
Adelaida, USA, California, 819
Adelsheim, USA, Oregon, 820
Adler Fels, USA, California, 820
Aetna Springs, USA, California, 820
Africa Collection, The, South Africa, 765
Agapito Rico, Bodegas, Spain, 776
Agassac, Château D', France, 283
Age, Bodegas, Spain, 776
Agostina, Pieri, Italy, 644
Agricola, La, Argentina, 799
Ahern, USA, California, 820
Ahlgren, USA, California, 820
Aiglon, Maison L', France, 283
Aiguelière, Domaine L', France, 283
Aiguilloux, Château, France, 283
Aiola, Italy, 644
Airlie, USA, Oregon, 820
Aja, L', Italy, 644
Aladame, Stephane, France, 283
Alameda, Chile, 263
Alamos Ridge, Argentina, 799
Alary, Domaine, France, 283
Alatera, USA, California, 821
Alavesas, Bodegas, Spain, 776
Alban, USA, California, 821
Albet I Noya, Spain, 776
Albini, USA, California, 821
Albola, Castello D', Italy, 644
Albrecht, Lucien, France, 283
Alderbrook, USA, California, 821
Alella, Marqués De, Spain, 776
Aleramici, Marchesato Degli, Italy, 644
Alessandria, Italy, 644
Alessi, Italy, 644
Alessia, Agricola, Italy, 644
Alexander Valley Fruit & Trading Co., USA, California, 822
Alexander Valley Vineyards, USA, California, 822
Alfieri, Italy, 644
Aliança, Caves, Portugal, 747
Alion, Bodegas y Viñedos, Spain, 776
All Saints, Australia, 212
Allaines, François D', France, 283
Allandale, Australia, 212
Allanmere, Australia, 212
Allegrini, Italy, 645
Allemand, Thierry, France, 283
Allesverloren, South Africa, 765
Alliet, Philippe, France, 283
Allinda, Australia, 212
Allouchery-Perseval, France, 283
Almaden, USA, California, 822
Almansa, Castillo De, Spain, 776
Almondo, Giovanni, Italy, 645
Alpen, USA, California, 822
Alpine, USA, Oregon, 822
Alquier, Gilbert, France, 284
Alta, Australia, 212
Altamura, USA, California, 822
Altare, Elio, Italy, 645
Altesino, Italy, 645
Altoviso, Caves, Portugal, 747
Alves De Sousa, Domingos, Portugal, 747
Alzinger, Austria, 249
Ama, Castello Di, Italy, 646
Amadieu, Pierre, France, 284
Amador Foothill, USA, California, 822
Ambra, Italy, 646
Ambroise, Bertrand, France, 284
Ambroise, Maison, France, 285
Ambrosini, Lorella, Italy, 646
Americana, USA, California, 823
Amerini, Cantina Colli, Italy, 646
Amezola De La Mora, Bodegas, Spain, 776
Amici, USA, California, 823
Amiot, Guy, France, 285
Amiot, Pierre, France, 285
Amiot-Bonfils, France, 285
Amiral De Beychevelle, France, 285
Amity, USA, Oregon, 823
Amizetta, USA, California, 823
Amouriers, Domaine Des, France, 285
Anapamu, USA, California, 823
Ancien Wines, USA, California, 823
Anderson Valley Vineyards, USA, New Mexico, 823
Anderson, S., USA, California, 824
Anderson's Conn Valley, USA, California, 824
Andre, USA, California, 825
André, Pierre, France, 286
Andrew Will, USA, Washington, 825
Andron-Blanquet, Château, France, 286
Angeline, USA, California, 825
Angelini, Italy, 646
Angélique De Monbousquet, Château, France, 286
Angelo, Dario D', Italy, 646
Angels Creek, USA, California, 825

Angélus, Château, France, 287
Angerhof, Austria, 249
Angerville, Marquis D', France, 287
Angludet, Château D', France, 287
Anselme, Pere, France, 287
Anselmi, Roberto, Italy, 646
Antares, USA, California, 825
Antario, Italy, 647
Antelope Valley, USA, California, 825
Antinori, Italy, 647
Antipodean, Australia, 212
Antonin, Auguste, France, 287
Antoniolo, Italy, 648
Antonopoulos Vineyards, Greece, 804
Apex, USA, Washington, 825
Apolline, Château L', France, 287
Aquéria, Château D', France, 287
Aquino, Gaetano D', Italy, 648
Ararimu, New Zealand, 807
Araujo, USA, California, 825
Arbios, USA, California, 825
Arbor Crest, USA, Washington, 825
Arcachon, USA, Oregon, 826
Arcaute, J.M., France, 288
Archambault, Pierre, France, 288
Archambeau, Château, France, 288
Arche, Château D', France, 288
Arche-Lafaurie, Château D', France, 288
Archery Summit, USA, Oregon, 826
Arciero, USA, California, 826
Arcins, Château D', France, 288
Ardechois, Vignerons, France, 288
Arfeulière, Domaine De L', France, 288
Argiano, Italy, 648
Argiolas, Italy, 648
Argonaut, USA, California, 827
Argyle, USA, Oregon, 827
Arienzo, Marques De, Spain, 776
Aries, USA, California, 827
Arjolle, Domaine De L', France, 288
Arlot, Domaine De L', France, 288
Armailhac, Château D', France, 288
Armand, Comte, France, 289
Armida, USA, California, 827
Arnaldo Caprai, Italy, 648
Arnauld, Château, France, 289
Arnoux, Robert, France, 289
Arnoux Père & Fils, France, 290
Arns, USA, California, 827
Arrigorriaga, Chile, 263
Arromans, Château Les, France, 290
Arrosée, Château L', France, 290
Arrowfield, Australia, 212
Arrowood, USA, California, 828
Arroyo, Bodegas Ismael, Spain, 776
Arroyo, Vincent, USA, California, 828
Arruda Dos Vinhos, Portugal, 747
Arsac, Château D', France, 290
Artadi, Spain, 776
Arterberry, USA, Oregon, 828
Arthur, David, USA, California, 829
Arunda, Australia, 212
Arvigny, Château D', France, 290
Arzobispo, Cooperativa Agricola Villar Del, Spain, 777
Arzuaga, Bodegas, Spain, 777
As Laxas, Bodegas, Spain, 777
Ascheri, Cantine Giacomo, Italy, 648
Ashby, Hunter, USA, California, 829
Ashland Park, USA, California, 829
Ashland Vineyards, USA, Oregon, 829
Ashwood Grove, Australia, 212
Ata Rangi, New Zealand, 807
Atlas Peak, USA, California, 829
Au Bon Climat, USA, California, 829
Aubert, Domaine Max, France, 290
Aubuisières, Domaine Des, France, 290
Audubon, USA, California, 830
Augey, France, 290
Aujoux, Jean-Marc, France, 290
Aupilhac, Domaine D', France, 291
Aurora, USA, Oregon, 830
Ausone, Château, France, 291
Austin, USA, California, 831
Ausvetia, Australia, 212
Autard, Domaine Paul, France, 291
Autumn Hill, USA, Virginia, 831
Autumn Wind, USA, Oregon, 831
Auvenay, Domaine D', France, 291
Auvernier, Château D', Switzerland, 812
Auvigue & Revel, France, 292
Auvigue, André, France, 292
Aveleda, Portugal, 747
Avery, France, 292
Avignonesi, Italy, 648
Avril, Pascal & Catherine, France, 292
Ayala, France, 292
Ayala Lete E Hijos, R. De, Spain, 777
Aydie, Château D', France, 292
Azalea Springs, USA, California, 831
Azelia, Italy, 649
Azo, Hervé, France, 292
Azpilicueta, Bodegas Felix, Spain, 777
Babcock, USA, California, 831
Babich, New Zealand, 807
Bacalhoa, Quinta Da, Portugal, 747
Bachelet, Denis, France, 292
Bachelet-Ramonet, France, 293
Backsberg, South Africa, 765
Badger Mountain, USA, Washington, 832
Badia A Coltibuono, Italy, 649
Badoux, Henri, Switzerland, 813
Baggiolino, Fattoria, Italy, 649
Bagnoli, Italy, 649
Bahans Haut-Brion, Château, France, 293
Baileyana, USA, California, 832
Baillat, Domaine, France, 293
Bailly, Alexis, USA, Minnesota, 832
Bailly, Franck & Jean-François, France, 293
Bainbridge Island, USA, Washington, 832
Baiocchi, Cantine, Italy, 649
Bajamar, Marques De, Spain, 777
Bakondi, Hungary, 805
Balac, Château, France, 293
Balbach, Germany, 615
Balbas, Bodegas, Spain, 777
Balbino Fernandez, Spain, 777
Balcom & Moe, USA, Washington, 832
Bald Mountain, USA, California, 832
Baldinelli, USA, California, 832
Baldivis, Australia, 212
Balestard, Château, France, 293
Balestard-La-Tonnelle, Château, France, 293
Balland, Domaine Jean-Paul, France, 293
Ballatore, USA, California, 832
Ballena, France, 293
Ballentine, USA, California, 832
Ballot-Millot & Fils, R., France, 293
Balmont, Jean, France, 293
Balverne, USA, California, 832
Bandiera, USA, California, 832
Banear, Italy, 649
Banfi, Castello, Italy, 650
Bannister, USA, California, 833
Bannockburn, Australia, 212
Banrock Station, Australia, 213
Bara, Paul, France, 293

Baracco De Baracho, Italy, 651
Barale, Fratelli, Italy, 651
Barancourt, France, 294
Barat, Michel, France, 294
Barbadillo, Antonio, Spain, 777
Barbi, Fattoria Dei, Italy, 651
Barbier, René, Spain, 777
Barboursville, USA, Virginia, 833
Barcelo, Hijos De Antonio, Spain, 777
Barco, Casa, Spain, 777
Barefoot, France, 294
Barefoot, USA, California, 833
Baret, Château, France, 294
Barge, Gilles, France, 294
Barge, Pierre, France, 294
Bargetto, Lawrence J., USA, California, 833
Barnett, USA, California, 834
Barolet, Dr., France, 294
Barolo, Marchesi Di, Italy, 651
Baron Herzog, USA, California, 834
Barone, Italy, 651
Baronia De Turís, Spain, 777
Baronne, Château De La, France, 294
Barossa Valley Estate, Australia, 213
Barrabaque, Château, France, 294
Barradis, Château Le, France, 294
Barral, Domaine Leon, France, 294
Barratt, Australia, 213
Barraud, Daniel, France, 294
Barré, Domaine, France, 295
Barreyres, Château, France, 295
Barrier Reef, Australia, 213
Barrocão, Caves Do, Portugal, 747
Barros, Portugal, 747
Barrot, Domaine Lucien, France, 295
Barrow Green, USA, California, 834
Barry, Brian, Australia, 213
Barry, Jim, Australia, 213
Barryes, Château, France, 295
Bartet, G., France, 295
Barthod, Ghislaine, France, 295
Bartholomew Park, USA, California, 834
Bartoli, Marco De, Italy, 651
Barton & Guestier, France, 295
Barwang, Australia, 213
Basciano, Fattoria Di, Italy, 651
Basedow, Australia, 213
Basque, Château Du, France, 296
Bass Phillip, Australia, 213
Basse, Case, Italy, 652
Bassermann-Jordan, Germany, 615
Bastide Blanche, La, France, 296
Bastide Dauzac, La, France, 296
Bastide De Siran, La, France, 296
Bastide, Cellier De La, France, 296
Bastor-Lamontagne, Château, France, 296
Batacchi, Philippe, France, 296
Batailley, Château, France, 296
Batard, Serge, France, 297
Batardière, Domaine De La, France, 297
Batasiolo, Beni Di, Italy, 652
Battaglini, USA, California, 834
Baubiac, Domaine De, France, 297
Bauchet Père & Fils, France, 297
Baudry, Domaine Bernard, France, 297
Bauget-Jouette, France, 297
Baumard, Domaine Des, France, 297
Baume, Domaine De La, France, 297
Bava, Italy, 652
Bay Cellars, USA, California, 834
Bayview Cellars, USA, California, 834
Bazan, Agro De, Spain, 778
Bearboat, USA, California, 834
Beaucanon, USA, California, 834
Beaucastel, Château De, France, 298
Beaudet, Paul, France, 298
Beaulieu Vineyard, USA, California, 835
Beault-Forgeot, France, 298
Beaumet, France, 298
Beaumont, Château, France, 298
Beaumont Des Crayères, France, 298
Beauregard, Château, France, 299
Beauregard, Château De, France, 299
Beaurenard, Domaine De, France, 299
Beauséjour, Château, France, 299
Beau-Séjour Bécot, Château, France, 299
Beau-Site, Château, France, 299
Beau-Soleil, Château, France, 300
Beau-Vallon, Château Du, France, 300
Beauvolage, France, 300
Beaux Frères, USA, Oregon, 837
Beck, Graham, South Africa, 765
Beckmen, USA, California, 837
Bedell, USA, New York, 837
Bedford Thompson, USA, California, 838
Behrens & Hitchcock, USA, California, 838
Bel Air, Château, France, 300
Bel Air, Château, France, 300
Bel Air, Château, France, 300
Bel-Air, Château, France, 300
Bélair, Château, France, 300
Bel Arbor, Chile, 263
Bel Arbor, USA, California, 838
Bel Colle, Italy, 652
Bel Evêque, Château, France, 300
Belcier, Château De, France, 300
Belgrave, Château, France, 300
Belin, Jules, France, 300
Belingard, Château, France, 300
Bell, USA, California, 838
Bell Mountain, USA, Texas, 838
Belland, Adrien, France, 300
Belland, Jean-Claude, France, 300
Belland, Roger, France, 300
Bellanova, Italy, 652
Bellavista, Italy, 652
Belle Père & Fils, France, 301
Bellefont-Belcier, Château, France, 301
Bellegarde, Château, France, 301
Bellegrave, Château, France, 301
Bellegrave-Van Der Voort, Château, France, 301
Bellerose, USA, California, 838
Bellevue-Figeac, Château, France, 301
Bellingham, South Africa, 765
Belondrade y Lurton, Spain, 778
Bel-Orme-Tronquoy-De-Lalande, Château, France, 301
Belvedere, USA, California, 838
Belvezel, Domaine Du, France, 301
Bénazeth, Domaine, France, 301
Benessere, USA, California, 839
Benham, USA, California, 839
Benicia, USA, California, 839
Benjamin, Australia, 213
Benjamin De Beauregard, Le, France, 301
Benton-Lane, USA, Oregon, 839
Benziger, USA, California, 839
Bera, Italy, 653
Berard Père & Fils, France, 301
Berberana, Bodegas, Spain, 778
Beretta, Cecilia, Italy, 653
Beretta, Gussalli, Italy, 653
Bergadano, Enrico, Italy, 653
Bergaglio, Nicola, Italy, 653
Bergat, Château, France, 301

Berger, E .& M., Austria, 249
Bergerie, Domaine De La, France, 301
Bergfeld, USA, California, 841
Bergsig, South Africa, 765
Beringer, USA, California, 841
Berliquet, Château, France, 302
Bernard, Domaine Michel, France, 302
Bernard, Guy, France, 302
Bernard, Jean, France, 302
Bernard, Paul, France, 302
Bernardus, USA, California, 842
Berneau, C., France, 302
Beronia, Bodegas, Spain, 778
Berri Estates, Australia, 213
Bersano, Italy, 653
Bertagna, Domaine, France, 302
Bertani, Italy, 653
Bertelli, Italy, 654
Bertheau, Domaine, France, 302
Berthet-Rayne, Domaine, France, 302
Bertinerie, Château, France, 302
Bertolla, Alfred Gino, France, 302
Bertrams, South Africa, 765
Bertrand, Domaine Georges, France, 303
Bertrand, Maurice, France, 303
Bessière, Daniel, France, 303
Best's, Australia, 214
Bethany Creek, Australia, 214
Bethel Heights, USA, Oregon, 843
Bettinelli, USA, California, 843
Beychevelle, Château, France, 303
Beyer, Léon, France, 303
Beyerskloof, South Africa, 765
Biale, Robert, USA, California, 843
Bianchi, A., Italy, 654
Bianchi, Valentin, Argentina, 799
Bibbiano, Tenuta, Italy, 654
Bibian, Domaine, France, 303
Bichot, Albert, France, 303
Bidwell, USA, New York, 843
Bienfaisance, Château La, France, 304
Bieville, Domaine De, France, 304
Biffar, Josef, Germany, 615
Bigi, Italy, 654
Bilbainas, Bodegas, Spain, 778
Billard-Gonnet, France, 305
Billaud-Simon, France, 305
Billecart-Salmon, France, 305
Billiot, Henri, France, 305
Biltmore Estate, USA, North Carolina, 843
Bindella, Rudolf, Italy, 654
Binet, France, 305
Biondi-Santi, Italy, 654
Biondi-Santi, Jacopo, Italy, 654
Birot, Château De, France, 305
Bisol & Figli, Desiderio, Italy, 654
Biston-Brillette, Château, France, 306
Bitouzet, Pierre, France, 306
Bitouzet-Prieur, France, 306
Bize & Fils, Simon, France, 306
Blaauwklippen, South Africa, 765
Blachon, Roger, France, 307
Black Mountain, USA, California, 843
Black Opal, Australia, 214
Black Rock, Australia, 214
Black Rock, USA, California, 843
Black Sheep, USA, California, 844
Black Silk, Australia, 214
Blackstone, USA, California, 844
Blagueurs, Domaine Des, France, 307
Blain-Gagnard, France, 307
Blake, USA, California, 844
Blanc, Georges, France, 307
Blanchet, Bernard, France, 307
Blanchet, Francis, France, 307
Blanck, Domaine Paul, France, 307
Blanck Frères, France, 307
Blandys, Portugal, 748
Blason D' Issan, France, 308
Blass, Wolf, Australia, 214
Bleasdale, Australia, 215
Blend Storming, France, 308
Blockheadia Ringnosii, USA, California, 844
Blomac, Château De, France, 308
Blossom Hill, USA, California, 844
Blue Nun, Argentina, 799
Blue Nun, Germany, 615
Blue Pyrenees, Australia, 215
Boada, Bodegas, Spain, 778
Boatina, La, Italy, 654
Bocage, USA, California, 844
Bocage, Château Le, France, 308
Bocard, Guy, France, 308
Bocce, Fattoria Le, Italy, 654
Bockfliess, Austria, 249
Bodrog Vàrhegy, Hungary, 805
Boeger, USA, California, 844
Bogle, USA, California, 845
Boglietti, Enzo, Italy, 655
Boileau, Etienne, France, 308
Boillot, Jean, France, 308
Boillot, Jean-Marc, France, 309
Boillot, Lucien, France, 310
Boillot, Pierre, France, 311
Bois Dauphin, Domaine Du, France, 311
Bois De La Garde, Château Du, France, 311
Boissan, Domaine De, France, 311
Boisset, USA, California, 845
Boisset, Château, France, 311
Boisset, Jean-Claude, France, 311
Boisson, J.P., France, 312
Boizel, France, 312
Boland Wynkelder, South Africa, 765
Boldos, Chateau Los, Chile, 263
Bolla, Italy, 655
Bollinger, France, 312
Bollini, Italy, 655
Bologna, Giacomo, Italy, 656
Bon Marche, USA, California, 845
Bonalgue, Château, France, 313
Bonci, Vallerosa, Italy, 656
Bonfio, Federico, Italy, 656
Bongran, Domaine De La, France, 313
Bonhomme, Château De, France, 313
Bonnaire, France, 313
Bonnat, Château Le, France, 313
Bonneau Du Martray, France, 313
Bonnet, Château, Bordeaux, France, 313
Bonnet, Château, Languedoc, France, 313
Bonnigal, M., France, 313
Bonny Doon, USA, California, 846
Bon-Pasteur, Château Le, France, 314
Bonterra, USA, California, 846
Bonverre, USA, California, 847
Bonvin, Charles, Switzerland, 813
Bookwalter, USA, Washington, 847
Boordy, USA, Maryland, 847
Boplaas, South Africa, 765
Borba, Adega Cooperativa De, Portugal, 748
Bord, Château De, France, 314
Bordoni, USA, California, 847
Borgeot, Domaine, France, 314
Borges, Portugal, 748
Borgo Al Castello, Italy, 656

Borgo Conventi, Italy, 656
Borgo Delle Rose, Italy, 656
Borgo Magredo, Italy, 656
Borgo Scopeto, Tenuta, Italy, 656
Borgo Tintor, Italy, 656
Borgogno, Lodovico, Italy, 656
Borgogno & Figli, Giacomo, Italy, 657
Borie De Maurel, Domaine, France, 314
Borie La Vitarèle, France, 314
Borja, Agricola De, Spain, 778
Borne, Domaine De La, France, 314
Bortoluzzi, Italy, 657
Boscaini, Paolo, Italy, 657
Boscarelli, Poderi, Italy, 657
Boschendal, South Africa, 765
Bosco, Castiglion Del, Italy, 657
Bosco, Tenuta Il, Italy, 657
Boscq, Château Le, France, 314
Boscq, Château Le, France, 314
Bosquet Des Papes, France, 314
Bossi, Castello Di, Italy, 657
Bott-Geyl, Domaine, France, 314
Bouachon, Henry, France, 315
Bouchacourt, Roland, France, 315
Bouchaine, USA, California, 847
Bouchard Finlayson, South Africa, 765
Bouchard, Pascal, France, 315
Bouchard-Aîné & Fils, France, 315
Bouchard Père & Fils, France, 315
Bouchon, Viñedos J., Chile, 263
Bouchotte, Valentin, France, 319
Bougrier, Jean-Claude, France, 319
Bouissière, Domaine La, France, 319
Boukandoura, Henri, France, 319
Boulder Opal, Australia, 215
Bouley, Jean-Marc, France, 319
Bour, Domaine, France, 319
Bourée Père & Fils, France, 319
Bourgeois, Henri, France, 319
Bourgeois, Richard, France, 320
Bourgeon, Paul, France, 320
Bourgeon, René, France, 320
Bourgneuf, Château, France, 320
Bourillon-Dorléans, Domaine, France, 320
Bouscassé, Château, France, 320
Bouscaut, Château, France, 321
Bousquet, Château Du, France, 321
Bousquette, Château, France, 321
Bousquette, Domaine De La, France, 321
Boussagol, Domaine, France, 321
Boutari, Greece, 804
Bouverie, La, France, 321
Bouvet, France, 321
Bouzereau & Fils, Michel, France, 321
Bovard, Switzerland, 813
Bovlei Winery, South Africa, 766
Bowen Estate, Australia, 215
Boxler, Albert, France, 322
Boyd-Cantenac, Château, France, 322
Boynton's Of Bright, Australia, 215
Brac De La Perrière, France, 322
Branaire-Ducru, Château, France, 322
Branavieja, Bodegas, Spain, 778
Brancaia, Podere La, Italy, 657
Brancott, New Zealand, 807
Brandborg, USA, California, 848
Brander, USA, California, 848
Brandolini D'Adda, Conti, Italy, 658
Brands Laira, Australia, 215
Brane, Château Baron De, France, 322
Brane-Cantenac, Château, France, 322
Branger, Claude, France, 323
Braren Pauli, USA, California, 848
Bredell's, South Africa, 766
Brédif, Marc, France, 323
Brégeon, Andre-Michel, France, 323
Bretón, Bodegas, Spain, 778
Bréton, Guy, France, 323
Breton, P., France, 323
Bretonnière, Yves, France, 323
Breuer, Georg, Germany, 615
Breuil, Château Du, France, 323
Brezza & Figli, Giacomo, Italy, 658
Briar Ridge, Australia, 215
Brick House, USA, Oregon, 848
Bricout, France, 323
Bridão, Portugal, 748
Briday, Michel, France, 323
Bridgehampton, USA, New York, 848
Bridgeview, USA, Oregon, 849
Bridgewater Mill, Australia, 215
Bridgman, W.B., USA, Washington, 849
Brien, Australia, 215
Brigands, Domaine De, France, 323
Briggs, August, USA, California, 849
Brillette, Château, France, 323
Brindiamo, USA, California, 849
Brisebarre, Philippe, France, 323
Britthill, USA, California, 850
Broadley, USA, Oregon, 850
Brocard, Jean-Marc, France, 323
Brochard, Hubert, France, 324
Broke Estate, Australia, 215
Broke Fordwich, Australia, 215
Brokenwood, Australia, 215
Brolio, Italy, 658
Brotherhood, USA, New York, 850
Brotte, Laurent Charles, France, 324
Broustet, Château, France, 324
Brovia, Fratelli, Italy, 658
Brown, Château, France, 324
Brown, Stillman, USA, California, 850
Brown Brothers, Australia, 215
Brown-Lamartine, Château, France, 324
Browns' Of Padthaway, Australia, 216
Bruce, David, USA, California, 850
Brucher, USA, California, 850
Brugo, Italy, 658
Brully, Domaine De, France, 324
Brun Labrie, Château, France, 325
Brun, Jean-Paul, France, 324
Brundlmayer, Austria, 249
Brunet, Patrick, France, 325
Bruno, Domaine Paul, Chile, 263
Brusset, Daniel, France, 325
Brusset, Domaine, France, 325
Brut Dargent, France, 325
Brutocao, USA, California, 850
Bryant Family, USA, California, 851
Bucci, Italy, 658
Bucy, Maison Joseph De, France, 325
Buehler, USA, California, 851
Buena Vista, USA, California, 851
Buffet, François, France, 325
Buhl, Reichsrat Von, Germany, 616
Buitenverwachting, South Africa, 766
Bulgare, Bulgaria, 802
Buller & Son, R.L., Australia, 216
Bulletin Place, Australia, 216
Bully Hill, USA, New York, 852
Bunan, Domaines, France, 325
Buon Donno, Italy, 658
Buoninsegna, La, Italy, 658
Buracchi, Italy, 659
Burgaud, Bernard, France, 325
Burgess, USA, California, 852
Burguet, Alain, France, 325
Burier, Jacques, France, 325
Bürklin-Wolf, Dr., Germany, 616

Burmester, Portugal, 748
Burn, Ernest, France, 326
Burrell School, USA, California, 853
Burrier, Georges, France, 326
Butterfly Creek, USA, California, 853
Buttonwood, USA, California, 853
Buzzinelli, Carlo, Italy, 659
Byington, USA, California, 853
Bynum, Davis, USA, California, 854
Byron, USA, California, 854
Ca' Bianca, Italy, 659
Ca' Bolani, Italy, 659
Ca' De Monte, Italy, 659
Ca' Dei Gancia, Italy, 659
Ca' Del Bosco, Italy, 659
Ca' Del Re, Italy, 659
Ca' Del Solo, USA, California, 855
Ca' Neuva, Italy, 659
Ca' Romé Di Romano Marengo, Italy, 659
Ca' Rugate, Italy, 660
Ca' Vit, Italy, 660
Caballero De Chile, Chile, 263
Cabanne, Château La, France, 326
Cabasse, Domaine De, France, 326
Caboche, Domaine Du Père, France, 326
Cabriac, Château De, France, 326
Cabrières, Château, France, 326
Cabutto, Italy, 660
Cacchiano, Castello Di, Italy, 660
Cáceres, Marqués De, Spain, 779
Cachazo, Bodegas Angel Lorenzo, Spain, 779
Cachazo, Bodegas Felix Lorenzo, Spain, 779
Cacheux, Jacques, France, 326
Cadaval, Casa, Portugal, 749
Cadeaux, France, 326
Cadet-Bon, Château, France, 326
Cadet-Piola, Château, France, 326
Cady, Domaine, France, 326
Cafaro, USA, California, 855
Cailbourdin, Domaine A., France, 326
Caillot, Roger, France, 327
Caillou, Château, France, 327
Caillou, Domaine Du, France, 327
Caillou Blanc Du Château Talbot, France, 327
Cailloux, Les, France, 327
Cain, USA, California, 855
Cairanne, Cave Des Coteaux, France, 327
Cakebread, USA, California, 855
Calage, Château De, France, 327
Calatrasi, Italy, 660
Cale, USA, California, 856
Cálem, Portugal, 749
Calera, USA, California, 856
Calhandriz, Portugal, 749
Calina, Chile, 263
Calissanne, Château, France, 327
Calissano, Luigi, Italy, 660
Caliterra, Chile, 263
Callaghan, USA, Arizona, 857
Callahan Ridge, USA, Oregon, 857
Callaway, USA, California, 857
Calle Cielo, USA, California, 857
Callejo, Bodegas Felix, Spain, 779
Calmasino, Italy, 660
Calo & Sons, Michele, Italy, 660
Calonica, La, Italy, 660
Calon-Segur, Château, France, 328
Calot, Domaine, France, 328
Camaraderie, USA, Washington, 858
Camarate, Quinta De, Portugal, 749
Cambria, USA, California, 858
Camelot, USA, California, 858
Camensac, Château De, France, 328
Camerano, Italy, 660
Cameron, USA, Oregon, 858
Camigliano, Castello Di, Italy, 660
Campacci, Italy, 661
Campanas, Las, Spain, 779
Campanile, Italy, 661
Camperos, Château, France, 328
Campillo, Bodegas, Spain, 779
Camplazens, Château, France, 328
Campo, Bodega Cooperativa Del, Spain, 779
Campo Viejo, Bodegas, Spain, 779
Campogiovanni, Italy, 661
Campredon, Château De, France, 328
Campriano, Italy, 661
Can Feixes, Spain, 780
Can Rafols Dels Caus, Spain, 780
Canale, Tenuta, Italy, 661
Canaletto, Italy, 661
Canalicchio De Sotto, Italy, 661
Canalicchio Di Sopra, Italy, 661
Canard, USA, California, 858
Canard-Duchene, France, 328
Candido, Francesco, Italy, 661
Canella, Italy, 661
Canepa, Chile, 264
Canepa, USA, California, 858
Canet, Château, France, 328
Canet Valette, France, 328
Canoe Ridge, USA, Washington, 858
Canon, Château, France, 328
Canon, Château, France, 328
Canon-De-Brem, Château, France, 329
Canon-La Gaffelière, Château, France, 329
Canon-Moueix, Château, France, 329
Canorgue, Château La, France, 329
Cantagallo, Tenuta, Italy, 662
Cantalupo, Antichi Vigneti Di, Italy, 662
Canteloup, Château, France, 329
Cantelys, Château, France, 330
Cantemerle, Château, France, 330
Cantenac-Brown, Château, France, 330
Canterbury, USA, California, 859
Cantrie, Château De La, France, 330
Canuet, Château, France, 330
Canyon Road, USA, California, 859
Cap De Haut, Château, France, 330
Cap De Mourlin, Château, France, 330
Cap Rock, USA, Texas, 859
Capaccia, Podere, Italy, 662
Capanna, Italy, 662
Capanna Fattoi, Italy, 662
Capannelle, Italy, 662
Caparone, USA, California, 859
Caparzo, Italy, 662
Capbern-Gasqueton, Château, France, 330
Cape Country, South Africa, 766
Cape Indaba, South Africa, 766
Cape Mentelle, Australia, 216
Cape Selection, South Africa, 766
Capel Vale, Australia, 216
Capendu, Château, France, 330
Capezzana, Italy, 663
Capiaux, USA, California, 859
Cappellano, Giuseppe, Italy, 663
Cappuccina, La, Italy, 663
Carasu, Romania, 812
Caratello, Italy, 663
Carbonnières, Domaine Des, France, 331
Carbonnieux, Château, France, 331

Cardinale, USA, California, 859
Cardo, Quinta Do, Portugal, 749
Cardonne, Château La, France, 331
Cardonnet, Château, France, 331
Cardus, Château, France, 331
Carey Cellars, USA, California, 859
Carillon, Château Du, France, 331
Carillon, Louis, France, 331
Carles, Château De, France, 331
Carmen, Chile, 264
Carmenet, USA, California, 859
Carmes-Haut-Brion, Château Les, France, 332
Carmo, Quinta Do, Portugal, 749
Carmody Mcknight, USA, California, 860
Carnasciale, Italy, 663
Carneros Bighorn Ranch, USA, California, 860
Carneros Creek, USA, California, 860
Carneros Quality Alliance, USA, California, 860
Carnevale, Giorgio, Italy, 663
Carobbio, Italy, 664
Caronne-Ste.-Gemme, Château, France, 332
Caroso, Italy, 664
Carpe Diem, USA, California, 860
Carpenè Malvolti, Italy, 664
Carpineto, Italy, 664
Carreras, Bodegas Jaime, Spain, 780
Carretta, Italy, 664
Carruades De Lafite Rothschild, France, 332
Carsin, Château, France, 332
Carta Vieja, Chile, 265
Cartillon, Château Du, France, 332
Cartlidge & Browne, USA, California, 860
Carvalhinho, Quinta Do, Portugal, 749
Carvalho, Ribeiro & Ferreira, Portugal, 749
Casa, La, Italy, 664
Casa Emma, Italy, 664
Casa Francesco, Italy, 664
Casa Girelli, Italy, 665
Casa Sola, Italy, 665
Casal De Tonda, Portugal, 749
Casal Figueira, Portugal, 749
Casal Thaulero, Italy, 665
Casaloste, Italy, 665
Casalte, Fattoria Le, Italy, 665
Casanova, La, France, 332
Casanova Di Neri, Italy, 665
Casas Del Toqui, Las, Chile, 265
Cascina Ballarin, Italy, 665
Cascina Bongiovanni, Italy, 665
Cascina Castle't, Italy, 665
Cascina Galleto, Italy, 665
Cascina La Barbatella, Italy, 665
Cascina La Pertica, Italy, 665
Cascina Luisin, Italy, 665
Cascinetta, Italy, 666
Case, USA, California, 861
Casenove, Domaine De La, France, 332
Casetta, Italy, 666
Casina Di Cornia, Italy, 666
Casisano-Colombaio, Italy, 666
Cask One, USA, California, 861
Casòn Hirschprunn, Italy, 666
Cassagne-Haut-Canon, Château, France, 332
Cassan, Domaine De, France, 332
Cassegrain, Australia, 216
Castagnier, Guy, France, 332
Castalia, USA, California, 861
Castaño, Bodegas, Spain, 780
Castel Ruggero, Italy, 666
Castelgiocondo, Italy, 666
Castelgreve, Italy, 666
Castell, Furst Zu, Germany, 617
Castell'in Villa, Italy, 666
Castellane, De, France, 333
Castellare Di Castellina, Italy, 666
Castellarin, Italy, 667
Castellblanch, Spain, 780
Castelli Martinozzi, Italy, 667
Castelluccio, Italy, 667
Castelnau De Suduiraut, France, 333
Castelot, Château Le, France, 333
Castelvecchio, Italy, 667
Castenet-Greffier, Château, France, 333
Castillo Del Rio, Chile, 265
Castle Creek, USA, California, 861
Castle Hill, New Zealand, 807
Castle Hill Cellars, Hungary, 805
Castle Rock, USA, California, 861
Castle Vineyards, USA, California, 861
Castleview, USA, California, 861
Castoro, USA, California, 861
Cataldi Madonna, Tenuta, Italy, 667
Caterina, USA, Washington, 861
Cathedral Cellar, South Africa, 766
Catherine De St.-Juery, France, 333
Catoctin, USA, Maryland, 862
Caton, Domaine, France, 333
Cattier, France, 333
Cava Tsantalis, Greece, 804
Cavalchina, Italy, 667
Cavallotto, Italy, 667
Cavas Hill, Spain, 780
Cavatappi, USA, Washington, 862
Cavazza, Italy, 667
Caymus, USA, California, 862
Cazal-Viel, Château, France, 333
Cazanove, Charles De, France, 333
Cazes, Domaine, France, 333
Cazin, François, France, 334
Cecchetti Sebastiani Cellar, USA, California, 863
Cecchi, Italy, 667
Ceci, Domaine, France, 334
Cedar Brook, USA, California, 863
Cedar Creek, Australia, 216
Cedar Creek, USA, Wisconsin, 863
Cedar Mountain, USA, California, 863
Cèdre, Château Du, France, 334
Cellier Des Baronnies, France, 334
Cellole, Italy, 668
Cenalsa-Murchante, Bodegas, Spain, 780
Cennatoio, Italy, 668
Centaurus, South Africa, 766
Cerbaia, Italy, 668
Cerbaiola, Italy, 668
Cerbaiona, Italy, 668
Ceretto, Fratelli, Italy, 668
Cerro, Fattoria Del, Italy, 669
Certan De May, Château, France, 334
Certan-Giraud, Château, France, 334
Cerveteri, Cantina Cooperativa Di, Italy, 669
Cesare, Pio, Italy, 669
Cesari, Umberto, Italy, 670
Cesari E Figli, Franco, Italy, 670
Chablis, Cave De, France, 334
Chablisienne, La, France, 334
Chabot, Patrick, France, 335
Chadds Ford, USA, Pennsylvania, 863
Chain of Ponds, Australia, 217
Chainier, Domaine, France, 335
Chaintré, Cave De, France, 335

Chais Baumière, France, 335
Chaize, Château De La, France, 335
Chalk Hill, USA, California, 863
Challon, Domaine, France, 335
Chalone, USA, California, 864
Chambers, Australia, 217
Chambert-Marbuzet, Château, France, 335
Chameleon, USA, California, 864
Chamfort, Bernard, France, 336
Chamirey, Château De, France, 336
Chamoux, Jean-Pierre, France, 336
Champalimaud, Portugal, 749
Champalou, France, 336
Champault, Domaine, France, 336
Champet, Emile, France, 336
Champoeg, USA, Oregon, 864
Champs, Jeanne-Marie De, France, 336
Champs Clos, Les, France, 336
Chandon De Briailles, France, 336
Chanrion, Nicole, France, 336
Chanson Père & Fils, France, 336
Chante Cigale, France, 337
Chante-Alouette, Château, France, 337
Chantefleur, France, 337
Chantegrive, Château De, France, 337
Chanteleuserie, Domaine De La, France, 337
Chante-Perdrix, Cave De, France, 337
Chante-Perdrix, Domaine, France, 337
Chapel Hill, Australia, 217
Chapelle, Domaine De La, France, 337
Chapelle De La Mission-Haut-Brion, La, France, 337
Chapoutier, M., France, 337
Chappell Family, USA, California, 864
Chappellet, USA, California, 864
Charbaut & Fils, A., France, 339
Charbaut Frères, France, 339
Charbonnière, Domaine De La, France, 339
Charlemagne, Château, France, 339
Charlopin-Parizot, Philippe, France, 339
Charmail, Château, France, 340
Charme Labory, Le, France, 340
Charmes De Kirwan, Les, France, 340
Charmes De Liversan, Les, France, 340
Charmes-Godard, Château Les, France, 340
Charron, Château De, France, 340
Chartogne-Taillet, France, 340
Chartreuse, Château De La, France, 340
Chartron, Jean, France, 340
Chartron & Trébuchet, France, 341
Chapelle, Domaine De La, France, 337
Chartrons, USA, California, 865
Chasse, Marquis De, France, 343
Chasse-Spleen, Château, France, 342
Chasseur, USA, California, 865
Chastan, Claude, France, 343
Château, Domaine De, France, 343
Chateau Benoit, USA, Oregon, 865
Chateau Bianca, USA, Oregon, 865
Chateau Chevalier, USA, California, 865
Chateau Chevre, USA, California, 865
Chateau Christina, USA, California, 865
Chateau De Baun, USA, California, 865
Chateau De Leu, USA, California, 866
Chateau Diana, USA, California, 866
Chateau Elan, USA, California, 866
Chateau Frank, USA, New York, 866
Chateau Grand Traverse, USA, Michigan, 866
Chateau Julien, USA, California, 866
Chateau La Grande Roche, USA, California, 866
Chateau Lafayette Reneau, USA, New York, 866
Chateau Libertas, South Africa, 766
Chateau Margarite, USA, California, 866
Chateau Montelena, USA, California, 866
Chateau Morrisette, USA, Virginia, 867
Chateau Potelle, USA, California, 867
Chateau Reynella, Australia, 217
Chateau St. Jean, USA, California, 867
Chateau Ste. Michelle, USA, Washington, 869
Chateau Souverain, USA, California, 870
Chateau Tahbilk, Australia, 217
Chateau Woltner, USA, California, 871
Chatelain, Jean-Claude, France, 343
Chatenoy, Domaine De, France, 343
Chatom, USA, California, 871
Chauffe-Eau, USA, California, 871
Chauvenet, F., France, 343
Chauvenet, Jean, France, 344
Chauvenet-Chopin, France, 344
Chauvin, Château, France, 344
Chave, Bernard, France, 344
Chave, Jean-Louis, France, 345
Chavy, Gérard, France, 345
Chavy, Philippe, France, 345
Chavy-Chouet, Claude & Hubert, France, 345
Chazelles, Domaine Des, France, 345
Cheetah Valley, South Africa, 766
Cheffieux, Domaine De, France, 345
Chehalem, USA, Oregon, 872
Chénas, Château De, France, 345
Chene, Domaine Du, France, 345
Cheneau, Paul, Spain, 780
Chenonceau, Château De, France, 345
Chéreau-Carré, France, 345
Chéreau Pere & Fils, B., France, 345
Cheret-Pitres, Château, France, 346
Cherrier & Fils, Pierre, France, 346
Cherry Hill, USA, Washington, 872
Cherubin, Italy, 670
Chesnaie, Château De La, France, 346
Chestnut Hill, USA, California, 872
Chestnut Mountain, USA, Georgia, 872
Cheval-Blanc, Château, France, 346
Chevalier, Domaine De, France, 347
Chevalier, Guy, France, 347
Chevalier De Rodilan, France, 347
Chevalier Pere & Fils, France, 347
Chevalière, Domaine La, France, 347
Chevillon, Denis, France, 347
Chevillon, Robert, France, 347
Chèze, Domaine, France, 348
Chezeaux, Domaine Des, France, 348
Chiarlo, Michele, Italy, 670
Chidaine, François, France, 348
Chiesa Di S. Restituta, La, Italy, 671
Chignard, Michel, France, 348
Chimere, USA, California, 872
Chimney Rock, USA, California, 872
China Bend, USA, Washington, 873
Chinook, USA, Washington, 873
Chionetti & Figlio, Quinto, Italy, 671
Chiquet, Gaston, France, 348
Chittering, Australia, 217
Chivite, Bodegas Julián, Spain, 780
Choblet, Luc & Andrée-Marie, France, 348
Chofflet-Valdenaire, France, 348
Chon Et Fils, Gilbert, France, 349
Chopin, A., France, 349
Chopin-Groffier, France, 349
Choppin, A.R., France, 349
Chorherren Klosterneuberg, Austria, 249

Chouinard, USA, California, 873
Christian Brothers, USA, California, 873
Christine Woods, USA, California, 873
Christoffel, Joh. Jos., Germany, 617
Christoffel Erben, Joh. Jos., Germany, 617
Christophe, USA, California, 873
Christopher Creek, USA, California, 873
Church Road, New Zealand, 807
Churchill, Portugal, 749
Ciabot Berton, Italy, 671
Ciacci Piccolomini D'Aragona, Italy, 671
Cielo, Italy, 671
Cigliuti, Fratelli, Italy, 671
Cilurzo, USA, California, 873
Cima, Portugal, 750
Cimicky, Charles, Australia, 217
Cinciole, Le, Italy, 671
Cinnabar, USA, California, 873
Cinquin, Paul, France, 349
Cirri, USA, California, 874
Cispiano, Italy, 671
Cissac, Château, France, 349
Citran, Château, France, 349
Claiborne & Churchill, USA, California, 874
Clair, Bruno, France, 350
Clair, Françoise & Denis, France, 351
Clairefont, Château De, France, 351
Clairfont, Domaine De, France, 351
Clairvaux, USA, California, 874
Clancy's, Australia, 218
Clape, A., France, 351
Clarendon Hills, Australia, 218
Clark-Claudon, USA, California, 874
Clarke, Château, France, 351
Claudia Springs, USA, California, 874
Clavel, Domaine, France, 351
Claverie, Château La, France, 352
Clement, Abel, France, 352
Clément, Bernard & Pierre, France, 352
Clément Pichon, Château, France, 352
Clemente & Figli, Guasti, Italy, 671
Clerc & Fils, Henri, France, 352
Clerc Milon, Château, France, 353
Clerc, Laurent, France, 352
Clerget, Yvon, France, 353
Clerico, Domenico, Italy, 671
Cleveland, Australia, 218
Climens, Château, France, 353
Cline, USA, California, 874
Clinet, Château, France, 353
Cloninger, USA, California, 875
Clos Beauregard, France, 353
Clos Chaumont, Château, France, 353
Clos Danielle, USA, California, 875
Clos De L'Eglise, France, 353
Clos De L'Escandil, France, 354
Clos De L'Oratoire, France, 354
Clos De La Roilette, France, 354
Clos De Paulilles, Les, France, 354
Clos De Villemajou, France, 354
Clos Des Jacobins, Château, France, 354
Clos Des Papes, France, 354
Clos Du Bois, USA, California, 875
Clos Du Chêne, Le, France, 354
Clos Du Clocher, Château, France, 354
Clos Du Lac, USA, California, 876
Clos Du Marquis, France, 354
Clos Du Mont-Olivet, France, 354
Clos Du Pavillon, Domaine Du, France, 355
Clos Du Val, USA, California, 877
Clos Fourtet, France, 355
Clos Frantin, Domaine Du, France, 355
Clos Garbo, USA, Oregon, 878
Clos Haut-Peyraguey, Château, France, 355
Clos L'Abeilley, France, 356
Clos L'Eglise, France, 356
Clos La Coutale, France, 356
Clos La Fleur Figeac, France, 356
Clos Lachance, USA, California, 878
Clos Larcis, France, 356
Clos Malverne, South Africa, 766
Clos Marsalette, France, 356
Clos Naudin, Domaine Du, France, 356
Clos Noir, France, 356
Clos Pegase, USA, California, 878
Clos René, Château, France, 356
Clos Robert, USA, California, 878
Clos Roche Blanche, France, 356
Clos St.-Martin, France, 356
Clos St.-Michel, France, 356
Clos St.-Poncian, France, 357
Clos St. Thomas, USA, California, 878
Clos Triguedina, France, 357
Closel, Domaine Du, France, 357
Cloudy Bay, New Zealand, 807
Cloverdale Ranch, USA, California, 878
Clusel, Domaine, France, 357
Clusel Roch, France, 357
Clusière, Château La, France, 357
Clyde Park, Australia, 218
Coastal Cellars, Argentina, 799
Coastal Cellars, Bulgaria, 802
Coastal Cellars, USA, Washington, 878
Cobblestone, USA, California, 878
Cocci Grifoni, Italy, 672
Coche-Dury, J.-F., France, 357
Cockatoo Ridge, Australia, 218
Cockburn, Portugal, 750
Cocora Ortona, Italy, 672
Codorniu, Spain, 780
Codorniu Napa, USA, California, 879
Coffaro, David, USA, California, 879
Cogno, Elvio, Italy, 672
Cohn, B.R., USA, California, 879
Coing De St.-Fiacre, Château Du, France, 357
Col D'Orcia, Italy, 672
Col Des Vents, France, 357
Colbois, Domaine Daniel, France, 357
Colby, USA, California, 879
Cold Heaven, USA, California, 879
Coldridge, Australia, 218
Coldstream Hills, Australia, 218
Colgin, USA, California, 879
Colin, Madame François, France, 358
Colin, Marc, France, 358
Colin, Pierre, France, 359
Colin-Deléger, Michel, France, 359
Colio, Canada, 803
Colio, USA, Michigan, 883
Colla, Poderi, Italy, 673
Collards, New Zealand, 807
Collavini, Italy, 673
Colle, Il, Italy, 673
Colle Bereto, Italy, 673
Colle Di Trequanda, Il, Italy, 673
Collemattoni, Italy, 673
Collet, Jean, France, 359
Collin & Bourisset, France, 360
Collin Du Pin, France, 360
Collonge, Domaine De La, France, 360
Collosorbo, Italy, 673
Colmello Di Grotta, Italy, 673
Colognole, Italy, 673
Colombier, Domaine Du, France, 360

Colombier De Château Brown, Le, France, 360
Colombier-Monpelou, Château, France, 360
Colombo, Cantine, Italy, 673
Colombo, Jean-Luc, France, 360
Colony, USA, California, 880
Colorado Cellars, USA, Colorado, 880
Colosi, Italy, 674
Colour Volant, France, 360
Colterenzio, Italy, 674
Colue, Tenute, Italy, 674
Columbia, USA, Washington, 880
Columbia Crest, USA, Washington, 881
Combe, Pierre, France, 360
Combebelle, Château De, France, 361
Combier, Domaine, France, 361
Commanderie, Château La, France, 361
Compass, Argentina, 799
Comte De Beltour, Argentina, 799
Concadoro, Italy, 674
Concannon, USA, California, 882
Concavins, Bodegas, Spain, 781
Concha y Toro, Chile, 265
Condado De Haza, Spain, 781
Confuron, Jean-Jacques, France, 361
Confuron-Cotetidot, J., France, 361
Congress Springs, USA, California, 883
Conn Creek, USA, California, 883
Connétable De Talbot, France, 362
Cono Sur, Chile, 266
Conseillante, Château La, France, 362
Contadi Castaldi, Italy, 674
Conterno, Aldo, Italy, 674
Conterno, Giacomo, Italy, 675
Conterno, Paolo, Italy, 675
Conterno-Fantino, Italy, 674
Contino, Spain, 781
Contratto, Giuseppe, Italy, 675
Cook, R & J, USA, California, 883
Cook's, USA, California, 883
Cooper Mountain, USA, Oregon, 883
Cooper-Garrod, USA, California, 884
Coopers Creek, New Zealand, 808
Coopers' Legacy, USA, California, 884
Copertino, Cantina Sociale Cooperativa Del, Italy, 675
Coppo, Luigi, Italy, 675
Corbans, New Zealand, 808
Corbett Canyon, USA, California, 884
Corbin-Michotte, Château, France, 362
Corcia, France, 362
Cordeillan-Bages, Château, France, 362
Cordero Di Montezemolo, Paolo, Italy, 675
Cordier Père & Fils, France, 363
Corey Creek, USA, New York, 884
Corino, Italy, 675
Coriole, Australia, 218
Corison, USA, California, 884
Cormeil-Figeac, Château, France, 363
Cornacchia, Barone, Italy, 676
Cornarea, Italy, 676
Corneau, Domaine Paul, France, 363
Cornerstone, USA, California, 885
Cornu, Edmond, France, 363
Coron Père & Fils, France, 364
Coroncino, Fattoria, Italy, 676
Corral, Bodegas, Spain, 781
Correggia, Matteo, Italy, 676
Corsin, France, 364
Cortaccia, Cantina Sociale Di, Italy, 676
Corte Pavone, Italy, 676
Corte Sant'alda, Italy, 676
Corte Vecchia, Italy, 676
Cortese, Giuseppe, Italy, 676
Corti, Le, Italy, 676
Cortile, Il, Italy, 677
Corton André, Château, France, 365
Corvo, Italy, 677
Cos-D'Estournel, Château, France, 365
Cosentino, USA, California, 885
Coser, Fabio, Italy, 677
Cosi, Italy, 677
Cosimi, Rodolfo, Italy, 677
Cos-Labory, Château, France, 365
Cossart Gordon, Portugal, 750
Costanti, Conti, Italy, 677
Coste, Domaine De La, France, 365
Costeau, Madame, France, 366
Coste-Caumartin, France, 365
Costers Del Siurana, Spain, 781
Costières De Pomerols, Les, France, 366
Cotat, Paul, France, 366
Côte De Baleau, Château, France, 366
Côte De Rol, Château, France, 366
Côte Montpezat, Château, France, 366
Cotes De Sonoma, USA, California, 886
Cottin, Domaine, France, 366
Côtto, Quinta Do, Portugal, 750
Cottonwood Canyon, USA, California, 886
Coturri, USA, California, 886
Coucheroy, Château, France, 366
Coudert, Fernand, France, 366
Couëdic, Paul Du, France, 367
Coufran, Château, France, 367
Couhins-Lurton, Château, France, 367
Couillaud, Les Frères, France, 367
Coujan, Domaine De, France, 367
Coulon & Fils, Paul, France, 367
Coulson, USA, California, 886
Couly-Dutheil, France, 367
Cour Pavillon, La, France, 368
Couranconne, Château La, France, 368
Courbis, Maurice & Dominique, France, 368
Courcel, Domaine De, France, 368
Couronne, Château La, France, 368
Couroulu, Domaine Le, France, 368
Coursodon, Pierre, France, 368
Courtade, La, France, 368
Courtault, Jean-Claude, France, 368
Courteillac, Domaine De, France, 368
Courtesses, Domaine De, France, 369
Courtial, Michel, France, 369
Cousiño-Macul, Chile, 266
Couspaude, Château La, France, 369
Coussergues, Domaine De, France, 369
Couteiro-Mor, Portugal, 750
Coutet, Château, France, 369
Couvent Des Jacobins, France, 369
Covela, Quinta De, Portugal, 750
Covey Run, USA, Washington, 886
Covisa, Spain, 781
Cowra, Australia, 219
Coyeux, Domaine Des, France, 369
Coyne, Thomas, USA, California, 887
Craig, Robert, USA, California, 887
Crane Canyon, USA, California, 887
Crane Lake, Chile, 266
Cranswick, Australia, 219
Crasto, Quinta Do, Portugal, 750
Crawford, Kim, New Zealand, 808
Cremaschi Furlotti, Chile, 266
Creston, USA, California, 888
Crichton Hall, USA, California, 888
Cristom, USA, Washington, 888
Crittenden, Garry, Australia, 219
Crochet, Gilles, France, 369
Crochet, Lucien, France, 369

Crock, Château Le, France, 369
Croft, Portugal, 751
Croix, Château La, France, 369
Croix Canon, Château La, France, 369
Croix De Figeac, Château La, France, 369
Croix-De-Gay, Château La, France, 370
Croix Du Casse, Château La, France, 370
Croix-Millorit, Château De La, France, 370
Croix St.-Georges, Château La, France, 370
Croix Senaillet, Domaine De La, France, 370
Croizet-Bages, Château, France, 370
Cronin, USA, California, 888
Cros, Domaine, France, 370
Crosswoods, USA, New York, 889
Cruchet, Régis, France, 370
Crusius, Germany, 617
Crusius & Sohn, Hans, Germany, 618
Cruvinet, USA, California, 889
Cruzeau, Château De, France, 370
Crystal Valley, USA, California, 889
Cuckoo Hill, France, 370
Cueva Del Granero, Bodegas, Spain, 781
Cuilleron, Yves, France, 371
Cuisine Cellars, USA, California, 889
Culbertson, USA, California, 889
Cullen, Australia, 219
Cune, Spain, 781
Cuneo, Richard, USA, California, 889
Cuneo Cellars, USA, Washington, 889
Curé-Bon, Château, France, 371
Curé-Bon-La-Madeleine, Château, France, 371
Curros, Los, Spain, 782
Curson, Château, France, 371
Curtis, USA, California, 889
Cutler Cellar, USA, California, 890
Cuvaison, USA, California, 890
Cuvée Les Bastides, France, 371
Cuvée Pierre Rouge, France, 371
Cygne Blanc De Fonréaud, Le, France, 371
Cyprès De Climens, France, 371
Cyrano, France, 371
D'Angelo Vineyards, Canada, 803
D'Angelo Vineyards, USA, Michigan, 891
D'Angelo, Italy, 677
D'Arenberg, Australia, 219
D'Attimis, Conti, Italy, 677
Da Silva, C., Portugal, 751
Da Vinci, USA, California, 890
Dabin, Jean, France, 371
Dagueneau, Didier, France, 371
Dagueneau, Jean-Claude, France, 372
Dagueneau, Serge, France, 372
Dal Forno, Romano, Italy, 677
Dalem, Château, France, 372
Dalfarras, Australia, 219
Dalicieux, France, 372
Dalina, Chateau, Bulgaria, 803
Dalla Valle, USA, California, 890
Dalwhinnie, Australia, 219
Dame, Château De La, France, 372
Damoy, Pierre, France, 372
Dampierre, Comte Audoin De, France, 372
Daniel, USA, California, 891
Dard & Ribo, France, 372
Dark Star, USA, California, 891
Darting, Kurt, Germany, 618
Darviot, Yves, France, 372
Dashwood, New Zealand, 808
Dassault, Château, France, 372
Dauny, Nicole & Christian, France, 372
Dauphine, Château De La, France, 372
Dauvissat, Jean, France, 372
Dauvissat, René & Vincent, France, 373
Dauzac, Château, France, 373
Dauzan La Vergne, Château, France, 373
Davenay, Château De, France, 373
Davidson, USA, Oregon, 891
Daydream, USA, California, 891
D-Cubed Cellars, USA, California, 890
De Bortoli, Australia, 220
De Leuwen Jagt, South Africa, 766
De Loach, USA, California, 891
De Martino, Chile, 266
De Redcliffe, New Zealand, 808
De Rose, USA, California, 892
De Wetshof, South Africa, 766
Deakin, Australia, 220
Deaver, USA, California, 892
Debonne, USA, Ohio, 893
Decelle, Château La, France, 373
Decoy, USA, California, 893
Deer Park, USA, California, 893
Deer Valley, USA, California, 893
Deerfield Ranch, USA, California, 893
Defaix, Bernard, France, 373
Dehlinger, USA, California, 893
Dei, Italy, 677
Deinhard, Germany, 618
Deiss, Domaine Marcel, France, 373
Del Dotto, USA, California, 894
Delaby-Génot, Marie, France, 374
Delaforce, Portugal, 751
Delamotte, France, 374
Delaporte, Domaine Vincent, France, 374
Delarche Père & Fils, Marius, France, 374
Delas, France, 374
Delaunay, Edouard, France, 375
Delbeck, France, 375
Delectus, USA, California, 894
Delegat's, New Zealand, 808
Delesvaux, Philippe, France, 375
Deletang, Domaine, France, 375
Delheim, South Africa, 767
Delille, USA, Washington, 894
Delizia, La, Italy, 677
Delmas, Y. & D., France, 375
Delorimier, USA, California, 894
Demeraulmont, Château, France, 376
Demessey, France, 376
Demoor, USA, California, 894
Denatale, USA, California, 895
Dervieux-Thaize, A., France, 376
Deschamps, Domaine Claudine, France, 376
Deschamps, Marc, France, 376
Deschaux, Lucien, France, 376
Deshenrys, Domaine, France, 377
Desmeures, Domaine, France, 377
Desmirail, Château, France, 377
Desserre, Domaine, France, 377
Dessilani, Italy, 677
Destieux, Château, France, 377
Destinare, South Africa, 767
Desvignes, Louis-Claude, France, 377
Desvignes Aîné & Fils, France, 377
Deurre, Domaine De, France, 377
Deutz, France, 377
Deux Amis, USA, California, 895
Deux Roches, Domaine Des, France, 378
Devil's Lair, Australia, 220
Devise De Lilian, La, France, 378
Devlin, USA, California, 895
Devon Cellars, USA, Washington, 895

Devoy Martine, Château Le, France, 378
Deydier & Fils, Domaine Jean, France, 378
Deyrem-Valentin, Château, France, 378
Di Bruno, USA, California, 895
Di Majo Norante, Italy, 678
Di Stefano, USA, Washington, 895
Diamond Creek, USA, California, 895
Diane De Belgrave, France, 378
Diaz, J., Spain, 782
Dickerson, USA, California, 897
Diconne, Jean-Pierre, France, 378
Diel, Schlossgut, Germany, 618
Dietrich, Domaine Robert, France, 378
Dievole, Italy, 678
Diez Hermanos, Portugal, 751
Dillon, Château, France, 378
Dimerie, Château De La, France, 378
Diochon, Domaine, France, 378
Dirler, France, 378
Disznókö, Hungary, 805
Doctors Creek, New Zealand, 808
Doisy-Daëne, Château, France, 379
Doisy-Védrines, Château, France, 379
Dolan, USA, California, 897
Dolce, USA, California, 897
Dom Hermano, Portugal, 751
Domaine Breton, USA, California, 898
Domaine Carneros, USA, California, 898
Domaine Chandon, USA, California, 898
Domaine Charbay, USA, California, 898
Domaine De Clarck, USA, California, 898
Domaine De La Terre Rouge, USA, California, 898
Domaine Drouhin, USA, Oregon, 898
Domaine Michel, USA, California, 899
Domaine Napa, USA, California, 899
Domaine Philippe, USA, California, 899
Domaine Saint George, USA, California, 899
Domaine Ste. Michelle, USA, Washington, 899
Domaine Ste. Vincent, USA, California, 899
Domaine San Martin, USA, California, 899
Domaine Santa Barbara, USA, California, 899
Domaine Serene, USA, Oregon, 899
Domecq, Bodegas, Argentina, 799
Domecq, Pedro, Spain, 782
Dominique, Château La, France, 379
Dominus Estate, USA, California, 899
Dona, Cellier De La, France, 379
Dona Baissas, Château, France, 379
Doña Sol, Chile, 267
Donats, Château Les, France, 379
Donjon, Château Du, France, 379
Donna Maria, USA, California, 899
Dönnhoff, H., Germany, 619
Donoso, Casa, Chile, 267
Dopff & Irion, France, 379
Dopff Au Moulin, France, 380
Dorcich Cellars, USA, California, 899
Dore, USA, California, 899
Dos Cabezas, USA, Arizona, 899
Dosio, Italy, 678
Doudet-Naudin, France, 380
Douglass Hill, USA, California, 900
Dourthe, Pierre, France, 380
Doutres, Robert, France, 380
Dover Canyon, USA, California, 900
Dow, Portugal, 751
Doyenné, Château Le, France, 380
Dozon, Domaine, France, 380
Dracy, Château De, France, 380
Drago, Cascino, Italy, 678
Drappier, France, 380
Draxton, USA, California, 900
Drayton's, Australia, 220
Dreyer Sonoma, USA, California, 900
Droin, Jean-Paul, France, 380
Dromana, Australia, 220
Drostdyhof, South Africa, 767
Drouhin, Joseph, France, 381
Drouhin, Robert, France, 386
Drouhin-Laroze, France, 386
Drouin, Béatrice & Jean-Michel, France, 386
Druet, Pierre-Jacques, France, 386
Dry Creek, USA, California, 900
Duboeuf, Georges, France, 387
Dubois, Jean-Luc, France, 389
Dubreuil-Fontaine Père & Fils, P., France, 389
Duchi Di Castelluccio, Italy, 678
Duck Pond, USA, Washington, 901
Duck Walk, USA, New York, 901
Duckhorn, USA, California, 901
Ducla, Château, France, 390
Ducluzeau, Château, France, 390
Ducru-Beaucaillou, Château, France, 390
Duff Gordon, Portugal, 752
Dufouleur, Lois, France, 391
Dufouleur Père & Fils, France, 391
Dugat, Claude, France, 391
Dugat-Py, Bernard, France, 391
Duhart-Milon Rothschild, Château, France, 391
Dujac, France, 391
Dulong, France, 392
Duluc, Château, France, 392
Dumangin, Jean, France, 392
Dumas, Laurent, France, 392
Dunavár, Hungary, 806
Duncan Peak, USA, California, 902
Dundee Springs, USA, Oregon, 902
Dunham, USA, Washington, 902
Dunn, USA, California, 902
Dunnewood, USA, California, 903
Dunning, USA, California, 903
Duplessis, Château, France, 392
Duplessis-Fabre, Château, France, 393
Dupuis, André, France, 393
Durand, Nöel & Jöel, France, 393
Durban, Domaine De, France, 393
Durdilly, Pierre & Paul, France, 393
Durfort-Vivens, Château, France, 393
Durieu, Domaine, France, 393
Durney, USA, California, 903
Duron, Bodegas, Spain, 782
Duval-Leroy, France, 393
Duvergey-Taboureau, France, 393
Duvernay, France, 393
Duxoup, USA, California, 903
Eagle Ridge, USA, California, 903
Easton, USA, California, 903
Eaton Hill, USA, Washington, 903
Eberbach, Staatsweingüter Kloster, Germany, 619
Eberle, USA, California, 904
Ecard, Maurice, France, 393
Ecco Domani, Italy, 678
Echeverria, Chile, 267
Ecu, Domaine De L', France, 393
Eddy, Tom, USA, California, 904
Eden Roc, USA, California, 904
Edgefield, USA, Oregon, 904
Edgewood, USA, California, 904
Edmeades, USA, California, 905

Edmunds St. John, USA, California, 905
Edna Valley, USA, California, 905
Edwards, Luis Felipe, Chile, 267
Eglise Clinet, Château L', France, 393
Eglise, Château Du Domaine De L', France, 393
Egly-Ouriet, France, 394
Ehlen, Stephan, Germany, 620
Ehlers Grove, USA, California, 905
Eikendal, South Africa, 767
Einaudi, Luigi, Italy, 678
Eira Velha, Quinta Da, Portugal, 752
Eiras, Adegas Das, Spain, 782
Eisele, Volker, USA, California, 905
Eklund, USA, California, 906
El Cep, Spain, 782
El Coto, Spain, 782
El Molino, USA, California, 906
Elan, USA, California, 906
Elderton, Australia, 220
Elena Talier, Spain, 782
Elget, Château, France, 394
Elizabeth, USA, California, 906
Elk Cove, USA, Oregon, 906
Elkhorn Peak, USA, California, 907
Elkton Valley, USA, Oregon, 907
Ellendale, USA, Oregon, 907
Elliott, USA, California, 907
Ellis, Neil, South Africa, 767
Elliston, USA, California, 907
Elyse, USA, California, 907
Emmolo, USA, California, 907
Enclos, Château L', France, 394
Endrizzi, Italy, 678
Engarran, Château De L', France, 394
Engel, René, France, 394
Eno-Friulia, Italy, 678
Entre Nous, France, 394
Envero, Spain, 782
Eola Hills, USA, Oregon, 907
Eos, USA, California, 908
Epayrié, L', France, 394
Epiré, Château D', France, 394
Epoch, USA, California, 908
Equinox, USA, California, 908
Erath Vineyards, USA, Oregon, 908
Erbaluna, Italy, 679
Eric Ross, USA, California, 908
Ermita De Pio, Spain, 782
Ermitage De Pic St.-Loup, France, 394
Errazuriz, Chile, 267
Eser, August, Germany, 620
Esk Valley, New Zealand, 808
Esmeralda, Bodegas, Argentina, 799
Esmonin, Frédéric, France, 394
Esmonin, Michel, France, 395
Espérance, Château L', France, 395
Espigouette, Domaine De L', France, 395
Esporão, Herdade Do, Portugal, 752
Esprit De Chevalier, France, 395
Estancia, USA, California, 908
Estate Baccala, USA, California, 909
Estiac, Baron D', France, 395
Estola, Spain, 782
Estournel, Maitre-D', France, 395
Estrella River, USA, California, 909
Estremieres, Domaine Des, France, 395
Etang Des Colombes, Château, France, 395
Etang Du Moulin, France, 395
Etchart, Argentina, 800
Etude, USA, California, 909
Etxaniz Txakolina, Spain, 782
Evangile, Château L', France, 395
Evans & Tate, Australia, 220
Evans Wine Company, Australia, 220
Everest, USA, California, 909
Evesham Wood, USA, Oregon, 909
Expressions, USA, California, 910
Eye Of The Swan, USA, California, 910
Eyrie, USA, Oregon, 910
Facelli, USA, Washington, 910
Fairview Estate, South Africa, 767
Faiveley, J., France, 395
Faizeau, Château, France, 397
Falchini, Riccardo, Italy, 679
Falcoaria, Portugal, 752
Falconer, USA, California, 910
Falesco, Italy, 679
Fall Creek, USA, Texas, 910
Fanti, Italy, 679
Fantinel, Italy, 679
Fanucchi, USA, California, 911
Far Niente, USA, California, 911
Faraud, Michel, France, 397
Farella-Park, USA, California, 911
Fargues, Château De, France, 397
Fariña, Bodegas, Spain, 782
Farina, Remo, Italy, 679
Farina, Stefano, Italy, 679
Farnese, Italy, 680
Farneta, Tenuta, Italy, 680
Farnete, Le, Italy, 680
Farnetella, Castello Di, Italy, 680
Farrell, Gary, USA, California, 911
Fassati, Italy, 680
Fastelli, Italy, 680
Fathom, USA, California, 912
Fattoi, Italy, 680
Faugères, Château, France, 397
Faure, Château Jean, France, 397
Faurie, Bernard, France, 397
Faury, Phillippe, France, 397
Faustino Martinez, Bodegas, Spain, 783
Fausto Gemme, Italy, 680
Fauterie, Domaine De, France, 397
Faux Frog, Le, France, 398
Favray, Château De, France, 398
Favreau, Yannick, France, 398
Fayolle, France, 398
Fazi-Battaglia, Italy, 680
Fazio, Nicolás E., Argentina, 800
Feiler-Artinger, Austria, 250
Feist, Portugal, 752
Felluga, Livio, Italy, 680
Felluga, Marco, Italy, 681
Felsina, Fattoria Di, Italy, 681
Fenestra, USA, California, 912
Fenn Valley, USA, Michigan, 912
Fenouillet, Domaine De, France, 398
Fensalir, USA, California, 912
Ferme St.-Martin, Domaine De La, France, 398
Fermentations & More, USA, California, 912
Fernandez, Bodegas Alejandro, Spain, 783
Feronia, Italy, 681
Ferrand, Château, France, 398
Ferrande, Château, France, 398
Ferrari, Italy, 681
Ferrari-Carano, USA, California, 912
Ferrari-Corradi, Italy, 682
Ferraton, Michel, France, 398
Ferraud & Fils, Pierre, France, 398
Ferreira, Portugal, 752
Ferreira, Antonio Esteves, Portugal, 752
Ferreirinha, Casa, Portugal, 752
Ferret, J.-A., France, 398
Ferrière, Château, France, 399

Fesles, Château De, France, 399
Fessy, Henry, France, 399
Fessy, Sylvain, France, 399
Fetzer, USA, California, 913
Feudi Di San Gregorio, Italy, 682
Feuerheerd, Portugal, 752
Feuillatte, Nicolas, France, 399
Fèvre, William, France, 399
Feytit-Clinet, Château, France, 399
Ficklin, USA, California, 915
Fiddlehead, USA, California, 915
Fiefs De Lagrange, Les, France, 400
Field Stone, USA, California, 915
Fieldbrook, USA, California, 915
Fields Of Fair, USA, Kansas, 916
Fieuzal, Château De, France, 400
Fife, USA, California, 916
Fifth Leg, Australia, 221
Figaro, France, 400
Figeac, Château, France, 400
Figeat, Colette, France, 400
Filhot, Château, France, 400
Filigare, Le, Italy, 682
Filippi, Jeanne Paule, France, 401
Filippi, Joseph, USA, California, 916
Filiputti, Walter, Italy, 682
Fillaboa, Granja, Spain, 783
Filliatreau, L., France, 401
Fines Roches, Château Des, France, 401
Fini, Barone, Italy, 682
Fioriae, Le, Italy, 682
Fiorina, Franco, Italy, 682
Firelands, USA, Ohio, 916
Firesteed, Italy, 682
Firesteed, USA, Oregon, 916
Firestone, USA, California, 917
Fisher, USA, California, 917
Fitch Mountain, USA, California, 918
Fitz-Ritter, Germany, 620
Five Mile Hollow, Australia, 221
Flame Opal, Australia, 221
Fleur, Château La, France, 401
Fleur-Cardinale, Château, France, 401
Fleur Cravignac, Château La, France, 402
Fleur De Carneros Cellars, USA, California, 918
Fleur De Gay, Château La, France, 402
Fleur Du Cap, South Africa, 767
Fleur Lartigue, Château, France, 402
Fleur-Pétrus, Château La, France, 401
Fleur-Pourret, Château La, France, 401
Fleur-St.-Georges, Château La, France, 401
Flichman, Finca, Argentina, 800
Flora Springs, USA, California, 918
Flowers, USA, California, 919
Flynn, USA, Oregon, 919
Fogarty, Thomas, USA, California, 919
Foillard, Jean, France, 402
Folie a Deux, USA, California, 919
Follin-Arbelet, Franck, France, 402
Folonari, Italy, 682
Fombrauge, Château, France, 402
Fonbadet, Château, France, 402
Fonné, Domaine, France, 402
Fonplégade, Château, France, 402
Fonréaud, Château, France, 402
Fonroque, Château, France, 402
Fonsalette, Château De, France, 403
Fonseca, Portugal, 753
Fonseca, José Maria Da, Portugal, 753
Font D'Estévenas, La, France, 403
Font De Michelle, Domaine, France, 403
Font Du Loup, Château De La, France, 403
Font Villac, France, 403
Fontaine St.-Martin, Château La, France, 404
Fontaine, Château La, France, 403
Fontaine-Gagnard, France, 403
Fontana Candida, Italy, 682
Fontanabianca, Italy, 682
Fontanafredda, Italy, 683
Fontanche, Château De, France, 404
Fontanelles, Domaine Des, France, 404
Fontenay, Henry De, France, 404
Fontenil, Château, France, 404
Fontenille, Château De, France, 404
Fonterutoli, Castello Di, Italy, 683
Fontevino, Italy, 683
Fonti, Fattoria Le, Italy, 684
Fontjun, Domaine Du, France, 404
Fontodi, Italy, 684
Fontsainte, Domaine De, France, 404
Font-Sane, Domaine De, France, 403
Foote, E.B., USA, Washington, 919
Foppiano, USA, California, 919
Foradori, Italy, 684
Foreau, France, 404
Forest Glen, USA, California, 920
Forest Hill, USA, California, 920
Forest Lake, USA, California, 920
Forest Ville, USA, California, 920
Forêt, Château La, France, 405
Forey Père & Fils, France, 405
Forge, La, France, 405
Forgeron, USA, Oregon, 920
Foris, USA, Oregon, 920
Forman, USA, California, 921
Formentini, Conti, Italy, 684
Fornelos, Lagar De, Spain, 783
Forrest, New Zealand, 808
Fortant De France, France, 405
Fortia, Château, France, 405
Fortnum & Mason, France, 405
Forts De Latour, Les, France, 405
Fortuna, La, Italy, 684
Fortune, Domaine, France, 405
Forum Prior Do Crato, Portugal, 753
Foss Creek, USA, California, 921
Fossi, Italy, 684
Fouassier Père & Fils, France, 406
Fougeray De Beauclair, France, 406
Fougeray, Domaine, France, 406
Fountain Grove, USA, California, 921
Four Corners, USA, California, 921
Four Sisters, Australia, 221
Fourcas-Dupré, Château, France, 406
Fourcas-Hosten, Château, France, 406
Fourcas-Loubaney, Château, France, 406
Fournas-Bernadotte, Château, France, 406
Fowler, USA, California, 921
Fox Creek, Australia, 221
Fox Mountain, USA, California, 921
Fox River, Australia, 221
Fox Run, USA, New York, 921
Foxen, USA, California, 922
Foxhollow, USA, California, 922
Fracassi, Umberto, Italy, 685
Framingham, New Zealand, 808
Francal, USA, California, 923
Franc-Bigaroux, Château, France, 406
France, Château De, France, 406
Francesco, Italy, 685
Franciscan Oakville Estate, USA, California, 923
Franc-Jaugue-Blanc, Château, France, 406
Franc-Mayne, Château, France, 406

Franco, Nino, Italy, 685
Frank, Dr. Konstantin, USA, New York, 923
Frank Phélan, France, 407
Frankhof, Germany, 620
Frankland, Australia, 221
Frank-Rombauer Larkmead, USA, California, 923
Franus, USA, California, 924
Frazier, USA, California, 924
Freemark Abbey, USA, California, 924
Freestone, USA, California, 925
Freie Weingartner Wachau, Austria, 250
Freixenet, Spain, 783
Frejau, Domaine Lou, France, 407
Fremont Creek, USA, California, 925
French Creek, USA, Washington, 925
French Farm, New Zealand, 808
Frescobaldi, Marchesi De', Italy, 685
Frey, USA, California, 925
Freynelle, Château La, France, 407
Frick, USA, California, 925
Frick, Pierre, France, 407
Friedrich-Wilhelm-Gymnasium, Germany, 620
Friggiali, Tenuta, Italy, 685
Frimaio, Italy, 686
Fritsch, Weinberghof, Austria, 250
Fritz, J., USA, California, 925
Frog's Leap, USA, California, 926
Fuentes, J.M., Spain, 783
Fuga, Tenuta La, Italy, 686
Fuissé, Château, France, 407
Fuligni, Eredi, Italy, 686
Furlan Castelcosa, Italy, 686
Fussiacus, France, 407
G'Sell, USA, California, 926
Gabbiano, Castello Di, Italy, 686
Gabrielli, USA, California, 926
Gaffelière, Château La, France, 407
Gagliardo, Gianni, Italy, 687
Gagnard, Jean-Noël, France, 407
Gagnerot & Fils, François, France, 408
Gaierhof, Italy, 687
Gaillard, Pierre, France, 408
Gainey, USA, California, 926
Gaja, Italy, 687
Galante, USA, California, 927
Galardi, Fattoria, Italy, 688
Galegas, Adegas, Spain, 783
Galet Des Papes, Domaine Du, France, 408
Galet Vineyards, France, 408
Galichets, Les, France, 408
Gallais, Le, Germany, 620
Gallant, Australia, 221
Galleron, USA, California, 927
Galliffet, Château De, France, 408
Gallo, E. & J., USA, California, 927
Gallo of Sonoma, USA, California, 927
Gamage, Château, France, 408
Gambier, Jean, France, 408
Gamla, Israel, 807
Gan Eden, USA, California, 928
Gancia, Italy, 688
Gandia, Spain, 783
Garaudet, Jean, France, 408
Garaudet, Paul, France, 409
Garde, Château La, France, 409
Gardine, Château De La, France, 409
Garenne, Domaine De La, France, 410
Garland Ranch, USA, California, 928
Garmont, France, 410
Garofoli, Italy, 688
Garrett, Andrew, Australia, 221
Garrigues, Les, France, 410
Garzas, Las, Chile, 268
Gastaldi, Italy, 688
Gattavecchi, Italy, 688
Gauby, Domaine, France, 410
Gaudet, Jean-François, France, 410
Gaudry, Domaine Denis, France, 410
Gauer Estate, USA, California, 928
Gaunoux, Jean-Michel, France, 410
Gauthier, Pierre, France, 410
Gautier, Benoit, France, 410
Gavoty, Domaines, France, 410
Gay, Château Le, France, 410
Gazin, Château, France, 410
Geantet-Pansiot, France, 411
Gehrs, Daniel, USA, California, 928
Geisweller & Fils, France, 411
Gemello, USA, California, 928
Gendrier, Michel, France, 411
Genillon, Domaine De, France, 411
Gentaz-Dervieux, France, 411
Geoffroy, Alain, France, 411
Geoffroy, René, France, 411
Geografico, Italy, 688
Georis, USA, California, 928
Gerard, François, France, 411
Gerin, Jean-Michel, France, 411
Gerla, La, Italy, 688
Germain, Henri, Burgundy, France, 412
Germain, Henri, Champagne, France, 412
Germain, Jacques, France, 412
Germain, Marie-Pierre, France, 412
Germain, Thierry, France, 412
Germanier-Balavaud, Switzerland, 813
Germano, Ettore, Italy, 688
Geymuller, Domaine Baron, Austria, 250
Geyser Peak, USA, California, 929
Ghisolfi, Attilio, Italy, 688
Ghizzano, Tenuta Di, Italy, 689
Giacosa, Bruno, Italy, 689
Giacosa, Carlo, Italy, 689
Giacosa Fratelli, Italy, 689
Gibalaux, Domaine, France, 412
Gibbston Valley, New Zealand, 808
Gicoma, USA, California, 930
Giesen, New Zealand, 808
Gilbert, Portugal, 754
Gilette, Château, France, 412
Gillet, Emilian, France, 413
Gilliard, Robert, Switzerland, 813
Giloux, Isabelle & Patrick, France, 413
Gimonnet & Fils, Pierre, France, 413
Ginglinger, Paul, France, 413
Gini, Italy, 689
Gioiosa, La, Italy, 689
Giovello, Italy, 689
Girard, USA, California, 930
Girard, Domaine, France, 413
Girard, Robert, France, 413
Girardet, USA, Oregon, 930
Girardin, Aleth, France, 413
Girardin, Armand, France, 413
Girardin, Jean, France, 413
Girardin, Vincent, France, 413
Giribaldi, Azienda, Italy, 689
Giscours, Château, France, 414
Giustiniana, La, Italy, 689
Glana, Château Du, France, 414
Glass Mountain Quarry, USA, California, 930
Glatzer, W., Austria, 250
Gleeson's Ridge, Australia, 221
Glen Carlou, South Africa, 767
Glen Ellen, USA, California, 930

Glen Fiona, USA, Washington, 931
Glenora, USA, New York, 931
Gleon Montanie, Château, France, 415
Glicine, Cantina Del, Italy, 689
Gloria, Château, France, 415
Gloria Ferrer, USA, California, 931
Glorian, Daphne, Spain, 784
Gobelsburg, Schloss, Austria, 251
Gobet, P., France, 415
Godeau, Château, France, 415
Godspeed, USA, California, 931
Godwin, USA, California, 931
Goerg, Paul, France, 415
Goisot, Ghislaine & Jean-Hugues, France, 415
Golan, Israel, 807
Gold Hill, USA, California, 931
Golden Creek, USA, California, 931
Goldwater, New Zealand, 808
Gomerie, Château La, France, 415
Gondi, Marchese, Italy, 690
Gonet, Michel, France, 416
Gonon, Pierre, France, 416
Gonzalez Byass, Spain, 784
Good Hope Wines, South Africa, 768
Gordon Brothers, USA, Washington, 931
Gorelli, Italy, 690
Goretti Miniati, Italy, 690
Gossamer Bay, USA, California, 932
Gosset, France, 416
Goubard, Michel, France, 416
Goubert, Domaine Les, France, 416
Gouges, Henri, France, 416
Goulaine, Marquis De, France, 417
Gould Campbell, Portugal, 754
Goulet, George, France, 417
Goundrey, Australia, 221
Gour De Chaule, Domaine Du, France, 417
Gourgazaud, Château De, France, 417
Gouzotte D'Or, La, France, 417
Gracciano Della Seta, Tenuta Di, Italy, 690
Grace Family, USA, California, 932
Graceland, USA, California, 932
Graeser, USA, California, 932
Graf Hardegg, Austria, 251
Graff, Carl, Germany, 620
Graff, Richard, USA, California, 932
Graham, Gregory, USA, California, 932
Graham, Portugal, 754
Graillot, Alain, France, 417
Gramenon, Domaine, France, 417
Gran Condal, Spain, 784
Gran Corpas, Spain, 784
Grand Barrail Lamarzelle Figeac, Château, France, 417
Grand Caumont, Château Du, France, 417
Grand Chariot, France, 417
Grand Chemin, Château, France, 418
Grand Claret, Château, France, 418
Grand Cres, Domaine Du, France, 418
Grand Cru, USA, California, 932
Grand-Corbin-Despagne, Château, France, 418
Grand Maison, Domaine De, France, 418
Grand-Mayne, Château, France, 418
Grand Montmirail, Domaine Du, France, 418
Grand Moulas, Château Du, France, 418
Grand Moulin, Château, France, 418
Grand-Moulinet, Château, France, 418
Grand-Pontet, Château, France, 418
Grand-Puy-Ducasse, Château, France, 418
Grand-Puy-Lacoste, Château, France, 418
Grand-Romane, Domaine, France, 419
Grand Tinel, Domaine Du, France, 418
Grand Village, Château, France, 418
Grandes Bodegas, Spain, 784
Grandes Murailles, Château Les, France, 419
Grands Chênes, Château Les, France, 419
Grands Devers, Domaine Des, France, 419
Grands Maréchaux, Château Les, France, 419
Grange Clinet, Château La, France, 419
Grange De Grenet, Château La, France, 419
Grangehurst, South Africa, 768
Grangeneuve, Domaine De, France, 419
Grangeotte, Château La, France, 419
Grangère, Château La, France, 419
Granges, Château Les, France, 419
Granges, Les, France, 419
Granges D'Or, Château Des, France, 419
Granite Creek, South Africa, 768
Granite Springs, USA, California, 932
Grans-Fassian, Germany, 621
Grant Smith Ltd., Australia, 222
Gras, Alain, France, 419
Grasso, Elio, Italy, 690
Grasso, Silvio, Italy, 690
Gratien, Alfred, France, 419
Gratien & Meyer, France, 420
Grattamacco, Italy, 690
Grave, Château De La, France, 420
Grave à Pomerol, Château La, France, 420
Gravner, Italy, 690
Green, Douglas, South Africa, 768
Green & Red, USA, California, 932
Green Point, Australia, 222
Greenstone, USA, California, 933
Greenvale, USA, New England, 933
Greenwood Ridge, USA, California, 933
Greffet, Domaine, France, 420
Greffière, Château De La, France, 420
Grenouilles, Château, France, 420
Greppone Mazzi, Tenuta Il, Italy, 690
Gressier-Grand-Poujeaux, Château, France, 420
Gresy, Marchesi Di, Italy, 690
Gretole, Poderi Di, Italy, 691
Grevepesa, Castelli Del, Italy, 691
Greysac, Château, France, 420
Grgich Hills, USA, California, 933
Griffin, Barnard, USA, Washington, 934
Grille, Château De La, France, 420
Griñon, Marqués De, Spain, 784
Gripa, Bernard, France, 420
Grippat, J.L., France, 420
Gristina, USA, New York, 934
Grivault, Albert, France, 420
Grivière, Château, France, 421
Grivot, Jean, France, 421
Groffier, Robert, France, 421
Grolet, Château La, France, 421
Grolle, Père La, France, 422
Gromis, Italy, 691
Groot Constantia, South Africa, 768
Gros, A.-F., France, 422
Gros, Anne, France, 422
Gros, Anne & François, France, 422
Gros, Jean, France, 423
Gros, Michel, France, 423
Gros Frère & Soeur, France, 423

Grosset, Australia, 222
Grossombre, Château, France, 424
Grossot, Jean-Pierre, France, 424
Groth, USA, California, 934
Grothé, Caves Jean, France, 424
Groupement De Producteurs De Prissé, France, 425
Grove Mill, New Zealand, 809
Grove Street, Argentina, 800
Grove Street, USA, California, 935
Gruaud-Larose, Château, France, 425
Gruet, USA, New Mexico, 935
Gsellmann & Gsellmann, Austria, 251
Gualdo Del Re, Italy, 691
Guelbenzu, Bodegas, Spain, 784
Guenoc, USA, California, 935
Guérin, André, France, 425
Guérin, René, France, 425
Guérin, Thierry, France, 425
Guerra Luigi, Italy, 691
Guffens-Heynen, France, 426
Guglielmo, USA, California, 936
Guibon, Château, France, 426
Guicciardini Strozzi, Italy, 691
Guicciardini, Conte Ferdinando, Italy, 691
Guigal, E., France, 426
Guilbaud, Heritiers, France, 428
Guillemot, Pierre, France, 428
Guilliams, USA, California, 936
Guillot-Clauzel, Château, France, 428
Guimonière, Château De La, France, 428
Guiraud, Château, France, 428
Guiraud-Cheval-Blanc, Château, France, 428
Gunderloch, Germany, 621
Gundlach Bundschu, USA, California, 936
Gunes, Château Des, France, 428
Guntrum, Louis, Germany, 621
Gurgue, Château La, France, 428
Gurpegui Muga, Bodegas Luis, Spain, 784
Gutierrez De La Vega, Bodegas, Spain, 784
Guy, Bernard, France, 428
Guyard, Alain, France, 428
Guyon, Antonin, France, 428
Guyot, Jean-Claude, France, 429
Haag, Domaine Jean-Marie, France, 429
Haag, Fritz, Germany, 621
Haart, Johann, Germany, 621
Haart, Reinhold, Germany, 621
Haas, Franz, Italy, 691
Hacienda, USA, California, 937
Haderburg, Italy, 691
Haegelen-Jayer, France, 429
Hagafen, USA, California, 937
Hahn, USA, California, 938
Hallcrest, USA, California, 938
Hamacher, USA, Oregon, 938
Hambrecht, USA, California, 938
Hamel, USA, California, 938
Hamelin, E.A.R.L., France, 429
Hamelin, Thierry, France, 429
Hamilton Russell, South Africa, 768
Hamilton, Richard, Australia, 222
Handley, USA, California, 938
Hanna, USA, California, 939
Hanteillan, Château, France, 429
Hanwood, Australia, 222
Hanzell, USA, California, 939
Happs, Australia, 222
Harbor, USA, California, 940
Hardys, Australia, 222
Hargrave, USA, New York, 940
Harlan Estate, USA, California, 940
Harmony Cellars, USA, California, 940
Harris, Randall, USA, Washington, 940
Harrison, USA, California, 940
Hart, USA, California, 940
Hart's Desire, USA, California, 941
Hartford Court, USA, California, 941
Hartwell, USA, California, 941
Harvard, Australia, 223
Haselgrove, Australia, 223
Haskovo Winery, Bulgaria, 803
Hatzimichalis, Domaine, Greece, 804
Haut-Bages-Avérous, Château, France, 429
Haut-Bages-Libéral, Château, France, 429
Haut-Bailly, Château, France, 430
Haut-Batailley, Château, France, 430
Haut-Beauséjour, Château, France, 430
Haut-Bergeron, Château, France, 430
Haut-Bergey, Château, France, 430
Haut-Bernat, Château, France, 430
Haut-Brie-Caillou, Château, France, 430
Haut-Brion, Château, France, 430
Haut Bommes, Château, France, 430
Haut-Corbin, Château, France, 431
Haut De La Bécade, Château, France, 431
Haut Des Terres Blanches, Domaine Du, France, 431
Haut Faugères, Château, France, 431
Haut-Gardère, Château, France, 432
Haut-Lagrange, Château, France, 432
Haut-Lariveau, Château, France, 432
Haut-Maillet, Château, France, 432
Haut-Marbuzet, Château, France, 432
Haut-Mazières, Château, France, 432
Haut-Nouchet, Château, France, 432
Haut-Redon, Château, France, 432
Haut-Rian, Château, France, 432
Haute Galine, Domaine, France, 431
Haute Provence Vineyards, South Africa, 768
Hauterive Le Haut, Château, France, 431
Hautes Ouches, Domaine Des, France, 433
Haut Sarpe, Château, France, 432
Haute-Serre, Château De, France, 432
Hauts-Conseillants, Château Les, France, 433
Haut-Surget, Château, France, 433
Haut-Vigneau, Château, France, 433
Hauts De Brame, Château Les, France, 433
Hauts De Plaisance, Château Les, France, 433
Hauts De Pontet, Les, France, 433
Hauts De Smith, Les, France, 433
Haux, Château De, France, 433
Havens, USA, California, 941
Hawk Crest, USA, California, 941
Hawley, USA, California, 941
Hawthorn Hill, Australia, 223
Haywood, USA, California, 941
Hazlitt 1852, USA, New York, 942
Hébrart, Marc, France, 433
Hecker Pass, USA, California, 942
Hedges, USA, Washington, 942
Heggies, Australia, 224
Heidsieck, Charles, France, 433
Heidsieck Monopole, France, 433
Heinrich, Austria, 251
Heitz, USA, California, 942
Helena View, USA, California, 943
Hélène, Château, France, 434

Helms, H.W., USA, California, 943
Hendry Ranch, USA, California, 943
Henriot, France, 434
Henriques & Henriques, Portugal, 754
Henry Estate, USA, Oregon, 944
Henschke, Australia, 224
Herbeaux, Château Des, France, 434
Heresztyn, Bernard, France, 434
Heresztyn, Stanislas, France, 434
Heritage, Australia, 224
Héritier-Guyot, L', France, 434
Hermanos Del Villar, Bodega, Spain, 784
Hermitage, Château L', France, 435
Hermitage Road, Australia, 224
Heron, France, 435
Heron Hill, USA, New York, 944
Heron Lake, USA, California, 944
Herrnsheim, Heyl Zu, Germany, 622
Herzog, France, 435
Hess Collection, The, USA, California, 944
Hess Select, USA, California, 945
Hetszolo, Hungary, 806
Hewn, Hans, USA, California, 945
Hickok, USA, California, 945
Hickory Ridge, Hungary, 806
Hidden Cellars, USA, California, 945
Hidden Springs, USA, Oregon, 946
Hiedler, Austria, 251
High Pass, USA, Oregon, 946
Highbank, Australia, 224
Highfield, New Zealand, 809
Hill, William, USA, California, 946
Hill & Thoma Winegrowers, USA, California, 946
Hill-Smith Estate, Australia, 224
Hillstowe, Australia, 225
Hinman, USA, Oregon, 946
Hirtzberger, Franz, Austria, 251
Hitching Post, USA, California, 946
Hobbs, Paul, USA, California, 947
Hogue, USA, Washington, 947
Homewood, USA, California, 948
Honig, USA, California, 949
Hoodsport, USA, Washington, 949
Hooper, Portugal, 755
Hop Kiln, USA, California, 949
Hope Farms, USA, California, 949
Hopler, Austria, 251
Horizon's Edge, USA, Washington, 949
Horte, Château De L', France, 435
Horton, USA, Virginia, 950
Hortus, Domaine De L', France, 435
Houghton, Australia, 225
Hövel, Von, Germany, 622
Howard Park, Australia, 225
Howell Mountain Vineyard, USA, California, 950
Huët, S.A., France, 435
Hugel, France, 435
Hugo, Australia, 225
Huguet, Spain, 784
Hungerford Hill, Australia, 225
Hunold, Domaine Bruno, France, 435
Hunt Country Vineyards, USA, New York, 950
Hunter, Robert, USA, California, 950
Hunter Park, Australia, 225
Hunter Ridge, Australia, 225
Hunters, Australia, 225
Hunter's, New Zealand, 809
Huntington, USA, California, 950
Husch, USA, California, 950
Hutcheson, Portugal, 755
Hyatt, USA, Washington, 951
Hyot Beauséjour, Château, France, 436
I Due Cipressi, Italy, 692
I Selvatici, Italy, 692
I Sodi, Italy, 692
I Verbi, Italy, 692
Ibernoble, Spain, 785
Ici/La-Bas, USA, Oregon, 951
Igristoje, Hungary, 806
Il Cuore, USA, California, 951
Il Greppone Mazzi, Tenuta, Italy, 692
Il Podere Dell'olivos, USA, California, 951
Ile, Domaine De L', France, 436
Illuminati, Italy, 692
Impala, South Africa, 768
Indian Springs, USA, California, 951
Indigo Hills, USA, California, 951
Infantado, Quinta Do, Portugal, 755
Infernotto, Italy, 692
Inglenook, USA, California, 951
Inglenook-Napa Valley, USA, California, 951
Ingleside Plantation, USA, Virginia, 952
Innisfree, USA, California, 952
Inniskillin Niagara, Canada, 803
Inniskillin Okanagan, Canada, 803
Innocenti, Vittorio, Italy, 692
Intaglio, USA, California, 952
Inviosa, Bodegas, Spain, 785
Irache, Bodegas, Spain, 785
Iron Horse, USA, California, 952
Ironstone, USA, California, 953
Isole E Olena, Italy, 692
Issan, Château D', France, 436
J, USA, California, 953
J.P. Vinhos, Portugal, 755
Jabiru, Australia, 226
Jaboulet Aîné, Paul, France, 436
Jackson, New Zealand, 809
Jackson-Triggs, Canada, 803
Jackson Valley, USA, California, 953
Jacob, Robert & Raymond, France, 437
Jacobsdal, South Africa, 768
Jacquart, France, 437
Jacques, Château Des, France, 437
Jacques De Merial, France, 437
Jacques-Blanc, Château, France, 437
Jacqueson, Domaine René, France, 437
Jacqueson, H & P, France, 437
Jacquesson, France, 437
Jacuzzi, USA, California, 953
Jade Mountain, USA, California, 953
Jadot, Louis, France, 438
Jaeger, USA, California, 954
Jaffelin, France, 442
Jaffurs, USA, California, 954
Jamek, Josef, Austria, 252
Jamelles, Les, France, 443
James Scott, USA, Oregon, 954
Jamesport, USA, New York, 954
Jamet, Jean-Paul & Jean-Luc, France, 444
Jamiesons Run, Australia, 226
Janasse, Domaine De La, France, 444
Janin, Paul, France, 444
Jankris, USA, California, 954
Janodet, Jacky, France, 444
Jarvis, USA, California, 954
Jasmin, Robert, France, 444
Jason, USA, California, 954
Jasper Hill, Australia, 226
Jau, Château De, France, 444
Jaumier, Denis, France, 445
Javillier, Patrick, France, 445
Jayer, Henri, France, 445
Jayer, J., France, 446

Jayer-Gilles, Robert, France, 446
JC Cellars, USA, California, 954
Jean, Pierre, France, 447
Jefferson Vineyards, USA, Virginia, 955
Jekel, USA, California, 955
Jenard, France, 447
Jenner, USA, California, 955
Jepson, USA, California, 955
Jermann, Italy, 692
Jessandra Vittoria, USA, California, 955
Jessiaume Père & Fils, France, 447
Joao Pato, Portugal, 755
Jobard, Charles & Remi, France, 447
Jobard, François, France, 447
Jobard, Rémi, France, 447
Joblot, France, 447
Joguet, Charles, France, 447
Johannisberg, Schloss, Germany, 623
Johannishof, Germany, 623
Johns, USA, Washington, 955
Johnson Turnbull, USA, California, 955
Joliesse, France, 448
Joliesse, USA, California, 956
Joliette, Domaine, France, 448
Jolivet, Pascal, France, 448
Joly, N., France, 448
Jolys, Château, France, 448
Jonqueyres, Château, France, 448
Jonquières, Château, France, 448
Jonquières, Domaine Des, France, 448
Jordan, USA, California, 956
Jory, USA, California, 956
Josmeyer, France, 449
Jost, Toni, Germany, 623
Joubert, C. & M., France, 449
Jougla, Domaine Des, France, 449
Joullian, USA, California, 956
Joya, USA, California, 956
Joya, Chateau La, Chile, 268
Judd's Hill, USA, California, 956
Juge, Marcel, France, 449
Juillot, Emile, France, 449
Juillot, Michel, France, 449
Julia, Casa, Chile, 268
Jumilla, Castillo, Spain, 785
Junot, René, France, 449
Jurat, Château Le, France, 449
Juris, Austria, 252
Justices, Château Les, France, 449
Justin, USA, California, 956
Juve y Camps, Spain, 785
Kaesler, Australia, 226
Kalin, USA, California, 957
Kalinda, USA, California, 957
Kanonkop, South Africa, 768
Karl Lawrence, USA, California, 957
Karlsmuhle, Germany, 623
Karly, USA, California, 957
Karthäuserhof, Germany, 623
Katnook, Australia, 226
Kaz, USA, California, 957
Keber, Edi, Italy, 693
Keeble, Robert, USA, California, 957
Keegan, USA, California, 957
Keenan, USA, California, 958
Keltie Brook, USA, California, 958
Kendall-Jackson, USA, California, 958
Kennedy, Kathryn, USA, California, 959
Kenwood, USA, California, 960
Kerr, J., USA, California, 961
Kesseler, August, Germany, 624
Kesselstatt, Reichsgraf Von, Germany, 624
Kestrel, USA, California, 961
Kientzler, André, France, 450
Kimich, Julius Ferdinand, Germany, 625
Kinderwood, USA, California, 961
King Estate, USA, Oregon, 961
Kings Ridge, USA, Oregon, 962
Kingston Estate, Australia, 226
Kiona, USA, Washington, 962
Kirwan, Château, France, 450
Kistler, USA, California, 962
Kittling Ridge, Canada, 804
Klein, USA, California, 963
Kleinbosch, South Africa, 768
Kleindal, South Africa, 769
Klug, France, 450
Knapp, USA, New York, 963
Knipprath, USA, Washington, 963
Knoll, Austria, 252
Knudsen Erath, USA, Oregon, 963
Knyphausen, Baron Zu, Germany, 625
Knyphausen, Freiherr Zu, Germany, 625
Koala Ridge, Australia, 226
Koehler-Ruprecht, Germany, 625
Konocti, USA, California, 964
Konrad, USA, California, 964
Kookaburra, Australia, 226
Kopke, Portugal, 755
Korbel, USA, California, 964
Kornell, Hanns, USA, California, 964
Kourtakis, D., Greece, 804
Kracher, Austria, 252
Kraft, Austria, 253
Kramer, USA, Oregon, 964
Kreusch, Leonard, Germany, 626
Kreydenweiss, Marc, France, 450
Kris, Italy, 693
Kristone, USA, California, 964
Krizia, Italy, 693
Krohn, Portugal, 755
Kronendal, South Africa, 769
Krug, France, 450
Krug, Charles, USA, California, 965
Kruger-Rumpf, Germany, 626
Kuentz-Bas, France, 451
Kühling-Gillot, Germany, 626
Kumeu River, New Zealand, 809
Kunde, USA, California, 966
Künstler, Franz, Germany, 626
KWV, South Africa, 769
Kynsi, USA, California, 966
L De La Louvière, France, 451
L'Ecole No. 41, USA, Washington, 966
L'Ecosse, USA, California, 967
L'Héritage, Chile, 268
L'Ormarins, South Africa, 769
La Boheme, USA, Oregon, 967
La Casa Sena, USA, California, 967
La Crema, USA, California, 967
La Crosse, USA, California, 967
La Ferronniere, USA, California, 967
La Garza, USA, Oregon, 967
La Jota, USA, California, 968
La Motte, South Africa, 769
La Petite Vigne, USA, California, 968
La Rougette, USA, California, 968
La Sirena, USA, California, 968
La Vieille Montagne, USA, California, 968
Labat, Château, France, 451
Labégorce, Château, France, 451
Labégorce-Zédé, Château, France, 451
Labet & N. Dechelette, J., France, 452
Labet, Pierre, France, 451
Laborotte, La, France, 452
Labouré-Roi, France, 452
Labry, A. & B., France, 453

Lacaussade-St.-Martin, Château, France, 453
Lachesnaye, Château, France, 453
Lacheteau, France, 453
Laclaverie, Château, France, 453
Lacombe-Noaillac, Château, France, 453
Lacoste-Borie, France, 453
Ladau, Château De, France, 453
Ladoucette, De, France, 453
Laetitia, USA, California, 968
Lafarge, Michel, France, 453
Lafaurie-Peyraguey, Château, France, 454
Laferrere, Hubert, France, 454
Lafite Rothschild, Château, France, 454
Lafleur, Château, France, 455
Lafleur-Gazin, Château, France, 455
Lafon, Domaine Des Comtes, France, 455
Lafon-Rochet, Château, France, 456
Lafont Menaut, Château, France, 457
Lagarde, Henry, Argentina, 800
Lagaria, Italy, 693
Lageder, Alois, Italy, 693
Lagoalva, Quinta Da, Portugal, 755
Lagrange, Château, France, 457
Lagrange, Château, France, 457
Lagrezette, Château, France, 457
Lagune, Château La, France, 457
Laissus, Château, France, 458
Lake Sonoma, USA, California, 969
Lakespring, USA, California, 969
Lakewood, USA, California, 969
Lalande, Domaine De, France, 458
Lalande-Borie, Château, France, 458
Laleure-Piot, France, 458
Lamarche, François, France, 459
Lamarque, Château De, France, 459
Lamartine, Château, France, 459
Lamarzelle, Château, France, 459
Lambert Bridge, USA, California, 969
Lamberti, Italy, 693
Lamblin & Fils, France, 459
Lamborn Family, USA, California, 969
Lambrays, Domaine Des, France, 459
Lamole Di Lamole, Italy, 693
Lamoreaux Landing, USA, New York, 970
Lamothe, Château, France, 459
Lamothe De Haux, Château, France, 459
Lamothe-Despujols, Château, France, 459
Lamothe-Guignard, Château, France, 459
Lamy, Henry, France, 459
Lamy, Hubert, France, 459
Lan, Bodegas, Spain, 785
Lancelot-Royer, P., France, 460
Lanciola, Italy, 694
Lançon Père & Fils, France, 460
Lancyre, Château De, France, 460
Lande, Domaine De La, France, 460
Landiras, Château De, France, 460
Landmark, USA, California, 970
Landrat-Guyollot, Domaine, France, 460
Landskroon, South Africa, 769
Lanessan, Château, France, 460
Lang, Austria, 253
Lang, USA, California, 970
Lang & Reed, USA, California, 970
Lange, USA, Oregon, 970
Lange, Château, France, 460
Langlois-Château, France, 460
Langoa Barton, Château, France, 460
Langoureau, Sylvain, France, 461
Lanson, France, 461
Lanzerac, South Africa, 769
Lapelletrie, Château, France, 461
Lapierre, M., France, 461
Laplace, Domaine Fleury, France, 461
Laplace, Domaine Frédéric, France, 461
Laporte, Domaine, France, 461
Lapostolle, Casa, Chile, 268
Lar De Lares, Spain, 785
Larcis-Ducasse, Château, France, 461
Large, A., France, 461
Larmande, Château, France, 461
Larmandier-Bernier, France, 462
Laroche, France, 462
Larose-Perganson, Château, France, 462
Larose-Trintaudon, Château, France, 462
Larrivet, Domaine De, France, 462
Larrivet-Haut-Brion, Château, France, 463
Las Vinas, USA, California, 970
Lascaux, Château De, France, 463
Lascombes, Château, France, 463
Lassalle, J., France, 463
Lassarat, Roger, France, 463
Lasserre Du Haut, Domaine, France, 463
Lassime, Marquise De, France, 463
Lastours, Château, France, 463
Latah Creek, USA, Washington, 970
Latham, Château, France, 464
Latham, Collection Eric, France, 464
Latini, Il, Italy, 694
Latour, Château, France, 464
Latour, Louis, France, 465
Latour, Pierre, France, 467
Latour à Pomerol, Château, France, 467
Latour-Giraud, France, 468
Lauerburg, Germany, 627
Launay, Château, France, 468
Laurel Estate, USA, California, 971
Laurel Glen, USA, California, 971
Laurel Ridge, USA, Oregon, 971
Laurens, France, 468
Laurens, Domaine J., France, 468
Laurent Cellars, USA, California, 972
Laurent, Dominique, France, 468
Laurent, Jean, France, 469
Laurent-Perrier, France, 469
Laurier, USA, California, 972
Lauze, Comte De, France, 469
Lava Cap, USA, California, 972
Lavabre, Château, France, 469
Lavernoya, Cavas, Spain, 785
Laville Bertrou, Château, France, 469
Laville Haut Brion, Château, France, 469
Lawrence, Daniel, USA, California, 972
Lawsons Dry Hills, New Zealand, 809
Lazaridi, Domaine Constantin, Greece, 804
Lazy Creek, USA, California, 972
Le Ducq, USA, California, 972
Leacock's, Portugal, 755
Leasingham, Australia, 226
Lebegue & Co., J, France, 469
Lebegue-Bichot, France, 469
Lebensraum, South Africa, 769
Leblanc Estate, Canada, 804
Leblanc Estate, USA, Michigan, 972
Leccia, Castello La, Italy, 694
Lecciaia, Le, Italy, 694
Lécheneault, France, 469
Lechere, France, 470
Leclerc, Philippe, France, 470
Leclerc, René, France, 471
Leclerc-Briant, France, 471
Leeuwin, Australia, 227
Leeward, USA, California, 972
Leflaive, Domaine, France, 471
Leflaive Frères, Olivier, France, 471
Lefranc, Charles, USA, California, 972

Legacy, Romania, 812
Léger-Plumet, Bernard, France, 473
Légland, Bernard, France, 474
Legras, R & L, France, 474
Legros, François, France, 474
Lehmann, Peter, Australia, 227
Leitz, Josef, Germany, 627
Lejeune, France, 474
Lembey, Spain, 785
Lemenicier, Jacques, France, 474
Lenoble, A.R., France, 474
Lenswood, Australia, 228
Lento, Cantine, Italy, 694
Lenz, USA, New York, 972
Lenz Moser, Austria, 253
Leon, Jean, Spain, 785
Léonard De St.-Aubin, France, 474
Leonardini, Italy, 694
Leonardo Da Vinci, Italy, 694
Leone De Castris, Italy, 694
Leonetti, USA, Washington, 973
Léoville Barton, Château, France, 475
Léoville Las Cases, Château, France, 475
Léoville Poyferré, Château, France, 475
Lepitre, Abel, France, 476
Lequin-Roussot, France, 476
Leroy, Domaine, France, 479
Leroy, France, 476
Les Hauts De Smith, France, 481
Lescure, Chantal, France, 481
Lestage, Château, France, 481
Lestage-Simon, Château, France, 481
Levet, B., France, 481
Lewelling, USA, California, 973
Lewellyn Estates, Argentina, 800
Lewis Cellars, USA, California, 973
Ley, Baron De, Spain, 785
Leydens Vale, Australia, 228
Leyrat, France, 481
Liaison, La, France, 481
Libarde, Domaine De, France, 481
Liberty School, USA, California, 973
Librandi, Italy, 694
Lichine, Alexis, France, 481
Lieser, Schloss, Germany, 627
Lievland, South Africa, 769
Liger-Belair, France, 481
Lignier, Georges, France, 481
Lignier, Hubert, France, 481
Lilian Ladouys, Château, France, 482
Lilliano, Castello Di, Italy, 694
Lillydale, Australia, 228
Limerick Lane, USA, California, 973
Limnos, Greece, 805
Lindemans, Australia, 228
Linden, USA, Virginia, 974
Lingenfelder, Germany, 627
Lionnet, Jean, France, 482
Liot, Château, France, 482
Liparita, USA, California, 974
Liquiere, Château De La, France, 482
Lisini, Italy, 694
Little's, Australia, 229
Littorai, USA, California, 974
Liversan, Château, France, 482
Livingston, 974
Livingstone, Steven Thomas, USA, Washington, 975
Livon, Italy, 695
Ljutomer Winery, Slovenia, 812
Llano Estacado, USA, Texas, 975
Llanos, Bodegas Los, Spain, 785
Llopart, P., Spain, 785
Lockwood, USA, California, 975
Logan, USA, California, 975
Loggia, Fattoria La, Italy, 695
Logis De La Giraudière, France, 482
Lohr, J., USA, California, 975
Loiben, Dinstlgut, Austria, 253
Loimer, Austria, 254
Loiseau, Yves, France, 482
Lolonis, USA, California, 976
Lombardo, Antonino, Italy, 695
Lone Oak, USA, California, 977
Lones, Domaine Des, France, 482
Lonetree, USA, California, 977
Long, USA, California, 977
Long-Depaquit, A., France, 482
Longoria, USA, California, 977
Longridge, New Zealand, 809
Longridge, South Africa, 769
Loosen, Dr., Germany, 627
López De Heredia Viña Tondonia, R., Spain, 785
Lorane Valley, USA, Oregon, 977
Lorentz, Gustave, France, 483
Lorenza-Lake, USA, California, 977
Lorieux, Alain, France, 483
Lornet, Frederic, France, 483
Los Encantos, USA, California, 977
Los Olivos, USA, California, 977
Losi, Paolo & Pietro, Italy, 695
Loudenne, Château, France, 483
Louisvale, South Africa, 769
Louvière, Château La, France, 483
Lowenstein, Fürst, Germany, 628
Luberri, Bodegas, Spain, 786
Luc, Château De, France, 483
Luce, Italy, 695
Lucia, Galasso, Italy, 695
Luciani, Italy, 695
Ludeman-La-Côte, Château, France, 483
Lugny, Cave De, France, 483
Lumpp, François, France, 484
Luna, USA, California, 978
Luneau-Papin, Pierre, France, 484
Lungarotti, Italy, 695
Lupé-Cholet, France, 484
Luquet, Roger, France, 484
Lurton, J. & F., Argentina, 800
Lurton, J. & F., Australia, 229
Lurton, J. & F., Chile, 268
Lurton, J. & F., France, 484
Lurton, J. & F., Spain, 786
Lusco Do Miño, Spain, 786
Lusseau, Château, France, 485
Lustau, Emilio, Spain, 786
Lyeth, USA, California, 978
Lynch, Michel, France, 485
Lynch-Bages, Blanc De, France, 485
Lynch-Bages, Château, France, 485
Lynch-Moussas, Château, France, 485
Lynmar, USA, California, 978
Lytton Springs, USA, California, 978
M & G, France, 486
Maacama Creek, USA, California, 978
Macchiole, Le, Italy, 696
Macgregor, Cathy, USA, California, 978
Machard De Gramont, France, 486
Machiavelli, Antica Fattoria, Italy, 696
Macioche, Le, Italy, 696
Mackenzie Estates, Australia, 229
Mackinaw, USA, California, 978
Macmahon, Marquis De, France, 486
Macmillan, USA, California, 978
Macrostie, USA, California, 978
Maculan, Italy, 696
Maddalena, USA, California, 979
Madfish Bay, Australia, 229

Madigan, USA, California, 979
Madrevinhos, Portugal, 755
Madron Lake Hills, USA, Michigan, 979
Madrona, USA, California, 979
Maese Joan, Bodegas, Spain, 786
Magaña, Bodegas, Spain, 786
Magdelaine, Château, France, 486
Mage, Domaine Du, France, 486
Magneau, Château, France, 486
Magni, Domaine, France, 486
Magnien, Henri, France, 486
Magnol, Château, France, 486
Magnotta, Canada, 804
Mahler Besse & Co., France, 486
Maillard Père & Fils, France, 487
Maire, Jean, France, 487
Maison Blanche, Domaine De, France, 487
Maison Charme, France, 487
Maison De Lamartine, France, 487
Maison Deutz, USA, California, 979
Maison Du Lac, Chile, 268
Makor, USA, California, 979
Malagar, Château, France, 487
Malaire, Château, France, 487
Malandes, Domaine Des, France, 487
Malartic-Lagraviere, Château, France, 487
Malat, Austria, 254
Malescasse, Château, France, 487
Malescot-St.-Exupery, Château, France, 487
Malestroit, Comte De, France, 488
Maligny, Château De, France, 488
Malle, Château De, France, 488
Malleret, Château De, France, 488
Malmaison, Château, France, 488
Malpaga, Italy, 696
Malrome, Château, France, 488
Malteser Ritterorden, Austria, 254
Maltroye, Château De La, France, 488
Manciat, Jean, France, 488
Manciat-Poncet, France, 488
Mandagot, Château, France, 489
Mandos, Portugal, 755
Mangualde, Adega Cooperativa De, Portugal, 755
Manischewitz, USA, California, 979
Mann, Albert, France, 489
Manora, Italy, 696
Mantlerhof, Austria, 254
Manuel, Domaine Réne, France, 489
Manzanita Ridge, USA, California, 979
Manzano, Fattoria Di, Italy, 696
Manzone, Giovanni, Italy, 696
Mar, Senorio Del, Spain, 786
Marai, Foss, Italy, 697
Marble Crest, USA, Washington, 979
Marbuzet, Château, France, 489
Marca, La, Italy, 697
Marcarini, Italy, 697
Marcassin, USA, California, 979
Marcelina, USA, California, 979
Marchand, Claude, France, 489
Marchand, Domaine Jean-Philippe, France, 489
Marchand, Jean, France, 489
Marchand-Grillot & Fils, France, 489
Marche-Canon, Château La, France, 489
Marchive, Lyne & Jean-Bernard, France, 489
Marcoux, Domaine De, France, 489
Mardon, Domaine, France, 489
Marega, Italy, 697
Marengo-Marenda, Poderi E, Italy, 697
Mares, Roger, France, 489
Margaine, A., France, 490
Margaux, Château, France, 490
Margon, Domaine De, France, 490
Marienberg, Australia, 230
Marietta, USA, California, 980
Marilyn Merlot, France, 490
Marilyn Merlot, USA, California, 980
Marino, A. Y B., Spain, 786
Marion, USA, California, 980
Mariposa, Argentina, 800
Maris, Domaine, France, 490
Maritsa, Bulgaria, 803
Marjosse, Château, France, 490
Mark Ridge, USA, California, 980
Mark West, USA, California, 980
Markham, USA, California, 980
Markko, USA, Ohio, 981
Markowitsch, Austria, 254
Marlunghe, Italy, 697
Maroslavac-Leger, France, 491
Marot, Château, France, 491
Marotte, Domaine De, France, 491
Marquam Hill, USA, Oregon, 981
Marroneto, Il, Italy, 697
Marsau, Château, France, 491
Martialis, Domaine De, France, 491
Martin, Jean-Jacques, France, 491
Martin, Robert, France, 491
Martin Brothers, USA, California, 981
Martinborough, New Zealand, 809
Martine, France, 491
Martinelli, USA, California, 981
Martinengo, Italy, 697
Martinengo, Rino, Italy, 697
Martinetti, Franco, Italy, 697
Martinez, Portugal, 755
Martinez Bujanda, Bodegas, Spain, 786
Martini, Louis M., USA, California, 982
Martini & Prati, USA, California, 982
Martini Di Cigala, Italy, 697
Martinolles, Domaine De, France, 491
Martinsancho, Spain, 787
Marwood, Italy, 698
Mas Blanc, Domaine Du, France, 491
Mas Champart, France, 492
Mas Cremat, Domaine Du, France, 492
Mas De Daumas Gassac, France, 492
Mas De Gourgonnier, France, 492
Mas De La Dame, France, 492
Mas Des Bressades, France, 492
Mas Des Chimères, France, 492
Mas Jullien, France, 492
Mas Martinet Viticultors, Spain, 787
Mas Neuf, Château, France, 492
Mas Neuf, Domaine Du, France, 492
Mas Ste.-Berthe, France, 492
Mascarello, Bartolo, Italy, 698
Mascarello & Figlio, Giuseppe, Italy, 698
Masciarelli, Italy, 698
Masi, Italy, 698
Masi, Renzo, Italy, 699
Masia Barril, Spain, 787
Maso, USA, California, 983
Maso Cantanghel, Italy, 699
Maso Poli, Italy, 699
Mason, USA, California, 983
Massa, La, Italy, 699
Massara, Fattoria, Italy, 699
Masse Di Greve, Le, Italy, 700
Massolino, Italy, 700
Masson, USA, California, 983
Masson-Blondelet, Domaine J.-M., France, 492
Mastantuono, USA, California, 984

Mastroberardino, Italy, 700
Mastrojanni, Italy, 700
Matanzas Creek, USA, California, 984
Mathier-Kuchler, Switzerland, 813
Mathieu, Domaine, France, 492
Mathieu, Serge, France, 492
Matibat, Domaine De, France, 493
Mato Miranda, Quinta De, Portugal, 756
Matronèo, Italy, 700
Matrot, Joseph, France, 493
Matrot, Pierre, France, 493
Matta, John, Italy, 700
Matthews, USA, Washington, 984
Mattituck Hills, USA, New York, 984
Matua, New Zealand, 809
Mau, Yvon, France, 493
Maucaillou, Château, France, 493
Maucoil, Château, France, 493
Maume, France, 493
Maurice Car'rie, USA, California, 984
Mauro, Bodegas, Spain, 787
Mavette, Domaine De La, France, 494
Mayacamas, USA, California, 984
Mayard, Jean-Luc, France, 494
Mayer, Franz, Austria, 254
Mayne Des Carmes, Château, France, 494
Mayne, Château Du, France, 494
Mayo, USA, California, 984
Mazeris, Château, France, 494
Mazeris-Bellevue, Château, France, 494
Mazzi, Italy, 700
Mazzocco, USA, California, 985
Mazzolino, Tenuta, Italy, 700
Mcalister, Australia, 230
Mccoy, Peter, USA, California, 985
Mcdowell, USA, California, 985
Mcgregor, USA, New York, 986
Mcguigan, Australia, 230
Mcilroy, USA, California, 986
Mckinlay, USA, Oregon, 986
Mclarens, Australia, 230
Mcwilliam's, Australia, 230
Meadow Glen, USA, California, 986
Meadowbank, Australia, 230
Medici, USA, Oregon, 986
Medici Ermete, Italy, 700
Méditéo, France, 494
Meeker, USA, California, 986
Meerendal, South Africa, 770
Meerlust, South Africa, 770
Megyer, Chateau, Hungary, 806
Meitz, USA, California, 986
Melini, Italy, 701
Mellot, Domaine Alphonse, France, 494
Meloterie, Domaine De La, France, 494
Melton, Charles, Australia, 230
Menada, Bulgaria, 803
Mendiani, Spain, 787
Mendocino Estate, USA, California, 987
Mendocino Hill, USA, California, 987
Menzies, Australia, 231
Méo-Camuzet, France, 494
Mer Soleil, USA, California, 987
Meredyth, USA, Virginia, 987
Meric, Château, France, 496
Meric, De, France, 496
Meridian, USA, California, 987
Merkelbach, Alfred, Germany, 628
Merlion, USA, California, 987
Mérode, Prince Florent De, France, 496
Merrill, Geoff, Australia, 231
Merryvale, USA, California, 987
Messia, Portugal, 756
Messina Hof, USA, Texas, 988
Mestre-Michelot, France, 497
Métaireau, Louis, France, 497
Metairie, La, France, 497
Meuliere, Château De La, France, 497
Meunier St.-Louis, Château, France, 497
Meursault, Château De, France, 497
Meyer-Fonné, France, 497
Meyney, Château, France, 498
Méziat, Pierre, France, 498
Mezzacorona, Cantine, Italy, 701
Miaudoux, Château, France, 498
Miccine, Le, Italy, 701
Michael, Peter, USA, California, 988
Michael-Scott, USA, California, 988
Michaud, Alain, France, 498
Michaud, J.F., France, 498
Michel, Louis, France, 498
Michel, Robert, France, 498
Michel Frères, France, 499
Michele, Robert, France, 498
Michelot, Alain, France, 499
Michelot, C., France, 499
Michelot, Domaine, France, 499
Michelot, G., France, 499
Michelot, Jean, France, 499
Michelot-Buisson, France, 499
Michel-Schlumberger, USA, California, 989
Michlits-Stadlmann, Austria, 254
Middelvlei, South Africa, 770
Midnight Cellars, USA, California, 989
Mietz, USA, California, 989
Milano, USA, California, 989
Milat, USA, California, 989
Milburn Park, Australia, 231
Mildara, Australia, 231
Milhau-Lacugue, Château, France, 500
Mill Creek, USA, California, 989
Millbrook, USA, California, 990
Millegrand, Château, France, 500
Millet-Doucet, Domaine, France, 500
Millot, Jean-Marc, France, 500
Mills Reef, New Zealand, 810
Millstream, USA, California, 990
Minet, Régis, France, 500
Minho, Quinta Do, Portugal, 756
Miolane, Christian, France, 500
Miquel, Château, France, 500
Miquel, Domaine, France, 500
Mirabelle, USA, California, 990
Mirassou, USA, California, 990
Mirefleurs, Château, France, 500
Misserey, P., France, 500
Mission, New Zealand, 810
Mission Canyon, USA, California, 992
Mission Mountain, USA, Washington, 992
Mission View, USA, California, 992
Mission-Haut-Brion, Château La, France, 500
Mistral, Cave Du, France, 501
Misty Mountain, USA, Virginia, 992
Mitchell, Australia, 231
Mitchell, Charles B., USA, California, 992
Mitchelton, Australia, 231
Moc Et Baril, France, 501
Mocali, Italy, 701
Moccagatta, Italy, 701
Moceri, France, 501
Moët & Chandon, France, 501
Moillard, France, 501
Moingeon, France, 503
Moletto, Italy, 702
Molino, Franco, Italy, 702
Molino, Mauro, Italy, 702

Mollina, Bodegas De, Spain, 787
Mommessin, France, 503
Monardière, Domaine La, France, 506
Monasterio, Hacienda, Spain, 787
Monbadon, Château, France, 506
Monbousquet, Château, France, 507
Monbrison, Château, France, 507
Monção, Adega Cooperativa Regional De, Portugal, 756
Moncontour, Château, France, 507
Mondavi, Ck, USA, California, 992
Mondavi, La Famiglia Di Robert, USA, California, 995
Mondavi, Robert, USA, California, 993
Mondot, France, 507
Mondotte, Château La, France, 507
Mongeard-Mugneret, France, 507
Monistrol, Marqués De, Spain, 787
Monmoussin, France, 508
Monnier, René, France, 508
Monpertuis, Domaine De, France, 508
Monsanto, Fattoria, Italy, 702
Monsordo, Italy, 702
Mont Belair, Château, France, 509
Mont Clair, France, 509
Mont Rose, Domaine, France, 509
Mont St. John, USA, California, 995
Mont St.-Michel, France, 509
Mont Tauch, Les Producteurs Du, France, 509
Montagliari, Fattoria Di, Italy, 702
Montana, New Zealand, 810
Montaudon, France, 509
Montbayon, Domaine De, France, 509
Montdomaine, USA, Virginia, 995
Monte Antico, Italy, 702
Monte Bernardi, Italy, 702
Monte Carasso, USA, California, 995
Monte Vannos, Spain, 787
Monte Verde, USA, California, 995
Monte Volpe, USA, California, 995
Montecalvi, Italy, 703
Montecchio, Fattoria Di, Italy, 703
Montecillo, Bodegas, Spain, 787
Montegiachi, Tenuta, Italy, 703
Montegrossi, Castello Di, Italy, 703
Monteleiva, Bodegas, Spain, 788
Montellori, Fattoria, Italy, 703
Montenidoli, Italy, 703
Monterey Peninsula, USA, California, 995
Monterey Vineyard, USA, California, 996
Monterra, USA, California, 996
Montes, Chile, 269
Montespertoli, Castello Di, Italy, 703
Montesquieu, Domaines H. De, France, 509
Montevannos, Bodegas, Spain, 788
Montevertine, Italy, 703
Montevina, USA, California, 996
Montfort, Château De, France, 509
Montgras, Chile, 269
Montgueret, Château De, France, 509
Monthaven, USA, California, 997
Monthélie-Douhairet, France, 510
Monti, Antonio & Elio, Italy, 703
Monticello, USA, California, 997
Montinore, USA, Oregon, 998
Montiverdi, Italy, 703
Mont-Marçal, Spain, 787
Montmirail, Château De, France, 510
Montmollin, Domaine De, Switzerland, 813
Montori, Camillo, Italy, 703
Montpatey, Château De, France, 510
Montpellier, USA, California, 998
Montreaux, USA, California, 999
Mont-Redon, Château, France, 509
Mont-Tana, France, 511
Montresor, Italy, 704
Montrose, Australia, 231
Montrose, Château, France, 510
Montrose, La Dame De, France, 511
Montsarra, Spain, 788
Montus, Château, France, 511
Montvac, Domaine De, France, 511
Montviel, Château, France, 511
Moondance, USA, California, 999
Moonshine Vineyard, Chile, 269
Moonshine Vineyard, USA, California, 999
Moore, Z, USA, California, 999
Moraga, USA, California, 999
Morales, Bodegas Hermanos, Spain, 788
Morandell, Austria, 254
Morasutti, Italy, 704
Moreau, Bernard, France, 511
Moreau, Louis, France, 511
Moreau & Fils, J., France, 512
Moreux, Patrice, France, 512
Moreux, Roger, France, 512
Morey, Albert, France, 512
Morey, Bernard, France, 512
Morey, Marc, France, 512
Morey, Pierre, France, 513
Morey-Blanc, France, 513
Morey-Coffinet, Michel, France, 513
Morgadío, Adegas, Spain, 788
Morgan, Portugal, 756
Morgan, USA, California, 999
Morgenhof, South Africa, 770
Morilleau, Michel, France, 514
Morin, Gérard, France, 514
Morning Star, Chile, 269
Morot, Albert, France, 514
Morovino, USA, California, 1000
Morris, J.W., USA, California, 1000
Morro Bay, USA, California, 1000
Mortet, Charles, France, 514
Mortet, Denis, France, 514
Mortet, Thierry, France, 515
Mortet & Fils, France, 515
Morton, Château, France, 516
Morton, New Zealand, 810
Mosby, USA, California, 1000
Mosca, Italy, 704
Moshin, USA, California, 1000
Mosnier, Sylvain, France, 516
Motte, Domaine De La, France, 516
Mouchet, Château De, France, 516
Moueix, Christian, France, 516
Moueix, Jean-Pierre, France, 516
Moulin Bousquet, Château, France, 516
Moulin De Bel-Air, Château, France, 516
Moulin De Citran, Château, France, 516
Moulin De Duhart, France, 516
Moulin De La Gardette, France, 516
Moulin De Launay, Château, France, 516
Moulin Du Cadet, Château, France, 516
Moulin Du Pont, Le, France, 516
Moulin Haut-Laroque, Château, France, 517
Moulin Pey-Labrie, Château, France, 517
Moulin Riche, Château, France, 517
Moulin Rouge, Château Du, France, 517
Moulin-St.-Georges, Château, France, 517
Moulin-Tacussel, Domaine, France, 517
Mouline, Château La, France, 517
Moulinet, Château, France, 517
Moulinier, G., France, 517

Mount Baker, USA, Washington, 1000
Mount Eden, USA, California, 1000
Mount Horrocks, Australia, 232
Mount Konocti, USA, California, 1001
Mount Langi Ghiran, Australia, 232
Mount Maroma, USA, California, 1001
Mount Mary, Australia, 232
Mount Palomar, USA, California, 1001
Mount Pleasant, Australia, 232
Mount Veeder, USA, California, 1001
Mountadam, Australia, 232
Mountain Dome, USA, Washington, 1001
Mountain Valley, USA, Tennessee, 1001
Mountain View, USA, California, 1001
Moure, Adegas, Spain, 788
Mourgue Du Gres, Château, France, 517
Mousset, Louis, France, 517
Mouton D'Armailhacq, Château, France, 517
Mouton-Baronne-Philippe, Château, France, 517
Mouton-Cadet, France, 517
Mouton-Rothschild, Château, France, 518
Movia Estates, Slovenia, 812
Mt. Madonna, USA, California, 1001
Mueller, USA, California, 1002
Muerza, Bodegas, Spain, 788
Muga, Bodegas, Spain, 788
Muga-Villfranca, Bodegas, Spain, 788
Mugneret, Georges, France, 518
Mugneret, Gérard, France, 519
Mugneret, René, France, 519
Mugneret-Gibourg, France, 519
Mugneret-Gouachon, B., France, 519
Mugnier, Jacques-Frédéric, France, 519
Mulderbosch, South Africa, 770
Müller, Egon, Germany, 628
Müller-Catoir, Germany, 628
Mumm, G.H., France, 519
Mumm Cuvée Napa, USA, California, 1002
Munzenrieder, Austria, 254
Muraglia Estate, La, Italy, 704
Murcas, Quinta De, Portugal, 756
Muré, France, 520
Murettes, Domaine Des, France, 520
Murgas, Quinta Das, Portugal, 756
Murisaltien, Le Manoir, France, 520
Murphy-Goode, USA, California, 1002
Murray, Andrew, USA, California, 1003
Murrieta, Bodegas Marqués De, Spain, 788
Murrieta's Well, USA, California, 1003
Murrindindi, Australia, 232
Musar, Chateau, Lebanon, 807
Mussy, France, 520
Muts, Château Les, France, 521
Muzard & Fils, Lucien, France, 521
Mylord, Château, France, 521
Myrat, Château De, France, 521
Nada, Fiorenzo, Italy, 704
Naddef, Philippe, France, 521
Nages, Château De, France, 521
Naigeon-Chauveau, France, 521
Nairac, Château, France, 521
Nalle, USA, California, 1003
Napa Cellars, USA, California, 1003
Napa Creek, USA, California, 1003
Napa Ridge, USA, California, 1003
Nardi, Silvio, Italy, 704
Nardique La Gravière, Château, France, 522
Nathanson Creek, USA, California, 1004
Natter, Henry, France, 522
Naudin-Ferrand, Henri, France, 522
Nautilus, New Zealand, 810
Navarra, Vinicola, Spain, 789
Navarro, USA, California, 1004
Navarro Correas, Argentina, 800
Navega, Antonio Afonso, Portugal, 756
Naylor, USA, Pennsylvania, 1005
Nazdrave, Bulgaria, 803
Nederburg, South Africa, 770
Neethlingshof, South Africa, 770
Negly, Château De La, France, 522
Negociants, The, USA, California, 1005
Negri, Nino, Italy, 704
Negro, Italy, 704
Neipperg, Graf Von , Germany, 629
Neirano, Italy, 704
Neive, Castello Di, Italy, 704
Nekeas, Bodega, Spain, 789
Nekowitsch, Austria, 255
Nelson Estate, USA, California, 1005
Nenin, Château, France, 522
Nerthe, Château La, France, 522
Nervi, Luigi & Italo, Italy, 704
Neudorf, New Zealand, 810
Neuharth, USA, Washington, 1005
Neuhaus, Ludwig, Germany, 629
Nevada City, USA, California, 1005
Nevada County Wine Guild, USA, California, 1005
New Land, USA, New York, 1005
Newlan, USA, California, 1005
Newton, USA, California, 1006
Neyers, USA, California, 1006
Ngatarawa, New Zealand, 810
Niccolini, Italy, 704
Nichelini, USA, California, 1007
Nichol's, Dave, USA, California, 1007
Nichols, USA, California, 1007
Nicolas, France, 522
Nicolay, Peter, Germany, 629
Nicole, Cuvée, France, 523
Nicolis, Italy, 704
Niebaum, Gustave, USA, California, 1008
Niebaum-Coppola, USA, California, 1008
Niellon, Michel, France, 523
Niepoort, Portugal, 756
Nigl, Austria, 255
Nikolaihof, Austria, 255
Nittardi, Casanuova Di, Italy, 705
Noarna, Castel, Italy, 705
Nobilis, France, 523
Nobilo, New Zealand, 810
Noble, Domaine La, France, 523
Noceto, USA, California, 1008
Nominee, USA, California, 1008
Noon's, Australia, 232
Norman, USA, California, 1008
Normans, Australia, 232
Northstar, USA, Washington, 1009
Norton, Bodega, Argentina, 801
Nottola, Italy, 705
Nouveau, Claude, France, 523
Nova Era, Bulgaria, 803
Novacella, Abbazia Di, Italy, 705
Noval, Quinta Do, Portugal, 756
Nozzole, Italy, 705
Numero 2 De Lafon-Rochet, Le, France, 523
O'shea, Maurice, Australia, 233
Oak Falls, USA, California, 1009
Oak Knoll, USA, Oregon, 1009
Oak Lane, USA, California, 1009
Oak Ridge, USA, California, 1009
Oakford, USA, California, 1009
Oakville Bench, USA, California, 1009
Oakville Ranch, USA, California, 1009

Oakwood, USA, Washington, 1010
Oasis, USA, Virginia, 1010
Oberto, Andrea, Italy, 705
Oberto, Egidio, Italy, 706
Oberto, Luigi, Italy, 706
Obester, USA, California, 1010
Ochoa, Bodegas, Spain, 789
Octopus Mountain, USA, California, 1010
Oddero, Fratelli, Italy, 706
Offley, Portugal, 757
Ogereau, Domaine, France, 523
Ogier, Michel, France, 523
Ogier & Fils, A., France, 524
Oinothekie, Greece, 805
Ojai, USA, California, 1010
Ol' Blue Jay, USA, California, 1010
Olarra, Bodegas, Spain, 789
Old Brookville, USA, New York, 1010
Olek-Mery, France, 524
Oliver, USA, Indiana, 1010
Olivet Lane, USA, California, 1010
Oliveto, Italy, 706
Olivier, Château, France, 524
Ollieux, Château Les, France, 524
Olmo, Podere, Italy, 706
Olson, USA, California, 1011
Oña, Torre De, Spain, 789
Ondarre, Bodegas, Spain, 789
One Vineyard, USA, California, 1011
One World Winery, USA, California, 1011
Onix, Spain, 789
Opitz, Willi, Austria, 255
Optima, USA, California, 1011
Opus One, USA, California, 1011
Oratoire St.-Martin, Domaine De L', France, 524
Oregon Vineyards, USA, Oregon, 1011
Oremus, Hungary, 806
Orfila, USA, California, 1011
Organic Wine Works, USA, California, 1011
Orlando, Australia, 232
Ormes-De-Pez, Château Les, France, 524
Ormes-Sorbet, Château Les, France, 524
Ormieres, Château, France, 524
Ornellaia, Tenuta Dell', Italy, 706
Orschwihr, Château D', France, 524
Orval, L', France, 524
Osborne, Portugal, 757
Osprey's Dominion, USA, New York, 1012
Ostange, Domaine D', France, 524
Ostertag, Domaine, France, 524
Othegraven, Von, Germany, 629
Ott, Domaines, France, 525
Oudinot, France, 525
Oupia, Château D', France, 525
Overgaauw, South Africa, 770
Oxford Landing, Australia, 233
Oyster Bay, New Zealand, 810
P.L.D. Viticoltori, Italy, 706
Pabiot, Didier, France, 525
Pabiot, Dominique, France, 525
Pabiot, J.A.D., France, 525
Pabiot & Fils, Jean, France, 525
Pacenti, Siro, Italy, 706
Pacheco Ranch, USA, California, 1012
Pacific Echo, USA, California, 1012
Pacina, Italy, 706
Paço, Quinta Do, Portugal, 757
Padaelecti, Italy, 707
Padelletti, Italy, 707
Padere, Château De, France, 525
Padin, Bodegas Pablo, Spain, 789
Padornina, Spain, 789
Page Mill, USA, California, 1012
Paggio, Italy, 707
Pagliarese, Italy, 707
Pagodes De Cos, Les, France, 525
Pagor, USA, California, 1012
Pahlmeyer, USA, California, 1012
Paillard, Bruno, France, 525
Paillas, Château, France, 525
Paillet-Quancard, Château De, France, 525
Paitin, Italy, 707
Pajzos, Château, Hungary, 806
Palacio, Bodegas, Spain, 790
Palacio Da Brejoeira, Portugal, 757
Palacio De La Vega, Spain, 789
Palacios, Alvaro, Spain, 790
Palacios Remondo, Bodegas, Spain, 790
Palagio, Il, Italy, 707
Palazzetta, La, Italy, 707
Palazzino, Podere Il, Italy, 707
Palazzo Vecchio, Fattoria Di, Italy, 707
Palazzone, Il, Italy, 707
Palladino, Italy, 707
Pallavicini, Italy, 707
Pallieres, Domaine Les, France, 525
Palliser, New Zealand, 810
Palme, Château La, France, 525
Palmer, Château, France, 525
Palmer, USA, New York, 1012
Palmer & Co., France, 526
Paloma, USA, California, 1013
Paloumey, Château, France, 526
Pancas, Quinta De, Portugal, 757
Pancrazi, Marchesi, Italy, 707
Paneretta, Castello Della, Italy, 708
Panizzi, Giovanni, Italy, 708
Pannier, France, 526
Pannier, Remy, France, 526
Panther Creek, USA, Oregon, 1013
Panzano, Italy, 708
Paoletti, USA, California, 1013
Paolis, Castel De, Italy, 708
Pape, Château Le, France, 526
Pape Clement, Château, France, 526
Papes, Caves Des, France, 526
Paquet, François, France, 527
Paquet, Jean-Paul, France, 527
Paradigm, USA, California, 1013
Paradise Ridge, USA, California, 1014
Paradise Valley, USA, Arizona, 1014
Paradiso, Fattoria, Italy, 708
Paradiso, Il, Italy, 708
Paraduxx, USA, California, 1014
Paraiso Springs, USA, California, 1014
Paran-Justice, Château, France, 527
Paraza, Château De, France, 527
Parce, Docteur, France, 527
Parde De Haut-Bailly, La, France, 527
Parducci, USA, California, 1014
Parent, France, 527
Parigot Père & Fils, France, 528
Parker, Fess, USA, California, 1015
Parker Coonawarra Estate, Australia, 233
Parrotes, Quinta De, Portugal, 757
Partager, Chile, 270
Parusso, Armando, Italy, 708
Pascal, Jean, France, 528
Pascaud-Villefranche, Château, France, 528
Pasini, Volpe, Italy, 708
Pask, C.J., New Zealand, 810
Paso Robles, USA, California, 1015
Pasqua, Fratelli, Italy, 708
Pasquale, Veglio, Italy, 708
Pasquero, Elia, Italy, 708
Passadouro, Quinta Do, Portugal, 758

Passat, Andre, France, 528
Pastou, Paul & Jean-Marc, France, 528
Patache D'Aux, Château, France, 528
Paternina, Bodegas Federico, Spain, 790
Paterno, Fattoria Di, Italy, 708
Paternoster, Italy, 709
Patissier, G., France, 528
Patissier, P., France, 528
Pato, Luis, Portugal, 758
Patriarche Père & Fils, France, 528
Patrick, Baron, France, 528
Patz & Hall, USA, California, 1015
Pauillac De Château Latour, France, 528
Paul, Patrick M., USA, Washington, 1015
Paulsen, Pat, USA, California, 1016
Pauly-Bergweiler, Dr., Germany, 629
Paumanok, USA, New York, 1016
Pavelot, Jean-Marc, France, 528
Pavie, Château, France, 529
Pavie-Decesse, Château, France, 529
Pavie-Macquin, Château, France, 529
Pavillon Blanc Du Château Margaux, France, 529
Pavillon La Croix Figeac, Château, France, 529
Pavillon La Grange, France, 529
Pavillon Rouge Du Château Margaux, France, 530
Pavillon-Mercurol, Domaine Du, France, 529
Pavona, USA, California, 1016
Paysage, France, 530
Pazo De Barrantes, Bodegas, Spain, 790
Pazo De Senorans, Spain, 790
Pazo De Villarei, Spain, 790
Peachy Canyon, USA, California, 1016
Pebblewood, USA, California, 1017
Pecchenino, Fratelli, Italy, 709
Pech De Jammes, Château, France, 530
Pech Redon, Château De, France, 530
Peconic Bay, USA, New York, 1017
Pecorari, Francesco, Italy, 709
Pecorari, Pierpaolo, Italy, 709
Pecota, Robert, USA, California, 1017
Pédauque, La Reine, France, 530
Pédesclaux, Château, France, 530
Pedroncelli, USA, California, 1018
Pégau, Domaine Du, France, 530
Peirano Estate, USA, California, 1018
Peju, USA, California, 1018
Pélaquié, Domaine, France, 530
Pelissero, Italy, 709
Pellada, Quinta Da, Portugal, 758
Pellé, Domaine Henry, France, 530
Pellegrini, USA, California, 1019
Pellegrini Vineyards, USA, New York, 1019
Peller Estates, Canada, 804
Pelletier & Fils, M., France, 531
Peloux, Du, France, 531
Peña, Château De, France, 531
Penalba, Spain, 790
Penfolds, Australia, 233
Penley, Australia, 235
Pennautier, Château De, France, 531
Pensees De Lafleur, France, 531
Pepi, Robert, USA, California, 1019
Pépière, Domaine De La, France, 531
Pepper Tree, Australia, 236
Pepperwood Grove, USA, California, 1020
Pepperwood Springs, USA, California, 1020
Per Sempre, USA, California, 1020
Pereira, Manuel Salvador, Portugal, 758
Perelada, Castillo, Spain, 790
Perelli-Minetti, Mario, USA, California, 1020
Pérenne, Château, France, 531
Perez Pascuas, Bodegas Hnos., Spain, 791
Périllierè, Domaine De, France, 531
Pernot, Paul, France, 531
Peron, Jules, France, 531
Perouse, La, France, 531
Perrachon, Pierre-Yves, France, 531
Perret, André, France, 531
Perrier, Joseph, France, 531
Perrier, Pascal, France, 532
Perrière, Domaine, France, 532
Perrière, Domaine De La, France, 532
Perrier-Jouët, France, 532
Perrin Réserve, France, 532
Perrot-Minot, Henri, France, 532
Perry Creek, USA, California, 1020
Pertimali, Italy, 709
Pescaia, La, Italy, 709
Pescatori, Casa Di, Italy, 709
Pesenti, USA, California, 1020
Pesquier, Domaine Du, France, 532
Petaluma, Australia, 236
Peters' Hill, Hungary, 806
Petershof, Germany, 630
Peterson, USA, California, 1020
Petit Cheval, Le, France, 533
Petit-Faurie-De-Soutard, Château, France, 533
Petit-Figeac, Château, France, 533
Petit-Puch, Château Du, France, 533
Petit-Village, Château, France, 533
Petite Eglise, La, France, 533
Petits Quarts, Domaine Des, France, 533
Petrognano, Italy, 709
Petroio, Fattoria Di, Italy, 709
Petrolo, Fattoria, Italy, 710
Pétrus, Château, France, 533
Peu De La Moriette, Domaine Le, France, 533
Pewsey Vale, Australia, 236
Peybonhomme-Les-Tours, Château, France, 533
Peyrade, La Vicomte De La, France, 533
Peyraud, Château, France, 534
Peyre Rose, Domaine, France, 534
Peyros, Château, France, 534
Peyrou, Château, France, 534
Pez, Château De, France, 534
Pezzi King, USA, California, 1020
Pfaffl, Austria, 255
Pfeffingen, Germany, 630
Phantom Hill, USA, Oregon, 1021
Pheasant Ridge, USA, Texas, 1021
Phélan-Ségur, Château, France, 534
Phelps, Joseph, USA, California, 1021
Philippe, Jean, France, 534
Philippe-Lorraine, USA, California, 1022
Philipponnat, France, 534
Phillips, R.H., USA, California, 1022
Phoenix, USA, California, 1023
Piada, Château, France, 535
Pialade, La, France, 535
Pian Cornello, Italy, 710
Pianpolvere Soprano, Italy, 710
Piaugier, Domaine De, France, 535
Piazzo, Armando, Italy, 710
Pibarnon, Château De, France, 535
Pibbin, Australia, 236
Pibran, Château, France, 535
Picard, Château, France, 535
Picard, Jean-Paul, France, 535

Picard, Michel, France, 535
Piccini, Italy, 710
Piccinini, Domaine, France, 536
Pichler, F.X., Austria, 255
Pichler, Rudolf, Austria, 256
Pichon, Château, France, 536
Pichon, France, 536
Pichon, Philippe, France, 536
Pichon-Longueville-Baron, Château, France, 536
Pichon-Longueville-Lalande, Château, France, 536
Pichot, J.-C., France, 537
Pici, Le, Italy, 710
Pico, Georges, France, 537
Picq, Gilbert, France, 537
Picque-Caillou, Château, France, 537
Piduco Creek, Chile, 270
Piedemonte, Bodegas, Spain, 791
Piedmont, USA, Virginia, 1023
Pieropan, Leonildo, Italy, 710
Pierriere, Château La, France, 538
Pierro, Australia, 236
Pietra Santa, USA, California, 1023
Pietroso, Italy, 710
Pieve Santa Restituta, Italy, 710
Pighin, Fratelli, Italy, 710
Pignan, France, 538
Piguet-Girardin, France, 538
Pikes, Australia, 236
Pillot, Fernand, France, 538
Pillot, Fernand & Laurent, France, 538
Pillot, Jean, France, 538
Pillot, Jean-Marc, France, 539
Pillot, Paul, France, 539
Pin, Château Le, France, 539
Pinard, Vincent, France, 539
Pindar, USA, New York, 1023
Pine Ridge, USA, California, 1023
Pinede, Domaine De La, France, 539
Piney, Château, France, 539
Pinnacles, USA, California, 1024
Pins, Château Les, France, 539
Pinson, Louis, France, 539
Pintler, USA, Idaho, 1024
Pintos Dos Santos, A., Portugal, 758
Piper Sonoma, USA, California, 1024
Piper-Heidsieck, France, 539
Pipers Brook, Australia, 236
Piquemal, Domaine, France, 540
Piqueras, Bodegas, Spain, 791
Pique-Sègue, Château, France, 540
Pira, Italy, 711
Pirineos, Bodega, Spain, 791
Pirlet, Luc, France, 540
Pistone, Luigi, Italy, 711
Pitray, Château De, France, 540
Pizay, Château De, France, 540
Place D'Argent, France, 540
Plagnac, Château, France, 540
Plaimont, France, 540
Plaisance, Château, France, 540
Plam, USA, California, 1025
Planels, Château Des, France, 540
Planeres, Château, France, 540
Plantey, Château, France, 540
Plantiers Du Haut-Brion, Les, France, 540
Playa, La, Chile, 270
Plince, Château, France, 540
Ployez-Jacquemart, France, 541
Plozner, Italy, 711
Plum Creek, USA, Colorado, 1025
Plumet Héritiers, Henri, France, 541
Plumpjack, USA, California, 1025
Plunkett, Australia, 236
Poboleda, Spain, 791
Pocas, Porto, Portugal, 758
Pocas Junior, Portugal, 758
Pocé, Château De, France, 541
Pockl, Austria, 256
Poderina, La, Italy, 711
Poderuccio, Il, Italy, 711
Poggerino, Italy, 711
Poggio, Castello Del, Italy, 712
Poggio, Il, Italy, 712
Poggio A 'Frati, Italy, 711
Poggio Al Sole, Italy, 711
Poggio Al Sorbo, Italy, 711
Poggio Al Vento, Italy, 711
Poggio Antico, Italy, 711
Poggio Bonelli, Italy, 712
Poggio Degli Ulivi, Italy, 712
Poggio Di Sotto, Italy, 712
Poggio Reale, Italy, 712
Poggio Salvi, Italy, 712
Poggio San Polo, Italy, 712
Poggio Scalette, Podere, Italy, 712
Poggiolino, Il, Italy, 712
Poggiolo, Il, Italy, 713
Poggione, Il, Italy, 713
Pointe, Château La, France, 541
Poiron, Henri, France, 541
Pojer & Sandri, Italy, 713
Pol Roger, France, 541
Poliziano, Italy, 713
Polz, Erich & Walter, Austria, 256
Pomarèdes, Les, France, 541
Pommard, Château De, France, 542
Pommery, France, 542
Pommier, Denis, France, 542
Poniatowski, Prince, France, 542
Ponnelle, Domaine, France, 542
Ponnelle, Pierre, France, 542
Ponsot, Christine, France, 543
Ponsot, France, 542
Pontac-Lynch, Château, France, 543
Pontet-Canet, Château, France, 543
Ponti, Lanza Ginori, Italy, 713
Pontifical, Domaine, France, 543
Pontin Del Roza, USA, Washington, 1025
Pontormo, Italy, 713
Ponzi, USA, Oregon, 1025
Pope Valley, USA, California, 1025
Poppy Hill, USA, California, 1025
Porta, Casa, Chile, 270
Porta Da Ravessa, Portugal, 758
Porta Rossa, Cantina Della, Italy, 713
Portal Del Alto, Chile, 270
Portalegre, Adega Cooperativa De, Portugal, 758
Porter Creek, USA, California, 1025
Portteus, USA, Washington, 1025
Potensac, Château, France, 543
Pothier-Emonin, France, 543
Pothier-Rieusset, France, 543
Pouget, Château, France, 543
Pouilly, Château, France, 544
Poujeaux, Château, France, 544
Poujol, Domaine Du, France, 544
Poumey, Château, France, 544
Pousse D'Or, Domaine De La, France, 544
Poussie, La, France, 545
Poveda, Salvador, Spain, 791
Powers, USA, Washington, 1026
Pra' Di Pradis, Italy, 714
Pra, Fratelli, Italy, 714
Pradeaux, Château, France, 545
Pradel, Bernard, USA, California, 1026
Prager, Austria, 256

Pratola, Le, Italy, 714
Prats, Bruno, France, 545
Pravini, Italy, 714
Preece, Australia, 236
Preiss-Henny, France, 545
Prejean, USA, New York, 1026
Presidente, Domaine De La, France, 545
Preston, USA, California, 1026
Preston Premium Wines, USA, Washington, 1027
Preys, France, 545
Pride, USA, California, 1027
Prieur, Jacques, France, 545
Prieur & Fils, Paul, France, 547
Prieur-Brunet, France, 546
Prieuré De St.-Jean De Bebian, France, 547
Prieuré Des Mourges, Château Du, France, 547
Prieuré, Château De, France, 547
Prieuré, Château Du, France, 547
Prieuré, Château Le, France, 547
Prieuré-Lichine, Blanc Du Château, France, 548
Prieuré-Lichine, Château, France, 547
Prieuré-Roch, France, 548
Prieurs De La Commanderie, Château, France, 548
Primavera, Caves, Portugal, 758
Primicia, Bodegas, Spain, 791
Prince Michel, USA, Virginia, 1028
Princic, Doro, Italy, 714
Principato, Italy, 714
Principe Corsini, Italy, 714
Principe De Viana, Bodegas, Spain, 791
Prissé, Cave De, France, 548
Produttori Del Barbaresco, Italy, 714
Prosperity, Chile, 270
Prosper-Maufoux, France, 548
Protheau & Fils, Maurice, France, 548
Protos, Bodegas, Spain, 791
Prova Regia, Portugal, 758
Proviar, Argentina, 801
Providence, New Zealand, 810
Provins Valais, Switzerland, 813
Prüm, Joh. Jos., Germany, 630
Prunier, Michel, France, 548
Prunier, Vincent, France, 549
Prunotto, Alfredo, Italy, 714
Puech Cocut, Domaine, France, 549
Puech-Haut, Château, France, 549
Puerto, Marqués Del, Spain, 791
Puget, Domaine Du, France, 549
Pugliese, USA, New York, 1028
Pugnane, Italy, 715
Puiatti, Giovanni, Italy, 715
Puiatti, Vittorio, Italy, 715
Puig & Roca, Cellers, Spain, 791
Pulden, Bulgaria, 803
Puligny-Montrachet, Domaine Du Château De, France, 549
Punset, Italy, 715
Pupille, Fattoria Le, Italy, 715
Puy-Blanquet, Château, France, 550
Puygueraud, Château, France, 550
Puzelat, J.-M. & T, France, 550
Pyramids, USA, California, 1028
Quady, USA, California, 1028
Quaff, USA, California, 1029
Quail Ridge, USA, California, 1029
Quails' Gate, Canada, 804
Quantin, Château De, France, 550
Quarles Harris, Portugal, 758
Quatro, USA, California, 1029
Queen Adelaide, Australia, 236
Querce, Fattoria La, Italy, 716
Quercecchio, Italy, 716
Querceto, Castello Di, Italy, 716
Quercia Al Poggio, Italy, 716
Querciabella, Fattoria, Italy, 716
Querciavalle, Italy, 716
Quilceda Creek, USA, Washington, 1029
Quilla, Domaine De La, France, 550
Quinault, Château, France, 550
Quintarelli, Giuseppe, Italy, 716
Quintessa, USA, California, 1029
Quivira, USA, California, 1029
Qupé, USA, California, 1029
R De Rieussec, France, 550
Rabasse Charavin, Domaine, France, 550
Rabat, Domaine, Chile, 270
Rabaud-Promis, Château, France, 550
Rabbit Ridge, USA, California, 1030
Raco, Cavas Del, Chile, 270
Radanovich, USA, California, 1031
Rafael, Argentina, 801
Rafanelli, A., USA, California, 1031
Raffault, Olga, France, 550
Ragose, Le, Italy, 716
Rahoul, Château, France, 550
Raimat, Spain, 791
Rainsong, USA, Oregon, 1032
Raja, La, Italy, 716
Ramafort, Château, France, 550
Ramage La Batisse, Château, France, 551
Rame, Château La, France, 551
Ramonet, France, 551
Ramos-Pinto, Portugal, 758
Rampolla, Castello Dei, Italy, 717
Ramsay, USA, California, 1032
Ramspeck, USA, California, 1032
Rancho Sisquoc, USA, California, 1032
Randall Bridge, Australia, 236
Random Ridge, USA, California, 1032
Rapet Pére & Fils, France, 551
Rapidan River, USA, Virginia, 1032
Rapitala, Italy, 717
Rapsani, Greece, 805
Rasmussen, Kent, USA, California, 1032
Raspail, Château, France, 552
Raspail-Ay, Domaine, France, 552
Rateau, Jean-Claude, France, 552
Ratti, Renato, Italy, 717
Rattlesnake Ridge, USA, Washington, 1032
Rausan-Segla, Château, France, 552
Rauzan, Château, France, 552
Rauzan-Despagne, Château, France, 552
Rauzan-Gassies, Château, France, 552
Rauzan-Segla, Château, France, 552
Ravaut, Gaston & Pierre, France, 552
Ravenswood, USA, California, 1032
Ravier, Olivier, France, 552
Ravier, Simone & Olivier, France, 552
Ray, Martin, USA, California, 1034
Rayas, Château, France, 553
Raymond, USA, California, 1034
Raymond-Lafon, Château, France, 553
Rayne, Château De, France, 553
Rayne-Vigneau, Château De, France, 553
Real Martin, Château, France, 553
Real Sitio De Ventosilla, Bodegas, Spain, 792
Real Vinícola, Portugal, 759
Rebello-Valente, Portugal, 759
Rebenhof, Austria, 257
Rectorie, Domaine De La, France, 553
Red Hill, South Africa, 770

Red Hill, USA, California, 1035
Redbank, Australia, 237
Redde, Michel, France, 553
Redhawk, USA, Oregon, 1035
Redhill, South Africa, 770
Redi, Italy, 717
Redwood Canyon, USA, California, 1035
Redwood Valley, New Zealand, 811
Regaleali, Italy, 717
Reguengos De Monsaraz, Cooperativa, Portugal, 759
Reif Estate, Canada, 804
Reignac, Château De, France, 553
Reinhartshausen, Schloss, Germany, 630
Reinisch, Johanneshof, Austria, 257
Relais De Patache D'Aux, Le, France, 553
Remejeanne, Domaine De La, France, 553
Remelluri, La Granja Nuestra Señora De, Spain, 792
Remick Ridge, USA, California, 1035
Remoissenet Père & Fils, France, 554
Remparts De Bastor, Les, France, 554
Renaissance, USA, California, 1035
Renaudie, Château La, France, 554
Renjarde, Domaine De La, France, 554
Renoir, René, France, 554
Renwood, USA, California, 1036
Réserve De La Comtesse, France, 554
Réserve De Léoville Barton, La, France, 554
Réserve J.-J. De Bethmann, France, 554
Réserve St.-Martin, France, 554
Ress, Balthasar, Germany, 631
Retuerta, Abadia, Spain, 792
Retzlaff, USA, California, 1036
Revelette, Château, France, 554
Reverdy, Bernard, France, 554
Reverdy, Hippolyte, France, 554
Reverdy, Jean, France, 555
Reverend, Domaine Du, France, 555
Rex Hill, USA, Oregon, 1036
Rey Sol, USA, California, 1036
Reyes, Bodegas, Spain, 792
Reynardière, Domaine De La, France, 555
Reynolds, Australia, 237
Reyssac, Château Le, France, 555
Rheinart, Germany, 631
Ribera, Vinicola De La, Spain, 792
Riberalta, Bodegas, Spain, 792
Ricasoli, Barone, Italy, 717
Ricavi, Spain, 792
Rich Passage, USA, Oregon, 1036
Rich, Andrew, USA, Washington, 1037
Richard, Château, France, 555
Richardson, USA, California, 1037
Richaud, Domaine, France, 555
Richeaume, Domaine, France, 555
Richemont, France, 555
Richter, Max Ferd., Germany, 631
Riddoch, Australia, 237
Ridge, USA, California, 1037
Riecine, Italy, 718
Rietine, Italy, 718
Rieussec, Château, France, 555
Righetti, Luigi, Italy, 718
Rinaldi, Giuseppe, Italy, 719
Rinaldi & Figli, Francesco, Italy, 718
Rio Grande, Italy, 719
Rioja Alta, La, Spain, 792
Rioja Santiago, Bodegas, Spain, 792
Riojanas, Bodegas, Spain, 793
Rion, Armelle & Bernard, France, 555
Rion, Daniel, France, 555
Rion, Michele & Patrice, France, 557
Rion Père & Fils, France, 555
Ripa, Fattoria La, Italy, 719
Ripeau, Château, France, 557
Riscal, Marqués De, Spain, 793
Ritchie Creek, USA, California, 1039
Ritratti, Italy, 719
River Falls, Chile, 270
River Road, USA, California, 1039
River Run, USA, California, 1039
Riverside, New Zealand, 811
Riverside Farm, USA, California, 1039
Riverview, USA, New York, 1039
Rivetti, Fratelli, Italy, 719
Rivetti & Figli, Giuseppe, Italy, 719
Rivière, Château De La, France, 557
Rizza, USA, Oregon, 1039
Rizzardi, Guerrieri, Italy, 719
Rizzo, Luigi, Italy, 719
Roagna, Alfredo & Giovanni, Italy, 719
Roally, Domaine De, France, 557
Robert, Alain, France, 557
Robert, Domaine, France, 557
Robert, Domaine De, France, 557
Robert Alison, USA, California, 1039
Robert-Denogent, France, 557
Robertson's Well, Australia, 237
Robin, Château, France, 558
Roble, Abadia Del, Spain, 793
Roblet-Monnot, F., France, 558
Roblin & Fils, Georges, France, 558
Robson, Murray, Australia, 237
Rocca Bernarda, Italy, 719
Rocca Delle Macie, Italy, 719
Rocca Di Castagnoli, Italy, 720
Rocca Di Montegrossi, Italy, 720
Rocca, Albino, Italy, 720
Rocca, Bruno, Italy, 720
Roccadoro, Italy, 720
Rocche Costamagna, Italy, 720
Rocche Dei Brovia, Italy, 721
Rocche Dei Manzoni, Poderi, Italy, 721
Roch, Clusel, France, 558
Rocha, Portugal, 759
Roche, USA, California, 1039
Roche, Yves, Germany, 632
Rochemorin, Château De, France, 558
Rocher Bellevue Figeac, Château, France, 558
Roches Neuves, Domaine Des, France, 558
Rochevine, Domaine, France, 558
Rochioli, USA, California, 1039
Rocking Horse, USA, California, 1040
Rockland, USA, California, 1041
Rodano, Italy, 721
Rodet, Antonin, France, 558
Roederer, Louis, France, 559
Roederer Estate, USA, California, 1041
Roger, Domaine Jean-Max, France, 559
Rogue, La, France, 559
Rois, Château De, France, 559
Rolin, Nicolas, USA, Oregon, 1041
Rolland-Maillet, Château, France, 560
Rolland, Château, France, 559
Rollet, Catherine & Pascal, France, 560
Romandiola, Italy, 721
Romanée-Conti, Domaine De La, France, 560
Romaneira, Quinta Da, Portugal, 759
Romanin, Château, France, 561
Rombauer, USA, California, 1041
Romefort, Château, France, 561

Romer Du Hayot, Château, France, 561
Romero, Bodega, Spain, 793
Romitorio, Castello, Italy, 721
Roncade, Castello Di, Italy, 721
Roncée, Domaine Du, France, 561
Ronco Dei Tassi, Italy, 721
Ronco Del Gnemiz, Italy, 721
Rongopai, New Zealand, 811
Roo's Leap, Australia, 237
Rooiberg Wynmakery, South Africa, 770
Roosenveldt, South Africa, 771
Ropiteau Frères, France, 561
Ropiteau-Mignon, France, 562
Roq Dur, France, 562
Roque, Château De La, France, 562
Roque, Château La, France, 562
Roquebrun, Château, France, 562
Roquenegade, Domaine De, France, 562
Roquetaillade, Châteaufort De, France, 562
Roquette, Domaine De La, Bordeaux, France, 562
Roquette, Domaine De La, Rhône, France, 562
Roquevale, Portugal, 759
Roquevignan, Domaine De, France, 562
Rosa, Quinta De La, Portugal, 759
Rosazzo, Abbazia Di, Italy, 721
Rose Figeac, Château La, France, 562
Rosemount, Australia, 237
Rosenblum, USA, California, 1041
Rosenhof, Austria, 257
Rosenthal-The Malibu Estate, USA, California, 1043
Roseti, Dei, Italy, 722
Rosewood, USA, California, 1043
Rosiere, Domaine La, France, 562
Ross Valley, USA, California, 1043
Rossi, G., France, 562
Rossignol, Michel & Marc, France, 562
Rossignol, Philippe, France, 563
Rossignol-Fevrier, France, 563
Rossignol-Trapet, France, 563
Rosso, Cantina Gigi, Italy, 722
Rostaing, R., France, 563
Rotari, Italy, 722
Rothbury, Australia, 238
Rothschild, Baron Philippe De, France, 564
Rothschild, Barons Edmond & Benjamin, France, 564
Roty, Joseph, France, 564
Roudon-Smith, USA, California, 1044
Rouget, Château, France, 564
Rouget, Emmanuel, France, 564
Roulerie, Château De, France, 565
Roulot, Guy, France, 565
Roumier, Christophe, France, 565
Roumier, G., France, 565
Roumieu, Château, France, 566
Roumieu-Lacoste, Château, France, 566
Round Hill, USA, California, 1044
Rousseau, Armand, France, 566
Rousseau, Jeanne, France, 567
Rousselle, Château La, France, 567
Routas, Château, France, 567
Routier, Château De, France, 567
Rouvier Selections, France, 567
Rouvinez, Switzerland, 814
Roux, Armand, France, 567
Roux, Charles, France, 567
Roux Père & Fils, France, 567
Rouzé, Jacques, France, 568
Rovalley Ridge, Australia, 238
Rovira, Bodegas Pedro, Spain, 793
Royal Oporto, Portugal, 759
Royal Tokaji Wine Co., The, Hungary, 806
Royce, USA, California, 1044
Royes, Domaine Des, France, 568
Roylland, Château, France, 568
Roy-Thevenin, Alain, France, 568
Rozendal Farm, South Africa, 771
Rozes, Portugal, 760
Rubentino, Italy, 722
Rubissow-Sargent, USA, California, 1044
Rudel, Comte De, France, 568
Ruet, France, 568
Ruffino, Italy, 722
Ruggeri & C., Italy, 723
Ruinart, France, 568
Ruiz, Santiago, Spain, 794
Rully, Château De, France, 569
Rumball, Peter, Australia, 239
Runquist, J., USA, California, 1044
Russiz Superiore, Italy, 723
Rust En Vrede, South Africa, 771
Rustenberg, South Africa, 771
Rustridge, USA, California, 1045
Rutherford Estate, USA, California, 1045
Rutherford Grove, USA, California, 1045
Rutherford Hill, USA, California, 1045
Rutherford Ranch, USA, California, 1045
Rutherford Vintners, USA, California, 1045
Rutz, USA, California, 1046
Ryan, Seth, USA, Washington, 1046
Ryecroft, Australia, 239
Rymill, Australia, 239
S. Biagio, Italy, 723
S. Stefano, Italy, 723
Saarstein, Schloss, Germany, 632
Sable View, South Africa, 771
Sabon & Fils, Domaine Roger, France, 569
Saccardi, Italy, 723
Sacred Hill, New Zealand, 811
Saddleback, USA, California, 1046
Saddler's Creek, Australia, 239
Sade, Marquis De, France, 569
Saes, Quinta De, Portugal, 760
Saffirio, Josetta, Italy, 723
Sagpond, USA, New York, 1046
Saier, France, 569
Saint Gregory, USA, California, 1048
Saint Morillon, Chile, 270
Saint-Yzans, Château, France, 571
Saintsbury, USA, California, 1049
Sakonnet, USA, New England, 1050
Sala, La, Italy, 723
Salamandre, USA, California, 1050
Salaparuta, Duca Di, Italy, 723
Salcetino, Italy, 724
Sales, Château De, France, 571
Salette, Le, Italy, 724
Salisbury, Australia, 239
Salishan, USA, Washington, 1050
Salitage, Australia, 239
Salle, Castello Di, Italy, 724
Salle, Domaine De La, France, 571
Salle De Coeurs, France, 571
Salle De Poujeaux, Château La, France, 571
Salm-Dalberg, Prinz Zu, Germany, 632
Salmon Creek, USA, California, 1050
Salnesur, Bodegas, Spain, 794
Salomon-Weingut Undhof, Erich, Austria, 257
Salon, France, 571
Saltram, Australia, 239

Salvard, Domaine Du, France, 571
Salvat, Domaine, France, 571
Salvestrin, USA, California, 1050
Salviano, Italy, 724
Sammicheli, Italy, 724
San Carlos, Chile, 271
San Fabiano Calcinaia, Italy, 724
San Felice, Italy, 724
San Filippo, Italy, 725
San Giorgio, Italy, 725
San Giuseppe, Italy, 725
San Guido, Tenuta, Italy, 725
San Jorge, Bodega, Spain, 794
San Jose De Santiago, Chile, 271
San Leonardo, Tenuta, Italy, 725
San Leonino, Fattoria, Italy, 726
San Luigi, Italy, 726
San Michele, Italy, 726
San Pedro, Chile, 271
San Pietro, Italy, 726
San Polo In Rosso, Castello Di, Italy, 726
San Quirico, Italy, 726
San Saba, USA, California, 1050
San Telmo, Bodegas, Argentina, 801
San Vicente, Senorio De, Spain, 794
San Vincenti, Italy, 726
Sancerre, Château De, France, 571
Sancho, Bodegas Manuel, Spain, 794
Sandalford, Australia, 239
Sandeman, Portugal, 760
Sandrone, Luciano, Italy, 726
Sanford, USA, California, 1051
Sang Des Cailloux, Domaine Le, France, 571
Sant'anna, Italy, 726
Santa Alicia, Chile, 271
Santa Amelia, Chile, 271
Santa Ana, Argentina, 801
Santa Ana De Curico, Chile, 271
Santa Anita, Italy, 726
Santa Barbara Winery, USA, California, 1051
Santa Cruz Mountain, USA, California, 1052
Santa Daria, Spain, 794
Santa Duc, Domaine, France, 571
Santa Ema, Chile, 271
Santa Julia, Argentina, 801
Santa Margherita, Italy, 726
Santa Marvista, Chile, 271
Santa Monica, Chile, 272
Santa Rita, Chile, 272
Santa Sofia, Italy, 726
Santa Ynez Valley, USA, California, 1052
Santadi, Cantina, Italy, 727
Santangelo, Italy, 727
Santar, Casa De, Portugal, 760
Santé, Bernard, France, 571
Santi, Italy, 727
Santino, USA, California, 1052
Santo Stefano, Italy, 727
São João, Caves, Portugal, 760
Sao Pedro, Portugal, 760
Sarafornia, USA, California, 1053
Sarah's Vineyard, USA, California, 1053
Sardà, Bodegas J., Spain, 794
Sardelli, A., Italy, 727
Sarget De Gruaud-Larose, France, 571
Sarrau, Robert, France, 571
Sarry, Domaine De, France, 572
Sartori, Italy, 727
Sartre, Château Le, France, 572
Sassetti, Livio, Italy, 727
Satta, Michele, Italy, 728
Sattlerhof, Austria, 257
Sattui, V., USA, California, 1053
Saucelito Canyon, USA, California, 1053
Saugère, Lyliane, France, 572
Sault, Domaine Du, France, 572
Saumaize, Jacques, France, 572
Saumaize-Michelin, France, 572
Sausal, USA, California, 1053
Sautereau, Domaine, France, 573
Sauvageonne, Château La, France, 573
Sauvanes, Domaine Guy De, France, 573
Sauvion & Fils, France, 573
Sauzet, Etienne, France, 573
Savanha, South Africa, 771
Savary, Francine & Olivier, France, 574
Savignola Paolina, Italy, 728
Savoye, R., France, 574
Saxenburg, South Africa, 771
Scala Dei, Spain, 794
Scaramouche, France, 574
Scarborough, Australia, 240
Scarlatta, Italy, 728
Scarpa, Italy, 728
Scavino, Paolo, Italy, 728
Schaefer, Willi, Germany, 632
Scharffenberger, USA, California, 1053
Scheid, USA, California, 1054
Scherrer, F., USA, California, 1054
Schiopetto, Italy, 728
Schlumberger, Austria, 257
Schlumberger, Domaines, France, 574
Schmitges, Germany, 632
Schmitt Schenk, Germany, 632
Schmitt Söhne, Germany, 632
Schneider, USA, New York, 1054
Schoffit, Domaine, France, 575
Schonborn, Schloss, Germany, 633
School House, USA, California, 1054
Schramsberg, USA, California, 1054
Schrock, Heidi, Austria, 257
Schubert, C. Von, Germany, 633
Schuetz Oles, USA, California, 1055
Schug, USA, California, 1055
Schulz, Gerhard, Germany, 634
Schumann-Nagler, Germany, 634
Schwarzenberg, USA, Oregon, 1055
Scotchmans Hill, Australia, 240
Scotland Craig, USA, California, 1055
Scott, Allan, New Zealand, 811
Screaming Eagle, USA, California, 1055
Scrimaglio, Italy, 729
Sea Ridge, USA, California, 1055
Seavey, USA, California, 1056
Seaview, Australia, 240
Sebaste, Italy, 729
Sebastiani, USA, California, 1056
Sebastopol, USA, California, 1057
Second De Carnet, Le, France, 575
Secret House, USA, Oregon, 1057
Seebrich, Heinrich, Germany, 634
Seghesio, Fratelli, Italy, 729
Seghesio, USA, California, 1057
Segin-Manuel, France, 575
Ségla, France, 575
Seguin, Hervé, France, 575
Ségur, Château, France, 575
Seigendorf, Klosterkeller, Austria, 258
Seigneurie De Gicon, France, 575
Seigneurs Du Perigord, France, 575
Selaks, New Zealand, 811
Selbach-Oster, Germany, 634
Selby, USA, California, 1058
Selene, USA, California, 1058
Sella & Mosca, Tenute, Italy, 729
Selosse, Jacques, France, 575
Selva, Tenuta Della, Italy, 729

Selvapiana, Italy, 729
Selvole, Italy, 730
Selwyn River, New Zealand, 811
Senard, Daniel, France, 575
Senda Galiana, Bodegas, Spain, 794
Senechaux, Domaine Des, France, 576
Sénéjac, Château, France, 576
Senez, Christian, France, 576
Senra, Casa Da, Portugal, 760
Sepp Moser, Austria, 258
Seppelt, Australia, 240
Septimanie, France, 576
Sequoia Grove, USA, California, 1058
Sérafin Père & Fils, France, 576
Serafino, Italy, 730
Serena, La, Italy, 730
Sergue, Château La, France, 577
Serra, Jaume, Spain, 794
Serre, Château La, France, 577
Serristori, Conti, Italy, 730
Serveau, Bernard, France, 577
Servin, France, 577
Servus, Austria, 258
Sesta, Tenuta Di, Italy, 730
Setten, Tenuta, Italy, 730
Settimo, Aurelio, Italy, 730
Setzer, Austria, 258
Seven Hills, USA, Oregon, 1058
Seven Peaks, USA, California, 1059
Sevenhill, Australia, 241
Sezim, Casa De, Portugal, 760
Shadow Brook, USA, California, 1059
Shafer, USA, California, 1059
Shafer Vineyard Cellars, USA, Oregon, 1060
Shale Ridge, USA, California, 1060
Shaw & Smith, Australia, 241
Sheldrake, Australia, 242
Shenandoah, USA, California, 1060
Shingle Peak, New Zealand, 811
Shooting Star, USA, California, 1060
Siaurac, Château, France, 577
Sichel, Germany, 634
Siduri, USA, California, 1061
Sienna Ridge, Australia, 242
Sierra Cantabria, Bodegas, Spain, 794
Sierra Vista, USA, California, 1061
Sigalas-Rabaud, Château, France, 577
Sigaut, Hervé, France, 578
Signatures, France, 578
Signorello, USA, California, 1061
Sillage De Malartic, Le, France, 578
Silvan Ridge, USA, Oregon, 1062
Silver Cloud, France, 578
Silver Falls, USA, Oregon, 1062
Silver Horse, USA, California, 1062
Silver Lake, USA, Washington, 1062
Silver Oak, USA, California, 1063
Silver Ridge, USA, California, 1063
Silverado Hill Cellars, USA, California, 1064
Silverado Vineyards, USA, California, 1064
Silverwood, USA, California, 1065
Simard, Château, France, 578
Simi, USA, California, 1065
Simian, Château, France, 578
Simmern, Langwerth Von, Germany, 634
Simonnet-Febvre, France, 578
Simonsig, South Africa, 772
Simonsvlei Wynkelder, South Africa, 772
Sine Qua Non, USA, California, 1065
Sineann, USA, Washington, 1065
Singing Creek, Australia, 242
Sinskey, Robert, USA, California, 1066
Siran, Château, France, 578
Sirène De Giscours, La, France, 578
Sirius, France, 578
Sirugue & Fils, Jean-Louis, France, 579
Siskiyou, USA, Oregon, 1066
Skeffington, Portugal, † 747
Skouras, Greece, 805
Sky, USA, California, 1066
Slaughter Leftwich, USA, Texas, 1066
Smith & Hook, USA, California, 1066
Smith Wines, W.H., USA, California, 1066
Smith Woodhouse, Portugal, 760
Smith-Haut-Lafitte, Château, France, 579
Smith-Madrone, USA, California, 1066
Smothers Brothers, USA, California, 1066
Snoqualmie, USA, Washington, 1066
Snowden, 1067
Sobon Estate, USA, California, 1067
Sociando-Mallet, Château, France, 579
Sociando-Mallet, La Demoiselle De, France, 579
Sogrape, Portugal, 761
Sokol Blosser, USA, Oregon, 1067
Solana, Spain, 795
Solar, Casa, Spain, 795
Solar De Libano, Spain, 795
Solari, USA, California, 1068
Solatione, Italy, 730
Soldera, Italy, 730
Soleo, USA, California, 1068
Solis, USA, California, 1068
Solitude, Domaine De La, Bordeaux, France, 579
Solitude, Domaine De La, Rhone, France, 579
Solitude, USA, California, 1068
Solouro, Portugal, 761
Songmeadow, Argentina, 802
Sonnhof, Austria, 258
Sonnino, Fattoria, Italy, 730
Sonoita, USA, Arizona, 1068
Sonoma Creek, USA, California, 1068
Sonoma Mission, USA, California, 1069
Sonoma-Cutrer, USA, California, 1068
Sonoma-Loeb, USA, California, 1069
Sonsierra, Spain, 795
Sonvico, Italy, 730
Soos Creek, USA, Washington, 1069
Sopé Da Encosta, Portugal, 761
Soquel, USA, California, 1069
Soraval, Italy, 730
Sorgvliet, South Africa, 772
Sorin, Domaine, France, 579
Sorrel, H., France, 579
Sorrel, M., France, 580
Sorte, La, Italy, 730
Soudars, Château, France, 580
Soufrandise, Domaine De La, France, 580
Soulez, Pierre & Yves, France, 580
Soumade, Domaine La, France, 580
Sours, Château De, France, 580
Souselas, Adega Cooperativa De, Portugal, 761
Soutard, Château, France, 580
South Valley, Chile, 272
Spalletti, Italy, 731
Sparr, Pierre, France, 580
Sparrow Lane, USA, California, 1069
Spencer Hill, New Zealand, 811
Spenker, USA, California, 1069
Speri, Fratelli, Italy, 731
Spessa, Castello Di, Italy, 731

Spiliotopoulos, Christos, Greece, 805
Spottswoode, USA, California, 1069
Spring Mountain, USA, California, 1070
Springbok, South Africa, 772
Springhill, USA, Oregon, 1070
St. Amant, USA, California, 1046
St. Andrew's Vineyard, USA, California, 1046
St. Andrew's Winery, USA, California, 1046
St. Antony, Germany, 632
St. Clair, New Zealand, 811
St. Clement, USA, California, 1047
St. Donatus, Hungary, 807
St. Francis, USA, California, 1047
St. Hallett, Australia, 239
St. Innocent, USA, Oregon, 1048
St. Josef's, USA, Oregon, 1048
St. Julian, USA, Michigan, 1049
St. Supéry, USA, California, 1049
St.-André, Château, France, 569
St.-André-Corbin, Château, France, 569
St.-Antonin, Domaine, France, 569
St.-Désirat, Cave De, France, 569
St.-Esteve D'Uchaux, Château, France, 569
St.-Florin, Château, France, 569
St.-Georges, Château, France, 569
St.-Georges, Domaine, France, 570
St.-Germain, Château, France, 570
St.-Jacques, Château, France, 570
St.-James, Château, France, 570
St.-Laurent, Château, France, 570
St.-Laurent-L'Abbaye, Domaine De, France, 570
St.-Louis La Perdrix, Château, France, 570
St.-Luc, Domaine, France, 570
St.-Maurice, Château, France, 570
St.-Michel, Château, France, 570
St.-Pierre, Château, France, 570
St.-Pierre, Les Caves, France, 570
St.-Robert, Château, France, 571
St.-Sauveur, Domaine, France, 571
St.-Sulpice, Château, France, 571
Stafford Ridge, Australia, 242
Stag Hollow, USA, Oregon, 1070
Stag's Leap Wine Cellars, USA, California, 1070
Staglin Family, USA, California, 1071
Stags' Leap Winery, USA, California, 1071
Staiger, P. & M., USA, California, 1072
Staley, Philip, USA, California, 1072
Standing Stone, USA, New York, 1072
Stangeland, USA, Oregon, 1072
Stanley Brothers, Australia, 242
Stanton & Killeen, Australia, 242
Star Hill, USA, California, 1072
Starr, USA, Oregon, 1072
Staton Hills, USA, Washington, 1072
Staub, Rusty, USA, California, 1072
Ste. Chapelle, USA, Idaho, 1049
Ste. Claire, USA, California, 1049
Ste. Genevieve, USA, Texas, 1049
Ste.-Anne, Domaine, France, 569
Ste.-Eulalie, Château, France, 569
Ste.-Maire, Château, France, 570
Ste.-Paule, Domaine, France, 570
Steele, USA, California, 1072
Stellenryck, South Africa, 772
Stellenzicht, South Africa, 772
Steltzner, USA, California, 1074
Stemmler, Robert, USA, California, 1074
Stephen Ross, USA, California, 1074
Sterling, USA, California, 1075
Stevenot, USA, California, 1076
Stewart, USA, Washington, 1077
Stich Den Buben, Germany, 635
Stival, Italy, 731
Stone Cellars, USA, Washington, 1077
Stone Creek, USA, California, 1077
Stone Hill, USA, Missouri, 1077
Stonechurch, Canada, 804
Stonegate, USA, California, 1077
Stonehedge, USA, California, 1077
Stonelake, Chile, 272
Stoneleigh, New Zealand, 811
Stonestreet, 1078
Stoney Ridge, Canada, 804
Stonier's, Australia, 242
Stonington, USA, New England, 1078
Stony Hill, USA, California, 1078
Stony Hollow, Chile, 272
Stony Ridge, USA, California, 1078
Stonyridge, New Zealand, 811
Storrs, USA, California, 1078
Story, USA, California, 1078
Storybook Mountain, USA, California, 1079
Stra & Figlio, Giovanni, Italy, 731
Straccali, Italy, 731
Stratford, USA, California, 1079
Straus, USA, California, 1079
Streblow, USA, California, 1079
Striffiling, Bernard, France, 581
Strong, Rodney, USA, California, 1079
Stuhlmuller, USA, California, 1080
Sturm, Italy, 731
Sturt, Charles, Australia, 242
Subida Di Monte, Italy, 731
Suduiraut, Château, France, 581
Sugarloaf Ridge, USA, California, 1080
Sullberg, Michael, USA, California, 1080
Sullivan, USA, California, 1080
Summerfield, USA, California, 1081
Summerhill, Canada, 804
Summers Ranch, USA, California, 1081
Summit Lake, USA, California, 1081
Suncrest, USA, Washington, 1081
Sunflower Valley, France, 582
Sunny St. Helena, USA, California, 1081
Sunnycliff, Australia, 242
Sunridge, USA, California, 1081
Sunstone, USA, California, 1081
Suronde, Château De, France, 582
Sutter Home, USA, California, 1081
Sutter Ridge, USA, California, 1082
Svevo, Italy, 731
Svishtov, Vinprom, Bulgaria, 803
Swan, Joseph, USA, California, 1082
Swann, Mark, Australia, 242
Swanson, USA, California, 1082
Swartland Winery, South Africa, 772
Swedish Hill, USA, New York, 1083
Sycamore Creek, USA, California, 1083
Sylvester, USA, California, 1083
Sylviane, USA, California, 1083
Symington, Portugal, 761
T Vine, USA, California, 1083
Tablas Hills, USA, California, 1083
Tabordet, Yvon & Pascal, France, 582
Tabula Rasa, USA, Washington, 1083
Taft Street, USA, California, 1083
Tagaris, USA, Washington, 1084
Tailhas, Château, France, 582
Taillefer, Château, France, 582
Taillevent, France, 582
Tain L'Hermitage, Cave De, France, 582
Taittinger, France, 582

Taja, Spain, 795
Talbot, Château, France, 583
Talbott, USA, California, 1084
Talenti, Italy, 731
Talley, USA, California, 1084
Talmard, Domaine, France, 583
Talosa, Italy, 732
Taltarni, Australia, 242
Taluau, Joël & Clarisse, France, 583
Talus, USA, California, 1085
Tamas, Ivan, USA, California, 1085
Tamborini, Carlo, Switzerland, 814
Tamburlaine, Australia, 243
Tanesse, Château, France, 583
Tanner, Lane, USA, California, 1085
Tantalus, USA, California, 1085
Tarara, USA, Virginia, 1085
Tardieu-Laurent, France, 583
Tarente, Duc De, France, 584
Targé, Château De, France, 584
Tariquet, Domaine Du, France, 584
Tarlant, France, 584
Tarrawarra, Australia, 243
Tartuguière, Château, France, 584
Tasman Bay, New Zealand, 811
Tassarolo, Castello Di, Italy, 732
Tatoux, J., France, 584
Taupenot-Merme, Domaine, France, 584
Taurino, Dr. Cosimo, Italy, 732
Tay, USA, California, 1085
Tayac, Château, France, 584
Taylor Fladgate, Portugal, 761
Te Awa Farm, New Zealand, 812
Te Mata, New Zealand, 812
Teal Lake, USA, California, 1085
Tedeschi Vineyards, USA, Hawaii, 1085
Tedeschi, Italy, 732
Tefft, USA, Washington, 1085
Teldeschi, USA, California, 1086
Telmont, J. De, France, 584
Tement, E. & M., Austria, 258
Tempier, Domaine, France, 584
Temple Bruer, Australia, 243
Tenaglia, Tenuta La, Italy, 732
Tennessee Valley, USA, Tennessee, 1086
Tenrebac, USA, Washington, 1086
Teodósio, Caves Dom, Portugal, 761
Terlano, Cantina Sociale, Italy, 732
Terme, Château Marquis De, France, 585
Terme, Domaine Du, France, 585
Terra, USA, California, 1086
Terra De Lobos, Portugal, 762
Terra Galos, Austria, 258
Terra Nova, Chile, 273
Terra Rosa, Chile, 273
Terra Rosa, USA, California, 1086
Terra Vin, USA, California, 1086
Terrabianca, Italy, 732
Terraces, USA, California, 1086
Terranoble, Chile, 273
Terrasse, Château La, France, 585
Terrasses De Guilhem, Les, France, 585
Terre Da Vino, Italy, 732
Terre Del Barolo, Italy, 732
Terre Del Principe, Italy, 732
Terre Di Ginestra, Italy, 733
Terre Ferme, Domaine De, France, 585
Terreno, Italy, 733
Terres Vineuses, Domaine Des, France, 585
Terricci, Italy, 733
Terriccio, Tenuta Del, Italy, 733
Terrière, Château De La, France, 585
Terroir De Lagrave, France, 585
Tertre, Château Du, France, 585
Tertre Daugay, Château, France, 585
Tertre De Launay, Château, France, 585
Tertre Roteboeuf, Château Le, France, 585
Teruzzi & Puthod, Italy, 733
Tessera, USA, California, 1086
Testarossa, USA, California, 1087
Testuz, Jean & Pierre, Switzerland, 814
Tête, Louis, France, 585
Tête, Michel, France, 586
Tewksbury, USA, New Jersey, 1087
Teysha, USA, Texas, 1087
Teyssier, Château, France, 586
Thackrey, Sean H., USA, California, 1087
Thanisch (Müller-Burggraef), Dr. H., Germany, 635
Thanisch, Dr. H., Germany, 635
Thelema, South Africa, 772
Thévenet, Jean, France, 586
Thévenet, Jean-Claude, France, 586
Thévenet, Jean-Paul, France, 586
Thévenot-Machal, Jacques, France, 586
Thibault, Jean-Baptiste, France, 586
Thibert Père & Fils, France, 586
Thiel, Richard, Austria, 258
Thienpont, François, France, 586
Thieuley, Château, France, 586
Thistle Hill, Australia, 243
Thivin, Château, France, 587
Thomas, Claude, France, 587
Thomas, France, 587
Thomas, USA, Oregon, 1087
Thomas, John, USA, Oregon, 1087
Thomas, Lucien, France, 587
Thomas, Paul, France, 587
Thomas, Paul, USA, Washington, 1087
Thomas-Labaille, France, 587
Thomas-Moillard, Domaine, France, 587
Thorin, Maison, France, 587
Thornhill, USA, California, 1088
Thornton, USA, California, 1088
Thunder Mountain, USA, California, 1088
Tia Chica, Portugal, 762
Tiefenbrunner, Italy, 733
Tiezzi, Enzo, Italy, 733
Tigny, De, France, 588
Tijou, Pierre-Yves, France, 588
Tijsseling, USA, California, 1088
Timara, New Zealand, 812
Timberlay, Château, France, 588
Tinazzi, Italy, 733
Tinel-Blondelet, F., France, 588
Tinos, Bodega Los, Spain, 795
Titus, USA, California, 1088
Toad Hall, USA, California, 1088
Tobin James, USA, California, 1088
Togata, La, Italy, 733
Togni, Philip, USA, California, 1089
Tollot-Beaut & Fils, France, 588
Tolva, Domaine, Chile, 273
Tomaze, Château La, France, 589
Tommasi, Italy, 733
Tonnelle, Château La, France, 589
Tonnelle, Château La, France, 589
Topaz, USA, California, 1089
Topel, USA, California, 1089
Topolos, USA, California, 1089
Torii Mor, USA, Oregon, 1089
Toro, El Senorio De, Spain, 795
Torraccia, La, Italy, 734
Torre, La, Italy, 734
Torre Di Luna, Italy, 734
Torre Rosazza, Italy, 734
Torre Terza, Italy, 734
Torrecilla, Spain, 795

Torregiorgi, Italy, 734
Torrente, Spain, 795
Torreón De Paredes, Chile, 273
Torres, Marimar, USA, California, 1089
Torres, Miguel, Chile, 273
Torres, Spain, 795
Torres Filoso, Bodegas, Spain, 796
Torresella, Italy, 734
Tortoise Creek, France, 589
Toscolo, Italy, 734
Toso, Pascual, Argentina, 802
Totier Creek, USA, Virginia, 1090
Tott's, USA, California, 1090
Toumalin, Château, France, 589
Tour, Château De La, Bordeaux, France, 590
Tour, Château De La, Burgundy, France, 590
Tour Bellevue, Château, France, 590
Tour Blanche, Château La, France, 590
Tour Boisee, Domaine La, France, 590
Tour Calon, Château, France, 590
Tour Carnet, Château La, France, 590
Tour De Mirambeau, Château, France, 591
Tour De Mons, Château La, France, 591
Tour Du Mayne, Château, France, 591
Tour Figeac, Château La, France, 591
Tour Haut-Caussan, Château, France, 591
Tour Léognan, Château La, France, 591
Tour Martillac, Château La, France, 592
Tour-Baladoz, Château, France, 590
Tour-De-Bessan, Château La, France, 590
Tour-De-By, Château La, France, 590
Tour-Du-Haut-Moulin, Château, France, 591
Tour-Du-Mirail, Château, France, 591
Tour-Du-Pin-Figeac, Château La, France, 591
Tour-Du-Pin-Figeac-Believier, Château La, France, 591
Tour-Du-Roc, Château, France, 591
Tour-Haut-Brion, Château La, France, 591
Tour-Prignac, Château, France, 592
Tourelles, Domaine Des, France, 592
Tourelles De Longueville, France, 592
Tourette, Château La, France, 592
Tourier, Paul, France, 592
Tournons, Cellier Des, France, 592
Tours, Château Des, France, 592
Tours, Domaine Des, France, 592
Tour-St.-Bonnet, Château La, France, 592
Touzot, Jean, France, 592
Tracolle, Italy, 734
Tracy, Château De, France, 592
Trail Ridge, USA, Colorado, 1090
Trapadis, Domaine Du, France, 593
Trapet, Jean & Jean-Louis, France, 593
Trapet, Louis, France, 593
Trapiche, Argentina, 802
Traulsen, USA, California, 1090
Travaglini, Italy, 734
Traverso, Sergio, Chile, 273
Trefethen, USA, California, 1090
Treleaven, USA, New York, 1090
Tremblay, Gérard, France, 593
Trenel & Fils, France, 593
Trentadue, USA, California, 1090
Trentham, Australia, 243
Trerose, Tenuta, Italy, 734
Trevallon, Domaine De, France, 593
Tria, USA, California, 1090
Tribaut, USA, California, 1091
Tribut, Laurent, France, 593
Tricon, Olivier, France, 593
Triebaumer, Ernst, Austria, 259
Triennes, Domaine De, France, 593
Trignon, Château Du, France, 593
Trimbach, France, 594
Trimoulet, Château, France, 594
Trinchero, M., USA, California, 1091
Trinquevedel, Château De, France, 594
Tripoz, Didier, France, 594
Trollat, Raymond, France, 594
Tronquoy-Lalande, Château, France, 594
Troplong-Mondot, Château, France, 594
Troquato, USA, California, 1091
Trotanoy, Château, France, 595
Trottevieille, Château, France, 595
Trout Gulch, USA, California, 1091
Truchard, USA, California, 1091
Truchot, Jacky, France, 595
Trumpetvine, USA, California, 1091
Tualatin, USA, Oregon, 1091
Tucker, USA, Washington, 1092
Tudal, USA, California, 1092
Tuilerie, Domaine La, France, 595
Tuke Holdsworth, Portugal, 762
Tulocay, USA, California, 1092
Tunnel Hill, Australia, 243
Tuque, Domaine De La, France, 595
Turcaud, Château, France, 595
Turckheim, France, 595
Turgy, Michel, France, 596
Turkey Flat, Australia, 243
Turley, USA, California, 1092
Turnbull, USA, California, 1093
Turning Leaf, USA, California, 1093
Twin Hills, USA, California, 1093
Tyee, USA, Oregon, 1093
Tyrell, Germany, 636
Tyrrell's, Australia, 243
Uccelliera, Fattoria, Italy, 734
Uiterwyk, South Africa, 773
Ulecia, Faustino Rivero, Spain, 796
Umani Ronchi, Italy, 735
Umathum, Austria, 259
Unalii, USA, California, 1093
Unckrich, Germany, 636
Undurraga, Chile, 273
Union Champagne, France, 596
Union De Cosecheros De Labastida, Spain, 796
Union De Producteurs De St.-Emilion, L', France, 596
Union De Producteurs Plaimont, L', France, 596
Unionville Vineyards, USA, New Jersey, 1093
Unissent, USA, California, 1093
Unterebnerhof, Tenuta, Italy, 735
Urbion, Spain, 796
Usseglio, Pierre, France, 596
Uvavins, Switzerland, 814
Uve Cellars, USA, California, 1093
Uzzano, Castello Di, Italy, 735
Vacheron, Domaine, France, 596
Vachet-Rousseau, G., France, 596
Vadiaperti, Italy, 735
Vaisse, A., France, 596
Vajra, G.D., Italy, 735
Val D'Orbieu, France, 596
Val Da Figueira, Quinta De, Portugal, 762
Val Des Bruyères, Domaine, France, 596
Val Di Suga, Italy, 735
Val Joanis, Château, France, 597
Val St.-Jean, Domaine, France, 597
Valandraud, Château De, France, 597
Valckenberg, Germany, 636

Valcombe, Château, France, 597
Valdamor, Spain, 796
Valdarcos, Caves, Portugal, 762
Valdeobispo, Spain, 796
Valdicava, Italy, 735
Valdipiatta, Tenuta, Italy, 736
Valdivieso, Chile, 274
Valdumia, Spain, 796
Vale Da Mina, Quinta, Portugal, 762
Valentin, Château, France, 597
Valette, France, 597
Valfieri, Italy, 736
Valiano, Italy, 736
Vallana, Italy, 736
Vallania, Italy, 736
Vallarom, Italy, 736
Valle Chiara, Abbazia Di, Italy, 736
Valle De San Fernando, Chile, 274
Valle Selezione Araldica, Italy, 736
Vallée, Château La, France, 597
Vallejo, M.G., USA, California, 1093
Valley Of The Moon, USA, California, 1094
Valley Ridge, USA, California, 1094
Valley View, USA, Oregon, 1094
Vallformosa, Spain, 796
Vallongue, Château De, France, 597
Vallouit, L. De, France, 597
Valsangiacomo, Switzerland, 814
Valtellina, Fattoria, Italy, 736
Vampire, Romania, 812
Van Asperen, USA, California, 1094
Van Der Heyden, USA, California, 1094
Van Der Kamp, USA, California, 1094
Van Duzer, USA, Oregon, 1094
Van Loveren, South Africa, 773
Van Zeller, Portugal, 762
Varichon & Clerc, France, 597
Varone, Switzerland, 814
Vasconcellos, Portugal, 762
Vascos, Los, Chile, 274
Vaselli, Italy, 736
Vasse Felix, Australia, 244
Vatan, Edmond, France, 598
Vaucher, France, 598
Vaudon, Domaine De, France, 598
Vavasour, New Zealand, 812
Vecchie Terre Di Montefili, Italy, 736
Veedercrest, USA, California, 1094
Veenwouden, South Africa, 773
Vega De La Reina, Bodegas, Spain, 796
Vega De Moriz, Spain, 796
Vega Sicilia, Bodegas, Spain, 796
Vega Vieja, Spain, 797
Vegaval Plata, Spain, 797
Velanges, Domaine Des, France, 598
Velhas, Caves, Portugal, 762
Velich, Austria, 259
Vendange, USA, California, 1095
Venegazzù, Italy, 736
Venezia, USA, California, 1095
Venge, USA, California, 1095
Venica & Venica, Italy, 737
Venoge, De, France, 598
Ventana, USA, California, 1095
Veramonte, Chile, 274
Verbena, Italy, 737
Verdignan, Château, France, 598
Verdillac, France, 598
Verduno, Castello Di, Italy, 737
Vergelegen, South Africa, 773
Verger, Domaine Le, France, 598
Verget, France, 598
Vergnes, Château Des, France, 600
Verhaeghe & Fils, France, 600
Veritas, USA, Oregon, 1095
Vernay, Georges, France, 600
Vernede, Château La, France, 600
Verrazzano, Castello Di, Italy, 737
Verset, Noël, France, 600
Vescovado Di Murlo, Italy, 737
Vescovino, Il, Italy, 737
Vesselle, Georges, France, 600
Vessigaud Père & Fils, France, 600
Vesúvio, Quinta Do, Portugal, 763
Veuve Clicquot, France, 601
Viader, USA, California, 1095
Viala, Italy, 737
Viale, Domaine Gabriel, France, 601
Viano, USA, California, 1096
Viansa, USA, California, 1096
Viberti, Eraldo, Italy, 737
Viberti, Giovanni, Italy, 737
Vicchiomaggio, Castello Di, Italy, 738
Vicentini Orgnani, Francesco, Italy, 738
Vichon Mediterranean, France, 601
Vichon, USA, California, 1096
Vico, Giacomo, Italy, 738
Vidal, Angel Rodriguez, Spain, 797
Vidal, New Zealand, 812
Vidal-Fleury, J., France, 601
Vieille Cure, Château La, France, 602
Vieille Ferme, La, France, 602
Vieille Julienne, Domaine De La, France, 602
Vieilles Pierres, Domaine Des, France, 602
Vieira De Sousa, Portugal, 763
Vie-Magne, Domaine, France, 602
Vienot, Charles, France, 602
Viento, USA, Oregon, 1096
Vietti, Italy, 738
Vieux Chene, Domaine Du, France, 603
Vieux Donjon, Le, France, 603
Vieux Lazaret, Domaine Du, France, 603
Vieux St.-Sorlin, Domaine Du, France, 603
Vieux Télégraphe, Domaine Du, France, 603
Vieux-Château-Certan, France, 603
Vieux-Château-Négrit, France, 603
Vieux-Robin, Château, France, 603
Vigil, USA, California, 1096
Vigna Del Cassero, Italy, 738
Vigna Piccola, Italy, 738
Vigna Senza Nome, Italy, 738
Vignaioli Da San Floriano, Italy, 738
Vignale, Fattoria, Italy, 738
Vignale, Il, Italy, 739
Vignalta, Italy, 739
Vignamaggio, Fattoria Di, Italy, 739
Vignavecchia, Italy, 739
Vigne Dal Leon, Italy, 739
Vigneau-Chevreau, France, 603
Vignelaure, Château, France, 603
Vignerons D'Ige, Les, France, 604
Vignerons De Buzet, Les, France, 603
Vignerons De Mancey, Cave Des, France, 604
Vignerons De St.-Félix De Lodez, France, 604
Vignerons De St.-Gervais, France, 604
Vignerons De Saumur, Cave Des, France, 604
Vignerons Des Coteaux De St.-Jean, Les, France, 604
Vignobles Barde, France, 604
Vignole, Tenuta Di, Italy, 739
Vigouroux, Georges, France, 604

Vilarinho Do Bairro, Adega Cooperativa De, Portugal, 763
Vilariño-Cambados, Bodegas, Spain, 797
Vilarnau, Castell De, Spain, 797
Villa Aba, Italy, 739
Villa Andriana, USA, California, 1097
Villa Arceno, Italy, 739
Villa Bel-Air, France, 604
Villa Boscorotondo, Italy, 740
Villa Buonasera, Italy, 740
Villa Cafaggio, Italy, 740
Villa Calcinaia, Italy, 740
Villa Capodilista, Italy, 740
Villa Carra, Italy, 740
Villa Cerna, Italy, 740
Villa Cervia, Italy, 740
Villa Cilnia, Italy, 740
Villa Dal Ferro, Italy, 740
Villa De Monte, Italy, 740
Villa Dei Lecchi, Italy, 740
Villa Del Borgo, Italy, 741
Villa Di Vetrice, Italy, 741
Villa Fiore, Italy, 741
Villa Frattina, Italy, 741
Villa Helena, USA, California, 1097
Villa Il Poggiolo, Italy, 741
Villa La Pagliaia, Italy, 741
Villa La Selva, Italy, 741
Villa Maisano, Italy, 741
Villa Maria, New Zealand, 812
Villa Monte Rico, Italy, 741
Villa Montersino, Italy, 741
Villa Mt. Eden, USA, California, 1097
Villa Nicola, Italy, 741
Villa Pigna, Italy, 741
Villa Pillo, Italy, 741
Villa Rica, Chile, 274
Villa Rocca, Italy, 741
Villa Russiz, Italy, 741
Villa S. Anna, Italy, 742
Villa Sandi, Italy, 742
Villa Vittoria, Italy, 742
Villa Zapu, USA, California, 1098
Villa Zingale, Italy, 742
Villadoria, Italy, 742
Villaine, A. & P. De, France, 604
Villalta, Italy, 742
Villamont, Henri De, France, 605
Villard, Chile, 274
Villard, François, France, 605
Villars, Château, France, 605
Villegeorge, Château, France, 605
Villemaurine, Château, France, 605
Villeneuve, Arnaud De, France, 605
Villerambert, Château Julien, France, 605
Villiera Estate, South Africa, 773
Villotte, Château, France, 605
Vilmart, France, 605
Vimompor, Portugal, 763
Vin Du Soleil, France, 605
Viña, Casa De La, Spain, 797
Viña Berceo, Spain, 797
Viña Calina, Chile, 274
Viña Del Mar, Chile, 274
Viña Gracia, Chile, 275
Viña Ijalba, Spain, 797
Viña Morandé, Chile, 275
Viña Pedrosa, Spain, 797
Viña Porta, Chile, 275
Viña Salceda, Spain, 797
Viña Santa Carolina, Chile, 275
Viña Segú Ollé, Chile, 275
Viña Tarapacá, Chile, 276
Viña Terra Andina, Chile, 276
Viña Valoria, Spain, 797
Vina Vista, USA, California, 1098
Vinaporta, Chile, 276
Viñas De Gain, Spain, 797
Viñas Del Vero, Spain, 797
Vinattierri, Italy, 742
Vincent & Fils, J.J., France, 605
Vine Cliff, USA, California, 1098
Vinedos y Bodegas, Bodegas, Spain, 798
Vinegras, Bodegas, Spain, 798
Vineland Estates, Canada, 804
Vinet, Gérard, France, 606
Vineyard 29, USA, California, 1098
Vini, Bulgaria, 803
Vinival, France, 606
Viños De Chile, Chile, 276
Vinos De La Granja, Compania De, Spain, 798
Viños Exposicion, Chile, 276
Vinprom, Bulgaria, 803
Vins De Roquebrun, Cave Les, France, 606
Vinterra, Argentina, 802
Vinterra, Chile, 276
Vinum Bonum, Hungary, 807
Violet, Château, France, 606
Violette, Château La, France, 606
Viornery, Georges, France, 606
Viré, Cave De, France, 606
Virely-Rougeot, France, 606
Virgin Hills, Australia, 244
Virginie De Valandraud, France, 606
Vissoux, Domaine Du, France, 606
Vista Del Rey, USA, California, 1098
Vistarenni, Italy, 742
Vita Nova, USA, California, 1098
Vitallis, Château, France, 606
Viticcio, Italy, 742
Vitigliano, Italy, 742
Viu Manent, Chile, 276
Vivier, Château Le, France, 607
Viviers, Château De, France, 607
Voarick, Emile, France, 607
Voarick, Michel, France, 607
Vocoret & Fils, France, 607
Voerzio, Gianni, Italy, 742
Voerzio, Roberto, Italy, 743
Voge, Alain, France, 607
Vogüé, Comte Georges De, France, 607
Voila!, USA, California, 1098
Voillard, Joël, France, 608
Vollrads, Schloss, Germany, 636
Volpaia, Castello Di, Italy, 743
Volpato-Costaille, France, 608
Volpe Pasini, Italy, 743
Von Strasser, USA, California, 1098
Vose, USA, California, 1099
Voss, USA, California, 1099
Voulte Gasparet, Château La, France, 608
Vrai Caillou, Château, France, 608
Vranken, France, 608
Vraye-Croix-De-Gay, Château La, France, 609
Vriesenhof, South Africa, 773
Wagner, USA, New York, 1099
Wagner, Dr. Heinz, Germany, 636
Waimarama, New Zealand, 812
Wairau River, New Zealand, 812
Wakefield, Australia, 244
Walla Walla Vintners, USA, Washington, 1099
Walnut Crest, Chile, 276
Walzer, Ewald, Austria, 259
Warre, Portugal, 763

Warwick, South Africa, 773
Washington Hills, USA, Washington, 1099
Water Wheel, Australia, 244
Waterbrook, USA, Washington, 1100
Wattle Creek, USA, California, 1100
Wegeler Erben, J., Germany, 636
Wegeler-Deinhard, Germany, 637
Wehrheim, Eugen, Germany, 637
Weibel, USA, California, 1100
Weil, Robert, Germany, 637
Weinbach, Domaine, France, 609
Weinert, Bodega y Cavas De, Argentina, 802
Weinstock, USA, California, 1100
Weisinger's, USA, Oregon, 1100
Wellington, USA, California, 1100
Welmoed Winery, South Africa, 773
Weltevrede, South Africa, 773
Wente, USA, California, 1101
Werner'sches, Domdechant, Germany, 638
Westbend, USA, North Carolina, 1102
Westport Rivers, USA, New England, 1102
Westrey, USA, Oregon, 1102
Westwood, USA, California, 1102
Whaler, USA, California, 1102
Wheeler, France, 610
Wheeler, USA, California, 1102
Whidbey Island, USA, Washington, 1103
Whitcraft, USA, California, 1103
White Cottage, USA, California, 1103
White Hall, USA, Virginia, 1103
White Heron, USA, Washington, 1103
White Oak, USA, California, 1103
White Opal, Australia, 245
White Rock, USA, California, 1104
White, Alice, Australia, 245
Whitehall Lane, USA, California, 1104
Whittlesey Mark, USA, Oregon, 1105
Wiederkehr, USA, Arkansas, 1105
Wiemer, Hermann J., USA, New York, 1105
Wieninger, Austria, 259
Wiese & Krohn, Portugal, 763
Wild Hog Hill, USA, California, 1105
Wild Horse, USA, California, 1105
Wildcat, USA, California, 1106
Wilderness, Australia, 245
Wildhurst, USA, California, 1106
Wile & Sons, J., USA, California, 1106
Wilkinson, Audrey, Australia, 245
Willakenzie, USA, Oregon, 1106
Willamette Valley Vineyards, USA, Oregon, 1106
Willespie, Australia, 245
Williams Selyem, USA, California, 1107
Williamsburg, USA, Virginia, 1108
Willm, Alsace, France, 610
Willow Creek, USA, California, 1109
Wilridge, USA, Washington, 1109
Wilson Daniels, USA, California, 1109
Wilton, Australia, 245
Windemere, USA, California, 1109
Windsor, USA, California, 1109
Windwalker, USA, California, 1109
Windward, USA, California, 1109
Wineglass Cellars, USA, Washington, 1109
Winkler-Hermaden, Austria, 259
Winterbrook, USA, California, 1109
Winzer Krems, Austria, 259
Winzerhaus, Austria, 259
Wirilda Creek, Australia, 245
Witness Tree, USA, Oregon, 1109
Wolfe, Thurston, USA, Washington, 1110
Wollersheim, USA, Wisconsin, 1110
Woodbridge, USA, California, 1110
Woodbury, USA, New York, 1110
Woodley, Australia, 245
Woodside, USA, California, 1110
Woodward Canyon, USA, Washington, 1110
Worden, USA, Washington, 1111
Wright, Ken, USA, Oregon, 1111
Wurzburg, Staatlicher Hofkeller, Germany, 638
Wyndham, Australia, 245
Wynn, David, Australia, 245
Wynns Coonawarra Estate, Australia, 245
Yakima River, USA, Washington, 1111
Yalumba, Australia, 246
Yamhill Valley, USA, Oregon, 1112
Yarden, Israel, 807
Yarra Ridge, Australia, 246
Yarra Yering, Australia, 247
Yarraman Road, Australia, 247
Yarraman, Australia, 247
Yering Station, Australia, 247
Yeringberg, Australia, 247
Yon-Figeac, Château, France, 610
York Mountain, USA, California, 1112
Yorkville, USA, California, 1112
Youngberg Hill, USA, Oregon, 1112
Yquem, Château D', France, 610
Zabaco, USA, California, 1112
Zaca Mesa, USA, California, 1112
Zamò & Palazzolo, Italy, 743
Zandvliet, South Africa, 773
Zardetto, Italy, 743
Zayante, USA, California, 1113
Zd Wines, USA, California, 1113
Zellerbach Estates, USA, California, 1113
Zemmer, Peter, Italy, 743
Zenato, Italy, 744
Zerba, La, Italy, 744
Zia, USA, California, 1113
Zillah Oakes, USA, Washington, 1113
Zilliken, Germany, 638
Zimmermann, Austria, 260
Zind-Humbrecht, Domaine, France, 610
Zonin, Italy, 744
Zonnebloem, South Africa, 773
Zoom, USA, California, 1113
Zull, Familie, Austria, 260